Tozzotto

416-420-1069

The Oxford Dictionary for International Business

Compiled by
Market House Books Ltd

OXFORD UNIVERSITY PRESS
1998

Oxford University Press, Great Clarendon Street, Oxford OX2 6DP
Oxford New York
Athens Auckland Bangkok Bogotá Buenos Aires Calcutta
Cape Town Chennai Dar es Salaam Delhi Florence Hong Kong Istanbul
Karachi Kuala Lumpur Madrid Melbourne Mexico City Mumbai
Nairobi Paris São Paulo Singapore Taipei Tokyo Toronto Warsaw
and associated companies in Berlin Ibadan

Oxford is a registered trade mark of Oxford University Press

Published in the United States
by Oxford University Press Inc., New York

First published as The Oxford Dictionary for the Business World *1993*
Revised and retitled The Oxford Dictionary for International Business *1998*

British Library Cataloguing in Publication Data
Data available

Library of Congress Cataloging in Publication Data
Data available

ISBN 0-19-860163-8

10 9 8 7 6 5 4 3 2 1

Typeset by Market House Books Ltd
Printed in Great Britain
by Biddles Ltd
Guildford and King's Lynn

Preface to the First Edition

The Oxford Dictionary for the Business World is an entirely new dictionary, which has been compiled with the needs of business people in mind. In addition to a full English dictionary, with a pronunciation guide based on the International Phonetic Alphabet and notes on the derivation of words, it provides a number of useful features all in the same alphabetical list:

- lengthy entries covering terms commonly used in business and accounting as well as the commodity, financial, and stockbroking markets. These entries are shown between rules with a diamond in front of them.
- entries for place-names, including towns and cities, giving brief notes on their commercial and industrial activities. Extended descriptions of the world's countries are given in boxes at the foot of the pages nearest to their alphabetical place. These boxes contain a considerable amount of information (including population, GDP, literacy, etc.) some of which is in graphical form.
- computer terms are explained at some length to provide business people with an accessible explanation of many of the terms widely used in this field.
- a large number of the abbreviations, not usually included in standard English dictionaries, that are frequently used in the business world.
- brief profiles of leading figures in the business world.

In addition to these entries in the main body of the text, the dictionary includes much useful information in the form of eight Appendices, including notes on the usage of English and punctuation, general office information (Royal Mail services, world time zones, etc.), notes on compiling business plans, graphs, charts, etc., and hints on making business speeches.

We hope that this combination of information will be of value to the business community. Reactions and suggestions for subsequent editions will be welcome.

A.I. E.A.M.

1993

Preface to the Second Edition

The success of *The Oxford Dictionary for the Business World* has prompted the publishers to produce a second edition in which many of the entries have been expanded and updated. Moreover, the broadening of the content of this second edition and its wider interest for business people throughout the world has suggested a change of title to *The Oxford Dictionary for International Business*.

The new and revised business entries reflect the 1998 budgetary changes introduced into the UK by the Labour government, as well as many changes that have occurred in international trading.

The entries for the countries of the world have been revised and the statistical matter has been redrafted. At the same time, the profiles of leading figures in the business world have been enhanced by the addition of a selection from the international business community.

The editors of this new edition hope that it will continue to be of use to business people throughout the English-speaking world.

A.I. M.S.

1998

Market House Books Editors

General Editors	Dr Alan Isaacs
	Mr Mark Salad
Business Editor	Dr Alan Isaacs
Computing Editor	Ms Valerie Illingworth
Place-name Editor	Ms Fran Alexander
Biographical Editor	Mr Peter Blair
Back-matter Editor	Mr Mark Salad

Oxford University Press Editors

Managing Editor	Dr Della Thompson
General Editors	Mr Andrew Hodgson
	Mr Chris Stewart
Science Editor	Dr Alexandra Clayton
Freelance Editors	Mrs Barbara Burge
	Mrs Anna Howes
	Ms Louise Jones

Contents

Preface iii
Guide to the Use of the Dictionary vi
Pronunciation Symbols used in the Dictionary ix
Abbreviations used in the Dictionary x

DICTIONARY 1

Appendix I: Checklist for a Business Plan 995
Appendix II: Compiling Graphs and Charts 997
Appendix III: World Times 999
Appendix IV: Some Points of English Usage 1000
Apppendix V: Punctuation Marks 1017
Appendix VI: Royal Mail Services 1021
Appendix VII: Paper Sizes and Types 1025
Appendix VIII: Checklist for a Business Speech 1026

Guide to the Use of the Dictionary

1. HEADWORD

1.1 The headword is printed in bold type, or in bold italic type if the word is usually found in italics in printed matter.

1.2 Variant spellings, synonyms, and in some cases abbreviations are given before the definition; in all such cases the form given as the headword is the preferred form. When the variant form is alphabetically remote from the main form it is given at its proper place in the dictionary.

1.3 Words that have different meanings, origins, and sometimes pronunciations but are spelt the same way (homographs) are distinguished by superior figures (e.g. **bat**^{1} and **bat**^{2}).

1.4 Words that are normally spelt with a capital initial are given in this form as the headword; when they are in some senses spelt with a small initial and in others with a capital initial this is indicated by repetition of the full word in the appropriate form within the entry (as at **carboniferous**).

1.5 Variant American spellings are indicated by the designation *US* (e.g. **favour** ... *US* **favor**).

2. PRONUNCIATION

Guidance on pronunciation follows the system of the International Phonetic Alphabet (IPA). Only the pronunciation standard in southern England is given. A key to the symbols used appears on page xv.

3. PART-OF-SPEECH LABEL

3.1 This is given for all main entries and derivatives except for place-name and biographical entries.

3.2 Different parts of speech of a single word are listed separately.

3.3 Verbs, whether transitive, intransitive, or both, are given the designation *v.* The designation *absol.* (absolute) denotes use with an implied object (as at **abdicate**).

4. INFLECTION

4.1 *Plurals of Nouns*: Plural forms of nouns ending in *-o* (preceded by any letter other than another *o*) are always given. Other irregular forms are also given, except when the word is a compound of obvious formation (e.g. **footman, schoolchild**).

4.2 *Forms of Verbs*: A doubled consonant in verbal inflections (e.g. *rubbed, rubbing, sinned, sinning*) is shown in the form (**-bb-**, **-nn-**, etc.). Where practice differs in American usage this is noted (as at **cavil**).

5. DEFINITION

5.1 Definitions are separated by a number, or by a letter when the two senses are more closely related.

5.2 Round brackets enclose letters or words that are optional (as at **crash** *v.* where '(cause to) make a loud smashing noise' can mean either 'make a loud smashing noise' or 'cause to make a lound smashing noise'), and indicate typical objects of transitive verbs (such as '(milk)' and '(skin etc.)' in two senses of **cream** *v.*).

6. SUBJECT AND USAGE LABELS

6.1 These are used to clarify the particular context in which a word or phrase is normally used.

6.2 Words and phrases more common in informal spoken English than in formal written English are labelled *colloq.* (colloquial) or *slang* as appropriate.

6.3 Some subject labels are used to indicate the particular relevance of a term or subject with which it is associated (e.g. *Econ., Commerce, Finance, Computing, Law*). They are not used when this is sufficiently clear from the definition itself.

6.4 Usage notes found at the end of entries give guidance on the current norms of standard English. Some of the rules given may legitimately be broken in less formal English, and especially in conversation.

7. PHRASES

Phrases are listed in alphabetical order after the treatment of the main word. The words *a, the, one*, and person do not count for purposes of alphabetical order.

8. DERIVATIVES

Words formed by adding a suffix to another word are in many cases listed at the end of the entry for the main word (e.g. **chalkiness** and **chalky** at **chalk**). In this position they are not defined since they can be understood from the sense of the main word and that given at the suffix concerned; when further definition is called for they are given main entries in their own right (e.g. **changeable**).

9. ETYMOLOGY

9.1 This is given in square brackets [ ] at the end of the entry. In the space available it can only give the direct line of derivation in outline. Forms in other languages are not given if they are exactly or nearly the same as the English form.

9.2 'Old English' is used for words that are known to have been used before AD 1150.

9.3 'Anglo-French' denotes the variety of French current in the Middle Ages after the Norman Conquest.

9.4 'Latin' denotes classical and Late Latin up to about AD 600; 'medieval Latin' that of the period 600–1500; 'Anglo-Latin' denotes Latin as used in medieval England.

9.5 Where the origin of a word cannot be reliably ascertained, the form 'origin uncertain' or 'origin unknown' is used.

9.6 Names of the rare languages that have contributed to English (such as Balti at **polo**, and Cree at **wapiti**) are given in full without explanation; they may be found explained in larger dictionaries or encyclopedias.

9.7 An etymology is not given when it is identical in essentials with that of a neighbouring entry, when the word is an abbreviation or compound of obvious formation (such as **bathroom**), or when the derivation is clear from the definition (as at **burgundy**).

10. CROSS-REFERENCE

10.1 Cross-reference to main entries is indicated by small capitals (e.g. **calk** *US* var. of CAULK; **CGT** *abbr.* = CAPITAL-GAINS TAX; **credit brokerage** see ANCILLARY CREDIT BUSINESS).

10.2 Cross-reference in italics to a defined phrase or compound refers to the entry for the first word unless another is specified.

10.3 Cross-reference from main entries is given when useful information can be found in related entries.

Pronunciation Symbols used in the Dictionary

Consonants

b	*but*	l	*leg*	v	*voice*	ŋ	ri*ng*
d	*dog*	m	*man*	w	*we*	x	lo*ch*
f	*few*	n	*no*	z	*zoo*	tʃ	*ch*ip
g	*get*	p	*pen*	ʃ	*she*	dʒ	*j*ar
h	*he*	r	*red*	ʒ	vi*s*ion		
j	*yes*	s	*sit*	θ	*th*in		
k	cat	t	*top*	ð	*th*is		

Vowels

æ	*cat*	ɒ	h*o*t	aɪ	m*y*	ɔɪ	b*oy*
ɑ:	*ar*m	ɔ:	s*aw*	aʊ	h*ow*	ʊə	p*oor*
e	b*e*d	ʌ	r*u*n	eɪ	d*ay*	aɪə	*fire*
ɜ:	h*er*	ʊ	p*u*t	əʊ	n*o*	aʊə	s*our*
ɪ	s*i*t	u:	t*oo*	eə	h*air*		
i:	s*ee*	ə	*a*go	ɪə	n*ear*		

(ə) signifies the indeterminate sound as in gard*e*n, carn*a*l, and rhyth*m*.

(r) at the end of a word indicates an r that is sounded when a word beginning with a vowel follows, as in *clutter up* and *an acre of land.*

The mark ~ indicates a nasalized sound, as in the following sounds that are not natural in English:

æ̃ (t*im*bre)
ɑ̃ (él*an*)
ɔ̃ (b*on* voyage)

The main or primary stress of a word is shown by ˈ preceeding the relevant syllable; any secondary stress in words or phrases of three or more syllables is shown by ˌ preceding the relevant syllable.

Abbreviations used in the Dictionary

Abbreviations in general use (such as etc., i.e.) are explained in the Dictionary itself.

abbr.	abbreviation
absol.	absolute(ly)
adj.	adjective
adv.	adverb
Aeron.	Aeronautics
Anat.	Anatomy
Anglo-Ind.	Anglo Indian
Antiq.	Antiquity
Archaeol.	Archaeology
Archit.	Architecture
assim.	assimilated
Astrol.	Astrology
Astron.	Astronomy
Astronaut.	Astronautics
attrib.	attributive(ly)
attrib. adj.	attributive adjective
Austral.	Australian
aux.	auxiliary
Bibl.	Biblical
Biochem.	Biochemistry
Biol.	Biology
Bot.	Botany
Chem.	Chemistry
Cinematog.	Cinematography
collect.	collective(ly)
colloq.	colloquial(ly)
comb.	combination; combining
compar.	comparative
compl.	complement
conj.	conjunction
contr.	contraction
demons. adj.	demonstrative adjective
demons. pron.	demonstrative pronoun
derog.	derogatory
dial.	dialect
Eccl.	Ecclesiastical
Econ.	Economics
Electr.	Electricity
ellipt.	elliptical(ly)
emphat.	emphatic
esp.	especially
euphem.	euphemism
Exod.	Exodus
fem.	feminine
foll.	followed
Gen.	Genesis
Geol.	Geology
Geom.	Geometry
Gk	Greek
Gram.	Grammar
Hist.	History
hist.	with historical reference
imper.	imperative
Ind.	of the subcontinent comprising India, Pakistan, and Bangladesh
infin.	infinitive

int.	interjection
interrog.	interrogative
interrog. adj.	interrogative adjective
interrog. adv.	interrogative adverb
interrog. pron.	interrogative pronoun
Ir.	Irish
iron.	ironical
joc.	jocular
Judg.	Judges
Lev.	Leviticus
masc.	masculine
Math.	Mathematics
Matt.	Matthew
Mech.	Mechanics
Med.	Medicine
Meteorol.	Meteorology
Mil.	Military
Mineral.	Mineralogy
Mus.	Music
Mythol.	Mythology
n.	noun
Naut.	Nautical
neg.	negative
N.Engl.	Northern English
n.pl.	noun plural
NZ	New Zealand
obj.	objective (case)
offens.	offensive
opp.	as opposed to
orig.	originally
Parl.	Parliament(ary)
part.	participle
past part.	past participle
Pharm.	Pharmacy; Pharmacology
Philos.	Philosophy
Phonet.	Phonetics
Photog.	Photography
phr.	phrase
Physiol.	Physiology
pl.	plural
poet.	poetical
Polit.	Politics
poss.	possessive (case)
poss. pron.	possessive pronoun
prec.	preceded
predic.	predicative(ly)
predic. adj.	predicative adjective
prep.	preposition
pres.	present
pres. part.	present participle
pron.	pronoun
pronunc.	pronunciation
propr.	proprietary term
Psychol.	Psychology
RC Ch.	Roman Catholic Church
ref.	reference
refl.	reflexive
rel. adj.	relative adjective
rel. adv.	relative adverb
rel. pron.	relative pronoun
Relig.	Religion
Rev.	Revelation
rhet.	rhetorical
Rom.	Roman
S.Afr.	South African
Scot.	Scottish
Sci.	Science
sing.	singular
Stock Exch.	Stock Exchange
superl.	superlative
symb.	symbol
Telecom.	Telecommunications
Theatr.	Theatre
Theol.	Theology
US	American, in American use
usu.	usually

v.	verb	v.refl.	reflexive verb
var.	variant(s)		
v.aux.	auxiliary verb	Zool.	Zoology

Note on Proprietary Status

This dictionary includes some words which are, or are asserted to be, proprietary names or trade marks. Their inclusion does not imply that they have acquired for legal purposes a non-proprietary or general significance, nor is any other judgement implied concerning their legal status. In cases where the editor has some evidence that a word is used as a proprietary name or trade mark this is indicated by the designation *propr.*, but no judgement concerning the legal status of such words is made or implied thereby.

Aa

A[1] /eɪ/ *n.* (*pl.* **As** or **A's**) **1** (also **a**) first letter of the alphabet. **2** *Mus.* sixth note of the diatonic scale of C major. **3** first hypothetical person or example. **4** highest category (of roads, marks, etc.). **5** (usu. **a**) *Algebra* first known quantity. **6 a** occupational grade comprising those in managerial or senior professional positions. **b** person in this grade. □ **from A to B** from one place to another. **from A to Z** from beginning to end.

A[2] *abbr.* (also **A.**) ampere(s).

a[1] /ə, eɪ/ *adj.* (also **an** /æn, ən/ before a vowel sound) (called the indefinite article) **1** one, some, any. **2** one like (*a Judas*). **3** one single (*not a chance*). **4** the same (*all of a size*). **5** per (*twice a year; seven a side*). [Old English *ān* one]

a[2] /ə/ *prep.* (usu. as *prefix*) **1** to, towards (*ashore; aside*). **2** (with verb in pres. part. or infin.) doing or being (*a-hunting; abuzz*). **3** on (*afire*). **4** in (*nowadays*). [Old English *an, on,* ON]

Å *abbr.* angstrom.

a. *abbr.* **1** about. **2** (esp. on a bill of exchange) accepted. **3** acre(s).

a- *prefix* (also **an** before a vowel sound) not, without (*amoral*). [Greek]

A0 *n.* standard paper size, 841 × 1189 mm.

◆ **A1** *–n.* **standard paper size, 594 × 841 mm.** *–adj.* **describing a property or person that is in the best condition. In marine insurance, before a vessel can be insured, it has to be inspected. If it is 'maintained in good and efficient condition' it will be shown in Lloyd's Register of Shipping as 'A' and if the anchor moorings are in the same condition the number '1' is added. This description is also used in life assurance. After a medical examination a person in perfect health is described as 'an A1 life'.**

A2 *–n.* standard paper size, 420 × 594 mm. *–international civil aircraft marking* Botswana.

A3 *–n.* standard paper size, 297 × 420 mm. *–international civil aircraft marking* Tonga.

A4 *n.* standard paper size, 210 × 297 mm.

A5 *–n.* standard paper size, 148 × 210 mm. *–international civil aircraft marking* Bhutan.

A6 *–n.* standard paper size, 105 × 148 mm. *–international civil aircraft marking* United Arab Emirates.

A7 *–n.* standard paper size, 74 × 105 mm. *–international civil aircraft marking* Qatar.

A8 *n.* standard paper size, 52 × 74 mm.

A9 *n.* standard paper size, 37 × 52 mm.

A9C *international civil aircraft marking* Bahrain.

A10 *n.* standard paper size, 26 × 37 mm.

A40 *international civil aircraft marking* Oman.

AA *abbr.* **1** = ADVERTISING ASSOCIATION. **2** Alcoholics Anonymous. **3** anti-aircraft. **4** Automobile Association.

AA1 *n.* (also **AA-one**) very high quality rating for credit.

AAA[1] *n.* highest quality rating for credit.

AAA[2] *abbr.* **1** American Accounting Association. **2** Association of Average Adjusters. **3** Australian Association of Accountants.

AAAA *abbr.* **1** American Association of Advertising Agencies. **2** Australian Association of Advertising Agencies.

AAAM *abbr.* American Association of Aircraft Manufacturers.

AABL *abbr.* Associated Australian Banks in London.

AABM *abbr.* Australian Association of British Manufacturers.

AACB *abbr.* Association of African Central Banks.

Aachen /ˈɑːxən, ˈɑːk(ə)n/ (French **Aix-la-Chapelle** /ˌeɪkslæʃæˈpel/) industrial city and spa in W Germany, in North Rhine-Westphalia near the Belgian and Dutch borders; industries include iron and steel and textiles; pop. (1993) 246 100.

AAIA *abbr.* **1** Associate of the Association of International Accountants. **2** Associate of the Australian Institute of Advertising.

AAIB *abbr.* Associate of the Australian Institute of Bankers.

AAII *abbr.* Associate of the Australian Insurance Institute.

Aalborg /ˈɔːlbɔːg/ (also **Ålborg**) industrial city and port in Denmark, in N Jutland, one of the country's oldest towns; industries include shipbuilding and textiles; pop. (1995) 159 100.

Aalst /ɑːlst/ (French **Alost** /æˈlɒst/) industrial city in Belgium, in East Flanders, 22 km (14 miles) NW of Brussels; industries include textiles and brewing; pop. (1991) 76 140.

AANA *abbr.* Australian Association of National Advertisers.

A & A *abbr.* additions and amendments.

A & C *abbr.* addenda and corrigenda.

a.&h. *abbr. Insurance* accident and health.

a.&i. *abbr. Insurance* accident and indemnity.

A & NI *abbr.* Andaman and Nicobar Islands.

A & P *abbr.* advertising and promotion.

a.&s. *abbr. Insurance* accident and sickness.

AAP *abbr.* **1** Association of American Publishers. **2** affirmative action programme.

a.a.r. *abbr. Insurance* against all risks.

aardvark /ˈɑːdvɑːk/ *n.* mammal with a tubular snout and a long tongue, feeding on termites. [Afrikaans]

Aarhus /ˈɔːrhuːs/ (also **Århus**) second-largest city of Denmark, in E Jutland; a port with oil refineries, it has electronics, textiles, and engineering industries; pop. (1995) 277 500.

AASA *abbr.* Associate of the Australian Society of Accountants.

AASB *abbr.* American Association of Small Businesses.

A'asia *abbr.* Australasia.

AAT *abbr.* Association of Accounting Technicians.

AB *postcode* Aberdeen.

A/B *abbr.* (Swedish) Aktiebolaget (= joint-stock company).

a.B. *abbr. Commerce* (German) auf Bestellung (= on order).

ab- *prefix* off, away, from (*abduct*). [Latin]

ABA *abbr.* **1** American Bankers' Association. **2** American Bar Association. **3** American Booksellers Association. **4** Associate in Business Administration. **5** Australian Bankers' Association.

aback /əˈbæk/ *adv.* □ **take aback** surprise, disconcert. [Old English: related to A[2]]

abacus /ˈæbəkəs/ *n.* (*pl.* **-cuses**) **1** frame with wires along which beads are slid for calculating. **2** *Archit.* flat slab on top of a capital. [Latin from Greek from Hebrew]

Abadan /ˌæbəˈdɑːn/ city in W Iran, on an island of the same name on the Shatt al-Arab waterway, a port with oil refineries; pop. (1991) 84 800.

abaft /əˈbɑːft/ *Naut. –adv.* in the stern half of a ship. *–prep.* nearer the stern than. [from A[2], *-baft*: see AFT]

abandon /ə'bænd(ə)n/ *–v.* **1** give up. **2** forsake, desert. **3** (often foll by *to*; often *refl.*) yield to a passion, another's control, etc. *–n.* freedom from inhibitions. [French: related to AD–, BAN]

abandoned *adj.* **1** deserted, forsaken. **2** unrestrained, profligate.

♦ **abandonment** *n.* **1** giving up, desertion. **2** yielding. **3** *Insurance* giving up the ownership of something covered by an insurance policy and treating it as if it has been completely lost or destroyed. If the insurers agree to abandonment, they will pay a total-loss claim (see ACTUAL TOTAL LOSS; CONSTRUCTIVE TOTAL LOSS). The owner who wishes to declare a vessel and its cargo a total loss gives the insurer a **notice of abandonment**; if, subsequently, the vessel or its cargo are recovered, they become the property of the insurer.

---

abase /ə'beɪs/ *v.* (**-sing**) (also *refl.*) humiliate, degrade. □ **abasement** *n.* [French: related to AD–, BASE[2]]

abashed /ə'bæʃt/ *adj.* embarrassed, disconcerted. [French *es-* EX-[1], *baïr* astound]

abate /ə'beɪt/ *v.* (**-ting**) make or become less strong etc.; diminish. □ **abatement** *n.* [French *abatre* from Latin *batt(u)o* beat]

abattoir /'æbə,twɑː(r)/ *n.* slaughterhouse. [French *abatre* fell, as ABATE]

abbacy /'æbəsɪ/ *n.* (*pl.* **-ies**) office or jurisdiction of an abbot or abbess. [Latin: related to ABBOT]

abbé /'æbeɪ/ *n.* (in France) abbot or priest. [French from Latin: related to ABBOT]

abbess /'æbɪs/ *n.* head of a community of nuns.

abbey /'æbɪ/ *n.* (*pl.* **-s**) **1** building(s) occupied by a community of monks or nuns. **2** the community itself. **3** building that was once an abbey.

abbot /'æbət/ *n.* head of a community of monks. [Old English from Latin *abbas*]

abbreviate /ə'briːvɪ,eɪt/ *v.* (**-ting**) shorten, esp. represent (a word etc.) by a part of it. □ **abbreviation** /-'eɪʃ(ə)n/ *n.* [Latin: related to BRIEF]

ABC[1] /,eɪbiː'siː/ *n.* **1** the alphabet. **2** rudiments of a subject. **3** alphabetical guide.

ABC[2] *abbr.* **1** Advance Booking Charter (airline ticket). **2** = AUDIT BUREAU OF CIRCULATION. **3** Australian Broadcasting Commission.

ABCC *abbr.* Association of British Chambers of Commerce.

ABC Islands Dutch islands of Aruba, Bonaire, and Curaçao, which lie in the Caribbean Sea near the coast of Venezuela. [abbreviation]

abdicate /'æbdɪ,keɪt/ *v.* (**-ting**) **1** (usu. *absol.*) give up or renounce (the throne). **2** renounce (a duty, right, etc.). □ **abdication** /-'keɪʃ(ə)n/ *n.* [Latin *dico* declare]

abdomen /'æbdəmən/ *n.* **1** the belly, including the stomach, bowels, etc. **2** the hinder part of an insect etc. □ **abdominal** /æb'dɒmɪn(ə)l/ *adj.* [Latin]

abduct /əb'dʌkt/ *v.* carry off or kidnap illegally. □ **abduction** *n.* **abductor** *n.* [Latin *duco* lead]

abeam /ə'biːm/ *adv.* at right angles to a ship's or an aircraft's length.

ABERCOR /'æbə,kɔː/ *abbr.* Associated Banks of Europe Corporation.

Aberdeen /,æbə'diːn/ city and fishing-port in NE Scotland; industries include offshore-oil transportation, engineering, food processing, textiles, and shipbuilding; pop. (1992) 218 200.

Aberdeen Angus /'æŋgəs/ *n.* animal of Scottish breed of hornless black cattle.

Aberdonian /,æbə'dəʊnɪən/ *–adj.* of Aberdeen. *–n.* native or citizen of Aberdeen. [medieval Latin]

aberrant /ə'berənt/ *adj.* deviating from what is normal or accepted. [Latin: related to ERR]

aberration /,æbə'reɪʃ(ə)n/ *n.* **1** aberrant behaviour; moral or mental lapse. **2** *Biol.* deviation from a normal type. **3** distortion of an image because of a defect in a lens or mirror. **4** *Astron.* apparent displacement of a celestial body.

abet /ə'bet/ *v.* (**-tt-**) (usu. in **aid and abet**) encourage or assist (an offender or offence). [French: related to AD–, BAIT]

abeyance /ə'beɪəns/ *n.* (usu. prec. by *in*, *into*) temporary disuse. [French: related to AD–, *beer* gape]

ABFD *abbr.* Association of British Factors and Discounters.

abhor /əb'hɔː(r)/ *v.* (**-rr-**) detest; regard with disgust. [Latin: related to HORROR]

abhorrence /əb'hɒrəns/ *n.* disgust; detestation.

abhorrent /əb'hɒrənt/ *adj.* (often foll. by *to*) disgusting or hateful.

ABI *abbr.* = ASSOCIATION OF BRITISH INSURERS.

abide /ə'baɪd/ *v.* (**-ding**; *past* **abided** or rarely **abode** /ə'bəʊd/) **1** (usu. in *neg.*) tolerate, endure (*can't abide him*). **2** (foll. by *by*) **a** act in accordance with (*abide by the rules*). **b** keep (a promise). **3** *archaic* remain, continue. [Old English *a-* intensive, BIDE]

abiding *adj.* enduring, permanent.

Abidjan /,æbɪ'dʒɑːn/ former capital and chief port of Côte d'Ivoire; linked to the sea by the Vridi Canal; pop. (1988) 1 729 100.

ability /ə'bɪlɪtɪ/ *n.* (*pl.* **-ies**) **1** (often foll. by *to* + infin.) capacity or power. **2** cleverness, talent. [French: related to ABLE]

-ability *suffix* forming nouns of quality from, or corresponding to, adjectives in *-able*.

♦ **ability-to-pay taxation** *n.* taxation in which taxes are levied on the basis of the taxpayers' ability to pay. Typical taxes of this sort in the UK are income tax and inheritance tax. Cf. BENEFIT TAXATION.

---

ab initio /,æb ɪ'nɪʃɪəʊ/ *adv.* from the beginning. [Latin]

ABINZ *abbr.* Associate of the Bankers' Institute of New Zealand.

abject /'æbdʒekt/ *adj.* miserable, wretched; degraded; despicable. □ **abjection** /æb'dʒekʃ(ə)n/ *n.* [Latin *jacio -ject-* throw]

abjure /əb'dʒʊə(r)/ *v.* (**-ring**) renounce on oath (an opinion, cause, etc.). □ **abjuration** /,æbdʒʊ'reɪʃ(ə)n/ *n.* [Latin *juro* swear]

ablative /'æblətɪv/ *Gram. –n.* case (in Latin) of nouns and pronouns indicating an agent, instrument, or location. *–adj.* of or in the ablative. [Latin *ablatus* taken away]

ablaze /ə'bleɪz/ *predic. adj.* & *adv.* **1** on fire. **2** glittering, glowing. **3** greatly excited.

able /'eɪb(ə)l/ *adj.* (**abler, ablest**) **1** (often foll. by *to* + infin.; used esp. in *is able*, *will be able*, etc., replacing tenses of *can*) having the capacity or power (*not able to come*). **2** talented, clever. □ **ably** *adv.* [Latin *habilis*]

-able *suffix* forming adjectives meaning: **1** that may or must be (*eatable*; *payable*). **2** that can be made the subject of (*dutiable*; *objectionable*). **3** relevant to or in accordance with (*fashionable*; *seasonable*). [Latin *-abilis*]

able-bodied *adj.* fit, healthy.

able-bodied seaman *n.* ordinary trained seaman.

ablution /ə'bluːʃ(ə)n/ *n.* (usu. in *pl.*) **1** ceremonial washing of the hands, sacred vessels, etc. **2** *colloq.* **a** ordinary bodily washing. **b** place for this. [Latin *ablutio* from *luo lut-* wash]

-ably *suffix* forming adverbs corresponding to adjectives in *-able*.

ABM *abbr.* anti-ballistic missile.

ABMAC /'æbmæk/ *abbr.* Association of British Manufacturers of Agricultural Chemicals.

abnegate /'æbnɪ,geɪt/ *v.* (**-ting**) give up or renounce (a pleasure or right etc.). [Latin *nego* deny]

abnegation /,æbnɪ'geɪʃ(ə)n/ *n.* denial; renunciation of a doctrine.

abnormal /æb'nɔːm(ə)l/ *adj.* deviating from the norm; exceptional. □ **abnormality** /-'mælɪtɪ/ *n.* (*pl.* **-ies**). **abnormally** *adv.* [French: related to ANOMALOUS]

Abo /'æbəʊ/ (also **abo**) *Austral. slang* usu. *offens.* –*n.* (*pl.* **-s**) Aboriginal. –*adj.* Aboriginal. [abbreviation]

aboard /ə'bɔːd/ *adv.* & *prep.* on or into (a ship, aircraft, etc.). [from A[2]]

abode[1] /ə'bəʊd/ *n.* dwelling-place. [related to ABIDE]

abode[2] see ABIDE.

abolish /ə'bɒlɪʃ/ *v.* put an end to (esp. a custom or institution). [Latin *aboleo* destroy]

abolition /ˌæbə'lɪʃ(ə)n/ *n.* abolishing or being abolished. □ **abolitionist** *n.*

A-bomb /'eɪbɒm/ *n.* = ATOMIC BOMB. [*A* for ATOMIC]

Abomey /ə'bəʊmeɪ, ˌæbə'meɪ/ town in S Benin, formerly capital of the kingdom of Dahomey; pop. (1992) 65 700.

abominable /ə'bɒmɪnəb(ə)l/ *adj.* **1** detestable, loathsome. **2** *colloq.* very unpleasant (*abominable weather*). □ **abominably** *adv.* [Latin *abominor* deprecate]

Abominable Snowman *n.* supposed manlike or bear-like Himalayan animal; yeti.

abominate /ə'bɒmɪˌneɪt/ *v.* (**-ting**) detest, loathe. □ **abomination** /-'neɪʃ(ə)n/ *n.* [Latin: related to ABOMINABLE]

aboriginal /ˌæbə'rɪdʒɪn(ə)l/ –*adj.* **1** indigenous, inhabiting a land from the earliest times, esp. before the arrival of colonists. **2** (usu. **Aboriginal**) of Australian Aborigines. –*n.* **1** aboriginal inhabitant. **2** (usu. **Aboriginal**) aboriginal inhabitant of Australia. [Latin: related to ORIGIN]

aborigine /ˌæbə'rɪdʒɪnɪ/ *n.* (usu. in *pl.*) **1** aboriginal inhabitant. **2** (usu. **Aborigine**) aboriginal inhabitant of Australia.

■ **Usage** When referring to the people, *Aboriginal* is preferred for the singular form and *Aborigines* for the plural, although *Aboriginals* is also acceptable.

abort /ə'bɔːt/ *v.* **1** miscarry. **2 a** effect abortion of (a foetus). **b** effect abortion in (a mother). **3** end or cause (a project etc.) to end before completion. **4** halt a processing activity in a computer before some planned conclusion has been reached. [Latin *orior* be born]

abortion /ə'bɔːʃ(ə)n/ *n.* **1** natural or (esp.) induced expulsion of a foetus from the womb before it is able to survive independently. **2** stunted or deformed creature or thing. **3** failed project or action. □ **abortionist** *n.*

abortive /ə'bɔːtɪv/ *adj.* fruitless, unsuccessful.

abound /ə'baʊnd/ *v.* **1** be plentiful. **2** (foll. by *in, with*) be rich; teem. [Latin *unda* wave]

about /ə'baʊt/ –*prep.* **1 a** on the subject of (*a book about birds*). **b** relating to (*glad about it*). **c** in relation to (*symmetry about a plane*). **2** at a time near to (*about six*). **3 a** in, round (*walked about the town*; *a scarf about her neck*). **b** all round from a centre (*look about you*). **4** at points in (*strewn about the house*). **5** carried with (*no money about me*). **6** occupied with (*about her business*). –*adv.* **1 a** approximately (*about ten miles*). **b** *colloq.* in an understatement (*just about had enough*). **2** nearby (*a lot of flu about*). **3** in every direction (*look about*). **4** on the move; in action (*out and about*). **5** in rotation or succession (*turn and turn about*). □ **be about** (or **all about**) *colloq.* have as its essential nature (*life is all about having fun*). **be about to** be on the point of (*was about to laugh*). [Old English]

about-face *n.* & *int.* = ABOUT-TURN, ABOUT TURN.

about-turn –*n.* **1** turn made so as to face the opposite direction. **2** change of opinion or policy etc. –*int.* (*about turn*) *Mil.* command to make an about-turn.

above /ə'bʌv/ –*prep.* **1** over; on the top of; higher than; over the surface of (*head above water*; *above the din*). **2** more than (*above twenty people*). **3** higher in rank, importance, etc., than. **4 a** too great or good for (*not above cheating*). **b** beyond the reach of (*above my understanding*; *above suspicion*). –*adv.* **1** at or to a higher point; overhead (*the floor above*; *the sky above*). **2** earlier on a page or in a book (*as noted above*). –*adj.* preceding (*the above argument*). –*n.* (prec. by *the*) preceding text (*the above shows*). □ **above all** most of all, more than anything else. **above oneself** conceited, arrogant. [Old English: related to A[2]]

above-board *adj.* & *adv.* without concealment; open or openly.

◆ **above par** see PAR VALUE.

◆ **above-the-line** *adj.* **1** denoting entries above the horizontal line on a company's profit and loss account that separates the entries that establish the profit (or loss) from the entries that show how the profit is distributed. **2** denoting advertising expenditure on mass media advertising, including press, television, radio, and posters. It is traditionally regarded as all advertising expenditure on which a commission is payable to an advertising agency. **3** denoting transactions concerned with revenue, as opposed to capital, in national accounts. Cf. BELOW-THE-LINE.

◆ **ABP** *abbr.* = ASSOCIATED BRITISH PORTS.

---

abracadabra /ˌæbrəkə'dæbrə/ –*int.* supposedly magic word used in conjuring. –*n.* spell or charm. [Latin from Greek]

abrade /ə'breɪd/ *v.* (**-ding**) scrape or wear away (skin, rock, etc.) by rubbing. [Latin *rado* scrape]

abrasion /ə'breɪʒ(ə)n/ *n.* **1** scraping or wearing away (of skin, rock, etc.). **2** resulting damaged area.

abrasive /ə'breɪsɪv/ –*adj.* **1 a** tending to rub or graze. **b** capable of polishing by rubbing or grinding. **2** harsh or hurtful in manner. –*n.* abrasive substance.

abreast /ə'brest/ *adv.* **1** side by side and facing the same way. **2** (foll. by *of*) up to date with.

abridge /ə'brɪdʒ/ *v.* (**-ging**) shorten (a book, film, etc.). □ **abridgement** *n.* [Latin: related to ABBREVIATE]

abroad /ə'brɔːd/ *adv.* **1** in or to a foreign country or countries. **2** widely (*scatter abroad*). **3** in circulation (*rumour abroad*).

abrogate /'æbrəˌgeɪt/ *v.* (**-ting**) repeal, abolish (a law etc.). □ **abrogation** /-'geɪʃ(ə)n/ *n.* [Latin *rogo* propose a law]

abrupt /ə'brʌpt/ *adj.* **1** sudden, hasty (*abrupt end*). **2** (of manner etc.) curt. **3** steep, precipitous. □ **abruptly** *adv.* **abruptness** *n.* [Latin: related to RUPTURE]

Abruzzi /ə'brʊtsɪ/ mountainous region on the Adriatic coast of E central Italy; cereals are produced and there is a large fishing fleet; pop. (est. 1993) 1 255 550; capital, L'Aquila.

ABS *abbr.* **1** American Bureau of Shipping. **2** Australian Bureau of Statistics.

a.b.s. *abbr.* (French, on postal addresses) aux bon soins (de) (= care of).

abscess /'æbsɪs/ *n.* (*pl.* **abscesses**) swelling containing pus. [Latin: related to AB-, CEDE]

abscissa /əb'sɪsə/ *n.* (*pl.* **abscissae** /-siː/ or **-s**) *Math.* (in a system of coordinates) shortest distance from a point to the vertical or *y*-axis. [Latin *abscindo* cut off]

abscond /əb'skɒnd/ *v.* depart hurriedly and furtively, esp. to avoid arrest; escape. [Latin *abscondo* secrete]

abseil /'æbseɪl/ –*v.* descend by using a doubled rope coiled round the body and fixed at a higher point. –*n.* descent made by abseiling. [German *ab* down, *Seil* rope]

absence /'æbs(ə)ns/ *n.* **1** being away. **2** time of this. **3** (foll. by *of*) lack of. □ **absence of mind** inattentiveness. [Latin *absentia*]

absent –*adj.* /'æbs(ə)nt/ **1** not present. **2** not existing; lacking. **3** inattentive. –*v.refl.* /əb'sent/ go or stay away. □ **absently** *adv.* (in sense 3 of *adj.*).

absentee /ˌæbsən'tiː/ *n.* person not present.

absenteeism /ˌæbsən'tiːɪz(ə)m/ *n.* absenting oneself from work or school etc., esp. frequently or illicitly.

absentee landlord *n.* one who lets a property while living elsewhere.

absent-minded *adj.* forgetful or inattentive. □ **absent-mindedly** *adv.* **absent-mindedness** *n.*

absinth /'æbsɪnθ/ *n.* **1** wormwood. **2** (usu. **absinthe**) aniseed-flavoured liqueur based on this. [French from Latin]

absolute /'æbsəˌluːt/ –*adj.* **1** complete, utter (*absolute* *bliss*). **2** unconditional (*absolute authority*). **3** despotic (*absolute monarch*). **4** not relative or comparative (*absolute standard*). **5** *Gram.* **a** (of a construction) syntactically independent of the rest of the sentence, as in *dinner being over, we left the table*. **b** (of an adjective or transitive verb) without an expressed noun or object (e.g. *the deaf, guns kill*). **6** (of a legal decree etc.) final. –*n. Philos.* (prec. by *the*) that which can exist independently of anything else. [Latin: related to ABSOLVE]

absolute address *n. Computing* **1** address in a programming language, high-level or low-level, that identifies a storage location (or a device) without the use of any intermediate reference. **2** address permanently assigned by the machine designer to a storage location.

absolute addressing *n. Computing* addressing mode in which an absolute address is used in a machine instruction in order to identify a location or device to be accessed.

absolutely *adv.* **1** completely, utterly. **2** in an absolute sense (*God exists absolutely*). **3** /-ˈluːtlɪ/ *colloq.* (used in reply) quite so; yes.

absolute majority *n.* majority over all rivals combined.

absolute pitch *n.* ability to recognize or sound any given note.

absolute temperature *n.* one measured from absolute zero.

absolute zero *n.* theoretical lowest possible temperature calculated as –273.15° C (or 0 K).

absolution /ˌæbsəˈluːʃ(ə)n/ *n.* formal forgiveness of sins.

absolutism /ˈæbsəluːˌtɪz(ə)m/ *n.* principle or practice of absolute government. □ **absolutist** *n.*

absolve /əbˈzɒlv/ *v.* (**-ving**) (often foll. by *from, of*) set or pronounce free from blame or obligation etc. [Latin: related to SOLVE]

absorb /əbˈsɔːb/ *v.* **1** incorporate as part of itself or oneself. **2** take in, suck up (liquid, heat, knowledge, etc.). **3** reduce the effect or intensity of; deal easily with (an impact, sound, difficulty, etc.). **4** consume (resources etc.). **5** (often as **absorbing** *adj.*) engross the attention of. [Latin *sorbeo* suck in]

absorbent –*adj.* tending to absorb. –*n.* absorbent substance or organ.

absorption /əbˈsɔːpʃ(ə)n/ *n.* **1** absorbing or being absorbed. **2** mental engrossment. □ **absorptive** *adj.*

♦ **absorption costing** *n.* costing products or activities by taking into account the total costs incurred in producing the product or service. Absorption costing ensures that full costs are recovered provided that goods or services can be sold at the price implied. Cf. MARGINAL COSTING.

abstain /əbˈsteɪn/ *v.* **1** (usu. foll. by *from*) refrain from indulging (*abstained from smoking*). **2** decline to vote. [Latin *teneo tent-* hold]

abstemious /əbˈstiːmɪəs/ *adj.* moderate or ascetic, esp. in eating and drinking. □ **abstemiously** *adv.* [Latin: related to AB-, *temetum* strong drink]

abstention /əbˈstenʃ(ə)n/ *n.* abstaining, esp. from voting. [Latin: related to ABSTAIN]

abstinence /ˈæbstɪnəns/ *n.* abstaining, esp. from food or alcohol. □ **abstinent** *adj.* [French: related to ABSTAIN]

abstract –*adj.* /ˈæbstrækt/ **1 a** of or existing in thought or theory rather than matter or practice; not concrete. **b** (of a word, esp. a noun) denoting a quality, condition, etc., not a concrete object. **2** (of art) achieving its effect by form and colour rather than by realism. –*v.* /əbˈstrækt/ **1** (often foll. by *from*) extract, remove. **2** summarize. –*n.* /ˈæbstrækt/ **1** summary. **2** abstract work of art. **3** abstraction or abstract term. [Latin: related to TRACT[1]]

abstracted /əbˈstræktɪd/ *adj.* inattentive, distracted. □ **abstractedly** *adv.*

abstraction /əbˈstrækʃ(ə)n/ *n.* **1** abstracting or taking away. **2** abstract or visionary idea. **3** abstract qualities (esp. in art). **4** absent-mindedness.

♦ **abstract of title** *n.* document used in conveyancing land that is not registered, to show how the vendor derived good title. It consists of a summary of certain documents (e.g. conveyances of the land) and recitals of certain events (e.g. marriages and deaths of previous owners).

abstruse /əbˈstruːs/ *adj.* hard to understand, profound. □ **abstruseness** *n.* [Latin *abstrudo -trus-* conceal]

absurd /əbˈsɜːd/ *adj.* wildly illogical or inappropriate; ridiculous. □ **absurdity** *n.* (*pl.* **-ies**). **absurdly** *adv.* [Latin: related to SURD]

ABTA /ˈæbtə/ *abbr.* **1** Allied Brewery Traders' Association. **2** Association of British Travel Agents. **3** Australian British Trade Association.

Abu Dhabi /ˌæbuː ˈdɑːbɪ/ **1** largest of the member states of the United Arab Emirates (UAE); oil production and export are the main activities; pop. (1991) 798 000. **2** capital city of the UAE and Abu Dhabi state; pop. (1989) 363 432.

Abuja /əˈbuːdʒə/ federal capital of Nigeria, built in the centre of the country to replace Lagos as the capital; the seat of government since December 1991; pop. (1991) 379 000.

abundance /əˈbʌnd(ə)ns/ *n.* **1** plenty; more than enough; a lot. **2** wealth. [Latin: related to ABOUND]

abundant *adj.* **1** plentiful. **2** (foll. by *in*) rich (*abundant in fruit*). □ **abundantly** *adv.*

abuse –*v.* /əˈbjuːz/ (**-sing**) **1** use improperly, misuse. **2** insult verbally. **3** maltreat. –*n.* /əˈbjuːs/ **1** misuse. **2** insulting language. **3** unjust or corrupt practice. **4** maltreatment (*child abuse*). □ **abuser** /əˈbjuːzə(r)/ *n.* [Latin: related to USE]

abusive /əˈbjuːsɪv/ *adj.* insulting, offensive. □ **abusively** *adv.*

abut /əˈbʌt/ *v.* (**-tt-**) **1** (foll. by *on*) (of land) border on. **2** (foll. by *on, against*) (of a building) touch or lean upon (another). [Anglo-Latin *butta* strip of land: related to BUTT[1]]

abutment *n.* lateral supporting structure of a bridge, arch, etc.

abuzz /əˈbʌz/ *adv.* & *adj.* in a state of excitement or activity.

abysmal /əˈbɪzm(ə)l/ *adj.* **1** *colloq.* extremely bad (*abysmal food*). **2** profound, utter (*abysmal ignorance*). □ **abysmally** *adv.* [Latin: related to ABYSS]

abyss /əˈbɪs/ *n.* **1** deep chasm. **2** immeasurable depth (*abyss of despair*). [Latin from Greek, = bottomless]

Abyssinia /ˌæbɪˈsɪnɪə/ see ETHIOPIA. □ **Abyssinian** *adj.* & *n.*

AC –*abbr.* **1** (also **ac**) alternating current. **2** aircraftman. –*airline flight code* Air Canada.

Ac *symb.* actinium.

a.c. *abbr.* (also **à.c.**) (French) à compte (= on account).

a/c *abbr.* account. [*account current*]

-ac *suffix* forming adjectives often (or only) used as nouns (*cardiac; maniac*). [Latin *-acus*, Greek *-akos*]

ACA *abbr.* **1** Associate of the Institute of Chartered Accountants. **2** Australian Consumers' Association.

acacia /əˈkeɪʃə/ *n.* tree with yellow or white flowers, esp. one yielding gum arabic. [Latin from Greek]

academia /ˌækəˈdiːmɪə/ *n.* the academic world; scholastic life.

academic /ˌækəˈdemɪk/ –*adj.* **1** scholarly, of learning. **2** of no practical relevance; theoretical. –*n.* teacher or scholar in a university etc. □ **academically** *adv.*

academy /əˈkædəmɪ/ *n.* (*pl.* **-ies**) **1** place of specialized training (*military academy*). **2** (usu. **Academy**) society or institution of distinguished scholars, artists, scientists, etc. (*Royal Academy*). **3** *Scot.* secondary school. [Greek *akadēmeia* the place in Athens where Plato taught]

acanthus /əˈkænθəs/ *n.* (*pl.* **-thuses**) **1** herbaceous plant with spiny leaves. **2** *Archit.* representation of its leaf. [Latin from Greek]

a cappella /ˌɑː kəˈpelə, ˌæ-/ *adj.* & *adv.* (of choral music) unaccompanied. [Italian, = in church style]

Acapulco /ˌækəˈpʊlkəʊ/ port and holiday resort in S Mexico, on the Pacific coast; pop. (1990) 593 200.

ACAS /ˈeɪkæs/ *abbr.* = ADVISORY, CONCILIATION, AND ARBITRATION SERVICE.

ACBSI *abbr.* Associate of the Chartered Building Societies Institute.

♦ **ACC** *abbr.* = AGRICULTURAL CREDIT CORPORATION LTD.

---

acc. *abbr. Commerce* **1** acceptance. **2** accepted.

ACCA *abbr.* Associate of the Chartered Association of Certified Accountants.

accede /əkˈsiːd/ *v.* (**-ding**) (foll. by *to*) **1** take office, esp. as monarch. **2** assent or agree. [Latin: related to CEDE]

accelerate /əkˈseləˌreɪt/ *v.* (**-ting**) move or cause to move or happen more quickly. □ **acceleration** /-ˈreɪʃ(ə)n/ *n.* [Latin: related to CELERITY]

accelerator *n.* **1** device for increasing speed, esp. the pedal controlling the speed of a vehicle's engine. **2** *Physics* apparatus for imparting high speeds to charged particles.

accent *–n.* /ˈæks(ə)nt/ **1** particular (esp. local or national) mode of pronunciation. **2** distinctive feature or emphasis (*an accent on comfort*). **3** prominence given to a syllable by stress or pitch. **4** mark on a letter or word to indicate pitch, stress, or the quality of a vowel. *–v.* /ækˈsent/ **1** emphasize (a word or syllable etc.). **2** write or print accents on (words etc.). **3** accentuate. [Latin *cantus* song]

accentuate /əkˈsentʃʊˌeɪt/ *v.* (**-ting**) emphasize, make prominent. □ **accentuation** /-ˈeɪʃ(ə)n/ *n.* [medieval Latin: related to ACCENT]

accept /əkˈsept/ *v.* **1** (also *absol.*) willingly receive (a thing offered). **2** (also *absol.*) answer affirmatively (an offer etc.). **3** regard favourably; treat as welcome (*was readily accepted*). **4** believe, receive (an opinion, explanation, etc.) as adequate or valid. **5** take as suitable (*machine only accepts tokens*). **6** undertake (an office or responsibility). [Latin *capio* take]

acceptable *adj.* **1** worth accepting, welcome. **2** tolerable. □ **acceptability** /-ˈbɪlɪtɪ/ *n.* **acceptably** *adv.* [French: related to ACCEPT]

acceptance *n.* **1** willingness to accept. **2** affirmative answer to an invitation etc. **3** approval, belief (*found wide acceptance*). **4** signature on a bill of exchange indicating that the person on whom it is drawn accepts the conditions of the bill. **5** bill of exchange that has been so accepted.

♦ **acceptance credit** *n.* a means of financing the sale of goods, particularly in international trade. It involves a commercial bank or merchant bank extending credit to a foreign importer whom it deems creditworthy. An acceptance credit is opened against which the exporter can draw a bill of exchange. Once accepted by the bank, the bill can be discounted on the money market or allowed to run to maturity.

♦ **acceptance supra protest** *n.* (also **acceptance for honour**) acceptance or payment of a bill of exchange, after it has been dishonoured, by a person wishing to save the honour of the drawer or an endorser of the bill. [*supra protest*, from Italian *sopra protesto* upon protest]

♦ **accepting house** *n.* institution specializing in accepting or guaranteeing bills of exchange. A service fee is charged for guaranteeing payment, enabling the bill to be discounted at preferential rates on the money market.

♦ **Accepting Houses Committee** *n.* committee representing the 16 accepting houses in the City of London. Members of the committee are eligible for finer discounts on bills bought by the Bank of England, a privilege now extended to other banks.

♦ **acceptor** *n.* drawee of a bill of exchange after he or she has accepted the bill, i.e. has accepted liability by signing the face of the bill.

---

access /ˈækses/ *–n.* **1** way of approach or entry (*shop with rear access*). **2 a** right or opportunity to reach or use or visit; admittance (*access to secret files*; *access to the prisoner*). **b** accessibility. **3** *archaic* outburst (*an access of anger*). *–v.* **1** *Computing* gain access to (data, a computer system, etc.). **2** accession. [French: related to ACCEDE]

accessible /əkˈsesɪb(ə)l/ *adj.* (often foll. by *to*) **1** reachable or obtainable; readily available. **2** easy to understand. □ **accessibility** /-ˈbɪlɪtɪ/ *n.*

accession /əkˈseʃ(ə)n/ *–n.* **1** taking office, esp. as monarch. **2** thing added. *–v.* record the addition of (a new item) to a library etc.

accessory /əkˈsesərɪ/ *n.* (*pl.* **-ies**) **1** additional or extra thing. **2** (usu. in *pl.*) small attachment, fitting, or subsidiary item of dress (e.g. shoes, gloves). **3** (often foll. by *to*) person who abets or is privy to an (esp. illegal) act. [medieval Latin: related to ACCEDE]

access road *n.* road giving access only to the properties along it.

access time *n. Computing* time taken to retrieve data from storage.

accident /ˈæksɪd(ə)nt/ *n.* **1** unfortunate esp. harmful event, caused unintentionally. **2** event that is unexpected or without apparent cause. □ **by accident** unintentionally. [Latin *cado* fall]

accidental /ˌæksɪˈdent(ə)l/ *–adj.* happening by chance or accident. *–n. Mus.* sign indicating a note's momentary departure from the key signature. □ **accidentally** *adv.*

♦ **accident insurance** *n.* insurance policy that pays a specified amount of money to the policyholder in the event of the loss of one or more eyes or limbs in an accident. It pays a sum to the dependants of the policyholder in the event of his or her death.

---

accident-prone *adj.* clumsy.

acclaim /əˈkleɪm/ *–v.* **1** welcome or applaud enthusiastically. **2** hail as (*acclaimed him king*). *–n.* applause, welcome, public praise. [Latin *acclamo*: related to CLAIM]

acclamation /ˌækləˈmeɪʃ(ə)n/ *n.* **1** loud and eager assent. **2** (usu. in *pl.*) shouting in a person's honour.

acclimatize /əˈklaɪməˌtaɪz/ *v.* (also **-ise**) (**-zing** or **-sing**) adapt to a new climate or conditions. □ **acclimatization** /-ˈzeɪʃ(ə)n/ *n.* [French *acclimater*: related to CLIMATE]

accolade /ˈækəˌleɪd/ *n.* **1** praise given. **2** touch made with a sword at the conferring of a knighthood. [Latin *collum* neck]

accommodate /əˈkɒməˌdeɪt/ *v.* (**-ting**) **1** provide lodging or room for (*flat accommodates two*). **2** adapt, harmonize, reconcile (*must accommodate himself to new ideas*). **3 a** do favour to, oblige (a person). **b** (foll. by *with*) supply (a person) with. [Latin: related to COMMODE]

accommodating *adj.* obliging, compliant.

accommodation /əˌkɒməˈdeɪʃ(ə)n/ *n.* **1** lodgings. **2** adjustment, adaptation. **3** convenient arrangement; settlement, compromise.

accommodation address *n.* postal address used by a person unable or unwilling to give a permanent address.

♦ **accommodation bill** *n.* (also **windbill** or **windmill**) bill of exchange signed by a person (the accommodation party) who acts as a guarantor. The accommodation party is liable for the bill should the acceptor fail to pay at maturity.

---

accompaniment /əˈkʌmpənɪmənt/ *n.* **1** instrumental or orchestral support for a solo instrument, voice, or group. **2** accompanying thing. □ **accompanist** *n.* (in sense 1).

accompany /əˈkʌmpənɪ/ *v.* (**-ies, -ied**) **1** go with; escort. **2** (usu. in *passive*; foll. by *with, by*) be done or found with; supplement. **3** *Mus.* partner with accompaniment. [French: related to COMPANION]

accomplice /əˈkʌmplɪs/ *n.* partner in a crime etc. [Latin: related to COMPLEX]

accomplish /əˈkʌmplɪʃ/ *v.* succeed in doing; achieve, complete. [Latin: related to COMPLETE]

accomplished *adj.* clever, skilled.

accomplishment *n.* **1** completion (of a task etc.). **2** acquired, esp. social, skill. **3** thing achieved.

accord /əˈkɔːd/ *–v.* **1** (often foll. by *with*) be consistent or in harmony. **2** grant (permission, a request, etc.); give (a welcome etc.). *–n.* **1** agreement, consent. **2** *Mus. & Art* etc. harmony. □ **of one's own accord** on one's own initiative; voluntarily. **with one accord** unanimously. **accord and satisfaction** device enabling one party to a contract to avoid an obligation that arises under the contract, provided that the other party agrees. The accord is the agreement by which the contractual obligation is discharged and the satisfaction is the consideration making the agreement legally operative. [Latin *cor cord-* heart]

accordance *n.* □ **in accordance with** in conformity to. □ **accordant** *adj.*

according *adv.* **1** (foll. by *to*) **a** as stated by (*according to Mary*). **b** in proportion to (*lives according to his means*). **2** (foll. by *as* + clause) in a manner or to a degree that varies as (*pays according as he is able*).

accordingly *adv.* **1** as circumstances suggest or require (*please act accordingly*). **2** consequently (*accordingly, he left the room*).

accordion /əˈkɔːdɪən/ *n.* musical reed instrument with concertina-like bellows, keys, and buttons. □ **accordionist** *n.* [Italian *accordare* to tune]

accost /əˈkɒst/ *v.* **1** approach and address (a person), esp. boldly. **2** (of a prostitute) solicit. [Latin *costa* rib]

account /əˈkaʊnt/ *–n.* **1** narration, description (*account of his trip*). **2** arrangement at a bank etc. for depositing and withdrawing money, credit, etc. (*open an account*). See CHEQUE ACCOUNT; CURRENT ACCOUNT; DEPOSIT ACCOUNT; SAVINGS ACCOUNT. **3** record or statement of financial transactions with the balance (*kept detailed accounts*). See ANNUAL ACCOUNTS. **4** named segment of a ledger recording transactions relevant to the person or the matter named. **5** period during which dealings on the London Stock Exchange are made without immediate cash settlement, of which there are 24 in a year. Settlement of all transactions made within an account is made ten days after the account ends (see ACCOUNT DAY). Most other stock exchanges use rolling accounts in which settlement is made a fixed number of days after the transaction. **6** client of an advertising, marketing, or public-relations agency from whom a commission or fee is derived. *–v.* consider as (*account him wise, a fool*). □ **account for 1** serve as or provide an explanation for (*that accounts for his mood*). **2** answer for (money etc. entrusted, one's conduct, etc.). **3** kill, destroy, defeat. **4** make up a specified amount of (*rent accounts for 50% of expenditure*). **account payee** words used in crossing a cheque to ensure that it is paid into the bank account of the payee only. **by all accounts** in everyone's opinion. **call to account** require an explanation from. **give a good** (or **bad) account of oneself** impress (or fail to impress); be successful (or unsuccessful). **keep account of** keep a record of; follow closely. **of no account** unimportant. **of some account** important. **on account 1** (of goods) to be paid for later. **2** (of money) in part payment. **on one's account** on one's behalf (*not on my account*). **on account of** because of. **on no account** under no circumstances. **take account of** (or **take into account**) consider (*took their age into account*). **turn to account** (or **good account**) turn to one's advantage. [French: related to COUNT[1]]

accountable *adj.* **1** responsible; required to account for one's conduct. **2** explicable, understandable. □ **accountability** /-ˈbɪlɪtɪ/ *n.*

accountant *n.* person trained to keep books of account of a business or other organization, and to prepare periodic accounts. The accounts normally consist of a balance sheet; a profit and loss account or, in the case of a non-trading organization, an income and expenditure account; and sometimes a statement of sources and application of funds. Other roles of accountants are to audit the accounts of organizations and to give advice on taxation and other financial matters. Wherever accountants work, their responsibilities centre on the collating, recording, and communicating of financial information and the preparation of analyses for decision-making purposes. See CERTIFIED ACCOUNTANT; CHARTERED ACCOUNTANT; COST ACCOUNTANT; FINANCIAL ACCOUNTANT; MANAGEMENT ACCOUNTANT. □ **accountancy** *n.* **accounting** *n.*

◆ **account executive** *n.* person in an advertising, marketing, or public-relations agency who is responsible for implementing a client's business. This involves carrying out the programme agreed between the agency and client, coordinating the activities, and liaising with the client.

◆ **accounting entity** *n.* any unit for which accounting records are kept and for which financial statements are prepared.

◆ **accounting period** *n.* period for which an organization makes up its accounts, usu. an annual period, although an organization might make use of shorter accounting periods for internal management purposes. For taxation the accounting period is defined by the taxation acts.

◆ **accounting rate of return** *n.* (also **ARR**) accounting ratio that expresses the profit of an organization before interest and taxation, usually for a year, as a percentage of the capital employed at the end of the period. Variants of the measure include using profit after interest and taxation, equity capital employed, and the average of opening and closing capital employed for the period.

◆ **accounting technician** *n.* person qualified by membership of an appropriate body (such as the Association of Accounting Technicians) to undertake tasks in the accountancy field without being a qualified accountant.

◆ **account management group** *n.* **1** group within an advertising, marketing, or public-relations agency responsible for planning, supervising, and coordinating the work done for a client. **2** group in the sales department of an organization that is responsible for managing the relationship with existing clients.

◆ **account of profits** *n.* legal remedy available as an alternative to damages in certain circumstances, esp. in breach of copyright cases. The person whose copyright has been breached sues the person who breached it for a sum of money equal to the gain made as a result of the breach.

◆ **account rendered** *n.* unpaid balance appearing in a statement of account, details of which have been given in a previous statement.

◆ **account sale** *n.* statement giving details of a sale made, often by an agent, on behalf of another person or firm.

◆ **accounts payable** *n.pl.* amounts owed by a business to suppliers (e.g. for raw materials).

◆ **accounts receivable** *n.pl.* amounts of money owed to an organization for invoiced amounts.

---

accoutrements /əˈkuːtrəmənts/ *n.pl.* (*US* **accouterments** /-təmənts/) **1** equipment, trappings. **2** soldier's equipment excluding weapons and clothes. [French]

Accra /əˈkrɑː/ capital of Ghana, a port and commercial centre on the Gulf of Guinea; pop. (1988) 949 100; Greater Accra pop. (est. 1990) 1 781 100.

accredit /əˈkredɪt/ *v.* (**-t-**) **1** (foll. by *to*) attribute (a saying etc.) to. **2** (foll. by *with*) credit (a person) with (a saying etc.). **3** (usu. foll. by *to* or *at*) send (an ambassador etc.) with credentials. **4** gain influence for or make credible (an adviser, a statement, etc.). [French: related to CREDIT]

accredited *adj.* **1** officially recognized. **2** generally accepted.

accretion /əˈkriːʃ(ə)n/ *n.* **1** growth or increase by accumulation, addition, or organic enlargement. **2** the resulting whole. **3 a** matter so added. **b** adhesion of this to the core matter. [Latin *cresco cret-* grow]

◆ **accrual** /əˈkruːəl/ *n.* (also **accrued charge**) estimate in the accounts of a business of a liability that is not supported by an invoice or a request for payment at the time the accounts are prepared.

---

accrue /əˈkruː/ *v.* (**-ues, -ued, -uing**) (often foll. by *to*) come as a natural increase or advantage, esp. financial. [Latin: related to ACCRETION]

◆ **accrued benefits** *n.pl.* benefits that have accrued to a person in respect of his or her pension, for the service rendered up to a given date, whether or not that person continues in office.

ACCS *abbr.* Associate of the Corporation of Secretaries. [formerly *A*ssociate of the *C*orporation of *C*ertified *S*ecretaries]

accumulate /əˈkjuːmjʊˌleɪt/ *v.* (**-ting**) **1** acquire an increasing number or quantity of; amass, collect. **2** grow numerous; increase. [Latin: related to CUMULUS]

◆ **accumulated depreciation** *n.* total amount written off the value of an asset; the sum of the yearly instalments of depreciation since the asset was acquired.

◆ **accumulated dividend** *n.* dividend that has not been paid to a company's preference shareholders and is, therefore, shown as a liability in its accounts.

◆ **accumulated profits** *n.pl.* amount showing in the appropriation of profits account that can be carried forward to the next year's accounts, i.e. after paying dividends, taxes, and putting some to reserve.

◆ **accumulating shares** *n.pl.* ordinary shares issued, instead of a dividend, to holders of ordinary shares in a company. Accumulating shares are a way of replacing annual income with capital growth; they avoid income tax but not capital-gains tax. Tax is usu. deducted by the company from the declared dividend and the net dividend is then used to buy additional ordinary shares for the shareholder.

accumulation /əˌkjuːmjʊˈleɪʃ(ə)n/ *n.* **1** accumulating, being accumulated. **2** accumulated mass. **3** growth of capital by continued interest. □ **accumulative** /əˈkjuːmjʊlətɪv/ *adj.*

◆ **accumulation unit** *n.* unit in an investment trust in which dividends are ploughed back into the trust, after deducting income tax, enabling the value of the unit to increase.

accumulator *n.* **1** rechargeable electric cell. **2** bet placed on a sequence of events, with the winnings and stake from each placed on the next. **3** electronic device that acts as a temporary store in the arithmetic and logic unit of a computer.

accuracy /ˈækjʊrəsɪ/ *n.* exactness or careful precision. [Latin *cura* care]

accurate /ˈækjʊrət/ *adj.* careful, precise; conforming exactly with the truth or a standard. □ **accurately** *adv.*

accursed /əˈkɜːsɪd/ *adj.* **1** under a curse. **2** *colloq.* detestable, annoying. [Old English *a-* intensive, CURSE]

accusation /ˌækjuːˈzeɪʃ(ə)n/ *n.* accusing, being accused. [French: related to ACCUSE]

accusative /əˈkjuːzətɪv/ *Gram.* –*n.* case expressing the object of an action. –*adj.* of or in this case.

accusatory /əˈkjuːzətərɪ/ *adj.* of or implying accusation.

accuse /əˈkjuːz/ *v.* (**-sing**) (often foll. by *of*) charge with a fault or crime; blame. [Latin *accusare*: related to CAUSE]

accustom /əˈkʌstəm/ *v.* (foll. by *to*) make used to (*accustomed him to hardship*). [French: related to CUSTOM]

accustomed *adj.* **1** (usu. foll. by *to*) used to a thing. **2** customary, usual.

ace –*n.* **1** playing-card etc. with a single spot and generally signifying 'one'. **2 a** person who excels in some activity. **b** pilot who has shot down many enemy aircraft. **3** (in tennis) unreturnable stroke (esp. a service). –*adj. slang* excellent. □ **within an ace of** on the verge of. [Latin *as* unity]

acellular /eɪˈseljʊlə(r)/ *adj.* having no cells; not consisting of cells.

-aceous *suffix* forming adjectives in the sense 'of the nature of', esp. in the natural sciences (*herbaceous*). [Latin *-aceus*]

acerbic /əˈsɜːbɪk/ *adj.* harsh and sharp, esp. in speech or manner. □ **acerbity** *n.* (*pl.* **-ies**). [Latin *acerbus* sour]

acetaldehyde /ˌæsɪˈtældɪˌhaɪd/ *n.* colourless volatile liquid aldehyde. [from ACETIC, ALDEHYDE]

acetate /ˈæsɪˌteɪt/ *n.* **1** salt or ester of acetic acid, esp. the cellulose ester. **2** fabric made from this.

acetic /əˈsiːtɪk/ *adj.* of or like vinegar. [Latin *acetum* vinegar]

acetic acid *n.* clear liquid acid giving vinegar its characteristic taste.

acetone /ˈæsɪˌtəʊn/ *n.* colourless volatile liquid that dissolves organic compounds, esp. paints, varnishes, etc.

acetylene /əˈsetɪˌliːn/ *n.* hydrocarbon gas burning with a bright flame, used esp. in welding.

ACGI *abbr.* Associate of the City and Guilds Institute.

ACH *abbr.* automated clearing-house.

ache /eɪk/ –*n.* **1** continuous dull pain. **2** mental distress. –*v.* (**-ching**) suffer from or be the source of an ache. [Old English]

achieve /əˈtʃiːv/ *v.* (**-ving**) **1** reach or attain, esp. by effort (*achieved victory; achieved notoriety*). **2** accomplish (a feat or task). [French *achever*: related to CHIEF]

achievement *n.* **1** something achieved. **2** act of achieving.

Achilles' heel /əˈkɪliːz/ *n.* person's weak or vulnerable point. [*Achilles*, Greek hero in the *Iliad*]

Achilles' tendon *n.* tendon connecting the heel with the calf muscles.

achromatic /ˌækrəʊˈmætɪk/ *adj. Optics* **1** transmitting light without separation into constituent colours (*achromatic lens*). **2** without colour. □ **achromatically** *adv.* [French: related to A-, CHROME]

achy /ˈeɪkɪ/ *adj.* (**-ier, -iest**) full of or suffering from aches.

ACI *abbr.* Associate of the Institute of Commerce.

ACIA *abbr.* **1** Associate of the Corporation of Insurance Agents. **2** *Computing* asynchronous communications interface adapter (electronic device).

ACI.Arb. *abbr.* Associate of the Chartered Institute of Arbitrators.

ACIB *abbr.* **1** Associate of the Chartered Institute of Bankers. **2** Associate of the Corporation of Insurance Brokers.

acid /ˈæsɪd/ –*n.* **1 a** any of a class of substances that liberate hydrogen ions in water, are usu. sour and corrosive, turn litmus red, and have a pH of less than 7. **b** any compound or atom donating protons. **2** any sour substance. **3** *slang* the drug LSD. –*adj.* **1** sour. **2** biting, sharp (*an acid wit*). **3** *Chem.* having the essential properties of an acid. □ **acidic** /əˈsɪdɪk/ *adj.* **acidify** /əˈsɪdɪˌfaɪ/ *v.* (**-ies, -ied**). **acidity** /əˈsɪdɪtɪ/ *n.* **acidly** *adv.* [Latin *aceo* be sour]

acid house *n.* a type of synthesized music with a simple repetitive beat, often associated with hallucinogenic drugs.

acid rain *n.* acid, esp. from industrial waste gases, falling with rain.

acid test *n.* severe or conclusive test.

◆ **acid-test ratio** *n.* = LIQUID RATIO.

acidulous /əˈsɪdjʊləs/ *adj.* somewhat acid.

ACII *abbr.* Associate of the Chartered Insurance Institute.

ACIS *abbr.* Associate of the Institute of Chartered Secretaries and Administrators. [formerly *A*ssociate of the *C*hartered *I*nstitute of *S*ecretaries]

ACK *abbr.* (also **ack, ack.**) *Computing* & *Telecom.* acknowledgement.

ack-ack /ækˈkæk/ *colloq.* –*adj.* anti-aircraft. –*n.* anti-aircraft gun etc. [formerly signallers' term for *AA*]

acknowledge /əkˈnɒlɪdʒ/ *v.* (**-ging**) **1** recognize; accept the truth of (*acknowledged its failure*). **2** confirm the receipt of (a letter etc.). **3 a** show that one has noticed (*acknowledged my arrival with a grunt*). **b** express appreciation of (a service etc.). **4** recognize the validity of, own (*the acknowledged king*). [from AD-, KNOWLEDGE]

acknowledgement *n.* **1** act of acknowledging. **2 a** thing given or done in gratitude. **b** letter confirming receipt of something. **3** (usu. in *pl.*) author's statement of gratitude, prefacing a book. **4** *Computing* & *Telecom.* means by which a device receiving transmitted data can indicate to the sending device whether the data has been correctly received or not. The receiving device returns a confirming message, known as a **positive acknowledgement**, for each block of data received correctly. When an error is detected in a block of data, the receiver returns a **negative acknowledgement** to indicate that this block should be retransmitted by the sending device. See also TIMEOUT.

ACLU *abbr.* American College of Life Underwriters.

ACMA *abbr.* Associate of the Institute of Cost and Management Accountants.

acme /'ækmɪ/ *n.* highest point (of achievement etc.). [Greek]

acne /'æknɪ/ *n.* skin condition with red pimples. [Latin]

acolyte /'ækə,laɪt/ *n.* **1** person assisting a priest. **2** assistant; beginner. [Greek *akolouthos* follower]

aconite /'ækə,naɪt/ *n.* **1** any of various poisonous plants, esp. monkshood. **2** drug from these. [Greek *akoniton*]

ACORN /'eɪkɔːn/ *abbr. Computing* **1** associative content retrieval network. **2** automatic checkout and recording network.

♦ ***ACORN*** *n. A Classification of Residential Neighbourhoods*, directory that classifies 39 different types of neighbourhoods in the UK, assuming that people living in a particular neighbourhood will have similar behaviour patterns, disposable incomes, etc. It is used by companies to provide target areas for selling particular products or services (e.g. swimming pools, double glazing, etc.) or alternatively to exclude areas (particularly finance and insurance-related) from a sales drive. It is also used extensively for selecting representative samples for questionnaire surveys. [abbreviation]

---

acorn *n.* fruit of the oak, with a smooth nut in a cuplike base. [Old English]

acoustic /ə'kuːstɪk/ *adj.* **1** of sound or the sense of hearing. **2** (of a musical instrument etc.) without electrical amplification (*acoustic guitar*). □ **acoustically** *adv.* [Greek *akouō* hear]

♦ **acoustic coupler** *n.* device used to connect a computer to an ordinary telephone set so that the computer can send information along the telephone line and receive information sent along the line by other computers.

---

acoustics *n.pl.* **1** properties or qualities (of a room etc.) in transmitting sound. **2** (usu. as *sing.*) science of sound.

ACP *abbr.* **1** advanced computer program. **2** African, Caribbean, and Pacific (countries).

ACPA *abbr. US* Associate of the Institute of Certified Public Accountants.

acpt. *abbr. Commerce* acceptance.

acquaint /ə'kweɪnt/ *v.* (usu. foll. by *with*) make aware of or familiar with (*acquaint me with the facts*). □ **be acquainted with** have personal knowledge of; know slightly. [Latin: related to AD-, COGNIZANCE]

acquaintance *n.* **1** being acquainted. **2** person one knows slightly. □ **acquaintanceship** *n.*

acquiesce /,ækwɪ'es/ *v.* (**-cing**) **1** agree, esp. by default. **2** (foll. by *in*) accept (an arrangement etc.). □ **acquiescence** *n.* **acquiescent** *adj.* [Latin: related to AD-, QUIET]

acquire /ə'kwaɪə(r)/ *v.* (**-ring**) gain for oneself; come into possession of. [Latin: related to AD-, *quaero quisit-* seek]

acquired immune deficiency syndrome see AIDS.

acquired taste *n.* **1** liking developed by experience. **2** object of this.

acquirement *n.* thing acquired, esp. a mental attainment.

acquisition /,ækwɪ'zɪʃ(ə)n/ *n.* **1** thing acquired, esp. when useful. **2** acquiring or being acquired. [Latin: related to ACQUIRE]

♦ **acquisition accounting** *n.* accounting procedure adopted when one company is taken over by another. This often involves controversial issues as to the way in which goodwill is to be treated. See also GOODWILL 3.

---

acquisitive /ə'kwɪzɪtɪv/ *adj.* keen to acquire things.

acquit /ə'kwɪt/ *v.* (**-tt-**) **1** (often foll. by *of*) declare not guilty. **2** *refl.* **a** behave or perform in a specified way (*acquitted herself well*). **b** (foll. by *of*) discharge (a duty or responsibility). □ **acquittal** *n.* [Latin: related to AD-, QUIT]

acrd *abbr.* accrued.

Acre /'eɪkə(r)/ (also **Akko** /'ækəʊ/) seaport in Israel; industries include tourism, fishing, paint, plastics, and steel; pop. (est. 1989) 40 500.

acre /'eɪkə(r)/ *n.* measure of land, 4840 sq. yds., 0.405 ha. [Old English]

acreage /'eɪkərɪdʒ/ *n.* a number of acres; extent of land.

acrid /'ækrɪd/ *adj.* (**-er, -est**) bitterly pungent. □ **acridity** /ə'krɪdɪtɪ/ *n.* [Latin *acer* keen, pungent]

acrimonious /,ækrɪ'məʊnɪəs/ *adj.* bitter in manner or temper. □ **acrimony** /'ækrɪmənɪ/ *n.*

acrobat /'ækrə,bæt/ *n.* entertainer performing gymnastic feats. □ **acrobatic** /,ækrə'bætɪk/ *adj.* **acrobatically** /,ækrə'bætɪkəlɪ/ *adv.* [Greek *akrobatēs* from *akron* summit, *bainō* walk]

acrobatics /,ækrə'bætɪks/ *n.pl.* **1** acrobatic feats. **2** (as *sing.*) art of performing these.

acronym /'ækrənɪm/ *n.* word formed from the initial letters of other words (e.g. *laser*, *Nato*). [Greek *akron* end, *onoma* name]

acropolis /ə'krɒpəlɪs/ *n.* citadel of an ancient Greek city. [Greek *akron* summit, *polis* city]

across /ə'krɒs/ *–prep.* **1** to or on the other side of (*across the river*). **2** from one side to another side of (*spread across the floor*). **3** at or forming an angle with (*stripe across the flag*). *–adv.* **1** to or on the other side (*ran across*). **2** from one side to another (*stretched across*). □ **across the board** applying to all. **across the network** *Television* broadcast over all the ITV regions simultaneously. [French *à, en, croix*: related to CROSS]

acrostic /ə'krɒstɪk/ *n.* poem etc. in which certain letters (usu. the first and last in each line) form a word or words. [Greek *akron* end, *stikhos* row]

ACRS *abbr. Taxation* Accelerated Cost Recovery System.

acrylic /ə'krɪlɪk/ *–adj.* of synthetic material made from acrylic acid. *–n.* acrylic fibre or fabric. [Latin *acer* pungent, *oleo* to smell]

acrylic acid *n.* a pungent liquid organic acid.

ACS *abbr.* **1** *Computing* automated control system. **2** Association of Caribbean States.

a/cs pay. *abbr.* accounts payable.

a/cs rec. *abbr.* accounts receivable.

ACT *abbr.* **1** = ADVANCE CORPORATION TAX. **2** Association of Corporate Treasurers. **3** Australian Capital Territory.

act *–n.* **1** something done; a deed. **2** process of doing (*caught in the act*). **3** item of entertainment. **4** pretence (*all an act*). **5** main division of a play etc. **6 a** decree of a legislative body. **b** document attesting a legal transaction. *–v.* **1** behave (*acted wisely*). **2** perform an action or function; take action (*act as referee*; *brakes failed to act*; *he acted quickly*). **3** (also foll. by *on*) have an effect (*alcohol acts on the brain*). **4 a** perform a part in a play, film, etc. **b** pretend. **5 a** play the part of (*acted Othello*; *acts the fool*). **b** perform (a play etc.). **c** portray (an incident) by actions. □ **act for** be the (esp. legal) representative of. **act up** *colloq.* misbehave; give trouble (*car is acting up*). **get one's act together** *slang* become properly organized; prepare. **put on an act** *colloq.* make a pretence. See also ACT OF GOD; ACT OF WAR. [Latin *ago act-* do]

acting *–n.* art or occupation of an actor. *–attrib. adj.* serving temporarily or as a substitute (*acting manager*).

actinism /'æktɪ͵nɪz(ə)m/ *n.* property of short-wave radiation that produces chemical changes, as in photography. [Greek *aktis* ray]

actinium /æk'tɪnɪəm/ *n. Chem.* radioactive metallic element found in pitchblende. [as ACTINISM]

action /'ækʃ(ə)n/ *n.* **1** process of doing or acting (*demanded action*). **2** forcefulness or energy. **3** exertion of energy or influence (*action of acid on metal*). **4** deed, act (*not aware of his actions*). **5** (**the action**) **a** series of events in a story, play, etc. **b** *slang* exciting activity (*missed the action*). **6** battle, fighting (*killed in action*). **7 a** mechanism of an instrument. **b** style of movement of an animal or human. **8** lawsuit. □ **out of action** not working. [Latin: related to ACT]

actionable *adj.* giving cause for legal action.

action-packed *adj.* full of action or excitement.

action point *n.* proposal for action.

action replay *n.* playback of part of a television broadcast, esp. a sporting event, often in slow motion.

action stations *n.pl.* positions taken up by troops etc. ready for battle.

activate /'æktɪ͵veɪt/ *v.* (**-ting**) **1** make active. **2** *Chem.* cause reaction in. **3** make radioactive.

active /'æktɪv/ *–adj.* **1** marked by action; energetic; diligent (*an active life*). **2** working, operative (*active volcano*). **3** not merely passive or inert; positive (*active support; active ingredients*). **4** radioactive. **5** *Gram.* designating the form of a verb whose subject performs the action (e.g. the verb in *he saw a film*). *–n. Gram.* active form or voice of a verb. □ **actively** *adv.* [Latin: related to ACT]

♦ **active partner** *n.* partner who has contributed to the business capital of a partnership and who participates in its management. All partners are deemed to be active partners unless otherwise agreed. Cf. SLEEPING PARTNER.

---

active service *n.* military service during war.

♦ **active stocks** *n.pl.* stocks and shares that have been actively traded, as recorded in the Official List of the London Stock Exchange.

---

activism *n.* policy of vigorous action, esp. for a political cause. □ **activist** *n.*

activity /æk'tɪvɪtɪ/ *n.* (*pl.* **-ies**) **1** being active; busy or energetic action. **2** (often in *pl.*) occupation or pursuit (*outdoor activities*). **3** = RADIOACTIVITY.

♦ **act of God** *n.* natural event that is not caused by any human action and cannot be predicted. Insurance policies covering homes and businesses cover such natural events as storms, lightning, and floods. However, some contracts exclude liability for damage arising from acts of God (see FORCE MAJEURE 2).

♦ **act of war** *n.* anything that causes loss or damage as a result of hostilities or conflict. Such risks are excluded from all insurance policies (except life assurances). In marine and aviation insurance only, any extra premium may be paid to include war risks.

---

actor *n.* person who acts in a play, film, etc. [Latin: related to ACT]

actress *n.* female actor.

actual /'æktʃʊəl/ *–adj.* (usu. *attrib.*) **1** existing in fact; real. **2** current. *–n.* (in *pl.*) (also **physicals**) commodities that can be purchased and used, rather than goods traded on a futures contract, which are represented by documents. See also SPOT GOODS. [Latin: related to ACT]

actuality /͵æktʃʊ'ælɪtɪ/ *n.* (*pl.* **-ies**) **1** reality. **2** (in *pl.*) existing conditions.

actually /'æktʃʊəlɪ/ *adv.* **1** as a fact, really (*not actually very rich*). **2** strange as it may seem (*he actually refused!*).

♦ **actual total loss** *n.* complete destruction or loss of an insured item or one that has suffered an amount of damage that makes it cease to be the thing it originally was. For example, a motor car would be an actual total loss if it was destroyed, stolen and not recovered, or damaged so badly that the repair cost exceeded its insured value. See also CONSTRUCTIVE TOTAL LOSS.

♦ **actuary** /'æktʃʊərɪ/ *n.* (*pl.* **-ies**) statistician, esp. one employed by an insurance company to calculate probable lengths of life and advise insurers on the amounts that should be put aside to pay claims and the amount of premium to be charged for each type of risk. Actuaries also advise on the administration of pension funds; the government actuary is responsible for advising the government on National Insurance and other state pension schemes. See also INSTITUTE OF ACTUARIES. □ **actuarial** /-'eərɪəl/ *adj.* [Latin *actuarius* bookkeeper]

---

actuate /'æktʃʊ͵eɪt/ *v.* (**-ting**) **1** cause (a machine etc.) to move or function. **2** cause (a person) to act. [Latin]

acuity /ə'kju:ɪtɪ/ *n.* sharpness, acuteness. [medieval Latin: related to ACUTE]

acumen /'ækjʊmən/ *n.* keen insight or discernment. [Latin, = ACUTE thing]

acupuncture /'ækju:͵pʌŋktʃə(r)/ *n.* medical treatment using needles in parts of the body. □ **acupuncturist** *n.* [Latin *acu* with needle]

acute /ə'kju:t/ *–adj.* (**acuter, acutest**) **1** serious, severe (*acute hardship*). **2** (of senses etc.) keen, penetrating. **3** shrewd. **4** (of a disease) coming quickly to a crisis. **5** (of an angle) less than 90°. **6** (of a sound) high, shrill. *–n.* = ACUTE ACCENT. □ **acutely** *adv.* [Latin *acutus* pointed]

acute accent *n.* diacritical mark (´) placed over certain letters in French etc., esp. to show pronunciation.

ACV *abbr.* (also **a.c.v.**) actual cash value.

-acy *suffix* forming nouns of state or quality (*accuracy; piracy*), or an instance of it (*conspiracy; fallacy*). [French *-acie*, Latin *-acia*, *-atia*, Greek *-ateia*]

AD *abbr.* of the Christian era. [ANNO DOMINI]

A/D *abbr.* **1** (also **A/d, a.d.**) after date. **2** *Computing* analog–digital (conversion). See A/D CONVERTER.

ad *n. colloq.* advertisement. [abbreviation]

ad- *prefix* (altered or assimilated before some letters) implying motion or direction to, reduction or change into, addition, adherence, increase, or intensification. [Latin]

Ada /'eɪdə/ *n. propr. Computing* programming language developed at the behest of the US Department of Defense in the late 1970s. It was designed to be used in embedded systems, i.e. in situations where a computer forms part of a specialized system such as a cruise missile or a manufacturing plant. Ada is a large high-level language embodying concepts developed in earlier languages such as Pascal, but carrying them much further. There is now an international standard for Ada. [*Ada*, Lady Lovelace, name of first computer programmer]

adage /'ædɪdʒ/ *n.* traditional maxim, proverb. [French from Latin]

adagio /ə'dɑ:ʒɪəʊ/ *Mus. –adv.* & *adj.* in slow time. *–n.* (*pl.* **-s**) such a movement or passage. [Italian]

Adam /'ædəm/ *n.* the first man. □ **not know a person from Adam** be unable to recognize a person. [Hebrew, = man]

adamant /'ædəmənt/ *adj.* stubbornly resolute; unyielding. □ **adamantly** *adv.* [Greek *adamas adamant-* untameable]

Adam's apple *n.* projection of cartilage at the front of the neck.

Adam's Bridge chain of small islands stretching across the Palk Strait between NW Sri Lanka and SE India.

Adana /'ædənə/ city in S Turkey, the centre of a cotton-growing region; pop. (1990) 1 934 907.

adapt /ə'dæpt/ *v.* **1 a** (foll. by *to*) fit, adjust (one thing to another). **b** (foll. by *to, for*) make suitable for a purpose. **c** modify (esp. a text for broadcasting etc.). **2** (also *refl.*, usu. foll. by *to*) adjust to new conditions. □ **adaptable** *adj.* **adaptation** /͵ædæp'teɪʃ(ə)n/ *n.* [Latin: related to AD-, APT]

adaptor *n.* **1** device for making equipment compatible. **2** device for connecting several electrical plugs to one socket.

ADAS /'eɪdæs/ *abbr. Computing* automatic data acquisition system.

ADB *abbr.* **1** accidental death benefit. **2** African Development Bank. **3** Asian Development Bank.

ADC *abbr.* **1** advanced developing country (or countries). **2** = A/D CONVERTER. **3** *Computing* automated distribution control.

ADCCP *abbr. Computing* advanced data communication control procedure.

A/D converter *n.* (also **ADC**) device for sampling an analog signal and converting it into an equivalent digital signal, i.e. for converting a continuously varying signal, such as a voltage, into a series of binary values that are suitable for use by a computer. See also D/A CONVERTER.

add *v.* **1** join (one thing to another) as an increase or supplement. **2** put together (numbers) to find their total. **3** say further. □ **add in** include. **add up 1** find the total of. **2** (foll. by *to*) amount to. **3** *colloq.* make sense. [Latin *addo*]

addendum /ə'dendəm/ *n.* (*pl.* **-da**) **1** thing to be added. **2** material added at the end of a book.

adder *n.* small venomous snake, esp. the common viper. [Old English, originally *nadder*]

addict /'ædɪkt/ *n.* **1** person addicted, esp. to a drug. **2** *colloq.* devotee (*film addict*). [Latin: related to AD-, *dico* say]

addicted /ə'dɪktɪd/ *adj.* **1** (usu. foll. by *to*) dependent on a drug etc. as a habit. **2** devoted to an interest. □ **addiction** /ə'dɪkʃ(ə)n/ *n.*

addictive *adj.* causing addiction.

add-in card *n.* (also **add-in board**) = EXPANSION CARD.

Addis Ababa /ˌædɪs 'æbəbə/ capital of Ethiopia, situated at 2440 m (about 8000 ft); cement, tobacco, textiles, and shoes are produced, and the city houses the headquarters of the Organization of African Unity and the Economic Commission for Africa; pop. (est. 1989) 1 739 130.

addition /ə'dɪʃ(ə)n/ *n.* **1** adding. **2** person or thing added. □ **in addition** (often foll. by *to*) also, as well (as). [Latin: related to ADD]

additional *adj.* added, extra, supplementary. □ **additionally** *adv.*

♦ **additional personal allowance** *n.* income-tax allowance available, in addition to the personal allowance, to a single person who has a qualifying child living with him or her or to a married man with such a child and a totally incapacitated wife. A qualifying child is either under 16 at the beginning of the tax year or, if over 16, is in full-time education.

---

additive /'ædɪtɪv/ *n.* substance added to improve another, esp. to colour, flavour, or preserve food. [Latin: related to ADD]

addle /'æd(ə)l/ *v.* (**-ling**) **1** muddle, confuse. **2** (usu. as **addled** *adj.*) (of an egg) become rotten. [Old English, = filth]

address /ə'dres/ *–n.* **1 a** place where a person lives or an organization is situated. **b** particulars of this, esp. for postal purposes. **2** discourse to an audience. **3** *Computing* **a** number, label, or name used to specify a location within a computer memory or backing store, usu. to allow storage or retrieval of an item of information at this location. The reference to an address appears in a machine instruction. **b** means used to specify the location of a participant in a computer network. When a piece of information is to be carried on the network, the address is indicated by the sender and forms part of the transmitted signal. *–v.* **1** write postal directions on (an envelope etc.). **2** direct (remarks etc.). **3** speak or write to, esp. formally. **4** direct one's attention to. **5** *Golf* take aim at (the ball). □ **address oneself to 1** speak or write to. **2** attend to. [French: related to AD-, DIRECT]

addressee /ˌædre'siː/ *n.* person to whom a letter etc. is addressed.

addressing mode *n. Computing* method by which an address can be specified in the address part of a machine instruction.

adduce /ə'djuːs/ *v.* (**-cing**) cite as an instance, proof, or evidence. □ **adducible** *adj.* [Latin: related to AD-, *duco* lead]

ADEF *abbr.* French rating agency. [French *Agence d'Evaluation Financière*]

Adelaide /'ædəˌleɪd/ capital and chief port of South Australia, on the River Torrens; industries include car manufacturing, oil refining, electronics and textiles; pop. (est. 1994) 1 076 400.

Adélie Coast /æ'deɪlɪ/ (also **Adélie Land**, French **Terre Adélie**) French territory in Antarctica; site of a French research station.

Aden /'eɪd(ə)n/ chief port of Yemen, on the **Gulf of Aden** linking the Red Sea to the Indian Ocean, capital of South Yemen 1967–90; pop. (est. 1986) 270 000. Formerly under British rule, it is the country's commercial capital, with oil-refining and other industries.

adenoids /'ædɪˌnɔɪdz/ *n.pl.* area of enlarged lymphatic tissue between the nose and the throat, often hindering breathing in the young. □ **adenoidal** /-'nɔɪd(ə)l/ *adj.* [Greek *adēn* gland]

adept /'ædept/ *–adj.* (foll. by *at*, *in*) skilful. *–n.* adept person. [Latin *adipiscor adept-* attain]

adequate /'ædɪkwət/ *adj.* sufficient, satisfactory. □ **adequacy** *n.* **adequately** *adv.* [Latin: related to AD-, EQUATE]

à deux /ɑː 'dɜː/ *adv.* & *adj.* for or between two. [French]

ADF *abbr.* **1** *Austral. Finance* approved deposit fund. **2** Asian Development Fund.

adhere /əd'hɪə(r)/ *v.* (**-ring**) **1** (usu. foll. by *to*) stick fast to a substance etc. **2** (foll. by *to*) behave according to (a rule, undertaking, etc.). **3** (foll. by *to*) give allegiance. [Latin *haereo* stick]

adherent *–n.* supporter. *–adj.* sticking, adhering. □ **adherence** *n.*

adhesion /əd'hiːʒ(ə)n/ *n.* **1** adhering. **2** unnatural union of body tissues due to inflammation.

adhesive /əd'hiːsɪv/ *–adj.* sticky, causing adhesion. *–n.* adhesive substance. □ **adhesiveness** *n.*

ad hoc /æd 'hɒk/ *adv.* & *adj.* for one particular occasion or use. [Latin]

♦ **ad hocracy** /æd'hɒkrəsɪ/ *n.* form of management that is reluctant to make forward plans, preferring to respond to urgent problems as they arise.

---

adieu /ə'djuː/ *int.* goodbye. [French, = to God]

ad infinitum /æd ˌɪnfɪ'naɪtəm/ *adv.* without limit; for ever. [Latin]

adipose /'ædɪˌpəʊz/ *adj.* of fat; fatty (*adipose tissue*). □ **adiposity** /-'pɒsɪtɪ/ *n.* [Latin *adeps* fat]

adj. **1** adjourned. **2** *Insurance* & *Banking* etc. adjustment.

adjacent /ə'dʒeɪs(ə)nt/ *adj.* (often foll. by *to*) lying near; adjoining. □ **adjacency** *n.* [Latin *jaceo* lie]

adjective /'ædʒɪktɪv/ *n.* word used to describe or modify a noun or pronoun. □ **adjectival** /ˌædʒɪk'taɪv(ə)l/ *adj.* [Latin *jaceo* lie]

adjoin /ə'dʒɔɪn/ *v.* be next to and joined with. [Latin *jungo* join]

adjourn /ə'dʒɜːn/ *v.* **1** put off, postpone; break off (a meeting etc.) temporarily. **2** (of a meeting) break and disperse or (foll. by *to*) transfer to another place (*adjourned to the pub*). □ **adjournment** *n.* [Latin: related to AD-, *diurnum* day]

adjudge /ə'dʒʌdʒ/ *v.* (**-ging**) **1** pronounce judgement on (a matter). **2** pronounce or award judicially. □ **adjudgement** *n.* (also **adjudgment**). [Latin *judex* judge]

adjudicate /ə'dʒuːdɪˌkeɪt/ *v.* (**-ting**) **1** act as judge in a competition, court, etc. **2** adjudge. □ **adjudicative** *adj.* **adjudicator** *n.*

♦ **adjudication** /əˌdʒuːdɪ'keɪʃ(ə)n/ *n.* **1** judgement or decision of a court, esp. in bankruptcy proceedings. **2** assessment by the Commissioners of Inland Revenue of the amount of stamp-duty due on a document. A document sent for adjudication will either be stamped as having no duty to pay or the taxpayer will be advised how much is due. An appeal may be made to the High Court if the taxpayer disagrees with the adjudication.

adjunct /'ædʒʌŋkt/ *n.* **1** (foll. by *to*, *of*) subordinate or incidental thing. **2** *Gram.* word or phrase used to explain or amplify the predicate, subject, etc. [Latin: related to ADJOIN]

adjure /ə'dʒʊə(r)/ *v.* (**-ring**) (usu. foll. by *to* + infin.) beg or command. □ **adjuration** /ˌædʒʊə'reɪʃ(ə)n/ *n.* [Latin *adjuro* put to oath: related to JURY]

adjust /ə'dʒʌst/ *v.* **1** order or position; regulate; arrange. **2** (usu. foll. by *to*) become or make suited; adapt. **3** harmonize (discrepancies). **4** assess (loss or damages). □ **adjustable** *adj.* **adjustment** *n.* [Latin *juxta* near]

♦ **adjustable-rate mortgage** *n.* (also **ARM**) mortgage in which the interest rate is adjusted periodically in accordance with movements on the money market.

♦ **adjuster** *n.* person who adjusts. See LOSS ADJUSTER.

adjutant /'ædʒʊt(ə)nt/ *n.* **1 a** army officer assisting a superior in administrative duties. **b** assistant. **2** (in full **adjutant bird**) giant Indian stork. [Latin: related to AD-, *juvo jut-* help]

ADL *abbr. Computing* Ada design language.

ad lib /æd 'lɪb/ *–v.* (**-bb-**) improvise. *–adj.* improvised. *–adv.* as one pleases, to any desired extent. [abbreviation of Latin *ad libitum* according to pleasure]

ad. man. *abbr.* advertisement (or advertising) manager.

admin /'ædmɪn/ *n. colloq.* administration. [abbreviation]

administer /əd'mɪnɪstə(r)/ *v.* **1** manage (business affairs etc.). **2 a** deliver or dispense, esp. formally (a punishment, sacrament, etc.). **b** (usu. foll. by *to*) direct the taking of (an oath). [Latin: related to AD-, MINISTER]

administrate /əd'mɪnɪˌstreɪt/ *v.* (**-ting**) administer (esp. business affairs); act as an administrator.

administration /ədˌmɪnɪ'streɪʃ(ə)n/ *n.* **1** administering, esp. public affairs. **2** government in power.

♦ **administration order** *n.* **1** order made in a county court for the administration of the estate of a judgement debtor (see JUDGEMENT CREDITOR). The order normally requires the debtor to pay his or her debts by instalments; so long as this is done, the creditors referred to in the order cannot enforce their individual claims by other methods without the leave of the court. Administration orders are issued when the debtor has multiple debts but it is thought that bankruptcy can be avoided. **2** order of the court under the Insolvency Act (1986) made in relation to a company in financial difficulties with a view to securing its survival as a going concern or, failing that, to achieving a more favourable realization of its assets than would be possible on a liquidation. While the order is in force, the affairs of the company are managed by an administrator.

administrative /əd'mɪnɪstrətɪv/ *adj.* of the management of affairs.

♦ **administrative receiver** see RECEIVER 3b.

administrator /əd'mɪnɪˌstreɪtə(r)/ *n.* **1** manager of a business or public affairs. **2** person appointed by the courts, or by private arrangement, to manage the property of another. **3** person appointed by the courts to take charge of the affairs of a deceased person who died without making a will. This includes collection of assets, payment of debts, and distribution of the surplus to those persons entitled to inherit, according to the laws of intestacy.

admirable /'ædmərəb(ə)l/ *adj.* deserving admiration; excellent. □ **admirably** *adv.* [Latin: related to ADMIRE]

admiral /'ædmər(ə)l/ *n.* **1 a** commander-in-chief of a navy. **b** high-ranking naval officer, commander. **2** any of various butterflies. [Arabic: related to AMIR]

Admiralty *n.* (*pl.* **-ies**) (in full **Admiralty Board**) *hist.* committee superintending the Royal Navy.

Admiralty Islands island group of Papua New Guinea in the W Pacific Ocean; exports include copra and cocoa; pop. (1980) 25 844; chief town, Lorengau (on Manus island).

admiration /ˌædmə'reɪʃ(ə)n/ *n.* **1** respect; warm approval or pleasure. **2** object of this.

admire /əd'maɪə(r)/ *v.* (**-ring**) **1** regard with approval, respect, or satisfaction. **2** express admiration of. □ **admirer** *n.* **admiring** *adj.* [Latin: related to AD-, *miror* wonder at]

admissible /əd'mɪsɪb(ə)l/ *adj.* **1** (of an idea etc.) worth accepting or considering. **2** *Law* allowable as evidence. [Latin: related to ADMIT]

admission /əd'mɪʃ(ə)n/ *n.* **1** acknowledgement (*admission of error*). **2 a** process or right of entering. **b** charge for this (*admission is £5*).

admit /əd'mɪt/ *v.* (**-tt-**) **1** (often foll. by *to be*, or *that* + clause) acknowledge; recognize as true. **2** (foll. by *to*) confess to (a deed, fault, etc.). **3** allow (a person) entrance, access, etc. **4** take (a patient) into hospital. **5** (of an enclosed space) accommodate. **6** (foll. by *of*) allow as possible. [Latin *mitto miss-* send]

admittance *n.* admitting or being admitted, usu. to a place.

admittedly *adv.* as must be admitted.

admixture /æd'mɪkstʃə(r)/ *n.* **1** thing added, esp. a minor ingredient. **2** adding of this.

admonish /əd'mɒnɪʃ/ *v.* **1** reprove. **2** urge, advise. **3** (foll. by *of*) warn. □ **admonishment** *n.* **admonition** /ˌædmə'nɪʃ(ə)n/ *n.* **admonitory** *adj.* [Latin *moneo* warn]

ADN *international vehicle registration* Yemen.

ad nauseam /æd 'nɔːzɪˌæm/ *adv.* excessively; disgustingly. [Latin, = to sickness]

ADNOC *abbr.* Abu Dhabi National Oil Company.

ado /ə'duː/ *n.* fuss, busy activity; trouble. [from AT, DO[1]: originally in *much ado* = much to do]

adobe /ə'dəʊbɪ/ *n.* **1** sun-dried brick. **2** clay for making these. [Spanish]

adolescent /ˌædə'les(ə)nt/ *–adj.* between childhood and adulthood. *–n.* adolescent person. □ **adolescence** *n.* [Latin *adolesco* grow up]

Adonis /ə'dəʊnɪs/ *n.* handsome young man. [Latin, name of a youth loved by Venus]

adopt /ə'dɒpt/ *v.* **1** legally take (a person) into a relationship, esp. another's child as one's own. **2** choose (a course of action etc.). **3** take over (another's idea etc.). **4** choose as a candidate for office. **5** accept responsibility for the maintenance of (a road etc.). **6** accept or approve (a report, accounts, etc.). □ **adoption** *n.* [Latin: related to AD-, OPT]

adoptive *adj.* because of adoption (*adoptive son*). [Latin: related to ADOPT]

adorable /ə'dɔːrəb(ə)l/ *adj.* **1** deserving adoration. **2** *colloq.* delightful, charming.

adore /ə'dɔː(r)/ *v.* (**-ring**) **1** love intensely. **2** worship as divine. **3** *colloq.* like very much. □ **adoration** /ˌædə'reɪʃ(ə)n/ *n.* **adorer** *n.* [Latin *adoro* worship]

adorn /ə'dɔːn/ *v.* add beauty to; decorate. □ **adornment** *n.* [Latin: related to AD-, *orno* decorate]

ADPLAN /'ædˌplæn/ *abbr.* advanced planning.

ADPSO *abbr.* Association of Data Processing Service Organizations.

ADR *abbr.* **1** *Law* alternative dispute resolution. **2** = AMERICAN DEPOSITORY RECEIPT.

♦ **ad referendum** /æd refər'endəm/ *–adv.* for further consideration. *–adj.* denoting a contract that has been signed although minor points remain to be decided. [Latin]

adrenal /ə'driːn(ə)l/ *–adj.* **1** at or near the kidneys. **2** of the adrenal glands. *–n.* (in full **adrenal gland**) either of two ductless glands above the kidneys, secreting adrenalin. [from AD-, RENAL]

adrenalin /ə'drenəlɪn/ *n.* (also **adrenaline**) **1** stimulative hormone secreted by the adrenal glands. **2** this extracted or synthesized for medicinal use.

Adriatic /ˌeɪdrɪˈætɪk/ *–adj.* of the Adriatic Sea. *–n.* Adriatic Sea.

Adriatic Sea arm of the Mediterranean Sea lying between Italy and the Balkan Peninsula.

adrift /əˈdrɪft/ *adv.* & *predic.adj.* **1** drifting. **2** powerless; aimless. **3** *colloq.* **a** unfastened. **b** out of order, wrong (*plans went adrift*).

adroit /əˈdrɔɪt/ *adj.* dexterous, skilful. [French *à droit* according to right]

adsorb /ədˈsɔːb/ *v.* (usu. of a solid) hold (molecules of a gas or liquid etc.) to its surface, forming a thin film. □ **adsorbent** *adj.* & *n.* **adsorption** *n.* [from AD-, ABSORB]

ADST *abbr.* = APPROVED DEFERRED SHARE TRUST.

ADTS *abbr.* Automated Data and Telecommunications Service.

adulation /ˌædjʊˈleɪʃ(ə)n/ *n.* obsequious flattery. [Latin *adulor* fawn on]

adult /ˈædʌlt/ *–adj.* **1** mature, grown-up. **2** (*attrib.*) of or for adults (*adult education*). *–n.* adult person. □ **adulthood** *n.* [Latin *adolesco adultus* grow up]

adulterate /əˈdʌltəˌreɪt/ *v.* (**-ting**) debase (esp. foods) by adding other substances. □ **adulterant** *adj.* & *n.* **adulteration** /-ˈreɪʃ(ə)n/ *n.* [Latin *adultero* corrupt]

adulterer /əˈdʌltərə(r)/ *n.* (*fem.* **adulteress**) person who commits adultery.

adultery *n.* voluntary sexual intercourse between a married person and a person other than his or her spouse. □ **adulterous** *adj.*

adumbrate /ˈædʌmˌbreɪt/ *v.* (**-ting**) **1** indicate faintly or in outline. **2** foreshadow. **3** overshadow. □ **adumbration** /-ˈbreɪʃ(ə)n/ *n.* [Latin: related to AD-, *umbra* shade]

ad val. *abbr.* ad valorem.

♦ ***ad valorem*** /aed vəˈlɔːrəm/ *adj.* & *adv.* (of a tax or commission) calculated as a percentage of the total invoice value of goods rather than the number of items. For example, VAT is an *ad valorem* tax, calculated by adding a fixed percentage to an invoice value. [Latin, = according to value]

---

advance /ədˈvɑːns/ *–v.* (**-cing**) **1** move or put forward; progress. **2** pay or lend (money) beforehand. **3** promote (a person, cause, etc.). **4** present (a suggestion etc.). **5** (as **advanced** *adj.*) **a** well ahead. **b** socially progressive. *–n.* **1** going forward; progress. **2** prepayment; loan. **3** (in *pl.*) amorous approaches. **4** rise in price. *–attrib. adj.* done or supplied beforehand (*advance warning*). □ **advance on** approach threateningly. **in advance** ahead in place or time. [Latin: related to AB-, *ante* before]

♦ **advance corporation tax** *n.* (also **ACT**) feature of the imputation system of taxation that applied in the UK between 1972 and 1999, when it was abolished. For dividends (or other distributions) paid by UK companies in this period to their shareholders, the companies had to account to the Inland Revenue for advance corporation tax at a rate that would equal the basic rate of income tax on a figure consisting of the distribution plus the ACT. Thus, if the basic rate of income tax is 25%, the rate of ACT would be 1/3, so that a dividend of £750 with its ACT of 1/3 × £750 = £250 would total £1000, on which the tax at 25% would be £250 (the amount of the ACT). The ACT thus paid serves two purposes: (1) it is a payment on account of the individual shareholder's personal income tax on the dividend, and (2) for the paying company it constitutes a payment on account of that company's corporation tax for the period in which the dividend is paid. There are limits to the amount of ACT that may be set against corporation tax liabilities for any given period. Unrelieved ACT may also be carried backwards or forwards or surrendered to other companies. See also IMPUTATION SYSTEM OF TAXATION.

---

advanced level *n.* high level of GCE examination.

advancement *n.* promotion of a person, cause, or plan.

advantage /ədˈvɑːntɪdʒ/ *–n.* **1** beneficial feature. **2** benefit, profit. **3** (often foll. by *over*) superiority. **4** (in tennis) the next point after deuce. *–v.* (**-ging**) benefit, favour. □ **take advantage of 1** make good use of. **2** exploit, esp. unfairly. **3** *euphem.* seduce. □ **advantageous** /ˌædvənˈteɪdʒəs/ *adj.* [French: related to ADVANCE]

Advent /ˈædvent/ *n.* **1** season before Christmas. **2** coming of Christ. **3** (**advent**) important arrival. [Latin *adventus* from *venio* come]

Adventist *n.* member of a Christian sect believing in the imminent second coming of Christ.

adventitious /ˌædvenˈtɪʃəs/ *adj.* **1** accidental, casual. **2** added from outside. **3** *Biol.* formed accidentally or under unusual conditions. [Latin: related to ADVENT]

adventure /ədˈventʃə(r)/ *–n.* **1** unusual and exciting experience. **2** enterprise (*spirit of adventure*). **3** speculative commercial undertaking. *–v.* (**-ring**) dare, venture; engage in adventure. [Latin: related to ADVENT]

adventure playground *n.* playground with climbing-frames, building blocks, etc.

adventurer *n.* (*fem.* **adventuress**) **1** person who seeks adventure, esp. for personal gain or enjoyment. **2** financial speculator.

adventurous *adj.* venturesome, enterprising.

adverb /ˈædvɜːb/ *n.* word indicating manner, degree, circumstance, etc., used to modify an adjective, verb, or other adverb (e.g. *gently*, *quite*, *then*). □ **adverbial** /ədˈvɜːbɪəl/ *adj.* [Latin: related to AD-, *verbum* word, VERB]

adversary /ˈædvəsərɪ/ *n.* (*pl.* **-ies**) enemy, opponent. □ **adversarial** /-ˈseərɪəl/ *adj.*

adverse /ˈædvɜːs/ *adj.* unfavourable; harmful. □ **adversely** *adv.* [Latin: related to AD-, *verto vers-* turn]

♦ **adverse balance** *n.* deficit on an account, esp. a balance of payments account.

♦ **adverse selection** see MORAL HAZARD.

---

adversity /ədˈvɜːsɪtɪ/ *n.* misfortune, distress.

advert /ˈædvɜːt/ *n. colloq.* advertisement. [abbreviation]

advertise /ˈædvəˌtaɪz/ *v.* (**-sing**) **1** promote (goods or services) publicly to increase sales. See ADVERTISING. **2** make generally known. **3** (often foll. by *for*) seek by a notice in a newspaper etc. to buy, employ, sell, etc. [French *avertir*: related to ADVERSE]

advertisement /ədˈvɜːtɪsmənt/ *n.* **1** public announcement, esp. of goods etc. for sale or wanted, vacancies, etc. **2** advertising. [French *avertissement*: related to ADVERSE]

♦ **advertising** *n.* communication intended both to inform and persuade. The media that carry advertising range from the press, television, cinema, radio, and posters to company logos on apparel. Advertising creates awareness of a product, extensive advertising creates confidence in the product, and good advertising creates a desire to buy the product. This series of emotions is known mnemonically as AIDA (attention, interest, desire, action). Only half the money spent on advertising in the UK is accounted for by producers of goods and services; the remainder is spent by individuals (mostly on classified advertising), the government, charities, and marketing intermediaries (e.g. banks, institutions, and retailers). See ABOVE-THE-LINE 2; BELOW-THE-LINE 2; CLASSIFIED ADVERTISING; CONSUMER ADVERTISING; TRADE ADVERTISING.

♦ **advertising agency** *n.* business organization specializing in planning and handling advertising on behalf of clients. A full-service agency provides a range of services to clients, including booking advertising space, designing and producing advertisements, devising media schedules, commissioning research, providing sales promotion advice, and acting as a marketing consultant. The departments within an agency include research, planning, creative design, media bookings, production, and accounts. Most advertising agents work on the basis of a commission on the total sums spent by the client.

♦ **advertising allowance** *n.* price concession given by a manufacturer of a product to a retailer to allow him or her to pay for local advertising. It is an effective way of advertising both the product and the retail outlet.

◆ **Advertising Association** *n.* (also **AA**) organization representing the interests of advertisers, advertising agencies, and the media. Founded in 1926, it collects and assesses statistics on advertising expenditure as well as running an annual programme of seminars and training courses for people working in advertising, marketing, and sales promotion.

◆ **advertising brief** *n.* agreement between an advertising agency and a client on the objectives of an advertising campaign. It is important that the client knows exactly what the objectives are, helps to plan the overall strategy, and sets the budgets. Once the brief has been agreed the agency can prepare and evaluate the advertisements themselves and develop the media plan.

◆ **advertising rates** *n.pl.* basic charges made by the advertising media for use of their services or facilities.

◆ **Advertising Standards Authority** *n.* (also **ASA**) independent body set up and paid for by the advertising industry to ensure that its system of self-regulation works in the public interest. The ASA must have an independent chairman, who appoints individuals to serve on the council, two-thirds of which must be unconnected with the advertising industry. The ASA maintains close links with central and local government, consumer organizations, and trade associations. All advertising, apart from television and radio commercials, which are dealt with by the Independent Broadcasting Authority (IBA), must be legal, decent, honest, and truthful; it must adhere to the **British Code of Advertising Practice (BCAP)**, which provides the rules for all non-broadcast advertising. This applies not only to what is said in an advertisement, but also what is shown. The ASA controls the contents of advertisements by continuous monitoring of publications and by dealing with complaints from members of the public.

---

advice /əd'vaɪs/ *n.* **1** recommendation on how to act. **2** information given; news. **3** formal notice of a transaction. □ **as per advice** see PER.

◆ **advice note** *n.* note sent to a customer by a supplier of goods to advise the customer that an order has been fulfilled. The advice note may either accompany the goods or be sent separately, thus preceding the invoice and any delivery note. The advice note refers to a particular batch of goods, denoting them by their marks and numbers (if more than one package); it also details the date and method of dispatch.

---

advisable /əd'vaɪzəb(ə)l/ *adj.* to be recommended, expedient. □ **advisability** /-'bɪlɪtɪ/ *n.*

advise /əd'vaɪz/ *v.* (**-sing**) **1** (also *absol.*) give advice to. **2** recommend (*advised me to rest*). **3** (usu. foll. by *of*, or *that* + clause) inform. □ **advise fate** request by a collecting bank wishing to know, as soon as possible, whether a cheque will be paid on its receipt by the paying bank. The cheque is sent direct and not through a clearing-house, asking that its fate should be advised immediately. [Latin: related to AD-, *video vis-* see]

advisedly /əd'vaɪzɪdlɪ/ *adv.* after due consideration; deliberately.

adviser *n.* (also **advisor**) person who advises, esp. officially.

■ **Usage** The variant *advisor* is fairly common, but is considered incorrect by many people.

advisory *adj.* giving advice (*advisory body*).

◆ **Advisory, Conciliation, and Arbitration Service** *n.* (also **ACAS**) UK government body set up in 1975 to mediate in industrial disputes in both the public and private sectors. Its findings are not binding on either side but carry considerable weight with the government. It consists of a panel of ten members, three each appointed by the TUC and the CBI, who elect three academics and an independent chairman. It does not, itself, carry out arbitrations but may recommend an arbitration to be held by other bodies.

---

advocaat /ˌædvə'kɑːt/ *n.* liqueur of eggs, sugar, and brandy. [Dutch, = ADVOCATE]

advocacy /'ædvəkəsɪ/ *n.* support or argument for a cause, policy, etc.

advocate *–n.* /'ædvəkət/ **1** (foll. by *of*) person who supports or speaks in favour. **2** person who pleads for another, esp. in a lawcourt. *–v.* /'ædvəˌkeɪt/ (**-ting**) recommend by argument. [Latin: related to AD-, *voco* call]

advt. *abbr.* advertisement.

ADX *abbr.* **1** *Computing* automatic data exchange. **2** *Telecom.* automatic digital exchange.

adze /ædz/ *n.* (*US* **adz**) tool like an axe, with an arched blade at right angles to the handle. [Old English]

AE *–abbr.* account executive. *–n. Insurance* (in Lloyd's Register) third-class ship.

AEA *abbr.* Atomic Energy Authority.

AEC *abbr.* **1** *Insurance* additional extended coverage. **2** (in the US) Atomic Energy Commission (or Council).

AED *abbr. Computing* Algol Extended for Design.

AEEU *abbr.* Amalgamated Engineering and Electrical Union.

AEG *abbr.* (German) Allgemeine Elektrizitäts-Gesellschaft (= General Electric Company).

Aegean /ɪ'dʒiːən/ *–adj.* of the Aegean Sea. *–n.* Aegean Sea.

Aegean Islands group of islands in the Aegean Sea forming a region of Greece. The principal islands of the group are Chios (Khios), Samos, Lesbos, the Cyclades, and the Dodecanese; pop. (est. 1991) 455 763.

Aegean Sea part of the Mediterranean lying between Greece and Turkey.

aegis /'iːdʒɪs/ *n.* protection; support. [Greek *aigis* shield of Zeus or Athene]

AEI *abbr.* **1** American Express International. **2** Associated Electrical Industries.

AELE *abbr.* (French) Association européenne de libre-échange (= European Free Trade Association).

aeolian harp /iː'əʊlɪən/ *n.* stringed instrument or toy sounding when the wind passes through it. [Latin *Aeolus* wind-god, from Greek]

Aeolian Islands /iː'əʊlɪən/ see LIPARI ISLANDS.

aeon /'iːɒn/ *n.* (also **eon**) **1** long or indefinite period. **2** an age. [Latin from Greek]

aerate /'eəreɪt/ *v.* (**-ting**) **1** charge (a liquid) with carbon dioxide. **2** expose to air. □ **aeration** /-'reɪʃ(ə)n/ *n.* [Latin *aer* AIR]

aerial /'eərɪəl/ *–n.* device for transmitting or receiving radio waves. *–adj.* **1** by or from the air; involving aircraft (*aerial attack*). **2** existing in the air. **3** of or like air. [Greek: related to AIR]

aero- *comb. form* air; aircraft. [Greek *aero-* from *aēr* air]

aerobatics /ˌeərə'bætɪks/ *n.pl.* **1** spectacular flying of aircraft, esp. to entertain. **2** (as *sing.*) performance of these. [from AERO-, after ACROBATICS]

aerobics /eə'rəʊbɪks/ *n.pl.* vigorous exercises designed to increase oxygen intake. □ **aerobic** *adj.* [from AERO-, Greek *bios* life]

aerodrome /'eərəˌdrəʊm/ *n.* small airport or airfield. [from AERO-, Greek *dromos* course]

aerodynamics /ˌeərəʊdaɪ'næmɪks/ *n.pl.* (usu. treated as *sing.*) dynamics of solid bodies moving through air. □ **aerodynamic** *adj.*

aerofoil /'eərəˌfɔɪl/ *n.* structure with curved surfaces (e.g. a wing, fin, or tailplane) designed to give lift in flight.

aeronautics /ˌeərəʊ'nɔːtɪks/ *n.pl.* (usu. treated as *sing.*) science or practice of motion in the air. □ **aeronautic** *adj.* **aeronautical** *adj.* [from AERO-, NAUTICAL]

aeroplane /'eərəˌpleɪn/ *n.* powered heavier-than-air flying vehicle with fixed wings. [French: related to AERO-, PLANE[1]]

aerosol /'eərəˌsɒl/ *n.* **1** pressurized container releasing a substance as a fine spray. **2** system of minute particles suspended in gas (e.g. fog or smoke). [from AERO-, SOL]

aerospace /ˈeərəʊˌspeɪs/ *n.* **1** earth's atmosphere and outer space. **2** aviation in this.

aesthete /ˈiːsθiːt/ *n.* person who has or professes a special appreciation of beauty. [Greek *aisthanomai* perceive]

aesthetic /iːsˈθetɪk/ *–adj.* **1** of or sensitive to beauty. **2** artistic, tasteful. *–n.* (in *pl.*) philosophy of beauty, esp. in art. □ **aesthetically** *adv.* **aestheticism** /-ˌsɪz(ə)m/ *n.*

aetiology /ˌiːtɪˈɒlədʒɪ/ *n.* (*US* **etiology**) study of causation or of the causes of disease. □ **aetiological** /-əˈlɒdʒɪk(ə)l/ *adj.* [Greek *aitia* cause]

AF *–abbr.* audio frequency. *–symb.* afghani. *–airline flight code* Air France.

A/F *abbr.* as found (in auction catalogues).

Af *symb.* Aruban florin.

a.f. *abbr.* advanced freight.

AFA *abbr. Scot.* Associate of the Faculty of Actuaries.

afar /əˈfɑː(r)/ *adv.* at or to a distance.

affable /ˈæfəb(ə)l/ *adj.* **1** friendly. **2** courteous. □ **affability** /-ˈbɪlɪtɪ/ *n.* **affably** *adv.* [Latin *affabilis*]

affair /əˈfeə(r)/ *n.* **1** matter, concern, or matter to be attended to (*that is my affair*). **2 a** celebrated or notorious happening. **b** *colloq.* thing or event (*puzzling affair*). **3** = LOVE AFFAIR. **4** (in *pl.*) public or private business. [French *à faire* to do]

affect /əˈfekt/ *v.* **1 a** produce an effect on. **b** (of disease etc.) attack. **2** move emotionally. **3** pretend (*affected ignorance*). **4** pose as or use for effect (*affects the aesthete; affects fancy hats*). □ **affecting** *adj.* **affectingly** *adv.* [Latin *afficio affect-* influence]

■ **Usage** This word should not be confused with *effect*, meaning 'to bring about'. Note also that *effect* is used as a noun as well as a verb.

affectation /ˌæfekˈteɪʃ(ə)n/ *n.* **1** artificial manner. **2** (foll. by *of*) studied display. **3** pretence.

affected /əˈfektɪd/ *adj.* **1** pretended, artificial. **2** full of affectation.

affection /əˈfekʃ(ə)n/ *n.* **1** goodwill, fond feeling. **2** disease; diseased condition.

affectionate /əˈfekʃənət/ *adj.* loving, fond. □ **affectionately** *adv.*

♦ **affidavit** /ˌæfɪˈdeɪvɪt/ *n.* sworn written statement by a person (the deponent), who signs it in the presence of a commissioner for oaths. It sets out facts known to the deponent. In certain cases, particularly proceedings in the Chancery division of the High Court, evidence may be taken by affidavit rather than by the witness appearing in person. [Latin, = has stated on oath]

affiliate /əˈfɪlɪˌeɪt/ *–v.* (**-ting**) (foll. by *to, with*) attach, adopt, or connect as a member or branch. *–n.* affiliated person etc. [Latin: related to FILIAL]

affiliation /əˌfɪlɪˈeɪʃ(ə)n/ *n.* affiliating or being affiliated.

affiliation order *n.* legal order against the supposed father of an illegitimate child for support.

affinity /əˈfɪnɪtɪ/ *n.* (*pl.* **-ies**) **1** liking or attraction; feeling of kinship. **2** relationship, esp. by marriage. **3** similarity of structure or character suggesting a relationship. **4** *Chem.* the tendency of certain substances to combine with others. [Latin *finis* border]

♦ **affinity card** *n.* credit card issued to an affinity group, such as the members of a club or college, in which the bank or credit-card company donates a small percentage of the money spent using the card to a specified charity.

affirm /əˈfɜːm/ *v.* **1** assert, state as a fact. **2** *Law* make a solemn declaration in place of an oath. □ **affirmation** /ˌæfəˈmeɪʃ(ə)n/ *n.* [Latin: related to FIRM[1]]

♦ **affirmation of contract** *n.* treating a contract as being valid, rather than exercising a right to rescind it for a good reason. Affirmation can only occur if it takes place with full knowledge of the facts. It may take the form of a declaration of intention or be inferred from such conduct as selling goods purchased under the contract or allowing time to pass without seeking a remedy.

affirmative /əˈfɜːmətɪv/ *–adj.* affirming; expressing approval. *–n.* affirmative statement or word etc.

affix *–v.* /əˈfɪks/ **1** attach, fasten. **2** add in writing. *–n.* /ˈæfɪks/ **1** addition. **2** *Gram.* prefix or suffix. [Latin: related to FIX]

afflict /əˈflɪkt/ *v.* distress physically or mentally. [Latin *fligo flict-* strike down]

affliction /əˈflɪkʃ(ə)n/ *n.* **1** distress, suffering. **2** cause of this.

affluent /ˈæflʊənt/ *adj.* wealthy, rich. □ **affluence** *n.* [Latin: related to FLUENT]

afford /əˈfɔːd/ *v.* **1** (prec. by *can* or *be able to*) **a** have enough money, time, etc., for; be able to spare. **b** be in a position (*can't afford to be critical*). **2** provide (*affords a view of the sea*). [Old English *ge-* prefix implying completeness, FORTH]

afforest /əˈfɒrɪst/ *v.* **1** convert into forest. **2** plant with trees. □ **afforestation** /-ˈsteɪʃ(ə)n/ *n.* [Latin: related to FOREST]

affray /əˈfreɪ/ *n.* breach of the peace by fighting or rioting in public. [Anglo-French = 'remove from peace']

affront /əˈfrʌnt/ *–n.* open insult. *–v.* insult openly; offend, embarrass. [Latin: related to FRONT]

AFG *international vehicle registration* Afghanistan.

Afghanistan /æfˈgænɪˌstæn/, **Republic of** mountainous country in central Asia, bordered by Iran to the W, Pakistan to the S and E, and Turkmenistan, Uzbekistan, and Tajikistan to the N. The principal industries are agriculture and sheep-raising; exports include karakul lambskins, dried fruit and nuts, carpets and rugs, and raw cotton. In recent years political instability has led to a deepening economic crisis, with rising inflation and grave food shortages. Exportation of natural gas, formerly Afghanistan's main export, was halted in 1989 and has not been resumed.
History. Part of the Indian Mogul empire, Afghanistan became independent in the mid-18th century but in the 19th and early 20th centuries became the focal point for conflicting Russian and British interests on the Northwest Frontier and came under British control. Independence was regained in 1921 and a monarchy established in 1926. Afghanistan became progressively politically unstable in the 1970s: the monarchy was overthrown in 1973 and the country was invaded by the Soviets in December 1979. A puppet regime was set up in Kabul but large parts of the country remained disaffected; the occupying Soviet forces were subjected to continuing attacks by Afghan guerrillas (mujahidin) and finally withdrew in 1988–9, but the conflict persisted. In 1992 the mujahidin overthrew the government and an Islamic Council was established; meanwhile fighting continued between rival mujahidin factions. In 1995 the Taliban militia took control of southern Afghanistan and the following year took control of Kabul, which was subsequently beseiged by a coalition of anti-Taliban forces. President, Burhanuddin Rabbani; capital, Kabul.

languages	Pashto, Dari (a form of Persian)
currency	afghani (AF) of 100 puls
pop. (est. 1994)	20 500 000
GNP (1988)	US $ 3.1B
literacy	44.1% (m); 13.9% (f)
life expectancy	45

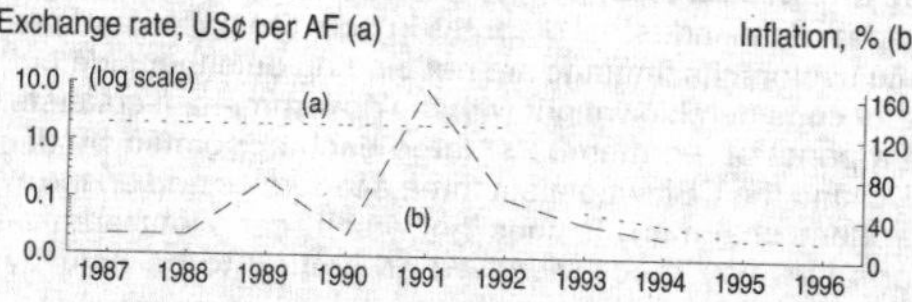

Afghan /'æfgæn/ *–n.* **1 a** native or national of Afghanistan. **b** person of Afghan descent. **2** official language of Afghanistan. *–adj.* of Afghanistan. [Pashto]

Afghan hound *n.* tall hunting dog with long silky hair.

afghani /'æfgɑːnɪ/ *n.* standard monetary unit of Afghanistan.

AFIA *abbr.* **1** American Foreign Insurance Association. **2** (in Australia) Associate of the Federal Institute of Accountants.

aficionado /əˌfɪsjə'nɑːdəʊ/ *n.* (*pl.* **-s**) devotee of a sport or pastime. [Spanish]

afield /ə'fiːld/ *adv.* to or at a distance (esp. *far afield*). [Old English: related to A[2]]

AFIMA *abbr.* Associate Fellow of the Institute of Mathematics and its Applications.

aflame /ə'fleɪm/ *adv.* & *predic.adj.* **1** in flames. **2** very excited.

AFL-CIO *abbr.* American Federation of Labor and Congress of Industrial Organizations.

afloat /ə'fləʊt/ *adv.* & *predic.adj.* **1** floating. **2 a** at sea. **b** (of goods, esp. commodities) on a ship from their port of origin to a specified port of destination. The price of goods afloat will usu. be between the price of spot goods and goods for immediate shipment from origin. **3** out of debt or difficulty. **4** current. [Old English: related to A[2]]

AFNOR /'æfˌnɔː(r)/ *abbr.* the standards organization of France. [French *Association Française de Normalisation*]

afoot /ə'fʊt/ *adv.* & *predic.adj.* in operation; progressing.

afore /ə'fɔː(r)/ *prep.* & *adv. archaic* before; previously; in front (of). [Old English: related to A[2]]

afore- *comb. form* before, previously (*aforementioned*; *aforesaid*).

aforethought *adj.* premeditated (following a noun: *malice aforethought*).

AFR *abbr.* accident frequency rate (in industry).

afraid /ə'freɪd/ *predic. adj.* alarmed, frightened. □ **be afraid** *colloq.* politely regret (*I'm afraid we're late*). [originally past part. of AFFRAY]

AFRASEC *abbr.* /'æfrəˌsek/ Afro-Asian Organization for Economic Cooperation.

afresh /ə'freʃ/ *adv.* anew; with a fresh beginning. [earlier *of fresh*]

Africa /'æfrɪkə/ second-largest of the world's continents, surrounded by sea except where the isthmus of Suez joins it to Asia. Much of the continent remained unknown to the outside world until voyages of discovery along the coast between the 15th and 17th centuries; the interior was explored and partitioned by European nations in the second half of the 19th century. Since the Second World War most of the former colonies have secured their independence.

African *–n.* **1** native (esp. dark-skinned) of Africa. **2** person of African descent. *–adj.* of Africa. [Latin]

African elephant *n.* the elephant of Africa, larger than that of India.

African violet *n.* house-plant with velvety leaves and blue, purple, or pink flowers.

Afrikaans /ˌæfrɪ'kɑːns/ *n.* language derived from Dutch, used in South Africa. [Dutch, = 'African']

Afrikaner /ˌæfrɪ'kɑːnə(r)/ *n.* Afrikaans-speaking White person in South Africa, esp. of Dutch descent.

Afro /'æfrəʊ/ *–adj.* (of hair) tightly-curled and bushy. *–n.* (*pl.* **-s**) Afro hairstyle.

Afro- *comb. form* African.

Afro-American /ˌæfrəʊə'merɪkən/ *–adj.* of American Blacks or their culture. *–n.* American Black.

Afro-Caribbean /ˌæfrəʊˌkærɪ'biːən/ *–n.* Caribbean person of African descent. *–adj.* of Afro-Caribbeans.

AFSBO *abbr.* American Federation of Small Business Organizations.

aft /ɑːft/ *adv. Naut.* & *Aeron.* at or towards the stern or tail. [earlier *baft*]

after /'ɑːftə(r)/ *–prep.* **1** following in time; later than (*after a week*). **2** in view of, in spite of (*after what you did what do you expect?*; *after all my efforts I still lost*). **3** behind (*shut the door after you*). **4** in pursuit or quest of (*run after them*). **5** about, concerning (*asked after her*). **6** in allusion to (*named after the prince*). **7** in imitation of (*a painting after Rubens*). **8** next in importance to (*best one after mine*). *–conj.* later than (*left after they arrived*). *–adv.* **1** later (*soon after*). **2** behind (*followed on after*). *–adj.* **1** later, following (*in after years*). **2** *Naut.* nearer the stern (*after cabins*). □ **after all** in spite of everything (*after all, what does it matter?*). **after date** see DATE. **after one's own heart** to one's taste. **after sight** see SIGHT. [Old English]

afterbirth *n.* placenta etc. discharged from the womb after childbirth.

after-care *n.* attention after leaving hospital etc.

after-effect *n.* delayed effect following an accident, trauma, etc.

afterglow *n.* glow remaining after its source has disappeared.

♦ **after-hours deals** *n.pl.* transactions made on the London Stock Exchange after its official close at the end of its mandatory quote period. Such deals are recorded as part of the following day's trading and are therefore also known as **early bargains**.

---

afterlife *n.* life after death.

aftermath /'ɑːftəˌmæθ/ *n.* **1** consequences, esp. unpleasant (*aftermath of war*). **2** new grass growing after mowing. [from AFTER, *math* mowing]

afternoon /ˌɑːftə'nuːn/ *n.* time from noon or lunch-time to evening.

afterpains *n.pl.* pains caused by contraction of the womb after childbirth.

afters *n.pl. colloq.* = DESSERT 1.

♦ **after-sales service** *n.* maintenance of a product by its manufacturer or the manufacturer's agent after it has been purchased. This often takes the form of a guarantee (see WARRANTY 3), which is effective for a stated period during which the service is free in respect of both parts and labour, followed by a maintenance contract for which the buyer of the product has to pay. Efficient and effective after-sales service is an essential component of good marketing policy, esp. for such consumer durables as cars and computers; in the case of exported goods it is of overriding importance.

---

aftershave *n.* lotion used after shaving.

aftertaste *n.* taste after eating or drinking.

afterthought *n.* thing thought of or added later.

afterwards /'ɑːftəwədz/ *adv.* (*US* **afterward**) later, subsequently. [Old English: related to AFTER, -WARD]

AFTR *abbr.* American Federal Tax Reports.

AG *abbr.* **1** (German) Aktiengesellschaft (= public limited company). **2** Attorney-General.

Ag *symb.* silver. [Latin *argentum*]

ag. *abbr.* **1** agent. **2** agreement.

Agadir /ˌægə'dɪə(r)/ seaport on the Atlantic coast of Morocco; industries include tourism, fishing, and fish canning; pop. (est. 1993) 137 000.

again /ə'gen/ *adv.* **1** another time; once more. **2** as previously (*home again*; *well again*). **3** in addition (*as much again*). **4** further, besides (*again, what about you?*). **5** on the other hand (*I might, and again I might not*). □ **again and again** repeatedly. [Old English]

against /ə'genst/ *prep.* **1** in opposition to (*fight against crime*). **2** into collision or in contact with (*lean against the wall*). **3** to the disadvantage of (*my age is against me*). **4** in contrast to (*against a dark background*). **5** in anticipation of (*against his coming*; *against the cold*). **6** as a compensating factor to (*income against expenditure*). **7** in return for (*issued against payment of the fee*). □ **against the grain** see GRAIN. **against time** see TIME. [from AGAIN, with inflectional *-s*]

agape /ə'geɪp/ *predic. adj.* gaping, open-mouthed. [from A[2]]

agaric /'ægərɪk/ *n.* fungus with a cap and stalk, e.g. the common mushroom. [Greek *agarikon*]

agate /'ægət/ *n.* hard usu. streaked chalcedony. [Greek *akhatēs*]

agave /ə'geɪvɪ/ *n.* plant with rosettes of narrow spiny leaves and flowers on tall stem. [*Agave*, name of a woman in Greek mythology]

age –*n.* **1** length of time that a person or thing has existed. **2 a** *colloq.* (often in *pl.*) a long time (*waited for ages*). **b** distinct historical period (*Bronze Age*). **3** old age. –*v.* (**ageing**) **1** show or cause to show signs of advancing age. **2** grow old. **3** mature. □ **come of age** reach adult status (esp. *Law* at 18, formerly 21). [Latin *aetas*]

-age *suffix* forming nouns denoting: **1** action (*breakage*). **2** condition (*bondage*). **3** aggregate or number (*coverage; acreage*). **4** cost (*postage*). **5** result (*wreckage*). **6** place or abode (*anchorage; orphanage*). [Latin *-aticus*]

♦ **age allowance** *n.* additional personal allowance set against income for income-tax purposes in the UK for both single people and married couples over 65. At the age of 75 both the personal allowance and the married couple's allowance are increased. See also PERSONAL ALLOWANCES.

♦ **age analysis** *n.* a list of the amounts owing to a business, often produced monthly, analysing the age of the debts.

---

aged *adj.* **1** /eɪdʒd/ (*predic.*) of the age of (*aged 3*). **2** /'eɪdʒɪd/ old.

ageism *n.* prejudice or discrimination on grounds of age. □ **ageist** *adj.* & *n.*

ageless *adj.* **1** never growing or appearing old. **2** eternal.

agelong *adj.* existing for a very long time.

agency /'eɪdʒənsɪ/ *n.* (*pl.* **-ies**) **1 a** business or premises of an agent. **b** relationship between an agent and his or her principal. **2** action; intervention (*free agency; by the agency of God*). [Latin: related to ACT]

agenda /ə'dʒendə/ *n.* (*pl.* **-s**) **1** list of items to be considered at a meeting. For the annual general meeting or an extraordinary general meeting of a company, the agenda is usu. sent to shareholders in advance. See also ORDER OF BUSINESS. **2** things to be done.

agent /'eɪdʒ(ə)nt/ *n.* **1** person who acts on behalf of another (the principal). In business, an agent is often appointed to negotiate a contract between the principal and a third party. If an agent discloses the principal's name (or at least the existence of a principal) to the third party with whom he or she is dealing, the agent is not normally liable on the contract. An undisclosed principal, whose existence is not revealed by the agent to a third party, may still be liable on the contract, but in such cases the agent is also liable. A general agent is one who has authority to act for his or her principal in all business of a particular kind, or who acts for the principal in the course of the agent's usual business or profession. A **special agent** is authorized to act only for a special purpose that is not in the ordinary course of the agent's business or profession. **2** spy. **3** person or thing that exerts power or produces an effect.

♦ ***agent de change*** /ˌɑːʒɑ̃ də 'ʃɑ̃dz/ *n.* (*pl.* ***agents de change*** pronunc. same) stockbroker on the Paris Bourse (see BOURSE 1). [French]

---

agent provocateur /ˌɑːʒɑ̃ prəˌvɒkə'tɜː(r)/ *n.* (*pl.* ***agents provocateurs*** pronunc. same) person used to tempt suspected offenders to self-incriminating action. [French, = provocative agent]

age of consent *n.* **1** age at which consent to sexual intercourse is valid in law. **2** age at which a person can enter a legally binding contract. For commercial purposes, it is set at 18 years by the Family Law Reform Act (1969). A contract entered into by a minor (i.e. someone below the age of consent) is not always capable of being enforced.

age-old *adj.* very long-standing.

agglomerate –*v.* (**-ting**) /ə'glɒməˌreɪt/ collect into a mass. –*n.* /ə'glɒmərət/ mass, esp. of fused volcanic fragments. –*adj.* /ə'glɒmərət/ collected into a mass. □ **agglomeration** /-'reɪʃ(ə)n/ *n.* [Latin *glomus -meris* ball]

agglutinate /ə'gluːtɪˌneɪt/ *v.* (**-ting**) stick as with glue. □ **agglutination** /-'neɪʃ(ə)n/ *n.* **agglutinative** /-nətɪv/ *adj.* [Latin: related to GLUTEN]

aggrandize /ə'grændaɪz/ *v.* (also **-ise**) (**-zing** or **-sing**) **1** increase the power, rank, or wealth of. **2** make seem greater. □ **aggrandizement** /-dɪzmənt/ *n.* [French: related to GRAND]

aggravate /'ægrəˌveɪt/ *v.* (**-ting**) **1** make worse or more serious. **2** annoy. □ **aggravation** /-'veɪʃ(ə)n/ *n.* [Latin *gravis* heavy]

■ **Usage** The use of *aggravate* in sense 2 is regarded by some people as incorrect, but it is common in informal use.

aggregate –*n.* /'ægrɪgət/ **1** sum total, amount assembled. **2** crushed stone etc. used in making concrete. **3** rock formed of a mass of different particles or minerals. –*adj.* /'ægrɪgət/ combined, collective, total. –*v.* /'ægrɪˌgeɪt/ (**-ting**) **1** collect, combine into one mass. **2** *colloq.* amount to. **3** unite. □ **in the aggregate** as a whole. □ **aggregation** /-'geɪʃ(ə)n/ *n.* **aggregative** /'ægrɪˌgeɪtɪv/ *adj.* [Latin *grex greg-* flock]

♦ **aggregate demand** *n.* sum of demands for all the goods and services in an economy at any particular time. Made a central concept in macroeconomics by Keynes, it is usu. defined as the sum of consumers' expenditure (see CONSUMPTION 6), investment, government expenditure, and imports less exports. Keynesian theory (see KEYNESIANISM) proposes that the free market will not always maintain a sufficient level of aggregate demand to ensure full employment and that at such times the government should seek to stimulate aggregate demand (see PUMP-PRIMING). The feasibility of such policies has been questioned. See also AGGREGATE SUPPLY.

♦ **aggregate supply** *n.* total supply of all the goods and services in an economy. Since the 1970s many economists have suggested that governments should concentrate on establishing conditions to encourage the supply of goods and services rather than focusing on aggregate demand. This could entail deregulation, encouraging competition, and removing restrictive practices in the labour market. See also AGGREGATE DEMAND.

---

aggression /ə'greʃ(ə)n/ *n.* **1** unprovoked attacking or attack. **2** hostile or destructive behaviour. [Latin *gradior gress-* walk]

aggressive /ə'gresɪv/ *adj.* **1** given to aggression; hostile. **2** forceful, self-assertive. □ **aggressively** *adv.*

aggressor *n.* person or party that attacks without provocation.

aggrieved /ə'griːvd/ *adj.* having a grievance. [French: related to GRIEF]

aggro /'ægrəʊ/ *n. slang* **1** aggressive hostility. **2** trouble, difficulty. [abbreviation of *aggravation* or *aggression*]

aghast /ə'gɑːst/ *predic. adj.* filled with dismay or consternation. [past part. of obsolete *(a)gast* frighten]

Aghios Nikolaos /'aɪɒs ˌnɪkɒ'laɪɒs/ (Greek **Ayios Nikólaos**) holiday resort in Greece, on the N coast of Crete E of Heraklion; pop. (1981) 8100.

AGI *abbr. US* adjusted gross income (on income-tax returns).

agile /'ædʒaɪl/ *adj.* quick-moving, nimble, active. □ **agility** /ə'dʒɪlɪtɪ/ *n.* [Latin *agilis*: related to ACT]

♦ **agio** /'ædʒɪəʊ/ *n.* **1** fee charged by a bank for changing money. **2** difference between a bank's lending and borrowing rates. [Italian, = 'ease']

AGIP *abbr.* (Italian) Agenzia Generale Italiana Petroli, Italian national oil company.

agitate /'ædʒɪˌteɪt/ *v.* (**-ting**) **1** disturb or excite (a person or feelings). **2** (often foll. by *for, against*) campaign, esp. politically (*agitated for tax reform*). **3** shake briskly. □ **agitation** /-'teɪʃ(ə)n/ *n.* **agitator** *n.* [Latin *agito*: related to ACT]

aglow /ə'gləʊ/ *predic. adj.* glowing.

AGM *abbr.* = ANNUAL GENERAL MEETING.

agnail /'ægneɪl/ *n.* piece of torn skin at the root of a fingernail; resulting soreness. [Old English, = tight (metal) nail, hard excrescence in flesh]

◆ **Agnelli** /'ægneli:/, **Giovanni** (1921–) Italian industrialist, grandson of Agnelli Giovanni — founder member of the Turin-based car manufacturer F.I.A.T. — and vice-chairman (1945–63), managing director (1963–66), and chairman (1966–96) of F.I.A.T. The 80 or so members of the Agnelli family controlled 32% of F.I.A.T. and together held net assets of $3.8 billion in 1997. Giovanni Agnelli was appointed a Senator for Life in 1991.

---

agnostic /æg'nɒstɪk/ *–n.* person who believes that the existence of God is not provable. *–adj.* of agnosticism. □ **agnosticism** /-ˌsɪz(ə)m/ *n.* [from A-, GNOSTIC]

ago /ə'gəʊ/ *adv.* (prec. by duration) earlier, in the past. [originally *agone* = gone by]

ago. *abbr.* (Italian) agosto (= August).

agog /ə'gɒg/ *predic. adj.* eager, expectant. [French *gogue* fun]

agonize /'ægəˌnaɪz/ *v.* (also **-ise**) (**-zing** or **-sing**) **1** undergo (esp. mental) anguish; suffer or cause to suffer agony. **2** (as **agonized** *adj.*) expressing agony (*an agonized look*).

agony /'ægənɪ/ *n.* (*pl.* **-ies**) **1** extreme mental or physical suffering. **2** severe struggle. [Greek *agōn* struggle]

agony aunt *n. colloq.* person (esp. a woman) who answers letters in an agony column.

agony column *n. colloq.* **1** column in a magazine etc. offering personal advice to correspondents. **2** = PERSONAL COLUMN.

agoraphobia /ˌægərə'fəʊbɪə/ *n.* abnormal fear of open spaces or public places. □ **agoraphobic** *adj.* & *n.* [Greek *agora* market-place]

Agra /'ɑːgrə/ city in India, in Uttar Pradesh, capital of the Mogul emperors from the early 16th century to the mid-17th century; pop. (1991) 892 000. A major commercial, industrial, and communications centre, it is the site of the Taj Mahal.

agrarian /ə'greərɪən/ *–adj.* **1** of the land or its cultivation. **2** of landed property. *–n.* advocate of the redistribution of land. [Latin *ager* field]

agree /ə'griː/ *v.* (**-ees, -eed, -eeing**) **1** hold the same opinion (*I agree with you*). **2** consent (*agreed to go*). **3** (often foll. by *with*) **a** become or be in harmony. **b** suit (*fish didn't agree with him*). **c** *Gram.* have the same number, gender, case, or person as. **4** reach agreement about (*agreed a price*). **5** (foll. by *on*) decide mutually on (*agreed on a compromise*). □ **be agreed** be of one opinion. [Latin: related to AD-, *gratus* pleasing]

agreeable *adj.* **1** pleasing, pleasant. **2** willing to agree. □ **agreeably** *adv.*

agreement *n.* **1** act or state of agreeing. **2** arrangement or contract.

agricultural /ˌægrɪ'kʌltʃər(ə)l/ *adj.* of or used in agriculture.

◆ **Agricultural Bank** *n.* (also **Land Bank**) credit bank specifically established to assist agricultural development, particularly by granting loans for longer periods than is usual with commercial banks.

◆ **Agricultural Credit Corporation Ltd.** *n.* (also **ACC**) corporation established in 1964 to extend the availability of medium-term bank credit for buildings, equipment, livestock, and working capital to farmers, growers, and cooperatives. The ACC offers a guarantee to the farmer's bank for such loans and promises to repay the bank should the farmer fail to do so. In return for this service the farmer pays a percentage charge to the ACC.

◆ **Agricultural Mortgage Corporation Ltd.** *n.* (also **AMC**) corporation established to grant loans to farmers against first mortgages on their land by the Agricultural Credits Act (1928). The AMC offers loans for periods of five to 40 years. The capital of the corporation is supplied by the Bank of England, the joint-stock banks, and by the issue of state-guaranteed debentures. The corporation's loans are irrevocable except in cases of default and are usu. made through the local branches of the commercial banking system.

---

agriculture /'ægrɪˌkʌltʃə(r)/ *n.* cultivation of the soil and rearing of animals. □ **agriculturalist** /-'kʌltʃərəlɪst/ *n.* [Latin *ager* field]

agrimony /'ægrɪmənɪ/ *n.* (*pl.* **-ies**) perennial plant with small yellow flowers. [Greek *argemōnē* poppy]

agronomy /ə'grɒnəmɪ/ *n.* science of soil management and crop production. □ **agronomist** *n.* [Greek *agros* land]

aground /ə'graʊnd/ *predic. adj.* & *adv.* on or on to the bottom of shallow water (*run aground*).

AGSM *abbr.* Australian Graduate of the School of Management.

ag[to] *abbr.* (Italian, Portuguese, Spanish) agosto (= August).

Aguascalientes /ˌɑːgwəskæl'jenteɪz/ **1** state of central Mexico; pop. (est. 1990) 719 659. **2** its capital city, the commercial centre of a surrounding fruit-growing region; industries include ceramics, tanning, and railway engineering; pop. (1990) 479 659.

ague /'eɪgjuː/ *n.* **1** *hist.* malarial fever. **2** shivering fit. [Latin: related to ACUTE]

a.g.w. (also **AGW**) *abbr.* actual gross weight.

AGWI *abbr. Marine insurance* Atlantic, Gulf, West Indies.

AH *–abbr.* (also **A/H**) *Marine insurance* Antwerp–Hamburg coastal ports. *–airline flight code* Air Algerie.

AH *abbr.* in the year of the Hegira (AD 622); of the Muslim era. [Latin *anno Hegirae*]

ah /ɑː/ *int.* expressing surprise, pleasure, realization, etc. [French *a*]

aha /ɑː'hɑː/ *int.* expressing surprise, triumph, mockery, etc. [from AH, HA]

AHC *abbr.* = ACCEPTING HOUSES COMMITTEE.

ahead /ə'hed/ *adv.* **1** further forward in space or time. **2** in the lead (*ahead on points*).

ahem /ə'həm/ *int.* used to attract attention, gain time, etc. [from HEM[2]]

Ahmadabad /'ɑːmædəˌbæd/ industrial city in W India, in the state of Gujarat; textiles are important; pop. (1991) 3 297 655.

ahoy /ə'hɔɪ/ *int. Naut.* call used in hailing. [from AH, HOY]

a.h.r. *abbr.* acceptable hazard rate (in risk analysis).

Ahvaz /ɑː'vɑːz/ (Arabic **Ahwāz**) city in W Iran, capital of the oil-producing province of Khuzestan; pop. (1991) 724 653.

AI *–abbr.* **1** artificial insemination. **2** = ARTIFICIAL INTELLIGENCE. *–airline flight code* Air India.

AIA *abbr.* **1** American Insurance Association. **2** Associate of the Institute of Actuaries.

AIAA *abbr.* Association of International Advertising Agencies.

AIB *abbr.* **1** accidents investigation branch (of insurance companies). **2** American Institute of Banking. **3** Association of Independent Businesses.

AIB.Scot. *abbr.* Associate of the Institute of Bankers in Scotland.

AICA *abbr.* Associate Member of the Commonwealth Institute of Accountants.

AICPA *abbr.* American Institute of Certified Public Accountants.

AICS *abbr.* Associate of the Institute of Chartered Shipbrokers.

AID *abbr.* **1** (in the US) Agency for International Development. **2** artificial insemination by donor.

aid *–n.* **1** help. **2** person or thing that helps. *–v.* **1** help. **2** promote (*sleep will aid recovery*). □ **in aid of 1** in support of. **2** *colloq.* for the purpose of (*what's it all in aid of?*). [Latin: related to AD–, *juvo* help]

AIDA *abbr.* attention, interest, desire, action (of the customer). See ADVERTISING.

AIDAS *abbr.* Agricultural Industry Development Advisory Service.

aide /eɪd/ *n.* **1** aide-de-camp. **2** esp. *US* assistant. [French]

aide-de-camp /ˌeɪd də ˈkɑ̃/ *n.* (*pl.* **aides-de-camp** pronunc. same) officer assisting a senior officer. [French]

AIDP *abbr.* Associate of the Institute of Data Processing.

Aids *n.* (also **AIDS**) acquired immune deficiency syndrome, an often fatal viral syndrome marked by severe loss of resistance to infection. [abbreviation]

◆ **aids to trade** *n.pl.* four aspects recognized in commerce as promoting trade: advertising, banking, insurance, and transport.

◆ **aid trade provision** *n.* (also **ATP**) major component of the British aid programme, which seeks to combine aid to developing countries with creating business for UK companies. Subsidized loans and credits are offered to developing countries on condition that goods and services are purchased from UK-based enterprises.

AIIA *abbr.* Associate of the Insurance Institute of America.

AIInf.Sc. *abbr.* Associate of the Institute of Information Scientists.

ail *v.* **1** *archaic* (only in 3rd person interrog. or indefinite constructions) trouble or afflict (*what ails him?*). **2** (usu. **be ailing**) be ill. [Old English]

aileron /ˈeɪləˌrɒn/ *n.* hinged flap on an aeroplane wing. [French *aile* wing]

ailing *adj.* **1** ill. **2** in poor condition.

ailment *n.* minor illness or disorder.

AIM *abbr.* **1** = ALTERNATIVE INVESTMENT MARKET. **2** Australian Institute of Management.

aim *–v.* **1** intend or try; attempt (*aim at winning*; *aim to win*). **2** (usu. foll. by *at*) direct or point (a weapon, remark, etc.). **3** take aim. *–n.* **1** purpose or object. **2** the directing of a weapon etc. at an object. □ **take aim** direct a weapon etc. at a target. [Latin *aestimare* reckon]

aimless *adj.* without aim or purpose. □ **aimlessly** *adv.*

AIMU *abbr.* American Institute of Marine Underwriters.

A.Inst.FF *abbr.* Associate of the Institute of Freight Forwarders Ltd.

A.Inst.PI *abbr.* Associate of the Institute of Patentees and Inventors.

ain't /eɪnt/ *contr. colloq.* **1** am, is, or are not. **2** have or has not.

■ **Usage** The use of *ain't* is usually regarded as unacceptable in spoken and written English.

AIP *abbr.* Association of Independent Producers.

AIPA *abbr.* Associate Member of the Institute of Practitioners in Advertising.

air /eə(r)/ *–n.* **1** mixture mainly of oxygen and nitrogen surrounding the earth. **2** earth's atmosphere; open space in it; this as a place for flying aircraft. **3 a** distinctive impression or manner (*air of mystery*). **b** (esp. in *pl.*) pretentiousness (*gave himself airs*). **4** tune. **5** light wind. *–v.* **1** expose (clothes, a room, etc.) to fresh air or warmth to remove damp. **2** express and discuss publicly (an opinion, question, grievance, etc.). □ **by air** by or in an aircraft. **in the air 1** (of opinions etc.) prevalent. **2** (of plans etc.) uncertain. **on** (or **off**) **the air** being (or not being) broadcast. [Greek *aēr*]

airbase *n.* base for military aircraft.

air-bed *n.* inflatable mattress.

airborne *adj.* **1** transported by air. **2** (of aircraft) in the air after taking off.

air-brick *n.* perforated brick used for ventilation.

Airbus *n. propr.* short-haul passenger aircraft.

Air Chief Marshal *n.* RAF officer of high rank, above Air Marshal.

Air Commodore *n.* RAF officer next above Group Captain.

air-conditioning *n.* **1** system for regulating the humidity, ventilation, and temperature in a building. **2** apparatus for this. □ **air-conditioned** *adj.*

◆ **air consignment note** *n.* = AIR WAYBILL.

aircraft *n.* (*pl.* same) machine capable of flight, esp. an aeroplane or helicopter.

aircraft-carrier *n.* warship carrying and used as a base for aircraft.

aircraftman *n.* lowest rank in the RAF.

aircraftwoman *n.* lowest rank in the WRAF.

aircrew *n.* crew of an aircraft.

air-cushion *n.* **1** inflatable cushion. **2** layer of air supporting a hovercraft etc.

◆ **air date** *n.* date of first transmission of a commercial or an advertising campaign on television.

Airedale /ˈeədeɪl/ *n.* large terrier of a rough-coated breed. [*Airedale* in Yorkshire]

airer *n.* stand for airing or drying clothes etc.

airfield *n.* area with runway(s) for aircraft.

air force *n.* branch of the armed forces fighting in the air.

◆ **air freight** *n.* **1** transport of goods by aircraft, either in a scheduled airliner or chartered airliner carrying passengers (an all-traffic service) or in a freight plane (an all-freight service). Air cargo usu. consists of goods that have a high value compared to their weight. **2** goods so transported. **3** cost of transporting goods by aircraft, usu. quoted on the basis of a price per kilogram.

airgun *n.* gun using compressed air to fire pellets.

airhead *n. slang* stupid person, esp. an empty-headed young woman.

air hostess *n.* stewardess in a passenger aircraft.

airless *adj.* stuffy; still, calm.

air letter *n.* sheet of light paper forming a letter for sending by airmail.

airlift *–n.* emergency transport of supplies etc. by air. *–v.* transport thus.

airline *n.* public air transport system or company.

airliner *n.* large passenger aircraft.

airlock *n.* **1** stoppage of the flow by an air bubble in a pump or pipe. **2** compartment permitting movement between areas at different pressures.

airmail *n.* **1** system of transporting mail by air. **2** mail carried by air.

airman *n.* pilot or member of an aircraft crew, esp. in an air force.

Air Marshal *n.* RAF officer of high rank, above Air Vice-Marshal.

airplane *n. US* = AEROPLANE.

air pocket *n.* apparent vacuum causing an aircraft to drop suddenly.

airport *n.* airfield with facilities for passengers and goods.

air raid *n.* attack by aircraft on ground targets.

air rifle *n.* rifle using compressed air to fire pellets.

airs and graces *n.pl.* affected manner.

airscrew *n.* aircraft propeller.

airship *n.* power-driven aircraft lighter than air.

airsick *adj.* nauseous due to air travel.

◆ **airspace** *n.* **1** air that lies above a state's land and sea territory and is subject to its exclusive jurisdiction. **2** air above a piece of land. The owner of the land is entitled to the ownership and possession of the airspace above this land. This is not exclusive, however, and is limited by the reasonable and necessary use of that airspace by neighbours as well as for the flight of aircraft.

air speed *n.* aircraft's speed relative to the air.
airstrip *n.* strip of ground for the take-off and landing of aircraft.
air terminal *n.* building with transport to and from an airport.
airtight *adj.* impermeable to air.

◆ **airtime** *n.* **1** amount of time allocated to an advertisement on radio or television. **2** time of transmission of an advertisement on radio or television.

---

air traffic controller *n.* official who controls air traffic by radio.
Air Vice-Marshal *n.* RAF officer of high rank, just below Air Marshal.
airwaves *n.pl. colloq.* radio waves used in broadcasting.
airway *n.* recognized route of aircraft.

◆ **air waybill** *n.* (also **air consignment note**) document made out by a consignor of goods by air freight to facilitate swift delivery of the goods to the consignee. It gives the name of the consignor and the loading airport, the consignee and the airport of destination, a description of the goods, the value of the goods, and the marks, number, and dimensions of the packages.

---

airwoman *n.* woman pilot or member of an aircraft crew, esp. in an air force.
airworthy *adj.* (of an aircraft) fit to fly.
airy *adj.* (**-ier, -iest**) **1** well-ventilated, breezy. **2** flippant, superficial. **3** light as air. **4** ethereal. □ **airily** *adv.*
airy-fairy *adj. colloq.* unrealistic, impractical.
AISA *abbr.* Associate of the Incorporated Secretaries Association.
aisle /aɪl/ *n.* **1** the part of a church on either side of the nave, divided from it by pillars. **2** passage between rows of pews, seats, etc. [Latin *ala* wing]
AIT *abbr.* Association of HM Inspectors of Taxes.
AITC *abbr.* Association of Investment Trust Companies.
aitch /eɪtʃ/ *n.* the letter H. [French *ache*]
aitchbone *n.* **1** rump bone of an animal. **2** cut of beef over this. [originally *nache-bone* from Latin *natis* buttock]
Aix-en-Provence /ˌeɪksɑ̃prɒ'vɑ̃s/ city in S France, in Provence; olive oil and fruit are produced; pop. (1990) 123 854.
Aix-la-Chapelle see AACHEN.
Ajaccio /æ'jætʃɪˌəʊ/ town in France, a seaport in W Corsica; tourism is important; pop. (est. 1990) 55 279.
ajar /ə'dʒɑː(r)/ *adv.* & *predic.adj.* (of a door) slightly open. [from A², obsolete *char* from Old English *cerr* a turn]
Ajman /ædʒ'mɑːn/ smallest of the seven emirates of the United Arab Emirates; pop. (est. 1991) 76 000; capital, Ajman.
AK *US postcode* Alaska.
a.k.a. *abbr.* (also **AKA**) also known as.
Akela /ɑː'keɪlə/ *n.* adult leader of Cub Scouts. [name of the leader of the wolf-pack in Kipling's *Jungle Book*]
akimbo /ə'kɪmbəʊ/ *adv.* (of the arms) with hands on the hips and elbows turned outwards. [originally *in kenebowe*, probably from Old Norse]
akin /ə'kɪn/ *predic. adj.* **1** related by blood. **2** similar.
Akmola /æk'məʊlə/ capital of Kazakhstan, in the north-west of the country. It is an important railway junction; pop. (est. 1995) 280 200.
Aksai Chin /ˌæksaɪ 'tʃɪn/ region of the Himalayas occupied by China but claimed by India as part of Kashmir.
Aksum /'ɑːksəm/ (also **Axum**) town in N Ethiopia, in the province of Tigre; pop. (est. 1984) 17 753. A religious centre and capital of a powerful kingdom during the 1st–6th centuries AD, it is now a tourist attraction. □ **Aksumite** *adj.* & *n.*
Aktb. *abbr.* (also **Akt., Aktieb.**) (Swedish) Aktiebolaget (= joint-stock company).
Akureyri /ˌækuː'reɪrɪ/ chief town of N Iceland; industries include fishing and textiles; pop. (1994) 14 914.
AL –*US postcode* Alabama. –*international vehicle registration* Albania. –*postcode* St Albans.
Al *symb.* aluminium.
a.l. *abbr.* **1** *Commerce* (French) après livraison (= after delivery). **2** autograph letter.
-al *suffix* **1** (also **-ial**) forming adjectives meaning 'relating to, of the kind of' (*central*; *tidal*; *dictatorial*). **2** forming nouns, esp. of verbal action (*removal*). [Latin *-alis*]
ALA *abbr.* (also **a.l.a.**) all letters answered.
Ala. *abbr.* Alabama.
à la /'æ lɑː/ *prep.* in the manner of (*à la russe*). [French from À LA MODE]
Alabama /ˌælə'bæmə/ state in the SE US bordering on the Gulf of Mexico; pop. (est. 1995) 4 274 000; capital, Montgomery. Industries include iron, steel, oil, chemicals, plastics, and defence projects; agriculture produces cotton, peanuts, soya beans, wheat, maize, cattle, and poultry.
alabaster /'æləˌbɑːstə(r)/ –*n.* translucent usu. white form of gypsum, used for carving etc. –*adj.* **1** of alabaster. **2** white or smooth. [Greek *alabastros*]
à la carte /ˌæ lɑː 'kɑːt/ *adv.* & *adj.* with individually priced dishes. [French]
alacrity /ə'lækrɪtɪ/ *n.* briskness; cheerful readiness. [Latin *alacer* brisk]

Albania /æl'beɪnɪə/, **Republic of** small country in SE Europe, bordering on the Adriatic Sea. Much of the land is mountainous and there are extensive forests, but the coastal areas are fertile. The economy is mainly agricultural but chemical and engineering industries are being developed and the rich mineral resources (which include oil, copper, and iron) exploited. Exports include tobacco, fruit and vegetables, crude oil, and minerals. All industry and land remained nationalized until 1991, when the government began a cautious programme of liberalization; this has since been accelerated. The country's economic crisis deepened in 1992, with thousands fleeing to Italy to escape food shortages. Albania now depends on foreign aid for survival. Remittances from the large numbers of Albanians working abroad are also an important source of income. *History*. Formerly part of the Turkish empire, it became independent in 1912 and a Communist state under Enver Hoxha after the Second World War. Although under the influence first of the USSR and later that of China, it remained generally isolationist in policy and outlook. Anti-Communist demonstrations in 1990–1 led to free elections and some liberalization. A non-Socialist government was elected in 1992. In 1997 civil unrest occurred (esp. in the south) as a result of the collapse of pyramid financial schemes; UN forces were deployed to the country in April to supervise foreign aid distribution. Elections held in July 1997 resulted in victory for the Socialists. President, Rexhep Medjani; capital, Tirana. □ **Albanian** *adj.* & *n.*

language	Albanian
currency	lek (Lk) of 100 qindars
pop. (est. 1991)	3 270 000
GNP (1993)	US $ 1.163B
literacy	91.8%
life expectancy	71 (m); 78 (f)

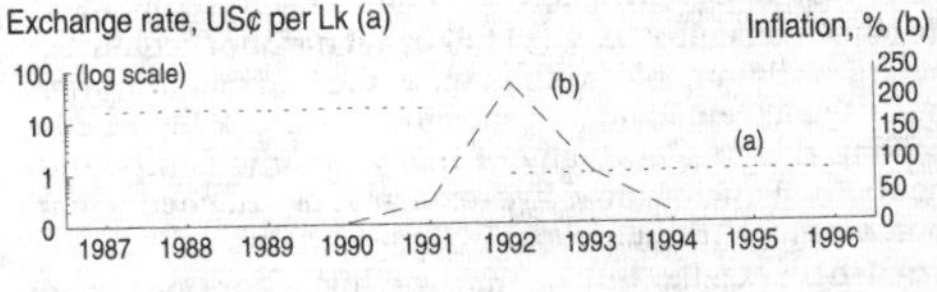

à la mode /ˌæ lɑː 'məʊd/ *adv.* & *adj.* in fashion; fashionable. [French]

Åland Islands /'ɔːlənd/ (Finnish **Ahvenanmaa**) group of islands in the Gulf of Bothnia forming an autonomous region of Finland; industries include farming and tourism; pop. (est. 1995) 25 158; capital, Mariehamn (Maarianhamina).

alarm /ə'lɑːm/ –*n.* **1** warning of danger etc. **2 a** warning sound or device. **b** = ALARM CLOCK. **3** apprehension (*filled with alarm*). –*v.* **1** frighten or disturb. **2** warn. [Italian *all'arme!* to arms]

alarm clock *n.* clock that rings at a set time.

alarmist *n.* person stirring up alarm.

alas /ə'læs/ *int.* expressing grief, pity, or concern. [French: related to AH, Latin *lassus* weary]

Alas. *abbr.* Alaska.

Alaska /ə'læskə/ largest state of the US, in the extreme NW of North America, with coasts in the Arctic Ocean, Bering Sea, and North Pacific; about one-third of it lies within the Arctic Circle; pop. (est. 1995) 634 000; capital, Juneau. The territory was purchased from Russia in 1867 and became the 49th state of the US in 1959; industries include oil, gas, fishing, and forestry; coal, gold, and copper are mined. □ **Alaskan** *adj.* & *n.*

alb *n.* long white vestment worn by Christian priests. [Latin *albus* white]

Alba Iulia /ˌælbə 'juːlɪə/ city in W Romania; wine and leather goods are produced; pop. (1985) 64 369.

Albany /'ɒlbənɪ/ city in the US, capital of New York state, on the Hudson River; electrical goods, textiles, chemicals, dental goods, and building materials are produced; pop. (est. 1994) 104 828.

albatross /'ælbəˌtrɒs/ *n.* **1 a** long-winged, stout bodied bird related to the petrel. **b** encumbrance. **2** *Golf* score of three strokes under par at any hole. [alteration of *alcatras*, from Spanish and Portuguese *alcatraz* from Arabic, = the jug]

albeit /ɔːl'biːɪt/ *conj. literary* though. [*all be it*]

Alberta /æl'bɜːtə/ prairie province in W Canada (from 1905), bounded on the S by the US and on the W by the Rocky Mountains; pop. (est. 1993) 2 662 000; capital, Edmonton. Oil, gas, and coal production are important; other industries include meat processing, chemicals, lumbering, and tourism.

albino /æl'biːnəʊ/ *n.* (*pl.* **-s**) **1** person or animal lacking pigment in the skin and hair (which are white), and the eyes (usu. pink). **2** plant lacking normal colouring. □ **albinism** /'ælbɪˌnɪz(ə)m/ *n.* [Spanish and Portuguese: related to ALB]

Ålborg var. of AALBORG.

Albufeira /ˌælbuː'feɪrə/ fishing village and holiday resort in S Portugal, on the Algarve coast; pop. (1981) 14 200.

album /'ælbəm/ *n.* **1** book for photographs, stamps, etc. **2 a** long-playing gramophone record. **b** set of these. [Latin, = blank tablet, from *albus* white]

albumen /'ælbjʊmɪn/ *n.* **1** egg-white. **2** substance found between the skin and germ of many seeds, usu. the edible part. [Latin: related to ALBUM]

albumin /'ælbjʊmɪn/ *n.* water-soluble protein found in egg-white, milk, blood, etc. □ **albuminous** /æl'bjuːmɪnəs/ *adj.*

Albuquerque /'ælbəˌkɜːkɪ/ city in the US, the largest city in the state of New Mexico; industries include food canning and meat processing; pop. (est. 1994) 411 994.

alchemy /'ælkəmɪ/ *n.* medieval chemistry, esp. seeking to turn base metals into gold. □ **alchemist** *n.* [Arabic]

alcohol /'ælkəˌhɒl/ *n.* **1** (in full **ethyl alcohol**) colourless volatile inflammable liquid, esp. as the intoxicant in wine, beer, spirits, etc., and as a solvent, fuel, etc. **2** liquor containing this. **3** *Chem.* any of many organic compounds containing one or more hydroxyl groups attached to carbon atoms. [Arabic: related to KOHL]

alcoholic /ˌælkə'hɒlɪk/ –*adj.* of, like, containing, or caused by alcohol. –*n.* person suffering from alcoholism.

alcoholism /'ælkəhɒˌlɪz(ə)m/ *n.* condition resulting from addiction to alcohol.

alcove /'ælkəʊv/ *n.* recess, esp. in the wall of a room. [Arabic, = the vault]

aldehyde /'ældɪˌhaɪd/ *n. Chem.* any of a class of compounds formed by the oxidation of alcohols. [from ALCOHOL, DE-, HYDROGEN]

al dente /æl 'dentɪ, -teɪ/ *adj.* (of pasta etc.) cooked so as to be still firm when bitten. [Italian, = 'to the tooth']

alder /'ɔːldə(r)/ *n.* tree related to the birch. [Old English]

alderman /'ɔːldəmən/ *n.* esp. *hist.* co-opted member of an English county or borough council, next in dignity to the mayor. [Old English *aldor* chief, MAN]

Alderney /'ɔːldənɪ/ one of the Channel Islands; dairy farming and tourism are important; pop. (est. 1994) 2375. –*n.* animal of a breed of small dairy cattle that came originally from Alderney.

ALE *abbr. Insurance* additional living expense.

ale *n.* beer. [Old English]

aleatory /'eɪlɪətərɪ/ *adj.* depending on chance. [Latin *alea* DIE[2]]

alehouse *n. hist.* tavern.

alembic /ə'lembɪk/ *n.* **1** *hist.* apparatus formerly used in distilling. **2** means of refining or extracting. [Greek *ambix*, *-ikos* cap of a still]

Alentejo /ˌælən'teɪʒəʊ/ historic region of central Portugal; industries include quarrying, mining, and cork production.

Aleppo /æ'lepəʊ/ (Arabic **Ḥalab** /hɑː'lɑːb/) second-largest city of Syria, in the N of the country; pop. (est. 1994) 1 591 400. The city is an ancient one, an important commercial and industrial centre between the Mediterranean and the countries of the East.

alert /ə'lɜːt/ –*adj.* **1** watchful, vigilant. **2** nimble, attentive. –*n.* **1** warning call or alarm. **2** state or period of special vigilance. –*v.* (often foll. by *to*) warn. [French *alerte* from Italian *all'erta* to the watch-tower]

Aleutian Islands /ə'ljuːʃ(ə)n/ (also **Aleutians**) group of islands in US possession, extending SW from Alaska; site of military bases; pop. (1980) 7768.

A level *n.* = ADVANCED LEVEL.

Alexander technique /ˌælɪg'zɑːndə(r)/ *n.* technique for controlling posture as an aid to well-being. [*Alexander*, name of a physiotherapist]

Alexandretta /ˌælɪgzɑːn'dretə/ see ISKENDERUN.

Alexandria /ˌælɪg'zɑːndrɪə/ chief port of Egypt; industries include oil refining and cotton ginning; pop. (est. 1994) 3 382 000.

alexandrine /ˌælɪg'zændraɪn/ –*adj.* (of a line of verse) having six iambic feet. –*n.* alexandrine line. [French *Alexandre*, title of a romance using this metre]

alfalfa /æl'fælfə/ *n.* clover-like plant used for fodder. [Arabic, = a green fodder]

♦ **Al Fayed** /æl 'faɪed/, **Mohammed** (1933–   ) Egyptian-born businessman resident in Britain, chairman of Harrods, the London store, (since 1985) and owner and chairman of the Ritz Hotel in Paris (since 1979). Al Fayed is also the owner of Fulham Football Club. Refused British citizenship, he acquired considerable fame and sympathy, when his son, 'Dodi' Fayed, was killed in a car crash with Diana, Princess of Wales in 1997.

---

alfresco /æl'freskəʊ/ *adv.* & *adj.* in the open air. [Italian]

alga /'ælgə/ *n.* (*pl.* **algae** /-dʒiː/) (usu. in *pl.*) non-flowering stemless water-plant, esp. seaweed and plankton. [Latin]

Algarve /æl'gɑːv/ southernmost province of Portugal, on the Atlantic coast; pop. (est. 1986) 339 200; capital, Faro. Industries include fishing and tourism; maize, figs, almonds, and olives are grown.

algebra /'ældʒɪbrə/ *n.* branch of mathematics that uses letters etc. to represent numbers and quantities. □ **algebraic** /-'breɪɪk/ *adj.* [ultimately from Arabic *al-jabr*, = reunion of broken parts]

Algeciras /ˌældʒɪ'sɪərəs/ ferry port in S Spain, opposite Gibraltar; exports include oranges and cork; pop. (est. 1994) 101 063.

Algiers /æl'dʒɪəz/ (French **Alger** /æl'ʒeɪ/, Arabic **El Djezair** /dʒe'zeə(r)/) capital of Algeria and a leading Mediterranean seaport; exports include wine, citrus fruit, and iron ore; pop. (1995) 2 168 000.

Algol /'ælgɒl/ *n.* high-level computer programming language. The version **Algol-60**, published in 1960, was designed to reflect mathematical algorithms rather than the architecture of computers and has strongly influenced many subsequent languages, such as Pascal and Ada. See also ALGORITHM. [from ALGO(RITHM), L(ANGUAGE)]

◆ **algorithm** /'ælgəˌrɪð(ə)m/ *n.* set of well-defined rules for solving a problem in a finite number of steps. Algorithms are extensively used in computer science. The steps in the algorithm are translated into a series of instructions that the computer can understand. These instructions form the computer program. □ **algorithmic** /-'rɪðmɪk/ *adj.* [Persian, name of a 9th-century mathematician *al-Kuwārizmī*]

---

alias /'eɪlɪəs/ *–adv.* also named or known as. *–n.* assumed name. [Latin, = at another time]

alibi /'ælɪˌbaɪ/ *n.* (*pl.* **-s**) **1** claim or proof that one was elsewhere when a crime etc. was committed. **2** *informal* excuse. [Latin, = elsewhere]

■ **Usage** The use of *alibi* in sense 2 is considered incorrect by some people.

Alicante /ˌælɪ'kænteɪ/ seaport on the Mediterranean coast of SE Spain; industries include oil refining, chemicals, soap, and tobacco; pop. (est. 1994) 274 964.

Alice Springs /'ælɪs/ town in central Australia, an administrative and supply centre, railway terminus, and tourist base serving the outback area of Northern Territory; pop. (1988) 23 600.

alien /'eɪlɪən/ *–adj.* **1** (often foll. by *to*) unfamiliar; unacceptable or repugnant. **2** foreign. **3** of beings from other worlds. *–n.* **1** foreign-born resident who is not naturalized. **2** a being from another world. [Latin *alius* other]

alienable *adj. Law* able to be transferred to new ownership.

alienate *v.* (**-ting**) **1** estrange, make hostile. **2** transfer ownership of. □ **alienation** /-'neɪʃ(ə)n/ *n.*

alight[1] /ə'laɪt/ *predic. adj.* **1** on fire. **2** lighted up; excited. [*on a light* (= lighted) *fire*]

alight[2] /ə'laɪt/ *v.* **1** (often foll. by *from*) descend from a vehicle. **2** come to earth, settle. [Old English]

align /ə'laɪn/ *v.* **1** put or bring into line. **2** (usu. foll. by *with*) ally (oneself etc.) with (a cause, party, etc.). □ **alignment** *n.* [French *à ligne* into line]

alike /ə'laɪk/ *–adj.* (usu. *predic.*) similar, like. *–adv.* in a similar way.

alimentary /ˌælɪ'mentərɪ/ *adj.* of or providing food or nourishment. [Latin *alo* nourish]

alimentary canal *n.* passage along which food passes during digestion.

alimony /'ælɪmənɪ/ *n.* money payable to a spouse or former spouse after separation or divorce.

■ **Usage** In UK usage this term has been replaced by *maintenance*.

aliphatic /ˌælɪ'fætɪk/ *adj. Chem.* of organic compounds in which carbon atoms form open chains, not aromatic rings. [Greek *aleiphar -phat-* fat]

aliquot /'ælɪˌkwɒt/ *–adj.* (of a part or portion) contained by the whole an integral number of times (*4 is an aliquot part of 12*). *–n.* **1** aliquot part. **2** (in general use) any known fraction of a whole; sample. [Latin, = several]

alive /ə'laɪv/ *adj.* (usu. *predic.*) **1** living. **2** lively, active. **3** (foll. by *to*) aware of; alert. **4** (foll. by *with*) swarming or teeming with. [Old English: related to A², LIFE]

alkali /'ælkəˌlaɪ/ *n.* (*pl.* **-s**) **1 a** any of a class of substances that liberate hydroxide ions in water, usu. form caustic or corrosive solutions, turn litmus blue, and have a pH of more than 7, e.g. caustic soda. **b** similar but weaker substance, e.g. sodium carbonate. **2** *Chem.* any substance that reacts with or neutralizes hydrogen ions. □ **alkaline** *adj.* **alkalinity** /-'lɪnɪtɪ/ *n.* [Arabic, = the calcined ashes]

alkaloid /'ælkəˌlɔɪd/ *n.* nitrogenous organic compound of plant origin, e.g. morphine, quinine.

alkane /'ælkeɪn/ *n. Chem.* saturated aliphatic hydrocarbon having the general formula C_nH_{2n+2}, including methane and ethane.

alkene /'ælkiːn/ *n. Chem.* unsaturated aliphatic hydrocarbon containing a double bond and having the general formula C_nH_{2n}, including ethylene.

alkyne /'ælkaɪn/ *n. Chem.* unsaturated aliphatic hydrocarbon containing a triple bond and having the general formula C_nH_{2n-2}, including acetylene.

all /ɔːl/ *–adj.* **1** whole amount, quantity, or extent of (*all day; all his life; take it all*). **2** any whatever (*beyond all doubt*). **3** greatest possible (*with all speed*). *–n.* **1** all persons or things concerned; everything (*all were present; all is lost*). **2** (foll. by *of*) **a** the whole of (*take all of it*). **b** every one of (*all of us*). **c** *colloq.* as much as (*all of six feet*). **d** *colloq.* in a state of (*all of a dither*). **3** one's whole strength or

---

Algeria /æl'dʒɪərɪə/, **Republic of** N African country on the Mediterranean coast, consisting chiefly of desert, with fertile areas near the coast. The people are mainly Arabs and Berbers and the economy is chiefly agricultural, though industrial development is proceeding; industries include oil, steel, motor vehicles, and chemicals. All major industries were under state control until 1991, when a policy of liberalization and restructuring began. The main exports are crude oil and (liquefied) natural gas, which are pumped from the Sahara to terminals on the coast. Refined petroleum is also exported.

History. Algeria was colonized by France in the mid-19th century and heavily settled by French immigrants. It was closely integrated with metropolitan France, but the refusal of the European settlers to grant equal rights to the native population led to increasing political instability and civil war in the 1950s, and in 1962 the country was granted independence and became a republic (one-party until November 1989). The departure of the French caused grave damage to the previously prosperous Algerian economy, with the result that the next two decades were characterized by slow attempts at economic recovery and limited external contacts. In 1991 the fundamentalist Islamic Salvation Front won a general election but the military prevented them from taking office, declaring a state of emergency. In 1992 President Mohamed Boudiaf was shot by Islamic extremists and the following year former prime minister Kasdi Merbah was also killed. Talks were held between the government and the Islamic Salvation Front in 1994, but violence has persisted, reaching a new peak in 1997–8. A general election in June 1997 resulted in victory for pro-government parties. Acting head of state, General Liamine Zeroual: capital, Algiers. □ **Algerian** *adj.* & *n.*

languages	Arabic (official), French
currency	dinar (DA) of 100 centimes
pop. (est. 1995)	27 939 000
GNP (1993)	US $ 44.35B
literacy	69.8% (m); 45.5% (f)
life expectancy	67 (m); 69 (f)

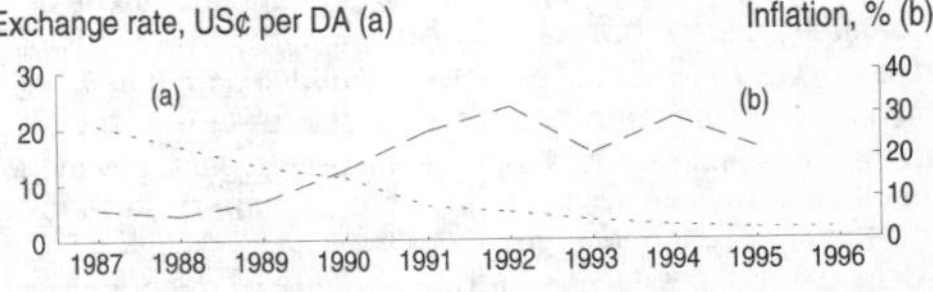

resources (prec. by *my*, *your*, etc.). **4** (in games) each (*two goals all*). *–adv.* **1 a** entirely, quite (*dressed all in black*). **b** as an intensifier (*stop all this grumbling*). **2** *colloq.* very (*went all shy*). **3** (foll. by *the* + compar.) to that, or the utmost, extent (*if they go, all the better; that makes it all the worse*). □ **all along** from the beginning. **all and sundry** everyone. **all but** very nearly. **all for** *colloq.* strongly in favour of. **all found** with board and lodging provided free. **all in** *colloq.* exhausted. **all in all** everything considered. **all manner of** every kind of. **all of a sudden** suddenly. **all one** (or **the same**) (usu. foll. by *to*) a matter of indifference. **all out** using all one's strength (also (with hyphen) *attrib.*: *all-out effort*). **all over 1** completely finished. **2** in or on all parts of (*mud all over the carpet*). **3** *colloq.* typically (*you all over*). **4** *slang* effusively attentive to (a person). **all right** (*predic.*) **1** satisfactory; safe and sound; in good condition. **2** satisfactorily (*it worked out all right*). **3 a** expressing consent. **b** as an intensifier (*that's the one all right*). **all round 1** in all respects. **2** for each person. **all the same** nevertheless. **all there** *colloq.* mentally alert or normal. **all the time** throughout (despite some contrary expectation etc.). **all together** all at once; all in one place or in a group (*came all together*) (cf. ALTOGETHER). **all up with** hopeless for (a person). **at all** (with *neg.* or *interrog.*) in any way; to any extent (*did not swim at all; did you like it at all?*). **in all** in total; altogether. [Old English]

■ **Usage** Note the differences in meaning between *all together* and *altogether*: see note at *altogether*.

Allah /'ælə/ *n.* the Muslim and Arab name of God. [Arabic]

Allahabad /'ɑːləhəˌbɑːd/ city in N India, a religious, educational, and administrative centre; pop. (est. 1991) 806 447.

allay /ə'leɪ/ *v.* **1** diminish (fear, suspicion, etc.). **2** alleviate (pain etc.). [Old English *a-* intensive, LAY[1]]

all-clear *n.* signal that danger etc. is over.

all comers *n.pl.* anyone who applies, takes up a challenge, etc.

allegation /ˌælɪ'geɪʃ(ə)n/ *n.* **1** assertion, esp. unproved. **2** alleging. [Latin *allego* adduce]

allege /ə'ledʒ/ *v.* **(-ging) 1** declare, esp. without proof. **2** advance as an argument or excuse. [Latin *lis lit-* lawsuit]

allegedly /ə'ledʒɪdlɪ/ *adv.* as is alleged.

allegiance /ə'liːdʒ(ə)ns/ *n.* **1** loyalty (to a person or cause etc.). **2** the duty of a subject. [French: related to LIEGE]

allegory /'ælɪgərɪ/ *n.* (*pl.* **-ies**) story whose moral etc. is represented symbolically. □ **allegorical** /ˌælɪ'gɒrɪk(ə)l/ *adj.* **allegorize** /'ælɪgəˌraɪz/ *v.* (also **-ise**). [Greek *allégoria* = other speaking]

allegretto /ˌælɪ'gretəʊ/ *Mus. –adv.* & *adj.* in a fairly brisk tempo. *–n.* (*pl.* **-s**) such a passage or movement. [Italian, diminutive of ALLEGRO]

allegro /ə'legrəʊ/ *Mus. –adv.* & *adj.* in a brisk tempo. *–n.* (*pl.* **-s**) such a passage or movement. [Italian, = lively]

alleluia /ˌælɪ'luːjə/ (also **hallelujah** /ˌhæl-/) *–int.* God be praised. *–n.* song or shout of praise to God. [Hebrew]

Allen key /'ælən/ *n. propr.* spanner designed to turn an Allen screw. [*Allen*, name of the US manufacturer]

Allen screw /'ælən/ *n. propr.* screw with a hexagonal socket in the head.

allergic /ə'lɜːdʒɪk/ *adj.* **1** (foll. by *to*) **a** having an allergy to. **b** *colloq.* having a strong dislike for. **2** caused by an allergy.

allergy /'ælədʒɪ/ *n.* (*pl.* **-ies**) **1** adverse reaction to certain substances, esp. particular foods, pollen, fur, or dust. **2** *colloq.* antipathy. [Greek *allos* other]

alleviate /ə'liːvɪˌeɪt/ *v.* **(-ting)** make (pain etc.) less severe. □ **alleviation** /-'eɪʃ(ə)n/ *n.* [Latin *levo* raise]

alley /'ælɪ/ *n.* (*pl.* **-s**) **1** narrow street or passageway. **2** enclosure for skittles, bowling, etc. **3** walk or lane in a park etc. [French *aller* go]

alliance /ə'laɪəns/ *n.* **1** union or agreement to cooperate, esp. of states by treaty or families by marriage. **2** (**Alliance**) political coalition party. **3** relationship; friendship. [French: related to ALLY]

allied /'ælaɪd/ *adj.* **1** (also **Allied**) associated in an alliance. **2** connected or related.

alligator /'ælɪˌgeɪtə(r)/ *n.* large reptile of the crocodile family with a head broader and shorter than a crocodile's. [Spanish *el lagarto* the lizard]

all-in *attrib. adj.* inclusive of all.

all'ingr. *abbr.* (Italian) all'ingrosso (= wholesale).

all-in wrestling *n.* wrestling with few or no restrictions.

alliteration /əˌlɪtə'reɪʃ(ə)n/ *n.* repetition of the same letter or sound at the beginning of adjacent or closely connected words (e.g. *cool, calm, and collected*). □ **alliterate** /ə'lɪtəˌreɪt/ *v.* **(-ting)**. **alliterative** /ə'lɪtərətɪv/ *adj.* [Latin: related to LETTER]

allocate /'æləˌkeɪt/ *v.* **(-ting)** (usu. foll. by *to*) assign or devote to (a purpose, person, or place). □ **allocation** /-'keɪʃ(ə)n/ *n.* [Latin: related to LOCAL]

◆ **allonge** /æ'lɒnʒ/ *n.* attachment to a bill of exchange to provide space for further endorsements when the back of the bill itself has been fully used. [French, = extension to document]

---

allot /ə'lɒt/ *v.* **(-tt-)** apportion or distribute to (a person), esp. as a share or task (*they were allotted equal sums*). [French *a* to, LOT]

allotment *n.* **1** small piece of land rented by a local authority for cultivation. **2** share. **3** allotting. **4** *Finance* method of distributing previously unissued shares in a limited company in exchange for a contribution of capital. An application for such shares will often be made after the issue of a prospectus on the flotation of a public company or on the privatization of a state-owned industry. The company accepts the application by dispatching a **letter of allotment** to the applicant stating how many shares he or she has been allotted; the applicant then has an unconditional right to be entered in the register of members in respect of those shares. If the number of shares applied for exceeds the number available (oversubscription), allotment is made by a random draw or by a proportional allocation. An applicant allotted fewer shares than were applied for receives a cheque for the unallotted balance (an application must be accompanied by a cheque for the full value of the shares applied for). See also MULTIPLE APPLICATION.

allotropy /ə'lɒtrəpɪ/ *n.* existence of two or more different physical forms of a chemical element. □ **allotropic** /ˌælə'trɒpɪk/ *adj.* [Greek *allos* different, *tropos* manner]

allow /ə'laʊ/ *v.* **1** (often foll. by *to* + infin.) permit. **2** assign a limited amount etc. (*was allowed £500*). **3** (usu. foll. by *for*) provide or set aside for a purpose; add or deduct in consideration (*allow £50 for expenses; allow for wastage*). [originally = commend, from French: related to AD-, Latin *laudo* praise, *loco* place]

allowance *n.* **1** amount or sum allowed, esp. regularly for a stated purpose. **2** amount allowed in reckoning. **3** tax-free amount that may be deducted before a particular tax is calculated. Typical allowances in assessing a person's liability to income tax are the personal allowance, the married-couple's allowance, and the additional personal allowance. It also includes tax-free annual amounts, such as the annual allowances available in respect of capital-gains tax or inheritance tax. **4** money paid to an employee for expenses incurred in the course of his or her business. **5** deduction from an invoice for substandard quality of goods, late delivery, or some other specified purpose. **6** price reduction or rebate given to a customer or intermediary on a large order or for some other specific reason. **7** agreed time used in work measurement; it is added to the basic time in calculating the standard time for a particular job. □ **make allowances** (often foll. by *for*) **1** consider (mitigating circumstances). **2** make excuses for (a person, bad behaviour, etc.).

alloy /'ælɔɪ/ *–n.* **1** mixture of two or more metals. **2** inferior metal mixed esp. with gold or silver. *–v.* **1** mix (metals). **2** debase by admixture. **3** moderate (*pleasure alloyed with pain*). [French: related to ALLY]

all-purpose *attrib. adj.* having many uses.

all-right *attrib. adj. colloq.* acceptable (*an all-right guy*).

♦ **all-risks policy** *n.* insurance policy covering personal possessions against many (but not all) risks. A policy of this kind does not list the risks covered; instead it lists only the exclusions. Such wide cover often merits very high premiums and items covered on this basis often include jewellery, photographic or electronic equipment, and other valuables.

---

all-round *attrib. adj.* (of a person) versatile.

all-rounder *n.* versatile person.

All Saints' Day *n.* 1 Nov., Christian festival in honour of saints.

All Souls' Day *n.* 2 Nov., Roman Catholic festival with prayers for the souls of the dead.

allspice *n.* **1** aromatic spice obtained from the berry of the pimento plant. **2** the berry.

all-time *attrib. adj.* (of a record etc.) unsurpassed.

allude /ə'luːd/ *v.* (**-ding**) (foll. by *to*) refer to, esp. indirectly or briefly. [Latin: related to AD-, *ludo* play]

allure /ə'ljʊə(r)/ *–v.* (**-ring**) attract, charm, or entice. *–n.* attractiveness, personal charm, fascination. □ **allurement** *n.* [French: related to AD-, LURE]

allusion /ə'luːʒ(ə)n/ *n.* (often foll. by *to*) passing or indirect reference. □ **allusive** /ə'luːsɪv/ *adj.* [Latin: related to ALLUDE]

alluvial /ə'luːvɪəl/ *–adj.* of alluvium. *–n.* alluvium, esp. containing a precious metal.

alluvium /ə'luːvɪəm/ *n.* (*pl.* **-via**) deposit of usu. fine fertile soil left behind by a flood, esp. in a river valley. [Latin *luo* wash]

ally /'ælaɪ/ *–n.* (*pl.* **-ies**) state, person, etc., formally cooperating or united with another, esp. (also **Ally**) in war. *–v.* also /ə'laɪ/ (**-ies, -ied**) (often *refl.* and foll. by *with*) combine in alliance. [Latin *alligo* bind]

Alma-Ata /ˌælmə 'ɑːtə/ (formerly **Vernyi**) former capital of Kazakhstan; industries include food and tobacco processing; pop. (est. 1991) 1 164 000. In 1997 the process of moving the capital to Akmola began.

Alma Mater /ˌælmə 'mɑːtə(r)/ *n.* one's university, school, or college. [Latin, = bounteous mother]

almanac /'ɔːlməˌnæk/ *n.* (also **almanack**) calendar, usu. with astronomical data. [medieval Latin from Greek]

almighty /ɔːl'maɪtɪ/ *adj.* **1** having complete power. **2** (**the Almighty**) God. **3** *slang* very great (*almighty crash*). [Old English: related to ALL, MIGHTY]

almond /'ɑːmənd/ *n.* **1** nutlike kernel of a fruit allied to the peach and plum. **2** tree bearing this. [Greek *amugdalē*]

almoner /'ɑːmənə(r)/ *n.* social worker attached to a hospital. [French: related to ALMS]

■ **Usage** The usual term now is *medical social worker.*

almost /'ɔːlməʊst/ *adv.* all but; very nearly. [Old English: related to ALL, MOST]

alms /ɑːmz/ *n.pl. hist.* donation of money or food to the poor. [Greek *eleēmosunē* pity]

almshouse *n. hist.* charitable institution for the poor.

aloe /'æləʊ/ *n.* **1** plant of the lily family with toothed fleshy leaves. **2** (in *pl.*) (in full **bitter aloes**) strong laxative from aloe juice. [Old English from Greek]

aloft /ə'lɒft/ *predic. adj. & adv.* **1** high up, overhead. **2** upwards. [Old Norse *á lopti* in air]

alone /ə'ləʊn/ *–predic. adj.* **1** without the presence or help of others. **2** lonely (*felt alone*). *–adv.* only, exclusively. [earlier *al one*: related to ALL, ONE]

along /ə'lɒŋ/ *–prep.* beside or through (part of) the length of. *–adv.* **1** onward, into a more advanced state (*come along; getting along nicely*). **2** with oneself or others (*bring a book along*). **3** beside or through part or the whole length of a thing. □ **along with** in addition to; together with. [Old English, originally adj. = facing against]

alongside /əlɒŋ'saɪd/ *–adv.* at or to the side. *–prep.* close to the side of.

aloof /ə'luːf/ *–adj.* distant, unsympathetic. *–adv.* away, apart (*he kept aloof*). [originally *Naut.*, from A² + LUFF]

Alost see AALST.

aloud /ə'laʊd/ *adv.* audibly.

alp *n.* **1 a** high mountain. **b** (**the Alps**) high range of mountains in Switzerland and adjoining countries. **2** pasture land on a Swiss mountainside. [originally *alps*, from Greek *alpeis*]

alpaca /æl'pækə/ *n.* **1** shaggy South American mammal related to the llama. **2** its wool; fabric made from this. [Spanish from Quechua]

alpha /'ælfə/ *n.* **1** first letter of the Greek alphabet (Α, α). **2** first-class mark for a piece of work etc. □ **alpha and omega** beginning and end. [Latin from Greek]

alphabet /'ælfəˌbet/ *n.* **1** set of letters used in writing a language. **2** symbols or signs for these. □ **alphabetical** /-'betɪk(ə)l/ *adj.* [Greek ALPHA, BETA]

alphanumeric /ˌælfənjuː'merɪk/ *adj.* containing or consisting of both letters and numbers (*alphanumeric keyboard*).

alphanumeric characters *n.pl. Computing* the 26 letters of the alphabet, capital or lower case, and any of the digits 0–9. An **alphanumeric character set** (see CHARACTER SET) contains the alphanumeric characters and may in addition include some special characters and the space character. A computer may have an **alphanumeric display**, which shows only alphanumeric characters, as opposed to a display with a full graphics capability, which can show such drawings as bar charts.

alpha particle *n.* helium nucleus emitted by a radioactive substance.

alpine /'ælpaɪn/ *–adj.* of mountainous regions or (**Alpine**) the Alps. *–n.* **1** plant growing in mountainous regions. **2** = ROCK-PLANT. [Latin: related to ALP]

already /ɔːl'redɪ/ *adv.* **1** before the time in question (*I knew that already*). **2** as early or as soon as this (*is back already*). [from ALL, READY]

alright /ɔːl'raɪt/ *adv.* = *all right* (see ALL).

■ **Usage** Although widely used, *alright* is still nonstandard and is considered incorrect by many people.

ALS *abbr.* (also **a.l.s.**) autograph letter signed.

Alsace /æl'sæs/ French region W of the Rhine; tobacco, sugar beet, and hops are produced and potassium is mined; pop. (est. 1993) 1 649 400; capital, Strasbourg. It was annexed by Prussia in 1871 and restored to France after the First World War.

Alsatian /æl'seɪʃ(ə)n/ *n.* (also **German shepherd**) large dog of a breed used as guard dogs etc. [Latin *Alsatia* = ALSACE]

♦ **Alsaud** /æl'saʊd/, **Prince Alwaleed Bin Talal Bin Abdulaziz** (1956/7–) Saudi businessman, nephew of oil-rich King Faud Bin Abdul Ayig, he has made large investments in TWA Airlines, Citicorp, Four Seasons hotels, Apple Computers, and top advertising agency Saatchi & Saatchi.

---

also /'ɔːlsəʊ/ *adv.* in addition, besides. [Old English: related to ALL, SO¹]

also-ran *n.* **1** loser in a race. **2** undistinguished person.

Alta. *abbr.* Alberta.

Altai /'æltaɪ/ Russian territory in SW Siberia; pop. (1985) 2 744 000; capital, Barnaul.

altar /'ɔːltə(r)/ *n.* **1** table or flat block for sacrifice or offering to a deity. **2** Communion table. [Latin *altus* high]

altarpiece *n.* painting etc. above or behind an altar.

alter /'ɔːltə(r)/ *v.* make or become different; change. □ **alteration** /-'reɪʃ(ə)n/ *n.* [Latin *alter* other]

♦ **alteration of share capital** *n.* increase, reduction, or any other change in the authorized capital of a company (see SHARE CAPITAL). If permitted by the articles of association, a limited company can increase its authorized capital as appropriate. It can also rearrange its existing authorized capital (e.g. by consolidating 100 shares of £1 into 25 shares of £4 or by subdividing 100 shares of £1 into 200 of 50p) and cancel unissued shares. These are reserved powers, passed (unless the articles of association provide otherwise) by an ordinary resolution.

---

altercate /ˈɔːltəˌkeɪt/ *v.* (**-ting**) (often foll. by *with*) dispute, wrangle. □ **altercation** /-ˈkeɪʃ(ə)n/ *n.* [Latin]

alter ego /ˌɔːltər ˈiːgəʊ/ *n.* (*pl.* **-s**) **1** one's hidden or second self. **2** intimate friend. [Latin, = other self]

alternate –*v.* /ˈɔːltəˌneɪt/ (**-ting**) **1** (often foll. by *with*) occur or cause to occur by turns. **2** (foll. by *between*) go repeatedly from one to another (*alternated between hope and fear*). –*adj.* /ɔːlˈtɜːnət/ **1** (with noun in *pl.*) every other (*on alternate days*). **2** (of things of two kinds) alternating (*alternate joy and misery*). □ **alternately** /-ˈtɜːnətlɪ/ *adv.* **alternation** /-ˈneɪʃ(ə)n/ *n.* [Latin *alterno* do by turns: related to ALTER]

■ **Usage** See note at *alternative*.

alternate angles *n.pl.* two angles formed alternately on two sides of a line.

◆ **alternate director** *n.* person who can act temporarily in place of a named director of a company in his or her absence. An alternate director can only be present at a meeting of the board of directors if the articles of association provide for this eventuality and if the other directors agree that the person chosen is acceptable to undertake this role.

---

alternating current *n.* electric current reversing its direction at regular intervals.

alternative /ɔːlˈtɜːnətɪv/ –*adj.* **1** available as another choice (*alternative route*). **2** unconventional (*alternative medicine*). –*n.* **1** any of two or more possibilities. **2** choice (*had no alternative but to go*). □ **alternatively** *adv.*

■ **Usage** The adjective *alternative* should not be confused with *alternate*, as in 'there will be a dance on alternate Saturdays'.

◆ **Alternative Investment Market** *n.* (also **AIM**) market of the London Stock Exchange, opened in 1995, to enable small companies to raise capital and have their shares traded without the expense of a main market listing.

---

alternator /ˈɔːltəˌneɪtə(r)/ *n.* dynamo that generates an alternating current.

although /ɔːlˈðəʊ/ *conj.* = THOUGH. [from ALL, THOUGH]

altimeter /ˈæltɪˌmiːtə(r)/ *n.* instrument indicating altitude reached.

altitude /ˈæltɪˌtjuːd/ *n.* height, esp. of an object above sea level or above the horizon. [Latin *altus* high]

alto /ˈæltəʊ/ *n.* (*pl.* **-s**) **1** = CONTRALTO. **2 a** highest adult male singing-voice, above tenor. **b** singer with this voice. **3** instrument pitched second- or third-highest in its family. [Italian *alto* (*canto*) high (singing)]

altogether /ˌɔːltəˈgeðə(r)/ *adv.* **1** totally, completely. **2** on the whole. **3** in total. □ **in the altogether** *colloq.* naked. [from ALL, TOGETHER]

■ **Usage** Note that *altogether* means 'in total', whereas *all together* means 'all at once' or 'all in one place'. The phrases *six rooms altogether* (in total) and *six rooms all together* (in one place) illustrate the difference.

altruism /ˈæltruːˌɪz(ə)m/ *n.* unselfishness as a principle of action. □ **altruist** *n.* **altruistic** /ˌæltruːˈɪstɪk/ *adj.* [Italian *altrui* somebody else]

ALU *abbr.* = ARITHMETIC AND LOGIC UNIT.

alum /ˈæləm/ *n.* double sulphate of aluminium and potassium. [Latin *alumen -min-*]

alumina /əˈluːmɪnə/ *n.* aluminium oxide occurring naturally as corundum and emery.

aluminium /ˌæljʊˈmɪnɪəm/ *n.* (*US* **aluminum** /əˈluːmɪnəm/) silvery light and malleable metallic element resistant to tarnishing by air.

aluminize /əˈluːmɪˌnaɪz/ *v.* (also **-ise**) (**-zing** or **-sing**) coat with aluminium.

alumnus /əˈlʌmnəs/ *n.* (*pl.* **alumni** /-naɪ/; *fem.* **alumna**, *pl.* **alumnae** /-niː/) former pupil or student. [Latin, = nursling, pupil]

always /ˈɔːlweɪz/ *adv.* **1** at all times; on all occasions. **2** whatever the circumstances. **3** repeatedly, often. [from ALL, WAY]

alyssum /ˈælɪsəm/ *n.* plant with small usu. yellow or white flowers. [Greek, = curing madness]

Alzheimer's disease /ˈæltsˌhaɪməz/ *n.* brain disorder causing senility. [*Alzheimer*, name of a neurologist]

AM *abbr.* **1** airmail. **2** amplitude modulation. **3** area manager. **4** assistant manager. **5** Associate Member. **6** *Insurance* (French) assurance mutuelle (= mutual insurance).

Am *symb.* americium.

Am. *abbr.* America(n).

am *1st person sing. present* of BE.

a.m. *abbr.* before noon. [Latin *ante meridiem*]

a/m *abbr.* above mentioned.

AMA *abbr.* **1** American Management Association. **2** Association of Metropolitan Authorities.

Amalfi /əˈmælfɪ/ port and holiday resort about 40 km (25 miles) SE of Naples, on the Gulf of Salerno; pop. (1981) 6000.

amalgam /əˈmælgəm/ *n.* **1** mixture or blend. **2** alloy of mercury and another metal, used esp. in dentistry. [Greek *malagma* an emollient]

amalgamate /əˈmælgəˌmeɪt/ *v.* (**-ting**) **1** mix, unite. **2** (of metals) alloy with mercury. [medieval Latin: related to AMALGAM]

◆ **amalgamation** /əˌmælgəˈmeɪʃ(ə)n/ *n.* **1** mixture. **2** uniting, combining, esp. of two or more businesses (see MERGER).

---

amanuensis /əˌmænjuːˈensɪs/ *n.* (*pl.* **-enses** /-siːz/) literary assistant, esp. writing from dictation. [Latin *a manu* 'at hand']

amaranth /ˈæməˌrænθ/ *n.* **1** plant with small green, red, or purple tinted flowers. **2** imaginary unfading flower. **3** purple colour. □ **amaranthine** /-ˈrænθaɪn/ *adj.* [Greek *amarantos* unfading]

amaryllis /ˌæməˈrɪlɪs/ *n.* bulbous plant with lily-like flowers. [Greek, a girl's name]

amass /əˈmæs/ *v.* heap together; accumulate. [French: related to AD-, MASS[1]]

amateur /ˈæmətə(r)/ *n.* person who engages in a pursuit as a pastime rather than a profession, or performs with limited skill. □ **amateurish** *adj.* **amateurism** *n.* [Latin *amator* lover: related to AMATORY]

amatory /ˈæmətərɪ/ *adj.* of sexual love. [Latin *amo* love]

amaze /əˈmeɪz/ *v.* (**-zing**) surprise greatly, fill with wonder. □ **amazement** *n.* **amazing** *adj.* [earlier *amase* from Old English *āmasod*]

Amazon[1] /ˈæməz(ə)n/ *n.* **1** female warrior of a mythical race in the Black Sea area. **2** (**amazon**) large, strong, or athletic woman. □ **Amazonian** /-ˈzəʊnɪən/ *adj.* [Latin from Greek]

Amazon[2] /ˈæməz(ə)n/ river in South America, 6570 km (4080 miles) long, rising in Peru, in the Andes, and flowing into the Atlantic Ocean on the N coast of Brazil. It drains two-fifths of the continent and in terms of waterflow it is the largest river in the world. □ **Amazonian** /-ˈzəʊnɪən/ *adj.*

ambassador /æmˈbæsədə(r)/ *n.* **1** diplomat sent to live abroad to represent his or her country's interests. **2** promoter (*ambassador of peace*). □ **ambassadorial** /-ˈdɔːrɪəl/ *adj.* [Latin *ambactus* servant]

Ambato /æmˈbɑːtəʊ/ market town and transportation centre in central Ecuador; pop. (est. 1990) 229 200. The town was almost totally destroyed by an earthquake in 1949.

amber –*n.* **1 a** yellow translucent fossilized resin used in jewellery. **b** colour of this. **2** yellow traffic-light meaning caution. –*adj.* of or like amber. [French from Arabic]

ambergris /ˈæmbəgrɪs/ *n.* waxlike secretion of the sperm whale, found floating in tropical seas and used in perfumes. [French, = grey amber]

ambidextrous /ˌæmbɪˈdekstrəs/ *adj.* able to use either hand equally well. [Latin *ambi-* on both sides, DEXTER]

ambience /ˈæmbɪəns/ *n.* surroundings or atmosphere. [Latin *ambio* go round]

ambient *adj.* surrounding.

ambiguous /æmˈbɪgjʊəs/ *adj.* **1** having an obscure or double meaning. **2** difficult to classify. □ **ambiguity** /-ˈgjuːɪtɪ/ *n.* (*pl.* **-ies**). [Latin *ambi-* both ways, *ago* drive]

ambit /ˈæmbɪt/ *n.* scope, extent, or bounds. [Latin: related to AMBIENCE]

ambition /æmˈbɪʃ(ə)n/ *n.* **1** determination to succeed. **2** object of this. [Latin, = canvassing: related to AMBIENCE]

ambitious *adj.* **1** full of ambition or high aims. **2** (foll. by *of*, or *to* + infin.) strongly determined.

ambivalence /æmˈbɪvələns/ *n.* coexistence of opposing feelings. □ **ambivalent** *adj.* [Latin *ambo* both, EQUIVALENCE]

amble /ˈæmb(ə)l/ *–v.* (**-ling**) move at an easy pace. *–n.* such a pace. [Latin *ambulo* walk]

ambrosia /æmˈbrəʊzɪə/ *n.* **1** (in classical mythology) the food of the gods. **2** sublimely delicious food etc. [Greek, = elixir of life]

ambulance /ˈæmbjʊləns/ *n.* **1** vehicle equipped for conveying patients to hospital. **2** mobile hospital serving an army. [Latin: related to AMBLE]

♦ **ambulance stocks** *n.pl.* high-performance stocks recommended by a broker to a client whose portfolio has not fulfilled expectations. They either refresh the portfolio (and the relationship between broker and client) or they confirm the client's worst fears.

---

ambulatory /ˈæmbjʊlətərɪ/ *–adj.* **1** of or for walking. **2** movable. *–n.* (*pl.* **-ies**) arcade or cloister. [Latin: related to AMBLE]

ambuscade /ˌæmbəˈskeɪd/ *n.* & *v.* (**-ding**) = AMBUSH.

ambush /ˈæmbʊʃ/ *–n.* **1** surprise attack by persons hiding. **2** hiding-place for this. *–v.* attack from an ambush; waylay. [French: related to IN-[1], BUSH[1]]

AMC *abbr.* **1** = AGRICULTURAL MORTGAGE CORPORATION LTD. **2** Association of Management Consultants.

AMCIB *abbr.* Associate Member of the Corporation of Insurance Brokers.

ameliorate /əˈmiːlɪəˌreɪt/ *v.* (**-ting**) make or become better. □ **amelioration** /əˌmiːlɪəˈreɪʃ(ə)n/ *n.* **ameliorative** *adj.* [from AD-, Latin *melior* better]

amen /ɑːˈmen/ *int.* (esp. at the end of a prayer etc.) so be it. [Church Latin from Hebrew, = certainly]

amenable /əˈmiːnəb(ə)l/ *adj.* **1** responsive, docile. **2** (often foll. by *to*) answerable to law etc. [French: related to AD-, Latin *mino* drive animals]

amend /əˈmend/ *v.* **1** make minor alterations in to improve. **2** correct an error in (a document etc.). [Latin: related to EMEND]

■ **Usage** *Amend* is often confused with *emend*, a more technical word used in the context of textual correction.

amendment *n.* minor alteration or addition in a document, resolution, etc.

amends *n.* □ **make amends** (often foll. by *for*) compensate (for).

amenity /əˈmiːnɪtɪ/ *n.* (*pl.* **-ies**) **1** pleasant or useful feature or facility. **2** pleasantness (of a place etc.). [Latin *amoenus* pleasant]

America /əˈmerɪkə/ **1** continent of the W hemisphere consisting of two great land masses, North and South America, joined by the narrow isthmus of Central America. **2** United States of America. [name of navigator *Amerigo* Vespucci]

American /əˈmerɪkən/ *–adj.* of America, esp. the United States. *–n.* **1** native, citizen, or inhabitant of America, esp. the US. **2** English as used in the US. □ **Americanize** *v.* (also **-ise**) (**-zing** or **-sing**).

♦ **American depository receipt** *n.* (also **ADR**) receipt issued by a US bank to a member of the US public who has bought shares in a foreign country. The certificates are denominated in US dollars and can be traded as a security in US markets.

American dream *n.* ideal of democracy and prosperity.

American football *n.* football evolved from Rugby.

American Indian see INDIAN.

Americanism *n.* word etc. of US origin or usage.

American National Standards Institute *n.* (also **ANSI**) organization that determines US industrial standards, including some used in computing, and ensures that these correspond to those set by the International Standards Organization.

♦ **American option** see OPTION 3.

---

americium /ˌæməˈrɪsɪəm/ *n.* artificial radioactive metallic element. [*America*, where first made]

Amerind /ˈæmərɪnd/ *adj.* & *n.* (also **Amerindian** /-ˈrɪndɪən/) = AMERICAN INDIAN (see INDIAN).

amethyst /ˈæməθɪst/ *n.* semiprecious stone of a violet or purple variety of quartz. [Greek, = preventing drunkenness]

Amex /ˈæmɛks/ *n.* **1** American Express. **2** American Stock Exchange. [abbreviation]

Amharic /æmˈhærɪk/ *–n.* official and commercial language of Ethiopia. *–adj.* of this language. [*Amhara*, region of Ethiopia]

amiable /ˈeɪmɪəb(ə)l/ *adj.* (esp. of a person) friendly and pleasant, likeable. □ **amiably** *adv.* [Latin: related to AMICABLE]

AMIAP *abbr.* Associate Member of the Institution of Analysts and Programmers.

amicable /ˈæmɪkəb(ə)l/ *adj.* (esp. of an arrangement, relations, etc.) friendly. □ **amicably** *adv.* [Latin *amicus* friend]

amid /əˈmɪd/ *prep.* in the middle of, among. [Old English: related to ON, MID]

amidships *adv.* in or into the middle of a ship. [from AMID, alternative form *midships*]

amidst var. of AMID.

Amiens /ˈæmjæ̃/ city in N France; the capital of Picardy; industries include textiles, chemicals, and tyres; pop. (est. 1990) 136 358.

AMI.Ex. *abbr.* Associate Member of the Institute of Export.

amine /ˈeɪmiːn/ *n.* compound formed from ammonia by replacement of one or more hydrogen atoms by an organic radical or radicals.

amino acid /əˈmiːnəʊ/ *n. Biochem.* any of a group of nitrogenous organic acids occurring naturally in plant and animal tissues and forming the basic constituents of proteins. [from AMINE, ACID]

AMIPA *abbr.* Associate Member of the Institute of Practitioners in Advertising.

AMIQM *abbr.* Associate Member of the Institute of Quality Assurance.

amir var. of EMIR.

Amirante Islands /ˈæmɪˌrænt/ group of coral islands in the W Indian Ocean, forming part of the Seychelles; pop. (1985) 144.

amiss /əˈmɪs/ *–predic. adj.* wrong, out of order. *–adv.* wrong(ly), inappropriately (*everything went amiss*). □ **take amiss** be offended by. [Old Norse *à mis* so as to miss]

amity /ˈæmɪtɪ/ *n.* friendship. [Latin *amicus* friend]

Amman /əˈmɑːn/ capital of Jordan; industries include communications and manufacturing; pop. (est. 1994) 1 300 040.

ammeter /ˈæmɪtə(r)/ *n.* instrument for measuring electric current in amperes. [from AMPERE, -METER]

ammo /ˈæməʊ/ *n. slang* ammunition. [abbreviation]

ammonia /əˈməʊnɪə/ *n.* **1** pungent strongly alkaline gas.

2 (in general use) solution of ammonia in water. [as SAL AMMONIAC]

ammonite /'æmə,naɪt/ *n.* coil-shaped fossil shell. [Latin, = horn of Jupiter Ammon]

ammunition /,æmjʊ'nɪʃ(ə)n/ *n.* **1** supply of bullets, shells, grenades, etc. **2** information usable in an argument. [French *la* MUNITION taken as *l'ammu-*]

amnesia /æm'ni:zɪə/ *n.* loss of memory. □ **amnesiac** /-zɪ,æk/ *n.* [Latin from Greek]

amnesty /'æmnɪstɪ/ –*n.* (*pl.* **-ies**) general pardon, esp. for political offences. –*v.* (**-ies**, **-ied**) grant an amnesty to. [Greek *amnēstia* oblivion]

amniocentesis /,æmnɪəʊsen'ti:sɪs/ *n.* (*pl.* **-teses** /-si:z/) sampling of amniotic fluid to detect foetal abnormality. [from AMNION, Greek *kentēsis* pricking]

amnion /'æmnɪən/ *n.* (*pl.* **amnia**) innermost membrane enclosing an embryo. □ **amniotic** /-'ɒtɪk/ *adj.* [Greek, = caul]

amoeba /ə'mi:bə/ *n.* (*pl.* **-s**) microscopic aquatic amorphous one-celled organism. □ **amoebic** *adj.* [Greek, = change]

amok /ə'mɒk/ *adv.* □ **run amok** run wild. [Malay]

among /ə'mʌŋ/ *prep.* (also **amongst**) **1** surrounded by, with (*lived among the trees*; *be among friends*). **2** included in (*among us were dissidents*). **3** in the category of (*among his best works*). **4 a** between; shared by (*divide it among you*). **b** from the joint resources of (*among us we can manage it*). **5** with one another (*talked among themselves*). □ **among matter** position of an advertisement within a newspaper or magazine so that it is among editorial material. [Old English, = in a crowd]

amoral /eɪ'mɒr(ə)l/ *adj.* **1** beyond morality. **2** without moral principles.

amorous /'æmərəs/ *adj.* of, showing, or feeling sexual love. [Latin *amor* love]

amorphous /ə'mɔ:fəs/ *adj.* **1** of no definite shape. **2** vague. **3** *Mineral.* & *Chem.* non-crystalline. [Greek *a-* not, *morphē* form]

♦ **amortize** /ə'mɔ:taɪz/ *v.* (also **-ise**) (**-zing** or **-sing**) **1** gradually extinguish (a debt) by regular instalments. **2** *Accounting* **a** treat as an expense the annual amount deemed to waste away from (a wasting asset, esp. a lease). It is customary to divide the cost of a lease by the number of years of its term and treat the result as an annual charge against profit. While this method does not necessarily reflect the value of the lease at any given time, it is an equitable way of allocating the original cost between periods. **b** write off (purchased goodwill), either in its year of purchase by a single charge to the reserves or by regular charges to the profit and loss account over the period of its economic life. □ **amortization** /-'zeɪʃ(ə)n/ *n.* [Latin *ad mortem* to death]

♦ **amortizing mortgage** *n.* mortgage in which all the principal and all the interest has been repaid by the end of the mortgage agreement period.

---

amount /ə'maʊnt/ –*n.* quantity, esp. a total in number, size, value, extent, etc. –*v.* (foll. by *to*) be equivalent to in number, significance, etc. □ **amounts differ** words written or stamped on a cheque or bill of exchange by a banker who returns it unpaid because the amount in words differs from that in figures. [Latin *ad montem* upward]

amour /ə'mʊə(r)/ *n.* (esp. secret) love affair. [French, = love]

amour propre /æ,mʊə 'prɒpr/ *n.* self-respect. [French]

amp[1] *n.* ampere. [abbreviation]

amp[2] *n. colloq.* amplifier. [abbreviation]

ampelopsis /,æmpɪ'lɒpsɪs/ *n.* (*pl.* same) climbing plant related to the vine. [Greek *ampelos* vine, *opsis* appearance]

amperage /'æmpərɪdʒ/ *n.* strength of an electric current in amperes.

ampere /'æmpeə(r)/ *n.* SI base unit of electric current. [*Ampère*, name of a physicist]

ampersand /'æmpə,sænd/ *n.* the sign & (= *and*). [corruption of *and* PER SE *and*]

amphetamine /æm'fetə,mi:n/ *n.* synthetic drug used esp. as a stimulant. [abbreviation of chemical name]

amphibian /æm'fɪbɪən/ –*adj.* of a class of vertebrates (e.g. frogs) with an aquatic larval stage followed by a terrestrial adult stage. –*n.* **1** vertebrate of this class. **2** vehicle able to operate both on land and in water. [Greek *amphi-* both, *bios* life]

amphibious *adj.* **1** living or operating on land and in water. **2** involving military forces landed from the sea.

amphitheatre /'æmfɪ,θɪətə(r)/ *n.* esp. circular unroofed building with tiers of seats surrounding a central space. [Greek *amphi-* round]

amphora /'æmfərə/ *n.* (*pl.* **-phorae** /-,ri:/) narrow-necked Greek or Roman vessel with two handles. [Greek *amphoreus*]

ample /'æmp(ə)l/ *adj.* (**ampler**, **amplest**) **1 a** plentiful, abundant, extensive. **b** *euphem.* large, stout. **2** more than enough. □ **amply** *adv.* [Latin *amplus*]

amplifier /'æmplɪ,faɪə(r)/ *n.* electronic device for increasing the strength of electrical signals, esp. for conversion into sound.

amplify /'æmplɪ,faɪ/ *v.* (**-ies**, **-ied**) **1** increase the strength of (sound, electrical signals, etc.). **2** add detail to, expand (a story etc.). □ **amplification** /-fɪ'keɪʃ(ə)n/ *n.* [Latin: related to AMPLE]

amplitude /'æmplɪ,tju:d/ *n.* **1** maximum departure from average of an oscillation, alternating current, etc. **2** spaciousness; abundance. [Latin: related to AMPLE]

amplitude modulation *n.* modulation of a wave by variation of its amplitude.

ampoule /'æmpu:l/ *n.* small sealed capsule holding a solution for injection. [French: related to AMPULLA]

ampulla /æm'pʊlə/ *n.* (*pl.* **-pullae** /-li:/) **1** Roman globular flask with two handles. **2** ecclesiastical vessel. [Latin]

amputate /'æmpjʊ,teɪt/ *v.* (**-ting**) cut off surgically (a limb etc.). □ **amputation** /-'teɪʃ(ə)n/ *n.* **amputee** /-'ti:/ *n.* [Latin *amb-* about, *puto* prune]

Amritsar /æm'rɪtsə(r)/ city in NW India, in Punjab; industries include textiles and silk; pop. (1991) 709 000. It is the centre of the Sikh faith and the site of its holiest temple.

♦ **AMSO** *abbr.* = ASSOCIATION OF MARKET SURVEY ORGANIZATIONS.

Amsterdam /,æmstə'dæm/ capital and largest city of the Netherlands, one of the major ports and commercial centres of Europe, built on about 100 islands separated by canals; pop. (1995) 1 101 400. Its many industries include diamond-cutting and shipbuilding.

AMT 1 (also **a.m.t.**) airmail transfer. **2** *US* alternative minimum tax.

AMTRI *abbr.* Advanced Manufacturing Technology Research Institute.

amuck var. of AMOK.

amulet /'æmjʊlɪt/ *n.* charm worn against evil. [Latin]

amuse /ə'mju:z/ *v.* (**-sing**) **1** cause to laugh or smile. **2** interest or occupy. □ **amusing** *adj.* [French *a* cause to, *muser* stare]

amusement *n.* **1** thing that amuses. **2** being amused. **3** mechanical device (e.g. a roundabout) for entertainment at a fairground etc.

amusement arcade *n.* indoor area with slot-machines.

AN *airline flight code* Ansett Australia.

an see A[1].

an- see A-.

-an *suffix* (also **-ian**) forming adjectives and nouns, esp. from names of places, systems, classes, etc. (*Mexican*; *Anglican*; *crustacean*). [French *-ain*, Latin *-anus*]

ANA *abbr.* All Nippon Airways.

Anabaptist /,ænə'bæptɪst/ *n.* member of a religious

group believing in baptism only of adults. [Greek *ana* again]

anabolic steroid /ˌænəˈbɒlɪk/ *n.* synthetic steroid hormone used to increase muscle size.

anabolism /əˈnæbəˌlɪz(ə)m/ *n.* synthesis of complex molecules in living organisms from simpler ones together with the storage of energy. [Greek *anabolē* ascent]

anachronism /əˈnækrəˌnɪz(ə)m/ *n.* **1 a** attribution of a custom, event, etc., to the wrong period. **b** thing thus attributed. **2** out-of-date person or thing. □ **anachronistic** /-ˈnɪstɪk/ *adj.* [Greek *ana-* against, *khronos* time]

anaconda /ˌænəˈkɒndə/ *n.* large non-poisonous snake killing its prey by constriction. [Sinhalese]

anaemia /əˈniːmɪə/ *n.* (*US* **anemia**) deficiency of red blood cells or their haemoglobin, causing pallor and weariness. [Greek, = want of blood]

anaemic /əˈniːmɪk/ *adj.* (*US* **anemic**) **1** of or suffering from anaemia. **2** pale, listless.

anaesthesia /ˌænɪsˈθiːzɪə/ *n.* (*US* **anes-**) absence of sensation, esp. artificially induced before surgery. [Greek]

anaesthetic /ˌænɪsˈθetɪk/ (*US* **anes-**) –*n.* substance producing anaesthesia. –*adj.* producing anaesthesia.

anaesthetist /əˈniːsθətɪst/ *n.* (*US* **anes-**) specialist in the administration of anaesthetics.

anaesthetize /əˈniːsθəˌtaɪz/ *v.* (*US* **anes-**) (also **-ise**) (**-zing** or **-sing**) administer an anaesthetic to.

anagram /ˈænəˌgræm/ *n.* word or phrase formed by transposing the letters of another. [Greek *ana* again, *gramma* letter]

anal /ˈeɪn(ə)l/ *adj.* of the anus.

analgesia /ˌænəlˈdʒiːzɪə/ *n.* absence or relief of pain. [Greek]

analgesic –*adj.* relieving pain. –*n.* analgesic drug.

analog var. of ANALOGUE.

■ **Usage** *Analog* is the US spelling of *analogue* in all its senses and is the preferred British spelling in computing and electronics.

◆ **analog computer** *n.* computer that accepts and processes data in the form of a continuously variable quantity whose magnitude is made proportional to the value of the data. An analog computer solves problems by physical analogy, usu. electrical. Each quantity (e.g. temperature, speed, displacement) that occurs in the problem is represented in the computer by a continuously variable quantity such as voltage. Circuit elements in the computer are interconnected in such a way that the voltages fed to them interact in the same way as the quantities in the real-life problem interact. The output voltage then represents the numerical solution of the problem.

Analog computers are used in situations where a continuous representation of data is more convenient or more useful than the discrete representation that is required by a digital computer. Their major application is in simulation, i.e. in imitating the behaviour of some existing or intended system, or some aspect of that behaviour, for purposes of design, research, etc. Another important application is process control in industry or manufacturing, where data has to be continuously monitored.

An analog computer can be used in conjunction with a digital computer, forming what is known as a **hybrid computer**. A hybrid computer, which can process both analog and discrete data, often has advantages over an analog computer in process control etc.

---

analogize /əˈnæləˌdʒaɪz/ *v.* (also **-ise**) (**-zing** or **-sing**) use, or represent or explain by, analogy.

analogous /əˈnæləgəs/ *adj.* (usu. foll. by *to*) partially similar or parallel. [Greek *analogos* proportionate]

analog signal *n.* continuously varying value of voltage or current. Cf. DIGITAL SIGNAL.

analog to digital converter see A/D CONVERTER.

analogue /ˈænəˌlɒg/ *n.* (*US* **analog**) **1** analogous thing. **2** (*attrib.*) (usu. **analog**) (of a computer etc.) using physical variables, e.g. voltage, to represent numbers. See also ANALOG COMPUTER.

analogy /əˈnælədʒɪ/ *n.* (*pl.* **-ies**) **1** correspondence; partial similarity. **2** arguing or reasoning from parallel cases. □ **analogical** /ˌænəˈlɒdʒɪk(ə)l/ *adj.* [Greek *analogia* proportion]

analyse /ˈænəˌlaɪz/ *v.* (*US* **analyze**) (**-sing** or **-zing**) **1** examine in detail; ascertain the constituents of (a substance, sentence, etc.). **2** psychoanalyse.

analysis /əˈnælɪsɪs/ *n.* (*pl.* **-lyses** /-ˌsiːz/) **1 a** detailed examination of elements or structure. **b** statement of the result of this. **2** *Chem.* determination of the constituent parts of a mixture or compound. **3** psychoanalysis. [Greek *ana* up, *luō* loose]

analyst /ˈænəlɪst/ *n.* **1** person skilled in (esp. chemical or computer) analysis. **2** psychoanalyst.

analytical /ˌænəˈlɪtɪk(ə)l/ *adj.* (also **analytic**) of or using analysis.

analyze *US* var. of ANALYSE.

anapaest /ˈænəˌpiːst/ *n.* metrical foot consisting of two short syllables followed by one long syllable (⏑⏑–). [Greek *anapaistos* reversed (dactyl)]

anarchism /ˈænəˌkɪz(ə)m/ *n.* political theory that all government and laws should be abolished. [French: related to ANARCHY]

anarchist /ˈænəkɪst/ *n.* advocate of anarchism. □ **anarchistic** /-ˈkɪstɪk/ *adj.*

anarchy /ˈænəkɪ/ *n.* disorder, esp. political. □ **anarchic** /əˈnɑːkɪk/ *adj.* [Greek *an-* without, *arkhē* rule]

anathema /əˈnæθəmə/ *n.* (*pl.* **-s**) **1** detested thing (*is anathema to me*). **2** ecclesiastical curse. [Greek, = thing devoted (i.e. to evil)]

anathematize *v.* (also **-ise**) (**-zing** or **-sing**) curse.

Anatolia /ˌænəˈtəʊlɪə/ (formerly **Asia Minor**) westernmost peninsula of Asia, which now forms the Asian part of Turkey. □ **Anatolian** *adj.* & *n.* [Greek *anatolē* east]

anatomy /əˈnætəmɪ/ *n.* (*pl.* **-ies**) **1** science of animal or plant structure. **2** such a structure. **3** analysis. □ **anatomical** /ˌænəˈtɒmɪk(ə)l/ *adj.* **anatomist** *n.* [Greek *ana-* up, *temnō* cut]

anatto var. of ANNATTO.

ANC *abbr.* African National Congress.

-ance *suffix* forming nouns expressing: **1** quality or state or an instance of one (*arrogance*; *resemblance*). **2** action (*assistance*). [French *-ance*, Latin *-antia*]

ancestor /ˈænsestə(r)/ *n.* **1** person, animal, or plant from which another has descended or evolved. **2** prototype or forerunner. [Latin *ante-* before, *cedo* go]

ancestral /ænˈsestr(ə)l/ *adj.* belonging to or inherited from one's ancestors.

ancestry /ˈænsestrɪ/ *n.* (*pl.* **-ies**) **1** family descent, lineage. **2** ancestors collectively.

anchor /ˈæŋkə(r)/ –*n.* **1** heavy metal weight used to moor a ship or a balloon. **2** stabilizing thing. –*v.* **1** secure with an anchor. **2** fix firmly. **3** cast anchor. **4** be moored by an anchor. [Greek *agkura*]

Anchorage /ˈæŋkərɪdʒ/ port in the US, the largest city in Alaska; industries include defence projects and coal- and gold-mining; pop. (est. 1994) 253 650.

anchorage *n.* **1** place for anchoring. **2** anchoring or lying at anchor.

anchorite /ˈæŋkəˌraɪt/ *n.* hermit; religious recluse. [Greek *anakhōreō* retire]

anchorman *n.* coordinator, esp. as compère in a broadcast.

anchovy /ˈæntʃəvɪ/ *n.* (*pl.* **-ies**) small strong-flavoured fish of the herring family. [Spanish and Portuguese *anchova*]

ancien régime /ɒ̃ˌsjæ̃ reˈʒiːm/ *n.* (*pl.* ***anciens régimes*** pronunc. same) **1** political and social system of pre-Revolutionary (before 1787) France. **2** any superseded regime. [French, = old rule]

ancient /ˈeɪnʃ(ə)nt/ *adj.* **1** of long ago, esp. before the fall of the Roman Empire in the West. **2** having lived or existed long. □ **the ancients** people of ancient times, esp. the Greeks and Romans. [Latin *ante* before]

♦ **ancient lights** *n.* (usu. treated as *sing.*) light enjoyed for 20 years or more through a defined aperture (e.g. a window) in a building. Under the Prescription Act (1832) the owner of the building has a right to such light, which may not thereafter be obstructed. Before the passing of this act it was very difficult to obtain rights to any light, as the common law recognizes no natural right to light.

ancillary /æn'sɪlərɪ/ *–adj.* **1** (esp. of health workers) providing essential support. **2** (often foll. by *to*) subordinate, subservient. *–n.* (*pl.* **-ies**) **1** ancillary worker. **2** auxiliary or accessory. [Latin *ancilla* handmaid]

♦ **ancillary credit business** *n.* business involved in credit brokerage, debt adjusting, debt counselling, debt collecting, or the operation of a credit-reference agency (see COMMERCIAL AGENCY). **Credit brokerage** includes the effecting of introductions of individuals wishing to obtain credit to persons carrying on a consumer-credit business. **Debt adjusting** is the process by which a third party negotiates terms for the discharge of a debt due under consumer-credit agreements or consumer-hire agreements with the creditor or owner on behalf of the debtor or hirer. The latter may also pay a third party to take over his obligation to discharge a debt or to undertake any similar acitivity concerned with its liquidation. **Debt counselling** is the giving of advice (other than by the original creditor and certain others) to debtors or hirers about the liquidation of debts due under consumer-credit agreements or consumer-hire agreements. A **credit-reference agency** collects information concerning the financial standing of individuals and supplies this information to those seeking it. The Consumer Credit Act (1974) provides for the licensing of ancillary credit businesses and regulates their activities.

-ancy *suffix* forming nouns denoting a quality (*constancy*) or state (*infancy*). [Latin *-antia*]

AND *international vehicle registration* Andorra.

and /ænd, ənd/ *conj.* **1 a** connecting words, clauses, or sentences, to be taken jointly (*you and I*). **b** implying progression (*better and better*). **c** implying causation (*she hit him and he cried*). **d** implying great duration (*cried and cried*). **e** implying a great number (*miles and miles*). **f** implying addition (*two and two*). **g** implying variety (*there are books and books*). **2** *colloq.* to (*try and come*). **3** in relation to (*Britain and the EC*). □ **and/or** either or both of two stated alternatives. [Old English]

Andalusia /ˌændə'luːsɪə/ (also **Andalucia**) southernmost region of Spain, bordering on the Atlantic Ocean and the Mediterranean Sea; pop. (est. 1994) 7 053 050; capital, Seville. Industries include tourism; wine, olive oil, and citrus fruit are produced. □ **Andalusian** *adj.* & *n.*

Andaman and Nicobar Islands /'ændəmən, 'nɪkəˌbɑː(r)/ Union Territory of India, consisting of two groups of islands in the Bay of Bengal; pop. (est. 1994) 322 000; capital, Port Blair, in the Andaman Islands. There are plywood, match, and fishing industries; coconuts, areca nuts, rubber, and coffee are produced.

andante /æn'dæntɪ/ *Mus. –adv.* & *adj.* in a moderately slow tempo. *–n.* such a passage or movement. [Italian, = going]

Andes /'ændiːz/ major mountain range running the length of the Pacific coast of South America. It includes many volcanoes, and several peaks top 6150 m (20 000 ft). □ **Andean** /æn'diːən, 'æn-/ *adj.*

Andhra Pradesh /ˌɑːndrə prə'deʃ/ state in SE India; industries include forestry, mining, farming, shipbuilding, machinery, and textiles; pop. (est. 1994) 71 800 000; capital, Hyderabad.

andiron /'ændˌaɪən/ *n.* metal stand (usu. one of a pair) for supporting logs in a fireplace. [French *andier*]

androgynous /æn'drɒdʒɪnəs/ *adj.* **1** hermaphrodite. **2** *Bot.* with stamens and pistils in the same flower. [Greek *anēr andr-* man, *gunē* woman]

android /'ændrɔɪd/ *n.* robot with a human appearance. [Greek *anēr andr-* man, -OID]

anecdote /'ænɪkˌdəʊt/ *n.* short, esp. true, account or story. □ **anecdotal** /-'dəʊt(ə)l/ *adj.* [Greek *anekdota* things unpublished]

anemia *US* var. of ANAEMIA.

anemic *US* var. of ANAEMIC.

anemometer /ˌænɪ'mɒmɪtə(r)/ *n.* instrument for measuring wind force. [Greek *anemos* wind]

anemone /ə'nemənɪ/ *n.* plant of the buttercup family, with vividly-coloured flowers. [Greek, = wind-flower]

aneroid /'ænəˌrɔɪd/ *–adj.* (of a barometer) measuring air-pressure by its action on the lid of a box containing a vacuum. *–n.* aneroid barometer. [Greek *a-* not, *nēros* water]

anesthesia etc. *US* var. of ANAESTHESIA etc.

aneurysm /'ænjʊˌrɪz(ə)m/ *n.* (also **aneurism**) excessive localized enlargement of an artery. [Greek *aneurunō* widen]

anew /ə'njuː/ *adv.* **1** again. **2** in a different way. [earlier *of newe*]

angel /'eɪndʒ(ə)l/ *n.* **1 a** attendant or messenger of God. **b** representation of this in human form with wings. **2** virtuous or obliging person. **3** *slang* financial backer of a play etc. [Greek *aggelos* messenger]

angel cake *n.* light sponge cake.

angel-fish *n.* fish with winglike fins.

angelic /æn'dʒelɪk/ *adj.* of or like an angel. □ **angelically** *adv.*

angelica /æn'dʒelɪkə/ *n.* aromatic plant or its candied stalks. [medieval Latin, = angelic (herb)]

angelus /'ændʒɪləs/ *n.* **1** Roman Catholic prayers commemorating the Incarnation, said at morning, noon, and sunset. **2** bell announcing this. [Latin *Angelus domini* (= the angel of the Lord), opening words]

anger /'æŋgə(r)/ *–n.* extreme or passionate displeasure. *–v.* make angry. [Old Norse *angr* grief]

Angers /'ɑ̃ʒeɪ/ city in W France, the capital of the former province of Anjou in the Pays de la Loire region; industries include wine, textiles, and agricultural machinery; pop. (1990) 146 163.

angina /æn'dʒaɪnə/ *n.* (in full **angina pectoris** /'pektərɪs/) chest pain brought on by exertion, caused by an inadequate blood supply to the heart. [Greek *agkhonē* strangling]

angiosperm /'ændʒɪəˌspɜːm/ *n.* plant producing flowers and reproducing by seeds enclosed within a carpel, including herbaceous plants, grasses, and most trees. [Greek *aggeion* vessel]

Angle /'æŋg(ə)l/ *n.* (usu. in *pl.*) member of a N German tribe that settled in E Britain in the 5th century. [Latin *Anglus*, from the name *Angul* in Germany]

angle[1] /'æŋg(ə)l/ *–n.* **1** space between two meeting lines

---

Andorra /æn'dɒrə/, **Principality of** small autonomous principality in the S Pyrenees, between France and Spain. The economy is based on agriculture (producing mainly tobacco and potatoes), forestry, and tourism. Clothes and motor vehicles are among the main exports. A customs union with the EC has been in force since 1991. Under a treaty of 1278 the sovereignty of Andorra is shared between the president of France and the bishop of Urgel in Spain. In 1993 the population voted in favour of a new democratic constitution, allowing them full sovereignty and reducing the powers of the co-princes. The first elections under this new system were held in late 1993. Head of government, Marc Forné Molné; capital, Andorra la Vella, pop. (est. 1993) 22 387. □ **Andorran** *adj.* & *n.*

languages	Catalan (official), French
currency	French franc (F) of 100 centimes, Spanish peseta (Pta) of 100 céntimos
pop. (est. 1994)	62 500
GNP (est. 1990)	US $ 1.2B
literacy	100%
life expectancy	76 (m); 82 (f)

or surfaces, esp. as measured in degrees. **2** corner. **3** point of view. –*v.* (**-ling**) **1** move or place obliquely. **2** present (information) in a biased way. [Latin *angulus*]

angle[2] /'æŋg(ə)l/ *v.* (**-ling**) **1** fish with hook and line. **2** (foll. by *for*) seek an objective indirectly (*angled for a loan*). □ **angler** *n.* [Old English]

Anglican /'æŋglıkən/ –*adj.* of the Church of England. –*n.* member of the Anglican Church. □ **Anglicanism** *n.* [Latin *Anglicanus*: related to ANGLE]

Anglicism /'æŋglı,sız(ə)m/ *n.* peculiarly English word or custom. [Latin *Anglicus*: related to ANGLE]

Anglicize /'æŋglı,saız/ *v.* (also **-ise**) (**-zing** or **-sing**) make English in character etc.

Anglo- *comb. form* **1** English. **2** of English origin. **3** English or British and. [Latin: related to ANGLE]

Anglo-Catholic /,æŋgləʊ'kæθəlık/ –*adj.* of a High Church Anglican wing emphasizing its Catholic tradition. –*n.* member of this group.

Anglo-French /,æŋgləʊ'frentʃ/ –*adj.* English (or British) and French. –*n.* French language as developed in England after the Norman Conquest.

Anglo-Indian /,æŋgləʊ'ındıən/ –*adj.* **1** of England and India. **2** of British descent but Indian residence. –*n.* Anglo-Indian person.

Anglo-Norman /,æŋgləʊ'nɔːmən/ –*adj.* English and Norman. –*n.* Norman dialect used in England after the Norman Conquest.

Anglophile /'æŋgləʊ,faıl/ *n.* person who greatly admires England or the English.

Anglo-Saxon /,æŋgləʊ'sæks(ə)n/ –*adj.* **1** of the English Saxons before the Norman Conquest. **2** of English descent. –*n.* **1** Anglo-Saxon person. **2** Old English. **3** *colloq.* plain (esp. crude) English.

angora /æŋ'gɔːrə/ *n.* **1** fabric or wool from the hair of the angora goat or rabbit. **2** long-haired variety of cat, goat, or rabbit. [*Angora* (= Ankara) in Turkey]

angostura /,æŋgə'stjʊərə/ *n.* aromatic bitter bark used as a flavouring. [*Angostura* (= Ciudad Bolívar) in Venezuela]

angry /'æŋgrı/ *adj.* (**-ier, -iest**) **1** feeling, showing, or suggesting anger (*angry sky*). **2** (of a wound etc.) inflamed, painful. □ **angrily** *adv.*

angst /æŋst/ *n.* anxiety, neurotic fear; guilt, remorse. [German]

angstrom /'æŋstrəm/ *n.* unit of length equal to 10^{-10} metre. [*Ångström*, name of a physicist]

Anguilla /æŋ'gwılə/ island in the West Indies, the most northerly of the Leeward Islands, a British dependency with full self-government (see ST KITTS AND NEVIS); pop. (1992) 8800; capital, The Valley, pop. (1992) 1400. The economy is based on tourism, fishing, and stock raising.

anguish /'æŋgwıʃ/ *n.* **1** severe mental suffering. **2** pain, agony. □ **anguished** *adj.* [Latin *angustia* tightness]

angular /'æŋgjʊlə(r)/ *adj.* **1** having sharp corners or (of a person) features. **2** forming an angle. **3** measured by angle (*angular distance*). □ **angularity** /-'lærıtı/ *n.* [Latin: related to ANGLE[1]]

Anhui /'ɑːnhweı/ (also **Anhwei**) province in E China; tea, rice, silk, steel, and soya beans are produced; pop. (est. 1994) 58 970 000; capital, Hefie (Hofei).

anhydrous /æn'haıdrəs/ *adj. Chem.* without water, esp. water of crystallization. [Greek *an-* without, *hudōr* water]

aniline /'ænı,liːn/ *n.* colourless oily liquid used in making dyes, drugs, and plastics. [German *Anil* indigo, former source]

animadvert /,ænımæd'vɜːt/ *v.* (foll. by *on*) *literary* criticize, censure. □ **animadversion** *n.* [Latin *animus* mind, ADVERSE]

animal /'ænım(ə)l/ –*n.* **1** living organism, esp. other than man, which feeds and usu. has sense-organs and a nervous system and can move quickly. **2** brutish person. –*adj.* **1** of or like an animal. **2** bestial; carnal. [Latin *animalis* having breath]

animalism *n.* **1** nature and activity of animals. **2** belief that humans are mere animals.

animality /,ænı'mælıtı/ *n.* **1** the animal world. **2** animal behaviour.

animalize /'ænımə,laız/ *v.* (also **-ise**) (**-zing** or **-sing**) make (a person) bestial, sensualize.

animate –*adj.* /'ænımət/ **1** having life. **2** lively. –*v.* /'ænı,meıt/ (**-ting**) **1** enliven. **2** give life to. [Latin *anima* breath]

animated /'ænı,meıtıd/ *adj.* **1** lively, vigorous. **2** having life. **3** (of a film etc.) using animation.

animation /,ænı'meıʃ(ə)n/ *n.* **1** vivacity, ardour. **2** being alive. **3** technique of producing a moving picture from a sequence of drawings or puppet poses etc.

animism /'ænı,mız(ə)m/ *n.* belief that inanimate and natural phenomena have souls. □ **animist** *n.* **animistic** /-'mıstık/ *adj.*

animosity /,ænı'mɒsıtı/ *n.* (*pl.* **-ies**) spirit or feeling of hostility. [Latin: related to ANIMUS]

animus /'ænıməs/ *n.* animosity, ill feeling. [Latin, = spirit, mind]

anion /'æn,aıən/ *n.* negatively charged ion. □ **anionic** /-'ɒnık/ *adj.* [Greek *ana* up, ION]

anise /'ænıs/ *n.* plant with aromatic seeds. [Greek *anison*]

aniseed /'ænı,siːd/ *n.* seed of the anise, used for flavouring.

Anjou /ɑ̃'ʒuː/ former province of W France, on the Loire.

Ankara /'æŋkərə/ (formerly **Angora**) capital of Turkey since 1923; an important trading centre in the W of the country; pop. (1990) 3 236 626.

Angola /æŋ'gəʊlə/, **People's Republic of** country in SW Africa, on the Atlantic coast N of Namibia. It is rich in mineral resources, including diamonds and oil, which account for most of its export revenue; other exports include coffee, sisal, and fish. A programme of economic reform, including widespread privatization, was scheduled to begin in 1992 but has been disrupted by civil war. *History.* The area was colonized by the Portuguese in the 16th century and remained in their possession until it achieved independence in 1975 after a bitter anti-colonial war. The years following independence were marked by civil war between the ruling Marxist MPLA party and the rival Unita movement. A ceasefire was agreed in 1991 and multi-party elections in 1992 resulted in victory for the MPLA; the result was not accepted by Unita supporters and the civil war resumed the following year. In late 1994 UNITA and the MPLA, under UN mediation, signed a peace agreement. In April 1997 a government of national reconciliation was formed; however, the UNITA leader refused the vice-presidency and would not enter the capital. In mid-1997 fighting resumed following the overthrow of President Mobutu in Zaïre (now Democratic Republic of Congo), a key ally of UNITA. President, José Eduardo dos Santos; capital, Luanda. □ **Angolan** *adj.* & *n.*

languages	Portuguese (official), Bantu dialects
currency	readjusted kwanza (Nkz) of 100 lwei
pop. (est. 1995)	11 558 000
GNP (1989)	US $ 6.01B
literacy	41.7%
life expectancy	45 (m); 48 (f)

Exchange rate, US¢ per Nkz

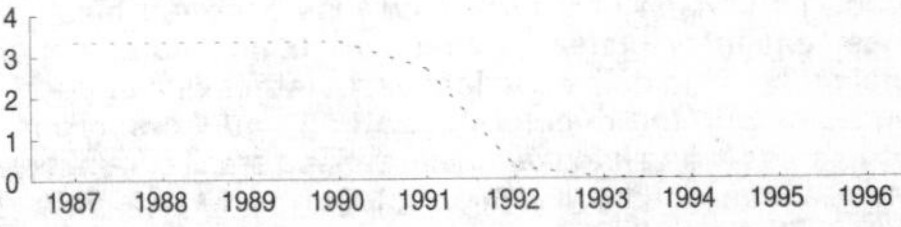

ankle /'æŋk(ə)l/ *n.* **1** joint connecting the foot with the leg. **2** this part of the leg. [Old Norse]

anklet /'æŋklɪt/ *n.* ornament or fetter worn round the ankle.

ankylosis /ˌæŋkɪ'ləʊsɪs/ *n.* stiffening of a joint by fusion of the bones. [Greek *agkulos* crooked]

Annaba /'ænəbə/ (formerly **Bône**) port in NE Algeria, on the Mediterranean coast, exporting chiefly minerals; industries include flour milling and iron and steel processing; pop. (1987) 453 951.

annals /'æn(ə)lz/ *n.pl.* **1** narrative of events year by year. **2** historical records. □ **annalist** *n.* [Latin *annus* year]

Annapolis /ə'næpəˌlɪs/ city and port in the US, capital of Maryland; pop. (1990) 33 187. The home of the US Naval Academy, it is a tourist resort with seafood industries.

annatto /ə'nætəʊ/ *n.* (also **anatto**) orange-red dye from the pulp of a tropical fruit, used for colouring foods. [Carib name of the fruit-tree]

anneal /ə'ni:l/ *v.* heat (metal or glass) and cool slowly, esp. to toughen it. [Old English *ǣlan* bake]

annelid /'ænəlɪd/ *n.* segmented worm, e.g. the earthworm. [Latin *anulus* ring]

annex /æ'neks/ *v.* **1** (often foll. by *to*) add as a subordinate part. **2** incorporate (territory) into one's own. **3** add as a condition or consequence. **4** *colloq.* take without right. □ **annexation** /-'seɪʃ(ə)n/ *n.* [Latin *necto* bind]

annexe /'æneks/ *n.* **1** separate or added building. **2** addition to a document.

annihilate /ə'naɪəˌleɪt/ *v.* (**-ting**) completely destroy or defeat. □ **annihilation** /-'leɪʃ(ə)n/ *n.* [Latin *nihil* nothing]

anniversary /ˌænɪ'vɜ:sərɪ/ *n.* (*pl.* **-ies**) **1** date of an event in a previous year. **2** celebration of this. [Latin *annus* year, *verto vers-* turn]

Annobón /'ænəˌbɔ:n/ (formerly (1973–9) **Pagalu**) island of Equatorial Guinea, in the Gulf of Guinea; pop. (est. 1987) 2360.

Anno Domini /ˌænəʊ 'dɒmɪˌnaɪ/ *adv.* years after Christ's birth. [Latin, = in the year of the Lord]

annotate /'ænəˌteɪt/ *v.* (**-ting**) add explanatory notes to. [Latin *nota* mark]

annotation /ˌænə'teɪʃ(ə)n/ *n.* **1** explanatory note. **2** *Computing* explanation added to a program to assist the reader. It may take the form of handwritten additions to the program listing, but more often is in the form of comments included in the program text.

announce /ə'naʊns/ *v.* (**-cing**) **1** make publicly known. **2** make known the arrival or imminence of (a guest, dinner, etc.). **3** be a sign of. □ **announcement** *n.* [Latin *nuntius* messenger]

announcer *n.* person who announces, esp. in broadcasting.

annoy /ə'nɔɪ/ *v.* **1** (often in *passive*) anger or distress slightly (*am annoyed with you*). **2** molest, harass. □ **annoyance** *n.* [Latin *in odio* hateful]

annual /'ænjʊəl/ *–adj.* **1** reckoned by the year. **2** occurring yearly. **3** living or lasting (only) a year. *–n.* **1** book etc. published yearly. **2** plant that lives only a year. □ **annually** *adv.* [Latin *annus* year]

♦ ***Annual Abstract of Statistics*** *n.* annual publication of the Central Statistical Office giving UK industrial, vital, legal, and social statistics. Cf. MONTHLY DIGEST OF STATISTICS.

♦ **annual accounts (annual report; report and accounts)** *n.pl.* financial statements of an organization, generally published annually. In the UK, incorporated bodies have a legal obligation to publish annual accounts and file them at Companies House. Annual accounts consist of a profit and loss account, balance sheet, cash-flow statement (if required), and statement of total recognized gains and losses, together with supporting notes and the directors' report and auditors' report. Companies falling into the legally defined small companies and medium-sized companies categories may file abbreviated accounts that may not have been audited. Some bodies are regulated by other statutes; for example, many financial institutions and their accounts will have to comply with their own regulations. Non-incorporated bodies, such as partnerships, are not legally obliged to produce accounts but may do so for their own information, for their banks if funding is being sought, and for the Inland Revenue for taxation purposes.

♦ **annual depreciation allowance** *n.* reduction in the book value of an asset at a specified annual percentage rate.

♦ **annual general meeting** *n.* (also **AGM**) annual meeting of the shareholders of a company, which must be held every year; the meetings may not be more than 15 months apart. Shareholders must be given 21 days' notice of the meeting. The usual business transacted at an AGM is the presentation of the audited accounts, the appointment of directors and auditors, the fixing of their remuneration, and recommendations for the payment of dividends. Other business may be transacted if notice of it has been given to the shareholders. See also AGENDA 1; ORDER OF BUSINESS.

---

annualized *adj.* (of rates of interest etc.) calculated on an annual basis, as a projection from figures obtained for a shorter period.

♦ **annual percentage rate** *n.* (also **APR**) annual equivalent rate of return on a loan or investment in which the rate of interest specified is chargeable or payable more frequently than annually. Most investment institutions are now required by law to specify the APR when the interest intervals are more frequent than annual. Similarly those charge cards that advertise monthly rates of interest (say, 2%) must state the equivalent APR; in this case it would be $[(1.02)^{12} - 1] \times 100 = 26.8\%$.

♦ **annual report** *n.* see ANNUAL ACCOUNTS.

♦ **annual return** *n.* document that must be filed with the Registrar of Companies within 14 days of the annual general meeting of a company. Information required on the annual return includes the address of the registered office of the company and the names, addresses, nationality, and occupations of its directors. The financial statements, directors' report, and auditors' report must be annexed to the return. Legally defined small companies and medium-sized companies may file abbreviated accounts. Unlimited companies are exempt from filing the financial statements and dormant companies may not have to be audited. There are penalties for late filing of accounts.

♦ **annuitant** /ə'nju:ɪtənt/ *n.* person who receives an annuity.

♦ **annuity** /ə'nju:ɪtɪ/ *n.* (*pl.* **-ies**) **1** yearly grant or allowance. **2 a** contract in which a person pays a premium to an insurance company, usu. in one lump sum, and in return receives periodic payments for an agreed period or for the rest of his or her life. An annuity has been described as the opposite of a life assurance as the policyholder pays the lump sum and the insurer makes the regular payments. Annuities are often purchased at a time of prosperity to convert capital into an income during old age. See also ANNUITY CERTAIN; DEFERRED ANNUITY. **b** payment made on such a contract.

♦ **annuity certain** *n.* annuity in which payments continue for a specified period irrespective of the life or death of the person covered. In general, annuities cease on the death of the policyholder unless they are annuities certain.

---

annul /ə'nʌl/ *v.* (**-ll-**) **1** declare invalid. **2** cancel, abolish. □ **annulment** *n.* [Latin *nullus* none]

annular /'ænjʊlə(r)/ *adj.* ring-shaped. [Latin *anulus* ring]

annular eclipse *n.* solar eclipse in which a ring of light remains visible.

annulate /'ænjʊlət/ *adj.* marked with or formed of rings.

annunciation /əˌnʌnsɪ'eɪʃ(ə)n/ *n.* **1** announcement, esp. (**Annunciation**) that made by the angel Gabriel to Mary. **2** festival of this. [Latin: related to ANNOUNCE]

anode /'ænəʊd/ *n.* positive electrode in an electrolytic cell etc. [Greek *anodos* way up]

anodize /'ænə,daɪz/ *v.* (also **-ise**) (**-zing** or **-sing**) coat (metal) with a protective layer by electrolysis.

anodyne /'ænə,daɪn/ *–adj.* **1** pain-relieving. **2** mentally soothing. *–n.* anodyne drug etc. [Greek *an-* without, *odunē* pain]

anoint /ə'nɔɪnt/ *v.* **1** apply oil or ointment to, esp. ritually. **2** (usu. foll. by *with*) smear. [Latin *inungo* anoint]

anomalous /ə'nɒmələs/ *adj.* irregular, deviant, abnormal. [Greek *an-* not, *homalos* even]

anomaly /ə'nɒməlɪ/ *n.* (*pl.* **-ies**) anomalous thing; irregularity.

anon /ə'nɒn/ *adv. archaic* soon, shortly. [Old English *on ān* into one]

anon. /ə'nɒn/ *abbr.* anonymous.

anonymous /ə'nɒnɪməs/ *adj.* **1** of unknown name or authorship. **2** without character; featureless. □ **anonymity** /,ænə'nɪmɪtɪ/ *n.* [Greek *an-* without, *onoma* name]

anorak /'ænə,ræk/ *n.* waterproof usu. hooded jacket. [Eskimo]

anorexia /,ænə'reksɪə/ *n.* lack of appetite, esp. (in full **anorexia nervosa** /nɜː'vəʊsə/) an obsessive desire to lose weight by refusing to eat. □ **anorexic** *adj.* & *n.* [Greek *an-* without, *orexis* appetite]

another /ə'nʌðə(r)/ *–adj.* **1** an additional; one more (*another cake*). **2** person like (*another Hitler*). **3** a different (*another matter*). **4** some other (*another man's work*). *–pron.* additional, other, or different person or thing. [earlier *an other*]

ANSI /'ænsɪ/ *abbr.* = AMERICAN NATIONAL STANDARDS INSTITUTE.

♦ **Ansoff matrix** /'ænsɒf/ *n.* = PRODUCT-MARKET STRATEGY. [*Ansoff*, name of an economist]

---

answer /'ɑːnsə(r)/ *–n.* **1** something said or done in reaction to a question, statement, or circumstance. **2** solution to a problem. *–v.* **1** make an answer or response (to) (*answer the door*). **2** suit (a purpose or need). **3** (foll. by *to, for*) be responsible (*you will answer to me for your conduct*). **4** (foll. by *to*) correspond, esp. to a description. □ **answer back** answer insolently. [Old English, = swear against (a charge)]

answerable *adj.* **1** (usu. foll. by *to, for*) responsible (*answerable to them for any accident*). **2** that can be answered.

answering machine *n.* tape recorder which answers telephone calls and takes messages.

answerphone *n.* = ANSWERING MACHINE.

ant *n.* small usu. wingless insect living in complex social colonies and proverbial for industry. [Old English]

-ant *suffix* **1** forming adjectives denoting attribution of an action (*repentant*) or state (*arrogant*). **2** forming agent nouns (*assistant*). [Latin *-ant-*, present participial stem of verbs]

antacid /ænt'æsɪd/ *–adj.* preventing or correcting acidity. *–n.* antacid agent.

antagonism /æn'tægə,nɪz(ə)m/ *n.* active hostility. [French: related to AGONY]

antagonist *n.* opponent or adversary. □ **antagonistic** /-'nɪstɪk/ *adj.*

antagonize /æn'tægə,naɪz/ *v.* (also **-ise**) (**-zing** or **-sing**) make hostile; provoke.

Antakya see ANTIOCH.

Antalya /æn'tæljə/ seaport and tourist resort in S Turkey, on the Mediterranean coast; pop. (1985) 258 139.

Antananarivo /,æntə,nænə'riːvəʊ/ capital of Madagascar; industries include tobacco and leather goods; pop. (est. 1993) 1 052 800.

Antarctic /ænt'ɑːktɪk/ *–adj.* of the S polar regions. *–n.* this region. [Latin: related to ARCTIC]

Antarctica /ænt'ɑːktɪkə/ continent round the South Pole, situated mainly within the Antarctic Circle and almost entirely covered by ice-sheet. Although there is no permanent human habitation Norway, Australia, France, New Zealand, and the UK claim sectors of the continent (Argentina and Chile claim parts of the British sector); its exploitation is governed by an international treaty of 1959.

Antarctic Circle *n.* parallel of latitude 66° 32′ S, forming an imaginary line round the Antarctic region.

Antarctic Ocean see SOUTHERN OCEAN.

ante /'æntɪ/ *–n.* **1** stake put up by a player in poker etc. before receiving cards. **2** amount payable in advance. *–v.* (**-tes, -ted**) **1** put up as an ante. **2** *US* **a** bet, stake. **b** (foll. by *up*) pay.

ante- *prefix* before, preceding. [Latin, = before]

anteater *n.* any of various mammals feeding on ants and termites.

antecedent /,æntɪ'siːd(ə)nt/ *–n.* **1** preceding thing or circumstance. **2** *Gram.* word or phrase etc. to which another word (esp. a relative pronoun) refers. **3** (in *pl.*) person's past history or ancestors. *–adj.* previous. [Latin *cedo* go]

antechamber /'æntɪ,tʃeɪmbə(r)/ *n.* ante-room.

antedate /,æntɪ'deɪt/ *v.* (**-ting**) **1** precede in time. **2** assign an earlier than actual date to. It is not necessarily illegal or improper to date a document before the date on which it is drawn up. For instance, an antedated cheque is not in law invalid. Cf. POSTDATE 1.

antediluvian /,æntɪdɪ'luːvɪən/ *adj.* **1** of the time before the Flood. **2** *colloq.* very old or out of date. [from ANTE-, Latin *diluvium* deluge]

antelope /'æntɪ,ləʊp/ *n.* (*pl.* same or **-s**) swift-moving deerlike ruminant e.g. the gazelle and gnu. [Greek *antholops*]

antenatal /,æntɪ'neɪt(ə)l/ *adj.* **1** before birth. **2** of pregnancy.

antenna /æn'tenə/ *n.* **1** (*pl.* **-tennae** /-niː/) each of a pair of feelers on the heads of insects, crustaceans, etc. **2** (*pl.* **-s**) = AERIAL *n.* [Latin, = sail-yard]

antepenultimate /,æntɪpɪ'nʌltɪmət/ *adj.* last but two.

ante-post /,æntɪ'pəʊst/ *adj.* (of betting) done at odds determined at the time of betting, in advance of the event concerned. [from ANTE-, POST[1]]

anterior /æn'tɪərɪə(r)/ *adj.* **1** nearer the front. **2** (often foll. by *to*) prior. [Latin from *ante* before]

ante-room /'æntɪ,ruːm/ *n.* small room leading to a main one.

anthem /'ænθəm/ *n.* **1** elaborate choral composition usu. based on a passage of scripture. **2** solemn hymn of praise etc., esp. = NATIONAL ANTHEM. [Latin: related to ANTIPHON]

anther /'ænθə(r)/ *n.* part of a stamen containing pollen. [Greek *anthos* flower]

anthill *n.* moundlike nest built by ants or termites.

anthology /æn'θɒlədʒɪ/ *n.* (*pl.* **-ies**) collection of poems, essays, stories, etc. □ **anthologist** *n.* [Greek *anthos* flower, *-logia* collection]

anthracite /'ænθrə,saɪt/ *n.* hard type of coal burning with little flame and smoke. [Greek: related to ANTHRAX]

anthrax /'ænθræks/ *n.* disease of sheep and cattle transmissible to humans. [Greek, = coal, carbuncle]

anthropocentric /,ænθrəpəʊ'sentrɪk/ *adj.* regarding mankind as the centre of existence. [Greek *anthrōpos* man]

anthropoid /'ænθrə,pɔɪd/ *–adj.* human in form. *–n.* anthropoid ape.

anthropology /,ænθrə'pɒlədʒɪ/ *n.* study of mankind, esp. its societies and customs. □ **anthropological** /-pə'lɒdʒɪk(ə)l/ *adj.* **anthropologist** *n.*

anthropomorphism /,ænθrəpə'mɔːfɪz(ə)m/ *n.* attribution of human characteristics to a god, animal, or thing. □ **anthropomorphic** *adj.* [Greek *morphē* form]

anthropomorphous /,ænθrəpə'mɔːfəs/ *adj.* human in form.

anti /'æntɪ/ *–prep.* opposed to. *–n.* (*pl.* **-s**) person opposed to a policy etc.

anti- *prefix* **1** opposed to (*anticlerical*). **2** preventing (*antifreeze*). **3** opposite of (*anticlimax*). **4** unconventional (*anti-hero*). [Greek]

anti-abortion /ˌæntɪəˈbɔːʃ(ə)n/ *adj.* opposing abortion. □ **anti-abortionist** *n.*

anti-aircraft /ˌæntɪˈeəkrɑːft/ *adj.* (of a gun or missile) used to attack enemy aircraft.

Antibes /ɑ̃ˈtiːb/ fishing-port and resort on the French Riviera; pop. (1982) 63 248.

antibiotic /ˌæntɪbaɪˈɒtɪk/ *–n.* substance (e.g. penicillin) that can inhibit or destroy susceptible micro-organisms. *–adj.* functioning as an antibiotic. [Greek *bios* life]

antibody /ˈæntɪˌbɒdɪ/ *n.* (*pl.* **-ies**) a blood protein produced in response to and then counteracting antigens. [translation of German *Antikörper*]

antic /ˈæntɪk/ *n.* (usu. in *pl.*) foolish behaviour or action. [Italian *antico* ANTIQUE]

Antichrist /ˈæntɪˌkraɪst/ *n.* enemy of Christ. □ **antichristian** /-ˈkrɪstʃ(ə)n/ *adj.*

anticipate /ænˈtɪsɪˌpeɪt/ *v.* (**-ting**) **1** deal with or use before the proper time. **2** expect, foresee (*did not anticipate a problem*). **3** forestall (a person or thing). **4** look forward to. □ **anticipation** /-ˈpeɪʃ(ə)n/ *n.* **anticipatory** *adj.* [Latin *anti-* before, *capio* take]

■ **Usage** The use of *anticipate* in sense 2, 'expect', 'foresee', is well-established in informal use, but is regarded as incorrect by some people.

anticlerical /ˌæntɪˈklerɪk(ə)l/ *adj.* opposed to clerical influence, esp. in politics.

anticlimax /ˌæntɪˈklaɪmæks/ *n.* disappointingly trivial conclusion to something significant.

anticlockwise /ˌæntɪˈklɒkwaɪz/ *adj.* & *adv.* moving in a curve opposite in direction to the hands of a clock.

anticyclone /ˌæntɪˈsaɪkləʊn/ *n.* system of winds rotating outwards from an area of high pressure, producing fine weather.

antidepressant /ˌæntɪdɪˈpres(ə)nt/ *–n.* drug etc. that alleviates depression. *–adj.* alleviating depression.

antidote /ˈæntɪˌdəʊt/ *n.* **1** medicine etc. used to counteract poison. **2** anything counteracting something unpleasant. [Greek *antidotos* given against]

antifreeze /ˈæntɪˌfriːz/ *n.* substance added to water to lower its freezing-point, esp. in a vehicle's radiator.

antigen /ˈæntɪdʒ(ə)n/ *n.* foreign substance (e.g. toxin) which causes the body to produce antibodies. [Greek *-genēs* of a kind]

Antigua /ænˈtiːgwə/ **1** (also **Antigua Guatemala**) city in the central highlands of Guatemala, the capital of Guatemala until destroyed by an earthquake in 1773; pop. (est. 1991) 30 000. **2** see ANTIGUA AND BARBUDA.

anti-hero /ˈæntɪˌhɪərəʊ/ *n.* (*pl.* **-es**) central character in a story, lacking conventional heroic qualities.

antihistamine /ˌæntɪˈhɪstəˌmiːn/ *n.* drug that counteracts the effects of histamine, used esp. in treating allergies.

antiknock /ˈæntɪˌnɒk/ *n.* substance added to motor fuel to prevent premature combustion.

Antilles /ænˈtɪliːz/ group of islands forming the greater part of the West Indies. The **Greater Antilles**, extending roughly E to W, comprise Cuba, Jamaica, Hispaniola (Haiti and the Dominican Republic), and Puerto Rico; the **Lesser Antilles**, to the SE, include the Virgin Islands, Leeward Islands, Windward Islands, and various small islands to the N of Venezuela. See also NETHERLANDS ANTILLES.

anti-lock /ˈæntɪˌlɒk/ *attrib. adj.* (of brakes) set up so as to prevent locking and skidding when applied suddenly.

antilog /ˈæntɪˌlɒg/ *n. colloq.* = ANTILOGARITHM. [abbreviation]

antilogarithm /ˌæntɪˈlɒgəˌrɪð(ə)m/ *n.* number to which a logarithm belongs.

antimacassar /ˌæntɪməˈkæsə(r)/ *n.* detachable protective cloth for the back of a chair etc.

antimatter /ˈæntɪˌmætə(r)/ *n.* matter composed solely of antiparticles.

antimony /ˈæntɪmənɪ/ *n.* brittle silvery metallic element used esp. in alloys. [medieval Latin]

antinomian /ˌæntɪˈnəʊmɪən/ *–adj.* believing that Christians need not obey the moral law. *–n.* (**Antinomian**) *hist.* person believing this. [Greek *nomos* law]

antinomy /ænˈtɪnəmɪ/ *n.* (*pl.* **-ies**) contradiction between two reasonable beliefs or conclusions.

antinovel /ˈæntɪˌnɒv(ə)l/ *n.* novel avoiding the conventions of the form.

anti-nuclear /ˌæntɪˈnjuːklɪə(r)/ *adj.* opposed to the development of nuclear weapons or power.

Antioch /ˈæntɪˌɒk/ (Turkish **Antakya** /ænˈtækjæ/) town in S Turkey near the Syrian border, ancient capital of Syria under the Seleucid kings; it has food and other processing industries; pop. (est. 1990) 123 871.

antiparticle /ˈæntɪˌpɑːtɪk(ə)l/ *n.* elementary particle with the same mass but opposite charge etc. to another particle.

antipathy /ænˈtɪpəθɪ/ *n.* (*pl.* **-ies**) (often foll. by *to, for, between*) strong aversion or dislike. □ **antipathetic** /-ˈθetɪk/ *adj.* [Greek: related to PATHETIC]

antiperspirant /ˌæntɪˈpɜːspərənt/ *n.* substance preventing or reducing perspiration.

antiphon /ˈæntɪf(ə)n/ *n.* **1** hymn sung alternately by two groups. **2** versicle or phrase from this. □ **antiphonal** /-ˈtɪfən(ə)l/ *adj.* [Greek *phōnē* sound]

antipodes /ænˈtɪpəˌdiːz/ *n.pl.* places diametrically opposite to one another on the earth, esp. (also **Antipodes**) Australasia in relation to Europe. □ **antipodean** /-ˈdiːən/ *adj.* & *n.* [Greek, = having the feet opposite]

antipope /ˈæntɪˌpəʊp/ *n.* pope set up in opposition to one chosen by canon law.

antipyretic /ˌæntɪpaɪəˈretɪk/ *–adj.* preventing or reducing fever. *–n.* antipyretic drug.

antiquarian /ˌæntɪˈkweərɪən/ *–adj.* of or dealing in antiques or rare books. *–n.* antiquary. □ **antiquarianism** *n.*

antiquary /ˈæntɪkwərɪ/ *n.* (*pl.* **-ies**) student or collector of antiques etc. [Latin: related to ANTIQUE]

antiquated /ˈæntɪˌkweɪtɪd/ *adj.* old-fashioned.

antique /ænˈtiːk/ *–n.* old object, esp. a piece of furniture,

---

Antigua and Barbuda /ænˈtiːgə, bɑːˈbuːdə/, **State of** country in the West Indies comprising three of the Leeward Islands (Antigua, Barbuda, and Redonda). The economy, formerly dependent on sugar, is now based mainly on tourism and related services. Agriculture has diversified, producing cotton, fruit, and vegetables, as well as sugar, and there is some fishing. An oil refinery opened in 1982. Antigua was a British colony with Barbuda as its dependency until the islands gained full independence as a member state of the Commonwealth in 1981. It is a member of CARICOM. Prime minister, Lester Bird; capital, St Johns. □ **Antiguan** *adj.* & *n.* **Barbudan** *adj.* & *n.*

language	English
currency	East Caribbean dollar (EC$) of 100 cents

pop. (1991)	59 355
GNP (est. 1993)	US $ 425M
literacy	90%
life expectancy	71 (m); 75 (f)

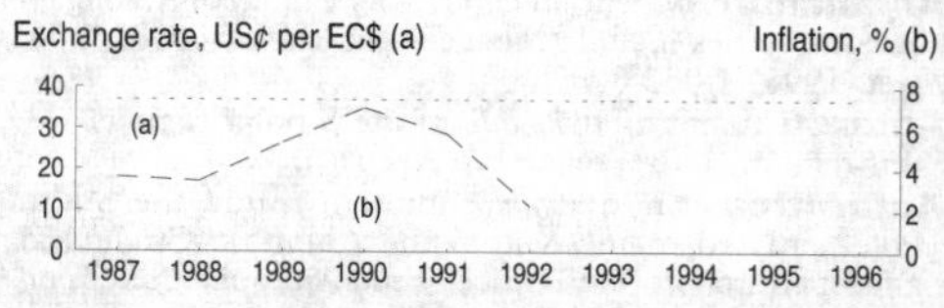

of high value. *–adj.* **1** of or from an early date. **2** old-fashioned. [Latin *antiquus*]

antiquity /æn'tɪkwətɪ/ *n.* (*pl.* **-ies**) **1** ancient times, esp. before the Middle Ages. **2** great age. **3** (usu. in *pl.*) relics from ancient times. [Latin: related to ANTIQUE]

antirrhinum /ˌæntɪ'raɪnəm/ *n.* plant with two-lipped flowers, esp. the snapdragon. [Greek, = snout]

anti-Semite /ˌæntɪ'siːmaɪt/ *n.* person prejudiced against Jews. □ **anti-Semitic** /-sɪ'mɪtɪk/ *adj.* **anti-Semitism** /-'semɪˌtɪz(ə)m/ *n.*

antiseptic /ˌæntɪ'septɪk/ *–adj.* **1** counteracting sepsis, esp. by destroying germs. **2** sterile, uncontaminated. **3** lacking character. *–n.* antiseptic agent.

antiserum /'æntɪˌsɪərəm/ *n.* serum with a high antibody content.

antisocial /ˌæntɪ'səʊʃ(ə)l/ *adj.* **1** opposed or harmful to society. **2** not sociable.

■ **Usage** *Antisocial* is sometimes used mistakenly instead of *unsocial* in the phrase *unsocial hours*. This should be avoided.

antistatic /ˌæntɪ'stætɪk/ *adj.* counteracting the effects of static electricity.

anti-tank /ˌæntɪ'tæŋk/ *attrib. adj.* used against tanks.

antitetanus /ˌæntɪ'tetənəs/ *adj.* effective against tetanus.

antithesis /æn'tɪθɪsɪs/ *n.* (*pl.* **-theses** /-ˌsiːz/) **1** (foll. by *of, to*) direct opposite. **2** contrast. **3** rhetorical use of strongly contrasted words. □ **antithetical** /-'θetɪk(ə)l/ *adj.* [Greek *antitithēmi* set against]

antitoxin /ˌæntɪ'tɒksɪn/ *n.* antibody counteracting a toxin. □ **antitoxic** *adj.*

antitrades /'æntɪˌtreɪdz/ *n.pl.* winds blowing in the opposite direction to (and usu. above) trade winds.

◆ **anti-trust laws** *n.pl.* laws passed in the US, from 1890 onwards, making it illegal to do anything in restraint of trade, set up monopolies, or otherwise interfere with free trade and competition.

---

antiviral /ˌæntɪ'vaɪər(ə)l/ *adj.* effective against viruses.

antler *n.* branched horn of a stag or other deer. □ **antlered** *adj.* [French]

Antofagasta /ˌæntəʊfə'gæstə/ port in N Chile, on the Pacific coast, capital of the Antofagasta region; industries include metal refining and founding; pop. (1992) 226 749.

◆ **Anton Piller order** /'æntɒn 'pɪlə/ *n.* court injunction ordering the defendant to allow the plaintiff to enter named premises to search for and take copies of specified articles and documents. This order is obtained by the plaintiff *ex parte* (without the other party being present in court) to enable the preservation of evidence in cases in which the plaintiff has grounds to think it will be destroyed. It is particularly useful in 'pirating' cases. The order is not a search warrant, so entry cannot be forced, but the defendant will be in contempt of court if entry is refused. A solicitor must serve the order. [*Anton Piller*, against whom the first such order was made]

---

antonym /'æntənɪm/ *n.* word opposite in meaning to another. [Greek *onoma* name]

Antrim /'æntrɪm/ **1** county of Northern Ireland; county town, Belfast. Industries include textiles; oats, potatoes, flax, and livestock are produced. **2** district in Northern Ireland, in Co. Antrim; pop. (1991) 44 516.

antrum /'æntrəm/ *n.* (*pl.* **antra**) natural cavity in the body, esp. in a bone. [Greek, = cave]

Antwerp /'æntwɜːp/ (French **Anvers** /'ɑ̃veə(r)/, Flemish **Antwerpen** /'ɑːntveərpən/) city and seaport in Belgium; industries include shipbuilding, oil refining, diamond-cutting, textiles, and electronics; pop. (est. 1994) 462 880.

Anuradhapura /əˌnʊərədə'pʊərə/ town in Sri Lanka, the ancient capital of the island, site of the sacred bo tree (descended from Buddha's original tree) and of numerous Buddhist foundations; pop. (1981) 36 248.

anus /'eɪnəs/ *n.* (*pl.* **anuses**) excretory opening at the end of the alimentary canal. [Latin]

Anvers see ANTWERP.

anvil /'ænvɪl/ *n.* iron block on which metals are worked. [Old English]

anxiety /æŋ'zaɪətɪ/ *n.* (*pl.* **-ies**) **1** being anxious. **2** worry or concern. **3** eagerness, troubled desire. [Latin *anxietas* from *ango* choke]

anxious /'æŋkʃəs/ *adj.* **1** mentally troubled. **2** causing or marked by anxiety (*anxious moment*). **3** eager, uneasily wanting (*anxious to please*). □ **anxiously** *adv.* [Latin *anxius*]

any /'enɪ/ *–adj.* **1 a** one, no matter which, of several (*cannot find any answer*). **b** some, no matter how much or many or of what sort (*if any books arrive*; *have you any sugar?*). **2** a minimal amount of (*hardly any difference*). **3** whichever is chosen (*any fool knows*). **4** appreciable or significant (*did not stay for any length of time*; *has any amount of money*). *–pron.* **1** any one (*did not know any of them*). **2** any number or amount (*are any of them yours?*). *–adv.* (usu. with *neg.* or *interrog.*) at all (*is that any good?*). [Old English *ǣnig*: related to ONE, -Y[1]]

anybody *n.* & *pron.* **1** any person. **2** person of importance (*is he anybody?*).

anyhow *adv.* **1** anyway. **2** in a disorderly manner or state (*does his work anyhow*).

anyone *pron.* anybody.

■ **Usage** *Anyone* is written as two words to emphasize a numerical sense, as in *any one of us can do it*.

anything *pron.* any thing; thing of any sort. □ **anything but** not at all.

anyway *adv.* **1** in any way or manner. **2** at any rate. **3** to resume (*anyway, as I was saying*).

anywhere *–adv.* in or to any place. *–pron.* any place (*anywhere will do*).

ANZ *abbr.* Australia and New Zealand Banking Group.

A/O *abbr.* (also **a/o**) **1** *Accounting* account of. **2** and others.

aO *abbr.* (also **a/O**) (German, after place-names) an der Oder (= on the River Oder).

AOB *abbr.* (also **a.o.b.**) any other business.

AOCB *abbr.* any other competent business.

Aorangi /aʊ'ræŋɪ/ administrative region of New Zealand, in the Canterbury Plains of South Island; pop. (1986) 81 300; chief town, Timaru.

aorta /eɪ'ɔːtə/ *n.* (*pl.* **-s**) main artery, giving rise to the arterial network carrying oxygenated blood to the body from the heart. □ **aortic** *adj.* [Greek *aeirō* raise]

AP *–abbr.* **1** (also **A/P, a.p.**) *Insurance* additional premium. **2** *Commerce* (French, on a bill of exchange) à protester (= to be protested). **3** *Computing* array processor. **4** (also **A/p**) authority to pay (or purchase). **5** *Insurance* average payable. *–international civil aircraft marking* Pakistan.

APA *abbr.* **1** *Taxation* additional personal allowance. **2** Associate in Public Administration.

apace /ə'peɪs/ *adv. literary* swiftly. [French *à pas*]

Apache /ə'pætʃɪ/ *n.* member of a North American Indian tribe. [Mexican Spanish]

APACS *abbr.* = ASSOCIATION FOR PAYMENT CLEARING SERVICES.

apart /ə'pɑːt/ *adv.* **1** separately, not together (*keep your feet apart*). **2** into pieces (*came apart*). **3** to or on one side. **4** to or at a distance. □ **apart from 1** excepting, not considering. **2** in addition to (*apart from roses we grow irises*). [French *à part* to one side]

apartheid /ə'pɑːteɪt/ *n.* (esp. in South Africa) racial segregation or discrimination. [Afrikaans]

apartment /ə'pɑːtmənt/ *n.* **1** (in *pl.*) suite of rooms. **2** single room. **3** *US* flat. [Italian *a parte*, apart]

apathy /'æpəθɪ/ *n.* lack of interest; indifference. □ **apathetic** /-'θetɪk/ *adj.* [Greek *a-* without, PATHOS]

◆ **APCIMS** *abbr.* = ASSOCIATION OF PRIVATE CLIENT INVESTMENT MANAGERS AND STOCKBROKERS.

APE *abbr.* Amalgamated Power Engineering.

ape *–n.* **1** tailless monkey-like primate, e.g. the gorilla, chimpanzee, orang-utan, or gibbon. **2** imitator. *–v.* (**-ping**) imitate, mimic. [Old English]

Apeldoorn /ˈæpəlˌdɔːn/ town in the E central Netherlands, in the province of Gelderland; industries include electronics and the manufacture of blankets, cloth, and paper; pop. (1994) 149 450.

apeman *n.* extinct primate held to be the forerunner of present-day man.

aperient /əˈpɪərɪənt/ *–adj.* laxative. *–n.* laxative medicine. [Latin *aperio* open]

aperitif /əˌperɪˈtiːf/ *n.* alcoholic drink taken before a meal. [Latin *aperio* open]

aperture /ˈæpəˌtʃə(r)/ *n.* opening or gap, esp. a variable opening in a camera for admitting light. [Latin *aperio* open]

Apex /ˈeɪpeks/ *n.* (also **APEX**) (often *attrib.*) system of reduced fares for scheduled airline flights or rail travel. Return airline tickets are offered at a discount to the standard fare, provided that bookings both ways are made 21 days in advance for international flights and 7–14 days for European flights, with no facilities for stopoffs or cancellations. [*A*dvance *P*urchase *Ex*cursion]

apex /ˈeɪpeks/ *n.* (*pl.* **-es**) **1** highest point. **2** tip or pointed end. [Latin]

aphasia /əˈfeɪzɪə/ *n.* loss of verbal understanding or expression, owing to brain damage. [Greek *aphatos* speechless]

aphelion /əˈfiːlɪən/ *n.* (*pl.* **-lia**) point in a celestial body's orbit where it is furthest from the sun. [Greek *aph' hēliou* from the sun]

aphid /ˈeɪfɪd/ *n.* small insect infesting and damaging plants, e.g. the greenfly.

aphis /ˈeɪfɪs/ *n.* (*pl.* **aphides** /-ˌdiːz/) aphid. [invented by Linnaeus: perhaps a misreading of Greek *koris* bug]

aphorism /ˈæfəˌrɪz(ə)m/ *n.* short pithy maxim. □ **aphoristic** /-ˈrɪstɪk/ *adj.* [Greek *aphorismos* definition]

aphrodisiac /ˌæfrəˈdɪzɪˌæk/ *–adj.* arousing sexual desire. *–n.* aphrodisiac substance. [Greek *Aphroditē* goddess of love]

API *abbr.* **1** American Petroleum Institute. **2** *Computing* application programmer interface.

Apia /ˈɑːpɪə/ capital of Independent State of Samoa, situated on the N coast of the island of Upolu; copra, bananas, and cocoa are produced; pop. (1986) 32 196.

apiary /ˈeɪpɪərɪ/ *n.* (*pl.* **-ies**) place where bees are kept. □ **apiarist** *n.* [Latin *apis* bee]

apical /ˈeɪpɪk(ə)l/ *adj.* of, at, or forming an apex.

apiculture /ˈeɪpɪˌkʌltʃə(r)/ *n.* bee-keeping. □ **apiculturist** /-ˈkʌltʃərɪst/ *n.* [Latin *apis* bee, CULTURE]

apiece /əˈpiːs/ *adv.* for each one; severally (*five pounds apiece*). [originally *a piece*]

apish /ˈeɪpɪʃ/ *adj.* **1** of or like an ape. **2** foolishly imitating.

♦ **APL** *n.* programming language developed in the 1960s for interactive computing. Its main feature is its unusual syntax, in which single character operators perform complex tasks. APL is a powerful tool for the scientist or engineer and is sometimes used for business programs. [*A* *P*rogramming *L*anguage]

---

aplomb /əˈplɒm/ *n.* skilful self-assurance. [French, = straight as a plummet]

APMI *abbr.* Associate of the Pensions Management Institute.

apocalypse /əˈpɒkəlɪps/ *n.* **1** violent or destructive event. **2** (**the Apocalypse**) Revelation, the last book of the New Testament. **3** revelation, esp. about the end of the world. □ **apocalyptic** /-ˈlɪptɪk/ *adj.* [Greek *apokaluptō* reveal]

Apocrypha /əˈpɒkrɪfə/ *n.pl.* **1** books included in the Septuagint and Vulgate versions of the Old Testament but not in the Hebrew Bible. **2** (**apocrypha**) writings etc. not considered genuine. [Greek *apokruptō* hide away]

apocryphal *adj.* of doubtful authenticity.

apogee /ˈæpəˌdʒiː/ *n.* **1** highest point; climax. **2** point in a celestial body's orbit where it is furthest from the earth. [Greek *apogeion*]

apolitical /ˌeɪpəˈlɪtɪk(ə)l/ *adj.* not interested in or concerned with politics.

apologetic /əˌpɒləˈdʒetɪk/ *–adj.* **1** showing or expressing regret. **2** of apologetics. *–n.* (usu. in *pl.*) reasoned defence, esp. of Christianity. □ **apologetically** *adv.*

apologia /ˌæpəˈləʊdʒɪə/ *n.* formal defence of opinions or conduct. [Greek: see APOLOGY]

apologist /əˈpɒlədʒɪst/ *n.* person who defends something by argument.

apologize /əˈpɒləˌdʒaɪz/ *v.* (also **-ise**) (**-zing** or **-sing**) make an apology, express regret.

apology /əˈpɒlədʒɪ/ *n.* (*pl.* **-ies**) **1** statement of regret for an offence or failure. **2** explanation or defence. **3** (foll. by *for*) poor specimen of. [Greek *apologia* from *apologeomai* speak in defence]

apophthegm /ˈæpəˌθem/ *n.* = APHORISM. [Latin from Greek]

apoplectic /ˌæpəˈplektɪk/ *adj.* **1** of or causing apoplexy. **2** *colloq.* enraged.

apoplexy /ˈæpəˌpleksɪ/ *n.* sudden paralysis caused by blockage or rupture of a brain artery; stroke. [Greek *apoplēssō* disable by stroke]

apostasy /əˈpɒstəsɪ/ *n.* (*pl.* **-ies**) renunciation of a belief or faith, abandoning of principles, etc. [Greek, = defection]

apostate /əˈpɒsteɪt/ *n.* person who renounces a belief etc. □ **apostatize** *v.* (also **-ise**) (**-zing** or **-sing**).

a posteriori /ˌeɪ pɒˌsterɪˈɔːraɪ/ *–adj.* (of reasoning) proceeding from effects to causes; inductive. *–adv.* inductively. [Latin, = from what comes after]

apostle /əˈpɒs(ə)l/ *n.* **1** (**Apostle**) any of the twelve men sent out by Christ to preach the gospel. **2** leader, esp. of a new movement. [Greek *apostolos* messenger]

apostolate /əˈpɒstələt/ *n.* **1** position or authority of an Apostle. **2** leadership in reform.

apostolic /ˌæpəˈstɒlɪk/ *adj.* **1** of the Apostles or their teaching. **2** of the Pope.

apostolic succession *n.* supposed uninterrupted transmission of spiritual authority from the Apostles through popes and bishops.

apostrophe /əˈpɒstrəfɪ/ *n.* **1** punctuation mark (') indicating: **a** omission of letters or numbers (e.g. *can't*; *May '92*). **b** possessive case (e.g. *Harry's book*; *boys' coats*). **2** exclamatory passage addressed to (an often absent) person or thing. □ **apostrophize** *v.* (also **-ise**) (**-zing** or **-sing**) (in sense 2). [Greek, = turning away]

apothecaries' measure *n.* (also **apothecaries' weight**) units formerly used in pharmacy.

apothecary /əˈpɒθəkərɪ/ *n.* (*pl.* **-ies**) *archaic* dispensing chemist. [Greek *apothēkē* storehouse]

apotheosis /əˌpɒθɪˈəʊsɪs/ *n.* (*pl.* **-theoses** /-siːz/) **1** elevation to divine status, deification. **2** glorification of a thing; sublime example (*apotheosis of chivalry*). [Greek *theos* god]

appal /əˈpɔːl/ *v.* (**-ll-**) **1** greatly dismay or horrify. **2** (as **appalling** *adj.*) *colloq.* very bad, shocking. [French *apalir* grow pale: related to PALE[1]]

apparatus /ˌæpəˈreɪtəs/ *n.* **1** equipment for a particular function, esp. scientific or technical. **2** political or other complex organization. [Latin *paro* prepare]

apparel /əˈpær(ə)l/ *n.* *formal* clothing, dress. □ **apparelled** *adj.* [Romanic, = make fit, from Latin *par* equal]

apparent /əˈpærənt/ *adj.* **1** readily visible; obvious. **2** seeming. □ **apparently** *adv.* [Latin: related to APPEAR]

apparition /ˌæpəˈrɪʃ(ə)n/ *n.* remarkable or unexpected thing that appears; ghost or phantom.

appeal /əˈpiːl/ *–v.* **1** request earnestly or formally; plead. **2** (usu. foll. by *to*) attract, be of interest. **3** (foll. by *to*) resort to for support. **4** *Law* **a** (often foll. by *to*) apply (to a higher court) for reconsideration of a legal decision. **b** refer (a case) to a higher court. **5** *Cricket* call on the umpire to declare whether a batsman is out. *–n.* **1** act of appealing. **2** request for public support, esp. financial. **3** *Law* referral of a case to a higher court. **4** attractiveness. [Latin *appello* address]

appear /əˈpɪə(r)/ *v.* **1** become or be visible. **2** seem (*appeared unwell*). **3** present oneself publicly or formally. **4** be published. [Latin *appareo*]

appearance /əˈpɪərəns/ *n.* **1** act of appearing. **2** outward form as perceived (*appearance of prosperity*). **3** semblance. □ **keep up appearances** maintain an impression or pretence of virtue, affluence, etc. **make** (or **put in**) **an appearance** be present, esp. briefly.

appease /əˈpiːz/ *v.* (**-sing**) **1** make calm or quiet, esp. conciliate (a potential aggressor) by making concessions. **2** satisfy (an appetite, scruples). □ **appeasement** *n.* [French *à* to, *pais* PEACE]

appellant /əˈpelənt/ *n.* person or organization that appeals against the decision of a court. [Latin *appello* address]

appellate /əˈpelət/ *attrib. adj.* (esp. of a court) concerned with appeals.

appellation /ˌæpəˈleɪʃ(ə)n/ *n. formal* name or title; nomenclature.

appellative /əˈpelətɪv/ *adj.* **1** naming. **2** *Gram.* (of a noun) designating a class, common.

append /əˈpend/ *v.* (usu. foll. by *to*) attach, affix, add, esp. to a written document. [Latin *appendo* hang]

appendage /əˈpendɪdʒ/ *n.* thing attached; addition.

appendectomy /ˌæpenˈdektəmɪ/ *n.* (also **appendicectomy** /-dɪˈsektəmɪ/) (*pl.* **-ies**) surgical removal of the appendix. [from APPENDIX, -ECTOMY]

appendicitis /əˌpendɪˈsaɪtɪs/ *n.* inflammation of the appendix.

appendix /əˈpendɪks/ *n.* (*pl.* **-dices** /-ˌsiːz/) **1** tissue forming a tube-shaped sac attached to the large intestine. **2** addition to a book etc. [Latin: related to APPEND]

appertain /ˌæpəˈteɪn/ *v.* (foll. by *to*) relate, belong, or be appropriate. [Latin: related to PERTAIN]

appetite /ˈæpɪˌtaɪt/ *n.* **1** natural craving, esp. for food or sexual activity. **2** (usu. foll. by *for*) inclination or desire. [Latin *peto* seek]

appetizer /ˈæpɪˌtaɪzə(r)/ *n.* (also **-iser**) small amount, esp. of food or drink, to stimulate the appetite.

appetizing *adj.* (also **-ising**) stimulating the appetite, esp. for food; tasty.

applaud /əˈplɔːd/ *v.* **1** express strong approval (of), esp. by clapping. **2** commend, approve (a person or action). [Latin *applaudo* clap hands]

applause /əˈplɔːz/ *n.* **1** approval shown by clapping the hands. **2** warm approval.

apple /ˈæp(ə)l/ *n.* **1** roundish firm fruit with crisp flesh. **2** tree bearing this. □ **apple of one's eye** cherished person or thing. [Old English]

apple-pie bed *n.* bed made (as a joke) with sheets folded so as to prevent a person lying flat.

apple-pie order *n.* extreme neatness.

appliance /əˈplaɪəns/ *n.* device etc. for a specific task. [related to APPLY]

applicable /ˈæplɪkəb(ə)l/ *adj.* (often foll. by *to*) that may be applied; relevant; appropriate. □ **applicability** /-ˈbɪlɪtɪ/ *n.* [medieval Latin: related to APPLY]

applicant /ˈæplɪkənt/ *n.* person who applies for something, esp. a job.

application /ˌæplɪˈkeɪʃ(ə)n/ *n.* **1** formal request. **2** act of applying. **3** substance applied. **4 a** relevance. **b** use (*has many applications*). **5** diligence.

♦ **application form** *n.* **1** form on which a formal request may be made. **2** form, issued by a newly-floated company with its prospectus, on which members of the public apply for shares in the company. See also ALLOTMENT 4; MULTIPLE APPLICATION; PINK FORM.

♦ **application for quotation** *n.* application by a public limited company for a quotation on the London Stock Exchange. The company is scrutinized by the Quotations Committee to see if it complies with the regulations and if its directors have a high reputation. If the application is accepted the company is given a quotation on one of the Stock Exchange's markets.

---

application package *n.* (also **software package**) set of computer programs directed at some application in general, e.g. computer graphics, word processing, CAD (computer-aided design), or statistics. Application packages are often driven by a series of commands, which make the packages perform the specific items of their repertoires that are required in a particular situation.

♦ **applications software** *n.* computer programs designed for a particular purpose or application. For example, accounts programs, games programs, and educational programs are all applications software. An **applications program** is a particular piece of applications software. Applications software is written for end-users of a computer system. Cf. SYSTEMS SOFTWARE.

---

applicator /ˈæplɪˌkeɪtə(r)/ *n.* device for applying ointment etc.

applied /əˈplaɪd/ *adj.* practical, not merely theoretical (*applied science*).

appliqué /əˈpliːkeɪ/ *–n.* cutting out of fabric patterns and attaching them to another fabric. *–v.* (**-qués**, **-quéd**, **-quéing**) decorate with appliqué. [French, = applied]

apply /əˈplaɪ/ *v.* (**-ies**, **-ied**) **1** (often foll. by *for*, *to*, or *to* + infin.) formally request. **2** (often foll. by *to*) be relevant. **3 a** make use of; employ (*apply the rules*; *apply common sense*). **b** operate (*apply the brakes*). **4** (often foll. by *to*) put or spread on. **5** *refl.* (often foll. by *to*) devote oneself. [Latin *applico* fasten to]

appoint /əˈpɔɪnt/ *v.* **1** assign a job or office to. **2** (often foll. by *for*) fix (a time, place, etc.). **3** (as **appointed** *adj.*) equipped, furnished (*well-appointed*). □ **appointee** /-ˈtiː/ *n.* [French *à point* to a point]

appointment *n.* **1** appointing or being appointed. **2** arrangement for meeting or consultation. **3 a** post or office open to applicants. **b** person appointed. **4** (usu. in *pl.*) furniture, fittings; equipment.

apportion /əˈpɔːʃ(ə)n/ *v.* (often foll. by *to*) share out; assign as a share. □ **apportionment** *n.* [medieval Latin: related to PORTION]

apposite /ˈæpəzɪt/ *adj.* (often foll. by *to*) apt, appropriate; well expressed. [Latin *appono* apply]

apposition /ˌæpəˈzɪʃ(ə)n/ *n.* juxtaposition, esp. *Gram.* of elements sharing a syntactic function (e.g. William the Conqueror; my friend Sue).

appraisal /əˈpreɪz(ə)l/ *n.* appraising or being appraised.

appraise /əˈpreɪz/ *v.* (**-sing**) **1** estimate the value or quality of. **2** set a price on (esp. officially). [earlier *apprize*, assimilated to PRAISE]

appreciable /əˈpriːʃəb(ə)l/ *adj.* significant, considerable. [French: related to APPRECIATE]

appreciate /əˈpriːʃɪˌeɪt/ *v.* (**-ting**) **1 a** esteem highly; value. **b** be grateful for. **2** understand, recognize (*appreciate the danger*). **3** rise or raise in value. □ **appreciative** /-ʃətɪv/ *adj.* **appreciatory** /-ʃjətərɪ/ *adj.* [Latin *pretium* price]

appreciation /əˌpriːʃɪˈeɪʃ(ə)n/ *n.* **1** favourable or grateful recognition. **2** sensitive estimation or judgement. **3** increase in the value of an asset, through inflation, a rise in market price, or interest earned. This usu. occurs with land and buildings; the directors of a company have an obligation to adjust the nominal value of land and buildings and other assets in balance sheets to take account of appreciation. See ASSET-STRIPPING. **4** increase in the value of a currency with a floating exchange rate relative to another currency. Cf. DEPRECIATION 3; DEVALUATION 1. [French: related to APPRECIATE]

apprehend /ˌæprɪˈhend/ *v.* **1** seize, arrest. **2** understand, perceive. [Latin *prehendo* grasp]

apprehension /ˌæprɪˈhenʃ(ə)n/ *n.* **1** uneasiness, dread. **2** understanding. **3** arrest, capture.

apprehensive /ˌæprɪˈhensɪv/ *adj.* uneasily fearful. □ **apprehensively** *adv.*

apprentice /əˈprentɪs/ *–n.* **1** young employee who signs a contract (an **indenture** or **articles of apprenticeship**) agreeing to be trained in a particular skill for a set amount of time by a specific employer. During this time the wages will be relatively low but on completion of the apprenticeship they increase to reflect the increased status of the employee and to recognize the skills acquired. **2** novice. *–v.* (**-cing**) (usu. foll. by *to*) engage as an apprentice (*apprenticed to a builder*). □ **apprenticeship** *n.* [French *apprendre* learn]

apprise /əˈpraɪz/ *v.* (**-sing**) *formal* inform. [French *appris(e)* learnt, taught]

appro /ˈæprəʊ/ *n. colloq.* □ **on appro** = *on approval* (see APPROVAL). [abbreviation]

approach /əˈprəʊtʃ/ *–v.* **1** come near or nearer (to) in space or time. **2** tentatively make a proposal to. **3** be similar or approximate to (*approaching 5 million*). **4** set about (a task etc.). *–n.* **1** act or means of approaching. **2** approximation. **3** technique (*try a new approach*). **4** *Golf* stroke from the fairway to the green. **5** *Aeron.* part of a flight before landing. [Latin *prope* near]

approachable *adj.* **1** friendly, easy to talk to. **2** able to be approached.

approbation /ˌæprəˈbeɪʃ(ə)n/ *n.* approval, consent. [Latin *probo* test]

appropriate *–adj.* /əˈprəʊprɪət/ suitable, proper. *–v.* /əˈprəʊprɪˌeɪt/ (**-ting**) **1** take, esp. without authority. **2** devote (money etc.) to special purposes. □ **appropriately** *adv.* [Latin *proprius* own]

♦ **appropriation** /əˌprəʊprɪˈeɪʃ(ə)n/ *n.* **1** taking; setting apart. **2** allocation of the net profit of an organization in its accounts. Some payments may be treated as expenses and deducted before arriving at net profit; other payments are deemed to be appropriations of profit, once that profit has been ascertained. Examples of the former are such normal trade expenses as wages and salaries of employees, motor running expenses, light and heat, and most interest payments on external finance. Appropriations of the net profit include payments of income tax or corporation tax, dividends to shareholders, transfers to reserves, and, in the case of partnerships, salaries and interest on capital paid to the partners. See also ACCUMULATED PROFITS. **3** allocation of payments to a particular debt out of several owed by a debtor to one creditor. The right to make the appropriation belongs first to the debtor but if he or she fails to make the appropriation the creditor has the right to do so. **4** document identifying a particular batch of goods to be supplied in fulfilment of a forward contract for a commodity.

---

approval /əˈpruːv(ə)l/ *n.* **1** approving. **2** consent; favourable opinion. □ **on approval** (of goods supplied) returnable if not satisfactory. The potential buyer is a bailee (see BAILMENT) and is obliged to return the goods in perfect condition if they are not purchased.

approve /əˈpruːv/ *v.* (**-ving**) **1** confirm; sanction. **2** (often foll. by *of*) regard with favour. [Latin *probo* test]

♦ **approved deferred share trust** *n.* (also **ADST**) trust fund set up by a British company, and approved by the Inland Revenue, that purchases shares in that company for the benefit of its employees. Tax on dividends is deferred until the shares are sold and is then paid at a reduced rate.

---

approx. *abbr.* approximate(ly).

approximate *–adj.* /əˈprɒksɪmət/ fairly correct, near to the actual (*approximate price*). *–v.* /əˈprɒksɪˌmeɪt/ (**-ting**) (often foll. by *to*) bring or come near (esp. in quality, number, etc.). □ **approximately** *adv.* **approximation** /-ˈmeɪʃ(ə)n/ *n.* [Latin *proximus* nearest]

appurtenance /əˈpɜːtɪnəns/ *n.* (usu. in *pl.*) belonging; accessory. [Latin *pertineo* belong to]

APR *abbr.* **1** Accredited Public Relations Practitioner. **2** = ANNUAL PERCENTAGE RATE.

Apr. *abbr.* April.

après-ski /ˌæpreɪˈskiː/ *–n.* social activities following a day's skiing. *–attrib. adj.* (of clothes, drinks, etc.) suitable for these. [French]

APRI *abbr.* Associate of the Plastics and Rubber Institute.

apricot /ˈeɪprɪˌkɒt/ *–n.* **1 a** small juicy soft orange-yellow peachlike fruit. **b** tree bearing it. **2** its colour. *–adj.* orange-yellow. [Portuguese and Spanish from Arabic, ultimately from Latin *praecox* early-ripe]

April /ˈeɪpr(ə)l/ *n.* fourth month of the year. [Latin]

April Fool *n.* person successfully tricked on 1 April.

a priori /ˌeɪ praɪˈɔːraɪ/ *–adj.* **1** (of reasoning) from causes to effects; deductive. **2** (of concepts etc.) logically independent of experience; not derived from experience. **3** assumed without investigation (*an a priori conjecture*). *–adv.* **1** deductively. **2** as far as one knows. [Latin, = from what is before]

apron /ˈeɪprən/ *n.* **1** garment for covering and protecting the front of the clothes. **2** *Theatr.* part of a stage in front of the curtain. **3** area on an airfield for manoeuvring or loading. □ **tied to a person's apron-strings** dominated by or dependent on that person (usu. a woman). [originally *napron*, from French *nape* table-cloth]

apropos /ˌæprəˈpəʊ/ *–adj.* **1** appropriate. **2** *colloq.* (often foll. by *of*) in respect of. *–adv.* **1** appropriately. **2** (*absol.*) incidentally. [French *à propos*]

APS *abbr.* Advanced Photo System.

APSE /æps/ *abbr. Computing* Ada programming support environment.

apse /æps/ *n.* large arched or domed recess, esp. at the end of a church. [related to APSIS]

apsis /ˈæpsɪs/ *n.* (*pl.* **apsides** /-ˌdiːz/) either of two points on the orbit of a planet etc. nearest to or furthest from the body round which it moves. [Greek *(h)apsis* arch, vault]

APT *abbr.* advanced passenger train.

apt *adj.* **1** appropriate, suitable. **2** tending (*apt to break down*). **3** clever; quick to learn. [Latin *aptus* fitted]

♦ **Apthorp** /ˈæpθɔːp/, **John Dorrington** (1935–) British businessman. In 1968 Apthorp founded the frozen-food chain Bejam and rapidly built it up into a multimillion-pound business with branches all over the country; he was named Guardian Young Businessman of the Year in 1974. Following an acrimonious take-over battle the company was acquired for £238 million by Iceland Frozen Foods in 1989. In the same year Apthorp became chairman of Wizard Wine (now Wharfeside Wines); the company took over Majestic Wines in a £2.5 million deal in 1991.

---

aptitude /ˈæptɪˌtjuːd/ *n.* **1** natural talent. **2** ability or fitness, esp. specified. [French: related to APT]

Apulia /əˈpjuːlɪə/ (Italian **Puglia** /ˈpjuːlɪeɪ/) region forming the SE 'heel' of Italy; wheat, tobacco, vegetables, olives, figs, vines, and almonds are produced; pop. (est. 1993) 4 049 972; capital, Bari.

Aqaba /ˈækəbə/ Jordan's only port, in the SW at the head of the Gulf of Aqaba (an inlet of the Red Sea); pop. (est. 1986) 40 500.

aqua /ˈækwə/ *n.* the colour aquamarine. [abbreviation]

aqua fortis /ˌækwə ˈfɔːtɪs/ *n.* nitric acid. [Latin, = strong water]

aqualung /ˈækwəˌlʌŋ/ *n.* portable breathing-apparatus for divers. [Latin *aqua* water]

aquamarine /ˌækwəməˈriːn/ *–n.* **1** bluish-green beryl. **2** its colour. *–adj.* bluish-green. [Latin *aqua marina* sea water]

aquaplane /ˈækwəˌpleɪn/ *–n.* board for riding on water, pulled by a speedboat. *–v.* (**-ning**) **1** ride on this. **2** (of a vehicle) glide uncontrollably on a wet surface. [Latin *aqua* water, PLANE[1]]

aqua regia /ˌækwə ˈriːdʒɪə/ *n.* highly corrosive mixture of acids, attacking many substances unaffected by other reagents. [Latin, = royal water]

aquarelle /ˌækwəˈrel/ *n.* painting in thin usu. transparent water-colours. [French from Italian]

aquarium /əˈkweərɪəm/ *n.* (*pl.* **-s**) tank of water for keeping and showing fish etc. [Latin *aquarius* of water]

Aquarius /əˈkweərɪəs/ *n.* (*pl.* **-es**) **1** constellation and eleventh sign of the zodiac (the Water-carrier). **2** person born when the sun is in this sign. [Latin: related to AQUARIUM]

aquatic /əˈkwætɪk/ *–adj.* **1** growing or living in water. **2** (of a sport) played in or on water. *–n.* **1** aquatic plant or animal. **2** (in *pl.*) aquatic sports. [Latin *aqua* water]

aquatint /ˈækwətɪnt/ *n.* etched print resembling a water-colour. [Italian *acqua tinta* coloured water]

aqua vitae /ˌækwə ˈviːtaɪ/ *n.* strong alcoholic spirit, esp. brandy. [Latin, = water of life]

aqueduct /ˈækwɪˌdʌkt/ *n.* water channel, esp. a bridge on columns across a valley. [Latin *aquae ductus* conduit]

aqueous /ˈeɪkwɪəs/ *adj.* of or like water. [Latin *aqua* water]

aqueous humour *n.* clear fluid in the eye between the lens and the cornea.

aquilegia /ˌækwɪˈliːdʒə/ *n.* (usu. blue-flowered) columbine. [Latin]

aquiline /ˈækwɪˌlaɪn/ *adj.* **1** of or like an eagle. **2** (of a nose) curved. [Latin *aquila* eagle]

Aquitaine /ˌækwɪˈteɪn/ **1** ancient province of SW France, comprising at some periods the whole country from the Loire to the Pyrenees. **2** region in SW France; viticulture is important; pop. (est. 1993) 2 841 400; capital, Bordeaux.

AR *–abbr.* **1** (also **A/R**) account receivable. **2** *Taxation* annual return. **3** Autonomous Republic. *–US postcode* Arkansas. *–airline flight code* Aerolineas Argentinas.

Ar *symb.* argon.

a.r. *abbr.* (also **a/r, A/r**) *Insurance* all risks.

-ar *suffix* forming adjectives (*angular, linear*). [Latin *-aris*]

Arab /ˈærəb/ *–n.* **1** member of a Semitic people originating in Saudi Arabia and neighbouring countries, now widespread throughout the Middle East. **2** horse of a breed originally native to Arabia. *–adj.* of Arabia or the Arabs (esp. with ethnic reference). [Arabic *araps*]

arabesque /ˌærəˈbesk/ *n.* **1** *Ballet* posture with one leg extended horizontally backwards and arms outstretched. **2** design of intertwined leaves, scrolls, etc. **3** *Mus.* florid piece. [French from Italian from *arabo* Arab]

Arabia /əˈreɪbɪə/ peninsula of SW Asia, largely desert, lying between the Red Sea and the Persian Gulf and bounded in the N by Jordan and Iraq.

Arabian /əˈreɪbɪən/ *–adj.* of or relating to Arabia (esp. in geographical contexts) (*Arabian Desert*). *–n.* native of Arabia.

■ **Usage** In the sense 'native of Arabia', the usual term is now *Arab*.

Arabian Gulf see PERSIAN GULF.

Arabian Sea NW part of the Indian Ocean, between Arabia and India.

Arabic /ˈærəbɪk/ *–n.* Semitic language of the Arabs. *–adj.* of the Arabs (esp. their language or literature).

arabic numeral *n.* any of the numerals 0-9.

Arabistan /ˌærəbɪˈstɑːn/ Iraqi name for the Iranian province of Khuzestan.

arable /ˈærəb(ə)l/ *adj.* (of land) suitable for crop production. [Latin *aro* to plough]

arachnid /əˈræknɪd/ *n.* arthropod of a class comprising spiders, scorpions, etc. [Greek *arakhnē* spider]

Aragon /ˈærəgən/ region of Spain, bounded in the N by the Pyrenees and in the E by Catalonia and Valencia; industries include sugar refining, metal working, and motor-vehicle production; pop. (est. 1994) 1 183 576; capital, Saragossa.

arak var. of ARRACK.

Araldite /ˈærəlˌdaɪt/ *n. propr.* epoxy resin for mending china etc. [origin unknown]

Aral Sea /ˈær(ə)l/ salt-water lake in Kazahkstan and Uzbekistan. It has been reduced to less than half its original size by excessive use of its source water for irrigation, and is heavily polluted.

Aramaic /ˌærəˈmeɪɪk/ *–n.* branch of the Semitic family of languages, esp. the language of Syria used as a lingua franca in the Near East from the sixth century BC. *–adj.* of or in Aramaic. [Greek *Aramaios* of Aram (Hebrew name of Syria)]

Aran Islands /ˈærən/ group of three islands off the W coast of Ireland. Chief town, Kilronan (on Inishmore).

ARB *abbr.* arbitrageur.

arbiter /ˈɑːbɪtə(r)/ *n.* **1** arbitrator in a dispute. **2** person influential in a specific field (*arbiter of taste*). [Latin from *arbitror* to judge]

◆ **arbitrage** /ˈɑːbɪˌtrɑːʒ, ˈɑːbɪtrɪdʒ/ *n.* non-speculative transfer of funds from one market to another to take advantage of differences in interest rates, exchange rates, or commodity prices between the two markets. It is non-speculative because an arbitrageur will only switch from one market to another if he or she knows exactly what the rates or prices are in both markets and if the profit to be gained outweighs the costs of the operation. Thus, a large stock of a commodity in a user country may force its price below that in a producing country; if the difference is greater than the cost of shipping the goods back to the producing country, this could provide a profitable opportunity for arbitrage. Similar opportunities arise with bills of exchange and foreign currencies. □ **arbitrageur** /ˌɑːbɪtræˈʒɜː(r)/ *n.* [French: related to ARBITRATE]

---

arbitrary /ˈɑːbɪtrərɪ/ *adj.* random; capricious; despotic. □ **arbitrarily** *adv.*

arbitrate /ˈɑːbɪˌtreɪt/ *v.* (**-ting**) decide by arbitration.

◆ **arbitration** /ˌɑːbɪˈtreɪʃ(ə)n/ *n.* settlement of a dispute by an impartial third party (an arbitrator) rather than by a court of law. Any civil (i.e. non-criminal) matter may be settled in this way; commercial contracts often contain **arbitration clauses** providing for this to be done in a specified way. If each side appoints its own arbitrator, as is usual, and the arbitrators fail to agree, the arbitrators are often empowered to appoint an umpire, whose decision is final. Arbitration is made binding on the parties by the Arbitration Acts (1950 and 1975). Various industries and chambers of commerce have set up tribunals for dealing with disputes in their particular trade or business. See AWARD *n.* 2.

---

arbitrator *n.* person appointed to arbitrate.

arbor[1] /ˈɑːbə(r)/ *n.* axle or spindle. [Latin, = tree]

arbor[2] *US* var. of ARBOUR.

arboreal /ɑːˈbɔːrɪəl/ *adj.* of or living in trees. [Latin *arbor* tree]

arborescent /ˌɑːbəˈres(ə)nt/ *adj.* treelike in growth or form.

arboretum /ˌɑːbəˈriːtəm/ *n.* (*pl.* **-ta**) place cultivating and displaying rare trees.

arboriculture /ˈɑːbərɪˌkʌltʃə(r)/ *n.* cultivation of trees and shrubs. [Latin *arbor* tree, after *agriculture*]

arbor vitae /ˌɑːbə ˈviːtaɪ/ *n.* any of various evergreen conifers. [Latin, = tree of life]

arbour /ˈɑːbə(r)/ *n.* (*US* **arbor**) shady garden alcove enclosed by trees etc. [Latin *herba* herb: assimilated to Latin *arbor* tree]

arbutus /ɑːˈbjuːtəs/ *n.* tree or shrub with clusters of flowers and strawberry-like berries. [Latin]

ARC *abbr.* = ARCHITECTS REGISTRATION COUNCIL OF THE UK.

arc *–n.* **1** part of the circumference of a circle or other curve. **2** *Electr.* luminous discharge between two electrodes. *–v.* (**arced; arcing** /ˈɑːkɪŋ/) form an arc; move in a curve. [Latin *arcus* bow]

arcade /ɑːˈkeɪd/ *n.* **1** covered walk, esp. lined with shops. **2** series of arches supporting or set along a wall. [Romanic: related to ARC]

Arcadian /ɑːˈkeɪdɪən/ *–n.* idealized country dweller. *–adj.* poetically rural. [Greek *Arkadia* in the Peloponnese]

arcane /ɑːˈkeɪn/ *adj.* mysterious, secret. [Latin *arceo* shut up]

arch[1] *–n.* **1** curved structure as an opening, as a support for a bridge, floor, etc., or as an ornament. **2** any arch-shaped curve. *–v.* **1** provide with or form into an arch. **2** span like an arch. **3** form an arch. [Latin *arcus* arc]

arch[2] *adj.* self-consciously or affectedly playful. □ **archly** *adv.* [from ARCH-, originally in *arch rogue* etc.]

arch- *comb. form* **1** chief, superior (*archbishop*). **2** pre-eminent, esp. unfavourably (*arch-enemy*). [Greek *arkhos* chief]

Archaean /ɑːˈkiːən/ (*US* **Archean**) *–adj.* of the earliest geological era. *–n.* this time. [Greek *arkhaios* ancient]

archaeology /ˌɑːkɪˈɒlədʒɪ/ *n.* (*US* **archeology**) study of ancient cultures, esp. by the excavation and analysis of physical remains. □ **archaeological** /-ˈlɒdʒɪk(ə)l/ *adj.* **archaeologist** *n.* [Greek *arkhaiologia* ancient history]

archaeopteryx /ˌɑːkɪˈɒptərɪks/ *n.* fossil bird with teeth, feathers, and a reptilian tail. [Greek *arkhaios* ancient, *pterux* wing]

archaic /ɑːˈkeɪɪk/ *adj.* **1 a** antiquated. **b** (of a word etc.) no longer in ordinary use. **2** of an early period of culture. □ **archaically** *adv.* [Greek *arkhē* beginning]

archaism /ˈɑːkeɪˌɪz(ə)m/ *n.* **1** use of the archaic esp. in language or art. **2** archaic word or expression. □ **archaistic** /-ˈɪstɪk/ *adj.*

Archangel /ˈɑːkˌeɪndʒ(ə)l/ (Russian **Arkhangelsk** /ɑːˈxæŋgelsk/) port in N Russia, on the White Sea; industries include timber processing, shipbuilding, and fishing; pop. (est. 1994) 407 100.

archangel /ˈɑːkˌeɪndʒ(ə)l/ *n.* angel of the highest rank.

archbishop /ɑːtʃˈbɪʃəp/ *n.* chief bishop of a province.

archbishopric *n.* office or diocese of an archbishop.

archdeacon /ɑːtʃˈdiːkən/ *n.* church dignitary next below a bishop. □ **archdeaconry** *n.* (*pl.* **-ies**).

archdiocese /ɑːtʃˈdaɪəsɪs/ *n.* diocese of an archbishop. □ **archdiocesan** /-daɪˈɒsɪs(ə)n/ *adj.*

archduke /ɑːtʃˈdjuːk/ *n. hist.* chief duke (esp. as the title of a son of the Emperor of Austria). □ **archduchy** /-ˈdʌtʃɪ/ *n.* (*pl.* **-ies**). [medieval Latin *archidux*]

Archean *US* var. of ARCHAEAN.

arch-enemy /ɑːtʃˈenəmɪ/ *n.* (*pl.* **-ies**) **1** chief enemy. **2** the Devil.

archeology *US* var. of ARCHAEOLOGY.

archer *n.* **1** person who shoots with a bow and arrows. **2** (**the Archer**) zodiacal sign or constellation Sagittarius. [Latin *arcus* bow]

archery *n.* shooting with a bow and arrows, esp. as a sport.

archetype /ˈɑːkɪˌtaɪp/ *n.* **1** original model; prototype. **2** typical specimen. □ **archetypal** /-ˈtaɪp(ə)l/ *adj.* [Greek *tupon* stamp]

archidiaconal /ˌɑːkɪdaɪˈækən(ə)l/ *adj.* of an archdeacon. [medieval Latin]

archiepiscopal /ˌɑːkɪɪˈpɪskəp(ə)l/ *adj.* of an archbishop. [Church Latin from Greek]

archimandrite /ˌɑːkɪˈmændraɪt/ *n.* **1** superior of a large monastery in the Orthodox Church. **2** honorary title of a monastic priest. [Greek *arkhi-* chief, *mandritēs* monk]

archipelago /ˌɑːkɪˈpeləˌgəʊ/ *n.* (*pl.* **-s**) **1** group of islands. **2** sea with many islands. [Greek *arkhi-* chief, *pelagos* sea]

architect /ˈɑːkɪˌtekt/ *n.* **1** designer of buildings etc., supervising their construction. **2** (foll. by *of*) person who brings about a specified thing (*architect of peace*). [Greek *arkhi-* chief, *tektōn* builder]

architectonic /ˌɑːkɪtekˈtɒnɪk/ *adj.* **1** of architecture. **2** of the systematization of knowledge.

♦ **Architects Registration Council of the UK** *n.* council established under the Architects (Registration) Act (1931) to maintain a register of persons entitled to practise as architects, to recognize the qualifying examinations for registration, to provide scholarships and maintenance grants for students of architecture, and to act as a disciplinary body for the profession.

---

architecture /ˈɑːkɪˌtektʃə(r)/ *n.* **1** design and construction of buildings. **2** style of a building. **3** buildings etc. collectively. **4** *Computing* description of a computer system at a general level, including details of the instruction set and user interface, input/output operation and control, the organization of memory and the available addressing modes, and the interconnection of the major units. A particular architecture may be implemented by a computer manufacturer in the form of several different machines with different performance and cost. □ **architectural** /-ˈtektʃər(ə)l/ *adj.*

architrave /ˈɑːkɪˌtreɪv/ *n.* **1** (in classical architecture) main beam resting across the tops of columns. **2** moulded frame around a doorway or window. [Italian *archi-* ARCH-, Latin *trabs* beam]

archive /ˈɑːkaɪv/ *–n.* (usu. in *pl.*) **1** collection of documents or records. **2** store for these. **3** *Computing* store for magnetic disks or tapes containing files that are seldom used. Most computer users maintain an archive holding copies of disks or tapes containing vital information. If the original disk or tape becomes damaged, the archive copy is used to reinstate the information. **4** *Computing* computer file, usually in a compressed format, holding data that is no longer current. *–v.* (**-ving**) **1** place or store in an archive. **2** *Computing* transfer (data) to a less frequently used file. [Greek *arkheia* public records]

archivist /ˈɑːkɪvɪst/ *n.* keeper of archives.

archway *n.* arched entrance or passage.

arc lamp *n.* (also **arc light**) light using an electric arc.

Arctic /ˈɑːktɪk/ *–adj.* **1** of the N polar regions. **2** (**arctic**) *colloq.* very cold. *–n.* Arctic regions. [Greek *arktos* Great Bear]

Arctic Circle *n.* parallel of latitude 66° 33′ N, forming an imaginary line round the Arctic region.

Arctic Ocean the world's smallest ocean, surrounding the North Pole and almost completely enclosed by North America, Greenland, and Eurasia.

ARCUK *abbr.* = ARCHITECTS REGISTRATION COUNCIL OF THE UK.

arc welding *n.* use of an electric arc to melt metals to be welded.

Ardennes /ɑːˈden/ forested upland region in S Belgium, Luxembourg, and NE France, the scene of fierce fighting in both World Wars.

ardent /ˈɑːd(ə)nt/ *adj.* **1** eager, fervent, passionate. **2** burning. □ **ardently** *adv.* [Latin *ardeo* burn]

ardour /ˈɑːdə(r)/ *n.* (*US* **ardor**) zeal, enthusiasm, passion.

arduous /ˈɑːdjuːəs/ *adj.* hard to accomplish; laborious, strenuous. [Latin, = steep]

are[1] *2nd sing. present* & *1st, 2nd, 3rd pl. present* of BE.

are[2] /ɑː(r)/ *n.* metric unit of measure, 100 square metres. [Latin: related to AREA]

area /ˈeərɪə/ *n.* **1** extent or measure of a surface (*over a large area*). **2** region (*southern area*). **3** space for a specific purpose (*dining area*). **4** scope or range. **5** space in front of the basement of a building. [Latin, = vacant space]

arena /əˈriːnə/ *n.* **1** central part of an amphitheatre etc. **2** scene of conflict; sphere of action. [Latin, = sand]

aren't /ɑːnt/ *contr.* **1** are not. **2** (in *interrog.*) am not (*aren't I coming too?*).

areola /æˈriːələ/ *n.* (*pl.* **-lae** /-liː/) circular pigmented area, esp. around a nipple. □ **areolar** *adj.* [Latin diminutive of AREA]

Arequipa /ˌæreɪˈkiːpə/ second-largest city in Peru, situated at the foot of the snow-capped El Misti volcano; industries include wool processing; pop. (est. 1993) 619 156.

arête /æˈreɪt/ *n.* sharp mountain ridge. [Latin *arista* spine]

argent /ˈɑːdʒ(ə)nt/ *n.* & *adj. Heraldry* silver; silvery-white. [Latin *argentum*]

Argentine /ˈɑːdʒənˌtaɪn, -ˌtiːn/ (also **Argentinian**

/-'tɪnɪən/) *–adj.* of or relating to Argentina. *–n.* **1** native or national of Argentina. **2** person of Argentine descent. **3** (**the Argentine**) Argentina.

argon /'ɑːgɒn/ *n.* inert gaseous element. [Greek *argos* idle]

Argos /'ɑːgɒs/ **1** ancient Greek town of the NE Peloponnese, from which the peninsula of Argolis derived its name. **2** modern Greek town in the same area, centre of a fruit- and vegetable-growing district with food-processing industries; pop. (1981) 20 702.

argosy /'ɑːgəsɪ/ *n.* (*pl.* **-ies**) *poet.* large merchant ship. [Italian *Ragusea nave* ship of Ragusa (in Dalmatia)]

argot /'ɑːgəʊ/ *n.* jargon of a group or class. [French]

argue /'ɑːgjuː/ *v.* (**-ues, -ued, -uing**) **1** (often foll. by *with, about,* etc.) exchange views forcefully or contentiously. **2** (often foll. by *that*) maintain by reasoning; indicate. **3** (foll. by *for, against*) reason. **4** treat (a matter) by reasoning. **5** (foll. by *into, out of*) persuade. □ **argue the toss** *colloq.* dispute a choice already made. □ **arguable** *adj.* **arguably** *adv.* [Latin *arguo* make clear, prove]

argument /'ɑːgjʊmənt/ *n.* **1** (esp. contentious) exchange of views; dispute. **2** (often foll. by *for, against*) reason given; reasoning process. **3** summary of a book etc.

argumentation /,ɑːgjʊmen'teɪʃ(ə)n/ *n.* methodical reasoning; arguing.

argumentative /,ɑːgjʊ'mentətɪv/ *adj.* given to arguing.

Argus /'ɑːgəs/ *n.* watchful guardian. [Greek *Argos* mythical giant with 100 eyes]

argy-bargy /,ɑːdʒɪ'bɑːdʒɪ/ *n.* (*pl.* **-ies**) *joc.* dispute, wrangle. [originally Scots]

a. Rh. *abbr.* (also **a/Rh, a.R.**) (German, after place-names) am Rhein (= on the River Rhine).

Århus see AARHUS.

aria /'ɑːrɪə/ *n.* long accompanied solo song in an opera etc. [Italian]

ARICS *abbr.* Professional Associate of the Royal Institution of Chartered Surveyors.

arid /'ærɪd/ *adj.* **1** dry, parched. **2** uninteresting. □ **aridity** /ə'rɪdɪtɪ/ *n.* [Latin *areo* be dry]

Aries /'eəriːz/ *n.* (*pl.* same) **1** constellation and first sign of the zodiac (the Ram). **2** person born when the sun is in this sign. [Latin, = ram]

aright /ə'raɪt/ *adv.* rightly.

ARIMA *abbr. Computing* autoregressive integrated moving average.

arise /ə'raɪz/ *v.* (**-sing**; *past* **arose**; *past part.* **arisen** /ə'rɪz(ə)n/) **1** originate. **2** (usu. foll. by *from, out of*) result. **3** come to one's notice; emerge. **4** rise, esp. from the dead or from kneeling. [Old English *a-* intensive]

aristocracy /,ærɪ'stɒkrəsɪ/ *n.* (*pl.* **-ies**) **1** ruling class or élite; nobility. **2 a** government by an élite. **b** state so governed. **3** (often foll. by *of*) best representatives. [Greek *aristokratia* rule by the best]

aristocrat /'ærɪstə,kræt/ *n.* member of the aristocracy.

aristocratic /,ærɪstə'krætɪk/ *adj.* **1** of or like the aristocracy. **2 a** distinguished. **b** grand, stylish.

Aristotelian /,ærɪstə'tiːlɪən/ *–n.* disciple or student of Aristotle. *–adj.* of Aristotle or his ideas. [Greek *Aristotelēs* (4th century BC), name of a Greek philosopher]

arithmetic *–n.* /ə'rɪθmətɪk/ **1** science of numbers. **2** use of numbers; computation. *–adj.* /,ærɪθ'metɪk/ (also **arithmetical**) of arithmetic. [Greek *arithmos* number]

arithmetic and logic unit *n.* (also **ALU**) electronic component of the processing unit of a computer in which arithmetic operations, logic operations, and related operations are performed. The ALU is thus able, for example, to add or subtract two numbers, negate a number, or compare two numbers. The operations are performed on items of data transferred from main store into registers (temporary stores) within the ALU. The result of the operation is subsequently transferred back to the main store. The movement of data between main store and ALU is under the direction of the control unit.

arithmetic mean *n.* = AVERAGE *n.* 2.

arithmetic operation *n.* operation that follows the rules of arithmetic, e.g. addition, subtraction, multiplication, and division. In computing, arithmetic operations are normally performed in the arithmetic and logic unit of a computer. See also OPERAND.

arithmetic progression *n.* sequence of numbers with constant intervals (e.g. 9, 7, 5, 3, etc.).

arithmetic unit *n.* = ARITHMETIC AND LOGIC UNIT.

Ariz. *abbr.* Arizona.

Arizona /,ærɪ'zəʊnə/ state in the SW US; pop. (est. 1995) 4 072 000; capital, Phoenix. Industries include the manufacture of electrical goods and aircraft; copper, cotton, citrus fruits, and livestock are produced.

Ark. *abbr.* Arkansas.

ark *n.* ship in which Noah escaped the Flood with his family and animals. [Old English from Latin *arca*]

Arkansas /'ɑːkən,sɔː/ state in the S central US, bordering on the Mississippi; pop. (est. 1995) 2 468 000; capital, Little Rock. Products include bauxite, natural gas, and timber; tourism is important.

Arkhangelsk see ARCHANGEL.

Ark of the Covenant *n.* chest or cupboard containing the tables of Jewish Law.

ARM *abbr.* = ADJUSTABLE-RATE MORTGAGE.

arm[1] *n.* **1** upper limb of the human body from shoulder to hand. **2** forelimb or tentacle of an animal. **3 a** sleeve of a garment. **b** arm support of a chair etc. **c** thing

---

Argentina /,ɑːdʒən'tiːnə/, **Republic of** country occupying much of the S part of South America, characterized by heavily Europeanized cities and a population largely of European descent. The economy is chiefly agricultural, and meat-packing is one of the principal industries, but there has been recent growth in textile, plastic, and engineering industries and development of natural mineral resources, particularly copper. Substantial deposits of oil and natural gas occur in various parts of the country and are of major importance to Argentina's industries. Main exports are meat and meat products, livestock, wool, cereals, minerals, metals, machinery, and petroleum and petroleum products. Since 1991 there has been considerable economic progress; inflation, previously an uncontrollable problem, has fallen dramatically and there has been a recovery in output. Argentina is a member of LAIA.

History. Colonized by the Spanish in the 16th century, Argentina declared its independence in 1816. Recent political leaders have been mainly military dictators, notably Juan Peron (1946–55; 1973–4) and Leopoldo Galtieri (1981–2), whose attempt to recover the Falkland Islands from the UK led to his military defeat and a return to civilian rule (1983). In 1994 Argentina signed a pact with the UK concerning arrangements for oil exploration in the Falkland Islands. President, Carlos Menem; capital and main port, Buenos Aires.

languages	Spanish (official), English, Italian, French
currency	peso ($) of 100 centavos (replaced the austral in 1992; 1 peso = 10,000 australes)
pop. (1995)	34 587 000
GNP (est. 1990)	US$244B
literacy	96%
life expectancy	68 (m); 71 (f)

Exchange rate, US¢ per austral and peso (a) Inflation, % (b)

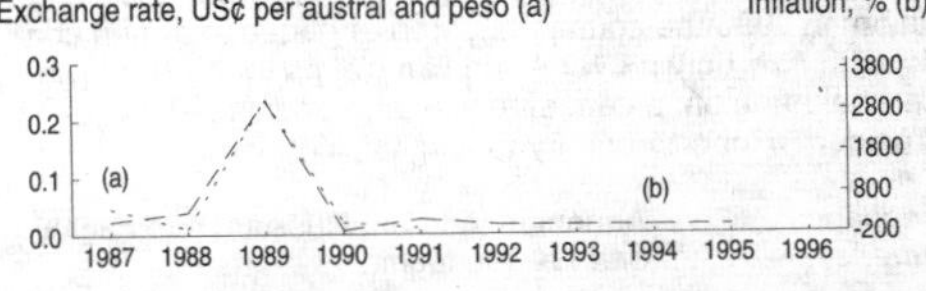

branching from a main stem (*an arm of the sea*). **d** control, means of reaching (*arm of the law*). □ **arm in arm** with arms linked. **with open arms** cordially. □ **armful** *n.* (*pl.* **-s**). [Old English]

arm[2] *–n.* **1** (usu. in *pl.*) weapon. **2** (in *pl.*) military profession. **3** branch of the military (e.g. infantry, cavalry). **4** (in *pl.*) heraldic devices (*coat of arms*). *–v.* **1** supply, or equip oneself, with weapons etc., esp. in preparation for war. **2** make (a bomb etc.) ready. □ **take up arms** go to war. **under arms** equipped for war. **up in arms** (usu. foll. by *against*, *about*) actively resisting, highly indignant. [Latin *arma* arms]

ARMA *abbr. Computing* autoregressive moving average.

armada /ɑː'mɑːdə/ *n.* fleet of warships, esp. (**Armada**) that sent by Spain against England in 1588. [Spanish from Romanic]

armadillo /ˌɑːmə'dɪləʊ/ *n.* (*pl.* **-s**) South American mammal with a plated body and large claws. [Spanish *armado* armed man]

Armageddon /ˌɑːmə'ged(ə)n/ *n.* huge battle or struggle, esp. marking the end of the world. [Rev. 16:16]

Armagh /ɑː'mɑː/ **1** county in S Northern Ireland; potatoes, flax, and apples are produced. **2** city in Northern Ireland, county town of Co. Armagh; industries include textiles, chemicals, optical equipment, and food processing; pop. (1981) 12 700. **3** district in Northern Ireland, in Co. Armagh; pop. (est. 1993) 51 700.

Armagnac /'ɑːmənˌjæk/ district in SW France; brandy is produced.

armament /'ɑːməmənt/ *n.* **1** (often in *pl.*) military equipment. **2** equipping for war. **3** force equipped. [Latin: related to ARM[2]]

armature /'ɑːmətʃə(r)/ *n.* **1** rotating coil or coils of a dynamo or electric motor. **2** iron bar placed across the poles of a horseshoe magnet to preserve its power. **3** metal framework on which a sculpture is moulded. [Latin *armatura*, = armour]

armband *n.* band worn around the upper arm to hold up a shirtsleeve or as identification etc.

armchair *n.* **1** chair with arm supports. **2** (*attrib.*) theoretical rather than active (*armchair critic*).

Armenian *–n.* **1** native or national of Armenia. **2** language of Armenia. *–adj.* of Armenia or its people or language.

armhole *n.* each of two holes for arms in a garment.

armistice /'ɑːmɪstɪs/ *n.* truce, esp. permanent. [Latin *arma* arms, *sisto* make stand]

Armistice Day *n.* anniversary of the armistice of 11 Nov. 1918.

armlet *n.* ornamental band worn round the arm.

armor etc. *US* var. of ARMOUR etc.

armorial /ɑː'mɔːrɪəl/ *adj.* of heraldry or coats of arms. [related to ARMOUR]

armour /'ɑːmə(r)/ *–n.* **1** protective usu. metal covering formerly worn in fighting. **2 a** (in full **armour-plate**) protective metal covering for an armed vehicle, ship, etc. **b** armed vehicles collectively. **3** protective covering or shell of an animal or plant. **4** heraldic devices. *–v.* (usu. as **armoured** *adj.*) provide with protective covering, and often guns (*armoured car*; *armoured train*). [Latin *armatura*: related to ARM[2]]

armourer *n.* **1** maker of arms or armour. **2** official in charge of arms.

armoury *n.* (*pl.* **-ies**) arsenal.

armpit *n.* hollow under the arm at the shoulder.

armrest *n.* = ARM[1] 3b.

♦ **arm's length** *adj.* **1** denoting a transaction in which the transacting parties have no financial connection. **2** denoting a relationship that lacks intimacy. □ **at arm's length** at a distance.

---

arms race *n.* competitive accumulation of weapons by nations.

arm-wrestling *n.* trial of strength in which each party tries to force the other's arm down.

army *n.* (*pl.* **-ies**) **1** organized armed land force. **2** (prec. by *the*) the military profession. **3** (often foll. by *of*) very large number (*army of locusts*). **4** organized civilian body (*Salvation Army*). [French: related to ARM[2]]

Arnhem /'ɑːnəm/ city in E Netherlands, capital of the province of Gelderland; industries include engineering and pharmaceuticals; pop. (est. 1994) 133 670.

Arnhem Land region in Northern Territory, Australia; bauxite and uranium are mined. Much of the region is an aboriginal reserve.

arnica /'ɑːnɪkə/ *n.* **1** plant of the daisy family with yellow flowers. **2** medicine prepared from this. [origin unknown]

aroma /ə'rəʊmə/ *n.* **1** esp. pleasing smell, often of food. **2** subtle pervasive quality. [Greek, = spice]

aromatherapy *n.* use of aromatic plant extracts and oils in massage.

aromatic /ˌærə'mætɪk/ *–adj.* **1** fragrant, spicy. **2** *Chem.* of organic compounds having an unsaturated ring, esp. containing a benzene ring. *–n.* aromatic substance. [Latin: related to AROMA]

arose *past* of ARISE.

around /ə'raʊnd/ *–adv.* **1** on every side; all round; round about. **2** *colloq.* **a** in existence; available. **b** near at hand. **3** here and there (*shop around*). *–prep.* **1** on or along the circuit of. **2** on every side of. **3** here and there in or near (*chairs around the room*). **4 a** round (*church around the corner*). **b** at a time near to (*came around four o'clock*). □ **have been around** *colloq.* be widely experienced.

arouse /ə'raʊz/ *v.* (**-sing**) **1** induce (esp. an emotion). **2** awake from sleep. **3** stir into activity. **4** stimulate sexually. □ **arousal** *n.* [*a-* intensive prefix]

ARP *abbr. US Finance* adjustable rate preferred stock.

ARPANET /'ɑːpəˌnet/ *abbr.* (also **Arpanet**) *Computing* Advanced Research Projects Agency Network.

arpeggio /ɑː'pedʒɪəʊ/ *n.* (*pl.* **-s**) *Mus.* notes of a chord played in succession. [Italian *arpa* harp]

♦ **ARR** *abbr.* = ACCOUNTING RATE OF RETURN.

---

arrack /'ærək/ *n.* (also **arak**) alcoholic spirit, esp. made from coco sap or rice. [Arabic]

arraign /ə'reɪn/ *v.* **1** indict, accuse. **2** find fault with; call

---

Armenia /ɑː'miːnɪə/, **Republic of** republic in central Asia, lying S of the Caucasus; there are food-processing, metallurgical, and chemical industries and mineral deposits of copper, lead, and zinc. Agriculture is centred on livestock rearing; crops include wine grapes and tobacco. Armenia was struck by severe earthquakes during the late 1980s. Until 1991 Armenia was a constituent republic of the Soviet Union; in 1990 the country became engaged in armed conflict with Azerbaijan over Armenian claims to the Nagorno-Karabakh region; a ceasefire was agreed in 1994.
President, Robert Kocharyon; capital, Yerevan.

languages	Armenian (official), Russian, Azerbaijani
currency	dram of 100 louma
pop. (est. 1995)	3 348 000
GNP (1993)	US$2.4B
life expectancy	68 (m); 75 (f)

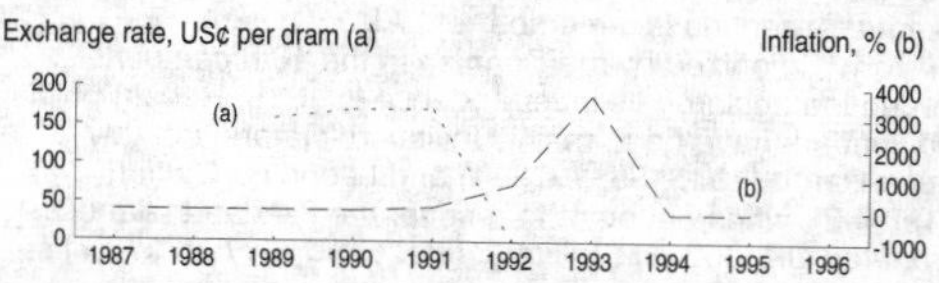

Exchange rate, US¢ per dram (a)
Inflation, % (b)
200
150
100
50
0
(a)
(b)
4000
3000
2000
1000
0
-1000
1987 1988 1989 1990 1991 1992 1993 1994 1995 1996

into question (an action or statement). □ **arraignment** *n.* [Latin *ratio* reason]

Arran /'ærən/ island in W Scotland in the Firth of Clyde, a popular tourist centre; pop. (1985) 4007.

arrange /ə'reɪndʒ/ *v.* (**-ging**) **1** put into order; classify. **2** plan or provide for; take measures (*arranged a meeting; arrange to see him; arranged for a taxi*). **3** agree (*arranged it with her*). **4** *Mus.* adapt (a composition) for a particular manner of performance. [French: related to RANGE]

arrangement *n.* **1** arranging or being arranged. **2** manner of this. **3** something arranged. **4** (in *pl.*) plans, measures (*made my own arrangements*). **5** *Mus.* composition adapted for performance in a particular way. **6** *Finance* **a** method of enabling a debtor to enter into an agreement with his or her creditors (either privately or through the courts) to discharge the debts by partial payment, as an alternative to bankruptcy. This is generally achieved by a **scheme of arrangement**, which involves applying the assets and income of the debtor in proportionate payment to the creditors. For instance, a scheme of arrangement may stipulate that the creditors will receive 20 pence for every pound that is owed to them. This is sometimes also known as **composition**. Once a scheme of arrangement has been agreed a **deed of arrangement** is drawn up, which must be registered with the Department of Trade and Industry within seven days. **b** see VOLUNTARY ARRANGEMENT.

arrant /'ærənt/ *adj. literary* downright, utter (*arrant liar*). [var. of ERRANT, originally in *arrant* (= outlawed, roving) *thief* etc.]

arras /'ærəs/ *n. hist.* rich tapestry or wall-hanging. [*Arras* in France]

array /ə'reɪ/ *–n.* **1** imposing or well-ordered series or display. **2** ordered arrangement, esp. of troops (*battle array*). **3** *Computing* one form in which a collection of data items can be stored in computer memory. The data items are arranged in a particular order or pattern. They are all of the same type, e.g. all integers or all real numbers. Each element in an array (i.e. a location in memory or its contents) can be specified uniquely. The simplest array is a single sequence of elements with each element specified by its position in the sequence. This is a **vector**. In a **matrix** the elements are arranged in the form of a table with a fixed number of rows and a fixed number of columns. Each element is specified by its row and column number. *–v.* **1** deck, adorn. **2** set in order; marshal (forces). [Latin *ad-*, READY]

arrears /ə'rɪəz/ *n.pl.* amount (esp. of work, rent, etc.) still outstanding or uncompleted. □ **in arrears** behind, esp. in payment. [medieval Latin *adretro* behindhand]

arrest /ə'rest/ *–v.* **1** lawfully seize (a suspect etc.). **2** stop or check the progress of. **3** attract (a person's attention). *–n.* **1** arresting or being arrested. **2** stoppage (*cardiac arrest*). [Latin *resto* remain]

arrester *n.* device for slowing an aircraft after landing.

arrière-pensée /ˌærjerpɑ̃'seɪ/ *n.* **1** secret motive. **2** mental reservation. [French]

arris /'ærɪs/ *n. Archit.* sharp edge at the junction of two surfaces. [French *areste*, = ARÊTE]

arrival /ə'raɪv(ə)l/ *n.* **1** arriving; appearance on the scene. **2** person or thing that has arrived.

arrive /ə'raɪv/ *v.* (**-ving**) **1** (often foll. by *at, in*) reach a destination. **2** (foll. by *at*) reach (a conclusion etc.). **3** *colloq.* become successful. **4** *colloq.* (of a child) be born. **5** (of a time) come. [Latin *ripa* shore]

arriviste /ˌæri:'vi:st/ *n.* ambitious or ruthless person. [French: related to ARRIVE]

arrogant /'ærəgənt/ *adj.* aggressively assertive or presumptuous. □ **arrogance** *n.* **arrogantly** *adv.* [related to ARROGATE]

arrogate /'ærəˌgeɪt/ *v.* (**-ting**) **1** (often foll. by *to* oneself) claim (power etc.) without right. **2** (often foll. by *to*) attribute unjustly (to a person). □ **arrogation** /-'geɪʃ(ə)n/ *n.* [Latin *rogo* ask]

arrow /'ærəʊ/ *n.* **1** pointed slender missile shot from a bow. **2** representation of this, esp. indicating direction. [Old English]

arrowhead *n.* **1** pointed tip of an arrow. **2** water-plant with arrow-shaped leaves.

arrow keys *n.pl. Computing* four keys on a keyboard that are labelled with up, down, left, and right arrow symbols and can be used for control of the cursor on a display screen.

arrowroot *n.* **1** nutritious starch. **2** plant yielding this.

arse /ɑ:s/ *n.* (*US* **ass** /æs/) *coarse slang* buttocks. [Old English]

arsehole *n.* (*US* **asshole**) *coarse slang* **1** anus. **2** *offens.* contemptible person.

arsenal /'ɑ:sən(ə)l/ *n.* **1** store, esp. of weapons. **2** place for the storage and manufacture of weapons and ammunition. [Arabic, = workshop]

arsenic *–n.* /'ɑ:sənɪk/ **1** nonscientific name for arsenic trioxide, a highly poisonous white powder used in weed-killers etc. **2** *Chem.* brittle semimetallic element. *–adj.* /ɑ:'senɪk/ of or containing arsenic. [French, ultimately from Persian *zar* gold]

arson /'ɑ:s(ə)n/ *n.* crime of deliberately setting fire to property. □ **arsonist** *n.* [Latin *ardeo ars-* burn]

art *n.* **1 a** human creative skill or its application. **b** work showing this. **2 a** (in *pl.*; prec. by *the*) branches of creative activity concerned with the production of imaginative designs, sounds, or ideas, e.g. painting, music, writing. **b** any one of these. **3** creative activity resulting in visual representation (*good at music but not art*). **4** human skill as opposed to nature (*art and nature combined*). **5** (often foll. by *of*) **a** skill, knack. **b** cunning; trick, stratagem. **6** (in *pl.*; usu. prec. by *the*) supposedly creative subjects (esp. languages, literature, and history) as opposed to scientific, technical, or vocational subjects. [Latin *ars art-*]

art deco /ɑ:t 'dekəʊ/ *n.* decorative art style of 1910–30, with geometric motifs and strong colours.

artefact /'ɑ:tɪˌfækt/ *n.* (also **artifact**) man-made object, esp. a tool or vessel as an archaeological item. [Latin *arte* by art, *facio* make]

arterial /ɑ:'tɪərɪəl/ *adj.* **1** of or like an artery. **2** (esp. of a road) main, important. [French: related to ARTERY]

arteriosclerosis /ɑ:ˌtɪərɪəʊsklɪə'rəʊsɪs/ *n.* loss of elasticity and thickening of artery walls, esp. in old age. [from ARTERY, SCLEROSIS]

artery /'ɑ:tərɪ/ *n.* (*pl.* **-ies**) **1** any of the blood-vessels carrying blood from the heart. **2** main road or railway line. [Greek, probably from *airō* raise]

artesian well /ɑ:'ti:zɪən/ *n.* well in which water rises to the surface by natural pressure through a vertically drilled hole. [*Artois*, old French province]

artful *adj.* crafty, deceitful. □ **artfully** *adv.*

arthritis /ɑ:'θraɪtɪs/ *n.* inflammation of a joint or joints. □ **arthritic** /-'θrɪtɪk/ *adj.* & *n.* [Greek *arthron* joint]

arthropod /'ɑ:θrəˌpɒd/ *n.* invertebrate with a segmented body and jointed limbs, e.g. an insect, spider, or crustacean. [Greek *arthron* joint, *pous pod-* foot]

artichoke /'ɑ:tɪˌtʃəʊk/ *n.* **1** plant allied to the thistle. **2** (in full **globe artichoke**) its partly edible flower-head (see also JERUSALEM ARTICHOKE). [Italian from Arabic]

article /'ɑ:tɪk(ə)l/ *–n.* **1** item or thing. **2** non-fictional journalistic essay. **3** clause or item in an agreement or contract. **4** definite or indefinite article. *–v.* (**-ling**) employ under contract as a trainee. [Latin *articulus* from *artus* joint]

♦ **articled clerk** *n.* trainee solicitor. The Law Society lays down provisions regulating the training of solicitors. All trainees are now graduates and will have taken professional examinations. They are then required to be articled to (i.e. to sign an agreement to learn from) a qualified solicitor for two years before being admitted as solicitors themselves.

♦ **articles of apprenticeship** see APPRENTICE *n.* 1.

♦ **articles of association** *n.pl.* document that governs the running of a company. It sets out voting rights of shareholders, conduct of shareholders' and directors' meetings, powers of the management, etc. Either the articles are submitted with the memorandum of association when application is made for incorporation or the relevant model articles contained in the Companies Regulations (Tables A to F) are adopted. Table A contains the model articles for companies limited by shares. The articles constitute a contract between the company and its members but this applies only to the rights of shareholders in their capacity as members. Therefore directors or company solicitors (for example) cannot use the articles to enforce their rights. The articles may be altered by a special resolution of the members in a general meeting.

---

articular /ɑːˈtɪkjʊlə(r)/ *adj.* of a joint or joints. [Latin: related to ARTICLE]

articulate –*adj.* /ɑːˈtɪkjʊlət/ **1** fluent and clear in speech. **2** (of sound or speech) having clearly distinguishable parts. **3** having joints. –*v.* /ɑːˈtɪkjʊˌleɪt/ (**-ting**) **1 a** pronounce distinctly. **b** speak or express clearly. **2** (usu. in *passive*) connect by joints. **3** mark with apparent joints. **4** (often foll. by *with*) form a joint. □ **articulately** *adv.*

articulated lorry *n.* one with sections connected by a flexible joint.

articulation /ɑːˌtɪkjʊˈleɪʃ(ə)n/ *n.* **1 a** speaking or being spoken. **b** articulate utterance; speech. **2 a** act or mode of jointing. **b** joint. [Latin: related to ARTICULATE]

artifact var. of ARTEFACT.

artifice /ˈɑːtɪfɪs/ *n.* **1** trick or clever device. **2** cunning. **3** skill, ingenuity. [Latin *ars art-* art, *facio* make]

artificer /ɑːˈtɪfɪsə(r)/ *n.* **1** craftsman. **2** skilled military mechanic.

artificial /ˌɑːtɪˈfɪʃ(ə)l/ *adj.* **1** not natural (*artificial lake*). **2** imitating nature (*artificial flowers*). **3** affected, insincere. □ **artificiality** /-ʃɪˈælɪtɪ/ *n.* **artificially** *adv.* [Latin: related to ARTIFICE]

artificial insemination *n.* non-sexual injection of semen into the uterus.

artificial intelligence *n.* (also **AI**) concept or area of study concerned with the production of computer programs that perform tasks normally associated with human intelligence. These tasks are usu. intellectual, e.g. the playing of chess and other games, the solving of problems, the formation of plans, the proving of theorems, and the understanding of speech and of natural language (as opposed to programming languages). The programs can have applications in science and technology and in computer-assisted learning, and may assist in the study of the workings of the human brain. See also EXPERT SYSTEM; ROBOT 2.

♦ **artificial person** *n.* person whose identity is recognized by the law but who is not an individual. For example, a company is an artificial person as it can sue and be sued, hold property, etc. in its own name.

---

artificial respiration *n.* manual or mechanical stimulation of breathing.

artillery /ɑːˈtɪlərɪ/ *n.* (*pl.* **-ies**) **1** heavy guns used in land warfare. **2** branch of the army using these. □ **artilleryman** *n.* [French *artiller* equip]

artisan /ˌɑːtɪˈzæn/ *n.* skilled manual worker or craftsman. [Latin *artio* instruct in the arts]

artist /ˈɑːtɪst/ *n.* **1** practitioner of any of the arts, esp. painting. **2** artiste. **3** person using skill or taste. □ **artistry** *n.* [French *artiste* from Italian]

artiste /ɑːˈtiːst/ *n.* professional performer, esp. a singer or dancer.

artistic /ɑːˈtɪstɪk/ *adj.* **1** having natural skill in art. **2** skilfully or tastefully done. **3** of art or artists. □ **artistically** *adv.*

artless *adj.* **1** guileless, ingenuous. **2** natural. **3** clumsy. □ **artlessly** *adv.*

art nouveau /ˌɑː nuːˈvəʊ/ *n.* art style of the late 19th century, with flowing lines.

Artois /ˈɑːtwæ/ former province of NW France, roughly equivalent to the department of Pas-de-Calais.

artwork *n.* **1** illustrative material in printed matter. **2** works of art collectively (*exhibition of children's artwork*).

arty *adj.* (**-ier, -iest**) *colloq.* pretentiously or affectedly artistic.

ARU *abbr. Computing* audio response unit.

Aruba /əˈruːbə/ Dutch island in the Caribbean Sea, 24 km (15 miles) N of the Venezuelan coast; currency, Aruban florin; pop. (1991) 68 897; capital, Oranjestad. Formerly part of the Netherlands Antilles, it separated from that group in 1986. Industries include tourism and light manufacturing; petroleum products form the main exports.

arum /ˈeərəm/ *n.* plant with arrow-shaped leaves. [Greek *aron*]

Arunachal Pradesh /ɑːrəˈnɑːtʃ(ə)l prəˈdeʃ/ state of NE India; forestry and timber-related industries are important; pop. (est. 1994) 965 000; capital, Itanagar.

-ary *suffix* forming adjectives (*contrary*; *primary*). [French *-aire*, Latin *-ari(u)s*]

Aryan /ˈeərɪən/ –*n.* **1** speaker of any of the languages of the Indo-European family. **2** *improperly* (in Nazi ideology) non-Jewish Caucasian. –*adj.* of Aryans. [Sanskrit]

A/S *abbr.* **1** account sales. **2** *Banking* after sight. **3** (Danish) Aktieselskab (= joint-stock company). **4** (Norwegian) Aktjeselskap (= limited company).

As *symb.* arsenic.

as[1] /æz, əz/ –*adv.* & *conj.* (*adv.* as antecedent in main sentence; *conj.* in relative clause expressed or implied) to the extent to which ... is or does etc. (*am as tall as he*; *am as tall as he is*; (*colloq.*) *am as tall as him*; *as recently as last week*). –*conj.* (with relative clause expressed or implied) **1** (with antecedent *so*) expressing result or purpose (*came early so as to meet us*). **2** (with antecedent adverb omitted) although (*good as it is* = although it is good). **3** (without antecedent adverb) **a** in the manner in which (*do as you like*; *rose as one man*). **b** in the capacity or form of (*I speak as your friend*; *Olivier as Hamlet*). **c** while (*arrived as I was eating*). **d** since, seeing that (*as you are here, we can talk*). **e** for instance (*cathedral cities, as York*). –*rel. pron.* (with verb of relative clause expressed or implied) **1** that, who, which (*I had the same trouble as you*; *he is a writer, as is his wife*; *such countries as France*). **2** (with a sentence as antecedent) a fact that (*he lost, as you know*). □ **as for** with regard to (*as for you, I think you are wrong*). **as from** on and after (a specified date). **as if** (or **though**) as would be the case if (*acts as if he were in charge*). **as it were** in a way; to some extent (*he is, as it were, infatuated*). **as long as** see LONG[1]. **as much** see MUCH. **as of 1** = *as from*. **2** as at (a specified time). **as per** see PER. **as regards** see REGARD. **as soon as** see SOON. **as such** see SUCH. **as though** see *as if*. **as to** with regard to. **as well 1** in addition. **2** advisable, desirable, reasonably. **as well as** in addition to. **as yet** until now or up to a particular time (*have received no news as yet*). [Old English, = ALSO]

as[2] /æs/ *n.* (*pl.* **asses**) Roman copper coin. [Latin]

ASA *abbr.* **1** Advertising Standards Authority. **2** Associate Member of the Society of Actuaries. **3** *US* Associate of the Society of Actuaries. **4** Australian Society of Accountants.

ASAA *abbr.* Associate of the Society of Incorporated Accountants and Auditors.

asafoetida /ˌæsəˈfetɪdə/ *n.* (*US* **asafetida**) resinous pungent plant gum used in cooking and formerly in medicine. [Persian *azā* mastic; FETID]

a.s.a.p. *abbr.* as soon as possible.

asbestos /æsˈbestɒs/ *n.* **1** fibrous silicate mineral. **2** this as a heat-resistant or insulating material. [Greek, = unquenchable]

ASCA *abbr.* Associate of the Society of Company and Commercial Accountants.

ascend /əˈsend/ *v.* **1** move or slope upwards, rise. **2** climb; go up. □ **ascend the throne** become king or queen. [Latin *scando* climb]

ascendancy *n.* (often foll. by *over*) dominant power or control.

ascendant –*adj.* **1** rising. **2** *Astron.* rising towards the zenith. **3** *Astrol.* just above the eastern horizon. **4** predominant. *–n. Astrol.* ascendant point of the sun's apparent path. □ **in the ascendant** gaining or having power or authority.

ascension /ə'senʃ(ə)n/ *n.* **1** ascent. **2** (**Ascension**) ascent of Christ into heaven.

Ascension Island small island in the S Atlantic, a dependency of St Helena; pop. (1993) 1117 (excluding military personnel). It is a British telecommunications centre and a US air base.

ascent /ə'sent/ *n.* **1** ascending, rising, or progressing. **2** upward slope or path etc.

ascertain /ˌæsə'teɪn/ *v.* find out for certain. □ **ascertainment** *n.* [French: related to CERTAIN]

ascetic /ə'setɪk/ *–adj.* severely abstinent; self-denying. *–n.* ascetic, esp. religious, person. □ **asceticism** /-tɪˌsɪz(ə)m/ *n.* [Greek *askeō* exercise]

ASCII /'æskɪ/ *n.* standard code for the interchange of information between computer systems, data communication systems, and associated equipment. It allows equipment of different manufacturers to exchange information and is thus widely used. ASCII encoding produces 128 characters that make up the ASCII character set: they consist of alphanumeric characters, the space character, special characters, and control characters. [*A*merican *S*tandard *C*ode for *I*nformation *I*nterchange]

ascorbic acid /ə'skɔːbɪk/ *n.* vitamin C, which prevents scurvy. [from A-, SCORBUTIC]

ascribe /ə'skraɪb/ *v.* (**-bing**) (usu. foll. by *to*) **1** attribute (*ascribes his health to exercise*). **2** regard as belonging. □ **ascription** /ə'skrɪpʃ(ə)n/ *n.* [Latin *scribo* write]

ASE *abbr.* American Stock Exchange.

Asean /'æsɪˌæn/ *abbr.* = ASSOCIATION OF SOUTH-EAST ASIAN NATIONS.

asepsis /eɪ'sepsɪs/ *n.* **1** absence of sepsis or harmful micro-organisms. **2** method of achieving asepsis in surgery. □ **aseptic** *adj.*

asexual /eɪ'sekʃʊəl/ *adj.* **1** without sex, sexual organs, or sexuality. **2** (of reproduction) not involving the fusion of gametes. □ **asexually** *adv.*

ASF *abbr.* Associate of the Institute of Shipping and Forwarding Agents.

ash[1] *n.* **1** (often in *pl.*) powdery residue left after burning. **2** (*pl.*) human remains after cremation. **3** (**the Ashes**) *Cricket* trophy competed for by Australia and England. [Old English]

ash[2] *n.* **1** tree with silver-grey bark. **2** its hard, pale wood. [Old English]

ashamed /ə'ʃeɪmd/ *adj.* (usu. *predic.*) **1** embarrassed by shame (*ashamed of myself*). **2** (foll. by *to* + infin.) hesitant, reluctant out of shame (*am ashamed to say*). [Old English *a-* intensive prefix]

Ashanti /ə'ʃæntɪ/ (also **Asante**) region of central Ghana; industries include metalworking and textiles; cocoa is the chief crop; pop. (est. 1991) 2 485 770; capital, Kumasi. The former Ashanti confederation, a tribal union (covering a wider area) that was forged in the 17th century, became part of the British colony of the Gold Coast in 1902.

♦ **A shares** *n.pl.* ordinary shares in a company that usu. do not carry voting rights. **Non-voting shares** are issued by a company when it wishes to raise additional capital without committing itself to a fixed dividend and without diluting control of the company. They are, however, unpopular with institutional investors (who like to have a measure of control with their investments) and are therefore now rarely issued.

---

ashcan *n. US* dustbin.

Ashdod /'æʃdɒd/ seaport in Israel, S of Tel Aviv on the Mediterranean coast; pop. (est. 1982) 66 000.

ashen *adj.* like ashes, esp. grey or pale.

Ashkenazi /ˌæʃkə'nɑːzɪ/ *n.* (*pl.* **-zim**) East European Jew. [Hebrew]

Ashkhabad /ˌæʃkə'bæd/ capital of Turkmenistan; food, glass, carpets, and machinery are produced; pop. (est. 1994) 518 000.

ashlar /'æʃlə(r)/ *n.* **1** large square-cut stone used in building; masonry made of these. **2** thin slabs of masonry used for facing walls. [Latin *axis* board]

Ashmore and Cartier Islands /'æʃmɔː(r), 'kɑːtɪeɪ/ external territory of Australia, in the Indian Ocean NW of Western Australia, comprising the uninhabited Cartier Island and the Ashmore Reef and islets, one of which is the site of an automatic weather station.

ashore /ə'ʃɔː(r)/ *adv.* towards or on the shore or land.

Ashquelon /'æʃkələn/ resort on the Mediterranean coast of Israel, S of Tel Aviv; pop. (est. 1989) 56 000. It is the site of an ancient Philistine city (called *Ashkelon* in the Bible).

ashram /'æʃrəm/ *n.* place of religious retreat for Hindus. [Sanskrit]

ashtray *n.* small receptacle for cigarette ash, stubs, etc.

ashy *adj.* (**-ier, -iest**) **1** = ASHEN. **2** covered with ashes.

Asia /'eɪʃə/ largest of the world's continents, constituting nearly one-third of the land mass, lying entirely N of the equator except for some SE Asian islands. It is connected to Africa by the isthmus of Suez, and generally divided from Europe (which forms part of the same land mass) by a line running through the Ural Mountains (in Russia) and the Caspian Sea.

Asia Minor *hist.* westernmost part of Asia. See ANATOLIA.

Asian /'eɪʃ(ə)n/ *–n.* **1** native of Asia. **2** person of Asian descent. *–adj.* of Asia. [Latin from Greek]

Asiatic /ˌeɪʃɪ'ætɪk/ *–n. offens.* Asian. *–adj.* Asian. [Latin from Greek]

aside /ə'saɪd/ *–adv.* to or on one side; away, apart. *–n.* words spoken aside, esp. confidentially to the audience by an actor.

asinine /'æsɪˌnaɪn/ *adj.* like an ass, esp. stupid or stubborn. □ **asininity** /-'nɪnɪtɪ/ *n.* [Latin *asinus* ass]

ask /ɑːsk/ *v.* **1** call for an answer to or about (*ask her about it; ask him his name*). **2** seek to obtain from someone (*ask a favour of*). **3** (usu. foll. by *out, in,* or *over,* or *to* (a function etc.)) invite (*must ask them over; asked her to dinner*). **4** (foll. by *for*) seek to obtain, meet, or be directed to (*ask for help; asking for you; ask for the bar*). □ **ask after** inquire about (esp. a person). **ask for it** *slang* invite trouble. [Old English]

askance /ə'skæns/ *adv.* sideways or squinting. □ **look askance at** regard suspiciously. [origin unknown]

askew /ə'skjuː/ *–adv.* awry, crookedly. *–predic. adj.* oblique; awry.

aslant /ə'slɑːnt/ *–adv.* obliquely or at a slant. *–prep.* obliquely across.

asleep /ə'sliːp/ *predic. adj.* & *adv.* **1 a** in or into a state of sleep. **b** inactive, inattentive. **2** (of a limb etc.) numb. **3** *euphem.* dead.

ASLEF /'æzlef/ *abbr.* (also **Aslef**) Associated Society of Locomotive Engineers and Firemen.

ASLIB /'æzlɪb/ *n.* (also **Aslib**) Association for Information Management. [formerly *A*ssociation of *S*pecial *Lib*raries and *I*nformation *B*ureaux]

ASM *abbr. Computing* algorithmic state machine (hardware design technique).

Asmara /æs'mɑːrə/ capital of Eritrea; industries include meat processing, distilling, and clothing; pop. (est. 1991) 367 300.

ASP *abbr.* **1** *Commerce* (French) accepté sous protêt (= accepted under protest). **2** American selling price.

asp *n.* small venomous snake of N Africa or S Europe. [Greek *aspis*]

asparagus /ə'spærəgəs/ *n.* **1** plant of the lily family. **2** edible shoots of this. [Latin from Greek]

ASPC *abbr. Commerce* (French) accepté sous protêt, pour compté (= accepted under protest for account).

aspect /'æspekt/ *n.* **1** viewpoint, feature, etc. to be considered (*one aspect of the problem*). **2** appearance or look (*cheerful aspect*). **3** side of a building or location facing a particular direction (*southern aspect*). [Latin *adspicio* look at]

aspen /'æspən/ *n.* poplar with very tremulous leaves. [Old English: originally adj.]

♦ **as per advice** see PER.

---

asperity /ə'sperɪtɪ/ *n.* (*pl.* **-ies**) **1** sharpness of temper or tone. **2** roughness; rough excrescence. [Latin *asper* rough]

aspersion /ə'spɜːʃ(ə)n/ *n.* □ **cast aspersions on** attack the reputation of. [Latin *aspergo* besprinkle]

asphalt /'æsfælt/ –*n.* **1** dark bituminous pitch. **2** mixture of this with sand, gravel, etc., for surfacing roads etc. –*v.* surface with asphalt. [Latin from Greek]

asphodel /'æsfəˌdel/ *n.* **1** plant of the lily family. **2** *poet.* immortal flower growing in Elysium. [Latin from Greek]

asphyxia /æs'fɪksɪə/ *n.* lack of oxygen in the blood, causing unconsciousness or death; suffocation. □ **asphyxiant** *adj.* & *n.* [Greek *a-* not, *sphuxis* pulse]

asphyxiate /æs'fɪksɪˌeɪt/ *v.* (**-ting**) suffocate. □ **asphyxiation** /-'eɪʃ(ə)n/ *n.*

aspic /'æspɪk/ *n.* savoury jelly used esp. to contain game, eggs, etc. [French, = ASP, suggested by the colours of the jelly]

aspidistra /ˌæspɪ'dɪstrə/ *n.* house-plant with broad tapering leaves. [Greek *aspis* shield]

aspirant /'æspɪrənt/ –*adj.* aspiring. –*n.* person who aspires. [Latin: related to ASPIRE]

aspirate /'æspərət/ –*adj.* pronounced with an exhalation of breath; blended with the sound of *h*. –*n.* sound of *h*; consonant pronounced in this way. –*v.* /-ˌreɪt/ (**-ting**) **1** pronounce with breath or with initial *h*. **2** draw (fluid) by suction from a cavity etc.

aspiration /ˌæspɪ'reɪʃ(ə)n/ *n.* **1** ambition or desire. **2** drawing breath or *Phonet.* aspirating.

aspirator /'æspɪˌreɪtə(r)/ *n.* apparatus for aspirating fluid. [Latin: related to ASPIRE]

aspire /ə'spaɪə(r)/ *v.* (**-ring**) (usu. foll. by *to* or *after*, or *to* + infin.) have ambition or a strong desire. [Latin *aspiro* breathe upon]

aspirin /'æsprɪn/ *n.* (*pl.* same or **-s**) **1** white powder, acetylsalicylic acid, used to reduce pain and fever. **2** tablet of this. [German]

♦ **Asprey** /'æsprɪ/, **John** (1938–) British businessman, chairman of Asprey, the London jewellers. The Asprey company has been selling jewels for 200 years and are jewellers to the royal family. John Asprey owns over 48% of the shares of the business.

---

ass[1] *n.* **1 a** four-legged long-eared mammal related to the horse. **b** donkey. **2** stupid person. [Old English from Latin]

ass[2] *US* var. of ARSE.

assagai var. of ASSEGAI.

assail /ə'seɪl/ *v.* **1** attack physically or verbally. **2** tackle (a task) resolutely. □ **assailant** *n.* [Latin *salio* leap]

Assam /æ'sæm/ state in NE India, formed in 1947; tea and oil production are important; pop. (est. 1994) 24 200 000; capital, Dispur. Since it was established, parts have since been separated off as the states of Meghalaya and Nagaland and the Union Territories of Arunachal Pradesh and Mizoram. □ **Assamese** /-'miːz/ *adj.* & *n.*

assassin /ə'sæsɪn/ *n.* killer, esp. of a political or religious leader. [Arabic, = hashish-eater]

assassinate /ə'sæsɪˌneɪt/ *v.* (**-ting**) kill for political or religious motives. □ **assassination** /-'neɪʃ(ə)n/ *n.*

assault /ə'sɔːlt/ –*n.* **1** violent physical or verbal attack. **2** *Law* threat or display of violence against a person. –*v.* make an assault on. □ **assault and battery** *Law* threatening act resulting in physical harm to a person. [Latin: related to ASSAIL]

assay /ə'seɪ/ –*n.* testing of a metal or ore to determine its ingredients and quality. In the UK assays are carried out by Official Assay Offices, the marks of which appear in the hallmarks of silver and gold articles. –*v.* make an assay of (a metal or ore). [French, var. of *essai* ESSAY]

ASSC *abbr.* Accounting Standards Steering Committee.

assegai /'æsɪˌgaɪ/ *n.* (also **assagai**) light iron-tipped S African spear. [Arabic, = the spear]

assemblage /ə'semblɪdʒ/ *n.* **1** assembling. **2** assembled group.

assemble /ə'semb(ə)l/ *v.* (**-ling**) **1** gather together; collect. **2** esp. *Mech.* fit together (components, a whole). [Latin *ad* to, *simul* together]

assembler /ə'semblə(r)/ *n.* **1** person who assembles a machine etc. **2** *Computing* **a** program for converting instructions written in low-level symbolic code (see ASSEMBLY LANGUAGE) into machine code. **b** the code itself.

assembly /ə'semblɪ/ *n.* (*pl.* **-ies**) **1** assembling. **2** assembled group, esp. as a deliberative body. **3** assembling of components.

assembly language *n.* type of computer programming language that is a readable and convenient notation (in human terms) for representing programs in machine code. A program (the assembler) translates the assembly language program into machine code. It can then be executed by the computer. Assembly language is the most commonly used low-level language. It was originally devised to alleviate the tedious and time-consuming task of writing programs in machine code. It may be used nowadays, in preference to a high-level language, for reasons of speed or compactness.

assembly line *n.* machinery arranged so that a product can be progressively assembled.

assent /ə'sent/ –*v.* (usu. foll. by *to*) **1** express agreement. **2** consent. –*n.* consent or approval, esp. official. □ **assenter** *n.* [Latin *sentio* think]

♦ **assented stock** *n.* security, usu. an ordinary share, the owner of which has agreed to the terms of a take-over bid. During the take-over negotiations, different prices may be quoted for assented and **non-assented stock**.

---

assert /ə'sɜːt/ *v.* **1** declare, state clearly. **2** *refl.* insist on one's rights. **3** enforce a claim to (*assert one's rights*). [Latin *assero -sert-*]

assertion /ə'sɜːʃ(ə)n/ *n.* declaration, forthright statement.

assertive /ə'sɜːtɪv/ *adj.* tending to assert oneself; forthright, positive. □ **assertively** *adv.* **assertiveness** *n.*

assess /ə'ses/ *v.* **1** estimate the size or quality of. **2** estimate the value of (property etc.) for taxation. [Latin *assideo -sess-* sit by]

♦ **assessment** *n.* **1** estimation. **2** method by which a tax authority raises a bill for a particular tax and sends it to the taxpayer or the taxpayer's agent. The assessment may be based on figures already agreed between the authority and the taxpayer or it may be an estimate by the tax authorities. The taxpayer normally has a right of appeal against an assessment within a specified time limit. See also DEFERRED ASSET.

---

assessor *n.* **1** person who assesses (esp. for tax or insurance). See LOSS ASSESSOR. **2** legal adviser on technical questions.

♦ **asset** /'æset/ *n.* **1** useful or valuable person or thing. **2** (usu. in *pl.*) property and possessions, esp. that can be set against debts etc. In most cases assets are cash or can be turned into cash; exceptions include prepayments, which may represent payments made for rent, rates, or motor licences, in cases in which the time paid for has not yet expired. Tangible assets include land and buildings, plant and machinery, fixtures and fittings, trading stock, investments, debtors, and cash; intangible assets include goodwill, patents, copyrights, and trade marks. See also DEFERRED ASSET. [French *asez* from Latin *ad satis* to enough]

♦ **asset-backed fund** *n.* fund in which the money is invested in tangible or corporate assets, e.g. property or shares, rather than being treated as savings loaned to a bank or other institution. Asset-backed funds can be expected to grow with inflation in a way that bank savings cannot. See also EQUITY-LINKED POLICY; UNIT-LINKED POLICY.

♦ **asset stripping** *n.* acquisition of a firm for a price that is well below its total asset value, and the subsequent sale of these assets. This may occur either because a particular asset, such as property, is valued in the firm's balance sheet at well below its potential market price, or because the firm has been poorly managed, in which case the low share price does not reflect the true value of the firm. After acquisition the assets of the firm are sold to third parties for significantly more than the purchase price of the assets. Little or no consideration is given to the interests of other stakeholders, such as employees, suppliers, or customers, and therefore the practice is viewed critically.

♦ **asset value** *n.* (per share) total value of the assets of a company less its liabilities, divided by the number of ordinary shares in issue. This represents in theory, although probably not in practice, the amount attributable to each share if the company was wound up. The asset value may not necessarily be the total of the values shown by a company's balance sheet, since it is not the function of balance sheets to value assets. It may therefore be necessary to substitute the best estimate that can be made of the market values of the assets (including goodwill) for the values shown in the balance sheet. If there is more than one class of share, it may be necessary to deduct amounts due to shareholders with a priority on winding up before arriving at the amounts attributable to shareholders with a lower priority. If a company goes into liquidation or receivership, the break-up value of the assets may well be below their book value, esp. if the assets include specialized or obsolete machinery saleable only for its scrap value.

---

asseverate /əˈsevəˌreɪt/ *v.* (**-ting**) declare solemnly. □ **asseveration** /-ˈreɪʃ(ə)n/ *n.* [Latin *severus* serious]

asshole *US* var. of ARSEHOLE.

assiduous /əˈsɪdjʊəs/ *adj.* **1** persevering, hard-working. **2** attending closely. □ **assiduity** /ˌæsɪˈdjuːɪtɪ/ *n.* **assiduously** *adv.* [Latin: related to ASSESS]

assign /əˈsaɪn/ *–v.* **1** (usu. foll. by *to*) **a** allot as a share or responsibility. **b** appoint to a position, task, etc. **2** fix (a time, place, etc.). **3** (foll. by *to*) ascribe to (a reason, date, etc.) (*assigned the manuscript to 1832*). **4** (foll. by *to*) *Law* transfer formally (esp. property) to (another). *–n.* assignee. □ **assigner** *n.* **assignor** *n.* *Law.* [Latin *assigno* mark out]

assignation /ˌæsɪgˈneɪʃ(ə)n/ *n.* **1** appointment to meet, esp. by lovers in secret. **2** assigning or being assigned.

assignee /ˌæsaɪˈniː/ *n.* *Law* person to whom a right or property is assigned.

assignment /əˈsaɪnmənt/ *n.* **1** task or mission. **2** assigning or being assigned. **3** *Law* **a** legal transfer of property to some other person. Examples of assignment include the transfer of rights under a contract or benefits under a trust to another person. **b** (also **deed of assignment**) document transferring property.

♦ **assignment of copyright** see COPYRIGHT.

♦ **assignment of insurable interest** *n.* assigning to another party the rights and obligations of the insurable interest in an item of property, life, or a legal liability to be insured. This enables the person to whom the interest is assigned to arrange insurance cover, which would not otherwise be legally permitted.

♦ **assignment of lease** *n.* transfer of a lease by the tenant (assignor) to some other person (assignee). Leases are freely transferable at common law although it is common practice to restrict assignment by conditions (covenants) in the lease. An assignment that takes place in breach of such a covenant is valid but it may entitle the landlord to put an end to the lease and re-enter the premises. An assignment of a legal lease must be by deed. An assignment puts the assignee into the shoes of the assignor, so that there is 'privity of estate' between the landlord and the new tenant. This is important with regard to the enforceability of covenants in the lease (see COVENANT). An assignment transfers the assignor's whole estate to the assignee, unlike a sublease (see HEAD LEASE).

♦ **assignment of life policies** *n.* transfer of the legal right under a life-assurance policy to collect the proceeds. Assignment is only valid if the life insurer is advised and agrees; life assurance is the only form of insurance in which the assignee need not possess an insurable interest. In recent years policy auctions have become a popular alternative to surrendering endowment assurances. In these auctions, a policy is sold to the highest bidder and then assigned to him or her by the original policyholder.

---

assignment statement *n.* *Computing* program statement that assigns a new value to a variable. Each variable is associated with a particular location or group of locations in memory. An assignment statement will thus cause a new value to be placed at the appropriate storage location(s). The assignment statement is fundamental to most programming languages. It is indicated by a special symbol, (e.g. = or :=) called the **assignment operator**. It may be read as 'becomes' since the expression on the right of the assignment operator is given to the variable whose name appears on the left.

assimilate /əˈsɪmɪˌleɪt/ *v.* (**-ting**) **1** absorb or be absorbed, either physically or mentally. **2** (usu. foll. by *to*, *with*) make like; cause to resemble. □ **assimilable** *adj.* **assimilation** /-ˈleɪʃ(ə)n/ *n.* **assimilative** /-lətɪv/ *adj.* **assimilator** *n.* [Latin *similis* like]

Assisi /əˈsiːsɪ/ town in central Italy, in Umbria, famous as the birthplace of St Francis; pop. (est. 1989) 24 567.

assist /əˈsɪst/ *v.* (often foll. by *in* + verbal noun) help. □ **assistance** *n.* [Latin *assisto* stand by]

assistant *n.* **1** (often *attrib.*) person who helps, esp. as a subordinate. **2** = SHOP ASSISTANT.

assizes /əˈsaɪzɪz/ *n.pl.* *hist.* court periodically administering the civil and criminal law. [French: related to ASSESS]

■ **Usage** In 1972 the civil jurisdiction of assizes in England and Wales was transferred to the High Court and the criminal jurisdiction to the Crown Court.

assn *abbr.* association.

Assoc. *abbr.* Association.

associate *–v.* /əˈsəʊʃɪˌeɪt/ (**-ting**) **1** connect mentally (*associate holly with Christmas*). **2** join or combine, esp. for a common purpose. **3** *refl.* declare oneself or be in agreement. **4** (usu. foll. by *with*) meet frequently or deal. *–n.* /əˈsəʊʃɪət/ **1** partner, colleague. **2** friend, companion. **3** subordinate member of a society etc. *–adj.* /əˈsəʊʃɪət/ **1** joined or allied. **2** of lower status (*associate member*). □ **associative** /-ʃɪətɪv/ *adj.* [Latin *socius* allied]

♦ **Associated British Ports** *n.pl.* (treated as *sing.*) (also **ABP**) statutory corporation set up by the Transport Act (1981) to administer the 19 ports previously controlled by the British Transport Docks Board. ABP now administers 21 ports and is controlled by Associated British Ports Holding plc.

---

association /əˌsəʊsɪˈeɪʃ(ə)n/ *n.* **1** group organized for a joint purpose; society. **2** associating or being associated. **3** companionship. **4** mental connection of ideas. [medieval Latin: related to ASSOCIATE]

Association Football *n.* football played with a round ball which may not be handled except by the goalkeepers.

♦ **Association for Payment Clearing Services** *n.* (also **APACS**) association set up by the UK banks in 1985 to manage payment clearing and overseas money transmission in the UK. The three operating companies under its aegis are: BACS Ltd., which provides an automated service for interbank clearing in the UK; Cheque and Credit Clearing Co. Ltd., which operates a bulk clearing system for interbank cheques and paper credits; and CHAPS and Town Clearing, which provides same-day clearing for high value cheques and electronic funds transfer. In addition EftPos UK Ltd. is a company set up to develop electronic funds transfer at the point of sale. APACS also oversees London Dollar Clearing, the London Currency Settlement Scheme, and the cheque card and Eurocheque schemes in the UK.

♦ **Association of British Insurers** *n.* (also **ABI**) trade association representing over 440 insurance companies offering any class of insurance business, whose members transact over 90% of the business of the British insurance market. It was formed in 1985 by a merger the British Insurance Association, the Accident Offices Association, the Fire Offices Committee, the Life Offices Association, and the Industrial Life Offices Association.

♦ **Association of Market Survey Organizations** *n.* (also **AMSO**) association of 27 of the largest UK survey research organizations. Member companies adhere to a strict code of conduct to ensure the highest standards of market research.

♦ **Association of Private Client Investment Managers and Stockbrokers** *n.* (also **APCIMS**) representative body formed in 1990 to supervise and expand private investors' business.

♦ **Association of South-East Asian Nations** *n.* (also **Asean**) political and economic grouping of the capitalist nations of South-East Asia, formed in 1967 and comprising Thailand, Malaysia, Singapore, Philippines, Indonesia, Brunei, Burma, Laos, and Vietnam. The countries are very diverse and interests often diverge accordingly. While committed to strengthening economic ties, progress has been limited. There has also been political cooperation, for example over policy towards Indochina. There are regular consultations between Asean and the major industrialized countries.

---

assonance /'æsənəns/ *n.* partial resemblance of sound between two syllables e.g. *sonnet, porridge,* and *killed, cold, culled.* □ **assonant** *adj.* [Latin *sonus* sound]

assort /ə'sɔːt/ *v.* **1** classify or arrange in sorts. **2** (usu. foll. by *with*) suit or harmonize with. [French: related to SORT]

assorted *adj.* **1** of various sorts, mixed. **2** classified. **3** matched (*ill-assorted pair*).

assortment *n.* diverse group or mixture.

assuage /ə'sweɪdʒ/ *v.* (**-ging**) **1** calm or soothe. **2** appease (an appetite). □ **assuagement** *n.* [Latin *suavis* sweet]

assume /ə'sjuːm/ *v.* (**-ming**) **1** (usu. foll. by *that*) take to be true. **2** simulate (ignorance etc.). **3** undertake (an office etc.). **4** take or put on (an aspect, attribute, etc.) (*assumed immense importance*). [Latin *sumo* take]

assuming *adj.* arrogant, presumptuous.

assumption /ə'sʌmpʃ(ə)n/ *n.* **1** assuming. **2** thing assumed. **3** (**Assumption**) reception of the Virgin Mary bodily into heaven.

assurance /ə'ʃʊərəns/ *n.* **1** emphatic declaration; guarantee. **2** insurance against an eventuality (esp. death) that must occur. See LIFE ASSURANCE. **3** certainty. **4** self-confidence; assertiveness.

assure /ə'ʃʊə(r)/ *v.* (**-ring**) **1** (often foll. by *of*) **a** convince. **b** tell (a person) confidently (*assured him all was well*). **2** ensure; guarantee (a result etc.). **3** insure (esp. a life). [Latin *securus* safe]

assured *–adj.* **1** guaranteed. **2** self-confident. *–n.* (usu. prec. by *the*) person named in a life-assurance policy to receive the proceeds in the event of maturity or the death of the life assured.

assuredly /ə'ʃʊərɪdlɪ/ *adv.* certainly.

♦ **assured tenancy** see REGULATED TENANCY.

AST *abbr.* **1** Atlantic Standard Time. **2** = AUTOMATED SCREEN TRADING.

astatine /'æstə,tiːn/ *n.* radioactive element, the heaviest of the halogens. [Greek *astatos* unstable]

aster *n.* plant with bright daisy-like flowers. [Greek, = star]

asterisk /'æstərɪsk/ *–n.* symbol (*) used to mark words or to indicate omission etc. *–v.* mark with an asterisk. [Greek, = little star]

astern /ə'stɜːn/ *adv.* (often foll. by *of*) **1** in or to the rear of a ship or aircraft. **2** backwards.

asteroid /'æstə,rɔɪd/ *n.* **1** any of the minor planets orbiting the sun, mainly between the orbits of Mars and Jupiter. **2** starfish. [Greek: related to ASTER]

asthma /'æsmə/ *n.* respiratory condition marked by wheezing. [Greek *azō* breathe hard]

asthmatic /æs'mætɪk/ *–adj.* of or suffering from asthma. *–n.* asthmatic person.

astigmatism /ə'stɪgmə,tɪz(ə)m/ *n.* eye or lens defect resulting in distorted images. □ **astigmatic** /,æstɪg'mætɪk/ *adj.* [from A-[1], STIGMA]

astir /ə'stɜː(r)/ *predic. adj.* & *adv.* **1** in motion. **2** out of bed.

astonish /ə'stɒnɪʃ/ *v.* surprise greatly, amaze. □ **astonishment** *n.* [Latin *ex-* forth, *tono* thunder]

astound /ə'staʊnd/ *v.* astonish greatly.

astraddle /ə'stræd(ə)l/ *adv.* astride.

Astrakhan /,æstrə'kɑːn/ city in SE Russia, on the delta of the River Volga; fishing is important; pop. (1994) 512 000.

astrakhan /,æstrə'kæn/ *n.* **1** dark curly fleece of young Astrakhan lambs. **2** cloth imitating this. [ASTRAKHAN]

astral /'æstr(ə)l/ *adj.* of the stars; starry. [Latin *astrum* star]

astray /ə'streɪ/ *adv.* & *predic. adj.* out of the right way, erring. □ **go astray** be missing. [Latin *extra* away, *vagor* wander]

astride /ə'straɪd/ *–adv.* **1** (often foll. by *of*) with a leg on each side. **2** with legs apart. *–prep.* astride of; extending across.

astringent /ə'strɪndʒ(ə)nt/ *–adj.* **1** checking bleeding by contracting body tissues. **2** severe, austere. *–n.* astringent substance. □ **astringency** *n.* [Latin *astringo* draw tight]

astrolabe /'æstrə,leɪb/ *n.* instrument formerly used to measure the altitude of stars etc. [Greek, = star-taking]

astrology /ə'strɒlədʒɪ/ *n.* study of supposed planetary influence on human affairs. □ **astrologer** *n.* **astrological** /,æstrə'lɒdʒɪk(ə)l/ *adj.* **astrologist** *n.* [Greek *astron* star]

astronaut /'æstrə,nɔːt/ *n.* crew member of a spacecraft. [Greek *astron* star, *nautēs* sailor]

astronautics /,æstrə'nɔːtɪks/ *n.pl.* (treated as *sing.*) science of space travel. □ **astronautical** *adj.*

astronomical /,æstrə'nɒmɪk(ə)l/ *adj.* (also **astronomic**) **1** of astronomy. **2** vast, gigantic. □ **astronomically** *adv.*

astronomy /ə'strɒnəmɪ/ *n.* the scientific study of celestial bodies. □ **astronomer** *n.* [Greek *astron* star, *nemō* arrange]

astrophysics /,æstrəʊ'fɪzɪks/ *n.pl.* (treated as *sing.*) the study of the physics and chemistry of celestial bodies. □ **astrophysical** *adj.* **astrophysicist** /-sɪst/ *n.* [Greek *astron* star]

Asturias /æs'tjʊərɪəs/ region of NW Spain; pop. (est. 1994) 1 083 388; capital, Oviedo.

astute /ə'stjuːt/ *adj.* shrewd. □ **astutely** *adv.* **astuteness** *n.* [Latin *astus* craft]

Asunción /ə,sʊnsɪ'ɒn/ capital and chief port of Paraguay; industries include flour milling, food processing, and textiles; pop. (1992) 637 700.

asunder /ə'sʌndə(r)/ *adv. literary* apart.

ASVA *abbr.* Associate of the Incorporated Society of Valuers and Auctioneers.

Aswan /æs'wɑːn/ city in S Egypt near which are two dams across the Nile; pop. (est. 1986) 195 700. The **Aswan Dam** was built in 1898–1902 to regulate the flooding of the Nile and control the supply of water for irrigation and other purposes. It is now superseded by the **Aswan High Dam**, built in 1960–70 with Soviet aid, about 3.6 km (2¼ miles) long and 111 m (364 ft) high. Behind it is the reservoir of Lake Nasser, and its controlled release not only ensures a steady supply of water for irrigation and domestic and industrial use but produces hydroelectric power sufficient to supply the greater part of Egypt's electricity.

asylum /ə'saɪləm/ *n.* **1** sanctuary; protection, esp. for fugitives from the law (*seek asylum*). **2** *hist.* institution for the mentally ill or destitute. [Greek *a-* not, *sulon* right of seizure]

asymmetry /æ'sɪmɪtrɪ/ *n.* lack of symmetry. □ **asymmetric** /-'metrɪk/ *adj.* **asymmetrical** /-'metrɪk(ə)l/ *adj.* [Greek]

AT *–abbr.* **1** alternative technology. **2** *US* appropriate technology. **3** Atlantic Time. *–airline flight code* Royal Air Maroc.

At *symb.* astatine.

at /æt, ət/ *prep.* **1** expressing position (*wait at the corner; at school*). **2** expressing a point in time (*at dawn*). **3** expressing a point in a scale (*at his best*). **4** expressing engagement in an activity etc. (*at war*). **5** expressing a value or rate (*sell at £10 each*). **6 a** with or with reference to (*annoyed at losing; came at a run*). **b** in response to (*starts at a touch*). **7** expressing motion or aim towards (*aim at the target; laughed at us*). □ **at and from** denoting a marine hull insurance cover that begins when the vessel is in dock before a voyage, continues during the voyage, and ends 24 hours after it has reached its port of destination. **at all** see ALL. **at best** see BEST. **at call** see CALL. **at hand** see HAND. **at home** see HOME. **at it** engaged in an activity; working hard. **at limit** see LIMIT. **at once** see ONCE. **at par** see PAR VALUE. **at sight** see SIGHT. **at that 1** moreover (*a good one at that*). **2** then (*at that he left*). **at times** see TIME. **at warehouse** see WAREHOUSE. [Old English]

atavism /'ætəˌvɪz(ə)m/ *n.* **1** reappearance of a remote ancestral characteristic, throwback. **2** reversion to an earlier type. □ **atavistic** /-'vɪstɪk/ *adj.* [Latin *atavus* ancestor]

ataxia /ə'tæksɪə/ *n. Med.* imperfect control of bodily movements. [Greek *a-* without, *taxis* order]

ATC *abbr.* **1** air-traffic control. **2** *Computing* authorization to copy (of software).

ate *past* of EAT.

-ate[1] *suffix* forming nouns denoting status, function, or office (*doctorate; consulate*). [Latin]

-ate[2] *suffix* forming adjectives with the sense 'having, full of' (*foliate; passionate*). [Latin participial ending *-atus*]

atelier /ə'telɪˌeɪ/ *n.* workshop or artist's studio. [French]

atheism /'eɪθɪˌɪz(ə)m/ *n.* belief that there is no God. □ **atheist** *n.* **atheistic** /-'ɪstɪk/ *adj.* [Greek *a-* not, *theos* god]

Athens /'æθɪnz/ (Greek **Athínai** /æ'θiːneɪ/) capital of Greece, lying 6 km (nearly 4 miles) from its port and main industrial centre, Piraeus; pop. (1991) 748 110; metropolitan area pop. 3 096 775. Industries include tourism, shipping, publishing, pottery, and textiles; marble and bauxite are mined nearby. □ **Athenian** /ə'θiːnɪən/ *adj.* & *n.*

atherosclerosis /ˌæθərəʊsklə'rəʊsɪs/ *n.* degeneration of the arteries caused by a build-up of fatty deposits. [Greek *athērē* groats]

Athínai see ATHENS.

athirst /ə'θɜːst/ *predic. adj. poet.* **1** (usu. foll. by *for*) eager. **2** thirsty.

athlete /'æθliːt/ *n.* person who engages in athletics, exercise, etc. [Greek *athlon* prize]

athlete's foot *n.* fungal foot condition.

athletic /æθ'letɪk/ *adj.* **1** of athletes or athletics. **2** physically strong or agile. □ **athletically** *adv.* **athleticism** /-ˌsɪz(ə)m/ *n.* [Latin: related to ATHLETE]

athletics *n.pl.* (usu. treated as *sing.*) physical exercises, esp. track and field events.

at-home *n.* social reception in a person's home.

ATI *abbr.* Associate of the Textile Institute.

ATII *abbr.* Associate Member of the Institute of Taxation.

-ation *suffix* **1** forming nouns denoting an action or an instance of it (*flirtation; hesitation*). **2** forming nouns denoting a result or product of action (*plantation; starvation*). [Latin *-atio*]

ATL *abbr.* **1** *Insurance* actual total loss. **2** *Computing* automated (or automatic) tape library.

Atlanta /ət'læntə/ city in the US, capital of Georgia; manufactures include aircraft, machinery, cottonseed oil, textiles, clothing, and chemicals; pop. (est. 1994) 396 052.

Atlantic /ət'læntɪk/ *–n.* (**the Atlantic**) the Atlantic Ocean. *–adj.* of or adjoining the Atlantic Ocean. [Greek: related to ATLAS]

Atlantic Ocean ocean between Europe and Africa to the E, and North and South America to the W.

Atlantic Time *n.* standard time used in the most E parts of Canada and Central America.

atlas /'ætləs/ *n.* book of maps or charts. [Greek *Atlas*, the Titan who held up the universe]

ATM *abbr.* = AUTOMATED TELLER MACHINE.

atmosphere /'ætməsfɪə(r)/ *n.* **1 a** gases enveloping the earth, any other planet, etc. **b** air in a room etc., esp. if fetid. **2** pervading tone or mood of a place, situation, or work of art. **3** unit of pressure equal to mean atmospheric pressure at sea level, 101 325 pascals. □ **atmospheric** /-'ferɪk/ *adj.* [Greek *atmos* vapour, SPHERE]

atmospherics /ˌætməs'ferɪks/ *n.pl.* **1** electrical atmospheric disturbance, esp. caused by lightning. **2** interference with telecommunications caused by this.

atoll /'ætɒl/ *n.* ring-shaped coral reef enclosing a lagoon. [Maldive]

atom /'ætəm/ *n.* **1 a** smallest particle of a chemical element that can take part in a chemical reaction. **b** this as a source of nuclear energy. **2** minute portion or thing (*atom of pity*). [Greek *atomos* indivisible]

atom bomb *n.* bomb in which energy is released by nuclear fission.

atomic /ə'tɒmɪk/ *adj.* **1** of or using atomic energy or atomic bombs. **2** of atoms.

atomic bomb *n.* = ATOM BOMB.

atomic energy *n.* nuclear energy.

atomic mass *n.* mass of an atom measured in atomic mass units.

atomic mass unit *n.* unit of mass used to express atomic and molecular weights, equal to one twelfth of the mass of an atom of carbon-12.

atomic number *n.* number of protons in the nucleus of an atom.

atomic theory *n.* theory that all matter consists of atoms.

atomic weight *n.* = RELATIVE ATOMIC MASS.

atomize /ˌætə'maɪz/ *v.* (also **-ise**) (**-zing** or **-sing**) reduce to atoms or fine particles.

atomizer *n.* (also **-iser**) = AEROSOL 1.

atonal /eɪ'təʊn(ə)l/ *adj. Mus.* not written in any key or mode. □ **atonality** /-'nælɪtɪ/ *n.*

atone /ə'təʊn/ *v.* (**-ning**) (usu. foll. by *for*) make amends (for a wrong). [from ATONEMENT]

atonement *n.* **1** atoning. **2** (**the Atonement**) expiation by Christ of mankind's sins. [*at one* + -MENT]

♦ **ATP** abbr. = AID TRADE PROVISION.

---

atrium /'eɪtrɪəm/ *n.* (*pl.* **-s** or **atria**) **1 a** central court of an ancient Roman house. **b** (usu. skylit) central court rising through several storeys. **2** each of the two upper cavities of the heart. [Latin]

atrocious /ə'trəʊʃəs/ *adj.* **1** very bad or unpleasant (*atrocious manners*). **2** wicked (*atrocious cruelty*). □ **atrociously** *adv.* [Latin *atrox* cruel]

atrocity /ə'trɒsɪtɪ/ *n.* (*pl.* **-ies**) **1** wicked or cruel act. **2** extreme wickedness. [Latin: related to ATROCIOUS]

atrophy /'ætrəfɪ/ *–n.* wasting away, esp. through disuse; emaciation. *–v.* (**-ies, -ied**) suffer atrophy or cause atrophy in. [Greek *a-* without, *trophē* food]

atropine /'ætrəˌpiːn/ *n.* poisonous alkaloid in deadly

nightshade. [Greek *Atropos*, the Fate who cut the thread of life]

ATS *abbr.* **1** (in Australia) Amalgamated Television Services. **2** American Transport Service. **3** automated trade system.

att. *abbr.* **1** attached. **2** attention.

attach /ə'tætʃ/ *v.* **1** fasten, affix, join. **2** (in *passive*; foll. by *to*) be very fond of. **3** attribute or be attributable; assign (*can't attach a name to it; no blame attaches to us*). **4** accompany; form part of (*no conditions are attached*). **5** *refl.* (usu. foll. by *to*) take part in; join (*attached himself to the team*). **6** seize by legal authority. [French from Germanic]

attaché /ə'tæʃeɪ/ *n.* specialist member of an ambassador's staff.

attaché case *n.* small rectangular document case.

attachment *n.* **1** thing attached, esp. for a purpose. **2** affection, devotion. **3** attaching or being attached. **4** temporary position in an organization. **5** court order enabling a creditor, who has obtained judgement in the courts (the judgement creditor), to secure payment of the amount due from his or her debtor. The judgement creditor may obtain a further court order enabling money or property due from a third party to the debtor to be frozen and paid instead to the judgement creditor to satisfy the debt (see GARNISHEE ORDER).

attack /ə'tæk/ *–v.* **1** try to hurt or defeat using force. **2** criticize adversely. **3** act harmfully upon (*rust attacks metal*). **4** vigorously apply oneself to. **5** *Sport* try to gain ground or score (against). *–n.* **1** act of attacking. **2** offensive operation. **3** sudden onset of an illness. □ **attacker** *n.* [French from Italian]

attain /ə'teɪn/ *v.* **1** reach, gain, accomplish (a goal etc.). **2** (foll. by *to*) arrive at by effort or development. [Latin *attingo* reach]

attainment *n.* **1** (often in *pl.*) accomplishment or achievement. **2** attaining.

attar /'ætɑː(r)/ *n.* perfume made from rose-petals. [Persian]

attempt /ə'tempt/ *–v.* **1** (often foll. by *to* + infin.) try to do or achieve (*attempted to explain*). **2** try to conquer (a mountain etc.). *–n.* (often foll. by *at, on,* or *to* + infin.) attempting; endeavour (*attempt at winning; attempt on his life*). [Latin *tempto* try]

attend /ə'tend/ *v.* **1 a** be present (at) (*attended the meeting*). **b** go regularly to (*attends church*). **2** escort. **3 a** (often foll. by *to*) turn or apply one's mind. **b** (foll. by *to*) deal with (*attend to the matter*). [Latin *tendo* stretch]

attendance *n.* **1** attending or being present. **2** number present (*high attendance*).

attendant *–n.* person escorting or providing a service (*cloakroom attendant*). *–adj.* **1** accompanying (*attendant costs*). **2** (often foll. by *on*) waiting (*attendant on the queen*).

attendee /ˌæten'diː/ *n.* person who attends (a meeting etc.).

attention /ə'tenʃ(ə)n/ *n.* **1** act or faculty of applying one's mind; notice (*attention wandered; attract his attention*). **2** consideration, care. **3** (in *pl.*) **a** courtesies. **b** sexual advances. **4** erect esp. military attitude of readiness.

attentive /ə'tentɪv/ *adj.* **1** concentrating; paying attention. **2** assiduously polite. □ **attentively** *adv.* **attentiveness** *n.*

attenuate /ə'tenjʊˌeɪt/ *v.* (**-ting**) **1** make thin. **2** reduce in force, value, etc. □ **attenuation** /-'eɪʃ(ə)n/ *n.* [Latin *tenuis* thin]

attest /ə'test/ *v.* **1** certify the validity of. **2** (foll. by *to*) bear witness to an act or event. The law requires that some documents are only valid and binding if the signatures on them have been attested to by a third party. This also requires the third party's signature on the document. For instance, the signature of the purchaser of land under a contract must be attested to by a witness. □ **attestation** /ˌæte'steɪʃ(ə)n/ *n.* [Latin *testis* witness]

◆ **at-the-money option** see INTRINSIC VALUE 2.

Attic /'ætɪk/ *–adj.* of ancient Athens or Attica, or the form of Greek used there. *–n.* Greek as used by the ancient Athenians. [Greek *Attikos*]

attic /'ætɪk/ *n.* space or room at the top of a house, usu. under the roof. [from ATTIC, with ref. to an architectural feature]

Attica /'ætɪkə/ region of E central Greece; pop. (est. 1991) 3 522 769. Its chief city is Athens, whose territory it was in ancient times.

attire /ə'taɪə(r)/ *formal –n.* clothes, esp. formal. *–v.* (**-ring**) (usu. as **attired** *adj.*) dress, esp. formally. [French *à tire* in order]

attitude /'ætɪˌtjuːd/ *n.* **1** opinion or way of thinking; behaviour reflecting this (*don't like his attitude*). **2** bodily posture; pose. **3** position of an aircraft etc. relative to given points. [Latin *aptus* fitted]

◆ **attitude research** *n.* investigation into the attitudes of people towards an organization or its products. Attitude research is important to advertising specialists in planning campaigns. For example, it might reveal a 'Buy British' attitude among respondents, which would present a marketing and advertising problem to a US manufacturer.

attitudinize /ˌætɪ'tjuːdɪˌnaɪz/ *v.* (also **-ise**) (**-zing** or **-sing**) adopt (esp. affected) attitudes; pose.

attn. *abbr.* **1** attention. **2** for the attention of.

attorney /ə'tɜːnɪ/ *n.* (*pl.* **-s**) **1** lawyer etc. appointed to act for another in business or legal matters. **2** *US* qualified lawyer. [French *atorner* assign]

Attorney-General *n.* (*pl.* **Attorneys-General**) chief legal officer in some countries.

attract /ə'trækt/ *v.* **1** (also *absol.*) (of a magnet etc.) draw to itself or oneself. **2** arouse interest or admiration in. [Latin *traho* draw]

attraction /ə'trækʃ(ə)n/ *n.* **1 a** attracting or being attracted. **b** attractive quality (*can't see the attraction in it*). **c** person or thing that attracts. **2** *Physics* tendency of bodies to attract each other.

attractive /ə'træktɪv/ *adj.* **1** attracting (esp. interest or admiration). **2** aesthetically pleasing; good-looking. □ **attractively** *adv.*

attribute *–v.* /ə'trɪbjuːt/ (**-ting**) (usu. foll. by *to*) **1** regard as belonging to, written or said by, etc. (*a poem attributed to Milton*). **2** ascribe to (a cause) (*delays attributed to snow*). *–n.* /'ætrɪˌbjuːt/ **1** esp. characteristic quality ascribed to a person or thing. **2** object symbolizing or appropriate to a person, office, or status. □ **attributable** /ə'trɪbjʊtəb(ə)l/ *adj.* **attribution** /ˌætrɪ'bjuːʃ(ə)n/ *n.* [Latin *tribuo* allot]

attributive /ə'trɪbjʊtɪv/ *adj. Gram.* (of an adjective or noun) preceding the word described, as *old* in *the old dog.*

attrition /ə'trɪʃ(ə)n/ *n.* **1** gradual wearing down (*war of attrition*). **2** abrasion, friction. [Latin *tero trit-* rub]

attune /ə'tjuːn/ *v.* (**-ning**) **1** (usu. foll. by *to*) adjust to a situation etc. **2** *Mus.* tune. [related to TUNE]

atypical /eɪ'tɪpɪk(ə)l/ *adj.* not typical. □ **atypically** *adv.*

AU *abbr. Computing* arithmetic unit.

Au *symb.* gold. [Latin *aurum*]

AUA *abbr. Finance* agricultural unit of account (in the EC).

aubergine /'əʊbəˌʒiːn/ *n.* plant with white or purple egg-shaped fruit used as a vegetable; eggplant. [French, ultimately from Sanskrit]

aubrietia /ɔː'briːʃə/ *n.* (also **aubretia**) dwarf perennial rock-plant with purple or pink flowers. [*Aubriet*, name of an artist]

auburn /'ɔːbən/ *adj.* reddish-brown (usu. of hair). [originally = yellowish white: from Latin *albus* white]

Auckland /'ɔːklənd/ **1** largest city and chief seaport of New Zealand; pop. (1994) 929 300. Industries include engineering, food processing, shipbuilding, and chemicals; iron, steel, dairy products, and meat are exported. **2** province of New Zealand comprising the N part of North Island.

♦ **auction** /ˈɔːkʃ(ə)n/ –*n.* sale in which goods are sold in public to the highest bidder. Auctions are used for any property for which there are likely to be a number of competing buyers (e.g. houses, second-hand and antique furniture, works of art, etc.) as well as for certain commodities (e.g. tea, bristles, wool, furs) which must be sold as individual lots, rather than on the basis of a standard sample or grading procedure. In most auctions the goods to be sold are available for viewing before the sale and it is usual for the seller to put a reserve price on the articles offered, i.e. the articles are withdrawn from sale unless more than a specified price is bid. The auctioneer acts as agent for the seller in most cases and receives a commission on the sale price. See also DUTCH AUCTION. –*v.* sell by auction. [Latin *augeo auct-* increase]

auction bridge *n.* game in which players bid for the right to name trumps.

auctioneer /ˌɔːkʃəˈnɪə(r)/ *n.* person who conducts auctions, esp. for a living.

aud. *abbr.* **1** audit. **2** auditor.

audacious /ɔːˈdeɪʃəs/ *adj.* **1** daring, bold. **2** impudent. □ **audacity** /ɔːˈdæsɪtɪ/ *n.* [Latin *audax* bold]

audible /ˈɔːdɪb(ə)l/ *adj.* able to be heard. □ **audibility** /-ˈbɪlɪtɪ/ *n.* **audibly** *adv.* [Latin *audio* hear]

audience /ˈɔːdɪəns/ *n.* **1 a** assembled listeners or spectators, esp. at a play, concert, etc. **b** people addressed by a film, book, etc. **2** formal interview with a superior. [Latin: related to AUDIBLE]

♦ **audience research** *n.* research to establish readership, audience, and circulation data, which is vital information in advertising. Research into television audiences is undertaken by the Broadcasters Audience Research Board (BARB) and into commercial radio audiences by the Joint Industry Committee for Radio Audience Research (JICRAR). The BBC undertakes its own research through the BBC Audience Research Unit. See also TELEVISION RATING.

audio /ˈɔːdɪəʊ/ *n.* (usu. *attrib.*) sound or its reproduction. [Latin *audio* hear]

audio- *comb. form* hearing or sound.

♦ **audioconferencing** *n.* national and international telephone service enabling several users in different places to conduct a business meeting over the telephone. Connections can be made between callers in several different countries. See also VIDEOCONFERENCING.

audio frequency *n.* frequency able to be perceived by the human ear.

♦ **audio response device** *n.* output device, connected to a computer, that produces human speech. These devices are used, for example, in computerized telephone enquiry systems. They work by storing words, syllables, or phrases in the computer and linking them together to form more-or-less recognizable speech.

audiotape *n.* **1 a** magnetic tape for recording sound. **b** a length of this. **2** a sound recording on tape.

audio typist *n.* person who types from a tape-recording.

audiovisual /ˌɔːdɪəʊˈvɪʒʊəl/ *adj.* (of teaching methods etc.) using both sight and sound.

♦ **audit** /ˈɔːdɪt/ –*n.* inspection of an organization's annual accounts. An **external audit** is carried out by a qualified accountant, in order to obtain an opinion as to the veracity of the accounts. Under the Companies Acts, companies are required to appoint an auditor to express an opinion as to whether the annual accounts give a true and fair view of the company's affairs and whether they comply with the provisions of the Companies Acts. To give such an opinion, the auditor needs to examine the company's internal accounting systems, inspect its assets, make tests of accounting transactions, etc. Some bodies have different requirements for audit; for example, accountants report to the Law Society on solicitors' accounts under the Accountants' Report Rules. Many companies and organizations now appoint internal auditors to carry out an **internal audit**, with the object of reporting to management on the efficacy and security of internal systems. In some cases these systems may not even be financial; they may include, for example, an audit of health and safety in the workplace or an audit of compliance with equal opportunities legislation. See also AUDITOR; AUDITORS' REPORT. –*v.* (**-t-**) conduct an audit of.

♦ **Audit Bureau of Circulation** *n.* (also **ABC**) organization to which most newspaper, magazine, and periodical publishers belong. Its function is to collect and audit sales figures from publishers regularly and to publish monthly circulation figures in its quarterly *Circulation Review*, a publication of great value to advertisers. A newspaper, magazine, or periodical must have been publishing for a minimum of six months before joining the ABC.

audition /ɔːˈdɪʃ(ə)n/ –*n.* test of a performer's suitability or ability. –*v.* assess or be assessed at an audition. [Latin *audio* hear]

♦ **auditor** *n.* person who carries out an audit. **External auditors** are normally members of a body of accountants authorized by the Companies Acts, such as the Institute of Chartered Accountants or the Chartered Association of Certified Accountants. The principal requirement for an external audit is that the auditor should be independent of the organization audited and professionally qualified. The same is not true of **internal auditors,** who may be members of such professional bodies as the Institute of Internal Auditors or any of the accountancy bodies, but who may also be appropriately trained employees of the organizations being audited. Every company must have properly qualified auditors. If none have been appointed, the Secretary of State for Trade and Industry must be informed within one week. Failure to do so may result in the company and its officers being liable to a fine. Auditors are usu. appointed at the annual general meeting of the company; the appointment of a new auditor or the removal of an auditor requires special notice. An auditor's notice of resignation must contain a statement of any matters that should be brought to the notice of the shareholders or creditors or a statement that there are no such matters. An auditor's duties must be carried out with due care and skill; an auditor may be liable to negligence to the company, the members, and third parties relying on the audited accounts. The **auditors' remuneration** has to be approved at a general meeting of the company and should be distinguished in the accounts from the cost of other accounting work. See also AUDITORS' REPORT. [French from Latin]

auditorium /ˌɔːdɪˈtɔːrɪəm/ *n.* (*pl.* **-s**) part of a theatre etc. for the audience. [Latin]

♦ **auditors' remuneration** see AUDITOR.

♦ **auditors' report** *n.* report by the auditors appointed to audit the accounts of a company or other organization. Auditors' reports may take many forms depending on who has appointed the auditors and for what purposes. Some auditors are engaged in an internal audit while others are appointed for various statutory purposes. The auditors of a limited company are required to form an opinion as to whether the annual accounts of the company give a true and fair view of its profit or loss for the period under review and of its state of affairs at the end of the period; they are also required to certify that the accounts are prepared in accordance with the requirements of the Companies Act (1985). The auditors' report is technically a report to the members of the company and it must be filed together with the accounts with the Registrar of Companies under the Companies Act (1985). Under this act, the auditors' report must also include an audit of the directors' report. See also QUALIFIED REPORT.

auditory /ˈɔːdɪtərɪ/ *adj.* of hearing.

audit trail *n. Computing* record showing the occurrence of specified events relevant to the security of a computer system. For example, an entry might be made in an audit trail whenever a user logs on or accesses a file. Examination of the audit trail may detect attempts at violating the security of the system, e.g. by unauthorized reading or writing of data in a file, and help to identify the culprit. See also SECURITY 4.

au fait /əʊ 'feɪ/ *predic. adj.* (usu. foll. by *with*) conversant (*au fait with the rules*). [French]

Aug. *abbr.* August.

Augean /ɔː'dʒiːən/ *adj.* filthy. [Greek *Augeas*, a mythical king: his filthy stables were cleaned by Hercules diverting a river through them]

auger /'ɔːgə(r)/ *n.* tool with a screw point for boring in wood. [Old English]

aught /ɔːt/ *n. archaic* anything. [Old English]

augment /ɔːg'ment/ *v.* make or become greater; increase. □ **augmentation** /-'teɪʃ(ə)n/ *n.* [Latin: related to AUCTION]

augmentative /ɔːg'mentətɪv/ *adj.* augmenting.

au gratin /əʊ 'grætæ̃/ *adj.* cooked with a crust of breadcrumbs or melted cheese. [French]

Augsburg /'aʊgzbɜːg/ city in Germany, in Bavaria; manufactures include cars, aircraft, chemicals, textiles, and printing machinery; pop. (1993) 265 000.

augur /'ɔːgə(r)/ *–v.* portend, serve as an omen (*augur well* or *ill*). *–n. hist.* Roman religious official interpreting natural phenomena in order to pronounce on proposed actions. [Latin]

augury /'ɔːgjərɪ/ *n.* (*pl.* **-ies**) **1** omen. **2** interpretation of omens.

August /'ɔːgəst/ *n.* eighth month of the year. [Latin *Augustus*, first Roman emperor]

august /ɔː'gʌst/ *adj.* venerable, imposing. [Latin]

Augusta /ɔː'gʌstə/ city in the US, capital of Maine; its timber industry is important; pop. (1990) 21 325.

Augustan /ɔː'gʌst(ə)n/ *adj.* **1** of the reign of Augustus, esp. as a flourishing literary period. **2** (of literature) refined and classical in style. [Latin: see AUGUST]

auk /ɔːk/ *n.* black and white sea bird with short wings e.g. the guillemot, puffin, etc. [Old Norse]

auld lang syne /ˌɔːld læŋ 'saɪn/ *n.* times long past. [Scots, = old long since]

aunt /ɑːnt/ *n.* **1** sister of one's father or mother. **2** uncle's wife. **3** *colloq.* (form of address by a child to) parent's female friend. [Latin *amita*]

auntie /'ɑːntɪ/ *n.* (also **aunty**) (*pl.* **-ies**) *colloq.* = AUNT.

Aunt Sally *n.* **1** game in which sticks or balls are thrown at a wooden dummy. **2** target of general abuse.

au pair /əʊ 'peə(r)/ *n.* young foreigner, esp. a woman, helping with housework etc. in exchange for board and lodging. [French]

aura /'ɔːrə/ *n.* (*pl.* **-s**) **1** distinctive atmosphere. **2** subtle emanation. [Greek, = breeze]

aural /'ɔːr(ə)l/ *adj.* of the ear or hearing. □ **aurally** *adv.* [Latin *auris* ear]

aureate /'ɔːrɪət/ *adj. literary* **1** golden. **2** resplendent. [Latin *aurum* gold]

aureole /'ɔːrɪˌəʊl/ *n.* (also **aureola** /ɔː'riːələ/) **1** halo or circle of light, esp. in a religious painting. **2** corona round the sun or moon. [Latin, = golden (crown)]

au revoir /ˌəʊ rə'vwɑː(r)/ *int.* & *n.* goodbye (until we meet again). [French]

auricle /'ɔːrɪk(ə)l/ *n.* **1** each atrium of the heart. **2** external ear of animals. □ **auricular** /-'rɪk-/ *adj.* [related to AURICULA]

auricula /ɔː'rɪkjʊlə/ *n.* (*pl.* **-s**) primula with ear-shaped leaves. [Latin, diminutive of *auris* ear]

auriferous /ɔː'rɪfərəs/ *adj.* yielding gold. [Latin *aurifer* from *aurum* gold]

aurochs /'ɔːrɒks/ *n.* (*pl.* same) extinct wild ox. [German]

aurora /ɔː'rɔːrə/ *n.* (*pl.* **-s** or **aurorae** /-riː/) luminous phenomenon, usu. of streamers of light in the night sky above the northern (**aurora borealis** /ˌbɒrɪ'eɪlɪs/) or southern (**aurora australis** /ɔː'streɪlɪs/) magnetic pole. [Latin, = dawn, goddess of dawn]

AUS *international vehicle registration* Australia.

Auschwitz /'aʊʃvɪts/ (Polish **Oświęcim**) town in S Poland, site of a Nazi concentration camp in the Second World War; pop. (est. 1989) 45 500.

auscultation /ˌɔːskəl'teɪʃ(ə)n/ *n.* listening, esp. to sounds from the heart, lungs, etc., for purposes of diagnosis. [Latin *ausculto* listen]

auspice /'ɔːspɪs/ *n.* **1** (in *pl.*) patronage (esp. *under the auspices of*). **2** omen, premonition. [originally 'observation of bird-flight': Latin *avis* bird]

auspicious /ɔː'spɪʃəs/ *adj.* promising well; favourable.

Aussie /'ɒzɪ/ *slang –n.* **1** Australian. **2** Australia. *–adj.* Australian. [abbreviation]

austere /ɒ'stɪə(r)/ *adj.* (**-terer**, **-terest**) **1** severely simple. **2** morally strict. **3** stern, grim. [Greek *austēros*]

austerity /ɒ'sterɪtɪ/ *n.* (*pl.* **-ies**) being austere; hardship.

Austin /'ɒstɪn/ city in the US, capital of Texas; industries include tourism, meat packing, and food processing; pop. (1994) 514 000.

austral /'ɔːstr(ə)l/ *adj.* **1** southern. **2** (**Austral**) of Australia or Australasia. [Latin *auster* south]

Australasia /ˌɒstrə'leɪʒə, -ʃə/ region consisting of Australia, New Zealand, and neighbouring islands of the SW Pacific. □ **Australasian** *adj.* & *n.*

Australia /ɒ'streɪlɪə/, **Commonwealth of** island country and continent of the S hemisphere in the SW Pacific, a member state of the Commonwealth. The people are mainly of European descent but there are about 160 000 Aborigines. Much of the continent has a hot dry climate and a large part of the central area is desert or semi-desert; the most fertile areas are the E coastal plains and the SW corner of Western Australia. Agriculture has always been of vital importance to the economy, with cereals grown over wide areas and livestock producing wool, meat, and dairy products for export. There are significant mineral resources (including bauxite, coal, copper, iron, lead, uranium, and zinc), and 14 oilfields produce nearly 70% of the country's requirements. Mineral fuels, textile fibres, and meat are among the principal exports. Since the Second World War trade with Asia has increased, Japan now taking a third of Australia's exports.

History. The Commonwealth of Australia was formed in 1901 and supported Great Britain heavily in each of the two World Wars. Since then, constitutional links with the UK have been severed and Australia has pursued her own interests both domestically and internationally, the latter with particular reference to SE Asia and the South Pacific: Japan is now a major trading partner. In 1993 Elizabeth II agreed to Australia becoming a republic within the Commonwealth if this was approved by a referendum. In 1998 a committee was established to look into the constitution. Prime minister, John Howard; capital, Canberra.

languages	English (official), Aboriginal languages
currency	dollar ($A) of 100 cents
pop. (1995)	18 025 000
GNP (1993)	US$310B
literacy	100%
life expectancy	74 (m); 80 (f)

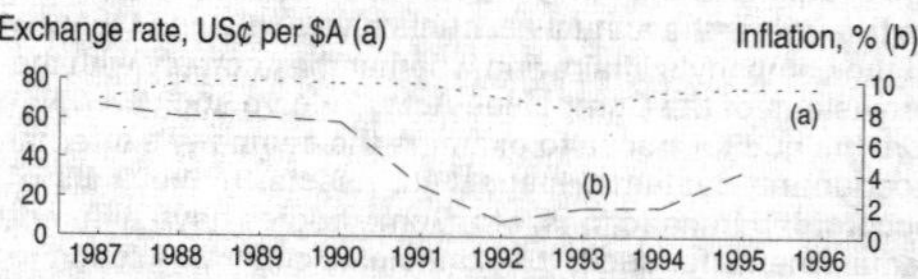

Australian /ɒ'streɪlɪən/ *–n.* **1** native or national of Australia. **2** person of Australian descent. *–adj.* of Australia.

Australian Capital Territory federal territory in New South Wales consisting of two enclaves ceded by New South Wales: one in 1911 to contain Canberra, the other in 1915 containing Jervis Bay; pop. (est. 1995) 303 000.

Austral Islands see TUBUAI ISLANDS.

autarchy /'ɔːtɑːkɪ/ *n.* absolute rule; despotism. [Greek *autos* self, *arkhē* rule]

♦ **autarky** /'ɔːtɑːkɪ/ *n.* self-sufficiency, esp. economic. An economic policy of autarky aims to prevent a country from engaging in international trade. It has been condemned by economists since Adam Smith, although some countries have chosen autarky for political reasons, notably the Soviet Union before the Second World War, on the ground that an underdeveloped country will be better able to build up its industries if it is free from international competition. [Greek *autos* self, *arkeō* suffice]

---

authentic /ɔː'θentɪk/ *adj.* **1** of undisputed origin; genuine. **2** reliable, trustworthy. □ **authentically** *adv.* **authenticity** /-'tɪsɪtɪ/ *n.* [Greek *authentikos*]

authenticate /ɔː'θentɪˌkeɪt/ *v.* (**-ting**) establish as true, genuine, or valid. □ **authentication** /-'keɪʃ(ə)n/ *n.*

author /'ɔːθə(r)/ *n.* (*fem.* **authoress** /'ɔːθrɪs/) **1** writer, esp. of books. **2** originator of an idea, event, etc. [Latin *auctor*]

authoritarian /ɔːˌθɒrɪ'teərɪən/ *–adj.* favouring or enforcing strict obedience to authority. *–n.* authoritarian person.

authoritative /ɔː'θɒrɪtətɪv/ *adj.* **1** reliable, esp. having authority. **2** official.

authority /ɔː'θɒrɪtɪ/ *n.* (*pl.* **-ies**) **1 a** power or right to enforce obedience. **b** (often foll. by *for*, or *to* + infin.) delegated power. **2** (esp. in *pl.*) body having authority. **3** influence based on recognized knowledge or expertise. **4** expert. [Latin *auctoritas*]

authorize /'ɔːθəˌraɪz/ *v.* (also **-ise**) (**-zing** or **-sing**) **1** officially approve, sanction. **2** (foll. by *to* + infin.) give authority to (a person to do a thing). □ **authorization** /-'zeɪʃ(ə)n/ *n.*

♦ **authorized share capital** see SHARE CAPITAL.

Authorized Version *n.* English translation of the Bible made in 1611.

authorship *n.* **1** origin of a book etc. **2** profession of an author.

autism /'ɔːtɪz(ə)m/ *n.* condition characterized by self-absorption and social withdrawal. □ **autistic** /ɔː'tɪstɪk/ *adj.* [related to AUTO-]

auto /'ɔːtəʊ/ *n.* (*pl.* **-s**) *US colloq.* car. [abbreviation of AUTOMOBILE]

auto- *comb. form* **1** self. **2** one's own. **3** of or by oneself or itself. [Greek *autos*]

autobahn /'ɔːtəʊˌbɑːn/ *n.* (*pl.* **-s**) German, Austrian, or Swiss motorway. [German]

autobiography /ˌɔːtəʊbaɪ'ɒgrəfɪ/ *n.* (*pl.* **-ies**) **1** written account of one's own life. **2** this as a literary genre. □ **autobiographer** *n.* **autobiographical** /-ˌbaɪə'græfɪk(ə)l/ *adj.*

autoclave /'ɔːtəˌkleɪv/ *n.* sterilizer using high-pressure steam. [Latin *clavus* nail or *clavis* key]

autocracy /ɔː'tɒkrəsɪ/ *n.* (*pl.* **-ies**) **1** rule by an autocrat. **2** dictatorship. [Greek *kratos* power]

autocrat /'ɔːtəˌkræt/ *n.* **1** absolute ruler. **2** dictatorial person. □ **autocratic** /-'krætɪk/ *adj.* **autocratically** /-'krætɪkəlɪ/ *adv.*

autocross /'ɔːtəʊˌkrɒs/ *n.* motor racing across country or on unmade roads.

Autocue /'ɔːtəʊˌkjuː/ *n. propr.* screen etc. from which a speaker reads a television script.

auto-da-fé /ˌɔːtəʊdɑː'feɪ/ *n.* (*pl.* ***autos-da-fé*** /ˌɔːtəʊz-/) **1** *hist.* ceremonial judgement of heretics by the Spanish Inquisition. **2** public burning of heretics. [Portuguese, = act of the faith]

autograph /'ɔːtəˌgrɑːf/ *–n.* **1** signature, esp. that of a celebrity. **2** note, letter, document, etc. handwritten by its author. *–v.* sign or write on in one's own hand. [Greek *graphō* write]

autoimmune /ˌɔːtəʊɪ'mjuːn/ *adj.* (of a disease) caused by antibodies produced against substances naturally present in the body.

automat /'ɔːtəˌmæt/ *n. US* **1** slot-machine. **2** cafeteria dispensing food and drink from slot-machines. [French: related to AUTOMATON]

automate /'ɔːtəˌmeɪt/ *v.* (**-ting**) convert to or operate by automation.

♦ **automated screen trading** *n.* (also **AST**) electronic dealing in securities using visual-display units to display prices and associated computer equipment to enter, match, and execute deals.

♦ **automated teller machine** *n.* (also **ATM**) computerized machine, usu. attached to the outside wall of a bank or building society, that enables customers to withdraw cash from current accounts, pay in cash or cheques, effect transfers, and obtain statements.

---

automatic /ˌɔːtə'mætɪk/ *–adj.* **1** working by itself, without direct human intervention. **2 a** done spontaneously (*automatic reaction*). **b** following inevitably (*automatic penalty*). **3** (of a firearm) able to be loaded and fired continuously. **4** (of a vehicle or its transmission) using gears that change automatically. *–n.* **1** automatic machine, firearm, or tool. **2** vehicle with automatic transmission. □ **automatically** *adv.* [related to AUTOMATON]

♦ **automatic debit transfer** see GIRO *n.* 1a.

♦ **automatic identification** *n.* means of identifying a product and entering the data obtained automatically into

---

Austria /'ɒstrɪə/, **Republic of** (German **Republik Österreich** /'ɜːstəˌraɪk/) country in central Europe, much of it mountainous, with the River Danube flowing through the NE. Agriculture and forestry are important (timber is a valuable source of export revenue) and there are considerable heavy industries providing iron and steel, machinery, transport equipment, and other manufactures for export. Hydroelectric power has been developed and is exported. The early 1990s have seen increased trade with the former Communist countries of E Europe. Tourism is a significant source of income.

History. The republic was established in 1918, on the breakup of the Austro-Hungarian Empire. After the Second World War the country remained under Allied military occupation until 1955. Since regaining her sovereignty Austria has emerged as a prosperous and stable democratic republic with decidedly westward leanings. In 1995 Austria, previously a member of EFTA, became a member of the EU. President, Thomas Klestil; chancellor, Viktor Klima; capital, Vienna. □ **Austrian** *adj.* & *n.*

language	German
currency	schilling (S) of 100 groschen
pop. (est. 1995)	8 063 000
GNP (est. 1993)	US$183.5B
literacy	100%
life expectancy	73 (m); 79 (f)

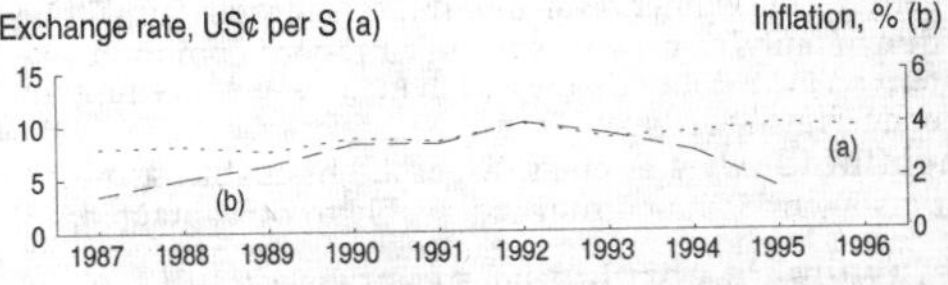

a computer. The most widely used method involves bar codes. Other methods include optical character recognition (OCR), magnetic ink character recognition (MICR), magnetic stripes, and voice systems.

automatic pilot *n.* device for keeping an aircraft or ship on a set course.

♦ **automatic stabilizers** *n.pl. Finance* adjustments to fiscal policy that occur automatically during business cycles and smooth the path of economic growth. For example, in a recession the government will pump money into the economy by paying more in unemployment benefit without a change in policy. Automatic stabilizers counterbalance the effect of the multiplier on economic activity, although in practice their effectiveness is limited.

♦ **automative vending** *n.* selling products by means of a vending machine.

automation /ˌɔːtəˈmeɪʃ(ə)n/ *n.* use or introduction of automatic methods or equipment in place of manual labour.

automatism /ɔːˈtɒməˌtɪz(ə)m/ *n.* **1** involuntary action. **2** unthinking routine. [French: related to AUTOMATON]

automaton /ɔːˈtɒmət(ə)n/ *n.* (*pl.* **-mata** or **-s**) **1** machine controlled automatically; robot. **2** person acting like a robot. [Greek, = acting of itself]

automobile /ˈɔːtəməˌbiːl/ *n. US* motor car. [French]

automotive /ˌɔːtəˈməʊtɪv/ *adj.* of motor vehicles.

autonomous /ɔːˈtɒnəməs/ *adj.* **1** having self-government. **2** acting or free to act independently. [Greek *nomos* law]

autonomy *n.* **1** self-government. **2** personal freedom.

autopilot *n.* = AUTOMATIC PILOT.

autopsy /ˈɔːtɒpsɪ/ *n.* (*pl.* **-ies**) post-mortem. [Greek *autoptēs* eye-witness]

autoroute /ˈɔːtəʊˌruːt/ *n.* French motorway. [French]

autostrada /ˈɔːtəʊˌstrɑːdə/ *n.* (*pl.* ***-s*** or ***-strade*** /-deɪ/) Italian motorway. [Italian]

auto-suggestion /ˌɔːtəʊsəˈdʒestʃ(ə)n/ *n.* hypnotic or subconscious suggestion made to oneself.

autumn /ˈɔːtəm/ *n.* **1** (often *attrib.*) season between summer and winter. **2** time of incipient decline. □ **autumnal** /ɔːˈtʌmn(ə)l/ *adj.* [Latin *autumnus*]

autumn equinox *n.* (also **autumnal equinox**) equinox about 22 Sept.

Auvergne /əʊˈvɜːn/ **1** ancient province of S central France. **2** region of modern France; wheat, wine, cheese, and cattle are produced; pop. (est. 1993) 1 315 200; capital, Clermont-Ferrand.

auxiliary /ɔːgˈzɪljərɪ/ *–adj.* **1** subsidiary, additional. **2** giving help. *–n.* (*pl.* **-ies**) **1** auxiliary person or thing. **2** (in *pl.*) foreign or allied troops in the service of a nation at war. **3** verb used to form tenses or moods of other verbs (e.g. *have* in *I have seen*). [Latin *auxilium* help]

♦ **auxiliary storage** *n. Computing* = BACKING STORE.

auxin /ˈɔːksɪn/ *n.* plant hormone that regulates growth.

AV *–abbr.* **1** (also **A/V, a.v., a/v**) ad valorem. **2** audiovisual. **3** Authorized Version. *–airline flight code* Avianca.

av. *abbr.* **1** average. **2** avoirdupois. **3** (French) avril (= April).

avail /əˈveɪl/ *–v.* **1** help; be of use. **2** *refl.* (foll. by *of*) make use of, profit by. *–n.* use, profit (*of no avail*). [Latin *valeo* be strong]

availability /əˌveɪləˈbɪlɪtɪ/ *n.* **1** accessibility; obtainability. **2** *Computing* actual available time expressed as a percentage of planned available time. Any shortfall will be due to faults or breakdowns. In a modern computer system an availability that is less than, say, 98% is cause for concern.

available *adj.* **1** at one's disposal, obtainable. **2 a** (of a person) free, not committed. **b** able to be contacted.

♦ **available earnings** *n.* = EARNINGS PER SHARE.

available time *n. Computing* amount of time in a given period that a computer system can be used by its normal users. During this period the system must be functioning correctly, have power supplied to it, and not be undergoing repair or maintenance.

avalanche /ˈævəˌlɑːntʃ/ *n.* **1** rapidly sliding mass of snow and ice on a mountain. **2** sudden abundance (*avalanche of work*). [French]

avant-garde /ˌævɑ̃ˈgɑːd/ *–n.* pioneers or (esp. artistic) innovators. *–adj.* new; pioneering. [French, = vanguard]

avarice /ˈævərɪs/ *n.* extreme greed for wealth. □ **avaricious** /-ˈrɪʃəs/ *adj.* [Latin *avarus* greedy]

avatar /ˈævəˌtɑː(r)/ *n.* (in Hindu mythology) descent of a deity etc. to earth in bodily form. [Sanskrit, = descent]

AVC *abbr.* additional voluntary contribution (in pension schemes).

Ave /ˈɑːveɪ/ *n.* (in full **Ave Maria**) prayer to the Virgin Mary (Luke 1:28). [Latin]

Ave. *abbr.* Avenue.

avenge /əˈvendʒ/ *v.* (**-ging**) **1** inflict retribution on behalf of. **2** take vengeance for (an injury). □ **be avenged** avenge oneself. [Latin *vindico*]

avenue /ˈævəˌnjuː/ *n.* **1 a** broad esp. tree-lined road or street. **b** tree-lined path etc. **2** approach (*explored every avenue*). [French *avenir* come to]

aver /əˈvɜː(r)/ *v.* (**-rr-**) *formal* assert, affirm. □ **averment** *n.* [Latin *verus* true]

average /ˈævərɪdʒ/ *–n.* **1** usual amount, extent, or rate. **2** (also **arithmetic mean**) amount obtained by adding two or more numbers and dividing by how many there are. See also GEOMETRIC MEAN; MEDIAN *n.* 2. **3** (with ref. to speed etc.) ratio obtained by subtracting the initial from the final value of each element of the ratio (*average of 50 miles per hour*). **4** partial loss in marine insurance. In **general average (GA)**, a loss resulting from a deliberate act of the master of the ship (e.g. throwing overboard all or part of the cargo to save the ship) is shared by all the parties involved, i.e. by the shipowners and all the cargo owners (see AVERAGE ADJUSTER; AVERAGE BOND). In a **particular average (PA)**, an accidental loss is borne by the owners of the particular thing lost or damaged, e.g. the ship, an individual cargo, etc. Cargo can be insured either **free of particular average (FPA)** or **with average (WA)**. An FPA policy covers the cargo against loss by perils of the sea, fire, or collision and includes cover for any contribution payable in the event of a general average. A WA policy gives better cover as it also includes damage by heavy seas and sea-water damage. In addition, marine cargo can be covered by an all-risks policy. See also FREE OF ALL AVERAGES; INSTITUTE CARGO CLAUSES. **5** method of sharing losses in property insurance to combat underinsurance. This is usu. applied in an **average clause** in a fire insurance policy, in which it is stated that the sum payable in the event of a claim shall not be more than the proportion that the insured value of an item bears to its actual value. *–adj.* **1 a** usual, ordinary. **b** mediocre. **2** constituting an average (*the average age is 72*). *–v.* (**-ging**) **1** amount on average to. **2** do on average. **3** estimate the average of. □ **average out (at)** result in an average (of). **law of averages** principle that if one of two extremes occurs the other will also. **on** (or **on an) average** as an average rate or estimate. [Arabic, = damaged goods]

♦ **average adjuster** *n.* person who handles marine insurance claims on behalf of the insurers. If there is a claim that involves general average (see AVERAGE *n.* 4) and contributions have to be made by all the parties involved it is the average adjuster who is responsible for apportioning payment.

♦ **average bond** *n.* promise to pay general-average contributions, if required (see AVERAGE *n.* 4). If a general-average loss occurs during a marine voyage the carrier has a right to take part of the cargo as payment of the cargo owners' contribution to the loss. As an alternative to the possibility of losing part of his cargo, the cargo owner may take out an average bond with insurers, who agree to pay any losses arising in this way.

♦ **average clause** see AVERAGE *n.* 5.

♦ **average cost** *n.* (also **average unit cost**) budgeted cost of a unit of production. A unit of production is whatever is being produced by a manufacturer at any given time; it might be a complete car or a car component (e.g. a carburettor). Costs of production will vary from time to time and for budgeting purposes it may be convenient to take an average.

♦ **average fixed cost** *n.* average taken over a specified period of the fixed costs incurred by a cost centre. It may seem to be a contradiction that if costs are fixed they remain the same and there can therefore be no average. However, for some purposes such costs as rents are taken as fixed, although they may vary from time to time; in such cases, for budgeting purposes, it is reasonable to take an average. A fixed cost in this sense is not necessarily a cost that will never change from one accounting period to the next, although it is one that will not change solely with the level of production. Cf. AVERAGE VARIABLE COST.

♦ **average stock method** *n.* method of accounting for stock movements that assumes goods are taken out of stock at the average cost of the goods in stock. See BASE STOCK METHOD; FIRST IN, FIRST OUT 1; LAST IN, FIRST OUT.

♦ **average variable cost** *n.* average taken over a specified period of the variable cost of producing units of production (see AVERAGE FIXED COST; AVERAGE COST). The variable costs (e.g. the cost of raw materials, direct labour, machine time, etc.) of producing a unit are those that vary directly with the number of units produced. As they are likely to change from time to time it may be convenient for budgeting purposes to take an average.

♦ **averaging** *n. Finance* adding to a holding of particular securities or commodities when the price falls, in order to reduce the average cost of the whole holding. **Averaging in** consists of buying at various price levels in order to build up a substantial holding of securities or commodities over a period. **Averaging out** is the opposite process, of selling a large holding at various price levels over a long period.

---

averse /əˈvɜːs/ *predic. adj.* (usu. foll. by *to*) opposed, disinclined. [Latin *verto vers-* turn]

aversion /əˈvɜːʃ(ə)n/ *n.* **1** (usu. foll. by *to, for*) dislike or unwillingness. **2** object of this.

avert /əˈvɜːt/ *v.* (often foll. by *from*) **1** turn away (one's eyes or thoughts). **2** prevent or ward off (esp. danger).

Avesta /əˈvestə/ *n.* (usu. prec. by *the*) sacred writings of Zoroastrianism (cf. ZEND). [Persian]

aviary /ˈeɪvɪərɪ/ *n.* (*pl.* **-ies**) large cage or building for keeping birds. [Latin *avis* bird]

aviation /ˌeɪvɪˈeɪʃ(ə)n/ *n.* science or practice of flying aircraft. [Latin: related to AVIARY]

♦ **aviation broker** *n.* broker who arranges chartering of aircraft, air-freight bookings, insurance of air cargo and aircraft, etc.

♦ **aviation insurance** *n.* insurance of aircraft, including accident or damage to aircraft, insurance of air cargo, loss of life or injury while flying, and loss or damage to baggage.

---

aviator /ˈeɪvɪˌeɪtə(r)/ *n.* person who flies aircraft.

avid /ˈævɪd/ *adj.* eager, greedy. □ **avidity** /əˈvɪdɪtɪ/ *n.* **avidly** *adv.* [Latin *aveo* crave]

Avignon /ˈæviːjɒ̃/ city on the Rhône in S France; industries include tourism, chemicals, soap, and cement; pop. (est. 1990) 89 440.

avionics /ˌeɪvɪˈɒnɪks/ *n.pl.* (usu. treated as *sing.*) electronics as applied to aviation. [from AVIATION, ELECTRONICS]

avocado /ˌævəˈkɑːdəʊ/ *n.* (*pl.* **-s**) **1** (in full **avocado pear**) dark green edible pear-shaped fruit with yellowish-green creamy flesh. **2** tree bearing it. [Spanish from Aztec]

avocet /ˈævəˌset/ *n.* long-legged wading bird with an upward-curved bill. [French from Italian]

avoid /əˈvɔɪd/ *v.* **1** keep away or refrain from. **2** escape; evade. **3** *Law* quash, annul. □ **avoidable** *adj.* **avoidance** *n.* [French]

avoirdupois /ˌævədəˈpɔɪz/ *n.* (in full **avoirdupois weight**) system of weights based on a pound of 16 ounces or 7000 grains. [French, = goods of weight]

Avon /ˈeɪvən/ former county of SW England; its county town was Bristol. Dairy farming was important; industries included engineering, printing, financial services, and aircraft manufacture. Following the abolition of Avon county council in 1996 administrative powers were devolved to four unitary authorities.

avow /əˈvaʊ/ *v. formal* declare, confess. □ **avowal** *n.* **avowedly** /əˈvaʊɪdlɪ/ *adv.* [Latin *voco* call]

avuncular /əˈvʌŋkjʊlə(r)/ *adj.* like or of an uncle, esp. in manner. [Latin *avunculus* uncle]

a.w. *abbr.* **1** (also **A/W**) actual weight. **2** *Shipping* all water.

await /əˈweɪt/ *v.* **1** wait for. **2** be in store for. [French: related to WAIT]

awake /əˈweɪk/ *–v.* (**-king**; *past* **awoke**; *past part.* **awoken**) **1** cease to sleep or arouse from sleep. **2** (often foll. by *to*) become or make alert, aware, or active. *–predic. adj.* **1** not asleep. **2** (often foll. by *to*) alert, aware. [Old English: related to A[2]]

awaken *v.* = AWAKE *v.*

■ **Usage** *Awake* and *awaken* are interchangeable but *awaken* is much rarer as an intransitive verb.

award /əˈwɔːd/ *–v.* give or order to be given as a payment or prize. *–n.* **1** thing or amount awarded. **2** judgement delivered as a result of an arbitration. This is binding on the parties concerned unless an appeal is lodged. On a question of law an arbitrator's award can be the subject of an appeal to the High Court under the provisions of the Arbitration Act (1979). [French]

aware /əˈweə(r)/ *predic. adj.* **1** (often foll. by *of* or *that*) conscious; having knowledge. **2** well-informed. □ **awareness** *n.* [Old English]

■ **Usage** *Aware* is also found used attributively in sense 2, as in '*a very aware person*', but this should be avoided in formal contexts.

awash /əˈwɒʃ/ *predic. adj.* **1** level with the surface of, and just covered by, water. **2** (foll. by *with*) overflowing, abounding.

away /əˈweɪ/ *–adv.* **1** to or at a distance from the place, person, or thing in question (*go, give, look, away*; *5 miles away*). **2** into non-existence (*explain, fade, away*). **3** constantly, persistently (*work away*). **4** without delay (*ask away*). *–attrib. adj. Sport* not played on one's own ground (*away match*). *–n. Sport* away match or win. [Old English: related to A[2], WAY]

AWB *abbr. US* air waybill.

awe /ɔː/ *–n.* reverential fear or wonder. *–v.* (**awing**) inspire with awe. [Old Norse]

aweigh /əˈweɪ/ *predic. adj.* (of an anchor) clear of the bottom.

awe-inspiring *adj.* awesome; magnificent.

awesome /ˈɔːsəm/ *adj.* inspiring awe; dreaded.

awful /ˈɔːfʊl/ *adj.* **1** *colloq.* very bad or unpleasant (*has awful writing*; *awful weather*). **2** (*attrib.*) as an intensifier (*awful lot of money*). **3** *poet.* inspiring awe.

awfully *adv.* **1** badly; unpleasantly (*played awfully*). **2** *colloq.* very (*awfully pleased*).

awhile /əˈwaɪl/ *adv.* for a short time. [*a while*]

awkward /ˈɔːkwəd/ *adj.* **1** difficult to use or deal with. **2** clumsy, ungainly. **3 a** embarrassed. **b** embarrassing. [obsolete *awk* perverse]

awl *n.* small tool for piercing holes, esp. in leather. [Old English]

awn *n.* bristly head of a sheath of barley and other grasses. [Old Norse]

awning *n.* sheet of canvas etc. stretched on a frame as a shelter against the sun or rain. [origin uncertain]

awoke *past* of AWAKE.

awoken *past part.* of AWAKE.

AWOL /'eɪwɒl/ *abbr. colloq.* (also **awol**) absent without leave.

awry /ə'raɪ/ *–adv.* **1** crookedly, askew. **2** amiss, wrong. *–predic. adj.* crooked; unsound.

axe /æks/ (*US* **ax**) *–n.* **1** chopping-tool with a handle and heavy blade. **2** (**the axe**) dismissal (of employees); abandonment of a project etc. *–v.* (**axing**) cut (esp. costs or staff) drastically; abandon (a project). □ **an axe to grind** private ends to serve. [Old English]

axial /'æksɪəl/ *adj.* of, forming, or placed round an axis.

axil /'æksɪl/ *n.* upper angle between a leaf and stem. [Latin *axilla* armpit]

axiom /'æksɪəm/ *n.* **1** established or accepted principle. **2** self-evident truth. □ **axiomatic** /-'mætɪk/ *adj.* [Greek *axios* worthy]

axis /'æksɪs/ *n.* (*pl.* **axes** /-siːz/) **1 a** imaginary line about which a body rotates. **b** line which divides a regular figure symmetrically. **2** fixed reference line for the measurement of coordinates etc. **3** (**the Axis**) alliance of Germany, Italy, and later Japan, in the war of 1939–45. [Latin, = axle]

axle /'æks(ə)l/ *n.* spindle on which a wheel is fixed or turns. [Old Norse]

axolotl /'æksə,lɒt(ə)l/ *n.* newtlike salamander, which in natural conditions retains its larval form of life. [Nahuatl, = water-servant]

Axum var. of AKSUM.

AY *airline flight code* Finnair.

Ayacucho /,ɑːjɑː'kuːtʃəʊ/ commercial city in S central Peru; agriculture and tourism are important; pop. (1993) 105 900. The Sendero Luminoso (Shining Path) guerrilla movement first emerged in the vicinity of Ayacucho during the 1980s.

ayatollah /,aɪə'tɒlə/ *n.* Shiite religious leader in Iran. [Persian from Arabic, = token of God]

aye /aɪ/ *–adv. archaic* or *dial.* yes. *–n.* affirmative answer or vote. [probably from *I*, expressing assent]

Ayios Nikólaos see AGHIOS NIKOLAOS.

AZ *–US postcode* Arizona. *–airline flight code* Alitalia.

azalea /ə'zeɪlɪə/ *n.* a kind of rhododendron. [Greek *azaleos* dry]

Azerbaijani *–n.* **1** (also **Azeri** /ə'zeərɪ/) native of Azerbaijan. **2** language of Azerbaijan. *–adj.* of the people or language of Azerbaijan.

azimuth /'æzɪməθ/ *n.* angular distance from a N or S point of the horizon to the intersection with the horizon of a vertical circle passing through a given celestial body. □ **azimuthal** /-'mʌθ(ə)l/ *adj.* [French from Arabic]

Azores /ə'zɔːz/ group of volcanic islands in the North Atlantic, 1287 km (800 miles) W of Portugal, in Portuguese possession but partially autonomous; fruit, tobacco, and wine are produced; pop. (est. 1993) 237 800; capital, Ponta Delgada (on São Miguel).

Azov /'æzɒf/, **Sea of** inland sea in S Russia, communicating with the Black Sea by a narrow strait.

AZT *abbr.* drug used against the Aids virus. [from the chemical name]

Aztec /'æztek/ *–n.* **1** member of the native Mexican people overthrown by the Spanish in 1519. **2** language of this people. *–adj.* of the Aztecs or their language. [Nahuatl, = men of the north]

azure /'æʒə(r)/ *–n.* **1** deep sky-blue colour. **2** *poet.* clear sky. *–adj.* deep sky-blue. [Arabic]

Azerbaijan /,æzəbaɪ'dʒɑːn/, **Republic of** republic in central Asia, lying between the Black and Caspian Seas and containing the Baku oilfields; oil and gas are the most important industries. Crops include cotton, tea, tobacco, and wheat. Food products and machinery are the main exports. Until 1991 Azerbaijan was a constituent republic of the Soviet Union. The country is currently embroiled in armed conflict with neighbouring Armenia over Armenian claims to the Nagorno-Karabakh region. In 1993, unrest caused by government indecisiveness and Armenian victories in Nagorno-Karabakh culminated in a military revolt after which the former Communist leader, Heidar Aliyev, became provisional head of government. In 1994 a ceasefire was signed between Azerbaijan and Armenia over the disputed territory of Nagorno-Karabakh. President, Gaidar Aliev; capital, Baku.

languages	Azerbaijani (official), Russian, Armenian
currency	manat of 100 gopik
pop. (est. 1995)	7 525 000
GNP (1993)	US$5.4B
literacy	97%
life expectancy	67 (m); 75 (f)

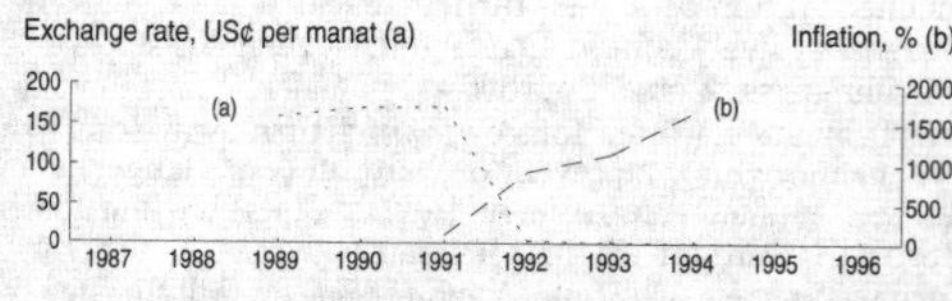

Bb

B[1] /biː/ *n.* (*pl.* **Bs** or **B's**) **1** (also **b**) second letter of the alphabet. **2** *Mus.* seventh note of the diatonic scale of C major. **3** second hypothetical person or example. **4** second highest category (of roads, academic marks, etc.). **5** (usu. **b**) *Algebra* second known quantity. **6 a** occupational grade comprising those in administrative or professional positions. **b** person in this grade.

B[2] *–symb.* **1** *Currency* **a** baht. **b** balboa. **c** bolívar. **2** boron. *–international vehicle registration* Belgium. *–international civil aircraft marking* China or Taiwan. *–postcode* Birmingham.

B[3] *abbr.* (also **B.**) **1** billion. **2** black (pencil-lead).

b. *abbr.* **1** bag. **2** bale. **3** born. **4** *Cricket* **a** bowled by. **b** bye.

B0 *n.* standard paper size, 1000 × 1414 mm.

B1 *n.* standard paper size, 707 × 1000 mm.

B2 *n.* standard paper size, 500 × 707 mm.

B3 *n.* standard paper size, 353 × 500 mm.

B4 *n.* standard paper size, 250 × 353 mm.

B5 *n.* standard paper size, 176 × 250 mm.

B6 *n.* standard paper size, 125 × 176 mm.

B7 *n.* standard paper size, 88 × 125 mm.

B8 *n.* standard paper size, 62 × 88 mm.

B9 *n.* standard paper size, 44 × 62 mm.

B10 *n.* standard paper size, 31 × 44 mm.

BA *abbr.* **1** Bachelor of Arts. **2** bank (or banker's) acceptance. **3** British Airways. **4** *Computing* bus automaton. *–postcode* Bath.

Ba *symb.* barium.

♦ **BAA** *abbr.* = BRITISH AIRPORTS AUTHORITY PLC.

baa /bɑː/ *–v.* (**baas, baaed** or **baa'd**) bleat. *–n.* sheep's cry. [imitative]

babble /ˈbæb(ə)l/ *–v.* (**-ling**) **1 a** talk, chatter, or say incoherently or excessively. **b** (of a stream etc.) murmur. **2** repeat or divulge foolishly. *–n.* **1** babbling. **2** murmur of voices, water, etc. [imitative]

babe *n.* **1** *literary* baby. **2** innocent or helpless person. **3** *US slang* young woman. [as BABY]

babel /ˈbeɪb(ə)l/ *n.* **1** confused noise, esp. of voices. **2** scene of confusion. [Hebrew, = Babylon (Gen. 11)]

baboon /bəˈbuːn/ *n.* large long-nosed African and Arabian monkey. [French or medieval Latin]

baby /ˈbeɪbɪ/ *–n.* (*pl.* **-ies**) **1** very young child. **2** childish person. **3** youngest member of a family etc. **4** (often *attrib.*) **a** very young animal. **b** small specimen. **5** *slang* sweetheart. **6** one's special concern etc. *–v.* (**-ies, -ied**) treat like a baby; pamper. □ **babyhood** *n.* **babyish** *adj.* [imitative of child's *ba ba*]

♦ **baby bond** *n.* bond offered by tax-exempt Friendly Society producing a fund for an infant, usu. over a ten-year period. The maximum investment allowed by UK tax regulations is £200 per annum.

baby boom *n. colloq.* temporary increase in the birthrate.

Baby Buggy *n. propr.* a kind of child's pushchair.

baby carriage *n. US* pram.

baby grand *n.* small grand piano.

Babygro *n.* (*pl.* **-s**) *propr.* stretchy all-in-one baby suit.

babysit *v.* (**-tt-**; *past* and *past part.* **-sat**) look after a child while its parents are out. □ **babysitter** *n.*

BAC *abbr.* **1** British Aircraft Corporation. **2** Business Archives Council.

B.Acc. *abbr.* Bachelor of Accountancy.

baccalaureate /ˌbækəˈlɔːrɪət/ *n.* final secondary school examination in France and many international schools. [medieval Latin *baccalaureus* bachelor]

baccarat /ˈbækəˌrɑː/ *n.* gambling card-game. [French]

bacchanal /ˈbækən(ə)l/ *–n.* **1** drunken revelry or reveller. **2** priest or follower of Bacchus. *–adj.* **1** of or like Bacchus. **2** drunkenly riotous. [Latin *Bacchus* from Greek, god of wine]

Bacchanalia /ˌbækəˈneɪlɪə/ *n.pl.* **1** Roman festival of Bacchus. **2** (**bacchanalia**) drunken revelry.

bacchant /ˈbækənt/ *–n.* (*fem.* **bacchante** /bəˈkæntɪ/) **1** priest or follower of Bacchus. **2** drunken reveller. *–adj.* **1** of or like Bacchus or his rites. **2** drunkenly riotous, roistering.

Bacchic /ˈbækɪk/ *adj.* = BACCHANAL *adj.*

baccy /ˈbækɪ/ *n.* (*pl.* **-ies**) *colloq.* tobacco. [abbreviation]

bachelor /ˈbætʃələ(r)/ *n.* **1** unmarried man. **2** person with a university first degree. □ **bachelorhood** *n.* [related to BACCALAUREATE]

bachelor girl *n.* independent young single woman.

bacillus /bəˈsɪləs/ *n.* (*pl.* **bacilli** /-laɪ/) rod-shaped bacterium, esp. one causing disease. □ **bacillary** *adj.* [Latin, diminutive of *baculus* stick]

back *–n.* **1 a** rear surface of the human body from shoulder to hip. **b** upper surface of an animal's body. **c** spine (*broke his back*). **d** keel of a ship. **2** backlike surface (*back of the head, chair, shirt*). **3** reverse or more distant part (*back of the room; sat in the back; write it on the back*). **4** defensive player in football etc. *–adv.* **1** to the rear (*go back a bit; looked back*). **2** in or into a previous state, place, or time (*came back; put it back; back in June*). **3** at a distance (*stand back*). **4** in return (*pay back*). **5** in check (*hold him back*). *–v.* **1 a** give moral or financial support to. **b** bet on (a horse etc.). **2** (often foll. by *up*) move backwards. **3 a** put or serve as a back, background, or support to. **b** *Mus.* accompany. **4** lie at the back of (*beach backed by cliffs*). **5** (of the wind) move anticlockwise. *–adj.* **1** situated to the rear: remote, subsidiary (*back teeth*). **2** past; not current (*back pay; back issue*). **3** reversed (*back flow*). □ **back and forth** to and fro. **back down** withdraw from confrontation. **the back of beyond** very remote place. **back off 1** draw back, retreat. **2** = *back down.* **back on to** have its back adjoining (*backs on to a field*). **back out** (often foll. by *of*) withdraw from a commitment. **back-pedal** reverse one's action or opinion. **back to back** with backs adjacent and facing each other (*stood back to back*). **back up 1** give (esp. moral) support to. **2** *Computing* make a backup of (data, a disk, etc.). **get** (or **put**) **a person's back up** annoy a person. **get off a person's back** stop troubling a person. **turn one's back on** abandon; ignore. □ **backer** *n.* (in sense 1 of *v.*). **backless** *adj.* [Old English]

backache *n.* ache in the back.

back-bencher *n.* MP not holding a senior office.

backbiting *n.* malicious talk. □ **backbite** *v.*

back-boiler *n.* boiler behind a domestic fire.

backbone *n.* **1** spine. **2** chief support. **3** firmness of character.

back-breaking *adj.* (esp. of manual work) extremely hard.

backchat *n. colloq.* verbal insolence.

backcloth *n.* **1** painted cloth at the back of a stage. **2** background to a scene or situation.

backcomb *v.* comb (the hair) towards the scalp to give it fullness.

back-crawl *n.* = BACKSTROKE.

backdate *v.* (**-ting**) **1** make retrospectively valid. **2** put an earlier date to than the actual one.

back door *n.* **1** secret or ingenious means. **2** method by which the Bank of England injects cash into the money market. The bank purchases treasury bills at the market rate rather than by lending money directly to the discount houses (the **front door** method) when it acts as lender of last resort.

backdrop *n.* = BACKCLOTH.

backend *n.* computer program that is used to convert output from a general-purpose program into a specific form.

♦ **backend load** *n.* final charge made by an investment trust when an investor sells shares in the fund.

---

backfire *v.* (**-ring**) **1** (of an engine or vehicle) ignite or explode too early in the cylinder or exhaust. **2** (of a plan etc.) rebound adversely on its originator.

back-formation *n.* **1** formation of a word from its seeming derivative (e.g. *laze* from *lazy*). **2** word so formed.

♦ **back freight** *n.* cost of shipping goods back to the port of destination after they have been overcarried. If the goods were overcarried for reasons beyond the master's control, the shipowner may be responsible for paying the back freight. If delivery was not accepted in reasonable time at the port of destination and the master took the goods on or sent them back to the port of shipment, the back freight would be the responsibility of the cargo owner.

---

backgammon *n.* board-game with pieces moved according to throws of the dice. [from BACK + obsolete form of GAME[1]]

background *n.* **1** part of a scene or picture furthest from the observer. **2** (often *attrib.*) inconspicuous position (*kept in the background*; *background music*). **3** person's education, social circumstances, etc. **4** explanatory or contributory information or events. **5** *Computing* low-priority work performed when computer facilities are not otherwise required. Background work may not be less important than other work: it is more likely to be a large or time-consuming program whose operation is interrupted for a series of small tasks that require immediate attention.

backhand *–attrib. adj.* (of a stroke) made with the hand across one's body. *–n.* such a stroke.

backhanded /bæk'hændɪd/ *adj.* **1** made with the back of the hand. **2** indirect; ambiguous (*backhanded compliment*).

backhander *n.* **1 a** backhand stroke. **b** backhanded blow. **2** *slang* bribe.

backing *n.* **1 a** support, esp. financial or moral. **b** material used for a thing's back or support. **2** musical accompaniment, esp. to a pop singer.

backing store *n.* computer storage devices in which programs and data are kept when not required by the processor of a computer. The use of backing store means that a computer has access to a large repertoire of programs and to large amounts of data, and can call on these only when it needs them. The information is then copied from backing store into the computer's main store, which is of much lower storage capacity (see MAIN STORE). Hard disks and floppy disks are extensively used for on-line backing storage. Magnetic tapes are used as off-line backing store. Programs and data can be transferred from tape to disk for processing.

backing track *n.* recorded musical accompaniment.

backlash *n.* **1** violent, usu. hostile, reaction. **2** sudden recoil in a mechanism.

backlist *n.* publisher's list of books still in print.

backlog *n.* arrears of work.

back number *n.* **1** out-of-date issue of a periodical. **2** *slang* out-of-date person or thing.

backpack *–n.* rucksack. *–v.* travel or hike with this. □ **backpacker** *n.*

back passage *n. colloq.* rectum.

backrest *n.* support for the back.

back room *n.* (often, with hyphen, *attrib.*) place where secret work is done.

back seat *n.* less prominent or important position.

back-seat driver *n.* person eager to advise without taking responsibility.

backside *n. colloq.* buttocks.

back slang *n.* slang using words spelt backwards (e.g. *yob*).

backslide *v.* (**-ding**; *past* **-slid**; *past part.* **-slid** or **-slidden**) return to bad habits etc.

backspace *v.* (**-cing**) move a typewriter carriage etc. back one or more spaces.

backspin *n.* backward spin making a ball bounce erratically.

backstage *adv.* & *adj.* behind the scenes.

backstairs *–n.pl.* rear or side stairs of a building. *–attrib. adj.* (also **backstair**) underhand; secret.

backstitch *n.* sewing with each stitch starting behind the end of the previous one.

back-stop *n.* **1** *Cricket* etc. **a** position directly behind the wicket-keeper. **b** fielder in this position. **2** last resort.

backstreet *–n.* side-street, alley. *–attrib. adj.* illicit; illegal (*backstreet abortion*).

backstroke *n.* swimming stroke done on the back.

back-to-back *adj.* (of houses) with a party wall at the rear.

♦ **back-to-back credit** *n.* (also **countervailing credit**) method used to conceal the identity of the seller from the buyer in a credit arrangement. When the credit is arranged by a British finance house, the foreign seller provides the relevant documentation. The finance house, acting as an intermediary, issues its own documents to the buyer, omitting the seller's name and so concealing the seller's identity.

---

back to front *adj.* **1** with back and front reversed. **2** in disorder.

back-to-nature *attrib. adj.* seeking a simpler way of life.

backtrack *v.* **1** retrace one's steps. **2** reverse one's policy or opinion.

backup *n.* (often *attrib.*) **1** support; reserve (*backup team*). **2** *Computing* file, device, or system that can be used as a substitute in the event of a loss of data, development of a fault, etc. A backup file, for example, is a copy of a file that is taken in case the original is unintentionally altered or destroyed and the data lost. It is not stored on-line. A floppy disk may be copied for the same reason. The backup copy should be on a completely different disk, or tape, and stored in a separate location from the original. Backup copies should be made of all information held on computer. How frequently the copies are made will depend upon how rapidly the information changes, its difficulty of replacement, and its importance.

backward /'bækwəd/ *–adv.* = BACKWARDS. *–adj.* **1** towards the rear or starting-point (*backward look*). **2** reversed (*backward roll*). **3** slow to develop or progress. **4** hesitant, shy.

♦ **backwardation** /ˌbækwə'deɪʃ(ə)n/ *n.* **1** difference between the spot price of a commodity, including rent, insurance, and interest accrued, and the forward price when the spot price is the higher. Cf. FORWARDATION. **2** situation that occasionally occurs on the London Stock Exchange when a market maker quotes a buying price for a share that is lower than the selling price quoted by another market maker. However, with prices now displayed on screens, this situation does not now last long.

♦ **backward integration** see INTEGRATION 3.

---

backwards *adv.* **1** away from one's front (*lean backwards*). **2 a** with the back foremost (*walk backwards*). **b** in reverse of the usual way (*count backwards*). **3 a** into a worse state. **b** into the past. **c** (of motion) back towards the starting-point (*roll backwards*). □ **backwards and forwards** to and fro. **bend** (or **fall** or **lean) over backwards** *colloq.* make every effort, esp. to be fair or helpful.

backwash *n.* **1** receding waves made by a ship etc. **2** repercussions.

backwater *n.* **1** peaceful, secluded, or dull place. **2** stagnant water fed from a stream.

backwoods *n.pl.* **1** remote uncleared forest land. **2** remote region. □ **backwoodsman** *n.*

backyard *n.* yard behind a house etc.

BACO *abbr.* British Aluminium Company Ltd.

Bacolod /bɑːˈkəʊlɒd/ port in the central Philippines, the chief city of the island of Negros; industries include sugar refining; pop. (est. 1994) 343 048.

bacon /ˈbeɪkən/ *n.* cured meat from the back or sides of a pig. [French from Germanic]

BACS *abbr.* Bankers' Automated Clearing Service. See ASSOCIATION FOR PAYMENT CLEARING SERVICES.

bacteriology /ˌbæktɪərɪˈɒlədʒɪ/ *n.* the study of bacteria.

bacterium /bækˈtɪərɪəm/ *n.* (*pl.* **-ria**) unicellular micro-organism lacking an organized nucleus, esp. of a kind causing disease. □ **bacterial** *adj.* [Greek, = little stick]

■ **Usage** A common mistake is the use of the plural form *bacteria* as the singular. This should be avoided.

bad *–adj.* (**worse, worst**) **1** inadequate, defective (*bad work, light*). **2** unpleasant (*bad weather*). **3** harmful (*is bad for you*). **4** (of food) decayed. **5** *colloq.* ill, injured (*feeling bad today; a bad leg*). **6** *colloq.* regretful, guilty (*feels bad about it*). **7** serious, severe (*a bad headache, mistake*). **8 a** morally unacceptable (*bad man; bad language*). **b** naughty. **9** not valid (*a bad cheque*). **10** (**badder, baddest**) esp. *US slang* excellent. *–n.* ill fortune; ruin. *–adv. US colloq.* badly. □ **not** (or **not so) bad** *colloq.* fairly good. **too bad** *colloq.* regrettable. [Old English]

bad blood *n.* ill feeling.

bad books see BOOK.

bad breath *n.* unpleasant-smelling breath.

♦ **bad debt** *n.* debt that is very unlikely to be paid. Such an amount can be treated as a loss and written off in the profit and loss account. Doubtful debts may appear in the accounts of an organization as a provision for bad debts.

---

baddy *n.* (*pl.* **-ies**) *colloq.* villain in a story, film, etc.

bade see BID.

bad egg see EGG[1].

Baden /ˈbɑːd(ə)n/ spa town in SE Austria; industries include textiles; pop. (est. 1991) 23 998.

Baden-Württemberg /ˌbɑːdənˈvʊətəmˌberk/ state (*Land*) in SW Germany; pop. (est. 1995) 10 272 100; capital, Stuttgart. There are textile, chemical, and car industries; jewellery and watches are manufactured.

bad faith *n.* intent to deceive.

badge *n.* **1** small flat emblem worn to signify office, membership, etc., or as decoration. **2** thing that reveals a condition or quality. [origin unknown]

badger *–n.* nocturnal burrowing mammal with a black and white striped head. *–v.* pester, harass. [origin uncertain]

♦ **badges of trade** *n.pl.* criteria distinguishing trading from investment for taxation purposes as set out by the Royal Commission on the Taxation of Profits and Income (1954).

---

badinage /ˈbædɪˌnɑːʒ/ *n.* playful ridicule. [French]

bad lot *n.* person of bad character.

badly *adv.* (**worse, worst**) **1** in a bad manner. **2** *colloq.* very much (*wants it badly*). **3** severely (*badly defeated*).

badminton /ˈbædmɪnt(ə)n/ *n.* game with rackets and a shuttlecock. [*Badminton* in S England]

bad-mouth *v.* esp. *US slang* abuse verbally, put down.

bad news *n. colloq.* unpleasant or troublesome person or thing.

bad-tempered *adj.* irritable.

BAe *abbr.* British Aerospace.

BA(Econ.) *abbr.* Bachelor of Arts in Economics.

baffle /ˈbæf(ə)l/ *–v.* (**-ling**) **1** perplex. **2** frustrate, hinder. *–n.* device that checks flow esp. of fluid or sound waves. □ **bafflement** *n.* [origin uncertain]

BAFTA /ˈbæftə/ *abbr.* British Academy of Film and Television Arts.

bag *–n.* **1** soft open-topped receptacle. **2 a** piece of luggage. **b** woman's handbag. **3** (in *pl.*; usu. foll. by *of*) *colloq.* large amount (*bags of time*). **4** *slang derog.* woman. **5** animal's sac. **6** amount of game shot by one person. **7** (usu. in *pl.*) baggy skin under the eyes. **8** *slang* particular interest (*folk music is not my bag*). *–v.* (**-gg-**) **1** *colloq.* **a** secure (*bagged the best seat*). **b** (often in phr. **bags I**) *colloq.* claim as being the first (*bags I go next*). **2** put in a bag. **3** (cause to) hang loosely; bulge. □ **in the bag** *colloq.* achieved, secured. □ **bagful** *n.* (*pl.* **-s**). [origin unknown]

bagatelle /ˌbægəˈtel/ *n.* **1** game in which small balls are struck into holes on a board. **2** mere trifle. **3** short piece of esp. piano music. [French from Italian]

bagel /ˈbeɪg(ə)l/ *n.* hard ring-shaped bread roll. [Yiddish]

baggage /ˈbægɪdʒ/ *n.* **1** luggage. **2** portable military equipment. **3** *joc.* or *derog.* girl or woman. [French]

baggy *adj.* (**-ier, -iest**) hanging loosely. □ **baggily** *adv.* **bagginess** *n.*

Baghdad /bægˈdæd/ capital of Iraq, on the River Tigris; pop. (est. 1995) 4 478 600. It has chemical, textile, and food-processing industries; manufactures include cement, bricks, and leather goods.

bagpipe *n.* (usu. in *pl.*) musical instrument consisting of a windbag connected to reeded pipes.

baguette /bæˈget/ *n.* long thin French loaf. [French]

bah *int.* expressing contempt or disbelief. [French]

Baha'i /bəˈhaɪ/ *n.* (*pl.* **-s**) member of a monotheistic religion emphasizing religious unity and world peace. [Persian *bahá* splendour]

Bahawalpur /bəˈhɑːwəlˌpʊə(r)/ city in central Pakistan; cotton and soap are produced; pop. (1981) 180 000.

Bahamas /bəˈhɑːməz/, **Commonwealth of the** country consisting of an archipelago off the SE coast of Florida, part of the West Indies. The subtropical climate and extensive beaches make tourism, which provides over half the country's revenue and employment, the main industry. 90% of companies are foreign-owned. Offshore financial services are also important, but have suffered in recent years following accusations of money laundering. The country's chief exports are rum, pharmaceuticals, mineral fuels, and crawfish. Formerly a British colony, the Bahamas gained independence, as a member of the Commonwealth, in 1973. It is a member of CARICOM. Prime minister, Hubert Ingraham; capital, Nassau. □ **Bahamian** /bəˈeɪmɪən/ *adj.* & *n.*

language	English
currency	dollar (B$) of 100 cents
pop. (est. 1996)	280 000
GNP (est. 1994)	US$3.2B
literacy	98%
life expectancy	67 (m); 77 (f)

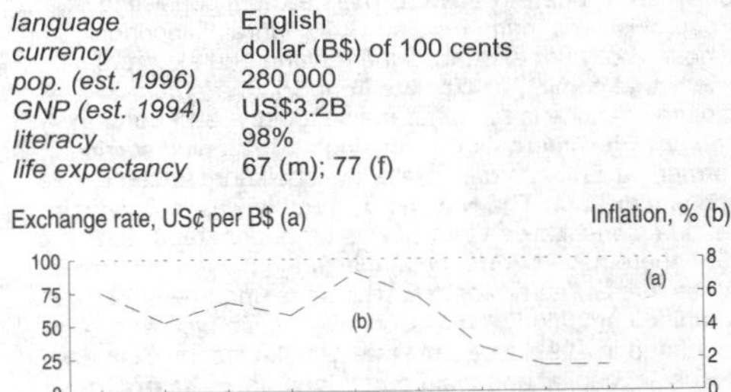

Bahia see SALVADOR 1.

Bahía Blanca /bəˈhiːə ˈblæŋkə/ port in central Argentina, serving the S Pampas; exports include wool, meat, and grain; pop. (1991) 260 090.

baht /bɑːt/ *n.* standard monetary unit of Thailand. [Thai]

bail[1] *–n.* **1** money etc. pledged against the temporary release of an untried prisoner. **2** person(s) giving this. *–v.* (usu. foll. by *out*) **1** release or secure the release of (a prisoner) on payment of bail. **2** release from a difficulty; rescue. □ **on bail** released after payment of bail. [Latin *bajulus* carrier]

bail[2] *n.* **1** *Cricket* either of two crosspieces bridging the stumps. **2** bar holding the paper against a typewriter platen. **3** bar separating horses in an open stable. [French]

bail[3] *v.* (also **bale**) **1** (usu. foll. by *out*) scoop water out of (a boat etc.). **2** scoop (water etc.) out. □ **bail out** var. of *bale out* 1 (see BALE[1]). [French]

bailey /ˈbeɪlɪ/ *n.* (*pl.* **-s**) **1** outer wall of a castle. **2** court enclosed by it. [French: related to BAIL[2]]

Bailey bridge /ˈbeɪlɪ/ *n.* prefabricated military bridge for rapid assembly. [Sir D. *Bailey*, name of its designer]

bailiff /ˈbeɪlɪf/ *n.* **1** sheriff's officer who executes writs and carries out distraints. **2** landlord's agent or steward. [French: related to BAIL[1]]

bailiwick /ˈbeɪlɪwɪk/ *n.* **1** *Law* district of a bailiff. **2** *joc.* person's particular interest. [as BAILIFF, obsolete *wick* district]

♦ **bailment** *n.* delivery of good from the **bailor** (the owner of the goods) to the **bailee** (the recipient of the goods), on the condition that the goods will ultimately be returned to the bailor. The goods may thus be hired, lent, pledged, or deposited for safe custody. A delivery of this nature is usu. also the subject of a contract, e.g. a contract with a bank for the deposit of valuables for safekeeping. Nonetheless, in English law a bailment retains its distinguishing characteristic of a business relationship that arises outside the law of contract and is therefore not governed by it.

bain-marie /ˌbænməˈriː/ *n.* (*pl.* **bains-marie** pronunc. same) pan of hot water holding a pan containing sauce etc. for slow heating. [French, translation of medieval Latin *balneum Mariae* bath of Maria (a supposed alchemist)]

bairn *n. Scot. & N.Engl.* child. [Old English: related to BEAR[1]]

Bairrada /baɪˈrɑːdə/ wine-producing region of Portugal, in the coastal province of Beira Litoral.

bait *–n.* **1** food used to entice prey. **2** allurement. *–v.* **1** harass, torment, or annoy (a person or chained animal). **2** put bait on (a hook, trap, etc.). [Old Norse]

baize *n.* usu. green woollen felted material, used for coverings. [French pl. *baies* chestnut-coloured]

Baja California /ˈbæxə/ (also **North Baja**) state of NW Mexico; industries include mining; pop. (est. 1995) 2 108 118; capital, Mexicali.

Baja California Sur /ˈbæxə, sʊə(r)/ (also **South Baja**) state of NW Mexico; pop. (est. 1995) 375 450; capital, La Paz. It has cotton-processing, fish-packing, and tourist industries.

bake *v.* (**-king**) **1** cook or become cooked by dry heat, esp. in an oven. **2** *colloq.* (usu. as **be baking**) (of weather, a person, etc.) be very hot. **3** harden by heat. [Old English]

baked beans *n.pl.* baked haricot beans, usu. tinned in tomato sauce.

Bakelite /ˈbeɪkəˌlaɪt/ *n. propr.* plastic made from formaldehyde and phenol, used formerly for buttons, plates, etc. [German from *Baekeland*, name of its inventor]

baker *n.* person who bakes and sells bread, cakes, etc., esp. for a living.

Baker day *n. colloq.* day set aside for in-service training of teachers. [*Baker*, name of the Education Secretary responsible for introducing them]

baker's dozen *n.* thirteen.

bakery *n.* (*pl.* **-ies**) place where bread and cakes are made or sold.

Bakewell tart /ˈbeɪkwel/ *n.* open pastry case lined with jam and filled with almond paste. [*Bakewell* in Derbyshire]

baking-powder *n.* mixture of sodium bicarbonate, cream of tartar, etc., as a raising agent.

baking-soda *n.* sodium bicarbonate.

baklava /ˈbækləvə/ *n.* rich sweetmeat of flaky pastry, honey, and nuts. [Turkish]

baksheesh /ˈbækʃiːʃ/ *n.* gratuity, tip. [Persian]

Baku /bæˈkuː/ capital of Azerbaijan, on the Caspian Sea; pop. (est. 1991) 1 713 700. It is an industrial port and centre of the oil industry.

bal. *abbr. Bookkeeping* balance.

Balaclava /ˌbæləˈklɑːvə/ *n.* (in full **Balaclava helmet**) usu. woollen covering for the whole head and neck, except for the face. [*Balaclava* in the Crimea, the site of a battle in 1854]

balalaika /ˌbæləˈlaɪkə/ *n.* guitar-like stringed instrument with a triangular body. [Russian]

balance /ˈbæləns/ *–n.* **1 a** even distribution of weight or amount. **b** stability of body or mind. **2** apparatus for weighing, esp. one with a central pivot, beam, and two scales. **3 a** counteracting weight or force. **b** (in full **balance-wheel**) regulating device in a clock etc. **4** decisive weight or amount (*balance of opinion*). **5 a** agreement or difference between credits and debits in an account. **b** amount still owing or outstanding (*will pay the balance*). **c** amount left over. **6 a** *Art* harmony and proportion. **b** *Mus.* relative volume of sources of sound. **7** (**the Balance**) zodiacal sign or constellation Libra. *–v.* (**-cing**) **1** bring into, keep, or be in equilibrium (*balanced a book on her head*; *balanced on one leg*). **2** (often foll. by *with*, *against*) offset or compare (one thing) with another (*balance the pros and cons*). **3** counteract, equal, or neutralize the weight or importance of. **4** (usu. as **balanced** *adj.*) make well-proportioned and harmonious (*balanced diet*; *balanced opinion*). **5 a** compare and esp. equalize the deb-

Bahrain /bɑːˈreɪn/, **State of** sheikdom consisting of a group of islands in the Persian Gulf. Bahrain's economy is almost wholly dependent on the refining and export of oil, chiefly that coming by pipeline from Saudi Arabia. Aluminium smelting is the other main industry, and Bahrain also provides international banking and shipping services. Formerly a British protectorate, the sheikdom became independent in 1971. The National Assembly was dissolved in 1975; a Consultative Council was formed in 1993. Since 1994 there have been regular clashes between the armed forces and Shi'ite protestors, who have undertaken a bombing campaign. A new Consultative Council was appointed in 1996. Head of state, Sheikh Isa ibn Sulman al-Khalifa; capital and main port, Manama. □ **Bahraini** *adj.* & *n.*

languages	Arabic (official), Farsi, Urdu, English
currency	dinar (BD) of 1000 fils
pop. (est. 1996)	598 000
GNP (est. 1994)	US$4.1B
literacy	76.5% (m); 58.6% (f)
life expectancy	69 (m); 72.5 (f)

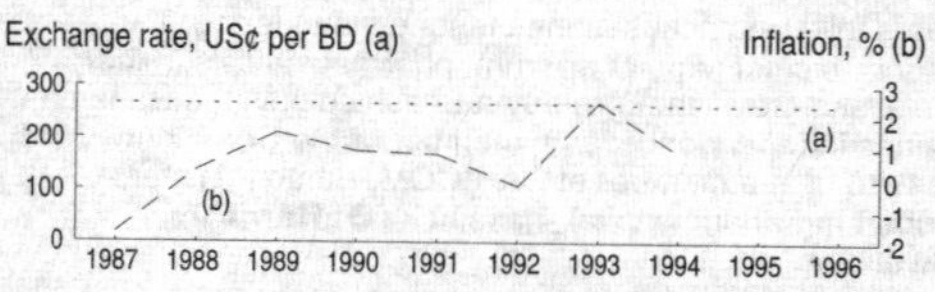

its and credits of (an account). **b** (of an account) have credits and debits equal. □ **in the balance** uncertain; at a critical stage. **on balance** all things considered. [Latin *bilanx* scales]

◆ **balanced-budget multiplier** *n.* effect on national income caused by a change in government expenditure that has been offset by an equal change in taxation. For example, an increase in government spending will inject more demand into the economy than the equal increase in taxation takes out, since some of the income absorbed by the tax would have been used for savings and therefore did not contribute to the aggregate demand. In effect, individuals have reduced savings, they feel worse off, and therefore work harder to build up their savings again. The balanced-budget multiplier is not usu. pursued explicitly as an instrument of fiscal policy as taxation is generally unpopular.

◆ **balance of payments** *n.* accounts setting out a country's transactions with the outside world. They are divided into various sub-accounts, notably the **current account** and the **capital account**. The former includes the trade account, which records the balance of imports and exports (see BALANCE OF TRADE). Overall, the accounts must always be in balance. A deficit or surplus on the balance of payments refers to an imbalance on a sub-account, usu. the amount by which the foreign-exchange reserves of the government have been depleted or increased. The conventions used for presenting balance-of-payments statistics are those recommended by the International Monetary Fund.

balance of power *n.* **1** situation of roughly equal power among the chief states of the world. **2** power held by a small group when larger groups are of equal strength.

◆ **balance of trade** *n.* accounts setting out the results of a country's trading position. It is a component of the balance of payments, forming part of the current account. It includes both the visibles (i.e. imports and exports in physical merchandise) and the invisible balance (receipts and expenditure on such services as insurance, finance, freight, and tourism).

◆ **balance sheet** *n.* one of the principal statements comprising a set of accounts, showing the financial state of affairs of an organization on a given date, usu. the last day of an accounting period. A balance sheet has three main headings: assets, liabilities, and capital. The assets must always equal the sum of the liabilities and the capital, as the statement can be looked at in either of two ways: (1) as a statement of the organization's wealth, in which case the assets less the liabilities equal the capital (the amount of wealth attributable to the proprietors); or (2) as a statement of how the assets have been funded, i.e. partly by borrowing (the liabilities) and partly by the proprietors (the capital). Although a balance sheet balances, i.e. its two sides are equal, it is actually so named since it comprises balances from the accounts in the ledgers.

balboa /bæl'bəʊə/ *n.* standard monetary unit of Panama. [Vasco de *Balboa*, Spanish explorer]

balcony /'bælkənɪ/ *n.* (*pl.* **-ies**) **1** usu. balustraded platform on the outside of a building with access from an upper floor. **2** upper tier of seats in a theatre etc. □ **balconied** *adj.* [Italian]

bald /bɔːld/ *adj.* **1** lacking some or all hair on the scalp. **2** lacking the usual hair, feathers, leaves, etc. **3** *colloq.* with a worn surface (*bald tyre*). **4** plain, direct (*bald statement, style*). □ **balding** *adj.* (in senses 1–3). **baldly** *adv.* (in sense 4). **baldness** *n.* [Old English]

balderdash /'bɔːldə,dæʃ/ *n.* nonsense. [origin unknown]

bale[1] *–n.* tightly bound bundle of merchandise or hay. *–v.* (**-ling**) make up into bales. □ **bale out 1** (also **bail out**) (of an airman) make an emergency parachute descent. **2** var. of BAIL[1] *v.* 2. [Dutch: related to BALL[1]]

bale[2] var. of BAIL[3].

Balearic Islands /,bælɪ'ærɪk/ (also **Balearics**) group of Mediterranean islands off the E coast of Spain, forming a province of that country, with four large islands (Majorca, Minorca, Ibiza, Formentera) and seven smaller ones; pop. (1994) 736 860; capital, Palma (on Majorca). The economy is largely dependent on tourism, but there is some farming.

baleen /bə'liːn/ *n.* whalebone. [Latin *balaena* whale]

baleful /'beɪlfʊl/ *adj.* **1** menacing in look, manner, etc. **2** malignant, destructive. □ **balefully** *adv.* [archaic *bale* evil]

Bali /'bɑːlɪ/ island of Indonesia; industries include tourism and craftwork; pop. (est. 1995) 2 902 200; capital, Denpasar.

balk var. of BAULK.

Balkan /'bɔːlkən/ *adj.* of the Balkan Peninsula or States. [Turkish]

Balkan Peninsula peninsula of SE Europe, bounded by the Adriatic, Aegean, and Black Seas.

Balkan States (also **the Balkans**) the countries of the Balkan Peninsula: Greece, Albania, the former Yugoslav republics, Bulgaria, Romania, and the European part of Turkey.

ball[1] /bɔːl/ *–n.* **1** sphere, esp. for use in a game. **2 a** ball-shaped object; material in the shape of a ball (*ball of snow, wool*). **b** rounded part of the body (*ball of the foot*). **3** cannon-ball. **4** single delivery or pass of a ball in cricket, baseball, football, etc. **5** (in *pl.*) *coarse slang* **a** testicles. **b** (usu. as *int.*) nonsense. **c** = BALLS-UP. **d** courage, 'guts'. *–v.* form into a ball. □ **balls up** *coarse slang* bungle; make a mess of. **on the ball** *colloq.* alert. [Old Norse]

ball[2] /bɔːl/ *n.* **1** formal social gathering for dancing. **2** *slang* enjoyable time (esp. *have a ball*). [Greek *ballō* throw]

ballad /'bæləd/ *n.* **1** poem or song narrating a popular story. **2** slow sentimental song. [Provençal: related to BALL[2]]

balladry *n.* ballad poetry.

ball-and-socket joint *n.* joint in which a rounded end lies in a concave socket.

Ballarat /'bælə,ræt/ city in the state of Victoria, Australia, a sheep-farming (and formerly mining) centre; manufactures include textiles and machinery; pop. (1986) 78 300.

ballast /'bæləst/ *–n.* **1** heavy material stabilizing a ship, the car of a balloon, etc. **2** coarse stone etc. as the bed of a railway track or road. **3** mixture of coarse and fine aggregate for making concrete. *–v.* provide with ballast. [Low German or Scandinavian]

ball-bearing *n.* **1** bearing in which the two halves are separated by a ring of small balls. **2** one of these balls.

ballboy *n.* (*fem.* **ballgirl**) (in tennis) boy or girl who retrieves balls.

ballcock *n.* floating ball on a hinged arm controlling the water level in a cistern.

ballerina /,bælə'riːnə/ *n.* female ballet-dancer. [Italian: related to BALL[2]]

ballet /'bæleɪ/ *n.* **1** dramatic or representational style of dancing to music. **2** particular piece or performance of ballet. □ **balletic** /bə'letɪk/ *adj.* [French: related to BALL[2]]

ballet-dancer *n.* dancer of ballet.

ball game *n.* **1 a** game played with a ball. **b** *US* baseball game. **2** esp. *US colloq.* affair; matter (*a whole new ball game*).

ballista /bə'lɪstə/ *n.* (*pl.* **-stae** /-stiː/) (in ancient warfare) catapult for hurling large stones etc. [Latin from Greek *ballō* throw]

ballistic /bə'lɪstɪk/ *adj.* of projectiles.

ballistic missile *n.* missile that is powered and guided but falls by gravity.

ballistics *n.pl.* (usu. treated as *sing.*) science of projectiles and firearms.

ballocking var. of BOLLOCKING.

ballocks var. of BOLLOCKS.

balloon /bə'luːn/ *–n.* **1** small inflatable rubber toy or decoration. **2** large usu. round inflatable flying bag, often carrying a basket for passengers. **3** *colloq.* balloon shape enclosing dialogue etc. in a comic strip or cartoon. **4** *Finance* large sum repaid as an irregular instalment of a loan repayment. *–v.* **1** (cause to) swell out like a balloon. **2** travel by balloon. □ **balloonist** *n.* [French or Italian, = large ball]

♦ **balloon loan** *n.* loan in which repayments are made, as funds become available, in balloons.

♦ **balloon mortgage** *n.* mortgage in which some of the original principal and some interest is still outstanding at the end of the mortgage agreement period; a lump sum has to be paid to cover the remaining debt.

ballot /'bælət/ *–n.* **1** occasion or system of voting, in writing and usu. secret. **2** total of such votes. **3** paper etc. used in voting. **4** *Finance* random selection of applications for an oversubscribed new issue of shares (see also FLOTATION). The successful applicants may be granted the full number of shares for which they have applied or a specified proportion of their applications. *–v.* (**-t-**) **1** (usu. foll. by *for*) **a** hold a ballot; give a vote. **b** draw lots for precedence etc. **2** take a ballot of (*balloted the members*). [Italian *ballotta*: related to BALLOON]

ballot-box *n.* sealed box for completed ballot-papers.

ballot-paper *n.* = BALLOT *n.* 3.

ballpark *n. US* **1** baseball ground. **2** *colloq.* sphere of activity etc. **3** (*attrib.*) *colloq.* approximate. □ **in the right ballpark** *colloq.* approximately correct.

ball-point *n.* (in full **ball-point pen**) pen with a tiny ball as its writing point.

ballroom *n.* large room for dancing.

ballroom dancing *n.* formal social dancing.

balls-up *n. coarse slang* bungle, mess.

bally /'bælɪ/ *adj.* & *adv. slang* mild form of *bloody* (see BLOODY *adj.* 3). [alteration of BLOODY]

ballyhoo /ˌbælɪ'huː/ *n.* **1** loud noise or fuss. **2** extravagant publicity. [origin unknown]

Ballymena /ˌbælɪ'miːnə/ **1** town in NE Northern Ireland, in Co. Antrim; industries include textiles; pop. (1981) 18 150. **2** district in Northern Ireland, in Co. Antrim; pop. (1990) 57 300.

balm /bɑːm/ *n.* **1** aromatic ointment. **2** fragrant oil or resin exuded from certain trees and plants. **3** thing that heals or soothes. **4** aromatic herb. [Latin: related to BALSAM]

balmy /'bɑːmɪ/ *adj.* (**-ier**, **-iest**) **1** mild and fragrant; soothing. **2** *slang* = BARMY. □ **balmily** *adv.* **balminess** *n.*

baloney var. of BOLONEY.

balsa /'bɔːlsə/ *n.* **1** (in full **balsa-wood**) tough lightweight wood used for making models etc. **2** tropical American tree yielding it. [Spanish, = raft]

balsam /'bɔːlsəm/ *n.* **1** resin exuded from various trees and shrubs. **2** ointment, esp. containing oil or turpentine. **3** tree or shrub yielding balsam. **4** any of several flowering plants. □ **balsamic** /-'sæmɪk/ *adj.* [Latin *balsamum*]

Baltic /'bɔːltɪk/ *–n.* (**the Baltic**) the Baltic Sea. *–adj.* of or relating to the Baltic Sea or Baltic States.

♦ **Baltic Exchange** *n.* former freight-chartering exchange in the City of London. It took its name from the trade in grain with Baltic ports that was the mainstay of its business in the 18th century. Most of its commodity trade, including the **Baltic International Freight Futures Market** (formerly **Exchange**) (**BIFFEX**), has been taken over by the London Commodity Exchange.

Baltic Sea sea in N Europe, connected with the North Sea by a channel and bordered by Sweden, Finland, Latvia, Lithuania, Estonia, Russia, Poland, Germany, and Denmark.

Baltic States the republics of Estonia, Latvia, and Lithuania.

Baltimore /'bɔːltɪˌmɔː(r), 'bɒl-/ seaport in the US, in N Maryland; pop. (est. 1994) 702 979. Its industries include shipbuilding, steel, food processing, oil refining, and chemicals.

Baltistan /ˌbɔːltɪ'stɑːn, ˌbɒl-/ (also **Little Tibet**) region in N Pakistan, in the Himalayas; barley and fruit farming support the local population; chief town, Skardu.

Baluchistan /bəˌluːkɪ'stɑːin/ **1** region of W Asia that includes part of SE Iran, SW Afghanistan, and W Pakistan. **2** province of W Pakistan; industries include craft, textiles and food processing; pop. (est. 1985) 4 908 000; capital, Quetta.

baluster /'bæləstə(r)/ *n.* short post or pillar supporting a rail. [Greek *balaustion* wild-pomegranate flower]

■ **Usage** This word is often confused with *banister*. A baluster is usu. part of a balustrade whereas a banister supports a stair handrail.

balustrade /ˌbælə'streɪd/ *n.* railing supported by balusters, esp. on a balcony etc.

Bamako /'bæməˌkəʊ/ capital of Mali; industries include chemicals and pharmaceuticals; pop. (est. 1995) 800 000.

bamboo /bæm'buː/ *n.* **1** tropical giant woody grass. **2** its stem, used for canes, furniture, etc. [Dutch from Malay]

bamboozle /bæm'buːz(ə)l/ *v.* (**-ling**) *colloq.* cheat; mystify. □ **bamboozlement** *n.* [origin unknown]

♦ **Bamford** /'bæmfəd/, **Joseph Cyril** (1916–) British businessman, former chairman and managing director of J. C. Bamford Excavators Ltd., makers of construction equipment. Bamford founded the company in 1945; it has been run by his son, **Sir Anthony (Paul) Bamford** (1945–), since 1975. The family owns 100% of JCB. In 1991 J. C. Bamford Excavators signed a deal with the Japanese company Sumitomo Construction Machinery. Between 1992 and 1997 sales more than doubled, with over 70% of the total going to the export market; Sir Anthony Bamford was named Top Exporter of the Year in 1995. The trade mark 'JCB' (the firm's initials) has become a generic name for all earth-moving equipment.

Bamian /ˌbæmɪ'ɑːn/ **1** province of central Afghanistan. **2** its capital city; pop. (est. 1984) 8000.

ban *–v.* (**-nn-**) forbid, prohibit, esp. formally. *–n.* formal prohibition (*ban on smoking*). [Old English, = summon]

banal /bə'nɑːl/ *adj.* trite, commonplace. □ **banality** /-'nælɪtɪ/ *n.* (*pl.* **-ies**). **banally** *adv.* [French, related to BAN: originally = compulsory, hence = common]

banana /bə'nɑːnə/ *n.* **1** long curved soft fruit with a yellow skin. **2** treelike plant bearing it. □ **go bananas** *slang* go mad. [Portuguese or Spanish, from an African name]

banana republic *n. derog.* small state, esp. in Central America, dependent on foreign capital.

♦ **bancassurance** /'bæŋkəˌʃʊərəns/ *n.* a combination of traditional loan and savings bank services with such assurance products as life assurance and pensions, which are now provided by many banks.

♦ **Bancogiro** /'bæŋkəʊˌdʒaɪrəʊ/ see GIRO *n.* 1c.

band *–n.* **1** flat, thin strip or loop of paper, metal, cloth, etc., put round something esp. to hold or decorate it. **2** **a** strip of material on a garment. **b** stripe. **3** group of esp. non-classical musicians. **4** organized group of criminals etc. **5** range of frequencies, wavelengths, or values. **6** belt connecting wheels or pulleys. *–v.* **1** (usu. foll. by *together*) unite. **2** put a band on. **3** mark with stripes. [Old Norse (related to BIND) and French]

bandage /'bændɪdʒ/ *–n.* strip of material used to bind a wound etc. *–v.* (**-ging**) bind with a bandage. [French: related to BAND]

bandanna /bæn'dænə/ *n.* large patterned handkerchief or neckerchief. [Portuguese from Hindi]

Bandar Seri Begawan /'bændə ˌseri bə'gɑːwən/ capital of Brunei, a port in the NE of the country; pop. (est. 1991) 46 229.

Banda Sea /'bændə/ sea in E Indonesia, between the central and S Molucca Islands.

b. & b. *abbr.* (also **B & B**) bed and breakfast.

bandbox *n.* hatbox.

B & C *abbr. Insurance* building and contents.

bandeau /ˈbændəʊ/ *n.* (*pl.* **-x** /-dəʊz/) narrow headband. [French]

◆ **banded pack** *n.* special offer of goods in which two or more related (or sometimes unrelated) items are bound together to form a single pack. This pack is offered at a lower price than the combined price of the individual items.

---

banderole /ˌbændəˈrəʊl/ *n.* **1** long narrow flag with a cleft end. **2** ribbon-like inscribed scroll. [Italian: related to BANNER]

bandicoot /ˈbændɪˌkuːt/ *n.* **1** catlike Australian marsupial. **2** (in full **bandicoot rat**) destructive rat in India. [Telugu, = pig-rat]

bandit /ˈbændɪt/ *n.* robber or outlaw, esp. one attacking travellers etc. □ **banditry** *n.* [Italian]

Bandjarmasin see BANJARMASIN.

bandmaster *n.* conductor of a band.

bandog /ˈbændɒg/ *n.* fighting-dog bred for its strength and ferocity. [from BAND, DOG]

bandolier /ˌbændəˈlɪə(r)/ *n.* (also **bandoleer**) shoulder belt with loops or pockets for cartridges. [Dutch or French]

band-saw *n.* mechanical saw with a blade formed by an endless toothed band.

bandsman *n.* player in a band.

bandstand *n.* outdoor platform for musicians.

Bandung /ˈbændʊŋ/ city in Indonesia, capital of the province of West Java; industries include chemicals, plastics, and metal processing; pop. (est. 1990) 1 462 637.

bandwagon *n.* □ **climb** (or **jump) on the bandwagon** join a popular or successful cause etc.

bandwidth *n.* range of frequencies within a given band.

bandy[1] *adj.* (**-ier, -iest**) **1** (of the legs) curved so as to be wide apart at the knees. **2** (also **bandy-legged**) having bandy legs. [perhaps from obsolete *bandy* curved stick]

bandy[2] *v.* (**-ies, -ied**) **1** (often foll. by *about*) **a** pass (a story, rumour, etc.) to and fro. **b** discuss disparagingly (*bandied her name about*). **2** (often foll. by *with*) exchange (blows, insults, etc.). [perhaps from French]

bane *n.* **1** cause of ruin or trouble. **2** *poet.* ruin. **3** *archaic* (except in *comb.*) poison (*ratsbane*). □ **baneful** *adj.* [Old English]

bang *–n.* **1** loud short explosive sound. **2** sharp blow. **3** *coarse slang* act of sexual intercourse. *–v.* **1** strike or shut noisily (*banged the door shut*). **2** (cause to) make a bang. **3** *coarse slang* have sexual intercourse (with). *–adv.* **1** with a bang. **2** *colloq.* exactly (*bang in the middle*). □ **bang on** *colloq.* exactly right. **go bang 1** shut noisily. **2** explode. **3** (as **bang goes** etc.) *colloq.* be suddenly lost (*bang go my chances*). [imitative]

Bangalore /ˌbæŋgəˈlɔː(r)/ city in southern India, capital of the state of Karnataka; industries include aircraft assembly and electronics; pop. (est. 1995) 4 749 000.

banger *n.* **1** *slang* sausage. **2** *slang* noisy old car. **3** firework designed to go bang.

Bangkok /bæŋˈkɒk/ capital and chief port of Thailand, the country's commercial and industrial centre; pop. (est. 1987) 5 609 350.

bangle /ˈbæŋg(ə)l/ *n.* rigid bracelet or anklet. [Hindi *bangri*]

Bangui /ˈbæŋgiː/ capital of the Central African Republic; a port in the SW exporting chiefly cotton and coffee; pop. (1994) 524 000.

banian var. of BANYAN.

banish /ˈbænɪʃ/ *v.* **1** condemn to exile. **2** dismiss (esp. from one's mind). □ **banishment** *n.* [Germanic: related to BAN]

banister /ˈbænɪstə(r)/ *n.* (also **bannister**) (usu. in *pl.*) uprights and handrail beside a staircase. [corruption of BALUSTER]

■ **Usage** See note at *baluster*.

Banjarmasin /ˌbændʒəˈmɑːsɪn, ˌbɑː-/ (also **Bandjarmasin**) port in Indonesia, capital of the province of South Kalimantan; pop. (est. 1990) 381 286.

banjo /ˈbændʒəʊ/ *n.* (*pl.* **-s** or **-es**) guitar-like stringed instrument with a circular body. □ **banjoist** *n.* [US southern corruption of *bandore* from Greek *pandoura* lute]

Banjul /bænˈdʒuːl/ (formerly **Bathurst**) capital of The Gambia, a port in the W of the country; pop. (1993) 42 400.

bank[1] *–n.* **1** sloping ground beside a river. **2** raised area, esp. in the sea; slope. **3** mass of cloud, fog, snow, etc. *–v.* **1** (often foll. by *up*) heap or rise into banks. **2** pack (a fire) tightly for slow burning. **3 a** (of a vehicle, aircraft, etc.) round a curve with one side higher than the other. **b** cause to do this. [Old Norse: related to BENCH]

bank[2] *–n.* **1** commercial institution concerned mainly with making and receiving payments on behalf of its customers, accepting deposits, and making short-term loans to private individuals, companies, and other organizations. In the UK, the banking system comprises the Bank of England (the central bank), the commercial banks, merchant banks, branches of foreign and Commonwealth banks, the TSB Group, the National Savings Bank, and the National Girobank. See also BUILDING SOCIETY. **2** kitty in some gambling games. **3** storage place (*blood bank*). *–v.* **1** deposit (money etc.) in a bank. **2** (often foll. by *at, with*) keep money (at a bank). □ **bank on** *colloq.* rely on (*I'm banking on you*). [French *banque* or Italian *banca*: related to BANK[1]]

bank[3] *n.* row of similar objects, e.g. lights, switches, oars. [French *banc* from Germanic: related to BANK[1]]

bankable *adj.* certain to bring profit.

Bangladesh /ˌbæŋgləˈdeʃ/, **People's Republic of** country in the Indian subcontinent, in the Ganges delta. Bangladesh is the world's chief producer of jute, which is a major export; tea, hides, and fish are also exported. Most industry is nationalized; it includes clothing manufacture (a major export), jute and cotton textiles, chemical fertilizers, and light engineering. The country is one of the poorest in the world and subject to frequent cyclones, which cause immense damage and loss of life and crops.

History. Formerly (as East Pakistan) one of the two geographical units of Pakistan, it became an independent republic in 1971 and a member state of the Commonwealth in 1972. Bangladesh became an Islamic state in 1977. Bangladesh was a one-party state under martial law from 1975–78; President Rahman lifted these restrictions but was assassinated in 1981. Gen. Ershad was elected president in 1986, having come to power in a coup in 1982. Following popular unrest Ershad resigned in 1990. Parliamentary elections were held in 1991. In 1994 the opposition parties resigned and organized rallies and strikes to demand fresh elections. Elections in early 1996 had a very low turnout, and fresh elections were held in June. President, Shahabuddin Ahmed; prime minister, Sheikh Hasina Wajed; capital, Dhaka. □ **Bangladeshi** *adj.* & *n.*

languages	Bengali (official), English
currency	taka (Tk) of 100 paisa
pop. (est. 1996)	123 063 000
GNP (est. 1994)	US$26.6B
literacy	45% (m); 23% (f)
life expectancy	57 (m); 57 (f)

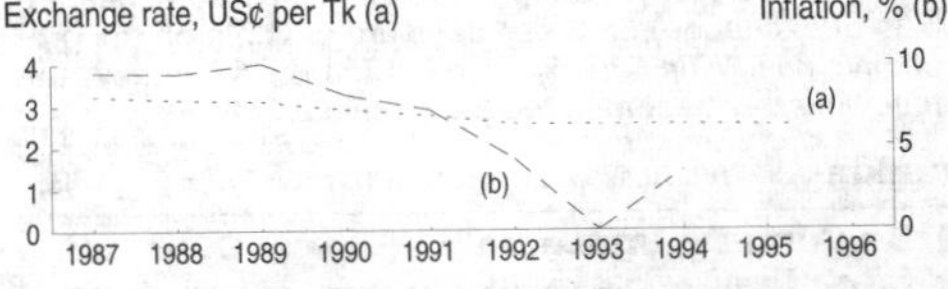

♦ **bank account** see CHEQUE ACCOUNT; CURRENT ACCOUNT 1; DEPOSIT ACCOUNT; SAVINGS ACCOUNT.

♦ **bank advance** *n.* = BANK LOAN.

♦ **bank bill** *n.* bill of exchange issued or guaranteed (accepted) by a bank. It is more acceptable than a trade bill as there is less risk of non-payment and hence it can be discounted at a more favourable rate.

bank card *n.* (also **banker's card**) = CHEQUE CARD.

♦ **bank certificate** *n.* certificate, signed by a bank manager, stating the balance held to a company's credit on a specified date. It may be asked for by a company's auditors if there is any reason for them to doubt the figures given by the company.

♦ **bank charges** *n.pl.* amount charged to a customer's account by a bank, usu. for a specific transaction, e.g. paying in a cheque or withdrawing cash. However, modern practice is to provide periods of commission-free banking by waiving most charges on current accounts.

♦ **bank draft** *n.* (also **banker's cheque**, **banker's draft**) cheque drawn by a bank on itself or its agent. A person who owes money to another buys the draft from a bank for cash and hands it to the creditor who need have no fear that it might be dishonoured. A bank draft is used if the creditor is unwilling to accept an ordinary cheque.

banker *n.* **1** owner or manager of a bank. **2** keeper of the bank in some gambling games.

♦ **banker's cheque** *n.* = BANK DRAFT.

♦ **banker's order** see STANDING ORDER 1.

♦ **banker's reference** *n.* report on the creditworthiness of an individual supplied by a bank to a third party.

♦ **Bank for International Settlements** *n.* (also **BIS**) international bank originally established in 1930 as a financial institution to coordinate the payment of war reparations between European central banks. It was hoped that the BIS, with headquarters in Basle, would develop into a European central bank but many of its functions were taken over by the International Monetary Fund (IMF) after World War II. Since then the BIS has fulfilled several roles, including acting as a trustee and agent for the OECD, European Monetary Agreement, and other international groups. The frequent meetings of the BIS directors have been a useful means of cooperation between central banks, esp. in combating short-term speculative monetary movements. Since 1986 the BIS has acted as a clearing house for interbank transactions in the form of European Currency Units.

♦ **Bank Giro** see GIRO *n.* 1b.

♦ **bank guarantee** *n.* undertaking given by a bank to settle a debt should the debtor fail to do so. A bank guarantee can be used as a security for a loan but the banks themselves will require good cover before they issue a guarantee.

♦ **bank holiday** *n.* public holiday, when banks are officially closed. The UK bank holidays are New Year's Day, Easter Monday, May Day (the first Monday in May), Spring Bank Holiday (the last Monday in May), August Bank Holiday (last Monday in August), and Boxing Day. In Scotland, Easter Monday is replaced by 2 January and the August Bank Holiday is on the first Monday in August. In Northern Ireland St Patrick's Day (17 March) is added. In the Channel Islands Liberation Day (9 May) is included. Bank holidays have a similar status to Sundays in that bills of exchange falling due on a bank holiday are postponed until the following day and also they do not count in working out days of grace. Good Friday and Christmas Day are also public holidays, but payments falling due (including bills of exchange) on these days are payable on the preceding day. When bank holidays fall on a Sunday, the following day becomes the bank holiday.

banking *n.* business of running a bank.

♦ **Banking Ombudsman** *n.* = FINANCIAL OMBUDSMAN 1.

♦ **bank loan** *n.* (also **bank advance**) specified sum of money lent by a bank to a customer, usu. for a specified time, at a specified rate of interest. In most cases banks require some form of security for loans, esp. if the loan is to a commercial enterprise. See also LOAN ACCOUNT; OVERDRAFT 1; PERSONAL LOAN.

♦ **banknote** *n.* item of paper currency issued by a central bank. Banknotes developed in England from the receipts issued by London goldsmiths in the 17th century for gold deposited with them for safe keeping. These receipts came to be used as money and their popularity as a medium of exchange encouraged the goldsmiths to issue their own banknotes, largely to increase their involvement in banking and, particularly, moneylending. Now only the Bank of England and the Scottish and Irish banks in the UK have the right to issue notes. Originally all banknotes were fully backed by gold and could be exchanged on demand for gold; however, since 1931 the promise on a note to 'pay the bearer on demand' simply indicates that the note is legal tender. See also PROMISSORY NOTE.

♦ **Bank of England** *n.* central bank of the UK. It was established in 1694 as a private bank by London merchants in order to lend money to the state and to deal with the national debt. It came under public ownership in 1946 with the passing of the Bank of England Act. The Bank of England acts as the government's bank, providing loans through ways and means advances and arranging borrowing through the issue of gilt-edged securities. The bank helps to implement the government's financial and monetary policy in conjunction with the Treasury and since 1997 has been responsible for setting the level of interest rates. It also has wide statutory powers to supervise the banking system, including the commercial banks to which, through the discount market, it acts as lender of last resort. The Bank Charter Act (1844) divided the bank into an issue department and a banking department. The issue department is responsible for the issue of banknotes and coins as supplied by the Royal Mint. The banking department provides banking services (including accounts) to commercial banks, foreign banks, other central banks, and government departments. The bank manages the national debt, acting as registrar of government stocks. It also administers exchange control, when in force, and manages the exchange equalization account. The bank is controlled by a governor, deputy governor and a court (board) of 16 directors, appointed by the Crown for periods of four to five years.

♦ **bank rate** *n. hist.* rate of interest at which a central bank (in the UK, the Bank of England) lent to the banking system, which in practice meant the rate charged for either rediscounting 'eligible paper' or making loans to the discount market. See BASE RATE; MINIMUM LENDING RATE.

♦ **bank reconciliation statement** *n.* statement, often in a firm's cash-book, showing how the entries in the cash-book can be reconciled with the firm's bank statement. Differences will arise owing to the record in the cash-book of cheques drawn that have not yet passed through the banking system, cheques paid in but not credited, and bank charges, interest payments, and standing orders not yet recorded.

bankrupt /ˈbæŋkrʌpt/ *–adj.* **1** legally declared insolvent. **2** (often foll. by *of*) exhausted or drained (of emotion etc.). *–n.* insolvent person, esp. one whose assets are used to repay creditors. *–v.* make bankrupt. [Italian *banca rotta* broken bench: related to BANK[2]]

♦ **bankruptcy** *n.* (*pl.* **-ies**) state of an individual who is unable to pay his or her debts and against whom a **bankruptcy order** has been made by a court. The order deprives the bankrupt of his or her property, which is then used to pay the debts. Bankruptcy proceedings are started by a petition, which may be presented to the court by a creditor or creditors, a person affected by a voluntary arrangement to pay debts set up by the debtor under the Insolvency Act (1986), the Director of Public Prosecutions, or the debtor. The grounds for a creditors' petition are that the debtor appears to be unable to pay his or her debts or to have reasonable prospects of doing so, i.e. that the debtor has failed to make arrangements to pay a debt for which a statutory demand has been made or that a judgement debt has not been satisifed. The debts must amount to at least £750. The grounds for a petition by a person bound by a voluntary arrangement are that the debtor has not complied with the terms of the arrangement or has withheld material information. The Director of Public Prosecutions may present a petition in the public interest under the Powers of Criminal Courts Act (1973). The debtor may present a petition on the ground of inability to pay the debts. Once a petition has been presented, the debtor may not dispose of any property. The court may halt any other legal proceedings against the debtor. An interim receiver may be appointed. This will usu. be the official receiver, who will take any necessary action to protect the debtor's estate. A special manager may be appointed if the nature of the debtor's business requires it.

The court may make a **bankruptcy order** at its discretion. Once this has happened, the debtor is an undischarged bankrupt. The debtor is deprived of the ownership of all property and must assist the official receiver in listing it, recovering it, protecting it, etc. The official receiver becomes manager and receiver of the estate until the appointment of a **trustee in bankruptcy**. The bankrupt must prepare a statement of affairs for the official receiver within 21 days of the bankruptcy order. A **public examination** of the bankrupt may be ordered on the application of the official receiver or the creditors, in which the bankrupt will be required to answer questions about his or her affairs in court.

Within 12 weeks the official receiver must decide whether to call a **meeting of creditors** to appoint a trustee in bankruptcy. The trustee's duties are to collect, realize, and distribute the bankrupt's estate. The trustee, who may be appointed by the creditors, the court, or the Secretary of State, must be a qualified insolvency practitioner or the official receiver. All the property of the bankrupt is available to pay the creditors, except for the following: necessary equipment in employment or business, necessary domestic equipment, and income required for the reasonable domestic needs of the bankrupt and his or her family. The court has discretion whether to order sale of a house in which a spouse or children are living. All creditors must prove their claims to the trustees. Only unsecured claims can be proved in bankruptcy. When all expenses have been paid, the trustee will divide the estate. The Insolvency Act (1986) sets out the order in which creditors will be paid (see PREFERENTIAL CREDITOR). The bankruptcy may end automatically after two or three years, but in some cases a court order is required. The bankrupt is discharged and receives a certificate of discharge from the court.

♦ **bankruptcy order** see BANKRUPTCY.

---

banksia /'bæŋksɪə/ *n.* Australian evergreen flowering shrub. [*Banks*, name of a naturalist]

♦ **bank statement** *n.* regular record, issued by a bank or building society, showing the credit and debit entries in a customer's cheque account, together with the current balance. The frequency of issue will vary with the customer's needs and the volume of transactions going through the account. Modern cash dispensers (see AUTOMATED TELLER MACHINE) can present the customer with a statement.

---

banner *n.* **1** large sign bearing a slogan or design, esp. in a demonstration or procession; flag. **2** slogan, esp. political. [Latin *bandum* standard]

banner headline *n.* large, esp. front-page, newspaper headline.

bannister var. of BANISTER.

bannock /'bænək/ *n. Scot.* & *N.Engl.* round flat loaf, usu. unleavened. [Old English]

banns *n.pl.* notice announcing an intended marriage, read out in a parish church. [pl. of BAN]

♦ ***banque d'affaires*** *n.* French investment bank, merchant bank, or issuing house. [French]

---

banquet /'bæŋkwɪt/ *–n.* sumptuous, esp. formal, feast or dinner. *–v.* (**-t-**) attend, or entertain with, a banquet; feast. [French diminutive of *banc* bench]

banquette /bæŋ'ket/ *n.* upholstered bench, esp. in a restaurant or bar. [French from Italian]

banshee /'bænʃi:/ *n. Ir.* & *Scot.* wailing female spirit warning of death in a house. [Irish, = woman of the fairies]

bantam /'bæntəm/ *n.* **1** a kind of small domestic fowl. **2** small but aggressive person. [apparently from *Bāntān* in Java]

bantamweight *n.* **1** weight in certain sports between flyweight and featherweight, in amateur boxing 51–54 kg. **2** sportsman of this weight.

banter *–n.* good-humoured teasing. *–v.* **1** tease. **2** exchange banter. [origin unknown]

Bantu /bæn'tu:/ *–n.* (*pl.* same or **-s**) **1** often *offens.* member of a large group of central and southern African Blacks. **2** group of languages spoken by them. *–adj.* of these peoples or languages. [Bantu, = people]

Bantustan /ˌbæntu:'stɑ:n/ *n. S.Afr.* often *offens.* = HOMELAND 2.

banyan /'bænjən/ *n.* (also **banian**) Indian fig tree with self-rooting branches. [Portuguese from Sanskrit, = trader]

baobab /'beɪəʊˌbæb/ *n.* African tree with a massive trunk and large pulpy fruit. [probably African dial.]

bap *n.* soft flattish bread roll. [origin unknown]

b. à p. *abbr.* (French) billets à payer (= bills payable).

baptism /'bæptɪz(ə)m/ *n.* symbolic admission to the Christian Church, with water and usu. name-giving. □ **baptismal** /-'tɪzm(ə)l/ *adj.* [Greek *baptizō* baptize]

baptism of fire *n.* **1** initiation into battle. **2** painful initiation into an activity.

baptist *n.* **1** person who baptizes, esp. John the Baptist. **2** (**Baptist**) Christian advocating baptism by total immersion.

baptistery /'bæptɪstərɪ/ *n.* (*pl.* **-ies**) **1 a** part of a church used for baptism. **b** *hist.* separate building used for baptism. **2** (in a Baptist chapel) receptacle used for immersion.

baptize /bæp'taɪz/ *v.* (also **-ise**) (**-zing** or **-sing**) **1** administer baptism to. **2** give a name or nickname to.

bar[1] *–n.* **1** long piece of rigid material, esp. used to confine or obstruct. **2 a** something of similar form (*bar of soap*; *bar of chocolate*). **b** band of colour or light. **c** heating element of an electric fire. **d** metal strip below the clasp of a medal, awarded as an extra distinction. **e** *Heraldry* narrow horizontal stripe across a shield. **3 a** counter for serving alcohol etc. on. **b** room or building containing it. **c** small shop or stall serving refreshments (*snack bar*). **d** counter for a special service (*heel bar*). **4 a** barrier. **b** restriction (*colour bar*; *bar to promotion*). **5** prisoner's enclosure in a lawcourt. **6** any of the sections into which a piece of music is divided by vertical lines. **7** (**the Bar**) *Law* **a** barristers collectively. **b** profession of barrister. **8** *Business slang* one million. *–v.* (**-rr-**) **1 a** fasten with a bar or bars. **b** (usu. foll. by *in*, *out*) shut or keep in or out. **2** obstruct, prevent. **3** (usu. foll. by *from*) prohibit, exclude. **4** mark with stripes. *–prep.* except. □ **be called to the Bar** be admitted as barrister. **behind bars** in prison. [French]

bar[2] *n.* esp. *Meteorol.* unit of pressure, 10^5 newtons per square metre, approx. one atmosphere. [Greek *baros* weight]

b. à r. *abbr.* (French) billets à recevoir (= bills receivable).

barathea /ˌbærə'θi:ə/ *n.* fine wool cloth. [origin unknown]

BARB *abbr.* Broadcasters Audience Research Board. See AUDIENCE RESEARCH; TELEVISION RATING.

barb *–n.* **1** secondary backward-facing projection from an arrow, fish-hook etc. **2** hurtful remark. **3** fleshy filament at the mouth of some fish. *–v.* **1** fit with a barb. **2** (as

barbed *adj.*) (of a remark etc.) deliberately hurtful. [Latin *barba* beard]

barbarian /bɑːˈbeərɪən/ *–n.* **1** uncultured or brutish person. **2** member of a primitive tribe etc. *–adj.* **1** rough and uncultured. **2** uncivilized. [Greek *barbaros* foreign]

barbaric /bɑːˈbærɪk/ *adj.* **1** uncultured; brutal, cruel. **2** primitive.

barbarism /ˈbɑːbəˌrɪz(ə)m/ *n.* **1** barbaric state or act. **2** non-standard word or expression.

barbarity /bɑːˈbærɪtɪ/ *n.* (*pl.* **-ies**) **1** savage cruelty. **2** brutal act.

barbarous /ˈbɑːbərəs/ *adj.* = BARBARIC 1.

barbecue /ˈbɑːbɪˌkjuː/ *–n.* **1 a** meal cooked over charcoal etc. out of doors. **b** party for this. **2** grill etc. used for this. *–v.* (**-ues**, **-ued**, **-uing**) cook on a barbecue. [Spanish from Haitian]

barbed wire *n.* wire with interwoven sharp spikes, used in fences and barriers.

barbel /ˈbɑːb(ə)l/ *n.* **1** freshwater fish with barbs. **2** = BARB *n.* 3. [Latin: related to BARB]

barbell *n.* iron bar with removable weights at each end, used for weightlifting.

barber *n.* person who cuts men's hair etc. by profession. [medieval Latin *barba* beard]

barberry /ˈbɑːbərɪ/ *n.* (*pl.* **-ies**) **1** shrub with yellow flowers and red berries. **2** its berry. [French *berberis*]

barber-shop *n. colloq.* close harmony singing for four male voices.

barber's pole *n.* pole with spiral red and white stripes as a barber's sign.

barbican /ˈbɑːbɪkən/ *n.* outer defence, esp. a double tower above a gate or drawbridge. [French]

barbie /ˈbɑːbɪ/ *n. Austral. slang* barbecue. [abbreviation]

bar billiards *n.pl.* form of billiards with holes in the table.

barbiturate /bɑːˈbɪtjʊrət/ *n.* soporific or sedative drug from barbituric acid. [German, from the name *Barbara*]

barbituric acid /ˌbɑːbɪˈtjʊərɪk/ *n.* organic acid from which barbiturates are derived.

Barbour /ˈbɑːbə(r)/ *n. propr.* type of green waxed jacket. [*Barbour*, name of a draper]

Barbuda see ANTIGUA AND BARBUDA.

barcarole /ˌbɑːkəˈrəʊl/ *n.* **1** gondoliers' song. **2** music imitating this. [Italian *barca* boat]

Barcelona /bɑːsɪˈləʊnə/ city in NE Spain; locomotives, aircraft, and electrical equipment are manufactured; pop. (est. 1994) 1 630 867.

bar-code *n.* pattern of parallel lines of variable width and spacing that provides coded information about the item on which it appears. The codes are read by relatively simple equipment using optical or magnetic sensing techniques. Bar-codes are found, for example, on goods sold in supermarkets, where they are used to identify the product and its cost at the checkout point and to update stock and sales records. They are also used in library books for identification purposes.

bard *n.* **1** *poet.* poet. **2 a** *hist.* Celtic minstrel. **b** prizewinner at an Eisteddfod. □ **bardic** *adj.* [Celtic]

Bardo /ˈbɑːdəʊ/ (also **Le Bardo**) town in N Tunisia; pop. (1994) 72 700.

bare *–adj.* **1** unclothed or uncovered. **2** leafless; unfurnished; empty. **3** plain, unadorned (*the bare truth*; *bare facts*). **4** (*attrib.*) scanty, just sufficient (*a bare majority*; *bare necessities*). *–v.* (**-ring**) uncover, reveal (*bared his teeth*; *bared his soul*). [Old English]

bareback *adj.* & *adv.* without a saddle.

♦ **bareboat charter** *n.* (also **demise charter**) charter of a ship in which the expenses incurred during the period of the charter are paid by the hirer, including the hiring of the master and crew, the provision of fuel and stores, etc. All the hirer gets is the ship.

---

barefaced *adj.* shameless, impudent.

barefoot *adj.* & *adv.* (also **barefooted** /-ˈfʊtɪd/) wearing nothing on the feet.

bareheaded /beəˈhedɪd/ *adj.* & *adv.* wearing nothing on the head.

barely *adv.* **1** scarcely (*barely escaped*). **2** scantily (*barely furnished*).

bargain /ˈbɑːgɪn/ *–n.* **1 a** agreement on the terms of a sale etc. **b** this from the buyer's viewpoint (*a bad bargain*). **c** transaction on the London Stock Exchange. The bargains made during the day are included in the *Daily Official List*. **2** cheap thing. *–v.* (often foll. by *with*, *for*) discuss the terms of a sale etc. (*bargained with me*; *bargain for the table*). □ **bargain for** (or *colloq.* **on**) be prepared for; expect. **bargain on** rely on. **into the bargain** moreover. [French from Germanic]

♦ **bargaining theory** *n.* theory that analyses economic outcomes between individuals possessing market power. Under conditions of perfect competition no individual has any market power; in most situations of practical interest, however, individuals have some influence over the prices at which they buy and sell. Bargaining theory can be applied to the determination of wages (see BILATERAL MONOPOLY), competition between oligopolists, or even the relationship between the government and the electorate. Modern bargaining theory mainly centres on game theory and focuses on some of the main problems in contemporary economies. See also GAME THEORY; NASH EQUILIBRIUM; PREDATORY PRICING; PRISONERS' DILEMMA; STRATEGIC BEHAVIOUR.

---

barge *–n.* **1** long flat-bottomed cargo boat on a canal or river. **2** long ornamental pleasure boat. *–v.* (**-ging**) **1** (foll. by *in*, *into*) **a** intrude rudely or awkwardly (*barged in on him*). **b** collide with (*barged into her*). **2** (often foll. by *around*) move clumsily about. [French: related to BARQUE]

bargeboard *n.* board fixed to the gable-end of a roof to hide the ends of the roof timbers. [perhaps from medieval Latin *bargus* gallows]

bargee /bɑːˈdʒiː/ *n.* person sailing a barge.

bargepole *n.* □ **would not touch with a bargepole** refuse to be associated or concerned with.

Bari /ˈbɑːrɪ/ seaport in SE Italy, capital of Apulia region; industries include chemicals and oil refining; pop. (1990) 353 032.

Barbados /bɑːˈbeɪdɒs/, island state in the Caribbean, E of the Windward Islands. The economy is based on tourism, sugar, and light manufacturing industries. Exports include sugar and sugar products, petroleum and petroleum products, and electrical goods. Formerly a British colony, it gained independence as a member state of the Commonwealth in 1966. It is a member of CARICOM. Prime minister, Owen Arthur; capital and main port, Bridgetown. □ **Barbadian** *adj.* & *n.*

language	English
currency	dollar (BDS$) of 100 cents
pop. (est. 1996)	265 000
GNP (est. 1994)	US$1.7B
literacy	98% (m); 97% (f)
life expectancy	73 (m); 77 (f)

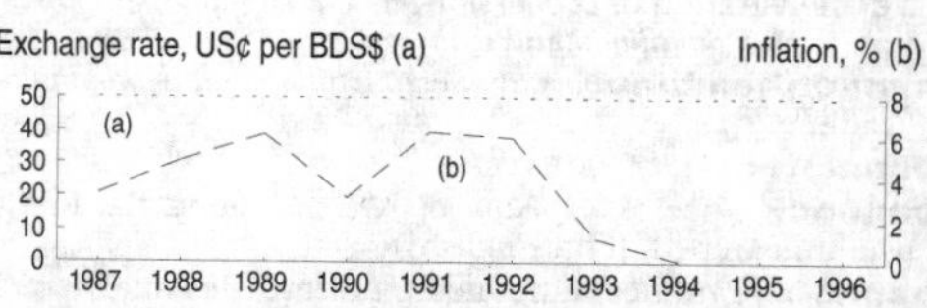

Bariloche see SAN CARLOS DE BARILOCHE.

Barisal /'bʌrɪˌsæl/ port in S Bangladesh; pop. (1991) 188 000.

baritone /'bærɪˌtəʊn/ *n.* **1 a** second-lowest adult male singing voice. **b** singer with this voice. **2** instrument pitched second-lowest in its family. [Greek *barus* heavy, *tonos* tone]

barium /'beərɪəm/ *n.* white soft metallic element. [from BARYTA]

barium meal *n.* mixture swallowed to reveal the abdomen in X-rays.

bark[1] *–n.* **1** sharp explosive cry of a dog, fox, etc. **2** sound like this. *–v.* **1** (of a dog etc.) give a bark. **2** speak or utter sharply or brusquely. **3** *colloq.* cough harshly. □ **bark up the wrong tree** make false assumptions. [Old English]

bark[2] *–n.* tough outer skin of tree-trunks, branches, etc. *–v.* **1** graze (one's shin etc.). **2** strip bark from. [Scandinavian]

barker *n.* tout at an auction, sideshow, etc. [from BARK[1]]

barley /'bɑːlɪ/ *n.* **1** cereal used as food and in spirits. **2** (also **barleycorn**) its grain. [Old English]

barley sugar *n.* sweet made from sugar, usu. in twisted sticks.

barley water *n.* drink made from a boiled barley mixture.

barm *n.* froth on fermenting malt liquor. [Old English]

barmaid *n.* woman serving in a pub etc.

barman *n.* man serving in a pub etc.

bar mitzvah /bɑː 'mɪtsvə/ *n.* **1** religious initiation ceremony of a Jewish boy at 13. **2** boy undergoing this. [Hebrew, = son of the commandment]

barmy /'bɑːmɪ/ *adj.* (**-ier, -iest**) *slang* crazy, stupid. [from BARM: earlier, = frothy]

barn *n.* large farm building for storing grain etc. [Old English, = barley house]

barnacle /'bɑːnək(ə)l/ *n.* **1** marine crustacean clinging to rocks, ships' bottoms, etc. **2** tenacious attendant or follower. [French or medieval Latin]

barnacle goose *n.* Arctic goose.

Barnaul /ˌbɑːnɑː'uːl/ city in S Russia, capital of Altai region; mining, engineering and the timber industry are important; pop. (est. 1995) 596 000.

barn dance *n.* **1** informal gathering for country dancing. **2** a kind of country dance.

barney /'bɑːnɪ/ *n.* (*pl.* **-s**) *colloq.* noisy quarrel. [perhaps dial.]

barn-owl *n.* a kind of owl frequenting barns.

barnstorm *v.* tour rural areas as an actor or political campaigner. □ **barnstormer** *n.*

barnyard *n.* area around a barn.

Baroda see VADODARA.

barograph /'bærəˌgrɑːf/ *n.* barometer equipped to record its readings. [Greek *baros* weight]

barometer /bə'rɒmɪtə(r)/ *n.* **1** instrument measuring atmospheric pressure, used in meteorology. **2** anything which reflects change. □ **barometric** /ˌbærə'metrɪk/ *adj.* [related to BAROGRAPH]

♦ **barometer stock** *n.* security whose price is regarded as an indicator of the state of the market. It will be a widely-held blue chip with a stable price record.

baron /'bærən/ *n.* **1** member of the lowest order of the British or foreign nobility. **2** powerful businessman, entrepreneur, etc. **3** *hist.* person holding lands from the sovereign. □ **baronial** /bə'rəʊnɪəl/ *adj.* [medieval Latin, = man]

baroness /'bærənɪs/ *n.* **1** woman holding the rank of baron. **2** baron's wife or widow.

baronet /'bærənɪt/ *n.* member of the lowest hereditary titled British order. □ **baronetcy** *n.* (*pl.* **-ies**).

baron of beef *n.* double sirloin.

barony /'bærənɪ/ *n.* (*pl.* **-ies**) domain or rank of a baron.

baroque /bə'rɒk/ *–adj.* **1** highly ornate and extravagant in style, esp. of European art etc. of the 17th and 18th centuries. **2** of this period. *–n.* baroque style or art. [Portuguese, originally = misshapen pearl]

bar person *n.* barmaid or barman.

barque /bɑːk/ *n.* **1** sailing-ship with the rear mast fore-and-aft-rigged and other masts square-rigged. **2** *poet.* boat. [Provençal from Latin *barca*]

barrack[1] /'bærək/ *–n.* (usu. in *pl.*, often treated as *sing.*) **1** housing for soldiers. **2** large bleak building. *–v.* lodge (soldiers etc.) in barracks. [Italian or Spanish]

barrack[2] /'bærək/ *v.* **1** shout or jeer at (players, a speaker, etc.). **2** (foll. by *for*) cheer for, encourage (a team etc.). [perhaps from Australian slang *borak* banter]

barracouta /ˌbærə'kuːtə/ *n.* (*pl.* same or **-s**) long slender fish of southern oceans. [var. of BARRACUDA]

barracuda /ˌbærə'kuːdə/ *n.* (*pl.* same or **-s**) large tropical marine fish. [Spanish]

barrage /'bærɑːʒ/ *n.* **1** concentrated artillery bombardment. **2** rapid succession of questions or criticisms. **3** artificial barrier in a river etc. [French *barrer* BAR[1]]

barrage balloon *n.* large anchored balloon used as a defence against low-flying aircraft.

Barranquilla /ˌbærən'kiːjə/ chief port of Colombia; manufactures include textiles, vegetable oils, and chemicals; pop. (est. 1995) 1 064 250.

barratry /'bærətrɪ/ *n.* fraud or gross negligence by a ship's master or crew, e.g. scuttling a ship, embezzling the cargo. Illegal activities (e.g. carrying prohibited persons) leading to the forfeiture of the ship also constitute barratry. Barratry is one of the risks covered by marine insurance policies. [French *barat* deceit]

barre /bɑː(r)/ *n.* horizontal bar at waist level, used in dance exercises. [French]

barré /'bæreɪ/ *n.* method of playing a chord on the guitar etc. with a finger laid across the strings at a particular fret. [French *barrer* bar]

barrel /'bær(ə)l/ *–n.* **1** cylindrical usu. convex container. **2** its contents. **3 a** unit of capacity used in the oil industry equal to 42 US gallons (35 Imperial gallons). **b** unit of capacity used in the brewing industry equal to 36 Imperial gallons. **4** cylindrical tube forming part of an object, e.g. a gun or a pen. *–v.* (**-ll-**; *US* **-l-**) put into a barrel or barrels. □ **over a barrel** *colloq.* helpless, at a person's mercy. [French]

barrel-organ *n.* mechanical musical instrument with a rotating pin-studded cylinder.

barren /'bærən/ *adj.* (**-er, -est**) **1 a** unable to bear young. **b** (of land, a tree, etc.) unproductive. **2** unprofitable, dull. □ **barrenness** *n.* [French]

barricade /ˌbærɪ'keɪd/ *–n.* barrier, esp. improvised. *–v.* (**-ding**) block or defend with this. [French *barrique* cask]

barrier /'bærɪə(r)/ *n.* **1** fence etc. that bars advance or access. **2** obstacle (*class barriers*). [Romanic: related to BAR[1]]

barrier cream *n.* protective skin cream.

barrier reef *n.* coral reef separated from the shore by a channel.

♦ **barriers to entry** *n.pl.* factors that prevent competitors from entering a particular market. These factors may be innocent, e.g. an absolute cost advantage on the part of the firm that dominates the market, or deliberate, such as high spending on advertising to make it very expensive for new firms to enter the market and establish themselves. Barriers to entry reduce the level of competition in a market, enabling incumbents to charge higher-than-competitive prices. See also CONTESTABLE MARKETS THEORY; LIMIT PRICE.

barring /'bɑːrɪŋ/ *prep.* except, not including.

barrister /'bærɪstə(r)/ *n.* advocate entitled to practise in the higher courts. [from BAR[1]: cf. MINISTER]

barrow[1] /'bærəʊ/ *n.* **1** two-wheeled handcart. **2** = WHEELBARROW. [Old English: related to BEAR[1]]

barrow[2] /'bærəʊ/ *n.* ancient grave-mound. [Old English]

BARS *abbr. Management* behaviourally anchored rating scales.

bar sinister *n.* = BEND SINISTER.

bartender *n.* person serving in a pub etc.

barter *–v.* **1** trade in goods or services without using money. **2** exchange (goods). *–n.* trade by bartering. [perhaps from French]

baryon /ˈbærɪˌɒn/ *n.* heavy elementary particle (i.e. a nucleon or a hyperon). [Greek *barus* heavy]

baryta /bəˈraɪtə/ *n.* barium oxide or hydroxide. [from BARYTES]

barytes /bəˈraɪtiːz/ *n.* mineral form of barium sulphate. [Greek *barus* heavy]

basal /ˈbeɪs(ə)l/ *adj.* of, at, or forming a base.

basalt /ˈbæsɔːlt/ *n.* a dark volcanic rock. □ **basaltic** /bəˈsɔːltɪk/ *adj.* [Latin *basaltes* from Greek]

base[1] *–n.* **1 a** part supporting from beneath or serving as a foundation. **b** notional support or foundation (*power base*). **2** principle or starting-point. **3** esp. *Mil.* headquarters. **4** main or important ingredient. **5 a** number in terms of which other numbers or logarithms are expressed. **b** number of distinct digits (and possibly letters) used in a particular number system. Decimal notation has base 10, binary notation has base 2. **6** substance capable of combining with an acid to form a salt. **7** *Baseball* etc. each of the four stations on a pitch. *–v.* **(-sing) 1** (usu. foll. by *on, upon*) found or establish (a theory, hope, etc.). **2** station (*troops based in Malta*). [Greek *basis* stepping]

base[2] *adj.* **1** cowardly, despicable. **2** menial. **3** alloyed (*base coin*). **4** (of a metal) low in value. [Latin *bassus*]

baseball *n.* **1** game played esp. in the US with a circuit of four bases which batsmen must complete. **2** ball used in this.

♦ **base date** *n.* = BASE YEAR.

Basel see BASLE.

baseless *adj.* unfounded, groundless.

baseline *n.* **1** line used as a base or starting-point. **2** line marking each end of a tennis-court.

basement /ˈbeɪsmənt/ *n.* floor of a building below ground level.

♦ **base metals** *n.pl.* copper, lead, zinc, and tin. Cf. PRECIOUS METALS. See also LONDON METAL EXCHANGE.

♦ **base rate** *n.* **1** rate of interest used as a basis by banks for the rates they charge their customers. **2** *colloq.* rate at which the Bank of England lends to the discount houses, which effectively controls the lending rate throughout the banking system. The abolition of the minimum lending rate in 1981 heralded a loosening of government control over the banking system, but the need to increase interest rates in the late 1980s (to control inflation and the balance of payments deficit) led to the use of this term in this sense. Since 1997 the Bank of England has the authority to set the base rate without reference to the Chancellor of the Exchequer.

---

bases *pl.* of BASE[1], BASIS.

♦ **base stock method** *n.* method of accounting for stock movements that assumes a given amount of the stock never moves and therefore retains its original cost. See AVERAGE STOCK METHOD; FIRST IN, FIRST OUT 1; LAST IN, FIRST OUT.

♦ **base year** *n.* (also **base date**) first of a series of years in an index. It is often denoted by the number 100, enabling percentage rises (or falls) to be seen at a glance. For example, if a price index indicates that the current value is 120, this will only be meaningful if it is compared to an earlier figure. This may be written: 120 (base year 1985 = 100), making it clear that there has been a 20% increase in prices since 1985.

---

bash *–v.* **1 a** strike bluntly or heavily. **b** (often foll. by *up*) *colloq.* attack violently. **c** (often foll. by *down, in,* etc.) damage or break by striking forcibly. **2** (foll. by *into*) collide with. *–n.* **1** heavy blow. **2** *slang* attempt. [imitative]

bashful /ˈbæʃfʊl/ *adj.* shy, diffident. □ **bashfully** *adv.* [as ABASHED]

♦ **BASIC** /ˈbeɪsɪk/ *n.* (also **Basic**) simple computer programming language that uses familiar English words in instructions to the computer and allows easy modification of programs. Since its introduction in the mid-1960s many computer manufacturers have developed their own dialects, and the emergence of the microcomputer has increased the diversification to the point where BASIC is now often extremely difficult to move from one computer to another. [*B*eginner's *A*ll-purpose *S*ymbolic *I*nstruction *C*ode]

---

basic /ˈbeɪsɪk/ *–adj.* **1** serving as a base; fundamental. **2 a** simplest or lowest in level (*basic pay, needs*). **b** vulgar (*basic humour*). *–n.* (usu. in *pl.*) fundamental facts or principles. □ **basically** *adv.*

♦ **basic rate** *n.* income-tax rate applied between the lower-rate band and the higher-rate band.

---

basic slag *n.* fertilizer containing phosphates formed as a by-product in steel manufacture.

basil /ˈbæz(ə)l/ *n.* aromatic herb used as flavouring. [Greek *basilikos* royal]

basilica /bəˈzɪlɪkə/ *n.* **1** ancient Roman hall with an apse and colonnades, used as a lawcourt etc. **2** similar building as a Christian church. [Greek *basilikē* (*stoa*) royal (portico)]

Basilicata /bəˌsɪlɪˈkɑːtə/ region of S Italy, lying between the 'heel' of Apulia and the 'toe' of Calabria; pop. (est. 1994) 611 150; capital, Potenza. Agricultural products include wheat and olive oil.

basilisk /ˈbæzɪlɪsk/ *n.* **1** mythical reptile with lethal breath and glance. **2** small American crested lizard. [Greek, diminutive of *basileus* king]

basin /ˈbeɪs(ə)n/ *n.* **1** round open vessel forholding liquids or preparing food in. **2** = WASH-BASIN. **3** hollow depression. **4** sheltered mooring area. **5** round valley. **6** area drained by a river. □ **basinful** *n.* (*pl.* **-s**). [medieval Latin *ba(s)cinus*]

basis /ˈbeɪsɪs/ *n.* (*pl.* **bases** /-siːz/) **1** foundation or support. **2** main principle or ingredient (*on a friendly basis*). **3** starting-point for a discussion etc. [Greek: related to BASE[1]]

bask /bɑːsk/ *v.* **1** relax in warmth and light. **2** (foll. by *in*) revel in (*basking in glory*). [Old Norse: related to BATHE]

basket /ˈbɑːskɪt/ *n.* **1** container made of interwoven cane, reed, wire, etc. **2** amount held by this. **3** the goal in basketball, or a goal scored. **4** *Econ.* group or range (of currencies). [French]

basketball *n.* **1** game in which goals are scored by putting the ball through high nets. **2** ball used in this.

♦ **basket of currencies** *n.* group of selected currencies used to establish a value for some other unit of currency. The European Currency Unit's value is determined by taking a weighted average of a basket of European currencies.

---

basketry *n.* **1** art of weaving cane etc. **2** work so produced.

basket weave *n.* weave like wickerwork.

basketwork *n.* = BASKETRY.

basking shark *n.* large shark which lies near the surface.

Basle /bɑːl/ (German **Basel** /ˈbɑːz(ə)l/) commercial and industrial city in NE Switzerland; pop. (1995) 406 400. It is the focal point of the three-nation Regio Basiliensis, which was set up in 1963 to coordinate the cultural and economic development of the French, German, and Swiss districts in the Upper Rhine Valley. The chemical and pharmaceutical industries are important.

Basque /bæsk/ *–n.* **1** member of a people of the W Pyrenees. **2** their language. *–adj.* of the Basques or their language. [Latin *Vasco*]

Basra /'bæzrə/ oil-port in Iraq, on the Shatt al-Arab waterway; pop. (1987) 406 300.

bas-relief /'bæsrɪˌli:f/ *n.* sculpture or carving with figures projecting slightly from the background. [French and Italian]

bass[1] /beɪs/ *–n.* **1 a** lowest adult male singing voice. **b** singer with this voice. **2** instrument pitched lowest in its family. **3** *colloq.* bass guitar or double-bass. **4** low-frequency output of a radio, record-player etc. *–adj.* **1** lowest in musical pitch. **2** deep-sounding. □ **bassist** *n.* (in sense 3). [from BASE[2] altered after Italian *basso*]

bass[2] /bæs/ *n.* (*pl.* same or **-es**) **1** common perch. **2** other spiny-finned fish of the perch family. [Old English]

bass clef *n.* clef placing F below middle C on the second highest line of the staff.

Bassein /bæ'seɪn/ port in SW Burma, on the Irrawaddy delta; pop. (1983) 144 100.

basset /'bæsɪt/ *n.* (in full **basset-hound**) sturdy hunting-dog with a long body and short legs. [French diminutive of *bas* low]

Basseterre /bæs'teə(r)/ capital of St Kitts and Nevis, a port in St Kitts; industries include data processing; pop. (est. 1990) 15 000.

Basse-Terre /bæs'teə(r)/ **1** main island of Guadeloupe in the West Indies. **2** its capital city and main port; pop. (1995) 18 000.

bass guitar *n.* electric guitar tuned as a double-bass.

bassinet /ˌbæsɪ'net/ *n.* child's wicker cradle, usu. hooded. [French diminutive of *bassin* BASIN]

basso /'bæsəʊ/ *n.* (*pl.* **-s**) singer with a bass voice. [Italian, = BASS[1]]

bassoon /bə'su:n/ *n.* bass instrument of the oboe family. □ **bassoonist** *n.* [Italian: related to BASS[1]]

Bass Strait /bæs/ channel separating the island of Tasmania from the mainland of Australia.

bast /bæst/ *n.* fibre from the inner bark of a tree (esp. the lime). [Old English]

bastard /'bɑ:stəd/ often *offens.* *–n.* **1** person born of an unmarried mother. **2** *slang* **a** unpleasant or despicable person. **b** person of a specified kind (*poor, lucky, bastard*). **3** *slang* difficult or awkward thing. *–attrib. adj.* **1** illegitimate by birth. **2** unauthorized, counterfeit, hybrid. □ **bastardy** *n.* (in sense 1 of *n.*). [French from medieval Latin]

bastardize *v.* (also **-ise**) (**-zing** or **-sing**) **1** corrupt, debase. **2** declare (a person) illegitimate.

baste[1] /beɪst/ *v.* (**-ting**) **1** moisten (meat) with fat etc. during cooking. **2** beat, thrash. [origin unknown]

baste[2] /beɪst/ *v.* (**-ting**) sew with large loose stitches, tack. [French from Germanic]

Bastia /bæ'sti:ə/ chief port and commercial centre of Corsica; pop. (est. 1990) 45 081.

bastinado /ˌbæstɪ'neɪdəʊ/ *–n.* beating with a stick on the soles of the feet. *–v.* (**-es, -ed**) punish in this way. [Spanish *baston* stick]

bastion /'bæstɪən/ *n.* **1** projecting part of a fortification. **2** thing regarded as protecting (*bastion of freedom*). [Italian *bastire* build]

Basutoland /bə'su:təʊˌlænd/ see LESOTHO.

bat[1] *–n.* **1** implement with a handle, used for hitting balls in games. **2** turn with this. **3** batsman. *–v.* (**-tt-**) **1** hit with or as with a bat. **2** take a turn at batting. □ **off one's own bat** unprompted, unaided. [Old English from French]

bat[2] *n.* mouselike nocturnal flying mammal. [Scandinavian]

bat[3] *v.* (**-tt-**) □ **not** (or **never**) **bat an eyelid** *colloq.* show no reaction or emotion. [var. of obsolete *bate* flutter]

Bata /'bɑ:tə/ seaport in Equatorial Guinea; pop. (est. 1986) 17 000.

Batavia /bə'teɪvɪə/ see JAKARTA.

batch *–n.* **1** group of things or persons considered or dealt with together; instalment. **2** loaves produced at one baking. **3** *Computing* group of records processed as one unit. *–v.* arrange or deal with in batches. [related to BAKE]

♦ **batch costing** *n.* method of attributing costs to batches of items being produced rather than individual items. This method is mainly used where it is not appropriate to attribute cost to a single unit of production.

---

batch processing *n.* method of organizing work for a computer in which items of work are put in a **batch queue** and the operating system takes one job at a time from the queue and processes it. Each job must be entirely self-contained, not requiring any intervention from the person who submitted it. The order in which the jobs are run is at the discretion of the operating system, which will take into account the estimated time to run the job and its demands on such resources as main store or tape drives.

Batdambang see BATTAMBANG.

bated /'beɪtɪd/ *adj.* □ **with bated breath** very anxiously. [as ABATE]

bath /bɑ:θ/ *–n.* (*pl.* **-s** /bɑ:ðz/) **1 a** container for sitting in and washing the body. **b** its contents. **2** act of washing in it (*have a bath*). **3** (usu. in *pl.*) public building with baths or a swimming-pool. **4 a** vessel containing liquid for immersing something, e.g. a film for developing. **b** its contents. *–v.* **1** wash (esp. a baby) in a bath. **2** take a bath. [Old English]

Bath bun /bɑ:θ/ *n.* round spiced bun with currants, often iced. [*Bath* in S England]

Bath chair /bɑ:θ/ *n.* wheelchair for invalids.

bath cube *n.* cube of soluble substance for scenting or softening bath-water.

bathe /beɪð/ *–v.* (**-thing**) **1** immerse oneself in water, esp. to swim or wash oneself. **2** immerse in, wash, or treat with liquid. **3** (of sunlight etc.) envelop. *–n.* swim. [Old English]

bathhouse *n.* public building with baths.

bathing-costume *n.* (also **bathing-suit**) garment worn for swimming.

bathos /'beɪθɒs/ *n.* lapse in mood from the sublime to the absurd or trivial; anticlimax. □ **bathetic** /bə'θetɪk/ *adj.* **bathotic** /bə'θɒtɪk/ *adj.* [Greek, = depth]

bathrobe *n.* esp. *US* dressing-gown, esp. of towelling.

bathroom *n.* **1** room with a bath, wash-basin etc. **2** *US* room with a lavatory.

bath salts *n.pl.* soluble powder or crystals for scenting or softening bath-water.

Bathurst /'bæθɜ:st/ see BANJUL.

bathyscaphe /'bæθɪˌskæf/ *n.* manned vessel for deep-sea diving. [Greek *bathus* deep, *skaphos* ship]

bathysphere /'bæθɪˌsfɪə(r)/ *n.* vessel for deep-sea observation. [Greek *bathus* deep, SPHERE]

batik /bə'ti:k/ *n.* **1** method of dyeing textiles by applying wax to parts to be left uncoloured. **2** cloth so treated. [Javanese, = painted]

batiste /bæ'ti:st/ *n.* fine linen or cotton cloth. [French from *Baptiste*, name of the first maker]

batman /'bætmən/ *n.* army officer's servant. [*bat* pack-saddle, from French]

baton /'bæt(ə)n/ *n.* **1** thin stick for conducting an orchestra etc. **2** short stick passed on in a relay race. **3** stick carried by a drum major. **4** staff of office. [French from Latin]

Baton Rouge /ˌbæt(ə) 'ru:ʒ/ city in the US, capital of the state of Louisiana; industries include oil and sugar refining; pop. (1994) 227 482.

baton round *n.* rubber or plastic bullet.

batrachian /bə'treɪkɪən/ *–n.* amphibian that discards its gills and tail, esp. a frog or toad. *–adj.* of batrachians. [Greek *batrakhos* frog]

bats *predic. adj. slang* crazy. [originally pl. of BAT[2]]

batsman *n.* person who bats, esp. in cricket.

battalion /bə'tæljən/ *n.* **1** army unit usu. of 300–1000 men. **2** large group with a common aim. [Italian *battaglia* BATTLE]

Battambang /ˈbætəmˌbæŋ/ (also **Batdambang**) **1** agricultural region of Cambodia. **2** its capital city; pop. (1987) 45 000.

batten[1] /ˈbæt(ə)n/ *–n.* **1 a** long flat strip of squared timber. **b** horizontal strip of wood to which laths, tiles, etc., are fastened. **2** strip for securing tarpaulin over a ship's hatchway. *–v.* strengthen or (often foll. by *down*) fasten with battens. [French: related to BATTER]

batten[2] /ˈbæt(ə)n/ *v.* (foll. by *on*) thrive at the expense of (another). [Old Norse]

Battenberg /ˈbæt(ə)nˌbɜːg/ *n.* oblong sponge cake, usu. of two colours and covered with marzipan. [*Battenberg* in Germany]

batter[1] *v.* **1 a** strike hard and repeatedly. **b** (often foll. by *against, at,* etc.) pound insistently (*batter at the door*). **2** (often in *passive*) **a** subject to long-term violence (*battered baby, wife*). **b** criticize severely. □ **batterer** *n.* [French *battre* beat: related to BATTLE]

batter[2] *n.* mixture of flour, egg, and milk or water, used for pancakes etc. [French: related to BATTER[1]]

battered *adj.* coated in batter and deep-fried.

battering-ram *n. hist.* beam used in breaching fortifications.

battery /ˈbætərɪ/ *n.* (*pl.* **-ies**) **1** usu. portable container of an electrically charged cell or cells as a source of current. **2** (often *attrib.*) series of cages for the intensive breeding and rearing of poultry or cattle. **3** set of similar units of equipment, esp. connected. **4** emplacement for heavy guns. **5** *Law* unlawful physical violence against a person. [Latin: related to BATTLE]

Batticaloa /ˌbætɪkəˈləʊə/ city in E Sri Lanka; pop. (1981) 42 900.

battle /ˈbæt(ə)l/ *–n.* **1** prolonged fight between armed forces. **2** difficult struggle; contest (*battle for supremecy; battle of wits*). *–v.* (**-ling**) engage in battle; fight. □ **half the battle** key to the success of an undertaking. [Latin *battuo* beat]

battleaxe *n.* **1** large axe used in ancient warfare. **2** *colloq.* formidable older woman.

battlebus *n. colloq.* bus used by a politician during an election campaign as a mobile centre of operations.

battle-cruiser *n. hist.* warship of higher speed and lighter armour than a battleship.

battle-cry *n.* cry or slogan used in a battle or contest.

battledore /ˈbæt(ə)lˌdɔː(r)/ *n. hist.* **1** (in full **battledore and shuttlecock**) game played with a shuttlecock and rackets. **2** racket used in this. [perhaps from Provençal *batedor* beater]

battledress *n.* everyday uniform of a soldier.

battlefield *n.* (also **battleground**) scene of a battle.

battlement /ˈbæt(ə)lmənt/ *n.* (usu. in *pl.*) recessed parapet along the top of a wall, as part of a fortification. [French *batailler* fortify]

battle royal *n.* **1** battle of many combatants; free fight. **2** heated argument.

battleship *n.* heavily armoured warship.

batty /ˈbætɪ/ *adj.* (**-ier**, **-iest**) *slang* crazy. [from BAT[2]]

batwing *attrib. adj.* (esp. of a sleeve) shaped like a bat's wing.

bauble /ˈbɔːb(ə)l/ *n.* showy worthless trinket or toy. [French *ba(u)bel* toy]

♦ **baud** *n.* unit that measures the rate at which information is transmitted along a communications link. In normal computer usage, it is equivalent to one bit per second (see BIT[4]). Thus, a 3000 baud communications link between, say, a terminal and a computer sends 3000 bits of information per second.

---

baulk /bɔːlk, bɔːk/ (also **balk**) *–v.* **1** (often foll. by *at*) jib, hesitate. **2 a** thwart, hinder. **b** disappoint. **3** miss, let slip (a chance etc.). *–n.* **1** hindrance; stumbling-block. **2** roughly-squared timber beam. [Old English]

bauxite /ˈbɔːksaɪt/ *n.* claylike mineral, the chief source of aluminium. [French from *Les Baux* in S France]

b. à v. *abbr. Finance* (French) bon à vue (= good at sight).

Bavaria /bəˈveərɪə/ (German **Bayern** /ˈbaɪɜːn/) state (*Land*) of Germany; manufactures include beer, cars, glass, and plastics; pop. (est. 1990) 11 200 000; capital, Munich. □ **Bavarian** *adj.* & *n.*

bawdy /ˈbɔːdɪ/ *–adj.* (**-ier**, **-iest**) humorously indecent. *–n.* such talk or writing. [*bawd* brothel-keeper from French *baudetrot*]

bawdy-house *n.* brothel.

bawl /bɔːl/ *v.* **1** speak or shout noisily. **2** weep loudly. □ **bawl out** *colloq.* reprimand angrily. [imitative]

♦ **Baxter** /ˈbækstə(r)/, **Gordon** (1918–) Scottish businessman, chairman of the Baxter food group. Some 96% of the shares of this up-market food company are owned by the Baxter family, despite many take-over approaches. The business was started in 1877 by Baxter's grandfather as a small grocery shop.

---

bay[1] *n.* broad curving inlet of the sea. [Spanish *bahia*]

bay[2] *n.* **1** laurel with deep green leaves. **2** (in *pl.*) bay wreath, for a victor or poet. [Latin *baca* berry]

bay[3] *n.* **1** recess; alcove in a wall. **2** compartment (*bomb bay*). **3** area specially allocated (*loading bay*). [French *baer* gape]

bay[4] *–adj.* (esp. of a horse) dark reddish-brown. *–n.* bay horse. [Latin *badius*]

bay[5] *–v.* bark or howl loudly and plaintively. *–n.* sound of this, esp. of hounds in close pursuit. □ **at bay** cornered, unable to escape. **keep at bay** hold off (a pursuer). [French *bayer* to bark]

bayberry *n.* (*pl.* **-ies**) fragrant North American tree.

Bayern see BAVARIA.

bay-leaf *n.* leaf of the bay-tree, used for flavouring.

Bay of Plenty region of North Island, New Zealand; pop. (1996) 228 839; chief town, Tauranga.

bayonet /ˈbeɪəˌnet/ *–n.* **1** stabbing blade attachable to the muzzle of a rifle. **2** electrical fitting pushed into a socket and twisted. *–v.* (**-t-**) stab with bayonet. [French, perhaps from *Bayonne* in SW France]

Bayreuth /ˈbaɪrɔɪt, -ˈrɔɪt/ town in Germany, in Bavaria; industries include textiles and machinery; pop. (1991) 72 780.

bay rum *n.* perfume distilled orig. from bayberry leaves in rum.

♦ **Bay Street** *n.* **1** street in Toronto in which the Toronto Stock Exchange is situated. **2** Toronto Stock Exchange itself. **3** financial institutions of Toronto collectively.

---

bay window *n.* window projecting outwards from a wall.

bazaar /bəˈzɑː(r)/ *n.* **1** oriental market. **2** fund-raising sale of goods, esp. for charity. [Persian]

bazooka /bəˈzuːkə/ *n.* anti-tank rocket-launcher. [origin unknown]

BB *–abbr.* **1** bail bond. **2** Blue Book. **3** (also **2B**) double black (pencil lead). *–postcode* Blackburn.

BBA *abbr.* **1** Bachelor of Business Administration. **2** = BRITISH BANKERS ASSOCIATION.

BBC *abbr.* British Broadcasting Corporation.

BBS *abbr.* **1** Bachelor of Business Science (or Studies). **2** *Computing* bulletin board system.

BBV *abbr.* Banco Bilbao Vizcaya (Spanish bank).

BC *–abbr.* **1** Bachelor of Commerce. **2** bank clearing. **3** bankruptcy court. **4** (also **B/C**) bills for collection. **5** British Columbia. *–airline flight code* Brymon Airways.

BC *abbr.* before Christ.

BCA *abbr. NZ* Bachelor of Commerce and Administration.

♦ **BCAP** *abbr.* British Code of Advertising Practice. See ADVERTISING STANDARDS AUTHORITY.

♦ **BCC** *abbr.* = BRITISH COAL CORPORATION.

b.c.c. *abbr.* blind carbon copy.

BCCI *abbr.* Bank of Credit and Commerce International.

BCE *abbr.* Board of Customs and Excise.

BCG *abbr.* **1** Bacillus Calmette-Guérin, an anti-tuberculosis vaccine. **2** Boston Consulting Group, a firm of business consultants.

B.Com. *abbr.* (also **B.Comm.**) Bachelor of Commerce.

B.Com.Sc. *abbr.* Bachelor of Commercial Science.

BCPIT *abbr.* British Council for the Promotion of International Trade.

BCS *abbr.* **1** Bachelor of Commercial Science. **2** British Computer Society.

BD *–abbr.* **1** *Commerce* bill(s) discounted. **2** Bachelor of Divinity. *–symb.* Bahrain dinar. *–international vehicle registration* Bangladesh. *–postcode* Bradford. *–airline flight code* British Midland.

B/D *abbr.* **1** bank draft. **2** *Commerce* bill(s) discounted. **3** *Bookkeeping* brought down.

Bd *symb.* baud.

b.d. *abbr. Commerce* bill(s) discounted.

bdellium /ˈdelɪəm/ *n.* **1** tree yielding resin. **2** this used in perfumes. [Latin from Greek]

BDI *abbr.* (German) Bundesverband der Deutschen Industrie (= Federal Association of German Industry).

BDS *international vehicle registration* Barbados.

BE *abbr.* **1** Bachelor of Economics. **2** Bank of England. **3** bill of exchange.

B/E *abbr.* **1** bill of entry. **2** bill of exchange.

Be *symb.* beryllium.

be /biː, bɪ/ *v.* (*sing. present* **am**; **are** /ɑː(r)/; **is** /ɪz/; *past* **was** /wɒz/; **were** /wɜː(r)/; *pres. part.* **being**; *past part.* **been**) **1** exist, live (*I think, therefore I am*; *there is no God*). **2 a** occur; take place (*dinner is at eight*). **b** occupy a position (*he is in the garden*). **3** remain, continue (*let it be*). **4** linking subject and predicate, expressing: **a** identity (*she is the person*). **b** condition (*he is ill today*). **c** state or quality (*he is kind*; *they are my friends*). **d** opinion (*I am against hanging*). **e** total (*two and two are four*). **f** cost or significance (*it is £5 to enter*; *it is nothing to me*). **5** *v.aux.* **a** with a past participle to form the passive (*it was done*; *it is said*). **b** with a present participle to form continuous tenses (*we are coming*; *it is being cleaned*). **c** with an infinitive to express duty or commitment, intention, possibility, destiny, or hypothesis (*I am to tell you*; *we are to wait here*; *he is to come at four*; *it was not to be found*; *they were never to meet again*; *if I were to die*). □ **be at** occupy oneself with (*what is he at?*; *mice have been at the food*). **be off** *colloq.* go away; leave. **-to-be** of the future (in *comb.*: *bride-to-be*). [Old English]

b.e. *abbr.* bill of exchange.

be- *prefix* forming verbs: **1** (from transitive verbs) **a** all over; all round (*beset*). **b** thoroughly, excessively (*begrudge*). **2** (from intransitive verbs) expressing transitive action (*bemoan*; *bestride*). **3** (from adjectives and nouns) expressing transitive action (*becalm*). **4** (from nouns) **a** affect with (*befog*). **b** treat as (*befriend*). **c** (forming adjectives in *-ed*) having (*bejewelled*). [Old English, = BY]

BEA *abbr. hist.* British European Airways.

beach *–n.* pebbly or sandy shore esp. of the sea. *–v.* run or haul (a boat etc.) on to a beach. [origin unknown]

beachcomber *n.* person who searches beaches for articles of value.

beachhead *n.* fortified position set up on a beach by landing forces.

beacon /ˈbiːkən/ *n.* **1** fire or light set up high as a warning etc. **2** visible warning or guiding device (e.g. a lighthouse, navigation buoy, etc.). **3** radio transmitter whose signal helps fix the position of a ship or aircraft. **4** = BELISHA BEACON. [Old English]

bead *–n.* **1 a** small usu. rounded piece of glass, stone, etc., for threading to make necklaces etc., or sewing on to fabric, etc. **b** (in *pl.*) bead necklace; rosary. **2** drop of liquid. **3** small knob in the foresight of a gun. **4** inner edge of a pneumatic tyre gripping the rim of the wheel. *–v.* adorn with or as with beads. □ **draw a bead on** take aim at. [Old English, = prayer]

beading *n.* **1** moulding or carving like a series of beads. **2** bead of a tyre.

beadle /ˈbiːd(ə)l/ *n.* **1** ceremonial officer of a church, college, etc. **2** *Scot.* church officer serving the minister. **3** *hist.* minor parish disciplinary officer. [French from Germanic]

beady *adj.* (**-ier, -iest**) (esp. of the eyes) small, round, and bright.

beady-eyed *adj.* **1** with beady eyes. **2** observant.

beagle /ˈbiːg(ə)l/ *n.* small short-haired hound used for hunting hares. [French]

beak[1] *n.* **1 a** bird's horny projecting jaws. **b** similar jaw of a turtle etc. **2** *slang* hooked nose. **3** *hist.* pointed prow of a warship. **4** spout. [French from Celtic]

beak[2] *n. slang* **1** magistrate. **2** schoolmaster. [probably thieves' cant]

beaker *n.* **1** tall cup or tumbler. **2** lipped glass vessel for scientific experiments. [Old Norse]

be-all and end-all *n. colloq.* (often foll. by *of*) whole being, essence.

beam *–n.* **1** long sturdy piece of squared timber or metal used in house-building etc. **2** ray or shaft of light or radiation. **3** bright look or smile. **4** series of radio or radar signals as a guide to a ship or aircraft. **5** crossbar of a balance. **6 a** ship's breadth. **b** width of a person's hips. **7** (in *pl.*) horizontal cross-timbers of a ship. *–v.* **1** emit or direct (light, approval, etc.). **2 a** shine. **b** look or smile radiantly. □ **off** (or **off the**) **beam** *colloq.* mistaken. **on the beam** *colloq.* on the right track. [Old English, = tree]

bean *n.* **1 a** climber with edible seeds in long pods. **b** seed or pod of this. **2** similar seed of coffee etc. □ **full of beans** *colloq.* lively, exuberant. **not a bean** *slang* no money. [Old English]

beanbag *n.* **1** small bag filled with dried beans and used as a ball. **2** large bag filled usu. with polystyrene pieces and used as a chair.

beanfeast *n.* **1** *colloq.* celebration. **2** workers' annual dinner.

beano /ˈbiːnəʊ/ *n.* (*pl.* **-s**) *slang* celebration, party.

beanpole *n.* **1** support for bean plants. **2** *colloq.* tall thin person.

bean sprout *n.* sprout of a bean seed as food.

beanstalk *n.* stem of a bean plant.

bear[1] /beə(r)/ *v.* (*past* **bore**; *past part.* **borne** or **born**) **1** carry, bring, or take (esp. visibly) (*bear gifts*). **2** show; have, esp. characteristically (*bear marks of violence*; *bears no relation to the case*; *bore no name*). **3 a** produce, yield (fruit etc.). **b** give birth to (*has borne a son*; *was born last week*). **4 a** sustain (a weight, responsibility, cost, etc.). **b** endure (an ordeal, difficulty, etc.). **5** (usu. with *neg.* or *interrog.*) **a** tolerate (*can't bear him*). **b** admit of (*does not bear thinking about*). **6** carry mentally (*bear a grudge*). **7** veer in a given direction (*bear left*). **8** bring or provide (something needed) (*bear him company*). □ **bear down** press downwards. **bear down on** approach inexorably. **bear on** (or **upon**) be relevant to. **bear out** support or confirm as evidence. **bear up** not despair. **bear with** tolerate patiently. **bear witness** testify. [Old English]

bear[2] /beə(r)/ *n.* **1** any of several large heavy mammals with thick fur. **2** rough or uncouth person. **3** dealer on a stock exchange, currency market, or commodity market who expects prices to fall. A **bear market** is one in which a dealer is more likely to sell securities, currency, or goods than to buy them. Securities, currency, or goods that the bear does not have may even be sold. This is known as selling short or establishing a **bear position**. The bear hopes to close (or cover) this short position by buying in at a lower price the securities, currency, or goods that the bear has contracted to deliver. The difference between the purchase price and the original sale price represents the successful bear's profit. A concerted attempt to force prices down by one or more bears by sustained selling is called a **bear raid**. In a **bear squeeze**, sellers force prices up against someone known to have a bear position that has to be covered. See also COVERED BEAR. Cf. BULL[1] 4. □ **bearish** *adj.* □ **the Great Bear, the Little Bear** constellations near the North Pole. [Old English]

bearable *adj.* endurable.

beard –*n.* **1** facial hair on the chin etc. **2** similar tuft etc. on an animal. –*v.* oppose; defy. □ **bearded** *adj.* **beardless** *adj.* [Old English]

bearer *n.* **1** person or thing that bears, carries, or brings. **2** person who presents a cheque or bill of exchange marked 'pay bearer'. As a bearer cheque or bill does not require endorsement it is considered a high-risk form of transfer.

♦ **bearer security** *n.* (also **bearer bond**) security for which proof of ownership is possession of the security certificate; this enables such bonds to be transferred from one person to another without registration. This is unusual as most securities are registered, so that proof of ownership is the presence of the owner's name on the security register. Eurobonds are bearer securities, enabling their owners to preserve their anonymity, which can have taxation advantages. Bearer bonds are usu. kept under lock and key, often deposited in a bank. Dividends are usu. claimed by submitting coupons attached to the certificate.

---

beargarden *n.* rowdy scene.

♦ **bear-hug** *n.* **1** tight embrace. **2** approach to the board of a company by another company indicating that an offer is about to be made for their shares. If the target company indicates that it is not against the merger, but wants a higher price, this is known as a **teddy-bear hug**.

---

bearing *n.* **1** bodily attitude; general manner. **2** (foll. by *on, upon*) relevance to (*has no bearing on it*). **3** endurability (*beyond bearing*). **4** part of a machine supporting a rotating part. **5 a** direction or position relative to a fixed point. **b** (in *pl.*) knowledge of one's relative position. **6** *Heraldry* device or charge.

Béarnaise sauce /ˌbeɪəˈneɪz/ *n.* rich thick sauce with egg-yolks. [French]

♦ **bear market** see BEAR[2] 3.

♦ **bear note** see BULL NOTE.

♦ **bear position, bear raid, bear squeeze** see BEAR[2] 3.

---

bearskin *n.* **1** skin of a bear, esp. as a wrap etc. **2** tall furry hat worn by some regiments.

beast *n.* **1** animal, esp. a wild mammal. **2 a** brutal person. **b** *colloq.* objectionable person or thing. **3** (prec. by *the*) the animal nature in man. [Latin *bestia*]

beastly –*adj.* (**-ier, -iest**) **1** *colloq.* objectionable, unpleasant. **2** like a beast; brutal. –*adv. colloq.* very, extremely.

beast of prey *n.* animal which hunts animals for food.

beat –*v.* (*past* **beat**; *past part.* **beaten**) **1 a** strike persistently and violently. **b** strike (a carpet, drum, etc.) repeatedly. **2** (foll. by *against, at, on*, etc.) pound or knock repeatedly. **3 a** overcome; surpass. **b** be too hard for; perplex. **4** (often foll. by *up*) whisk (eggs etc.) vigorously. **5** (often foll. by *out*) shape (metal etc.) by blows. **6** (of the heart etc.) pulsate rhythmically. **7** (often foll. by *out*) **a** indicate (a tempo etc.) by tapping etc. **b** sound (a signal etc.) by striking a drum etc. (*beat a tattoo*). **8** move or cause (wings) to move up and down. **9** make (a path etc.) by trampling. **10** strike (bushes etc.) to rouse game. –*n.* **1 a** main accent in music or verse. **b** rhythm indicated by a conductor (*watch the beat*). **c** (in popular music) strong rhythm. **2 a** stroke or blow or measured sequence of strokes. **b** throbbing movement or sound. **3 a** police officer's route or area. **b** person's habitual round. –*predic. adj. slang* exhausted, tired out. □ **beat about the bush** not come to the point. **beat the bounds** mark parish boundaries by striking certain points with rods. **beat down 1** cause (a seller) to lower the price by bargaining. **2** strike to the ground (*beat the door down*). **3** (of the sun, rain, etc.) shine or fall relentlessly. **beat it** *slang* go away. **beat off** drive back (an attack etc.). **beat a person to it** arrive or do something before another person. **beat up** beat, esp. with punches and kicks. □ **beatable** *adj.* [Old English]

beater *n.* **1** implement for beating (esp. eggs). **2** person who rouses game at a shoot.

beatific /ˌbiːəˈtɪfɪk/ *adj.* **1** *colloq.* blissful (*beatific smile*). **2** making blessed. [Latin *beatus* blessed]

beatify /biːˈætɪˌfaɪ/ *v.* (**-ies, -ied**) **1** *RC Ch.* declare (a person) to be 'blessed', often as a step towards canonization. **2** make happy. □ **beatification** /-fɪˈkeɪʃ(ə)n/ *n.*

beatitude /biːˈætɪˌtjuːd/ *n.* **1** perfect bliss or happiness. **2** (in *pl.*) blessings in Matt. 5:3-11.

beatnik /ˈbiːtnɪk/ *n.* member of a movement of socially unconventional young people in the 1950s.

beat-up *adj. colloq.* dilapidated.

beau /bəʊ/ *n.* (*pl.* **-x** /bəʊz/) **1** esp. *US* admirer; boyfriend. **2** fop; dandy. [Latin *bellus* pretty]

Beaufort scale /ˈbəʊfət/ *n.* scale of wind speed ranging from 0 (calm) to 12 (hurricane). [Sir F. *Beaufort*, name of an admiral]

Beaufort Sea part of the Arctic Ocean lying to the N of Alaska and Canada.

Beaujolais /ˈbəʊʒəˌleɪ/ *n.* red or white wine from the Beaujolais district of France.

Beaujolais Nouveau /nuːˈvəʊ/ *n.* Beaujolais wine sold in the first year of a vintage.

beauteous /ˈbjuːtɪəs/ *adj. poet.* beautiful.

beautician /bjuːˈtɪʃ(ə)n/ *n.* specialist in beauty treatment.

beautiful /ˈbjuːtɪˌfʊl/ *adj.* **1** having beauty, pleasing to the eye, ear, or mind etc. (*beautiful voice*). **2** pleasant, enjoyable (*had a beautiful time*). **3** excellent (*beautiful specimen*). □ **beautifully** *adv.*

beautify /ˈbjuːtɪˌfaɪ/ *v.* (**-ies, -ied**) make beautiful; adorn. □ **beautification** /-fɪˈkeɪʃ(ə)n/ *n.*

beauty /ˈbjuːtɪ/ *n.* (*pl.* **-ies**) **1** combination of shape, colour, sound, etc., that pleases the senses. **2** *colloq.* **a** excellent specimen (*what a beauty!*). **b** attractive feature; advantage (*that's the beauty of it!*). **3** beautiful woman. [Latin *bellus* pretty]

beauty parlour *n.* (also **beauty salon**) establishment for cosmetic treatment.

beauty queen *n.* woman judged most beautiful in a contest.

beauty spot *n.* **1** place of scenic beauty. **2** small facial mark considered to enhance the appearance.

beaux *pl.* of BEAU.

beaver[1] –*n.* **1 a** amphibious broad-tailed rodent which cuts down trees with its teeth and dams rivers. **b** its fur. **c** hat of this. **2** (**Beaver**) boy aged six or seven affiliated to the Scouts. –*v. colloq.* (usu. foll. by *away*) work hard. [Old English]

beaver[2] *n. hist.* lower face-guard of a helmet. [French, = bib]

beaver lamb *n.* lamb's wool made to look like beaver fur.

bebop /ˈbiːbɒp/ *n.* type of 1940s jazz with complex harmony and rhythms. [imitative]

B.Ec. *abbr.* Bachelor of Economics.

becalm /bɪˈkɑːm/ *v.* (usu. in *passive*) deprive (a ship) of wind.

became *past* of BECOME.

because /bɪˈkɒz/ *conj.* for the reason that; since. □ **because of** on account of; by reason of. [from BY, CAUSE]

béchamel /ˈbeʃəˌmel/ *n.* a kind of thick white sauce. [Marquis de *Béchamel*, name of a courtier]

♦ **Bechtel** /ˈbektel/, **Stephen Davidson** (1900–89) US construction engineer and businessman, president (1935–60), chairman (1960–65), and a senior director (1965–89) of Bechtel Group (formerly Bechtel Corporation). Taking over the family business two years after his father's death, he transformed it from a regional builder of roads, railways, pipelines, and dams into one of the world's most successful construction companies. Diversifying into power plants and oil refineries, Bechtel built the first commercial nuclear power plant and established his company as a leading contractor in the Middle East. His son, **Stephen Davidson Bechtel Jr.** (1925–), succeeded him as president (1960–65), chairman (1965–90), and chairman emeritus (from 1990). The company, now run by Bechtel Jr.'s. son, **Riley P. Bechtel**, has recently been involved in the construction of the Channel Tunnel rail link and Hong Kong's new airport. The family's net worth was $3 billion in 1997.

Bechuanaland /ˌbetʃʊˈɑːnəˌlænd/ see BOTSWANA.

beck[1] *n. N.Engl.* brook; mountain stream. [Old Norse]

beck[2] *n.* □ **at a person's beck and call** subject to a person's constant orders. [from BECKON]

beckon /ˈbekən/ *v.* **1** (often foll. by *to*) summon by gesture. **2** entice. [Old English]

become /bɪˈkʌm/ *v.* (**-ming**; *past* **became**; *past part.* **become**) **1** begin to be (*became king, famous*). **2** (often as **becoming** *adj.*) **a** look well on; suit (*blue becomes him*). **b** befit (*it ill becomes you to complain*; *becoming modesty*). □ **become of** happen to (*what became of her?*). [Old English: related to BE-]

B.Econ. *abbr.* Bachelor of Economics.

becquerel /ˈbekəˌrel/ *n.* SI unit of radioactivity. [*Becquerel*, name of a physicist]

B.Ed. *abbr.* Bachelor of Education.

bed *–n.* **1** piece of furniture for sleeping on. **2** any place used for sleep or rest. **3** garden plot, esp. for flowers. **4 a** bottom of the sea, a river, etc. **b** foundations of a road or railway. **5** stratum, layer. *–v.* (**-dd-**) **1** (usu. foll. by *down*) put or go to bed. **2** *colloq.* have sexual intercourse with. **3** (usu. foll. by *out*) plant in a garden bed. **4** cover up or fix firmly. **5** arrange as a layer. □ **bed of roses** life of ease. **go to bed 1** retire to sleep. **2** (often foll. by *with*) have sexual intercourse. [Old English]

bed and board *n.* lodging and food.

♦ **bed and breakfast** *n.* **1** room and breakfast in a hotel etc. **2** establishment providing this. **3** operation on the London Stock Exchange in which a shareholder sells a holding one evening and makes an agreement with the broker to buy the same holding back again when the market opens the next morning. The object is to establish a loss, which can be set against other profits for calculating capital-gains tax. In the event of an unexpected change in the market, the deal is scrapped. In the 1998 budget this practice was scrapped.

♦ **bed and PEP** *n.* operation on the London Stock Exchange that complies with regulations for self-select PEPs in which a shareholding is sold in the evening and bought back the next morning for the shareholder's own PEP. See also PERSONAL EQUITY PLAN.

---

bedaub /bɪˈdɔːb/ *v.* smear or daub.

bedazzle /bɪˈdæz(ə)l/ *v.* (**-ling**) **1** dazzle. **2** confuse.

bedbug *n.* wingless parasite infesting beds etc.

bedclothes *n.pl.* sheets, blankets, etc., for a bed.

bedding *n.* **1** mattress and bedclothes. **2** litter for animals. **3** geological strata.

bedding plant *n.* plant suitable for a garden bed.

bedeck /bɪˈdek/ *v.* adorn.

bedevil /bɪˈdev(ə)l/ *v.* (**-ll-**; *US* **-l-**) **1** trouble, vex. **2** confound, confuse. **3** torment, abuse. □ **bedevilment** *n.*

bedew /bɪˈdjuː/ *v.* cover or sprinkle (as) with dew.

bedfellow *n.* **1** person who shares a bed. **2** associate.

Bedfordshire /ˈbedfədˌʃɪə(r)/ county in SE England; pop. (est. 1994) 543 100; county town, Bedford. Electrical goods are manufactured and agriculture is important.

bedizen /bɪˈdaɪz(ə)n/ *v. poet.* deck out gaudily. [from BE-, obsolete *dizen* deck out]

bedjacket *n.* jacket worn when sitting up in bed.

bedlam /ˈbedləm/ *n.* uproar and confusion. [St Mary of *Bethlehem*, name of a hospital in London]

bedlinen *n.* sheets and pillowcases.

Bedlington terrier /ˈbedlɪŋt(ə)n/ *n.* terrier with a narrow head, long legs, and curly grey hair. [*Bedlington* in Northumberland]

Bedouin /ˈbedʊɪn/ *n.* (also **Beduin**) (*pl.* same) **1** nomadic desert Arab. **2** wandering person. [Arabic, = dwellers in the desert]

bedpan *n.* portable toilet for use in bed.

bedpost *n.* each of four upright supports of a bed.

bedraggled /bɪˈdræg(ə)ld/ *adj.* dishevelled, untidy.

bedrest *n.* recuperation in bed.

bedridden *adj.* confined to bed by infirmity.

bedrock *n.* **1** solid rock underlying alluvial deposits etc. **2** basic principles.

bedroom *n.* room for sleeping in.

Beds. *abbr.* Bedfordshire.

bedside *n.* space beside esp. a patient's bed. □ **bedside manner** (esp. doctor's) way with patients.

bedsit *n.* (also **bedsitter, bedsitting room**) combined bedroom and sitting-room with cooking facilities.

bedsock *n.* warm sock worn in bed.

bedsore *n.* sore developed by lying in bed.

bedspread *n.* cover for a bed.

bedstead *n.* framework of a bed.

bedstraw *n.* small herbaceous plant.

bedtime *n.* (often *attrib.*) usual time for going to bed (*bedtime drink*).

Beduin var. of BEDOUIN.

bedwetting *n.* involuntary urination when asleep in bed.

bee *n.* **1** four-winged stinging insect, collecting nectar and pollen and producing wax and honey. **2** (usu. **busy bee**) busy person. **3** esp. *US* meeting for work or amusement. □ **a bee in one's bonnet** obsession. [Old English]

Beeb *n.* (prec. by *the*) *colloq.* BBC. [abbreviation]

beech *n.* **1** large smooth grey tree with glossy leaves. **2** its hard wood. [Old English]

beechmast *n.* (*pl.* same) fruit of the beech.

beef *–n.* **1** flesh of the ox, bull, or cow for eating. **2** *colloq.* male muscle. **3** (*pl.* **beeves** or *US* **-s**) ox etc. bred for beef. **4** (*pl.* **-s**) *slang* complaint. *–v. slang* complain. □ **beef up** *slang* strengthen, reinforce. [Latin *bos bovis* ox]

beefburger *n.* = HAMBURGER.

beefcake *n.* esp. *US slang* male muscle.

beefeater *n.* **1** warder at the Tower of London. **2** Yeoman of the Guard.

beefsteak *n.* thick slice of beef for grilling or frying.

beef tea *n.* stewed beef extract for invalids.

beef tomato *n.* large tomato.

beefy *adj.* (**-ier, -iest**) **1** like beef. **2** solid, muscular. □ **beefiness** *n.*

beehive *n.* **1** artificial shelter for a colony of bees. **2** busy place.

bee-keeper *n.* keeper of bees. □ **bee-keeping** *n.*

beeline *n.* □ **make a beeline for** go directly to.

Beelzebub /biːˈelzɪˌbʌb/ *n.* the Devil. [Hebrew, = lord of the flies]

been *past part.* of BE.

beep *–n.* sound of a (esp. motor-car) horn. *–v.* emit a beep. [imitative]

beer *n.* **1** alcoholic drink made from fermented malt etc., flavoured with hops. **2** glass of this. □ **beer and skittles** amusement. [Old English]

beer-cellar *n.* cellar for storing, or selling and drinking, beer.

beer garden *n.* (also **beer hall**) garden (or large room) where beer is sold and drunk.

beer-mat *n.* small mat for a beer-glass.

Beersheba /bɪəˈʃiːbə/ town in S Israel; chemicals and glass are produced; pop. (est. 1996) 152 600.

beery *adj.* (**-ier, -iest**) **1** affected by beer-drinking. **2** like beer.

beeswax *–n.* **1** wax secreted by bees to make honeycombs. **2** this used to polish wood. *–v.* polish with beeswax.

beeswing *n.* filmy second crust on old port.

beet *n.* plant with an edible root (see BEETROOT, SUGAR BEET). [Old English]

beetle[1] /'biːt(ə)l/ *–n.* insect, esp. black, with hard protective outer wings. *–v.* (**-ling**) *colloq.* (foll. by *about, off, etc.*) hurry, scurry. [Old English: related to BITE]

beetle[2] /'biːt(ə)l/ *–adj.* projecting, shaggy, scowling (*beetle brows*). *–v.* (usu. as **beetling** *adj.*) (of brows, cliffs, etc.) project, overhang. [origin unknown]

beetle[3] /'biːt(ə)l/ *n.* heavy tool for ramming, crushing, etc. [Old English: related to BEAT]

beetle-browed *adj.* with shaggy, projecting, or scowling eyebrows.

beetroot *n.* beet with an edible dark-red root.

beeves *pl.* of BEEF 3.

befall /bɪ'fɔːl/ *v.* (*past* **befell**; *past part.* **befallen**) *poet.* happen; happen to. [Old English: related to BE-]

befit /bɪ'fɪt/ *v.* (**-tt-**) be appropriate for; be incumbent on.

befog /bɪ'fɒg/ *v.* (**-gg-**) **1** confuse, obscure. **2** envelop in fog.

before /bɪ'fɔː(r)/ *–conj.* **1** earlier than the time when (*see me before you go*). **2** rather than that (*would die before he stole*). *–prep.* **1** earlier than (*before noon*). **2 a** in front of, ahead of (*before her in the queue*). **b** in the face of (*recoil before the attack*). **c** awaiting (*the future before them*). **3** rather than (*death before dishonour*). **4 a** in the presence of (*appear before the judge*). **b** for the attention of (*put before the committee*). *–adv.* **1** previously; already (*happened long before; done it before*). **2** ahead (*go before*). **3** on the front (*hit before and behind*). [Old English: related to BY, FORE]

Before Christ *adv.* (of a date) reckoned backwards from the birth of Christ.

beforehand *adv.* in advance, in readiness.

befriend /bɪ'frend/ *v.* act as a friend to; help.

befuddle /bɪ'fʌd(ə)l/ *v.* (**-ling**) **1** make drunk. **2** confuse.

beg *v.* (**-gg-**) **1 a** (usu. foll. by *for*) ask for (food, money, etc.). **b** live by begging. **2** ask earnestly, humbly, or formally (for) (*begged for mercy; beg your indulgence; beg leave*). **3** (of a dog etc.) sit up with the front paws raised expectantly. **4** (foll. by *to* + infin.) take leave (*I beg to differ*). □ **beg off 1** ask to be excused from something. **2** get (a person) excused a penalty etc. **beg pardon** see PARDON. **beg the question** assume the truth of a proposition needing proof. **go begging** be unwanted or refused. [related to BID]

■ **Usage** The expression *beg the question* is often used incorrectly to mean (1) to avoid giving a straight answer, or (2) to invite the obvious question (that ...). These uses should be avoided.

began *past* of BEGIN.

beget /bɪ'get/ *v.* (**-tt-**; *past* **begot**; *archaic* **begat**; *past part.* **begotten**) *literary* **1** father, procreate. **2** cause (*anger begets violence*). [Old English: related to BE-]

beggar /'begə(r)/ *–n.* **1** person who lives by begging. **2** *colloq.* person (*cheeky beggar*). *–v.* **1** make poor. **2** be too extraordinary for (*beggar description*). □ **beggarly** *adj.*

begin /bɪ'gɪn/ *v.* (**-nn-**; *past* **began**; *past part.* **begun**) **1** perform the first part of; start (*begin work; begin crying; begin to understand*). **2** come into being (*war began in 1939; Wales begins here*). **3** (usu. foll. by *to* + infin.) start at a certain time (*soon began to feel ill*). **4** be begun (*meeting began at 7*). **5 a** start speaking (*'No,' he began*). **b** take the first step, be the first (*shall I begin?*). **6** (usu. with *neg.*) *colloq.* show any likelihood (*can't begin to compete*). [Old English]

beginner *n.* trainee, learner. □ **beginner's luck** supposed good luck of a beginner.

beginning *n.* **1** time or place at which anything begins. **2** source or origin. **3** first part.

begone /bɪ'gɒn/ *int. poet.* go away at once! [*be gone*]

begonia /bɪ'gəʊnɪə/ *n.* garden plant with bright flowers and leaves. [*Bégon*, name of a patron of science]

begot *past* of BEGET.

begotten *past part.* of BEGET.

begrudge /bɪ'grʌdʒ/ *v.* (**-ging**) **1** resent; be dissatisfied at. **2** envy (a person) the possession of. □ **begrudgingly** *adv.*

beguile /bɪ'gaɪl/ *v.* (**-ling**) **1** charm; amuse. **2** wilfully divert, seduce. **3** (usu. foll. by *of, out of,* or *into* + verbal noun) delude; cheat. □ **beguilement** *n.* **beguiling** *adj.*

beguine /bɪ'giːn/ *n.* popular dance of West Indian origin. [French *béguin* infatuation]

begum /'beɪgəm/ *n.* in India or Pakistan: **1** Muslim woman of high rank. **2** (**Begum**) title of a married Muslim woman. [Turkish *bīgam* princess]

begun *past part.* of BEGIN.

behalf /bɪ'hɑːf/ *n.* □ **on behalf of** (or **on a person's behalf**) in the interests of; as representative of. [earlier *bihalve* on the part of]

behave /bɪ'heɪv/ *v.* (**-ving**) **1** act or react (in a specified way) (*behaved well*). **2** (often *refl.*) conduct oneself properly (*behave yourself!*). **3** (of a machine etc.) work well (or in a specified way). [from BE-, HAVE]

behaviour /bɪ'heɪvjə(r)/ *n.* (*US* **behavior**) way of behaving or acting. □ **behavioural** *adj.*

behavioural science *n.* (*US* **behavioral**) the study of human behaviour.

behaviourism *n.* (*US* **behaviorism**) *Psychol.* theory that human behaviour is determined by conditioned response to stimuli, and that psychological disorders are best treated by altering behaviour. □ **behaviourist** *n.*

behead /bɪ'hed/ *v.* cut the head off (a person), esp. as execution. [Old English: related to BE-]

beheld *past* and *past part.* of BEHOLD.

behemoth /bɪ'hiːmɒθ/ *n.* huge creature or thing. [Hebrew (Job 40:15)]

Belarus /'belərʊs/, **Republic of** (also **Belorussia, Byelorussia, White Russia**) country in E Europe, bounded by Russia to the E and Poland to the W. Manufacturing industry is an important element of the economy, producing machinery, metals, cars and other vehicles, and textiles, and the peat industry is being developed. Cereal growing is the principal agricultural activity. Belarus was a constituent republic of the Soviet Union from 1922 until 1991, and most of its exports are still to other former Soviet republics, esp. Russia. The country is seeking new markets in Europe, but efforts to reform and liberalize the economy were opposed by the former Communists, who retained control of the government. However, in 1994, Aleksandr Lukashenko won the presidential elections and appointed a more reformist government. A referendum in 1996 greatly increased the powers of the president. President, Aleksandr Lukashenko; capital, Minsk.

languages	Belarussian (official), Russian, Polish
currency	rouble of 100 copecks
pop. (est. 1996)	10 442 000
GNP (est. 1994)	US$21.9B
literacy	99% (m); 96% (f)
life expectancy	64 (m); 74 (f)

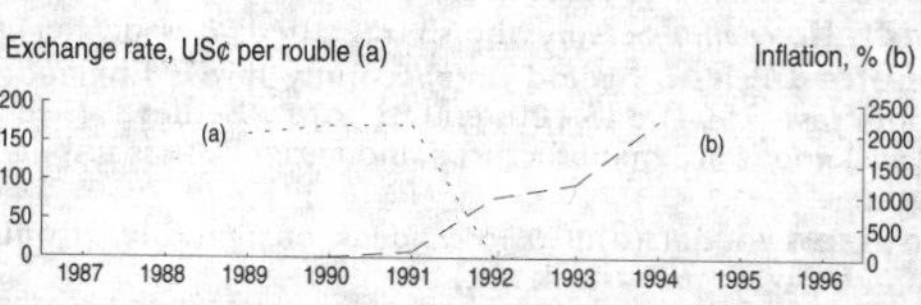

behest /bɪ'hest/ *n. literary* command; request. [Old English]

behind /bɪ'haɪnd/ *–prep.* **1 a** in or to the rear of. **b** on the far side of (*behind the bush*). **c** hidden or implied by (*something behind that remark*). **2 a** in the past in relation to (*trouble is behind me now*). **b** late regarding (*behind schedule*). **3** inferior to; weaker than (*behind the others in maths*). **4 a** in support of (*she's behind us*). **b** responsible for (*the man behind the project*). **5** in the tracks of; following. *–adv.* **1 a** in or to the rear; further back (*the street behind; glance behind*). **b** on the further side (*wall with a field behind*). **2** remaining after others' departure (*stay behind*). **3** (usu. foll. by *with*) **a** in arrears. **b** late in finishing a task etc. (*getting behind*). **4** in a weak position; backward (*behind in Latin*). **5** following (*dog running behind*). *–n. colloq.* buttocks. □ **behind the scenes** see SCENE. **behind time** late. **behind the times** old-fashioned, antiquated. [Old English]

behindhand *adv.* & *predic. adj.* **1** (usu. foll. by *with, in*) late; in arrears. **2** out of date.

behold /bɪ'həʊld/ *v.* (*past* & *past part.* **beheld**) (esp. in *imper.*) *literary* see, observe. [Old English: related to BE-, HOLD]

beholden *predic. adj.* (usu. foll. by *to*) under obligation.

behove /bɪ'həʊv/ *v.* (**-ving**) *formal* **1** be incumbent on. **2** befit (*it ill behoves him to protest*). [Old English: related to BE, HEAVE]

beige /beɪʒ/ *–n.* pale sandy fawn colour. *–adj.* of this colour. [French]

Beijing /beɪ'dʒɪŋ/ see PEKING.

being /'biːɪŋ/ *n.* **1** existence. **2** nature or essence (of a person etc.) (*his whole being revolted*). **3** person or creature.

Beira /'beɪrə/ seaport in E Mozambique; pop. (est. 1991) 298 847. A railway, road, and oil pipeline along the so-called 'Beira Corridor' link landlocked Zimbabwe with Beira.

Beirut /beɪ'ruːt/ capital of Lebanon, a port on the E coast of the Mediterranean; pop. (est. 1991) 1 100 000.

bejewelled /bɪ'dʒuːəld/ *adj.* (*US* **bejeweled**) adorned with jewels.

Bel. *abbr.* **1** Belgian. **2** Belgium.

bel *n.* unit of relative power level, esp. of sound, corresponding to an intensity ratio of 10 to 1 (cf. DECIBEL). [*Bell*, name of the inventor of the telephone]

belabour /bɪ'leɪbə(r)/ *v.* (*US* **belabor**) **1** attack physically or verbally. **2** labour (a subject).

Belarussian /ˌbelə'rʌʃ(ə)n/ (also **Belorussian, Byelorussian** /ˌbyelə-/) *–n.* native or language of Belarus. *–adj.* of Belarus, its people, or language.

belated /bɪ'leɪtɪd/ *adj.* late or too late. □ **belatedly** *adv.*

Belau see PALAU.

belay /bɪ'leɪ/ *–v.* secure (a rope) by winding it round a peg etc. *–n.* act of belaying. [Dutch *beleggen*]

bel canto /bel 'kæntəʊ/ *n.* lyrical rich-toned style of operatic singing. [Italian, = fine song]

belch *–v.* **1** emit wind noisily through the mouth. **2** (of a chimney, gun, etc.) send (smoke etc.) out or up. *–n.* act of belching. [Old English]

beleaguer /bɪ'liːgə(r)/ *v.* **1** besiege. **2** vex; harass. [Dutch *leger* camp]

Belém /be'lem/ (also **Pará** /pə'rɑː/) port and commercial city in N Brazil; exports include nuts, jute, and rubber; pop. (est. 1995) 1 574 000.

Belfast /bel'fɑːst/ **1** capital of Northern Ireland, a port with shipbuilding and engineering industries; pop. (1987) 303 800. **2** district in Northern Ireland, in Co. Antrim and Co. Down; pop. (1991) 283 746.

belfry /'belfrɪ/ *n.* (*pl.* **-ies**) **1** bell tower. **2** space for bells in a church tower. [Germanic, probably = peace-protector]

Belgian Congo see DEMOCRATIC REPUBLIC OF CONGO.

Belgrade /bel'greɪd/ (Serbian **Beograd**) capital of Serbia and of the Federal Republic of Yugoslavia, at the junction of the Rivers Sava and Danube; industries include light engineering, food processing, and textiles; pop. (1991) 1 168 454.

Belial /'biːlɪəl/ *n.* the Devil. [Hebrew, = worthless]

belie /bɪ'laɪ/ *v.* (**belying**) **1** give a false impression of (*its appearance belies its age*). **2** fail to fulfil or justify. [Old English: related to BE-]

belief /bɪ'liːf/ *n.* **1** firm opinion; acceptance (*that is my belief*). **2** religious conviction (*belief in the afterlife; has no belief*). **3** (usu. foll. by *in*) trust or confidence. [related to BELIEVE]

believe /bɪ'liːv/ *v.* (**-ving**) **1** accept as true or as conveying the truth (*I believe it; don't believe him*). **2** think, suppose. **3** (foll. by *in*) **a** have faith in the existence of (*believes in God*). **b** have confidence in (*believes in homoeopathy*). **c** have trust in as a policy (*believes in telling the truth*). **4** have (esp. religious) faith. □ **believable** *adj.* **believer** *n.* [Old English]

Belisha beacon /bə'liːʃə/ *n.* flashing orange ball on a striped post, marking some pedestrian crossings. [Hore-*Belisha*, who introduced it]

belittle /bɪ'lɪt(ə)l/ *v.* (**-ling**) disparage, make appear insignificant. □ **belittlement** *n.*

Belitung /bɪ'liːtʊŋ/ Indonesian island in the Java Sea between Borneo and Sumatra; industries include tin mining; chief town, Tanjungpandan.

Belize City chief port and former capital (until 1970) of Belize; pop. (1994) 48 655.

bell[1] *–n.* **1** hollow esp. cup-shaped usu. metal object sounding a note when struck. **2** such a sound, esp. as a signal. **3** thing resembling a bell, esp. in sound or shape. *–v.* provide with a bell. □ **give a person a bell** *colloq.* telephone a person. [Old English]

Belgium /'beldʒəm/, **Kingdom of** country in W Europe on the S shore of the North Sea. Belgium is a highly industrialized manufacturing nation: textiles, food processing, engineering, and chemicals are major industries; coal production, once a major industry, has now stopped. Agriculture is also important, producing esp. cereals, sugar beet, and livestock. Export revenue accounts for a high proportion of the country's income: chief exports include machinery and transport equipment, chemicals, food products, iron and steel, and textiles. Some 75% of Belgium's trade is with other members of the EC.

History. Ruled at various times by Spain, Austria, France, and the Netherlands, Belgium gained formal independence in 1839. Occupied and devastated during both world wars, Belgium made a quick recovery after 1945, taking the first step towards European economic integration with the formation of the Benelux customs union with the Netherlands and Luxembourg in 1947; Belgium was a founder member of the EC (now EU). The country is divided into autonomous French- and Flemish-speaking regions and the bilingual Brussels; the powers of these regions are being increased at the expense of national government. Head of state: King Albert II; prime minister, Jean-Luc Dehaene; capital, Brussels. □ **Belgian** *adj.* & *n.*

languages	French, Flemish, German
currency	franc (BF) of 100 centimes
pop. (1996)	10 185 500
GNP (est. 1994)	US$231B
literacy	99%
life expectancy	73 (m); 79 (f)

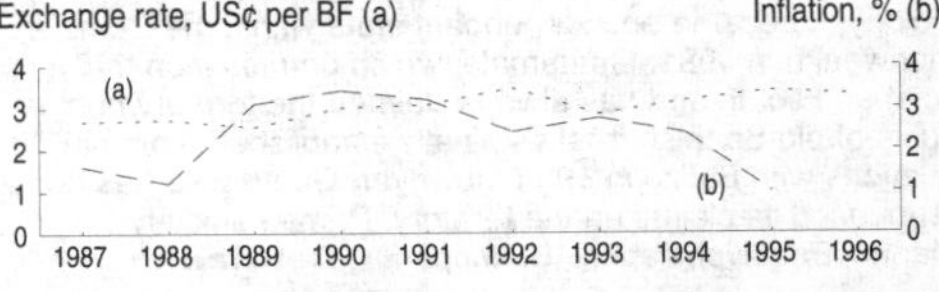

bell[2] *–n.* cry of a stag. *–v.* make this cry. [Old English]

belladonna /ˌbelə'dɒnə/ *n.* **1** deadly nightshade. **2** drug from this. [Italian, = fair lady]

bell-bottom *n.* **1** marked flare below the knee (of a trouser-leg). **2** (in *pl.*) trousers with these. □ **bell-bottomed** *adj.*

bellboy *n.* esp. *US* page in a hotel or club.

belle /bel/ *n.* beautiful or most beautiful woman. [French, feminine of BEAU]

belles-lettres /bel 'letr/ *n.pl.* (also treated as *sing.*) literary writings or studies. [French, = fine letters]

bellicose /'belɪˌkəʊs/ *adj.* eager to fight; warlike. [Latin *bellum* war]

belligerence /bɪ'lɪdʒərəns/ *n.* **1** aggressive behaviour. **2** status of a belligerent.

belligerent *–adj.* **1** engaged in war or conflict. **2** pugnacious. *–n.* belligerent nation or person. [Latin *belligero* wage war]

bell-jar *n.* bell-shaped glass cover or container for use in a laboratory.

bellow /'beləʊ/ *–v.* **1** emit a deep loud roar. **2** utter loudly. *–n.* loud roar. [origin uncertain]

bellows *n.pl.* (also treated as *sing.*) **1** device for driving air into or through something. **2** expandable part, e.g. of a camera. [related to BELLY]

bell-pull *n.* handle etc. sounding a bell when pulled.

bell-push *n.* button operating an electric bell.

bell-ringer *n.* ringer of church bells or handbells. □ **bell-ringing** *n.*

♦ **bells and whistles** *n.pl.* **1** superfluous but attractive trappings. **2** additions, such as an option or warranty, appended to a financial product to increase its appeal.

---

bell-wether *n.* **1** leading sheep of a flock. **2** ringleader.

belly /'belɪ/ *–n.* (*pl.* **-ies**) **1** trunk below the chest, containing the stomach and bowels. **2** stomach. **3** front of the body from waist to groin. **4** underside of an animal. **5** cavity or bulging part. *–v.* (**-ies**, **-ied**) (often foll. by *out*) swell; bulge. [Old English, = bag]

bellyache *–n. colloq.* stomach pain. *–v.* (**-ching**) *slang* complain noisily or persistently.

belly button *n. colloq.* navel.

belly-dance *n.* oriental dance performed by a woman, with voluptuous belly movements. □ **belly-dancer** *n.* **belly-dancing** *n.*

bellyflop *n. colloq.* dive with the belly landing flat on the water.

bellyful *n.* (*pl.* **-s**) **1** enough to eat. **2** *colloq.* more than one can tolerate.

belly-laugh *n.* loud unrestrained laugh.

Belmopan /ˌbelməʊ'pæn/ river port and (since 1970) capital city of Belize; pop. (est. 1994) 3927.

Belo Horizonte /'beləʊ ˌhɒrɪ'zɒnteɪ/ city in E Brazil, capital of the state of Minas Gerais, situated at the centre of a rich mining and agricultural region; pop. (est. 1991) 3 899 000.

belong /bɪ'lɒŋ/ *v.* **1** (foll. by *to*) **a** be the property of. **b** be correctly assigned to. **c** be a member of. **2** fit socially (*just doesn't belong*). **3** (foll. by *in*, *under*) be correctly placed or classified. [from BE-, obsolete *long* belong]

belongings *n.pl.* possessions or luggage.

Belorussia /ˌbeləʊ'rʌʃə/ see BELARUS.

Belorussian var. of BELARUSSIAN.

beloved /bɪ'lʌvɪd/ *–adj.* much loved. *–n.* much loved person.

below /bɪ'ləʊ/ *–prep.* **1** lower in position, amount, status, etc., than. **2** beneath the surface of (*head below water*). **3** unworthy of. *–adv.* **1** at or to a lower point or level. **2** downstream. **3** further forward on a page or in a book (*as noted below*). [*be* BY, LOW[1]]

♦ **below par** see PAR VALUE.

♦ **below-the-line** *adj.* **1** denoting entries below the horizontal line on a company's profit and loss account that separates the entries that establish the profit (or loss) from the entries that show how the profit is distributed or where the funds to finance the loss have come from. **2** denoting advertising expenditure in which no commission is payable to an advertising agency. For example, direct mail, exhibitions, point-of-sale material, and free samples are regarded as below-the-line advertising. **3** denoting transactions concerned with capital, as opposed to revenue, in national accounts. Cf. ABOVE-THE-LINE.

---

belt *–n.* **1** strip of leather etc. worn esp. round the waist. **2** circular band in machinery; conveyor belt. **3** distinct strip of colour etc. **4** region or extent (*cotton belt*). **5** *slang* heavy blow. *–v.* **1** put a belt round; fasten with a belt. **2** *slang* hit hard. **3** *slang* rush, hurry. □ **below the belt** unfair(ly). **belt out** *slang* sing or play (music) loudly or vigorously. **belt up 1** *slang* be quiet. **2** *colloq.* put on a seat belt. **tighten one's belt** economize. **under one's belt** securely acquired. [Old English]

beluga /bɪ'lu:gə/ *n.* (*pl.* same or **-s**) **1 a** large kind of sturgeon. **b** caviare from it. **2** white whale. [Russian]

belvedere /'belvɪˌdɪə(r)/ *n.* raised summer-house or gallery for viewing scenery. [Italian, = beautiful view]

BEM *abbr.* British Empire Medal.

BEMA *abbr.* Business Equipment Manufacturers' Association.

bemoan /bɪ'məʊn/ *v.* lament; complain about.

bemuse /bɪ'mju:z/ *v.* (**-sing**) puzzle, bewilder. [from BE-, MUSE[1]]

Benares see VARANASI.

bench *n.* **1** long seat of wood or stone. **2** strong worktable. **3** (prec. by *the*) **a** judge's seat. **b** lawcourt. **c** judges and magistrates collectively. [Old English]

bencher *n.* senior member of an Inn of Court.

benchmark *n.* **1** surveyor's mark cut in a wall etc. as a reference point in measuring altitudes. **2** standard or point of reference. **3** standard set of computer programs used to measure what a computer can do and how fast it can do it. The benchmark programs are designed to accomplish simple tasks, such as performing a large number of additions or retrieving data from memory.

bend[1] *–v.* (*past* and *past part.* **bent** exc. in *bended knee*) **1 a** force or adapt (something straight) into a curve or angle. **b** (of an object) be so altered. **2** (often foll. by

---

Belize /be'li:z/ (formerly **British Honduras**) country in Central America, on the Caribbean coast. The economy is mainly agricultural; there are also important forestry and clothing industries. Sugar is the chief export earner, followed by citrus products, bananas, and timber. Belize, which is a member of CARICOM, has the fastest growing economy in the Caribbean. Formerly a British Crown Colony, it became an independent state within the Commonwealth in 1981. Guatemala, which bounds it on the west and south and has always claimed the territory on the basis of old Spanish treaties, finally established diplomatic relations with Belize in 1992; however, Guatemala has not renounced its claims on the territory. Prime minister, Manuel Esquivel; capital, Belmopan. □ **Belizian** *adj.* & *n.*

languages	English (official), Spanish, Creole
currency	dollar (BZ$) of 100 cents
pop. (1996)	219 000
GNP (est. 1994)	US$535M
literacy	93%
life expectancy	66 (m); 70 (f)

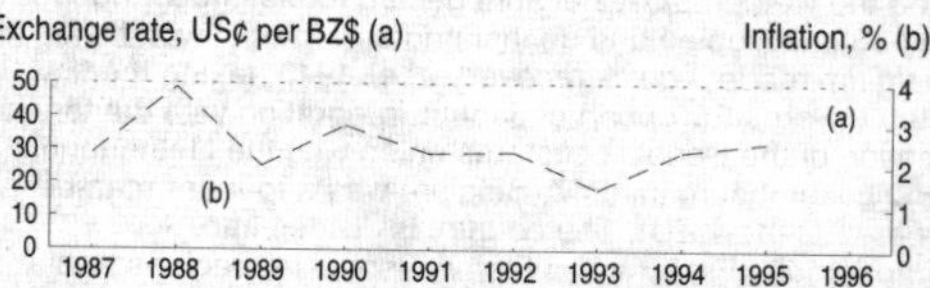

down, over, etc.) curve, incline, or stoop (*road bends; bent down to pick it up; bent her head*). **3** interpret or modify (a rule) to suit oneself. **4** turn (one's steps, eyes, or energies) in a new direction. **5** be flexible, submit, or force to submit. *–n.* **1** curve; departure from a straight course. **2** bent part. **3** (in *pl.*; prec. by *the*) *colloq.* decompression sickness. □ **bend over backwards** see BACKWARDS. **round the bend** *colloq.* crazy, insane. □ **bendy** *adj.* (**-ier, -iest**). [Old English]

bend[2] *n.* **1** any of various knots. **2** *Heraldry* diagonal stripe from top right to bottom left of a shield (from its wearer's position). [Old English: related to BIND]

bender *n. slang* wild drinking-spree. [from BEND[1]]

Bendigo /ˈbendɪˌgəʊ/ former gold-mining town in Australia, in the state of Victoria; pop. (est. 1991) 70 360. It is now a centre for livestock trading and wine production.

bend sinister *n. Heraldry* diagonal stripe from top left to bottom right of a shield, as a sign of bastardy.

beneath /bɪˈniːθ/ *–prep.* **1** unworthy of (*beneath him to reply*). **2** below, under. *–adv.* below, underneath. [Old English: related to BE-, NETHER]

Benedictine /ˌbenɪˈdɪktɪn/ *–n.* **1** monk or nun of an order following the rule of St Benedict. **2** /-ˌtiːn/ *propr.* liqueur orig. made by Benedictines. *–adj.* of St Benedict or the Benedictines. [Latin *Benedictus* Benedict]

benediction /ˌbenɪˈdɪkʃ(ə)n/ *n.* blessing, esp. at the end of a religious service or as a special Roman Catholic service. □ **benedictory** *adj.* [Latin *benedico* bless]

benefaction /ˌbenɪˈfækʃ(ə)n/ *n.* **1** donation, gift. **2** giving or doing good. [Latin: related to BENEFIT]

benefactor /ˈbenɪˌfæktə(r)/ *n.* (*fem.* **benefactress**) person giving (esp. financial) support.

benefice /ˈbenɪfɪs/ *n.* a living from a church office.

beneficent /bɪˈnefɪs(ə)nt/ *adj.* doing good; generous, kind. □ **beneficence** *n.*

beneficial /ˌbenɪˈfɪʃ(ə)l/ *adj.* advantageous; having benefits. □ **beneficially** *adv.*

♦ **beneficial interest** *n.* right to the use and enjoyment of property, rather than to its bare legal ownership. For example, if property is held in trust, the trustee has the legal title but the beneficiaries have the beneficial interest in equity. The beneficiaries, not the trustee, are entitled to any income from the property.

♦ **beneficial owner** *n.* owner of a beneficial interest in property.

---

beneficiary /ˌbenɪˈfɪʃərɪ/ *n.* (*pl.* **-ies**) **1** person who benefits, esp. from a will. **2** person for whose benefit a trust exists. **3** person who receives payment from the proceeds of a letter of credit etc. **4** holder of a benefice.

benefit /ˈbenɪfɪt/ *–n.* **1** favourable or helpful factor etc. **2** (often in *pl.*) insurance or social security payment (*sickness benefit*). **3** public performance or game in aid of a charitable cause etc. *–v.* (**-t-**; *US* **-tt-**) **1** help; bring advantage to. **2** (often foll. by *from, by*) receive benefit. □ **the benefit of the doubt** concession that a person is innocent, correct, etc., although doubt exists. [Latin *benefactum* from *bene* well, *facio* do]

♦ **benefit segmentation** see MARKET SEGMENTATION.

♦ **benefits in kind** *n.pl.* (also **income in kind**) remuneration other than wages and salaries, e.g. company cars, free lunches, health insurance, cheap loans, etc. In an economy in which the main form of taxation is an income tax, benefits in kind become common because, without special provisions, they avoid tax. There is usu. therefore a substantial body of legislation to enable the authorities to tax these benefits.

♦ **benefit taxation** *n.* form of taxation in which taxpayers pay tax according to the amounts of benefit that they receive from the system. Such a system of taxation is, in practice, very difficult to apply unless specific charges are made for specific services (e.g. metered electricity charges). Cf. ABILITY-TO-PAY TAXATION.

♦ **Benelux** /ˈbenɪˌlʌks/ *n.* association of countries in W Europe, consisting of Belgium, the Netherlands, and Luxembourg. Apart from geographical proximity these countries have particularly close economic interests, recognized in their 1947 customs union. In 1958 the Benelux countries joined the European Economic Community. [*Be*lgium, *Ne*therlands, *Lux*embourg]

♦ **Benetton** /ˈbenɪˌtɒn/, **Luciano** (1935–) Italian businessman, founder (1978) of clothing company Benetton and now vice-president and managing director of the multinational Benetton Group, 71% of which is owned by Luciano and his three siblings. The original Benetton company, Fratelli Benetton, was founded by Luciano and his brothers in 1965 and began selling sweaters designed by his sister, Giuliana Benetton, to clothing retailers, opening the first Bentton shop in 1968. Luciano's Benetton Group now has thousands of shops around the world and has added sportswear to its clothing range to complement its Rollerblade and Prince (racket sports) brands. The family's net worth was $3.6 billion in 1997.

---

benevolent /bɪˈnevələnt/ *adj.* **1** well-wishing; actively friendly and helpful. **2** charitable (*benevolent fund*). □ **benevolence** *n.* [French from Latin *bene volens* well wishing]

Bengal /beŋˈgɔːl/ former province of NE India, partitioned in 1947 into West Bengal (a state of India) and East Bengal (East Pakistan, now Bangladesh).

Bengal, Bay of arm of the Indian Ocean, between India and Burma.

Bengali /beŋˈgɔːlɪ/ *–n.* (*pl.* **-s**) **1** native of Bengal. **2** language of Bengal. *–adj.* of Bengal, its people, or language.

Benghazi /benˈgɑːzɪ/ port in NE Libya; pop. (est. 1991) 500 000. The co-capital of Libya from 1951 to 1972, it has oil and light-engineering industries.

Benin /beˈnɪn/, **Republic of** (formerly, until 1975, **Dahomey**) country in W Africa, immediately W of Nigeria. The economy is mainly agricultural, cotton, coffee, palm oil and kernels, cocoa, and sugar being the principal exports; maize, rice, and cassava are grown as food crops. Offshore oil is also exported and processed. Most other industry is geared to the processing of agricultural produce. Stable democratic government has enabled development and growth of the economy.
History. The country was part of French West Africa until 1960, when it became fully independent. After a succession of military coups, Mathieu Kerekou came to power in 1972 at the head of a military government and in 1974 proclaimed Benin a Marxist state, the People's Republic of Benin. In response to increasing unrest at the failure of the economy, Marxism was abandoned in 1989 and a new democratic constitution approved in 1990 and the country's name became Republic of Benin. In elections in 1991 Nicéphore Soglo was elected president; however, he was defeated by the former military ruler, Mathieu Kerekon in the 1996 presidential elections. President, Mathieu Kerekon; capital, Porto Novo. □ **Beninese** /ˌbenɪˈniːz/ *adj.* & *n.*

languages	French (official), African languages
currency	CFA franc (CFAF) of 100 centimes
pop. (est. 1996)	5 574 000
GNP (est. 1994)	US$1.9B
literacy	48% (m); 25% (f)
life expectancy	50 (m); 54 (f)

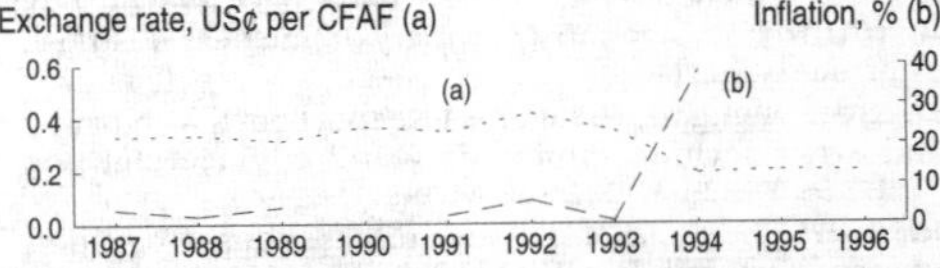

Benguela /beŋ'gwelə/ port and railway terminal of Angola, on the Atlantic coast; pop. (1988) 155 000. The railway provides an outlet for copper exports from the African interior.

benighted /bɪ'naɪtɪd/ *adj.* intellectually or morally ignorant.

benign /bɪ'naɪn/ *adj.* **1** gentle, mild, kindly. **2** fortunate, salutary. **3** (of a tumour etc.) not malignant. □ **benignly** *adv.* [Latin *benignus*]

benignant /bɪ'nɪgnənt/ *adj.* **1** kindly, esp. to inferiors. **2** salutary, beneficial. □ **benignancy** *n.*

benignity /bɪ'nɪgnɪtɪ/ *n.* (*pl.* **-ies**) kindliness.

Benin, Bight of wide bay on the coast of Africa N of the Gulf of Guinea, bordered by Togo, Benin, and SW Nigeria. Lagos is its chief port.

bent[1] *past* and *past part.* of BEND[1] *v.* *–adj.* **1** curved, angular. **2** *slang* dishonest, illicit. **3** *slang* sexually deviant. **4** (foll. by *on*) set on doing or having. *–n.* **1** inclination or bias. **2** (foll. by *for*) talent.

bent[2] *n.* **1** reedy grass with stiff stems. **2** stiff flower stalk of a grass. [Old English]

bentwood *n.* wood artificially shaped for making furniture.

benumb /bɪ'nʌm/ *v.* **1** make numb; deaden. **2** paralyse (the mind or feelings).

benzene /'benziːn/ *n.* colourless liquid found in coal tar and used as a volatile solvent etc. [as BENZOIN]

benzine /'benziːn/ *n.* mixture of liquid hydrocarbons obtained from petroleum.

benzoin /'benzəʊɪn/ *n.* fragrant gum resin from an E Asian tree. □ **benzoic** /-'zəʊɪk/ *adj.* [ultimately from Arabic *lubān jāwī* incense of Java]

benzol /'benzɒl/ *n.* benzene, esp. unrefined.

Beograd see BELGRADE.

bequeath /bɪ'kwiːð/ *v.* **1** leave to a person in a will. **2** hand down to posterity. [from BE-: related to QUOTH]

bequest /bɪ'kwest/ *n.* **1** bequeathing; bestowal by will. **2** thing bequeathed. [from BE-, obsolete *quiste* saying]

berate /bɪ'reɪt/ *v.* (**-ting**) scold, rebuke.

Berber /'bɜːbə(r)/ *–n.* **1** member of the indigenous mainly Muslim Caucasian peoples of N Africa. **2** language of these peoples. *–adj.* of the Berbers or their language. [Arabic]

Berbera /'bɜːbərə/ seaport in N Somalia, on the oil route from the Middle East to Europe; pop. (est. 1988) 65 000.

berceuse /beə'sɜːz/ *n.* (*pl.* **-s** pronunc. same) **1** lullaby. **2** instrumental piece in this style. [French]

bereave /bɪ'riːv/ *v.* (**-ving**) (esp. as **bereaved** *adj.*) (often foll. by *of*) deprive of a relation, friend, etc., esp. by death. □ **bereavement** *n.* [Old English: related to BE-, REAVE]

bereft /bɪ'reft/ *adj.* (foll. by *of*) deprived (*bereft of hope*). [past part. of BEREAVE]

beret /'bereɪ/ *n.* round flattish brimless cap of felt etc. [French: related to BIRETTA]

♦ **Berezovsky** /ˌbɪrɪ'zɒvskɪ/, **Boris** (1946–) Russian businessman. He has controlling interests in Russia's former national airline Aeroflot, in oil company Silneft, and in media and real estate companies, as well as owning Russia's largest auto trader. Financial backer of Russian president Boris Yeltsin, he was appointed deputy national head of security in 1996. His net assets were valued at $3 billion in 1997.

---

berg *n.* = ICEBERG. [abbreviation]

bergamot[1] /'bɜːgəˌmɒt/ *n.* **1** perfume from the fruit of a dwarf orange tree. **2** aromatic herb. [*Bergamo* in Italy]

bergamot[2] /'bɜːgəˌmɒt/ *n.* variety of fine pear. [Turkish, = prince's pear]

Bergen /'bɜːgən, 'beəgən/ **1** seaport in SW Norway; industries include shipbuilding and engineering; pop. (est. 1996) 223 100. **2** see MONS.

beriberi /ˌberɪ'berɪ/ *n.* nervous disease caused by a deficiency of vitamin B_1. [Sinhalese]

berk *n. slang* stupid person. [*Berkshire Hunt*, rhyming slang for *cunt*]

berkelium /bɜː'kiːlɪəm/ *n.* artificial radioactive metallic element. [*Berkeley* in US, where first made]

Berks. /bɑːks/ *abbr.* Berkshire.

Berkshire /'bɑːkʃɪə(r)/ county in S England; pop. (est. 1994) 769 200; county town, Reading. It is mainly agricultural, producing barley and other cereals, dairy produce, and livestock; industries include plastics and pharmaceuticals. Berkshire county council was abolished in 1998, when its administrative powers were devolved to a number of unitary authorities.

Berlin /bɜː'lɪn/ capital of Germany; manufactures include electrical equipment, machinery, chemicals, and clothing and there are also printing and publishing industries; pop. (est. 1995) 3 472 000. From 1948 until 1990 it was divided into two parts: West Berlin (an enclave of the Federal Republic of Germany within the German Democratic Republic) and East Berlin (capital of the German Democratic Republic). In 1990 it became capital of reunited Germany, although Bonn remained the seat of government.

Bermuda /bɜː'mjuːdə/ (also **Bermuda Islands, Bermudas**) British dependency with full internal self-government, comprising a group of about 150 small islands off the coast of North Carolina; pop. (1994) 60 500; capital, Hamilton. Vegetables and bananas are grown and there is some light manufacturing, but the principal industries are finance and tourism, which has declined recently because of the US recession, higher air fares, and competition from Caribbean resorts. □ **Bermudian** /bɜː'mjuːdɪən/ *adj.* & *n.*

Bermuda shorts *n.pl.* (also **Bermudas**) close-fitting knee-length shorts. [BERMUDA]

Berne /beən/ (also **Bern**) capital of Switzerland; manufactures include textiles, chocolate, pharmaceuticals, and electrical goods. pop. (est. 1995) 128 422.

♦ **Berne Union** *n. colloq.* International Union of Credit and Investment Insurers, an association of credit insurers from the main industrial countries, except Japan. Its main function is to facilitate an exchange of information, esp. over credit terms. The Export Credits Guarantee Department of the UK government is a member.

---

berry *n.* (*pl.* **-ies**) **1** any small roundish juicy stoneless fruit. **2** *Bot.* fruit with its seeds enclosed in pulp (e.g. a banana or tomato). [Old English]

berserk /bə'zɜːk/ *adj.* (esp. in **go berserk**) wild, frenzied; in a rage. [originally = Norse warrior: Icelandic, = bear-coat]

berth *–n.* **1** bunk on a ship, train, etc. **2** place for a ship to moor or be at anchor. **3** adequate room for a ship. **4** *colloq.* job. *–v.* **1** moor (a ship); be moored. **2** provide a sleeping place for. □ **give a wide berth to** stay away from. [probably from a special use of BEAR[1]]

Berwick-upon-Tweed /'berɪk/ town and fishing-port in NE England; pop. (est. 1991) 26 400.

beryl /'berɪl/ *n.* **1** transparent precious stone, esp. pale green. **2** mineral species including this, emerald, and aquamarine. [Greek *bērullos*]

beryllium /bə'rɪlɪəm/ *n.* hard white metallic element.

BES *abbr.* = BUSINESS EXPANSION SCHEME.

Besançon /bezɑ̃'sɔ̃/ town in NE France, regional capital of Franche-Comté; industries include textiles and clock-making; pop. (est. 1990) 119 194.

beseech /bɪ'siːtʃ/ *v.* (*past* and *past part.* **besought** /-'sɔːt/ or **beseeched**) **1** (foll. by *for*, or *to* + infin.) entreat. **2** ask earnestly for. [from BE-, SEEK]

beset /bɪ'set/ *v.* (**-tt-**; *past* and *past part.* **beset**) **1** attack or harass persistently (*beset by worries*). **2** surround (a person etc.). [Old English: related to BE-]

beside /bɪ'saɪd/ *prep.* **1** at the side of; near. **2** compared with. **3** irrelevant to (*beside the point*). □ **beside oneself** frantic with worry etc. [Old English: related to BY, SIDE]

besides *–prep.* in addition to; apart from. *–adv.* also; moreover.

besiege /bɪ'siːdʒ/ *v.* (**-ging**) **1** lay siege to. **2** crowd round eagerly. **3** harass with requests.

besmirch /bɪ'smɜːtʃ/ *v.* **1** soil, discolour. **2** dishonour.

BESO *abbr.* British Executive Service Overseas.

besom /'biːz(ə)m/ *n.* broom of twigs. [Old English]

besotted /bɪ'sɒtɪd/ *adj.* **1** infatuated. **2** intoxicated, stupefied.

besought *past* and *past part.* of BESEECH.

bespangle /bɪ'spæŋg(ə)l/ *v.* (**-ling**) adorn with spangles.

bespatter /bɪ'spætə(r)/ *v.* **1** spatter all over. **2** slander, defame.

bespeak /bɪ'spiːk/ *v.* (*past* **bespoke**; *past part.* **bespoken** or as *adj.* **bespoke**) **1** engage in advance. **2** order (goods). **3** suggest; be evidence of.

bespectacled /bɪ'spektək(ə)ld/ *adj.* wearing spectacles.

bespoke *past* and *past part.* of BESPEAK. *adj.* **1** made to order. **2** making goods to order.

bespoken *past part.* of BESPEAK.

Bessarabia /ˌbesə'reɪbɪə/ region in E Europe, in Moldova and Ukraine. The chief economic activities are agriculture and agricultural processing. Crops include grapes, fruit, and wheat. Formerly part of Russia, in 1918 Bessarabia chose union with Romania, which was forced to cede it to the Soviet Union in 1940. □ **Bessarabian** *adj.* & *n.*

best *–adj.* (*superl.* of GOOD) of the most excellent or desirable kind. *–adv.* (*superl.* of WELL[1]). **1** in the best manner. **2** to the greatest degree. **3** most usefully (*is best ignored*). *–n.* **1** that which is best (*the best is yet to come*). **2** chief merit or advantage (*brings out the best in him*). **3** (foll. by *of*) winning majority of (games played etc.) (*the best of five*). **4** one's best clothes. *–v. colloq.* defeat, outwit, outbid, etc. □ **at best 1** on the most optimistic view. **2** *Finance* at the best possible price: an instruction to a broker to buy or sell shares, stocks, commodities, currencies, etc., as specified, that must be executed immediately, irrespective of market movements. Cf. *at limit* (see LIMIT). **best bib and tucker** one's best clothes. **the best part of** most of. **do one's best** do all one can. **get the best of** defeat, outwit. **had best** would find it wisest to. **make the best of** derive what limited advantage one can from. [Old English]

bestial /'bestɪəl/ *adj.* **1** brutish, cruel. **2** of or like a beast. [Latin: related to BEAST]

bestiality /ˌbestɪ'ælɪtɪ/ *n.* **1** bestial behaviour. **2** sexual intercourse between a person and an animal.

bestiary /'bestɪərɪ/ *n.* (*pl.* **-ies**) medieval treatise on beasts. [medieval Latin: related to BEAST]

bestir /bɪ'stɜː(r)/ *v.refl.* (**-rr-**) exert or rouse oneself.

best man *n.* bridegroom's chief attendant.

bestow /bɪ'stəʊ/ *v.* (foll. by *on, upon*) confer (a gift, right, etc.). □ **bestowal** *n.* [Old English *stow* a place]

bestrew /bɪ'struː/ *v.* (*past part.* **bestrewed** or **bestrewn**) **1** (usu. foll. by *with*) strew (a surface). **2** lie scattered over.

bestride /bɪ'straɪd/ *v.* (**-ding**; *past* **-strode**; *past part.* **-stridden**) **1** sit astride on. **2** stand astride over.

best seller *n.* **1** book etc. sold in large numbers. **2** author of such a book.

bet *–v.* (**-tt-**; *past* and *past part.* **bet** or **betted**) **1** risk a sum of money on the result of a race, contest, etc. (*I don't bet on horses*). **2** risk (a sum) thus, or risk (a sum) against (a person) (*bet £10 on a horse; he bet me £10 I'd lose*). **3** *colloq.* feel sure. *–n.* **1** act of betting (*make a bet*). **2** money etc. staked (*put a bet on*). **3** *colloq.* opinion (*that's my bet*). **4** *colloq.* choice or possibility (*she's our best bet*). □ **you bet** *colloq.* you may be sure. [origin uncertain]

beta /'biːtə/ *n.* **1** second letter of the Greek alphabet (Β, β). **2** second-class mark for a piece of work etc. [Latin from Greek]

beta-blocker *n.* drug preventing unwanted stimulation of the heart, used to treat angina and high blood pressure.

betake /bɪ'teɪk/ *v.refl.* (**-king**; *past* **betook**; *past part.* **betaken**) (foll. by *to*) go to (a place or person).

beta particle *n.* fast-moving electron emitted by the radioactive decay of substances.

betatron /'biːtəˌtrɒn/ *n.* apparatus for accelerating electrons in a circular path. [from BETA, ELECTRON]

betel /'biːt(ə)l/ *n.* leaf chewed in the East with the betel-nut. [Portuguese from Malayalam]

betel-nut *n.* seed of a tropical palm.

bête noire /beɪt 'nwɑː(r)/ *n.* (*pl.* ***bêtes noires*** pronunc. same) person or thing one hates or fears. [French, literally = 'black beast']

bethink /bɪ'θɪŋk/ *v.refl.* (*past* and *past part.* **bethought**) *formal* **1** reflect; stop to think. **2** be reminded by reflection. [Old English: related to BE-]

Bethlehem /'beθlɪˌhem/ **1** small town S of Jerusalem, the reputed birthplace of Jesus Christ; pop. (est. 1984) 20 000. **2** city in the US, in E Pennsylvania, an important steel centre; chemicals, textiles, and machinery are also produced; pop. (1990) 71 428.

betide /bɪ'taɪd/ *v.* □ **woe betide a person** used as a warning (*woe betide us if we fail*). [from BE-, *tide* befall]

betimes /bɪ'taɪmz/ *adv. literary* early, in good time. [related to BY]

betoken /bɪ'təʊkən/ *v.* be a sign of; indicate. [Old English: related to BE-]

betony /'betənɪ/ *n.* (*pl.* **-ies**) purple-flowered plant. [French from Latin]

betook *past* of BETAKE.

betray /bɪ'treɪ/ *v.* **1** be disloyal or treacherous to (a friend, one's country, a person's trust, etc.). **2** reveal involuntarily or treacherously; be evidence of. **3** lead astray. □ **betrayal** *n.* [from BE-, obsolete *tray* from Latin *trado* hand over]

betroth /bɪ'trəʊð/ *–v.* (usu. as **betrothed** *–adj.*) engage to marry. □ **betrothal** *n.* [from BE-, TRUTH]

better *–adj.* (*compar.* of GOOD). **1** of a more excellent or desirable kind. **2** partly or fully recovered from illness (*feeling better*). *–adv.* (*compar.* of WELL[1]). **1** in a better manner. **2** to a greater degree. **3** more usefully (*is better forgotten*). *–n.* **1** better thing etc. (*the better of the two*). **2** (in *pl.*) one's superiors. *–v.* **1** improve on; surpass. **2** improve. **3** *refl.* improve one's position etc. □ **the better part of** most of. **get the better of** defeat, outwit. **had better** would find it prudent to. [Old English]

better half *n. colloq.* one's spouse.

betterment *n.* improvement.

better off *adj.* **1** in a better situation. **2** having more money.

betting *n.* **1** gambling by risking money on an unpredictable outcome. **2** odds offered on this. □ **what's the betting?** *colloq.* it is likely or to be expected (*what's the betting he'll be late?*).

betting-shop *n.* bookmaker's shop or office.

between /bɪ'twiːn/ *–prep.* **1 a** at a point in the area bounded by two or more other points in space, time, etc. (*between London and Dover; between now and Friday*). **b** along the extent of such an area (*no shops between here and the centre; numbers between 10 and 20*). **2** separating (*difference between right and wrong*). **3 a** shared by (*£5 between us*). **b** by joint action (*agreement between us*). **4** to and from (*runs between London and Oxford*). **5** taking one of (*choose between them*). *–adv.* (also **in between**) at a point or in the area bounded by two or more other points (*not fat or thin but in between*). □ **between ourselves** (or **you and me**) in confidence. [Old English: related to BY, TWO]

betwixt /bɪ'twɪkst/ *adv.* □ **betwixt and between** *colloq.* neither one thing nor the other. [Old English]

bevel /'bev(ə)l/ *–n.* **1** slope from the horizontal or vertical in carpentry etc.; sloping surface or edge. **2** tool for marking angles. *–v.* (**-ll-**; *US* **-l-**) **1** reduce (a square edge) to a sloping edge. **2** slope at an angle. [French]

bevel gear *n.* gear working another at an angle to it.

beverage /'bevərɪdʒ/ *n. formal* drink. [Latin *bibo* drink]

Beverly Hills /'bevəlɪ/ affluent and largely residential city in the US, in California to the W of Los Angeles; pop. (1990) 31 970.

bevy /ˈbevɪ/ *n.* (*pl.* **-ies**) company (of quails, larks, women, etc.). [origin unknown]

bewail /bɪˈweɪl/ *v.* lament; wail over.

beware /bɪˈweə(r)/ *v.* (only in *imper.* or *infin.*; often foll. by *of*) be cautious (of) (*beware of the dog*; *beware the Ides of March*). [from BE, *ware* cautious]

bewilder /bɪˈwɪldə(r)/ *v.* perplex, confuse. □ **bewildering** *adj.* **bewilderment** *n.* [from BE-, obsolete *wilder* lose one's way]

bewitch /bɪˈwɪtʃ/ *v.* **1** enchant. **2** cast a spell on.

BEXA /ˈbeksə/ *abbr.* = BRITISH EXPORTERS ASSOCIATION.

beyond /bɪˈjɒnd/ *–prep.* **1** at or to the further side of. **2** outside the scope or understanding of (*beyond repair*; *it is beyond me*). **3** more than. *–adv.* **1** at or to the further side. **2** further on. *–n.* (prec. by *the*) the unknown after death. [Old English: related to BY, YON]

bezel /ˈbez(ə)l/ *n.* **1** sloped edge of a chisel. **2** oblique faces of a cut gem. **3** groove holding a watch-glass or gem. [French]

bezique /bɪˈziːk/ *n.* card-game for two. [French]

BF *–abbr.* (French) Banque de France (= Bank of France). *–symb.* Belgian franc.

b.f. *abbr.* **1** *colloq.* bloody fool. **2** (also **B/f, B/F**) *Bookkeeping* brought forward.

BFBPW *abbr.* British Federation of Business and Professional Women.

BFCA *abbr.* British Federation of Commodity Associations.

BFr *abbr.* Belgian franc.

BG *–international vehicle registration* Bulgaria. *–airline flight code* Biman Bangladesh Airlines.

bg *abbr. Commerce* bag.

b/g *abbr.* bonded goods.

BGC *abbr.* bank giro credit.

BH *–international vehicle registration* Belize. *–postcode* Bournemouth.

bhang /bæŋ/ *n.* Indian hemp used as a narcotic. [Portuguese from Sanskrit]

Bharat /ˈbərət/ see INDIA.

Bhopal /bəʊˈpɑːl/ city in central India, the capital of Madhya Pradesh with various manufacturing industries; pop. (1991) 1 604 000. In 1984 leakage of poisonous gas from an American-owned pesticide factory caused the death of about 2500 people and thousands suffered injury.

BHP *abbr.* (in Australia) Broken Hill Proprietary.

b.h.p. *abbr.* (also **bhp**) brake horsepower.

BHS *abbr.* British Home Stores.

BI *airline flight code* Royal Brunei Airlines.

Bi *symb.* bismuth.

bi- *comb. form* forming nouns, adjectives, and verbs, meaning: **1** division into two (*biplane*; *bisect*). **2 a** occurring twice in every one or once in every two (*bi-weekly*). **b** lasting for two (*biennial*). **3** *Chem.* substance having a double proportion of what is indicated by the simple word (*bicarbonate*). **4** *Bot.* & *Zool.* having divided parts which are themselves similarly divided (*bipinnate*). [Latin]

Biafra /bɪæˈfrə/ see NIGERIA.

biannual /baɪˈænjʊəl/ *adj.* occurring etc. twice a year.

Biarritz /bɪəˈrɪts/ seaside resort in SW France, on the Bay of Biscay; pop. (1990) 28 890.

bias /ˈbaɪəs/ *–n.* **1** (often foll. by *towards, against*) predisposition or prejudice. **2** *Statistics* distortion of a statistical result due to a neglected factor. **3** edge cut obliquely across the weave of a fabric. **4** *Sport* **a** irregular shape given to a bowl. **b** oblique course this causes it to run. *–v.* (**-s-** or **-ss-**) **1** (esp. as **biased** *adj.*) influence (usu. unfairly); prejudice. **2** give a bias to. □ **on the bias** obliquely, diagonally. [French]

bias binding *n.* strip of fabric cut obliquely and used to bind edges.

biathlon /baɪˈæθlən/ *n.* athletic contest in skiing and shooting or cycling and running. [from BI-, after PENTATHLON]

bib *n.* **1** piece of cloth etc. fastened round a child's neck while eating. **2** top front part of an apron, dungarees, etc. [origin uncertain]

bib-cock *n.* tap with a bent nozzle. [perhaps from BIB]

Bible /ˈbaɪb(ə)l/ *n.* **1 a** (prec. by *the*) Christian scriptures of Old and New Testaments. **b** (**bible**) copy of these. **2** (**bible**) *colloq.* authoritative book. □ **biblical** /ˈbɪblɪk(ə)l/ *adj.* [Greek *biblia* books]

Bible-bashing *n.* (also **Bible-thumping**) *slang* aggressive fundamentalist preaching. □ **Bible-basher** *n.* (also **-thumper**).

bibliography /ˌbɪblɪˈɒgrəfɪ/ *n.* (*pl.* **-ies**) **1** list of books on a specific subject, by a particular author, etc.; book containing this. **2** the study of books, their authorship, editions, etc. □ **bibliographer** *n.* **bibliographical** /-əˈgræfɪk(ə)l/ *adj.* [Greek: related to BIBLE]

bibliophile /ˈbɪblɪəˌfaɪl/ *n.* lover or collector of books.

bibulous /ˈbɪbjʊləs/ *adj.* tending to drink alcohol. [Latin *bibo* drink]

bicameral /baɪˈkæmər(ə)l/ *adj.* (of a legislative body) having two chambers. [from BI-, Latin *camera* chamber]

bicarb /ˈbaɪkɑːb/ *n. colloq.* = BICARBONATE 2. [abbreviation]

bicarbonate /baɪˈkɑːbənɪt/ *n.* **1** any acid salt of carbonic acid. **2** (in full **bicarbonate of soda**) sodium bicarbonate used as an antacid or in baking powder.

bicentenary /ˌbaɪsenˈtiːnərɪ/ *n.* (*pl.* **-ies**) **1** two-hundredth anniversary. **2** celebration of this.

bicentennial /ˌbaɪsenˈtenɪəl/ esp. *US –n.* bicentenary. *–adj.* occurring every two hundred years.

biceps /ˈbaɪseps/ *n.* (*pl.* same) muscle with two heads or attachments, esp. that bending the elbow. [Latin *caput* head]

bicker *v.* argue pettily. [origin unknown]

bicuspid /baɪˈkʌspɪd/ *–adj.* having two cusps. *–n.* the premolar tooth in humans. [from BI-, CUSP]

bicycle /ˈbaɪsɪk(ə)l/ *–n.* pedal-driven two-wheeled vehicle. *–v.* (**-ling**) ride a bicycle. [Greek *kuklos* wheel]

Bhutan /buːˈtɑːn/, **Kingdom of** country in SE Asia, in the Himalayas between India and Tibet. Most of the population supports itself by farming and forestry, but there is some mining (esp. of limestone) and manufacturing (food processing, chemicals, and cement), hydroelectric power stations are being established, and tourism is being developed. Exports include electricity, cardamom and other agricultural produce, timber, and cement. Head of state, King Jigme Singye Wangchuk; capital, Thimphu. □ **Bhutanese** /ˌbuːtəˈniːz/ *adj.* & *n.*

languages	Dzongkha (a form of Tibetan; official), Nepali, English
currency	ngultrum (Nu) of 100 chetrums, Indian rupee
pop. (est. 1996)	842 000
GNP (est. 1994)	US$272M
literacy	31% (m); 9% (f)
life expectancy	51 (m); 54 (f)

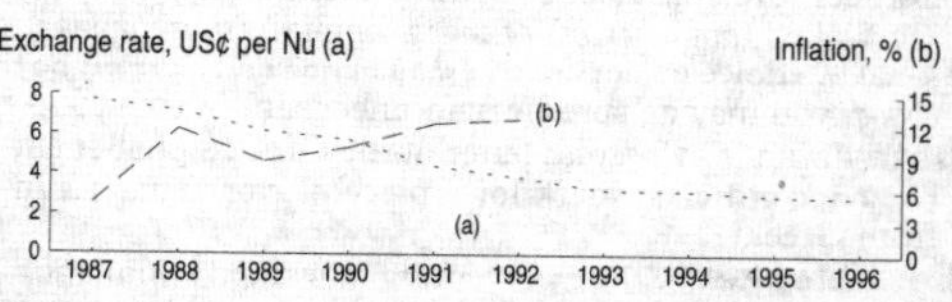

bid –*v.* (**-dd-**; *past* **bid**, *archaic* **bade** /beɪd, bæd/; *past part.* **bid**, *archaic* **bidden**) **1** (*past* and *past part.* **bid**) **a** (esp. at an auction) make an offer (of) (*bid for the vase; bid £20*). **b** offer a service for a stated price. **2** *literary* command; invite (*bid the soldiers shoot; bade her start*). **3** *literary* utter (a greeting or farewell) to (*I bade him welcome*). **4** (*past* and *past part.* **bid**) *Cards* state before play how many tricks one intends to make. –*n.* **1** act of bidding. **2 a** price at which a buyer is willing to close a deal. If the seller has made an offer which the buyer considers too high, the buyer may make a bid at a lower price (or on more advantageous terms). Having received a bid, the seller may accept it, withdraw, or make a counter-offer. Once the buyer has made a bid the original offer no longer stands. **b** see TAKE-OVER BID. **3** *colloq.* attempt; effort (*bid for power*). □ **bidder** *n.* [Old English]

biddable *adj.* obedient.

bidding *n.* **1** command, request, or invitation. **2** bids at an auction or in a card-game.

biddy *n.* (*pl.* **-ies**) *slang* woman (esp. *old biddy*). [a form of the name *Bridget*]

bide *v.* (**-ding**) □ **bide one's time** wait for a good opportunity. [Old English]

bidet /ˈbiːdeɪ/ *n.* low basin for sitting on to wash the genital area. [French, = pony]

bidirectional printer see CHARACTER PRINTER.

♦ **bid price** *n.* lower of the two prices quoted by a market maker or institution marketing shares or units in a unit trust, i.e. the price at which the market maker or institution will buy shares or units from an investor. Cf. OFFER PRICE.

Bielefeld /ˈbiːlə͵felt/ city in Germany, in North Rhine-Westphalia; motorcycles and machinery are manufactured; pop. (1987) 299 400.

biennial /baɪˈenɪəl/ –*adj.* lasting, or recurring every, two years. –*n.* plant that grows from seed one year and flowers and dies the following. [Latin *annus* year]

bier *n.* movable frame on which a coffin or corpse rests. [Old English]

BIF *abbr.* British Industries Fair.

biff *slang* –*n.* sharp blow. –*v.* strike (a person). [imitative]

♦ **BIFFEX** /ˈbɪfeks/ *abbr.* Baltic International Freight Futures Market (formerly Exchange). See BALTIC EXCHANGE.

---

bifid /ˈbaɪfɪd/ *adj.* divided by a deep cleft into two parts. [Latin *findo* cleave]

bifocal /baɪˈfəʊk(ə)l/ –*adj.* having two focuses, esp. of a lens with a part for distant and a part for near vision. –*n.* (in *pl.*) bifocal spectacles.

BIFU /ˈbɪfuː/ *abbr.* Banking, Insurance, and Finance Union.

bifurcate /ˈbaɪfə͵keɪt/ –*v.* (**-ting**) fork. –*adj.* forked; branched. □ **bifurcation** /-ˈkeɪʃ(ə)n/ *n.* [Latin *furca* fork]

big –*adj.* (**bigger, biggest**) **1 a** of considerable size, amount, intensity, etc. **b** of a large or the largest size (*big toe*). **2** important (*my big day*). **3** adult, elder (*big sister*). **4** *colloq.* **a** boastful (*big words*). **b** often *iron.* generous (*big of him*). **c** ambitious (*big ideas*). **5** (usu. foll. by *with*) advanced in pregnancy (*big with child*). –*adv. colloq.* impressively or grandly (*think big*). □ **in a big way** *colloq.* with great enthusiasm, display, etc. □ **biggish** *adj.* [origin unknown]

bigamy /ˈbɪgəmɪ/ *n.* (*pl.* **-ies**) crime of marrying while still married to another person. □ **bigamist** *n.* **bigamous** *adj.* [Greek *gamos* marriage]

Big Apple *n. US slang* New York City.

♦ **Big Bang** *n.* modernization of the London Stock Exchange (LSE), which took place on 27 October 1986. The major changes enacted on that date were the abolition of LSE rules enforcing a dual-capacity system and the abolition of fixed commission rates charged by stockbrokers to their clients.

---

big bang theory *n.* theory that the universe began with the explosion of dense matter.

Big Brother *n.* supposedly benevolent watchful dictator.

♦ **Big Eight** *n.* eight largest firms of accountants in the world, i.e. Arthur Andersen, Coopers and Lybrand, Deloitte Haskins and Sells, Ernst and Whinney, Peat Marwick Mitchell, Price Waterhouse, Touche Ross, and Arthur Young.

---

big end *n.* (in a vehicle) end of the connecting-rod, encircling the crankpin.

big-head *n. colloq.* conceited person. □ **big-headed** *adj.*

big-hearted *adj.* generous.

bight /baɪt/ *n.* **1** bay, inlet, etc. **2** loop of rope. [Old English]

big money *n.* large amounts of money.

big noise *n.* (also **big shot**) *colloq.* = BIGWIG.

bigot /ˈbɪgət/ *n.* obstinate believer who is intolerant of others. □ **bigoted** *adj.* **bigotry** *n.* [French]

big stick *n. colloq.* display of force.

big time *n.* (prec. by *the*) *slang* success, esp. in show business. □ **big-timer** *n.*

big top *n.* main tent in a circus.

big wheel *n.* Ferris wheel.

bigwig *n. colloq.* important person.

Bihar /bɪˈhɑː(r)/ state in NE India; pop. (1991) 86 338 853; capital, Patna. The economy is based on mining and farming.

BIIBA *abbr.* = BRITISH INSURANCE AND INVESTMENT BROKERS ASSOCIATION.

Bijagos, Ilhas dos see BISSAGOS ISLANDS.

bijou /ˈbiːʒuː/ –*n.* (*pl.* **-x** pronunc. same) jewel; trinket. –*attrib. adj.* (**bijou**) small and elegant. [French]

bike *colloq.* –*n.* bicycle or motor cycle. –*v.* (**-king**) ride a bike. □ **biker** *n.* [abbreviation]

bikini /bɪˈkiːnɪ/ *n.* (*pl.* **-s**) two-piece swimsuit for women. [*Bikini*, Pacific atoll]

bilateral /baɪˈlætər(ə)l/ *adj.* **1** of, on, or with two sides. **2** affecting or between two parties, countries, etc. □ **bilaterally** *adv.*

♦ **bilateral monopoly** *n.* situation in which a monopoly seller bargains with a monopoly buyer (see MONOPSONY). The classic application of bilateral monopoly is to the negotiation of wages between a union and a firm. The most famous solution (1950) is that stated by John Nash (see NASH EQUILIBRIUM), which suggests that both sides will settle for the wage that maximizes the benefits from cooperation.

♦ **bilateral trade agreement** *n.* agreement on trade policy between two countries, usu. concerning a reduction in tariffs or other protective barriers. Although bilateral deals tend to fragment world trade, governments are attracted by their relative simplicity. The US, in particular, has used such deals in free-trade agreements with Mexico and Canada and to hasten the resolution of problems with particular trading partners, notably Japan and other Asian countries.

Bilbao /bɪlˈbɑːəʊ/ seaport in N Spain; industries include metallurgy and chemicals; pop. (est. 1994) 371 787.

bilberry /ˈbɪlbərɪ/ *n.* (*pl.* **-ies**) **1** hardy N European shrub of heaths and mountains. **2** its small dark-blue edible berry. [Scandinavian]

bile *n.* **1** bitter digestive fluid secreted by the liver. **2** bad temper; peevish anger. [Latin *bilis*]

bilge /bɪldʒ/ *n.* **1 a** the almost flat part of a ship's bottom. **b** (in full **bilge-water**) filthy water that collects there. **2** *slang* nonsense. [probably var. of BULGE]

bilharzia /bɪlˈhɑːtsɪə/ *n.* chronic tropical disease caused by a parasitic flatworm. [*Bilharz*, name of a physician]

biliary /ˈbɪlɪərɪ/ *adj.* of the bile. [French: related to BILE]

bilingual /baɪˈlɪŋgw(ə)l/ –*adj.* **1** able to speak two languages. **2** spoken or written in two languages. –*n.* bilingual person. □ **bilingualism** *n.* [Latin *lingua* tongue]

bilious /ˈbɪlɪəs/ *adj.* **1** affected by a disorder of the bile. **2** bad-tempered. [Latin: related to BILE]

bilk *v. slang* **1** cheat. **2** elude. **3** avoid paying (a creditor or debt). [origin uncertain]

bill[1] –*n.* **1** statement of charges for goods or services. **2** draft of a proposed law. **3** poster or placard. **4** programme of entertainment. **5** = BILL OF EXCHANGE. **6** *US* banknote. –*v.* **1** send a statement of charges to. **2** put in the programme; announce. **3** (foll. by *as*) advertise as. [medieval Latin *bulla* seal]

bill[2] –*n.* **1** bird's beak. **2** narrow promontory. –*v.* (of doves etc.) stroke bills. □ **bill and coo** exchange caresses. [Old English]

bill[3] *n.* **1** *hist.* weapon with a hook-shaped blade. **2** = BILLHOOK. [Old English]

billabong /ˈbɪləˌbɒŋ/ *n.* (in Australia) backwater of a river. [Aboriginal]

billboard *n.* large outdoor advertising hoarding.

♦ **bill broker** *n.* (also **discount broker**) broker who buys bills of exchange from traders and sells them to banks and discount houses or holds them to maturity. Many now deal exclusively in treasury bills.

---

billet[1] /ˈbɪlɪt/ –*n.* **1 a** place where troops etc. are lodged. **b** order to provide this. **2** *colloq.* job. –*v.* (**-t-**) (usu. foll. by *on, in, at*) quarter (soldiers etc.). [Anglo-French diminutive of BILL[1]]

billet[2] /ˈbɪlɪt/ *n.* **1** thick piece of firewood. **2** small metal bar. [French diminutive of *bille* tree-trunk]

billet-doux /ˌbɪlɪˈduː/ *n.* (*pl.* **billets-doux** /-ˈduːz/) often *joc.* love-letter. [French, = sweet note]

billhook *n.* pruning tool with a hooked blade.

billiards /ˈbɪljədz/ *n.* **1** game played on a table, with three balls struck with cues. **2** (**billiard**) (in *comb.*) used in billiards (*billiard-ball*). [French: related to BILLET[2]]

Billingsgate /ˈbɪlɪŋzˌgeɪt/ London fish-market dating from the 16th century, moved from its original site near London Bridge to the Isle of Dogs in 1982 and known for the invective traditionally ascribed to the fish-porters.

billion /ˈbɪljən/ *adj.* & *n.* (*pl.* same or (in sense 3) **-s**) **1** a thousand million (10^9). **2** (now less often) a million million (10^{12}). **3** (in *pl.*) *colloq.* a very large number (*billions of years*). □ **billionth** *adj.* & *n.* [French]

billionaire /ˌbɪljəˈneə(r)/ *n.* person who has over a billion pounds, dollars, etc. [after MILLIONAIRE]

♦ **bill of entry** *n.* detailed statement of the nature and value of a consignment of goods prepared by the shipper of the consignment for customs entry.

♦ **bill of exchange** *n.* unconditional order in writing, addressed by one person (the drawer) to another (the drawee) and signed by the person giving it, requiring the drawee to pay on demand or at a fixed or determinable future time a specified sum of money to or to the order of a specified person (the payee) or to the bearer. If the bill is payable at a future time the drawee signifies his or her acceptance, which makes the drawee the party primarily liable upon the bill; the drawer and endorsers may also be liable upon a bill. The use of bills of exchange enables one person to transfer to another an enforceable right to a sum of money. A bill of exchange is not only transferable but also negotiable, since if a person without an enforceable right to the money transfers a bill to a holder in due course, the latter obtains a good title to it. Much of the law on bills of exchange is codified by the Bills of Exchange Act (1882). See ACCOMMODATION BILL; BILLS IN A SET; DISHONOUR *v.* 3; HOLDER 3.

---

bill of fare *n.* menu.

♦ **bill of lading** *n.* document acknowledging the shipment of a consignor's goods for carriage by sea. It is used primarily when the ship is carrying goods belonging to a number of consignors (a general ship). In this case, each consignor receives a bill issued (normally by the master of the ship) on behalf of either the shipowner or a charterer under a charter-party. The bill serves three functions: it is a receipt for the goods; it summarizes the terms of the contract of carriage; and it acts as a document of title to the goods. A bill of lading is also issued by a shipowner to a charterer who is using the ship for the carriage of his or her own goods. In this case, the terms of the contract of carriage are in the charter-party and the bill serves only as a receipt and a document of title. During transit, ownership of the goods may be transferred by delivering the bill to another if it is drawn to bearer or by endorsing it if it is drawn to order. It is not, however, a negotiable instrument. The bill gives details of the goods; if the packages are in good order a **clean bill** is issued; if they are not, the bill will say so (see DIRTY BILL OF LADING). See also CONTAINERIZATION.

♦ **bill of quantities** *n.* document drawn up by a quantity surveyor showing in detail the materials and parts required to build a structure (e.g. factory, house, office block), together with the price of each component and the labour costs. The bill of quantities is one of the tender documents that goes out to contractors who wish to quote for carrying out the work.

♦ **bill of sale** *n.* **1** document by which a person transfers the ownership of goods to another. Commonly the goods are transferred conditionally, as security for a debt, and a **conditional bill of sale** is thus a mortgage of goods. The mortgager has a right to redeem the goods on repayment of the debt and usu. remains in possession of them; he or she may thus obtain false credit by appearing to own them. An **absolute bill of sale** transfers ownership of the goods absolutely. The Bills of Sale Acts (1878 and 1882) regulate the registration and form of bills of sale. **2** document recording the change of ownership when a ship is sold; it is regarded internationally as legal proof of ownership.

♦ **bill of sight** *n.* document that an importer, who is unable fully to describe an imported cargo, gives to the Customs and Excise authorities to authorize them to inspect the goods on landing. After the goods have been landed and the importer supplies the missing information the entry is completed and the importer is said to have **perfected the sight**.

♦ **bill of sufferance** *n.* document issued by the Customs and Excise enabling goods to be landed in the absence of detailed documentation, subject to the Customs being able to examine the goods at any time.

---

billow /ˈbɪləʊ/ –*n.* **1** wave. **2** any large mass. –*v.* rise, fill, or surge in billows. □ **billowy** *adj.* [Old Norse]

billposter *n.* (also **billsticker**) person who pastes up advertisements on hoardings.

♦ **bill rate** *n.* (also **discount rate**) rate on the discount market at which bills of exchange are discounted (i.e. purchased for less than they are worth when they mature). The rate will depend on the quality of the bill and the risk the purchaser takes. First-class bills, i.e. those backed by banks or well-respected finance houses, will be discounted at a lower rate than bills involving greater risk.

♦ **bills in a set** *n.pl.* two, or more usu. three, copies of a foreign bill of exchange. Payment is made on any one of the three, the others becoming invalid on the payment of any one of them. All are made out in the same way, except that each refers to the others. The first copy is called the **first of exchange**, the next is the **second of exchange**, and so on. The duplication or triplication is to reduce the risk of loss in transit.

♦ **bills payable** *n.pl.* item that may appear in a firm's accounts under current liabilities, summarizing the bills of exchange being held, which will have to be paid when they mature.

♦ **bills receivable** *n.pl.* item that may appear in a firm's accounts under current assets, summarizing the bills of exchange being held until the funds become available when they mature.

---

billy[1] /ˈbɪlɪ/ *n.* (*pl.* **-ies**) (in full **billycan**) *Austral.* tin or enamel outdoor cooking-pot. [perhaps from Aboriginal *billa* water]

billy[2] /ˈbɪlɪ/ *n.* (*pl.* **-ies**) (in full **billy-goat**) male goat. [from the name *Billy*]

♦ **BIM** *abbr.* = BRITISH INSTITUTE OF MANAGEMENT.

bimbo /ˈbɪmbəʊ/ *n.* (*pl.* **-s** or **-es**) *slang* usu. *derog.* attractive but unintelligent young woman. [Italian, = little child]

bimetallic /ˌbaɪmɪˈtælɪk/ *adj.* using or made of two metals. [French]

bin *n.* large receptacle for rubbish or storage. [Old English]

binary /ˈbaɪnərɪ/ *–adj.* **1** of two parts, dual. **2** of the binary system. *–n.* (*pl.* **-ies**) **1** something having two parts. **2** binary number. [Latin *bini* two together]

binary code *n. Computing* rule for transforming data, program instructions, or other information into a symbolic form in which only the two binary digits 0 and 1 are used. Once encoded there is no way of distinguishing an instruction from a piece of data. The binary notation used to represent numbers in a computer is a binary encoding. The representation of letters and other characters using the ASCII scheme is another example.

binary digit *n.* either of the two digits 0 and 1. See BIT[4]; BINARY NOTATION.

♦ **binary notation** *n.* way of writing numbers using two symbols only. The symbols are usu. written as 0 and 1, and called **bits** (or **binary digits**). A **binary number** is composed of a sequence of bits, e.g. 1001. The value of a binary number depends not only on the bits it contains but also on their position in the number. The positional value increases from right to left by powers of 2, i.e. positions from the right represent 'units', 'twos', 'fours', 'eights', and so on. Binary notation is used in computing to represent numbers internally.

binary number see BINARY NOTATION.

binary star *n.* system of two stars orbiting each other.

binary system *n.* system involving just two possible values, two alternatives, or two items. One example is binary notation, in which numbers are represented by means of the two digits 0 and 1 (see BINARY NOTATION; BIT[4]).

binaural /baɪˈnɔːr(ə)l/ *adj.* **1** of or used with both ears. **2** (of sound) recorded using two microphones and usu. transmitted separately to the two ears. [from BI-, AURAL]

bind /baɪnd/ *–v.* (*past* and *past part.* **bound**) **1** tie or fasten tightly. **2** restrain forcibly. **3** (cause to) cohere. **4** compel; impose a duty on. **5 a** edge with braid etc. **b** fasten (the pages of a book) in a cover. **6** constipate. **7** ratify (a bargain, agreement, etc.). **8** (often foll. by *up*) bandage. *–n. colloq.* nuisance; restriction. □ **bind over** *Law* order (a person) to do something, esp. keep the peace. [Old English]

binder *n.* **1** cover for loose papers etc. **2** substance that binds things together. **3** *hist.* reaping-machine that binds grain into sheaves. **4** bookbinder.

bindery *n.* (*pl.* **-ies**) bookbinder's workshop.

binding *–n.* thing that binds, esp. the covers, glue, etc., of a book. *–adj.* obligatory.

bindweed *n.* **1** convolvulus. **2** honeysuckle or other climber.

bine *n.* **1** twisting stem of a climbing plant, esp. the hop. **2** flexible shoot. [dial. form of BIND]

bin end *n.* one of the last bottles from a bin of wine, usu. sold at a reduced price.

binge /bɪndʒ/ *slang –n.* bout of excessive eating, drinking, etc.; spree. *–v.* (**-ging**) indulge in a binge. [probably dial., = soak]

bingo /ˈbɪŋgəʊ/ *n.* gambling game in which each player has a card with numbers to be marked off as they are called. [origin uncertain]

bin-liner *n.* bag for lining a rubbish bin.

binman *n. colloq.* dustman.

binnacle /ˈbɪnək(ə)l/ *n.* case for a ship's compass. [Latin *habitaculum* dwelling]

binocular /baɪˈnɒkjʊlə(r)/ *adj.* for both eyes. [Latin *bini* two together, *oculus* eye]

binoculars /bɪˈnɒkjʊləz/ *n.pl.* instrument with a lens for each eye, for viewing distant objects.

binomial /baɪˈnəʊmɪəl/ *–n.* algebraic expression of the sum or the difference of two terms. *–adj.* of two terms. [Greek *nomos* part]

binomial theorem *n.* formula for finding any power of a binomial.

bint *n. slang*, usu. *offens.* girl or woman. [Arabic]

bio- *comb. form* **1** life (*biography*). **2** biological; of living things. [Greek *bios* life]

biochemistry /ˌbaɪəʊˈkemɪstrɪ/ *n.* the study of the chemistry of living organisms. □ **biochemical** *adj.* **biochemist** *n.*

biodegradable /ˌbaɪəʊdɪˈgreɪdəb(ə)l/ *adj.* capable of being decomposed by bacteria or other living organisms.

bioengineering /ˌbaɪəʊˌendʒɪˈnɪərɪŋ/ *n.* **1** the application of engineering techniques to biological processes. **2** the use of artificial tissues, organs, etc. to replace parts of the body, e.g. artificial limbs, pacemakers, etc.

biogenesis /ˌbaɪəʊˈdʒenɪsɪs/ *n.* **1** hypothesis that a living organism arises only from a similar living organism. **2** synthesis of substances by living organisms.

biography /baɪˈɒgrəfɪ/ *n.* (*pl.* **-ies**) **1** account of a person's life, written usu. by another. **2** these as a literary genre. □ **biographer** *n.* **biographical** /ˌbaɪəˈgræfɪk(ə)l/ *adj.* [French: related to BIO-]

Bioko /bɪˈəʊkəʊ/ (formerly **Fernando Po**, **Macías Nguema Bijogo**) island in the Gulf of Guinea, forming part of Equatorial Guinea; coffee, cacao, and copra are produced; pop. (est. 1987) 67 920.

biological /ˌbaɪəˈlɒdʒɪk(ə)l/ *adj.* of biology or living organisms. □ **biologically** *adv.*

biological clock *n.* innate mechanism controlling an organism's rhythmic physiological activities.

biological warfare *n.* use of toxins or micro-organisms against an enemy.

biology /baɪˈɒlədʒɪ/ *n.* the study of living organisms. □ **biologist** *n.* [German: related to BIO-]

bionic /baɪˈɒnɪk/ *adj.* having electronically operated body parts or the resulting superhuman powers. [from BIO- after ELECTRONIC]

bionics *n.pl.* (treated as *sing.*) the study of mechanical systems that function like living organisms.

biophysics /ˌbaɪəʊˈfɪzɪks/ *n.pl.* (treated as *sing.*) science of the application of the laws of physics to biological phenomena. □ **biophysical** *adj.* **biophysicist** *n.*

biopsy /ˈbaɪɒpsɪ/ *n.* (*pl.* **-ies**) examination of severed tissue for diagnosis. [Greek *bios* life, *opsis* sight]

biorhythm /ˈbaɪəʊˌrɪð(ə)m/ *n.* any recurring biological cycle thought to affect one's physical or mental state.

BIOS /ˈbaɪɒs/ *abbr. Computing* basic input-output system.

biosphere /ˈbaɪəʊˌsfɪə(r)/ *n.* regions of the earth's crust and atmosphere occupied by living things. [German: related to BIO-]

biosynthesis /ˌbaɪəʊˈsɪnθɪsɪs/ *n.* production of organic molecules by living organisms. □ **biosynthetic** /-ˈθetɪk/ *adj.*

biotechnology /ˌbaɪəʊtekˈnɒlədʒɪ/ *n.* branch of technology exploiting biological processes, esp. using micro-organisms, in industry, medicine, etc.

biotin /ˈbaɪətɪn/ *n.* vitamin of the B complex, found in egg-yolk, liver, and yeast. [Greek *bios* life]

BIP *abbr.* British Industrial Plastics.

bipartisan /ˌbaɪpɑːtɪˈzæn/ *adj.* of or involving two parties.

bipartite /baɪˈpɑːtaɪt/ *adj.* **1** of two parts. **2** shared by or involving two parties. [Latin *bipartio* divide in two]

biped /ˈbaɪped/ *–n.* two-footed animal. *–adj.* two-footed. □ **bipedal** *adj.* [Latin *bipes -edis*]

biplane /ˈbaɪpleɪn/ *n.* aeroplane with two sets of wings, one above the other.

bipolar /baɪˈpəʊlə(r)/ *adj.* having two poles or extremities.

BIR *abbr.* = BOARD OF INLAND REVENUE.

birch *–n.* **1** tree with pale hard wood and thin peeling bark, bearing catkins. **2** bundle of birch twigs used for flogging. *–v.* beat with a birch. [Old English]

bird *n.* **1** two-legged feathered winged vertebrate, egg-laying and usu. able to fly. **2** *slang* young woman. **3** *slang* person. □ **a bird in the hand** something secured or certain. **the birds and the bees** *euphem.* sexual activity and reproduction. **birds of a feather** similar people. **for the birds** *colloq.* trivial, uninteresting. **get the bird** *slang* be rejected, esp. by an audience. [Old English]

bird-bath *n.* basin with water for birds to bathe in.

birdbrain *n. colloq.* stupid or flighty person. □ **bird-brained** *adj.*

birdcage *n.* cage for birds.

birdie *n.* **1** *colloq.* little bird. **2** *Golf* hole played in one under par.

birdlime *n.* sticky substance spread to trap birds.

bird-nesting *n.* hunting for birds' eggs.

bird of paradise *n.* bird, the male of which has brilliant plumage.

bird of passage *n.* **1** migrant. **2** habitual traveller.

bird of prey *n.* bird which hunts animals for food.

birdseed *n.* blend of seeds for caged birds.

bird's-eye view *n.* detached view from above.

birdsong *n.* musical cry of birds.

bird table *n.* platform on which food for birds is placed.

bird-watcher *n.* person who observes wild birds as a hobby. □ **bird-watching** *n.*

biretta /bɪˈretə/ *n.* square usu. black cap worn by Roman Catholic priests. [Latin *birrus* cape]

Birmingham /ˈbɜːmɪŋəm/ **1** industrial city and the county town of West Midlands; pop. (est. 1994) 1 008 400. Major industries include motor vehicles and general engineering, and Birmingham is the site of the National Exhibition Centre. **2** city in the US, the largest city in Alabama and a main industrial centre of the South; pop. (1994) 264 527.

Biro /ˈbaɪərəʊ/ *n.* (*pl.* **-s**) *propr.* a kind of ball-point pen. [*Biró*, name of its inventor]

birr /bɜː/ *n.* standard monetary unit of Ethiopia. [Amharic]

birth *n.* **1** emergence of a baby or young from its mother's body. **2** beginning (*birth of civilization*). **3 a** ancestry (*of noble birth*). **b** high or noble birth; inherited position. □ **give birth to 1** produce (young). **2** be the cause of. [Old Norse]

birth certificate *n.* official document detailing a person's birth.

birth control *n.* contraception.

birthday *n.* **1** day on which one was born. **2** anniversary of this.

birthing pool *n.* large bath for giving birth in.

birthmark *n.* unusual coloured mark on one's body at or from birth.

birthplace *n.* place where one was born.

birth rate *n.* number of live births per thousand of population per year.

birthright *n.* inherited, esp. property, rights.

birthstone *n.* gem popularly associated with the month of one's birth.

♦ **BIS** *abbr.* = BANK FOR INTERNATIONAL SETTLEMENTS.

Biscay /ˈbɪskeɪ/, **Bay of** part of the North Atlantic between the N coast of Spain and the W coast of France, notorious for storms.

biscuit /ˈbɪskɪt/ *n.* **1** flat thin unleavened cake, usu. crisp and sweet. **2** fired unglazed pottery. **3** light brown colour. [Latin *bis* twice, *coquo* cook]

bisect /baɪˈsekt/ *v.* divide into two (strictly, equal) parts. □ **bisection** *n.* **bisector** *n.* [from BI-, Latin *seco sect-* cut]

bisexual /baɪˈsekʃʊəl/ *–adj.* **1** feeling or involving sexual attraction to people of both sexes. **2** hermaphrodite. *–n.* bisexual person. □ **bisexuality** /-ˈælɪtɪ/ *n.*

BISF *abbr.* British Iron and Steel Federation.

Bishkek see PISHPEK.

bishop /ˈbɪʃəp/ *n.* **1** senior clergyman in charge of a diocese. **2** mitre-shaped chess piece. [Greek *episkopos* overseer]

bishopric /ˈbɪʃəprɪk/ *n.* office or diocese of a bishop.

Bismarck /ˈbɪzmɑːk/ city in the US, the capital of North Dakota; pop. (1990) 49 256. It is an agricultural market centre.

Bismarck Sea arm of the Pacific Ocean NE of New Guinea and N of New Britain.

bismuth /ˈbɪzməθ/ *n.* **1** reddish-white metallic element used in alloys etc. **2** compound of it used medicinally. [German]

bison /ˈbaɪs(ə)n/ *n.* (*pl.* same) wild hump-backed ox of Europe or North America. [Latin from Germanic]

BISPA *abbr.* British Independent Steel Producers' Association.

bisque[1] /bɪsk/ *n.* rich soup, esp. of lobster. [French]

bisque[2] /bɪsk/ *n.* advantage of one free point or stroke in certain games. [French]

bisque[3] /bɪsk/ *n.* = BISCUIT 2.

Bissagos Islands /bɪˈsɑːgəs/ (Portuguese **Ilhas dos Bijagós** /ˌviːʒəˈgɒʃ/) group of islands off the coast of Guinea-Bissau, W Africa.

Bissau /bɪˈsəʊ/ capital and chief port of Guinea-Bissau; pop. (est. 1991) 197 610.

bistre /ˈbɪstə(r)/ *n.* (*US* **bister**) brownish pigment from wood soot. [French]

bistro /ˈbiːstrəʊ/ *n.* (*pl.* **-s**) small informal restaurant. [French]

BISYNC /ˈbaɪˌsɪŋk/ *abbr. Computing* binary synchronous communications.

bit[1] *n.* **1** small piece or quantity. **2** (prec. by *a*) fair amount (*sold quite a bit*). **3** often *colloq.* short or small time, distance, or amount (*wait a bit*; *move up a bit*; *a bit tired*; *a bit of an idiot*). □ **bit by bit** gradually. **do one's bit** *colloq.* make a useful contribution. [Old English]

bit[2] *past* of BITE.

bit[3] *n.* **1** metal mouthpiece of a bridle. **2** tool or piece for boring or drilling. **3** cutting or gripping part of a plane, pincers, etc. [Old English]

bit[4] *n. Computing* either of the two digits 0 and 1 used for the internal representation of numbers, characters, and machine instructions. The bit is the smallest unit of information and of storage in any binary system within a computer. See BINARY NOTATION. [*binary digit*]

bitch *–n.* **1** female dog or other canine animal. **2** *slang offens.* spiteful woman. **3** *slang* unpleasant or difficult thing. *–v.* **1** speak scathingly or spitefully. **2** complain. [Old English]

bitchy *adj.* (**-ier, -iest**) *slang* spiteful. □ **bitchily** *adv.* **bitchiness** *n.*

bit density *Computing* see DENSITY 4.

bite *–v.* (**-ting**; *past* **bit**; *past part.* **bitten**) **1** cut or puncture with the teeth. **2** (foll. by *off*, *away*, etc.) detach thus. **3** (of an insect etc.) sting. **4** (of a wheel etc.) grip, penetrate. **5** accept bait or an inducement. **6** be harsh in effect, esp. intentionally. **7** (in *passive*) **a** swindle. **b** (foll. by *by*, *with*, etc.) be infected by (enthusiasm etc.). **8** *colloq.* worry, perturb. **9** cause smarting pain (*biting wind*). **10** be sharp or effective (*biting wit*). **11** (foll. by *at*) snap at. *–n.* **1** act of biting. **2** wound etc. made by biting. **3 a** mouthful of food. **b** snack. **4** taking of bait by a fish. **5** pungency (esp. of flavour). **6** incisiveness, sharpness. **7** position of the teeth when the jaws are closed. □ **bite the dust** *slang* die. **bite a person's head off** *colloq.* respond angrily. **bite one's lip** repress emotion etc. [Old English]

bit on the side *n. slang* sexual relationship involving infidelity.

bit part *n.* minor role.

bit rate *n. Computing* number of bits transmitted or

transferred per unit of time. The unit of time is usu. the second; the bit rate is then the number of bits per second (bps).

bitter –*adj.* **1** having a sharp pungent taste; not sweet. **2** causing, showing, or feeling mental pain or resentment (*bitter memories*). **3 a** harsh; virulent (*bitter animosity*). **b** piercingly cold. –*n.* **1** beer flavoured with hops and tasting slightly bitter. **2** (in *pl.*) liquor flavoured esp. with wormwood, used in cocktails. □ **to the bitter end** to the very end in spite of difficulties. □ **bitterly** *adv.* **bitterness** *n.* [Old English]

bittern /ˈbɪt(ə)n/ *n.* wading bird of the heron family. [French *butor* from Latin *butio*]

bitter-sweet –*adj.* sweet with a bitter aftertaste. –*n.* **1** such sweetness. **2** = WOODY NIGHTSHADE.

bitty *adj.* (**-ier, -iest**) made up of bits; scrappy.

bitumen /ˈbɪtjʊmɪn/ *n.* tarlike mixture of hydrocarbons derived from petroleum. [Latin]

bituminous /bɪˈtjuːmɪnəs/ *adj.* of or like bitumen.

bituminous coal *n.* coal burning with a smoky flame.

bivalve /ˈbaɪvælv/ –*n.* aquatic mollusc with a hinged double shell, e.g. the oyster and mussel. –*adj.* with such a shell.

bivouac /ˈbɪvʊˌæk/ –*n.* temporary open encampment without tents. –*v.* (**-ck-**) make, or camp in, a bivouac. [French, probably from German]

biz *n. colloq.* business. [abbreviation]

bizarre /bɪˈzɑː(r)/ *adj.* strange; eccentric; grotesque. [French]

Bizerta /bɪˈzɜːtə/ (also **Bizerte**) seaport on the N coast of Tunisia; industries include oil refining and metalwork; pop. (1994) 98 970.

Bk *symb.* berkelium.

bk. *abbr.* **1** backwardation. **2** bank.

bkcy. *abbr.* bankruptcy.

bkg. *abbr.* **1** banking. **2** (also **bkkg.**) bookkeeping.

bkpt. *abbr.* (also **bkrpt.**) bankrupt.

BL –*abbr.* (also **B/L, b/l, b.l.**) **1** bill of lading. **2** *hist.* British Leyland. **3** British Library. –*postcode* Bolton.

blab *v.* (**-bb-**) **1** talk foolishly or indiscreetly. **2** reveal (a secret etc.); confess. [imitative]

blabber –*n.* (also **blabbermouth**) person who blabs. –*v.* (often foll. by *on*) talk foolishly or inconsequentially.

♦ **Black, Conrad Moffat** (1944–) Canadian businessman, deputy chairman of Hollinger International, Canada's largest newspaper company, through which he is chairman of Daily Telegraph plc (since 1987) and a director of Jerusalem Post Publications Ltd. He is also chief executive of Argus Corporation Ltd. (since 1985) and a director of the Canadian Imperial Bank of Commerce.

---

black –*adj.* **1** reflecting no light, colourless from lack of light (like coal or soot); completely dark. **2** (**Black**) of the human group with dark-coloured skin, esp. African. **3** (of the sky etc.) heavily overcast. **4** angry; gloomy (*black look, mood*). **5** implying disgrace etc. (*in his black books*). **6** wicked, sinister, deadly. **7** portending trouble (*things look black*). **8** comic but sinister (*black comedy*). **9** (of tea or coffee) without milk. **10** (of industrial labour or its products) boycotted, esp. by a trade union, in a strike etc. –*n.* **1** black colour or pigment. **2** black clothes or material (*dressed in black*). **3 a** (in a game) black piece, ball, etc. **b** player of this. **4** credit side of an account (*in the black*). **5** (**Black**) member of a dark-skinned race, esp. an African. –*v.* **1** make black (*blacked his boots*). **2** declare (goods etc.) 'black'. □ **black out 1** effect a blackout on. **2** undergo a blackout. [Old English]

black and blue *adj.* bruised.

black and white –*n.* writing or printing (*in black and white*). –*adj.* **1** (of a film etc.) monochrome. **2** consisting of extremes only, oversimplified.

black art *n.* = BLACK MAGIC.

blackball *v.* reject (a candidate) in a ballot.

black beetle *n.* the common cockroach.

black belt *n.* **1** highest grade of proficiency in judo, karate, etc. **2** holder of this grade, entitled to wear a black belt.

blackberry *n.* (*pl.* **-ies**) black fleshy edible fruit of the bramble.

blackbird *n.* common thrush of which the male is black with an orange beak.

blackboard *n.* board with a smooth dark surface for writing on with chalk.

black box *n.* **1** flight-recorder. **2** self-contained unit in, for example, a computer system or a communications system, whose function can be understood without any knowledge or reference to its electronic components or circuitry.

blackcap *n.* small warbler, the male of which has a black-topped head.

Black Country *n.* (prec. by *the*) industrial area of the Midlands.

blackcurrant *n.* **1** cultivated flowering shrub. **2** its small dark edible berry.

Black Death *n.* (prec. by *the*) 14th-century plague in Europe.

♦ **black economy** *n.* economic activity that is undisclosed, as to disclose it would render the earnings involved liable to taxation or even cause those engaged to be imprisoned (if they are claiming state benefits and have lied about their earnings). In economies in which production and exchange are regulated by the state (see COMMAND ECONOMY), the black economy is generally considered to be very large, although by its nature it is unmeasurable. Even in mixed economies, however, the black economy is thought to be significant, largely due to the benefits of evading tax. Earnings made in the black economy do not appear in national statistics.

---

blacken *v.* **1** make or become black or dark. **2** defame, slander.

black eye *n.* bruised skin around the eye.

black flag *n.* flag of piracy.

blackfly *n.* **1** dark coloured thrips or aphid. **2** these collectively.

Black Forest gateau *n.* chocolate sponge with cherries and whipped cream. [originally from the *Black Forest* region of SW Germany]

Black Friar *n.* Dominican friar.

blackguard /ˈblægɑːd/*n.* villain, scoundrel. □ **blackguardly** *adj.* [originally = menial]

blackhead *n.* black-topped pimple on the skin.

black hole *n.* region of space from which matter and radiation cannot escape.

black ice *n.* thin hard transparent ice on a road etc.

blacking *n.* black polish, esp. for shoes.

blackjack *n.* = PONTOON[1].

♦ **black knight** *n.* person or firm that makes an unwelcome take-over bid for a company. Cf. GREY KNIGHT; WHITE KNIGHT.

---

blacklead *n.* graphite.

blackleg –*n. derog.* person refusing to join a strike etc. –*v.* (**-gg-**) act as a blackleg.

blacklist –*n.* list of people in disfavour etc. –*v.* put on a blacklist.

black magic *n.* magic supposed to invoke evil spirits.

blackmail –*n.* **1 a** extortion of payment in return for silence. **b** payment so extorted. **2** use of threats or moral pressure. –*v.* **1** (try to) extort money etc. from by blackmail. **2** threaten, coerce. □ **blackmailer** *n.* [obsolete *mail* rent]

Black Maria /məˈraɪə/ *n. slang* police van.

black mark *n.* mark of discredit.

♦ **black market** *n.* illegal market for a particular good or service. It can occur when regulations control a particular trade (as in arms dealing) or a particular period (as in wartime). Cf. GREY MARKET 1. □ **black marketeer** *n.*

Black Mass *n.* travesty of the Mass, in worship of Satan.

♦ **Black Monday** *n.* either of the two Mondays on which the two largest stock market crashes occurred in this century. The original Wall Street crash occurred on Monday, 28 October 1929, when the Dow Jones Industrial Average fell by 13%. On Monday, 19 October 1987, the Dow Jones Average lost 23%. In both cases Black Monday in the US triggered heavy stock market falls around the world.

blackout *n.* **1** temporary loss of consciousness or memory. **2** loss of electric power, radio reception, etc. **3** compulsory darkness as a precaution against air raids. **4** temporary suppression of news. **5** sudden darkening of a theatre stage.

black pepper *n.* pepper made by grinding the whole dried pepper berry including the outer husk.

Blackpool /ˈblækpuːl/ seaside resort in NE England, on the coast of Lancashire; pop. (est. 1994) 153 600.

Black Power *n.* movement for Black rights and political power.

black pudding *n.* sausage of pork, dried pig's blood, suet, etc.

Black Rod *n.* principal usher of the House of Lords etc.

Black Sea virtually landlocked sea bounded by Russia, Georgia, Turkey, Bulgaria, Romania, Moldova, and Ukraine, connected to the Mediterranean Sea through the Bosporus and Sea of Marmara.

black sheep *n. colloq.* member of a family, group, etc. regarded as a disgrace or failure.

blackshirt *n. hist.* member of a Fascist organization.

blacksmith *n.* smith who works in iron.

black spot *n.* **1** place of danger or trouble. **2** plant disease producing black spots.

black tea *n.* tea that is fully fermented before drying.

blackthorn *n.* thorny shrub bearing white blossom and sloes.

black tie *n.* **1** black bow-tie worn with a dinner jacket. **2** *colloq.* man's formal evening dress.

black velvet *n.* mixture of stout and champagne.

Black Watch *n.* (prec. by *the*) Royal Highland Regiment.

♦ **Black Wednesday** *n.* Wednesday, 16 September 1992, the day on which sterling left the Exchange Rate Mechanism leading to a 15% fall in its value against the Deutschmark.

black widow *n.* venomous spider of which the female devours the male.

bladder *n.* **1 a** sac in some animals, esp. that holding urine. **b** this adapted for various uses. **2** inflated blister in seaweed etc. [Old English]

bladderwrack *n.* brown seaweed with air bladders.

blade *n.* **1** cutting part of a knife etc. **2** flattened part of an oar, propeller, etc. **3 a** flat narrow leaf of grass etc. **b** broad thin part of a leaf. **4** flat bone, e.g. in the shoulder. [Old English]

♦ **Blakenham** /ˈbleɪkənəm/, **Michael John Hare, 2nd Viscount** (1938–) British businessman, chairman of Pearson plc (since 1983) and nephew of Lord Cowdray, a former chairman of the group. Pearson's wide interests include merchant banking (Lazard Brothers), publishing (Addison Wesley Longman, Penguin, *Financial Times*), entertainment (The Tussauds Group, which includes Madame Tussauds and Alton Towers), and industry (Royal Doulton). The Pearson family own 20% of the company's shares.

blame –*v.* (**-ming**) **1** assign fault or responsibility to. **2** (foll. by *on*) fix responsibility for (an error etc.) on (*blamed it on his brother*). –*n.* **1** responsibility for an error etc. **2** blaming or attributing of responsibility (*got all the blame*). □ **be to blame** be responsible; deserve censure. □ **blameable** *adj.* **blameless** *adj.* **blameworthy** *adj.* [French: related to BLASPHEME]

blanch /blɑːntʃ/ *v.* **1** make or become white or pale. **2 a** peel (almonds etc.) by scalding. **b** immerse (vegetables etc.) briefly in boiling water. **3** whiten (a plant) by depriving it of light. [French: related to BLANK]

blancmange /bləˈmɒndʒ/ *n.* sweet opaque jelly of flavoured cornflour and milk. [French, = white food]

bland *adj.* **1 a** mild, not irritating. **b** tasteless; insipid. **2** gentle in manner; suave. □ **blandly** *adv.* **blandness** *n.* [Latin *blandus* smooth]

blandish /ˈblændɪʃ/ *v.* flatter; coax. □ **blandishment** *n.* (usu. in *pl.*). [Latin: related to BLAND]

blank –*adj.* **1 a** (of paper) not written or printed on. **b** (of a document) with spaces left for a signature or details. **2 a** empty (*blank space*). **b** unrelieved (*blank wall*). **3 a** without interest, result, or expression (*blank face*). **b** having (temporarily) no knowledge etc. (*mind went blank*). **4** complete (*a blank refusal*; *blank despair*). –*n.* **1 a** unfilled space, esp. in a document. **b** document having blank spaces. **2** (in full **blank cartridge**) cartridge containing gunpowder but no bullet. **3** dash written instead of a word or letter. –*v.* (usu. foll. by *off, out*) screen, obscure. □ **draw a blank** get no response; fail. □ **blankly** *adv.* **blankness** *n.* [French *blanc* white, from Germanic]

♦ **blank bill** *n.* bill of exchange in which the name of the payee is left blank.

blank cheque *n.* **1** see CHEQUE. **2** *colloq.* unlimited freedom of action.

♦ **blank endorsement** see ENDORSEMENT 2.

blanket /ˈblæŋkɪt/ –*n.* **1** large esp. woollen sheet used as a bed-covering etc. **2** thick covering mass or layer. –*attrib. adj.* covering everything; inclusive. –*v.* (**-t-**) **1** cover. **2** stifle, suppress. [French: related to BLANK]

blanket bath *n.* body wash given to a bedridden patient.

♦ **blanket policy** *n.* insurance policy that covers a number of items but has only one total sum insured and no insured sums for individual items. The policy can be of any type, e.g. covering a fleet of vehicles or a group of buildings.

blanket stitch *n.* stitch used to finish the edges of a blanket etc.

♦ **blank transfer** *n.* share transfer form in which the name of the transferee and the transfer date are left blank. The form is signed by the registered holder of the shares so that the holder of the blank transfer has only to fill in the missing details to become the registered owner of the shares. Blank transfers can be deposited with a bank, when shares are being used as a security for a loan. A blank transfer can also be used when shares are held by nominees, the beneficial owner holding the blank transfer (see NOMINEE).

blank verse *n.* unrhymed verse, esp. iambic pentameters.

Blantyre /blænˈtaɪə(r)/ (also **Blantyre-Limbe**) chief commercial and industrial city of Malawi; industries include textiles and distilling; pop. (1994) 446 800 (with Limbe).

blare –*v.* (**-ring**) **1** sound or utter loudly. **2** make the sound of a trumpet. –*n.* blaring sound. [Low German or Dutch, imitative]

blarney /ˈblɑːnɪ/ –*n.* cajoling talk; flattery. –*v.* (**-eys, -eyed**) flatter, cajole. [*Blarney*, castle near Cork]

blasé /ˈblɑːzeɪ/ *adj.* bored or indifferent through over-familiarity. [French]

blaspheme /blæsˈfiːm/ *v.* (**-ming**) **1** use religious names irreverently; treat a religious or sacred subject irreverently. **2** talk irreverently about; use blasphemy against. [Greek *blasphēmeō*]

blasphemy /ˈblæsfəmɪ/ *n.* (*pl.* **-ies**) **1** irreverent talk or treatment of a religious or sacred thing. **2** instance of this. □ **blasphemous** *adj.*

blast /blɑːst/ *–n.* **1** strong gust of air. **2 a** explosion. **b** destructive wave of air from this. **3** loud note from a wind instrument, car horn, etc. **4** *colloq.* severe reprimand. *–v.* **1** blow up with explosives. **2** wither, blight (*blasted oak*; *blasted her hopes*). **3** (cause to) make a loud noise. *–int.* expressing annoyance. □ **at full blast** *colloq.* at maximum volume, speed, etc. **blast off** take off from a launching site. [Old English]

blasted *colloq. –attrib. adj.* damned; annoying. *–adv.* damned; extremely.

blast-furnace *n.* smelting furnace into which hot air is driven.

blast-off *n.* launching of a rocket etc.

blatant /ˈbleɪt(ə)nt/ *adj.* **1** flagrant, unashamed. **2** loudly obtrusive. □ **blatantly** *adv.* [coined by Spenser]

blather /ˈblæðə(r)/ *–n.* foolish chatter. *–v.* chatter foolishly. [Old Norse]

blaze[1] *–n.* **1** bright flame or fire. **2** violent outburst (of passion etc.). **3** brilliant display (*blaze of scarlet, of glory*). *–v.* **(-zing) 1** burn or shine brightly or fiercely. **2** be consumed with anger, excitement, etc. □ **blaze away** (often foll. by *at*) **1** shoot continuously. **2** work vigorously. [Old English, = torch]

blaze[2] *–n.* **1** white mark on an animal's face. **2** mark cut on a tree, esp. to show a route. *–v.* **(-zing)** mark (a tree or a path) with blazes. □ **blaze a trail** show the way for others. [origin uncertain]

blazer *n.* jacket without matching trousers, esp. lightweight and often part of a uniform. [from BLAZE[1]]

blazon /ˈbleɪz(ə)n/ *–v.* **1** proclaim (esp. *blazon abroad*). **2** *Heraldry* describe or paint (arms). *–n. Heraldry* shield or coat of arms. □ **blazonment** *n.* **blazonry** *n.* [French, originally = shield]

bleach *–v.* whiten in sunlight or by a chemical process. *–n.* bleaching substance or process. [Old English]

bleak *adj.* **1** exposed, windswept. **2** dreary, grim. [Old Norse]

bleary /ˈblɪərɪ/ *adj.* **(-ier, -iest) 1** dim; blurred. **2** indistinct. [Low German]

bleary-eyed *adj.* having dim sight.

bleat *–v.* **1** (of a sheep, goat, or calf) make a wavering cry. **2** (often foll. by *out*) speak or say plaintively. *–n.* bleating cry. [Old English]

bleed *–v.* (*past* and *past part.* **bled**) **1** emit blood. **2** draw blood from surgically. **3** *colloq.* extort money from. **4** (often foll. by *for*) suffer wounds or violent death. **5 a** emit sap. **b** (of dye) come out in water. **6** empty (a system) of excess air or fluid. *–n.* act of bleeding. □ **one's heart bleeds** usu. *iron.* one is very sorrowful. [Old English]

bleeder *n. coarse slang* unpleasant or contemptible person.

bleeding *adj.* & *adv. coarse slang* expressing annoyance or antipathy.

bleep *–n.* intermittent high-pitched electronic sound. *–v.* **1** make a bleep. **2** summon with a bleeper. [imitative]

bleeper *n.* small electronic device bleeping to contact the carrier.

blemish /ˈblemɪʃ/ *–n.* flaw, defect, or stain. *–v.* spoil, mark, or stain. [French]

blench *v.* flinch, quail. [Old English]

blend *–v.* **1** mix together as required. **2** become one. **3** (often foll. by *with, in*) mingle; mix thoroughly. **4** (esp. of colours) merge imperceptibly; harmonize. *–n.* mixture. [Old Norse]

blender *n.* machine for liquidizing, chopping, or puréeing food.

blenny /ˈblenɪ/ *n.* (*pl.* **-ies**) small spiny-finned scaleless marine fish. [Greek *blennos* mucus]

bless *v.* (*past* and *past part.* **blessed**, *poet.* **blest**) **1** ask God to look favourably on, esp. by making the sign of the cross over. **2** consecrate (food etc.). **3** glorify (God). **4** attribute one's good luck to (stars etc.); thank. **5** (usu. in *passive*) make happy or successful (*blessed with children*). □ **bless me** (or **my soul**) exclamation of surprise etc. **bless you!** exclamation of endearment, gratitude, etc., or to a person who has just sneezed. [Old English]

blessed /ˈblesɪd, blest/ *adj.* (also *poet.* **blest**) **1** holy. **2** *euphem.* cursed (*blessed nuisance!*). **3** *RC Ch.* beatified. □ **blessedness** *n.*

blessing *n.* **1** invocation of (esp. divine) favour. **2** grace said at a meal. **3** benefit.

blether var. of BLATHER.

BLEU *abbr.* Belgo-Luxembourg Economic Union.

blew *past* of BLOW[1].

blight /blaɪt/ *–n.* **1** plant disease caused by insects etc. **2** such an insect etc. **3** harmful or destructive force. **4** ugly urban area. *–v.* **1** affect with blight. **2** harm, destroy. **3** spoil. [origin unknown]

blighter *n. colloq.* contemptible or annoying person.

Blighty /ˈblaɪtɪ/ *n. Mil. slang* England; home. [Hindustani, = foreign]

blimey /ˈblaɪmɪ/ *int. coarse slang* expression of surprise, contempt, etc. [(*God*) *blind me!*]

blimp *n.* **1** (also **(Colonel) Blimp**) reactionary person. **2** small non-rigid airship. **3** soundproof cover for a cine-camera. [origin uncertain]

blind /blaɪnd/ *–adj.* **1** lacking the power of sight. **2 a** without adequate foresight, discernment, or information (*blind effort*). **b** (often foll. by *to*) unwilling or unable to appreciate a factor etc. (*blind to argument*). **3** not governed by purpose or reason (*blind forces*). **4** reckless (*blind hitting*). **5 a** concealed (*blind ditch*). **b** closed at one end. **6** (of flying) using instruments only. **7** *Cookery* (of a flan case etc.) baked without a filling. *–v.* **1** deprive of sight. **2** rob of judgement; deceive; overawe. **3** *slang* go recklessly. *–n.* **1** screen for a window; awning. **2** thing used to hide the truth. **3** obstruction to sight or light. *–adv.* blindly. □ **blindly** *adv.* **blindness** *n.* [Old English]

blind alley *n.* **1** alley closed at one end. **2** futile course.

blind date *n. colloq.* date between two people who have not previously met.

blind drunk *adj. colloq.* extremely drunk.

blindfold *–v.* cover the eyes of (a person) with a tied cloth etc. *–n.* cloth etc. so used. *–adj.* & *adv.* **1** with eyes covered. **2** without due care. [originally *blindfelled* = struck blind]

blind man's buff *n.* game in which a blindfold player tries to catch others.

blind spot *n.* **1** point on the retina insensitive to light. **2** area where vision or understanding is lacking.

♦ **blind testing** *n.* market-research technique in which unidentified products are tested by consumers in order to determine their preference. It is often used to test a new product against an established product, esp. one with a strong market position.

---

blindworm *n.* = SLOW-WORM.

blink *–v.* **1** shut and open the eyes quickly. **2** (often foll. by *back*) prevent (tears) by blinking. **3** shine unsteadily, flicker. *–n.* **1** act of blinking. **2** momentary gleam or glimpse. □ **blink at 1** look at while blinking. **2** ignore, shirk. **on the blink** *slang* not working properly; out of order. [Dutch, var. of BLENCH]

blinker *–n.* **1** (usu. in *pl.*) each of two screens on a bridle preventing lateral vision. **2** device that blinks. *–v.* **1** obscure with blinkers. **2** (as **blinkered** *adj.*) having narrow and prejudiced views.

blinking *adj.* & *adv. slang* expressing annoyance etc. (*it's blinking stupid*).

blip *–n.* **1** minor deviation or error. **2** quick popping sound. **3** small image on a radar screen. *–v.* **(-pp-)** make a blip. [imitative]

bliss *n.* **1** perfect joy. **2** being in heaven. □ **blissful** *adj.* **blissfully** *adv.* [Old English]

blister *–n.* **1** small bubble on the skin filled with watery fluid and caused by heat or friction. **2** similar swelling on plastic, wood, etc. *–v.* **1** come up in blisters. **2** raise a blister on. **3** attack sharply. [origin uncertain]

blithe /blaɪð/ *adj.* **1** cheerful, happy. **2** careless, casual. □ **blithely** *adv.* [Old English]

blithering /ˈblɪðərɪŋ/ *attrib. adj. colloq.* hopeless; contemptible (esp. in *blithering idiot*). [*blither*, var. of BLATHER]

BLitt. *abbr.* Bachelor of Letters. [Latin *Baccalaureus Litterarum*]

blitz /blɪts/ *colloq.* –*n.* **1 a** intensive or sudden (esp. aerial) attack. **b** intensive period of work etc. (*must have a blitz on this room*). **2** (**the Blitz**) German air raids on London in 1940. –*v.* inflict a blitz on. [abbreviation of BLITZKRIEG]

blitzkrieg /ˈblɪtskriːg/ *n.* intense military campaign intended to bring about a swift victory. [German, = lightning war]

blizzard /ˈblɪzəd/ *n.* severe snowstorm. [origin unknown]

bloat *v.* **1** inflate, swell. **2** (as **bloated** *adj.*) inflated with pride, wealth, or food. **3** cure (a herring) by salting and smoking lightly. [Old Norse]

bloater *n.* bloated herring.

blob *n.* small drop or spot. [imitative]

bloc *n.* group of governments etc. sharing a common purpose. [French: related to BLOCK]

block –*n.* **1** solid piece of hard material, esp. stone or wood. **2** this as a base for chopping etc., as a stand, or for mounting a horse from. **3 a** large building, esp. when subdivided. **b** group of buildings between streets. **4** obstruction. **5** two or more pulleys mounted in a case. **6** piece of wood or metal engraved for printing. **7** *slang* head. **8** (often *attrib.*) number of things as a unit, e.g. shares, theatre seats (*block booking*). **9** sheets of paper glued along one edge. **10** *Computing* group of numbers, characters, or words that is transferred as a unit between the parts of a computer system, e.g. between the computer terminal and a disk drive. Information stored on tape is divided into blocks for convenience in handling the tape and for error management. –*v.* **1 a** (often foll. by *up*) obstruct. **b** impede. **2** restrict the use of. **3** *Cricket* stop (a ball) with a bat defensively. □ **block in 1** sketch roughly; plan. **2** confine. **block out 1** shut out (light, noise, a memory, view, etc.). **2** sketch roughly; plan. **block up** confine; enclose. [Low German or Dutch]

blockade /blɒˈkeɪd/ –*n.* surrounding or blocking of a place by an enemy to prevent entry and exit. –*v.* (**-ding**) subject to a blockade.

blockage *n.* obstruction.

block and tackle *n.* system of pulleys and ropes, esp. for lifting.

blockbuster *n. slang* **1** thing of great power, esp. a very successful film, book, etc. **2** highly destructive bomb.

block capitals *n.pl.* (also **block letters**) letters printed without serifs, or written with each letter separate and in capitals.

♦ **blocked account** *n.* **1** bank account from which money cannot be withdrawn, usu. because the affairs of the holder of the account are in the hands of a receiver owing to bankruptcy or (in the case of a company) liquidation. **2.** bank account held by an exporter of goods in another country into which the proceeds of the sale of the exporter's goods have been paid but from which they cannot be transferred to the exporter's own country. This is usu. a result of a government order, when that government is so short of foreign currency that it has to block all accounts that require the use of a foreign currency.

♦ **blocked currency** *n.* currency that cannot be removed from a country as a result of exchange controls.

---

blockhead *n.* stupid person.

blockhouse *n.* **1** reinforced concrete shelter. **2** *hist.* small fort of timber.

block vote *n.* vote proportional in power to the number of people a delegate represents.

Bloemfontein /ˈbluːmfɒnˌteɪn/ judicial capital of the Republic of South Africa and capital of Free State province; products include canned fruit, glass, plastics, and furniture; pop. (1991) 300 150.

bloke *n. slang* man, fellow. [Shelta]

blond (of a woman usu. **blonde**) –*adj.* (of a person, hair, or complexion) light-coloured, fair. –*n.* blond person. [Latin *blondus* yellow]

blood /blʌd/ –*n.* **1** usu. red fluid circulating in the arteries and veins of animals. **2** bloodshed, esp. killing. **3** passion, temperament. **4** race, descent, parentage (*of the same blood*). **5** relationship; relations (*blood is thicker than water*). **6** dandy. –*v.* **1** give (a hound) a first taste of blood. **2** initiate (a person). □ **in one's blood** inherent in one's character. [Old English]

blood bank *n.* store of blood for transfusion.

blood bath *n.* massacre.

blood count *n.* number of corpuscles in a specific amount of blood.

blood-curdling *adj.* horrifying.

blood donor *n.* person giving blood for transfusion.

blood group *n.* any of the types of human blood.

blood-heat *n.* normal human temperature, about 37 °C or 98.4 °F.

bloodhound *n.* large keen-scented dog used in tracking.

bloodless *adj.* **1** without blood or bloodshed. **2** unemotional. **3** pale. **4** feeble.

blood-letting *n.* surgical removal of blood.

blood-money *n.* **1** money paid as compensation for a death. **2** money paid to a killer.

blood orange *n.* red-fleshed orange.

blood-poisoning *n.* diseased condition caused by micro-organisms in the blood.

blood pressure *n.* pressure of the blood in the arteries etc., measured for diagnosis.

blood relation *n.* (also **blood relative**) relative by birth.

bloodshed *n.* killing.

bloodshot *adj.* (of an eyeball) inflamed.

blood sport *n.* sport involving the killing or wounding of animals.

bloodstain *n.* stain caused by blood. □ **bloodstained** *adj.*

bloodstream *n.* blood in circulation.

bloodsucker *n.* **1** leech. **2** extortioner. □ **bloodsucking** *adj.*

blood sugar *n.* amount of glucose in the blood.

blood test *n.* examination of blood, esp. for diagnosis.

bloodthirsty *adj.* (**-ier, -iest**) eager for bloodshed.

blood-vessel *n.* vein, artery, or capillary carrying blood.

bloody –*adj.* (**-ier, -iest**) **1** of, like, running with, or smeared with blood. **2 a** involving bloodshed. **b** bloodthirsty, cruel. **3** *coarse slang* expressing annoyance or antipathy, or as an intensive (*bloody fool*; *a bloody sight better*). **4** red. –*adv. coarse slang* as an intensive (*bloody awful*). –*v.* (**-ies, -ied**) stain with blood.

Bloody Mary *n.* mixture of vodka and tomato juice.

bloody-minded *adj. colloq.* deliberately uncooperative.

bloom –*n.* **1 a** flower, esp. cultivated. **b** state of flowering (*in bloom*). **2** one's prime (*in full bloom*). **3 a** healthy glow of the complexion. **b** fine powder on fresh fruit and leaves. –*v.* **1** bear flowers; be in flower. **2** be in one's prime; flourish. [Old Norse]

bloomer[1] *n.* **1** *slang* blunder. **2** plant that blooms in a specified way.

bloomer[2] *n.* long loaf with diagonal marks. [origin uncertain]

bloomers *n.pl.* **1** women's long loose knickers. **2** *hist.* women's loose knee-length trousers. [Mrs A. *Bloomer*, name of the originator]

blooming –*adj.* **1** flourishing; healthy. **2** *slang* an intensive (*blooming miracle*). –*adv. slang* an intensive (*blooming difficult*).

blossom /ˈblɒsəm/ –*n.* **1** flower or mass of flowers, esp. of a fruit-tree. **2** promising stage (*blossom of youth*). –*v.* **1** open into flower. **2** mature, thrive. [Old English]

blot –*n.* **1** spot or stain of ink etc. **2** disgraceful act or quality. **3** blemish. –*v.* (**-tt-**) **1** make a blot on, stain. **2** dry with blotting-paper. □ **blot one's copybook** damage one's reputation. **blot out 1** obliterate. **2** obscure (a view, sound, etc.). [probably Scandinavian]

blotch –*n.* **1** discoloured or inflamed patch on the skin. **2** irregular patch of colour. –*v.* cover with blotches. □ **blotchy** *adj.* (**-ier, -iest**). [obsolete *plotch*, BLOT]

blotter *n.* pad of blotting-paper.

blotting-paper *n.* absorbent paper for drying wet ink.

blotto /ˈblɒtəʊ/ *adj. slang* very drunk. [origin uncertain]

blouse /blaʊz/ –*n.* **1** woman's garment like a shirt. **2** upper part of a military uniform. –*v.* (**-sing**) make (a bodice etc.) full like a blouse. [French]

blouson /ˈbluːzɒn/ *n.* short blouse-shaped jacket. [French]

blow[1] /bləʊ/ –*v.* (*past* **blew**; *past part.* **blown**) **1** direct a current of air (at) esp. from the mouth. **2** drive or be driven by blowing (*blew the door open*). **3** (esp. of the wind) move rapidly. **4** expel by breathing (*blew smoke*). **5** sound or be sounded by blowing. **6** (*past part.* **blowed**) *slang* (esp. in *imper.*) curse, confound (*I'm blowed if I know*; *blow it!*). **7** clear (the nose) by blowing. **8** puff, pant. **9** *slang* depart suddenly (from). **10** shatter etc. by an explosion. **11** make or shape (glass or a bubble) by blowing. **12 a** melt from overloading (*the fuse has blown*). **b** break or burst suddenly. **13** (of a whale) eject air and water. **14** break into with explosives. **15** *slang* **a** squander (*blew £20*). **b** bungle (an opportunity etc.). **c** reveal (a secret etc.). –*n.* **1** act of blowing. **2 a** gust of wind or air. **b** exposure to fresh air. □ **be blowed if one will** *colloq.* be unwilling to. **blow a gasket** *slang* lose one's temper. **blow hot and cold** *colloq.* vacillate. **blow in 1** break inwards by an explosion. **2** *colloq.* arrive unexpectedly. **blow a person's mind** *slang* cause to have hallucinations etc.; astound. **blow off 1** escape or allow (steam etc.) to escape forcibly. **2** *slang* break wind noisily. **blow out 1** extinguish by blowing. **2** send outwards by an explosion. **blow over** (of trouble etc.) fade away. **blow one's top** *colloq.* explode in rage. **blow up 1** explode. **2** *colloq.* rebuke strongly. **3** inflate (a tyre etc.). **4** *colloq.* **a** enlarge (a photograph). **b** exaggerate. **5** *colloq.* arise, happen. **6** *colloq.* lose one's temper. [Old English]

blow[2] /bləʊ/ *n.* **1** hard stroke with a hand or weapon. **2** sudden shock or misfortune. [origin unknown]

blow-by-blow *attrib. adj.* (of a narrative) detailed.

blow-dry *v.* arrange (the hair) while drying it.

blower *n.* **1** device for blowing. **2** *colloq.* telephone.

blowfly *n.* bluebottle.

blow-hole *n.* **1** nostril of a whale. **2** hole (esp. in ice) for breathing or fishing through. **3** vent for air, smoke, etc.

blow-job *n. coarse slang* instance of fellatio or cunnilingus.

blowlamp *n.* device with a very hot flame for burning off paint, plumbing, etc.

blown *past part.* of BLOW[1].

blow-out *n. colloq.* **1** burst tyre. **2** melted fuse. **3** huge meal.

blowpipe *n.* **1** tube for blowing air through, esp. to intensify a flame or to blow glass. **2** tube for propelling poisoned darts etc. by blowing.

blowtorch *n. US* = BLOWLAMP.

blow-up *n.* **1** *colloq.* enlargement (of a photograph etc.). **2** explosion.

blowy /ˈbləʊɪ/ *adj.* (**-ier, -iest**) windy.

blowzy /ˈblaʊzɪ/ *adj.* (**-ier, -iest**) **1** coarse-looking; red-faced. **2** slovenly. [obsolete *blowze* beggar's wench]

BLOX /blɒks/ *abbr. Finance* block order exposure system.

blub *v.* (**-bb-**) *slang* sob. [shortening of BLUBBER]

blubber –*n.* whale fat. –*v.* **1** sob loudly. **2** sob out (words). –*adj.* swollen, thick. [probably imitative]

bludgeon /ˈblʌdʒ(ə)n/ –*n.* heavy club. –*v.* **1** beat with this. **2** coerce. [origin unknown]

blue /bluː/ –*adj.* (**bluer, bluest**) **1** having the colour of a clear sky. **2** sad, depressed. **3** pornographic (*a blue film*). **4** politically conservative. –*n.* **1** blue colour or pigment. **2** blue clothes or material (*dressed in blue*). **3** person who represents a university in a sport, esp. Oxford or Cambridge. **4** Conservative party supporter. –*v.* (**blues, blued, bluing** or **blueing**) **1** make blue. **2** *slang* squander. □ **once in a blue moon** very rarely. **out of the blue** unexpectedly. [French from Germanic]

blue baby *n.* baby with a blue complexion due to a congenital heart defect.

bluebell *n.* woodland plant with bell-shaped blue flowers.

blueberry *n.* (*pl.* **-ies**) small blue-black edible fruit of various plants.

blue blood *n.* noble birth.

Blue Book *n.* **1** report issued by Parliament or the Privy Council. **2** = UK NATIONAL ACCOUNTS.

bluebottle *n.* large buzzing fly; blowfly.

blue cheese *n.* cheese with veins of blue mould.

♦ **blue chip** *n.* ordinary share in a substantial company with a well-known name, a good growth record, and large assets. Blue chips are not precisely definable, but the main part of an institution's equity portfolio will consist of blue chips.

---

blue-collar *attrib. adj.* (of a worker or work) manual or industrial.

blue-eyed boy *n. colloq.* favourite.

Bluefields /ˈbluːfiːldz/ port in SE Nicaragua, on the SE coast, the country's chief Caribbean port; pop. (est. 1990) 21 500.

blue funk *n. colloq.* terror or panic.

bluegrass *n.* a kind of instrumental country-and-western music.

blue-pencil *v.* censor or cut (a manuscript, film, etc.).

Blue Peter *n.* blue flag with a white square flown by a ship about to leave port.

blueprint *n.* **1** photographic print of plans in white on a blue background. **2** detailed plan.

blue rinse *n.* bluish dye for grey hair.

blues *n.pl.* **1** (prec. by *the*) bout of depression. **2 a** (prec. by *the*; often treated as *sing.*) melancholic music of Black American origin, usu. in a twelve-bar sequence. **b** (*pl.* same) (as *sing.*) piece of such music (*played a blues*).

bluestocking *n.* usu. *derog.* intellectual or literary woman. [18th-century Blue Stocking Society]

blue tit *n.* common tit with a blue crest.

blue whale *n.* rorqual, the largest known living mammal.

bluff[1] –*v.* pretend strength, confidence, etc. –*n.* act of bluffing. □ **call a person's bluff** challenge a person to prove a claim. [Dutch *bluffen* brag]

bluff[2] –*adj.* **1** blunt, frank, hearty. **2** vertical or steep and broad in front. –*n.* steep cliff or headland. [origin unknown]

bluish /ˈbluːɪʃ/ *adj.* fairly blue.

blunder –*n.* serious or foolish mistake. –*v.* **1** make a blunder. **2** move clumsily; stumble. [probably Scandinavian]

blunderbuss /ˈblʌndəˌbʌs/ *n. hist.* short large-bored gun. [Dutch *donderbus* thunder gun]

blunt –*adj.* **1** not sharp or pointed. **2** direct, outspoken. –*v.* make blunt or less sharp. □ **bluntly** *adv.* (in sense 2 of *adj.*). **bluntness** *n.* [probably Scandinavian]

blur –*v.* (**-rr-**) make or become unclear or less distinct; smear. –*n.* blurred object, sound, memory, etc. [perhaps related to BLEARY]

blurb *n.* promotional description, esp. of a book. [coined by G. Burgess 1907]

blurt *v.* (usu. foll. by *out*) utter abruptly, thoughtlessly, or tactlessly. [imitative]

blush –*v.* **1 a** become pink in the face from embarrassment or shame. **b** (of the face) redden thus. **2** feel embarrassed or ashamed. **3** redden. –*n.* **1** act of blushing. **2** pink tinge. [Old English]

blusher *n.* rouge.

bluster –*v.* **1** behave pompously or boisterously. **2** (of the wind etc.) blow fiercely. –*n.* bombastic talk; empty threats. □ **blustery** *adj.* [imitative]

BM *abbr.* **1** British Museum. **2** Bachelor of Medicine.

BMA *abbr.* **1** British Manufacturers' Association. **2** British Medical Association.

BMRB *abbr.* British Market Research Bureau.

B.Mus. *abbr.* Bachelor of Music.

BMW *abbr.* Bavarian Motor Works. [German *Bayerische Motorenwerke*]

BMX /ˌbiːem'eks/ *n.* **1** organized bicycle-racing on a dirt-track. **2** bicycle used for this. [abbreviation of *bi*cycle *moto-cross*]

BN –*abbr.* banknote. –*postcode* Brighton.

BNA *abbr. Insurance* British North Atlantic.

BNEC *abbr.* British National Export Council.

BNF *abbr.* (also **BNFL**) British Nuclear Fuels Limited.

bnkg. *abbr.* banking.

BNMAU *international civil aircraft marking* Mongolia.

BNOC *abbr.* British National Oil Corporation.

BNP *abbr.* National Bank of Paris. [French *Banque nationale de Paris*]

BNS *abbr. Stock Exch.* buyer no seller.

BO *abbr. colloq.* body odour.

B/O *abbr.* (also **b/o**) **1** *Bookkeeping* brought over. **2** buyer's option.

b.o. *abbr.* **1** back order. **2** branch office. **3** broker's order. **4** buyer's option.

boa /'bəʊə/ *n.* **1** large snake which kills by crushing and suffocating. **2** long stole of feathers or fur. [Latin]

boa constrictor *n.* species of boa.

boar *n.* **1** male wild pig. **2** uncastrated male pig. [Old English]

board –*n.* **1 a** flat thin piece of sawn timber, usu. long and narrow. **b** material resembling this, of compressed fibres. **c** thin slab of wood etc. **d** thick stiff card used in bookbinding. **e** printed circuit board used in electronics. **2** provision of regular meals, usu. with accommodation, for payment. **3** directors of a company; official administrative body. **4** (in *pl.*) stage of a theatre. **5** side of a ship. –*v.* **1** go on board (a ship, train, etc.). **2** receive, or provide with, meals and usu. lodging. **3** (usu. foll. by *up*) cover with boards; seal or close. □ **go by the board** be neglected or discarded. **on board** on or on to a ship, aircraft, oil rig, etc. **take on board** consider, take notice of; accept. [Old English]

boarder *n.* **1** person who boards, esp. at a boarding-school. **2** person who boards a ship, esp. an enemy.

board-game *n.* game played on a board.

boarding-house *n.* unlicensed establishment providing board and lodging, esp. to holiday-makers.

boarding-school *n.* school in which pupils live in term-time.

♦ **Board of Customs and Excise** *n.* (also **BOCE**) government department responsible for collecting and administering customs and excise duties and VAT. The Commissioners of Customs were first appointed in 1671 by Charles II; the Excise department, formerly part of the Inland Revenue Department, was merged with the Customs in 1909. The Customs and Excise have an investigation division responsible for preventing and detecting evasions of revenue laws and for enforcing restrictions on the importation of certain goods (e.g. arms, drugs, etc.). Their statistical office compiles overseas trade statistics from customs import and export documents.

♦ **board of directors** see DIRECTOR 1.

♦ **Board of Inland Revenue** *n.* (also **BIR**) group of higher civil servants, known individually as Commissioners of Inland Revenue, responsible to the Treasury for the administration and collection of the principal direct taxes in the UK, but not the indirect VAT and excise duties. They are responsible for income tax, capital-gains tax, corporation tax, inheritance tax, petroleum revenue tax, and stamp duties. They also advise on new legislation and prepare statistical information.

---

boardroom *n.* room in which a board of directors etc. meets regularly.

boast –*v.* **1** declare one's virtues, wealth, etc. with excessive pride. **2** own or have with pride (*hotel boasts a ballroom*). –*n.* **1** act of boasting. **2** thing one is proud of. [Anglo-French]

boastful *adj.* given to boasting. □ **boastfully** *adv.*

boat –*n.* **1** small vessel propelled on water by an engine, oars, or sails. **2** any ship. **3** long low jug for sauce etc. –*v.* go in a boat, esp. for pleasure. □ **in the same boat** having the same problems. [Old English]

boater *n.* flat-topped straw hat with a brim.

boat-hook *n.* long hooked pole for moving boats.

boat-house *n.* waterside shed for housing boats.

boating *n.* rowing or sailing as recreation.

boatman *n.* person who hires out boats or provides transport by boat.

boat people *n.pl.* refugees travelling by sea.

boatswain /'bəʊs(ə)n/ *n.* (also **bosun, bo'sun**) ship's officer in charge of equipment and crew.

boat-train *n.* train scheduled to meet or go on a boat.

bob[1] –*v.* (**-bb-**) **1** move quickly up and down. **2** (usu. foll. by *back, up*) bounce or emerge buoyantly or suddenly. **3** cut (the hair) in a bob. **4** curtsy. –*n.* **1** jerking or bouncing movement, esp. upward. **2** hairstyle with the hair hanging evenly above the shoulders. **3** weight on a pendulum etc. **4** horse's docked tail. **5** curtsy. [imitative]

bob[2] *n.* (*pl.* same) *hist. slang* shilling (now = 5 pence). [origin unknown]

bob[3] *n.* □ **bob's your uncle** *slang* expression of completion or success. [pet form of *Robert*]

bobbin /'bɒbɪn/ *n.* spool or reel for thread etc. [French]

bobble /'bɒb(ə)l/ *n.* small woolly ball on a hat etc. [diminutive of BOB[1]]

bobby *n.* (*pl.* **-ies**) *colloq.* police officer. [Sir *Robert* Peel, 19th-century statesman]

bob-sled *n. US* = BOB-SLEIGH.

bob-sleigh –*n.* mechanically-steered and -braked racing sledge. –*v.* race in a bob-sleigh.

bobtail *n.* **1** docked tail. **2** horse or dog with this.

BOC *abbr. Computing* beginning of cycle.

BOCE *abbr.* = BOARD OF CUSTOMS AND EXCISE.

Boche /bɒʃ/ *n. slang derog.* German, esp. a soldier. [French]

Bochum /'bəʊxʊm/ city in Germany, in North Rhine-Westphalia; industries include metallurgy and chemicals; pop. (est. 1995) 401 129.

bod *n. colloq.* person. [shortening of BODY]

bode *v.* (**-ding**) be a sign of, portend. □ **bode well** (or **ill**) be a good (or bad) sign. [Old English]

bodega /bəʊ'diːgə/ *n.* cellar or shop selling wine. [Spanish]

bodge var. of BOTCH.

bodice /'bɒdɪs/ *n.* **1** part of a woman's dress above the waist. **2** woman's vest-like undergarment. [originally *pair of bodies*]

bodily /'bɒdɪlɪ/ –*adj.* of the body. –*adv.* **1** as a whole body (*threw them bodily*). **2** in the flesh, in person.

bodkin /'bɒdkɪn/ *n.* blunt thick needle for drawing tape etc. through a hem. [origin uncertain]

body /'bɒdɪ/ *n.* (*pl.* **-ies**) **1** whole physical structure, including the bones, flesh, and organs, of a person or an animal, whether dead or alive. **2** = TRUNK *n.* 2. **3** main or central part; bulk or majority (*body of opinion*). **4 a** group regarded as a unit. **b** (usu. foll. by *of*) collection (*body of facts*). **5** quantity (*body of water*). **6** piece of matter (*heavenly body*). **7** *colloq.* person. **8** full or substantial quality of flavour, tone, etc. □ **in a body** all together. [Old English]

body-blow *n.* severe setback.

body-building *n.* exercises to enlarge and strengthen the muscles.

bodyguard *n.* person or group escorting and protecting another.

body language *n.* communication through gestures and poses.

body odour *n.* smell of the human body, esp. when unpleasant.

body politic *n.* nation or state as a corporate body.

body shop *n.* workshop where bodywork is repaired.

body stocking *n.* woman's undergarment covering the torso.

bodysuit *n.* close-fitting all-in-one garment for women, worn esp. for sport.

bodywork *n.* outer shell of a vehicle.

Boeotia /bɪ'əʊʃə/ region of central Greece, N of Attica, dominated in ancient times by Thebes and now forming a department of Greece; pop (1991) 134 108. □ **Boeotian** *adj.* & *n.*

Boer /bɔː(r)/ *–n.* South African of Dutch descent. *–adj.* of the Boers. [Dutch, = farmer]

BOF *abbr. Computing* beginning of file.

B of E *abbr.* Bank of England.

boffin /'bɒfɪn/ *n. colloq.* research scientist. [origin unknown]

bog *–n.* **1 a** wet spongy ground. **b** stretch of this. **2** *slang* lavatory. *–v.* **(-gg-)** (foll. by *down*; usu. in *passive*) impede (*bogged down by snow*). □ **boggy** *adj.* **(-ier, -iest)**. [Irish or Gaelic *bogach*]

bogey[1] /'bəʊgɪ/ *n.* (*pl.* **-eys**) *Golf* **1** score of one stroke more than par at any hole. **2** (formerly) par. [perhaps from *Bogey*, as an imaginary player]

bogey[2] /'bəʊgɪ/ *n.* (also **bogy**) (*pl.* **-eys** or **-ies**) **1** evil or mischievous spirit; devil. **2** awkward thing. **3** *slang* piece of dried nasal mucus. [originally (*Old*) *Bogey* the Devil]

bogeyman *n.* (also **bogyman**) frightening person etc.

boggle /'bɒg(ə)l/ *v.* **(-ling)** *colloq.* be startled or baffled (esp. *the mind boggles*). [probably dial. *boggle* BOGEY[2]]

bogie /'bəʊgɪ/ *n.* wheeled undercarriage below a locomotive etc. [origin unknown]

Bogotá /ˌbɒgə'tɑː/ capital of Colombia, situated in the E Andes; pop. (est. 1995) 5 237 635.

bogus /'bəʊgəs/ *adj.* sham, spurious. [origin unknown]

bogy var. of BOGEY[2].

bogyman var. of BOGEYMAN.

Bohemia /bəʊ'hiːmɪə/ industrial area of the Czech Republic, a former province (1919–49) of Czechoslovakia. It has mineral resources, including uranium, and agriculture is important.

Bohemian *–n.* **1** native of Bohemia, a Czech. **2** (also **bohemian**) socially unconventional person, esp. an artist or writer. *–adj.* **1** of Bohemia or its people. **2** (also **bohemian**) socially unconventional. □ **bohemianism** *n.*

Bohol /bəʊ'hɒl/ island in the central Philippines; pop. (1990) 948 000; chief town, Tagbilaran.

boil[1] *–v.* **1 a** (of a liquid) start to bubble up and turn into vapour on reaching a certain temperature. **b** (of a vessel) contain boiling liquid (*kettle is boiling*). **2 a** bring to boiling-point. **b** cook in boiling liquid. **c** subject to boiling water, e.g. to clean. **3 a** move or seethe like boiling water. **b** be very angry. *–n.* act or process of boiling; boiling-point (*on the boil; bring to the boil*). □ **boil down 1** reduce in volume by boiling. **2** reduce to essentials. **3** (foll. by *to*) amount to. **boil over 1** spill over in boiling. **2** lose one's temper. [Latin *bullio* to bubble]

boil[2] *n.* inflamed pus-filled swelling under the skin. [Old English]

boiler *n.* **1** apparatus for heating a hot-water supply. **2** tank for heating water or turning it to steam. **3** tub for boiling laundry etc.

◆ **boilerplate** *n.* **1** copy intended for use in making other copies. **2** group of instructions incorporated in different places in a computer program. **3** detailed standard form of words used in a contract, guarantee, etc.

---

boiler-room *n.* **1** room with a boiler and other heating equipment, esp. in a basement. **2** *colloq.* firm selling securities that functions from a small room selling by telephone.

boiler suit *n.* protective outer garment of trousers and jacket in one.

boiling *adj. colloq.* very hot.

boiling-point *n.* **1** temperature at which a liquid begins to boil. **2** great excitement.

Boise /'bɔɪsɪ/ city in the US, capital of Idaho; industries include timber and food processing; pop. (est. 1994) 145 987.

Bois-le-Duc see 'S-HERTOGENBOSCH.

boisterous /'bɔɪstərəs/ *adj.* **1** noisily exuberant, rough. **2** (of the sea etc.) stormy. [origin unknown]

BoJ *abbr.* (also **BOJ**) Bank of Japan.

Bokhara see BUKHARA.

bold /bəʊld/ *adj.* **1** confidently assertive; adventurous, brave. **2** impudent. **3** vivid (*bold colours*). □ **make** (or **be**) **so bold as to** presume to; venture to. □ **boldly** *adv.* **boldness** *n.* [Old English]

boldface *n.* style of typeface in which the characters are printed in heavy black ink.

bole *n.* trunk of a tree. [Old Norse]

bolero *n.* (*pl.* **-s**) **1** /bə'leərəʊ/ Spanish dance, or the music for it, in triple time. **2** /'bɒlərəʊ/ woman's short open jacket. [Spanish]

Bolivia /bə'lɪvɪə/, **Republic of** landlocked country in central South America. Mining is the most important industry, accounting for over 70% of foreign-exchange earnings: zinc, tin, silver, and gold are the main mineral exports, and oil and natural gas are also sources of revenue. The agricultural sector produces hides and skins, timber, soya beans, sugar, and coffee for export; other crops include cereals and the coca plant (in which an illegal trade with Colombia exists). Bolivia is a member of LAIA and in 1996 signed an agreement with Mercosaur concerning the creation of a free trade zone.

History. Once part of the Spanish empire, Bolivia became independent in 1825, since when it has lost much of its original territory (including access to the sea) to neighbouring countries. For much of the 20th century Bolivia has been crippled by endemic poverty and political instability, suffering from almost continual coups and changes of government. Following a period of military government (1964–82), civilian rule was restored. Lozada became president following elections in 1993. President, Gonzálo Sánchez de Lozada; capital, La Paz (seat of government), Sucre (legal capital and seat of judiciary). □ **Bolivian** *adj.* & *n.*

languages	Spanish, Quechua, Aymara
currency	boliviano ($b) of 100 centavos
pop. (est. 1996)	7 592 000
GNP (est. 1994)	US$5.6B
literacy	87% (m); 72% (f)
life expectancy	61 (m); 66 (f)

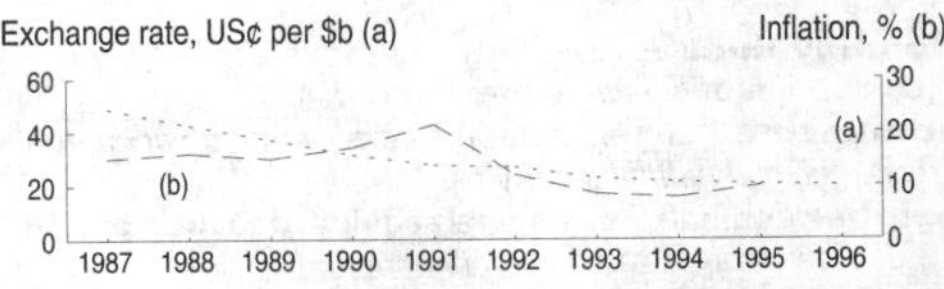

bolívar /ˈbɒlɪˌvɑː/ *n.* standard monetary unit of Venezuela. [Simon *Bolívar*, South American liberator]

boliviano /bəˌlɪvɪˈɑːnəʊ/ *n.* standard monetary unit of Bolivia. [BOLIVIA]

boll /bəʊl/ *n.* round seed-vessel of cotton, flax, etc. [Dutch]

bollard /ˈbɒlɑːd/ *n.* **1** short post in the road, esp. on a traffic island. **2** short post on a quay or ship for securing a rope. [perhaps related to BOLE]

bollocking /ˈbɒləkɪŋ/ *n.* (also **ballocking**) *coarse slang* severe reprimand.

bollocks /ˈbɒləks/ *n.* (also **ballocks**) *coarse slang* **1** (usu. as *int.*) nonsense. **2** testicles. [Old English: related to BALL[1]]

Bologna /bəˈləʊnjə/ city in N Italy, capital of the region of Emilia-Romagna; industries include engineering and food processing; pop. (est, 1994) 394 969.

boloney /bəˈləʊnɪ/ *n.* (also **baloney**) *slang* nonsense. [origin uncertain]

Bolshevik /ˈbɒlʃəvɪk/ –*n.* **1** *hist.* member of the radical faction of the Russian Social Democratic Party becoming the Communist Party in 1918. **2** Russian Communist. **3** any revolutionary socialist. –*adj.* **1** of the Bolsheviks. **2** communist. □ **Bolshevism** *n.* **Bolshevist** *n.* [Russian, = member of the majority]

Bolshie /ˈbɒlʃɪ/ (also **Bolshy**) *slang* –*adj.* (usu. **bolshie**) **1** uncooperative; bad-tempered. **2** left-wing. –*n.* (*pl.* **-ies**) Bolshevik. [abbreviation]

bolster /ˈbəʊlstə(r)/ –*n.* long cylindrical pillow. –*v.* (usu. foll. by *up*) encourage, support, prop up. [Old English]

bolt[1] /bəʊlt/ –*n.* **1** sliding bar and socket used to fasten a door etc. **2** large metal pin with a thread, usu. used with a nut, to hold things together. **3** discharge of lightning. **4** act of bolting. –*v.* **1** fasten with a bolt. **2** (foll. by *in, out*) keep (a person etc.) in or out by bolting a door. **3** fasten together with bolts. **4 a** dash off suddenly. **b** (of a horse) suddenly gallop out of control. **5** gulp down (food) unchewed. **6** (of a plant) run to seed. –*adv.* (usu. in **bolt upright**) rigidly, stiffly. □ **bolt from the blue** complete surprise. [Old English]

bolt[2] /bəʊlt/ *v.* (also **boult**) sift (flour etc.). [French]

bolt-hole *n.* means of escape.

Bolzano /bɒlˈtsɑːnəʊ/ **1** province in N Italy, in Trentino-Alto Adige region. **2** its capital city; industries include tourism, steel, and textiles; pop. (est. 1990) 100 380.

b.o.m. *abbr.* (in manufacturing) bill of materials.

bomb /bɒm/ –*n.* **1** container filled with explosive, incendiary material, etc., designed to explode and cause damage. **2** (prec. by *the*) the atomic or hydrogen bomb. **3** *slang* large sum of money (*cost a bomb*). –*v.* **1** attack with bombs; drop bombs on. **2** (usu. foll. by *along, off*) *colloq.* go very quickly. □ **like a bomb** *colloq.* **1** very successfully. **2** very fast. [Greek *bombos* hum]

bombard /bɒmˈbɑːd/ *v.* **1** attack with bombs, shells, etc. **2** (often foll. by *with*) question or abuse persistently. **3** *Physics* direct a stream of high-speed particles at. □ **bombardment** *n.* [Latin: related to BOMB]

bombardier /ˌbɒmbəˈdɪə(r)/ *n.* **1** non-commissioned officer in the artillery. **2** *US* crew member in an aircraft who aims and releases bombs.

bombast /ˈbɒmbæst/ *n.* pompous language; hyperbole. □ **bombastic** /-ˈbæstɪk/ *adj.* [earlier *bombace* cotton wool]

Bombay /bɒmˈbeɪ/ city and port in W India, a commercial centre long noted for its textile industry; pop. (1991) 9 909 547.

Bombay duck *n.* dried fish as a relish, esp. with curry. [corruption of *bombil*, native name of fish]

bombazine /ˈbɒmbəˌziːn/ *n.* twilled worsted dress-material. [Greek *bombux* silk]

bomber /ˈbɒmə(r)/ *n.* **1** aircraft equipped to drop bombs. **2** person using bombs, esp. illegally.

bomber jacket *n.* jacket gathered at the waist and cuffs.

bombshell *n.* **1** overwhelming surprise or disappointment. **2** artillery bomb. **3** *slang* very attractive woman.

bomb-site *n.* area where bombs have caused destruction.

♦ **bona fide** /ˌbəʊnə ˈfaɪdɪ/ –*adj.* genuine; sincere; without collusion or fraud. A bona fide purchaser for value without notice is a person who has bought property in good faith, without being aware of prior claims to it (e.g. that it is subject to a trust). The purchaser will not be bound by those claims unless (if the property is land) they were registered. –*adv.* genuinely; sincerely. [Latin]

Bonaire /bɒˈneə(r)/ one of the two principal islands of the Netherlands Antilles; pop. (est. 1990) 11 060; chief town, Kralendijk.

bonanza /bəˈnænzə/ *n.* **1** source of wealth or prosperity. **2** large output (esp. of a mine). [Spanish, = fair weather]

♦ ***bona vacantia*** /ˈbəʊnə vəˈkæntɪə/ *n.pl.* goods without an owner. By royal prerogative, the Crown is entitled to any personal property that has no owner, e.g. the goods of a person who dies intestate with no living relatives. The prerogative does not apply to real property, but the Crown may be entitled to that as well under the doctrine of escheat (the return of ownerless land to the superior landowner). See FEE SIMPLE. [Latin, = empty goods]

---

bon-bon *n.* sweet. [French *bon* good]

bond –*n.* **1** thing or force that unites or (usu. in *pl.*) restrains. **2** binding agreement. **3** *Finance* IOU issued by a borrower to a lender. Bonds usu. take the form of fixed-interest securities issued by governments, local authorities, or companies. However, bonds come in many forms: with fixed or variable rates of interest, redeemable or irredeemable, short- or long-term, secured or unsecured, and marketable or unmarketable. See also DEBENTURE 1; DEPOSIT BONDS; INCOME BOND; PREMIUM BOND. **4** adhesiveness. **5** *Law* deed binding a person to make payment to another. **6** *Chem.* linkage between atoms in a molecule. –*v.* **1** hold or tie together. **2** connect or reinforce with a bond. **3** place (goods) in bond. □ **in bond** denoting imported goods available for immediate delivery but held in a bonded warehouse until the buyer has paid the customs duty due. The buyer must also pay the cost of loading from the warehouse and any further on-carriage costs. [var. of BAND]

bondage *n.* **1** slavery. **2** subjection to constraint etc. **3** sexual practices involving constraint. [Anglo-Latin: related to BONDSMAN]

bonded *adj.* **1** stored in or for storing in bond (*bonded whisky*). **2** (of a debt) secured by bonds.

♦ **bonded warehouse** *n.* warehouse, usu. close to a seaport or airport, in which goods that attract customs or excise duty are stored after being imported, pending payment of the duty or the re-export of the goods. The owners of the warehouse are held responsible for ensuring that the goods remain in bond until the duty is paid; they may only be released in the presence of a Customs officer.

♦ **bond note** *n.* document, signed by an officer of the Customs and Excise, that enables goods to be released from a bonded warehouse, usu. for re-export.

---

bond paper *n.* high-quality writing-paper.

bondsman *n.* serf, slave. [Old English *bonda* husbandman]

♦ **bond washing** *n.* = DIVIDEND STRIPPING.

---

bone –*n.* **1** any piece of hard tissue making up the skeleton in vertebrates. **2** (in *pl.*) **a** skeleton, esp. as remains. **b** body. **3** material of bones or similar material, e.g. ivory. **4** thing made of bone. **5** (in *pl.*) essentials (*the bones of an agreement*). **6** strip of stiffening in a corset etc. –*v.* (**-ning**) **1** remove the bones from. **2** stiffen with bone etc.

□ **bone up** (often foll. by *on*) *colloq.* study intensively. **have a bone to pick** (usu. foll. by *with*) have cause for dispute (with a person). **make no bones about 1** be frank about. **2** not hesitate or scruple. □ **boneless** *adj.* [Old English]

bone china *n.* fine china made of clay mixed with bone ash.

bone-dry *adj.* completely dry.

bone-idle *adj.* utterly idle.

bone-marrow *n.* = MARROW 2.

bone-meal *n.* crushed bones, esp. as a fertilizer.

boneshaker *n.* decrepit or uncomfortable old vehicle.

bonfire *n.* large open-air fire, esp. for burning rubbish. [from BONE (because bones were once used), FIRE]

bongo /ˈbɒŋgəʊ/ *n.* (*pl.* **-s** or **-es**) either of a pair of small drums usu. held between the knees and played with the fingers. [American Spanish]

bonhomie /ˌbɒnɒˈmiː/ *n.* good-natured friendliness. [French]

bonk *–v.* **1** bang, bump. **2** *coarse slang* have sexual intercourse (with). *–n.* instance of bonking (*bonk on the head*). [imitative]

bonkers /ˈbɒŋkəz/ *predic. adj. slang* crazy. [origin unknown]

bon mot /bɔ̃ ˈməʊ/ *n.* (*pl.* ***bons mots*** /-məʊz/) witty saying. [French]

Bonn /bɒn/ city in NW Germany, situated on the Rhine; industries include chemicals, plastics, and textiles; pop. (1994) 295 300. From 1949 until 1990 Bonn was the capital of West Germany; it is the temporary seat of government of the reunited country, although Berlin is the capital.

bonnet /ˈbɒnɪt/ *n.* **1 a** hat tied under the chin, worn esp. by babies. **b** Scotsman's floppy beret. **2** hinged cover over a vehicle's engine. [French]

bonny /ˈbɒnɪ/ *adj.* (**-ier, -iest**) esp. *Scot.* & *N.Engl.* **1 a** physically attractive. **b** healthy-looking. **2** good, pleasant. [perhaps from French *bon* good]

bonsai /ˈbɒnsaɪ/ *n.* (*pl.* same) **1** dwarfed tree or shrub. **2** art of growing these. [Japanese]

BONUS /ˈbəʊnəs/ *abbr. Finance* Borrower's Option for Notes and Underwritten Standby.

♦ **bonus** /ˈbəʊnəs/ *n.* **1** extra payment made to employees by management, usu. as a reward for good work, to compensate for something (e.g. dangerous work), or to share out the profits of a good year's trading. **2** extra amount of money, additional to the proceeds, which is distributed to a policyholder by an insurer who has made a profit on the investment of a life-assurance fund. Only holders of with-profits policies are entitled to a share in these profits and the payment of this bonus is conditional on the life assurer having surplus funds after claims, costs, and expenses have been paid in a particular year. **3.** extra benefit. See also NO-CLAIM BONUS; REVERSIONARY BONUS; TERMINAL BONUS. [Latin, = good]

♦ **bonus issue** *n.* = SCRIP ISSUE.

---

bon vivant /ˌbɔ̃ viːˈvɑ̃/ *n.* (*pl.* ***bon*** or ***bons vivants*** pronunc. same) person fond of good food and drink. [French]

bon voyage /ˌbɔ̃ vwɑːˈjɑːʒ/ *int.* expression of good wishes to a departing traveller. [French]

bony /ˈbəʊnɪ/ *adj.* (**-ier, -iest**) **1** thin with prominent bones. **2** having many bones. **3** of or like bone. □ **boniness** *n.*

boo *–int.* **1** expression of disapproval etc. **2** sound intended to surprise. *–n.* utterance of *boo*, esp. to a performer etc. *–v.* (**boos, booed**) **1** utter boos. **2** jeer at by booing. [imitative]

boob[1] *colloq. –n.* **1** silly mistake. **2** foolish person. *–v.* make a silly mistake. [shortening of BOOBY]

boob[2] *n. slang* woman's breast. [origin uncertain]

booby *n.* (*pl.* **-ies**) stupid or childish person. [Spanish *bobo*]

booby prize *n.* prize given for coming last.

booby trap *n.* **1** practical joke in the form of a trap. **2** disguised explosive device triggered by the unknowing victim.

boodle /ˈbuːd(ə)l/ *n. slang* money, esp. gained or used dishonestly. [Dutch *boedel* possessions]

boogie /ˈbuːgɪ/ *v.* (**-ies, -ied, -ieing**) *slang* dance to pop music.

boogie-woogie /ˌbuːgɪˈwuːgɪ/ *n.* style of playing blues or jazz on the piano. [origin unknown]

book /bʊk/ *–n.* **1 a** written or printed work with pages bound along one side. **b** work intended for publication. **2** bound blank sheets for notes, records, etc. **3** bound set of tickets, stamps, matches, etc. **4** (in *pl.*) set of records or accounts. **5** main division of a large literary work. **6** telephone directory. **7** *colloq.* magazine. **8** libretto, script, etc. **9** record of bets. *–v.* **1 a** (also *absol.*) reserve (a seat etc.) in advance. **b** engage (an entertainer etc.). **2 a** take the personal details of (an offender or rule-breaker). **b** enter in a book or list. □ **book in** register at a hotel etc. **book up 1** buy tickets in advance. **2** (as **booked up**) with all places reserved. **bring to book** call to account. **go by the book** proceed by the rules. **in a person's good** (or **bad) books** in (or out of) favour with a person. [Old English]

bookbinder *n.* person who binds books for a living. □ **bookbinding** *n.*

bookcase *n.* cabinet of shelves for books.

book club *n.* society in which selected books are available cheaply.

book-end *n.* prop used to keep books upright.

bookie /ˈbʊkɪ/ *n. colloq.* = BOOKMAKER. [abbreviation]

booking *n.* reservation or engagement.

booking-hall *n.* (also **booking-office**) ticket office at a railway station etc.

bookish *adj.* **1** studious; fond of reading. **2** having knowledge mainly from books.

♦ **bookkeeping** *n.* keeping of the books of account of a business. The records kept enable a profit and loss account and the balance sheet to be compiled. Most firms now use business software packages of programs to enable the books to be kept by computer. See also BOOK OF PRIME ENTRY; DOUBLE-ENTRY BOOKKEEPING. □ **bookkeeper** *n.*

---

booklet /ˈbʊklɪt/ *n.* small book usu. with a paper cover.

bookmaker *n.* professional taker of bets. □ **bookmaking** *n.*

bookmark *n.* thing used to mark a reader's place.

♦ **book of prime entry** *n.* book or record in which certain types of transaction are recorded before becoming part of the double-entry bookkeeping system. The most common books of prime entry are the day books, the cash-book, and the journal.

---

book-plate *n.* decorative personalized label stuck in a book.

bookseller *n.* dealer in books.

bookshop *n.* shop selling books.

♦ **books of account** *n.pl.* books in which a business records its transactions. See BOOK OF PRIME ENTRY; DOUBLE-ENTRY BOOKKEEPING.

---

bookstall *n.* stand selling books, newspapers, etc.

book token *n.* voucher exchangeable for books.

♦ **book value** *n.* value of an asset as recorded in the books of account of an organization, usu. the historical cost of the asset reduced by amounts written off for depreciation. If the asset has ever been revalued, the book value will be the amount of the revaluation less amounts subsequently written off for depreciation. Except at the time of purchase of the asset, the book value will rarely be the same as the market value of the asset.

bookworm *n.* **1** *colloq.* devoted reader. **2** larva feeding on the paper and glue in books.

Boolean algebra /ˈbuːlɪən/ *n.* system of algebraic notation used to represent logical propositions and now of particular importance in computing. The methods of algebra are applied to problems in logic involving statements and conclusions that can be given a truth value (either 'true' or 'false') and thus have a binary nature. These true or false expressions can be combined by the logical operations 'and' and 'or' and negated by the operation 'not' to give a conclusion whose truth or falsity can be determined from the rules of Boolean algebra. [*Boole*, name of a mathematician]

Boolean logic *n.* use of 'and', 'or', and 'not' in retrieving information from a database.

boom[1] *–n.* deep resonant sound. *–v.* make or speak with a boom. [imitative]

♦ **boom**[2] *–n.* period of economic prosperity or activity, esp. part of the business cycle that follows a recovery, in which the economy is working at full capacity. Demand, prices, and wages rise, while unemployment falls. If government control of the economy is not sufficiently tight a boom can lead to a recession and ultimately to a slump. *–v.* be suddenly prosperous. [perhaps from BOOM[1]]

---

boom[3] *n.* **1** pivoted spar to which a sail is attached. **2** long pole carrying a microphone, camera, etc. **3** barrier across a harbour etc. [Dutch, = BEAM]

boomerang /ˈbuːməˌræŋ/ *–n.* **1** flat V-shaped hardwood missile used esp. by Australian Aboriginals, able to return to its thrower. **2** plan that recoils on its originator. *–v.* (of a plan etc.) backfire. [Aboriginal]

boon[1] *n.* advantage; blessing. [Old Norse]

boon[2] *adj.* intimate, favourite (usu. *boon companion*). [French *bon* from Latin *bonus* good]

boor *n.* ill-mannered person. □ **boorish** *adj.* [Low German or Dutch]

boost *colloq. –v.* **1** promote or encourage. **2** increase, assist. **3** push from below. *–n.* act or result of boosting. [origin unknown]

booster *n.* **1** device for increasing power or voltage. **2** auxiliary engine or rocket for initial speed. **3** dose, injection, etc. renewing the effect of an earlier one.

boot[1] *–n.* **1** outer foot-covering reaching above the ankle. **2** luggage compartment of a car. **3** *colloq.* **a** firm kick. **b** (prec. by *the*) dismissal (*got the boot*). *–v.* **1** kick. **2** (often foll. by *out*) eject forcefully. **3** (usu. foll. by *up*) make (a computer) ready. See also BOOTSTRAP 2. □ **put the boot in 1** kick brutally. **2** harm a person. [Old Norse]

boot[2] *n.* □ **to boot** as well, in addition. [Old English]

bootblack *n. US* person who polishes boots and shoes.

bootee /buːˈtiː/ *n.* baby's soft shoe.

booth /buːð/ *n.* **1** small temporary structure used esp. as a market stall. **2** enclosure for telephoning, voting, etc. **3** cubicle in a restaurant etc. [Old Norse]

bootleg *–adj.* (esp. of alcohol) smuggled, illicit. *–v.* (**-gg-**) illicitly make or deal in (alcohol etc.). □ **bootlegger** *n.*

bootlicker *n. colloq.* toady.

boots *n.* hotel servant who cleans shoes etc.

bootstrap *n.* **1** loop used to pull a boot on. **2** *Computing* short program whose function is to load another longer program into a computer, e.g. when a computer is first switched on. **3** cash offer for a controlling interest in a company. This is followed by an offer to acquire the rest of the company's shares at a lower price. The purpose is to establish control of the company and to reduce the cost of the purchase. □ **pull oneself up by one's bootstraps** better oneself.

booty /ˈbuːtɪ/ *n.* **1** loot, spoil. **2** *colloq.* prize or gain. [German]

booze *colloq. –n.* alcoholic drink. *–v.* (**-zing**) drink alcohol, esp. to excess. □ **boozy** *adj.* (**-ier, -iest**). [Dutch]

boozer *n. colloq.* **1** habitual drinker. **2** public house.

booze-up *n. slang* drinking bout.

bop[1] *colloq. –n.* **1 a** spell of dancing, esp. to pop music. **b** social occasion for this. **2** = BEBOP. *–v.* (**-pp-**) dance, esp. to pop music. □ **bopper** *n.* [abbreviation]

bop[2] *colloq. –v.* (**-pp-**) hit or punch, esp. lightly. *–n.* esp. light blow or hit. [imitative]

Bophuthatswana /bəʊˌpuːtəˈtswɑːnə/ former Bantu homeland in South Africa, comprising six separate territories, designated an independent republic in 1977 but not recognized as such outside South Africa (see HOMELAND 2). In 1994 Bophuthatswana was integrated into the provinces of Free State, Mpumalanga, and North-West. Mmabatho, formerly the capital of Bophuthatswana, is now the capital of North-West province. Rich deposits of chrome, platinum, asbestos, vanadium, and other minerals are mined in the area; there is also subsistence agriculture, esp. livestock farming.

Bora-Bora /ˌbɔːrəˈbɔːrə/ island in French Polynesia, part of the Leeward group of the Society Islands; exports include mother-of-pearl and tobacco.

boracic /bəˈræsɪk/ *adj.* of borax.

boracic acid *n.* = BORIC ACID.

borage /ˈbɒrɪdʒ/ *n.* plant with leaves used as flavouring. [French ultimately from Arabic]

Borås /bʊˈrɔːs/ city in SW Sweden; industries include textiles and engineering; pop. (1994) 96 123.

borax /ˈbɔːræks/ *n.* salt used in making glass and china, and as an antiseptic. [French ultimately from Persian]

Bordeaux /bɔːˈdəʊ/ inland port and major wine centre in SW France, on the River Garonne; industries include oil refining and aeronautics; pop. (est. 1990) 213 274. *–n.* (*pl.* same /-ˈdəʊz/) red, white, or rosé wine from the district of Bordeaux.

border *–n.* **1** edge or boundary, or the part near it. **2 a** line or region separating two countries. **b** (**the Border**) boundary between Scotland and England (usu. **the Borders**), or Northern Ireland and the Irish Republic. **3** esp. ornamental strip round an edge. **4** long narrow flower-bed (*herbaceous border*). *–v.* **1** be a border to. **2** provide with a border. **3** (usu. foll. by *on, upon*) **a** adjoin; come close to being. **b** resemble. [French from Germanic: related to BOARD]

Border collie *n.* sheepdog of the North Country.

borderer *n.* person living near a border.

borderland *n.* **1** district near a border. **2** condition between two extremes. **3** area for debate.

borderline *–n.* **1** line dividing two conditions. **2** line marking a boundary. *–adj.* **1** on the borderline. **2** barely acceptable.

Borders former administrative region of S Scotland; pop. (est. 1994) 105 700; capital, Newtown St Boswells. In 1996 it became a unitary authority and was renamed Scottish Borders. Tweed and other textiles are produced.

Border terrier *n.* small rough-haired terrier.

bore[1] *–v.* (**-ring**) **1** make (a hole), esp. with a revolving tool. **2** make a hole in, hollow out. *–n.* **1** hollow of a firearm barrel or of a cylinder in an internal-combustion engine. **2** diameter of this. **3** deep hole made esp. to find water. [Old English]

bore[2] *–n.* tiresome or dull person or thing. *–v.* (**-ring**) weary by tedious talk or dullness. □ **bored** *adj.* **boring** *adj.* [origin unknown]

bore[3] *n.* high tidal wave in an estuary. [Scandinavian]

bore[4] *past* of BEAR[1].

boredom *n.* state of being bored. [from BORE[2]]

boric acid /ˈbɔːrɪk/ *n.* acid derived from borax, used as an antiseptic.

born *adj.* **1** existing as a result of birth. **2 a** of natural ability or quality (*a born leader*). **b** (usu. foll. by *to* + infin.) destined (*born lucky; born to be king*). **3** (in *comb.*) of a certain status by birth (*French-born; well-born*). [past part. of BEAR[1]]

born-again *attrib. adj.* converted (esp. to fundamentalist Christianity).

borne /bɔːn/ **1** *past part.* of BEAR[1]. **2** (in *comb.*) carried by (*airborne*).

Bornholm /ˈbɔːnhəʊm/ Danish island in the Baltic Sea; dairy farming and tourism are important; pop. (est. 1995) 44 936.

boron /ˈbɔːrɒn/ *n.* non-metallic usu. crystalline element. [from BORAX, after *carbon*]

borough /ˈbʌrə/ *n.* **1 a** town represented in the House of Commons. **b** town or district granted the status of a borough. **2** *hist.* town with a municipal corporation conferred by a royal charter. [Old English]

borrow /ˈbɒrəʊ/ *v.* **1 a** acquire temporarily, promising or intending to return. **b** obtain money thus. **2** use (another's idea, invention, etc.); plagiarize. □ **borrower** *n.* [Old English]

Borstal /ˈbɔːst(ə)l/ *n. hist.* residential institution for youth custody. [*Borstal* in Kent]

■ **Usage** This term has now been replaced by *detention centre* and *youth custody centre*.

bortsch /bɔːtʃ/ *n.* Russian soup of beetroot, cabbage, etc. [Russian]

borzoi /ˈbɔːzɔɪ/ *n.* large silky-coated dog. [Russian, = swift]

bosh *n.* & *int. slang* nonsense. [Turkish, = empty]

bosom /ˈbʊz(ə)m/ *n.* **1 a** person's (esp. woman's) breast. **b** *colloq.* each of a woman's breasts. **c** enclosure formed by the breast and arms. **2** emotional centre (*bosom of one's family*). [Old English]

bosom friend *n.* intimate friend.

Bosporus /ˈbɒspərəs/ (also **Bosphorus** /-fərəs/) strait connecting the Black Sea and the Sea of Marmara, and separating Europe from Asia.

boss[1] *colloq.* –*n.* employer, manager, or supervisor. –*v.* (usu. foll. by *about, around*) give orders to; order about. [Dutch *baas*]

boss[2] *n.* **1** round knob, stud, etc., esp. on the centre of a shield. **2** *Archit.* ornamental carving etc. at the junction of the ribs in a vault. [French]

bossa nova /ˌbɒsə ˈnəʊvə/ *n.* **1** dance like the samba. **2** music for this. [Portuguese, = new flair]

boss-eyed *adj. colloq.* **1** cross-eyed; blind in one eye. **2** crooked. [*boss* = bad shot, origin unknown]

bossy *adj.* (**-ier, -iest**) *colloq.* domineering. □ **bossiness** *n.*

Boston /ˈbɒst(ə)n/ city and seaport in the US, the capital of Massachusetts and a major financial and service centre; industries include publishing, food processing, and machinery; pop. (est. 1994) 547 725.

◆ **Boston matrix** *n.* means of analysing the performance of business units in large diversified firms by reference to market share and growth rates. Four main categories are displayed in a two-dimensional matrix, which identifies the business units that generate cash and those that use it, enabling an overall business strategy to be formulated. The matrix was developed by the Boston Consultancy Group, a leading firm of strategic consultants.

bosun (also **bo'sun**) var. of BOATSWAIN.

BOT *abbr.* **1** *Computing* beginning of tape. **2** (also **BoT**) Board of Trade.

botany /ˈbɒtənɪ/ *n.* the study of plants. □ **botanic** /bəˈtænɪk/ *adj.* **botanical** /bəˈtænɪk(ə)l/ *adj.* **botanist** *n.* [Greek *botanē* plant]

BOTB *abbr.* = BRITISH OVERSEAS TRADE BOARD.

botch (also **bodge**) –*v.* **1** bungle; do badly. **2** patch clumsily. –*n.* bungled or spoilt work. [origin unknown]

both /bəʊθ/ –*adj.* & *pron.* the two, not only one (*both boys; both the boys; both of the boys; I like both*). –*adv.* with equal truth in two cases (*is both hot and dry*). [Old Norse]

bother /ˈbɒðə(r)/ –*v.* **1** trouble; worry, disturb. **2** (often foll. by *about, with,* or *to* + infin.) take the time or trouble (*didn't bother to tell me; shan't bother with dessert*). –*n.* **1 a** person or thing that bothers. **b** minor nuisance. **2** trouble, worry. –*int.* expressing irritation. [Irish *bodhraim* deafen]

botheration /ˌbɒðəˈreɪʃ(ə)n/ *n.* & *int. colloq.* = BOTHER *n., int.*

bothersome /ˈbɒðəsəm/ *adj.* causing bother.

Bothnia /ˈbɒθnɪə/, **Gulf of** arm of the N Baltic Sea, between Sweden and Finland.

bottle /ˈbɒt(ə)l/ –*n.* **1** container, esp. glass or plastic, for storing liquid. **2** amount filling it. **3** baby's feeding-bottle. **4** = HOT-WATER BOTTLE. **5** metal cylinder for liquefied gas. **6** *slang* courage. –*v.* (**-ling**) **1** put into, or preserve in, bottles or jars. **2** (foll. by *up*) conceal or restrain (esp. a feeling). □ **hit the bottle** *slang* drink heavily. [medieval Latin: related to BUTT[4]]

bottle bank *n.* place for depositing bottles for recycling.

bottle-feed *v.* (*past* and *past part.* **-fed**) feed (a baby) from a bottle.

bottle green *adj.* & *n.* (as adj. often hyphenated) dark green.

bottleneck *n.* **1** narrow congested area, esp. on a road. **2** impeding thing.

bottlenose dolphin *n.* dolphin with a bottle-shaped snout.

bottle party *n.* party to which guests bring bottles of drink.

Bosnia-Hercegovina /ˈbɒznɪə, ˌhɜːtsɪgəˈviːnə/, **Republic of** country in SE Europe, formerly a constitutent republic of Yugoslavia. It is an agricultural region, producing wheat, maize, potatoes, plums, tobacco, and livestock (esp. sheep). Industries include iron and steel and textiles. Bosnia is ethnically mixed, with large Muslim, Serb, and Croat minorities. In 1992 some two-thirds of the population voted for independence from Yugoslavia, and the republic, with a Muslim-led presidency, was granted official recognition by the EC and other states. However, areas occupied by the Serb and Croat minorities proclaimed independence from the Muslim-dominated government and in 1992 fighting began, with Serbian forces quickly occupying over two-thirds of the country and laying siege to Sarajevo. Prompted by the brutal "ethnic cleansing" the UN declared a number of "safe areas" and "no-fly zones". In 1994 NATO carried out air strikes against Serbian positions and later that year Bosnian Muslims and Bosnian Croats formed an allegiance. Supported by the Croatian army they managed to regain a large amount of territory from the Bosnian Serbs in 1995. In September 1995, following further NATO air strikes, the siege of Sarajevo was lifted. In December 1995 a US-brokered peace agreement was signed, agreeing that Bosnia-Hercegovina would remain a single state but would consist of two entities: a Muslim–Croat Federation in the west and a Bosnian Serb Republic in the north and east. In 1996 Izetbegovic, the sitting president, became chairman of a tripartite presidency, serving alongside a Croat and a Serb. President, Alija Izetbegovic; capital, Sarajevo. □ **Bosnian** *adj* & *n.*

language	Serbo-Croat
currency	Bosnian dinar of 100 paras
pop. (est. 1996)	3 200 000 (excluding refugees in other countries)
GNP (1992)	US$5.9B
literacy	96% (m); 76% (f)
life expectancy	51 (m); 54 (f)

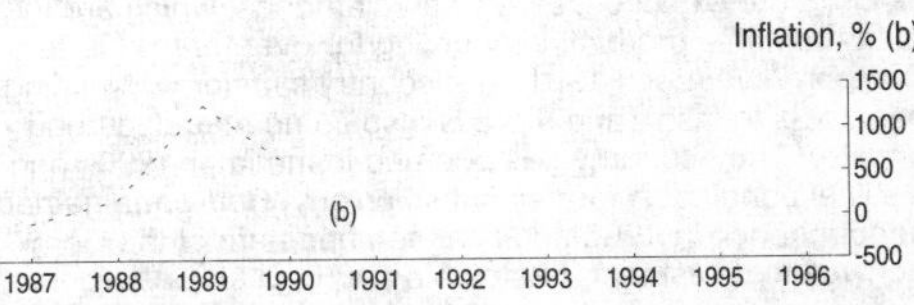

bottom /ˈbɒtəm/ *–n.* **1 a** lowest point or part. **b** base. **c** underneath part. **d** furthest or inmost part. **2** *colloq.* **a** buttocks. **b** seat of a chair etc. **3 a** less honourable end of a table, class, etc. **b** person occupying this (*he's bottom of the class*). **4** ground below water. **5** basis or origin. **6** essential character. **7** *Commerce* ship (*cargo made in one bottom*). *–adj.* lowest, last. *–v.* **1** put a bottom to (a chair etc.). **2** find the extent of. **3** touch the bottom or lowest point (of). □ **at bottom** basically. **be at the bottom of** have caused. **bottom out** reach the lowest level. **get to the bottom of** fully investigate and explain. [Old English]

bottom drawer *n.* linen etc. stored by a woman for marriage.

bottomless *adj.* **1** without a bottom. **2** inexhaustible.

bottom line *n. colloq.* underlying truth; ultimate, esp. financial, criterion.

♦ **bottomry** /ˈbɒtəmrɪ/ see HYPOTHECATION 2. [from BOTTOM, = ship, -RY]

botulism /ˈbɒtjʊˌlɪz(ə)m/ *n.* poisoning caused by a bacillus in badly preserved food. [Latin *botulus* sausage]

bouclé /ˈbuːkleɪ/ *n.* **1** looped or curled yarn (esp. wool). **2** fabric made of this. [French, = curled]

boudoir /ˈbuːdwɑː(r)/ *n.* woman's private room. [French *bouder* sulk]

bouffant /ˈbuːfɑ̃/ *adj.* (of a dress, hair, etc.) puffed out. [French]

bougainvillaea /ˌbuːgənˈvɪlɪə/ *n.* tropical plant with large coloured bracts. [*Bougainville*, name of a navigator]

Bougainville /ˈbuːgənˌvɪl/ island of Papua New Guinea, forming part of North Solomons province; it is the largest of the Solomon Islands archipelago; pop. (est. 1990) 128 000. Secessionist militants forced the closure of its giant copper mine in 1989.

bough /baʊ/ *n.* main branch of a tree. [Old English]

bought *past* and *past part.* of BUY.

♦ **bought deal** *n.* method of raising capital for acquisitions or other purposes, used by quoted companies as an alternative to a rights issue or placing. The company invites market makers or banks to bid for new shares, selling them to the highest bidder, who then sells them to the rest of the market in the expectation of making a profit. Bought deals originated in the US and are becoming increasingly popular in the UK, although they remain controversial as they violate the principle of pre-emption rights. See also VENDOR PLACING.

♦ **bought note** see CONTRACT NOTE.

bouillon /ˈbuːjɒn/ *n.* clear broth. [French *bouillir* to boil]

boulder /ˈbəʊldə(r)/ *n.* large smooth rock. [Scandinavian]

boule /buːl/ *n.* (also **boules** pronunc. same) French form of bowls played on rough ground. [French]

boulevard /ˈbuːləˌvɑːd/ *n.* **1** broad tree-lined avenue. **2** esp. *US* broad main road. [French from German]

Boulogne /bʊˈlɔɪn/ (also **Boulogne-sur-Mer** /sjʊə ˈmer/) fishing-port on the NW coast of France, also operating a ferry service to England; industries include textiles and steel; pop. (1990) 44 240.

boult var. of BOLT².

bounce *–v.* (**-cing**) **1** (cause to) rebound. **2** *slang* (of a cheque) be returned by a bank when there are no funds to meet it. **3** (foll. by *about, up, in, out*, etc.) jump, move, or rush boisterously. *–n.* **1 a** rebound. **b** power of rebounding. **2** *colloq.* **a** swagger, self-confidence. **b** liveliness. □ **bounce back** recover well after a setback. □ **bouncy** *adj.* (**-ier, -iest**). [imitative]

bouncer *n.* **1** *slang* doorman ejecting troublemakers from a dancehall, club, etc. **2** = BUMPER 3.

bouncing *adj.* (esp. of a baby) big and healthy.

bound¹ *–v.* **1** spring, leap. **2** (of a ball etc.) bounce. *–n.* **1** springy leap. **2** bounce. [French *bondir* from Latin *bombus* hum]

bound² *–n.* (usu. in *pl.*) **1** limitation; restriction. **2** border, boundary. *–v.* **1** limit. **2** be the boundary of. □ **out of bounds** outside a permitted area. [French from medieval Latin]

bound³ *adj.* **1** (usu. foll. by *for*) starting or having started (*bound for stardom*). **2** (in *comb.*) in a specified direction (*northbound*). [Old Norse, = ready]

bound⁴ *past* and *past part.* of BIND. □ **bound to** certain to (*he's bound to come*). **bound up with** closely associated with.

boundary /ˈbaʊndərɪ/ *n.* (*pl.* **-ies**) **1** line marking the limits of an area etc. **2** *Cricket* hit crossing the limits of the field, scoring 4 or 6 runs. [related to BOUND²]

♦ **bounded rationality** *n. Econ.* form of rationality in which it is assumed that some economic agents will not go to the lengths of calculation required by full rationality in order to attain either utility or profit maximization but will instead follow various empirical rules determined by the complexity of the real situations they encounter. Bounded rationality produces different predictions about economic behaviour from strict rationality, although it has proved extremely difficult to specify how far the bounds of rationality extend. See also RATIONALITY 3.

bounden duty /ˈbaʊnd(ə)n/ *n. formal* solemn responsibility. [archaic past part. of BIND]

bounder *n. colloq.* cad.

boundless *adj.* unlimited.

bounteous /ˈbaʊntɪəs/ *adj. poet.* = BOUNTIFUL. [French: related to BOUNTY]

bountiful /ˈbaʊntɪˌfʊl/ *adj.* **1** generous. **2** ample.

bounty /ˈbaʊntɪ/ *n.* (*pl.* **-ies**) **1** generosity. **2** reward, esp. from the state. **3** gift. [French from Latin *bonus* good]

bouquet /buːˈkeɪ/ *n.* **1** bunch of flowers, esp. professionally arranged. **2** scent of wine etc. **3** compliment. [French *bois* wood]

bouquet garni /ˈgɑːnɪ/ *n.* (*pl.* **bouquets garnis** /ˌbuːkeɪz ˈgɑːnɪ/) bunch or bag of herbs for seasoning.

bourbon /ˈbɜːbən/ *n. US* whisky from maize and rye. [*Bourbon* County, Kentucky]

bourgeois /ˈbʊəʒwɑː/ often *derog.* *–adj.* **1 a** conventionally middle-class. **b** materialistic. **2** capitalist. *–n.* (*pl.* same) bourgeois person. [French]

Botswana /bɒtˈswɑːnə/, **Republic of** (formerly **Bechuanaland**) landlocked country in S Africa, surrounded by Zambia, Zimbabwe, South Africa, and Namibia. Agriculture, esp. the raising of beef cattle, is the main occupation, providing beef and beef products for export, but minerals are the chief exports. Nickel, copper, and coal deposits are exploited, along with diamonds, which are the most profitable product, accounting for over three-quarters of export revenue in 1991. The country's major non-mining industry is tourism, and there is also some manufacturing industry. The economy has boomed in the later 1990s and is still expanding. A former British colony, Botswana gained independence in 1966 and is a member state of the Commonwealth. President, Festus Mogae; capital, Gaborone.

languages	English (official), Tswana
currency	pula (P) of 100 thebe
pop. (est. 1996)	1 594 000
GNP (est. 1994)	US$4B
literacy	83% (m); 65% (f)
life expectancy	59 (m); 65 (f)

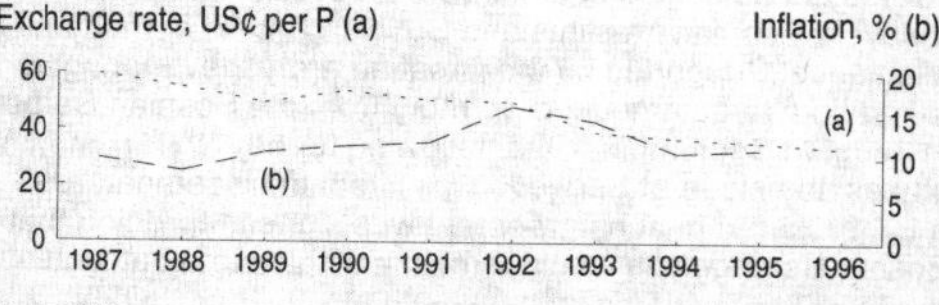

bourgeoisie /ˌbʊəʒwɑːˈziː/ *n.* **1** capitalist class. **2** middle class. [French]

Bourgogne see BURGUNDY.

bourn /bɔːn/ *n.* small stream. [var. of BURN[2]]

♦ **bourse** /bʊəs/ *n.* **1 (Bourse)** Paris Stock Exchange. Members of the Paris Bourse, who have to buy their membership for a large sum, are known as *agents de change*. **2** any continental stock exchange. [French: related to PURSE]

---

bout *n.* **1** (often foll. by *of*) **a** spell (of work or activity). **b** attack (*bout of flu*). **2** wrestling- or boxing-match. [obsolete *bought* bending]

boutique /buːˈtiːk/ *n.* **1** small shop selling esp. fashionable clothes. **2** office, usu. with a shop front and located in a shopping parade, that offers financial advice to investors, often on a walk-in basis. [French]

bouzouki /buːˈzuːkɪ/ *n.* (*pl.* **-s**) Greek form of mandolin. [modern Greek]

bovine /ˈbəʊvaɪn/ *adj.* **1** of cattle. **2** stupid, dull. [Latin *bos* ox]

bovine spongiform encephalopathy see BSE.

bow[1] /bəʊ/ *–n.* **1 a** slip-knot with a double loop. **b** ribbon etc. so tied. **2** curved piece of wood etc. with a string stretched across its ends, for shooting arrows. **3** rod with horsehair stretched along its length, for playing the violin etc. **4** shallow curve or bend; thing of this form. *–v.* (also *absol.*) use a bow on (a violin etc.). [Old English]

bow[2] /baʊ/ *–v.* **1** incline the head or body, esp. in greeting or acknowledgement. **2** submit (*bowed to the inevitable*). **3** cause (the head etc.) to incline. *–n.* act of bowing. □ **bow and scrape** toady. **bow down 1** bend or kneel esp. in submission or reverence. **2** make stoop; crush (*bowed down by care*). **bow out 1** exit (esp. formally). **2** withdraw; retire. **take a bow** acknowledge applause. [Old English]

bow[3] /baʊ/ *n.* **1** (often in *pl.*) front end of a boat. **2** rower nearest this. [Low German or Dutch: related to BOUGH]

bowdlerize /ˈbaʊdləˌraɪz/ *v.* (also **-ise**) (**-zing** or **-sing**) expurgate (a book etc.). □ **bowdlerization** /-ˈzeɪʃ(ə)n/ *n.* [*Bowdler*, name of an expurgator of Shakespeare]

bowel /ˈbaʊəl/ *n.* **1** (often in *pl.*) = INTESTINE. **2** (in *pl.*) innermost parts. [Latin *botulus* sausage]

bower /ˈbaʊə(r)/ *n.* **1** arbour; summer-house. **2** *poet.* inner room. [Old English, = dwelling]

bowerbird *n.* Australasian bird, the male of which constructs elaborate runs.

bowie /ˈbəʊɪ/ *n.* (in full **bowie knife**) a kind of long hunting-knife. [*Bowie*, name of an American soldier]

bowl[1] /bəʊl/ *n.* **1 a** usu. round deep basin for food or liquid. **b** contents of a bowl. **2** hollow part of a tobacco-pipe, spoon, etc. □ **bowlful** *n.* (*pl.* **-s**). [Old English]

bowl[2] /bəʊl/ *–n.* **1** hard heavy ball, made with a bias to run in a curve. **2** (in *pl.*; usu. treated as *sing.*) game played with these on grass. **3** spell or turn of bowling in cricket. *–v.* **1 a** roll (a ball etc.). **b** play bowls. **2** (also *absol.*) *Cricket* etc. **a** deliver (a ball, over, etc.). **b** (often foll. by *out*) dismiss (a batsman) by knocking down the wicket with a ball. **3** (often foll. by *along*) go along rapidly. □ **bowl out** *Cricket* etc. dismiss (a batsman or a side). **bowl over 1** knock down. **2** *colloq.* impress greatly, overwhelm. [Latin *bulla* bubble]

bow-legs *n.pl.* bandy legs. □ **bow-legged** *adj.*

bowler[1] *n.* **1** *Cricket* etc. player who bowls. **2** bowls-player.

bowler[2] *n.* (in full **bowler hat**) man's hard round felt hat. [*Bowler*, name of a hatter]

bowline /ˈbəʊlɪn/ *n.* **1** rope from a ship's bow keeping the sail taut against the wind. **2** knot forming a non-slipping loop at the end of a rope.

bowling *n.* the game of skittles, tenpin bowling, or bowls.

bowling-alley *n.* **1** long enclosure for skittles or tenpin bowling. **2** building with these.

bowling-green *n.* lawn for playing bowls.

bowman *n.* archer.

bowsprit /ˈbəʊsprɪt/ *n.* spar running forward from a ship's bow.

bowstring *n.* string of an archer's bow.

bow-tie *n.* necktie in the form of a bow.

bow-window *n.* curved bay window.

bow-wow *–int.* /baʊˈwaʊ/ imitation of a dog's bark. *–n.* /ˈbaʊwaʊ/ *colloq.* dog. [imitative]

box[1] *–n.* **1** container, usu. flat-sided and firm. **2** amount contained in a box. **3** compartment, e.g. in a theatre or lawcourt. **4** receptacle or kiosk for a special purpose (often in *comb.*: *money box*; *telephone box*). **5** facility at a newspaper office for receiving replies to an advertisement. **6** (prec. by *the*) *colloq.* television. **7** enclosed area or space. **8** area of print enclosed by a border. **9** light shield for the genitals in cricket etc. **10** (prec. by *the*) *Football colloq.* penalty area. *–v.* **1** put in or provide with a box. **2** (foll. by *in*, *up*) confine. [Latin *buxis*: related to BOX[3]]

box[2] *–v.* **1 a** take part in boxing. **b** fight (an opponent) at boxing. **2** slap (esp. a person's ears). *–n.* hard slap, esp. on the ears. [origin unknown]

box[3] *n.* **1** small evergreen tree with dark green leaves. **2** its fine hard wood. [Latin *buxus*, Greek *puxos*]

Box and Cox *n.* two people sharing accommodation etc. in shifts. [names of characters in a play (1847)]

box camera *n.* simple box-shaped camera.

boxer *n.* **1** person who boxes, esp. as a sport. **2** medium-size short-haired dog with a puglike face.

boxer shorts *n.pl.* men's loose underpants like shorts.

box girder *n.* hollow girder square in cross-section.

boxing *n.* fighting with the fists, esp. as a sport.

Boxing Day *n.* first weekday after Christmas. [from BOX[1], from the custom of giving Christmas-boxes]

boxing glove *n.* each of a pair of heavily padded gloves worn in boxing.

box junction *n.* road area marked with a yellow grid, which a vehicle should enter only if its exit is clear.

box number *n.* number for replies to a private advertisement in a newspaper.

box office *n.* ticket-office at a theatre etc.

box pleat *n.* arrangement of parallel pleats folding in alternate directions.

boxroom *n.* small room for storing boxes, cases, etc.

box spring *n.* each of a set of vertical springs in a frame, e.g. in a mattress.

boxwood *n.* = BOX[3] 2.

boxy *adj.* (**-ier, -iest**) cramped.

boy *–n.* **1** male child, son. **2** young man. **3** male servant etc. *–int.* expressing pleasure, surprise, etc. □ **boyhood** *n.* **boyish** *adj.* [origin uncertain]

boycott /ˈbɔɪkɒt/ *–v.* **1** refuse to have social or commercial relations with (a person, country, etc.). **2** refuse to handle (goods). *–n.* such a refusal. [Capt. *Boycott*, so treated from 1880]

boyfriend *n.* person's regular male companion or lover.

boyo /ˈbɔɪəʊ/ *n.* (*pl.* **-s**) *Welsh* & *Ir. colloq.* (esp. as a form of address) boy, mate.

boy scout *n.* = SCOUT *n.* 4 .

BP *abbr.* **1** *Finance* basis point. **2** before the present (era). **3** (also **B/P, b.p., b/p**) bills payable. **4** blood pressure. **5** boiling-point. **6** British Petroleum. **7** British Pharmacopoeia.

bpi *abbr. Computing* bits per inch.

BPR *abbr.* = BUSINESS PROCESS RE-ENGINEERING.

bps *abbr. Computing* bits per second.

Bq *symb. Physics* becquerel.

BR *–abbr.* **1** (also **B/R**) bills receivable. **2** British Rail. *–international vehicle registration* Brazil. *–postcode* Bromley.

Br *symb.* **1** *Currency* birr. **2** bromine.

b.r. *abbr.* **1** bank rate. **2** (also **b/r**) bills receivable.

bra /brɑː/ *n.* undergarment worn by women to support the breasts. [abbreviation]

Brabant /brəˈbænt/ **1** former duchy in W Europe, now

divided between Belgium (forming the provinces of Brabant and Antwerp) and the Netherlands (see NORTH BRABANT). **2** former province in central Belgium; in 1995 it was divided into Flemish Brabant and Walloon Brabant. The area is highly industrialized and agriculture (both dairy and arable farming) is important.

brace –*n.* **1** device that clamps or fastens tightly. **2** timber etc. strengthening a framework. **3** (in *pl.*) straps supporting trousers from the shoulders. **4** wire device for straightening the teeth. **5** (*pl.* same) pair (esp. of game). **6** rope for trimming a sail. **7** connecting mark { or } in printing. –*v.* (**-cing**) **1** make steady by supporting. **2** fasten tightly to make firm. **3** (esp. as **bracing** *adj.*) invigorate, refresh. **4** (often *refl.*) prepare for a difficulty, shock, etc. [Latin *bracchia* arms]

brace and bit *n.* revolving tool for boring, with a D-shaped central handle.

bracelet /ˈbreɪslɪt/ *n.* **1** ornamental band or chain worn on the wrist or arm. **2** *slang* handcuff.

brachiosaurus /ˌbreɪkɪəˈsɔːrəs, ˌbræk-/ *n.* (*pl.* **-ruses**) plant-eating dinosaur with forelegs longer than its hind legs. [Latin from Greek *brakhiōn* arm, *sauros* lizard]

bracken /ˈbrækən/ *n.* **1** large coarse fern. **2** mass of these. [Old Norse]

bracket /ˈbrækɪt/ –*n.* **1** (esp. angled) support projecting from a vertical surface. **2** shelf fixed to a wall with this. **3** each of a pair of marks () [] {} enclosing words or figures. **4** group or classification (*income bracket*). –*v.* (**-t-**) **1** enclose in brackets. **2** group or classify together. [Latin *bracae* breeches]

♦ **bracket indexation** *n.* change in the upper and lower limits of any particular taxation bracket in line with an index of inflation. This is needed in times of inflation to avoid fiscal drag (the tax system collecting unduly large amounts of tax).

---

brackish /ˈbrækɪʃ/ *adj.* (of water etc.) slightly salty. [Low German or Dutch]

bract *n.* leaf-like and often brightly coloured part of a plant, growing before the flower. [Latin *bractea* thin sheet]

♦ ***BRAD*** *abbr.* = BRITISH RATES AND DATA.

---

brad *n.* thin flat nail with a head on only one side. [Old Norse]

bradawl /ˈbrædɔːl/ *n.* small pointed tool for boring holes by hand.

Bradford /ˈbrædfəd/ city in N England, in West Yorkshire; industries include engineering, electronics, printing, and textiles; pop. (est. 1994) 481 700.

brae /breɪ/ *n. Scot.* hillside. [Old Norse]

brag –*v.* (**-gg-**) talk boastfully. –*n.* **1** card-game like poker. **2** boastful statement or talk. [origin unknown]

Braga /ˈbrɑːgə/ **1** mountainous district of northern Portugal; pop. (est. 1993) 754 700. **2** its capital city; manufactures include jewellery, textiles, and vehicles; pop. (1991) 90 535.

Braganza /brəˈgænsə/ (Portuguese **Bragança**) **1** district of NE Portugal; pop. (est. 1993) 154 700. **2** its capital city; pop. (1991) 16 550.

braggart /ˈbrægət/ –*n.* boastful person. –*adj.* boastful.

Brahma /ˈbrɑːmə/ *n.* **1** Hindu Creator. **2** supreme divine Hindu reality. [Sanskrit, = creator]

Brahman /ˈbrɑːmən/ *n.* (also **brahman**) (*pl.* **-s**) **1** (also **Brahmin**) member of the highest or priestly Hindu caste. **2** = BRAHMA 2. □ **Brahmanic** /-ˈmænɪk/ *adj.* **Brahmanism** *n.*

Brahmaputra /ˌbrɑːməˈpuːtrə/ river of S Asia, rising in Tibet and flowing through the Himalayas and NE India to join the Ganges at its delta (in Bangladesh) on the Bay of Bengal.

braid –*n.* **1** woven band as edging or trimming. **2** *US* plait of hair. –*v.* **1** *US* plait. **2** trim with braid. □ **braiding** *n.* [Old English]

Brăila /brəˈiːlə/ city and port in E Romania, on the Danube; machinery, paper, and synthetic fibres are manufactured; pop. (est. 1993) 236 344.

Braille /breɪl/ –*n.* system of writing and printing for the blind, with patterns of raised dots. –*v.* (**-ling**) print or transcribe in Braille. [*Braille*, name of its inventor]

brain –*n.* **1** organ of soft nervous tissue in the skull of vertebrates, the centre of sensation and of intellectual and nervous activity. **2 a** *colloq.* intelligent person. **b** (often in *pl.*) intelligence. **3** (usu. in *pl.*; prec. by *the*) *colloq.* cleverest person in a group; mastermind. **4** electronic device functioning like a brain. –*v.* **1** dash out the brains of. **2** *colloq.* strike hard on the head. □ **on the brain** *colloq.* obsessively in one's thoughts. [Old English]

brainchild *n. colloq.* person's clever idea or invention.

brain death *n.* irreversible brain damage causing the end of independent respiration, regarded as indicative of death. □ **brain-dead** *adj.*

brain drain *n. colloq.* loss of skilled personnel by emigration.

brainless *adj.* foolish.

brainpower *n.* mental ability or intelligence.

brainstorm *n.* **1** sudden mental disturbance. **2** *colloq.* mental lapse. **3** *US* brainwave.

♦ **brainstorming** *n.* group discussion in order to invoke ideas and solve business problems. No idea is rejected, no matter how irrelevant it appears, until it has been thoroughly discussed and evaluated. A major rule of brainstorming is that the discussion of ideas should not be inhibited.

---

brains trust *n.* group of experts answering questions, usu. publicly and impromptu.

brainwash *v.* implant ideas or esp. ideology into (a person) by repetition etc. □ **brainwashing** *n.*

brainwave *n.* **1** (usu. in *pl.*) electrical impulse in the brain. **2** *colloq.* sudden bright idea.

brainy *adj.* (**-ier**, **-iest**) intellectually clever.

braise /breɪz/ *v.* (**-sing**) stew slowly with a little liquid in a closed container. [French *braise* live coals]

brake[1] –*n.* **1** (often in *pl.*) device for stopping or slowing a wheel, vehicle, etc. **2** thing that impedes. –*v.* (**-king**) **1** apply a brake. **2** slow or stop with a brake. [probably obsolete *brake* = curb]

brake[2] *n.* large estate car. [var. of BREAK]

brake[3] –*n.* **1** toothed instrument for crushing flax and hemp. **2** (in full **brake harrow**) heavy harrow. –*v.* (**-king**) crush (flax or hemp). [Low German or Dutch: related to BREAK]

brake[4] *n.* thicket or clump of brushwood. [Old English]

brake drum *n.* cylinder attached to a wheel, on which the brake shoes press to brake.

brake horsepower *n.* power of an engine measured by the force needed to brake it.

brake lining *n.* strip of fabric increasing the friction of a brake shoe.

brake shoe *n.* long curved block which presses on a brake drum to brake.

bramble /ˈbræmb(ə)l/ *n.* wild thorny shrub, esp. the blackberry. □ **brambly** *adj.* [Old English]

brambling /ˈbræmblɪŋ/ *n.* the speckled finch. [German: related to BRAMBLE]

bran *n.* grain husks separated from flour. [French]

branch /brɑːntʃ/ –*n.* **1** limb of a tree or bough. **2** lateral extension or subdivision, esp. of a river, road, or railway. **3** subdivision of a family, knowledge, etc. **4** local office etc. of a large business. –*v.* (often foll. by *off*) **1** diverge. **2** divide into branches. □ **branch out** extend one's field of interest. [Latin *branca* paw]

brand –*n.* **1 a** particular make of goods. **b** (also **brand name**) trade name used to identify a specific product, manufacturer, or distributor. The sale of most branded products began in the UK at the turn of the century (some, e.g. Bovril (trade mark) and Horlicks (trade mark), were mid-Victorian) when manufacturers wanted to distinguish their goods from those of their competitors. As consumers became more sophisticated, manufacturers placed more emphasis upon promoting their brands directly to consumers (rather than to distributors), spending considerable sums on advertising the high quality of their products. Manufacturers believe that if they invest in the quality of their brands, consumers will respond by asking for their goods by their brand names and by being willing to pay a premium for them; manufacturers also believe they will be less susceptible to demands from distributors for extra discounts to stock their brands. For some products (e.g. perfumes and alcoholic drinks), considerable effort has gone into promoting brands to reflect the personality of their likely purchasers; market research has shown that for these products consumers can be persuaded to buy brands that enhance the image they have of themselves. See GENERIC *n.*; OWN BRAND. **2** (usu. foll. by *of*) characteristic kind (*brand of humour*). **3** identifying mark burned esp. on livestock. **4** iron used for this. **5** piece of burning or charred wood. **6** stigma; mark of disgrace. **7** *poet.* torch. –*v.* **1** mark with a hot iron. **2** stigmatize (*branded him a liar*). **3** impress unforgettably. **4** assign a trade mark etc. to. [Old English]

Brandenburg /ˈbrændənˌbɜːg/ **1** state (*Land*) of E Germany, a former electorate of Prussia; pop. (est. 1995) 2 536 700; capital, Potsdam. **2** city in E Germany; industries include steel, machinery, and textile manufacturing; pop. (est. 1989) 93 660.

brandish /ˈbrændɪʃ/ *v.* wave or flourish as a threat or display. [French from Germanic]

♦ **brand loyalty** *n.* support by consumers for a particular brand or product, usu. the result of continued satisfaction with a product or its price and reinforced by effective and heavy advertising. Strong brand loyalty, which is often subjective or subconscious, reduces the impact of competitive brand promotions and discourages switching between brands, unless it is for an improved product.

♦ **brand manager** *n.* (also **product manager**) executive responsible for the overall marketing and promotion of a particular branded product. The responsibilities range from setting objectives for the product to managing and coordinating its sale.

♦ **brand name** *n.* = BRAND *n.* 1b.

brand-new *adj.* completely new.

brandy /ˈbrændɪ/ *n.* (*pl.* **-ies**) strong alcoholic spirit distilled from wine or fermented fruit juice. [Dutch *brandewijn*]

brandy butter *n.* mixture of brandy, butter, and sugar.

brandy-snap *n.* crisp rolled gingerbread wafer usu. filled with cream.

♦ **Branson** /ˈbrænsən/, **Richard** (1950–) British entrepreneur; founder and chairman of the Virgin group of companies. Branson's business career began when he left school at 16 to start a mail-order record service; he opened the first Virgin records store in 1971, founding the Virgin recording company in the same year. Virgin Atlantic Airlines was founded in 1984 and the group has now diversified into publishing, broadcasting, construction, holidays, British rail travel, mutual funds, and soft drinks (Virgin Cola). Branson floated the business in 1986 but bought it back in 1988. In 1992 the Virgin music business was sold to EMI for some £560 million.

bran-tub *n.* lucky dip with prizes hidden in bran.

brash *adj.* vulgarly self-assertive; impudent. □ **brashly** *adv.* **brashness** *n.* [dial.]

Brasília /brəˈzɪlɪə/ capital (since 1960) of Brazil, built on a site in the central plateau in an attempt to draw people away from the crowded coastal areas; pop. (1991) 1 601 094.

Braşov /bræˈʃɒv/ (Hungarian **Brassó**, German **Kronstadt**) second-largest city of Romania; industries include machinery, textiles, chemicals, and cement; pop. (est. 1994) 324 310.

brass /brɑːs/ –*n.* **1** yellow alloy of copper and zinc. **2** brass objects collectively. **3** brass wind instruments. **4** *slang* money. **5** brass memorial tablet. **6** *colloq.* effrontery. –*adj.* made of brass. □ **brassed off** *slang* fed up. [Old English]

brass band *n.* band of brass instruments.

brasserie /ˈbræsərɪ/ *n.* restaurant, orig. one serving beer with food. [French *brasser* brew]

brassica /ˈbræsɪkə/ *n.* plant of the cabbage family. [Latin, = cabbage]

brassière /ˈbræzɪə(r)/ *n.* = BRA. [French]

brass monkey *n. coarse slang* used in various phrases to indicate extreme cold.

brass-rubbing *n.* **1** practice of taking impressions by rubbing heelball etc. over paper laid on engraved brasses. **2** impression obtained by this.

brass tacks *n.pl. slang* essential details.

brassy /ˈbrɑːsɪ/ *adj.* (**-ier**, **-iest**) **1** of or like brass. **2** impudent. **3** vulgarly showy. **4** loud and blaring.

Brazil /brəˈzɪl/, **Federative Republic of** country in NE South America, the largest of that continent, comprising almost half its total area. Agriculture is still the main occupation, with coffee, soya products, cocoa, orange juice, and meat being significant exports. Fishing also provides employment and income. Many of the country's mineral resources, which include gold, quartz, copper, and manganese, remain untapped, but substantial amounts of iron ore and iron and steel products are exported. Machinery and road vehicles are also exported. Uranium deposits are being exploited for use in nuclear power stations, according to an agreement with Germany. Textiles are the main manufacture, but car production is increasing and efforts to encourage greater industrialization in the interior are likely to lead to a diversification of products. Plentiful hydroelectric power is helping these efforts. The domestic economy has been troubled by high inflation and a low rate of economic growth; the latest of a series of plans to combat these includes the implementation of a broad privatization programme. In 1994 Brazil signed an agreement to reschedule a large amount of foreign debt. By the mid-1990s inflation had been reduced and the economy stabilized somewhat.

History. Colonized by the Portuguese in the 16th century, Brazil became an independent empire in 1822 and a republic in 1889. The 20th century has seen military dictatorship and political unrest, but the country is now more settled as a federal democratic republic than many of its neighbours. Following 20 years of military rule, democratic elections were held in 1985. In 1990 Fernando Collar de Mello became president, succeeding José Sarney (president 1985–90). The presidency of de Mello ended in 1992 with his resignation following charges of corruption. It is a member of LAIA. President, Fernando Henrique Cardoso; capital, Brasília. □ **Brazilian** *adj.* & *n.*

languages	Portuguese (official), Spanish, Indian languages
currency	real of 100 centavos
pop. (est. 1996)	157 872 000
GNP (1994)	US$536B
literacy	83% (m); 83% (f)
life expectancy	56 (m); 67 (f)

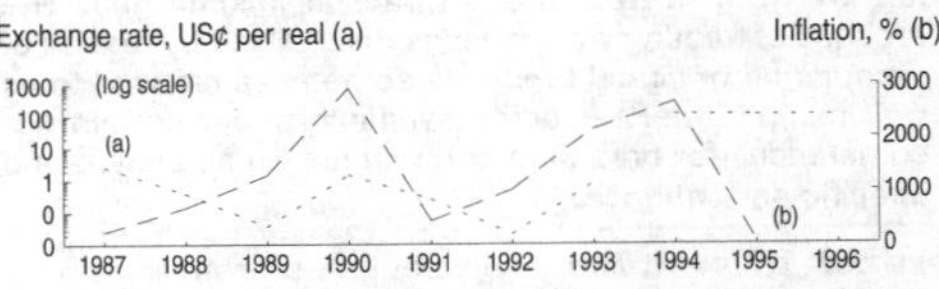

brat *n.* usu. *derog.* child, esp. an ill-behaved one. [origin unknown]

Bratislava /ˌbrætɪˈslɑːvə/ (Hungarian **Pozsony**, German **Pressburg**) capital of Slovakia, a port on the Danube; industries include oil refining, engineering, and chemicals; pop. (1985) 450 776.

Braunschweig see BRUNSWICK.

bravado /brəˈvɑːdəʊ/ *n.* show of boldness. [Spanish]

brave *–adj.* **1** able or ready to face and endure danger, disgrace, or pain. **2** *formal* splendid, spectacular. *–n.* American Indian warrior. *–v.* (**-ving**) face bravely or defiantly. □ **bravely** *adv.* **braveness** *n.* **bravery** *n.* [ultimately Latin *barbarus* barbarian]

bravo /brɑːˈvəʊ/ *–int.* expressing approval. *–n.* (*pl.* **-s**) cry of 'bravo'. [French from Italian]

bravura /brəˈvjʊərə/ *n.* **1** brilliance of execution. **2** (often *attrib.*) passage of (esp. vocal) music requiring brilliant technique. [Italian]

brawl *–n.* noisy quarrel or fight. *–v.* **1** engage in a brawl. **2** (of a stream) run noisily. [Provençal]

brawn *n.* **1** muscular strength. **2** muscle; lean flesh. **3** jellied meat made from a pig's head. □ **brawny** *adj.* (**-ier, -iest**). [French from Germanic]

bray *–n.* **1** cry of a donkey. **2** harsh sound like this. *–v.* **1** make a bray. **2** utter harshly. [French *braire*]

braze *v.* (**-zing**) solder with an alloy of brass and zinc. [French *braser*]

brazen /ˈbreɪz(ə)n/ *–adj.* **1** shameless; insolent. **2** of or like brass. **3** harsh in sound. *–v.* (foll. by *out*) face or undergo defiantly (*brazen it out*). □ **brazenly** *adv.* [Old English]

brazier[1] /ˈbreɪzɪə(r)/ *n.* metal pan or stand holding burning coals etc. [French: related to BRAISE]

brazier[2] /ˈbreɪzɪə(r)/ *n.* worker in brass. [probably from BRASS]

Brazil nut *n.* (also **Brazil**) **1** large three-sided nut of a tall South American tree. **2** the tree itself.

Brazzaville /ˈbræzəvɪl/ capital and a major port of the Republic of the Congo; industries include shipbuilding; pop. (est. 1992) 937 579.

breach *–n.* **1** (often foll. by *of*) breaking or non-observation of a law, contract, etc. **2** breaking of relations; quarrel. **3** opening, gap. *–v.* **1** break through; make a gap in. **2** break (a law, contract, etc.). □ **step into the breach** help in a crisis, esp. as a replacement. [Germanic: related to BREAK]

♦ **breach of contract** *n.* failure by a party to a contract to perform the obligations under that contract or an indication of the party's intention not to do so. An indication that a contract will be breached in the future is called **repudiation** or an **anticipatory breach**; it may be either expressed in words or implied from conduct. For example, an anticipatory breach occurs if a person contracts to sell his or her car to A but sells and delivers it to B before the delivery date agreed with A. The repudiation of a contract entitles the injured party to treat the contract as discharged and to sue immediately for damages for the loss sustained. The same procedure only applies to an actual breach if it constitutes a **fundamental breach**, i.e. a breach of a major term (see CONDITION *n.* 2) of the contract. In either an anticipatory or an actual breach, the injured party may, however, decide to affirm the contract instead (see AFFIRMATION OF CONTRACT). When an actual breach relates only to a minor term of the contract (a **breach of warranty**) the injured party may sue for damages but has no right to treat the contract as discharged. The process of treating a contract as discharged by reason of repudiation or actual breach is sometimes referred to as rescission. Other remedies available under certain circumstances for breach of contract are an injunction and specific performance.

---

breach of promise *n.* breaking of a promise, esp. to marry.

breach of the peace *n.* crime of causing a public disturbance.

♦ **breach of warranty** see BREACH OF CONTRACT.

---

bread /bred/ *–n.* **1** baked dough of flour and water, usu. leavened with yeast. **2** necessary food. **3** *slang* money. *–v.* coat with breadcrumbs for cooking. [Old English]

bread and butter *–n.* one's livelihood. *–attrib. adj.* (**bread-and-butter**) done or produced to earn a basic living.

breadboard *n.* **1** board for cutting bread on. **2** board for making an experimental model of an electric circuit.

breadcrumb *n.* small fragment of bread, esp. (in *pl.*) for use in cooking.

breadfruit *n.* **1** fruit which resembles new bread when roasted. **2** tropical evergreen tree bearing it.

breadline *n.* subsistence level (esp. *on the breadline*).

bread sauce *n.* white sauce thickened with breadcrumbs.

breadth /bredθ/ *n.* **1** distance or measurement from side to side of a thing. **2** freedom from prejudice or intolerance. [Old English: related to BROAD]

breadwinner *n.* person who works to support a family.

break /breɪk/ *–v.* (*past* **broke**; *past part.* **broken** /ˈbrəʊkən/) **1 a** separate into pieces under a blow or strain; shatter. **b** make or become inoperative. **c** break a bone in or dislocate (part of the body). **2 a** interrupt (*broke our journey*). **b** have an interval (*broke for tea*). **3** fail to keep (a law, promise, etc.). **4 a** make or become subdued or weak; (cause to) yield; destroy. **b** weaken the effect of (a fall, blow, etc.). **c** = *break in* 3c. **5** surpass (a record). **6** (foll. by *with*) end a friendship with (a person etc.). **7 a** be no longer subject to (a habit). **b** (foll. by *of*) free (a person) from a habit (*broke them of their addiction*). **8** reveal or be revealed (*broke the news*; *story broke*). **9 a** (of fine weather) change suddenly. **b** (of waves) curl over and foam. **c** (of the day) dawn. **d** (of clouds) move apart. **e** (of a storm) begin violently. **10** *Electr.* disconnect (a circuit). **11 a** (of the voice) change with emotion. **b** (of a boy's voice) change at puberty. **12 a** (often foll. by *up*) divide (a set etc.). **b** change (a banknote etc.) for coins. **13** ruin financially (see also BROKE *adj.*). **14** penetrate (e.g. a safe) by force. **15** decipher (a code). **16** make (a way, path, etc.) by force. **17** burst forth (*sun broke through*). **18 a** (of troops) disperse in confusion. **b** rupture (ranks). **19 a** (usu. foll. by *free*, *loose*, *out*, etc.) escape by a sudden effort. **b** escape or emerge from (prison, bounds, cover, etc.). **20** *Tennis etc.* win a game against (an opponent's service). **21** (of boxers etc.) come out of a clinch. **22** *Billiards* etc. disperse the balls at the start of a game. *–n.* **1 a** act or instance of breaking. **b** point of breaking; gap. **2** interval, interruption; pause. **3** sudden dash (esp. to escape). **4** *colloq.* piece of luck; fair chance. **5** *Cricket* deflection of a bowled ball on bouncing. **6** *Billiards* etc. **a** series of points scored during one turn. **b** opening shot dispersing the balls. □ **break away** make or become free or separate. **break the back of** do the hardest or greatest part of. **break down 1 a** fail mechanically; cease to function. **b** (of human relationships etc.) fail, collapse. **c** fail in (esp. mental) health. **d** collapse in tears or emotion. **2 a** demolish, destroy. **b** suppress (resistance). **c** force to yield. **3** analyse into components. **break even** make neither profit nor loss. See BREAK-EVEN POINT. **break a person's heart** see HEART. **break the ice** begin to overcome formality or shyness. **break in 1** enter by force, esp. with criminal intent. **2** interrupt. **3 a** accustom to a habit etc. **b** wear etc. until comfortable. **c** tame (an animal); accustom (a horse) to a saddle etc. **break in on** disturb; interrupt. **break into 1** enter forcibly. **2 a** burst forth with (a song, laughter, etc.). **b** change pace for (a faster one) (*broke into a gallop*). **3** interrupt. **break off 1** detach by breaking. **2** bring to an end. **3** cease talking etc. **break open** open forcibly. **break out 1** escape by force, esp. from prison. **2** begin suddenly. **3** (foll. by *in*) become covered in (a rash etc.). **4** exclaim. **break up 1** break into small pieces. **2** disperse; disband. **3** end the school term.

4 (cause to) terminate a relationship; disband. **break wind** release gas from the anus. [Old English]

breakable –*adj.* easily broken. –*n.* (esp. in *pl.*) breakable thing.

breakage *n.* **1 a** broken thing. **b** damage caused by breaking. **2** act or instance of breaking.

breakaway *n.* (often *attrib.*) breaking away; secession (*breakaway group*).

break-dancing *n.* acrobatic style of street-dancing.

breakdown *n.* **1 a** mechanical failure. **b** loss of (esp. mental) health. **2** collapse (*breakdown of communication*). **3** analysis (of statistics etc.).

breaker *n.* **1** heavy breaking wave. **2** person or thing that breaks something, esp. disused machinery.

◆ **break-even point** *n.* level of sales of a product required to produce an income to cover costs of overheads and production without profit or loss. Once the break-even point is passed the producer will be making a profit.

breakfast /'brekfəst/ –*n.* first meal of the day. –*v.* have breakfast.

◆ **break-forward** *n.* contract on the money market that combines the features of a forward-exchange contract and a currency option (see FORWARD-EXCHANGE CONTRACT). The forward contract can be undone at a previously agreed rate of exchange, enabling the consumer to be free if the market moves in the consumer's favour. There is no premium on the option; the cost is built into the fixed rate of exchange.

break-in *n.* illegal forced entry, esp. with criminal intent.

◆ **breaking a leg** see STRADDLE *n.*

breaking and entering *n.* (formerly) the illegal entering of a building with intent to commit a felony.

breaking-point *n.* point of greatest strain.

breakneck *attrib. adj.* (of speed) dangerously fast.

break-out *n.* forcible escape.

breakthrough *n.* **1** major advance or discovery. **2** act of breaking through an obstacle etc.

breakup *n.* **1** disintegration or collapse. **2** dispersal.

◆ **breakup value** *n.* **1** value of an asset on the assumption that an organization will not continue in business. On this assumption the assets are likely to be sold piecemeal and probably in haste. **2** asset value per share of a company.

breakwater *n.* barrier breaking the force of waves.

bream *n.* (*pl.* same) **1** yellowish arch-backed freshwater fish. **2** (in full **sea bream**) similar marine fish. [French from Germanic]

breast /brest/ –*n.* **1 a** either of two milk-secreting organs on a woman's chest. **b** corresponding part of a man's body. **2 a** chest. **b** corresponding part of an animal. **3** part of a garment that covers the breast. **4** breast as a source of nourishment or emotion. –*v.* **1** contend with. **2** reach the top of (a hill). □ **make a clean breast of** confess fully. [Old English]

breastbone *n.* thin flat vertical bone in the chest between the ribs.

breast-feed *v.* feed (a baby) from the breast.

breastplate *n.* armour covering the breast.

breast-stroke *n.* swimming stroke made by extending both arms forward and sweeping them back.

breastwork *n.* low temporary defence or parapet.

breath /breθ/ *n.* **1 a** air drawn into or expelled from the lungs. **b** one respiration of air. **c** breath as perceived by the senses. **2 a** slight movement of air. **b** whiff (of perfume etc.). **3** whisper, murmur (esp. of scandal). □ **catch one's breath 1** cease breathing momentarily in surprise etc. **2** rest to restore normal breathing. **hold one's breath** cease breathing temporarily. **out of breath** gasping for air, esp. after exercise. **take one's breath away** surprise, delight, etc. **under one's breath** in a whisper. [Old English]

Breathalyser /'breθə,laɪzə(r)/ *n.* (also **-lyzer**) *propr.* instrument for measuring alcohol levels in the breath exhaled into it. □ **breathalyse** *v.* (also **-lyze**) (**-sing** or **-zing**). [from BREATH, ANALYSE]

breathe /bri:ð/ *v.* (**-thing**) **1** draw air into and expel it from the lungs. **2** be or seem alive. **3 a** utter or sound (esp. quietly). **b** express (*breathed defiance*). **4** pause. **5** send out or take in (as if) with the breath (*breathed new life into them*; *breathed whisky*). **6** (of wine etc.) be exposed to the air. □ **breathe again** (or **freely**) feel relief.

breather /'bri:ðə(r)/ *n.* **1** *colloq.* brief pause for rest. **2** brief period in the fresh air.

breathing-space *n.* time to recover; pause.

breathless *adj.* **1** panting, out of breath. **2** holding the breath. **3** still, windless. □ **breathlessly** *adv.*

breathtaking *adj.* astounding; awe-inspiring. □ **breathtakingly** *adv.*

breath test *n.* test with a Breathalyser.

b. rec. *abbr.* bills receivable.

bred *past* and *past part.* of BREED.

Breda /'breɪdə/ manufacturing town in the SW Netherlands; pop. (1987) 120 212.

breech *n.* back part of a rifle or gun barrel. [Old English]

breech birth *n.* (also **breech delivery**) delivery of a baby with the buttocks or feet foremost.

breeches /'brɪtʃɪz/ *n.pl.* short trousers, esp. fastened below the knee.

breeches buoy *n.* lifebuoy with canvas breeches for the user's legs.

breed –*v.* (*past* and *past part.* **bred**) **1** (of animals) produce young. **2** propagate; raise (animals). **3** yield; result in. **4** arise; spread. **5** bring up; train. **6** create (fissile material) by nuclear reaction. –*n.* **1** stock of similar animals or plants within a species, usu. developed by deliberate selection. **2** race; lineage. **3** sort, kind. □ **breeder** *n.* [Old English]

breeder reactor *n.* nuclear reactor creating surplus fissile material.

breeding *n.* **1** raising of offspring; propagation. **2** social behaviour; ancestry.

breeze[1] –*n.* **1** gentle wind. **2** *colloq.* quarrel. **3** esp. *US colloq.* easy task. –*v.* (**-zing**) (foll. by *in*, *out*, *along*, etc.) *colloq.* saunter casually. [probably Spanish and Portuguese *briza*]

breeze[2] *n.* small cinders. [French: related to BRAISE]

breeze-block *n.* lightweight building block, esp. of breeze mixed with sand and cement.

breezy *adj.* (**-ier, -iest**) **1** slightly windy. **2** *colloq.* cheerful, light-hearted, casual.

Bremen /'breɪmən/ **1** state (*Land*) of Germany; pop. (est. 1995) 680 000. **2** its capital city and a major German port; industries include iron and steel, shipbuilding, oil refining, and chemicals; pop. (est. 1994) 551 000.

Bren *n.* (in full **Bren gun**) lightweight quick-firing machine-gun. [*Br*no in the Czech Republic, *En*field in England]

brent *n.* (in full **brent-goose**) small migratory goose. [origin unknown]

Brescia /'breʃə/ industrial city in N Italy, in Lombardy; manufactures include machinery and firearms; pop. (est. 1994) 191 875.

Breslau see WROCLAW.

Brest /brest/ **1** port and naval base in NW France, on the Atlantic coast of Brittany; pop. (est. 1990) 153 099. **2** (formerly **Brest-Litovsk**, Polish **Brześć nad Bu-giem**) inland port in Belarus, near the Polish border, a major industrial, commercial, and transportation centre; pop. (est. 1996) 293 000.

Bretagne see BRITTANY.

brethren see BROTHER.

Breton /'bret(ə)n/ –*n.* **1** native of Brittany. **2** Celtic language of Brittany. *–adj.* of Brittany, its people, or language. [French, = BRITON]

breve *n.* **1** *Mus.* note twice the length of a semibreve. **2** mark (˘) indicating a short or unstressed vowel. [var. of BRIEF]

breviary /'bri:vɪərɪ/ *n.* (*pl.* **-ies**) book containing the Roman Catholic daily office. [Latin: related to BRIEF]

brevity /'brevɪtɪ/ *n.* **1** economy of expression; conciseness. **2** shortness (of time etc.). [Anglo-French: related to BRIEF]

brew /bru:/ *–v.* **1 a** make (beer etc.) by infusion, boiling, and fermentation. **b** make (tea etc.) by infusion. **2** undergo these processes. **3** gather force; threaten (*trouble is brewing*). **4** concoct (a plan etc.). *–n.* **1** liquid or amount brewed. **2** process of brewing. □ **brew up** make tea. □ **brewer** *n.* [Old English]

brewery /'bru:ərɪ/ *n.* (*pl.* **-ies**) factory for brewing beer etc.

brew-up *n.* instance of making tea.

briar[1] var. of BRIER[1].

briar[2] var. of BRIER[2].

bribe *–v.* (**-bing**) (often foll. by *to* + infin.) persuade to act improperly in one's favour by a gift of money etc. *–n.* money or services offered in bribing. [French *briber* beg]

♦ **bribery** *n.* offering or receiving bribes. The offences commonly grouped under the expression 'bribery and corruption' relate to the improper influencing of people in positions of trust and are now statutory. Under the Public Bodies Corrupt Practices Act (1889), amended by the Prevention of Corruption Act (1916), it is an offence corruptly to offer to a member, officer, or servant of a public body any reward or advantage to do anything in relation to any matter with which that body is concerned; it is also an offence for a public servant or officer to corruptly receive or solicit such a reward. The Prevention of Corruption Act (1906) amended by the 1916 act is wider in scope. Under this act it is an offence corruptly to give or offer any valuable consideration to an agent to do any act or show any favour in relation to his or her principal's affairs.

bric-à-brac /'brɪkə,bræk/ *n.* (also **bric-a-brac**) cheap ornaments, trinkets, etc. [French]

brick *–n.* **1 a** small usu. rectangular block of fired or sun-dried clay used in building. **b** material of this. **2** child's toy block. **3** brick-shaped thing. **4** *slang* generous or loyal person. *–v.* (foll. by *in, up*) close or block with brickwork. *–adj.* **1** built of brick (*brick wall*). **2** (also **brick-red**) dull red. [Low German or Dutch]

brickbat *n.* **1** piece of brick, esp. as a missile. **2** insult.

brickie *n. slang* bricklayer.

bricklayer *n.* person who builds with bricks, esp. for a living. □ **bricklaying** *n.*

brickwork *n.* building or work in brick.

brickyard *n.* place where bricks are made.

bridal /'braɪd(ə)l/ *adj.* of a bride or wedding. [Old English]

bride *n.* woman on her wedding day and during the period just before and after it. [Old English]

bridegroom *n.* man on his wedding day and during the period just before and after it. [Old English]

bridesmaid *n.* girl or unmarried woman attending a bride at her wedding.

bridge[1] *–n.* **1 a** structure providing a way across a river, road, railway, etc. **b** thing joining or connecting. **2** operational superstructure on a ship. **3** upper bony part of the nose. **4** piece of wood on a violin etc. over which the strings are stretched. **5** = BRIDGEWORK. *–v.* (**-ging**) **1** be or make a bridge over. **2** reduce (a gap, deficiency, etc.). [Old English]

bridge[2] *n.* card-game derived from whist. [origin unknown]

bridgehead *n.* fortified position held on the enemy's side of a river etc.

bridge roll *n.* small soft bread roll.

Bridgetown /'brɪdʒtaʊn/ capital of Barbados, a port in the SW exporting mainly sugar and rum; pop. (1990) 6070.

bridgework *n. Dentistry* dental structure covering a gap, joined to the teeth on either side.

♦ **bridging loan** *n.* loan taken on a short-term basis to bridge the gap between the purchase of one asset and the sale of another. It is particularly common in the property and housing market.

bridle /'braɪd(ə)l/ *–n.* **1** headgear for controlling a horse, including reins and bit. **2** restraining thing. *–v.* (**-ling**) **1** put a bridle on. **2** curb, restrain. **3** (often foll. by *up*) express anger, offence, etc., esp. by throwing up the head and drawing in the chin. [Old English]

bridle-path *n.* (also **bridle-way**) rough path for riders or walkers.

Brie /bri:/ *n.* a kind of soft cheese. [*Brie* in N France]

brief *–adj.* **1** of short duration. **2** concise; abrupt, brusque. **3** scanty (*brief skirt*). *–n.* **1** (in *pl.*) short pants. **2 a** summary of a case drawn up for counsel. **b** piece of work for a barrister. **3** instructions for a task. **4** papal letter on discipline. *–v.* **1** instruct (a barrister) by brief. **2** inform or instruct in advance. □ **hold a brief for** argue in favour of. **in brief** to sum up. □ **briefly** *adv.* **briefness** *n.* [Latin *brevis* short]

briefcase *n.* flat document case.

brier[1] /'braɪə(r)/ *n.* (also **briar**) wild rose or other prickly bush. [Old English]

brier[2] /'braɪə(r)/ *n.* (also **briar**) **1** white heath of S Europe. **2** tobacco pipe made from its root. [French *bruyère*]

Brig. *abbr.* Brigadier.

brig[1] *n.* two-masted square-rigged ship. [abbreviation of BRIGANTINE]

brig[2] *n. Scot.* & *N.Engl.* bridge. [var. of BRIDGE[1]]

brigade /brɪ'geɪd/ *n.* **1** military unit, usu. three battalions, as part of a division. **2** group organized for a special purpose. [Italian *briga* strife]

brigadier /,brɪgə'dɪə(r)/ *n.* **1** officer commanding a brigade. **2** staff officer of similar standing.

brigand /'brɪgənd/ *n.* member of a robber band; bandit. □ **brigandage** *n.* [Italian *brigante*: related to BRIGADE]

brigantine /'brɪgən,ti:n/ *n.* two-masted ship with a square-rigged foremast and a fore-and-aft rigged mainmast. [French or Italian: related to BRIGAND]

bright /braɪt/ *–adj.* **1** emitting or reflecting much light; shining. **2** intense, vivid. **3** clever. **4** cheerful. *–adv.* esp. *poet.* brightly. □ **brightly** *adv.* **brightness** *n.* [Old English]

brighten *v.* make or become brighter.

Brighton /'braɪt(ə)n/ resort in S England, in East Sussex; pop. (est. 1994) 154 400.

Bright's disease /braɪts/ *n.* kidney disease. [*Bright*, name of a physician]

brill[1] *n.* (*pl.* same) European flat-fish. [origin unknown]

brill[2] *adj. colloq.* = BRILLIANT *adj.* 4. [abbreviation]

brilliant /'brɪlɪənt/ *–adj.* **1** very bright; sparkling. **2** outstandingly talented. **3** showy. **4** *colloq.* excellent. *–n.* diamond of the finest cut with many facets. □ **brilliance** *n.* **brilliantly** *adv.* [French *briller* shine, from Italian]

brilliantine /'brɪljən,ti:n/ *n.* dressing for making the hair glossy. [French: related to BRILLIANT]

brim *–n.* **1** edge or lip of a vessel. **2** projecting edge of a hat. *–v.* (**-mm-**) fill or be full to the brim. □ **brim over** overflow. [origin unknown]

brim-full *adj.* (also **brimful**) filled to the brim.

brimstone *n. archaic* sulphur. [from BURN[1], STONE]

brindled /'brɪnd(ə)ld/ *adj.* (esp. of domestic animals) brown or tawny with streaks of another colour. [Scandinavian]

brine *n.* **1** water saturated or strongly impregnated with salt. **2** sea water. [Old English]

bring *v.* (*past* and *past part.* **brought** /brɔ:t/) **1** come carrying; lead, accompany; convey. **2** cause or result in (*war* *brings misery*). **3** be sold for; produce as income. **4 a** prefer (a charge). **b** initiate (legal action). **5** cause to become or to reach a state (*brings me alive*; *cannot bring myself to agree*). **6** adduce (evidence, an argument, etc.). □ **bring about** cause to happen. **bring back** call to mind. **bring down 1** cause to fall. **2** lower (a price). **bring forth 1** give birth to. **2** cause. **bring forward 1** move to an earlier time. **2** transfer from the previous page or account. **3** draw attention to. **bring home to** cause to realize fully. **bring the house down** receive rapturous applause. **bring in 1** introduce. **2** yield as income or profit. **bring off** achieve successfully. **bring on** cause to happen, appear, or make progress. **bring out 1** emphasize; make evident. **2** publish. **bring over** convert to one's own side. **bring round 1** restore to consciousness. **2** persuade. **bring through** aid (a person) through adversity, esp. illness. **bring to** restore to consciousness (*brought him to*). **bring up 1** rear (a child). **2** vomit. **3** call attention to. **4** (*absol.*) stop suddenly. [Old English]

bring-and-buy sale *n.* charity sale at which people bring items for sale and buy those brought by others.

brink *n.* **1** extreme edge of land before a precipice, river, etc. **2** furthest point before danger, discovery, etc. □ **on the brink of** about to experience or suffer; in imminent danger of. [Old Norse]

brinkmanship *n.* pursuit (esp. habitual) of danger etc. to the brink of catastrophe.

briny –*adj.* (**-ier**, **-iest**) of brine or the sea; salty. –*n.* (prec. by *the*) *slang* the sea.

briquette /brɪ'ket/ *n.* block of compressed coal-dust as fuel. [French diminutive: related to BRICK]

Brisbane /'brɪzbən/ seaport in E Australia, capital of Queensland; industries include brewing, tanning, and engineering; pop. (est. 1995) 1 489 100.

brisk –*adj.* **1** quick, lively, keen (*brisk pace, trade*). **2** enlivening (*brisk wind*). –*v.* (often foll. by *up*) make or grow brisk. □ **briskly** *adv.* **briskness** *n.* [probably French BRUSQUE]

brisket /'brɪskɪt/ *n.* animal's breast, esp. as a joint of meat. [French]

brisling /'brɪzlɪŋ/ *n.* small herring or sprat. [Norwegian and Danish]

bristle /'brɪs(ə)l/ –*n.* short stiff hair, esp. one on an animal's back, used in brushes. –*v.* (**-ling**) **1 a** (of hair) stand upright. **b** make (hair) do this. **2** show irritation. **3** (usu. foll. by *with*) be covered or abundant (in). □ **bristly** *adj.* (**-ier**, **-iest**). [Old English]

Bristol /'brɪst(ə)l/ city and port in SW England; industries include engineering (esp. aircraft engines), electronics, chemicals, and printing; pop. (est. 1994) 399 200.

Brit *n. colloq.* British person. [abbreviation]

Britain /'brɪt(ə)n/ Great Britain or the United Kingdom.

Britannia /brɪ'tænjə/ *n.* personification of Britain, esp. as a helmeted woman with shield and trident. [Latin]

♦ **Britannia coins** *n.pl.* four British gold coins (£100, £50, £25, and £10 denominations) introduced in October 1987 for investment purposes, in competition with the krugerrand. Although all sales of gold coins attract VAT, Britannia coins are widely dealt in as bullion coins.

Britannia metal *n.* silvery alloy of tin, antimony, and copper.

Britannic /brɪ'tænɪk/ *adj.* (esp. in **His** or **Her Britannic Majesty**) of Britain.

Briticism /'brɪtɪ,sɪz(ə)m/ *n.* idiom used only in Britain. [after *Gallicism*]

British /'brɪtɪʃ/ –*adj.* of Great Britain, the United Kingdom or its dependencies, or their people. –*n.* (prec. by *the*; treated as *pl.*) the British people. [Old English]

♦ **British Airports Authority plc** *n.* (also **BAA**) public limited company floated on the London Stock Exchange in 1987 and formed from the former British Airports Authority (founded in 1966). It owns and operates London airports (Heathrow, Gatwick, and Stansted) as well as Aberdeen, Edinburgh, Prestwick, and Glasgow airports. It is responsible for the construction and maintenance of buildings, fire and security services, passenger services, and terminal management.

British Antarctic Territory part of Antarctica claimed by Britain, together with the adjacent South Orkney Islands and South Shetland Islands.

♦ **British Bankers Association** *n.* (also **BBA**) organization founded in 1920 to represent the views of the recognized UK banks (approximately 300). Membership is open to all banks established under British law with head offices in the UK. The Association is a member of the European Community Banking Federation.

♦ **British Coal Corporation** *n.* (also **BCC**) nationalized corporation, formerly called the **National Coal Board** (**NCB**), which owns and runs all British coalmines. The NCB itself took control of the mines in 1947.

♦ **British Code of Advertising Practice** (also **BCAP**) see ADVERTISING STANDARDS AUTHORITY.

British Columbia /kə'lʌmbɪə/ province of W Canada; pop. (est. 1995) 3 766 000; capital, Victoria. Forestry and mining (esp. of copper, coal, natural gas, and petroleum) are important and most manufacturing industry is concentrated on processing timber products and minerals; there is also a major fishing industry.

British English *n.* English as used in Great Britain.

♦ **British Exporters Association** *n.* (also **BEXA**) association, formerly the British Export Houses Association (BEHA), that puts UK suppliers in touch with association members, who trade and finance trade throughout the world.

British Honduras /hɒn'djʊərəs/ see BELIZE.

British Indian Ocean Territory British dependency in the Indian Ocean, comprising the islands of the Chagos Archipelago. British and US naval personnel occupy the island of Diego Garcia.

♦ **British Institute of Management** *n.* (also **BIM**) *hist.* institution set up in 1974 by the then Board of Trade to promote professionalism in management practice and courses in management and to provide information for its members. In 1992 it merged with the Institution of Industrial Managers to form the Institute of Management.

♦ **British Insurance and Investment Brokers Association** *n.* (also **BIIBA**) trade association for insurance brokers registered with the Insurance Brokers Registration Council and investment brokers registered under the Financial Services Act (1986). Formed in 1977 as the British Insurance Brokers Association by the amalgamation of a number of insurance broking associations, it changed to its current name in 1988 to widen its membership to include investment advisers. It provides public relations, free advice, representation in parliament, and a conciliation service for consumers.

British Legion *n.* = ROYAL BRITISH LEGION.

♦ **British Overseas Trade Board** *n.* (also **BOTB**) organization set up by the Department of Trade and Industry, whose members are drawn mainly from industry and commerce. The BOTB was formed in 1972 to advise on overseas trade and the official export-promotion programme. It liaises between government and private industry to expand overseas trade, advises new exporters on foreign tariffs and regulations, assists exporters in displaying products in trade fairs, etc.

♦ ***British Rates and Data*** *n.* (also ***BRAD***) monthly publication listing addresses, cover price, circulation, frequency, rate cards, copy and cancellation requirements, and advertising representatives for national and provincial newspapers, consumer, trade, technical, and professional publications, and for television and radio stations.

♦ **British Standards 5750** *n.* quality assurance standard applying to processes and procedures. BS 5750 accreditation is now indispensable in many industries.

♦ **British Standards Institution** *n.* (also **BSI**) institution founded in 1901, which received a royal charter in 1929 and took its present name in 1931. Its function is to formulate standards for building, engineering, chemical, textile, and electrical products, ensuring that they maintain a specified quality. Products so standardized make use of the **Kitemark** logo as a symbol of quality. Manufacturers who use the Kitemark do so under licence from the BSI on condition that products are subject to regular inspection. Apart from maintaining quality standards in this way, the BSI attempts to ensure that the design of goods is restricted to a sensible number of patterns and sizes for one purpose, to avoid unnecessary variety. The BSI, which collaborates closely with the International Standards Organization, is also actively concerned in metrology, providing information on units of measurement and issuing glossaries defining technical words.

British summer time *n.* = SUMMER TIME.

♦ **British Technology Group** *n.* (also **BTG**) government-appointed organization formed in 1981 by the merger of the **National Enterprise Board** (**NEB**) and the **National Research and Development Corporation** (**NRDC**). Its purpose is to encourage technological development by providing finance for new scientific and engineering products and processes discovered through research at UK universities, polytechnics, research councils, and government research establishments.

♦ **British Telecom** *n.* (also **BT**, in full **British Telecommunications plc**) public limited company licensed to run telecommunications throughout the UK. Its forerunner was the British Telecommunications Corporation, formed in 1981 as a public corporation to control the UK telephone and telecommunications system, which had previously been the responsibility of the Post Office. In 1984 this corporation became British Telecommunications plc, when 51% of the shares were sold to the public.

♦ **British Textile Confederation** *n.* (also **BTC**) organization formed in 1972 to represent the interests of textile manufacturers, on issues of trading and economic policies, to the UK government and within the European Community.

British thermal unit *n.* amount of heat needed to raise 1 lb of water through one degree Fahrenheit, equivalent to 1.055×10^3 joules.

♦ **British Waterways Board** *n.* (also **BWB**) board set up under the Transport Act (1962) to provide services and facilities for UK inland waterways. Its responsibilities extend over approximately 2000 miles of waterways and 90 reservoirs.

Briton /ˈbrɪt(ə)n/ *n.* **1** inhabitant of S Britain before the Roman conquest. **2** native or inhabitant of Great Britain. [Latin *Britto -onis*]

Brittany /ˈbrɪtənɪ/ (French **Bretagne** /breˈtænj/) region of NW France forming a peninsula between the Bay of Biscay and the English Channel; tourism is important; pop. (est. 1994) 2 840 600; capital, Rennes.

brittle /ˈbrɪt(ə)l/ *adj.* hard and fragile; apt to break. □ **brittlely** *adv.* (also **brittly**). [Old English]

brittle-bone disease *n.* = OSTEOPOROSIS.

BRN *international vehicle registration* Bahrain.

Brno /ˈbɜːnəʊ/ city in the SE Czech Republic; manufactures include machinery and firearms; pop. (est. 1994) 390 100.

broach *–v.* **1** raise for discussion. **2** pierce (a cask) to draw liquor. **3** open and start using. *–n.* **1** bit for boring. **2** roasting-spit. [Latin *broccus* projecting]

broad /brɔːd/ *–adj.* **1** large in extent from one side to the other; wide. **2** in breadth (*two metres broad*). **3** extensive (*broad acres*). **4** full and clear (*broad daylight*). **5** explicit (*broad hint*). **6** general (*broad intentions, facts*). **7** tolerant, liberal (*broad view*). **8** coarse (*broad humour*). **9** markedly regional (*broad Scots*). *–n.* **1** broad part (*broad of the back*). **2** *US slang* woman. **3** (**the Broads**) large areas of water in East Anglia, formed where rivers widen. □ **broadly** *adv.* **broadness** *n.* [Old English]

broad bean *n.* **1** bean with large edible flat seeds. **2** one such seed.

broadcast *–v.* (*past* and *past part.* **broadcast**) **1** transmit by radio or television. **2** take part in such a transmission. **3** scatter (seed etc.). **4** disseminate (information) widely. *–n.* radio or television programme or transmission. □ **broadcaster** *n.* **broadcasting** *n.*

broadcast network see NETWORK *n.* 6.

broadcloth *n.* fine cloth of wool, cotton, or silk.

broaden *v.* make or become broader.

broad gauge *n.* railway track with a wider than standard gauge.

broad-leaved *adj.* (of a tree) deciduous and hard-timbered.

broadloom *adj.* (esp. of carpet) woven in broad widths.

broad-minded *adj.* tolerant, liberal.

♦ **broad money** *n. colloq.* M3 (see MONEY SUPPLY). Cf. NARROW MONEY.

broadsheet *n.* **1** large-sized newspaper. **2** large sheet of paper printed on one side only.

broadside *n.* **1** vigorous verbal attack. **2** simultaneous firing of all guns from one side of a ship. **3** side of a ship above the water between the bow and quarter. □ **broadside on** sideways on.

broadsword *n.* broad-bladed sword, for cutting rather than thrusting.

brocade /brəˈkeɪd/ *–n.* rich fabric woven with a raised pattern. *–v.* (**-ding**) weave in this way. [Italian *brocco* twisted thread]

broccoli /ˈbrɒkəlɪ/ *n.* brassica with greenish flower-heads. [Italian]

brochure /ˈbrəʊʃə(r)/ *n.* pamphlet or booklet, esp. with descriptive information. [French *brocher* stitch]

broderie anglaise /ˌbrəʊdərɪ ɑ̃ˈgleɪz/ *n.* open embroidery on white linen etc. [French, = English embroidery]

brogue[1] /brəʊg/ *n.* **1** strong outdoor shoe with ornamental perforations. **2** rough shoe of untanned leather. [Gaelic and Irish *brōg* from Old Norse]

brogue[2] /brəʊg/ *n.* marked accent, esp. Irish. [perhaps related to BROGUE[1]]

broil *v.* esp. *US* **1** grill (meat). **2** make or become very hot, esp. from the sun. [French *bruler* burn]

broiler *n.* young chicken for broiling or roasting.

broke *past* of BREAK. *predic. adj. colloq.* having no money.

broken *past part.* of BREAK. *adj.* **1** having been broken. **2** reduced to despair; beaten. **3** (of language) badly spoken, esp. by a foreigner. **4** interrupted (*broken sleep*).

broken-down *adj.* **1** worn out by age, use, etc. **2** not functioning.

broken-hearted *adj.* overwhelmed with grief.

Broken Hill **1** mining town in SE Australia, in New South Wales; pop. (est. 1987) 24 170. **2** see KABWE.

broken home *n.* family disrupted by divorce or separation.

♦ **broker** *n.* **1** agent who brings two parties together, enabling them to enter into a contract to which the broker is not a principal. Brokers are used because they have specialized knowledge of certain markets or to conceal the identity of a principal; they also introduce buyers to sellers. See AVIATION BROKER; BILL BROKER; BROKER/DEALER; COMMODITY BROKER; INSURANCE BROKER; SHIPBROKER; STOCKBROKER. **2** middleman. **3** official appointed to sell or appraise distrained goods. □ **broking** *n.* [Anglo-French]

♦ **brokerage** *n.* broker's fee or commission, which is usu. calculated as a percentage of the sum involved in the contract but may be fixed according to a tariff.

♦ **broker/dealer** *n.* member of the London Stock

Exchange who, since 1986 (see BIG BANG), has functioned both as a stockbroker and a jobber, but only in a single capacity in one particular transaction.

---

brolly /ˈbrɒlɪ/ *n.* (*pl.* **-ies**) *colloq.* umbrella. [abbreviation]

Bromberg see BYDGOSZCZ.

bromide /ˈbrəʊmaɪd/ *n.* **1** any binary compound of bromine. **2** trite remark. **3** reproduction or proof on paper coated with silver bromide emulsion.

bromine /ˈbrəʊmiːn/ *n.* poisonous liquid element with a choking smell. [Greek *brōmos* stink]

bronchial /ˈbrɒŋkɪəl/ *adj.* of the bronchi (see BRONCHUS) or of the smaller tubes into which they divide.

bronchitis /brɒŋˈkaɪtɪs/ *n.* inflammation of the mucous membrane in the bronchial tubes.

bronchus /ˈbrɒŋkəs/ *n.* (*pl.* **-chi** /-kaɪ/) either of the two main divisions of the windpipe. [Latin from Greek]

bronco /ˈbrɒŋkəʊ/ *n.* (*pl.* **-s**) wild or half-tamed horse of the western US. [Spanish, = rough]

♦ **Bronfman** /ˈbrɒnfmən/ **Edgar Miles** (1929–) Canadian industrialist, chairman (since 1975) of the Seagram Company Ltd., a leading producer of alcoholic and non-alcoholic beverages. His brother, **Charles Rosner Bronfman** (1931–), is co-chairman (since 1986) of the company. Together the brothers own 16% of Seagram. **Edgar Miles Bronfman, Jr.**, (1955–) is chief operating officer (since 1989) of Seagram and now runs the company. He sold Seagram's large profitable stake in DuPont to fund the purchase of 80% of Hollywood's MCA Inc., of which he is acting president (since 1995).

---

brontosaurus /ˌbrɒntəˈsɔːrəs/ *n.* (*pl.* **-ruses**) large plant-eating dinosaur with a long whiplike tail. [Greek *brontē* thunder, *sauros* lizard]

bronze *–n.* **1** alloy of copper and tin. **2** its brownish colour. **3** thing of bronze, esp. a sculpture. *–adj.* made of or coloured like bronze. *–v.* (**-zing**) make or become brown; tan. [French from Italian]

Bronze Age *n. Archaeol.* period when weapons and tools were usu. made of bronze.

bronze medal *n.* medal, usu. awarded as third prize.

brooch /brəʊtʃ/ *n.* ornamental hinged pin. [French *broche*: related to BROACH]

brood *–n.* **1** young of esp. a bird born or hatched at one time. **2** *colloq.* children in a family. *–v.* **1** worry or ponder (esp. resentfully). **2** (of a bird) sit on eggs to hatch them. [Old English]

broody *adj.* (**-ier, -iest**) **1** (of a hen) wanting to brood. **2** sullenly thoughtful. **3** *colloq.* (of a woman) wanting pregnancy.

brook[1] /brʊk/ *n.* small stream. [Old English]

brook[2] /brʊk/ *v.* (usu. with *neg.*) *literary* tolerate, allow. [Old English]

broom *n.* **1** long-handled brush for sweeping. **2** shrub with bright yellow flowers. [Old English]

broomstick *n.* handle of a broom.

Bros. *abbr.* Brothers (esp. in the name of a firm).

broth *n.* thin soup of meat or fish stock. [Old English]

brothel /ˈbrɒθ(ə)l/ *n.* premises for prostitution. [originally = worthless fellow, from Old English]

brother /ˈbrʌðə(r)/ *n.* **1** man or boy in relation to his siblings. **2** close male friend or associate. **3** (*pl.* also **brethren** /ˈbreðrɪn/) **a** member of a male religious order, esp. a monk. **b** fellow Christian etc. **4** fellow human being. □ **brotherly** *adj.* [Old English]

brother german see GERMAN.

brotherhood *n.* **1** relationship between brothers. **2** association of people with a common interest. **3** community of feeling between human beings.

brother-in-law *n.* (*pl.* **brothers-in-law**) **1** one's wife's or husband's brother. **2** one's sister's or sister-in-law's husband.

brought *past* and *past part.* of BRING.

brouhaha /ˈbruːhɑːˌhɑː/ *n.* commotion; sensation. [French]

brow /braʊ/ *n.* **1** forehead. **2** eyebrow. **3** summit of a hill etc. **4** edge of a cliff etc. [Old English]

browbeat *v.* (*past* **-beat**; *past part.* **-beaten**) intimidate, bully.

brown /braʊn/ *–adj.* **1** having the colour of dark wood or rich soil. **2** dark-skinned or suntanned. **3** (of bread) made from wholemeal or wheatmeal flour. *–n.* **1** brown colour or pigment. **2** brown clothes or material. *–v.* make or become brown. □ **browned off** *colloq.* fed up, disheartened. □ **brownish** *adj.* [Old English]

brown bear *n.* large North American brown bear.

brown coal *n.* = LIGNITE.

♦ **brown goods** *n.pl.* televisions, hi-fi equipment, etc., which are usu. housed in wood or imitation wood cabinets. Cf. WHITE GOODS.

Brownie *n.* **1** (in full **Brownie Guide**) junior Guide. **2** (**brownie**) small square of chocolate cake with nuts. **3** (**brownie**) benevolent elf.

Brownie point *n. colloq.* notional mark awarded for good conduct etc.

browning *n.* additive to colour gravy.

brown owl *n.* **1** any of various owls, esp. the tawny owl. **2** (**Brown Owl**) adult leader of Brownie Guides.

brown rice *n.* unpolished rice.

brown sugar *n.* unrefined or partially refined sugar.

browse /braʊz/ *–v.* (**-sing**) **1** read desultorily or look over goods for sale. **2** (often foll. by *on*) feed on leaves, twigs, etc. *–n.* **1** twigs, shoots, etc. as fodder. **2** act of browsing. [French *brost* bud]

BRS *abbr.* British Road Services.

BRU *international vehicle registration* Brunei.

brucellosis /ˌbruːsɪˈləʊsɪs/ *n.* bacterial disease, esp. of cattle. [Sir D. *Bruce*, name of a physician]

Bruges /bruːʒ/ (Flemish **Brugge** /ˈbrʊxə/) city in NW Belgium, capital of the province of West Flanders; textiles, lace, beer, and furniture are produced; pop. (est. 1995) 116 273.

bruise /bruːz/ *–n.* **1** discolouration of the skin caused esp. by a blow. **2** similar damage on a fruit etc. *–v.* (**-sing**) **1**

Brunei /ˈbruːnaɪ/, **State of** Islamic sultanate on the NW coast of Borneo. The economy is dominated by the oil industry, with new offshore oilfields being developed; the chief exports are crude petroleum and petroleum products. A deep-water port and a natural-gas liquefaction plant have been built to diversify the economy, and liquefied natural gas contributes to export revenue; agriculture is being improved with the intention that Brunei should become self-sufficient in food production. Formerly a British protectorate, the country came under the sultan's rule following a revolution in 1962; full independence was achieved in 1984. Head of state, Sultan Hassanal Bolkia Mu'izuddin Waddaulah; capital, Bandar Seri Begawan. □ **Bruneian** *adj.*

languages	Malay (official), Chinese, English
currency	dollar (B$) of 100 cents
pop. (est. 1996)	300 000
GNP (est. 1994)	US$3.9B
literacy	92% (m); 82% (f)
life expectancy	72 (m); 77 (f)

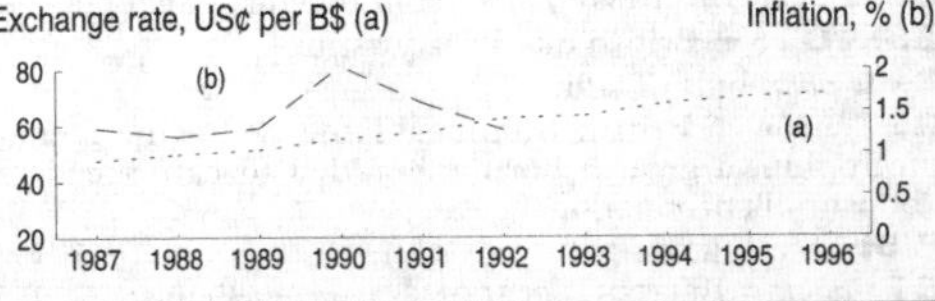

a inflict a bruise on. **b** hurt mentally. **2** be susceptible to bruising. [originally = crush, from Old English]

bruiser *n. colloq.* **1** large tough-looking person. **2** professional boxer.

bruit /bruːt/ *v.* (often foll. by *abroad, about*) spread (a report or rumour). [French, = noise]

brunch *n.* combined breakfast and lunch. [portmanteau word]

brunette /bruː'net/ *n.* woman with dark brown hair. [French diminutive]

Brunswick /'brʌnzwɪk/ (German **Braunschweig**) city in N Germany, in Lower Saxony; industries include precision engineering, motor vehicles, chemicals, and food processing; pop. (est. 1995) 254 130.

brunt *n.* chief impact of an attack, task, etc. (esp. *bear the brunt of*). [origin unknown]

brush *–n.* **1** implement with bristles, hair, wire, etc. set into a block, for cleaning, painting, arranging the hair, etc. **2** act of brushing. **3** (usu. foll. by *with*) short esp. unpleasant encounter. **4** fox's bushy tail. **5** piece of carbon or metal as an electrical contact esp. with a moving part. **6** = BRUSHWOOD 2. *–v.* **1** sweep, scrub, treat, or tidy with a brush. **2** remove or apply with a brush. **3** graze in passing. □ **brush aside** dismiss curtly or lightly. **brush off** dismiss abruptly. **brush up 1** clean up or smarten. **2** revise (a subject). [French]

brush-off *n.* abrupt dismissal.

brush-up *n.* act of brushing up.

brushwood *n.* **1** undergrowth, thicket. **2** cut or broken twigs etc.

brushwork *n.* **1** use of the brush in painting. **2** painter's style in this.

brusque /brʊsk/ *adj.* abrupt or offhand. □ **brusquely** *adv.* **brusqueness** *n.* [Italian *brusco* sour]

Brussels /'brʌs(ə)lz/ (French **Bruxelles** /bruː'sel/, Flemish **Brüssel**) capital of Belgium; industries include textiles and machinery; pop. (est. 1995) 951 580. The Commission of the European Communities and the international secretariat of NATO have their headquarters here.

Brussels sprout *n.* **1** brassica with small cabbage-like buds on a stem. **2** such a bud.

brutal /'bruːt(ə)l/ *adj.* **1** savagely cruel. **2** harsh, merciless. □ **brutality** /-'tælɪtɪ/ *n.* (*pl.* **-ies**). **brutally** *adv.* [French: related to BRUTE]

brutalize /'bruːtə,laɪz/ *v.* (also **-ise**) (**-zing** or **-sing**) **1** make brutal. **2** treat brutally.

brute /bruːt/ *–n.* **1 a** brutal or violent person. **b** *colloq.* unpleasant person or difficult thing. **2** animal. *–attrib. adj.* **1** unthinking (*brute force*). **2** cruel; stupid; sensual. □ **brutish** *adj.* **brutishly** *adv.* **brutishness** *n.* [Latin *brutus* stupid]

bryony /'braɪənɪ/ *n.* (*pl.* **-ies**) climbing plant with red berries. [Latin from Greek]

BS *–abbr.* **1** Bachelor of Surgery. **2** bill of sale. **3** British Standard(s). See also BRITISH STANDARDS INSTITUTION. **4** building society. *–international vehicle registration* Bahamas. *–postcode* Bristol.

B/S *abbr.* **1** bill of sale. **2** bill of store.

b.s. *abbr.* **1** balance sheet. **2** bill of sale.

BSC *abbr.* **1** *Computing* binary synchronous communications. **2** British Sugar Corporation.

B.Sc. *abbr.* Bachelor of Science.

B.Sc.(Econ.) *abbr.* Bachelor of Science in Economics.

BSE *abbr.* bovine spongiform encephalopathy, a usu. fatal cattle disease.

BSI *abbr.* = BRITISH STANDARDS INSTITUTION.

BSIS *abbr.* Business Sponsorship Incentive Scheme.

BSkyB *abbr.* British Sky Broadcasting.

Bs/L *abbr.* bills of lading.

BST *abbr.* **1** British Summer Time. **2** bovine somatotrophin, a growth hormone added to cattle-feed to boost milk production.

B/St *abbr.* bill of sight.

BT *–abbr.* = BRITISH TELECOM. *–postcode* Belfast.

Bt. *abbr.* Baronet.

BTC *abbr.* = BRITISH TEXTILE CONFEDERATION.

◆ **BTEC** *abbr.* Business and Technology Education Council. See VOCATIONAL TRAINING.

BTG *abbr.* = BRITISH TECHNOLOGY GROUP.

BTN *abbr.* Brussels Tariff Nomenclature.

BTU *abbr.* **1** Board of Trade unit. **2** *US* British thermal unit.

Btu *abbr.* British thermal unit.

bubble /'bʌb(ə)l/ *–n.* **1 a** thin sphere of liquid enclosing air etc. **b** air-filled cavity in a liquid or solidified liquid. **2** transparent domed canopy. **3** visionary or unrealistic project. *–v.* (**-ling**) **1** rise in or send up bubbles. **2** make the sound of boiling. □ **bubble over** (often foll. by *with*) be exuberant. [imitative]

bubble and squeak *n.* cooked cabbage etc. fried with cooked potatoes.

bubble bath *n.* foaming preparation for adding to bath water.

bubble car *n.* small domed car.

bubble gum *n.* chewing-gum that can be blown into bubbles.

bubble-jet printer see INK-JET PRINTER.

bubbly *–adj.* (**-ier**, **-iest**) **1** having or like bubbles. **2** exuberant. *–n. colloq.* champagne.

bubo /'bjuːbəʊ/ *n.* (*pl.* **-es**) inflamed swelling in the armpit or groin. [Greek *boubōn* groin]

bubonic plague /bjuː'bɒnɪk/ *n.* contagious disease with buboes.

buccaneer /,bʌkə'nɪə(r)/ *n.* **1** pirate. **2** unscrupulous adventurer. □ **buccaneering** *n.* & *adj.* [French]

Bucharest /,buːkə'rest/ capital of Romania; industries include flour milling, textiles, and oil refining; pop. (est. 1993) 2 343 824.

buck[1] *–n.* **1** male deer, hare, rabbit, etc. **2** *archaic* dandy. **3** (*attrib.*) *slang* male. *–v.* **1** (of a horse) jump upwards with its back arched. **2** (usu. foll. by *off*) throw (a rider) in this way. **3** (usu. foll. by *up*) *colloq.* **a** cheer up. **b** hurry up; make an effort. [Old English]

buck[2] *n. US slang* dollar. [origin unknown]

buck[3] *n. slang* (in poker) article placed before the next dealer. □ **pass the buck** *colloq.* shift responsibility (to another). [origin unknown]

bucket /'bʌkɪt/ *–n.* **1 a** round open container with a handle, for carrying or drawing water etc. **b** amount contained in this. **2** (in *pl.*) *colloq.* large quantities, esp. of rain or tears. **3** scoop in a water wheel, dredger, etc. *–v.* (**-t-**) *colloq.* **1** (often foll. by *down*) (esp. of rain) pour heavily. **2** (often foll. by *along*) move or drive fast or bumpily. [Anglo-French]

bucket seat *n.* seat with a rounded back for one person, esp. in a car.

bucket-shop *n. colloq.* **1** firm of brokers, dealers, agents, etc., of questionable standing and frail resources, that is unlikely to be a member of an established trade organization. **2** travel agency specializing in cheap air tickets.

Buckinghamshire /'bʌkɪŋəm,ʃɪə(r)/ county in S central England; pop. (est. 1994) 658 400; county town, Aylesbury. It is mainly agricultural, but there is some manufacturing, esp. of furniture.

buckle /'bʌk(ə)l/ *–n.* clasp with a hinged pin for securing a belt, strap etc. *–v.* (**-ling**) **1** (often foll. by *up, on,* etc.) fasten with a buckle. **2** (often foll. by *up*) (cause to) crumple under pressure. □ **buckle down** make a determined effort. [Latin *buccula* cheek-strap]

buckler *n. hist.* small round shield.

buckram /'bʌkrəm/ *n.* coarse linen etc. stiffened with paste etc. [French *boquerant*]

Bucks. /bʌks/ *abbr.* Buckinghamshire.

Buck's Fizz *n.* cocktail of champagne and orange juice. [*Buck's* Club in London]

buckshee /bʌk'ʃiː/ *adj.* & *adv. slang* free of charge. [corruption of BAKSHEESH]

buckshot *n.* coarse lead shot.

buckskin *n.* **1** leather from a buck's skin. **2** thick smooth cotton or woollen cloth.

buckthorn *n.* thorny shrub with berries formerly used as a purgative.

buck-tooth *n.* upper projecting tooth.

buckwheat *n.* seed of a plant related to the rhubarb, used to make flour, or as an alternative to rice. [Dutch, = beech-wheat]

bucolic /bjuː'kɒlɪk/ *–adj.* of shepherds; rustic, pastoral. *–n.* (usu. in *pl.*) pastoral poem or poetry. [Greek *boukolos* herdsman]

bud *–n.* **1 a** knoblike shoot from which a stem, leaf, or flower develops. **b** flower or leaf not fully open. **2** asexual outgrowth from an organism separating to form a new individual. *–v.* (**-dd-**) **1** form buds. **2** begin to grow or develop (*budding artist*). **3** graft a bud of (a plant) on to another. [origin unknown]

bud. *abbr.* budget.

Budapest /ˌbuːdə'pest/ capital of Hungary; industries include metalworking, chemicals, and textiles; pop. (est. 1996) 1 909 000.

Buddha /'bʊdə/ *n.* **1** title of the Indian philosopher Gautama (5th century BC) and his successors. **2** sculpture etc. of Buddha. [Sanskrit, = enlightened]

Buddhism /'bʊdɪz(ə)m/ *n.* Asian religion or philosophy founded by Gautama Buddha. □ **Buddhist** *n.* & *adj.*

buddleia /'bʌdlɪə/ *n.* shrub with fragrant flowers attractive to butterflies. [*Buddle*, name of a botanist]

buddy /'bʌdɪ/ *n.* (*pl.* **-ies**) esp. *US colloq.* friend or mate. [perhaps from BROTHER]

budge *v.* (**-ging**) (usu. with *neg.*) **1** move slightly. **2** (cause to) change an opinion. □ **budge up** (or **over**) make room for another person by moving. [French *bouger*]

budgerigar /'bʌdʒərɪˌgɑː(r)/ *n.* small parrot, often kept as a cage-bird. [Aboriginal]

budget /'bʌdʒɪt/ *–n.* **1** amount of money needed or available. **2** financial plan setting targets for the revenues, expenditures, etc. of an organization for a specified period. **3** (**the Budget**) UK financial plan for the coming year, presented to Parliament by the Chancellor of the Exchequer. It reveals the Chancellor's predictions for the economy and the taxation changes for the coming year. **4** (*attrib.*) inexpensive. *–v.* (**-t-**) (often foll. by *for*) allow or arrange for in a budget. □ **budgetary** *adj.* [Latin *bulga* bag]

♦ **budgetary control** *n.* means of controlling the progress of a business in which budgets submitted by each department are agreed by senior management and subsequently compared with actual results during the course of the ensuing accounting period. The use of computers enables any discrepancies to be rapidly noted so that the appropriate action can be taken, or the budget altered, without waiting for the accounts to be prepared at the end of the accounting period. The budgets will normally include output, sales revenue, expenses, efficiency, cash flow, etc. and it is regarded as a principle of budgetary control that departmental managers should only be held responsible for those revenues or expenditures that they can themselves control.

♦ **budget constraint** *n.* different combinations of goods that can be bought with a given income at prevailing prices; this can be represented as a curve on a graph. In consumer theory the point on a curve of an individual's budget constraint that touches the highest indifference curve represents the point of utility maximization. It is also possible to think of governments or firms as facing a budget constraint when choosing their level of expenditure.

♦ **budget deficit** *n.* excess of government expenditure over government income, which must be financed either by borrowing or by printing money. Keynesians have advocated that governments should run budget deficits during recessions in order to stimulate aggregate demand (see PUMP-PRIMING). Monetarists and new classical macroeconomists, however, argue that budget deficits simply stimulate inflation and crowd out private investment. Most economists now argue that, at least on average, governments should seek a balanced budget and that persistent deficits should be eliminated, either by reducing expenditure or increasing taxation. In some cases a **budget surplus** can be used during a boom to collect more revenue than is being spent.

♦ **budget surplus** see BUDGET DEFICIT.

---

budgie /'bʌdʒɪ/ *n. colloq.* = BUDGERIGAR. [abbreviation]

Buenaventura /ˌbweɪnəven'tʊərə/ port in Colombia; exports include tobacco, sugar, and coffee; pop. (est. 1995) 266 988.

Buenos Aires /'bweɪnəs 'aɪriːz/ capital and chief port of Argentina; exports include beef and wool; pop. (1991) 2 988 006.

buff *–adj.* of a yellowish beige colour (*buff envelope*). *–n.* **1** this colour. **2** *colloq.* enthusiast (*railway buff*). **3** velvety dull-yellow ox-leather. *–v.* **1** polish (metal etc.). **2** make (leather) velvety. □ **in the buff** *colloq.* naked. [originally = buffalo, from French *buffle*]

Buffalo /'bʌfəˌləʊ/ industrial city in the US, in New York state, and a major port of the St Lawrence Seaway, at the E end of Lake Erie; manufactures include motor vehicles and electrical equipment; pop. (est. 1994) 312 965.

buffalo /'bʌfəˌləʊ/ *n.* (*pl.* same or **-es**) **1** wild ox of Africa or Asia. **2** North American bison. [Greek *boubalos* ox]

buffer[1] *n.* **1** thing that deadens impact, esp. a device on a train or at the end of a track. **2** substance that maintains the constant acidity of a solution. **3** *Computing* temporary store for data in transfer, usu. used to compensate for the difference in the rates at which two devices can handle data during a transfer. It allows the two devices to operate independently, without the faster device being delayed by the slower device. [imitative]

buffer[2] *n. slang* silly or incompetent old man. [perhaps from BUFFER[1]]

buffer state *n.* small state between two larger ones, regarded as reducing friction.

♦ **buffer stock** *n.* stock of a commodity owned by a government or trade organization and used to stabilize the price of the commodity. The manager of the buffer stock is usu. authorized to buy the commodity in question if its price falls below a certain level, which is itself reviewed periodically, to enable producers to find a ready market for their goods at a profitable level. If the price rises above another fixed level, the buffer stock manager is authorized to sell the commodity on the open market. Thus, producers are encouraged to keep up a steady supply of the commodity and users are reassured that its price has a ceiling.

---

buffet[1] /'bʊfeɪ/ *n.* **1** room or counter where refreshments are sold. **2** self-service meal of several dishes set out at once. **3** also /bʌfɪt/ sideboard or recessed cupboard. [French, = stool]

buffet[2] /'bʌfɪt/ *–v.* (**-t-**) **1** strike repeatedly. **2** contend with (waves etc.). *–n.* **1** blow, esp. of the hand. **2** shock. [French diminutive of *bufe* blow]

buffet car *n.* railway coach serving refreshments.

buffoon /bə'fuːn/ *n.* clownish or stupid person. □ **buffoonery** *n.* [Latin *buffo* clown]

bug *–n.* **1 a** any of various insects with mouthparts modified for piercing and sucking. **b** esp. *US* small insect. **2** *slang* virus; infection. **3** *slang* concealed microphone. **4** *slang* error in a computer program or system etc. **5** *slang* obsession, enthusiasm, etc. *–v.* (**-gg-**) **1** *slang* conceal a microphone in. **2** *slang* annoy. [origin unknown]

bugbear *n.* **1** cause of annoyance. **2** object of baseless fear. [*bug* = bogey]

bugger *coarse slang* (except in sense 2 of *n.* and 3 of *v.*) *–n.* **1 a** unpleasant or awkward person or thing. **b** person of a specified kind (*clever bugger!*). **2** person who commits buggery. *–v.* **1** as an exclamation of annoyance (*bugger it!*). **2** (often foll. by *up*) **a** ruin; spoil. **b** exhaust. **3** commit buggery with. *–int.* expressing annoyance. □ **bug-**

ger-all nothing. **bugger about** (or **around**) (often foll. by *with*) mess about. **bugger off** (often in *imper.*) go away. [Latin *Bulgarus* Bulgarian heretic]

buggery *n.* **1** anal intercourse. **2** = BESTIALITY 2.

buggy /'bʌgɪ/ *n.* (*pl.* **-ies**) **1** small, sturdy, esp. open, motor vehicle. **2** lightweight push-chair. **3** light, horse-drawn vehicle for one or two people. [origin unknown]

bugle /'bju:g(ə)l/ *–n.* brass military instrument like a small trumpet. *–v.* (**-ling**) **1** sound a bugle. **2** sound (a call etc.) on a bugle. □ **bugler** *n.* [Latin *buculus* young bull]

bugloss /'bju:glɒs/ *n.* plant with bright blue tubular flowers, related to borage. [French *buglosse* from Greek, = ox-tongued]

build /bɪld/ *–v.* (*past* and *past part.* **built** /bɪlt/) **1** construct or cause to be constructed. **2 a** (often foll. by *up*) establish or develop (*built the business up*). **b** (often foll. by *on*) base (hopes, theories, etc.). **3** (as **built** *adj.*) of specified build (*sturdily built*). *–n.* **1** physical proportions (*slim build*). **2** style of construction; make. □ **build in** incorporate. **build on** add (an extension etc.). **build up 1** increase in size or strength. **2** praise; boost. **3** gradually become established. [Old English]

builder *n.* person who builds, esp. a building contractor.

building *n.* **1** permanent fixed structure e.g. a house, factory, or stable. **2** constructing of these.

♦ **Building Societies Ombudsman** *n.* = FINANCIAL OMBUDSMAN 2.

♦ **building society** *n.* financial institution traditionally offering a variety of saving accounts to attract deposits, which are used to fund long-term mortgages for house buyers or for house improvement (see MORTGAGE *n.* 1. Building societies developed from the Friendly Society movement in the late 17th century and are non-profit-making. They are regulated by the Building Societies Act (1986). The societies accept deposits into a variety of accounts, which offer different interest rates and different withdrawal terms, or into 'shares', which often require longer notice of withdrawal. Interest on all building-society accounts is paid net of income tax, the society paying the tax direct to the Inland Revenue unless the investor is not a taxpayer. Since the Building Societies Act (1986), societies have been able to widen the range of services they offer; this has enabled them to compete with the high-street banks in many areas. They offer cheque accounts, which pay interest on all credit balances, cash-cards, credit cards, debit cards, loans, money transmission, foreign exchange, personal financial planning services (shares, insurance, pensions, etc.), estate agency, and valuation and conveyancing services. The distinction between banks and building societies is fast disappearing: some building societies have obtained the sanction of their members to become public limited companies to enable them to actually become banks. These changes have led to the merger of many building societies to provide a national network that can compete with the Big Four banks.

---

build-up *n.* **1** favourable advance publicity. **2** gradual approach to a climax. **3** accumulation or increase.

built *past* and *past part.* of BUILD.

built-in *adj.* integral.

♦ **built-in obsolescence** see OBSOLESCENCE 2.

♦ **built-in software** *n.* computer programs that are built into a computer and available automatically when the computer is switched on. Examples include the word processors, spreadsheets, and graphics programs that are built into some desktop terminals.

---

built-up *adj.* **1** (of a locality) densely developed. **2** increased in height etc. by addition. **3** made of prefabricated parts.

Bujumbura /ˌbu:dʒəm'bʊərə/ capital of Burundi, on Lake Tanganyika; pop. (est. 1994) 300 000.

Bukhara /bʊ'kɑ:rə/ (also **Bokhara**) city in S Uzbekistan; pop. (est. 1993) 236 000. Situated in a large cotton-growing district, it is one of the oldest trade centres in central Asia.

Bukovina /ˌbʊkə'vi:nə/ region of SE Europe, divided between Romania and Ukraine.

Bulawayo /ˌbu:lə'weɪəʊ/ industrial city in W Zimbabwe; manufactures include agricultural and electrical equipment; pop. (1992) 620 936.

bulb *n.* **1 a** globular base of the stem of some plants, sending roots downwards and leaves upwards. **b** plant grown from this, e.g. a daffodil. **2** = LIGHT-BULB. **3** object or part shaped like a bulb. [Latin *bulbus* from Greek, = onion]

bulbous *adj.* bulb-shaped; fat or bulging.

Bulgarian *–n.* **1** native or national of Bulgaria. **2** language of Bulgaria. *–adj.* of Bulgaria or its people or language.

bulge *–n.* **1** irregular swelling. **2** *colloq.* temporary increase (*baby bulge*). *–v.* (**-ging**) swell outwards. □ **bulgy** *adj.* [Latin *bulga* bag]

bulimia /bju:'lɪmɪə/ *n.* (in full **bulimia nervosa**) disorder in which overeating alternates with self-induced vomiting, fasting, etc. [Greek *bous* ox, *limos* hunger]

bulk *–n.* **1 a** size; magnitude (esp. large). **b** large mass, body, etc. **c** large quantity. **2** (treated as *pl.* & usu. prec. by *the*) greater part or number (*the bulk of the applicants are women*). **3** roughage. *–v.* **1** seem (in size or impor-

---

Bulgaria /bʌl'geərɪə/, **Republic of** country in SE Europe on the W shore of the Black Sea. With an economy formerly based on agriculture, Bulgaria underwent rapid industrialization after 1945. Engineering, metal processing, and food processing are major industries and mining is important; exports include machinery, consumer goods, metals, minerals, chemicals, rubber, and textiles. Oilfields in the Black Sea and natural-gas deposits are exploited. Agriculture has been mechanized; crops include cereals and tobacco. Bulgaria is struggling to implement market-oriented economic reforms and privatization programmes. The immediate effects of this have been a drop in trade and rises in inflation and unemployment, causing a deep recession.

History. Under Turkish rule until the 20th century, Bulgaria became independent in 1908 but was occupied by the Soviets in 1944. It became a Communist state in 1946, remaining one of the most consistently pro-Soviet members of the Warsaw Pact until the general collapse of Communism in E Europe at the end of 1989. Free elections in 1991 resulted in victory for an anti-Communist coalition. In 1992 another coalition held power; however, the former Communists (now Socialists) were re-elected in 1994. A non-socialist president was elected in 1996. During 1996–97 there were protests about falling standards of living, which resulted in the resignation of the socialist prime minister. Subsequent legislative elections in 1997 were won by a centre-right coalition. Economic problems, notably high unemployment and inflation, have persisted. President, Zhelyu Zhelev; prime minister, Ivan Kostov; capital, Sofia.

languages	Bulgarian (official), Turkish
currency	lev of 100 stotinki
pop. (est. 1996)	8 366 000
GNP (1994)	US$10.2B
literacy	95%
life expectancy	69 (m); 75 (f)

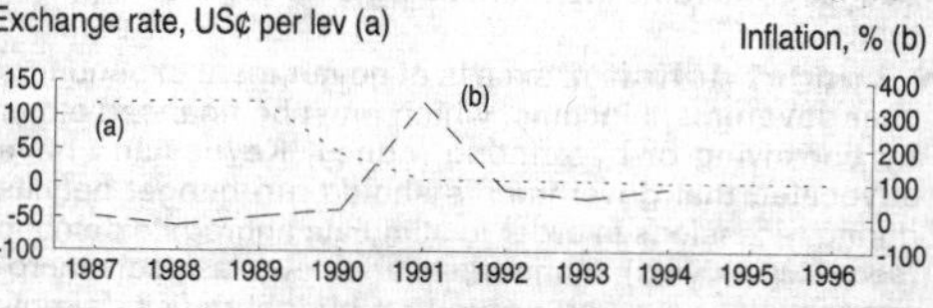

tance) (*bulks large*). **2** make (a book etc.) thicker etc. □ **in bulk** in large quantities. [Old Norse]

bulk buying *n.* buying in quantity at a discount.

◆ **bulk carrier** *n.* ship in which the cargo is carried in bulk, rather than in bags, containers, etc. Bulk cargoes are usu. homogeneous and capable of being loaded by gravity; examples include ores, coal, wheat, etc.

bulkhead *n.* upright partition in a ship, aircraft, etc.

bulky *adj.* (**-ier, -iest**) awkwardly large. □ **bulkiness** *n.*

bull[1] /bʊl/ *n.* **1 a** uncastrated male bovine animal. **b** male of the whale, elephant, etc. **2** (**the Bull**) zodiacal sign or constellation Taurus. **3** bull's-eye of a target. **4** dealer on a stock exchange, currency market, or commodity market who expects prices to rise. A **bull market** is one in which a dealer is more likely to be a buyer than a seller, even to the extent of buying without having made a corresponding sale, thus establishing a **bull position**. A bull with a long position hopes to sell his purchases at a higher price after the market has risen. Cf. BEAR[2] 3. □ **take the bull by the horns** face danger or a challenge boldly. □ **bullish** *adj.* [Old Norse]

bull[2] /bʊl/ *n.* papal edict. [Latin *bulla* seal]

bull[3] /bʊl/ *n.* **1** *slang* **a** nonsense. **b** unnecessary routine tasks. **2** absurdly illogical statement. [origin unknown]

bulldog *n.* **1** short-haired heavy-jowled sturdy dog. **2** tenacious and courageous person.

◆ **bulldog bond** *n.* fixed-interest sterling bond issued in the UK by a foreign borrower.

bulldog clip *n.* strong sprung clip for papers.

bulldoze *v.* (**-zing**) **1** clear with a bulldozer. **2** *colloq.* **a** intimidate. **b** make (one's way) forcibly.

bulldozer *n.* powerful tractor with a broad vertical blade at the front for clearing ground.

bullet /ˈbʊlɪt/ *n.* **1** small pointed missile fired from a rifle, revolver, etc. **2** *Finance* security offering a fixed interest and maturing on a fixed date. **3** final repayment of a loan, which consists of the whole of sum borrowed. In a **bullet loan**, interim repayments are interest-only repayments, the principal sum being repaid in the final bullet. [French diminutive of *boule* ball]

bulletin /ˈbʊlɪtɪn/ *n.* **1** short official news report. **2** society's regular list of information etc. [Italian diminutive: related to BULL[2]]

bulletin board *n.* general facility on a computer network allowing any user of the network to leave messages that can be read by all the other users. Cf. ELECTRONIC MAIL.

bulletproof *adj.* designed to protect from bullets.

bullfight *n.* public baiting, and usu. killing, of bulls. □ **bullfighter** *n.* **bullfighting** *n.*

bullfinch *n.* pink and black finch.

bullfrog *n.* large North American frog with a booming croak.

bull-headed *n.* obstinate, blundering.

◆ **bullion** /ˈbʊlɪən/ *n.* gold, silver, or some other precious metal used in bulk, i.e. in the form of bars or ingots rather than in coin. Central banks use gold bullion in the settlement of international debts. In the **London bullion market**, bullion brokers act as agents for both buyers and sellers and also trade as principals. [French: related to BOIL[1]]

◆ **bull market** see BULL[1] 4.

◆ **bull note** *n.* bond whose redemption value is linked to a price index (e.g. the FT-SE 100) or a commodity price (e.g. the price of gold). Thus, a holder of a bull note will receive on redemption an amount greater than the principal of the bond if the relevant index or price has risen (but less if it has fallen). With a **bear note** the reverse happens. Bull and bear notes are therefore akin to an ordinary bond plus an option, providing opportunities for hedging and speculating.

bullock /ˈbʊlək/ *n.* castrated male of domestic cattle. [Old English diminutive of BULL[1]]

◆ **bull position** see BULL[1] 4.

bullring *n.* arena for bullfights.

bull's-eye *n.* **1** centre of a target. **2** hard minty sweet. **3** hemispherical ship's window. **4** small circular window. **5 a** hemispherical lens. **b** lantern with this. **6** boss of glass in a blown glass sheet.

bullshit *coarse slang* –*n.* (often as *int.*) nonsense; pretended knowledge. –*v.* (**-tt-**) talk nonsense or as if one has specialist knowledge (to). □ **bullshitter** *n.* [from BULL[3]]

bull-terrier *n.* cross between a bulldog and a terrier.

bully[1] /ˈbʊlɪ/ –*n.* (*pl.* **-ies**) person coercing others by fear. –*v.* (**-ies, -ied**) persecute or oppress by force or threats. –*int.* (foll. by *for*) often *iron.* expressing approval (*bully for you*). [Dutch]

bully[2] /ˈbʊlɪ/ (in full **bully off**) –*n.* (*pl.* **-ies**) start of play in hockey in which two opponents strike each other's sticks three times and then go for the ball. –*v.* (**-ies, -ied**) start play in this way. [origin unknown]

bully[3] /ˈbʊlɪ/ *n.* (in full **bully beef**) corned beef. [French: related to BOIL[1]]

buloga /bʊˈləʊgə/ *n.* business logistics game. [abbreviation]

bulrush /ˈbʊlrʌʃ/ *n.* **1** a kind of tall rush. **2** *Bibl.* papyrus. [perhaps from BULL[1] = coarse + RUSH[2]]

bulwark /ˈbʊlwək/ *n.* **1** defensive wall, esp. of earth. **2** protecting person or thing. **3** (usu. in *pl.*) ship's side above deck. [Low German or Dutch]

bum[1] *n. slang* buttocks. [origin uncertain]

bum[2] *US slang* –*n.* loafer or tramp; dissolute person. –*v.* (**-mm-**) **1** (often foll. by *around*) loaf or wander around. **2** cadge. –*attrib. adj.* of poor quality. [German *Bummler* loafer]

bum-bag *n. slang* small pouch worn on a belt round the waist or hips.

bumble /ˈbʌmb(ə)l/ *v.* (**-ling**) **1** (foll. by *on*) speak in a rambling way. **2** (often as **bumbling** *adj.*) be inept; blunder. [from BOOM[1]]

bumble-bee *n.* large bee with a loud hum.

bumf *n. colloq.* usu. *derog.* papers, documents. [abbreviation of *bum-fodder* = toilet-paper]

bump –*n.* **1** dull-sounding blow or collision. **2** swelling or dent so caused. **3** uneven patch on a road etc. **4** prominence on the skull thought to indicate a mental faculty. –*v.* **1 a** hit or come against with a bump. **b** (often foll. by *against, into*) collide. **2** (often foll. by *against, on*) hurt or damage by striking (*bumped my head, the car*). **3** (usu. foll. by *along*) move along with jolts. –*adv.* with a bump; suddenly; violently. □ **bump into** *colloq.* meet by chance. **bump off** *slang* murder. **bump up** *colloq.* increase (prices etc.). □ **bumpy** *adj.* (**-ier, -iest**). [imitative]

bumper *n.* **1** horizontal bar at the front or back of a motor vehicle, reducing damage in a collision. **2** (usu. *attrib.*) unusually large or fine example (*bumper crop*). **3** *Cricket* ball rising high after pitching. **4** brim-full glass.

bumper car *n.* = DODGEM.

bumpkin /ˈbʌmpkɪn/ *n.* rustic or socially inept person. [Dutch]

bumptious /ˈbʌmpʃəs/ *adj.* offensively self-assertive or conceited. [from BUMP, after *fractious*]

bun *n.* **1** small sweet bread roll or cake, often with dried fruit. **2** hair coiled and pinned to the head. [origin unknown]

Bunbury /ˈbʌnbərɪ/ seaport and resort in S Western Australia; pop. (est. 1987) 25 250.

BUNCH *abbr.* Burroughs, Univac, NCR, Control Data, Honeywell (computer manufacturers).

bunch –*n.* **1** things gathered together. **2** collection; lot (*best of the bunch*). **3** *colloq.* group; gang. –*v.* **1** make into a bunch; gather into close folds. **2** form into a group or crowd. [origin unknown]

♦ **Bundesbank** /ˈbʊndəs,bæŋk/ *n.* German central bank. [German, = federal bank]

bundle /ˈbʌnd(ə)l/ –*n.* **1** things tied or fastened together. **2** set of nerve fibres etc. **3** *slang* large amount of money. –*v.* (**-ling**) **1** (usu. foll. by *up*) tie or make into a bundle. **2** (usu. foll. by *into*) throw or move carelessly. **3** (usu. foll. by *out*, *off*, *away*, etc.) send away hurriedly. □ **be a bundle of nerves** (or **fun** etc.) be extremely nervous (or amusing etc.). **go a bundle on** *slang* admire; like. [Low German or Dutch]

♦ **bundling** *n.* marketing ploy of giving away a relatively cheap product with a relatively expensive one to attract customers; for example, giving a number of free audio cassettes with each purchase of a music centre.

bun fight *n. slang* tea party.

bung –*n.* stopper, esp. for a cask. –*v.* **1** stop with a bung. **2** *slang* throw. □ **bunged up** blocked up. [Dutch]

bungalow /ˈbʌŋgə,ləʊ/ *n.* one-storeyed house. [Gujarati, = of Bengal]

bungee /ˈbʌndʒɪ/ *n.* (in full **bungee cord, rope**) elasticated cord or rope used for securing baggage or in bungee jumping.

bungee jumping *n.* sport of jumping from a height while secured by a bungee from the ankles or a harness.

bungle /ˈbʌŋg(ə)l/ –*v.* (**-ling**) **1** mismanage or fail at (a task). **2** work badly or clumsily. –*n.* bungled attempt or work. [imitative]

bunion /ˈbʌnjən/ *n.* swelling on the foot, esp. on the big toe. [French]

bunk[1] *n.* shelflike bed against a wall, esp. in a ship. [origin unknown]

bunk[2] *slang* –*v.* (often foll. by *off*) play truant (from). –*n.* (in **do a bunk**) leave or abscond hurriedly. [origin unknown]

bunk[3] *n. slang* nonsense, humbug. [shortening of BUNKUM]

bunk-bed *n.* each of two or more tiered beds forming a unit.

bunker *n.* **1** container for fuel. **2** reinforced underground shelter. **3** sandy hollow in a golf-course. [origin unknown]

bunkum /ˈbʌŋkəm/ *n.* nonsense, humbug. [*Buncombe* in US]

bunny /ˈbʌnɪ/ *n.* (*pl.* **-ies**) **1** child's name for a rabbit. **2** (in full **bunny girl**) club hostess, waitress, etc., wearing rabbit ears and tail. [dial. *bun* rabbit]

Bunsen burner /ˈbʌns(ə)n/ *n.* small adjustable gas burner used in a laboratory. [*Bunsen*, name of a chemist]

bunting[1] /ˈbʌntɪŋ/ *n.* small bird related to the finches. [origin unknown]

bunting[2] /ˈbʌntɪŋ/ *n.* **1** flags and other decorations. **2** loosely-woven fabric for these. [origin unknown]

buoy /bɔɪ/ –*n.* **1** anchored float as a navigation mark etc. **2** lifebuoy. –*v.* **1** (usu. foll. by *up*) **a** keep afloat. **b** encourage, uplift. **2** (often foll. by *out*) mark with a buoy. [Dutch, perhaps from Latin *boia* collar]

buoyant /ˈbɔɪənt/ *adj.* **1** able or apt to keep afloat. **2** resilient; exuberant. □ **buoyancy** *n.* [French or Spanish: related to BUOY]

BUPA /ˈbuːpə/ *abbr.* British United Provident Association, a private health insurance organization.

BUR *international vehicle registration* Burma (Myanmar).

bur *n.* **1 a** prickly clinging seed-case or flower-head. **b** any plant having these. **2** clinging person. **3** var. of BURR *n.* 2. [Scandinavian]

Burbank /ˈbɜːbæŋk/ city in the US, in California, a centre of the film and television industries; pop. (1990) 93 643.

burble /ˈbɜːb(ə)l/ *v.* **1** talk ramblingly. **2** make a bubbling sound. [imitative]

burbot /ˈbɜːbət/ *n.* (*pl.* same) eel-like freshwater fish. [French]

burden /ˈbɜːd(ə)n/ –*n.* **1** load, esp. a heavy one. **2** oppressive duty, expense, emotion, etc. **3** bearing of loads (*beast of burden*). **4 a** refrain of a song. **b** chief theme of a speech, book, etc. –*v.* load with a burden; oppress. □ **burdensome** *adj.* [Old English: related to BIRTH]

burden of proof *n.* obligation to prove one's case.

burdock /ˈbɜːdɒk/ *n.* plant with prickly flowers and docklike leaves. [from BUR, DOCK[3]]

bureau /ˈbjʊərəʊ/ *n.* (*pl.* **-x** or **-s** /-z/) **1 a** desk with drawers and usu. an angled hinged top. **b** *US* chest of drawers. **2 a** office, department, or agency for specific business. **b** government department. [French, originally = baize]

bureaucracy /bjʊəˈrɒkrəsɪ/ *n.* (*pl.* **-ies**) **1 a** government by central administration. **b** state etc. so governed. **2** government officials, esp. regarded as oppressive and inflexible. **3** conduct typical of these.

bureaucrat /ˈbjʊərə,kræt/ *n.* **1** official in a bureaucracy. **2** inflexible administrator. □ **bureaucratic** /-ˈkrætɪk/ *adj.* **bureaucratically** /-ˈkrætɪkəlɪ/ *adv.*

♦ **Bureau of Customs** *n.* (in the US) part of the Department of the Treasury, which functions as the US equivalent of the British Board of Customs and Excise.

burette /bjʊəˈret/ *n.* (*US* **buret**) graduated glass tube with an end-tap for measuring liquid in chemical analysis. [French]

Burgas /bʊəˈgæs/ port and health resort in Bulgaria, on the coast of the Black Sea; industries include mining and oil refining; pop. (est. 1995) 199 869.

Burgenland /ˈbʊəgən,lænt/ agricultural province of E Austria; pop. (est. 1994) 267 613; capital, Eisenstadt.

burgeon /ˈbɜːdʒ(ə)n/ *v. literary* grow rapidly; flourish. [Latin *burra* wool]

burger /ˈbɜːgə(r)/ *n. colloq.* hamburger. [abbreviation]

Burkina Faso /bɜːˈkiːnə fæsəʊ/ (formerly **Upper Volta**) landlocked country in W Africa. Agriculture is the main economic activity, but manufacturing industry and mining are also important; cotton, gold, oil-seeds, livestock, and hides and skins are among the main exports and millet, sorghum, and rice are important food crops. Economic growth is hampered by political instability, and in recent years poor harvests have weakened the economy. However, an agreement with Canada to exploit manganese deposits should bring some improvement.
History. Part of French West Africa from 1896, the area was made a separate protectorate in 1919. It became an autonomous republic within the French Community in 1958 and a fully independent republic in 1960. Burkina Faso has been subject to a succession of military coups and, although moves towards democracy have been made (presidential and legislative elections were held in 1991 and 1992, respectively), political unrest is likely to continue. The 1991 elections, and those held in 1992, were boycotted by the opposition parties. Head of state, Blaise Compaoré; capital, Ougadougou. □ **Burkinan** *adj.* & *n.*

languages	French (official), tribal languages
currency	CFA franc (CFAF) of 100 centimes
pop. (est. 1996)	10 615 000
GNP (est. 1994)	US$2.9B
literacy	29% (m); 9% (f)
life expectancy	44 (m); 43 (f)

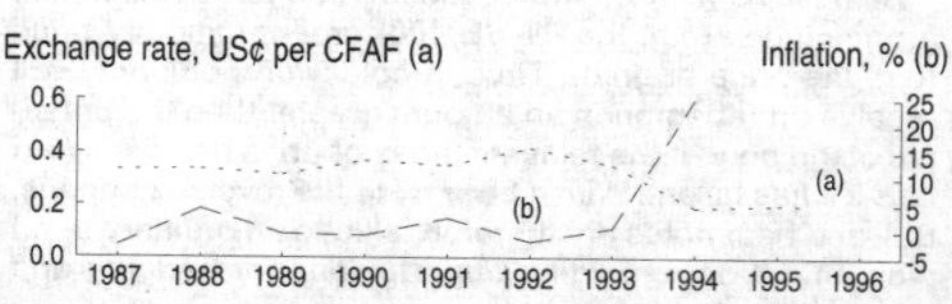

burgher /ˈbɜːgə(r)/ *n.* citizen of a Continental town. [German or Dutch]

burglar /ˈbɜːglə(r)/ *n.* person who commits burglary. [Anglo-French]

burglary *n.* (*pl.* **-ies**) **1** illegal entry with intent to commit theft, do bodily harm, or do damage. **2** instance of this.

■ **Usage** Before 1968 in English law, burglary was a crime under statute and common law; since 1968 it has been a statutory crime only; cf. HOUSEBREAKING.

burgle /ˈbɜːg(ə)l/ *v.* (**-ling**) commit burglary (on).

burgomaster /ˈbɜːgəˌmɑːstə(r)/ *n.* mayor of a Dutch or Flemish town. [Dutch]

Burgundy /ˈbɜːgəndɪ/ (French **Bourgogne** /buəˈgɒnj/) wine-producing region of E central France; pop. (est. 1994) 1 622 567; capital, Dijon.

burgundy /ˈbɜːgəndɪ/ *n.* (*pl.* **-ies**) **1** (also **Burgundy**) **a** red or white wine from Burgundy. **b** *hist.* similar wine from elsewhere. **2** dark red colour of this.

burial /ˈberɪəl/ *n.* **1 a** burying of a corpse. **b** funeral. **2** *Archaeol.* grave or its remains.

burin /ˈbjʊərɪn/ *n.* **1** tool for engraving copper or wood. **2** *Archaeol.* chisel-pointed flint tool. [French]

burk var. of BERK.

burlesque /bɜːˈlesk/ *–n.* **1 a** comic imitation, parody. **b** this as a genre. **2** *US* variety show, esp. with striptease. *–adj.* of or using burlesque. *–v.* (**-ques**, **-qued**, **-quing**) parody. [Italian *burla* mockery]

burly /ˈbɜːlɪ/ *adj.* (**-ier**, **-iest**) large and sturdy. [Old English]

Burmese /bɜˈmiːz/ *–n.* native or language of Burma. *–adj.* of Burma, its people, or language.

burn[1] *–v.* (*past* and *past part.* **burnt** or **burned**) **1** (cause to) be consumed or destroyed by fire. **2** blaze or glow with fire. **3** (cause to) be injured or damaged by fire, heat, radiation, acid, etc. **4** use or be used as fuel etc. **5** char in cooking. **6** produce (a hole, mark, etc.) by fire or heat. **7 a** heat (clay, chalk, etc.). **b** harden (bricks) by fire. **8** colour, tan, or parch with heat or light. **9** (be) put to death by fire. **10** cauterize, brand. **11** make, be, or feel hot, esp. painfully. **12** (often foll. by *with*) (cause to) feel great emotion or passion (*burn with shame*). **13** *slang* drive fast. *–n.* mark or injury caused by burning. □ **burn one's boats** (or **bridges**) commit oneself irrevocably. **burn the candle at both ends** work etc. excessively. **burn down** destroy or be destroyed by burning. **burn one's fingers** suffer for meddling or rashness. **burn the midnight oil** read or work late. **burn out 1** be reduced to nothing by burning. **2** (cause to) fail by burning. **3** (usu. *refl.*) suffer exhaustion. **burn up 1** get rid of by fire. **2** begin to blaze. [Old English]

burn[2] *n. Scot.* brook. [Old English]

burner *n.* part of a gas cooker, lamp, etc. that emits the flame.

burning *adj.* **1** ardent, intense. **2** hotly discussed, vital, urgent.

burning-glass *n.* lens for concentrating the sun's rays to produce a flame.

burnish /ˈbɜːnɪʃ/ *v.* polish by rubbing. [French *brunir* from *brun* brown]

burnous /bɜːˈnuːs/ *n.* Arab or Moorish hooded cloak. [Arabic from Greek]

burn-out *n.* exhaustion. □ **burnt-out** *adj.*

◆ **burn-out turn-around** *n.* restructuring a company that is in trouble by producing new finance to save it from liquidation, at the cost of diluting the shareholding of existing investors.

◆ **burn rate** *n.* rate at which a new company uses up its venture capital to fund fixed overheads before cash begins to come in from its trading activities.

---

burnt see BURN[1].

burnt ochre *n.* (also **burnt sienna** or **umber**) pigment darkened by burning.

burnt offering *n.* offering burnt on an altar as a sacrifice.

burp *colloq. –v.* **1** belch. **2** make (a baby) belch. *–n.* belch. [imitative]

burr *–n.* **1 a** whirring sound. **b** rough sounding of the letter *r*. **2** (also **bur**) **a** rough edge on metal or paper. **b** surgeon's or dentist's small drill. **3** var. of BUR 1, 2. *–v.* make a burr. [imitative]

burrow /ˈbʌrəʊ/ *–n.* hole or tunnel dug by a rabbit etc. as a dwelling or shelter. *–v.* **1** make a burrow. **2** make (a hole, one's way, etc.) (as) by digging. **3** (foll. by *into*) investigate, search. [apparently var. of BOROUGH]

Bursa /ˈbɜːsə/ city in NW Turkey, capital of the Ottoman Empire until 1413; pop. (est. 1994) 996 000.

bursar /ˈbɜːsə(r)/ *n.* **1** treasurer, esp. of a college. **2** holder of a bursary. [medieval Latin *bursarius* from *bursa* purse]

bursary *n.* (*pl.* **-ies**) grant, esp. a scholarship. [medieval Latin: related to BURSAR]

burst *–v.* (*past* and *past part.* **burst**) **1** (cause to) break violently apart; open forcibly from within. **2 a** (usu. foll. by *in, out*) make one's way suddenly or by force. **b** break away from or through (*river burst its banks*). **3** be full to overflowing. **4** appear or come suddenly (*burst into flame*). **5** (foll. by *into*) suddenly begin to shed (tears) or utter. **6** seem about to burst from effort, excitement, etc. *–n.* **1** act of bursting. **2** sudden issue or outbreak (*burst of flame*; *burst of applause*). **3** sudden effort, spurt. □ **burst out 1** suddenly begin (*burst out laughing*). **2** exclaim. [Old English]

burster *n. Computing* device that separates into sheets

Burma /ˈbɜːmə/ (officially **Union of Myanmar**) country in SE Asia, on the Bay of Bengal. Rice has traditionally been the mainstay of the country's economy, and teak is a valuable export; other agricultural exports include rubber, oil-seeds, and jute. Burma is rich in minerals, including oil, zinc, lead, tin, and tungsten; gemstones and metals contribute to export revenue. The economy is weak, with only half-hearted efforts being made to reform it. Sanctions imposed by Japan, Australia, the EC, and the US over human rights violations have left China and Thailand as Burma's only important trading partners.

History. Part of British India until the Second World War, Burma was occupied by the Japanese in 1942 and became an independent republic in 1948. In 1962 an army coup led by U Ne Win overthrew the government and established an authoritarian state; Ne Win remained the effective leader of the country until 1988. In the late 1980s the pro-democracy movement gathered momentum and, led by Aung San Suu Kyi, who had been under house arrest since 1989, won the election held in May 1990; however, the military refused to hand over power. Aung San Suu Kyi was released in 1995. Head of state and government, General Than Shwe; capital, Rangoon.

language	Burmese
currency	kyat (k) of 100 pyas
pop. (est. 1996)	45 976 000
GNP (1993)	US$30B
literacy	85% (m); 71% (f)
life expectancy	58 (m); 61 (f)

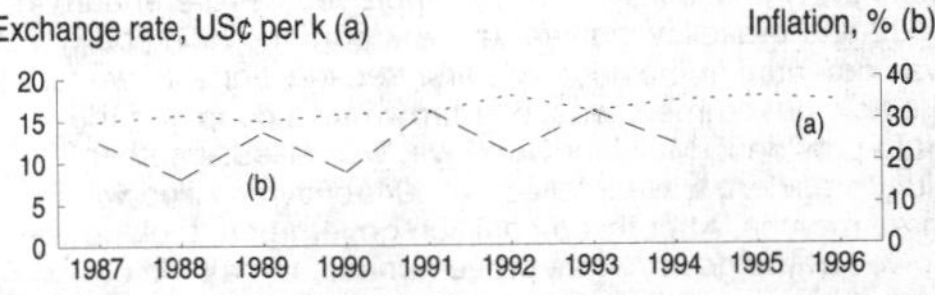

continuous stationery produced as output from a printer. The paper is split at the perforations across its width. With multipart stationery a burster frequently also acts as a decollator, separating the copies and possibly sorting them into stacks and removing the interleaved carbon paper. A burster may also trim the edges of the stationery, removing the ragged edges left by the perforations and the sprocket holes down each side.

burton /'bɜːt(ə)n/ *n.* □ **go for a burton** *slang* be lost, destroyed, or killed. [origin uncertain]

bury /'berɪ/ *v.* (**-ies**, **-ied**) **1** place (a corpse) in the earth, a tomb, or the sea. **2** lose by death (*buried two sons*). **3 a** put or hide under ground. **b** cover up; conceal. **4** consign to obscurity; forget. **5** (*refl.* or *passive*) involve deeply (*buried in a book*). □ **bury the hatchet** cease to quarrel. [Old English]

bus –*n.* (*pl.* **buses** or *US* **busses**) **1** large esp. public passenger vehicle, usu. travelling a fixed route. **2** *colloq.* car, aeroplane, etc. **3** set of conducting wires connecting several components of a computer and allowing the components to send signals to each other. –*v.* (**buses** or **busses**, **bussed**, **bussing**) **1** go by bus. **2** *US* transport by bus, esp. to aid racial integration. [abbreviation of OMNIBUS]

busby /'bʌzbɪ/ *n.* (*pl.* **-ies**) tall fur hat worn by hussars etc. [origin unknown]

bush[1] /bʊʃ/ *n.* **1** shrub or clump of shrubs. **2** thing like a bush, esp. a clump of hair. **3** (esp. in Australia and Africa) uncultivated area; woodland or forest. [Old English and Old Norse]

bush[2] /bʊʃ/ –*n.* **1** metal lining for a hole enclosing a revolving shaft etc. **2** sleeve giving electrical insulation. –*v.* fit with a bush. [Dutch *busse* box]

bush-baby *n.* (*pl.* **-ies**) small African lemur.

bushed *adj. colloq.* tired out.

bushel /'bʊʃ(ə)l/ *n.* former measure of capacity for corn, fruit, etc. (8 gallons or 36.4 litres). [French]

bushfire *n.* forest or scrub fire often spreading widely.

bushman *n.* **1** traveller or dweller in the Australian bush. **2** (**Bushman**) member or language of a S African aboriginal people.

bush telegraph *n.* rapid spreading of information, rumour, etc.

bushy *adj.* (**-ier**, **-iest**) **1** growing thickly like a bush. **2** having many bushes.

business /'bɪznɪs/ *n.* **1** one's regular occupation or profession. **2** one's own concern. **3** task or duty. **4** serious work or activity. **5** (difficult or unpleasant) matter or affair. **6** thing(s) needing attention or discussion. **7** buying and selling; trade. **8** commercial firm. □ **mind one's own business** not meddle. [Old English: related to BUSY]

◆ **Business and Technology Education Council** (also **BTEC**) see VOCATIONAL TRAINING.

◆ **business cycle** *n.* (also **trade cycle**) process by which investment, output, and employment in an economy tend to fluctuate up and down in a regular pattern causing booms and depressions, with recession and recovery as intermediate stages. The business cycle is one of the major unsolved phenomena in economics. Both market-clearing and Keynesian theories have failed to account convincingly for the facts, and fine-tuning policies aimed at smoothing over business cycles have rarely been successful. One explanation of business cycles is that they operate as a result of political activity. The earliest suggestion of the political aspect came from Karl Marx and was developed by Michal Kelecki. He suggested that in a boom period workers become economically powerful and demand higher wages: the subsequent recession is engineered by capitalists in order to create unemployment and reduce the power of the workers. More recent political theories ascribe the cause to the desire of political parties to achieve re-election; it is easier for a party to impose hard decisions shortly after an election and then stimulate demand in the run-up to the next election, thus creating a business cycle.

◆ **business-interruption policy** *n.* (also **consequential-loss policy, loss-of-profits policy**) insurance policy that pays claims for financial losses occurring if a business has to stop or reduce its activities as a result of a fire or any other insurable risk. Claims can be made for lost profit, rent, rates, and other unavoidable overhead costs that continue even when trading has temporarily ceased.

◆ **business judgement rule** *n.* rule that the courts will not generally interfere in the conduct of a business. For example, the courts will not substitute their judgement for that of the directors of a company unless the directors are acting improperly. The rule is often invoked when directors are accused of acting out of self-interest in take-over bids.

businesslike *adj.* efficient, systematic.

businessman *n.* (*fem.* **businesswoman**) man or woman engaged in trade or commerce.

◆ **business marketing research** *n.* = INDUSTRIAL MARKETING RESEARCH.

◆ ***Business Monitor*** *n.* government publication produced by the Business Statistics Office giving information and data on production, services and distribution, civil aviation, car registrations, and cinema audiences.

◆ **business name** *n.* name under which a business trades. According to the Business Names Act (1985), if a business is conducted under a name other than that of the

Burundi /bʊ'rʌndɪ/, **Republic of** country in central Africa on the E side of Lake Tanganyika. The economy is based on agriculture, with coffee as the main export; tea, cotton, and hides and skins are also exported and cassava, maize, peas, and sorghum are grown for food. There are reserves of minerals (including gold and nickel) and peat, but these resources remain largely untapped. Political instability and targets set by the IMF have hindered economic growth.

History. The area formed part of German East Africa until the First World War, after which it was administered by Belgium. It became an independent monarchy in 1962 and a republic in 1966. After a series of military coups a military junta seized power in 1987; in response to tribal unrest, a multi-party political system was approved by referendum in 1992 and the following year the leader of the ruling party was defeated in the country's first free elections; however, the new government was overthrown by a coup and the Hutu president, Melchior Ndadaye, was killed. Another Hutu president was installed in 1994, but was killed within three months. After this a coalition government took power; however, the government proved unable to halt the ethnic violence. In 1996 a Tutsi-led military coup overthrew the government. A multi-ethnic government of national unity took power in late 1996, but ethnic violence continues. President, Pierre Buyoya; capital, Bujumbura. □ **Burundian** *adj.* & *n.*

languages	Kirundi (a Bantu language) & French (official), Swahili
currency	franc (FBu) of 100 centimes
pop. (est. 1996)	5 943 000
GNP (est. 1994)	US$904M
literacy	49% (m); 22% (f)
life expectancy	48 (m); 50 (f)

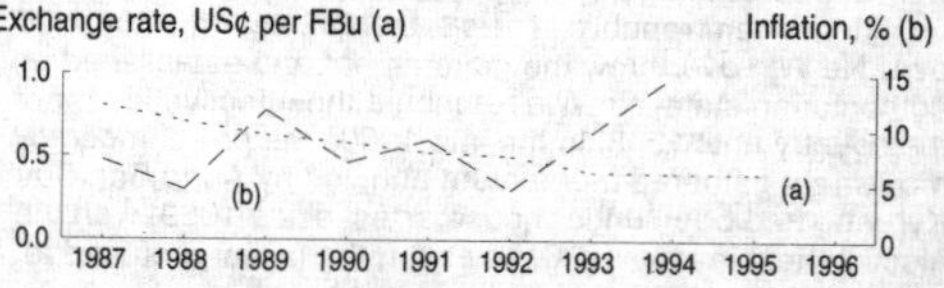

proprietor, it must display at its place of business the business name, its activity, and the name of the proprietor. All business stationery must carry both the business name and the names of the owners. The name of the business must be registered with the Registrar of Companies.

business park *n.* area designed for commerce and light industry.

business person *n.* businessman or businesswoman.

◆ **business plan** *n.* detailed plan setting out the objectives of a business over a stated period, often three, five, or ten years. A business plan is drawn up by many businesses, esp. if the business has passed through a bad period or if it has had a major change of policy. For new businesses it is an essential document for raising capital or loans. The plan should quantify as many of the objectives as possible, providing monthly cash flows and production figures for at least the first two years, with diminishing detail in subsequent years; it must also outline its strategy and the tactics it intends to use in achieving its objectives. Anticipated profit and loss accounts should form part of the business plan on a quarterly basis for at least two years, and an annual basis thereafter. For a group of companies the business plan is often called a **corporate plan**.

◆ **business process re-engineering** (also **BPR**) *n.* restructuring an organization by radically reassessing its main core businesses and predominant strengths, esp. by making use of modern technology and information technology.

◆ **business reply service** *n.* service offered by the Post Office enabling a company to supply its customers with a prepaid business reply card, envelope, or label (either first- or second-class postage) so that they can reply to mailshots, ask for follow-up literature, pay bills promptly, etc. free of postal charges.

◆ **business software package** *n.* one of a wide range of software programs sold in packages to enable computers to be used for a variety of business uses. Packages range in complexity and expense from those needed to operate a PC to the suite of programs required by a mainframe. A typical package would include one or more of: bookkeeping programs, which provide facilities for keeping sales, purchase, and nominal ledgers; accounting packages, enabling balance sheets, budgetary control, and sale and purchase analysis to be undertaken automatically; payroll packages, dealing with wages, salaries, PAYE, National Insurance, pensions, etc.; database management systems to maintain company records; communications software to allow two or more computers to work together; and word processors. The programs comprising the package are designed to work together and use each other's data; sometimes a single program provides one or more of these functions.

◆ **Business Statistics Office** *n.* department of the Central Statistical Office since 1989 (formerly a department of the Department of Trade and Industry). It collects statistics of British businesses and publishes *Business Monitor*.

busk *v.* perform esp. music in the street etc. for tips. □ **busker** *n.* [obsolete *busk* peddle]

bus lane *n.* part of a road mainly for use by buses.

busman *n.* bus driver.

busman's holiday *n.* holiday spent in an activity similar to one's regular work.

bus shelter *n.* shelter beside a bus-stop.

bus station *n.* centre where buses depart and arrive.

bus-stop *n.* **1** regular stopping-place of a bus. **2** sign marking this.

bust[1] *n.* **1** human chest, esp. of a woman; bosom. **2** sculpture of a person's head, shoulders, and chest. □ **busty** *adj.* (**-ier, -iest**). [French from Italian]

bust[2] *–v.* (*past* and *past part.* **busted** or **bust**) *colloq.* **1** break, burst. **2 a** raid, search. **b** arrest. *–adj.* (also **busted**) **1** broken, burst. **2** bankrupt. □ **bust up 1** collapse. **2** (esp. of a married couple) separate. [var. of BURST]

bustard /ˈbʌstəd/ *n.* large land bird that can run very fast. [Latin *avis tarda* slow bird ('slow' unexplained)]

buster *n.* esp. *US slang* mate; fellow. [from BUST[2]]

bustier /ˈbʌstɪˌeɪ/ *n.* strapless close-fitting bodice. [French]

bustle[1] /ˈbʌs(ə)l/ *–v.* (**-ling**) **1** (often foll. by *about*) (cause to) move busily and energetically. **2** (as **bustling** *adj.*) active, lively. *–n.* excited or energetic activity. [perhaps from obsolete *busk* prepare]

bustle[2] /ˈbʌs(ə)l/ *n. hist.* padding worn under a skirt to puff it out behind. [origin unknown]

bust-up *n.* **1** quarrel. **2** collapse.

busy /ˈbɪzɪ/ *–adj.* (**-ier, -iest**) **1** occupied or engaged in work etc. **2** full of activity; fussy (*busy evening, street; busy design*). **3** esp. *US* (of a telephone line) engaged. *–v.* (**-ies, -ied**) (often *refl.*) keep busy; occupy. □ **busily** *adv.* [Old English]

busybody *n.* (*pl.* **-ies**) meddlesome person.

busy Lizzie *n.* plant with abundant esp. red, pink, or white flowers.

but /bʌt, bət/ *–conj.* **1 a** nevertheless, however (*tried but failed*). **b** on the other hand; on the contrary (*I am old but you are young*). **2** except, otherwise than (*cannot choose but do it; what could we do but run?*). **3** without the result that (*it never rains but it pours*). *–prep.* except; apart from; other than (*all cried but me; nothing but trouble*). *–adv.* **1** only; no more than; only just (*we can but try; is but a child; had but arrived*). **2** in emphatic repetition; definitely (*would see nobody, but nobody*). *–rel. pron.* who not; that not (*not a man but feels pity*). *–n.* objection (*ifs and buts*). □ **but for** without the help or hindrance etc. of (*but for you I'd be rich*). **but one** (or **two** etc.) excluding one (or two etc.) from the number (*next door but one; last but one*). **but then** however (*I won, but then I am older*). [Old English]

butane /ˈbjuːteɪn/ *n.* gaseous alkane hydrocarbon, used in liquefied form as fuel. [from BUTYL]

butch /bʊtʃ/ *adj. slang* masculine; tough-looking. [origin uncertain]

butcher /ˈbʊtʃə(r)/ *–n.* **1 a** person who deals in meat. **b** slaughterer. **2** brutal murderer. *–v.* **1** slaughter or cut up (an animal) for food. **2** kill wantonly or cruelly. **3** *colloq.* ruin through incompetence. [French *boc* BUCK[1]]

butchery *n.* (*pl.* **-ies**) **1** needless or cruel slaughter (of people). **2** butcher's trade.

butler *n.* principal manservant of a household. [French *bouteille* bottle]

butt[1] *–v.* **1** push or strike with the head or horns. **2** (cause to) meet edge to edge. *–n.* **1** push with the head. **2** join of two edges. □ **butt in** interrupt, meddle. [French from Germanic]

butt[2] *n.* **1** (often foll. by *of*) object of ridicule etc. **2 a** mound behind a target. **b** (in *pl.*) shooting-range. [French *but* goal]

butt[3] *n.* **1** thicker end, esp. of a tool or weapon. **2** stub of a cigarette etc. **3** esp. *US slang* buttocks. [Dutch]

butt[4] *n.* cask. [Latin *buttis*]

butter *–n.* **1** solidified churned cream, used as a spread and in cooking. **2** substance of similar texture (*peanut butter*). *–v.* spread, cook, or serve with butter. □ **butter up** *colloq.* flatter. [Greek *bouturon*]

butter-bean *n.* **1** flat, dried, white lima bean. **2** yellow-podded bean.

butter-cream *n.* mixture of butter, icing sugar, etc., as a filling etc. for a cake.

buttercup *n.* wild plant with yellow cup-shaped flowers.

butterfat *n.* essential fats of pure butter.

butter-fingers *n. colloq.* person prone to drop things.

butterfly *n.* (*pl.* **-flies**) **1** insect with four usu. brightly coloured wings. **2** (in *pl.*) *colloq.* nervous sensation in the stomach. **3** *Finance* strategy used by dealers in traded options. It involves simultaneously purchasing and selling call options (the right to buy) at different exercise prices or different expiry dates. A butterfly is most profitable when the price of the underlying security fluctuates within narrow limits. Cf. STRADDLE *n.*

butterfly nut *n.* a kind of wing-nut.

butterfly stroke *n.* stroke in swimming, with arms raised and lifted forwards together.

butter-icing *n.* = BUTTER-CREAM.

buttermilk *n.* liquid left after churning butter.

butter muslin *n.* thin loosely-woven cloth, orig. for wrapping butter.

butterscotch *n.* brittle toffee made from butter, brown sugar, etc.

buttery[1] /'bʌtərɪ/ *n.* (*pl.* **-ies**) food store, esp. in a college; snack-bar etc. [related to BUTT[4]]

buttery[2] *adj.* like or containing butter.

buttock /'bʌtək/ *n.* **1** each of the two fleshy protuberances at the rear of the human trunk. **2** corresponding part of an animal. [*butt* ridge]

button /'bʌt(ə)n/ *–n.* **1** small disc etc. sewn to a garment as a fastener or worn as an ornament. **2** small round knob etc. pressed to operate electronic equipment. *–v.* = *button up* 1. □ **button up 1** fasten with buttons. **2** *colloq.* complete satisfactorily. **3** *colloq.* be silent. [French from Germanic]

buttonhole *–n.* **1** slit in cloth for a button. **2** flower etc. worn in a lapel buttonhole. *–v.* (**-ling**) *colloq.* accost and detain (a reluctant listener).

button mushroom *n.* young unopened mushroom.

buttress /'bʌtrɪs/ *–n.* **1** projecting support built against a wall. **2** source of help etc. *–v.* (often foll. by *up*) **1** support with a buttress. **2** support by argument etc. (*buttressed by facts*). [related to BUTT[1]]

butty /'bʌtɪ/ *n.* (*pl.* **-ies**) *N.Engl.* sandwich. [from BUTTER]

butyl /'bju:taɪl/ *n.* the univalent alkyl radical C_4H_9. [Latin *butyrum* BUTTER]

buxom /'bʌksəm/ *adj.* (esp. of a woman) plump and rosy; busty. [earlier = *pliant*: related to BOW[2]]

buy /baɪ/ *–v.* (**buys, buying**; *past* and *past part.* **bought** /bɔ:t/) **1 a** obtain for money etc. **b** serve to obtain (*money can't buy happiness*; *the best that money can buy*). **2 a** procure by bribery etc. **b** bribe. **3** get by sacrifice etc. **4** *slang* believe in, accept. **5** be a buyer for a store etc. *–n.* *colloq.* purchase. □ **buy earnings** invest in a company that has a low yield but whose earnings are increasing, so that a substantial capital gain can be expected. **buy in 1** buy a stock of. **2** *Stock Exch.* (of a broker) buy securities, commodities, etc. because the original seller has failed to deliver, which invariably happens after a rise in a market price (the seller would be able to buy in himself if the market had fallen). The broker buys at the best price available and the original seller is responsible for any difference between the buying-in price and the original buying price, plus the cost of buying in. Cf. *sell out (see* SELL). **buy into** pay for a share in (an enterprise). **buy off** pay to get rid of. **buy oneself out** obtain one's release (esp. from the armed services) by payment. **buy out** pay (a person) for ownership, an interest etc. **buy up 1** buy as much as possible of. **2** absorb (a firm etc.) by purchase. [Old English]

♦ **buy-back** *n.* buying back by a company of its shares from an investor, who put venture capital up for the formation of the company. The shares are bought back at a price that satisfies the investor, which has to be the price the company is willing to pay for its independence. The buy-back may occur if the company is publicly floated or is taken over.

---

buyer *n.* **1** person employed to purchase stock for a large store etc. **2** purchaser, customer. □ **buyers over** condition of a market in securities, commodities, etc. in which the sellers have sold all they wish to sell but there are still buyers. This is clearly a strong market, with an inclination for prices to rise.

♦ **buyer's market** *n.* (also **buyers' market**) market in which the supply exceeds the demand, so that buyers can force prices down. At some point, however, sellers will withdraw from the market if prices fall too low; when this happens the supply will fall off and prices will begin to rise again. Cf. SELLER'S MARKET.

♦ **buy-grid** *n.* the three classes of industrial buying: rebuying, which usu. entails reordering from existing suppliers; modified rebuying, which involves reassessing existing policy, often seeking improved quality; and new-task buying, in which an organization buys something it has not bought before.

♦ **buyout** *n.* **1** option, open to a member of an occupational pension scheme on leaving, of transferring the benefits already purchased to an insurance company of his or her own choice. **2** see LEVERAGED BUYOUT. **3** see MANAGEMENT BUYOUT.

---

buzz *–n.* **1** hum of a bee etc. **2** sound of a buzzer. **3 a** low murmur as of conversation. **b** stir; hurried activity (*buzz of excitement*). **4** *slang* telephone call. **5** *slang* thrill. *–v.* **1** hum. **2 a** summon with a buzzer. **b** *slang* telephone. **3 a** (often foll. by *about*) move busily. **b** (of a place) appear busy or full of excitement. □ **buzz off** *slang* go or hurry away. [imitative]

buzzard /'bʌzəd/ *n.* large bird of the hawk family. [Latin *buteo* falcon]

buzzer *n.* electrical buzzing device as a signal.

buzz-word *n.* *colloq.* fashionable technical or specialist word; catchword.

BV *abbr.* **1** (Dutch) Besloten Vennootschap (= private limited company). **2** (French) Bureau Veritas (ship-classification society).

b.v. *abbr.* *Accounting* book value.

BW *–abbr.* bonded warehouse. *–airline flight code* BWIA International.

BWB *abbr.* = BRITISH WATERWAYS BOARD.

BWIA *abbr.* British West Indian Airways.

BY *airline flight code* Britannia Airways.

by /baɪ/ *–prep.* **1** near, beside (*sit by me*; *path by the river*). **2** through the agency or means of (*by proxy*; *poem by Donne*; *by bus*; *by cheating*; *divide by two*; *killed by robbers*). **3** not later than (*by next week*). **4 a** past, beyond (*drove by the church*). **b** through; via (*went by Paris*). **5** during (*by day*; *by daylight*). **6** to the extent of (*missed by a foot*; *better by far*). **7** according to; using as a standard or unit (*judge by appearances*; *paid by the hour*). **8** with the succession of (*worse by the minute*; *day by day*). **9** concerning; in respect of (*did our duty by them*; *Smith by name*). **10** used in mild oaths (*by God*). **11** expressing dimensions of an area etc. (*three feet by two*). **12** avoiding, ignoring (*passed us by*). **13** inclining to (*north by north-west*). *–adv.* **1** near (*sat by*). **2** aside; in reserve (*put £5 by*). **3** past (*marched by*). *–n.* (*pl.* **byes**) = BYE[1]. □ **by and by** before long; eventually. **by and large** on the whole. **by the by** (or **bye**) incidentally. **by oneself 1 a** unaided. **b** unprompted. **2** alone. [Old English]

by- *prefix* subordinate, incidental (*by-effect*; *by-road*).

Bydgoszcz /bɪd'gɒʃtʃ/ (German **Bromberg** /'brɒmbeək/) inland port in N central Poland; industries include engineering, printing, and timber processing; pop. (est. 1995) 385 700.

bye[1] /baɪ/ *n.* **1** *Cricket* run scored from a ball that passes the batsman without being hit. **2** status of an unpaired competitor in a sport, who proceeds to the next round by default. [from BY as a noun]

bye[2] /baɪ/ *int.* (also **bye-bye**) *colloq.* = GOODBYE. [abbreviation]

by-election *n.* election to fill a vacancy arising between general elections.

Byelorussia see BELARUS.

Byelorussian var. of BELARUSSIAN.

bygone *–adj.* past, antiquated. *–n.* (in phr. **let bygones be bygones**) forgive and forget past quarrels.

by-law *n.* regulation made by a local authority or corporation. [obsolete *by* town]

byline *n.* **1** line naming the writer of a newspaper article etc. **2** secondary line of work. **3** goal-line or touch-line.

bypass –*n.* **1** main road passing round a town or its centre. **2 a** secondary channel or pipe etc. used in emergencies. **b** alternative passage for the circulation of blood through the heart. –*v.* avoid, go round (a town, difficulty, etc.).

byplay *n.* secondary action, esp. in a play.

by-product *n.* **1** incidental product made in the manufacture of something else. **2** secondary result.

byre /ˈbaɪə(r)/ *n.* cowshed. [Old English]

byroad *n.* minor road.

byssinosis /ˌbɪsɪˈnəʊsɪs/ *n.* lung disease caused by textile fibre dust. [Greek *bussinos* made of linen]

bystander *n.* person present but not taking part; onlooker.

byte /baɪt/ *n. Computing* fixed number of bits (usu. 8) that can be handled and stored as a unit by a computer. Since characters are often represented in the form of an 8-bit binary code, the byte can be regarded as the storage space required to hold a single character.

byway *n.* **1** byroad or secluded path. **2** minor activity.

byword *n.* **1** person or thing as a notable example (*is a byword for luxury*). **2** familiar saying.

Byzantine /bɪˈzæntaɪn/ –*adj.* **1** of Byzantium or the E Roman Empire. **2** of its highly decorated style of architecture. **3** (of a political situation etc.) complex, inflexible, or underhand. –*n.* citizen of Byzantium or the E Roman Empire. □ **Byzantinism** *n.* **Byzantinist** *n.* [Latin *Byzantium*, now Istanbul]

Cc

C[1] /siː/ *n.* (*pl.* **Cs** or **C's**) **1** (also **c**) third letter of the alphabet. **2** *Mus.* first note of the diatonic scale of C major. **3** third hypothetical person or example. **4** third highest category etc. **5** *Algebra* (usu. **c**) third known quantity. **6** (as a roman numeral) 100. **7** (also ©) copyright. **8** *Computing* programming language developed in the early 1970s for systems software, esp. for writing the operating system UNIX. C has the control structures usu. found in high-level languages but has features that make it suitable for writing systems software. Many of the most widely used business applications programs are written in C.

C[2] *–symb.* **1** carbon. **2** coulomb(s). **3** capacitance. *–international vehicle registration* Cuba.

C[3] *abbr.* (also **C.**) **1** Celsius, centigrade. **2** century.

c *symb.* cent(s).

c. *abbr.* **1** century. **2** cent(s). **3** centavo(s). **4** centime(s).

c. *abbr. circa.*

c/- *abbr.* **1** *Austral.* & *NZ* care of. **2** currency.

C1 *n.* **1** occupational grade comprising supervisory or clerical workers. **2** person in this grade.

C2 *–n.* **1** occupational grade comprising skilled manual workers. **2** person in this grade. *–international civil aircraft marking* Nauru.

C3 *international civil aircraft marking* Andorra.

C4 *abbr. Television* Channel Four.

C5 *–abbr. Television.* Channel Five. *–international civil aircraft marking* Gambia.

C6 *international civil aircraft marking* Bahamas.

C9 *international civil aircraft marking* Mozambique.

CA *–abbr.* **1** (also **C/A**) capital account. **2** = CAPITAL ALLOWANCES. **3** = CHARTERED ACCOUNTANT. **4** chief accountant. **5** commercial agent. **6** Companies Act. **7** = CONSUMERS' ASSOCIATION. **8** (also **C/A**) credit account. **9** Crown Agent. **10** (also **C/A**) current account. **11** current assets. *–postcode* Carlisle. *–US postcode* California. *–airline flight code* Air China.

Ca *symb.* calcium.

Ca. *abbr.* (Italian) compagnia (= company).

Cª *abbr.* **1** (Portuguese) companhia (= company). **2** (Spanish) compañia (= company).

ca. *abbr. circa.*

c.a. *abbr.* capital asset.

CAA *abbr.* **1** = CIVIL AVIATION AUTHORITY. **2** Cost Accountants' Association.

CAAA *abbr.* Canadian Association of Advertising Agencies.

cab *n.* **1** taxi. **2** driver's compartment in a lorry, train, or crane etc. [abbreviation of CABRIOLET]

cabal /kə'bæl/ *n.* **1** secret intrigue. **2** political clique. [French from Latin]

cabaret /'kæbə,reɪ/ *n.* entertainment in a nightclub or restaurant. [French, = tavern]

cabbage /'kæbɪdʒ/ *n.* **1** vegetable with a round head and green or purple leaves. **2** = VEGETABLE 2. [French *caboche* head]

cabbage white *n.* butterfly whose caterpillars feed on cabbage leaves.

cabby *n.* (also **cabbie**) (*pl.* **-ies**) *colloq.* taxi-driver.

CABEI *abbr.* (also **Cabei**) Central American Bank for Economic Integration.

caber /'keɪbə(r)/ *n.* trimmed tree-trunk tossed as a sport in the Scottish Highlands. [Gaelic]

cabin /'kæbɪn/ *n.* **1** small shelter or house, esp. of wood. **2** room or compartment in an aircraft or ship for passengers or crew. **3** driver's cab. [French from Latin]

cabin-boy *n.* boy steward on a ship.

cabin cruiser *n.* large motor boat with accommodation.

Cabinda /kə'bɪndə/ **1** district of Angola at the mouth of the Congo, separated from the rest of Angola by a wedge of the Democratic Republic of Congo; pop. (est. 1996) 199 000. It has offshore oil deposits and also produces coffee and cocoa. **2** its capital city; pop. (1970) 21 120.

cabinet /'kæbɪnɪt/ *n.* **1 a** cupboard or case for storing or displaying things. **b** casing of a radio, television, etc. **2** (**Cabinet**) committee of senior ministers in a government. [diminutive of CABIN]

cabinet-maker *n.* skilled joiner.

cable /'keɪb(ə)l/ *–n.* **1** encased group of insulated wires for transmitting electricity etc. **2** thick rope of wire or hemp. **3** international telegram. See also TELEGRAPHIC ADDRESS; TELEX; FAX. **4** (in full **cable stitch**) knitting stitch resembling twisted rope. *–v.* (**-ling**) transmit (a message) or inform (a person) by cable. [Latin *caplum* halter, from Arabic]

cable-car *n.* small cabin suspended on a looped cable, for carrying passengers up and down a mountain etc.

cablegram *n.* = CABLE *n.* 3.

cable television *n.* television transmission by cable to subscribers.

cabman *n.* driver of a cab.

caboodle /kə'buːd(ə)l/ *n.* □ **the whole caboodle** *slang* the whole lot. [origin uncertain]

caboose /kə'buːs/ *n.* **1** kitchen on a ship's deck. **2** *US* guard's van on a train etc. [Dutch]

cabriole /'kæbrɪ,əʊl/ *n.* a kind of esp. 18th-century curved table or chair leg. [French: related to CAPRIOLE]

cabriolet /,kæbrɪəʊ'leɪ/ *n.* **1** car with a folding top. **2** light two-wheeled one-horse carriage with a hood. [French: related to CAPRIOLE]

CAC *abbr.* **1** = CENTRAL ARBITRATION COMMITTEE. **2** (in France) **a** Compagnie des Agents de Change (French stockbrokers' association). **b** Cotation Assistée en Continue (quotation system on the Paris Bourse). [sense 2 French]

cacao /kə'kaʊ/ *n.* (*pl.* **-s**) **1** seed from which cocoa and chocolate are made. **2** tree bearing these. [Spanish from Nahuatl]

cache /kæʃ/ *–n.* **1** hiding-place for treasure, stores, guns, etc. **2** things so hidden. *–v.* (**-ching**) put in a cache. [French *cacher* hide]

cachet /'kæʃeɪ/ *n.* **1** prestige. **2** distinguishing mark or seal. **3** flat capsule of medicine. [French *cacher* press]

cachou /'kæʃuː/ *n.* lozenge to sweeten the breath. [Portuguese *cachu* from Malay *kāchu*]

cack-handed /kæk'hændɪd/ *adj. colloq.* **1** clumsy. **2** left-handed. [dial. *cack* excrement]

cackle /'kæk(ə)l/ *–n.* **1** clucking of a hen etc. **2** raucous laugh. **3** noisy chatter. *–v.* (**-ling**) **1** emit a cackle. **2** chatter noisily. [imitative]

CACM *abbr.* Central American Common Market.

cacophony /kə'kɒfənɪ/ *n.* (*pl.* **-ies**) harsh discordant sound. □ **cacophonous** *adj.* [Greek *kakos* bad, *phōnē* sound]

cactus /'kæktəs/ *n.* (*pl.* **-ti** /-taɪ/ or **cactuses**) plant with a thick fleshy stem and usu. spines but no leaves. [Latin from Greek]

◆ **CAD** *abbr.* **1** (also **c.a.d.**) = CASH AGAINST DOCUMENTS. **2** = COMPUTER-AIDED DESIGN.

cad *n.* man who behaves dishonourably. □ **caddish** *adj.* [abbreviation of CADDIE]

cadaver /kə'dævə(r)/ *n.* esp. *Med.* corpse. [Latin *cado* fall]

cadaverous /kə'dævərəs/ *adj.* corpselike; very pale and thin.

CADCAM /'kæd,kæm/ *abbr.* (also **CAD/CAM**) computer-aided design, computer-aided manufacturing.

CADD *abbr.* computer-aided drafting and design.

caddie /'kædɪ/ (also **caddy**) *–n.* (*pl.* **-ies**) person who carries a golfer's clubs during play. *–v.* (**-ies, -ied, caddying**) act as a caddie. [French CADET]

caddis-fly /'kædɪs/ *n.* small nocturnal insect living near water. [origin unknown]

caddis-worm /'kædɪs/ *n.* (also **caddis**) larva of the caddis-fly. [origin unknown]

caddy[1] /'kædɪ/ *n.* (*pl.* **-ies**) small container for tea. [Malay]

caddy[2] var. of CADDIE.

CADE *abbr.* computer-assisted data evaluation.

cadence /'keɪd(ə)ns/ *n.* **1** rhythm; the measure or beat of a sound or movement. **2** fall in pitch of the voice. **3** tonal inflection. **4** close of a musical phrase. [Latin *cado* fall]

cadenza /kə'denzə/ *n.* virtuoso passage for a soloist. [Italian: related to CADENCE]

cadet /kə'det/ *n.* young trainee for the armed services or police force. □ **cadetship** *n.* [French, ultimately from Latin *caput* head]

cadge *v.* (**-ging**) *colloq.* get or seek by begging. [origin unknown]

cadi /'kɑːdɪ/ *n.* (*pl.* **-s**) judge in a Muslim country. [Arabic]

Cádiz /kə'dɪz/ city, fishing-port, and naval base in SW Spain, on the Andalusian coast; pop. (est. 1994) 155 438.

CADMAT /'kæd,mæt/ *abbr.* computer-aided design, manufacturing, and testing.

cadmium /'kædmɪəm/ *n.* soft bluish-white metallic element. [Greek *kadmia* Cadmean (earth)]

CADPO *abbr.* communications and data-processing operation.

cadre /'kɑːdə(r)/ *n.* **1** basic unit, esp. of servicemen. **2** group of esp. Communist activists. [French from Latin *quadrus* square]

CADS *abbr.* computer-aided design system.

CAE *abbr.* **1** computer-aided education. **2** computer-aided engineering.

caecum /'siːkəm/ *n.* (*US* **cecum**) (*pl.* **-ca**) blind-ended pouch at the junction of the small and large intestines. [Latin *caecus* blind]

Caen /kã/ port in NW France, on the coast of Normandy, capital of Basse-Normandie region; pop. (est. 1990) 115 624. It produces iron, silk, leather, and electrical goods.

Caenozoic var. of CENOZOIC.

Caernarfon /kə'nɑːvən/ (also **Caernarvon**) market town and port in NW Wales, administrative centre of Gwynedd; pop. (1981) 9400.

Caerphilly /keə'fɪlɪ/ *n.* a kind of mild white cheese. [*Caerphilly* in Wales]

Caesar /'siːzə(r)/ *n.* **1** title of Roman emperors. **2** autocrat. [Latin (C. Julius) *Caesar*]

Caesarean /sɪ'zeərɪən/ (*US* **Cesarean, Cesarian**) *–adj.* (of birth) effected by Caesarean section. *–n.* Caesarean section. [from CAESAR: Julius Caesar was supposedly born this way]

Caesarean section *n.* delivery of a child by cutting through the mother's abdomen.

caesium /'siːzɪəm/ *n.* (*US* **cesium**) soft silver-white element. [Latin *caesius* blue-grey]

caesura /sɪ'zjʊərə/ *n.* (*pl.* **-s**) pause in a line of verse. □ **caesural** *adj.* [Latin *caedo* cut]

CAF *abbr.* (also **c.a.f.**) *Commerce* **1** cost and freight. **2** (French) coût, assurance, fret (= cost, insurance, freight).

café /'kæfeɪ/ *n.* small coffee-house or restaurant. [French]

cafeteria /,kæfɪ'tɪərɪə/ *n.* self-service restaurant. [American Spanish, = coffee-shop]

caffeine /'kæfiːn/ *n.* alkaloid stimulant in tea-leaves and coffee beans. [French *café* coffee]

CAFS *abbr. Computing* content-addressable file system.

caftan /'kæftæn/ *n.* (also **kaftan**) **1** long tunic worn by men in the Near East. **2** long loose dress or shirt. [Turkish]

cage *–n.* **1** structure of bars or wires, esp. for confining animals or birds. **2** similar open framework, esp. a lift in mine etc. *–v.* (**-ging**) place or keep in a cage. [Latin *cavea*]

cagey /'keɪdʒɪ/ *adj.* (also **cagy**) (**-ier, -iest**) *colloq.* cautious and non-committal. □ **cagily** *adv.* **caginess** *n.* [origin unknown]

Cagliari /kæl'jɑːrɪ/ seaport in Italy, the capital of Sardinia; pop. (est. 1994) 178 063. It has milling, tanning, and fishing industries and exports lead, zinc, and salt.

cagoule /kə'guːl/ *n.* thin hooded windproof jacket. [French]

cahoots /kə'huːts/ *n.pl.* □ **in cahoots** *slang* in collusion. [origin uncertain]

CAI *abbr.* computer-assisted instruction. See COMPUTER-ASSISTED LEARNING.

CAIB *abbr.* Certified Associate of the Institute of Bankers.

caiman var. of CAYMAN.

Cain *n.* □ **raise Cain** *colloq.* = *raise the roof.* [*Cain*, eldest son of Adam (Gen. 4)]

Cainozoic var. of CENOZOIC.

cairn *n.* **1** mound of stones as a monument or landmark. **2** (in full **cairn terrier**) small shaggy short-legged terrier. [Gaelic]

cairngorm /'keəngɔːm/ *n.* semi-precious form of quartz. [*Cairngorms*, in Scotland]

Cairo /'kaɪrəʊ/ capital of Egypt, a port on the Nile; city pop. (est. 1992) 6 849 000. Industries include textile manufacturing, food processing, metallurgy, plastics, and iron and steel working.

caisson /'keɪs(ə)n/ *n.* watertight chamber for underwater construction work. [Italian *cassone*]

cajole /kə'dʒəʊl/ *v.* (**-ling**) persuade by flattery, deceit, etc. □ **cajolery** *n.* [French]

cake *–n.* **1** mixture of flour, butter, eggs, sugar, etc., baked in the oven and often iced and decorated. **2** other food in a flat round shape (*fish cake*). **3** flattish compact mass (*cake of soap*). *–v.* (**-king**) **1** form into a compact mass. **2** (usu. foll. by *with*) cover (with a hard or sticky mass). □ **have one's cake and eat it** *colloq.* enjoy both of two mutually exclusive alternatives. **a piece of cake** *colloq.* something easily achieved. **sell** (or **go) like hot cakes** *colloq.* be sold (or go) quickly; be popular. [Old Norse]

cakewalk *n.* **1** obsolete American Black dance. **2** *colloq.* easy task. **3** fairground entertainment consisting of a promenade moved by machinery.

CAL *abbr.* = COMPUTER-ASSISTED LEARNING.

Cal *abbr.* large calorie(s).

Cal. *abbr.* California.

cal *abbr.* small calorie(s).

Calabar /'kælə,bɑː(r)/ port in SE Nigeria, the capital of Cross River state; pop. (est. 1995) 170 000. Exports include palm oil, rubber, timber, and cocoa.

calabash /'kælə,bæʃ/ *n.* **1** gourd-bearing tree of tropical America. **2** such a gourd, esp. as a vessel for water, etc. [French from Spanish]

calabrese /,kælə'briːs/ *n.* variety of broccoli. [Italian, = Calabrian]

Calabria /kə'læbrɪə/ SW promontory of Italy, an agricultural region producing olives, citrus fruits, and cereals; pop. (est. 1994) 2 079 588; capital, Catanzaro. □ **Calabrian** *adj.* & *n.*

Calais /'kæleɪ/ ferry-port in NW France, on the coast of the English Channel, with textile industries; pop. (est. 1990) 75 836. The French terminal of the Channel Tunnel is at Fréthun, near Calais.

calamine /'kælə,maɪn/ *n.* powdered form of zinc carbonate and ferric oxide used as a skin lotion. [French from Latin]

calamity /kə'læmɪtɪ/ *n.* (*pl.* **-ies**) disaster, great misfortune. □ **calamitous** *adj.* [French from Latin]

calcareous /kæl'keərɪəs/ *adj.* of or containing calcium carbonate. [related to CALX]

calceolaria /,kælsɪə'leərɪə/ *n.* plant with slipper-shaped flowers. [Latin *calceus* shoe]

calces *pl.* of CALX.

calciferol /kæl'sɪfə,rɒl/ *n.* vitamin (D_2) promoting calcium deposition in the bones. [related to CALX]

calciferous /kæl'sɪfərəs/ *adj.* yielding calcium salts, esp. calcium carbonate.

calcify /'kælsɪ,faɪ/ *v.* (**-ies, -ied**) **1** harden by the depositing of calcium salts. **2** convert or be converted to calcium carbonate. □ **calcification** /-fɪ'keɪʃ(ə)n/ *n.*

calcine /'kælsaɪn/ *v.* (**-ning**) decompose or be decomposed by strong heat. □ **calcination** /-'neɪʃ(ə)n/ *n.* [French or medieval Latin: related to CALX]

calcite /'kælsaɪt/ *n.* natural crystalline calcium carbonate. [Latin: related to CALX]

calcium /'kælsɪəm/ *n.* soft grey metallic element occurring in limestone, marble, chalk, etc. [related to CALX]

calcium carbide *n.* greyish solid used in the production of acetylene.

calcium carbonate *n.* white insoluble solid occurring as chalk, marble, etc.

calcium hydroxide *n.* white crystalline powder used in the manufacture of mortar.

calcium oxide *n.* white crystalline solid from which many calcium compounds are manufactured.

calculate /'kælkjʊ,leɪt/ *v.* (**-ting**) **1** ascertain or forecast esp. by mathematics or reckoning. **2** plan deliberately. **3** (foll. by *on*) rely on; reckon on. □ **calculable** *adj.* [Latin: related to CALCULUS]

calculated *adj.* **1** (of an action) done deliberately or with foreknowledge. **2** (foll. by *to* + infin.) designed or suitable; intended.

calculating *adj.* scheming, mercenary.

calculation /,kælkjʊ'leɪʃ(ə)n/ *n.* act, process, or result of calculating. [Latin: related to CALCULUS]

calculator *n.* electronic device that can perform simple arithmetic (and often other) operations on numbers entered from a keyboard. Final solutions and intermediate numbers are displayed on a small screen. More sophisticated calculators can perform complex mathematical and statistical operations and may be programmed. Add-on memory modules containing specialist programs can often be used, as can small printers.

calculus /'kælkjʊləs/ *n.* (*pl.* **-luses** or **-li** /-,laɪ/) **1** particular method of mathematical calculation or reasoning. **2** stone or mineral mass in the body. [Latin, = small stone (used on an abacus)]

Calcutta /kæl'kʌtə/ city in India, the capital of West Bengal, an important port and industrial centre with engineering, textile, and chemical industries; pop. (1995) 11 673 000.

caldron var. of CAULDRON.

Caledonian /,kælɪ'dəʊnɪən/ *literary* –*adj.* of Scotland. –*n.* Scotsman. [Latin *Caledonia* N Britain]

calendar /'kælɪndə(r)/ –*n.* **1** system fixing the year's beginning, length, and subdivision. **2** chart etc. showing such subdivisions. **3** timetable of dates, events, etc. –*v.* enter in a calendar; register (documents). [Latin: related to CALENDS]

calender /'kælɪndə(r)/ –*n.* machine in which cloth, paper, etc. is rolled to glaze or smooth it. –*v.* press in a calender. [French]

calends /'kælendz/ *n.pl.* (also **kalends**) first of the month in the ancient Roman calendar. [Latin *Kalendae*]

calendula /kə'lendjʊlə/ *n.* plant with large yellow or orange flowers, esp. the marigold. [Latin diminutive of *Kalendae*]

calf[1] /kɑːf/ *n.* (*pl.* **calves** /kɑːvz/) **1** young cow or bull. **2** young of other animals, e.g. the elephant, deer, and whale. **3** calfskin. [Old English]

calf[2] /kɑːf/ *n.* (*pl.* **calves**) fleshy hind part of the human leg below the knee. [Old Norse]

calf-love *n.* romantic adolescent love.

calfskin *n.* calf-leather, esp. in bookbinding and shoemaking.

Calgary /'kælgərɪ/ city in SW Canada, in S Alberta, on the edge of a rich agricultural and stock-raising area; city pop. (1995) 828 500; metropolitan area pop. 754 033.

Cali /'kɑːlɪ/ industrial city and transportation centre in W Colombia, capital of the Valle del Cauca department; pop. (est. 1995) 1 718 871.

calibrate /'kælɪ,breɪt/ *v.* (**-ting**) **1** mark (a gauge) with a scale of readings. **2** correlate the readings of (an instrument or system of measurement) with a standard. **3** determine the calibre of (a gun). □ **calibration** /-'breɪʃ(ə)n/ *n.*

calibre /'kælɪbə(r)/ *n.* (*US* **caliber**) **1 a** internal diameter of a gun or tube. **b** diameter of a bullet or shell. **2** strength or quality of character; ability, importance. [French from Italian from Arabic, = mould]

calices *pl.* of CALIX.

calico /'kælɪ,kəʊ/ –*n.* (*pl.* **-es** or *US* **-s**) **1** cotton cloth, esp. plain white or unbleached. **2** *US* printed cotton fabric. –*adj.* **1** of calico. **2** *US* multicoloured. [*Calicut* (now KOZHIKODE]

Calicut /'kælɪ,kʌt/ see KOZHIKODE.

Calif. *abbr.* California.

California /,kælɪ'fɔːnɪə/ state on the Pacific coast of the US; pop. (est. 1996) 31 878 234; capital, Sacramento. Fruit and cattle farming are important, together with film, television, aerospace, and high-technology industries. □ **Californian** *adj.* & *n.*

californium /,kælɪ'fɔːnɪəm/ *n.* artificial radioactive metallic element. [CALIFORNIA, where first made]

caliper var. of CALLIPER.

caliph /'keɪlɪf/ *n.* esp. *hist.* chief Muslim civil and religious ruler. □ **caliphate** *n.* [Arabic, = successor (of Muhammad)]

calisthenics var. of CALLISTHENICS.

calix var. of CALYX.

calk *US* var. of CAULK.

call /kɔːl/ –*v.* **1 a** (often foll. by *out*) cry, shout; speak loudly. **b** (of a bird etc.) emit its characteristic sound. **2** communicate with by telephone or radio. **3** summon. **4** (often foll. by *at, in, on*) pay a brief visit. **5** order to take place (*called a meeting*). **6** name; describe as. **7** regard as (*I call that silly*). **8** rouse from sleep. **9** (foll. by *for*) demand. **10** (foll. by *on, upon*) appeal to (*called on us to be quiet*). **11** name (a suit) in bidding at cards. **12** guess the outcome of tossing a coin etc. –*n.* **1** shout, cry. **2 a** characteristic cry of a bird etc. **b** instrument for imitating it. **3** brief visit. **4 a** act of telephoning. **b** telephone conversation. **5 a** invitation, summons. **b** vocation. **6** need, occasion (*no call for rudeness*). **7** demand (*a call on one's time*). **8** signal on a bugle etc. **9** (also **call option**) option to buy stock at a fixed price on a given date. See OPTION 3. **10** demand from a company to its shareholders to pay a specified sum on a specified date in respect of their partly paid shares. **11** *Cards* **a** player's right or turn to make a bid. **b** bid made. □ **at call** *Finance* denoting money that has been lent on a short-term basis and must be repaid on demand. Discount houses are the main borrowers of money at call. **call in 1** withdraw from circulation. **2** seek the advice or services of. **call off 1** cancel (an arrangement). **2** order (an attacker or pursuer) to desist. **call out 1** summon to action. **2** order (workers) to strike. **call the shots** (or **tune**) *colloq.* be in control; take the initiative. **call up 1** telephone. **2** recall. **3** summon to military service. **on call** ready or available if required. [Old English from Old Norse]

Callao /kəl'jɑːəʊ/ principal seaport in Peru; exports include minerals, metals, and fish-meal; pop. (1993) 369 768.

◆ **call bird** *n.* low-priced article used in the retail trade to encourage members of the public to come into a shop, in the hope that purchases for higher-priced goods will follow.

call-box *n.* telephone box.

◆ **call-cost indicator** *n.* device installed by a telephone company on business premises to monitor calls as they are being made or over a prescribed period. A printout provides information on the duration and cost of each call (which is identified by date, time, and the number called).

◆ **called-up capital** see SHARE CAPITAL.

caller *n.* person who calls, esp. one who pays a visit or makes a telephone call.

call-girl *n.* prostitute accepting appointments by telephone.

calligraphy /kə'lɪgrəfɪ/ *n.* **1** handwriting, esp. when fine. **2** art of this. □ **calligrapher** *n.* **calligraphic** /-'græfɪk/ *adj.* **calligraphist** *n.* [Greek *kallos* beauty]

calling *n.* **1** profession or occupation. **2** vocation.

calliper /'kælɪpə(r)/ *n.* (also **caliper**) **1** (in *pl.*) compasses for measuring diameters. **2** metal splint to support the leg. [var. of CALIBRE]

callisthenics /ˌkælɪs'θenɪks/ *n.pl.* (also **calisthenics**) exercises for fitness and grace. □ **callisthenic** *adj.* [Greek *kallos* beauty, *sthenos* strength]

◆ **call money** *n.* **1** money put into the money market that can be called at short notice (see also MONEY AT CALL AND SHORT NOTICE). **2** see OPTION MONEY.

◆ **call-of-more option** see OPTION TO DOUBLE 2.

◆ **call option** *n.* = CALL *n.* 9.

callosity /kə'lɒsɪtɪ/ *n.* (*pl.* **-ies**) area of hard thick skin. [Latin: related to CALLOUS]

callous /'kæləs/ *adj.* **1** unfeeling, insensitive. **2** (also **calloused**) (of skin) hardened. □ **callously** *adv.* **callousness** *n.* [Latin: related to CALLUS]

◆ **call-over** *n.* meeting of commodity brokers and dealers at fixed times during the day in order to form a market in that commodity. The call-over is usu. used for trading in futures, in fixed quantities on a standard contract, payments usu. being settled by differences through a clearing-house. Because traders usu. form a ring around the person calling out the prices, this form of market is often called **ring trading**. This method of trading is also called **open outcry**, as bids and offers are shouted out during the course of the call-over.

callow /'kæləʊ/ *adj.* inexperienced, immature. [Old English, = bald]

call-up *n.* summons to do military service.

callus /'kæləs/ *n.* (*pl.* **calluses**) **1** area of hard thick skin or tissue. **2** hard tissue formed round bone ends after a fracture. [Latin]

calm /kɑːm/ *–adj.* **1** tranquil, quiet, windless. **2** serene; not agitated. *–n.* calm condition or period. *–v.* (often foll. by *down*) make or become calm. □ **calmly** *adv.* **calmness** *n.* [Greek *kauma* heat]

calomel /'kæləˌmel/ *n.* compound of mercury used as a cathartic. [Greek *kalos* beautiful, *melas* black]

Calor gas /'kælə/ *n. propr.* liquefied butane gas stored under pressure in containers for domestic use. [Latin *calor* heat]

caloric /'kælərɪk/ *adj.* of heat or calories.

calorie /'kælərɪ/ *n.* (*pl.* **-ies**) unit of quantity of heat, the amount needed to raise the temperature of one gram (**small calorie**) or one kilogram (**large calorie** or **kilocalorie**) of water by 1 °C. [Latin *calor* heat]

calorific /ˌkælə'rɪfɪk/ *adj.* producing heat.

calorimeter /ˌkælə'rɪmɪtə(r)/ *n.* instrument for measuring quantity of heat.

calumniate /kə'lʌmnɪˌeɪt/ *v.* (**-ting**) slander. [Latin]

calumny /'kæləmnɪ/ *n.* (*pl.* **-ies**) slander; malicious representation. □ **calumnious** /kə'lʌmnɪəs/ *adj.* [Latin]

calvados /'kælvəˌdɒs/ *n.* apple brandy. [*Calvados* in France]

calve /kɑːv/ *v.* (**-ving**) give birth to a calf. [Old English: related to CALF[1]]

calves *pl.* of CALF[1], CALF[2].

Calvinism /'kælvɪˌnɪz(ə)m/ *n.* theology of Calvin or his followers, stressing predestination and divine grace. □ **Calvinist** *n.* & *adj.* **Calvinistic** /-'nɪstɪk/ *adj.* [*Calvin*, name of a theologian]

calx *n.* (*pl.* **calces** /'kælsiːz/) powdery substance formed when an ore or mineral has been heated. [Latin *calx calc-* lime]

calypso /kə'lɪpsəʊ/ *n.* (*pl.* **-s**) West Indian song with improvised usu. topical words and a syncopated rhythm. [origin unknown]

calyx /'keɪlɪks/ *n.* (*pl.* **calyces** /-lɪˌsiːz/ or **-es**) (also **calix**)

Cambodia /kæm'bəʊdɪə/, **State of** (formerly (1976–89) **Kampuchea**) country in SE Asia between Thailand and Vietnam. The economy is chiefly agricultural, with rice as the staple crop; there is also some forestry and fishing, but little industry. Products include rice, rubber, livestock, pepper, maize, and dried fish, but the economy has been devastated by civil war and recent political upheavals; both production and exports have been adversely affected and inflation is high.

History. The country became a French protectorate in 1863 and remained under French influence until it became fully independent in 1953. Civil war in 1970–5 undermined and finally overthrew the government, but the victorious Communist Khmer Rouge regime was itself toppled by a Vietnamese invasion in 1979; the country continued to be plagued by intermittent guerrilla activity. Vietnam withdrew its forces in 1989 but guerrilla warfare intensified. In 1991 UN-sponsored peace talks brought together the four main factions, who established an interim governing coalition, the Supreme National Council, working with the UN Transitional Authority for Cambodia. In 1993, after free elections (boycotted by the Khmer Rouge) were held, the leaders of the two main parties agreed to form an interim coalition administration pending the drafting of a new constitution. In 1994 the Khmer Rouge were outlawed, many defected, but some remain active in the north. In June 1997 Pol Pot was captured by a group of Khmer Rouge defectors. In 1997, troops loyal to one of the premiers (Hun Sen) seized Phnom Penh and forced the other premier (Prince Ranariddh) into exile; he was replaced as co-premier by Ung Huot. Head of state, Prince Norodim Sihanouk; capital, Phnom Penh. □ **Cambodian** *adj.* & *n.*

languages	Khmer (official), French
currency	riel of 100 sen
pop. (est. 1996)	10 081 000
GNP (est. 1995)	US$2.7B
literacy	85% (m); 65% (f)
life expectancy	52 (m); 55 (f)

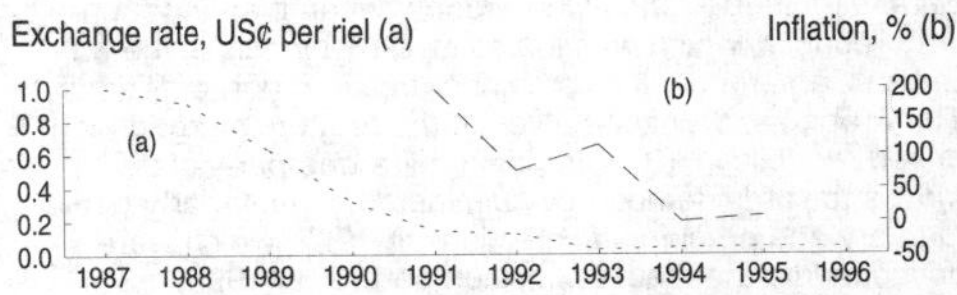

1 sepals forming the protective case of a flower in bud. **2** cuplike cavity or structure. [Greek, = husk]

CAM *abbr.* **1** communication, advertising, and marketing. **2** = COMPUTER-AIDED MANUFACTURING. **3** *Computing* content-addressable memory.

cam *n.* projection on a wheel etc., shaped to convert circular into reciprocal or variable motion. [Dutch *kam* comb]

camaraderie /ˌkæməˈrɑːdərɪ/ *n.* friendly comradeship. [French]

Camargue /kæˈmɑːg/, **the** region of the Rhône delta in SE France, known for its white horses; cattle are also reared.

Camb. *abbr.* Cambridge.

camber *–n.* convex surface of a road, deck, etc. *–v.* build with a camber. [Latin *camurus* curved]

Cambrian /ˈkæmbrɪən/ *–adj.* **1** Welsh. **2** *Geol.* of the first period in the Palaeozoic era. *–n.* this period. [Welsh: related to CYMRIC]

cambric /ˈkeɪmbrɪk/ *n.* fine linen or cotton fabric. [*Cambrai* in France]

Cambridge /ˈkeɪmbrɪdʒ/ **1** city in E central England, county town of Cambridgeshire; industries include electronics, printing, paper, flour milling, and the manufacture of scientific instruments; pop. (est. 1994) 113 800. **2** city in the US, in Massachusetts; the printing and publishing industries are important; pop. (est. 1994) 99 890.

Cambridge blue *adj.* & *n.* (as adj. often hyphenated) pale blue. [CAMBRIDGE in England]

Cambridgeshire /ˈkeɪmbrɪdʒʃə(r)/ county in E central England; pop. (est. 1994) 686 900; county town, Cambridge. It is mainly agricultural, with some light industry.

Cambs. *abbr.* Cambridgeshire.

camcorder /ˈkæmˌkɔːdə(r)/ *n.* combined video camera and sound recorder. [from CAMERA, RECORDER]

came *past* of COME.

camel /ˈkæm(ə)l/ *n.* **1** long-legged ruminant with one hump (**Arabian camel**) or two humps (**Bactrian camel**). **2** fawn colour. [Greek]

camel-hair *n.* fine soft hair used in artists' brushes or for fabric.

camellia /kəˈmiːlɪə/ *n.* evergreen shrub with shiny leaves and showy flowers. [*Camellus*, name of a botanist]

Camembert /ˈkæməmˌbeə(r)/ *n.* a kind of soft creamy pungent cheese. [*Camembert* in France]

cameo /ˈkæmɪəʊ/ *n.* (*pl.* **-s**) **1** small piece of hard stone carved in relief with a background of a different colour. **2 a** short descriptive literary sketch or acted scene. **b** small character part in a play or film, usu. brief and played by a distinguished actor. [French and medieval Latin]

camera /ˈkæmrə/ *n.* **1** apparatus for taking photographs or moving film. **2** equipment for converting images into electrical signals. □ **in camera** *Law* in private. [Latin: related to CHAMBER]

cameraman *n.* person who operates a camera professionally, esp. in film-making or television.

♦ **camera-ready copy** *n.* (also **CRC**) text and illustrations printed in such a form that they are ready for photographing to make the film from which printing plates are made. The CRC may be produced by a phototypesetter for high-class work or for less high quality it may be produced by a laser printer or daisywheel printer driven by a word processor.

---

camiknickers /ˈkæmɪˌnɪkəz/ *n.pl.* women's knickers and vest combined. [from CAMISOLE, KNICKERS]

camisole /ˈkæmɪˌsəʊl/ *n.* women's lightweight vest. [Italian or Spanish: related to CHEMISE]

CAMM *abbr.* computer-aided (or -assisted) maintenance management.

camomile /ˈkæməˌmaɪl/ *n.* (also **chamomile**) aromatic plant with daisy-like flowers used esp. to make tea. [Greek, = earth-apple]

camouflage /ˈkæməˌflɑːʒ/ *–n.* **1 a** disguising of soldiers, tanks, etc. so that they blend into the background. **b** such a disguise. **2** the natural blending colouring of an animal. **3** misleading or evasive behaviour etc. *–v.* (**-ging**) hide by camouflage. [French *camoufler* disguise]

camp[1] *–n.* **1** place where troops are lodged or trained. **2** temporary accommodation of huts, tents, etc., for detainees, holiday-makers, etc. **3** ancient fortified site. **4** party supporters etc. regarded collectively. *–v.* set up or spend time in a camp. [Latin *campus* level ground]

camp[2] *colloq.* *–adj.* **1** affected, effeminate, theatrically exaggerated. **2** homosexual. *–n.* camp manner or style. *–v.* behave or do in a camp way. □ **camp it up** overact; behave affectedly. □ **campy** *adj.* (**-ier**, **-iest**). [origin uncertain]

♦ ***Campaign*** /kæmˈpeɪn/ *n.* weekly magazine that gives details of new advertising campaigns, job vacancies, personnel moves in advertising agencies, and general advertising gossip.

---

campaign /kæmˈpeɪn/ *–n.* **1** organized course of action, esp. to gain publicity (*advertising campaign, marketing campaign, sales campaign*). **2** military operations towards a particular objective. *–v.* take part in a campaign. □ **campaigner** *n.* [Latin: related to CAMP[1]]

Campania /kæmˈpeɪnɪə/ region of W central Italy; pop. (est. 1994) 5 708 657; capital, Naples. The region is mainly agricultural, producing wheat, citrus fruits, and grains.

campanile /ˌkæmpəˈniːlɪ/ *n.* bell-tower (usu. free-standing), esp. in Italy. [Italian *campana* 'bell', from Latin]

Cameroon /ˌkæməˈruːn/, **Republic of** country on the W coast of Africa between Nigeria and Gabon. Subsistence agriculture is the main occupation; cocoa, coffee, and cotton are valuable cash crops and timber is also exported. The main industrial activity is aluminium smelting and oil is a major source of export revenue. Recent political turmoil has weakened the economy; there is little investment and revenue from exports has decreased, due to the fall in world oil prices.

History. From 1884 to 1916 the territory was a German protectorate; it was then administered under League of Nations, later UN, trusteeship, part by France and part by Britain. In 1960 French Cameroons became an independent republic, which was joined in 1961 by part of the British Cameroons; the remainder became part of Nigeria. The French and British halves of the territory merged as a united republic in 1972 and became a one-party state. Moves towards democracy culminated in multi-party parliamentary and presidential elections in 1992, which were boycotted by the main opposition parties. In 1995, Cameroon became a member of the British Commonwealth. Head of state, Paul Biya; capital, Yaoundé. □ **Cameroonian** *adj.* & *n.*

languages	French & English (official), African languages
currency	CFA franc (CFAF) of 100 centimes
pop. (est. 1996)	13 609 000
GNP (est. 1994)	US$8.7B
literacy	75% (m); 52% (f)
life expectancy	51 (m); 54 (f)

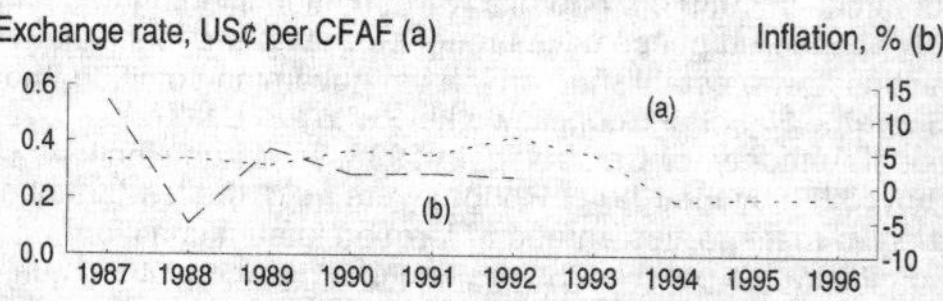

campanology /ˌkæmpəˈnɒlədʒɪ/ *n.* **1** the study of bells. **2** bell-ringing. □ **campanologist** *n.* [Latin *campana* bell]

campanula /kæmˈpænjʊlə/ *n.* plant with bell-shaped usu. blue, purple, or white flowers. [diminutive: related to CAMPANOLOGY]

camp-bed *n.* folding canvas bed.

Campeche /kæmˈpeɪtʃeɪ/ **1** state in SE Mexico, on the Yucatán peninsula; pop. (est. 1995) 642 082. **2** its capital city, a seaport; pop. (1990) 172 208.

camper *n.* **1** person who camps. **2** large motor vehicle with beds etc.

camp-follower *n.* **1** civilian worker in a military camp. **2** disciple or adherent.

camphor /ˈkæmfə(r)/ *n.* pungent white crystalline substance used in making celluloid, medicine, and mothballs. [French ultimately from Sanskrit]

camphorate *v.* (**-ting**) impregnate or treat with camphor.

campion /ˈkæmpɪən/ *n.* wild plant with usu. pink or white notched flowers. [origin uncertain]

campsite *n.* place for camping.

campus /ˈkæmpəs/ *n.* (*pl.* **-es**) **1** grounds of a university or college. **2** esp. *US* a university. [Latin, = field]

CAMRA /ˈkæmrə/ *abbr.* Campaign for Real Ale.

camshaft *n.* shaft with one or more cams.

Can. *abbr.* **1** Canada. **2** Canadian.

can[1] /kæn, kən/ *v.aux.* (*3rd sing. present* **can**; *past* **could** /kʊd/) **1 a** be able to; know how to. **b** be potentially capable of (*these storms can last for hours*). **2** be permitted to. [Old English, = know]

can[2] –*n.* **1** metal vessel for liquid. **2** sealed tin container for the preservation of food or drink. **3** (in *pl.*) *slang* headphones. **4** (prec. by *the*) *slang* **a** prison. **b** *US* lavatory. –*v.* (**-nn-**) put or preserve in a can. □ **in the can** *colloq.* completed, ready. [Old English]

Canada goose *n.* wild North American goose with a brownish-grey body and white neck and breast.

canaille /kəˈnɑːɪ/ *n.* rabble; populace. [French from Italian]

canal /kəˈnæl/ *n.* **1** artificial inland waterway. **2** tubular duct in a plant or animal. [Latin *canalis*]

canalize /ˈkænəˌlaɪz/ *v.* (also **-ise**) (**-zing** or **-sing**) **1** provide with or convert into a canal or canals. **2** channel. □ **canalization** /-ˈzeɪʃ(ə)n/ *n.* [French: related to CANAL]

canapé /ˈkænəˌpeɪ/ *n.* small piece of bread or pastry with a savoury topping. [French]

canard /ˈkænɑːd/ *n.* unfounded rumour or story. [French, = duck]

canary /kəˈneərɪ/ *n.* (*pl.* **-ies**) small songbird with yellow feathers. [CANARY ISLANDS]

Canary Islands /kəˈneərɪ/ (also **Canaries**) group of islands off the NW coast of Africa, an autonomous region of Spain; fruit and vegetables (esp. tomatoes) are grown for export and tourism is important; pop. (est. 1994) 1 534 897.

canasta /kəˈnæstə/ *n.* card-game using two packs and resembling rummy. [Spanish, = basket]

Canberra /ˈkænbərə/ capital and seat of the federal government of Australia, in Australian Capital Territory; pop. (est. 1994) 328 000.

cancan /ˈkænkæn/ *n.* lively stage-dance with high kicking. [French]

cancel /ˈkæns(ə)l/ *v.* (**-ll-**; *US* **-l-**) **1** revoke or discontinue (an arrangement). **2** delete (writing etc.). **3** mark (a ticket, stamp, etc.) to invalidate it. **4** annul; make void. **5** (often foll. by *out*) neutralize or counterbalance. **6** *Math.* strike out (an equal factor) on each side of an equation etc. □ **cancellation** /-ˈleɪʃ(ə)n/ *n.* [Latin: related to CHANCEL]

cancer *n.* **1 a** malignant tumour of body cells. **b** disease caused by this. **2** evil influence or corruption. **3** (**Cancer**) **a** constellation and fourth sign of the zodiac (the Crab). **b** person born when the sun is in this sign. □ **cancerous** *adj.* **cancroid** *adj.* [Latin, = crab]

Cancún /kænˈkuːn/ Caribbean resort in SE Mexico; pop. (1990) 172 425.

c. & d. *abbr.* collection and delivery.

C & E *abbr.* Customs and Excise.

candela /kænˈdiːlə/ *n.* SI unit of luminous intensity. [Latin, = candle]

candelabrum /ˌkændɪˈlɑːbrəm/ *n.* (also **-bra**) (*pl.* **-bra**, *US* **-brums, -bras**) large branched candlestick or lampholder. [Latin: related to CANDELA]

■ **Usage** The form *candelabra* is, strictly speaking, the plural. However, *candelabra* (singular) and *candelabras* (plural) are often found in informal use.

◆ **c. & f.** *abbr.* cost and freight, denoting a price for goods that includes the cost of shipping the goods to the port of destination but not the cost of insuring the goods once they have been loaded onto a ship or aircraft. It is, in other respects, similar to a c.i.f. contract. See C.I.F. Cf. F.O.B.

C & G *abbr.* City and Guilds.

C & I *abbr.* **1** commerce and industry. **2** commercial and industrial.

c. & i. *abbr.* cost and insurance.

candid /ˈkændɪd/ *adj.* **1** frank; open. **2** (of a photograph) taken informally, usu. without subject's knowledge. □ **candidly** *adv.* **candidness** *n.* [Latin *candidus* white]

candida /ˈkændɪdə/ *n.* fungus causing thrush. [Latin *candidus*: related to CANDID]

Canada /ˈkænədə/ country covering the entire N half of North America with the exception of Alaska. Industry is highly developed; manufactures such as motor vehicles, paper, and iron and steel products are important exports. Deposits of gold, silver, uranium, molybdenum, asbestos, nickel, and zinc are profitably exploited, and oil and natural gas are major sources of revenue. The more traditional activities of farming, fishing, and forestry have become highly mechanized. The majority of Canada's trade is with the US; free trade between the two countries was established in 1989 and in 1992 a free-trade agreement was established with Mexico (NAFTA; see NORTH AMERICAN FREE TRADE AGREEMENT).

History. Settled by the French and English during the 17th century, the region was ceded to Britain after the Seven Years War (Treaty of Paris, 1763). It became a federation of provinces, the Dominion of Canada, in 1867 and an independent constitutional monarchy in the Commonwealth in 1931; the last step in the attainment of its legal independence from the UK was taken with the signing of the Constitution Act of 1982. Since then Quebec has acted outside the constitution, and agreement on a new federal constitution, in which more powers are devolved to individual provinces, has not yet been reached. In 1995 a referendum calling for sovereignty was defeated in Quebec. Prime minister, Jean Chrétien; capital, Ottawa. □ **Canadian** /kəˈneɪdɪən/ *adj.* & *n.*

languages	English & French (official), Indian languages
currency	dollar (Can$) of 100 cents
pop. (est. 1996)	29 784 000
GNP (est. 1994)	US$569B
literacy	95%
life expectancy	74 (m); 81 (f)

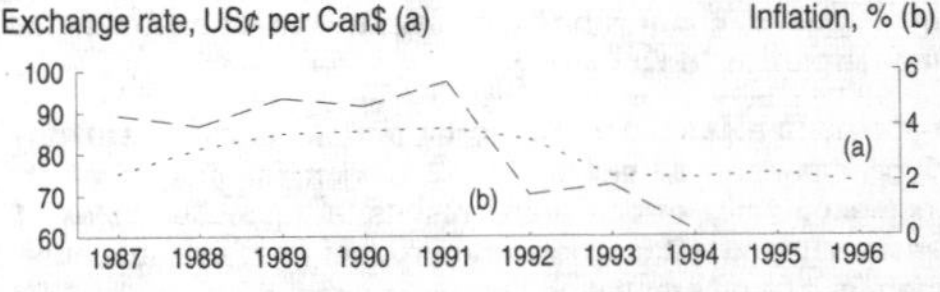

candidate /'kændɪdət/ *n.* **1** person nominated for or seeking office, an award, etc. **2** person or thing likely to gain some distinction or position. **3** person entered for an examination. □ **candidacy** *n.* **candidature** *n.* [Latin, = white-robed]

candle /'kænd(ə)l/ *n.* cylinder or block of wax or tallow with a central wick which gives light when burning. □ **cannot hold a candle to** is much inferior to. **not worth the candle** not justifying cost or trouble. [Latin *candela*]

candlelight *n.* light from candles. □ **candlelit** *adj.*

Candlemas /'kænd(ə)lˌmæs/ *n.* feast of the Purification of the Virgin Mary (2 Feb.). [Old English: related to MASS[2]]

candlestick *n.* holder for one or more candles.

candlewick *n.* **1** thick soft cotton yarn. **2** tufted material from this.

c. & m. *abbr.* = CARE AND MAINTENANCE.

candour /'kændə(r)/ *n.* (*US* **candor**) frankness; openness. [Latin *candor*]

c. & p. *abbr.* carriage and packing.

C & W *abbr.* country-and-western (music).

candy /'kændɪ/ *–n.* (*pl.* **-ies**) **1** (in full **sugar-candy**) sugar crystallized by repeated boiling and slow evaporation. **2** *US* sweets; a sweet. *–v.* (**-ies, -ied**) (usu. as **candied** *adj.*) preserve (fruit etc.) in candy. [French from Arabic]

candyfloss *n.* fluffy mass of spun sugar round a stick.

candystripe *n.* alternate stripes of white and a colour. □ **candystriped** *adj.*

candytuft /'kændɪˌtʌft/ *n.* plant with white, pink, or purple flowers in tufts. [*Candia* Crete, TUFT]

cane *–n.* **1 a** hollow jointed stem of giant reeds or grasses. **b** solid stem of slender palms. **2** = SUGAR CANE. **3** cane used for wickerwork etc. **4** cane used as a walking-stick, plant support, for punishment, etc. *–v.* (**-ning**) **1** beat with a cane. **2** weave cane into (a chair etc.). [Greek *kanna* reed]

Canea /kə'niːə/ (Greek **Khaniá** /xɑːn'jɑː/) major port on the NW coast of Crete; pop. (est. 1981) 47 451.

cane-sugar *n.* sugar from sugar-cane.

canine /'keɪnaɪn/ *–adj.* of a dog or dogs. *–n.* **1** dog. **2** (in full **canine tooth**) pointed tooth between incisors and premolars. [Latin *canis* dog]

canister /'kænɪstə(r)/ *n.* **1** small container for tea etc. **2** cylinder of shot, tear-gas, etc., exploding on impact. [Greek *kanastron* wicker basket]

canker *–n.* **1** destructive disease of trees and plants. **2** ulcerous ear disease of animals. **3** corrupting influence. *–v.* **1** infect with canker. **2** corrupt. **3** (as **cankered** *adj.*) soured, malignant. □ **cankerous** *adj.* [Latin: related to CANCER]

canna /'kænə/ *n.* tropical plant with bright flowers and ornamental leaves. [Latin: related to CANE]

cannabis /'kænəbɪs/ *n.* **1** hemp plant. **2** parts of it used as a narcotic. [Latin from Greek]

canned *adj.* **1** pre-recorded (*canned music*). **2** sold in a can (*canned beer*). **3** *slang* drunk.

cannelloni /ˌkænə'ləʊnɪ/ *n.pl.* tubes of pasta stuffed with a savoury mixture. [Italian]

cannery /'kænərɪ/ *n.* (*pl.* **-ies**) canning-factory.

Cannes /kæn/ coastal resort in S France, on the Riviera; pop. (est. 1990) 69 363. There are aircraft and textile industries, and an important international film festival is held here annually.

cannibal /'kænɪb(ə)l/ *n.* person or animal that eats its own species. □ **cannibalism** *n.* **cannibalistic** /-bə'lɪstɪk/ *adj.* [Spanish from Carib]

◆ **cannibalization** /ˌkænɪbəlaɪ'zeɪʃ(ə)n/ *n.* (also **-isation**) **1** cannibalizing a machine etc. **2** market situation in which increased sales of one brand results in decreased sales of another brand within the same product line, usu. because there is little differentiation between them.

cannibalize /'kænɪbəˌlaɪz/ *v.* (also **-ise**) (**-zing** or **-sing**) use (a machine etc.) as a source of spare parts.

cannon /'kænən/ *–n.* **1** *hist.* (*pl.* usu. same) large heavy esp. mounted gun. **2** *Billiards* hitting of two balls successively by the player's ball. *–v.* (usu. foll. by *against, into*) collide. [Italian: related to CANE]

cannonade /ˌkænə'neɪd/ *–n.* period of continuous heavy gunfire. *–v.* (**-ding**) bombard with a cannonade. [Italian: related to CANNON]

cannon-ball *n. hist.* large ball fired by a cannon.

cannon-fodder *n.* soldiers regarded as expendable.

cannot /'kænɒt/ *v.aux.* can not.

canny /'kænɪ/ *adj.* (**-ier, -iest**) **1** shrewd, worldly-wise; thrifty. **2** *Scot.* & *N.Engl.* pleasant, agreeable. □ **cannily** *adv.* **canniness** *n.* [from CAN[1]]

canoe /kə'nuː/ *–n.* small narrow boat with pointed ends, usu. paddled. *–v.* (**-noes, -noed, -noeing**) travel in a canoe. □ **canoeist** *n.* [Spanish and Haitian]

canon /'kænən/ *n.* **1 a** general law, rule, principle, or criterion. **b** church decree or law. **2** (*fem.* **canoness**) member of a cathedral chapter. **3** body of (esp. sacred) writings accepted as genuine. **4** the part of the Roman Catholic Mass containing the words of consecration. **5** *Mus.* piece with different parts taking up the same theme successively. [Greek *kanōn* rule]

cañon var. of CANYON.

canonical /kə'nɒnɪk(ə)l/ *–adj.* (also **canonic**) **1 a** according to canon law. **b** included in the canon of Scripture. **2** authoritative, accepted. **3** of a cathedral chapter or a member of it. *–n.* (in *pl.*) canonical dress of clergy. [medieval Latin: related to CANON]

canonist /'kænənɪst/ *n.* expert in canon law.

canonize /'kænəˌnaɪz/ *v.* (also **-ise**) (**-zing** or **-sing**) **1 a** declare officially to be a saint, usu. with a ceremony. **b** regard as a saint. **2** admit to the canon of Scripture. **3** sanction by Church authority. □ **canonization** /-'zeɪʃ(ə)n/ *n.* [medieval Latin: related to CANON]

canon law *n.* ecclesiastical law.

canoodle /kə'nuːd(ə)l/ *v.* (**-ling**) *colloq.* kiss and cuddle. [origin unknown]

canopy /'kænəpɪ/ *–n.* (*pl.* **-ies**) **1 a** covering suspended over a throne, bed, etc. **b** sky. **c** overhanging shelter. **2** *Archit.* rooflike projection over a niche etc. **3** expanding part of a parachute. *–v.* (**-ies, -ied**) supply or be a canopy to. [Greek, = mosquito-net]

canst *archaic 2nd person sing.* of CAN[1].

cant[1] *–n.* **1** insincere pious or moral talk. **2** language peculiar to a class, profession, etc.; jargon. *–v.* use cant. [probably from Latin: related to CHANT]

cant[2] *–n.* **1** slanting surface, bevel. **2** oblique push or jerk. **3** tilted position. *–v.* push or pitch out of level; tilt. [Low German or Dutch, = edge]

can't /kɑːnt/ *contr.* can not.

Cantab. /'kæntæb/ *abbr.* of Cambridge University. [Latin *Cantabrigiensis*]

cantabile /kæn'tɑːbɪˌleɪ/ *Mus.* *–adv.* & *adj.* in smooth flowing style. *–n.* cantabile passage or movement. [Italian, = singable]

Cantabria /kæn'tæbrɪə/ autonomous region of N Spain; pop. (est. 1994) 526 090; capital, Santander. □ **Cantabrian** *adj.* & *n.*

Cantabrigian /ˌkæntə'brɪdʒɪən/ *–adj.* of Cambridge or its university. *–n.* person from Cambridge or its university. [*Cantabrigia*, Latinized name of Cambridge]

cantaloup /'kæntəˌluːp/ *n.* (also **cantaloupe**) small round ribbed melon. [*Cantaluppi* near Rome, where it was first grown in Europe]

cantankerous /kæn'tæŋkərəs/ *adj.* bad-tempered, quarrelsome. □ **cantankerously** *adv.* **cantankerousness** *n.* [origin uncertain]

cantata /kæn'tɑːtə/ *n. Mus.* composition with vocal solos and usu. choral and orchestral accompaniment. [Italian: related to CHANT]

canteen /kæn'tiːn/ *n.* **1 a** restaurant for employees in an office, factory, etc. **b** shop for provisions in a barracks or camp. **2** case of cutlery. **3** soldier's or camper's water-flask. [Italian, = cellar]

canter –*n.* horse's pace between a trot and a gallop. –*v.* go or make go at a canter. [*Canterbury gallop* of medieval pilgrims]

Canterbury /ˈkæntəbərɪ/ city in SE England, in Kent, seat of the archbishop, Primate of All England; pop. (1991) 36 464.

Canterbury Plains region in New Zealand, on the central E coast of South Island, important for sheep farming; chief town, Christchurch.

canticle /ˈkæntɪk(ə)l/ *n.* song or chant with a biblical text. [Latin *canticum* CHANT]

cantilever /ˈkæntɪˌliːvə(r)/ *n.* **1** bracket or beam etc. projecting from a wall to support a balcony etc. **2** beam or girder fixed at one end only. □ **cantilevered** *adj.* [origin unknown]

cantilever bridge *n.* bridge made of cantilevers projecting from piers and connected by girders.

canto /ˈkæntəʊ/ *n.* (*pl.* **-s**) division of a long poem. [Latin *cantus*: related to CHANT]

Canton /kænˈtɒn/ (also **Guangzhou** /kwæŋˈdʒəʊ/) city in S China, capital of Guangdong province; pop. (1993) 3 560 000. It is the leading industrial and commercial centre of S China, with engineering, textile, and chemical industries.

canton –*n.* /ˈkæntɒn/ subdivision of a country, esp. of Switzerland. –*v.* /kænˈtuːn/ put (troops) into quarters. [French, = corner: related to CANT[2]]

cantonment /kænˈtuːnmənt/ *n.* **1** lodging assigned to troops. **2** *hist.* permanent military station in India. [French: related to CANTON]

cantor /ˈkæntɔː(r)/ *n.* **1** church choir leader. **2** precentor in a synagogue. [Latin, = singer]

canvas /ˈkænvəs/ –*n.* **1** strong coarse cloth used for sails and tents etc. and for oil-painting. **2** a painting on canvas, esp. in oils. –*v.* (**-ss-**; *US* **-s-**) cover with canvas. □ **under canvas 1** in tents. **2** with sails spread. [Latin: related to CANNABIS]

canvass /ˈkænvəs/ –*v.* **1** solicit votes, esp. from a constituency electorate. **2 a** ascertain the opinions of. **b** seek custom from. **3** propose (an idea or plan etc.). –*n.* canvassing, esp. of electors. □ **canvasser** *n.* [originally = toss in sheet, from CANVAS]

canyon /ˈkænjən/ *n.* (also **cañon**) deep gorge. [Spanish *cañón* tube]

CAP *abbr.* **1** Code of Advertising Practice. **2** = COMMON AGRICULTURAL POLICY. **3** computer-aided planning. **4** computer-aided production.

cap –*n.* **1 a** soft brimless hat, usu. with a peak. **b** head-covering worn in a particular profession. **c** cap as a sign of membership of a sports team. **d** mortarboard. **2 a** cover like a cap (*kneecap*). **b** top for a bottle, jar, pen, camera lens, etc. **3** = DUTCH CAP. **4** = PERCUSSION CAP. **5** dental crown. **6** *Finance* see COLLAR *n.* 5. –*v.* (**-pp-**) **1 a** put a cap on. **b** cover the top or end of. **c** set a limit to (*charge-capping*). **2** award a sports cap to. **3** form the top of. **4** surpass, excel. □ **cap in hand** humbly. **if the cap fits** (of a remark) if it applies to you, so be it. **to cap it all** after everything else. [Latin *cappa*]

capability /ˌkeɪpəˈbɪlɪtɪ/ *n.* (*pl.* **-ies**) **1** ability, power. **2** undeveloped or unused faculty.

capable /ˈkeɪpəb(ə)l/ *adj.* **1** competent, able, gifted. **2** (foll. by *of*) **a** having the ability, fitness, etc. for. **b** admitting of (explanation, improvement, etc.). □ **capably** *adv.* [Latin *capio* hold]

capacious /kəˈpeɪʃəs/ *adj.* roomy. □ **capaciousness** *n.* [Latin *capax*: related to CAPABLE]

capacitance /kəˈpæsɪt(ə)ns/ *n.* **1** ability to store electric charge. **2** ratio of change in the electric charge in a system to the corresponding change in its potential.

capacitor /kəˈpæsɪtə(r)/ *n.* device able to store electric charge.

capacity /kəˈpæsɪtɪ/ *n.* (*pl.* **-ies**) **1 a** power to contain, receive, experience, or produce (*capacity for heat, pain,* etc.). **b** maximum amount that can be contained or produced etc. **c** *Computing* (also **storage capacity**) amount of information that can be held in a storage device, usu. measured in bytes or in bits. **d** (*attrib.*) fully occupying the available space etc. (*capacity crowd*). **2** mental power. **3** position or function. **4** legal competence. □ **to capacity** fully. [Latin: related to CAPACIOUS]

caparison /kəˈpærɪs(ə)n/ *literary* –*n.* **1** (usu. in *pl.*) horse's trappings. **2** equipment, finery. –*v.* adorn. [Spanish, = saddle-cloth]

cape[1] *n.* **1** sleeveless cloak. **2** this worn over or as part of a longer cloak or coat. [Latin *cappa* CAP]

cape[2] *n.* **1** headland, promontory. **2** (**the Cape**) the Cape of Good Hope. [Latin *caput* head]

Cape Breton Island /ˈbret(ə)n/ Canadian island in NE Nova Scotia; pop (1988) 170 000; chief town, Sydney. Its industries include coal, steel, and oil refining.

Cape Canaveral /kəˈnævər(ə)l/ cape in the SE US, on the E coast of Florida, the location of the John F. Kennedy Space Center.

Cape Cod peninsula in the NE US, in SE Massachusetts; industries include tourism; and agriculture, esp. the cultivation of cranberries.

Cape Horn southernmost point of South America, on a Chilean island forming part of Tierra del Fuego.

Cape of Good Hope mountainous promontory near the S extremity of Africa.

Cape Province former province of the Republic of South Africa; its capital was Cape Town. In 1994 it was divided into the provinces of Eastern Cape, Western Cape, Northern Cape, and part of North-West Province. Diamonds and copper were mined; canning, food processing, textiles, and motor-vehicle production were the major industries.

caper[1] –*v.* jump or run playfully. –*n.* **1** playful leap. **2 a** prank. **b** *slang* illicit activity. □ **cut a caper** frolic. [abbreviation of CAPRIOLE]

caper[2] *n.* **1** bramble-like shrub. **2** (in *pl.*) its pickled buds used esp. in a sauce. [Greek *kapparis*]

Cape Verde /vɜːd/, **Republic of** country consisting of a group of islands in the Atlantic off the coast of Senegal. The economy is based on subsistence agriculture and fishing is important; fish products and bananas are the main exports. Ship refuelling is a major source of revenue and employment. The economy is stable, and foreign aid is likely to increase if the transition to democracy continues to be successful. Since 1994 the government has been pursuing a programme of economic reform, including the privatization of much industry. The islands formed a Portuguese colony until 1975, when they became an independent one-party state. The first multi-party elections, held in 1991, saw the defeat of the ruling party by the Movement for Democracy, which won the 1995 elections. President, Antonio Mascarenhas Monteiro; prime minister, Carlos Veiga; capital, Praia. □ **Cape Verdean** /ˈvɜːdɪən/ *adj.* & *n.*

languages	Portuguese (official), Creole
currency	escudo (CV Esc) of 100 centavos
pop. (est. 1996)	403 000
GNP (est. 1994)	US$346M
literacy	52% (m); 47% (f)
life expectancy	61 (m); 65 (f)

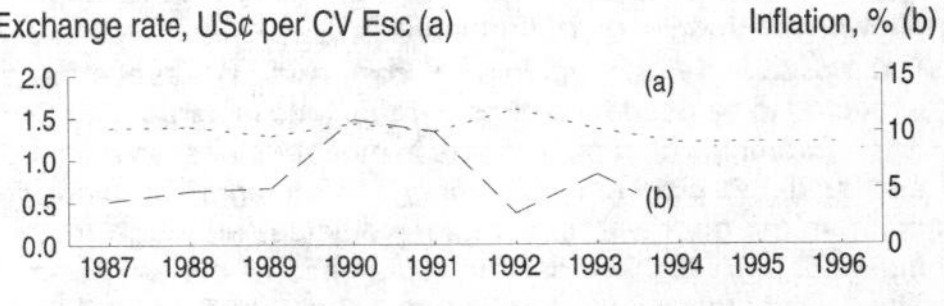

capercaillie /ˌkæpə'keɪlɪ/ *n.* (also **capercailzie** /-lzɪ/) large European grouse. [Gaelic, = horse of the forest]

Cape Town legislative capital of the Republic of South Africa, a port in the S of the country; industries include oil refining, textiles, chemicals, and motor-vehicle production; pop. (1991) 854 616.

x**Cape York** peninsula forming the most northerly point of the Australian mainland, on the Torres Strait. Bauxite is mined.

capillarity /ˌkæpɪ'lærɪtɪ/ *n.* the rise or depression of a liquid in a narrow tube. [French: related to CAPILLARY]

capillary /kə'pɪlərɪ/ *–attrib. adj.* **1** of or like a hair, esp. (of a tube) of very small diameter. **2** of the branching blood-vessels connecting arteries and veins. *–n.* (*pl.* **-ies**) **1** capillary tube. **2** capillary blood vessel. [Latin *capillus* hair]

capillary action *n.* = CAPILLARITY.

capital /'kæpɪt(ə)l/ *–n.* **1** chief town or city of a country or region. **2** total value of the assets of a person less liabilities. **3** amount of the proprietors' interests in the assets of an organization, less its liabilities. **4** money contributed by the proprietors to an organization to enable it to function; thus **share capital** is the amount provided by way of shares and the **loan capital** is the amount provided by way of loans. However, the capital of the proprietors of companies not only consists of the share and loan capital, it also includes retained profit, which accrues to the holders of the ordinary shares. See also RESERVE CAPITAL. **5** *Econ.* factor of production, usu. either machinery and plant (**physical capital**) or money (**financial capital**). Capital is generally used to enhance the productivity of other factors of production (e.g. combine harvesters enhance the productivity of land, tools enhance the value of labour) and its return is the reward following from this enhancement. In general, the rate of return on capital is called profit. **6** capitalists collectively. **7** capital letter. **8** head of a column or pillar. *–adj.* **1 a** principal, most important. **b** *colloq.* excellent. **2 a** involving punishment by death. **b** (of an error etc.) vitally harmful, fatal. **3** (of letters of the alphabet) large in size, used to begin sentences and names etc. □ **make capital out of** use to one's advantage. [Latin *caput -itis* head]

♦ **capital account** *n.* **1** account recording capital expenditure on such items as land and buildings, plant and machinery, etc. **2** budgeted amount that can only be spent on major items, esp. in public-sector budgeting. Cf. REVENUE ACCOUNT 2. **3** account showing the interest of a sole trader in the net assets of the trader's business. **4** series of accounts recording the interests of the partners in the net assets of a partnership. Capital accounts can embrace both the amounts originally contributed and the current accounts; it may also refer, more narrowly, to the amounts originally contributed, adjusted where necessary by agreement between the partners.

♦ **capital allowances** *n.pl.* income tax reliefs given against business and some other profits to reflect the depreciation of certain types of asset owned by the business. Because the Inland Revenue cannot control the amount of depreciation of fixed assets that traders charge in their accounts against profits, it is customary for the trader's own depreciation charge to be disallowed for tax purposes and the Revenue's own charges (the capital allowances) substituted. These may be targeted to some types of asset (e.g. plant and machinery) and not others (office buildings); where the authorities want to create incentives for traders to invest, the allowances may be accelerated (i.e. allowed at a higher rate than would be expected if normal depreciation rates were applied), even to the extent of allowing 100% capital allowances in the year of purchase.

♦ **capital asset** *n.* (also **fixed asset**) asset that is expected to be used for a considerable time in a trade or business. Examples of capital assets in most businesses are land and buildings, plant and machinery, investments in subsidiary companies, goodwill, and motor vehicles, although in the hands of dealers these assets would become current assets. The costs of these assets are normally written off against profits over their expected useful life spans by deducting an item for depreciation from their book value each year. Cf. CURRENT ASSETS.

♦ **capital budget** *n.* sums allocated by an organization for future capital expenditure. The capital budget may well encompass a longer period than the next accounting period.

♦ **capital commitments** *n.pl.* firm plans, usu. approved by the board of directors in the case of companies, to spend sums of money on capital assets. Capital commitments must by law be shown by way of a note, or otherwise, on company balance sheets.

♦ **capital consumption** *n.* total depreciation in the value of the capital goods in an economy during a specified period. It is difficult to calculate this figure, but it is needed as it has to be deducted from the gross national product and the gross domestic product to obtain the net figures.

♦ **capital-conversion plan** *n.* annuity that converts capital into income. Capital-conversion policies are often used to provide an income later in life for a person who might be liable to capital-gains tax if capital is not reinvested in some way.

♦ **capital duty** *n.* stamp-duty payable in the UK on the formation of companies, the issue of shares, or the immigration to Great Britain of companies other than from within the EC.

♦ **capital expenditure** *n.* expenditure on capital assets. Capital expenditure is not deducted from profits, as an asset is acquired rather than a loss being made. However, as a capital asset loses value by depreciation, the amount of the depreciation is charged against profit.

♦ **capital gain** *n.* gain on an asset not bought and sold in the normal course of trade by the person making the gain. These gains are taxed in the UK and in many other countries by means of a capital-gains tax.

♦ **capital-gains tax** *n.* (also **CGT**) tax on capital gains. Most countries have a form of income tax under which they tax the profits from trading and a different tax to tax substantial disposals of assets either by traders for whom the assets are not trading stock (e.g. a trader's factory) or by individuals who do not trade (e.g. sales of shares by an investor). The latter type of tax is a capital-gains tax. Short-term gains taxes are taxes sometimes applied to an asset that has only been held for a limited time. In these cases the rates tend to be higher than for the normal capital-gains tax. In the UK, capital-gains tax applies to the net gains (after deducting losses) accruing to an individual in any tax year, with an exemption to liability if the individual's gains do not exceed a specified figure (£6800 in 1998–9); this exemption has applied separately to husbands and wives since April 1990. Other exemptions include gains on private cars, government securities and savings certificates, loan stocks, options, gambling, life-assurance and deferred-annuity contracts, main dwelling house, and works of art. The rate of tax is 40% for assets held for two years, tapering down to 24% for non-business assets held for 10 years or more. Gains on business assets pay less capital-gains tax. The former indexation allowance was scrapped from 1998–9.

♦ **capital gearing** *n.* (*US* **leverage**) ratio of the amount of fixed interest loan stock and preference shares in a company to its ordinary share capital. A company with a preponderance of ordinary share capital is **low-geared** while one in which fixed-interest capital dominates is **high-geared**. With high gearing, when profits are rising, the amounts available to ordinary shareholders rise, in percentage terms, faster than the percentage rise in profits. However, when profits are falling shareholders in high-geared companies suffer a larger percentage drop in their dividends than the percentage fall in profits. See also DEGEARING.

♦ **capital goods** *n.pl.* (also **producer goods**) goods used to produce other goods rather than being bought by consumers (see CONSUMER GOODS). Capital goods include plant and machinery, industrial buildings, and raw materials.

♦ **capital growth** *n.* increase in the value of invested capital. Investment in fixed-interest securities or bonds provides income but limited capital growth (which may be improved in index-linked gilts). Substantial capital growth requires investment in equities (see ORDINARY SHARE), the value of which should increase with inflation. Investing in equities is thus said to be a hedge against inflation. See GROWTH STOCK.

♦ **capital-intensive** see LABOUR-INTENSIVE.

♦ **capital investment** *n.* = INVESTMENT 3.

♦ **capitalism** *n.* economic and political system in which individual owners of capital are free to dispose of it as they please, esp. for their own profit. Most economies are now capitalistic, even though governments do interfere significantly with the movements of capital. Neoclassical economics is usu. associated with capitalism because of its traditional advocacy of free trade. However, neoclassical economists have little to say about redistribution of capital. Marxist economists see capitalism as a stage in the development of society – a stage to be superseded by socialism, in which private capital will be abolished.

---

capitalist *–n.* **1** person investing or possessing capital. **2** advocate of capitalism. *–adj.* of or favouring capitalism. □ **capitalistic** /-ˈlɪstɪk/ *adj.*

♦ **capitalization** /ˌkæpɪtəlaɪˈzeɪʃ(ə)n/ *n.* (also **-isation**) **1** taking advantage of. **2** providing capital for a company or other organization. **3** structure of the capital of a company or other organization, i.e. the extent to which its capital is divided into share or loan capital and the extent to which share capital is divided into ordinary and preference shares. See also THIN CAPITALIZATION. **4** conversion of the reserves of a company into capital by means of a scrip issue. **5** writing in capital letters.

♦ **capitalization issue** *n.* = SCRIP ISSUE.

---

capitalize *v.* (also **-ise**) (**-zing** or **-sing**) **1** (foll. by *on*) use to one's advantage. **2** convert into or provide with capital. **3 a** write (a letter of the alphabet) as a capital. **b** begin (a word) with a capital letter. [French: related to CAPITAL]

♦ **capitalized value** *n.* **1** value at which an asset has been recorded in the balance sheet of a company or other organization, usu. before the deduction of depreciation. **2** capital equivalent of an asset that yields a regular income, calculated at the prevailing rate of interest. For example, a piece of land bringing in an annual income of £1000, when the prevailing interest rate is 10%, would have a notional capitalized value of £10,000 (i.e. £1000/0.1). This may not reflect its true value.

---

capital levy *n.* tax on wealth or property.

♦ **capital loss** *n.* loss arising from the disposal, loss, or destruction of a capital asset or from a long-term liability. For tax purposes a capital loss can be set off against a capital profit. See CAPITAL-GAINS TAX.

♦ **capital maintenance** *n.* maintaining the value of the share capital of an organization or of its share capital and reserves. More vaguely, it could refer to maintaining the operating capacity of an organization, regardless of the composition of its assets.

♦ **capital market** *n.* market in which long-term capital is raised by industry and commerce, the government, and local authorities. The money comes from private investors, insurance companies, pension funds, and banks and is usu. arranged by issuing houses and merchant banks. Stock exchanges are also part of the capital market in that they provide a market for the shares and loan stocks that represent the capital once it has been raised. It is the presence and sophistication of their capital markets that distinguish the industrial countries from the developing countries.

♦ **capital movement** *n.* transfer of capital between countries, either by companies or individuals. Restrictions on exchange controls and capital transfers between countries have been greatly reduced in recent years. Capital movements seeking long-term gains are usu. those made by companies investing abroad, e.g. to set up a factory. Capital movements seeking short-term gains are often more speculative, such as those taking advantage of temporarily high interest rates in another country or an expected change in the exchange rate.

♦ **capital profit** *n.* profit arising from the disposal of a capital asset. Capital profits, if taxable at all, are normally subject to capital-gains tax, which applies both to individuals and to companies. The Companies Act (1980) allows capital profits made by limited companies to be distributed as revenue profits, provided that they are real, realized, have not been previously capitalized, and take into account any accumulated realized capital losses.

♦ **capital-redemption reserve** *n.* reserve fund required to be created by the UK Companies Act (1985) when shares are redeemed out of retained profits and not out of a new issue of share capital (see RETAINED PROFITS). The reserve is created by making a transfer out of the profit and loss account to a specially designated account, the **capital-redemption reserve account**. Amounts held in this account cannot be distributed to shareholders by way of dividend, although they may be used to make bonus issues of share capital. The purpose of the reserve is to ensure that the company's capital is not diluted by the redemption of some of the shares.

♦ **capital reserves** *n.pl.* undistributed profits of a company that for various reasons are not regarded as distributable to shareholders as dividends. These include certain profits on the revaluation of capital assets and any sums received from share issues in excess of the nominal value of the shares, which are shown in a share premium account. Capital reserves are known as **undistributable reserves** under the Companies Act (1985). See also RESERVE *n.* 4.

♦ **capital stock** *n.* aggregate of an organization's capital assets. Cf. CURRENT ASSETS; STOCK-IN-TRADE 1.

♦ **capital structure** *n.* elements, such as shares, loan stock, etc., from which the capital of a company or other organization is composed.

---

capital sum *n.* lump sum, esp. payable to an insured person.

♦ **capital-transfer tax** *n.* (also **CTT**) tax levied when capital is transferred from one person's estate usu. into that of another, as by lifetime gifts or inheritances. Levied in the UK 1974–86, it continued in a truncated form as inheritance tax.

♦ **capital turnover** *n.* ratio of sales of a company or other organization to its capital employed (i.e. its assets less liabilities). It is presumed that the higher this ratio, the better the use that is being made of the assets in generating sales.

---

capitation /ˌkæpɪˈteɪʃ(ə)n/ *n.* tax or fee paid per person. [Latin: related to CAPITAL]

capitular /kəˈpɪtjʊlə(r)/ *adj.* of a cathedral chapter. [Latin *capitulum* CHAPTER]

capitulate /kəˈpɪtjʊˌleɪt/ *v.* (**-ting**) surrender. □ **capitulation** /-ˈleɪʃ(ə)n/ *n.* [medieval Latin, = put under headings]

capo /ˈkæpəʊ/ *n.* (*pl.* **-s**) device fitted across the strings of a guitar etc. to raise their pitch equally. [Italian *capo tasto* head stop]

capon /ˈkeɪpən/ *n.* castrated cock fattened for eating. [Latin *capo*]

CAPP *abbr.* computer-aided process planning.

♦ **capped mortgage** *n.* mortgage with a variable rate of interest in which the maximum rate of interest is specified, often for a specified number of years.

---

cappuccino /ˌkæpʊˈtʃiːnəʊ/ *n.* (*pl.* **-s**) frothy milky coffee. [Italian, = CAPUCHIN]

Capri /ˈkæpriː, kəˈpriː/ island off the W coast of Italy, in the Bay of Naples, a popular tourist resort; pop. (est. 1987) 7750.

caprice /kəˈpriːs/ *n.* **1 a** whim. **b** tendency to this. **2** lively or fanciful work of art, music, etc. [Italian *capriccio* sudden start]

capricious /kəˈprɪʃəs/ *adj.* subject to whims; unpredictable. □ **capriciously** *adv.* **capriciousness** *n.*

Capricorn /ˈkæprɪˌkɔːn/ *n.* **1** constellation and tenth sign of the zodiac (the Goat). **2** person born when the sun is in this sign. [Latin *caper -pri* goat, *cornu* horn]

capriole /ˈkæprɪˌəʊl/ *–n.* leap, caper, esp. of a trained horse. *–v.* (**-ling**) perform this. [Italian: related to CAPRICORN]

Caprivi Strip /kə'priːvɪ/ narrow strip of Namibia, in the NE, providing access to the Zambezi River.

capsicum /'kæpsɪkəm/ *n.* **1** plant with edible fruits, esp. any of several varieties of pepper. **2** red, green, or yellow fruit of these. [Latin *capsa* case]

capsize /kæp'saɪz/ *v.* (**-zing**) (of a boat etc.) be overturned; overturn. [Spanish *capuzar* sink]

capstan /'kæpst(ə)n/ *n.* **1** thick revolving cylinder for winding a cable etc. **2** revolving spindle carrying the spool on a tape recorder. [Provençal]

capstan lathe *n.* lathe with a revolving tool-holder.

capsule /'kæpsjuːl/ *n.* **1** small edible soluble case enclosing medicine. **2** detachable compartment of a spacecraft or nose of a rocket. **3** enclosing membrane in the body. **4** dry fruit that releases its seeds when ripe. **5** (*attrib.*) concise; condensed. □ **capsular** *adj.* [Latin *capsa* case]

capsulize *v.* (also **-ise**) (**-zing** or **-sing**) put (information etc.) in compact form.

Capt. *abbr.* Captain.

captain /'kæptɪn/ *–n.* **1 a** chief, leader. **b** leader of a team. **2 a** commander of a ship. **b** pilot of a civil aircraft. **3** army officer next above lieutenant. *–v.* be captain of; lead. □ **captaincy** *n.* (*pl.* **-ies**). [Latin *caput* head]

caption /'kæpʃ(ə)n/ *–n.* **1** wording appended to an illustration, cartoon, etc. **2** wording on a cinema or television screen. **3** heading of a chapter, article, etc. *–v.* provide with a caption. [Latin *capio* take]

captious /'kæpʃəs/ *adj.* fault-finding. [Latin: related to CAPTION]

captivate /'kæptɪ,veɪt/ *v.* (**-ting**) fascinate; charm. □ **captivation** /-'veɪʃ(ə)n/ *n.* [Latin: related to CAPTIVE]

captive /'kæptɪv/ *–n.* confined or imprisoned person or animal. *–adj.* **1** taken prisoner; restrained. **2** unable to escape. □ **captivity** /-'tɪvɪtɪ/ *n.* [Latin *capio capt-* take]

◆ **captive audience** *n.* audience that is unlikely to be able to escape being exposed to an advertising message *in toto*. Examples include cinema audiences and conference audiences.

◆ **captive insurance company** *n.* insurance company that is totally owned by another organization and insures only, or mostly, the parent company's risks. In this way the parent organization is able to obtain insurance cover (esp. those classes that are compulsory by law) without having to pay premiums to an organization outside its trading group.

◆ **captive market** *n.* group of purchasers who are obliged to buy a particular product as a result of some special circumstance, such as the absence of an alternative supplier or product.

captor /'kæptə(r)/ *n.* person who captures. [Latin: related to CAPTIVE]

capture /'kæptʃə(r)/ *–v.* (**-ring**) **1 a** take prisoner; seize. **b** obtain by force or trickery. **2** portray; record on film etc. **3** absorb (a subatomic particle). **4** record (data) for use in a computer. *–n.* **1** act of capturing. **2** thing or person captured. [Latin: related to CAPTIVE]

Capuchin /'kæpjʊtʃɪn/ *n.* **1** Franciscan friar. **2** (**capuchin**) **a** monkey with cowl-like head hair. **b** pigeon with a cowl-like head and neck. [Italian *cappuccio* cowl]

capybara /,kæpɪ'bɑːrə/ *n.* large semi-aquatic South American rodent. [Tupi]

◆ **CAR** *abbr.* **1** Central African Republic. **2** = COMPOUND ANNUAL RETURN.

car *n.* **1** (in full **motor car**) motor vehicle for a driver and small number of passengers. **2** (in *comb.*) road vehicle or railway carriage esp. of a specified kind (*tramcar; dining-car*). **3** *US* any railway carriage or van. **4** passenger compartment of a lift, balloon, etc. [French from Latin]

car. *abbr.* carat.

c.a.r. *abbr.* compounded annual rate (of interest).

Caracas /kə'rækəs/ capital of Venezuela; pop. (est. 1990) 2 784 000. It is an industrial and commercial centre, esp. for the oil industry.

caracul var. of KARAKUL.

carafe /kə'ræf/ *n.* glass container for water or wine. [French from Arabic]

Carajás /,kærə'ʒɑːs/ mining region in N Brazil, the site of one of the richest deposits of iron ore in the world.

caramel /'kærə,mel/ *n.* **1 a** burnt sugar or syrup as a flavouring or colouring. **b** a kind of soft toffee. **2** light-brown colour. □ **caramelize** /-mə,laɪz/ *v.* (also **-ise**) (**-zing** or **-sing**). [French from Spanish]

carapace /'kærə,peɪs/ *n.* upper shell of a tortoise or crustacean. [French from Spanish]

◆ **carat** /'kærət/ *n.* **1** measure of the purity (fineness) of gold. Pure gold is defined as 24 carat; 14-carat gold contains 14/24ths gold, the remainder usu. being copper. **2** unit for measuring the weight of a diamond or other gemstone, equal to 0.2 gram. [French ultimately from Greek *keras* horn]

caravan /'kærə,væn/ *–n.* **1** vehicle equipped for living in and usu. towed by a car. **2** people travelling together, esp. across a desert. *–v.* (**-nn-**) travel or live in a caravan. □ **caravanner** *n.* [French from Persian]

caravanserai /,kærə'vænsə,raɪ/ *n.* Eastern inn with a central court. [Persian, = caravan place]

caravel /'kærə,vel/ *n.* (also **carvel** /'kɑːv(ə)l/) *hist.* small light fast ship. [Greek *karabos*, literally 'horned beetle']

caraway /'kærə,weɪ/ *n.* plant with tiny white flowers. [Spanish from Arabic]

caraway seed *n.* fruit of the caraway as flavouring and a source of oil.

carb *n. colloq.* carburettor. [abbreviation]

carbide /'kɑːbaɪd/ *n.* **1** binary compound of carbon. **2** = CALCIUM CARBIDE.

carbine /'kɑːbaɪn/ *n.* short rifle orig. for cavalry use. [French]

carbohydrate /,kɑːbə'haɪdreɪt/ *n.* energy-producing organic compound of carbon, hydrogen, and oxygen (e.g. starch, sugar).

carbolic /kɑː'bɒlɪk/ *n.* (in full **carbolic acid**) phenol. [from CARBON]

carbolic soap *n.* soap containing carbolic.

car bomb *n.* terrorist bomb placed in or under a parked car.

carbon /'kɑːbən/ *n.* **1** non-metallic element occurring naturally as diamond, graphite, and charcoal, and in all organic compounds. **2 a** = CARBON COPY. **b** = CARBON PAPER. **3** rod of carbon in an arc lamp. [Latin *carbo* charcoal]

carbonaceous /,kɑːbə'neɪʃəs/ *adj.* **1** consisting of or containing carbon. **2** of or like coal or charcoal.

carbonate /'kɑːbə,neɪt/ *–n. Chem.* salt of carbonic acid. *–v.* (**-ting**) fill with carbon dioxide. [French: related to CARBON]

carbon copy *n.* **1** copy made with carbon paper. **2** exact copy.

carbon dating *n.* determination of the age of an organic object from the ratio of isotopes, which changes as carbon-14 decays.

carbon dioxide *n.* gas occurring naturally in the atmosphere and formed by respiration.

carbon fibre *n.* thin strong crystalline filament of carbon used as a strengthening material.

carbon-14 *n.* radioisotope of mass 14, used in carbon dating.

carbonic /kɑː'bɒnɪk/ *adj.* containing carbon.

carbonic acid *n.* weak acid formed from carbon dioxide in water.

carboniferous /,kɑːbə'nɪfərəs/ *–adj.* **1** producing coal. **2** (**Carboniferous**) of the fifth period in the Palaeozoic era, with extensive formation of coal. *–n.* (**Carboniferous**) this period.

carbonize /'kɑːbə,naɪz/ *v.* (also **-ise**) (**-zing** or **-sing**) **1** convert into carbon. **2** reduce to charcoal or coke. **3** coat with carbon. □ **carbonization** /-'zeɪʃ(ə)n/ *n.*

carbon monoxide *n.* toxic gas formed by the incomplete burning of carbon.

carbon paper *n.* thin carbon-coated paper used for making copies.

carbon tetrachloride *n.* colourless liquid used as a solvent.

carbon-12 *n.* stable isotope of carbon, used as a standard.

car-boot sale *n.* sale of goods from (tables stocked from) the boots of cars.

carborundum /ˌkɑːbəˈrʌndəm/ *n.* compound of carbon and silicon used esp. as an abrasive. [from CARBON, CORUNDUM]

carboy /ˈkɑːbɔɪ/ *n.* large globular glass bottle usu. in a frame. [Persian]

carbuncle /ˈkɑːbʌŋk(ə)l/ *n.* **1** severe skin abscess. **2** bright-red gem. [Latin: related to CARBON]

carburettor /ˌkɑːbəˈretə(r)/ *n.* (*US* **carburetor**) apparatus in an internal-combustion engine for mixing petrol and air to make an explosive mixture.

carcass /ˈkɑːkəs/ *n.* (also **carcase**) **1** dead body of an animal, esp. as meat. **2** bones of a cooked bird. **3** *colloq.* human body; corpse. **4** framework. **5** worthless remains. [French]

Carcassonne /ˌkɑːkəˈsɒn/ historic city in SW France, centre of a wine-growing region; pop. (1990) 44 990.

carcinogen /kɑːˈsɪnədʒ(ə)n/ *n.* substance producing cancer. □ **carcinogenic** /-ˈdʒenɪk/ *adj.* [related to CARCINOMA]

carcinoma /ˌkɑːsɪˈnəʊmə/ *n.* (*pl.* **-s** or **-mata**) cancerous tumour. [Greek *karkinos* crab]

card[1] *n.* **1** thick stiff paper or thin pasteboard. **2 a** piece of this for writing or printing on, esp. to send greetings, to identify a person, or to record information. **b** small rectangular piece of plastic used for identity etc. **3 a** = PLAYING-CARD. **b** (in *pl.*) card-playing. **4** (in *pl.*) *colloq.* tax and national insurance documents etc., held by an employer. **5** programme of events at a race-meeting etc. **6** *colloq.* odd or amusing person. □ **card up one's sleeve** plan or secret weapon in reserve. **get one's cards** *colloq.* be dismissed from one's employment. **on the cards** possible or likely. **put** (or **lay**) **one's cards on the table** reveal one's resources, intentions, etc. [Greek *khartēs* papyrus-leaf]

card[2] *–n.* wire brush etc. for raising a nap on cloth etc. *–v.* brush or comb with a card. [Latin *caro* card (v.)]

cardamom /ˈkɑːdəməm/ *n.* seeds of an aromatic SE Asian plant used as a spice. [Latin from Greek]

cardboard *n.* pasteboard or stiff paper, esp. for making boxes.

cardboard city *n.* area where homeless people make shelters from cardboard boxes etc.

card-carrying *adj.* registered as a member (esp. of a political party or trade union).

card-game *n.* game using playing-cards.

cardiac /ˈkɑːdɪˌæk/ *adj.* of the heart. [Greek *kardia* heart]

Cardiff /ˈkɑːdɪf/ capital of Wales; pop. (est. 1994) 300 000. Once an important industrial port, Cardiff now relies heavily on the service industries to provide employment.

cardigan /ˈkɑːdɪgən/ *n.* knitted jacket. [Earl of *Cardigan*]

cardinal /ˈkɑːdɪn(ə)l/ *–adj.* **1** chief, fundamental. **2** deep scarlet. *–n.* **1** (as a title **Cardinal**) leading Roman Catholic dignitary, one of the college electing the Pope. **2** small scarlet American songbird. [Latin *cardo -din-* hinge]

cardinal number *n.* number denoting quantity (1, 2, 3, etc.), as opposed to an ordinal number.

cardinal points *n.pl.* four main points of the compass (N, S, E, W).

cardinal virtues *n.pl.* justice, prudence, temperance, and fortitude.

card index *n.* index with a card for each entry.

cardiogram /ˈkɑːdɪəʊˌgræm/ *n.* record of heart movements. [Greek *kardia* heart]

cardiograph /ˈkɑːdɪəʊˌgrɑːf/ *n.* instrument recording heart movements. □ **cardiographer** /-ˈɒgrəfə(r)/ *n.* **cardiography** /-ˈɒgrəfɪ/ *n.*

cardiology /ˌkɑːdɪˈɒlədʒɪ/ *n.* branch of medicine concerned with the heart. □ **cardiologist** *n.*

cardiovascular /ˌkɑːdɪəʊˈvæskjʊlə(r)/ *adj.* of the heart and blood-vessels.

cardoon /kɑːˈduːn/ *n.* thistle-like plant with leaves used as a vegetable. [French from Latin]

cardphone *n.* public telephone operated by a machine-readable card instead of money.

card reader *n.* device that reads data encoded on cards and converts it into binary code for processing by a computer. The data is represented by magnetic patterns in, say, a magnetic stripe on a plastic card or by patterns of holes in a punched card.

card-sharp *n.* (also **card-sharper**) swindler at card-games.

card-table *n.* (esp. folding) table for card-playing.

card vote *n.* = BLOCK VOTE.

CARE /keə/ *abbr.* **1** computer-aided risk evaluation. **2** Cottage and Rural Enterprises.

care *–n.* **1** worry, anxiety. **2** cause of this. **3** serious attention; caution. **4 a** protection, looking after, charge. **b** = CHILD CARE. **5** thing to be done or seen to. *–v.* (**-ring**) **1** (usu. foll. by *about*, *for*, *whether*) feel concern or interest. **2** (usu. foll. by *for*) like, be fond of (*don't care for jazz*). **3** (foll. by *to* + infin.) wish or be willing (*would you care to try?*). □ **care for** provide for; look after. **care of** at the address of. **in care** (of a child) in local authority care. **not care a damn** etc. = *not give a damn* etc. (see GIVE). **take care 1** be careful. **2** (foll. by *to* + infin.) not fail or neglect. **take care of 1** look after. **2** deal with, dispose of. [Old English, = sorrow]

◆ **care and maintenance** *n.* (also **c. & m.**) (*attrib.*) denoting the status of a building, machinery, ship, etc. that is not currently in active use, usu. as a result of a fall in demand, but which is being kept in a good state of repair so that it can be brought back into use quickly, if needed.

---

careen /kəˈriːn/ *v.* **1** turn (a ship) on one side for repair etc. **2** tilt, lean over. **3** swerve about. [Latin *carina* keel]

■ **Usage** Sense 3 of *careen* is influenced by the verb *career*.

career /kəˈrɪə(r)/ *–n.* **1** one's professional etc. progress through life. **2** profession or occupation, esp. as offering advancement. **3** (*attrib.*) **a** pursuing or wishing to pursue a career (*career woman*). **b** working permanently in a specified profession (*career diplomat*). **4** swift course (*in full career*). *–v.* **1** move or swerve about wildly. **2** go swiftly. [Latin: related to CAR]

careerist *n.* person predominantly concerned with personal advancement.

carefree *adj.* light-hearted; joyous.

careful *adj.* **1** painstaking, thorough. **2** cautious. **3** taking care; not neglecting (*careful to remind them*). □ **carefully** *adv.* **carefulness** *n.*

careless *adj.* **1** lacking care or attention. **2** unthinking, insensitive. **3** light-hearted. **4** (foll. by *of*) not concerned about. □ **carelessly** *adv.* **carelessness** *n.*

carer *n.* person who cares for a sick or elderly person, esp. a relative at home.

caress /kəˈres/ *–v.* touch or stroke gently or lovingly. *–n.* loving or gentle touch. [Latin *carus* dear]

caret /ˈkærət/ *n.* mark (∧,) indicating a proposed insertion in printing or writing. [Latin, = is lacking]

caretaker *n.* **1** person employed to look after a house, building, etc. **2** (*attrib.*) exercising temporary authority (*caretaker government*).

careworn *adj.* showing the effects of prolonged worry.

cargo /ˈkɑːgəʊ/ *n.* (*pl.* **-es** or **-s**) goods carried on a ship, aircraft, etc. [Spanish: related to CHARGE]

♦ **cargo insurance** *n.* insurance covering cargoes carried by ships, aircraft, or other forms of transport. On an f.o.b. contract the responsibility for insuring the goods for the voyage rests with the buyer. The seller's responsibility ends once the goods have been loaded onto the ship or aircraft (or train in the case of f.o.r. contracts). On a c.i.f. contract, insurance is the responsibility of the seller up to the port of destination. On a c. & f. contract, the seller arranges the shipment and pays the freight but the buyer is responsible for the insurance during the voyage (as in an f.o.b. contract). See F.O.B.; C.I.F.; C. & F. See also AVERAGE *n.* 4; FLOATING POLICY; OPEN COVER.

Carib /'kærɪb/ *–n.* **1** aboriginal inhabitant of the southern West Indies or adjacent coasts. **2** their language. *–adj.* of the Caribs. [Spanish from Haitian]

CARIBANK /'kærɪˌbæŋk/ *abbr.* Caribbean Investment Bank.

Caribbean /ˌkærə'biːən/ *–adj.* of the Caribs, the Caribbean Sea, or the West Indies generally. *–n.* the Caribbean Sea.

♦ **Caribbean Community and Common Market** *n.* (also **CARICOM**) association of Caribbean states established in 1973 to further economic cooperation, coordinate foreign policy among member states, and to provide common services in health, education and culture, communications, and industrial relations. The organs are the Conference of Heads of Government and the Common Market Council of Ministers (usu. trade ministers). The members are Antigua and Barbuda, the Bahamas, Barbados, Belize, Dominica, Grenada, Guyana, Jamaica, Montserrat, St Kitts and Nevis, St Lucia, St Vincent and the Grenadines, Suriname, and Trinidad and Tobago. Its headquarters are in Georgetown, Guyana.

Caribbean Sea part of the Atlantic Ocean lying between the Antilles and the mainland of Central and South America.

caribou /'kærɪˌbuː/ *n.* (*pl.* same) North American reindeer. [French from American Indian]

caricature /'kærɪkətʃʊə(r)/ *–n.* **1** grotesque usu. comically exaggerated representation esp. of a person. **2** ridiculously poor imitation or version. *–v.* (**-ring**) make or give a caricature of. □ **caricaturist** *n.* [Italian *caricare* exaggerate]

CARICOM /'kærɪˌkɒm/ *abbr.* = CARIBBEAN COMMUNITY AND COMMON MARKET.

caries /'keəriːz/ *n.* (*pl.* same) decay of a tooth or bone. [Latin]

carillon /kə'rɪljən/ *n.* **1** set of bells sounded either from a keyboard or mechanically. **2** tune played on bells. [French]

caring *adj.* **1** kind, humane. **2** (*attrib.*) concerned with looking after people (*caring professions*).

Carinthia /kə'rɪnθɪə/ (German **Kärnten** /'keənt(ə)n/) Alpine province of S Austria; pop. (est. 1991) 552 421; capital, Klagenfurt. Farming, forestry, mining, and tourism are the main sources of income.

carioca /ˌkærɪ'əʊkə/ *n.* **1** Brazilian dance like the samba. **2** music for this. [Portuguese]

Carlow /'kɑːləʊ/ **1** agricultural county in the E Republic of Ireland, in the province of Leinster; crops include barley, wheat, and sugar beet; pop. (est. 1991) 40 946. **2** its capital city; pop. (1981) 11 720.

Carlsbad see KARLOVY VARY.

Carmelite /'kɑːməˌlaɪt/ *–n.* **1** friar of the order of Our Lady of Carmel. **2** nun of a similar order. *–adj.* of the Carmelites. [Mt. *Carmel* in Palestine, where the order was founded]

carminative /'kɑːmɪnətɪv/ *–adj.* relieving flatulence. *–n.* carminative drug. [Latin *carmino* heal by CHARM]

carmine /'kɑːmaɪn/ *–adj.* of vivid crimson colour. *–n.* **1** this colour. **2** carmine pigment made from cochineal. [probably from Latin *carmesinum* CRIMSON]

carnage /'kɑːnɪdʒ/ *n.* great slaughter, esp. in battle. [Latin: related to CARNAL]

carnal /'kɑːn(ə)l/ *adj.* **1** of the body or flesh; worldly. **2** sensual, sexual. □ **carnality** /-'nælɪtɪ/ *n.* [Latin *caro carn-* flesh]

carnation /kɑː'neɪʃ(ə)n/ *–n.* **1** clove-scented pink. **2** rosy-pink colour. *–adj.* rosy-pink. [Italian: related to CARNAL because of the flesh-colour]

carnelian var. of CORNELIAN.

carnet /'kɑːneɪ/ *n.* permit to drive across a frontier, use a camp-site, etc. [French, = notebook]

carnival /'kɑːnɪv(ə)l/ *n.* **1 a** annual festivities including a parade through the streets in fancy dress. **b** festival preceding Lent. **2** merrymaking. **3** *US* funfair or circus. [Latin *carnem levo* put away meat]

carnivore /'kɑːnɪˌvɔː(r)/ *n.* carnivorous animal or plant, esp. a mammal of the order including cats, dogs, and bears.

carnivorous /kɑː'nɪvərəs/ *adj.* (of an animal or plant) feeding on flesh. [Latin: related to CARNAL, *voro* devour]

carob /'kærəb/ *n.* seed pod of a Mediterranean tree used as a chocolate substitute. [Arabic *ḳarrūba*]

carol /'kær(ə)l/ *–n.* joyous song, esp. a Christmas hymn. *–v.* (**-ll-**; *US* **-l-**) **1** sing carols. **2** sing joyfully. [French]

Caroline Islands /'kærəˌlaɪn/ (also **Carolines**) group of islands in the W Pacific Ocean, forming (with the exception of Palau and some smaller islands) the Federated States of Micronesia.

Carolingian /ˌkærə'lɪndʒɪən/ *–adj.* of the Frankish dynasty founded by Charlemagne. *–n.* member of this dynasty. [Latin *Carolus* Charles]

carotene /'kærəˌtiːn/ *n.* orange-coloured pigment found in carrots, tomatoes, etc., acting as a source of vitamin A. [Latin: related to CARROT]

carotid /kə'rɒtɪd/ *–n.* each of the two main arteries carrying blood to the head and neck. *–adj.* of these arteries. [Latin from Greek]

carouse /kə'raʊz/ *–v.* (**-sing**) have a lively drinking-party. *–n.* such a party. □ **carousal** *n.* **carouser** *n.* [German *gar aus* (drink) right out]

carousel /ˌkærə'sel/ *n.* **1** *US* merry-go-round. **2** rotating luggage delivery system at an airport etc. [French from Italian]

carp[1] *n.* (*pl.* same) freshwater fish often bred for food. [Provençal or Latin]

carp[2] *v.* find fault; complain pettily. □ **carper** *n.* [Old Norse, = brag]

carpal /'kɑːp(ə)l/ *–adj.* of the bones in the wrist. *–n.* wrist-bone. [from CARPUS]

car park *n.* area for parking cars.

carpel /'kɑːp(ə)l/ *n.* female reproductive organ of a flower. [Greek *karpos* fruit]

carpenter /'kɑːpɪntə(r)/ *–n.* person skilled in woodwork. *–v.* **1** make or construct in wood. **2** construct; fit together. □ **carpentry** *n.* [Latin *carpentum* wagon]

carpet /'kɑːpɪt/ *–n.* **1 a** thick fabric for covering floor or stairs. **b** piece of this. **2** thing resembling this etc. (*carpet of snow*). *–v.* (**-t-**) **1** cover with or as with carpet. **2** *colloq.* reprimand. □ **on the carpet** *colloq.* **1** being reprimanded. **2** under consideration. **sweep under the carpet** conceal (a problem or difficulty). [Latin *carpo* pluck]

carpet-bag *n.* travelling-bag, orig. made of carpet-like material.

carpet-bagger *n. colloq.* **1** esp. *US* political candidate etc. without local connections. **2** unscrupulous opportunist.

carpeting *n.* **1** material for carpets. **2** carpets collectively.

carpet slipper *n.* soft slipper.

carpet-sweeper *n.* household implement for sweeping carpets.

car phone *n.* (also **car telephone**) radio-telephone for use in a car etc. See CELLULAR NETWORK.

carport *n.* roofed open-sided shelter for a car.

carpus /'kɑːpəs/ *n.* (*pl.* **-pi** /-paɪ/) small bones forming the wrist in humans and similar parts in other mammals. [Latin from Greek]

carrageen /'kærə,giːn/ *n.* (also **carragheen**) edible red seaweed. [origin uncertain]

Carrara /kə'rɑːrə/ town in NW Italy, in Tuscany, famous for its white marble; pop. (est. 1987) 69 230.

carrel /'kær(ə)l/ *n.* small cubicle for a reader in a library. [French from medieval Latin]

carr. fwd. *abbr.* carriage forward. See CARRIAGE COST.

carriage /'kærɪdʒ/ *n.* **1** railway passenger vehicle. **2** wheeled horse-drawn passenger vehicle. **3 a** conveying of goods. **b** cost of this. See CARRIAGE COST. **4** carrying part of a machine (e.g. a typewriter). **5** gun-carriage. **6** bearing, deportment. [French: related to CARRY]

carriage clock *n.* portable clock with a handle.

◆ **carriage cost** *n.* cost of delivering goods within the UK. **Carriage forward** means that the cost of delivery has to be paid by the buyer. **Carriage paid** or **carriage free** means that it is paid by the seller.

---

carriageway *n.* the part of a road intended for vehicles.

carrier /'kærɪə(r)/ *n.* **1** person or thing that carries. **2** person or firm that carries goods or people from place to place, usu. under a contract and for a fee. A **common carrier**, who has to have an A licence in the UK, provides a public service and must carry any goods or people on the carrier's regular routes, must charge a reasonable rate, and is liable for all loss or damage to goods in transit. A **limited carrier**, who requires a B licence, carries only certain types of goods (e.g. liquid chemicals in tankers) and may refuse to carry anything else. A **private carrier**, with a C licence, carries only his or her own goods. **3** = CARRIER BAG. **4** framework on a bicycle for luggage or a passenger. **5** person or animal that may transmit disease etc. without suffering from it. **6** = AIRCRAFT-CARRIER.

carrier bag *n.* plastic or paper bag with handles.

carrier pigeon *n.* pigeon trained to carry messages.

carrier wave *n.* high-frequency electromagnetic wave modulated in amplitude or frequency to convey a signal.

carrion /'kærɪən/ *n.* **1** dead putrefying flesh. **2** something vile or filthy. [Latin *caro* flesh]

carrion crow *n.* crow feeding on carrion.

carrot /'kærət/ *n.* **1 a** plant with a tapering orange-coloured root. **b** this as a vegetable. **2** incentive. □ **carroty** *adj.* [Greek *karōton*]

carry /'kærɪ/ *–v.* (**-ies, -ied**) **1** support or hold up, esp. while moving. **2** convey with one or have on one's person. **3** conduct or transmit (*pipe carries water*). **4** (often foll. by *to*) take (a process etc.) to a specified point; continue; prolong (*carry into effect*; *carry a joke too far*). **5** involve, imply (*carries 6% interest*). **6** *Math.* transfer (a figure) to a column of higher value. **7** hold in a specified way (*carry oneself erect*). **8 a** (of a newspaper etc.) publish. **b** (of a radio or television station) broadcast. **9** keep a regular stock of. **10 a** (of sound) be audible at a distance. **b** (of a missile or gun etc.) travel or propel to a specified distance. **11 a** win victory or acceptance for (a proposal etc.). **b** win acceptance from (*carried the audience with her*). **c** win, capture (a prize, fortress, etc.). **12 a** endure the weight of; support. **b** be the driving force in (*you carry the department*). **13** be pregnant with. *–n.* (*pl.* **-ies**) **1** act of carrying. **2** *Golf* distance a ball travels before reaching the ground. □ **carry away 1** remove. **2** inspire. **3** deprive of self-control (*got carried away*). **carry the can** *colloq.* bear the responsibility or blame. **carry the day** be victorious or successful. **carry forward** transfer to a new page or account. **carry it off** do well under difficulties. **carry off 1** take away, esp. by force. **2** win (a prize). **3** (esp. of a disease) kill. **carry on 1** continue. **2** engage in (conversation or business). **3** *colloq.* behave strangely or excitedly. **4** (often foll. by *with*) *colloq.* flirt or have a love affair. **carry out** put (an idea etc.) into practice. **carry over 1** = *carry forward*. **2** postpone. See also CARRY-OVER 1. **carry through 1** complete successfully. **2** bring safely out of difficulties. **carry weight** be influential or important. [Anglo-French: related to CAR]

carry-cot *n.* portable cot for a baby.

carryings-on *n.pl.* = CARRY-ON.

carry-on *n. slang* **1** fuss, excitement. **2** questionable behaviour. **3** flirtation or love affair.

carry-out *attrib. adj.* & *n.* esp. *Scot.* & *US* = TAKE-AWAY.

◆ **carry-over** *n.* **1** quantity of a commodity that is carried over from one crop to the following one. The price of some commodities, e.g. grain, coffee, cocoa, and jute, which grow in annual or biannual crops, is determined by the supply and the demand. The supply consists of the quantity produced by the current crop added to the quantity in the hands of producers and traders that is carried over from the previous crop. Thus, in some circumstances the carry-over can strongly influence the market price. **2** see CONTANGO.

---

carsick *adj.* nauseous from car travel. □ **carsickness** *n.*

Carson City /'kɑːs(ə)n/ city in the US, capital of Nevada; gambling is the main industry; pop. (est. 1995) 46 770.

cart *–n.* **1** open usu. horse-drawn vehicle for carrying loads. **2** light vehicle for pulling by hand. *–v.* **1** convey in a cart. **2** *slang* carry or convey with effort. □ **put the cart before the horse** reverse the proper order or procedure. [Old English and Old Norse]

Cartagena /,kɑːtə'dʒiːnə, -'xenə/ **1** port and naval base in SW Spain, on the Mediterranean Sea; pop. (est. 1994) 179 659. **2** port, resort, and oil-refining centre in NW Colombia, on the Caribbean Sea; pop. (est. 1995) 745 689.

◆ **car tax** *n.* excise duty levied on motor cars at the wholesale stage. It applies to both home-produced and imported cars and is additional to VAT.

---

carte blanche /kɑːt 'blɑ̃ʃ/ *n.* full discretionary power. [French, = blank paper]

◆ **cartel** /kɑː'tel/ *n.* association of independent companies formed to regulate the price and sales conditions of the products or services they offer. A cartel may be national or international, although some countries, including the UK and the US, have legislation forbidding cartels to be formed on the grounds that they are monopolies that function against the public interest. The International Air Transport Association is an example of an international price-fixing cartel that is regarded as acceptable because of fears that price-cutting of fares between airlines would jeopardize safety. [Italian diminutive: related to CARD[1]]

◆ **car telephone** *n.* = CAR PHONE. See CELLULAR NETWORK.

Cartesian /kɑː'tiːzɪən/ *–adj.* of Descartes or his philosophy. *–n.* follower of Descartes. [Latin *Cartesius* Descartes]

Cartesian coordinates *n.pl.* system for locating a point by reference to its distance from axes intersecting at right angles.

cart-horse *n.* thickset horse.

Carthusian /kɑː'θjuːzɪən/ *–n.* monk of a contemplative order founded by St Bruno. *–adj.* of this order. [Latin: related to CHARTREUSE]

cartilage /'kɑːtɪlɪdʒ/ *n.* firm flexible connective tissue, mainly replaced by bone in adulthood. □ **cartilaginous** /-'lædʒɪnəs/ *adj.* [French from Latin]

cartography /kɑː'tɒgrəfɪ/ *n.* map-drawing. □ **cartographer** *n.* **cartographic** /-tə'græfɪk/ *adj.* [French *carte* map]

carton /'kɑːt(ə)n/ *n.* light esp. cardboard box or container. [French: related to CARTOON]

cartoon /kɑː'tuːn/ *n.* **1** humorous, esp. topical, drawing in a newspaper etc. **2** sequence of drawings telling a story. **3** animated sequence of these on film. **4** full-size preliminary design for a tapestry etc. □ **cartoonist** *n.* [Italian: related to CARD[1]]

cartouche /kɑː'tuːʃ/ *n.* **1** scroll-like ornamentation. **2** oval ring enclosing the name and title of a pharaoh. [French: related to CARTOON]

cartridge /'kɑːtrɪdʒ/ *n.* **1** case containing an explosive charge or bullet for firearms or blasting. **2** sealed container of film, magnetic tape, electronic circuitry, etc. **3** component carrying the stylus on a record-player. **4** ink-container for insertion in a pen. [French: related to CARTOON]

cartridge-belt *n.* belt with pockets or loops for cartridges.

cartridge paper *n.* thick paper for drawing etc.

cartwheel *n.* **1** wheel of a cart. **2** circular sideways handspring with arms and legs extended.

cart-wright *n.* maker of carts.

carve *v.* (**-ving**) **1** produce or shape by cutting. **2 a** cut patterns etc. in. **b** (foll. by *into*) form a pattern etc. from (*carved it into a bust*). **3** (*absol.*) cut (meat etc.) into slices. □ **carve out 1** take from a larger whole. **2** establish (a career etc.) purposefully. **carve up 1** subdivide. **2** drive aggressively into the path of (another vehicle). [Old English]

carvel var. of CARAVEL.

carvel-built *adj.* (of a boat) made with planks flush, not overlapping.

carver *n.* **1** person who carves. **2** carving knife. **3** chair with arms, for a person carving.

carvery *n.* (*pl.* **-ies**) buffet or restaurant with joints displayed for carving.

carve-up *n. slang* sharing-out, esp. of spoils.

carving *n.* carved object, esp. as a work of art.

carving knife *n.* knife for carving meat.

CA(SA) *abbr.* Chartered Accountant (South Africa).

Casablanca /ˌkæsəˈblæŋkə/ largest city in Morocco, a seaport and trading centre on the Atlantic coast; industries include textiles, electronics, food processing, and tourism; pop. (est. 1993) 2 943 000.

Casanova /ˌkæsəˈnəʊvə/ *n.* notorious womanizer. [Italian adventurer]

cascade /kæsˈkeɪd/ *–n.* **1** small waterfall, esp. one of series. **2** thing falling or arranged like a cascade. *–v.* (**-ding**) fall in or like a cascade. [Latin: related to CASE[1]]

Cascais /kæʃˈkaɪʃ/ fishing-port and resort on the Atlantic coast of central Portugal, W of Lisbon; pop. (1981) 12 500.

cascara /kæsˈkɑːrə/ *n.* bark of a Californian buckthorn, used as a laxative. [Spanish]

CASE /keɪs/ *abbr.* computer-aided (or -assisted) software (or system) engineering.

case[1] *n.* **1** instance of something occurring. **2** hypothetical or actual situation. **3 a** person's illness, circumstances, etc., as regarded by a doctor, social worker, etc. **b** such a person. **4** matter under esp. police investigation. **5** suit at law. **6 a** sum of the arguments on one side, esp. in a lawsuit. **b** set of arguments (*have a good case*). **c** valid set of arguments (*have no case*). **7** *Gram.* **a** relation of a word to other words in a sentence. **b** form of a noun, adjective, or pronoun expressing this. **8** *colloq.* comical person. □ **in any case** whatever the truth is; whatever may happen. **in case 1** in the event that; if. **2** lest; in provision against a possibility (*took it in case*). **in case of** in the event of. **is** (or **is not) the case** is (or is not) so. [Latin *casus* from *cado* fall]

case[2] *–n.* **1** container or enclosing covering. **2** this with its contents. **3** protective outer covering. **4** item of luggage, esp. a suitcase. *–v.* (**-sing**) **1** enclose in a case. **2** (foll. by *with*) surround. **3** *slang* reconnoitre (a house etc.) before burgling it. [Latin *capsa* box]

case-harden *v.* **1** harden the surface of (esp. iron by carbonizing). **2** make callous.

case history *n.* record of a person's life or medical history for use in professional treatment.

casein /ˈkeɪsiːn/ *n.* the main protein in milk and cheese. [Latin *caseus* cheese]

case-law *n.* law as established by the outcome of former cases.

casemate /ˈkeɪsmeɪt/ *n.* **1** embrasured room in a fortress wall. **2** armoured enclosure for guns on a warship. [French and Italian]

casement /ˈkeɪsmənt/ *n.* window or part of a window hinged to open like a door. [Anglo-Latin: related to CASE[2]]

◆ **case of need** *n.* endorsement written on a bill of exchange giving the name of someone to whom the holder may apply if the bill is not honoured at maturity.

---

case statement *n. Computing* conditional control structure that appears in many programming languages and allows a selection to be made between several choices; the choice is dependent on the value of some expression. A case statement could be used in selecting, say, a month in the year or one age group out of six age groups. It is often employed in programming menus.

casework *n.* social work concerned with studying a person's family and background. □ **caseworker** *n.*

cash *–n.* **1** money in coins or notes, readily acceptable for the settlement of debts. See also LEGAL TENDER. **2** (also **cash down**) full payment at the time of purchase. **3** *colloq.* wealth. *–v.* give or obtain cash for (a note, cheque, etc.). □ **cash in 1** obtain cash for. **2** *colloq.* (usu. foll. by *on*) profit (from); take advantage (of). **cash up** count and check the day's takings. [Latin: related to CASE[2]]

◆ **cash against documents** *n.* (also **CAD, c.a.d.**) means of obtaining payment for exported goods in which the shipping documents are sent to a bank, agent, etc. in the country to which the goods are being shipped, and the buyer then obtains the documents by paying the invoice amount in cash to the bank, agent, etc. Having the shipping documents enables the buyer to take possession of the goods when they arrive at their port of destination; this is known as **documents against presentation**. Cf. DOCUMENTS AGAINST ACCEPTANCE.

◆ **cash and carry** *n.* **1 a** wholesaler, esp. of groceries, who sells to retailers and others with businesses at discounted prices on condition that they pay in cash, collect the goods themselves, and buy in bulk. **b** payment system operated by such a wholesaler. **2** operation that is sometimes possible on the futures market, esp. in the London Metal Exchange. In some circumstances the spot price of a metal, including the cost of insurance, warehousing, and interest for three months, is less than the futures-market price for delivery in three months. Under these conditions it is possible to buy the spot metal, simultaneously sell the forward goods, and make a profit in excess of the yield the capital would have earned on the money market.

◆ **cash-book** *n.* book of prime entry in which are recorded receipts into and payments out of an organization's bank account (cf. PETTY CASH). The cash-book, unlike most other books of prime entry, is also an account, as its balance shows the amount due to or from the bank.

◆ **cash budget** see CASH FLOW.

---

cashcard *n.* embossed plastic card for withdrawing money from an automated teller machine in conjunction with a personal identification number. See also MULTI-FUNCTION CARD 1.

◆ **cash cow** *n.* product, with a well-known brand name, that commands a high market share in old-established markets and therefore produces a steady flow of cash.

---

cash crop *n.* crop produced for sale.

◆ **cash deal** *n.* transaction (either buying or selling) on the London Stock Exchange in which settlement is made immediately, i.e. usu. on the following day.

---

cash desk *n.* counter etc. where payment is made in a shop.

◆ **cash discount** *n.* **1** reduction in the price of goods offered by a seller to a buyer who pays promptly (usu. within seven days). **2** reduction in the price of goods bought from a wholesaler and paid for in cash.

---

cash dispenser *n. colloq.* automated teller machine.

cashew /ˈkæʃuː/ *n.* **1** evergreen tree bearing kidney-shaped nuts. **2** this edible nut. [Portuguese from Tupi]

♦ **cash flow** *n.* movement of money into and out of a business. The amount of cash is often analysed into its various components. A **cash-flow projection** (or **cash budget**) sets out all the expected payments and receipts in a given period. This is different from the projected profit and loss account and, in times of cash shortage, may be more important. It is on the basis of the cash-flow projection that managers arrange for employees and creditors to be paid at appropriate times. See also DISCOUNTED CASH FLOW.

cashier[1] /kæ'ʃɪə(r)/ *n.* person dealing with cash transactions in a shop, bank, etc.

cashier[2] /kæ'ʃɪə(r)/ *v.* dismiss from service, esp. with disgrace. [French: related to QUASH]

♦ **cash management account** *n.* bank account in which deposits are invested by the bank, usu. on the money market; it is, however, a cheque account and the client is able to obtain loans if required.

cashmere /'kæʃmɪə(r)/ *n.* **1** fine soft wool, esp. that of a Kashmir goat. **2** material made from this. [KASHMIR]

cash on delivery *n.* (also **COD**; *US* **collect on delivery**) payment for goods when they are delivered, the customer paying the deliverer the full invoice amount. It was extensively used in mail order but the use of telephone ordering using credit cards has reduced the amount of COD business.

cashpoint *n. colloq.* automated teller machine.

♦ **cash price** *n.* price at which a seller is prepared to sell goods provided there is immediate payment in cash, i.e. the seller does not have to give credit or give a commission to a credit-card company. This is invariably below the price that includes a hire-purchase agreement.

♦ **cash ratio** *n.* (also **liquidity ratio**) ratio of the cash reserve that a bank keeps in coin, banknotes, etc. to its total liabilities to its customers, i.e. the amount deposited with it in current accounts and deposit accounts. Because cash reserves earn no interest, bankers try to keep them to a minimum, consistent with being able to meet customers' demands. The usual figure for the cash ratio is 8%.

cash register *n.* till recording sales, totalling receipts, etc.

♦ **cash settlements** *n.pl.* (also **cash deals**) deals on the London Stock Exchange in which gilt-edged securities or new issues are bought by investors. These have to be paid for immediately (normally by the next business day) rather than on the next account day.

casing /'keɪsɪŋ/ *n.* protective or enclosing cover or material.

casino /kə'siːnəʊ/ *n.* (*pl.* **-s**) public room or building for gambling. [Italian diminutive of *casa* house]

cask /kɑːsk/ *n.* **1** barrel, esp. for alcohol. **2** its contents. [French *casque* or Spanish *casco* helmet]

casket /'kɑːskɪt/ *n.* **1** small often ornamental box for jewels etc. **2** *US* coffin. [Latin: related to CASE[2]]

Caspian Sea /'kæspɪən/ landlocked salt lake, the world's largest body of inland water, bounded by Iran, Russia, Azerbaijan, Kazakhstan, and Turkmenistan.

cassata /kə'sɑːtə/ *n.* ice-cream containing fruit and nuts. [Italian]

cassava /kə'sɑːvə/ *n.* **1** plant with starchy roots. **2** starch or flour from these, used e.g. in tapioca. [Taino]

casserole /'kæsəˌrəʊl/ *–n.* **1** covered dish for cooking food in the oven. **2** food cooked in this. *–v.* (**-ling**) cook in a casserole. [Greek *kuathion* little cup]

cassette /kə'set/ *n.* sealed case containing magnetic tape, film, etc., ready for insertion in a tape recorder, camera, computer, etc. [French diminutive: related to CASE[2]]

cassia /'kæsɪə/ *n.* **1** tree from the leaves of which senna is extracted. **2** cinnamon-like bark of this used as a spice. [Greek *kasia* from Hebrew]

cassis /kæ'siːs/ *n.* blackcurrant flavouring for drinks etc. [French]

cassock /'kæsək/ *n.* long usu. black or red clerical garment. □ **cassocked** *adj.* [French from Italian]

cassoulet /'kæsʊˌleɪ/ *n.* ragout of meat and beans. [French]

cassowary /'kæsəˌweərɪ/ *n.* (*pl.* **-ies**) large flightless Australasian bird. [Malay]

cast /kɑːst/ *–v.* (*past* and *past part.* **cast**) **1** throw, esp. deliberately or forcefully. **2** (often foll. by *on, over*) **a** direct or cause (one's eyes, a glance, light, a shadow, a spell, etc.) to fall. **b** express (doubts, aspersions, etc.). **3** throw out (a fishing-line etc.) into the water. **4** let down (an anchor etc.). **5 a** throw off, get rid of. **b** shed or lose (horns, skin, a horseshoe, etc.). **6** register (a vote). **7 a** shape (molten metal etc.) in a mould. **b** make thus. **8 a** (usu. foll. by *as*) assign (an actor) to a role. **b** allocate roles in (a play etc.). **9** (foll. by *in, into*) arrange (facts etc.) in a specified form. **10** reckon, add up (accounts or figures). **11** calculate (a horoscope). *–n.* **1** throwing of a missile, dice, line, net, etc. **2 a** object made in a mould. **b** moulded mass of solidified material, esp. plaster for a broken limb. **3** actors in a play etc. **4** form, type, or quality. **5** tinge or shade of colour. **6** slight squint. **7** worm-cast. □ **cast about** (or **around**) search. **cast adrift** leave to drift. **cast aside** abandon. **cast loose** detach (oneself). **cast lots** see LOT. **cast off 1** abandon. **2** finish a piece of knitting. **3** set a ship free from a quay etc. **cast on** make the first row of a piece of knitting. **cast up 1** deposit on the shore. **2** add up (figures etc.). [Old Norse]

castanet /ˌkæstə'net/ *n.* (usu. in *pl.*) each of a pair of hand-held pieces of wood etc., clicked together as an accompaniment, esp. by Spanish dancers. [Latin: related to CHESTNUT]

castaway /'kɑːstəˌweɪ/ *–n.* shipwrecked person. *–adj.* shipwrecked.

caste /kɑːst/ *n.* **1** any of the Hindu hereditary classes whose members have no social contact with other classes. **2** exclusive social class or system of classes. □ **lose caste** descend in social order. [Spanish and Portuguese: related to CHASTE]

casteism /'kɑːstɪz(ə)m/ *n.* caste system.

castellated /'kæstəˌleɪtɪd/ *adj.* **1** having battlements. **2** castle-like. □ **castellation** /-'leɪʃ(ə)n/ *n.* [medieval Latin: related to CASTLE]

caster var. of CASTOR.

castigate /'kæstɪˌgeɪt/ *v.* (**-ting**) rebuke or punish severely. □ **castigation** /-'geɪʃ(ə)n/ *n.* **castigator** *n.* [Latin *castus* pure]

Castile /kæ'stiːl/ central plateau of the Iberian peninsula, a former Spanish kingdom. □ **Castilian** /-'stɪlɪən/ *adj.*

Castilla-La Mancha /kæˌstiːljə lɑː 'mæntʃə/ autonomous province, chiefly agricultural, in central Spain; pop. (1994) 1 656 179; administrative centre, Toledo.

Castilla-León /kæ'stiːləleɪ'ɒn/ autonomous region of N Spain; livestock rearing and arable farming are important; pop. (1994) 2 504 371; capital, Valladolid.

casting /'kɑːstɪŋ/ *n.* cast, esp. of molten metal.

casting vote *n.* second or deciding vote when the votes on two sides are equal. It is common practice to give the chair of a meeting a second vote to be used to resolve a deadlock. In the case of a company meeting, the chair is usu. given this right by the articles of association, but has no common-law right to a casting vote. [from an obsolete sense of *cast*, = turn the scale]

cast iron *n.* hard alloy of iron, carbon, and silicon cast in a mould.

cast-iron *adj.* **1** of cast iron. **2** very strong; rigid; unchallengeable.

castle /'kɑːs(ə)l/ *–n.* **1** large fortified building with towers and battlements. **2** *Chess* = ROOK[2]. *–v.* (**-ling**) *Chess* move a rook next to the king and the king to the other side of the rook. □ **castles in the air** day-dream; impractical scheme. [Latin *castellum*]

cast-off *–adj.* abandoned, discarded. *–n.* **1** cast-off thing, esp. a garment. **2** estimate of the number of characters, words, or pages that text for printing contains. If the cast-off is given in pages, this will include any illustrations.

castor /ˈkɑːstə(r)/ *n.* (also **caster**) **1** small swivelled wheel on the leg or underside of a piece of furniture. **2** small perforated container for sprinkling sugar, flour, etc. [from CAST]

castor oil /ˈkɑːstə(r)/ *n.* oil from the seeds of a tropical plant, used as a purgative and lubricant. [origin uncertain]

castor sugar *n.* finely granulated white sugar.

castrate /kæˈstreɪt/ *v.* (**-ting**) **1** remove the testicles of; geld. **2** deprive of vigour. □ **castration** *n.* [Latin *castro*]

castrato /kæˈstrɑːtəʊ/ *n.* (*pl.* **-ti** /-tɪ/) *hist.* castrated male soprano or alto singer. [Italian: related to CASTRATE]

Castries /ˈkæstriːs/ capital and main port of St Lucia, in the Windward Islands; textiles, chemicals, and tobacco are produced; pop. (1992) 13 615.

casual /ˈkæʒʊəl/ *–adj.* **1** accidental; chance. **2** not regular or permanent (*casual work*). **3 a** unconcerned. **b** careless; unthinking. **4** (of clothes) informal. *–n.* **1** casual worker. **2** (usu. in *pl.*) casual clothes or shoes. □ **casually** *adv.* **casualness** *n.* [French and Latin: related to CASE[1]]

casualty /ˈkæʒʊəltɪ/ *n.* (*pl.* **-ies**) **1** person killed or injured in a war or accident. **2** thing lost or destroyed. **3** = CASUALTY DEPARTMENT. **4** accident, mishap. [medieval Latin: related to CASUAL]

casualty department *n.* part of a hospital where casualties are dealt with.

casuist /ˈkæʒʊɪst/ *n.* **1** person who uses clever but false reasoning in matters of conscience etc. **2** sophist, quibbler. □ **casuistic** /-ˈɪstɪk/ *adj.* **casuistry** *n.* [Latin: related to CASE[1]]

CAT /kæt/ *abbr.* **1** computer-aided (or assisted) teaching (or training). **2** computer-aided (or assisted) trading. **3** computer-aided (or assisted) typesetting.

cat *n.* **1** small soft-furred four-legged domesticated animal. **2** wild animal of the same family, e.g. lion, tiger. **3** *colloq.* malicious or spiteful woman. **4** = CAT-O'-NINE-TAILS. □ **the cat's whiskers** *colloq.* excellent person or thing. **let the cat out of the bag** reveal a secret. **like a cat on hot bricks** very agitated. **put** (or **set**) **the cat among the pigeons** cause trouble. **rain cats and dogs** rain hard. [Latin *cattus*]

cata- *prefix* **1** down. **2** wrongly. [Greek]

catabolism /kəˈtæbəˌlɪz(ə)m/ *n.* breakdown of complex molecules in living organisms to release energy; destructive metabolism. □ **catabolic** /ˌkætəˈbɒlɪk/ *adj.* [Greek *katabolē* throwing down]

catachresis /ˌkætəˈkriːsɪs/ *n.* (*pl.* **-chreses** /-siːz/) incorrect use of words. □ **catachrestic** /-ˈkriːstɪk/ *adj.* [Greek *khraomai* use]

cataclysm /ˈkætəˌklɪz(ə)m/ *n.* **1 a** violent upheaval or disaster. **b** great change. **2** great flood. □ **cataclysmic** /-ˈklɪzmɪk/ *adj.* [Greek *kluzō* wash]

catacomb /ˈkætəˌkuːm/ *n.* (often in *pl.*) underground cemetery, esp. Roman. [French from Latin]

catafalque /ˈkætəˌfælk/ *n.* decorated bier, used esp. in state funerals or for lying in state. [French from Italian]

Catalan /ˈkætəˌlæn/ *–n.* native or language of Catalonia. *–adj.* of Catalonia. [French from Spanish]

catalepsy /ˈkætəˌlepsɪ/ *n.* trance or seizure with unconsciousness and rigidity of the body. □ **cataleptic** /-ˈleptɪk/ *adj.* & *n.* [Greek *lēpsis* seizure]

catalogue /ˈkætəˌlɒg/ (*US* **catalog**) *–n.* **1** complete alphabetical or otherwise ordered list of items, often with a description of each. **2** extensive list (*catalogue of disasters*). *–v.* (**-logues, -logued, -loguing**; *US* **-logs, -loged, -loging**) **1** make a catalogue of. **2** enter in a catalogue. [Greek *legō* choose]

♦ **catalogue store** *n.* store that combines the techniques of selling by catalogue with those of a discount house. The stores themselves are not designed for customer comfort but by keeping the premises simple they achieve competitive prices.

Catalonia /ˌkætəˈləʊnɪə/ autonomous region of NE Spain; pop. (est. 1994) 6 090 107; capital, Barcelona. It is highly industrialized, producing hydroelectricity; agriculture and tourism are also important.

catalpa /kəˈtælpə/ *n.* tree with long pods and showy flowers. [North American Indian]

catalyse /ˈkætəˌlaɪz/ *v.* (*US* **-yze**) (**-sing** or **-zing**) produce (a reaction) by catalysis.

catalysis /kəˈtælɪsɪs/ *n.* (*pl.* **-lyses** /-ˌsiːz/) acceleration of a chemical reaction by a catalyst. [Greek *luō* set free]

catalyst /ˈkætəlɪst/ *n.* **1** substance that does not itself change, but speeds up a chemical reaction. **2** person or thing that precipitates change.

catalytic /ˌkætəˈlɪtɪk/ *adj.* of or involving catalysis.

catalytic converter *n.* device incorporated in a vehicle's exhaust system, with a catalyst for converting pollutant gases into harmless products.

catamaran /ˌkætəməˈræn/ *n.* **1** boat with parallel twin hulls. **2** raft of yoked logs or boats. [Tamil]

catamite /ˈkætəˌmaɪt/ *n.* passive partner (esp. a boy) in homosexual practices. [Latin, = Ganymede]

cat-and-dog *adj.* (of a relationship etc.) quarrelsome.

Catania /kəˈtɑːnɪə/ seaport in Italy, on the E coast of Sicily; industries include sulphur refining; pop. (est. 1994) 327 163.

catapult /ˈkætəˌpʌlt/ *–n.* **1** forked stick etc. with elastic for shooting stones. **2** *Mil hist.* machine for hurling large stones etc. **3** device for launching a glider etc. *–v.* **1 a** hurl from or launch with a catapult. **b** fling forcibly. **2** leap or be hurled forcibly. [Latin from Greek]

cataract /ˈkætəˌrækt/ *n.* **1 a** large waterfall. **b** downpour; rush of water. **2** eye condition in which the lens becomes progressively opaque. [Greek *katarrhaktēs*, = down-rushing]

catarrh /kəˈtɑː(r)/ *n.* **1** inflammation of the mucous membrane of the nose, air-passages, etc. **2** mucus caused by this. □ **catarrhal** *adj.* [Greek *rheō* flow]

catastrophe /kəˈtæstrəfɪ/ *n.* **1** great and usu. sudden disaster. **2** dénouement of a drama. □ **catastrophic** /-ˈstrɒfɪk/ *adj.* **catastrophically** /-ˈstrɒfɪkəlɪ/ *adv.* [Greek *strephō* turn]

♦ **catastrophe risk** *n.* risk in which the potential loss is of the greatest size, such as the explosion of a nuclear power station or a major earthquake.

---

catatonia /ˌkætəˈtəʊnɪə/ *n.* **1** schizophrenia with intervals of catalepsy and sometimes violence. **2** catalepsy. □ **catatonic** /-ˈtɒnɪk/ *adj.* & *n.* [Greek: related to CATA-, TONE]

cat burglar *n.* burglar who enters by climbing to an upper storey.

catcall *–n.* shrill whistle of disapproval. *–v.* make a catcall.

catch *–v.* (*past* and *past part.* **caught** /kɔːt/) **1** capture in a trap, one's hands, etc. **2** detect or surprise (esp. a guilty person). **3 a** intercept and hold (a moving thing) in the hands etc. **b** *Cricket* dismiss (a batsman) by catching the ball before it reaches the ground. **4 a** contract (a disease) from an infected person. **b** acquire (a quality etc.) from another. **5 a** reach in time and board (a train, bus, etc.). **b** be in time to see etc. (a person or thing about to leave or finish). **6** apprehend with the senses or mind (esp. a thing occurring quickly or briefly). **7** (of an artist etc.) reproduce faithfully. **8 a** (cause to) become fixed, entangled, or checked. **b** (often foll. by *on*) hit, deal a blow to (*caught his elbow on the table*). **9** draw the attention of; captivate (*caught his eye*; *caught her fancy*). **10** begin to burn. **11** reach or overtake (a person etc. ahead). **12** (foll. by *at*) try to grasp. *–n.* **1 a** act of catching. **b** *Cricket* etc. chance or act of catching the ball. **2 a** amount of a thing caught, esp. of fish. **b** thing or person caught or worth catching, esp. in marriage. **3 a** question, trick, etc., intended to deceive, incriminate, etc. **b** unexpected or hidden difficulty or disadvantage. **4** device for fastening a door or window etc. **5** *Mus.* round, esp. with words arranged to produce a humorous effect. □ **catch fire** see FIRE. **catch hold of** grasp, seize. **catch it** *slang* be punished. **catch on** *colloq.* **1** become popular. **2** understand what is meant. **catch out 1** detect in a mistake etc. **2** take unawares. **3** = sense 3b of *v.* **catch up 1 a** (often foll. by *with*) reach a person etc. ahead (*caught us up*; *caught up with us*). **b** (often foll. by *with, on*) make up arrears. **2** pick up hurriedly. **3** (often in *passive*) **a** involve; entangle (*caught up in crime*). **b** fasten up (*hair caught up in a ribbon*). [Latin *capto* try to catch]

catch-all *n.* (often *attrib.*) thing designed to be all-inclusive.

catch-as-catch-can *n.* wrestling with few holds barred.

♦ **catch crop** *n.* quick-growing crop planted on land that is available for a short period, as between main crops, or sometimes planted between the rows of a main crop.

catching *adj.* (of a disease, practice, etc.) infectious.

♦ **catching bargain** *n.* (also **unconscionable bargain**) unfair contract, often one in which one party has been taken advantage of by the other. Such a contract may be set aside or modified by a court.

catchline *n.* short line of type, esp. at the head of copy or as a running headline.

catchment *n.* collection of rainfall.

catchment area *n.* **1** area served by a school, hospital, etc. **2** area from which rainfall flows into a river etc.

catchpenny *attrib. adj.* intended merely to sell quickly; superficially attractive.

catch-phrase *n.* phrase in frequent use.

catch-22 *n.* (often *attrib.*) *colloq.* unresolvable situation containing conflicting or mutually dependent conditions.

catchweight *–adj.* unrestricted as regards weight. *–n.* unrestricted weight category in sports.

catchword *n.* **1** phrase, word, or slogan in frequent current use. **2** word so placed as to draw attention.

catchy *adj.* (**-ier, -iest**) (of a tune) easy to remember, attractive.

cat door var. of CAT FLAP.

catechism /ˈkætɪˌkɪz(ə)m/ *n.* **1 a** principles of a religion in the form of questions and answers. **b** book containing this. **2** series of questions. [Church Latin: related to CATECHIZE]

catechist /ˈkætɪkɪst/ *n.* religious teacher, esp. one using a catechism.

catechize /ˈkætɪˌkaɪz/ *v.* (also **-ise**) (**-zing** or **-sing**) instruct by using a catechism. [Greek *katēkheō* cause to hear]

catechumen /ˌkætɪˈkjuːmən/ *n.* Christian convert under instruction before baptism. [Church Latin *catechumenus*]

categorical /ˌkætɪˈgɒrɪk(ə)l/ *adj.* unconditional, absolute; explicit. □ **categorically** *adv.* [related to CATEGORY]

categorize /ˈkætɪgəˌraɪz/ *v.* (also **-ise**) (**-zing** or **-sing**) place in a category. □ **categorization** /-ˈzeɪʃ(ə)n/ *n.*

category /ˈkætɪgərɪ/ *n.* (*pl.* **-ies**) class or division (of things, ideas, etc.). [Greek, = statement]

cater /ˈkeɪtə(r)/ *v.* **1** supply food. **2** (foll. by *for*) provide what is needed or desired (*caters for all tastes*). **3** (foll. by *to*) pander to (esp. low tastes). [Anglo-French *acatour* buyer, from Latin *capto*: related to CATCH]

caterer *n.* professional supplier of food for social events.

caterpillar /ˈkætəˌpɪlə(r)/ *n.* **1** larva of a butterfly or moth. **2** (**Caterpillar**) **a** (in full **Caterpillar track** or **tread**) *propr.* steel band passing round the wheels of a tractor etc. for travel on rough ground. **b** vehicle with these. [Anglo-French, = hairy cat]

caterwaul /ˈkætəˌwɔːl/ *–v.* make the shrill howl of a cat. *–n.* this noise. [from CAT, *-waul* imitative]

catfish *n.* (*pl.* same) freshwater fish with whisker-like barbels round the mouth.

cat flap *n.* (also **cat door**) small swinging flap in an outer door, for a cat to pass in and out.

catgut *n.* material used for the strings of musical instruments and surgical sutures, made of intestines of the sheep, horse, etc. (but not cat).

catharsis /kəˈθɑːsɪs/ *n.* (*pl.* **catharses** /-siːz/) **1** emotional release in drama or art. **2** *Psychol.* freeing and elimination of repressed emotion. **3** emptying of the bowels. [Greek *katharos* clean]

cathartic /kəˈθɑːtɪk/ *–adj.* **1** effecting catharsis. **2** laxative. *–n.* laxative.

cathedral /kəˈθiːdr(ə)l/ *n.* principal church of a diocese. [Greek *kathedra* seat]

Catherine wheel /ˈkæθrɪn/ *n.* flat coiled firework spinning when lit. [St *Catherine*, who was martyred on a spiked wheel]

catheter /ˈkæθɪtə(r)/ *n.* tube inserted into a body cavity for introducing or removing fluid. [Greek *kathiēmi* send down]

cathode /ˈkæθəʊd/ *n. Electr.* **1** negative electrode in an electrolytic cell. **2** positive terminal of a battery etc. [Greek *kathodos* way down]

cathode ray *n.* beam of electrons from the cathode of a vacuum tube.

cathode-ray tube *n.* (also **CRT**) vacuum tube in which cathode rays produce a luminous image on a fluorescent screen, used esp. in television receivers and computer display devices.

catholic /ˈkæθlɪk/ *–adj.* **1** all-embracing; of wide sympathies or interests. **2** of interest or use to all; universal. **3** (**Catholic**) **a** Roman Catholic. **b** including all Christians, or all of the Western Church. *–n.* (**Catholic**) Roman Catholic. □ **Catholicism** /kəˈθɒlɪˌsɪz(ə)m/ *n.* **catholicity** /ˌkæθəˈlɪsɪtɪ/ *n.* [Greek *holos* whole]

CATI *abbr.* = COMPUTER-ASSISTED TELEPHONE INTERVIEWING.

cation /ˈkætˌaɪən/ *n.* positively charged ion. □ **cationic** /-ˈɒnɪk/ *adj.* [from CATA-, ION]

catkin *n.* small spike of usu. hanging flowers on a willow, hazel, etc. [Dutch, = kitten]

catlick *n. colloq.* perfunctory wash.

catmint *n.* pungent plant attractive to cats.

catnap *–n.* short sleep. *–v.* (**-pp-**) have a catnap.

catnip *n.* = CATMINT. [from CAT, dial. *nip* catmint]

cat-o'-nine-tails *n. hist.* whip with nine knotted lashes.

cat's cradle *n.* child's game of forming patterns from a loop of string.

Cat's-eye *n. propr.* reflector stud set into a road.

cat's-eye *n.* precious stone.

cat's-paw *n.* **1** person used as a tool by another. **2** slight breeze.

catsuit *n.* close-fitting garment with trouser legs, covering the whole body.

catsup *US* var. of KETCHUP.

cattery *n.* (*pl.* **-ies**) place where cats are boarded or bred.

cattle /ˈkæt(ə)l/ *n.pl.* large ruminant animals with horns and cloven hoofs, esp. bred for milk or meat. [Anglo-French *catel*: related to CAPITAL]

cattle-grid *n.* grid over a ditch, allowing people and vehicles but not livestock to pass over.

catty *adj.* (**-ier, -iest**) spiteful. □ **cattily** *adv.* **cattiness** *n.*

CATV *abbr.* cable television.

catwalk *n.* narrow footway or platform.

Caucasian /kɔːˈkeɪʒ(ə)n/ *–adj.* **1** of the White or light-skinned race. **2** of the Caucasus. *–n.* Caucasian person.

Caucasoid /ˈkɔːkəˌsɔɪd/ *adj.* of Caucasians.

Caucasus /ˈkɔːkəsəs/ mountain range in SE Europe and W Asia, between the Black and Caspian Seas.

caucus /ˈkɔːkəs/ *n.* (*pl.* **-es**) **1** *US* meeting of party members, esp. in the Senate etc., to decide policy. **2** often *derog.* **a** meeting of a group within a larger organization or party. **b** such a group. [perhaps from Algonquian]

caudal /'kɔːd(ə)l/ *adj.* **1** of or like a tail. **2** of the posterior part of the body. [Latin *cauda* tail]

caudate /'kɔːdeɪt/ *adj.* tailed.

caught *past* and *past part.* of CATCH.

caul /kɔːl/ *n.* **1** membrane enclosing a foetus. **2** part of this occasionally found on a child's head at birth. [French]

cauldron /'kɔːldrən/ *n.* (also **caldron**) large deep vessel used for boiling. [Latin *caldarium* hot bath]

cauliflower /'kɒlɪˌflaʊə(r)/ *n.* cabbage with a large white flower-head. [French *chou fleuri* flowered cabbage]

cauliflower ear *n.* ear thickened by repeated blows.

caulk /kɔːk/ *v.* (also **calk**) **1** stop up (the seams of a boat etc.). **2** make (esp. a boat) watertight. [Latin *calco* tread]

causal /'kɔːz(ə)l/ *adj.* **1** of or forming a cause. **2** relating to cause and effect. □ **causally** *adv.*

causality /kɔː'zælɪtɪ/ *n.* **1** relation of cause and effect. **2** principle that everything has a cause.

causation /kɔː'zeɪʃ(ə)n/ *n.* **1** act of causing. **2** = CAUSALITY.

causative /'kɔːzətɪv/ *adj.* acting as or expressing a cause.

cause /kɔːz/ *–n.* **1 a** thing that produces an effect. **b** person or thing that occasions or produces something. **c** reason or motive. **2** adequate reason (*show cause*). **3** principle, belief, or purpose. **4 a** matter to be settled at law. **b** case offered at law (*plead a cause*). *–v.* (**-sing**) be the cause of, produce, make happen. [Latin *causa*]

cause célèbre /ˌkɔːz se'lebr/ *n.* (*pl.* ***causes célèbres*** pronunc. same) lawsuit that attracts much interest. [French]

causerie /'kəʊzərɪ/ *n.* (*pl.* **-s** pronunc. same) informal article or talk. [French]

causeway /'kɔːzweɪ/ *n.* **1** raised road across low ground or water. **2** raised path by a road. [Anglo-French *caucée* from Latin CALX]

caustic /'kɔːstɪk/ *–adj.* **1** corrosive; burning. **2** sarcastic, biting. *–n.* caustic substance. □ **caustically** *adv.* **causticity** /-'tɪsɪtɪ/ *n.* [Greek *kaiō* burn]

caustic soda *n.* sodium hydroxide.

cauterize /'kɔːtəˌraɪz/ *v.* (also **-ise**) (**-zing** or **-sing**) burn (tissue), esp. to stop bleeding. [French: related to CAUSTIC]

caution /'kɔːʃ(ə)n/ *–n.* **1** attention to safety; prudence, carefulness. **2 a** *Law* warning, esp. a formal one. **b** warning and reprimand. **3** *colloq.* amusing or surprising person or thing. *–v.* **1** warn or admonish. **2** issue a caution to. [Latin *caveo* take heed]

cautionary *adj.* giving or serving as a warning.

cautious *adj.* having or showing caution. □ **cautiously** *adv.* **cautiousness** *n.*

cavalcade /ˌkævəl'keɪd/ *n.* procession or assembly of riders, vehicles, etc. [Italian: related to CHEVALIER]

cavalier /ˌkævə'lɪə(r)/ *–n.* **1** *hist.* (**Cavalier**) supporter of Charles I in the Civil War. **2** courtly gentleman. **3** *archaic* horseman. *–adj.* offhand, supercilious, curt. [related to CAVALCADE]

cavalry /'kævəlrɪ/ *n.* (*pl.* **-ies**) (usu. treated as *pl.*) soldiers on horseback or in armoured vehicles. [related to CAVALCADE]

Cavan /'kævən/ **1** agricultural county in the NE Republic of Ireland, in the province of Ulster; pop. (est. 1991) 52 756. **2** its capital city; pop. (1981) 3240.

cave *–n.* large hollow in the side of a cliff, hill, etc., or underground. *–v.* (**-ving**) explore caves. □ **cave in 1** (cause to) subside or collapse. **2** yield, give up. [Latin *cavus* hollow]

caveat /'kævɪˌæt/ *n.* **1** proviso or warning that limits liability by putting another party on notice. For example, a retailer may sell goods subject to the caveat that their suitability for a particular purpose is not guaranteed. The purchaser is thereby put on notice that there is no remedy against the retailer should the goods in fact turn out to be unsuitable for that particular purpose. **2** *Law* process in court to suspend proceedings. [Latin, = let him beware]

♦ ***caveat emptor*** /'emptɔː(r)/ *n.* principle that the purchaser of goods must take care to ensure that they are free from defects of quality, fitness, or title, i.e. that the risk is borne by the purchaser and not by the seller. If the goods turn out to be defective, the purchaser has no remedy against the seller. The rule does not apply if the purchaser is unable to examine the goods, if the defects are not evident from a reasonable examination, or if the seller has behaved fraudulently. Some measure of protection for the unwary purchaser is afforded by a number of statutes, including the Unfair Contract Terms Act (1977), the Sale of Goods Act (1979), and the Consumer Protection Act (1987). [Latin, = let the buyer beware]

---

caveman *n.* **1** prehistoric person living in caves. **2** crude person.

cavern /'kæv(ə)n/ *n.* cave, esp. a large or dark one. □ **cavernous** *adj.* [Latin *caverna*: related to CAVE]

♦ **CAVIAR** /'kævɪˌɑː(r)/ *abbr.* Cinema and Video Industry Audience Research.

---

caviare /'kævɪˌɑː(r)/ *n.* (*US* **caviar**) pickled roe of sturgeon or other large fish. [Italian from Turkish]

cavil /'kævɪl/ *–v.* (**-ll-**, *US* **-l-**) (usu. foll. by *at*, *about*) make petty objections; carp. *–n.* trivial objection. [Latin *cavillor*]

cavity /'kævɪtɪ/ *n.* (*pl.* **-ies**) **1** hollow within a solid body. **2** decayed part of a tooth. [Latin: related to CAVE]

cavity wall *n.* double wall with a space between.

cavort /kə'vɔːt/ *v.* caper excitedly. [origin uncertain]

cavy /'keɪvɪ/ *n.* (*pl.* **-ies**) small South American rodent, esp. the guinea pig. [Latin from Galibi]

caw *–n.* harsh cry of a rook, crow, etc. *–v.* utter this cry. [imitative]

Cawnpore see KANPUR.

Cayenne /keɪ'en/ capital and chief port of French Guiana; pop. (1990) 41 600.

cayenne /keɪ'en/ *n.* (in full **cayenne pepper**) powdered red pepper. [Tupi]

cayman /'keɪmən/ *n.* (also **caiman**) (*pl.* **-s**) South American alligator-like reptile. [Spanish and Portuguese from Carib]

Cayman Islands /'keɪmən/ (also **Caymans**) British colony comprising three islands in the Caribbean Sea; pop. (est. 1994) 31 930; capital, George Town. Turtle shell and meat are the main exports but the economy depends on tourism; financial service industries are developing, as the colony is a tax haven.

♦ **Cayzer** /'keɪzə(r)/, **William Nicholas, Baron Cayzer** (1910–) British businessman and financier, president and director (since 1994) of Caledonia Investments plc, of which he was chairman (1958–94), and life president (since 1987) of British and Commonwealth Shipping Co. Ltd., of which he was chairman (1958–87). Lord Cayzer sold the family's holdings in British and Commonwealth in 1987 for about £427 million. The money from this sale has been invested in various companies, including Bristow Helicopters, in which Caledonia now has a 45% holding.

CB *–abbr.* **1** citizens' band. **2** Companion of the Order of the Bath. **3** cost benefit. **4** currency bond. *–postcode* Cambridge. *–airline flight code* Suckling Airways.

c.b. *abbr.* cash-book.

CBA *abbr.* **1** Commercial Bank of Australia. **2** cost benefit analysis.

CBD *abbr.* **1** cash before delivery. **2** central business district.

CBE *abbr.* Commander of the Order of the British Empire.

CBI *abbr.* **1** computer-based information. **2** computer-based instruction. **3** = CONFEDERATION OF BRITISH INDUSTRY.

CBIS *abbr.* computer-based information system.
CBIV *abbr.* computer-based interactive videodisc.
CBL *abbr.* computer-based learning. See COMPUTER-ASSISTED LEARNING.
c.b.l. *abbr.* commercial bill of lading.
CBMIS *abbr.* computer-based management information system.
CBO *abbr.* (in the US) Congressional Budget Office.
CBOE *abbr.* Chicago Board of Options Exchange.
CBOT *abbr.* Chicago Board of Trade.
CBS *abbr.* (in the US) Columbia Broadcasting System.
CBSI *abbr.* Chartered Building Societies Institute.
CBT *abbr.* **1** Chicago Board of Trade. **2** = COMPUTER-BASED TRAINING.
c.b.u. *abbr.* (also **CBU**) *Commerce* (of goods for immediate use) completely built-up.
CBX *abbr.* company branch (telephone) exchange.
CC *abbr.* **1** Chamber of Commerce. **2** *Commerce* continuation clause. **3** credit card. *–international civil aircraft marking* Chile.
c.c. *abbr.* **1** (also **cc**) carbon copy or copies (to). **2** cash credit. **3** (also **c/c**) (French) compte courant (= current account). **4** (also **c/c**) (Italian) conto corrente (= current account). **5** contra credit. **6** (also **cc**) cubic centimetre(s).

◆ **CCA** *abbr.* = CURRENT-COST ACCOUNTING.

CCAB *abbr.* Consultative Committee of Accountancy Bodies.
CCC *abbr.* **1** Canadian Chamber of Commerce. **2** Commodity Credit Corporation.
c.c.c. *abbr.* (Welsh) cwmni cyfyngedig cyhoeddus (= public limited company).
c.c.e.i. *abbr.* composite cost effectiveness index.
CCF *abbr.* central computing facility.
CCITT *abbr.* International Telegraph and Telephone Consultative Committee, an agency of the International Telecommunication Union that provides worldwide coordination for telephone and data communication systems. [French *Comité Consultatif International Télégraphique et Téléphonique*]
CCST *abbr.* (in the US) Center for Computer Sciences and Technology.
CCT *abbr.* (in the EC) common customs tariff.
CCTA *abbr.* Central Computer and Telecommunications Agency.
CCUS *abbr.* Chamber of Commerce of the United States.
CD *abbr.* **1** = CERTIFICATE OF DEPOSIT. **2** Civil Defence. **3** closing date. **4** commercial dock. **5** compact disc. **6** *Corps Diplomatique.*
C/D *abbr.* **1** consular declaration. **2** customs declaration.
Cd *symb.* cadmium.
cd *symb.* candela.
c.d. *abbr.* **1** (also **c/d**) *Bookkeeping* carried down. **2** cash discount. **3** cum dividend (see EX[1] 2).
CDB *abbr. Computing* comprehensive database.
CDC *abbr.* **1** Commonwealth Development Corporation. **2** Control Data Corporation (computer manufacturer).
CDE *abbr.* (also **CD-E**) compact-disc erasable.
CDF *abbr. Computing* central database facility.
CDFC *abbr.* Commonwealth Development Finance Company.
cd. fwd. *abbr. Bookkeeping* carried forward.
CDI *abbr.* (also **CD-I**) compact-disc interactive.
C.Dip.A.F. *abbr.* Certified Diploma in Accounting and Finance.
CDN *international vehicle registration* Canada.
CDR *abbr.* (also **CD-R**) compact-disc recordable.
CD-ROM /ˌsiːdiːˈrɒm/ *abbr. Computing* compact disc read-only memory, a storage device, based on the audio compact disc, in which information is impressed during manufacture by optical means and cannot subsequently be altered (see ROM). The user can only read (i.e. retrieve) data, text, etc. Many commercial databases are now available on CD-ROM.
CDT *abbr.* craft, design, and technology.
CD-video /ˌsiːdiːˈvɪdɪəʊ/ *n.* (*pl.* **-s**) **1** system of simultaneously reproducing high-quality sound and video pictures from a compact disc. **2** such a compact disc.
CDW *abbr. US* (in car insurance) collision damage waiver.
CE *abbr.* **1** Chancellor of the Exchequer. **2** (French) Communauté européenne (= European Community). **3** Council of Europe.
Ce *symb.* cerium.
c.e. *abbr.* = CAVEAT EMPTOR.
CEA *abbr.* **1** commodity exchange authority. **2** (in the US) Council of Economic Advisers.
cease *formal –v.* (**-sing**) stop; bring or come to an end. *–n.* (in **without cease**) unending. [Latin *cesso*]
cease-fire *n.* **1** period of truce. **2** order to stop firing.
ceaseless *adj.* without end. □ **ceaselessly** *adv.*
Cebu /seɪˈbuː/ **1** island in the S central Philippines; pop. (1980) 2 091 600. Coal and copper are mined and farming is important. **2** its chief city and port; pop. (est. 1991) 641 042.
CEC *abbr.* **1** Commission of the European Communities. **2** Commonwealth Economic Committee.
cecum *US* var. of CAECUM.
CED *abbr.* **1** Committee for Economic Development. **2** computer entry device. **3** (in the US) Council for Economic Development.
CEDA *abbr.* Committee for Economic Development of Australia.
cedar /ˈsiːdə(r)/ *n.* **1** spreading evergreen conifer. **2** its hard fragrant wood. [Greek *kedros*]
cede *v.* (**-ding**) *formal* give up one's rights to or possession of. [Latin *cedo cess-* yield]
cedi /ˈseɪdɪ/ *n.* (*pl.* same) standard monetary unit of Ghana. [Fanti]
cedilla /sɪˈdɪlə/ *n.* **1** mark written under *c*, esp. in French, to show it is sibilant (as in *façade*). **2** similar mark under *s* in Turkish etc. [Spanish diminutive of *zeda* Z]
CEE *abbr.* (French) Communauté économique européenne (= European Economic Community).
CEEC *abbr.* Council for European Economic Cooperation.
CEED *abbr.* Centre for Economic and Environment Development.
Ceefax /ˈsiːfæks/ *n. propr.* teletext service provided by the BBC. See TELETEXT. [representing a pronunciation of *see*ing + *fac*simile]
CEIF *abbr.* Council of European Industrial Federations.
ceilidh /ˈkeɪlɪ/ *n.* informal gathering for music, dancing, etc. [Gaelic]
ceiling /ˈsiːlɪŋ/ *n.* **1** upper interior surface of a room or other compartment. **2** upper limit. **3** maximum altitude a given aircraft can reach. [origin uncertain]
CEIR *abbr.* Corporation for Economic and Industrial Research.
CELA *abbr.* Council for Exports to Latin America.
celandine /ˈselənˌdaɪn/ *n.* yellow-flowered plant. [Greek *khelidōn* a swallow]
Celebes see SULAWESI.
celebrant /ˈselɪbrənt/ *n.* person who performs a rite, esp. the priest at the Eucharist.
celebrate /ˈselɪˌbreɪt/ *v.* (**-ting**) **1** mark with or engage in festivities. **2** perform (a rite or ceremony). **3** praise publicly. □ **celebration** /-ˈbreɪʃ(ə)n/ *n.* **celebrator** *n.* **celebratory** /-ˈbreɪtərɪ/ *adj.* [Latin *celeber* renowned]
celebrity /sɪˈlebrɪtɪ/ *n.* (*pl.* **-ies**) **1** well-known person. **2** fame. [Latin: related to CELEBRATE]
celeriac /sɪˈlerɪˌæk/ *n.* variety of celery. [from CELERY]
celerity /sɪˈlerɪtɪ/ *n. archaic* or *literary* swiftness. [Latin *celer* swift]

celery /ˈselərɪ/ *n.* plant with crisp long whitish leaf-stalks used as a vegetable. [Greek *selinon* parsley]

celesta /sɪˈlestə/ *n.* small keyboard instrument with steel plates struck to give a bell-like sound. [French: related to CELESTIAL]

celestial /sɪˈlestɪəl/ *adj.* **1** of the sky or heavenly bodies. **2** heavenly; divinely good; sublime. [Latin *caelum* sky]

celestial equator *n.* the great circle of the sky in the plane perpendicular to the earth's axis.

celestial sphere *n.* imaginary sphere, of any radius, of which the observer is the centre and in which celestial bodies are represented as lying.

CELEX /ˈseleks/ *n.* computerized documentation system for European Community law. [abbreviation of Latin *Communitatis Europeae Lex*]

celibate /ˈselɪbət/ *–adj.* **1** unmarried or committed to sexual abstention, esp. for religious reasons. **2** having no sexual relations. *–n.* celibate person. □ **celibacy** *n.* [Latin *caelebs* unmarried]

cell *n.* **1** small room, esp. in a prison or monastery. **2** small compartment, e.g. in a honeycomb. **3** small, active, esp. subversive, political group. **4 a** smallest structural and functional unit of living matter, consisting of cytoplasm and a nucleus enclosed in a membrane. **b** enclosed cavity in an organism etc. **5** vessel containing electrodes for current-generation or electrolysis. [Latin *cella*]

cellar /ˈselə(r)/ *–n.* **1** storage room below ground level in a house. **2** stock of wine in a cellar. *–v.* store in a cellar. [Latin *cellarium*: related to CELL]

♦ **Cellnet** /ˈselˌnet/ *propr.* see CELLULAR NETWORK.

---

cello /ˈtʃeləʊ/ *n.* (*pl.* **-s**) bass instrument of the violin family, held between the legs of the seated player. □ **cellist** *n.* [abbreviation of VIOLONCELLO]

Cellophane /ˈseləˌfeɪn/ *n. propr.* thin transparent viscose wrapping material. [from CELLULOSE: cf. DIAPHANOUS]

cellphone *n.* small portable radio-telephone. See CELLULAR NETWORK.

cellular /ˈseljʊlə(r)/ *adj.* consisting of cells, of open texture; porous. □ **cellularity** /-ˈlærɪtɪ/ *n.* [French: related to CELL]

♦ **cellular network** *n.* radio-telephone network for mobile subscribers that connects them to the main telephone system. Operated in the UK jointly by British Telecom and Securicor (as **Cellnet**), it consists of a number of adjacent 'cells', each containing a transmit/receive station connected to the main telephone network and reached by the mobile subscriber using a battery-operated portable radio-telephone (**cellphone**). As subscribers move from one geographical cell to another (e.g. by car), they are automatically switched to receive signals from the new area. Car phones, operating on this **cellular radio** system, have been a great boon to business people who can remain in contact with their offices while travelling.

---

cellulite /ˈseljʊˌlaɪt/ *n.* lumpy fat, esp. on the hips and thighs of women. [French: related to CELL]

celluloid /ˈseljʊˌlɔɪd/ *n.* **1** plastic made from camphor and cellulose nitrate. **2** cinema film.

cellulose /ˈseljʊˌləʊs/ *n.* **1** carbohydrate forming plant-cell walls, used in textile fibres. **2** (in general use) paint or lacquer consisting of esp. cellulose acetate or nitrate in solution. [Latin: related to CELL]

Celsius /ˈselsɪəs/ *adj.* of a scale of temperature on which water freezes at 0° and boils at 100°. [name of an astronomer]

■ **Usage** See note at *centigrade*.

Celt /kelt/ *n.* (also **Kelt**) member of an ethnic group, including the inhabitants of Ireland, Wales, Scotland, Cornwall, and Brittany. [Latin from Greek]

Celtic /ˈkeltɪk/ *–adj.* of the Celts. *–n.* group of Celtic languages, including Gaelic and Irish, Welsh, Cornish, and Breton.

cement /sɪˈment/ *–n.* **1** powdery substance of calcined lime and clay, mixed with water to form mortar or used in concrete. **2** similar substance. **3** uniting factor or principle. **4** substance used in filling teeth, doing hip replacements, etc. *–v.* **1 a** unite with or as with cement. **b** establish or strengthen (a friendship etc.). **2** apply cement to. **3** line or cover with cement. □ **cementation** /ˌsiːmenˈteɪʃ(ə)n/ *n.* [Latin *caedo* cut]

cemetery /ˈsemɪtrɪ/ *n.* (*pl.* **-ies**) burial ground, esp. one not in a churchyard. [Greek *koimaō* put to sleep]

CEN /sen/ *abbr.* official standards body of the European Community. [French *Comité Européen de Normalisation*]

CENELEC /ˈsenəˌlek/ *abbr.* EC standards body for electrical goods. [French *Comité Européen Normalisation Électrotechnique*]

cenobite *US* var. of COENOBITE.

cenotaph /ˈsenəˌtɑːf/ *n.* tomblike monument to a person whose body is elsewhere. [Greek *kenos* empty, *taphos* tomb]

Cenozoic /ˌsiːnəˈzəʊɪk/ (also **Cainozoic** /ˌkaɪnə-/, **Caenozoic** /ˌsiːn-/) *–adj.* of the most recent geological era, marked by the evolution and development of mammals etc. *–n.* this era. [Greek *kainos* new, *zōion* animal]

censer /ˈsensə(r)/ *n.* vessel for burning incense. [Anglo-French: related to INCENSE[1]]

censor /ˈsensə(r)/ *–n.* official authorized to suppress or expurgate books, films, news, etc., on grounds of obscenity, threat to security, etc. *–v.* **1** act as a censor of. **2** make deletions or changes in. □ **censorial** /-ˈsɔːrɪəl/ *adj.* **censorship** *n.* [Latin *censeo* assess]

■ **Usage** As a verb, *censor* is often confused with *censure*.

censorious /senˈsɔːrɪəs/ *adj.* severely critical. □ **censoriously** *adv.*

censure /ˈsenʃə(r)/ *–v.* (**-ring**) criticize harshly; reprove. *–n.* hostile criticism; disapproval. [Latin: related to CENSOR]

■ **Usage** As a verb, *censure* is often confused with *censor*.

♦ **census** /ˈsensəs/ *n.* (*pl.* **-suses**) official count of a population for demographic, social, or economic purposes. In the UK, population censuses have been held every ten years since 1801 and since 1966 supplementary censuses have been held halfway through the ten-year period. A **census of distribution**, quantifying the wholesale and retail distribution, has been carried out approximately every five years since 1950. A **census of production**, recording the output of all manufacturing, mining, quarrying, and building industries, together with that of all public services, has been held every year since 1968. [Latin: related to CENSOR]

---

cent *n.* **1 a** one-hundredth of a dollar or other decimal currency unit. **b** coin of this value. **2** *colloq.* very small amount. [Latin *centum* 100]

centaur /ˈsentɔː(r)/ *n.* creature in Greek mythology with the upper half of a man and the lower half of a horse. [Latin from Greek]

centenarian /ˌsentɪˈneərɪən/ *–n.* person a hundred or more years old. *–adj.* a hundred or more years old.

centenary /senˈtiːnərɪ/ *–n.* (*pl.* **-ies**) **1** hundredth anniversary. **2** celebration of this. *–adj.* **1** of a centenary. **2** occurring every hundred years. [Latin *centeni* 100 each]

centennial /senˈtenɪəl/ *–adj.* **1** lasting for a hundred years. **2** occurring every hundred years. *–n.* *US* = CENTENARY *n.* [Latin *centum* 100: cf. BIENNIAL]

center *US* var. of CENTRE.

centerboard *US* var. of CENTREBOARD.

centerfold *US* var. of CENTREFOLD.

centesimal /senˈtesɪm(ə)l/ *adj.* reckoning or reckoned by hundredths. [Latin *centum* 100]

centi- *comb. form* **1** one-hundredth. **2** hundred. [Latin *centum* 100]

centigrade /ˈsentɪˌgreɪd/ *adj.* **1** = CELSIUS. **2** having a scale of a hundred degrees. [Latin *gradus* step]

■ **Usage** In sense 1, *Celsius* is usu. preferred in technical contexts.

centigram /'sentɪˌgræm/ *n.* (also **centigramme**) metric unit of mass, equal to 0.01 gram.

centilitre /'sentɪˌli:tə(r)/ *n.* (*US* **centiliter**) 0.01 litre.

centime /'sɑ̃ti:m/ *n.* **1** one-hundredth of a franc. **2** coin of this value. [Latin *centum* 100]

centimetre /'sentɪˌmi:tə(r)/ *n.* (*US* **centimeter**) 0.01 metre.

centipede /'sentɪˌpi:d/ *n.* arthropod with a segmented wormlike body and many legs. [Latin *pes ped-* foot]

Central local government region in central Scotland; industries include brewing, distilling, and tourism, and dairy and livestock farming are important; pop. (est. 1987) 272 077; capital, Stirling.

central /'sentr(ə)l/ *adj.* **1** of, at, or forming the centre. **2** from the centre. **3** chief, essential, most important. □ **centrality** /-'trælɪtɪ/ *n.* **centrally** *adv.*

Central America isthmus joining North and South America, extending from the S border of Mexico to the NW border of Colombia.

♦ **Central Arbitration Committee** *n.* (also **CAC**) committee set up by the Employment Protection Act (1975) to arbitrate on matters voluntarily submitted to it through ACAS by the parties to a trade dispute. It has powers to enforce the disclosure of certain bargaining information in these disputes and to arbitrate when a statutory joint industrial council is deadlocked. It does not charge for its services and cannot award costs.

♦ **central bank** *n.* bank that provides financial and banking services for the government of a country and its commercial banking system as well as implementing the government's monetary policy. The main functions of a central bank are: to manage the government's accounts, to accept deposits and grant loans to the commercial banks, to control the issue of banknotes, to manage the public debt, to help manage the exchange rate when necessary, to influence the interest rate structure and control the money supply, to hold the country's reserves of gold and foreign currency, to manage dealings with other central banks, and to act as lender of last resort to the banking system. Examples of major central banks include the Bank of England in the UK, the Federal Reserve Bank of the US, the Deutsche Bundesbank in Germany, and France's Banque de France.

♦ **Central Government Borrowing Requirement** *n.* (also **CGBR**) Public Sector Borrowing Requirement (PSBR) less any borrowings by local authorities and public corporations from the private sector. Since local authorities and public corporations both have a measure of freedom in deciding how much they borrow, the government does not have the complete control over the PSBR that is has over the CGBR.

---

central heating *n.* method of heating a building by pipes, radiators, etc., fed from a central source.

centralism *n.* system that centralizes (esp. administration). □ **centralist** *n.*

centralize *v.* (also **-ise**) (**-zing** or **-sing**) **1** concentrate (esp. administration) at a single centre. **2** subject (a state) to this system. □ **centralization** /-'zeɪʃ(ə)n/ *n.*

central nervous system *n.* brain and spinal cord.

central processor *n.* (also **central processing unit, CPU**) principal operating part of a computer. It consists of the arithmetic and logic unit and the control unit, i.e. the units in which program instructions are interpreted and executed. Sometimes main store is considered a component of the central processor. See also PROCESSOR 3.

♦ **Central Statistical Office** *n.* (also **CSO**) statistical department of the UK government. Among its publications are the *Monthly Digest of Statistics*, *Financial Statistics* (monthly), *Economic Trends* (monthly), *UK National Accounts* (the Blue Book; annual), *UK Balance of Payments* (the Pink Book; annual), and the *Annual Abstract of Statistics*. It is also responsible for the Business Statistics Office.

---

centre /'sentə(r)/ (*US* **center**) –*n.* **1** middle point. **2** pivot or axis of rotation. **3 a** place or buildings forming a central point or a main area for an activity (*shopping centre; town centre*). **b** (with a preceding word) equipment for a number of connected functions (*music centre*). **4** point of concentration or dispersion; nucleus, source. **5** political party or group holding moderate opinions. **6** filling in chocolate etc. **7** *Sport* **a** middle player in a line in some field games. **b** kick or hit from the side to the centre of a pitch. **8** (*attrib.*) of or at the centre. –*v.* (**-ring**) **1** (foll. by *in, on, round*) have as its main centre. **2** place in the centre. **3** (foll. by *in* etc.) concentrate. [Greek *kentron* sharp point]

■ **Usage** The use of the verb in sense 1 with *round* is common and used by good writers, but is still considered incorrect by some people.

centre back *n. Sport* middle player or position in a half-back line.

centreboard *n.* (*US* **centerboard**) board lowered through a boat's keel to prevent leeway.

centrefold *n.* (*US* **centerfold**) centre spread of a magazine etc., esp. with nude photographs.

centre forward *n. Sport* middle player or position in a forward line.

centre half *n.* = CENTRE BACK.

centre of gravity *n.* (also **centre of mass**) point at which the weight of a body may be considered to act.

centre-piece *n.* **1** ornament for the middle of a table. **2** principal item.

centre spread *n.* two facing middle pages of a newspaper etc.

centric *adj.* **1** at or near the centre. **2** from a centre. □ **centrical** *adj.* **centrically** *adv.*

centrifugal /ˌsentrɪ'fju:g(ə)l/ *adj.* moving or tending to

Central African Republic country in central Africa, bounded by Chad, Sudan, Democratic Republic of Congo, and Cameroon. Subsistence agriculture supports most of the population; coffee is the main cash crop, though earnings from this are decreasing. Other important sources of revenue are diamonds (the most profitable export), cotton, and timber. Wildlife tourism is a developing industry. Economic growth will depend on a successful transition to democracy.

History. Formerly the French colony of Ubanghi Shari, it became a republic within the French Community in 1958 and a fully independent state in 1960. In 1976 its president, Jean Bédel Bokassa, who had come to power after a military coup in 1966, declared himself emperor and changed the country's name to Central African Empire, but it reverted to its original name and status after he had been ousted in 1979 and became a one-party state in 1986. Opposition parties were legalized in 1991. Multiparty elections were held in 1992, but were subsequently annulled. A coalition government ruled in 1992–93. More elections were held in 1993, following which another coalition government was formed. In 1996 the country faced an economic crisis; soldiers demanding their wages mutinied and an insurrection began. Order was restored later in the year. President, Ange-Félux Patassé; capital, Bangui.

languages	French, Sangho (national language)
currency	CFA franc (CFAF) of 100 centimes
pop. (est. 1996)	3 274 000
GNP (est. 1994)	US$1.1B
literacy	68% (m); 52% (f)
life expectancy	47 (m); 52 (f)

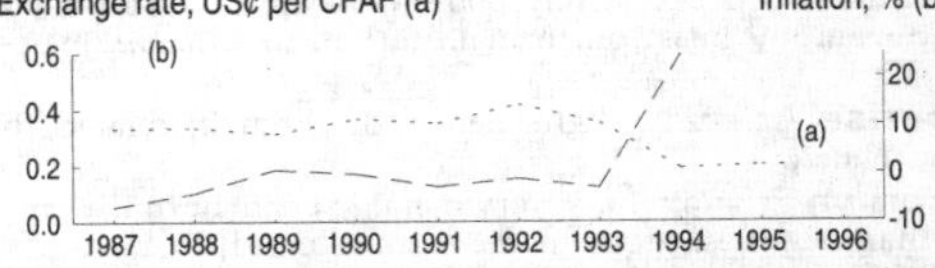

move from a centre. □ **centrifugally** *adv.* [from CENTRE, Latin *fugio* flee]

centrifugal force *n.* apparent force that acts outwards on a body moving about a centre.

centrifuge /ˈsentrɪˌfjuːdʒ/ *n.* rapidly rotating machine designed to separate liquids from solids etc.

centripetal /senˈtrɪpɪt(ə)l/ *adj.* moving or tending to move towards a centre. □ **centripetally** *adv.* [Latin *peto* seek]

centripetal force *n.* force acting on a body causing it to move towards a centre.

centrist *n. Polit.* often *derog.* person holding moderate views. □ **centrism** *n.*

centurion /senˈtjʊərɪən/ *n.* commander of a century in the ancient Roman army. [Latin: related to CENTURY]

century /ˈsentʃərɪ/ *n.* (*pl.* **-ies**) **1 a** 100 years. **b** any century reckoned from the birth of Christ (*twentieth century* = 1901–2000; *fifth century* BC = 500–401 BC). **2** score etc. of 100 esp. by one batsman in cricket. **3** company in the ancient Roman army, orig. of 100 men. [Latin *centuria*: related to CENT]

■ **Usage** Strictly speaking, since the first century ran from the year 1–100, the first year of a given century should be that ending in 01. However, in popular use this has been moved back a year, and so the twenty-first century will commonly be regarded as running from 2000–2099.

CEO *abbr.* **1** Chief Executive Officer. **2** Confederation of Employee Organizations.

cephalic /səˈfælɪk/ *adj.* of or in the head. [Greek *kephalē* head]

Cephalonia /ˌsefəˌləʊnɪə/ (Greek **Kefallinía** /ˌkefəlɪˈniːə/) Greek island in the Ionian Sea; pop. (1990) 32 314; capital, Argostolion. Olives and grapes are grown.

cephalopod /ˈsefələˌpɒd/ *n.* mollusc with a distinct tentacled head, e.g. the octopus. [from CEPHALIC, Greek *pous pod-* foot]

ceramic /sɪˈræmɪk/ *–adj.* **1** made of (esp.) baked clay. **2** of ceramics. *–n.* ceramic article or product. [Greek *keramos* pottery]

ceramics *n.pl.* **1** ceramic products collectively. **2** (usu. treated as *sing.*) art of making ceramic articles.

cereal /ˈsɪərɪəl/ *–n.* **1 a** grain used for food. **b** wheat, maize, rye, etc. producing this. **2** breakfast food made from a cereal. *–adj.* of edible grain. [Latin *Ceres* goddess of agriculture]

cerebellum /ˌserɪˈbeləm/ *n.* (*pl.* **-s** or **-bella**) part of the brain at the back of the skull. [Latin diminutive of CEREBRUM]

cerebral /ˈserɪbr(ə)l/ *adj.* **1** of the brain. **2** intellectual; unemotional. [related to CEREBRUM]

cerebral palsy *n.* paralysis resulting from brain damage before or at birth, involving spasm of the muscles and involuntary movements.

cerebration /ˌserɪˈbreɪʃ(ə)n/ *n.* working of the brain.

cerebrospinal /ˌserɪbrəʊˈspaɪn(ə)l/ *adj.* of the brain and spine.

cerebrum /ˈserɪbrəm/ *n.* (*pl.* **-bra**) principal part of the brain in vertebrates, at the front of the skull. [Latin]

ceremonial /ˌserɪˈməʊnɪəl/ *–adj.* of or with ceremony; formal. *–n.* system of rites or ceremonies. □ **ceremonially** *adv.*

ceremonious /ˌserɪˈməʊnɪəs/ *adj.* fond of or characterized by ceremony; formal. □ **ceremoniously** *adv.*

ceremony /ˈserɪmənɪ/ *n.* (*pl.* **-ies**) **1** formal procedure, esp. at a public event or anniversary. **2** formalities, esp. ritualistic. **3** excessively polite behaviour. □ **stand on ceremony** insist on formality. [Latin *caerimonia* worship]

cerise /səˈriːz/ *n.* light clear red. [French: related to CHERRY]

cerium /ˈsɪərɪəm/ *n.* silvery metallic element of the lanthanide series. [*Ceres*, name of an asteroid]

CERN /sɜːn/ *abbr.* European Laboratory for Particle Physics, formerly called European Organization for Nuclear Research. [French *Conseil Européen pour la Recherche Nucléaire*, original title]

cert *n.* (esp. **dead cert**) *slang* a certainty. [abbreviation]

cert. *abbr.* **1** certificate. **2** certification. **3** certified.

certain /ˈsɜːt(ə)n/ *–adj.* **1 a** confident, convinced. **b** indisputable (*it is certain that he is guilty*). **2** (often foll. by *to* + infin.) sure; destined (*it is certain to rain; certain to win*). **3** unerring, reliable. **4** that need not be specified or may not be known to the reader or hearer (*of a certain age; a certain John Smith*). **5** some but not much (*a certain reluctance*). *–pron.* (as *pl.*) some but not all (*certain of them knew*). □ **for certain** without doubt. [Latin *certus*]

certainly *adv.* **1** undoubtedly. **2** (in answer) yes; by all means.

certainty *n.* (*pl.* **-ies**) **1 a** undoubted fact. **b** indubitable prospect. **2** absolute conviction. **3** reliable thing or person.

Cert. CAM *abbr.* Certificate in Communication, Advertising, and Marketing.

Cert. Ed. *abbr.* (also **Cert Ed**) Certificate in Education.

certifiable /ˈsɜːtɪˌfaɪəb(ə)l/ *adj.* **1** able or needing to be certified. **2** *colloq.* insane.

certificate /səˈtɪfɪkət/ *–n.* formal document attesting a fact, esp. birth, marriage, or death, a medical condition, or a qualification. *–v.* /-ˌkeɪt/ (**-ting**) (esp. as **certificated** *adj.*) provide with, license, or attest by a certificate. □ **certification** /ˌsɜːtɪfɪˈkeɪʃ(ə)n/ *n.* [Latin: related to CERTIFY]

♦ **certificate of damage** *n.* certificate issued by a dock or wharfage company when it takes in damaged goods. The certificate, signed for or on behalf of the dock surveyor, states the nature of the damage and the cause, if known.

♦ **certificate of deposit** *n.* (also **CD**) negotiable certificate issued by a bank in return for a term deposit of up to five years. CDs originated in the US in the 1960s. From 1968, a sterling CD was issued by UK banks. They were intended to enable the merchant banks to attract funds away from the clearing banks with the offer of competitive interest rates. However, in 1971 the clearing banks also began to issue CDs as their negotiability and higher average yield had made them increasingly popular with the larger investors. A secondary market in CDs has developed, made up of the discount houses and the banks in the interbank market. They are issued in various amounts between £10,000 and £50,000, although they may be subdivided into units of the lower figure to facilitate negotiation of part holdings.

♦ **certificate of incorporation** *n.* certificate that brings a company into existence, issued to the shareholders of a company by the Registrar of Companies. It is issued when the memorandum and articles of association have been submitted to the Registrar of Companies, together with other documents that disclose the proposed registered address of the company, details of the proposed directors and company secretary, the nominal and issued share capital, and the capital duty.

♦ **certificate of insurance** *n.* certificate giving abbreviated details of the cover provided by an insurance policy. In a motor-insurance policy or an employers'-liability policy, the information that must be shown on the certificate of insurance is laid down by law and in both cases the policy cover does not come into force until the certificate has been delivered to the policyholder.

♦ **certificate of origin** *n.* document that states the country from which a particular parcel of goods originated. In international trade it is one of the shipping documents and will often determine whether or not an import duty has to be paid on the goods and, if it has, on what tariff. Such certificates are usu. issued by a chamber of commerce in the country of origin.

Certificate of Secondary Education *n. hist.* secondary-school leaving examination in England, Wales, and Northern Ireland.

■ **Usage** This examination was replaced in 1988 by the *General Certificate of Secondary Education* (GCSE).

◆ **certified accountant** *n.* member of the Chartered Association of Certified Accountants. Its members are trained in industry, in the public service, and in the offices of practising accountants. They often attend sandwich courses in technical colleges while still working and take the Association's exams. Members are recognized by the UK Department of Trade and Industry as qualified to audit the accounts of companies. They may be associates (ACCA) or fellows (FCCA) of the Association and although they are not chartered accountants, they fulfil much the same role. In the US the equivalent is a **certified public accountant** (CPA), who is a member of the Institute of Certified Public Accountants.

◆ **certified check** *n. US* = MARKED CHEQUE.

◆ **certified stock** *n.* (also **certificated stock**) stocks of a commodity that have been examined and passed as acceptable for delivery in fulfilment of contracts on a futures market.

certify /'sɜːtɪˌfaɪ/ *v.* (**-ies, -ied**) **1** attest; attest to, esp. formally. **2** declare by certificate. **3** officially declare insane. [Latin *certus*]

certitude /'sɜːtɪˌtjuːd/ *n.* feeling of certainty. [Latin: related to CERTAIN]

cerulean /sə'ruːlɪən/ *adj.* & *n. literary* deep sky-blue. [Latin *caeruleus*]

cervical /sə'vaɪk(ə)l, 'sɜːvɪk(ə)l/ *adj.* of the neck or the cervix (*cervical vertebrae*). [related to CERVIX]

cervical screening *n.* mass routine examination for cervical cancer.

cervical smear *n.* specimen from the neck of the womb for examination.

cervix /'sɜːvɪks/ *n.* (*pl.* **cervices** /-ˌsiːz/) **1** necklike structure, esp. the neck of the womb. **2** the neck. [Latin]

CES *abbr.* cost-estimating system.

Cesarean (also **Cesarian**) *US* var. of CAESAREAN.

cesium *US* var. of CAESIUM.

cessation /se'seɪʃ(ə)n/ *n.* ceasing or pause. [Latin: related to CEASE]

◆ **cesser clause** /'sesə/ *n.* clause in a charter-party, inserted when the charterer's right to have goods carried is to be transferred to a shipper. It provides that the shipowner is to have a lien over the shipper's goods for the freight payable under the charter-party and that the charterer's liability for freight ceases on shipment of a full cargo.

cession /'seʃ(ə)n/ *n.* **1** ceding. **2** territory etc. ceded. [Latin: related to CEDE]

cesspit /'sespɪt/ *n.* (also **cesspool**) covered pit for the temporary storage of liquid waste or sewage. [origin uncertain]

CET *abbr.* **1** Central European Time. **2** = COMMON EXTERNAL TARIFF.

cetacean /sɪ'teɪʃ(ə)n/ *–n.* marine mammal, e.g. the whale. *–adj.* of cetaceans. [Greek *kētos* whale]

cetane /'siːteɪn/ *n.* liquid hydrocarbon used in standardizing ratings of diesel fuel. [from SPERMACETI]

◆ ***ceteris paribus*** /'ketəris 'pɑːrɪbʊs/ *n.* widely used assumption in economics that the variables under consideration have no other effects on the economy than those specified and are not themselves affected by any other variables. Usu. hopelessly unrealistic, the *ceteris paribus* assumption is the basis of partial equilibrium analysis from which most economic theories are derived. On the other hand, general-equilibrium analysis excludes the *ceteris paribus* assumption but has difficulty in reaching any worthwhile conclusions. [Latin, = other things being equal]

Ceuta /seɪ'uːtə, 'θe-/ Spanish enclave in Morocco; pop. (est. 1994) 68 867. It is a military post and free port.

Ceylon /sɪ'lɒn/ see SRI LANKA.

CF *–abbr.* **1** carriage forward. **2** Comorian franc. **3** compensation fee. **4** cost and freight. *–international civil aircraft marking* Canada. *–postcode* Cardiff. *–airline flight code* Faucett Peruvian Airlines.

Cf *symb.* californium.

cf. *abbr.* compare. [Latin *confer*]

c.f. *abbr.* (also **c/f**) **1** *Bookkeeping* carried forward. **2** cost and freight.

CFA *abbr.* **1** *US* Chartered Financial Analyst. **2** (French) Communauté financière africaine (= African Financial Community).

CFA franc *n.* (also **CFAF**) standard monetary unit of the African Financial Community, i.e. Benin, Burkina Faso, Cameroon, Central African Republic, Chad, Congo, Côte d'Ivoire, Equatorial Guinea, Gabon, Mali, Niger, Senegal, and Togo.

CFC *abbr.* **1** chloro-fluorocarbon, a usu. gaseous compound of carbon, hydrogen, chlorine, and fluorine, used in refrigerants, aerosol propellants, etc., and thought to harm the ozone layer. **2** Common Fund for Commodities. See UNITED NATIONS CONFERENCE ON TRADE AND DEVELOPMENT.

CFE *abbr.* College of Further Education.

CFI *abbr.* (also **c.f.i.**) cost, freight, and insurance. See C.I.F.

CFP *abbr.* **1** = COMMON FISHERIES POLICY. **2** (French) Communauté financière du Pacifique (= Pacific Financial Community).

CFS *abbr. Computing* common file system.

◆ **CFTC** *abbr.* = COMMODITY FUTURES TRADING COMMISSION.

CG *abbr.* computer graphics.

cg *abbr.* centigram(s).

CGA *abbr.* **1** *Commerce* cargo's proportion of general average. **2** Certified General Accountant. **3** *Computing* colour graphics adapter.

CGBR *abbr.* = CENTRAL GOVERNMENT BORROWING REQUIREMENT.

Chad /tʃæd/, **Republic of** inland country in N central Africa, bordered in the N by Libya. Most of the population survive by subsistence agriculture and fishing; raw cotton, live cattle, and meat are the main exports. Some oil and minerals are mined but there is little industry. Political instability has almost halted the growth of the economy, which has been severely weakened by years of civil war, but the cotton industry is showing signs of recovery.

History. Chad gained full independence from France in 1960, but conflict between Muslims in the N, supported by Libya, and Black Africans in the S, supported by France, has been violent and disruptive. The present government has plans to phase in a multi-party system, but continuing political instability indicates that progress will be slow. A new constitution was approved by referendum in 1996. Multi-party elections were held that same year, resulting in the election of standing president Idriss Déby, amid allegations of electoral fraud. Peace agreements were reached between the government and several rebel groups. President, Idriss Déby; capital, N'djamena. □ **Chadian** *adj.* & *n.*

languages	French & Arabic (official), African languages
currency	CFA franc (CFAF) of 100 centimes
pop. (est. 1996)	6 543 000
GNP (est. 1994)	US$1.1B
literacy	23% (m); 5% (f)
life expectancy	45 (m); 49 (f)

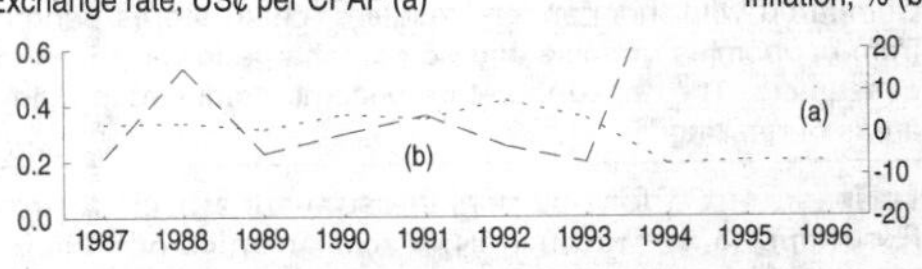

cge. *abbr.* **1** carriage. **2** charge.

CGI *abbr.* **1** City and Guilds Institute. **2** commercial grade item. **3** computer graphics interface.

CGLI *abbr.* City and Guilds of London Institute.

CGM *abbr.* computer graphics metafile, standardized file format for transmission of pictures, also widely used as file format for PC drawing programs.

cgo. *abbr.* **1** cargo. **2** contango.

CGT *abbr.* **1** = CAPITAL-GAINS TAX. **2** (French) Confédération générale du travail (= General Confederation of Labour).

CGT-FO *abbr.* (French) Confédération générale du travail–force ouvrière (= General Confederation of Labour–Workers' Force).

CH *–abbr.* **1** (also **c.h.**) clearing-house. **2** Companion of Honour. **3** (also **c.h.**) custom(s) house. *–international vehicle registration* Switzerland. *–postcode* Chester.

ch. *abbr.* **1** chapter. **2** charge(s).

Chablis /ˈʃæbliː/ *n.* (*pl.* same /-liːz/) very dry white wine from Chablis in E France.

cha-cha /ˈtʃɑːtʃɑː/ *n.* (also **cha-cha-cha** /ˌtʃɑːtʃɑːˈtʃɑː/) **1** Latin American dance. **2** music for this. [American Spanish]

chaconne /ʃəˈkɒn/ *n.* **1** musical variations over a ground bass. **2** dance performed to this. [French from Spanish]

chad *n.* (*pl.* same) *Computing* piece of paper, plastic, etc. removed when a hole is punched in a data medium. For example, the punching of sprocket holes along the edges of continuous stationery produces chad.

chafe *–v.* (**-fing**) **1** make or become sore or damaged by rubbing. **2** make or become annoyed; fret. **3** rub (esp. the skin to restore warmth or sensation). *–n.* sore caused by rubbing. [Latin *calefacio* make warm]

chaff /tʃɑːf/ *–n.* **1** separated husks of corn etc. **2** chopped hay or straw. **3** light-hearted teasing. **4** worthless things. *–v.* tease, banter. [Old English]

chaffinch /ˈtʃæfɪntʃ/ *n.* a common European finch. [Old English: related to CHAFF, FINCH]

chafing-dish *n.* vessel in which food is cooked or kept warm at table.

Chagos Archipelago /ˈtʃeɪgəs/ island group in the Indian Ocean, formerly a dependency of Mauritius and now part of the strategic British Indian Ocean Territory.

chagrin /ˈʃægrɪn/ *–n.* acute annoyance or disappointment. *–v.* affect with chagrin. [French]

chain *–n.* **1 a** connected flexible series of esp. metal links. **b** thing resembling this. **2** (in *pl.*) fetters; restraining force. **3** sequence, series, or set. **4** group of associated hotels, shops, etc. **5** badge of office in the form of a chain worn round the neck. **6** unit of length (66 ft). *–v.* (often foll. by *up*) secure or confine with a chain. [Latin *catena*]

chain-gang *n. hist.* team of convicts chained together to work out of doors.

chain-mail *n.* armour made of interlaced rings.

chain reaction *n.* **1** chemical or nuclear reaction forming products which initiate further reactions. **2** series of events, each caused by the previous one.

chain-saw *n.* motor-driven saw with teeth on an endless chain.

chain-smoke *v.* smoke continually, esp. by lighting the next cigarette etc. from the previous one. □ **chain-smoker** *n.*

♦ **chain store** *n.* (also **multiple store, multiple shop**) one of a series of similar shops owned by the same retailer. Compared with independent retailers, chain stores benefit from economies of scale and so can charge lower prices to consumers. They have therefore become dominant in many areas of retailing.

---

chair *–n.* **1** seat for one person usu. with a back. **2** professorship. **3 a** = CHAIRMAN. **b** seat or office of a chairman. **4** *US* = ELECTRIC CHAIR. *–v.* **1** preside over (a meeting). **2** carry (a person) aloft in triumph. □ **take the chair** preside over a meeting. [Greek *kathedra*]

chair-lift *n.* series of chairs on a looped cable, for carrying passengers up and down a mountain etc.

chairman *n.* (also **chair, chairperson**; *fem.* also **chairwoman**) **1** person who presides over a meeting, committee, etc. **2** most senior officer in a company, who presides at the annual general meeting of the company and usu. also at meetings of the board of directors. The chairman may also be the managing director, esp. in a small company of which he or she is the majority shareholder, or merely a figurehead, without executive participation in the day-to-day running of the company. The chairman is often a retired managing director. See also PRESIDENT 4b, 5.

♦ **chairman's report** *n.* report, often included in the annual report of a company, giving a summary of the year's activities and a brief survey of what can be expected in the coming year. It is signed by the chairman, who usu. reads it at the annual general meeting.

---

chairperson *n.* chairman or chairwoman.

chaise /ʃeɪz/ *n.* esp. *hist.* horse-drawn usu. open carriage for one or two persons. [French]

chaise longue /ʃeɪz ˈlɒŋ/ *n.* (*pl.* ***chaise longues*** or ***chaises longues*** pronunc. same) sofa with only one arm rest. [French, = long chair]

chalcedony /kælˈsedənɪ/ *n.* (*pl.* **-ies**) type of quartz with many varieties, e.g. onyx. [Latin from Greek]

Chalcis /ˈkælsɪs/ (Greek **Khalkís** /xælˈkiːs/) chief town on the Greek island of Euboea; pop. (1981) 44 800.

chalet /ˈʃæleɪ/ *n.* **1** Swiss mountain hut or cottage with overhanging eaves. **2** house in a similar style. **3** small cabin in a holiday camp etc. [Swiss French]

chalice /ˈtʃælɪs/ *n.* **1** goblet. **2** Eucharistic cup. [Latin CALIX]

chalk /tʃɔːk/ *–n.* **1** white soft limestone. **2 a** similar substance, sometimes coloured, for writing or drawing. **b** piece of this. *–v.* **1** rub, mark, draw, or write with chalk. **2** (foll. by *up*) **a** write or record with chalk. **b** register or gain (success etc.). □ **by a long chalk** by far. □ **chalky** *adj.* (**-ier, -iest**). **chalkiness** *n.* [Latin CALX]

challenge /ˈtʃælɪndʒ/ *–n.* **1** summons to take part in a contest etc. or to prove or justify something. **2** demanding or difficult task. **3** objection made to a jury member. **4** call to respond. *–v.* (**-ging**) **1** issue a challenge to. **2** dispute, deny. **3** (as **challenging** *adj.*) stimulatingly difficult. **4** object to (a jury member, evidence, etc.). □ **challenger** *n.* [Latin *calumnia* calumny]

chalybeate /kəˈlɪbɪət/ *adj.* (of water etc.) impregnated with iron salts. [Latin *chalybs* steel, from Greek]

chamber /ˈtʃeɪmbə(r)/ *n.* **1 a** hall used by a legislative or judicial body. **b** body that meets in it, esp. any of the houses of a parliament. **2** (in *pl.*) **a** rooms used by a barrister or barristers, esp. in Inns of Court. **b** judge's room for hearing cases not needing to be taken in court. **3** *archaic* room, esp. a bedroom. **4** *Mus.* (*attrib.*) of or for a small group of instruments. **5** cavity or compartment in the body, machinery, etc. (esp. the part of a gun-bore that contains the charge). [Greek *kamara* vault]

chamberlain /ˈtʃeɪmbəlɪn/ *n.* **1** officer managing a royal or noble household. **2** treasurer of a corporation etc. [Germanic: related to CHAMBER]

chambermaid *n.* woman who cleans hotel bedrooms.

♦ **chamber of commerce** *n.* voluntary organization of commercial, industrial, and trading business people who represent their joint interests to local and central government. The London Chamber of Commerce is the largest such organization in the UK; it also fulfils an educational role, running several commercial courses, for which it also sets examinations. Most UK chambers of commerce are affiliated to the Association of British Chambers of Commerce.

♦ **chamber of trade** *n.* organization of local retailers set up to protect their interests in local matters. It is a much narrower organization than a chamber of commerce and most chambers of trade in the UK are affiliated to the National Chamber of Trade.

chamber-pot *n.* receptacle for urine etc., used in the bedroom.

♦ **Chambre Agent General Index** *n.* arithmetically weighted index of 430 shares on the Paris Bourse. [French]

chameleon /kəˈmiːlɪən/ *n.* **1** small lizard able to change colour for camouflage. **2** variable or inconstant person. [Greek, = ground-lion]
chamfer /ˈtʃæmfə(r)/ *–v.* bevel symmetrically (a right-angled edge or corner). *–n.* bevelled surface at an edge or corner. [French *chant* edge, *fraint* broken]
chamois *n.* (*pl.* same /-wɑːz/, /-mɪz/) **1** /ˈʃæmwɑː/ agile European and Asian mountain antelope. **2** /ˈʃæmɪ/ (in full **chamois leather**) **a** soft leather from sheep, goats, deer, etc. **b** piece of this. [French]
chamomile var. of CAMOMILE.
champ[1] *–v.* munch or chew noisily. *–n.* chewing noise. □ **champ at the bit** be restlessly impatient. [imitative]
champ[2] *n. slang* champion. [abbreviation]
champagne /ʃæmˈpeɪn/ *n.* **1 a** white sparkling wine from Champagne. **b** similar wine from elsewhere. **2** pale cream colour. [*Champagne*, former province in E France]
■ **Usage** The use of this word in sense 1b is, strictly speaking, incorrect.
Champagne-Ardenne /ʃæmˌpeɪnɑːˈden/ region of NE France comprising part of the Ardennes forest and the vine-growing Plain of Champagne; pop. (est. 1994) 1 351 869; capital, Reims.
champers /ˈʃæmpəz/ *n. slang* champagne.
champion /ˈtʃæmpɪən/ *–n.* **1** (often *attrib.*) person or thing that has defeated or surpassed all rivals. **2** person who fights or argues for a cause or another person. *–v.* support the cause of, defend. *–adj. colloq.* splendid. *–adv. colloq.* splendidly. [medieval Latin *campio* fighter]
championship *n.* **1** (often in *pl.*) contest to decide the champion in a sport etc. **2** position of champion.
chance /tʃɑːns/ *–n.* **1** possibility. **2** (often in *pl.*) probability. **3** unplanned occurrence. **4** opportunity. **5** fortune; luck. **6** (often **Chance**) course of events regarded as a power; fate. *–attrib. adj.* fortuitous, accidental. *–v.* (**-cing**) **1** *colloq.* risk. **2** happen (*I chanced to find it*). □ **by any chance** perhaps. **by chance** fortuitously. **chance one's arm** try though unlikely to succeed. **chance on** (or **upon**) happen to find, meet, etc. **game of chance** one decided by luck, not skill. **on the off chance** just in case (the unlikely occurs). **stand a chance** have a prospect of success etc. **take a chance** (or **chances**) risk failure; behave riskily. **take a** (or **one's**) **chance on** (or **with**) risk the consequences of. [Latin *cado* fall]
chancel /ˈtʃɑːns(ə)l/ *n.* part of a church near the altar. [Latin *cancelli* grating]
chancellery /ˈtʃɑːnsələrɪ/ *n.* (*pl.* **-ies**) **1** chancellor's department, staff, or residence. **2** *US* office attached to an embassy or consulate.
chancellor /ˈtʃɑːnsələ(r)/ *n.* **1** state or legal official. **2** head of government in some European countries. **3** non-resident honorary head of a university. [Latin *cancellarius* secretary]
Chancellor of the Exchequer *n.* UK finance minister.
chancery /ˈtʃɑːnsərɪ/ *n.* (*pl.* **-ies**) **1** (**Chancery**) Lord Chancellor's division of the High Court of Justice. **2** records office. **3** chancellery. [contraction of CHANCELLERY]
chancy /ˈtʃɑːnsɪ/ *adj.* (**-ier**, **-iest**) uncertain; risky. □ **chancily** *adv.*
chandelier /ˌʃændəˈlɪə(r)/ *n.* ornamental branched hanging support for lighting. [French: related to CANDLE]
Chandigarh /ˌtʃʌndɪˈgɑː(r)/ **1** Union Territory in India, created in 1966; pop. (1991) 642 015. **2** city in this Territory, capital of both Punjab and Haryana states; pop. (1991) 504 094. It is a major road and rail junction; its industries include engineering.
chandler /ˈtʃɑːndlə(r)/ *n.* dealer in candles, oil, soap, paint, etc. [French: related to CANDLE]
Changchun /ˌtʃæŋˈtʃʊn/ city in NE China, capital of Jilin province; machinery and motor vehicles are manufactured; pop. (est. 1991) 2 110 000.
change /tʃeɪndʒ/ *–n.* **1 a** making or becoming different. **b** alteration or modification. **2 a** money exchanged for money in larger units or a different currency. **b** money returned as the balance of that given in payment. **3** new experience; variety (*need a change*). **4** substitution of one thing for another (*change of scene*). **5** (in full **change of life**) *colloq.* menopause. **6** (usu. in *pl.*) one of the different orders in which bells can be rung. *–v.* (**-ging**) **1** undergo, show, or subject to change; make or become different. **2 a** take or use another instead of; go from one to another (*change one's socks*; *changed trains*). **b** (usu. foll. by *for*) give up or get rid of in exchange (*changed the car for a van*). **3** give or get money in exchange for. **4** put fresh clothes or coverings on. **5** (often foll. by *with*) give and receive, exchange. **6** change trains etc. **7** (of the moon) arrive at a fresh phase. □ **change down** engage a lower gear. **change gear** engage a different gear. **change hands 1** pass to a different owner. **2** substitute one hand for the other. **change one's mind** adopt a different opinion or plan. **change over** change from one system or situation to another. **change one's tune 1** voice a different opinion from before. **2** become more respectful. **change up** engage a higher gear. **get no change out of** *slang* **1** get no information or help from. **2** fail to outwit (in business etc.). □ **changeful** *adj.* **changeless** *adj.* [Latin *cambio* barter]
changeable *adj.* **1** inconstant. **2** that can change or be changed.
changeling *n.* child believed to be substituted for another.
change of clothes *n.* second outfit in reserve.
change of heart *n.* conversion to a different view.
change-over *n.* change from one system to another.
Changsha /tʃæŋˈʃɑː/ river port in SE China, capital of Hunan province; industries include chemicals, electronics, textiles, and metalwork; pop. (est. 1991) 1 330 000.
channel /ˈtʃæn(ə)l/ *–n.* **1 a** piece of water wider than a strait, joining esp. two seas. **b** (**the Channel**) the English Channel. **2 a** medium of communication; agency. **b** route along which information etc. can be sent. See also DISTRIBUTION CHANNEL. **3** band of frequencies used in radio and television transmission, esp. by a particular station. **4** course in which anything moves. **5 a** hollow bed of water. **b** navigable part of a waterway. **6** passage for liquid. **7** lengthwise strip on recording tape etc. *–v.* (**-ll-**; *US* **-l-**) **1** guide, direct. **2** form channel(s) in. [Latin: related to CANAL]

♦ **channel captain** *n.* most powerful member in the distribution channel of goods. The channel consists of the manufacturer, wholesaler, and retailer, the channel captain usu. being the manufacturer. There are, however, exceptions, most notably when the retailer is a major department store or chain, whose buying power enables it to become the channel captain. See also CHANNEL CONFLICT.

♦ **channel conflict** *n.* disagreement between members of a distribution channel (see CHANNEL CAPTAIN). Horizontal channel conflict can occur among retailers, if one retailer feels another is competing too vigorously through pricing or is invading the retailer's sales territory by means of advertising. Vertical conflict occurs between retailers and their suppliers when either side feels dominated by the other.

Channel Islands group of islands forming a British dependency in the English Channel off the NW coast of France, of which the largest are Jersey, Guernsey, and Alderney; pop. (1986) 144 494. Tourism, banking, and agriculture are of economic importance; exports include flowers, potatoes, and tomatoes.

♦ **Channel Tunnel** *n.* (also **Chunnel, Eurotunnel**) Anglo-French railway tunnel beneath the English Channel. It opened in 1994 and has greatly facilitated the transport of goods between the UK and mainland Europe. Its terminals are near Folkestone in England and near Calais in France.

chant /tʃɑːnt/ *–n.* **1** spoken singsong phrase. **2 a** simple tune used for singing unmetrical words, e.g. psalms. **b** song, esp. monotonous or repetitive. *–v.* **1** talk or repeat monotonously. **2** sing or intone (a psalm etc.). [Latin *canto* from *cano* sing]

chanter *n.* melody-pipe of bagpipes.

chanticleer /ˌtʃæntɪ'klɪə(r)/ *n.* name given to a domestic cock in stories. [French: related to CHANT, CLEAR]

chantry /'tʃɑːntrɪ/ *n.* (*pl.* **-ies**) **1** endowment for the singing of masses. **2** priests, chapel, etc., so endowed. [French: related to CHANT]

chaos /'keɪɒs/ *n.* **1** utter confusion. **2** formless matter supposed to have existed before the creation of the universe. □ **chaotic** /keɪ'ɒtɪk/ *adj.* **chaotically** /-'ɒtɪkəlɪ/ *adv.* [Latin from Greek]

chap[1] *n. colloq.* man, boy, fellow. [abbreviation of CHAPMAN]

chap[2] *–v.* (**-pp-**) **1** (esp. of the skin) develop cracks or soreness. **2** (of the wind, cold, etc.) cause to chap. *–n.* (usu. in *pl.*) crack in the skin etc. [origin uncertain]

chaparral /ˌʃæpə'ræl/ *n. US* dense tangled brushwood. [Spanish]

chapatti /tʃə'pɑːtɪ/ *n.* (also **chapati, chupatty**) (*pl.* **chapat(t)is** or **chupatties**) flat thin cake of unleavened bread. [Hindi]

chapel /'tʃæp(ə)l/ *n.* **1 a** place for private Christian worship in a Cathedral or large church, with its own altar. **b** this attached to a private house etc. **2 a** place of worship for Nonconformists. **b** chapel service. **3** members or branch of a printers' trade union at a place of work. [medieval Latin *cappa* cloak: the first chapel was a sanctuary in which St Martin's cloak (*cappella*) was preserved]

chaperon /'ʃæpəˌrəʊn/ *–n.* person, esp. an older woman, ensuring propriety by accompanying a young unmarried woman on social occasions. *–v.* act as chaperon to. □ **chaperonage** /-rənɪdʒ/ *n.* [French from *chape* cope: related to CAPE[1]]

chaplain /'tʃæplɪn/ *n.* member of the clergy attached to a private chapel, institution, ship, regiment, etc. □ **chaplaincy** *n.* (*pl.* **-ies**). [Latin: related to CHAPEL]

chaplet /'tʃæplɪt/ *n.* **1** garland or circlet for the head. **2** short string of beads; rosary. [Latin: related to CAP]

chapman /'tʃæpmən/ *n. hist.* pedlar. [Old English: related to CHEAP, MAN]

chappie *n. colloq.* = CHAP[1].

♦ **CHAPS** *abbr.* Clearing House Automatic Payments System. See ASSOCIATION FOR PAYMENT CLEARING SERVICES.

chapter *n.* **1** main division of a book. **2** period of time (in a person's life etc.). **3 a** canons of a cathedral or members of a religious community. **b** meeting of these. [Latin diminutive of *caput* head]

♦ **Chapter 7** *n. US* statute empowering a court to appoint a trustee to operate a business in liquidation to prevent further loss. [Chapter 7 of the Bankruptcy Reform Act (1978)]

♦ **Chapter 11** *n. US* statute empowering a court to allow the debtors of a failing business to remain in control to attempt to save it. [Chapter 11 of the Bankruptcy Reform Act (1978)]

chapter and verse *n.* exact reference or details.

chapter of accidents *n.* series of misfortunes.

char[1] *v.* (**-rr-**) **1** make or become black by burning; scorch. **2** burn to charcoal. [from CHARCOAL]

char[2] *colloq. –n.* = CHARWOMAN. *–v.* (**-rr-**) work as a charwoman. [Old English, = turn]

char[3] *n. slang* tea. [Chinese *cha*]

char[4] *n.* (*pl.* same) a kind of small trout. [origin unknown]

charabanc /'ʃærəˌbæŋ/ *n. hist.* early form of motor coach. [French *char à bancs* seated carriage]

character /'kærɪktə(r)/ *n.* **1** collective qualities or characteristics that distinguish a person or thing. **2 a** moral strength. **b** reputation, esp. good reputation. **3 a** person in a novel, play, etc. **b** part played by an actor; role. **4** *colloq.* person, esp. an eccentric one. **5 a** printed or written letter, symbol, etc. **b** *Computing* letter, digit, punctuation mark, or other symbol used in representing data and in organizing and possibly controlling data. See also CHARACTER SET 2. **6** written description of a person's qualities. **7** characteristic (esp. of a biological species). □ **in** (or **out of) character** consistent (or inconsistent) with a person's character. □ **characterless** *adj.* [Greek *kharaktēr*]

characteristic /ˌkærɪktə'rɪstɪk/ *–adj.* typical, distinctive. *–n.* characteristic feature or quality. □ **characteristically** *adv.*

characterize /'kærɪktəˌraɪz/ *v.* (also **-ise**) (**-zing** or **-sing**) **1 a** describe the character of. **b** (foll. by *as*) describe as. **2** be characteristic of. **3** impart character to. □ **characterization** /-'zeɪʃ(ə)n/ *n.*

♦ **character printer** *n.* device that prints one letter, digit, etc. at a time. An ordinary typewriter is a type of character printer. Most character printers used in computing are bidirectional: the printing mechanism prints as it moves from left to right along one line and then prints on the following line as it returns from right to left; this increases printing speed. In many designs the printing mechanism can be made to move at high speed over areas that are to remain blank. See also DAISY-WHEEL PRINTER; INK-JET PRINTER. Cf. LINE PRINTER.

♦ **character set** *n.* **1** collection of letters, numbers, symbols, etc. that can be produced by a device (e.g. a printer or typewriter). **2** collection of characters that a computer can handle, including the characters of the one or more programming languages used on the computer. It usu. includes the alphanumeric characters (letters and digits), the space character, **special characters** (e.g. punctuation marks, brackets, and the symbols used in arithmetic and logic operations), and **control characters** (producing a new line, backspace, etc.). Within a computer all these characters must be represented in binary form. Two widely used encoding schemes for characters are EBCDIC, used on IBM machines, and ASCII, which is in more general use.

charade /ʃə'rɑːd/ *n.* **1** (usu. in *pl.*, treated as *sing.*) game of guessing a word from acted clues. **2** absurd pretence. [Provençal *charra* chatter]

charcoal /'tʃɑːkəʊl/ *n.* **1 a** form of carbon consisting of black residue from partially burnt wood etc. **b** piece of this for drawing. **c** a drawing in charcoal. **2** (in full **charcoal grey**) dark grey. [origin unknown]

charge *–v.* (**-ging**) **1 a** ask (an amount) as a price. **b** ask (a person) for an amount as a price. **2 a** (foll. by *to*, *up to*) debit the cost of to (a person or account). **b** debit (a person or account). **3 a** (often foll. by *with*) accuse (of an offence). **b** (foll. by *that* + clause) make an accusation that. **4** (foll. by *to* + infin.) instruct or urge. **5** (foll. by *with*) entrust with. **6** make a rushing attack (on). **7** (often foll. by *up*) **a** give an electric charge to. **b** store energy in (a battery). **8** (often foll. by *with*) load or fill (a vessel, gun, etc.) to the full or proper extent. **9** (usu. as **charged** *adj.*) **a** (foll. by *with*) saturated with. **b** (usu. foll. by *with*) pervaded (with strong feelings etc.). *–n.* **1** price asked for services or goods. **2** legal or equitable interest in land, securing the payment of money. It gives the creditor in whose favour the charge is created (the **chargee**) the right to payment from the income or proceeds of sale of the land charged, in priority to claims against the debtor by unsecured creditors. **3** an interest in company property created in favour of a creditor (e.g. as a debenture holder) to secure the amount owing. Most charges must be registered by the Registrar of Companies (see also REGISTER OF CHARGES 1). A fixed charge is attached to a specific item of property (e.g. land); a floating charge is created in respect of circulating assets (e.g. cash, stock in trade), to which it will not attach until **crystallization**, i.e. until some event (e.g. winding-up) causes it to become fixed. Before crystallization, unsecured debts can be paid out of the assets charged. After, the charge is treated as a fixed charge. A charge can also be created upon shares. **4** accusation. **5 a** task, duty, commission. **b** care, custody. **c** person or thing entrusted. **6 a** impetuous rush or attack, esp. in battle. **b** signal for this. **7** appropriate amount of material to be put into a receptacle, mechanism, etc. at one time, esp. of explosive for a gun. **8 a** property of matter causing electrical phenomena. **b** quantity of this carried by the body. **c** energy stored chemically for conversion into electricity. **9** exhortation; directions, orders. **10** heraldic device or bearing. □ **charges forward** instruction indicating that all carriage charges on a consignment of goods will be paid by the consignee after receiving the goods. **in charge** having command. **take charge** (often foll. by *of*) assume control. □ **chargeable** *adj.* [Latin *carrus* CAR]

♦ **chargeable asset** *n.* any asset that can incur capital-gains tax when it is sold. Exempt assets include cars, government securities, and principal private residences.

♦ **chargeable event** *n.* transaction or event that gives rise to a liability to income tax or to capital-gains tax.

♦ **charge account** *n.* (also **credit account**) account held by a customer at a retail shop that allows the customer to pay for any goods purchased at the end of a stated period (usu. one month). Interest is usu. charged on any amounts unpaid after the stated period. The customer is identified by a plastic **charge card**.

charge-capping *n. hist.* imposition of an upper limit on the community charge levied by a local authority.

♦ **charge card** see CHARGE ACCOUNT.

chargé d'affaires /ˌʃɑːʒeɪ dæˈfeə(r)/ *n.* (*pl.* **chargés** pronunc. same) **1** ambassador's deputy. **2** envoy to a minor country. [French]

charger *n.* **1** cavalry horse. **2** apparatus for charging a battery.

♦ **charges register** *n.* **1** = REGISTER OF CHARGES 1, 2. **2** see LAND REGISTRATION.

chariot /ˈtʃærɪət/ *n. hist.* two-wheeled vehicle drawn by horses, used in ancient warfare and racing. [French: related to CAR]

charioteer /ˌtʃærɪəˈtɪə(r)/ *n.* chariot-driver.

charisma /kəˈrɪzmə/ *n.* **1** power to inspire or attract others; exceptional charm. **2** divinely conferred power or talent. □ **charismatic** /-ˈmætɪk/ *adj.* [Greek *kharis* grace]

charitable /ˈtʃærɪtəb(ə)l/ *adj.* **1** generous in giving to those in need. **2** of or relating to a charity or charities. **3** generous in judging others. □ **charitably** *adv.*

♦ **charitable trust** *n.* trust set up for a charitable purpose that is registered with the **Charity Commissioners**, a body responsible to parliament. Charitable trusts do not have to pay income tax if they comply with the regulations of the Charity Commissioners.

charity /ˈtʃærɪtɪ/ *n.* (*pl.* **-ies**) **1** giving voluntarily to those in need. **2** organization set up to help those in need or for the common good. **3 a** kindness, benevolence. **b** tolerance in judging others. **c** love of fellow men. [Latin *caritas* from *carus* dear]

charlady *n.* = CHARWOMAN.

charlatan /ˈʃɑːlət(ə)n/ *n.* person falsely claiming knowledge or skill. □ **charlatanism** *n.* [Italian, = babbler]

Charleroi /ˈʃɑːləˌrwɑː/ city in SW Belgium, in the province of Hainaut; industries include iron founding; pop. (1995) 206 491.

Charleston /ˈtʃɑːlst(ə)n/ **1** city in the US, capital of West Virginia; industries include chemicals, coal, glass, and timber; pop. (1990) 57 287. **2** city in the US, the main port of South Carolina; manufactures include paper products, textiles, and clothing; pop. (est. 1994) 76 854.

charleston /ˈtʃɑːlst(ə)n/ *n.* (also **Charleston**) lively dance of the 1920s with side-kicks from the knee. [CHARLESTON in South Carolina]

Charlotte /ˈʃɑːlət/ city in the US, principal commercial centre of North Carolina; industries include data processing, chemicals, and textiles; pop. (est. 1994) 437 797.

charlotte /ˈʃɑːlɒt/ *n.* pudding of stewed fruit covered with bread etc. [French]

Charlotte Amalie /ˌʃɑːlət əˈmɑːljə/ capital of the US Virgin Islands, a tourist resort on the island of St Thomas; pop. (1990) 12 331.

Charlottetown /ˈʃɑːlətˌtaʊn/ city in Canada, capital and chief port of Prince Edward Island; pop. (est. 1991) 30 000.

charm *–n.* **1** power or quality of delighting, arousing admiration, or influencing; fascination, attractiveness. **2** trinket on a bracelet etc. **3** object, act, or word(s) supposedly having magic power. *–v.* **1** delight, captivate. **2** influence or protect as if by magic (*a charmed life*). **3** obtain or gain by charm (*charmed his way into the BBC*). □ **charmer** *n.* [Latin *carmen* song]

charming *adj.* delightful. □ **charmingly** *adv.*

charnel-house /ˈtʃɑːn(ə)lˌhaʊs/ *n.* repository of corpses or bones. [Latin: related to CARNAL]

chart *–n.* **1** geographical map or plan, esp. for navigation. **2** sheet of information in the form of a table, graph, or diagram. **3** (usu. in *pl.*) *colloq.* listing of the currently best-selling pop records. *–v.* make a chart of, map. [Latin *charta*: related to CARD[1]]

charter *–n.* **1 a** document granting rights, issued esp. by a sovereign or legislature. **b** written constitution or description of an organization's functions etc. **2 a** hire of an aircraft, ship, etc., for a special purpose. **b** contract regulating this. See CHARTER-PARTY; BAREBOAT CHARTER; OPEN CHARTER; TIME CHARTER; VOYAGE CHARTER. *–v.* **1** grant a charter to. **2** hire (an aircraft, ship, etc.). □ **charterer** *n.* [Latin *chartula*: related to CHART]

chartered *attrib. adj.* (of an accountant, engineer, librarian, etc.) qualified as a member of a professional body that has a royal charter.

♦ **chartered accountant** *n.* (in the UK) qualified member of the Institute of Chartered Accountants in England and Wales, the Institute of Chartered Accountants of Scotland, or the Institute of Chartered Accountants in Ireland. These were the original bodies to be granted royal charters. Other bodies of accountants now have charters (the Chartered Association of Certified Accountants, the Chartered Institute of Management Accountants, and the Chartered Institute of Public Finance and Accountancy) but their members are not known as chartered accountants. Most firms of chartered accountants are engaged in public practice concerned with auditing, taxation, and other financial advice; however, many trained chartered accountants fulfil management roles in industry.

♦ **Chartered Association of Certified Accountants** see CERTIFIED ACCOUNTANT; CHARTERED ACCOUNTANT.

♦ **chartered company** *n.* company formed under royal charter, the earliest type of company to exist but now rare.

♦ **Chartered Institute of Management Accountants** see CHARTERED ACCOUNTANT; MANAGEMENT ACCOUNTANT.

♦ **Chartered Institute of Public Finance and Accountancy** see CHARTERED ACCOUNTANT.

♦ **Chartered Insurance Institute** *n.* (also **CII**) association of insurers and brokers in the insurance industry. Its origins date back to 1873; its first Royal Charter was granted in 1912. It provides training by post and at its own college, examinations leading to its associateship diploma (ACII) and fellowship diploma (FCII), and sets high standards of ethical behaviour in the industry.

♦ **chartered secretary** see INSTITUTE OF CHARTERED SECRETARIES AND ADMINISTRATORS.

♦ **chartered surveyor** see ROYAL INSTITUTION OF CHARTERED SURVEYORS.

charter flight *n.* flight by chartered aircraft.

◆ **charter-party** *n.* document setting out the terms and conditions of a contract of charter.

Chartism *n. hist.* UK Parliamentary reform movement of 1837–48. □ **Chartist** *n.* [from CHARTER: name taken from 'People's Charter']

◆ **chartist** *n.* investment analyst who uses charts and graphs to record past movements of the share prices, P/E ratios, turnover, etc. of individual companies to anticipate the future share movements of these companies. Claiming that history repeats itself and that the movements of share prices conform to a small number of repetitive patterns, chartists have been popular, esp. in the US, in the past. It is now more usual for analysts to use broader techniques in addition to those used by chartists.

Chartres /ʃɑːtr/ town and agricultural centre in NW France, noted for its Gothic cathedral; pop. (1990) 41 850.

chartreuse /ʃɑːˈtrɜːz/ *n.* pale green or yellow brandy-based liqueur. [*Chartreuse*, monastery in S France]

charwoman *n.* woman employed as a cleaner in a house.

chary /ˈtʃeərɪ/ *adj.* (**-ier, -iest**) **1** cautious, wary. **2** sparing; ungenerous. [Old English: related to CARE]

Charybdis see SCYLLA AND CHARYBDIS.

chase[1] *–v.* (**-sing**) **1** run after; pursue. **2** (foll. by *from*, *out of*, *to*, etc.) force to run away or flee. **3 a** (foll. by *after*) hurry in pursuit of. **b** (foll. by *round* etc.) *colloq.* act or move about hurriedly. **4** (usu. foll. by *up*) *colloq.* pursue (a thing overdue). **5** *colloq.* **a** try to attain. **b** court persistently. *–n.* **1** pursuit. **2** unenclosed hunting-land. **3** (prec. by *the*) hunting, esp. as a sport. [Latin *capto*: related to CATCH]

chase[2] *v.* (**-sing**) emboss or engrave (metal). [French: related to CASE[2]]

chaser *n.* **1** horse for steeplechasing. **2** *colloq.* drink taken after another of a different kind.

chasm /ˈkæz(ə)m/ *n.* **1** deep cleft or opening in the earth, rock, etc. **2** wide difference of feeling, interests, etc. [Latin from Greek]

chassis /ˈʃæsɪ/ *n.* (*pl.* same /-sɪz/) **1** base-frame of a motor vehicle, carriage, etc. **2** frame to carry radio etc. components. [Latin: related to CASE[2]]

chaste /tʃeɪst/ *adj.* **1** abstaining from extramarital, or from all, sexual intercourse. **2** pure, virtuous. **3** simple, unadorned. □ **chastely** *adv.* **chasteness** *n.* [Latin *castus*]

chasten /ˈtʃeɪs(ə)n/ *v.* **1** (esp. as **chastening, chastened** *adjs.*) subdue, restrain. **2** discipline, punish.

chastise /tʃæsˈtaɪz/ *v.* (**-sing**) **1** rebuke severely. **2** punish, esp. by beating. □ **chastisement** *n.*

chastity /ˈtʃæstɪtɪ/ *n.* being chaste.

chasuble /ˈtʃæzjʊb(ə)l/ *n.* loose sleeveless usu. ornate outer vestment worn by a celebrant at Mass or the Eucharist. [Latin *casubla*]

chat *–v.* (**-tt-**) talk in a light familiar way. *–n.* **1** pleasant informal talk. **2** any of various songbirds. □ **chat up** *colloq.* chat to, esp. flirtatiously or with an ulterior motive. [shortening of CHATTER]

château /ˈʃætəʊ/ *n.* (*pl.* **-x** /-təʊz/) large French country house or castle. [French: related to CASTLE]

chatelaine /ˈʃætəˌleɪn/ *n.* **1** mistress of a large house. **2** *hist.* set of short chains attached to a woman's belt, for carrying keys etc. [medieval Latin *castellanus*: related to CASTLE]

Chatham Islands /ˈtʃætəm/ group of two islands, Pitt and Chatham, in the SW Pacific Ocean, comprising part of New Zealand; pop. (1991) 769. Sheep farming is the main occupation.

chatline *n.* telephone service which sets up a social conference call among youngsters.

chat show *n.* television or radio broadcast in which celebrities are interviewed informally.

◆ **chattels** /ˈtʃæt(ə)lz/ *n.pl.* all property of whatever kind, excluding freehold land and anything permanently affixed to freehold land. Interests in land (e.g. leaseholds) are **chattels real**. **Chattels personal** are all movable and tangible articles of property. Chattels include timber growing on land (whether freehold or leasehold) and articles of personal use. [French: related to CATTLE]

chatter *–v.* **1** talk quickly, incessantly, trivially, or indiscreetly. **2** (of a bird, monkey, etc.) emit short quick sounds. **3** (of teeth) click repeatedly together. *–n.* chattering talk or sounds. [imitative]

chatterbox *n.* talkative person.

chatty *adj.* (**-ier, -iest**) **1** fond of chatting. **2** resembling chat. □ **chattily** *adv.* **chattiness** *n.*

chauffeur /ˈʃəʊfə(r)/ *–n.* (*fem.* **chauffeuse** /-ˈfɜːz/) person employed to drive a car. *–v.* drive (a car or person) as a chauffeur. [French, = stoker]

chauvinism /ˈʃəʊvɪˌnɪz(ə)m/ *n.* **1** exaggerated or aggressive patriotism. **2** excessive or prejudiced support or loyalty for one's cause or group. [*Chauvin*, name of a character in a French play 1831]

chauvinist *n.* **1** person exhibiting chauvinism. **2** (in full **male chauvinist**) man showing prejudice against women. □ **chauvinistic** /-ˈnɪstɪk/ *adj.* **chauvinistically** /-ˈnɪstɪkəlɪ/ *adv.*

CHDL *abbr.* computer hardware description language.

cheap *–adj.* **1** low in price; worth more than its cost. **2** charging low prices; offering good value. **3** of poor quality; inferior. **4** costing little effort and hence of little worth. *–adv.* cheaply. □ **on the cheap** cheaply. □ **cheaply** *adv.* **cheapness** *n.* [Old English, = price, bargain]

cheapen *v.* make or become cheap; depreciate, degrade.

cheapjack *–n.* seller of inferior goods at low prices. *–adj.* inferior, shoddy.

◆ **cheap money** *n.* (also **easy money**) money that can be borrowed at a low rate of interest. The policy of keeping interest rates at a low level is normally adopted to encourage an expansion in the level of economic activity by reducing the costs of borrowing and investment. It was used in the 1930s to help recovery after the Great Depression and during the Second World War to reduce the cost of government borrowing. Cf. DEAR MONEY.

cheapskate *n.* esp. *US colloq.* stingy person.

cheat *–v.* **1 a** (often foll. by *into*, *out of*) deceive or trick. **b** (foll. by *of*) deprive of. **2** gain an unfair advantage by deception or breaking rules. *–n.* **1** person who cheats. **2** trick, deception. □ **cheat on** *colloq.* be sexually unfaithful to. [from ESCHEAT]

check *–v.* **1 a** examine the accuracy or quality of. **b** make sure, verify. **2 a** stop or slow the motion of; curb. **b** *colloq.* rebuke. **3** *Chess* directly threaten (the opposing king). **4** *US* agree on comparison. **5** *US* mark with a tick etc. **6** *US* deposit (luggage etc.). *–n.* **1** means or act of testing or ensuring accuracy, quality, etc. **2 a** stopping or slowing of motion. **b** rebuff or rebuke. **c** person or thing that restrains. **3 a** pattern of small squares. **b** fabric so patterned. **c** (*attrib.*) so patterned. **4** (*also as int.*) *Chess* exposure of a king to direct attack. **5** *US* restaurant bill. **6** *US* = CHEQUE. **7** esp. *US* token of identification for left luggage etc. **8** *US Cards* counter used in games. **9** temporary loss of the scent in hunting. □ **check in 1** arrive or register at a hotel, airport, etc. **2** record the arrival of. **check into** register one's arrival at (a hotel etc.). **check off** mark on a list etc. as having been examined. **check on** examine, verify, keep watch on. **check out 1** (often foll. by *of*) leave a hotel etc. with due formalities. **2** esp. *US* investigate. **check up** make sure, verify. **check up on** = *check on*. [Persian, = king]

checked *adj.* having a check pattern.

checker[1] *n.* person etc. that examines, esp. in a factory etc.

checker[2] *n.* **1** var. of CHEQUER. **2** *US* **a** (in *pl.*, usu. treated as *sing.*) draughts. **b** piece used in this game.

check-in *n.* act or place of checking in.

checkmate –*n.* (also as *int.*) *Chess* check from which a king cannot escape. –*v.* (**-ting**) **1** *Chess* put into checkmate. **2** frustrate. [French: related to CHECK, Persian *māt* is dead]

checkout *n.* **1** act of checking out. **2** pay-desk in a supermarket etc.

checkpoint *n.* **1** place, esp. a barrier or entrance, where documents, vehicles, etc., are inspected. **2** *Computing* point in some processing activity, or a place in a program, at which a copy is taken of data associated with the active program. It is hence the point or place from which the program can subsequently be restarted. The use of checkpoints guards against system failure during very long program executions.

check-up *n.* thorough (esp. medical) examination.

Cheddar /'tʃedə(r)/ *n.* a kind of firm smooth cheese. [*Cheddar* in Somerset]

cheek –*n.* **1 a** side of the face below the eye. **b** side-wall of the mouth. **2 a** impertinence; cool confidence. **b** impertinent speech. **3** *slang* buttock. –*v.* be impertinent to. □ **cheek by jowl** close together; intimate. [Old English]

cheek-bone *n.* bone below the eye.

cheeky *adj.* (**-ier**, **-iest**) impertinent. □ **cheekily** *adv.* **cheekiness** *n.*

cheep –*n.* weak shrill cry of a young bird. –*v.* make such a cry. [imitative]

cheer –*n.* **1** shout of encouragement or applause. **2** mood, disposition (*full of good cheer*). **3** (in *pl.*; as *int.*) *colloq.* **a** expressing good wishes on parting or before drinking. **b** expressing gratitude. –*v.* **1 a** applaud with shouts. **b** (usu. foll. by *on*) urge with shouts. **2** shout for joy. **3** gladden; comfort. □ **cheer up** make or become less depressed. [Latin *cara* face, from Greek]

cheerful *adj.* **1** in good spirits, noticeably happy. **2** bright, pleasant. □ **cheerfully** *adv.* **cheerfulness** *n.*

cheerio /,tʃɪrɪ'əʊ/ *int. colloq.* expressing good wishes on parting.

cheer-leader *n.* person who leads cheers of applause etc.

cheerless *adj.* gloomy, dreary.

cheery *adj.* (**-ier**, **-iest**) cheerful. □ **cheerily** *adv.* **cheeriness** *n.*

cheese /tʃi:z/ *n.* **1 a** food made from curds of milk. **b** cake of this with rind. **2** conserve with the consistency of soft cheese. □ **cheesy** *adj.* [Latin *caseus*]

cheeseburger *n.* hamburger with cheese in or on it.

cheesecake *n.* **1** tart filled with sweetened curds etc. **2** *slang* portrayal of women in a sexually stimulating manner.

cheesecloth *n.* thin loosely-woven cloth.

cheesed /tʃi:zd/ *adj. slang* (often foll. by *off*) bored, fed up. [origin unknown]

cheese-paring *adj.* stingy.

cheese plant *n.* climbing plant with holes in its leaves.

cheetah /'tʃi:tə/ *n.* swift-running spotted leopard-like feline. [Hindi]

chef /ʃef/ *n.* (usu. male) cook, esp. the chief cook in a restaurant. [French]

Chekiang see ZHEJIANG.

Chelsea bun /'tʃelsɪ/ *n.* currant bun in the form of a flat spiral. [*Chelsea* in London]

Chelsea pensioner *n.* inmate of the Chelsea Royal Hospital for old or disabled soldiers.

Chelyabinsk /,tʃel'jæbɪnsk/ industrial city in SW Russia; manufactures include vehicles, steel, and chemicals; pop. (est. 1995) 1 086 000.

chemical /'kemɪk(ə)l/ –*adj.* of, made by, or employing chemistry or chemicals. –*n.* substance obtained or used in chemistry. □ **chemically** *adv.* [French or medieval Latin: related to ALCHEMY]

chemical engineering *n.* creation and operation of industrial chemical plants. □ **chemical engineer** *n.*

chemical warfare *n.* warfare using poison gas and other chemicals.

chemise /ʃə'mi:z/ *n. hist.* woman's loose-fitting undergarment or dress. [Latin *camisia* shirt]

chemist /'kemɪst/ *n.* **1** dealer in medicinal drugs etc. **2** expert in chemistry. [French: related to ALCHEMY]

chemistry /'kemɪstrɪ/ *n.* (*pl.* **-ies**) **1** branch of science dealing with the elements and the compounds they form and the reactions they undergo. **2** chemical composition and properties of a substance. **3** *colloq.* sexual attraction.

Chemnitz /'kemnɪts/ (formerly **Karl-Marx-Stadt**) industrial city in SE Germany; products include textiles and machinery; pop. (est. 1995) 274 162.

chemotherapy /,ki:məʊ'θerəpɪ/ *n.* treatment of disease, esp. cancer, by chemical substances.

Chengchow see ZHENGZHOU.

Chengdu /tʃeŋ'du:/ city in central China, capital of Sichuan province; industries include textiles, chemicals, and machinery; pop. (est. 1991) 2 810 000.

chenille /ʃə'ni:l/ *n.* **1** tufty velvety cord or yarn. **2** fabric of this. [French, = caterpillar, from Latin *canicula* little dog]

♦ **cheque** /tʃek/ *n.* (*US* **check**) printed form on which instructions are given to an account holder (a bank or building society) to pay a stated sum to a named recipient. It is the most common form of payment of debts of all kinds (see also CHEQUE ACCOUNT; CURRENT ACCOUNT 1). In a **crossed cheque** two parallel lines across the face of the cheque indicate that it must be paid into a bank account and not cashed over the counter (a **general crossing**). A **special crossing** may be used in order to further restrict the negotiability of the cheque, for example by adding the name of the payee's bank. According to the Cheque Act (1992) a cheque endorsed 'account payee' is non-transferable; banks require the customer's express permission to cash an endorsed cheque. An **open cheque** is an uncrossed cheque that can be cashed at the bank of origin. An **order cheque** is one made payable to a named recipient 'or order', enabling the payee to either deposit it in an account or endorse it to a third party, i.e. transfer the rights to the cheque by signing it on the reverse. In a **blank cheque** the amount is not stated; it is often used if the exact debt is not known and the payee is left to complete it. However, the drawer may impose a maximum by writing 'under £...' on the cheque. See also MARKED CHEQUE; RETURNED CHEQUE; STALE CHEQUE. [from CHECK]

♦ **cheque account** *n.* account with a bank or building society on which cheques can be drawn. In general, building societies pay interest on the daily credit balances in a cheque account but banks traditionally did not; they are now often doing so to meet competition from building societies. See also CURRENT ACCOUNT 1.

---

cheque-book *n.* book of detachable cheques issued by a bank or building society to holders of cheque accounts.

cheque card *n.* card issued by a UK bank or building society to an approved customer, guaranteeing any cheque drawn by that customer up to an amount stated on the cheque card (usu. either £50 or £100). Cf. MULTIFUNCTION CARD 1.

chequer /'tʃekə(r)/ –*n.* **1** (often in *pl.*) pattern of squares often alternately coloured. **2** var. of CHECKER[2] 2. –*v.* **1** mark with chequers. **2** variegate; break the uniformity of. **3** (as **chequered** *adj.*) with varied fortunes (*chequered career*). [from EXCHEQUER]

Cherbourg /'ʃɜ:bʊəg, 'feə-/ seaport and naval base in NW France; city pop. (est. 1983) 32 415; metropolitan area pop. (est. 1990) 92 045.

cherish /'tʃerɪʃ/ *v.* **1** protect or tend lovingly. **2** hold dear, cling to (hopes, feelings, etc.). [French *cher* dear, from Latin *carus*]

Chernobyl /tʃə'nɒbɪl, -'nəʊbɪl/ city in N Ukraine, near Kiev, where in 1986 explosions at a nuclear power station resulted in a serious escape of radioactivity which spread to contaminate many parts of Europe.

cheroot /ʃə'ru:t/ *n.* cigar with both ends open. [French from Tamil]

cherry /ˈtʃerɪ/ *–n.* (*pl.* **-ies**) **1 a** small soft round stone-fruit. **b** tree bearing this or grown for its ornamental flowers. **c** its wood. **2** light red colour. *–adj.* of light red colour. [Greek *kerasos*]

cherub /ˈtʃerəb/ *n.* **1** (*pl.* **-im**) angelic being of the second order of the celestial hierarchy. **2 a** representation of a winged child or its head. **b** beautiful or innocent child. □ **cherubic** /tʃɪˈruːbɪk/ *adj.* [ultimately from Hebrew]

chervil /ˈtʃɜːvɪl/ *n.* herb used for flavouring. [Greek *khairephullon*]

Ches. *abbr.* Cheshire.

Chesapeake Bay /ˈtʃesəˌpiːk/ large inlet of the Atlantic Ocean on the coast of the US, bordering on Virginia and Maryland.

Cheshire /ˈtʃeʃə(r)/ county in NW England; products include chemicals, textiles, and dairy produce; pop. (est. 1994) 975 600; county town, Chester. *–n.* crumbly cheese originally made in Cheshire. □ **like a Cheshire cat** with a broad fixed grin.

chess *n.* game for two with 16 men each, played on a chessboard. [French: related to CHECK]

chessboard *n.* chequered board of 64 squares on which chess and draughts are played.

chessman *n.* any of the 32 pieces and pawns with which chess is played.

chest *n.* **1** large strong box. **2 a** part of the body enclosed by the ribs. **b** front surface of the body from the neck to the bottom of the ribs. **3** small cabinet for medicines etc. □ **get a thing off one's chest** *colloq.* disclose a secret etc. to relieve one's anxiety about it. [Latin *cista*]

Chester /ˈtʃestə(r)/ town in NW central England, county town of Cheshire; industries include engineering; pop. (1991) 80 110.

chesterfield /ˈtʃestəˌfiːld/ *n.* sofa with arms and back of the same height and curved outwards at the top. [Earl of *Chesterfield*]

chestnut /ˈtʃesnʌt/ *–n.* **1 a** glossy hard brown edible nut. **b** tree bearing it. **2** = HORSE CHESTNUT. **3** wood of any chestnut. **4** horse of a reddish-brown colour. **5** *colloq.* stale joke etc. **6** reddish-brown. *–adj.* reddish-brown. [Greek *kastanea* nut]

chest of drawers *n.* piece of furniture consisting of a set of drawers in a frame.

chesty *adj.* (**-ier**, **-iest**) *colloq.* inclined to or symptomatic of chest disease. □ **chestily** *adv.* **chestiness** *n.*

cheval-glass /ʃəˈvæl/ *n.* tall mirror swung on an upright frame. [Latin *caballus* horse]

chevalier /ˌʃevəˈlɪə(r)/ *n.* member of certain orders of knighthood, or of the French Legion of Honour etc. [medieval Latin *caballarius* horseman]

chevron /ˈʃevrən/ *n.* V-shaped line or stripe. [Latin *caper* goat]

chew *–v.* work (food etc.) between the teeth. *–n.* **1** act of chewing. **2** chewy sweet. □ **chew on 1** work continuously between the teeth. **2** think about. **chew over 1** discuss, talk over. **2** think about. [Old English]

chewing-gum *n.* flavoured gum for chewing.

chewy *adj.* (**-ier**, **-iest**) **1** needing much chewing. **2** suitable for chewing. □ **chewiness** *n.*

Cheyenne /ʃaɪˈæn/ city in the US, capital of Wyoming and an agricultural trading centre; pop. (1990) 50 008.

chez /ʃeɪ/ *prep.* at the home of. [French from Latin *casa* cottage]

ch. fwd. *abbr.* charges forward.

chg. *abbr.* (also **chge.**) charge.

chi /kaɪ/ *n.* twenty-second letter of the Greek alphabet (Χ, χ). [Greek]

Chianti /kɪˈæntɪ/ *n.* (*pl.* **-s**) red wine from the Chianti area in Italy.

Chiapas /tʃɪˈɑːpəs/ state of S Mexico; pop. (est. 1995) 3 606 828; capital, Tuxtla Gutiérrez.

chiaroscuro /kɪˌɑːrəˈskʊərəʊ/ *n.* **1** treatment of light and shade in drawing and painting. **2** use of contrast in literature etc. [Italian, = clear dark]

chic /ʃiːk/ *–adj.* (**chic-er**, **chic-est**) stylish, elegant. *–n.* stylishness, elegance. [French]

Chicago /ʃɪˈkɑːgəʊ/ city in the US, in Illinois on Lake Michigan, an important commercial, financial, and industrial centre; pop. (1994) 2 731 743. Manufactures include steel, textiles, chemicals, and cars.

chicane /ʃɪˈkeɪn/ *–n.* **1** artificial barrier or obstacle on a motor racecourse. **2** chicanery. *–v.* (**-ning**) *archaic* **1** use chicanery. **2** (usu. foll. by *into*, *out of*, etc.) cheat (a person). [French]

chicanery /ʃɪˈkeɪnərɪ/ *n.* (*pl.* **-ies**) **1** clever but misleading talk. **2** trickery, deception. [French]

chick *n.* **1** young bird. **2** *slang* young woman. [Old English: related to CHICKEN]

chicken /ˈtʃɪkɪn/ *–n.* **1 a** domestic fowl. **b** its flesh as food. **2** young bird of a domestic fowl. **3** youthful person (*is no chicken*). *–adj. colloq.* cowardly. *–v.* (foll. by *out*) *colloq.* withdraw through cowardice. [Old English]

chicken-feed *n.* **1** food for poultry. **2** *colloq.* trivial amount, esp. of money.

chickenpox *n.* infectious disease, esp. of children, with a rash of small blisters.

chicken-wire *n.* light wire netting with a hexagonal mesh.

chick-pea *n.* yellow pea-like seed used as a vegetable. [Latin *cicer*]

chickweed *n.* small weed with tiny white flowers.

chicle /ˈtʃɪk(ə)l/ *n.* milky juice of a tropical tree, used in chewing-gum. [Spanish from Nahuatl]

chicory /ˈtʃɪkərɪ/ *n.* (*pl.* **-ies**) **1** plant with leaves used in salads. **2** its root, roasted and ground and used with or instead of coffee. **3** esp. *US* = ENDIVE. [Greek *kikhorion*]

chide *v.* (*past* **chided** or **chid**; *past part.* **chided** or **chidden**) *archaic* scold, rebuke. [Old English]

Chile /ˈtʃɪlɪ/, **Republic of** country occupying a long coastal strip in the S half of W South America. The country's considerable mineral wealth includes copper, iron, nitrates, coal, and oil; Chile is one of the world's chief exporters of copper. Stable democratic rule is allowing the economy to expand: revenue from exports other than copper, including paper and wood products, chemical and petroleum products, and fish-meal, is increasing, and agricultural industry is being encouraged; cereals, sugar beet, vegetables, and vines are extensively grown. Chile is a member of LAIA.

History. Chilean independence from Spain was achieved in 1818. In 1973 the democratically elected Marxist president, Salvador Allende, was overthrown by a coup led by General Pinochet, who headed the subsequent military dictatorship. He was defeated in elections held in 1989. In 1996 the US Congress refused to allow Chile to join NAFTA; however, it did become a member of the Southern Cone Common Market (Mercosur). President, Eduardo Frei; capital, Santiago. □ **Chilean** *adj.* & *n.*

language	Spanish
currency	peso (Ch$) of 100 centavos
pop. (est. 1996)	14 376 000
GNP (1994)	US$50B
literacy	81%
life expectancy	71 (m); 77 (f)

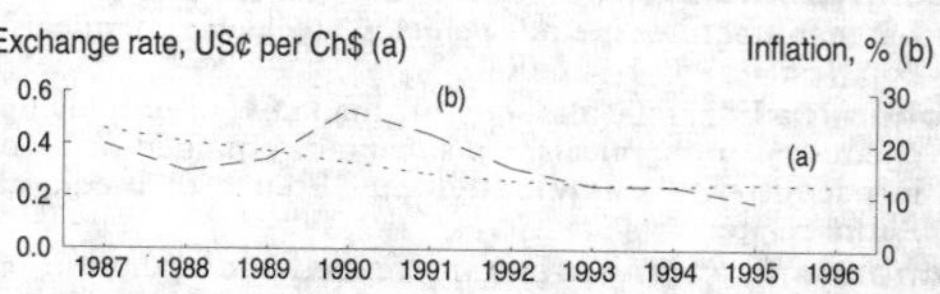

---

chief –*n.* **1 a** leader or ruler. **b** head of a tribe, clan, etc. **2** head of a department; highest official. –*adj.* **1** first in position, importance, influence, etc. **2** prominent, leading. [Latin *caput* head]

Chief Constable *n.* head of the police force of a county etc.

◆ **chief executive** *n.* person with responsibility for ensuring that an organization functions efficiently if it is non-profit-making and makes a profit acceptable to the shareholders if it is profit-making. Although the term was formerly more common in North America than the UK, it is now sometimes used in place of managing director in the UK.

chiefly *adv.* above all; mainly but not exclusively.

Chief of Staff *n.* senior staff officer of a service or command.

chieftain /ˈtʃiːft(ə)n/ *n.* leader of a tribe, clan, etc. □ **chieftaincy** *n.* (*pl.* **-ies**). [Latin: related to CHIEF]

Chiengmai /tʃɪeŋˈmaɪ/ (also **Chiang Mai**) city in NW Thailand, a trading centre with teak, silk, and handicraft industries; pop. (1991) 161 541.

chiffchaff /ˈtʃɪftʃæf/ *n.* small European warbler. [imitative]

chiffon /ˈʃɪfɒn/ *n.* light diaphanous fabric of silk, nylon, etc. [French *chiffe* rag]

chignon /ˈʃiːnjɔ̃/ *n.* coil of hair at the back of a woman's head. [French]

Chihuahua /tʃɪˈwɑːwə/ **1** state in Mexico; industries include mining, smelting, and meat packing; pop. (est. 1995) 2 792 989. **2** its capital city; pop. (1990) 516 153.

chihuahua /tʃɪˈwɑːwə/ *n.* dog of a very small smooth-haired breed. [CHIHUAHUA]

chilblain /ˈtʃɪlbleɪn/ *n.* painful itching swelling on a hand, foot, etc., caused by exposure to cold. [from CHILL, *blain* inflamed sore, blister]

child /tʃaɪld/ *n.* (*pl.* **children** /ˈtʃɪldrən/) **1 a** young human being below the age of puberty. **b** unborn or newborn human being. **2** one's son or daughter. **3** (foll. by *of*) descendant, follower, or product of. **4** childish person. □ **childless** *adj.* [Old English]

child abuse *n.* maltreatment of a child, esp. by physical violence or sexual molestation.

child benefit *n.* regular payment made direct to a parent in the UK by the Department of Social Security through a post office in respect of each child under the age of 16 (or 18 if they are in full-time education). This payment replaces the former family allowance set against the parents' income tax.

childbirth *n.* giving birth to a child.

child care *n.* the care of children, esp. by a local authority or (for children of working parents) by a child-minder.

childhood *n.* state or period of being a child.

childish *adj.* **1** of, like, or proper to a child. **2** immature, silly. □ **childishly** *adv.* **childishness** *n.*

childlike *adj.* having the good qualities of a child, such as innocence, frankness, etc.

child-minder *n.* person looking after children for payment.

◆ **children's assurance** *n.* insurance arranged on the life of a child or a minor (anyone aged below 18). The main use of life assurance is to replace income lost following the death of a breadwinner. As a child does not usu. earn any income, the law insists that children's assurance policies only pay the sum assured when the policy matures or death occurs after the child reaches the age of 18. If the child dies before reaching this age no payment is made but the premiums are refunded in full. This restriction was applied to policies of this kind to prevent unscrupulous parents from murdering their children to claim the benefit.

child's play *n.* easy task.

chili var. of CHILLI.

chill –*n.* **1 a** unpleasant cold sensation; lowered body temperature. **b** feverish cold. **2** unpleasant coldness (of air, water, etc.). **3** depressing influence. **4** coldness of manner. –*v.* **1** make or become cold. **2** depress; horrify. **3** preserve (food or drink) by cooling. –*adj. literary* chilly. [Old English]

chilli /ˈtʃɪlɪ/ *n.* (also **chili**) (*pl.* **-es**) hot-tasting dried red capsicum pod. [Spanish from Aztec]

chilli con carne /kɒn ˈkɑːnɪ/ *n.* dish of chilli-flavoured mince and beans.

chilly *adj.* (**-ier, -iest**) **1** somewhat cold. **2** sensitive to the cold. **3** unfriendly; unemotional.

Chiltern Hundreds /ˈtʃɪlt(ə)n/ *n.pl.* Crown manor, whose administration is a nominal office for which an MP applies as a way of resigning from the House of Commons. [*Chiltern* Hills in S England]

chime –*n.* **1** set of attuned bells. **2** sounds made by this. –*v.* (**-ming**) **1** (of bells) ring. **2** show (the time) by chiming. **3** (usu. foll. by *together, with*) be in agreement. □ **chime in 1** interject a remark. **2** join in harmoniously. **3**

China /ˈtʃaɪnə/, **People's Republic of** country in E Asia, the third-largest and most populous in the world. It is essentially an agricultural country, cereals being produced in the N provinces and rice and sugar in the S; cotton, tea, hemp, jute, and flax are the most important crops, while the culture of silkworms is one of the oldest industries. Mineral resources are considerable and include coal, iron ore, and oil, in which the country has been self-sufficient since 1973. China is the world's main producer of tungsten, and antimony, lead, bauxite, and manganese are also mined. Hydroelectricity is a developing power source. Manufactured products include consumer goods, industrial products, chemicals, textiles, and steel. The economy is healthy, and the government is committed to market-orientated reforms, with expansion of the private sector and closer trade links with Taiwan, Hong Kong, and the US. A third of China's exports are sold to the US, but trade agreements are under threat if human rights in China continue to be violated.

History. China was ruled by a series of dynasties until the Ch'ing (or Manchu) dynasty was overthrown in 1912. From the 1920s the country was stricken by civil war and Japanese invasion, and soon after the end of the Second World War the corrupt and ineffective Kuomintang (Nationalist People's Party) government was overthrown by the Communists, the People's Republic of China being declared in 1949. Until quite recently, China remained generally closed to Western economic or political penetration. The 1980s saw a period of economic liberalization, but a pro-democracy movement was ruthlessly repressed by the army in 1989, since when any signs of political dissent have been vigorously suppressed. Following the death of Deng Xiaoping in 1997, Jiang Zemin became China's new supreme leader. Also in 1997 the colony of Hong Kong reverted to Chinese control, becoming a Special Administrative Region. President, Jiang Zemin; prime minister, Li Peng; capital, Peking.

languages	Mandarin Chinese (official), Cantonese
currency	yuan (Y) of 10 jiao or 100 fen
pop. (est. 1996)	1 218 700 000
GNP (1994)	US$630B
literacy	87% (m); 68% (f)
life expectancy	69 (m); 72 (f)

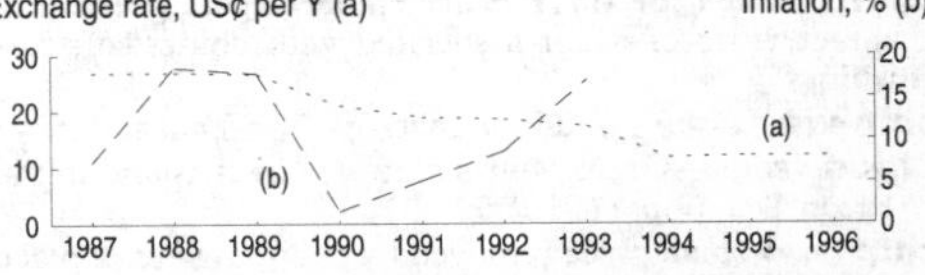

(foll. by *with*) agree with. [Old English: related to CYMBAL]

chimera /kaɪˈmɪərə/ *n.* **1** (in Greek mythology) monster with a lion's head, goat's body, and serpent's tail. **2** bogey. **3** wild or fantastic conception. □ **chimerical** /-ˈmerɪk(ə)l/ *adj.* [Latin from Greek]

chimney /ˈtʃɪmnɪ/ *n.* (*pl.* **-s**) **1** channel conducting smoke etc. up and away from a fire, engine, etc. **2** part of this above a roof. **3** glass tube protecting the flame of a lamp. **4** narrow vertical crack in a rock-face. [Latin *caminus* oven, from Greek]

chimney-breast *n.* projecting wall surrounding a chimney.

chimney-pot *n.* earthenware or metal pipe at the top of a chimney.

chimney-stack *n.* number of chimneys grouped in one structure.

chimney-sweep *n.* person who removes soot from inside chimneys.

chimp *n. colloq.* = CHIMPANZEE. [abbreviation]

chimpanzee /ˌtʃɪmpənˈziː/ *n.* small African manlike ape. [French from Kongo]

chin *n.* front of the lower jaw. □ **keep one's chin up** *colloq.* remain cheerful. **take on the chin** suffer a severe blow from; endure courageously. [Old English]

china /ˈtʃaɪnə/ *–n.* **1** fine white or translucent ceramic ware, porcelain, etc. **2** things made of this. *–adj.* made of china. [CHINA]

china clay *n.* kaolin.

Chinaman /ˈtʃaɪnəmən/ *n.* **1** *archaic* or *derog.* (now usu. *offens.*) native of China. **2** *Cricket* ball bowled by a left-handed bowler that spins from off to leg.

China Sea part of the Pacific Ocean off the coast of China. See EAST CHINA SEA; SOUTH CHINA SEA.

chinchilla /tʃɪnˈtʃɪlə/ *n.* **1 a** small South American rodent. **b** its soft grey fur. **2** breed of cat or rabbit. [Spanish *chinche* bug]

chine *–n.* **1 a** backbone. **b** joint of meat containing all or part of this. **2** ridge. *–v.* (**-ning**) cut (meat) through the backbone. [Latin *spina* SPINE]

Chinese /tʃaɪˈniːz/ *–adj.* of China. *–n.* **1** Chinese language. **2** (*pl.* same) **a** native or national of China. **b** person of Chinese descent.

Chinese lantern *n.* **1** collapsible paper lantern. **2** plant with an orange-red papery calyx.

Chinese leaf *n.* lettuce-like cabbage.

♦ **Chinese wall** *n.* notional information barrier between the parts of a business, esp. between the market-making part of a stockbroking firm and the broking part. It would clearly not be in investors' interests for brokers to persuade their clients to buy investments from them for no other reason than that the market makers in the firm, expecting a fall in price, were anxious to sell them.

Chink *n. slang offens.* a Chinese. [abbreviation]

chink[1] *n.* narrow opening; slit. [related to *chine* narrow ravine]

chink[2] *–v.* (cause to) make a sound like glasses or coins striking together. *–n.* this sound. [imitative]

chinless *adj. colloq.* weak or feeble in character.

chinless wonder *n.* ineffectual esp. upper-class person.

chinoiserie /ʃɪnˈwɑːzərɪ/ *n.* **1** imitation of Chinese motifs in painting and in decorating furniture. **2** object(s) in this style. [French]

chintz /tʃɪnts/ *n.* printed multicoloured usu. glazed cotton fabric. [Hindi from Sanskrit]

chintzy *adj.* (**-ier, -iest**) **1** like chintz. **2** gaudy, cheap. **3** characteristic of décor associated with chintz soft furnishings.

chin-wag *slang –n.* talk or chat. *–v.* (**-gg-**) chat.

Chios /ˈkaɪɒs/ (Greek **Khios** /ˈkiːɒs/) Greek island in the Aegean Sea; pop. (1990) 52 691.

chip *–n.* **1** small piece removed by chopping etc. **2** place or mark where a piece has been broken off. **3 a** strip of potato, usu. deep-fried. **b** *US* potato crisp. **4** counter used in some games to represent money. **5** = MICROCHIP. *–v.* (**-pp-**) **1** (often foll. by *off, away*) cut or break (a piece) from a hard material. **2** (often foll. by *at, away at*) cut pieces off (a hard material) to alter its shape etc. **3** be apt to break at the edge. **4** (usu. as **chipped** *adj.*) make (potatoes) into chips. □ **chip in** *colloq.* **1** interrupt. **2** contribute (money etc.). **a chip off the old block** child resembling its parent, esp. in character. **a chip on one's shoulder** *colloq.* inclination to feel resentful or aggrieved. **when the chips are down** *colloq.* when it comes to the point. [Old English]

chipboard *n.* board made from compressed wood chips.

chipmunk /ˈtʃɪpmʌŋk/ *n.* striped North American ground squirrel. [Algonquian]

chipolata /ˌtʃɪpəˈlɑːtə/ *n.* small thin sausage. [French from Italian]

Chippendale /ˈtʃɪpənˌdeɪl/ *adj.* (of furniture) of an elegantly ornate 18th-century style. [name of a cabinet-maker]

CHIPS /tʃɪps/ *abbr.* = CLEARING HOUSE INTERBANK PAYMENTS SYSTEM.

chiro- *comb. form* hand. [Greek *kheir*]

chiromancy /ˈkaɪərəʊˌmænsɪ/ *n.* palmistry. [Greek *mantis* seer]

chiropody /kɪˈrɒpədɪ/ *n.* treatment of the feet and their ailments. □ **chiropodist** *n.* [Greek *pous podos* foot]

chiropractic /ˌkaɪərəʊˈpræktɪk/ *n.* treatment of disease by manipulation of esp. the spinal column. □ **chiropractor** /ˈkaɪərəʊ-/ *n.* [Greek *prattō* do]

chirp *–v.* **1** (of small birds, grasshoppers, etc.) utter a short sharp note. **2** speak or utter merrily. *–n.* chirping sound. [imitative]

chirpy *adj. colloq.* (**-ier, -iest**) cheerful, lively. □ **chirpily** *adv.* **chirpiness** *n.*

chirrup /ˈtʃɪrəp/ *–v.* (**-p-**) chirp, esp. repeatedly. *–n.* chirruping sound. [imitative]

chisel /ˈtʃɪz(ə)l/ *–n.* hand tool with a squared bevelled blade for shaping wood, stone, or metal. *–v.* **1** (**-ll-**; *US* **-l-**) cut or shape with a chisel. **2** (as **chiselled** *adj.*) (of facial features) clear-cut, fine. **3** *slang* cheat. [Latin *caedo* cut]

chit[1] *n.* **1** *derog.* or *joc.* young small woman (esp. *a chit of a girl*). **2** young child. [originally = whelp, cub]

chit[2] *n.* **1** note of requisition, of a sum owed, etc. **2** note or memorandum. [Hindi from Sanskrit]

chit-chat *n. colloq.* light conversation; gossip. [reduplication of CHAT]

Chittagong /ˈtʃɪtəˌgɒŋ/ major industrial city and seaport in SE Bangladesh; industries include steel, engineering, chemicals, and textiles; pop. (1991) 2 040 663.

chivalrous /ˈʃɪvəlrəs/ *adj.* **1** gallant, honourable. **2** of or showing chivalry. □ **chivalrously** *adv.* [Latin: related to CHEVALIER]

chivalry /ˈʃɪvəlrɪ/ *n.* **1** medieval knightly system with its religious, moral, and social code. **2** honour, courtesy, and readiness to help the weak. □ **chivalric** *adj.*

chive *n.* small plant with long onion-flavoured leaves. [Latin *cepa* onion]

chivvy /ˈtʃɪvɪ/ *v.* (**-ies, -ied**) urge persistently, nag. [probably from ballad of *Chevy Chase*]

chloral /ˈklɔːr(ə)l/ *n.* **1** colourless liquid aldehyde used in making DDT. **2** (in full **chloral hydrate**) *Pharm.* crystalline solid made from this and used as a sedative. [French: related to CHLORINE, ALCOHOL]

chloride /ˈklɔːraɪd/ *n.* **1** compound of chlorine and another element or group. **2** bleaching agent containing this.

chlorinate /ˈklɔːrɪˌneɪt/ *v.* (**-ting**) impregnate or treat with chlorine. □ **chlorination** /-ˈneɪʃ(ə)n/ *n.*

chlorine /ˈklɔːriːn/ *n.* poisonous gaseous element used for purifying water etc. [Greek *khlōros* green]

chloro-fluorocarbon see CFC.

chloroform /ˈklɒrəˌfɔːm/ *–n.* colourless volatile liquid formerly used as a general anaesthetic. *–v.* render unconscious with this. [from CHLORINE, FORMIC ACID]

chlorophyll /'klɒrəfɪl/ *n.* green pigment found in most plants. [Greek *khlōros* green, *phullon* leaf]

choc *n. colloq.* chocolate. [abbreviation]

choc-ice *n.* bar of ice-cream covered with chocolate.

chock *–n.* block or wedge to check the motion of a wheel etc. *–v.* make fast with chocks. [French]

chock-a-block *predic. adj.* (often foll. by *with*) crammed together or full.

chock-full *predic. adj.* (often foll. by *of*) crammed full.

chocolate /'tʃɒklət/ *–n.* **1 a** food preparation in the form of a paste or solid block made from ground cacao seeds and usu. sweetened. **b** sweet made of or coated with this. **c** drink containing this. **2** deep brown. *–adj.* **1** made from chocolate. **2** deep brown. [Aztec *chocolatl*]

choice *–n.* **1 a** act of choosing. **b** thing or person chosen. **2** range from which to choose. **3** power or opportunity to choose. *–adj.* of superior quality. [Germanic: related to CHOOSE]

choir /'kwaɪə(r)/ *n.* **1** regular group of singers, esp. in a church. **2** part of a cathedral or large church between the altar and nave. [Latin: related to CHORUS]

choirboy *n.* (*fem.* **choirgirl**) boy singer in a church choir.

choke *–v.* (**-king**) **1** stop the breathing of (a person or animal), esp. by constricting the windpipe or (of gas, smoke, etc.) by being unbreathable. **2** suffer a stoppage of breath. **3** make or become speechless from emotion. **4** retard the growth of or kill (esp. plants) by depriving of light etc. **5** (often foll. by *back*) suppress (feelings) with difficulty. **6** block or clog (a passage, tube, etc.). **7** (as **choked** *adj.*) *colloq.* disgusted, disappointed. *–n.* **1** valve in a carburettor controlling the intake of air. **2** device for smoothing the variations of an alternating current. □ **choke up** block (a channel etc.). [Old English]

choker *n.* close-fitting necklace.

cholecalciferol /ˌkɒlɪkæl'sɪfəˌrɒl/ *n.* a vitamin (D_3) produced by the action of sunlight on a steroid in the skin. [from CHOLER, CALCIFEROL]

choler /'kɒlə(r)/ *n.* **1** *hist.* one of the four humours, bile. **2** *poet.* or *archaic* anger, irascibility. [Greek *kholē* bile]

cholera /'kɒlərə/ *n.* infectious often fatal bacterial disease of the small intestine. [related to CHOLER]

choleric /'kɒlərɪk/ *adj.* irascible, angry.

cholesterol /kə'lestəˌrɒl/ *n.* sterol found in most body tissues, including the blood where high concentrations promote arteriosclerosis. [from CHOLER, Greek *stereos* stiff]

chomp *v.* = CHAMP[1]. [imitative]

Chongqing /tʃʊŋ'kɪŋ/ (also **Chungking**) city in central China; industries include iron, steel, rubber, and textiles; pop. (est. 1991) 2 980 000.

choose /tʃu:z/ *v.* (**-sing**; *past* **chose** /tʃəʊz/; *past part.* **chosen**) **1** select out of a greater number. **2** (usu. foll. by *between, from*) take or select one or another. **3** (usu. foll. by *to* + infin.) decide, be determined. **4** select as (*was chosen leader*). □ **nothing** (or **little**) **to choose between them** they are very similar. [Old English]

choosy /'tʃu:zɪ/ *adj.* (**-ier**, **-iest**) *colloq.* fastidious. □ **choosiness** *n.*

chop[1] *–v.* (**-pp-**) **1** (usu. foll. by *off, down,* etc.) cut or fell by the blow of an axe etc. **2** (often foll. by *up*) cut into small pieces. **3** strike (esp. a ball) with a short heavy edgewise blow. *–n.* **1** cutting blow. **2** thick slice of meat (esp. pork or lamb) usu. including a rib. **3** short chopping stroke in cricket etc. **4** (prec. by *the*) *slang* **a** = SACK[1] *n.* 2. **b** killing or being killed. [related to CHAP[2]]

chop[2] *n.* (usu. in *pl.*) jaw. [origin unknown]

chop[3] *v.* (**-pp-**) □ **chop and change** vacillate; change direction frequently. **chop logic** argue pedantically. [perhaps related to CHEAP]

chopper *n.* **1 a** short axe with a large blade. **b** butcher's cleaver. **2** *colloq.* helicopter. **3** *colloq.* type of bicycle or motor cycle with high handlebars.

choppy *adj.* (**-ier**, **-iest**) (of the sea etc.) fairly rough. □ **choppily** *adv.* **choppiness** *n.* [from CHOP[1]]

chopstick *n.* each of a pair of sticks held in one hand as eating utensils by the Chinese, Japanese, etc. [pidgin English from Chinese, = nimble ones]

chopsuey /tʃɒp'su:ɪ/ *n.* (*pl.* **-s**) Chinese-style dish of meat fried with vegetables and rice. [Chinese, = mixed bits]

choral /'kɔ:r(ə)l/ *adj.* of, for, or sung by a choir or chorus. [medieval Latin: related to CHORUS]

chorale /kɒ'rɑ:l/ *n.* **1** simple stately hymn tune; harmonized form of this. **2** esp. *US* choir. [German: related to CHORAL]

chord[1] /kɔ:d/ *n.* group of notes sounded together. [originally *cord* from ACCORD]

chord[2] /kɔ:d/ *n.* **1** straight line joining the ends of an arc or curve. **2** *poet.* string of a harp etc. □ **strike a chord** elicit sympathy. [var. of CORD]

chordate /'kɔ:deɪt/ *–n.* animal having a cartilaginous skeletal rod at some stage of its development. *–adj.* of chordates. [Latin *chorda* CHORD[2] after *Vertebrata* etc.]

chore *n.* tedious or routine task, esp. domestic. [from CHAR[2]]

choreograph /'kɒrɪəˌgrɑ:f/ *v.* compose choreography for (a ballet etc.). □ **choreographer** /-ɪ'ɒgrəfə(r)/ *n.*

choreography /ˌkɒrɪ'ɒgrəfɪ/ *n.* design or arrangement of a ballet etc. □ **choreographic** /-ə'græfɪk/ *adj.* [Greek *khoreia* dance]

chorister /'kɒrɪstə(r)/ *n.* member of a choir, esp. a choirboy. [French: related to CHOIR]

chortle /'tʃɔ:t(ə)l/ *–n.* gleeful chuckle. *–v.* (**-ling**) utter or express with a chortle. [probably from CHUCKLE, SNORT]

chorus /'kɔ:rəs/ *–n.* (*pl.* **-es**) **1** group of singers; choir. **2** music composed for a choir. **3** refrain or main part of a song. **4** simultaneous utterance. **5** group of singers and dancers performing together. **6** *Gk Antiq.* **a** group of performers who comment on the action in a Greek play. **b** utterance made by it. **7** character speaking the prologue in a play. *–v.* (**-s-**) speak or utter simultaneously. [Latin from Greek]

chose[1] *past* of CHOOSE.

◆ **chose**[2] /ʃəʊz/ *n.* thing; article of property. [French]

◆ **chose in action** *n.* right of proceeding in a court of law to obtain a sum of money or to recover damages. Examples include rights under an insurance policy, a debt, and rights under a contract. A chose in action is a form of property and can be assigned, sold, held in trust, etc.

◆ **chose in possession** *n.* moveable item of property in a person's possession. Examples include goods and merchandise. All assets are either choses in possession or choses in action.

---

chosen *past part.* of CHOOSE.

chough /tʃʌf/ *n.* bird with glossy blue-black plumage and red legs. [imitative]

choux pastry /ʃu:/ *n.* very light pastry enriched with eggs. [French]

chow *n.* **1** *slang* food. **2** dog of a Chinese breed with long woolly hair. [Chinese *chow-chow*]

chow mein /tʃaʊ 'meɪn/ *n.* Chinese-style dish of fried noodles with shredded meat or shrimps etc. and vegetables. [Chinese *chao mian* fried flour]

ch. ppd. *abbr.* charges prepaid.

Christ /kraɪst/ *–n.* **1** title, also now treated as a name, given to Jesus. **2** Messiah as prophesied in the Old Testament. *–int. slang* expressing surprise, anger, etc. [Greek, = anointed]

Christchurch /'kraɪstˌtʃɜ:tʃ/ city in New Zealand, on South Island, capital of Canterbury region; industries include meat processing, tanning, fertilizers, and chemicals; pop. (1996) 313 969.

christen /'krɪs(ə)n/ *v.* **1** baptize as a sign of admission to the Christian Church. **2** give a name to. **3** *colloq.* use for the first time. □ **christening** *n.* [Latin: related to CHRISTIAN]

Christendom /ˈkrɪsəndəm/ *n.* Christians worldwide.

Christian /ˈkrɪstʃ(ə)n/ *–adj.* **1** of Christ's teaching. **2** believing in or following the religion of Christ. **3** showing the associated qualities. **4** *colloq.* kind. *–n.* adherent of Christianity. [Latin *Christianus* of CHRIST]

Christian era *n.* era reckoned from Christ's birth.

Christianity /ˌkrɪstɪˈænɪtɪ/ *n.* **1** Christian religion. **2** being a Christian; Christian quality or character.

Christian name *n.* forename, esp. as given at baptism.

Christian Science *n.* Christian sect believing in the power of healing by prayer alone. □ **Christian Scientist** *n.*

Christmas /ˈkrɪsməs/ *n.* **1** (also **Christmas Day**) annual festival of Christ's birth, celebrated on 25 Dec. **2** period around this. □ **Christmassy** *adj.* [Old English: related to CHRIST, MASS[2]]

Christmas-box *n.* present or gratuity given at Christmas.

Christmas Eve *n.* 24 Dec.

Christmas Island 1 island in the Indian Ocean administered as an external territory of Australia since 1958; phosphate mining is the only industrial activity; pop. (1986) 2000. **2** see KIRITIMATI.

Christmas pudding *n.* rich boiled pudding of flour, suet, dried fruit, etc.

Christmas rose *n.* white-flowered winter-blooming hellebore.

Christmas tree *n.* evergreen tree or imitation of this set up and decorated at Christmas.

chromatic /krəˈmætɪk/ *adj.* **1** of colour; in colours. **2** *Mus.* **a** of or having notes not belonging to a particular diatonic scale. **b** (of a scale) ascending or descending by semitones. □ **chromatically** *adv.* [Greek *khrōma -mat-* colour]

chromatin /ˈkrəʊmətɪn/ *n.* chromosome material in a cell nucleus which stains with basic dyes. [Greek: related to CHROME]

chromatography /ˌkrəʊməˈtɒgrəfɪ/ *n.* separation of the components of a mixture by slow passage through or over material which adsorbs them differently. [Greek: related to CHROME]

chrome /krəʊm/ *n.* **1** chromium, esp. as plating. **2** (in full **chrome yellow**) yellow pigment got from a certain compound of chromium. [Greek *khrōma* colour]

chromite /ˈkrəʊmaɪt/ *n.* mineral of chromium and iron oxides.

chromium /ˈkrəʊmɪəm/ *n.* metallic element used as a shiny decorative or protective coating.

chromium plate *n.* protective coating of chromium.

chromosome /ˈkrəʊməˌsəʊm/ *n.* threadlike structure, usu. found in the cell nucleus of animals and plants, carrying genes. [Greek: related to CHROME, *sōma* body]

chronic /ˈkrɒnɪk/ *adj.* **1** (esp. of an illness) long-lasting. **2** having a chronic complaint. **3** *colloq.* very bad; intense, severe. **4** *colloq.* habitual, inveterate (*a chronic liar*). □ **chronically** *adv.* [Greek *khronos* time]

■ **Usage** The use of *chronic* in sense 3 is very informal, and its use in sense 4 is considered incorrect by some people.

chronicle /ˈkrɒnɪk(ə)l/ *–n.* register of events in order of occurrence. *–v.* (**-ling**) record (events) thus. [Greek *khronika*: related to CHRONIC]

chronological /ˌkrɒnəˈlɒdʒɪk(ə)l/ *adj.* **1** according to order of occurrence. **2** of chronology. □ **chronologically** *adv.*

chronology /krəˈnɒlədʒɪ/ *n.* (*pl.* **-ies**) **1** science of determining dates. **2 a** arrangement of events etc. in order of occurrence. **b** table or document displaying this. [Greek *khronos* time, -LOGY]

chronometer /krəˈnɒmɪtə(r)/ *n.* time-measuring instrument, esp. one used in navigation. [from CHRONOLOGY, -METER]

chrysalis /ˈkrɪsəlɪs/ *n.* (*pl.* **-lises**) **1** pupa of a butterfly or moth. **2** case enclosing it. [Greek *khrusos* gold]

chrysanthemum /krɪˈsænθəməm/ *n.* garden plant of the daisy family blooming in autumn. [Greek, = gold flower]

chrysoberyl /ˈkrɪsəˌberɪl/ *n.* yellowish-green gem. [Greek *khrusos* gold, BERYL]

chrysolite /ˈkrɪsəˌlaɪt/ *n.* precious variety of olivine. [Greek *khrusos* gold, *lithos* stone]

chrysoprase /ˈkrɪsəˌpreɪz/ *n.* apple-green variety of chalcedony. [Greek *khrusos* gold, *prason* leek]

chub *n.* (*pl.* same) thick-bodied river fish. [origin unknown]

Chubb *n.* (in full **Chubb lock**) *propr.* lock with a device for fixing the bolt immovably should someone try to pick it. [*Chubb*, name of a locksmith]

chubby *adj.* (**-ier, -iest**) plump and rounded. [from CHUB]

Chubu /ˈtʃuːbuː/ region of Japan on the island of Honshu; pop. (1995) 21 400 462; capital, Nagoya.

chuck[1] *–v.* **1** *colloq.* fling or throw carelessly or casually. **2** (often foll. by *in, up*) *colloq.* give up; reject. **3** touch playfully, esp. under the chin. *–n.* **1** playful touch under the chin. **2** toss.□ **the chuck** *slang* dismissal; rejection. **chuck out** *colloq.* **1** expel (a person) from a gathering etc. **2** get rid of, discard. [perhaps from French *chuquer* knock]

chuck[2] *–n.* **1** cut of beef from neck to ribs. **2** device for holding a workpiece or bit. *–v.* fix to a chuck. [var. of CHOCK]

chuckle /ˈtʃʌk(ə)l/ *–v.* (**-ling**) laugh quietly or inwardly. *–n.* quiet or suppressed laugh. [*chuck* cluck]

chuff *v.* (of an engine etc.) work with a regular sharp puffing sound. [imitative]

chuffed *adj. slang* delighted. [dial. *chuff*]

chug *–v.* (**-gg-**) **1** emit a regular muffled explosive sound, as of an engine running slowly. **2** move with this sound. *–n.* chugging sound. [imitative]

Chugoku /tʃuːˈgəʊkuː/ region of Japan on the island of Honshu; pop. (1996) 7 774 841; capital, Hiroshima.

Chukchi Sea /ˈtʃuːktʃɪ/ arm of the Arctic Ocean lying between North America and NE Asia, N of the Bering Strait.

chukka boot *n.* ankle-high leather boot.

chukker *n.* (also **chukka**) period of play in polo. [Sanskrit *cakra* wheel]

chum *n. colloq.* close friend. □ **chum up** (**-mm-**) (often foll. by *with*) become a close friend (of). □ **chummy** *adj.* (**-ier, -iest**). **chummily** *adv.* **chumminess** *n.* [abbreviation of *chamber-fellow*]

chump *n.* **1** *colloq.* foolish person. **2** thick end of a loin of lamb or mutton (*chump chop*). **3** short thick block of wood. □ **off one's chump** *slang* crazy. [blend of CHUNK, LUMP[1]]

Chungking see CHONGQING.

chunk *n.* **1** thick piece cut or broken off. **2** substantial amount. [var. of CHUCK[2]]

chunky *adj.* (**-ier, -iest**) **1** consisting of or resembling chunks; thick, substantial. **2** small and sturdy. □ **chunkiness** *n.*

♦ **Chunnel** /ˈtʃʌnəl/ *n. colloq.* = CHANNEL TUNNEL.

---

chunter *v. colloq.* mutter, grumble. [probably imitative]

chupatty var. of CHAPATTI.

church *n.* **1** building for public Christian worship. **2** public worship (*met after church*). **3** (**Church**) **a** body of all Christians. **b** clergy or clerical profession. **c** organized Christian society (*the early Church*). [Greek *kuriakon* Lord's (house)]

churchgoer *n.* person attending church regularly.

churchman *n.* member of the clergy or of a Church.

Church of England *n.* English Protestant Church.

churchwarden *n.* either of two elected lay representatives of an Anglican parish.

churchyard *n.* enclosed ground around a church used for burials.

churl *n.* **1** ill-bred person. **2** *archaic* peasant. [Old English, = man]

churlish *adj.* surly; mean. □ **churlishly** *adv.* **churlishness** *n.* [from CHURL]

churn –*n.* **1** large milk-can. **2** butter-making machine. –*v.* **1** agitate (milk or cream) in a churn. **2** produce (butter) in a churn. **3** (usu. foll. by *up*) upset, agitate. □ **churn out** produce in large quantities. [Old English]

♦ **churning** *n.* **1** practice by a broker of encouraging an investor to change investments frequently in order to enable the broker to earn excessive commissions. **2** practice by a bank, building society, insurance broker, etc. of encouraging a householder with an endowment mortgage to surrender the policy and to take out a new one when seeking to increase a mortgage or to raise extra funds, instead of topping up the existing mortgage. The purpose is to increase charges and commissions at the expense of the policyholder. **3** government policy of paying a benefit to a wide category of persons and taxing it so that those paying little or no taxes receive it while the well-off return it through the tax system. There have been suggestions that a higher child benefit is suitable for churning.

chute[1] /ʃuːt/ *n.* sloping channel or slide for sending things to a lower level. [Latin *cado* fall]

chute[2] /ʃuːt/ *n. colloq.* parachute. [abbreviation]

chutney /'tʃʌtnɪ/ *n.* (*pl.* **-s**) pungent condiment of fruits, vinegar, spices, etc. [Hindi]

chutzpah /'xʊtspə/ *n. slang* shameless audacity. [Yiddish]

chyle /kaɪl/ *n.* milky fluid of food materials formed in the intestine after digestion. [Greek *khulos* juice]

chyme /kaɪm/ *n.* acid pulp formed from partly-digested food. [Greek *khumos* juice]

CI –*abbr.* **1** Channel Islands. **2** (in management) continuous improvement. –*international vehicle registration* Côte d'Ivoire. –*airline flight code* China Airlines.

CIA *abbr.* **1** cash in advance. **2** (in the US) Central Intelligence Agency. **3** Corporation of Insurance Agents.

Cia. *abbr.* **1** (Italian) compagnia (= company). **2** (Portuguese) companhia (= company). **3** (Spanish) compañia (= company).

ciao /tʃaʊ/ *int. colloq.* **1** goodbye. **2** hello. [Italian]

CIArb. *abbr.* Chartered Institute of Arbitrators.

CIB *abbr.* **1** Chartered Institute of Bankers. **2** Corporation of Insurance Brokers.

CICA *abbr.* Canadian Institute of Chartered Accountants.

cicada /sɪ'kɑːdə/ *n.* large transparent-winged insect making a rhythmic chirping sound. [Latin]

cicatrice /'sɪkətrɪs/ *n.* scar left by a wound. [Latin]

cicely /'sɪsəlɪ/ *n.* (*pl.* **-ies**) flowering plant related to parsley and chervil. [Greek *seselis*]

cicerone /ˌtʃɪtʃə'rəʊnɪ/ *n.* (*pl.* **-roni** pronunc. same) person who guides sightseers. [Latin *Cicero*, name of a Roman statesman]

CID *abbr.* **1** computer-assisted imaging device. **2** Council of Industrial Design. **3** Criminal Investigation Department.

-cide *suffix* **1** person or substance that kills (*regicide*; *insecticide*). **2** killing of (*infanticide*). [Latin *caedo* kill]

cider *n.* drink of fermented apple juice. [Hebrew, = strong drink]

Cie. *abbr.* (French) compagnie (= company).

♦ **c.i.f.** *abbr.* (also **CIF**) cost, insurance, and freight, denoting a price for goods that includes the cost of shipping the goods to the port of destination and of insuring the goods up to this point. On a c.i.f. contract, the seller sends the documents giving title to the goods to the buyer, usu. through a bank. These documents include the bill of lading, the insurance policy, the commercial invoice, and sometimes such additional documents as a certificate of origin, quality certificate, or export licence. In order to obtain the goods the buyer is obliged to pay for the documents when they are presented. It is said that with a c.i.f. contract the buyer is paying for documents rather than goods because, provided the documents are in order, the buyer is obliged to pay for them even if the goods themselves have been lost at sea during the voyage. In these circumstances the buyer would hold the insurance policy entitling the policyholder to recompense for the lost goods. Cf. C. & F.; C.I.F.C.I.; F.O.B.

c.i.f.c. *abbr.* cost, insurance, and freight, plus commission.

♦ **c.i.f.c.i.** *abbr.* cost, insurance, and freight, plus commission and interest. A price quoted c.i.f.c.i. is a c.i.f. price that also includes an agreed commission payable by the seller to the buyer and the interest charged by the seller's bank for negotiating the documents.

c.i.f.i. *abbr.* cost, insurance, and freight, plus interest.

cigar /sɪ'gɑː(r)/ *n.* tight roll of tobacco-leaves for smoking. [French or Spanish]

cigarette /ˌsɪgə'ret/ *n.* finely-cut tobacco rolled in paper for smoking. [French diminutive]

♦ **CII** *abbr.* = CHARTERED INSURANCE INSTITUTE.

cilium /'sɪlɪəm/ *n.* (*pl.* **cilia**) **1** minute hairlike structure on the surface of many animal cells. **2** eyelash. □ **ciliary** *adj.* **ciliate** *adj.* [Latin, = eyelash]

CIM *abbr.* **1** computer input on (or from) microfilm. **2** computer-integrated manufacture (or manufacturing). **3** Cooperative Investment Management.

CIMA *abbr.* Chartered Institute of Management Accountants. See CHARTERED ACCOUNTANT; MANAGEMENT ACCOUNTANT.

cinch *n. colloq.* **1** sure thing; certainty. **2** easy task. [Spanish *cincha* saddle-girth]

cinchona /sɪŋ'kəʊnə/ *n.* **1 a** South American evergreen tree or shrub. **b** its bark, containing quinine. **2** drug from this. [Countess of *Chinchón*]

Cincinnati /ˌsɪnsɪ'nætɪ/ industrial city and port in the US, in Ohio; industries include machinery, clothing, furniture making, and meat packing; pop. (est. 1994) 358 170.

cincture /'sɪŋktʃə(r)/ *n. literary* girdle, belt, or border. [Latin *cingo* gird]

cinder *n.* **1** residue of coal or wood etc. after burning. **2** (in *pl.*) ashes. [Old English *sinder* = slag]

Cinderella /ˌsɪndə'relə/ *n.* person or thing of unrecognized or disregarded merit or beauty. [name of a girl in a fairy tale]

cine- *comb. form* cinematographic (*cine-camera*). [abbreviation]

cinema /'sɪnəmə/ *n.* **1** theatre where films are shown. **2 a** films collectively. **b** art or industry of producing films. □ **cinematic** /-'mætɪk/ *adj.* [French: related to KINEMATICS]

cinematography /ˌsɪnɪmə'tɒgrəfɪ/ *n.* art of making films. □ **cinematographer** *n.* **cinematographic** /-ˌmætə'græfɪk/ *adj.*

cineraria /ˌsɪnə'reərɪə/ *n.* composite plant with bright flowers and ash-coloured down on its leaves. [Latin *cinis -ner-* ashes]

cinnabar /'sɪnəˌbɑː(r)/ *n.* **1** bright red mercuric sulphide. **2** vermilion. **3** moth with reddish-marked wings. [Latin from Greek]

cinnamon /'sɪnəmən/ *n.* **1** aromatic spice from the bark of a SE Asian tree. **2** this tree. **3** yellowish-brown. [Greek *kinnamon*]

cinque /sɪŋk/ *n.* the five on dice. [Latin *quinque* five]

cinquefoil /'sɪŋkfɔɪl/ *n.* **1** plant with compound leaves of five leaflets. **2** *Archit.* five-cusped ornament in a circle or arch. [Latin: related to CINQUE, *folium* leaf]

Cinque Ports *n.pl.* group of (orig. five) ports in SE England with ancient privileges. [Latin *quinque portus* five ports]

CIO *abbr.* (in the US) Congress of Industrial Organizations.

CIPA *abbr.* Chartered Institute of Patent Agents.

CIPFA *abbr.* Chartered Institute of Public Finance and Accountancy. See CHARTERED ACCOUNTANT.

cipher /ˈsaɪfə(r)/ (also **cypher**) –*n.* **1 a** secret or disguised writing. **b** thing so written; code. **c** key to it. See also CRYPTOGRAPHY. **2** arithmetical symbol (0) used to occupy a vacant place in decimal etc. numeration. **3** person or thing of no importance. –*v.* write in cipher. [Arabic *ṣifr*]

CIPM *abbr.* **1** (French) Commission internationale des poids et mésures (= International Committee on Weights and Measures). **2** Companion of the Institute of Personnel Management.

CIR *abbr.* **1** Commission (or Council) on Industrial Relations. **2** Commissioners of Inland Revenue.

circa /ˈsɜːkə/ *prep.* (preceding a date) about. [Latin]

circadian /sɜːˈkeɪdɪən/ *adj. Physiol.* occurring about once per day. [from CIRCA, Latin *dies* day]

circle /ˈsɜːk(ə)l/ –*n.* **1** round plane figure whose circumference is everywhere equidistant from its centre. **2** circular or roundish enclosure or structure. **3** curved upper tier of seats in a theatre etc. **4** circular route. **5** persons grouped round a centre of interest. **6** set or restricted group (*literary circles*). –*v.* (**-ling**) **1** (often foll. by *round, about*) move in a circle. **2 a** revolve round. **b** form a circle round. □ **come full circle** return to the starting-point. [Latin diminutive: related to CIRCUS]

circlet /ˈsɜːklɪt/ *n.* **1** small circle. **2** circular band, esp. as an ornament.

circuit /ˈsɜːkɪt/ *n.* **1** line or course enclosing an area; the distance round. **2 a** path of an electric current. **b** apparatus through which a current passes. **3 a** judge's itinerary through a district to hold courts. **b** such a district. **c** lawyers following a circuit. **4** chain of theatres, cinemas, etc. under a single management. **5** motor-racing track. **6** itinerary or specific sphere of operation (*election circuit; cabaret circuit*). **7** sequence of sporting events or athletic exercises. [Latin: related to CIRCUM-, *eo it-* go]

circuit board *n.* rigid board of insulating material on which an electric circuit has been or can be built. See PRINTED CIRCUIT.

circuit-breaker *n.* automatic device for interrupting an electric circuit.

circuitous /sɜːˈkjuːɪtəs/ *adj.* **1** indirect. **2** going a long way round. □ **circuity** /-ˈkjuːɪtɪ/ *n.*

circuitry /ˈsɜːkɪtrɪ/ *n.* (*pl.* **-ies**) **1** system of electric circuits. **2** equipment forming this.

♦ **circuity of action** *n.* return of a bill of exchange, prior to maturity, to the person who first signed it. Under these circumstances it may be renegotiated, but the person forfeits any right of action against those who put their names to it in the intervening period.

circular /ˈsɜːkjʊlə(r)/ –*adj.* **1 a** having the form of a circle. **b** moving (roughly) in a circle, finishing at the starting-point (*circular walk*). **2** (of reasoning) using the point it is trying to prove as evidence for its conclusion, hence invalid. **3** (of a letter etc.) distributed to a number of people. –*n.* circular letter, leaflet, etc. □ **circularity** /-ˈlærɪtɪ/ *n.* [Latin: related to CIRCLE]

circularize *v.* (also **-ise**) (**-zing** or **-sing**) distribute circulars to.

♦ **circular flow of income** *n.* process by which money and goods pass between different groups in the economy. The concept is used as the basis for studying macroeconomic relationships. In its simplest forms, it postulates that households provide labour to firms in exchange for money, which the households use to buy the goods produced by firms. Household savings represent a leakage from the economy, as money saved is removed from the circular flow, but this is partially compensated for by investment, which is an injection into the circular flow. In the real world, circular flow is complicated by such factors as taxation (leakage) and government spending (injection), exports (leakage), and imports (injection). National income accounts are based on the concept of the circular flow.

circular saw *n.* power saw with a rapidly rotating toothed disc.

circulate /ˈsɜːkjʊˌleɪt/ *v.* (**-ting**) **1** be in circulation; spread. **2 a** put into circulation. **b** send circulars to. **3** move about among guests etc. [Latin: related to CIRCLE]

♦ **circulating capital** *n.* (also **working capital**) part of the capital of a company or other organization that is used in the activities of trading, as distinct from its fixed capital. The circulation of this capital occurs thus: suppliers provide stock; the stock is sold to customers who become debtors, eventually paying cash; the cash is used to pay suppliers, who provide more stock, etc.

circulation /ˌsɜːkjʊˈleɪʃ(ə)n/ *n.* **1** movement to and fro, or from and back to a starting-point, esp. that of the blood from and to the heart. **2 a** transmission or distribution. **b** number of copies sold. □ **in** (or **out of) circulation** active (or not active) socially.

circulatory /ˌsɜːkjʊˈleɪtərɪ/ *adj.* of circulation, esp. of the blood.

circum- *comb. form* round, about. [Latin]

circumcise /ˈsɜːkəmˌsaɪz/ *v.* (**-sing**) cut off the foreskin or clitoris of. □ **circumcision** /-ˈsɪʒ(ə)n/ *n.* [Latin *caedo* cut]

circumference /səˈkʌmfərəns/ *n.* **1** enclosing boundary, esp. of a circle. **2** distance round. □ **circumferential** /-ˈrenʃ(ə)l/ *adj.* [Latin *fero* carry]

circumflex /ˈsɜːkəmˌfleks/ *n.* (in full **circumflex accent**) mark (^) placed over a vowel to show contraction, length, etc. [Latin: related to FLEX[1]]

circumlocution /ˌsɜːkəmləˈkjuːʃ(ə)n/ *n.* **1 a** roundabout expression. **b** evasive talk. **2** verbosity. □ **circumlocutory** /-ˈlɒkjʊtərɪ/ *adj.*

circumnavigate /ˌsɜːkəmˈnævɪˌgeɪt/ *v.* (**-ting**) sail round (esp. the world). □ **circumnavigation** /-ˈgeɪʃ(ə)n/ *n.*

circumscribe /ˈsɜːkəmˌskraɪb/ *v.* (**-bing**) **1** (of a line etc.) enclose or outline. **2** lay down the limits of; confine, restrict. **3** *Geom.* draw (a figure) round another, touching it at points but not cutting it. □ **circumscription** /-ˈskrɪpʃ(ə)n/ *n.* [Latin *scribo* write]

circumspect /ˈsɜːkəmˌspekt/ *adj.* cautious; taking everything into account. □ **circumspection** /-ˈspekʃ(ə)n/ *n.* **circumspectly** *adv.* [Latin *specio spect-* look]

circumstance /ˈsɜːkəmst(ə)ns/ *n.* **1** fact, occurrence, or condition, esp. (in *pl.*) connected with or influencing an event; (bad) luck (*victim of circumstance(s)*). **2** (in *pl.*) one's financial condition. **3** ceremony, fuss. □ **in** (or **under) the circumstances** the state of affairs being what it is. **in** (or **under) no circumstances** not at all; never. □ **circumstanced** *adj.* [Latin *sto* stand]

circumstantial /ˌsɜːkəmˈstænʃ(ə)l/ *adj.* **1** giving full details (*circumstantial account*). **2** (of evidence etc.) indicating a conclusion by inference from known facts hard to explain otherwise. □ **circumstantiality** /-ʃɪˈælɪtɪ/ *n.*

circumvent /ˌsɜːkəmˈvent/ *v.* **1** evade, find a way round. **2** baffle, outwit. □ **circumvention** *n.* [Latin *venio vent-* come]

circus /ˈsɜːkəs/ *n.* (*pl.* **-es**) **1** travelling show of performing acrobats, clowns, animals, etc. **2** *colloq.* **a** scene of lively action. **b** group of people in a common activity, esp. sport. **3** open space in a town, where several streets converge. **4** *Rom. Antiq.* arena for sports and games. [Latin, = ring]

cirrhosis /sɪˈrəʊsɪs/ *n.* chronic liver disease, as a result of alcoholism etc. [Greek *kirrhos* tawny]

cirrus /ˈsɪrəs/ *n.* (*pl.* **cirri** /-raɪ/) **1** white wispy cloud at high altitude. **2** tendril or appendage of a plant or animal. [Latin, = curl]

CIS *abbr.* **1** Commonwealth of Independent States, a loose association of former Soviet republics. **2** Cooperative Insurance Society.

cisalpine /sɪsˈælpaɪn/ *adj.* on the south side of the Alps. [Latin *cis-* on this side of]

CISC *abbr.* complex instruction-set computer.

CIS–COBOL *abbr. Computing* compact interactive standard COBOL.

Ciskei /sɪsˈkaɪ/ former Bantu homeland in South Africa, designated an independent republic in 1981 but not recognized as such outside South Africa (see HOMELAND 2); its capital was Bisho. In 1994 Ciskei was integrated into the province of Eastern Cape.

CISL *abbr.* **1** (French) Confédération internationale des syndicats libres (= International Confederation of Free Trade Unions). **2** (Italian) Confederazione italiana sindacati lavoratori (= Italian Confederation of Workers' Trade Unions).

cissy var. of SISSY.

Cistercian /sɪˈstɜːʃ(ə)n/ *–n.* monk or nun of the order founded as a stricter branch of the Benedictines. *–adj.* of the Cistercians. [French *Cîteaux* in France]

cistern /ˈsɪst(ə)n/ *n.* **1** tank for storing water. **2** underground reservoir. [Latin *cista* box, from Greek]

cistus /ˈsɪstəs/ *n.* shrub with large white or red flowers. [Latin from Greek]

citadel /ˈsɪtəd(ə)l/ *n.* fortress, usu. on high ground, protecting or dominating a city. [French *citadelle*]

citation /saɪˈteɪʃ(ə)n/ *n.* **1** citing; passage cited. **2** *Mil.* mention in dispatches. **3** description of the reasons for an award.

cite *v.* **(-ting) 1** mention as an example etc. **2** quote (a book etc.) in support. **3** *Mil.* mention in dispatches. **4** summon to appear in court. [Latin *cieo* set in motion]

CITES /ˈsaɪtiːz/ *abbr.* Convention on International Trade in Endangered Species.

citizen /ˈsɪtɪz(ə)n/ *n.* **1** member of a state, either native or naturalized. **2** inhabitant of a city. **3** *US* civilian. □ **citizenry** *n.* **citizenship** *n.* [Anglo-French: related to CITY]

citizen's band *n.* system of local intercommunication by individuals on special radio frequencies.

citrate /ˈsɪtreɪt/ *n.* a salt of citric acid.

citric /ˈsɪtrɪk/ *adj.* derived from citrus fruit.

citric acid *n.* sharp-tasting acid in citrus fruits.

citron /ˈsɪtrən/ *n.* **1** tree with large lemon-like fruits. **2** this fruit. [French from Latin CITRUS]

citronella /ˌsɪtrəˈnelə/ *n.* **1** a fragrant oil. **2** grass from S Asia yielding it.

citrus /ˈsɪtrəs/ *n.* (*pl.* **-es**) **1** tree of a group including the lemon, orange, and grapefruit. **2** (in full **citrus fruit**) fruit of such a tree. [Latin]

city /ˈsɪtɪ/ *n.* (*pl.* **-ies**) **1** large town, strictly one created by charter and containing a cathedral. **2** (**the City**) **a** part of central London governed by the Lord Mayor and Corporation. **b** financial district of central London in which are situated the head offices of the banks, the money markets, the foreign exchange markets, the commodity and metal exchanges, the insurance market (including Lloyd's), the London Stock Exchange, and the offices of the representatives of foreign financial institutions. **c** commercial circles. [Latin *civitas*: related to CIVIC]

♦ **City Call** *n.* financial information service provided by Prestel over the telephone in the UK. It gives nine bulletins of updated information each day.

♦ **City Code on Take-overs and Mergers** *n.* code first laid down in 1968, and subsequently modified, giving the practices to be observed in company take-overs and mergers. Encouraged by the Bank of England, the code was compiled by a panel (the **Take-over Panel**) including representatives from the London Stock Exchange Association, the Issuing Houses Association, the London Clearing Bankers, and others. The code does not have the force of law but the panel can admonish offenders and refer them to their own professional bodies for disciplinary action. The code attempts to ensure that all shareholders, including minority shareholders, are treated equally, are kept advised of the terms of all bids and counter-bids, and are advised fairly by the directors of the company receiving the bid on the likely outcome if the bid succeeds. Its many other recommendations are aimed at preventing directors from acting in their own interests rather than those of their shareholders, ensuring that the negotiations are conducted openly and honestly, and preventing a spurious market arising in the shares of either side.

city-state *n.* esp. *hist.* city that with its surrounding territory forms an independent state.

Ciudad Bolívar /θjuːðɑːð bɒˈliːvɑː(r), sjuː-/ (formerly **Angostura**) city in SE Venezuela, capital of the state of Bolívar; exports include gold and diamonds; pop. (1990) 225 340.

civet /ˈsɪvɪt/ *n.* **1** (in full **civet-cat**) catlike animal of central Africa. **2** strong musky perfume obtained from it. [French ultimately from Arabic]

civic /ˈsɪvɪk/ *adj.* **1** of a city. **2** of citizens or citizenship. □ **civically** *adv.* [Latin *civis* citizen]

civic centre *n.* **1** area where municipal offices etc. are situated. **2** the offices themselves.

civics *n.pl.* (usu. treated as *sing.*) the study of the rights and duties of citizenship.

civil /ˈsɪv(ə)l/ *adj.* **1** of or belonging to citizens. **2** of ordinary citizens; non-military. **3** polite, obliging, not rude. **4** *Law* concerning private rights and not criminal offences. See CIVIL LAW. **5** (of the length of a day, year, etc.) fixed by custom or law, not natural or astronomical. □ **civilly** *adv.* [Latin *civilis*: related to CIVIC]

♦ **Civil Aviation Authority** *n.* (also **CAA**) independent UK body set up in 1971 to be responsible for the development and economic regulation of the UK civil air-transport industry, safety regulations by certification of airlines and aircraft, and the provision of air-traffic control and telecommunications.

civil defence *n.* organizing of civilians for protection during wartime attacks.

civil disobedience *n.* refusal to comply with certain laws as a peaceful protest.

civil engineer *n.* one who designs or maintains roads, bridges, dams, etc.

civilian /sɪˈvɪlɪən/ *–n.* person not in the armed services or police force. *–adj.* of or for civilians.

civility /sɪˈvɪlɪtɪ/ *n.* (*pl.* **-ies**) **1** politeness. **2** act of politeness. [Latin: related to CIVIL]

civilization /ˌsɪvɪlaɪˈzeɪʃ(ə)n/ *n.* (also **-isation**) **1** advanced stage or system of social development. **2** peoples of the world that are regarded as having this. **3** a people or nation (esp. of the past) regarded as an element of social evolution (*Inca civilization*).

civilize /ˈsɪvɪˌlaɪz/ *v.* (also **-ise**) (**-zing** or **-sing**) **1** bring out of a barbarous or primitive stage of society. **2** enlighten; refine and educate. [French: related to CIVIL]

♦ **civil law** *n.* **1** the law applied by the civil courts in the UK, as opposed to ecclesiastical, criminal, or military law. It is therefore the law that regulates dealings between private citizens who are not subject to interference by the state. Its chief divisions include the law of contract, torts, and trusts. **2** Roman law. **3** the law generally in force on the Continent, which has its basis in Roman law.

civil liberty *n.* (often in *pl.*) freedom of action subject to the law.

civil list *n.* annual allowance voted by Parliament for the royal family's household expenses.

civil marriage *n.* one solemnized without religious ceremony.

civil rights *n.pl.* rights of citizens to freedom and equality.

civil servant *n.* member of the civil service.

civil service *n.* branches of state administration, excluding military and judicial branches and elected politicians.

civil war *n.* war between citizens of the same country.

civvies *n.pl. slang* civilian clothes. [abbreviation]

Civvy Street *n. slang* civilian life. [abbreviation]

CJA *abbr.* Criminal Justice Act.

CKD *abbr.* (also **c.k.d.**) (of goods for sale) completely knocked down (i.e. in parts).

CL –*abbr.* **1** civil law. **2** common law. –*international vehicle registration* Sri Lanka.

Cl *symb.* chlorine.

cl *abbr.* centilitre(s).

cl. *abbr.* **1** claim. **2** clause.

clack –*v.* **1** make a sharp sound as of boards struck together. **2** chatter. –*n.* clacking noise or talk. [imitative]

clad *adj.* **1** clothed. **2** provided with cladding. [past part. of CLOTHE]

cladding *n.* covering or coating on a structure or material etc.

cladistics /klə'dɪstɪks/ *n.pl.* (usu. treated as *sing.*) *Biol.* method of classifying animals and plants on the basis of shared characteristics. [Greek *klados* branch]

claim –*v.* **1** state, declare, assert. **2** demand as one's due or property. **3** represent oneself as having or achieving (*claim victory*). **4** (foll. by *to* + infin.) profess. **5** have as an achievement or consequence (*fire claimed two victims*). **6** (of a thing) deserve (attention etc.). –*n.* **1** demand or request for a thing considered one's due (*lay claim to*; *put in a claim*). **2** (foll. by *to, on*) right or title to a thing. **3** assertion. **4** thing claimed. [Latin *clamo* call out]

claimant *n.* person making a claim, esp. in a lawsuit, or claiming state benefit.

clairvoyance /kleə'vɔɪəns/ *n.* supposed faculty of perceiving the future or things beyond normal sensory perception. □ **clairvoyant** *n.* & *adj.* [French: related to CLEAR, *voir* see]

clam –*n.* edible bivalve mollusc. –*v.* (**-mm-**) (foll. by *up*) *colloq.* refuse to talk. [related to CLAMP[1]]

clamber –*v.* climb laboriously using hands and feet. –*n.* difficult climb. [from CLIMB]

clammy /'klæmɪ/ *adj.* (**-ier**, **-iest**) unpleasantly damp and sticky. □ **clammily** *adv.* **clamminess** *n.* [*clam* to daub]

clamour /'klæmə(r)/ (*US* **clamor**) –*n.* **1** loud or vehement shouting or noise. **2** protest, demand. –*v.* **1** make a clamour. **2** utter with a clamour. □ **clamorous** *adj.* [Latin: related to CLAIM]

clamp[1] –*n.* **1** device, esp. a brace or band of iron etc., for strengthening or holding things together. **2** device for immobilizing an illegally parked vehicle. –*v.* **1** strengthen or fasten with a clamp; fix firmly. **2** immobilize (a vehicle) with a clamp. □ **clamp down** (usu. foll. by *on*) become stricter (about); suppress. [Low German or Dutch]

clamp[2] *n.* potatoes etc. stored under straw or earth. [Dutch: related to CLUMP]

clamp-down *n.* sudden policy of suppression.

clan *n.* **1** group of people with a common ancestor, esp. in the Scottish Highlands. **2** large family as a social group. **3** group with a strong common interest. [Gaelic]

clandestine /klæn'destɪn/ *adj.* surreptitious, secret. [Latin]

clang –*n.* loud resonant metallic sound. –*v.* (cause to) make a clang. [imitative: cf. Latin *clango* resound]

clanger *n. slang* mistake, blunder.

clangour /'klæŋgə(r)/ *n.* (*US* **clangor**) prolonged clanging. □ **clangorous** *adj.*

clank –*n.* sound as of metal on metal. –*v.* (cause to) make a clank. [imitative]

clannish *adj.* often *derog.* (of a family or group) associating closely with each other; inward-looking.

clansman *n.* (*fem.* **clanswoman**) member or fellow-member of a clan.

clap[1] –*v.* (**-pp-**) **1 a** strike the palms of one's hands together, esp. repeatedly as applause. **b** strike (the hands) together in this way. **2** applaud thus. **3** put or place quickly or with determination (*clapped him in prison*; *clap a tax on whisky*). **4** (foll. by *on*) give a friendly slap (*clapped him on the back*). –*n.* **1** act of clapping, esp. as applause. **2** explosive sound, esp. of thunder. **3** slap, pat. □ **clap eyes on** *colloq.* see. [Old English]

clap[2] *n. coarse slang* venereal disease, esp. gonorrhoea. [French]

clapped out *adj. slang* worn out; exhausted.

clapper *n.* tongue or striker of a bell. □ **like the clappers** *slang* very fast or hard.

clapperboard *n.* device in film-making of hinged boards struck together to synchronize the starting of picture and sound machinery.

claptrap *n.* insincere or pretentious talk, nonsense.

claque /klæk/ *n.* group of people hired to applaud. [French]

Clare /kleə(r)/ county in the W Republic of Ireland, in the province of Munster; agriculture and salmon fisheries provide the main occupations; pop. (est. 1991) 90 826; capital, Ennis.

claret /'klærət/ *n.* **1** red wine, esp. from Bordeaux. **2** purplish-red. [French: related to CLARIFY]

clarify /'klærɪ,faɪ/ *v.* (**-ies**, **-ied**) **1** make or become clearer. **2 a** free (liquid etc.) from impurities. **b** make transparent. □ **clarification** /-fɪ'keɪʃ(ə)n/ *n.* [Latin: related to CLEAR]

clarinet /,klærɪ'net/ *n.* woodwind instrument with a single reed. □ **clarinettist** *n.* (*US* **clarinetist**). [French diminutive of *clarine*, a kind of bell]

clarion /'klærɪən/ *n.* **1** clear rousing sound. **2** *hist.* shrill war-trumpet. [Latin: related to CLEAR]

clarity /'klærɪtɪ/ *n.* clearness.

clash –*n.* **1 a** loud jarring sound as of metal objects struck together. **b** collision. **2 a** conflict. **b** discord of colours etc. –*v.* **1** (cause to) make a clashing sound. **2** collide; coincide awkwardly. **3** (often foll. by *with*) **a** come into conflict or be at variance. **b** (of colours) be discordant. [imitative]

clasp /klɑːsp/ –*n.* **1** device with interlocking parts for fastening. **2 a** embrace. **b** grasp, handshake. **3** bar on a medal-ribbon. –*v.* **1** fasten with or as with a clasp. **2 a** grasp, hold closely. **b** embrace. [Old English]

clasp-knife *n.* folding knife, usu. with a catch to hold the blade open.

class /klɑːs/ –*n.* **1** any set of persons or things grouped together, or graded or differentiated from others esp. by quality (*first class*; *economy class*). **2** division or order of society (*upper class*). **3** *colloq.* distinction, high quality. **4 a** group of students taught together. **b** occasion when they meet. **c** their course of instruction. **5** division of candidates by merit in an examination. **6** *Biol.* next grouping of organisms below a division or phylum. –*v.* assign to a class or category. □ **in a class of** (or **on) its** (or **one's) own** unequalled. □ **classless** *adj.* [Latin *classis* assembly]

class-conscious *adj.* aware of social divisions or one's place in them. □ **class-consciousness** *n.*

classic /'klæsɪk/ –*adj.* **1** first-class; of lasting value and importance. **2** very typical (*a classic case*). **3 a** of ancient Greek and Latin literature, art, etc. **b** (of style) simple, harmonious. **4** famous because long-established. –*n.* **1** classic writer, artist, work, or example. **2** (in *pl.*) ancient Greek and Latin. [Latin *classicus*: related to CLASS]

classical *adj.* **1 a** of ancient Greek or Roman literature or art. **b** (of a language) having the form used by ancient standard authors. **2** (of music) serious or conventional, or of the period from *c.*1750–1800. **3** restrained in style. □ **classicality** /-'kælɪtɪ/ *n.* **classically** *adv.*

♦ **Classical school** *n.* school of economics founded by Adam Smith. Smith was primarily concerned with explaining the origins of wealth creation and with advocating the benefits of free trade. He achieved this by analysing the economic relationships between the classes: workers, who earn their living by wage labour; capitalists, who derive income from profits; and landlords, whose income derives from rent. Supply and demand in each class determined prices. David Ricardo extended this analysis, in particular elucidating the concept of value, which in the Classical school is seen as a product of labour. The labour theory of value was used by Marx as a basis for his analysis of the capitalist economy and Marxists have remained firmly wedded to the Classical school. The Marginalists of the late 19th century overturned this thinking by defining value in relation to scarcity alone; this remains the basis of the neoclassical school.

♦ **classical system of corporation tax** *n.* system of taxing companies in which the company is treated as a taxable entity separate from its own shareholders. The profits of companies under this system are therefore taxed twice, first when made by the company and again when distributed to the shareholders as dividends. Cf. IMPUTATION SYSTEM OF TAXATION.

classicism /'klæsɪˌsɪz(ə)m/ *n.* **1** following of a classic style. **2** classical scholarship. **3** ancient Greek or Latin idiom. □ **classicist** *n.*

♦ **classified advertising** *n.* form of advertising that consists of small typeset or semi-display advertisements grouped together in such categories as cars for sale, furniture for sale, flats to let, etc., usu. in a paper or magazine. They are usu. inserted by direct contact between the advertiser and the advertising department of the publication.

♦ **classified directory** *n.* (also, *propr.*, **Yellow Pages**) UK trade directory, printed on yellow paper, issued by British Telecom for each business area. Businesses are listed by trade.

classify /'klæsɪˌfaɪ/ *v.* (**-ies, -ied**) **1 a** arrange in classes or categories. **b** assign to a class or category. **2** designate as officially secret or not for general disclosure. □ **classifiable** *adj.* **classification** /-fɪ'keɪʃ(ə)n/ *n.* **classificatory** /-'keɪtərɪ/ *adj.* [French: related to CLASS]

classmate *n.* person in the same class at school.

classroom *n.* room where a class of students is taught.

classy *adj.* (**-ier, -iest**) *colloq.* superior, stylish. □ **classily** *adv.* **classiness** *n.*

clatter *–n.* sound as of hard objects struck together. *–v.* (cause to) make a clatter. [Old English]

clause /klɔːz/ *n.* **1** *Gram.* part of a sentence, including a subject and predicate. **2** single statement in a treaty, law, contract, etc. □ **clausal** *adj.* [Latin *clausula*: related to CLOSE]

Clause 28 *n.* clause in the Local Government Bill (and later Act) banning local authorities from promoting homosexuality.

♦ **claused bill of lading** *n.* = DIRTY BILL OF LADING.

claustrophobia /ˌklɔːstrə'fəʊbɪə/ *n.* abnormal fear of confined places. □ **claustrophobic** *adj.* [Latin *claustrum* CLOISTER, -PHOBIA]

clavichord /'klævɪˌkɔːd/ *n.* small keyboard instrument with a very soft tone. [medieval Latin: related to CLAVICLE]

clavicle /'klævɪk(ə)l/ *n.* collar-bone. [Latin *clavis* key]

claw *–n.* **1 a** pointed nail on an animal's foot. **b** foot armed with claws. **2** pincers of a shellfish. **3** device for grappling, holding, etc. *–v.* scratch, maul, or pull with claws or fingernails. [Old English]

claw back *v.* regain laboriously or gradually.

♦ **claw-back** *n.* **1** money that a government takes back from members of the public by higher-rate tax, having given the money away in benefits (e.g. increased retirement pensions). **2** recovery of such money.

claw-hammer *n.* hammer with one side of the head forked for extracting nails.

clay *n.* **1** stiff sticky earth, used for making bricks, pottery, etc. **2** *poet.* substance of the human body. □ **clayey** *adj.* [Old English]

claymore /'kleɪmɔː(r)/ *n. hist.* Scottish two-edged broadsword. [Gaelic, = great sword]

clay pigeon *n.* breakable disc thrown up from a trap as a target for shooting.

clean *–adj.* **1** free from dirt or impurities, unsoiled. **2** clear; unused; pristine (*clean air*; *clean page*). **3** not obscene or indecent. **4** attentive to personal hygiene and cleanliness. **5** complete, clear-cut. **6** showing no record of crime, disease, etc. **7** fair (*a clean fight*). **8** streamlined; well-formed. **9** adroit, skilful. **10** (of a nuclear weapon) producing relatively little fallout. *–adv.* **1** completely, outright, simply. **2** in a clean manner. *–v.* make or become clean. *–n.* act or process of cleaning. □ **clean out 1** clean thoroughly. **2** *slang* empty or deprive (esp. of money). **clean up 1 a** clear away (a mess). **b** (also *absol.*) put (things) tidy. **c** make (oneself) clean. **2** restore order or morality to. **3** *slang* acquire as or make a profit. **come clean** *colloq.* confess fully. **make a clean breast of** see BREAST. [Old English]

clean bill of health *n.* declaration that there is no disease or defect.

♦ **clean bill of lading** see BILL OF LADING.

clean-cut *adj.* **1** sharply outlined or defined. **2** (of a person) clean and tidy.

cleaner *n.* **1** person employed to clean rooms etc. **2** establishment for cleaning clothes etc. **3** device or substance for cleaning. □ **take a person to the cleaners** *slang* **1** defraud or rob a person. **2** criticize severely.

♦ **clean floating** *n.* government policy allowing a country's currency to fluctuate without direct intervention in the foreign-exchange markets. In practice, clean floating is rare as governments are frequently tempted to manage exchange rates by direct intervention by means of the official reserves, a policy sometimes called **managed floating** (see also MANAGED CURRENCY). However, clean floating does not necessarily mean that there is no control of exchange rates, as they can still be influenced by the government's monetary policy.

cleanly[1] *adv.* in a clean way.

cleanly[2] /'klenlɪ/ *adj.* (**-ier, -iest**) habitually clean; with clean habits. □ **cleanliness** *n.*

♦ **clean price** *n.* price of a gilt-edged security excluding the accrued interest since the previous dividend payment. Interest on gilt-edged stocks accrues continuously although dividends are paid at fixed intervals (usu. six months). Prices quoted in newspapers are usu. clean prices, although a buyer will normally pay for and receive the accrued income as well as the stock itself.

cleanse /klenz/ *v.* (**-sing**) make clean or pure. □ **cleanser** *n.*

clean-shaven *adj.* without beard or moustache.

clean sheet *n.* (also **clean slate**) freedom from commitments or imputations; removal of these from one's record.

clean-up *n.* act of cleaning up.

clear *–adj.* **1** free from dirt or contamination. **2** (of weather, the sky, etc.) not dull. **3** transparent. **4 a** easily perceived; distinct; evident (*a clear voice*; *it is clear that*). **b** easily understood. **5** discerning readily and accurately (*clear mind*). **6** confident, convinced. **7** (of a conscience) free from guilt. **8** (of a road etc.) unobstructed. **9 a** net, without deduction. **b** complete (*three clear days*). **10** (often foll. by *of*) free, unhampered; unencumbered. *–adv.* **1** clearly. **2** completely (*got clear away*). **3** apart, out of contact (*keep clear*). *–v.* **1** make or become clear. **2** (often foll. by *of*) make or become free from obstruction etc. **3** (often foll. by *of*) show (a person) to be innocent. **4** approve (a person etc.) for a special duty, access, etc. **5** pass over or by, safely or without touching. **6** make (an amount of money) as a net gain or to balance expenses. **7** pass (a cheque) through a clearing-house. **8** pass through (customs etc.). **9** disappear (*mist cleared*). □ **clear the air** remove suspicion, tension, etc. **clear away 1** remove (esp. dishes etc.). **2** disappear. **clear the decks** prepare for action. **clear off** *colloq.* go away. **clear out 1** empty, tidy by emptying. **2** remove. **3** *colloq.* go away. **clear up 1** tidy up. **2** solve. **3** (of weather) become fine. **4** disappear (*acne has cleared up*). **clear a thing with** get approval or authorization for it from (a person). **in the clear** free from suspicion or difficulty. □ **clearly** *adj.* **clearness** *n.* [Latin *clarus*]

clearance *n.* **1** removal of obstructions etc. **2** space allowed for the passing of two objects or parts in machinery etc. **3** special authorization. **4 a** clearing by customs. **b** certificate showing this. **5** clearing of cheques.

clear-cut *adj.* sharply defined.

♦ **clear days** *n.pl.* full days referred to in a contract, i.e. not including the days on which the contract period starts or finishes.

---

clear-headed *adj.* thinking clearly, sensible.

clearing *n.* open area in a forest.

clearing bank *n.* **1** (in the UK) bank which is a member of a bankers' clearing-house. **2** any major high-street or joint-stock bank.

♦ **clearing-house** *n.* centralized and computerized system for settling indebtedness between members. The best known in the UK is the Association for Payment Clearing Services (APACS), which enables the member banks to offset claims against one another for cheques and orders paid into banks other than those upon which they were drawn. Similar arrangements exist in some commodity exchanges, in which sales and purchases are registered with the clearing-house for settlement at the end of the accounting period. See LONDON CLEARING HOUSE. **2** agency for collecting and distributing information etc.

♦ **Clearing House Interbank Payments System** *n.* (also **CHIPS**) US electronic clearing house, situated in New York, that clears most dollar cheques between US banks.

---

clear-out *n.* tidying by emptying and sorting.

clear-sighted *adj.* seeing, thinking, or understanding clearly.

clear-up *n.* **1** tidying up. **2** (usu. *attrib.*) solving of crimes (*clear-up rates*).

clearway *n.* main road (other than a motorway) on which vehicles may not normally stop.

cleat *n.* **1** piece of metal, wood, etc., bolted on for fastening ropes to, or to strengthen woodwork etc. **2** projecting piece on a spar, gangway, etc. to prevent slipping. [Old English]

cleavage /'kli:vɪdʒ/ *n.* **1** hollow between a woman's breasts. **2** division, splitting. **3** line along which rocks, crystals, etc. split.

cleave[1] *v.* (**-ving**; *past* **clove** or **cleft** or **cleaved**; *past part.* **cloven** or **cleft** or **cleaved**) *literary* **1** chop or break apart; split, esp. along the grain or line of cleavage. **2** make one's way through (air or water). [Old English]

cleave[2] *v.* (**-ving**) (foll. by *to*) *literary* stick fast; adhere. [Old English]

cleaver *n.* butcher's heavy chopping tool.

clef *n. Mus.* symbol indicating the pitch of notes on a staff. [Latin *clavis* key]

cleft[1] *adj.* split, partly divided. [past part. of CLEAVE[1]]

cleft[2] *n.* split, fissure. [Old English: related to CLEAVE[1]]

cleft lip *n.* congenital cleft in the upper lip.

cleft palate *n.* congenital split in the roof of the mouth.

clematis /'klemətɪs/ *n.* climbing plant with white, pink, or purple flowers. [Greek]

clement /'klemənt/ *adj.* **1** (of weather) mild. **2** merciful. □ **clemency** *n.* [Latin *clemens*]

clementine /'klemən,ti:n/ *n.* small tangerine-like citrus fruit. [French]

clench *–v.* **1** close (the teeth, fingers, etc.) tightly. **2** grasp firmly. *–n.* clenching action; clenched state. [Old English]

clerestory /'klɪə,stɔ:rɪ/ *n.* (*pl.* **-ies**) upper row of windows in a cathedral or large church, above the level of the aisle roofs. [*clear storey*]

clergy /'klɜ:dʒɪ/ *n.* (*pl.* **-ies**) (usu. treated as *pl.*) those ordained for religious duties. [French (related to CLERIC) and Church Latin]

clergyman *n.* member of the clergy.

cleric /'klerɪk/ *n.* member of the clergy. [Greek *klērikos* from *klēros* lot, heritage]

clerical *adj.* **1** of clergy or clergymen. **2** of or done by clerks.

clerical collar *n.* stiff upright white collar fastening at the back.

clerihew /'klerɪ,hju:/ *n.* short comic biographical verse in two rhyming couplets. [E. *Clerihew* Bentley, name of its inventor]

clerk /klɑ:k/ *–n.* **1** person employed to keep records, accounts, etc. **2** secretary or agent of a local council, court, etc. **3** lay officer of a church. *–v.* work as clerk. [Old English and French: related to CLERIC]

Clermont-Ferrand /,kleəmɔ̃fe'rɑ̃/ city in central France, capital of the Auvergne region; pop. (est. 1990) 140 167. The rubber industry is important; manufactures include chemicals, foodstuffs, and textiles.

Cleveland /'kli:vlənd/ **1** former county of NE England; industries included iron and steel, chemicals, and engineering; its county town was Middlesbrough. **2** major port and industrial city in the US, in NE Ohio; industries include iron and steel, oil refining, and food processing; pop. (est. 1994) 492 901.

clever /'klevə(r)/ *adj.* (**-er, -est**) **1** skilful, talented; quick to understand and learn. **2** adroit, dextrous. **3** ingenious. □ **cleverly** *adv.* **cleverness** *n.* [Old English]

cliché /'kli:ʃeɪ/ *n.* **1** hackneyed phrase or opinion. **2** metal casting of a stereotype or electrotype. □ **clichéd** *adj.* (also **cliché'd**). [French]

click *–n.* slight sharp sound. *–v.* **1** (cause to) make a click. **2** *colloq.* **a** become clear or understood. **b** be popular. **c** (foll. by *with*) strike up a rapport. [imitative]

client /'klaɪənt/ *n.* **1** person using the services of a lawyer, architect, or other professional person. **2** customer. [Latin *cliens*]

♦ **client account** *n.* bank or building society account operated by a professional person (solicitor, stockbroker, agent, etc.) on behalf of a client. A client account is legally required for any company handling investments on a client's behalf; it protects the client's money in case the company becomes insolvent and makes dishonest appropriation of the client's funds more difficult. For this reason money in client accounts should be quite separate from the business transactions of the company or the professional person.

---

clientele /,kli:ɒn'tel/ *n.* **1** clients collectively. **2** customers. [French and Latin: related to CLIENT]

cliff *n.* steep rock-face, esp. on a coast. [Old English]

cliff-hanger *n.* story etc. with a strong element of suspense.

climacteric /klaɪ'mæktərɪk/ *n.* period of life when fertility and sexual activity are in decline. [Greek: related to CLIMAX]

climate /'klaɪmɪt/ *n.* **1** prevailing weather conditions of an area. **2** region with particular weather conditions. **3** prevailing trend of opinion or feeling. □ **climatic** /-'mætɪk/ *adj.* **climatically** /-'mætɪkəlɪ/ *adv.* [Greek *klima*]

climax /'klaɪmæks/ *–n.* **1** event or point of greatest intensity or interest; culmination. **2** orgasm. *–v. colloq.* reach or bring to a climax. □ **climactic** /-'mæktɪk/ *adj.* [Greek, = ladder]

climb /klaɪm/ *–v.* **1** (often foll. by *up*) ascend, mount, go or come up. **2** grow up a wall etc. by clinging or twining. **3** progress, esp. in social rank. *–n.* **1** ascent by climbing. **2** hill etc. climbed or to be climbed. □ **climb down 1** descend, esp. using hands. **2** withdraw from a stance taken up in an argument etc. □ **climber** *n.* [Old English]

climb-down *n.* withdrawal from a stance taken up.

climbing-frame *n.* structure of joined bars etc. for children to climb on.

clime *n. literary* **1** region. **2** climate. [Latin: related to CLIMATE]

clinch *–v.* **1** confirm or settle (an argument, bargain, etc.) conclusively. **2** (of boxers etc.) become too closely engaged. **3** secure (a nail or rivet) by driving the point sideways when through. *–n.* **1 a** clinching action. **b** clinched state. **2** *colloq.* embrace. [var. of CLENCH]

clincher *n. colloq.* point or remark that settles an argument etc.

cling *v.* (*past* and *past part.* **clung**) **1** (often foll. by *to*) adhere. **2** (foll. by *to*) be unwilling to give up; be emotionally dependent on (a habit, idea, friend, etc.). **3** (often foll. by *to*) maintain grasp; keep hold; resist separation. □ **clingy** *adj.* (**-ier, -iest**). [Old English]

cling film *n.* thin transparent plastic covering for food.

clinic /'klɪnɪk/ *n.* **1** private or specialized hospital. **2** place or occasion for giving medical treatment or specialist advice. **3** gathering at a hospital bedside for medical teaching. [Greek *klinē* bed]

clinical *adj.* **1** of or for the treatment of patients. **2** dispassionate, coolly detached. **3** (of a room, building, etc.) bare, functional. □ **clinically** *adv.* [Greek: related to CLINIC]

clinical death *n.* death judged by professional observation of a person's condition.

clink[1] *–n.* sharp ringing sound. *–v.* (cause to) make a clink. [Dutch: imitative]

clink[2] *n. slang* prison. [origin unknown]

clinker *n.* **1** mass of slag or lava. **2** stony residue from burnt coal. [Dutch: related to CLINK[1]]

clinker-built *adj.* (of a boat) having external planks overlapping downwards and secured with clinched nails. [*clink*, Northern English var. of CLINCH]

♦ **cliometrics** /ˌklaɪəʊ'metrɪks/ *n.pl.* (treated as *sing.*) application of econometrics to the study of history, a technique developed in the 1960s and 1970s. [from *Clio*, muse of history]

---

clip[1] *–n.* **1** device for holding things together or for attaching something. **2** piece of jewellery fastened by a clip. **3** set of attached cartridges for a firearm. *–v.* (**-pp-**) fix with a clip. [Old English]

clip[2] *–v.* (**-pp-**) **1** cut (hair, wool, etc.) short with shears or scissors. **2** trim or remove the hair or wool of. **3** *colloq.* hit smartly. **4 a** omit (a letter etc.) from a word. **b** omit letters or syllables of (words uttered). **5** punch a hole in (a ticket) to show it has been used. **6** cut from a newspaper etc. **7** *slang* swindle, rob. *–n.* **1** act of clipping. **2** *colloq.* smart blow. **3** sequence from a motion picture. **4** yield of wool etc. **5** *colloq.* speed, esp. rapid. [Old Norse]

clipboard *n.* small board with a spring clip for holding papers etc.

clip-joint *n. slang* club etc. charging exorbitant prices.

clip-on *adj.* attached by a clip.

clipper *n.* **1** (usu. in *pl.*) instrument for clipping hair etc. **2** *hist.* fast sailing-ship.

clipping *n.* piece clipped, esp. from a newspaper.

clique /kliːk/ *n.* small exclusive group of people. □ **cliquey** *adj.* (**cliquier, cliquiest**). **cliquish** *adj.* [French]

clitoris /'klɪtərɪs/ *n.* small erectile part of the female genitals at the upper end of the vulva. □ **clitoral** *adj.* [Latin from Greek]

Cllr. *abbr.* Councillor.

CLNS *abbr. Computing* connectionless network service.

cloak *–n.* **1** outdoor usu. long and sleeveless over-garment. **2** covering (*cloak of snow*). *–v.* **1** cover with a cloak. **2** conceal, disguise. □ **under the cloak of** using as pretext. [ultimately from medieval Latin *clocca* bell]

cloak-and-dagger *adj.* involving intrigue and espionage.

cloakroom *n.* **1** room where outdoor clothes or luggage may be left. **2** *euphem.* lavatory.

clobber[1] *v. slang* **1** hit; beat up. **2** defeat. **3** criticize severely. [origin unknown]

clobber[2] *n. slang* clothing, belongings. [origin unknown]

cloche /klɒʃ/ *n.* **1** small translucent cover for protecting outdoor plants. **2** (in full **cloche hat**) woman's close-fitting bell-shaped hat. [French, = bell, medieval Latin *clocca*]

clock[1] *–n.* **1** instrument for measuring and showing time. **2 a** measuring device resembling this. **b** *colloq.* speedometer, taximeter, or stopwatch. **3** electronic device providing an extremely regular signal that is used to synchronize related pieces of computer equipment. **4** *slang* person's face. **5** seed-head of the dandelion. *–v.* **1** *colloq.* **a** (often foll. by *up*) attain or register (a stated time, distance, or speed). **b** time (a race) with a stopwatch. **2** *slang* hit. □ **clock in** (or **on**) register one's arrival at work. **clock off** (or **out**) register one's departure from work. **round the clock** all day and (usu.) night. [medieval Latin *clocca* bell]

clock[2] *n.* ornamental pattern on the side of a stocking or sock near the ankle. [origin unknown]

clockwise *adj.* & *adv.* in a curve corresponding in direction to that of the hands of a clock.

clockwork *n.* **1** mechanism like that of a clock, with a spring and gears. **2** (*attrib.*) driven by clockwork. □ **like clockwork** smoothly, regularly, automatically.

clod *n.* lump of earth, clay, etc. [var. of CLOT]

cloddish *adj.* loutish, foolish, clumsy.

clodhopper *n.* (usu. in *pl.*) *colloq.* large heavy shoe.

clog *–n.* shoe with a thick wooden sole. *–v.* (**-gg-**) **1** (often foll. by *up*) obstruct or become obstructed; choke. **2** impede. [origin unknown]

cloister *–n.* **1** covered walk round a quadrangle, esp. in a college or ecclesiastical building. **2** monastic life or seclusion. *–v.* seclude. □ **cloistered** *adj.* **cloistral** *adj.* [Latin *claustrum*: related to CLOSE[2]]

clomp var. of CLUMP *v.* 2.

clone *–n.* **1 a** group of organisms produced asexually from one stock or ancestor. **b** one such organism. **2** *colloq.* person or thing regarded as identical to another. *–v.* (**-ning**) propagate as a clone. □ **clonal** *adj.* [Greek *klōn* twig]

clonk *–n.* abrupt heavy sound of impact. *–v.* **1** make this sound. **2** *colloq.* hit. [imitative]

close[1] /kləʊs/ *–adj.* **1** (often foll. by *to*) situated at a short distance or interval. **2 a** having a strong or immediate relation or connection (*close friend*). **b** in intimate friendship or association. **c** corresponding almost exactly (*close resemblance*). **3** in or almost in contact (*close combat*). **4** dense, compact, with no or only slight intervals. **5** (of a contest etc.) in which competitors are almost equal. **6** leaving no gaps or weaknesses, rigorous (*close reasoning*). **7** concentrated, searching. **8** (of air etc.) stuffy, humid. **9** closed, shut. **10** limited to certain persons etc. (*close corporation*). **11** hidden, secret; secretive. **12** niggardly. *–adv.* at only a short distance or interval. *–n.* **1** street closed at one end. **2** precinct of a cathedral. □ **at close quarters** very close together. □ **closely** *adv.* **closeness** *n.* [Latin *clausus* from *claudo* shut]

close[2] /kləʊz/ *–v.* (**-sing**) **1 a** shut. **b** block up. **2** bring or come to an end. **3** end the day's business. **4** bring or come closer or into contact. **5** make (an electric circuit etc.) continuous. *–n.* conclusion, end. □ **close down** (of a shop etc.) discontinue business. **close in 1** enclose. **2** come nearer. **3** (of days) get successively shorter. **close out** *Finance* etc. close an open position, usu. on a futures market by buying to cover a short sale or by selling a long purchase. See FUTURES CONTRACT; OPEN POSITION. **close up 1** (often foll. by *to*) move closer. **2** shut. **3** block up. **4** (of an aperture) grow smaller. [Latin: related to CLOSE[1]]

♦ **close company** *n.* (*US* **closed company**) company resident in the UK that is under the control of five or fewer participators or any number of participators who are also directors. There is also an alternative asset-based test, which applies if five or fewer participators, or any number who are directors, would be entitled to more than 50% of the company's assets on liquidation. The principal consequences of being a close company are that certain payments made to shareholders can be treated by the Inland Revenue as a distribution, as can loans or quasi-loans. Close investment companies do not qualify for the reduced rate of corporation tax.

---

closed book *n.* subject one does not understand.

closed-circuit *adj.* (of television) transmitted by wires to a restricted set of receivers.

♦ **closed economy** *n.* theoretical model of an economy that neither imports nor exports and is therefore independent of economic factors in the outside world. No such economy exists, although the foreign sector of the US economy is relatively small and most economic decisions are taken by the US government independently of the rest of the world.

♦ **closed indent** see OPEN INDENT.

♦ **closed shop** *n.* business etc. in which there is an agreement between the employers and a trade union that only members of that union will be taken on as employees. Under the Employment Protection (Consolidation) Act (1978), as amended by the Employment Acts (1980, 1982, and 1988), all employees are free to join a trade union or not, as they wish. While closed-shop agreements are not in themselves illegal, they are unenforceable by either employers or unions. In an **open shop** the employer is free to take on employees of any trade union or employees who belong to no trade union.

---

close harmony *n.* harmony in which the notes of a chord are close together.

close-knit *adj.* tightly interlocked; closely united in friendship.

♦ **close price** *n.* price of a share or commodity when the margin between the bid and offer prices is narrow.

---

close season *n.* season when the killing of game etc. is illegal.

close shave *n.* (also **close thing**) *colloq.* narrow escape.

closet /'klɒzɪt/ –*n.* **1** small room. **2** cupboard. **3** = WATER-CLOSET. **4** (*attrib.*) secret (*closet homosexual*). –*v.* (**-t-**) shut away, esp. in private conference or study. [French diminutive: related to CLOSE[2]]

close-up *n.* photograph etc. taken at close range.

♦ **closing deal** *n.* transaction on a commodity market or stock exchange that closes a long or short position or terminates the liability of an option holder.

♦ **closing prices** *n.pl.* buying and selling prices recorded at the end of a day's trading on a commodity market or stock exchange. See AFTER-HOURS DEALS.

---

closure /'kləʊʒə(r)/ *n.* **1** closing. **2** closed state. **3** procedure for ending a debate and taking a vote. [Latin: related to CLOSE[2]]

clot –*n.* **1** thick mass of coagulated liquid etc., esp. of blood. **2** *colloq.* foolish person. –*v.* (**-tt-**) form into clots. [Old English]

cloth *n.* **1** woven or felted material. **2** piece of this, esp. for a particular purpose; tablecloth, dishcloth, etc. **3** fabric for clothes. **4 a** status, esp. of the clergy, as shown by clothes. **b** (prec. by *the*) the clergy. [Old English]

clothe /kləʊð/ *v.* (**-thing**; *past* and *past part.* **clothed** or *formal* **clad**) **1** put clothes on; provide with clothes. **2** cover as with clothes. [Old English]

clothes /kləʊðz/ *n.pl.* **1** garments worn to cover the body and limbs. **2** bedclothes. [Old English]

clothes-horse *n.* frame for airing washed clothes.

clothes-line *n.* rope etc. on which clothes are hung to dry.

clothes-peg *n.* clip etc. for securing clothes to a clothes-line.

♦ **Clothier** /'kləʊðɪə(r)/, **John** (1947–) British businessman, managing director of C & J Clark, the shoe manufacturing and retailing group, and great-great-grandson of the founder. A family business, which began in Street, Somerset, 150 years ago, it now employs more than 20 000 people worldwide.

---

clothier /'kləʊðɪə(r)/ *n.* seller of men's clothes.

clothing /'kləʊðɪŋ/ *n.* clothes collectively.

clotted cream *n.* thick cream obtained by slow scalding.

cloud –*n.* **1** visible mass of condensed watery vapour floating high above the ground. **2** mass of smoke or dust. **3** (foll. by *of*) mass of insects etc. moving together. **4** state of gloom, trouble, or suspicion. –*v.* **1** cover or darken with clouds or gloom or trouble. **2** (often foll. by *over*, *up*) become overcast or gloomy. **3** make unclear. □ **on cloud nine** *colloq.* extremely happy. **under a cloud** out of favour, under suspicion. **with one's head in the clouds** day-dreaming. □ **cloudless** *adj.* [Old English]

cloudburst *n.* sudden violent rainstorm.

cloud chamber *n.* device containing vapour for tracking the paths of charged particles, X-rays, and gamma rays.

cloud-cuckoo-land *n.* fanciful or ideal place. [translation of Greek *Nephelokokkugia* in Aristophanes' *Birds*]

cloudy *adj.* (**-ier, -iest**) **1** (of the sky, weather) covered with clouds, overcast. **2** not transparent; unclear. □ **cloudily** *adv.* **cloudiness** *n.*

clout –*n.* **1** heavy blow. **2** *colloq.* influence, power of effective action. **3** *dial.* piece of cloth or clothing. –*v.* hit hard. [Old English]

clove[1] *n.* dried bud of a tropical plant used as a spice. [Latin *clavus* nail (from its shape)]

clove[2] *n.* small segment of a compound bulb, esp. of garlic. [Old English: related to CLEAVE[1]]

clove[3] *past* of CLEAVE[1].

clove hitch *n.* knot by which a rope is secured to a spar etc. [*clove*, old past part. of CLEAVE[1]]

cloven /'kləʊv(ə)n/ *adj.* split, partly divided. [past part. of CLEAVE[1]]

cloven hoof *n.* (also **cloven foot**) divided hoof, esp. of oxen, sheep, or goats, or of the Devil.

clover *n.* trefoil fodder plant. □ **in clover** in ease and luxury. [Old English]

clown –*n.* **1** comic entertainer, esp. in a circus. **2** foolish or playful person. –*v.* (often foll. by *about*, *around*) behave like a clown. [origin uncertain]

cloy *v.* satiate or sicken with sweetness, richness, etc. [obsolete *acloy* from Anglo-French: related to ENCLAVE]

CLT *abbr.* computer-language translator.

club –*n.* **1** heavy stick with a thick end, esp. as a weapon. **2** stick with a head used in golf. **3** association of persons meeting periodically for a shared activity. **4** organization or premises offering members social amenities, meals, temporary residence, etc. **5 a** playing-card of the suit denoted by a black trefoil. **b** (in *pl.*) this suit. **6** commercial organization offering subscribers special deals (*book club*). –*v.* (**-bb-**) **1** beat with or as with a club. **2** (foll. by *together*, *with*) combine, esp. to raise a sum of money for a purpose. [Old Norse]

clubbable *adj.* sociable; fit for club membership.

club class *n.* class of fare on an aircraft etc. designed for business travellers.

club-foot *n.* congenitally deformed foot.

clubhouse *n.* premises of a (usu. sporting) club.

clubland *n.* area where there are many nightclubs.

club-root *n.* disease of cabbages etc. with swelling at the base of the stem.

club sandwich *n.* sandwich with two layers of filling between three slices of toast or bread.

cluck –*n.* guttural cry like that of a hen. –*v.* emit cluck(s). [imitative]

clue /kluː/ –*n.* **1** fact or idea that serves as a guide, or suggests a line of inquiry, in a problem or investigation. **2** piece of evidence etc. in the detection of a crime. **3** verbal formula as a hint to what is to be inserted in a crossword. –*v.* (**clues, clued, cluing** or **clueing**) provide a clue to. □ **clue in** (or **up**) *slang* inform. **not have a clue** *colloq.* be ignorant or incompetent. [var. of Old English *clew*]

clueless *adj. colloq.* ignorant, stupid.

Cluj /kluːʒ/ city in W central Romania; manufactures include machinery, furniture, and knitwear; pop. (est. 1993) 321 850.

clump –*n.* (foll. by *of*) cluster or mass, esp. of trees. –*v.* **1 a** form a clump. **b** heap or plant together. **2** (also **clomp**) walk with a heavy tread. [Low German or Dutch]

clumsy /'klʌmzɪ/ *adj.* (**-ier, -iest**) **1** awkward in movement or shape; ungainly. **2** difficult to handle or use. **3** tactless. □ **clumsily** *adv.* **clumsiness** *n.* [obsolete *clumse* be numb with cold]

clung *past* and *past part.* of CLING.

clunk –*n.* dull sound as of thick pieces of metal meeting. –*v.* make such a sound. [imitative]

cluster –*n.* close group or bunch of similar people or things growing or occurring together. –*v.* **1** bring into, come into, or be in cluster(s). **2** (foll. by *round, around*) gather. [Old English]

♦ **cluster sampling** *n.* type of sampling used in market research, in which the respondents are selected in groups, often chosen according to their geographical areas in order to reduce travelling costs.

clutch[1] –*v.* **1** seize eagerly; grasp tightly. **2** (foll. by *at*) try desperately to seize. –*n.* **1** tight grasp. **2** (in *pl.*) grasping hands; cruel or relentless grasp or control. **3 a** (in a vehicle) device for connecting and disconnecting the engine and the transmission. **b** pedal operating this. [Old English]

clutch[2] *n.* **1** set of eggs for hatching. **2** brood of chickens. [Old Norse, = hatch]

clutch bag *n.* slim flat handbag without handles.

clutter –*n.* **1** crowded and untidy collection of things. **2** untidy state. –*v.* (often foll. by *up, with*) crowd untidily, fill with clutter. [related to CLOT]

Clwyd /'klu:ɪd/ former county in NE Wales; manufactures included glass, plastics, and microprocessors; its county town was Mold.

CM *postcode* Chelmsford.

Cm *symb.* curium.

cm *abbr.* centimetre(s).

CMA *abbr.* **1** *US* Certificate of Management Accounting. **2** *NZ* cost and management accountant.

CMC *abbr. US* certified management consultant.

CME *abbr.* **1** Chicago Mercantile Exchange. **2** *US* cost and manufacturability expert.

♦ **CMEA** *abbr. hist.* Council for Mutual Economic Assistance. See COMECON.

CMG *abbr.* Companion (of the Order) of St Michael and St George.

CMI *abbr.* computer-managed instruction. See COMPUTER-ASSISTED LEARNING.

cml. *abbr.* commercial.

CMO *abbr. US* collateralized mortgage-backed obligation.

CMS *abbr.* **1** Certificate in Management Studies. **2** *Computing* conversational monitor system.

CN *international civil aircraft marking* Morocco.

C/N 1 consignment note. **2** contract note. **3** *Insurance* cover note. **4** credit note.

♦ **CNAR** *abbr.* compound net annual rate. See COMPOUND ANNUAL RETURN.

CNC *abbr.* computer numerical control.

CND *abbr.* Campaign for Nuclear Disarmament.

CNN *abbr.* Cable News Network.

CNT *abbr.* (Spanish) Confederación nacional del trabajo (= National Confederation of Labour).

CO –*abbr.* **1** Clerical Officer. **2** Commanding Officer. –*international vehicle registration* Colombia. –*postcode* Colchester. –*US postcode* Colorado. –*airline flight code* Continental Airlines.

C/O *abbr.* **1** cash order. **2** = CERTIFICATE OF ORIGIN.

Co *symb.* cobalt.

Co. *abbr.* **1** company. **2** county. **3** Colorado.

co- *prefix* added to: **1** nouns, with the sense 'joint, mutual, common' (*co-author, coequality*). **2** adjectives and adverbs, with the sense 'jointly, mutually' (*coequal*). **3** verbs, with the sense 'together with another or others' (*cooperate*). [var. of COM-]

c/o *abbr.* **1** care of. **2** *Bookkeeping* carried over.

coach –*n.* **1** single-decker bus, usu. comfortably equipped for long journeys. **2** railway carriage. **3** closed horse-drawn carriage. **4 a** instructor or trainer in a sport. **b** private tutor. –*v.* train or teach as a coach. [French from Magyar]

coachload *n.* group of tourists etc. taken by coach.

coachman *n.* driver of a horse-drawn carriage.

coachwork *n.* bodywork of a road or rail vehicle.

coagulate /kəʊ'ægjʊ,leɪt/ *v.* (**-ting**) **1** change from a fluid to a semisolid. **2** clot, curdle. □ **coagulant** *n.* **coagulation** /-'leɪʃ(ə)n/ *n.* [Latin *coagulum* rennet]

Coahuila /,kəʊə'wi:lə/ state in N Mexico; pop. (est. 1995) 2 172 136; capital, Saltillo.

coal *n.* **1** hard black rock, mainly carbonized plant matter, found underground and used as a fuel. **2** piece of this, esp. one that is burning. □ **coals to Newcastle** something brought to a place where it is already plentiful. **haul** (or **call) over the coals** reprimand. [Old English]

coalesce /,kəʊə'les/ *v.* (**-cing**) come together and form a whole. □ **coalescence** *n.* **coalescent** *adj.* [Latin *alo* nourish]

coalface *n.* exposed working surface of coal in a mine.

coalfield *n.* extensive area yielding coal.

coal gas *n.* mixed gases formerly extracted from coal and used for lighting and heating.

coalition /,kəʊə'lɪʃ(ə)n/ *n.* **1** temporary alliance, esp. of political parties. **2** fusion into one whole. [medieval Latin: related to COALESCE]

coalman *n.* man who carries or delivers coal.

coalmine *n.* mine in which coal is dug. □ **coalminer** *n.* **coalmining** *n.*

coal-scuttle *n.* container for coal for a domestic fire.

coal tar *n.* thick black oily liquid distilled from coal and used as a source of benzene.

coal-tit *n.* small greyish bird with a black head.

coaming /'kəʊmɪŋ/ *n.* raised border round a ship's hatches etc. to keep out water. [origin unknown]

coarse *adj.* **1** rough or loose in texture; made of large particles. **2** lacking refinement; crude, obscene. □ **coarsely** *adv.* **coarseness** *n.* [origin unknown]

coarse fish *n.* freshwater fish other than salmon and trout.

coarsen *v.* make or become coarse.

coast –*n.* border of land near the sea; seashore. –*v.* **1** ride or move, usu. downhill, without the use of power. **2** make progress without much effort. **3** sail along the coast. □ **the coast is clear** there is no danger of being observed or caught. □ **coastal** *adj.* [Latin *costa* side]

coaster *n.* **1** small cargo ship that travels along the coast from port to port. **2** small tray or mat for a bottle or glass.

coastguard *n.* **1** member of a group of people employed to keep watch on coasts to save life, prevent smuggling, etc. **2** such a group.

coastline *n.* line of the seashore, esp. with regard to its shape.

coat –*n.* **1** outer garment with sleeves, usu. extending below the hips; overcoat or jacket. **2** animal's fur or hair. **3** covering of paint etc. laid on a surface at one time. –*v.* **1** (usu. foll. by *with, in*) cover with a coat or layer. **2** (of paint etc.) form a covering to. [French from Germanic]

coat-hanger see HANGER 2.

coating *n.* **1** layer of paint etc. **2** material for coats.

coat of arms *n.* heraldic bearings or shield of a person, family, or corporation.

coat of mail *n.* jacket covered with mail.

coat-tail *n.* each of the flaps formed by the back of a tailcoat.

coax *v.* **1** persuade gradually or by flattery. **2** (foll. by *out of*) obtain (a thing from a person) thus. **3** manipulate (a thing) carefully or slowly. [obsolete *cokes* a fool]

coaxial /kəʊ'æksɪəl/ *adj.* **1** having a common axis. **2** *Electr.* (of a cable or line) transmitting by means of two concentric conductors separated by an insulator.

cob *n.* **1** roundish lump. **2** domed loaf. **3** = CORN-COB. **4** large hazelnut. **5** sturdy riding-horse with short legs. **6** male swan. [origin unknown]

cobalt /ˈkəʊbɔːlt/ *n.* **1** silvery-white metallic element. **2 a** pigment made from this. **b** its deep-blue colour. [German, probably = *Kobold* demon in mines]

cobber *n. Austral.* & *NZ colloq.* companion, friend. [origin uncertain]

cobble[1] /ˈkɒb(ə)l/ *–n.* (in full **cobblestone**) small rounded stone used for paving. *–v.* (**-ling**) pave with cobbles. [from COB]

cobble[2] /ˈkɒb(ə)l/ *v.* (**-ling**) **1** mend or patch up (esp. shoes). **2** (often foll. by *together*) join or assemble roughly. [from COBBLER]

cobbler *n.* **1** person who mends shoes professionally. **2** stewed fruit topped with scones. **3** (in *pl.*) *slang* nonsense. [origin unknown]

♦ **COBOL** /ˈkəʊbɒl/ *n.* (also **Cobol**) computer programming language widely used for commercial data processing, such as invoice and payroll production. It is an easy-to-learn high-level language that uses a limited number of English words. Programs written in COBOL can be run on different computers, provided that the standard version has been used. Because the language was designed to make program writing easy, a program occupies considerable amounts of computer memory, making COBOL more popular on larger systems than on microcomputers. However, microcomputer versions of COBOL are available. [*co*mmon *b*usiness *o*riented *l*anguage]

---

cobra /ˈkəʊbrə/ *n.* venomous hooded snake of Africa and Asia. [Latin *colubra* snake]

cobweb *n.* **1** fine network spun by a spider from liquid it secretes. **2** thread of this. □ **cobwebby** *adj.* [obsolete *coppe* spider]

coca /ˈkəʊkə/ *n.* **1** South American shrub. **2** its dried leaves, chewed as a stimulant. [Spanish from Quechua]

cocaine /kəʊˈkeɪn/ *n.* drug from coca, used as a local anaesthetic and as a stimulant.

coccyx /ˈkɒksɪks/ *n.* (*pl.* **coccyges** /-ˌdʒiːz/) small triangular bone at the base of the spinal column. [Greek, = cuckoo (from shape of its bill)]

Cochabamba /ˌkɒtʃəˈbæmbə/ city in Bolivia, at the centre of a rich agricultural region; industries include oil refining; pop. (1992) 404 100.

Cochin /ˈkəʊtʃɪn/ major seaport and naval base in SW India, in the state of Kerala; industries include oil refining; pop. (1991) 564 589.

cochineal /ˌkɒtʃɪˈniːl/ *n.* **1** scarlet dye used esp. for colouring food. **2** insects whose dried bodies yield this. [Latin *coccinus* scarlet, from Greek]

cock[1] *–n.* **1** male bird, esp. of the domestic fowl. **2** *slang* (as a form of address) friend; fellow. **3** *coarse slang* penis. **4** *slang* nonsense. **5 a** firing lever in a gun, raised to be released by the trigger. **b** cocked position of this. **6** tap or valve controlling flow. *–v.* **1** raise or make upright or erect. **2** turn or move (the eye or ear) attentively or knowingly. **3** set aslant; turn up the brim of (a hat). **4** raise the cock of (a gun). □ **at half cock** only partly ready. **cock a snook** see SNOOK. **cock up** *sl.* bungle; make a mess of. [Old English and French]

cock[2] *n.* conical heap of hay or straw. [perhaps from Scandinavian]

cockade /kɒˈkeɪd/ *n.* rosette etc. worn in the hat as a badge. [French: related to COCK[1]]

cock-a-doodle-doo *n.* cock's crow.

cock-a-hoop *adj.* exultant.

cock-a-leekie *n.* Scottish soup of boiling fowl and leeks.

cock-and-bull story *n.* absurd or incredible account.

cockatoo /ˌkɒkəˈtuː/ *n.* crested parrot. [Dutch from Malay]

cockchafer /ˈkɒkˌtʃeɪfə(r)/ *n.* large pale-brown beetle. [from COCK[1]]

cock crow *n.* dawn.

cocker *n.* (in full **cocker spaniel**) small spaniel with a silky coat. [related to COCK[1]]

cockerel /ˈkɒkər(ə)l/ *n.* young cock. [diminutive of COCK[1]]

cock-eyed *adj. colloq.* **1** crooked, askew. **2** absurd, not practical. [from COCK[1]]

cock-fight *n.* fight between cocks as sport.

cockle /ˈkɒk(ə)l/ *n.* **1 a** edible bivalve shellfish. **b** its shell. **2** (in full **cockle-shell**) small shallow boat. **3** pucker or wrinkle in paper, glass, etc. □ **warm the cockles of one's heart** make one contented. [French *coquille* from Greek: related to CONCH]

cockney /ˈkɒknɪ/ *–n.* (*pl.* **-s**) **1** native of London, esp. of the East End. **2** dialect or accent used there. *–adj.* of cockneys or their dialect. [*cokeney* 'cock's egg']

cockpit *n.* **1 a** compartment for the pilot (and crew) of an aircraft or spacecraft. **b** driver's seat in a racing car. **c** space for the helmsman in some yachts. **2** arena of war or other conflict. **3** place for cock-fights.

cockroach /ˈkɒkrəʊtʃ/ *n.* flat dark-brown beetle-like insect infesting kitchens, bathrooms, etc. [Spanish *cucaracha*]

cockscomb /ˈkɒkskəʊm/ *n.* crest of a cock.

cocksure /ˌkɒkˈʃɔː(r)/ *adj.* arrogantly confident. [from COCK[1]]

cocktail /ˈkɒkteɪl/ *n.* **1** drink made of various spirits, fruit juices, etc. **2** appetizer containing shellfish or fruit. **3** any hybrid mixture. [origin unknown]

cocktail dress *n.* short evening dress worn at a drinks party.

cocktail stick *n.* small pointed stick for serving an olive, cherry, etc.

cock-up *n. slang* muddle or mistake.

cocky *adj.* (**-ier, -iest**) *colloq.* conceited, arrogant. □ **cockily** *adv.* **cockiness** *n.* [from COCK[1]]

coco /ˈkəʊkəʊ/ *n.* (*pl.* **-s**) coconut palm. [Portuguese and Spanish, = grimace]

cocoa /ˈkəʊkəʊ/ *n.* **1** powder made from crushed cacao seeds, often with other ingredients. **2** drink made from this. [altered from CACAO]

cocoa bean *n.* cacao seed.

cocoa butter *n.* fatty substance obtained from the cocoa bean.

COCOM /ˈkəʊˌkɒm/ *abbr.* (also **CoCom**) Coordinating Committee for Multinational Export Controls.

COCOMO /kɒˈkəʊməʊ/ *abbr. Computing* (also **CoCoMo**) constructive cost model.

coconut /ˈkəʊkəˌnʌt/ *n.* large brown seed of the coco, with a hard shell and edible white lining enclosing milky juice.

coconut matting *n.* matting made of fibre from coconut husks.

coconut shy *n.* fairground sideshow where balls are thrown to dislodge coconuts.

cocoon /kəˈkuːn/ *–n.* **1** silky case spun by insect larvae for protection as pupae. **2** protective covering. *–v.* wrap or coat in a cocoon. [Provençal *coca* shell]

Cocos Islands /ˈkəʊkəs/ (also **Keeling Islands** /ˈkiːlɪŋ/) group of 27 small coral islands in the Indian Ocean, an external territory of Australia; pop. (1986) 616. Copra is produced, and there is a meteorological station.

cocotte /kəˈkɒt/ *n.* small fireproof dish for cooking and serving an individual portion. [French]

COD *abbr.* cash (*US* collect) on delivery.

cod[1] *n.* (*pl.* same) large sea fish. [origin unknown]

cod[2] *slang –n.* **1** parody. **2** hoax. *–v.* (**-dd-**) **1** perform a hoax. **2** parody. [origin unknown]

cod[3] *n. slang* nonsense. [abbreviation of CODSWALLOP]

coda /ˈkəʊdə/ *n.* **1** *Mus.* final additional passage of a piece or movement. **2** concluding section of a ballet. [Latin *cauda* tail]

coddle /ˈkɒd(ə)l/ *v.* (**-ling**) **1** treat as an invalid; protect attentively; pamper. **2** cook (an egg) in water below boiling point. □ **coddler** *n.* [a dialect form of *caudle* invalids' gruel]

code *–n.* **1** system of words, letters, symbols, etc., used to represent others for secrecy or brevity. **2** system of prearranged signals used to ensure secrecy in transmitting messages. **3** *Computing* **a** piece of program text. **b** rule for transforming data or other information from one symbolic form into another. **4** systematic set of laws etc. **5** prevailing standard of moral behaviour. –*v.* (**-ding**) put into code. [Latin CODEX]

codec /'kəʊdek/ *n. Computing* coder-decoder. [abbreviation]

codeine /'kəʊdiːn/ *n.* alkaloid derived from morphine, used to relieve pain. [Greek *kōdeia* poppy-head]

codependency /ˌkəʊdɪ'pendənsɪ/ *n.* addiction to a supportive role in a relationship. □ **codependent** *adj.* & *n.*

codex /'kəʊdeks/ *n.* (*pl.* **codices** /-dɪˌsiːz/) **1** ancient manuscript text in book form. **2** collection of descriptions of drugs etc. [Latin, = tablet, book]

codfish *n.* (*pl.* same) = COD[1].

codger /'kɒdʒə(r)/ *n.* (usu. in **old codger**) *colloq.* person, esp. a strange one. [origin uncertain]

codicil /'kəʊdɪsɪl/ *n.* addition to a will. [Latin diminutive of CODEX]

codify /'kəʊdɪˌfaɪ/ *v.* (**-ies, -ied**) arrange (laws etc.) systematically into a code. □ **codification** /-fɪ'keɪʃ(ə)n/ *n.* **codifier** *n.*

♦ **coding notice** *n.* document issued by the Inland Revenue as part of the PAYE system showing the amount of income-tax allowances to be set against an individual's taxable pay. The total of allowances is reduced to a code by dropping the last digit and adding a letter depending on the taxpayer's circumstances (e.g. H for higher personal allowance, L for lower single person's allowance).

---

codling[1] /'kɒdlɪŋ/ *n.* (also **codlin**) **1** a kind of cooking apple. **2** moth whose larva feeds on apples. [Anglo-French *quer de lion* lion-heart]

codling[2] *n.* small codfish.

cod-liver oil *n.* oil from cod livers, rich in vitamins D and A.

codpiece *n. hist.* bag or flap at the front of a man's breeches. [*cod* scrotum]

codswallop /'kɒdzˌwɒləp/ *n. slang* nonsense. [origin unknown]

coed /kəʊ'ed/ *colloq.* –*n.* **1** school for both sexes. **2** esp. *US* female pupil of a coed school. –*adj.* coeducational. [abbreviation]

coeducation /ˌkəʊedjuː'keɪʃ(ə)n/ *n.* education of pupils of both sexes together. □ **coeducational** *adj.*

coefficient /ˌkəʊɪ'fɪʃ(ə)nt/ *n.* **1** *Math.* quantity placed before and multiplying an algebraic expression. **2** *Physics* multiplier or factor by which a property is measured (*coefficient of expansion*). [related to CO-, EFFICIENT]

coelacanth /'siːləˌkænθ/ *n.* large sea fish formerly thought to be extinct. [Greek *koilos* hollow, *akantha* spine]

coelenterate /siː'lentəˌreɪt/ *n.* marine animal with a simple tube-shaped or cup-shaped body, e.g. jellyfish, corals, and sea anemones. [Greek *koilos* hollow, *enteron* intestine]

coeliac disease /'siːlɪˌæk/ *n.* disease of the small intestine, brought on by contact with dietary gluten. [Latin *coeliacus* from Greek *koilia* belly]

♦ **coemption** /kəʊ'empʃ(ə)n/ *n.* buying up the whole stock of a commodity. See CORNER *n.* 7. [Latin *coemptionem* buying together]

---

coenobite /'siːnəˌbaɪt/ *n.* (*US* **cenobite**) member of a monastic community. [Greek *koinos bios* common life]

coequal /kəʊ'iːkw(ə)l/ *adj.* & *n. archaic* or *literary* equal.

coerce /kəʊ'ɜːs/ *v.* (**-cing**) persuade or restrain by force. □ **coercible** *adj.* **coercion** /-'ɜːʃ(ə)n/ *n.* **coercive** *adj.* [Latin *coerceo* restrain]

coeval /kəʊ'iːv(ə)l/ *formal* –*adj.* of the same age; existing at the same time; contemporary. –*n.* coeval person or thing. □ **coevally** *adv.* [Latin *aevum* age]

coexist /ˌkəʊɪg'zɪst/ *v.* (often foll. by *with*) **1** exist together. **2** (esp. of nations) exist in mutual tolerance of each other's ideologies etc. □ **coexistence** *n.* **coexistent** *adj.*

coextensive /ˌkəʊɪk'stensɪv/ *adj.* extending over the same space or time.

COFACE *abbr.* French export credit guarantee company. [French *Compagnie Française pour l'Assurance du Commerce Extérieur*]

C. of C. *abbr.* Chamber of Commerce.

C. of E. *abbr.* **1** Church of England. **2** Council of Europe.

coffee /'kɒfɪ/ *n.* **1 a** drink made from roasted and ground beanlike seeds of a tropical shrub. **b** cup of this. **2 a** the shrub. **b** its seeds. **3** pale brown. [Turkish from Arabic]

coffee bar *n.* bar or café serving coffee and light refreshments from a counter.

coffee-mill *n.* small machine for grinding roasted coffee beans.

coffee morning *n.* morning gathering, esp. for charity, at which coffee is served.

coffee shop *n.* small informal restaurant, esp. in a hotel or department store.

coffee-table *n.* small low table.

coffee-table book *n.* large lavishly illustrated book.

coffer *n.* **1** large strong box for valuables. **2** (in *pl.*) treasury, funds. **3** sunken panel in a ceiling etc. [Latin *cophinus* basket]

coffer-dam *n.* watertight enclosure pumped dry to permit work below the water-line, e.g. building bridges etc. or repairing a ship.

coffin /'kɒfɪn/ *n.* box in which a corpse is buried or cremated. [Latin: related to COFFER]

cog *n.* **1** each of a series of projections on the edge of a wheel or bar transferring motion by engaging with another series. **2** unimportant member of an organization etc. [probably Scandinavian]

cogent /'kəʊdʒ(ə)nt/ *adj.* (of an argument etc.) convincing, compelling. □ **cogency** *n.* **cogently** *adv.* [Latin *cogo* drive]

cogitate /'kɒdʒɪˌteɪt/ *v.* (**-ting**) ponder, meditate. □ **cogitation** /-'teɪʃ(ə)n/ *n.* **cogitative** /-tətɪv/ *adj.* [Latin *cogito*]

cognac /'kɒnjæk/ *n.* high-quality brandy, properly that distilled in Cognac in W France.

cognate /'kɒgneɪt/ –*adj.* **1** related to or descended from a common ancestor. **2** (of a word) having the same linguistic family or derivation. –*n.* **1** relative. **2** cognate word. [Latin *cognatus*]

cognate object *n. Gram.* object related in origin and sense to its verb (as in *live a good life*).

cognition /kɒg'nɪʃ(ə)n/ *n.* **1** knowing, perceiving, or conceiving as an act or faculty distinct from emotion and volition. **2** result of this. □ **cognitional** *adj.* **cognitive** /'kɒg-/ *adj.* [Latin *cognitio*: related to COGNIZANCE]

♦ **cognitive dissonance** *n.* state of mental conflict caused by the difference between a consumer's expectations of a product and its actual performance. As expectations are largely formed by advertising, the dissonance may be reduced by making only realistic and consistent claims about a product's performance.

---

cognizance /'kɒgnɪz(ə)ns/ *n. formal* **1** knowledge or awareness; perception. **2** sphere of observation or concern. **3** *Heraldry* distinctive device or mark. [Latin *cognosco* get to know]

cognizant *adj.* (foll. by *of*) *formal* having knowledge or being aware of.

cognomen /kɒg'nəʊmen/ *n.* **1** nickname. **2** ancient Roman's third or fourth name designating a branch of a family, as in Marcus Tullius *Cicero*, or as an epithet, as in P. Cornelius Scipio *Africanus*. [Latin]

cognoscente /ˌkɒnjə'ʃentɪ/ *n.* (*pl.* ***-ti*** /-tɪ/) connoisseur. [Italian]

cog-wheel *n.* wheel with cogs.

cohabit /kəʊ'hæbɪt/ *v.* (**-t-**) (esp. of an unmarried couple) live together as husband and wife. □ **cohabitation** /-'teɪʃ(ə)n/ *n.* **cohabitee** /-'tiː/ *n.* [Latin *habito* dwell]

cohere /kəʊˈhɪə(r)/ *v.* (**-ring**) **1** (of parts or a whole) stick together, remain united. **2** (of reasoning etc.) be logical or consistent. [Latin *haereo haes-* stick]

coherent *adj.* **1** intelligible and articulate. **2** (of an argument etc.) consistent; easily followed. **3** cohering. **4** *Physics* (of waves) having a constant phase relationship. □ **coherence** *n.* **coherently** *adv.*

cohesion /kəʊˈhiːʒ(ə)n/ *n.* **1 a** sticking together. **b** tendency to cohere. **2** *Chem.* force with which molecules cohere. □ **cohesive** *adj.*

cohort /ˈkəʊhɔːt/ *n.* **1** ancient Roman military unit, one-tenth of a legion. **2** band of warriors. **3 a** persons banded together. **b** group of persons with a common statistical characteristic. [Latin]

COHSE /ˈkəʊzɪ/ *abbr.* (also **Cohse**) Confederation of Health Service Employees.

COI *abbr.* Central Office of Information.

coif *n. hist.* close-fitting cap. [Latin *cofia* helmet]

coiff /kwɑːf/ *–v.* (usu. as **coiffed** *–adj.*) dress or arrange (the hair). [French *coiffer*]

coiffeur /kwɑːˈfɜː(r)/ *n.* (*fem.* ***coiffeuse*** /-ˈfɜːz/) hairdresser. [French]

coiffure /kwɑːˈfjʊə(r)/ *n.* hairstyle. [French]

coil *–v.* **1** arrange or be arranged in spirals or concentric rings. **2** move sinuously. *–n.* **1** coiled arrangement. **2** coiled length of rope etc. **3** single turn of something coiled. **4** flexible loop as a contraceptive device in the womb. **5** coiled wire for the passage of an electric current and acting as an inductor. [Latin: related to COLLECT[1]]

Coimbatore /ˌkəʊɪmbəˈtɔː(r)/ city in S India, in Tamil Nadu; industries include textiles; pop. (1991) 816 321.

Coimbra /kəʊˈɪmbrə/ city in central Portugal; products include pottery, wine, and beer; pop. (1991) 96 140.

coin *–n.* **1** stamped disc of metal as official money. **2** (*collect.*) metal money. *–v.* **1** make (coins) by stamping. **2** make (metal) into coins. **3** invent (esp. a new word or phrase). □ **coin money** make much money quickly. [Latin *cuneus* wedge]

coinage *n.* **1** coining. **2 a** coins. **b** system of coins in use. **3** invention, esp. of a word.

coin-box *n.* **1** telephone operated by inserting coins. **2** receptacle for these.

coincide /ˌkəʊɪnˈsaɪd/ *v.* (**-ding**) **1** occur at the same time. **2** occupy the same portion of space. **3** (often foll. by *with*) agree or be identical. [Latin: related to INCIDENT]

coincidence /kəʊˈɪnsɪd(ə)ns/ *n.* **1** coinciding. **2** remarkable concurrence of events etc. apparently by chance. □ **coincident** *adj.*

coincidental /kəʊˌɪnsɪˈdent(ə)l/ *adj.* in the nature of or resulting from a coincidence. □ **coincidentally** *adv.*

♦ **co-insurance** *n.* sharing an insurance risk between several insurers. An insurer may find a particular risk too large to accept because the potential losses may be out of proportion to their claims funds. Rather than turning the insurance away, the insurer can offer to split the risk with a number of other insurers, each of whom would be asked to cover a percentage of the risk in return for the same percentage of the premium. The policyholder deals only with the first or leading insurer, who issues all the documents, collects all the premiums, and distributes shares to the others involved. A co-insurance policy includes a schedule of all the insurers involved and shows the percentage of the risk each one is accepting.

---

coir /ˈkɔɪə(r)/ *n.* coconut fibre used for ropes, matting, etc. [Malayalam *kāyar* cord]

coition /kəʊˈɪʃ(ə)n/ *n.* = COITUS. [Latin *coitio* from *eo* go]

coitus /ˈkəʊɪtəs/ *n.* sexual intercourse. □ **coital** *adj.* [Latin: related to COITION]

coitus interruptus /ˌɪntəˈrʌptəs/ *n.* sexual intercourse with withdrawal of the penis before ejaculation.

coke[1] *–n.* solid substance left after gases have been extracted from coal. *–v.* (**-king**) convert (coal) into coke. [dial. *colk* core]

coke[2] *n. slang* cocaine. [abbreviation]

COL *abbr.* **1** computer-oriented language. **2** cost of living.

Col. *abbr.* **1** Colonel. **2** Colorado.

col *n.* depression in a chain of mountains. [Latin *collum* neck]

col. *abbr.* column.

col- see COM-.

COLA /ˈkəʊlə/ *abbr. US* cost of living adjustment, a clause in employment contracts.

cola /ˈkəʊlə/ *n.* (also **kola**) **1** W African tree bearing seeds containing caffeine. **2** carbonated drink usu. flavoured with these. [W African]

colander /ˈkʌləndə(r)/ *n.* perforated vessel used to strain off liquid in cookery. [Latin *colo* strain]

cold /kəʊld/ *–adj.* **1** of or at a low temperature. **2** not heated; cooled after heat. **3** feeling cold. **4** lacking ardour, friendliness, or affection. **5 a** depressing, uninteresting. **b** (of colour) suggestive of cold. **6 a** dead. **b** *colloq.* unconscious. **7** (of a scent in hunting) grown faint. **8** (in games) far from finding what is sought. *–n.* **1 a** prevalence of low temperature. **b** cold weather or environment. **2** infection of the nose or throat with sneezing, catarrh, etc. *–adv.* unrehearsed. □ **in cold blood** without emotion, deliberately. **out in the cold** ignored, neglected. **throw** (or **pour) cold water on** be discouraging about. □ **coldly** *adv.* **coldness** *n.* [Old English]

cold-blooded *adj.* **1** having a body temperature varying with that of the environment. **2** callous; deliberately cruel. □ **cold-bloodedly** *adv.* **cold-bloodedness** *n.*

♦ **cold call** *–n.* marketing approach, face to face or by telephone, to a person who has previously not shown interest in the product. In view of the high cost of maintaining a sales force, many companies direct their sales representatives to those potential customers who are favourably disposed to the supplier (either as an existing customer or by replying to a press advertisement). The primary objective of cold calls is to establish a favourable relationship quickly, enabling the representatives to explain the benefits of their products or services before being dismissed. *–v.* visit or telephone (a person) in this way.

---

cold chisel *n.* chisel for cutting metal, stone, or brick.

cold comfort *n.* poor consolation.

cold cream *n.* ointment for cleansing and softening the skin.

cold feet *n.pl. colloq.* loss of nerve.

cold frame *n.* unheated glass-topped frame for growing small plants.

cold-hearted *adj.* lacking sympathy or kindness. □ **cold-heartedly** *adv.* **cold-heartedness** *n.*

cold shoulder *–n.* (prec. by *the*) intentional unfriendliness. *–v.* (**cold-shoulder**) be deliberately unfriendly towards.

cold sore *n.* inflammation and blisters in and around the mouth, caused by a virus infection.

cold storage *n.* **1** storage in a refrigerator. **2** temporary putting aside (of an idea etc.), postponement.

cold sweat *n.* sweating induced by fear or illness.

cold table *n.* selection of dishes of cold food.

cold turkey *n. slang* abrupt withdrawal from addictive drugs.

cold war *n.* hostility between nations without actual fighting.

cole *n.* (usu. in *comb.*) cabbage. [Latin *caulis*]

coleopteron /ˌkɒlɪˈɒptəˌrɒn/ *n.* insect with front wings serving as sheaths, e.g. the beetle and weevil. □ **coleopterous** *adj.* [Greek *koleon* sheath, *pteron* wing]

Coleraine /kəʊlˈreɪn/ **1** town in N Northern Ireland, in Co. Londonderry; manufactures include synthetic fibres; pop. (est. 1987) 47 700. **2** district in Northern Ireland, in Co. Londonderry; pop. (1990) 48 600.

coleslaw /ˈkəʊlslɔː/ *n.* dressed salad of sliced raw cabbage etc. [from COLE, Dutch *sla* salad]

coleus /ˈkəʊlɪəs/ *n.* plant with variegated leaves. [Greek *koleon* sheath]

coley /'kəʊlɪ/ *n.* (*pl.* **-s**) any of several fish used as food, e.g. the rock-salmon. [origin uncertain]

colic /'kɒlɪk/ *n.* severe spasmodic abdominal pain. □ **colicky** *adj.* [Latin: related to COLON[2]]

Colima /kɒ'li:mə/ **1** state in SW Mexico, on the Pacific coast; pop. (est. 1995) 487 324. **2** its capital city; pop. (1990) 106 967.

colitis /kə'laɪtɪs/ *n.* inflammation of the lining of the colon.

collaborate /kə'læbə,reɪt/ *v.* (**-ting**) (often foll. by *with*) **1** work together. **2** cooperate with an enemy. □ **collaboration** /-'reɪʃ(ə)n/ *n.* **collaborative** /-rətɪv/ *adj.* **collaborator** *n.* [Latin: related to LABOUR]

collage /'kɒlɑ:ʒ/ *n.* form or work of art in which various materials are fixed to a backing. [French, = gluing]

collagen /'kɒlədʒ(ə)n/ *n.* protein found in animal connective tissue, yielding gelatin on boiling. [Greek *kolla* glue]

collapse /kə'læps/ *–n.* **1** falling down or in of a structure; folding up; giving way. **2** sudden failure of a plan etc. **3** physical or mental breakdown; exhaustion. *–v.* (**-sing**) **1** (cause to) undergo collapse. **2** *colloq.* lie or sit down and relax, esp. after prolonged effort. **3** fold up. □ **collapsible** *adj.* [Latin *labor laps-* slip]

collar /'kɒlə(r)/ *–n.* **1** neckband, upright or turned over. **2** band of leather etc. round an animal's neck. **3** band or ring or pipe in machinery. **4** piece of meat rolled up and tied. **5** *Finance* combination of two interest-rate options designed to protect an investor against wide fluctuations in interest rates. One, the **cap**, covers the investor if the interest rate rises against him or her; the other, the **floor**, provides cover if the rate of interest falls too far. *–v.* **1** capture, seize. **2** *colloq.* accost. **3** *slang* appropriate. [Latin *collum* neck]

collar-bone *n.* bone joining the breastbone and shoulder-blade.

collate /kə'leɪt/ *v.* (**-ting**) **1** assemble and arrange systematically. **2** compare (texts, statements, etc.). □ **collator** *n.* [Latin: related to CONFER]

collateral /kə'lætər(ə)l/ *–n.* **1** form of security, esp. an impersonal form such as life-assurance policies or shares, used to secure a bank loan. In some senses such impersonal securities are referred to as 'secondary securities', to distinguish them from primary securities (e.g. guarantees). **2** person having the same ancestor as another but by a different line. *–adj.* **1** descended from the same ancestor but by a different line. **2** side by side; parallel. **3 a** additional but subordinate. **b** contributory. **c** connected but aside from the main subject, course, etc. □ **collaterally** *adv.* [Latin: related to LATERAL]

collating sequence *n.* ordering of characters in a character set used within a computer. It is employed, for example, in sorting into alphabetic or alphanumeric order.

collation /kə'leɪʃ(ə)n/ *n.* **1** collating. **2** thing collated. **3** light meal. [Latin: related to CONFER]

colleague /'kɒli:g/ *n.* fellow worker, esp. in a profession or business. [Latin *collega*]

collect[1] /kə'lekt/ *–v.* **1** bring or come together; assemble, accumulate. **2** systematically seek and acquire, esp. as a hobby. **3** obtain (contributions etc.) from a number of people. **4** call for; fetch. **5 a** *refl.* regain control of oneself. **b** concentrate (one's thoughts etc.). **c** (as **collected** *adj.*) not perturbed or distracted. *–adj.* & *adv.* *US* (of a telephone call, parcel, etc.) to be paid for by the receiver. [Latin *lego lect-* pick]

collect[2] /'kɒlekt/ *n.* short prayer of the Anglican or Roman Catholic Church. [Latin *collecta*: related to COLLECT[1]]

collectable /kə'lektɪb(ə)l/ (also **collectible**) *–adj.* worth collecting. *–n.* item sought by collectors.

collection /kə'lekʃ(ə)n/ *n.* **1** collecting or being collected. **2** things collected, esp. systematically. **3** money collected, esp. at a meeting or church service.

collective /kə'lektɪv/ *–adj.* of, by, or relating to a group or society as a whole; joint; shared. *–n.* **1** cooperative enterprise; its members. **2** = COLLECTIVE NOUN. □ **collectively** *adv.*

♦ **collective bargaining** *n.* negotiation between employers and employees over wages, terms of employment, etc. when the employees are represented by a trade union or some other collective body.

collective farm *n.* jointly-operated esp. state-owned amalgamation of several smallholdings.

collective noun *n.* singular noun denoting a collection or number of individuals (e.g. *assembly, family, troop*).

collective ownership *n.* ownership of land etc., by all for the benefit of all.

♦ **collectivism** *n.* economic system in which much of the planning is carried out by a central government and the means of production owned by the community. Collectivism was practised in several formerly Communist states in E Europe. □ **collectivist** *n.* & *adj.*

collectivize *v.* (also **-ise**) (**-zing** or **-sing**) organize on the basis of collective ownership. □ **collectivization** /-'zeɪʃ(ə)n/ *n.*

collector *n.* **1** person who collects things of interest. **2** person who collects money etc. due.

♦ **Collector of Taxes** *n.* civil servant responsible for the collection of taxes for which assessments have been raised by Inspectors of Taxes and for the collection of tax under PAYE.

collector's item *n.* (also **collector's piece**) thing of interest to collectors.

colleen /kɒ'li:n/ *n.* *Ir.* girl. [Irish *cailín*]

college /'kɒlɪdʒ/ *n.* **1** establishment for further, higher, or professional education. **2** college premises (*lived in college*). **3** students and teachers in a college. **4** school. **5** organized body of persons with shared functions and privileges. [Latin: related to COLLEAGUE]

collegiate /kə'li:dʒɪət/ *adj.* **1** of, or constituted as, a college; corporate. **2** (of a university) consisting of different colleges.

collegiate church *n.* church endowed for a chapter of canons but without a bishop's see.

collide /kə'laɪd/ *v.* (**-ding**) (often foll. by *with*) come into collision or conflict. [Latin *collido -lis-* clash]

collie /'kɒlɪ/ *n.* sheepdog of an orig. Scottish breed. [perhaps from *coll* COAL]

collier /'kɒlɪə(r)/ *n.* **1** coalminer. **2 a** coal ship. **b** member of its crew. [from COAL]

colliery *n.* (*pl.* **-ies**) coalmine and its buildings.

collision /kə'lɪʒ(ə)n/ *n.* **1** violent impact of a moving body with another or with a fixed object. **2** clashing of interests etc. [Latin: related to COLLIDE]

collocate /'kɒlə,keɪt/ *v.* (**-ting**) juxtapose (a word etc.) with another. □ **collocation** /-'keɪʃ(ə)n/ *n.* [Latin: related to LOCUS]

colloid /'kɒlɔɪd/ *n.* **1** substance consisting of ultramicroscopic particles. **2** mixture of such particles dispersed in another substance. □ **colloidal** /kə'lɔɪd(ə)l/ *adj.* [Greek *kolla* glue]

colloquial /kə'ləʊkwɪəl/ *adj.* of ordinary or familiar conversation, informal. □ **colloquially** *adv.* [Latin: related to COLLOQUY]

colloquialism *n.* **1** colloquial word or phrase. **2** use of these.

colloquium /kə'ləʊkwɪəm/ *n.* (*pl.* **-s** or **-quia**) academic conference or seminar. [Latin: related to COLLOQUY]

colloquy /'kɒləkwɪ/ *n.* (*pl.* **-quies**) *literary* conversation, talk. [Latin *loquor* speak]

collude /kə'lu:d/ *v.* (**-ding**) conspire together. □ **collusive** *adj.* [Latin *ludo lus-* play]

♦ **collusion** *n.* **1** agreement between two or more parties in order to prejudice a third party, or for any improper purpose. Collusion to carry out an illegal (not merely improper) purpose is punishable as a conspiracy. **2** secret agreement between two parties involved in legal proceedings, as a result of which one of them agrees to bring an action against the other in order to obtain a judicial decision for an improper purpose. **3** secret agreement between the parties to a legal action to do or to refrain from doing something in order to influence the judicial decision. For instance, an agreement between the plaintiff and the defendant to supress certain evidence would amount to collusion. Any judgement obtained by collusion is a nullity and may be set aside.

♦ **collusive duopoly** *n.* form of duopoly in which producers collude with each other in a price-fixing agreement, thus forming a virtual monopoly, and negotiate a profit-sharing arrangement. See MONOPOLIES AND MERGERS COMMISSION.

---

collywobbles /'kɒlɪˌwɒb(ə)lz/ *n.pl. colloq.* **1** rumbling or pain in the stomach. **2** apprehensive feeling. [from COLIC, WOBBLE]

Colo. *abbr.* Colorado.

Cologne /kə'ləʊn/ (German **Köln** /kɜːln/) city and port in W Germany, on the W bank of the Rhine; pop. (est. 1995) 963 817. A major commercial and industrial centre, famous for its toilet water, it has textile, iron and steel, chemical, and motor industries.

cologne /kə'ləʊn/ *n.* eau-de-Cologne or similar toilet water. [abbreviation]

Colombo /kə'lʌmbəʊ/ capital and chief port of Sri Lanka, with iron and steel industries; exports include tea, spices, and rubber; pop. (est. 1990) 615 000.

Colón /kɒ'lɒn/ chief port of Panama and a major commercial centre; industries include oil refining; pop. (est. 1994) 137 825.

colon[1] /'kəʊlən/ *n.* punctuation mark (:), used esp. to mark illustration or antithesis. [Greek, = clause]

colon[2] /'kəʊlən/ *n.* lower and greater part of the large intestine. [Latin from Greek]

colón /kɒ'lɒn/ *n.* standard monetary unit of Costa Rica and El Salvador. [Spanish *Colón* (Christopher) Columbus]

colonel /'kɜːn(ə)l/ *n.* army officer in command of a regiment, ranking next below brigadier. □ **colonelcy** *n.* (*pl.* **-ies**). [Italian *colonnello*: related to COLUMN]

colonial /kə'ləʊnɪəl/ *–adj.* **1** of a colony or colonies. **2** of colonialism. *–n.* inhabitant of a colony.

colonialism *n.* **1** policy of acquiring or maintaining colonies. **2** *derog.* exploitation of colonies. □ **colonialist** *n.* & *adj.*

colonist /'kɒlənɪst/ *n.* settler in or inhabitant of a colony.

colonize /'kɒləˌnaɪz/ *v.* (also **-ise**) (**-zing** or **-sing**) **1** establish a colony in. **2** join a colony. □ **colonization** /-'zeɪʃ(ə)n/ *n.*

colonnade /ˌkɒlə'neɪd/ *n.* row of columns, esp. supporting an entablature or roof. □ **colonnaded** *adj.* [French: related to COLUMN]

colony /'kɒlənɪ/ *n.* (*pl.* **-ies**) **1 a** settlement or settlers in a new country, fully or partly subject to the mother country. **b** their territory. **2 a** people of one nationality, occupation, etc., esp. forming a community in a city. **b** separate or segregated group (*nudist colony*). **3** group of animals, plants, etc., living close together. [Latin *colonia* farm]

colophon /'kɒləˌf(ə)n/ *n.* **1** publisher's identifying emblem on a book or other published material. **2** tailpiece in a manuscript or book, giving the writer's or printer's name, date, etc. [Greek, = summit]

color etc. *US* var. of COLOUR etc.

Colorado /ˌkɒlə'rɑːdəʊ/ state in the central US; pop. (est. 1996) 3 822 676; capital, Denver. Manufactures include iron, steel, machinery, military equipment, and chemicals; agriculture produces cattle and other livestock and cereals.

Colorado beetle *n.* yellow and black beetle, with larva destructive to the potato plant. [COLORADO]

coloration /ˌkʌlə'reɪʃ(ə)n/ *n.* (*US* **colouration**) **1** appearance as regards colour. **2** act or mode of colouring. [Latin: related to COLOUR]

coloratura /ˌkɒlərə'tʊərə/ *n.* **1** elaborate ornamentation of a vocal melody. **2** soprano skilled in this. [Italian: related to COLOUR]

colossal /kə'lɒs(ə)l/ *adj.* **1** huge. **2** *colloq.* splendid. □ **colossally** *adv.* [related to COLOSSUS]

colossus /kə'lɒsəs/ *n.* (*pl.* **-ssi** /-saɪ/ or **-ssuses**) **1** statue much bigger than life size. **2** gigantic or remarkable person etc. **3** imperial power personified. [Latin from Greek]

colostomy /kə'lɒstəmɪ/ *n.* (*pl.* **-ies**) operation on the colon to make an opening in the abdominal wall to provide an artificial anus. [from COLON[2]]

colour /'kʌlə(r)/ (*US* **color**) *–n.* **1** sensation produced on the eye by rays of light when resolved as by a prism into different wavelengths. **2** one, or any mixture, of the constituents into which light can be separated as in a spectrum or rainbow, sometimes including (loosely) black and white. **3** colouring substance, esp. paint. **4** use of all colours in photography etc. **5 a** pigmentation of the skin, esp. when dark. **b** this as ground for discrimination. **6** ruddiness of complexion. **7** (in *pl.*) appearance or aspect (*saw them in their true colours*). **8** (in *pl.*) **a** coloured ribbon or uniform etc. worn to signify membership of a school, club, team, etc. **b** flag of a regiment or ship. **9** quality, mood, or variety in music, literature, etc. **10** show of reason; pretext (*lend colour to*; *under colour of*). *–v.* **1** apply colour to, esp. by painting, dyeing, etc. **2** influence. **3** misrepresent, exaggerate. **4** take on colour; blush.

Colombia /kə'lɒmbɪə/, **Republic of** country in the extreme NW of South America, having a coastline on both the Atlantic and the Pacific Oceans. The economy is mainly agricultural, coffee being a major export. Colombia's rich mineral resources include oil, natural gas, gold, silver, platinum, emeralds, and salt; crude oil and petroleum products are an important source of export revenue. Manufacturing industries have been developed and production of textiles, leather goods, and chemicals for export is increasing. The government has succeeded in reducing drug-related violence, but the drugs trade is still thriving. Inflation and interest rates are high, and although changes to the constitution allow more government control of the economy the rate of GDP growth has slowed. Colombia is a member of LAIA.
History. Colombia achieved independence from Spain in the early 19th century with the formation of the Republic of Great Colombia, consisting of Colombia, Venezuela, Ecuador, and Panama. The present name was adopted in 1866, after Venezuela and Ecuador became independent states; Panama seceded in 1903. The country was stricken by civil war between 1949 and 1953, since when it has struggled with endemic poverty and social problems. A new constitution was introduced in 1991 to reduce political corruption, reduce social unrest, and liberalize the economy. Ernesto Samper, who became president in 1994, was charged with accepting money from drug cartels the following year; charges were later dropped. President, Ernesto Samper; capital, Bogotá. □ **Colombian** *adj.* & *n.*

language	Spanish
currency	peso (Col$) of 100 centavos
pop. (1996)	35 652 000
GNP (1994)	US$58.9B
literacy	87% (m); 85% (f)
life expectancy	69 (m); 75 (f)

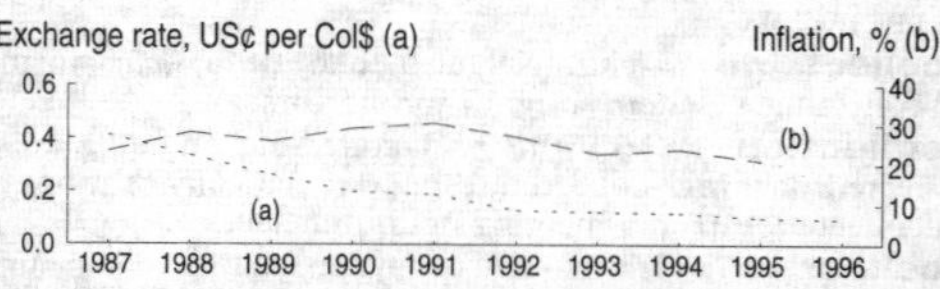

□ **show one's true colours** reveal one's true character or intentions. [Latin *color*]

colouration var. of COLORATION.

colour bar *n.* racial discrimination against non-White people.

colour-blind *adj.* unable to distinguish certain colours. □ **colour-blindness** *n.*

colour code –*n.* use of colours as a means of identification. –*v.* (*colour-code*) identify by means of a colour code.

coloured (*US* **colored**) –*adj.* **1** having colour. **2** (**Coloured**) **a** wholly or partly of non-White descent. **b** *S.Afr.* of mixed White and non-White descent. –*n.* **1** (**Coloured**) **a** Coloured person. **b** *S.Afr.* person of mixed descent speaking Afrikaans or English as his or her mother tongue. **2** (in *pl.*) coloured clothing etc. for washing.

colourful *adj.* (*US* **color-**) **1** full of colour; bright. **2** full of interest; vivid. □ **colourfully** *adv.*

colouring *n.* (*US* **color-**) **1** appearance as regards colour, esp. facial complexion. **2** use or application of colour. **3** substance giving colour.

colourless *adj.* (*US* **color-**) **1** without colour. **2** lacking character or interest.

colour scheme *n.* arrangement of colours, esp. in interior design.

colour-sergeant *n.* senior sergeant of an infantry company.

colour supplement *n.* magazine with colour printing, as a supplement to a newspaper.

colposcopy /kɒl'pɒskəpɪ/ *n.* examination of the vagina and neck of the womb. □ **colposcope** /'kɒlpəˌskəʊp/ *n.* [Greek *kolpos* womb]

COLS *abbr. Computing* communications for online systems.

colt /kəʊlt/ *n.* **1** young male horse. **2** *Sport* inexperienced player. □ **coltish** *adj.* [Old English]

colter *US* var. of COULTER.

coltsfoot *n.* (*pl.* **-s**) wild plant with large leaves and yellow flowers.

Columbia /kə'lʌmbɪə/ **1** city in the US, capital of South Carolina; manufactures include textiles, plastics, and electrical goods; pop. (est. 1994) 104 100. **2** see DISTRICT OF COLUMBIA.

columbine /'kɒləmˌbaɪn/ *n.* garden plant with purple-blue flowers like a cluster of doves. [Latin *columba* dove]

Columbus /kə'lʌmbəs/ city in the US, capital of Ohio; manufactures include aircraft, machinery, and footwear; pop. (est. 1994) 635 910.

column /'kɒləm/ *n.* **1** pillar, usu. of circular section and with a base and capital. **2** column-shaped object. **3** vertical cylindrical mass of liquid or vapour. **4** vertical division of a printed page. **5** part of a newspaper etc. regularly devoted to a particular subject. **6** vertical row of figures in accounts etc. **7** narrow-fronted arrangement of troops or armoured vehicles in successive lines. □ **columnar** /kə'lʌmnə(r)/ *adj.* **columned** *adj.* [French and Latin]

♦ **column inch** *n.* unit of measurement of an area of typeset matter, esp. advertising matter, one inch deep and one column wide. **Column centimetres** are now replacing column inches in practice, although most public relations consultancies still refer to column inches when measuring the coverage their activities have achieved.

---

columnist /'kɒləmnɪst/ *n.* journalist contributing regularly to a newspaper etc.

♦ **COM** *abbr.* **1** computerized operations management. **2** = COMPUTER OUTPUT MICROFILM.

---

com. *abbr.* **1** commercial. **2** commission. **3** communication(s).

com- *prefix* (also **co-**, **col-**, **con-**, **cor-**) with, together, jointly, altogether. [Latin *com-*, *cum* with]

■ **Usage** *Com-* is used before *b*, *m*, *p*, and occasionally before vowels and *f*; *co-* esp. before vowels, *h*, and *gn*; *col-* before *l*, *cor-* before *r*, and *con-* before other consonants.

coma /'kəʊmə/ *n.* (*pl.* **-s**) prolonged deep unconsciousness. [Latin from Greek]

comatose /'kəʊməˌtəʊs/ *adj.* **1** in a coma. **2** drowsy, sleepy.

comb /kəʊm/ –*n.* **1 a** toothed strip of rigid material for tidying the hair. **b** similar curved decorative strip worn in the hair. **2** thing like a comb, esp. a device for tidying and straightening wool etc. **3** red fleshy crest of a fowl, esp. a cock. **4** honeycomb. –*v.* **1** draw a comb through (the hair). **2** dress (wool etc.) with a comb. **3** *colloq.* search (a place) thoroughly. □ **comb out 1** arrange the hair loosely by combing. **2** remove with a comb. **3** search out and get rid of. [Old English]

combat /'kɒmbæt/ –*n.* fight, struggle, contest. –*v.* (**-t-**) **1** engage in combat (with). **2** oppose; strive against. [Latin: related to BATTLE]

combatant /'kɒmbət(ə)nt/ –*n.* person engaged in fighting. –*adj.* **1** fighting. **2** for fighting.

combative /'kɒmbətɪv/ *adj.* pugnacious.

combe var. of COOMB.

combination /ˌkɒmbɪ'neɪʃ(ə)n/ *n.* **1** combining or being combined. **2** combined set of things or people. **3** sequence of numbers or letters used to open a combination lock. **4** motor cycle with a side-car attached. **5** (in *pl.*) single undergarment for the body and legs. [Latin: related to COMBINE]

combination lock *n.* lock that can be opened only by a specific sequence of movements.

combine –*v.* /kəm'baɪn/ (**-ning**) **1** join together; unite for a common purpose. **2** possess (qualities usu. distinct) together. **3** form or cause to form a chemical compound. **4** /'kɒmbaɪn/ harvest with a combine harvester. –*n.* /'kɒmbaɪn/ combination of esp. commercial interests. [Latin *bini* a pair]

♦ **combined-transport bill of lading** see CONTAINERIZATION.

---

combine harvester *n.* machine that reaps and threshes in one operation.

combings /'kəʊmɪŋz/ *n.pl.* hairs combed off.

combining form *n.* linguistic element used in combination with another to form a word (e.g. *Anglo-* = English).

combo /'kɒmbəʊ/ *n.* (*pl.* **-s**) *slang* small jazz or dance band. [abbreviation of COMBINATION]

combustible /kəm'bʌstɪb(ə)l/ –*adj.* capable of or used for burning. –*n.* combustible substance. □ **combustibility** /-'bɪlɪtɪ/ *n.* [Latin *comburo -bust-* burn up]

combustion /kəm'bʌstʃ(ə)n/ *n.* **1** burning. **2** development of light and heat from the chemical combination of a substance with oxygen.

come /kʌm/ –*v.* (**-ming**; *past* **came**; *past part.* **come**) **1** move, be brought towards, or reach a place. **2** reach a specified situation or result (*came to no harm*). **3** reach or extend to a specified point. **4** traverse or accomplish (with compl.: *have come a long way*). **5** occur, happen; (of time) arrive in due course (*how did you come to break your leg?*; *the day soon came*). **6** take or occupy a specified position in space or time (*Nero came after Claudius*). **7** become perceptible or known (*it will come to me*). **8** be available (*comes in three sizes*). **9** become (*come loose*). **10** (foll. by *from*, *of*) **a** be descended from. **b** be the result of (*that comes of complaining*). **11** *colloq.* play the part of; behave like (*don't come the bully with me*). **12** *slang* have an orgasm. **13** (in *subj.*) *colloq.* when a specified time is reached (*come next month*). **14** (as *int.*) expressing mild protest or encouragement (*come, it cannot be that bad*). –*n.* *slang* semen ejaculated. □ **come about** happen. **come across 1** meet or find by chance. **2** *colloq.* be effective or understood; give a specified impression. **come again** *colloq.* **1** make a further effort. **2** (as *imper.*) what did you say? **come along 1** make progress. **2** (as *imper.*) hurry up. **come apart** disintegrate. **come at 1** attack. **2** reach, get access to. **come away 1** become detached. **2** (foll. by *with*) be left with (an impression etc.). **come back 1** return. **2** recur to one's memory. **3** (often foll. by *in*) become fashionable or popular again. **come between 1** interfere with the relationship of. **2** separate. **come by 1** call on a visit. **2** obtain. **come clean** see CLEAN. **come down 1** lose position or wealth. **2** be handed down by tradition. **3** be reduced. **4** (foll. by *against, in favour of*) reach a decision. **5** (foll. by *to*) amount basically. **6** (foll. by *on*) criticize harshly; rebuke, punish. **7** (foll. by *with*) begin to suffer from (a disease). **come for 1** come to collect. **2** attack. **come forward 1** advance. **2** offer oneself for a task, post, etc. **come in 1** enter. **2** take a specified position in a race etc. (*came in third*). **3** become fashionable or seasonable. **4** (with compl.) prove to be (useful etc.) (*came in handy*). **5** have a part to play (*where do I come in?*). **6** be received (*news has just come in*). **7** begin speaking, interrupt. **8** return to base (*come in, number 9*). **9** (foll. by *for*) receive. **come into 1** enter, be brought into (collision, prominence, etc.). **2** receive, esp. as an heir. **come of age** see AGE. **come off 1** (of an action) succeed, occur. **2** fare (badly, well, etc.). **3** be detached or detachable (from). **come off it** *colloq.* expression of disbelief, disapproval, etc. **come on 1** advance. **2** make progress. **3** begin (*came on to rain*). **4** appear on a stage, field of play, etc. **5** (as *imper.*) expressing encouragement or disbelief. **6** = *come upon*. **come out 1** emerge; become known. **2** be published. **3 a** declare oneself. **b** openly declare that one is a homosexual. **4** go on strike. **5** (of a photograph or thing photographed) be produced satisfactorily and clearly. **6** attain a specified result in an examination etc. **7** (of a stain etc.) be removed. **8** make one's début in society etc. **9** (foll. by *in*) become covered with (*came out in spots*). **10** be solved. **11** (foll. by *with*) declare openly; disclose. **come over 1 a** come from some distance to visit etc. **b** come nearer. **2** change sides or one's opinion. **3 a** (of a feeling etc.) overtake or affect (a person). **b** *colloq.* feel suddenly (*came over faint*). **4** appear or sound in a specified way. **come round 1** pay an informal visit. **2** recover consciousness. **3** be converted to another person's opinion. **4** (of a date) recur. **come through** survive. **come to 1** recover consciousness. **2** amount to. **come to one's senses** see SENSE. **come up 1** arise; present itself; be mentioned or discussed. **2** attain position or wealth. **3** (often foll. by *to*) approach. **4** (foll. by *to*) match (a standard etc.). **5** (foll. by *with*) produce (an idea etc.). **6** (of a plant etc.) spring up out of the ground. **7** become brighter (e.g. with polishing). **come up against** be faced with or opposed by. **come upon 1** meet or find by chance. **2** attack by surprise. [Old English]

comeback *n.* **1** return to a previous (esp. successful) state. **2** *slang* retaliation or retort.

Comecon /ˈkɒmɪˌkɒn/ *n. hist.* economic association of Communist countries, formed in 1949 and disbanded in 1991. [abbreviation of *Council for Mutual Economic Assistance*]

comedian /kəˈmiːdɪən/ *n.* **1** humorous entertainer. **2** comedy actor. **3** *slang* buffoon. [French]

comedienne /kəˌmiːdɪˈen/ *n.* female comedian. [French feminine]

comedown *n.* **1** loss of status. **2** disappointment.

comedy /ˈkɒmədɪ/ *n.* (*pl.* **-ies**) **1 a** play, film, etc., of amusing character, usu. with a happy ending. **b** such works as a dramatic genre. **2** humour; amusing aspects. □ **comedic** /kəˈmiːdɪk/ *adj.* [Greek: related to COMIC]

comedy of manners *n.* satirical play portraying the social behaviour of the upper classes.

come-hither *attrib. adj. colloq.* flirtatious, inviting.

comely /ˈkʌmlɪ/ *adj.* (**-ier**, **-iest**) *literary* handsome, good-looking. □ **comeliness** *n.* [Old English]

come-on *n. slang* enticement.

comer /ˈkʌmə(r)/ *n.* person who comes as an applicant etc. (*offered it to the first comer*).

comestibles /kəˈmestɪb(ə)lz/ *n.pl. formal* or *joc.* food. [French from Latin]

comet /ˈkɒmɪt/ *n.* hazy object moving in a path about the sun, usu. with a nucleus of ice surrounded by gas and with a tail pointing away from the sun. [Greek *komētēs*]

comeuppance /kʌmˈʌpəns/ *n. colloq.* deserved punishment. [*come up*, -ANCE]

♦ **COMEX** /ˈkəʊmeks/ *abbr.* Commodity Exchange Inc. of New York, a US commodity exchange that specializes in trading in metal futures and options.

---

comfit /ˈkʌmfɪt/ *n. archaic* sweet consisting of a nut etc. in sugar. [Latin: related to CONFECTION]

comfort /ˈkʌmfət/ *–n.* **1 a** state of physical well-being. **b** (usu. in *pl.*) things that make life easy or pleasant. **2** relief of suffering or grief, consolation. **3** person or thing giving consolation. *–v.* soothe in grief; console. [Latin *fortis* strong]

comfortable *adj.* **1** giving ease. **2** free from discomfort; at ease. **3** having an easy conscience. **4 a** having an adequate standard of living; free from financial worry. **b** sufficient (*comfortable income*). **5 a** with a wide margin (*comfortable win*). **b** appreciable (*comfortable margin*). □ **comfortably** *adv.*

comforter *n.* **1** person who comforts. **2** baby's dummy. **3** *archaic* woollen scarf.

comfortless *adj.* **1** dreary, cheerless. **2** without comfort.

comfort station *n. US euphem.* public lavatory.

comfrey /ˈkʌmfrɪ/ *n.* (*pl.* **-s**) tall bell-flowered plant growing in damp, shady places. [French from Latin]

comfy /ˈkʌmfɪ/ *adj.* (**-ier**, **-iest**) *colloq.* comfortable. [abbreviation]

comic /ˈkɒmɪk/ *–adj.* **1** of or like comedy. **2** funny. *–n.* **1** comedian. **2** periodical in the form of comic strips. □ **comical** *adj.* **comically** *adv.* [Greek *kōmos* revel]

comic strip *n.* sequence of drawings telling a story.

coming /ˈkʌmɪŋ/ *–attrib. adj.* **1** approaching, next (*the coming week*). **2** of potential importance (*coming man*). *–n.* arrival.

Comino /kɒˈmiːnəʊ/ smallest of the three main islands of Malta.

comity /ˈkɒmɪtɪ/ *n.* (*pl.* **-ies**) *formal* **1** courtesy, friendship. **2 a** association of nations etc. **b** (in full **comity of nations**) mutual recognition by nations of the laws and customs of others. [Latin *comis* courteous]

comm. *abbr.* commerce.

comma /ˈkɒmə/ *n.* punctuation mark (,) indicating a pause or break between parts of a sentence etc. [Greek, = clause]

command /kəˈmɑːnd/ *–v.* **1** (often foll. by *to* + infin., or *that* + clause) give a formal order or instruction to. **2** (also *absol.*) have authority or control over. **3** have at one's disposal or within reach (a skill, resources, etc.). **4** deserve and get (sympathy, respect, etc.). **5** dominate (a strategic position) from a superior height; look down over. *–n.* **1** order, instruction. See also COMMAND LANGUAGE. **2** mastery, control, possession. **3** exercise or tenure of authority, esp. naval or military. **4 a** body of troops etc. **b** district under a commander. [Latin: related to MANDATE]

commandant /ˈkɒmənˌdænt/ *n.* commanding officer, esp. of a military academy. [French or Italian or Spanish: related to COMMAND]

♦ **command economy** *n.* (also **planned economy**) economy in which the activities of firms and the allocation of productive resources is determined by government direction rather than market forces. China and the former USSR are typical examples. Western economists have always pointed out that command economies are likely to lead to inefficiency because the bureaucrats who run them will not have sufficient information to allocate resources in a way that will satisfy consumer demands. Command economists have argued that the system prevents the exploitation of workers by capitalists.

---

commandeer /ˌkɒmənˈdɪə(r)/ *v.* **1** seize (esp. goods) for military use. **2** take arbitrary possession of. [Afrikaans *kommanderen*]

commander /kə'mɑːndə(r)/ *n.* **1** person who commands, esp. a naval officer next below captain. **2** (in full **knight commander**) member of a higher class in some orders of knighthood.

commander-in-chief *n.* (*pl.* **commanders-in-chief**) supreme commander, esp. of a nation's forces.

commanding *adj.* **1** exalted, impressive. **2** (of a position) giving a wide view. **3** (of an advantage etc.) substantial (*commanding lead*).

command language *n.* programming language enabling a user to communicate with the operating system of a computer. Statements in such a language are called **commands**. They are requests from someone using a terminal or a microcomputer for the performance of some operation or the execution of some program, examples being 'list', 'sort', 'delete', 'load', 'run'.

commandment *n.* divine command.

command module *n.* control compartment in a spacecraft.

commando /kə'mɑːndəʊ/ *n.* (*pl.* **-s**) **1** unit of shock troops. **2** member of this. [Portuguese: related to COMMAND]

Command Paper *n.* paper laid before Parliament by royal command.

command performance *n.* theatrical or film performance given at royal request.

commemorate /kə'memə,reɪt/ *v.* (**-ting**) **1** preserve in memory by a celebration or ceremony. **2** be a memorial of. □ **commemoration** /-'reɪʃ(ə)n/ *n.* **commemorative** /-rətɪv/ *adj.* [Latin: related to MEMORY]

commence /kə'mens/ *v.* (**-cing**) *formal* begin. [Latin: related to COM-, INITIATE]

commencement *n. formal* beginning.

commend /kə'mend/ *v.* **1** praise. **2** entrust, commit. **3** recommend. □ **commendation** /,kɒmen'deɪʃ(ə)n/ *n.* [Latin: related to MANDATE]

commendable *adj.* praiseworthy. □ **commendably** *adv.*

commensurable /kə'menʃərəb(ə)l/ *adj.* **1** (often foll. by *with*, *to*) measurable by the same standard. **2** (foll. by *to*) proportionate to. **3** *Math.* (of numbers) in a ratio equal to the ratio of integers. □ **commensurability** /-'bɪlɪtɪ/ *n.* [Latin: related to MEASURE]

commensurate /kə'menʃərət/ *adj.* **1** (usu. foll. by *with*) coextensive. **2** (often foll. by *to*, *with*) proportionate.

comment /'kɒment/ *–n.* **1** brief critical or explanatory remark or note; opinion. **2** commenting; criticism (*aroused much comment; his art is a comment on society*). *–v.* (often foll. by *on* or *that*) make (esp. critical) remarks. □ **no comment** *colloq.* I decline to answer your question. [Latin]

commentary /'kɒməntərɪ/ *n.* (*pl.* **-ies**) **1** descriptive spoken esp. broadcast account of an event or performance as it happens. **2** set of explanatory notes on a text etc. [Latin]

commentate /'kɒmən,teɪt/ *v.* (**-ting**) act as a commentator.

commentator *n.* **1** person who provides a commentary. **2** person who comments on current events. [Latin]

commerce /'kɒmɜːs/ *n.* financial transactions, esp. buying and selling; trading. [Latin: related to MERCER]

commercial /kə'mɜːʃ(ə)l/ *–adj.* **1** of or engaged in commerce. **2** having financial profit as its primary aim. **3** (of chemicals) for industrial use. *–n.* television or radio advertisement. □ **commercially** *adv.*

♦ **commercial agency** *n.* (also **credit-reference agency**) organization giving a credit reference on businesses or persons and specializing in collating information regarding debtors, bankruptcies, and court judgements. See also ANCILLARY CREDIT BUSINESS; BANKER'S REFERENCE.

♦ **commercial bank** *n.* privately-owned bank that provides a wide range of financial services both to the general public and to firms. The principal activities are operating cheque current accounts, receiving deposits, taking in and paying out notes and coin, and making loans. Additional services include trustee and executor facilities, the supply of foreign currency, the purchase and sale of securities, insurance, a credit-card system, and personal pensions. Commercial banks also compete with the finance houses and merchant banks by providing venture capital and with building societies by providing mortgages. The number of commercial banks in the UK has gradually reduced following a series of mergers. The main banks with national networks of branches are the Big Four (National Westminster, Barclays, Lloyds, and the Midland), the Royal Bank of Scotland, the Bank of Scotland, the Ulster Bank, and the TSB Group plc. See also CLEARING BANK; JOINT-STOCK BANK.

---

commercial broadcasting *n.* broadcasting financed by advertising.

♦ **commercial code** *n.* code used, esp. before telex and fax, to reduce the cost of sending cables. Single five-letter code words can represent long phrases.

♦ **commercial invoice** see INVOICE *n.*

---

commercialism *n.* **1** commercial practices. **2** emphasis on financial profit.

commercialize *v.* (also **-ise**) (**-zing** or **-sing**) **1** exploit or spoil for profit. **2** make commercial. □ **commercialization** /-'zeɪʃ(ə)n/ *n.*

♦ **commercial law** see MERCANTILE LAW.

♦ **commercial paper** *n.* (also **CP**) relatively low-risk short-term (maturing at 60 days or less in the US but longer in the UK) unsecured form of borrowing. Commercial paper is often regarded as a reasonable substitute for treasury bills, certificates of deposit, etc. The main issuers are large creditworthy institutions, e.g. insurance companies, bank trust departments, and pension funds. In the UK, sterling commercial paper was first issued in 1986. Commercial paper is now available in Australia, France, Hong Kong, the Netherlands, Singapore, Spain, and Sweden.

---

commercial traveller *n.* firm's representative visiting shops etc. to get orders.

Commie /'kɒmɪ/ *n. slang derog.* Communist. [abbreviation]

commination /,kɒmɪ'neɪʃ(ə)n/ *n. literary* threatening of divine vengeance. □ **comminatory** /'kɒmɪnətərɪ/ *adj.* [Latin: related to MENACE]

commingle /kə'mɪŋg(ə)l/ *v.* (**-ling**) *literary* mingle together.

comminute /'kɒmɪ,njuːt/ *v.* (**-ting**) **1** reduce to small fragments. **2** divide (property) into small portions. □ **comminution** /-'njuːʃ(ə)n/ *n.* [Latin: related to MINUTE²]

comminuted fracture *n.* fracture producing multiple bone splinters.

commiserate /kə'mɪzə,reɪt/ *v.* (**-ting**) (usu. foll. by *with*) express or feel sympathy. □ **commiseration** /-'reɪʃ(ə)n/ *n.* [Latin: related to MISER]

commissar /'kɒmɪ,sɑː(r)/ *n. hist.* **1** official of the Soviet Communist Party responsible for political education and organization. **2** head of a government department in the USSR. [Latin: related to COMMIT]

commissariat /,kɒmɪ'seərɪət/ *n.* **1** esp. *Mil.* **a** department for the supply of food etc. **b** food supplied. **2** *hist.* government department of the USSR. [related to COMMISSARY]

commissary /'kɒmɪsərɪ/ *n.* (*pl.* **-ies**) **1** deputy, delegate. **2** *US Mil.* store for supplies of food etc. [Latin: related to COMMIT]

commission /kə'mɪʃ(ə)n/ *–n.* **1 a** authority to perform a task etc. **b** person(s) entrusted with such authority. **c** task etc. given to such person(s). **2** order for something to be produced specially. **3 a** warrant conferring the rank of officer in the armed forces. **b** rank so conferred. **4** payment made to an intermediary, e.g. an agent, salesman, or broker, usu. calculated as a percentage of the value of the goods sold. Sometimes the whole of the commission is paid by the seller (e.g. an estate agent's commission in the UK) but in other cases (e.g. some commodity markets) it is shared equally between buyer and seller. In advertising, the commission is the discount (usu. between 10% and 15%) allowed to an advertising agency by owners of the advertising medium for the space or time purchased on behalf of their clients. **5** act of committing (a crime etc.). *–v.* **1** empower by commission. **2 a** give (an artist etc.) a commission for a piece of work. **b** order (a work) to be written etc. **3 a** give (an officer) command of a ship. **b** prepare (a ship) for active service. **4** bring (a machine etc.) into operation. □ **in** (or **out of**) **commission** ready (or not ready) for service. [Latin: related to COMMIT]

commission-agent *n.* **1** bookmaker. **2** agent specializing in buying or selling goods for a principal in another country for a commission.

commissionaire /kəˌmɪʃəˈneə(r)/ *n.* uniformed door-attendant. [French: related to COMMISSIONER]

commissioner *n.* **1** person appointed by a commission to perform a specific task, e.g. the head of the London police etc. **2** member of a government commission. **3** representative of government in a district, department, etc. [medieval Latin: related to COMMISSION]

♦ **Commissioner for Local Administration** *n.* local ombudsman responsible for investigating complaints from the public against local authorities in England, Wales, or Scotland. Complaints relating to personnel and commercial matters are excluded. Cf. FINANCIAL OMBUDSMAN; PARLIAMENTARY COMMISSIONER FOR ADMINISTRATION.

Commissioner for Oaths *n.* solicitor authorized to administer an oath in an affidavit etc.

♦ **Commissioners of Customs and Excise** see BOARD OF CUSTOMS AND EXCISE.

♦ **Commissioners of Inland Revenue** see BOARD OF INLAND REVENUE; GENERAL COMMISSIONERS; SPECIAL COMMISSIONERS.

commit /kəˈmɪt/ *v.* (**-tt-**) **1** do or make (a crime, blunder, etc.). **2** (usu. foll. by *to*) entrust or consign for safe keeping or treatment. **3** send (a person) to prison. **4** pledge or bind (esp. oneself) to a certain course or policy. **5** (as **committed** *adj.*) (often foll. by *to*) **a** dedicated. **b** obliged. □ **commit to memory** memorize. **commit to paper** write down. [Latin *committo -miss-*]

commitment *n.* **1** engagement or obligation. **2** committing or being committed. **3** dedication; committing oneself.

♦ **commitment fee** *n.* amount charged by a bank to keep open a line of credit or to continue to make unused loan facilities available to a potential borrower.

committal *n.* act of committing, esp. to prison.

♦ **committed facility** *n.* bank loan to a customer up to a specified limit at a specified rate of interest.

committee /kəˈmɪtɪ/ *n.* **1** body of persons appointed for a special function by (and usu. out of) a larger body. **2** (**Committee**) House of Commons sitting as a committee. [from COMMIT, -EE]

♦ **Committee of Marketing Organizations** *n.* (also **COMO**) body formed to encourage the development of marketing in all sectors of UK business. COMO represents all the main organizations concerned with marketing, including the Advertising Authority, the Association of Market Survey Organizations, the Incorporated Advertising Management Association, the Incorporated Society of British Advertisers, the Industrial Marketing Research Association, the Institute of Marketing, the Institute of Practitioners in Advertising, the Institute of Public Relations, the Institute of Sales Promotion, the Market Research Society, and the Public Relations Consultants Society.

committee stage *n.* third of five stages of a bill's progress through Parliament.

commode /kəˈməʊd/ *n.* **1** chamber-pot in a chair with a cover. **2** chest of drawers. [Latin *commodus* convenient]

commodious /kəˈməʊdɪəs/ *adj.* roomy.

♦ **commodity** /kəˈmɒdɪtɪ/ *n.* (*pl.* **-ies**) **1** a raw material traded on a commodity market, such as grain, coffee, cocoa, wool, cotton, jute, rubber, or pork bellies (sometimes known as **soft commodities**) or metals and other solid raw materials (known as **hard commodities**). In some contexts soft commodities are referred to as **produce**. **2** a good regarded in economics as the basis of production and exchange characterized by its physical attributes and where and when it is available. Cf. SERVICE *n.* 5. [Latin: related to COMMODE]

♦ **commodity broker** *n.* broker who deals in commodities, esp. one who trades on behalf of his principals in a commodity market (see also FUTURES CONTRACT). The rules governing the procedure adopted in each market vary from commodity to commodity and the function of brokers may also vary. In some markets brokers pass on the names of their principals, in others they do not, and in yet others they are permitted to act as principals. Commodity brokers, other than those dealing in metals, are often called **produce brokers**. See LONDON FOX; LONDON METAL EXCHANGE; SECURITIES AND FUTURES AUTHORITY LTD.

♦ **commodity exchange** see COMMODITY MARKET.

♦ **Commodity Futures Trading Commission** *n.* (also **CFTC**) US government body set up in 1975 in Washington to control trading in commodity futures and options.

♦ **commodity market** *n.* market in which commodities are traded. The main terminal markets in commodities are in London and New York, but in some commodities there are markets in the country of origin. Some commodities are dealt with at auctions (e.g. tea), each auctioned lot having been examined by dealers, but most dealers deal with goods that have been classified according to established quality standards (see CERTIFIED STOCK). In these commodities both actuals and futures are traded on **commodity exchanges**, often with daily call-overs, in which dealers are represented by commodity brokers. Many commodity exchanges offer option dealing in futures, and settlement of differences on futures through a clearing house. As commodity prices fluctuate widely, commodity exchanges provide users and producers with hedging facilities with outside speculators and investors helping to make an active market, although amateurs are advised not to gamble on commodity exchanges. The fluctuations in commodity prices have caused considerable problems in developing countries, from which many commodities originate, as they are often important sources of foreign currency. Various measures have been used to restrict price fluctuations but none have been completely successful. See also LONDON CLEARING HOUSE; LONDON COMMODITY EXCHANGE; LONDON METAL EXCHANGE.

commodore /ˈkɒməˌdɔː(r)/ *n.* **1** naval officer above captain and below rear-admiral. **2** commander of a squadron or other division of a fleet. **3** president of a yacht-club. [French: related to COMMANDER]

common /ˈkɒmən/ *–adj.* (**-er, -est**) **1 a** occurring often. **b** ordinary; without special rank or position. **2 a** shared by, coming from, more than one (*common knowledge*). **b** belonging to the whole community; public. **3** *derog.* low-class; vulgar; inferior. **4** of the most familiar type (*common cold*). **5** *Math.* belonging to two or more quantities (*common denominator*). **6** *Gram.* (of gender) referring to individuals of either sex. *–n.* **1** piece of open public land. **2** *slang* = COMMON SENSE. □ **in common 1** in joint use; shared. **2** of joint interest. **in common with** in the same way as. [Latin *communis*]

♦ **Common Agricultural Policy** *n.* (also **CAP**) policy set up in 1957 by the European Economic Community to support free trade within the Common Market and to protect farmers in the member states. The European Commission fixes a **threshold price**, below which cereals may not be imported into the European Community (EC), and also buys surplus cereals at an agreed **intervention price** in order to help farmers achieve a reasonable average price, called the **target price**. Prices are also agreed for meats, poultry, eggs, fruit, and vegetables, with arrangements similar to those for cereals. The European Commission is also empowered by the CAP to subsidize the modernization of farms within the community. The common policy for exporting agricultural products to non-member countries is laid down by the CAP. In the UK, the Intervention Board for Agricultural Produce is responsible for the implementation of EC regulations regarding the CAP. See also COMMON BUDGET.

commonality /ˌkɒməˈnælɪtɪ/ *n.* (*pl.* **-ies**) **1** sharing of an attribute. **2** common occurrence. **3** = COMMONALTY. [var. of COMMONALTY]

commonalty /ˈkɒmənəltɪ/ *n.* (*pl.* **-ies**) **1** the common people. **2** the general body (esp. of mankind). [medieval Latin: related to COMMON]

♦ **Common Budget** *n.* fund, administered by the European Commission, into which all levies and customs duties on goods entering the European Community are paid and from which all subsidies due under the Common Agricultural Policy are taken.

♦ **common carrier** see CARRIER 2.

commoner *n.* **1** one of the common people (below the rank of peer). **2** university student without a scholarship. [medieval Latin: related to COMMON]

♦ **Common External Tariff** *n.* (also **CET**) tariff of import duties payable on certain goods entering any country in the European Community from non-member countries. Income from these duties is paid into the Common Budget.

♦ **Common Fisheries Policy** *n.* (also **CFP**) fishing policy agreed between members of the European Community in 1983. It lays down annual catch limits for major species of fish, a 12-mile exclusive fishing zone for each state, and an equal-access zone of 200 nautical miles from its coast, within which any member state is allowed to fish. There are also some exceptions to these regulations.

common ground *n.* point or argument accepted by both sides in a dispute.

♦ **common law** *n.* **1** law common to the whole of the UK, as opposed to local law. **2** case law as opposed to legislation, i.e. the law that has evolved by judicial precedent rather than by statute. For instance, the rules relating to the formation of contracts is a product of the common law and is not contained in any act of parliament. **3** law of the UK as opposed to foreign law. In this sense, the common law would include case law as well as legislation.

common-law husband *n.* (also **common-law wife**) partner recognized by common (unwritten) law without formal marriage.

commonly *adv.* usually; frequently; ordinarily.

♦ **Common Market** see EUROPEAN UNION.

common noun *n. Gram.* name denoting a class of objects or a concept, not a particular individual.

common or garden *adj. colloq.* ordinary.

commonplace *–adj.* lacking originality; trite; ordinary. *–n.* **1** event, topic, etc. that is ordinary or usual. **2** trite remark. [translation of Latin *locus communis*]

common-room *n.* room for the social use of students or teachers at a college etc.

commons *n.pl.* **1** (**the Commons**) = HOUSE OF COMMONS. **2** the common people.

common sense *n.* sound practical sense.

commonsensical /ˌkɒmənˈsensɪk(ə)l/ *adj.* having or marked by common sense.

♦ **common stock** *n. US* = ORDINARY SHARE.

common time *n. Mus.* four crotchets in a bar.

commonwealth *n.* **1** independent state or community, esp. a democratic republic. **2** (**the Commonwealth**) **a** association of the UK with states that were previously part of the British Empire. **b** republican government of Britain 1649–60. **3** federation of states.

♦ **Commonwealth Development Corporation** *n.* (also **CDC**) public corporation set up in 1948 to assist commercial and industrial development in any Commonwealth or other developing country. It is authorized to borrow up to £850M from the Treasury and the minimum investment permitted is £1M. Investments are in the form of low-interest loans.

Commonwealth of Independent States see CIS.

♦ **Commonwealth preference** see PREFERENTIAL DUTY.

commotion /kəˈməʊʃ(ə)n/ *n.* confused and noisy disturbance, uproar. [Latin: related to COM-]

communal /ˈkɒmjʊn(ə)l/ *adj.* **1** shared between members of a group or community; for common use. **2** (of conflict etc.) between esp. ethnic or religious communities. □ **communally** *adv.* [Latin: related to COMMUNE[1]]

commune[1] /ˈkɒmjuːn/ *n.* **1** group of people sharing accommodation, goods, etc. **2** small district of local government in France etc. [medieval Latin: related to COMMON]

commune[2] /kəˈmjuːn/ *v.* (**-ning**) (usu. foll. by *with*) **1** speak intimately. **2** feel in close touch (with nature etc.). [French: related to COMMON]

communicable /kəˈmjuːnɪkəb(ə)l/ *adj.* (esp. of a disease) able to be passed on. [Latin: related to COMMUNICATE]

communicant /kəˈmjuːnɪkənt/ *n.* **1** person who receives Holy Communion. **2** person who imparts information. [related to COMMUNICATE]

communicate /kəˈmjuːnɪˌkeɪt/ *v.* (**-ting**) **1** impart, transmit (news, heat, motion, feelings, disease, ideas, etc.). **2** succeed in conveying information. **3** (often foll. by *with*) relate socially; have dealings. **4** be connected (*they have communicating rooms*). □ **communicator** *n.* **communicatory** *adj.* [Latin: related to COMMON]

communication /kəˌmjuːnɪˈkeɪʃ(ə)n/ *n.* **1 a** communicating or being communicated. **b** information etc. communicated. **c** letter, message, etc. **2** connection or means of access. **3** social dealings. **4** (in *pl.*) science and practice of transmitting information.

♦ **Communication, Advertising and Marketing Education Foundation** *n.* educational charity funded and supported by the Advertising Association and the Institute of Public Relations. It provides education and training in communications, public relations, advertising, and marketing, operating diploma courses in these subjects.

communication card *Computing* see EXPANSION CARD.

communication cord *n.* cord or chain pulled to stop a train in an emergency.

communication(s) satellite *n.* artificial satellite used to relay telephone circuits or broadcast programmes.

communicative /kəˈmjuːnɪkətɪv/ *adj.* ready to talk and impart information.

communion /kəˈmjuːnɪən/ *n.* **1** sharing, esp. of thoughts etc.; fellowship. **2** participation; sharing in common (*communion of interests*). **3** (**Communion** or **Holy Communion**) Eucharist. **4** body or group within the Christian faith (*the Methodist communion*). [Latin: related to COMMON]

communiqué /kəˈmjuːnɪˌkeɪ/ *n.* official communication, esp. a news report. [French, = communicated]

communism /ˈkɒmjʊˌnɪz(ə)m/ *n.* **1 a** social system in which most property is publicly owned and each person works for the common benefit. **b** political theory advocating this. **2** (usu. **Communism**) the form of socialist society established in Cuba, China, etc., and previously, the USSR. [French: related to COMMON]

communist /ˈkɒmjʊnɪst/ *–n.* **1** person advocating communism. **2** (**Communist**) member of a Communist Party. *–adj.* of or relating to communism. □ **communistic** /-ˈnɪstɪk/ *adj.*

community /kəˈmjuːnɪtɪ/ *n.* (*pl.* **-ies**) **1** body of people living in one place, district, or country. **2** body of people having religion, ethnic origin, profession, etc., in common. **3** fellowship (*community of interest*). **4** commune. **5** joint ownership or liability. [Latin: related to COMMON]

community centre *n.* place providing social etc. facilities for a neighbourhood.

◆ **community charge** *n.* (also **poll tax**) *hist.* annual lump-sum tax levied on every adult in a community with some allowances for personal circumstances. It was introduced by the Conservative government in the late 1980s as an alternative to domestic rates for local-government finance, and was itself replaced by the council tax in 1993.

community home *n.* centre for housing young offenders and other juveniles.

community service *n.* unpaid work in the community esp. by an offender.

community singing *n.* singing by a large group, esp. of old popular songs or hymns.

community spirit *n.* feeling of belonging to a community, expressed in mutual support etc.

◆ **commutation** /ˌkɒmjʊˈteɪʃ(ə)n/ *n.* **1** substitution; exchange. **2** reduction in severity of a punishment or penalty. **3** *Finance* right to receive an immediate cash sum in return for accepting smaller annual payments at some time in the future. This is usu. associated with a pension in which certain life-assurance policyholders can, on retirement, elect to take a cash sum from the pension fund immediately and a reduced annual pension.

commute /kəˈmjuːt/ *v.* (**-ting**) **1** travel some distance to and from work. **2** (usu. foll. by *to*) change (a punishment) to one less severe. **3** (often foll. by *into*, *for*) change (one kind of payment or obligation) for another. **4** exchange. □ **commutable** *adj.* [Latin *muto* change]

commuter *n.* person who commutes to and from work.

◆ **COMO** *abbr.* = COMMITTEE OF MARKETING ORGANIZATIONS.

Comodoro Rivadavia /ˌkəʊməˈdɔːrəʊ ˌriːvəˈdɑːvɪə/ seaport in SE Argentina, in Patagonia, and the country's chief centre of oil and gas production; pop. (1991) 124 104.

compact[1] *–adj.* /kəmˈpækt/ **1** closely or neatly packed together. **2** small and economically designed. **3** concise. **4** (of a person) small but well-proportioned. *–v.* /kəmˈpækt/ make compact. *–n.* /ˈkɒmpækt/ (in full **powder compact**) small flat case for face-powder. □ **compactly** *adv.* **compactness** *n.* [Latin *pango* fasten]

compact[2] /ˈkɒmpækt/ *n.* agreement, contract. [Latin: related to PACT]

compact disc /ˈkɒmpækt/ *n.* disc on which information or sound is recorded digitally and reproduced by reflection of laser light.

◆ **Companies House** *n.* (also **Companies Registration Office**) office of the Registrar of Companies, formerly in London but now in Cardiff. It contains a register of all UK private and public companies, their directors, shareholders, and balance sheets. All this information has to be provided by companies by law and is available to any member of the public for a small charge.

companion /kəmˈpænjən/ *n.* **1 a** person who accompanies or associates with another. **b** (foll. by *in*, *of*) partner, sharer. **c** person employed to live with and assist another. **2** handbook or reference book. **3** thing that matches another. **4** (**Companion**) member of some orders of knighthood. [Latin *panis* bread]

companionable *adj.* sociable, friendly. □ **companionably** *adv.*

companionship *n.* friendship; being together.

companion-way *n.* staircase from a ship's deck to the saloon or cabins.

company /ˈkʌmpənɪ/ *n.* (*pl.* **-ies**) **1 a** number of people assembled. **b** guest(s). **2** person's associate(s). **3** corporate enterprise that has a legal identity separate from that of its members and operates as one single unit, in the success of which all the members participate. An **incorporated company** is a legal person in its own right, able to own property and to sue and be sued in its own name. See also CHARTERED COMPANY; JOINT-STOCK COMPANY; LIMITED COMPANY; PRIVATE LIMITED COMPANY; PUBLIC LIMITED COMPANY; REGISTERED COMPANY; STATUTORY COMPANY. **4** actors etc. working together. **5** subdivision of an infantry battalion. **6** body of people combined for a common purpose (*the ship's company*). **7** being with another or others. □ **in company with** together with. **keep a person company** remain with a person to be sociable. **part company** (often foll. by *with*) cease to associate; separate; disagree. [French: related to COMPANION]

◆ **company doctor** *n.* **1** business person or accountant with wide commercial experience who specializes in analysing and rectifying the problems of ailing companies. A company doctor may either act as a consultant or be given executive powers to implement the policies he or she recommends. **2** medical doctor employed by a company to look after its staff, esp. its senior executives, and to advise on medical and public-health matters.

◆ **company formation** *n.* procedure to be adopted for forming a company in the UK. The subscribers to the company must send to the Registrar of Companies a statement giving details of the registered address of the new company together with the names and addresses of the first directors and secretary, with their written consent to act in these capacities. They must also give a declaration (**declaration of compliance**) that the provisions of the Companies acts have been complied with and provide the memorandum of association and the articles of association. Provided all these documents are in order the Registrar will issue a certificate of incorporation and a certificate enabling it to start business. In the case of a public limited company additional information is required.

Comoros /kɒˈmɔːrəʊz/, **Federal Islamic Republic of the** country consisting of a group of islands in the Indian Ocean N of Madagascar. The economy is almost entirely dependent on agriculture, the main exports being vanilla, cloves, copra, and ylang-ylang and other essential oils. The market for these products is vulnerable, and tourism is an increasing source of employment and revenue, esp. as the environment cannot sustain increased agricultural production. Formerly a French colony, the country became independent in 1975. In 1992, after a succession of military coups, a new constitution was approved and multi-party elections were held at the end of the year; a coalition government was established in 1993. In 1997 secessionists on two islands declared independence from the Republic of Comoros, demanding a resumption of French rule. Clashes ensued between the secessionists and government forces. President, Mohamed Taki Abdoulkarim; prime minister, Tadjidine Ben Said Massounde; capital, Moroni. □ **Comorian** *adj.* & *n.*

languages	Comorian, French & Arabic (official), Swahili dialect
currency	Comorian franc (CF) of 100 centimes, CFA franc
pop. (1996)	562 000
GNP (1994)	US$249M
literacy	64% (m); 50% (f)
life expectancy	56 (m); 60 (f)

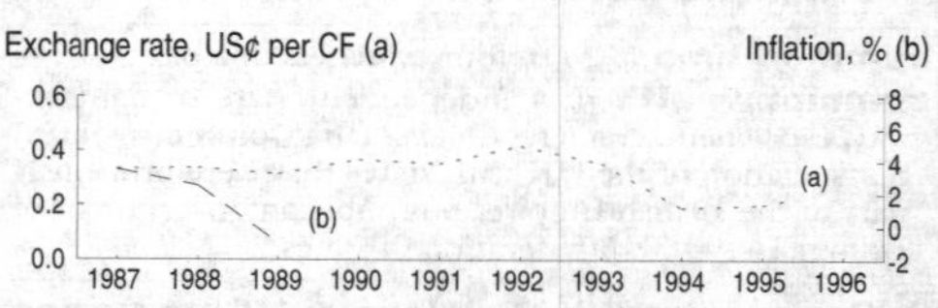

◆ **company law** *n.* collection of laws governing the formation, conduct, and control of companies. These are largely statute-based law; the principal acts are the Companies Act (1985), the Insolvency Act (1986), the Company Directors' Disqualification Act (1986), and the Financial Services Act (1986).

◆ **company seal** *n.* (also **common seal**) seal with a company's name engraved on it in legible characters, used to authenticate share certificates and other important documents issued by the company. Unless it is affixed to any contract required by English law to be made under seal, the company will not be bound by that contract.

◆ **company secretary** *n.* one of the officers of a company, usu. appointed by the directors. The secretary's duties are mainly administrative, including preparation of the agenda for directors' meetings. However, the modern company secretary may also manage the office and enter into contracts on behalf of the company. Duties imposed by law include the submission of the annual return and the keeping of minutes. The secretary of a public company is required to have certain qualifications, set out in the Companies Act (1985). See INSTITUTE OF CHARTERED SECRETARIES AND ADMINISTRATORS.

---

comparable /'kɒmpərəb(ə)l/ *adj.* (often foll. by *with*, *to*) able or fit to be compared. □ **comparability** /-'bɪlɪtɪ/ *n.* **comparably** *adv.* [Latin: related to COMPARE]

■ **Usage** Use *comparable* with *to* and *with* corresponds to the senses of *compare*: *to* is more common.

comparative /kəm'pærətɪv/ *–adj.* **1** perceptible or estimated by comparison; relative (*in comparative comfort*). **2** of or involving comparison (*a comparative study*). **3** *Gram.* (of an adjective or adverb) expressing a higher degree of a quality (e.g. *braver, more quickly*). *–n. Gram.* comparative expression or word. □ **comparatively** *adv.* [Latin: related to COMPARE]

◆ **comparative advantage** *n.* relative efficiency in a particular economic activity of an individual or group of individuals over another economic activity, compared to another individual or group. One of the fundamental propositions of economics is that if individuals or groups specialize in activities in which their comparative advantage lies, then there are gains from trade. This is one of the main arguments for free trade and against such restrictions as tariffs and quotas. It still holds even if one group holds an absolute advantage in all economic activities over another group.

---

compare /kəm'peə(r)/ *–v.* (**-ring**) **1** (usu. foll. by *to*) express similarities in; liken. **2** (often foll. by *to, with*) estimate the similarity of. **3** (often foll. by *with*) bear comparison. **4** *Gram.* form comparative and superlative degrees of (an adjective or adverb). *–n. literary* comparison (*beyond compare*). □ **compare notes** exchange ideas or opinions. [Latin *compar* equal]

■ **Usage** In current use, *to* and *with* are generally interchangeable, but *with* often implies a greater element of formal analysis.

comparison /kəm'pærɪs(ə)n/ *n.* **1** comparing. **2** illustration or example of similarity. **3** capacity for being likened (*there's no comparison*). **4** (in full **degrees of comparison**) *Gram.* positive, comparative, and superlative forms of adjectives and adverbs. □ **bear** (or **stand**) **comparison** (often foll. by *with*) be able to be compared favourably. **beyond comparison 1** totally different in quality. **2** greatly superior; excellent.

compartment /kəm'pɑːtmənt/ *n.* **1** space within a larger space, separated by partitions. **2** watertight division of a ship. **3** area of activity etc. kept apart from others in a person's mind. [Latin: related to PART]

compartmental /ˌkɒmpɑːt'ment(ə)l/ *adj.* of or divided into compartments or categories.

compartmentalize *v.* (also **-ise**) (**-zing** or **-sing**) divide into compartments or categories.

compass /'kʌmpəs/ *n.* **1** instrument showing the direction of magnetic north and bearings from it. **2** (usu. in *pl.*) instrument for taking measurements and describing circles, with two arms connected at one end by a hinge. **3** circumference or boundary. **4** area, extent; scope; range. [Latin *passus* pace]

compassion /kəm'pæʃ(ə)n/ *n.* pity inclining one to help or be merciful. [Church Latin: related to PASSION]

compassionate /kəm'pæʃənət/ *adj.* showing compassion, sympathetic. □ **compassionately** *adv.*

compassionate leave *n.* leave granted on grounds of bereavement etc.

compatibility /kəmˌpætə'bɪlɪtɪ/ *n.* **1** ability to coexist. **2** ability of a computer to directly execute program code originally produced for another computer. This generally occurs for successive computers in a family of machines made by a particular manufacturer. Since later computers are almost always more capable (have a larger instruction set and/or more memory), a computer that is able to run a program of a less capable machine is said to be **upward compatible**. Computers from different manufacturers are rarely compatible, unless this is a deliberate feature of the design. For example, many microcomputers are designed to be compatible with the IBM PC. **3** ability of a piece of computing hardware (e.g. a storage device or a terminal) to be used in place of the equipment originally specified or selected. If the equipment substituted is made by another manufacturer, and fits into the computer without any modifications and works straight away, it is said to be **plug compatible**.

compatible /kəm'pætəb(ə)l/ *adj.* **1 a** able to coexist; well-suited. **b** (often foll. by *with*) consistent. **2** (of equipment etc.) able to be used in combination. [medieval Latin: related to PASSION]

compatriot /kəm'pætrɪət/ *n.* fellow-countryman. [Latin *compatriota*]

compel /kəm'pel/ *v.* (**-ll-**) **1** force, constrain. **2** arouse irresistibly (*compels admiration*). **3** (as **compelling** *adj.*) rousing strong interest, conviction, or admiration. □ **compellingly** *adv.* [Latin *pello puls-* drive]

compendious /kəm'pendɪəs/ *adj.* comprehensive but brief. [Latin: related to COMPENDIUM]

compendium /kəm'pendɪəm/ *n.* (*pl.* **-s** or **-dia**) **1** concise summary or abridgement. **2** collection of table-games etc. [Latin]

compensate /'kɒmpenˌseɪt/ *v.* (**-ting**) **1 a** (often foll. by *for*) recompense (a person). **b** recompense (loss, damage, etc.). **2** (usu. foll. by *for* a thing) make amends. **3** counterbalance. **4** offset disability or frustration by development in another direction. □ **compensatory** /-'seɪtərɪ/ *adj.* [Latin *pendo pens-* weigh]

◆ **compensated demand function** *n.* = HICKSIAN DEMAND FUNCTION.

---

compensation /ˌkɒmpen'seɪʃ(ə)n/ *n.* **1** compensating or being compensated. **2** money etc. given as recompense.

◆ **compensation for loss of office** *n.* (also *colloq.* **golden handshake**) payment, often tax-free, made by a company to a director, senior executive, or consultant who is forced to retire before the expiry of his or her service contract, as a result of a merger, take-over, or any other reason. This form of **severance payment** (see also REDUNDANCY 1) may be additional to a retirement pension or in place of it; it must also be shown separately in the company's accounts. See also GOLDEN PARACHUTE.

◆ **compensation fund** *n.* fund set up by the London Stock Exchange, to which member firms contribute. It provides compensation to investors who suffer loss as a result of a member firm failing to meet its financial obligations.

---

compère /'kɒmpeə(r)/ *–n.* person who introduces a variety show etc. *–v.* (**-ring**) act as compère (to). [French, = godfather]

compete /kəm'piːt/ *v.* (**-ting**) **1** take part in a contest etc. **2** (often foll. by *with, against* a person, *for* a thing) strive. [Latin *peto* seek]

competence /'kɒmpɪt(ə)ns/ *n.* (also **competency**) **1** ability; being competent. **2** income large enough to live on. **3** legal capacity.

competent *adj.* **1** adequately qualified or capable. **2** effective. □ **competently** *adv.* [Latin: related to COMPETE]

competition /ˌkɒmpəˈtɪʃ(ə)n/ *n.* **1** (often foll. by *for*) competing. **2** event in which people compete. **3** the other people competing; opposition. **4** *Econ.* rivalry between suppliers providing goods or services for a market, usu. considered beneficial in the sense of achieving Pareto optimality. Governments usu. pursue policies aimed at increasing competition in markets (see REGULATION 3; DEREGULATE), although there may often be a conflict between policies that increase competition and those that promote purely national interest. See also IMPERFECT COMPETITION; MONOPOLY 1; PERFECT COMPETITION. [Latin: related to COMPETE]

♦ **competition and credit control** *n.* subject of an important paper issued in 1971 by the Bank of England. It outlined a number of changes affecting the banking system and the means of controlling credit. From October 1971 a new system of reserve requirements was implemented, the banks agreed to abandon collusion on setting interest rates, and the Bank of England changed its operations in the gilt-edged securities market. The main aim of these changes was to stimulate more active competition between the banks and to move towards greater reliance upon interest rates as a means of credit control. Further changes were made in 1981 with the abolition of the minimum lending rate and the reserve asset ratio.

competitive /kəmˈpetɪtɪv/ *adj.* **1** of or involving competition. **2** (of prices etc.) comparing favourably with those of rivals. **3** having a strong urge to win.

♦ **competitive advantage** *n.* group of factors that give a company an advantage over its rivals. For companies marketing similar products, one may achieve a competitive advantage by creative and memorable advertising, innovative package design, or superior distribution methods.

♦ **competitiveness** *n.* **1** strong urge to win. **2** ability of an economy to supply increasing aggregate demand and maintain exports. A loss of competitiveness is usu. signalled by increasing imports and falling exports. Competitiveness is often measured in a narrower sense by comparing relative inflation rates. For instance, if the sterling-dollar exchange rate remains constant, but prices rise faster in the UK than in the US, UK goods will become relatively more expensive, reflecting a loss in competitiveness; this in turn may lead to a falling demand for exports.

competitor /kəmˈpetɪtə(r)/ *n.* person who competes; rival, esp. in business.

compile /kəmˈpaɪl/ *v.* (**-ling**) **1 a** collect and arrange (material) into a list, book, etc. **b** produce (a book etc.) thus. **2** *Computing* translate (a program) into machine code. □ **compilation** /ˌkɒmpɪˈleɪʃ(ə)n/ *n.* [Latin *compilo* plunder]

compiler *n.* **1** person who compiles. **2** computer program that translates a program written in a high-level language into the detailed instructions (see MACHINE CODE) that the computer can execute (cf. INTERPRETER 2). The program must be translated in its entirety before it can be executed; however, it can then be executed any number of times. Program run times are much faster when a compiler is used rather than an interpreter.

complacent /kəmˈpleɪs(ə)nt/ *adj.* smugly self-satisfied or contented. □ **complacence** *n.* **complacency** *n.* **complacently** *adv.* [Latin *placeo* please]

■ **Usage** *Complacent* is often confused with *complaisant*.

complain /kəmˈpleɪn/ *v.* **1** express dissatisfaction. **2** (foll. by *of*) **a** say that one is suffering from (an ailment). **b** state a grievance concerning. **3** creak under strain. [Latin *plango* lament]

complainant *n.* plaintiff in certain lawsuits.

complaint *n.* **1** complaining. **2** grievance, cause of dissatisfaction. **3** ailment. **4** formal accusation.

complaisant /kəmˈpleɪz(ə)nt/ *adj. formal* **1** deferential. **2** willing to please; acquiescent. □ **complaisance** *n.* [French: related to COMPLACENT]

■ **Usage** *Complaisant* is often confused with *complacent*.

complement *–n.* /ˈkɒmplɪmənt/ **1** thing that completes; counterpart. **2** full number needed. **3** word(s) added to a verb to complete the predicate of a sentence. **4** amount by which an angle is less than 90°. **5** *Commerce* a good for which the demand changes in the same direction as the demand for some other good whose price has changed. For example, a rise in the price of bread may lead to a fall in demand for bread; if the demand for butter fell at the same time, butter would be called a complement of bread. Cf. SUBSTITUTE *n.* 3. *–v.* /ˈkɒmplɪˌment/ **1** complete. **2** form a complement to. [Latin *compleo* fill up]

complementary /ˌkɒmplɪˈmentərɪ/ *adj.* **1** completing; forming a complement. **2** (of two or more things) complementing each other.

complementary medicine *n.* alternative medicine.

complete /kəmˈpliːt/ *–adj.* **1** having all its parts; entire. **2** finished. **3** total, in every way. *–v.* (**-ting**) **1** finish. **2** make complete. **3** fill in (a form etc.). **4** conclude the sale or purchase of property. □ **complete with** having (as an important feature) (*comes complete with instructions*). □ **completely** *adv.* **completeness** *n.* [Latin: related to COMPLEMENT]

♦ **completion** *n.* **1** end, finish; conclusion. **2** *Law* conveyance of land in fulfilment of a contract of sale. The purchaser will have obtained an equitable interest in the land at the date of the exchange of contracts but will not become the full legal owner until completion. If the seller refuses to complete, the court may grant a decree of specific performance.

complex /ˈkɒmpleks/ *–n.* **1** building, series of rooms, etc., made up of related parts (*shopping complex*). **2** *Psychol.* group of usu. repressed feelings or thoughts which cause abnormal behaviour or mental states. **3** preoccupation; feeling of inadequacy. *–adj.* **1** complicated. **2** consisting of related parts; composite. □ **complexity** /kəmˈpleksɪtɪ/ *n.* (*pl.* **-ies**). [Latin *complexus*]

complexion /kəmˈplekʃ(ə)n/ *n.* **1** natural colour, texture, and appearance of the skin, esp. of the face. **2** aspect, character (*puts a different complexion on the matter*). [Latin: related to COMPLEX]

compliance /kəmˈplaɪəns/ *n.* **1** obedience to a request, command, etc. **2** capacity to yield. □ **in compliance with** according to.

compliant *adj.* obedient; yielding. □ **compliantly** *adv.*

complicate /ˈkɒmplɪˌkeɪt/ *v.* (**-ting**) **1** make difficult or complex. **2** (as **complicated** *adj.*) complex; intricate. [Latin *plico* to fold]

complication /ˌkɒmplɪˈkeɪʃ(ə)n/ *n.* **1 a** involved or confused condition or state. **b** complicating circumstance; difficulty. **2** (often in *pl.*) disease or condition aggravating or arising out of a previous one. [Latin: related to COMPLICATE]

complicity /kəmˈplɪsɪtɪ/ *n.* partnership in wrongdoing. [French: related to COMPLEX]

compliment *–n.* /ˈkɒmplɪmənt/ **1 a** polite expression of praise. **b** act implying praise. **2** (in *pl.*) **a** formal greetings accompanying a present etc. **b** praise. *–v.* /ˈkɒmplɪˌment/ (often foll. by *on*) congratulate; praise. [Latin: related to COMPLEMENT]

complimentary /ˌkɒmplɪˈmentərɪ/ *adj.* **1** expressing a compliment. **2** given free of charge.

♦ **compliments slip** *n.* slip of paper with the words 'With the compliments of...' printed on it, followed by the name and address of the firm sending it. It is enclosed with material sent to another person or firm to identify the sender, when a letter is not necessary.

compline /ˈkɒmplɪn/ *n.* **1** last of the canonical hours of prayer. **2** service during this. [Latin: related to COMPLY]

comply /kəmˈplaɪ/ *v.* (**-ies, -ied**) (often foll. by *with*) act in accordance (with a request or command). [Latin *compleo* fill up]

component /kəm'pəʊnənt/ *–n.* part of a larger whole. *–adj.* being part of a larger whole. [Latin: related to COMPOUND[1]]

comport /kəm'pɔːt/ *v.refl. literary* conduct oneself; behave. □ **comport with** suit, befit. □ **comportment** *n.* [Latin *porto* carry]

compose /kəm'pəʊz/ *v.* (**-sing**) **1** create in music or writing. **2** constitute; make up. **3** arrange artistically, neatly, or for a specified purpose. **4 a** (often *refl.*) calm; settle. **b** (as **composed** *adj.*) calm, self-possessed. **5** *Printing* **a** set up (type). **b** arrange (an article etc.) in type. □ **composed of** made up of, consisting of. □ **composedly** /-zɪdlɪ/ *adv.* [French: related to POSE]

■ **Usage** See note at *comprise*.

composer *n.* person who composes (esp. music).

composite /'kɒmpəzɪt/ *–adj.* **1** made up of parts. **2** of mixed Ionic and Corinthian style. **3** (of a plant) having a head of many flowers forming one bloom. *–n.* composite thing or plant. [Latin: related to COMPOSE]

♦ **composite rate tax** *n.* (also **CRT**) *hist.* special rate of tax, levied in the UK from 1951 to April 1991, that building societies and banks had to deduct from interest paid to investors (resident in the UK). The rate of tax was some figure (about 3% in 1991) below the basic rate of income tax, but this tax could not be claimed back under any circumstances. Basic-rate taxpayers with such deposits thus made a gain while non-taxpayers were worse off. Taxpayers now pay the full basic rate (deducted at source) and non-taxpayers can opt to be paid gross interest or to reclaim the tax.

composition /ˌkɒmpə'zɪʃ(ə)n/ *n.* **1 a** act or method of putting together; composing. **b** thing composed, esp. music. **2** constitution of a substance. **3** school essay. **4** arrangement of the parts of a picture etc. **5** compound artificial substance. □ **compositional** *adj.*

compositor /kəm'pɒzɪtə(r)/ *n.* person who sets type, esp. metal type, for printing. [Latin: related to COMPOSE]

compos mentis /ˌkɒmpɒs 'mentɪs/ *adj.* sane. [Latin]

compost /'kɒmpɒst/ *–n.* **1** mixture of decayed organic matter. **2** loam soil with fertilizer for growing plants. *–v.* **1** treat with compost. **2** make into compost. [Latin: related to COMPOSE]

composure /kəm'pəʊʒə(r)/ *n.* tranquil manner. [from COMPOSE]

compote /'kɒmpəʊt/ *n.* fruit preserved or cooked in syrup. [French: related to COMPOSE]

compound[1] /'kɒmpaʊnd/ *–n.* **1** mixture of two or more things. **2** word made up of two or more existing words. **3** substance formed from two or more elements chemically united in fixed proportions. *–adj.* **1** made up of two or more ingredients or parts. **2** combined; collective. *–v.* /kəm'paʊnd/ **1** mix or combine (ingredients or elements). **2** increase or complicate (difficulties etc.). **3** make up (a composite whole). **4** settle (a matter) by mutual agreement. **5** *Law* condone or conceal (a liability or offence) for personal gain. **6** (usu. foll. by *with*) *Law* come to terms with a person. [Latin *compono -pos-* put together]

compound[2] /'kɒmpaʊnd/ *n.* **1** enclosure or fenced-in space. **2** enclosure, esp. in India, China, etc., in which a factory or house stands. [Malay *kampong*]

♦ **compound annual return** *n.* (also **CAR**) total return available from an investment or deposit in which the interest is used to augment the investment. The more frequently the interest is credited, the higher the CAR. The CAR is usu. quoted on a gross basis. The return, taking into account the deduction of tax at the basic rate on the interest, is known as the **compound net annual rate** (**CNAR**).

compound fracture *n.* fracture complicated by a wound.

compound interest *n.* interest payable on capital and its accumulated interest. See INTEREST RATE.

♦ **compound net annual rate** see COMPOUND ANNUAL RETURN.

comprehend /ˌkɒmprɪ'hend/ *v.* **1** grasp mentally; understand. **2** include. [Latin *comprehendo* seize]

comprehensible *adj.* that can be understood. [Latin: related to COMPREHEND]

comprehension *n.* **1 a** understanding. **b** text set as a test of understanding. **2** inclusion.

comprehensive *–adj.* including all or nearly all, inclusive. *–n.* (in full **comprehensive school**) secondary school for children of all abilities. □ **comprehensively** *adv.* **comprehensiveness** *n.*

♦ **comprehensive income tax** *n.* income tax for which the tax base consists not only of income but also of capital gains as well as other accretions of wealth (e.g. legacies). Although this is not a tax currently levied in the UK, tax theorists find it attractive since sometimes clear distinctions between income, capital gains, etc. are difficult to sustain.

♦ **comprehensive insurance** see MOTOR INSURANCE.

compress *–v.* /kəm'pres/ **1** squeeze together. **2** bring into a smaller space or shorter time. *–n.* /'kɒmpres/ pad of lint etc. pressed on to part of the body to relieve inflammation, stop bleeding, etc. □ **compressible** /kəm'presɪb(ə)l/ *adj.* [Latin: related to PRESS[1]]

compression /kəm'preʃ(ə)n/ *n.* **1** compressing. **2** reduction in volume of the fuel and air mixture in an internal-combustion engine before ignition.

compressor /kəm'presə(r)/ *n.* machine for compressing air or other gases.

comprise /kəm'praɪz/ *v.* (**-sing**) **1** include. **2** consist of. **3** make up, compose. [French: related to COMPREHEND]

■ **Usage** The use of this word in sense 3 is considered incorrect and *compose* is generally preferred.

compromise /'kɒmprəˌmaɪz/ *–n.* **1** settlement of a dispute by mutual concession. **2** (often foll. by *between*) intermediate state between conflicting opinions, actions, etc. *–v.* (**-sing**) **1 a** settle a dispute by mutual concession. **b** modify one's opinions, demands, etc. **2** bring into disrepute or danger by indiscretion. [Latin: related to PROMISE]

comp slip *n. colloq.* = COMPLIMENTS SLIP.

♦ **comptroller** /kən'trəʊlə(r)/ *n.* title of the financial director in some companies or chief financial officer of a group of companies. The title is more widely used in the US than in the UK. [var. of CONTROLLER]

compulsion /kəm'pʌlʃ(ə)n/ *n.* **1** compelling or being compelled; obligation. **2** irresistible urge. [Latin: related to COMPEL]

compulsive /kəm'pʌlsɪv/ *adj.* **1** compelling. **2** resulting or acting (as if) from compulsion (*compulsive gambler*). **3** irresistible (*compulsive entertainment*). □ **compulsively** *adv.* [medieval Latin: related to COMPEL]

compulsory /kəm'pʌlsərɪ/ *adj.* **1** required by law or a rule. **2** essential. □ **compulsorily** *adv.*

♦ **compulsory liquidation** *n.* (also **compulsory winding-up**) winding-up of a company by a court. A petition must be presented, both at the court and the registered office of the company. Those by whom it may be presented include: the company, the directors, a creditor, an official receiver, and the Secretary of State for Trade and Industry. The grounds on which a company may be wound up by the court include: a special resolution of the company that it be wound up by the court; that the company is unable to pay its debts; that the number of members is reduced below two; or that the court is of the opinion that it would be just and equitable for the company to be wound up. The court may appoint a provisional liquidator after the winding-up petition has been presented; it may also appoint a special manager to manage the company's property. On the grant of the order for winding-up, the official receiver becomes the liquidator and continues in office until some other person is appointed, either by the creditors or the members. See also PROVISIONAL LIQUIDATOR. Cf. MEMBERS' VOLUNTARY LIQUIDATION.

compulsory purchase *n.* enforced sale of land or

property to a local authority etc. when it is required for some purpose under the Town and Country Planning legislation. Compensation is paid on the basis of market value. Cf. REQUISITION *n.* 1.

♦ **compulsory purchase annuity** *n.* annuity that must be purchased with the fund built up from certain types of pension arrangements. When retirement age is reached, a person who has been paying premiums into this type of pension fund is obliged to use the fund to purchase an annuity to provide an income for the rest of his or her life. The fund may not be used in any other way (except for a small portion, which may be taken in cash).

compunction /kəm'pʌŋkʃ(ə)n/ *n.* **1** pricking of conscience. **2** slight regret; scruple. [Church Latin: related to POINT]

compute /kəm'pjuːt/ *v.* (**-ting**) **1** reckon or calculate. **2** use a computer. □ **computation** /ˌkɒmpjuː'teɪʃ(ə)n/ *n.* [Latin *puto* reckon]

♦ **computer** *n.* electronic tool that manipulates information in accordance with a predefined sequence of instructions. Computers have a simple 'brain' (see CENTRAL PROCESSOR) that interprets and executes the instructions, and a memory (see MAIN STORE), which stores the instructions and information. In addition, all computers have at least: an input device (e.g. a keyboard), where the information and instructions are fed in; an output device (e.g. a screen or printer), where results are given; and extra memory in the form of magnetic disks or magnetic tape (see BACKING STORE). Inside a computer, both information and instructions are in binary form, encoded as combinations of binary digits (bits; see BINARY NOTATION) and all processing is done using these strings of bits. A computer needs to be given detailed instructions, called a program, before it can perform even the simplest task (see COMPUTER PROGRAMMING). The general term for the programs that a computer needs in order to operate is software, while the computer and devices attached to it are called hardware. Computers come in three main sizes. The largest is the mainframe, used typically for large-scale corporate data processing; and the smallest is the microcomputer, designed for a single user. Between these extremes is the minicomputer. These distinctions are becoming blurred, as minicomputers and microcomputers become more powerful. All three groups may be used as general-purpose machines, capable of solving a wide variety of problems. Alternatively they may be designed for a special purpose or for a limited range of problems. See also NETWORK *n.* 6.

♦ **computer-aided design** *n.* (also **CAD**) use of computers for a variety of design projects, including determining the contours of car bodies, investigating the behaviour of bridges in windy conditions, and the creation of home interiors. There are two elements to CAD. On-the-screen drawing, using light pens or similar devices, allows the designer a similar versatility to that given by word processing to the typist. Designs can be amended easily, rotated and looked at from different angles, and printed out as working drawings. Other programs can systematically analyse the design and test it against appropriate technical data. The final output of CAD is often transferred directly to computer-aided manufacturing systems.

♦ **computer-aided manufacturing** *n.* (also **computer-assisted manufacturing**, **CAM**) use of computers to control industrial processes (e.g. brewing, chemical manufacture, oil refining, and steel making) or to control automatic machines that can be programmed to carry out different tasks, esp. in the car-manufacturing industry.

computer architecture see ARCHITECTURE 4.

computer-assisted learning *n.* (also **CAL**, **computer-assisted instruction**, **computer-based learning**) use of computers to aid or support education. CAL can test attainment at any point, providing faster or slower routes through the material as necessary, and can produce a progress record.

♦ **computer-assisted telephone interviewing** *n.* (also **CATI**) system in which a telephone interviewer conducts a sales or marketing interview, using a computer and a computerized questionnaire. This system reduces the number of errors as the interviewer keys in the respondent's answers as they are given and the computer follows a complex questionnaire routing efficiently, enabling the required statistics to be extracted automatically.

♦ **computer-assisted trading** *n.* (also **CAT**) use of computers by brokers and traders on a market, e.g. a stock exchange or foreign-exchange market, to facilitate trading by displaying prices, recording deals, etc.

computer-based learning *n.* (also **CBL**) = COMPUTER-ASSISTED LEARNING.

♦ **computer-based training** *n.* (also **CBT**, **computer-assisted training**) use of computers and video films in training. Exercises are shown on the video screen and participants have to key in answers to questions, which are assessed by the computer.

computer graphics *n.pl.* **1** (treated as *sing.*) mode of computer processing in which a large part of the output information is in pictorial form. **2** images so produced. These can range from a simple graph to a highly complicated engineering design, molecular structure, etc., in one or more colours, and may be labelled. They can be displayed on a VDU screen or may be in the form of a permanent record produced by a plotter or printer. Information is input to the computer by various means, e.g. a mouse or light pen. The computer can be made to straighten lines, move or erase specified areas, and expand or contract details. Images may be two-dimensional or, in the case of designs, models, etc., may appear three-dimensional. It is sometimes possible to display or draw three-dimensional images from different viewpoints. It is also possible to simulate motion in a displayed image.

computerize *v.* (also **-ise**) (**-zing** or **-sing**) **1** equip with a computer. **2** store, perform, or produce by computer. □ **computerization** /-'zeɪʃ(ə)n/ *n.*

computer-literate *adj.* able to use computers.

computer network see NETWORK *n.* 6.

♦ **computer output microfilm** *n.* (also **COM**) system that produces computer output on microfilm or microfiche. The information is recorded on film either by a camera that photographs a miniature screen displaying the computer output, or by a laser beam recorder, which writes directly onto the film. COM is used where there is a large volume of output, particularly where immediate reference is not required: for example, to produce updated copies of a bank's customer account at the end of each day's business.

♦ **computer programming** *n.* (also **programming**) process of writing the list of instructions (program) that a computer must follow to solve a problem. The program must be complete in every detail, since the computer cannot think for itself. The steps involved in writing a program are: understanding the problem, planning the solution, preparing the program, testing the program and removing errors, and documenting the program. A systems analyst will often help the programmer understand the problem and produce a detailed specification of the required program. This specification is further resolved into a sequence of logical steps, often by drawing a flow chart. The program itself is a translation of these steps into a programming language, which can be fed into the computer. Once the program is complete the errors, or bugs, must be located and corrected. Finally, a manual for the users of the program must be written. See also PROGRAMMING LANGUAGE; SYSTEMS ANALYSIS. □ **computer programmer** *n.*

computer science *n.* the study of the principles and use of computers.

computer system *n.* (also **computing system**) self-contained set of computing equipment consisting of a computer, or possibly several computers, together with associated software. Computer systems are designed to fulfil particular requirements.

computer virus *n.* self-replicating code maliciously introduced into a computer program and intended to corrupt the system or destroy data.

comrade /'kɒmreɪd/ *n.* **1** associate or companion in some activity. **2** fellow socialist or communist. □ **comradely** *adj.* **comradeship** *n.* [Spanish: related to CHAMBER]

Con. *abbr.* = CONSOLS.

con[1] *slang* –*n.* confidence trick. –*v.* (**-nn-**) swindle; deceive. [abbreviation]

con[2] –*n.* (usu. in *pl.*) reason against. –*prep.* & *adv.* against (cf. PRO[2]). [Latin *contra* against]

con[3] *n. slang* convict. [abbreviation]

con[4] *v.* (*US* **conn**) (**-nn-**) direct the steering of (a ship). [originally *cond* from French: related to CONDUCT]

con- see COM-.

Conakry /'kɒnəˌkriː/ capital and chief port of Guinea; pop. (est. 1995) 1 508 000.

concatenation /ˌkɒnkætɪ'neɪʃ(ə)n/ *n.* series of linked things or events. [Latin *catena* chain]

concave /'kɒnkeɪv/ *adj.* curved like the interior of a circle or sphere. □ **concavity** /-'kævɪtɪ/ *n.* [Latin: related to CAVE]

conceal /kən'siːl/ *v.* **1** keep secret. **2** hide. □ **concealment** *n.* [Latin *celo* hide]

♦ **concealed unemployment** *n.* = HIDDEN UNEMPLOYMENT.

---

concede /kən'siːd/ *v.* (**-ding**) **1** admit to be true. **2** admit defeat in. **3** grant (a right, privilege, etc.). [Latin: related to CEDE]

conceit /kən'siːt/ *n.* **1** personal vanity; pride. **2** *literary* **a** far-fetched comparison. **b** fanciful notion. [from CONCEIVE]

conceited *adj.* vain. □ **conceitedly** *adv.*

conceivable /kən'siːvəb(ə)l/ *adj.* capable of being grasped or imagined. □ **conceivably** *adv.*

conceive /kən'siːv/ *v.* (**-ving**) **1** become pregnant (with). **2 a** (often foll. by *of*) imagine, think. **b** (usu. in *passive*) formulate (a belief, plan, etc.). [Latin *concipio -cept-*]

concentrate /'kɒnsənˌtreɪt/ –*v.* (**-ting**) **1** (often foll. by *on*) focus one's attention or thought. **2** bring together to one point. **3** increase the strength of (a liquid etc.) by removing water etc. **4** (as **concentrated** *adj.*) intense, strong. –*n.* concentrated substance. [Latin: related to CENTRE]

♦ **concentrated segmentation** *n.* (also **niche marketing**) identification of a comparatively small segment of a market, usu. by a small company, in which to concentrate their efforts. For example, a company might decide to offer a service converting cine films to video tapes; as long as this activity does not threaten the profitability of the manufacturers of either video tapes or cine films, it can establish a profitable niche in the market.

---

concentration /ˌkɒnsən'treɪʃ(ə)n/ *n.* **1** concentrating or being concentrated. **2** mental attention. **3** something concentrated. **4** weight of a substance in a given amount of material.

concentration camp *n.* camp where political prisoners etc. are detained.

concentric /kən'sentrɪk/ *adj.* having a common centre. □ **concentrically** *adv.* [French or medieval Latin: related to CENTRE]

Concepción /kɒnˌsepsɪ'əʊn/ city in S central Chile; industries include steel processing and textiles; pop. (est. 1995) 350 268. Its port, on the Pacific coast, is Talcahuano.

concept /'kɒnsept/ *n.* general notion; abstract idea. [Latin: related to CONCEIVE]

conception /kən'sepʃ(ə)n/ *n.* **1** conceiving or being conceived. **2** idea, plan. **3** understanding (*has no conception*).□ **conceptional** *adj.* [French from Latin: related to CONCEPT]

♦ **concept test** *n.* technique used in marketing research to assess the reactions of consumers to a new product or a proposed change to an existing product (see NEW PRODUCT DEVELOPMENT). Before an organization invests in production facilities for a new product it writes a **concept statement** describing the proposed product and commissions a market researcher to interview a small number of potential consumers (see GROUP DISCUSSION; DEPTH INTERVIEW). Respondents are shown the concept statement and their reactions are explored in considerable detail. The results of these interviews help the organization to understand what it should do with the proposed product if it is to be successful.

---

conceptual /kən'septʃʊəl/ *adj.* of mental conceptions or concepts. □ **conceptually** *adv.*

conceptualize *v.* (also **-ise**) (**-zing** or **-sing**) form a concept or idea of. □ **conceptualization** /-'zeɪʃ(ə)n/ *n.*

concern /kən'sɜːn/ –*v.* **1 a** be relevant or important to. **b** relate to; be about. **2** (*refl.*; often foll. by *with, about, in*) interest or involve oneself. **3** worry, affect. –*n.* **1** anxiety, worry. **2 a** matter of interest or importance to one. **b** interest, connection (*has a concern in politics*). **3** business, firm. **4** *colloq.* complicated thing, contrivance. [Latin *cerno* sift]

concerned *adj.* **1** involved, interested. **2** troubled, anxious. □ **be concerned** (often foll. by *in*) take part. □ **concernedly** /-ɪdlɪ/ *adv.* **concernedness** /-ɪdnɪs/ *n.*

concerning *prep.* about, regarding.

concert /'kɒnsət/ *n.* **1** musical performance of usu. several separate compositions. **2** agreement. **3** combination of voices or sounds. [Italian: related to CONCERTO]

concerted /kən'sɜːtɪd/ *adj.* **1** jointly arranged or planned. **2** *Mus.* arranged in parts for voices or instruments.

concertina /ˌkɒnsə'tiːnə/ –*n.* musical instrument like an accordion but smaller. –*v.* (**-nas, -naed** /-nəd/ or **-na'd, -naing**) compress or collapse in folds like those of a concertina.

concerto /kən'tʃeətəʊ/ *n.* (*pl.* **-s** or **-ti** /-tɪ/) composition for solo instrument(s) and orchestra. [Italian]

♦ **concert party** *n.* group of apparently unconnected shareholders who make secret agreements (**concert-party agreements**) to act together to manipulate the share price of a company or to influence its management. The Companies Act (1981) laid down that the shares of the parties to such an agreement should be treated as if they were owned by one person, from the point of view of disclosing interests in a company's shareholding.

---

concert pitch *n.* pitch internationally agreed whereby the A above middle C = 440 Hz.

concession /kən'seʃ(ə)n/ *n.* **1 a** conceding. **b** thing conceded. **2** reduction in price for a certain category of persons. **3 a** right to use land etc. **b** right to sell goods in a particular territory. □ **concessionary** *adj.* [Latin: related to CONCEDE]

concessive /kən'sesɪv/ *adj. Gram.* (of a preposition or conjunction) introducing a phrase or clause which contrasts with the main clause (e.g. *in spite of, although*). [Latin: related to CONCEDE]

conch /kɒntʃ/ *n.* **1** thick heavy spiral shell of various marine gastropod molluscs. **2** any such gastropod. [Latin *concha*]

conchology /kɒŋ'kɒlədʒɪ/ *n.* the study of shells. [from CONCH]

concierge /ˌkɔ̃sɪ'eəʒ/ *n.* (esp. in France) door-keeper or porter of a block of flats etc. [French]

conciliate /kən'sɪlɪˌeɪt/ *v.* (**-ting**) **1** make calm and amenable; pacify; gain the goodwill of. **2** reconcile. □ **conciliator** *n.* **conciliatory** /-'sɪlɪətərɪ/ *adj.* [Latin: related to COUNCIL]

♦ **conciliation** /kənˌsɪlɪ'eɪʃ(ə)n/ *n.* conciliating; reconciling, esp. in industrial disputes. See MEDIATION 2; ADVISORY, CONCILIATION, AND ARBITRATION SERVICE.

---

concise /kən'saɪs/ *adj.* brief but comprehensive in expression. □ **concisely** *adv.* **conciseness** *n.* **concision** /-'sɪʒ(ə)n/ *n.* [Latin *caedo* cut]

conclave /ˈkɒnkleɪv/ *n.* **1** private meeting. **2** *RC Ch.* **a** assembly of cardinals for the election of a pope. **b** meeting-place for this. [Latin *clavis* key]

conclude /kənˈkluːd/ *v.* (**-ding**) **1** bring or come to an end. **2** (often foll. by *from* or *that*) infer. **3** settle (a treaty etc.). [Latin *concludo*: related to CLOSE[1]]

conclusion /kənˈkluːʒ(ə)n/ *n.* **1** ending, end. **2** judgement reached by reasoning. **3** summing-up. **4** settling (of peace etc.). **5** *Logic* proposition reached from given premisses. □ **in conclusion** lastly, to conclude. [Latin: related to CONCLUDE]

conclusive /kənˈkluːsɪv/ *adj.* decisive, convincing. □ **conclusively** *adv.* [Latin: related to CONCLUDE]

concoct /kənˈkɒkt/ *v.* **1** make by mixing ingredients. **2** invent (a story, lie, etc.). □ **concoction** /-ˈkɒkʃ(ə)n/ *n.* [Latin *coquo coct-* cook]

concomitant /kənˈkɒmɪt(ə)nt/ *–adj.* (often foll. by *with*) accompanying; occurring together. *–n.* accompanying thing. □ **concomitance** *n.* [Latin *comes comit-* companion]

Concord /ˈkɒŋkɔːd/ **1** city in the US, capital of New Hampshire; industries include printing and publishing; pop. (1990) 36 006. **2** town in the US, in NE Massachusetts; pop. (1990) 17 076.

concord /ˈkɒŋkɔːd/ *n.* agreement, harmony. □ **concordant** /kənˈkɔːd(ə)nt/ *adj.* [Latin *cor cord-* heart]

concordance /kənˈkɔːd(ə)ns/ *n.* **1** agreement. **2** alphabetical index of words used in a book or by an author. [medieval Latin: related to CONCORD]

concordat /kənˈkɔːdæt/ *n.* agreement, esp. between the Church and a state. [Latin: related to CONCORD]

concourse /ˈkɒŋkɔːs/ *n.* **1** crowd, gathering. **2** large open area in a railway station etc. [Latin: related to CONCUR]

con. cr. *abbr. Bookkeeping* contra credit.

concrete /ˈkɒŋkriːt/ *–adj.* **1 a** existing in a material form; real. **b** specific, definite (*concrete evidence*; *a concrete proposal*). **2** *Gram.* (of a noun) denoting a material object as opposed to a quality, state, etc. *–n.* (often *attrib.*) mixture of gravel, sand, cement, and water, used for building. *–v.* (**-ting**) cover with or embed in concrete. [Latin *cresco cret-* grow]

concretion /kənˈkriːʃ(ə)n/ *n.* **1** hard solid mass. **2** forming of this by coalescence. [Latin: related to CONCRETE]

concubine /ˈkɒŋkjʊˌbaɪn/ *n.* **1** *literary* or *joc.* mistress. **2** (among polygamous peoples) secondary wife. □ **concubinage** /kənˈkjuːbɪnɪdʒ/ *n.* [Latin *cubo* lie]

concupiscence /kənˈkjuːpɪs(ə)ns/ *n. formal* lust. □ **concupiscent** *adj.* [Latin *cupio* desire]

concur /kənˈkɜː(r)/ *v.* (**-rr-**) **1** (often foll. by *with*) have the same opinion. **2** coincide. [Latin *curro* run]

concurrent /kənˈkʌrənt/ *adj.* **1** (often foll. by *with*) existing or in operation at the same time or together. **2** (of three or more lines) meeting at or tending towards one point. **3** agreeing, harmonious. □ **concurrence** *n.* **concurrently** *adv.*

♦ **concurrent engineering** *n.* method of designing and marketing new products in which development takes place in parallel stages in order to reduce lead times and costs.

---

concuss /kənˈkʌs/ *v.* subject to concussion. [Latin *quatio* shake]

concussion /kənˈkʌʃ(ə)n/ *n.* **1** temporary unconsciousness or incapacity due to a blow to the head, a fall, etc. **2** violent shaking.

condemn /kənˈdem/ *v.* **1** express utter disapproval of. **2 a** find guilty; convict. **b** (usu. foll. by *to*) sentence to (a punishment). **3** pronounce (a building etc.) unfit for use. **4** (usu. foll. by *to*) doom or assign (to something unpleasant). □ **condemnation** /ˌkɒndemˈneɪʃ(ə)n/ *n.* **condemnatory** /-ˈdemnətərɪ/ *adj.* [Latin: related to DAMN]

condensation /ˌkɒndenˈseɪʃ(ə)n/ *n.* **1** condensing or being condensed. **2** condensed liquid (esp. water on a cold surface). **3** abridgement. [Latin: related to CONDENSE]

condense /kənˈdens/ *v.* (**-sing**) **1** make denser or more concentrated. **2** express in fewer words. **3** reduce or be reduced from a gas or vapour to a liquid. [Latin: related to DENSE]

condensed milk *n.* milk thickened by evaporation and sweetened.

condenser *n.* **1** apparatus or vessel for condensing vapour. **2** *Electr.* = CAPACITOR. **3** lens or system of lenses for concentrating light.

condescend /ˌkɒndɪˈsend/ *v.* **1** be gracious enough (to do a thing) esp. while showing one's sense of dignity or superiority (*condescended to attend*). **2** (foll. by *to*) pretend to be on equal terms with (an inferior). **3** (as **condescending** *adj.*) patronizing. □ **condescendingly** *adv.* **condescension** /-ˈsenʃ(ə)n/ *n.* [Latin: related to DESCEND]

condign /kənˈdaɪn/ *adj.* (of a punishment etc.) severe and well-deserved. [Latin *dignus* worthy]

condiment /ˈkɒndɪmənt/ *n.* seasoning or relish for food. [Latin *condio* pickle]

condition /kənˈdɪʃ(ə)n/ *–n.* **1** stipulation; thing upon the fulfilment of which something else depends. **2** *Law* major term of a contract that, if unfulfilled, constitutes a fundamental breach of contract and may invalidate it. Cf. WARRANTY 1. See also CONDITION PRECEDENT. **3 a** state of being or fitness of a person or thing. **b** ailment, abnormality (*heart condition*). **4** (in *pl.*) circumstances, esp. those affecting the functioning or existence of something (*good working conditions*). *–v.* **1 a** bring into a good or desired state. **b** make fit (esp. dogs or horses). **2** teach or accustom. **3 a** impose conditions on. **b** be essential to. □ **in** (or **out of**) **condition** in good (or bad) condition. **on condition that** with the stipulation that. [Latin *dico* say]

conditional *adj.* **1** (often foll. by *on*) dependent; not absolute; containing a condition. **2** *Gram.* (of a clause, mood, etc.) expressing a condition. □ **conditionally** *adv.* [Latin: related to CONDITION]

♦ **conditional bid** see TAKE-OVER BID.

♦ **conditionality** *n.* terms under which the International Monetary Fund (IMF) provides balance-of-payments support to member states. The principle is that support will only be given on the condition that it is accompanied by steps to solve the underlying problem. Programmes of economic reform are agreed with the member; these emphasize the attainment of a sustainable balance-of-payments position and boosting the supply side of the economy. The most recent review of general guidelines of conditionality principles was undertaken in 1988. Lending by commercial banks is frequently linked to IMF conditionality.

♦ **conditional sale agreement** *n.* contract of sale under which the price is payable by instalments and ownership does not pass to the buyer (who nevertheless is in possession of the goods) until specified conditions relating to the payment have been fulfilled. The seller retains ownership of the goods as security until paid in full. A conditional sale agreement is a form of consumer credit regulated by the Consumer Credit Act (1974) if the buyer is an individual, the credit does not exceed £15,000, and the agreement is not otherwise exempt.

---

conditioned reflex *n.* reflex response to a non-natural stimulus, established by training.

conditioner *n.* agent that conditions, esp. the hair.

♦ **condition precedent** *n.* provision that does not form part of a contract but suspends it until a specified event has happened. A **condition subsequent** is a similar provision that brings a contract to an end in specified circumstances. An example of a condition precedent is an agreement to buy a particular car if it passes its MOT test; an example of a condition subsequent is an agreement that entitles the purchaser of goods to return them if he is dissatisfied with them.

---

condole /kənˈdəʊl/ *v.* (**-ling**) (foll. by *with*) express sympathy with (a person) over a loss etc. [Latin *condoleo* grieve with another]

■ **Usage** *Condole* is often confused with *console*[1].

condolence *n.* (often in *pl.*) expression of sympathy.

condom /'kɒndɒm/ *n.* contraceptive sheath worn by men. [origin unknown]

condominium /ˌkɒndə'mɪnɪəm/ *n.* **1** joint rule or sovereignty. **2** *US* building containing individually owned flats. [Latin *dominium* lordship]

condone /kən'dəʊn/ *v.* (**-ning**) forgive or overlook (an offence or wrongdoing). [Latin *dono* give]

condor /'kɒndɔː(r)/ *n.* large South American vulture. [Spanish from Quechua]

conduce /kən'djuːs/ *v.* (**-cing**) (foll. by *to*) contribute to (a result). [Latin: related to CONDUCT]

conducive *adj.* (often foll. by *to*) contributing or helping (towards something).

conduct *–n.* /'kɒndʌkt/ **1** behaviour. **2** activity or manner of directing or managing (a business, war, etc.). *–v.* /kən'dʌkt/ **1** lead or guide. **2** direct or manage (a business etc.). **3** (also *absol.*) be the conductor of (an orchestra etc.). **4** transmit (heat, electricity, etc.) by conduction. **5** *refl.* behave. [Latin *duco duct-* lead]

conductance /kən'dʌkt(ə)ns/ *n.* power of a specified material to conduct electricity.

conduction /kən'dʌkʃ(ə)n/ *n.* transmission of heat, electricity, etc. through a substance. [Latin: related to CONDUCT]

conductive /kən'dʌktɪv/ *adj.* transmitting (esp. heat, electricity, etc.). □ **conductivity** /ˌkɒndʌk'tɪvɪtɪ/ *n.*

conductor *n.* **1** person who directs an orchestra etc. **2** (*fem.* **conductress**) person who collects fares in a bus etc. **3** thing that conducts heat or electricity. [Latin: related to CONDUCT]

conduit /'kɒndɪt, -djʊɪt/ *n.* **1** channel or pipe conveying liquids. **2** tube or trough protecting insulated electric wires. [medieval Latin: related to CONDUCT]

cone *n.* **1** solid figure with a circular (or other curved) plane base, tapering to a point. **2** thing of similar shape. **3** dry fruit of a conifer. **4** ice-cream cornet. [Latin from Greek]

coney var. of CONY.

Coney Island /'kəʊnɪ/ resort in the US, in New York City, forming part of Long Island; its amusement parks attract many tourists.

confab /'kɒnfæb/ *colloq.* *–n.* = CONFABULATION (see CONFABULATE). *–v.* (**-bb-**) = CONFABULATE. [abbreviation]

confabulate /kən'fæbjʊˌleɪt/ *v.* (**-ting**) converse, chat. □ **confabulation** /-'leɪʃ(ə)n/ *n.* [Latin: related to FABLE]

confection /kən'fekʃ(ə)n/ *n.* dish or delicacy made with sweet ingredients. [Latin *conficio* prepare]

confectioner *n.* maker or retailer of confectionery.

confectionery *n.* confections, esp. sweets.

confederacy /kən'fedərəsɪ/ *n.* (*pl.* **-ies**) league or alliance, esp. of confederate states. [French: related to CONFEDERATE]

confederate /kən'fedərət/ *–adj.* esp. *Polit.* allied. *–n.* **1** ally, esp. (in a bad sense) accomplice. **2** (**Confederate**) supporter of the Confederate States. *–v.* /-ˌreɪt/ (**-ting**) (often foll. by *with*) bring or come into alliance. [Latin: related to FEDERAL]

Confederate States *n.pl.* states which seceded from the US in 1860–1.

confederation /kənˌfedə'reɪʃ(ə)n/ *n.* **1** union or alliance, esp. of states. **2** confederating or being confederated.

♦ **Confederation of British Industry** *n.* (also **CBI**) independent non-party organization formed in 1965, by a merger of the National Association of British Manufacturers, the British Employers Confederation, and the Federation of British Industry, to promote prosperity in British industry and to represent industry in dealings with the government. The CBI represents, directly or indirectly, some 250 000 companies. The governing body is the Confederation of British Industry Council, which meets monthly; there are 13 Regional Councils that deal with local industrial problems.

---

confer /kən'fɜː(r)/ *v.* (**-rr-**) **1** (often foll. by *on*, *upon*) grant or bestow. **2** (often foll. by *with*) converse, consult. □ **conferrable** *adj.* [Latin *confero collat-* bring together]

conference /'kɒnfərəns/ *n.* **1** consultation. **2** meeting for discussion. [French or medieval Latin: related to CONFER]

♦ **conference lines** see SHIPPING CONFERENCE.

♦ **conferencing** see AUDIOCONFERENCING; TELECONFERENCE; VIDEOCONFERENCING.

---

conferment /kən'fɜːmənt/ *n.* conferring of a degree, honour, etc.

confess /kən'fes/ *v.* **1 a** (also *absol.*) acknowledge or admit (a fault, crime, etc.). **b** (foll. by *to*) admit to. **2** admit reluctantly. **3 a** (also *absol.*) declare (one's sins) to a priest. **b** (of a priest) hear the confession of. [Latin *confiteor -fess-*]

confessedly /kən'fesɪdlɪ/ *adv.* by one's own or general admission.

confession /kən'feʃ(ə)n/ *n.* **1 a** act of confessing. **b** thing confessed. **2** (in full **confession of faith**) declaration of one's beliefs or principles.

confessional *–n.* enclosed stall in a church in which the priest hears confessions. *–adj.* of confession.

confessor *n.* priest who hears confessions and gives spiritual counsel.

confetti /kən'fetɪ/ *n.* small pieces of coloured paper thrown by wedding guests at the bride and groom. [Italian]

confidant /'kɒnfɪˌdænt/ *n.* (*fem.* **confidante** pronunc. same) person trusted with knowledge of one's private affairs. [related to CONFIDE]

confide /kən'faɪd/ *v.* (**-ding**) **1** (foll. by *in*) talk confidentially to. **2** (usu. foll. by *to*) tell (a secret etc.) in confidence. **3** (foll. by *to*) entrust (an object of care, a task, etc.) to. [Latin *confido* trust]

confidence /'kɒnfɪd(ə)ns/ *n.* **1** firm trust. **2 a** feeling of reliance or certainty. **b** sense of self-reliance; boldness. **3** something told as a secret. □ **in confidence** as a secret. **in a person's confidence** trusted with a person's secrets. **take into one's confidence** confide in. [Latin: related to CONFIDE]

confidence trick *n.* swindle in which the victim is persuaded to trust the swindler. □ **confidence trickster** *n.*

confident *adj.* feeling or showing confidence; bold. □ **confidently** *adv.* [Italian: related to CONFIDE]

confidential /ˌkɒnfɪ'denʃ(ə)l/ *adj.* **1** spoken or written in confidence. **2** entrusted with secrets (*confidential secretary*). **3** confiding. □ **confidentiality** /-ʃɪ'ælɪtɪ/ *n.* **confidentially** *adv.*

♦ **confidentiality clause** *n.* clause in a contract of employment that details certain types of information the employee will acquire on joining the firm that may not be passed on to anyone outside the firm.

---

configuration /kənˌfɪgjʊ'reɪʃ(ə)n/ *n.* **1** arrangement in a particular form. **2** form or figure resulting from this. **3** *Computing* hardware and its arrangement of connections etc. [Latin: related to FIGURE]

configure *v.* (**-ring**) *Computing* select various optional settings of (a program) so that it will run to best advantage on a particular computer. The program may need to know whether the display is monochrome or colour, what sort of printer is available, how many disks are available, and so on. Once the program has been configured, the initial settings will be stored and used the next time the program is run. All kinds of programs, from word-processing programs on microcomputers to mainframe operating systems, need to be configured.

confine *–v.* /kən'faɪn/ (**-ning**) **1** keep or restrict (within certain limits). **2** imprison. *–n.* /'kɒnfaɪn/ (usu. in *pl.*) limit, boundary. [Latin *finis* limit]

confinement *n.* **1** confining or being confined. **2** time of childbirth.

confirm /kən'fɜːm/ *v.* **1** provide support for the truth or correctness of. **2** (foll. by *in*) encourage (a person) in (an opinion etc.). **3** establish more firmly (power, possession, etc.). **4** make formally valid. **5** administer the religious rite of confirmation to. [Latin: related to FIRM[1]]

confirmation /ˌkɒnfə'meɪʃ(ə)n/ *n.* **1** confirming or being confirmed. **2** rite confirming a baptized person as a member of the Christian Church.

confirmed *adj.* firmly settled in some habit or condition (*confirmed bachelor*).

♦ **confirmed letter of credit** see LETTER OF CREDIT.

♦ **confirming house** *n.* organization that purchases goods from local exporters on behalf of overseas buyers. It may act as a principal or an agent, invariably pays for the goods in the exporters' own currency, and purchases on a contract that is enforceable in the exporters' own country. The overseas buyer, who usu. pays the confirming house a commission or its equivalent, regards the confirming house as a local buying agent, who will negotiate the best prices on its behalf, arrange for the shipment and insurance of the goods, and provide information regarding the goods being sold and the status of the various exporters.

confiscate /'kɒnfɪˌskeɪt/ *v.* (**-ting**) take or seize by authority. □ **confiscation** /-'skeɪʃ(ə)n/ *n.* [Latin: related to FISCAL]

conflagration /ˌkɒnflə'greɪʃ(ə)n/ *n.* great and destructive fire. [Latin: related to FLAGRANT]

conflate /kən'fleɪt/ *v.* (**-ting**) blend or fuse together (esp. two variant texts into one). □ **conflation** /-'fleɪʃ(ə)n/ *n.* [Latin *flo flat-* blow]

conflict *–n.* /'kɒnflɪkt/ **1 a** state of opposition. **b** fight, struggle. **2** (often foll. by *of*) disagreement, clashing. See CONFLICT OF INTERESTS. *–v.* /kən'flɪkt/ clash; be incompatible. [Latin *fligo flict-* strike]

♦ **conflict of interests** *n.* situation that can arise if a person (or firm) acts in two or more separate capacities and the objectives in these capacities are not identical. The conflict may be between self-interest and the interest of a company for which a person works or it could arise when a person is a director of two companies, which find themselves competing. The proper course of action in the case of a conflict of interests is for these interests to be declared by the person concerned, who should make known the way in which they conflict and abstain from voting or sharing in the decision-making procedure involving these interests.

confluence /'kɒnfluəns/ *n.* **1** place where two rivers meet. **2 a** coming together. **b** crowd of people. [Latin *fluo* flow]

confluent *–adj.* flowing together, uniting. *–n.* stream joining another.

conform /kən'fɔːm/ *v.* **1** comply with rules or general custom. **2** (foll. by *to, with*) comply with; be in accordance with. **3** (often foll. by *to*) be or make suitable. [Latin: related to FORM]

conformable *adj.* **1** (often foll. by *to*) similar. **2** (often foll. by *with*) consistent. **3** (often foll. by *to*) adaptable.

conformation /ˌkɒnfɔː'meɪʃ(ə)n/ *n.* way a thing is formed; shape.

conformist /kən'fɔːmɪst/ *–n.* person who conforms to an established practice. *–adj.* conforming, conventional. □ **conformism** *n.*

conformity *n.* **1** accordance with established practice. **2** agreement, suitability.

confound /kən'faʊnd/ *–v.* **1** perplex, baffle. **2** confuse (in one's mind). **3** *archaic* defeat, overthrow. *–int.* expressing annoyance (*confound you!*). [Latin *confundo -fus-* mix up]

confounded *attrib. adj. colloq.* damned.

♦ **Confravision** *propr.* see VIDEOCONFERENCING.

confront /kən'frʌnt/ *v.* **1 a** face in hostility or defiance. **b** face up to and deal with. **2** (of a difficulty etc.) present itself to. **3** (foll. by *with*) bring (a person) face to face with (an accusation etc.). **4** meet or stand facing. □ **confrontation** /ˌkɒnfrʌn'teɪʃ(ə)n/ *n.* **confrontational** /ˌkɒnfrʌn'teɪʃən(ə)l/ *adj.* [French from medieval Latin]

Confucian /kən'fjuːʃ(ə)n/ *adj.* of Confucius or his philosophy. □ **Confucianism** *n.* [*Confucius*, name of a Chinese philosopher]

confuse /kən'fjuːz/ *v.* (**-sing**) **1** perplex, bewilder. **2** mix up in the mind; mistake (one for another). **3** make indistinct (*confuse the issue*). **4** (often as **confused** *adj.*) throw into disorder. □ **confusedly** /-zɪdlɪ/ *adv.* **confusing** *adj.* [related to CONFOUND]

confusion *n.* confusing or being confused.

confute /kən'fjuːt/ *v.* (**-ting**) prove (a person or argument) to be in error. □ **confutation** /ˌkɒnfjuː'teɪʃ(ə)n/ *n.* [Latin]

conga /'kɒŋgə/ *–n.* **1** Latin-American dance, with a line of dancers one behind the other. **2** tall narrow drum beaten with the hands. *–v.* (**congas, congaed** /-gəd/ or **conga'd, congaing** /-gəɪŋ/) perform the conga. [Spanish *conga* (feminine), = of the Congo]

congeal /kən'dʒiːl/ *v.* **1** make or become semi-solid by

Congo /'kɒŋgəʊ/ **Democratic Republic of** (formerly (1908–60) **Belgian Congo**; (1971–97) **Republic of Zaïre**) country in central Africa with a short coastline on the Atlantic Ocean. The economy is largely based on mineral exports, particularly of diamonds, copper, and the country is one of the world's major producers of cobalt. There are also deposits of manganese, uranium, zinc, gold, and other minerals. Offshore oil, exploited since 1975, is also exported and the Congo River is an important source of hydroelectric power. Agricultural production has been adversely affected by drought and political unrest in recent years. Coffee, rubber, cotton, and palm oil are exported and cassava, bananas, sugar cane, and maize are the principal food crops. Manufacturing industry produces textiles, leather goods, building materials, wood products, food and drink, and tobacco.

History. The area became a Belgian colony in the late 19th and early 20th centuries. Independence as the Republic of the Congo in 1960 was followed by civil war and UN intervention; the present name was adopted in 1971. President Mobutu, who came to power in 1965, bowed to pressure for political reform in 1990, but delays in the drafting of a new constitution and the implementation of a multi-party system of democratic government has led to violent riots and political and economic crisis. A transitional government was elected in 1992; however, Mobutu set up a rural government during the period 1993–94. Civil war erupted in 1996 following conflict between Zaïrean Tutsi rebels and Hutu militia who had fled from Rwanda. By mid-1997 rebels held most of the country and Mobutu fled. Laurent Kabila, the rebel leader became head of state. President, Laurent Kabila; prime minister, Faustin Birindwa; capital, Kinshasa. □ **Congolese** /ˌkɒŋgə'liːz/ *adj.* & *n.*

languages	French (official), Swahili, Lingala
currency	Congolese franc
pop. (1996)	45 259 000
GNP (1991)	US$8.1B
literacy	86% (m); 67% (f)
life expectancy	50 (m); 53 (f)

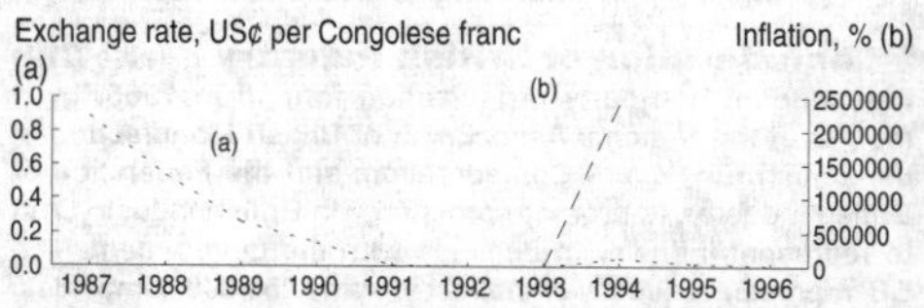

cooling. **2** (of blood etc.) coagulate. □ **congelation** /ˌkɒndʒɪˈleɪʃ(ə)n/ *n.* [French from Latin *gelo* freeze]

congenial /kənˈdʒiːnɪəl/ *adj.* **1** (often foll. by *with*, *to*) pleasant because like-minded. **2** (often foll. by *to*) suited or agreeable. □ **congeniality** /-ˈælɪtɪ/ *n.* **congenially** *adv.* [from COM-, GENIAL]

congenital /kənˈdʒenɪt(ə)l/ *adj.* **1** (esp. of disease) existing from birth. **2** as such from birth (*congenital liar*). □ **congenitally** *adv.* [Latin: related to COM-]

conger /ˈkɒŋgə(r)/ *n.* (in full **conger eel**) large marine eel. [Greek *goggros*]

congeries /kənˈdʒɪəriːz/ *n.* (*pl.* same) disorderly collection; mass, heap. [Latin *congero* heap together]

■ **Usage** The form *congery*, formed under the misapprehension that *congeries* is plural only, is incorrect.

congest /kənˈdʒest/ *–v.* (esp. as **congested** *–adj.*) affect with congestion. [Latin *congero -gest-* heap together]

congestion /kənˈdʒestʃ(ə)n/ *n.* abnormal accumulation or obstruction, esp. of traffic etc. or of blood or mucus in part of the body.

conglomerate /kənˈglɒmərət/ *–adj.* gathered into a rounded mass. *–n.* **1** heterogeneous mass. **2** group of companies merged into one entity, although active in totally different fields. A conglomerate is usu. formed by a company wishing to diversify so that it is not totally dependent on one industry. Many tobacco firms and brewers have diversified in this way. *–v.* /kənˈglɒməˌreɪt/ (**-ting**) collect into a coherent mass. □ **conglomeration** /kənˌglɒməˈreɪʃ(ə)n/ *n.* [Latin *glomus -eris* ball]

Congo River (formerly **Zaïre River**) major river in central Africa, flowing largely within the Democratic Republic of Congo before entering the Atlantic. It is a potential source of hydroelectricity.

congratulate /kənˈgrætʃʊˌleɪt/ *v.* (**-ting**) (often foll. by *on*) **1** express pleasure at the happiness, good fortune, or excellence of (a person). **2** *refl.* think oneself fortunate or clever. □ **congratulatory** /-lətərɪ/ *adj.* [Latin *gratus* pleasing]

congratulation /kənˌgrætʃʊˈleɪʃ(ə)n/ *n.* **1** congratulating. **2** (usu. in *pl.*) expression of this.

congregate /ˈkɒŋgrɪˌgeɪt/ *v.* (**-ting**) collect or gather into a crowd. [Latin *grex greg-* flock]

congregation /ˌkɒŋgrɪˈgeɪʃ(ə)n/ *n.* **1** gathering of people, esp. for religious worship. **2** body of persons regularly attending a particular church etc. [Latin: related to CONGREGATE]

congregational *adj.* **1** of a congregation. **2** (**Congregational**) of or adhering to Congregationalism.

Congregationalism *n.* system whereby individual churches are largely self-governing. □ **Congregationalist** *n.*

congress /ˈkɒŋgres/ *n.* **1** formal meeting of delegates for discussion. **2** (**Congress**) national legislative body, esp. of the US. □ **congressional** /kənˈgreʃən(ə)l/ *adj.* [Latin *gradior gress-* walk]

congressman *n.* (*fem.* **congresswoman**) member of the US Congress.

congruent /ˈkɒŋgrʊənt/ *adj.* **1** (often foll. by *with*) suitable, agreeing. **2** *Geom.* (of figures) coinciding exactly when superimposed. □ **congruence** *n.* **congruency** *n.* [Latin *congruo* agree]

congruous /ˈkɒŋgrʊəs/ *adj.* suitable, agreeing; fitting. □ **congruity** /kənˈgruːɪtɪ/ *n.* [Latin: related to CONGRUENT]

conic /ˈkɒnɪk/ *adj.* of a cone. [Greek: related to CONE]

conical *adj.* cone-shaped.

conifer /ˈkɒnɪfə(r)/ *n.* tree usu. bearing cones. □ **coniferous** /kəˈnɪfərəs/ *adj.* [Latin: related to CONE]

con. inv. *abbr.* = CONSULAR INVOICE.

conjectural /kənˈdʒektʃər(ə)l/ *adj.* based on conjecture.

conjecture /kənˈdʒektʃə(r)/ *–n.* **1** formation of an opinion on incomplete information; guessing. **2** guess. *–v.* (**-ring**) guess. [Latin *conjectura* from *jacio* throw]

conjoin /kənˈdʒɔɪn/ *v. formal* join, combine.

conjoint /kənˈdʒɔɪnt/ *adj. formal* associated, conjoined.

conjugal /ˈkɒndʒʊg(ə)l/ *adj.* of marriage or the relationship of husband and wife. [Latin *conjux* consort]

conjugate *–v.* /ˈkɒndʒuˌgeɪt/ (**-ting**) **1** *Gram.* list the different forms of (a verb). **2 a** unite. **b** become fused. *–adj.* /ˈkɒndʒʊgət/ **1** joined together, paired. **2** fused. [Latin *jugum* yoke]

conjugation /ˌkɒndʒʊˈgeɪʃ(ə)n/ *n. Gram.* system of verbal inflection.

conjunct /kənˈdʒʌŋkt/ *adj.* joined together; combined; associated. [Latin from *juntus* joined]

conjunction /kənˈdʒʌŋkʃ(ə)n/ *n.* **1** joining; connection. **2** *Gram.* word used to connect clauses or sentences or words in the same clause (e.g. *and*, *but*, *if*). **3** combination (of events or circumstances). **4** apparent proximity to each other of two bodies in the solar system.

conjunctiva /ˌkɒndʒʌŋkˈtaɪvə/ *n.* (*pl.* **-s**) mucous membrane covering the front of the eye and the lining inside the eyelids.

conjunctive /kənˈdʒʌŋktɪv/ *adj.* **1** serving to join. **2** *Gram.* of the nature of a conjunction.

conjunctivitis /kənˌdʒʌŋktɪˈvaɪtɪs/ *n.* inflammation of the conjunctiva.

conjure /ˈkʌndʒə(r)/ *v.* (**-ring**) **1** perform tricks which are seemingly magical, esp. by movements of the hands. **2** summon (a spirit or demon) to appear. □ **conjure up 1** produce as if by magic. **2** evoke. [Latin *juro* swear]

conjuror *n.* (also **conjurer**) performer of conjuring tricks.

conk[1] *v.* (usu. foll. by *out*) *colloq.* **1** (of a machine etc.) break down. **2** (of a person) become exhausted and give up; fall asleep; faint; die. [origin unknown]

Congo /ˈkɒŋgəʊ/, **Republic of** country in W central Africa, with a short Atlantic coastline, lying on the Equator with Democratic Republic of Congo to the E. Agriculture is the principal occupation, sugar cane, cocoa, coffee, tobacco, and palm oil being the main cash crops. The country is a major reserve of virgin rain forest and timber is an important export. Oil and petroleum products are the largest source of revenue; other mineral resources include lead, zinc, copper, and gold. The economy is weak, with many loss-making state companies and much bureaucratic wastage. Foreign debt is high and recent strikes have led to a decrease in GDP.

History. Formerly a French colony, the country became fully independent in 1960 and a Marxist state in 1970. A new constitution was agreed in 1991 and the first multi-party elections were held in 1993. In 1997 there were violent clashes, centred on Brazzaville, between forces loyal to the elected president, Pascal Lissouba, and the forces of former dictator Denis Sassou-Nguesso, who, with the aid of Angolan troops, emerged victorious. Sassou-Nguesso was sworn in as president in late 1997. President, Denis Sassou-Nguesso; capital, Brazzaville. □ **Congolese** /ˌkɒŋgəˈliːz/ *adj.* & *n.*

languages	French (official), African languages
currency	CFA franc (CFAF) of 100 centimes
pop. (1996)	2 665 000
GNP (1994)	US$1.6B
literacy	83% (m); 67% (f)
life expectancy	49 (m); 54 (f)

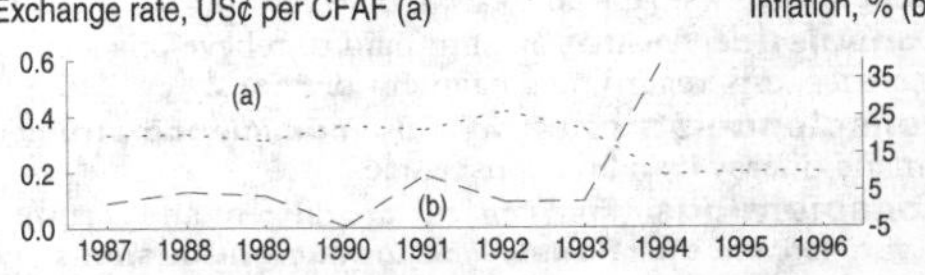

---

conk[2] *slang* –*n.* **1** nose or head. **2** punch on the nose or head. –*v.* hit on the nose or head. [perhaps = CONCH]

conker *n.* **1** fruit of the horse chestnut. **2** (in *pl.*) children's game played with conkers on strings. [dial. *conker* snail-shell]

con man *n.* confidence trickster.

Conn. *abbr.* Connecticut.

conn *US* var. of CON[4].

Connacht see CONNAUGHT.

Connaught /kəˈnɔːt/ (also **Connacht**) mainly agricultural province of the Republic of Ireland; pop. (1991) 423 031.

connect /kəˈnekt/ *v.* **1** (often foll. by *to, with*) join (two things, or one thing with another). **2** be joined or joinable. **3** (often foll. by *with*) associate mentally or practically. **4** (foll. by *with*) (of a train etc.) be timed to arrive with another, so passengers can transfer. **5** put into communication by telephone. **6 a** (usu. in *passive*; foll. by *with*) associate with others in relationships etc. **b** be meaningful or relevant. **7** *colloq.* hit or strike effectively. [Latin *necto nex-* bind]

Connecticut /kəˈnetɪkət/ state in the NE US; pop. (est. 1996) 3 274 238; capital, Hartford. Manufactures include clocks, silver and brassware, engines, submarines, and helicopters; insurance is a major industry.

connecting-rod *n.* rod between the piston and crankpin etc. in an internal combustion engine.

connection /kəˈnekʃ(ə)n/ *n.* (also **connexion**) **1** connecting or being connected. **2** point at which two things are connected. **3** link, esp. by telephone. **4** connecting train etc. **5** (often in *pl.*) relative or associate, esp. one with influence. **6** relation of ideas. □ **in connection with** with reference to.

connective *adj.* connecting, esp. of body tissue connecting, separating, etc., organs etc.

connector *n.* thing that connects.

conning tower *n.* **1** superstructure of a submarine containing the periscope. **2** armoured wheel-house of a warship. [from CON[4]]

connive /kəˈnaɪv/ *v.* (**-ving**) **1** (foll. by *at*) disregard or tacitly consent to (a wrongdoing). **2** (usu. foll. by *with*) conspire. □ **connivance** *n.* [Latin *conniveo* shut the eyes]

connoisseur /ˌkɒnəˈsɜː(r)/ *n.* (often foll. by *of, in*) expert judge in matters of taste. [French *connaître* know]

connote /kəˈnəʊt/ *v.* (**-ting**) **1** (of a word etc.) imply in addition to the literal or primary meaning. **2** mean, signify. □ **connotation** /ˌkɒnəˈteɪʃ(ə)n/ *n.* **connotative** /ˈkɒnəˌteɪtɪv/ *adj.* [medieval Latin: related to NOTE]

connubial /kəˈnjuːbɪəl/ *adj.* of marriage or the relationship of husband and wife. [Latin *nubo* marry]

conquer /ˈkɒŋkə(r)/ *v.* **1 a** overcome and control militarily. **b** be victorious. **2** overcome by effort. □ **conqueror** *n.* [Latin *conquiro* win]

conquest /ˈkɒŋkwest/ *n.* **1** conquering or being conquered. **2 a** conquered territory. **b** something won. **3** person whose affection has been won.

CONS *abbr. Computing* connection-oriented network service.

consanguineous /ˌkɒnsæŋˈgwɪnɪəs/ *adj.* descended from the same ancestor; akin. □ **consanguinity** *n.* [Latin *sanguis* blood]

conscience /ˈkɒnʃ(ə)ns/ *n.* moral sense of right and wrong, esp. as affecting behaviour. □ **in all conscience** *colloq.* by any reasonable standard. **on one's conscience** causing one feelings of guilt. **prisoner of conscience** person imprisoned by the state for his or her political or religious views. [Latin: related to SCIENCE]

conscience money *n.* sum paid to relieve one's conscience, esp. regarding a payment previously evaded.

conscience-stricken *adj.* (also **conscience-struck**) made uneasy by a bad conscience.

conscientious /ˌkɒnʃɪˈenʃəs/ *adj.* diligent and scrupulous. □ **conscientiously** *adv.* **conscientiousness** *n.* [medieval Latin: related to CONSCIENCE]

conscientious objector *n.* person who for reasons of conscience objects to military service etc.

conscious /ˈkɒnʃəs/ –*adj.* **1** awake and aware of one's surroundings and identity. **2** (usu. foll. by *of* or *that*) aware, knowing. **3** (of actions, emotions, etc.) realized or recognized by the doer; intentional. **4** (in *comb.*) aware of; concerned with (*fashion-conscious*). –*n.* (prec. by *the*) the conscious mind. □ **consciously** *adv.* **consciousness** *n.* [Latin *scio* know]

conscript –*v.* /kənˈskrɪpt/ summon for compulsory state (esp. military) service. –*n.* /ˈkɒnskrɪpt/ conscripted person. □ **conscription** /kənˈskrɪpʃ(ə)n/ *n.* [Latin *scribo* write]

consecrate /ˈkɒnsɪˌkreɪt/ *v.* (**-ting**) **1** make or declare sacred; dedicate formally to religious or divine purpose. **2** (foll. by *to*) devote to (a purpose). □ **consecration** /-ˈkreɪʃ(ə)n/ *n.* [Latin: related to SACRED]

consecutive /kənˈsekjʊtɪv/ *adj.* **1 a** following continuously. **b** in an unbroken or logical order. **2** *Gram.* expressing a consequence. □ **consecutively** *adv.* [Latin *sequor secut-* follow]

consensus /kənˈsensəs/ *n.* (often foll. by *of*; often *attrib.*) general agreement or opinion. [Latin: related to CONSENT]

consent /kənˈsent/ –*v.* (often foll. by *to*) express willingness, give permission, agree. –*n.* voluntary agreement, permission. [Latin *sentio* feel]

consequence /ˈkɒnsɪkwəns/ *n.* **1** result or effect of what has gone before. **2** importance. □ **in consequence** as a result. **take the consequences** accept the results of one's choice or action. [Latin: related to CONSECUTIVE]

consequent *adj.* **1** (often foll. by *on, upon*) following as a result or consequence. **2** logically consistent.

consequential /ˌkɒnsɪˈkwenʃ(ə)l/ *adj.* **1** consequent; resulting indirectly. **2** important.

♦ **consequential-loss policy** *n.* = BUSINESS-INTERRUPTION POLICY.

---

consequently *adv.* & *conj.* as a result; therefore.

conservancy /kənˈsɜːvənsɪ/ *n.* (*pl.* **-ies**) **1** body controlling a port, river, etc., or preserving the environment. **2** official environmental conservation. [Latin: related to CONSERVE]

conservation /ˌkɒnsəˈveɪʃ(ə)n/ *n.* preservation, esp. of the natural environment. [Latin: related to CONSERVE]

conservationist *n.* supporter of environmental conservation.

conservation of energy *n.* principle that the total quantity of energy in any system that is not subject to external action remains constant.

♦ **conservatism** /kənˈsɜːvəˌtɪzəm/ *n.* **1 a** moderation; prudence. **b** aversion to rapid change. **2** *Finance* prudent and not overoptimistic view of the state of affairs of a company or other organization. Because it is regarded as imprudent to distribute to shareholders profits that may not materialize, it is a general principle of accounting not to anticipate profits before they are realized but to anticipate losses as soon as they become foreseeable. See also TRUE AND FAIR VIEW; PRUDENCE CONCEPT.

---

conservative –*adj.* **1 a** averse to rapid change. **b** (of views, taste, etc.) moderate, avoiding extremes. **2** (of an estimate etc.) purposely low. **3** (**Conservative**) of Conservatives or the Conservative Party. **4** tending to conserve. –*n.* **1** conservative person. **2** (**Conservative**) supporter or member of the Conservative Party. [Latin: related to CONSERVE]

Conservative Party *n.* political party promoting free enterprise and private ownership.

conservatoire /kənˈsɜːvəˌtwɑː(r)/ *n.* (usu. European) school of music or other arts. [French from Italian]

conservatory /kənˈsɜːvətərɪ/ *n.* (*pl.* **-ies**) **1** greenhouse for tender plants, esp. attached to a house. **2** esp. *US* = CONSERVATOIRE. [Latin and Italian: related to CONSERVE]

conserve –*v.* /kənˈsɜːv/ (**-ving**) keep from harm or damage, esp. for later use. –*n.* /'kɒnsɜːv/ fresh fruit jam. [Latin *servo* keep]

consider /kən'sɪdə(r)/ *v.* **1** contemplate mentally, esp. in order to reach a conclusion. **2** examine the merits of. **3** look attentively at. **4** take into account; show consideration or regard for. **5** (foll. by *that*) have the opinion. **6** regard as. **7** (as **considered** *adj.*) formed after careful thought (*a considered opinion*). □ **all things considered** taking everything into account. [French from Latin]

considerable *adj.* **1** much; a lot of (*considerable pain*). **2** notable, important. □ **considerably** *adv.*

considerate /kən'sɪdərət/ *adj.* thoughtful towards others; careful not to cause hurt or inconvenience. □ **considerately** *adv.* [Latin: related to CONSIDER]

consideration /kən,sɪdə'reɪʃ(ə)n/ *n.* **1** careful thought. **2** thoughtfulness for others; being considerate. **3** fact or thing taken into account. **4** compensation; payment or reward. **5** *Law* promise by one party to a contract that constitutes the price for buying a promise from the other party to the contract. A consideration is essential if a contract, other than a deed, is to be valid. It usu. consists of a promise to do or not to do something or to pay a sum of money. **6** money value of a contract for the purchase or sale of securities on the London Stock Exchange, before commissions, charges, stamp-duty, and any other expenses have been deducted. □ **in consideration of** in return for; on account of. **take into consideration** make allowance for. **under consideration** being considered.

considering –*prep.* in view of; taking into consideration. –*adv. colloq.* taking everything into account (*not so bad, considering*).

consign /kən'saɪn/ *v.* (often foll. by *to*) **1** hand over; deliver. **2** assign; commit. **3** transmit or send (goods). [Latin: related to SIGN]

◆ **consignee** /,kɒnsaɪ'niː/ *n.* **1** any person or organization to whom goods are sent. **2** agent who sells goods on consignment (see CONSIGNMENT).

---

consignment *n.* **1** consigning or being consigned. **2** shipment or delivery of goods sent at one time. □ **on consignment** (of goods) sent by a principal (consignor) to an agent (consignee), usu. in a foreign country, for sale either at an agreed price or at the best market price. The agent, who usu. works for a commission, does not normally pay for the goods until they are sold and does not own them, but usu. has possession of them. The final settlement, often called a **consignment account**, details the cost of the goods, the expenses incurred, the agent's commission, and the proceeds of the sale.

◆ **consignment note** *n.* document accompanying a consignment of goods in transit. It is signed by the consignee on delivery and acts as evidence that the goods have been received. It gives the names and addresses of both consignor and consignee, details the goods, usu. gives their gross weight, and states who has responsibility for insuring them while in transit. It is not a negotiable document (cf. BILL OF LADING) and in some circumstances is called a **waybill**.

◆ **consignor** *n.* **1** any person or organization that sends goods to a consignee. **2** principal who sells goods on consignment (see CONSIGNMENT).

---

consist /kən'sɪst/ *v.* **1** (foll. by *of*) be composed; have as ingredients. **2** (foll. by *in, of*) have its essential features as specified. [Latin *sisto* stop]

consistency /kən'sɪstənsɪ/ *n.* (*pl.* **-ies**) **1** degree of density, firmness, or viscosity, esp. of thick liquids. **2** being consistent. [Latin: related to CONSIST]

◆ **consistency concept** *n.* concept of applying the same accounting principles to successive accounting periods. It is possible to quantify profit in a variety of ways. If different methods are used in different periods, one period cannot be compared with another and no clear trend can emerge; thus similar methods should be maintained from year to year. This may still make it difficult to compare one company with another, a problem to which accounting standards are a partial solution (see STATEMENT OF STANDARD ACCOUNTING PRACTICE).

---

consistent *adj.* **1** (usu. foll. by *with*) compatible or in harmony. **2** (of a person) constant to the same principles. □ **consistently** *adv.* [Latin: related to CONSIST]

consistory /kən'sɪstərɪ/ *n.* (*pl.* **-ies**) *RC Ch.* council of cardinals (with or without the pope). [Latin: related to CONSIST]

consolation /,kɒnsə'leɪʃ(ə)n/ *n.* **1** consoling or being consoled. **2** consoling thing or person. □ **consolatory** /kən'sɒlətərɪ/ *adj.*

consolation prize *n.* prize given to a competitor who just fails to win a main prize.

console[1] /kən'səʊl/ *v.* (**-ling**) comfort, esp. in grief or disappointment. [Latin: related to SOLACE]

■ **Usage** *Console* is often confused with *condole*, which is different in that it is always followed by *with*.

console[2] /'kɒnsəʊl/ *n.* **1** panel for switches, controls, etc. **2** cabinet for a television etc. **3** cabinet with the keyboards and stops of an organ. **4** bracket supporting a shelf etc. [French]

consolidate /kən'sɒlɪ,deɪt/ *v.* (**-ting**) **1** make or become strong or secure. **2** combine (territories, companies, debts, etc.) into one whole. □ **consolidator** *n.* [Latin: related to SOLID]

◆ **consolidated accounts** *n.pl.* combined accounts of a group of companies. Although a parent company and its subsidiaries (the companies it owns and controls) are separate companies, it is customary to combine their results in a single set of accounts, which eliminates inter-company shareholdings and inter-company indebtedness; it also aggregates the assets and liabilities of all the companies. Parent companies of groups are required by law to prepare and file consolidated accounts in addition to individual accounts of the subsidiary companies. See also HOLDING COMPANY.

◆ **consolidated annuities** see CONSOLS.

◆ **Consolidated Fund** *n.* the Exchequer account, held at the Bank of England and controlled by the Treasury, into which taxes are paid and from which government expenditure is made. It was formed in 1787 by the consolidation of several government funds.

◆ **consolidation** /kən,sɒlɪ'deɪʃ(ə)n/ *n.* **1** consolidating, combining. **2** increase in the nominal price of a company's shares, by combining a specified number of lower-price shares into one higher-priced share. For example five 20p shares may be consolidated into one £1 share.

◆ **Consols** /'kɒnsɒlz/ *n.pl.* government securities that pay interest but have no redemption date. The present bonds, called **consolidated annuities** or **consolidated stock**, are the result of merging several loans at various different times going back to the 18th century. Their original interest rate was 3% on the nominal price of £100; most now pay 2½% and therefore stand at a price that makes their annual yield comparable to long-dated gilt-edged securities.

---

consommé /kən'sɒmeɪ/ *n.* clear soup from meat stock. [French]

consonance /'kɒnsənəns/ *n.* agreement, harmony. [Latin *sono* SOUND[1]]

consonant –*n.* **1** speech sound in which the breath is at least partly obstructed, and which forms a syllable by combining with a vowel. **2** letter(s) representing this. –*adj.* (foll. by *with, to*) consistent; in agreement or harmony. □ **consonantal** /-'nænt(ə)l/ *adj.*

consort[1] –*n.* /'kɒnsɔːt/ wife or husband, esp. of royalty. –*v.* /kən'sɔːt/ **1** (usu. foll. by *with, together*) keep company. **2** harmonize. [Latin: related to SORT]

consort[2] /'kɒnsɔːt/ *n. Mus.* small group of players, singers, or instruments. [var. of CONCERT]

consortium /kən'sɔːtɪəm/ *n.* (*pl.* **-tia** or **-s**) association, esp. of two or more large companies formed on a temporary basis to quote for a large project, e.g. a new power station or dam. The companies would then work together, on agreed terms, if they were successful in obtaining the work. The purpose of forming a consortium may be to eliminate competition between the members or to pool skills, not all of which may be available to the individual companies. [Latin: related to CONSORT[1]]

♦ **consortium relief** *n.* means of enabling companies owned by a consortium to transfer to members of the consortium (or vice versa) the benefit of their tax losses or certain other payments for which they are unable to obtain tax relief in their own right. The relief is not available for all losses and the requirements for consortium status are rigidly defined.

conspicuous /kən'spɪkjʊəs/ *adj.* **1** clearly visible; attracting notice. **2** noteworthy. □ **conspicuously** *adv.* [Latin *specio* look]

conspiracy /kən'spɪrəsɪ/ *n.* (*pl.* **-ies**) **1** secret plan to commit a crime; plot. **2** conspiring. [Latin: related to CONSPIRE]

conspiracy of silence *n.* agreement to say nothing.

conspirator /kən'spɪrətə(r)/ *n.* person who takes part in a conspiracy. □ **conspiratorial** /-'tɔːrɪəl/ *adj.*

conspire /kən'spaɪə(r)/ *v.* (**-ring**) **1** combine secretly for an unlawful or harmful act. **2** (of events) seem to be working together. [Latin *spiro* breathe]

constable /'kʌnstəb(ə)l/ *n.* **1** (also **police constable**) police officer of the lowest rank. **2** governor of a royal castle. [Latin *comes stabuli* count of the stable]

constabulary /kən'stæbjʊlərɪ/ *n.* (*pl.* **-ies**) police force. [medieval Latin: related to CONSTABLE]

constancy /'kɒnstənsɪ/ *n.* being unchanging and dependable; faithfulness. [Latin: related to CONSTANT]

constant *–adj.* **1** continuous (*constant attention*). **2** occurring frequently (*constant complaints*). **3** unchanging, faithful, dependable. *–n.* **1** anything that does not vary. **2** *Math.* & *Physics* quantity or number that remains the same. □ **constantly** *adv.* [Latin *sto* stand]

Constanţa /kɒn'stæntsə/ (also **Constanza**) chief port of Romania, on the Black Sea, and the country's centre for refining and exporting oil; pop. (est. 1993) 348 985.

Constantine /'kɒnstən,taɪn/ (formerly **Cirta, Kirtha**) city in NE Algeria, manufacturing carpets and leather goods; pop. (1987) 440 842. Its port is Skikda.

Constantinople /,kɒnstæntɪ'nəʊp(ə)l/ see ISTANBUL.

constellation /,kɒnstə'leɪʃ(ə)n/ *n.* **1** group of fixed stars. **2** group of associated persons etc. [Latin *stella* star]

consternation /,kɒnstə'neɪʃ(ə)n/ *n.* anxiety, dismay. [Latin *sterno* throw down]

constipate /'kɒnstɪ,peɪt/ *v.* (**-ting**) (esp. as **constipated** *adj.*) affect with constipation. [Latin *stipo* cram]

constipation /,kɒnstɪ'peɪʃ(ə)n/ *n.* difficulty in emptying the bowels.

constituency /kən'stɪtjʊənsɪ/ *n.* (*pl.* **-ies**) **1** body of voters who elect a representative. **2** area so represented.

constituent /kən'stɪtjʊənt/ *–adj.* **1** composing or helping to make a whole. **2** able to make or change a constitution (*constituent assembly*). **3** electing. *–n.* **1** member of a constituency. **2** component part. [Latin: related to CONSTITUTE]

constitute /'kɒnstɪ,tjuːt/ *v.* (**-ting**) **1** be the components or essence of; compose. **2 a** amount to (*this constitutes a warning*). **b** formally establish (*constitutes a precedent*). **3** give legal or constitutional form to. [Latin *constituo* establish]

constitution /,kɒnstɪ'tjuːʃ(ə)n/ *n.* **1** act or method of constituting; composition. **2** body of fundamental principles by which a state or other body is governed. **3** person's inherent state of health, strength, etc. [Latin: related to CONSTITUTE]

constitutional *–adj.* **1** of or in line with the constitution. **2** inherent (*constitutional weakness*). *–n.* walk taken regularly as healthy exercise. □ **constitutionality** /-'nælɪtɪ/ *n.* **constitutionally** *adv.*

constitutive /'kɒnstɪ,tjuːtɪv/ *adj.* **1** able to form or appoint. **2** component. **3** essential.

constrain /kən'streɪn/ *v.* **1** compel. **2 a** confine forcibly; imprison. **b** restrict severely. **3** (as **constrained** *adj.*) forced, embarrassed. [Latin *stringo strict-* tie]

constraint /kən'streɪnt/ *n.* **1** constraining or being constrained. **2** restriction. **3** self-control.

constrict /kən'strɪkt/ *v.* make narrow or tight; compress. □ **constriction** *n.* **constrictive** *adj.* [Latin: related to CONSTRAIN]

constrictor *n.* **1** snake that kills by compressing. **2** muscle that contracts an organ or part of the body.

construct *–v.* /kən'strʌkt/ **1** make by fitting parts together; build, form. **2** *Geom.* delineate (a figure). *–n.* /'kɒnstrʌkt/ thing constructed, esp. by the mind. □ **constructor** /kən'strʌktə(r)/ *n.* [Latin *struo struct-* build]

construction /kən'strʌkʃ(ə)n/ *n.* **1** constructing or being constructed. **2** thing constructed. **3** interpretation or explanation. **4** syntactical arrangement of words. □ **constructional** *adj.*

constructive /kən'strʌktɪv/ *adj.* **1 a** tending to form a basis for ideas. **b** helpful, positive. **2** derived by inference. □ **constructively** *adv.*

♦ **constructive dismissal** *n.* situation that arises when an employer's behaviour towards an employee is so intolerable that the employee is left with no option but resignation. In these circumstances the employee can still claim compensation for wrongful dismissal.

♦ **constructive total loss** *n.* (also **CTL**) loss of an insured ship or cargo in which the item insured is not totally destroyed but is so severely damaged that it is not financially worth repairing. For insurance purposes it is treated as if it were an actual total loss.

construe /kən'struː/ *v.* (**-strues, -strued, -struing**) **1** interpret. **2** (often foll. by *with*) combine (words) grammatically. **3** analyse the syntax of (a sentence). **4** translate literally. [Latin: related to CONSTRUCT]

consubstantial /,kɒnsəb'stænʃ(ə)l/ *adj. Theol.* of one substance. [Church Latin: related to SUBSTANCE]

consubstantiation /,kɒnsəb,stænʃɪ'eɪʃ(ə)n/ *n. Theol.* presence of Christ's body and blood together with the bread and wine in the Eucharist.

consul /'kɒns(ə)l/ *n.* **1** official appointed by a state to protect its citizens and interests in a foreign city. **2** *hist.* either of two chief magistrates in ancient Rome. □ **consular** /-sjʊlə(r)/ *adj.* **consulship** *n.* [Latin]

♦ **consulage** see CONSULAR INVOICE.

♦ **consular invoice** *n.* export invoice that has been certified in the exporting country by the consul of the importing country. This form of invoice is required by the customs of certain countries (esp. South American countries) to enable them to charge the correct import duties. A certificate of origin may also be required. The fee charged by the consul for this or any other commercial service is called the **consulage**.

consulate /'kɒnsjʊlət/ *n.* **1** official building of a consul. **2** position of consul.

consult /kən'sʌlt/ *v.* **1** seek information or advice from. **2** (often foll. by *with*) refer to a person for advice etc. **3** take into account (feelings, interests, etc.). □ **consultative** *adj.* [Latin *consulo consult-* take counsel]

consultancy *n.* (*pl.* **-ies**) practice or position of a consultant.

consultant *n.* **1** person providing professional advice etc. **2** senior medical specialist in a hospital.

consultation /,kɒnsəl'teɪʃ(ə)n/ *n.* **1** meeting arranged to consult. **2** act or process of consulting.

consume /kən'sjuːm/ *v.* (**-ming**) **1** eat or drink. **2** destroy. **3** preoccupy, possess (*consumed with rage*). **4** use up. □ **consumable** *adj.* & *n.* [Latin *consumo -sumpt-*]

consumer *n.* **1** person who consumes, esp. one who uses a product. **2** purchaser of goods or services.

♦ **consumer advertising** *n.* advertising of goods or services specifically aimed at the potential end-user, rather than at an intermediary in the selling chain. Cf. TRADE ADVERTISING.

♦ **consumer credit** *n.* short-term loans to the public for the purchase of goods, usu. in the form of credit accounts at retail outlets, personal loans from banks and finance houses, hire purchase, and credit cards. Since the Consumer Credit Act (1974), the borrower has been given greater protection, esp. with regard to regulations establishing the true rate of interest being charged when loans are made (see ANNUAL PERCENTAGE RATE). The act also made it necessary for anyone giving credit in a business (with minor exceptions) to obtain a licence. See CONSUMER-CREDIT REGISTER.

♦ **consumer-credit register** *n.* register kept by the Director General of Fair Trading (see CONSUMER PROTECTION), as required by the Consumer Credit Act (1974), relating to the licensing or carrying on of consumer-credit businesses or consumer-hire businesses. The register contains particulars of undetermined applications, licences that are in force or have at any time been suspended or revoked, and decisions given by the Director under the act and any appeal from them. The public is entitled to inspect the register on payment of a fee.

♦ **consumer durable** see CONSUMER GOODS.

consumer goods *n.pl.* goods purchased by members of the public, not for producing other goods. **Consumer durables** are consumer goods (e.g. cars, refrigerators, and television sets), whose useful life extends over a relatively long period. The purchase of a consumer durable falls between consumption and investment, which tends to complicate macroeconomic analysis of these two variables. **Consumer non-durables** or **disposables** are goods that are used up within a short time after purchase (e.g. food, drink, newspapers, etc.). Personal services, such as those provided by doctors, hairdressers, etc., are also classed by economists as consumer goods.

consumerism *n.* **1** protection of consumers' interests. **2** (often *derog.*) continual increase in the consumption of goods. □ **consumerist** *adj.*

♦ **consumer market** *n.* market for consumer goods, as opposed to the industrial market, in which buyers of goods are not the end users.

♦ **consumer non-durable** see CONSUMER GOODS.

♦ **consumer preference** *n.* way in which consumers in a free market choose to divide their total expenditure in purchasing goods and services; these preferences constitute the basis of consumer theory. Using a limited number of assumptions, an individual's preferences can be built up into a utility function. Applying price theory to the utility functions of individuals enables a model to be constructed of the behaviour of markets in an economy.

♦ **consumer price index** *n.* (also **CPI**) *US* = RETAIL PRICE INDEX.

♦ **consumer profile** *n.* profile of a typical consumer of a product, in terms of age, sex, social class, and other characteristics.

♦ **consumer protection** *n.* protection, esp. by legal means, of consumers. In the UK, consumers are protected by the Unfair Contract Terms Act (1977) and the Sale of Goods Act (1979) against terms that attempt to restrict the seller's implied undertakings that he or she has a right to sell the goods, that the goods conform with either description or sample (see TRADE DESCRIPTION), and that they are of merchantable quality and fit for their particular purpose. There is also provision for the banning of unfair consumer trade practices in the Fair Trading Act (1973). This act provides for a **Director General of Fair Trading**, who is responsible for reviewing commercial activities relating to the supply of goods to consumers and discovering any practices against the economic interest of the consumer. The Director may refer certain practices to the **Consumer Protection Advisory Committee** or take legal action. Consumers (including individual business people) are also protected when obtaining credit by the Consumer Credit Act (1974); see CONSUMER-CREDIT REGISTER. There is provision for the imposition of standards relating to the safety of goods under the Consumer Protection Act (1987), which also makes the producer of a product liable for any damage it causes (see PRODUCTS LIABILITY).

♦ **consumer research** *n.* any form of marketing research undertaken among the final consumers of a product or service. Cf. INDUSTRIAL MARKETING RESEARCH.

♦ **Consumers' Association** *n.* (also **CA**) charitable organization formed in 1957 to provide independent and technically based guidance on the goods and services available to the public. The Consumers' Association tests and investigates products and services and publishes comparative reports on performance, quality, and value in its monthly magazine *Which?*. It also publishes *Holiday Which?* and *Gardening From Which?* as well as various books.

♦ **consumers' expenditure** *n.* = CONSUMPTION 6.

♦ **consumer theory** *n. Econ.* theory explaining the choices made by individuals and households in terms of the concept of utility. Consumers are assumed to be able to order their preferences (see CONSUMER PREFERENCE) in such a way that they can choose a basket of goods that maximize their utility, subject to the constraint that their income is limited. The application of price theory and demand theory to this problem forms the basis of microeconomics (together with the theory of the firm) and also of macroeconomics.

consummate *–v.* /'kɒnsəˌmeɪt/ (**-ting**) **1** complete; make perfect. **2** complete (a marriage) by sexual intercourse. *–adj.* /kən'sʌmɪt/ complete, perfect; fully skilled. □ **consummation** /-'meɪʃ(ə)n/ *n.* [Latin *summus* utmost]

consumption /kən'sʌmpʃ(ə)n/ *n.* **1** consuming or being consumed. **2** amount consumed. **3** use by a particular group (*a film unsuitable for children's consumption*). **4** *archaic* tuberculosis of the lungs. **5** using up of consumer goods and services for the satisfaction of the present needs of individuals, organizations, and governments. **6** (also **consumers' expenditure**) *Econ.* amount of money spent by the whole of an economy on consumer goods and services. In most economies about 80% of national income is spent on consumption, the balance going to investment (which provides for future consumption). However, the distinction between consumption and investment is not always clear as some goods, e.g. consumer durables, provide for both present and future consumption. [French: related to CONSUME]

consumptive /kən'sʌmptɪv/ *archaic –adj.* suffering or tending to suffer from consumption. *–n.* consumptive person. [medieval Latin: related to CONSUMPTION]

cont. *abbr.* **1** contents. **2** continued. **3** contract.

contact /'kɒntækt/ *–n.* **1** state or condition of touching, meeting, or communicating. **2** person who is or may be communicated with for information, assistance, etc. **3** connection for the passage of an electric current. **4** person likely to carry a contagious disease through being near an infected person. *–v.* **1** get in touch with (a person). **2** begin correspondence or personal dealings with. [Latin *tango tact-* touch]

contact lens *n.* small lens placed directly on the eyeball to correct vision.

contact print photographic print made by placing a negative directly on to printing paper and exposing it to light.

contagion /kən'teɪdʒ(ə)n/ *n.* **1 a** spreading of disease by bodily contact. **b** contagious disease. **2** moral corruption. [related to CONTACT]

contagious /kən'teɪdʒəs/ *adj.* **1 a** (of a person) likely to transmit a disease by contact. **b** (of a disease) transmitted in this way. **2** (of emotions etc.) likely to spread (*contagious enthusiasm*).

contain /kən'teɪn/ *v.* **1** hold or be capable of holding within itself; include, comprise. **2** (of measures) be equal to (*a gallon contains eight pints*). **3** prevent from moving or extending. **4** control or restrain (feelings etc.). **5** (of a number) be divisible by (a factor) without a remainder. [Latin *teneo* hold]

container *n.* **1** box, jar, etc., for holding things. **2** large metal box for transporting goods.

♦ **containerization** *n.* use of large rectangular containers for the shipment of goods. Goods are packed into the containers at the factory or loading depot and transported by road in these containers to the port of shipment, where they are loaded direct onto the ship without unpacking. At the port of destination they can again be transported by road to the final user. It is usual for such shipments to be covered by a **container bill of lading** (or **combined-transport bill of lading**).

---

containerize *v.* (also **-ise**) (**-zing** or **-sing**) pack in or transport by container.

containment *n.* action or policy of preventing the expansion of a hostile country or influence.

contaminate /kən'tæmɪˌneɪt/ *v.* (**-ting**) **1** pollute, esp. with radioactivity. **2** infect. □ **contaminant** *n.* **contamination** /-'neɪʃ(ə)n/ *n.* **contaminator** *n.* [Latin *tamen*- related to *tango* touch]

♦ **contango** /kən'tæŋgəʊ/ *n.* (*pl.* **-s**) former practice of carrying the purchase of stocks and shares over from one account day on the London Stock Exchange to the next. See CASH AND NEW. [probably an arbitrary formation]

---

contemplate /'kɒntəmˌpleɪt/ *v.* (**-ting**) **1** survey visually or mentally. **2** regard (an event) as possible. **3** intend (*he is not contemplating retiring*). **4** meditate. □ **contemplation** /-'pleɪʃ(ə)n/ *n.* [Latin]

contemplative /kən'templətɪv/ *–adj.* of or given to (esp. religious) contemplation; thoughtful. *–n.* person devoted to religious contemplation. [Latin: related to CONTEMPLATE]

contemporaneous /kənˌtempə'reɪnɪəs/ *adj.* (usu. foll. by *with*) existing or occurring at the same time. □ **contemporaneity** /-'niːɪtɪ/ *n.* [Latin: related to COM-, *tempus* time]

contemporary /kən'tempərərɪ/ *–adj.* **1** living or occurring at the same time. **2** of approximately the same age. **3** modern in style or design. *–n.* (*pl.* **-ies**) contemporary person or thing. [medieval Latin: related to CONTEMPORANEOUS]

contempt /kən'tempt/ *n.* **1** feeling that a person or thing deserves scorn or extreme reproach. **2** condition of being held in contempt. **3** = CONTEMPT OF COURT. [Latin *temno tempt-* despise]

contemptible *adj.* deserving contempt. □ **contemptibly** *adv.*

♦ **contempt of court** *n.* act that hinders the course of justice or that constitutes disrespect to the lawful authority of the court. Contempt may be divided into acts committed in court (e.g. unseemly behaviour or refusing to answer a question as a witness) and acts committed out of court (e.g. intimidating a witness or refusing to obey a court order). Contempt of court is punishable by fine or imprisonment or both.

---

contemptuous *adj.* (often foll. by *of*) feeling or showing contempt. □ **contemptuously** *adv.*

♦ **contemptuous damages** see DAMAGES.

---

contend /kən'tend/ *v.* **1** (usu. foll. by *with*) fight, argue. **2** compete. **3** assert, maintain. □ **contender** *n.* [Latin: related to TEND[1]]

content[1] /kən'tent/ *–predic. adj.* **1** satisfied; adequately happy. **2** (foll. by *to* + infin.) willing. *–v.* make content; satisfy. *–n.* contented state; satisfaction. □ **to one's heart's content** as much as one wishes. [Latin: related to CONTAIN]

content[2] /'kɒntent/ *n.* **1** (usu. in *pl.*) what is contained, esp. in a vessel, book, or house. **2** amount (of a constituent) contained (*high fat content*). **3** substance (of a speech etc.) as distinct from form. **4** capacity or volume. [medieval Latin: related to CONTAIN]

contented /kən'tentɪd/ *adj.* showing or feeling content; happy, satisfied. □ **contentedly** *adv.* **contentedness** *n.*

contention /kən'tenʃ(ə)n/ *n.* **1** dispute or argument; rivalry. **2** point contended for in an argument. [Latin: related to CONTEND]

contentious /kən'tenʃəs/ *adj.* **1** quarrelsome. **2** likely to cause an argument.

contentment *n.* satisfied state; tranquil happiness.

contest *–n.* /'kɒntest/ **1** contending; strife. **2** a competition. *–v.* /kən'test/ **1** dispute (a decision etc.). **2** contend or compete for; compete in (an election). [Latin *testis* witness]

♦ **contestable markets theory** *n. Econ.* theory that prices in oligopolies may be close to the perfectly competitive level due to the threat of entry by maverick firms. In the airline industry, for example, although there are a relatively small number of competitors, prices tend to remain low, since as soon as the airlines try to raise their prices entrepreneurs enter the market and undercut existing fares. This leads to the suggestion that governments need not try to encourage perfect competition in markets as long as they ensure that they are contestable.

---

contestant /kən'test(ə)nt/ *n.* person taking part in a contest.

context /'kɒntekst/ *n.* **1** parts that surround a word or passage and clarify its meaning. **2** relevant circumstances. □ **in** (or **out of**) **context** with (or without) the surrounding words or circumstances. □ **contextual** /kən'tekstjʊəl/ *adj.* **contextualize** /kən'tekstjʊəˌlaɪz/ *v.* (also **-ise**) (**-zing** or **-sing**). [Latin: related to TEXT]

contiguous /kən'tɪgjʊəs/ *adj.* (usu. foll. by *with*, *to*) touching; in contact. □ **contiguity** /ˌkɒntɪ'gjuːɪtɪ/ *n.* [Latin: related to CONTACT]

continent[1] /'kɒntɪnənt/ *n.* **1** any of the main continuous expanses of land (Europe, Asia, Africa, North and South America, Australia, Antarctica). **2** (**the Continent**) mainland of Europe as distinct from the British Isles. [Latin: related to CONTAIN]

continent[2] /'kɒntɪnənt/ *adj.* **1** able to control one's bowels and bladder. **2** exercising self-restraint, esp. sexually. □ **continence** *n.* [Latin: related to CONTAIN]

continental /ˌkɒntɪ'nent(ə)l/ *adj.* **1** of or characteristic of a continent. **2** (**Continental**) of or characteristic of mainland Europe.

continental breakfast *n.* light breakfast of coffee, rolls, etc.

continental quilt *n.* duvet.

continental shelf *n.* area of shallow seabed bordering a continent.

contingency /kən'tɪndʒənsɪ/ *n.* (*pl.* **-ies**) **1** event that may or may not occur. **2** something dependent on another uncertain event. [Latin: related to CONTINGENT]

♦ **contingency insurance** *n.* insurance policy covering financial losses occurring as a result of a specified event happening. The risks covered by policies of this kind are various and often unusual, such as a missing documents indemnity, the birth of twins, or pluvial insurance.

♦ **contingency plan** *n.* plan formulated to cope with some event or circumstances that may occur in the future. For example, the contingency may be an increase in sales, in which case the plan would include means of increasing production very quickly.

---

contingent *–adj.* **1** (usu. foll. by *on*, *upon*) conditional, dependent (on an uncertain event or circumstance). **2 a** that may or may not occur. **b** fortuitous. *–n.* **1** body (of troops, ships, etc.) forming part of a larger group. **2** group of people sharing an interest, origin, etc. (*the Oxford contingent*). [Latin: related to CONTACT]

♦ **contingent annuity** *n.* (also **reversionary annuity**) annuity in which the payment is conditional on a specified event happening, esp. an annuity purchased jointly by a husband and wife that begins payment after the death of one of the parties. See JOINT-LIFE ANNUITY.

♦ **contingent interest** see VESTED INTEREST 2.

♦ **contingent liability** *n.* liability that, at a balance sheet date, can be anticipated to arise if a particular event occurs. Typical examples include a court case pending against the company, the outcome of which is uncertain, or loss of earnings as a result of a customer invoking a penalty clause in a contract that may not be completed on time. Under the Companies Act (1985), such liabilities must be explained by a note on the company balance sheet.

continual /kən'tɪnjʊəl/ *adj.* constantly or frequently recurring; always happening. □ **continually** *adv.* [French: related to CONTINUE]

■ **Usage** *Continual* is often confused with *continuous*. *Continual* is used of something that happens very frequently (e.g. *there were continual interruptions*) while *continuous* is used of something that happens without a pause (e.g. *continuous rain all day*).

continuance /kən'tɪnjʊəns/ *n.* **1** continuing in existence or operation. **2** duration.

continuation /kən,tɪnjʊ'eɪʃ(ə)n/ *n.* **1** continuing or being continued. **2** part that continues something else. **3** arrangement between an investor and a stockbroker in which the broker reduces his commission for a series of purchases by that investor of the same stock over a stated period.

continue /kən'tɪnjuː/ *v.* **(-ues, -ued, -uing) 1** maintain, not stop (an action etc.) (*continued to read, reading*). **2** (also *absol.*) resume or prolong (a narrative, journey, etc.). **3** be a sequel to. **4** remain, stay (*will continue as manager; weather continued fine*). [Latin: related to CONTAIN]

continuity /,kɒntɪ'njuːɪtɪ/ *n.* (*pl.* **-ies**) **1** state of being continuous. **2** a logical sequence. **3** detailed scenario of a film or broadcast. **4** linking of broadcast items.

continuo /kən'tɪnjʊəʊ/ *n.* (*pl.* **-s**) *Mus.* accompaniment providing a bass line, played usu. on a keyboard instrument. [Italian]

continuous /kən'tɪnjʊəs/ *adj.* uninterrupted, connected throughout in space or time. □ **continuously** *adv.* [Latin: related to CONTAIN]

■ **Usage** See note at *continual*.

continuous assessment *n.* evaluation of a pupil's progress throughout a course of study.

continuous stationery *n.* paper that can be printed in a continuous roll. It is perforated at regular intervals across its width, enabling it to be fan-folded into a stack of 'pages', and has a row of regularly spaced sprocket holes down each side so that it can be fed automatically through a computer printer etc. Before printing, the paper may be blank or preprinted (e.g. headed notepaper or invoice forms). It may be multipart stationery, consisting of two or more lots of paper with interleaved carbon paper and folded into a single stack.

continuum /kən'tɪnjʊəm/ *n.* (*pl.* **-nua**) thing having a continuous structure. [Latin: related to CONTINUOUS]

contort /kən'tɔːt/ *v.* twist or force out of its normal shape. □ **contortion** *n.* [Latin *torqueo tort-* twist]

contortionist /kən'tɔːʃənɪst/ *n.* entertainer who adopts contorted postures.

contour /'kɒntʊə(r)/ *–n.* **1** outline. **2** (in full **contour line**) line on a map joining points of equal altitude. *–v.* mark with contour lines. [Italian *contornare* draw in outline]

contra[1] /'kɒntrə/ *n.* (*pl.* **-s**) member of a counter-revolutionary force in Nicaragua. [abbreviation of Spanish *contrarevolucionario* counter-revolutionary]

♦ **contra**[2] /'kɒntrə/ *n.* (*pl.* **-s**) bookkeeping entry on the opposite side of an account to an earlier entry, with the object of cancelling the effect of the earlier entry. See also PER CONTRA. [Latin, = opposite]

---

contra- *comb. form* against, opposite. [Latin]

contraband /'kɒntrə,bænd/ *–n.* **1** smuggled goods. **2** smuggling; illegal trade. *–adj.* forbidden to be imported or exported. [Spanish from Italian]

contraception /,kɒntrə'sepʃ(ə)n/ *n.* prevention of pregnancy; use of contraceptives. [from CONTRA-, CONCEPTION]

contraceptive /,kɒntrə'septɪv/ *–adj.* preventing pregnancy. *–n.* contraceptive device or drug.

contract *–n.* /'kɒntrækt/ **1** written or spoken agreement, esp. one enforceable by law. Agreement arises as a result of an offer and acceptance, but a number of other requirements must be satisfied for an agreement to be legally binding. There must be a promise of consideration (see CONSIDERATION 5), unless the contract is by deed; the parties must have an intention to create legal relations; the parties must have capacity to contract (i.e. they must be competent to enter a legal obligation, by not being a minor, mentally disordered, or drunk); the agreement must comply with any formal legal requirements; the agreement must be legal (see ILLEGAL CONTRACT); and the agreement must not be rendered void either by some common-law or statutory rule or by some inherent defect. In general, no particular formality is required for the creation of a valid contract. However, certain contracts are valid only if made by deed (e.g. transfers of shares in statutory companies, transfers of shares in British ships) or in writing (e.g. hire-purchase agreements, bills of exchange, promissory notes) and certain others, though valid, can only be enforced if evidenced in writing (e.g. guarantees). See also AFFIRMATION OF CONTRACT; BREACH OF CONTRACT; CONTRACT OF EMPLOYMENT. **2** document recording a contract. *–v.* /kən'trækt/ **1** make or become smaller. **2 a** (usu. foll. by *with*) make a contract. **b** (often foll. by *out*) arrange (work) to be done by contract. **3** become affected by (a disease). **4** enter into (marriage). **5** incur (a debt etc.). **6** draw together (the muscles, brow, etc.), or be drawn together. □ **contract in** (or **out**) choose to enter (or withdraw from or not enter) a scheme or commitment. See also STATE EARNINGS-RELATED PENSION SCHEME. [Latin *contractus*: related to TRACT[1]]

contractable *adj.* (of a disease) that can be contracted.

contract bridge *n.* bridge in which only tricks bid and won count towards the game.

♦ **contract guarantee insurance** *n.* insurance policy designed to guarantee the financial solvency of a contractor during the performance of a contract. If the contractor becomes financially insolvent and cannot complete the work the insurer makes a payment equivalent to the contract price, which enables another contractor to be paid to complete the work. See also CREDIT INSURANCE.

---

contractible *adj.* that can be shrunk or drawn together.

contractile /kən'træktaɪl/ *adj.* capable of or producing contraction. □ **contractility** /,kɒntræk'tɪlɪtɪ/ *n.*

contraction /kən'trækʃ(ə)n/ *n.* **1** contracting or being contracted. **2** *Med.* shortening of the uterine muscles during childbirth. **3** shrinking, diminution. **4** shortened form of a word or words (e.g. *he's*).

♦ **contract note** *n.* document sent by a stockbroker or commodity broker to his client as evidence that he has bought (a **bought note**) or sold (a **sold note**) securities or commodities in accordance with the client's instructions. It will state the quantity of securities or goods, the price, the date (and sometimes the time of day at which the bargain was struck), the rate of commission, the cost of the transfer stamp and VAT (if any), and (finally) the amount due and the settlement date.

♦ **contract of employment** *n.* (also **contract of service**) legally enforceable agreement entered into orally or in writing by an employer and an employee. There is no requirement in UK law that a contract of employment must be in writing; however, the basic terms and conditions of employment are normally written and signed by both parties to ensure that each knows their rights and obligations. The Employment Protection (Consolidation) Act (1978) states that every employee must be given, within 13 weeks of joining, a note giving the date of joining, job title, salary, pay day, holiday entitlement, sick pay, pensions, notice requirements, and disciplinary procedures. Most employers expand this statement to provide as detailed a contract as possible in order to avoid misunderstandings. Larger organizations provide a company handbook giving a detailed account of company policies, disciplinary rules, and any other relevant matters. A contract can be varied by mutual agreement but neither an employee nor an employer can contract out of obligations covered by normal common-law rights.

---

contractor /kən'træktə(r)/ *n.* person who makes a contract, esp. to conduct building operations.

contractual /kən'træktʃʊəl/ *adj.* of or in the nature of a contract. □ **contractually** *adv.*

contradict /ˌkɒntrə'dɪkt/ *v.* **1** deny (a statement). **2** deny a statement made by (a person). **3** be in opposition to or in conflict with. □ **contradiction** *n.* **contradictory** *adj.* [Latin *dico dict-* say]

contradistinction /ˌkɒntrədɪ'stɪŋkʃ(ə)n/ *n.* distinction made by contrasting.

contraflow /'kɒntrəˌfləʊ/ *n.* transfer of traffic from its usual half of the road to the other half by borrowing one or more of the other half's lanes.

contralto /kən'træltəʊ/ *n.* (*pl.* **-s**) **1** lowest female singing-voice. **2** singer with this voice. [Italian: related to CONTRA-, ALTO]

◆ ***contra proferentem*** /'kɒntrə prɒfə'rentəm/ *n. Law* rule of interpretation primarily applying to documents. If any doubt or ambiguity arises in the interpretation of a document, the rule requires that the doubt or ambiguity should be resolved against the party who drafted it or who uses it as a basis for a claim against another. For instance, a plaintiff who sues for breach of a written contract can expect that any ambiguity in the terms of the contract will be resolved against him. [Latin, = against the person proclaiming them (i.e. the words of a contract)]

contraption /kən'træpʃ(ə)n/ *n.* machine or device, esp. a strange or cumbersome one. [origin unknown]

contrapuntal /ˌkɒntrə'pʌnt(ə)l/ *adj. Mus.* of or in counterpoint. □ **contrapuntally** *adv.* [Italian]

contrariwise /kən'treərɪˌwaɪz/ *adv.* **1** on the other hand. **2** in the opposite way. **3** perversely.

contrary /'kɒntrərɪ/ *–adj.* **1** (usu. foll. by *to*) opposed in nature or tendency. **2** /kən'treərɪ/ perverse, self-willed. **3** (of a wind) unfavourable, impeding. **4** opposite in position or direction. *–n.* (prec. by *the*) the opposite. *–adv.* (foll. by *to*) in opposition or contrast (*contrary to expectations*). □ **on the contrary** expressing denial of what has just been implied or stated. **to the contrary** to the opposite effect. □ **contrariness** /kən'treərɪnɪs/ *n.* [Latin: related to CONTRA-]

contrast *–n.* /'kɒntrɑːst/ **1 a** juxtaposition or comparison showing differences. **b** difference so revealed. **2** (often foll. by *to*) thing or person having different qualities. **3** degree of difference between the tones in a television picture or photograph. *–v.* /kən'trɑːst/ (often foll. by *with*) **1** set together so as to reveal a contrast. **2** have or show a contrast. [Italian from Latin *sto* stand]

contravene /ˌkɒntrə'viːn/ *v.* (**-ning**) **1** infringe (a law etc.). **2** (of things) conflict with. □ **contravention** /-'venʃ(ə)n/ *n.* [Latin *venio* come]

contretemps /'kɒntrəˌtɔ̃/ *n.* (*pl.* same /-ˌtɔ̃z/) **1** unfortunate occurrence. **2** unexpected mishap. [French]

contribute /kən'trɪbjuːt, 'kɒntrɪˌbjuːt/ *v.* (**-ting**) (often foll. by *to*) **1** give (time, money, etc.) towards a common purpose. **2** help to bring about a result etc. **3** (also *absol.*) supply (an article etc.) for publication with others. □ **contributor** /kən'trɪb-/ *n.* [Latin: related to TRIBUTE]

■ **Usage** The second pronunciation, stressed on the first syllable, is considered incorrect by some people.

contribution /ˌkɒntrɪ'bjuːʃ(ə)n/ *n.* **1** act of contributing. **2** thing contributed. **3** *Finance* amount that, under marginal-costing principles, a given transaction produces to cover fixed overheads and to provide profit. The contribution is normally taken to be the selling price of a given unit of merchandise, less the variable costs of producing it. Once the total contributions exceed the fixed overheads, all further contribution represents pure profit. **4** *Insurance* sharing of claim payments between two or more insurers who find themselves insuring the same item, against the same risks, for the same person. As that person is not entitled to claim more than the full value of the item, each insurer pays a share. For example, if a coat was stolen from a car, it might be insured under both a personal-effects insurance and a motor policy. As the policyholder is only entitled to the value of the coat (he or she cannot profit from the theft), each insurer contributes half of the loss.

contributory /kən'trɪbjʊtərɪ/ *–adj.* **1** that contributes. **2** using contributions. *–n.* (*pl.* **-ries**) person liable to contribute towards the assets of a company on liquidation. The list of contributories will be settled by the liquidator or by the court and will include all shareholders, although those who hold fully paid-up shares will not be liable to pay any more.

◆ **contributory pension** *n.* pension in which the employee as well as the employer contribute to the pension fund. Cf. NON-CONTRIBUTORY PENSION.

contrite /'kɒntraɪt/ *adj.* penitent, feeling great guilt. □ **contritely** *adv.* **contrition** /kən'trɪʃ(ə)n/ *n.* [Latin: related to TRITE]

contrivance /kən'traɪv(ə)ns/ *n.* **1** something contrived, esp. a plan or mechanical device. **2** act of contriving.

contrive /kən'traɪv/ *v.* (**-ving**) **1** devise; plan or make resourcefully or with skill. **2** (often foll. by *to* + infin.) manage. [French from Latin]

contrived *adj.* artificial, forced.

control /kən'trəʊl/ *–n.* **1** power of directing. **2** power of restraining, esp. self-restraint. **3** means of restraint. **4** (usu. in *pl.*) means of regulating. **5** (usu. in *pl.*) switches and other devices by which a machine is controlled. **6** place where something is controlled or verified. **7** standard of comparison for checking the results of an experiment. *–v.* (**-ll-**) **1** have control of, regulate. **2** hold in check. **3** check, verify. □ **in control** (often foll. by *of*) directing an activity. **out of control** no longer manageable. **under control** being controlled; in order. □ **controllable** *adj.* [medieval Latin, = keep copy of accounts: related to CONTRA-, ROLL]

◆ **control accounts** *n.pl.* accounts in which the balances are designed to equal the aggregate of the balances on a substantial number of subsidiary accounts. Examples are the sales ledger control account (or total debtors account), in which the balance equals the aggregate of all the individual debtors' accounts, the purchase ledger control account (or total creditors account), which performs the same function for creditors, and the stock control account, whose balance should equal the aggregate of the balances on the stock accounts for each item of stock. This is achieved by entering in the control accounts the totals of all the individual entries made in the subsidiary accounts. The purpose is twofold: to obtain total figures of debtors, creditors, stock, etc. at any given time, without adding up all the balances on the individual records, and to have a cross-check on the accuracy of the subsidiary records.

control character see CHARACTER SET 2.

control key see KEYBOARD *n.* 1.

controller *n.* **1** person or thing that controls. **2** person in charge of expenditure.

◆ **controlling interest** *n.* an interest in a company that gives a person control of it. To have a controlling interest, a shareholder would normally need to own or control more than half the voting shares. However, in practice, a shareholder might control the company with considerably less than half the shares, if the remaining shares are held by a large number of people. For legal purposes, a director is said to have a controlling interest in a company if that director alone, or together with his or her spouse, minor children, and the trustees of any settlement in which the director has an interest, owns more than 20% of the voting shares in a company or in a company that controls that company.

control tower *n.* tall building at an airport etc. from which air traffic is controlled.

control unit *n.* part of a computer that supervises the execution of a program. It is a component of the processing unit and is wholly electronic. Before a program can be executed it must be translated into a sequence of machine instructions. The control unit receives the machine instructions in the order in which they are to be executed. It interprets each instruction and causes it to be executed by sending command signals to the arithmetic and logic unit (ALU) and other appropriate parts of the computer. The data required for the execution is moved between main store, ALU, and other portions of the computer in accordance with the sequence of instructions and under the direction of the control unit.

controversial /ˌkɒntrə'vɜːʃ(ə)l/ *adj.* causing or subject to controversy. [Latin: related to CONTROVERT]

controversy /'kɒntrəˌvɜːsɪ, kən'trɒvəsɪ/ *n.* (*pl.* **-ies**) prolonged argument or dispute. [Latin: related to CONTROVERT]

■ **Usage** The second pronunciation, stressed on the second syllable, is considered incorrect by some people.

controvert /'kɒntrəˌvɜːt/ *v.* dispute, deny. [Latin *verto vers-* turn]

contumacious /ˌkɒntjuː'meɪʃəs/ *adj.* stubbornly or wilfully disobedient. □ **contumacy** /'kɒntjʊməsɪ/ *n.* (*pl.* **-ies**). [Latin *tumeo* swell]

contumely /'kɒntjuːmlɪ/ *n.* **1** insolent language or treatment. **2** disgrace. [Latin: related to CONTUMACIOUS]

contuse /kən'tjuːz/ *v.* (**-sing**) bruise. □ **contusion** *n.* [Latin *tundo tus-* thump]

conundrum /kə'nʌndrəm/ *n.* **1** riddle, esp. one with a pun in its answer. **2** hard question. [origin unknown]

conurbation /ˌkɒnɜː'beɪʃ(ə)n/ *n.* extended urban area, esp. consisting of several towns and merging suburbs. [Latin *urbs* city]

convalesce /ˌkɒnvə'les/ *v.* (**-cing**) recover health after illness. [Latin *valeo* be well]

convalescent *–adj.* recovering from an illness. *–n.* convalescent person. □ **convalescence** *n.*

convection /kən'vekʃ(ə)n/ *n.* heat transfer by upward movement of a heated and less dense medium. [Latin *veho vect-* carry]

convector /kən'vektə(r)/ *n.* heating appliance that circulates warm air by convection.

convene /kən'viːn/ *v.* (**-ning**) **1** summon or arrange (a meeting etc.). **2** assemble. [Latin *venio vent-* come]

convener *n.* (also **convenor**) **1** person who convenes a meeting. **2** senior trade union official at a workplace.

convenience /kən'viːnɪəns/ *n.* **1** state of being convenient; suitability. **2** useful thing. **3** advantage. **4** lavatory, esp. a public one. □ **at one's convenience** at a time or place that suits one. [Latin: related to CONVENE]

convenience food *n.* food requiring little preparation.

♦ **convenience store** *n.* store that trades primarily on the convenience it offers to customers. The products stocked may be influenced by local tastes or ethnic groups and the stores are often open long hours as well as being conveniently placed for customers in local shopping parades.

---

convenient *adj.* **1 a** serving one's comfort or interests. **b** suitable. **c** free of trouble or difficulty. **2** available or occurring at a suitable time or place. **3** well situated (*convenient for the shops*). □ **conveniently** *adv.*

convent /'kɒnv(ə)nt/ *n.* **1** religious community, esp. of nuns, under vows. **2** premises occupied by this. [Latin: related to CONVENE]

conventicle /kən'ventɪk(ə)l/ *n.* esp. *hist.* secret or unlawful religious meeting, esp. of dissenters. [Latin: related to CONVENE]

convention /kən'venʃ(ə)n/ *n.* **1 a** general agreement on social behaviour etc. by implicit majority consent. **b** a custom or customary practice. **2** conference of people with a common interest. **3** a formal agreement, esp. between states. [Latin: related to CONVENE]

conventional *adj.* **1** depending on or according with convention. **2** (of a person) bound by social conventions. **3** usual; of agreed significance. **4** not spontaneous or sincere or original. **5** (of weapons etc.) non-nuclear. □ **conventionalism** *n.* **conventionality** /-'nælɪtɪ/ *n.* (*pl.* **-ies**). **conventionally** *adv.*

converge /kən'vɜːdʒ/ *v.* (**-ging**) **1** come together or towards the same point. **2** (foll. by *on, upon*) approach from different directions. □ **convergence** *n.* **convergent** *adj.* [Latin *vergo* incline]

conversant /kən'vɜːs(ə)nt/ *adj.* (foll. by *with*) well acquainted with. [French: related to CONVERSE[1]]

conversation /ˌkɒnvə'seɪʃ(ə)n/ *n.* **1** informal spoken communication. **2** instance of this. [Latin: related to CONVERSE[1]]

conversational *adj.* **1** of or in conversation. **2** colloquial. **3** *Computing* interactive. □ **conversationally** *adv.*

conversationalist *n.* person good at or fond of conversation.

converse[1] /kən'vɜːs/ *v.* (**-sing**) (often foll. by *with*) talk. [Latin: related to CONVERT]

converse[2] /'kɒnvɜːs/ *–adj.* opposite, contrary, reversed. *–n.* something, esp. a statement or proposition, that is opposite or reversed. □ **conversely** *adv.* [Latin: related to CONVERT]

conversion /kən'vɜːʃ(ə)n/ *n.* **1** converting or being converted. **2** converted building or part of this. **3** tort (i.e. civil wrong) equivalent to the crime of theft. It is possible to bring an action in respect of conversion to recover damages, but this is uncommon. [Latin: related to CONVERT]

convert *–v.* /kən'vɜːt/ **1** (usu. foll. by *into*) change in form or function. **2** cause (a person) to change belief etc. **3** change (moneys etc.) into others of a different kind. **4** make structural alterations in (a building) for a new purpose. **5** (also *absol.*) *Rugby* score extra points from (a try) by a successful kick at the goal. *–n.* /'kɒnvɜːt/ (often foll. by *to*) person converted to a different belief etc. [Latin *verto vers-* turn]

♦ **convertibility** /kənˌvɜːtɪ'bɪlɪtɪ/ *n.* **1** ability to be converted. **2** extent to which one currency can be freely exchanged for another. Since 1979 sterling has been freely convertible. The International Monetary Fund encourages free convertibility, although many governments try to maintain some direct control over foreign-exchange transactions involving their own currency, esp. if there is a shortage of hard-currency foreign-exchange reserves.

---

convertible /kən'vɜːtɪb(ə)l/ *–adj.* able to be converted. *–n.* **1** car with a folding or detachable roof. **2** (also **conversion issue**) *Finance* **a** security, usu. a bond or debenture, that can be converted into the ordinary shares or preference shares of the company at a fixed date or dates at a fixed price. In effect, **convertible loan stock** is equivalent to a bond plus a stock option. **b** government security in which the holder has the right to convert a holding into new stock instead of obtaining repayment. [Latin: related to CONVERT]

♦ **convertible term assurance** *n.* life assurance for a specified period that gives the policyholder the option to widen the policy to become a whole life policy or an endowment assurance policy, without having to provide any further evidence of good health. All that is required is the payment of the extra premium. The risk of Aids has meant that policies of this kind are no longer available, as insurers are not now prepared to offer any widening of life cover without evidence of good health.

---

convex /'kɒnveks/ *adj.* curved like the exterior of a circle or sphere. □ **convexity** /-'veksɪtɪ/ *n.* [Latin]

convey /kən'veɪ/ *v.* **1** transport or carry (goods, passengers, etc.). **2** communicate (an idea, meaning, etc.). **3** transfer the title to (a property). **4** transmit (sound etc.). □ **conveyable** *adj.* [Latin *via* way]

conveyance *n.* **1** conveying or being conveyed. **2** means of transport; vehicle. **3** *Law* **a** transfer of property. **b** document effecting this. □ **conveyancer** *n.* (in sense 3). **conveyancing** *n.* (in sense 3).

conveyor *n.* (also **conveyer**) person or thing that conveys.

conveyor belt *n.* endless moving belt for conveying articles, esp. in a factory.

convict *–v.* /kən'vɪkt/ **1** (often foll. by *of*) prove to be guilty (of a crime etc.). **2** declare guilty by a legal process. *–n.* /'kɒnvɪkt/ chiefly *hist.* person serving a prison sentence. [Latin *vinco vict-* conquer]

conviction /kən'vɪkʃ(ə)n/ *n.* **1** convicting or being convicted. **2 a** being convinced. **b** firm belief. [Latin: related to CONVICT]

convince /kən'vɪns/ *v.* (**-cing**) firmly persuade. □ **convincible** *adj.* **convincing** *adj.* **convincingly** *adv.* [Latin: related to CONVICT]

convivial /kən'vɪvɪəl/ *adj.* fond of good company; sociable and lively. □ **conviviality** /-'ælɪtɪ/ *n.* [Latin *vivo* live]

convocation /ˌkɒnvə'keɪʃ(ə)n/ *n.* **1** convoking or being convoked. **2** large formal gathering. [Latin: related to CONVOKE]

convoke /kən'vəʊk/ *v.* (**-king**) *formal* call together; summon to assemble. [Latin *voco* call]

convoluted /'kɒnvəˌluːtɪd/ *adj.* **1** coiled, twisted. **2** complex. [Latin *volvo volut-* roll]

convolution /ˌkɒnvə'luːʃ(ə)n/ *n.* **1** coiling. **2** coil or twist. **3** complexity. **4** sinuous fold in the surface of the brain.

convolvulus /kən'vɒlvjʊləs/ *n.* (*pl.* **-luses**) twining plant, esp. bindweed. [Latin]

convoy /'kɒnvɔɪ/ *–n.* group of ships, vehicles, etc., travelling together or under escort. *–v.* escort, esp. with armed force. □ **in convoy** as a group. [French: related to CONVEY]

convulse /kən'vʌls/ *v.* (**-sing**) **1** (usu. in *passive*) affect with convulsions. **2** cause to laugh uncontrollably. □ **convulsive** *adj.* **convulsively** *adv.* [Latin *vello vuls-* pull]

convulsion /kən'vʌlʃ(ə)n/ *n.* **1** (usu. in *pl.*) violent irregular motion of the limbs or body caused by involuntary contraction of muscles. **2** violent disturbance. **3** (in *pl.*) uncontrollable laughter.

cony /'kəʊnɪ/ *n.* (also **coney**) rabbit fur. [Latin *cuniculus*]

coo *–n.* soft murmuring sound as of a dove. *–v.* (**coos, cooed**) **1** emit a coo. **2** talk or say in a soft or amorous voice. *–int. slang* expressing surprise or disbelief. [imitative]

cooee /'kuːiː/ *n.* & *int. colloq.* call used to attract attention. [imitative]

cook /kʊk/ *–v.* **1** prepare (food) by heating it. **2** (of food) undergo cooking. **3** *colloq.* falsify (accounts etc.). **4** (as **be cooking**) *colloq.* be happening or about to happen. *–n.* person who cooks, esp. professionally or in a specified way (*a good cook*). □ **cook up** *colloq.* concoct (a story, excuse, etc.). [Latin *coquus*]

cookbook *n. US* cookery book.

cook-chill *attrib. adj.* (of food, meals, etc.) sold in precooked and refrigerated form.

cooker *n.* **1** appliance or vessel for cooking food. **2** fruit (esp. an apple) suitable for cooking.

cookery *n.* art or practice of cooking.

cookery book *n.* book containing recipes.

cookie /'kʊkɪ/ *n. US* **1** sweet biscuit. **2** *colloq.* person (*a tough cookie*). [Dutch *koekje*]

Cook Islands group of islands in the SW Pacific Ocean, a self-governing territory of New Zealand; exports include copra and fruit; pop. (1990) 18 187.

Cook Strait passage separating the North and South Islands of New Zealand.

cool *–adj.* **1** of or at a fairly low temperature, fairly cold. **2** suggesting or achieving coolness. **3** calm, unexcited. **4** lacking enthusiasm. **5** unfriendly (*a cool reception*). **6** calmly audacious. **7** (prec. by *a*) *colloq.* at least (*cost a cool thousand*). **8** *slang* esp. *US* marvellous. *–n.* **1** coolness. **2** cool air or place. **3** *slang* calmness, composure. *–v.* (often foll. by *down, off*) make or become cool. □ **cool it** *slang* relax, calm down. □ **coolly** /'kuːllɪ/ *adv.* **coolness** *n.* [Old English]

coolant *n.* cooling agent, esp. fluid.

cool-bag *n.* (also **cool-box**) insulated container for keeping food cool.

cooler *n.* **1** vessel in which a thing is cooled. **2** *US* refrigerator. **3** *slang* prison cell.

coolie /'kuːlɪ/ *n.* unskilled native labourer in Eastern countries. [perhaps from *Kulī*, tribe in India]

cooling-off period *n.* **1** interval to allow for a change of mind. **2** interval (14 days) that begins when a life-assurance policy is received, during which a new policy-holder can elect to cancel the policy and is then entitled to receive a full refund of premiums.

cooling tower *n.* tall structure for cooling hot water before reuse, esp. in industry.

coomb /kuːm/ *n.* (also **combe**) **1** valley on the side of a hill. **2** short valley running up from the coast. [Old English]

coon *n.* **1** *US* racoon. **2** *slang offens.* Black. [abbreviation]

coop *–n.* cage for keeping poultry. *–v.* (often foll. by *up, in*) confine (a person). [Latin *cupa* cask]

co-op /'kəʊɒp/ *n. colloq.* cooperative society or shop. [abbreviation]

cooper *n.* maker or repairer of casks, barrels, etc. [Low German or Dutch: related to COOP]

cooperate /kəʊ'ɒpəˌreɪt/ *v.* (also **co-operate**) (**-ting**) **1** (often foll. by *with*) work or act together. **2** be helpful and do as one is asked. □ **cooperation** /-'reɪʃ(ə)n/ *n.* [related to CO-]

cooperative /kəʊ'ɒpərətɪv/ (also **co-operative**) *–adj.* **1** willing to cooperate. **2** of or characterized by cooperation. **3** (of a business) owned and run jointly by its members, with all profits shared. *–n.* **1** (also **worker cooperative**) business organization common in labour-intensive industries (e.g. agriculture) and often associated with Communist countries. Agricultural cooperatives are encouraged in the developing countries, where individual farmers are too poor to take advantage of expensive machinery and large-scale production. In this case several farms pool resources to jointly purchase and use agricultural machinery. The principle has been extended to other industries in which factory employees have arranged a worker buyout in order to secure threatened employment. The overall management of such cooperatives is usu. vested in a committee of the employee-owners. **2** (**consumer cooperative**) movement launched in 1844 by 28 Rochdale weavers who combined to establish retail outlets where members enjoyed not only the benefits of good-quality products at fair prices but also a share of the profits (a dividend) based on the amount of each member's purchases.

co-opt /kəʊ'ɒpt/ *v.* appoint to membership of a body by invitation of the existing members. □ **co-option** *n.* **co-optive** *adj.* [Latin *coopto* from *opto* choose]

coordinate (also **co-ordinate**) *–v.* /kəʊ'ɔːdɪˌneɪt/ (**-ting**) **1** cause (parts, movements, etc.) to function together efficiently. **2** work or act together effectively. *–adj.* /kəʊ'ɔːdɪnət/ equal in rank or importance. *–n.* /kəʊ'ɔːdɪnət/ **1** *Math.* each of a system of values used to fix the position of a point, line, or plane. **2** (in *pl.*) matching items of clothing. □ **coordination** /-'neɪʃ(ə)n/ *n.* **coordinator** /-ˌneɪtə(r)/ *n.* [Latin *ordino*: related to ORDER]

coot *n.* **1** black aquatic bird with a white horny plate on its forehead. **2** *colloq.* stupid person. [probably Low German]

cop *slang –n.* **1** police officer. **2** capture or arrest (*it's a fair cop*). *–v.* (**-pp-**) **1** catch or arrest (an offender). **2** receive, suffer. **3** take, seize. □ **cop it** get into trouble; be punished. **cop out 1** withdraw; give up. **2** go back on a promise. **not much cop** of little value or use. [French *caper* seize]

copal /'kəʊp(ə)l/ *n.* resin of a tropical tree, used for varnish. [Spanish from Aztec]

copartner /kəʊ'pɑːtnə(r)/ *n.* partner or associate. □ **copartnership** *n.*

cope[1] *v.* (**-ping**) (often foll. by *with*) deal effectively or contend; manage. [French: related to COUP]

cope[2] *–n.* priest's long cloaklike vestment. *–v.* (**-ping**) cover with a cope or coping. [Latin *cappa* CAP]

copeck /'kəʊpek/ *n.* (also **kopek, kopeck**) Soviet coin worth one-hundredth of a rouble. [Russian *kopeĭka*]

Copenhagen /ˌkəʊpən'heɪgən/ (Danish **København** /'kopənˌhaʊn/) capital and chief port of Denmark; industries include engineering, brewing, and food processing; city pop. (1995) 625 810; metropolitan area pop. 1 353 333.

Copernican system /kə'pɜːnɪkən/ *n.* universally accepted theory that the planets (including the earth) move round the sun. [*Copernicus*, name of an astronomer]

copier /'kɒpɪə(r)/ *n.* machine that copies (esp. documents).

copilot /'kəʊˌpaɪlət/ *n.* second pilot in an aircraft.

coping *n.* top (usu. sloping) course of masonry in a wall. [from COPE²]

coping saw *n.* D-shaped saw for cutting curves in wood. [from COPE¹]

coping-stone *n.* stone used in coping.

copious /'kəʊpɪəs/ *adj.* **1** abundant. **2** producing much. □ **copiously** *adv.* [Latin *copia* plenty]

cop-out *n.* cowardly evasion.

copper¹ *–n.* **1** malleable red-brown metallic element. **2** bronze coin. **3** large metal vessel for boiling esp. laundry. *–adj.* made of or coloured like copper. *–v.* cover with copper. [Latin *cuprum*]

copper² *n. slang* police officer. [from COP]

copper beech *n.* variety of beech with copper-coloured leaves.

Copperbelt /'kɒpəˌbelt/ province of central Zambia; pop. (1990) 1 579 542; capital, Ndola. Copper, cobalt, and uranium are mined here.

copper-bottomed *adj.* **1** having a bottom sheathed with copper. **2** genuine or reliable.

copperhead *n.* venomous North American or Australian snake.

copperplate *n.* **1 a** polished copper plate for engraving or etching. **b** print made from this. **2** ornate style of handwriting.

coppice /'kɒpɪs/ *n.* area of undergrowth and small trees. [medieval Latin: related to COUP]

copra /'kɒprə/ *n.* dried coconut-kernels. [Portuguese from Malayalam]

copse *n.* = COPPICE. [shortened form]

Copt *n.* **1** native Egyptian in the Hellenistic and Roman periods. **2** native Christian of the independent Egyptian Church. [French from Arabic]

Coptic *–n.* language of the Copts. *–adj.* of the Copts.

copula /'kɒpjʊlə/ *n.* (*pl.* **-s**) connecting word, esp. part of the verb *be* connecting subject and predicate. [Latin]

copulate /'kɒpjʊˌleɪt/ *v.* (**-ting**) (often foll. by *with*) have sexual intercourse. □ **copulation** /-'leɪʃ(ə)n/ *n.*

copy /'kɒpɪ/ *–n.* (*pl.* **-ies**) **1** thing made to imitate another. **2** single specimen of a publication or issue. **3 a** matter to be printed, e.g. text, tables, illustrations. **b** material for a newspaper or magazine article, esp. regarded as good etc. reading matter (*the crisis will make exciting copy*). *–v.* (**-ies, -ied**) **1** make a copy of. **2** imitate, do the same as. [Latin *copia* transcript]

copybook *n.* **1** book containing models of handwriting for learners to imitate. **2** (*attrib.*) **a** tritely conventional. **b** exemplary.

copycat *n. colloq.* person who copies another, esp. slavishly.

copyist *n.* person who makes (esp. written) copies.

♦ **copyright** *–n.* exclusive legal right to reproduce or authorize others to reproduce artistic, dramatic, literary, or musical works. It is conferred by the Copyright Act (1988), which also extends to sound broadcasting, cinematograph films, and television broadcasts. Computer programs in the UK and US are protected as literary works. In EU countries it now lasts for the author's lifetime plus 70 years from the end of the year in which the author died (or from the end of the year in which a film or broadcast was made); it can be assigned or transmitted on death. The principal remedies for breach of copyright (see PIRACY 2) are an action for damages and account of profits or an injunction. It is a criminal offence to make or deal in articles that infringe a copyright. *–adj.* protected by copyright. *–v.* secure copyright for (material).

---

copy-typist *n.* typist who types from documents rather than dictation.

copywriter *n.* person who writes or prepares advertising copy for publication, usu. as an employee of an advertising agency.

coq au vin /ˌkɒk əʊ 'væ̃/ *n.* casserole of chicken pieces in wine. [French]

coquette /kɒ'ket/ *n.* woman who flirts. □ **coquetry** /'kɒkɪtrɪ/ *n.* (*pl.* **-ies**). **coquettish** *adj.* [French diminutive: related to COCK¹]

cor *int. slang* expressing surprise etc. [corruption of *God*]

cor- see COM-.

coracle /'kɒrək(ə)l/ *n.* small boat of wickerwork covered with watertight material. [Welsh]

coral /'kɒr(ə)l/ *–n.* hard red, pink, or white calcareous substance secreted by marine polyps for support and habitation. *–adj.* **1** red or pink, like coral. **2** made of coral. [Greek *korallion*]

coral island *n.* (also **coral reef**) island (or reef) formed by the growth of coral.

coralline /'kɒrəˌlaɪn/ *–n.* seaweed with a hard jointed stem. *–adj.* of or like coral. [French and Italian: related to CORAL]

Coral Sea part of the Pacific Ocean lying between Australia, New Guinea, and Vanuatu.

cor anglais /kɔːr 'ɒŋgleɪ/ *n.* (*pl.* **cors anglais** /kɔːz/) alto woodwind instrument of the oboe family. [French]

corbel /'kɔːb(ə)l/ *n.* projection of stone, timber, etc., jutting out from a wall to support a weight. □ **corbelled** *adj.* [Latin *corvus* crow]

cord *–n.* **1 a** flexible material like thick string, made from twisted strands. **b** piece of this. **2** similar structure in the body. **3 a** ribbed fabric, esp. corduroy. **b** (in *pl.*) corduroy trousers. **4** electric flex. *–v.* **1** fasten or bind with cord. **2** (as **corded** *adj.*) (of cloth) ribbed. [Greek *khordē* string]

cordial /'kɔːdɪəl/ *–adj.* **1** heartfelt. **2** friendly. *–n.* fruit-flavoured drink. □ **cordiality** /-'ælɪtɪ/ *n.* **cordially** *adv.* [Latin *cor cord-* heart]

cordite /'kɔːdaɪt/ *n.* smokeless explosive. [from CORD, because of its appearance]

cordless *adj.* (of a hand-held electrical device) usable without a power cable because working from an internal source of energy or battery.

Córdoba /'kɔːdəbə/ **1** city in S Spain; industries include silverware and textiles; pop. (est. 1994) 315 948. **2** city in central Argentina, capital of Córdoba province; industries include textiles, chemicals, glass, and cement; pop. (est. 1995) 2 914 972.

córdoba /'kɔːdəbə/ *n.* standard monetary unit of Nicaragua. [Francisco de *Córdoba*, Spanish explorer]

cordon /'kɔːd(ə)n/ *–n.* **1** line or circle of police, soldiers, guards, etc., esp. preventing access. **2** ornamental cord or braid. **3** fruit-tree trained to grow as a single stem. *–v.* (often foll. by *off*) enclose or separate with a cordon of police etc. [Italian and French: related to CORD]

cordon bleu /ˌkɔːdɒn 'blɜː/ *Cookery –adj.* of the highest class. *–n.* cook of this class. [French]

cordon sanitaire /ˌkɔːdɔ̃ ˌsænɪ'teə(r)/ *n.* **1** guarded line between infected and uninfected districts. **2** measure designed to prevent the spread of undesirable influences.

corduroy /'kɔːdəˌrɔɪ/ *n.* **1** thick cotton fabric with velvety ribs. **2** (in *pl.*) corduroy trousers. [*cord* = ribbed fabric]

core *–n.* **1** horny central part of certain fruits, containing the seeds. **2** central or most important part of anything (also *attrib.*: *core curriculum*). **3** inner central region of the earth. **4** part of a nuclear reactor containing fissile material. **5 a** *hist.* structural unit in a computer memory, storing one bit of data (see BIT⁴). **b** main store memory, esp. the type composed of cores. **6** inner strand of an electric cable. **7** piece of soft iron forming the centre of an electromagnet or induction coil. –*v.* (**-ring**) remove the core from. □ **corer** *n.* [origin unknown]

♦ **CORES** *abbr.* (in Japan) Computer-Assisted Order Routing and Execution System, through which dealing occurs on the Tokyo Stock Exchange.

♦ **core skills** *n. pl.* distinctive abilities that give a competitive advantage to an organization.

---

co-respondent /ˌkəʊrɪˈspɒnd(ə)nt/ *n.* person cited in a divorce case as having committed adultery with the respondent.

Corfu /kɔːˈfuː/ (Greek **Kérkira** /ˈkeəkɪrə/) **1** island off the W coast of Greece, one of the Ionian Islands; citrus fruits and olives are grown and tourism is important; pop. (1990) 105 043. **2** its chief town; pop. (est. 1991) 36 901.

corgi /ˈkɔːgɪ/ *n.* (*pl.* **-s**) dog of a short-legged breed with a foxlike head. [Welsh]

coriander /ˌkɒrɪˈændə(r)/ *n.* **1** aromatic plant. **2** its seeds used for flavouring. [Greek *koriannon*]

Corinthian /kəˈrɪnθɪən/ *adj.* **1** of ancient Corinth in S Greece. **2** *Archit.* of the order characterized by ornate decoration and acanthus leaves. [Latin from Greek]

Cork /kɔːk/ **1** county in the SW Republic of Ireland, in the province of Munster; pop. (1991) 410 369. It is agricultural, with both dairy and arable farming, and fishing is important. **2** its capital city, a trading centre and port with a fine harbour; industries include brewing and distilling and car assembly; pop. (est. 1991) 127 024.

cork –*n.* **1** buoyant light-brown bark of a S European oak. **2** bottle-stopper of cork etc. **3** float of cork. **4** (*attrib.*) made of cork. –*v.* (often foll. by *up*) **1** stop or confine. **2** restrain (feelings etc.). [Spanish *alcorque*]

corkage *n.* charge made by a restaurant etc. for serving a customer's own wine etc.

corked *adj.* **1** stopped with a cork. **2** (of wine) spoilt by a decayed cork.

corker *n. slang* excellent person or thing.

corkscrew –*n.* **1** spiral device for extracting corks from bottles. **2** (often *attrib.*) thing with a spiral shape. –*v.* move spirally; twist.

corm *n.* underground swollen stem base of some plants. [Greek *kormos* lopped tree-trunk]

cormorant /ˈkɔːmərənt/ *n.* diving sea bird with black plumage. [Latin *corvus marinus* sea-raven]

corn[1] *n.* **1 a** cereal before or after harvesting, esp. the chief crop of a region. **b** grain or seed of a cereal plant. **2** *colloq.* something corny or trite. [Old English]

corn[2] *n.* small tender area of horny skin, esp. on the toe. [Latin *cornu* horn]

corn-cob *n.* cylindrical centre of a maize ear on which the grains grow.

corncrake *n.* rail inhabiting grassland and nesting on the ground.

corn dolly *n.* figure of plaited straw.

cornea /ˈkɔːnɪə/ *n.* transparent circular part of the front of the eyeball. □ **corneal** *adj.* [medieval Latin: related to CORN[2]]

corned *adj.* (esp. of beef) preserved in salt or brine. [from CORN[1]]

cornelian /kɔːˈniːlɪən/ *n.* (also **carnelian** /kɑː-/) dull red variety of chalcedony. [French]

corner –*n.* **1** place where converging sides or edges meet. **2** projecting angle, esp. where two streets meet. **3** internal space or recess formed by the meeting of two sides, esp. of a room. **4** difficult position, esp. one with no escape. **5** secluded place. **6** region or quarter, esp. a remote one. **7** action or result of controlling the total supply of a commodity, service, etc. The action establishes a monopoly forcing the price up until further supplies or substitutes can be found. A corner can now rarely be attempted as government restrictions on monopolies and antitrust laws prevent it. **8** *Boxing* & *Wrestling* corner of the ring where a contestant rests between rounds. **9** *Football* & *Hockey* free kick or hit from the corner of a pitch. –*v.* **1** force into a difficult or inescapable position. **2** establish a corner in (a commodity etc.). **3** (esp. of or in a vehicle) go round a corner. [Latin: related to CORN[2]]

cornerstone *n.* **1 a** stone in the projecting angle of a wall. **b** foundation-stone. **2** indispensable part or basis.

cornet /ˈkɔːnɪt/ *n.* **1** brass instrument resembling a trumpet but shorter and wider. **2** conical wafer for holding ice-cream. □ **cornetist** /kɔːˈnetɪst/ *n.* (also **cornettist**). [Latin *cornu*: related to CORN[2]]

cornflake *n.* **1** (in *pl.*) breakfast cereal of toasted maize flakes. **2** flake of this cereal.

cornflour *n.* fine-ground flour, esp. of maize or rice.

cornflower *n.* plant with deep-blue flowers originally growing among corn.

cornice /ˈkɔːnɪs/ *n.* ornamental moulding, esp. round a room just below the ceiling or as the topmost part of an entablature. [French from Italian]

Cornish /ˈkɔːnɪʃ/ –*adj.* of Cornwall. –*n.* Celtic language of Cornwall.

Cornish pasty *n.* pastry envelope containing meat and vegetables.

corn on the cob *n.* maize cooked and eaten from the corn-cob.

cornucopia /ˌkɔːnjʊˈkəʊpɪə/ *n.* **1** horn overflowing with flowers, fruit, and corn, as a symbol of plenty. **2** abundant supply. [Latin: related to CORN[2], COPIOUS]

Cornwall /ˈkɔːnw(ə)l/ county in the extreme SW of England; pop. (with Isles of Scilly) (est. 1994) 479 600; county town, Truro. Tourism is a major industry; there is also dairy farming and market gardening.

corny *adj.* (**-ier**, **-iest**) *colloq.* **1** banal. **2** feebly humorous. **3** sentimental. □ **cornily** *adv.* **corniness** *n.* [from CORN[1]]

corolla /kəˈrɒlə/ *n.* whorl of petals forming the inner envelope of a flower. [Latin diminutive of CORONA]

corollary /kəˈrɒlərɪ/ *n.* (*pl.* **-ies**) **1** proposition that follows from one already proved. **2** (often foll. by *of*) natural consequence. [Latin, = gratuity: related to COROLLA]

corona /kəˈrəʊnə/ *n.* (*pl.* **-nae** /-niː/) **1 a** halo round the sun or moon. **b** gaseous envelope of the sun, seen as an area of light around the moon during a total solar eclipse. **2** *Anat.* crownlike structure. **3** crownlike outgrowth from the inner side of a corolla. **4** glow around an electric conductor. □ **coronal** *adj.* [Latin, = crown]

coronary /ˈkɒrənərɪ/ –*adj. Anat.* resembling or encircling like a crown. –*n.* (*pl.* **-ies**) = CORONARY THROMBOSIS. [Latin: related to CORONA]

coronary artery *n.* artery supplying blood to the heart.

coronary thrombosis *n.* blockage caused by a blood clot in a coronary artery.

coronation /ˌkɒrəˈneɪʃ(ə)n/ *n.* ceremony of crowning a sovereign or consort. [medieval Latin: related to CORONA]

coroner /ˈkɒrənə(r)/ *n.* official holding inquests on deaths thought to be violent or accidental. [Anglo-French: related to CROWN]

coronet /ˈkɒrənɪt/ *n.* **1** small crown. **2** circlet of precious materials, esp. as a headdress. [French diminutive: related to CROWN]

corpora *pl.* of CORPUS.

corporal[1] /ˈkɔːpr(ə)l/ *n.* non-commissioned army or air-force officer ranking next below sergeant. [French from Italian]

corporal[2] /ˈkɔːpər(ə)l/ *adj.* of the human body. □ **corporality** /-ˈrælɪtɪ/ *n.* [Latin *corpus* body]

corporal punishment *n.* physical punishment.

corporate /ˈkɔːpərət/ *adj.* **1** forming a corporation. **2** of, belonging to, or united in a group. [Latin: related to CORPORAL[2]]

♦ **corporate anorexia** *n. colloq.* sickness that can befall a business if too many creative people are made redundant as a result of cost cutting and downsizing.

♦ **corporate image** *n.* image that a company projects of itself. To gain a benevolent image for the way a company treats its employees or the environment, for example, can be as important to its sales as its individual brand images.

◆ **corporate plan** see BUSINESS PLAN.

◆ **corporate raider** *n.* person or company that buys a substantial proportion of the equity of another company (the target company) with the object of either taking it over or of forcing the management of the target company to take certain steps to improve the image of the company sufficiently for the share price to rise enough for the raider to sell at a profit.

◆ **corporate restructuring** *n.* change in the corporate strategy of an organization resulting in diversification in some areas, closing other areas to concentrate on core skills, etc., to increase long-term profitability.

◆ **corporate venturing** *n.* provision of risk capital by one company for another, either in order to obtain information about the activities of the company requiring the capital or its markets or as a preliminary step towards acquiring that company. It may often be a means of moving into a fresh market cheaply and without needing to acquire the necessary expertise and personnel required to do so on its own.

◆ **corporation** /ˌkɔːpəˈreɪʃ(ə)n/ *n.* **1** group of people authorized by law to act as one person, esp. in business, and having rights and liabilities distinct from the individuals forming it. A corporation may be created by royal charter, statute, or common law. The most important type is the registered company formed under the Companies Act. **Corporations sole** are those having only one individual forming them, e.g. a bishop, the sovereign, or the Treasury Solicitor. **Corporations aggregate** are composed of more than one individual, e.g. a limited company. They may be formed for special purposes by statute; the BBC is an example. Corporations can hold property, carry on business, bring legal actions, etc., in their own name. Their actions may, however, be limited by the doctrine of *ultra vires*. See also PUBLIC CORPORATION. **2** municipal authorities of a borough, town, or city. **3** *joc.* large stomach.

◆ **corporation tax** *n.* (also **CT**) tax levied on the trading profits and other income of companies and other incorporated bodies. The rate of corporation tax in the UK is 30% (from April 1999), but for small companies with profits below £300,000 it is reduced to 20%. For profits between £300,000 and £1,500,000 there is an increasing rate, until the full rate applies at the higher figure. With the abolition of advance corporation tax from April 1999, small companies will pay the full amount of tax at the end of the year, but large companies will pay in quarterly instalments.

---

corporative /ˈkɔːpərətɪv/ *adj.* **1** of a corporation. **2** governed by or organized in corporations.

corporeal /kɔːˈpɔːrɪəl/ *adj.* bodily, physical, material. □ **corporeality** /-ˈælɪtɪ/ *n.* **corporeally** *adv.* [Latin: related to CORPORAL[2]]

corps /kɔː(r)/ *n.* (*pl.* **corps** /kɔːz/) **1 a** body of troops with special duties (*intelligence corps*). **b** main subdivision of an army in the field. **2** body of people engaged in a special activity (*diplomatic corps*). [French: related to CORPSE]

corps de ballet /ˌkɔː də ˈbæleɪ/ *n.* group of ensemble dancers in a ballet. [French]

corpse *n.* dead body. [Latin: related to CORPUS]

corpulent /ˈkɔːpjʊlənt/ *adj.* physically bulky; fat. □ **corpulence** *n.* [Latin: related to CORPUS]

corpus /ˈkɔːpəs/ *n.* (*pl.* **-pora**) body or collection of writings, texts, etc. [Latin, = body]

corpuscle /ˈkɔːpʌs(ə)l/ *n.* minute body or cell in an organism, esp. (in *pl.*) the red or white cells in the blood of vertebrates. □ **corpuscular** /-ˈpʌskjʊlə(r)/ *adj.* [Latin diminutive of CORPUS]

corral /kəˈrɑːl/ *–n.* **1** *US* pen for cattle, horses, etc. **2** enclosure for capturing wild animals. *–v.* (**-ll-**) put or keep in a corral. [Spanish and Portuguese: related to KRAAL]

correct /kəˈrekt/ *–adj.* **1** true, accurate. **2** proper, in accordance with taste or a standard. *–v.* **1** set right; amend. **2** mark errors in. **3** substitute a right thing for (a wrong one). **4 a** admonish (a person). **b** punish (a person or fault). **5** counteract (a harmful quality). **6** adjust (an instrument etc.). □ **correctly** *adv.* **correctness** *n.* **corrector** *n.* [Latin *rego rect-* guide]

correction /kəˈrekʃ(ə)n/ *n.* **1** correcting or being corrected. **2** thing substituted for what is wrong. **3** *archaic* punishment. □ **correctional** *adj.* [Latin: related to CORRECT]

correctitude /kəˈrektɪˌtjuːd/ *n.* consciously correct behaviour. [from CORRECT, RECTITUDE]

corrective *–adj.* serving to correct or counteract something harmful. *–n.* corrective measure or thing. [Latin: related to CORRECT]

correlate /ˈkɒrəˌleɪt/ *–v.* (**-ting**) (usu. foll. by *with*, *to*) have or bring into a mutual relation or dependence. *–n.* each of two related or complementary things. □ **correlation** /-ˈleɪʃ(ə)n/ *n.* [medieval Latin *correlatio*]

correlative /kəˈrelətɪv/ *–adj.* **1** (often foll. by *with*, *to*) having a mutual relation. **2** (of words) corresponding to each other and used together (as *neither* and *nor*). *–n.* correlative word or thing.

correspond /ˌkɒrɪˈspɒnd/ *v.* **1 a** (usu. foll. by *to*) be similar or equivalent. **b** (usu. foll. by *with*, *to*) be in agreement, not contradict. **2** (usu. foll. by *with*) exchange letters. □ **correspondingly** *adv.* [French from medieval Latin]

correspondence *n.* **1** agreement or similarity. **2 a** exchange of letters. **b** letters.

correspondence course *n.* course of study conducted by post.

correspondent *n.* **1** person who writes letters. **2** person employed to write or report for a newspaper or for broadcasting etc.

corridor /ˈkɒrɪˌdɔː(r)/ *n.* **1** passage giving access into rooms. **2** passage in a train giving access into compartments. **3** strip of territory of one state passing through that of another. **4** route which an aircraft must follow, esp. over a foreign country. [French from Italian]

corridors of power *n.pl.* places where covert influence is said to be exerted in government.

corrigendum /ˌkɒrɪˈgendəm/ *n.* (*pl.* **-da**) error to be corrected. [Latin *corrigo*: related to CORRECT]

corrigible /ˈkɒrɪdʒɪb(ə)l/ *adj.* **1** able to be corrected. **2** submissive. □ **corrigibly** *adv.* [medieval Latin: related to CORRIGENDUM]

corroborate /kəˈrɒbəˌreɪt/ *v.* (**-ting**) confirm or give support to (a statement or belief etc.). □ **corroboration** /-ˈreɪʃ(ə)n/ *n.* **corroborative** /-rətɪv/ *adj.* **corroborator** *n.* [Latin *robur* strength]

corrode /kəˈrəʊd/ *v.* (**-ding**) **1 a** wear away, esp. by chemical action. **b** decay. **2** destroy gradually. [Latin *rodo ros-* gnaw]

corrosion /kəˈrəʊʒ(ə)n/ *n.* **1** corroding or being corroded. **2** corroded area. □ **corrosive** *adj.* & *n.*

corrugate /ˈkɒrəˌgeɪt/ *v.* (**-ting**) (esp. as **corrugated** *adj.*) form into alternate ridges and grooves, esp. to strengthen (*corrugated iron*). □ **corrugation** /-ˈgeɪʃ(ə)n/ *n.* [Latin *ruga* wrinkle]

corrupt /kəˈrʌpt/ *–adj.* **1** dishonest, esp. using bribery. See BRIBERY. **2** immoral; wicked. **3** (of a text etc.) made unreliable by errors or alterations. *–v.* **1** make or become corrupt. **2** alter data stored in a computer system, usu. accidently, and hence introduce errors. See also INTEGRITY 3. □ **corruptible** *adj.* **corruptibility** /-ˈbɪlɪtɪ/ *n.* **corruption** *n.* **corruptive** *adj.* **corruptly** *adv.* **corruptness** *n.* [Latin *rumpo rupt-* break]

corsage /kɔːˈsɑːʒ/ *n.* small bouquet worn by women. [French: related to CORPSE]

corsair /ˈkɔːseə(r)/ *n.* **1** pirate ship. **2** pirate. [French: related to COURSE]

corselette /ˈkɔːslɪt/ *n.* combined corset and bra. [French *corslet* armour covering trunk]

corset /ˈkɔːsɪt/ *n.* **1** closely-fitting undergarment worn to shape the body or to support it after injury. **2** restriction imposed on currency values, bank lending, etc., esp. by a government. □ **corsetry** *n.* [French diminutive: related to CORPSE]

Corsica /ˈkɔːsɪkə/ French island off the W coast of Italy; pop. (est. 1994) 258 879; capital, Ajaccio. Tourism is a major source of revenue; exports include wine and olive oil. □ **Corsican** *adj.* & *n.*

cortège /kɔː'teɪʒ/ *n.* procession, esp. for a funeral. [French]

cortex /'kɔːteks/ *n.* (*pl.* **-tices** /-tɪˌsiːz/) outer part of an organ, esp. of the brain or kidneys. □ **cortical** /-tɪk(ə)l/ *adj.* [Latin, = bark]

cortisone /'kɔːtɪˌzəʊn/ *n.* hormone used esp. in treating inflammation and allergy. [abbreviation of chemical name]

corundum /kə'rʌndəm/ *n.* extremely hard crystallized alumina, used esp. as an abrasive. [Tamil from Sanskrit]

Corunna /kə'rʌnə/ (Spanish **La Coruña** /læ kɒ'ruːnjə/) seaport in NW Spain; fishing is important and tobacco and linen are produced; pop. (est. 1994) 255 087.

coruscate /'kɒrəˌskeɪt/ *v.* (**-ting**) sparkle. □ **coruscation** /-'skeɪʃ(ə)n/ *n.* [Latin]

corvette /kɔː'vet/ *n.* **1** small naval escort-vessel. **2** *hist.* warship with one tier of guns. [French from Dutch]

corymb /'kɒrɪmb/ *n.* flat-topped cluster of flowers with the outer flower-stalks proportionally longer. [Latin from Greek]

COS *abbr.* (also **c.o.s.**) cash on shipment.

Cos /kɒs/ (Greek **Kós**) Greek island in the SE Aegean Sea; products include fruit, silk, and tobacco; pop. (1981) 20 350.

cos[1] *n.* lettuce with crisp narrow leaves. [Cos]

cos[2] /kɒz/ *abbr.* cosine.

cos[3] /kəz/ *conj. colloq.* because. [abbreviation]

cosec /'kəʊsek/ *abbr.* cosecant.

cosecant /kəʊ'siːkənt/ *n. Math.* ratio of the hypotenuse (in a right-angled triangle) to the side opposite an acute angle.

cosh[1] *colloq.* –*n.* heavy blunt weapon. –*v.* hit with a cosh. [origin unknown]

cosh[2] /kɒʃ, kɒs'eɪtʃ/ *abbr.* hyperbolic cosine.

co-signatory /kəʊ'sɪgnətərɪ/ *n.* (*pl.* **-ies**) person or state signing a treaty etc. jointly with others.

cosine /'kəʊsaɪn/ *n.* ratio of the side adjacent to an acute angle (in a right-angled triangle) to the hypotenuse.

CoSIRA /kəʊ'saɪrə/ *abbr.* Council for Small Industries in Rural Areas.

cosmetic /kɒz'metɪk/ –*adj.* **1** beautifying, enhancing. **2** superficially improving or beneficial. **3** (of surgery or a prosthesis) imitating, restoring, or enhancing normal appearance. –*n.* cosmetic preparation, esp. for the face. □ **cosmetically** *adv.* [Greek, = ornament]

cosmic /'kɒzmɪk/ *adj.* **1** of the cosmos or its scale; universal (*of cosmic significance*). **2** of or for space travel.

cosmic rays *n.pl.* high-energy atomic nuclei from space.

cosmogony /kɒz'mɒgənɪ/ *n.* (*pl.* **-ies**) **1** origin of the universe. **2** theory about this. [Greek *-gonia* -begetting]

cosmology /kɒz'mɒlədʒɪ/ *n.* science or theory of the universe. □ **cosmological** /-mə'lɒdʒɪk(ə)l/ *adj.* **cosmologist** *n.* [from COSMOS, -LOGY]

cosmonaut /'kɒzməˌnɔːt/ *n.* Soviet astronaut. [from COSMOS, Greek *nautēs* sailor]

cosmopolitan /ˌkɒzmə'pɒlɪt(ə)n/ –*adj.* **1** of, from, or knowing many parts of the world. **2** free from national limitations or prejudices. –*n.* cosmopolitan person. □ **cosmopolitanism** *n.* [Greek *politēs* citizen]

cosmos /'kɒzmɒs/ *n.* the universe as a well-ordered whole. [Greek]

Cossack /'kɒsæk/ *n.* member of a people of S Russia. [Turki *quzzāq*]

cosset /'kɒsɪt/ *v.* (**-t-**) pamper. [dialect *cosset* = pet lamb, probably from Old English, = cottager]

cost –*v.* (*past* and *past part.* **cost**) **1** be obtainable for (a sum of money); have as a price. **2** involve as a loss or sacrifice (*it cost him his life*). **3** (*past* and *past part.* **costed**) fix or estimate the cost of. –*n.* **1** expenditure, usu. of money, required for the purchase of goods or services or incurred in achieving a goal, e.g. producing certain goods, building a factory, or closing down a branch. See also ECONOMIC COST; OPPORTUNITY COST. **2** loss or sacrifice. **3** (in *pl.*) legal expenses. □ **at all costs** (or **at any cost**) whatever the cost or risk may be. **at cost** at the original price paid, with nothing added for profit etc.; at cost price. [Latin *consto* stand at a price]

Costa Brava /'kɒstə 'brɑːvə/ resort region on the Mediterranean coast of NE Spain.

♦ **cost accountant** *n.* accountant whose principal function is to gather and manipulate data on the costs and efficiency of industrial processes and thus to advise management on the profitability of ventures. It is the cost accountant who operates budgetary control of departments, estimates unit costs, and provides the information required for preparing tenders. □ **cost accounting** *n.*

Costa del Sol /'kɒstə del 'sɒl/ resort region on the Mediterranean coast of S Spain. Marbella and Torremolinos are the principal resort towns.

costal /'kɒst(ə)l/ *adj.* of the ribs. [Latin *costa* rib]

♦ **cost and freight** see C. & F.

♦ **cost-benefit analysis** *n.* method of deciding whether or not a particular project should be undertaken, by comparing the relevant economic costs and the potential benefits. It can be used for private investment projects, calculating outlays and returns, and estimating the net present value of the project: if this is positive the project would be profitable. Cost-benefit analysis is also frequently used by governments in an attempt to evaluate all the social costs and benefits of a project (e.g. road building), which is much more problematic, involving such considerations as externalities, public goods, macroeconomic consequences, etc. See also SHADOW PRICE.

♦ **cost centre** *n.* unit of a business or other organization, e.g. a department in a school or a single machine in a workshop, that generates identifiable expenditure for cost-account-

---

Costa Rica /ˌkɒstə 'riːkə/, **Republic of** country in Central America on the Isthmus of Panama, with Nicaragua to the N and Panama to the SE. The economy is based mainly on agriculture; bananas, coffee, cattle, sugar, and cocoa are major exports. Manufactured goods, including foodstuffs, textiles, plastic goods, and pharmaceuticals, comprise the largest category of exports. There are mineral resources of gold, haematite ore, and sulphur and valuable hardwoods, such as mahogany and rosewood. Tourism is the major source of foreign exchange revenue.

History. Costa Rica achieved independence from Spain in 1823 and finally emerged as a separate country in 1838 after 14 years within the Federation of Central America. A new constitution in 1948 introduced more democratic rule, including abolition of the army. Since then the country has been one of the most stable and prosperous states in the region. In 1996 the country was badly affected by a hurricane, which damaged the Pan-American Highway. President, Miguel Angel Rodriguez; capital, San José. □ **Costa Rican** *adj.* & *n.*

language	Spanish
currency	colón of 100 céntimos
pop. (1996)	3 400 000
GNP (1994)	US$7.8B
literacy	94% (m); 95% (f)
life expectancy	72 (m); 77 (f)

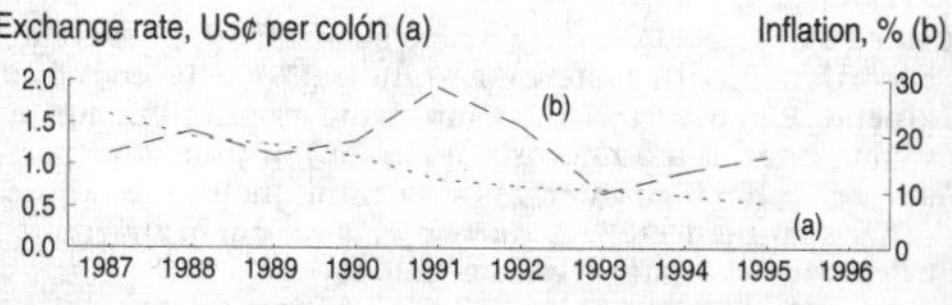

---

ing purposes. Each cost centre is frequently given its own budget, which is subsequently compared with the actual costs incurred. In some organizations central overheads, which the cost centre cannot control, are apportioned appropriately to cost centres. This may be necessary when one cost centre services other cost centres and it is required to assess the total cost of products or services for pricing purposes.

◆ **cost-effective** *adj.* **1** able to achieve a goal with the minimum of expenditure. **2** able to achieve a goal with an expenditure that makes the achievement viable in commercial terms. The M25, for example, could have been built as an eight-lane, rather than a six-lane, motorway but this was erroneously thought not to be cost-effective. □ **cost-effectiveness** *n.*

costermonger /ˈkɒstəˌmʌŋgə(r)/ *n.* person who sells produce from a barrow. [*costard* large apple: related to COSTAL]

◆ **cost function** *n. Econ.* function that defines the costs of different combinations of inputs for each level of output. In producer theory, by making certain assumptions, a unique cost-minimizing combination of inputs for each level of output can be derived from the cost function.

◆ **cost, insurance, and freight** see C.I.F.

costive /ˈkɒstɪv/ *adj.* constipated. [Latin: related to CONSTIPATE]

costly *adj.* (**-ier, -iest**) costing much; expensive. □ **costliness** *n.*

◆ **cost minimization** *n. Econ.* behavioural assumption that an individual or firm will seek to purchase a given amount of goods or inputs at the least cost, other things being equal (see CETERIS PARIBUS). In producer theory, making certain assumptions, there will exist a single cost-minimizing combination of inputs for any level of output. Assuming that firms or entrepreneurs choose to minimize costs, their behaviour can be predicted. It can be shown that the profit-maximizing level of output for a firm (see PROFIT MAXIMIZATION) is also cost-minimizing; however, it need not be assumed that firms actually maximize profits, which is a different behavioural assumption. See also MANAGERIAL THEORY OF THE FIRM; SATISFICING BEHAVIOUR.

cost of living *n.* level of prices esp. of basic necessities.

◆ **cost-plus** *attrib. adj.* **1** calculated as cost price plus an agreed fee or percentage. A contract supplying goods or services on these terms is sometimes used if it is difficult to estimate costs in advance, as in the building trade, but it is unpopular because the supplier is motivated to increase the costs rather than to reduce them and the buyer has to enter into an open-ended commitment. **2** denoting a method of pricing work in which the cost of doing the work is marked up by a fixed percentage to cover either overheads or profit or both.

cost price *n.* price paid for a thing by one who later sells it.

◆ **cost-push inflation** *n.* increase in the prices of goods caused by increases in the cost of inputs, esp. wages and raw materials. As an explanation of inflation, cost-push theories became popular in the 1970s when they appeared to explain the rapid inflation of that period, which followed on from very rapid rises in wages and the increases in oil prices. However, the theory is now widely criticized as it describes only changes in relative prices (e.g. oil), rather than rises in the general price level (which is how inflation is defined), and most economists now agree that price rises can only continue if there is an accompanying increase in the money supply.

costume /ˈkɒstjuːm/ *–n.* **1** style of dress, esp. of a particular place or time. **2** set of clothes. **3** clothing for a particular activity (*swimming-costume*). **4** actor's clothes for a part. *–v.* (**-ming**) provide with a costume. [Latin: related to CUSTOM]

costume jewellery *n.* artificial jewellery.

costumier /kɒˈstjuːmɪə(r)/ *n.* person who makes or deals in costumes. [French: related to COSTUME]

◆ **cost unit** *n.* item of production or a specific service provided to which costs can be attributed. In a company making refrigerators a cost unit might be one refrigerator although in a company making refrigerator parts, each part might be a cost unit.

cosy /ˈkəʊzɪ/ (*US* **cozy**) *–adj.* (**-ier, -iest**) comfortable and warm; snug. *–n.* (*pl.* **-ies**) cover to keep a teapot etc. hot. □ **cosily** *adv.* **cosiness** *n.* [origin unknown]

cot[1] *n.* **1** small bed with high sides for a baby. **2** small light bed. [Hindi]

cot[2] *n.* **1** small shelter; cote. **2** *poet.* cottage. [Old English]

cot[3] *abbr.* cotangent.

cotangent /kəʊˈtændʒ(ə)nt/ *n.* ratio of the side adjacent to an acute angle (in a right-angled triangle) to the opposite side.

cot-death *n.* unexplained death of a sleeping baby.

cote *n.* shelter for animals or birds. [Old English]

coterie /ˈkəʊtərɪ/ *n.* exclusive group of people sharing interests. [French]

cotoneaster /kəˌtəʊnɪˈæstə(r)/ *n.* shrub bearing usu. bright red berries. [Latin *cotoneum* QUINCE]

Cotonou /ˌkɒtəˈnuː/ largest city and chief port of Benin, a commercial and financial centre with textile and brewing industries; pop. (1992) 533 212.

cottage /ˈkɒtɪdʒ/ *n.* small simple house, esp. in the country. [Anglo-French: related to COT[2]]

cottage cheese *n.* soft white lumpy cheese made from skimmed milk curds.

cottage industry *n.* business activity carried on at home.

cottage pie *n.* dish of minced meat topped with mashed potato.

cottager *n.* person who lives in a cottage.

Cottbus /ˈkɒtbʊs/ industrial city and railway junction in SE Germany; industries include textiles and carpet making; pop. (est. 1995) 125 643.

Côte d'Ivoire /kəʊt diːˈvɑː(r)/, **Republic of** (formerly **Ivory Coast**) country in W Africa, on the Gulf of Guinea, between Liberia and Ghana. Agriculture and forestry are the mainstays of the economy, coffee and cocoa being major exports; timber (notably mahogany), pineapples, palm oil, and bananas are also exported. There is some mining of manganese and diamonds. Tourism and manufacturing industries are being developed.

History. Formerly a French colony, it became an autonomous republic within the French Community in 1958 and a fully independent republic outside it in 1960. Multiparty elections were held for the first time in 1990 and the ruling party was returned to power. Félix Houphouet-Boigny, who had been president since independence, died in 1993 and was replaced by Henri Konan Bédié, who won the 1995 presidential election. President, Henri Konan Bédié; capital, Yamoussoukro.

languages	French (official), African languages
currency	CFA franc (CFAF) of 100 centimes
pop. (1996)	14 733 000
GNP (1994)	US$7B
literacy	49% (m); 30% (f)
life expectancy	49 (m); 52 (f)

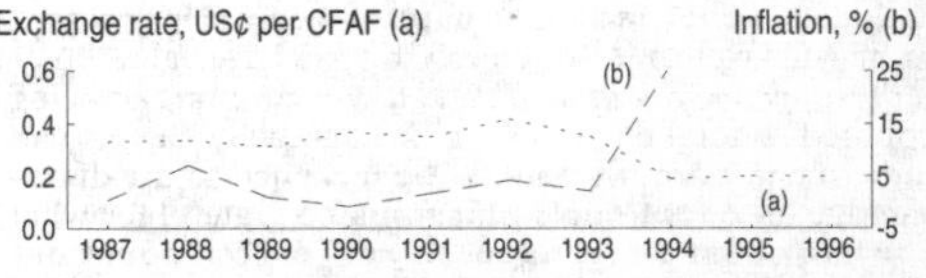

cotter *n.* **1** bolt or wedge for securing parts of machinery etc. **2** (in full **cotter pin**) split pin that can be opened after passing through a hole. [origin unknown]

cotton /'kɒt(ə)n/ *n.* **1** soft white fibrous substance covering the seeds of certain plants. **2** such a plant. **3** thread or cloth from this. □ **cotton on** (often foll. by *to*) *colloq.* begin to understand. [French from Arabic]

cotton wool *n.* fluffy wadding of a kind orig. made from raw cotton.

cotyledon /ˌkɒtɪ'liːd(ə)n/ *n.* embryonic leaf in seed-bearing plants. [Greek *kotulē* cup]

couch[1] *–n.* **1** upholstered piece of furniture for several people; sofa. **2** long padded seat with a headrest at one end. *–v.* **1** (foll. by *in*) express in (certain terms). **2** *archaic* (of an animal) lie, esp. in its lair. [Latin *colloco* lay in place]

couch[2] /kaʊtʃ, kuːtʃ/ *n.* (in full **couch grass**) a grass with long creeping roots. [var. of QUITCH]

couchette /kuː'ʃet/ *n.* **1** railway carriage with seats convertible into sleeping-berths. **2** berth in this. [French, = little bed]

couch potato *n. US slang* person who likes lazing at home.

cougar /'kuːgə(r)/ *n. US* puma. [French from Guarani]

cough /kɒf/ *–v.* **1** expel air etc. from the lungs with a sudden sharp sound. **2** (of an engine etc.) make a similar sound. **3** *slang* confess. *–n.* **1** act of coughing. **2** condition of respiratory organs causing coughing. □ **cough up 1** eject with coughs. **2** *slang* bring out or give (money or information) reluctantly. [imitative, related to Dutch *kuchen*]

cough mixture *n.* liquid medicine to relieve a cough.

could *past* of CAN[1]. *v. colloq.* feel inclined to (*I could murder him*).

couldn't /'kʊd(ə)nt/ *contr.* could not.

coulomb /'kuːlɒm/ *n.* SI unit of electric charge. [*Coulomb*, name of a physicist]

coulter /'kəʊltə(r)/ *n.* (*US* **colter**) vertical blade in front of a ploughshare. [Latin *culter* knife]

council /'kaʊns(ə)l/ *n.* **1 a** advisory, deliberative, or administrative body. **b** meeting of such a body. **2 a** local administrative body of a parish, district, town, etc. **b** (*attrib.*) provided by a local council (*council flat*). [Latin *concilium*]

♦ **Council for Mutual Economic Assistance** *hist.* see COMECON.

---

councillor *n.* member of a (esp. local) council.

council tax *n.* local tax based on the value of a property and the number of people living in it. It replaced the community charge in April 1993.

counsel /'kaʊns(ə)l/ *–n.* **1** advice, esp. formally given. **2** consultation for advice. **3** (*pl.* same) legal adviser, esp. a barrister; body of these. *–v.* (**-ll-**; *US* **-l-**) **1** advise (a person). **2** give esp. professional advice to (a person) on personal problems. **3** recommend (a course of action). □ **keep one's own counsel** not confide in others. **take counsel** (usu. foll. by *with*) consult. □ **counselling** *n.* [Latin *consilium*]

counsellor *n.* (*US* **counselor**) **1** adviser. **2** person giving professional guidance on personal problems. **3** *US* barrister.

counsel of perfection *n.* ideal but impracticable advice.

count[1] *–v.* **1** determine the total number of, esp. by assigning successive numbers. **2** repeat numbers in ascending order. **3** (often foll. by *in*) include or be included in one's reckoning or plan. **4** consider or regard to be (lucky etc.). **5** (often foll. by *for*) have value; matter (*my opinion counts for little*). *–n.* **1 a** counting or being counted. **b** total of reckoning. **2** *Law* each charge in an indictment. □ **count against** be reckoned to the disadvantage of. **count one's blessings** be grateful for what one has. **count on** (or **upon**) rely on; expect. **count out 1** count while taking from a stock. **2** complete a count of ten seconds over (a fallen boxer etc.). **3** *colloq.* exclude, disregard. **4** *Polit.* procure the adjournment of (the House of Commons) when fewer than 40 members are present. **count up** find the sum of. **keep count** take note of how many there have been etc. **lose count** forget the number etc. counted. **out for the count 1** defeated. **2** unconscious; asleep. [Latin: related to COMPUTE]

count[2] *n.* foreign noble corresponding to an earl. [Latin *comes* companion]

countable *adj.* **1** that can be counted. **2** *Gram.* (of a noun) that can form a plural or be used with the indefinite article.

countdown *n.* **1** act of counting backwards to zero, esp. at the launching of a rocket etc. **2** period immediately before an event.

countenance /'kaʊntɪnəns/ *–n.* **1** the face or facial expression. **2** composure. **3** moral support. *–v.* (**-cing**) support, approve. [French: related to CONTAIN]

counter[1] *n.* **1** long flat-topped fitment in a shop etc., across which business is conducted. **2 a** small disc for playing or scoring in board-games etc. **b** token representing a coin. **3** apparatus for counting. □ **under the counter** surreptitiously, esp. illegally. [related to COUNT[1]]

counter[2] *–v.* **1 a** oppose, contradict. **b** meet by countermove. **2** *Boxing* give a return blow while parrying. *–adv.* in the opposite direction or manner. *–adj.* opposite. *–n.* parry; countermove. [related to COUNTER-]

counter- *comb. form* denoting: **1** retaliation, opposition, or rivalry (*counter-threat*). **2** opposite direction (*counter-clockwise*). **3** correspondence (*counterpart*; *countersign*). [Latin *contra* against]

counteract /ˌkaʊntə'rækt/ *v.* hinder or neutralize by contrary action. □ **counteraction** *n.* **counteractive** *adj.*

counter-attack *–n.* attack in reply to a preceding attack. *–v.* attack in reply.

counterbalance *–n.* weight or influence balancing another. *–v.* (**-cing**) act as a counterbalance to.

♦ **counter-bid** *–n.* **1** bid made in an auction that exceeds a bid already made (which then becomes the **underbid**). **2** second bid made in reply to a counter-offer. *–v.* (**-dd-**; *past* **-bid**; *past part.* **-bid**) make a counter-bid.

---

counter-clockwise /ˌkaʊntə'klɒkwaɪz/ *adv.* & *adj. US* = ANTICLOCKWISE.

counter-espionage /ˌkaʊntər'espɪəˌnɑːʒ/ *n.* action taken against enemy spying.

counterfeit /'kaʊntəfɪt/ *–adj.* made in imitation; not genuine; forged. *–n.* a forgery or imitation. *–v.* imitate fraudulently; forge. [French]

counterfoil *n.* part of a cheque, receipt, etc., retained by the payer as a record. [from FOIL[2]]

counter-intelligence /ˌkaʊntərɪn'telɪdʒ(ə)ns/ *n.* = COUNTER-ESPIONAGE.

countermand /ˌkaʊntə'mɑːnd/ *–v.* **1** revoke (a command). **2** recall by a contrary order. *–n.* order revoking a previous one. [Latin: related to MANDATE]

countermeasure *n.* action taken to counteract a danger, threat, etc.

countermove *n.* move or action in opposition to another.

♦ **counter-offer** *n.* reply made to a bid. If a seller makes an offer of goods on specified terms at a specified price, the buyer may accept it or make a bid against the offer. If the seller finds the bid unacceptable he or she may make a counter-offer, usu. on terms or at a price that are a compromise between those in the offer and bid. If the buyer still finds the counter-offer unacceptable he or she may make a counter-bid.

---

counterpane /'kaʊntəˌpeɪn/ *n.* bedspread. [medieval Latin *culcita puncta* quilted mattress]

counterpart *n.* **1** person or thing like another or forming the complement or equivalent to another. **2** duplicate.

♦ **counterparty** *n.* a person who is a party to a contract.

♦ **counterparty risk** *n.* the risk that any of the parties to a contract will fail to honour their obligations under it.

---

counterpoint /'kaʊntə,pɔɪnt/ *n.* **1 a** art or practice of combining melodies according to fixed rules. **b** melody combined with another. **2** contrasting argument, plot, literary theme, etc. [medieval Latin *contrapunctum* marked opposite]

counterpoise /'kaʊntə,pɔɪz/ *–n.* **1** counterbalance. **2** state of equilibrium. *–v.* (**-sing**) counterbalance. [Latin *pensum* weight]

counter-productive /,kaʊntəprə'dʌktɪv/ *adj.* having the opposite of the desired effect.

counter-revolution /,kaʊntə,revə'lu:ʃ(ə)n/ *n.* revolution opposing a former one or reversing its results.

countersign *–v.* add a signature to (a document already signed by another). *–n.* **1** password spoken to a person on guard. **2** mark used for identification etc. [Italian: related to SIGN]

countersink *v.* (*past* and *past part.* **-sunk**) **1** shape (the rim of a hole) so that a screw or bolt can be inserted flush with the surface. **2** sink (a screw etc.) in such a hole.

counter-tenor *n.* **1** male alto singing-voice. **2** singer with this voice. [Italian: related to CONTRA-]

♦ **countertrade** *–n.* international trading in which goods are paid for in a form other than hard currency. For example, a South American country wishing to buy aircraft may pay for them (usu. through a third party) in coffee beans. *–v.* (**-ding**) engage in countertrade. □ **countertrading** *n.*

---

countervail /'kaʊntə,veɪl/ *v. literary* **1** counterbalance. **2** (often foll. by *against*) oppose, usu. successfully. [Latin *valeo* have worth]

♦ **countervailing credit** *n.* = BACK-TO-BACK CREDIT.

♦ **countervailing tariff** *n.* (also **countervailing duty**) extra import duty imposed by a country on certain imports. It is usu. used to prevent dumping or to counteract export subsidies given by foreign countries.

---

counterweight *n.* counterbalancing weight.

countess /'kaʊntɪs/ *n.* **1** wife or widow of a count or earl. **2** woman holding the rank of count or earl. [Latin *comitissa*: related to COUNT²]

countless *adj.* too many to be counted.

countrified /'kʌntrɪ,faɪd/ *adj.* rustic in manner or appearance.

country /'kʌntrɪ/ *n.* (*pl.* **-ies**) **1** territory of a nation; state. **2** (often *attrib.*) rural districts as opposed to towns or the capital. **3** land of a person's birth or citizenship. **4** region with regard to its aspect, associations, etc. (*mountainous country*; *Hardy country*). **5** national population, esp. as voters. [medieval Latin *contrata* (*terra*) (land) lying opposite]

country-and-western *n.* type of folk music originated by Whites in the southern US.

country club *n.* sporting and social club in a rural setting.

country dance *n.* traditional dance, esp. English, usu. with couples facing each other in lines.

countryman *n.* (*fem.* **countrywoman**) **1** person living in a rural area. **2** (also **fellow-countryman**) person of one's own country.

country music *n.* = COUNTRY-AND-WESTERN.

countryside *n.* rural areas.

country-wide *adj.* & *adv.* extending throughout a nation.

county /'kaʊntɪ/ *–n.* (*pl.* **-ies**) **1** territorial division in some countries, forming the chief unit of local administration. **2** *US* political and administrative division of a state. *–adj.* of or like the gentry. [Latin *comitatus*: related to COUNT²]

county council *n.* elected governing body of an administrative county.

county court *n.* judicial court for civil cases.

county town *n.* administrative capital of a county.

coup /ku:/ *n.* (*pl.* **-s** /ku:z/) **1** successful stroke or move. **2** = COUP D'ÉTAT. [medieval Latin *colpus* blow]

coup de grâce /,ku: də 'grɑ:s/ *n.* finishing stroke. [French]

coup d'état /,ku: deɪ'tɑ:/ *n.* (*pl.* ***coups d'état*** pronunc. same) violent or illegal seizure of power. [French]

coupé /'ku:peɪ/ *n.* (*US* **coupe** /ku:p/) car with a hard roof, two doors, and usu. a sloping rear. [French *couper* cut]

couple /'kʌp(ə)l/ *–n.* **1 a** two (*a couple of girls*). **b** about two (*a couple of hours*). **2 a** two people who are married to, or in a sexual relationship with, each other. **b** pair of partners in a dance etc. *–v.* (**-ling**) **1** link together. **2** associate in thought or speech. **3** copulate. [Latin COPULA]

couplet /'kʌplɪt/ *n.* two successive lines of verse, usu. rhyming and of the same length. [French diminutive: related to COUPLE]

coupling /'kʌplɪŋ/ *n.* **1** link connecting railway carriages etc. **2** device for connecting parts of machinery.

coupon /'ku:pɒn/ *n.* **1** form etc. as an application for a purchase etc. **2** entry form for a football pool or other competition. **3** discount voucher given with a purchase. **4** *Finance* **a** one of several dated slips attached to a bond, which must be presented to the agents of the issuer or the company to obtain an interest payment or dividend. They are usu. used with bearer bonds; the **coupon yield** is the yield provided by a bearer bond. **b** rate of interest paid by a fixed-interest bearer bond. A 5% coupon implies that the bond pays 5% interest. [French *couper* cut]

♦ **coupon yield** see COUPON 4a.

---

courage /'kʌrɪdʒ/ *n.* ability to disregard fear; bravery. □ **courage of one's convictions** courage to act on one's beliefs. [Latin *cor* heart]

courageous /kə'reɪdʒəs/ *adj.* brave. □ **courageously** *adv.*

courgette /kʊə'ʒet/ *n.* small vegetable marrow. [French]

courier /'kʊrɪə(r)/ *n.* **1** person employed to guide and assist tourists. **2** special messenger. **3** organization that provides a special delivery service for parcels, documents, etc. [Latin *curro curs-* run]

course /kɔ:s/ *–n.* **1** onward movement or progression. **2** direction taken (*changed course*). **3** stretch of land or water for races; golf-course. **4** series of lessons etc. in a particular subject. **5** each successive part of a meal. **6** sequence of medical treatment etc. **7** line of conduct. **8** continuous horizontal layer of masonry, brick, etc. **9** channel in which water flows. *–v.* (**-sing**) **1** (esp. of liquid) run, esp. fast. **2** (also *absol.*) use hounds to hunt (esp. hares). □ **in course of** in the process of. **in the course of** during. **of course** naturally; as is or was to be expected; admittedly. [Latin *cursus*: related to COURIER]

courser *n. poet.* swift horse.

court /kɔ:t/ *–n.* **1** (in full **court of law**) **a** judicial body hearing legal cases. **b** = COURTROOM. **2** quadrangular area for games (*tennis-court*; *squash-court*). **3 a** yard surrounded by houses with entry from the street. **b** = COURTYARD. **4 a** the residence, retinue, and courtiers of a sovereign. **b** sovereign and councillors, constituting the ruling power. **c** assembly held by a sovereign; state reception. **5** attention paid to a person whose favour etc. is sought (*paid court to her*). *–v.* **1 a** try to win affection or favour of. **b** pay amorous attention to. **2** seek to win (applause, fame, etc.). **3** invite (misfortune) by one's actions. □ **go to court** take legal action. **out of court 1** without reaching trial. **2** not worthy of consideration. [Latin: related to COHORT]

court-card *n.* playing-card that is a king, queen, or jack.

courteous /'kɜ:tɪəs/ *adj.* polite, considerate. □ **courteously** *adv.* **courteousness** *n.* [French: related to COURT]

courtesan /ˌkɔːtɪˈzæn/ *n.* prostitute, esp. one with wealthy or upper-class clients. [Italian: related to COURT]

courtesy /ˈkɜːtəsɪ/ *n.* (*pl.* **-ies**) courteous behaviour or act. □ **by courtesy of** with the formal permission of. [French: related to COURTEOUS]

courtesy light *n.* light in a car switched on by opening a door.

court-house *n.* **1** building in which a judicial court is held. **2** *US* building containing the administrative offices of a county.

courtier /ˈkɔːtɪə(r)/ *n.* person who attends a sovereign's court. [Anglo-French: related to COURT]

courtly *adj.* (**-ier**, **-iest**) dignified, refined. □ **courtliness** *n.*

court martial /ˌkɔːt ˈmɑːʃ(ə)l/ *–n.* (*pl.* **courts martial**) judicial court trying members of the armed services. *–v.* (**court-martial**) (**-ll-**; *US* **-l-**) try by this.

court order *n.* direction issued by a court or judge.

Courtrai see KORTRIJK.

courtroom *n.* room in which a court of law meets.

courtship *n.* **1** courting, wooing. **2** courting behaviour of animals, birds, etc.

court shoe *n.* woman's light, usu. high-heeled, shoe with a low-cut upper.

courtyard *n.* area enclosed by walls or buildings.

couscous /ˈkuːskuːs/ *n.* N African dish of crushed wheat or coarse flour steamed over broth, often with meat or fruit added. [French from Arabic]

cousin /ˈkʌz(ə)n/ *n.* **1** (also **first cousin**) child of one's uncle or aunt. **2** person of a kindred race or nation. [Latin *consobrinus*]

■ **Usage** There is often some confusion as to the difference between *cousin, first cousin, second cousin, first cousin once removed*, etc. For definitions see *cousin, second cousin* and *remove v.* 5.

couture /kuːˈtjʊə(r)/ *n.* design and manufacture of fashionable clothes. [French]

couturier /kuːˈtjʊərɪˌeɪ/ *n.* fashion designer.

cove[1] *–n.* **1** small bay or creek. **2** sheltered recess. **3** moulding, esp. at the junction of a wall and a ceiling. *–v.* (**-ving**) **1** provide (a room etc.) with a cove. **2** slope (the sides of a fireplace) inwards. [Old English]

cove[2] *n. slang* fellow, chap. [cant: origin unknown]

coven /ˈkʌv(ə)n/ *n.* assembly of witches. [related to CONVENT]

covenant /ˈkʌvənənt/ *–n.* **1** agreement; contract. **2** *Law* promise made in a deed under seal (see also DEED OF COVENANT). Such a promise can be enforced by the parties to it as a contract, even if the promise is gratuitous: for example, if A covenants to pay B £100 per month, B can enforce this promise even though he has done nothing in return. Covenants may also be used to minimize income tax, by transferring income from higher-rate taxpayers to non-taxpayers (e.g. children or charities). However, since the Finance Act (1988), only covenants made to charities offer much scope for tax planning. Covenants may be entered into concerning the use of land, frequently to restrict the activities of a new owner or tenant (e.g. a covenant not to sell alcohol or run a fish-and-chip shop). Such covenants may be enforceable by persons deriving title from the original parties. This is an exception to the general rule that a contract cannot bind persons who are not parties to it. If the land is leasehold, a covenant 'touching and concerning land' may be enforced by persons other than the original parties if there is 'privity of estate' between them, i.e. if they are in the position of landlord and tenant. If the land is freehold, the benefit of any covenant (i.e. the rights under it) may be assigned together with the land. The burden of the covenant (i.e. the duties under it) will pass with the land only if it is a restrictive covenant. This means that it must be negative in nature, such as a covenant not to build on land. **3** (**Covenant**) *Bibl.* agreement between God and the Israelites. *–v.* agree, esp. by legal covenant. [French: related to CONVENE]

Coventry /ˈkɒvəntrɪ/ industrial city in central England in West Midlands; manufactures include cars, machinery, and electrical equipment; pop. (est. 1994) 302 500. □ **send a person to Coventry** refuse to associate with or speak to a person.

cover /ˈkʌvə(r)/ *–v.* **1** (often foll. by *with*) protect or conceal with a cloth, lid, etc. **2 a** extend over; occupy the whole surface of. **b** (often foll. by *with*) strew thickly or thoroughly. **c** lie over. **3 a** protect; clothe. **b** (as **covered** *adj.*) wearing a hat; having a roof. **4** include; comprise; deal with. **5** travel (a specified distance). **6** describe as a reporter. **7** be enough to defray (*£20 should cover it*). **8 a** *refl.* take measures to protect oneself. **b** (*absol.*; foll. by *for*) stand in for. **9 a** aim a gun etc. at. **b** (of a fortress, guns, etc.) command (territory). **c** protect (an exposed person etc.) by being able to return fire. **10 a** esp. *Cricket* stand behind (another player) to stop any missed balls. **b** mark (an opposing player). **11** (of a stallion etc.) copulate with. *–n.* **1** thing that covers, esp.: **a** lid. **b** book's binding. **c** either board of this. **d** envelope or wrapping (*under separate cover*). **2** shelter. **3 a** pretence; screen. **b** pretended identity. **c** *Mil.* supporting force protecting an advance party from attack. **4 a** funds, esp. obtainable from insurance to meet a liability or secure against loss. **b** insurance protection (*third-party cover*). **5** *Finance* **a** see DIVIDEND COVER. **b** collateral given against a loan or credit, as in option dealing. **c** hedge purchased to safeguard an open position in commodity futures or currency dealing. **6** place-setting at table. **7** *Cricket* = COVER-POINT. □ **cover up** completely cover or conceal. **take cover** find shelter. [Latin *cooperio*]

coverage *n.* **1** area or amount covered. **2** amount of publicity received by an event etc.

coverall *n.* esp. *US* **1** thing that covers entirely. **2** (usu. in *pl.*) full-length protective garment.

cover charge *n.* service charge per head in a restaurant, nightclub, etc.

♦ **covered bear** *n.* (also **protected bear**) person who has sold securities, commodities, or currency that they do not have, although they do have a hedge that they could sell at a profit if the market moves upwards, preventing them from covering their bear sale at a profit. See also HEDGE *v.* 4.

---

cover girl *n.* female model appearing on magazine covers etc.

covering letter *n.* (also **covering note**) explanatory letter sent with an enclosure.

coverlet /ˈkʌvəlɪt/ *n.* bedspread. [Anglo-French: related to COVER, *lit* bed]

♦ **cover note** *n.* temporary proof of cover issued prior to the main insurance-policy documents. Motor-insurance cover notes are temporary versions of the certificate of insurance; as motor insurers are rarely able to issue the full policy and certificate immediately, a cover note is issued as an abbreviated version for a short period (usu. 30 or 60 days).

---

cover-point *n. Cricket* **1** fielding position covering point. **2** fielder at this position.

cover story *n.* news story in a magazine that is advertised etc. on the front cover.

covert /ˈkʌvət/ *–adj.* secret or disguised (*covert glance*). *–n.* **1** shelter, esp. a thicket hiding game. **2** feather covering the base of a bird's flight-feather. □ **covertly** *adv.* [French: related to COVER]

cover-up *n.* concealment of facts.

covet /ˈkʌvɪt/ *v.* (**-t-**) desire greatly (esp. a thing belonging to another person). [French: related to CUPID]

covetous /ˈkʌvɪtəs/ *adj.* (usu. foll. by *of*) coveting; grasping. □ **covetously** *adv.*

covey /ˈkʌvɪ/ *n.* (*pl.* **-s**) **1** brood of partridges. **2** small group of people. [Latin *cubo* lie]

cow[1] *n.* **1** fully grown female of any esp. domestic bovine animal, used as a source of milk and beef. **2** female of other large animals, esp. the elephant, whale, and seal. **3** *derog. slang* woman. [Old English]

cow[2] *v.* intimidate or dispirit. [Old Norse]

coward /'kaʊəd/ *n.* person who is easily frightened. [Latin *cauda* tail]

cowardice /'kaʊədɪs/ *n.* lack of bravery.

cowardly *adj.* **1** of or like a coward; lacking courage. **2** (of an action) done against one who cannot retaliate.

cowbell *n.* bell worn round a cow's neck.

cowboy *n.* **1** (*fem.* **cowgirl**) person who tends cattle, esp. in the western US. **2** *colloq.* unscrupulous or incompetent person in business.

cower *v.* crouch or shrink back in fear or distress. [Low German]

Cowes /kaʊz/ town on the Isle of Wight, famous internationally as a yachting centre; industries include boat- and hovercraft-building and marine engineering; pop. (1991) 16 335.

cowherd *n.* person who tends cattle.

cowhide *n.* **1** cow's hide. **2** leather or whip made from this.

cowl *n.* **1** monk's cloak. **2** hood-shaped covering of a chimney or ventilating shaft. [Latin *cucullus*]

cow-lick *n.* projecting lock of hair.

cowling *n.* removable cover of a vehicle or aircraft engine.

co-worker /kəʊ'wɜːkə(r)/ *n.* person who works with another.

cow-parsley *n.* hedgerow plant with lacelike umbels of flowers.

cow-pat *n.* flat round piece of cow-dung.

cowpox *n.* disease of cows, whose virus was formerly used in smallpox vaccination.

cowrie /'kaʊrɪ/ *n.* **1** tropical mollusc with a bright shell. **2** its shell as money in parts of Africa and S Asia. [Urdu and Hindi]

co-write /kəʊ'raɪt/ *v.* write with another person. □ **co-writer** *n.*

cowslip /'kaʊslɪp/ *n.* primula with small yellow flowers. [obsolete *slyppe* dung]

cox –*n.* coxswain, esp. of a racing-boat. –*v.* act as cox (of). [abbreviation]

coxcomb /'kɒkskəʊm/ *n.* ostentatiously conceited man. □ **coxcombry** *n.* (*pl.* **-ies**). [= *cock's comb*]

Cox's Bazaar /'kɒksɪz/ seaport in SE Bangladesh, near Chittagong; pop. (1981) 29 600.

coxswain /'kɒks(ə)n/ –*n.* **1** person who steers, esp. a rowing-boat. **2** senior petty officer in a small ship. –*v.* act as coxswain (of). [*cock* ship's boat, SWAIN]

coy *adj.* **1** affectedly shy. **2** irritatingly reticent. □ **coyly** *adv.* **coyness** *n.* [French: related to QUIET]

coyote /kɔɪ'əʊtɪ/ *n.* (*pl.* same or **-s**) North American wolflike wild dog. [Mexican Spanish]

coypu /'kɔɪpuː/ *n.* (*pl.* **-s**) aquatic beaver-like rodent native to South America. [Araucan]

cozen /'kʌz(ə)n/ *v. literary* **1** cheat, defraud. **2** beguile. **3** act deceitfully. □ **cozenage** *n.* [cant]

Cozumel /ˌkəʊzə'mel/ resort island in the Caribbean, off the NE Coast of Mexico.

cozy *US* var. of COSY.

CP –*abbr.* **1** carriage paid. **2** *Computing* central processor. **3** (also **C/P**) charter-party. **4** = COMMERCIAL PAPER. –*international civil aircraft marking* Bolivia. –*airline flight code* Canadian Airlines International.

c.p. *abbr.* candlepower.

CPA *abbr.* **1** *US* certified public accountant (see CERTIFIED ACCOUNTANT). **2** chartered patent agent. **3** *Insurance* claims payable abroad. **4** cost planning and appraisal. **5** = CRITICAL-PATH ANALYSIS.

CPAC *abbr.* Consumer Protection Advisory Committee.

CPI *abbr.* consumer price index.

cpi *abbr.* (also **c.p.i.**) *Printing* characters per inch.

Cpl. *abbr.* Corporal.

CPM *abbr.* critical-path method. See CRITICAL-PATH ANALYSIS.

◆ **CP/M** *abbr. propr.* Control Program for Microcomputers, an operating system developed by Digital Research Inc. in 1976 and now widely used on microcomputers. There are hundreds of programs available to computers using CP/M.

CPP *abbr.* current purchasing power. See CURRENT PURCHASING POWER ACCOUNTING.

CPS *abbr.* **1** Centre for Policy Studies. **2** cents per share. **3** *US* certified professional secretary.

cps *abbr.* (also **c.p.s.**) **1** *Computing* characters per second. **2** *Sci.* cycles per second.

CPSA *abbr.* Civil and Public Services Association, clerical civil servants' union.

CPSC *abbr.* (in the US) Consumer Product Safety Commission.

CPT *abbr.* cost per thousand.

CPU *abbr.* (also **c.p.u.**) central processing unit. See CENTRAL PROCESSOR.

CR –*abbr.* **1** carrier's risk. **2** cash receipts. **3** company's risk. **4** credit rating. **5** credit reference. **6** current rate. –*international vehicle registration* Costa Rica. –*postcode* Croydon.

Cr *symb.* chromium.

cr. *abbr.* (also **Cr.**) credit.

c.r. *abbr. Finance* cum rights.

crab[1] *n.* **1 a** ten-footed crustacean, with the first pair of legs as pincers. **b** crab as food. **2** (**Crab**) sign or constellation Cancer. **3** (in full **crab-louse**) (often in *pl.*) parasitic louse transmitted sexually to esp. pubic hair. **4** machine for hoisting heavy weights. □ **catch a crab** *Rowing* jam an oar or miss the water. □ **crablike** *adj.* [Old English]

crab[2] *n.* **1** (in full **crab-apple**) small sour apple. **2** (in full **crab tree** or **crab-apple tree**) tree (esp. uncultivated) bearing this. **3** sour person. [origin unknown]

crab[3] *v.* (**-bb-**) *colloq.* **1** criticize; grumble. **2** spoil. [Low German *krabben*]

crabbed /'kræbɪd/ *adj.* **1** = CRABBY. **2** (of handwriting) ill-formed; illegible. [from CRAB[2]]

crabby *adj.* (**-ier, -iest**) irritable, morose. □ **crabbily** *adv.* **crabbiness** *n.*

crabwise *adv.* & *attrib.adj.* sideways or backwards.

crack –*n.* **1 a** sharp explosive noise. **b** sudden harshness or change in vocal pitch. **2** sharp blow. **3 a** narrow opening; break or split. **b** chink. **4** *colloq.* joke or malicious remark. **5** *colloq.* attempt. **6** *slang* crystalline form of cocaine broken into small pieces. –*v.* **1** break without separating the parts. **2** make or cause to make a sharp explosive sound. **3** break with a sharp sound. **4** give way or cause to give way (under torture etc.). **5** (of the voice) change pitch sharply; break. **6** *colloq.* find the solution to. **7** tell (a joke etc.). **8** *colloq.* hit sharply. **9** (as **cracked** *adj.*) crazy. **10** break (wheat) into coarse pieces. –*attrib. adj. colloq.* excellent; first-rate (*crack shot*). □ **crack a bottle** open a bottle, esp. of wine, and drink it. **crack down on** *colloq.* take severe measures against. **crack of dawn** daybreak. **crack up** *colloq.* **1** collapse under strain. **2** praise. **get cracking** *colloq.* begin promptly and vigorously. [Old English]

crack-brained *adj.* crazy.

crack-down *n. colloq.* severe measures (esp. against lawbreakers).

cracker *n.* **1** paper cylinder pulled apart, esp. at Christmas, with a sharp noise and releasing a hat, joke, etc. **2** loud firework. **3** (usu. in *pl.*) instrument for cracking. **4** thin dry savoury biscuit. **5** *slang* attractive or admirable person. **6** *US* biscuit.

crackers *predic. adj. slang* crazy.

cracking *slang* –*adj.* **1** excellent. **2** (*attrib.*) fast and exciting. –*adv.* outstandingly.

crackle /'kræk(ə)l/ –*v.* (**-ling**) make repeated slight cracking sound (*radio crackled; fire was crackling*). –*n.* such a sound. □ **crackly** *adj.* [from CRACK]

crackling /'kræklɪŋ/ *n.* crisp skin of roast pork.

cracknel /ˈkrækn(ə)l/ *n.* light crisp biscuit. [Dutch: related to CRACK]

crackpot *slang –n.* eccentric person. *–adj.* mad, unworkable.

crack-up *n. colloq.* mental breakdown.

Cracow /ˈkrækaʊ/ (Polish **Kraków** /ˈkrɑːkuːf/) industrial city in S Poland; manufactures include railway wagons, paper, chemicals, and tobacco; pop. (est. 1995) 746 000.

-cracy *comb. form* denoting a particular form of government etc. (*bureaucracy*). [Latin *-cratia*]

cradle /ˈkreɪd(ə)l/ *–n.* **1 a** baby's bed or cot, esp. on rockers. **b** place in which something begins, esp. civilization (*cradle of democracy*). **2** supporting framework or structure. *–v.* (**-ling**) **1** contain or shelter as in a cradle. **2** place in a cradle. [Old English]

cradle-snatcher *n. slang* admirer or lover of a much younger person.

cradle-song *n.* lullaby.

craft /krɑːft/ *–n.* **1** special skill or technique. **2** occupation needing this. **3** (*pl.* **craft**) **a** boat or vessel. **b** aircraft or spacecraft. **4** cunning or deceit. *–v.* make in a skilful way. [Old English]

craftsman *n.* (*fem.* **craftswoman**) **1** skilled worker. **2** person who practises a craft. □ **craftsmanship** *n.*

♦ **craft union** see TRADE UNION.

---

crafty *adj.* (**-ier, -iest**) cunning, artful, wily. □ **craftily** *adv.* **craftiness** *n.*

crag *n.* steep or rugged rock. [Celtic]

craggy *adj.* (**-ier, -iest**) (of facial features, landscape, etc.) rugged; rough-textured. □ **cragginess** *n.*

Craiova /krəˈjəʊvə/ city in SW Romania, in the mineral-rich Oltenia region; industries include heavy engineering and textiles; pop. (est. 1993) 303 033.

crake *n.* bird of the rail family, esp. the corncrake. [Old Norse, imitative of cry]

cram *v.* (**-mm-**) **1 a** fill to bursting; stuff. **b** (foll. by *in, into*; also *absol.*) force (a thing) in or into. **2** prepare intensively for an examination. **3** (often foll. by *with*) feed to excess. [Old English]

crammer *n.* person or institution that crams pupils for examinations.

cramp *–n.* **1** painful involuntary muscular contraction. **2** (also **cramp-iron**) metal bar with bent ends for holding masonry etc. together. *–v.* **1** affect with cramp. **2** (often foll. by *up*) confine narrowly. **3** restrict. **4** fasten with a cramp. □ **cramp a person's style** prevent a person from acting freely or naturally. [Low German or Dutch]

cramped *adj.* **1** (of a space) too small. **2** (of handwriting) small and with the letters close together.

crampon /ˈkræmpən/ *n.* (*US* **crampoon** /-ˈpuːn/) (usu. in *pl.*) spiked iron plate fixed to a boot for climbing on ice. [French: related to CRAMP]

cranberry /ˈkrænbərɪ/ *n.* (*pl.* **-ies**) **1** shrub with small red acid berries. **2** this berry used in cookery. [German *Kranbeere* crane-berry]

crane *–n.* **1** machine with a long projecting arm for moving heavy objects. **2** tall wading bird with long legs, neck, and bill. *–v.* (**-ning**) (also *absol.*) stretch out (one's neck) in order to see something. [Old English]

crane-fly *n.* two-winged long-legged fly: also called DADDY-LONG-LEGS.

cranesbill *n.* wild geranium.

cranium /ˈkreɪnɪəm/ *n.* (*pl.* **-s** or **-nia**) **1** skull. **2** part of the skeleton enclosing the brain. □ **cranial** *adj.* **craniology** /-ˈɒlədʒɪ/ *n.* [medieval Latin from Greek]

crank *–n.* **1** part of an axle or shaft bent at right angles for converting reciprocal into circular motion or vice versa. **2** eccentric person. *–v.* cause to move by means of a crank. □ **crank up** start (a car engine) with a crank. [Old English]

crankcase *n.* case enclosing a crankshaft.

crankpin *n.* pin by which a connecting-rod is attached to a crank.

crankshaft *n.* shaft driven by a crank.

cranky *adj.* (**-ier, -iest**) **1** *colloq.* eccentric. **2** working badly; shaky. **3** esp. *US* crotchety. □ **crankily** *adv.* **crankiness** *n.*

cranny /ˈkrænɪ/ *n.* (*pl.* **-ies**) chink, crevice. □ **crannied** *adj.* [French]

crap *coarse slang –n.* **1** (often as *int.* or *attrib.*) nonsense, rubbish. **2** faeces. *–v.* (**-pp-**) defecate. □ **crappy** *adj.* (**-ier, -iest**). [Dutch]

crape *n.* crêpe, usu. of black silk, formerly used for mourning. [from CRÊPE]

craps *n.pl. US* gambling dice game. [origin uncertain]

crapulent /ˈkræpjʊlənt/ *adj.* suffering the effects of drunkenness. □ **crapulence** *n.* **crapulous** *adj.* [Latin *crapula* inebriation]

crash[1] *–v.* **1** (cause to) make a loud smashing noise. **2** throw, drive, move, or fall with a loud smash. **3** (often foll. by *into*) collide or fall, or cause (a vehicle etc.) to collide or fall, violently; overturn at high speed. **4** collapse financially. **5** *colloq.* gatecrash. **6** *Computing* **a** suffer failure (*the system crashed*). **b** terminate abnormally (*the program crashed*). **7** *colloq.* pass (a red traffic-light etc.). **8** (often foll. by *out*) *slang* sleep, esp. on a floor etc. *–n.* **1** loud and sudden smashing noise. **2** violent collision or fall, esp. of a vehicle. **3** ruin, esp. financial. **4** rapid and serious fall in the level of prices in a financial market. **5** *Computing* **a** (also **system crash**) system failure that requires at least operator intervention and often some maintenance before system running can resume. **b** see HEAD CRASH. **6** (*attrib.*) done rapidly or urgently (*crash course in first aid*). *–adv.* with a crash (*go crash*). [imitative]

crash[2] *n.* coarse plain fabric of linen, cotton, etc. [Russian]

crash barrier *n.* barrier at the side or centre of a road etc.

crash-dive *–v.* **1 a** (of a submarine or its pilot) dive hastily in an emergency. **b** (of an aircraft or airman) dive and crash. **2** cause to crash-dive. *–n.* such a dive.

crash-helmet *n.* helmet worn esp. by motor cyclists.

crashing *adj. colloq.* overwhelming (*crashing bore*).

crash-land *v.* land or cause (an aircraft etc.) to land hurriedly with a crash. □ **crash landing** *n.*

crass *adj.* gross; grossly stupid. □ **crassly** *adv.* **crassness** *n.* [Latin *crassus* thick]

-crat *comb. form* member or supporter of a type of government etc.

crate *–n.* **1** slatted wooden case etc. for conveying esp. fragile goods. **2** *slang* old aircraft or other vehicle. *–v.* (**-ting**) pack in a crate. [perhaps from Dutch]

crater *–n.* **1** mouth of a volcano. **2** bowl-shaped cavity, esp. that made by a shell or bomb. **3** hollow on the surface of a planet or moon, caused by impact. *–v.* form a crater in. [Greek, = mixing-bowl]

-cratic *comb. form* (also **-cratical**) denoting a type of government etc. (*autocratic*). □ **-cratically** *comb. form* forming adverbs. [forming adverbs]

cravat /krəˈvæt/ *n.* man's scarf worn inside an open-necked shirt. [Serbo-Croatian, = Croat]

crave *v.* (**-ving**) (often foll. by *for*) long or beg for. [Old English]

craven /ˈkreɪv(ə)n/ *adj.* cowardly, abject. [probably French *cravanté* defeated]

craving *n.* strong desire or longing.

craw *n.* crop of a bird or insect. □ **stick in one's craw** be unacceptable. [Low German or Dutch]

crawfish /ˈkrɔːfɪʃ/ *n.* (*pl.* same) large marine spiny lobster. [var. of CRAYFISH]

crawl *–v.* **1** move slowly, esp. on hands and knees or with the body close to the ground etc. **2** walk or move slowly. **3** *colloq.* behave obsequiously. **4** (often foll. by *with*) be or appear to be covered or filled with crawling or moving things or people. **5** (esp. of the skin) creep. *–n.* **1** crawling. **2** slow rate of movement. **3** high-speed overarm swimming stroke. [origin unknown]

♦ **crawling peg** *n.* (also **sliding peg**) method of exchange-rate control that accepts the need for stability given by fixed (or pegged) exchange rates, while recognizing that fixed rates can be prone to serious misalignments, which in turn can cause periods of financial upheaval. Under crawling-peg arrangements, countries alter their pegs by small amounts at frequent intervals, rather than making large infrequent changes. This procedure provides flexibility and, in conjunction with the manipulation of interest rates, reduces the possibility of destabilizing speculative flows of capital. However, it is exposed to the criticism made against all fixed-rate regimes, that they are an inefficient alternative to the free play of market forces. At the same time, the crawling peg loses a major advantage of fixed rates, which is to inject certainty into the international trading system.

---

crayfish /ˈkreɪfɪʃ/ *n.* (*pl.* same) **1** small lobster-like freshwater crustacean. **2** crawfish. [French *crevice*]

crayon /ˈkreɪən/ *–n.* stick or pencil of coloured chalk, wax, etc. *–v.* draw with crayons. [French *craie* chalk]

craze *–v.* **(-zing) 1** (usu. as **crazed** *adj.*) make insane (*crazed with grief*). **2** produce fine surface cracks on (pottery glaze etc.); develop such cracks. *–n.* **1** usu. temporary enthusiasm (*craze for skateboarding*). **2** object of this. [perhaps from Old Norse]

crazy *adj.* **(-ier, -iest) 1** *colloq.* insane or mad; foolish. **2** (usu. foll. by *about*) *colloq.* extremely enthusiastic. **3** (*attrib.*) (of paving etc.) made up of irregular pieces. □ **crazily** *adv.* **craziness** *n.*

CRC *abbr.* **1** = CAMERA-READY COPY. **2** *Computing* cyclic redundancy check (or code), a widely used error-detecting code.

creak *–n.* harsh scraping or squeaking sound. *–v.* **1** make a creak. **2 a** move stiffly or with a creaking noise. **b** be poorly constructed (*plot creaks*). [imitative]

creaky *adj.* **(-ier, -iest) 1** liable to creak. **2 a** stiff or frail. **b** decrepit, outmoded. □ **creakiness** *n.*

cream *–n.* **1** fatty part of milk. **2** its yellowish-white colour. **3** creamlike cosmetic etc. **4** food or drink like or containing cream. **5** (usu. prec. by *the*) best part of something. *–v.* **1** take cream from (milk). **2** make creamy. **3** treat (the skin etc.) with cosmetic cream. **4** form a cream or scum. *–adj.* pale yellowish white. □ **cream off** take (esp. the best part) from a whole. [Latin *cramum* and Church Latin *chrisma* chrism]

cream cheese *n.* soft rich cheese made from cream and unskimmed milk.

creamer *n.* **1** cream-substitute for adding to coffee. **2** jug for cream.

creamery *n.* (*pl.* **-ies**) **1** factory producing butter and cheese. **2** dairy.

cream of tartar *n.* purified tartar, used in medicine, baking powder, etc.

cream soda *n.* carbonated vanilla-flavoured soft drink.

cream tea *n.* afternoon tea with scones, jam, and cream.

creamy *adj.* **(-ier, -iest) 1** like cream. **2** rich in cream. □ **creamily** *adv.* **creaminess** *n.*

crease *–n.* **1** line caused by folding or crushing. **2** *Cricket* line marking the position of a bowler or batsman. *–v.* **(-sing) 1** make creases in. **2** develop creases. **3** *slang* (often foll. by *up*) make or become incapable through laughter. [from CREST]

create /kriːˈeɪt/ *v.* **(-ting) 1** bring into existence; cause. **2** originate (*actor creates a part*). **3** invest with rank (*created him a lord*). **4** *slang* make a fuss. [Latin *creo*]

creation /kriːˈeɪʃ(ə)n/ *n.* **1** creating or being created. **2 a** (usu. **the Creation**) God's creating of the universe. **b** (usu. **Creation**) all created things, the universe. **3** product of the imagination, art, etc.

creative *adj.* **1** inventive, imaginative. **2** able to create. □ **creatively** *adv.* **creativeness** *n.* **creativity** /-ˈtɪvɪtɪ/ *n.*

creative accounting *n.* exploitation of loopholes in financial legislation to gain maximum advantage or present figures in a misleadingly favourable light.

creator *n.* **1** person who creates. **2** (as **the Creator**) God.

creature /ˈkriːtʃə(r)/ *n.* **1** any living being, esp. an animal. **2** person of a specified kind (*poor creature*). **3** subservient person. □ **creaturely** *adj.* [French from Latin: related to CREATE]

creature comforts *n.pl.* good food, warmth, etc.

crèche /kreʃ/ *n.* day nursery. [French]

credence /ˈkriːd(ə)ns/ *n.* belief. □ **give credence to** believe. [medieval Latin: related to CREDO]

credential /krɪˈdenʃ(ə)l/ *n.* (usu. in *pl.*) **1** certificates, references, etc., attesting to a person's education, character, etc. **2** letter(s) of introduction. [medieval Latin: related to CREDENCE]

credibility /ˌkredɪˈbɪlɪtɪ/ *n.* **1** being credible. **2** reputation, status.

credibility gap *n.* apparent difference between what is said and what is true.

credible /ˈkredɪb(ə)l/ *adj.* believable or worthy of belief. [Latin: related to CREDO]

■ **Usage** *Credible* is sometimes confused with *credulous*.

credit /ˈkredɪt/ *–n.* **1** source of honour, pride, etc. (*is a credit to the school*). **2** acknowledgement of merit. **3** good reputation. **4** belief or trust. **5 a** financial standing of a person or organization, esp. as regards money in the bank etc. **b** power to obtain goods etc. before payment with money borrowed from finance companies, banks, or other money lenders. **c** sum of money that a trader allows a customer before requiring payment. **6** (usu. in *pl.*) acknowledgement of a contributor's services to a film etc. **7** grade above pass in an examination. **8** reputation for solvency and honesty in business. **9 a** entry on the right-hand side of an account in double-entry bookkeeping, showing a positive asset. **b** sum entered. **c** right-hand side of an account. **10** educational course counting towards a degree. *–v.* **(-t-) 1** believe (*cannot credit it*). **2** (usu. foll. by *to, with*) enter on the credit side of an account. □ **credit a person with** ascribe (a good quality) to a person. **do credit to** (or **do a person credit**) enhance the reputation of. **on credit** with an arrangement to pay later. **to one's credit** in one's favour. [Italian or Latin: related to CREDO]

creditable *adj.* bringing credit or honour. □ **creditably** *adv.*

♦ **credit account** *n.* = CHARGE ACCOUNT.

♦ **credit brokerage** see ANCILLARY CREDIT BUSINESS.

♦ **credit call** *n.* national or international telephone call that is charged to the caller's credit card.

♦ **credit card** *n.* plastic card issued by a bank or finance organization to enable holders to obtain credit in shops, hotels, restaurants, petrol stations, etc. The retailer or trader receives monthly payments from the credit-card company equal to its total sales in the month by means of that credit card, less a service charge. The customer also receives monthly statements from the credit-card company; this may be paid in full within a certain number of days with no interest charged, or by means of a specified minimum payment plus a high rate of interest (usu. between 24% and 30% p.a.) on the outstanding balance. In the UK the main cards are **Barclaycard**, **Access**, **American Express**, and **Diners Club**. See also DEBIT CARD; GOLD CARD.

♦ **credit control** *n.* any system used by an organization to ensure that its outstanding debts are paid within a reasonable period. It involves establishing a **credit policy**, credit rating of clients, and chasing accounts that become overdue. See also CREDIT RATING; FACTORING.

♦ **credit guarantee** see CREDIT INSURANCE 2.

♦ **credit insurance** *n.* **1** insurance policy that continues the repayments of a particular debt in the event of the policyholder being financially unable to do so because of illness, death, redundancy, or any other specified cause. **2** form of insurance or **credit guarantee** against losses arising from bad debts, usu. undertaken not by normal insurance policies but by factors (see FACTORING). See also EXPORT CREDITS GUARANTEE DEPARTMENT.

♦ **credit line** *n.* **1** extent of the credit available to the user of a credit card. **2** facility to borrow money up to a specified amount for a specified period.

♦ **credit note** *n.* note with a specific monetary value given by a shop etc. for goods returned. When goods are supplied to a customer an invoice is issued; if the customer returns all or part of the goods the invoice is wholly or partially cancelled by a credit note.

♦ **creditor** *n.* one to whom an organization or person owes money. The balance sheet of a company shows the total owed to creditors and a distinction has to be made between creditors who will be paid during the coming accounting period and those who will not be paid until later than this. [Latin: related to CREDIT]

♦ **creditors' committee** *n.* committee of creditors of an insolvent company or a bankrupt individual that represents all the creditors. The committee supervises the conduct of the administration of a company or the bankruptcy of an individual or receives reports from an administrative receiver.

♦ **creditors' voluntary liquidation** *n.* (also **creditors' voluntary winding-up**) *n.* winding-up of a company by special resolution of the members when it is insolvent. A **meeting of creditors** must be held within 14 days of such a resolution and the creditors must be given seven days' notice of the meeting. Notices must also be posed in the *Gazette* and two local newspapers. The creditors also have certain rights to information before the meeting. A liquidator may be appointed by the members before the meeting of creditors or at the meeting by the creditors. If two different liquidators are appointed, an application may be made to the court to resolve the matter.

♦ **credit rating** *n.* assessment of the creditworthiness of an individual or a firm, i.e. the extent to which they can safely be granted credit. Traditionally, banks have provided confidential trade references, but recently **credit-reference agencies** have grown up, which gather information from a wide range of sources, including the county courts, bankruptcy proceedings, hire-purchase companies, and professional debt collectors. This information is then provided, for a fee, to interested parties. The consumer was given some protection from such activities in the Consumer Credit Act (1974), which allows an individual to obtain a copy of all information held by such agencies relating to that individual, as well as the right to correct any discrepancies.

♦ **credit-reference agency** *n.* = COMMERCIAL AGENCY. See also CREDIT RATING; ANCILLARY CREDIT BUSINESS.

♦ **credit-sale agreement** see HIRE PURCHASE.

♦ **credit squeeze** *n.* government measure, or set of measures, to reduce economic activity by restricting the money supply. Measures used include increasing the interest rate (to restrain borrowing), controlling moneylending by banks and others, and increasing down payments or making other changes to hire-purchase regulations.

♦ **credit transfer** *n.* (also **bank giro**) method of settling a debt by transferring money through a bank or post office, useful for persons who do not have bank accounts. The debtor completes written instructions naming the creditor, his address, and account number. Several creditors may be listed and settled by a single transaction. The popularity of this system led the banks to introduce a credit-clearing system in 1961 and the post office in 1968.

---

creditworthy *adj.* considered suitable to receive commercial credit. □ **creditworthiness** *n.*

credo /ˈkriːdəʊ, ˈkreɪ-/ *n.* (*pl.* **-s**) creed. [Latin, = I believe]

credulous /ˈkredjʊləs/ *adj.* too ready to believe; gullible. □ **credulity** /krɪˈdjuːlɪtɪ/ *n.* **credulously** *adv.* [Latin: related to CREDO]

■ **Usage** *Credulous* is sometimes confused with *credible.*

creed *n.* **1** set of principles or beliefs. **2** system of religious belief. **3** (often **the creed**) formal summary of Christian doctrine. [Latin: related to CREDO]

creek *n.* **1 a** inlet on a sea-coast. **b** short arm of a river. **2** esp. *US*, *Austral.*, & *NZ* tributary of a river; stream. □ **up the creek** *slang* **1** in difficulties. **2** crazy. [Old Norse and Dutch]

creel *n.* fisherman's large wicker basket. [origin unknown]

creep *–v.* (*past* and *past part.* **crept**) **1** move with the body prone and close to the ground. **2** move stealthily or timidly. **3** advance very gradually (*a feeling crept over her*). **4** *colloq.* act obsequiously in the hope of advancement. **5** (of a plant) grow along the ground or up a wall etc. **6** (as **creeping** *adj.*) developing slowly and steadily. **7** (of flesh) shiver or shudder from fear, horror, etc. *–n.* **1** act or spell of creeping. **2** (in *pl.*; prec. by *the*) *colloq.* feeling of revulsion or fear. **3** *slang* unpleasant person. **4** (of metals etc.) gradual change of shape under stress. [Old English]

creeper *n.* **1** climbing or creeping plant. **2** bird that climbs, esp. the treecreeper. **3** *slang* soft-soled shoe.

♦ **creeping take-over** *n.* accumulation of a company's shares, by purchasing them openly over a period on a stock exchange, as a preliminary to a take-over.

---

creepy *adj.* (**-ier**, **-iest**) *colloq.* feeling or causing horror or fear. □ **creepily** *adv.* **creepiness** *n.*

creepy-crawly /ˌkriːpɪˈkrɔːlɪ/ *n.* (*pl.* **-ies**) *colloq.* small crawling insect etc.

cremate /krɪˈmeɪt/ *v.* (**-ting**) burn (a corpse etc.) to ashes. □ **cremation** *n.* [Latin *cremo* burn]

crematorium /ˌkreməˈtɔːrɪəm/ *n.* (*pl.* **-ria** or **-s**) place where corpses are cremated.

crème /krem/ *n.* **1** = CREAM *n.* 4. **2** liqueur (*crème de cassis*). [French, = cream]

crème brûlée /bruːˈleɪ/ *n.* baked cream or custard pudding coated with caramel.

crème caramel *n.* custard coated with caramel.

crème de cassis /də kæˈsiːs/ *n.* blackcurrant liqueur.

crème de la crème /də lɑː ˈkrem/ *n.* best part; élite.

crème de menthe /də ˈmɑ̃t, ˈmɒnt/ *n.* peppermint liqueur.

crenellate /ˈkrenəˌleɪt/ *v.* (*US* **crenelate**) (**-ting**) provide (a tower etc.) with battlements. □ **crenellation** /-ˈleɪʃ(ə)n/ *n.* [French *crenel* embrasure]

Creole /ˈkriːəʊl/ *–n.* **1 a** descendant of European settlers in the West Indies or Central or South America. **b** White descendant of French settlers in the southern US. **c** person of mixed European and Black descent. **2** language formed from a European language and another (esp. African) language. *–adj.* **1** of Creoles. **2** (usu. **creole**) of Creole origin etc. (*creole cooking*). [French from Spanish]

creosote /ˈkriːəˌsəʊt/ *–n.* **1** dark-brown oil distilled from coal tar, used as a wood-preservative. **2** oily fluid distilled from wood tar, used as an antiseptic. *–v.* (**-ting**) treat with creosote. [Greek *kreas* flesh, *sōtēr* preserver, because of its antiseptic properties]

crêpe /kreɪp/ *n.* **1** fine gauzy wrinkled fabric. **2** thin pancake with a savoury or sweet filling. **3** hard-wearing wrinkled sheet rubber used for the soles of shoes etc. □ **crêpey** *adj.* **crêpy** *adj.* [Latin: related to CRISP]

crêpe de Chine /də ˈʃiːn/ *n.* fine silk crêpe.

crêpe paper *n.* thin crinkled paper.

crêpe Suzette /suːˈzet/ *n.* small dessert pancake flamed in alcohol.

crept *past* and *past part.* of CREEP.

crepuscular /krɪˈpʌskjʊlə(r)/ *adj.* **1 a** of twilight. **b** dim. **2** *Zool.* appearing or active in twilight. [Latin *crepusculum* twilight]

Cres. *abbr.* Crescent.

cresc. *abbr.* (also **cres.**) *Mus.* = CRESCENDO.

crescendo /krɪˈʃendəʊ/ *–n.* (*pl.* **-s**) **1** *Mus.* gradual increase in loudness. **2** progress towards a climax. *–adv.* & *adj.* increasing in loudness. [Italian: related to CRESCENT]

■ **Usage** *Crescendo* is sometimes wrongly used to mean the climax itself rather than progress towards it.

crescent /ˈkrez(ə)nt/ *–n.* **1** curved sickle shape as of the waxing or waning moon. **2** thing of this shape, esp. a street forming an arc. *–adj.* crescent-shaped. [Latin *cresco* grow]

cress *n.* any of various plants with pungent edible leaves. [Old English]

◆ **CREST** *n.* electronic share-settlement system created by the Bank of England and owned by 69 firms. It began operations in 1996 and has replaced TALISMAN.

crest *–n.* **1 a** comb or tuft etc. on a bird's or animal's head. **b** plume etc. on a helmet etc. **2** top of a mountain, wave, roof, etc. **3** *Heraldry* **a** device above a coat of arms. **b** such a device on writing-paper etc. *–v.* **1** reach the crest of. **2** provide with a crest or serve as a crest to. **3** (of a wave) form a crest. □ **crested** *adj.* [Latin *crista*]

crestfallen *adj.* dejected, dispirited.

cretaceous /krɪˈteɪʃəs/ *–adj.* **1** of or like chalk. **2** (**Cretaceous**) *Geol.* of the last period of the Mesozoic era, with deposits of chalk. *–n.* (**Cretaceous**) *Geol.* this era or system. [Latin *creta* chalk]

Crete /kriːt/ (Greek **Kríti** /ˈkriːtɪ/) Greek island in the E Mediterranean; pop. (1991) 540 054. It produces citrus fruit, olives, and wine; tourism is important. □ **Cretan** *adj.* & *n.*

cretin /ˈkretɪn/ *n.* **1** deformed and mentally retarded person, esp. as the result of thyroid deficiency. **2** *colloq.* stupid person. □ **cretinism** *n.* **cretinous** *adj.* [French *crétin*: related to CHRISTIAN]

cretonne /kreˈtɒn/ *n.* (often *attrib.*) heavy cotton upholstery fabric, usu. with a floral pattern. [*Creton* in Normandy]

crevasse /krəˈvæs/ *n.* deep open crack, esp. in a glacier. [Latin *crepo* crack]

crevice /ˈkrevɪs/ *n.* narrow opening or fissure, esp. in rock etc. [French: related to CREVASSE]

crew[1] /kruː/ *–n.* (often treated as *pl.*) **1 a** people manning a ship, aircraft, train, etc. **b** these as distinct from the captain or officers. **c** people working together; team. **2** *colloq.* gang. *–v.* **1** supply or act as a crew or crew member for. **2** act as a crew. [Latin *cresco* increase]

crew[2] *past* of CROW[2].

crew cut *n.* close-cropped hairstyle.

crewel /ˈkruːəl/ *n.* thin worsted yarn for tapestry and embroidery. [origin unknown]

crewel-work *n.* design in crewel.

crew neck *n.* round close-fitting neckline.

crib *–n.* **1 a** baby's small bed or cot. **b** model of the Nativity with a manger. **2** rack for animal fodder. **3** *colloq.* **a** translation of a text used by students. **b** plagiarized work etc. **4** *colloq.* **a** cribbage. **b** set of cards given to the dealer at cribbage. *–v.* (**-bb-**) (also *absol.*) **1** *colloq.* copy unfairly. **2** confine in a small space. **3** *colloq.* pilfer. [Old English]

cribbage /ˈkrɪbɪdʒ/ *n.* card-game for up to four players. [origin unknown]

crick *–n.* sudden painful stiffness, esp. in the neck. *–v.* cause this in. [origin unknown]

cricket[1] /ˈkrɪkɪt/ *n.* team game played on a grass pitch, with bowling at a wicket defended by a batting player of the other team. □ **not cricket** *colloq.* unfair behaviour. □ **cricketer** *n.* [origin uncertain]

cricket[2] /ˈkrɪkɪt/ *n.* grasshopper-like chirping insect. [French, imitative]

cri de cœur /ˌkriː də ˈkɜː(r)/ *n.* (*pl.* ***cris de cœur*** pronunc. same) passionate appeal, protest, etc. [French, = cry from the heart]

cried *past* and *past part.* of CRY.

crier /ˈkraɪə(r)/ *n.* (also **cryer**) **1** person who cries. **2** official making public announcements in a lawcourt or street. [related to CRY]

crikey /ˈkraɪkɪ/ *int. slang* expression of astonishment. [from CHRIST]

crime *n.* **1 a** offence punishable by law. **b** illegal acts (*resorted to crime*). **2** evil act (*crime against humanity*). **3** *colloq.* shameful act. [Latin *crimen*]

Crimea /kraɪˈmɪə/ peninsula and autonomous region of Ukraine, lying between the Sea of Azov and the Black Sea. □ **Crimean** *adj.*

criminal /ˈkrɪmɪn(ə)l/ *–n.* person guilty of a crime. *–adj.* **1** of, involving, or concerning crime. **2** guilty of crime. **3** *Law* of or concerning criminal offences (*criminal code*; *criminal lawyer*). **4** *colloq.* scandalous, deplorable. □ **criminality** /-ˈnælɪtɪ/ *n.* **criminally** *adv.* [Latin: related to CRIME]

criminology /ˌkrɪmɪˈnɒlədʒɪ/ *n.* the study of crime. □ **criminologist** *n.*

crimp *–v.* **1** press into small folds; corrugate. **2** make waves in (hair). *–n.* crimped thing or form. [Low German or Dutch]

Crimplene /ˈkrɪmpliːn/ *n. propr.* synthetic crease-resistant fabric.

crimson /ˈkrɪmz(ə)n/ *–adj.* of a rich deep red. *–n.* this colour. [ultimately from Arabic: related to KERMES]

cringe /krɪndʒ/ *v.* (**-ging**) **1** shrink in fear; cower. **2** (often foll. by *to*) behave obsequiously. [related to CRANK]

crinkle /ˈkrɪŋk(ə)l/ *–n.* wrinkle or crease. *–v.* (**-ling**) form crinkles (in). □ **crinkly** *adj.* [related to CRINGE]

crinkle-cut *adj.* (of vegetables) with wavy edges.

crinoline /ˈkrɪnəlɪn/ *n.* **1** *hist.* stiffened or hooped petticoat. **2** stiff fabric of horsehair etc. used for linings, hats, etc. [French from Latin *crinis* hair, *linum* thread]

cripple /ˈkrɪp(ə)l/ *–n.* permanently lame person. *–v.* (**-ling**) **1** make a cripple of; lame. **2** disable, weaken, or damage seriously (*crippled by strikes*). [Old English]

crisis /ˈkraɪsɪs/ *n.* (*pl.* **crises** /-siːz/) **1** time of danger or great difficulty. **2** decisive moment; turning-point. [Greek, = decision]

crisp *–adj.* **1** hard but brittle. **2 a** (of air) bracing. **b** (of style or manner) lively, brisk and decisive. **c** (of features etc.) neat, clear-cut. **d** (of paper) stiff and crackling. **e** (of hair) closely curling. *–n.* (in full **potato crisp**) potato sliced thinly, fried, and sold in packets. *–v.* make or become crisp. □ **crisply** *adv.* **crispness** *n.* [Latin *crispus* curled]

crispbread *n.* **1** thin crisp biscuit of crushed rye etc. **2** these collectively (*packet of crispbread*).

crispy *adj.* (**-ier, -iest**) crisp. □ **crispiness** *n.*

criss-cross *–n.* pattern of crossing lines. *–adj.* crossing; in cross lines. *–adv.* crosswise; at cross purposes. *–v.* **1 a** intersect repeatedly. **b** move crosswise. **2** mark or make with a criss-cross pattern. [*Christ's cross*]

criterion /kraɪˈtɪərɪən/ *n.* (*pl.* **-ria**) principle or standard of judgement. [Greek, = means of judging]

■ **Usage** The plural form of *criterion*, *criteria*, is often used incorrectly as the singular. In the singular *criterion* should always be used.

critic /ˈkrɪtɪk/ *n.* **1** person who criticizes. **2** person who reviews literary, artistic, etc. works. [Latin *criticus* from Greek *kritēs* judge]

critical *adj.* **1 a** fault-finding, censorious. **b** expressing or involving criticism. **2** skilful at or engaged in criticism. **3** providing textual criticism (*critical edition of Milton*). **4 a** of or at a crisis; dangerous, risky (*in a critical condition*). **b** decisive, crucial (*at the critical moment*). **5 a** *Math.* & *Physics* marking a transition from one state etc. to another (*critical angle*). **b** (of a nuclear reactor) maintaining a self-sustaining chain reaction. □ **critically** *adv.* **criticalness** *n.*

critical path see CRITICAL-PATH ANALYSIS.

◆ **critical-path analysis** *n.* (also **CPA, critical-path method, CPM**) technique for planning a complicated operation so that it can be completed as quickly and cheaply as possible. The total operation (e.g. building a power station) is broken down into separate steps, each represented by arrows on a chart; the length of the arrow is related to the time anticipated that each step will take. Many arrows will be parallel, but there will also be points of intersection. The chain of arrows representing the longest time is the **critical path**, as this determines the total time that must elapse before the job is completed. The chart is arranged to show how each step dovetails with others, when supplies of materials are required, when plant and equipment is needed, as well as details of the managers and workforce involved. The technique can be applied to many commercial operations.

---

criticism /ˈkrɪtɪˌsɪz(ə)m/ *n.* **1 a** fault-finding; censure. **b** critical remark etc. **2 a** work of a critic. **b** analytical article, essay, etc.

criticize /ˈkrɪtɪˌsaɪz/ *v.* (also **-ise**) (**-zing** or **-sing**) (also *absol.*) **1** find fault with; censure. **2** discuss critically.

critique /krɪˈtiːk/ *n.* critical analysis. [French: related to CRITIC]

croak *–n.* deep hoarse sound, esp. of a frog. *–v.* **1** utter or speak with a croak. **2** *slang* die. [imitative]

croaky *adj.* (**-ier**, **-iest**) croaking; hoarse. □ **croakily** *adv.* **croakiness** *n.*

Croat /ˈkrəʊæt/ *–n.* **1** native of Croatia. **2** person of Croatian descent. *–adj.* & *n.* = CROATIAN. [Serbo-Croat *Hrvat*]

Croatian *–adj.* of Croatia, its people, or language. *–n.* dialect of Serbo-Croat spoken in Croatia.

crochet /ˈkrəʊʃeɪ/ *–n.* needlework in which yarn is hooked to make a lacy patterned fabric. *–v.* (**crocheted** /-ʃeɪd/; **crocheting** /-ʃeɪɪŋ/) (also *absol.*) make using crochet. [French: related to CROTCHET]

crock[1] *n. colloq.* old or worn-out person or vehicle. [originally Scots]

crock[2] *n.* **1** earthenware pot or jar. **2** broken piece of this. [Old English]

crockery *n.* earthenware or china dishes, plates, etc. [related to CROCK[2]]

crocodile /ˈkrɒkəˌdaɪl/ *n.* **1 a** large tropical amphibious reptile with thick scaly skin, a long tail, and long jaws. **b** (often *attrib.*) its skin. **2** *colloq.* line of schoolchildren etc. walking in pairs. [Greek *krokodilos*]

crocodile tears *n.pl.* insincere grief.

crocus /ˈkrəʊkəs/ *n.* (*pl.* **-cuses**) small plant with white, yellow, or purple flowers, growing from a corm. [Latin from Greek]

Croesus /ˈkriːsəs/ *n.* person of great wealth. [name of a king of ancient Lydia]

croft *–n.* **1** enclosed piece of (usu. arable) land. **2** small rented farm in Scotland or N England. *–v.* farm a croft; live as a crofter. [Old English]

crofter *n.* person who farms a croft.

Crohn's disease /krəʊnz/ *n.* chronic inflammatory disease of the alimentary tract. [*Crohn*, name of a US pathologist]

croissant /ˈkrwʌsɑ̃/ *n.* crescent-shaped breakfast roll. [French: related to CRESCENT]

cromlech /ˈkrɒmlek/ *n.* **1** dolmen. **2** prehistoric stone circle. [Welsh]

crone *n.* withered old woman. [Dutch *croonje* carcass]

crony /ˈkrəʊnɪ/ *n.* (*pl.* **-ies**) friend, companion. [Greek *khronios* long-lasting]

crook /krʊk/ *–n.* **1** hooked staff of a shepherd or bishop. **2 a** bend, curve, or hook. **b** hooked or curved thing. **3** *colloq.* rogue; swindler; criminal. *–v.* bend, curve. [Old Norse]

crooked /ˈkrʊkɪd/ *adj.* (**-er**, **-est**) **1** not straight or level; bent. **2** *colloq.* not straightforward; dishonest, criminal. □ **crookedly** *adv.* **crookedness** *n.*

croon *–v.* sing, hum, or say in a low sentimental voice. *–n.* such singing etc. □ **crooner** *n.* [Low German or Dutch]

crop *–n.* **1 a** produce of cultivated plants, esp. cereals. **b** season's yield. **2** group, yield, etc., of one time or place (*a new crop of students*). **3** handle of a whip. **4 a** very short haircut. **b** cropping of hair. **5** pouch in a bird's gullet where food is prepared for digestion. *–v.* (**-pp-**) **1 a** cut off. **b** bite off. **2** cut (hair etc.) short. **3** (foll. by *with*) sow or plant (land) with a crop. **4** (of land) bear a crop. □ **crop up** occur unexpectedly. [Old English]

crop circle *n.* circle of crops that has been inexplicably flattened.

crop-eared *adj.* with the ears (esp. of animals) or hair cut short.

cropper *n.* crop-producing plant of a specified quality. □ **come a cropper** *slang* fall heavily; fail badly.

croquet /ˈkrəʊkeɪ/ *–n.* **1** lawn game in which wooden balls are driven through hoops with mallets. **2** act of croqueting a ball. *–v.* (**croqueted** /-keɪd/; **croqueting** /-keɪɪŋ/) drive away (an opponent's ball) by placing and then striking one's own against it. [perhaps a dial. form of French *crochet* hook]

croquette /krəˈket/ *n.* ball of breaded and fried mashed potato etc. [French *croquer* crunch]

♦ **crore** /krɔː/ *n.* (in India, Pakistan, and Bangladesh; usu. foll. by *of*) hundred lakhs, i.e. ten million. It usu. refers to a number of rupees. [Hindi *karōr*]

---

crosier /ˈkrəʊzɪə(r)/ *n.* (also **crozier**) bishop's ceremonial hooked staff. [French *croisier* cross-bearer and *crossier* crook-bearer]

cross *–n.* **1** upright post with a transverse bar, as used in antiquity for crucifixion. **2 a** (**the Cross**) cross on which Christ was crucified. **b** representation of this as an emblem of Christianity. **c** = SIGN OF THE CROSS. **3** staff surmounted by a cross, carried in a religious procession. **4** thing or mark like a cross, esp. two short intersecting lines (+ or x). **5** cross-shaped military etc. decoration. **6 a** hybrid. **b** crossing of breeds etc. **7** (foll. by *between*) mixture of two things. **8** crosswise movement, pass in football, etc. **9** trial or affliction. *–v.* **1** (often foll. by *over*) go across. **2** intersect; (cause to) be across (*roads cross*; *cross one's legs*). **3 a** draw line(s) across. **b** mark (a cheque) with two parallel lines to indicate that it cannot be cashed. **4**

Croatia /krəʊˈeɪʃə/, **Republic of** (Croatian **Hrvatska** /ˈhɜːvætskə/) country in SE Europe, on the Adriatic Sea, formerly (until 1992) a constituent republic of Yugoslavia. Agriculture produces wheat, maize, fruit (esp. plums and grapes), potatoes, tobacco, and livestock, and fishing is important. Industries include metallurgy and the manufacture of machinery, transport equipment, chemicals, clothing and textiles, and food products, which all contribute to export earnings. Tourism, formerly a major source of hard-currency income, was badly affected by the civil wars in the former Yugoslavia and has not recovered. The war in neighbouring Bosnia-Hercegovina (1992–5) produced a massive influx of refugees, adding to those from the Serb-occupied territories (Krajina) of Croatia itself. In 1995 Croatian forces seized Krajina, prompting the flight of a large number of Serbs, and East Slavonia, the last Serb-held part of Croatia, agreed to eventual reintegration. Despite the ending of the war in late 1995, economic growth and stability have yet to return. In 1996 an agreement was signed with the Federal Republic of Yugoslavia (i.e. Serbia and Montenegro) to normalize relations between the two countries. President, Franjo Tudjman; capital, Zagreb.

language	Croatian
currency	kuna of 100 lipa
pop. (1996)	4 775 000
GDP (1994)	US$11.8B
literacy	99% (m); 96% (f)
life expectancy	68 (m); 76 (f)

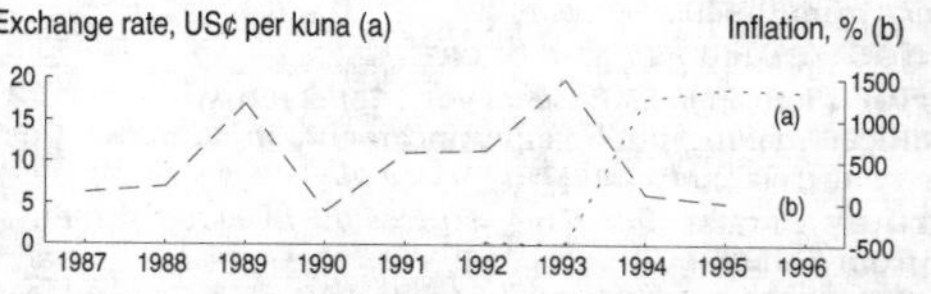

(foll. by *off*, *out*, *through*) cancel etc. by drawing lines across. **5** (often *refl.*) make the sign of the cross on or over. **6 a** pass in opposite or different directions. **b** (of letters etc.) be sent at the same time. **c** (of telephone lines) be connected to an unwanted conversation. **7 a** cause to interbreed. **b** cross-fertilize (plants). **8** oppose or thwart (*crossed in love*). –*adj.* **1** (often foll. by *with*) peevish, angry. **2** (usu. *attrib.*) transverse; reaching from side to side. **3** (usu. *attrib.*) intersecting. **4** (usu. *attrib.*) contrary, opposed, reciprocal. □ **at cross purposes** misunderstanding; conflicting. **cross one's fingers** (or **keep one's fingers crossed**) **1** put one finger across another to ward off bad luck. **2** trust in good luck. **cross one's heart** make a solemn pledge, esp. by crossing one's front. **cross one's mind** occur to one, esp. transiently. **cross swords** (often foll. by *with*) argue or dispute. **cross wires** (or **get one's wires crossed**) **1** become wrongly connected by telephone. **2** have a misunderstanding. **on the cross** diagonally. □ **crossly** *adv.* **crossness** *n.* [Latin *crux*]

crossbar *n.* horizontal bar, esp. that on a man's bicycle.

cross-bench *n.* seat in the House of Lords for non-party members. □ **cross-bencher** *n.*

crossbill *n.* finch with a bill with crossed mandibles for opening pine cones.

crossbones see SKULL AND CROSSBONES.

crossbow *n.* bow fixed on a wooden stock, with a groove for an arrow.

cross-breed –*n.* **1** hybrid breed of animals or plants. **2** individual hybrid. –*v.* produce by crossing.

cross-check –*v.* check by alternative method(s). –*n.* such a check.

cross-country –*adj.* & *adv.* **1** across open country. **2** not keeping to main roads. –*n.* (*pl.* **-ies**) cross-country race.

cross-cut –*adj.* cut across the main grain. –*n.* diagonal cut, path, etc.

cross-cut saw *n.* saw for cross-cutting.

cross-dressing *n.* practice of dressing in the clothes of the opposite sex. □ **cross-dress** *v.*

crosse *n.* lacrosse stick. [French]

♦ **crossed cheque** see CHEQUE.

---

cross-examine *v.* question (esp. an opposing witness in a lawcourt). □ **cross-examination** *n.*

cross-eyed /ˈkrɒsaɪd/ *adj.* having one or both eyes turned inwards.

cross-fertilize *v.* (also **-ise**) **1** fertilize (an animal or plant) from one of a different species. **2** interchange ideas etc. □ **cross-fertilization** *n.*

crossfire *n.* **1** firing in two crossing directions simultaneously. **2 a** attack or criticism from all sides. **b** combative exchange of views etc.

cross-grain *n.* grain in timber, running across the regular grain.

cross-grained *adj.* **1** having a cross-grain. **2** perverse, intractable.

cross-hatch *v.* shade with crossing parallel lines.

crossing *n.* **1** place where things (esp. roads) cross. **2** place for crossing a street etc. **3** journey across water. **4** printing and writing that converts an open cheque to a crossed cheque. See CHEQUE.

cross-legged /krɒsˈlegd/ *adj.* (sitting) with legs folded one across the other.

crossover –*n.* **1** point or place of crossing. **2** process of crossing over, esp. from one style or genre to another. –*attrib. adj.* that crosses over, esp. from one style or genre to another.

crosspatch *n. colloq.* bad-tempered person.

crosspiece *n.* transverse beam etc.

cross-ply *adj.* (of a tyre) having fabric layers with crosswise cords.

cross-question *v.* = CROSS-EXAMINE.

cross-refer *v.* (**-rr-**) refer from one part of a book etc. to another.

cross-reference –*n.* reference from one part of a book etc. to another. –*v.* provide with cross-references.

crossroad *n.* (usu. in *pl.*) intersection of two or more roads. □ **at the crossroads** at the critical point.

cross-section *n.* **1 a** a cutting across a solid. **b** plane surface so produced. **c** drawing etc. of this. **2** representative sample. □ **cross-sectional** *adj.*

cross-stitch *n.* cross-shaped stitch.

crosstalk *n.* **1** unwanted signals between communication channels. **2** witty repartee.

crossways *adv.* = CROSSWISE.

crosswind *n.* wind blowing across one's path etc.

crosswise *adj.* & *adv.* **1** in the form of a cross; intersecting. **2** diagonal or diagonally.

crossword *n.* (also **crossword puzzle**) printed grid of squares and blanks for vertical and horizontal words to be filled in from clues.

crotch *n.* fork, esp. between legs (of a person, trousers, etc.). [related to CROOK]

crotchet /ˈkrɒtʃɪt/ *n. Mus.* note equal to a quarter of a semibreve and usu. one beat. [French diminutive of *croc*: related to CROOK]

crotchety *adj.* peevish, irritable.

crouch –*v.* lower the body with limbs close to the chest; be in this position. –*n.* crouching; crouching position. [Old Norse: related to CROOK]

croup[1] /kruːp/ *n.* childhood inflammation of the larynx etc., with a hard cough. [imitative]

croup[2] /kruːp/ *n.* rump, esp. of a horse. [French: related to CROP]

croupier /ˈkruːpɪə(r)/ *n.* person running a gaming-table, raking in and paying out money etc. [French: related to CROUP[2]]

croûton /ˈkruːtɒn/ *n.* small cube of fried or toasted bread served with soup etc. [French: related to CRUST]

crow[1] /krəʊ/ *n.* **1** large black bird with a powerful black beak. **2** similar bird, e.g. the raven, rook, and jackdaw. □ **as the crow flies** in a straight line. [Old English]

crow[2] /krəʊ/ –*v.* **1** (*past* **crowed** or **crew** /kruː/) (of a cock) utter a loud cry. **2** (of a baby) utter happy cries. **3** (usu. foll. by *over*) gloat; show glee. –*n.* cry of a cock or baby. [Old English]

crowbar *n.* iron bar with a flattened end, used as a lever.

crowd –*n.* **1** large gathering of people. **2** spectators; audience. **3** *colloq.* particular set of people. **4** (prec. by *the*) majority. –*v.* **1 a** (cause to) come together in a crowd. **b** force one's way (*crowded into the cinema*). **2 a** (foll. by *into*) force or compress into a confined space. **b** (often foll. by *with*; usu. in *passive*) fill or make full of. **3** *colloq.* come aggressively close to. □ **crowd out** exclude by crowding. □ **crowdedness** *n.* [Old English]

♦ **crowding-out** *n. Econ.* concept suggesting that a reduction in private expenditure results from an increase in government expenditure. For example, if the government stimulates aggregate demand by maintaining a budget deficit, the increase in government borrowing will raise interest rates, which will inhibit private investment. Keynesians tend to believe that the effect of crowding-out is limited, while new classical macroeconomists believe it is complete, i.e. that every additional £1 of government expenditure causes a fall of £1 in private expenditure.

---

crown –*n.* **1** monarch's jewelled headdress. **2** (**the Crown**) **a** monarch as head of state. **b** power or authority of the monarchy. **3 a** wreath for the head as an emblem of victory. **b** award or distinction, esp. in sport. **4** crown-shaped ornament etc. **5** top part of the head, a hat, etc. **6 a** highest or central part (*crown of the road*). **b** thing that completes or forms a summit. **7 a** part of a tooth visible outside the gum. **b** artificial replacement for this. **8** former British coin worth five shillings. –*v.* **1** put a crown on (a person or head). **2** invest with a royal crown or authority. **3** be a crown to; rest on top of. **4 a** (often as **crowning** *adj.*) (cause to) be the reward, summit, or finishing touch to (*crowning glory*). **b** bring to a happy outcome. **5** fit a crown to (a tooth). **6** *slang* hit on the head. **7** promote (a piece in draughts) to king. [Latin *corona*]

Crown Colony *n.* British colony controlled by the Crown.

Crown Court *n.* court of criminal jurisdiction in England and Wales.

Crown Derby *n.* porcelain made at Derby and often marked with a crown.

crown glass *n.* glass without lead or iron used formerly in windows, now as optical glass of low refractive index.

crown jewels *n.pl.* sovereign's state regalia etc.

Crown prince *n.* male heir to a throne.

Crown princess *n.* **1** wife of a Crown prince. **2** female heir to a throne.

crown wheel *n.* wheel with teeth at right angles to its plane.

crow's-foot *n.* wrinkle near the eye.

crow's-nest *n.* shelter at a sailing-ship's masthead for a lookout man.

crozier var. of CROSIER.

CRS *abbr.* Cooperative Retail Society.

CRT *abbr.* **1** = CATHODE-RAY TUBE. **2** = COMPOSITE RATE TAX.

cru /kruː/ *n.* **1** French vineyard or wine region. **2** grade of wine. [French *crû* grown]

cruces *pl.* of CRUX.

crucial /ˈkruːʃ(ə)l/ *adj.* **1** decisive, critical. **2** very important. □ **crucially** *adv.* [Latin *crux crucis* cross]

■ **Usage** The use of *crucial* in sense 2 should be restricted to informal contexts.

crucible /ˈkruːsɪb(ə)l/ *n.* **1** melting-pot for metals etc. **2** severe test. [medieval Latin: related to CRUCIAL]

cruciferous /kruːˈsɪfərəs/ *adj.* having flowers with four petals arranged in a cross. [Latin: related to CRUCIAL]

crucifix /ˈkruːsɪfɪks/ *n.* model of a cross with the figure of Christ on it. [Latin *cruci fixus* fixed to a cross]

crucifixion /ˌkruːsɪˈfɪkʃ(ə)n/ *n.* **1** crucifying or being crucified. **2** (**Crucifixion**) crucifixion of Christ. [Church Latin: related to CRUCIFIX]

cruciform /ˈkruːsɪˌfɔːm/ *adj.* cross-shaped. [Latin *crux crucis* cross]

crucify /ˈkruːsɪˌfaɪ/ *v.* (**-ies**, **-ied**) **1** put to death by fastening to a cross. **2** persecute, torment. **3** *slang* defeat thoroughly; humiliate. [French: related to CRUCIFIX]

crud *n. slang* **1** deposit of grease etc. **2** unpleasant person. □ **cruddy** *adj.* (**-ier**, **-iest**). [var. of CURD]

crude /kruːd/ *–adj.* **1 a** in the natural state; not refined. **b** unpolished; lacking finish. **2 a** rude, blunt. **b** offensive, indecent. **3** inexact. *–n.* natural mineral oil. □ **crudely** *adv.* **crudeness** *n.* **crudity** *n.* [Latin *crudus* raw]

crudités /ˌkruːdɪˈteɪ/ *n.pl.* hors d'œuvre of mixed raw vegetables. [French]

cruel /ˈkruːəl/ *adj.* (**crueller**, **cruellest** or **crueler**, **cruelest**) **1** causing pain or suffering, esp. deliberately. **2** harsh, severe (*a cruel blow*). □ **cruelly** *adv.* **cruelness** *n.* **cruelty** *n.* (*pl.* **-ies**). [Latin: related to CRUDE]

cruet /ˈkruːɪt/ *n.* **1** set of small salt, pepper, etc. containers for use at table. **2** such a container. [Anglo-French diminutive: related to CROCK[2]]

cruise /kruːz/ *–v.* (**-sing**) **1 a** travel by sea for pleasure, calling at ports. **b** sail about. **2** travel at a relaxed or economical speed. **3** achieve an objective, esp. win a race etc. with ease. **4** *slang* search for a sexual (esp. homosexual) partner in bars, streets, etc. *–n.* cruising voyage. [Dutch: related to CROSS]

cruise missile *n.* one able to fly low and guide itself.

cruiser *n.* **1** high-speed warship. **2** = CABIN CRUISER.

cruiserweight *n.* = LIGHT HEAVYWEIGHT.

crumb /krʌm/ *–n.* **1 a** small fragment, esp. of bread. **b** small particle (*crumb of comfort*). **2** bread without crusts. **3** *slang* objectionable person. *–v.* cover with or break into breadcrumbs. [Old English]

crumble /ˈkrʌmb(ə)l/ *–v.* (**-ling**) **1** break or fall into small fragments. **2** (of power etc.) gradually disintegrate. *–n.* dish of stewed fruit with a crumbly topping.

crumbly *adj.* (**-ier**, **-iest**) consisting of, or apt to fall into, crumbs or fragments. □ **crumbliness** *n.*

crumbs /krʌmz/ *int. slang* expressing dismay or surprise. [euphemism for CHRIST]

crumby *adj.* (**-ier**, **-iest**) **1** like or covered in crumbs. **2** = CRUMMY.

crumhorn var. of KRUMMHORN.

crummy *adj.* (**-ier**, **-iest**) *slang* dirty, squalid; inferior, worthless. □ **crumminess** *n.* [var. of CRUMBY]

crumpet /ˈkrʌmpɪt/ *n.* **1** soft flat yeasty cake toasted and buttered. **2** *joc.* or *offens.* sexually attractive woman or women. [origin uncertain]

crumple /ˈkrʌmp(ə)l/ *–v.* (**-ling**) (often foll. by *up*) **1** crush or become crushed into creases or wrinkles. **2** collapse, give way. *–n.* crease or wrinkle. [obsolete *crump* curl up]

crunch *–v.* **1 a** crush noisily with the teeth. **b** grind under foot, wheels, etc. **2** (often foll. by *up*, *through*) make a crunching sound. *–n.* **1** crunching; crunching sound. **2** *colloq.* decisive event or moment. [imitative]

crunchy *adj.* (**-ier**, **-iest**) hard and crisp. □ **crunchiness** *n.*

crupper *n.* **1** strap looped under a horse's tail to hold the harness back. **2** hindquarters of a horse. [French: related to CROUP[2]]

crusade /kruːˈseɪd/ *–n.* **1** *hist.* any of several medieval military expeditions made by Europeans to recover the Holy Land from the Muslims. **2** vigorous campaign for a cause. *–v.* (**-ding**) engage in a crusade. □ **crusader** *n.* [French: related to CROSS]

cruse /kruːz/ *n. archaic* earthenware pot. [Old English]

crush *–v.* **1** compress with force or violence, so as to break, bruise, etc. **2** reduce to powder by pressure. **3** crease or crumple. **4** defeat or subdue completely. *–n.* **1** act of crushing. **2** crowded mass of people. **3** drink from the juice of crushed fruit. **4** (usu. foll. by *on*) *colloq.* infatuation. [French]

crust *–n.* **1 a** hard outer part of bread. **b** hard dry scrap of bread. **c** *slang* livelihood. **2** pastry covering of a pie. **3** hard casing over a soft thing. **4** outer portion of the earth. **5** deposit, esp. from wine on a bottle. *–v.* cover or become covered with or form into a crust. [Latin *crusta* rind, shell]

crustacean /krʌˈsteɪʃ(ə)n/ *–n.* esp. aquatic arthropod with a hard shell, e.g. the crab, lobster, and shrimp. *–adj.* of crustaceans.

crusty *adj.* (**-ier**, **-iest**) **1** having a crisp crust. **2** irritable, curt. □ **crustily** *adv.* **crustiness** *n.*

crutch *n.* **1** usu. T-shaped support for a lame person fitting under the armpit. **2** support, prop. **3** crotch. [Old English]

crux *n.* (*pl.* **cruxes** or **cruces** /ˈkruːsiːz/) decisive point at issue. [Latin, = cross]

cruzeiro /kruːˈzeərəʊ/ *n.* (*pl.* **-s**) former standard monetary unit of Brazil; replaced by the REAL. [Portuguese]

cry /kraɪ/ *–v.* (**cries**, **cried**) **1** (often foll. by *out*) make a loud or shrill sound, esp. to express pain, grief, etc., or to appeal for help. **2** shed tears; weep. **3** (often foll. by *out*) say or exclaim loudly or excitedly. **4** (foll. by *for*) appeal, demand, or show a need for. **5** (of an animal, esp. a bird) make a loud call. *–n.* (*pl.* **cries**) **1** loud shout or scream of grief, pain, etc. **2** spell of weeping. **3** loud excited utterance. **4** urgent appeal. **5 a** public demand or opinion. **b** rallying call. **6** call of an animal. □ **cry down** disparage. **cry off** withdraw from an undertaking. **cry out for** need as an obvious requirement or solution. **cry wolf** see WOLF. [Latin *quirito*]

cry-baby *n.* person who weeps frequently.

cryer var. of CRIER.

crying *attrib. adj.* (of injustice etc.) flagrant, demanding redress.

cryogenics /ˌkraɪəʊˈdʒenɪks/ *n.* branch of physics dealing with very low temperatures. □ **cryogenic** *adj.* [Greek *kruos* frost, *-genēs* born]

crypt /krɪpt/ *n.* vault, esp. beneath a church, used usu. as a burial-place. [Latin *crypta* from Greek *kruptos* hidden]

cryptic *adj.* obscure in meaning; secret, mysterious. □ **cryptically** *adv.*

cryptogam /'krɪptə,gæm/ *n.* plant with no true flowers or seeds, e.g. ferns, mosses, and fungi. □ **cryptogamous** /-'tɒgəməs/ *adj.* [as CRYPT, Greek *gamos* marriage]

cryptogram /'krɪptə,græm/ *n.* text written in cipher. [related to CRYPT]

cryptography /krɪp'tɒgrəfɪ/ *n.* **1** art of writing or solving ciphers. **2** *Computing* protection of a message so as to make it unintelligible to anybody not authorized to receive it. The sender of a message renders it into an unintelligible form, known as **cipher** or **code**, by a process known as **encryption**. The original message is recovered by processing the encrypted message, which is expected to be impossible without prior knowledge of the secret key to the encryption. □ **cryptographer** *n.* **cryptographic** /-tə'græfɪk/ *adj.*

crystal /'krɪst(ə)l/ *–n.* **1 a** transparent colourless mineral, esp. rock crystal. **b** piece of this. **2 a** highly transparent glass; flint glass. **b** articles of this. **3** crystalline piece of semiconductor. **4** aggregation of molecules with a definite internal structure and the external form of a solid enclosed by symmetrically arranged plane faces. *–adj.* (usu. *attrib.*) made of, like, or clear as crystal. [Greek *krustallos*]

crystal ball *n.* glass globe used in crystal-gazing.

crystal-gazing *n.* supposed foretelling of the future by gazing into a crystal ball.

crystalline /'krɪstə,laɪn/ *adj.* **1** of, like, or clear as crystal. **2** having the structure and form of a crystal. □ **crystallinity** /-'lɪnɪtɪ/ *n.*

crystallize /'krɪstə,laɪz/ *v.* (also **-ise**) (**-zing** or **-sing**) **1** form into crystals. **2** (of ideas, plans, etc.) make or become definite or fixed. **3** See CHARGE *n.* 3; FLOATING CHARGE. **4** make or become coated or impregnated with sugar (*crystallized fruit*). □ **crystallization** /-'zeɪʃ(ə)n/ *n.*

crystallography /,krɪstə'lɒgrəfɪ/ *n.* science of crystal formation and structure. □ **crystallographer** *n.*

crystalloid /'krɪstə,lɔɪd/ *n.* substance that in solution is able to pass through a semipermeable membrane.

CS *–abbr.* **1** chartered surveyor. **2** Civil Service. *–international vehicle registration* Czech Republic and Slovakia. *–international civil aircraft marking* Portugal.

Cs *symb.* caesium.

c/s *abbr.* **1** cases. **2** cycles per second.

CSA *abbr.* Child Support Agency.

CSE *abbr. hist.* Certificate of Secondary Education.

■ **Usage** The CSE examination was replaced in 1988 by GCSE.

CS gas *n.* tear-gas used to control riots etc. [*C*arson and *S*taughton, names of chemists]

CSIRO *abbr.* Commonwealth Scientific and Industrial Research Organization.

CSMA/CD *abbr. Computing* carrier sense multiple access, collision detection (network protocol).

CSO *abbr.* Central Statistical Office.

CST *abbr. US* Central Standard Time.

CT *–abbr.* **1** *US* Central Time. **2** = CORPORATION TAX. **3** counter trade. *–postcode* Canterbury. *–US postcode* Connecticut.

C/T *abbr.* Californian Terms (in the grain trade).

ct. *abbr.* cent.

CTA *abbr. US* commodities trading adviser.

CTC *abbr.* City Technology College.

CTL *abbr.* = CONSTRUCTIVE TOTAL LOSS.

cts *abbr.* cents.

CTT *abbr.* = CAPITAL-TRANSFER TAX.

CU *–international civil aircraft marking* Cuba. *–airline flight code* Cubana De Aviacion.

Cu *symb.* copper. [Latin *cuprum*]

cu. *abbr.* cubic.

cub *–n.* **1** young of a fox, bear, lion, etc. **2** (**Cub**) (in full **Cub Scout**) junior Scout. **3** *colloq.* young newspaper reporter. *–v.* (**-bb-**) (also *absol.*) give birth to (cubs). [origin unknown]

cubby-hole /'kʌbɪ,həʊl/ *n.* **1** very small room. **2** snug space. [Low German]

cube *–n.* **1** solid contained by six equal squares. **2** cube-shaped block. **3** product of a number multiplied by its square. *–v.* (**-bing**) **1** find the cube of (a number). **2** cut (food etc.) into small cubes. [Latin from Greek]

cube root *n.* number which produces a given number when cubed.

cubic *adj.* **1** cube-shaped. **2** of three dimensions. **3** involving the cube (and no higher power) of a number (*cubic equation*).

cubical *adj.* cube-shaped.

cubicle /'kju:bɪk(ə)l/ *n.* **1** small screened space. **2** small separate sleeping-compartment. [Latin *cubo* lie]

cubic metre etc. *n.* volume of a cube whose edge is one metre etc.

cubism /'kju:bɪz(ə)m/ *n.* style in art, esp. painting, in which objects are represented geometrically. □ **cubist** *n.* & *adj.*

cubit /'kju:bɪt/ *n.* ancient measure of length, approximating to the length of a forearm. [Latin *cubitum* elbow]

cuboid /'kju:bɔɪd/ *–adj.* cube-shaped; like a cube. *–n. Geom.* rectangular parallelepiped.

cuckold /'kʌkəʊld/ *–n.* husband of an adulteress. *–v.* make a cuckold of. □ **cuckoldry** *n.* [French]

cuckoo /'kʊku:/ *–n.* bird having a characteristic cry, and

Cuba /'kju:bə/, **Republic of** Caribbean country, the largest and westernmost of the islands of the West Indies, situated S of Florida. Sugar is the mainstay of the economy (which is state-controlled) and the principal export; other exports include nickel, tobacco, citrus fruits, seafood, and rum. Meat production is important for the domestic economy. Metallurgy, textiles, construction, and tourism are developing industries. Formerly reliant on imports and aid from the Soviet Union, Cuba is now faced with fuel and other shortages since the demise of Communism in E Europe and the destabilization of Russia's economy. Only limited concessions to a free-market economy have been made. The economy has also been badly affected by long-term trade sanctions imposed by the US.
History. Under Spanish rule until 1898, it was thereafter nominally independent but heavily under American influence, until granted full autonomy in 1934. In 1959 the dictatorship of General Batista was overthrown in a rebellion led by Fidel Castro, who installed a socialist government; the Communist Party remains the only authorized political party. President, Fidel Castro Ruz; capital, Havana. □ **Cuban** *adj.* & *n.*

language	Spanish
currency	peso (CUP) of 100 centavos
pop. (1996)	11 117 000
GNP (1991)	US$17B
literacy	95% (m); 96% (f)
life expectancy	74 (m); 77 (f)

Exchange rate, US¢ per CUP

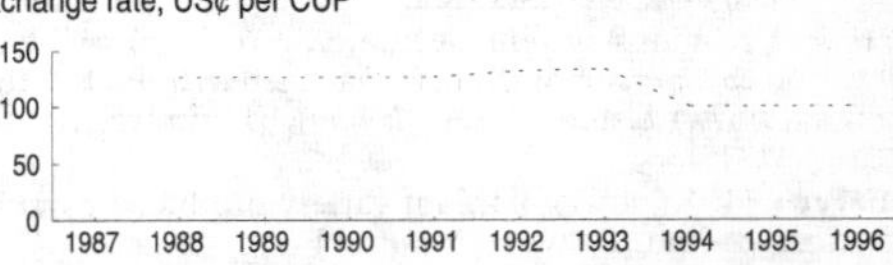

---

laying its eggs in the nests of small birds. *–predic. adj. slang* crazy. [French, imitative]

cuckoo clock *n.* clock with the figure of a cuckoo emerging to make a call on the hour.

cuckoo-pint *n.* wild arum.

cuckoo-spit *n.* froth exuded by insect larvae on leaves, stems, etc.

cucumber /'kjuːkʌmbə(r)/ *n.* **1** long green fleshy fruit, used in salads. **2** climbing plant yielding this. [French from Latin]

cud *n.* half-digested food returned to the mouth of ruminants for further chewing. [Old English]

cuddle /'kʌd(ə)l/ *–v.* (**-ling**) **1** hug, fondle. **2** nestle together, lie close and snug. *–n.* prolonged and fond hug. □ **cuddlesome** *adj.* [origin uncertain]

cuddly *adj.* (**-ier, -iest**) **1** (of a person, toy, etc.) soft and yielding. **2** given to cuddling.

cudgel /'kʌdʒ(ə)l/ *–n.* short thick stick used as a weapon. *–v.* (**-ll-**; *US* **-l-**) beat with a cudgel. [Old English]

cue[1] *–n.* **1 a** last words of an actor's speech as a signal to another to enter or speak. **b** similar signal to a musician etc. **2 a** stimulus to perception etc. **b** signal for action. **c** hint on appropriate behaviour. **3** cueing audio equipment (see sense 2 of *v.*). *–v.* (**cues, cued, cueing** or **cuing**) **1** give a cue to. **2** put (audio equipment) in readiness to play a particular section. □ **cue in 1** insert a cue for. **2** give information to. **on cue** at the correct moment. [origin unknown]

cue[2] *Billiards* etc. *–n.* long rod for striking a ball. *–v.* (**cues, cued, cueing** or **cuing**) strike (a ball) with or use a cue. [var. of QUEUE]

cue-ball *n.* ball to be struck with a cue.

Cuenca /'kweŋkə/ city in S central Ecuador and commercial centre of the region, trading in marble, agricultural products, and hides; industries include chemicals, machinery, and textiles; pop. (est. 1996) 247 421.

cuff[1] *n.* **1** end part of a sleeve. **2** *US* trouser turn-up. **3** (in *pl.*) *colloq.* handcuffs. □ **off the cuff** *colloq.* without preparation, extempore. [origin unknown]

cuff[2] *–v.* strike with an open hand. *–n.* such a blow. [perhaps imitative]

cuff-link *n.* two joined studs etc. for fastening a cuff.

Cufic var. of KUFIC.

cuirass /kwɪ'ræs/ *n.* armour breastplate and back-plate fastened together. [Latin *corium* leather]

cuisine /kwɪ'ziːn/ *n.* style or method of cooking. [French]

cul-de-sac /'kʌldəˌsæk/ *n.* (*pl.* **culs-de-sac** pronunc. same) **1** road etc. with a dead end. **2** futile course. [French, = sack-bottom]

-cule *suffix* forming (orig. dimin.) nouns (*molecule*). [Latin *-culus*]

culinary /'kʌlɪnərɪ/ *adj.* of or for cooking. [Latin *culina* kitchen]

cull *–v.* **1** select or gather (*knowledge culled from books*). **2** gather (flowers etc.). **3 a** select (animals), esp. for killing. **b** reduce the population of (an animal) by selective slaughter. *–n.* **1** culling or being culled. **2** animal(s) culled. [French: related to COLLECT[1]]

culminate /'kʌlmɪˌneɪt/ *v.* (**-ting**) (usu. foll. by *in*) reach its highest or final point (*culminate in war*). □ **culmination** /-'neɪʃ(ə)n/ *n.* [Latin *culmen* top]

culottes /kjuː'lɒts/ *n.pl.* women's trousers cut like a skirt. [French, = knee-breeches]

culpable /'kʌlpəb(ə)l/ *adj.* deserving blame. □ **culpability** /-'bɪlɪtɪ/ *n.* [Latin *culpo* blame]

culprit /'kʌlprɪt/ *n.* guilty person. [perhaps from Anglo-French *culpable*: see CULPABLE]

cult *n.* **1** religious system, sect, etc., esp. ritualistic. **2 a** devotion to a person or thing (*cult of aestheticism*). **b** fashion. **c** (*attrib.*) fashionable (*cult film*). [Latin: related to CULTIVATE]

cultivar /'kʌltɪˌvɑː(r)/ *n.* plant variety produced by cultivation. [from CULTIVATE, VARIETY]

cultivate /'kʌltɪˌveɪt/ *v.* (**-ting**) **1** prepare and use (soil etc.) for crops or gardening. **2 a** raise (crops). **b** culture (bacteria etc.). **3 a** (often as **cultivated** *adj.*) improve (the mind, manners, etc.). **b** nurture (a person, friendship, etc.). □ **cultivable** *adj.* **cultivation** /-'veɪʃ(ə)n/ *n.* [Latin *colo cult-* till, worship]

cultivator *n.* **1** mechanical implement for breaking up the ground etc. **2** person or thing that cultivates.

cultural /'kʌltʃər(ə)l/ *adj.* of or relating to intellectual or artistic matters, or to a specific culture. □ **culturally** *adv.*

culture /'kʌltʃə(r)/ *–n.* **1 a** intellectual and artistic achievement or expression (*city lacking in culture*). **b** refined appreciation of the arts etc. (*person of culture*). **2** customs, achievements, etc. of a particular civilization or group (*Chinese culture*). **3** improvement by mental or physical training. **4** cultivation of plants; rearing of bees etc. **5** quantity of micro-organisms and nutrient material supporting their growth. *–v.* (**-ring**) maintain (bacteria etc.) in suitable growth conditions. [Latin: related to CULTIVATE]

cultured *adj.* having refined taste etc.

cultured pearl *n.* pearl formed by an oyster after the insertion of a foreign body into its shell.

culture shock *n.* disorientation felt by a person subjected to an unfamiliar way of life.

culture vulture *n. colloq.* person eager for cultural pursuits.

culvert /'kʌlvət/ *n.* underground channel carrying water under a road etc. [origin unknown]

cum *prep.* (usu. in *comb.*) **1** with, combined with, also used as (*bedroom-cum-study*). **2** *Finance* including (specified benefits when a security is quoted) (*cum dividend*). See EX[1] 2. [Latin]

cum. *abbr. Finance* cumulative.

cumbersome /'kʌmbəsəm/ *adj.* (also **cumbrous** /'kʌmbrəs/) inconveniently bulky etc.; unwieldy. [*cumber* hinder]

Cumbria /'kʌmbrɪə/ county of NW England; pop. (est. 1994) 490 200; county town, Carlisle. Sheep, dairy, and arable farming are important; industries include plastics and electronics. □ **Cumbrian** *adj.* & *n.*

cum div. *abbr. Finance* cum dividend. See EX[1] 2.

cumin /'kʌmɪn/ *n.* (also **cummin**) **1** plant with aromatic seeds. **2** these as flavouring. [Greek *kuminon*]

cummerbund /'kʌməˌbʌnd/ *n.* waist sash. [Hindustani and Persian]

♦ **cum new** *adj.* denoting a share that is offered for sale with the right to take up any scrip issue or rights issue. Cf. EX NEW.

---

cum. pref. *abbr.* cumulative preference (share).

cumulative /'kjuːmjʊlətɪv/ *adj.* **1** increasing or increased progressively in amount, force, etc. (*cumulative evidence*). **2** formed by successive additions (*learning is a cumulative process*). □ **cumulatively** *adv.*

♦ **cumulative preference share** *n.* preference share that entitles the owner to receive any dividends not paid in previous years. Companies are not obliged to pay dividends on preference shares if there are insufficient earnings in any particular year. Cumulative preference shares guarantee the eventual payment of these dividends in arears before the payment of dividends on ordinary shares, provided that the company returns to profit in subsequent years.

---

cumulus /'kjuːmjʊləs/ *n.* (*pl.* **-li** /-ˌlaɪ/) cloud formation of rounded masses heaped up on a flat base. [Latin, = heap]

cuneiform /'kjuːnɪˌfɔːm/ *–adj.* **1** wedge-shaped. **2** of or using wedge-shaped writing. *–n.* cuneiform writing. [Latin *cuneus* wedge]

cunnilingus /ˌkʌnɪ'lɪŋgəs/ *n.* oral stimulation of the female genitals. [Latin *cunnus* vulva, *lingo* lick]

cunning *–adj.* (**-er, -est**) **1** deceitful, clever, or crafty. **2** ingenious (*cunning device*). **3** *US* attractive, quaint. *–n.* **1** craftiness; deception. **2** skill, ingenuity. □ **cunningly** *adv.* [Old Norse: related to CAN[1]]

cunt *n. coarse slang* **1** female genitals. **2** *offens.* unpleasant person. [origin uncertain]

CUP *symb.* Cuban peso.

cup *–n.* **1** small bowl-shaped container for drinking from. **2 a** its contents. **b** = CUPFUL. **3** cup-shaped thing. **4** flavoured wine, cider, etc., usu. chilled. **5** cup-shaped trophy as a prize. **6** one's fate or fortune (*a bitter cup*). *–v.* (**-pp-**) **1** form (esp. the hands) into the shape of a cup. **2** take or hold as in a cup. □ **one's cup of tea** *colloq.* what interests or suits one. [medieval Latin *cuppa*]

cupboard /'kʌbəd/ *n.* recess or piece of furniture with a door and (usu.) shelves.

cupboard love *n.* false affection for gain.

Cup Final *n.* final match in a (esp. football) competition.

cupful *n.* (*pl.* **-s**) **1** amount held by a cup, esp. *US* a half-pint or 8-ounce measure. **2** full cup.

■ **Usage** A *cupful* is a measure, and so *three cupfuls* is a quantity regarded in terms of a cup; *three cups full* denotes the actual cups as in *brought us three cups full of water.*

Cupid /'kju:pɪd/ *n.* **1** Roman god of love, represented as a naked winged boy archer. **2** (also **cupid**) representation of Cupid. [Latin *cupio* desire]

cupidity /kju:'pɪdɪtɪ/ *n.* greed; avarice. [Latin: related to CUPID]

Cupid's bow *n.* upper lip etc. shaped like an archery bow.

cupola /'kju:pələ/ *n.* **1** dome forming or adorning a roof. **2** revolving dome protecting mounted guns. **3** furnace for melting metals. □ **cupolaed** /-ləd/ *adj.* [Italian from Latin *cupa* cask]

cuppa /'kʌpə/ *n. colloq.* **1** cup of. **2** cup of tea. [corruption]

cupreous /'kju:prɪəs/ *adj.* of or like copper. [Latin: related to COPPER[1]]

cupric /'kju:prɪk/ *adj.* of copper.

cupro-nickel /ˌkju:prəʊ'nɪk(ə)l/ *n.* alloy of copper and nickel.

cup-tie *n.* match in a competition for a cup.

cur *n.* **1** mangy ill-tempered dog. **2** contemptible person. [perhaps from Old Norse *kurr* grumbling]

cur. *abbr.* currency.

curable /'kjʊərəb(ə)l/ *adj.* able to be cured. □ **curability** /-'bɪlɪtɪ/ *n.*

Curaçao /ˌkjʊərə'səʊ/ largest island of the Netherlands Antilles, in the Caribbean Sea; pop. (est. 1992) 143 816; chief town, Willemstad. Industry is centred around the refining of oil from Venezuela, ship repairing, and the production of curaçao liqueur.

curaçao /'kjʊərəˌsəʊ/ *n.* (*pl.* **-s**) orange-flavoured liqueur. [CURAÇAO]

curacy /'kjʊərəsɪ/ *n.* (*pl.* **-ies**) curate's office or tenure of it.

curare /kjʊə'rɑ:rɪ/ *n.* extract of various plants, used by American Indians to poison arrows. [Carib]

curate /'kjʊərət/ *n.* assistant to a parish priest. [medieval Latin *curatus*: related to CURE]

curate's egg *n.* thing that is good in parts.

curative /'kjʊərətɪv/ *–adj.* tending or able to cure. *–n.* curative agent. [medieval Latin: related to CURATE]

curator /kjʊə'reɪtə(r)/ *n.* keeper or custodian of a museum etc. □ **curatorship** *n.* [Anglo-Latin: related to CURE]

curb *–n.* **1** check, restraint. **2** strap etc. passing under a horse's lower jaw, used as a check. **3** enclosing border, e.g. the frame round a well or a fender round a hearth. **4** = KERB. *–v.* **1** restrain. **2** put a curb on (a horse). [French: related to CURVE]

curd *n.* (often in *pl.*) coagulated acidic milk product made into cheese or eaten as food. [origin unknown]

curd cheese *n.* soft smooth cheese made from skimmed milk curds.

curdle /'kɜ:d(ə)l/ *v.* (**-ling**) form into curds; congeal. □ **make one's blood curdle** horrify one. [from CURD]

cure *–v.* (**-ring**) **1** (often foll. by *of*) restore to health; relieve (*cured of pleurisy*). **2** eliminate (disease, evil, etc.). **3** preserve (meat, fruit, etc.) by salting, drying, etc. **4** vulcanize (rubber); harden (plastic etc.). *–n.* **1** restoration to health. **2** thing effecting a cure. **3** course of treatment. **4** curacy. [Latin *cura* care]

curé /'kjʊəreɪ/ *n.* parish priest in France etc. [French]

cure-all *n.* panacea.

curette /kjʊə'ret/ *–n.* small scraping-instrument used by a surgeon. *–v.* (**-tting**) clean or scrape with this. □ **curettage** /-'retɪdʒ/ *n.* [French: related to CURE]

curfew /'kɜ:fju:/ *n.* **1** signal or time after which people must remain indoors. **2** *hist.* signal for extinction of fires at a fixed hour. [French: related to COVER, Latin FOCUS]

Curia /'kjʊərɪə/ *n.* (also **curia**) papal court; government departments of the Vatican. [Latin]

curie /'kjʊərɪ/ *n.* unit of radioactivity. [P. *Curie*, name of a scientist]

curio /'kjʊərɪəʊ/ *n.* (*pl.* **-s**) rare or unusual object. [abbreviation of CURIOSITY]

curiosity /ˌkjʊərɪ'ɒsɪtɪ/ *n.* (*pl.* **-ies**) **1** eager desire to know; inquisitiveness. **2** strange, rare, etc. object. [Latin: related to CURIOUS]

curious /'kjʊərɪəs/ *adj.* **1** eager to learn; inquisitive. **2** strange, surprising, odd. □ **curiously** *adv.* [Latin: related to CURE]

Curitiba /ˌkʊərɪ'ti:bə/ commercial and industrial city in SE Brazil, capital of Paraná state; furniture, paper, maté, and chemicals are produced; pop. (1991) 2 270 000.

curium /'kjʊərɪəm/ *n.* artificial radioactive metallic element. [M. and P. *Curie*, name of scientists]

curl *–v.* **1** (often foll. by *up*) bend or coil into a spiral. **2** move in a spiral form. **3 a** (of the upper lip) be raised contemptuously. **b** cause (the lip) to do this. **4** play curling. *–n.* **1** lock of curled hair. **2** anything spiral or curved inwards. **3 a** curling movement. **b** being curled. □ **curl one's lip** express scorn. **curl up 1** lie or sit with the knees drawn up. **2** *colloq.* writhe in embarrassment etc. [Dutch]

curler *n.* pin or roller etc. for curling the hair.

curlew /'kɜ:lju:/ *n.* wading bird, usu. with a long slender bill. [French]

curlicue /'kɜ:lɪˌkju:/ *n.* decorative curl or twist. [from CURLY, CUE[2] or Q[1]]

curling *n.* game resembling bowls, played on ice with round flat stones.

curly *adj.* (**-ier, -iest**) **1** having or arranged in curls. **2** moving in curves. □ **curliness** *n.*

curly kale *n.* = KALE.

curmudgeon /kə'mʌdʒ(ə)n/ *n.* bad-tempered person. □ **curmudgeonly** *adj.* [origin unknown]

currant /'kʌrənt/ *n.* **1** small seedless dried grape. **2 a** any of various shrubs producing red, white, or black berries. **b** such a berry. [Anglo-French from *Corinth* in Greece]

currency /'kʌrənsɪ/ *n.* (*pl.* **-ies**) **1** money in circulation in an economy. **2** anything that functions as a medium of exchange, including coins, banknotes, cheques, bills of exchange, promissory notes, etc. **3** money in use in a particular country. See FOREIGN EXCHANGE. **4** time that has to elapse before a bill of exchange matures. **5** being current; prevalence (e.g. of words or ideas).

♦ **currency future** *n.* financial futures contract in which a currency is bought or sold for forward delivery at a specified rate of exchange.

---

current *–adj.* **1** belonging to the present; happening now (*current events*). **2** (of money, opinion, rumour, etc.) in general circulation or use. *–n.* **1** body of moving water, air, etc., esp. passing through still water etc. **2 a** ordered movement of electrically charged particles. **b** quantity representing the intensity of this. **3** (usu. foll. by *of*) general tendency or course (of events, opinions, etc.). □ **currentness** *n.* [Latin *curro curs-* run]

♦ **current account** *n.* **1** active account at a bank or building society into which deposits can be paid and from which withdrawals can be made by cheque (see also CHEQUE ACCOUNT). The bank or building society supplies regular statements listing all transactions and the current balance. Building societies usu. make no charges and pay interest on balances maintained in a current account. Banks, in order to remain competitive, are following this practice. **2** part of the balance of payments account that records non-capital transactions. **3** account in which intercompany or interdepartmental balances are recorded. **4** account recording the transactions of a partner in a partnership that do not relate directly to his capital in the partnership (see CAPITAL ACCOUNT 4).

◆ **current assets** *n.pl.* assets that form part of the circulating capital of a business and are turned over frequently in the course of trade. The most common current assets are stock in trade, debtors, and cash. Cf. CAPITAL ASSET.

◆ **current-cost accounting** *n.* (also **CCA**) method of accounting, recommended by the Sandilands Committee, to deal with the problem of showing the effects of inflation on business profits. Instead of showing assets at their historical cost (i.e. their original purchase price), less depreciation where appropriate, the assets are shown at their current cost (see REPLACEMENT COST 2) at the time of producing the accounts. However, it does not strictly show the effects of inflation because it can confuse the effects of inflation with price changes caused by other factors. CAA was much used in the UK in the late 1970s and early 1980s, when inflation was high; it was not popular, however, and as inflation reduced many companies abandoned it. See SANDILANDS COMMITTEE. Cf. CURRENT PURCHASING POWER ACCOUNTING.

◆ **current liabilities** *n.pl.* amounts due to the creditors of an organization that are due to be paid within twelve months.

---

currently *adv.* at the present time; now.

◆ **current purchasing power accounting** *n.* (also **CPP accounting**) method of accounting designed to deal with the problem of showing the effects of inflation on business profits: the historical cost of an asset (i.e. its original purchase price) is increased by indexation using, for example, the retail price index. See also SANDILANDS COMMITTEE. Cf. CURRENT-COST ACCOUNTING.

◆ **current ratio** *n.* proportion of the current assets to the current liabilities of an organization. This ratio is used in the analysis of balance sheets to gauge the likelihood that an organization can pay its debts regularly. No absolute figure for the ratio is deemed desirable, although clearly an excess of current liabilities over current assets would be a cause for concern; different ratios might be appropriate to different sorts of business. In analysing successive balance sheets, trends might be more important than the absolute figures.

◆ **current yield** see YIELD *n.* 2.

---

curriculum /kə'rɪkjʊləm/ *n.* (*pl.* **-la**) subjects included in a course of study. [Latin, = course]

curriculum vitae /'vi:taɪ/ *n.* (also **CV, c.v.**) brief account of one's education, career, etc., prepared by a candidate for a job and given to a prospective employer.

curry[1] /'kʌrɪ/ *–n.* (*pl.* **-ies**) meat, vegetables, etc., cooked in a spicy sauce, usu. served with rice. *–v.* (**-ies, -ied**) prepare or flavour with a curry sauce. [Tamil]

curry[2] /'kʌrɪ/ *v.* (**-ies, -ied**) **1** groom (a horse) with a curry-comb. **2** treat (tanned leather) to improve it. □ **curry favour** ingratiate oneself. [Germanic: related to READY]

curry-comb *n.* metal serrated device for grooming horses.

curry-powder *n.* mixture of turmeric, cumin, etc. for making curry.

curse *–n.* **1** solemn invocation of divine wrath on a person or thing. **2** supposed resulting evil. **3** violent or profane exclamation or oath. **4** thing causing evil or harm. **5** (prec. by *the*) *colloq.* menstruation. *–v.* (**-sing**) **1 a** utter a curse against. **b** (in *imper.*) may God curse. **2** (usu. in *passive*; foll. by *with*) afflict with. **3** swear profanely. [Old English]

cursed /'kɜ:sɪd/ *attrib. adj.* damned.

cursive /'kɜ:sɪv/ *–adj.* (of writing) with joined characters. *–n.* cursive writing. [medieval Latin, = running: related to CURRENT]

cursor /'kɜ:sə(r)/ *n.* **1** *Math.* etc. transparent slide with a hairline, forming part of a slide-rule. **2** *Computing* indicator on a VDU screen identifying the 'active' position, e.g. the position at which the next character to be entered will appear. The cursor is typically a bright character-sized rectangle, possibly flashing on and off, or an underline. [Latin, = runner: related to CURSIVE]

cursor keys *n.pl.* keys on a computer keyboard that can be used to move the cursor to a new position on a display screen. They may be arrow keys.

cursory /'kɜ:sərɪ/ *adj.* hasty, hurried. □ **cursorily** *adv.* **cursoriness** *n.* [Latin: related to CURSOR]

curt *adj.* noticeably or rudely brief. □ **curtly** *adv.* **curtness** *n.* [Latin *curtus* short]

curtail /kɜ:'teɪl/ *v.* cut short; reduce. □ **curtailment** *n.* [corruption of obsolete adj. *curtal*: related to CURT]

curtain /'kɜ:t(ə)n/ *–n.* **1** piece of cloth etc. hung as a screen, esp. at a window. **2 a** rise or fall of a stage curtain between acts or scenes. **b** = CURTAIN-CALL. **3** partition or cover. **4** (in *pl.*) *slang* the end. *–v.* **1** provide or cover with curtain(s). **2** (foll. by *off*) shut off with curtain(s). [Latin *cortina*]

curtain-call *n.* audience's applause summoning actors to take a bow.

curtain-raiser *n.* **1** short play before the main performance. **2** preliminary event.

curtilage /'kɜ:tɪlɪdʒ/ *n.* esp. *Law* area attached to a house and forming one enclosure with it. [French: related to COURT]

curtsy /'kɜ:tsɪ/ (also **curtsey**) *–n.* (*pl.* **-ies** or **-eys**) bending of the knees and lowering of the body made by a girl or woman in acknowledgement of applause or as a respectful greeting etc. *–v.* (**-ies, -ied** or **-eys, -eyed**) make a curtsy. [var. of COURTESY]

curvaceous /kɜ:'veɪʃəs/ *adj. colloq.* (esp. of a woman) having a shapely figure.

curvature /'kɜ:vətʃə(r)/ *n.* **1** curving. **2** curved form. **3** deviation of a curve or curved surface from a plane. [French from Latin: related to CURVE]

curve *–n.* **1** line or surface of which no part is straight or flat. **2** curved form or thing. **3** curved line on a graph. *–v.* (**-ving**) bend or shape to form a curve. □ **curved** *adj.* [Latin *curvus* curved]

curvet /kɜ:'vet/ *–n.* horse's frisky leap. *–v.* (**-tt-** or **-t-**) perform a curvet. [Italian diminutive: related to CURVE]

curvilinear /ˌkɜ:vɪ'lɪnɪə(r)/ *adj.* contained by or consisting of curved lines. □ **curvilinearly** *adv.* [from CURVE after *rectilinear*]

curvy *adj.* (**-ier, -iest**) **1** having many curves. **2** (of a woman's figure) shapely. □ **curviness** *n.*

cushion /'kʊʃ(ə)n/ *–n.* **1** bag stuffed with soft material, for sitting or leaning on etc. **2** protection against shock; measure to soften a blow. **3** padded rim of a billiard-table etc. **4** air supporting a hovercraft etc. *–v.* **1** provide or protect with cushion(s). **2** mitigate the adverse effects of. [Latin *culcita* mattress]

cushy /'kʊʃɪ/ *adj.* (**-ier, -iest**) *colloq.* (of a job etc.) easy and pleasant. [Hindi *ḳhūsh* pleasant]

('kju:səʊ) Canadian University Services Overseas.

cusp *n.* point at which two curves meet, e.g. the horn of a crescent moon etc. [Latin *cuspis -id-* point, apex]

cuss *colloq. –n.* **1** curse. **2** usu. *derog.* person; creature. *–v.* curse. [var. of CURSE]

cussed /'kʌsɪd/ *adj. colloq.* stubborn. □ **cussedness** *n.*

custard /'kʌstəd/ *n.* pudding or sweet sauce of eggs or flavoured cornflour and milk. [obsolete *crustade*: related to CRUST]

custodian /kʌ'stəʊdɪən/ *n.* guardian or keeper. □ **custodianship** *n.*

custody /'kʌstədɪ/ *n.* **1** guardianship; protective care. **2** imprisonment. □ **take into custody** arrest. □ **custodial** /kʌ'stəʊdɪəl/ *adj.* [Latin *custos -od-* guard]

custom /'kʌstəm/ *n.* **1 a** usual behaviour. **b** particular established way of behaving. **2** *Law* established usage having the force of law. See also CUSTOM OF THE TRADE. **3** regular business dealings or customers. **4** (in *pl.*; also treated as *sing.*) **a** duty on imports and exports. **b** (usu. **Customs**) official department administering this. See BOARD OF CUSTOMS AND EXCISE. **c** area at a port, frontier, etc., dealing with customs etc. [Latin *consuetudo*]

customary *adj.* in accordance with custom, usual. □ **customarily** *adv.* **customariness** *n.* [medieval Latin: related to CUSTOM]

custom-built *adj.* (also **custom-made**) made to order.

customer *n.* **1** person who buys goods or services from a shop or business. **2** *colloq.* person of a specified kind (*awkward customer*). [Anglo-French: related to CUSTOM]

♦ **customer services** *n.pl.* services an organization offers to its customers, esp. of industrial goods and expensive consumer goods (e.g. computers or cars). Customer services cover a wide variety of forms, including after-sales servicing (e.g. a repair and replacement service), extended guarantees, regular mailings of information, and, more recently, freephone telephone calls in case of complaints. The appeal of a company's products are greatly influenced by the customer services it offers.

---

custom-house *n.* customs office at a port or frontier etc.

customize *v.* (also **-ise**) (**-zing** or **-sing**) make or modify to order; personalize.

♦ **custom of the trade** *n.* practice that has been used in a particular trade for a long time and is understood to apply by all engaged in that trade. Such practices may influence the way in which a term in a contract is interpreted and courts will generally take into account established customs of a trade in settling a dispute over the interpretation of a contract.

♦ **Customs and Excise** *n.* = BOARD OF CUSTOMS AND EXCISE.

♦ **customs entry** *n.* record kept by the Customs of goods imported into or exported from a country. In the UK a bill of entry is used for either imports (**entry in**) or exports (**entry out**). If no duty is involved with a consignment it is given **free entry**.

♦ **customs tariff** *n.* listing of the goods on which a country's government requires customs duty to be paid on being imported into that country, together with the rate of customs duty applicable. For the UK it is published by the Stationery Office.

♦ **customs union** *n.* union of two or more states to form a region in which there are no import or export duties between members but goods imported into the region bear the same import duties. The European Community is an example.

---

cut *–v.* (**-tt-**; *past* and *past part.* **cut**) **1** (also *absol.*) penetrate or wound with a sharp-edged instrument. **2** (often foll. by *into*) divide or be divided with a knife etc. **3** trim or detach by cutting. **4** (foll. by *loose*, *open*, etc.) loosen etc. by cutting. **5** (esp. as **cutting** *adj.*) wound (*cutting remark*). **6** (often foll. by *down*) reduce (wages, time, etc.) or cease (services etc.). **7 a** make (a coat, gem, key, record, etc.) by cutting. **b** make (a path, tunnel, etc.) by removing material. **8** perform, make (*cut a caper*; *cut a sorry figure*). **9** (also *absol.*) cross, intersect. **10** (foll. by *across*, *through*, etc.) traverse, esp. as a shorter way (*cut across the grass*). **11 a** deliberately ignore (a person one knows). **b** renounce (a connection). **12** esp. *US* deliberately miss (a class etc.). **13** *Cards* **a** divide (a pack) into two parts. **b** do this to select a dealer etc. **14 a** edit (film or tape). **b** (often in *imper.*) stop filming or recording. **c** (foll. by *to*) go quickly to (another shot). **15** switch off (an engine etc.). **16** chop (a ball). *–n.* **1** cutting. **2** division or wound made by cutting. **3** stroke with a knife, sword, whip, etc. **4 a** reduction (in wages etc.). **b** cessation (of power supply etc.). **5** removal of lines etc. from a play, film, etc. **6** wounding remark or act. **7** style of hair, garment, etc. achieved by cutting. **8** particular piece of butchered meat. **9** *colloq.* commission; share of profits. **10** stroke made by cutting. **11** deliberate ignoring of a person. **12** = WOODCUT. □ **a cut above** *colloq.* noticeably superior to. **be cut out** (foll. by *for*, or *to* + infin.) be suited. **cut across 1** transcend (normal limitations etc.). **2** see sense 10 of *v.* **cut and run** *slang* run away. **cut back 1** reduce (expenditure etc.). **2** prune (a tree etc.). **cut both ways 1** serve both sides of an argument etc. **2** (of an action) have both good and bad effects. **cut a corner** go across it. **cut corners** do perfunctorily or incompletely, esp. to save time. **cut a dash** make a brilliant show. **cut a person dead** deliberately ignore (a person one knows). **cut down 1 a** bring or throw down by cutting. **b** kill by sword or disease. **2** see sense 6 of *v.* **3** reduce the length of (*cut down trousers to make shorts*). **4** (often foll. by *on*) reduce consumption (*cut down on beer*). **cut a person down to size** *colloq.* deflate a person's pretensions. **cut in 1** interrupt. **2** pull in too closely in front of another vehicle. **cut it fine** allow very little margin of time etc. **cut it out** (usu. in *imper.*) *slang* stop doing that. **cut one's losses** abandon an unprofitable scheme. **cut no ice** *slang* have no influence. **cut off 1** remove by cutting. **2 a** (often in *passive*) bring to an abrupt end or (esp. early) death. **b** intercept, interrupt. **c** disconnect (a person on the telephone). **3 a** prevent from travelling. **b** (as **cut off** *adj.*) isolated or remote. **4** disinherit. **cut out 1** remove from inside by cutting. **2** make by cutting from a larger whole. **3** omit. **4** *colloq.* stop doing or using (something) (*cut out chocolate*). **5** (cause to) cease functioning (*engine cut out*). **6** outdo or supplant (a rival). **cut short** interrupt; terminate. **cut one's teeth on** acquire experience from. **cut a tooth** have it appear through the gum. **cut up 1** cut into pieces. **2** (usu. in *passive*) distress greatly. **cut up rough** *slang* show anger or resentment. [Old English]

cut and dried *adj.* **1** completely decided; inflexible. **2** (of opinions etc.) ready-made, lacking freshness.

♦ **cut and paste** *n.* technique used in word processing whereby a section of text (e.g. a paragraph) can be moved within a document: the section is 'cut' (i.e. removed) from its original position and then 'pasted' (i.e. inserted) into the new position.

---

cut and thrust *n.* lively argument etc.

cutaneous /kjuːˈteɪnɪəs/ *adj.* of the skin. [Latin: related to CUTICLE]

cutaway *adj.* (of a diagram etc.) with parts of the exterior left out to reveal the interior.

cut-back *n.* cutting back, esp. a reduction in expenditure.

cute *adj. colloq.* **1** esp. *US* attractive, quaint. **2** clever, ingenious. □ **cutely** *adv.* **cuteness** *n.* [shortening of ACUTE]

cut glass *n.* glass with patterns cut on it.

cuticle /ˈkjuːtɪk(ə)l/ *n.* dead skin at the base of a fingernail or toenail. [Latin diminutive of *cutis* skin]

cutis /ˈkjuːtɪs/ *n.* true skin, beneath the epidermis. [Latin]

cutlass /ˈkʌtləs/ *n. hist.* short sword with a slightly curved blade. [Latin *cultellus*: related to CUTLER]

cutler *n.* person who makes or deals in knives etc. [Latin *cultellus* diminutive: related to COULTER]

cutlery /ˈkʌtlərɪ/ *n.* knives, forks, and spoons for use at table. [Anglo-French: related to CUTLER]

cutlet /ˈkʌtlɪt/ *n.* **1** neck-chop of mutton or lamb. **2** small piece of veal etc. for frying. **3** flat cake of minced meat or nuts and breadcrumbs etc. [French diminutive from Latin *costa* rib]

cut-off *n.* **1** point at which something is cut off. **2** device for stopping a flow.

cut-out *n.* **1** figure cut out of paper etc. **2** device for automatic disconnection, the release of exhaust gases, etc.

cut-price *adj.* (also **cut-rate**) at a reduced price.

CUTS /kʌts/ *abbr.* Computer Users' Tape System.

cutter *n.* **1 a** person or thing that cuts. **b** (in *pl.*) cutting tool. **2 a** small fast sailing-ship. **b** small boat carried by a large ship.

cutthroat *–n.* **1** murderer. **2** (in full **cutthroat razor**)

razor with a long unguarded blade set in a handle. *–adj.* **1** (of competition) ruthless and intense. **2** (of a card-game) three-handed.

cutting *–n.* **1** piece cut from a newspaper etc. **2** piece cut from a plant for propagation. **3** excavated channel in a hillside etc. for a railway or road. *–adj.* see CUT *v.* 5. □ **cuttingly** *adv.*

cuttlefish /ˈkʌt(ə)lfɪʃ/ *n.* (*pl.* same or **-es**) mollusc with ten arms and ejecting a black fluid when threatened. [Old English]

cutwater *n.* **1** forward edge of a ship's prow. **2** wedge-shaped projection from a pier or bridge.

cuvée /kjuːˈveɪ/ *n.* blend or batch of wine. [French, = vatful]

Cuzco /ˈkʌskəʊ/ city in S Peru, commercial centre of an agricultural region; pop. (est. 1988) 255 300.

CV *–abbr.* **1** *Finance* convertible. **2** (also **c.v.**) = CURRICULUM VITAE. *–postcode* Coventry.

c.v.d. *abbr. Commerce* cash versus documents.

CV Esc *symb.* Cape Verde escudo.

CW *postcode* Crewe.

cwm /kuːm/ *n.* **1** (in Wales) = COOMB. **2** *Geog.* cirque. [Welsh]

c.w.o. *abbr.* (also **cwo**) cash with order.

CWS *abbr.* Cooperative Wholesale Society.

cwt. *abbr.* (also **cwt**) hundredweight.

CX *international civil aircraft marking* Uruguay.

CY *–international vehicle registration* Cyprus. *–airline flight code* Cyprus Airways.

cy. *abbr.* currency.

-cy *suffix* denoting state, condition, or status (*idiocy*; *captaincy*). [Latin *-cia*, Greek *-kia*]

cyanic acid /saɪˈænɪk/ *n.* unstable colourless pungent acid gas. [Greek *kuanos* a blue mineral]

cyanide /ˈsaɪəˌnaɪd/ *n.* highly poisonous substance used in the extraction of gold and silver.

cyanogen /saɪˈænədʒ(ə)n/ *n.* highly poisonous gas used in fertilizers.

cyanosis /ˌsaɪəˈnəʊsɪs/ *n.* bluish skin due to oxygen-deficient blood.

cybernetics /ˌsaɪbəˈnetɪks/ *n.pl.* (usu. treated as *sing.*) science of communications and control systems in machines and living things. □ **cybernetic** *adj.* [Greek *kubernētēs* steersman]

cyberpunk /ˈsaɪbəˌpʌŋk/ *n.* science fiction writing combining high-tech plots with unconventional or nihilistic social values. [from CYBERNETICS, PUNK]

cycad /ˈsaɪkæd/ *n.* palmlike plant often growing to a great height. [Greek *koix* Egyptian palm]

Cyclades /ˈsɪkləˌdiːz/ (Greek **Kikládhes** /kɪkˈlɑːðiːs/) group of islands in the Aegean Sea, a department of Greece; pop. (1990) 95 083; capital, Síros. Tourism is the main industry. □ **Cycladic** /saɪˈklædɪk, sɪ-/ *adj.*

cyclamate /ˈsaɪkləˌmeɪt/ *n.* former artificial sweetener. [chemical name]

cyclamen /ˈsɪkləmən/ *n.* **1** plant with pink, red, or white flowers with backward-turned petals. **2** cyclamen red or pink. [Latin from Greek]

cycle /ˈsaɪk(ə)l/ *–n.* **1 a** recurrent round or period (of events, phenomena, etc.). **b** time needed for this. **2 a** *Physics* etc. recurrent series of operations or states. **b** *Electr.* = HERTZ. **3** series of related songs, poems, etc. **4** bicycle, tricycle, etc. *–v.* (**-ling**) **1** ride a bicycle etc. **2** move in cycles. [Greek *kuklos* circle]

cycle-track *n.* (also **cycle-way**) path or road for bicycles.

cyclic /ˈsaɪklɪk/ *adj.* (also **cyclical** /ˈsɪklɪk(ə)l/) **1 a** recurring in cycles. **b** belonging to a chronological cycle. **2** with constituent atoms forming a ring. □ **cyclically** *adv.*

cyclist /ˈsaɪklɪst/ *n.* rider of a bicycle.

cyclo- *comb. form* circle, cycle, or cyclic.

cyclone /ˈsaɪkləʊn/ *n.* **1** winds rotating inwards to an area of low barometric pressure; depression. **2** violent hurricane of limited diameter. □ **cyclonic** /-ˈklɒnɪk/ *adj.* [Greek *kuklōma* wheel]

cyclotron /ˈsaɪkləˌtrɒn/ *n.* apparatus for the acceleration of charged atomic and subatomic particles revolving in a magnetic field.

cygnet /ˈsɪgnɪt/ *n.* young swan. [Latin *cygnus* swan from Greek]

cylinder /ˈsɪlɪndə(r)/ *n.* **1** uniform solid or hollow body with straight sides and a circular section. **2** thing of this shape, e.g. a container for liquefied gas, a piston-chamber in an engine. □ **cylindrical** /-ˈlɪndrɪk(ə)l/ *adj.* [Latin *cylindrus* from Greek]

cymbal /ˈsɪmb(ə)l/ *n.* concave disc, struck usu. with another to make a ringing sound. □ **cymbalist** *n.* [Latin from Greek]

cyme /saɪm/ *n.* flower cluster with a single terminal flower that develops first. □ **cymose** *adj.* [Greek *kuma* wave]

Cymric /ˈkɪmrɪk/ *adj.* Welsh. [Welsh *Cymru* Wales]

cynic /ˈsɪnɪk/ *n.* **1** person with a pessimistic view of human nature. **2** (**Cynic**) one of a school of ancient Greek philosophers showing contempt for ease and pleasure. □ **cynical** *adj.* **cynically** *adv.* **cynicism** /-ˌsɪz(ə)m/ *n.* [Greek *kuōn* dog]

cynosure /ˈsaɪnəˌzjʊə(r)/ *n.* centre of attraction or admiration. [Greek, = dog's tail (name for Ursa Minor)]

cypher var. of CIPHER.

cypress /ˈsaɪprəs/ *n.* conifer with hard wood and dark foliage. [Greek *kuparissos*]

Cypriot /ˈsɪprɪət/ (also **Cypriote** /-əʊt/) *–n.* native or national of Cyprus. *–adj.* of Cyprus.

Cyrillic /sɪˈrɪlɪk/ *–adj.* of the alphabet used by the Slavonic

---

Cyprus /ˈsaɪprəs/, **Republic of** island state in the E Mediterranean, about 80 km (50 miles) S of the Turkish coast. Agriculture is important, esp. in the N, producing potatoes, citrus fruits, grapes, and wine for export. Mining of copper ores, iron pyrites, asbestos, and chromite has declined. Manufacturing (esp. of food, beverages, textiles and clothing, and mineral products), construction, and service industries are expanding but tourism is the main growth industry. Cyprus formed a customs union with the European Community in 1988, and has since been formally invited to join the EU early in the next century.

History. The island was occupied by the Turks from 1571 until 1878, when it was placed under British administration; it became a Crown Colony in 1925 and an independent republic within the Commonwealth in 1960. However, the constitution failed to reconcile the opposing Greek and Turkish communities and in 1974 Turkey invaded the island, establishing a 'Turkish Federated State' in N Cyprus with Rauf Denktash as president. In 1983 it was declared an independent state, the Turkish Republic of Northern Cyprus, but this has not been internationally recognized. A series of UN-sponsored discussions on reunifying the island have so far failed to produce any agreement. President, Glafcos Clerides; capital, Nicosia.

languages	Greek & Turkish (official), English
currency	pound (£C) of 100 cents
pop. (1996)	657 000
GNP (1994)	US$7B
literacy	97% (m); 92% (f)
life expectancy	74 (m); 79 (f)

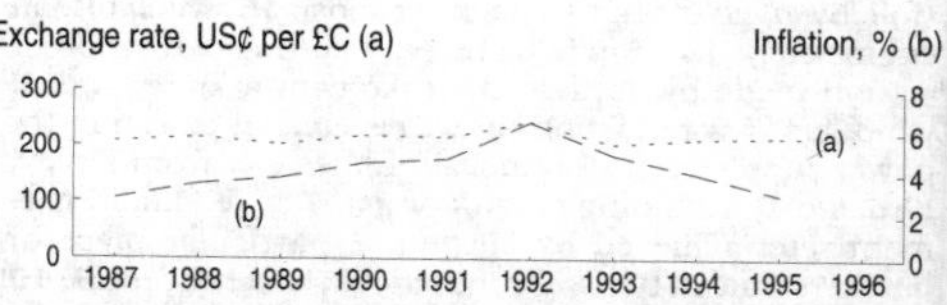

---

peoples of the Orthodox Church, now used esp. for Russian and Bulgarian. –*n.* this alphabet. [St *Cyril*, d. 869]

cyst /sɪst/ *n.* sac formed in the body, containing liquid matter. [Greek *kustis* bladder]

cystic *adj.* **1** of the bladder. **2** like a cyst.

cystic fibrosis *n.* hereditary disease usu. with respiratory infections.

cystitis /sɪ'staɪtɪs/ *n.* inflammation of the bladder usu. causing frequent painful urination.

-cyte *comb. form* mature cell (*leucocyte*). [Greek *kutos* vessel]

cytology /saɪ'tɒlədʒɪ/ *n.* study of biological cells. □ **cytological** /-tə'lɒdʒɪk(ə)l/ *adj.* **cytologist** *n.* [Greek *kutos* vessel]

cytoplasm /'saɪtəʊ,plæz(ə)m/ *n.* protoplasmic content of a cell apart from its nucleus. □ **cytoplasmic** /-'plæzmɪk/ *adj.*

czar var. of TSAR

Czech /tʃek/ –*n.* **1** native or national of the Czech Republic. **2** official language of the Czech Republic. –*adj.* of the Czech Republic, its people, or language. [Bohemian *Čech*]

Czechoslovakia /,tʃekəslə'vækɪə/ former country in central Europe. Czechoslovakia was created out of the N part of the old Austro-Hungarian empire after the latter's collapse at the end of the First World War. It incorporated the Czechs of Bohemia and Moravia in the W with the Slovaks of Slovakia in the E. After the Second World War, power was seized by the Communists and Czechoslovakia remained under Soviet domination until the Communist government was overthrown in 1989. A new government was formed, with Václav Havel as president, followed by the introduction of democratic reforms. In August 1990 the official name of the country was changed to the Czech and Slovak Federal Republic; at the end of 1992 the federation was dissolved (see CZECH REPUBLIC; SLOVAKIA). □ **Czechoslovakian** *adj.* & *n.*

Czech Republic landlocked country in central Europe, formerly (until January 1993) a federal republic of Czechoslovakia. The economy is highly industrialized; major exports include machinery, motor vehicles, glass, ceramics, textiles, and footwear. Lignite and coal are mined and the timber industry is important. Agriculture produces sugar beet, potatoes, and cereals. Reforms have been introduced to create a free-market economy, but progress was initially slow as the introduction of privatization led to administrative problems; foreign investment offers the best chance of security. Production and exports dropped in the early 1990s, largely owing to the loss of trade with other former Communist countries, but the country is seeking new markets in W Europe. In 1996 the Privatization Ministry closed; having privatized several thousand state enterprises, its work was complete. The Czech Republic applied for EU membership in 1996 and has since been formally invited to join early in the next century. President, Václav Havel; prime minister, Josef Tosovsky; capital, Prague.

languages	Czech (official), Slovak
currency	koruna (Kčs) of 100 haléřů
pop. (1996)	10 315 842
GNP (1994)	US$33B
literacy	99%
life expectancy	69 (m); 76 (f)

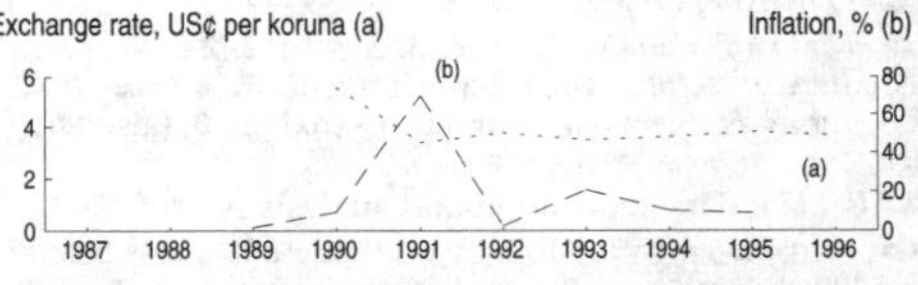

Dd

D[1] /diː/ *n.* (also **d**) (*pl.* **Ds** or **D's**) **1** fourth letter of the alphabet. **2** *Mus.* second note of the diatonic scale of C major. **3** (as a roman numeral) 500. **4** = DEE. **5** fourth highest class or category (of academic marks etc.). **6 a** occupational grade comprising semiskilled or unskilled workers. **b** person in this grade.

D[2] *–symb.* **1** deuterium. **2** *Currency* **a** dalasi. **b** dông. *–international vehicle registration & civil aircraft marking* Germany.

d. *abbr.* **1** died. **2** departs. **3** daughter. **4** date. **5** dividend. **6** dollar(s). **7** *hist.* (pre-decimal) penny. [sense 7 from Latin DENARIUS]

'd *v. colloq.* (usu. after pronouns) had, would (*I'd*; *he'd*). [abbreviation]

D2 *international civil aircraft marking* Angola.

D4 *international civil aircraft marking* Cape Verde Islands.

D6 *international civil aircraft marking* Comoros.

DA *–abbr.* **1** deed of arrangement. **2** *US* District Attorney. *–symb.* Algerian dinar. *–postcode* Dartford. *–airline flight code* Dan-Air Services.

D/A *abbr.* **1** (also **d/a**) days after acceptance. **2** delivery on acceptance. **3** (also **D/a**) deposit account. **4** (also **D-A**) *Computing* & *Electronics* digital-to-analog. **5** (also **d/a**) DOCUMENTS AGAINST ACCEPTANCE.

DAAS *abbr.* data acquisition and analysis system.

dab[1] *–v.* (**-bb-**) **1** (often foll. by *at*) repeatedly press briefly and lightly with a cloth etc. (*dabbed at her eyes*). **2** press (a cloth etc.) thus. **3** (foll. by *on*) apply by dabbing. **4** (often foll. by *at*) aim a feeble blow; strike lightly. *–n.* **1** dabbing. **2** small amount thus applied (*dab of paint*). **3** light blow. **4** (in *pl.*) *slang* fingerprints. [imitative]

dab[2] *n.* (*pl.* same) a kind of marine flat-fish. [origin unknown]

dabble /'dæb(ə)l/ *v.* (**-ling**) **1** (usu. foll. by *in, at*) engage (in an activity etc.) superficially. **2** move the feet, hands, etc. in esp. shallow liquid. **3** wet partly; stain, splash. □ **dabbler** *n.* [from DAB[1]]

dabchick /'dæbtʃɪk/ *n.* = LITTLE GREBE. [Old English]

dab hand *n.* (usu. foll. by *at*) *colloq.* expert. [*dab* adept, origin unknown]

DAC *abbr.* **1** data analysis and control. **2** Development Assistance Committee (of the OECD). **3** = D/A CONVERTER.

d.a.c. *abbr. Insurance* deductible average clause.

da capo /dɑː 'kɑːpəʊ/ *adv. Mus.* repeat from the beginning. [Italian]

Dacca see DHAKA.

dace *n.* (*pl.* same) small freshwater fish related to the carp. [French *dars*: related to DART]

dacha /'dætʃə/ *n.* Russian country cottage. [Russian]

dachshund /'dækshʊnd/ *n.* dog of a short-legged long-bodied breed. [German, = badger-dog]

D/A converter *n.* (also **DAC**) device for converting the output from a computer (in the form of a series of binary values) into a continuous representation. [digital-to-analog converter]

dactyl /'dæktɪl/ *n.* metrical foot consisting of one long syllable followed by two short syllables (¯˘˘). □ **dactylic** /-'tɪlɪk/ *adj.* [Greek, = finger]

dad *n. colloq.* father. [imitative of a child's *da da*]

Dada /'dɑːdɑː/ *n.* early 20th-century artistic and literary movement repudiating conventions. □ **Dadaism** /-dəˌɪz(ə)m/ *n.* **Dadaist** /-dəɪst/ *n.* & *adj.* **Dadaistic** /-'ɪstɪk/ *adj.* [French *dada* hobby-horse]

daddy /'dædɪ/ *n.* (*pl.* **-ies**) *colloq.* father. [from DAD]

daddy-long-legs *n.* (*pl.* same) crane-fly.

dado /'deɪdəʊ/ *n.* (*pl.* **-s**) **1** lower, differently decorated, part of an interior wall. **2** plinth of a column. **3** cube of a pedestal between the base and the cornice. [Italian: related to DIE[2]]

Dadra and Nagar Haveli /'dɑːdrə, ˌnɑːgə hə'veɪlɪ/ Union Territory of W India, an agricultural region producing cereals and pulses; pop. (1991) 138 477; capital, Silvassa.

daemon var. of DEMON 4.

daff *n. colloq.* = DAFFODIL. [abbreviation]

daffodil /'dæfədɪl/ *n.* spring bulb with a yellow trumpet-shaped flower. [related to ASPHODEL]

daft /dɑːft/ *adj. colloq.* silly, foolish, crazy. [Old English, = meek]

Dagestan /ˌdægɪ'stɑːn/ autonomous republic of S Russia, on the Caspian Sea; pop. (est. 1995) 2 067 000; capital, Makhachkala. Engineering, food-processing, oil, and chemical industries are important.

dagger *n.* **1** short pointed knife used as a weapon. **2** *Printing* = OBELUS. □ **at daggers drawn** in bitter enmity. **look daggers at** glare angrily at. [origin uncertain]

◆ **DAGMAR** /'dægmɑː(r)/ *n.* principle, developed in the US in the 1960s, that the function of advertising is to communicate and that its success or failure should be measured against the specific objectives defined for it. [*d*efining *a*dvertising *g*oals for *m*easured *a*dvertising *r*esults]

dago /'deɪgəʊ/ *n.* (*pl.* **-s**) *slang offens.* foreigner, esp. a Spaniard, Portuguese, or Italian. [Spanish *Diego* = James]

daguerreotype /də'gerəʊˌtaɪp/ *n.* early photograph using a silvered plate and mercury vapour. [*Daguerre*, name of its inventor]

dahlia /'deɪlɪə/ *n.* large-flowered showy garden plant. [*Dahl*, name of a botanist]

Dahomey /də'həʊmɪ/ see BENIN.

Dáil /dɔɪl/ *n.* (in full **Dáil Éireann** /'eɪrən/) lower house of parliament in the Republic of Ireland. [Irish, = assembly (of Ireland)]

daily /'deɪlɪ/ *–adj.* done, produced, or occurring every day or every weekday. *–adv.* **1** every day. **2** constantly. *–n.* (*pl.* **-ies**) *colloq.* **1** daily newspaper. **2** cleaning woman.

daily bread *n.* necessary food; livelihood.

◆ **daimyo bond** /'deəmjəʊ/ *n.* bearer bond issued in Japan and the eurobond market by the World Bank. [Japanese, = 10th-19th-century territorial magnate]

dainty /'deɪntɪ/ *–adj.* (**-ier, -iest**) **1** delicately pretty. **2** delicate or small. **3** (of food) choice. **4** fastidious; discriminating. *–n.* (*pl.* **-ies**) choice delicacy. □ **daintily** *adv.* **daintiness** *n.* [Latin *dignitas* DIGNITY]

daiquiri /'daɪkərɪ/ *n.* (*pl.* **-s**) cocktail of rum, lime juice, etc. [*Daiquiri* in Cuba]

dairy /'deərɪ/ *n.* (*pl.* **-ies**) **1** place for processing, distributing, or selling milk and its products. **2** (*attrib.*) of, containing, or used for dairy products (and sometimes eggs) (*dairy cow*). [Old English]

dairying *n.* dairy farming and distribution.

dairymaid *n.* woman employed in a dairy.

dairyman *n.* dealer in dairy products.

dais /'deɪɪs/ *n.* low platform, usu. at the upper end of a hall. [Latin DISCUS disc, (later) table]

daisy /'deɪzɪ/ *n.* (*pl.* **-ies**) **1** small wild plant with white-petalled flowers. **2** plant with similar flowers. [Old English, = *day's eye*]

♦ **daisy-wheel printer** *n.* printer that carries its font on a plastic disc (**daisy wheel**) with characters on the end of stalks radiating from the centre. The wheel is rotated until the required letter etc. is in position, when a hammer strikes it against the paper through an inked ribbon. The wheel moves along the line as it prints. These printers produce a high-quality print at a reasonable cost, but they are not as fast as other types of printers and cannot produce graphics. The daisy wheels are removable, and different ones can be used to provide alternative fonts, print styles (e.g. italic), and character sets.

Dak. *abbr.* Dakota.

Dakar /'dækɑː(r)/ capital and chief port of Senegal, on the Atlantic coast of W Africa; industries include sugar refining and peanut-oil production; pop. (est. 1994) 1 014 036.

dal var. of DHAL.

Dalai Lama /ˌdælaɪ 'lɑːmə/ *n.* spiritual head of Tibetan Buddhism. [Mongolian *dalai* ocean]

dalasi /də'lɑːsɪ/ *n.* standard monetary unit of The Gambia. [W African language]

dale *n.* valley. [Old English]

Dalian /ˌdɑːlɪ'æn/ see LÜDA.

Dallas /'dæləs/ city in the US, in NE Texas; city pop. (est. 1994) 1 022 830; metropolitan area pop. 2 731 503. It is a financial and commercial centre; industries include aircraft manufacture, electronics, and oil refining.

dally /'dælɪ/ *v.* (**-ies, -ied**) **1** delay; waste time. **2** (often foll. by *with*) flirt, trifle. □ **dalliance** *n.* [French]

Dalmatian /dæl'meɪʃ(ə)n/ *n.* large white spotted short-haired dog. [*Dalmatia* in Croatia]

dal segno /dæl 'seɪnjəʊ/ *adv. Mus.* repeat from the point marked by a sign. [Italian, = from the sign]

dam[1] *–n.* **1** barrier across river etc., forming a reservoir or preventing flooding. **2** barrier made by beaver. *–v.* (**-mm-**) **1** provide or confine with a dam. **2** (often foll. by *up*) block up; obstruct. [Low German or Dutch]

dam[2] *n.* mother, esp. of a four-footed animal. [var. of DAME]

damage /'dæmɪdʒ/ *–n.* **1** harm or injury; loss. **2** (prec. by *the*) *slang* cost. *–v.* (**-ging**) inflict damage on. [Latin *damnum*]

♦ **damages** *n.pl. Law* financial compensation for a loss or injury, breach of contract, tort, or infringement of a right. The award of damages is an attempt, as far as money can, to restore the injured party to the position he was in before the event in question took place; i.e. the object is to provide restitution rather than profit. Damages are not assessed in an arbitrary fashion but are subject to various judicial guidelines. In general, damages capable of being quantified in monetary terms are known as **liquidated damages**. These include instances in which a genuine pre-estimate can be given of the loss that will be caused to one party if a contract is broken by the other party; this will be the amount recoverable for the breach (cf. penalty). Another form of liquidated damages is that expressly made recoverable under a statute. These may also be known as **statutory damages** if they involve a breach of statutory duty or are regulated or limited by statute. **Unliquidated damages** are those fixed by a court rather than those that have been estimated in advance. **General damages** are compensation for general damage, which is the kind of damage the law presumes to exist in any given situation. It is recoverable even without being specifically claimed and is awarded for the usual or probable consequences of the wrongful act complained of. For example, in an action for medical negligence, pain and suffering is presumed to exist, therefore if the action is successful, general damages would be awarded as compensation even though not specifically claimed or proved. Loss of earnings by the injured party, however, must be specifically claimed and proved, in which case they are known as **specific damages**. **Nominal** and **contemptuous damages** are those awarded for trifling amounts. These are awarded either when the court is of the opinion that although the plaintiff's rights have been infringed no real loss has been suffered, or, although actual loss has resulted, the loss has been caused by the conduct of the plaintiff. The prospect of receiving only nominal or contemptuous damages prevents frivolous actions being brought. The award is usu. accompanied by an order that each party bears his or her own legal costs. **Exemplary damages**, on the other hand, are punitive damages awarded not merely as a means of compensation but also to punish the party responsible for the loss or injury. This usu. occurs when the party causing the damage has done so wilfully or has received financial gain from this wrongful conduct. Exemplary damages will be greater than the amount that would have been payable purely as compensation. **Prospective damages** are awarded to a plaintiff, not as compensation for any loss suffered at the time of a legal action but in respect of a loss it is reasonably anticipated the plaintiff will suffer at some future time. Such an injury or loss may sometimes be considered to be too remote and therefore not recoverable. See REMOTENESS OF DAMAGE.

Daman and Diu /dəˌmɑːn, 'diːuː/ Union Territory of India; industries include tourism and fishing; pop. (1991) 101 586. Until 1987 the district of Daman and the island of Diu were administered with Goa, which now forms a separate state.

damascene /'dæməˌsiːn/ *–v.* (**-ning**) decorate (metal) by etching or inlaying esp. with gold or silver. *–n.* design or article produced in this way. *–adj.* of this process. [DAMASCUS]

Damascus /də'mɑːskəs/ capital of Syria, in the SE of the country; pop. (1994) 1 549 932. It has existed as a city for over 4000 years and has always been a centre of trade and travel.

damask /'dæməsk/ *–n.* reversible figured woven fabric, esp. white table linen. *–adj.* **1** made of damask. **2** velvety pink. *–v.* weave with figured designs. [as DAMASCENE]

damask rose *n.* old sweet-scented rose used to make attar.

dame *n.* **1** (**Dame**) **a** title given to a woman holding any of several orders of chivalry. **b** woman holding this title. **2** comic middle-aged female pantomime character, usu. played by a man. **3** *US slang* woman. [Latin *domina* lady]

dame-school *n. hist.* primary school kept by an elderly woman.

Damietta /ˌdæmɪ'etə/ (Arabic **Dumyât** /dʊm'jɑːt/) port in Egypt, on the Nile delta; manufactures include cotton and silk; pop. (1991) 113 000.

dammit /'dæmɪt/ *int. colloq.* damn it.

damn /dæm/ *–v.* **1** (often *absol.* or as *int.* of anger or annoyance, = *may God damn*) curse (a person or thing). **2** doom to hell; cause the damnation of. **3** condemn, censure (*review damning the book*). **4 a** (often as **damning** *adj.*) (of circumstance, evidence, etc.) show or prove to be guilty. **b** be the ruin of. *–n.* **1** uttered curse. **2** *slang* negligible amount. *–adj. & adv. colloq.* = DAMNED. □ **damn all** *slang* nothing at all. **damn well** *colloq.* (for emphasis) simply (*damn well do as I say*). **damn with faint praise** commend feebly, and so imply disapproval. **I'm** (or **I'll be) damned if** *colloq.* I certainly do not, will not, etc. **not give a damn** see GIVE. **well I'm** (or **I'll be) damned** *colloq.* exclamation of surprise etc. [Latin *damnum* loss]

damnable /'dæmnəb(ə)l/ *adj.* hateful, annoying. □ **damnably** *adv.*

damnation /dæm'neɪʃ(ə)n/ *–n.* eternal punishment in hell. *–int.* expressing anger.

damned /dæmd/ *colloq. –attrib. adj.* damnable. *–adv.* extremely (*damned hot*). □ **damned well** = *damn well*. **do one's damnedest** do one's utmost.

damp *–adj.* slightly wet. *–n.* slight diffused or condensed moisture, esp. when unwelcome. *–v.* **1** make damp;

moisten. **2** (often foll. by *down*) **a** temper; mute (*damps my enthusiasm*). **b** make (a fire) burn less strongly by reducing the flow of air to it. **3** reduce or stop the vibration of (esp. strings of a musical instrument). □ **damply** *adv.* **dampness** *n.* [Low German]

damp course *n.* (also **damp-proof course**) layer of waterproof material in a wall near the ground, to prevent rising damp.

dampen *v.* **1** make or become damp. **2** (often foll. by *down*) = DAMP *v.* 2a.

damper *n.* **1** discouraging person or thing. **2** device that reduces shock or noise. **3** metal plate in a flue to control the draught. **4** *Mus.* pad silencing a piano string. □ **put a damper on** take the vigour or enjoyment out of.

damp squib *n.* unsuccessful attempt to impress etc.

damsel /ˈdæmz(ə)l/ *n. archaic* or *literary* young unmarried woman. [French diminutive: related to DAME]

damselfly *n.* insect like a dragonfly but with wings folded when resting.

damson /ˈdæmz(ə)n/ *n.* **1** (in full **damson plum**) small dark-purple plum. **2** dark-purple colour. [Latin: related to DAMASCENE]

dan *n.* **1** grade of proficiency in judo. **2** holder of such a grade. [Japanese]

Da Nang /dɑː ˈnæŋ/ (formerly **Tourane**) port and city in central Vietnam, on the South China Sea; industries include textile manufacturing; pop. (est. 1992) 382 674.

dance /dɑːns/ –*v.* (**-cing**) **1** move rhythmically, usu. to music. **2** skip or jump about. **3** perform (a specified dance, role, etc.). **4** bob up and down. **5** dandle (a child). –*n.* **1 a** dancing as an art form. **b** style or form of this. **2** social gathering for dancing. **3** single round or turn of a dance. **4** music for dancing to. **5** lively motion. □ **dance attendance on** serve obsequiously. **lead a person a dance** (or **merry dance**) cause a person much trouble. □ **danceable** *adj.* **dancer** *n.* [French]

dancehall *n.* public hall for dancing.

d. and c. *n.* (also **D&C**) dilatation (of the cervix) and curettage (of the uterus).

dandelion /ˈdændɪˌlaɪən/ *n.* wild plant with jagged leaves, a yellow flower, and a fluffy seed-head. [French *dent-de-lion*, = lion's tooth]

dander *n. colloq.* temper, indignation. □ **get one's dander up** become angry. [origin uncertain]

D & HAA *abbr.* Dock and Harbour Authorities' Association.

dandify /ˈdændɪˌfaɪ/ *v.* (**-ies, -ied**) make a dandy.

dandle /ˈdænd(ə)l/ *v.* (**-ling**) bounce (a child) on one's knees etc. [origin unknown]

dandruff /ˈdændrʌf/ *n.* **1** flakes of dead skin in the hair. **2** this as a condition. [origin uncertain]

d. & s. *abbr.* demand and supply.

dandy /ˈdændɪ/ –*n.* (*pl.* **-ies**) **1** man greatly devoted to style and fashion. **2** *colloq.* excellent thing. –*adj.* (**-ier, -iest**) esp. *US colloq.* splendid. [perhaps from the name *Andrew*]

dandy-brush *n.* brush for grooming a horse.

◆ **dandy note** *n.* delivery order issued by an exporter and countersigned by HM Customs and Excise, authorizing a bonded warehouse to release goods for export.

Dane *n.* **1** native or national of Denmark. **2** *hist.* Viking invader of England in the 9th–11th centuries. [Old Norse]

danger /ˈdeɪndʒə(r)/ *n.* **1** liability or exposure to harm. **2** thing that causes or may cause harm. □ **in danger of** likely to incur or to suffer from. [earlier = 'power', from Latin *dominus* lord]

danger list *n.* list of those dangerously ill.

danger money *n.* extra payment for dangerous work. See also OCCUPATIONAL HAZARD.

dangerous *adj.* involving or causing danger. □ **dangerously** *adv.*

dangle /ˈdæŋg(ə)l/ *v.* (**-ling**) **1** be loosely suspended and able to sway. **2** hold or carry thus. **3** hold out (hope, temptation, etc.) enticingly. [imitative]

Danish /ˈdeɪnɪʃ/ –*adj.* of Denmark or the Danes. –*n.* **1** Danish language. **2** (prec. by *the*; treated as *pl.*) the Danish people. [Latin: related to DANE]

Danish blue *n.* white blue-veined cheese.

Danish pastry *n.* yeast cake topped with icing, fruit, nuts, etc.

dank *adj.* disagreeably damp and cold. □ **dankly** *adv.* **dankness** *n.* [probably Scandinavian]

Danube /ˈdænjuːb/ (German **Donau**, Czech **Dunaj**, Hungarian **Duna**, Romanian **Dunarea**) river that rises in SW Germany and flows into the Black Sea. It is Europe's second longest river and is commercially important; the capital cities of Vienna, Budapest, and Belgrade are situated on it.

Danzig see GDAŃSK.

DAP *abbr. Computing* distributed array processor.

d.a.p. *abbr.* documents against payment.

daphne /ˈdæfnɪ/ *n.* any of various flowering shrubs. [Greek]

dapper *adj.* **1** neat and precise, esp. in dress. **2** sprightly. [Low German or Dutch *dapper* strong]

dapple /ˈdæp(ə)l/ –*v.* (**-ling**) mark or become marked with spots of colour or shade. –*n.* dappled effect. [origin unknown]

dapple-grey *adj.* (of an animal's coat) grey or white with darker spots.

dapple grey *n.* dapple-grey horse.

Darby and Joan /ˌdɑːbɪ ənd ˈdʒəʊn/ *n.* devoted old married couple. [names of a couple in an 18th-century poem]

Darby and Joan club *n.* club for pensioners.

Dardanelles /ˌdɑːdəˈnelz/ narrow strait between Europe and Asiatic Turkey, linking the Sea of Marmara with the Aegean Sea.

DARE *abbr.* demand and resource evaluation.

dare –*v.* (**-ring**; *3rd sing. present* usu. **dare** before an expressed or implied infinitive without *to*) **1** (foll. by infin. with or without *to*) have the courage or impudence (to) (*dare he do it?*; *if they dare to come*; *how dare you?*). **2** (usu. foll. by *to* + infin.) defy or challenge (*I dare you to own up*). –*n.* **1** act of daring. **2** challenge, esp. to prove courage. □ **I dare say 1** (often foll. by *that*) it is probable. **2** probably; I grant that much. [Old English]

daredevil –*n.* recklessly daring person. –*adj.* recklessly daring. □ **daredevilry** *n.*

Dar es Salaam /dɑːr es səˈlɑːm/ former capital and chief port of Tanzania, an economic and administrative centre and terminus of the Tanzania–Zambia railway; pop. (1988) 1 360 850.

Darfur /dɑːˈfʊə(r)/ former region of W Sudan; products included gum arabic.

Darien /ˈdeərɪən, ˈdæ-/ province of E Panama; pop. (est. 1994) 53 725.

daring –*n.* adventurous courage. –*adj.* adventurous, bold; prepared to take risks. □ **daringly** *adv.*

dariole /ˈdærɪˌəʊl/ *n.* dish cooked and served in a small mould. [French]

Darjeeling /dɑːˈdʒiːlɪŋ/ town in India, in West Bengal; pop. (1991) 73 090. It is a tourist resort and the centre of a tea-growing region. –*n.* high-quality tea from this region.

dark –*adj.* **1** with little or no light. **2** of deep or sombre colour. **3** (of a person) with dark colouring. **4** gloomy, dismal. **5** evil, sinister. **6** sullen, angry. **7** secret, mysterious. **8** ignorant, unenlightened. –*n.* **1** absence of light. **2** lack of knowledge. **3** dark area or colour, esp. in painting. □ **after dark** after nightfall. **the Dark Ages** (or **Age**) **1** period of European history from the 5th–10th centuries. **2** period of supposed unenlightenment. **in the dark 1** lacking information. **2** with no light. □ **darkish** *adj.* **darkly** *adv.* **darkness** *n.* [Old English]

darken *v.* make or become dark or darker. □ **never**

darken a person's door keep away permanently. □ **darkener** *n.*

dark glasses *n.pl.* spectacles with dark-tinted lenses.

Darkhan /dɑː'kɑːn/ (also **Darhan**) industrial and mining city in N Mongolia, established in 1961; pop. (1990) 80 100.

dark horse *n.* little-known person who is unexpectedly successful.

darkie var. of DARKY.

darkroom *n.* darkened room for photographic work.

darky *n.* (also **darkie**) (*pl.* **-ies**) *slang offens.* Black person.

darling /'dɑːlɪŋ/ *–n.* **1** beloved, lovable, or endearing person or thing. **2** favourite. *–adj.* **1** beloved, lovable. **2** *colloq.* charming or pretty. [Old English: related to DEAR]

darn[1] *–v.* mend (cloth etc.) by filling a hole with stitching. *–n.* darned area. [origin uncertain]

darn[2] *v., int., adj., & adv. colloq.* = DAMN (in imprecatory senses). [corruption]

darned *adj. & adv. colloq.* = DAMNED.

darnel /'dɑːn(ə)l/ *n.* grass growing in cereal crops. [origin unknown]

darner *n.* needle for darning.

darning *n.* **1** act of darning. **2** things to be darned.

dart *–n.* **1** small pointed missile. **2** (in *pl.*; usu. treated as *sing.*) indoor game of throwing darts at a dartboard to score points. **3** sudden rapid movement. **4** dartlike structure, e.g. an insect's sting. **5** tapering tuck in a garment. *–v.* (often foll. by *out, in, past,* etc.) move, send, or go suddenly or rapidly. [French from Germanic]

dartboard *n.* circular target in darts.

Darwin /'dɑːwɪn/ port in N Australia, capital of the Northern Territory; exports include uranium ore; pop. (1991) 67 950.

Darwinian /dɑː'wɪnɪən/ *–adj.* of Darwin's theory of evolution. *–n.* adherent of this. □ **Darwinism** /'dɑː-/ *n.* **Darwinist** /'dɑː-/ *n.* [*Darwin,* name of a naturalist]

DAS *abbr.* **1** *Computing* data-acquisition system. **2** development advisory service.

d.a.s. *abbr.* delivered alongside ship.

DASD *abbr. Computing* direct-access storage device.

dash *–v.* **1** rush. **2** strike or fling forcefully, esp. so as to shatter (*dashed it to the ground*). **3** frustrate, dispirit (*dashed their hopes*). **4** *colloq.* (esp. **dash it** or **dash it all**) = DAMN *v.* 1. *–n.* **1** rush or onset; sudden advance. **2** horizontal stroke (–) in writing or printing to mark a pause etc. **3** impetuous vigour; capacity for or appearance of this. **4** *US* sprinting-race. **5** longer signal of two in Morse code (cf. DOT *n.* 2). **6** slight admixture, esp. of a liquid. **7** = DASHBOARD. □ **dash off** write or draw hurriedly. [imitative]

dashboard *n.* instrument panel of a vehicle or aircraft.

dashing *adj.* **1** spirited, lively. **2** showy. □ **dashingly** *adv.* **dashingness** *n.*

dastardly /'dæstədlɪ/ *adj.* cowardly, despicable. □ **dastardliness** *n.* [origin uncertain]

DAT /dæt/ *abbr.* digital audio tape.

data /'deɪtə/ *n.pl.* (also treated as *sing.*, although the singular form is strictly *datum*) **1** known facts used for inference or in reckoning. **2** *Computing* **a** basic facts (numbers, digits, words, and characters) that are fed into a computer system (in the required form) to be stored and processed for some purpose; input. **b** numbers or quantities that a program handles and upon which arithmetic and logic operations are performed, as distinct from program instructions. [Latin *data* from *do* give]

■ **Usage** (1) In scientific, philosophical, and general use, this word is usu. considered to denote a number of items and is thus treated as plural with *datum* as the singular. (2) In computing and allied subjects (and sometimes in general use), it is treated as a mass (or collective) noun and used with words like *this, that,* and *much,* with singular verbs, e.g. *useful data has been collected.* Some people consider use (2) to be incorrect but it is more common than use (1). However, *data* is not a singular countable noun and cannot be preceded by *a, every, each, either,* or *neither,* or be given a plural form *datas.*

data bank *n.* system that offers facilities to a community of users for the deposit and withdrawal of data on a particular topic, trade statistics or share prices. The user community is usu. widespread and the data bank itself may be a public facility. The data to be accessed may be organized as a database or as one or more files.

database *n.* structured set of related data stored on magnetic disk and accessed by means of a computer. A set of computer programs, called a **database management system (DBMS)**, is used to organize the data held in the database according to a specified schema, to update the data, and to help users find the data they seek. There are two kinds of DBMS: simple DBMS, which are the electronic equivalents of a card index; and programmable DBMS, which provide a **database language** that allows the user to analyse the data held in the database. DBMS software is available on small as well as large computers. On large systems, other programs can generally communicate with the DBMS and use its facilities.

database management system see DATABASE.

datable /'deɪtəb(ə)l/ *adj.* (often foll. by *to*) capable of being dated.

data capture *n.* process by which data can be extracted during some operation or activity and can then be fed into a computer. The equipment involved may be connected directly to a computer, allowing the incoming data to be monitored automatically. The use of electronic point-of-sale terminals in a supermarket involves data capture.

data cleaning *n.* (also **data vetting**) *Computing* process of checking raw data for completeness, consistency, and validity. Any bad characters, out-of-range values, and inconsistencies are either removed or brought to the attention of someone for a decision.

data compression *n. Computing* process whereby data can be stored in a compact form to reduce the storage space required.

data corruption see CORRUPT *v.* 2.

data entry *n.* process by which an operator feeds data into a computer by means of an input device.

♦ **data file** *n.* file on a computer system that contains data, i.e. the numbers, text, etc. upon which operations are performed by the computer. A data file is normally organized as a set of records. See also FILE[1] *n.* 3.

---

data integrity see INTEGRITY 3.

data link *n.* physical medium, e.g. a telephone line or electric cable, by which two locations are connected for the purpose of transmitting and receiving computer data, together with the agreed procedures (see PROTOCOL *n.* 4) by which the data is to be exchanged and any associated devices or programs.

♦ **Datapost** *n. propr.* Royal Mail fast service for packages weighing up to 27.5 kg. The same-day door-to-door service by radio-controlled motorcycles and vans is more expensive than the overnight service, which guarantees next-day delivery to any point in the UK. There is also a Datapost International Service, which operates to many countries.

---

data processing *n.* (also **DP**) series of computing operations conducted mainly in business, industrial, and government organizations whereby data is collected, stored, and processed on a routine basis in order to produce information, regularly or on request. A DP system usu. handles large quantities of data organized in a complex way. Typical applications include production of payslips, accounting, market research and sales forecasting, stock control, and the handling of orders. Data processing forms a major use of computers in business, and many firms have full-time data-processing departments. □ **data processor** *n.*

data protection *n.* protection of data handled in a

computer, esp. confidential **personal data**, i.e. data concerning a living person who can be identified from that information, and possibly including some opinion expressed about that person. Credit ratings produced by banks, donations received by charities, transactions by mail-order firms, and personal records kept by government agencies and the police all involve data concerning the individual; for ease of access, ease of updating, saving of space, and other reasons, this kind of information is now usu. stored in computers. Legislation exists or is being introduced in many countries to protect personal data when it is stored in computers. The aim is to control the potential for misuse of such information. The information contained in personal data should be obtained fairly and lawfully, and the data processed fairly and lawfully. Personal data should be held only for specified and lawful purposes and not used or disclosed in any manner incompatible with those purposes. Personal data held for any purpose should be relevant to that purpose, accurate, and, where necessary, kept up to date; it should not be kept longer than necessary for that purpose. Appropriate security measures should be taken against unauthorized access to, or alteration, disclosure, or destruction of personal data and against accidental loss or destruction of personal data. The UK enacted the Data Protection Act (1984) to comply with a convention signed by all member countries of the Council of Europe. The act is concerned only with personal data. **Data users** are people holding personal data on computers. In the UK they are legally obliged to register their activities with the **Data Protection Registrar** by means of a registration form obtained from a post office. This requires the data user to give: a description of the personal data held and the purposes for which the data is held; a description of the sources used for this data; a description of any persons to whom the data could be disclosed; the names or a description of any countries or territories outside the UK to which the user could transfer the data. An individual is entitled to be informed by any data user whether the user holds personal data of which that individual is the subject. Such a **data subject** is also entitled to obtain a printout from a registered data user of any personal data held by the user and to demand that any inaccurate or misleading information is corrected or erased. If a court is satisfied on the application of a data subject that personal data held by a data user is inaccurate it may order the rectification or erasure of the data. Additionally it may order the rectification or erasure of any data held by the data user that contains an expression of opinion that appears to the court to be based on the inaccurate data.

data retrieval *n.* computer process by which data is selected and extracted from a file, a group of files, a database, or some other area of memory. See also INFORMATION RETRIEVAL.

data user see DATA PROTECTION.

data vetting *n.* = DATA CLEANING.

date[1] *–n.* **1** day of the month, esp. as a number. **2** particular, esp. historical, day or year. **3** day, month, and year of writing etc., at the head of a document etc. **4** period to which a work of art etc. belongs. **5** time when an event takes place. **6** *colloq.* **a** appointment, esp. social with a person of the opposite sex. **b** *US* person to be met at this. *–v.* (**-ting**) **1** mark with a date. **2 a** assign a date to (an object, event, etc.). **b** (foll. by *to*) assign to a particular time, period, etc. **3** (often foll. by *from*, *back to*, etc.) have its origins at a particular time. **4** appear or expose as old-fashioned (*design that does not date*; *that hat dates you*). **5** *US colloq.* **a** make a date with. **b** go out together as sexual partners. □ **after date** words used in a bill of exchange to indicate that the period of the bill should commence from the date inserted on the bill (*30 days after date, we promise to pay…*). **out of date** (*attrib.* **out-of-date**) old-fashioned, obsolete. **to date** until now. **up to date** (*attrib.* **up-to-date**) modern; fashionable; current. [French: related to DATA]

date[2] *n.* **1** dark oval single-stoned fruit. **2** (in full **date-palm**) tree bearing it. [Greek: related to DACTYL, from the shape of the leaf]

◆ **dated security** *n.* a stock that has a fixed redemption date.

Datel /ˈdeɪˌtel/ *n. propr.* data transmission service. [*da*ta *tel*ex]

date-line *n.* **1** north-south line partly along the meridian 180° from Greenwich, to the east of which the date is a day earlier than to the west. **2** date and place of writing at the head of a newspaper article etc.

date-stamp *–n.* **1** adjustable rubber stamp etc. used to record a date. **2** impression made by a date-stamp. A date stamped on the packaging of prepacked perishable food indicates either the date by which it must be sold by a retailer (**sell-by date**) or the date by which it must be consumed by the consumer (**consume-by date**). This is a legal requirement for prepacked perishable food sold in the UK. *–v.* mark with a date-stamp.

dative /ˈdeɪtɪv/ *Gram. –n.* case expressing the indirect object or recipient. *–adj.* of or in this case. [Latin: related to DATA]

Datong /dɑːˈtʊŋ/ city in N China, in Shanxi province; pop. (est. 1990) 1 110 000.

datum /ˈdeɪtəm/ see DATA.

daub /dɔːb/ *–v.* **1** spread (paint etc.) crudely or roughly. **2** coat or smear (a surface) with paint etc. **3** paint crudely or unskilfully. *–n.* **1** paint etc. daubed on a surface. **2** plaster, clay, etc., esp. coating laths or wattles to form a wall. **3** crude painting. [Latin: related to DE-, ALB]

daughter /ˈdɔːtə(r)/ *n.* **1** girl or woman in relation to her parent(s). **2** female descendant. **3** (foll. by *of*) female member of a family etc. **4** (foll. by *of*) female descendant or inheritor of a quality etc. □ **daughterly** *adj.* [Old English]

daughter-in-law *n.* (*pl.* **daughters-in-law**) son's wife.

daunt /dɔːnt/ *v.* discourage, intimidate. □ **daunting** *adj.* [Latin *domito* from *domo* tame]

dauntless *adj.* intrepid, persevering.

dauphin /ˈdɔːfɪn/ *n. hist.* eldest son of the King of France. [French from Latin *delphinus* DOLPHIN, as a family name]

Davao /ˈdɑːvaʊ/ seaport and commercial centre in the SE Philippines, the largest city on the island of Mindanao; pop. (est. 1994) 960 910. There are fishing and timber industries; exports include hemp and coffee.

Davenport /ˈdævənˌpɔːt/ *n.* **1** small writing-desk with a sloping top. **2** *US* large sofa. [name of the maker]

David /dɑːˈviːd/ principal city of W Panama; pop. (1990) 102 517.

davit /ˈdævɪt/ *n.* small crane on board ship, esp. for moving or holding a lifeboat. [French diminutive of *David*]

Davos /dɑːˈvəʊs/ resort and winter-sports centre in E Switzerland; pop. (1990) 10 500.

Davy /ˈdeɪvɪ/ *n.* (*pl.* **-ies**) (in full **Davy lamp**) miner's safety lamp. [name of its inventor]

Davy Jones /ˌdeɪvɪ ˈdʒəʊnz/ *n. slang* (in full **Davy Jones's locker**) bottom of the sea, esp. as the sailors' graveyard. [origin unknown]

daw *n.* = JACKDAW. [Old English]

dawdle /ˈdɔːd(ə)l/ *v.* (**-ling**) **1** walk slowly and idly. **2** waste time; procrastinate. [origin unknown]

dawn *–n.* **1** daybreak. **2** beginning or birth of something. *–v.* **1** (of a day) begin; grow light. **2** (often foll. by *on*, *upon*) begin to become obvious (to). [Old English]

dawn chorus *n.* bird-song at daybreak.

◆ **dawn raid** *n.* **1** unexpected early-morning attack, visit, etc. **2** *Finance* attempt by one company or investor to acquire a significant holding in the equity of another company by instructing brokers to buy all the shares available in that company as soon as the stock exchange opens, usu. before the target company knows that it is, in fact, a target. The dawn raid may provide a significant stake from which to launch a take-over bid. The conduct of dawn raids is now restricted by the City Code on Takeovers and Mergers.

DAX *abbr.* Deutsche Aktienindex, a share index on the Frankfurt Stock Exchange.

day *n.* **1** time between sunrise and sunset. **2 a** 24 hours as a unit of time. **b** corresponding period on other planets (*Martian day*). **3** daylight (*clear as day*). **4** time during which work is normally done (*eight-hour day*). **5 a** (also *pl.*) historical period (*in those days*). **b** (prec. by *the*) present time (*issues of the day*). **6** prime of a person's life (*have had my day*; *in my day*). **7** a future time (*will do it one day*). **8** date of a specific festival or event etc. (*graduation day*; *Christmas day*). **9** battle or contest (*win the day*). □ **all in a day's work** part of the normal routine. **at the end of the day** when all is said and done. **call it a day** end a period of activity. **day after day** without respite. **day and night** all the time. **day by day** gradually. **day in, day out** routinely, constantly. **not one's day** day when things go badly (for a person). **one of these days** soon. **one of those days** day when things go badly. **that will be the day** *colloq.* that will never happen. [Old English]

day-bed *n.* bed for daytime rest.

◆ **day books** *n.pl.* books of prime entry that provide a record of series of similar documents (see BOOK OF PRIME ENTRY); the sales day book records details of invoices rendered to customers, while the purchase day book records invoices issued to the organization by suppliers. Other day books might record credit notes issued by suppliers or credit notes issued to customers. These books are then used as a source for making double-entry postings (see POST *v.* 3) to the individual accounts of customers or suppliers as appropriate, while periodic totals are posted to the sales or the purchases account as appropriate.

---

day-boy *n.* (also **day-girl**) non-boarding pupil, esp. at a boarding school.

daybreak *n.* first light in the morning.

day care *n.* care of young children, the elderly, the handicapped, etc. during the working day.

day centre *n.* place for care of the elderly or handicapped during the day.

day-dream *–n.* pleasant fantasy or reverie. *–v.* indulge in this. □ **day-dreamer** *n.*

daylight *n.* **1** light of day. **2** dawn. **3** visible gap, e.g. between boats in a race. **4** (usu. in *pl.*) *slang* life or consciousness (*scared the daylights out of me*; *beat the living daylights out of them*).

daylight robbery *n. colloq.* blatantly excessive charge.

daylight saving *n.* longer summer evening daylight, achieved by putting clocks forward.

day nursery *n.* nursery for children of working parents.

day off *n.* day's holiday.

day of reckoning *n.* time when something must be atoned for or avenged.

◆ **day order** *n.* order to a stockbroker, commodity broker, etc. to buy or sell a specified security or commodity at a fixed price or within fixed limits; the order is valid for the day on which it is given and automatically becomes void at the close of trading on that day.

---

day release *n.* part-time education for employees.

day return *n.* reduced fare or ticket for a return journey in one day.

day-room *n.* room, esp. in an institution, used during the day.

day-school *n.* school for pupils living at home.

◆ **days of grace** *n.pl.* extra time allowed for payment of a bill of exchange or insurance premium after the actual due date. With bills of exchange the usual custom is to allow three days of grace (not including Sundays and Bank Holidays) and 14 days for insurance policies.

---

daytime *n.* part of the day when there is natural light.

day-to-day *adj.* mundane, routine.

day-trip *n.* trip completed in one day. □ **day-tripper** *n.*

daze *–v.* (**-zing**) stupefy, bewilder. *–n.* state of bewilderment. [Old Norse]

dazzle /ˈdæz(ə)l/ *–v.* (**-ling**) **1** blind or confuse temporarily with a sudden bright light. **2** impress or overpower with knowledge, ability, etc. *–n.* bright confusing light. □ **dazzling** *adj.* **dazzlingly** *adv.* [from DAZE]

DB *abbr.* **1** *Computing* database. **2** (also **D/B**) *Bookkeeping* day book. **3** (German) Deutsche Bundesbank (= German Federal Bank).

Db *symb. Currency* dobra.

dB *abbr.* decibel(s).

DBA *abbr.* **1** *Computing* database administrator (or administration). **2** Doctor of Business Administration. **3** (also **d.b.a.**) doing business as (or at).

DBEATS *abbr.* dispatch payable both ends all time saved.

DBELTS *abbr.* dispatch payable both ends on lay time saved.

DBIU *abbr.* (in Canada) Dominion Board of Insurance Underwriters.

DBM *abbr.* Diploma in Business Management.

DBMS *abbr. Computing* database management system. See DATABASE.

DBS *abbr.* **1** direct-broadcast satellite. **2** direct broadcasting by satellite.

DC *abbr.* **1** (also **dc**) direct current. **2** District of Columbia. **3** *Commerce* documents (against) cash. **4** da capo.

D/C *abbr. Marine insurance* deviation clause.

DCE *abbr.* **1** *Computing* data-communication equipment. **2** domestic credit expansion.

◆ **DCF** *abbr.* = DISCOUNTED CASH FLOW.

DCI *abbr.* (also **d.c.i.**) double column inch (in advertisements).

d.col. *abbr.* double column (in advertisements).

D.Comm. *abbr.* Doctor of Commerce.

DCS *abbr.* Doctor of Commercial Sciences.

DD *–abbr.* **1** *Insurance* damage done. **2** *Banking* demand draft. **3** direct debit. **4** Doctor of Divinity. *–postcode* Dundee.

D/D *abbr.* **1** delivered at docks. **2** demand draft. **3** dock dues.

D/d *abbr.* **1** days after date. **2** *Commerce* delivered.

dd. **1** dated. **2** delivered.

d.d. *abbr.* **1** days after date. **2** delayed delivery. **3** *Commerce* delivered dock. **4** demand draft. **5** due date (or day). **6** today's date [sense 6 Latin *de dato*].

D-Day /ˈdiːdeɪ/ *n.* **1** day (6 June 1944) on which Allied forces invaded N France. **2** important or decisive day. [*D* for *day*]

DDC *abbr. Computing* direct digital control.

DDD *abbr.* deadline delivery date.

DDE *abbr. Computing* direct data entry.

DDL *abbr. Computing* data description language(s).

DDP *abbr. Computing* distributed data processing.

dd/s *abbr.* delivered sound.

DDT *n.* colourless chlorinated hydrocarbon used as insecticide. [abbreviation from the chemical name]

DE *–abbr.* = DEPARTMENT OF EMPLOYMENT. *–US postcode* Delaware. *–postcode* Derby.

d.e. *abbr. Bookkeeping* double entry.

de- *prefix* **1** forming verbs and their derivatives: **a** down, away (*descend*; *deduct*). **b** completely (*denude*). **2** added to verbs and their derivatives to form verbs and nouns implying removal or reversal (*de-ice*; *decentralization*). [Latin]

deacon /ˈdiːkən/ *n.* (*fem.* (in senses 2 and 3) **deaconess** /-ˈnes/) **1** (in Episcopal churches) minister below bishop and priest. **2** (in Nonconformist churches) lay officer. **3** (in the early Church) minister of charity. [Greek *diakonos* servant]

deactivate /diːˈæktɪˌveɪt/ *v.* (**-ting**) make inactive or less reactive.

dead /ded/ *–adj.* **1** no longer alive. **2** *colloq.* extremely tired or unwell. **3** numb (*fingers are dead*). **4** (foll. by *to*) insensitive to. **5** no longer effective or in use; extinct. **6** (of a match, coal, etc.) extinguished. **7** inanimate. **8 a** lacking force or vigour. **b** (of sound) not resonant. **9** quiet; lacking activity (*dead season*). **10** (of a microphone, telephone, etc.) not transmitting sounds. **11** (of a ball in a game) out of play. **12** abrupt, complete (*come to a dead stop*; *a dead calm*; *dead certainty*). *–adv.* **1** absolutely, completely (*dead on target*; *dead tired*). **2** *colloq.* very, extremely (*dead easy*). *–n.* time of silence or inactivity (*dead of night*). □ **as dead as the** (or **a) dodo** entirely obsolete. **dead to the world** *colloq.* fast asleep; unconscious. [Old English]

dead beat *adj. colloq.* exhausted.

dead-beat *n. colloq.* derelict, tramp.

♦ **dead-cat bounce** *n. colloq.* temporary recovery on a stock exchange, caused by short covering after a substantial fall (see SHORT COVERING). It does not imply a reversal of the downward trend.

---

dead duck *n. slang* unsuccessful or useless person or thing.

deaden *v.* **1** deprive of or lose vitality, force, brightness, sound, feeling, etc. **2** (foll. by *to*) make insensitive.

dead end *n.* **1** closed end of road, passage, etc. **2** (often, with hyphen, *attrib.*) hopeless situation, job, etc.

♦ **dead freight** *n.* freight charge incurred by a shipper for space reserved but not used.

---

deadhead *–n.* **1** faded flower-head. **2** non-paying passenger or spectator. **3** useless person. *–v.* remove deadheads from (a plant).

dead heat *n.* **1** race in which competitors tie. **2** result of such a race.

dead language *n.* language no longer spoken, e.g. Latin.

dead letter *n.* law or practice no longer observed or recognized.

deadline *n.* time-limit.

deadlock *–n.* **1** state of unresolved conflict. **2** lock requiring a key to open or close it. *–v.* bring or come to standstill.

dead loss *n. colloq.* useless person or thing.

deadly *–adj.* (**-ier, -iest**) **1** causing or able to cause fatal injury or serious damage. **2** intense, extreme (*deadly dullness*). **3** (of aim etc.) true; effective. **4** deathlike (*deadly pale*). **5** *colloq.* dreary, dull. *–adv.* **1** like death; as if dead (*deadly faint*). **2** extremely (*deadly serious*).

deadly nightshade *n.* poisonous plant with purple-black berries.

dead man's handle *n.* (also **dead man's pedal**) device on an electric train disconnecting the power supply if released.

dead march *n.* funeral march.

dead on *adj.* exactly right.

deadpan *adj.* & *adv.* lacking expression or emotion.

dead reckoning *n.* calculation of a ship's position from the log, compass, etc., when visibility is bad.

Dead Sea salt lake or inland sea in the Jordan valley, on the Israel–Jordan border.

dead set *n.* determined attack. □ **be dead set against** strongly oppose. **be dead set on** be determined to do or get.

dead shot *n.* person who shoots extremely accurately.

dead weight *n.* (also **dead-weight**) **1 a** inert mass. **b** heavy burden. **2** debt not covered by assets. **3** total weight carried on a ship.

♦ **dead-weight cargo** *n.* cargo, e.g. minerals and coal, for which the freight is charged on the basis of weight rather than volume.

♦ **dead-weight debt** *n.* debt that is incurred to meet current needs without the security of an enduring asset, usu. a debt incurred by a government. The national debt is a dead-weight debt incurred by the UK government during the two World Wars.

♦ **dead-weight loss** *n.* loss to society arising from an inefficient allocation of resources, as in monopoly or taxation. However, in the case of taxation the loss may be justified by reference to some other (say, political) principle. Economists frequently attempt to measure dead-weight losses when they are thought to exist although their estimates are usu. controversial.

♦ **dead-weight tonnage** see TONNAGE 1.

---

dead wood *n. colloq.* useless person(s) or thing(s).

deaf /def/ *adj.* **1** wholly or partly unable to hear. **2** (foll. by *to*) refusing to listen or comply. □ **turn a deaf ear** (usu. foll. by *to*) be unresponsive. □ **deafness** *n.* [Old English]

deaf-aid *n.* hearing-aid.

deaf-and-dumb alphabet *n.* (also **deaf-and-dumb language**) = SIGN LANGUAGE.

■ **Usage** *Sign language* is the preferred term in official use.

deafen *v.* (often as **deafening** *adj.*) overpower with noise or make deaf by noise, esp. temporarily. □ **deafeningly** *adv.*

deaf mute *n.* deaf and dumb person.

deal[1] *–v.* (*past* and *past part.* **dealt** /delt/) **1** (foll. by *with*) **a** take measures to resolve, placate, etc. **b** do business with; associate with. **c** discuss or treat (a subject). **2** (often foll. by *by*, *with*) behave in specified way (*dealt honourably by them*). **3** (foll. by *in*) sell (*deals in insurance*). **4** (often foll. by *out*, *round*) distribute to several people etc. **5** (also *absol.*) distribute (cards) to players. **6** administer (*was dealt a blow*). **7** assign, esp. providentially (*were dealt much happiness*). *–n.* **1** (usu. **a good** or **great deal**) *colloq.* **a** large amount (*good deal of trouble*). **b** considerably (*great deal better*). **2** *colloq.* business arrangement; transaction. **3** specified treatment (*a rough deal*). **4 a** dealing of cards. **b** player's turn to do this. [Old English]

deal[2] *n.* **1** fir or pine timber, esp. as boards of a standard size. **2** board of this. [Low German]

dealer *n.* **1** trader in (esp. retail) goods (*car-dealer*; *dealer in tobacco*). **2** player dealing at cards. **3** person who deals as a principal, such as a market maker on a stock exchange, a commodity merchant, etc., rather than as a broker or agent. See also BROKER/DEALER; JOBBER 3.

♦ **dealer brand** *n.* product on which a middleman, usu. a retailer, puts his own brand name. For example, St Michael is the dealer brand for Marks and Spencer's products.

---

dealings *n.pl.* contacts, conduct, or transactions.

dealt *past* and *past part.* of DEAL[1].

dean[1] *n.* **1 a** head of the chapter of a cathedral or collegiate church. **b** (usu. **rural dean**) clergyman supervising parochial clergy. **2 a** college or university official with disciplinary and advisory functions. **b** head of a university faculty or department or of a medical school. [Latin *decanus*]

dean[2] var. of DENE.

deanery *n.* (*pl.* **-ies**) **1** dean's house or position. **2** parishes presided over by a rural dean.

dear *–adj.* **1 a** beloved or much esteemed. **b** as a merely polite or ironic form (*my dear man*). **2** as a formula of address, esp. beginning a letter (*Dear Sir*). **3** (often foll. by *to*) precious; cherished. **4** (usu. in *superl.*) earnest (*my dearest wish*). **5 a** expensive. **b** having high prices. *–n.* (esp. as a form of address) dear person. *–adv.* at great cost (*will pay dear*). *–int.* expressing surprise, dismay, pity, etc. (*dear me!*; *oh dear!*). □ **for dear life** desperately. □ **dearly** *adv.* [Old English]

dearie *n.* my dear. □ **dearie me!** *int.* expressing surprise, dismay, etc.

♦ **dear money** *n.* (also **tight money**) money that is

difficult to borrow as it is available only at high rates of interest. Cf. CHEAP MONEY.

---

dearth /dɜːθ/ *n.* scarcity, lack.

death /deθ/ *n.* **1** irreversible ending of life; dying or being killed. **2** instance of this. **3** destruction; ending (*death of our hopes*). **4** being dead (*eyes closed in death*). **5** (usu. **Death**) personification of death, esp. as a skeleton. **6** lack of spiritual life. □ **at death's door** close to death. **be the death of 1** cause the death of. **2** be annoying or harmful to. **catch one's death** *colloq.* catch a serious chill etc. **do to death 1** kill. **2** overdo. **fate worse than death** *colloq.* very unpleasant experience. **put to death** kill or cause to be killed. **to death** to the utmost, extremely (*bored to death*). □ **deathlike** *adj.* [Old English]

deathbed *n.* bed where a person dies.

deathblow *n.* **1** blow etc. causing death. **2** event etc. that destroys or ends something.

death certificate *n.* official statement of a person's death.

♦ **death duty** *n.* tax levied on a person's estate at the time of death. The principal death duty in the UK was estate duty, which was introduced in 1894. This became capital-transfer tax in 1974, which itself became inheritance tax in 1986. See INHERITANCE TAX.

♦ **death futures** *n.pl.* life assurance policies of terminally ill people bought speculatively by a company for a lump sum so that the company can collect the proceeds on the death of the sufferer.

---

deathly *–adj.* (**-ier, -iest**) suggestive of death (*deathly silence*). *–adv.* in a deathly way (*deathly pale*).

death-mask *n.* cast taken of a dead person's face.

death penalty *n.* punishment by death.

death rate *n.* number of deaths per thousand of population per year.

death-rattle *n.* gurgling in the throat sometimes heard at death.

death row *n. US* part of a prison for those sentenced to death.

death squad *n.* armed paramilitary group.

death-trap *n. colloq.* dangerous building, vehicle, etc.

♦ **death-valley curve** *n.* graph of a new company's capital plotted against time, showing a sharp fall as the venture capital becomes exhausted before income reaches predicted levels.

---

death-warrant *n.* **1** order of execution. **2** anything that causes the end of an established practice etc.

death-watch *n.* (in full **death-watch beetle**) small beetle which makes a ticking sound, said to portend death.

death-wish *n. Psychol.* alleged usu. unconscious desire for death.

deb *n. colloq.* débutante. [abbreviation]

deb. *abbr.* **1** debenture. **2** debit.

débâcle /deɪˈbɑːk(ə)l/ *n.* (*US* **debacle**) **1 a** utter defeat or failure. **b** sudden collapse. **2** confused rush or rout. [French]

debag /diːˈbæg/ *v.* (**-gg-**) *slang* remove the trousers of (a person), esp. as a joke.

debar /dɪˈbɑː(r)/ *v.* (**-rr-**) (foll. by *from*) exclude; prohibit (*debarred from the club*). □ **debarment** *n.* [French: related to BAR[1]]

debark /diːˈbɑːk/ *v.* land from a ship. □ **debarkation** /-ˈkeɪʃ(ə)n/ *n.* [French *débarquer*]

debase /dɪˈbeɪs/ *v.* (**-sing**) **1** lower in quality, value, or character. **2** depreciate (a coin) by alloying etc. □ **debasement** *n.* [from DE-, (A)BASE]

debatable /dɪˈbeɪtəb(ə)l/ *adj.* questionable; disputable. [related to DEBATE]

debate /dɪˈbeɪt/ *–v.* (**-ting**) **1** (also *absol.*) discuss or dispute, esp. formally. **2** consider aspects of (a question); ponder. *–n.* **1** formal discussion on a particular matter. **2** discussion (*open to debate*). [French: related to BATTLE]

debauch /dɪˈbɔːtʃ/ *–v.* **1** (as **debauched** *adj.*) dissolute. **2** corrupt, deprave. **3** debase (taste or judgement). *–n.* bout of sensual indulgence. [French]

debauchee /ˌdɪbɔːˈtʃiː/ *n.* debauched person.

debauchery *n.* excessive sensual indulgence.

♦ **debenture** /dɪˈbentʃə(r)/ *n.* **1** acknowledgement of indebtedness, esp. a long-term loan taken by a company and repayable at a fixed date. Some debentures are irredeemable securities; these are sometimes called **perpetual debentures.** Most debentures also pay a fixed rate of interest, which must be paid before a dividend is paid to shareholders. Most debentures are also secured on the borrower's assets, although some, known as **naked** (or **unsecured) debentures**, are not. In the US debentures are usu. unsecured, relying only on the reputation of the borrower. In a **secured debenture,** the bond may have a fixed charge (i.e. a charge over a particular asset) or a floating charge. If debentures are issued to a large number of people (for example in the form of **debenture stock** or **loan stock**) trustees may be appointed to act on behalf of the debenture holders. There may be a premium on redemption and some debentures are convertible, i.e. they can be converted into ordinary shares on a specified date, usu. at a specified price. The advantage of debentures to companies is that they carry lower interest rates than, e.g., overdrafts and are usu. repayable a long time into the future. For an investor, they are usu. saleable on a stock exchange and involve less risk than equities. **2** deed under seal setting out the main terms of such a loan. [Latin *debentur* are owed]

---

debilitate /dɪˈbɪlɪˌteɪt/ *v.* (**-ting**) enfeeble, enervate. □ **debilitation** /-ˈteɪʃ(ə)n/ *n.* [Latin *debilis* weak]

debility /dɪˈbɪlɪtɪ/ *n.* feebleness, esp. of health.

debit /ˈdebɪt/ *–n.* **1** entry on the left-hand side of an account in double-entry bookkeeping, showing an amount owed by the organization keeping the book. In the case of a bank account, a debit shows an outflow of funds from the account. **2** sum recorded. **3** total of such sums. **4** debit side of an account. *–v.* (**-t-**) **1** (foll. by *against, to*) enter on the debit side of an account (*debit £50 to my account*). **2** (foll. by *with*) charge (a person) with a debt (*debited me with £500*). [Latin *debitum* DEBT]

♦ **debit card** *n.* plastic card issued by a bank or building society to enable its customers with cheque accounts to pay for goods or services at certain retail outlets by using the telephone network to debit their cheque accounts directly. The retail outlets, e.g. petrol stations and some large stores, need to have the necessary computerized input device, into which the card is inserted; the customer may be required to tap in a personal identification number before entering the amount to be debited. Some debit cards also function as cheque cards and cashcards.

♦ **debit note** *n.* document sent by an organization to a person showing that the recipient is indebted to the organization for the amount shown in the debit note. It might be used when an invoice would not be appropriate, e.g. for some form of inter-company transfer other than a sale of goods or services.

---

debonair /ˌdebəˈneə(r)/ *adj.* **1** cheerful, self-assured. **2** pleasant-mannered. [French]

debouch /dɪˈbaʊtʃ/ *v.* **1** (of troops or a stream) come out into open ground. **2** (often foll. by *into*) (of a river, road, etc.) merge into a larger body or area. □ **debouchment** *n.* [French *bouche* mouth]

Debrecen /ˈdebrətˌsen/ industrial and commercial city in E Hungary; manufactures include machinery and pharmaceuticals; pop. (est. 1996) 211 000.

debrief /diːˈbriːf/ *v. colloq.* question (a diplomat, pilot, etc.) about a completed mission or undertaking. □ **debriefing** *n.*

debris /ˈdebriː/ *n.* **1** scattered fragments, esp. of wreckage. **2** accumulation of loose rock etc. [French *briser* break]

debt /det/ *n.* **1** money owed by one person to another. In commerce, it is usual for debts to be settled within one month of receiving an invoice, after which interest may be incurred. A long-term debt may be covered by a bill of exchange, which can be a negotiable instrument. See also DEBENTURE. **2** obligation; something owed (*debt of gratitude*). **3** state of owing (*in debt*; *get into debt*). □ **in a person's debt** under obligation to a person. [Latin *debeo debit-* owe]

◆ **debt adjusting** see ANCILLARY CREDIT BUSINESS.

◆ **debt-collection agency** *n.* organization that specializes in collecting the outstanding debts of its clients, charging a commission for doing so. See also ANCILLARY CREDIT BUSINESS.

◆ **debt counselling** see ANCILLARY CREDIT BUSINESS.

◆ **debt neutrality** see RICARDIAN EQUIVALENCE THEOREM.

debt of honour *n.* debt not legally recoverable, esp. a sum lost in gambling.

debtor *n.* person owing money etc. In balance sheets, debtors are those who owe money to the organization and a distinction has to be made between those who are expected to pay their debts during the next accounting period and those who will not pay until later.

◆ **debt rescheduling** *n.* negotiation concerning outstanding loans in which the debtor has repayment difficulties; it can take the form of a new loan or an extension of the existing payment period.

◆ **debt service ratio** *n.* (also **DSR**) proportion of annual export earnings needed to service a country's external debts, including both interest payments and repayment of principal. The DSR is an important statistic, indicating the severity of a country's indebtedness. The effect of rescheduling programmes can be examined by comparing pre- and post-rescheduling DSRs.

debug /diːˈbʌg/ *v.* (**-gg-**) *colloq.* **1** remove concealed microphones from (a room etc.). **2** identify and remove errors from (a computer program or system). **3** = DELOUSE.

debunk /diːˈbʌŋk/ *v. colloq.* expose (a person, claim, etc.) as spurious or false. □ **debunker** *n.*

début /ˈdeɪbjuː/ *n.* (*US* **debut**) first public appearance (as a performer etc.). [French]

débutante /ˈdebjuːˌtɑːnt/ *n.* (*US* **debutante**) (usu. wealthy) young woman making her social début.

DEC *abbr. Computing* Digital Equipment Corporation.

Dec. *abbr.* December.

deca- *comb. form* ten. [Greek *deka* ten]

decade /ˈdekeɪd, dɪˈkeɪd/ *n.* **1** period of ten years. **2** series or group of ten. [Greek: related to DECA-]

■ **Usage** The second pronunciation given, with the stress on the second syllable, is considered incorrect by some people even though it is much used in broadcasting.

decadence /ˈdekəd(ə)ns/ *n.* **1** moral or cultural decline. **2** immoral behaviour. □ **decadent** *adj.* & *n.* **decadently** *adv.* [Latin: related to DECAY]

decaffeinated /diːˈkæfɪˌneɪtɪd/ *adj.* with caffeine removed or reduced.

decagon /ˈdekəgən/ *n.* plane figure with ten sides and angles. □ **decagonal** /dɪˈkægən(ə)l/ *adj.* [Greek: related to DECA-, *-gōnos* -angled]

decahedron /ˌdekəˈhiːdrən/ *n.* solid figure with ten faces. □ **decahedral** *adj.* [after POLYHEDRON]

decalitre /ˈdekəˌliːtə(r)/ *n.* (*US* **-liter**) metric unit of capacity, equal to 10 litres.

Decalogue /ˈdekəˌlɒg/ *n.* Ten Commandments. [Greek: related to DECA-, *logos* word, reason]

decametre /ˈdekəˌmiːtə(r)/ *n.* (*US* **-meter**) metric unit of length, equal to 10 metres.

decamp /dɪˈkæmp/ *v.* **1** depart suddenly; abscond. **2** break up or leave camp. □ **decampment** *n.* [French: related to CAMP[1]]

decanal /dɪˈkeɪn(ə)l/ *adj.* **1** of a dean. **2** of the south side of a choir (where the dean sits). [Latin: related to DEAN[1]]

decant /dɪˈkænt/ *v.* **1** gradually pour off (esp. wine), esp. leaving the sediment behind. **2** transfer as if by pouring. [Greek *kanthos* lip of jug]

decanter *n.* stoppered glass container for decanted wine or spirit.

decapitate /dɪˈkæpɪˌteɪt/ *v.* (**-ting**) behead. □ **decapitation** /-ˈteɪʃ(ə)n/ *n.* [Latin: related to CAPITAL]

decapod /ˈdekəˌpɒd/ *n.* **1** crustacean with ten limbs for walking, e.g. the shrimp. **2** ten-tentacled mollusc, e.g. the squid. [Greek: related to DECA-, *pous pod-* foot]

decarbonize /diːˈkɑːbəˌnaɪz/ *v.* (also **-ise**) (**-zing** or **-sing**) remove the carbon etc. from (an internal-combustion engine etc.). □ **decarbonization** /-ˈzeɪʃ(ə)n/ *n.*

decathlon /dɪˈkæθlən/ *n.* athletic contest of ten events for all competitors. □ **decathlete** /-liːt/ *n.* [from DECA-, Greek *athlon* contest]

decay /dɪˈkeɪ/ *–v.* **1** (cause to) rot or decompose. **2** decline or cause to decline in quality, power, etc. **3** (usu. foll. by *to*) (of a substance) undergo change by radioactivity. *–n.* **1** rotten state; wasting away. **2** decline in health, quality, etc. **3** radioactive change. [Latin *cado* fall]

decease /dɪˈsiːs/ *formal* esp. *Law –n.* death. *–v.* (**-sing**) die. [Latin *cedo* go]

deceased *formal –adj.* dead. *–n.* (usu. prec. by *the*) person who has died, esp. recently.

deceit /dɪˈsiːt/ *n.* **1** deception, esp. by concealing the truth. **2** dishonest trick. [Latin *capio* take]

deceitful *adj.* using deceit. □ **deceitfully** *adv.* **deceitfulness** *n.*

deceive /dɪˈsiːv/ *v.* (**-ving**) **1** make (a person) believe what is false, purposely mislead. **2** be unfaithful to, esp. sexually. **3** use deceit. □ **deceive oneself** persist in a mistaken belief. □ **deceiver** *n.*

decelerate /diːˈseləˌreɪt/ *v.* (**-ting**) (cause to) reduce speed. □ **deceleration** /-ˈreɪʃ(ə)n/ *n.* [from DE-, ACCELERATE]

December /dɪˈsembə(r)/ *n.* twelfth month of the year. [Latin *decem* ten, originally 10th month of Roman year]

decency /ˈdiːsənsɪ/ *n.* (*pl.* **-ies**) **1** correct, honourable, or modest behaviour. **2** (in *pl.*) proprieties; manners. [Latin: related to DECENT]

decennial /dɪˈsenɪəl/ *adj.* lasting, recurring every, ten years. [Latin *decem* ten, *annus* year]

decent /ˈdiːs(ə)nt/ *adj.* **1 a** conforming with standards of decency. **b** avoiding obscenity. **2** respectable. **3** acceptable, good enough. **4** kind, obliging. □ **decently** *adv.* [Latin *decet* is fitting]

decentralize /diːˈsentrəˌlaɪz/ *v.* (also **-ise**) (**-zing** or **-sing**) **1** transfer (power etc.) from central to local authority. **2** reorganize to give greater local autonomy. □ **decentralization** /-ˈzeɪʃ(ə)n/ *n.*

deception /dɪˈsepʃ(ə)n/ *n.* **1** deceiving or being deceived. **2** thing that deceives. [Latin: related to DECEIVE]

deceptive /dɪˈseptɪv/ *adj.* likely to deceive; misleading. □ **deceptively** *adv.* **deceptiveness** *n.*

deci- *comb. form* one-tenth. [Latin *decimus* tenth]

decibel /ˈdesɪˌbel/ *n.* unit used in the comparison of sound levels or power levels of electrical signals.

decide /dɪˈsaɪd/ *v.* (**-ding**) **1** (usu. foll. by *to*, *that*, or *on*, *about*) resolve after consideration (*decided to stay*; *decided quickly*; *weather decided me*; *decided on a blue hat*). **2** resolve or settle (an issue etc.). **3** (usu. foll. by *between*, *for*, *against*, *in favour of*, or *that*) give a judgement. □ **decidable** *adj.* [Latin *caedo* cut]

decided *adj.* **1** (usu. *attrib.*) definite, unquestionable (*decided tilt*). **2** positive, wilful, resolute.

decidedly *adv.* undoubtedly, undeniably.

decider *n.* **1** game, race, etc., as a tie-break. **2** person or thing that decides.

deciduous /dɪˈsɪdjʊəs/ *adj.* **1** (of a tree) shedding leaves annually. **2** (of leaves, horns, teeth, etc.) shed periodically. [Latin *cado* fall]

decigram /'desɪ,græm/ *n.* (also **decigramme**) metric unit of mass, equal to 0.1 gram.

decilitre /'desɪ,li:tə(r)/ *n.* (*US* **-liter**) metric unit of capacity, equal to 0.1 litre.

decimal /'desɪm(ə)l/ *–adj.* **1** (of a system of numbers, weights, measures, etc.) based on the number ten (*decimal notation*). **2** of tenths or ten; reckoning or proceeding by tens. *–n.* decimal fraction. [Latin *decem* ten]

◆ **decimal currency** *n.* currency system, now used in most countries, in which the standard unit is subdivided into 100 parts. Decimalization was introduced in the UK on 15 Feb. 1971, following the recommendations of the Halesbury Committee of 1961. The UK now has eight decimal coins, the 1p, 2p, 5p, 10p, 20p, 50p, £1 (introduced in 1983), and £2 (introduced in 1989). The ½p was introduced to ease the transition from a system based on 240 units to one based on 100 units but was abandoned in 1984.

decimal fraction *n.* fraction expressed in tenths, hundredths, etc., esp. by units to the right of the decimal point (e.g. 0.61).

decimalize *v.* (also **-ise**) (**-zing** or **-sing**) **1** express as a decimal. **2** convert to a decimal system (esp. of coinage). □ **decimalization** /-'zeɪʃ(ə)n/ *n.*

decimal point *n.* dot placed before the fraction in a decimal fraction.

decimate /'desɪ,meɪt/ *v.* (**-ting**) **1** destroy a large proportion of. **2** orig. *Rom. Hist.* kill or remove one in every ten of. □ **decimation** /-'meɪʃ(ə)n/ *n.*

■ **Usage** Sense 1 is now the usual sense, but it is considered inappropriate by some people. This word should not be used to mean 'defeat utterly'.

decimetre /'desɪ,mi:tə(r)/ *n.* (*US* **-meter**) metric unit of length, equal to 0.1 metre.

decipher /dɪ'saɪfə(r)/ *v.* **1** convert (coded information) into intelligible language. **2** determine the meaning of (unclear handwriting etc.). □ **decipherable** *adj.*

decision /dɪ'sɪʒ(ə)n/ *n.* **1** act or process of deciding. **2** resolution made after consideration (*made my decision*). **3** (often foll. by *of*) **a** settlement of a question. **b** formal judgement. **4** resoluteness. [Latin: related to DECIDE]

◆ **decision-making unit** *n.* (also **DMU**) informal group of individuals within an organization that decides which items the organization should buy. Commercial buying is undertaken by a group of people, rather than by individuals; it is important for the seller to discover the composition of this group within each of his potential customers, and to recognize that membership changes periodically. The group's composition varies according to the cost and complexity of the item being bought, but might comprise the company's purchasing manager, the proposed user of the item (the **internal user**), the **influencer** (one or more people, such as the production scheduler, indirectly associated with the use of the item), and the **decider** (one or more people, such as a director, who authorize the purchase).

decision table *n.* table used in computer programming to indicate all the conditions that could arise in the description of a problem, together with the actions to be taken for each set of conditions. It thus shows precisely what action is to be taken under a particular set of circumstances. Decision tables can be used in specifying what a program is to do (but not how it is to achieve this).

◆ **decision tree** *n.* diagram used in business to map the various possible courses of action that flow from a decision and the subsequent decisions that have to be made as a result of it. It consists of a series of levels at each of which the possible courses of action are represented by branches arising from decision points. It is often used in analysing financial situations and possible investments.

decisive /dɪ'saɪsɪv/ *adj.* **1** conclusive, settling an issue. **2** quick to decide. □ **decisively** *adv.* **decisiveness** *n.* [medieval Latin: related to DECIDE]

deck *–n.* **1 a** platform in a ship serving as a floor. **b** the accommodation on a particular deck of a ship. **2** floor or compartment of a bus etc. **3** section for playing discs or tapes etc. in a sound system. **4** *US* pack of cards. **5** *slang* ground. *–v.* **1** (often foll. by *out*) decorate. **2** provide with or cover as a deck. □ **below deck(s)** in or into the space below the main deck. [Dutch, = cover]

◆ **deck cargo** *n.* cargo that is carried on the deck of a ship rather than in a hold. This may increase the insurance premium, depending on the nature of the cargo.

deck-chair *n.* folding garden chair of wood and canvas.

-decker *comb. form* having a specified number of decks or layers (*double-decker*).

deck-hand *n.* cleaner on a ship's deck.

declaim /dɪ'kleɪm/ *v.* **1** speak or say as if addressing an audience. **2** (foll. by *against*) protest forcefully. □ **declamation** /,deklə'meɪʃ(ə)n/ *n.* **declamatory** /dɪ'klæmətərɪ/ *adj.* [Latin: related to CLAIM]

declaration /,deklə'reɪʃ(ə)n/ *n.* **1** declaring. **2** formal, emphatic, or deliberate statement. [Latin: related to DECLARE]

◆ **declaration of compliance** see COMPANY FORMATION.

◆ **declaration of solvency** *n.* declaration made by the directors of a company seeking voluntary liquidation that it will be able to pay its debts within a specified period, not exceeding 12 months from the date of the declaration. It must contain a statement of the company's assets and liabilities, and a copy must be sent to the Registrar of Companies. A director who participates in a declaration of solvency without reasonable grounds will be liable to a fine or imprisonment on conviction. See MEMBERS' VOLUNTARY LIQUIDATION.

declare /dɪ'kleə(r)/ *v.* (**-ring**) **1** announce openly or formally (*declare war*). **2** pronounce (*declared it invalid*). **3** (usu. foll. by *that*) assert emphatically. **4** acknowledge possession of (dutiable goods, income, etc.). **5** (as **declared** *adj.*) admitting to be such (*declared atheist*). **6** (also *absol.*) *Cricket* close (an innings) voluntarily before the team is out. **7** (also *absol.*) *Cards* name (the trump suit). □ **declare oneself** reveal one's intentions or identity. □ **declarative** /-'klærətɪv/ *adj.* **declaratory** /-'klærətərɪ/ *adj.* **declarer** *n.* [Latin *clarus* clear]

declassify /di:'klæsɪ,faɪ/ *v.* (**-ies, -ied**) declare (information etc.) to be no longer secret. □ **declassification** /-fɪ'keɪʃ(ə)n/ *n.*

declension /dɪ'klenʃ(ə)n/ *n.* **1** *Gram.* **a** variation of the form of a noun, pronoun, or adjective to show its grammatical case etc. **b** class of nouns with the same inflections. **2** deterioration, declining. [Latin: related to DECLINE]

declination /,deklɪ'neɪʃ(ə)n/ *n.* **1** downward bend or turn. **2** angular distance of a star etc. north or south of the celestial equator. **3** deviation of a compass needle from true north. □ **declinational** *adj.* [Latin: related to DECLINE]

decline /dɪ'klaɪn/ *–v.* (**-ning**) **1** deteriorate; lose strength or vigour; decrease. **2** (also *absol.*) politely refuse (an invitation, challenge, etc.). **3** slope or bend downwards, droop. **4** *Gram.* state the forms of (a noun, pronoun, or adjective). *–n.* **1** gradual loss of vigour or excellence. **2** deterioration. [Latin *clino* bend]

declining years *n.pl.* old age.

declivity /dɪ'klɪvɪtɪ/ *n.* (*pl.* **-ies**) downward slope. [Latin *clivus* slope]

declutch /di:'klʌtʃ/ *v.* disengage the clutch of a motor vehicle.

decoction /dɪ'kɒkʃ(ə)n/ *n.* **1** boiling down to extract an essence. **2** the resulting liquid. [Latin *coquo* boil]

decode /di:'kəʊd/ *v.* (**-ding**) decipher. □ **decoder** *n.*

decoke *colloq.* –*v.* /diːˈkəʊk/ (**-king**) decarbonize. –*n.* /ˈdiːkəʊk/ process of this.

décolletage /ˌdeɪkɒlˈtɑːʒ/ *n.* low neckline of a woman's dress etc. [French *collet* collar]

décolleté /deɪˈkɒlteɪ/ *adj.* (also ***décolletée***) (of a dress, woman, etc.) having or wearing a low neckline.

decompose /ˌdiːkəmˈpəʊz/ *v.* (**-sing**) **1** rot. **2** separate (a substance, light, etc.) into its elements. □ **decomposition** /ˌdiːkɒmpəˈzɪʃ(ə)n/ *n.*

decompress /ˌdiːkəmˈpres/ *v.* subject to decompression.

decompression /ˌdiːkəmˈpreʃ(ə)n/ *n.* **1** release from compression. **2** gradual reduction of high pressure on a deep-sea diver etc.

decompression chamber *n.* enclosed space for decompression.

decompression sickness *n.* condition caused by the sudden lowering of air pressure.

decongestant /ˌdiːkənˈdʒest(ə)nt/ *n.* medicine etc. that relieves nasal congestion.

decontaminate /ˌdiːkənˈtæmɪˌneɪt/ *v.* (**-ting**) remove contamination from. □ **decontamination** /-ˈneɪʃ(ə)n/ *n.*

décor /ˈdeɪkɔː(r)/ *n.* furnishing and decoration of a room, stage set, etc. [French: related to DECORATE]

decorate /ˈdekəˌreɪt/ *v.* (**-ting**) **1** beautify, adorn. **2** paint, wallpaper, etc. (a room or building). **3** give a medal or award to. [Latin *decus -oris* beauty]

Decorated style *n. Archit.* highly ornamented late English Gothic style (14th century).

decoration /ˌdekəˈreɪʃ(ə)n/ *n.* **1** decorating. **2** thing that decorates. **3** medal etc. worn as an honour. **4** (in *pl.*) flags, tinsel, etc., put up on a festive occasion.

decorative /ˈdekərətɪv/ *adj.* pleasing in appearance. □ **decoratively** *adv.*

decorator *n.* person who decorates for a living.

decorous /ˈdekərəs/ *adj.* having or showing decorum. □ **decorously** *adv.* **decorousness** *n.* [Latin *decorus* seemly]

decorum /dɪˈkɔːrəm/ *n.* polite dignified behaviour. [as DECOROUS]

decoy –*n.* /ˈdiːkɔɪ/ person or thing used as a lure; bait, enticement. –*v.* /dɪˈkɔɪ/ lure, esp. using a decoy. [Dutch]

decrease –*v.* /dɪˈkriːs/ (**-sing**) make or become smaller or fewer. –*n.* /ˈdiːkriːs/ **1** decreasing. **2** amount of this. □ **decreasingly** *adv.* [Latin: related to DE-, *cresco* grow]

♦ **decreasing returns to scale** see RETURNS TO SCALE.

♦ **decreasing term assurance** *n.* form of term assurance in which the amount to be paid in the event of the death of the life assured reduces with the passage of time. These policies are usu. arranged in conjunction with a cash loan or mortgage and are designed to repay the loan if the life assured dies. As the amount of the loan decreases with successive repayments the sum assured reduces at the same rate.

---

decree /dɪˈkriː/ –*n.* **1** official legal order. **2** legal judgement or decision, esp. in divorce cases. –*v.* (**-ees, -eed, -eeing**) ordain by decree. [Latin *decretum* from *cerno* sift]

decree absolute *n.* final order for completion of a divorce.

decree nisi /ˈnaɪsaɪ/ *n.* provisional order for divorce, made absolute after a fixed period. [Latin *nisi* unless]

decrepit /dɪˈkrepɪt/ *adj.* **1** weakened by age or infirmity. **2** dilapidated. □ **decrepitude** *n.* [Latin *crepo* creak]

decrescendo /ˌdiːkrɪˈʃendəʊ/ *adv., adj.,* & *n.* (*pl.* **-s**) = DIMINUENDO. [Italian: related to DECREASE]

decretal /dɪˈkriːt(ə)l/ *n.* papal decree. [Latin: related to DECREE]

decriminalize /diːˈkrɪmɪnəˌlaɪz/ *v.* (also **-ise**) (**-zing** or **-sing**) cease to treat as criminal. □ **decriminalization** /-ˈzeɪʃ(ə)n/ *n.*

decry /dɪˈkraɪ/ *v.* (**-ies, -ied**) disparage, belittle.

dedicate /ˈdedɪˌkeɪt/ *v.* (**-ting**) (often foll. by *to*) **1** devote (esp. oneself) to a special task or purpose. **2** address (a book etc.) to a friend, patron, etc. **3** devote (a building etc.) to a deity, saint, etc. **4** (as **dedicated** *adj.*) **a** (of a person) single-mindedly loyal to an aim, vocation, etc. **b** (of equipment, esp. a computer) designed for or assigned to a specific task. □ **dedicator** *n.* **dedicatory** *adj.* [Latin *dico* declare]

dedication /ˌdedɪˈkeɪʃ(ə)n/ *n.* **1** dedicating or being dedicated. **2** words with which a book etc. is dedicated. [Latin: related to DEDICATE]

deduce /dɪˈdjuːs/ *v.* (**-cing**) (often foll. by *from*) infer logically. □ **deducible** *adj.* [Latin *duco duct-* lead]

deduct /dɪˈdʌkt/ *v.* (often foll. by *from*) subtract, take away, or withhold (an amount, portion, etc.). [related to DEDUCE]

deductible –*adj.* that may be deducted, esp. from tax or taxable income. –*n.* amount deducted from a claim in a large commercial excess policy (cf. EXCESS *n.* 4). It is an amount that is deducted from every claim that is paid. If a claim is made for a figure below the deductible no payment is made. Deductibles are usu. applied to policies in return for a premium reduction.

deduction /dɪˈdʌkʃ(ə)n/ *n.* **1 a** deducting. **b** amount deducted. **2 a** inferring of particular instances from a general law or principle. **b** conclusion deduced. [Latin: related to DEDUCE]

♦ **deductions at source** *n.pl.* amounts deducted for tax from a person's income by the payer of the income, who is responsible for paying the tax to the authorities. Tax authorities have found that, in general, it is easier to collect tax from the payer rather than the recipient of income, esp. if paying the tax is made a condition of the payer's obtaining tax relief for the payment. The payee receives a credit against his tax liability for the tax already suffered. Examples of this in the UK tax system are PAYE, sharehold dividends, interest on government securities, deeds of covenant, trust income, and subcontractors in the building industry. Normally, tax is deducted at the basic rate of income tax only, although in certain cases, such as PAYE and payments from discretionary trusts, other rates might be used.

---

deductive *adj.* of or reasoning by deduction. □ **deductively** *adv.* [medieval Latin: related to DEDUCE]

dee *n.* **1** letter D. **2** thing shaped like this. [name of the letter D]

deed *n.* **1** thing done intentionally or consciously. **2** brave, skilful, or conspicuous act. **3** action (*kind in word and deed*). **4** legal document that has been signed, sealed, and delivered. The seal and the delivery make it different from an ordinary written agreement. The former use of sealing wax and a signet to effect the seal is now usu. replaced by using a small paper disc; delivery may now be informal, i.e. by carrying out some act to show that the deed is intended to be operative. Some transactions, e.g. conveyances of land, must be carried out by deed to be effective. [Old English: related to DO[1]]

deed-box *n.* strong box for deeds etc.

♦ **deed of arrangement** see ARRANGEMENT 6a.

♦ **deed of assignment** see ASSIGNMENT 3b.

♦ **deed of covenant** *n.* legal document, which must be in a specified form, used to transfer income from one person to another with a view to making a saving in tax. It authorizes regular annual payments to be made, which must normally be at least six (except in the case of payments to charities, when it can be three). The person making the payment deducts income tax at the basic rate from the payment, in most cases obtaining tax relief on it. Any recipient who is exempt from tax (e.g. a charity) can reclaim the tax deducted. In certain cases, such as payments to charities, tax relief at higher rates may be available to the payer; this does not apply to student children.

---

deed poll *n.* deed made by one party only, esp. to change one's name.

deem *v. formal* consider, judge (*deem it my duty*). [Old English]

deemster *n.* judge in the Isle of Man. [from DEEM]

deep *–adj.* **1** extending far down or in (*deep water*; *deep wound*; *deep shelf*). **2** (*predic.*) **a** to or at a specified depth (*water 6 feet deep*). **b** in a specified number of ranks (*soldiers drawn up six deep*). **3** situated or coming from far down, back, or in (*deep in his pockets*; *deep sigh*). **4** low-pitched, full-toned (*deep voice*). **5** intense, extreme (*deep sleep*; *deep colour*; *deep interest*). **6** (*predic.*) fully absorbed or overwhelmed (*deep in a book*; *deep in debt*). **7** profound; difficult to understand (*too deep for me*). *–n.* **1** (prec. by *the*) *poet.* sea, esp. when deep. **2** abyss, pit, cavity. **3** (prec. by *the*) *Cricket* position of a fielder distant from the batsman. **4** deep state (*deep of the night*). *–adv.* deeply; far down or in (*dig deep*). □ **go off the deep end** *colloq.* give way to anger or emotion. **in deep water** in trouble or difficulty. □ **deeply** *adv.* [Old English]

deep breathing *n.* breathing with long breaths, esp. as exercise.

♦ **deep-discount bond** *n.* fixed-interest security paying little or no interest (see also ZERO-COUPON BOND). Because it provides little or no income it is offered at a substantial discount to its redemption value, providing a large capital gain in place of income. This may have tax advantages in certain circumstances.

---

deepen *v.* make or become deep or deeper.

deep-freeze *–n.* cabinet for freezing and keeping food for long periods. *–v.* freeze or store in a deep-freeze.

deep-fry *v.* immerse in boiling fat to cook.

deep-laid *adj.* (of a scheme) secret and elaborate.

deep-rooted *adj.* (also **deep-seated**) firmly established, profound.

deer *n.* (*pl.* same) four-hoofed grazing animal the male of which usu. has antlers. [Old English]

deerskin *n.* (often *attrib.*) leather from a deer's skin.

deerstalker *n.* soft cloth peaked cap with ear-flaps.

de-escalate /diːˈeskəˌleɪt/ *v.* make or become less intense. □ **de-escalation** /-ˈleɪʃ(ə)n/ *n.*

def *adj. slang* excellent. [perhaps from DEFINITE or DEFINITIVE]

deface /dɪˈfeɪs/ *v.* (**-cing**) disfigure. □ **defacement** *n.* [French: related to FACE]

de facto /deɪ ˈfæktəʊ/ *–adv.* in fact (whether by right or not). *–adj.* existing as a matter of fact rather than by right (*a de facto ruler; de facto control of a property*). Cf. DE JURE. [Latin]

defalcate /ˈdiːfælˌkeɪt/ *v.* (**-ting**) *formal* misappropriate, esp. money. □ **defalcator** *n.* [Latin *defalcare* lop, from *falx* sickle]

defalcation /ˌdiːfælˈkeɪʃ(ə)n/ *n. formal* **1 a** misappropriation of money. **b** amount misappropriated. **2** shortcoming.

defame /dɪˈfeɪm/ *v.* (**-ming**) libel; slander; speak ill of. □ **defamation** /ˌdefəˈmeɪʃ(ə)n/ *n.* **defamatory** /dɪˈfæmətərɪ/ *adj.* [Latin *fama* report]

default /dɪˈfɔːlt/ *–n.* **1** failure to do something that is required by law, esp. failure to comply with the rules of legal procedure. **2** failure to comply with the terms of a contract. A seller is in default when failing to supply the right quality goods at the contracted time. A buyer is in default when failing to take up documents or pay for goods when there is a contract to do so. Before taking legal action against a defaulter a **default notice** must be served on that person. **3** preselected option adopted by a computer program when no alternative is specified. *–v.* fail to fulfil (esp. a legal) obligation. □ **by default** because of lack of an alternative or opposition. **in default of** because of the absence of. □ **defaulter** *n.* [French: related to FAIL]

defeat /dɪˈfiːt/ *–v.* **1** overcome in battle, a contest, etc. **2** frustrate, baffle. **3** reject (a motion etc.) by voting. *–n.* defeating or being defeated. [Latin: related to DIS-, FACT]

defeatism *n.* excessive readiness to accept defeat. □ **defeatist** *n.* & *adj.*

defecate /ˈdefɪˌkeɪt/ *v.* (**-ting**) evacuate the bowels. □ **defecation** /-ˈkeɪʃ(ə)n/ *n.* [Latin *faex faecis* dregs]

defect *–n.* /ˈdiːfekt/ fault, imperfection, shortcoming. *–v.* /dɪˈfekt/ leave one's country or cause for another. □ **defection** *n.* **defector** *n.* [Latin *deficio -fect-* fail]

defective /dɪˈfektɪv/ *adj.* having defect(s); imperfect. [Latin: related to DEFECT]

defence /dɪˈfens/ *n.* (*US* **defense**) **1** defending, protection. **2** means of this. **3** (in *pl.*) fortifications. **4** justification, vindication. **5** defendant's case or counsel in a lawsuit. **6** defending play or players. □ **defenceless** *adj.* **defencelessly** *adv.* **defencelessness** *n.* [related to DEFEND]

defence mechanism *n.* **1** body's resistance to disease. **2** usu. unconscious mental process to avoid anxiety.

defend /dɪˈfend/ *v.* (also *absol.*) **1** (often foll. by *against*, *from*) resist an attack made on; protect. **2** uphold by argument. **3** conduct a defence in a lawsuit. **4** compete to retain (a title etc.) in a contest. □ **defender** *n.* [Latin *defendo -fens-*]

defendant *n.* person etc. sued or accused in a lawcourt. [French: related to DEFEND]

defense *US* var. of DEFENCE.

defensible /dɪˈfensɪb(ə)l/ *adj.* **1** justifiable; supportable by argument. **2** able to be defended militarily. □ **defensibility** /-ˈbɪlɪtɪ/ *n.* **defensibly** *adv.* [Latin: related to DEFEND]

defensive *adj.* **1** done or intended for defence. **2** over-reacting to criticism. □ **on the defensive 1** expecting criticism. **2** *Mil* ready to defend. □ **defensively** *adv.* **defensiveness** *n.* [medieval Latin: related to DEFEND]

defer[1] /dɪˈfɜː(r)/ *v.* (**-rr-**) postpone. □ **deferment** *n.* **deferral** *n.* [originally the same as DIFFER]

defer[2] /dɪˈfɜː(r)/ *v.* (**-rr-**) (foll. by *to*) yield or make concessions to. [Latin *defero* carry away]

deference /ˈdefərəns/ *n.* **1** courteous regard, respect. **2** compliance with another's wishes. □ **in deference to** out of respect for.

deferential /ˌdefəˈrenʃ(ə)l/ *adj.* respectful. □ **deferentially** *adv.*

♦ **deferred annuity** *n.* annuity in which payments do not start at once but either at a specified later date or when the policyholder reaches a specified age.

♦ **deferred asset** *n.* asset the realization of which is likely to be considerably delayed. An example might be a payment of advance corporation tax (ACT), which can be used to offset a future payment of corporation tax. If there is no possibility of a liability to corporation tax in the near future, the ACT is a deferred asset rather than an actual asset.

♦ **deferred liability** *n.* prospective liability that will only become a definite liability if some future event occurs. See also CONTINGENT LIABILITY.

♦ **deferred ordinary share** *n.* **1** ordinary share, formerly often issued to founder members of a company, in which dividends are only paid after all other types of ordinary share have been paid. Such shares often entitle their owners to a large share of the profit. **2** share on which little or no dividend is paid for a fixed number of years, after which it ranks with other ordinary shares for dividend.

---

deferred payment *n.* payment by instalments.

♦ **deferred-payment agreement** see HIRE PURCHASE.

♦ **deferred rebate** *n.* rebate offered by a supplier of goods or services to customers on the understanding that further goods and services are purchased from the same supplier. The rebate is usu. paid periodically, after the supplier is convinced of the customer's continued support. Some shipping companies offer a deferred rebate to shippers.

♦ **deferred taxation** *n.* sum set aside for tax in the accounts of an organization that will become payable in a period other than that under review. It arises because of timing differences between tax rules and accounting conventions. The principle of **deferred-tax accounting** is to re-allocate a tax payment to the same period as that in which the relevant amount of income or expenditure is shown. Historically, the timing difference has arisen in company accounts because the percentages used for the calculation of capital allowances have differed from those used for depreciation.

---

defiance /dɪˈfaɪəns/ *n.* open disobedience; bold resistance. [French: related to DEFY]

defiant *adj.* showing defiance; disobedient. □ **defiantly** *adv.*

deficiency /dɪˈfɪʃənsɪ/ *n.* (*pl.* **-ies**) **1** being deficient. **2** (usu. foll. by *of*) lack or shortage. **3** thing lacking. **4** deficit, esp. financial.

deficiency disease *n.* disease caused by the lack of an essential element of diet.

deficient *adj.* (often foll. by *in*) incomplete or insufficient in quantity, quality, etc. [Latin: related to DEFECT]

deficit /ˈdefɪsɪt/ *n.* **1** amount by which a thing (esp. money) is too small. **2** excess of liabilities over assets. [French from Latin: related to DEFECT]

♦ **deficit financing** *n.* creation of a government budget deficit for the purpose of influencing economic activity.

---

defile[1] /dɪˈfaɪl/ *v.* (**-ling**) **1** make dirty; pollute. **2** desecrate, profane. □ **defilement** *n.* [earlier *defoul*, from French *defouler* trample down]

defile[2] /dɪˈfaɪl/ *–n.* narrow gorge or pass. *–v.* (**-ling**) march in file. [French: related to FILE[1]]

define /dɪˈfaɪn/ *v.* (**-ning**) **1** give the meaning of (a word etc.). **2** describe or explain the scope of (*define one's position*). **3** outline clearly (*well-defined image*). **4** mark out the boundary of. □ **definable** *adj.* [Latin *finis* end]

definite /ˈdefɪnɪt/ *adj.* **1** certain, sure. **2** clearly defined; not vague; precise. □ **definitely** *adv.* [Latin: related to DEFINE]

■ **Usage** See note at *definitive*.

definite article *n.* the word (*the* in English) preceding a noun and implying a specific instance.

definition /ˌdefɪˈnɪʃ(ə)n/ *n.* **1 a** defining. **b** statement of the meaning of a word etc. **2** distinctness in outline esp. of a photographic image. [Latin: related to DEFINE]

definitive /dɪˈfɪnɪtɪv/ *adj.* **1** (of an answer, verdict, etc.) decisive, unconditional, final. **2** (of a book etc.) most authoritative.

■ **Usage** In sense 1, this word is often confused with *definite*, which does not imply authority and conclusiveness. A *definite no* is a firm refusal, while a *definitive no* is an authoritative judgement or decision that something is not the case.

deflate /dɪˈfleɪt/ *v.* (**-ting**) **1** empty (a tyre, balloon, etc.) of air, gas, etc.; be so emptied. **2** (cause to) lose confidence or conceit. **3 a** subject (a currency or economy) to deflation. **b** pursue this as a policy. [from DE-, INFLATE]

deflation /dɪˈfleɪʃ(ə)n/ *n.* **1** deflating or being deflated. **2** general fall in the price level (cf. INFLATION 2). As with inflation, a general change in the price level should, in theory, have no real effect. However, if traders are holding goods whose prices fall, they may suffer such large losses that they are forced into bankruptcy. Conversely, agents holding money are simultaneously better off, although there may be a lag in increasing expenditure, during which a recession may occur. The only major deflation in this century occurred during the Great Depression in the 1920s and 1930s. Since then, governments have avoided deflation wherever possible. See also PRICE LEVEL; DISINFLATION. □ **deflationary** *adj.*

deflect /dɪˈflekt/ *v.* **1** bend or turn aside from a course or purpose. **2** (often foll. by *from*) (cause to) deviate. □ **deflection** *n.* (also **deflexion**). **deflector** *n.* [Latin *flecto* bend]

deflower /diːˈflaʊə(r)/ *v. literary* **1** deprive of virginity. **2** ravage, spoil. [Latin: related to FLOWER]

defoliate /diːˈfəʊlɪˌeɪt/ *v.* (**-ting**) destroy the leaves of (trees or plants). □ **defoliant** *n.* **defoliation** /-ˈeɪʃ(ə)n/ *n.* [Latin: related to FOIL[2]]

deforest /diːˈfɒrɪst/ *v.* clear of forests or trees. □ **deforestation** /-ˈsteɪʃ(ə)n/ *n.*

deform /dɪˈfɔːm/ *v.* make ugly or misshapen, disfigure. □ **deformation** /ˌdiːfɔːˈmeɪʃ(ə)n/ *n.* [Latin: related to FORM]

deformed *adj.* (of a person or limb) misshapen.

deformity *n.* (*pl.* **-ies**) **1** being deformed. **2** malformation, esp. of a body or limb.

defraud /dɪˈfrɔːd/ *v.* (often foll. by *of*) cheat by fraud. [Latin: related to FRAUD]

defray /dɪˈfreɪ/ *v.* provide money for (a cost or expense). □ **defrayal** *n.* **defrayment** *n.* [medieval Latin *fredum* fine]

defrock /diːˈfrɒk/ *v.* deprive (esp. a priest) of office. [French: related to DE-, FROCK]

defrost /diːˈfrɒst/ *v.* **1** remove frost or ice from (a refrigerator, windscreen, etc.). **2** unfreeze (frozen food). **3** become unfrozen.

deft *adj.* neat; dextrous; adroit. □ **deftly** *adv.* **deftness** *n.* [var. of DAFT = 'meek']

defunct /dɪˈfʌŋkt/ *adj.* **1** no longer existing or used. **2** dead or extinct. □ **defunctness** *n.* [Latin *fungor* perform]

♦ **defunct company** *n.* company that has been wound up and has therefore ceased to exist.

---

defuse /diːˈfjuːz/ *v.* (**-sing**) **1** remove the fuse from (a bomb etc.). **2** reduce tension etc. in (a crisis, difficulty, etc.).

defy /dɪˈfaɪ/ *v.* (**-ies, -ied**) **1** resist openly; refuse to obey. **2** (of a thing) present insuperable obstacles to (*defies solution*). **3** (foll. by *to* + infin.) challenge (a person) to do or prove something. [Latin *fides* faith]

♦ **degearing** /diːˈgɪərɪŋ/ *n.* process in which some of the fixed-interest loan stock of a company is replaced by ordinary share capital. See CAPITAL GEARING.

---

degenerate *–adj.* /dɪˈdʒenərət/ **1** having lost its usual or good qualities; immoral, degraded. **2** *Biol.* having changed to a lower type. *–n.* /dɪˈdʒenərət/ degenerate person or animal. *–v.* /dɪˈdʒenəˌreɪt/ (**-ting**) become degenerate. □ **degeneracy** *n.* [Latin *genus* race]

degeneration /dɪˌdʒenəˈreɪʃ(ə)n/ *n.* **1** becoming degenerate. **2** *Med.* morbid deterioration of body tissue etc. [Latin: related to DEGENERATE]

degrade /dɪˈgreɪd/ *v.* (**-ding**) **1** humiliate, dishonour. **2** reduce to a lower rank. **3** *Chem.* reduce to a simpler molecular structure. □ **degradation** /ˌdegrəˈdeɪʃ(ə)n/ *n.* **degrading** *adj.* [Latin: related to GRADE]

degree /dɪˈgriː/ *n.* **1** stage in a scale, series, or process. **2** stage in intensity or amount (*in some degree*). **3** unit of measurement of an angle or arc. **4** unit in a scale of temperature, hardness, etc. **5** extent of burns. **6** academic rank conferred by a polytechnic, university, etc. **7** grade of crime (*first-degree murder*). **8** step in direct genealogical descent. **9** social rank. □ **by degrees** gradually. [Latin *gradus* step]

degrees of comparison see COMPARISON 4.

dehisce /diːˈhɪs/ *v.* (**-cing**) (esp. of a pod, cut, etc.) gape or burst open. □ **dehiscence** *n.* **dehiscent** *adj.* [Latin *hio* gape]

dehumanize /diːˈhjuːməˌnaɪz/ *v.* (also **-ise**) (**-zing** or **-sing**) **1** take human qualities away from. **2** make impersonal. □ **dehumanization** /-ˈzeɪʃ(ə)n/ *n.*

dehydrate /diːˈhaɪdreɪt/ *v.* (**-ting**) **1** remove water from (esp. foods). **2** make or become dry, esp. too dry. □ **dehydration** /-ˈdreɪʃ(ə)n/ *n.* [Greek *hudōr* water]

de-ice /diːˈaɪs/ *v.* **1** remove ice from. **2** prevent the formation of ice on. □ **de-icer** *n.*

deify /ˈdiːɪˌfaɪ, ˈdeɪ-/ *v.* (**-ies, -ied**) make a god or idol of. □ **deification** /-fɪˈkeɪʃ(ə)n/ *n.* [Latin *deus* god]

deign /deɪn/ *v.* (foll. by *to* + infin.) think fit, condescend. [Latin *dignus* worthy]

♦ **deindustrialization** /diːɪnˌdʌstrɪəlaɪˈzeɪʃ(ə)n/ *n.* (also **-isation**) substantial fall in the importance of the manufacturing sector in the economy of an industrialized nation as it becomes uncompetitive with its neighbours. This may result from bad industrial relations, poor management, inadequate investment in capital goods, or short-sighted government economic policies. In many cases each of these factors contributes to deindustrialization. □ **deindustrialize** /-ˌlaɪz/ *v.* (also **-ise) (-zing** or **-sing**).

deinstitutionalize /diːˌɪnstɪˈtjuːʃənəˌlaɪz/ *v.* (also **-ise**) (**-zing** or **-sing**) (usu. as **deinstitutionalized** *adj.*) remove from an institution or help recover from the effects of institutional life. □ **deinstitutionalization** /-ˈzeɪʃ(ə)n/ *n.*

deism /ˈdiːɪz(ə)m, ˈdeɪ-/ *n.* reasoned belief in the existence of a god. □ **deist** *n.* **deistic** /-ˈɪstɪk/ *adj.* [Latin *deus* god]

deity /ˈdiːɪtɪ, ˈdeɪɪ-/ *n.* (*pl.* **-ies**) **1** god or goddess. **2** divine status or nature. **3** (**the Deity**) God. [French from Church Latin]

déjà vu /ˌdeɪʒɑː ˈvuː/ *n.* **1** feeling of having already experienced the present situation. **2** something tediously familiar. [French, = already seen]

deject /dɪˈdʒekt/ *–v.* (usu. as **dejected** *adj.*) make sad; depress. □ **dejectedly** *adv.* **dejection** *n.* [Latin *jacio* throw]

de jure /deɪ ˈjʊərɪ/ *–adj.* rightful; existing as a matter of legal right (*de jure recognition of a government*). Cf. DE FACTO. *–adv.* rightfully; by right. [Latin]

dekko /ˈdekəʊ/ *n.* (*pl.* **-s**) *slang* look, glance. [Hindi]

Del. *abbr.* Delaware.

Delaware /ˈdeləˌweə(r)/ state in the US, on the Atlantic coast; manufactures include chemicals, motor vehicles, synthetic rubber, and textiles; pop. (est. 1996) 724 842; capital, Dover.

delay /dɪˈleɪ/ *–v.* **1** postpone; defer. **2** make or be late; loiter. *–n.* **1** delaying or being delayed. **2** time lost by this. **3** hindrance. [French]

delayed-action *attrib. adj.* (esp. of a bomb, camera, etc.) operating after a set interval.

♦ **del credere agent** /del ˈkreɪdərɪ/ *n.* agent who sells goods on behalf of another (the principal) and guarantees to pay for any goods sold on the principal's behalf if the customer fails to do so. The agent charges an extra commission for covering this risk. [Italian *del credere* of trust]

delectable /dɪˈlektəb(ə)l/ *adj.* esp. *literary* delightful, delicious. □ **delectably** *adv.* [Latin: related to DELIGHT]

delectation /ˌdiːlekˈteɪʃ(ə)n/ *n. literary* pleasure, enjoyment.

delegate *–n.* /ˈdelɪgət/ **1** elected representative sent to a conference. **2** member of a committee or delegation. *–v.* /ˈdelɪˌgeɪt/ (**-ting**) **1** (often foll. by *to*) **a** commit (power etc.) to an agent or deputy. **b** entrust (a task) to another. **2** send or authorize (a person) as a representative. [Latin: related to LEGATE]

delegation /ˌdelɪˈgeɪʃ(ə)n/ *n.* **1** group representing others. **2** delegating or being delegated.

♦ ***delegatus non potest delegare*** /delɪˈgɑːtʊs nɒn ˈpəʊtest delɪˈgɑːrɪ/ *n.* rule that a person to whom a power, trust, or authority is given to act on behalf, or for the benefit of, another, cannot delegate this obligation unless expressly authorized to do so. For instance, an auditor who has been appointed to audit the accounts of a company cannot delegate the task to another unless expressly allowed to do so. If express authorization has not been granted the person will have acted *ultra vires*. [Latin, = a delegate cannot further delegate]

delete /dɪˈliːt/ *v.* (**-ting**) remove (a letter, word, etc.), esp. by striking out or by operating a function key or cursor on a computer keyboard. □ **deletion** *n.* [Latin *deleo*]

deleterious /ˌdelɪˈtɪərɪəs/ *adj.* harmful. [Latin from Greek]

Delft /delft/ town in the W Netherlands, in the province of South Holland, noted since the 17th century for its pottery (see DELFT); pop. (1987) 87 736.

delft *n.* (also **delftware**) glazed, usu. blue and white, earthenware. [DELFT]

Delhi /ˈdelɪ/ **1** Union Territory of India; grain, sugar cane, and fruits are produced; pop. (1991) 9 420 644. **2** capital of India, comprising Old and New Delhi; it is an important commercial and industrial centre of N India; pop. (1991) 7 206 704.

deli /ˈdelɪ/ *n.* (*pl.* **-s**) *colloq.* delicatessen shop. [abbreviation]

deliberate *–adj.* /dɪˈlɪbərət/ **1 a** intentional. **b** considered; careful. **2** (of movement, thought, etc.) unhurried; cautious. *–v.* /dɪˈlɪbəˌreɪt/ (**-ting**) **1** think carefully; consider. **2** discuss (*jury deliberated*). □ **deliberately** /dɪˈlɪbərətlɪ/ *adv.* [Latin *libra* balance]

deliberation /ˌdɪlɪbəˈreɪʃ(ə)n/ *n.* **1** careful consideration; discussion. **2** careful slowness.

deliberative /dɪˈlɪbərətɪv/ *adj.* (esp. of an assembly etc.) of or for deliberation or debate.

delicacy /ˈdelɪkəsɪ/ *n.* (*pl.* **-ies**) **1** being delicate (in all senses). **2** a choice food. [from DELICATE]

delicate /ˈdelɪkət/ *adj.* **1 a** fine in texture, quality, etc.; slender, slight. **b** (of a colour, flavour, etc.) subtle, hard to discern. **2** susceptible; weak, tender. **3 a** requiring tact; tricky (*delicate situation*). **b** (of an instrument) highly sensitive. **4** deft (*delicate touch*). **5** modest. **6** (esp. of actions) considerate. □ **delicately** *adv.* [Latin]

delicatessen /ˌdelɪkəˈtes(ə)n/ *n.* **1** shop selling esp. exotic cooked meats, cheeses, etc. **2** (often *attrib.*) such foods. [French: related to DELICATE]

delicious /dɪˈlɪʃəs/ *adj.* highly enjoyable, esp. to taste or smell. □ **deliciously** *adv.* [Latin *deliciae* delights]

delight /dɪˈlaɪt/ *–v.* **1** (often as **delighted** *adj.*) please greatly (*her singing delighted us*; *delighted to help*). **2** (foll. by *in*) take great pleasure in (*delights in surprising everyone*). *–n.* **1** great pleasure. **2** thing that delights. □ **delighted** *adj.* **delightful** *adj.* **delightfully** *adv.* [Latin *delecto*]

delimit /dɪˈlɪmɪt/ *v.* (**-t-**) fix the limits or boundary of. □ **delimiter** *n.* **delimitation** /-ˈteɪʃ(ə)n/ *n.* [Latin: related to LIMIT]

delineate /dɪˈlɪnɪˌeɪt/ *v.* (**-ting**) portray by drawing etc. or in words. □ **delineation** /-ˈeɪʃ(ə)n/ *n.* [Latin: related to LINE[1]]

delinquent /dɪˈlɪŋkwənt/ *–n.* offender (*juvenile delinquent*). *–adj.* **1** guilty of a minor crime or misdeed. **2** failing in one's duty. □ **delinquency** *n.* [Latin *delinquo* offend]

deliquesce /ˌdelɪˈkwes/ *v.* (**-cing**) **1** become liquid, melt. **2** dissolve in water absorbed from the air. □ **deliquescence** *n.* **deliquescent** *adj.* [Latin: related to LIQUID]

delirious /dɪˈlɪrɪəs/ *adj.* **1** affected with delirium. **2** wildly excited, ecstatic. □ **deliriously** *adv.*

delirium /dɪˈlɪrɪəm/ *n.* **1** disorder involving incoherent speech, hallucinations, etc., caused by intoxication, fever, etc. **2** great excitement, ecstasy. [Latin *lira* ridge between furrows]

delirium tremens /ˈtriːmenz/ *n.* psychosis of chronic alcoholism involving tremors and hallucinations.

deliver /dɪˈlɪvə(r)/ *v.* **1 a** distribute (letters, goods, etc.) to their destination(s). **b** (often foll. by *to*) hand over. **2** (often foll. by *from*) save, rescue, or set free. **3 a** give birth to (*delivered a girl*). **b** assist at the birth of or in giving birth (*delivered six babies*). **4** utter (an opinion, speech, etc.). **5** (often foll. by *up*, *over*) abandon; resign (*delivered his soul up*). **6** launch or aim (a blow etc.). □ **be delivered of** give birth to. **deliver the goods** *colloq.* carry out an undertaking. [Latin *liber* free]

deliverance *n.* rescuing or being rescued.

♦ **delivered price** *n.* quoted price that includes the cost of packing, insurance, and delivery to the destination given by the buyer.

delivery *n.* (*pl.* **-ies**) **1** delivering or being delivered. **2** regular distribution of letters etc. (*two deliveries a day*). **3** thing delivered. **4** childbirth. **5** deliverance. **6** style of throwing a ball, delivering a speech, etc. [Anglo-French: related to DELIVER]

♦ **delivery note** *n.* document, usu. made out in duplicate, that is given to the consignee of goods when they are delivered. The consignee, or a representative, signs one copy of the delivery note as evidence that the goods have been received. See also ADVICE NOTE.

♦ **delivery order** *n.* written document from the owner of goods to the holder of the goods (e.g. a warehouse company) instructing them to release the goods to the firm named on the delivery order or to the bearer (if made out to 'bearer'). A delivery order backed by a dock or warehouse warrant may be accepted by a bank as security for a loan.

dell *n.* small usu. wooded valley. [Old English]

♦ **Dellal** /dəˈlæl/, **Jack** (1923–) British businessman and financier, chairman of Allied Commercial Exporters Ltd., from which his salary in 1990 was £6.2 million. Dellal sold his merchant bank, Dalton Barton, in 1972 to Keyser Ullmann for £58 million. A well-known entrepreneur, he is currently seeking investments in E Europe.

delouse /diːˈlaʊs/ *v.* (**-sing**) rid of lice.

Delphic /ˈdelfɪk/ *adj.* (also **Delphian** /-fɪən/) **1** obscure, ambiguous, or enigmatic. **2** of the ancient Greek oracle at Delphi.

delphinium /delˈfɪnɪəm/ *n.* (*pl.* **-s**) garden plant with tall spikes of usu. blue flowers. [Greek: related to DOLPHIN]

♦ **Delphi technique** *n.* technique used in decision making in which written questionnaires replace committee discussions to eliminate the effects of personal relationships and domination of committees by strong personalities.

delta /ˈdeltə/ *n.* **1** triangular area of earth, alluvium etc. at the mouth of a river, formed by its diverging outlets. **2 a** fourth letter of the Greek alphabet (Δ, δ). **b** fourth-class mark for work etc. [Greek]

delta wing *n.* triangular swept-back wing of an aircraft.

delude /dɪˈluːd/ *v.* (**-ding**) deceive, mislead. [Latin *ludo* mock]

deluge /ˈdeljuːdʒ/ *–n.* **1** great flood. **2** (**the Deluge**) biblical Flood (Gen. 6–8). **3** overwhelming rush. **4** heavy fall of rain. *–v.* (**-ging**) flood or inundate (*deluged with complaints*). [Latin *diluvium*]

delusion /dɪˈluːʒ(ə)n/ *n.* **1** false belief, hope, etc. **2** hallucination. □ **delusive** *adj.* **delusory** *adj.* [related to DELUDE]

de luxe /də ˈlʌks/ *adj.* luxurious; superior; sumptuous. [French, = of luxury]

delve *v.* (**-ving**) **1** (often foll. by *in, into*) search or research energetically or deeply (*delved into his pocket, his family history*). **2** *poet.* dig. [Old English]

demagnetize /diːˈmægnɪˌtaɪz/ *v.* (also **-ise**) (**-zing** or **-sing**) remove the magnetic properties of. □ **demagnetization** /-ˈzeɪʃ(ə)n/ *n.*

demagogue /ˈdeməˌgɒg/ *n.* (*US* **-gog**) political agitator appealing to mob instincts. □ **demagogic** /-ˈgɒgɪk/ *adj.* **demagogy** *n.* [Greek, = leader of the people]

demand /dɪˈmɑːnd/ *–n.* **1** insistent and peremptory request. **2** *Econ.* **a** willingness and ability to purchase goods and services. **b** amount of a commodity that consumers are willing and able to purchase at a specified price. **3** urgent claim (*makes demands on her*). *–v.* **1** (often foll. by *of, from,* or *to* + infin., or *that* + clause) ask for insistently (*demanded to know*). **2** require (*task demanding skill*). **3** insist on being told (*demanded her age*). **4** (as **demanding** *adj.*) requiring skill, effort, attention, etc. (*demanding job; demanding child*). □ **in demand** sought after. **on demand** as soon as requested (*payable on demand*). [French from Latin: related to MANDATE]

♦ **demand curve** *n. Econ.* curve on a graph relating the quantity of a good demanded to its price. Economists usu. expect the demand curve to slope downwards, i.e. an increase in the price of a good brings a lower level of demand. Demand curves are useful in developing theories describing the way in which an economy behaves. See also DEMAND THEORY; PRICE THEORY; SUPPLY CURVE.

demand feeding *n.* feeding a baby when it cries.

♦ **demand for money** *n. Econ.* concept that has been the core of monetarism. If the existence of a stable demand for money is accepted, it can be shown that fiscal policy is neutral, i.e. when government expenditure pushes up interest rates private investment is reduced accordingly. Furthermore, changes in the supply of money are a necessary and sufficient condition for changes in the nominal value of the gross domestic product or for inflation. However, econometric evidence has failed to establish whether or not the demand for money is, in fact, stable.

♦ **demand function** *n. Econ.* function relating a good or service demanded to the preferences of an individual (see CONSUMER PREFERENCE). See also HICKSIAN DEMAND FUNCTION; MARSHALLIAN DEMAND FUNCTION.

♦ **demand management** *n. Econ.* use of economic policy instruments (see INSTRUMENT 5) by government to influence the level of aggregate demand. These instruments include government expenditure, tax cuts (see FISCAL POLICY), interest rates, and the money supply (see MONETARY POLICY). Demand management may consist of expanding aggregate demand when, e.g., unemployment is rising or inhibiting aggregate demand when there is inflation. Demand management is favoured by Keynesians, but became discredited to some extent during the 1970s when governments seemed unable to prevent prices and unemployment rising simultaneously (see STAGFLATION).

♦ **demand-pull inflation** *n. Econ.* rise in prices caused by an excess of demand over supply in the economy as a whole. When the labour force and all resources are fully employed extra demand will only disappear as a result of rising prices. Popular in the 1960s and 1970s as a Keynesian theory of inflation, the demand-pull theory appeared to be supported by the Phillips curve. This turned out not to be the case, however, and alternative, esp. monetarist, theories of inflation have since dominated. See also COST-PUSH INFLATION; QUANTITY THEORY OF MONEY.

♦ **demand theory** *n. Econ.* theory that concerns the relationship between the demand for goods and their prices; it forms the core of microeconomics (see also PRICE THEORY). By plotting the quantities that an individual would purchase at different prices, a demand curve can be drawn. Summing the demand curves of individuals will yield a market demand curve, while summing the demands for all goods will in turn give an aggregate demand curve for an economy. In this way, a macroeconomic model can be built up from microeconomic data.

demarcation /ˌdiːmɑːˈkeɪʃ(ə)n/ *n.* **1** marking of a boundary or limits. **2** trade-union practice of restricting a specific job to one union. □ **demarcate** /ˈdiː-/ *v.* (**-ting**). [Spanish *marcar* MARK[1]]

♦ **demarcation dispute** *n.* industrial dispute between trade unions or between members of the same union regarding the allocation of work between different types of tradespeople or workers. The **Demarcation Dispute Tribunal** set up by the TUC has effectively dealt with many of these disputes.

♦ **demarketing** *n.* process of discouraging consumers from either buying or consuming a particular product, e.g. cigarettes. It may also be used if a product is found to be faulty and the producers do not wish to risk their reputation by continuing to sell it.

dematerialize /ˌdiːməˈtɪərɪəˌlaɪz/ *v.* (also **-ise**) (**-zing** or **-sing**) make or become non-material; vanish. □ **dematerialization** /-ˈzeɪʃ(ə)n/ *n.*

demean /dɪ'miːn/ *v.* (usu. *refl.*) lower the dignity of (*would not demean myself*). [from MEAN[2]]

demeanour /dɪ'miːnə(r)/ *n.* (*US* **demeanor**) outward behaviour or bearing. [Latin *minor* threaten]

demented /dɪ'mentɪd/ *adj.* mad. □ **dementedly** *adv.* [Latin *mens* mind]

dementia /dɪ'menʃə/ *n.* chronic insanity. [Latin: related to DEMENTED]

dementia praecox /'priːkɒks/ *n. formal* schizophrenia.

demerara /ˌdemə'reərə/ *n.* light-brown cane sugar. [*Demerara* in Guyana]

demerger /diː'mɜːdʒə(r)/ *n.* dissolution of a commercial merger. □ **demerge** *v.* (**-ging**).

demerit /diː'merɪt/ *n.* fault; blemish.

demesne /dɪ'miːn, -'meɪn/ *n.* **1 a** territory; domain. **b** land attached to a mansion etc. **c** landed property. **2** (usu. foll. by *of*) region or sphere. **3** *Law hist.* possession (of real property) as one's own. [Latin *dominicus* from *dominus* lord]

demi- *prefix* half; partly. [Latin *dimidius* half]

demigod /'demɪˌgɒd/ *n.* **1 a** partly divine being. **b** child of a god or goddess and a mortal. **2** *colloq.* godlike person.

demijohn /'demɪˌdʒɒn/ *n.* large bottle usu. in a wicker cover. [French]

demilitarize /diː'mɪlɪtəˌraɪz/ *v.* (also **-ise**) (**-zing** or **-sing**) remove an army etc. from (a frontier, zone, etc.). □ **demilitarization** /-'zeɪʃ(ə)n/ *n.*

demi-monde /'demɪˌmɒnd/ *n.* **1** class of women considered to be of doubtful morality. **2** any semi-respectable group. [French, = half-world]

demise /dɪ'maɪz/ *–n.* **1** death; termination. **2** *Law* transfer of an estate, title, etc. by demising. *–v.* (**-sing**) *Law* transfer (an estate, title, etc.) by will, lease, or death. [Anglo-French: related to DISMISS]

♦ **demise charter** *n.* = BAREBOAT CHARTER.

---

demisemiquaver /ˌdemɪ'semɪˌkweɪvə(r)/ *n. Mus.* note equal to half a semiquaver.

demist /diː'mɪst/ *v.* clear mist from (a windscreen etc.). □ **demister** *n.*

demo /'deməʊ/ *n.* (*pl.* **-s**) *colloq.* = DEMONSTRATION 2, 3. [abbreviation]

demob /diː'mɒb/ *colloq. –v.* (**-bb-**) demobilize. *–n.* demobilization. [abbreviation]

demobilize /diː'məʊbɪˌlaɪz/ *v.* (also **-ise**) (**-zing** or **-sing**) disband (troops, ships, etc.). □ **demobilization** /-'zeɪʃ(ə)n/ *n.*

democracy /dɪ'mɒkrəsɪ/ *n.* (*pl.* **-ies**) **1 a** government by the whole population, usu. through elected representatives. **b** state so governed. **2** classless and tolerant society. [Greek *dēmokratia* rule of the people]

democrat /'deməˌkræt/ *n.* **1** advocate of democracy. **2** (**Democrat**) (in the US) member of the Democratic Party.

democratic /ˌdemə'krætɪk/ *adj.* **1** of, like, practising, or being a democracy. **2** favouring social equality. □ **democratically** *adv.*

Democratic Party *n.* more liberal of the two main US political parties.

democratize /dɪ'mɒkrəˌtaɪz/ *v.* (also **-ise**) (**-zing** or **-sing**) make democratic. □ **democratization** /-'zeɪʃ(ə)n/ *n.*

demodulate /diː'mɒdjʊˌleɪt/ *v.* (**-ting**) extract (a modulating signal) from its carrier. □ **demodulation** /ˌdiːmɒdjʊ'leɪʃ(ə)n/ *n.* **demodulator** *n.*

demography /dɪ'mɒgrəfɪ/ *n.* the study of the statistics of births, deaths, population size and composition (by age, sex, occupation, etc.), disease, etc. □ **demographic** /ˌdemə'græfɪk/ *adj.* **demographically** /ˌdemə'græfɪkəlɪ/ *adv.* [Greek *dēmos* the people, -GRAPHY]

demolish /dɪ'mɒlɪʃ/ *v.* **1 a** pull down (a building). **b** destroy. **2** overthrow (an institution). **3** refute (an argument, theory, etc.). **4** *joc.* eat up voraciously. □ **demolition** /ˌdemə'lɪʃ(ə)n/ *n.* [Latin *moles* mass]

demon /'diːmən/ *n.* **1 a** evil spirit or devil. **b** personification of evil passion. **2** (often *attrib.*) forceful or skilful performer (*demon player*). **3** cruel person. **4** (also **daemon**) supernatural being in ancient Greece. □ **demonic** /dɪ'mɒnɪk/ *adj.* [Greek *daimōn* deity]

demonetize /diː'mʌnɪˌtaɪz/ *v.* (also **-ise**) (**-zing** or **-sing**) withdraw (a coin etc.) from use. □ **demonetization** /-'zeɪʃ(ə)n/ *n.* [French: related to DE-, MONEY]

demoniac /dɪ'məʊnɪˌæk/ *–adj.* **1** fiercely energetic or frenzied. **2** supposedly possessed by an evil spirit. **3** of or like demons. *–n.* demoniac person. □ **demoniacal** /ˌdiːmə'naɪək(ə)l/ *adj.* **demoniacally** /ˌdiːmə'naɪəkəlɪ/ *adv.* [Church Latin: related to DEMON]

demonism /'diːməˌnɪz(ə)m/ *n.* belief in demons.

demonolatry /ˌdiːmə'nɒlətrɪ/ *n.* worship of demons. [from DEMON, Greek *latreuō* worship]

demonology /ˌdiːmə'nɒlədʒɪ/ *n.* the study of demons etc.

demonstrable /'demɒnstrəb(ə)l, dɪ'mɒnstrəb(ə)l/ *adj.* able to be shown or proved. □ **demonstrably** *adv.*

demonstrate /'demənˌstreɪt/ *v.* (**-ting**) **1** show (feelings etc.). **2** describe and explain by experiment, practical use, etc. **3** logically prove or be proof of the truth or existence of. **4** take part in a public demonstration. **5** act as a demonstrator. [Latin *monstro* show]

demonstration /ˌdemən'streɪʃ(ə)n/ *n.* **1** (foll. by *of*) show of feeling etc. **2** (esp. political) public meeting, march, etc. **3** the exhibiting etc. of specimens or experiments in esp. scientific teaching. **4** proof by logic, argument, etc. **5** *Mil.* display of military force.

demonstrative /dɪ'mɒnstrətɪv/ *adj.* **1** showing feelings readily; affectionate. **2** (usu. foll. by *of*) logically conclusive; giving proof (*demonstrative of their skill*). **3** *Gram.* (of an adjective or pronoun) indicating the person or thing referred to (e.g. *this*, *that*, *those*). □ **demonstratively** *adv.* **demonstrativeness** *n.*

demonstrator *n.* **1** person who demonstrates politically. **2** person who demonstrates machines etc. to prospective customers. **3** person who teaches by esp. scientific demonstration.

demoralize /dɪ'mɒrəˌlaɪz/ *v.* (also **-ise**) (**-zing** or **-sing**) destroy the morale of; dishearten. □ **demoralization** /-'zeɪʃ(ə)n/ *n.* [French]

demote /dɪ'məʊt/ *v.* (**-ting**) reduce to a lower rank or class. □ **demotion** /-'məʊʃ(ə)n/ *n.* [from DE-, PROMOTE]

demotic /dɪ'mɒtɪk/ *–n.* **1** colloquial form of a language. **2** simplified form of ancient Egyptian writing (cf. HIERATIC). *–adj.* **1** (esp. of language) colloquial or vulgar. **2** of ancient Egyptian or modern Greek demotic. [Greek *dēmos* the people]

demotivate /ˌdiː'məʊtɪˌveɪt/ *v.* (**-ting**) (also *absol.*) cause to lose motivation or incentive. □ **demotivation** /-'veɪʃ(ə)n/ *n.*

demountable disk *n.* = EXCHANGEABLE DISK STORE.

demur /dɪ'mɜː(r)/ *–v.* (**-rr-**) **1** (often foll. by *to*, *at*) raise objections. **2** *Law* put in a demurrer. *–n.* (usu. in *neg.*) objection; objecting (*agreed without demur*). [Latin *moror* delay]

demure /dɪ'mjʊə(r)/ *adj.* (**demurer, demurest**) **1** quiet, reserved; modest. **2** coy. □ **demurely** *adv.* **demureness** *n.* [French: related to DEMUR]

♦ **demurrage** /dɪ'mʌrɪdʒ/ *n.* **1** liquidated damages payable under a charter-party at a specified daily rate for any days (**demurrage days**) required for completing the loading or discharging of cargo after the lay days have expired. **2** unliquidated damages to which a shipowner is entitled if, when no lay days are specified, the ship is detained for loading or unloading beyond a reasonable time. **3** liquidated damages included in any contract to compensate one party if the other is late in fulfilling his or her obligations. This occurs frequently in building contracts. Even if the loss caused by the delay is less than the demurrage, the demurrage must be paid in full.

---

demurrer /dɪˈmʌrə(r)/ *n. Law* objection raised or exception taken.

demystify /diːˈmɪstɪˌfaɪ/ *v.* (**-ies**, **-ied**) remove the mystery from; clarify. □ **demystification** /-fɪˈkeɪʃ(ə)n/ *n.*

Den. *abbr.* Denmark.

den *n.* **1** wild animal's lair. **2** place of crime or vice (*opium den*). **3** small private room. [Old English]

denar /ˈdiːnɑː(r)/ *n.* standard monetary unit of the Former Yugoslav Republic of Macedonia.

denarius /dɪˈneərɪəs/ *n.* (*pl.* **denarii** /-rɪˌaɪ/) ancient Roman silver coin. [Latin *deni* by tens]

denary /ˈdiːnərɪ/ *adj.* of ten; decimal.

denationalize /diːˈnæʃənəˌlaɪz/ *v.* (also **-ise**) (**-zing** or **-sing**) transfer (an industry etc.) from public to private ownership; privatize. □ **denationalization** /-ˈzeɪʃ(ə)n/ *n.*

denature /diːˈneɪtʃə(r)/ *v.* (**-ring**) **1** change the properties of (a protein etc.) by heat, acidity, etc. **2** make (alcohol) undrinkable. [French]

dendrochronology /ˌdendrəʊkrəˈnɒlədʒɪ/ *n.* **1** dating of trees by their annual growth rings. **2** the study of these. [Greek *dendron* tree]

dendrology /denˈdrɒlədʒɪ/ *n.* the study of trees. □ **dendrological** /-drəˈlɒdʒɪk(ə)l/ *adj.* **dendrologist** *n.* [Greek *dendron* tree]

dene *n.* (also **dean**) narrow wooded valley. [Old English]

dengue /ˈdeŋgɪ/ *n.* infectious tropical viral fever. [West Indian Spanish from Swahili]

Den Haag see the HAGUE.

deniable /dɪˈnaɪəb(ə)l/ *adj.* that may be denied.

denial /dɪˈnaɪəl/ *n.* **1** denying the truth or existence of a thing. **2** refusal of a request or wish. **3** disavowal of a leader etc.

denier /ˈdenjə(r)/ *n.* unit of weight measuring the fineness of silk, nylon, etc. [originally the name of a small coin, from Latin DENARIUS]

denigrate /ˈdenɪˌgreɪt/ *v.* (**-ting**) blacken the reputation of. □ **denigration** /-ˈgreɪʃ(ə)n/ *n.* **denigrator** *n.* **denigratory** /-ˈgreɪtərɪ/ *adj.* [Latin *niger* black]

denim /ˈdenɪm/ *n.* **1** (often *attrib.*) hard-wearing usu. blue cotton twill used for jeans, overalls, etc. **2** (in *pl.*) *colloq.* jeans etc. made of this. [French *de* of, *Nîmes* in France]

denizen /ˈdenɪz(ə)n/ *n.* **1** (usu. foll. by *of*) inhabitant or occupant. **2** foreigner having certain rights in an adopted country. **3** naturalized foreign word, animal, or plant. [Latin *de intus* from within]

denominate /dɪˈnɒmɪˌneɪt/ *v.* (**-ting**) give a name to, call, describe as. [Latin: related to NOMINATE]

denomination /dɪˌnɒmɪˈneɪʃ(ə)n/ *n.* **1** Church or religious sect. **2** class of measurement or money. **3** name, esp. a characteristic or class name. □ **denominational** *adj.* [Latin: related to DENOMINATE]

denominator /dɪˈnɒmɪˌneɪtə(r)/ *n.* number below the line in a vulgar fraction; divisor. [Latin *nomen* name]

denote /dɪˈnəʊt/ *v.* (**-ting**) **1** (often foll. by *that*) be a sign of; indicate; mean. **2** stand as a name for; signify. □ **denotation** /ˌdiːnəˈteɪʃ(ə)n/ *n.* [Latin: related to NOTE]

denouement /deɪˈnuːmɑ̃/ *n.* (also **dénouement**) **1** final unravelling of a plot or complicated situation. **2** final scene in a play, novel, etc. [French, from Latin *nodus* knot]

denounce /dɪˈnaʊns/ *v.* (**-cing**) **1** accuse publicly; condemn. **2** inform against. **3** announce withdrawal from (an armistice, treaty, etc.). □ **denouncement** *n.* [Latin *nuntius* messenger]

de novo /diː ˈnəʊvəʊ/ *adv.* starting again; anew. [Latin]

Denpasar /denˈpɑːsɑː(r)/ city in Indonesia, the chief city and seaport of the island of Bali; pop. (1990) 261 263.

dense *adj.* **1** closely compacted; crowded together; thick. **2** *colloq.* stupid. □ **densely** *adv.* **denseness** *n.* [Latin *densus*]

density *n.* (*pl.* **-ies**) **1** compactness of a substance. **2** *Physics* degree of consistency measured by the quantity of mass per unit volume. **3** opacity of a photographic image. **4** *Computing* amount of data that can be stored per unit length or per unit area of a computer disk, tape, etc.

dent –*n.* **1** slight hollow as made by a blow or pressure. **2** noticeable adverse effect (*dent in our funds*). –*v.* **1** mark with a dent. **2** adversely affect. [from INDENT]

dental /ˈdent(ə)l/ *adj.* **1** of the teeth or dentistry. **2** (of a consonant) produced with the tongue-tip against the upper front teeth (as *th*) or the ridge of the teeth (as *n*, *s*, *t*). [Latin *dens dent-* tooth]

dental floss *n.* thread used to clean between the teeth.

dental surgeon *n.* dentist.

dentate /ˈdenteɪt/ *adj. Bot.* & *Zool.* toothed; with toothlike notches.

dentifrice /ˈdentɪfrɪs/ *n.* toothpaste or tooth powder. [Latin: related to DENTAL, *frico* rub]

dentine /ˈdentiːn/ *n.* (*US* **dentin** /-tɪn/) hard dense tissue forming the bulk of a tooth.

dentist /ˈdentɪst/ *n.* person qualified to treat, extract, etc., teeth. □ **dentistry** *n.*

dentition /denˈtɪʃ(ə)n/ *n.* **1** type, number, and arrangement of teeth in a species etc. **2** teething.

denture /ˈdentʃə(r)/ *n.* removable artificial tooth or teeth.

denuclearize /diːˈnjuːklɪəˌraɪz/ *v.* (also **-ise**) (**-zing** or **-sing**) remove nuclear weapons from (a country etc.). □ **denuclearization** /-ˈzeɪʃ(ə)n/ *n.*

denude /dɪˈnjuːd/ *v.* (**-ding**) **1** make naked or bare. **2** (foll. by *of*) strip of (covering, property, etc.). □ **denudation** /ˌdiːnjuːˈdeɪʃ(ə)n/ *n.* [Latin *nudus* naked]

denunciation /dɪˌnʌnsɪˈeɪʃ(ə)n/ *n.* denouncing; public condemnation. [Latin: related to DENOUNCE]

Denmark /ˈdenmɑːk/, **Kingdom of** Scandinavian country consisting of the greater part of the Jutland peninsula and neighbouring islands, between the North Sea and the Baltic, together with Greenland and the Faeroe Islands. Industry has expanded since the Second World War, including manufacturing, engineering, brewing, and food processing; manufactures for export include furniture, machinery, chemicals, textiles, metal goods, glass, and porcelain. Agriculture and fishing remain important, exports including meat and meat products, dairy produce, cereals, and fish, but are likely to be adversely affected by EC reforms. In a referendum in 1993 Denmark voted to accept the Maastricht treaty, amended to exempt the country from adopting a common European currency, citizenship, and defence policy.

History. Denmark emerged as a separate country during the Viking period of the 10th and 11th centuries; it attained its present form in 1920. Its present constitution was established in 1953, instituting a single-chamber parliament elected by proportional representation, and executive power vested in the monarch, acting through the ministers. Head of state, Queen Margrethe II; prime minister, Poul Nyrup Rasmussen; capital, Copenhagen.

language	Danish
currency	krone (Dkr) of 100 øre
pop. (1996)	5 244 000
GNP (1994)	US$145B
literacy	99%
life expectancy	72 (m); 78 (f)

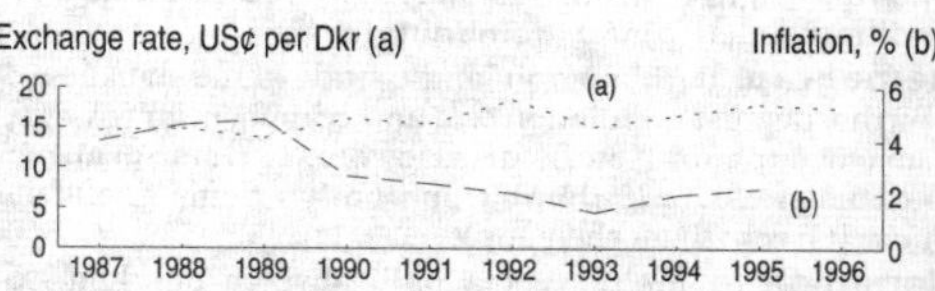

Denver /ˈdenvə(r)/ city in the US, capital of Colorado; pop. (est. 1994) 493 559. The industrial and commercial centre for a large agricultural area, it is also the site of a US mint.

deny /dɪˈnaɪ/ *v.* (**-ies, -ied**) **1** declare untrue or non-existent. **2** repudiate or disclaim. **3** (often foll. by *to*) withhold (a thing) from (*denied him the satisfaction*; *denied it to me*). □ **deny oneself** be abstinent. [Latin: related to NEGATE]

deodar /ˈdiːəˌdɑː(r)/ *n.* Himalayan cedar. [Sanskrit, = divine tree]

deodorant /diːˈəʊdərənt/ *n.* (often *attrib.*) substance applied to the body or sprayed into the air to conceal smells. [related to ODOUR]

deodorize /diːˈəʊdəˌraɪz/ *v.* (also **-ise**) (**-zing** or **-sing**) remove or destroy the smell of. □ **deodorization** /-ˈzeɪʃ(ə)n/ *n.*

deoxyribonucleic acid /ˌdiːɒksɪˌraɪbəʊnjʊˈkleɪɪk/ see DNA. [from DE-, OXYGEN, RIBONUCLEIC]

dep. *abbr.* **1** departs. **2** deposit. **3** depositor. **4** deputy.

depart /dɪˈpɑːt/ *v.* **1 a** (often foll. by *from*) go away; leave. **b** (usu. foll. by *for*) start; set out. **2** (usu. foll. by *from*) deviate (*departs from good taste*). **3** esp. *formal* or *literary* leave by death; die (*departed this life*). [Latin *dispertio* divide]

departed *–adj.* bygone. *–n.* (prec. by *the*) *euphem.* dead person or people.

department *n.* **1** separate part of a complex whole, esp.: **a** a branch of administration (*Housing Department*). **b** a division of a school, college, etc., by subject (*physics department*). **c** a section of a large store (*hardware department*). **2** *colloq.* area of special expertise. **3** administrative district, esp. in France. [French: related to DEPART]

departmental /ˌdiːpɑːtˈment(ə)l/ *adj.* of a department. □ **departmentally** *adv.*

♦ **Department of Education and Employment** *n.* UK government department formed in 1995 from the former Department of Education and the former Department of Employment. It is responsible for all education services, the labour market, helping the unemployed find work, encouraging training in industry, and assisting small firms.

♦ **Department of Trade and Industry** *n.* (also **DTI**) UK government department responsible for: international trade policy; the promotion of exports (under the direction of the British Overseas Trade Board); industrial policy; competition policy and consumer protection, including relations with the Office of Fair Trading and the Monopolies and Mergers Commission; policy in relation to all forms of energy; policy on scientific research and development; company legislation and the Companies Registration Office; patents and the Patent Office; the insolvency service; and the regulation of the insurance industry.

---

department store *n.* large shop with many departments.

departure /dɪˈpɑːtʃə(r)/ *n.* **1** departing. **2** (often foll. by *from*) deviation (from the truth, a standard, etc.). **3** (often *attrib.*) departing of a train, aircraft, etc. (*departure lounge*). **4** new course of action or thought (*driving is rather a departure for him*).

depend /dɪˈpend/ *v.* **1** (often foll. by *on, upon*) be controlled or determined by (*it depends on luck*). **2** (foll. by *on, upon*) **a** need (*depends on his car*). **b** rely on (*I'm depending on good weather*). [Latin *pendeo* hang]

dependable *adj.* reliable. □ **dependability** /-ˈbɪlɪtɪ/ *n.* **dependableness** *n.* **dependably** *adv.*

dependant *n.* (*US* **dependent**) person supported, esp. financially, by another. [French: related to DEPEND]

dependence *n.* **1** depending or being dependent, esp. financially. **2** reliance; trust.

dependency *n.* (*pl.* **-ies**) country or province controlled by another.

dependent *–adj.* **1** (usu. foll. by *on, upon*) depending, conditional. **2** unable to do without (esp. a drug). **3** maintained at another's cost. **4** (of a clause etc.) subordinate to a sentence or word. *–n. US* var. of DEPENDANT.

depict /dɪˈpɪkt/ *v.* **1** represent in drawing or painting etc. **2** portray in words; describe. □ **depicter** *n.* (also **-tor**). **depiction** *n.* [Latin: related to PICTURE]

depilate /ˈdepɪˌleɪt/ *v.* (**-ting**) remove hair from. □ **depilation** /-ˈleɪʃ(ə)n/ *n.* [Latin *pilus* hair]

depilatory /dɪˈpɪlətərɪ/ *–adj.* removing unwanted hair. *–n.* (*pl.* **-ies**) depilatory substance.

deplete /dɪˈpliːt/ *v.* (**-ting**) (esp. in *passive*) reduce in numbers, force, or quantity; exhaust. □ **depletion** *n.* [Latin *pleo* fill]

deplorable /dɪˈplɔːrəb(ə)l/ *adj.* exceedingly bad. □ **deplorably** *adv.*

deplore /dɪˈplɔː(r)/ *v.* (**-ring**) **1** regret deeply. **2** find exceedingly bad. [Latin *ploro* wail]

deploy /dɪˈplɔɪ/ *v.* **1** spread out (troops) into a line ready for action. **2** use (arguments, forces, etc.) effectively. □ **deployment** *n.* [Latin *plico* fold]

depoliticize /ˌdiːpəˈlɪtɪˌsaɪz/ *v.* (also **-ise**) (**-zing** or **-sing**) make non-political. □ **depoliticization** /-ˈzeɪʃ(ə)n/ *n.*

deponent /dɪˈpəʊnənt/ *–adj.* (of esp. a Latin or Greek verb) passive in form but active in meaning. *–n.* **1** deponent verb. **2** person making deposition under oath. [Latin *depono* put down, lay aside]

depopulate /diːˈpɒpjʊˌleɪt/ *v.* (**-ting**) reduce the population of. □ **depopulation** /-ˈleɪʃ(ə)n/ *n.*

deport /dɪˈpɔːt/ *v.* **1** remove forcibly or exile to another country; banish. **2** *refl.* behave (in a specified manner) (*deported himself well*). □ **deportation** /ˌdiːpɔːˈteɪʃ(ə)n/ *n.* (in sense 1). [Latin *porto* carry]

deportee /ˌdiːpɔːˈtiː/ *n.* deported person.

deportment /dɪˈpɔːtmənt/ *n.* bearing, demeanour. [French: related to DEPORT]

depose /dɪˈpəʊz/ *v.* (**-sing**) **1** remove from office, esp. dethrone. **2** *Law* (usu. foll. by *to*, or *that* + clause) testify, esp. on oath. [French from Latin: related to DEPOSIT]

deposit /dɪˈpɒzɪt/ *–n.* **1 a** money left with an organization, e.g. a bank, for safe keeping or to earn interest or with a broker, dealer, etc., as a security to cover any trading losses incurred. **b** anything stored for safe keeping. **2 a** payment made as a pledge for a contract or as an initial part payment for a thing bought. See also HIRE PURCHASE. **b** returnable sum paid on the hire of an item etc. **3 a** natural layer of sand, rock, coal, etc. **b** layer of accumulated matter on a surface. *–v.* (**-t-**) **1 a** put or lay down (*deposited the book on the shelf*). **b** (of water etc.) leave (matter etc.) lying. **2 a** store or entrust for keeping. **b** pay (a sum of money) into a bank account. **3** pay (a sum) as part of a larger sum or as a pledge for a contract. [Latin *pono posit-* put]

♦ **deposit account** *n.* bank account that pays interest but is not usu. immediately accessible (cf. CHEQUE ACCOUNT). The interest paid will depend on the current rate of interest and the notice required by the bank before money can be withdrawn, but it will always be higher than that on a current account.

---

depositary *n.* (*pl.* **-ies**) person to whom a thing is entrusted. [Latin: related to DEPOSIT]

♦ **deposit bonds** *n.pl.* (in full **National Savings Deposit Bonds**) bonds introduced by the Department for National Savings in 1983 and withdrawn from sale in 1989, offering a premium rate of interest on lump sums between £100 and £100,000. They will continue to earn interest until the tenth anniversary of their purchase; interest is taxable, but not deducted at source.

---

deposition /ˌdepəˈzɪʃ(ə)n/ *n.* **1** deposing, esp. dethronement. **2** sworn evidence; giving of this. **3** (**the Deposition**) taking down of Christ from the Cross. **4** depositing or being deposited. [Latin: related to DEPOSIT]

depositor *n.* person who deposits money, property, etc.

depository *n.* (*pl.* **-ies**) **1 a** storehouse. **b** store (of wisdom, knowledge, etc.). **2** = DEPOSITARY. [Latin: related to DEPOSIT]

depot /ˈdepəʊ/ *n.* **1 a** storehouse, esp. for military supplies. **b** headquarters of a regiment. **2 a** place where vehicles, e.g. buses, are kept. **b** *US* railway or bus station. [French: related to DEPOSIT]

deprave /dɪˈpreɪv/ *v.* (**-ving**) corrupt, esp. morally. [Latin *pravus* crooked]

depravity /dɪˈprævɪtɪ/ *n.* (*pl.* **-ies**) moral corruption; wickedness.

deprecate /ˈdeprɪˌkeɪt/ *v.* (**-ting**) express disapproval of; deplore. □ **deprecation** /-ˈkeɪʃ(ə)n/ *n.* **deprecatory** /-ˈkeɪtərɪ/ *adj.* [Latin: related to PRAY]

■ **Usage** *Deprecate* is often confused with *depreciate*.

depreciate /dɪˈpriːʃɪˌeɪt/ *v.* (**-ting**) **1** diminish in value. **2** belittle. □ **depreciatory** /dɪˈpriːʃɪətərɪ/ *adj.* [Latin: related to PRICE]

■ **Usage** *Depreciate* is often confused with *deprecate*.

◆ **depreciation** /dɪˌpriːʃɪˈeɪʃ(ə)n/ *n.* **1 a** decline in value, esp. due to wear and tear. **b** allowance made for this. **2** amount charged to the profit and loss account of an organization to represent the wearing out or diminution in value of an asset. The amount charged is normally based on a percentage of the value of the asset as shown in the books; however, the way in which the percentage is used reflects different views of depreciation. **Straight-line depreciation** allocates a given percentage of the cost of the asset each year, thus suggesting an even spread of the cost of the asset over its useful life. **Reducing-balance depreciation** applies a constant percentage reduction first to the cost of the asset and subsequently to the cost as reduced by previous depreciations. In this way reducing amounts are charged periodically to the profit and loss account; by this method the depreciated value of the asset in the balance sheet may approximate more nearly to its true value, in that many assets depreciate more quickly early and more slowly later in their life. See also ACCUMULATED DEPRECIATION. **3** fall in the value of a currency with a floating exchange rate relative to another. Depreciation can refer both to day-to-day movements and to long-term realignments in value. For currencies with a fixed exchange rate a devaluation or revaluation of currency is required to change the relative value. Cf. APPRECIATION 4. **4** belittlement.

---

depredation /ˌdeprɪˈdeɪʃ(ə)n/ *n.* (usu. in *pl.*) despoiling, ravaging. [Latin: related to PREY]

depress /dɪˈpres/ *v.* **1** make dispirited or sad. **2** push down; lower. **3** reduce the activity of (esp. trade). **4** (as **depressed** *adj.*) **a** miserable. **b** suffering from depression. □ **depressing** *adj.* **depressingly** *adv.* [Latin: related to PRESS[1]]

depressant *–adj.* reducing activity, esp. of a body function. *–n.* depressant substance.

depressed area *n.* area of economic depression.

depression /dɪˈpreʃ(ə)n/ *n.* **1** extreme melancholy, often with a reduction in vitality and physical symptoms. **2** *Econ.* extended or severe period of recession; slump. Depressions occur infrequently and possibly in cycles (see KONDRATIEFF WAVES): the most recent occurred in the 1930s; prior to that they occurred in the periods 1873–96, 1844–51, and 1810–7. Depressions are usu. associated with falling prices (see DEFLATION 2) and large-scale involuntary unemployment. They are often preceded by major financial crashes, e.g. the Wall Street crash of 1929. Keynes advocated fiscal reflation to resolve depressions by raising employment. Monetarists have claimed that excessively restrictive monetary policy causes depressions and that monetary expansion will alleviate them. **3** lowering of atmospheric pressure; winds etc. caused by this. **4** hollow on a surface. **5** pressing down.

depressive *–adj.* **1** tending to depress (*depressive drug, influence*). **2** of or tending towards depression (*depressive illness; depressive father*). *–n.* person suffering from depression.

deprivation /ˌdeprɪˈveɪʃ(ə)n/ *n.* depriving or being deprived (*suffered many deprivations*).

deprive /dɪˈpraɪv/ *v.* (**-ving**) **1** (usu. foll. by *of*) prevent from having or enjoying. **2** (as **deprived** *adj.*) lacking what is needed for well-being; underprivileged. □ **deprival** *n.* [Latin: related to PRIVATION]

Dept. *abbr.* Department.

depth *n.* **1 a** deepness. **b** measurement from the top down, from the surface inwards, or from front to back. **2** difficulty; abstruseness. **3 a** wisdom. **b** intensity of emotion etc. **4** intensity of colour, darkness, etc. **5** (usu. in *pl.*) **a** deep water or place; abyss. **b** low, depressed state. **c** lowest, central, or inmost part (*depths of the country; depth of winter*). □ **in depth** thoroughly. **out of one's depth 1** in water over one's head. **2** engaged in a task etc. too difficult for one. [related to DEEP]

depth-charge *n.* bomb exploding under water.

◆ **depth interview** *n.* unstructured interview that explores a marketing issue for purposes of marketing research. The interviewer, a specialist acting on behalf of a client, will have previously compiled a topic guide that identifies the points to be explored; the respondent is part of a sample chosen to match certain criteria (e.g. if the problem concerned tea all respondents would be tea drinkers). The interview is conducted informally and the interviewer adopts a passive role, encouraging the respondent to talk and ask questions, while ensuring that all the points on the topic guide are covered. After a minimum of ten such interviews, the interviewer reports back to the client with marketing recommendations. See also QUALITATIVE MARKETING RESEARCH.

---

deputation /ˌdepjʊˈteɪʃ(ə)n/ *n.* delegation. [Latin: related to DEPUTE]

depute /dɪˈpjuːt/ *v.* (**-ting**) (often foll. by *to*) **1** delegate (a task, authority, etc.). **2** authorize as representative. [Latin *puto* think]

deputize /ˈdepjʊˌtaɪz/ *v.* (also **-ise**) (**-zing** or **-sing**) (usu. foll. by *for*) act as deputy.

deputy /ˈdepjʊtɪ/ *n.* (*pl.* **-ies**) **1** person appointed to act for another (also *attrib.*: *deputy manager*). **2** parliamentary representative in some countries. [var. of DEPUTE]

derail /diːˈreɪl/ *v.* (usu. in *passive*) cause (a train etc.) to leave the rails. □ **derailment** *n.* [French: related to RAIL[1]]

derange /dɪˈreɪndʒ/ *v.* (**-ging**) **1** make insane. **2** disorder, disturb. □ **derangement** *n.* [French: related to RANK[1]]

Derbent /dəˈbent/ city in S Russia, in Dagestan, on the Caspian Sea; pop. (1987) 84 000.

Derby[1] /ˈdɑːbɪ/ industrial city in central England, in Derbyshire; manufactures include Rolls Royce aero engines, rail locomotives, and engineering equipment; pop. (est. 1994) 230 500.

Derby[2] /ˈdɑːbɪ/ *n.* (*pl.* **-ies**) **1 a** annual flat horse-race at Epsom. **b** similar race elsewhere. **2** important sporting contest. **3** (**derby**) *US* bowler hat. [Earl of *Derby*]

Derby. *abbr.* Derbyshire.

Derbyshire /ˈdɑːbɪʃɪə(r)/ county in N central England; pop. (est. 1994) 954 100; county town, Matlock. The coal, iron, and steel industries have declined, but sheep and dairy farming remain important.

derecognize /diːˈrekəgˌnaɪz/ *v.* (also **-ise**) (**-zing** or **-sing**) cease to recognize the status of (esp. a trade union). □ **derecognition** /-ˈnɪʃ(ə)n/ *n.*

deregulate /diːˈregjʊˌleɪt/ *v.* (**-ting**) remove regulations or controls from (esp. a market). Many economists and politicians believe that during this century governments have imposed controls over markets that have little or no justification in economic theory; some have even been economically harmful. For example, in the postwar era, as a result of the Bretton Woods agreements, many governments imposed controls on the flow of capital between countries. In the belief that this was harmful to economic growth, many governments have recently eliminated these restrictions. However, most economists still argue that certain markets should be regulated, esp. if a monopoly is involved. □ **deregulation** /-ˈleɪʃ(ə)n/ *n.*

derelict /'derəlɪkt/ *–adj.* **1** (esp. of a property) dilapidated. **2** abandoned, ownerless. *–n.* **1** vagrant. **2** abandoned property. [Latin: related to RELINQUISH]

dereliction /ˌderə'lɪkʃ(ə)n/ *n.* **1** (usu. foll. by *of*) neglect; failure to carry out obligations. **2** abandoning or being abandoned.

derestrict /ˌdiːrɪ'strɪkt/ *v.* remove restrictions (esp. speed limits) from. □ **derestriction** *n.*

deride /dɪ'raɪd/ *v.* (**-ding**) mock. □ **derision** /-'rɪʒ(ə)n/ *n.* [Latin *rideo* laugh]

de rigueur /də rɪ'gɜː(r)/ *predic. adj.* required by fashion or etiquette (*drugs were de rigueur*). [French]

derisive /dɪ'raɪsɪv/ *adj.* = DERISORY. □ **derisively** *adv.* [from DERIDE]

derisory /dɪ'raɪsərɪ/ *adj.* **1** scoffing, ironical (*derisory cheers*). **2** ridiculously small (*derisory offer*).

derivation /ˌderɪ'veɪʃ(ə)n/ *n.* **1** deriving or being derived. **2 a** formation of a word from another or from a root. **b** tracing of the origin of a word. **c** statement of this.

derivative /dɪ'rɪvətɪv/ *–adj.* derived; not original (*his music is derivative*). *–n.* **1** derived word or thing. **2** *Math.* quantity measuring the rate of change of another. **3** *Finance* financial instrument valued according to the expected price movements of an underlying asset, e.g. a commodity, currency, etc.

♦ **derivative action** *n.* legal action brought by a shareholder on behalf of a company, when the company cannot itself decide to sue. A company will usu. sue in its own name but if those against whom it has a cause of action are in control of the company (i.e. directors or majority shareholders) a shareholder may bring a derivative action. The company will appear as defendant so that it will be bound by, and able to benefit from, the decision. The need to bring such an action must be proved to the court before it can proceed.

♦ **derivative market** *n.* futures or options market derived from a cash market. For example, the traded options market on LIFFE is a derivative market of the London Stock Exchange.

---

derive /dɪ'raɪv/ *v.* (**-ving**) **1** (usu. foll. by *from*) get or trace from a source (*derived satisfaction from work*). **2** (foll. by *from*) arise from, originate in (*happiness derives from many things*). **3** (usu. foll. by *from*) show or state the origin or formation of (a word etc.). [Latin *rivus* stream]

dermatitis /ˌdɜːmə'taɪtɪs/ *n.* inflammation of the skin. [Greek *derma* skin, -ITIS]

dermatology /ˌdɜːmə'tɒlədʒɪ/ *n.* the study of skin diseases. □ **dermatological** /-tə'lɒdʒɪk(ə)l/ *adj.* **dermatologist** *n.* [from DERMATITIS, -LOGY]

dermis /'dɜːmɪs/ *n.* **1** (in general use) the skin. **2** layer of living tissue below the epidermis. [from EPIDERMIS]

derogate /'derəˌgeɪt/ *v.* (**-ting**) (foll. by *from*) *formal* detract from (merit, right, etc.). □ **derogation** /-'geɪʃ(ə)n/ *n.* [Latin *rogo* ask]

derogatory /dɪ'rɒgətərɪ/ *adj.* disparaging; insulting (*derogatory remark*). □ **derogatorily** *adv.*

derrick /'derɪk/ *n.* **1** crane for heavy weights, with a movable pivoted arm. **2** framework over an oil well etc., holding the drilling machinery. [*Derrick*, name of a hangman]

derring-do /ˌderɪŋ'duː/ *n. literary joc.* heroic courage or actions. [*daring to do*]

derris /'derɪs/ *n.* **1** tropical climbing plant. **2** insecticide made from its root. [Latin from Greek]

Derry /'derɪ/ **1** district of Northern Ireland, in Co. Londonderry; pop. (1990) 100 500. **2** see LONDONDERRY.

derv *n.* diesel oil for road vehicles. [*d*iesel-*e*ngined *r*oad-*v*ehicle]

dervish /'dɜːvɪʃ/ *n.* member of a Muslim fraternity vowed to poverty and austerity. [Turkish from Persian, = poor]

DES *abbr.* Department of Education and Science.

desalinate /diː'sælɪˌneɪt/ *v.* (**-ting**) remove the salt from (esp. sea water). □ **desalination** /-'neɪʃ(ə)n/ *n.* [from SALINE]

descale /diː'skeɪl/ *v.* (**-ling**) remove scale from.

descant *–n.* /'deskænt/ **1** harmonizing treble melody above the basic melody, esp. of a hymn tune. **2** *poet.* melody; song. *–v.* /dɪs'kænt/ (foll. by *on, upon*) talk prosily, esp. in praise of. [Latin *cantus* song: related to CHANT]

descend /dɪ'send/ *v.* **1** go or come down. **2** sink, fall. **3** slope downwards. **4** (usu. foll. by *on*) make a sudden attack or visit. **5** (of property etc.) be passed on by inheritance. **6 a** sink in rank, quality, etc. **b** (foll. by *to*) stoop to (an unworthy act). □ **be descended from** have as an ancestor. □ **descendent** *adj.* [Latin *scando* climb]

descendant *n.* person or thing descended from another. [French: related to DESCEND]

descent /dɪ'sent/ *n.* **1** act or way of descending. **2** downward slope. **3** lineage, family origin. **4** decline; fall. **5** sudden attack.

describe /dɪ'skraɪb/ *v.* (**-bing**) **1 a** state the characteristics, appearance, etc. of. **b** (foll. by *as*) assert to be; call (*described him as a liar*). **2 a** draw (esp. a geometrical figure). **b** move in (a specified way, esp. a curve) (*described a parabola through the air*). [Latin *scribo* write]

description /dɪ'skrɪpʃ(ə)n/ *n.* **1 a** describing or being described. **b** representation, esp. in words. **2** sort, kind (*no food of any description*). [Latin: related to DESCRIBE]

descriptive /dɪ'skrɪptɪv/ *adj.* describing, esp. vividly. [Latin: related to DESCRIBE]

descry /dɪ'skraɪ/ *v.* (**-ies, -ied**) *literary* catch sight of; discern. [French: related to CRY]

desecrate /'desɪˌkreɪt/ *v.* (**-ting**) violate (a sacred place etc.) with violence, profanity, etc. □ **desecration** /-'kreɪʃ(ə)n/ *n.* **desecrator** *n.* [from DE-, CONSECRATE]

desegregate /diː'segrɪˌgeɪt/ *v.* (**-ting**) abolish racial segregation in. □ **desegregation** /-'geɪʃ(ə)n/ *n.*

deselect /ˌdiːsɪ'lekt/ *v.* reject (a selected candidate, esp. a sitting MP) in favour of another. □ **deselection** *n.*

desensitize /diː'sensɪˌtaɪz/ *v.* (also **-ise**) (**-zing** or **-sing**) reduce or destroy the sensitivity of. □ **desensitization** /-'zeɪʃ(ə)n/ *n.*

desert[1] /dɪ'zɜːt/ *v.* **1** leave without intending to return. **2** (esp. as **deserted** *adj.*) forsake, abandon. **3** run away (esp. from military service). □ **deserter** *n.* (in sense 3). **desertion** *n.* [Latin *desero -sert-* leave]

desert[2] /'dezət/ *–n.* dry barren, esp. sandy, tract. *–adj.* uninhabited, desolate, barren. [Latin *desertus*: related to DESERT[1]]

desert[3] /dɪ'zɜːt/ *n.* **1** (in *pl.*) deserved reward or punishment (*got his deserts*). **2** being worthy of reward or punishment. [French: related to DESERVE]

desert boot *n.* suede etc. ankle-high boot.

desertification /dɪˌzɜːtɪfɪ'keɪʃ(ə)n/ *n.* making or becoming a desert.

desert island *n.* (usu. tropical) uninhabited island.

deserve /dɪ'zɜːv/ *v.* (**-ving**) (often foll. by *to* + infin.) be worthy of (a reward, punishment, etc.) (*deserves a prize*). □ **deservedly** /-vɪdlɪ/ *adv.* [Latin *servio* serve]

deserving *adj.* (often foll. by *of*) worthy (esp. of help, praise, etc.).

déshabillé /ˌdezæ'biːeɪ/ *n.* (also ***déshabille*** /ˌdeɪzæ'biːl/, **dishabille** /ˌdɪsə'biːl/) state of partial undress. [French, = undressed]

desiccate /'desɪˌkeɪt/ *v.* (**-ting**) remove moisture from (esp. food) (*desiccated coconut*). □ **desiccation** /-'keɪʃ(ə)n/ *n.* [Latin *siccus* dry]

desideratum /dɪˌzɪdə'rɑːtəm/ *n.* (*pl.* **-ta**) something lacking but desirable. [Latin: related to DESIRE]

design /dɪ'zaɪn/ *–n.* **1 a** preliminary plan or sketch for making something. **b** art of producing these. **2** lines or shapes forming a pattern or decoration. **3** plan, purpose, or intention. **4 a** arrangement or layout of a product. **b** established version of a product. *–v.* **1** produce a design for (a building, machine, etc.). **2** intend or plan (*designed for beginners*). **3** be a designer. □ **by design** on purpose. **have designs on** plan to appropriate, seduce, etc. [Latin *signum* mark]

designate *–v.* /'dezɪgˌneɪt/ (**-ting**) **1** (often foll. by *as*) appoint to an office or function. **2** specify (*designated *times*). **3** (often foll. by *as*) describe as; style. **4** serve as the name or symbol of. *–adj.* /ˈdezɪgnət/ (after the noun) appointed to office but not yet installed. [Latin: related to DESIGN]

designation /ˌdezɪgˈneɪʃ(ə)n/ *n.* **1** name, description, or title. **2** designating.

designedly /dɪˈzaɪnɪdlɪ/ *adv.* on purpose.

designer *n.* **1** person who designs e.g. clothing, machines, theatre sets; draughtsman. **2** (*attrib.*) bearing the label of a famous designer; prestigious.

designer drug *n.* synthetic analogue of an illegal drug.

designing *adj.* crafty, scheming.

desirable /dɪˈzaɪərəb(ə)l/ *adj.* **1** worth having or doing. **2** sexually attractive. □ **desirability** /-ˈbɪlɪtɪ/ *n.* **desirableness** *n.* **desirably** *adv.*

desire /dɪˈzaɪə(r)/ *–n.* **1 a** unsatisfied longing or wish. **b** expression of this; request. **2** sexual appetite. **3** something desired (*achieved his heart's desire*). *–v.* (**-ring**) **1** (often foll. by *to* + infin., or *that* + clause) long for; wish. **2** request (*desires a rest*). [Latin *desidero* long for]

desirous *predic. adj.* **1** (usu. foll. by *of*) desiring, wanting (*desirous of stardom*). **2** wanting; hoping (*desirous to do the right thing*).

desist /dɪˈzɪst/ *v.* (often foll. by *from*) abstain; cease. [Latin *desisto*]

desk *n.* **1** piece of furniture with a surface for writing on, and often drawers. **2** counter in a hotel, bank, etc. **3** specialized section of a newspaper office (*sports desk*). **4** unit of two orchestral players sharing a stand. [Latin: related to DISCUS]

◆ **deskill** *v.* remove the need for skills in the performance of a particular task.

◆ **desk research** *n.* marketing-research study using mainly external published data and material but also including some internal reports, company records, etc. See also OFF-THE-PEG RESEARCH.

---

desktop *n.* **1** working surface of a desk. **2** (*attrib.*) (esp. of a microcomputer) for use on an ordinary desk.

◆ **desktop evaluation** *n.* process of deciding whether a computer system or program can perform a particular task by testing it in realistic circumstances. This contrasts with evaluation on a theoretical basis, using technical data supplied by the manufacturer.

◆ **desktop publishing** *n.* (also **DTP**) application of computers that enables small companies and individuals to produce reports, advertising, magazines, etc. to near-typeset quality. A typical system comprises a microcomputer, using DTP software, and a laser printer. The capabilities of the software vary with price, although all offer basic page formatting and the ability to use several founts with a choice of typesize. More elaborate systems enable graphics to be incorporated into the text and simulate many of the functions of professional typesetting systems. A common feature is the ability to preview each page on the computer's screen before it is printed; many DTP systems therefore require a computer with a superior graphics capability. The laser printer is usu. capable of printing text and graphics at a resolution of 300 dots per inch, although some programs are capable also of driving typesetting machines, which use resolutions of over 1000 dots per inch.

Des Moines /dɪ ˈmɔɪn/ city in the US, capital of Iowa; pop. (est. 1994) 193 965. It is the commercial centre of the corn belt and has many manufacturing industries.

desolate *–adj.* /ˈdesələt/ **1** left alone; solitary. **2** uninhabited, ruined, dreary (*desolate moor*). **3** forlorn; wretched. *–v.* /ˈdesəˌleɪt/ (**-ting**) **1** depopulate, devastate; lay waste. **2** (esp. as **desolated** *adj.*) make wretched. □ **desolately** /-lətlɪ/ *adv.* **desolateness** /-lətnɪs/ *n.* [Latin *solus* alone]

desolation /ˌdesəˈleɪʃ(ə)n/ *n.* **1** desolating or being desolated. **2** loneliness, grief, etc., esp. caused by desertion. **3** neglected, ruined, or empty state.

despair /dɪˈspeə(r)/ *–n.* **1** complete loss or absence of hope. **2** cause of this. *–v.* (often foll. by *of*) lose or be without hope (*despaired of ever winning*). [Latin *spero* hope]

despatch var. of DISPATCH.

desperado /ˌdespəˈrɑːdəʊ/ *n.* (*pl.* **-es** or *US* **-s**) desperate or reckless criminal etc. [as DESPERATE]

desperate /ˈdespərət/ *adj.* **1** reckless from despair; violent and lawless. **2 a** extremely dangerous, serious, or bad (*desperate situation*). **b** staking all on a small chance (*desperate remedy*). **3** (usu. foll. by *for*) needing or desiring very much (*desperate for recognition*). □ **desperately** *adv.* **desperateness** *n.* **desperation** /-ˈreɪʃ(ə)n/ *n.* [Latin: related to DESPAIR]

despicable /ˈdespɪkəb(ə)l, dɪˈspɪk-/ *adj.* vile; contemptible, esp. morally. □ **despicably** *adv.* [Latin *specio spect-* look at]

despise /dɪˈspaɪz/ *v.* (**-sing**) regard as inferior, worthless, or contemptible. [Latin: related to DESPICABLE]

despite /dɪˈspaɪt/ *prep.* in spite of. [Latin: related to DESPICABLE]

despoil /dɪˈspɔɪl/ *v. literary* (often foll. by *of*) plunder; rob; deprive. □ **despoliation** /dɪˌspəʊlɪˈeɪʃ(ə)n/ *n.* [Latin: related to SPOIL]

despondent /dɪˈspɒnd(ə)nt/ *adj.* in low spirits, dejected. □ **despondence** *n.* **despondency** *n.* **despondently** *adv.* [Latin: related to SPONSOR]

despot /ˈdespɒt/ *n.* **1** absolute ruler. **2** tyrant. □ **despotic** /-ˈspɒtɪk/ *adj.* **despotically** /-ˈspɒtɪkəlɪ/ *adv.* [Greek *despotēs* master]

despotism /ˈdespəˌtɪz(ə)m/ *n.* **1** rule by a despot; tyranny. **2** country ruled by a despot.

des res /dez ˈrez/ *n. slang* desirable residence. [abbreviation]

Dessau /ˈdesaʊ/ industrial city in E Germany; vehicles, armaments, and machinery are produced; pop. (1986) 103 500.

dessert /dɪˈzɜːt/ *n.* **1** sweet course of a meal. **2** fruit, nuts, etc., served at the end of a meal. [French: related to DIS-, SERVE]

dessertspoon *n.* **1** medium-sized spoon for dessert. **2** amount held by this. □ **dessertspoonful** *n.* (*pl.* **-s**).

destabilize /diːˈsteɪbɪˌlaɪz/ *v.* (also **-ise**) (**-zing** or **-sing**) **1** make unstable. **2** subvert (esp. a foreign government). □ **destabilization** /-ˈzeɪʃ(ə)n/ *n.*

destination /ˌdestɪˈneɪʃ(ə)n/ *n.* place a person or thing is bound for. [Latin: related to DESTINE]

destine /ˈdestɪn/ *v.* (**-ning**) (often foll. by *to*, *for*, or *to* + infin.) appoint; preordain; intend (*destined him for the navy*). □ **be destined to** be fated or preordained to. [French from Latin]

destiny /ˈdestɪnɪ/ *n.* (*pl.* **-ies**) **1 a** fate. **b** this regarded as a power. **2** particular person's fate etc. [French from Latin]

destitute /ˈdestɪˌtjuːt/ *adj.* **1** without food, shelter, etc. **2** (usu. foll. by *of*) lacking (*destitute of friends*). □ **destitution** /-ˈtjuːʃ(ə)n/ *n.* [Latin]

destroy /dɪˈstrɔɪ/ *v.* **1** pull or break down; demolish. **2** kill (esp. an animal). **3** make useless; spoil. **4** ruin, esp. financially. **5** defeat. [Latin *struo struct-* build]

destroyer *n.* **1** person or thing that destroys. **2** fast armed warship escorting other ships.

destruct /dɪˈstrʌkt/ *US* esp. *Astronaut.* *–v.* destroy (one's own rocket etc.) or be destroyed deliberately, esp. for safety. *–n.* destructing.

destructible *adj.* able to be destroyed. [Latin: related to DESTROY]

destruction /dɪˈstrʌkʃ(ə)n/ *n.* **1** destroying or being destroyed. **2** cause of this. [Latin: related to DESTROY]

destructive *adj.* **1** (often foll. by *to*, *of*) destroying or tending to destroy. **2** negatively critical. □ **destructively** *adv.* **destructiveness** *n.*

desuetude /dɪˈsjuːɪˌtjuːd/ *n. formal* state of disuse (*fell into desuetude*). [Latin *suesco* be accustomed]

desultory /ˈdezəltərɪ/ *adj.* **1** constantly turning from one subject to another. **2** disconnected; unmethodical. □ **desultorily** *adv.* [Latin *desultorius* superficial]

detach /dɪˈtætʃ/ *v.* **1** (often foll. by *from*) unfasten or disengage and remove. **2** send (troops etc.) on a separate mission. **3** (as **detached** *adj.*) **a** impartial; unemotional. **b** (esp. of a house) standing separate. □ **detachable** *adj.* [French: related to ATTACH]

detachment *n.* **1 a** aloofness; indifference. **b** impartiality. **2** detaching or being detached. **3** troops etc. detached for a specific purpose. [French: related to DETACH]

detail /ˈdiːteɪl/ –*n.* **1** small particular; item. **2 a** these collectively (*eye for detail*). **b** treatment of them (*detail was unconvincing*). **3 a** minor decoration on a building etc. **b** small part of a picture etc. shown alone. **4** small military detachment. –*v.* **1** give particulars of. **2** relate circumstantially. **3** assign for special duty. **4** (as **detailed** *adj.*) **a** (of a picture, story, etc.) containing many details. **b** itemized (*detailed list*). □ **in detail** item by item, minutely. [French: related to TAIL[2]]

detain /dɪˈteɪn/ *v.* **1** keep waiting; delay. **2** keep in custody, lock up. □ **detainment** *n.* [Latin *teneo* hold]

detainee /ˌdiːteɪˈniː/ *n.* person kept in custody, esp. for political reasons.

detect /dɪˈtekt/ *v.* **1** discover or perceive (*detected a note of sarcasm*). **2** (often foll. by *in*) discover (a criminal); solve (a crime). □ **detectable** *adj.* **detector** *n.* [Latin *tego tect-* cover]

detection /dɪˈtekʃ(ə)n/ *n.* **1** detecting or being detected. **2** work of a detective.

detective /dɪˈtektɪv/ *n.* person, esp. a police officer, investigating crimes.

détente /deɪˈtɑ̃t/ *n.* easing of strained, esp. international, relations. [French, = relaxation]

detention /dɪˈtenʃ(ə)n/ *n.* **1** detaining or being detained. **2** being kept late in school as a punishment. [Latin: related to DETAIN]

detention centre *n.* short-term prison for young offenders.

deter /dɪˈtɜː(r)/ *v.* (**-rr-**) (often foll. by *from*) discourage or prevent esp. through fear. □ **determent** *n.* [Latin *terreo* frighten]

detergent /dɪˈtɜːdʒ(ə)nt/ –*n.* synthetic cleansing agent used with water. –*adj.* cleansing. [Latin *tergeo* wipe]

deteriorate /dɪˈtɪərɪəˌreɪt/ *v.* (**-ting**) become worse. □ **deterioration** /-ˈreɪʃ(ə)n/ *n.* [Latin *deterior* worse]

determinant /dɪˈtɜːmɪnənt/ –*adj.* determining. –*n.* **1** determining factor etc. **2** quantity obtained by the addition of products of the elements of a square matrix according to a given rule. [Latin: related to DETERMINE]

determinate /dɪˈtɜːmɪnət/ *adj.* limited, of definite scope or nature.

determination /dɪˌtɜːmɪˈneɪʃ(ə)n/ *n.* **1** firmness of purpose; resoluteness. **2** process of deciding or determining.

determine /dɪˈtɜːmɪn/ *v.* (**-ning**) **1** find out or establish precisely. **2** decide or settle; resolve. **3** be the decisive factor in regard to (*demand determines supply*). □ **be determined** be resolved. [Latin *terminus* boundary]

determined *adj.* showing determination; resolute, unflinching. □ **determinedly** *adv.*

determinism *n.* doctrine that human actions, events, etc. are determined by causes external to the will. □ **determinist** *n.* & *adj.* **deterministic** /-ˈnɪstɪk/ *adj.* **deterministically** /-ˈnɪstɪkəlɪ/ *adv.*

deterrent /dɪˈterənt/ –*adj.* deterring. –*n.* deterrent thing or factor (esp. nuclear weapons). □ **deterrence** *n.*

detest /dɪˈtest/ *v.* hate violently, loathe. □ **detestation** /ˌdiːteˈsteɪʃ(ə)n/ *n.* [Latin *detestor* from *testis* witness]

detestable *adj.* intensely disliked; hateful.

dethrone /diːˈθrəʊn/ *v.* (**-ning**) remove from a throne, depose. □ **dethronement** *n.*

detonate /ˈdetəˌneɪt/ *v.* (**-ting**) set off (an explosive charge); be set off. □ **detonation** /-ˈneɪʃ(ə)n/ *n.* [Latin *tono* thunder]

detonator *n.* device for detonating explosives.

detour /ˈdiːtʊə(r)/ *n.* divergence from a usual route; roundabout course. [French: related to TURN]

detoxify /diːˈtɒksɪˌfaɪ/ *v.* (**-ies, -ied**) remove poison or harmful substances from. □ **detoxification** /-fɪˈkeɪʃ(ə)n/ *n.* [Latin *toxicum* poison]

detract /dɪˈtrækt/ *v.* (foll. by *from*) take away (a part); diminish; make seem less valuable or important. [Latin *traho tract-* draw]

detractor *n.* person who criticizes unfairly. □ **detraction** *n.*

detriment /ˈdetrɪmənt/ *n.* **1** harm, damage. **2** cause of this. □ **detrimental** /-ˈment(ə)l/ *adj.* [Latin: related to TRITE]

detritus /dɪˈtraɪtəs/ *n.* gravel, sand, etc. produced by erosion; debris. [Latin: related to DETRIMENT]

Detroit /dɪˈtrɔɪt/ industrial city in the US, in NE Michigan, and a major port serving the Great Lakes; city pop. (1994) 992 038. It is the centre of the US automobile industry, containing the headquarters of Ford, Chrysler, and General Motors; other industries include chemicals, steel, and oil refining.

de trop /də ˈtrəʊ/ *predic. adj.* not wanted, in the way. [French, = excessive]

deuce[1] /djuːs/ *n.* **1** two on dice or playing-cards. **2** *Tennis* score of 40 all. [Latin *duo duos* two]

deuce[2] /djuːs/ *n.* the Devil, esp. as an exclamation of surprise or annoyance (*who the deuce are you?*). [Low German *duus* two (being the worst throw at dice)]

deus ex machina /ˌdeɪʊs eks ˈmækɪnə/ *n.* unlikely agent resolving a seemingly hopeless situation, esp. in a play or novel. [Latin, = god from the machinery, i.e. in a theatre]

deuterium /djuːˈtɪərɪəm/ *n.* stable isotope of hydrogen with a mass about double that of the usual isotope. [Greek *deuteros* second]

Deutschmark /ˈdɔɪtʃmɑːk/ *n.* (also **Deutsche Mark** /ˈdɔɪtʃə mɑːk/) standard monetary unit of Germany. [German: related to MARK[2]]

◆ **devaluation** /diːˌvæljuːˈeɪʃ(ə)n/ *n.* **1** fall in the value of a currency relative to gold or to other currencies. Governments engage in devaluation when they feel that their currency has become overvalued, for example through high rates of inflation making exports uncompetitive or because of a substantially adverse balance of trade. The intention is that devaluation will make exports cheaper and imports dearer, although the loss of confidence in an economy forced to devalue invariably has an adverse effect. Devaluation is a measure that need only concern governments with a fixed exchange rate for their currency. With a floating exchange rate, devaluation or revaluation takes place continuously and automatically (see DEPRECIATION 3; REVALUATION OF CURRENCY). **2** reduction in value.

devalue /diːˈvæljuː/ *v.* (**-ues, -ued, -uing**) **1** reduce the value of. **2** reduce the value of (a currency) in relation to others or to gold.

devastate /ˈdevəˌsteɪt/ *v.* (**-ting**) **1** lay waste; cause great destruction to. **2** (often in *passive*) overwhelm with shock or grief. □ **devastation** /-ˈsteɪʃ(ə)n/ *n.* [Latin *vasto* lay waste]

devastating *adj.* crushingly effective; overwhelming. □ **devastatingly** *adv.*

develop /dɪˈveləp/ *v.* (**-p-**) **1 a** make or become bigger, fuller, more elaborate, etc. **b** bring or come to an active, visible, or mature state. **2** begin to exhibit or suffer from (*developed a rattle*). **3 a** build on (land). **b** convert (land) to new use. **4** treat (photographic film etc.) to make the image visible. □ **developer** *n.* [French]

developing country *n.* poor or primitive country. Developing countries often have abundant natural resources but lack the capital and entrepreneurial and technical skills required to develop them. The average income per head and the standard of living in these countries is therefore far below that of the industrial nations. Often known as the **Third World**, these countries are being supported by various nations and United Nations organizations. The developing countries, in which some 70% of the world's population lives, are characterized by poverty, poor diet, the prevalence of disease, high fertility, overpopulation, illiteracy, poor educational facilities, and an agricultural economy. Many depend on a single product for their exports and are therefore vulnerable in world markets. The Third World consists of most of Africa (except the Republic of South Africa), much of Asia (exceptions include Japan and the former Soviet republics), and much of South America.

development *n.* **1** developing or being developed. **2 a** stage of growth or advancement. **b** thing that has developed; new event or circumstance etc. (*latest developments*). **3** full-grown state. **4** developed land; group of buildings. □ **developmental** /-'ment(ə)l/ *adj.*

development area *n.* area where new industries are encouraged by the state.

deviant /'di:vɪənt/ *–adj.* deviating from what is normal, esp. sexually. *–n.* deviant person or thing. □ **deviance** *n.* **deviancy** *n.*

deviate /'di:vɪ,eɪt/ *v.* (**-ting**) (often foll. by *from*) turn aside or diverge (from a course of action, rule, etc.). □ **deviation** /-'eɪʃ(ə)n/ *n.* [Latin *via* way]

device /dɪ'vaɪs/ *n.* **1** thing made or adapted for a special purpose. **2** plan, scheme, or trick. **3** design, esp. heraldic. □ **leave a person to his** or **her own devices** leave a person to do as he or she wishes. [French: related to DEVISE]

devil /'dev(ə)l/ *–n.* **1** (usu. **the Devil**) (in Christian and Jewish belief) supreme spirit of evil; Satan. **2 a** evil spirit; demon. **b** personified evil. **3 a** wicked person. **b** mischievously clever person. **4** *colloq.* person of a specified kind (*lucky devil*). **5** fighting spirit, mischievousness (*devil is in him tonight*). **6** *colloq.* awkward thing. **7** (**the devil** or **the Devil**) *colloq.* used as an exclamation of surprise or annoyance (*who the devil are you?*). **8** literary hack. **9** junior legal counsel. *–v.* (**-ll-**; *US* **-l-**) **1** cook (food) with hot seasoning. **2** act as devil for an author or barrister. **3** *US* harass, worry. □ **between the devil and the deep blue sea** in a dilemma. **a devil of** *colloq.* considerable, difficult, or remarkable. **devil's own** *colloq.* very difficult or unusual (*the devil's own job*). **the devil to pay** trouble to be expected. **speak** (or **talk) of the devil** said when person appears just after being mentioned. [Greek *diabolos* accuser, slanderer]

devilish *–adj.* **1** of or like a devil; wicked. **2** mischievous. *–adv. colloq.* very. □ **devilishly** *adv.*

devil-may-care *adj.* cheerful and reckless.

devilment *n.* mischief, wild spirits.

devilry *n.* (*pl.* **-ies**) **1** wickedness; reckless mischief. **2** black magic.

devil's advocate *n.* person who argues against a proposition to test it.

devils-on-horseback *n.pl.* savoury of prunes or plums wrapped in bacon.

devious /'di:vɪəs/ *adj.* **1** not straightforward, underhand. **2** winding, circuitous. □ **deviously** *adv.* **deviousness** *n.* [Latin *via* way]

devise /dɪ'vaɪz/ *v.* (**-sing**) **1** carefully plan or invent. **2** *Law* leave (real estate) by will. [Latin: related to DIVIDE]

devoid /dɪ'vɔɪd/ *predic. adj.* (foll. by *of*) lacking or free from. [French: related to VOID]

devolution /,di:və'lu:ʃ(ə)n/ *n.* delegation of power, esp. to local or regional administration. □ **devolutionist** *n.* & *adj.* [Latin: related to DEVOLVE]

devolve /dɪ'vɒlv/ *v.* (**-ving**) **1** (foll. by *on*, *upon*, etc.) pass (work or duties) or be passed to (a deputy etc.). **2** (foll. by *on*, *to*, *upon*) (of property etc.) descend to. □ **devolvement** *n.* [Latin *volvo volut-* roll]

Devon /'devən/ county in SW England; pop. (est. 1994) 1 053 400; county town, Exeter. It is mainly agricultural, products including clotted cream and cider; tourism is also important.

Devonian /dɪ'vəʊnɪən/ *–adj.* of the fourth period of the Palaeozoic era. *–n.* this period. [*Devon* in England]

Devonshire /'devənʃɪə(r)/ = DEVON.

devote /dɪ'vəʊt/ *v.* (**-ting**) (often *refl.*; foll. by *to*) apply or give over to (a particular activity etc.). [Latin *voveo vot-* vow]

devoted *adj.* loving; loyal. □ **devotedly** *adv.*

devotee /,devə'ti:/ *n.* **1** (usu. foll. by *of*) zealous enthusiast or supporter. **2** pious person.

devotion /dɪ'vəʊʃ(ə)n/ *n.* **1** (usu. foll. by *to*) great love or loyalty. **2 a** religious worship. **b** (in *pl.*) prayers. □ **devotional** *adj.* [Latin: related to DEVOTE]

devour /dɪ'vaʊə(r)/ *v.* **1** eat voraciously. **2** (of fire etc.) engulf, destroy. **3** take in eagerly (*devoured the play*). **4** preoccupy (*devoured by fear*). [Latin *voro* swallow]

devout /dɪ'vaʊt/ *adj.* earnestly religious or sincere. □ **devoutly** *adv.* **devoutness** *n.* [Latin: related to DEVOTE]

dew *n.* **1** condensed water vapour forming on cool surfaces at night. **2** similar glistening moisture. □ **dewy** *adj.* (**-ier, -iest**). [Old English]

dewberry *n.* (*pl.* **-ies**) bluish fruit like the blackberry.

dew-claw *n.* rudimentary inner toe on some dogs.

dewdrop *n.* drop of dew.

Dewey system /'dju:ɪ/ *n.* decimal system of library classification. [*Dewey*, name of a librarian]

dewlap *n.* loose fold of skin hanging from the throat of cattle, dogs, etc. [from DEW, LAP[1]]

dew-point *n.* temperature at which dew forms.

dexter *adj.* esp. *Heraldry* on or of the right-hand side (observer's left) of a shield etc. [Latin, = on the right]

dexterity /dek'sterɪtɪ/ *n.* **1** skill in using one's hands. **2** mental adroitness. [Latin: related to DEXTER]

dexterous /'dekstrəs/ *adj.* (also **dextrous**) having or showing dexterity. □ **dexterously** *adv.* **dexterousness** *n.*

dextrin /'dekstrɪn/ *n.* soluble gummy substance used as a thickening agent, adhesive, etc. [Latin *dextra* on or to the right]

dextrose /'dekstrəʊs/ *n.* form of glucose. [Latin *dextra* on or to the right]

DF *symb.* Djibouti franc.

d.f. *abbr.* dead freight.

DFC *abbr.* Distinguished Flying Cross.

DFD *abbr. Computing* dataflow diagram.

DfEE *abbr.* Department for Education and Employment.

DFM *abbr.* Distinguished Flying Medal.

DG *postcode* Dumfries.

DH *symb.* dirham (of Morocco). *–postcode* Durham.

Dh *symb.* dirham (of United Arab Emirates).

Dhaka /'dækə/ (formerly **Dacca**) capital of Bangladesh, a river port and commercial centre on the Ganges delta; textiles and chemicals are manufactured; metropolitan area pop. (1991) 6 105 160.

dhal /dɑ:l/ *n.* (also **dal**) **1** a kind of split pulse common in India. **2** dish made with this. [Hindi]

Dhanbad /'dɑ:nbɑ:d/ city in NE India, in the state of Bihar; pop. (1991) 815 000.

dharma /'dɑ:mə/ *n. Ind.* **1** social custom; correct behaviour. **2** the Buddhist truth. **3** the Hindu moral law. [Sanskrit, = decree, custom]

Dhofar /dəʊ'fɑ:(r)/ fertile S province of Oman; pop. (1993) 158 787; chief town, Salalah.

dhoti /'dəʊtɪ/ *n.* (*pl.* **-s**) loincloth worn by male Hindus. [Hindi]

di-[1] *comb. form* two-, double. [Greek *dis* twice]

di-[2] *prefix* = DIS-.

di-[3] *prefix* form of DIA- before a vowel.

dia. *abbr.* diameter.

dia- *prefix* (also **di-** before a vowel) **1** through (*diaphanous*). **2** apart (*diacritical*). **3** across (*diameter*). [Greek *dia* through]

diabetes /,daɪə'bi:ti:z/ *n.* disease in which sugar and starch are not properly absorbed by the body. [Latin from Greek]

diabetic /,daɪə'betɪk/ *–adj.* **1** of or having diabetes. **2** for diabetics. *–n.* person suffering from diabetes.

diabolical /ˌdaɪə'bɒlɪk(ə)l/ *adj.* (also **diabolic**) **1** of the Devil. **2** devilish; inhumanly cruel or wicked. **3** extremely bad, clever, or annoying. □ **diabolically** *adv.* [Latin: related to DEVIL]

diabolism /daɪ'æbəˌlɪz(ə)m/ *n.* **1** worship of the Devil. **2** sorcery. [Greek: related to DEVIL]

diachronic /ˌdaɪə'krɒnɪk/ *adj.* of a thing's historical development. □ **diachronically** *adv.* [Greek *khronos* time]

diaconal /daɪ'ækən(ə)l/ *adj.* of a deacon. [Church Latin: related to DEACON]

diaconate /daɪ'ækənət/ *n.* **1** position of deacon. **2** body of deacons.

diacritic /ˌdaɪə'krɪtɪk/ *n.* sign (e.g. an accent or cedilla) indicating different sounds or values of a letter. [Greek: related to CRITIC]

diacritical *–adj.* distinguishing, distinctive. *–n.* (in full **diacritical mark** or **sign**) = DIACRITIC.

diadem /'daɪəˌdem/ *n.* **1** crown or headband as a sign of sovereignty. **2** sovereignty. **3** crowning distinction. [Greek *deō* bind]

diaeresis /daɪ'ɪərəsɪs/ *n.* (*pl.* **diaereses** /-ˌsiːz/) (*US* **dieresis**) mark (as in *naïve*) over a vowel to indicate that it is sounded separately. [Greek, = separation]

diagnose /'daɪəgˌnəʊz/ *v.* (**-sing**) make a diagnosis of (a disease, fault, etc.).

diagnosis /ˌdaɪəg'nəʊsɪs/ *n.* (*pl.* **diagnoses** /-ˌsiːz/) **1 a** identification of a disease from its symptoms. **b** formal statement of this. **2** identification of the cause of a mechanical fault etc. [Greek *gignōskō* recognize]

diagnostic /ˌdaɪəg'nɒstɪk/ *–adj.* of or assisting diagnosis. *–n.* symptom. □ **diagnostically** *adv.* **diagnostician** /-nɒ'stɪʃ(ə)n/ *n.* [Greek: related to DIAGNOSIS]

diagnostics *n.* **1** (treated as *pl.*) *Computing* programs etc. used to identify faults in hardware or software. **2** (treated as *sing.*) science of diagnosing disease.

diagonal /daɪ'ægən(ə)l/ *–adj.* **1** crossing a straight-sided figure from corner to corner. **2** slanting, oblique. *–n.* straight line joining two opposite corners. □ **diagonally** *adv.* [Greek *gōnia* angle]

diagram /'daɪəˌgræm/ *n.* outline drawing, plan, or graphic representation of a machine, structure, process, etc. □ **diagrammatic** /-grə'mætɪk/ *adj.* **diagrammatically** /-grə'mætɪkəlɪ/ *adv.* [Greek: related to -GRAM]

dial /'daɪ(ə)l/ *–n.* **1** plate with a scale for measuring weight, volume, etc., indicated by a pointer. **2** movable numbered disc on a telephone for making connection. **3** face of a clock or watch, marking the hours etc. **4 a** plate or disc etc. on a radio or television for selecting a wavelength or channel. **b** similar device on other equipment. *–v.* (**-ll-**; *US* **-l-**) **1** (*also absol.*) select (a telephone number) with dial. **2** measure, indicate, or regulate with dial. [medieval Latin *diale* from *dies* day]

dialect /'daɪəˌlekt/ *n.* **1** regional form of speech. **2** variety of language with non-standard vocabulary, pronunciation, or grammar. □ **dialectal** /-'lekt(ə)l/ *adj.* [Greek *legō* speak]

dialectic /ˌdaɪə'lektɪk/ *n.* **1** art of investigating the truth by discussion and logical argument. **2** process whereby contradictions merge to form a higher truth. **3** any situation or discussion involving the juxtaposition or conflict of opposites. [Greek: related to DIALECT]

dialectical *adj.* of dialectic. □ **dialectically** *adv.*

dialectical materialism *n.* Marxist theory that political and historical events are due to the conflict of social forces arising from economic conditions.

dialectics *n.* (treated as *sing.* or *pl.*) = DIALECTIC 1.

dialling tone *n.* sound indicating that a telephone caller may dial.

dialogue /'daɪəˌlɒg/ *n.* (*US* **dialog**) **1 a** conversation. **b** this in written form. **2** discussion between people with different opinions. [Greek *legō* speak]

dialysis /daɪ'ælɪsɪs/ *n.* (*pl.* **dialyses** /-ˌsiːz/) **1** separation of particles in a liquid by differences in their ability to pass through a membrane into another liquid. **2** purification of the blood by this technique. [Greek *luō* set free]

diamanté /dɪə'mɑ̃teɪ/ *adj.* decorated with synthetic diamonds or another sparkling substance. [French *diamant* diamond]

diamat /'daɪəˌmæt/ *n. Econ.* dialectical materialism. [abbreviation]

diameter /daɪ'æmɪtə(r)/ *n.* **1** straight line passing through the centre of a circle or sphere to its edges; length of this. **2** transverse measurement; width, thickness. **3** unit of linear magnifying power. [Greek: related to -METER]

diametrical /ˌdaɪə'metrɪk(ə)l/ *adj.* (also **diametric**) **1** of or along a diameter. **2** (of opposites etc.) absolute. □ **diametrically** *adv.* [Greek: related to DIAMETER]

diamond /'daɪəmənd/ *n.* **1** very hard transparent precious stone of pure crystallized carbon. **2** rhombus. **3 a** playing-card of the suit denoted by a red rhombus. **b** (in *pl.*) this suit. [Greek: related to ADAMANT]

diamond wedding *n.* 60th (or 75th) wedding anniversary.

DIANE /daɪ'æn/ *abbr. Computing* Direct Information Access Network for Europe.

dianthus /daɪ'ænθəs/ *n.* flowering plant of the genus including the carnation. [Greek, = flower of Zeus]

diapason /ˌdaɪə'peɪz(ə)n/ *n.* **1** compass of a voice or musical instrument. **2** fixed standard of musical pitch. **3** either of two main organ-stops. [Greek, = through all (notes)]

diaper /'daɪəpə(r)/ *n. US* baby's nappy. [Greek *aspros* white]

diaphanous /daɪ'æfənəs/ *adj.* (of fabric etc.) light, delicate, and almost transparent. [Greek *phainō* show]

diaphragm /'daɪəˌfræm/ *n.* **1** muscular partition between the thorax and abdomen in mammals. **2** = DUTCH CAP. **3 a** *Photog.* plate or disc pierced with a circular hole to cut off marginal beams of light. **b** vibrating disc in a microphone, telephone, loudspeaker, etc. **4** device for varying the lens aperture in a camera etc. **5** thin sheet as a partition etc. [Greek *phragma* fence]

diapositive /ˌdaɪə'pɒzɪtɪv/ *n.* positive photographic slide or transparency.

diarist /'daɪərɪst/ *n.* person who keeps a diary.

diarrhoea /ˌdaɪə'rɪə/ *n.* (esp. *US* **diarrhea**) condition of excessively frequent and loose bowel movements. [Greek *rheō* flow]

diary /'daɪərɪ/ *n.* (*pl.* **-ies**) **1** daily record of events or thoughts. **2** book for this or for noting future engagements. [Latin *dies* day]

♦ diary panel *n.* group of shops and shoppers who keep a regular record of all purchases or purchases of selected products, for the purpose of marketing research.

Diaspora /daɪ'æspərə/ *n.* **1** the dispersion of the Jews after their exile in 538 BC. **2** the dispersed Jews. [Greek]

diastase /'daɪəˌsteɪz/ *n.* enzyme converting starch to sugar. [Greek *diastasis* separation]

diatom /'daɪətəm/ *n.* one-cell alga found as plankton and forming fossil deposits. [Greek, = cut in half]

diatomic /ˌdaɪə'tɒmɪk/ *adj.* consisting of two atoms.

diatonic /ˌdaɪə'tɒnɪk/ *adj. Mus.* (of a scale, interval, etc.) involving only notes belonging to the prevailing key. [Greek: related to TONIC]

diatribe /'daɪəˌtraɪb/ *n.* forceful verbal attack or criticism; invective. [Greek *tribō* rub]

diazepam /daɪ'æzɪˌpæm/ *n.* a tranquillizing drug. [benzo*diaze*pine + *am*]

dibble /'dɪb(ə)l/ *–n.* (also **dibber** /'dɪbə(r)/) hand tool for making holes for planting. *–v.* (**-ling**) sow, plant, or prepare (soil) with a dibble. [origin uncertain]

dice *–n.pl.* **1 a** small cubes with faces bearing 1–6 spots, used in games or gambling. **b** (treated as *sing.*) one of these cubes (see DIE[2]). **2** game played with dice. *–v.* (**-cing**) **1** take great risks, gamble (*dicing with death*). **2** cut into small cubes. [pl. of DIE[2]]

■ **Usage** See note at DIE[2].

dicey *adj.* (**dicier, diciest**) *slang* risky, unreliable.

♦ **dichotomous question** *n.* question to which there can only be one of two answers, often "yes" or "no".

dichotomy /daɪˈkɒtəmɪ/ *n.* (*pl.* **-ies**) division into two, esp. a sharply defined one. [Greek *dikho-* apart: related to TOME]

■ **Usage** *Dichotomy* should not be used to mean *dilemma* or *ambivalence*.

dichromatic /ˌdaɪkrəʊˈmætɪk/ *adj.* **1** two-coloured. **2** having vision sensitive to only two of the three primary colours.

dick[1] *n.* **1** *colloq.* (in certain set phrases) person (*clever dick*). **2** *coarse slang* penis. [*Dick*, pet form of *Richard*]

dick[2] *n. slang* detective. [perhaps an abbreviation]

dickens /ˈdɪkɪnz/ *n.* (usu. prec. by *how, what, why*, etc., *the*) *colloq.* (esp. in exclamations) deuce; the Devil (*what the dickens is it*). [probably the name *Dickens*]

Dickensian /dɪˈkenzɪən/ *adj.* **1** of the 19th-century novelist Dickens or his work. **2** resembling situations in Dickens's work, esp. poverty.

dickhead *n. coarse slang* idiot. [from DICK[1]]

dicky /ˈdɪkɪ/ *–n.* (*pl.* **-ies**) *colloq.* false shirt-front. *–adj.* (**-ier, -iest**) *slang* unsound; unhealthy. [*Dicky*, pet form of *Richard*]

dicky-bird *n.* **1** child's word for a little bird. **2** word (*didn't say a dicky-bird*).

dicky bow *n. colloq.* bow-tie.

dicotyledon /ˌdaɪkɒtɪˈliːd(ə)n/ *n.* flowering plant having two cotyledons. □ **dicotyledonous** *adj.*

dicta *pl.* of DICTUM.

Dictaphone /ˈdɪktəˌfəʊn/ *n. propr.* machine for recording and playing back dictated words. [from DICTATE, PHONE]

dictate *–v.* /dɪkˈteɪt/ (**-ting**) **1** say or read aloud (material to be written down or recorded). **2** state or order authoritatively or peremptorily. *–n.* /ˈdɪk-/ (usu. in *pl.*) authoritative instruction or requirement (*dictates of conscience, fashion*). □ **dictation** /dɪkˈteɪʃ(ə)n/ *n.* [Latin *dicto* from *dico* say]

dictator /dɪkˈteɪtə(r)/ *n.* **1** usu. unelected omnipotent ruler. **2** omnipotent person in any sphere. **3** domineering person. □ **dictatorship** *n.* [Latin: related to DICTATE]

dictatorial /ˌdɪktəˈtɔːrɪəl/ *adj.* **1** of or like a dictator. **2** overbearing. □ **dictatorially** *adv.* [Latin: related to DICTATOR]

diction /ˈdɪkʃ(ə)n/ *n.* manner of enunciation in speaking or singing. [Latin *dictio* from *dico dict-* say]

dictionary /ˈdɪkʃənərɪ/ *n.* (*pl.* **-ies**) **1** book listing (usu. alphabetically) and explaining the words of a language or giving corresponding words in another language. **2** reference book explaining the terms of a particular subject. [medieval Latin: related to DICTION]

dictum /ˈdɪktəm/ *n.* (*pl.* **dicta** or **-s**) **1** formal expression of opinion. **2** a saying. [Latin, neuter past part. of *dico* say]

did *past* of DO[1].

didactic /daɪˈdæktɪk/ *adj.* **1** meant to instruct. **2** (of a person) tediously pedantic. □ **didactically** *adv.* **didacticism** /-tɪˌsɪz(ə)m/ *n.* [Greek *didaskō* teach]

diddle /ˈdɪd(ə)l/ *v.* (**-ling**) *colloq.* swindle. [probably from *Diddler*, name of a character in a 19th-century play]

diddums /ˈdɪdəmz/ *int.* often *iron.* expressing commiseration. [= *did 'em*, i.e. did they (tease you etc.)?]

didgeridoo /ˌdɪdʒərɪˈduː/ *n.* long tubular Australian Aboriginal musical instrument. [imitative]

didn't /ˈdɪd(ə)nt/ *contr.* did not.

die[1] /daɪ/ *v.* (**dies, died, dying** /ˈdaɪɪŋ/) **1** cease to live; expire, lose vital force. **2 a** come to an end, fade away (*his interest died*). **b** cease to function. **c** (of a flame) go out. **3** (foll. by *on*) die or cease to function while in the presence or charge of (a person). **4** (usu. foll. by *of, from, with*) be exhausted or tormented (*nearly died of boredom*). □ **be dying** (foll. by *for*, or *to* + infin.) wish for longingly or intently (*was dying for a drink*). **die away** fade to the point of extinction. **die back** (of a plant) decay from the tip towards the root. **die down** become fainter or weaker. **die hard** die reluctantly (*old habits die hard*). **die off** die one after another. **die out** become extinct, cease to exist. [Old Norse]

die[2] /daɪ/ *n.* **1** = DICE *n.* 1b. **2** (*pl.* **dies**) **a** engraved device for stamping coins, medals, etc. **b** device for stamping, cutting, or moulding material. □ **the die is cast** an irrevocable step has been taken. [Latin *datum* from *do* give]

■ **Usage** *Dice*, rather than *die*, is now the standard singular as well as plural form in the games sense (*one dice, two dice*).

die-casting *n.* process or product of casting from metal moulds.

Diego Garcia /dɪˌeɪgəʊ gɑːˈsiːə/ largest island of the Chagos Archipelago and comprising part of British Indian Ocean Territory. It is the site of a strategic Anglo-American naval base established in 1973.

die-hard *n.* conservative or stubborn person.

Diekirch /ˈdiːkɜːx/ resort town in Luxembourg; pop. (1991) 5650.

dielectric /ˌdaɪɪˈlektrɪk/ *–adj.* not conducting electricity. *–n.* dielectric substance.

Dieppe /dɪˈep/ channel port in N France, from which ferries run to Newhaven and elsewhere; industries include shipbuilding and chemicals; pop. (1990) 36 600.

dieresis *US* var. of DIAERESIS.

diesel /ˈdiːz(ə)l/ *n.* **1** (in full **diesel engine**) internal-combustion engine in which heat produced by the compression of air in the cylinder ignites the fuel. **2** vehicle driven by a diesel engine. **3** fuel for a diesel engine. [*Diesel*, name of an engineer]

diesel-electric *adj.* (of a locomotive etc.) driven by an electric current from a diesel-engined generator.

diesel oil *n.* heavy petroleum fraction used in diesel engines.

die-sinker *n.* engraver of dies.

♦ ***dies non*** /daɪiːz nɒn/ *n.* day on which no legal business can be transacted; a non-business day. [Latin, short for *dies non juridicus* non-juridical day]

die-stamping *n.* embossing paper etc. with die.

diet[1] /ˈdaɪət/ *–n.* **1** range of foods habitually eaten by a person or animal. **2** limited range of food to which a person is restricted. **3** thing regularly offered (*diet of half-truths*). *–v.* (**-t-**) restrict oneself to a special diet, esp. to slim. □ **dietary** *adj.* **dieter** *n.* [Greek *diaita* way of life]

diet[2] /ˈdaɪət/ *n.* **1** legislative assembly in certain countries. **2** *hist.* congress. [Latin *dieta*]

dietetic /ˌdaɪəˈtetɪk/ *adj.* of diet and nutrition. [Greek: related to DIET[1]]

dietetics *n.pl.* (usu. treated as *sing.*) the study of diet and nutrition.

dietitian /ˌdaɪəˈtɪʃ(ə)n/ *n.* (also **dietician**) expert in dietetics.

dif- *prefix* = DIS-.

differ *v.* **1** (often foll. by *from*) be unlike or distinguishable. **2** (often foll. by *with*) disagree. [Latin *differo, dilat-* bring apart]

difference /ˈdɪfrəns/ *n.* **1** being different or unlike. **2** degree of this. **3** way in which things differ. **4 a** quantity by which amounts differ. **b** remainder left after subtraction. **5** disagreement, dispute. □ **make a** (or **all the, no,** etc.) **difference** have a significant (or a very significant, or no) effect. **with a difference** having a new or unusual feature.

different *adj.* **1** (often foll. by *from* or *to*) unlike, of another nature. **2** distinct, separate. **3** unusual. □ **differently** *adv.*

■ **Usage** In sense 1, *different from* is more widely acceptable than *different to*, which is common in less formal use.

differential /ˌdɪfəˈrenʃ(ə)l/ *–adj.* **1** of, exhibiting, or depending on a difference. **2** *Math.* relating to infinitesimal differences. **3** constituting or relating to a specific difference. *–n.* **1** difference between things of the same kind. **2** difference in wages between industries or categories of employees in the same industry. **3** difference between rates of interest etc.

differential calculus *n.* method of calculating rates of change, maximum or minimum values, etc.

differential gear *n.* gear enabling a vehicle's rear wheels to revolve at different speeds on corners.

differentiate /ˌdɪfəˈrenʃɪˌeɪt/ *v.* (**-ting**) **1** constitute a difference between or in. **2** recognize as different; distinguish. **3** become different during development. **4** *Math.* calculate the derivative of. □ **differentiation** /-ˈeɪʃ(ə)n/ *n.*

♦ **differentiated marketing** *n.* marketing in which provision is made to meet the special needs of consumers. For example, weight watchers require diet drinks and left-handed people require left-handed scissors.

---

difficult /ˈdɪfɪkəlt/ *adj.* **1 a** needing much effort or skill. **b** troublesome, perplexing. **2** (of a person) demanding. **3** problematic.

difficulty *n.* (*pl.* **-ies**) **1** being difficult. **2 a** difficult thing; problem, hindrance. **b** (often in *pl.*) distress, esp. financial (*in difficulties*). [Latin *difficultas*: related to FACULTY]

diffident /ˈdɪfɪd(ə)nt/ *adj.* shy, lacking self-confidence; excessively reticent. □ **diffidence** *n.* **diffidently** *adv.* [Latin *diffido* distrust]

diffract /dɪˈfrækt/ *v.* break up (a beam of light) into a series of dark and light bands or coloured spectra, or (a beam of radiation or particles) into a series of high and low intensities. □ **diffraction** *n.* **diffractive** *adj.* [Latin *diffringo*: related to FRACTION]

diffuse *–adj.* /dɪˈfjuːs/ **1** spread out, not concentrated. **2** not concise, wordy. *–v.* /dɪˈfjuːz/ (**-sing**) **1** disperse or spread widely. **2** intermingle by diffusion. □ **diffusible** /dɪˈfjuːzɪb(ə)l/ *adj.* **diffusive** /dɪˈfjuːsɪv/ *adj.* [Latin: related to FOUND[3]]

diffusion /dɪˈfjuːʒ(ə)n/ *n.* **1** diffusing or being diffused. **2** interpenetration of substances by natural movement of their particles. [Latin: related to DIFFUSE]

♦ **diffusion of innovation** *n.* process by which the sale of new products and services spreads among customers. Initially, only those with confidence in the new product or who like taking risks will try it out. Once the innovators have accepted the product, a larger group of early adopters will come into the market. These **opinion leaders** will in turn bring about a wider acceptance by consumers. The diffusion process can be speeded up by making new products more attractive, e.g. by giving away free samples or by special introductory prices.

---

dig *–v.* (**-gg-**; *past* and *past part.* **dug**) **1** (also *absol.*) break up and remove or turn over (ground etc.). **2** (foll. by *up*) break up the soil of (fallow land). **3** make (a hole, tunnel, etc.) by digging. **4** (often foll. by *up, out*) **a** obtain by digging. **b** (foll. by *up, out*) find or discover. **c** (foll. by *into*) search for information in (a book etc.). **5** (also *absol.*) excavate (an archaeological site). **6** *slang* like; understand. **7** (foll. by *in, into*) thrust (a sharp object); prod or nudge. **8** (foll. by *into, through, under*) make one's way by digging. *–n.* **1** piece of digging. **2** thrust or poke. **3** *colloq.* pointed remark. **4** archaeological excavation. **5** (in *pl.*) *colloq.* lodgings. □ **dig one's heels in** be obstinate. **dig in** *colloq.* begin eating. **dig oneself in 1** prepare a defensive trench or pit. **2** establish one's position. [Old English]

digest *–v.* /daɪˈdʒest/ **1** assimilate (food) in the stomach and bowels. **2** understand and assimilate mentally. **3** summarize. *–n.* /ˈdaɪdʒest/ **1** periodical synopsis of current literature or news. **2** methodical summary esp. of laws. □ **digestible** *adj.* [Latin *digero -gest-*]

digestion /daɪˈdʒestʃ(ə)n/ *n.* **1** process of digesting. **2** capacity to digest food.

digestive *–adj.* of or aiding digestion. *–n.* **1** substance aiding digestion. **2** (in full **digestive biscuit**) wholemeal biscuit.

digger *n.* **1** person or machine that digs, esp. a mechanical excavator. **2** *colloq.* Australian or New Zealander.

digit /ˈdɪdʒɪt/ *n.* **1** any numeral from 0 to 9. **2** finger or toe. [Latin, = finger, toe]

digital *adj.* **1** of digits. **2** (of a clock, watch, etc.) giving a reading by displayed digits. **3** (of a computer) operating on data represented by a series of digits. See COMPUTER. **4** (of a recording) with sound-information represented by digits for more reliable transmission. □ **digitally** *adv.* [Latin: related to DIGIT]

digital audio tape *n.* magnetic tape on which sound is recorded digitally.

♦ **digital computer** *n.* = COMPUTER. Cf. ANALOG COMPUTER.

---

digitalis /ˌdɪdʒɪˈteɪlɪs/ *n.* drug prepared from foxgloves, used to stimulate the heart. [related to DIGIT, from the form of the flowers]

digital signal *n.* electrical signal whose voltage at any particular time will be at any one of a group of discrete (distinct) levels, usu. two. The voltage therefore does not vary continuously. Digital signals are used in computers.

digital to analog converter *n.* = D/A CONVERTER.

digitize *v.* (also **-ise**) (**-zing** or **-sing**) convert (data etc.) into digital form, esp. for a computer. □ **digitization** /-ˈzeɪʃ(ə)n/ *n.*

digitizing pad *n.* (also **digitizing tablet**) flat surface that can be placed on a desk and is used together with a penlike device for the input of data to a computer graphics system. Larger surfaces are also available and are known as **digitizing tables** or **boards**. The main use of a digitizing pad plus pen is to convert an existing picture, e.g. a map or engineering design, into a digital form that can be fed into a computer; the picture is placed or projected on the pad and the pen is moved along the outlines etc., so generating a digital signal.

dignified /ˈdɪgnɪˌfaɪd/ *adj.* having or showing dignity.

dignify /ˈdɪgnɪˌfaɪ/ *v.* (**-ies, -ied**) **1** confer dignity on; ennoble. **2** give a fine name to. [Latin *dignus* worthy]

dignitary /ˈdɪgnɪtərɪ/ *n.* (*pl.* **-ies**) person of high rank or office. [from DIGNITY]

dignity /ˈdɪgnɪtɪ/ *n.* (*pl.* **-ies**) **1** composed and serious manner. **2** worthiness, nobleness (*dignity of work*). **3** high rank or position. □ **beneath one's dignity** not worthy enough for one. **stand on one's dignity** insist on being treated with respect. [Latin *dignus* worthy]

digraph /ˈdaɪgrɑːf/ *n.* two letters representing one sound, e.g. *ph, ey* as in *ph*one, k*ey*. [from DI-[1], -GRAPH]

■ **Usage** *Digraph* is sometimes confused with *ligature*, which means two or more letters joined together.

digress /daɪˈgres/ *v.* depart from the main subject in speech or writing. □ **digression** *n.* [Latin *digredior -gress-*]

digs see DIG *n.* 5.

Dijon /ˌdiːʒɔ̃/ industrial city in E central France, the former capital of Burgundy, noted for its mustard; pop. (1990) 151 636.

dike[1] var. of DYKE[1].

dike[2] var. of DYKE[2].

diktat /ˈdɪktæt/ *n.* categorical statement or decree. [German, = DICTATE]

dilapidated /dɪˈlæpɪˌdeɪtɪd/ *adj.* in disrepair or ruin. □ **dilapidation** /-ˈdeɪʃ(ə)n/ *n.* [Latin: related to DI-[2], *lapis* stone]

♦ **dilapidations** *n.pl. Law* disrepair of leasehold premises. The landlord may be liable to repair certain parts of domestic premises (e.g. the structure and exterior and the sanitary appliances) under the Landlord and Tenant Act (1985) if the lease is for less than seven years. Otherwise, the lease will usu. contain a covenant by either the landlord or the tenant obliging them to keep the premises in repair. Under the Landlord and Tenant Act (1985), a landlord cannot enforce a repairing covenant against a tenant by ending the lease prematurely unless a notice is first served on the tenant specifying the disrepair and giving time for the repairs to be carried out. If there is no covenant in the lease, the tenant is under a common-law duty not to damage the premises and must keep them from falling down.

---

dilatation /ˌdaɪləˈteɪʃ(ə)n/ *n.* **1** dilating of the cervix, e.g. for surgical curettage. **2** dilation. [from DILATE]

dilate /daɪˈleɪt/ *v.* (**-ting**) **1** make or become wider or larger. **2** speak or write at length. □ **dilation** *n.* [Latin *latus* wide]

dilatory /ˈdɪlətərɪ/ *adj.* given to or causing delay. [Latin *dilatorius*: related to DIFFER]

dildo /ˈdɪldəʊ/ *n.* (*pl.* **-s**) artificial erect penis for sexual stimulation. [origin unknown]

dilemma /daɪˈlemə/ *n.* **1** situation in which a difficult choice has to be made. **2** difficult situation, predicament. [Greek *lēmma* premiss]

■ **Usage** The use of *dilemma* in sense 2 is considered incorrect by some people.

dilettante /ˌdɪlɪˈtæntɪ/ *n.* (*pl.* **dilettanti** /-tɪ/ or **-s**) dabbler in a subject. □ **dilettantism** *n.* [Italian *dilettare* DELIGHT]

Dili /ˈdɪlɪ/ seaport in Indonesia, on the island of Timor, capital of the province of East Timor; pop. (1980) 60 150.

diligent /ˈdɪlɪdʒ(ə)nt/ *adj.* **1** hard-working. **2** showing care and effort. □ **diligence** *n.* **diligently** *adv.* [French from Latin *diligo* love]

dill *n.* herb with aromatic leaves and seeds. [Old English]

dilly-dally /ˌdɪlɪˈdælɪ/ *v.* (**-ies**, **-ied**) *colloq.* **1** dawdle. **2** vacillate. [reduplication of DALLY]

dilute /daɪˈljuːt/ *–v.* (**-ting**) **1** reduce the strength of (a fluid) by adding water etc. **2** weaken or reduce in effect. *–adj.* diluted. □ **dilution** *n.* [Latin *diluo -lut-* wash away]

♦ **dilution of equity** *n.* increase in the number of ordinary shares in a company without a corresponding increase in its assets or profitability. The result is a fall in the value of the shares.

---

diluvial /daɪˈluːvɪəl/ *adj.* of a flood, esp. of the Flood in Genesis. [Latin: related to DELUGE]

dim *–adj.* (**dimmer**, **dimmest**) **1 a** faintly luminous or visible; not bright. **b** indistinct. **2** not clearly perceived or remembered. **3** *colloq.* stupid. **4** (of the eyes) not seeing clearly. *–v.* (**-mm-**) make or become dim. □ **take a dim view of** *colloq.* disapprove of. □ **dimly** *adv.* **dimness** *n.* [Old English]

dime *n. US* ten-cent coin. [Latin *decima* tenth (part)]

dimension /daɪˈmenʃ(ə)n/ *–n.* **1** measurable extent, as length, breadth, depth, etc. **2** (in *pl.*) size (*of huge dimensions*). **3** aspect, facet (*gained a new dimension*). *–v.* (usu. as **dimensioned** *adj.*) mark dimensions on (a diagram etc.). □ **dimensional** *adj.* [Latin *metior mens-* measure]

diminish /dɪˈmɪnɪʃ/ *v.* **1** make or become smaller or less. **2** (often as **diminished** *adj.*) lessen the reputation of (a person); humiliate. □ **law of diminishing returns** fact that expenditure etc. beyond a certain point ceases to produce a proportionate yield. See also RETURNS TO SCALE. [Latin: related to MINUTE[1]]

♦ **diminishing-balance depreciation** *n.* reducing-balance depreciation. See DEPRECIATION 2.

---

diminuendo /dɪˌmɪnjʊˈendəʊ/ *Mus. –n.* (*pl* **-s**) gradual decrease in loudness. *–adv.* & *adj.* decreasing in loudness. [Italian: related to DIMINISH]

diminution /ˌdɪmɪˈnjuːʃ(ə)n/ *n.* **1** diminishing or being diminished. **2** decrease. [Latin: related to DIMINISH]

diminutive /dɪˈmɪnjʊtɪv/ *–adj.* **1** tiny. **2** (of a word or suffix) implying smallness or affection. *–n.* diminutive word or suffix.

dimmer *n.* **1** (in full **dimmer switch**) device for varying the brightness of an electric light. **2** *US* **a** (in *pl.*) small parking lights on a vehicle. **b** headlight on low beam.

dimple /ˈdɪmp(ə)l/ *–n.* small hollow, esp. in the cheek or chin. *–v.* (**-ling**) form dimples (in). □ **dimply** *adj.* [probably Old English]

DIMS *abbr. Computing* Data and Information Management System.

dim-wit *n. colloq.* stupid person. □ **dim-witted** *adj.*

DIN *n.* any of a series of German technical standards designating electrical connections, film speeds, and paper sizes. [German, from *D*eutsche *I*ndustrie-*N*orm]

Din *symb.* dinar (of Yugoslavia).

din *–n.* prolonged loud confused noise. *–v.* (**-nn-**) (foll. by *into*) force (information) into a person by constant repetition; make a din. [Old English]

dinar /ˈdiːnɑː(r)/ *n.* **1** standard monetary unit of Algeria, Bahrain, Bosnia-Hercegovina, Iraq, Jordan, Kuwait, Libya, Tunisia, and the Federal Republic of Yugoslavia. **2** monetary unit of Iran worth one hundredth of a rial. [Arabic and Persian from Latin DENARIUS]

dine *v.* (**-ning**) **1 a** eat dinner. **b** (foll. by *on*, *upon*) eat for dinner. **2** give dinner to, esp. socially. □ **dine out** dine away from home. [French *diner* as DIS-, Latin *jejunus* fasting]

diner *n.* **1** person who dines. **2** dining-car. **3** *US* small restaurant. **4** small dining-room.

dinette /daɪˈnet/ *n.* small room or alcove for eating meals.

ding *–v.* make a ringing sound. *–n.* ringing sound. [imitative]

dingbat /ˈdɪŋbæt/ *n. slang US* & *Austral.* stupid or eccentric person. [perhaps from *ding* to beat + BAT[1]]

ding-dong /ˈdɪŋdɒŋ/ *n.* **1** sound of two chimes, esp. as a doorbell. **2** *colloq.* heated argument or fight. [imitative]

dinghy /ˈdɪŋɪ/ *n.* (*pl.* **-ies**) **1** small boat carried by a ship. **2** small sailing boat. **3** small inflatable rubber boat. [Hindi]

dingle /ˈdɪŋg(ə)l/ *n.* deep wooded valley or dell. [origin unknown]

dingo /ˈdɪŋgəʊ/ *n.* (*pl.* **-es**) wild Australian dog. [Aboriginal]

dingy /ˈdɪndʒɪ/ *adj.* (**-ier**, **-iest**) dirty-looking, drab. □ **dingily** *adv.* **dinginess** *n.* [origin uncertain]

dining-car *n.* restaurant on a train.

dining-room *n.* room in which meals are eaten.

dinkum /ˈdɪŋkəm/ *adj. Austral.* & *NZ colloq.* genuine, honest, true. □ **dinkum oil** the honest truth. **fair dinkum** **1** fair play. **2** genuine(ly), honest(ly), true, truly. [origin unknown]

dinky[1] /ˈdɪŋkɪ/ *adj.* (**-ier**, **-iest**) *colloq.* neat and attractive; small, dainty. [Scots *dink*]

♦ **dinky**[2] /ˈdɪŋkɪ/ *n. colloq.* affluent married couple who may be expected to be extensive purchasers of consumer goods. [from *d*ouble *i*ncome *n*o *k*ids, -Y[2]]

---

dinner *n.* **1** main meal of the day, either at midday or in the evening. **2** (in full **dinner-party**) formal evening meal, esp. with guests. [French: related to DINE]

dinner-dance *n.* formal dinner followed by dancing.

dinner-jacket *n.* man's short usu. black formal jacket for evening wear.

dinner lady *n.* woman who supervises school dinners.

dinner service *n.* set of matching crockery for dinner.

dinosaur /ˈdaɪnəˌsɔː(r)/ *n.* **1** extinct, often enormous, reptile of the Mesozoic era. **2** unwieldy or unchanging system or organization. [Greek *deinos* terrible, SAURIAN]

dint *–n.* dent. *–v.* mark with dints. □ **by dint of** by force or means of. [Old English and Old Norse]

diocese /ˈdaɪəsɪs/ *n.* district under the pastoral care of a bishop. □ **diocesan** /daɪˈɒsɪs(ə)n/ *adj.* [Greek *dioikēsis* administration]

diode /ˈdaɪəʊd/ *n.* **1** semiconductor allowing the flow of current in one direction only and having two terminals.

2 *hist.* thermionic valve having two electrodes. [from DI-[1], ELECTRODE]

Dionysian /ˌdaɪəˈnɪzɪən/ *adj.* wildly sensual; unrestrained. [Greek *Dionusos* god of wine]

dioptre /daɪˈɒptə(r)/ *n.* (*US* **diopter**) unit of refractive power of a lens. [Greek: related to DIA-, *opsis* sight]

diorama /ˌdaɪəˈrɑːmə/ *n.* **1** scenic painting lit to simulate sunrise etc. **2** small scene with three-dimensional figures, viewed through a window etc. **3** small-scale model or film-set. [from DIA-, Greek *horaō* see]

dioxide /daɪˈɒksaɪd/ *n.* oxide containing two atoms of oxygen (*carbon dioxide*).

Dip. *abbr.* Diploma.

dip –*v.* (**-pp-**) **1** put or lower briefly into liquid etc.; immerse. **2 a** go below a surface or level. **b** (of income, activity, etc.) decline slightly, esp. briefly. **3** slope or extend downwards (*road dips*). **4** go under water and emerge quickly. **5** (foll. by *into*) look cursorily into (a book, subject, etc.). **6 a** (foll. by *into*) put a hand, ladle, etc., into (a container) to take something out. **b** use part of (one's resources) (*dipped into our savings*). **7** lower or be lowered, esp. in salute. **8** lower the beam of (headlights) to reduce dazzle. **9** colour (a fabric) by immersing it in dye. **10** wash (sheep) in disinfectant. –*n.* **1** dipping or being dipped. **2** liquid for dipping. **3** brief bathe in the sea etc. **4** downward slope or hollow in a road, skyline, etc. **5** sauce into which food is dipped. **6** candle made by dipping the wick in tallow. [Old English]

Dip. BA *abbr.* Diploma in Business Administration.

Dip. CAM *abbr.* Diploma in Communication, Advertising, and Marketing.

Dip. Com. *abbr.* Diploma in Commerce.

Dip. Econ. *abbr.* Diploma in Economics.

Dip. Ed. *abbr.* Diploma in Education.

diphtheria /dɪfˈθɪərɪə, dɪp-/ *n.* acute infectious bacterial disease with inflammation of a mucous membrane esp. of the throat. [Greek *diphthera* skin, hide]

■ **Usage** The second pronunciation is considered incorrect by some people.

diphthong /ˈdɪfθɒŋ/ *n.* two written or spoken vowels pronounced in one syllable (as in *coin*, *loud*, *toy*). [Greek *phthoggos* voice]

diplodocus /dɪˈplɒdəkəs/ *n.* (*pl.* **-cusus**) giant plant-eating dinosaur with a long neck and tail. [Greek *diplous* double, *dokos* wooden beam]

diploma /dɪˈpləʊmə/ *n.* **1** certificate of qualification awarded by a college etc. **2** document conferring an honour or privilege. [Greek, = folded paper, from *diplous* double]

diplomacy /dɪˈpləʊməsɪ/ *n.* **1 a** management of international relations. **b** skill in this. **2** tact. [French: related to DIPLOMATIC]

diplomat /ˈdɪpləˌmæt/ *n.* **1** member of a diplomatic service. **2** tactful person.

diplomatic /ˌdɪpləˈmætɪk/ *adj.* **1** of or involved in diplomacy. **2** tactful. □ **diplomatically** *adv.* [French: related to DIPLOMA]

diplomatic bag *n.* container for dispatching official mail etc. to or from an embassy, usu. exempt from customs inspection.

diplomatic immunity *n.* exemption of diplomatic staff abroad from arrest, taxation, etc.

diplomatic service *n.* branch of the civil service concerned with the representation of a country abroad.

diplomatist /dɪˈpləʊmətɪst/ *n.* diplomat.

Dip. M *abbr.* Diploma in Marketing.

dipole /ˈdaɪpəʊl/ *n.* **1** two equal and oppositely charged or magnetized poles separated by a distance. **2** molecule in which a concentration of positive charges is separated from a concentration of negative charges. **3** aerial consisting of a horizontal metal rod with a connecting wire at its core.

dipper *n.* **1** diving bird, esp. the water ouzel. **2** ladle.

dippy /ˈdɪpɪ/ *adj.* (**-ier**, **-iest**) *slang* crazy, silly. [origin uncertain]

DIPS *abbr.* digital image-processing system.

dipso /ˈdɪpsəʊ/ *n.* (*pl.* **-s**) *colloq.* alcoholic. [abbreviation]

dipsomania /ˌdɪpsəˈmeɪnɪə/ *n.* alcoholism. □ **dipsomaniac** /-nɪˌæk/ *n.* [Greek *dipsa* thirst]

dipstick *n.* rod for measuring the depth of esp. oil in a vehicle's engine.

dip-switch *n.* switch for dipping a vehicle's headlights.

dipterous /ˈdɪptərəs/ *adj.* (of an insect) having two wings. [Greek *pteron* wing]

diptych /ˈdɪptɪk/ *n.* painting, esp. an altarpiece, on two hinged panels closing like a book. [Greek, = pair of writing-tablets, from *ptukhē* fold]

dire *adj.* **1 a** calamitous, dreadful. **b** ominous. **c** (*predic.*) *colloq.* very bad. **2** urgent (*in dire need*). [Latin]

direct /daɪˈrekt, dɪ-/ –*adj.* **1** extending or moving in a straight line or by the shortest route; not crooked or circuitous. **2** straightforward; frank. **3** with nothing or no-one in between; personal (*direct line*). **4** (of descent) lineal, not collateral. **5** complete, greatest possible (*the direct opposite*). –*adv.* **1** in a direct way or manner (*dealt with them direct*). **2** by the direct route (*sent direct to London*). –*v.* **1** control; govern or guide (*duty directs me*). **2** (foll. by *to* + infin., or *that* + clause) order (a person) to. **3** (foll. by *to*) **a** address (a letter etc.). **b** tell or show (a person) the way to (a place). **4** (foll. by *at*, *to*, *towards*) point, aim, or turn (a blow, attention, or remark). **5** (also *absol.*) supervise the performing, staging, etc., of (a film, play, etc.). □ **directness** *n.* [Latin *dirigo* from *rego rect-* guide]

direct access *n.* *Computing* random access to a storage device, esp. a magnetic disk. See RANDOM ACCESS.

♦ **direct costs** *n.pl.* costs, e.g. materials and labour, that can be attributed directly to a cost unit, usu. without the necessity of apportionment (see COST UNIT). The labour cost would be measured as the length of time needed to produce the cost unit at a given rate per hour. Cf. OVERHEAD COSTS.

direct current *n.* electric current flowing in one direction only.

direct data entry *n.* (also **DDE**) any process by which data is fed directly into a computer and is written in the computer's on-line files stored on disk. The data is usu. entered by an operator at a keyboard.

♦ **direct debit** *n.* form of standing order given to a bank by an account holder to pay regular amounts from his or her cheque account to a third party. Unlike a normal standing order, however, the amount to be paid is not specified; the account holder trusts the third party to claim an appropriate sum from the bank.

direct-grant school *n.* school funded by the government and not a local authority.

direction /daɪˈrekʃ(ə)n, dɪ-/ *n.* **1** directing; supervision. **2** (usu. in *pl.*) order or instruction. **3** line along which, or point to or from which, a person or thing moves or looks. **4** tendency or scope of a theme, subject, etc.

directional *adj.* **1** of or indicating direction. **2** sending or receiving radio or sound waves in one particular direction.

directive /daɪˈrektɪv, dɪ-/ –*n.* **1** order from an authority. **2** legislative decision by the EC Council of Ministers and Parliament that is binding on member states. –*adj.* serving to direct.

♦ **direct labour** *n.* **1** employees of an organization who carry out work for that organization, rather than employees of a contractor used to carry out the work. For example, some councils use direct labour to collect refuse, while others use a contractor. **2** labour involved in producing goods or providing services, rather than the ancillary costs of supporting the producers and providers. Cf. INDIRECT LABOUR.

directly –*adv.* **1 a** at once; without delay, immediately (*directly after lunch*). **b** presently, shortly. **2** exactly (*directly* *opposite*). **3** in a direct manner. *–conj. colloq.* as soon as (*will tell you directly they come*).

♦ **direct-mail selling** *n.* form of direct marketing in which sales literature or other promotional material is mailed directly to selected potential purchasers. The seller may be the producer of the products or a business that specializes in this form of marketing. The seller may either build up a list of potential customers or buy or rent a list (see LIST RENTING). See also MAIL-ORDER HOUSE.

♦ **direct marketing** *n.* selling directly to consumers rather than through retailers. Methods include mail order, direct-mail selling, cold calling, telephone selling, door-to-door calling, etc.

direct object *n.* primary object of the action of a transitive verb.

director *n.* **1** person who directs or controls, esp. a person appointed to carry out the day-to-day management of a company. A public company must have at least two directors, a private company at least one. The directors of a company, collectively known as the **board of directors**, usu. act together, although power may be conferred (by the articles of association) on one or more directors to exercise executive powers; in particular there is often a managing director with considerable executive power. The first directors of a company are usu. named in its articles of association or are appointed by the subscribers; they are required to give a signed undertaking to act in that capacity, which must be sent to the Registrar of Companies. Subsequent directors are appointed by the company at a general meeting, although in practice they may be appointed by the other directors for ratification by the general meeting. Directors may be discharged from office by an ordinary resolution with special notice at a general meeting, whether or not they have a service contract in force. They may be disqualified for fraudulent trading or wrongful trading or for any conduct that makes them unfit to manage the company. Directors owe duties of honesty and loyalty to the company (fiduciary duties) and a duty of care; their liability in negligence depends upon their personal qualifications (e.g. a chartered accountant must exercise more skill than an unqualified person). Directors need no formal qualifications. Directors may not put their own interests before those of the company, may not make contracts (other than service contracts) with the company, and must declare any personal interest in work undertaken by the company. Their formal responsibilities include: presenting to members of the company, at least annually, the accounts of the company and a directors' report (see ACCOUNT *n.* 3; DIRECTORS' REPORT); keeping a register of directors, a register of directors' shareholdings, and a register of shares; calling an annual general meeting; sending all relevant documents to the Registrar of Companies; and submitting a statement of affairs if the company is wound up (see LIQUIDATOR). Directors' remuneration consists of a salary and in some cases **directors' fees**, paid to them for being a director, and an expense allowance to cover their expenses incurred in the service of the company. Directors' remuneration must be disclosed in the company's accounts and shown separately from any pension payments or compensation for loss of office. See also EXECUTIVE DIRECTOR; MANAGING DIRECTOR. **2** person who directs a film, play, etc. □ **directorial** /-'tɔːrɪəl/ *adj.* **directorship** *n.*

directorate /daɪ'rektərət, dɪ-/ *n.* **1** board of directors. **2** office of director.

director-general *n.* chief executive of a large organization.

♦ **Director General of Fair Trading** see CONSUMER PROTECTION.

♦ **directors' report** *n.* annual report by the directors of a company to its shareholders, which forms part of the company's accounts required to be filed with the Registrar of Companies under the Companies Act (1985). The information that must be given includes the principal activities of the company, a fair review of the developments and position of the business with likely future developments, details of research and development, significant issues on the sale, purchase, or valuation of assets, recommended dividends, transfers to reserves, names of the directors and their interests in the company during the period, employee statistics, and any political or charitable gifts made during the period. See also MEDIUM-SIZED COMPANY; SMALL COMPANY.

directory /daɪ'rektərɪ, dɪ-/ *n.* (*pl.* **-ies**) **1** book with a list of telephone subscribers, inhabitants of a district, or members of a profession etc. **2** file in a computer system (see FILE[1] *n.* 3) containing a list of file names, their locations on backing store, and their size, as well as other information, e.g. creation date, author, date of last access, and file protection code. A computer system may have many directories. On a multi-access system each user has a directory and the operating system also has one or more. On a microcomputer system each disk has its own directory. Directories are used by the operating system to locate files when given their names, and by computer users to keep track of what files are available. [Latin: related to DIRECT]

directory enquiries *n.pl.* telephone service providing a subscriber's number on request.

directress *n.* woman director.

direct speech *n.* words actually spoken, not reported.

♦ **direct taxation** *n.* taxation, the effect of which is intended to be borne by the person or organization that pays it (cf. INDIRECT TAXATION). The principal **direct tax** is income tax, in which the person who receives the income pays the tax. Corporation tax is a direct tax but there is evidence that its incidence can be shifted to consumers by higher prices or to employees by lower wages. Inheritance tax could also be thought of as a direct tax on the deceased, although its incidence falls on the heirs of the estate.

♦ **direct utility function** *n. Econ.* type of utility function that expresses the preferences of individuals (see CONSUMER PREFERENCE) in terms of the goods and services that they choose to purchase. Cf. INDIRECT UTILITY FUNCTION.

dirge *n.* **1** lament for the dead. **2** any dreary piece of music. [Latin imperative *dirige* = direct, used in the Office for the Dead]

dirham /'dɪəræm/ *n.* **1** standard monetary unit of Morocco and the United Arab Emirates. **2** monetary unit of Libya worth one thousandth of a dinar. **3** monetary unit of Qatar worth one hundredth of a riyal. **4** monetary unit of Kuwait worth one tenth of a dinar. [Arabic]

dirigible /'dɪrɪdʒɪb(ə)l/ *–adj.* capable of being guided. *–n.* dirigible balloon or airship. [related to DIRECT]

dirk *n.* short dagger. [origin unknown]

dirndl /'dɜːnd(ə)l/ *n.* **1** dress with a close-fitting bodice and full skirt. **2** full skirt of this kind. [German]

dirt *n.* **1** unclean matter that soils. **2 a** earth, soil. **b** earth, cinders, etc., used to make the surface for a road etc. (usu. *attrib.*: *dirt track*). **3** foul or malicious words or talk. **4** excrement. □ **treat like dirt** treat with contempt. [Old Norse *drit* excrement]

dirt cheap *adj.* & *adv. colloq.* extremely cheap.

dirty *–adj.* (**-ier, -iest**) **1** soiled, unclean. **2** causing dirtiness (*dirty job*). **3** sordid, lewd, obscene. **4** unpleasant, dishonourable, unfair (*dirty trick*). **5** (of weather) rough, squally. **6** (of colour) muddied, dingy. *–adv. slang* **1** very (*a dirty great diamond*). **2** in a dirty manner (*talk dirty*; *act dirty*) (esp. in senses 3 and 4 of *adj.*). *–v.* (**-ies, -ied**) make or become dirty. □ **do the dirty on** *colloq.* play a mean trick on. □ **dirtily** *adv.* **dirtiness** *n.*

♦ **dirty bill of lading** *n.* (also **foul** or **claused bill of lading**) bill of lading carrying a clause or endorsement by the master or mate of the ship on which goods are carried to the effect that the goods (or their packing) arrived for loading in a damaged condition.

♦ **dirty float** *n. Finance* technique for managing the exchange rate in which a government publicly renounces direct intervention in the foreign exchange markets while continuing to engage in intervention surreptitiously. This technique was widely used after the collapse of the Bretton Woods fixed exchange rate system in the early 1970s as governments were unable to agree programmes of explicitly managed floating but were not prepared to accept fully floating rates.

---

dirty look *n. colloq.* look of disapproval or disgust.
dirty old man *n. colloq.* lecherous man.
dirty weekend *n. colloq.* weekend spent with a lover.
dirty word *n.* **1** offensive or indecent word. **2** word for something disapproved of (*profit is a dirty word*).
dirty work *n.* dishonourable or illegal activity.
dis- *prefix* forming nouns, adjectives, and verbs implying: **1** negation or direct opposite (*dishonest*; *discourteous*). **2** reversal (*disengage*; *disorientate*). **3** removal of a thing or quality (*dismember*; *disable*). **4** separation (*distinguish*). **5** completeness or intensification (*disgruntled*). **6** expulsion from (*disbar*). [French *des-* or Latin *dis-*]
disability /ˌdɪsəˈbɪlɪtɪ/ *n.* (*pl.* **-ies**) **1** permanent physical or mental incapacity. **2** lack of some capacity etc., preventing action.
disable /dɪsˈeɪb(ə)l/ *v.* (**-ling**) **1** deprive of an ability or function. **2** (often as **disabled** *adj.*) physically incapacitate. □ **disablement** *n.*
disabuse /ˌdɪsəˈbjuːz/ *v.* (**-sing**) (usu. foll. by *of*) free from a mistaken idea; disillusion.
disadvantage /ˌdɪsədˈvɑːntɪdʒ/ *–n.* **1** unfavourable circumstance or condition. **2** damage; loss. *–v.* (**-ging**) cause disadvantage to. □ **at a disadvantage** in an unfavourable position or aspect. □ **disadvantageous** /-ˌædvənˈteɪdʒəs/ *adj.*
disadvantaged *adj.* lacking normal opportunities through poverty, disability, etc.
disaffected /ˌdɪsəˈfektɪd/ *adj.* discontented (esp. politically); no longer loyal. □ **disaffection** *n.*
disagree /ˌdɪsəˈgriː/ *v.* (**-ees, -eed, -eeing**) (often foll. by *with*) **1** hold a different opinion. **2** (of factors) not correspond. **3** upset (*onions disagree with me*). □ **disagreement** *n.*
disagreeable *adj.* **1** unpleasant. **2** bad-tempered. □ **disagreeably** *adv.*
disallow /ˌdɪsəˈlaʊ/ *v.* refuse to allow or accept; prohibit.
disappear /ˌdɪsəˈpɪə(r)/ *v.* **1** cease to be visible. **2** cease to exist or be in circulation or use. **3** (of a person) go missing. □ **disappearance** *n.*
disappoint /ˌdɪsəˈpɔɪnt/ *v.* **1** fail to fulfil the desire or expectation of. **2** frustrate (a hope etc.). □ **disappointed** *adj.* **disappointing** *adj.*
disappointment *n.* **1** person or thing that disappoints. **2** being disappointed.
disapprobation /dɪsˌæprəˈbeɪʃ(ə)n/ *n. formal* disapproval.
disapprove /ˌdɪsəˈpruːv/ *v.* (**-ving**) (usu. foll. by *of*) have or express an unfavourable opinion. □ **disapproval** *n.*
disarm /dɪsˈɑːm/ *v.* **1** take weapons etc. away from. **2** reduce or give up one's own weapons. **3** defuse (a bomb etc.). **4** make less angry, hostile, etc; charm, win over. □ **disarming** *adj.* (esp. in sense 4). **disarmingly** *adv.*
disarmament /dɪsˈɑːməmənt/ *n.* reduction by a state of its armaments.
disarrange /ˌdɪsəˈreɪndʒ/ *v.* (**-ging**) bring into disorder. □ **disarrangement** *n.*
disarray /ˌdɪsəˈreɪ/ *–n.* disorder. *–v.* throw into disorder.
disassociate /ˌdɪsəˈsəʊʃɪˌeɪt/ *v.* (**-ting**) = DISSOCIATE. □ **disassociation** /-ˈeɪʃ(ə)n/ *n.*
disaster /dɪˈzɑːstə(r)/ *n.* **1** great or sudden misfortune; catastrophe. **2** *colloq.* complete failure. □ **disastrous** *adj.* **disastrously** *adv.* [Latin *astrum* star]
disavow /ˌdɪsəˈvaʊ/ *v.* disclaim knowledge of or responsibility for. □ **disavowal** *n.*
disband /dɪsˈbænd/ *v.* break up; disperse. □ **disbandment** *n.*
disbar /dɪsˈbɑː(r)/ *v.* (**-rr-**) deprive (a barrister) of the right to practise. □ **disbarment** *n.*
disbelieve /ˌdɪsbɪˈliːv/ *v.* (**-ving**) be unable or unwilling to believe; be sceptical. □ **disbelief** *n.* **disbelievingly** *adv.*
disburse /dɪsˈbɜːs/ *v.* (**-sing**) pay out (money). □ **disbursal** *n.* [French: related to DIS-, BOURSE]

♦ **disbursement** *n.* payment made by a professional person, e.g. a solicitor or banker, on behalf of a client. This is claimed back when the client receives an account for the professional services.

---

disc *n.* (also esp. *US* **disk**) **1 a** flat thin circular object. **b** round flat or apparently flat surface or mark. **2** layer of cartilage between vertebrae. **3** gramophone record. **4** *Computing* var. of DISK 2. [Latin DISCUS]
discard /dɪsˈkɑːd/ *v.* **1** reject as unwanted. **2** remove or put aside. [from DIS-, CARD[1]]
disc brake *n.* brake employing the friction of pads against a disc.
discern /dɪˈsɜːn/ *v.* **1** perceive clearly with the mind or senses. **2** make out with effort. □ **discernible** *adj.* [Latin *cerno cret-* separate]
discerning *adj.* having good judgement. □ **discerningly** *adv.* **discernment** *n.*
discharge *–v.* /dɪsˈtʃɑːdʒ/ (**-ging**) **1** release (a prisoner); allow (a patient, jury) to leave. **2** dismiss from office or employment. **3** fire (a gun etc.). **4** throw; eject. **5** emit, pour out (pus etc.). **6** (foll. by *into*) (of a river etc.) flow into (esp. the sea). **7 a** carry out (a duty or obligation). **b** relieve oneself of (a debt etc.). **c** relieve (a bankrupt) of residual liability. **8** *Law* cancel (an order of court). **9** release an electrical charge from. **10 a** relieve (a ship etc.) of cargo. **b** unload (cargo). *–n.* /ˈdɪstʃɑːdʒ/ **1** discharging or being discharged. **2** certificate of release, dismissal, etc. **3** matter discharged; pus etc. **4** release of an electric charge, esp. with a spark.
disciple /dɪˈsaɪp(ə)l/ *n.* follower of a leader, teacher, etc., esp. of Christ. [Latin *disco* learn]
disciplinarian /ˌdɪsɪplɪˈneərɪən/ *n.* enforcer of or believer in firm discipline.
disciplinary /ˈdɪsɪplɪnərɪ/ *adj.* of or enforcing discipline.
discipline /ˈdɪsɪplɪn/ *–n.* **1 a** control or order exercised over people or animals, e.g. over members of an organization. **b** system of rules for this. **2** training or way of life aimed at self-control and conformity. **3** branch of learning. **4** punishment. *–v.* (**-ning**) **1** punish. **2** control by training in obedience. [Latin *disciplina* from *disco* learn]
disc jockey *n.* presenter of recorded pop music.
disclaim /dɪsˈkleɪm/ *v.* **1** deny or disown. **2** renounce legal claim to.
disclaimer *n.* renunciation; statement disclaiming something.
disclose /dɪsˈkləʊz/ *v.* (**-sing**) make known; expose.

♦ **disclosure** *n.* **1** something disclosed. **2** revealing; exposing. **3** *Law* **a** obligation that each party to a contract has to the other to disclose all the facts relevant to the subject matter of the contract. See UTMOST GOOD FAITH. **b** obligation that a company has to disclose all relevant information and results of trading to its shareholders. See DIRECTORS' REPORT.

---

disco /ˈdɪskəʊ/ *colloq. –n.* (*pl.* **-s**) = DISCOTHÈQUE. *–v.* (**-es, -ed**) dance to disco music. [abbreviation]
discolour /dɪsˈkʌlə(r)/ *v.* (*US* **discolor**) cause to change from its normal colour; stain; tarnish. □ **discoloration** /-ˈreɪʃ(ə)n/ *n.*
discomfit /dɪsˈkʌmfɪt/ *v.* (**-t-**) disconcert, baffle, frustrate. □ **discomfiture** *n.* [French: related to DIS-, CONFECTION]
■ **Usage** *Discomfit* is sometimes confused with *discomfort*.

discomfort /dɪs'kʌmfət/ *–n.* **1** lack of comfort; slight pain or unease. **2** cause of this. *–v.* make uncomfortable.
■ **Usage** As a verb, *discomfort* is sometimes confused with *discomfit*.

discompose /ˌdɪskəm'pəʊz/ *v.* (**-sing**) disturb the composure of. □ **discomposure** *n.*

disco music *n.* popular dance music with a heavy bass rhythm.

disconcert /ˌdɪskən'sɜːt/ *v.* disturb the composure of; fluster.

disconnect /ˌdɪskə'nekt/ *v.* **1** break the connection of. **2** put out of action by disconnecting the parts. □ **disconnection** *n.*

disconnected *adj.* incoherent and illogical.

disconsolate /dɪs'kɒnsələt/ *adj.* forlorn, unhappy, disappointed. □ **disconsolately** *adv.* [Latin: related to DIS-, SOLACE]

discontent /ˌdɪskən'tent/ *–n.* lack of contentment; dissatisfaction, grievance. *–v.* (esp. as **discontented** *adj.*) make dissatisfied. □ **discontentment** *n.*

discontinue /ˌdɪskən'tɪnjuː/ *v.* (**-ues**, **-ued**, **-uing**) **1** come or bring to an end (*a discontinued line*). **2** give up, cease from (doing something). □ **discontinuance** *n.*

discontinuous *adj.* lacking continuity; intermittent. □ **discontinuity** /-ˌkɒntɪ'njuːɪtɪ/ *n.*

discord /'dɪskɔːd/ *n.* **1** disagreement; strife. **2** harsh noise; clashing sounds. **3** lack of harmony in a chord. [Latin: related to DIS-, *cor cord-* heart]

discordant /dɪ'skɔːd(ə)nt/ *adj.* **1** disagreeing. **2** not in harmony; dissonant. □ **discordance** *n.* **discordantly** *adv.*

discothèque /'dɪskəˌtek/ *n.* **1** nightclub etc. for dancing to pop records. **2** professional lighting and sound equipment used for this. **3** party with such equipment. [French, = record-library]

discount *–n.* /'dɪskaʊnt/ **1** amount deducted from the list price of goods for buyers who pay cash (**cash discount**), for members of the trade (**trade discount**), for buying in bulk (**bulk** or **quantity discount**), etc. **2** deduction from a bill of exchange when it is purchased before its maturity date. The party that purchases the bill pays less than its face value and therefore makes a profit when it matures. The amount of the discount consists of interest calculated at the bill rate for the length of time that the bill has to run. See DISCOUNT MARKET. **3** amount by which the market price of a security is below its par value. A £100 par value loan stock with a market price of £95 is said to be at a 5% discount. *–v.* /dɪs'kaʊnt/ **1** disregard as unreliable or unimportant. **2** deduct an amount from (a price etc.). **3** buy or sell (a bill of exchange which has yet to mature) at less than the face value. □ **at a discount** below the usual price or true value. **discount back** see DISCOUNTED CASH FLOW.

♦ **discount broker** *n.* = BILL BROKER.

♦ **discounted cash flow** *n.* (also **DCF**) method of appraising capital-investment projects by comparing their income in the future and their present and future costs with the current equivalents. The current equivalents take account of the fact that future receipts are less valuable than current receipts, in that interest can be earned on current receipts; on the other hand future payments are less onerous than current payments, as interest can be earned on money retained for future payments. Accordingly, future receipts and payments are **discounted back**, i.e. discounted to their present values by applying discount factors, taking account of interest that could be earned for the relevant number of years to the date of payment or receipt. See also NET PRESENT VALUE.

---

discountenance /dɪ'skaʊntɪnəns/ *v.* (**-cing**) **1** disconcert. **2** refuse to approve of.

♦ **discount house** *n.* **1** (also **discount store**) shop that is open to members of the public, or in some cases to members of a trade, and sells goods, usu. consumer durables, at prices close to wholesale prices. **2** company or bank on the discount market that specializes in discounting bills of exchange, esp. treasury bills.

♦ **discount market** *n.* component of the money market consisting of banks, discount houses, and bill brokers. By borrowing money at short notice from commercial banks or discount houses, bill brokers are able to discount bills of exchange, esp. treasury bills, and make a profit. The loans are secured on unmatured bills.

♦ **discount rate** *n.* **1** = BILL RATE. **2** rate of interest charged by the US Federal Reserve Banks when lending to other banks.

---

discourage /dɪ'skʌrɪdʒ/ *v.* (**-ging**) **1** deprive of courage or confidence. **2** dissuade, deter. **3** show disapproval of. □ **discouragement** *n.*

discourse *–n.* /'dɪskɔːs/ **1** conversation. **2** lengthy treatment of a subject. **3** lecture, speech. *–v.* /dɪ'skɔːs/ (**-sing**) **1** converse. **2** speak or write at length on a subject. [Latin *curro curs-* run]

discourteous /dɪs'kɜːtɪəs/ *adj.* lacking courtesy. □ **discourteously** *adv.* **discourtesy** *n.* (*pl.* **-ies**).

discover /dɪ'skʌvə(r)/ *v.* **1 a** find out or become aware of, by intention or chance. **b** be first to find or find out (*who discovered America?*). **2** find and promote as a new performer. □ **discoverer** *n.* [Latin *discooperio*: related to DIS-, COVER]

discovery *n.* (*pl.* **-ies**) **1** discovering or being discovered. **2** person or thing discovered.

discredit /dɪs'kredɪt/ *–n.* **1** harm to reputation. **2** person or thing causing this. **3** lack of credibility. *–v.* (**-t-**) **1** harm the good reputation of. **2** cause to be disbelieved. **3** refuse to believe.

discreditable *adj.* bringing discredit; shameful. □ **discreditably** *adv.*

discreet /dɪ'skriːt/ *adj.* (**-er**, **-est**) **1 a** circumspect. **b** tactful; judicious, prudent. **2** unobtrusive. □ **discreetly** *adv.* **discreetness** *n.* [Latin: related to DISCERN]

discrepancy /dɪs'krepənsɪ/ *n.* (*pl.* **-ies**) difference; inconsistency. □ **discrepant** *adj.* [Latin *discrepo* be discordant]

discrete /dɪ'skriːt/ *adj.* individually distinct; separate, discontinuous. □ **discreteness** *n.* [Latin: related to DISCERN]

discretion /dɪ'skreʃ(ə)n/ *n.* **1** being discreet. **2** prudence; good judgement. **3** freedom or authority to act according to one's judgement. □ **use one's discretion** act according to one's own judgement. □ **discretionary** *adj.* [Latin: related to DISCERN]

♦ **discretionary order** *n.* **1** order given to a stockbroker, commodity broker, etc. to buy or sell a stated quantity of specified securities or commodities, leaving the broker discretion to deal at the best price. **2** similar order given to a stockbroker in which the sum of money is specified but the broker has discretion as to which security to buy.

♦ **discretionary trust** *n.* financial trust in which the shares of each beneficiary are not fixed by the settlor in the trust deed but may be varied at the discretion of some person or persons (often the trustees). In an **exhaustive discretionary trust** all the income arising in any year must be paid out during that year, although no beneficiary has a right to any specific sum. In a **non-exhaustive discretionary trust**, income may be carried forward to subsequent years and no beneficiary need receive anything. Such trusts are useful when the needs of the beneficiaries are likely to change, for example in the case of children.

---

discriminate /dɪ'skrɪmɪˌneɪt/ *v.* (**-ting**) **1** (often foll. by *between*) make or see a distinction. **2** (usu. foll. by *against* or *in favour of*) treat unfavourably or favourably, esp on the basis of race, gender, etc. □ **discriminatory** /-nətərɪ/ *adj.* [Latin *discrimino*: related to DISCERN]

discriminating *adj.* showing good judgement or taste.

♦ **discriminating monopoly** *n.* monopoly in which the supplier sells products or services to consumers at different prices; by dividing the market into segments and charging each market segment the price it will bear, the monopolist profit is increased. For example, different domestic and industrial tariffs are operated by suppliers of electricity in many countries.

♦ **discriminating tariff** *n.* tariff that is not imposed equally by a country or group of countries on all its trading partners. The abolition of discriminating tariffs is one of the purposes of the General Agreement on Tariffs and Trade and other trading blocs.

---

discrimination /dɪˌskrɪmɪˈneɪʃ(ə)n/ *n.* **1** unfavourable treatment based on racial, sexual, etc. prejudice. See also EQUAL PAY. **2** good taste or judgement.

discursive /dɪˈskɜːsɪv/ *adj.* tending to digress, rambling. [Latin *curro curs-* run]

discus /ˈdɪskəs/ *n.* (*pl.* **-cuses**) heavy thick-centred disc thrown in athletic events. [Latin from Greek]

discuss /dɪˈskʌs/ *v.* **1** talk about (*discussed their holidays*). **2** talk or write about (a subject) in detail. □ **discussion** *n.* [Latin *discutio -cuss-* disperse]

disdain /dɪsˈdeɪn/ *–n.* scorn, contempt. *–v.* **1** regard with disdain. **2** refrain or refuse out of disdain. □ **disdainful** *adj.* **disdainfully** *adv.* [Latin: related to DE-, DEIGN]

disease /dɪˈziːz/ *n.* **1** unhealthy condition of the body or mind, plants, society, etc. **2** particular kind of disease. □ **diseased** *adj.* [French: related to DIS-, EASE]

♦ **diseconomies of scale** see ECONOMIES OF SCALE.

---

disembark /ˌdɪsɪmˈbɑːk/ *v.* put or go ashore; get off an aircraft, bus, etc. □ **disembarkation** /-ˈkeɪʃ(ə)n/ *n.*

disembarrass /ˌdɪsɪmˈbærəs/ *v.* **1** (usu. foll. by *of*) relieve (of a load etc.). **2** free from embarrassment. □ **disembarrassment** *n.*

disembodied /ˌdɪsɪmˈbɒdɪd/ *adj.* **1** (of the soul etc.) freed from the body or concrete form. **2** lacking a body. □ **disembodiment** *n.*

disembowel /ˌdɪsɪmˈbaʊəl/ *v.* (**-ll-**; *US* **-l-**) remove the bowels or entrails of. □ **disembowelment** *n.*

disenchant /ˌdɪsɪnˈtʃɑːnt/ *v.* disillusion. □ **disenchantment** *n.*

disencumber /ˌdɪsɪnˈkʌmbə(r)/ *v.* free from encumbrance.

disenfranchise /ˌdɪsɪnˈfræntʃaɪz/ *v.* (also **disfranchise**) (**-sing**) **1** deprive of the right to vote or to be represented. **2** deprive of rights as a citizen or of a franchise held. □ **disenfranchisement** *n.*

disengage /ˌdɪsɪnˈgeɪdʒ/ *v.* (**-ging**) **1** detach, loosen, release. **2** remove (troops) from battle etc. **3** become detached. **4** (as **disengaged** *adj.*) **a** at leisure. **b** uncommitted. □ **disengagement** *n.*

disentangle /ˌdɪsɪnˈtæŋg(ə)l/ *v.* (**-ling**) free or become free of tangles or complications. □ **disentanglement** *n.*

disestablish /ˌdɪsɪˈstæblɪʃ/ *v.* **1** deprive (a Church) of state support. **2** terminate the establishment of. □ **disestablishment** *n.*

disfavour /dɪsˈfeɪvə(r)/ (*US* **disfavor**) *–n.* **1** disapproval or dislike. **2** being disliked. *–v.* regard or treat with disfavour.

disfigure /dɪsˈfɪgə(r)/ *v.* (**-ring**) spoil the appearance of. □ **disfigurement** *n.*

disfranchise var. of DISENFRANCHISE.

disgorge /dɪsˈgɔːdʒ/ *v.* (**-ging**) **1** eject from the throat. **2** pour forth. □ **disgorgement** *n.*

disgrace /dɪsˈgreɪs/ *–n.* **1** shame; ignominy. **2** shameful or very bad person or thing (*bus service is a disgrace*). *–v.* (**-cing**) **1** bring shame or discredit on. **2** dismiss from a position of honour or favour. □ **in disgrace** out of favour. [Latin: related to DIS-, GRACE]

disgraceful *adj.* shameful; causing disgrace. □ **disgracefully** *adv.*

disgruntled /dɪsˈgrʌnt(ə)ld/ *adj.* discontented; sulky. □ **disgruntlement** *n.* [from DIS-, GRUNT]

disguise /dɪsˈgaɪz/ *–v.* (**-sing**) **1** conceal the identity of; make unrecognizable. **2** conceal (*disguised my anger*). *–n.* **1 a** costume, make-up, etc., used to disguise. **b** action, manner, etc., used to deceive. **2** disguised state. **3** practice of disguising. [French: related to DIS-]

disgust /dɪsˈgʌst/ *–n.* strong aversion; repugnance. *–v.* cause disgust in. □ **disgusting** *adj.* **disgustingly** *adv.* [French or Italian: related to DIS-, GUSTO]

dish *–n.* **1 a** shallow flat-bottomed container for food. **b** its contents. **c** particular kind of food or food prepared to a particular recipe (*meat dish*). **2** (in *pl.*) crockery, pans, etc. after a meal (*wash the dishes*). **3 a** dish-shaped object or cavity. **b** = SATELLITE DISH. **4** *colloq.* sexually attractive person. *–v.* **1** *colloq.* outmanoeuvre, frustrate. **2** make dish-shaped. □ **dish out** *colloq.* distribute. **dish up** **1** put (food) in dishes for serving. **2** *colloq.* present as a fact or argument. [Old English from Latin DISCUS]

dishabille var. of DÉSHABILLÉ.

disharmony /dɪsˈhɑːmənɪ/ *n.* lack of harmony; discord. □ **disharmonious** /-ˈməʊnɪəs/ *adj.*

dishcloth *n.* cloth for washing dishes.

dishearten /dɪsˈhɑːt(ə)n/ *v.* cause to lose courage, hope, or confidence. □ **disheartenment** *n.*

dishevelled /dɪˈʃev(ə)ld/ *adj.* (*US* **disheveled**) untidy; ruffled. □ **dishevelment** *n.* [from DIS-, *chevel* 'hair', from Latin *capillus*]

dishonest /dɪsˈɒnɪst/ *adj.* fraudulent or insincere. □ **dishonestly** *adv.* **dishonesty** *n.*

dishonour /dɪsˈɒnə(r)/ (*US* **dishonor**) *–n.* **1** loss of honour or respect; disgrace. **2** thing causing this. *–v.* **1** disgrace (*dishonoured his name*). **2** fail to pay (a cheque) when the account of the drawer does not have sufficient funds to cover it. When a bank dishonours a cheque it marks it 'refer to drawer' and returns it to the payee through his or her bank. **3** fail either to accept (**dishonour by non-acceptance**) or to pay (**dishonour by non-payment**) (a bill of exchange). See PROTEST *n.* 2.

dishonourable *adj.* (*US* **dishonorable**) **1** causing disgrace; ignominious. **2** unprincipled. □ **dishonourably** *adv.*

dishwasher *n.* machine or person that washes dishes.

dishy *adj.* (**-ier, -iest**) *colloq.* sexually attractive.

disillusion /ˌdɪsɪˈluːʒ(ə)n/ *–v.* free from an illusion or mistaken belief. *–n.* disillusioned state. □ **disillusionment** *n.*

disincentive /ˌdɪsɪnˈsentɪv/ *n.* thing discouraging action, effort, etc.

disincline /ˌdɪsɪnˈklaɪn/ *v.* (**-ning**) make unwilling or reluctant. □ **disinclination** /-klɪˈneɪʃ(ə)n/ *n.*

disinfect /ˌdɪsɪnˈfekt/ *v.* cleanse of infection, esp. with disinfectant. □ **disinfection** *n.*

disinfectant *–n.* substance that destroys germs etc. *–adj.* disinfecting.

♦ **disinflation** /ˌdɪsɪnˈfleɪʃ(ə)n/ *n.* gentle form of deflation, to restrain inflation without creating unemployment. Measures include restricting consumer spending by raising the interest rate, imposing restrictions on hire-purchase agreements, and introducing price controls on commodities in short supply. □ **disinflationary** *adj.*

---

disinformation /ˌdɪsɪnfəˈmeɪʃ(ə)n/ *n.* false information, propaganda.

disingenuous /ˌdɪsɪnˈdʒenjʊəs/ *adj.* insincere, not candid. □ **disingenuously** *adv.*

disinherit /ˌdɪsɪnˈherɪt/ *v.* (**-t-**) reject as one's heir; deprive of the right of inheritance. □ **disinheritance** *n.*

disintegrate /dɪsˈɪntɪˌgreɪt/ *v.* (**-ting**) **1** separate into component parts or fragments, break up. **2** *colloq.* break down, esp. mentally. **3** (of an atomic nucleus) emit particles or divide into smaller nuclei. □ **disintegration** /-ˈgreɪʃ(ə)n/ *n.*

disinter /ˌdɪsɪnˈtɜː(r)/ *v.* (**-rr-**) dig up (esp. a corpse). □ **disinterment** *n.*

disinterested /dɪsˈɪntrɪstɪd/ *adj.* **1** impartial. **2** uninterested. □ **disinterest** *n.* **disinterestedly** *adv.*

■ **Usage** Use of *disinterested* in sense 2 is common in informal use, but is widely regarded as incorrect. The use of the noun *disinterest* to mean 'lack of interest' is also objected to but it is rarely used in any other sense and the alternative *uninterest* is rare.

◆ **disintermediation** /dɪsˌɪntəˌmiːdɪ'eɪʃ(ə)n/ *n.* elimination of financial intermediaries, e.g. brokers and bankers, from transactions between borrowers and lenders or buyers and sellers in financial markets. An example is the securitization of debt. Disintermediation has been a consequence of improved technology and deregulation (see also GLOBALIZATION 1). It allows both parties to a financial transaction to reduce costs by eliminating payments of commissions and fees. It often occurs when governments attempt to impose direct controls on the banking system, such as reserve asset ratios and lending ceilings. In response, the market develops new instruments and institutions that are not covered by the direct controls. When these controls are relaxed, funds may return to the normal banking system, i.e. there may be **reintermediation.**

disinvest /ˌdɪsɪn'vest/ *v.* reduce or dispose of one's investment.

◆ **disinvestment** *n.* **1** reducing one's investment. **2** reduction in the capital stock of an economy, usu. following an economic depression during which there has not been sufficient investment to match the loss in the value of capital goods caused by normal wear and tear.

disjoint /dɪs'dʒɔɪnt/ *v.* **1** take apart at the joints. **2** (as **disjointed** *adj.*) incoherent; disconnected. **3** disturb the working of; disrupt.

disjunction /dɪs'dʒʌŋkʃ(ə)n/ *n.* separation.

disjunctive /dɪs'dʒʌŋktɪv/ *adj.* **1** involving separation. **2** (of a conjunction) expressing an alternative, e.g. *or* in *is it wet or dry?*

disk *n.* **1** *US* var. of DISC. **2** *Computing* flat circular storage device. See MAGNETIC DISK; OPTICAL DISK.

◆ **disk capacity** *n. Computing* amount of data that can be stored on a magnetic disk, described in terms of bytes, where one byte will hold one character of the computer's character set.

disk cartridge *n. Computing* module consisting of a single hard magnetic disk permanently housed inside a protective plastic cover. It is used in a specially designed disk drive, from which it can be removed and replaced by another cartridge. See also EXCHANGEABLE DISK STORE.

disk crash *n.* = HEAD CRASH.

◆ **disk drive** *n.* (also **disk unit**) *Computing* peripheral device that transfers information to or from a magnetic disk (see HARD DISK; FLOPPY DISK). The disk is turned at high speed under a read/write head that is similar to the head on a tape recorder. Information is stored on the disk as a pattern of magnetic spots, which are read or written as the appropriate part of the spinning disk passes under the head. In disk drives using hard disks, the disks are either fixed in position or are removable and replaceable (see EXCHANGEABLE DISK STORE). Hard disks must always be carefully protected from the slightest physical damage. In fixed disk drives the disks and read/write heads are hermetically sealed inside the device. A fixed disk has a higher storage capacity than a similar-sized removable disk. In floppy disk drives the disks are always removable and do not require such careful protection as hard disks. Disk plus protective envelope is fed into the disk drive by hand through a slot, and is automatically mounted on the rotation mechanism. Rotation speeds are considerably lower than for hard disk drives. The read/write head or heads operate through slots in the envelope. Floppy disk drives are extensively used in small computers.

◆ **diskette** /dɪ'sket/ *n. Computing* = FLOPPY DISK.

disk format *Computing* see FORMAT *n.* 3.

Disko /'dɪskəʊ/ island off the W coast of Greenland, with extensive coal resources. Its chief settlement is Godhavn.

◆ **disk operating system** *n.* (also **DOS**) operating system designed for use on a computer that has one or more disk drives.

disk pack *n. Computing* form of disk storage used in a specially designed disk drive, from which it can be removed and replaced by another pack of the same type (see EXCHANGEABLE DISK STORE). It is an assembly of identical hard disks permanently mounted on a single spindle. When not mounted on a disk drive the assembly is kept in plastic covers to protect it from damage and dust. Once the pack is mounted, the read/write mechanism moves automatically into position and the pack is set into rotation. A read/write head is provided for each recording surface.

disk unit *n.* = DISK DRIVE.

dislike /dɪs'laɪk/ –*v.* (**-king**) have an aversion to; not like. –*n.* **1** feeling of repugnance or not liking. **2** object of this.

dislocate /'dɪsləˌkeɪt/ *v.* (**-ting**) **1** disturb the normal connection of (esp. a joint in the body). **2** disrupt. □ **dislocation** /-'keɪʃ(ə)n/ *n.*

dislodge /dɪs'lɒdʒ/ *v.* (**-ging**) disturb or move. □ **dislodgement** *n.*

disloyal /dɪs'lɔɪəl/ *adj.* not loyal; unfaithful. □ **disloyally** *adv.* **disloyalty** *n.*

dismal /'dɪzm(ə)l/ *adj.* **1** gloomy; miserable. **2** dreary; sombre. **3** *colloq.* feeble, inept (*dismal attempt*). □ **dismally** *adv.* [medieval Latin *dies mali* unlucky days]

dismantle /dɪs'mænt(ə)l/ *v.* (**-ling**) **1** take to pieces; pull down. **2** deprive of defences or equipment.

dismay /dɪs'meɪ/ –*n.* intense disappointment or despair. –*v.* fill with dismay. [French from Germanic: related to DIS-, MAY]

dismember /dɪs'membə(r)/ *v.* **1** remove the limbs from. **2** partition or divide up. □ **dismemberment** *n.*

dismiss /dɪs'mɪs/ *v.* **1** send away, esp. from one's presence; disperse. **2** terminate the employment of, esp. dishonourably; sack. **3** put from one's mind or emotions. **4** consider not worth talking or thinking about; treat summarily. **5** *Law* refuse further hearing to (a case). **6** *Cricket* put (a batsman or side) out (usu. for a stated score). □ **dismissal** *n.* [Latin *mitto miss-* send]

dismissive *adj.* dismissing rudely or casually; disdainful. □ **dismissively** *adv.* **dismissiveness** *n.*

dismount /dɪs'maʊnt/ *v.* **1 a** alight from a horse, bicycle, etc. **b** unseat. **2** remove (a thing) from its mounting.

disobedient /ˌdɪsə'biːdɪənt/ *adj.* disobeying; rebellious. □ **disobedience** *n.* **disobediently** *adv.*

disobey /ˌdɪsə'beɪ/ *v.* refuse or fail to obey.

disoblige /ˌdɪsə'blaɪdʒ/ *v.* (**-ging**) refuse to help or cooperate with (a person).

disorder /dɪs'ɔːdə(r)/ *n.* **1** lack of order; confusion. **2** public disturbance; riot. **3** ailment or disease. □ **disordered** *adj.*

disorderly *adj.* **1** untidy; confused. **2** riotous, unruly. □ **disorderliness** *n.*

disorganize /dɪs'ɔːgəˌnaɪz/ *v.* (also **-ise**) (**-zing** or **-sing**) **1** throw into confusion or disorder. **2** (as **disorganized** *adj.*) badly organized; untidy. □ **disorganization** /-'zeɪʃ(ə)n/ *n.*

disorient /dɪs'ɔːrɪənt/ *v.* = DISORIENTATE.

disorientate /dɪs'ɔːrɪənˌteɪt/ *v.* (also **disorient**) (**-ting**) confuse (a person), esp. as to his or her bearings. □ **disorientation** /-'teɪʃ(ə)n/ *n.*

disown /dɪs'əʊn/ *v.* deny or give up any connection with; repudiate.

disparage /dɪ'spærɪdʒ/ *v.* (**-ging**) **1** criticize; belittle. **2** bring discredit on. □ **disparagement** *n.* [French: related to DIS-, *parage* rank]

disparate /'dɪspərət/ *adj.* essentially different; not comparable. □ **disparateness** *n.* [Latin *disparo* separate]

disparity /dɪ'spærɪtɪ/ *n.* (*pl.* **-ies**) inequality; difference; incongruity.

dispassionate /dɪ'spæʃ(ə)nət/ *adj.* free from emotion; impartial. □ **dispassionately** *adv.*

dispatch /dɪ'spætʃ/ (also **despatch**) *–v.* **1** send off to a destination or for a purpose. **2** perform (a task etc.) promptly; finish off. **3** kill, execute. **4** *colloq.* eat quickly. *–n.* **1** dispatching or being dispatched. **2 a** official written message, esp. military. **b** news report to a newspaper etc. **3** promptness, efficiency. [Italian *dispacciare* or Spanish *despachar*]

dispatch-box *n.* case for esp. parliamentary documents.

dispatch-rider *n.* messenger on a motor cycle.

dispel /dɪ'spel/ *v.* (**-ll-**) drive away; scatter (fears etc.). [Latin *pello* drive]

dispensable /dɪ'spensəb(ə)l/ *adj.* that can be dispensed with.

dispensary /dɪ'spensərɪ/ *n.* (*pl.* **-ies**) place where medicines are dispensed.

dispensation /ˌdɪspen'seɪʃ(ə)n/ *n.* **1** dispensing or distributing. **2** exemption from penalty, rule, etc. **3** ordering or management of the world by Providence.

dispense /dɪ'spens/ *v.* (**-sing**) **1** distribute; deal out. **2** administer. **3** make up and give out (medicine etc.). **4** (foll. by *with*) do without; make unnecessary. [French from Latin *pendo pens-* weigh]

dispenser *n.* **1** person or thing that dispenses e.g. medicine, good advice. **2** automatic machine dispensing a specific amount.

disperse /dɪ'spɜːs/ *v.* (**-sing**) **1** go, send, drive, or scatter widely or in different directions. **2** send to or station at different points. **3** disseminate. **4** *Chem.* distribute (small particles) in a medium. **5** divide (white light) into its coloured constituents. □ **dispersal** *n.* **dispersive** *adj.* [Latin: related to DIS-, SPARSE]

dispersion /dɪ'spɜːʃ(ə)n/ *n.* **1** dispersing or being dispersed. **2** (**the Dispersion**) = DIASPORA.

dispirit /dɪ'spɪrɪt/ *v.* (esp. as **dispiriting, dispirited** *adjs.*) make despondent, deject.

displace /dɪs'pleɪs/ *v.* (**-cing**) **1** move from its place. **2** remove from office. **3** take the place of; oust.

displaced person *n.* refugee in war etc., or from persecution.

displacement *n.* **1** displacing or being displaced. **2** amount of fluid displaced by an object floating or immersed in it.

◆ **displacement tonnage** see TONNAGE 1.

display /dɪ'spleɪ/ *–v.* **1** exhibit; show. **2** reveal; betray. **3** make (information) visible on a computer screen etc. *–n.* **1** displaying. **2 a** exhibition or show. **b** thing(s) displayed. **3** ostentation. **4** mating rituals of some birds etc. **5 a** device that enables textual or pictorial information to be seen but not permanently recorded. In computing, the most widely used technology involves a cathode-ray tube. See also LED; LIQUID CRYSTAL DISPLAY; PLASMA DISPLAY; VDU. **b** information so displayed. [Latin *plico* fold]

◆ **display advertising** *n.* form of advertising typically using full-page or quarter-page advertisements, often containing logos or illustrations. Cf. CLASSIFIED ADVERTISING.

displease /dɪs'pliːz/ *v.* (**-sing**) make upset or angry; annoy. □ **displeasure** /-'pleʒ(ə)r/ *n.*

disport /dɪ'spɔːt/ *v.* (often *refl.*) play, frolic, enjoy oneself. [Anglo-French *porter* carry, from Latin]

disposable /dɪ'spəʊzəb(ə)l/ *–adj.* **1** intended to be used once and discarded. **2** able to be disposed of. *–n.* **1** disposable article. **2** (in *pl.*) see CONSUMER GOODS.

◆ **disposable income** *n.* **1** income available for spending after payment of taxes, National Insurance contributions, and other deductions, e.g. pension contributions. **2** item in national income accounts consisting of the total value of income of individuals and households available for consumer expenditure and savings, after deducting income tax, National Insurance contributions, and remittances overseas.

disposal /dɪ'spəʊz(ə)l/ *n.* disposing of, e.g. waste. □ **at one's disposal** available.

■ **Usage** *Disposal* is the noun corresponding to the verb *dispose of* (get rid of, deal with, etc.). *Disposition* is the noun from *dispose* (arrange, incline).

dispose /dɪ'spəʊz/ *v.* (**-sing**) **1** (usu. foll. by *to*, or *to* + infin.) **a** make willing; incline (*was disposed to agree*). **b** tend (*wheel was disposed to buckle*). **2** arrange suitably. **3** (as **disposed** *adj.*) have a specified inclination (*ill-disposed; well-disposed*). **4** determine events (*man proposes, God disposes*). □ **dispose of 1 a** deal with. **b** get rid of. **c** finish. **d** kill. **2** sell. **3** prove (an argument etc.) incorrect. [French: related to POSE]

disposition /ˌdɪspə'zɪʃ(ə)n/ *n.* **1** natural tendency; temperament. **2 a** ordering; arrangement (of parts etc.). **b** arrangement. **3** (usu. in *pl.*) preparations; plans.

■ **Usage** See note at *disposal*.

dispossess /ˌdɪspə'zes/ *v.* **1** (usu. foll. by *of*) (esp. as **dispossessed** *adj.*) deprive (a person) of. **2** dislodge; oust. □ **dispossession** /-'zeʃ(ə)n/ *n.*

disproof /dɪs'pruːf/ *n.* refutation.

disproportion /ˌdɪsprə'pɔːʃ(ə)n/ *n.* lack of proportion; being out of proportion. □ **disproportional** *adj.* **disproportionally** *adv.*

disproportionate *adj.* **1** out of proportion. **2** relatively too large or small etc. □ **disproportionately** *adv.*

disprove /dɪs'pruːv/ *v.* (**-ving**) prove false.

disputable /dɪ'spjuːtəb(ə)l/ *adj.* open to question; uncertain. □ **disputably** *adv.*

disputant /dɪ'spjuːt(ə)nt/ *n.* person in a dispute.

disputation /ˌdɪspjuː'teɪʃ(ə)n/ *n.* **1** debate, esp. formal. **2** argument; controversy.

disputatious *adj.* argumentative.

dispute /dɪ'spjuːt/ *–v.* (**-ting**) **1** debate, argue. **2** discuss, esp. heatedly; quarrel. **3** question the truth or validity of (a statement etc.). **4** contend for (*disputed territory*). **5** resist, oppose. *–n.* **1** controversy; debate. **2** quarrel. **3** disagreement leading to industrial action. □ **in dispute 1** being argued about. **2** (of a workforce) involved in industrial action. [Latin *puto* reckon]

disqualify /dɪs'kwɒlɪˌfaɪ/ *v.* (**-ies, -ied**) **1** debar from a competition or pronounce ineligible as a winner. **2** make or pronounce ineligible, unsuitable, or unqualified (*disqualified from driving*). □ **disqualification** /-fɪ'keɪʃ(ə)n/ *n.*

disquiet /dɪs'kwaɪət/ *–v.* make anxious. *–n.* anxiety; uneasiness.

disquietude *n.* disquiet.

disquisition /ˌdɪskwɪ'zɪʃ(ə)n/ *n.* discursive treatise or discourse. [Latin *quaero quaesit-* seek]

disregard /ˌdɪsrɪ'gɑːd/ *–v.* **1** ignore. **2** treat as unimportant. *–n.* indifference; neglect.

disrepair /ˌdɪsrɪ'peə(r)/ *n.* poor condition due to lack of repairs.

disreputable /dɪs'repjʊtəb(ə)l/ *adj.* **1** of bad reputation. **2** not respectable in character or appearance. □ **disreputably** *adv.*

disrepute /ˌdɪsrɪ'pjuːt/ *n.* lack of good reputation; discredit.

disrespect /ˌdɪsrɪ'spekt/ *n.* lack of respect; discourtesy. □ **disrespectful** *adj.* **disrespectfully** *adv.*

disrobe /dɪs'rəʊb/ *v.* (**-bing**) *literary* undress.

disrupt /dɪs'rʌpt/ *v.* **1** interrupt the continuity of; bring disorder to. **2** break apart. □ **disruption** *n.* **disruptive** *adj.* **disruptively** *adv.* [Latin: related to RUPTURE]

dissatisfy /dɪ'sætɪsˌfaɪ/ *v.* (**-ies, -ied**) make discontented; fail to satisfy. □ **dissatisfaction** /-'fækʃ(ə)n/ *n.*

dissect /dɪ'sekt/ *v.* **1** cut into pieces, esp. for examination or post mortem. **2** analyse or criticize in detail. □ **dissection** *n.* [Latin: related to SECTION]

dissemble /dɪ'semb(ə)l/ *v.* (**-ling**) **1** be hypocritical or insincere. **2** disguise or conceal (a feeling, intention, etc.). [Latin *simulo* SIMULATE]

disseminate /dɪ'semɪˌneɪt/ *v.* (**-ting**) scatter about, spread (esp. ideas) widely. □ **dissemination** /-ˈneɪʃ(ə)n/ *n.* [Latin: related to DIS-, SEMEN]

dissension /dɪˈsenʃ(ə)n/ *n.* angry disagreement. [Latin: related to DISSENT]

dissent /dɪˈsent/ *–v.* (often foll. by *from*) **1** disagree, esp. openly. **2** differ, esp. from the established or official opinion. *–n.* **1** such difference. **2** expression of this. [Latin: related to DIS-, *sentio* feel]

dissenter *n.* **1** person who dissents. **2** (**Dissenter**) Protestant dissenting from the Church of England.

dissentient /dɪˈsenʃ(ə)nt/ *–adj.* disagreeing with the established or official view. *–n.* person who dissents.

dissertation /ˌdɪsəˈteɪʃ(ə)n/ *n.* detailed discourse, esp. one submitted towards an academic degree. [Latin *disserto* discuss]

disservice /dɪsˈsɜːvɪs/ *n.* harmful action, harm.

dissident /ˈdɪsɪd(ə)nt/ *–adj.* disagreeing, esp. with the established government, system, etc. *–n.* dissident person. □ **dissidence** *n.* [Latin: related to DIS-, *sedeo* sit]

dissimilar /dɪˈsɪmɪlə(r)/ *adj.* unlike, not similar. □ **dissimilarity** /-ˈlærɪtɪ/ *n.* (*pl.* **-ies**).

dissimulate /dɪˈsɪmjʊˌleɪt/ *v.* (**-ting**) dissemble. □ **dissimulation** /-ˈleɪʃ(ə)n/ *n.* [Latin: related to DISSEMBLE]

dissipate /ˈdɪsɪˌpeɪt/ *v.* (**-ting**) **1** disperse, disappear, dispel. **2** squander. **3** (as **dissipated** *adj.*) dissolute. [Latin *dissipare -pat-*]

dissipation /ˌdɪsɪˈpeɪʃ(ə)n/ *n.* **1** dissolute way of life. **2** dissipating or being dissipated.

dissociate /dɪˈsəʊʃɪˌeɪt/ *v.* (**-ting**) **1** disconnect or separate. **2** become disconnected. □ **dissociate oneself from** declare oneself unconnected with. □ **dissociation** /-ˈeɪʃ(ə)n/ *n.* **dissociative** /-ətɪv/ *adj.* [Latin: related to DIS-, ASSOCIATE]

dissoluble /dɪˈsɒljʊb(ə)l/ *adj.* that can be disintegrated, loosened, or disconnected.

dissolute /ˈdɪsəˌluːt/ *adj.* lax in morals; licentious. [Latin: related to DISSOLVE]

dissolution /ˌdɪsəˈluːʃ(ə)n/ *n.* **1** dissolving or being dissolved, esp. of a partnership or of parliament for a new election. **2** breaking up, abolition (of an institution). **3** death.

dissolve /dɪˈzɒlv/ *v.* (**-ving**) **1** make or become liquid, esp. by immersion or dispersion in a liquid. **2** (cause to) disappear gradually. **3** dismiss (an assembly, esp. Parliament). **4** annul or put an end to (a partnership, marriage, etc.). **5** (often foll. by *into*) be overcome (by tears, laughter, etc.). [Latin: related to DIS-, *solvo solut-* loosen]

dissonant /ˈdɪsənənt/ *adj.* **1** harsh-toned; unharmonious. **2** incongruous. □ **dissonance** *n.* [Latin: related to DIS-, *sono* SOUND[1]]

dissuade /dɪˈsweɪd/ *v.* (**-ding**) (often foll. by *from*) discourage (a person); persuade against. □ **dissuasion** /-ˈsweɪʒ(ə)n/ *n.* **dissuasive** *adj.* [Latin: related to DIS-, *suadeo* advise]

dissyllable var. of DISYLLABLE.

distaff /ˈdɪstɑːf/ *n.* cleft stick holding wool or flax for spinning by hand. [Old English]

distaff side *n.* female branch of a family.

distance /ˈdɪst(ə)ns/ *–n.* **1** being far off; remoteness. **2** space between two points. **3** distant point or place. **4** aloofness; reserve. **5** remoter field of vision (*in the distance*). **6** interval of time. *–v.* (**-cing**) (often *refl.*) **1** place or cause to seem far off; be aloof. **2** leave far behind in a race etc. □ **at a distance** far off. **keep one's distance** remain aloof. [Latin: related to DIS-, *sto* stand]

distant *adj.* **1** far away; at a specified distance (*three miles distant*). **2** remote in time, relationship, etc. (*distant prospect; distant relation*). **3** aloof. **4** abstracted (*distant stare*). **5** faint (*distant memory*). □ **distantly** *adv.*

distaste /dɪsˈteɪst/ *n.* (usu. foll. by *for*) dislike; aversion. □ **distasteful** *adj.* **distastefully** *adv.* **distastefulness** *n.*

distemper[1] /dɪˈstempə(r)/ *hist. –n.* paint using glue or size as a base, for use on walls. *–v.* paint with this. [Latin, = soak: see DISTEMPER[2]]

distemper[2] /dɪˈstempə(r)/ *n.* disease of esp. dogs, with coughing and weakness. [Latin: related to DIS-, *tempero* mingle]

distend /dɪˈstend/ *v.* swell out by pressure from within (*distended stomach*). □ **distensible** /-ˈstensɪb(ə)l/ *adj.* **distension** /-ˈstenʃ(ə)n/ *n.* [Latin: related to TEND[1]]

distich /ˈdɪstɪk/ *n.* verse couplet. [Greek *stikhos* line]

distil /dɪˈstɪl/ *v.* (*US* **distill**) (**-ll-**) **1** purify or extract the essence from (a substance) by vaporizing and condensing it and collecting the resulting liquid. **2** extract the essential meaning of (an idea etc.). **3** make (whisky, essence, etc.) by distilling raw materials. **4** fall or cause to fall in drops. □ **distillation** /-ˈleɪʃ(ə)n/ *n.* [Latin: related to DE-, *stillo* drip]

distiller *n.* person who distils, esp. alcoholic liquor.

distillery *n.* (*pl.* **-ies**) place where alcoholic liquor is distilled.

distinct /dɪˈstɪŋkt/ *adj.* **1** (often foll. by *from*) not identical; separate; different. **2** clearly perceptible. **3** unmistakable, decided (*distinct advantage*). □ **distinctly** *adv.* [Latin: related to DISTINGUISH]

distinction /dɪˈstɪŋkʃ(ə)n/ *n.* **1** discriminating or distinguishing. **2** difference between two things. **3** thing that differentiates or distinguishes. **4** special consideration or honour (*treat with distinction*). **5** excellence (*person of distinction*). **6** title or mark of honour. [Latin: related to DISTINGUISH]

distinctive *adj.* distinguishing, characteristic. □ **distinctively** *adv.* **distinctiveness** *n.*

distingué /dɪˈstæŋgeɪ/ *adj.* distinguished in appearance, manner, etc. [French]

distinguish /dɪˈstɪŋgwɪʃ/ *v.* **1** (often foll. by *from, between*) differentiate; see or draw distinctions. **2** be a mark or property of; characterize. **3** discover by listening, looking, etc. **4** (usu. *refl.*; often foll. by *by*) make prominent (*distinguished himself by winning*). □ **distinguishable** *adj.* [Latin: related to DIS-, *stinguo stinct-* extinguish]

distinguished *adj.* **1** eminent; famous. **2** dignified.

distort /dɪˈstɔːt/ *v.* **1** pull or twist out of shape. **2** misrepresent (facts etc.). **3** transmit (sound etc.) inaccurately. □ **distortion** *n.* [Latin *torqueo tort-* twist]

distract /dɪˈstrækt/ *v.* **1** (often foll. by *from*) draw away the attention of. **2** bewilder, perplex. **3** (as **distracted** *adj.*) confused, mad, or angry. **4** amuse, esp. to divert from pain etc. [Latin: related to DIS-, *traho tract-* draw]

distraction /dɪˈstrækʃ(ə)n/ *n.* **1 a** distracting or being distracted. **b** thing that distracts. **2** relaxation; amusement. **3** confusion; frenzy, madness.

distrain /dɪˈstreɪn/ *v.* (usu. foll. by *upon*) impose distraint (on a person, goods, etc.). [Latin: related to DIS-, *stringo strict-* draw tight]

distraint /dɪˈstreɪnt/ *n.* seizure of goods to enforce payment, esp. seizure of goods by a landlord because a tenant is in arrears with his or her rent.

distrait /dɪˈstreɪ/ *adj.* (*fem.* ***distraite*** /-ˈstreɪt/) inattentive; distraught. [French: related to DISTRACT]

distraught /dɪˈstrɔːt/ *adj.* distracted with worry, fear, etc.; extremely agitated. [related to DISTRAIT]

distress /dɪˈstres/ *–n.* **1** anguish or suffering caused by pain, sorrow, worry, etc. **2** poverty. **3** *Law* = DISTRAINT. *–v.* cause distress to, make unhappy. □ **in distress** suffering or in danger. □ **distressful** *adj.* [Romanic: related to DISTRAIN]

distressed *adj.* **1** suffering from distress. **2** impoverished. **3** (of furniture, clothing, etc.) aged, torn, etc. artificially.

distressed area *n.* region of high unemployment and poverty.

♦ **distributable profits** *n.pl.* profits of a company that are legally available for distribution as dividends. They consist of a company's accumulated realized profits after deducting all realized losses, except for any part of these net realized profits that have been previously distributed or capitalized. Public companies, however, may not distribute profits to such an extent that their net assets are reduced to less than the sum of their called-up capital (see SHARE CAPITAL) and their undistributable reserves (see CAPITAL RESERVES).

◆ **distributable reserves** *n.pl.* retained profits of a company that it may legally distribute by way of dividends. See DISTRIBUTABLE PROFITS.

---

distribute /dɪ'strɪbjuːt, 'dɪs-/ *v.* (**-ting**) **1** give shares of; deal out. **2** scatter; put at different points. **3** arrange; classify. □ **distributable** *adj.* [Latin *tribuo -but-* assign]

■ **Usage** The second pronunciation given, with the stress on the first syllable, is considered incorrect by some people.

◆ **distributed logic** *n.* computer system that supplements the main computer with remote terminals capable of doing some of the computing, or with electronic devices capable of making simple decisions, distributed throughout the system. See also DISTRIBUTED PROCESSING.

---

distributed processing *n.* processing of data in a system in which a number of independent but interconnected computers can cooperate. The system itself is known as a **distributed system**, an example of which is a local area network. The processors involved may be situated at different places and are connected by communication lines. They normally have their own peripherals, i.e. terminals, disks, printers, so that 'local' data can be processed and 'local' decisions made. Data with a wider application can be exchanged over the communication lines.

distributed system see DISTRIBUTED PROCESSING.

distribution /ˌdɪstrɪ'bjuːʃ(ə)n/ *n.* **1** distributing or being distributed. **2** commercial dispersal of goods etc. by means of wholesalers and retailers. **3** payment by a company from its distributable profits, usu. by means of a dividend. **4** dividend or quasi-dividend on which advance corporation tax is payable. **5** *Econ.* allocation of resources among agents in an economy. The Classical school investigated the distribution of wealth between classes, workers, capitalists, and landlords. Economists of the neoclassical school have tended to accept initial endowments of wealth and to analyse the distribution of income resulting from the production process, operating through the laws of supply and demand (see MARKET FORCES). Mainstream economists do not prejudge the issue of whether or not income and wealth should be redistributed, providing instead theories of optimal taxation, to establish how any redistribution could be achieved efficiently. **6** *Statistics* representation of the possible values that can be taken by a random variable. A distribution can be thought of as a curve in which each point represents the probability of the random variable taking that particular value. A **distribution function** must define all the possible values that a random variable may take, so that the sum of all probabilities of that function will equal one. In the **normal distribution** the largest probabilities are clustered around a central point, the mean, while the probabilities become smaller as the distance from the mean increases; this gives the curve a bell-like shape. **7** *Law* division of property and assets of a bankrupt person, deceased person, etc. according to law.

◆ **distribution centre** *n.* warehouse, usu. owned by a manufacturer, that receives goods in bulk and dispatches them to retailers.

◆ **distribution channel** *n.* network of firms necessary to distribute goods or services from the manufacturers to the consumers. It consists primarily of wholesalers and retailers.

---

distributive /dɪ'strɪbjʊtɪv/ *–adj.* **1** of or produced by distribution. **2** *Logic & Gram.* referring to each individual of a class, not to the class collectively (e.g. *each*, *either*). *–n. Gram.* distributive word.

distributor *n.* **1** person or thing that distributes, esp. an intermediary, or one of a chain of intermediaries, that specializes in transferring a manufacturer's goods or services to the consumers. **2** device in an internal-combustion engine for passing current to each spark-plug in turn.

district /'dɪstrɪkt/ *n.* **1** (often *attrib.*) area regarded as a geographical or administrative unit (*the Peak District*; *postal district*; *wine-growing district*). **2** administrative division of a county etc. [Latin: related to DISTRAIN]

district attorney *n.* (in the US) prosecuting officer of a district.

district nurse *n.* nurse who makes home visits in an area.

District of Columbia federal district of the US, coextensive with the city of Washington; pop. (est. 1996) 543 213.

distrust /dɪs'trʌst/ *–n.* lack of trust; suspicion. *–v.* have no trust in. □ **distrustful** *adj.* **distrustfully** *adv.*

disturb /dɪ'stɜːb/ *v.* **1** break the rest, calm, or quiet of. **2** agitate; worry. **3** move from a settled position (*disturbed my papers*). **4** (as **disturbed** *adj.*) emotionally or mentally unstable. [Latin: related to DIS-, *turba* tumult]

disturbance *n.* **1** disturbing or being disturbed. **2** tumult; uproar; agitation.

disunion /dɪs'juːnɪən/ *n.* lack of union; separation; dissension.

disunite /ˌdɪsjuː'naɪt/ *v.* (**-ting**) **1** remove the unity from. **2** separate. □ **disunity** /-'juːnɪtɪ/ *n.*

disuse *–n.* /dɪs'juːs/ disused state. *–v.* /-'juːz/ (**-sing**) cease to use.

disyllable /daɪ'sɪləb(ə)l/ *n.* (also **dissyllable**) *Prosody* word or metrical foot of two syllables. □ **disyllabic** /-'læbɪk/ *adj.*

DIT *abbr.* double income tax (*DIT relief*).

ditch *–n.* long narrow excavation esp. for drainage or as a boundary. *–v.* **1** make or repair ditches (*hedging and ditching*). **2** *slang* abandon; discard. □ **dull as ditch-water** extremely dull. [Old English]

dither /'dɪðə(r)/ *–v.* **1** hesitate; be indecisive. **2** tremble; quiver. *–n. colloq.* state of agitation or hesitation. □ **ditherer** *n.* **dithery** *adj.* [var. of *didder* DODDER[1]]

dithyramb /'dɪθɪˌræm/ *n.* **1** wild choral hymn in ancient Greece. **2** passionate or inflated poem etc. □ **dithyrambic** /-'ræmbɪk/ *adj.* [Latin from Greek]

ditto /'dɪtəʊ/ *n.* (*pl.* **-s**) **1** (in accounts, inventories, etc.) the aforesaid, the same. **2** *colloq.* (used to avoid repetition) the same (*came late today and ditto yesterday*). [Latin DICTUM]

■ **Usage** In sense 1, the word *ditto* is often replaced by " under the word or sum to be repeated.

ditto marks *n.pl.* inverted commas etc. representing 'ditto'.

ditty /'dɪtɪ/ *n.* (*pl.* **-ies**) short simple song. [Latin: related to DICTATE]

Diu /'diːuː/ see DAMAN AND DIU.

diuretic /ˌdaɪjʊ'retɪk/ *–adj.* causing increased output of urine. *–n.* diuretic drug. [Greek: related to DIA-, *oureō* urinate]

diurnal /daɪ'ɜːn(ə)l/ *adj.* **1** of the day or daytime. **2** daily. **3** occupying one day. □ **diurnally** *adv.* [Latin *diurnalis* from *dies* day]

div. *abbr.* (also **div**) dividend.

diva /'diːvə/ *n.* (*pl.* **-s**) great woman opera singer; prima donna. [Italian from Latin, = goddess]

divalent /daɪ'veɪlənt/ *adj. Chem.* having a valency of two.

divan /dɪ'væn/ *n.* low couch or bed without a back or ends. [ultimately from Persian *dīvān* bench]

dive *–v.* (**-ving**) **1** plunge head first into water. **2 a** (of an aircraft, person, etc.) plunge steeply downwards. **b** (of a submarine) submerge; go deeper. **3** (foll. by *into*) *colloq.* **a** put one's hand into (a pocket, handbag, etc.). **b** become enthusiastic about (a subject, meal, etc.). **4** move suddenly (*dived into a shop*). *–n.* **1** act of diving; plunge. **2** steep descent or fall. **3** *colloq.* disreputable nightclub, bar, etc. [Old English]

dive-bomb *v.* bomb (a target) from a diving aircraft. □ **dive-bomber** *n.*

diver *n.* **1** person who dives, esp. working under water. **2** diving bird.

diverge /daɪˈvɜːdʒ/ *v.* (**-ging**) **1 a** spread out from a central point, become dispersed. **b** take different courses (*their interests diverged*). **2 a** (often foll. by *from*) depart from a set course. **b** (of opinions etc.) differ. □ **divergence** *n.* **divergent** *adj.* [Latin: related to DI-[2], *vergo* incline]

divers /ˈdaɪvɜːz/ *adj. archaic* various; several. [Latin: related to DIVERSE]

diverse /daɪˈvɜːs/ *adj.* varied. [Latin: related to DI-[2], *verto vers-* turn]

♦ **diversification** /daɪˌvɜːsɪfɪˈkeɪʃ(ə)n/ *n.* **1** varying; diversifying. **2** movement by a manufacturer or trader into a wider field of products, e.g. by buying firms already serving the target markets or by expanding existing facilities. It is often undertaken to reduce reliance on one market, which may be diminishing (e.g. tobacco), to balance a seasonal market (e.g. ice cream), or to provide scope for general growth.

diversify /daɪˈvɜːsɪˌfaɪ/ *v.* (**-ies, -ied**) **1** make diverse; vary. **2** spread (investment portfolio) over a wide range of companies to avoid serious losses if a recession is localized to one sector of the market. **3** (often foll. by *into*) expand one's range of products.

diversion /daɪˈvɜːʃ(ə)n/ *n.* **1** diverting or being diverted. **2 a** diverting of attention. **b** stratagem for this. **3** recreation, pastime. **4** alternative route when a road is temporarily closed. □ **diversionary** *adj.*

diversity /daɪˈvɜːsɪtɪ/ *n.* variety.

divert /daɪˈvɜːt/ *v.* **1 a** turn aside; deflect. **b** distract (attention). **2** (often as **diverting** *adj.*) entertain; amuse. [Latin: related to DIVERSE]

divest /daɪˈvest/ *v.* (usu. foll. by *of*) **1** unclothe; strip. **2** deprive, rid. [Latin: related to VEST]

divide /dɪˈvaɪd/ –*v.* (**-ding**) **1** (often foll. by *in, into*) separate into parts; break up; split. **2** (often foll. by *out*) distribute; deal; share. **3 a** separate (one thing) from another. **b** classify into parts or groups. **4** cause to disagree. **5 a** find how many times (a number) contains or is contained in another (*divide 20 by 4*; *divide 4 into 20*). **b** (of a number) be contained in (a number) without remainder (*4 divides into 20*). **6** *Parl.* vote (by members entering either of two lobbies) (*the House divided*). –*n.* **1** dividing line. **2** watershed. [Latin *divido -vis-*]

♦ **dividend** /ˈdɪvɪˌdend/ *n.* **1** share of part of the earnings of a company to its shareholders, usu. expressed as an amount per share on the par value of the share. Thus a 15% dividend on a £1 share will pay 15p. However, investors are usu. more interested in the **dividend yield**, i.e. the dividend expressed as a percentage of the share value; thus if the market value of these £1 shares is now £5, the dividend yield would be 1/5 × 15% = 3%. The size of the dividend payment is determined by the board of directors of a company, who must decide how much to pay out to shareholders and how much to retain in the business; these amounts may vary from year to year. In the UK it is usual for companies to pay a dividend every six months, the largest portion (the **final dividend**) being announced at the company's AGM together with the annual financial results. A smaller **interim dividend** usu. accompanies the interim statement of the company's affairs, six months before the AGM. In the US dividends are usu. paid quarterly. See also DIVIDEND COVER; YIELD *n.* 2. **2** payment made by a cooperative society out of profits to its members, usu. related to the amount the member spends and expressed as a number of pence in the pound. **3** share of profits paid to winners in a football pool etc. **4** number to be divided. **5** benefit from an action. [Anglo-French: related to DIVIDE]

♦ **dividend cover** *n.* number of times a company's dividends to ordinary shareholders could be paid out of its net profits after tax in the same period. For example, a net dividend of £400,000 paid by a company showing a net profit of £1M is said to be covered 2½ times. Dividend cover is a measure of the probability that dividend payments will be sustained (low cover might make it difficult to pay the same level of dividends in a bad year's trading) and of a company's commitment to investment and growth (high cover implies that the company retains its earnings for investment in the business). Negative dividend cover is unusual, and is taken as a sign that a company is in difficulties. See also PRICE–DIVIDEND RATIO.

♦ **dividend equalization reserve** *n. hist.* reserve created to smooth out fluctuations in the incidence of taxation so that dividends could be maintained. Such reserves are now usu. referred to as **deferred-tax accounts** (see DEFERRED TAXATION).

♦ **dividend limitation** *n.* (also **dividend restraint**) economic policy in which the dividends a company can pay to its shareholders are limited by government order. It is usu. part of a prices and income policy to defeat inflation, providing a political counterpart to a wage freeze.

♦ **dividend mandate** *n.* document in which a shareholder of a company notifies the company to whom dividends are to be paid.

♦ **dividend stripping** *n.* (also **bond washing**) practice of buying gild-edged securities after they have gone ex-dividend and selling them cum-dividend just before the next dividend is due (see EX[1] 2). This procedure enables the investor to avoid receiving dividends, which in the UK are taxable as income, and to make a tax-free capital gain. This activity has mainly been indulged in by high-rate taxpayers but has now become of little interest since the rules regulating the taxation of accrued interest were changed.

♦ **dividend waiver** *n.* decision by a major shareholder in a company not to take a dividend, usu. because the company cannot afford to pay it.

♦ **dividend warrant** *n.* cheque issued by a company to its shareholders when paying dividends. It states the tax deducted and the net amount paid. This document must be sent by non-taxpayers to the Inland Revenue when claiming back the tax.

♦ **dividend yield** see DIVIDEND 1.

divider *n.* **1** screen etc. dividing a room. **2** (in *pl.*) measuring-compasses.

divination /ˌdɪvɪˈneɪʃ(ə)n/ *n.* supposed supernatural insight into the future etc. [Latin: related to DIVINE]

divine /dɪˈvaɪn/ –*adj.* (**diviner, divinest**) **1 a** of, from, or like God or a god. **b** sacred. **2** *colloq.* excellent; delightful. –*v.* (**-ning**) **1** discover by intuition or guessing. **2** foresee. **3** practise divination. –*n.* theologian or clergyman. □ **divinely** *adv.* [Latin *divinus*]

diviner *n.* person who practises divination.

diving-bell *n.* open-bottomed enclosure, supplied with air, for descent into deep water.

diving-board *n.* elevated board for diving from.

diving-suit *n.* watertight suit, usu. with helmet and air-supply, for work under water.

divining-rod *n.* = DOWSING-ROD.

divinity /dɪˈvɪnɪtɪ/ *n.* (*pl.* **-ies**) **1** being divine. **2** god; godhead. **3** theology.

divisible /dɪˈvɪzɪb(ə)l/ *adj.* capable of being divided. □ **divisibility** /-ˈbɪlɪtɪ/ *n.*

division /dɪˈvɪʒ(ə)n/ *n.* **1** dividing or being divided. **2** dividing one number by another. **3** disagreement (*division of opinion*). **4** *Parl.* separation of members for counting votes. **5** one of two or more parts into which a thing is divided. **6** unit of administration, esp. a group of army brigades, regiments, or teams in a sporting league. □ **divisional** *adj.*

♦ **division of labour** *n.* specialization of workers in the processes of production (or any other economic activity). Division of labour was identified by Adam Smith in *The Wealth of Nations* as one of the greatest contributions to the advancement of national wealth then (early in the Industrial Revolution) being experienced in the UK. The idea that specialization permits higher production and therefore improved economic welfare is the basis for one of the fundamental principles of economics, the theory of comparative advantage, and for the almost universal support amongst economists for free trade. See COMPARATIVE ADVANTAGE.

division sign *n.* sign (÷) indicating that one quantity is to be divided by another.

divisive /dɪ'vaɪsɪv/ *adj.* causing disagreement. □ **divisively** *adv.* **divisiveness** *n.* [Latin: related to DIVIDE]

divisor /dɪ'vaɪzə(r)/ *n.* number by which another is divided.

divorce /dɪ'vɔːs/ *–n.* **1** legal dissolution of a marriage. **2** separation (*divorce between thought and feeling*). *–v.* (**-cing**) **1 a** (usu. as **divorced** *adj.*) (often foll. by *from*) legally dissolve the marriage of. **b** separate by divorce. **c** end one's marriage with. **2** separate (*divorced from reality*). [Latin: related to DIVERSE]

divorcee /ˌdɪvɔː'siː/ *n.* divorced person.

divot /'dɪvət/ *n.* piece of turf cut out by a blow, esp. by the head of a golf club. [origin unknown]

divulge /daɪ'vʌldʒ/ *v.* (**-ging**) disclose, reveal (a secret etc.). □ **divulgence** *n.* [Latin *divulgo* publish]

divvy /'dɪvɪ/ *colloq. –n.* (*pl.* **-ies**) dividend. *–v.* (**-ies, -ied**) (often foll. by *up*) share out. [abbreviation]

Diwali /diː'wɑːlɪ/ *n.* Hindu and Jainist festival with illuminations, held between September and November. [Sanskrit *dīpa* lamp]

Dixie /'dɪksɪ/ *n.* southern states of the US. [origin uncertain]

dixie /'dɪksɪ/ *n.* large iron cooking-pot used by campers etc. [Hindustani from Persian]

Dixieland *n.* **1** = DIXIE. **2** traditional kind of jazz.

DIY *abbr.* do-it-yourself.

dizzy /'dɪzɪ/ *–adj.* (**-ier, -iest**) **1 a** giddy. **b** feeling confused. **2** causing giddiness. *–v.* (**-ies, -ied**) **1** make dizzy. **2** bewilder. □ **dizzily** *adv.* **dizziness** *n.* [Old English]

DJ *abbr.* **1** dinner-jacket. **2** disc jockey.

Djakarta var. of JAKARTA.

djellaba /'dʒeləbə/ *n.* (also **jellaba**) loose hooded cloak (as) worn by Arab men. [Arabic]

Djerba /'dʒɜːbə/ (also **Jerba**) Tunisian resort island in the Gulf of Gabès, N of the mainland.

DJIA *abbr.* = DOW JONES INDUSTRIAL AVERAGE.

DJTA *abbr.* Dow Jones Transportation Average.

DJUA *abbr.* Dow Jones Utilities Average.

DK *international vehicle registration* Denmark.

DKB *abbr. Computing* distributed knowledge base.

Dkr *symb.* krone (of Denmark).

DL *–postcode* Darlington. *–airline flight code* Delta Airlines.

D/L *abbr.* **1** data link. **2** demand loan.

dl *abbr.* decilitre(s).

D-layer *n.* lowest layer of the ionosphere. [*D* arbitrary]

DLES *abbr.* Doctor of Letters in Economic Studies.

D.Litt. *abbr.* Doctor of Letters. [Latin *Doctor Litterarum*]

DLO *abbr.* (also **d.l.o.**) dispatch (money payable) loading only.

DM *symb.* Deutschmark.

dm *abbr.* decimetre(s).

DMA *abbr. Computing* direct memory access.

D-mark *abbr.* Deutschmark.

DMC *abbr.* direct manufacturing costs.

DML *abbr. Computing* data-manipulation language.

DMS *abbr.* **1** *Computing* data-management system. **2** Diploma in Management Studies.

♦ **DMU** *abbr.* = DECISION-MAKING UNIT.

D.Mus. *abbr.* Doctor of Music.

DN *–abbr.* (also **D/N**) debit note. *–postcode* Doncaster.

DNA *abbr.* deoxyribonucleic acid, esp. carrying genetic information in chromosomes.

DNC *abbr. Computing* distributed numerical control.

Dnepropetrovsk /ˌdniːprəpe'trɒfsk/ (formerly **Ekaterinoslav**) industrial port in Ukraine; industries include iron, steel, chemicals, and engineering; pop. (est. 1996) 1 147 000.

Dnieper /'dniːpə(r)/ (also **Dnepr**) river in NE Europe flowing through Belarus and Ukraine to the Black Sea. Dams have been built at a number of points to provide hydroelectric power and water for Ukraine's industries.

Dniester /'dniːstə(r)/ (also **Dnestr**) river in NE Europe flowing through Moldova to the Black Sea.

D-notice *n.* government notice to news editors not to publish certain items for security reasons. [defence, NOTICE]

DO *abbr.* **1** deferred ordinary (shares). **2** (also **d/o**) delivery order. **3** (also **D/O**) direct order.

do[1] /duː/ *–v.* (*3 sing. pres.* **does** /dʌz/; *past* **did**; *past part.* **done** /dʌn/; *pres. part.* **doing**) **1** perform, carry out, achieve, complete (work etc.) (*did his homework*; *a lot to do*). **2** produce, make, provide (*doing a painting*; *we do lunches*). **3** grant; impart (*does you good*; *do me a favour*). **4** act, behave, proceed (*do as I do*; *would do well to wait*). **5** work at (*do carpentry*; *do chemistry*). **6** be suitable or acceptable; satisfy (*will never do*; *will do me nicely*). **7** deal with; attend to (*do one's hair*). **8** fare; get on (*did badly in the test*). **9** solve; work out (*did the sum*). **10 a** traverse (a certain distance) (*did 50 miles today*). **b** travel at a specified speed (*was doing eighty*). **11** *colloq.* act or behave like; play the part of. **12** produce (a play, opera, etc.) (*will*

Djibouti /dʒɪ'buːtɪ/, **Republic of** (formerly **French Territory of the Afars and the Issas, French Somaliland**) country on the NE coast of Africa. The economy relies on transshipment trade through the free port of Djibouti, which handles about half of Ethiopia's trade (there is a railway line to Addis Ababa). Most employment is provided by transport service industries, such as ship repairing, refuelling, and the expansion of berthing and container facilities. Subsistence agriculture, esp. livestock herding, supports the inland population. Djibouti's economy has been adversely affected by war in neighbouring Somaliland and Ethiopia, and French budgetary aid will be reduced if political reforms are not speeded up. The country, which gained independence from France in 1977, was a one-party state from 1981 until 1992, when a new multi-party constitution was approved by a referendum and the country's first multi-party legislative elections were held. These were boycotted by the mainly Afar opposition parties and resulted in victory for the ruling Issa-dominated party. The Front for the Restoration of Unity and Democracy (FRUD), an Afar rebel movement, have been fighting in protest at the concentration of power in the Issa-dominated Popular Rally for Progress (PRP). In 1996 a formal peace agreement was signed and FRUD was recognized as a political party. However, small factions continue fighting. President, Hassan Gouled Aptidon; capital, Djibouti, pop. (est. 1989) 450 000. □ **Djiboutian** *adj.* & *n.*

languages	French & Arabic (official), Somali, Afar
currency	franc (DF) of 100 centimes
pop. (1996)	603 000
GNP (1993)	US$448M
literacy	60% (m); 32% (f)
life expectancy	46 (m); 50 (f)

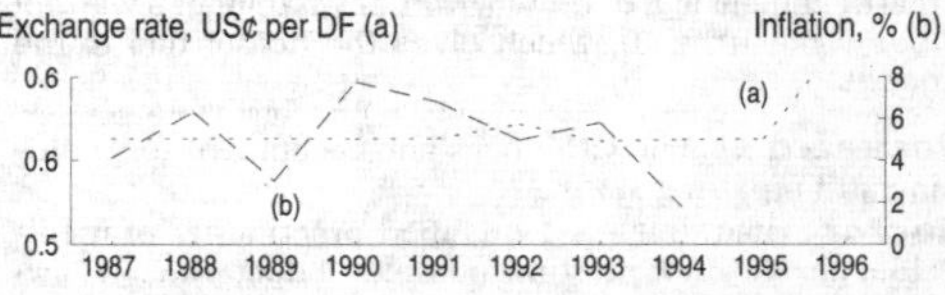

do Shakespeare). **13 a** *colloq.* finish (*I've done in the garden*). **b** (as **done** *adj.*) be finished (*day is done*). **14** cook, esp. completely (*do it in the oven*; *potatoes aren't done*). **15** be in progress (*what's doing?*). **16** *colloq.* visit (*did the museums*). **17** *colloq.* **a** (often as **done** *adj.*) exhaust; tire out. **b** defeat, kill, ruin. **18** (foll. by *into*) translate or transform. **19** *colloq.* cater for (*they do one very well here*). **20** *slang* **a** rob (*did a big bank*). **b** swindle. **21** *slang* prosecute, convict (*done for shoplifting*). **22** *slang* undergo (a term of imprisonment). **23** *slang* take (an illegal drug). *–v.aux.* **1** in questions and negative statements or commands (*do you understand?*; *I don't smoke*; *don't be silly*). **2** *ellipt.* or in place of a verb (*you know her better than I do*; *I wanted to go and I did*; *tell me, do!*). **3** for emphasis (*I do want to*; *do tell me*; *they did go*). **4** in inversion (*rarely does it happen*). *–n.* (*pl.* **dos** or **do's**) *colloq.* elaborate party, operation, etc. □ **be done with** see DONE. **be nothing to do with 1** be no business of. **2** be unconnected with. **be to do with** be concerned or connected with. **do away with** *colloq.* **1** get rid of; abolish. **2** kill. **do down** *colloq.* **1** cheat, swindle. **2** overcome. **do for 1** be satisfactory or sufficient for. **2** *colloq.* (esp. as **done for** *adj.*) destroy, ruin, kill. **3** *colloq.* act as cleaner etc. for. **do in 1** *slang* **a** kill. **b** ruin. **2** *colloq.* exhaust, tire out. **do justice to** see JUSTICE. **do nothing for** (or **to**) *colloq.* not flatter or enhance. **do or die** persist recklessly. **do out** *colloq.* clean or redecorate (a room). **do a person out of** *colloq.* cheat of. **do over 1** *slang* attack; beat up. **2** *colloq.* redecorate, refurbish. **do proud** see PROUD. **dos and don'ts** rules of behaviour. **do something for** (or **to**) *colloq.* enhance the appearance or quality of. **do up 1** fasten. **2** *colloq.* **a** refurbish, renovate. **b** adorn, dress up. **do with** (prec. by *could*) would be glad of; would profit by (*could do with a rest*). **do without** manage without; forgo. **to do with** in connection with, related to (*what has that to do with it?*; *something to do with the weather*). □ **doable** *adj.* [Old English]

do[2] var. of DOH.

do. *abbr.* ditto.

Dobermann pinscher /ˌdəʊbəmən ˈpɪnʃə(r)/ *n.* large dog of a smooth-coated German breed with a docked tail. [German]

dobra /ˈdəʊbrə/ *n.* standard monetary unit of São Tomé and Príncipe. [Portuguese]

Dobruja /ˈdɒbrejə/ district in SE Romania and NE Bulgaria, bounded on the E by the Black Sea and on the N and W by the Danube.

doc *n. colloq.* doctor. [abbreviation]

doc. *abbr.* document(s).

docile /ˈdəʊsaɪl/ *adj.* submissive, easily managed. □ **docilely** *adv.* **docility** /-ˈsɪlɪtɪ/ *n.* [Latin *doceo* teach]

dock[1] *–n.* **1** enclosed harbour for the loading, unloading, and repair of ships. **2** (in *pl.*) docks with wharves and offices. *–v.* **1** bring or come into dock. **2 a** join (spacecraft) together in space. **b** be joined thus. [Dutch *docke*]

dock[2] *n.* enclosure in a criminal court for the accused. [Flemish *dok* cage]

dock[3] *n.* weed with broad leaves. [Old English]

dock[4] *v.* **1** cut short (an animal's tail). **2** take away part of, reduce (wages, supplies, etc.). [Old English]

docker *n.* person employed to load and unload ships.

docket /ˈdɒkɪt/ *–n.* document or label listing goods delivered, jobs done, contents of a package, etc. *–v.* (**-t-**) label with, or enter on, a docket. [origin unknown]

dockland *n.* district near docks or former docks.

♦ **dock receipt** *n.* (also **wharfinger's receipt**) receipt for goods given by a dock warehouse or wharf, acknowledging that the goods are awaiting shipment. A more formal document is a **dock warrant** or wharfinger's warrant (see WARRANT *n.* 3), which gives the holder title to the goods.

---

dockyard *n.* area with docks and equipment for building and repairing ships.

doctor /ˈdɒktə(r)/ *–n.* **1** qualified practitioner of medicine; physician. **2** person who holds a doctorate. *–v. colloq.* **1** treat medically. **2** castrate or spay. **3** patch up (machinery etc.). **4** adulterate. **5** tamper with, falsify. □ **what the doctor ordered** *colloq.* something welcome. [Latin *doceo* teach]

doctoral *adj.* of or for the degree of doctor.

doctorate /ˈdɒktərət/ *n.* highest university degree in any faculty, often honorary.

doctrinaire /ˌdɒktrɪˈneə(r)/ *adj.* applying theory or doctrine dogmatically. [French: related to DOCTRINE]

doctrine /ˈdɒktrɪn/ *n.* **1** what is taught; body of instruction. **2 a** principle of religious or political etc. belief. **b** set of such principles. □ **doctrinal** /-ˈtraɪn(ə)l/ *adj.* [Latin: related to DOCTOR]

docudrama /ˈdɒkjʊˌdrɑːmə/ *n.* television drama based on real events. [from DOCUMENTARY, DRAMA]

document *–n.* /ˈdɒkjʊmənt/ thing providing a record or evidence of events, agreement, ownership, identification, etc. *–v.* /ˈdɒkjʊˌment/ **1** prove by or support with documents. **2** record in a document. [Latin: related to DOCTOR]

documentary /ˌdɒkjʊˈmentərɪ/ *–adj.* **1** consisting of documents (*documentary evidence*). **2** providing a factual record or report. *–n.* (*pl.* **-ies**) documentary film etc.

♦ **documentary bill** *n.* bill of exchange attached to the shipping documents of a parcel of goods. These documents include the bill of lading, insurance policy, dock warrant, invoice, etc.

♦ **documentary credit** *n.* credit arrangement in which a bank agrees to accept bills of exchange drawn by an exporter of goods on the foreign buyer for a stated sum, provided that the bill of exchange has specified shipping documents attached to it.

---

documentation /ˌdɒkjʊmenˈteɪʃ(ə)n/ *n.* **1** collection and classification of information. **2** material so collected. **3** *Computing* etc. material explaining a system, usu. in the form of manuals, often in loose-leaf format to make amendments and additions simple, or accessible from a computer terminal. Software documentation normally includes a tutorial guide to new users, a reference section, an explanation of error messages, an installation guide, and perhaps a small detachable summary card. Hardware documentation is similar but includes a technical specification and a trouble-shooting and maintenance-engineers manual.

♦ **document merge** *n.* process of combining two or more documents to produce a single document, a common operation in word processing. An example is the combining of data produced by a spreadsheet program into a document produced by a word-processing program.

---

document reader *n.* device that reads data directly from a document and feeds it, in coded form, into a computer. The document reader has to recognize characters on the document, or to sense marks on it. It operates by OCR (optical character recognition), MICR (magnetic ink character recognition), or OMR (optical mark reading). The documents can generally be read not only by the input device but also by people, and may involve more than one reading process, for instance OCR and OMR.

♦ **documents against acceptance** *n.* (also **D/A**) method of payment for goods that have been exported in which the exporter sends the shipping documents with a bill of exchange to a bank or agent at the port of destination. The bank or agent releases the goods when the bill has been accepted by the consignee. Cf. CASH AGAINST DOCUMENTS.

♦ **documents against presentation** see CASH AGAINST DOCUMENTS.

---

dodder[1] *v.* tremble or totter, esp. from age. □ **dodderer** *n.* **doddery** *adj.* [obsolete dial. *dadder*]

dodder[2] *n.* threadlike climbing parasitic plant. [origin uncertain]

doddle /ˈdɒd(ə)l/ *n. colloq.* easy task. [perhaps from *doddle* = TODDLE]

dodecagon /dəʊˈdekəgən/ *n.* plane figure with twelve sides. [Greek *dōdeka* twelve, *-gōnos* angled]

dodecahedron /ˌdəʊdekəˈhiːdrən/ *n.* solid figure with twelve faces. [from DODECAGON, Greek *hedra* base]

Dodecanese /ˌdəʊdɪkəˈniːz/ group of Greek islands in the SE Aegean; capital, Rhodes.

dodge *–v.* (**-ging**) **1** (often foll. by *about*, *behind*, *round*) move quickly to elude a pursuer, blow, etc. **2** evade by cunning or trickery. *–n.* **1** quick movement to avoid something. **2** clever trick or expedient. □ **dodger** *n.* [origin unknown]

dodgem /ˈdɒdʒəm/ *n.* small electrically-driven car in an enclosure at a funfair, bumped into others for fun. [from DODGE, 'EM]

dodgy *adj.* (**-ier**, **-iest**) *colloq.* unreliable, risky.

dodo /ˈdəʊdəʊ/ *n.* (*pl.* **-s**) large extinct bird of Mauritius etc. [Portuguese *doudo* simpleton]

Dodoma /dəˈdəʊmə/ capital of Tanzania since 1983, replacing Dar es Salaam; pop. (1988) 203 833.

DOE *abbr.* (also **d.o.e.**) depends on experience (referring to salary in job advertisements).

DoE *abbr.* Department of the Environment.

doe *n.* (*pl.* same or **-s**) female fallow deer, reindeer, hare, or rabbit. [Old English]

doer /ˈduːə(r)/ *n.* **1** person who does something. **2** person who acts rather than theorizing.

does see DO[1].

doesn't /ˈdʌz(ə)nt/ *contr.* does not.

doff *v.* remove (a hat or clothes). [from *do off*]

dog *–n.* **1** four-legged flesh-eating animal akin to the fox and wolf, and of many breeds. **2** male of this, or of the fox or wolf. **3** *colloq.* **a** despicable person. **b** person of a specified kind (*lucky dog*). **4** mechanical device for gripping. **5** (in *pl.*; prec. by *the*) *colloq.* greyhound-racing. **6** (in *pl.*) goods with a low share of a market, esp. those in new or slow markets, which are therefore unlikely to yield attractive profits. *–v.* (**-gg-**) follow closely; pursue, track. □ **go to the dogs** *slang* deteriorate, be ruined. **like a dog's dinner** *colloq.* smartly or flashily (dressed etc.). **not a dog's chance** no chance at all. [Old English]

dogcart *n.* two-wheeled driving-cart with cross seats back to back.

dog-collar *n.* **1** collar for a dog. **2** *colloq.* clerical collar.

dog days *n.pl.* hottest period of the year.

doge /dəʊdʒ/ *n. hist.* chief magistrate of Venice or Genoa. [Italian from Latin *dux* leader]

dog-eared *adj.* (of a book etc.) with bent or worn corners.

dog-eat-dog *adj. colloq.* ruthlessly competitive.

dog-end *n. slang* cigarette-end.

dogfight *n.* **1** close combat between fighter aircraft. **2** rough fight.

dogfish *n.* (*pl.* same or **-es**) a kind of small shark.

dogged /ˈdɒgɪd/ *adj.* tenacious; grimly persistent. □ **doggedly** *adv.* **doggedness** *n.*

doggerel /ˈdɒgər(ə)l/ *n.* poor or trivial verse. [apparently from DOG]

doggo /ˈdɒgəʊ/ *adv.* □ **lie doggo** *slang* lie motionless or hidden.

doggy *–adj.* **1** of or like a dog. **2** devoted to dogs. *–n.* (also **doggie**) (*pl.* **-ies**) pet name for a dog.

doggy bag *n.* bag for leftovers given to a customer in a restaurant etc.

doggy-paddle *n.* (also **dog-paddle**) elementary swimming stroke like that of a dog.

doghouse *n. US* & *Austral.* dog's kennel. □ **in the doghouse** *slang* in disgrace.

dog in the manger *n.* person who stops others using a thing for which he or she has no use.

dogma /ˈdɒgmə/ *n.* **1** principle, tenet, or system of these, esp. of a Church or political party. **2** arrogant declaration of opinion. [Greek, = opinion]

dogmatic /dɒgˈmætɪk/ *adj.* asserting or imposing personal opinions; intolerantly authoritative; arrogant. □ **dogmatically** *adv.*

dogmatism /ˈdɒgməˌtɪz(ə)m/ *n.* tendency to be dogmatic. □ **dogmatist** *n.*

dogmatize /ˈdɒgməˌtaɪz/ *v.* (also **-ise**) (**-zing** or **-sing**) **1** speak dogmatically. **2** express (a principle etc.) as dogma.

do-gooder *n.* well-meaning but unrealistic or patronizing philanthropist or reformer.

dog-paddle var. of DOGGY-PADDLE.

dog-rose *n.* wild hedge-rose.

dogsbody *n.* (*pl.* **-ies**) *colloq.* drudge.

dog's breakfast *n.* (also **dog's dinner**) *colloq.* mess.

dog's life *n.* life of misery etc.

dog-star *n.* chief star of the constellation Canis Major or Minor, esp. Sirius.

dog-tired *adj.* tired out.

dog-tooth *n.* V-shaped pattern or moulding; chevron.

dogtrot *n.* gentle easy trot.

dogwatch *n.* either of two short watches on a ship (4–6 or 6–8 p.m.).

dogwood *n.* shrub with dark-red branches, greenish-white flowers, and purple berries.

DoH *abbr.* Department of Health.

doh /dəʊ/ *n.* (also **do**) *Mus.* first note of a major scale. [Italian *do*]

Doha /ˈdəʊhə/ capital of Qatar; industries include oil refining and engineering; pop. (1992) 313 639.

doily /ˈdɔɪlɪ/ *n.* (also **doyley**) (*pl.* **-ies** or **-eys**) small lacey usu. paper mat used on a plate for cakes etc. [*Doiley*, name of a draper]

doing /ˈduːɪŋ/ *pres. part.* of DO[1]. *n.* **1 a** action (*famous for his doings*). **b** effort (*takes a lot of doing*). **2** (in *pl.*) *slang* unspecified things (*have we got all the doings?*).

doing-over *n. slang* attack, beating-up.

do-it-yourself *–adj.* (of work) done or to be done by a householder etc. *–n.* such work.

DOL *abbr.* (in the US) Department of Labor.

dol. *abbr.* dollar.

Dolby /ˈdɒlbɪ/ *n. propr.* electronic noise-reduction system used esp. in tape-recording to reduce hiss. [name of its inventor]

doldrums /ˈdɒldrəmz/ *n.pl.* (usu. prec. by *the*) **1** low spirits. **2** period of inactivity. **3** equatorial ocean region with little or no wind. [perhaps after *dull*, *tantrum*]

dole *–n.* **1** (usu. prec. by *the*) *colloq.* unemployment benefit. **2 a** charitable distribution. **b** thing given sparingly or reluctantly. *–v.* (**-ling**) (usu. foll. by *out*) distribute sparingly. □ **on the dole** *colloq.* receiving unemployment benefit. [Old English]

doleful /ˈdəʊlfʊl/ *adj.* **1** mournful, sad. **2** dreary, dismal. □ **dolefully** *adv.* **dolefulness** *n.* [Latin *doleo* grieve]

doll *–n.* **1** small model of esp. a baby or child as a child's toy. **2** *colloq.* **a** pretty but silly young woman. **b** attractive woman. **3** ventriloquist's dummy. *–v.* (foll. by *up*) *colloq.* dress smartly. [pet form of *Dorothy*]

dollar /ˈdɒlə(r)/ *n.* standard monetary unit of Antigua and Barbuda, Australia, Bahamas, Barbados, Belize, Bermuda, Brunei, Canada, Dominica, Fiji, Grenada, Guyana, Hong Kong, Jamaica, Kiribati, Liberia, Montserrat, Nauru, New Zealand, Puerto Rico, St Kitts and Nevis, Singapore, Solomon Islands, Taiwan, Trinidad and Tobago, Tuvalu, the US, Virgin Islands, and Zimbabwe. [Low German *daler* from German *Taler*]

♦ **dollar stocks** *n.pl.* US or Canadian securities.

---

dollop /ˈdɒləp/ *–n.* shapeless lump of food etc. *–v.* (**-p-**) (usu. foll. by *out*) serve in dollops. [perhaps from Scandinavian]

dolly *n.* (*pl.* **-ies**) **1** child's name for a doll. **2** movable platform for a cine-camera etc. **3** easy catch in cricket.

dolly-bird *n. colloq.* attractive and stylish young woman.

dolma /ˈdɒlmə/ *n.* (*pl.* **-s** or **dolmades** /-ˈmɑːðez/) E European delicacy of spiced rice or meat etc. wrapped in vine or cabbage leaves. [modern Greek]

dolman sleeve /ˈdɒlmən/ *n.* loose sleeve cut in one piece with a bodice. [Turkish]

dolmen /ˈdɒlmən/ *n.* megalithic tomb with a large flat stone laid on upright ones. [French]

dolomite /ˈdɒləˌmaɪt/ *n.* mineral or rock of calcium magnesium carbonate. [de *Dolomieu*, name of a French geologist]

dolour /ˈdɒlə(r)/ *n.* (*US* **dolor**) *literary* sorrow, distress. □ **dolorous** *adj.* [Latin *dolor* pain]

dolphin /ˈdɒlfɪn/ *n.* large porpoise-like sea mammal with a slender pointed snout. [Greek *delphis -in-*]

dolphinarium /ˌdɒlfɪˈneərɪəm/ *n.* (*pl.* **-s**) public aquarium for dolphins.

dolt /dəʊlt/ *n.* stupid person. □ **doltish** *adj.* [apparently related to obsolete *dol* = DULL]

DOM *international vehicle registration* Dominican Republic.

Dom *n.* title of some Roman Catholic dignitaries, and Benedictine and Carthusian monks. [Latin *dominus* master]

-dom *suffix* forming nouns denoting: **1** condition (*freedom*). **2** rank, domain (*earldom*; *kingdom*). **3** class of people (or associated attitudes etc.) regarded collectively (*officialdom*). [Old English]

domain /dəˈmeɪn/ *n.* **1** area under one rule; realm. **2** estate etc. under one control. **3** sphere of control or influence. [French: related to DEMESNE]

dome *–n.* **1** rounded (usu. hemispherical) vault forming a roof. **2** dome-shaped thing. *–v.* (**-ming**) (usu. as **domed** *adj.*) cover with or shape as a dome. [Latin *domus* house]

domestic /dəˈmestɪk/ *–adj.* **1** of the home, household, or family affairs. **2** of one's own country. **3** (of an animal) tamed, not wild. **4** fond of home life. *–n.* household servant. □ **domestically** *adv.* [Latin *domus* home]

domesticate /dəˈmestɪˌkeɪt/ *v.* (**-ting**) **1** tame (an animal) to live with humans. **2** accustom to housework etc. □ **domestication** /-ˈkeɪʃ(ə)n/ *n.* [medieval Latin: related to DOMESTIC]

domesticity /ˌdɒməˈstɪsɪtɪ/ *n.* **1** being domestic. **2** domestic or home life.

domestic science *n.* = HOME ECONOMICS.

domicile /ˈdɒmɪˌsaɪl/ (also **domicil**) *–n.* **1** dwelling-place. **2** *Law* **a** country or place of a person's permanent home, which may differ from that of the person's nationality or place of residence. Domicile is determined by both the physical fact of residence and the continued intention of remaining there. **b** country or place of a corporation's place of registration. *–v.* (**-ling**) (usu. as **domiciled** *adj.*) (usu. foll. by *at, in*) settle in a place. [Latin *domus* home]

domiciliary /ˌdɒmɪˈsɪlɪərɪ/ *adj. formal* (esp. of a doctor's etc. visit) to, at, or of a person's home. [medieval Latin: related to DOMICILE]

dominant /ˈdɒmɪnənt/ *–adj.* **1** dominating, prevailing. **2** (of an inherited characteristic) appearing in offspring even when the opposite characteristic is also inherited. *–n. Mus.* fifth note of the diatonic scale of any key. □ **dominance** *n.* **dominantly** *adv.*

dominate /ˈdɒmɪˌneɪt/ *v.* (**-ting**) **1** command, control. **2** be the most influential or obvious. **3** (of a high place) overlook. □ **domination** /-ˈneɪʃ(ə)n/ *n.* [Latin *dominor* from *dominus* lord]

domineer /ˌdɒmɪˈnɪə(r)/ *–v.* (often as **domineering** *adj.*) behave arrogantly or tyrannically. [French: related to DOMINATE]

Dominican /dəˈmɪnɪkən/ *–adj.* of St Dominic or his order. *–n.* Dominican friar or nun. [Latin *Dominicus* Dominic]

dominion /dəˈmɪnjən/ *n.* **1** sovereignty, control. **2** realm; domain. **3** *hist.* self-governing territory of the British Commonwealth. [Latin *dominus* lord]

domino /ˈdɒmɪˌnəʊ/ *n.* (*pl.* **-es**) **1** any of 28 small oblong pieces marked with 0–6 pips in each half. **2** (in *pl.*) game played with these. **3** loose cloak with a mask. [French, probably as DOMINION]

domino effect *n.* (also **domino theory**) effect whereby (or theory that) one event precipitates others in causal sequence.

don[1] *n.* **1** university teacher, esp. a senior member of a college at Oxford or Cambridge. **2** (**Don**) Spanish title prefixed to a forename. [Spanish from Latin *dominus* lord]

don[2] *v.* (**-nn-**) put on (clothing). [= *do on*]

donate /dəʊˈneɪt/ *v.* (**-ting**) give (money etc.), esp. to charity. [from DONATION]

donation /dəʊˈneɪʃ(ə)n/ *n.* **1** donating or being donated. **2** thing, esp. money, donated. [Latin *donum* gift]

Donau see DANUBE.

Donbas, Donbass see DONETS BASIN.

done /dʌn/ *adj.* **1** completed. **2** cooked. **3** *colloq.* socially acceptable (*the done thing*). **4** (often with *in*) *colloq.* tired out. **5** (esp. as *int.* in reply to an offer etc.) accepted. □ **be done with** have or be finished with. **done for** *colloq.* in serious trouble. **have done with** be rid of; finish dealing with. [past part. of DO[1]]

donee /dəʊˈniː/ *n.* recipient of a gift. [DONOR, -EE]

Donegal /ˌdɒnɪˈgɔːl/ county in the NW Republic of Ireland, in the province of Ulster; linen and tweed are manufactured and agriculture is important; pop. (1991) 128 117; capital, Lifford.

doner kebab /ˈdɒnə, ˈdəʊ-/ *n.* spiced lamb cooked on a spit and served in slices, often with pitta bread. [Turkish: related to KEBAB]

Donets Basin /dɒˈnjets/ (also **Donbas, Donbass** /dɒnˈbæs/) coalmining region in E Ukraine, in the valley of the Donets and lower Dnieper Rivers.

Donetsk /dɒˈnjetsk/ leading city of the Donets Basin in E Ukraine, having important coalmining and metallurgical industries; pop. (est. 1996) 1 088 000.

dông /dɒŋ/ *n.* standard monetary unit of Vietnam. [Vietnamese]

donjon /ˈdɒndʒ(ə)n/ *n.* great tower or innermost keep of a castle. [archaic spelling of DUNGEON]

Don Juan /ˈdʒuːən, ˈwɑːn/ *n.* seducer of women.

Dominica /ˌdɒmɪˈniːkə/, **Commonwealth of** island country in the West Indies, the largest of the Windward Islands. The economy is agricultural, exporting bananas, lime juice, lime oil, coconut-based soap, copra, and rum. Export performance is improving, but foreign debt is large and absorbs most of the export profits. There are plans to diversify the economy (e.g. by tourism) and increase foreign investment.

History. The island came into British possession at the end of the 18th century, becoming an independent republic within the Commonwealth in 1978. It is a member of CARICOM. In 1996 the government sold a number of state-owned enterprises in an attempt to reduce debts. President, Crispen Sorhaindo; prime minister, Edison James; capital, Roseau. □ **Dominican** *adj.* & *n.*

languages	English (official), French patois
currency	East Caribbean dollar (EC$) of 100 cents
pop. (1996)	73 800
GNP (1994)	US$201M
literacy	90%
life expectancy	74 (m); 80 (f)

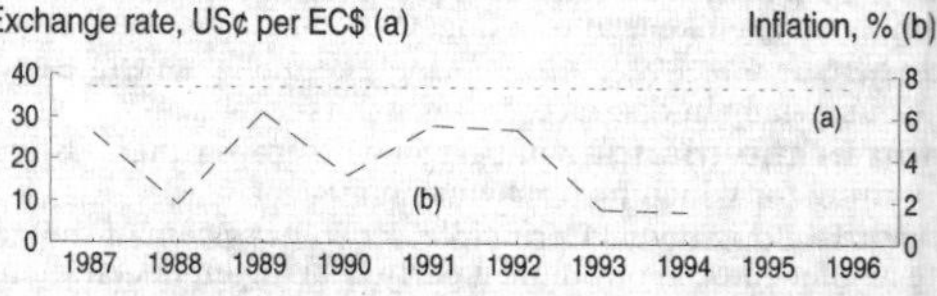

donkey /ˈdɒŋkɪ/ *n.* (*pl.* **-s**) **1** domestic ass. **2** *colloq.* stupid person. [perhaps from *Duncan*: cf. NEDDY]

donkey jacket *n.* thick weatherproof workman's jacket or fashion garment.

donkey's years *n.pl. colloq.* very long time.

donkey-work *n.* laborious part of a job.

Donna /ˈdɒnə/ *n.* title of an Italian, Spanish, or Portuguese lady. [Latin *domina* mistress]

donnish *adj.* like a college don; pedantic.

donor /ˈdəʊnə(r)/ *n.* **1** person who makes a gift or transfers property to another (the donee). **2** person who provides blood, semen, or an organ or tissue for medical use.

donor card *n.* official card authorizing the use of organs, carried by a donor.

don't /dəʊnt/ *–contr.* do not. *–n.* prohibition (*dos and don'ts*).

donut *US* var. of DOUGHNUT.

doodle /ˈduːd(ə)l/ *–v.* (**-ling**) scribble or draw, esp. absent-mindedly. *–n.* such a scribble or drawing. [originally = foolish person]

doom *–n.* **1 a** grim fate or destiny. **b** death or ruin. **2** condemnation. *–v.* **1** (usu. foll. by *to*) condemn or destine. **2** (esp. as **doomed** *adj.*) consign to misfortune or destruction. [Old English, = STATUTE]

doomsday *n.* day of the Last Judgement. □ **till doomsday** for ever.

door *n.* **1 a** esp. hinged barrier for closing and opening the entrance to a building, room, cupboard, etc. **b** this as representing a house etc. (*lives two doors away*). **2 a** entrance or exit; doorway. **b** means of access. □ **close** (or **open) the door to** exclude (or create) an opportunity for. [Old English]

doorbell *n.* bell on a door rung by visitors to signal arrival.

door-keeper *n.* = DOORMAN.

doorknob *n.* knob turned to open a door.

doorman *n.* person on duty at the door to a large building.

doormat *n.* **1** mat at an entrance, for wiping shoes. **2** *colloq.* submissive person.

Doornik see TOURNAI.

doorpost *n.* upright of a door-frame, on which the door is hung.

doorstep *–n.* **1** step or area in front of the outer door of a house etc. **2** *slang* thick slice of bread. *–v. colloq.* **1** go from door to door canvassing, selling, etc. **2** call upon or wait on the doorstep for (a person) in order to interview etc. □ **on one's doorstep** very near.

doorstop *n.* device for keeping a door open or to prevent it from striking the wall.

door-to-door *adj.* (of selling etc.) done at each house in turn.

doorway *n.* opening filled by a door.

dope *–n.* **1 a** *slang* narcotic. **b** drug etc. given to a horse, athlete, etc., to improve performance. **2** thick liquid used as a lubricant etc. **3** varnish. **4** *slang* stupid person. **5** *slang* information. *–v.* (**-ping**) **1** give or add a drug to. **2** apply dope to. [Dutch, = sauce]

dopey *adj.* (also **dopy**) (**dopier**, **dopiest**) *colloq.* **1** half asleep or stupefied as if by a drug. **2** stupid. □ **dopily** *adv.* **dopiness** *n.*

doppelgänger /ˈdɒp(ə)l,geŋə(r)/ *n.* apparition of a living person. [German, = double-goer]

Doppler effect *n.* increase (or decrease) in the frequency of sound, light, etc. waves caused by moving nearer to (or further from) the source. [*Doppler*, name of a physicist]

dorado /dəˈrɑːdəʊ/ *n.* (*pl.* same or **-s**) sea-fish showing brilliant colours when dying out of water. [Spanish, = gilded]

Dordogne /dɔːˈdɔɪn/ department of SW France containing important prehistoric remains. Tourism is the main industry, and hydroelectricity is produced.

Dordrecht /ˈdɔːdrext/ (also **Dort** /dɔːt/) industrial city and river port in the Netherlands, in the province of South Holland; pop. (est. 1995) 114 152. Situated on one of the busiest river junctions in the world, it has shipbuilding, metallurgical, and chemical industries.

Doric /ˈdɒrɪk/ *–adj.* **1** *Archit.* of the oldest and simplest of the Greek orders. **2** (of a dialect) broad, rustic. *–n.* rustic English or esp. Scots. [from *Dōris* in Greece]

dormant /ˈdɔːmənt/ *adj.* **1** lying inactive; sleeping. **2** temporarily inactive. **3** (of plants) alive but not growing. □ **dormancy** *n.* [Latin *dormio* sleep]

♦ **dormant company** *n.* company that has had no significant accounting transactions for the accounting period in question. Such a company need not appoint auditors.

---

dormer *n.* (in full **dormer window**) projecting upright window in a sloping roof. [French: related to DORMANT]

dormitory /ˈdɔːmɪtərɪ/ *n.* (*pl.* **-ies**) **1** sleeping-room with several beds, esp. in a school or institution. **2** (in full **dormitory town** etc.) small commuter town or suburb. [Latin: related to DORMER]

Dormobile /ˈdɔːmə,biːl/ *n. propr.* motor caravan. [from DORMITORY, AUTOMOBILE]

dormouse /ˈdɔːmaʊs/ *n.* (*pl.* **-mice**) small mouselike hibernating rodent. [origin unknown]

Dors. *abbr.* Dorset.

dorsal /ˈdɔːs(ə)l/ *adj.* of or on the back (*dorsal fin*). [Latin *dorsum* back]

Dorset /ˈdɔːsɪt/ county in SW England; pop. (est. 1994) 673 000; county town, Dorchester. Livestock farming and tourism are important.

Dort see DORDRECHT.

Dortmund /ˈdɔːtmʊnd/ industrial city in NW Germany, terminus of the Dortmund–Ems Canal, which links the Ruhr industrial area with the North Sea; manufactures include steel, textiles, furniture, and beer; pop. (est. 1995) 600 918.

Dominican Republic /dəˈmɪnɪkən/ country in the Caribbean, comprising the E portion of the island of Hispaniola. Agriculture is the main occupation; agricultural exports include: sugar, coffee, cocoa, and tobacco. Mineral exports include ferro-nickel, gold, and bauxite. Tourism is a major source of revenue, and there is a growing number of light industries. The economy is in recession, but inflation has been reduced with a change of government policy. A programme to improve the electricity supply, financed by the World Bank and the Inter-American Development Bank, should help to boost the manufacturing industries.
History. A former Spanish colony, it was proclaimed a republic in 1844. After a period of military dictatorship (1930–61) and civil war, a new constitution was introduced in 1966, establishing a democratic system. President, Leonel Fernández; capital, Santo Domingo. □ **Dominican** *adj.* & *n.*

language	Spanish
currency	peso of 100 centavos
pop. (1996)	7 502 000
GNP (1994)	US$10B
literacy	82%(m); 82% (f)
life expectancy	66 (m); 71 (f)

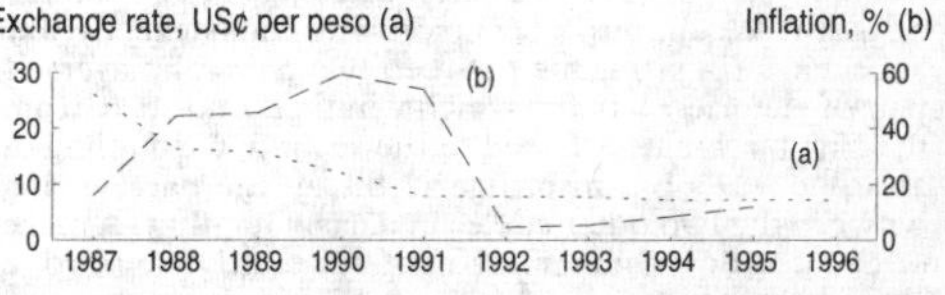

dory /ˈdɔːrɪ/ *n.* (*pl.* same or **-ies**) any of various edible marine fish, esp. the John Dory. [French *dorée* = gilded]

DOS /dɒs/ *abbr. Computing* disk operating system. See also MS-DOS.

dosage /ˈdəʊsɪdʒ/ *n.* **1** size of a dose. **2** giving of a dose.

dose *–n.* **1** single portion of medicine. **2** quantity of work, punishment, etc. **3** amount of radiation received. **4** *slang* venereal infection. *–v.* (**-sing**) treat with or give doses of medicine to. [Greek *dosis* gift]

do-se-do /ˌdəʊsɪˈdəʊ/ *n.* (also **do-si-do**) (*pl.* **-s**) figure in which two dancers pass round each other back to back. [French *dos-à-dos*, = back to back]

dosh *n. slang* money. [origin unknown]

doss *v.* **1** (often foll. by *down*) *slang* sleep roughly or in a doss house. **2** (often foll. by *about, around*) spend time idly. [probably originally = 'seat-back cover': from Latin *dorsum* back]

dosser *n. slang* **1** person who dosses. **2** = DOSS-HOUSE.

doss-house *n.* cheap lodging-house for vagrants.

dossier /ˈdɒsɪˌeɪ, -sɪə(r)/ *n.* file containing information about a person, event, etc. [French]

DOT *abbr.* designated order turn-around (on the New York Stock Exchange).

DoT *abbr.* Department of Transport.

dot *–n.* **1 a** small spot or mark. **b** this as part of *i* or *j*, or as a decimal point etc.. **2** shorter signal of the two in Morse code. *–v.* (**-tt-**) **1 a** mark with dot(s). **b** place a dot over (a letter). **2** (often foll. by *about*) scatter like dots. **3** partly cover as with dots (*sea dotted with ships*). **4** *slang* hit. □ **dot the i's and cross the t's** *colloq.* **1** be minutely accurate. **2** add the final touches to a task etc. **on the dot** exactly on time. **the year dot** *colloq.* far in the past. [Old English]

dotage *n.* feeble-minded senility (*in his dotage*).

dotard /ˈdəʊtəd/ *n.* senile person.

dote *v.* (**-ting**) (foll. by *on*) be excessively fond of. □ **dotingly** *adv.* [origin uncertain]

♦ **dot matrix printer** *n.* printer that is used with a computer, printing characters as a pattern of dots produced by fine needles striking the paper through a normal typewriter ribbon. There are usu. seven or nine needles on the print head; as they move across the paper they build up the required matrix to form each character. Dot matrix printers can print a large selection of shapes and styles of letters and digits, and may also print Arabic characters or the idiograms of oriental languages. Some printers can also produce graphs and other illustrations. They are fast and cheap, but the output is not of the highest quality.

---

dotted line *n.* line of dots on a document etc., esp. for writing a signature on.

dotterel /ˈdɒtər(ə)l/ *n.* small migrant plover. [from DOTE]

dottle /ˈdɒt(ə)l/ *n.* remnant of unburnt tobacco in a pipe. [from DOT]

dotty *adj.* (**-ier, -iest**) *colloq.* **1** crazy; eccentric. **2** (foll. by *about*) infatuated with. □ **dottiness** *n.*

Douala /duːˈælə/ chief port and largest city of Cameroon; industries include textiles, brewing, and food processing; pop. (est. 1992) 1 200 000.

double /ˈdʌb(ə)l/ *–adj.* **1** consisting of two parts or things; twofold. **2** twice as much or many (*double thickness*). **3** having twice the usual size, quantity, strength, etc. (*double bed*). **4 a** being double in part. **b** (of a flower) with two or more circles of petals. **5** ambiguous, deceitful (*double meaning*; *a double life*). *–adv.* **1** at or to twice the amount etc. (*counts double*). **2** two together (*sleep double*). *–n.* **1** double quantity (of spirits etc.) or thing; twice as much or many. **2** counterpart; person who looks exactly like another. **3** (in *pl.*) game between two pairs of players. **4** pair of victories. **5** bet in which winnings and stake from the first bet are transferred to the second. **6** doubling of an opponent's bid in bridge. **7** hit on the narrow ring between the two outer circles in darts. *–v.* (**-ling**) **1** make or become double; increase twofold; multiply by two. **2** amount to twice as much as. **3** fold or bend over on itself; become folded. **4 a** act (two parts) in the same play etc. **b** (often foll. by *for*) be understudy etc. **5** (usu. foll. by *as*) play a twofold role. **6** turn sharply in flight or pursuit. **7** sail round (a headland). **8** make a call in bridge increasing the value of the points to be won or lost on (an opponent's bid). □ **at the double** running, hurrying. **bent double** stooping. **double back** turn back in the opposite direction. **double or quits** gamble to decide whether a player's loss or debt be doubled or cancelled. **double up 1** (cause to) bend or curl up with pain or laughter. **2** share or assign to a shared room, quarters, etc. □ **doubly** *adv.* [Latin *duplus*]

double act *n.* comedy act by a duo.

double agent *n.* spy working for rival countries.

double-barrelled *adj.* **1** (of a gun) having two barrels. **2** (of a surname) hyphenated.

double-bass *n.* largest instrument of the violin family.

double bluff *n.* genuine action or statement disguised as a bluff.

double-book *v.* reserve (the same seat, room, etc.) for two people at once.

double-breasted *adj.* (of a coat etc.) overlapping across the body.

double-check *v.* verify twice.

double chin *n.* chin with a fold of loose flesh below it.

double cream *n.* thick cream with a high fat-content.

double-cross *–v.* deceive or betray (a supposed ally). *–n.* act of doing this. □ **double-crosser** *n.*

double-dealing *–n.* deceit, esp. in business. *–adj.* practising deceit.

double-decker *n.* **1** bus having an upper and lower deck. **2** *colloq.* sandwich with two layers of filling.

double-density disk see FLOPPY DISK.

double Dutch *n. colloq.* gibberish.

double eagle *n.* figure of a two-headed eagle.

double-edged *adj.* **1** presenting both a danger and an advantage. **2** (of a knife etc.) having two cutting-edges.

double entendre /ˌduːb(ə)l ɑːnˈtɑːndrə/ *n.* ambiguous phrase open to usu. indecent interpretation. [obsolete French]

♦ **double-entry bookkeeping** *n.* (also **double entry**) method of recording the transactions of a business in a set of accounts, such that every transaction has a dual aspect and therefore needs to be recorded in at least two accounts. For example, when a person (debtor) pays cash to a business for goods purchased, the cash held by the business is increased and the amount due from the debtor is decreased by the same amount; similarly, when a purchase is made on credit, the stock is decreased and the amount owing to creditors is increased by the same amount. This double aspect enables the business to be controlled because all the books of accounts must balance.

---

double feature *n.* cinema programme with two full-length films.

double figures *n.pl.* numbers from 10 to 99.

double glazing *n.* two layers of glass in a window.

double helix *n.* pair of parallel helices with a common axis, esp. in the structure of a DNA molecule.

double-jointed *adj.* having joints that allow unusual bending.

double negative *n. Gram.* negative statement containing two negative elements (e.g. *he didn't say nothing*).

■ **Usage** The double negative is considered incorrect in standard English.

♦ **double-page spread** Two facing pages in a magazine or newspaper used in advertising as if they were a single page.

---

double-park *v.* (also *absol.*) park (a vehicle) alongside one already parked at the roadside.

double pneumonia *n.* pneumonia affecting both lungs.

double-quick *adj.* & *adv. colloq.* very quick or quickly.

double-sided disk see FLOPPY DISK.

double standard *n.* rule or principle not impartially applied.

doublet /'dʌblɪt/ *n.* **1** *hist.* man's short close-fitting jacket. **2** one of a pair of similar things. [French: related to DOUBLE]

double take *n.* delayed reaction to a situation etc.

double-talk *n.* (usu. deliberately) ambiguous or misleading speech.

♦ **double taxation** *n.* taxation that falls on the same source of income in more than one country. Taxation is normally levied on a person's worldwide income in that person's country of residence. A person may also be taxed in other countries in which he or she has a permanent trading establishment. Because this would inhibit trade, arrangements are usu. made to mitigate or abolish this double taxation. This is often achieved by double-taxation treaties between countries; it may also be imposed by a country unilaterally. The principal methods of **double-taxation relief** are: inclusion of the income in one country after deduction of the tax levied in the other; agreement between countries that only one of them will tax the income; and double-tax credits, enabling one country to allow a credit against its own tax for the tax paid in the other country.

double-think *n.* capacity to accept contrary opinions at the same time.

double time *n.* wages paid at twice the normal rate.

doubloon /dʌ'bluːn/ *n. hist.* Spanish gold coin. [French or Spanish: related to DOUBLE]

doubt /daʊt/ *–n.* **1** uncertainty; undecided state of mind. **2** cynicism. **3** uncertain state. **4** lack of full proof or clear indication. *–v.* **1** feel uncertain or undecided about. **2** hesitate to believe. **3** call in question. □ **in doubt** open to question. **no doubt** certainly; probably; admittedly. **without doubt** (or **a doubt**) certainly. [Latin *dubito* hesitate]

doubtful *adj.* **1** feeling doubt. **2** causing doubt. **3** unreliable. □ **doubtfully** *adv.* **doubtfulness** *n.*

doubtless *adv.* certainly; probably.

douche /duːʃ/ *–n.* **1** jet of liquid applied to part of the body for cleansing or medicinal purposes. **2** device for producing such a jet. *–v.* (**-ching**) **1** treat with a douche. **2** use a douche. [Latin: related to DUCT]

dough /dəʊ/ *n.* **1** thick mixture of flour etc. and liquid for baking. **2** *slang* money. □ **doughy** *adj.* (**-ier, -iest**). [Old English]

doughnut *n.* (*US* **donut**) small fried cake of sweetened dough.

doughnutting *n.* the clustering of politicians round a speaker during a televised debate to make him or her appear well supported.

doughty /'daʊtɪ/ *adj.* (**-ier, -iest**) *archaic* valiant. □ **doughtily** *adv.* **doughtiness** *n.* [Old English]

Douglas /'dʌgləs/ capital of the Isle of Man, a port and resort on the E coast; pop. (1991) 22 214.

dour /dʊə(r)/ *adj.* severe, stern, obstinate. [probably Gaelic *dúr* dull, obstinate]

douse *v.* (also **dowse**) (**-sing**) **1 a** throw water over. **b** plunge into water. **2** extinguish (a light). [origin uncertain]

dove /dʌv/ *n.* **1** bird with short legs, a small head, and a large breast. **2** gentle or innocent person. **3** advocate of peace or peaceful policies. [Old Norse]

dovecote /'dʌvkɒt/ *n.* (also **dovecot**) shelter with nesting-holes for domesticated pigeons.

Dover /'dəʊvə(r)/ **1** ferry port in SE England, in Kent on the coast of the English Channel; pop. (est. 1994) 34 179. It is mainland Britain's nearest point to the Continent, being only 35 km (21 miles) from Calais. **2** city in the US, capital of Delaware; pop. (1990) 27 630.

dovetail *–n.* mortise and tenon joint shaped like a dove's spread tail. *–v.* **1** join with dovetails. **2** fit together; combine neatly.

dowager /'daʊədʒə(r)/ *n.* **1** widow with a title or property from her late husband (*dowager duchess*). **2** *colloq.* dignified elderly woman. [French: related to DOWER]

dowdy /'daʊdɪ/ *adj.* (**-ier, -iest**) **1** (of clothes) unattractively dull. **2** dressed dowdily. □ **dowdily** *adv.* **dowdiness** *n.* [origin unknown]

dowel /'daʊəl/ *–n.* cylindrical peg for holding structural components together. *–v.* (**-ll-**; *US* **-l-**) fasten with a dowel. [Low German]

dowelling *n.* rods for cutting into dowels.

dower *n.* **1** widow's share for life of a husband's estate. **2** *archaic* dowry. [Latin *dos* dowry]

dower house *n.* smaller house near a big one, as part of a widow's dower.

♦ **Dow Jones Industrial Average** /daʊ 'dʒəʊnz/ *n.* (also **DJIA**) index of security prices issued by Dow Jones & Co. (a US firm providing financial information), used on the New York Stock Exchange. It is a narrowly based index, comparable to the London Financial Times Ordinary Share Index, having 30 constituent companies. The index was founded in 1884, based then on 11 stocks (mostly in railways), but was reorganized in 1928 when it was given the value of 100. Its lowest point was on 2 July 1932, when it reached 41. In 1987 it exceeded 2400. There are three other Dow Jones indexes, representing price movements in US home bonds, transportation stocks, and utilities. Cf. STANDARD AND POOR'S 500 STOCK INDEX. [*Dow* and *Jones*, names of American economists]

down[1] *–adv.* **1** into or towards a lower place, esp. to the ground (*fall down*). **2** in a lower place or position (*blinds were down*). **3** to or in a place regarded as lower, esp.: **a** southwards. **b** away from a major city or a university. **4 a** in or into a low or weaker position or condition (*hit a man when he's down; down with a cold*). **b** losing by (*three goals down; £5 down*). **c** (of a computer system) out of action. **5** from an earlier to a later time (*down to 1600*). **6** to a finer or thinner consistency or smaller amount or size (*grind down; water down; boil down*). **7** cheaper (*bread is down; shares are down*). **8** into a more settled state (*calm down*). **9** in writing or recorded form (*copy it down; down on tape; down to speak next*). **10** paid or dealt with as a deposit or part (*£5 down, £20 to pay; three down, six to go*). **11** with the current or wind. **12** (of a crossword clue or answer) read vertically (*five down*). *–prep.* **1** downwards along, through, or into. **2** from the top to the bottom of. **3** along (*walk down the road*). **4** at or in a lower part of (*lives down the road*). *–attrib. adj.* **1** directed downwards (*a down draught*). **2** from a capital or centre (*down train; down platform*). *–v. colloq.* **1** knock or bring down. **2** swallow. *–n.* **1** act of putting down. **2** reverse of fortune (*ups and downs*). **3** *colloq.* period of depression. □ **be down to 1** be the responsibility of. **2** have nothing left but (*down to my last penny*). **3** be attributable to. **down on one's luck** *colloq.* temporarily unfortunate. **down to the ground** *colloq.* completely. **down tools** *colloq.* cease work, go on strike. **down with** expressing rejection of a specified person or thing. **have a down on** *colloq.* show hostility towards. [earlier *adown*: related to DOWN[3]]

down[2] *n.* **1 a** first covering of young birds. **b** bird's underplumage. **c** fine soft feathers or hairs. **2** fluffy substance. [Old Norse]

down[3] *n.* **1** open rolling land. **2** (in *pl.*) chalk uplands, esp. in S England. [Old English]

Down /daʊn/ **1** county in Northern Ireland; county town, Downpatrick. Dairy farming is the chief occupation. **2** district of Northern Ireland, in Co. Down; pop. (1990) 57 700.

down-and-out *n.* destitute person. □ **down and out** *attrib. adj.*

downbeat *–n. Mus.* accented beat, usu. the first of the bar. *–adj.* **1** pessimistic, gloomy. **2** relaxed.

downcast *adj.* **1** dejected. **2** (of eyes) looking downwards.

downer *n. slang* **1** depressant or tranquillizing drug. **2**

depressing person or experience; failure. **3** = DOWNTURN.

downfall *n.* **1** fall from prosperity or power. **2** cause of this.

downgrade *v.* (**-ding**) reduce in rank or status.

downhearted *adj.* dejected. □ **downheartedly** *adv.* **downheartedness** *n.*

downhill *–adv.* in a descending direction. *–adj.* sloping down, declining. *–n.* **1** downhill race in skiing. **2** downward slope. □ **go downhill** *colloq.* deteriorate.

down in the mouth *adj.* looking unhappy.

downland *n.* = DOWN[3].

download *v.* send (programs or data) from a central or controlling computer to a remote terminal or to a microcomputer.

down-market *adj.* & *adv. colloq.* of or to the cheaper sector of the market.

down payment *n.* partial initial payment.

downpipe *n.* pipe to carry rainwater from a roof.

downpour *n.* heavy fall of rain.

downright *–adj.* **1** plain, straightforward. **2** utter (*downright nonsense*). *–adv.* thoroughly (*downright rude*).

downsize *v.* (**-zing**) **1** replace a mainframe or minicomputer (in a computer system) by a network of microcomputers. **2** reduce the size (of an organization), esp. by reducing the number of employees. See also RIGHTSIZE.

Down's syndrome *n.* congenital disorder with mental retardation and physical abnormalities. [*Down*, name of a physician]

downstage *adv.* nearer the front of a theatre stage.

downstairs *–adv.* **1** down the stairs. **2** to or on a lower floor. *–attrib. adj.* situated downstairs. *–n.* lower floor.

downstream *adv.* & *adj.* in the direction in which a stream etc. flows.

downtime *n.* (also **down time**) time, or the percentage of time, during which a computer is not available for use, usu. as a result of regular preventative maintenance or because the computer breaks down and has to be taken out of service for repairs.

down-to-earth *adj.* practical, realistic.

downtown esp. *US –attrib. adj.* of the lower or more central part of a town or city. *–n.* downtown area. *–adv.* in or into the downtown area.

downtrodden *adj.* oppressed; badly treated.

downturn *n.* decline, esp. in economic activity.

down under *adv. colloq.* in the antipodes, esp. Australia.

downward /ˈdaʊnwəd/ *–adv.* (also **downwards**) towards what is lower, inferior, less important, or later. *–adj.* moving or extending downwards.

downwind *adj.* & *adv.* in the direction in which the wind is blowing.

downy *adj.* (**-ier, -iest**) **1** of, like, or covered with down. **2** soft and fluffy.

dowry /ˈdaʊərɪ/ *n.* (*pl.* **-ies**) property or money brought by a bride to her husband. [Anglo-French = French *douaire* DOWER]

dowse[1] /daʊs/ *v.* (**-sing**) search for underground water or minerals by holding a stick or rod which dips abruptly when over the right spot. □ **dowser** *n.* [origin unknown]

dowse[2] var. of DOUSE.

dowsing-rod *n.* rod for dowsing.

doxology /dɒkˈsɒlədʒɪ/ *n.* (*pl.* **-ies**) liturgical hymn etc. of praise to God. □ **doxological** /-səˈlɒdʒɪk(ə)l/ *adj.* [Greek *doxa* glory]

doyen /ˈdɔɪən/ *n.* (*fem.* **doyenne** /dɔɪˈen/) senior member of a group. [French: related to DEAN[1]]

doyley var. of DOILY.

doz. *abbr.* dozen.

doze *–v.* (**-zing**) sleep lightly; be half asleep. *–n.* short light sleep. □ **doze off** fall lightly asleep. [origin unknown]

dozen /ˈdʌz(ə)n/ *n.* **1** (prec. by *a* or a number) (*pl.* **dozen**) twelve (*a dozen eggs*; *two dozen eggs*). **2** set of twelve (*sold in dozens*). **3** (in *pl.*; usu. foll. by *of*) *colloq.* very many (*dozens of errors*). □ **talk nineteen to the dozen** talk incessantly. [Latin *duodecim* twelve]

dozy *adj.* (**-ier, -iest**) **1** drowsy. **2** *colloq.* stupid or lazy.

DP *abbr.* **1** data processing. **2** delivery point. **3** duty paid. **4** *Computing* dynamic programming.

D/P *abbr.* documents against presentation. See CASH AGAINST DOCUMENTS.

d.p. *abbr.* direct port.

DPA *abbr.* Diploma in Public Administration.

DPB *abbr. Finance* deposit pass book.

DPD *abbr.* Data Protection Directive.

D.P.Ec. *abbr.* Doctor of Political Economy.

D.Phil. *abbr.* Doctor of Philosophy.

dpi *abbr.* (also **d.p.i.**) *Computing* dots per inch.

DPM *abbr.* data-processing manager.

DPMI *abbr. Computing* DOS/Protected Mode Interface.

DPP *abbr.* **1** *Insurance* deferred payment plan. **2** Director of Public Prosecutions.

DPR *abbr.* Data Protection Register.

DPS *abbr.* dividend per share.

dpt. *abbr.* **1** department. **2** deposit. **3** depot.

DQ *international civil aircraft marking* Fiji.

DR *abbr.* discount rate.

D/R *abbr.* deposit receipt.

Dr *–abbr.* Doctor. *–symb.* drachma.

dr. *abbr.* **1** debit. **2** debtor. **3** drachma. **4** draw (or drawn). **5** drawer.

drab *adj.* (**drabber, drabbest**) **1** dull, uninteresting. **2** of a dull brownish colour. □ **drably** *adv.* **drabness** *n.* [obsolete *drap* cloth]

drachm /dræm/ *n.* weight formerly used by apothecaries, = $^{1}/_{8}$ ounce. [Latin from Greek]

drachma /ˈdrækmə/ *n.* (*pl.* **-s**) **1** standard monetary unit of Greece. **2** silver coin of ancient Greece. [Greek *drakhmē*]

Draconian /drəˈkəʊnɪən/ *adj.* (of laws) very harsh, cruel. [*Drakōn*, name of an Athenian lawgiver]

draft /drɑːft/ *–n.* **1** preliminary written version of a speech, document, etc., or outline of a scheme. **2 a** written order for payment of money, esp. by a bank (see BANK DRAFT). **b** drawing of money by this. **3 a** detachment from a larger group. **b** selection of this. **4** *US* conscription. **5** *US* = DRAUGHT. *–v.* **1** prepare a draft of (a document, scheme, etc.). **2** select for a special duty or purpose. **3** *US* conscript. [phonetic spelling of DRAUGHT]

draftsman *n.* **1** person who drafts documents. **2** = DRAUGHTSMAN 1. [phonetic spelling of DRAUGHTSMAN]

drafty *US* var. of DRAUGHTY.

drag *–v.* (**-gg-**) **1** pull along with effort. **2 a** trail or allow to trail along the ground. **b** (often foll. by *on*) (of time, a meeting, etc.) go or pass slowly or tediously. **3 a** use a grapnel. **b** search the bottom of (a river etc.) with grapnels, nets, etc. **4** (often foll. by *to*) *colloq.* take (an esp. unwilling person) with one. **5** (foll. by *on, at*) draw on (a cigarette etc.). *–n.* **1 a** obstruction to progress. **b** retarding force or motion. **2** *colloq.* boring or tiresome person, duty, etc. **3 a** lure before hounds as a substitute for a fox. **b** hunt using this. **4** apparatus for dredging. **5** = DRAG-NET. **6** *slang* inhalation. **7** *slang* women's clothes worn by men. □ **drag one's feet** be deliberately slow or reluctant to act. **drag in** introduce (an irrelevant subject). **drag out** protract. **drag up** *colloq.* introduce or revive (an unwelcome subject). [Old English or Old Norse]

draggle /ˈdræg(ə)l/ *v.* (**-ling**) **1** make dirty, wet, or limp by trailing. **2** hang trailing. [from DRAG]

drag-net *n.* **1** net drawn through a river or across the ground to trap fish or game. **2** systematic hunt for criminals etc.

dragon /ˈdrægən/ *n.* **1** mythical usu. winged monster like a reptile, able to breathe fire. **2** fierce woman. [Greek, = serpent]

dragonfly *n.* large insect with a long body and two pairs of transparent wings.

♦ **dragon markets** *n.pl. colloq.* emerging markets and economies of the Pacific basin, e.g. Indonesia, Malaysia, and Thailand. See also TIGER MARKETS.

dragoon /drəˈguːn/ *–n.* **1** cavalryman. **2** fierce fellow. *–v.* (foll. by *into*) coerce or bully into. [French *dragon*: related to DRAGON]

drag queen *n. slang derog.* male homosexual transvestite.

drain *–v.* **1** draw off liquid from. **2** draw off (liquid). **3** flow or trickle away. **4** dry or become dry as liquid flows away. **5** exhaust of strength or resources. **6 a** drink to the dregs. **b** empty (a glass etc.) by drinking the contents. *–n.* **1 a** channel, conduit, or pipe carrying off liquid, sewage, etc. **b** tube for drawing off discharge etc. **2** constant outflow or expenditure. □ **down the drain** *colloq.* lost, wasted. [Old English: related to DRY]

drainage *n.* **1** draining. **2** system of drains. **3** what is drained off.

draining-board *n.* sloping grooved surface beside a sink for draining washed dishes.

drainpipe *n.* **1** pipe for carrying off water etc. **2** (*attrib.*) (of trousers) very narrow. **3** (in *pl.*) very narrow trousers.

drake *n.* male duck. [origin uncertain]

Dralon /ˈdreɪlɒn/ *n. propr.* **1** synthetic acrylic fibre. **2** fabric made from this. [invented word, after NYLON]

DRAM /dræm/ *abbr. Computing* dynamic random-access memory.

dram *n.* standard monetary unit of Armenia.

dram *n.* **1** small drink of spirits, esp. whisky. **2** = DRACHM. [Latin *drama*: related to DRACHM]

drama /ˈdrɑːmə/ *n.* **1** play for stage or broadcasting. **2** art of writing and presenting plays. **3** dramatic event or quality (*the drama of the situation*). [Latin from Greek *draō* do]

dramatic /drəˈmætɪk/ *adj.* **1** of drama. **2** sudden and exciting or unexpected. **3** vividly striking. **4** (of a gesture etc.) theatrical. □ **dramatically** *adv.* [Greek: related to DRAMA]

dramatics *n.pl.* (often treated as *sing.*) **1** performance of plays. **2** exaggerated behaviour.

dramatis personae /ˌdræmətɪs pɜːˈsəʊnaɪ/ *n.pl.* **1** characters in a play. **2** list of these. [Latin, = persons of the drama]

dramatist /ˈdræmətɪst/ *n.* writer of dramas.

dramatize /ˈdræməˌtaɪz/ *v.* (also **-ise**) (**-zing** or **-sing**) **1** turn (a novel etc.) into a play. **2** make a dramatic scene of. **3** behave dramatically. □ **dramatization** /-ˈzeɪʃ(ə)n/ *n.*

Drammen /ˈdrɑːmən/ seaport in SE Norway; exports include timber, wood pulp, and paper; pop. (1991) 51 900.

drank *past* of DRINK.

drape *–v.* (**-ping**) **1** hang or cover loosely, adorn with cloth etc. **2** arrange (hangings etc.) esp. in folds. *–n.* (in *pl.*) *US* curtains. [Latin *drappus* cloth]

draper *n.* dealer in textile fabrics.

drapery *n.* (*pl.* **-ies**) **1** clothing or hangings arranged in folds. **2** draper's trade or fabrics.

drastic /ˈdræstɪk/ *adj.* far-reaching in effect; severe. □ **drastically** *adv.* [Greek *drastikos*: related to DRAMA]

drat *colloq. –v.* (**-tt-**) (usu. as *int.*) curse (*drat the thing!*). *–int.* expressing anger or annoyance. □ **dratted** *adj.* [*(Go)d rot*]

draught /drɑːft/ *n.* (*US* **draft**) **1** current of air in a room or chimney etc. **2** pulling, traction. **3** depth of water needed to float a ship. **4** drawing of liquor from a cask etc. **5 a** single act of drinking or inhaling. **b** amount drunk thus. **6** (in *pl.*) game for two with 12 pieces each on a draughtboard. **7 a** drawing in of a fishing-net. **b** fish so caught. □ **feel the draught** *colloq.* suffer from esp. financial hardship. [related to DRAW]

draught beer *n.* beer from the cask, not bottled or canned.

draughtboard *n.* = CHESSBOARD.

draught-horse *n.* horse for heavy work.

draughtsman *n.* **1** person who makes drawings, plans, or sketches. **2** piece in draughts. □ **draughtsmanship** *n.*

draughty *adj.* (*US* **drafty**) (**-ier, -iest**) (of a room etc.) letting in sharp currents of air. □ **draughtiness** *n.*

DRAW /drɔː/ *abbr. Computing* direct read after write.

draw *–v.* (*past* **drew** /druː/; *past part.* **drawn**) **1** pull or cause to move towards or after one. **2** pull (a thing) up, over, or across. **3** pull (curtains etc.) open or shut. **4** take (a person) aside. **5** attract; bring; take in (*drew a deep breath*; *felt drawn to her*; *drew my attention*; *drew a crowd*). **6** (foll. by *at, on*) inhale from (a cigarette, pipe, etc.). **7** (also *absol.*) take out; remove (a tooth, gun, cork, card, etc.). **8** obtain or take from a source (*draw a salary*; *draw inspiration*; *drew £100 out*). **9 a** (also *absol.*) make (a line or mark). **b** produce (a picture) thus. **c** represent (something) thus. **10** (also *absol.*) finish (a contest or game) with equal scores. **11** proceed (*drew near the bridge*; *draw to a close*; *drew level*). **12** infer (a conclusion). **13 a** elicit, evoke (*draw criticism*). **b** induce (a person) to reveal facts etc. **14** haul up (water) from a well. **15** bring out (liquid from a tap etc. or blood from a wound). **16** extract a liquid essence from. **17** (of a chimney etc.) promote or allow a draught. **18** (of tea) infuse. **19 a** obtain by lot (*drew the winner*). **b** *absol.* draw lots. **20** (foll. by *on*) call on (a person or a person's skill etc.). **21** write out or compose (a cheque, document, etc.). **22** formulate or perceive (a comparison or distinction). **23** disembowel. **24** search (cover) for game. **25** drag (a badger or fox) from a hole. *–n.* **1** act of drawing. **2** person or thing attracting custom, attention, etc. **3** drawing of lots, raffle. **4** drawn game. **5** inhalation of smoke etc. □ **draw back** withdraw from an undertaking. **draw a bead on** see BEAD. **draw a blank** see BLANK. **draw in 1** (of days) become shorter. **2** persuade to join. **3** (of a train) arrive at a station. **draw in one's horns** become less assertive or ambitious. **draw the line at** set a limit of tolerance etc. at. **draw lots** see LOT. **draw on 1** approach, come near. **2** lead to. **3** allure. **4** put (gloves, boots, etc.) on. **draw out 1** prolong. **2** elicit. **3** induce to talk. **4** (of days) become longer. **5** (of a train) leave a station. **draw up 1** draft (a document etc.). **2** bring into order. **3** come to a halt. **4** make (oneself) erect. **quick on the draw** quick to react. [Old English]

drawback *n.* **1** disadvantage. **2** refund of import duty by the Customs and Excise when imported goods are re-exported. Payment of the import duty and claiming the drawback can be avoided if the goods are stored in a bonded warehouse immediately after unloading from the incoming ship or aircraft until re-export.

drawbridge *n.* hinged retractable bridge, esp. over a moat.

♦ **drawdown** *n.* drawing of funds against a line of credit.

♦ **drawee** /drɔːˈiː/ *n.* **1** person on whom a bill of exchange is drawn (i.e. to whom it is addressed). The drawee will accept it (see ACCEPTANCE 4) and pay it on maturity. **2** bank on whom a cheque is drawn, i.e. the bank holding the account of the individual or company that wrote it. **3** bank named in a bank draft. Cf. DRAWER 2.

drawer /ˈdrɔːə(r)/ *n.* **1** person or thing that draws. **2 a** person who signs a bill of exchange ordering the drawee to pay the specified sum at the specified time. **b** person who signs a cheque ordering the drawee bank to pay a specified sum of money on demand. Cf. DRAWEE. **3** also /drɔː(r)/ lidless boxlike storage compartment, sliding in and out of a table etc. (*chest of drawers*). **4** (in *pl.*) knickers, underpants.

drawing *n.* **1** art of representing by line with a pencil etc. **2** picture etc. made thus.

drawing-board *n.* board on which paper is fixed for drawing on.

drawing-pin *n.* flat-headed pin for fastening paper etc. to a surface.

drawing-room *n.* **1** room in a private house for sitting or entertaining in. **2** (*attrib.*) restrained, polite (*drawing-room manners*). [earlier *withdrawing-room*]

drawl –*v.* speak with drawn-out vowel sounds. –*n.* drawling utterance or way of speaking. [Low German or Dutch]

drawn *adj.* looking strained and tense.

drawstring *n.* string or cord threaded through a waistband, bag opening, etc.

dray *n.* low cart without sides for heavy loads, esp. beer-barrels. [related to DRAW]

dread /dred/ –*v.* fear greatly, esp. in advance. –*n.* great fear or apprehension. –*adj.* **1** dreaded. **2** *archaic* awe-inspiring, dreadful. [Old English]

dreadful *adj.* **1** terrible. **2** *colloq.* troublesome, very bad. □ **dreadfully** *adv.*

dreadlocks *n.pl.* Rastafarian hairstyle with hair hanging in tight braids on all sides.

dream –*n.* **1** series of scenes or feelings in the mind of a sleeping person. **2** day-dream or fantasy. **3** ideal, aspiration. **4** beautiful or ideal person or thing. –*v.* (*past* and *past part.* **dreamt** /dremt/ or **dreamed**) **1** experience a dream. **2** imagine as in a dream. **3** (with *neg.*) consider possible (*never dreamt that he would come*; *would not dream of it*). **4** (foll. by *away*) waste (time). **5** be inactive or unpractical. □ **dream up** imagine, invent. **like a dream** *colloq.* easily, effortlessly. □ **dreamer** *n.* [Old English]

dreamboat *n. colloq.* sexually attractive or ideal person.

dreamland *n.* ideal or imaginary land.

dreamy *adj.* (**-ier**, **-iest**) **1** given to day-dreaming or fantasy. **2** dreamlike; vague. **3** *colloq.* delightful. □ **dreamily** *adv.* **dreaminess** *n.*

dreary *adj.* (**-ier**, **-iest**) dismal, dull, gloomy. □ **drearily** *adv.* **dreariness** *n.* [Old English]

dredge[1] –*n.* apparatus used to scoop up oysters etc., or to clear mud etc., from a river or sea bed. –*v.* (**-ging**) **1** (often foll. by *up*) **a** bring up or clear (mud etc.) with a dredge. **b** bring up (something forgotten) (*dredged it all up*). **2** clean with or use a dredge. [origin uncertain]

dredge[2] *v.* (**-ging**) sprinkle with flour, sugar, etc. [earlier = sweetmeat, from French]

dredger[1] *n.* **1** boat with a dredge. **2** dredge.

dredger[2] *n.* container with a perforated lid, for sprinkling flour, sugar, etc.

dregs *n.pl.* **1** sediment; grounds, lees. **2** = SCUM *n.* 2 (*dregs of humanity*). [Old Norse]

drench –*v.* **1** wet thoroughly. **2** force (an animal) to take medicine. –*n.* dose of medicine for an animal. [Old English]

Drenthe /'drentə/ sparsely populated agricultural province in the NE Netherlands; pop. (est. 1995) 454 864; capital, Assen.

Dresden /'drezd(ə)n/ city in E Germany, the capital of Saxony, a centre for light industry and market gardening; pop. (est. 1995) 474 443. Its porcelain industry moved to Meissen in 1710.

dress –*v.* **1 a** (also *absol.*) put clothes on. **b** have and wear clothes (*dresses well*). **2** put on evening dress. **3** arrange or adorn (hair, a shop window, etc.). **4** treat (a wound) esp. with a dressing. **5 a** prepare (poultry, crab, etc.) for cooking or eating. **b** add dressing to (a salad etc.). **6** apply manure to. **7** finish the surface of (fabric, leather, stone, etc.). **8** correct the alignment of (troops). **9** make (an artificial fly) for fishing. –*n.* **1** woman's garment of a bodice and skirt. **2** clothing, esp. a whole outfit. **3** formal or ceremonial costume. **4** external covering; outward form. □ **dress down** *colloq.* **1** reprimand or scold. **2** dress informally. **dress up 1** put on special clothes. **2** make (a thing) more attractive or interesting. [French *dresser*, ultimately related to DIRECT]

dressage /'dresɑːʒ/ *n.* training of a horse in obedience and deportment; display of this. [French]

dress circle *n.* first gallery in a theatre.

dress coat *n.* man's swallow-tailed evening coat.

dresser[1] *n.* kitchen sideboard with shelves for plates etc. [French *dresser* prepare]

dresser[2] *n.* **1** person who helps to dress actors or actresses. **2** surgeon's assistant in operations. **3** person who dresses in a specified way (*snappy dresser*).

dressing *n.* **1** putting one's clothes on. **2 a** sauce, esp. of oil and vinegar etc., for salads (*French dressing*). **b** sauce or stuffing etc. for food. **3** bandage, ointment, etc., for a wound. **4** size or stiffening used to coat fabrics. **5** compost etc. spread over land.

dressing-down *n. colloq.* scolding.

dressing-gown *n.* loose robe worn when one is not fully dressed.

dressing-room *n.* room for changing one's clothes, esp. in a theatre, or attached to a bedroom.

dressing-table *n.* table with a flat top, mirror, and drawers, used while applying make-up etc.

dressmaker *n.* person who makes women's clothes, esp. for a living. □ **dressmaking** *n.*

dress rehearsal *n.* final rehearsal in full costume.

dress-shield *n.* waterproof material in the armpit of a dress to protect it from sweat.

dress-shirt *n.* man's shirt worn with evening dress, usu. white with concealed buttons or studs.

dressy *adj.* (**-ier**, **-iest**) *colloq.* (of clothes or a person) smart, elaborate, elegant. □ **dressiness** *n.*

drew *past* of DRAW.

drey /dreɪ/ *n.* squirrel's nest. [origin unknown]

dribble /'drɪb(ə)l/ –*v.* (**-ling**) **1** allow saliva to flow from the mouth. **2** flow or allow to flow in drops. **3** (also *absol.*) esp. *Football & Hockey* move (the ball) forward with slight touches of the feet or stick. –*n.* **1** act of dribbling. **2** dribbling flow. [obsolete *drib* = DRIP]

driblet /'drɪblɪt/ *n.* small quantity.

dribs and drabs *n.pl. colloq.* small scattered amounts.

dried *past* and *past part.* of DRY.

drier[1] *compar.* of DRY.

drier[2] /'draɪə(r)/ *n.* (also **dryer**) device for drying hair, laundry, etc.

driest *superl.* of DRY.

drift –*n.* **1 a** slow movement or variation. **b** this caused by a current. **2** intention, meaning, etc. of what is said etc. **3** mass of snow etc. heaped up by the wind. **4** esp. *derog.* state of inaction. **5** slow deviation of a ship, aircraft, etc., from its course. **6** fragments of rock heaped up (*glacial drift*). **7** *S.Afr.* ford. –*v.* **1** be carried by or as if by a current of air or water. **2** progress casually or aimlessly (*drifted into teaching*). **3** pile or be piled into drifts. **4** (of a current) carry, cause to drift. [Old Norse and Germanic *trift* movement of cattle]

drifter *n.* **1** aimless person. **2** boat used for drift-net fishing.

drift-net *n.* net for sea fishing, allowed to drift.

driftwood *n.* wood floating on moving water or washed ashore.

drill[1] –*n.* **1** tool or machine for boring holes, sinking wells, etc. **2** instruction in military exercises. **3** routine procedure in an emergency (*fire-drill*). **4** thorough training, esp. by repetition. **5** *colloq.* recognized procedure (*what's the drill?*). –*v.* **1 a** make a hole in or through with a drill. **b** make (a hole) with a drill. **2** train or be trained by drill. [Dutch]

drill[2] –*n.* **1** machine for making furrows, sowing, and covering seed. **2** small furrow. **3** row of seeds sown by a drill. –*v.* plant in drills. [origin unknown]

drill[3] *n.* coarse twilled cotton or linen fabric. [Latin *trilix* having three threads]

drill[4] *n.* W African baboon related to the mandrill. [probably native]

drily *adv.* (also **dryly**) in a dry manner.

drink –*v.* (*past* **drank**; *past part.* **drunk**) **1 a** (also *absol.*) swallow (liquid). **b** swallow the contents of (a vessel). **2** take alcohol, esp. to excess. **3** (of a plant, sponge, etc.) absorb (moisture). **4** bring (oneself etc.) to a specified condition by drinking. **5** wish (a person good health etc.) by drinking (*drank his health*). –*n.* **1 a** liquid for drinking. **b** draught or specified amount of this. **2 a** alcoholic liquor. **b** portion, glass, etc. of this. **c** excessive use of alcohol (*took to drink*). **3** (**the drink**) *colloq.* the sea. □ **drink in** listen eagerly to. **drink to** toast; wish success to. **drink up** (also *absol.*) drink all or the remainder of. □ **drinkable** *adj.* **drinker** *n.* [Old English]

drink-driver *n.* person who drives with excess alcohol in the blood. □ **drink-driving** *n.*

drip –*v.* (**-pp-**) **1** fall or let fall in drops. **2** (often foll. by *with*) be so wet as to shed drops. –*n.* **1 a** liquid falling in drops (*steady drip of rain*). **b** drop of liquid. **c** sound of dripping. **2** *colloq.* dull or ineffectual person. **3** = DRIP-FEED. □ **be dripping with** be full of or covered with. [Danish: cf. DROP]

drip-dry –*v.* dry or leave to dry crease-free when hung up. –*adj.* able to be drip-dried.

drip-feed –*v.* **1** feed intravenously in drops. **2** fund (a new company) in stages rather than by making a large capital sum available at the start. –*n.* **1** feeding thus. **2** apparatus for doing this.

dripping *n.* fat melted from roasted meat.

drippy *adj.* (**-ier**, **-iest**) *slang* ineffectual; sloppily sentimental.

drive –*v.* (**-ving**; *past* **drove**; *past part.* **driven** /'drɪv(ə)n/) **1** urge forward, esp. forcibly. **2 a** compel (*was driven to complain*). **b** force into a specified state (*drove him mad*). **c** (often *refl.*) urge to overwork. **3 a** operate and direct (a vehicle, locomotive, etc.). **b** convey or be conveyed in a vehicle. **c** be competent to drive (a vehicle) (*does he drive?*). **d** travel in a private vehicle. **4** (of wind etc.) carry along, propel, esp. rapidly (*driven snow*; *driving rain*). **5 a** (often foll. by *into*) force (a stake, nail, etc.) into place by blows. **b** bore (a tunnel etc.). **6** effect or conclude forcibly (*drove a hard bargain*; *drove his point home*). **7** (of power) operate (machinery). **8** (usu. foll. by *at*) work hard; dash, rush. **9** hit (a ball) forcibly. –*n.* **1** journey or excursion in a vehicle. **2 a** (esp. scenic) street or road. **b** private road through a garden to a house. **3 a** motivation and energy. **b** inner urge (*sex-drive*). **4** forcible stroke of a bat etc. **5** organized effort (*membership drive*). **6 a** transmission of power to machinery, wheels, etc. **b** position of the steering-wheel in a vehicle (*left-hand drive*). **c** *Computing* = DISK DRIVE. **7** organized whist, bingo, etc. competition. □ **drive at** seek, intend, or mean (*what is he driving at?*). [Old English]

drive-in –*attrib. adj.* (of a bank, cinema, etc.) used while sitting in one's car. –*n.* such a bank, cinema, etc.

drivel /'drɪv(ə)l/ –*n.* silly talk; nonsense. –*v.* (**-ll-**; *US* **-l-**, **-ling**) **1** talk drivel. **2** run at the mouth or nose. [Old English]

driven *past part.* of DRIVE.

drive-on *adj.* (of a ship) on to which vehicles may be driven.

driver *n.* **1** person who drives a vehicle. **2** golf-club for driving from a tee.

driveway *n.* = DRIVE *n.* 2b.

driving-licence *n.* licence permitting one to drive a vehicle.

driving test *n.* official test of competence to drive.

driving-wheel *n.* wheel communicating motive power in machinery.

drizzle /'drɪz(ə)l/ –*n.* very fine rain. –*v.* (**-ling**) (of rain) fall in very fine drops. □ **drizzly** *adj.* [Old English]

droll /drəʊl/ *adj.* quaintly amusing; strange, odd. □ **drollery** *n.* (*pl.* **-ies**). **drolly** /'drəʊllɪ/ *adv.* [French]

dromedary /'drɒmɪdərɪ/ *n.* (*pl.* **-ies**) one-humped (esp. Arabian) camel bred for riding. [Greek *dromas -ados* runner]

drone –*n.* **1** non-working male of the honey-bee. **2** idler. **3** deep humming sound. **4** monotonous speaking tone. **5** bass-pipe of bagpipes or its continuous note. –*v.* (**-ning**) **1** make a deep humming sound. **2** speak or utter monotonously. [Old English]

drool *v.* **1** slobber, dribble. **2** (often foll. by *over*) admire extravagantly. [from DRIVEL]

droop –*v.* **1** bend or hang down, esp. from weariness; flag. **2** (of the eyes) look downwards. –*n.* **1** drooping attitude. **2** loss of spirit. □ **droopy** *adj.* [Old Norse: related to DROP]

drop –*n.* **1 a** globule of liquid that hangs, falls, or adheres to a surface. **b** very small amount of liquid (*just a drop left*). **c** glass etc. of alcohol. **2 a** abrupt fall or slope. **b** amount of this (*drop of fifteen feet*). **c** act of dropping. **d** fall in prices, temperature, etc. **e** deterioration (*drop in status*). **3** drop-shaped thing, esp. a pendant or sweet. **4** curtain or scenery let down on to a stage. **5** (in *pl.*) liquid medicine used in drops (*eye drops*). **6** minute quantity. **7** *slang* hiding-place for stolen goods etc. **8** *slang* bribe. –*v.* (**-pp-**) **1** fall or let fall in drops, shed (tears, blood). **2** fall or allow to fall; let go. **3 a** sink down from exhaustion or injury. **b** die. **c** fall naturally (*drop asleep*; *drop into the habit*). **4 a** (cause to) cease or lapse; abandon. **b** *colloq.* cease to associate with or discuss. **5** set down (a passenger etc.) (*drop me here*). **6** utter or be uttered casually (*dropped a hint*). **7** send casually (*drop a line*). **8 a** fall or allow to fall in direction, amount, condition, degree, pitch, etc. (*voice dropped*; *wind dropped*; *we dropped the price*). **b** (of a person) jump down lightly; let oneself fall. **c** allow (trousers etc.) to fall to ground. **9** omit (a letter etc.) in speech (*drop one's h's*). **10** (as **dropped** *adj.*) in a lower position than usual (*dropped handlebars*; *dropped waist*). **11** give birth to (esp. a lamb). **12** lose (a game, point, etc.). **13** deliver by parachute etc. **14** *Football* send (a ball), or score (a goal), by a drop-kick. **15** *colloq.* dismiss or omit (*dropped from the team*). □ **at the drop of a hat** promptly, instantly. **drop back** (or **behind**) fall back; get left behind. **drop a brick** *colloq.* make an indiscreet or embarrassing remark. **drop a curtsy** curtsy. **drop in** (or **by**) *colloq.* visit casually. **drop off 1** fall asleep. **2** drop (a passenger). **drop out** *colloq.* cease to participate. □ **droplet** *n.* [Old English]

drop-curtain *n.* painted curtain lowered on to a stage.

◆ **drop-dead fee** *n.* fee paid by an individual or company that is bidding for another company to the organization lending the money required to finance the bid. The fee is only paid if the bid fails and the loan is not required. Thus, for the price of the drop-dead fee, the bidder ensures that he only incurs the interest charges if the money is required.

---

drop-kick *n.* *Football* kick as the ball touches the ground having been dropped.

◆ **drop lock** *n.* *Finance* form of issue in the bond market that combines the benefits of a bank loan with the benefits of a bond. The borrower arranges a variable-rate bank loan on the understanding that if long-term interest rates fall to a specified level, the bank loan will be automatically refinanced by a placing of fixed-rate long-term bonds with a group of institutions. Drop locks are most commonly used on the international market.

---

drop-out *n.* *colloq.* person who has dropped out of conventional society, a course of study, etc.

dropper *n.* device for releasing liquid in drops.

droppings *n.pl.* **1** dung of animals or birds. **2** thing that falls or has fallen in drops.

drop scone *n.* scone made by dropping a spoonful of mixture into the pan etc.

drop-shot *n.* (in tennis) shot dropping abruptly over the net.

dropsy /'drɒpsɪ/ *n.* = OEDEMA. □ **dropsical** *adj.* [earlier *hydropsy* from Greek *hudrōps*: related to HYDRO-]

drosophila /drə'sɒfɪlə/ *n.* fruit fly used in genetic research. [Greek, = dew-loving]

dross *n.* **1** rubbish. **2 a** scum from melted metals. **b** impurities. [Old English]

drought /draʊt/ *n.* prolonged absence of rain. [Old English]

drove[1] *past* of DRIVE.

drove[2] *n.* **1 a** moving crowd. **b** (in *pl.*) *colloq.* great number (*people arrived in droves*). **2** herd or flock driven or moving together. [Old English: related to DRIVE]

drover *n.* herder of cattle.

drown *v.* **1** kill or die by submersion in liquid. **2** submerge; flood; drench. **3** deaden (grief etc.) by drinking. **4** (often foll. by *out*) overpower (sound) with louder sound. [probably Old English]

drowse /draʊz/ *v.* (**-sing**) be lightly asleep. [from DROWSY]

drowsy /'draʊzɪ/ *adj.* (**-ier**, **-iest**) very sleepy, almost asleep. □ **drowsily** *adv.* **drowsiness** *n.* [probably Old English]

DRP *abbr.* dividend reinvestment plan.

drub *v.* (**-bb-**) **1** beat, thrash. **2** defeat thoroughly. □ **drubbing** *n.* [Arabic *ḍaraba* beat]

drudge –*n.* person who does dull, laborious, or menial work. –*v.* (**-ging**) work laboriously, toil. □ **drudgery** *n.* [origin uncertain]

drug –*n.* **1** medicinal substance. **2** (esp. addictive) narcotic, hallucinogen, or stimulant. –*v.* (**-gg-**) **1** add a drug to (food or drink). **2 a** give a drug to. **b** stupefy. [French]

drugget /'drʌgɪt/ *n.* coarse woven fabric used for floor coverings etc. [French]

druggist *n.* pharmacist. [related to DRUG]

drugstore *n. US* combined chemist's shop and café.

Druid /'dru:ɪd/ *n.* **1** priest of an ancient Celtic religion. **2** member of a modern Druidic order, esp. the Gorsedd. □ **Druidic** /-'ɪdɪk/ *adj.* **Druidism** *n.* [Latin from Celtic]

drum –*n.* **1** hollow esp. cylindrical percussion instrument covered at the end(s) with plastic etc. **2** (often in *pl.*) percussion section of an orchestra etc. **3** sound made by a drum. **4** thing resembling a drum, esp. a container, etc. **5** segment of a pillar. **6** eardrum. –*v.* (**-mm-**) **1** play a drum. **2** beat or tap continuously with the fingers etc. **3** (of a bird or insect) make a loud noise with the wings. □ **drum into** drive (a lesson or facts) into (a person) by persistence. **drum out** dismiss with ignominy. **drum up** summon or get by vigorous effort (*drum up support*). [Low German]

drumbeat *n.* stroke or sound of a stroke on a drum.

drum brake *n.* brake in which brake shoes on a vehicle press against the brake drum on a wheel.

drumhead *n.* part of a drum that is hit.

drum kit *n.* set of drums in a band etc.

drum machine *n.* electronic device that simulates percussion.

drum major *n.* leader of a marching band.

drum majorette *n.* female baton-twirling member of a parading group.

drummer *n.* player of drums.

drumstick *n.* **1** stick for beating drums. **2** lower leg of a dressed fowl.

drunk –*adj.* **1** lacking control from drinking alcohol. **2** (often foll. by *with*) overcome with joy, success, power, etc. –*n.* person who is drunk, esp. habitually. [past part. of DRINK]

drunkard /'drʌŋkəd/ *n.* person who is habitually drunk.

drunken *adj.* (usu. *attrib.*) **1** = DRUNK *adj.* 1. **2** caused by or involving drunkenness (*drunken brawl*). **3** often drunk. □ **drunkenly** *adv.* **drunkenness** *n.*

drupe /dru:p/ *n.* fleshy stone-fruit, e.g. the olive and plum. [Latin from Greek]

dry /draɪ/ –*adj.* (**drier**; **driest**) **1** free from moisture, esp.: **a** with moisture having evaporated, drained away, etc. (*clothes are not dry yet*). **b** (of eyes) free from tears. **c** (of a climate etc.) with insufficient rain; not rainy (*dry spell*). **d** (of a river, well, etc.) dried up. **e** using or producing no moisture (*dry shampoo*; *dry cough*). **f** (of a shave) with an electric razor. **2** (of wine) not sweet (*dry sherry*). **3 a** plain, unelaborated (*dry facts*). **b** uninteresting (*dry book*). **4** (of a sense of humour) subtle, ironic, understated. **5** prohibiting the sale of alcohol (*a dry State*). **6** (of bread) without butter etc. **7** (of provisions etc.) solid, not liquid. **8** impassive. **9** (of a cow) not yielding milk. **10** *colloq.* thirsty (*feel dry*). –*v.* (**dries, dried**) **1** make or become dry. **2** (usu. as **dried** *adj.*) preserve (food etc.) by removing moisture. **3** (often foll. by *up*) *colloq.* forget one's lines. –*n.* (*pl.* **dries**) **1** act of drying. **2** dry ginger ale. **3** dry place (*come into the dry*). □ **dry out 1** make or become fully dry. **2** treat or be treated for alcoholism. **dry up 1** make or become utterly dry. **2** dry dishes. **3** *colloq.* (esp. in *imper.*) cease talking. **4** become unproductive. **5** (of supplies) run out. □ **dryness** *n.* [Old English]

dryad /'draɪæd/ *n.* wood nymph. [Greek *drus* tree]

dry battery *n.* (also **dry cell**) electric battery or cell in which electrolyte is absorbed in a solid.

dry-clean *v.* clean (clothes etc.) with solvents without water. □ **dry-cleaner** *n.*

dry dock *n.* dock that can be pumped dry for building or repairing ships.

dryer var. of DRIER².

dry-fly *attrib. adj.* (of fishing) with a floating artificial fly.

dry ice *n.* solid carbon dioxide used as a refrigerant.

dry land *n.* land as distinct from sea etc.

dryly var. of DRILY.

dry measure *n.* measure for dry goods.

dry rot *n.* decayed state of unventilated wood; fungi causing this.

dry run *n. colloq.* rehearsal; trial.

dry-shod *adj.* & *adv.* without wetting one's shoes.

drystone *attrib. adj.* (of a wall etc.) built without mortar.

DS *abbr.* debenture stock.

DSC *abbr.* Distinguished Service Cross.

D.Sc. *abbr.* Doctor of Science.

DSIR *abbr.* (in New Zealand) Department of Scientific and Industrial Research.

DSM *abbr.* Distinguished Service Medal.

DSO *abbr.* Distinguished Service Order.

DSP *abbr.* dye sublimation printing.

♦ **DSR** *abbr.* = DEBT SERVICE RATIO.

DSS *abbr.* **1** *Computing* decision-support system. **2** Department of Social Security.

DT –*abbr.* (also **DT's** /di:'ti:z/) delirium tremens. –*postcode* Dorchester.

d.t.b.a. *abbr. Commerce* date to be advised.

DTE *abbr. Computing* data terminal equipment.

DTI *abbr.* = DEPARTMENT OF TRADE AND INDUSTRY.

DTP *abbr.* = DESKTOP PUBLISHING.

DTR *abbr.* double-taxation relief. See DOUBLE TAXATION.

dual /'dju:əl/ –*adj.* **1** in two parts; twofold. **2** double (*dual ownership*). –*n. Gram.* dual number or form. □ **duality** /-'ælɪtɪ/ *n.* [Latin *duo* two]

♦ **dual-capacity system** *n.* system of trading on a stock exchange in which the functions of stockjobber and stockbroker are carried out by separate firms. In a **single-capacity system** the two functions can be combined by firms known as market makers. Dual capacity existed on the London Stock Exchange prior to October 1986 (see BIG BANG), since when a single-capacity system has been introduced, bringing London into line with most foreign international stock markets. The major advantage of single capacity is that it cuts down on the costs to the investor, although it can also create more opportunity for unfair dealing (see CHINESE WALL).

---

dual carriageway *n.* road with a dividing strip between traffic flowing in opposite directions.

dual control *n.* two linked sets of controls, enabling operation by either of two persons.

dub¹ *v.* (**-bb-**) **1** make (a person) a knight by touching his shoulders with a sword. **2** give (a person) a name, nickname, etc. **3** smear (leather) with grease. [French]

dub² *v.* (**-bb-**) **1** provide (a film etc.) with an, esp. translated, alternative soundtrack. **2** add (sound effects or music) to a film or broadcast. **3** transfer or make a copy of (recorded sound or images). [abbreviation of DOUBLE]

Dubai /du:'baɪ/ **1** member state of the United Arab Emirates (UAE); the oil industry is its main source of income;

pop. (1993) 548 000. **2** its capital city, chief port of the UAE; pop. (1980) 265 700.

dubbin /ˈdʌbɪn/ *n.* (also **dubbing**) thick grease for softening and waterproofing leather. [see DUB[1] 3]

dubiety /djuːˈbaɪətɪ/ *n. literary* doubt. [Latin: related to DUBIOUS]

dubious /ˈdjuːbɪəs/ *adj.* **1** hesitating, doubtful. **2** questionable; suspicious. **3** unreliable. □ **dubiously** *adv.* **dubiousness** *n.* [Latin *dubium* doubt]

Dublin /ˈdʌblɪn/ capital and chief port of the Republic of Ireland; industries include brewing, whiskey distilling, textiles, and pharmaceuticals; pop. (1991) 478 389.

Dubrovnik /dʊˈbrɒvnɪk/ (Italian **Ragusa** /ræˈguːzə/) port and resort in Croatia, on the Adriatic coast; pop. (1991) 49 730.

ducal /ˈdjuːk(ə)l/ *adj.* of or like a duke. [French: related to DUKE]

ducat /ˈdʌkət/ *n.* gold coin, formerly current in most of Europe. [medieval Latin *ducatus* DUCHY]

duchess /ˈdʌtʃɪs/ *n.* **1** duke's wife or widow. **2** woman holding the rank of duke. [medieval Latin *ducissa*: related to DUKE]

duchesse potatoes /duːˈʃes/ *n.pl.* mashed potatoes mixed with egg, baked or fried, and served as small cakes or used for piping. [French]

duchy /ˈdʌtʃɪ/ *n.* (*pl.* **-ies**) territory of a duke or duchess; royal dukedom of Cornwall or Lancaster. [medieval Latin *ducatus*: related to DUKE]

duck[1] *–n.* (*pl.* same or **-s**) **1 a** swimming-bird, esp. the domesticated form of the mallard or wild duck. **b** female of this. **c** its flesh as food. **2** score of 0 in cricket. **3** (also *ducks*) *colloq.* (esp. as a form of address) dear. *–v.* **1** bob down, esp. to avoid being seen or hit. **2 a** dip one's head briefly under water. **b** plunge (a person) briefly in water. **3** *colloq.* dodge (a task etc.). □ **like water off a duck's back** *colloq.* producing no effect. [Old English]

duck[2] *n.* **1** strong linen or cotton fabric. **2** (in *pl.*) trousers made of this. [Dutch]

duckbill *n.* (also **duck-billed platypus**) = PLATYPUS.

duckboard *n.* (usu. in *pl.*) path of wooden slats over muddy ground, in a trench, etc.

duckling *n.* young duck.

ducks and drakes *n.pl.* (usu. treated as *sing.*) game of making a flat stone skim the surface of water. □ **play ducks and drakes with** *colloq.* squander.

duckweed *n.* any of various plants growing on the surface of still water.

ducky *n.* (*pl.* **-ies**) *colloq.* (esp. as a form of address) dear.

duct *–n.* channel or tube for conveying a fluid, cable, bodily secretions, etc. (*tear ducts*). *–v.* convey through a duct. [Latin *ductus* from *duco duct-* lead]

ductile /ˈdʌktaɪl/ *adj.* **1** (of metal) capable of being drawn into wire; pliable. **2** easily moulded. **3** docile. □ **ductility** /-ˈtɪlɪtɪ/ *n.* [Latin: related to DUCT]

ductless gland *n.* gland secreting directly into the bloodstream.

dud *slang –n.* **1** useless or broken thing. **2** counterfeit article. **3** (in *pl.*) clothes, rags. *–adj.* useless, defective. [origin unknown]

dude /duːd/ *n. slang* **1** fellow. **2** *US* dandy. **3** *US* city-dweller staying on a ranch. [German dial. *dude* fool]

dudgeon /ˈdʌdʒ(ə)n/ *n.* resentment, indignation. □ **in high dudgeon** very angry. [origin unknown]

due *–adj.* **1** owing or payable. **2** (often foll. by *to*) merited; appropriate. **3** (foll. by *to*) that ought to be given or ascribed to (a person, cause, etc.) (*first place is due to Milton*; *difficulty due to ignorance*). **4** (often foll. by *to* + infin.) expected or under an obligation at a certain time (*due to speak tonight*; *train due at 7.30*). **5** suitable, right, proper (*in due time*). *–n.* **1** what one owes or is owed (*give him his due*). **2** (usu. in *pl.*) fee or amount payable. *–adv.* (of a compass point) exactly, directly (*went due east*). □ **due to** because of (*he was late due to an accident*). [French from Latin *debeo* owe]

■ **Usage** The use of *due to* to mean 'because of' as in the example given is regarded as unacceptable by some people and could be avoided by substituting *his lateness was due to an accident*. Alternatively, *owing to* could be used.

♦ **due date** *n.* date on which a debt is due to be settled, such as the maturity date of a bill of exchange.

---

duel /ˈdjuːəl/ *–n.* **1** armed contest between two people, usu. to the death. **2** two-sided contest. *–v.* (**-ll-**; *US* **-l-**) fight a duel. □ **duellist** *n.* [Latin *duellum* war]

duenna /djuːˈenə/ *n.* older woman acting as a chaperon to girls, esp. in Spain. [Spanish from Latin *domina* DON[1]]

duet /djuːˈet/ *n.* musical composition for two performers. □ **duettist** *n.* [Latin *duo* two]

duff[1] *–n.* boiled pudding. *–adj. slang* worthless, counterfeit, useless. [var. of DOUGH]

duff[2] *v.* □ **duff up** *slang* beat; thrash. [perhaps from DUFFER]

duffer *n. colloq.* inefficient or stupid person. [origin uncertain]

duffle /ˈdʌf(ə)l/ *n.* (also **duffel**) heavy woollen cloth. [*Duffel* in Belgium]

duffle bag *n.* cylindrical canvas bag closed by a drawstring.

duffle-coat *n.* hooded overcoat of duffle, fastened with toggles.

dug[1] *past* and *past part.* of DIG.

dug[2] *n.* udder, teat. [origin unknown]

dugong /ˈduːgɒŋ/ *n.* (*pl.* same or **-s**) Asian sea-mammal. [Malay]

dugout *n.* **1 a** roofed shelter, esp. for troops in trenches. **b** underground shelter. **2** canoe made from a tree-trunk.

Duisburg /ˈduːsbʊəg/ city in NW Germany, the largest inland port in Europe, situated at the junction of the Rhine and Ruhr rivers; industries include steel production; pop. (est. 1995) 536 106.

duke /djuːk/ *n.* **1** person holding the highest hereditary title of the nobility. **2** sovereign prince ruling a duchy or small state. □ **dukedom** *n.* [Latin *dux* leader]

dulcet /ˈdʌlsɪt/ *adj.* sweet-sounding. [Latin *dulcis* sweet]

dulcimer /ˈdʌlsɪmə(r)/ *n.* metal stringed instrument struck with two hand-held hammers. [Latin: related to DULCET, *melos* song]

dull *–adj.* **1** tedious; not interesting. **2** (of the weather) overcast. **3** (of colour, light, sound, etc.) not bright, vivid, or clear. **4** (of a pain) indistinct; not acute (*a dull ache*). **5** slow-witted; stupid. **6** (of a knife-edge etc.) blunt. **7 a** (of trade etc.) sluggish, slow. **b** listless; depressed. **8** (of the ears, eyes, etc.) lacking keenness. *–v.* make or become dull. □ **dullness** *n.* **dully** /ˈdʌllɪ/ *adv.* [Low German or Dutch]

dullard /ˈdʌləd/ *n.* stupid person.

duly /ˈdjuːlɪ/ *adv.* **1** in due time or manner. **2** rightly, properly.

dumb /dʌm/ *adj.* **1 a** unable to speak. **b** (of an animal) naturally dumb. **2** silenced by surprise, shyness, etc. **3** taciturn, reticent (*dumb insolence*). **4** suffered or done in silence (*dumb agony*). **5** *colloq.* stupid; ignorant. **6** disenfranchised; inarticulate (*dumb masses*). **7** (of a computer terminal etc.) able to transmit or receive but unable to process data. **8** giving no sound. [Old English]

dumb-bell *n.* **1** short bar with a weight at each end, for muscle-building etc. **2** *slang* stupid person, esp. a woman.

dumbfound /dʌmˈfaʊnd/ *v.* nonplus, make speechless with surprise. [from DUMB, CONFOUND]

dumbo /ˈdʊmbəʊ/ *n.* (*pl.* **-s**) *slang* stupid person. [from DUMB, -O]

dumb show *n.* gestures; mime.

dumbstruck *adj.* speechless with surprise.

dumb waiter *n.* small hand-operated lift for conveying food from kitchen to dining-room.

dumdum /ˈdʌmdʌm/ *n.* (in full **dumdum bullet**) soft-nosed bullet that expands on impact. [*Dum-Dum* in India]

Dumfries and Galloway /ˌdʌmfriːs, ˈgæləˌweɪ/ local government region of SW Scotland; pop. (est. 1994) 147 800; capital, Dumfries. Sheep farming and stock raising are the main occupations.

dummy /ˈdʌmɪ/ *–n.* (*pl.* **-ies**) **1** model of a human figure, esp. as used to display clothes or by a ventriloquist or as a target. **2** (often *attrib.*) imitation object used to replace a real or normal one. **3** baby's rubber or plastic teat. **4** *colloq.* stupid person. **5** figurehead. **6** imaginary player in bridge etc., whose cards are exposed and played by a partner. *–attrib. adj.* sham; imitation. *–v.* (**-ies, -ied**) make a pretended pass or swerve in football etc. [from DUMB]

dummy run *n.* trial attempt; rehearsal.

dump *–n.* **1** place or heap for depositing rubbish. **2** *colloq.* unpleasant or dreary place. **3** temporary store of ammunition etc. *–v.* **1** put down firmly or clumsily. **2** deposit as rubbish. **3** *colloq.* abandon or get rid of. **4** sell (goods) to a foreign market at a low price. Under the General Agreement on Tariffs and Trade, tariffs can be imposed on goods that are being dumped, although it is always difficult to establish conclusively that a particular price level constitutes dumping. Dumping is prohibited in the EC. **5** copy (the contents of a computer memory etc.), usu. to safeguard against loss of data or as a diagnostic aid. For example, in a system handling large numbers of users' files stored on magnetic disks, the contents of the disks are dumped periodically on magnetic tape. This provides a reference copy of the data in the event of, e.g., accidental overwriting or damage of the disks. □ **dump on** esp. *US* criticize or abuse; get the better of. □ **dumping** *n.* [origin uncertain]

dumpling /ˈdʌmplɪŋ/ *n.* **1** ball of dough boiled in stew or containing apple etc. **2** small fat person. [*dump* small round object]

dumps *n.pl.* (usu. in **down in the dumps**) *colloq.* low spirits. [Low German or Dutch: related to DAMP]

dump truck *n.* truck that tilts or opens at the back for unloading.

dumpy *adj.* (**-ier, -iest**) short and stout. □ **dumpily** *adv.* **dumpiness** *n.* [related to DUMPLING]

dun *–adj.* greyish-brown. *–n.* **1** dun colour. **2** dun horse. [Old English]

Duna, Dunarea, Dunav see DANUBE.

dunce *n.* person slow at learning; dullard. [*Duns* Scotus, name of a philosopher]

dunce's cap *n.* paper cone worn by a dunce.

Dundee /dʌnˈdiː/ city and port in E Scotland; pop. (est. 1994) 167 600. It provides services and supplies for the North Sea oil industry; other industries include textiles and electronics.

dunderhead /ˈdʌndəˌhed/ *n.* stupid person. [origin unknown]

dune *n.* drift of sand etc. formed by the wind. [Dutch: related to DOWN³]

Dunedin /dʌˈniːdɪn/ city and port in New Zealand, on South Island; industries include engineering and textiles; pop. (1996) 121 100.

Dunfermline /dʌnˈfɜːmlɪn/ industrial city of Scotland; manufactures include electronic equipment; pop. (est. 1988) 42 720.

dung *–n.* excrement of animals; manure. *–v.* apply dung to (land). [Old English]

dungaree /ˌdʌŋgəˈriː/ *n.* **1** coarse cotton cloth. **2** (in *pl.*) overalls or trousers of this. [Hindi]

dung-beetle *n.* beetle whose larvae develop in dung.

dungeon /ˈdʌndʒ(ə)n/ *n.* underground prison cell. [earlier *donjon* keep of a castle; ultimately from Latin *dominus* lord]

dunghill *n.* heap of dung or refuse.

dunk *v.* **1** dip (food) into liquid before eating. **2** immerse. [German *tunken* dip]

Dunkirk /dʌnˈkɜːk/ (French **Dunquerque**) port in N France, on the coast of the English Channel; industries include oil refining, textiles, and fishing; pop. (1990) 71 070.

dunlin /ˈdʌnlɪn/ *n.* red-backed sandpiper. [probably from DUN]

dunnock /ˈdʌnək/ *n.* hedge sparrow. [apparently from DUN]

Dunquerque see DUNKIRK.

duo /ˈdjuːəʊ/ *n.* (*pl.* **-s**) **1** pair of performers. **2** duet. [Italian from Latin, = two]

duodecimal /ˌdjuːəʊˈdesɪm(ə)l/ *adj.* **1** of twelfths or twelve. **2** in or by twelves. [Latin *duodecim* twelve]

duodenum /ˌdjuːəʊˈdiːnəm/ *n.* (*pl.* **-s**) first part of the small intestine immediately below the stomach. □ **duodenal** *adj.* [medieval Latin: related to DUODECIMAL]

duologue /ˈdjuːəˌlɒg/ *n.* dialogue between two people. [from DUO, MONOLOGUE]

◆ **duopoly** /djʊˈɒpəlɪ/ *n.* (*pl.* **-ies**) market in which there are only two producers or sellers of a particular product or service and many buyers. The profits are in practice usu. less than could be achieved if the two suppliers merged to form a monopoly but more than if the two allowed competition to force them into marginal costing. See also COLLUSIVE DUOPOLY. □ **duopolistic** /-ˈlɪstɪk/ *adj.*

---

dupe *–n.* victim of deception. *–v.* (**-ping**) deceive, trick. [French]

duple /ˈdjuːp(ə)l/ *adj.* of two parts. [Latin *duplus*]

duple time *n. Mus.* rhythm with two beats to the bar.

duplex /ˈdjuːpleks/ *–n.* (often *attrib.*) esp. *US* **1** flat on two floors. **2** house subdivided for two families; semi-detached house. *–adj.* **1** of two parts. **2** *Computing* (of a circuit) allowing simultaneous two-way transmission of signals. [Latin, = double]

duplicate *–adj.* /ˈdjuːplɪkət/ **1** identical. **2 a** having two identical parts. **b** doubled. **3** (of card-games) with the same hands played by different players. *–n.* /ˈdjuːplɪkət/ **1** identical thing, esp. a copy. **2** copy of a letter etc. *–v.* /ˈdjuːplɪˌkeɪt/ (**-ting**) **1** multiply by two; double. **2** make or be an exact copy of. **3** repeat (an action etc.), esp. unnecessarily. □ **in duplicate** in two exact copies. □ **duplication** /-ˈkeɪʃ(ə)n/ *n.* [Latin: related to DUPLEX]

duplicator *n.* machine for making multiple copies of a text etc.

duplicity /djuːˈplɪsɪtɪ/ *n.* double-dealing; deceitfulness. □ **duplicitous** *adj.* [Latin: related to DUPLEX]

durable /ˈdjʊərəb(ə)l/ *–adj.* **1** lasting; hard-wearing. **2** (of goods) with a relatively long useful life. *–n.* (in *pl.*) durable goods. See CONSUMER GOODS. □ **durability** /-ˈbɪlɪtɪ/ *n.* [Latin *durus* hard]

dura mater /ˌdjʊərə ˈmeɪtə(r)/ *n.* tough outermost membrane enveloping the brain and spinal cord. [medieval Latin = hard mother, translation of Arabic]

Durango /dʊəˈræŋgəʊ/ **1** state in N central Mexico; pop. (est. 1995) 1 430 964. **2** (in full **Victoria de Durango**) its capital city; industries include iron founding and sugar refining; pop. (1990) 413 835.

duration /djʊəˈreɪʃ(ə)n/ *n.* **1** time taken by an event. **2** specified length of time (*duration of a minute*). □ **for the duration 1** until the end of an event. **2** for a very long time. [medieval Latin: related to DURABLE]

Durban /ˈdɜːbən/ seaport and resort in the Republic of South Africa, on the coast of KwaZulu/Natal province; industries include car assembly and sugar refining; pop. (1991) 715 669.

duress /djʊəˈres/ *n.* **1** compulsion, esp. illegal use of threats or violence (*under duress*). **2** imprisonment. [Latin *durus* hard]

Durex /ˈdjʊəreks/ *n. propr.* condom. [origin uncertain]

Durham /ˈdʌrəm/ **1** county in NE England; pop. (est. 1994) 607 800. With the decline of the coalmining and steel industries, manufacturing and tourism are becoming more important sources of income. **2** its county town, having varied manufacturing and service industries; pop. (1991) 36 937.

during /ˈdjʊərɪŋ/ *prep.* throughout or at some point in. [Latin: related to DURABLE]

Durrës /ˈdʊres/ port and resort in E Albania; pop. (1990) 85 400. It has flour mills, distilleries, and soap factories.

Dushanbe /duːˈʃænbeɪ/ (formerly **Stalinabad**) capital of Tajikistan; industries include textiles and food processing; pop. (est. 1994) 524 000.

dusk *n.* darker stage of twilight. [Old English]

dusky *adj.* (**-ier**, **-iest**) **1** shadowy; dim. **2** dark-coloured; dark-skinned. □ **duskily** *adv.* **duskiness** *n.*

Düsseldorf /ˈdʊsəlˌdɔːf/ industrial city in NW Germany, on the Rhine; pop. (est. 1995) 572 638. It is the commercial and industrial centre of the Ruhr region, with iron and steel industries; manufactures include agricultural machinery and textiles.

dust *–n.* **1** finely powdered earth or other material etc. (*pollen dust*). **2** dead person's remains. **3** confusion, turmoil. *–v.* **1** wipe the dust from (furniture etc.). **2 a** sprinkle with powder, sugar, etc. **b** sprinkle (sugar, powder, etc.). □ **dust down 1** dust the clothes of. **2** *colloq.* reprimand. **3** = *dust off*. **dust off 1** remove the dust from. **2** use again after a long period. **when the dust settles** when things quieten down. [Old English]

dustbin *n.* container for household refuse.

dust bowl *n.* desert made by drought or erosion.

dustcart *n.* vehicle collecting household refuse.

dust cover *n.* **1** = DUST-SHEET. **2** = DUST-JACKET.

duster *n.* cloth for dusting furniture etc.

dust-jacket *n.* paper cover on a hardback book.

dustman *n.* person employed to collect household refuse.

dustpan *n.* pan into which dust is brushed from the floor.

dust-sheet *n.* protective cloth over furniture.

dust-up *n. colloq.* fight, disturbance.

dusty *adj.* (**-ier**, **-iest**) **1** full of or covered with dust. **2** (of a colour) dull or muted. □ **not so dusty** *slang* fairly good. □ **dustily** *adv.* **dustiness** *n.*

dusty answer *n. colloq.* curt refusal.

Dutch *–adj.* of the Netherlands or its people or language. *–n.* **1** the Dutch language. **2** (prec. by *the*; treated as *pl.*) the people of the Netherlands. □ **go Dutch** share expenses on an outing etc. [Dutch]

dutch *n. slang* wife. [abbreviation of DUCHESS]

Dutch auction *n.* one in which the auctioneer starts by calling a very high price and reduces it until a bid is received.

Dutch barn *n.* roof for hay etc., set on poles.

Dutch cap *n.* dome-shaped contraceptive device fitting over the cervix.

Dutch courage *n.* courage induced by alcohol.

♦ **Dutch disease** *n.* deindustrialization of an economy as a result of the discovery of a natural resource, as occurred in the Netherlands after the discovery of North Sea gas. The discovery of such a resource lifts the value of the country's currency, making manufactured goods less competitive; exports therefore decline and imports rise.

Dutch elm disease *n.* fungus disease of elms.

Dutch Guiana see SURINAME.

Dutchman *n.* (*fem.* **Dutchwoman**) person of Dutch birth or nationality.

Dutch oven *n.* **1** metal box with the open side facing a fire. **2** covered cooking-pot for braising etc.

Dutch treat *n.* party, outing, etc., at which people pay for themselves.

Dutch uncle *n.* kind but firm adviser.

duteous /ˈdjuːtɪəs/ *adj. literary* dutiful. □ **duteously** *adv.*

dutiable /ˈdjuːtɪəb(ə)l/ *adj.* requiring the payment of duty.

dutiful /ˈdjuːtɪˌfʊl/ *adj.* doing one's duty; obedient. □ **dutifully** *adv.*

duty /ˈdjuːtɪ/ *n.* (*pl.* **-ies**) **1 a** moral or legal obligation; responsibility. **b** binding force of what is right. **2** government tax on certain goods or services. See DEATH DUTY; EXCISE[1] *n.* 1; IMPORT DUTY; STAMP-DUTY. **3** job or function arising from a business or office (*playground duty*). **4** deference; respect due to a superior. □ **do duty for** serve as or pass for (something else). **on** (or **off**) **duty** working (or not working). [Anglo-French: related to DUE]

duty-bound *adj.* obliged by duty.

duty-free *adj.* (of goods) on which duty is not payable.

duty-free shop *n.* shop at an airport etc. selling duty-free goods.

♦ **duty of care** see NEGLIGENCE 3.

---

duvet /ˈduːveɪ/ *n.* thick soft quilt used instead of sheets and blankets. [French]

DVI *abbr. Computing* digital video imaging.

DW *abbr.* (also **D/W**) dock warrant.

d.w. *abbr.* **1** dead weight. **2** delivered weight.

dwarf /dwɔːf/ *–n.* (*pl.* **-s** or **dwarves** /dwɔːvz/) **1** person, animal, or plant much below normal size. **2** small mythological being with magical powers. **3** small usu. dense star. *–v.* **1** stunt in growth. **2** make seem small. □ **dwarfish** *adj.* [Old English]

■ **Usage** In sense 1, with regard to people, the term *person of restricted growth* is now often preferred.

d.w.c. *abbr.* deadweight capacity.

dwell *v.* (*past* and *past part.* **dwelt** or **dwelled**) live, reside. □ **dwell on** (or **upon**) think, write, or speak at length on. □ **dweller** *n.* [Old English, = lead astray]

dwelling *n.* house, residence.

dwindle /ˈdwɪnd(ə)l/ *v.* (**-ling**) **1** become gradually less or smaller. **2** lose importance. [Old English]

d.w.t. *abbr.* (also **DWT**) deadweight tonnage.

DY *–international vehicle registration* Benin. *–postcode* Dudley.

Dy *symb.* dysprosium.

dy. *abbr.* delivery.

dye /daɪ/ *–n.* **1** substance used to change the colour of hair, fabric, etc. **2** colour so produced. *–v.* (**dyeing**, **dyed**) **1** colour with dye. **2** dye a specified colour (*dyed it yellow*). □ **dyer** *n.* [Old English]

dyed-in-the-wool *adj.* (usu. *attrib.*) out and out; unchangeable.

Dyfed /ˈdʌvɪd/ former county in SW Wales; its county town was Carmarthen. It was predominantly agricultural; industries included tourism and oil refining.

dying /ˈdaɪɪŋ/ *attrib. adj.* of, or at the time of, death (*dying words*).

dyke[1] /daɪk/ (also **dike**) *–n.* **1** embankment built to prevent flooding. **2** low wall of turf or stone. *–v.* (**-king**) provide or protect with dyke(s). [related to DITCH]

dyke[2] /daɪk/ *n.* (also **dike**) *slang* lesbian. [origin unknown]

dynamic /daɪˈnæmɪk/ *adj.* **1** energetic; active. **2** *Physics* **a** of motive force. **b** of force in actual operation. **3** of dynamics. **4** *Computing* occurring, changing, or capable of being changed over a period of time, usu. while a system or device is in operation or a program is running. □ **dynamically** *adv.* [Greek *dunamis* power]

dynamics *n.pl.* **1** (usu. treated as *sing.*) **a** mathematical study of motion and the forces causing it. **b** branch of any science concerned with forces or changes. **2** motive forces in any sphere. **3** *Mus.* variation in loudness.

dynamism /ˈdaɪnəˌmɪz(ə)m/ *n.* energy; dynamic power.

dynamite /ˈdaɪnəˌmaɪt/ *–n.* **1** high explosive mixture containing nitroglycerine. **2** potentially dangerous person etc. *–v.* (**-ting**) charge or blow up with dynamite.

dynamo /ˈdaɪnəˌməʊ/ *n.* (*pl.* **-s**) **1** machine converting mechanical into electrical energy, esp. by rotating coils of copper wire in a magnetic field. **2** *colloq.* energetic person. [abbreviation of *dynamo-electric machine*]

dynamometer /ˌdaɪnəˈmɒmɪtə(r)/ *n.* instrument measuring energy expended. [Greek: related to DYNAMIC]

dynast /ˈdɪnəst/ *n.* **1** ruler. **2** member of a dynasty. [Latin from Greek]

dynasty /ˈdɪnəstɪ/ *n.* (*pl.* **-ies**) **1** line of hereditary rulers. **2** succession of leaders in any field. □ **dynastic** /-ˈnæstɪk/ *adj.* [Latin from Greek]

dyne /daɪn/ *n. Physics* force required to give a mass of one gram an acceleration of one centimetre per second per second. [Greek *dunamis* force]

dys- *prefix* bad, difficult. [Greek]

dysentery /ˈdɪsəntrɪ/ *n.* inflammation of the intestines, causing severe diarrhoea. [Greek *entera* bowels]

dysfunction /dɪsˈfʌŋkʃ(ə)n/ *n.* abnormality or impairment of functioning.

dyslexia /dɪsˈleksɪə/ *n.* abnormal difficulty in reading and spelling. □ **dyslectic** /-ˈlektɪk/ *adj.* & *n.* **dyslexic** *adj.* & *n.* [Greek *lexis* speech]

dysmenorrhoea /ˌdɪsmenəˈrɪə/ *n.* painful or difficult menstruation.

dyspepsia /dɪsˈpepsɪə/ *n.* indigestion. □ **dyspeptic** *adj.* & *n.* [Greek *peptos* digested]

dysphasia /ˌdɪsˈfeɪzɪə/ *n.* lack of coordination in speech, owing to brain damage. [Greek *dusphatos* hard to utter]

dysprosium /dɪsˈprəʊzɪəm/ *n.* metallic element of the lanthanide series. [Greek *dusprositos* hard to get at]

dystrophy /ˈdɪstrəfɪ/ *n.* defective nutrition. [Greek *-trophē* nourishment]

DZ *international vehicle registration* Algeria.

E[1] /iː/ *n.* (also **e**) (*pl.* **Es** or **E's**) **1** fifth letter of the alphabet. **2** *Mus.* third note of the diatonic scale of C major. **3 a** occupational grade comprising casual workers and state pensioners. **b** person in this grade.

E[2] *–abbr.* (also **E.**) **1** east, eastern. **2** see E-NUMBER. *–symb.* **1** emalangeni (see LILANGENI). **2** second-class merchant ship (in Lloyd's Register). *–international vehicle registration* Spain. *–postcode* East London.

e- *prefix* see EX-[1] before some consonants.

EA *abbr.* enterprise allowance.

EAC *abbr.* East African Community.

each *–adj.* every one of two or more persons or things, regarded separately (*five in each class*). *–pron.* each person or thing (*each of us*). [Old English]

each other *pron.* one another.

each way *adj.* (of a bet) backing a horse etc. either to win or to come second or third.

eager /ˈiːgə(r)/ *adj.* keen, enthusiastic (*eager to learn*; *eager for news*). □ **eagerly** *adv.* **eagerness** *n.* [Latin *acer* keen]

eager beaver *n. colloq.* very diligent person.

EAGGF *abbr.* (in the EC) European Agricultural Guidance and Guarantee Fund.

eagle /ˈiːg(ə)l/ *n.* **1 a** large bird of prey with keen vision and powerful flight. **b** this as a symbol, esp. of the US. **2** score of two strokes under par at any hole in golf. [Latin *aquila*]

eagle eye *n.* keen sight, watchfulness. □ **eagle-eyed** *adj.*

eaglet /ˈiːglɪt/ *n.* young eagle.

EAK *international vehicle registration* Kenya.

EAN *abbr. Computing* European Academic Network.

E. & O. E. *abbr.* errors and omissions excepted: often printed on invoice forms to safeguard the sender in case of an error made in the recipient's favour.

ear[1] *n.* **1** organ of hearing, esp. its external part. **2** faculty for discriminating sounds (*an ear for music*). **3** attention, esp. sympathetic (*give ear to*; *have a person's ear*). **4** advertising space at the top left or right corner of a newspaper's front page. □ **all ears** listening attentively. **have** (or **keep) an ear to the ground** be alert to rumours or trends. **up to one's ears** (often foll. by *in*) *colloq.* deeply involved or occupied. [Old English]

ear[2] *n.* seed-bearing head of a cereal plant. [Old English]

earache *n.* pain in the inner ear.

eardrum *n.* membrane of the middle ear.

earful *n.* (*pl.* **-s**) *colloq.* **1** prolonged amount of talking. **2** strong reprimand.

earl /ɜːl/ *n.* British nobleman ranking between marquis and viscount. □ **earldom** *n.* [Old English]

Earl Marshal *n.* president of the College of Heralds, with ceremonial duties.

early /ˈɜːlɪ/ *–adj. & adv.* (**-ier, -iest**) **1** before the due, usual, or expected time. **2 a** not far on in the day or night, or in time (*early evening*; *at the earliest opportunity*). **b** prompt (*early payment appreciated*). **3** not far on in a period, development, or process of evolution; being the first stage (*Early English architecture*; *early spring*). **4** forward in flowering, ripening, etc. (*early peaches*). *–n.* (*pl.* **-ies**) (usu. in *pl.*) early fruit or vegetable. □ **earliness** *n.* [Old English: related to ERE]

♦ **early bargains** *n.pl.* = AFTER-HOURS DEALS.

---

early bird *n. colloq.* person who arrives, gets up, etc. early.

early days *n.pl.* too soon to expect results etc.

early on *adv.* at an early stage.

earmark *–v.* set aside for a special purpose. *–n.* identifying mark.

EARN /ɜːn/ *abbr. Computing* European Academic and Research Network.

earn /ɜːn/ *v.* **1** bring in as income or interest. **2** be entitled to or obtain as the reward for work or merit. □ **earner** *n.* [Old English]

♦ **earned income** *n.* income generally acquired by the personal exertion of the taxpayer as distinct from such passive income as dividends from investments. It is often thought by tax theorists that earned income should be taxed at a lower rate than unearned income, since the latter accrues without the expenditure of the taxpayer's time. This has been reflected in different ways in the UK, with such measures as earned-income relief, wife's earned-income relief, and investment-income surcharge. Earned income consists primarily of wages and salaries, business profits, royalties, and some pensions. There are currently no differences between the rates of taxation for earned and unearned income.

---

earnest /ˈɜːnɪst/ *adj.* intensely serious. □ **in earnest** serious, seriously, with determination. □ **earnestly** *adv.* **earnestness** *n.* [Old English]

earnings *n.pl.* money earned.

♦ **earnings per share** *n.pl.* (also **e.p.s.**) earnings of a company over a stated period (usu. one year) divided by the number of ordinary shares issued by the company. The earnings (sometimes called **available earnings**) are calculated as annual profits, after allowing for tax and any exceptional items. **Fully diluted earnings per share** include any shares that the company is committed to issuing but has not yet issued (e.g. through convertibles). See also PRICE–EARNINGS RATIO.

♦ **earnings-related pension** see PENSION[1] *n.* 1; STATE EARNINGS-RELATED PENSION SCHEME.

♦ **earnings yield** see YIELD *n.* 2.

EAROM /ˈɪərɒm/ *abbr. Computing* electrically alterable read-only memory.

earphone *n.* device applied to the ear to receive a radio etc. communication.

earpiece *n.* part of a telephone etc. applied to the ear.

ear-piercing *–adj.* shrill. *–n.* piercing of the ears for wearing earrings.

earplug *n.* piece of wax etc. placed in the ear to protect against water, noise, etc.

earring *n.* jewellery worn on the ear.

earshot *n.* hearing-range (*within earshot*).

ear-splitting *adj.* excessively loud.

earth /ɜːθ/ *–n.* **1 a** (also **Earth**) the planet on which we live. **b** land and sea, as distinct from sky. **2 a** the ground (*fell to earth*). **b** soil, mould. **3** *Relig.* this world, as distinct from heaven or hell. **4** connection to the earth as the completion of an electrical circuit. **5** hole of a fox etc. **6** (prec. by *the*) *colloq.* huge sum; everything (*cost the earth*; *want the earth*). *–v.* **1** cover (plant-roots) with earth. **2** connect (an electrical circuit) to the earth. □ **come back** (or **down) to earth** return to realities. **gone to earth** in hiding. **on earth** *colloq.* existing anywhere; emphatically (*the happiest man on earth*; *looked like nothing on earth*; *what on earth have you done?*). **run to earth** find after a long search. □ **earthward** *adj.* & *adv.* **earthwards** *adv.* [Old English]

earthbound *adj.* **1** attached to the earth or earthly things. **2** moving towards the earth.

earthen *adj.* made of earth or baked clay.

earthenware *n.* pottery made of fired clay.

earthling *n.* inhabitant of the earth, esp. in science fiction.

earthly *adj.* **1** of the earth or human life on it; terrestrial. **2** (usu. with *neg.*) *colloq.* remotely possible (*is no earthly use*; *there wasn't an earthly reason*). □ **not an earthly** *colloq.* no chance or idea whatever.

earth mother *n.* sensual and maternal woman.

earthquake *n.* convulsion of the earth's surface as a result of faults in strata or volcanic action.

earth sciences *n.pl.* those concerned with the earth or part of it.

earth-shattering *adj. colloq.* traumatic, devastating. □ **earth-shatteringly** *adv.*

earthwork *n.* artificial bank of earth in fortification or road-building etc.

earthworm *n.* common worm living in the ground.

earthy *adj.* (**-ier, -iest**) **1** of or like earth or soil. **2** coarse, crude (*earthy humour*). □ **earthiness** *n.*

ear-trumpet *n.* trumpet-shaped device formerly used as a hearing-aid.

earwig *n.* small insect with pincers at its rear end. [from EAR[1], because they were once thought to enter the head through the ear]

ease /iːz/ *–n.* **1** facility, effortlessness. **2 a** freedom from pain or trouble. **b** freedom from constraint. *–v.* (**-sing**) **1** relieve from pain or anxiety. **2** (often foll. by *off*, *up*) **a** become less burdensome or severe. **b** begin to take it easy. **c** slow down; moderate one's behaviour etc. **3 a** relax; slacken; make a less tight fit. **b** move or be moved carefully into place (*eased it into position*). □ **at ease 1** free from anxiety or constraint. **2** *Mil.* in a relaxed attitude, with the feet apart. [Latin: related to ADJACENT]

easel /ˈiːz(ə)l/ *n.* stand for an artist's work, a blackboard, etc. [Dutch *ezel* ass]

♦ **easement** *n.* legal right, e.g. a right of way, right of water, or right of support, that one owner of one piece of land (the dominant tenement) may have over the land of another (the servient tenement). The right must benefit the dominant tenement and the two pieces of land must be reasonably near each other. The right must not involve expenditure by the owner of the servient tenement and must be analogous to those rights accepted in the past as easements. An easement may be granted by deed or it may be acquired by prescription (lapse of time, during which it is exercised without challenge); it may also be acquired of necessity (for example, if A sells B a piece of land that B cannot reach without crossing A's land) or when 'continuous and apparent' rights have been enjoyed with the part of the land sold before it was divided. Existing easements over the land of third parties pass with a conveyance of the dominant tenement. [French: related to EASE]

---

easily /ˈiːzɪlɪ/ *adv.* **1** without difficulty. **2** by far (*easily the best*). **3** very probably (*it could easily snow*).

east *–n.* **1 a** point of the horizon where the sun rises at the equinoxes. **b** compass point corresponding to this. **c** direction in which this lies. **2** (usu. *the East*) **a** countries to the east of Europe. **b** states of eastern Europe. **3** eastern part of a country, town, etc. *–adj.* **1** towards, at, near, or facing the east. **2** from the east (*east wind*). *–adv.* **1** towards, at, or near the east. **2** (foll. by *of*) further east than. □ **to the east** (often foll. by *of*) in an easterly direction. [Old English]

East Anglia /ˈæŋglɪə/ region of E England consisting of the counties of Norfolk, Suffolk, and parts of Essex and Cambridgeshire.

eastbound *adj.* travelling or leading eastwards.

East Cape peninsula on the E coast of North Island, New Zealand, in Gisborne administrative region.

East China Sea section of the Pacific Ocean between China, Taiwan, and South Korea.

East End *n.* part of London east of the City. □ **East Ender** *n.*

Easter *n.* festival (held on a variable Sunday in March or April) commemorating Christ's resurrection. [Old English]

Easter egg *n.* artificial usu. chocolate egg given at Easter.

Easter Island island in the SE Pacific, administered by Chile; wool is exported; pop. (est. 1988) 2000.

easterly *–adj.* & *adv.* **1** in an eastern position or direction. **2** (of a wind) from the east. *–n.* (*pl.* **-ies**) such a wind.

eastern *adj.* of or in the east. □ **easternmost** *adj.*

Eastern Church *n.* Orthodox Church.

easterner *n.* native or inhabitant of the east.

East Indies islands off the SE coast of Asia, now usu. called the Malay Archipelago.

East London port and resort in the Republic of South Africa, on the SE coast of Eastern Cape province; pop. (1991) 102 325.

east-north-east *n.* point or direction midway between east and north-east.

east-south-east *n.* point or direction midway between east and south-east.

East Sussex /ˈsʌsɪks/ county in SE England; pop. (est. 1994) 726 500; county town, Lewes. It is primarily agricultural, producing cereals, fruit, and vegetables; industries include light engineering and electronics.

eastward *–adj.* & *adv.* (also **eastwards**) towards the east. *–n.* eastward direction or region.

easy /ˈiːzɪ/ *–adj.* (**-ier, -iest**) **1** not difficult; not requiring great effort. **2** free from pain, trouble, or anxiety. **3** free from constraint; relaxed and pleasant. **4** compliant. *–adv.* with ease; in an effortless or relaxed manner. *–int.* go or move carefully. □ **easy on the eye** (or **ear** etc.) *colloq.* pleasant to look at (or listen to etc.). **go easy** (foll. by *with*, *on*) be sparing or cautious. **I'm easy** *colloq.* I have no preference. **take it easy 1** proceed gently. **2** relax; work less. □ **easiness** *n.* [French: related to EASE]

easy chair *n.* large comfortable armchair.

easygoing *adj.* placid and tolerant.

♦ **easy money** *n.* **1** money obtained with little effort. **2** = CHEAP MONEY.

Easy Street *n. colloq.* affluence.

EAT *international vehicle registration* Tanzania.

eat *–v.* (*past* **ate** /et, eɪt/; *past part.* **eaten**) **1 a** take into the mouth, chew, and swallow (food). **b** consume food; take a meal. **c** devour (*eaten by a lion*). **2** (foll. by *away*, *at*, *into*) **a** destroy gradually, esp. by corrosion, disease, etc. **b** begin to consume or diminish (resources etc.). **3** *colloq.* trouble, vex (*what's eating you?*). *–n.* (in *pl.*) *colloq.* food. □ **eat one's heart out** suffer from excessive longing or envy. **eat out** have a meal away from home, esp. in a restaurant. **eat up 1** eat completely. **2** use or deal with rapidly or wastefully (*eats up petrol*; *eats up the miles*). **3** preoccupy (*eaten up with envy*). **eat one's words** retract them abjectly. [Old English]

eatable *–adj.* fit to be eaten. *–n.* (usu. in *pl.*) food.

eater *n.* **1** person who eats (*a big eater*). **2** eating apple etc.

eating apple etc. *n.* apple etc. suitable for eating raw.

EAU *international vehicle registration* Uganda.

eau-de-Cologne /ˌəʊdəkəˈləʊn/ *n.* toilet water orig. from Cologne. [French, = water of COLOGNE]

eaves /iːvz/ *n.pl.* underside of a projecting roof. [Old English]

eavesdrop *v.* (**-pp-**) listen to a private conversation. □ **eavesdropper** *n.*

EAZ *international vehicle registration* Tanzania (Zanzibar).

ebb *–n.* movement of the tide out to sea. *–v.* (often foll. by *away*) **1** flow out to sea; recede. **2** decline (*life was ebbing away*). [Old English]

EBCDIC /ˈepsɪˌdɪk/ *abbr. Computing* extended binary-coded decimal-interchange code, for equipment manufactured by or associated with IBM.

ebonite /ˈebəˌnaɪt/ *n.* vulcanite. [from EBONY]

ebony /ˈebənɪ/ *–n.* heavy hard dark wood of a tropical tree. *–adj.* **1** made of ebony. **2** black like ebony. [Greek *ebenos* ebony tree]

EBRD *abbr.* European Bank for Reconstruction and Development.

ebullient /ɪˈbʌlɪənt/ *adj.* exuberant. □ **ebullience** *n.* **ebulliency** *n.* **ebulliently** *adv.* [Latin: related to BOIL[1]]

EC *–abbr.* **1** = European Community. **2** European Commission. **3** executive committee. *–postcode* East Central London. *–international vehicle registration* Ecuador. *–international civil aircraft marking* Spain.

ECA *abbr.* Economic Commission for Africa, a UN agency.

♦ **ECB** *abbr.* EUROPEAN CENTRAL BANK.

---

eccentric /ɪkˈsentrɪk/ *–adj.* **1** odd or capricious in behaviour or appearance. **2** (also **excentric**) **a** not placed, not having its axis placed, centrally. **b** (often foll. by *to*) (of a circle) not concentric (to another). **c** (of an orbit) not circular. *–n.* **1** eccentric person. **2** disc at the end of a shaft for changing rotatory into backward-and-forward motion. □ **eccentrically** *adv.* **eccentricity** /ˌeksenˈtrɪsətɪ/ *n.* [Greek: related to CENTRE]

Eccles cake /ˈek(ə)lz/ *n.* round cake of pastry filled with currants etc. [*Eccles* in N England]

ecclesiastic /ɪˌkliːzɪˈæstɪk/ *–n.* clergyman. *–adj.* = ECCLESIASTICAL. [Greek *ekklēsia* church]

ecclesiastical *adj.* of the Church or clergy.

ECE *abbr.* Economic Commission for Europe, a UN agency.

ECG *abbr.* electrocardiogram.

♦ **ECGD** *abbr.* = EXPORT CREDITS GUARANTEE DEPARTMENT.

---

echelon /ˈeʃəˌlɒn/ *n.* **1** level in an organization, in society, etc.; those occupying it (often in *pl.*: *upper echelons*). **2** wedge-shaped formation of troops, aircraft, etc. [French, = ladder, from Latin *scala*]

echidna /ɪˈkɪdnə/ *n.* Australian egg-laying spiny mammal. [Greek, = viper]

echinoderm /ɪˈkaɪnəˌdɜːm/ *n.* (usu. spiny) sea animal of the group including the starfish and sea urchin. [Greek *ekhinos* sea-urchin, *derma* skin]

echo /ˈekəʊ/ *–n.* (*pl.* **-es**) **1 a** repetition of a sound by the reflection of sound waves. **b** sound so produced. **2 a** reflected radio or radar beam. **b** reflection of transmitted computer data. **3** close imitation or imitator. **4** circumstance or event reminiscent of an earlier one. *–v.* (**-es, -ed**) **1 a** (of a place) resound with an echo. **b** (of a sound) be repeated; resound. **2 a** repeat (a sound) thus. **b** reflect (transmitted data etc.). **3 a** repeat (another's words). **b** imitate the opinions etc. of. [Latin from Greek]

echo chamber *n.* enclosure with sound-reflecting walls.

echoic /eˈkəʊɪk/ *adj.* (of a word) onomatopoeic.

echo location *n.* location of objects by reflected sound.

echo-sounder *n.* depth-sounding device using timed echoes.

echt /ext/ *adj.* genuine. [German]

ECLAC /ˈeklæk/ *abbr.* Economic Commission for Latin America and the Caribbean, a UN agency.

éclair /ɪˈkleə(r)/ *n.* small elongated iced cake of choux pastry filled with cream. [French, = lightning]

eclampsia /ɪˈklæmpsɪə/ *n.* convulsive condition occurring esp. in pregnant women. [ultimately from Greek]

éclat /eɪˈklɑː/ *n.* **1** brilliant display. **2** social distinction; conspicuous success. [French]

eclectic /ɪˈklektɪk/ *–adj.* selecting ideas, style, etc., from various sources. *–n.* eclectic person or philosopher. □ **eclectically** *adv.* **eclecticism** /-ˌsɪz(ə)m/ *n.* [Greek *eklegō* pick out]

eclipse /ɪˈklɪps/ *–n.* **1** obscuring of light from one heavenly body by another. **2** loss of light, importance, or prominence. *–v.* (**-sing**) **1** (of a heavenly body) cause the eclipse of (another). **2** intercept (light). **3** outshine, surpass. [Greek *ekleipsis*]

ecliptic /ɪˈklɪptɪk/ *n.* sun's apparent path among the stars during the year.

eclogue /ˈeklɒg/ *n.* short pastoral poem. [Greek: related to ECLECTIC]

ECMA /ˈekmə/ *abbr.* European Computer Manufacturers' Association, in Geneva.

eco- *comb. form* ecology, ecological (*ecoclimate*).

ecocentric /ˌiːkəʊˈsentrɪk/ *adj.* having a serious concern for the environment.

ECODU *abbr.* European Control Data Users.

ecofriendly /ˌiːkəʊˈfrendlɪ/ *adj.* not damaging the environment.

ecology /ɪˈkɒlədʒɪ/ *n.* **1** the study of the relations of organisms to one another and to their surroundings. **2** the study of the interaction of people with their environment. □ **ecological** /ˌiːkəˈlɒdʒɪk(ə)l/ *adj.* **ecologically** /ˌiːkəˈlɒdʒɪkəlɪ/ *adv.* **ecologist** *n.* [Greek *oikos* house]

♦ **econometrics** /ɪˌkɒnəˈmetrɪks/ *n.pl.* (treated as *sing.*) study of economic phenomena based on observed data. Its aim is sometimes described as the statistical verification of economic theories, in much the same way as experiments are used to verify theories in the natural sciences. However, this is only a partial analogy as the object of the economist's research is not always amenable to experiment. In addition, the results of econometric analysis are usu. open to more than one interpretation. The main tool of the econometrician is regression analysis. This establishes the statistical relationship between two or more sets of economic data. These results can then be used for forecasting. To achieve this the economic theorist relates one economic variable (the dependent variable) to one or more other economic variables (the independent variables). The regression establishes the nature of the relationship by yielding coefficients of the relevant parameters. One of the problems of econometrics is to ensure that data adequately reflect the underlying variable in question. For example, a monetarist will claim that the demand for money is determined by, amongst other things, the interest rate. The econometrician can regress some measure of the money stock on some particular interest rate, but must be aware that the data may not exactly represent the variables suggested by the theory. □ **econometric** *adj.* **econometrician** /-məˈtrɪʃ(ə)n/ *n.*

---

economic /ˌiːkəˈnɒmɪk/ *adj.* **1** of economics. **2** profitable (*not economic to run buses on a Sunday*). **3** connected with trade and industry (*economic geography*). □ **economically** *adv.* [Greek: related to ECONOMY]

economical *adj.* sparing; avoiding waste. □ **economically** *adv.*

♦ **economic cost** *n. Econ.* total sacrifice involved in doing something. It will include the opportunity cost and therefore is greater than the accounting cost, which is restricted to the total outlay of money.

♦ **Economic Development Council** see NATIONAL ECONOMIC DEVELOPMENT OFFICE.

♦ **economic effects of taxation** *n.pl.* ways in which taxation can affect the taxpayer's behaviour. When a tax is imposed, some people will alter their behaviour to minimize the effects the tax has on them. They may work harder or less hard, they may buy different sorts of goods from those they bought previously, or they may even emigrate. Taxes that most distort consumer choices are said to impose the heaviest 'excess burden'.

♦ **economic good** see GOOD *n.* 3.

♦ **economic growth** *n.* expansion of the output of an economy, usu. expressed in terms of the increase of national income. Nations experience different rates of economic growth mainly because of differences in population growth, investment, and technical progress.

♦ **economic profit** *n.* = PROFIT *n.* 2d.

♦ **economic rent** *n.* extra amount earned by a factor of production (land, labour, or capital) in order to keep that factor from being used elsewhere.

economics *n.pl.* (as *sing.*) **1** social science concerning behaviour in the fields of production, consumption, distribution, and exchange. Economists analyse the processes involved and investigate the consequences for the individual, such organizations as the firm, and society as a whole. There are many competing schools of thought in economics (see CLASSICAL SCHOOL; MARXIST ECONOMICS; NEOCLASSICAL SCHOOL; MARGINALISTS; MACROECONOMICS; MICROECONOMICS). **2** application of this to a particular subject (*the economics of publishing*).

♦ **economic sanctions** *n.pl.* actions taken by one country or group of countries to harm the economic interest of another country or group of countries, usu. to bring about pressure for social or political change. Sanctions normally take the form of restrictions on imports or exports, or on financial transactions. They may be applied to specific items or they may be comprehensive trade bans. There is considerable disagreement over their effectiveness. Critics point out that they are easily evaded and often inflict more pain on those they are designed to help than on the governments they are meant to influence. They can also harm the country that imposes sanctions, through the loss of export markets or raw material supplies. In addition the target country may impose retaliatory sanctions. See also EMBARGO *n.* 2.

♦ ***Economic Trends*** *n.* monthly publication of the UK Central Statistical Office devoted to economic statistics.

♦ **economies of scale** *n.pl.* reductions in the average cost of production, and hence in the unit costs, when output is increased; this results in a **scale effect**. If the average costs of production rise with output, this is known as **diseconomies of scale**. Economies of scale can enable a producer to offer a product at more competitive prices and thus to capture a larger share of the market. **Internal economies of scale** occur when better use is made of the factors of production and by using the increased output to pay for a higher proportion of the costs of marketing, financing, development, etc. Internal diseconomies can occur when a plant exceeds its optimum size, requiring a disproportionate unwieldy administrative staff. **External economies** and diseconomies arise from the effects of a firm's expansion on market conditions and on technological advance.

economist /ɪˈkɒnəmɪst/ *n.* expert on or student of economics.

economize /ɪˈkɒnəˌmaɪz/ *v.* (also **-ise**) (**-zing** or **-sing**) **1** be economical; make economies; reduce expenditure. **2** (foll. by *on*) use sparingly.

economy /ɪˈkɒnəmɪ/ *n.* (*pl.* **-ies**) **1 a** community's system of wealth creation. **b** particular kind of this (*a capitalist economy*). **c** administration or condition of this. **2 a** careful management of (esp. financial) resources; frugality. **b** instance of this (*made many economies*). **3** sparing or careful use (*economy of language*). [Greek *oikonomia* household management]

economy class *n.* cheapest class of air travel.

economy-size *adj.* (of goods) consisting of a larger quantity for a proportionally lower cost.

ECOSOC /ˈekəʊsɒk/ *abbr.* **1** (in the EC) Economic and Social Committee. **2** (in the UN) Economic and Social Council.

ecosystem /ˈiːkəʊˌsɪstəm/ *n.* biological community of interacting organisms and their physical environment.

ECOWAS /eˈkəʊəs/ *abbr.* Economic Community of West African States.

ECP *abbr.* = EURO-COMMERCIAL PAPER.

ECR *abbr.* electronic cash register.

ECSC *abbr.* = EUROPEAN COAL AND STEEL COMMUNITY.

ecstasy /ˈekstəsɪ/ *n.* (*pl.* **-ies**) **1** overwhelming joy or rapture. **2** *slang* type of hallucinogenic drug. □ **ecstatic** /-ˈstætɪk/ *adj.* **ecstatically** /-ˈstætɪkəlɪ/ *adv.* [Greek *ekstasis* standing outside oneself]

ECT *abbr.* electroconvulsive therapy.

ecto- *comb. form* outside. [Greek *ektos*]

ectomorph /ˈektəʊˌmɔːf/ *n.* person with a lean body. [Greek *morphē* form]

-ectomy *comb. form* denoting the surgical removal of part of the body (*appendectomy*). [Greek *ektomē* excision]

ectoplasm /ˈektəʊˌplæz(ə)m/ *n.* supposed viscous substance exuding from the body of a spiritualistic medium during a trance. [from ECTO-, PLASMA]

ecu /ˈeɪkjuː, -kuː/ *n.* (also **Ecu**) (*pl.* **-s**) = EUROPEAN CURRENCY UNIT. [abbreviation]

ecumenical /ˌiːkjuːˈmenɪk(ə)l/ *adj.* **1** of or representing the whole Christian world. **2** seeking worldwide Christian unity. □ **ecumenically** *adv.* **ecumenism** /iːˈkjuːməˌnɪz(ə)m/ *n.* [Greek *oikoumenikos* of the inhabited earth]

eczema /ˈeksɪmə/ *n.* inflammation of the skin, with itching and discharge. [Latin from Greek]

ED *abbr.* ex dividend (see EX[1] 2).

ed. *abbr.* **1** edited by. **2** edition. **3** editor. **4** educated.

-ed[1] *suffix* forming adjectives: **1** from nouns, meaning 'having, wearing, etc.' (*talented*; *trousered*). **2** from phrases of adjective and noun (*good-humoured*). [Old English]

Ecuador /ˈekwəˌdɔː(r)/, **Republic of** equatorial country in South America, on the Pacific coast. Oil has been a major source of revenue since 1972, when the oilfields were discovered. Agriculture and fishing are important, supporting nearly half the population; the main agricultural exports are bananas, coffee, cocoa, shrimps, and timber (esp. balsa-wood). Industry is being encouraged, with the manufacture of petrochemicals, pharmaceuticals, steel, and cement. In 1992 the government instituted a programme of free-market reforms, including the privatization of inefficient state enterprises, aimed at boosting the economy. Plans to resume interest payments on its large foreign debts were agreed at the end of the year. Ecuador is a member of LAIA.

History. Ecuador was under Spanish rule from the 16th century until independence was won in 1822. The country has remained independent since leaving the Federation of Grand Colombia in 1830, but has since lost territory in border disputes with its more powerful neighbours. Following a period of military rule, a new constitution in 1979 established Ecuador as a democracy. Elections in 1992 resulted in victory for right-wing parties. In 1995 Ecuador was involved in a brief border war with Peru. A demilitarized zone was agreed between the two countries. In 1996, recently elected president Abdala Bucaram was removed from office on grounds of insanity. President, Fabián Alarcón; capital, Quito. □ **Ecuadorean** *adj.* & *n.*

languages	Spanish (official), Quechua and other Indian languages
currency	sucre (S/.) of 100 centavos
pop. (1996)	11 698 000
GNP (1994)	US$14.7B
literacy	90% (m); 86% (f)
life expectancy	67 (m); 72 (f)

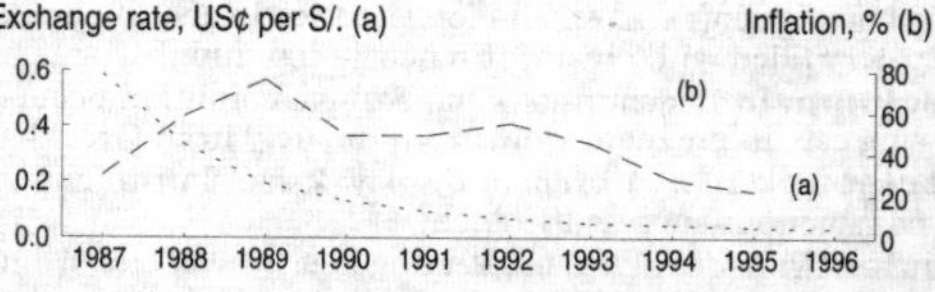

-ed[2] *suffix* forming: **1** past tense and past participle of weak verbs (*needed*). **2** participial adjectives (*escaped prisoner*). [Old English]

EDA *abbr.* (in the US) Economic Development Administration.

Edam /ˈiːdæm/ market town in the Netherlands, in the province of North Holland; pop. (1989) 24 572 (with Volendam). *–n.* round Dutch cheese, usu. pale yellow with a red rind.

EDAS /ˈiːdæs/ *abbr. Computing* enhanced data-acquisition system.

EDBS *abbr. Computing* expert database system.

EDC *abbr.* **1** Economic Development Committee. **2** Engineering Design Centre. **3** (also **e.d.c.**) *Computing* error detection and correction.

eddy /ˈedɪ/ *–n.* (*pl.* **-ies**) **1** circular movement of water causing a small whirlpool. **2** movement of wind, smoke, etc. resembling this. *–v.* (**-ies, -ied**) whirl round in eddies. [Old English *ed-* again, back]

edelweiss /ˈeɪd(ə)lˌvaɪs/ *n.* Alpine plant with white flowers. [German, = noble-white]

edema *US* var. of OEDEMA.

Eden /ˈiːd(ə)n/ *n.* place or state of great happiness, with reference to the abode of Adam and Eve at the Creation. [Hebrew, originally = delight]

edentate /ɪˈdenteɪt/ *–adj.* having no or few teeth. *–n.* such a mammal. [Latin *dens dent-* tooth]

EDF *abbr.* European Development Fund.

edge *–n.* **1** boundary-line or margin of an area or surface. **2** narrow surface of a thin object. **3** meeting-line of surfaces. **4 a** sharpened side of a blade. **b** sharpness. **5** brink of a precipice. **6** edge-like thing, esp. the crest of a ridge. **7** effectiveness, incisiveness; excitement. *–v.* (**-ging**) **1** advance, esp. gradually or furtively. **2 a** provide with an edge or border. **b** form a border to. **3** sharpen (a tool etc.). □ **have the edge on** (or **over**) have a slight advantage over. **on edge** tense and irritable. **set a person's teeth on edge** (of taste or sound) cause an unpleasant nervous sensation. **take the edge off** make less intense. [Old English]

edgeways *adv.* (also **edgewise**) with edge uppermost or foremost. □ **get a word in edgeways** contribute to a conversation when the dominant speaker pauses.

edging *n.* thing forming an edge or border.

edgy *adj.* (**-ier, -iest**) irritable; anxious. □ **edgily** *adv.* **edginess** *n.*

EDI *abbr.* = ELECTRONIC DATA INTERCHANGE.

edible /ˈedɪb(ə)l/ *adj.* fit to be eaten. □ **edibility** /-ˈbɪlɪtɪ/ *n.* [Latin *edo* eat]

edict /ˈiːdɪkt/ *n.* order proclaimed by authority. [Latin *edico* proclaim]

edifice /ˈedɪfɪs/ *n.* building, esp. an imposing one. [Latin *aedis* dwelling]

edify /ˈedɪˌfaɪ/ *v.* (**-ies, -ied**) improve morally or intellectually. □ **edification** /-fɪˈkeɪʃ(ə)n/ *n.* [Latin *aedifico* build]

Edinburgh /ˈedɪnbərə/ capital of Scotland; pop. (est. 1994) 447 600. A cultural centre, it has service and manufacturing (esp. food, drink, and printing) industries.

edit /ˈedɪt/ *v.* (**-t-**) **1** assemble, prepare, or modify (written material for publication). **2** be editor of (a newspaper etc.). **3** take extracts from and collate (a film etc.) to form a unified sequence. **4 a** prepare (data) for processing by a computer. **b** alter (a text entered in a word processor etc.). **5 a** reword in order to correct, or to alter the emphasis. **b** (foll. by *out*) remove (a part) from a text etc. [Latin *edo edit-* give out]

edition /ɪˈdɪʃ(ə)n/ *n.* **1** edited or published form of a book etc. **2** copies of a book, newspaper, etc. issued at one time. **3** instance of a regular broadcast. **4** person or thing similar to another (*a miniature edition of her mother*).

editor *n.* **1** person who edits. **2** person who directs the preparation of a newspaper or broadcast news programme or a particular section of one (*sports editor*). **3** person who selects or commissions material for publication. **4** computer program for entering and modifying textual data. See TEXT EDITOR. □ **editorship** *n.*

editorial /ˌedɪˈtɔːrɪəl/ *–adj.* **1** of editing or editors. **2** written or approved by an editor. *–n.* article giving a newspaper's views on a current topic. □ **editorially** *adv.*

♦ **editorial advertisement** *n.* advertisement in a newspaper or magazine written in the form of an editorial feature but clearly labelled 'advertisement'.

Edmonton /ˈedmənt(ə)n/ city in Canada, capital of Alberta; city pop. (1991) 616 741; metropolitan area pop. (est. 1995) 882 900. Oil-refining and mining industries are important; it is also the commercial centre of an agricultural region.

EDNS *abbr.* expected demand not supplied.

EDP *abbr.* electronic data processing.

EDS *abbr.* **1** Electronic Data Systems Corporation. **2** *Computing* exchangeable disk store.

♦ **EDSP** *abbr.* Exchange Delivery Settlement Price. See SETTLEMENT PRICE.

EDSS *abbr. Computing* expert decision-support system.

EDT *abbr. US* & *Canadian* Eastern Daylight Time.

educate /ˈedjʊˌkeɪt/ *v.* (**-ting**) **1** give intellectual, moral, and social instruction to. **2** provide education for. □ **educable** /-kəb(ə)l/ *adj.* **educability** /-kəˈbɪlɪtɪ/ *n.* **educative** /-kətɪv/ *adj.* **educator** *n.* [Latin *educo -are* rear]

educated *adj.* **1** having had an (esp. good) education. **2** resulting from this (*educated accent*). **3** based on experience or study (*educated guess*).

education /ˌedjʊˈkeɪʃ(ə)n/ *n.* **1** systematic instruction. **2** particular kind of or stage in education (*a classical education*; *further education*). **3** development of character or mental powers. □ **educational** *adj.* **educationally** *adv.*

educationist *n.* (also **educationalist**) expert in educational methods.

educe /ɪˈdjuːs/ *v.* (**-cing**) *literary* bring out or develop from latency. □ **eduction** /ɪˈdʌkʃ(ə)n/ *n.* [Latin *educo -ere* draw out]

Edwardian /edˈwɔːdɪən/ *–adj.* of or characteristic of the reign of Edward VII (1901–10). *–n.* person of this period.

-ee *suffix* forming nouns denoting: **1** person affected by the verbal action (*employee*; *payee*). **2** person concerned with or described as (*absentee*; *refugee*). **3** object of smaller size (*bootee*). [French *-é* in past part.]

EEA *abbr.* European Economic Area. See EUROPEAN FREE TRADE ASSOCIATION.

EEB *abbr.* European Environmental Bureau.

EEC *abbr.* = EUROPEAN ECONOMIC COMMUNITY.

■ **Usage** EC is the more correct term when referring to the Community in its present form.

EEG *abbr.* electroencephalogram.

eel *n.* snakelike fish. [Old English]

EEMS *abbr. Computing* enhanced expanded memory specification.

EEO *abbr.* equal employment opportunity.

EEOC *abbr.* (in the US) Equal Employment Opportunities Commission.

-eer *suffix* forming: **1** nouns meaning 'person concerned with' (*auctioneer*). **2** verbs meaning 'be concerned with' (*electioneer*). [French *-ier* from Latin *-arius*]

eerie /ˈɪərɪ/ *adj.* (**eerier, eeriest**) gloomy and strange; weird (*eerie silence*). □ **eerily** *adv.* **eeriness** *n.* [Old English]

EEROM /ˈɪərɒm/ *abbr. Computing* electrically erasable read-only memory.

EET *abbr.* Eastern European Time.

EETPU *abbr.* Electrical, Electronic, Telecommunications, and Plumbing Union.

EEZ *abbr.* exclusive economic zone.

ef- see EX-[1].

efface /ɪˈfeɪs/ *v.* (**-cing**) **1** rub or wipe out (a mark, recollection, etc.). **2** surpass, eclipse. **3** *refl.* (usu. as **self-**

effacing *adj.*) treat oneself as unimportant. □ **effacement** *n.* [French: related to FACE]

effect /ɪˈfekt/ –*n.* **1** result or consequence of an action etc. **2** efficacy (*had little effect*). **3** impression produced on a spectator, hearer, etc. (*lights gave a pretty effect; said it just for effect*). **4** (in *pl.*) property. **5** (in *pl.*) lighting, sound, etc., giving realism to a play, film, etc. **6** physical phenomenon (*Doppler effect; greenhouse effect*). –*v.* bring about (a change, cure, etc.). □ **bring** (or **carry) into effect** accomplish. **give effect to** make operative. **in effect** for practical purposes. **take effect** become operative. **to the effect that** the gist being that. **to that effect** having that result or implication. **with effect from** coming into operation at (a stated time). [Latin: related to FACT]

■ **Usage** *Effect* should not be confused with *affect* which, as a verb, has more meanings and is more common, but which does not exist as a noun.

effective *adj.* **1** producing the intended result. **2** impressive, striking. **3** actual, existing. **4** operative. □ **effectively** *adv.* **effectiveness** *n.*

♦ **effective demand** *n.* demand for goods and services for which money is available to convert them into actual purchases. In Keynesian theory it is often argued that in a recession or a depression there will be inadequate effective demand as unemployed workers demand goods but have no means to pay for them. Similarly, firms would demand labour if only there was someone to buy their goods. Pump priming can add to effective demand and move the economy towards full employment by means of the multiplier process (see PUMP-PRIMING).

♦ **effective tax rate** *n.* average tax rate applicable in a given circumstance. In many cases the actual rate of tax applying to an amount of income or to a gift may not, for various reasons, be the published rate of the tax; these reasons include the necessity to gross up, the complex effects of some reliefs, and peculiarities in scales of rates. The effective rate is therefore found by dividing the additional tax payable as a result of the transaction by the amount of the income, gift, or whatever else is involved in the transaction.

effectual /ɪˈfektʃʊəl/ *adj.* **1** producing the required effect. **2** valid. □ **effectually** *adv.*

effeminate /ɪˈfemɪnət/ *adj.* (of a man) womanish in appearance or manner. □ **effeminacy** *n.* **effeminately** *adv.* [Latin *femina* woman]

effervesce /ˌefəˈves/ *v.* **(-cing) 1** give off bubbles of gas. **2** be lively. □ **effervescence** *n.* **effervescent** *adj.* [Latin: related to FERVENT]

effete /ɪˈfiːt/ *adj.* feeble, lanquid; effeminate. □ **effeteness** *n.* [Latin]

efficacious /ˌefɪˈkeɪʃəs/ *adj.* producing the desired effect. □ **efficacy** /ˈefɪkəsɪ/ *n.* [Latin *efficax*: related to EFFICIENT]

♦ **efficiency** *n.* **1** competence; effectiveness. **2** (also **technical efficiency**) measure of the ability of a manufacturer to produce the maximum output of acceptable quality with the minimum of inputs. One company is said to be more efficient than another if it can produce the same output as the other with less inputs, irrespective of the price factor. **3** (also **economic efficiency**) measure of the ability of an organization to produce and distribute its product at the lowest possible cost. A firm can have a high technical efficiency but a low economic efficiency because its prices are too high to meet competition. **4** ratio of useful work done by an engine, machine, etc. to the energy supplied to it.

♦ **efficiency variance** *n. Finance* variance arising when the actual productivity of an organization is greater or less than that budgeted for.

♦ **efficiency wage theory** *n. Econ.* theory that the productivity of a worker increases with the wages paid to that worker. It was first applied in the late 1950s to developing economies; in this context it became clear that higher wages enable poor workers to improve their diets and thus to become more productive. Recently, however, the argument has been applied in developed economies to explain involuntary unemployment. Higher wages raise morale and company loyalty, attract better quality workers, and result in less shirking. Thus, even in a recession, when some workers are being made redundant, firms will be unwilling to reduce wages levels to reflect the balance of supply and demand.

efficient /ɪˈfɪʃ(ə)nt/ *adj.* **1** productive with minimum waste or effort. **2** (of a person) capable; acting effectively. □ **efficiently** *adv.* [Latin *facio* make]

effigy /ˈefɪdʒɪ/ *n.* (*pl.* **-ies**) sculpture or model of a person. □ **burn in effigy** burn a model of a person. [Latin *effigies* from *fingo* fashion]

effloresce /ˌeflɔːˈres/ *v.* **(-cing) 1** burst into flower. **2 a** (of a substance) turn to a fine powder on exposure to air. **b** (of salts) come to the surface and crystallize. **c** (of a surface) become covered with salt particles. □ **efflorescence** *n.* **efflorescent** *adj.* [Latin *flos flor-* FLOWER]

effluence /ˈeflʊəns/ *n.* **1** flowing out of light, electricity, etc. **2** that which flows out. [Latin *fluo flux-* flow]

effluent –*adj.* flowing out. –*n.* **1** sewage or industrial waste discharged into a river etc. **2** stream or lake flowing from a larger body of water.

effluvium /ɪˈfluːvɪəm/ *n.* (*pl.* **-via**) unpleasant or noxious outflow. [Latin: related to EFFLUENCE]

effort /ˈefət/ *n.* **1** use of physical or mental energy. **2** determined attempt. **3** force exerted. **4** *colloq.* something accomplished. [Latin *fortis* strong]

effortless *adj.* easily done, requiring no effort. □ **effortlessly** *adv.* **effortlessness** *n.*

effrontery /ɪˈfrʌntərɪ/ *n.* (*pl.* **-ies**) impudent audacity. [Latin *frons front-* forehead]

effulgent /ɪˈfʌldʒ(ə)nt/ *adj. literary* radiant. □ **effulgence** *n.* [Latin *fulgeo* shine]

effuse /ɪˈfjuːz/ *v.* **(-sing) 1** pour forth (liquid, light, etc.). **2** give out (ideas etc.). [Latin *fundo fus-* pour]

effusion /ɪˈfjuːʒ(ə)n/ *n.* **1** outpouring. **2** *derog.* unrestrained flow of words. [Latin: related to EFFUSE]

effusive /ɪˈfjuːsɪv/ *adj.* gushing, demonstrative. □ **effusively** *adv.* **effusiveness** *n.*

EFL *abbr.* **1** English as a foreign language. **2** external financial limit.

EFT *abbr.* = ELECTRONIC FUNDS TRANSFER.

eft *n.* newt. [Old English]

Efta /ˈeftə/ *n.* (also **EFTA**) = EUROPEAN FREE TRADE ASSOCIATION. [abbreviation]

♦ **EFTPOS** /ˈeftpɒs/ *abbr.* = ELECTRONIC FUNDS TRANSFER AT POINT OF SALE.

♦ **EftPos UK Ltd.** see ASSOCIATION FOR PAYMENT CLEARING SERVICES.

EFTS *abbr.* electronic funds transfer system.

e.g. *abbr.* for example. [Latin *exempli gratia*]

EGA *abbr. Computing* enhanced graphics adapter. See GRAPHICS ADAPTER.

egalitarian /ɪˌgælɪˈteərɪən/ –*adj.* of or advocating equal rights for all. –*n.* egalitarian person. □ **egalitarianism** *n.* [French *égal* EQUAL]

EGCI *abbr.* Export Group for the Construction Industries.

Eger /ˈegə(r)/ spa town in N Hungary, noted for its red 'Bull's Blood' wine; pop. (1993) 63 365.

egg[1] *n.* **1 a** body produced by females of birds, insects, etc. and capable of developing into a new individual. **b** egg of the domestic hen, used for food. **2** *Biol.* ovum. **3** *colloq.* person or thing of a specified kind (*good egg*). □ **with egg on one's face** *colloq.* looking foolish. □ **eggy** *adj.* [Old Norse]

egg[2] *v.* (foll. by *on*) urge. [Old Norse: related to EDGE]

eggcup *n.* cup for holding a boiled egg.

egg-flip *n.* (also **egg-nog**) drink of alcoholic spirit with beaten egg, milk, etc.

egghead *n. colloq.* intellectual; expert.

eggplant *n.* = AUBERGINE.

eggshell –*n.* shell of an egg. –*adj.* **1** (of china) thin and fragile. **2** (of paint) with a slight gloss.

egg-white *n.* white part round the yolk of an egg.

eglantine /ˈeglənˌtaɪn/ *n.* sweet-brier. [Latin *acus* needle]

◆ **EGM** *abbr.* = EXTRAORDINARY GENERAL MEETING.

EGmbH *abbr.* (German) Eingetragene Gesellschaft mit beschränkter Haftung (= registered limited company).

ego /ˈiːgəʊ/ *n.* (*pl.* **-s**) **1** the self; the part of the mind that reacts to reality and has a sense of individuality. **2** self-esteem; self-conceit. [Latin, = I]

egocentric /ˌiːgəʊˈsentrɪk/ *adj.* self-centred.

egoism /ˈiːgəʊˌɪz(ə)m/ *n.* **1** self-interest as the moral basis of behaviour. **2** systematic selfishness. **3** = EGOTISM. □ **egoist** *n.* **egoistic** /-ˈɪstɪk/ *adj.* **egoistical** /-ˈɪstɪk(ə)l/ *adj.* **egoistically** /-ˈɪstɪkəlɪ/ *adv.*

■ **Usage** The senses of *egoism* and *egotism* overlap, but *egoism* alone is used as a term in philosophy and psychology to mean self-interest (often contrasted with *altruism*).

egotism /ˈiːgəˌtɪz(ə)m/ *n.* **1** self-conceit. **2** selfishness. □ **egotist** *n.* **egotistic** /-ˈtɪstɪk/ *adj.* **egotistical** /-ˈtɪstɪk(ə)l/ *adj.* **egotistically** /-ˈtɪstɪkəlɪ/ *adv.*

■ **Usage** See note at *egoism*.

ego-trip *n. colloq.* activity to boost one's own self-esteem or self-conceit.

EGR *abbr. Finance* earned growth rate.

egregious /ɪˈgriːdʒəs/ *adj.* **1** extremely bad. **2** *archaic* remarkable. [Latin *grex greg-* flock]

egress /ˈiːgres/ *n. formal* **1** exit. **2** right of going out. [Latin *egredior -gress-* walk out]

egret /ˈiːgrɪt/ *n.* a kind of heron with long white feathers. [French *aigrette*]

Egyptian /ɪˈdʒɪpʃ(ə)n/ –*adj.* of Egypt. –*n.* **1** native of Egypt. **2** language of the ancient Egyptians.

Egyptology /ˌiːdʒɪpˈtɒlədʒɪ/ *n.* the study of the language, history, and culture of ancient Egypt. □ **Egyptologist** *n.*

EH *postcode* Edinburgh.

eh /eɪ/ *int. colloq.* **1** expressing enquiry or surprise. **2** inviting assent. **3** asking for repetition or explanation. [instinctive exclamation]

EI –*international civil aircraft marking* Republic of Ireland. –*airline flight code* Aer Lingus.

EIA *abbr.* **1** Engineering Industries Association. **2** environmental impact analysis (or assessment).

EIB *abbr.* = EUROPEAN INVESTMENT BANK.

eider /ˈaɪdə(r)/ *n.* any of various large northern ducks. [Icelandic]

eiderdown *n.* quilt stuffed with soft material, esp. down.

eight /eɪt/ *adj.* & *n.* **1** one more than seven. **2** symbol for this (8, viii, VIII). **3** size etc. denoted by eight. **4** eight-oared rowing-boat or its crew. **5** eight o'clock. [Old English]

eighteen /eɪˈtiːn/ *adj.* & *n.* **1** one more than seventeen. **2** symbol for this (18, xviii, XVIII). **3** size etc. denoted by eighteen. **4** (*18*) (of films) suitable only for persons of 18 years and over. □ **eighteenth** *adj.* & *n.* [Old English]

eightfold *adj.* & *adv.* **1** eight times as much or as many. **2** consisting of eight parts.

eighth *adj.* & *n.* **1** next after seventh. **2** one of eight equal parts of a thing. □ **eighthly** *adv.*

eightsome *n.* (in full **eightsome reel**) lively Scottish dance for eight people.

eighty /ˈeɪtɪ/ *adj.* & *n.* (*pl.* **-ies**) **1** eight times ten. **2** symbol for this (80, lxxx, LXXX). **3** (in *pl.*) numbers from 80 to 89, esp. the years of a century or of a person's life. □ **eightieth** *adj.* & *n.* [Old English]

Eilat /eɪˈlæt/ (also **Elat**) town in Israel, a port at the head of the Gulf of Aqaba; pop. (est. 1989) 26 010. It is Israel's only outlet to the Red Sea and has an oil-refining industry.

Eindhoven /ˈaɪnthəʊv(ə)n/ industrial city in the Netherlands, in the province of North Brabant; pop. (est. 1995) 197 055. The city is a major producer of electrical and electronic goods.

einsteinium /aɪnˈstaɪnɪəm/ *n.* artificial radioactive metallic element. [*Einstein*, name of a physicist]

EISA *abbr. Computing* extended industry standard architecture (for microcomputers).

Eisenstadt /ˈaɪzənˌʃtɑːt/ city in E Austria, capital of the province of Burgenland; pop. (1991) 10 500.

eisteddfod /aɪˈstedfəd/ *n.* congress of Welsh poets and musicians; festival for musical competitions etc. [Welsh]

either /ˈaɪðə(r), ˈiːðə(r)/ –*adj.* & *pron.* **1** one or the other of two (*either of you can go; you may have either book*). **2** each of two (*houses on either side of the road*). –*adv.* & *conj.* **1** as one possibility (*is either right or wrong*). **2** as one

Egypt /ˈiːdʒɪpt/, **Arab Republic of** country in NE Africa bordering on the Mediterranean Sea, consisting largely of desert, with its population concentrated chiefly along the fertile valley of the River Nile. The economy is primarily agricultural; land reclamation schemes and improved irrigation have boosted production, but the country is still a net importer of foodstuffs. Crops include cotton (a major export), citrus fruits, vegetables, and cereals. Oil is an important export and there are iron, steel, and electricity industries; manufactured products include motor vehicles, electrical goods, chemicals, and textiles. Tourism is an expanding industry, but has been disrupted in 1992–3 by terrorist activities of Islamic fundamentalists. The government is in the process of implementing fiscal and monetary reforms agreed with the IMF.

History. The ancient kingdoms of Upper and Lower Egypt were united in about 3100 BC and the country was ruled by a succession of 31 dynasties until 332 BC, when it was conquered by Alexander the Great. For three centuries after Alexander's death Egypt was a centre of Hellenistic culture; it subsequently became a Roman province and, after the Arab conquest in 642, an Islamic country. From 1517 it formed part of the Ottoman empire except for a brief period (1798–1801) under French rule following Napoleon's invasion. The opening of the Suez Canal in 1869 made Egypt strategically important, and when the Turks became allies of Germany in the First World War the British (who had installed themselves following an Egyptian nationalist revolt in 1882) declared the country a British protectorate. Independence was granted in 1922 and a kingdom was established, becoming a republic after the overthrow of the monarchy in 1953. In 1979 Egypt signed a peace treaty with Israel ending 31 years of war and was expelled from the Arab League; it was readmitted to the League in 1989 and is now taking a leading role in Arab-Israeli peace talks. Since 1992 political stability has been threatened by opposition from militant Islamic fundamentalists, who have targeted civil servants, tourists, and government ministers. In November 1997 Islamic extremists shot dead more than 60 tourists at the temple of Luxor. President, Hosni Mubarak; capital, Cairo.

languages	Arabic (official), English, French
currency	pound (£E) of 100 piastres
pop. (1996)	60 896 000
GNP (1994)	US$40.9B
literacy	63% (m); 38% (f)
life expectancy	65 (m); 69 (f)

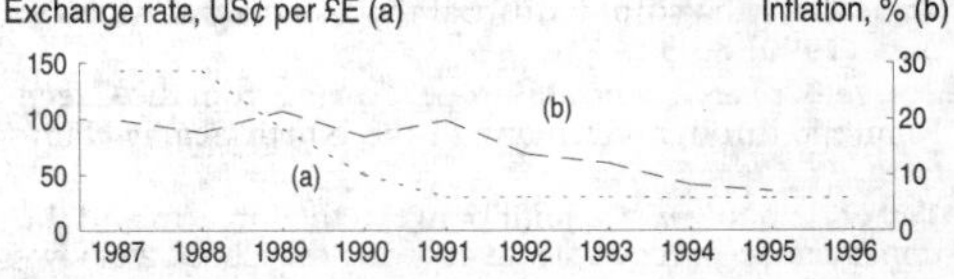

choice or alternative; which way you will (*either come in or go out*). **3** (with *neg.*) **a** any more than the other (*if you do not go, I shall not either*). **b** moreover (*there is no time to lose, either*). [Old English]

EIU *abbr.* Economist Intelligence Unit.

ejaculate /ɪ'dʒækjʊ,leɪt/ *v.* (**-ting**) (also *absol.*) **1** exclaim. **2** emit (semen) in orgasm. □ **ejaculation** /-'leɪʃ(ə)n/ *n.* **ejaculatory** *adj.* [Latin *ejaculor* dart out]

eject /ɪ'dʒekt/ *v.* **1** expel, compel to leave. **2** (of a pilot etc.) cause oneself to be propelled from an aircraft as an emergency measure. **3** cause to be removed, drop out, or pop up automatically from a gun, cassette-player, etc. **4** dispossess (a tenant). **5** emit, send out. □ **ejection** *n.* [Latin *ejicio eject-* throw out]

ejector *n.* device for ejecting.

ejector seat *n.* device in an aircraft for the emergency ejection of a pilot etc.

EK *airline flight code* Emirates.

Ekaterinburg /ɪ'kætərɪnbɜːg/ (formerly (1924–90) **Sverdlovsk** /sveəd'lɒfsk/) city in NW Russia, with engineering, metallurgical, and chemical industries; pop. (est. 1995) 1 280 000.

eke *v.* (**eking**) □ **eke out 1** supplement (income etc.). **2** make (a living) or support (an existence) with difficulty. [Old English]

EL *international civil aircraft marking* Liberia.

El Aaiún see LA'YOUN.

elaborate *–adj.* /ɪ'læbərət/ **1** minutely worked out. **2** complicated. *–v.* /ɪ'læbə,reɪt/ (**-ting**) work out or explain in detail. □ **elaborately** /-rətlɪ/ *adv.* **elaborateness** /-rətnɪs/ *n.* **elaboration** /-'reɪʃ(ə)n/ *n.* [Latin: related to LABOUR]

élan /eɪ'lɑ̃/ *n.* vivacity, dash. [French]

eland /'iːlənd/ *n.* (*pl.* same or **-s**) large African antelope. [Dutch]

elapse /ɪ'læps/ *v.* (**-sing**) (of time) pass by. [Latin *elabor elaps-* slip away]

elastic /ɪ'læstɪk/ *–adj.* **1** able to resume its normal bulk or shape after contraction, dilation, or distortion. **2** springy. **3** flexible, adaptable. *–n.* elastic cord or fabric, usu. woven with strips of rubber. □ **elastically** *adv.* [Greek *elastikos* propulsive]

elasticated /ɪ'læstɪ,keɪtɪd/ *adj.* (of fabric) made elastic by weaving with rubber thread.

elastic band *n.* = RUBBER BAND.

♦ **elasticity** /,iːlæ'stɪsətɪ/ *n.* **1** quality of being elastic; flexibility. **2** *Econ.* percentage change in a variable resulting from unit change of another variable. The price **elasticity of demand**, for example, represents the percentage change in demand for a good resulting from a change in its price; this is usu. negative, reflecting the shape of the demand curve. However, by convention elasticities are usu. represented as positive numbers. For an elasticity of zero the relationship is said to be **perfectly inelastic**; if the elasticity is infinite, it is said to be **perfectly elastic**; if it is one it is said to be **unit elastic**. Elasticities greater than one are called **relatively elastic**; less than one, **relatively inelastic**.

---

elastomer /ɪ'læstəmə(r)/ *n.* natural or synthetic rubber or rubber-like plastic. [from ELASTIC, after *isomer*]

Elat see EILAT.

elate /ɪ'leɪt/ *v.* (**-ting**) (esp. as **elated** *adj.*) make delighted or proud. □ **elatedly** *adv.* **elation** *n.* [Latin *effero elat-* raise]

Elba /'elbə/ small Italian island off the W coast of Italy; iron ore is exported; pop. (est. 1984) 28 907.

Elbasan /,elbə'sɑːn/ industrial town in central Albania; pop. (1990) 83 300.

Elbe /elb/ river in central Europe, flowing from the Czech Republic through Germany to the North Sea at Hamburg.

elbow /'elbəʊ/ *–n.* **1 a** joint between the forearm and the upper arm. **b** part of a sleeve covering the elbow. **2** elbow-shaped bend etc. *–v.* (foll. by *in, out, aside,* etc.) **1** jostle or thrust (a person or oneself). **2** make (one's way) thus. □ **give a person the elbow** *colloq.* dismiss or reject a person. [Old English: related to ELL, BOW[1]]

elbow-grease *n. colloq.* vigorous polishing; hard work.

elbow-room *n.* sufficient room to move or work in.

elder[1] *–attrib. adj.* (of persons, esp. when related) senior; of greater age. *–n.* **1** older of two persons (*is my elder by ten years*). **2** (in *pl.*) persons of greater age or venerable because of age. **3** official in the early Christian Church and some modern Churches. [Old English: related to OLD]

elder[2] *n.* tree with white flowers and dark berries. [Old English]

elderberry *n.* (*pl.* **-ies**) berry of the elder tree.

elderly *adj.* rather old; past middle age.

elder statesman *n.* influential experienced older person, esp. a politician.

eldest *adj.* first-born; oldest surviving.

eldorado /,eldə'rɑːdəʊ/ *n.* (*pl.* **-s**) **1** imaginary land of great wealth. **2** place of abundance or opportunity. [Spanish *el dorado* the gilded]

elecampane /,elɪkæm'peɪn/ *n.* plant with bitter aromatic leaves and roots. [Latin *enula* this plant, *campana* of the fields]

elect /ɪ'lekt/ *–v.* (usu. foll. by *to* + infin.) **1** choose. **2** choose by voting. *–adj.* **1** chosen. **2** select, choice. **3** (after the noun) chosen but not yet in office (*president elect*). [Latin *eligo elect-* pick out]

election /ɪ'lekʃ(ə)n/ *n.* **1** electing or being elected. **2** occasion of this.

electioneer /ɪ,lekʃə'nɪə(r)/ *v.* take part in an election campaign.

elective /ɪ'lektɪv/ *adj.* **1** chosen by or derived from election. **2** (of a body) having the power to elect. **3** optional, not urgently necessary.

elector *n.* **1** person who has the right to vote in an election. **2** (**Elector**) *hist.* (in the Holy Roman Empire) any of the German princes entitled to elect the Emperor. □ **electoral** *adj.*

electorate /ɪ'lektərət/ *n.* **1** body of all electors. **2** *hist.* office or territories of a German Elector.

electric /ɪ'lektrɪk/ *–adj.* **1** of, worked by, or charged with electricity; producing or capable of generating electricity. **2** causing or charged with excitement. *–n.* (in *pl.*) *colloq.* electrical equipment. [Greek *ēlektron* amber]

electrical *adj.* of electricity. □ **electrically** *adv.*

electric blanket *n.* blanket heated by an internal electric element.

electric chair *n.* electrified chair used for capital punishment.

electric eel *n.* eel-like fish able to give an electric shock.

electric eye *n. colloq.* photoelectric cell operating a relay when a beam of light is broken.

electric fire *n.* electrically operated portable domestic heater.

electric guitar *n.* guitar with a solid body and built-in pick-up rather than a soundbox.

electrician /,ɪlek'trɪʃ(ə)n/ *n.* person who installs or maintains electrical equipment for a living.

electricity /,ɪlek'trɪsɪtɪ/ *n.* **1** form of energy occurring in elementary particles (electrons, protons, etc.) and hence in larger bodies containing them. **2** science of electricity. **3** supply of electricity. **4** excitement.

electric shock *n.* effect of a sudden discharge of electricity through the body of a person etc.

electrify /ɪ'lektrɪ,faɪ/ *v.* (**-ies, -ied**) **1** charge with electricity. **2** convert to the use of electric power. **3** cause sudden excitement (*news was electrifying*). □ **electrification** /-fɪ'keɪʃ(ə)n/ *n.*

electro- *comb. form* of, by, or caused by electricity.

electrocardiogram /ɪ,lektrəʊ'kɑːdɪə,græm/ *n.* record traced by an electrocardiograph. [German: related to ELECTRO-]

electrocardiograph /ɪ,lektrəʊ'kɑːdɪə,grɑːf/ *n.* instrument recording the electric currents generated by a heartbeat.

electroconvulsive /ɪˌlektrəʊkən'vʌlsɪv/ *adj.* (of therapy) using convulsive response to electric shocks.

electrocute /ɪ'lektrəˌkjuːt/ *v.* (**-ting**) kill by electric shock. □ **electrocution** /-'kjuːʃ(ə)n/ *n.* [from ELECTRO-, after *execute*]

electrode /ɪ'lektrəʊd/ *n.* conductor through which electricity enters or leaves an electrolyte, gas, vacuum, etc. [from ELECTRIC, Greek *hodos* way]

electrodynamics /ɪˌlektrəʊdaɪ'næmɪks/ *n.pl.* (usu. treated as *sing.*) the study of electricity in motion. □ **electrodynamic** *adj.*

electroencephalogram /ɪˌlektrəʊɪn'sefələˌgræm/ *n.* record traced by an electroencephalograph. [German: related to ELECTRO-]

electroencephalograph /ɪˌlektrəʊɪn'sefələˌgrɑːf/ *n.* instrument recording the electrical activity of the brain.

electrolyse /ɪ'lektrəˌlaɪz/ *v.* (*US* **-yze**) (**-sing**, *US* **-zing**) subject to or treat by electrolysis.

electrolysis /ˌɪlek'trɒlɪsɪs/ *n.* **1** chemical decomposition by electric action. **2** destruction of tumours, hairroots, etc., by this process. □ **electrolytic** /ɪˌlektrəʊ'lɪtɪk/ *adj.*

electrolyte /ɪ'lektrəˌlaɪt/ *n.* **1** solution able to conduct electricity, esp. in an electric cell or battery. **2** substance that can dissolve to produce this.

electromagnet /ɪˌlektrəʊ'mægnɪt/ *n.* soft metal core made into a magnet by passing an electric current through a coil surrounding it.

electromagnetic /ɪˌlektrəʊmæg'netɪk/ *adj.* having both electrical and magnetic properties. □ **electromagnetically** *adv.*

electromagnetism /ɪˌlektrəʊ'mægnɪˌtɪz(ə)m/ *n.* **1** magnetic forces produced by electricity. **2** the study of these.

electromotive /ɪˌlektrəʊ'məʊtɪv/ *adj.* producing or tending to produce an electric current.

electromotive force *n.* force set up in an electric circuit by a difference in potential.

electron /ɪ'lektrɒn/ *n.* stable elementary particle with a charge of negative electricity, found in all atoms and acting as the primary carrier of electricity in solids.

electronic /ˌɪlek'trɒnɪk/ *adj.* **1 a** produced by or involving the flow of electrons. **b** of electrons or electronics. **2** (of music) produced by electronic means and usu. recorded on tape. □ **electronically** *adv.*

♦ **electronic banking** *n.* the facility of being able to use banking services by remote instructions using a computer, modem, and telephone line. This facility is largely made use of by business firms, while individual customers use TELEPHONE BANKING arrangements.

♦ **electronic data interchange** *n.* (also **EDI**) exchange by electronic means between banks and their customers and between suppliers and purchasers in industry of invoices, payment instructions, and funds.

---

electronic filing *n.* computer-based system for the storage, cataloguing, and retrieval of documents. It plays a major role in an electronic office. The 'objects' in an electronic filing system are usu. stored on magnetic disk or tape and can be organized using a variety of methods. They may be letters, complex reports, charts, graphs, pictures, etc., which are created, manipulated, or deleted as required.

♦ **electronic funds transfer** *n.* (also **EFT**) transfer of money from one bank account to another by means of computers and communications links. Banks routinely transfer funds between accounts using computers; another variety of EFT is the telebanking service enabling the videotex network to be used for banking in a customer's home. See also ELECTRONIC FUNDS TRANSFER AT POINT OF SALE.

♦ **electronic funds transfer at point of sale** *n.* (also **EFTPOS**) automatic debiting of a purchase price from the customer's bank or credit-card account by a computer link between a retailer's checkout till and the bank or credit-card company. The system depends on a magnetic strip on the customer's card which is 'wiped' through a terminal reader at the point of sale. This gives authorization and prints a voucher for the customer to sign. Transfer of funds to the retailer can take place within 48 hours.

---

electronic mail *n.* (also **e-mail, email**) messages sent between users of computer systems, the computer systems being used to transport and hold the messages. Sender and recipient(s) need not be on the same computer to communicate, or be on-line at the same time. The mail-handling program will have facilities for typing in messages, selecting one or more recipients, and checking for incoming mail. It may also be able to forward copies of incoming messages to other people, provide teleconferencing facilities, or delay messages until a given time or date. A single message may possibly combine text, graphics, and other forms of information.

electronic office *n.* computer-based system designed for office tasks and involving, for example, the use of electronic filing, word processing, databases, computer graphics, electronic mail, and teleconferencing.

♦ **electronic point of sale** *n.* (also **EPOS**) computerized method of recording sales in retail outlets, using a laser scanner at the checkout till to read bar-codes printed on the items' packages (see BAR-CODE). Other advantages over conventional checkout points include a more efficient use of checkout staff time and the provision of a more detailed receipt to the customer.

---

electronics *n.pl.* (treated as *sing.*) science of the movement of electrons in a vacuum, gas, semiconductor, etc., esp. in devices in which the flow is controlled and utilized.

electronic tagging *n.* the attaching of electronic markers to people or goods, enabling them to be tracked down.

electron lens *n.* device for focusing a stream of electrons by means of electric or magnetic fields.

electron microscope *n.* microscope with high magnification and resolution, using electron beams instead of light.

electronvolt /ɪ'lektrɒnˌvəʊlt/ *n.* a unit of energy, the amount gained by an electron when accelerated through a potential difference of one volt.

electroplate /ɪ'lektrəʊˌpleɪt/ –*v.* (**-ting**) coat with a thin layer of chromium, silver, etc., by electrolysis. –*n.* electroplated articles.

electroscope /ɪ'lektrəˌskəʊp/ *n.* instrument for detecting and measuring electricity, esp. as an indication of the ionization of air by radioactivity. □ **electroscopic** /-'skɒpɪk/ *adj.*

electro-shock /ɪˌlektrəʊ'ʃɒk/ *attrib. adj.* (of therapy) by means of electric shocks.

electrostatics /ɪˌlektrəʊ'stætɪks/ *n.pl.* (treated as *sing.*) the study of electricity at rest.

electrotechnology /ɪˌlektrəʊtek'nɒlədʒɪ/ *n.* science of the application of electricity in technology.

electrotherapy /ɪˌlektrəʊ'θerəpɪ/ *n.* treatment of diseases by use of electricity.

elegant /'elɪgənt/ *adj.* **1** tasteful, refined, graceful. **2** ingeniously simple. □ **elegance** *n.* **elegantly** *adv.* [Latin: related to ELECT]

elegiac /ˌelɪ'dʒaɪək/ –*adj.* **1** used for elegies. **2** mournful. –*n.* (in *pl.*) elegiac verses. □ **elegiacally** *adv.*

elegy /'elɪdʒɪ/ *n.* (*pl.* **-ies**) **1** sorrowful poem or song, esp. for the dead. **2** poem in elegiac metre. [Latin from Greek]

element /'elɪmənt/ *n.* **1** component part; contributing factor. **2** any of the substances that cannot be resolved by chemical means into simpler substances. **3 a** any of the four substances (earth, water, air, and fire) in ancient and medieval philosophy. **b** a being's natural abode or environment. **4** *Electr.* wire that heats up in an electric heater, kettle, etc. **5** (in *pl.*) atmospheric agencies, esp. wind and storm. **6** (in *pl.*) rudiments of learning or of an art etc. **7** (in *pl.*) bread and wine of the Eucharist. □ **in one's element** in one's preferred situation, doing what one does well and enjoys. [French from Latin]

elemental /ˌelɪ'ment(ə)l/ *adj.* **1** of or like the elements or the forces of nature; powerful. **2** essential, basic.

elementary /ˌelɪ'mentərɪ/ *adj.* **1** dealing with the simplest facts of a subject. **2** unanalysable.

elementary particle *n. Physics* subatomic particle, esp. one not known to consist of simpler ones.

elephant /'elɪf(ə)nt/ *n.* (*pl.* same or **-s**) largest living land animal, with a trunk and ivory tusks. [Greek *elephas*]

elephantiasis /ˌelɪfən'taɪəsɪs/ *n.* skin disease causing gross enlargement of limbs etc.

elephantine /ˌelɪ'fæntaɪn/ *adj.* **1** of elephants. **2 a** huge. **b** clumsy.

elevate /'elɪˌveɪt/ *v.* (**-ting**) **1** raise, lift up. **2** exalt in rank etc. **3** (usu. as **elevated** *adj.*) raise morally or intellectually. [Latin *levo* lift]

elevation /ˌelɪ'veɪʃ(ə)n/ *n.* **1 a** elevating or being elevated. **b** angle with the horizontal. **c** height above sea level etc. **d** high position. **2** flat drawing or diagram showing one side of a building.

elevator *n.* **1** *US* lift. **2** movable part of a tailplane for changing an aircraft's altitude. **3** hoisting machine.

eleven /ɪ'lev(ə)n/ *adj.* & *n.* **1** one more than ten. **2** symbol for this (11, xi, XI). **3** size etc. denoted by eleven. **4** team of eleven players at cricket, football, etc. **5** eleven o'clock. [Old English]

elevenfold *adj.* & *adv.* **1** eleven times as much or as many. **2** consisting of eleven parts.

eleven-plus *n.* esp. *hist.* examination taken at age 11–12 to determine the type of secondary school a child would enter.

elevenses /ɪ'levənzɪz/ *n. colloq.* light refreshment taken at about 11 a.m.

eleventh *adj.* & *n.* **1** next after tenth. **2** each of eleven equal parts of a thing. □ **eleventh hour** last possible moment.

elf *n.* (*pl.* **elves** /elvz/) mythological being, esp. one that is small and mischievous. □ **elfish** *adj.* **elvish** *adj.* [Old English]

elfin *adj.* of elves; elflike.

elicit /ɪ'lɪsɪt/ *v.* (**-t-**) draw out (facts, a response, etc.), esp. with difficulty. [Latin *elicio*]

elide /ɪ'laɪd/ *v.* (**-ding**) omit (a vowel or syllable) in pronunciation. [Latin *elido elis-* crush out]

♦ **eligibility** /ˌelɪdʒɪ'bɪlɪtɪ/ *n.* **1** state of being eligible; suitability. **2** *Finance* criteria that determine which bills the Bank of England will discount, as lender of last resort. Such bills, known as **eligible paper**, include treasury bills, short-dated gilts, and first-class trade bills.

eligible /'elɪdʒɪb(ə)l/ *adj.* **1** (often foll. by *for*) fit or entitled to be chosen (*eligible for a rebate*). **2** desirable or suitable, esp. for marriage. [Latin: related to ELECT]

♦ **eligible paper** see ELIGIBILITY 2.

eliminate /ɪ'lɪmɪˌneɪt/ *v.* (**-ting**) **1** remove, get rid of. **2** exclude from consideration. **3** exclude from a further stage of a competition through defeat etc. □ **elimination** /-'neɪʃ(ə)n/ *n.* **eliminator** *n.* [Latin *limen limin-* threshold]

Elisabethville /ɪ'lɪzəbəθˌvɪl/ see LUBUMBASHI.

elision /ɪ'lɪʒ(ə)n/ *n.* omission of a vowel or syllable in pronunciation (e.g. in *we'll*). [Latin: related to ELIDE]

élite /ɪ'liːt/ *n.* **1** (prec. by *the*) the best (of a group). **2** select group or class. **3** size of letters in typewriting (12 per inch). [French: related to ELECT]

élitism *n.* recourse to or advocacy of leadership or dominance by a select group. □ **élitist** *n.* & *adj.*

elixir /ɪ'lɪksɪə(r)/ *n.* **1 a** alchemist's preparation supposedly able to change metals into gold or (in full **elixir of life**) to prolong life indefinitely. **b** remedy for all ills. **2** aromatic medicinal drug. [Latin from Arabic]

Elizabethan /ɪˌlɪzə'biːθ(ə)n/ –*adj.* of the time of Queen Elizabeth I or II. –*n.* person of this time.

elk *n.* (*pl.* same or **-s**) large deer of northern parts of Europe, North America, and Asia. [Old English]

ell *n. hist.* measure = 45 in. [Old English, = forearm]

Ellice Islands /'elɪs/ see TUVALU.

ellipse /ɪ'lɪps/ *n.* regular oval, resulting when a cone is cut obliquely by a plane. [Greek *elleipsis* deficit]

ellipsis /ɪ'lɪpsɪs/ *n.* (*pl.* **ellipses** /-siːz/) **1** omission of words needed to complete a construction or sense. **2** set of three dots etc. indicating omission.

ellipsoid /ɪ'lɪpsɔɪd/ *n.* solid of which all the plane sections through one axis are circles and all the other plane sections are ellipses.

elliptic /ɪ'lɪptɪk/ *adj.* (also **elliptical**) of or in the form of an ellipse. □ **elliptically** *adv.*

elm *n.* **1** tree with rough serrated leaves. **2** its wood. [Old English]

elocution /ˌelə'kjuːʃ(ə)n/ *n.* art of clear and expressive speech. [Latin *loquor* speak]

elongate /'iːlɒŋˌgeɪt/ *v.* (**-ting**) lengthen, extend. □ **elongation** /-'geɪʃ(ə)n/ *n.* [Latin *longus* long]

elope /ɪ'ləʊp/ *v.* (**-ping**) run away to marry secretly. □ **elopement** *n.* [Anglo-French]

eloquence /'eləkwəns/ *n.* fluent and effective use of language. [Latin *loquor* speak]

eloquent *adj.* **1** having eloquence. **2** (often foll. by *of*) expressive. □ **eloquently** *adv.*

El Paso /el 'pæsəʊ/ industrial city in the US, in W Texas; pop. (1990) 515 342. It is the commercial centre of an

El Salvador /el 'sælvəˌdɔː(r)/, **Republic of** country in Central America, on the Pacific coast. Its economy is mainly agricultural, coffee, cotton, sugar cane, shrimps, and sisal being the chief exports. Forestry is also important; mahogany, walnut, dye woods, and balsam are exported. The food-processing and textile industries provide employment and tourism is being developed. The economy has been adversely affected by civil war and drought. Firm monetary policy and improved public finances have helped to reduce inflation, but export revenues have not risen. *History*. Conquered by the Spanish in 1524, El Salvador gained its independence in 1821 and joined the Central American Federation in 1824, before finally emerging as an independent republic in 1839. After years of military rule, by the late 1970s and early 1980s the country had fallen into increasingly severe internal unrest, characterized by guerrilla warfare and harsh repressive measures. In 1992 a peace agreement was signed to end 12 years of civil war between government forces and the left-wing guerrilla movement FMLN; implementation of this was monitored by UN observers. In 1994 the FMLN took part in legislative and presidential elections, which were won by the right-wing National Republican Alliance Party (ARENA). President, Armando Calderón; capital, San Salvador. □ **Salvadorean** /ˌsælvə'dɔːrɪən/ *adj.* & *n.*

languages	Spanish (official), Nahua (an Indian language)
currency	colón of 100 centavos
pop. (1996)	5 897 000
GNP (1994)	US$8.3B
literacy	77% (m); 71% (f)
life expectancy	65 (m); 72 (f)

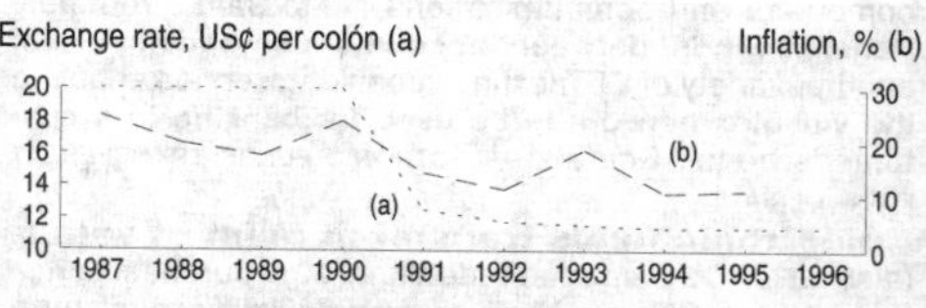

agricultural and mining region, with food-processing and oil-refining industries.

ELR *abbr.* export licensing regulations.

else *adv.* **1** (prec. by indef. or interrog. pron.) besides (*someone else*; *nowhere else*; *who else?*). **2** instead (*what else could I say?*). **3** otherwise; if not (*run, (or) else you will be late*). □ **or else** see OR[1]. [Old English]

elsewhere *adv.* in or to some other place.

Elsinore /'elsɪ,nɔː(r)/ (Danish **Helsingør** /'helsɪŋ,ɜː(r)/) seaport in Denmark, on the NE coast of the island of Zealand; industries include brewing, food processing, and shipbuilding; pop. (1990) 56 750.

elucidate /ɪ'luːsɪ,deɪt/ *v.* (**-ting**) throw light on; explain. □ **elucidation** /-'deɪʃ(ə)n/ *n.* **elucidatory** *adj.* [Latin: related to LUCID]

elude /ɪ'luːd/ *v.* (**-ding**) **1** escape adroitly from (danger, pursuit, etc.). **2** avoid compliance with (a law etc.) or fulfilment of (an obligation). **3** baffle (a person or memory etc.). □ **elusion** /-ʒ(ə)n/ *n.* [Latin *ludo* play]

elusive /ɪ'luːsɪv/ *adj.* **1** difficult to find or catch. **2** difficult to remember. **3** avoiding the point raised. □ **elusiveness** *n.*

elver /'elvə(r)/ *n.* young eel. [from EEL, FARE]

elves *pl.* of ELF.

elvish see ELF.

Elysium /ɪ'lɪzɪəm/ *n.* **1** (also **Elysian Fields**) (in Greek mythology) abode of the blessed after death. **2** place of ideal happiness. □ **Elysian** *adj.* [Latin from Greek]

em *n. Printing* unit of measurement equal to the width of an M. [name of the letter *M*]

em-[1,2] see EN-[1,2].

'em /əm/ *pron. colloq.* them.

EMA *abbr.* European Monetary Agreement.

emaciate /ɪ'meɪsɪ,eɪt/ *v.* (**-ting**) (esp. as **emaciated** *adj.*) make abnormally thin or feeble. □ **emaciation** /-'eɪʃ(ə)n/ *n.* [Latin *macies* leanness]

email /'iːmeɪl/ *n.* (also **e-mail**) = ELECTRONIC MAIL.

emalangeni *pl.* of LILANGENI.

emanate /'emə,neɪt/ *v.* (**-ting**) (usu. foll. by *from*) issue or originate (from a source). □ **emanation** /-'neɪʃ(ə)n/ *n.* [Latin *mano* flow]

emancipate /ɪ'mænsɪ,peɪt/ *v.* (**-ting**) **1** free from social or political restraint. **2** (usu. as **emancipated** *adj.*) free from the inhibitions of moral or social conventions. **3** free from slavery. □ **emancipation** /-'peɪʃ(ə)n/ *n.* **emancipatory** /-pətərɪ/ *adj.* [Latin, = free from possession, from *manus* hand, *capio* take]

emasculate –*v.* /ɪ'mæskjʊ,leɪt/ (**-ting**) **1** deprive of force or vigour. **2** castrate. –*adj.* /ɪ'mæskjʊlət/ **1** deprived of force. **2** castrated. **3** effeminate. □ **emasculation** /-'leɪʃ(ə)n/ *n.* [Latin: related to MALE]

embalm /ɪm'bɑːm/ *v.* **1** preserve (a corpse) from decay. **2** preserve from oblivion. **3** make fragrant. □ **embalmment** *n.* [French: related to BALM]

embankment /ɪm'bæŋkmənt/ *n.* bank constructed to keep back water or carry a road, railway, etc.

embargo /ɪm'bɑːgəʊ/ –*n.* (*pl.* **-es**) **1** order forbidding foreign ships to enter, or any ships to leave, a country's ports. **2** official suspension of an activity, esp. a ban on some or all of the trade with one or more countries, which is a form of economic sanction. Full embargoes are rare and difficult to apply in practice. –*v.* (**-es, -ed**) place under embargo. [Spanish: related to BAR[1]]

embark /ɪm'bɑːk/ *v.* **1** (often foll. by *for*) put or go on board a ship or aircraft (to a destination). **2** (foll. by *on, in*) begin an enterprise. □ **embarkation** /,embɑː'keɪʃ(ə)n/ *n.* (in sense 1). [French: related to BARQUE]

embarrass /ɪm'bærəs/ *v.* **1** make (a person) feel awkward or ashamed. **2** (as **embarrassed** *adj.*) encumbered with debts. **3** encumber. □ **embarrassment** *n.* [Italian *imbarrare* bar in]

embassy /'embəsɪ/ *n.* (*pl.* **-ies**) **1 a** residence or offices of an ambassador. **b** ambassador and staff. **2** deputation to a foreign government. [French: related to AMBASSADOR]

embattled /ɪm'bæt(ə)ld/ *adj.* **1** prepared or arrayed for battle. **2** fortified with battlements. **3** under heavy attack or in trying circumstances.

embed /ɪm'bed/ *v.* (also **imbed**) (**-dd-**) (esp. as **embedded** *adj.*) fix firmly in a surrounding mass.

embedded computer system *n.* system that uses a computer as a component dedicated to a particular task. Examples are programmable washing machines, arcade video games, and satellite navigation systems.

embellish /ɪm'belɪʃ/ *v.* **1** beautify, adorn. **2** enhance with fictitious additions. □ **embellishment** *n.* [French *bel*, BEAU]

ember *n.* (usu. in *pl.*) small piece of glowing coal etc. in a dying fire. [Old English]

ember days *n.pl.* days of fasting and prayer in the Christian Church, associated with ordinations. [Old English]

embezzle /ɪm'bez(ə)l/ *v.* (**-ling**) divert (money etc.) fraudulently to one's own use. □ **embezzlement** *n.* **embezzler** *n.* [Anglo-French]

embitter /ɪm'bɪtə(r)/ *v.* arouse bitter feelings in. □ **embitterment** *n.*

emblazon /ɪm'bleɪz(ə)n/ *v.* **1** portray or adorn conspicuously. **2** adorn (a heraldic shield). □ **emblazonment** *n.*

emblem /'embləm/ *n.* **1** symbol. **2** (foll. by *of*) type, embodiment (*the very emblem of courage*). **3** heraldic or representative device. □ **emblematic** /-'mætɪk/ *adj.* [Greek, = insertion]

embody /ɪm'bɒdɪ/ *v.* (**-ies, -ied**) **1** make (an idea etc.) actual or discernible. **2** (of a thing) be a tangible expression of. **3** include, comprise. □ **embodiment** *n.*

embolden /ɪm'bəʊld(ə)n/ *v.* make bold; encourage.

embolism /'embə,lɪz(ə)m/ *n.* obstruction of an artery by a clot, air-bubble, etc. [Latin from Greek]

embolus /'embələs/ *n.* (*pl.* **-li** /-,laɪ/) object causing an embolism.

emboss /ɪm'bɒs/ *v.* carve or decorate with a design in relief. □ **embossment** *n.* [related to BOSS[2]]

embouchure /'ɒmbʊ,ʃʊə(r)/ *n.* way of applying the mouth to the mouthpiece of a musical instrument. [French: related to EN-[1], *bouche* mouth]

embrace /ɪm'breɪs/ –*v.* (**-cing**) **1 a** hold closely in the arms. **b** (*absol.*, of two people) embrace each other. **2** clasp, enclose. **3** accept eagerly (an offer etc.). **4** adopt (a cause, idea, etc.). **5** include, comprise. **6** take in with the eye or mind. –*n.* act of embracing, clasp. □ **embraceable** *adj.* [Latin: related to BRACE]

embrasure /ɪm'breɪʒə(r)/ *n.* **1** bevelling of a wall at the sides of a window etc. **2** opening in a parapet for a gun etc. □ **embrasured** *adj.* [French *embraser* splay]

embrocation /,embrə'keɪʃ(ə)n/ *n.* liquid for rubbing on the body to relieve muscular pain. [Greek *embrokhē* lotion]

embroider /ɪm'brɔɪdə(r)/ *v.* **1** decorate (cloth etc.) with needlework. **2** embellish (a narrative). □ **embroiderer** *n.* [Anglo-French from Germanic]

embroidery *n.* (*pl.* **-ies**) **1** art of embroidering. **2** embroidered work. **3** inessential ornament. **4** fictitious additions (to a story etc.).

embroil /ɪm'brɔɪl/ *v.* (often foll. by *with*) involve (a person etc.) in a conflict or difficulties. □ **embroilment** *n.* [French *brouiller* mix]

embryo /'embrɪəʊ/ *n.* (*pl.* **-s**) **1 a** unborn or unhatched offspring. **b** human offspring in the first eight weeks from conception. **2** rudimentary plant in a seed. **3** thing in a rudimentary stage. **4** (*attrib.*) undeveloped, immature. □ **in embryo** undeveloped. □ **embryonic** /,embrɪ'ɒnɪk/ *adj.* [Greek *bruō* grow]

embryology /,embrɪ'ɒlədʒɪ/ *n.* the study of embryos.

EMCOF /'emkɒf/ *abbr.* = EUROPEAN MONETARY COOPERATION FUND.

emend /ɪ'mend/ *v.* edit (a text etc.) to make corrections. □ **emendation** /,iːmen'deɪʃ(ə)n/ *n.* [Latin *menda* fault]

■ **Usage** See note at *amend*.

emerald /ˈemər(ə)ld/ *n.* **1** bright-green gem. **2** colour of this. [Greek *smaragdos*]

Emerald Isle *n.* Ireland.

emerge /ɪˈmɜːdʒ/ *v.* (**-ging**) **1** come up or out into view. **2** (of facts etc.) become known, be revealed. **3** become recognized or prominent. **4** (of a question, difficulty, etc.) become apparent. □ **emergence** *n.* **emergent** *adj.* [Latin: related to MERGE]

emergency /ɪˈmɜːdʒənsɪ/ *n.* (*pl.* **-ies**) **1** sudden state of danger etc., requiring immediate action. **2 a** condition requiring immediate treatment. **b** patient with this. **3** (*attrib.*) for use in an emergency. [medieval Latin: related to EMERGE]

♦ **emerging market** *n.* financial or consumer market in a newly developing country or in a former communist country.

---

emeritus /ɪˈmerɪtəs/ *adj.* retired but retaining one's title as an honour (*emeritus professor*). [Latin *mereor* earn]

emery /ˈemərɪ/ *n.* coarse corundum for polishing metal etc. [Greek *smēris* polishing powder]

emery-board *n.* emery-coated nail-file.

emetic /ɪˈmetɪk/ *–adj.* that causes vomiting. *–n.* emetic medicine. [Greek *emeō* vomit]

EMF *abbr.* electromotive force.

EMI *abbr.* **1** Electric and Musical Industries. **2** *Computing* electromagnetic interference. **3** = EUROPEAN MONETARY INSTITUTE.

emigrant /ˈemɪgrənt/ *–n.* person who emigrates. *–adj.* emigrating.

emigrate /ˈemɪˌgreɪt/ *v.* (**-ting**) leave one's own country to settle in another. □ **emigration** /-ˈgreɪʃ(ə)n/ *n.* [Latin: related to MIGRATE]

émigré /ˈemɪˌgreɪ/ *n.* emigrant, esp. a political exile. [French]

eminence /ˈemɪnəns/ *n.* **1** distinction; recognized superiority. **2** piece of rising ground. **3** title used in addressing or referring to a cardinal (*Your Eminence*; *His Eminence*). [Latin: related to EMINENT]

éminence grise /ˌeɪmɪnɑ̃s ˈgriːz/ *n.* (*pl.* ***éminences grises*** pronunc. same) person who exercises power or influence without holding office. [French, = grey cardinal (originally of Richelieu's secretary)]

eminent /ˈemɪnənt/ *adj.* distinguished, notable, outstanding. [Latin *emineo* jut out]

emir /eˈmɪə(r)/ *n.* (also **amir** /əˈmɪə(r)/) title of various Muslim rulers. [French: related to AMIR]

emirate /ˈemɪrət/ *n.* rank, domain, or reign of an emir.

emissary /ˈemɪsərɪ/ *n.* (*pl.* **-ies**) person sent on a diplomatic mission. [Latin: related to EMIT]

emit /ɪˈmɪt/ *v.* (**-tt-**) give or send out (heat, light, a smell, sound, etc.); discharge. □ **emission** /-ʃ(ə)n/ *n.* [Latin *emitto emiss-*]

emollient /ɪˈmɒlɪənt/ *–adj.* that softens or soothes the skin, feelings, etc. *–n.* emollient substance. [Latin *mollis* soft]

emolument /ɪˈmɒljʊmənt/ *n.* fee from employment, salary. [Latin]

emote /ɪˈməʊt/ *v.* (**-ting**) show excessive emotion.

emotion /ɪˈməʊʃ(ə)n/ *n.* **1** strong instinctive feeling such as love or fear. **2** emotional intensity or sensibility (*spoke with emotion*). [French: related to MOTION]

emotional *adj.* **1** of or expressing emotions. **2** especially liable to emotion. **3** arousing emotion. □ **emotionalism** *n.* **emotionally** *adv.*

■ **Usage** See note at *emotive*.

emotive /ɪˈməʊtɪv/ *adj.* **1** arousing emotion. **2** of emotion. [Latin: related to MOTION]

■ **Usage** Although the senses of *emotive* and *emotional* overlap, *emotive* is more common in the sense 'arousing emotion', as in *an emotive issue*, and is not used at all in sense 2 of *emotional*.

empanel /ɪmˈpæn(ə)l/ *v.* (also **impanel**) (**-ll-**; *US* **-l-**) enter (a jury) on a panel.

empathize /ˈempəˌθaɪz/ *v.* (also **-ise**) (**-zing** or **-sing**) (usu. foll. by *with*) exercise empathy.

empathy /ˈempəθɪ/ *n.* ability to identify with a person or object. □ **empathetic** /-ˈθetɪk/ *adj.* [as PATHOS]

emperor /ˈempərə(r)/ *n.* sovereign of an empire. [Latin *impero* command]

emperor penguin *n.* largest known penguin.

emphasis /ˈemfəsɪs/ *n.* (*pl.* **emphases** /-ˌsiːz/) **1** importance or prominence attached to a thing (*emphasis on economy*). **2** stress laid on a word or syllable to make the meaning clear or show importance. **3** vigour or intensity of expression, feeling, etc. [Latin from Greek]

emphasize /ˈemfəˌsaɪz/ *v.* (also **-ise**) (**-zing** or **-sing**) put emphasis on, stress.

emphatic /ɪmˈfætɪk/ *adj.* **1** forcibly expressive. **2** of words: **a** bearing the stress. **b** used to give emphasis. □ **emphatically** *adv.*

emphysema /ˌemfɪˈsiːmə/ *n.* disease of the lungs causing breathlessness. [Greek *emphusaō* puff up]

empire /ˈempaɪə(r)/ *n.* **1** large group of states or countries under a single authority. **2** supreme dominion. **3** large commercial organization etc. owned or directed by one person. **4** (**the Empire**) *hist.* the British Empire. [Latin *imperium* dominion]

empire-building *n.* purposeful accumulation of territory, authority, etc.

empirical /ɪmˈpɪrɪk(ə)l/ *adj.* (also **empiric**) based on observation, experience, or experiment, not on theory. □ **empirically** *adv.* **empiricism** /-ˌsɪz(ə)m/ *n.* **empiricist** /-sɪst/ *n.* [Greek *empeiria* experience]

emplacement /ɪmˈpleɪsmənt/ *n.* **1** putting in position. **2** platform for guns. [French: related to PLACE]

employ /ɪmˈplɔɪ/ *–v.* **1** use the services of (a person) in return for payment. **2** use (a thing, time, energy, etc.) to good effect. **3** keep (a person) occupied. *–n.* (in phr. **in the employ of**) employed by. □ **employable** *adj.* **employer** *n.* [Latin *implicor* be involved]

employee /ˌemplɔɪˈiː, -ˈplɔɪiː/ *n.* person employed for wages.

♦ **employee buyout** *n.* acquisition of a controlling interest in the equity of a company by its employees, which may occur if the company is threatened with closure and the employees wish to secure their jobs. By obtaining financial backing, the employees acting as a group of individuals, or by means of a trust, can acquire a majority of the shares by offering existing shareholders more than their breakup value. An employee buyout has also taken place on privatization of a company.

♦ **employee participation** *n.* **1** encouragement of motivation in a workforce by giving shares in the company to employees. Employee shareholding (see EMPLOYEE SHARE-OWNERSHIP PLAN) is now an important factor in improving industrial relations. **2** appointment to a board of directors of a representative of the employees of a company, to enable the employees to take part in the direction of the company.

♦ **employee share-ownership plan** *n.* (also **ESOP**) method of giving employees shares in the business for which they work. Various ESOPs came into existence in the UK after their announcement in 1989; in 1990, in order to encourage their growth, company owners were given roll-over relief from capital-gains tax for sales of shares through ESOPs.

♦ **employers'-liability insurance** *n.* insurance policy covering an employer's legal liability to pay compensation to any employees suffering or contracting injury or disease during the course of their work. This type of insurance is compulsory by law for anyone who employs another person (other than members of their own family) under a contract of service. A certificate of insurance must be displayed at each place of work, confirming that employer's liability insurance is in force and giving details of the policy number and the insurer's name and address.

---

employment *n.* **1** employing or being employed. **2** person's trade or profession.

◆ **employment agency** *n.* organization that introduces suitable potential employees to employers, charging the employer a fee, usu. related to the initial salary, for the service. Employment agencies also provide temporary staff, in which they are the employers, the temporary staff member being charged out at an hourly rate. Employment agencies that specialize in finding suitable managers and executives for a firm, or finding suitable jobs for executives who want a change, are often known as **head-hunters**. Such agencies will often provide a short list of candidates in order to save their client's time in personnel selection. See also JOBCENTRE.

employment office *n.* (formerly **employment exchange**) state-run employment agency. See also JOBCENTRE.

◆ **employment protection** *n.* safeguarding of an employee's position with regard to employment. According to the Employment Protection (Consolidation) Act (1978), an employer must give an employee, within 13 weeks of the start of the employment, a contract stating the rate of pay, hours of work, holiday entitlement, details of sick pay and pension scheme (if any), and the length of notice to be given by either side to terminate the contract. See also REDUNDANCY 1; UNFAIR DISMISSAL.

emporium /em'pɔːrɪəm/ *n.* (*pl.* **-s** or **-ria**) **1** large shop or store. **2** centre of commerce, market. [Greek *emporos* merchant]

empower /ɪm'paʊə(r)/ *v.* give authority to.

empress /'emprɪs/ *n.* **1** wife or widow of an emperor. **2** woman emperor. [French: related to EMPEROR]

empty /'emptɪ/ *–adj.* (**-ier, -iest**) **1** containing nothing. **2** (of a house etc.) unoccupied or unfurnished. **3** (of a vehicle etc.) without passengers etc. **4 a** hollow, insincere (*empty threats*). **b** without purpose (*an empty existence*). **c** vacuous (*an empty head*). **5** *colloq.* hungry. *–v.* (**-ies, -ied**) **1** remove the contents of. **2** (often foll. by *into*) transfer (contents). **3** become empty. **4** (of a river) discharge itself. *–n.* (*pl.* **-ies**) *colloq.* empty bottle etc. □ **emptiness** *n.* [Old English]

empty-handed *adj.* (usu. *predic.*) **1** bringing or taking nothing. **2** having achieved nothing.

empty-headed *adj.* foolish; lacking sense.

empyrean /ˌempaɪ'riːən/ *–n.* the highest heaven, as the sphere of fire or abode of God. *–adj.* of the empyrean. □ **empyreal** *adj.* [Greek *pur* fire]

EMS *abbr.* **1** = EUROPEAN MONETARY SYSTEM. **2** *Computing* expanded memory support.

EMSA *abbr. Computing* expanded memory specification.

EMU /ˌiːem'juː, 'iːmjuː/ *abbr.* **1** economic and monetary union. **2** = EUROPEAN MONETARY UNION.

emu /'iːmjuː/ *n.* (*pl.* **-s**) large flightless Australian bird. [Portuguese]

emulate /'emjʊˌleɪt/ *v.* (**-ting**) **1** try to equal or excel. **2** imitate. □ **emulative** /-lətɪv/ *adj.* **emulator** *n.* [Latin *aemulus* rival]

emulation /ˌemjʊ'leɪʃ(ə)n/ *n.* **1** emulating. **2** imitation of all or part of one computer system by another computer system such that the imitating system executes the same programs, accepting the identical data and producing the identical results (but not necessarily in the same way), as the system imitated. A particular emulation could be used as a replacement for all or part of the system being emulated and could also be an improved version. For example, a new computer may emulate an obsolete one so that programs written for the old one will run without modification. Cf. SIMULATION 2.

emulsify /ɪ'mʌlsɪˌfaɪ/ *v.* (**-ies, -ied**) convert into an emulsion. □ **emulsification** /-fɪ'keɪʃ(ə)n/ *n.* **emulsifier** *n.*

emulsion /ɪ'mʌlʃ(ə)n/ *n.* **1** fine dispersion of one liquid in another, esp. as paint, medicine, etc. **2** mixture of a silver compound in gelatin etc. for coating photographic plate or film. [Latin *mulgeo* milk]

emulsion paint *n.* water-thinned paint.

EMV *abbr.* = EXPECTED MONETARY VALUE.

EN *postcode* Enfield.

en *n. Printing* unit of measurement equal to half an em. [name of the letter *N*]

en-[1] *prefix* (also **em-** before *b, p*) forming verbs, = IN-[2]: **1** from nouns, meaning 'put into or on' (*engulf*; *entrust*; *embed*). **2** from nouns or adjectives, meaning 'bring into the condition of' (*enslave*); often with the suffix *-en* (*enlighten*). **3** from verbs: **a** in the sense 'in, into, on' (*enfold*). **b** as an intensive (*entangle*). [French *en-*, Latin *in-*]

en-[2] *prefix* (also **em-** before *b, p*) in, inside (*energy*; *enthusiasm*). [Greek]

-en *suffix* forming verbs: **1** from adjectives, usu. meaning 'make or become so or more so' (*deepen*; *moisten*). **2** from nouns (*happen*; *strengthen*). [Old English]

enable /ɪ'neɪb(ə)l/ *v.* (**-ling**) **1** (foll. by *to* + infin.) give (a person etc.) the means or authority. **2** make possible. **3** esp. *Computing* make (a device) operational; switch on.

enact /ɪ'nækt/ *v.* **1 a** ordain, decree. **b** make (a bill etc.) law. **2** play (a part on stage or in life). □ **enactive** *adj.*

enactment *n.* **1** law enacted. **2** process of enacting.

enamel /ɪ'næm(ə)l/ *–n.* **1** glasslike opaque ornamental or preservative coating on metal etc. **2 a** smooth hard coating. **b** a kind of hard gloss paint. **c** cosmetic simulating this, esp. nail varnish. **3** hard coating of a tooth. **4** painting done in enamel. *–v.* (**-ll-**; *US* **-l-**) inlay, coat, or portray with enamel. [Anglo-French from Germanic]

enamour /ɪ'næmə(r)/ *v.* (*US* **enamor**) (usu. in *passive*; foll. by *of*) inspire with love or delight. [French *amour* love]

en bloc /ɑ̃ 'blɒk/ *adv.* in a block; all at the same time. [French]

encamp /ɪn'kæmp/ *v.* settle in a (esp. military) camp. □ **encampment** *n.*

encapsulate /ɪn'kæpsjʊˌleɪt/ *v.* (**-ting**) **1** enclose in or as in a capsule. **2** express briefly, summarize. □ **encapsulation** /-'leɪʃ(ə)n/ *n.* [related to CAPSULE]

encase /ɪn'keɪs/ *v.* (**-sing**) enclose in or as in a case. □ **encasement** *n.*

encaustic /ɪn'kɔːstɪk/ *–adj.* (of painting etc.) using pigments mixed with hot wax, which are burned in as an inlay. *–n.* **1** art of encaustic painting. **2** product of this. [Greek: related to CAUSTIC]

-ence *suffix* forming nouns expressing: **1** a quality or state or an instance of this (*patience*; *an impertinence*). **2** an action (*reference*). [French *-ence*, Latin *-erie*]

encephalitis /enˌkefə'laɪtɪs/ *n.* inflammation of the brain. [Greek *egkephalos* brain]

encephalogram /en'kefələʊˌgræm/ *n.* = ELECTROENCEPHALOGRAM.

encephalograph /en'kefələʊˌgrɑːf/ *n.* = ELECTROENCEPHALOGRAPH.

enchant /ɪn'tʃɑːnt/ *v.* **1** charm, delight. **2** bewitch. □ **enchantedly** *adv.* **enchanting** *adj.* **enchantingly** *adv.* **enchantment** *n.*

enchanter *n.* (*fem.* **enchantress**) person who enchants, esp. by using magic.

encircle /ɪn'sɜːk(ə)l/ *v.* (**-ling**) **1** surround. **2** form a circle round. □ **encirclement** *n.*

enclave /'enkleɪv/ *n.* territory of one state surrounded by that of another. [Latin *clavis* key]

enclose /ɪn'kləʊz/ *v.* (**-sing**) **1 a** surround with a wall, fence, etc. **b** shut in. **2** put in a receptacle (esp. in an envelope with a letter). **3** (usu. as **enclosed** *adj.*) seclude (a religious community) from the outside world. [Latin: related to INCLUDE]

enclosure /ɪn'kləʊʒə(r)/ *n.* **1** act of enclosing. **2** enclosed space or area, esp. at a sporting event. **3** thing enclosed with a letter. [French: related to ENCLOSE]

encode /ɪn'kəʊd/ *v.* (**-ding**) put into code. □ **encoder** *n.*

encomium /ɪn'kəʊmɪəm/ *n.* (*pl.* **-s**) formal or high-flown praise. [Greek *kōmos* revelry]

encompass /ɪn'kʌmpəs/ *v.* **1** contain; include. **2** surround.

encore /ˈɒŋkɔː(r)/ –*n.* **1** audience's demand for the repetition of an item, or for a further item. **2** such an item. –*v.* (**-ring**) **1** call for the repetition of (an item). **2** call back (a performer) for this. –*int.* /also -ˈkɔː(r)/ again, once more. [French, = once again]

encounter /ɪnˈkaʊntə(r)/ –*v.* **1** meet unexpectedly. **2** meet as an adversary. –*n.* meeting by chance or in conflict. [Latin *contra* against]

encourage /ɪnˈkʌrɪdʒ/ *v.* (**-ging**) **1** give courage or confidence to. **2** urge. **3** promote. □ **encouragement** *n.* [French: related to EN-[1]]

encroach /ɪnˈkrəʊtʃ/ *v.* **1** (foll. by *on*, *upon*) intrude on another's territory etc. **2** advance gradually beyond due limits. □ **encroachment** *n.* [French *croc* CROOK]

encrust /ɪnˈkrʌst/ *v.* **1** cover with or form a crust. **2** coat with a hard casing or deposit, sometimes for decoration. [French: related to EN-[1]]

encrypt /ɪnˈkrɪpt/ *v.* **1** convert (data) into code, esp. to prevent unauthorized access. **2** conceal by this means. See CRYPTOGRAPHY. □ **encryption** /-ˈkrɪpʃ(ə)n/ *n.* [from EN-[1], Greek *kruptos* hidden]

encumber /ɪnˈkʌmbə(r)/ *v.* **1** be a burden to. **2** hamper. [French from Romanic]

encumbrance /ɪnˈkʌmbrəns/ *n.* **1** burden. **2** impediment. **3** *Law* charge or liability, e.g. a mortgage or registered judgement, to which land is subject.

-ency *suffix* forming nouns denoting quality or state (*efficiency*; *fluency*; *presidency*). [Latin *-entia*]

encyclical /ɪnˈsɪklɪk(ə)l/ –*adj.* for wide circulation. –*n.* papal encyclical letter. [Greek: related to CYCLE]

encyclopedia /ɪnˌsaɪkləˈpiːdɪə/ *n.* (also **-paedia**) book, often in a number of volumes, giving information on many subjects, or on many aspects of one subject. [Greek *egkuklios* all-round, *paideia* education]

encyclopedic *adj.* (also **-paedic**) (of knowledge or information) comprehensive.

end –*n.* **1 a** extreme limit. **b** extremity (*to the ends of the earth*). **2** extreme part or surface of a thing (*strip of wood with a nail in one end*). **3 a** finish (*no end to his misery*). **b** latter part. **c** death, destruction (*met an untimely end*). **d** result. **4** goal (*will do anything to achieve his ends*). **5** remnant (*cigarette-end*). **6** (prec. by *the*) *colloq.* the limit of endurability. **7** half of a sports pitch etc. occupied by one team or player. **8** part with which a person is concerned (*no problem at my end*). –*v.* **1** bring or come to an end, finish. **2** (foll. by *in*) result. □ **end it all** (or **end it**) *colloq.* commit suicide. **end on** with the end facing one, or adjoining the end of the next object. **end to end** with the end of one adjoining the end of the next in a series. **end up** reach a specified state or action eventually (*ended up a drunkard*; *ended up making a fortune*). **in the end** finally. **keep one's end up** do one's part despite difficulties. **make ends meet** live within one's income. **no end** *colloq.* to a great extent. **no end of** *colloq.* much or many of. **on end 1** upright (*hair stood on end*). **2** continuously (*for three weeks on end*). **put an end to** stop, abolish, destroy. [Old English]

endanger /ɪnˈdeɪndʒə(r)/ *v.* place in danger.

endangered species *n.* species in danger of extinction.

endear /ɪnˈdɪə(r)/ *v.* (usu. foll. by *to*) make dear.

endearment *n.* **1** an expression of affection. **2** liking, affection.

endeavour /ɪnˈdevə(r)/ (*US* **endeavor**) –*v.* (foll. by *to* + infin.) try earnestly. –*n.* earnest attempt. [from EN-[1], French *devoir* owe]

endemic /enˈdemɪk/ *adj.* (often foll. by *to*) regularly or only found among a particular people or in a particular region. □ **endemically** *adv.* [Greek *en-* in, *dēmos* the people]

Enderby Land /ˈendəbɪ/ part of Antarctica, claimed by Australia.

ending *n.* **1** end or final part, esp. of a story. **2** inflected final part of a word.

endive /ˈendaɪv/ *n.* curly-leaved plant used in salads. [Greek *entubon*]

endless *adj.* **1** infinite; without end. **2** continual (*endless complaints*). **3** *colloq.* innumerable. **4** (of a belt, chain, etc.) having the ends joined for continuous action over wheels etc. □ **endlessly** *adv.* [Old English: related to END]

endmost *adj.* nearest the end.

endo- *comb. form* internal. [Greek *endon* within]

endocrine /ˈendəʊˌkraɪn/ *adj.* (of a gland) secreting directly into the blood. [Greek *krinō* sift]

endogenous /enˈdɒdʒɪnəs/ *adj.* growing or originating from within.

endometrium /ˌendəʊˈmiːtrɪəm/ *n.* membrane lining the womb. [Greek *mētra* womb]

endomorph /ˈendəʊˌmɔːf/ *n.* person with a soft round body. [Greek *morphē* form]

endorse /ɪnˈdɔːs/ *v.* (also **indorse**) (**-sing**) **1** approve. **2** sign or write on (a document), esp. sign the back of (a cheque). **3** enter details of a conviction for an offence on (a driving-licence). □ **endorsee** /-dɔːˈsiː/ *n.* [Latin *dorsum* back]

♦ **endorsement** (also **indorsement**) *n.* **1** approval; support. **2** signature on the back of a bill of exchange or cheque, making it payable to the person who signed it. A bill can have any number of endorsements, the presumption being that the endorsements were made in the order in which they appear, the last named being the holder to receive payment. A bill with a **blank endorsement**, i.e. one in which no endorsee is named, is payable to the bearer. In the case of a **restrictive endorsement** of the form 'Pay X only', it ceases to be a negotiable instrument. A **special endorsement**, when the endorsee is specified, becomes payable **to order**, which is short for 'in obedience to the order of'. **3** signature required on a document to make it valid in law. **4** amendment to an insurance policy or cover note, recording a change in the conditions of the insurance. **5** procedure of endorsing a driving licence.

---

endoscope /ˈendəʊˌskəʊp/ *n.* instrument for viewing internal parts of the body.

endow /ɪnˈdaʊ/ *v.* **1** bequeath or give a permanent income to (a person, institution, etc.). **2** (esp. as **endowed** *adj.*) provide with talent, ability, etc. [Anglo-French: related to DOWER]

endowment *n.* **1** endowing. **2** endowed income.

♦ **endowment assurance** *n.* form of assurance that pays a specified amount of money on an agreed date or on the death of the life assured, whichever is the earlier. As endowment assurance policies guarantee to make a payment (either to the policyholder or his or her dependants) they offer both life cover and a reasonable investment. A with-profits policy will also provide bonuses in addition to the sum assured. These policies are often used in the repayment of a personal mortgage or as a form of saving, although they lost their tax relief on premiums in the Finance Act (1984).

---

endowment mortgage *n.* mortgage linked to endowment assurance. See MORTGAGE *n.* 2.

endpaper *n.* either of the blank leaves of paper at the beginning and end of a book.

end-product *n.* final product of manufacture etc.

endue /ɪnˈdjuː/ *v.* (also **indue**) (**-dues**, **-dued**, **-duing**) (foll. by *with*) provide (a person) with (qualities etc.). [Latin *induo* put on clothes]

endurance /ɪnˈdjʊərəns/ *n.* **1** power of enduring. **2** ability to withstand prolonged strain. [French: related to ENDURE]

endure /ɪnˈdjʊə(r)/ *v.* (**-ring**) **1** undergo (a difficulty etc.). **2** tolerate. **3** last. □ **endurable** *adj.* [Latin *durus* hard]

endways *adv.* (also **endwise**) **1** with end uppermost or foremost. **2** end to end.

enema /ˈenɪmə/ *n.* **1** introduction of fluid etc. into the rectum, esp. to flush out its contents. **2** fluid etc. used for this. [Greek *hiēmi* send]

enemy /ˈenəmɪ/ *n.* (*pl.* **-ies**) **1** person actively hostile to another. **2 a** (often *attrib.*) hostile nation or army. **b** member of this. **3** adversary or opponent (*enemy of progress*). [Latin: related to IN-[2], *amicus* friend]

energetic /ˌenəˈdʒetɪk/ *adj.* full of energy, vigorous. □ **energetically** *adv.* [Greek: related to ENERGY]

energize /ˈenəˌdʒaɪz/ *v.* (also **-ise**) (**-zing** or **-sing**) **1** give energy to. **2** provide (a device) with energy for operation.

energy /ˈenədʒɪ/ *n.* (*pl.* **-ies**) **1** capacity for activity, force, vigour. **2** capacity of matter or radiation to do work. [Greek *ergon* work]

enervate /ˈenəˌveɪt/ *v.* (**-ting**) deprive of vigour or vitality. □ **enervation** /-ˈveɪʃ(ə)n/ *n.* [Latin: related to NERVE]

en famille /ˌɑ̃ fæˈmiː/ *adv.* in or with one's family. [French, = in family]

enfant terrible /ˌɑ̃fɑ̃ teˈriːbl/ *n.* (*pl.* ***enfants terribles*** pronunc. same) indiscreet or unruly person. [French, = terrible child]

enfeeble /ɪnˈfiːb(ə)l/ *v.* (**-ling**) make feeble. □ **enfeeblement** *n.*

enfilade /ˌenfɪˈleɪd/ –*n.* gunfire directed along a line from end to end. –*v.* (**-ding**) direct an enfilade at. [French: related to FILE[1]]

enfold /ɪnˈfəʊld/ *v.* **1** (usu. foll. by *in*, *with*) wrap; envelop. **2** clasp, embrace.

enforce /ɪnˈfɔːs/ *v.* (**-cing**) **1** compel observance of (a law etc.). **2** (foll. by *on*) impose (an action or one's will, etc.) on. □ **enforceable** *adj.* **enforcement** *n.* **enforcer** *n.* [Latin: related to FORCE[1]]

enfranchise /ɪnˈfræntʃaɪz/ *v.* (**-sing**) **1** give (a person) the right to vote. **2** give (a town) municipal rights, esp. representation in parliament. **3** *hist.* free (a slave etc.). □ **enfranchisement** /-ɪzmənt/ *n.* [French: related to FRANK]

Eng. *abbr.* **1** England. **2** English.

engage /ɪnˈgeɪdʒ/ *v.* (**-ging**) **1** employ or hire (a person). **2 a** (usu. in *passive*) occupy (*are you engaged tomorrow?*). **b** hold fast (a person's attention). **3** (usu. in *passive*) bind by a promise, esp. of marriage. **4** arrange beforehand to occupy (a room, seat, etc.). **5 a** interlock (parts of a gear etc.). **b** (of a gear etc.) become interlocked. **6 a** come into battle with. **b** bring (troops) into battle with. **c** come into battle with (an enemy etc.). **7** take part (*engage in politics*). **8** (foll. by *that* + clause or *to* + infin.) undertake. [French: related to GAGE[1]]

engaged *adj.* **1** pledged to marry. **2** (of a person) occupied, busy. **3** (of a telephone line, toilet, etc.) in use.

engagement *n.* **1** engaging or being engaged. **2** appointment with another person. **3** betrothal. **4** battle.

engaging *adj.* attractive, charming. □ **engagingly** *adv.*

♦ **Engel curve** /ˈeŋg(ə)l/ *n.* curve relating the expenditure on a good as income rises. **Engel's law** states that the proportion of expenditure on food will fall as income rises, i.e. food is a necessary good. Engel curves are useful for separating the effect of income on demand from the effects of changes in relative prices. [*Engel*, name of statistician]

♦ **Engel's law** see ENGEL CURVE.

---

engender /ɪnˈdʒendə(r)/ *v.* give rise to; produce (a feeling etc.). [related to GENUS]

engine /ˈendʒɪn/ *n.* **1** mechanical contrivance of parts working together, esp. as a source of power (*steam engine*). **2 a** railway locomotive. **b** = FIRE-ENGINE. [Latin *ingenium* device]

engineer /ˌendʒɪˈnɪə(r)/ –*n.* **1** person skilled in a branch of engineering. **2** person who makes or is in charge of engines etc. (*ship's engineer*). **3** person who designs and constructs military works; soldier so trained. **4** contriver. –*v.* **1** contrive, bring about. **2** act as an engineer. **3** construct or manage as an engineer. [medieval Latin: related to ENGINE]

engineering *n.* application of science to the design, building, and use of machines etc. (*civil engineering*).

England /ˈɪŋglənd/ largest division of the United Kingdom, consisting of the area of Great Britain S of Scotland and E of Wales; pop. (1991) 47 055 200; capital, London. England emerged as a distinct political entity in the 9th century before being conquered by William, Duke of Normandy, in 1066. The neighbouring principality of Wales was gradually conquered during the Middle Ages and politically incorporated in the 16th century. During the period of Tudor rule (1485–1603) England emerged as a Protestant state with a strong stable monarchy and as a naval power. Scotland and England have been ruled by one monarch from 1603, and the two crowns were formally united in 1707. (For subsequent history and economy, see UNITED KINGDOM.)

English /ˈɪŋglɪʃ/ –*adj.* of England or its people or language. –*n.* **1** language of England, now used in the UK, US, and most Commonwealth countries. **2** (prec. by *the*; treated as *pl.*) the people of England. [Old English]

Englishman *n.* (*fem.* **Englishwoman**) person who is English by birth or descent.

engorged /ɪnˈgɔːdʒd/ *adj.* **1** crammed full. **2** congested with blood. [French: related to EN-[1], GORGE]

engraft /ɪnˈgrɑːft/ *v.* (also **ingraft**) **1** *Bot.* (usu. foll. by *into*, *on*) graft. **2** implant. **3** (usu. foll. by *into*) incorporate.

engrave /ɪnˈgreɪv/ *v.* (**-ving**) **1** (often foll. by *on*) carve (a text or design) on a hard surface. **2** inscribe (a surface) thus. **3** (often foll. by *on*) impress deeply (on a person's memory). □ **engraver** *n.* [from GRAVE[2]]

engraving *n.* print made from an engraved plate.

engross /ɪnˈgrəʊs/ *v.* **1** absorb the attention of; occupy fully. **2** write out in larger letters or in legal form. □ **engrossment** *n.* [Anglo-French: related to EN-[1]]

engulf /ɪnˈgʌlf/ *v.* flow over and swamp; overwhelm. □ **engulfment** *n.*

enhance /ɪnˈhɑːns/ *v.* (**-cing**) intensify (qualities, powers, etc.); improve (something already good). □ **enhancement** *n.* [Anglo-French from Latin *altus* high]

enigma /ɪˈnɪgmə/ *n.* **1** puzzling thing or person. **2** riddle or paradox. □ **enigmatic** /ˌenɪgˈmætɪk/ *adj.* **enigmatically** /ˌenɪgˈmætɪkəlɪ/ *adv.* [Latin from Greek]

enjoin /ɪnˈdʒɔɪn/ *v.* **1** command or order. **2** (often foll. by *on*) impose (an action). **3** (usu. foll. by *from*) *Law* prohibit by injunction (from doing a thing). [Latin *injungo* attach]

enjoy /ɪnˈdʒɔɪ/ *v.* **1** take pleasure in. **2** have the use or benefit of. **3** experience (*enjoy good health*). □ **enjoy oneself** experience pleasure. □ **enjoyment** *n.* [French]

enjoyable *adj.* pleasant. □ **enjoyably** *adv.*

enkephalin /enˈkefəlɪn/ *n.* either of two morphine-like peptides in the brain thought to control levels of pain. [Greek *egkephalos* brain]

enkindle /ɪnˈkɪnd(ə)l/ *v.* (**-ling**) cause to flare up, arouse.

enlarge /ɪnˈlɑːdʒ/ *v.* (**-ging**) **1** make or become larger or wider. **2** (often foll. by *on*, *upon*) describe in greater detail. **3** reproduce a photograph on a larger scale. □ **enlargement** *n.* [French: related to LARGE]

enlarger *n.* apparatus for enlarging photographs.

enlighten /ɪnˈlaɪt(ə)n/ *v.* **1** (often foll. by *on*) inform (about a subject). **2** (as **enlightened** *adj.*) progressive.

enlightenment *n.* **1** enlightening or being enlightened. **2** (**the Enlightenment**) 18th-century philosophy of reason and individualism.

enlist /ɪnˈlɪst/ *v.* **1** enrol in the armed services. **2** secure as a means of help or support. □ **enlistment** *n.*

enliven /ɪnˈlaɪv(ə)n/ *v.* make lively or cheerful; brighten (a picture etc.); inspirit. □ **enlivenment** *n.*

en masse /ɑ̃ ˈmæs/ *adv.* all together. [French]

enmesh /ɪnˈmeʃ/ *v.* entangle in or as in a net.

enmity /ˈenmɪtɪ/ *n.* (*pl.* **-ies**) **1** state of being an enemy. **2** hostility. [Romanic: related to ENEMY]

Enniskillen /ˌenɪsˈkɪlɪn/ county town of Fermanagh, Northern Ireland; industries include engineering and food processing; pop. (1989) 10 500.

ennoble /ɪ'nəʊb(ə)l/ *v.* (**-ling**) **1** make noble. **2** make (a person) a noble. □ **ennoblement** *n.* [French: related to EN-[1]]

ennui /ɒ'nwiː/ *n.* mental weariness from idleness or lack of interest; boredom. [French: related to ANNOY]

enormity /ɪ'nɔːmɪtɪ/ *n.* (*pl.* **-ies**) **1** monstrous wickedness; monstrous crime. **2** serious error. **3** great size. [Latin *enormitas*]

■ **Usage** Sense 3 is commonly found, but is regarded as incorrect by some people.

enormous /ɪ'nɔːməs/ *adj.* extremely large. □ **enormously** *adv.* [Latin *enormis*: related to NORM]

enough /ɪ'nʌf/ *–adj.* as much or as many as required (*enough apples*). *–n.* sufficient amount or quantity (*we have enough*). *–adv.* **1** adequately (*warm enough*). **2** fairly (*sings well enough*). **3** quite (*you know well enough what I mean*). □ **have had enough of** want no more of; be satiated with or tired of. **sure enough** as expected. [Old English]

en passant /ˌɑ̃ pæ'sɑ̃/ *adv.* in passing; casually (*mentioned it en passant*). [French, = in passing]

enprint /'enprɪnt/ *n.* standard-sized photograph. [*en*larged *print*]

enquire /ɪn'kwaɪə(r)/ *v.* (**-ring**) **1** seek information; ask; ask a question. **2** = INQUIRE. **3** (foll. by *after, for*) ask about (a person, a person's health, etc.). □ **enquirer** *n.* [Latin *quaero quaesit-* seek]

enquiry *n.* (*pl.* **-ies**) **1** act of asking or seeking information. **2** = INQUIRY.

enrage /ɪn'reɪdʒ/ *v.* (**-ging**) make furious. [French: related to EN-[1]]

enrapture /ɪn'ræptʃə(r)/ *v.* (**-ring**) delight intensely.

enrich /ɪn'rɪtʃ/ *v.* **1** make rich or richer. **2** make more nutritive. **3** increase the strength, wealth, value, or contents of. □ **enrichment** *n.* [French: related to EN-[1]]

enrol /ɪn'rəʊl/ *v.* (*US* **enroll**) (**-ll-**) **1** enlist. **2 a** write the name of (a person) on a list. **b** incorporate as a member. **c** enrol oneself, esp. for a course of study. □ **enrolment** *n.* [French: related to EN-[1]]

en route /ɑ̃ 'ruːt/ *adv.* on the way. [French]

Enschede /'enskəˌdeɪ/ city in the Netherlands, in the province of Overijssel; pop. (est. 1995) 147 924. Since its founding (1325) it has been the focal point of the Dutch textile industry.

ensconce /ɪn'skɒns/ *v.* (**-cing**) (usu. *refl.* or in *passive*) establish or settle comfortably. [from *sconce* small fortification]

ensemble /ɒn'sɒmb(ə)l/ *n.* **1 a** thing viewed as the sum of its parts. **b** general effect of this. **2** set of clothes worn together. **3** group of performers working together. **4** *Mus.* concerted passage for an ensemble. [Latin *simul* at same time]

enshrine /ɪn'ʃraɪn/ *v.* (**-ning**) **1** enclose in a shrine. **2** protect, make inviolable. □ **enshrinement** *n.*

enshroud /ɪn'ʃraʊd/ *v. literary* **1** cover with or as with shroud. **2** obscure.

ensign /'ensaɪn, -s(ə)n/ *n.* **1** banner or flag, esp. the military or naval flag of a nation. **2** standard-bearer. **3 a** *hist.* lowest commissioned infantry officer. **b** *US* lowest commissioned naval officer. [French: related to INSIGNIA]

ensilage /'ensɪlɪdʒ/ *–n.* = SILAGE. *–v.* (**-ging**) preserve (fodder) by ensilage. [French: related to SILO]

enslave /ɪn'sleɪv/ *v.* (**-ving**) make (a person) a slave. □ **enslavement** *n.*

ensnare /ɪn'sneə(r)/ *v.* (**-ring**) catch in or as in a snare. □ **ensnarement** *n.*

ensue /ɪn'sjuː/ *v.* (**-sues, -sued, -suing**) happen later or as a result. [Latin *sequor* follow]

en suite /ɑ̃ 'swiːt/ *–adv.* forming a single unit (*bedroom with bathroom en suite*). *–adj.* **1** forming a single unit (*en suite bathroom*). **2** with a bathroom attached (*seven en suite bedrooms*). [French, = in sequence]

ensure /ɪn'ʃʊə(r)/ *v.* (**-ring**) **1** make certain. **2** (usu. foll. by *against*) make safe (*ensure against risks*). □ **ensurer** *n.* [Anglo-French: related to ASSURE]

ENT *abbr.* ear, nose, and throat.

-ent *suffix* **1** forming adjectives denoting attribution of an action (*consequent*) or state (*existent*). **2** forming agent nouns (*president*). [Latin *-ent-* present participial stem of verbs]

entablature /ɪn'tæblətʃə(r)/ *n.* upper part of a classical building supported by columns including an architrave, frieze, and cornice. [Italian: related to TABLE]

entail /ɪn'teɪl/ *–v.* **1** necessitate or involve unavoidably (*entails much effort*). **2** *Law* bequeath (an estate) to a specified line of beneficiaries so that it cannot be sold or given away. *–n.* *Law* **1** entailed estate. **2** succession to such an estate. [related to TAIL[2]]

entangle /ɪn'tæŋg(ə)l/ *v.* (**-ling**) **1** catch or hold fast in a snare, tangle, etc. **2** involve in difficulties. **3** complicate. □ **entanglement** *n.*

Entebbe /en'tebɪ/ town in Uganda, on the N shore of Lake Victoria, former administrative centre of the country and site of Uganda's international airport; pop. (1991) 41 638.

entente /ɒn'tɒnt/ *n.* friendly understanding between states. [French]

entente cordiale *n.* entente, esp. between Britain and France from 1904.

enter *v.* **1** go or come in or into. **2** come on stage (also as a direction: *enter Macbeth*). **3** penetrate (*bullet entered his arm*). **4** write (name, details, etc.) in a list, book, etc. **5** register, record the name of as a competitor (*entered for the long jump*). **6 a** become a member of (a society or profession). **b** enrol in a school etc. **7** make known; present for consideration (*enter a protest*). **8** record formally (before a court of law etc.). **9** (foll. by *into*) **a** engage in (conversation etc.). **b** subscribe to; bind oneself by (an agreement, contract, etc.). **c** form part of (a calculation, plan, etc.). **d** sympathize with (feelings). **10** (foll. by *on, upon*) **a** begin; begin to deal with. **b** assume the functions of (an office) or possession of (property). [Latin *intra* within]

enteric /en'terɪk/ *adj.* of the intestines. □ **enteritis** /ˌentə'raɪtɪs/ *n.* [Greek *enteron* intestine]

enter key *n.* = RETURN KEY.

enterprise /'entəˌpraɪz/ *n.* **1** undertaking, esp. a challenging one. **2** readiness to engage in such undertakings. **3** business firm or venture. [Latin *prehendo* grasp]

♦ **Enterprise Investment Scheme** *n.* investment scheme in the UK that in 1994 replaced the Business Expansion Scheme. It provides tax relief on investments in certain small companies.

♦ **enterprise zone** *n.* area, designated as such by the government, in which its aim is to restore private-sector activity by removing certain tax burdens and by relaxing certain statutory controls. Benefits, which are available for a ten-year period, include exemption from rates on industrial and commercial property, 100% allowances for corporation- and income-tax purposes for capital expenditure on industrial and commercial buildings, exemption from industrial training levies, and a simplified planning regime.

---

enterprising *adj.* showing enterprise; resourceful, energetic. □ **enterprisingly** *adv.*

entertain /ˌentə'teɪn/ *v.* **1** occupy agreeably. **2 a** receive as a guest. **b** receive guests. **3** cherish, consider (an idea etc.). [Latin *teneo* hold]

entertainer *n.* person who entertains, esp. professionally.

entertaining *adj.* amusing, diverting. □ **entertainingly** *adv.*

entertainment *n.* **1** entertaining or being entertained. **2** thing that entertains; performance.

enthral /ɪn'θrɔːl/ *v.* (*US* **enthrall**) (**-ll-**) captivate, please greatly. □ **enthralment** *n.* [from EN-[1], THRALL]

enthrone /ɪn'θrəʊn/ *v.* (**-ning**) place on a throne, esp. ceremonially. □ **enthronement** *n.*

enthuse /ɪn'θjuːz/ *v.* (**-sing**) *colloq.* be or make enthusiastic.

enthusiasm /ɪn'θju:zɪ,æz(ə)m/ *n.* **1** (often foll. by *for, about*) strong interest or admiration, great eagerness. **2** object of enthusiasm. [Greek *entheos* inspired by a god]

enthusiast *n.* person full of enthusiasm. [Church Latin: related to ENTHUSIASM]

enthusiastic /ɪn,θju:zɪ'æstɪk/ *adj.* having enthusiasm. □ **enthusiastically** *adv.*

entice /ɪn'taɪs/ *v.* (**-cing**) attract by the offer of pleasure or reward. □ **enticement** *n.* **enticing** *adj.* **enticingly** *adv.* [French *enticier* probably from Romanic]

entire /ɪn'taɪə(r)/ *adj.* **1** whole, complete. **2** unbroken. **3** unqualified, absolute. **4** in one piece; continuous. [Latin: related to INTEGER]

entirely *adv.* **1** wholly. **2** solely.

entirety /ɪn'taɪərətɪ/ *n.* (*pl.* **-ies**) **1** completeness. **2** (usu. foll. by *of*) sum total. □ **in its entirety** in its complete form.

entitle /ɪn'taɪt(ə)l/ *v.* (**-ling**) **1** (usu. foll. by *to*) give (a person) a just claim or right. **2** give a title to. □ **entitlement** *n.* [Latin: related to TITLE]

entity /'entɪtɪ/ *n.* (*pl.* **-ies**) **1** thing with distinct existence. **2** thing's existence in itself. [Latin *ens ent-* being]

entomb /ɪn'tu:m/ *v.* **1** place in a tomb. **2** serve as a tomb for. □ **entombment** *n.* [French: related to TOMB]

entomology /,entə'mɒlədʒɪ/ *n.* the study of insects. □ **entomological** /-mə'lɒdʒɪk(ə)l/ *adj.* **entomologist** *n.* [Greek *entomon* insect]

entourage /'ɒntʊə,rɑ:ʒ/ *n.* people attending an important person. [French]

entr'acte /'ɒntrækt/ *n.* **1** interval between acts of a play. **2** music or dance performed during this. [French]

entrails /'entreɪlz/ *n.pl.* **1** bowels, intestines. **2** innermost parts of a thing. [Latin *inter* among]

entrance[1] /'entrəns/ *n.* **1** place for entering. **2** going or coming in. **3** right of admission. **4** coming of an actor on stage. **5** (in full **entrance fee**) admission fee. [French: related to ENTER]

entrance[2] /ɪn'trɑ:ns/ *v.* (**-cing**) **1** enchant, delight. **2** put into a trance. □ **entrancement** *n.* **entrancing** *adj.* **entrancingly** *adv.*

entrant /'entrənt/ *n.* person who enters (an examination, profession, etc.). [French: related to ENTER]

entrap /ɪn'træp/ *v.* (**-pp-**) **1** catch in or as in a trap. **2** beguile. □ **entrapment** *n.* [related to EN-[1]]

entreat /ɪn'tri:t/ *v.* ask earnestly, beg. [related to EN-[1]]

entreaty *n.* (*pl.* **-ies**) earnest request.

entrecôte /'ɒntrə,kəʊt/ *n.* boned steak off the sirloin. [French, = between-rib]

entrée /'ɒntreɪ/ *n.* **1** dish served between the fish and meat courses. **2** *US* main dish. **3** right of admission. [French]

entrench /ɪn'trentʃ/ *v.* **1 a** establish firmly (in a position, office, etc.). **b** (as **entrenched** *adj.*) (of an attitude etc.) not easily modified. **2** surround with a trench as a fortification. □ **entrenchment** *n.*

entrepôt /'ɒntrə,pəʊ/ *n.* warehouse for goods in transit. [French]

♦ **entrepôt trade** *n.* trade that passes through a port, district, airport, etc. before being shipped on to some other country. The entrepôt trade may make use of such a port because it is conveniently situated on shipping lanes and has the warehouses and customs facilities required for re-export or because that port is the centre of the particular trade concerned and facilities are available there for sampling, testing, auctioning, breaking bulk, etc. Rotterdam, Singapore, and Hong Kong are centres of the entrepôt trade.

♦ **entrepreneur** /,ɒntrəprə'nɜ:(r)/ *n.* **1** person who undertakes to supply a good or service to the market for personal profit, usu. investing personal capital in the business and taking on the risks associated with the investment. It has been said that the initiative of entrepreneurs creates a society's wealth and that governments should therefore establish conditions in which they will thrive. **2** contractor acting as an intermediary. □ **entrepreneurial** *adj.* **entrepreneurialism** *n.* (also **entrepreneurism**). [French: related to ENTERPRISE]

---

entrism var. of ENTRYISM.

entropy /'entrəpɪ/ *n.* **1** *Physics* measure of the disorganization or degradation of the universe, resulting in a decrease in available energy. **2** *Physics* measure of the unavailability of a system's thermal energy for conversion into mechanical work. [Greek: related to EN-[2], *tropē* transformation]

entrust /ɪn'trʌst/ *v.* (also **intrust**) **1** (foll. by *to*) give (a person or thing) into the care of a person. **2** (foll. by *with*) assign responsibility for (a person or thing) to (a person) (*entrusted him with my camera*).

entry /'entrɪ/ *n.* (*pl.* **-ies**) **1 a** going or coming in. **b** liberty to do this. **2** place of entrance; door, gate, etc. **3** passage between buildings. **4 a** item entered in a diary, list, etc. **b** recording of this. **5 a** person or thing competing in a race etc. **b** list of competitors. [Romanic: related to ENTER]

Entryphone *n. propr.* intercom at the entrance of a building or flat for callers to identify themselves.

entwine /ɪn'twaɪn/ *v.* (**-ning**) twine round, interweave.

E-number /'i:,nʌmbə(r)/ *n.* E plus a number, the EC designation for food additives.

enumerate /ɪ'nju:mə,reɪt/ *v.* (**-ting**) **1** specify (items). **2** count. □ **enumeration** /-'reɪʃ(ə)n/ *n.* **enumerative** /-rətɪv/ *adj.* [Latin: related to NUMBER]

enumerator *n.* person employed in census-taking.

enunciate /ɪ'nʌnsɪ,eɪt/ *v.* (**-ting**) **1** pronounce (words) clearly. **2** express in definite terms. □ **enunciation** /-'eɪʃ(ə)n/ *n.* [Latin *nuntio* announce]

enuresis /,enjʊə'ri:sɪs/ *n.* involuntary urination. [Greek *enoureō* urinate in]

envelop /ɪn'veləp/ *v.* (**-p-**) **1** wrap up or cover completely. **2** completely surround. □ **envelopment** *n.* [French]

envelope /'envə,ləʊp/ *n.* **1** folded paper container for a letter etc. **2** wrapper, covering. **3** gas container of a balloon or airship.

enviable /'envɪəb(ə)l/ *adj.* likely to excite envy, desirable. □ **enviably** *adv.*

envious /'envɪəs/ *adj.* feeling or showing envy. □ **enviously** *adv.* [Anglo-French: related to ENVY]

environment /ɪn'vaɪərənmənt/ *n.* **1** surroundings, esp. as affecting lives. **2** circumstances of living. **3** *Computing* overall structure within which a user, computer, or program operates. □ **environmental** /-'ment(ə)l/ *adj.* **environmentally** /-'mentəlɪ/ *adv.* [French *environ* surroundings]

environmentalist /ɪn,vaɪərən'mentəlɪst/ *n.* person concerned with the protection of the natural environment. □ **environmentalism** *n.*

♦ **environmental scanning** *n.* examination of the environment of a business in order to identify its marketing opportunities, competition, etc.

---

environs /ɪn'vaɪərənz/ *n.pl.* district round a town etc.

envisage /ɪn'vɪzɪdʒ/ *v.* (**-ging**) **1** have a mental picture of (a thing not yet existing). **2** imagine as possible or desirable. [French: related to VISAGE]

envoy /'envɔɪ/ *n.* **1** messenger or representative. **2** (in full **envoy extraordinary**) diplomatic agent ranking below ambassador. [French *envoyer* send, from Latin *via* way]

envy /'envɪ/ –*n.* (*pl.* **-ies**) **1** discontent aroused by another's better fortune etc. **2** object of this feeling. –*v.* (**-ies, -ied**) feel envy of (a person etc.). [Latin *invidia*, from *video* see]

enwrap /ɪn'ræp/ *v.* (**-pp-**) (often foll. by *in*) *literary* wrap, enfold.

enzyme /'enzaɪm/ *n.* protein catalyst of a specific biochemical reaction. [Greek *enzumos* leavened]

EO *abbr.* **1** Equal Opportunities. **2** Executive Officer. **3** executive order.

EOB *abbr.* **1** *Computing* end of block. **2** Executive Office Building.

EOC *abbr.* Equal Opportunities Commission.

Eocene /ˈiːəʊˌsiːn/ *Geol. –adj.* of the second epoch of the Tertiary period. *–n.* this epoch. [Greek *ēōs* dawn, *kainos* new]

EOD *abbr. Computing* end of data.

EOE *abbr.* **1** equal opportunity employer. **2** = EUROPEAN OPTIONS EXCHANGE.

EOF *abbr. Computing* end of file.

EOJ *abbr. Computing* end of job.

eolian harp *US* var. of AEOLIAN HARP.

eolithic /ˌiːəˈlɪθɪk/ *adj.* of the period preceding the palaeolithic age. [Greek *ēōs* dawn, *lithos* stone]

e.o.m. *abbr. Commerce* end of the month.

eon var. of AEON.

e.o.o.e. *abbr.* (French) erreur ou omission exceptée (= errors and omissions excepted).

EOQC *abbr.* European Organization for Quality Control.

EOR *abbr. Computing* end of record.

EORI *abbr.* (in the US) Economic Opportunity Research Institute.

EOS *abbr. Computing* erasable optical storage.

EOT *abbr. Computing* **1** end of tape. **2** end of transmission.

EP *–abbr.* extended-play (gramophone record). *–international civil aircraft marking* Iran.

EPA *abbr.* Employment Protection Act.

epaulette /ˈepəˌlet/ *n.* (*US* **epaulet**) ornamental shoulder-piece on a coat etc., esp. on a uniform. [French *épaule* shoulder]

épée /eɪˈpeɪ/ *n.* sharp-pointed sword, used (with the end blunted) in fencing. [French: related to SPATHE]

ephedrine /ˈefədrɪn/ *n.* alkaloid drug used to relieve asthma, etc. [*Ephedra*, genus of plants yielding it]

ephemera /ɪˈfemərə/ *n.pl.* things of only short-lived relevance. [Latin: related to EPHEMERAL]

ephemeral /ɪˈfemər(ə)l/ *adj.* lasting or of use for only a short time; transitory. [Greek: related to EPI-, *hēmera* day]

epi- *prefix* **1** upon. **2** above. **3** in addition. [Greek]

epic /ˈepɪk/ *–n.* **1** long poem narrating the adventures or deeds of one or more heroic or legendary figures. **2** book or film based on an epic narrative. *–adj.* **1** of or like an epic. **2** grand, heroic. [Greek *epos* song]

epicene /ˈepɪˌsiːn/ *–adj.* **1** of, for, denoting, or used by both sexes. **2** having characteristics of both sexes or of neither sex. *–n.* epicene person. [Greek *koinos* common]

epicentre /ˈepɪˌsentə(r)/ *n.* (*US* **epicenter**) **1** point at which an earthquake reaches the earth's surface. **2** central point of a difficulty. [Greek: related to CENTRE]

epicure /ˈepɪˌkjʊə(r)/ *n.* person with refined tastes, esp. in food and drink. □ **epicurism** *n.* [medieval Latin: related to EPICUREAN]

Epicurean /ˌepɪkjʊəˈriːən/ *–n.* **1** disciple or student of the Greek philosopher Epicurus. **2** (**epicurean**) devotee of (esp. sensual) enjoyment. *–adj.* **1** of Epicurus or his ideas. **2** (**epicurean**) characteristic of an epicurean. □ **Epicureanism** *n.* [Latin from Greek]

epidemic /ˌepɪˈdemɪk/ *–n.* widespread occurrence of a disease in a community at a particular time. *–adj.* in the nature of an epidemic. [Greek *epi* against, *dēmos* the people]

epidemiology /ˌepɪdiːmɪˈɒlədʒɪ/ *n.* the study of epidemic diseases and their control. □ **epidemiologist** *n.*

epidermis /ˌepɪˈdɜːmɪs/ *n.* outer layer of the skin. □ **epidermal** *adj.* [Greek *derma* skin]

epidiascope /ˌepɪˈdaɪəˌskəʊp/ *n.* optical projector capable of giving images of both opaque and transparent objects. [from EPI-, DIA-, -SCOPE]

epidural /ˌepɪˈdjʊər(ə)l/ *–adj.* (of an anaesthetic) introduced into the space around the dura mater of the spinal cord. *–n.* epidural anaesthetic. [from EPI-, DURA MATER]

epiglottis /ˌepɪˈglɒtɪs/ *n.* flap of cartilage at the root of the tongue, depressed during swallowing to cover the windpipe. □ **epiglottal** *adj.* [Greek *glōtta* tongue]

epigram /ˈepɪˌgræm/ *n.* **1** short poem with a witty ending. **2** pointed saying. □ **epigrammatic** /-grəˈmætɪk/ *adj.* [Greek: related to -GRAM]

epigraph /ˈepɪˌgrɑːf/ *n.* inscription. [Greek: related to -GRAPH]

epilepsy /ˈepɪˌlepsɪ/ *n.* nervous disorder with convulsions and often loss of consciousness. [Greek *lambanō* take]

epileptic /ˌepɪˈleptɪk/ *–adj.* of epilepsy. *–n.* person with epilepsy. [French: related to EPILEPSY]

epilogue /ˈepɪˌlɒg/ *n.* **1** short piece ending a literary work. **2** speech addressed to the audience by an actor at the end of a play. [Greek *logos* speech]

epiphany /ɪˈpɪfənɪ/ *n.* (*pl.* **-ies**) **1** (**Epiphany**) **a** manifestation of Christ to the Magi. **b** festival of this on 6 January. **2** manifestation of a god or demigod. [Greek *phainō* show]

Epirus /ɪˈpaɪrəs/ (Greek **Ipiros** /ˈiːpɪˌrɒs/) administrative region of NW Greece; pop. (1991) 399 714; capital, Ioánnina.

episcopacy /ɪˈpɪskəpəsɪ/ *n.* (*pl.* **-ies**) **1** government by bishops. **2** (prec. by *the*) the bishops.

episcopal /ɪˈpɪskəp(ə)l/ *adj.* **1** of a bishop or bishops. **2** (of a Church) governed by bishops. □ **episcopally** *adv.* [Church Latin: related to BISHOP]

episcopalian /ɪˌpɪskəˈpeɪlɪən/ *–adj.* **1** of episcopacy. **2** of an episcopal Church or (**Episcopalian**) the Episcopal Church. *–n.* **1** adherent of episcopacy. **2** (**Episcopalian**) member of the Episcopal Church. □ **episcopalianism** *n.*

episcopate /ɪˈpɪskəpət/ *n.* **1** the office or tenure of a bishop. **2** (prec. by *the*) the bishops collectively. [Church Latin: related to BISHOP]

episiotomy /ɪˌpɪzɪˈɒtəmɪ/ *n.* (*pl.* **-ies**) surgical cut made at the vaginal opening during childbirth, to aid delivery. [Greek *epision* pubic region]

episode /ˈepɪˌsəʊd/ *n.* **1** event or group of events as part of a sequence. **2** each of the parts of a serial story or broadcast. **3** incident or set of incidents in a narrative. [Greek *eisodos* entry]

episodic /ˌepɪˈsɒdɪk/ *adj.* **1** consisting of separate episodes. **2** irregular, sporadic.□ **episodically** *adv.*

epistemology /ɪˌpɪstɪˈmɒlədʒɪ/ *n.* philosophy of knowledge. □ **epistemological** /-məˈlɒdʒɪk(ə)l/ *adj.* [Greek *epistēmē* knowledge]

epistle /ɪˈpɪs(ə)l/ *n.* **1** *joc.* letter. **2** (**Epistle**) any of the apostles' letters in the New Testament. **3** poem etc. in the form of a letter. [Greek *epistolē* from *stellō* send]

epistolary /ɪˈpɪstələrɪ/ *adj.* of or in the form of a letter or letters. [Latin: related to EPISTLE]

epitaph /ˈepɪˌtɑːf/ *n.* words written in memory of a dead person, esp. as a tomb inscription. [Greek *taphos* tomb]

epithelium /ˌepɪˈθiːlɪəm/ *n.* (*pl.* **-s** or **-lia** /-lɪə/) tissue forming the outer layer of the body and lining many hollow structures. □ **epithelial** *adj.* [Greek *thēlē* teat]

epithet /ˈepɪˌθet/ *n.* **1** adjective etc. expressing a quality or attribute. **2** this as a term of abuse. [Greek *tithēmi* place]

epitome /ɪˈpɪtəmɪ/ *n.* **1** person or thing embodying a quality etc. **2** thing representing another in miniature. [Greek *temnō* cut]

epitomize *v.* (also **-ise**) (**-zing** or **-sing**) make or be a perfect example of (a quality etc.).

EPLD *abbr. Computing* erasable programmable logic device.

EPNS *abbr.* electroplated nickel silver.

epoch /ˈiːpɒk/ *n.* **1** period of history etc. marked by notable events. **2** beginning of an era. **3** *Geol.* division of a period, corresponding to a set of strata. □ **epochal** /ˈepək(ə)l/ *adj.* [Greek, = pause]

epoch-making *adj.* remarkable; very important.

eponym /ˈepənɪm/ *n.* **1** word, place-name, etc., derived from a person's name. **2** person whose name is thus used. □ **eponymous** /ɪ'pɒnɪməs/ *adj.* [Greek *onoma* name]

EPOS /'iːpɒs/ *abbr.* = ELECTRONIC POINT OF SALE.

epoxy /ɪ'pɒksɪ/ *adj.* relating to or derived from a compound with one oxygen atom and two carbon atoms bonded in a triangle. [from EPI-, OXYGEN]

epoxy resin *n.* synthetic thermosetting resin.

♦ **EPP** *abbr.* = EXECUTIVE PENSION PLAN.

EPPT *abbr. Computing* European printer performance test (for office printers).

EPROM /'iːprɒm/ *abbr. Computing* erasable programmable read-only memory, semiconductor memory that is fabricated in a similar way to ROM, but with the contents added after rather than during manufacture and then if necessary erased and rewritten, possibly several times. The desired contents are added electronically and are erased usu. by exposure to ultraviolet radiation. It is only outside a computer that an EPROM can be programmed. Within a computer the contents cannot be changed; they can only be read. See also PROM; ROM.

EPS *abbr.* Encapsulated Postscript.

♦ **e.p.s.** *abbr.* = EARNINGS PER SHARE.

---

epsilon /'epsɪˌlɒn/ *n.* fifth letter of the Greek alphabet (Ε, ε). [Greek]

Epsom salts /'epsəm/ *n.* magnesium sulphate used as a purgative etc. [*Epsom* in S England]

EPT *abbr.* excess profits tax.

EPU *abbr.* European Payments Union.

EQA *abbr.* = EUROPEAN QUALITY AWARD.

EQC *abbr.* external quality control.

equable /'ekwəb(ə)l/ *adj.* **1** not varying. **2** moderate (*equable climate*). **3** (of a person) not easily disturbed. □ **equably** *adv.* [related to EQUAL]

equal /'iːkw(ə)l/ *–adj.* **1** (often foll. by *to*, *with*) the same in quantity, quality, size, degree, level, etc. **2** evenly balanced (*an equal contest*). **3** having the same rights or status (*human beings are essentially equal*). **4** uniform in application or effect. *–n.* person or thing equal to another, esp. in rank or quality. *–v.* (**-ll-**; *US* **-l-**) **1** be equal to. **2** achieve something that is equal to. □ **be equal to** have the ability or resources for. [Latin *aequalis*]

equality /ɪ'kwɒlɪtɪ/ *n.* being equal. [Latin: related to EQUAL]

equalize *v.* (also **-ise**) (**-zing** or **-sing**) **1** make or become equal. **2** reach one's opponent's score. □ **equalization** /-'zeɪʃ(ə)n/ *n.*

equalizer *n.* (also **-iser**) equalizing score or goal etc.

equally *adv.* **1** in an equal manner (*treated them equally*). **2** to an equal degree (*equally important*).

■ **Usage** In sense 2, construction with *as* (e.g. *equally as important*) is often found, but is considered incorrect by some people.

equal opportunity *n.* (often in *pl.*) opportunity to compete on equal terms, regardless of sex, race, etc. See also EQUAL PAY.

♦ **equal pay** *n.* requirement of the Equal Pay Act (1970), expressing the principle of equal opportunities, that men and women in the same employment must be paid at the same rate for like work or work rated as equivalent. Work is rated as equivalent when the employer has undertaken a study to evaluate employees' jobs in terms of the skill, effort, and responsibility demanded of them and the woman's job is given the same grade as the man's, or when an independent expert appointed by an industrial tribunal evaluates the two jobs as of equal value.

---

equanimity /ˌekwə'nɪmɪtɪ/ *n.* composure, evenness of temper, esp. in adversity. [Latin *aequus* even, *animus* mind]

equate /ɪ'kweɪt/ *v.* (**-ting**) **1** (usu. foll. by *to*, *with*) regard as equal or equivalent. **2** (foll. by *with*) be equal or equivalent to. □ **equatable** *adj.* [Latin *aequo aequat-*: related to EQUAL]

equation /ɪ'kweɪʒ(ə)n/ *n.* **1** equating or making equal; being equal. **2** statement that two mathematical expressions are equal (indicated by the sign =). **3** formula indicating a chemical reaction by means of symbols.

equator *n.* **1** imaginary line round the earth or other body, equidistant from the poles. **2** = CELESTIAL EQUATOR. [medieval Latin: related to EQUATE]

equatorial /ˌekwə'tɔːrɪəl/ *adj.* of or near the equator.

equerry /'ekwərɪ/ *n.* (*pl.* **-ies**) officer attending the British royal family. [French *esquierie* stable]

equestrian /ɪ'kwestrɪən/ *–adj.* **1** of horse-riding. **2** on horseback. *–n.* rider or performer on horseback. □ **equestrianism** *n.* [Latin *equestris* from *equus* horse]

equi- *comb. form* equal. [Latin: related to EQUAL]

equiangular /ˌiːkwɪ'æŋgjʊlə(r)/ *adj.* having equal angles.

equidistant /ˌiːkwɪ'dɪst(ə)nt/ *adj.* at equal distances.

equilateral /ˌiːkwɪ'lætər(ə)l/ *adj.* having all its sides equal in length.

equilibrium /ˌiːkwɪ'lɪbrɪəm/ *n.* (*pl.* **-ria** /-rɪə/ or **-s**) **1** state of physical balance. **2** state of composure. **3** *Econ.* situation in which the forces acting on an economic variable are exactly balanced, so that there is no tendency for that variable to change. Equilibrium is a fundamental tool of economic analysis, since without it there is no posssibility of predicting the value that a variable will take. Most of economics is concerned with defining the forces that act on a variable and establishing a process, such as supply and demand, by which equilibrium is reached. [Latin *libra* balance]

equine /'ekwaɪn/ *adj.* of or like a horse. [Latin *equus* horse]

Equatorial Guinea /'gɪnɪ/, **Republic of** small country in W Africa on the Gulf of Guinea, comprising several offshore islands and a coastal settlement (Río Muni) between Cameroon and Gabon. Agriculture, forestry, and fishing are the main occupations and account for most industrial activity, coffee, timber, and cocoa being the chief agricultural exports. Oil has been discovered, and is a major source of export revenue; oil exploration is continuing and in 1995 an oil strike off Bioko was announced. IMF restructuring of debts should ease pressure on the economy, but aid from France and Spain depends upon the impending transition to a multi-party democracy being successful. Formerly a Spanish colony, the country became fully independent in 1968. It has been under military rule since 1979 but moves to institute a democratic system were made in 1992, when a transitional government was formed pending multi-party elections. Elections were held in 1993, but most of the electorate and many opposition parties boycotted them. Similarly, most opposition parties boycotted the 1996 presidential elections. President, Teodoro Obiang Nguema Mbasogo; prime minister, Angel Serafin Seriche Dougan; capital, Malabo.

languages	Spanish (official), Fang and other native languages
currency	CFA franc (CFAF) of 100 centimes
pop. (1996)	406 000
GNP (1994)	US$167M
literacy	77% (m); 48% (f)
life expectancy	50 (m); 54 (f)

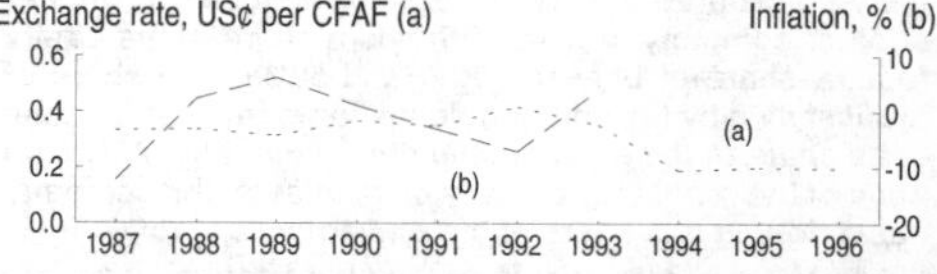

equinoctial /ˌiːkwɪˈnɒkʃ(ə)l/ *–adj.* happening at or near the time of an equinox. *–n.* (in full **equinoctial line**) = CELESTIAL EQUATOR. [Latin: related to EQUINOX]

equinox /ˈiːkwɪˌnɒks/ *n.* time or date (twice each year) at which the sun crosses the celestial equator, when day and night are of equal length. [Latin *nox noctis* night]

equip /ɪˈkwɪp/ *v.* **(-pp-)** supply with what is needed. [Old Norse *skipa* to man a ship]

equipage /ˈekwɪpɪdʒ/ *n.* **1** *archaic* **a** requisites. **b** outfit. **2** *hist.* carriage and horses with attendants. [French: related to EQUIP]

equipment *n.* **1** necessary articles, clothing, etc. **2** equipping or being equipped. [French: related to EQUIP]

equipoise /ˈekwɪˌpɔɪz/ *n.* **1** equilibrium. **2** counterbalancing thing.

equitable /ˈekwɪtəb(ə)l/ *adj.* **1** fair, just. **2** *Law* valid in equity as distinct from law. □ **equitably** *adv.* [French: related to EQUITY]

♦ **equitable interest** *n.* interest in, or ownership of, property that is recognized by equity but not by the common law. A beneficiary under a trust has an equitable interest. Any disposal of an equitable interest (e.g. a sale) must be in writing. Some equitable interests in land must be registered or they will be lost if the legal title to the land is sold. Similarly, equitable interests in other property will be lost if the legal title is sold to a bona fide purchaser for value who has no notice of the equitable interest. In such circumstances the owner of the equitable interest may claim damages from the person who sold the legal title.

---

equitation /ˌekwɪˈteɪʃ(ə)n/ *n.* horsemanship; horse-riding. [Latin *equito* ride a horse]

♦ **equity** /ˈekwɪtɪ/ *n.* (*pl.* **-ies**) **1** fairness. **2** system of law complementary to but separate from the common law and providing remedies unavailable at common law, such as specific performance of a contract rather than damages. Until 1873 equity was applied and administered by the Court of Chancery, and equitable remedies were not available in the common law courts (and vice versa). However, the Judicature Acts 1873 and 1875 merged the two systems so that any court may now apply both common law and equity. If the two sets of rules contradict each other, the equitable rule prevails. Equity has been particularly important in the development of the law of trusts, land law, administration of estates, and alternative remedies for breach of contract. **3** ordinary share capital of a company (see EQUITY CAPITAL). **4** (in *pl.*) ordinary shares of a company, esp. those of a publicly owned quoted company. In the event of a liquidation, the ordinary shareholders are entitled to share out the asssets remaining after all other creditors (including holders of preference shares) have been paid out. Investment in equities on a stock exchange represents the best opportunity for capital growth, although there is a high element of risk as only a small proportion (if any) of the investment is secured. Although equities pay relatively low profit-related dividends, unlike fixed-interest securities, they are popular in times of inflation as they tend to rise in value as the value of money falls. **5** beneficial interest in an asset. For example, a person having a house worth £100,000 with a mortgage of £20,000 may be said to have an equity of £80,000 in the house. **6** net assets of a company after all creditors (including the holders of preference shares) have been paid off. **7** amount of money returned to a borrower in a mortgage or hire-purchase agreement, after the sale of the specified asset and the full repayment of the lender of the money. [Latin *aequitas*: related to EQUAL]

♦ **equity accounting** *n.* practice of showing in a company's accounts a share of the undistributed profits of another company in which it holds a share of the equity (usu. a share of between 20% and 50%). The share of profit shown by the equity-holding company is usu. equal to its share of the equity in the other company. Although none of the profit may actually be paid over, the company has a right to this share of the undistributed profit.

♦ **equity capital** *n.* part of the share capital of a company owned by ordinary shareholders, although for certain purposes, such as pre-emption rights, other classes of shareholders may be deemed to share in the equity capital and therefore be entitled to share in the profits of the company or any surplus assets on winding up. See also A SHARES.

♦ **equity dilution** *n.* reduction in the percentage of the equity owned by a shareholder as a result of a new issue of shares in the company, which rank equally with the existing voting shares.

♦ **equity-linked policy** *n.* insurance or assurance policy in which a proportion of the premiums paid are invested in equities. The surrender value of the policy is therefore the selling price of the equities purchased; as more premiums are paid the portfolio gets larger. Although investment returns may be considerably better on this type of policy than on a traditional endowment policy, the risk is greater, as the price of equities can fall dramatically reducing the value of the policy. With unit-linked policies, a much wider range of investments can be achieved and the risk is correspondingly reduced.

---

equivalent /ɪˈkwɪvələnt/ *–adj.* **1** (often foll. by *to*) equal in value, amount, importance, etc. **2** corresponding. **3** having the same meaning or result. *–n.* equivalent thing, amount, etc. □ **equivalence** *n.* [Latin: related to VALUE]

equivocal /ɪˈkwɪvək(ə)l/ *adj.* **1** of double or doubtful meaning. **2** of uncertain nature. **3** (of a person etc.) questionable. □ **equivocally** *adv.* [Latin *voco* call]

equivocate /ɪˈkwɪvəˌkeɪt/ *v.* **(-ting)** use ambiguity to conceal the truth. □ **equivocation** /-ˈkeɪʃ(ə)n/ *n.* **equivocator** *n.* [Latin: related to EQUIVOCAL]

ER *abbr.* Queen Elizabeth. [Latin *Elizabetha Regina*]

Er *symb.* erbium.

er /ɜː(r)/ *int.* expressing hesitation. [imitative]

-er[1] *suffix* forming nouns from nouns, adjectives, and verbs, denoting: **1** person, animal, or thing that does (*cobbler*; *poker*). **2** person or thing that is (*foreigner*; *four-wheeler*). **3** person concerned with (*hatter*; *geographer*). **4** person from (*villager*; *sixth-former*). [Old English]

-er[2] *suffix* forming the comparative of adjectives (*wider*) and adverbs (*faster*). [Old English]

-er[3] *suffix* used in a slang distortion of the word (*rugger*). [probably an extension of -ER[1]]

era /ˈɪərə/ *n.* **1** system of chronology reckoning from a noteworthy event (*Christian era*). **2** large period, esp. regarded historically. **3** date at which an era begins. **4** major division of geological time. [Latin, = number (pl. of *aes* money)]

eradicate /ɪˈrædɪˌkeɪt/ *v.* **(-ting)** root out; destroy completely. □ **eradicable** *adj.* **eradication** /-ˈkeɪʃ(ə)n/ *n.* **eradicator** *n.* [Latin *radix -icis* root]

erase /ɪˈreɪz/ *v.* **(-sing) 1** rub out; obliterate. **2** remove all traces of. **3** remove recorded material from (magnetic tape or disk). [Latin *rado ras-* scrape]

eraser *n.* thing that erases, esp. a piece of rubber etc. for removing pencil etc. marks.

erasure /ɪˈreɪʒə(r)/ *n.* **1** erasing. **2** erased word etc.

erbium /ˈɜːbɪəm/ *n.* metallic element of the lanthanide series. [*Ytterby* in Sweden]

ERC *abbr.* Economic Research Council.

ERCS *abbr.* emergency response computer system.

ERDF *abbr.* European Regional Development Fund.

ERDS *abbr.* emergency response data system.

ere /eə(r)/ *prep.* & *conj. poet.* or *archaic* before (of time) (*ere noon*; *ere they come*). [Old English]

erect /ɪˈrekt/ *–adj.* **1** upright, vertical. **2** (of the penis etc.) enlarged and rigid, esp. in sexual excitement. **3** (of hair) bristling. *–v.* **1** set up; build. **2** establish. □ **erection** *n.* **erectly** *adv.* **erectness** *n.* [Latin *erigere erect-* set up]

erectile *adj.* that can become erect (esp. of body tissue in sexual excitement). [French: related to ERECT]

Erfurt /ˈeəfʊət/ industrial city in central Germany, the capital of Thuringia; manufactures include machinery, textiles, and footwear; pop. (est. 1995) 213 474.

erg *n.* unit of work or energy. [Greek *ergon* work]

ergo /ˈɜːgəʊ/ *adv.* therefore. [Latin]

ergonomics /ˌɜːgəˈnɒmɪks/ *n.* the study of the relationship between people and their working environment. □ **ergonomic** *adj.* [Greek *ergon* work]

ergot /ˈɜːgət/ *n.* disease of rye etc. caused by a fungus. [French]

Erin /ˈɪərɪn/ *n. poet.* Ireland. [Irish]

ERIS *abbr.* emergency response information system.

♦ **ERM** *abbr.* Exchange Rate Mechanism. See EUROPEAN MONETARY SYSTEM.

ermine /ˈɜːmɪn/ *n.* (*pl.* same or **-s**) **1** stoat, esp. when white in winter. **2** its white fur, used to trim robes etc. [French]

Ernie /ˈɜːnɪ/ *n.* device for drawing prize-winning numbers of Premium Bonds. [*e*lectronic *r*andom *n*umber *i*ndicator *e*quipment]

erode /ɪˈrəʊd/ *v.* (**-ding**) wear away, destroy gradually. □ **erosion** *n.* **erosive** *adj.* [Latin *rodo ros-* gnaw]

erogenous /ɪˈrɒdʒɪnəs/ *adj.* (of a part of the body) particularly sensitive to sexual stimulation. [Greek (as EROTIC), -GENOUS]

erotic /ɪˈrɒtɪk/ *adj.* of or causing sexual love, esp. tending to arouse sexual desire or excitement. □ **erotically** *adv.* [Greek *erōs* sexual love]

erotica *n.pl.* erotic literature or art.

eroticism /ɪˈrɒtɪˌsɪz(ə)m/ *n.* **1** erotic character. **2** use of or response to erotic images or stimulation.

err /ɜː(r)/ *v.* **1** be mistaken or incorrect. **2** do wrong; sin. [Latin *erro* stray]

errand /ˈerənd/ *n.* **1** short journey, esp. on another's behalf, to take a message, collect goods, etc. **2** object of such a journey. [Old English]

errand of mercy *n.* journey to relieve suffering etc.

errant /ˈerənt/ *adj.* **1** erring. **2** *literary* or *archaic* travelling in search of adventure (*knight errant*). □ **errantry** *n.* (in sense 2). [from ERR: sense 2 ultimately from Latin *iter* journey]

erratic /ɪˈrætɪk/ *adj.* **1** inconsistent in conduct, opinions, etc. **2** uncertain in movement. □ **erratically** *adv.* [Latin: related to ERR]

erratum /ɪˈrɑːtəm/ *n.* (*pl.* **errata**) error in printing or writing. [Latin: related to ERR]

erroneous /ɪˈrəʊnɪəs/ *adj.* incorrect. □ **erroneously** *adv.* [Latin: related to ERR]

error /ˈerə(r)/ *n.* **1** mistake. **2** condition of being morally wrong (*led into error*). **3** degree of inaccuracy in a calculation etc. (*2% error*). **4** *Computing* inaccuracy caused by some failure in the hardware of the system or by some condition occurring in the software. [Latin: related to ERR]

error-correcting code *n. Computing* code used to correct errors that occur during the transfer of data etc. The data is sent along a communication channel as a coded signal, with each element of the code constructed automatically by an encoder using a specific rule. A decoder at the other end of the channel detects any departure from this construction (i.e. any errors) and automatically corrects them, with a high probability of success. Error-correcting codes are more complex and hence more costly to implement than error-detecting codes but reduce the necessity for retransmission.

error-detecting code *n. Computing* code used to check data for certain kinds of errors that may have occurred, e.g. during transfer of the data or due to a data-writing or -reading process. The information is encoded automatically so that each element is constructed following a specific rule. A decoder can subsequently detect whether an error has arisen. If an error is detected then generally the sending device is requested to retransmit the affected set of bits. See also ERROR-CORRECTING CODE.

error diagnostics *n.pl. Computing* information that is presented following the detection of some condition causing an error, for example after an attempt to execute instructions in a program that are invalid or that operate on illegal data. The information is mainly to assist in identifying the cause of the error.

error message *n. Computing* message that reports the occurrence of an error. There may be some attempt to diagnose the cause of the error. The message appears on a VDU screen or on a printout, or is stored in an **error file**.

ERS *abbr.* earnings-related supplement.

ersatz /eəˈzæts/ *adj.* & *n.* substitute, imitation. [German]

Erse /ɜːs/ –*adj.* Irish or Highland Gaelic. –*n.* the Gaelic language. [early Scots form of IRISH]

erstwhile /ˈɜːstwaɪl/ –*adj.* former, previous. –*adv. archaic* formerly. [related to ERE]

ERT *abbr.* excess retention tax.

eructation /ˌiːrʌkˈteɪʃ(ə)n/ *n. formal* belching. [Latin *ructo* belch]

erudite /ˈeruːˌdaɪt/ *adj.* learned. □ **erudition** /-ˈdɪʃ(ə)n/ *n.* [Latin *eruditus* instructed: related to RUDE]

erupt /ɪˈrʌpt/ *v.* **1** break out suddenly or dramatically. **2** (of a volcano) eject lava etc. **3** (of a rash etc.) appear on the skin. □ **eruption** *n.* **eruptive** *adj.* [Latin *erumpo erupt-* break out]

-ery *suffix* (also **-ry**) forming nouns denoting: **1** class or kind (*greenery*; *machinery*; *citizenry*). **2** employment; state or condition (*dentistry*; *slavery*). **3** place of work or cultivation or breeding (*brewery*; *rookery*). **4** behaviour (*mimicry*). **5** often *derog.* all that has to do with (*popery*). [French *-erie*]

Eritrea /ˌerɪˈtreɪə/ small country in NE Africa, bordering on the Red Sea, formerly (until 1993) a province of Ethiopia. Subsistence agriculture supports most of the population; crops include sorghum, and livestock (esp. camels and goats) are raised. Red-Sea fishing is also important, and reserves of gold, copper, potash, and iron ore are mined. Exports include hides, salt, cement, and gum arabic. Reconstruction of Eritrea's war-torn economy will require substantial aid from foreign donors, which will require the implementation of plans for a multi-party democratic system.

History. An Italian colony from 1890, Eritrea federated with Ethiopia in 1952 and was integrated as a province in 1962. This resulted in an armed campaign for independence against the government of Ethiopia, which finally agreed to the establishment of a provisional Eritrean government in 1991. In a referendum in April 1993 Eritreans voted for independence, which was internationally recognized the following month. There was a brief conflict with Yemen in 1995 over the possession of three islands in the Red Sea. There have also been border tensions with Djibouti and the Sudan. President, Isaais Afeworki; capital, Asmara. □ **Eritrean** *adj.* & *n.*

languages	Afar, Bilen, Hadareb, Kunama, Nara, Rashida, Saho, Tigre, Tigrinya
currency	nafka
pop. (est. 1996)	3 627 000
GDP (1993)	US$393M
literacy	20%
life expectancy	48 (m); 51 (f)

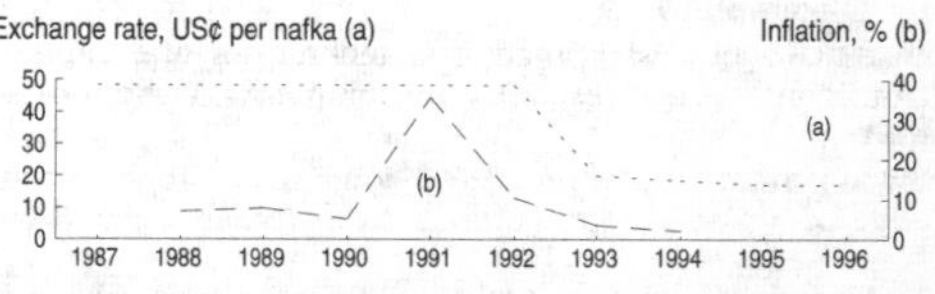

erysipelas /ˌerɪˈsɪpɪləs/ *n.* disease causing fever and a deep red inflammation of the skin. [Latin from Greek]

erythrocyte /ɪˈrɪθrəʊˌsaɪt/ *n.* red blood cell. [Greek *eruthros* red, -CYTE]

Erzurum /ˈeəzʊˌrʊm/ city in NE Turkey; manufactures include handmade jewellery; pop. (est. 1994) 250 100.

ES *–international vehicle registration* El Salvador. *–international civil aircraft marking* Estonia.

Es *symb.* einsteinium.

Esbjerg /ˈesbjɜːg/ ferry port and oil exploration centre in Denmark, on the SW coast of Jutland; pop. (1990) 81 500.

ESC *abbr.* **1** (in the EC) Economic and Social Committee. **2** (in the UN) Economic and Social Council.

Esc *–abbr. Computing* escape key. *–symb.* escudo.

escalate /ˈeskəˌleɪt/ *v.* (**-ting**) **1** increase or develop (usu. rapidly) by stages. **2** make or become more intense. □ **escalation** /-ˈleɪʃ(ə)n/ *n.* [from ESCALATOR]

♦ **escalation clause** *n.* clause in a contract authorizing the contractor to increase the price in specified conditions of all or part of the services or goods supplied under the contract. Escalation clauses are common in contracts involving work over a long period in times of high inflation. The escalation may refer to either or both labour and materials and may or may not state the way in which the price is permitted to escalate. An escalation clause does not convert a contract into a cost-plus contract, but it represents a move in that direction.

---

escalator *n.* moving staircase consisting of a circulating belt forming steps. [Latin *scala* ladder]

escalope /ˈeskəˌlɒp/ *n.* thin slice of boneless meat, esp. veal. [French, originally = shell]

ESCAP /ˈeskæp/ *abbr.* Economic and Social Commission for Asia and the Pacific, a UN agency.

escapade /ˈeskəˌpeɪd/ *n.* piece of reckless behaviour. [French from Provençal or Spanish: related to ESCAPE]

escape /ɪˈskeɪp/ *–v.* (**-ping**) **1** (often foll. by *from*) get free of restriction or control. **2** (of gas etc.) leak. **3** succeed in avoiding punishment etc. **4** get free of (a person, grasp, etc.). **5** avoid (a commitment, danger, etc.). **6** elude the notice or memory of (*nothing escapes you*; *name escaped me*). **7** (of words etc.) issue unawares from (a person etc.). *–n.* **1** act or instance of escaping. **2** means of escaping (often *attrib.*: *escape hatch*). **3** leakage of gas etc. **4** temporary relief from unpleasant reality. [Latin *cappa* cloak]

escape clause *n. Law* clause in a contract specifying conditions under which a contracting party is released from an obligation.

Esch-sur-Alzette /ˌeʃsʊəræl'zet/ town in Luxembourg, situated at the centre of a mining region; pop. (1995) 24 255.

♦ **escrow** /eˈskrəʊ/ *n. Law* deed that has been signed and sealed but is delivered on the condition that it will not become operative until some stated event happens. It will become effective as soon as that event occurs and it cannot be revoked in the meantime. [French from Latin *scroda* scroll]

---

escapee /ɪskeɪˈpiː/ *n.* person who has escaped.

escapement *n.* part of a clock etc. that connects and regulates the motive power. [French: related to ESCAPE]

escape velocity *n.* minimum velocity needed to escape from the gravitational field of a body.

escapism *n.* pursuit of distraction and relief from reality. □ **escapist** *n.* & *adj.*

escapology /ˌeskəˈpɒlədʒɪ/ *n.* techniques of escaping from confinement, esp. as entertainment. □ **escapologist** *n.*

escarpment /ɪˈskɑːpmənt/ *n.* long steep slope at the edge of a plateau etc. [French from Italian: related to SCARP]

eschatology /ˌeskəˈtɒlədʒɪ/ *n.* theology of death and final destiny. □ **eschatological** /-təˈlɒdʒɪk(ə)l/ *adj.* [Greek *eskhatos* last]

escheat /ɪsˈtʃiːt/ *hist. –n.* **1** reversion of property to the state etc. in the absence of legal heirs. **2** property so affected. *–v.* **1** hand over (property) as an escheat. **2** confiscate. **3** revert by escheat. [Latin *cado* fall]

eschew /ɪsˈtʃuː/ *v. formal* avoid; abstain from. □ **eschewal** *n.* [Germanic: related to SHY[1]]

escort *–n.* /ˈeskɔːt/ **1** one or more persons, vehicles, etc., accompanying a person, vehicle, etc., for protection or as a mark of status. **2** person accompanying a person of the opposite sex socially. *–v.* /ɪˈskɔːt/ act as an escort to. [French from Italian]

escritoire /ˌeskrɪˈtwɑː(r)/ *n.* writing-desk with drawers etc. [French from Latin *scriptorium* writing-room]

escudo /eˈskjuːdəʊ/ *n.* (*pl.* **-s**) standard monetary unit of Portugal and Cape Verde. [Spanish and Portuguese from Latin *scutum* shield]

escutcheon /ɪˈskʌtʃ(ə)n/ *n.* shield or emblem bearing a coat of arms. [Latin *scutum* shield]

Esfahan see ISFAHAN.

Eskimo /ˈeskɪˌməʊ/ *–n.* (*pl.* same or **-s**) **1** member of a people inhabiting N Canada, Alaska, Greenland, and E Siberia. **2** language of this people. *–adj.* of Eskimos or their language. [Algonquian]

■ **Usage** The Eskimos of North America prefer the name *Inuit*.

ESL *abbr.* English as a second language.

ESN *abbr.* educationally subnormal.

ESOL /ˈiːsɒl/ *abbr.* English for speakers of other languages.

ESOP /ˈiːsɒp/ *abbr.* = EMPLOYEE SHARE-OWNERSHIP PLAN.

esophagus *US* var. of OESOPHAGUS.

esoteric /ˌesəʊˈterɪk/ *adj.* intelligible only to those with special knowledge. □ **esoterically** *adv.* [Greek *esō* within]

ESP *abbr.* extrasensory perception.

espadrille /ˌespəˈdrɪl/ *n.* light canvas shoe with a plaited fibre sole. [Provençal: related to ESPARTO]

espalier /ɪˈspælɪə(r)/ *n.* **1** lattice-work along which the branches of a tree or shrub are trained. **2** tree or shrub so trained. [French from Italian]

esparto /eˈspɑːtəʊ/ *n.* (*pl.* **-s**) (in full **esparto grass**) coarse grass of Spain and N Africa, used to make good-quality paper etc. [Greek *sparton* rope]

especial /ɪˈspeʃ(ə)l/ *adj.* notable. [Latin: related to SPECIAL]

especially *adv.* **1** in particular. **2** much more than in other cases. **3** particularly.

Esperanto /ˌespəˈræntəʊ/ *n.* an artificial language designed for universal use. [Latin *spero* hope]

espionage /ˈespɪəˌnɑːʒ/ *n.* spying or use of spies. [French: related to SPY]

esplanade /ˌespləˈneɪd/ *n.* **1** long open level area for walking on, esp. beside the sea. **2** level space separating a fortress from a town. [Latin *planus* level]

espousal /ɪˈspaʊz(ə)l/ *n.* **1** (foll. by *of*) espousing of (a cause etc.). **2** *archaic* marriage, betrothal.

espouse /ɪˈspaʊz/ *v.* (**-sing**) **1** adopt or support (a cause, doctrine, etc.). **2** *archaic* **a** (usu. of a man) marry. **b** (usu. foll. by *to*) give (a woman) in marriage. [Latin *spondeo* betroth]

espresso /eˈspresəʊ/ *n.* (also **expresso** /ekˈspresəʊ/) (*pl.* **-s**) strong black coffee made under steam pressure. [Italian, = pressed out]

ESPRIT /ˈesprɪt/ *abbr.* European strategic programme for research and development in information technology.

esprit /eˈspriː/ *n.* sprightliness, wit. □ ***esprit de corps*** /də ˈkɔː(r)/ devotion to and pride in one's group. [French: related to SPIRIT]

espy /ɪˈspaɪ/ *v.* (**-ies, -ied**) catch sight of. [French: related to SPY]

Esq. *abbr.* Esquire.

-esque *suffix* forming adjectives meaning 'in the style of' or 'resembling' (*Kafkaesque*). [French from Latin *-iscus*]

esquire /ɪ'skwaɪə(r)/ *n.* **1** (usu. as abbr. **Esq.**) title added to a man's surname when no other title is used, esp. as a form of address for letters. **2** *archaic* = SQUIRE. [French from Latin *scutum* shield]

ESRC *abbr.* Economic and Social Research Council.

-ess *suffix* forming nouns denoting females (*actress*; *lioness*). [Greek *-issa*]

essay *–n.* /'eseɪ/ **1** short piece of writing on a given subject. **2** (often foll. by *at, in*) *formal* attempt. *–v.* /e'seɪ/ attempt. □ **essayist** *n.* [Latin *exigo* weigh: cf. ASSAY]

Essen /'es(ə)n/ city in NW Germany; pop. (est. 1995) 617 955. The administrative centre of the Ruhr region, it has textile and chemical industries.

essence /'es(ə)ns/ *n.* **1** fundamental nature; inherent characteristics. **2 a** extract got by distillation etc. **b** perfume. □ **in essence** fundamentally. **of the essence** indispensable. [Latin *esse* be]

essential /ɪ'senʃ(ə)l/ *–adj.* **1** necessary; indispensable. **2** of or constituting the essence of a person or thing. *–n.* (esp. in *pl.*) basic or indispensable element or thing. □ **essentially** *adv.* [Latin: related to ESSENCE]

essential oil *n.* volatile oil derived from a plant etc. with its characteristic odour.

Essex /'esɪks/ county in SE England; pop. (est. 1994) 1 569 900; county town, Chelmsford. Cereals, sugar beet, and vegetables are produced and there are various manufacturing industries.

EST *abbr.* **1** earliest start time. **2** *US* & *Canadian* Eastern Standard Time.

est. *abbr.* **1** established. **2** estimated.

-est *suffix* forming the superlative of adjectives (*widest*; *nicest*; *happiest*) and adverbs (*soonest*). [Old English]

establish /ɪ'stæblɪʃ/ *v.* **1** set up (a business, system, etc.) on a permanent basis. **2** (foll. by *in*) settle (a person or oneself) in some capacity. **3** (esp. as **established** *adj.*) **a** achieve permanent acceptance for (a custom, belief, etc.). **b** place (a fact etc.) beyond dispute. [Latin *stabilio* make firm]

Established Church *n.* the Church recognized by the state.

establishment *n.* **1** establishing or being established. **2 a** business organization or public institution. **b** place of business. **c** residence. **3 a** staff of an organization. **b** household. **4** organized body permanently maintained. **5** Church system organized by law. **6** (**the Establishment**) social group with authority or influence and resisting change.

estate /ɪ'steɪt/ *n.* **1** property consisting of much land and usu. a large house. **2** modern residential or industrial area with an integrated design or purpose. **3** sum total of a person's assets less liabilities, esp. at death. **4** property where rubber, tea, grapes, etc. are cultivated. **5** order or class forming (or regarded as) part of the body politic. **6** *archaic* or *literary* state or position in life (*the estate of holy matrimony*). □ **the Three Estates** Lords Spiritual (the heads of the Church), Lords Temporal (the peerage), and the Commons. [French *estat*, from Latin *sto stat-* stand]

estate agent *n.* person whose business is the sale or lease of buildings and land on behalf of others.

estate car *n.* car with a continuous area for rear passengers and luggage.

♦ **estate duty** *n. hist.* tax on the estate of a deceased person at the time of death. This tax applied in the UK from 1894 to 1974, when it was converted to capital-transfer tax. The latter tax became inheritance tax in 1986, when it reverted to a form of taxation similar to the former estate duty. See INHERITANCE TAX.

♦ **estate in land** *n. Law* nature and duration of a person's ownership of land. For example, a life estate would last only for the life of the owner. See FEE SIMPLE.

esteem /ɪ'stiːm/ *–v.* **1** (usu. in *passive*) have a high regard for. **2** *formal* consider (*esteemed it an honour*). *–n.* high regard; favour. [Latin: related to ESTIMATE]

ester /'estə(r)/ *n. Chem.* a compound produced by replacing the hydrogen of an acid by an alkyl etc. radical. [German]

estimable /'estɪməb(ə)l/ *adj.* worthy of esteem; admirable. [Latin: related to ESTEEM]

estimate *–n.* /'estɪmət/ **1** approximate judgement, esp. of cost, value, size, etc. **2** statement of approximate charge for work to be undertaken. *–v.* /'estɪˌmeɪt/ (**-ting**) (*also absol.*) **1** form an estimate or opinion of. **2** (foll. by *that*) make a rough calculation. **3** (often foll. by *at*) form an estimate; adjudge. □ **estimator** /-ˌmeɪtə(r)/ *n.* [Latin *aestimo* fix the price of]

estimation /ˌestɪ'meɪʃ(ə)n/ *n.* **1** estimating. **2** judgement of worth. [Latin: related to ESTIMATE]

Estonian /e'stəʊnɪən/ *–n.* **1 a** native or national of Estonia. **b** person of Estonian descent. **2** language of Estonia. *–adj.* of Estonia, its people, or language.

♦ **estoppel** /ɪ'stɒp(ə)l/ *n. Law* **1** rule of evidence by which a person is prevented from denying that a certain state of affairs exists if that person has previously asserted that it does. **2** (also **promissory estoppel**) rule that if a person has declared that he or she will not insist upon the strict legal rights under a contract, that person will not later be allowed to insist upon them if the other party has relied on that declaration. The person may, however, be allowed to enforce the strict legal rights, on giving reasonable notice, if this would not be inequitable. **3** (also **proprietary estoppel**) rule that if one person allows or encourages another person to act to his or her detriment in respect of land, that person will not later be able to refuse to grant something that the other person was led to expect. [Old French *estoupail* plug]

Estoril /ˌeʃtə'rɪl/ resort on the Atlantic coast of Portugal; pop. (1991) 24 850.

estrange /ɪ'streɪndʒ/ *v.* (**-ging**) **1** (usu. in *passive*; often foll. by *from*) alienate; make hostile or indifferent. **2** (as **estranged** *adj.*) (of a husband or wife) no longer living with his or her spouse. □ **estrangement** *n.* [Latin: related to STRANGE]

Estonia /ɪ'stəʊnɪə/, **Republic of** country in NE Europe, on the S coast of the Gulf of Finland, formerly (1940–91) a constituent republic of the Soviet Union. Agriculture and dairy farming are major occupations; the principal crops include rye, oats, barley, potatoes, and flax. There is also fishing, esp. of herring. Light industry, which is concentrated on textiles, clothing, and food processing, is important. The economy, which was formerly heavily dependent on the Soviet Union, has undergone free-market reforms; large-scale privatization of former state-run enterprises began in 1992 and there was a vast increase in foreign investment in the mid-1990s. Estonia has greatly reduced its economic dependence on former Soviet countries and much of its trade is now with EU countries, especially Germany and Scandinavia. It now has the strongest economy of the former Eastern bloc countries. Estonia has been formally invited to join the EU early in the next century. President, Lennart Meri; prime minister, Mart Siimaan; capital, Tallinn.

languages	Estonian (official), Russian, Finnish
currency	kroon of 100 cents
pop. (1996)	1 475 000
GNP (1994)	US$4.3B
literacy	99%
life expectancy	62 (m); 73 (f)

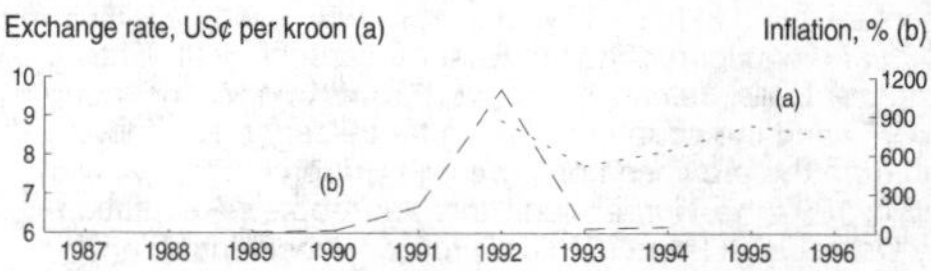

estrogen *US* var. of OESTROGEN.

estrus *US* var. of OESTRUS.

estuary /ˈestjʊərɪ/ *n.* (*pl.* **-ies**) wide tidal river mouth. [Latin *aestus* tide]

Esztergom /ˌestəˈgɒm/ town and river port in N Hungary, on the Danube; pop. (1993) 29 730.

ET *–abbr.* **1** *US* Eastern Time. **2** Employment Training (for the unemployed). *–international vehicle registration* Egypt. *–international civil aircraft marking* Ethiopia. *–airline flight code* Ethiopian Airlines.

ETA *abbr.* estimated time of arrival.

eta /ˈiːtə/ *n.* seventh letter of the Greek alphabet (Η, η). [Greek]

Étab. *abbr.* (French) établissement (= business establishment).

et al. /et ˈæl/ *abbr.* and others. [Latin *et alii*]

etc. *abbr.* = ET CETERA.

et cetera /et ˈsetrə/ (also **etcetera**) *–adv.* **1** and the rest. **2** and so on. *–n.* (in *pl.*) the usual extras. [Latin]

etch *v.* **1 a** reproduce (a picture etc.) by engraving it on a metal plate with acid (esp. to print copies). **b** engrave (a plate) in this way. **2** practise this craft. **3** (foll. by *on*, *upon*) impress deeply (esp. on the mind). □ **etcher** *n.* [Dutch *etsen*]

etching *n.* **1** print made from an etched plate. **2** art of producing these plates.

eternal /ɪˈtɜːn(ə)l/ *adj.* **1** existing always; without an end or (usu.) beginning. **2** unchanging. **3** *colloq.* constant; too frequent (*eternal nagging*). □ **eternally** *adv.* [Latin *aeternus*]

eternal triangle *n.* two people of one sex and one person of the other involved in a complex emotional relationship.

eternity /ɪˈtɜːnɪtɪ/ *n.* (*pl.* **-ies**) **1** infinite (esp. future) time. **2** endless life after death. **3** being eternal. **4** *colloq.* (often prec. by *an*) a very long time. [Latin: related to ETERNAL]

eternity ring *n.* finger-ring esp. set with gems all round.

◆ **ETF** *abbr.* electronic transfer of funds (see ELECTRONIC FUNDS TRANSFER).

ETH *international vehicle registration* Ethiopia.

-eth var. of -TH.

ethanal /ˈeθəˌnæl/ *n.* = ACETALDEHYDE.

ethane /ˈiːθeɪn/ *n.* gaseous hydrocarbon of the alkane series. [from ETHER]

ether /ˈiːθə(r)/ *n.* **1** *Chem.* colourless volatile organic liquid used as an anaesthetic or solvent. **2** clear sky; upper regions of the air. **3** *hist.* **a** medium formerly assumed to permeate all space. **b** medium through which electromagnetic waves were formerly thought to be transmitted. [Greek *aithō* burn]

ethereal /ɪˈθɪərɪəl/ *adj.* **1** light, airy. **2** highly delicate, esp. in appearance. **3** heavenly. □ **ethereally** *adv.* [Greek: related to ETHER]

ethic /ˈeθɪk/ *–n.* set of moral principles (*the Quaker ethic*). *–adj.* = ETHICAL. [Greek: related to ETHOS]

ethical *adj.* **1** relating to morals, esp. as concerning human conduct. **2** morally correct. **3** (of a drug etc.) not advertised to the general public, and usu. available only on prescription. □ **ethically** *adv.*

◆ **ethical investment** *n.* investment in an organization offering products or services that the investor considers to be morally acceptable.

---

ethics *n.pl.* (also treated as *sing.*) **1** moral philosophy. **2 a** moral principles. **b** set of these.

Ethiopian /ˌiːθɪˈəʊpɪən/ *–n.* **1** native or national of Ethiopia. **2** person of Ethiopian descent. *–adj.* of Ethiopia.

ethnic /ˈeθnɪk/ *adj.* **1 a** (of a social group) having a common national or cultural tradition. **b** (of music, clothing, etc.) inspired by or resembling those of an exotic people. **2** denoting origin by birth or descent rather than nationality (*ethnic Turks*). □ **ethnically** *adv.* [Greek *ethnos* nation]

ethnology /eθˈnɒlədʒɪ/ *n.* the comparative study of peoples. □ **ethnological** /-nəˈlɒdʒɪk(ə)l/ *adj.* **ethnologist** *n.*

ethos /ˈiːθɒs/ *n.* characteristic spirit or attitudes of a community etc. [Greek *ēthos* character]

ethyl /ˈeθɪl/ *n.* (*attrib.*) a radical derived from ethane, present in alcohol and ether. [German: related to ETHER]

ethylene /ˈeθɪˌliːn/ *n.* a hydrocarbon of the alkene series.

etiolate /ˈiːtɪəˌleɪt/ *v.* (**-ting**) **1** make (a plant) pale by excluding light. **2** give a sickly colour to (a person). □ **etiolation** /-ˈleɪʃ(ə)n/ *n.* [Latin *stipula* straw]

etiology *US* var. of AETIOLOGY.

etiquette /ˈetɪˌket/ *n.* conventional rules of social behaviour or professional conduct. [French: related to TICKET]

Etruscan /ɪˈtrʌskən/ *–adj.* of ancient Etruria in Italy. *–n.* **1** native of Etruria. **2** language of Etruria. [Latin *Etruscus*]

et seq. *abbr.* (also **et seqq.**) and the following (pages etc.). [Latin *et sequentia*]

-ette *suffix* forming nouns meaning: **1** small (*kitchenette*). **2** imitation or substitute (*flannelette*). **3** female (*usherette*). [French]

ETUC *abbr.* European Trade Union Confederation.

étude /ˈeɪtjuːd/ *n.* = STUDY *n.* 6. [French, = study]

etymology /ˌetɪˈmɒlədʒɪ/ *n.* (*pl.* **-ies**) **1 a** derivation and development of a word in form and meaning. **b** account

---

Ethiopia /ˌiːθɪˈəʊpɪə/ **Federal Democratic Republic of** (formerly **Abyssinia**) country in NE Africa, one of the poorest in the world. Agriculture is chiefly at subsistence level, and serious crop failures have resulted in widespread famines. Coffee is the main export; other exports include skins and hides and petroleum products. There are small largely unexploited resources of oil, gold, platinum, and potash. Manufacturing and food-processing industries are being encouraged. The economy has been devastated by drought, civil war, and political upheaval. Despite an agreed increase in foreign aid, recovery will depend on improved harvests and successful implementation of democratization and the market-based economic policy proposed by the provisional administration in 1991.

History. The country successfully resisted Italian attempts at colonization in the 1890s but was conquered by Italy in 1935 and was part of Italian East Africa until 1941. The Emperor Haile Selassie was overthrown in a Marxist coup in 1975 and the country came under military rule. Opposition from the provinces of Tigre and Eritrea led to civil war, and in 1991 the Tigrean-led Ethiopia People's Revolutionary Democratic Front (EPRDF) forced President Mengistu to resign and established a provisional government. This agreed to the autonomous administration of Eritrea (which became independent in 1993), but ethnic unrest continued with the Oromo people demanding greater autonomy. Multiparty elections were held in 1995. President, Negasso Gidada; capital, Addis Ababa.

languages	Amharic, English, local languages
currency	birr (Br) of 100 cents
pop. (1996)	56 713 000
GNP (1994)	US$6.9B
literacy	45% (m); 25% (f)
life expectancy	45 (m); 48 (f)

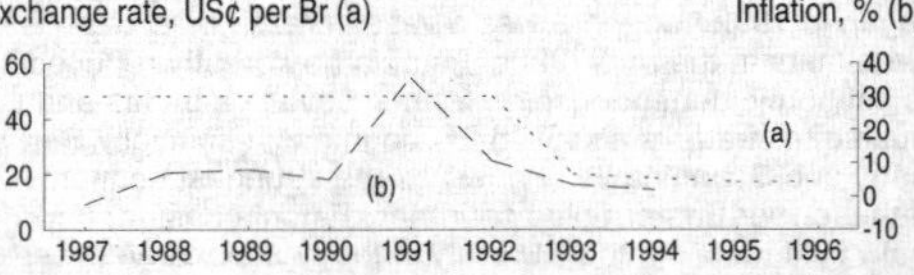

of these. **2** the study of word origins. □ **etymological** /-mə'lɒdʒɪk(ə)l/ *adj.* **etymologist** *n.* [Greek *etumos* true]

EU *abbr.* = EUROPEAN UNION.

Eu *symb.* europium.

eu- *comb. form* well, easily. [Greek]

EUA *abbr. Finance* European unit of account.

Euboea /juː'biːə/ (Greek **Évvoia** /'eɪvɪə/) Greek island in the W Aegean Sea, separated from the mainland by a narrow channel for most of its length; pop. (1991) 209 130; capital, Chalcis (Khalkis). Crops include grapes, figs, and olives; sheep and cattle are reared.

eucalyptus /ˌjuːkə'lɪptəs/ *n.* (*pl.* **-tuses** or **-ti** /-taɪ/) (also **eucalypt** *pl.* **-s**) **1** tall evergreen Australasian tree. **2** its oil, used as an antiseptic etc. [from EU-, Greek *kaluptos* covered]

Eucharist /'juːkərɪst/ *n.* **1** Christian sacrament in which consecrated bread and wine are consumed. **2** consecrated elements, esp. the bread. □ **Eucharistic** /-'rɪstɪk/ *adj.* [Greek, = thanksgiving]

eugenics /juː'dʒenɪks/ *n.pl.* (also treated as *sing.*) improvement of the qualities of a race by control of inherited characteristics. □ **eugenic** *adj.* **eugenically** *adv.* [from EU-, Greek *gen-* produce]

eukaryote /juː'kærɪˌəʊt/ *n.* organism consisting of a cell or cells in which the genetic material is contained within a distinct nucleus. □ **eukaryotic** /-'ɒtɪk/ *adj.* [from EU-, *karyo-* from Greek *karuon* kernel, *-ote* as in ZYGOTE]

eulogize /'juːləˌdʒaɪz/ *v.* (also **-ise**) (**-zing** or **-sing**) praise in speech or writing. □ **eulogistic** /-'dʒɪstɪk/ *adj.*

eulogy /'juːlədʒɪ/ *n.* (*pl.* **-ies**) **1** speech or writing in praise of a person. **2** expression of praise. [Latin from Greek]

eunuch /'juːnək/ *n.* castrated man, esp. one formerly employed at an oriental harem or court. [Greek, = bedchamber attendant]

euphemism /'juːfɪˌmɪz(ə)m/ *n.* **1** mild or vague expression substituted for a harsher or more direct one (e.g. *pass over* for *die*). **2** use of such expressions. □ **euphemistic** /-'mɪstɪk/ *adj.* **euphemistically** /-'mɪstɪkəlɪ/ *adv.* [Greek *phēmē* speaking]

euphonium /juː'fəʊnɪəm/ *n.* brass instrument of the tuba family. [related to EUPHONY]

euphony /'juːfənɪ/ *n.* (*pl.* **-ies**) **1** pleasantness of sound, esp. of a word or phrase. **2** pleasant sound. □ **euphonious** /-'fəʊnɪəs/ *adj.* [Greek *phōnē* sound]

euphoria /juː'fɔːrɪə/ *n.* intense feeling of well-being and excitement. □ **euphoric** /-'fɒrɪk/ *adj.* [Greek *pherō* bear]

Eurasian /jʊə'reɪʒ(ə)n/ *–adj.* **1** of mixed European and Asian parentage. **2** of Europe and Asia. *–n.* Eurasian person.

Euratom /jʊə'rætəm/ *n.* = EUROPEAN ATOMIC ENERGY COMMUNITY. [abbreviation]

eureka /jʊə'riːkə/ *int.* I have found it! (announcing a discovery etc.). [Greek *heurēka*]

Euro- *comb. form* Europe, European. [abbreviation]

◆ **euro** /jʊərəʊ/ *n.* the currency unit adopted by the European Union for European Monetary Union.

◆ **Euro-ad** *n.* advertisement designed to be used in all countries of the European Community, when the appeal of the product (e.g. cars) is equal in all the member countries.

◆ **Eurobond** /'jʊərəʊˌbɒnd/ *n.* bond that is issued in a Eurocurrency and is now one of the largest markets for raising money (it is much larger than the UK stock exchange). The reason for the popularity of the Eurobond market is that secondary market investors can remain anonymous, usu. for the purpose of avoiding tax. For this reason it is difficult to ascertain the exact size and scope of operation of the market. Issues of new Eurobonds usu. take place in London, largely through syndicates of US and Japanese investment banks; they are bearer securities, unlike the shares registered in most stock exchanges, and interest payments are free of any withholding taxes. There are various kinds of Eurobonds. An ordinary bond, called a **straight**, is a fixed-interest loan of three to eight years duration; others include **floating-rate notes**, which carry a variable interest rate based on the LIBOR, and perpetuals, which are never redeemed. Some carry warrants and some are convertible. See also BEARER SECURITY; BOND *n.* 3; EUROCURRENCY; NOTE ISSUANCE FACILITY; SWAP *n.* 3; ZERO-COUPON BOND.

◆ **Eurocheque** /'jʊərəʊˌtʃek/ *n.* cheque drawn on a European bank, which can be cashed at any bank or bureau de change in the world that displays the EC sign (of which there are some 200 000). It can also be used to pay for goods and services in shops, hotels, restaurants, garages, etc. that display the EC sign (over 4 million). The cheques are blank and are made out for any amount as required, usu. in the local currency. They have to be used with a **Eurocheque Card**, which guarantees cheques for up to about £100. In most cases, a commission of 1.25% is added to the foreign currency value of the cheque before it is converted to sterling and there is a 30p cheque charge (for cheques drawn on UK banks).

◆ **Euro-commercial paper** *n.* (also **ECP**) commercial paper issued in a Eurocurrency, the market for which is centred in London.

◆ **Eurocurrency** /'jʊərəʊˌkʌrənsɪ/ *n.* (*pl.* **-ies**) currency held in a European country other than its country of origin. For example, dollars deposited in a bank in Switzerland are Eurodollars (see EURODOLLAR), yen deposited in Germany are **Euroyen**, etc. Eurocurrency is used for lending and borrowing; the Eurocurrency market often provides a cheap and convenient form of liquidity for the financing of international trade and investment. The main borrowers and lenders are the commercial banks, large companies, and the central banks. By raising funds in Eurocurrencies it is possible to secure more favourable terms and rates of interest, and sometimes to avoid domestic regulations and taxation. Most of the deposits and loans are on a short-term basis but increasing use is being made of medium-term loans, particularly through the raising of Eurobonds. This has to some extent replaced the syndicated loan market, in which banks lent money as a group in order to share the risk. Euromarkets emerged in the 1950s.

◆ **Eurodollar** /'jʊərəʊˌdɒlə(r)/ *n.* dollar deposited in a financial institution outside the US, originally in Europe but now in any country. The Eurodollar market evolved in London in the late 1950s when the growing demand for dollars to finance international trade and investment coincided with a greater supply of dollars. See also EUROCURRENCY.

◆ **Euromarket** /'jʊərəʊˌmɑːkɪt/ *n.* **1** market that emerged in the 1950s for financing international trade. Its principal participants are commercial banks, large companies, and the central banks of members of the EC. Its main business is in Eurobonds issued in Eurocurrencies. The largest Euromarket is in London, but there are smaller ones in Paris and Brussels. **2** the European Community, regarded as one large market for goods.

Euronet /'jʊərəʊˌnet/ *n.* European data-transmission network. [abbreviation]

◆ **Euronote** /'jʊərəʊˌnəʊt/ *n.* form of Euro-commercial paper consisting of short-term negotiable bearer notes. They may be in any currency but are usu. in dollars or ecus.

Europe /'jʊərəp/ continent of the N hemisphere consisting of the W part of the land mass of which Asia forms the E (and greater) part, and including Scandinavia and the British Isles. It contains approximately 20% of the world's population. Politically and economically pre-eminent in the 18th and 19th centuries, Europe was overshadowed as a result of the rise of the superpowers in the mid-20th century. However, since the breakup of the Soviet Union, and with the movement towards political and economic union by member states of the European Community, its importance is once more increasing.

European /ˌjʊərə'pɪən/ *–adj.* **1** of or in Europe. **2** originating in, native to, or characteristic of Europe. *–n.* **1 a**

native or inhabitant of Europe. **b** person descended from natives of Europe. **2** person favouring European integration. [Greek *Eurōpē* Europe]

♦ **European Atomic Energy Community** *n.* (also **Euratom**) organization set up by the six members of the European Coal and Steel Community in 1957; the European Economic Community was established at the same time. Euratom was formed to create the technical and industrial conditions necessary to produce nuclear energy on an industrial scale. The UK, Denmark, and Ireland joined in 1973, Greece joined in 1981, and Spain and Portugal joined in 1986.

♦ **European Coal and Steel Community** *n.* (also **ECSC**) first of the European Communities (EC), founded in 1953. The ECSC created a common market in coal, steel, iron ore, and scrap between the original six members of the EC (Belgium, France, West Germany, Italy, Luxembourg, and the Netherlands). These six countries, in 1957, signed the Treaty of Rome setting up the European Economic Community.

♦ **European Commission** *n.* (also **Commission of the European Communities**) single executive body formed in 1967 from the three separate executive bodies of the European Coal and Steel Community, the European Atomic Energy Community, and the European Economic Community. It now consists of 17 Commissioners: two each from the UK, France, Germany, Spain, and Italy; and one each from Belgium, the Netherlands, Luxembourg, Ireland, Denmark, Greece, and Portugal. The Commissioners accept joint responsibility for their decisions, which are taken on the basis of a majority vote. The Commission initiates action in the European Community and mediates between member governments. See also EUROPEAN COMMUNITY.

♦ **European Community** *n.* see EUROPEAN UNION.

♦ **European Currency Unit** *n.* (also **ecu**, **Ecu**) currency medium and unit of account created in 1979 to act as the reserve asset and accounting unit of the European Monetary System. The value of the ecu is calculated as a weighted average of a basket of specified amounts of European Community (EC) currencies; its value is reviewed periodically as currencies change in importance and membership of the EC expands. It also acts as the unit of account for all EC transactions. It has some similarities with the special drawing rights of the International Monetary Fund; however, ecu reserves are not allocated to individual countries but are held in the European Monetary Cooperation Fund. See also EURO.

♦ **European Economic Community** *n.* see EUROPEAN UNION.

♦ **European Free Trade Association** *n.* (also **Efta**) trade association formed in 1960 between Austria, Denmark, Norway, Portugal, Sweden, Switzerland, and the UK. Finland, Iceland, and Liechtenstein joined later while the UK, Denmark, Portugal, Austria, Finland, and Sweden left on joining the EUROPEAN UNION (or its earlier forms). EFTA is a looser association than the EU, dealing only with trade barriers rather than generally coordinating economic policy. All tariffs between Efta and EU countries were abolished finally in 1984. Efta is governed by a council in which each member has one vote; decisions must normally be unanimous and are binding on all member countries. In 1992 the EUROPEAN ECONOMIC AREA (EEA) was formed to facilitate the movement of goods, services, capital, and labour between all EU and Efta countries. Efta has also signed economic cooperation treaties with some former eastern bloc countries.

♦ **European Investment Bank** *n.* (also **EIB**) bank set up under the Treaty of Rome in 1958 to finance capital-investment projects in the European Economic Community. It grants long-term loans to private companies and public institutions for projects that further the aims of the Community. The members of the EIB are the 15 member states of the EUROPEAN UNION, all of whom have subscribed to the Bank's capital of 62,013M ECU but most of the funds lent by the bank are borrowed on the EU and international capital markets. The bank is non-profit making and charges interest at a rate that reflects the rate at which it borrows. Its headquarters are in Luxembourg.

♦ **European Monetary Cooperation Fund** *n.* (also **EMCF**) fund organized by the European Monetary System in which members of the EUROPEAN UNION deposit reserves to provide a pool of resources to stabilize exchange rates and to finance balance of payments support. In return for depositing 20% of their gold and gross dollar reserves, member states have access to a wide variety of credit facilities, denominated in ECU, from the fund.

♦ **European Monetary Insititute** *n.* (also **EMI**) organization set up in 1991 by the Maastricht Treaty to coordinate economic and monetary policy within the EUROPEAN UNION.

♦ **European Monetary System** *n.* (also **EMS**) system of exchange-rate stabilization involving the countries of the EUROPEAN UNION, which began operations in 1979. There are two elements: the **Exchange Rate Mechanism** (**ERM**), under which participating countries commit themselves to maintaining the values of their currencies within agreed limits, and a balance of payments support mechanism, organized through the European Monetary Cooperation Fund. The ERM operates by giving each currency a value in ECUs and drawing up a **parity grid** giving exchange values in ECUs for each pair of currencies. In practice, the Deutschmark has replaced the ECU as the anchor currency. If market rates differ from the agreed parity by more than a permitted percentage (currently 2.25% or 6% depending on the currency), the relevant governments have to take action to correct the disparity. Three currencies, the UK pound, the Italian lira, and the Spanish peseta, were forced out of the ERM in 1992 and some of the currencies remaining in it are now allowed 15% fluctuations. The ultimate goal of the EMS is also controversial. To some its function is to facilitate monetary cooperation; to others, it is the first step towards **European Monetary Union** (EMU), with a single European currency and a European Central Bank. The decision to create a single currency was part of the Maastricht Treaty in 1991, provided that the participants fulfil certain conditions. Countries that fulfil the conditions for EMU will be named in 1998. Their currencies will be locked together in 1999, enabling the common European currency (the **euro**) to be in circulation by 2002.

♦ **European Monetary Union** *n.* see EUROPEAN MONETARY SYSTEM.

♦ **European option** see OPTION 3.

♦ **European Options Exchange** *n.* (also **EOE**) market based in Amsterdam that deals in traded options, mostly in currencies but also in some securities and precious metals.

♦ **European Quality Award** *n.* (also **EQA**) award instituted in 1992 by the European Foundation for Quality Management. It is given to companies that can demonstrate excellence in their management of quality and that their approach to TOTAL QUALITY MANAGEMENT has contributed to the satisfaction of customers, employees, and other stake-holders. The nine first-level categories of the EQA model are leadership, policy and strategy, people management, resources, processes, customer satisfaction, people satisfaction, impact on society, and business results.

♦ **European Union** *n.* (also **EU**) 15 nations (Belgium, Denmark, France, Germany, Greece, Ireland, Italy, Luxembourg, the Netherlands, Portugal, Spain, the UK, Austria, Finland, and Sweden) that have joined together to form an economic community, with some common monetary, political, and social aspirations. The EU was created in 1993 from the European Community, which itself grew from the European Coal and Steel Community, the European Atomic Energy Community, and the European Economic Community. Its executive body is the European Commission, which was formed in 1967 with the Council of the European Communities. EU policy emerges from a dialogue between the Commission, which initiates and implements the policy, and the Council, which takes the major policy decisions. The European Parliament, formed in 1957, exercises democratic control over policy, and the European Court of Justice imposes the rule of law on the EU, as set out in its various treaties.

europium /jʊˈrəʊpɪəm/ *n.* metallic element of the lanthanide series. [from EUROPE]

◆ **Europort** /ˈjʊərəʊˌpɔːt/ *n.* any of the main European ports, esp. Rotterdam.

◆ **Eurotunnel** /ˈjʊərəʊˌtʌn(ə)l/ *n.* = CHANNEL TUNNEL.

◆ **Euroyen** /ˈjʊərəʊˌjen/ see EUROCURRENCY.

Eustachian tube /juːˈsteɪʃ(ə)n/ *n.* tube from the pharynx to the cavity of the middle ear. [*Eustachio*, name of an anatomist]

euthanasia /ˌjuːθəˈneɪzɪə/ *n.* bringing about of a gentle death in the case of incurable and painful disease. [Greek *thanatos* death]

eV *symb.* electronvolt.

evacuate /ɪˈvækjʊˌeɪt/ *v.* (**-ting**) **1 a** remove (people) from a place of danger. **b** empty (a place) in this way. **2** make empty. **3** (of troops) withdraw from (a place). **4** empty (the bowels etc.). □ **evacuation** /-ˈeɪʃ(ə)n/ *n.* [Latin *vacuus* empty]

evacuee /ɪˌvækjuːˈiː/ *n.* person evacuated.

evade /ɪˈveɪd/ *v.* (**-ding**) **1 a** escape from, avoid, esp. by guile or trickery. **b** avoid doing (one's duty etc.). **c** avoid answering (a question). **2** avoid paying (tax). [Latin *evado* escape]

evaluate /ɪˈvæljʊˌeɪt/ *v.* (**-ting**) **1** assess, appraise. **2** find or state the number or amount of. □ **evaluation** /-ˈeɪʃ(ə)n/ *n.* [French: related to VALUE]

evanesce /ˌevəˈnes/ *v.* (**-cing**) *literary* fade from sight. [Latin *vanus* empty]

evanescent /ˌevəˈnes(ə)nt/ *adj.* quickly fading. □ **evanescence** *n.*

evangelical /ˌiːvænˈdʒelɪk(ə)l/ *–adj.* **1** of or according to the teaching of the gospel. **2** of the Protestant school maintaining the doctrine of salvation by faith. *–n.* member of this. □ **evangelicalism** *n.* **evangelically** *adv.* [Greek: related to EU-, ANGEL]

evangelism /ɪˈvændʒəˌlɪz(ə)m/ *n.* preaching or spreading of the gospel.

evangelist *n.* **1** writer of one of the four Gospels. **2** preacher of the gospel. □ **evangelistic** /-ˈlɪstɪk/ *adj.*

evangelize *v.* (also **-ise**) (**-zing** or **-sing**) **1** (also *absol.*) preach the gospel to. **2** convert to Christianity. □ **evangelization** /-ˈzeɪʃ(ə)n/ *n.*

evaporate /ɪˈvæpəˌreɪt/ *v.* (**-ting**) **1** turn from solid or liquid into vapour. **2** (cause to) lose moisture as vapour. **3** (cause to) disappear. □ **evaporable** *adj.* **evaporation** /-ˈreɪʃ(ə)n/ *n.* [Latin: related to VAPOUR]

evaporated milk *n.* unsweetened milk concentrated by evaporation.

evasion /ɪˈveɪʒ(ə)n/ *n.* **1** evading. **2** evasive answer. [Latin: related to EVADE]

evasive /ɪˈveɪsɪv/ *adj.* **1** seeking to evade. **2** not direct in one's answers etc. □ **evasively** *adv.* **evasiveness** *n.*

eve *n.* **1** evening or day before a festival etc. (*Christmas Eve*; *eve of the funeral*). **2** time just before an event (*eve of the election*). **3** *archaic* evening. [= EVEN[2]]

even[1] /ˈiːv(ə)n/ *–adj.* (**evener, evenest**) **1** level; smooth. **2 a** uniform in quality; constant. **b** equal in amount or value etc. **c** equally balanced. **3** (of a person's temper etc.) equable, calm. **4 a** (of a number) divisible by two without a remainder. **b** bearing such a number (*no parking on even dates*). **c** not involving fractions; exact (*in even dozens*). *–adv.* **1** inviting comparison of the assertion, negation, etc., with an implied one that is less strong or remarkable (*never even opened* [let alone read] *the letter*; *ran even faster* [not just as fast as before]). **2** introducing an extreme case (*even you must realize it*). *–v.* (often foll. by *up*) make or become even. □ **even now 1** now as well as before. **2** at this very moment. **even so** nevertheless. **even though** despite the fact that. **get** (or **be**) **even with** have one's revenge on. □ **evenly** *adv.* **evenness** *n.* [Old English]

even[2] /ˈiːv(ə)n/ *n. poet.* evening. [Old English]

even chance *n.* equal chance of success or failure.

even-handed *adj.* impartial.

evening /ˈiːvnɪŋ/ *n.* end part of the day, esp. from about 6 p.m. to bedtime. [Old English: related to EVEN[2]]

evening dress *n.* formal dress for evening wear.

evening primrose *n.* plant with pale-yellow flowers that open in the evening.

evening star *n.* planet, esp. Venus, conspicuous in the west after sunset.

even money *n.* betting odds offering the gambler the chance of winning the amount staked.

evens *n.pl.* = EVEN MONEY.

evensong *n.* service of evening prayer in the Church of England. [from EVEN[2]]

event /ɪˈvent/ *n.* **1** thing that happens. **2** fact of a thing's occurring. **3** item in a (esp. sports) programme. □ **at all events** (or **in any event**) whatever happens. **in the event** as it turns (or turned) out. **in the event of** if (a specified thing) happens. **in the event that** if it happens that. [Latin *venio vent-* come]

■ **Usage** The phrase *in the event that* is considered awkward by some people. It can usu. be avoided by rephrasing, e.g. *in the event that it rains* can be replaced by *in the event of rain*.

eventful *adj.* marked by noteworthy events. □ **eventfully** *adv.*

eventide /ˈiːv(ə)nˌtaɪd/ *n. archaic* or *poet.* = EVENING. [related to EVEN[2]]

eventing *n.* participation in equestrian competitions, esp. dressage and showjumping. [see EVENT 3]

eventual /ɪˈventʃʊəl/ *adj.* occurring in due course, ultimate. □ **eventually** *adv.* [from EVENT]

eventuality /ɪˌventʃʊˈælɪtɪ/ *n.* (*pl.* **-ies**) possible event or outcome.

eventuate /ɪˈventʃʊˌeɪt/ *v.* (**-ting**) (often foll. by *in*) result.

ever /ˈevə(r)/ *adv.* **1** at all times; always (*ever hopeful*; *ever after*). **2** at any time (*have you ever smoked?*). **3** (used for emphasis) in any way; at all (*how ever did you do it?*). **4** (in *comb.*) constantly (*ever-present*). **5** (foll. by *so, such*) *colloq.* very; very much (*ever so easy*; *thanks ever so*). □ **did you ever?** *colloq.* did you ever hear or see the like? **ever since** throughout the period since. [Old English]

■ **Usage** When *ever* is used with a question word for emphasis it is written separately (see sense 2). When used with a relative pronoun or adverb to give it indefinite or general force, *ever* is written as one word with the relative pronoun or adverb, e.g. *however it's done, it's difficult*.

evergreen *–adj.* retaining green leaves all year round. *–n.* evergreen plant.

◆ **evergreen fund** *n.* fund that provides capital for new companies and supports their development for a period with regular injections of capital.

everlasting *–adj.* **1** lasting for ever or for a long time. **2** (of flowers) keeping their shape and colour when dried. *–n.* **1** eternity. **2** everlasting flower.

evermore *adv.* for ever; always.

every /ˈevrɪ/ *adj.* **1** each single (*heard every word*). **2** each at a specified interval in a series (*comes every four days*). **3** all possible (*every prospect of success*). □ **every bit as** *colloq.* (in comparisons) quite as. **every now and again** (or **then**) from time to time. **every other** each second in a series (*every other day*). **every so often** occasionally. [Old English: related to EVER, EACH]

everybody *pron.* every person.

everyday *attrib. adj.* **1** occurring every day. **2** used on ordinary days. **3** commonplace.

Everyman *n.* ordinary or typical human being. [name of a character in a 15th-century morality play]

everyone *pron.* everybody.

every one *n.* each one.

everything *pron.* **1** all things. **2** most important thing (*speed is everything*).

everywhere *adv.* **1** in every place. **2** *colloq.* in many places.

evict /ɪ'vɪkt/ *v.* expel (a tenant etc.) by legal process. □ **eviction** *n.* [Latin *evinco evict-* conquer]

evidence /'evɪd(ə)ns/ *–n.* **1** (often foll. by *for, of*) available facts, circumstances, etc. indicating whether or not a thing is true or valid. **2** *Law* **a** information tending to prove a fact or proposition. **b** statements or proofs admissible as testimony in a lawcourt. *–v.* (**-cing**) be evidence of. □ **in evidence** conspicuous. **Queen's** (or **King's** or **state's**) **evidence** *Law* evidence for the prosecution given by a participant in the crime at issue. [Latin *video* see]

evident *adj.* plain or obvious; manifest. [Latin: related to EVIDENCE]

evidential /ˌevɪ'denʃ(ə)l/ *adj.* of or providing evidence.

evidently *adv.* **1** seemingly; as it appears. **2** as shown by evidence.

evil /'iːv(ə)l/ *–adj.* **1** morally bad; wicked. **2** harmful. **3** disagreeable (*evil temper*). *–n.* **1** evil thing. **2** wickedness. □ **evilly** *adv.* [Old English]

evildoer *n.* sinner. □ **evildoing** *n.*

evil eye *n.* gaze that is superstitiously believed to cause harm.

evince /ɪ'vɪns/ *v.* (**-cing**) indicate, display (a quality, feeling, etc.). [Latin: related to EVICT]

eviscerate /ɪ'vɪsəˌreɪt/ *v.* (**-ting**) disembowel. □ **evisceration** /-'reɪʃ(ə)n/ *n.* [Latin: related to VISCERA]

evocative /ɪ'vɒkətɪv/ *adj.* evoking (esp. feelings or memories). □ **evocatively** *adv.* **evocativeness** *n.*

evoke /ɪ'vəʊk/ *v.* (**-king**) inspire or draw forth (memories, a response, etc.). □ **evocation** /ˌevə'keɪʃ(ə)n/ *n.* [Latin *voco* call]

evolution /ˌiːvə'luːʃ(ə)n/ *n.* **1** gradual development. **2** development of species from earlier forms, as an explanation of their origins. **3** unfolding of events etc. (*evolution of the plot*). **4** change in the disposition of troops or ships. □ **evolutionary** *adj.* [Latin: related to EVOLVE]

evolutionist *n.* person who regards evolution as explaining the origin of species.

evolve /ɪ'vɒlv/ *v.* (**-ving**) **1** develop gradually and naturally. **2** devise (a theory, plan, etc.). **3** unfold. **4** give off (gas, heat, etc.). [Latin *volvo volut-* roll]

Évvoia see EUBOEA.

EW *international vehicle registration* Estonia.

ewe /juː/ *n.* female sheep. [Old English]

ewer /'juːə(r)/ *n.* water-jug with a wide mouth. [Latin *aqua* water]

EX *postcode* Exeter.

ex[1] *prep.* **1** (of goods) sold from. See EX QUAY; EX SHIP; EX WAREHOUSE; EX WORKS. **2** *Finance* excluding (specified benefits when a security is quoted). A share quoted **ex dividend** (**x.d.** or **ex div.**) means that a potential purchaser will no longer be entitled to receive the company's current dividend, the right to which remains with the vendor. Government stocks go ex dividend 36 days before the interest payment. Similarly, **ex rights**, **ex scrip**, **ex coupon**, **ex capitalization** (or **ex cap.**), and **ex bonus** (or **ex b.**) mean that each of these benefits belongs to the vendor rather than the buyer. **Ex all** means that all benefits belong to the vendor. **Cum** has exactly the opposite sense, meaning that the dividend or other benefits belong to the buyer rather than the seller. The price of a share that has gone ex dividend will usu. fall by the amount of the dividend, while one that is **cum dividend** will usu. rise by this amount. However, in practice market forces mean that these falls and rises are often slightly less than expected. [Latin, = out of]

ex[2] *n. colloq.* former husband or wife. [see EX-[1] 2]

ex-[1] *prefix* (also before some consonants **e-**, **ef-** before *f*) **1** forming verbs meaning: **a** out, forth (*exclude*; *exit*). **b** upward (*extol*). **c** thoroughly (*excruciate*). **d** bring into a state (*exasperate*). **e** remove or free from (*expatriate*; *exonerate*). **2** forming nouns from titles of office, status, etc., meaning 'formerly' (*ex-president*; *ex-wife*). [Latin from *ex* out of]

ex-[2] *prefix* out (*exodus*). [Greek]

exacerbate /ek'sæsəˌbeɪt/ *v.* (**-ting**) **1** make (pain etc.) worse. **2** irritate (a person). □ **exacerbation** /-'beɪʃ(ə)n/ *n.* [Latin *acerbus* bitter]

exact /ɪg'zækt/ *–adj.* **1** accurate; correct in all details (*exact description*). **2** precise. *–v.* **1** demand and enforce payment of (money etc.). **2** demand; insist on; require. □ **exactness** *n.* [Latin *exigo exact-* require]

exacting *adj.* **1** making great demands. **2** requiring much effort.

exaction /ɪg'zækʃ(ə)n/ *n.* **1** exacting or being exacted. **2 a** illegal or exorbitant demand; extortion. **b** sum or thing exacted.

exactitude *n.* exactness, precision.

exactly *adv.* **1** precisely. **2** (said in reply) I quite agree.

exact science *n.* a science in which absolute precision is possible.

exaggerate /ɪg'zædʒəˌreɪt/ *v.* (**-ting**) **1** (also *absol.*) make (a thing) seem larger or greater etc. than it really is. **2** increase beyond normal or due proportions (*exaggerated politeness*). □ **exaggeration** /-'reɪʃ(ə)n/ *n.* [Latin *agger* heap]

◆ **ex all** see EX[1] 2.

---

exalt /ɪg'zɔːlt/ *v.* **1** raise in rank or power etc. **2** praise highly. **3** (usu. as **exalted** *adj.*) make lofty or noble (*exalted aims*; *exalted style*). □ **exaltation** /ˌegzɔːl'teɪʃ(ə)n/ *n.* [Latin *altus* high]

exam /ɪg'zæm/ *n.* = EXAMINATION 3.

examination /ɪgˌzæmɪ'neɪʃ(ə)n/ *n.* **1** examining or being examined. **2** detailed inspection. **3** test of proficiency or knowledge by questions. **4** formal questioning of a witness etc. in court.

examine /ɪg'zæmɪn/ *v.* (**-ning**) **1** inquire into the nature or condition etc. of. **2** look closely at. **3** test the proficiency of. **4** check the health of (a patient). **5** formally question in court. □ **examinee** /-'niː/ *n.* **examiner** *n.* [Latin *examen* tongue of a balance]

example /ɪg'zɑːmp(ə)l/ *n.* **1** thing characteristic of its kind or illustrating a general rule. **2** person, thing, or piece of conduct, in terms of its fitness to be imitated. **3** circumstance or treatment seen as a warning to others. **4** problem or exercise designed to illustrate a rule. □ **for example** by way of illustration. [Latin *exemplum*: related to EXEMPT]

exasperate /ɪg'zɑːspəˌreɪt/ *v.* (**-ting**) irritate intensely. □ **exasperation** /-'reɪʃ(ə)n/ *n.* [Latin *asper* rough]

◆ **ex bonus** see EX[1] 2.

◆ **ex capitalization** see EX[1] 2.

---

ex cathedra /ˌeks kə'θiːdrə/ *adj.* & *adv.* with full authority (esp. of a papal pronouncement). [Latin, = from the chair]

excavate /'ekskəˌveɪt/ *v.* (**-ting**) **1 a** make (a hole or channel) by digging. **b** dig out material from (the ground). **2** reveal or extract by digging. **3** (also *absol.*) *Archaeol.* dig systematically to explore (a site). □ **excavation** /-'veɪʃ(ə)n/ *n.* **excavator** *n.* [Latin *excavo*: related to CAVE]

exceed /ɪk'siːd/ *v.* **1** (often foll. by *by* an amount) be more or greater than. **2** go beyond or do more than is warranted by (a set limit, esp. of one's authority, instructions, or rights). **3** surpass. [Latin *excedo -cess-* go beyond]

exceedingly /ɪk'siːdɪŋlɪ/ *adv.* extremely.

excel /ɪk'sel/ *v.* (**-ll-**) **1** surpass. **2** be pre-eminent. [Latin *excello* be eminent]

excellence /'eksələns/ *n.* outstanding merit or quality. [Latin: related to EXCEL]

Excellency *n.* (*pl.* **-ies**) (usu. prec. by *Your, His, Her, Their*) title used in addressing or referring to certain high officials.

excellent *adj.* extremely good.

excentric var. of ECCENTRIC (in technical senses).

except /ɪk'sept/ *–v.* exclude from a general statement, condition, etc. *–prep.* (often foll. by *for*) not including; other than (*all failed except him*; *is all right except that it is too long*). *–conj. archaic* unless (*except he be born again*). [Latin *excipio -cept-* take out]

♦ **excepted peril** see PERIL 2.

excepting *prep.* = EXCEPT *prep.*

■ **Usage** *Excepting* should be used only after *not* and *always*; otherwise, *except* should be used.

exception /ɪk'sepʃ(ə)n/ *n.* **1** excepting or being excepted. **2** thing that has been or will be excepted. **3** instance that does not follow a rule. □ **take exception** (often foll. by *to*) object. **with the exception of** except.

exceptionable *adj.* open to objection.

■ **Usage** *Exceptionable* is sometimes confused with *exceptional*.

exceptional *adj.* **1** forming an exception; unusual. **2** outstanding. □ **exceptionally** *adv.*

■ **Usage** See note at *exceptionable*.

♦ **exceptional items** *n.pl.* costs or income affecting a company's profit and loss account that arise from the normal activities of the company but are of exceptional magnitude, either large or small. These should be disclosed separately in arriving at the trading profit or loss but not after the normal trading profit or loss has been shown (cf. EXTRAORDINARY ITEMS).

excerpt *–n.* /'eksɜːpt/ short extract from a book, film, etc. *–v.* /ɪk'sɜːpt/ (also *absol.*) take excerpts from. □ **excerption** /-'sɜːpʃ(ə)n/ *n.* [Latin *carpo* pluck]

excess /ɪk'ses, 'ekses/ *–n.* **1** exceeding. **2** amount by which one thing exceeds another. **3 a** overstepping of accepted limits of moderation, esp. in eating or drinking. **b** (in *pl.*) immoderate behaviour. **4** part of an insurance claim to be paid by the insured, esp. in motor-vehicle and householders' insurance (cf. DEDUCTIBLE *n.*). See also EXCESS POLICY. *–attrib. adj.* usu. /'ekses/ **1** that exceeds a limited or prescribed amount. **2** required as extra payment (*excess postage*). □ **in** (or **to**) **excess** exceeding the proper amount or degree. **in excess of** more than; exceeding. [Latin: related to EXCEED]

excess baggage *n.* (also **excess luggage**) baggage exceeding a weight allowance and liable to an extra charge.

♦ **excess capacity** *n.* part of the output of a plant or process that is not currently being utilized but which, if it could be, would reduce the average cost of production. The excess capacity is thus the amount by which the present output must be increased to reduce the average cost per unit to a minimum.

♦ **excess demand** see EXCESS SUPPLY (OR DEMAND).

excessive /ɪk'sesɪv/ *adj.* too much or too great. □ **excessively** *adv.*

♦ **excess policy** *n.* insurance policy in which the insured is responsible for paying a specified sum (the **excess**) of each claim and cannot make claims of a lower value than this excess. For example, a £100 excess on a motor-insurance policy means that the insured has to pay the first £100 of any claim and cannot make a claim on the policy for less than £100. This arrangement enables the insurer to offer the insurance at a lower premium than would otherwise be the case as the administrative cost of small claims is avoided and a saving on claims paid out is made. See also DEDUCTIBLE *n.*; FRANCHISE *n.* 5.

♦ **excess supply** (or **demand**) *n.* amount by which the quantity of a good supplied (or demanded) in the market exceeds the quantity demanded (or supplied). It is a fundamental tenet of economics that excess supply (or demand) will be eliminated by falling (or rising) prices in a free market.

exchange /ɪks'tʃeɪndʒ/ *–n.* **1** giving of one thing and receiving of another in its place. **2** giving of money for its equivalent in the money of the same or another country. **3** centre where telephone connections are made. **4** place where merchants, bankers, etc. transact business. **5 a** office where information is given or a service provided. **b** employment office. **6** system of settling debts without the use of money, by bills of exchange. **7** *Econ.* process enabling values to be traded between individuals or groups. Values include physical goods, services, information, and even promises (e.g. options). The arena in which exchange takes place is a market; it is the focus of economic analysis. The achievement of the neoclassical school of economics has been to prove that under certain restrictive conditions the free exchange of values between individuals will yield a Pareto-optimal outcome (see PARETO OPTIMALITY), one that could not be improved upon by any other method of allocation. Much of modern economics is concerned with investigating the consequences of relaxing the restrictive conditions to take into account such real-world problems as monopoly, limited information, and the absence of certain markets. **8** short conversation. *–v.* (**-ging**) **1** (often foll. by *for*) give or receive (one thing) in place of another. **2** give and receive as equivalents. **3** (often foll. by *with*) make an exchange. □ **in exchange** (often foll. by *for*) as a thing exchanged (for). □ **exchangeable** *adj.* [French: related to CHANGE]

exchangeable disk store *n.* (also **EDS, demountable disk**) *Computing* disk pack or cartridge that can be removed from a disk drive and replaced by another of the same type and can be mounted on other disk drives of appropriate design. The use of EDS produces a 'library' of disks and greatly increases the amount of data that can be stored.

♦ **exchange control** *n.* process placing restrictions on the purchase and sale of foreign exchange. It is operated in various forms by many countries, esp. those who experience shortages of hard currencies; sometimes different regulations apply to transactions that would come under the capital account of the balance of payments. There has been a gradual movement toward dismantling exchange controls by many countries in recent years. The UK abolished all form of exchange control in 1979.

♦ **exchange equalization account** *n.* account set up in 1932 and managed by the Bank of England on behalf of the government. It contains the official gold and foreign-exchange reserves (including special drawing rights) of the UK and is used as a buyer of foreign exchange to support the value of sterling. Although all exchange controls were abolished in 1979, the Bank of England still makes use of this account to help to stabilize rates of exchange.

♦ **exchange of contracts** *n.* procedure adopted in the sale and purchase of land in which both parties sign their copies of the contract, having satisfied themselves as to the state of the property etc. and agreed that they wish to be bound. There need be no physical exchange of documents; the parties or their advisers can exchange contracts by agreeing to do so orally (e.g. by telephone). From that moment the contract is binding and can normally be enforced by specific performance. Contracts for the sale of land must be in writing.

exchange rate *n.* value of one currency in terms of another. See RATE OF EXCHANGE.

♦ **Exchange Rate Mechanism** see EUROPEAN MONETARY SYSTEM.

exchequer /ɪks'tʃekə(r)/ *n.* **1** former government department in charge of national revenue. **2** royal or national treasury. **3** money of a private individual or group. [medieval Latin *scaccarium* chessboard]

■ **Usage** With reference to sense 1, the functions of this department in the UK now belong to the Treasury, although the name formally survives, esp. in the title *Chancellor of the Exchequer*.

♦ **exchequer stocks** see GILT-EDGED SECURITY.

excise[1] /'eksaɪz/ *–n.* **1** (also **excise duty**) tax levied on certain goods, e.g. alcoholic drinks and tobacco products, produced and sold within the country of origin. Cf. CUSTOMS TARIFF. See also BOARD OF CUSTOMS AND EXCISE. **2** tax on certain licences. *–v.* (**-sing**) **1** charge excise on. **2** force (a person) to pay excise. [Dutch *excijs* from Romanic: related to Latin CENSUS tax]

excise[2] /ɪk'saɪz/ *v.* (**-sing**) **1** remove (a passage from a book etc.). **2** cut out (an organ etc.) by surgery. □ **excision** /ɪk'sɪʒ(ə)n/ *n.* [Latin *excido* cut out]

♦ **excise duty** *n.* = EXCISE[1] *n.* 1.

excitable /ɪk'saɪtəb(ə)l/ *adj.* easily excited. □ **excitability** /-'bɪlɪtɪ/ *n.* **excitably** *adv.*

excite /ɪk'saɪt/ *v.* (**-ting**) **1 a** rouse the emotions of (a person). **b** arouse (feelings etc.). **c** arouse sexually. **2** provoke (an action etc.). **3** stimulate (an organism, tissue, etc.) to activity. [Latin *cieo* stir up]

excitement *n.* **1** excited state of mind. **2** exciting thing.

exciting *adj.* arousing great interest or enthusiasm. □ **excitingly** *adv.*

exclaim /ɪk'skleɪm/ *v.* **1** cry out suddenly. **2** (foll. by *that*) utter by exclaiming. [Latin: related to CLAIM]

exclamation /ˌekskləˈmeɪʃ(ə)n/ *n.* **1** exclaiming. **2** word(s) exclaimed. [Latin: related to EXCLAIM]

exclamation mark *n.* punctuation mark (!) indicating exclamation.

exclamatory /ɪk'sklæmətərɪ/ *adj.* of or serving as an exclamation.

exclude /ɪk'skluːd/ *v.* (**-ding**) **1** keep out (a person or thing) from a place, group, privilege, etc. **2** remove from consideration (*no theory can be excluded*). **3** make impossible, preclude (*excluded all doubt*). □ **exclusion** *n.* [Latin *excludo -clus-* shut out]

exclusive /ɪk'skluːsɪv/ *–adj.* **1** excluding other things. **2** (*predic.*; foll. by *of*) not including; except for. **3** tending to exclude others, esp. socially. **4** high-class. **5** not obtainable elsewhere or not published elsewhere. *–n.* article etc. published by only one newspaper etc. □ **exclusively** *adv.* **exclusiveness** *n.* **exclusivity** /-'sɪvɪtɪ/ *n.* [medieval Latin: related to EXCLUDE]

♦ **exclusive economic zone** see TERRITORIAL WATERS.

excommunicate *–v.* /ˌekskəˈmjuːnɪˌkeɪt/ (**-ting**) officially exclude (a person) from membership and esp. sacraments of the Church. *–adj.* /ˌekskəˈmjuːnɪkət/ excommunicated. *–n.* /ˌekskəˈmjuːnɪkət/ excommunicated person. □ **excommunication** /-'keɪʃ(ə)n/ *n.* [Latin: related to COMMON]

excoriate /eks'kɔːrɪˌeɪt/ *v.* (**-ting**) **1 a** remove skin from (a person etc.) by abrasion. **b** strip off (skin). **2** censure severely. □ **excoriation** /-'eɪʃ(ə)n/ *n.* [Latin *corium* hide]

♦ **ex coupon** see EX[1] 2.

excrement /'ekskrɪmənt/ *n.* faeces. □ **excremental** /-'ment(ə)l/ *adj.* [Latin: related to EXCRETE]

excrescence /ɪk'skres(ə)ns/ *n.* **1** abnormal or morbid outgrowth on the body or a plant. **2** ugly addition. □ **excrescent** *adj.* [Latin *cresco* grow]

excreta /ɪk'skriːtə/ *n.pl.* faeces and urine. [Latin: related to EXCRETE]

excrete /ɪk'skriːt/ *v.* (**-ting**) (of an animal or plant) expel (waste matter). □ **excretion** *n.* **excretory** *adj.* [Latin *cerno cret-* sift]

excruciating /ɪk'skruːʃɪˌeɪtɪŋ/ *adj.* causing acute mental or physical pain. □ **excruciatingly** *adv.* [Latin *crucio* torment]

exculpate /'ekskʌlˌpeɪt/ *v.* (**-ting**) *formal* (often foll. by *from*) free from blame; clear of a charge. □ **exculpation** /-'peɪʃ(ə)n/ *n.* **exculpatory** /-'kʌlpətərɪ/ *adj.* [Latin *culpa* blame]

excursion /ɪk'skɜːʃ(ə)n/ *n.* journey (usu. a day-trip) to a place and back, made for pleasure. [Latin *excurro* run out]

excursive /ɪk'skɜːsɪv/ *adj. literary* digressive.

excuse *–v.* /ɪk'skjuːz/ (**-sing**) **1** try to lessen the blame attaching to (a person, act, or fault). **2** (of a fact) serve as a reason to judge (a person or act) less severely. **3** (often foll. by *from*) release (a person) from a duty etc. **4** forgive (a fault or offence). **5** (foll. by *for*) forgive (a person) for (a fault). **6** *refl.* leave with apologies. *–n.* /ɪk'skjuːs/ **1** reason put forward to mitigate or justify an offence. **2** apology (*made my excuses*). □ **be excused** be allowed to leave the room etc. or be absent. **excuse me** polite preface to an interruption etc., or to disagreeing. □ **excusable** /-'kjuːzəb(ə)l/ *adj.* [Latin *causa* accusation]

ex-directory /ˌeksdəˈrektərɪ/ *adj.* not listed in a telephone directory, at one's own request.

♦ **ex dividend** see EX[1] 2.

execrable /'eksɪkrəb(ə)l/ *adj.* abominable. [Latin: related to EXECRATE]

execrate /'eksɪˌkreɪt/ *v.* (**-ting**) **1** express or feel abhorrence for. **2** (also *absol.*) curse (a person or thing). □ **execration** /-'kreɪʃ(ə)n/ *n.* [Latin *exsecror* curse: related to SACRED]

execute /'eksɪˌkjuːt/ *v.* (**-ting**) **1** carry out, perform (a plan, duty etc.). **2** carry out a design for (a product of art or skill). **3** carry out a death sentence on. **4** make (a legal instrument) valid by signing, sealing, etc. **5** *Computing* carry out (a program); run. A program executes from the time that it is started until either it completes its task and returns control to the operating system or it encounters an error whose severity prevents it from continuing. See also CONTROL UNIT. [Latin *sequor* follow]

execution /ˌeksɪˈkjuːʃ(ə)n/ *n.* **1** carrying out; performance. **2** technique or style of performance in the arts, esp. music. **3** carrying out of a death sentence. [Latin: related to EXECUTE]

executioner *n.* official who carries out a death sentence.

executive /ɪg'zekjʊtɪv/ *–n.* **1** person or body with managerial or administrative responsibility. **2** branch of a government etc. concerned with executing laws, agreements, etc. *–adj.* concerned with executing laws, agreements, etc., or with other administration or management. [medieval Latin: related to EXECUTE]

♦ **executive director** *n.* (also **working director**) director of a company who is also an employee (usu. full-time) of that company. An executive director will often have a specified role in the management of the company, e.g. finance director, marketing director, production director. See also DIRECTOR 1. Cf. NON-EXECUTIVE DIRECTOR.

♦ **executive pension plan** *n.* (also **EPP**) pension for a senior executive or director of a company in which the company provides a tax-deductible contribution to the premium. An EPP may be additional to any group pension scheme provided by the company, as long as the pension limit of two-thirds of the working salary is not exceeded.

♦ **executive share option** *n.* form of profit-sharing scheme in which the executives of a company are given options to purchase shares in the company at preferential rates.

executor /ɪg'zekjʊtə(r)/ *n.* (*fem.* **executrix** /-trɪks/) person named in a will of another person (the testator) to gather in the assets of the testator's estate, pay any liabilities, and distribute any residue to the beneficiaries in accordance with the instructions contained in the will. □ **executorial** /-'tɔːrɪəl/ *adj.*

exegesis /ˌeksɪˈdʒiːsɪs/ *n.* (*pl.* **exegeses** /-siːz/) critical explanation of a text, esp. of Scripture. □ **exegetic** /-'dʒetɪk/ *adj.* [Greek *hēgeomai* lead]

exemplar /ɪg'zemplə(r)/ *n.* **1** model. **2** typical or parallel instance. [Latin: related to EXAMPLE]

exemplary *adj.* **1** fit to be imitated; outstandingly good.

2 serving as a warning. **3** illustrative. [Latin: related to EXAMPLE]

◆ **exemplary damages** see DAMAGES.

exemplify /ɪg'zemplɪˌfaɪ/ *v.* (**-ies, -ied**) **1** illustrate by example. **2** be an example of. □ **exemplification** /-fɪ'keɪʃ(ə)n/ *n.*

exempt /ɪg'zempt/ *–adj.* (often foll. by *from*) free from an obligation or liability etc. imposed on others. *–v.* (foll. by *from*) make exempt. □ **exemption** *n.* [Latin *eximo -empt-* take out]

◆ **exempt gilts** *n.pl.* government gilt-edged securities that pay interest gross, unlike ordinary gilts on which tax is deducted from interest payments. These gilts are of particular interest to foreign buyers and others, e.g. institutions, who do not pay income tax.

◆ **exempt transfers** *n.* transfers made as a gift during a person's lifetime that do not result in a liability to inheritance tax. They include gifts to spouses and charities, marriage gifts by a parent of up to £5000, gifts of up to £3000 per annum, and gifts to political parties.

exercise /'eksəˌsaɪz/ *–n.* **1** activity requiring physical effort, done to sustain or improve health. **2** mental or spiritual activity, esp. as practice to develop a faculty. **3** task devised as exercise. **4 a** use or application of a mental faculty, right, etc. **b** practice of an ability, quality, etc. **5** (often in *pl.*) military drill or manoeuvres. *–v.* (**-sing**) **1** use or apply (a faculty, right, etc.). **2** perform (a function). **3 a** take (esp. physical) exercise. **b** provide (an animal) with exercise. **4 a** tax the powers of. **b** perplex, worry. [Latin *exerceo* keep busy]

◆ **exercise date** *n.* date on which the holder of a traded option can be called upon to implement the option contract.

◆ **exercise notice** *n.* formal notification from the owner of an option to the person of the firm that has written it that the owner wishes to exercise the option to buy (for a call option) or sell (for a put option) at the exercise price. See also OPTION 3.

◆ **exercise price** *n.* (also **striking price**) price per share at which a traded option entitles the owner to buy the underlying security in a call option or to sell it in a put option. See also EXERCISE NOTICE; OPTION 3.

exert /ɪg'zɜːt/ *v.* **1** bring to bear, use (a quality, force, influence, etc.). **2** *refl.* (often foll. by *for*, or *to* + infin.) use one's efforts or endeavours; strive. □ **exertion** *n.* [Latin *exsero exsert-* put forth]

exeunt /'eksɪˌʌnt/ *v.* (as a stage direction) (actors) leave the stage. [Latin: related to EXIT]

◆ **ex factory** *adj.* & *adv.* = EX WORKS.

exfoliate /eks'fəʊlɪˌeɪt/ *v.* (**-ting**) **1** come off in scales or layers. **2** throw off layers of bark. □ **exfoliation** /-'eɪʃ(ə)n/ *n.* [Latin *folium* leaf]

ex gratia /eks 'greɪʃə/ *–adv.* as a favour; out of gratitude, kindness, etc. rather than from legal obligation. *–attrib. adj.* granted on this basis (*an ex gratia payment*). [Latin, = from favour]

◆ **ex growth** *adj.* (of a share or a company) having had substantial growth in the past but now not holding out prospects for immediate growth of earnings or value.

exhale /eks'heɪl/ *v.* (**-ling**) **1** breathe out. **2** give off or be given off in vapour. □ **exhalation** /ˌekshə'leɪʃ(ə)n/ *n.* [French from Latin *halo* breathe]

exhaust /ɪg'zɔːst/ *–v.* **1** consume or use up the whole of. **2** (often as **exhausted** *adj.* or **exhausting** *adj.*) tire out. **3** study or expound (a subject) completely. **4** (often foll. by *of*) empty (a vessel etc.) of its contents. *–n.* **1** waste gases etc. expelled from an engine after combustion. **2** (also **exhaust-pipe**) pipe or system by which these are expelled. **3** process of expulsion of these gases. □ **exhaustible** *adj.* [Latin *haurio haust-* drain]

exhaustion /ɪg'zɔːstʃ(ə)n/ *n.* **1** exhausting or being exhausted. **2** total loss of strength.

exhaustive /ɪg'zɔːstɪv/ *adj.* thorough, comprehensive. □ **exhaustively** *adv.* **exhaustiveness** *n.*

exhibit /ɪg'zɪbɪt/ *–v.* (**-t-**) **1** show or reveal, esp. publicly. **2** display (a quality etc.). *–n.* item displayed, esp. in an exhibition or as evidence in a lawcourt. □ **exhibitor** *n.* [Latin *exhibeo -hibit-*]

exhibition /ˌeksɪ'bɪʃ(ə)n/ *n.* **1** display (esp. public) of works of art etc. **2** exhibiting or being exhibited. **3** scholarship, esp. from the funds of a school, college, etc.

exhibitioner *n.* student who has been awarded an exhibition.

exhibitionism *n.* **1** tendency towards attention-seeking behaviour. **2** *Psychol.* compulsion to display one's genitals in public. □ **exhibitionist** *n.*

exhilarate /ɪg'zɪləˌreɪt/ *–v.* (often as **exhilarating** *–adj.* or **exhilarated** *–adj.*) enliven, gladden; raise the spirits of. □ **exhilaration** /-'reɪʃ(ə)n/ *n.* [Latin *hilaris* cheerful]

exhort /ɪg'zɔːt/ *v.* (often foll. by *to* + infin.) urge strongly or earnestly. □ **exhortation** /ˌegzɔː'teɪʃ(ə)n/ *n.* **exhortative** /-tətɪv/ *adj.* **exhortatory** /-tətərɪ/ *adj.* [Latin *exhortor* encourage]

exhume /eks'hjuːm/ *v.* (**-ming**) dig up (esp. a buried corpse). □ **exhumation** /-'meɪʃ(ə)n/ *n.* [Latin *humus* ground]

exigency /'eksɪdʒənsɪ/ *n.* (*pl.* **-ies**) (also **exigence**) **1** urgent need or demand. **2** emergency. □ **exigent** *adj.* [Latin *exigo* EXACT]

exiguous /eg'zɪgjʊəs/ *adj.* scanty, small. □ **exiguity** /-'gjuːɪtɪ/ *n.* [Latin]

exile /'eksaɪl/ *–n.* **1** expulsion from one's native land or (**internal exile**) native town etc. **2** long absence abroad. **3** exiled person. *–v.* (**-ling**) send into exile. [French from Latin]

◆ **Eximbank** /'eksɪmˌbæŋk/ *n.* = EXPORT-IMPORT BANK.

ex int. *abbr. Banking* without interest. [Latin *ex* without]

exist /ɪg'zɪst/ *v.* **1** have a place in objective reality. **2** (of circumstances etc.) occur; be found. **3** live with no pleasure. **4** continue in being. **5** live. [Latin *existo*]

existence *n.* **1** fact or manner of being or existing. **2** continuance in life or being. **3** all that exists. □ **existent** *adj.*

existential /ˌegzɪ'stenʃ(ə)l/ *adj.* **1** of or relating to existence. **2** *Philos.* concerned with existence, esp. with human existence as viewed by existentialism. □ **existentially** *adv.*

existentialism *n.* philosophical theory emphasizing the existence of the individual as a free and self-determining agent. □ **existentialist** *n.* & *adj.*

exit /'eksɪt/ *–n.* **1** passage or door by which to leave a room etc. **2** act or right of going out. **3** place where vehicles can leave a motorway etc. **4** actor's departure from the stage. *–v.* (**-t-**) **1** go out of a room etc. **2** leave the stage (also as a direction: *exit Macbeth*). **3** *Computing* transfer control away from a program etc. [Latin *exeo exit-* go out]

exit poll *n.* poll of people leaving a polling-station, asking how they voted.

◆ **ex new** *adv.* & *adj.* (also **ex n., x.n.**) (of a share) offered for sale without the right to take up any scrip issue or rights issue.

exo- *comb. form* external. [Greek *exō* outside]

exocrine /'eksəʊˌkraɪn/ *adj.* (of a gland) secreting through a duct. [Greek *krinō* sift]

exodus /'eksədəs/ *n.* **1** mass departure. **2** (**Exodus**) Biblical departure of the Israelites from Egypt. [Greek *hodos* way]

ex officio /ˌeks ə'fɪʃɪəʊ/ *adv.* & *attrib.adj.* by virtue of one's office. [Latin]

exonerate /ɪg'zɒnəˌreɪt/ *v.* (**-ting**) (often foll. by *from*) free or declare free from blame etc. □ **exoneration** /-'reɪʃ(ə)n/ *n.* [Latin *onus oner-* burden]

exorbitant /ɪg'zɔːbɪt(ə)nt/ *adj.* (of a price, demand, etc.) grossly excessive. [Latin: related to ORBIT]

exorcize /'eksɔːˌsaɪz/ *v.* (also **-ise**) (**-zing** or **-sing**) **1** expel (a supposed evil spirit) by prayers etc. **2** (often foll. by *of*) free (a person or place) in this way. □ **exorcism** *n.* **exorcist** *n.* [Greek *horkos* oath]

exordium /ek'sɔːdɪəm/ *n.* (*pl.* **-s** or **-dia**) introductory part, esp. of a discourse or treatise. [Latin *exordior* begin]

exotic /ɪg'zɒtɪk/ *–adj.* **1** introduced from or originating in a foreign country. **2** strange or unusual. *–n.* exotic person or thing. □ **exotically** *adv.* [Greek *exō* outside]

exotica *n.pl.* strange or rare objects.

expand /ɪk'spænd/ *v.* **1** increase in size or importance. **2** (often foll. by *on*) give a fuller account. **3** become more genial. **4** set or write out in full. **5** spread out flat. □ **expandable** *adj.* [Latin *pando pans-* spread]

expanse /ɪk'spæns/ *n.* wide continuous area of land, space, etc.

expansible *adj.* that can be expanded.

expansion /ɪk'spænʃ(ə)n/ *n.* **1** expanding or being expanded. **2** enlargement of the scale or scope of a business.

expansion card *n.* (also **expansion board, add-in card**) electronic circuit that can be added to the existing circuitry in a microcomputer in order to improve the performance and capability of the computer. The cards may supply a particular need, e.g. additional memory (**memory cards**), improved graphics (**graphics cards**), or the possibility of communications (**communication cards**). The popular **multifunction card** provides a range of functions, e.g. extra memory, a connection point for a printer, a connection point for communications, and a built-in digital clock.

expansionism *n.* advocacy of expansion, esp. of a state's territory. □ **expansionist** *n.*

expansive /ɪk'spænsɪv/ *adj.* **1** able or tending to expand. **2** extensive. **3** (of a person etc.) effusive, open. □ **expansively** *adv.* **expansiveness** *n.*

expatiate /ɪk'speɪʃɪˌeɪt/ *v.* (**-ting**) (usu. foll. by *on, upon*) speak or write at length. □ **expatiation** /-'eɪʃ(ə)n/ *n.* **expatiatory** /-ʃɪətərɪ/ *adj.* [Latin *spatium* SPACE]

expatriate *–adj.* /eks'pætrɪət/ **1** living abroad. **2** exiled. *–n.* /eks'pætrɪət, -'peɪtrɪət/ expatriate person. *–v.* /eks'pætrɪˌeɪt/ (**-ting**) **1** expel (a person) from his or her native country. **2** *refl.* renounce one's citizenship. □ **expatriation** /-'eɪʃ(ə)n/ *n.* [Latin *patria* native land]

expect /ɪk'spekt/ *v.* **1 a** regard as likely. **b** look for as appropriate or one's due (*I expect cooperation*). **2** *colloq.* think, suppose. □ **be expecting** *colloq.* be pregnant (with). [Latin *specto* look]

expectancy /ɪk'spektənsɪ/ *n.* (*pl.* **-ies**) **1** state of expectation. **2** prospect. **3** (foll. by *of*) prospective chance.

expectant /ɪk'spekt(ə)nt/ *adj.* **1** (often foll. by *of*) expecting. **2** having an expectation. **3** pregnant. □ **expectantly** *adv.*

expectation /ˌekspek'teɪʃ(ə)n/ *n.* **1** expecting or anticipation. **2** thing expected. **3** (foll. by *of*) probability of an event. **4** (in *pl.*) one's prospects of inheritance.

expectorant /ek'spektərənt/ *–adj.* causing expectoration. *–n.* expectorant medicine.

expectorate /ek'spektəˌreɪt/ *v.* (**-ting**) (also *absol.*) cough or spit out (phlegm etc.). □ **expectoration** /-'reɪʃ(ə)n/ *n.* [Latin *pectus pector-* breast]

expedient /ɪk'spiːdɪənt/ *–adj.* advantageous; advisable on practical rather than moral grounds. *–n.* means of attaining an end; resource. □ **expedience** *n.* **expediency** *n.* [related to EXPEDITE]

expedite /'ekspɪˌdaɪt/ *v.* (**-ting**) **1** assist the progress of. **2** accomplish (business) quickly. [Latin *expedio* from *pes ped-* foot]

expedition /ˌekspɪ'dɪʃ(ə)n/ *n.* **1** journey or voyage for a particular purpose, esp. exploration. **2** people etc. undertaking this. **3** speed. [Latin: related to EXPEDITE]

expeditionary *adj.* of or used in an expedition.

expeditious /ˌekspɪ'dɪʃəs/ *adj.* acting or done with speed and efficiency.

expel /ɪk'spel/ *v.* (**-ll-**) (often foll. by *from*) **1** deprive (a person) of membership etc. of a school, society, etc. **2** force out, eject. **3** order or force to leave a building etc. [Latin *pello puls-* drive]

expend /ɪk'spend/ *v.* spend or use up (money, time, etc.). [Latin *pendo pens-* weigh]

expendable *adj.* that may be sacrificed or dispensed with; not worth preserving or saving.

expenditure /ɪk'spendɪtʃə(r)/ *n.* **1** spending or using up. **2** thing expended, esp. money spent for goods or services. Expenditure may or may not become an expense in the profit and loss account, depending on whether any residual value remains for the purchasing organization.

♦ **expenditure tax** *n.* (also **outlay tax**) tax on the expenditure of individuals or households, e.g. VAT.

---

expense /ɪk'spens/ *n.* **1** cost incurred; payment of money. **2** (usu. in *pl.*) **a** costs incurred in doing a job etc. **b** amount paid to reimburse this. **c** sums spent for goods or services, usu. shown as charge against profit in the profit and loss account. **3** thing on which money is spent. □ **at the expense of** so as to cause loss or harm to; costing. [Latin *expensa*: related to EXPEND]

expense account *n.* list of an employee's expenses payable by the employer, which is submitted to the Inland Revenue on a P11D form for assessment of any taxable element.

expensive *adj.* costing or charging much. □ **expensively** *adv.* **expensiveness** *n.*

experience /ɪk'spɪərɪəns/ *–n.* **1** observation of or practical acquaintance with facts or events. **2** knowledge or skill resulting from this. **3** event or activity participated in or observed (*a rare experience*). *–v.* (**-cing**) **1** have experience of; undergo. **2** feel. [Latin *experior -pert-* try]

experienced *adj.* **1** having had much experience. **2** skilled from experience (*experienced driver*).

experiential /ɪkˌspɪərɪ'enʃ(ə)l/ *adj.* involving or based on experience. □ **experientially** *adv.*

experiment /ɪk'sperɪmənt/ *–n.* procedure adopted in the hope of success, or for testing a hypothesis etc., or to demonstrate a known fact. *–v.* /also -ˌment/ (often foll. by *on, with*) make an experiment. □ **experimentation** /-men'teɪʃ(ə)n/ *n.* **experimenter** *n.* [Latin: related to EXPERIENCE]

experimental /ɪkˌsperɪ'ment(ə)l/ *adj.* **1** based on or making use of experiment. **2** used in experiments. □ **experimentalism** *n.* **experimentally** *adv.*

expert /'ekspɜːt/ *–adj.* **1** (often foll. by *at, in*) having special knowledge of or skill in a subject. **2** (*attrib.*) involving or resulting from this (*expert advice*). *–n.* (often foll. by *at, in*) person with special knowledge or skill. □ **expertly** *adv.* [Latin: related to EXPERIENCE]

expertise /ˌekspɜː'tiːz/ *n.* expert skill, knowledge, or judgement. [French]

♦ **expert system** *n.* (also **intelligent knowledge-based system, IKBS**) computer program that simulates the knowledge and experience of an expert in a particular field enabling it to solve problems in that field. It can be questioned by a non-expert and will give the answer that the expert would give. Expert systems are an application of artificial intelligence techniques. They are finding increasing use in commerce for such tasks as evaluating loan applications and buying stocks and shares.

---

expiate /'ekspɪˌeɪt/ *v.* (**-ting**) pay the penalty for or make amends for (wrongdoing). □ **expiable** /'ekspɪəb(ə)l/ *adj.* **expiation** /-'eɪʃ(ə)n/ *n.* **expiatory** *adj.* [Latin *expio*: related to PIOUS]

expire /ɪk'spaɪə(r)/ *v.* (**-ring**) **1** (of a period of time, validity, etc.) come to an end. **2** cease to be valid. **3** die. **4** (also *absol.*) breathe out (air etc.). □ **expiration** /ˌekspɪ'reɪʃ(ə)n/ *n.* **expiratory** *adj.* (in sense 4). [Latin *spirare* breathe]

expiry *n.* end of validity or duration.

◆ **expiry date** *n.* **1** date on which a contract expires. **2** last day on which an option expires. In a European option the option must be taken up or allowed to lapse on this date. In an American option the decision can be taken at any time up to the expiry date.

---

explain /ɪk'spleɪn/ *v.* **1 a** make clear or intelligible (also *absol.*: *let me explain*). **b** make known in detail. **2** (foll. by *that*) say by way of explanation. **3** account for (one's conduct etc.). □ **explain away** minimize the significance of by explanation. **explain oneself 1** make one's meaning clear. **2** give an account of one's motives or conduct. [Latin *explano* from *planus* flat]

explanation /ˌeksplə'neɪʃ(ə)n/ *n.* **1** explaining. **2** statement or circumstance that explains something.

explanatory /ɪk'splænətərɪ/ *adj.* serving or designed to explain.

expletive /ɪk'spliːtɪv/ *n.* swear-word or exclamation. [Latin *expleo* fill out]

explicable /ɪk'splɪkəb(ə)l/ *adj.* that can be explained.

explicate /'ekspliˌkeɪt/ *v.* (**-ting**) **1** develop the meaning of (an idea etc.). **2** explain (esp. a literary text). □ **explication** /-'keɪʃ(ə)n/ *n.* [Latin *explico -plicat-* unfold]

explicit /ɪk'splɪsɪt/ *adj.* **1** expressly stated, not merely implied; stated in detail. **2** definite. **3** outspoken. □ **explicitly** *adv.* **explicitness** *n.* [Latin: related to EXPLICATE]

explode /ɪk'spləʊd/ *v.* (**-ding**) **1 a** expand suddenly with a loud noise owing to a release of internal energy. **b** cause (a bomb etc.) to explode. **2** give vent suddenly to emotion, esp. anger. **3** (of a population etc.) increase suddenly or rapidly. **4** show (a theory etc.) to be false or baseless. **5** (as **exploded** *adj.*) (of a drawing etc.) showing the components of a mechanism somewhat separated but in the normal relative positions. [Latin *explodo -plos-* hiss off the stage]

exploit *–n.* /'eksplɔɪt/ daring feat. *–v.* /ɪk'splɔɪt/ **1** make use of (a resource etc.). **2** usu. *derog.* utilize or take advantage of (esp. a person) for one's own ends. □ **exploitation** /ˌeksplɔɪ'teɪʃ(ə)n/ *n.* **exploitative** /ɪk'splɔɪtətɪv/ *adj.* **exploiter** *n.* [Latin: related to EXPLICATE]

explore /ɪk'splɔː(r)/ *v.* (**-ring**) **1** travel through (a country etc.) to learn about it. **2** inquire into. **3** *Surgery* examine (a part of the body) in detail. □ **exploration** /ˌeksplə'reɪʃ(ə)n/ *n.* **exploratory** /-'splɒrətrɪ/ *adj.* **explorer** *n.* [Latin *exploro* search out]

explosion /ɪk'spləʊʒ(ə)n/ *n.* **1** exploding. **2** loud noise caused by this. **3** sudden outbreak of feeling. **4** rapid or sudden increase. [Latin: related to EXPLODE]

explosive /ɪk'spləʊsɪv/ *–adj.* **1** able, tending, likely to explode. **2** likely to cause a violent outburst etc.; dangerously tense. *–n.* explosive substance. □ **explosiveness** *n.*

Expo /'ekspəʊ/ *n.* (also **expo**) (*pl.* **-s**) large international exhibition. [abbreviation of EXPOSITION 4]

exponent /ɪk'spəʊnənt/ *n.* **1** person who promotes an idea etc. **2** practitioner of an activity, profession, etc. **3** person who explains or interprets something. **4** type or representative. **5** raised symbol beside a numeral indicating how many of the number are to be multiplied together (e.g. $2^3 = 2 \times 2 \times 2$). [Latin *expono* EXPOUND]

exponential /ˌekspə'nenʃ(ə)l/ *adj.* **1** of or indicated by a mathematical exponent. **2** (of an increase etc.) more and more rapid.

export *–v.* /ɪk'spɔːt, 'ek-/ sell or send (goods or services) to another country. *–n.* /'ekspɔːt/ **1** exporting. **2 a** exported article or service. **b** (in *pl.*) amount of goods or services sold to foreign countries. In terms of the balance of payments, goods are classified as visibles, while such services as banking, insurance, and tourism are treated as invisibles. The UK has traditionally relied on its invisibles to achieve its trade balance as it tends to spend more on imports than it receives in exports. See also EXPORT CREDITS GUARANTEE DEPARTMENT. □ **exportation** /-'teɪʃ(ə)n/ *n.* **exporter** /ɪk'spɔːtə(r)/ *n.* [Latin *porto* carry]

◆ **Export Credits Guarantee Department** *n.* (also **ECGD**) UK government department, responsible to the Secretary of State for Trade and Industry, that operates under the Export Guarantees and Overseas Investment Act (1978). It encourages exports from the UK by making export credit insurance available to exporters and guaranteeing repayment to UK banks that provide finance for exports on credit terms of two years or more. It also insures British private investment overseas against war risk, expropriation, and restrictions on the making of remittances. It was largely privatized in 1991.

◆ **Export-Import Bank** *n.* (also **Eximbank**) US bank established by the US government to foster trade with the US. It provides export credit guarantees and guarantees loans made by commercial banks to US exporters.

◆ **export incentive** *n.* incentive offered by a government to exporters. These incentives can include subsidies, grants, tax concessions, credit facilities, etc.

◆ **export licence** *n.* licence required before goods can be exported from a country. Export licences are only required in the UK for certain works of art, antiques, etc., and certain types of arms and armaments.

---

expose /ɪk'spəʊz/ *v.* (**-sing**) (esp. as **exposed** *adj.*) **1** leave uncovered or unprotected, esp. from the weather. **2** (foll. by *to*) **a** put at risk of. **b** subject to (an influence etc.). **3** *Photog.* subject (a film) to light, esp. by operation of a camera. **4** reveal the identity or fact of. **5** exhibit, display. □ **expose oneself** display one's body, esp. one's genitals, indecently in public. [Latin *pono* put]

exposé /ek'spəʊzeɪ/ *n.* **1** orderly statement of facts. **2** revelation of something discreditable. [French]

exposition /ˌekspə'zɪʃ(ə)n/ *n.* **1** explanatory account. **2** explanation or commentary. **3** *Mus.* part of a movement in which the principal themes are presented. **4** large public exhibition. [Latin: related to EXPOUND]

ex post facto /ˌeks pəʊst 'fæktəʊ/ *adj.* & *adv.* with retrospective action or force. [Latin, = in the light of subsequent events]

expostulate /ɪk'spɒstjʊˌleɪt/ *v.* (**-ting**) (often foll. by *with* a person) make a protest; remonstrate. □ **expostulation** /-'leɪʃ(ə)n/ *n.* **expostulatory** /-lətərɪ/ *adj.* [Latin: related to POSTULATE]

exposure /ɪk'spəʊʒə(r)/ *n.* (foll. by *to*) **1** exposing or being exposed. **2** physical condition resulting from being exposed to the elements. **3** *Photog.* **a** exposing a film etc. to the light. **b** duration of this. **c** section of film etc. affected by it.

expound /ɪk'spaʊnd/ *v.* **1** set out in detail. **2** explain or interpret. [Latin *pono posit-* place]

express /ɪk'spres/ *–v.* **1** represent or make known in words or by gestures, conduct, etc. **2** *refl.* communicate what one thinks, feels, or means. **3** esp. *Math.* represent by symbols. **4** squeeze out (liquid or air). **5** send by express service. *–adj.* **1** operating at high speed. **2** also /'ekspres/ definitely stated. **3** delivered by a specially fast service. *–adv.* **1** at high speed. **2** by express messenger or train. *–n.* **1** express train etc. **2** *US* service for the rapid transport of parcels etc. □ **expressible** *adj.* **expressly** *adv.* (in sense 2 of *adj.*). [Latin *exprimo -press-* squeeze out]

expression /ɪk'spreʃ(ə)n/ *n.* **1** expressing or being expressed. **2** word or phrase expressed. **3** person's facial appearance, indicating feeling. **4** conveying of feeling in music, speaking, dance, etc. **5** depiction of feeling etc. in art. **6** *Math.* collection of symbols expressing a quantity. □ **expressionless** *adj.* [French: related to EXPRESS]

expressionism *n.* style of painting, music, drama, etc., seeking to express emotion rather than the external world. □ **expressionist** *n.* & *adj.*

expressive /ɪk'spresɪv/ *adj.* **1** full of expression (*expressive look*). **2** (foll. by *of*) serving to express. □ **expressively** *adv.* **expressiveness** *n.*

expresso var. of ESPRESSO.

expressway *n. US* motorway.

expropriate /ɪk'sprəʊprɪˌeɪt/ *v.* (**-ting**) **1** take away (property) from its owner. **2** (foll. by *from*) dispossess. □ **expropriation** /-'eɪʃ(ə)n/ *n.* **expropriator** *n.* [Latin *proprium* property]

expulsion /ɪk'spʌlʃ(ə)n/ *n.* expelling or being expelled. □ **expulsive** *adj.* [Latin: related to EXPEL]

expunge /ɪk'spʌndʒ/ *v.* (**-ging**) erase, remove (objectionable matter) from a book etc. [Latin *expungo* prick out (for deletion)]

expurgate /'ekspəˌgeɪt/ *v.* (**-ting**) **1** remove objectionable matter from (a book etc.). **2** remove (such matter). □ **expurgation** /-'geɪʃ(ə)n/ *n.* **expurgator** *n.* [Latin: related to PURGE]

♦ **ex quay** *adj.* & *adv.* denoting delivery terms for goods in which the seller pays all freight charges up to the port of destination, unloading onto the quay, and loading onto road or rail vehicles. Thereafter all transport charges must be paid by the buyer.

---

exquisite /'ekskwɪzɪt/ *adj.* **1** extremely beautiful or delicate. **2** keenly felt (*exquisite pleasure*). **3** highly sensitive (*exquisite taste*). □ **exquisitely** *adv.* [Latin *exquiro -quisit-* seek out]

♦ **ex rights** see EX[1] 2; EX NEW.

♦ **ex scrip** see EX[1] 2; EX NEW.

---

ex-serviceman /eks'sɜːvɪsmən/ *n.* man formerly a member of the armed forces.

ex-servicewoman /eks'sɜːvɪsˌwʊmən/ *n.* woman formerly a member of the armed forces.

♦ **ex ship** *adj.* & *adv.* (also **free overboard, free overside**) denoting delivery terms for goods shipped from one place to another in which the seller pays all charges up to the port of destination, including unloading from the ship. All subsequent charges (e.g. lighterage, loading charges, etc.) are paid by the buyer.

---

extant /ek'stænt/ *adj.* still existing. [Latin *ex(s)to* exist]

extemporaneous /ɪkˌstempə'reɪnɪəs/ *adj.* spoken or done without preparation. □ **extemporaneously** *adv.* [from EXTEMPORE]

extemporary /ɪk'stempərərɪ/ *adj.* = EXTEMPORANEOUS. □ **extemporarily** *adv.*

extempore /ɪk'stempərɪ/ *adj.* & *adv.* without preparation. [Latin]

extemporize /ɪk'stempəˌraɪz/ *v.* (also **-ise**) (**-zing** or **-sing**) improvise. □ **extemporization** /-'zeɪʃ(ə)n/ *n.*

extend /ɪk'stend/ *v.* **1** lengthen or make larger in space or time. **2** stretch or lay out at full length. **3** (foll. by *to*, *over*) reach or be or make continuous over a specified area. **4** (foll. by *to*) have a specified scope (*permit does not extend to camping*). **5** offer or accord (an invitation, hospitality, kindness, etc.). **6** (usu. *refl.* or in *passive*) tax the powers of (an athlete, horse, etc.). □ **extendible** *adj.* (also **extensible**). [Latin *extendo -tens-*: related to TEND[1]]

extended family *n.* family including relatives living near.

♦ **extended guarantee** *n.* servicing and maintenance cover that a manufacturer offers to a customer for a specified additional amount of time beyond the original guarantee. Extended guarantees usu. have to be paid for.

---

extended-play *adj.* (of a gramophone record) playing for somewhat longer than most singles.

extension /ɪk'stenʃ(ə)n/ *n.* **1** extending or being extended. **2** part enlarging or added on to a main building etc. **3** additional part. **4 a** subsidiary telephone on the same line as the main one. **b** its number. **5** additional period of time. **6** extramural instruction by a university or college.

extensive /ɪk'stensɪv/ *adj.* **1** covering a large area. **2** far-reaching. □ **extensively** *adv.* **extensiveness** *n.* [Latin: related to EXTEND]

extent /ɪk'stent/ *n.* **1** space over which a thing extends. **2** range, scope, degree. [Anglo-French: related to EXTEND]

extenuate /ɪk'stenjʊˌeɪt/ *–v.* (often as **extenuating** *adj.*) make (guilt or an offence) seem less serious by reference to another factor. □ **extenuation** /-'eɪʃ(ə)n/ *n.* [Latin *tenuis* thin]

exterior /ɪk'stɪərɪə(r)/ *–adj.* **1** of or on the outer side. **2** coming from outside. *–n.* **1** outward aspect or surface of a building etc. **2** outward demeanour. **3** outdoor scene in filming. [Latin]

exterminate /ɪk'stɜːmɪˌneɪt/ *v.* (**-ting**) destroy utterly (esp. a living thing). □ **extermination** /-'neɪʃ(ə)n/ *n.* **exterminator** *n.* [Latin: related to TERMINAL]

external /ɪk'stɜːn(ə)l/ *–adj.* **1 a** of or on the outside or visible part. **b** coming from the outside or an outside source. **2** relating to a country's foreign affairs. **3** outside the conscious subject (*the external world*). **4** (of medicine etc.) for use on the outside of the body. **5** for students taking the examinations of a university without attending it. *–n.* (in *pl.*) **1** outward features or aspect. **2** external circumstances. **3** inessentials. □ **externally** *adv.* [Latin *externus* outer]

♦ **external account** *n.* sterling bank account held by someone who resides outside the sterling area.

♦ **externality** /ˌekstɜː'nælɪtɪ/ *n.* **1** state of being external. **2** something external. **3** economic effect of a business that is not recorded in its accounts as it does not arise from individual transactions of the business. For example, local overcrowding may arise because a large number of employees have been attracted to the neighbourhood, thus incurring extra costs for roads, schools, health care, etc. More generally, an externality results from an economic choice that is not reflected in market prices. For example, siting a railway station close to a housing estate represents an externality to householders on that estate if they are not asked to pay for it. It is an external economy if the householders benefit from greater freedom to travel and an external diseconomy if the noise of trains keeps them awake at night. It is usu. argued that governments should internalize external diseconomies (e.g. pollution) by means of taxation.

---

externalize *v.* (also **-ise**) (**-zing** or **-sing**) give or attribute external existence to. □ **externalization** /-'zeɪʃ(ə)n/ *n.*

extinct /ɪk'stɪŋkt/ *adj.* **1** that has died out. **2 a** no longer burning. **b** (of a volcano) that no longer erupts. **3** obsolete. [Latin *ex(s)tinguo -stinct-* quench]

extinction /ɪk'stɪŋkʃ(ə)n/ *n.* **1** making or becoming extinct. **2** extinguishing or being extinguished. **3** total destruction or annihilation.

extinguish /ɪk'stɪŋgwɪʃ/ *v.* **1** cause (a flame, light, etc.) to die out. **2** destroy. **3** terminate. **4** wipe out (a debt). □ **extinguishable** *adj.*

extinguisher *n.* = FIRE EXTINGUISHER.

extirpate /'ekstəˌpeɪt/ *v.* (**-ting**) root out; destroy completely. □ **extirpation** /-'peɪʃ(ə)n/ *n.* [Latin *ex(s)tirpo* from *stirps* stem of tree]

extol /ɪk'stəʊl/ *v.* (**-ll-**) praise enthusiastically. [Latin *tollo* raise]

extort /ɪk'stɔːt/ *v.* obtain by coercion. [Latin *torqueo tort-* twist]

extortion /ɪk'stɔːʃ(ə)n/ *n.* **1** act of extorting, esp. money. **2** illegal exaction. □ **extortioner** *n.* **extortionist** *n.*

extortionate /ɪk'stɔːʃənət/ *adj.* (of a price etc.) exorbitant. □ **extortionately** *adv.*

extra /'ekstrə/ *–adj.* additional; more than usual or necessary or expected. *–adv.* **1** more than usually. **2** additionally (*was charged extra*). *–n.* **1** extra thing. **2** thing for which an extra charge is made. **3** person engaged temporarily for a minor part in a film. **4** special issue of a newspaper etc. **5** *Cricket* run scored other than from a hit with the bat. [probably from EXTRAORDINARY]

extra- *comb. form* **1** outside, beyond. **2** beyond the scope of. [Latin *extra* outside]

extra cover *n. Cricket* **1** fielding position on a line between cover-point and mid-off, but beyond these. **2** fielder at this position.

extract *–v.* /ɪk'strækt/ **1** remove or take out, esp. by effort or force. **2** obtain (money, an admission, etc.) against a person's will. **3** obtain (a natural resource) from the earth. **4** select or reproduce for quotation or performance. **5** obtain (juice etc.) by pressure, distillation, etc. **6** derive (pleasure etc.). **7** find (the root of a number). *–n.* /'ekstrækt/ **1** short passage from a book etc. **2** preparation containing a concentrated constituent of a substance (*malt extract*). [Latin *traho tract-* draw]

extraction /ɪk'strækʃ(ə)n/ *n.* **1** extracting or being extracted. **2** removal of a tooth. **3** lineage, descent (*of Indian extraction*). [Latin: related to EXTRACT]

extractive /ɪk'stræktɪv/ *adj.* of or involving extraction.

extractor /ɪk'stræktə(r)/ *n.* **1** person or machine that extracts. **2** (*attrib.*) (of a device) that extracts bad air etc.

extracurricular /ˌekstrəkə'rɪkjʊlə(r)/ *adj.* not part of the normal curriculum.

extraditable /'ekstrəˌdaɪtəb(ə)l/ *adj.* **1** liable to extradition. **2** (of a crime) warranting extradition.

extradite /'ekstrəˌdaɪt/ *v.* (**-ting**) hand over (a person accused or convicted of a crime) to the foreign state etc. in which the crime was committed. □ **extradition** /-'dɪʃ(ə)n/ *n.* [French: related to TRADITION]

extramarital /ˌekstrə'mærɪt(ə)l/ *adj.* (esp. of sexual relations) occurring outside marriage.

extramural /ˌekstrə'mjʊər(ə)l/ *adj.* additional to normal teaching or studies, esp. for non-resident students.

extraneous /ɪk'streɪnɪəs/ *adj.* **1** of external origin. **2** (often foll. by *to*) **a** separate from the object to which it is attached etc. **b** irrelevant, unrelated. [Latin *extraneus*]

extraordinary /ɪk'strɔːdɪnərɪ/ *adj.* **1** unusual or remarkable. **2** unusually great. **3** (of a meeting, official, etc.) additional; specially employed. □ **extraordinarily** *adv.* [Latin]

♦ **extraordinary general meeting** *n.* (also **EGM**) any general meeting of a company other than the annual general meeting. Most company's articles give the directors the right to call an EGM whenever they wish. Members have the right to requisition an EGM if they hold not less than 10% of the paid-up share capital; a resigning auditor may also requisition a meeting. Directors must call an EGM when there has been a serious loss of capital. The court may call an EGM if it is impracticable to call it in any other way. Those entitled to attend must be given 14 days' notice of the meeting (21 days if a special resolution is to be proposed). See also AGENDA 1; ORDER OF BUSINESS.

♦ **extraordinary items** *n.pl.* costs or income affecting a company's profit and loss account that do not derive from the normal activities of the company and, if undisclosed, would distort the normal trend of profits. Such items are therefore disclosed after the normal trading profit or loss has been shown. Cf. EXCEPTIONAL ITEMS.

♦ **extraordinary resolution** *n.* resolution submitted to a general meeting of a company; 14 days' notice of such a resolution is required, and the notice should state that it is an extraordinary resolution. 75% of those voting must approve the resolution for it to be passed.

---

extrapolate /ɪk'stræpəˌleɪt/ *v.* (**-ting**) (also *absol.*) calculate approximately from known data etc. (others which lie outside the range of those known), often by extending a curve on a graph. □ **extrapolation** /-'leɪʃ(ə)n/ *n.* [from EXTRA-, INTERPOLATE]

extrasensory /ˌekstrə'sensərɪ/ *adj.* derived by means other than the known senses, e.g. by telepathy.

extraterrestrial /ˌekstrətɪ'restrɪəl/ *–adj.* outside the earth or its atmosphere. *–n.* (in science fiction) being from outer space.

extravagant /ɪk'strævəgənt/ *adj.* **1** spending money excessively. **2** excessive; absurd. **3** costing much. □ **extravagance** *n.* **extravagantly** *adv.* [Latin *vagor* wander]

extravaganza /ɪkˌstrævə'gænzə/ *n.* **1** spectacular theatrical or television production. **2** fanciful literary, musical, or dramatic composition. [Italian]

Extremadura /ˌekstreɪmə'dʊərə ˌes-/ autonomous region of W Spain; pop. (est. 1994) 1 050 590; capital, Mérida. Irrigated land is used for growing cereals and as pasture.

extreme /ɪk'striːm/ *–adj.* **1** of a high, or the highest, degree (*extreme danger*). **2** severe (*extreme measures*). **3** outermost. **4** on the far left or right of a political party. **5** utmost; last. *–n.* **1** (often in *pl.*) either of two things as remote or as different as possible. **2** thing at either end. **3** highest degree. **4** *Math.* first or last term of a ratio or series. □ **go to extremes** take an extreme course of action. **in the extreme** to an extreme degree. □ **extremely** *adv.* [French from Latin]

extreme unction *n.* last rites in the Roman Catholic and Orthodox Churches.

extremist *n.* (also *attrib.*) person with extreme views. □ **extremism** *n.*

extremity /ɪk'stremɪtɪ/ *n.* (*pl.* **-ies**) **1** extreme point; very end. **2** (in *pl.*) the hands and feet. **3** condition of extreme adversity. [Latin: related to EXTREME]

extricate /'ekstrɪˌkeɪt/ *v.* (**-ting**) (often foll. by *from*) free or disentangle from a difficulty etc. □ **extricable** *adj.* **extrication** /-'keɪʃ(ə)n/ *n.* [Latin *tricae* perplexities]

extrinsic /ek'strɪnsɪk/ *adj.* **1** not inherent or intrinsic. **2** (often foll. by *to*) extraneous; not belonging. □ **extrinsically** *adv.* [Latin *extrinsecus* outwardly]

extrovert /'ekstrəˌvɜːt/ *–n.* **1** outgoing person. **2** person mainly concerned with external things. *–adj.* typical of or with the nature of an extrovert. □ **extroversion** /-'vɜːʃ(ə)n/ *n.* **extroverted** *adj.* [Latin *verto* turn]

extrude /ɪk'struːd/ *v.* (**-ding**) **1** (foll. by *from*) thrust or force out. **2** shape metal, plastics, etc. by forcing them through a die. □ **extrusion** *n.* **extrusive** *adj.* [Latin *extrudo -trus-* thrust out]

exuberant /ɪg'zjuːbərənt/ *adj.* **1** lively, high-spirited. **2** (of a plant etc.) prolific. **3** (of feelings etc.) abounding. □ **exuberance** *n.* **exuberantly** *adv.* [Latin *uber* fertile]

exude /ɪg'zjuːd/ *v.* (**-ding**) **1** ooze out. **2** emit (a smell). **3** display (an emotion etc.) freely. □ **exudation** /-'deɪʃ(ə)n/ *n.* [Latin *sudo* sweat]

exult /ɪg'zʌlt/ *v.* be joyful. □ **exultation** /-'teɪʃ(ə)n/ *n.* **exultant** *adj.* **exultantly** *adv.* [Latin *ex(s)ulto* from *salio salt-* leap]

♦ **ex warehouse** *adj.* & *adv.* denoting delivery terms for goods that are available for immediate delivery, in which the buyer pays for the delivery of the goods but the seller pays for loading them onto road or rail transport.

♦ **ex works** *adj.* & *adv.* (also **ex factory**) denoting delivery terms for goods in which the buyer has to pay for transporting them away from the factory that made them. In some cases, however, the seller will pay for loading them onto road or rail transport.

-ey var. of -Y².

eye /aɪ/ *–n.* **1** organ of sight. **2** eye characterized by the colour of the iris (*has blue eyes*). **3** region round the eye (*eyes swollen from weeping*). **4** (in *sing.* or *pl.*) sight. **5** particular visual ability (*a straight eye*). **6** thing like an eye, esp.: **a** a spot on a peacock's tail. **b** a leaf bud of a potato. **7** calm region at the centre of a hurricane etc. **8** hole of a needle. *–v.* (**eyes**, **eyed**, **eyeing** or **eying**) (often foll. by *up*) watch or observe closely, esp. admiringly or with suspicion. □ **all eyes** watching intently. **an eye for an eye** retaliation in kind. **have an eye for** be discerning about. **have one's eye on** wish or plan to procure. **have eyes for** be interested in; wish to acquire. **keep an eye on 1** watch. **2** look after. **keep an eye open** (or **out**) (often foll. by *for*) watch carefully. **keep one's eyes open** (or **peeled** or **skinned**) watch out; be on the alert. **make eyes** (or **sheep's eyes**) (foll. by *at*) look amorously or flirtatiously at. **one in the eye** (foll. by *for*) disappointment or setback. **see eye to eye** (often foll. by *with*) agree. **set eyes on** see. **up to the** (or **one's**)

eyes in deeply engaged or involved in. **with one's eyes shut** (or **closed**) with little effort. **with an eye to** with a view to. [Old English]

eyeball –*n.* ball of the eye within the lids and socket. –*v.* *US slang* look or stare (at).

eyeball to eyeball *adv. colloq.* confronting closely.

eyebath *n.* small vessel for applying lotion etc. to the eye.

eyebright *n.* plant used as a remedy for weak eyes.

eyebrow *n.* line of hair on the ridge above the eye-socket. □ **raise one's eyebrows** show surprise, disbelief, or disapproval.

eye-catching *adj. colloq.* striking.

eyeful *n.* (*pl.* **-s**) *colloq.* **1** (esp. in phr. **get an eyeful (of)**) good look; as much as the eye can take in. **2** visually striking person or thing. **3** thing thrown or blown into the eye.

eyeglass *n.* lens to assist defective sight.

eyehole *n.* hole to look through.

eyelash *n.* each of the hairs growing on the edges of the eyelids.

eyelet /ˈaɪlɪt/ *n.* **1** small hole for string or rope etc. to pass through. **2** metal ring strengthening this. [French *oillet* from Latin *oculus*]

eyelid *n.* either of the folds of skin closing to cover the eye.

eye-liner *n.* cosmetic applied as a line round the eye.

eye-opener *n. colloq.* enlightening experience; unexpected revelation.

eyepiece *n.* lens or lenses to which the eye is applied at the end of an optical instrument.

eye-shade *n.* device to protect the eyes, esp. from strong light.

eye-shadow *n.* coloured cosmetic applied to the eyelids.

eyesight *n.* faculty or power of seeing.

eyesore *n.* ugly thing.

eye strain *n.* fatigue of the eye muscles.

eye-tooth *n.* canine tooth in the upper jaw just under the eye.

eyewash *n.* **1** lotion for the eyes. **2** *slang* nonsense; insincere talk.

eyewitness *n.* person who saw a thing happen and can tell of it.

eyrie /ˈɪərɪ/ *n.* **1** nest of a bird of prey, esp. an eagle, built high up. **2** house etc. perched high up. [French *aire* lair, from Latin *agrum* piece of ground]

Ff

F[1] /ef/ *n.* (also **f**) (*pl.* **Fs** or **F's**) **1** sixth letter of the alphabet. **2** *Mus.* fourth note of the diatonic scale of C major.

F[2] *–abbr.* (also **F.**) **1** Fahrenheit. **2** farad(s). **3** fine (pencil-lead). **4** fresh water (see LOAD LINE). *–international vehicle registration* & *international civil aircraft marking* France.

F[3] *symb.* **1** fluorine. **2** franc.

f *–abbr.* (also **f.**) **1** female. **2** feminine. **3** following page etc. **4** *Mus.* forte. **5** folio. **6** focal length. *–symb.* guilder (of the Netherlands). [from its former name *florin*]

FA *abbr.* **1** Faculty of Actuaries. **2** Finance Act. **3** financial adviser. **4** Football Association. **5** freight agent.

fa var. of FAH.

f.a. *abbr. Commerce* free alongside.

f.a.a. *abbr.* = FREE OF ALL AVERAGES.

fab *adj. colloq.* fabulous, marvellous. [abbreviation]

f. à b. *abbr.* (French) franco à bord (= free on board).

fable /'feɪb(ə)l/ *n.* **1 a** fictional, esp. supernatural, story. **b** moral tale, esp. with animals as characters. **2** legendary tales collectively (*in fable*). **3 a** lie. **b** thing only supposed to exist. [Latin *fabula* discourse]

fabled *adj.* celebrated; legendary.

fabric /'fæbrɪk/ *n.* **1** woven material; cloth. **2** walls, floor, and roof of a building. **3** essential structure. [Latin *faber* metal-worker]

fabricate /'fæbrɪˌkeɪt/ *v.* (**-ting**) **1** construct, esp. from components. **2** invent (a story etc.). **3** forge (a document). □ **fabrication** /-'keɪʃ(ə)n/ *n.* **fabricator** *n.* [Latin: related to FABRIC]

fabulous /'fæbjʊləs/ *adj.* **1** incredible. **2** *colloq.* marvellous. **3** legendary. □ **fabulously** *adv.* [Latin: related to FABLE]

f.a.c. *abbr. Insurance* (French) franc d'avarie commune (= free of general average).

façade /fə'sɑːd/ *n.* **1** face or front of a building. **2** outward appearance, esp. a deceptive one. [French: related to FACE]

face *–n.* **1** front of the head from forehead to chin. **2** facial expression. **3** coolness, effrontery. **4** surface, esp.: **a** the side of a mountain etc. (*north face*). **b** = COALFACE. **c** *Geom.* each surface of a solid. **d** the façade of a building. **e** the dial of a clock etc. **5** functional side of a tool etc. **6** = TYPEFACE. **7** aspect (*unacceptable face of capitalism*). *–v.* (**-cing**) **1** look or be positioned towards or in a certain direction. **2** be opposite. **3** meet resolutely. **4** confront (*faces us with a problem*). **5 a** coat the surface of (a thing). **b** put a facing on (a garment). □ **face the music** *colloq.* take unpleasant consequences without flinching. **face up to** accept bravely. **have the face** be shameless enough. **in face** (or **the face) of** despite. **lose face** be humiliated. **on the face of it** apparently. **put a bold** (or **brave) face on it** accept difficulty etc. cheerfully. **save face** avoid humiliation. **set one's face against** oppose stubbornly. **to a person's face** openly in a person's presence. [Latin *facies*]

face-cloth *n.* cloth for washing one's face.

face-flannel *n.* = FACE-CLOTH.

faceless *adj.* **1** without identity; characterless. **2** purposely not identifiable.

face-lift *n.* **1** (also **face-lifting**) cosmetic surgery to remove wrinkles etc. **2** improvement to appearance, efficiency, etc.

face-pack *n.* skin preparation for the face.

facer *n. colloq.* sudden difficulty.

facet /'fæsɪt/ *n.* **1** aspect. **2** side of a cut gem etc. [French: related to FACT]

facetious /fə'siːʃəs/ *adj.* intending or intended to be amusing, esp. inappropriately. □ **facetiously** *adv.* [Latin *facetia* jest]

face to face *adv.* & *adj.* (also **face-to-face** when *attrib.*) (often foll. by *with*) facing; confronting each other.

♦ **face value** *n.* **1** value printed on a banknote or coin. **2** nominal value printed on the face of a security, which may be more or less than the market value. See PAR VALUE. **3** superficial appearance or implication.

---

facia var. of FASCIA.

facial /'feɪʃ(ə)l/ *–adj.* of or for the face. *–n.* beauty treatment for the face. □ **facially** *adv.*

facile /'fæsaɪl/ *adj.* usu. *derog.* **1** easily achieved but of little value. **2** glib, fluent. [Latin *facio* do]

facilitate /fə'sɪlɪˌteɪt/ *v.* (**-ting**) ease (a process etc.). □ **facilitation** /-'teɪʃ(ə)n/ *n.* [Italian: related to FACILE]

facility /fə'sɪlɪtɪ/ *n.* (*pl.* **-ies**) **1** ease; absence of difficulty. **2** fluency, dexterity. **3** (esp. in *pl.*) opportunity or equipment for doing something. [Latin: related to FACILE]

facing *n.* **1** layer of material covering part of a garment etc. for contrast or strength. **2** outer covering on a wall etc.

♦ **facing matter** *adj.* & *adv.* (of advertisement in a publication) positioned to appear opposite an editorial page, esp. when the advertisement is related to the text of the article.

---

facsimile /fæk'sɪmɪlɪ/ *n.* exact copy, esp. of writing, printing, a picture, etc. See also FAX. [Latin, = make like]

fact *n.* **1** thing that is known to exist or to be true. **2** (usu. in *pl.*) item of verified information. **3** truth, reality. **4** thing assumed as the basis for argument. □ **before** (or **after) the fact** before (or after) the committing of a crime. **in** (or **in point of) fact 1** in reality. **2** in short. [Latin *factum* from *facio* do]

♦ **fact book** *n.* file containing information on the history of a product, including data on sales, distribution, competition, customers, and relevant market research undertaken, as well as a detailed record of the product's performance in relation to the marketing effort made on its behalf.

---

faction /'fækʃ(ə)n/ *n.* small organized dissentient group within a larger one, esp. in politics. □ **factional** *adj.* [Latin: related to FACT]

-faction *comb. form* forming nouns of action from verbs in *-fy* (*satisfaction*). [Latin *-factio*]

factious /'fækʃəs/ *adj.* of, characterized by, or inclined to faction. [Latin: related to FACTION]

factitious /fæk'tɪʃəs/ *adj.* **1** specially contrived. **2** artificial. [Latin: related to FACT]

fact of life *n.* something that must be accepted.

factor /'fæktə(r)/ *n.* **1** circumstance etc. contributing to a result. **2** whole number etc. that when multiplied with another produces a given number. **3 a** individual or firm that acts as an agent (often called a **mercantile agent**) in certain trades, usu. receiving a **factorage** (commission or fee) based on the amount of sales achieved. Unlike some other forms of agent, a factor takes possession of the goods and sells them in his or her own name. **b** *Scot.* land-agent, steward. **c** agent, deputy. **4** firm that engages in factoring. [Latin: related to FACT]

factorial /fæk'tɔːrɪəl/ *–n.* product of a number and all the whole numbers below it. *–adj.* of a factor or factorial.

♦ **factoring** *n.* buying of the trade debts of a manufacturer, assuming the task of debt collection and accepting the credit risk, thus providing the manufacturer with working capital. **With service factoring** involves collecting the debts, assuming the credit risk, and passing on the funds as they are paid by the buyer. **With service plus finance factoring** involves paying the manufacturer up to 90% of the invoice value immediately after delivery of the goods, with the balance paid after the money has been collected. This form of factoring is clearly more expensive than with service factoring. In either case the factor, which may be a bank or finance house, has the right to select its debtors. See also UNDISCLOSED FACTORING.

factorize *v.* (also **-ise**) (**-zing** or **-sing**) resolve into factors. □ **factorization** /-'zeɪʃ(ə)n/ *n.*

♦ **factors of production** *n.pl.* resources required to produce economic goods. They are land (including all natural resources), labour (including all human work and skill), capital (including all money, assets, machinery, raw materials, etc.), and entrepreneurial ability (including organizational management skills, inventiveness, and the willingness to take risks). For each of these factors there is a price, i.e. rent for land, wages for labour, interest for capital, and profit for the entrepreneur.

factory /'fæktərɪ/ *n.* (*pl.* **-ies**) building(s) in which goods are manufactured. [ultimately from Latin *factorium*]

♦ **factory costs** *n.pl.* costs of producing goods, which have been incurred in the area of the factory; these include materials, factory labour, costs of machinery, and costs of factory buildings, but not mark-up or profit.

factory farm *n.* farm using intensive or industrial methods of livestock rearing. □ **factory farming** *n.*

factotum /fæk'təʊtəm/ *n.* (*pl.* **-s**) employee who does all kinds of work. [medieval Latin: related to FACT, TOTAL]

facts and figures *n.pl.* precise details.

factsheet *n.* information leaflet, esp. accompanying a television programme.

facts of life *n.pl.* (prec. by *the*) information about sexual functions and practices.

factual /'fæktʃʊəl/ *adj.* based on or concerned with fact. □ **factually** *adv.*

♦ **facultative reinsurance** /'fæk(ə)ltətɪv/ *n.* form of reinsurance in which the terms, conditions, and reinsurance premium are individually negotiated between the insurer and the reinsurer. There is no obligation on the reinsurer to accept the risk or on the insurer to reinsure it if it is not considered necessary. The policyholder has no indication that reinsurance has been arranged (cf. CO-INSURANCE).

faculty /'fækəltɪ/ *n.* (*pl.* **-ies**) **1** aptitude for a particular activity. **2** inherent mental or physical power. **3 a** group of related university departments. **b** *US* teaching staff of a university or college. **4** authorization, esp. by a Church authority. [Latin: related to FACILE]

♦ **Faculty of Actuaries** see INSTITUTE OF ACTUARIES.

fad *n.* **1** craze. **2** peculiar notion. □ **faddish** *adj.* [probably from *fiddle-faddle*]

faddy *adj.* (**-ier**, **-iest**) having petty likes and dislikes. □ **faddiness** *n.*

fade *–v.* (**-ding**) **1** lose or cause to lose colour, light, or sound; slowly diminish. **2** lose freshness or strength. **3** (foll. by *in*, *out*) *Cinematog.* etc. cause (a picture or sound) to appear or disappear, increase or decrease, gradually. *–n.* action of fading. □ **fade away 1** *colloq.* languish, grow thin. **2** die away; disappear. [French *fade* dull]

faeces /'fiːsiːz/ *n.pl.* (*US* **feces**) waste matter discharged from the bowels. □ **faecal** /'fiːk(ə)l/ *adj.* [Latin]

Faenza /fɑː'entsə/ town in N Italy that gave its name to the type of pottery known as 'faience'; pop. (1990) 54 050.

Faeroe Islands /'feərəʊ/ (also **Faeroes**) group of islands in the N Atlantic, belonging to Denmark but partly autonomous; pop. (est. 1992) 46 800; capital, Thorshavn. Fishing is a major source of income and there is some sheep-farming.

faff *v. colloq.* (often foll. by *about*, *around*) fuss, dither. [imitative]

fag[1] *–n.* **1** *colloq.* tedious task. **2** *slang* cigarette. **3** (at public schools) junior boy who runs errands for a senior. *–v.* (**-gg-**) **1** (often foll. by *out*) *colloq.* exhaust. **2** (at public schools) act as a fag. [origin unknown]

fag[2] *n. US slang offens.* male homosexual. [abbreviation of FAGGOT]

fag-end *n. slang* cigarette-end.

faggot /'fægət/ *n.* (*US* **fagot**) **1** ball of seasoned chopped liver etc., baked or fried. **2** bundle of sticks etc. **3** *slang offens.* **a** unpleasant woman. **b** *US* male homosexual. [French from Italian]

fah /fɑː/ *n.* (also **fa**) *Mus.* fourth note of a major scale. [Latin *famuli*: see GAMUT]

Fahrenheit /'færən,haɪt/ *adj.* of a scale of temperature on which water freezes at 32° and boils at 212°. [*Fahrenheit* name of a physicist]

faience /'faɪɑ̃s/ *n.* decorated and glazed earthenware and porcelain. [French from FAENZA]

F.A.I.Ex. *abbr.* Fellow of the Australian Institute of Export.

FAII *abbr.* Fellow of the Australian Insurance Institute.

fail *–v.* **1** not succeed (*failed to qualify*). **2** be or judge to be unsuccessful in (an examination etc.). **3** be unable; neglect (*failed to appear*). **4** disappoint. **5** be absent or insufficient. **6** become weaker; cease functioning (*health is failing*; *engine failed*). **7** become bankrupt. *–n.* failure in an examination. □ **without fail** for certain, whatever happens. [Latin *fallo* deceive]

failed *adj.* unsuccessful (*failed actor*).

failing *–n.* fault, weakness. *–prep.* in default of.

fail-safe *adj.* reverting to a safe condition when faulty etc.

failure /'feɪljə(r)/ *n.* **1** lack of success; failing. **2** unsuccessful person or thing. **3** non-performance. **4** breaking down or ceasing to function (*heart failure*). **5** running short of supply etc. [Anglo-French: related to FAIL]

FAIM *abbr.* Fellow of the Australian Institute of Management.

fain *archaic –predic. adj.* (foll. by *to* + infin.) willing or obliged to. *–adv.* gladly (esp. *would fain*). [Old English]

faint *–adj.* **1** indistinct, pale, dim. **2** weak or giddy. **3** slight. **4** feeble; timid. **5** (also **feint**) (of paper) with inconspicuous ruled lines. *–v.* **1** lose consciousness. **2** become faint. *–n.* act or state of fainting. □ **faintly** *adv.* **faintness** *n.* [French: related to FEIGN]

faint-hearted *adj.* cowardly, timid.

fair[1] *–adj.* **1** just, equitable; in accordance with the rules. **2** blond; light or pale. **3 a** moderate in quality or amount. **b** satisfactory. **4** (of weather) fine; (of the wind) favourable. **5** clean, clear (*fair copy*). **6** *archaic* beautiful. *–adv.* **1** in a just manner. **2** exactly, completely. □ **in a fair way to** likely to. □ **fairness** *n.* [Old English]

fair[2] *n.* **1** stalls, amusements, etc., for public entertainment. **2** periodical market, often with entertainments. **3** exhibition, esp. commercial. [Latin *feriae* holiday]

fair and square *adv.* exactly; straightforwardly.

♦ **fair average quality** see F.A.Q. 1.

fair dinkum see DINKUM.

fair dos *n.pl.* (esp. as *int.*) *colloq.* fair shares; fair treatment.

fair game *n.* legitimate target or object.

fairground *n.* outdoor area where a fair is held.
fairing *n.* streamlining structure added to a ship, aircraft, vehicle, etc.
Fair Isle *n.* (also *attrib.*) multicoloured knitwear design characteristic of Fair Isle. [*Fair Isle* in the Shetlands]
fairly *adv.* **1** in a fair manner. **2** moderately (*fairly good*). **3** quite, rather (*fairly narrow*).
fair play *n.* just treatment or behaviour.
fair sex *n.* (prec. by *the*) women.

♦ **fair trading** see CONSUMER PROTECTION.

---

fairway *n.* **1** navigable channel. **2** part of a golf-course between a tee and its green, kept free of rough grass.
fair-weather friend *n.* unreliable friend or ally.
fairy *n.* (*pl.* **-ies**) **1** (often *attrib.*) small winged legendary being. **2** *slang offens.* male homosexual. [French: related to FAY, -ERY]
fairy cake *n.* small iced sponge cake.
fairy godmother *n.* benefactress.
fairyland *n.* **1** home of fairies. **2** enchanted region.
fairy lights *n.pl.* small decorative coloured lights.
fairy ring *n.* ring of darker grass caused by fungi.
fairy story *n.* (also **fairy tale**) **1** tale about fairies. **2** incredible story; lie.
Faisalabad /ˌfaɪsælə'bæd/ industrial city in Pakistan, in Punjab province, the centre of a cotton- and wheat-producing region; pop. (est. 1995) 1 875 000.
fait accompli /ˌfeɪt ə'kɒmpliː/ *n.* thing that has been done and is not capable of alteration. [French]
faith *n.* **1** complete trust or confidence. **2** firm, esp. religious, belief. **3** religion or creed (*Christian faith*). **4** loyalty, trustworthiness. [Latin *fides*]
faithful *adj.* **1** showing faith. **2** (often foll. by *to*) loyal, trustworthy. **3** accurate (*faithful account*). **4** (**the Faithful**) the believers in a religion. □ **faithfulness** *n.*
faithfully *adv.* in a faithful manner. □ **Yours faithfully** formula for ending a formal letter when it begins 'Dear Sir' or 'Dear Madam'.
faithless *adj.* **1** false, unreliable, disloyal. **2** without religious faith.
fake –*n.* false or counterfeit thing or person. –*adj.* counterfeit; not genuine. –*v.* (**-king**) **1** make a fake or imitation of (*faked my signature*). **2** feign (a feeling, illness, etc.). [German *fegen* sweep]
fakir /'feɪkɪə(r)/ *n.* Muslim or (rarely) Hindu religious beggar or ascetic. [Arabic, = poor man]
falcon /'fɔːlkən/ *n.* small hawk sometimes trained to hunt. [Latin *falco*]
falconry *n.* breeding and training of hawks.
Falkland Islands /'fɔːlklənd, 'fɒl-/ (also **Falklands**, Spanish **Islas Malvinas**) British Crown Colony in the S Atlantic, comprising two main islands and nearly 100 smaller ones; pop. (1991) 2120; capital, Stanley. The economy is based on fishing and sheep-farming. The islands were colonized by Britain in 1832–3, following the expulsion of an Argentinian garrison, but Argentina refused to recognize British sovereignty and continued to refer to the islands by their Spanish name. In 1982 an Argentinian invasion led to a two-month war ending in a successful British reoccupation.
fall /fɔːl/ –*v.* (*past* **fell**; *past part.* **fallen**) **1** go or come down freely; descend. **2** (often foll. by *over*) come suddenly to the ground from loss of balance etc. **3 a** hang or slope down. **b** (foll. by *into*) (of a river etc.) discharge into. **4 a** sink lower; decline, esp. in power, status, etc. **b** subside. **5** occur (*falls on a Monday*). **6** (of the face) show dismay or disappointment. **7** yield to temptation. **8** take or have a particular direction or place (*his eye fell on me*; *accent falls on the first syllable*). **9 a** find a place; be naturally divisible. **b** (foll. by *under*, *within*) be classed among. **10** come by chance or duty (*it fell to me to answer*). **11 a** pass into a specified condition (*fell ill*). **b** become (*fall asleep*). **12** be defeated or captured. **13** die. **14** (foll. by *on*, *upon*) **a** attack. **b** meet with. **c** embrace or embark on avidly. **15** (foll. by *to* + verbal noun) begin (*fell to wondering*). –*n.* **1** act of falling. **2** that which falls or has fallen, e.g. snow. **3** recorded amount of rainfall etc. **4** overthrow (*fall of Rome*). **5 a** succumbing to temptation. **b** (**the Fall**) Adam's sin and its results. **6** (also **Fall**) *US* autumn. **7** (esp. in *pl.*) waterfall etc. **8** wrestling-bout; throw in wrestling. □ **fall about** *colloq.* be helpless with laughter. **fall away 1** (of a surface) incline abruptly. **2** become few or thin; gradually vanish. **3** desert. **fall back** retreat. **fall back on** have recourse to in difficulty. **fall behind 1** be outstripped; lag. **2** be in arrears. **fall down** (often foll. by *on*) *colloq.* fail. **fall for** *colloq.* be captivated or deceived by. **fall foul of** come into conflict with. **fall in 1** take one's place in military formation. **2** collapse inwards. **fall in with 1** meet by chance. **2** agree with. **3** coincide with. **fall off 1** become detached. **2** decrease, deteriorate. **fall out 1** quarrel. **2** (of the hair, teeth, etc.) become detached. **3** *Mil.* come out of formation. **4** result; occur. **fall over backwards** see BACKWARDS. **fall over oneself** *colloq.* **1** be eager. **2** stumble through haste, confusion, etc. **fall short** be deficient. **fall short of** fail to reach or obtain. **fall through** fail; miscarry. **fall to** begin, e.g. eating or working. [Old English]
fallacy /'fæləsɪ/ *n.* (*pl.* **-ies**) **1** mistaken belief. **2** faulty reasoning; misleading argument. □ **fallacious** /fə'leɪʃəs/ *adj.* [Latin *fallo* deceive]

♦ **fall-back price** see COMMON AGRICULTURAL POLICY.

---

fall guy *n. slang* easy victim; scapegoat.
fallible /'fælɪb(ə)l/ *adj.* capable of making mistakes. □ **fallibility** /-'bɪlɪtɪ/ *n.* **fallibly** *adv.* [medieval Latin: related to FALLACY]
falling star *n.* meteor.
Fallopian tube /fə'ləʊpɪən/ *n.* either of two tubes along which ova travel from the ovaries to the womb. [*Fallopius*, name of an anatomist]
fallout *n.* radioactive nuclear debris.
fallow /'fæləʊ/ –*adj.* **1** (of land) ploughed but left unsown. **2** uncultivated. –*n.* fallow land. [Old English]
fallow deer *n.* small deer with a white-spotted reddish-brown summer coat. [Old English *fallow* pale brownish or reddish yellow]
false /fɔːls/ *adj.* **1** wrong, incorrect. **2** spurious, artificial. **3** improperly so called (*false acacia*). **4** deceptive. **5** (foll. by *to*) deceitful, treacherous, or unfaithful. □ **falsely** *adv.* **falseness** *n.* [Latin *falsus*: related to FAIL]
false alarm *n.* alarm given needlessly.
falsehood *n.* **1** untrue thing. **2 a** act of lying. **b** lie.
false pretences *n.pl.* misrepresentations made with intent to deceive (esp. *under false pretences*).
falsetto /fɔːl'setəʊ/ *n.* male singing voice above the normal range. [Italian diminutive: related to FALSE]
falsies /'fɔːlsɪz/ *n.pl. colloq.* pads worn to make the breasts seem larger.

♦ **falsification of accounts** *n.* dishonest entry in a firm's books of account, made by an employee with the object of covering up the theft of goods or money from the firm.

---

falsify /'fɔːlsɪˌfaɪ/ *v.* (**-ies**, **-ied**) **1** fraudulently alter. **2** misrepresent. □ **falsification** /-fɪ'keɪʃ(ə)n/ *n.* [French or medieval Latin: related to FALSE]
falsity *n.* being false.
Falster /'fɑːlstə(r)/ Danish island in the Baltic Sea.
falter /'fɔːltə(r)/ *v.* **1** stumble; go unsteadily. **2** lose courage. **3** speak hesitatingly. [origin uncertain]
fame *n.* **1** renown; being famous. **2** *archaic* reputation. [Latin *fama*]
famed *adj.* (foll. by *for*) famous; much spoken of.
FAMI *abbr.* Fellow of the Australian Marketing Institute.
familial /fə'mɪlɪəl/ *adj.* of a family or its members.
familiar /fə'mɪlɪə(r)/ –*adj.* **1 a** (often foll. by *to*) well known. **b** often met (with). **2** (foll. by *with*) knowing a thing well. **3** (often foll. by *with*) well acquainted (with a

person). **4** informal, esp. presumptuously so. *–n.* **1** close friend. **2** (in full **familiar spirit**) supposed attendant of a witch etc. □ **familiarity** /-'ærɪtɪ/ *n.* **familiarly** *adv.* [Latin: related to FAMILY]

familiarize *v.* (also **-ise**) (**-zing** or **-sing**) (usu. foll. by *with*) make (a person or oneself) conversant or well acquainted. □ **familiarization** /-'zeɪʃ(ə)n/ *n.*

family /'fæmɪlɪ/ *n.* (*pl.* **-ies**) **1** set of relations, esp. parents and children. **2 a** members of a household. **b** person's children. **3** all the descendants of a common ancestor. **4** group of similar objects, people, etc. **5** group of related genera of animals or plants. □ **in the family way** *colloq.* pregnant. [Latin *familia*]

family allowance *n.* former name for CHILD BENEFIT.

♦ **family brand** *n.* group of brand names for the products of a company, all of which contain the same word to establish their relationship in the minds of the consumers. See also PRODUCT LINE.

family credit *n.* (also **family income supplement**) regular state payment to a low-income family.

♦ **family life cycle** *n.* series of stages of family life based on demographic data: (1) young single people; (2) young couples with no children; (3) young couples with youngest child under six years; (4) couples with dependent children; (5) older couples with no children at home; (6) older single people. These groups have been useful in marketing and advertising for defining the markets for certain goods and services, as each group has its own specific and distinguishable needs and interests.

family man *n.* man who has a wife and children, esp. one fond of family life.

family name *n.* surname.

family planning *n.* birth control.

family tree *n.* genealogical chart.

famine /'fæmɪn/ *n.* extreme scarcity, esp. of food. [Latin *fames* hunger]

famish /'fæmɪʃ/ *v.* (usu. in *passive*) make or become extremely hungry. □ **be famished** (or **famishing**) *colloq.* be very hungry. [Romanic: related to FAMINE]

famous /'feɪməs/ *adj.* **1** (often foll. by *for*) celebrated; well-known. **2** *colloq.* excellent. □ **famously** *adv.* [Latin: related to FAME]

fan[1] *–n.* **1** apparatus, usu. with rotating blades, for ventilation etc. **2** folding semicircular device waved to cool oneself. **3** thing spread out like a fan (*fan tracery*). *–v.* (**-nn-**) **1** blow air on, with or as with a fan. **2** (of a breeze) blow gently on. **3** (usu. foll. by *out*) spread out like a fan. [Latin *vannus* winnowing-basket]

fan[2] *n.* devotee of a particular activity, performer, etc. (*film fan*). [abbreviation of FANATIC]

fanatic /fə'nætɪk/ *–n.* person obsessively devoted to a belief, activity, etc. *–adj.* excessively enthusiastic. □ **fanatical** *adj.* **fanatically** *adv.* **fanaticism** /-tɪ,sɪz(ə)m/ *n.* [Latin *fanum* temple]

fan belt *n.* belt driving a fan to cool the radiator in a vehicle.

fancier /'fænsɪə(r)/ *n.* connoisseur (*dog-fancier*).

fanciful /'fænsɪ,fʊl/ *adj.* **1** imaginary. **2** indulging in fancies. □ **fancifully** *adv.*

fan club *n.* club of devotees.

fancy /'fænsɪ/ *–n.* (*pl.* **-ies**) **1** inclination. **2** whim. **3** supposition. **4 a** faculty of imagination. **b** mental image. *–adj.* (**-ier**, **-iest**) **1** ornamental. **2** extravagant. *–v.* (**-ies**, **-ied**) **1** (foll. by *that*) be inclined to suppose. **2** *colloq.* feel a desire for (*fancy a drink?*). **3** *colloq.* find sexually attractive. **4** *colloq.* value (oneself, one's ability, etc.) unduly highly. **5** (in *imper.*) exclamation of surprise. **6** imagine. □ **take a fancy to** become (esp. inexplicably) fond of. **take a person's fancy** suddenly attract or please. □ **fanciable** *adj.* (in sense 3 of *v.*). **fancily** *adv.* **fanciness** *n.* [contraction of FANTASY]

fancy dress *n.* costume for masquerading at a party.

fancy-free *adj.* without (esp. emotional) commitments.

fancy man *n. slang derog.* **1** woman's lover. **2** pimp.

fancy woman *n. slang derog.* mistress.

fandango /fæn'dæŋgəʊ/ *n.* (*pl.* **-es** or **-s**) **1** lively Spanish dance for two. **2** music for this. [Spanish]

F. & A.P. *abbr. Insurance* fire and allied perils.

f. & d. *abbr.* (also **F. & D.**) freight and demurrage.

f. & t. *abbr.* (also **F. & T.**) *Insurance* fire and theft.

fanfare /'fænfeə(r)/ *n.* short showy or ceremonious sounding of trumpets etc. [French]

fang *n.* **1** canine tooth, esp. of a dog or wolf. **2** tooth of a venomous snake. **3** root of a tooth or its prong. [Old English]

fan-jet *n.* = TURBOFAN.

fanlight *n.* small, orig. semicircular, window over a door or another window.

fan mail *n.* letters from fans.

fanny *n.* (*pl.* **-ies**) **1** *coarse slang* the female genitals. **2** *US slang* the buttocks. [origin unknown]

fantail *n.* pigeon with a broad tail.

fantasia /fæn'teɪzɪə/ *n.* free or improvisatory musical or other composition, or one based on familiar tunes. [Italian: related to FANTASY]

fantasize /'fæntə,saɪz/ *v.* (also **-ise**) (**-zing** or **-sing**) **1** day-dream. **2** imagine; create a fantasy about.

fantastic /fæn'tæstɪk/ *adj.* **1** *colloq.* excellent, extraordinary. **2** extravagantly fanciful. **3** grotesque, quaint. □ **fantastically** *adv.* [Greek: related to FANTASY]

fantasy /'fæntəsɪ/ *n.* (*pl.* **-ies**) **1** faculty of inventing images, esp. extravagant ones. **2** mental image, day-dream. **3** fantastic invention or composition. [Greek *phantasia* appearance]

♦ **FAO** *abbr.* = FOOD AND AGRICULTURAL ORGANIZATION.

f.a.p. *abbr. Insurance* (French) franc d'avarie particulière (= free of particular average).

♦ **f.a.q.** *abbr.* (also **faq**) **1** fair average quality, a trade description of certain commodities that are offered for sale on the basis that the goods supplied will be equal to the average quality of the current crop or recent shipments rather than on the basis of a specification or quality sample. **2** free alongside quay. See FREE ALONGSIDE SHIP.

FAR *abbr. Insurance* free (of claim) for accident reported.

far (**further**, **furthest** or **farther**, **farthest**) *–adv.* **1** at, to, or by a great distance (*far away*; *far off*; *far out*). **2** a long way (off) in space or time (*are you travelling far?*). **3** to a great extent or degree; by much (*far better*; *far too early*). *–adj.* **1** remote; distant (*far country*). **2** more distant (*far end of the hall*). **3** extreme (*far left*). □ **as far as 1** right up to (a place). **2** to the extent that. **by far** by a great amount. **a far cry** a long way. **far from** very different from being; almost the opposite of (*far from being fat*). **go far 1** achieve much. **2** contribute greatly. **go too far** overstep the limit (of propriety etc.). **so far 1** to such an extent; to this point. **2** until now. **so** (or **in so**) **far as** (or **that**) to the extent that. **so far so good** satisfactory up to now. [Old English]

farad /'færəd/ *n.* SI unit of capacitance. [*Faraday*, name of a physicist]

far and away *adv.* by a very large amount.

far and wide *adv.* over a large area.

far-away *adj.* **1** remote. **2** (of a look or voice) dreamy, distant.

farce *n.* **1 a** low comedy with a ludicrously improbable plot. **b** this branch of drama. **2** absurdly futile proceedings; pretence. □ **farcical** *adj.* [Latin *farcio* to stuff, used metaphorically of interludes etc.]

fare *–n.* **1 a** price of a journey on public transport. **b** fare-paying passenger. **2** range of food. *–v.* (**-ring**) progress; get on (*how did you fare?*). [Old English]

Far East *n.* (prec. by *the*) China, Japan, and other countries of E Asia.

fare-stage *n.* **1** section of bus etc. route for which a fixed fare is charged. **2** stop marking this.

farewell /feə'wel/ *–int.* goodbye. *–n.* leave-taking.

far-fetched *adj.* unconvincing, incredible.

far-flung *adj.* **1** widely scattered. **2** remote.

far gone *adj. colloq.* very ill, drunk, etc.

farina /fə'ri:nə/ *n.* **1** flour or meal of cereal, nuts, or starchy roots. **2** starch. □ **farinaceous** /ˌfærɪ'neɪʃəs/ *adj.* [Latin]

farm *–n.* **1** land and its buildings under one management for growing crops, rearing animals, etc. **2** such land etc. for a specified purpose (*trout-farm*). **3** = FARMHOUSE. *–v.* **1 a** use (land) for growing crops, rearing animals, etc. **b** be a farmer; work on a farm. **2** breed (fish etc.) commercially. **3** (often foll. by *out*) delegate or subcontract (work) to others. □ **farming** *n.* [French *ferme* from Latin *firma* fixed payment]

farmer *n.* owner or manager of a farm.

farm-hand *n.* worker on a farm.

farmhouse *n.* house attached to a farm.

farmstead /'fɑ:msted/ *n.* farm and its buildings.

farmyard *n.* yard attached to a farmhouse.

far-off *adj.* remote.

far-out *adj.* **1** distant. **2** *slang* avant-garde, unconventional. **3** *slang* excellent.

farrago /fə'rɑ:gəʊ/ *n.* (*pl.* **-s** or *US* **-es**) medley, hotchpotch. [Latin, = mixed fodder, from *far* corn]

far-reaching *adj.* widely influential or applicable.

farrier /'færɪə(r)/ *n.* smith who shoes horses. [Latin *ferrum* iron, horseshoe]

farrow /'færəʊ/ *–n.* **1** litter of pigs. **2** birth of a litter. *–v.* (also *absol.*) (of a sow) produce (pigs). [Old English]

far-seeing *adj.* showing foresight; wise.

Farsi /'fɑ:sɪ/ *n.* modern Persian language. [Persian]

far-sighted *adj.* **1** having foresight, prudent. **2** esp. *US* = LONG-SIGHTED.

fart *coarse slang –v.* **1** emit wind from the anus. **2** (foll. by *about, around*) behave foolishly. *–n.* **1** an emission of wind from the anus. **2** unpleasant or foolish person. [Old English]

farther var. of FURTHER (esp. of physical distance).

farthest var. of FURTHEST (esp. of physical distance).

farthing /'fɑ:ðɪŋ/ *n. hist.* coin and monetary unit worth a quarter of an old penny. [Old English: related to FOURTH]

■ **Usage** The farthing was withdrawn from circulation in 1961.

farthingale /'fɑ:ðɪŋˌgeɪl/ *n. hist.* hooped petticoat. [Spanish *verdugo* rod]

♦ **f.a.s.** *abbr.* (also **fas**) = FREE ALONGSIDE SHIP.

FASA *abbr.* Fellow of the Australian Society of Accountants.

FASB *abbr.* (in the US) Financial Accounting Standards Board.

fasces /'fæsi:z/ *n.pl.* **1** *Rom. Hist.* bundle of rods with a projecting axe-blade, as a magistrate's symbol of power. **2** emblems of authority. [Latin, pl. of *fascis* bundle]

fascia /'feɪʃə/ *n.* (also **facia**) (*pl.* **-s**) **1 a** instrument panel of a vehicle. **b** similar panel etc. for operating machinery. **2** strip with a name etc. over a shop-front. **3 a** long flat surface in classical architecture. **b** flat surface, usu. of wood, covering the ends of rafters. **4** stripe or band. [Latin, = band, door-frame]

fascicle /'fæsɪk(ə)l/ *n.* section of a book that is published in instalments. [Latin diminutive: related to FASCES]

fascinate /'fæsɪˌneɪt/ *v.* (**-ting**) **1** capture the interest of; attract. **2** paralyse (a victim) with fear. □ **fascination** /-'neɪʃ(ə)n/ *n.* [Latin *fascinum* spell]

Fascism /'fæʃɪz(ə)m/ *n.* **1** extreme totalitarian right-wing nationalist movement in Italy (1922–43). **2** (also **fascism**) any similar movement. □ **Fascist** *n.* & *adj.* (also **fascist**). **Fascistic** /-'ʃɪstɪk/ *adj.* (also **fascistic**). [Italian *fascio* bundle, organized group]

fashion /'fæʃ(ə)n/ *–n.* **1** current popular custom or style, esp. in dress. **2** manner of doing something. *–v.* (often foll. by *into*) make or form. □ **after** (or **in) a fashion** to some extent, barely acceptably. **in** (or **out of) fashion** fashionable (or not fashionable). [Latin *factio*: related to FACT]

fashionable *adj.* **1** following or suited to current fashion. **2** of or favoured by high society. □ **fashionableness** *n.* **fashionably** *adv.*

fast[1] /fɑ:st/ *–adj.* **1** rapid, quick-moving. **2** capable of or intended for high speed (*fast car; fast road*). **3** (of a clock etc.) ahead of the correct time. **4** (of a pitch etc.) causing the ball to bounce quickly. **5** firm; firmly fixed or attached (*fast knot; fast friendship*). **6** (of a colour) not fading. **7** pleasure seeking, dissolute. **8** (of photographic film etc.) needing only short exposure. *–adv.* **1** quickly; in quick succession. **2** firmly, tightly (*stand fast*). **3** soundly, completely (*fast asleep*). □ **pull a fast one** *colloq.* perpetrate deceit. [Old English]

fast[2] /fɑ:st/ *–v.* abstain from food, or certain food, for a time. *–n.* act or period of fasting. [Old English]

fastback *n.* **1** car with a sloping rear. **2** such a rear.

fast breeder *n.* (also **fast breeder reactor**) reactor using fast neutrons.

fasten /'fɑ:s(ə)n/ *v.* **1** make or become fixed or secure. **2** (foll. by *in, up*) lock securely; shut in. **3** (foll. by *on, upon*) direct (a look, thoughts, etc.) towards. **4** (foll. by *on, upon*) **a** take hold of. **b** single out. **5** (foll. by *off*) fix with a knot or stitches. □ **fastener** *n.* [Old English: related to FAST[1]]

fastening /'fɑ:snɪŋ/ *n.* device that fastens something; fastener.

♦ **fast food** *n.* **1** food that requires little or no preparation before serving. **2** restaurant food that is quickly produced and served, often in self-service establishments offering the same quality of product throughout the country or, in some cases, internationally.

---

fastidious /fæ'stɪdɪəs/ *adj.* **1** excessively discriminatory; fussy. **2** easily disgusted; squeamish. □ **fastidiously** *adv.* **fastidiousness** *n.* [Latin *fastidium* loathing]

♦ **fast-moving consumer goods** *n.pl.* (also **FMCG**) products that move off the shelves of retail shops quickly, and therefore require constant replenishing, including standard groceries etc. sold in supermarkets as well as records and tapes sold in music shops.

---

fastness /'fɑ:stnɪs/ *n.* stronghold. [Old English]

Fastnet /'fɑ:s(t)net/ rocky islet off the SW coast of the Republic of Ireland.

fast neutron *n.* neutron with high kinetic energy.

fast worker *n. colloq.* person who rapidly makes esp. sexual advances.

fat *–n.* **1** natural oily or greasy substance found esp. in animal bodies. **2** part of meat etc. containing this. *–adj.* (**fatter, fattest**) **1** corpulent; plump. **2** containing much fat. **3** fertile. **4 a** thick (*fat book*). **b** substantial (*fat cheque*). **5** *colloq. iron.* very little; not much (*a fat chance; a fat lot*). *–v.* (**-tt-**) make or become fat. □ **the fat is in the fire** trouble is imminent. **kill the fatted calf** celebrate, esp. at a prodigal's return (Luke 15). **live off** (or **on) the fat of the land** live luxuriously. □ **fatless** *adj.* **fatness** *n.* **fattish** *adj.* [Old English]

fatal /'feɪt(ə)l/ *adj.* **1** causing or ending in death (*fatal accident*). **2** (often foll. by *to*) ruinous (*fatal mistake*). **3** fateful. □ **fatally** *adv.* [Latin: related to FATE]

fatalism *n.* **1** belief in predetermination. **2** submissive acceptance. □ **fatalist** *n.* **fatalistic** /-'lɪstɪk/ *adj.* **fatalistically** /-'lɪstɪkəlɪ/ *adv.*

fatality /fə'tælətɪ/ *n.* (*pl.* **-ies**) **1** death by accident or in war etc. **2** fatal influence. **3** predestined liability to disaster.

fate *–n.* **1** supposed power predetermining events. **2 a** the future so determined. **b** individual's destiny or fortune. **3** death, destruction. *–v.* (**-ting**) **1** (usu. in *passive*) preordain (*fated to win*). **2** (as **fated** *adj.*) doomed. □ **advise fate** (of a bank) inform another bank whether or not a cheque or bill has been paid or dishonoured. **fate worse than death** see DEATH. [Italian and Latin *fatum*]

fateful *adj.* **1** important, decisive. **2** controlled by fate. □ **fatefully** *adv.*

fat-head *n. colloq.* stupid person.

fat-headed *adj.* stupid.

father /ˈfɑːðə(r)/ *–n.* **1** male parent. **2** (usu. in *pl.*) forefather. **3** originator, early leader. **4** (**Fathers** or **Fathers of the Church**) early Christian theologians. **5** (also **Father**) (often as a title or form of address) priest. **6** (**the Father**) (in Christian belief) first person of the Trinity. **7** (**Father**) venerable person, esp. as a title in personifications (*Father Time*). **8** (usu. in *pl.*) elders (*city fathers*). *–v.* **1** beget. **2** originate (a scheme etc.). □ **fatherhood** *n.* **fatherless** *adj.* [Old English]

father-figure *n.* older man respected and trusted like a father.

father file *Computing* see MASTER FILE.

father-in-law *n.* (*pl.* **fathers-in-law**) father of one's husband or wife.

fatherland *n.* one's native country.

fatherly *adj.* like or of a father.

Father's Day *n.* day on which cards and presents are given to fathers.

fathom /ˈfæð(ə)m/ *–n.* (*pl.* often **fathom** when prec. by a number) measure of six feet, esp. in depth soundings. *–v.* **1** comprehend. **2** measure the depth of (water). □ **fathomable** *adj.* [Old English]

fathomless *adj.* too deep to fathom.

fatigue /fəˈtiːg/ *–n.* **1** extreme tiredness. **2** weakness in metals etc. caused by repeated stress. **3 a** non-military army duty. **b** (in *pl.*) clothing worn for this. *–v.* (**-gues, -gued, -guing**) cause fatigue in. [Latin *fatigo* exhaust]

fatstock *n.* livestock fattened for slaughter.

fatten *v.* make or become fat.

fatty *adj.* (**-ier, -iest**) like or containing fat.

fatty acid *n.* organic compound consisting of a hydrocarbon chain and a terminal carboxyl group.

fatuous /ˈfætjʊəs/ *adj.* vacantly silly; purposeless, idiotic. □ **fatuity** /fəˈtjuːɪtɪ/ *n.* (*pl.* **-ies**). **fatuously** *adv.* **fatuousness** *n.* [Latin *fatuus*]

fatwa /ˈfætwɑː/ *n.* legal decision or ruling by an Islamic religious leader. [Arabic]

faucet /ˈfɔːsɪt/ *n.* esp. *US* tap. [French *fausset* vent-peg]

fault /fɔːlt/ *–n.* **1** defect or imperfection of character, structure, appearance, etc. **2** responsibility for wrongdoing, error, etc. (*your own fault*). **3 a** break in an electric circuit. **b** accidental condition that prevents some portion of a computer system from performing its prescribed function, usu. causing a failure. See also FAULT-TOLERANT. **4** transgression, offence. **5 a** *Tennis* etc. incorrect service. **b** (in showjumping) penalty for error. **6** break in rock strata. *–v.* **1** find fault with; blame. **2** *Geol.* **a** break the continuity of (strata). **b** show a fault. □ **at fault** guilty; to blame. **find fault** (often foll. by *with*) criticize; complain. **to a fault** excessively (*generous to a fault*). [Latin *fallo* deceive]

fault-finder *n.* complaining person.

fault-finding *n.* continual criticism.

faultless *adj.* perfect. □ **faultlessly** *adv.*

fault-tolerant *adj.* (of a computer system) capable of providing either a full or a reduced level of service in the event of a fault. If a disk were to develop a faulty track, then one of a number of spare tracks would automatically be brought into use in its place with minimum impact on the overall performance of the system.

faulty *adj.* (**-ier, -iest**) having faults; imperfect. □ **faultily** *adv.* **faultiness** *n.*

faun /fɔːn/ *n.* Latin rural deity with goat's horns, legs, and tail. [Latin *Faunus*]

fauna /ˈfɔːnə/ *n.* (*pl.* **-s** or **-nae** /-niː/) animal life of a region or period. [Latin *Fauna*, name of a rural goddess]

faux pas /fəʊ ˈpɑː/ *n.* (*pl.* same /ˈpɑːz/) tactless mistake; blunder. [French, = false step]

favour /ˈfeɪvə(r)/ (*US* **favor**) *–n.* **1** kind act (*did it as a favour*). **2** approval, goodwill; friendly regard (*gained their favour*). **3** partiality. **4** badge, ribbon, etc., as an emblem of support. *–v.* **1** regard or treat with favour or partiality. **2** support, promote, prefer. **3** be to the advantage of; facilitate. **4** tend to confirm (an idea etc.). **5** (foll. by *with*) oblige. **6** (as **favoured** *adj.*) having special advantages. □ **in favour 1** approved of. **2** (foll. by *of*) **a** in support of. **b** to the advantage of. **out of favour** disapproved of. [Latin *faveo* be kind to]

favourable /ˈfeɪvərəb(ə)l/ *adj.* (*US* **favorable**) **1** well-disposed; propitious; approving. **2** promising, auspicious. **3** helpful, suitable. □ **favourably** *adv.*

favourite /ˈfeɪvərɪt/ (*US* **favorite**) *–adj.* preferred to all others (*favourite book*). *–n.* **1** favourite person or thing. **2** *Sport* competitor thought most likely to win. [Italian: related to FAVOUR]

favouritism *n.* (*US* **favoritism**) unfair favouring of one person etc. at the expense of another.

fawn[1] *–n.* **1** deer in its first year. **2** light yellowish brown. *–adj.* fawn-coloured. *–v.* (also *absol.*) give birth to (a fawn). [Latin: related to FOETUS]

fawn[2] *v.* **1** (often foll. by *on*, *upon*) behave servilely, cringe. **2** (of esp. a dog) show extreme affection. [Old English]

fax *–n.* **1** transmission of an exact copy of a document etc. electronically, using a **fax machine** and a separate telephone line. Copies are transmitted for the cost of a telephone call of equal duration (approximately 30–60 seconds per A4 page), and communication can be worldwide. **2** copy produced by this. *–v.* transmit in this way. [abbreviation of FACSIMILE]

fay *n. literary* fairy. [Latin *fata* pl. Fates]

faze *v.* (**-zing**) (often as **fazed** *adj.*) *colloq.* disconcert, disorientate. [origin unknown]

FBA *abbr.* Fellow of the British Academy.

FBCS *abbr.* Fellow of the British Computer Society.

FBEC(S) *abbr.* Fellow of the Business Education Council (Scotland).

FBI *abbr.* Federal Bureau of Investigation.

FBIBA *abbr.* Fellow of the British Insurance Brokers' Association.

FBINZ *abbr.* Fellow of the Bankers' Institute of New Zealand.

FBT *abbr.* fringe benefit tax.

FBu *symb.* Burundi franc.

FC *abbr.* Football Club.

FCA *abbr.* Fellow of the Institute of Chartered Accountants. See INSTITUTE OF CHARTERED ACCOUNTANTS.

FCA(Aust.) *abbr.* Fellow of the Institute of Chartered Accountants in Australia.

FCAI *abbr.* Fellow of the New Zealand Institute of Cost Accountants.

FCAR *abbr. Insurance* free of claim for accident reported.

FCB *abbr. Computing* file control block.

FCBSI *abbr.* Fellow of the Chartered Building Societies Institute.

◆ **FCCA** *abbr.* Fellow of the Chartered Association of Certified Accountants. See CERTIFIED ACCOUNTANT; CHARTERED ACCOUNTANT.

FCCS *abbr.* Fellow of the Corporation of Secretaries. [formerly *F*ellow of the *C*orporation of *C*ertified *S*ecretaries]

FCI *abbr.* Fellow of the Institute of Commerce.

FCIA *abbr.* **1** Fellow of the Corporation of Insurance Agents. **2** Foreign Credit Insurance Association.

FCIB *abbr.* **1** Fellow of the Chartered Institute of Bankers. **2** Fellow of the Corporation of Insurance Brokers.

FCII *abbr.* Fellow of the Chartered Insurance Institute. See CHARTERED INSURANCE INSTITUTE.

FCILA *abbr.* Fellow of the Chartered Institute of Loss Adjusters.

FCIM *abbr.* Fellow of the Chartered Institute of Marketing.

FCIS *abbr.* Fellow of the Institute of Chartered Secretaries and Administrators. [formerly *F*ellow of the *C*hartered *I*nstitute of *S*ecretaries]

FCISA *abbr.* Fellow of the Chartered Institute of Secretaries and Administrators (Australia).

FCMA *abbr.* Fellow of the Institute of Cost and Management Accountants.

FCO *abbr.* Foreign and Commonwealth Office.

fco. *abbr. Commerce* (French) franco (= free of charge).

FCT *abbr.* Fellow of the Association of Corporate Treasurers.

FD *abbr.* **1** (also **f/d**) free-delivered (at docks). **2** (also **f/d, f.d.**) free delivery.

FDDI *abbr. Computing* fibre distributed data interface (high-speed local area network system).

FDIC *abbr.* (in the US) Federal Deposit Insurance Corporation.

FDM *abbr.* frequency-division multiplexing. See MULTIPLEXER.

FDO *abbr. Taxation* for declaration (purposes) only.

FDX *abbr. Computing* full duplex.

Fe *symb.* iron. [Latin *ferrum*]

fealty /'fiːəltɪ/ *n.* (*pl.* **-ies**) **1** *hist.* fidelity to a feudal lord. **2** allegiance. [Latin: related to FIDELITY]

fear *–n.* **1 a** panic or distress caused by a sense of impending danger, pain, etc. **b** cause of this. **c** state of alarm (*in fear*). **2** (often foll. by *of*) dread, awe (towards) (*fear of heights*). **3** danger (*little fear of failure*). *–v.* **1** feel fear about or towards. **2** (foll. by *for*) feel anxiety about (*feared for my life*). **3** (often foll. by *that*) foresee or expect with unease, fear, or regret (*fear the worst; I fear that you are wrong*). **4** (foll. by verbal noun) shrink from (*feared meeting his ex-wife*). **5** revere (esp. God). □ **for fear of** (or **that**) to avoid the risk of (or that). **no fear** *colloq.* certainly not! [Old English]

fearful *adj.* **1** (usu. foll. by *of* or *that*) afraid. **2** terrible, awful. **3** *colloq.* extreme, esp. unpleasant (*fearful row*). □ **fearfully** *adv.* **fearfulness** *n.*

fearless *adj.* **1** courageous, brave. **2** (foll. by *of*) without fear. □ **fearlessly** *adv.* **fearlessness** *n.*

fearsome *adj.* frightening. □ **fearsomely** *adv.*

♦ **feasibility study** *n.* **1** study of the financial factors involved in producing a new product, setting up a new process, etc. The study will analyse the technical feasibility with detailed costings of set-up expenses, running expenses, and raw-material costs, together with expected income. The capital required and the interest charges will also be analysed to enable an opinion to be given as to the commercial viability of product, process, etc. **2** study carried out before development of a proposed computer system in order to establish that the system is possible, practical, and can serve a useful purpose.

---

feasible /'fiːzɪb(ə)l/ *adj.* practicable, possible. □ **feasibility** /-'bɪlɪtɪ/ *n.* **feasibly** *adv.* [Latin *facio* do]

■ **Usage** *Feasible* should not be used to mean 'possible' or 'probable' in the sense 'likely'. 'Possible' or 'probable' should be used instead.

feast *–n.* **1** large or sumptuous meal. **2** sensual or mental pleasure. **3** religious festival. **4** annual village festival. *–v.* **1** (often foll. by *on*) partake of a feast; eat and drink sumptuously. **2** regale. □ **feast one's eyes on** look with pleasure at. [Latin *festus* joy]

feat *n.* remarkable act or achievement. [Latin: related to FACT]

feather /'feðə(r)/ *–n.* **1** one of the structures forming a bird's plumage, with a horny stem and fine strands. **2** (*collect.*) **a** plumage. **b** game-birds. *–v.* **1** cover or line with feathers. **2** turn (an oar) edgeways through the air. □ **feather in one's cap** a personal achievement. **feather one's nest** enrich oneself. **in fine** (or **high**) **feather** *colloq.* in good spirits. □ **feathery** *adj.* [Old English]

feather bed *n.* bed with a feather-stuffed mattress.

feather-bed *v.* (**-dd-**) cushion, esp. financially.

feather-brain *n.* (also **feather-head**) silly or absent-minded person. □ **feather-brained** *adj.* (also **feather-headed**).

feathering *n.* **1** bird's plumage. **2** feathers of an arrow. **3** feather-like structure or marking.

featherweight *n.* **1 a** weight in certain sports between bantamweight and lightweight, in amateur boxing 54–7kg. **b** sportsman of this weight. **2** very light person or thing. **3** (usu. *attrib.*) unimportant thing.

feature /'fiːtʃə(r)/ *–n.* **1** distinctive or characteristic part of a thing. **2** (usu. in *pl.*) part of the face. **3** (esp. specialized) article in a newspaper etc. **4** (in full **feature film**) main film in a cinema programme. *–v.* (**-ring**) **1** make a special display of; emphasize. **2** have as or be a central participant or topic in a film, broadcast, etc. □ **featureless** *adj.* [Latin *factura* formation: related to FACT]

Feb. *abbr.* February.

febrifuge /'febrɪˌfjuːdʒ/ *n.* medicine or treatment for fever. [Latin *febris* fever]

febrile /'fiːbraɪl/ *adj.* of fever; feverish. [Latin *febris* fever]

February /'februərɪ/ *n.* (*pl.* **-ies**) second month of the year. [Latin *februa* purification feast]

FEC *abbr.* Foreign Exchange Certificate (tourist currency used in China).

fecal *US* var. of FAECAL.

FECB *abbr.* Foreign Exchange Control Board.

feces *US* var. of FAECES.

FECI *abbr.* Fellow of the Institute of Employment Consultants.

feckless /'feklɪs/ *adj.* **1** feeble, ineffective. **2** unthinking, irresponsible. [Scots *feck* from *effeck* var. of EFFECT]

fecund /'fekənd/ *adj.* **1** prolific, fertile. **2** fertilizing. □ **fecundity** /fɪ'kʌndətɪ/ *n.* [Latin]

fecundate /'fekənˌdeɪt/ *v.* (**-ting**) **1** make fruitful. **2** fertilize. □ **fecundation** /-'deɪʃ(ə)n/ *n.*

fed *past* and *past part.* of FEED. □ **fed up** (often foll. by *with*) discontented or bored.

FED /fed/ *n.* (also **Fed**) = FEDERAL RESERVE SYSTEM. [abbreviation]

federal /'fedər(ə)l/ *adj.* **1** of a system of government in which self-governing states unite for certain functions etc. **2** of such a federation (*federal laws*). **3** of or favouring centralized government. **4** (**Federal**) *US* of the northern states in the Civil War. **5** comprising an association of largely independent units. □ **federalism** *n.* **federalist** *n.* **federalize** *v.* (also **-ise**) (**-zing** or **-sing**). **federalization** /-'zeɪʃ(ə)n/ *n.* **federally** *adv.* [Latin *foedus* covenant]

♦ **federal funding rate** *n.* rate of interest charged by the US Federal Reserve System when lending money to the rest of the banking system.

---

federal reserve *n.* (in the US) reserve cash available to banks.

♦ **Federal Reserve System** *n.* (also **FED, Fed**) (in the US) banking system that performs the functions of a central bank. The system consists of 12 Federal Reserve Districts, in each of which a **Federal Reserve Bank** acts as lender of last resort. The activities of the 12 Reserve Banks are controlled from Washington by the **Federal Reserve Board**. The Federal Reserve System is used to implement US monetary policy.

---

federate *–v.* /'fedəˌreɪt/ (**-ting**) unite on a federal basis. *–adj.* /'fedərət/ federally organized. □ **federative** /'fedərətɪv/ *adj.*

federation /ˌfedə'reɪʃ(ə)n/ *n.* **1** federal group. **2** act of federating. [Latin: related to FEDERAL]

fee *n.* **1** payment made for professional advice or services etc. **2 a** charge for a privilege, examination, admission to a society, etc. (*enrolment fee*). **b** money paid for the transfer to another employer of a footballer etc. **3** (in *pl.*) regular payments (esp. to a school). **4** *Law* inherited estate, unlimited (**fee simple**) or limited (**fee tail**) as to category of heir. See also FEE SIMPLE. [medieval Latin *feudum*]

feeble /ˈfiːb(ə)l/ *adj.* (**feebler, feeblest**) **1** weak, infirm. **2** lacking strength, energy, or effectiveness. □ **feebly** *adv.* [Latin *flebilis* lamentable]

feeble-minded *adj.* mentally deficient.

feed *–v.* (*past* and *past part.* **fed**) **1 a** supply with food. **b** put food into the mouth of. **2** give as food, esp. to animals. **3** (usu. foll. by *on*) (esp. of animals, or *colloq.* of people) eat. **4** (often foll. by *on*) nourish or be nourished by; benefit from. **5 a** keep (a fire, machine, etc.) supplied with fuel etc. **b** (foll. by *into*) supply (material) to a machine etc. **c** (often foll. by *into*) (of a river etc.) flow into a lake etc. **d** keep (a meter) supplied with coins to ensure continuity. **6** *slang* supply (an actor etc.) with cues. **7** *Sport* send passes to (a player). **8** gratify (vanity etc.). **9** provide (advice, information, etc.) to. *–n.* **1** food, esp. for animals or infants. **2** feeding; giving of food. **3** *colloq.* meal. **4 a** raw material for a machine etc. **b** provision of or device for this. □ **feed back** produce feedback. **feed up** fatten. [Old English]

feedback *n.* **1** public response to an event, experiment, etc. **2** *Electronics* **a** return of a fraction of an output signal to the input. **b** signal so returned.

feeder *n.* **1** person or thing that feeds, esp. in specified manner. **2** baby's feeding-bottle. **3** bib. **4** tributary stream. **5** branch road, railway line, etc. linking with a main system. **6** main carrying electricity to a distribution point. **7** feeding apparatus in a machine.

feel *–v.* (*past* and *past part.* **felt**) **1 a** examine or search by touch. **b** (*absol.*) have the sensation of touch (*unable to feel*). **2** perceive or ascertain by touch (*feel the warmth*). **3** experience, exhibit, or be affected by (an emotion, conviction, etc.) (*felt strongly about it*; *felt the rebuke*). **4** (foll. by *that*) have an impression (*I feel that I am right*). **5** consider, think (*I feel it useful*). **6** seem (*air feels chilly*). **7** be consciously; consider oneself (*I feel happy*). **8** (foll. by *for, with*) have sympathy or pity. **9** (often foll. by *up*) *slang* fondle sexually. *–n.* **1** feeling; testing by touch. **2** sensation characterizing a material, situation, etc. **3** sense of touch. □ **feel like** have a wish or inclination for. **feel up to** be ready to face or deal with. **feel one's way** proceed cautiously. **get the feel of** become accustomed to using. [Old English]

feeler *n.* **1** organ in certain animals for touching or searching for food. **2** tentative proposal (*put out feelers*).

feeling *–n.* **1 a** capacity to feel; sense of touch (*lost all feeling*). **b** physical sensation. **2 a** (often foll. by *of*) emotional reaction (*feeling of despair*). **b** (in *pl.*) emotional susceptibilities (*hurt my feelings*). **3** particular sensitivity (*feeling for literature*). **4 a** opinion or notion (*had a feeling she would*). **b** general sentiment. **5** sympathy or compassion. **6** emotional sensibility or intensity (*played with feeling*). *–adj.* sensitive, sympathetic; heartfelt. □ **feelingly** *adv.*

FEER *abbr. Finance* fundamental equilibrium exchange rate.

♦ **fee simple** *n. Law* most common form of freehold estate in land and the only type that can now exist in common law, as opposed to in equity. Although all land in England is theoretically held by the Crown, the owner of a fee simple, or the owner's heirs, will own the land forever and may dispose of it with complete freedom both during life and by will. The land will revert to the Crown only if the owner dies without leaving a will and with no surviving relatives.

---

feet *pl.* of FOOT.

feign /feɪn/ *v.* simulate; pretend (*feign madness*). [Latin *fingo fict-* mould, contrive]

feint /feɪnt/ *–n.* **1** sham attack or diversionary blow. **2** pretence. *–v.* make a feint. *–adj.* = FAINT *adj.* 5. [French: related to FEIGN]

feldspar /ˈfeldspɑː(r)/ *n.* (also **felspar**) common aluminium silicate of potassium, sodium, or calcium. □ **feldspathic** /-ˈspæθɪk/ *adj.* [German *Feld* field, *Spat(h)* SPAR[3]]

felicitate /fəˈlɪsɪˌteɪt/ *v.* (**-ting**) *formal* congratulate. □ **felicitation** /-ˈteɪʃ(ə)n/ *n.* (usu. in *pl.*). [Latin *felix* happy]

felicitous /fəˈlɪsɪtəs/ *adj. formal* apt; pleasantly ingenious; well-chosen.

felicity /fəˈlɪsɪtɪ/ *n.* (*pl.* **-ies**) *formal* **1** intense happiness. **2 a** capacity for apt expression. **b** well-chosen phrase. [Latin *felix* happy]

feline /ˈfiːlaɪn/ *–adj.* **1** of the cat family. **2** catlike. *–n.* animal of the cat family. □ **felinity** /fɪˈlɪnɪtɪ/ *n.* [Latin *feles* cat]

fell[1] *past* of FALL *v.*

fell[2] *v.* **1** cut down (esp. a tree). **2** strike or knock down. **3** stitch down (the edge of a seam). [Old English]

fell[3] *n. N.Engl.* **1** hill. **2** stretch of hills or moorland. [Old Norse]

fell[4] *adj. poet.* or *rhet.* ruthless, destructive. □ **at** (or **in**) **one fell swoop** in a single (orig. deadly) action. [French: related to FELON]

fell[5] *n.* animal's hide or skin with its hair. [Old English]

fellatio /fɪˈleɪʃɪəʊ/ *n.* oral stimulation of the penis. [Latin *fello* suck]

feller *n.* = FELLOW 1.

felloe /ˈfeləʊ/ *n.* (also **felly** /ˈfelɪ/) (*pl.* **-s** or **-ies**) outer circle (or a section of it) of a wheel. [Old English]

fellow /ˈfeləʊ/ *n.* **1** *colloq.* man or boy (*poor fellow!*). **2** (usu. in *pl.*) person in a group etc.; comrade (*separated from their fellows*). **3** counterpart; one of a pair. **4** equal; peer. **5 a** incorporated senior member of a college. **b** elected graduate paid to do research. **6** member of a learned society. **7** (*attrib.*) of the same group etc. (*fellow-countryman*). [Old English from Old Norse]

fellow-feeling *n.* sympathy.

fellowship *n.* **1** friendly association with others, companionship. **2** body of associates. **3** status or income of a fellow of a college or society.

fellow-traveller *n.* **1** person who travels with another. **2** sympathizer with the Communist Party.

felly var. of FELLOE.

felon /ˈfelən/ *n.* person who has committed a felony. [medieval Latin *fello*]

felony *n.* (*pl.* **-ies**) serious, usu. violent, crime. □ **felonious** /fɪˈləʊnɪəs/ *adj.*

felspar var. of FELDSPAR.

felt[1] *–n.* cloth of matted and pressed fibres of wool etc. *–v.* **1** make into felt; mat. **2** cover with felt. **3** become matted. [Old English]

felt[2] *past* and *past part.* of FEEL.

felt-tipped pen *n.* (also **felt-tip pen**) pen with a fibre point.

felucca /fɪˈlʌkə/ *n.* small Mediterranean coasting vessel with oars and/or sails. [Arabic *fulk*]

female /ˈfiːmeɪl/ *–adj.* **1** of the sex that can give birth or produce eggs. **2** (of plants) fruit-bearing. **3** of women or female animals or plants. **4** (of a screw, socket, etc.) hollow to receive an inserted part. *–n.* female person, animal, or plant. [Latin diminutive of *femina* woman, assimilated to *male*]

feminine /ˈfemɪnɪn/ *–adj.* **1** of women. **2** having womanly qualities. **3** of the gender proper to women's names. *–n.* feminine gender or word. □ **femininity** /-ˈnɪnɪtɪ/ *n.* [Latin: related to FEMALE]

feminism /ˈfemɪˌnɪz(ə)m/ *n.* advocacy of women's rights and sexual equality. □ **feminist** *n.* & *adj.*

femme fatale /ˌfæm fæˈtɑːl/ *n.* (*pl.* ***femmes fatales*** pronunc. same) dangerously seductive woman. [French]

femur /ˈfiːmə(r)/ *n.* (*pl.* **-s** or **femora** /ˈfemərə/) thigh-bone. □ **femoral** /ˈfemər(ə)l/ *adj.* [Latin]

fen *n.* **1** low marshy land. **2** (**the Fens**) low-lying areas in Cambridgeshire etc. [Old English]

fence –*n.* **1** barrier, railing, etc., enclosing a field, garden, etc. **2** large upright jump for horses. **3** *slang* receiver of stolen goods. **4** guard or guide in machinery. –*v.* (**-cing**) **1** surround with or as with a fence. **2** (foll. by *in, off, up*) enclose, separate, or seal, with or as with a fence. **3** practise fencing with a sword. **4** be evasive. **5** *slang* deal in (stolen goods). □ **fencer** *n.* [from DEFENCE]

fencing *n.* **1** set of, or material for, fences. **2** sword-fighting, esp. as a sport.

fend *v.* **1** (foll. by *for*) look after (esp. oneself). **2** (usu. foll. by *off*) ward off. [from DEFEND]

fender *n.* **1** low frame bordering a fireplace. **2** *Naut.* padding protecting a ship against impact. **3** *US* vehicle's bumper.

fennel /'fen(ə)l/ *n.* yellow-flowered fragrant herb used for flavouring. [Latin *fenum* hay]

fenugreek /'fenjuː,griːk/ *n.* leguminous plant with aromatic seeds used for flavouring. [Latin, = Greek hay]

feral /'fer(ə)l/ *adj.* **1** wild; uncultivated. **2** (of an animal) escaped and living wild. **3** brutal. [Latin *ferus* wild]

ferial /'fɪərɪəl/ *adj. Eccl.* (of a day) not a festival or fast. [Latin *feria* FAIR[2]]

Ferm. *abbr.* Fermanagh.

Fermanagh /fə'mænə/ **1** county in S Northern Ireland; county town, Enniskillen. It is agricultural, producing cereals and livestock, and has textile industries. **2** district in Northern Ireland, in Co. Fermanagh; pop. (1990) 50 600.

ferment –*n.* /'fɜːment/ **1** agitation, excitement. **2 a** fermentation. **b** fermenting-agent. –*v.* /fə'ment/ **1** undergo or subject to fermentation. **2** excite; stir up. [Latin *fermentum*: related to FERVENT]

fermentation /,fɜːmen'teɪʃ(ə)n/ *n.* **1** breakdown of a substance by yeasts and bacteria etc., esp. of sugar in making alcohol. **2** agitation, excitement. □ **fermentative** /-'mentətɪv/ *adj.* [Latin: related to FERMENT]

fermium /'fɜːmɪəm/ *n.* transuranic artificial radioactive metallic element. [*Fermi*, name of a physicist]

fern *n.* (*pl.* same or **-s**) flowerless plant usu. having feathery fronds. □ **ferny** *adj.* [Old English]

Fernando Po /fə'nændəʊ 'pəʊ/ see BIOKO.

ferocious /fə'rəʊʃəs/ *adj.* fierce, savage. □ **ferociously** *adv.* **ferocity** /fə'rɒsɪtɪ/ *n.* [Latin *ferox*]

-ferous *comb. form* (usu. **-iferous**) forming adjectives with the sense 'bearing', 'having' (*odoriferous*). [Latin *fero* bear]

ferrel var. of FERRULE.

ferret /'ferɪt/ –*n.* small polecat used in catching rabbits, rats, etc. –*v.* **1** hunt with ferrets. **2** (often foll. by *out, about*, etc.) rummage; search out (secrets, criminals, etc.). [Latin *fur* thief]

ferric /'ferɪk/ *adj.* **1** of iron. **2** containing iron in a trivalent form. [Latin *ferrum* iron]

Ferris wheel /'ferɪs/ *n.* tall revolving vertical wheel with passenger cars in fairgrounds etc. [*Ferris*, name of its inventor]

ferro- *comb. form* **1** iron. **2** (of alloys) containing iron. [related to FERRIC]

ferroconcrete /,ferəʊ'kɒŋkriːt/ –*n.* reinforced concrete. –*adj.* made of this.

ferrous /'ferəs/ *adj.* **1** containing iron. **2** containing iron in a divalent form.

ferrule /'feruːl/ *n.* (also **ferrel** /'fer(ə)l/) **1** ring or cap on the lower end of a stick, umbrella, etc. **2** band strengthening or forming a joint. [Latin *viriae* bracelet]

ferry –*n.* (*pl.* **-ies**) **1** boat or aircraft etc. for esp. regular transport, esp. across water. **2** place or service of ferrying. –*v.* (**-ies, -ied**) **1** convey or go in a ferry. **2** (of a boat etc.) cross water regularly. **3** transport, esp. regularly, from place to place. □ **ferryman** *n.* [Old Norse]

fertile /'fɜːtaɪl/ *adj.* **1 a** (of soil) abundantly productive. **b** fruitful. **2 a** (of a seed, egg, etc.) capable of growth. **b** (of animals and plants) able to reproduce. **3** (of the mind) inventive. **4** (of nuclear material) able to become fissile by the capture of neutrons. □ **fertility** /-'tɪlɪtɪ/ *n.* [French from Latin]

fertilize /'fɜːtɪ,laɪz/ *v.* (also **-ise**) (**-zing** or **-sing**) **1** make (soil etc.) fertile. **2** cause (an egg, female animal, etc.) to develop by mating etc. □ **fertilization** /-'zeɪʃ(ə)n/ *n.*

fertilizer *n.* (also **-iser**) substance added to soil to make it more fertile.

fervent /'fɜːv(ə)nt/ *adj.* ardent, intense (*fervent admirer*). □ **fervency** *n.* **fervently** *adv.* [Latin *ferveo* boil]

fervid /'fɜːvɪd/ *adj.* ardent, intense. □ **fervidly** *adv.* [Latin: related to FERVENT]

fervour /'fɜːvə(r)/ *n.* (*US* **fervor**) passion, zeal. [Latin: related to FERVENT]

Fès see FEZ.

fescue /'feskjuː/ *n.* a pasture and fodder grass. [Latin *festuca* stalk, straw]

festal /'fest(ə)l/ *adj.* **1** joyous, merry. **2** of a feast or festival. □ **festally** *adv.* [Latin: related to FEAST]

fester *v.* **1** make or become septic. **2** cause continuing anger or bitterness. **3** rot, stagnate. [Latin FISTULA]

festival /'festɪv(ə)l/ *n.* **1** day or period of celebration. **2** series of cultural events in a town etc. (*Bath Festival*). [French: related to FESTIVE]

festive /'festɪv/ *adj.* **1** of or characteristic of a festival. **2** joyous. □ **festively** *adv.* **festiveness** *n.* [Latin: related to FEAST]

festivity /fe'stɪvɪtɪ/ *n.* (*pl.* **-ies**) **1** gaiety, rejoicing. **2** (in *pl.*) celebration; party.

festoon /fe'stuːn/ –*n.* curved hanging chain of flowers, leaves, ribbons, etc. –*v.* (often foll. by *with*) adorn with or form into festoons; decorate elaborately. [Italian: related to FESTIVE]

Festschrift /'festʃrɪft/ *n.* (also **festschrift**) (*pl.* **-en** or **-s**) collection of writings published in honour of a scholar. [German, = festival-writing]

FET *abbr.* **1** *US* **a** federal estate tax. **b** federal excise tax. **2** field-effect transistor.

feta /'fetə/ *n.* soft white esp. ewe's-milk cheese made esp. in Greece. [Greek *pheta*]

fetal *US* var. of FOETAL.

fetch –*v.* **1** go for and bring back (*fetch a doctor*). **2** be sold for (a price) (*fetched £10*). **3** cause (blood, tears, etc.) to flow. **4** draw (breath), heave (a sigh). **5** *colloq.* give (a blow etc.) (*fetched him a slap*). –*n.* **1** act of fetching. **2** dodge, trick. □ **fetch and carry** do menial tasks. **fetch up** *colloq.* **1** arrive, come to rest. **2** vomit. [Old English]

fetching *adj.* attractive. □ **fetchingly** *adv.*

fête /feɪt/ –*n.* **1** outdoor fund-raising event with stalls and amusements etc. **2** festival. **3** saint's day. –*v.* (**-ting**) honour or entertain lavishly. [French: related to FEAST]

fetid /'fetɪd/ *adj.* (also **foetid**) stinking. [Latin *feteo* stink]

fetish /'fetɪʃ/ *n.* **1** *Psychol.* abnormal object of sexual desire. **2 a** object worshipped by primitive peoples. **b** obsessional cause (*makes a fetish of punctuality*). □ **fetishism** *n.* **fetishist** *n.* **fetishistic** /-'ʃɪstɪk/ *adj.* [Portuguese *feitiço* charm]

fetlock /'fetlɒk/ *n.* back of a horse's leg above the hoof with a tuft of hair. [ultimately related to FOOT]

fetter –*n.* **1** shackle for the ankles. **2** (in *pl.*) captivity. **3** restraint. –*v.* **1** put into fetters. **2** restrict. [Old English]

fettle /'fet(ə)l/ *n.* condition or trim (*in fine fettle*). [Old English]

fetus *US* var. of FOETUS.

feu /fjuː/ *Scot.* –*n.* **1** perpetual lease at a fixed rent. **2** land so held. –*v.* (**feus, feued, feuing**) grant (land) on feu. [French: related to FEE]

feud[1] /fjuːd/ –*n.* prolonged hostility, esp. between families, tribes, etc. –*v.* conduct a feud. [Germanic: related to FOE]

feud[2] /fjuːd/ *n.* = FIEF. [medieval Latin *feudum* FEE]

feudal /'fjuːd(ə)l/ *adj.* **1** of, like, or according to the feudal system. **2** reactionary (*feudal attitude*). □ **feudalism** *n.* **feudalistic** /-'lɪstɪk/ *adj.*

feudal system *n.* medieval system of land tenure with allegiance and service due to the landowner.

fever *–n.* **1 a** abnormally high temperature, often with delirium etc. **b** disease characterized by this (*scarlet fever*). **2** nervous excitement; agitation. *–v.* (esp. as **fevered** *adj.*) affect with fever or excitement. [Latin *febris*]

feverfew /ˈfiːvəˌfjuː/ *n.* aromatic bushy plant, used formerly to reduce fever, now to cure migraine. [Latin *febrifuga*: related to FEVER, *fugo* drive away]

feverish *adj.* **1** having symptoms of fever. **2** excited, restless. □ **feverishly** *adv.* **feverishness** *n.*

fever pitch *n.* state of extreme excitement.

few *–adj.* not many (*few doctors smoke*). *–n.* (as *pl.*) **1** (prec. by *a*) some but not many (*a few of his friends were there*). **2** not many (*few are chosen*). **3** (prec. by *the*) **a** the minority. **b** the elect. □ **a good few** *colloq.* fairly large number. **no fewer than** as many as (a specified number). **not a few** a considerable number. [Old English]

few and far between *predic. adj.* scarce.

fey /feɪ/ *adj.* **1 a** strange, other-worldly; whimsical. **b** clairvoyant. **2** *Scot.* fated to die soon. [Old English, = doomed to die]

Fez /fez/ (also **Fès**) city in N Morocco; textiles, carpets, and leather goods are manufactured; pop. (1994) 510 000.

fez *n.* (*pl.* **fezzes**) man's flat-topped conical red cap worn by some Muslims. [Turkish]

ff *abbr. Mus.* fortissimo.

ff. *abbr.* following pages etc.

FFA *abbr.* **1** *Scot.* Fellow of the Faculty of Actuaries. **2** Fellow of the Institute of Financial Accountants.

f.f.a. *abbr.* free from alongside (ship).

FFC *abbr.* Foreign Funds Control.

FFI *abbr.* Finance for Industry.

FFr *abbr.* (also **Ffr**) French franc.

f.g. *abbr. Commerce* fully good.

f.g.f. *abbr. Commerce* fully good, fair.

FGT *abbr. US* federal gift tax.

FHA *abbr.* Finance Houses Association.

FIA *abbr.* **1** (in the US) Federal Insurance Administration. **2** Fellow of the Institute of Actuaries (see INSTITUTE OF ACTUARIES). **3** (also **f.i.a.**) *Commerce* full interest admitted.

FIAA *abbr.* Fellow of the Institute of Actuaries of Australia.

FIAI *abbr.* Fellow of the Institute of Industrial and Commercial Accountants.

FIAM *abbr.* **1** Fellow of the Institute of Administrative Management. **2** Fellow of the International Academy of Management.

fiancé /fɪˈɒnseɪ/ *n.* (*fem.* **fiancée** pronunc. same) person one is engaged to. [French]

FIAP *abbr.* Fellow of the Institution of Analysts and Programmers.

fiasco /fɪˈæskəʊ/ *n.* (*pl.* **-s**) ludicrous or humiliating failure or breakdown. [Italian, = bottle]

fiat /ˈfaɪæt/ *n.* **1** authorization. **2** decree. [Latin, = let it be done]

♦ **fiat money** *n.* money, esp. paper money, that a government has declared to be legal tender, although it has no intrinsic value and is not backed by reserves. Most of the world's paper money is now fiat money. Cf. FIDUCIARY ISSUE 1.

---

fib *–n.* trivial lie. *–v.* (**-bb-**) tell a fib. □ **fibber** *n.* [perhaps from *fible-fable*, a reduplication of FABLE]

f.i.b. *abbr.* **1** free into barge. **2** free into bond. **3** free into bunker.

FIBA *abbr.* Fellow of the Institute of Business Administration (Australia).

FIBOR *abbr.* Frankfurt Inter Bank Offered Rate.

fibre /ˈfaɪbə(r)/ *n.* (*US* **fiber**) **1** thread or filament forming tissue or textile. **2** piece of threadlike glass. **3** substance formed of fibres, or able to be spun, woven, etc. **4** structure; character (*moral fibre*). **5** roughage. [French from Latin *fibra*]

fibreboard *n.* (*US* **fiberboard**) board of compressed wood or other plant fibres.

fibreglass *n.* (*US* **fiberglass**) **1** fabric made from woven glass fibres. **2** plastic reinforced by glass fibres.

fibre optics *n.pl.* optics using thin glass fibres, usu. for the transmission of modulated light to carry signals.

fibril /ˈfaɪbrɪl/ *n.* small fibre. [diminutive of FIBRE]

fibroid /ˈfaɪbrɔɪd/ *–adj.* of, like, or containing fibrous tissue or fibres. *–n.* benign fibrous tumour growing in the womb.

fibrosis /faɪˈbrəʊsɪs/ *n.* thickening and scarring of connective tissue. [from FIBRE, -OSIS]

fibrositis /ˌfaɪbrəˈsaɪtɪs/ *n.* rheumatic inflammation of fibrous tissue. [from FIBRE, -ITIS]

fibrous /ˈfaɪbrəs/ *adj.* of or like fibres.

F.I.B.Scot. *abbr.* Fellow of the Institute of Bankers in Scotland.

fibula /ˈfɪbjʊlə/ *n.* (*pl.* **fibulae** /-ˌliː/ or **-s**) small outer bone between the knee and the ankle. □ **fibular** *adj.* [Latin, = brooch]

-fic *suffix* (usu. as **-ific**) forming adjectives meaning 'producing', 'making' (*prolific*; *pacific*). [Latin *facio* make]

FICA *abbr.* Fellow of the Commonwealth Institute of Accountants.

FICAI *abbr.* Fellow of the Institute of Chartered Accountants in Ireland.

-fication *suffix* (usu. as **-ification**) forming nouns of action from verbs in *-fy* (*purification*; *simplification*).

fiche /fiːʃ/ *n.* (*pl.* same or **-s**) microfiche. [abbreviation]

fickle /ˈfɪk(ə)l/ *adj.* inconstant, changeable, disloyal. □ **fickleness** *n.* **fickly** *adv.* [Old English]

FICM *abbr.* Fellow of the Institute of Credit Management.

FICMA *abbr.* Fellow of the Institute of Cost and Management Accountants.

FICS *abbr.* Fellow of the Institute of Chartered Shipbrokers.

fiction /ˈfɪkʃ(ə)n/ *n.* **1** non-factual literature, esp. novels. **2** invented idea, thing, etc. **3** generally accepted falsehood (*polite fiction*). □ **fictional** *adj.* **fictionalize** *v.* (also **-ise**) (**-zing** or **-sing**). [Latin: related to FEIGN]

fictitious /fɪkˈtɪʃəs/ *adj.* imaginary, unreal; not genuine.

♦ **fictitious asset** *n.* asset, usu. as shown in a balance sheet, that does not exist. The reasons for showing it may be fraudulent, the asset may have ceased to exist but has not been taken out of the accounts, or it may be an asset, e.g. goodwill, that no longer has any value. Cf. INTANGIBLE ASSET.

FIDA *abbr.* Fellow of the Institute of Directors, Australia.

fiddle /ˈfɪd(ə)l/ *–n.* **1** *colloq.* or *derog.* stringed instrument played with a bow, esp. a violin. **2** *colloq.* cheat or fraud. **3** fiddly task. *–v.* (**-ling**) **1 a** (often foll. by *with*, *at*) play restlessly. **b** (often foll. by *about*) move aimlessly; waste time. **c** (usu. foll. by *with*) adjust, tinker; tamper. **2** *slang* **a** cheat, swindle. **b** falsify. **c** get by cheating. **3** play (a tune) on the fiddle. □ **as fit as a fiddle** in very good health. **play second** (or **first) fiddle** take a subordinate (or leading) role. [Old English]

fiddle-faddle *–n.* trivial matters. *–v.* (**-ling**) fuss, trifle. *–int.* nonsense! [reduplication of FIDDLE]

fiddler *n.* **1** fiddle-player. **2** *slang* swindler, cheat. **3** small North American crab.

fiddlesticks *int.* nonsense.

fiddling *adj.* **1** petty, trivial. **2** *colloq.* = FIDDLY.

fiddly *adj.* (**-ier, -iest**) *colloq.* awkward or tiresome to do or use.

fidelity /fɪˈdelɪtɪ/ *n.* **1** faithfulness, loyalty. **2** strict accuracy. **3** precision in sound reproduction (*high fidelity*). [Latin *fides* faith]

◆ **fidelity guarantee** *n.* insurance policy covering employers for any financial losses they may sustain as a result of the dishonesty of employees. Policies can be arranged to cover all employees or specific named persons. Insurers require full details of the procedure adopted by the organization in recruiting and vetting new employees.

fidget /ˈfɪdʒɪt/ –*v.* (**-t-**) **1** move or act restlessly or nervously. **2** be or make uneasy. –*n.* **1** person who fidgets. **2** (usu. in *pl.*) restless movements or mood. □ **fidgety** *adj.* [obsolete or dial. *fidge* twitch]

fiduciary /fɪˈdjuːʃərɪ/ –*adj.* **1** of a trust, trustee, or trusteeship. Persons acting in a fiduciary capacity do so not for their own profit but to safeguard the interests of some other person or persons. **2** held or given in trust. For example, a fiduciary loan is made on trust, rather than against some security. –*n.* (*pl.* **-ies**) trustee. [Latin *fiducia* trust]

◆ **fiduciary issue** *n.* **1** part of the issue of banknotes by the Bank of England that is backed by government securities, rather than by gold. Nearly the whole of the note issue is now fiduciary. Cf. FIAT MONEY. **2** *hist.* banknotes issued by a bank in the UK without backing in gold, the value of the issues relying entirely on the reputation of the issuing bank.

fie /faɪ/ *int. archaic* expressing disgust, shame, etc. [French from Latin]

fief *n.* **1** land held under the feudal system or in fee. **2** person's sphere of operation. [French: related to FEE]

field –*n.* **1** area of esp. cultivated enclosed land. **2** area rich in some natural product (*gas field*). **3** land for a game etc. (*football field*). **4** participants in a contest, race, or sport, or all except those specified. **5** *Cricket* **a** the side fielding. **b** fielder. **6** expanse of ice, snow, sea, sky, etc. **7 a** battlefield. **b** (*attrib.*) (of artillery etc.) light and mobile. **8** area of activity or study (*in his own field*). **9** *Physics* **a** region in which a force is effective (*gravitational field*). **b** force exerted in this. **10** range of perception (*field of view*). **11** (*attrib.*) **a** (of an animal or plant) wild (*field mouse*). **b** in the natural environment, not in a laboratory etc. (*field test*). **12 a** background of a picture, coin, flag, etc. **b** *Heraldry* surface of an escutcheon. **13** *Computing* part of a record, esp. in a file of data, holding a particular category of data. See RECORD *n.* 8. –*v.* **1 a** act as a fieldsman in cricket etc. **b** stop and return (the ball) in cricket etc. **2** select to play in a game. **3** deal with (questions, an argument, etc.). □ **hold the field** not be superseded. **play the field** *colloq.* date many partners. **take the field** begin a campaign. [Old English]

field-day *n.* **1** exciting or successful time. **2** military exercise or review.

fielder *n.* = FIELDSMAN.

field events *n.pl.* athletic events other than races.

fieldfare *n.* thrush with grey plumage.

field-glasses *n.pl.* outdoor binoculars.

field marshal *n.* army officer of the highest rank.

field mouse *n.* small long-tailed rodent.

field officer *n.* army officer of field rank.

field of honour *n.* battlefield.

field rank *n.* army rank above captain and below general.

fieldsman *n. Cricket, Baseball*, etc. member (other than the bowler or pitcher) of the fielding side.

field sports *n.pl.* outdoor sports, esp. hunting, shooting, and fishing.

field telegraph *n.* movable military telegraph.

fieldwork *n.* **1** practical surveying, science, sociology, etc. conducted in the natural environment. **2** temporary fortification. □ **fieldworker** *n.*

fiend *n.* **1** evil spirit, demon. **2 a** wicked or cruel person. **b** mischievous or annoying person. **3** *slang* devotee (*fitness fiend*). **4** difficult or unpleasant thing. □ **fiendish** *adj.* **fiendishly** *adv.* [Old English]

fierce *adj.* (**fiercer, fiercest**) **1** violently aggressive or frightening. **2** eager, intense. **3** unpleasantly strong or intense (*fierce heat*). □ **fiercely** *adv.* **fierceness** *n.* [Latin *ferus* savage]

fiery /ˈfaɪərɪ/ *adj.* (**-ier, -iest**) **1** consisting of or flaming with fire. **2** bright red. **3** hot; burning. **4 a** flashing, ardent (*fiery eyes*). **b** pugnacious; spirited (*fiery temper*). □ **fierily** *adv.* **fieriness** *n.*

fiesta /fɪˈestə/ *n.* holiday, festivity, or religious festival. [Spanish]

F.I.Ex. *abbr.* Fellow of the Institute of Export.

FIFA /ˈfiːfə/ *abbr.* International Football Federation. [French *Fédération Internationale de Football Association*]

Fife /faɪf/ local government region in E central Scotland; industries include light engineering, electronics, and aluminium refining; pop. (est. 1994) 352 100.

fife *n.* small shrill flute used in military music. □ **fifer** *n.* [German *Pfeife* PIPE or French *fifre*]

FIFF *abbr.* Fellow of the Institute of Freight Forwarders.

FIFO /ˈfaɪfəʊ/ *abbr.* = FIRST IN, FIRST OUT.

fifteen /fɪfˈtiːn/ *adj.* & *n.* **1** one more than fourteen. **2** symbol for this (15, xv, XV). **3** size etc. denoted by fifteen. **4** team of fifteen players, esp. in Rugby. **5** (**15**) (of a film) for persons of 15 and over. □ **fifteenth** *adj.* & *n.* [Old English: related to FIVE, -TEEN]

fifth *adj.* & *n.* **1** next after fourth. **2** any of five equal parts of a thing. **3** *Mus.* interval or chord spanning five consecutive notes in a diatonic scale (e.g. C to G). □ **fifthly** *adv.* [Old English: related to FIVE]

fifth column *n.* traitorous group within a country at war etc. □ **fifth-columnist** *n.*

fifty /ˈfɪftɪ/ *adj.* & *n.* (*pl.* **-ies**) **1** five times ten. **2** symbol for this (50, l, L). **3** (in *pl.*) numbers from 50 to 59, esp. the years of a century or of a person's life. □ **fiftieth** *adj.* & *n.* [Old English]

fifty-fifty –*adj.* equal. –*adv.* equally, half and half.

fig[1] *n.* **1** soft pulpy fruit with many seeds. **2** (in full **fig-tree**) tree bearing figs. □ **not care** (or **give**) **a fig** not care at all. [Latin *ficus*]

fig[2] *n.* **1** dress or equipment (*in full fig*). **2** condition or form (*in good fig*). [obsolete *feague*: related to FAKE]

fight /faɪt/ –*v.* (*past* and *past part.* **fought** /fɔːt/) **1** (often foll. by *against, with*) contend or contend with in war, battle, single combat, etc. **2** engage in (a battle, duel, etc.). **3** contend (an election); maintain (a lawsuit, cause, etc.) against an opponent. **4** strive to achieve something or to overcome (disease, fire, etc.). **5** make (one's way) by fighting. –*n.* **1 a** combat. **b** boxing-match. **c** battle. **2** conflict, struggle, or effort. **3** power or inclination to fight (*no fight left*). □ **fight back 1** counter-attack. **2** suppress (tears etc.). **fight for 1** fight on behalf of. **2** fight to secure. **fight a losing battle** struggle without hope of success. **fight off** repel with effort. **fight out** (usu. **fight it out**) settle by fighting. **fight shy of** avoid. **put up a fight** offer resistance. [Old English]

fighter *n.* **1** person or animal that fights. **2** fast military aircraft designed for attacking other aircraft.

fighting chance *n.* slight chance of success if an effort is made.

fighting fit *n.* fit and ready; at the peak of fitness.

fig-leaf *n.* **1** leaf of a fig-tree. **2** concealing device, esp. for the genitals (Gen. 3:7).

figment /ˈfɪgmənt/ *n.* invented or imaginary thing. [Latin: related to FEIGN]

figuration /ˌfɪgjʊˈreɪʃ(ə)n/ *n.* **1 a** act or mode of formation; form. **b** shape or outline. **2** ornamentation. [Latin: related to FIGURE]

figurative /ˈfɪgərətɪv/ *adj.* **1** metaphorical, not literal. **2** characterized by figures of speech. **3** of pictorial or sculptural representation. □ **figuratively** *adv.* [Latin: related to FIGURE]

figure /ˈfɪgə(r)/ –*n.* **1** external form or bodily shape. **2 a** silhouette, human form (*figure on the lawn*). **b** person of a specified kind or appearance (*public figure; cut a poor figure*). **3 a** human form in drawing, sculpture, etc. **b** image or likeness. **4** two- or three-dimensional space enclosed by lines or surface(s), e.g. a triangle or sphere. **5 a** numerical symbol or number, esp. 0–9. **b** amount; estimated value (*cannot put a figure on it*). **c** (in *pl.*) arithmetical calculations. **6** diagram or illustration. **7** decorative pattern. **8** movement or sequence in a set dance etc. **9** *Mus.* succession of notes from which longer passages are developed. **10** (in full **figure of speech**) metaphor, hyperbole, etc. *–v.* (**-ring**) **1** appear or be mentioned, esp. prominently. **2** represent pictorially. **3** imagine; picture mentally. **4** embellish with a pattern etc. (*figured satin*). **5** calculate; do arithmetic. **6** symbolize. **7** esp. *US* **a** understand, consider. **b** *colloq.* make sense; be likely (*that figures*). □ **figure on** *US* count on, expect. **figure out** work out by arithmetic or logic. [Latin *figura*: related to FEIGN]

figured bass *n. Mus.* = CONTINUO.

figurehead *n.* **1** nominal leader. **2** wooden bust or figure at a ship's prow.

figure-skating *n.* skating in prescribed patterns. □ **figure-skater** *n.*

figurine /ˌfɪɡjəˈriːn/ *n.* statuette. [Italian: related to FIGURE]

FIIA *abbr.* Fellow of the Institute of Internal Auditors.

FIIM *abbr.* Fellow of the Institution of Industrial Managers.

filament /ˈfɪləmənt/ *n.* **1** threadlike body or fibre. **2** conducting wire or thread in an electric bulb etc. □ **filamentous** /-ˈmentəs/ *adj.* [Latin *filum* thread]

filbert /ˈfɪlbət/ *n.* **1** the cultivated hazel with edible nuts. **2** this nut. [Anglo-French, because ripe about St *Philibert's* day]

filch *v.* pilfer, steal. [origin unknown]

file[1] *–n.* **1** folder, box, etc. for holding loose papers. **2** papers kept in this. **3** *Computing* named collection of information held on backing store. The **file name** is stored in a directory and is used to identify the file to the operating system of the computer. Files may hold data, programs, text, or any other information (see DATA FILE; PROGRAM FILE). Data files are normally organized as sets of related records. The type of organization used for the records is designed to support one or more **access methods** used for the storage and retrieval of records (see RANDOM ACCESS; SERIAL ACCESS). **4** line of people or things one behind another. *–v.* (**-ling**) **1** place (papers) in a file or among (esp. public) records. **2** submit (a petition for divorce, a patent application, etc.). **3** (of a reporter) send (copy) to a newspaper. **4** walk in a line. [Latin *filum* thread]

file[2] *–n.* tool with a roughened surface for smoothing or shaping wood, metal, fingernails, etc. *–v.* (**-ling**) smooth or shape with a file. [Old English]

file archive *Computing* see ARCHIVE *n.* 3.

file maintenance *n. Computing* maintenance of both the integrity of files, i.e. the correctness of all the data values, and an efficient internal organization of files. It is performed by software.

file management *n. Computing* overall management of files, including their allocation to space on backing store, control over file access, the writing of backup copies, the movement of files to the file archive, and the maintenance of directories. It is performed by software.

file protection *n. Computing* protection of files from mistaken or unauthorized access of information or, in the case of program files, from mistaken or unauthorized execution. File protection may be concerned with the security of the contents of files, or with the protection of the disks or tapes on which files are held. The former is implemented by software, the latter by operating procedures.

file server see SERVER 3.

filestore *n. Computing* portion of disk backing store used for storing permanent files, programs, data, etc.

file transfer *n. Computing* movement of entire files from one computer system to another, typically across a computer network. In order to transfer a file successfully there must be cooperating programs running on each system: the sender has to be able to specify the file name, ultimate destination, and authorization for the transfer to the receiver, and the receiver must agree to the transfer and inform the sender of its eventual success or failure.

filial /ˈfɪlɪəl/ *adj.* of or due from a son or daughter. □ **filially** *adv.* [Latin *filius*, *-a* son, daughter]

filibuster /ˈfɪlɪˌbʌstə(r)/ *–n.* **1** obstruction of progress in a legislative assembly, esp. by prolonged speaking. **2** esp. *US* person who engages in this. *–v.* act as a filibuster (against). □ **filibusterer** *n.* [Dutch: related to FREEBOOTER]

filigree /ˈfɪlɪˌɡriː/ *n.* **1** fine ornamental work in gold etc. wire. **2** similar delicate work. □ **filigreed** *adj.* [Latin *filum* thread, *granum* seed]

filing *n.* (usu. in *pl.*) particle rubbed off by a file.

filing cabinet *n.* cabinet with drawers for storing files.

Filipino /ˌfɪlɪˈpiːnəʊ/ *–n.* (*pl.* **-s**) native or national of the Philippines. *–adj.* of the Philippines or Filipinos. [Spanish, = Philippine]

fill *–v.* **1** (often foll. by *with*) make or become full. **2** occupy completely; spread over or through. **3** block up (a cavity in a tooth); drill and put a filling into (a decayed tooth). **4** appoint a person to hold or (of a person) hold (a post). **5** hold (an office). **6** carry out or supply (an order, commission, etc.). **7** occupy (vacant time). **8** (of a sail) be distended by wind. **9** (usu. as **filling** *adj.*) (esp. of food) satisfy, satiate. *–n.* **1** as much as one wants or can bear (*eat your fill*). **2** enough to fill something. □ **fill the bill** be suitable or adequate. **fill in 1** complete (a form, document, etc.). **2 a** complete (a drawing etc.) within an outline. **b** fill (an outline) in this way. **3** fill (a hole etc.) completely. **4** (often foll. by *for*) act as a substitute. **5** occupy oneself during (spare time). **6** *colloq.* inform (a person) more fully. **7** *slang* thrash, beat. **fill out 1** enlarge to the required size. **2** become enlarged or plump. **3** *US* fill in (a document etc.). **fill up 1** make or become completely full. **2** fill in (a document etc.). **3** fill the petrol tank of (a car etc.). [Old English]

Fiji /ˈfiːdʒɪ/, **Republic of** country in the S Pacific Ocean, comprising a group of about 840 islands of which about 100 are inhabited. Agriculture dominates the economy, sugar cane being the main cash crop, but forestry and fishing are expanding industries; fish, timber, coconut oil, ginger, and copra are all exported. Gold is mined on Viti Levu, boosting export revenue. Tourism is also an important source of income. The economy is stable and growth should continue at a steady rate. The islands became a British Crown Colony in 1874 and an independent state within the Commonwealth in 1970. In 1987, after two military coups, Fiji was declared a republic and withdrew from the Commonwealth. A new constitution drawn up in 1990 guaranteed native Fijians a government majority. In 1997 Fiji was readmitted to the Commonwealth. President, Ratu Sir Kamisese Mara; prime minister, Major-General Sitiveni Rabuka; capital, Suva. □ **Fijian** *adj.* & *n.*

languages	English (official), Fijian, Hindi
currency	dollar (F$) of 100 cents
pop. (1996)	802 000
GNP (1994)	US$1.7B
literacy	90% (m); 84% (f)
life expectancy	70 (m); 75 (f)

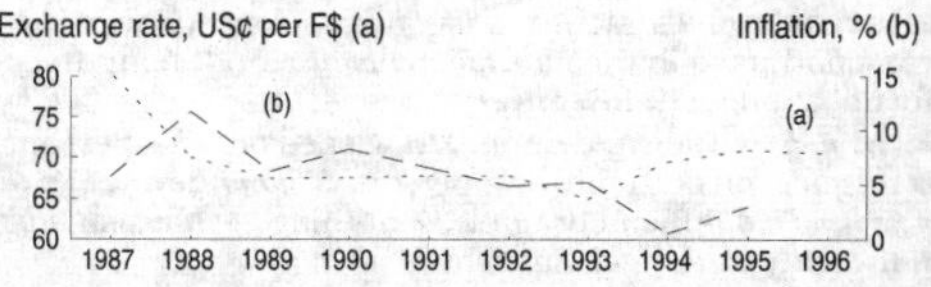

filler *n.* **1** material used to fill a cavity or increase bulk. **2** small item filling space in a newspaper etc.

fillet /ˈfɪlɪt/ *–n.* **1 a** boneless piece of meat or fish. **b** (in full **fillet steak**) undercut of a sirloin. **2** ribbon etc. binding the hair. **3** thin narrow strip or ridge. **4** narrow flat band between mouldings. *–v.* (**-t-**) **1** remove bones from (fish or meat) or divide into fillets. **2** bind or provide with fillet(s). [Latin *filum* thread]

filling *n.* material that fills a tooth, sandwich, pie, etc.

filling-station *n.* garage selling petrol etc.

fillip /ˈfɪlɪp/ *–n.* **1** stimulus, incentive. **2** flick with a finger or thumb. *–v.* (**-p-**) **1** stimulate. **2** flick. [imitative]

filly /ˈfɪlɪ/ *n.* (*pl.* **-ies**) **1** young female horse. **2** *colloq.* girl or young woman. [Old Norse]

film *–n.* **1** thin coating or covering layer. **2** strip or sheet of plastic etc. coated with light-sensitive emulsion for exposure in a camera. **3 a** story, episode, etc., on film, with the illusion of movement. **b** (in *pl.*) the cinema industry. **4** slight veil or haze etc. **5** dimness or morbid growth affecting the eyes. *–v.* **1** make a photographic film of (a scene, story, etc.). **2** cover or become covered with or as with a film. [Old English]

film-goer *n.* person who frequents the cinema.

filmsetting *n.* typesetting by projecting characters on to photographic film. □ **film-set** *v.* **film-setter** *n.*

film star *n.* celebrated film actor or actress.

film-strip *n.* series of transparencies in a strip for projection.

filmy *adj.* (**-ier**, **-iest**) **1** thin and translucent. **2** covered with or as with a film.

Filofax /ˈfaɪləʊˌfæks/ *n. propr.* a type of loose-leaf personal organizer. [from FILE[1], FACT]

filo pastry /ˈfiːləʊ, ˈfaɪ-/ *n.* (also **phyllo pastry**) leaved pastry like strudel pastry. [Greek *phullon* leaf]

filter *–n.* **1** porous device for removing impurities etc. from a liquid or gas passed through it. **2** = FILTER TIP. **3** screen or attachment for absorbing or modifying light, X-rays, etc. **4** device for suppressing unwanted electrical or sound waves. **5** arrangement for filtering traffic. *–v.* **1** (cause to) pass through a filter. **2** (foll. by *through*, *into*, etc.) make way gradually. **3** (foll. by *out*) (cause to) leak. **4** allow (traffic) or (of traffic) be allowed to pass to the left or right at a junction. [Germanic: related to FELT[1]]

filter-paper *n.* porous paper for filtering.

filter tip *n.* **1** filter on a cigarette removing some impurities. **2** cigarette with this. □ **filter-tipped** *adj.*

filth *n.* **1** repugnant or extreme dirt. **2** obscenity. [Old English: related to FOUL]

filthy *–adj.* (**-ier**, **-iest**) **1** extremely or disgustingly dirty. **2** obscene. **3** *colloq.* (of weather) very unpleasant. *–adv.* **1** filthily (*filthy dirty*). **2** *colloq.* extremely (*filthy rich*). □ **filthily** *adv.* **filthiness** *n.*

filthy lucre *n.* **1** dishonourable gain. **2** *joc.* money.

filtrate /ˈfɪltreɪt/ *–v.* (**-ting**) filter. *–n.* filtered liquid. □ **filtration** /-ˈtreɪʃ(ə)n/ *n.* [related to FILTER]

FIMA *abbr.* Fellow of the Institute of Mathematics and its Applications.

FIMC *abbr.* Fellow of the Institute of Management Consultants.

FIMS *abbr.* Fellow of the Institute of Mathematical Statistics.

FIN *international vehicle registration* Finland.

fin *n.* **1** (usu. thin) flat external organ of esp. fish, for propelling, steering, etc. (*dorsal fin*). **2** similar stabilizing projection on an aircraft, car, etc. **3** underwater swimmer's flipper. □ **finned** *adj.* [Old English]

fin. *abbr.* **1** finance. **2** financial. **3** financier.

finagle /fɪˈneɪg(ə)l/ *v.* (**-ling**) *colloq.* act or obtain dishonestly. □ **finagler** *n.* [dial. *fainaigue* cheat]

final /ˈfaɪn(ə)l/ *–adj.* **1** situated at the end, coming last. **2** conclusive, decisive. *–n.* **1** last or deciding heat or game in sports etc. (*Cup Final*). **2** last daily edition of a newspaper. **3** (usu. in *pl.*) examinations at the end of a degree course. □ **finally** *adv.* [Latin *finis* end]

♦ **final accounts** *n.pl.* accounts for a company produced at the end of its financial year (see ANNUAL ACCOUNTS), as opposed to any **interim accounts** produced during the year, often after six months. Interim accounts are for the guidance of management and are often not audited, whereas final accounts must be audited and are open for inspection by the public.

---

final cause *n. Philos.* ultimate purpose.

final clause *n. Gram.* clause expressing purpose.

♦ **final dividend** *Finance* see DIVIDEND 1.

---

finale /fɪˈnɑːlɪ/ *n.* last movement or section of a piece of music or drama etc. [Italian: related to FINAL]

♦ **final invoice** *n.* invoice that replaces a pro-forma invoice for goods. It contains any information missing from the pro-forma invoice and states the full amount still owing for the goods. See PRO FORMA *n.*

---

finalist *n.* competitor in the final of a competition etc.

finality /faɪˈnælɪtɪ/ *n.* (*pl.* **-ies**) **1** fact of being final. **2** final act etc. [Latin: related to FINAL]

finalize *v.* (also **-ise**) (**-zing** or **-sing**) put into final form; complete. □ **finalization** /-ˈzeɪʃ(ə)n/ *n.*

final solution *n.* Nazi policy (1941–5) of exterminating European Jews.

finance /ˈfaɪnæns/ *–n.* **1** management of (esp. public) money. **2** capital involved in a project, esp. capital that has to be raised to start a new business. **3** loan of money for a particular purpose, esp. by a finance house. **4** (in *pl.*) money resources of a state, company, or person. *–v.* (**-cing**) provide capital for. [French: related to FINE[2]]

♦ **finance house** *n.* (also **finance company**) organization providing finance for hire-purchase agreements. A consumer, who buys an expensive item (e.g. a car) from a trader and does not wish to pay cash, enters into a hire-purchase contract with the finance house, which collects the deposit and instalments. The finance house pays the trader the cash price in full, borrowing from the commercial banks (which own many of the finance houses). The finance house's profit is the difference between the low rate of interest it pays to the commercial banks to borrow and the high rate it charges the consumer.

♦ **Finance Houses Association** *n.* UK organization of finance houses, set up in 1945 to regulate the trade of hire purchase and to negotiate with the government on acceptable terms and conditions. Its members control most UK hire-purchase agreements.

---

financial /faɪˈnænʃ(ə)l/ *adj.* of finance. □ **financially** *adv.*

♦ **financial accountant** *n.* accountant whose primary responsibility is the management of the finances of an organization and the preparation of its annual accounts. Cf. COST ACCOUNTANT; MANAGEMENT ACCOUNTANT.

♦ **financial adviser** *n.* **1** person who offers financial advice to someone else, esp. one who advises on investments. See also INDEPENDENT FINANCIAL ADVISER. **2** organization, usu. a merchant bank, which advises the board of a company during a take-over.

♦ **financial futures** *n.pl.* futures contract in currencies or interest rates (see INTEREST-RATE FUTURES). Unlike simple forward contracts, futures contracts themselves can be bought and sold on specialized markets. Until about 1970 trading in financial futures did not exist, although futures and options were dealt in widely on commodity markets. However, instantaneous trading across the world coupled with accelerated international capital flows combined to produce great volatility in interest rates, stock-market prices, and currency exchanges. The result has been an environment in which organizations and individuals responsible for managing large sums need a financial futures and options market both to manage risks effectively and as a source of additional profit. In the UK financial futures and options are traded on the London

International Financial Futures and Options Exchange (LIFFE).

♦ **financial institution** *n.* organization, e.g. a bank, building society, or finance house, that collects funds from individuals, other organizations, or government agencies and invests these funds or lends them on to borrowers.

♦ **financial instrument** *n.* formal financial document. See also NEGOTIABLE INSTRUMENT.

♦ **Financial Intermediaries, Managers, and Brokers Regulatory Association Ltd.** (also **FIMBRA**) see SELF-REGULATING ORGANIZATION.

♦ **financial intermediary** *n.* **1** bank, building society, finance house, insurance company, investment trust, etc. that holds funds borrowed from lenders in order to make loans to borrowers. **2** person or organization that sells insurance but is not directly employed by an insurance company (e.g. a broker, insurance agent, bank). See also INDEPENDENT INTERMEDIARY.

♦ **financial investment** see INVESTMENT 2.

♦ **Financial Ombudsman** *n.* **1** (also **Banking Ombudsman**) official in charge of a service set up in 1986 by 19 banks, which fund the service, to investigate complaints from bank customers against the service provided by member banks. In 1993 the service was extended to deal with complaints from small businesses (turnover less than £1M). **2** (also **Building Societies Ombudsman**) official in charge of a service set up in 1987 by all the UK building societies, which fund the service, to investigate complaints from building-society customers against the services provided by the building societies. **3** (also **Insurance Ombudsman**) official in charge of a service set up in 1981 by some 200 insurance companies, which fund the service, to settle disputes between insurance policyholders and member insurance companies. The Insurance Ombudsman's Bureau also runs the **Unit Trusts Ombudsman Scheme** to settle disputes between unit-trust holders and unit-trust management companies. It was set up in 1988. **4** (also **Investment Ombudsman**) official in charge of a service set up in 1989 by IMRO to settle disputes between IMRO members and their customers. The Personal Investment Authority (PIA) Ombudsman is responsible for resolving complaints against PIA members. **5** (also **Pensions Ombudsman**) official responsible for resolving disputes between individuals and their pension schemes. It was set up under the Pension Schemes Act (1993).

♦ **Financial Reporting Council** *n.* (also **FRC**) UK company limited by guarantee, set up in 1989 to oversee and support the work of the Accounting Standards Board and the Financial Reporting Review Panel to encourage good financial reporting generally. Its chairman and three deputies are appointed jointly by the Secretary of State for Trade and Industry and the Governor of the Bank of England. It first met in May 1990.

♦ ***Financial Statistics*** *n.* monthly publication of the UK Central Statistical Office giving a full account of financial statistics.

♦ **Financial Times Share Indexes** *n.pl.* share indexes published by the *Financial Times*, daily except Sundays and Mondays, as a barometer of share prices on the London Stock Exchange. The **Financial Times Actuaries Share Indexes** are calculated by the Institute of Actuaries and the Faculty of Actuaries as weighted arithmetic averages for 54 sectors of the market (capital goods, consumer goods, etc.) and divided into various industries. They are widely used by investors and portfolio managers. The widest measure of the market comes from the **FTA All-Share Index** of some 800 shares and fixed-interest stocks, which includes a selection from the financial sector. Calculated after the end of daily business, it covers 98% of the market. The **FTA World Share Index** was introduced in 1987 and is based on 2400 share prices from 24 countries. The **Financial Times Industrial Ordinary Share Index** (or **FT-30**) represents the movements of shares in 30 leading industrial and commercial shares, chosen to be representative of British industry. It continues to be published but it has been superseded as the main index by the **Financial Times-Stock Exchange 100 Share Index** (**FT-SE 100** or **Footsie**), a weighted arithmetic index representing the price of 100 securities with a base of 1000 on 3 Jan. 1984. In 1992 the index series was extended to create two further real-time indexes, the **FT-SE Mid 250**, comprising companies capitalized between £150 million and £1 billion, and the **FT-SE Actuaries 350**, both based on 31 Dec. 1985. These indexes are further broken down into Industry Baskets, comprising all the shares of the industrial sectors, to provide an instant view of industry performance across the market, and corresponding roughly to sectors defined by markets in New York and Tokyo. A **FT-SE Small Cap Index** covers 500–600 companies capitalized between £20 million and £150 million, calculated at the end of the day's business, both including and excluding investment trusts. The **Financial Times Government Securities Index** measures the movements of government stocks (gilts). The newest indexes measure the performance of securities throughout the European market. The **Financial Times-Stock Exchange Eurotrack 100 Index** (or **FT-SE Eurotrack 100**) is a weighted average of 100 stocks in Europe, which started on 29 Oct. 1990, with a base of 1000 at the close of business on 26 Oct. 1990. Quoted in Deutschmarks, the index includes up-to-date currency exchange rates. On 25 Feb. 1991 the **Financial Times-Stock Exchange Eurotrack 200 Index** was first quoted, with the same base as the Eurotrack 100 to combine the constituents of the FT-SE 100 and the Eurotrack 100.

♦ **financial year** *n.* **1** any year connected with finance, e.g. a company's accounting period or a year for which budgets are made up. **2** specific period relating to corporation tax, i.e. the year beginning 1 April (the year beginning 1 April 1993 is the financial year 1993). Cf. FISCAL YEAR.

♦ **financier** /faɪˈnænsɪə(r)/ *n.* person who uses his own money to finance a business deal or venture or who makes arrangements for such a deal or venture to be financed by a merchant bank or other financial institution. [French: related to FINANCE]

♦ **financing gap** *n.* difference between a country's foreign exchange requirements, for imports and the servicing of its debts, and what it has available from export receipts and overseas earnings. This gap must be filled either by raising further foreign exchange (donor aid, loans, etc.) or by cutting back the requirements, either by reducing imports or rescheduling the repayment of debts. Forecasting the financing gap and negotiating means of bridging it are major elements in helping countries with balance of payments problems.

---

finch *n.* small seed-eating bird, esp. a crossbill, canary, or chaffinch. [Old English]

find /faɪnd/ *–v.* (*past* and *past part.* **found**) **1 a** discover or get by chance or effort (*found a key*). **b** become aware of. **2 a** obtain, succeed in obtaining; receive (*idea found acceptance*). **b** summon up (*found courage*). **3** seek out and provide or supply (*will find you a book*; *finds his own meals*). **4** discover by study etc. (*find the answer*). **5 a** perceive or experience (*find no sense in it*). **b** (often in *passive*) discover to be present (*not found in Shakespeare*). **c** discover from experience (*finds England too cold*). **6** *Law* (of a jury, judge, etc.) decide and declare (*found him guilty*). **7** reach by a natural process (*water finds its own level*). *–n.* **1** discovery of treasure etc. **2** valued thing or person newly discovered. □ **all found** (of wages) with board and lodging provided free. **find fault** see FAULT. **find favour** prove acceptable. **find one's feet 1** become able to walk. **2** develop independence. **find oneself 1** discover that one is (*found herself agreeing*). **2** discover one's vocation. **find out 1** discover or detect (a wrongdoer etc.). **2** (often foll. by *about*) get information. **3** discover (*find out where we are*). **4** (often foll. by *about*) discover the truth, a fact, etc. (*he never found out*). [Old English]

finder *n.* **1** person who finds. **2** small telescope attached to a large one to locate an object. **3** viewfinder.

finding *n.* (often in *pl.*) conclusion reached by an inquiry etc.

fine[1] *–adj.* **1 a** of high quality; excellent (*fine painting*). **b** good, satisfactory (*that will be fine*). **2 a** pure, refined. **b** (of gold or silver) containing a specified proportion of pure metal. **3** imposing, dignified (*fine buildings*). **4** in good health (*I'm fine*). **5** (of weather etc.) bright and clear. **6 a** thin; sharp. **b** in small particles. **c** worked in slender thread. **7** euphemistic; flattering (*fine words*). **8** ornate, showy. **9** fastidious, affectedly refined. *–adv.* **1** finely. **2** *colloq.* very well (*suits me fine*). *–v.* **(-ning) 1** (often foll. by *away, down, off*) make or become finer, thinner, more tapering, or less coarse. **2** (often foll. by *down*) make or become clear (esp. of beer etc.). □ **not to put too fine a point on it** to speak bluntly. □ **finely** *adv.* **fineness** *n.* [French *fin* from Latin *finio* FINISH]

fine[2] *–n.* money to be paid as a penalty. *–v.* **(-ning)** punish by a fine (*fined him £5*). □ **in fine** in short. [French *fin* settlement of a dispute, from Latin *finis* end]

fine arts *n.pl.* poetry, music, and the visual arts, esp. painting, sculpture, and architecture.

♦ **fine paper** *n.* = FIRST-CLASS PAPER.

---

finery /ˈfaɪnərɪ/ *n.* showy dress or decoration. [from FINE[1]]

fines herbes /fiːnz ˈeəb/ *n.pl.* mixed herbs used in cooking. [French, = fine herbs]

fine-spun *adj.* **1** delicate. **2** (of theory etc.) too subtle, unpractical.

finesse /fɪˈnes/ *–n.* **1** refinement. **2** subtle manipulation. **3** artfulness; tact. **4** *Cards* attempt to win a trick with a card that is not the highest held. *–v.* **(-ssing) 1** use or achieve by finesse. **2** *Cards* **a** make a finesse. **b** play (a card) as a finesse. [French: related to FINE[1]]

fine-tooth comb *n.* comb with close-set teeth. □ **go over with a fine-tooth comb** check or search thoroughly.

♦ **fine trade bill** *n.* bill of exchange that is acceptable to the Bank of England as security, when acting as lender of last resort. It will be backed by a first-class bank or finance house.

♦ **fine-tune** *v.* **1** make small adjustments to (a mechanism etc.). **2** (of a government) make small changes in (monetary and fiscal policy) to maintain a constant level of aggregate demand, usu. that associated with full employment. In the 1950s and 1960s it was widely believed that the government could raise employment during recessions and curb inflation during booms by fine-tuning; the policy is now discredited (see STAGFLATION). See also AGGREGATE DEMAND; DEMAND MANAGEMENT.

---

finger /ˈfɪŋɡə(r)/ *–n.* **1** any of the terminal projections of the hand (usu. excluding the thumb). **2** part of a glove etc. for a finger. **3** finger-like object or structure (*fish finger*). **4** *colloq.* small measure of liquor. *–v.* touch, feel, or turn about with the fingers. □ **get** (or **pull**) **one's finger out** *slang* start to act. **lay a finger on** touch, however slightly. **put one's finger on** locate or identify exactly. □ **fingerless** *adj.* [Old English]

finger-board *n.* part of the neck of a stringed instrument on which the fingers press to vary the pitch.

finger-bowl *n.* (also **finger-glass**) small bowl for rinsing the fingers during a meal.

finger-dry *v.* dry and style (the hair) by running one's fingers through it.

fingering *n.* **1** technique etc. of using the fingers, esp. in playing music. **2** indication of this in a musical score.

finger-mark *n.* mark left by a finger.

fingernail *n.* nail of each finger.

finger-plate *n.* plate fixed to a door to prevent finger-marks.

fingerprint *–n.* impression of a fingertip on a surface, used in detecting crime. *–v.* record the fingerprints of.

finger-stall *n.* protective cover for an injured finger.

fingertip *n.* tip of a finger. □ **have at one's fingertips** be thoroughly familiar with (a subject etc.).

finial /ˈfɪnɪəl/ *n.* ornamental top or end of a roof, gable, etc. [Anglo-French: related to FINE[1]]

finicky /ˈfɪnɪkɪ/ *adj.* (also **finical, finicking**) **1** over-particular, fastidious. **2** detailed; fiddly. □ **finickiness** *n.* [perhaps from FINE[1]]

finis /ˈfɪnɪs/ *n.* end, esp. of a book. [Latin]

finish /ˈfɪnɪʃ/ *–v.* **1 a** (often foll. by *off*) bring or come to an end or the end of; complete; cease. **b** (usu. foll. by *off*) *colloq.* kill; vanquish. **c** (often foll. by *off, up*) consume or complete consuming (food or drink). **2** treat the surface of (cloth, woodwork, etc.). *–n.* **1 a** end, last stage, completion. **b** point at which a race etc. ends. **2** method, material, etc. used for surface treatment of wood, cloth, etc. (*mahogany finish*). □ **finish up** (often foll. by *in, by*) end (*finished up by crying*). **finish with** have no more to do with, complete using etc. [Latin *finis* end]

finishing-school *n.* private college preparing girls for fashionable society.

finishing touch *n.* (also **finishing touches**) final enhancing details.

Finisterre /ˌfɪnɪˈsteə(r)/ westernmost point of mainland Spain, a promontory on its NW coast.

finite /ˈfaɪnaɪt/ *adj.* **1** limited; not infinite. **2** (of a part of a verb) having a specific number and person. [Latin: related to FINISH]

Finn *n.* native or national of Finland; person of Finnish descent. [Old English]

finnan /ˈfɪnən/ *n.* (in full **finnan haddock**) smoke-cured haddock. [*Findhorn, Findon*, in Scotland]

Finnic *adj.* of the group of peoples or languages related to the Finns or Finnish.

Finnish *–adj.* of the Finns or their language. *–n.* language of the Finns.

Finland /ˈfɪnlənd/, **Republic of** Scandinavian country with a coastline on the Baltic Sea and an extensive network of inland waterways. The country is highly industrialized, principal export earnings being from timber and the paper industry, shipbuilding, metal-working, chemicals, and engineering. Textiles and chemical industries are also important, and tourism provides extra income. Mineral resources include copper and iron ore, and hydroelectricity is the main power source.

History. A Grand Duchy from the 16th century, Finland was ceded to Russia in 1809, regaining full independence after the Russian Revolution. Wars with the USSR in 1939–40 and 1941–4 cost Finland Karelia and Petsamo, but a treaty of friendship between the two countries was signed in 1948. Finland is a member of Efta and has been a member of the European Community since 1995. The markka joined the ERM in 1996. President, Martti Ahtisaari; prime minister, Paavo Lipponen; capital, Helsinki.

languages	Finnish, Swedish
currency	markka (Fmk) of 100 penniä
pop. (1996)	5 132 000
GNP (1994)	US$95B
literacy	99%
life expectancy	72 (m); 79 (f)

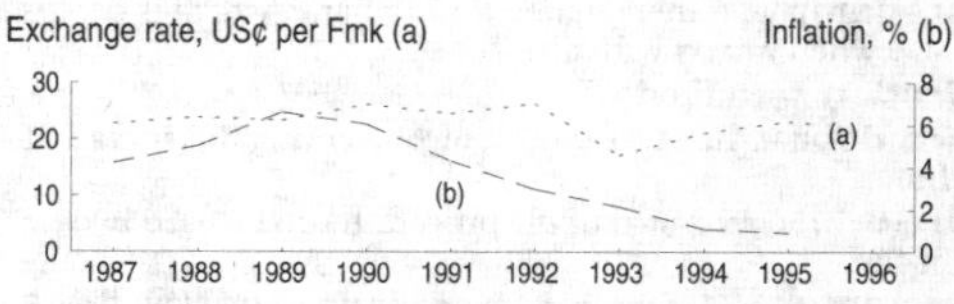

fino /ˈfiːnəʊ/ *n.* (*pl.* **-s**) light-coloured dry sherry. [Spanish, = fine]

F.Inst.A.M. *abbr.* Fellow of the Institute of Administrative Management.

F.Inst.D. *abbr.* Fellow of the Institute of Directors.

F.Inst.F.F. *abbr.* Fellow of the Institute of Freight Forwarders.

F.Inst.P.S. *abbr.* Fellow of the Institute of Purchasing and Supply.

F.Inst.S.M.M. *abbr.* Fellow of the Institute of Sales and Marketing Management.

f.i.o. *abbr. Commerce* free in and out.

fiord /fjɔːd/ *n.* (also **fjord**) long narrow sea inlet, as in Norway. [Norwegian]

FIPA *abbr.* Fellow of the Institute of Practitioners in Advertising.

FIPM *abbr.* Fellow of the Institute of Personnel Management.

fipple /ˈfɪp(ə)l/ *n.* plug at the mouth-end of a wind instrument. [origin unknown]

fipple flute *n.* flute played by blowing endwise, e.g. a recorder.

FIQA *abbr.* Fellow of the Institute of Quality Assurance.

fir *n.* **1** (in full **fir-tree**) evergreen coniferous tree with needles growing singly on the stems. **2** its wood. □ **firry** *adj.* [Old Norse]

fir-cone *n.* fruit of the fir.

fire –*n.* **1 a** combustion of substances with oxygen, giving out light and heat. **b** flame or incandescence. **2** destructive burning (*forest fire*). **3 a** burning fuel in a grate, furnace, etc. **b** = ELECTRIC FIRE. **c** = GAS FIRE. **4** firing of guns. **5 a** fervour, spirit, vivacity. **b** poetic inspiration. **6** burning heat, fever. –*v.* (**-ring**) **1** (often foll. by *at, into, on*) **a** shoot (a gun, missile, etc.). **b** shoot a gun or missile etc. **2** produce (a broadside, salute, etc.) by shooting guns etc. **3** (of a gun etc.) be discharged. **4** explode or kindle (an explosive). **5** deliver or utter rapidly (*fired insults at us*). **6** *slang* dismiss (an employee). **7** set fire to intentionally. **8** catch fire. **9** (of esp. an internal-combustion engine) undergo ignition. **10** supply (a furnace, engine, etc.) with fuel. **11** stimulate; enthuse. **12** bake, dry, or cure (pottery, bricks, tea, tobacco, etc.). **13** become or cause to become heated, excited, red, or glowing. □ **catch fire** begin to burn. **fire away** *colloq.* begin; go ahead. **on fire 1** burning. **2** excited. **set fire to** (or **set on fire**) ignite, kindle. **set the world** (or **Thames) on fire** do something remarkable or sensational. **under fire 1** being shot at. **2** being rigorously criticized or questioned. [Old English]

fire-alarm *n.* device warning of fire.

fire and brimstone *n.* supposed torments of hell.

firearm *n.* (usu. in *pl.*) gun, pistol, or rifle.

fire-ball *n.* **1** large meteor. **2** ball of flame or lightning. **3** energetic person.

fire-bomb *n.* incendiary bomb.

firebox *n.* place where fuel is burned in a steam engine or boiler.

firebrand *n.* **1** piece of burning wood. **2** person causing trouble or unrest.

fire-break *n.* obstacle to the spread of fire in a forest etc., esp. an open space.

fire-brick *n.* fireproof brick in a grate.

fire brigade *n.* body of professional firefighters.

fireclay *n.* clay used to make fire-bricks.

firecracker *n. US* explosive firework.

firedamp *n.* miners' name for methane, which is explosive when mixed with air.

firedog *n.* andiron.

fire door *n.* fire-resistant door preventing the spread of fire.

fire-drill *n.* rehearsal of the procedures to be used in case of fire.

fire-eater *n.* **1** conjuror who appears to swallow fire. **2** quarrelsome person.

fire-engine *n.* vehicle carrying hoses, firefighters, etc.

fire-escape *n.* emergency staircase etc. for use in a fire.

fire extinguisher *n.* apparatus discharging foam etc. to extinguish a fire.

firefighter *n.* = FIREMAN 1.

firefly *n.* beetle emitting phosphorescent light, e.g. the glow-worm.

fire-guard *n.* protective screen placed in front of a fireplace.

♦ **fire insurance** *n.* insurance against financial losses caused by damage to property by fires. Most fire insurance policies also include cover for damage caused by lightning and explosions of boilers or gas used for domestic purposes. Payment of an additional premium usu. allows additional risks, e.g. those arising from various weather-related or man-made causes, to be covered.

---

fire-irons *n.pl.* tongs, poker, and shovel for a domestic fire.

firelight *n.* light from a fire in a fireplace.

fire-lighter *n.* inflammable material used to start a fire in a grate.

fireman *n.* **1** member of a fire brigade. **2** person who tends a steam engine or steamship furnace.

Firenze see FLORENCE.

fireplace *n.* **1** place for a domestic fire, esp. a recess in a wall. **2** structure surrounding this.

fire-power *n.* destructive capacity of guns etc.

fire-practice *n.* fire-drill.

fireproof –*adj.* able to resist fire or great heat. –*v.* make fireproof.

fire-raiser *n.* arsonist. □ **fire-raising** *n.*

fire-screen *n.* **1** ornamental screen for a fireplace. **2** screen against the direct heat of a fire. **3** fire-guard.

fire-ship *n. hist.* ship set on fire and directed against an enemy's ships etc.

fireside *n.* **1** area round a fireplace. **2** home or home-life.

fire station *n.* headquarters of a fire brigade.

fire-storm *n.* high wind or storm following a fire caused by bombs.

fire-trap *n.* building without fire-escapes etc.

firewall *n.* system usu. inserted between a local area network and the Internet to filter incoming traffic, to try to eliminate viral infection, and to restrict the access of hackers to the system. It may create a bottleneck in the transmission of data to and from the system.

fire-watcher *n.* person keeping watch for fires, esp. those caused by bombs.

fire-water *n. colloq.* strong alcoholic liquor.

firewood *n.* wood as fuel.

firework *n.* **1** device that burns or explodes spectacularly when lit. **2** (in *pl.*) outburst of passion, esp. anger.

firing *n.* **1** discharge of guns. **2** fuel.

firing-line *n.* **1** front line in a battle. **2** centre of activity etc.

firing-squad *n.* **1** soldiers ordered to shoot a condemned person. **2** group firing the salute at a military funeral.

firm[1] –*adj.* **1 a** solid or compact. **b** fixed, stable, steady. **2 a** resolute, determined. **b** steadfast, constant (*firm belief; firm friend*). **3** (of an offer etc.) definite; not conditional. –*adv.* firmly (*stand firm*). –*v.* (often foll. by *up*) make or become firm, secure, compact, or solid. □ **firmly** *adv.* **firmness** *n.* [Latin *firmus*]

firm[2] *n.* business concern or its partners. [Latin *firma*: cf. FIRM[1]]

firmament /ˈfɜːməmənt/ *n. literary* the sky regarded as a vault or arch. [Latin: related to FIRM[1]]

♦ **firm commitment** *n.* undertaking by a bank to lend up to a maximum sum over a period at a specified rate; a commitment fee usu. has to be paid by the borrower, which is not returned if the loan is not taken up.

♦ **firm offer** *n.* **1** definite offer. **2** offer to sell goods that remains in force for a stated period. If the buyer makes a lower bid during the period that the offer is firm, the offer ceases to be valid.

♦ **firm order** *n.* **1** definite order. **2** order to a broker (for securities, commodities, currencies, etc.) that remains firm for a stated period or until cancelled. A broker who has a firm order from the principal does not have to refer back if the terms of the order can be executed in the stated period.

---

firmware /'fɜːmweə(r)/ *n. Computing* programs that do not have to be loaded into a computer but are permanently available in main store. They are held in ROM (read-only memory) and thus are fixed in content even when the power supply is removed.

firry see FIR.

first –*adj.* **1** earliest in time or order (*took the first bus*). **2** foremost in rank or importance (*First Lord of the Treasury*). **3** most willing or likely (*the first to admit it*). **4** basic or evident (*first principles*). –*n.* **1** (prec. by *the*) person or thing first mentioned or occurring. **2** first occurrence of something notable. **3** place in the first class in an examination. **4** first gear. **5 a** first place in a race. **b** winner of this. –*adv.* **1** before any other person or thing (*first of all*; *first and foremost*). **2** before someone or something else (*get this done first*). **3** for the first time (*when did you first see her?*). **4** in preference; rather (*will see him damned first*). □ **at first** at the beginning. **at first hand** directly from the original source. **first past the post** (of an electoral system) selecting a candidate or party by simple majority. **from the first** from the beginning. **in the first place** as first consideration. [Old English]

first aid *n.* emergency medical treatment.

first-born –*adj.* eldest. –*n.* person's eldest child.

first class –*n.* **1** best group or category. **2** best accommodation in a train, ship, etc. **3** mail given priority. **4** highest division in an examination. –*adj.* & *adv.* (*first-class*) **1** of or by the first class. **2** excellent.

♦ **first-class paper** *n.* (also **fine paper**) bill of exchange, cheque, etc. drawn on or accepted or endorsed by a first-class bank, finance house, etc.

---

first cousin see COUSIN.

first-day cover *n.* envelope with stamps postmarked on their first day of issue.

first-degree *adj.* denoting non-serious surface burns.

first finger *n.* finger next to the thumb.

first floor *n.* (*US* **second floor**) floor above the ground floor.

first-foot *Scot.* –*n.* first person to cross a threshold in the New Year. –*v.* be a first-foot.

first-fruit *n.* (usu. in *pl.*) **1** first agricultural produce of a season, esp. as offered to God. **2** first results of work etc.

firsthand *adj.* & *adv.* from the original source; direct.

♦ **first in, first out** *n.* (also **FIFO**) **1** *Accounting* method of charging homogeneous items of stock to production when the cost of the items has changed. It is assumed, both for costing and stock valuation purposes, that the earliest items taken into stock are those used in production although this may not necessarily correspond with the physical movement of the stock items. **2** *Computing* procedure by which the first item in a list of data items is the first to be removed.

First Lady *n.* (in the US) wife of the President.

first light *n.* dawn.

♦ **first-loss policy** *n.* property insurance policy in which the policyholder arranges cover for an amount below the full value of the items insured and the insurer agrees not to penalize the insured for under-insurance. The main use of these policies is in circumstances in which a total loss is virtually impossible. For example, a large warehouse may contain £2.5M worth of wines and spirits but the owner may feel that no more than £500,000 worth could be stolen at any one time. The solution is a first-loss policy that deals with all claims up to £500,000 but pays no more than this figure if more is stolen.

---

firstly *adv.* in the first place, first (cf. FIRST *adv.*).

first mate *n.* (on a merchant ship) second in command.

first name *n.* personal or Christian name.

first night *n.* first public performance of a play etc.

♦ **first of exchange** see BILLS IN A SET.

---

first offender *n.* criminal without previous convictions.

first officer *n.* = FIRST MATE.

first person see PERSON.

first post *n.* (also **last post**) bugle-call as a signal to retire for the night.

first-rate *adj.* **1** excellent. **2** *colloq.* very well (*feeling first-rate*).

first thing *adv. colloq.* before anything else; very early.

firth *n.* (also **frith**) **1** narrow inlet of sea. **2** estuary. [Old Norse: related to FIORD]

FIS *abbr.* **1** Family Income Supplement. **2** Fellow of the Institute of Statisticians. **3** (also **f.i.s.**) free into store.

FISA *abbr.* Fellow of the Incorporated Secretaries Association.

fiscal /'fɪsk(ə)l/ –*adj.* of public revenue. –*n.* **1** legal official in some countries. **2** *Scot.* = PROCURATOR FISCAL. [Latin *fiscus* treasury]

♦ **fiscal drag** *n.* restraint on the expansion of an economy as a consequence of government taxation policy. In a progressive tax system, a rise in inflation will cause wage-earners to pay a higher proportion of their income in tax, even though their real wages are unchanged; this is **nominal fiscal drag. Real fiscal drag** occurs when all taxpayers pay a higher proportion of their income in taxation, as a result of rising real wages. In these circumstances there is a rise in government tax revenues as a proportion of gross domestic product. The most widely advocated remedy for fiscal drag is the indexation of tax thresholds.

♦ **fiscal policy** *n.* use of government spending to influence macroeconomic conditions. Keynes advocated the encouragement of public works in order to create employment during recessions, arguing that fiscal policy would be more effective than monetary policy. Fiscal policy was actively pursued to sustain full employment in the postwar years; however, monetarists and others have claimed that this set off the inflation of the 1970s. Fiscal policy has remained 'tight' in most western countries in the 1980s, with governments actively attempting to reduce the level of public expenditure.

♦ **fiscal year** *n.* (also **tax year, year of assessment**) year beginning on 6 April in one year and ending on 5 April in the next. Income tax, capital-gains tax, and annual allowances for inheritance tax are calculated for fiscal years, and the UK Budget estimates refer to the fiscal year. In the US it runs from 1 July to the following 30 June. Cf. FINANCIAL YEAR.

---

fish[1] –*n.* (*pl.* same or **-es**) **1** vertebrate cold-blooded animal with gills and fins living wholly in water. **2** any of various non-vertebrate animals living wholly in water, e.g. the cuttlefish, shellfish, and jellyfish. **3** fish as food. **4** *colloq.* person of a specified, usu. unpleasant, kind (*an odd fish*). **5** (**the Fish** or **Fishes**) sign or constellation Pisces. –*v.* **1** try to catch fish. **2** fish in (a certain river, pool, etc.). **3** (foll. by *for*) **a** search for. **b** seek indirectly (*fishing for compliments*). **4** (foll. by *up*, *out*, etc.) retrieve with effort. □ **drink like a fish** drink alcohol excessively. **fish out of water** person out of his or her element. **other fish to fry** other matters to attend to. [Old English]

fish[2] *n.* flat or curved plate of iron, wood, etc., used to strengthen a beam, joint, or mast. [French *ficher* fix, from Latin *figere* FIX]

fish-bowl *n.* (usu. round) glass bowl for pet fish.

fish cake *n.* breaded cake of fish and mashed potato, usu. fried.

fisher *n.* **1** animal that catches fish. **2** *archaic* fisherman. [Old English]

fisherman *n.* man who catches fish as a livelihood or for sport.

fishery *n.* (*pl.* **-ies**) **1** place where fish are caught or reared. **2** industry of fishing or breeding fish.

fish-eye lens *n.* very wide-angle lens with a highly-curved front.

fish farm *n.* place where fish are bred for food.

fish finger *n.* small oblong piece of fish in batter or breadcrumbs.

fish-hook *n.* barbed hook for catching fish.

fishing *n.* catching fish.

fishing-line *n.* thread with a baited hook etc. for catching fish.

fishing-rod *n.* tapering usu. jointed rod for fishing.

fish-kettle *n.* oval pan for boiling fish.

fish-knife *n.* knife for eating or serving fish.

fish-meal *n.* ground dried fish as fertilizer or animal feed.

fishmonger *n.* dealer in fish.

fishnet *n.* (often *attrib.*) open-meshed fabric (*fishnet stockings*).

fish-plate *n.* flat piece of iron etc. connecting railway rails or positioning masonry.

fish-slice *n.* flat slotted cooking utensil.

fishtail *n.* device etc. shaped like a fish's tail.

fishwife *n.* **1** coarse-mannered or noisy woman. **2** woman who sells fish.

fishy *adj.* (**-ier**, **-iest**) **1** of or like fish. **2** *slang* dubious, suspect. □ **fishily** *adv.* **fishiness** *n.*

fissile /'fɪsaɪl/ *adj.* **1** capable of undergoing nuclear fission. **2** tending to split. [Latin: related to FISSURE]

fission /'fɪʃ(ə)n/ *–n.* **1** splitting of a heavy atomic nucleus, with a release of energy. **2** cell division as a mode of reproduction. *–v.* (cause to) undergo fission. □ **fissionable** *adj.* [Latin: related to FISSURE]

fission bomb *n.* atomic bomb.

fissure /'fɪʃə(r)/ *–n.* crack or split, usu. long and narrow. *–v.* (**-ring**) split, crack. [Latin *findo fiss-* cleave]

fist *n.* tightly closed hand. □ **fistful** *n.* (*pl.* **-s**). [Old English]

fisticuffs /'fɪstɪˌkʌfs/ *n.pl.* fighting with the fists. [probably from obsolete *fisty* (from FIST), CUFF[2]]

fistula /'fɪstjʊlə/ *n.* (*pl.* **-s** or **-lae** /-ˌliː/) abnormal or artificial passage between an organ and the body surface or between two organs. □ **fistular** *adj.* **fistulous** *adj.* [Latin, = pipe]

fit[1] *–adj.* (**fitter**, **fittest**) **1 a** well suited. **b** qualified, competent, worthy. **c** in suitable condition, ready. **d** (foll. by *for*) good enough (*fit for a king*). **2** in good health or condition. **3** proper, becoming, right (*it is fit that*). *–v.* (**-tt-**) **1 a** (also *absol.*) be of the right shape and size for (*dress fits her; key doesn't fit*). **b** (often foll. by *in, into*) be correctly positioned (*that bit fits here*). **c** find room for (*fit another on here*). **2** make suitable or competent; adapt (*fitted for battle*). **3** (usu. foll. by *with*) supply. **4** fix in place (*fit a lock on the door*). **5** = *fit on*. **6** befit, become (*it fits the occasion*). *–n.* way in which a garment, component, etc., fits (*tight fit*). *–adv.* (foll. by *to* + infin.) *colloq.* so that; likely (*laughing fit to bust*). □ **fit the bill** = *fill the bill*. **fit in 1** (often foll. by *with*) be compatible; accommodate (*tried to fit in with their plans*). **2** find space or time for (*dentist fitted me in*). **fit on** try on (a garment). **fit out** (or **up**) (often foll. by *with*) equip. **see** (or **think**) **fit** (often foll. by *to* + infin.) decide or choose (a specified action). □ **fitly** *adv.* **fitness** *n.* [origin unknown]

fit[2] *n.* **1** sudden esp. epileptic seizure with unconsciousness or convulsions. **2** sudden brief bout or burst (*fit of giggles; fit of coughing*). □ **by** (or **in**) **fits and starts** spasmodically. **have a fit** *colloq.* be greatly surprised or outraged. **in fits** laughing uncontrollably. [Old English]

f.i.t. *abbr.* free of income tax.

fitful *adj.* spasmodic or intermittent. □ **fitfully** *adv.*

fitment *n.* (usu. in *pl.*) fixed item of furniture.

fitted *adj.* **1** made to fit closely or exactly (*fitted carpet*). **2** provided with built-in fittings etc. (*fitted kitchen*). **3** built-in (*fitted cupboards*).

fitter *n.* **1** mechanic who fits together and adjusts machinery. **2** supervisor of the cutting, fitting, etc. of garments.

fitting *–n.* **1** trying-on of a garment etc. for adjustment before completion. **2** (in *pl.*) fixtures and fitments of a building. *–adj.* proper, becoming, right. □ **fittingly** *adv.*

Fiume see RIJEKA.

five *adj.* & *n.* **1** one more than four. **2** symbol for this (5, v, V). **3** size etc. denoted by five. **4** set or team of five. **5** five o'clock (*is it five yet?*). **6** *Cricket* hit scoring five runs. [Old English]

fivefold *adj.* & *adv.* **1** five times as much or as many. **2** consisting of five parts.

five o'clock shadow *n.* beard-growth visible in the latter part of the day.

fiver *n. colloq.* five-pound note.

fives *n.* game in which a ball is hit with a gloved hand or bat against the walls of a court.

five-star *adj.* of the highest class.

fivestones *n.* jacks played with five pieces of metal etc. and usu. no ball.

f.i.w. *abbr. Commerce* free in (or into) wagon(s).

fix *–v.* **1** make firm or stable; fasten, secure. **2** decide, settle, specify (a price, date, etc.). **3** mend, repair. **4** implant in the mind. **5 a** (foll. by *on, upon*) direct (the eyes etc.) steadily, set. **b** attract and hold (the attention, eyes, etc.). **c** (foll. by *with*) single out with one's look etc. **6** place definitely, establish. **7** determine the exact nature, position, etc., of; refer (a thing) to a definite place or time; identify, locate. **8 a** make (the eyes, features, etc.) rigid. **b** (of eyes, features, etc.) become rigid. **9** *US colloq.* prepare (food or drink). **10** congeal or become congealed. **11** *colloq.* punish, kill, deal with (a person). **12** *colloq.* **a** bribe or threaten into supporting. **b** gain a fraudulent result of (a race etc.). **13** *slang* inject a narcotic. **14** make (a colour, photographic image, etc.) fast or permanent. **15** (of a plant etc.) assimilate (nitrogen or carbon dioxide). *–n.* **1** *colloq.* dilemma, predicament. **2 a** finding one's position by bearings etc. **b** position found in this way. **3** *slang* dose of an addictive drug. □ **be fixed** (usu. foll. by *for*) *colloq.* be situated (regarding) (*how is he fixed for money?*). **fix on** (or **upon**) choose, decide on. **fix up 1** arrange, organize. **2** accommodate. **3** (often foll. by *with*) provide (a person) (*fixed me up with a job*). □ **fixable** *adj.* [Latin *figo fix-*]

fixate /fɪk'seɪt/ *v.* (**-ting**) **1** direct one's gaze on. **2** *Psychol.* (usu. in *passive*; often foll. by *on, upon*) cause (a person) to become abnormally attached to a person or thing. [Latin: related to FIX]

fixation /fɪk'seɪʃ(ə)n/ *n.* **1** state of being fixated. **2** obsession, monomania. **3** coagulation. **4** process of assimilating a gas to form a solid compound.

fixative /'fɪksətɪv/ *–adj.* tending to fix or secure. *–n.* fixative substance.

◆ **fixed asset** *n.* = CAPITAL ASSET.

◆ **fixed capital** *n.* amount of capital tied up in the capital assets of an organization. Cf. CIRCULATING CAPITAL.

◆ **fixed capital formation** *n.* investment over a given period, as used in the national income accounts. It consists primarily of investment in manufacturing and housing. **Gross fixed capital formation** is the total amount of expenditure on investment, while **net fixed capital formation** includes a deduction for the depreciation of existing capital.

◆ **fixed charge** *n.* (also **specific charge**) charge in which a creditor has the right to have a specific asset sold and applied to the repayment of his debt if the debtor defaults on any payments (see CHARGE 3). The debtor is not at liberty to deal with the asset without the charge-holder's consent. Cf. FLOATING CHARGE.

◆ **fixed costs** see OVERHEAD COSTS.

◆ **fixed debenture** *n.* debenture that has a fixed charge as security. Cf. FLOATING DEBENTURE.

◆ **fixed disk** *n. Computing* hard disk permanently attached to a computer.

◆ **fixed exchange rate** *n.* rate of exchange between one currency and another that is fixed by government and maintained by that government buying or selling its currency to support or depress its currency. Cf. FLOATING EXCHANGE RATE.

◆ **fixed-interest security** *n.* type of security that gives a fixed stated interest payment once or twice per annum. These assets include gilt-edged securities, bonds, preference shares, and debentures; as they entail less risk than equities they offer less scope for capital appreciation. They do, however, often give a better yield than equities. The prices of fixed-interest securities tend to move inversely with the general level of interest rates, reflecting changes in the value of their fixed yield relative to the market. Fixed-interest securities tend to be particularly poor investments at times of high inflation as their value does not adjust to changes in the price level. To overcome this problem some gilts now give index-linked interest payments.

fixedly /ˈfɪksɪdlɪ/ *adv.* intently.

◆ **fixed rate mortgage** *n.* mortgage in which the rate of interest paid by the borrower is fixed; usu. for the first few years of the loan.

◆ **fixed spot** *n.* television advertising spot for which a premium is paid (normally 15%) to ensure that it is transmitted in a preselected commercial break during a particular programme.

fixed star *n. Astron.* seemingly motionless star.

fixer *n.* **1** person or thing that fixes. **2** *Photog.* substance for fixing a photographic image etc. **3** *colloq.* person who makes esp. illicit deals.

fixings *n.pl. US* **1** apparatus or equipment. **2** trimmings for a dish, dress, etc.

fixity *n.* fixed state; stability; permanence.

fixture /ˈfɪkstʃə(r)/ *n.* **1 a** something fixed in position. **b** *colloq.* seemingly immovable person or thing (*seems to be a fixture*). **2 a** sporting event, esp. a match, race, etc. **b** date agreed for this. **3** (in *pl.*) articles attached to a building or land and regarded as legally part of it.

fizz –*v.* **1** make a hissing or spluttering sound. **2** (of a drink) effervesce. –*n.* **1** effervescence. **2** *colloq.* effervescent drink, esp. champagne. [imitative]

fizzle /ˈfɪz(ə)l/ –*v.* (**-ling**) make a feeble hiss. –*n.* such a sound. □ **fizzle out** end feebly. [imitative]

fizzy *adj.* (**-ier, -iest**) effervescent. □ **fizziness** *n.*

FJI *international vehicle registration* Fiji.

fjord var. of FIORD.

FK *postcode* Falkirk.

Fkr *symb.* Faeroese krone.

FL –*US postcode* Florida. –*international vehicle registration* Liechtenstein.

fl. *abbr.* **1** floruit. **2** fluid. **3** (in the Netherlands) guilder. [from its former name *florin*]

Fla. *abbr.* Florida.

flab *n. colloq.* fat; flabbiness. [imitative, or from FLABBY]

flabbergast /ˈflæbəˌgɑːst/ –*v.* (esp. as **flabbergasted** –*adj.*) *colloq.* astonish; dumbfound. [origin uncertain]

flabby /ˈflæbɪ/ *adj.* (**-ier, -iest**) **1** (of flesh etc.) limp; flaccid. **2** feeble. □ **flabbiness** *n.* [alteration of *flappy*: related to FLAP]

flaccid /ˈflæksɪd/ *adj.* limp, flabby, drooping. □ **flaccidity** /-ˈsɪdɪtɪ/ *n.* [Latin *flaccus* limp]

flag[1] –*n.* **1 a** usu. oblong or square piece of cloth, attachable by one edge to a pole or rope as a country's emblem or standard, a signal, etc. **b** small toy etc. resembling a flag. **2** adjustable strip of metal etc. indicating a taxi's availability for hire. –*v.* (**-gg-**) **1 a** grow tired; lag (*was soon flagging*). **b** hang down; droop. **2** mark out with or as if with a flag or flags. **3** (often foll. by *that*) inform or communicate by flag-signals. □ **flag down** signal to stop. [origin unknown]

flag[2] –*n.* (also **flagstone**) **1** flat usu. rectangular paving stone. **2** (in *pl.*) pavement of these. –*v.* (**-gg-**) pave with flags. [probably Scandinavian]

flag[3] *n.* plant with a bladed leaf (esp. the iris). [origin unknown]

flag-day *n.* fund-raising day for a charity, esp. with the sale of small paper flags etc. in the street.

flagellant /ˈflædʒələnt/ –*n.* person who scourges himself, herself, or others as a religious discipline or as a sexual stimulus. –*adj.* of flagellation. [Latin *flagellum* whip]

flagellate /ˈflædʒəˌleɪt/ *v.* (**-ting**) scourge, flog. □ **flagellation** /-ˈleɪʃ(ə)n/ *n.*

flagellum /fləˈdʒeləm/ *n.* (*pl.* **-gella**) **1** long lashlike appendage on some microscopic organisms. **2** runner; creeping shoot. [Latin, = whip]

flageolet /ˌflædʒəˈlet/ *n.* small flute blown at the end. [French from Provençal]

◆ **flag of convenience** *n.* national flag of a small country that is flown by a ship registered in this country, although the ship is owned by a national of another country. The object is to avoid taxation and the more stringent safety and humanitarian conditions imposed on ships and their crews by the larger seagoing nations.

flag-officer *n.* admiral, vice admiral, or rear admiral, or the commodore of a yacht-club.

flag of truce *n.* white flag requesting a truce.

flagon /ˈflægən/ *n.* **1** large bottle, usu. holding a quart (1.13 litres), esp. of wine, cider, etc. **2** large vessel for wine etc., usu. with a handle, spout, and lid. [Latin *flasco* FLASK]

flag-pole *n.* = FLAGSTAFF.

flagrant /ˈfleɪgrənt/ *adj.* blatant; notorious; scandalous. □ **flagrancy** *n.* **flagrantly** *adv.* [Latin *flagro* blaze]

flagship *n.* **1** ship with an admiral on board. **2** leader in a category etc.; exemplar.

flagstaff *n.* pole on which a flag may be hoisted.

flagstone *n.* = FLAG[2].

flag-waving *n.* populist agitation, chauvinism.

flail –*n.* wooden staff with a short heavy stick swinging from it, used for threshing. –*v.* **1** wave or swing wildly. **2** beat with or as with a flail. [Latin *flagellum* whip]

flair *n.* **1** natural talent in a specific area (*flair for languages*). **2** style, finesse. [French *flairer* to smell]

flak *n.* **1** anti-aircraft fire. **2** adverse criticism; abuse. [German, *Fl*ieger*a*bwehr*k*anone, 'aviator-defence-gun']

flake –*n.* **1** small thin light piece of snow etc. **2** thin broad piece peeled or split off. **3** dogfish etc. as food. –*v.* (**-king**) (often foll. by *away, off*) **1** take off or come away in flakes. **2** sprinkle with or fall in flakes. □ **flake out** *colloq.* fall asleep or drop from exhaustion; faint. [origin unknown]

flak jacket *n.* protective reinforced military jacket.

flaky *adj.* (**-ier, -iest**) **1** of, like, or in flakes. **2** esp. *US slang* crazy, eccentric.

flaky pastry *n.* crumblier version of puff pastry.

flambé /ˈflɒmbeɪ/ *adj.* (of food) covered with alcohol and set alight briefly (following a noun: *pancakes flambé*). [French: related to FLAME]

flamboyant /flæmˈbɔɪənt/ *adj.* **1** ostentatious; showy. **2** floridly decorated or coloured. □ **flamboyance** *n.* **flamboyantly** *adv.* [French: related to FLAMBÉ]

flame –*n.* **1 a** ignited gas. **b** portion of this (*flame flickered; burst into flames*). **2 a** bright light or colouring. **b** brilliant orange-red colour. **3 a** strong passion, esp. love (*fan the flame*). **b** *colloq.* sweetheart. –*v.* (**-ming**) **1** (often foll. by *away, forth, out, up*) burn; blaze. **2** (often foll. by *out, up*) **a** (of passion) break out. **b** (of a person) become angry. **3** shine or glow like flame. [Latin *flamma*]

flamenco /fləˈmeŋkəʊ/ *n.* (*pl.* **-s**) **1** style of Spanish gypsy guitar music with singing. **2** dance performed to this. [Spanish, = Flemish]

flame-thrower *n.* weapon for throwing a spray of flame.

flaming *adj.* **1** emitting flames. **2** very hot (*flaming June*). **3** *colloq.* **a** passionate (*flaming row*). **b** expressing annoyance (*that flaming dog*). **4** bright-coloured.

flamingo /flə'mɪŋgəʊ/ *n.* (*pl.* **-s** or **-es**) tall long-necked wading bird with mainly pink plumage. [Provençal: related to FLAME]

flammable /'flæməb(ə)l/ *adj.* inflammable. □ **flammability** /-'bɪlɪtɪ/ *n.* [Latin: related to FLAME]

■ **Usage** *Flammable* is often used because *inflammable* can be mistaken for a negative (the true negative being *non-flammable*).

flan *n.* **1** pastry case with a savoury or sweet filling. **2** sponge base with a sweet topping. [medieval Latin *flado -onis*]

Flanders /'flɑːndəz/ medieval principality in W Europe, now divided between Belgium (the provinces of East and West Flanders), N France, and the Netherlands.

flange /flændʒ/ *n.* projecting flat rim etc., for strengthening or attachment. [origin uncertain]

flank –*n.* **1** side of the body between ribs and hip. **2** side of a mountain, building, etc. **3** right or left side of an army etc. –*v.* (often in *passive*) be at or move along the side of (*road flanked by mountains*). [French from Germanic]

flannel /'flæn(ə)l/ –*n.* **1 a** woven woollen usu. napless fabric. **b** (in *pl.*) flannel garments, esp. trousers. **2** face-cloth, esp. towelling. **3** *slang* nonsense; flattery. –*v.* (**-ll-**; *US* **-l-**) **1** *slang* flatter. **2** wash with a flannel. [Welsh *gwlanen* from *gwlān* wool]

flannelette /ˌflænə'let/ *n.* napped cotton fabric like flannel.

flap –*v.* (**-pp-**) **1** move or be moved up and down; beat. **2** *colloq.* be agitated or panicky. **3** sway; flutter. **4** (usu. foll. by *away, off*) strike (flies etc.) with flat object; drive. **5** *colloq.* (of ears) listen intently. –*n.* **1** piece of cloth, wood, etc. attached by one side esp. to cover a gap, e.g. a pocket-cover, the folded part of an envelope, a table-leaf. **2** motion of a wing, arm, etc. **3** *colloq.* agitation; panic (*in a flap*). **4** aileron. **5** light blow with something flat. □ **flappy** *adj.* [probably imitative]

flapdoodle /flæp'duːd(ə)l/ *n. colloq.* nonsense. [origin unknown]

flapjack *n.* **1** sweet oatcake. **2** esp. *US* pancake.

flapper *n.* **1** person apt to panic. **2** *slang* (in the 1920s) young unconventional woman.

flare –*v.* (**-ring**) **1** widen gradually (*flared trousers*). **2** (cause to) blaze brightly and unsteadily. **3** burst out, esp. angrily. –*n.* **1 a** dazzling irregular flame or light. **b** sudden outburst of flame. **2** flame or bright light used as a signal or to illuminate a target etc. **3 a** gradual widening, esp. of a skirt or trousers. **b** (in *pl.*) wide-bottomed trousers. □ **flare up** burst into a sudden blaze, anger, activity, etc. [origin unknown]

flare-path *n.* line of lights on a runway to guide aircraft.

flare-up *n.* sudden outburst.

flash –*v.* **1** (cause to) emit a brief or sudden light; (cause to) gleam. **2** send or reflect like a sudden flame (*eyes flashed fire*). **3 a** burst suddenly into view or perception (*answer flashed upon me*). **b** move swiftly (*train flashed past*). **4 a** send (news etc.) by radio, telegraph, etc. **b** signal to (a person) with lights. **5** *colloq.* show ostentatiously (*flashed her ring*). **6** *slang* indecently expose oneself. –*n.* **1** sudden bright light or flame, e.g. of lightning. **2** an instant (*in a flash*). **3** sudden brief feeling, display of wit, etc. (*flash of hope*). **4** = NEWSFLASH. **5** *Photog.* = FLASHLIGHT 1. **6** *Mil.* coloured cloth patch on a uniform. **7** bright patch of colour. –*adj. colloq.* gaudy; showy; vulgar (*flash car*). [imitative]

flashback *n.* scene set in an earlier time than the main action.

flash bulb *n. Photog.* bulb for a flashlight.

flash-cube *n. Photog.* set of four flash bulbs in a cube, operated in turn.

flasher *n.* **1** *slang* man who indecently exposes himself. **2** automatic device for switching lights rapidly on and off.

flash-gun *n.* device operating a camera flashlight.

flashing *n.* (usu. metal) strip used to prevent water penetration at a roof joint etc. [dial.]

flash in the pan *n.* promising start followed by failure.

flash-lamp *n.* portable flashing electric lamp.

flashlight *n.* **1** light giving an intense flash, used for night or indoor photography. **2** *US* electric torch.

flashpoint *n.* **1** temperature at which vapour from oil etc. will ignite in air. **2** point at which anger etc. is expressed.

flashy *adj.* (**-ier, -iest**) showy; gaudy; cheaply attractive. □ **flashily** *adv.* **flashiness** *n.*

flask /flɑːsk/ *n.* **1** narrow-necked bulbous bottle for wine etc. or used in chemistry. **2** = HIP-FLASK. **3** = VACUUM FLASK. [Latin *flasca, flasco*: cf. FLAGON]

flat[1] –*adj.* (**flatter, flattest**) **1 a** horizontally level. **b** even; smooth; unbroken. **c** level and shallow (*flat cap*). **2** unqualified; downright (*flat refusal*). **3 a** dull; lifeless; monotonous (*in a flat tone*). **b** dejected. **4** (of a fizzy drink) having lost its effervescence. **5** (of an accumulator, battery, etc.) having exhausted its charge. **6** *Mus.* **a** below true or normal pitch (*violins are flat*). **b** (of a key) having a flat or flats in the signature. **c** (as **B, E,** etc. **flat**) semitone lower than B, E, etc. **7** (of a tyre) punctured; deflated. –*adv.* **1** at full length; spread out (*lay flat; flat against the wall*). **2** *colloq.* **a** completely, absolutely (*flat broke*). **b** exactly (*in five minutes flat*). **3** *Mus.* below the true or normal pitch (*sings flat*). –*n.* **1** flat part or thing (*flat of the hand*). **2** level ground, esp. a plain or swamp. **3** *Mus.* **a** note lowered a semitone below natural pitch. **b** sign (♭) indicating this. **4** (as **the flat**) flat racing or its season. **5** *Theatr.* flat scenery on a frame. **6** esp. *US colloq.* flat tyre. □ **flat out 1** at top speed. **2** using all one's strength etc. **that's flat** *colloq.* that is definite. □ **flatly** *adv.* **flatness** *n.* **flattish** *adj.* [Old Norse]

flat[2] *n.* set of rooms, usu. on one floor, as a residence. □ **flatlet** *n.* [obsolete *flet* floor, dwelling, from Germanic: related to FLAT[1]]

flat-fish *n.* sole, plaice, etc. with both eyes on one side of a flattened body.

flat foot *n.* foot with a flattened arch.

flat-footed *n.* **1** having flat feet. **2** *colloq.* **a** uninspired. **b** unprepared. **c** resolute.

flat-iron *n. hist.* domestic iron heated on a fire etc.

flatmate *n.* person sharing a flat.

flat race *n.* horse race without jumps, over level ground. □ **flat racing** *n.*

flat rate *n.* unvarying rate or charge.

flat screen *n. Computing* type of screen in the form of a thin flat panel rather than the protruding surface used in many display devices. Plasma panel displays and LCDs have flat screens.

flat spin *n.* **1** *Aeron.* a nearly horizontal spin. **2** *colloq.* state of panic.

flatten *v.* **1** make or become flat. **2** *colloq.* **a** humiliate. **b** knock down.

flatter *v.* **1** compliment unduly, esp. for gain or advantage. **2** (usu. *refl.*; usu. foll. by *that*) congratulate or delude (oneself etc.) (*he flatters himself that he can sing*). **3** (of colour, style, portrait, painter etc.) enhance the appearance of (*that blouse flatters you*). **4** cause to feel honoured. □ **flatterer** *n.* **flattering** *adj.* **flatteringly** *adv.* [French]

flattery *n.* exaggerated or insincere praise.

flatulent /'flætjʊlənt/ *adj.* **1 a** causing intestinal wind. **b** caused by or suffering from this. **2** (of speech etc.) inflated, pretentious. □ **flatulence** *n.* [Latin *flatus* blowing]

flatworm *n.* worm with a flattened body, e.g. flukes.

◆ **flat yield** *Finance* see YIELD *n.* 2.

flaunt *v.* (often *refl.*) display proudly; show off; parade. [origin unknown]

■ **Usage** *Flaunt* is often confused with *flout* which means 'to disobey contemptuously'.

flautist /'flɔːtɪst/ *n.* flute-player. [Italian: related to FLUTE]

flavour /'fleɪvə(r)/ (*US* **flavor**) *–n.* **1** mingled sensation of smell and taste (*cheesy flavour*). **2** characteristic quality (*romantic flavour*). **3** (usu. foll. by *of*) slight admixture (*flavour of failure*). *–v.* give flavour to; season. □ **flavourless** *adj.* **flavoursome** *adj.* [French]

flavouring *n.* (*US* **flavoring**) substance used to flavour food or drink.

flavour of the month *n.* (also **flavour of the week**) temporary trend or fashion.

flaw[1] *–n.* **1** imperfection; blemish. **2** crack, chip, etc. **3** invalidating defect. *–v.* crack; damage; spoil. □ **flawless** *adj.* **flawlessly** *adv.* [Old Norse]

flaw[2] *n.* squall of wind. [Low German or Dutch]

flax *n.* **1** blue-flowered plant cultivated for its textile fibre and its seeds. **2** flax fibres. [Old English]

flaxen *adj.* **1** of flax. **2** (of hair) pale yellow.

flax-seed *n.* linseed.

flay *v.* **1** strip the skin or hide off, esp. by beating. **2** criticize severely. **3** peel off (skin, bark, peel, etc.). **4** extort money etc. from. [Old English]

flea *n.* small wingless jumping parasitic insect. □ **a flea in one's ear** sharp reproof. [Old English]

fleabag *n. slang* shabby or unattractive person or thing.

flea-bite *n.* **1** bite of a flea. **2** trivial injury or inconvenience.

flea-bitten *adj.* **1** bitten by or infested with fleas. **2** shabby.

flea market *n.* street market selling second-hand goods etc.

flea-pit *n.* dingy dirty cinema etc.

fleck *–n.* **1** small patch of colour or light. **2** particle, speck. *–v.* mark with flecks. [Old Norse, or Low German or Dutch]

flection *US* var. of FLEXION.

fled *past* and *past part.* of FLEE.

fledge *v.* (**-ging**) **1** provide or deck (an arrow etc.) with feathers. **2** bring up (a young bird) until it can fly. **3** (as **fledged** *adj.*) **a** able to fly. **b** independent; mature. [obsolete adj. *fledge* fit to fly]

fledgling /'fledʒlɪŋ/ *n.* (also **fledgeling**) **1** young bird. **2** inexperienced person.

flee *v.* (*past* and *past part.* **fled**) **1** (often foll. by *from*, *before*) **a** run away (from); leave abruptly (*fled the room*). **b** seek safety by fleeing. **2** vanish. [Old English]

fleece *–n.* **1 a** woolly coat of a sheep etc. **b** wool sheared from a sheep at one time. **2** thing resembling a fleece, esp. soft fabric for lining etc. *–v.* (**-cing**) **1** (often foll. by *of*) strip of money, valuables, etc.; swindle. **2** shear (sheep etc.). **3** cover as if with a fleece (*sky fleeced with clouds*). □ **fleecy** *adj.* (**-ier, -iest**). [Old English]

fleet *–n.* **1 a** warships under one commander-in-chief. **b** (prec. by *the*) nation's warships etc.; navy. **2** number of vehicles in one company etc. *–adj. poet. literary* swift, nimble. [Old English]

fleeting *adj.* transitory; brief. □ **fleetingly** *adv.*

♦ **fleet rating** *n.* single special premium rate quoted by an insurer for covering the insurance on a number of ships or vehicles owned by one person or company, rather than considering each one individually. The fleet need not consist of identical vehicles or vessels but common ownership is essential.

Fleet Street London street between the Strand and the City, in or near which most of the leading national newspapers formerly (until the mid-1980s) had offices, whence the allusive use of its name to refer to the British press.

Fleming /'flemɪŋ/ *n.* **1** native of medieval Flanders. **2** member of a Flemish-speaking people of N and W Belgium. [Old English]

Flemish /'flemɪʃ/ *–adj.* of Flanders. *–n.* language of the Flemings. [Dutch]

Flemish Brabant province in central Belgium; pop. (est. 1995) 995 266; capital, Leuven. The province was created in 1995 following the division of Brabant into Flemish Brabant and Walloon Brabant.

flesh *n.* **1 a** soft, esp. muscular, substance between the skin and bones of an animal or a human. **b** plumpness; fat. **2** the body, esp. as sinful. **3** pulpy substance of a fruit etc. **4 a** visible surface of the human body. **b** (also **flesh-colour**) yellowish pink colour. **5** animal or human life. □ **all flesh** all animate creation. **flesh out** make or become substantial. **in the flesh** in person. **one's own flesh and blood** near relatives. [Old English]

flesh and blood *–n.* **1** the body or its substance. **2** humankind. **3** human nature, esp. as fallible. *–adj.* real, not imaginary.

fleshly *adj.* (**-lier, -liest**) **1** bodily; sensual. **2** mortal. **3** worldly.

fleshpots *n.pl.* luxurious living.

flesh-wound *n.* superficial wound.

fleshy *adj.* (**-ier, -iest**) of flesh; plump, pulpy. □ **fleshiness** *n.*

fleur-de-lis /ˌflɜːdə'liː/ *n.* (also **fleur-de-lys**) (*pl.* **fleurs-** pronunc. same) **1** iris flower. **2** *Heraldry* **a** lily of three petals. **b** former royal arms of France. [French, = flower of lily]

Flevoland /'fleɪʊəˌlɑːnt/ province of the Netherlands, created in 1986, comprising an area reclaimed from the Zuider Zee in 1950–7 and 1959–68; pop. (est. 1985) 262 324.

flew *past* of FLY[1].

flews *n.pl.* hanging lips of a bloodhound etc. [origin unknown]

flex[1] *v.* **1** bend (a joint, limb, etc.) or be bent. **2** move (a muscle) or (of a muscle) be moved to bend a joint. [Latin *flecto flex-* bend]

flex[2] *n.* flexible insulated electric cable. [abbreviation of FLEXIBLE]

flexible /'fleksɪb(ə)l/ *adj.* **1** capable of bending without breaking; pliable. **2** manageable. **3** adaptable; variable (*works flexible hours*). □ **flexibility** /-'bɪlɪtɪ/ *n.* **flexibly** *adv.* [Latin *flexibilis*: related to FLEX[1]]

flexion /'flekʃ(ə)n/ *n.* (*US* **flection**) **1** bending or being bent, esp. of a limb or joint. **2** bent part; curve. [Latin *flexio*: related to FLEX[1]]

flexitime /'fleksɪˌtaɪm/ *n.* system of flexible working hours, used esp. in offices. Provided employees work an agreed number of hours per day, they may start or finish work at different times and so reduce time spent in rush-hour travelling. [from FLEXIBLE]

FLIA *abbr.* Fellow of the Life Insurance Association.

flibbertigibbet /ˌflɪbətɪ'dʒɪbɪt/ *n.* gossiping, frivolous, or restless person. [imitative]

flick *–n.* **1 a** light sharp blow with a whip etc. **b** sudden release of a bent digit, esp. to propel a small object. **2** sudden movement or jerk, esp. of the wrist in throwing etc. **3** *colloq.* **a** cinema film. **b** (in *pl.*; prec. by *the*) the cinema. *–v.* **1** (often foll. by *away*, *off*) strike or move with a flick (*flicked the ash off*). **2** give a flick with (a whip etc.). □ **flick through 1** turn over (cards, pages, etc.). **2 a** turn over the pages etc. of, by a rapid movement of the fingers. **b** glance through (a book etc.). [imitative]

flicker *–v.* **1** (of light or flame) shine or burn unsteadily. **2** flutter. **3** (of hope etc.) waver. *–n.* **1** flickering movement or light. **2** brief spell (of hope etc.). □ **flicker out** die away. [Old English]

flick-knife *n.* knife with a blade that springs out when a button is pressed.

flier var. of FLYER.

flight[1] /flaɪt/ *n.* **1 a** act or manner of flying. **b** movement or passage through the air. **2 a** journey through the air or in space. **b** timetabled airline journey. **3** flock of birds, insects, etc. **4** (usu. foll. by *of*) series, esp. of stairs. **5** imaginative excursion or sally (*flight of fancy*). **6** (usu. foll. by *of*) volley (*flight of arrows*). **7** tail of a dart. [Old English: related to FLY[1]]

flight[2] /flaɪt/ *n.* fleeing, hasty retreat. □ **put to flight** cause to flee. **take** (or **take to) flight** flee. [Old English]

flight bag *n.* small zipped shoulder bag for air travel.

flight-deck *n.* **1** deck of an aircraft-carrier. **2** control room of a large aircraft.

flightless *adj.* (of a bird etc.) unable to fly.

flight lieutenant *n.* RAF officer next below squadron leader.

flight path *n.* planned course of an aircraft etc.

flight-recorder *n.* device in an aircraft recording technical details of a flight.

flight sergeant *n.* RAF rank next above sergeant.

flighty *adj.* (**-ier**, **-iest**) (usu. of a girl) frivolous, fickle, changeable. □ **flightiness** *n.*

flimsy /ˈflɪmzɪ/ *adj.* (**-ier**, **-iest**) **1** insubstantial, rickety (*flimsy structure*). **2** (of an excuse etc.) unconvincing. **3** (of clothing) thin. □ **flimsily** *adv.* **flimsiness** *n.* [origin uncertain]

flinch *v.* draw back in fear etc.; wince. [French from Germanic]

Flinders Island /ˈflɪndəz/ Australian island, the largest of the Furneaux Islands, situated in the Bass Strait between Tasmania and mainland Australia. Sheep-farming is the main occupation.

fling *–v.* (*past* and *past part.* **flung**) **1** throw or hurl forcefully or hurriedly. **2** (foll. by *on*, *off*) put on or take off (clothes) carelessly or rapidly. **3** put or send suddenly or violently (*was flung into jail*). **4** rush, esp. angrily (*flung out of the room*). **5** (foll. by *away*) discard rashly. *–n.* **1** act of flinging; throw. **2** bout of wild behaviour. **3** whirling Scottish dance, esp. the Highland fling. [Old Norse]

flint *n.* **1 a** hard grey siliceous stone. **b** piece of this, esp. as a primitive tool or weapon. **2** piece of hard alloy used to give a spark. **3** anything hard and unyielding. □ **flinty** *adj.* (**-ier**, **-iest**). [Old English]

flintlock *n. hist.* old type of gun fired by a spark from a flint.

flip[1] *–v.* (**-pp-**) **1** flick or toss (a coin, pellet, etc.) so that it spins in the air. **2** turn (a small object) over; flick. **3** *slang* = *flip one's lid*. *–n.* **1** act of flipping. **2** *colloq.* short trip. *–adj. colloq.* glib; flippant. □ **flip one's lid** *slang* lose self-control; go mad. **flip through** = *flick through*. [probably from FILLIP]

flip[2] *n.* **1** = EGG-FLIP. **2** drink of heated beer and spirit. [perhaps from FLIP[1]]

flip chart *n.* large pad of paper on a stand.

flip-flop *n.* (usu. rubber) sandal with a thong between the toes. [imitative]

flippant /ˈflɪpənt/ *adj.* frivolous; disrespectful; offhand. □ **flippancy** *n.* **flippantly** *adv.* [from FLIP[1]]

flipper *n.* **1** broad flat limb of a turtle, penguin, etc., used in swimming. **2** similar rubber foot attachment for underwater swimming. **3** *slang* hand.

flipping *adj.* & *adv. slang* expressing annoyance, or as an intensifier.

flip side *n. colloq.* **1** reverse side of a gramophone record. **2** reverse or less important side of something.

flirt *–v.* **1** (usu. foll. by *with*) try to attract sexually but without serious intent. **2** (usu. foll. by *with*) superficially engage in; trifle. *–n.* person who flirts. □ **flirtation** /-ˈteɪʃ(ə)n/ *n.* **flirtatious** /-ˈteɪʃəs/ *adj.* **flirtatiously** /-ˈteɪʃəslɪ/ *adv.* **flirtatiousness** /-ˈteɪʃəsnɪs/ *n.* [imitative]

flit *–v.* (**-tt-**) **1** move lightly, softly, or rapidly. **2** make short flights. **3** *colloq.* disappear secretly to escape creditors etc. *–n.* act of flitting. [Old Norse: related to FLEET]

flitch *n.* side of bacon. [Old English]

flitter *v.* flit about; flutter. [from FLIT]

flitter-mouse *n.* = BAT[2].

float *–v.* **1 a** (cause to) rest or move on the surface of a liquid. **b** set (a stranded ship) afloat. **2** *colloq.* **a** move in a leisurely way. **b** (often foll. by *before*) hover before the eye or mind. **3** (often foll. by *in*) move or be suspended freely in a liquid or gas. **4 a** start or launch (a company, scheme, etc.). **b** offer (stock, shares, etc.) on the stock market. **5** *Commerce* cause or allow to have a fluctuating exchange rate. **6** circulate or cause (a rumour or idea) to circulate. *–n.* **1** thing that floats, esp.: **a** a raft. **b** a light object as an indicator of a fish biting or supporting a fishing-net. **c** a hollow structure enabling an aircraft to float on water. **d** a floating device on water, petrol, etc., controlling the level. **2** small esp. electrically-powered vehicle or cart (*milk float*). **3** decorated platform or tableau on a lorry in a procession etc. **4 a** supply of loose change in a shop, at a fête, etc. **b** petty cash. **5** *Theatr.* (in *sing.* or *pl.*) footlights. **6** tool for smoothing plaster. □ **floatable** *adj.* [Old English]

floatation var. of FLOTATION.

floater *n* . **1** person or thing that floats. **2** *colloq.* floating-rate note. See EUROBOND.

floating *adj.* not settled; variable (*floating population*).

♦ **floating charge** *n.* charge over the assets of a company that floats over the charged assets until crystallized by some predetermined event (see CHARGE *n.* 3). For example, a floating charge may be created over all the assets of a company, including its trading stock. The assets may be freely dealt with until a crystallizing event occurs, such as the company going into liquidation. Thereafter no further dealing may take place but the debt may be satisfied from the charged assets. Such a charge ranks in priority after legal charges and after preferred creditors in the event of a winding-up. It must be registered (see REGISTER OF CHARGES). Cf. FIXED CHARGE.

♦ **floating debenture** *n.* debenture that has a floating charge as security. Cf. FIXED DEBENTURE.

♦ **floating debt** *n.* part of the national debt that consists primarily of short-term treasury bills. See also FUNDING OPERATIONS.

---

floating dock *n.* floating structure usable as a dry dock.

♦ **floating exchange rate** *n.* rate of exchange between one currency and others that is permitted to float according to market forces. Cf. FIXED EXCHANGE RATE.

---

floating kidney *n.* abnormally movable kidney.

♦ **floating policy** *n.* insurance policy that has only one sum insured although it may cover many items. No division of the total is shown on the policy and the policyholder is often able to add or remove items from the cover without reference to the insurers, provided that the total sum insured is not exceeded.

♦ **floating-rate interest** *n.* interest rate on certain bonds, certificates of deposit, etc. that changes with the market rate in a predetermined manner, usu. in relation to the base rate.

♦ **floating-rate note** (also **FRN**) see EUROBOND.

---

floating rib *n.* lower rib not attached to the breastbone.

floating voter *n.* voter without fixed allegiance.

♦ **floating warranty** *n.* guarantee given by one person to another that induces this other person to enter into a contract with a third party. For example, a car dealer may induce a customer to enter into a hire-purchase contract with a finance company. If the car does not comply with the dealer's guarantee, the customer may recover damages from the dealer, on the basis of the hire-purchase contract, even though the dealer is not a party to that contract.

---

floaty *adj.* (esp. of fabric) light and airy. [from FLOAT]

flocculent /ˈflɒkjʊlənt/ *adj.* like or in tufts of wool etc.; downy. □ **flocculence** *n.* [related to FLOCK[2]]

flock[1] *–n.* **1** animals of one kind as a group or unit. **2** large crowd of people. **3** people in the care of a priest or teacher etc. *–v.* (usu. foll. by *to*, *in*, *out*, *together*) congregate; mass; troop. [Old English]

flock[2] *n.* **1** lock or tuft of wool, cotton, etc. **2** (also in *pl.*; often *attrib.*) wool-refuse etc. used for quilting and stuffing. [Latin *floccus*]

flock-paper *n.* (also **flock-wallpaper**) wallpaper with a raised flock pattern.

floe *n.* sheet of floating ice. [Norwegian]

flog *v.* (**-gg-**) **1 a** beat with a whip, stick, etc. **b** make work through violent effort (*flogged the engine*). **2** (often foll. by *off*) *slang* sell. □ **flog a dead horse** waste one's efforts. **flog to death** *colloq.* talk about or promote at tedious length. [origin unknown]

flood /flʌd/ *–n.* **1 a** overflowing or influx of water, esp. over land; inundation. **b** the water that overflows. **2** outpouring; torrent (*flood of tears*). **3** inflow of the tide (also in *comb.*: *flood-tide*). **4** *colloq.* floodlight. **5** (**the Flood**) the flood described in Genesis. *–v.* **1** overflow, cover, or be covered with or as if with a flood (*bathroom flooded; flooded with enquiries*). **2** irrigate. **3** deluge (a mine etc.) with water. **4** (often foll. by *in, through*) come in great quantities (*complaints flooded in*). **5** overfill (a carburettor) with petrol. **6** have a uterine haemorrhage. □ **flood out** drive out (of one's home etc.) with a flood. [Old English]

floodgate *n.* **1** gate for admitting or excluding water, esp. in a lock. **2** (usu. in *pl.*) last restraint against tears, rain, anger, etc.

floodlight *–n.* large powerful light (usu. one of several) to illuminate a building, sports ground, etc. *–v.* illuminate with floodlights. □ **floodlit** *adj.*

flood-tide *n.* exceptionally high tide caused esp. by the moon.

floor /flɔː(r)/ *–n.* **1** lower supporting surface of a room. **2 a** bottom of the sea, a cave, etc. **b** any level area. **3** all the rooms etc. on one level of a building; storey. **4 a** (in a legislative assembly) place where members sit and speak. **b** right to speak next in a debate (*gave him the floor*). **5** *Finance* **a** room in a stock exchange, commodity exchange, Lloyd's, etc. in which dealing takes place. See also FLOOR TRADER. **b** see COLLAR *n.* 5. **6** minimum of prices, wages, etc. **7** *colloq.* ground. *–v.* **1** provide with a floor; pave. **2** knock or bring (a person) down. **3** *colloq.* confound, baffle. **4** *colloq.* overcome. **5** serve as the floor of (*lino floored the hall*). □ **from the floor** (of a speech etc.) given by a member of the audience. **take the floor 1** begin to dance. **2** speak in a debate. [Old English]

floorboard *n.* long wooden board used for flooring.

floorcloth *n.* cloth for washing the floor.

flooring *n.* material of which a floor is made.

floor manager *n.* stage-manager of a television production.

floor plan *n.* diagram of the rooms etc. on one storey.

floor show *n.* nightclub entertainment.

♦ **floor trader** *n.* member of a stock exchange, commodity market, Lloyd's, etc. who is permitted to enter the dealing room of these institutions and deal with other traders, brokers, underwriters, etc. Each institution has its own rules of exclusivity, but in many, computer dealing is replacing face-to-face floor trading.

---

floozie /ˈfluːzɪ/ *n.* (also **floozy**) (*pl.* **-ies**) *colloq.* esp. disreputable girl or woman. [origin unknown]

flop *–v.* (**-pp-**) **1** sway about heavily or loosely. **2** (often foll. by *down, on, into*) fall or sit etc. awkwardly or suddenly. **3** *slang* fail; collapse (*play flopped*). **4** make a dull soft thud or splash. *–n.* **1** flopping movement or sound. **2** *slang* failure. *–adv.* with a flop. [var. of FLAP]

floppy *–adj.* (**-ier, -iest**) tending to flop; flaccid. *–n.* (*pl.* **-ies**) = FLOPPY DISK. □ **floppiness** *n.*

floppy disk *n.* (also **floppy, diskette**) *Computing* flexible magnetic disk, enclosed within a stiff protective envelope and usu. 3½ inches in diameter. Floppy disks are extensively used in small computers as on-line backing store and off-line storage devices. They have much smaller storage capacities and much longer access times than hard disks, but are considerably cheaper and need less careful handling. As with other magnetic disks, data is recorded in concentric tracks in the magnetic coating (see also SECTOR 4). **Single-sided disks** use only one surface for recording data; **double-sided disks** use both sides. There are recording techniques whereby the storage capacity of each track can be doubled; this gives **double density** as opposed to **single density**. Storage capacities can exceed a megabyte. The floppy disk remains inside its envelope when it is fed into a disk drive for reading and writing purposes (see DISK DRIVE). A hole through the centre of the disk and envelope allows the disk to be positioned on the rotation mechanism and clamped in place. The disk rotates inside the envelope, becoming rigid as it spins. Radial slots in the envelope allow the read/write head (or heads in a double-sided disk) to make contact with the disk surface. The disk drive can be prevented from writing to the disk by means of the **write-protect notch** in one edge of the envelope.

flops /flɒps/ *n.* measure of computer performance for very powerful computers, usu. expressed in **megaflops**. [*fl*oating-point *op*erations per *s*econd]

flora /ˈflɔːrə/ *n.* (*pl.* **-s** or **florae** /-riː/) **1** plant life of a region or period. **2** list or book of these. [Latin *Flora*, name of the goddess of flowers]

floral *adj.* of, decorated with, or depicting flowers. □ **florally** *adv.* [Latin]

Florence /ˈflɒrəns/ (Italian **Firenze** /fɪəˈrentseɪ/) city in N Italy, capital of Tuscany; pop. (est. 1994) 392 800. Tourism is the main source of revenue; other industries include light engineering and the manufacture of luxury goods.

Florentine /ˈflɒrənˌtaɪn/ *–adj.* of Florence in Italy. *–n.* native or citizen of Florence. [Latin]

Flores /ˈflɔːrez/ Indonesian island, the largest of the Lesser Sunda group; copra and sandalwood are exported.

floret /ˈflɒrɪt/ *n.* **1** each of the small flowers making up a composite flower-head. **2** each stem of a head of cauliflower, broccoli, etc. **3** small flower. [Latin *flos* FLOWER]

floribunda /ˌflɒrɪˈbʌndə/ *n.* plant, esp. a rose, bearing dense clusters of flowers. [related to FLORET: cf. MORIBUND]

florid /ˈflɒrɪd/ *adj.* **1** ruddy (*florid complexion*). **2** elaborately ornate; showy. □ **floridly** *adv.* **floridness** *n.* [Latin: related to FLOWER]

Florida /ˈflɒrɪdə/ state in the SE US; pop. (est. 1990) 14 399 985; capital, Tallahassee. Fruit (esp. citrus fruit) is exported; tourism, manufacturing, and mining are major industries.

florin /ˈflɒrɪn/ *n.* **1** *hist.* British two-shilling coin now worth 10 pence. **2** English or foreign gold or silver coin. **3** standard monetary unit of Aruba. [Italian *fiorino*: related to FLORIST]

florist /ˈflɒrɪst/ *n.* person who deals in or grows flowers. [Latin *flos* FLOWER]

floruit /ˈflɒrʊɪt/ *–v.* flourished; lived and worked (of a painter, writer, etc., whose exact dates are unknown). *–n.* period or date of working etc. [Latin, = he or she flourished]

floss *–n.* **1** rough silk of a silkworm's cocoon. **2** silk thread used in embroidery. **3** = DENTAL FLOSS. *–v.* (also *absol.*) clean (teeth) with dental floss. □ **flossy** *adj.* [French *floche*]

♦ **flotation** /fləʊˈteɪʃ(ə)n/ *n.* (also **floatation**) initial sale of a private (or government-owned) company's stock to the general public, usu. by means of an introduction, issue by tender, offer for sale, placing, or public issue. Once flotation has taken place, the shares can be traded on a stock exchange. The purpose of a flotation is to raise new capital for the business or for the owners to realize their investment. In the UK, a flotation may be made on the main market of the London Stock Exchange or on the unlisted securities market, where less stringent regulations apply. [from FLOAT]

---

flotilla /fləˈtɪlə/ *n.* **1** small fleet. **2** fleet of small ships. [Spanish]

◆ **flotsam** /'flɒtsəm/ *n.* **1** items from a cargo or ship that is itself floating on the sea after a shipwreck. In British waters, it can be claimed by the ship's owners for 366 days after the shipwreck; thereafter it belongs to the Crown. Cf. JETSAM 2. **2** *Marine insurance* items or rights that are lost as a result of breach of warranty. In such cases the policyholder has no right to make an insurance claim. [Anglo-French: related to FLOAT]

flotsam and jetsam *n.* **1** odds and ends. **2** vagrants.
flounce[1] *–v.* (**-cing**) (often foll. by *away, about, off, out*) go or move angrily or impatiently (*flounced out in a huff*). *–n.* flouncing movement. [origin unknown]
flounce[2] *–n.* frill on a dress, skirt, etc. *–v.* (**-cing**) trim with flounces. [alteration of *frounce* pleat, from French]
flounder[1] *–v.* **1** struggle helplessly as if wading in mud. **2** do a task clumsily. *–n.* act of floundering. [imitative]
flounder[2] *n.* (*pl.* same) **1** edible European flat-fish. **2** North American flat-fish. [Anglo-French, probably Scandinavian]
flour *–n.* **1** meal or powder from ground wheat etc. **2** any fine powder. *–v.* sprinkle with flour. □ **floury** *adj.* (**-ier, -iest**). **flouriness** *n.* [different spelling of FLOWER 'best part']
flourish /'flʌrɪʃ/ *–v.* **1 a** grow vigorously; thrive. **b** prosper. **c** be in one's prime. **2** wave, brandish. *–n.* **1** showy gesture. **2** ornamental curve in handwriting. **3** *Mus.* ornate passage or fanfare. [Latin *floreo* from *flos* FLOWER]
flout *–v.* disobey (the law etc.) contemptuously; mock; insult. *–n.* flouting speech or act. [Dutch *fluiten* whistle: related to FLUTE]
■ **Usage** *Flout* is often confused with *flaunt* which means 'to display proudly, show off'.
flow /fləʊ/ *–v.* **1** glide along as a stream. **2** (of liquid, blood, etc.) gush out; be spilt. **3** (of blood, money, electric current, etc.) circulate. **4** move smoothly or steadily. **5** (of a garment, hair, etc.) hang gracefully. **6** (often foll. by *from*) be caused by. **7** (esp. of the tide) be in flood. **8** (of wine) be plentiful. **9** (foll. by *with*) *archaic* be plentifully supplied with (*flowing with milk and honey*). *–n.* **1 a** flowing movement or mass. **b** flowing liquid (*stop the flow*). **c** outpouring; stream (*flow of complaints*). **2** rise of a tide or river (*ebb and flow*). [Old English]
flow chart *n.* (also **flow diagram, flow sheet**) diagram of the movement or action in a complex activity. It is a useful tool for the computer programmer, showing the actions performed by a program and the flow of control, and can be used to plan a program. There are a number of conventional symbols used in flow charts. The important ones are the process box, which indicates a process taking place, and the decision lozenge, which indicates where a decision is needed.
flower /'flaʊə(r)/ *–n.* **1** part of a plant from which the fruit or seed is developed. **2** blossom, esp. used for decoration. **3** plant cultivated for its flowers. *–v.* **1** bloom or cause (a plant) to bloom; blossom. **2** reach a peak. □ **the flower of** the best of. **in flower** blooming. □ **flowered** *adj.* [Latin *flos flor-*]
flower-bed *n.* garden bed for flowers.
flower-head *n.* = HEAD *n.* 3 c.
flower people *n.* hippies with flowers as symbols of peace and love.
flowerpot *n.* pot for growing a plant in.
flower power *n.* peace and love, esp. as a political idea.
flowers of sulphur *n.* fine powder produced when sulphur evaporates and condenses.
flowery *adj.* **1** florally decorated. **2** (of style, speech, etc.) high-flown; ornate. **3** full of flowers. □ **floweriness** *n.*
flowing *adj.* **1** (of style etc.) fluent; easy. **2** (of a line, curve, etc.) smoothly continuous. **3** (of hair etc.) unconfined. □ **flowingly** *adv.*
flown *past part.* of FLY[1].
flu /flu:/ *n. colloq.* influenza. [abbreviation]
fluctuate /'flʌktʃʊ,eɪt/ *v.* (**-ting**) vary irregularly; rise and fall. □ **fluctuation** /-'eɪʃ(ə)n/ *n.* [Latin *fluctus* wave]
flue /flu:/ *n.* **1** smoke-duct in a chimney. **2** channel for conveying heat. [origin unknown]
fluent /'flu:ənt/ *adj.* **1** (of speech, style, etc.) flowing, natural. **2** verbally facile, esp. in a foreign language (*fluent in German*). □ **fluency** *n.* **fluently** *adv.* [Latin *fluo* flow]
fluff *–n.* **1** soft fur, feathers, or fabric particles etc. **2** *slang* mistake in a performance etc. *–v.* **1** (often foll. by *up*) shake into or become a soft mass. **2** *colloq.* make a fluff; bungle. □ **bit of fluff** *slang offens.* attractive woman. □ **fluffy** *adj.* (**-ier, -iest**). **fluffiness** *n.* [probably dial. alteration of *flue* fluff]
flugelhorn /'flu:g(ə)l,hɔ:n/ *n.* valved brass wind instrument like a cornet. [German *Flügel* wing, *Horn* horn]
fluid /'flu:ɪd/ *–n.* **1** substance, esp. a gas or liquid, whose shape is determined by its confines. **2** fluid part or secretion. *–adj.* **1** able to flow and alter shape freely. **2** constantly changing (*situation is fluid*). □ **fluidity** /-'ɪdɪtɪ/ *n.* **fluidly** *adv.* **fluidness** *n.* [Latin: related to FLUENT]
fluid ounce see OUNCE.
fluke[1] /flu:k/ *–n.* lucky accident (*won by a fluke*). *–v.* (**-king**) achieve by a fluke (*fluked that shot*). □ **fluky** *adj.* (**-ier, -iest**). [origin uncertain]
fluke[2] /flu:k/ *n.* **1** parasitic flatworm, e.g. the liver fluke. **2** flat-fish, esp. a flounder. [Old English]
fluke[3] /flu:k/ *n.* **1** broad triangular plate on an anchor arm. **2** lobe of a whale's tail. [perhaps from FLUKE[2]]
flummery /'flʌmərɪ/ *n.* (*pl.* **-ies**) **1** flattery; nonsense. **2** sweet dish made with beaten eggs, sugar, etc. [Welsh *llymru*]
flummox /'flʌməks/ *v. colloq.* bewilder, disconcert. [origin unknown]
flung *past* and *past part.* of FLING.
flunk *v. US colloq.* fail (esp. an exam). [origin unknown]
flunkey /'flʌŋkɪ/ *n.* (also **flunky**) (*pl.* **-eys** or **-ies**) usu. *derog.* **1** liveried footman. **2** toady; snob. **3** *US* cook, waiter, etc. [origin uncertain]
fluoresce /fluə'res/ *v.* (**-scing**) be or become fluorescent. [from FLUORESCENT]
fluorescence *n.* **1** light radiation from certain substances. **2** property of absorbing invisible light and emitting visible light. [from FLUORSPAR, after *opalescence*]
fluorescent *adj.* of, having, or showing fluorescence.
fluorescent lamp *n.* (also **fluorescent bulb**) esp. tubular lamp or bulb radiating largely by fluorescence.
fluoridate /,fluərɪ'deɪt/ *v.* (**-ting**) add fluoride to (drinking-water etc.), esp. to prevent tooth decay. □ **fluoridation** /-'deɪʃ(ə)n/ *n.*
fluoride /'fluəraɪd/ *n.* binary compound of fluorine.
fluorinate /'fluərɪ,neɪt/ *v.* (**-ting**) **1** = FLUORIDATE. **2** introduce fluorine into (a compound). □ **fluorination** /-'neɪʃ(ə)n/ *n.*
fluorine /'fluəri:n/ *n.* poisonous pale-yellow gaseous element. [French: related to FLUORSPAR]
fluorite /'fluəraɪt/ *n.* mineral form of calcium fluoride. [Italian: related to FLUORSPAR]
fluorocarbon /,fluərəʊ'kɑ:bən/ *n.* compound of a hydrocarbon with fluorine atoms.
fluorspar /'fluəspɑ:(r)/ *n.* = FLUORITE. [*fluor* a mineral used as flux, from Latin from *fluo* flow]
flurry /'flʌrɪ/ *–n.* (*pl.* **-ies**) **1** gust or squall (of snow, rain, etc.). **2** sudden burst of activity, excitement, etc.; commotion. *–v.* (**-ies, -ied**) confuse; agitate. [imitative]
flush[1] *–v.* **1** blush, redden, glow warmly (*he flushed with embarrassment*). **2** (usu. as **flushed** *adj.*) cause to glow or blush (often foll. by *with*: *he was flushed with pride*). **3 a** cleanse (a drain, lavatory, etc.) by a flow of water. **b** (often foll. by *away, down*) dispose of in this way. **4** rush out, spurt. *–n.* **1** blush or glow. **2 a** rush of water. **b** cleansing of a drain, lavatory, etc. thus. **3** rush of esp. elation or triumph. **4** freshness; vigour. **5 a** (also **hot flush**) sudden feeling of heat during menopause. **b** feverish redness or temperature etc. *–adj.* **1** level, in the same plane. **2** *colloq.* having plenty of money. [perhaps = FLUSH[3]]

flush[2] *n.* hand of cards all of one suit, esp. in poker. [Latin *fluxus* FLUX]

flush[3] *v.* **1** cause (esp. a game-bird) to fly up. **2** (of a bird) fly up and away. □ **flush out 1** reveal. **2** drive out. [imitative]

fluster *–v.* **1** make or become nervous or confused (*he flusters easily*). **2** bustle. *–n.* confused or agitated state. [origin unknown]

flute /fluːt/ *–n.* **1 a** high-pitched woodwind instrument held sideways. **b** any similar wind instrument. **2** ornamental vertical groove in a column. *–v.* (**-ting**) **1** play, or play (a tune etc.) on, the flute. **2** speak or sing etc. in a high voice. **3** make grooves in. □ **fluting** *n.* **fluty** *adj.* (in sense 1a of *n.*). [French]

flutter *–v.* **1** flap (the wings) in flying or trying to fly. **2** fall quiveringly (*fluttered to the ground*). **3** wave or flap quickly. **4** move about restlessly. **5** (of a pulse etc.) beat feebly or irregularly. *–n.* **1** act of fluttering. **2** tremulous excitement (*caused a flutter*). **3** *slang* small bet, esp. on a horse. **4** abnormally rapid heartbeat. **5** rapid variation of pitch, esp. of recorded sound. [Old English]

fluvial /ˈfluːvɪəl/ *adj.* of or found in rivers. [Latin *fluvius* river]

flux *n.* **1** process of flowing or flowing out. **2** discharge. **3** continuous change (*state of flux*). **4** substance mixed with a metal etc. to aid fusion. [Latin *fluxus* from *fluo flux-* flow]

fly[1] /flaɪ/ *–v.* (**flies**; *past* **flew** /fluː/; *past part.* **flown** /fləʊn/) **1 a** (of an aircraft, bird, etc.) move through the air or space under control, esp. with wings. **b** travel through the air or space. **2** control the flight of or transport in (esp. an aircraft). **3 a** cause to fly or remain aloft. **b** (of a flag, hair, etc.) wave or flutter. **4** pass, move, or rise quickly. **5 a** flee; flee from. **b** *colloq.* depart hastily. **6** be driven, forced, or scattered (*sent me flying*). **7** (foll. by *at, upon*) **a** hasten or spring violently. **b** attack or criticize fiercely. *–n.* (*pl.* **-ies**) **1** (usu. in *pl.*) **a** concealing flap, esp. over a trouser-fastening. **b** this fastening. **2** flap at a tent entrance. **3** (in *pl.*) space above a stage where scenery and lighting are suspended. **4** act of flying. □ **fly high** be ambitious; prosper. **fly in the face of** disregard or disobey. **fly a kite** test opinion. **fly off the handle** *colloq.* lose one's temper. [Old English]

fly[2] /flaɪ/ *n.* (*pl.* **flies**) **1** insect with two usu. transparent wings. **2** other winged insect, e.g. a firefly. **3** disease of plants or animals caused by flies. **4** (esp. artificial) fly as bait in fishing. □ **like flies** in large numbers (usu. of people dying etc.). **no flies on (him** etc.) *colloq.* (he is) very astute. [Old English]

fly[3] /flaɪ/ *adj. slang* knowing, clever, alert. [origin unknown]

fly-away *adj.* (of hair) fine and difficult to control.

fly-blown *adj.* tainted, esp. by flies.

fly-by-night *–adj.* unreliable. *–n.* unreliable person.

flycatcher *n.* bird catching insects during short flights from a chosen perch.

flyer *n.* (also **flier**) *colloq.* **1** airman or airwoman. **2** thing that flies in a specified way (*poor flyer*). **3** fast-moving animal or vehicle. **4** ambitious or outstanding person. **5** small handbill.

fly-fish *v.* fish with a fly.

fly-half *n. Rugby* stand-off half.

flying *–adj.* **1** fluttering, waving, or hanging loose. **2** hasty, brief (*flying visit*). **3** designed for rapid movement. **4** (of an animal) leaping with winglike membranes etc. *–n.* flight, esp. in an aircraft. □ **with flying colours** with distinction.

flying boat *n.* boatlike seaplane.

flying buttress *n.* (usu. arched) buttress running from the upper part of a wall to an outer support and transmitting the thrust of the roof or vault.

flying doctor *n.* doctor who uses an aircraft to visit patients.

flying fish *n.* tropical fish with winglike fins for gliding through the air.

flying fox *n.* fruit-eating bat with a foxlike head.

flying officer *n.* RAF rank next below flight lieutenant.

flying picket *n.* mobile industrial strike picket. See PICKET *n.* 1; PICKETING.

flying saucer *n.* supposed alien spaceship.

flying squad *n.* rapidly mobile police detachment etc.

flying start *n.* **1** start (of a race etc.) in which the starting-point is crossed at full speed. **2** vigorous start (of an enterprise etc.).

fly in the ointment *n.* minor irritation or setback.

flyleaf *n.* blank leaf at the beginning or end of a book.

fly on the wall *n.* unnoticed observer.

flyover *n.* bridge carrying one road or railway over another.

fly-paper *n.* sticky treated paper for catching flies.

fly-past *n.* ceremonial flight of aircraft.

fly-post *v.* (esp. of underground-magazine publishers, record companies, etc.) fix (posters etc.) illegally on walls, empty shop windows, etc., usu. at night. [FLY[1]]

flysheet *n.* **1** canvas cover over a tent for extra protection. **2** short tract or circular. [FLY[1]]

fly-tip *v.* illegally dump (waste). □ **fly-tipper** *n.* [FLY[1]]

fly-trap *n.* plant that catches flies.

flyweight *n.* **1** weight in certain sports between light flyweight and bantamweight, in amateur boxing 48-51 kg. **2** sportsman of this weight.

flywheel *n.* heavy wheel on a revolving shaft to regulate machinery or accumulate power.

FM *abbr.* **1** field marshal. **2** frequency modulation. **3** *Computing* facilities management.

Fm *symb.* fermium.

FMCG *abbr.* = FAST-MOVING CONSUMER GOODS.

FMG *symb.* Malagasy franc.

Fmk *symb.* (also **FMk**) markka.

FMS *abbr.* **1** Fellow of the Institute of Management Studies. **2** *Computing* flexible manufacturing system.

f-number /ˈefˌnʌmbə(r)/ *n.* ratio of the focal length to the effective diameter of a camera lens. [from *f*ocal]

FNZIM *abbr.* Fellow of the New Zealand Institute of Management.

FO *abbr.* **1** *Commerce* firm offer. **2** Flying Officer. **3** formal offer (to shareholders in business mergers).

f.o. *abbr. Commerce* free overside. See EX SHIP.

f/o *abbr. Commerce* for orders.

foal *–n.* young of a horse or related animal. *–v.* give birth to (a foal). □ **in** (or **with) foal** (of a mare etc.) pregnant. [Old English]

foam *–n.* **1** mass of small bubbles formed on or in liquid by agitation, fermentation, etc. **2** froth of saliva or sweat. **3** substance resembling these, e.g. spongy rubber or plastic. *–v.* emit or run with foam; froth. □ **foam at the mouth** be very angry. □ **foamy** *adj.* (**-ier, -iest**). [Old English]

fob[1] *n.* **1** chain of a pocket-watch. **2** small pocket for a watch etc. **3** tab on a key-ring. [German]

fob[2] *v.* (**-bb-**) □ **fob off 1** (often foll. by *with* a thing) deceive into accepting something inferior. **2** (often foll. by *on* or *on to* a person) offload (an unwanted thing). [cf. obsolete *fop* dupe]

♦ **f.o.b.** *abbr.* (also **FOB**) free on board, denoting a price for goods that includes the cost of sending them to the port of shipment and loading them on to the ship or aircraft, together with insurance costs up to this point. Thereafter the transport and insurance charges have to be paid by the buyer. If the goods are to travel by rail rather than by ship, the equivalent terms are **f.o.r.** (or **FOR, free on rail**).

FOC *abbr.* (also **f.o.c.**) **1** *Commerce* free of charge. **2** free of claims.

FoC *abbr.* father of the (trade-union) chapel.

focal /ˈfəʊk(ə)l/ *adj.* of or at a focus. [Latin: related to FOCUS]

focal distance *n.* (also **focal length**) distance between the centre of a mirror or lens and its focus.

focal point *n.* **1** = FOCUS *n.* 1. **2** centre of interest or activity.

fo'c's'le var. of FORECASTLE.

focus /ˈfəʊkəs/ *–n.* (*pl.* **focuses** or **foci** /ˈfəʊsaɪ/) **1 a** point at which rays or waves meet after reflection or refraction. **b** point from which rays etc. appear to proceed. **2 a** point at which an object must be situated for a lens or mirror to give a well-defined image. **b** adjustment of the eye or a lens to give a clear image. **c** state of clear definition (*out of focus*). **3** = FOCAL POINT 2. *–v.* (**-s-** or **-ss-**) **1** bring into focus. **2** adjust the focus of (a lens or eye). **3** concentrate or be concentrated on. **4** converge or make converge to a focus. [Latin, = hearth]

♦ **focused strategy** *n.* business strategy in which organizations divest themselves of all but their core activities, using the funds raised to enhance their core skills.

FOD *abbr.* (also **f.o.d.**) free of damage.

fodder *n.* dried hay or straw etc. as animal food. [Old English]

FOE /*colloq.* fəʊ/ *abbr.* Friends of the Earth.

foe *n.* esp. *poet.* enemy. [Old English]

foetid var. of FETID.

foetus /ˈfiːtəs/ *n.* (*US* **fetus**) (*pl.* **-tuses**) unborn mammalian offspring, esp. a human embryo of eight weeks or more. □ **foetal** *adj.* [Latin *fetus* offspring]

fog *–n.* **1** thick cloud of water droplets or smoke suspended at or near the earth's surface. **2** cloudiness on a photographic negative etc. **3** uncertain or confused position or state. *–v.* (**-gg-**) **1** cover or become covered with or as with fog. **2** perplex. [perhaps a back-formation from FOGGY]

fog-bank *n.* mass of fog at sea.

fog-bound *adj.* unable to travel because of fog.

fogey var. of FOGY.

foggy *adj.* (**-ier**, **-iest**) **1** full of fog. **2** of or like fog. **3** vague, indistinct. □ **not have the foggiest** *colloq.* have no idea at all. □ **fogginess** *n.* [perhaps from *fog* long grass]

foghorn *n.* **1** horn warning ships in fog. **2** *colloq.* loud penetrating voice.

fog-lamp *n.* powerful lamp for use in fog.

fogy /ˈfəʊgɪ/ *n.* (also **fogey**) (*pl.* **-ies** or **-eys**) dull old-fashioned person (esp. *old fogy*). [origin unknown]

foible /ˈfɔɪb(ə)l/ *n.* minor weakness or idiosyncrasy. [French: related to FEEBLE]

foil[1] *v.* frustrate, baffle, defeat. [perhaps from French *fouler* trample]

foil[2] *n.* **1** metal rolled into a very thin sheet. **2** person or thing setting off another to advantage. [Latin *folium* leaf]

foil[3] *n.* light blunt fencing sword. [origin unknown]

foist *v.* (foll. by *on*) force (a thing or oneself) on to an unwilling person. [Dutch *vuisten* take in the hand]

FOL *abbr.* (in New Zealand) Federation of Labour.

fold[1] /fəʊld/ *–v.* **1 a** bend or close (a flexible thing) over upon itself. **b** (foll. by *back, over, down*) bend part of (a thing) (*fold down the flap*). **2** become or be able to be folded. **3** (foll. by *away, up*) make compact by folding. **4** (often foll. by *up*) *colloq.* collapse, cease to function. **5** enfold (esp. *fold in the arms* or *to the breast*). **6** (foll. by *about, round*) clasp (the arms). **7** (foll. by *in*) mix (an ingredient with others) gently. *–n.* **1** folding. **2** line made by folding. **3** folded part. **4** hollow among hills. **5** curvature of geological strata. □ **fold one's arms** place or entwine them across the chest. **fold one's hands** clasp them. [Old English]

fold[2] /fəʊld/ *–n.* **1** = SHEEPFOLD. **2** religious group or congregation. *–v.* enclose (sheep) in a fold. [Old English]

-fold *suffix* forming adjectives and adverbs from cardinal numbers, meaning: **1** in an amount multiplied by (*repaid tenfold*). **2** with so many parts (*threefold blessing*). [originally = 'folded in so many layers']

folder *n.* folding cover or holder for loose papers.

foliaceous /ˌfəʊlɪˈeɪʃəs/ *adj.* **1** of or like leaves. **2** laminated. [Latin: related to FOIL[2]]

foliage /ˈfəʊlɪɪdʒ/ *n.* leaves, leafage. [French *feuillage* from *feuille* leaf]

foliar /ˈfəʊlɪə(r)/ *adj.* of leaves. [as FOLIATE]

foliar feed *n.* fertilizer supplied to the leaves of plants.

foliate *–adj.* /ˈfəʊlɪət/ **1** leaflike. **2** having leaves. *–v.* /ˈfəʊlɪˌeɪt/ (**-ting**) split or beat into thin layers. □ **foliation** /-ˈeɪʃ(ə)n/ *n.* [Latin *folium* leaf]

folio /ˈfəʊlɪəʊ/ *–n.* (*pl.* **-s**) **1** leaf of paper etc., esp. numbered only on the front. **2** sheet of paper folded once making two leaves of a book. **3** book of such sheets. *–adj.* (of a book) made of folios, of the largest size. □ **in folio** made of folios. [Latin, ablative of *folium* leaf]

folk /fəʊk/ *n.* (*pl.* same or **-s**) **1** (treated as *pl.*) people in general or of a specified class (*few folk about; townsfolk*). **2** (in *pl.*) (usu. **folks**) one's parents or relatives. **3** (treated as *sing.*) a people or nation. **4** (in full **folk-music**) (treated as *sing.*) *colloq.* traditional music or modern music in this style. **5** (*attrib.*) of popular origin (*folk art*). [Old English]

folk-dance *n.* dance of popular origin.

Folkestone /fəʊkst(ə)n/ seaport and resort in SE England, in Kent; pop. (1991) 45 587. The English terminal of the Channel Tunnel is at Cheriton, near Folkestone.

folklore *n.* traditional beliefs and stories of a people; the study of these.

folk-singer *n.* singer of folk-songs.

folk-song *n.* song of popular or traditional origin or style.

folksy /ˈfəʊksɪ/ *adj.* (**-ier**, **-iest**) **1** of or like folk art, culture, etc. **2** friendly, unpretentious. □ **folksiness** *n.*

folk-tale *n.* traditional story.

folkweave *n.* rough loosely woven fabric.

follicle /ˈfɒlɪk(ə)l/ *n.* small sac or vesicle in the body, esp. one containing a hair-root. □ **follicular** /fɒˈlɪkjʊlə(r)/ *adj.* [Latin diminutive of *follis* bellows]

follow /ˈfɒləʊ/ *v.* **1** (often foll. by *after*) go or come after (a person or thing ahead). **2** go along (a road etc.). **3** come after in order or time (*dessert followed; proceed as follows*). **4** take as a guide or leader. **5** conform to. **6** practise (a trade or profession). **7** undertake (a course of study etc.). **8** understand (a speaker, argument, etc.). **9** take an interest in (current affairs etc.). **10** (foll. by *with*) provide with a sequel or successor. **11** happen after something else; ensue. **12 a** be necessarily true as a consequence. **b** (foll. by *from*) result. □ **follow on 1** continue. **2** (of a cricket team) have to bat twice in succession. **follow out** carry out (instructions etc.). **follow suit 1** play a card of the suit led. **2** conform to another's actions. **follow through 1** continue to a conclusion. **2** continue the movement of a stroke after hitting the ball. **follow up** (foll. by *with*) **1** develop, supplement. **2** investigate further. [Old English]

follower *n.* **1** supporter or devotee. **2** person who follows.

following *–prep.* after in time; as a sequel to. *–n.* supporters or devotees. *–adj.* that follows or comes after. □ **the following 1** what follows. **2** now to be given or named (*answer the following*).

follow-on *n. Cricket* instance of following on.

follow-through *n.* action of following through.

follow-up *n.* subsequent or continued action.

folly *n.* (*pl.* **-ies**) **1** foolishness. **2** foolish act, behaviour, idea, etc. **3** fanciful ornamental building created for display. [French *folie* from *fol* mad, FOOL[1]]

foment /fəˈment/ *v.* instigate or stir up (trouble, discontent, etc.). □ **fomentation** /ˌfəʊmenˈteɪʃ(ə)n/ *n.* [Latin *foveo* heat, cherish]

fond *adj.* **1** (foll. by *of*) liking. **2 a** affectionate. **b** doting. **3** (of beliefs etc.) foolishly optimistic or credulous. □ **fondly** *adv.* **fondness** *n.* [obsolete *fon* fool, be foolish]

fondant /ˈfɒnd(ə)nt/ *n.* soft sugary sweet. [French = melting: related to FUSE[1]]

fondle /ˈfɒnd(ə)l/ *v.* (**-ling**) caress. [related to FOND]

fondue /ˈfɒndjuː/ *n.* dish of melted cheese. [French, = melted: related to FUSE[1]]

font[1] *n.* receptacle in a church for baptismal water. [Latin *fons font-* fountain]

font[2] var. of FOUNT[2].

fontanelle /ˌfɒntəˈnel/ *n.* (*US* **fontanel**) membranous space in an infant's skull at the angles of the parietal bones. [Latin *fontanella* little FOUNTAIN]

Foochow see FUZHOU.

food *n.* **1 a** substance taken in to maintain life and growth. **b** solid food (*food and drink*). **2** mental stimulus (*food for thought*). [Old English]

food additive *n.* substance added to food to colour or flavour it etc.

♦ **Food and Agricultural Organization** *n.* (also **FAO**) specialized United Nations agency, with headquarters in Rome, responsible for organizing world agriculture, esp. in developing countries, to improve nutrition and avoid famine.

---

food-chain *n.* series of organisms each dependent on the next for food.

foodie /ˈfuːdɪ/ *n. colloq.* person who is fond of food; gourmet.

food poisoning *n.* illness due to bacteria etc. in food.

food processor *n.* machine for chopping and mixing food.

foodstuff *n.* substance used as food.

food value *n.* nourishing power of a food.

fool[1] *–n.* **1** rash, unwise, or stupid person. **2** *hist.* jester; clown. **3** dupe. *–v.* **1** deceive. **2** (foll. by *into* or *out of*) trick; cheat. **3** joke or tease. **4** (foll. by *about, around*) play or trifle. □ **act** (or **play) the fool** behave in a silly way. **be no** (or **nobody's) fool** be shrewd or prudent. **make a fool of** make (a person or oneself) look foolish; trick, deceive. [Latin *follis* bellows]

fool[2] *n.* dessert of fruit purée with cream or custard. [perhaps from FOOL[1]]

foolery *n.* foolish behaviour.

foolhardy *adj.* (**-ier, -iest**) rashly or foolishly bold; reckless. □ **foolhardily** *adv.* **foolhardiness** *n.*

foolish *adj.* lacking good sense or judgement; unwise. □ **foolishly** *adv.* **foolishness** *n.*

foolproof *adj.* (of a procedure, mechanism, etc.) incapable of misuse or mistake.

foolscap /ˈfuːlskæp/ *n.* large size of paper, about 330 x 200 (or 400) mm. [from a watermark of a *fool's cap*]

fool's paradise *n.* illusory happiness.

foot *–n.* (*pl.* **feet**) **1 a** part of the leg below the ankle. **b** part of a sock etc. covering this. **2 a** lowest part of a page, stairs, etc. **b** end of a bed where the feet rest. **c** part of a chair, appliance, etc. on which it rests. **3** step, pace, or tread (*fleet of foot*). **4** (*pl.* **feet** or **foot**) linear measure of 12 inches (30.48 cm). **5** metrical unit of verse forming part of a line. **6** *hist.* infantry. *–v.* **1** pay (a bill). **2** (usu. as **foot it**) go or traverse on foot. □ **feet of clay** fundamental weakness in a respected person. **have one's** (or **both) feet on the ground** be practical. **have one foot in the grave** be near death or very old. **my foot!** *int.* expressing strong contradiction. **on foot** walking. **put one's feet up** *colloq.* take a rest. **put one's foot down** *colloq.* **1** insist firmly. **2** accelerate a vehicle. **put one's foot in it** *colloq.* make a tactless blunder. **under one's feet** in the way. **under foot** on the ground. □ **footless** *adj.* [Old English]

footage *n.* **1** a length of TV or cinema film etc. **2** length in feet.

foot-and-mouth disease *n.* contagious viral disease of cattle etc.

football *n.* **1** large inflated ball of leather or plastic. **2** outdoor team game played with this. □ **footballer** *n.*

football pool *n.* (also **football pools** *pl.*) large-scale organized gambling on the results of football matches.

footbrake *n.* foot-operated brake on a vehicle.

footbridge *n.* bridge for pedestrians.

footfall *n.* sound of a footstep.

foot-fault *n.* (in tennis) placing of the foot over the baseline while serving.

foothill *n.* any of the low hills at the base of a mountain or range.

foothold *n.* **1** secure place for a foot when climbing etc. **2** secure initial position.

footing *n.* **1** foothold; secure position (*lost his footing*). **2** operational basis. **3** relative position or status (*on an equal footing*). **4** (often in *pl.*) foundations of a wall.

footle /ˈfuːt(ə)l/ *v.* (**-ling**) (usu. foll. by *about*) *colloq.* potter or fiddle about. [origin uncertain]

footlights *n.pl.* row of floor-level lights at the front of a stage.

footling /ˈfuːtlɪŋ/ *adj. colloq.* trivial, silly.

footloose *adj.* free to act as one pleases.

footman *n.* liveried servant.

footmark *n.* footprint.

footnote *n.* note printed at the foot of a page.

footpad *n. hist.* unmounted highwayman.

footpath *n.* path for pedestrians; pavement.

footplate *n.* platform for the crew in a locomotive.

footprint *n.* **1** impression left by a foot or shoe. **2** area of floor, desk space, etc. occupied by a device.

footrest *n.* stool, rail, etc. for the feet.

Footsie /ˈfʊtsɪ/ *n.* Financial Times-Stock Exchange 100 Share Index (or FT-SE 100). See FINANCIAL TIMES SHARE INDEXES. [respelling of *FT-SE*]

footsie /ˈfʊtsɪ/ *n. colloq.* amorous play with the feet.

footsore *adj.* with sore feet, esp. from walking.

footstep *n.* **1** step taken in walking. **2** sound of this. □ **follow in a person's footsteps** do as another did before.

footstool *n.* stool for resting the feet on when sitting.

footway *n.* path for pedestrians.

footwear *n.* shoes, socks, etc.

footwork *n.* use or agility of the feet in sports, dancing, etc.

fop *n.* dandy. □ **foppery** *n.* **foppish** *adj.* [perhaps from obsolete *fop* fool]

♦ **f.o.q.** *abbr.* (also **FOQ**) free on quay. See FREE ALONGSIDE SHIP.

---

for /fə(r), fɔː(r)/ *–prep.* **1** in the interest or to the benefit of; intended to go to (*these flowers are for you; did it all for my country*). **2** in defence, support, or favour of. **3** suitable or appropriate to (*a dance for beginners; not for me to say*). **4** in respect of or with reference to; regarding (*usual for ties to be worn; ready for bed*). **5** representing or in place of (*MP for Lincoln; here for my uncle*). **6** in exchange with, at the price of, corresponding to (*swapped it for a cake; give me £5 for it; bought it for £5; word for word*). **7** as a consequence of (*fined for speeding; decorated for bravery; here's £5 for your trouble*). **8 a** with a view to; in the hope or quest of; in order to get (*go for a walk; send for a doctor; did it for the money*). **b** on account of (*could not speak for laughing*). **9** to reach; towards (*left for Rome*). **10** so as to start promptly at (*meet at seven for eight*). **11** through or over (a distance or period); during (*walked for miles*). **12** as being (*for the last time; I for one refuse*). **13** in spite of; notwithstanding (*for all your fine words*). **14** considering or making due allowance in respect of (*good for a beginner*). *–conj.* because, since, seeing that. □ **be for it** *colloq.* be about to be punished etc. **for all (that)** in spite of, although. **for ever** for all time (cf. FOREVER). [Old English reduced form of FORE]

♦ **f.o.r.** *abbr.* (also **FOR**) free on rail. See F.O.B.

---

for- *prefix* forming verbs etc. meaning: **1** away, off (*forget; forgive*). **2** prohibition (*forbid*). **3** abstention or neglect (*forgo; forsake*). [Old English]

forage /ˈfɒrɪdʒ/ *–n.* **1** food for horses and cattle. **2** searching for food. *–v.* **1** search for food; rummage. **2** collect food from. **3** get by foraging. [Germanic: related to FODDER]

forage cap *n.* infantry undress cap.

forasmuch as /ˌfɒrəz'mʌtʃ/ *conj. archaic* because, since. [from *for as much*]

foray /'fɒreɪ/ *–n.* sudden attack; raid. *–v.* make a foray. [French: related to FODDER]

forbade (also **forbad**) *past* of FORBID.

forbear[1] /fɔː'beə(r)/ *v.* (*past* **forbore**; *past part.* **forborne**) *formal* abstain or desist (from) (*could not forbear (from) speaking out*; *forbore to mention it*). [Old English: related to BEAR[1]]

forbear[2] var. of FOREBEAR.

forbearance *n.* patient self-control; tolerance.

forbid /fə'bɪd/ *v.* (**forbidding**; *past* **forbade** /-'bæd/ or **forbad**; *past part.* **forbidden**) **1** (foll. by *to* + infin.) order not (*I forbid you to go*). **2** refuse to allow (a thing, or a person to have a thing). **3** refuse a person entry to. □ **God forbid!** may it not happen! [Old English: related to BID]

forbidden degrees *n.pl.* (also **prohibited degrees**) family relationship too close for marriage to be permitted.

forbidden fruit *n.* something desired esp. because not allowed.

forbidding *adj.* stern, threatening. □ **forbiddingly** *adv.*

forbore *past* of FORBEAR[1].

forborne *past part.* of FORBEAR[1].

force[1] *–n.* **1** power; strength, impetus; intense effort. **2** coercion, compulsion. **3 a** military strength. **b** organized body of soldiers, police, etc. **4 a** moral, intellectual, or legal power, influence, or validity. **b** person etc. with such power (*force for good*). **5** effect; precise significance. **6 a** influence tending to cause the motion of a body. **b** intensity of this. *–v.* (**-cing**) **1** constrain or coerce (a person) by force. **2** make a forcible entry into; break open by force. **3** drive or propel violently or against resistance. **4** make (a way) by force. **5** (foll. by *on*, *upon*) impose or press on (a person). **6** cause, produce, or attain by effort (*forced a smile*; *forced an entry*). **7** strain or increase to the utmost. **8** artificially hasten the growth of (a plant). **9** seek quick results from; accelerate (*force the pace*). □ **force a person's hand** make a person act prematurely or unwillingly. **force the issue** make an immediate decision necessary. **in force 1** valid (*laws now in force*). **2** in great strength or numbers (*attacked in force*). [Latin *fortis* strong]

force[2] *n. N.Engl.* waterfall. [Old Norse]

forced labour *n.* compulsory labour, esp. in prison.

forced landing *n.* emergency landing of an aircraft.

forced march *n.* long and vigorous march, esp. by troops.

♦ **forced sale** *n.* sale that has to take place because it has been ordered by a court or because it is necessary to raise funds to avoid bankruptcy or liquidation.

♦ **forced saving** *n.* government measure imposed on an economy with a view to increasing savings and reducing expenditure on consumer goods. It is usu. implemented by raising taxes, increasing interest rates, or raising prices.

force-feed *v.* force (esp. a prisoner) to take food.

♦ **force-feed analysis** *n.* decision-making technique that seeks to identify all the positive and negative forces impinging on a problem, often using a graphical technique.

forceful *adj.* vigorous, powerful, impressive. □ **forcefully** *adv.* **forcefulness** *n.*

force majeure /ˌfɔːs mæ'ʒɜː(r)/ *n.* **1** irresistible force. **2** unforeseeable circumstances (e.g. a strike, riot, war, act of God) excusing either party from the fulfilment of a contract, provided that the contract contains a *force majeure* clause. If one party invokes the *force majeure* clause the other may either accept that it is applicable or challenge the interpretation (and so involve an arbitration). [French]

forcemeat *n.* minced seasoned meat for stuffing or garnish. [related to FARCE]

forceps /'fɔːseps/ *n.* (*pl.* same) surgical pincers. [Latin]

forcible *adj.* done by or involving force; forceful. □ **forcibly** *adv.* [French: related to FORCE[1]]

ford *–n.* shallow place where a river or stream may be crossed by wading, in a vehicle, etc. *–v.* cross (water) at a ford. □ **fordable** *adj.* [Old English]

fore *–adj.* situated in front. *–n.* front part; bow of a ship. *–int.* (in golf) warning to a person in the path of a ball. □ **to the fore** in or into a conspicuous position. [Old English]

fore- *prefix* forming: **1** verbs meaning: **a** in front (*foreshorten*). **b** beforehand (*forewarn*). **2** nouns meaning: **a** situated in front of (*forecourt*). **b** front part of (*forehead*). **c** of or near the bow of a ship (*forecastle*). **d** preceding (*forerunner*).

fore and aft *–adv.* at bow and stern; all over the ship. *–adj.* (**fore-and-aft**) (of a sail or rigging) lengthwise.

forearm[1] /'fɔːrɑːm/ *n.* the arm from the elbow to the wrist or fingertips.

forearm[2] /fɔːr'ɑːm/ *v.* arm beforehand, prepare.

forebear /'fɔːbeə(r)/ *n.* (also **forbear**) (usu. in *pl.*) ancestor. [from FORE, obsolete *beer*: related to BE]

forebode /fɔː'bəʊd/ *v.* (**-ding**) **1** be an advance sign of, portend. **2** (often foll. by *that*) have a presentiment of (usu. evil).

foreboding *n.* expectation of trouble.

forecast *–v.* (*past* and *past part.* **-cast** or **-casted**) predict; estimate beforehand. *–n.* prediction, esp. of weather. □ **forecaster** *n.*

forecastle /'fəʊks(ə)l/ *n.* (also **fo'c's'le**) forward part of a ship, formerly the living quarters.

foreclose /fɔː'kləʊz/ *v.* (**-sing**) **1** *Law* **a** stop (a mortgage) from being redeemable. **b** repossess the mortgaged property of (a person) when a loan is not duly repaid. See FORECLOSURE. **2** exclude, prevent. [Latin *foris* out, CLOSE[2]]

♦ **foreclosure** *n.* legal right of a lender of money if the borrower fails to repay the money or part of it on the due date. The lender must apply to a court to be permitted to sell the property that has been held as security for the debt. The court will order a new date for payment in an order called a **foreclosure nisi**. If the borrower again fails to pay, the lender may sell the property. This procedure can occur when a person fails to pay mortgage instalments, in which the security is the house in which the person lives. The mortgagee (building society, bank, etc.) then forecloses the mortgage, dispossessing the mortgager.

forecourt *n.* **1** part of a filling-station with petrol pumps. **2** enclosed space in front of a building.

forefather *n.* (usu. in *pl.*) ancestor of a family or people.

forefinger *n.* finger next to the thumb.

forefoot *n.* front foot of an animal.

forefront *n.* **1** leading position. **2** foremost part.

forego var. of FORGO.

foregoing /fɔː'gəʊɪŋ/ *adj.* preceding; previously mentioned.

foregone conclusion /'fɔːgɒn/ *n.* easily predictable result.

foreground *n.* **1** part of a view or picture nearest the observer. **2** most conspicuous position. [Dutch: related to FORE-, GROUND[1]]

foreground processing *n.* processing of a computer program that has been granted a high priority and can thus pre-empt the resources (main store, processor, etc.) of the computer from programs with a low priority.

forehand *n.* **1** (in tennis etc.) stroke played with the palm of the hand facing forward. **2** (*attrib.*) (also **forehanded**) of or made with a forehand.

forehead /ˈfɒrɪd/ *n.* the part of the face above the eyebrows.

foreign /ˈfɒrən/ *adj.* **1** of, from, in, or characteristic of, a country or language other than one's own. **2** dealing with other countries (*foreign service*). **3** of another district, society, etc. **4** (often foll. by *to*) unfamiliar, alien. **5** coming from outside (*foreign body*). □ **foreignness** *n.* [Latin *foris* outside]

Foreign and Commonwealth Office *n.* (also **FCO**) British government department dealing with foreign affairs.

♦ **foreign bill** see INLAND BILL.

---

foreigner *n.* person born in or coming from another country.

♦ **foreign exchange** *n.* currencies of foreign countries, bought and sold in foreign-exchange markets. Firms or organizations require foreign exchange to purchase goods from abroad or for purposes of investment or speculation.

♦ **foreign-exchange broker** *n.* broker who specializes in arranging deals in foreign currencies on the foreign-exchange markets, usu. between commercial banks and governments. Foreign-exchange brokers do not normally deal direct with the public or with firms who require foreign currencies for buying goods abroad (who buy from commercial banks). They earn their living from the brokerage paid on each deal.

♦ **foreign-exchange dealer** *n.* person who buys and sells foreign exchange on a foreign-exchange market, usu. as an employee of a commercial bank. Banks charge fees or commissions for buying and selling foreign exchange on behalf of their customers; dealers may also be authorized to speculate in forward exchange rates.

♦ **foreign-exchange market** *n.* international market in which foreign currencies are traded. It consists primarily of foreign-exchange dealers employed by commercial banks (acting as principals) and foreign-exchange brokers (acting as intermediaries). Although tight exchange controls have been abandoned by many governments, including the UK government, the market is not entirely free in that the market is to some extent manipulated by the Bank of England on behalf of the government, usu. by means of the exchange equalization account. Currency dealing has a spot currency market for delivery of foreign exchange immediately and a forward-exchange market in which transactions are made for foreign currencies to be delivered at agreed dates in the future. This enables dealers, and their customers who require foreign exchange in the future, to hedge their purchases and sales. Options on future exchange rates can also be traded in London through the London International Financial Futures and Options Exchange.

♦ **foreign investment** *n.* investment in the domestic economy by foreign individuals or companies, either direct investment in productive enterprises or investment in financial instruments, e.g. a portfolio of shares. Although increasingly important in the economy of the modern world, it frequently arouses antagonism both in the countries receiving foreign investment and in countries whose nationals invest overseas.

---

foreign legion *n.* body of foreign volunteers in the (esp. French) army.

foreign minister *n.* (also **foreign secretary**) government minister in charge of foreign affairs.

Foreign Office *n. hist.* or *informal* = FOREIGN AND COMMONWEALTH OFFICE.

♦ **foreign sector** *n.* part of a country's economy that is concerned with external trade (imports and exports) and capital flows (inward and outward).

♦ **foreign trade multiplier** *n.* effect that an increase in home demand has on a country's foreign trade. The primary effect is to increase that country's imports of raw materials. A secondary effect may be an increase in exports because the increased home demand enables manufacturers to be more competitive and also because the countries supplying the increased quantities of imports have more foreign exchange available to increase their imports.

♦ **foreign trade zone** see FREE PORT 1.

---

foreknow /fɔːˈnəʊ/ *v.* (*past* **-knew**, *past part.* **-known**) *literary* know beforehand. □ **foreknowledge** /fɔːˈnɒlɪdʒ/ *n.*

foreland *n.* cape, promontory.

foreleg *n.* front leg of an animal.

forelimb *n.* front limb of an animal.

forelock *n.* lock of hair just above the forehead. □ **touch one's forelock** defer to a person of higher social rank.

foreman *n.* **1** worker supervising others. **2** president and spokesman of a jury.

foremast *n.* mast nearest the bow of a ship.

foremost *–adj.* **1** most notable, best. **2** first, front. *–adv.* most importantly (*first and foremost*). [Old English]

forename *n.* first or Christian name.

forenoon *n.* morning.

forensic /fəˈrensɪk/ *adj.* **1** of or used in courts of law (*forensic science*; *forensic medicine*). **2** of or involving forensic science (*sent for forensic examination*).□ **forensically** *adv.* [Latin *forensis*: related to FORUM]

■ **Usage** Use of *forensic* in sense 2 is common but considered an illogical extension of sense 1 by some people.

foreordain /ˌfɔːrɔːˈdeɪn/ *v.* destine beforehand.

forepaw *n.* front paw of an animal.

foreplay *n.* stimulation preceding sexual intercourse.

forerunner *n.* **1** predecessor. **2** herald.

foresail /ˈfɔːseɪl/ *n.* principal sail on a foremast.

foresee /fɔːˈsiː/ *v.* (*past* **-saw**; *past part.* **-seen**) see or be aware of beforehand. □ **foreseeable** *adj.*

foreshadow /fɔːˈʃædəʊ/ *v.* be a warning or indication of (a future event).

foreshore *n.* shore between high- and low-water marks.

foreshorten /fɔːˈʃɔːt(ə)n/ *v.* show or portray (an object) with the apparent shortening due to visual perspective.

foresight *n.* **1** regard or provision for the future. **2** foreseeing. **3** front sight of a gun.

foreskin *n.* fold of skin covering the end of the penis.

forest *–n.* **1** (often *attrib.*) large area of trees and undergrowth. **2** trees in this. **3** large number or dense mass. *–v.* **1** plant with trees. **2** convert into a forest. [Latin *forestis*: related to FOREIGN]

forestall /fɔːˈstɔːl/ *v.* **1** prevent by advance action. **2** deal with beforehand. [from FORE-, STALL[1]]

forester *n.* **1** person managing a forest or skilled in forestry. **2** dweller in a forest.

forestry *n.* science or management of forests.

foretaste *n.* small preliminary experience of something.

foretell /fɔːˈtel/ *v.* (*past* and *past part.* **-told**) **1** predict, prophesy. **2** indicate the approach of.

forethought *n.* **1** care or provision for the future. **2** deliberate intention.

forever /fəˈrevə(r)/ *adv.* continually, persistently (*is forever complaining*) (cf. *for ever*).

forewarn /fɔːˈwɔːn/ *v.* warn beforehand.

forewoman *n.* **1** female worker with supervisory responsibilities. **2** president and spokeswoman of a jury.

foreword *n.* introductory remarks at the beginning of a book, often not by the author.

♦ **forfaiting** /ˈfɔːˌfeɪtɪŋ/ *n.* form of debt discounting for exporters in which a forfaiter accepts at a discount, and without recourse, a promissory note, bill of exchange, letter of credit, etc. received from a foreign buyer by an exporter. Maturities are normally from one to three years. Thus the exporter receives payment without risk at the cost of the discount. □ **forfaiter** *n.* [French *forfaire* FORFEIT]

---

forfeit /ˈfɔːfɪt/ *–n.* **1** penalty. **2** thing surrendered as a penalty. *–adj.* lost or surrendered as a penalty. *–v.* (**-t-**) lose the right to, surrender as a penalty. □ **forfeiture** *n.*

[French *forfaire* transgress, from Latin *foris* outside, *facio* do]

◆ **forfeited share** *n.* partly paid share in a company that the shareholder has to forfeit because of failure to pay a subsequent part- or final payment.

forgather /fɔːˈgæðə(r)/ *v.* assemble; associate. [Dutch]

forgave *past* of FORGIVE.

forge[1] –*v.* (**-ging**) **1** make or write in fraudulent imitation. **2** shape (metal) by heating and hammering. –*n.* **1** furnace or workshop etc. for melting or refining metal. **2** blacksmith's workshop; smithy. □ **forger** *n.* [Latin *fabrica*: related to FABRIC]

forge[2] *v.* (**-ging**) move forward gradually or steadily. □ **forge ahead 1** take the lead. **2** progress rapidly. [perhaps an alteration of FORCE[1]]

forgery /ˈfɔːdʒərɪ/ *n.* (*pl.* **-ies**) **1** act of forging. **2** *Law* offence of making a false instrument in order that it may be accepted as genuine, thereby causing harm to others. Under the Forgery and Counterfeiting Act (1981), an instrument may be a document or any device (e.g. magnetic tape) on which information is recorded. An instrument is considered false, for example, if it purports to have been made or altered by someone who did not do so, on a date or at a place when it was not, or by someone who does not exist. It is also an offence to copy or use a false instrument knowing it to be false or to make or possess any material meant to be used to produce such specified false instruments as money, cheques, share certificates, cheque cards, credit cards, passports, or registration certificates. **3** forged document etc.

forget /fəˈget/ *v.* (**forgetting**; *past* **forgot**; *past part.* **forgotten** or *US* **forgot**) **1** (often foll. by *about*) lose remembrance of; not remember. **2** neglect or overlook. **3** cease to think of. □ **forget oneself 1** act without dignity. **2** act selflessly. □ **forgettable** *adj.* [Old English]

forgetful *adj.* **1** apt to forget, absent-minded. **2** (often foll. by *of*) neglectful. □ **forgetfully** *adj.* **forgetfulness** *n.*

forget-me-not *n.* plant with small blue flowers.

forgive /fəˈgɪv/ *v.* (**-ving**; *past* **forgave**; *past part.* **forgiven**) **1** cease to feel angry or resentful towards; pardon. **2** remit (a debt). □ **forgivable** *adj.* [Old English]

forgiveness *n.* forgiving or being forgiven.

forgiving *adj.* inclined to forgive.

forgo /fɔːˈgəʊ/ *v.* (also **forego**) (**-goes**; *past* **-went**; *past part.* **-gone**) go without; relinquish. [Old English]

forgot *past* of FORGET.

forgotten *past part.* of FORGET.

forint /ˈfɒrɪnt/ *n.* standard monetary unit of Hungary. [Magyar from Italian *fiorino* FLORIN]

fork –*n.* **1** pronged item of cutlery. **2** similar large tool used for digging, lifting, etc. **3** forked support for a bicycle wheel. **4 a** divergence of a branch, road, etc. into two parts. **b** place of this. **c** either part. –*v.* **1** form a fork or branch by separating into two parts. **2** take one road at a fork. **3** dig, lift, etc., with a fork. □ **fork out** *slang* pay, esp. reluctantly. [Latin *furca* pitchfork]

fork-lift truck *n.* vehicle with a fork for lifting and carrying loads.

forlorn /fəˈlɔːn/ *adj.* **1** sad and abandoned. **2** in a pitiful state. □ **forlornly** *adv.* [*lorn* = past part. of obsolete *leese* LOSE]

forlorn hope *n.* faint remaining hope or chance. [Dutch *verloren hoop* lost troop]

form –*n.* **1** shape; arrangement of parts; visible aspect. **2** person or animal as visible or tangible. **3** mode of existence or manifestation. **4** kind or variety (*a form of art*). **5 a** printed document with blank spaces for information to be inserted. **b** page of computer-printer paper. **6** class in a school. **7** customary method. **8** set order of words. **9** etiquette or specified adherence to it (*good or bad form*). **10** (prec. by *the*) correct procedure (*knows the form*). **11 a** (of an athlete, horse, etc.) condition of health and training. **b** racing history of a horse etc. **12** state or disposition (*in great form*). **13** any of the spellings, inflections, etc. of a word. **14** arrangement and style in a literary or musical composition. **15** long low bench. **16** hare's lair. –*v.* **1** make or be made (*formed a straight line*; *puddles formed*). **2** make up or constitute. **3** develop or establish as a concept, institution, or practice (*form an idea*; *form a habit*). **4** (foll. by *into*) mould or organize to become (*formed ourselves into a circle*). **5** (often foll. by *up*) (of troops etc.) bring or move into formation. **6** train or instruct. □ **off form** not playing or performing well. **on form** playing or performing well. **out of form** not fit for racing etc. [Latin *forma*]

-form *comb. form* (usu. as **-iform**) forming adjectives meaning: **1** having the form of (*cruciform*). **2** having so many forms (*multiform*).

formal /ˈfɔːm(ə)l/ *adj.* **1** in accordance with rules, convention, or ceremony (*formal dress*; *formal occasion*). **2** precise or symmetrical (*formal garden*). **3** prim or stiff. **4** perfunctory, in form only. **5** drawn up etc. correctly; explicit (*formal agreement*). **6** of or concerned with (outward) form, not content or matter. □ **formally** *adv.* [Latin: related to FORM]

formaldehyde /fɔːˈmældɪˌhaɪd/ *n.* colourless pungent gas used as a disinfectant and preservative. [from FORMIC ACID, ALDEHYDE]

formalin /ˈfɔːməlɪn/ *n.* solution of formaldehyde in water.

formalism *n.* strict adherence to external form without regard to content, esp. in art. □ **formalist** *n.*

formality /fɔːˈmælɪtɪ/ *n.* (*pl.* **-ies**) **1 a** formal, esp. meaningless, act, regulation, or custom. **b** thing done simply to comply with a rule. **2** rigid observance of rules or convention.

formalize *v.* (also **-ise**) (**-zing** or **-sing**) **1** give definite (esp. legal) form to. **2** make formal. □ **formalization** /-ˈzeɪʃ(ə)n/ *n.*

format /ˈfɔːmæt/ –*n.* **1** shape and size (of a book, etc.). **2** style or manner of procedure etc. **3** *Computing* structure used in the arrangement of data, determined before use and in some cases set by industrial or international standards. **Printer format** defines the layout on paper of the output from a printer, e.g. the areas of a page where printing will occur and the spacing between words and between lines. **Tape format** and **disk format** define the arrangements in which data can be recorded on magnetic tape or disk. –*v.* (**-tt-**) **1** arrange or put into a format. **2** *Computing* **a** prepare (a storage medium) to receive data, e.g. divide (a magnetic disk) into sectors. **b** put (data) into a predetermined structure. [Latin *formatus* shaped: related to FORM]

formation /fɔːˈmeɪʃ(ə)n/ *n.* **1** forming. See also COMPANY FORMATION. **2** thing formed. **3** particular arrangement (e.g. of troops). **4** rocks or strata with a common characteristic. [Latin: related to FORM]

formative /ˈfɔːmətɪv/ *adj.* serving to form or fashion; of formation (*formative years*).

forme *n.* *Printing* body of type secured in a chase ready for printing. [var. of FORM]

former *attrib. adj.* **1** of the past, earlier, previous (*in former times*). **2** (**the former**) (often *absol.*) the first or first-mentioned of two. [related to FOREMOST]

-former *comb. form* pupil in a specified form (*fourth-former*).

formerly *adv.* in former times.

Formica /fɔːˈmaɪkə/ *n. propr.* hard durable plastic laminate used for surfaces. [origin uncertain]

formic acid /ˈfɔːmɪk/ *n.* colourless irritant volatile acid contained in fluid emitted by ants; methanoic acid. [Latin *formica* ant]

formidable /ˈfɔːmɪdəb(ə)l, fɔːˈmɪd-/ *adj.* **1** inspiring dread, awe, or respect. **2** hard to overcome or deal with. □ **formidably** *adv.* [Latin *formido* fear]

■ **Usage** The second pronunciation given, with the stress on the second syllable, is common but considered incorrect by some people.

formless *adj.* without definite or regular form. □ **formlessness** *n.*

Formosa /fɔːˈməʊsə/ see TAIWAN.

formula /ˈfɔːmjʊlə/ *n.* (*pl.* **-s** or (esp. in senses 1, 2) **-lae** /-ˌliː/) **1** chemical symbols showing the constituents of a substance. **2** mathematical rule expressed in symbols. **3 a** fixed form of esp. ceremonial or polite words. **b** words used to formulate a treaty etc. **4 a** list of ingredients. **b** *US* infant's food. **5** classification of a racing car, esp. by engine capacity. □ **formulaic** /-ˈleɪɪk/ *adj.* [Latin, diminutive of *forma* FORM]

formulary /ˈfɔːmjʊlərɪ/ *n.* (*pl.* **-ies**) **1** collection of esp. religious formulas or set forms. **2** *Pharm.* compendium of drug formulae. [French or medieval Latin: related to FORMULA]

formulate /ˈfɔːmjʊˌleɪt/ *v.* (**-ting**) **1** express in a formula. **2** express clearly and precisely. □ **formulation** /-ˈleɪʃ(ə)n/ *n.*

fornicate /ˈfɔːnɪˌkeɪt/ *v.* (**-ting**) *archaic* or *joc.* (of people not married to each other) have sexual intercourse. □ **fornication** /-ˈkeɪʃ(ə)n/ *n.* **fornicator** *n.* [Latin *fornix* brothel]

forsake /fɔːˈseɪk/ *v.* (**-king**; *past* **forsook** /-ˈsʊk/; *past part.* **forsaken**) *literary* **1** give up; renounce. **2** desert, abandon. [Old English]

forsooth /fəˈsuːθ/ *adv. archaic* or *joc.* truly; no doubt. [Old English: related to FOR, SOOTH]

forswear /fɔːˈsweə(r)/ *v.* (*past* **forswore**; *past part.* **forsworn**) **1** abjure; renounce. **2** (as **forsworn** *adj.*) perjured. □ **forswear oneself** perjure oneself. [Old English]

forsythia /fɔːˈsaɪθɪə/ *n.* shrub with bright yellow flowers in early spring. [*Forsyth*, name of a botanist]

fort *n.* fortified military building or position. [Latin *fortis* strong]

Fort-de-France /ˌfɔːdəˈfrɑ̃s/ capital and chief port of Martinique; exports include bananas and rum; pop. (1990) 100 080.

♦ **Forte** /ˈfɔːtɪ/, **Charles, Baron Forte** (1908–) British mass caterer and hotel-owner, born in Italy. He began his catering chain in 1935 with a £2000 loan and in 1970 merged it with the Trust House Group, which had been formed in 1903 to restore the standards of Britain's old coaching inns. The joint company was known as Trusthouse Forte until 1991, when it reverted to the name Forte. Lord Forte was chairman (1982–92), then president (1992–96). His son, **Hon. Sir Rocco (John Vincent) Forte** (1945–), succeeded him as chief executive in (1983–92) and chairman (1992–96); Rocco Forte is now chief executive officer (since 1993) of Forte plc and is a member of the chairman's committee of the Savoy Group (since 1994). The Fortes own a wide variety of hotels and restaurants throughout the world.

forte[1] /ˈfɔːteɪ/ *n.* person's strong point or speciality. [feminine of French FORT]

forte[2] /ˈfɔːteɪ/ *Mus. –adj.* loud. *–adv.* loudly. *–n.* loud playing or passage. [Italian: related to FORT]

forth *adv. archaic* except in set phrases **1** forward; into view (*bring forth*; *come forth*). **2** onwards in time (*from this time forth*). **3** forwards (*back and forth*). **4** out from a starting-point (*set forth*). □ **and so forth** see SO[1]. [Old English]

forthcoming /fɔːθˈkʌmɪŋ, ˈfɔːθ-/ *adj.* **1** coming or available soon. **2** produced when wanted. **3** (of a person) informative, responsive.

forthright *adj.* **1** outspoken; straightforward. **2** decisive. [Old English]

forthwith /fɔːθˈwɪθ/ *adv.* at once; without delay. [from FORTH]

fortification /ˌfɔːtɪfɪˈkeɪʃ(ə)n/ *n.* **1** act of fortifying. **2** (usu. in *pl.*) defensive works, walls, etc.

fortify /ˈfɔːtɪˌfaɪ/ *v.* (**-ies, -ied**) **1** provide with fortifications. **2** strengthen physically, mentally, or morally. **3** strengthen (wine) with alcohol. **4** increase the nutritive value of (food, esp. with vitamins). [Latin *fortis* strong]

fortissimo /fɔːˈtɪsɪˌməʊ/ *Mus. –adj.* very loud. *–adv.* very loudly. *–n.* (*pl.* **-s** or **-mi** /-ˌmiː/) very loud playing or passage. [Italian, superlative of FORTE[2]]

fortitude /ˈfɔːtɪˌtjuːd/ *n.* courage in pain or adversity. [Latin *fortis* strong]

Fort Knox /nɒks/ US military reservation in Kentucky, famous as the site of the US Depository (built in 1936) which holds the bulk of the nation's gold bullion in its vaults; pop. (est. 1989) 38 277.

Fort Lamy /læˈmiː/ see N'DJAMENA.

fortnight *n.* two weeks. [Old English, = *fourteen nights*]

fortnightly *–adj.* done, produced, or occurring once a fortnight. *–adv.* every fortnight. *–n.* (*pl.* **-ies**) fortnightly magazine etc.

Fortran /ˈfɔːtræn/ *n.* (also **FORTRAN**) computer language widely used for scientific and technical applications. First released by IBM in the mid-1950s, it has been under continuous development with each new release having more sophisticated features. [from *formula translation*]

fortress /ˈfɔːtrɪs/ *n.* fortified building or town. [Latin *fortis* strong]

fortuitous /fɔːˈtjuːɪtəs/ *adj.* happening by esp. lucky chance; accidental. □ **fortuitously** *adv.* **fortuitousness** *n.* **fortuity** *n.* (*pl.* **-ies**). [Latin *forte* by chance]

fortunate /ˈfɔːtʃənət/ *adj.* **1** lucky. **2** auspicious. □ **fortunately** *adv.* [Latin *fortunatus*: related to FORTUNE]

fortune /ˈfɔːtʃ(ə)n, -tʃuːn/ *n.* **1 a** chance or luck in human affairs. **b** person's destiny. **2** (in *sing.* or *pl.*) luck that befalls a person or enterprise. **3** good luck. **4** prosperity. **5** *colloq.* great wealth. □ **make a** (or **one's**) **fortune** become very rich. [Latin *fortuna*]

fortune-teller *n.* person who claims to foretell one's destiny. □ **fortune-telling** *n.*

Fort Worth /wɜːθ/ oil-refining city in the US, in N Texas; other industries include aircraft manufacture; pop. (est. 1994) 451 814.

forty /ˈfɔːtɪ/ *adj.* & *n.* (*pl.* **-ies**) **1** four times ten. **2** symbol for this (40, xl, XL). **3** (in *pl.*) numbers from 40 to 49, esp. the years of a century or of a person's life. □ **fortieth** *adj.* & *n.* [Old English: related to FOUR]

forty winks *n. colloq.* short sleep.

forum /ˈfɔːrəm/ *n.* **1** place of or meeting for public discussion. **2** court or tribunal. **3** *hist.* public square in an ancient Roman city used for judicial and other business. [Latin]

forward /ˈfɔːwəd/ *–adj.* **1** onward; towards the front. **2** lying in the direction in which one is moving. **3** precocious; bold; presumptuous. **4** relating to the future (*forward contract*). **5 a** approaching maturity or completion. **b** (of a plant etc.) early. *–n.* attacking player near the front in football, hockey, etc. *–adv.* **1** to the front; into prominence (*come forward*; *move forward*). **2** in advance; ahead (*sent them forward*). **3** onward so as to make progress (*no further forward*). **4** towards the future (*from this time forward*). **5** (also **forwards**) **a** towards the front in the direction one is facing. **b** in the normal direction of motion. **c** with continuous forward motion (*rushing forward*). *–v.* **1 a** send (a letter etc.) on to a further destination. **b** dispatch (goods etc.). **2** help to advance; promote. [Old English: related to FORTH, -WARD]

♦ **forwardation** /ˌfɔːwəˈdeɪʃ(ə)n/ *n.* situation in a commodity market in which spot goods can be bought more cheaply than goods for forward delivery, enabling a dealer to buy spot goods and carry them forward to deliver them against a forward contract. Cf. BACKWARDATION 1.

♦ **forward-dated** *adj.* post-dated.

♦ **forward dealing** *n.* dealing in commodities, securities, currencies, freight, etc. for delivery at some future date at a price agreed at the time the contract (called a **forward contract**) is made. This form of trading enables dealers and manufacturers to cover their future requirements by hedging their more immediate purchases. See FUTURES CONTRACT.

♦ **forward delivery** *n.* contracted delivery of goods at some time in the future. Commodities may be sold for forward delivery up to one year or more ahead, often involving shipment from their port of origin. Cf. SPOT GOODS.

♦ **forward-exchange contract** *n.* agreement to purchase foreign exchange at a specified date in the future at an agreed exchange rate. In international trade, with floating rates of exchange, the **forward-exchange market** provides an important way of eliminating risk on future transactions that will require foreign exchange. The buyer on the forward market gains by the certainty such a contract can bring; the seller, by buying and selling exchanges for future delivery, makes a market and earns a living partly from the profit made by selling at a higher price than the buying price and partly by speculation. There is also an active option market in forward foreign-exchange rates. See FOREIGN-EXCHANGE MARKET.

♦ **forwarding agent** see SHIPPING AND FORWARDING AGENT.

♦ **forward integration** see INTEGRATION 3.

♦ **forward price** *n.* fixed price at which a given amount of a commodity, currency, or financial instrument is to be delivered on a fixed date in the future.

f.o.s. *abbr. Commerce* **1** free on ship (or steamer). **2** free on station.

FOSDIC *Computing* film optical sensing device.

fosse /fɒs/ *n.* long ditch or trench, esp. in a fortification. [Latin *fossa*]

fossil /ˈfɒs(ə)l/ –*n.* **1** remains or impression of a (usu. prehistoric) plant or animal hardened in rock. **2** *colloq.* antiquated or unchanging person or thing. –*attrib. adj.* of or like a fossil; antiquated. □ **fossilize** *v.* (also **-ise**) (**-zing** or **-sing**). **fossilization** /-ˈzeɪʃ(ə)n/ *n.* [Latin *fodio foss-* dig]

fossil fuel *n.* natural fuel extracted from the ground.

foster –*v.* **1 a** promote the growth or development of. **b** encourage or harbour (a feeling). **2 a** bring up (another's child). **b** (of a local authority etc.) assign (a child) to be fostered. **3** (of circumstances) be favourable to. –*attrib. adj.* **1** having a family connection by fostering (*foster-brother; foster-parent*). **2** concerned with fostering a child (*foster care; foster home*). [Old English: related to FOOD]

f.o.t. *abbr.* (also **FOT**) *Commerce* **1** free of tax. **2** free on truck(s).

fought *past* and *past part.* of FIGHT.

foul –*adj.* **1** offensive; loathsome, stinking. **2** soiled, filthy. **3** *colloq.* disgusting, awful. **4 a** noxious (*foul air*). **b** clogged, choked. **5** obscenely abusive (*foul language*). **6** unfair; against the rules (*by fair means or foul*). **7** (of the weather) rough, stormy. **8** (of a rope etc.) entangled. –*n.* **1** *Sport* foul stroke or play. **2** collision, entanglement. –*adv.* unfairly. –*v.* **1** make or become foul. **2** (of an animal) foul with excrement. **3** *Sport* commit a foul against (a player). **4** (often foll. by *up*) **a** (cause to) become entangled or blocked. **b** bungle. **5** collide with. □ **foully** *adv.* **foulness** *n.* [Old English]

♦ **foul bill of lading** *n.* = DIRTY BILL OF LADING.

foul-mouthed *adj.* using obscene or offensive language.

foul play *n.* **1** unfair play in games. **2** treacherous or violent act, esp. murder.

foul-up *n.* muddle, bungle.

found[1] *past* and *past part.* of FIND.

found[2] *v.* **1** establish (an institution etc.); initiate, originate. **2** be the original builder of (a town etc.). **3** lay the base of (a building). **4** (foll. by *on, upon*) construct or base (a story, theory, rule, etc.) on. □ **founder** *n.* [Latin *fundus* bottom]

found[3] *v.* **1 a** melt and mould (metal). **b** fuse (materials for glass). **2** make by founding. □ **founder** *n.* [Latin *fundo fus-* pour]

foundation /faʊnˈdeɪʃ(ə)n/ *n.* **1 a** solid ground or base beneath a building. **b** (usu. in *pl.*) lowest part of a building, usu. below ground level. **2** material base. **3** basis, underlying principle. **4 a** establishing (esp. an endowed institution). **b** college, hospital, etc. so founded; its revenues. **5** (in full **foundation garment**) woman's supporting undergarment, e.g. a corset. [Latin: related to FOUND[2]]

foundation-stone *n.* **1** stone laid ceremonially at the founding of a building. **2** basis.

founder *v.* **1** (of a ship) fill with water and sink. **2** (of a plan etc.) fail. **3** (of a horse or its rider) stumble, fall lame, stick in mud etc. [related to FOUND[2]]

♦ **founders' shares** *n.pl.* shares issued to the founders of a company, who often have special rights to dividends. See also DEFERRED ORDINARY SHARE 1.

founding father *n.* American statesman at the time of the Revolution.

foundling /ˈfaʊndlɪŋ/ *n.* abandoned infant of unknown parentage. [related to FIND]

foundry /ˈfaʊndrɪ/ *n.* (*pl.* **-ies**) workshop for or business of casting metal.

fount[1] *n. poet.* spring or fountain; source. [back-formation from FOUNTAIN]

fount[2] /fɒnt/ *n.* (also **font**) set of printing-type of same face and size. [French: related to FOUND[3]]

fountain /ˈfaʊntɪn/ *n.* **1 a** spouting jet or jets of water as an ornament or for drinking. **b** structure for this. **2** spring. **3** (often foll. by *of*) source. [Latin *fontana* from *fons font-* spring]

fountain-head *n.* source.

fountain-pen *n.* pen with a reservoir or cartridge for ink.

four /fɔː(r)/ *adj.* & *n.* **1** one more than three. **2** symbol for this (4, iv, IV). **3** size etc. denoted by four. **4** team or crew of four; four-oared rowing-boat. **5** four o'clock. □ **on all fours** on hands and knees. [Old English]

fourfold *adj.* & *adv.* **1** four times as much or as many. **2** of four parts.

four-in-hand *n.* four-horse carriage with one driver.

four-letter word *n.* short obscene word.

♦ **four-plus cover** *n.* advertising campaign in which a particular advertisement is exposed to the public at least four times, four exposures being thought the most likely to persuade a person to buy a particular product.

four-poster *n.* bed with four posts supporting a canopy.

foursome *n.* **1** group of four people. **2** golf match between two pairs.

four-square –*adj.* **1** solidly based. **2** steady, resolute. –*adv.* steadily, resolutely.

four-stroke *adj.* (of an internal-combustion engine) having a cycle of four strokes of the piston with the cylinder firing once.

fourteen /fɔːˈtiːn/ *adj.* & *n.* **1** one more than thirteen. **2** symbol for this (14, xiv, XIV). **3** size etc. denoted by fourteen. □ **fourteenth** *adj.* & *n.* [Old English: related to FOUR, -TEEN]

fourth *adj.* & *n.* **1** next after third. **2** any of four equal parts of a thing. □ **fourthly** *adv.* [Old English: related to FOUR]

fourth estate *n.* the press.

four-wheel drive *n.* drive acting on all four wheels of a vehicle.

f.o.w. *abbr. Commerce* **1** first open water. **2** free on wagon.

fowl –*n.* (*pl.* same or **-s**) **1** chicken kept for eggs and meat. **2** poultry as food. **3** *archaic* (except in *comb.*) bird (*guineafowl; wildfowl*). –*v.* catch or hunt wildfowl. [Old English]

FOX /fɒks/ *abbr.* Futures and Options Exchange. See LONDON FOX.

fox –*n.* **1 a** wild canine animal with a bushy tail and red or grey fur. **b** its fur. **2** cunning person. –*v.* **1** deceive, baffle, trick. **2** (usu. as **foxed** *adj.*) discolour (leaves of a book etc.) with brownish marks. □ **foxlike** *adj.* [Old English]

foxglove *n.* tall plant with purple or white flowers like glove-fingers.

foxhole *n.* hole in the ground used as a shelter etc. in battle.

foxhound *n.* a kind of hound bred and trained to hunt foxes.

fox-hunting *n.* hunting foxes with hounds.

fox-terrier *n.* a kind of short-haired terrier.

foxtrot –*n.* **1** ballroom dance with slow and quick steps. **2** music for this. –*v.* **(-tt-)** perform this.

foxy *adj.* **(-ier, -iest) 1** foxlike. **2** sly or cunning. **3** reddish-brown. □ **foxily** *adv.* **foxiness** *n.*

foyer /'fɔɪeɪ/ *n.* entrance-hall in a hotel, theatre, etc. [French, = hearth, home, from Latin FOCUS]

FP *abbr.* **1** *Insurance* fire policy. **2** *Insurance* floating policy. **3** (also **f.p.**) (of shares) fully paid.

FPA *abbr.* **1** Family Planning Association. **2** *Computing* floating-point accelerator. **3** *Insurance* free of particular average (see AVERAGE *n.* 4).

FPLA *abbr. Computing* field-programmable logic array.

FPMI *abbr.* Fellow of the Pensions Management Institute.

FR –*abbr.* **1** (in the US) Federal Reserve (System). **2** freight release. –*international vehicle registration* Faeroe Islands. –*airline flight code* Ryanair.

Fr *symb.* francium.

Fr. *abbr.* **1** Father. **2** France. **3** French. **4** Friday.

fr. *abbr.* franc(s).

FRA *abbr. Finance* forward rate agreement.

fracas /'frækɑː/ *n.* (*pl.* same /-kɑːz/) noisy disturbance or quarrel. [French from Italian]

fraction /'frækʃ(ə)n/ *n.* **1** part of a whole number (e.g. $^1/_2$, 0.5). **2** small part, piece, or amount. **3** portion of a mixture obtained by distillation etc. □ **fractional** *adj.* **fractionally** *adv.* [Latin *frango fract-* break]

◆ **fractional banking** *n.* banking practice that some governments impose on their banks, calling for a fixed fraction between cash reserves and total liabilities.

fractious /'frækʃəs/ *adj.* irritable, peevish. [from FRACTION in obsolete sense 'brawling']

fracture /'fræktʃə(r)/ –*n.* breakage, esp. of a bone or cartilage. –*v.* **(-ring)** cause a fracture in; suffer fracture. [Latin: related to FRACTION]

fragile /'frædʒaɪl/ *adj.* **1** easily broken; weak. **2** delicate; not strong. □ **fragility** /frə'dʒɪlɪtɪ/ *n.* [Latin: related to FRACTURE]

fragment –*n.* /'frægmənt/ **1** part broken off. **2** extant remains or unfinished portion (of a book etc.). –*v.* /fræg'ment/ break or separate into fragments. □ **fragmental** /-'ment(ə)l/ *adj.* **fragmentary** /'frægməntərɪ/ *adj.* **fragmentation** /-'teɪʃ(ə)n/ *n.* [Latin: related to FRACTION]

fragrance /'freɪgrəns/ *n.* **1** sweetness of smell. **2** sweet scent. [Latin *fragro* smell sweet]

fragrant *adj.* sweet-smelling.

frail *adj.* **1** fragile, delicate. **2** morally weak. □ **frailly** *adv.* **frailness** *n.* [Latin: related to FRAGILE]

frailty *n.* (*pl.* **-ies**) **1** frail quality. **2** weakness, foible.

frame –*n.* **1** case or border enclosing a picture, window, door, etc. **2** basic rigid supporting structure of a building, vehicle, etc. **3** (in *pl.*) structure of spectacles holding the lenses. **4** human or animal body, esp. as large or small. **5 a** established order or system (*the frame of society*). **b** construction, build, structure. **6** temporary state (esp. in **frame of mind**). **7** single complete image on a cinema film or transmitted in a series of lines by television. **8 a** triangular structure for positioning balls in snooker etc. **b** round of play in snooker etc. **9** *Hort.* box-like structure of glass etc. for protecting plants. **10** *US slang* = FRAME-UP. –*v.* **(-ming) 1 a** set in a frame. **b** serve as a frame for. **2** construct, put together, devise. **3** (foll. by *to, into*) adapt or fit. **4** *slang* concoct a false charge or evidence against; devise a plot against. **5** articulate (words). [Old English, = be helpful]

frame of reference *n.* **1** set of standards or principles governing behaviour, thought, etc. **2** system of geometrical axes for defining position.

frame-up *n. slang* conspiracy to convict an innocent person.

framework *n.* **1** essential supporting structure. **2** basic system.

franc *n.* **1** (also **F**) standard monetary unit of France and French dependencies, Andorra, and Monaco. **2** (also **BF**) standard monetary unit of Belgium. **3** (also **SwF**) standard monetary unit of Switzerland and Liechtenstein. **4** (also **LF**) standard monetary unit of Luxembourg. **5** (also **FBu**) standard monetary unit of Burundi. **6** (also **CF**) standard monetary unit of Comoros. **7** (also **DF**) standard monetary unit of Djibouti. **8** (also **GF**) standard monetary unit of Guinea. **9** (also **FMG**) standard monetary unit of Madagascar. **10** (also **RF**) standard monetary unit of Rwanda. **11** (also **CFAF**) see CFA FRANC. [French: related to FRANK]

Franche-Comté /ˌfrɑ̃ʃkɒn'teɪ/ region of E France; pop. (est. 1994) 1 111 219; capital, Besançon. Dairy farming, cattle rearing, and forestry are important.

franchise /'fræntʃaɪz/ –*n.* **1** right to vote in state elections. **2** full membership of a corporation or state; citizenship. **3** licence given to a manufacturer, distributor, trader, etc. to enable them to manufacture or sell a named product or service in a particular area for a stated period. The holder of the licence (**franchisee**) usu. pays the grantor of the licence (**franchisor**) a royalty on sales, often with a lump sum as an advance against royalties. The franchisor may also supply the franchisee with finance and technical expertise. **4** right or privilege granted to a person or corporation. **5** clause in an insurance policy, often a marine-insurance policy, that

---

France /frɑːns/, **Republic of** country in W Europe, with coastlines on the Atlantic Ocean, the English Channel, and the Mediterranean Sea. Although it is an industrial country agriculture remains important; animal products, cereals, and fruit are produced and many regions are famous for their wines. Industrial activity is diversified, major industries including oil refining, iron and steel, mechanical and electrical engineering, and food processing; manufactures include machinery, motor vehicles, aircraft, textiles, and chemicals. Mineral resources of iron ore, potash, bauxite, coal, and sulphur are exploited. Natural gas is produced but hydroelectricity is a significant power supply. The economy has maintained modest growth, with a low rate of inflation, but unemployment has remained high for most of the 1990s.

History. France emerged as a permanently unified state at the end of the Middle Ages and briefly dominated Europe under Napoleon at the beginning of the 19th century. Defeated in the Franco-Prussian war (1870–1), severely handled in the First World War, and occupied by the Germans in the Second, France revived in the postwar era as a major European power; the country was a founder member of the EC (now EU). The Conservative Jacques Chirac was elected in 1996 but the Socialists were successful in parliamentary elections in 1997. President, Jacques Chirac; prime minister, Lionel Jospin; capital, Paris.

language	French
currency	franc (F) of 100 centimes
pop. (1996)	58 392 000
GNP (1994)	US$1317B
literacy	99%
life expectancy	73 (m); 81 (f)

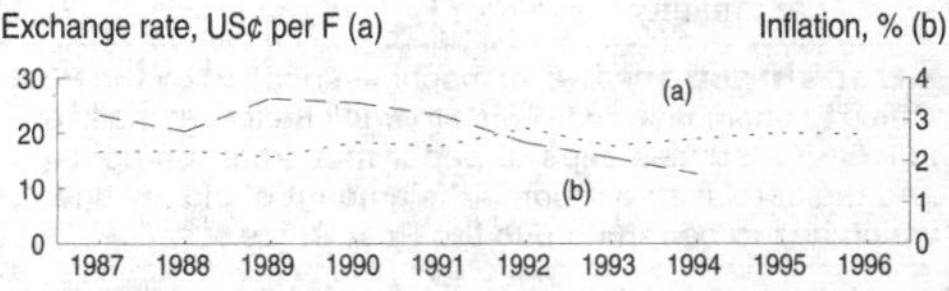

excludes the payment of claims up to a specified level but agrees to pay in full all claims above it. Insurers thus avoid administratively expensive small claims. –*v.* (**-sing**) grant a franchise to. [French *franc* FRANK]

Franciscan /fræn'sɪskən/ –*adj.* of St Francis or his order. –*n.* Franciscan friar or nun. [Latin *Franciscus* Francis]

francium /'frænkɪəm/ *n.* radioactive metallic element. [FRANCE, the discoverer's country]

◆ **franco** /'fræŋkəʊ/ *adj.* (of goods) delivered free of all transport and insurance charges to the buyer's warehouse, even when this is in a foreign country, the seller paying these charges. [Italian, = free]

Franco- *comb. form* French and (*Franco-German*). [Latin: related to FRANK]

f.r. & c.c. *abbr. Insurance* free of riot and civil commotions.

franglais /'frɑ̃gleɪ/ *n.* corrupt version of French using many English words and idioms. [French *français* French, *anglais* English]

Frank *n.* member of the Germanic people that conquered Gaul in the 6th century. □ **Frankish** *adj.* [Old English]

frank –*adj.* **1** candid, outspoken. **2** undisguised. **3** open. –*v.* mark (a letter) to record the payment of postage. See also FRANKING MACHINE. –*n.* franking signature or mark. □ **frankly** *adv.* **frankness** *n.* [Latin *francus* free: related to FRANK]

◆ **franked investment income** *n.* dividends and other distributions from UK companies that are received by other companies. The principle of the imputation system of taxation is that once one company has paid corporation tax, any dividends it pays can pass through any number of other companies without carrying a further corporation-tax charge. Thus franked investment is exempt from corporation tax in the recipient company; moreover, the amount of tax credit included in the franked investment income can reduce the amount of advance corporation tax that the recipient company has to pay on its own dividends.

◆ **franked payment** *n.* dividend or other distribution from a UK company together with the amount of advance corporation tax (ACT) attributable to the dividend. Thus, if the basic rate of income tax is 30%, a franked payment is the dividend actually paid plus three-sevenths of it, i.e. it is a grossed-up dividend. In any accounting period ACT is actually paid on franked payments less franked investment income at the basic rate of income tax.

Frankenstein /'fræŋkən,staɪn/ *n.* (in full **Frankenstein's monster**) thing that becomes terrifying to its maker. [*Frankenstein*, name of a character in and title of a novel by Mary Shelley]

Frankfort /'fræŋkfɜːt/ city in the US, capital of Kentucky; whiskey distilling is the main industry; pop. (1990) 25 968.

Frankfurt /'fræŋkfɜːt/ (in full **Frankfurt am Main** /æm 'maɪn/) commercial city and financial centre in W Germany; pop. (est. 1995) 652 412. It is the site of the headquarters of the Bundesbank and of an annual international book fair; manufactures include machinery, chemicals, and pharmaceuticals.

frankfurter /'fræŋk,fɜːtə(r)/ *n.* seasoned smoked sausage. [German from FRANKFURT]

frankincense /'fræŋkɪn,sens/ *n.* aromatic gum resin burnt as incense. [French: related to FRANK in obsolete sense 'high quality', INCENSE[1]]

◆ **franking machine** *n.* machine supplied by the Post Office to businesses who wish to frank their own mail. The machine produces slips of paper that state the postage and the date. It also records the amount of money spent, which has to be remitted to the Post Office.

frantic /'fræntɪk/ *adj.* **1** wildly excited; frenzied. **2** hurried, anxious; desperate, violent. **3** *colloq.* extreme. □ **frantically** *adv.* [Latin: related to FRENETIC]

frappé /'fræpeɪ/ *adj.* iced, cooled. [French]

fraternal /frə'tɜːn(ə)l/ *adj.* **1** of brothers, brotherly. **2** (of twins) developed from separate ova and not necessarily similar. □ **fraternally** *adv.* [Latin *frater* brother]

fraternity /frə'tɜːnɪtɪ/ *n.* (*pl.* **-ies**) **1** religious brotherhood. **2** group with common interests, or of the same professional class. **3** *US* male students' society. **4** brotherliness. [Latin: related to FRATERNAL]

fraternize /'frætə,naɪz/ *v.* (also **-ise**) (**-zing** or **-sing**) (often foll. by *with*) **1** associate; make friends. **2** enter into friendly relations with enemies etc. □ **fraternization** /-'zeɪʃ(ə)n/ *n.* [French and Latin: related to FRATERNAL]

fratricide /'frætrɪ,saɪd/ *n.* **1** killing of one's brother or sister. **2** person who does this. □ **fratricidal** /-'saɪd(ə)l/ *adj.* [Latin *frater* brother]

Frau /fraʊ/ *n.* (*pl.* **Frauen** /'fraʊən/) (often as a title) married or widowed German-speaking woman. [German]

fraud /frɔːd/ *n.* **1** criminal deception; false representation by means of a statement or conduct, in order to gain a material advantage. A contract obtained by fraud is voidable on the grounds of fraudulent misrepresentation. If a person uses fraud to induce someone to part with money, this may amount to theft. **2** dishonest artifice or trick. **3** person or thing that is not what it claims to be. [Latin *fraus fraud-*]

fraudulent /'frɔːdjʊlənt/ *adj.* of, involving, or guilty of fraud. □ **fraudulence** *n.* **fraudulently** *adv.* [Latin: related to FRAUD]

◆ **fraudulent conveyance** *n.* transfer of property to another person for the purposes of putting it beyond the reach of creditors. The transaction may be set aside by the court under the provisions of the Insolvency Act (1986).

◆ **fraudulent preference** *n.* paying money to a creditor of a company, or otherwise improving a creditor's position, at a time when the company is unable to pay its debts. If this occurs because of an act of the company within six months of winding-up (or two years if the preference is given to a person connected with the company), an application to the court may be made to cancel the transaction. The court may make any order that it thinks fit, but no order may prejudice the rights of a third party who has acquired property for value without notice of the preference.

◆ **fraudulent trading** *n.* carrying on of the business of a company with intent to defraud creditors or for any other fraudulent purpose. This includes accepting money from customers when the company is unable to pay its debts and cannot meet its obligations under the contract. The liquidator of a company may apply to the court for an order against any person who has been a party to fraudulent trading to make such contributions to the assets of the company as the court thinks fit. Thus an officer of the company may be made personally liable for some of its debts. 'Fraudulent' in this context implies actual dishonesty or real moral blame; this definition has limited the usefulness of the remedy as fraud is notoriously difficult to prove. See WRONGFUL TRADING.

fraught /frɔːt/ *adj.* **1** (foll. by *with*) filled or charged with (danger etc.). **2** *colloq.* distressing; tense. [Dutch *vracht* FREIGHT]

Fräulein /'frɔɪlaɪn/ *n.* (often as a title or form of address) unmarried German-speaking woman. [German]

fray[1] *v.* **1** wear through or become worn; esp. (of woven material) unravel at the edge. **2** (of nerves, temper, etc.) become strained. [Latin *frico* rub]

fray[2] *n.* **1** conflict, fight. **2** brawl. [related to AFFRAY]

Fray Bentos /fraɪ 'bentɒs/ port and meat-packing centre in W Uruguay, on the Uruguay River; pop. (1985) 20 091.

frazzle /'fræz(ə)l/ *colloq.* –*n.* worn, exhausted, or shrivelled state (*burnt to a frazzle*). –*v.* (**-ling**) (usu. as **frazzled** *adj.*) wear out; exhaust. [origin uncertain]

FRB *abbr.* (in the US) **1** Federal Reserve Bank. **2** Federal Reserve Board. See FEDERAL RESERVE SYSTEM.

♦ **FRC** *abbr.* = FINANCIAL REPORTING COUNCIL.

FRCD *abbr.* floating-rate certificate of deposit.
freak –*n.* **1** (often *attrib.*) monstrosity; abnormal person or thing (*freak storm*). **2** *colloq.* **a** unconventional person. **b** fanatic of a specified kind (*health freak*). **c** drug addict. –*v.* (often foll. by *out*) *colloq.* **1** become or make very angry. **2** (cause to) undergo hallucinations etc., esp. as a result of drug abuse. **3** adopt an unconventional lifestyle. □ **freakish** *adj.* **freaky** *adj.* (**-ier, -iest**). [probably from dial.]
freckle /'frek(ə)l/ –*n.* small light brown spot on the skin. –*v.* (**-ling**) (usu. as **freckled** *adj.*) spot or be spotted with freckles. □ **freckly** *adj.* [Old Norse]
F.R.Econ.S. *abbr.* Fellow of the Royal Economic Society.
Fredericton /'fredərɪkt(ə)n/ city in Canada, capital of New Brunswick; industries include plastics and tourism; pop. (1991) 45 364.
free –*adj.* (**freer** /'friːə(r)/; **freest** /'friːɪst/) **1** not a slave or under another's control; having personal rights and social and political liberty. **2** (of a state, its citizens, etc.) autonomous; democratic. **3 a** unrestricted; not confined or fixed. **b** not imprisoned. **c** released from duties etc. **d** independent (*free agent*). **4** (foll. by *of, from*) **a** exempt from (tax etc.). **b** not containing or subject to (*free of preservatives; free from disease*). **5** (foll. by *to* + infin.) permitted; at liberty to. **6** costing nothing. **7** *Commerce* (of a price for goods) including delivery and insurance costs up to a specified point. See F.O.B.; FREE ALONGSIDE SHIP; FREE DOCKS; FREE IN AND OUT. **8 a** clear of duties etc. (*am free tomorrow*). **b** not in use (*bathroom is free*). **9** spontaneous, unforced (*free offer*). **10** available to all. **11** lavish (*free with their money*). **12** frank, unreserved. **13** (of literary style) informal, unmetrical. **14** (of translation) not literal. **15** familiar, impudent. **16** (of stories etc.) slightly indecent. **17** *Chem.* not combined (*free oxygen*). **18** (of power or energy) disengaged, available. –*adv.* **1** freely. **2** without cost or payment. –*v.* (**frees, freed**) **1** make free; liberate. **2** (foll. by *of, from*) relieve from. **3** disentangle, clear. □ **for free** *colloq.* free of charge, gratis. □ **freely** *adv.* [Old English]
-free *comb. form* free of or from (*fancy-free; duty-free*).

♦ **free alongside ship** *adj.* (also **f.a.s.**) (of a price for goods) including the cost of sending the goods to the port of shipment, together with all insurance up to this point and any lighterage required, but excluding the cost of loading them onto the ship. This may be the same as **free on quay** (or **f.o.q.**) and **free alongside quay** (or **f.a.q.**) as long as the ship can reach the dock. If it is unable to, the buyer has to pay for lighterage.

free and easy *adj.* informal, relaxed.
freebie /'friːbɪ/ *n. colloq.* thing given free of charge.
freeboard *n.* part of a ship's side between the water-line and deck.
freebooter *n.* pirate. [Dutch *vrijbuiter*: related to FREE, BOOTY]
free-born *adj.* not born a slave.

♦ **free capital** *n.* capital in the form of cash. See also LIQUID ASSETS.

Free Church *n.* Nonconformist Church.

♦ **free competition** *n.* (also **free economy**) economy in which the market forces of supply and demand control prices, incomes, etc. without government interference. In such an economy private enterprise is dominant, the public sector being very small.
♦ **free depreciation** *n.* method of granting tax relief to organizations by allowing them to charge the cost of fixed assets against taxable profits in whatever proportions and over whatever period they choose. This gives businesses considerable flexibility, enabling them to choose the best method of depreciation depending on their anticipated cash flow, profit estimates, and taxation expectations.

freedman *n.* emancipated slave.

♦ **free docks** *adj.* (of a price for goods) including the cost of delivering the goods to the shipping dock, but not of loading and shipping them.

freedom /'friːdəm/ *n.* **1** condition of being free or unrestricted. **2** personal or civic liberty. **3** liberty of action (*freedom to leave*). **4** (foll. by *from*) exemption from. **5** (foll. by *of*) **a** honorary membership or citizenship (*freedom of the city*). **b** unrestricted use of (a house etc.). [Old English]
freedom fighter *n.* terrorist or rebel claiming to fight for freedom.

♦ **free economy** *n.* = FREE COMPETITION.

free enterprise *n.* = PRIVATE ENTERPRISE.
free fall *n.* movement under the force of gravity only.
free fight *n.* general fight in which all present join.
freefone *n.* (also **Freefone, -phone**) system provided by British Telecom whereby certain telephone calls, esp. on business, can be made without cost to the caller.
free-for-all *n.* free fight, unrestricted discussion, etc.
free-form *attrib. adj.* of irregular shape or structure.

♦ **free good** *Econ.* see GOOD *n.* 3.

freehand –*adj.* (of a drawing etc.) done without special instruments. –*adv.* in a freehand manner.
free hand *n.* freedom to act at one's own discretion.
free-handed *adj.* generous.
freehold –*n.* **1** complete ownership of property for an unlimited period. See also FEE SIMPLE. **2** such land or property. –*adj.* owned thus. Cf. LEASEHOLD. □ **freeholder** *n.*
free house *n.* public house not controlled by a brewery.

♦ **free in and out** *adj.* denoting a selling price that includes all costs of loading goods (into a container, road vehicle, ship, etc.) and unloading them (out of the transport).
♦ **free issue** *n.* = SCRIP ISSUE.

free kick *n.* kick granted in football as a minor penalty.
freelance –*n.* **1** (also **freelancer**) person, usu. self-employed, working for several employers on particular assignments. **2** (*attrib.*) (*freelance editor*). –*v.* (**-cing**) act as a freelance. –*adv.* as a freelance. [*free lance*, a medieval mercenary]

♦ **free list** *n.* list, issued by the Customs and Excise, of the goods that can be imported into the UK without paying duty.

freeloader *n. slang* sponger. □ **freeload** /-'ləʊd/ *v.*
free love *n.* sexual freedom.

♦ **free lunch** *n. colloq.* nonexistent benefit; an apparently free benefit for which someone, somewhere, always pays.

freeman *n.* **1** person who has the freedom of a city etc. **2** person who is not a slave or serf.

♦ **free market** *n.* **1** market that is free from government interference, prices rising and falling in accordance with supply and demand. **2** security that is widely traded on a stock exchange, there being sufficient stock on offer for the price to be uninfluenced by availability. **3** foreign-exchange market that is free from pegging of rates by governments, rates being free to rise and fall in accordance with supply and demand.

Freemason /'friːˌmeɪs(ə)n/ *n.* member of an international fraternity for mutual help, having elaborate secret rituals. □ **Freemasonry** *n.*

freephone var. of FREEFONE.

♦ **free of all averages** *adj.* (also **f.a.a.**) denoting a marine insurance that covers only a total loss, general average and particular average losses being excluded (see AVERAGE *n.* 4).

♦ **free of capture** *adj.* denoting a marine insurance (usu. taken out in wartime) in which capture, seizure, and mutiny are excluded.

♦ **free of particular average** (also **FPA**) see AVERAGE *n.* 4.

♦ **free on board** see F.O.B.

♦ **free on board and trimmed** *adj.* denoting an f.o.b. contract in the coal trade in which the seller is responsible for delivering the coal to the ship, paying for it to be loaded, and ensuring that it is correctly stowed. See F.O.B.

♦ **free on quay** see FREE ALONGSIDE SHIP.

♦ **free on rail** see F.O.B.

♦ **free overside** *adj.* (also **free overboard**) = EX SHIP.

♦ **free port** *n.* **1** port, such as Bremerhaven, Gdansk, Rotterdam, or Singapore, that is free of customs duties. The area around the port, known as a **foreign trade zone** or **free zone**, specializes in entrepôt trade, as goods can be landed and warehoused before re-export without the payment of customs duties. **2** port open to all traders.

freepost *n.* system of business post provided by the Post Office where postage is paid by the addressee, usu. an advertiser.

free radical *n. Chem.* atom or group of atoms with one or more unpaired electrons.

free-range *adj.* **1** (of hens etc.) roaming freely; not kept in a battery. **2** (of eggs) produced by such hens.

♦ **freesheet** *n.* local newspaper or magazine published and distributed without charge and entirely dependent upon advertising revenue.

freesia /ˈfriːzjə/ *n.* African bulb with fragrant flowers. [*Freese*, name of a physician]

free speech *n.* right of expression.

free spirit *n.* independent or uninhibited person.

free-spoken *adj.* forthright.

free-standing *adj.* not supported by another structure.

freestyle *n.* **1** swimming race in which any stroke may be used. **2** wrestling allowing almost any hold.

freethinker /friːˈθɪŋkə(r)/ *n.* person who rejects dogma or authority, esp. in religious belief. □ **freethinking** *n.* & *adj.*

Freetown /ˈfriːtaʊn/ capital and chief port of Sierra Leone; industries include fish processing, plastics, and oil refining; pop. (est. 1990) 669 000.

♦ **free trade** *n.* flow of goods and services across national frontiers without the interference of laws, tariffs, quotas, or other restrictions. Most economists believe that free trade is economically beneficial (see also COMPARATIVE ADVANTAGE); under the auspices of GATT, trade barriers have continuously, if slowly, fallen.

free vote *n.* parliamentary vote not subject to party discipline.

freeway *n. US* motorway.

free wheel *n.* driving wheel of a bicycle, able to revolve with the pedals at rest.

free-wheel *v.* **1** ride a bicycle with the pedals at rest. **2** act without constraint.

free will *n.* **1** power of acting independently of necessity or fate. **2** ability to act without coercion (*did it of my own free will*).

free world *n. hist.* non-Communist countries' collective name for themselves.

freeze –*v.* (**-zing**; *past* **froze**; *past part.* **frozen**) **1 a** turn into ice or another solid by cold. **b** make or become rigid from the cold. **2** be or feel very cold. **3** cover or become covered with ice. **4** (foll. by *to*, *together*) adhere by frost. **5** refrigerate (food) below freezing-point. **6 a** make or become motionless through fear, surprise, etc. **b** (as **frozen** *adj*) devoid of emotion (*frozen smile*). **7** make (assets etc.) unrealizable. **8** fix (prices, wages, etc.) at a certain level. **9** stop (the movement in a film). –*n.* **1** period or state of frost. **2** fixing or stabilization of prices, wages, etc. **3** (in full **freeze-frame**) still film-shot. □ **freeze up** obstruct or be obstructed by ice. [Old English]

freeze-dry *v.* preserve (food) by freezing and then drying in a vacuum.

♦ **freeze-out** *n.* pressure applied to minority shareholders of a company that has been taken over to sell their stock to the new owners.

freezer *n.* refrigerated cabinet etc. for preserving frozen food at very low temperatures.

freeze-up *n.* period or state of extreme cold.

freezing-point *n.* temperature at which a liquid, esp. water, freezes.

♦ **free zone** see FREE PORT 1.

♦ **freight** /freɪt/ –*n.* **1** transport of goods by sea (**sea freight**) or air (**air freight**), or (*US*) by land. **2** goods so transported; cargo, load. **3** charge for the transport of goods, based on their weight (see DEAD-WEIGHT CARGO) or the volume they occupy, described as **weight or measurement**. Certain cargoes are charged on an ad valorem basis, expressed as a percentage of the f.o.b. value. Freight is normally paid when the goods are delivered for shipment but in some cases it is paid at the destination (**freight forward**). –*v.* transport as or load with freight. [Low German or Dutch *vrecht*]

freighter *n.* **1** ship or aircraft for carrying freight. **2** *US* freight-wagon.

♦ **freight forward** see FREIGHT *n.* 3.

♦ **freight insurance** *n.* form of marine or aviation insurance in which a consignor or a consignee covers loss of sums paid in freight for the transport of goods.

♦ **freight note** *n.* invoice from a shipowner to a shipper showing the amount of freight due on a shipment of goods.

♦ **freight release** *n.* endorsement on a bill of lading made by a shipowner or his agent, stating that freight has been paid and the goods may be released on arrival. Sometimes the freight release is a separate document providing the same authority.

Fremantle /ˈfriːmænt(ə)l/ major port in Western Australia; industries include shipbuilding and iron founding; pop. (est. 1994) 23 834.

French –*adj.* **1** of France, its people, or language. **2** having French characteristics. –*n.* **1** the French language. **2** (**the French**) (*pl.*) the people of France. **3** *colloq.* dry vermouth. □ **Frenchness** *n.* [Old English: related to FRANK]

French bean *n.* kidney or haricot bean as unripe sliced pods or ripe seeds.

French bread *n.* long crisp loaf.

French Canadian *n.* Canadian whose principal language is French.

French chalk *n.* a kind of talc used for marking cloth, as a dry lubricant, etc.

French dressing *n.* salad dressing of seasoned vinegar and oil.

French fried potatoes *n.pl.* (also **French fries**) *US* potato chips.

French Guiana /gɪˈɑːnə/ overseas department of France, in N South America; exports include timber and sugar; pop. (1990) 114 808; capital, Cayenne.

French horn *n.* coiled brass wind instrument with a wide bell.

Frenchify /ˈfrentʃɪˌfaɪ/ *v.* (**-ies**, **-ied**) (usu. as **Frenchified** *adj.*) *colloq.* make French in form, manners, etc.

French kiss *n.* open-mouthed kiss.

French leave *n.* absence without permission.

French letter *n. colloq.* condom.

Frenchman *n.* man of French birth or nationality.

French polish *n.* shellac polish for wood. □ **French-polish** *v.*

French Polynesia overseas territory of France in the S Pacific, comprising five groups of islands (Society, Tuamotu, Gambier, Tubuai, and Marquesas); pop. (est. 1994) 216 600; capital, Papeete (on Tahiti). Tourism is the major industry, and pearls, copra, coffee, and vanilla are exported.

French window *n.* glazed door in an outside wall.

Frenchwoman *n.* woman of French birth or nationality.

frenetic /frə'netɪk/ *adj.* (also **phrenetic**) **1** frantic, frenzied. **2** fanatic. □ **frenetically** *adv.* [Greek *phrēn* mind]

frenzy /'frenzɪ/ *–n.* (*pl.* **-ies**) wild or delirious excitement, agitation, or fury. *–v.* (**-ies, -ied**) (usu. as **frenzied** *adj.*) drive to frenzy. □ **frenziedly** *adv.* [medieval Latin: related to FRENETIC]

frequency /'friːkwənsɪ/ *n.* (*pl.* **-ies**) **1** commonness of occurrence. **2** frequent occurrence. **3** rate of recurrence (of a vibration etc.); number of repetitions in a given time, esp. per second. **4** *Advertising* number of times an average person in a target audience is to be exposed to an advertising message within a specified period. [related to FREQUENT]

frequency division multiplexing (also **FDM**) see MULTIPLEXER.

frequency modulation *n. Electronics* modulation by varying carrier-wave frequency.

frequent *–adj.* /'friːkwənt/ **1** occurring often or in close succession. **2** habitual, constant. *–v.* /frɪ'kwent/ attend or go to habitually. □ **frequently** /'friːkwəntlɪ/ *adv.* [Latin *frequens -ent-* crowded]

frequentative /frɪ'kwentətɪv/ *Gram. –adj.* (of a verb etc.) expressing frequent repetition or intensity. *–n.* frequentative verb etc.

FRES *abbr.* Federation of Recruitment and Employment Services.

fresco /'freskəʊ/ *n.* (*pl.* **-s**) painting done in water-colour on a wall or ceiling before the plaster is dry. [Italian, = fresh]

fresh *–adj.* **1** newly made or obtained. **2 a** other, different; new (*start a fresh page; fresh ideas*). **b** additional (*fresh supplies*). **3** (foll. by *from*) lately arrived. **4** not stale, musty, or faded. **5** (of food) not preserved; newly caught, grown, etc. **6** not salty (*fresh water*). **7 a** pure, untainted, refreshing (*fresh air*). **b** bright and pure in colour (*fresh complexion*). **8** (of wind) brisk. **9** *colloq.* cheeky; amorously impudent. **10** inexperienced. *–adv.* newly, recently (esp. in *comb.*: *fresh-baked*). □ **freshly** *adv.* **freshness** *n.* [Old English *fersc* and French *freis*]

freshen *v.* **1** make or become fresh. **2** (foll. by *up*) **a** wash, tidy oneself, etc. **b** revive.

fresher *n. colloq.* first-year student at university or (*US*) high school.

freshet /'freʃɪt/ *n.* **1** rush of fresh water flowing into the sea. **2** flood of a river.

freshman *n.* = FRESHER.

freshwater *attrib. adj.* (of fish etc.) not of the sea.

fret[1] *–v.* (**-tt-**) **1** be worried or distressed. **2** worry, vex. **3** wear or consume by gnawing or rubbing. *–n.* worry, vexation. [Old English: related to FOR, EAT]

fret[2] *–n.* ornamental pattern of straight lines joined usu. at right angles. *–v.* (**-tt-**) embellish with a fret or with carved or embossed work. [French *freter*]

fret[3] *n.* each of a series of bars or ridges on the fingerboard of a guitar etc. to guide fingering. [origin unknown]

fretful *adj.* anxious, irritable. □ **fretfully** *adv.*

fretsaw *n.* narrow saw on a frame for cutting thin wood in patterns.

fretwork *n.* ornamental work in wood done with a fretsaw.

Freudian /'frɔɪdɪən/ *–adj.* of Freud, his theories, or his method of psychoanalysis. *–n.* follower of Freud.

Freudian slip *n.* unintentional verbal error revealing subconscious feelings.

FRG *abbr.* Federal Republic of Germany.

Fri. *abbr.* Friday.

friable /'fraɪəb(ə)l/ *adj.* easily crumbled. □ **friability** /-'bɪlɪtɪ/ *n.* [Latin *frio* crumble]

friar /'fraɪə(r)/ *n.* member of a male non-enclosed Roman Catholic order, e.g. Carmelites and Franciscans. [Latin *frater* brother]

friar's balsam *n.* tincture of benzoin etc. used esp. as an inhalant.

friary /'fraɪərɪ/ *n.* (*pl.* **-ies**) monastery for friars.

fricassee /'frɪkə,seɪ/ *–n.* pieces of meat served in a thick sauce. *–v.* (**fricassees, fricasseed**) make a fricassee of. [French]

fricative /'frɪkətɪv/ *–adj.* (of a consonant) sounded by friction of the breath in a narrow opening. *–n.* such a consonant (e.g. *f, th*). [Latin *frico* rub]

FRICS *abbr.* Fellow of the Royal Institution of Chartered Surveyors.

friction /'frɪkʃ(ə)n/ *n.* **1** rubbing of one object against another. **2** the resistance encountered in so moving. **3** clash of wills, opinions, etc. □ **frictional** *adj.* [Latin: related to FRICATIVE]

◆ **frictional unemployment** *n.* amount of unemployment consistent with the efficient operation of the economy, equivalent to the natural rate of unemployment. Frictional unemployment exists because of lags between workers leaving one job and taking up another and because there are times of the year when many new workers (e.g. school-leavers) enter the labour market; in these circumstances there is some delay in finding them all jobs. See also NATURAL RATE OF UNEMPLOYMENT.

Friday /'fraɪdeɪ/ *–n.* day of the week following Thursday. *–adv. colloq.* **1** on Friday. **2** (**Fridays**) on Fridays; each Friday. [Old English]

fridge *n. colloq.* = REFRIGERATOR. [abbreviation]

fridge-freezer *n.* combined refrigerator and freezer.

friend /frend/ *n.* **1** person one likes and chooses to spend time with (usu. without sexual or family bonds). **2** sympathizer, helper. **3** ally or neutral person (*friend or foe?*). **4** person already mentioned (*our friend at the bank*). **5** regular supporter of an institution. **6** (**Friend**) Quaker. [Old English]

friendly *–adj.* (**-ier, -iest**) **1** outgoing, well-disposed, kindly. **2 a** (often foll. by *with*) on amicable terms. **b** not hostile. **3** (in *comb.*) not harming; helping (*ozone-friendly; user-friendly*). **4** = USER-FRIENDLY. *–n.* (*pl.* **-ies**) = FRIENDLY MATCH. *–adv.* in a friendly manner. □ **friendliness** *n.*

Friendly Islands see TONGA.

friendly match *n.* match played for enjoyment rather than competition.

◆ **Friendly Society** *n.* non-profit-making association insuring against illness etc. Dating back to the 17th century, Friendly Societies were widespread in the 19th and early 20th centuries, but many closed in 1946 after the introduction of National Insurance. Some developed into trade unions and some large insurance companies are still registered as Friendly Societies. The Friendly Society Act (1992) extended the services permitted to the societies and established a commission to regulate them. This commission, in consultation with the Treasury, has made further recommendations regarding their regulation.

---

friendship *n.* friendly relationship or feeling.

frier var. of FRYER.

Friesian /'friːzɪən/ *n.* one of a breed of black and white dairy cattle orig. from Friesland. [var. of FRISIAN]

Friesland /'friːzlənd/ province in N Netherlands; pop.

(est. 1995) 609 579; capital, Leeuwarden. Cattle raising and dairy farming are the main occupations.

frieze /friːz/ *n.* **1** part of an entablature between the architrave and cornice. **2** horizontal band of sculpture filling this. **3** band of decoration, esp. at the top of a wall. [Latin *Phrygium* (*opus*) Phrygian (work)]

frig *v.* (**-gg-**) *coarse slang* **1** = FUCK *v.* **2** masturbate. [perhaps imitative]

frigate /ˈfrɪɡɪt/ *n.* **1** naval escort-vessel. **2** *hist.* warship. [French from Italian]

fright /fraɪt/ *n.* **1 a** sudden or extreme fear. **b** instance of this (*gave me a fright*). **2** grotesque-looking person or thing. □ **take fright** become frightened. [Old English]

frighten *v.* **1** fill with fright (*the bang frightened me*; *frightened of dogs*). **2** (foll. by *away*, *off*, *out of*, *into*) drive by fright. □ **frightening** *adj.* **frighteningly** *adv.*

frightful *adj.* **1 a** dreadful, shocking. **b** ugly. **2** *colloq.* extremely bad. **3** *colloq.* extreme (*frightful rush*). □ **frightfully** *adv.*

frigid /ˈfrɪdʒɪd/ *adj.* **1** unfriendly, cold (*frigid stare*). **2** (of a woman) sexually unresponsive. **3** (esp. of a climate or air) cold. □ **frigidity** /-ˈdʒɪdɪtɪ/ *n.* [Latin *frigus* (n.) cold]

frill –*n.* **1** strip of gathered or pleated material as an ornamental edging. **2** (in *pl.*) unnecessary embellishments. –*v.* decorate with a frill. □ **frilly** *adj.* (**-ier**, **-iest**). [origin unknown]

fringe –*n.* **1** border of tassels or loose threads. **2** front hair hanging over the forehead. **3** outer limit of an area, population, etc. (often *attrib.*: *fringe theatre*). **4** unimportant area or part. –*v.* (**-ging**) **1** adorn with a fringe. **2** serve as a fringe to. [Latin *fimbria*]

♦ **fringe benefit** *n.* **1** employee's benefit additional to salary. Fringe benefits include company cars, expense accounts, the opportunity to buy company products at reduced prices, private health plans, canteens with subsidized meals, luncheon vouchers, cheap loans, and social clubs. **2** benefit, other than a dividend, provided by a company for its shareholders, e.g. reduced prices for the company's products or services, Christmas gifts, and special travel facilities.

---

frippery /ˈfrɪpərɪ/ *n.* (*pl.* **-ies**) **1** showy finery, esp. in dress. **2** empty display in speech, literary style, etc. **3** (usu. in *pl.*) knick-knacks. [French *friperie*]

Frisbee /ˈfrɪzbɪ/ *n. propr.* concave plastic disc for skimming through the air as an outdoor game. [perhaps from *Frisbie* bakery pie-tins]

Frisian /ˈfrɪzɪən/ –*adj.* of Friesland. –*n.* native or language of Friesland. [Latin *Frisii* (n. pl.) from Old Frisian *Frīsa*]

Frisian Islands line of islands off the coast of Denmark, Germany, and the Netherlands, divided between these countries; farming, fishing, and tourism are the main sources of income.

frisk –*v.* **1** leap or skip playfully. **2** *slang* search (a person) for a weapon etc. by feeling. –*n.* **1** playful leap or skip. **2** *slang* frisking of a person. [French *frisque* lively]

frisky *adj.* (**-ier**, **-iest**) lively, playful. □ **friskily** *adv.* **friskiness** *n.*

frisson /ˈfriːsɒn/ *n.* emotional thrill. [French]

frith var. of FIRTH.

fritillary /frɪˈtɪlərɪ/ *n.* (*pl.* **-ies**) **1** plant with bell-like flowers. **2** butterfly with red-brown wings chequered with black. [Latin *fritillus* dice-box]

fritter[1] *v.* (usu. foll. by *away*) waste (money, time, etc.) triflingly. [obsolete *fritter(s)* fragments]

fritter[2] *n.* fruit, meat, etc. coated in batter and fried. [French *friture* from Latin *frigo* FRY[1]]

Friuli-Venezia Giulia /frɪˌuːlɪveˈnetsɪə ˈdʒuːlɪə/ autonomous region of NE Italy; pop. (est. 1994) 1 193 217; capital, Trieste. It has textile, chemical, and food-processing industries and produces wine.

frivolous /ˈfrɪvələs/ *adj.* **1** not serious, silly, shallow. **2** paltry, trifling. □ **frivolity** /-ˈvɒlɪtɪ/ *n.* (*pl.* **-ies**). **frivolously** *adv.* **frivolousness** *n.* [Latin]

frizz –*v.* form (hair) into tight curls. –*n.* frizzed hair or state. [French *friser*]

frizzle[1] /ˈfrɪz(ə)l/ *v.* (**-ling**) **1** fry or cook with a sizzling noise. **2** (often foll. by *up*) burn or shrivel. [obsolete *frizz*: related to FRY[1], with imitative ending]

frizzle[2] /ˈfrɪz(ə)l/ –*v.* (**-ling**) form into tight curls. –*n.* frizzled hair. [perhaps related to FRIZZ]

frizzy *adj.* (**-ier**, **-iest**) in tight curls.

FRN *abbr. Finance* floating-rate note. See EUROBOND.

FRO *abbr. Insurance* fire risk only.

fro *adv.* back (now only in *to and fro*: see TO). [Old Norse: related to FROM]

frock *n.* **1** woman's or girl's dress. **2** monk's or priest's gown. **3** smock. [French from Germanic]

frock-coat *n.* man's long-skirted coat.

frog[1] *n.* **1** small smooth tailless leaping amphibian. **2** (**Frog**) *slang offens.* Frenchman. □ **frog in one's throat** *colloq.* hoarseness. [Old English]

frog[2] *n.* horny substance in the sole of a horse's foot. [origin uncertain: perhaps a use of FROG[1]]

frog[3] *n.* ornamental coat-fastening of a button and loop. [origin unknown]

frogman *n.* person with a rubber suit, flippers, and an oxygen supply for underwater swimming.

frogmarch *v.* hustle forward with the arms pinned behind.

frog-spawn *n.* frog's eggs.

frolic /ˈfrɒlɪk/ –*v.* (**-ck-**) play about cheerfully. –*n.* **1** cheerful play. **2** prank. **3** merry party. [Dutch *vrolijk* (adj.) from *vro* glad]

frolicsome *adj.* merry, playful.

from /frəm, frɒm/ *prep.* expressing separation or origin, followed by: **1** person, place, time, etc., that is the starting-point (*dinner is served from 8*; *from start to finish*). **2** place, object, etc. at a specified distance etc. (*10 miles from Rome*; *far from sure*). **3 a** source (*gravel from a pit*; *quotations from Shaw*). **b** giver or sender (*not heard from her*). **4** thing or person avoided, deprived, etc. (*released him from prison*; *took his gun from him*). **5** reason, cause, motive (*died from fatigue*; *did it from jealousy*). **6** thing distinguished or unlike (*know black from white*). **7** lower limit (*from 10 to 20 boats*). **8** state changed for another (*from being poor he became rich*). **9** adverb or preposition of time or place (*from long ago*; *from abroad*; *from under the bed*). □ **from time to time** occasionally. [Old English]

fromage frais /ˌfrɒmɑːʒ ˈfreɪ/ *n.* smooth low-fat soft cheese.

frond *n.* leaflike part of a fern or palm. [Latin *frons frond-* leaf]

front /frʌnt/ –*n.* **1** side or part most prominent or important, or nearer the spectator or direction of motion (*front of the house*). **2 a** line of battle. **b** ground towards an enemy. **c** scene of actual fighting. **3 a** activity compared to a military front. **b** organized political group. **4** demeanour, bearing. **5** forward or conspicuous position. **6 a** bluff. **b** pretext. **7** person etc. as a cover for subversive or illegal activities. **8** promenade. **9** forward edge of advancing cold or warm air. **10** auditorium of a theatre. **11** breast of a garment (*spilt food down his front*). –*attrib. adj.* **1** of the front. **2** situated in front. –*v.* **1** (foll. by *on*, *to*, *towards*, *upon*) have the front facing or directed towards. **2** (foll. by *for*) *slang* act as a front or cover for. **3** provide with or have a front (*fronted with stone*). **4** lead (a band, organization, etc.). □ **in front** in an advanced or facing position. **in front of 1** ahead of, in advance of. **2** in the presence of. [Latin *frons front-* face]

frontage *n.* **1** front of a building. **2** land next to a street or water etc. **3** extent of a front. **4 a** the way a thing faces. **b** outlook.

frontal *adj.* **1** of or on the front (*frontal view*; *frontal attack*). **2** of the forehead (*frontal bone*).

front bench *n.* seats in Parliament occupied by leading members of the government and opposition.

front-bencher *n.* MP occupying the front bench.

♦ **front door** *Finance* see BACK DOOR 2.

♦ **front-end load** *n.* initial charge made by a unit trust, life-assurance company, or other investment fund to pay for administration and commission for any introducing agent. The investment made on behalf of the investor is, therefore, the total of his initial payment less the front-end load.

front-end processor *n.* small computer used to relieve a mainframe computer of some of the tasks associated with input/output. In a network, it may handle the control of communication lines, code conversion, error control, etc. It is more powerful than a multiplexer.

frontier /ˈfrʌntɪə(r)/ *n.* **1 a** border between two countries. **b** district on each side of this. **2** limits of attainment or knowledge in a subject. **3** *US* borders between settled and unsettled country. □ **frontiersman** *n.*

frontispiece /ˈfrʌntɪsˌpiːs/ *n.* illustration facing the title-page of a book. [Latin: related to FRONT, *specio* look]

front line *n.* foremost part of an army or group under attack.

front runner *n.* favourite in a race etc.

♦ **front running** *n.* practice by market makers on the London Stock Exchange of dealing on advance information provided by their brokers and investment analysis department before their clients have been given the information. See also CHINESE WALL.

frost *–n.* **1 a** frozen dew or vapour. **b** consistent temperature below freezing-point. **2** cold dispiriting atmosphere. *–v.* **1** (usu. foll. by *over, up*) become covered with frost. **2 a** cover with or as with frost. **b** injure (a plant etc.) with frost. **3** make (glass) non-transparent by roughening its surface. [Old English: related to FREEZE]

frostbite *n.* injury to body tissues due to freezing. □ **frostbitten** *adj.*

frosting *n.* icing.

frosty *adj.* (**-ier, -iest**) **1** cold with frost. **2** covered with or as with frost. **3** unfriendly in manner. □ **frostily** *adv.* **frostiness** *n.*

froth *–n.* **1** foam. **2** idle or amusing talk etc. *–v.* **1** emit or gather froth. **2** cause (beer etc.) to foam. □ **frothy** *adj.* (**-ier, -iest**). [Old Norse]

frown *–v.* **1** wrinkle one's brows, esp. in displeasure or concentration. **2** (foll. by *at, on*) disapprove of. *–n.* **1** act of frowning. **2** look of displeasure or concentration. [French]

frowsty /ˈfraʊstɪ/ *adj.* (**-ier, -iest**) fusty, stuffy. [var. of FROWZY]

frowzy /ˈfraʊzɪ/ *adj.* (also **frowsy**) (**-ier, -iest**) **1** fusty. **2** slatternly, dingy. [origin unknown]

froze *past* of FREEZE.

frozen *past part.* of FREEZE.

♦ **frozen assets** *n.pl.* assets that cannot be used or realized, for example because a government refuses to allow certain assets to be exported.

FRS *abbr.* **1** Fellow of the Royal Society. **2** = FEDERAL RESERVE SYSTEM.

Frt. fwd. *abbr.* freight forward.

Frt. ppd. *abbr.* freight prepaid.

fructify /ˈfrʌktɪˌfaɪ/ *v.* (**-ies, -ied**) **1** bear fruit. **2** make fruitful. [Latin: related to FRUIT]

fructose /ˈfrʌktəʊz/ *n.* sugar in honey, fruits, etc. [Latin: related to FRUIT]

frugal /ˈfruːg(ə)l/ *adj.* **1** sparing or thrifty, esp. as regards food. **2** meagre, cheap. □ **frugality** /-ˈgælɪtɪ/ *n.* **frugally** *adv.* [Latin]

fruit /fruːt/ *–n.* **1 a** seed-bearing part of a plant or tree; this as food. **b** these collectively. **2** (usu. in *pl.*) vegetables, grains, etc. as food (*fruits of the earth*). **3** (usu. in *pl.*) profits, rewards. *–v.* (cause to) bear fruit. [Latin *fructus* from *fruor* enjoy]

fruit cake *n.* cake containing dried fruit.

fruit cocktail *n.* diced fruit salad.

fruiterer *n.* dealer in fruit.

fruitful *adj.* **1** producing much fruit. **2** successful, profitable. □ **fruitfully** *adv.*

fruition /fruːˈɪʃ(ə)n/ *n.* **1** bearing of fruit. **2** realization of aims or hopes. [Latin: related to FRUIT]

fruit juice *n.* juice of fruit, esp. as a drink.

fruitless *adj.* **1** not bearing fruit. **2** useless, unsuccessful. □ **fruitlessly** *adv.*

fruit machine *n.* coin-operated gaming machine using symbols representing fruit.

fruit sugar *n.* fructose.

fruity *adj.* (**-ier, -iest**) **1 a** of fruit. **b** tasting or smelling like fruit. **2** (of a voice etc.) deep and rich. **3** *colloq.* slightly indecent or suggestive. □ **fruitily** *adv.* **fruitiness** *n.*

frump *n.* dowdy unattractive woman. □ **frumpish** *adj.* **frumpy** *adj.* (**-ier, -iest**). [perhaps dial. *frumple* wrinkle]

Frunze see PISHPEK.

frustrate /frʌˈstreɪt/ *v.* (**-ting**) **1** make (efforts) ineffective. **2** prevent (a person) from achieving a purpose. **3** (as **frustrated** *adj.*) **a** discontented because unable to achieve one's aims. **b** sexually unfulfilled. □ **frustrating** *adj.* **frustratingly** *adv.* **frustration** *n.* [Latin *frustra* in vain]

♦ **frustration of contract** *n.* termination of a contract as a result of an unforeseen event that makes its performance impossible or illegal. For example, an export contract could be frustrated if the importer was in a country that declared war on the country of the exporter.

frustum /ˈfrʌstəm/ *n.* (*pl.* **-ta** or **-s**) *Geom.* remaining part of a decapitated cone or pyramid. [Latin, = piece cut off]

fry[1] *–v.* (**fries, fried**) cook or be cooked in hot fat. *–n.* (*pl.* **fries**) **1** offal, usu. eaten fried (*lamb's fry*). **2** fried food, esp. meat. [Latin *frigo*]

fry[2] *n.pl.* young or newly hatched fishes. [Old Norse, = seed]

fryer *n.* (also **frier**) **1** person who fries. **2** vessel for frying esp. fish.

frying-pan *n.* shallow pan used in frying. □ **out of the frying-pan into the fire** from a bad situation to a worse one.

fry-up *n. colloq.* fried bacon, eggs, etc.

FS *abbr.* **1** feasibility study. **2** financial secretary. **3** financial statement. **4** Friendly Society.

FSA *abbr.* Financial Services Act (1986).

FSAA *abbr.* Fellow of the Society of Incorporated Accountants and Auditors.

FSBI *abbr.* Fellow of the Savings Bank Institute.

FSCA *abbr.* Fellow of the Society of Company and Commercial Accountants.

FSF *abbr.* Fellow of the Institute of Shipping and Forwarding Agents.

FSLIC *abbr.* (in the US) Federal Savings and Loan Insurance Corporation.

FSS *abbr.* Fellow of the Royal Statistical Society.

FSVA *abbr.* Fellow of the Incorporated Society of Valuers and Auctioneers.

FT *abbr. Financial Times.*

Ft *symb. Currency* forint.

ft *abbr.* foot, feet.

FT-30 *abbr.* Financial Times Ordinary Share Index. See FINANCIAL TIMES SHARE INDEXES.

FTA *abbr.* **1** Financial Times Actuaries (Share Indexes). See FINANCIAL TIMES SHARE INDEXES. **2** Free Trade Agreement.

FTAM *abbr. Computing* file transfer, access, and management.

FTASI *abbr.* Financial Times Actuaries All-Share Index. See FINANCIAL TIMES SHARE INDEXES.

FTC *abbr.* (in the US) Federal Trade Commission.

♦ **FT Cityline** *n.* telephone service giving information, updated seven times a day, on the Financial Times Ordinary Share Index.

FTII *abbr.* Fellow of the Institute of Taxation.

FTP *abbr. Computing* file-transfer protocol.

FT-SE 100 *abbr.* Financial Times-Stock Exchange 100 Share Index. See FINANCIAL TIMES SHARE INDEXES.

FT-SE Eurotrack Indexes see FINANCIAL TIMES SHARE INDEXES.

♦ **FT Share Indexes** *n.pl.* = FINANCIAL TIMES SHARE INDEXES.

FTZ *abbr.* free-trade zone.

fuchsia /'fjuːʃə/ *n.* shrub with drooping red, purple, or white flowers. [*Fuchs*, name of a botanist]

fuck *coarse slang –v.* **1** have sexual intercourse (with). **2** (often *absol.* or as *int.* expressing annoyance) curse (a person or thing). **3** (foll. by *about, around*) mess about; fool around. **4** (as **fucking** *adj., adv.*) expressing annoyance etc. *–n.* **1 a** act of sexual intercourse. **b** partner in this. **2** slightest amount (*don't give a fuck*). □ **fuck-all** nothing. **fuck off** go away. **fuck up** bungle. □ **fucker** *n.* (often as a term of abuse). [origin unknown]

■ **Usage** Although widely used, *fuck* is still considered to be the most offensive word in the English language by many people. In discussions about bad language it is frequently referred to as *the 'f' word*.

fuck-up *n. coarse slang* bungle or muddle.

fuddle /'fʌd(ə)l/ *–v.* (**-ling**) confuse or stupefy, esp. with alcohol. *–n.* **1** confusion. **2** intoxication. [origin unknown]

fuddy-duddy /'fʌdɪˌdʌdɪ/ *slang –adj.* old-fashioned or quaintly fussy. *–n.* (*pl.* **-ies**) such a person. [origin unknown]

fudge *–n.* **1** soft toffee-like sweet made of milk, sugar, butter, etc. **2** piece of dishonesty or faking. *–v.* (**-ging**) make or do clumsily or dishonestly; fake (*fudge the results*). [origin uncertain]

fuehrer var. of FÜHRER.

fuel /'fjuːəl/ *–n.* **1** material for burning or as a source of heat, power, or nuclear energy. **2** food as a source of energy. **3** thing that sustains or inflames passion etc. *–v.* (**-ll-**; *US* **-l-**) **1** supply with, take in, or get, fuel. **2** inflame (feeling etc.). [French from Latin]

fuel cell *n.* cell producing electricity direct from a chemical reaction.

fug *n. colloq.* close stuffy atmosphere. □ **fuggy** *adj.* [origin unknown]

fugitive /'fjuːdʒɪtɪv/ *–n.* (often foll. by *from*) person who flees, e.g. from justice or an enemy. *–adj.* **1** fleeing. **2** transient, fleeting. [Latin *fugio* flee]

fugue /fjuːg/ *n.* piece of music in which a short melody or phrase is introduced by one part and taken up and developed by others. □ **fugal** *adj.* [Latin *fuga* flight]

führer /'fjʊərə(r)/ *n.* (also **fuehrer**) tyrannical leader. [German]

Fujairah /fuː'dʒaɪrə/ **1** state of the United Arab Emirates; pop. (1993) 68 000. **2** its capital city.

Fujian /ˌfuːdʒɪ'æn/ (formerly **Fukien** /fuː'kjen/) province of SE China; pop. (est. 1995) 31 830 000; capital, Fuzhou. It produces sugar, rice, and tea, and there is some light industry.

Fukuoka /ˌfuːkuː'əʊkə/ commercial city and port in Japan, the chief city of Kyushu; industries include textiles and chemicals; pop. (est. 1995) 1 284 741.

-ful *comb. form* forming: **1** adjectives from **a** nouns, meaning full of or having qualities of (*beautiful*; *masterful*). **b** adjectives (*direful*). **c** verbs, meaning 'apt to' (*forgetful*). **2** nouns (*pl.* **-fuls**) meaning 'amount that fills' (*handful*; *spoonful*).

fulcrum /'fʌlkrəm/ *n.* (*pl.* **-cra** or **-s**) point on which a lever is supported. [Latin *fulcio* to prop]

fulfil /fʊl'fɪl/ *v.* (*US* **fulfill**) (**-ll-**) **1** carry out (a task, prophecy, promise, etc.). **2 a** satisfy (conditions, a desire, prayer, etc.). **b** (as **fulfilled** *adj.*) completely happy. **3** answer (a purpose). □ **fulfil oneself** realize one's potential. □ **fulfilment** *n.* [Old English: related to FULL[1], FILL]

full[1] /fʊl/ *–adj.* **1** holding all it can (*bucket is full*; *full of water*). **2** having eaten all one can or wants. **3** abundant, copious, satisfying (*a full life*; *full details*). **4** (foll. by *of*) having an abundance of (*full of vitality*). **5** (foll. by *of*) engrossed in (*full of himself*). **6** complete, perfect (*full membership*; *in full bloom*). **7** (of tone) deep and clear. **8** plump, rounded (*full figure*). **9** (of clothes) ample, hanging in folds. *–adv.* **1** very (*knows full well*). **2** quite, fully (*full six miles*). **3** exactly (*full on the nose*). □ **full up** *colloq.* completely full. **in full 1** without abridgement. **2** to or for the full amount. **in full view** entirely visible. **to the full** to the utmost extent. [Old English]

full[2] /fʊl/ *v.* clean and thicken (cloth). [from FULLER]

full back *n.* defensive player near the goal in football, hockey, etc.

full-blooded *adj.* **1** vigorous, hearty, sensual. **2** not hybrid.

full-blown *adj.* fully developed.

full board *n.* provision of bed and all meals at a hotel etc.

full-bodied *adj.* rich in quality, tone, etc.

♦ **full-cost pricing** *n.* method of pricing goods that takes account of their full cost, i.e. cost including fixed costs in addition to direct costs (cf. MARGINAL COST). Clearly a business must ultimately cover its full costs to be profitable, but there are some circumstances in which goods sold at less than their full cost could make some contribution, whereas if they remain unsold at a higher price they make no contribution.

♦ **full employment** *n.* state in which all the economic resources of a country (esp. its labour force) are fully utilized. It is generally regarded as the ultimate goal of economic policy, but there has been some recent debate on exactly what is meant by full employment and whether or not governments can achieve it. See FRICTIONAL UNEMPLOYMENT; INVOLUNTARY UNEMPLOYMENT; NATURAL RATE OF UNEMPLOYMENT; OVER-FULL EMPLOYMENT.

fuller *n.* person who fulls cloth. □ **fuller's earth** type of clay used in fulling. [Latin *fullo*]

full-frontal *adj.* **1** (of a nude figure) fully exposed at the front. **2** explicit, unrestrained.

full house *n.* **1** maximum attendance at a theatre etc. **2** hand in poker with three of a kind and a pair.

full-length *adj.* **1** not shortened. **2** (of a mirror, portrait, etc.) showing the whole figure.

full moon *n.* **1** moon with its whole disc illuminated. **2** time of this.

fullness *n.* being full. □ **the fullness of time** the appropriate or destined time.

full-scale *adj.* not reduced in size, complete.

full stop *n.* **1** punctuation mark (.) at the end of a sentence or an abbreviation. **2** complete cessation.

full term *n.* completion of a normal pregnancy.

full-time *–adj.* for or during the whole of the working week (*full-time job*). *–adv.* on a full-time basis (*work full-time*).

full-timer *n.* person who does a full-time job.

fully *adv.* **1** completely, entirely (*am fully aware*). **2** at least (*fully 60*).

fully-fashioned *adj.* (of clothing) shaped to fit closely.

♦ **fully-paid share capital** see SHARE CAPITAL.

fulmar /'fʊlmə(r)/ *n.* Arctic sea bird related to the petrel. [Old Norse: related to FOUL, *mar* gull]

fulminant /'fʊlmɪnənt/ *adj.* **1** fulminating. **2** (of a disease etc.) developing suddenly. [Latin: related to FULMINATE]

fulminate /'fʊlmɪˌneɪt/ *v.* (**-ting**) **1** criticize loudly and forcefully. **2** explode violently; flash. □ **fulmination** /-'neɪʃ(ə)n/ *n.* [Latin *fulmen -min-* lightning]

fulsome /'fʊlsəm/ *adj.* excessive, cloying, insincere (*fulsome praise*). □ **fulsomely** *adv.* [from FULL[1]]

■ **Usage** The phrase *fulsome praise* is sometimes wrongly used to mean generous praise rather than excessive praise.

fumble /ˈfʌmb(ə)l/ –*v.* (**-ling**) **1** use the hands awkwardly, grope about. **2** handle clumsily or nervously (*fumbled the ball*). –*n.* act of fumbling. [Low German *fummeln*]

fume –*n.* (usu. in *pl.*) exuded gas, smoke, or vapour, esp. when harmful or unpleasant. –*v.* (**-ming**) **1** emit fumes or as fumes. **2** be very angry. **3** subject (oak, film, etc.) to fumes to darken. [Latin *fumus* smoke]

fumigate /ˈfjuːmɪˌgeɪt/ *v.* (**-ting**) disinfect or purify with fumes. □ **fumigation** /-ˈgeɪʃ(ə)n/ *n.* **fumigator** *n.* [Latin: related to FUME]

fun –*n.* **1** lively or playful amusement. **2** source of this. **3** mockery, ridicule (*figure of fun*). –*attrib. adj. colloq.* amusing, enjoyable (*a fun thing to do*). □ **for fun** (or **for the fun of it**) not for a serious purpose. **in fun** as a joke, not seriously. **make fun of** (or **poke fun at**) ridicule, tease. [obsolete *fun, fon*: related to FOND]

■ **Usage** The use of *fun* as an attributive adjective is common in informal use, but is considered incorrect by some people.

Funafuti /ˌfuːnəˈfuːtɪ/ capital and sole port of Tuvalu, situated on the island of Funafuti; pop. (est. 1990) 2718.

Funchal /fʊnˈʃɑːl/ capital of the Madeira Islands and chief port of Madeira; pop. (est. 1987) 44 111. Madeira wines, embroidery, and wickerwork are exported; tourism is a major industry.

function /ˈfʌŋkʃ(ə)n/ –*n.* **1 a** proper or necessary role, activity, or purpose. **b** official or professional duty. **2** public or social occasion. **3** *Math.* quantity whose value depends on the varying values of others. –*v.* fulfil a function, operate. [Latin *fungor funct-* perform]

functional *adj.* **1** of or serving a function. **2** practical rather than attractive. **3** affecting the function of a bodily organ but not its structure. □ **functionally** *adv.*

functionalism *n.* belief that a thing's function should determine its design. □ **functionalist** *n.* & *adj.*

functionary *n.* (*pl.* **-ies**) official performing certain duties.

function key see KEYBOARD *n.* 1.

◆ **functions of money** *n.pl. Econ.* roles fulfilled by money acting as a medium of exchange, a unit of account, and a store of value, none of which occur in an economy based on barter.

---

fund –*n.* **1** permanently available stock (*fund of knowledge*). **2** reserve of money or investments held for a specific purpose, e.g. to provide a source of pensions (see PENSION FUND) or to sell as units (see FUND MANAGER; UNIT TRUST). **3** (in *pl.*) money resources. –*v.* **1** provide with money. **2** make (a debt) permanent at fixed interest. □ **in funds** *colloq.* having money to spend. [Latin *fundus* bottom]

fundamental /ˌfʌndəˈment(ə)l/ –*adj.* of or being a base or foundation; essential, primary. –*n.* **1** (usu. in *pl.*) fundamental principle. **2** *Mus.* fundamental note. □ **fundamentally** *adv.* [Latin: related to FOUND[2]]

fundamentalism *n.* strict adherence to traditional religious beliefs or doctrines. □ **fundamentalist** *n.* & *adj.*

fundamental note *n. Mus.* lowest note of a chord.

fundamental particle *n.* elementary particle.

◆ **fundamental term** *n. Law* term in a contract that is of such importance to the contract that to omit it would make the contract useless. Fundamental terms cannot be exempted from a contract, whereas lesser terms, known as conditions and warranties, can be exempted by mutual consent.

◆ **funded debt** *n.* part of the national debt that the government is under no obligation to repay by a specified date, consisting mostly of Consols. See also FUNDING OPERATIONS 1.

◆ **funded pension scheme** *n.* pension scheme that pays benefits to retired people from a pension fund invested in securities. The profits produced by such a fund are paid out as pensions to the members of the scheme.

◆ **funding operations** *n.pl.* **1** replacement of short-term fixed-interest debt (floating debt) by long-term fixed-interest debt (funded debt), usu. associated with the government's handling of the national debt through the operations of the Bank of England. The bank buys treasury bills and replaces them with an equal amount of longer-term government bonds, thus lengthening the average maturity of government debt. This has the effect of tightening the monetary system, as treasury bills are regarded by the commercial banks as liquid assets while bonds are not. See also OVERFUNDING. **2** change in the capital gearing of a company, in which short-term debts, such as overdrafts, are replaced by longer-term debts, such as debentures.

◆ **fund manager** *n.* (also **investment manager**) employee of one of the larger financial institutions, such as an insurance company, investment trust, or pension fund, who manages its investment fund. The fund manager decides which investments the fund shall hold in accordance with the specified aims of the fund, e.g. high income, maximum growth, etc.

◆ **fund of funds** *n.* unit trust belonging to an institution, most of its funds being invested in a selection of other unit trusts owned by that institution. It is designed to give maximum security to the small investor.

---

fund-raiser *n.* person raising money for a cause, enterprise, etc. □ **fund-raising** *n.*

Fundy /ˈfʌndɪ/, **Bay of** inlet of the Atlantic Ocean between the Canadian provinces of New Brunswick and Nova Scotia. It is subject to fast-running tides, which are now used to generate electricity.

funeral /ˈfjuːnər(ə)l/ –*n.* **1** ceremonial burial or cremation of a corpse. **2** *slang* one's (usu. unpleasant) concern (*that's your funeral*). –*attrib. adj.* of or used at funerals. [Latin *funus funer-*]

funeral director *n.* undertaker.

funeral parlour *n.* establishment where corpses are prepared for funerals.

funerary /ˈfjuːnərərɪ/ *adj.* of or used at funerals.

funereal /fjuːˈnɪərɪəl/ *adj.* **1** of or appropriate to a funeral. **2** dismal, dark. □ **funereally** *adv.*

funfair *n.* fair with amusements and sideshows.

◆ **fungibles** /ˈfʌndʒɪbəlʒ/ *n.pl.* **1** interchangeable goods, securities, etc. that allow one to be replaced by another without loss of value. Bearer bonds and banknotes are examples. **2** perishable goods the quantity of which can be estimated by number or weight.

---

fungicide /ˈfʌndʒɪˌsaɪd/ *n.* substance that kills fungus. □ **fungicidal** /-ˈsaɪd(ə)l/ *adj.*

fungoid /ˈfʌŋgɔɪd/ –*adj.* fungus-like. –*n.* fungoid plant.

fungus /ˈfʌŋgəs/ *n.* (*pl.* **-gi** /-gaɪ/ or **-guses**) **1** mushroom, toadstool, or allied plant, including moulds, feeding on organic matter. **2** *Med.* spongy morbid growth. □ **fungal** *adj.* **fungous** *adj.* [Latin]

funicular /fjuːˈnɪkjʊlə(r)/ –*adj.* (of a mountain railway) operating by cable with ascending and descending cars counterbalanced. –*n.* funicular railway. [Latin *funiculus* diminutive of *funis* rope]

funk[1] *slang* –*n.* **1** fear, panic. **2** coward. –*v.* **1** evade through fear. **2** be afraid (of). [origin uncertain]

funk[2] *n. slang* funky music. [origin uncertain]

funky *adj.* (**-ier, -iest**) *slang* (esp. of jazz or rock music) earthy, bluesy, with a heavy rhythm.

funnel /ˈfʌn(ə)l/ –*n.* **1** tube widening at the top, for pouring liquid etc. into a small opening. **2** metal chimney on a steam engine or steamship. –*v.* (**-ll-**; *US* **-l-**) guide or move through or as through a funnel. [Provençal *fonilh* from Latin *(in)fundibulum*]

funny /ˈfʌnɪ/ *adj.* (**-ier, -iest**) **1** amusing, comical. **2** strange, peculiar. **3** *colloq.* **a** slightly unwell. **b** eccentric. □ **funnily** *adv.* **funniness** *n.* [from FUN]

funny-bone *n.* part of the elbow over which a very sensitive nerve passes.

fun run *n. colloq.* uncompetitive sponsored run for charity.

fur *–n.* **1 a** short fine soft animal hair. **b** hide with fur on it, used esp. for clothing. **2** garment of or lined with fur. **3** (*collect.*) animals with fur. **4** fur-like coating on the tongue, in a kettle, etc. *–v.* (**-rr-**) **1** (esp. as **furred** *adj.*) line or trim with fur. **2** (often foll. by *up*) (of a kettle etc.) become coated with fur. □ **make the fur fly** *colloq.* cause a disturbance, stir up trouble. [French from Germanic]

furbelow /ˈfɜːbɪˌləʊ/ *n.* **1** (in *pl.*) showy ornaments. **2** *archaic* gathered strip or border of a skirt or petticoat. [French *falbala*]

furbish /ˈfɜːbɪʃ/ *v.* (often foll. by *up*) = REFURBISH. [French from Germanic]

furcate /ˈfɜːkeɪt/ *–adj.* forked, branched. *–v.* (**-ting**) fork, divide. □ **furcation** /fɜːˈkeɪʃ(ə)n/ *n.* [Latin: related to FORK]

furious /ˈfjʊərɪəs/ *adj.* **1** very angry. **2** raging, frantic. □ **furiously** *adv.* [Latin: related to FURY]

furl *v.* **1** roll up and secure (a sail etc.). **2** become furled. [French *ferler*]

furlong /ˈfɜːlɒŋ/ *n.* eighth of a mile. [Old English: related to FURROW, LONG[1]]

furlough /ˈfɜːləʊ/ *–n.* leave of absence, esp. military. *–v. US* **1** grant furlough to. **2** spend furlough. [Dutch: related to FOR-, LEAVE[1]]

furnace /ˈfɜːnɪs/ *n.* **1** enclosed structure for intense heating by fire, esp. of metals or water. **2** very hot place. [Latin *fornax* from *fornus* oven]

furnish /ˈfɜːnɪʃ/ *v.* **1** provide (a house, room, etc.) with furniture. **2** (often foll. by *with*) supply. [French from Germanic]

furnished *adj.* (of a house etc.) let with furniture.

furnisher *n.* **1** person who sells furniture. **2** person who furnishes.

furnishings *n.pl.* furniture and fitments in a house, room, etc.

furniture /ˈfɜːnɪtʃə(r)/ *n.* **1** movable equipment of a house, room, etc., e.g. tables, beds. **2** *Naut.* ship's equipment. **3** accessories, e.g. the handles and lock on a door. [French: related to FURNISH]

furore /fjʊəˈrɔːrɪ/ *n.* (*US* **furor** /ˈfjʊərɔː(r)/) **1** uproar; fury. **2** enthusiastic admiration. [Latin: related to FURY]

furrier /ˈfʌrɪə(r)/ *n.* dealer in or dresser of furs. [French]

furrow /ˈfʌrəʊ/ *–n.* **1** narrow trench made by a plough. **2** rut, groove, wrinkle. **3** ship's track. *–v.* **1** plough. **2** make furrows in. [Old English]

furry /ˈfɜːrɪ/ *adj.* (**-ier, -iest**) like or covered with fur.

further /ˈfɜːðə(r)/ *–adv.* (also **farther** /ˈfɑːðə(r)/) **1** more distant in space or time. **2** to a greater extent, more (*will enquire further*). **3** in addition (*I may add further*). *–adj.* (also **farther** /ˈfɑːðə(r)/) **1** more distant or advanced. **2** more, additional (*further details*). *–v.* promote or favour (a scheme etc.). [Old English: related to FORTH]

■ **Usage** The form *farther* is used esp. with reference to physical distance, although *further* is preferred by many people even in this sense.

furtherance *n.* furthering of a scheme etc.

further education *n.* education for those above school age.

furthermore /ˌfɜːðəˈmɔː(r)/ *adv.* in addition, besides.

furthest /ˈfɜːðɪst/ (also **farthest** /ˈfɑːðɪst/) *–adj.* most distant. *–adv.* to or at the greatest distance.

■ **Usage** The form *farthest* is used esp. with reference to physical distance, although *furthest* is preferred by many people even in this sense.

furtive /ˈfɜːtɪv/ *adj.* sly, stealthy. □ **furtively** *adv.* **furtiveness** *n.* [Latin *fur* thief]

fury /ˈfjʊərɪ/ *n.* (*pl.* **-ies**) **1 a** wild and passionate anger. **b** fit of rage. **2** violence of a storm, disease, etc. **3** (**Fury**) (usu. in *pl.*) (in Greek mythology) avenging goddess. **4** avenging spirit. **5** angry or malignant woman. □ **like fury** *colloq.* with great force or effort. [Latin *furia*]

furze *n.* = GORSE. □ **furzy** *adj.* [Old English]

fuse[1] /fjuːz/ *–v.* (**-sing**) **1** melt with intense heat. **2** blend into one whole by melting. **3** provide (an electric circuit) with a fuse. **4 a** (of an appliance) fail owing to the melting of a fuse. **b** cause to do this. *–n.* device with a strip or wire of easily melted metal placed in an electric circuit so as to interrupt an excessive current by melting. [Latin *fundo fus-* melt]

fuse[2] /fjuːz/ (also **fuze**) *–n.* **1** device of combustible matter for igniting a bomb or explosive charge. **2** component made of this in a shell, mine, etc. *–v.* (**-sing**) fit a fuse to. [Latin *fusus* spindle]

fuselage /ˈfjuːzəˌlɑːʒ/ *n.* body of an aeroplane. [French from *fuseau* spindle]

fusible /ˈfjuːzɪb(ə)l/ *adj.* that can be melted. □ **fusibility** /-ˈbɪlɪtɪ/ *n.* [Latin: related to FUSE[1]]

fusil /ˈfjuːzɪl/ *n. hist.* light musket. [Latin *focus* fire]

fusilier /ˌfjuːzɪˈlɪə(r)/ *n.* member of any of several British regiments formerly armed with fusils. [French: related to FUSIL]

fusillade /ˌfjuːzɪˈleɪd/ *n.* **1** period of continuous discharge of firearms. **2** sustained outburst of criticism etc.

fusion /ˈfjuːʒ(ə)n/ *n.* **1** fusing or melting. **2** blending. **3** coalition. **4** = NUCLEAR FUSION. [Latin: related to FUSE[1]]

fuss *–n.* **1** excited commotion, bustle. **2** excessive concern about a trivial thing. **3** sustained protest or dispute. *–v.* **1** behave with nervous concern. **2** agitate, worry. □ **make a fuss** complain vigorously. **make a fuss of** (or **over**) treat (a person or animal) affectionately. □ **fusser** *n.* [origin unknown]

fusspot *n. colloq.* person given to fussing.

fussy *adj.* (**-ier, -iest**) **1** inclined to fuss. **2** over-elaborate. **3** fastidious. □ **fussily** *adv.* **fussiness** *n.*

fustian /ˈfʌstɪən/ *–n.* **1** thick usu. dark twilled cotton cloth. **2** bombast. *–adj.* **1** made of fustian. **2** bombastic. **3** worthless. [French]

fusty /ˈfʌstɪ/ *adj.* (**-ier, -iest**) **1** musty, stuffy. **2** antiquated. □ **fustiness** *n.* [French *fust* cask, from Latin *fustis* cudgel]

fut. *abbr. Finance* futures.

futile /ˈfjuːtaɪl/ *adj.* **1** useless, ineffectual. **2** frivolous. □ **futility** /-ˈtɪlɪtɪ/ *n.* [Latin *futilis* leaky, futile]

futon /ˈfuːtɒn/ *n.* Japanese quilted mattress used as a bed; this sold with a wooden frame, often convertible into a couch. [Japanese]

future /ˈfjuːtʃə(r)/ *–adj.* **1** about to happen, be, or become. **2 a** of time to come. **b** *Gram.* (of a tense) describing an event yet to happen. *–n.* **1** time to come. **2** future events. **3** future condition of a person, country, etc. **4** prospect of success etc. (*no future in it*). **5** *Gram.* future tense. **6** (in *pl.*) see FUTURES CONTRACT. □ **in future** from now onwards. [Latin *futurus* future part. of *sum* be]

future perfect *n. Gram.* tense giving the sense 'will have done'.

♦ **futures contract** *n.* agreement to buy or sell a fixed quantity of a particular commodity, currency, or security for delivery at a fixed date in the future at a fixed price; the commodities etc. are known as **futures** (see also FINANCIAL FUTURES). Unlike an option, a futures contract involves a definite purchase or sale and not an option to buy or sell; it therefore may entail a potentially unlimited loss. However, futures provide an opportunity for those who must purchase goods regularly to hedge against changes in price. For hedging to be possible there must be speculators willing to offer these contracts; in fact trade between speculators usu. exceeds the amount of hedging taking place by a considerable amount. In London, futures are traded in a variety of markets. Financial futures are traded on the London International Financial Futures and Options Exchange; London FOX deals with cocoa, coffee, and other foodstuffs; the London Metal Exchange with metals; and the International Petroleum Exchange with oil. In these **futures markets**, in many cases actual goods do not pass between dealers, a bought contract being cancelled out by an equivalent sale contract, and vice versa; money differences arising as a result are usu. settled through a clearing-house (see also LONDON CLEARING HOUSE). In some futures markets only brokers are allowed to trade; in others, both dealers and brokers are permitted to do so. See also FORWARD-EXCHANGE CONTRACT.

◆ **futures market** see FUTURES CONTRACT.

◆ **future value** *n.* value that a sum of money (the **present value**) invested at compound interest will have in the future. If the future value is F, and the present value is P, at an annual rate of interest r, compounded annually for n years, $F = P(1 + r)^n$. Thus a sum with a present value of £1000 will have a future value of £1973.82 at 12% p.a., after six years.

---

futurism *n.* 20th-century artistic movement departing from traditional forms and celebrating technology and dynamism. □ **futurist** *n.* & *adj.*

futuristic /ˌfjuːtʃəˈrɪstɪk/ *adj.* **1** suitable for the future; ultra-modern. **2** of futurism.

futurity /fjuːˈtjʊərɪtɪ/ *n.* (*pl.* **-ies**) *literary* **1** future time. **2** (in *sing.* or *pl.*) future events.

futurology /ˌfjuːtʃəˈrɒlədʒɪ/ *n.* forecasting of the future, esp. from present trends.

fuze var. of FUSE².

Fuzhou /fuːˈdʒəʊ/ (also **Foochow**) city and port in E China, capital of Fujian province; industries include steel production and shipbuilding; pop. (est. 1995) 874 809.

fuzz *n.* **1** fluff. **2** fluffy or frizzed hair. **3** *slang* **a** the police. **b** police officer. [probably Low German or Dutch]

fuzzy *adj.* (**-ier**, **-iest**) **1** like fuzz, fluffy. **2** blurred, indistinct. □ **fuzzily** *adv.* **fuzziness** *n.*

f.w.t. *abbr.* (also **FWT**) fair wear and tear.

FX *abbr.* (also **f.x.**) foreign exchange.

FY *–abbr.* (also **f.y.**) fiscal year. *–postcode* Blackpool.

-fy *suffix* forming: **1** verbs from nouns, meaning: **a** make, produce (*pacify*). **b** make into (*deify*; *petrify*). **2** verbs from adjectives, meaning 'bring or come into a state' (*Frenchify*; *solidify*). **3** verbs in a causative sense (*horrify*; *stupefy*). [French *-fier* from Latin *facio* make]

FZ *abbr.* free zone.

Gg

G[1] /dʒiː/ *n.* (also **g**) (*pl.* **Gs** or **G's**) **1** seventh letter of the alphabet. **2** *Mus.* fifth note of the diatonic scale of C major.

G[2] *–abbr.* **1** gauss. **2** giga-. **3** gravitational constant. *–symb.* gourde. *–international civil aircraft marking* UK. *–postcode* Glasgow.

g *–abbr.* (also **g.**) **1** gram(s). **2** gravity. **3** guinea(s). *–symb.* acceleration due to gravity.

G3 *abbr.* = GROUP OF THREE.

G5 *abbr.* = GROUP OF FIVE.

G7 *abbr.* (also **G-7**) = GROUP OF SEVEN.

G10 *abbr.* = GROUP OF TEN.

G24 *abbr.* Group of Twenty Four (industrialized nations).

G77 *abbr.* = GROUP OF SEVENTY SEVEN.

GA *–abbr.* **1** general agent. **2** (also **G/A, g.a.**) *Insurance* general average (see AVERAGE *n.* 4). *–US postcode* Georgia. *–airline flight code* Garuda Indonesia.

Ga *symb.* gallium.

Ga. *abbr.* Georgia (US).

GAB *abbr.* general arrangements to borrow (in the IMF).

gab *n. colloq.* talk, chatter. [var. of GOB[1]]

gabardine /ˌgæbəˈdiːn/ *n.* (also **gaberdine**) **1** twill-woven cloth, esp. of worsted. **2** raincoat etc. made of this. [French *gauvardine*]

gabble /ˈgæb(ə)l/ *–v.* (**-ling**) talk or utter unintelligibly or too fast. *–n.* fast unintelligible talk. [Dutch, imitative]

gaberdine var. of GABARDINE.

Gabès /ˈgɑːbez/ industrial seaport in E Tunisia; pop. (1994) 98 900.

gable /ˈgeɪb(ə)l/ *n.* **1** triangular upper part of a wall at the end of a ridged roof. **2** gable-topped wall. □ **gabled** *adj.* [Old Norse and French]

Gaborone /ˌgæbəˈrəʊnɪ/ capital of Botswana (since 1965), in the SE of the country, mainly an administrative centre with some light industry; pop. (1993) 156 800.

gad *v.* (**-dd-**) (foll. by *about*) go about idly or in search of pleasure. [obsolete *gadling* companion]

gadabout *n.* person who gads about.

gadfly *n.* **1** fly that bites cattle and horses. **2** irritating person. [obsolete *gad* spike]

gadget /ˈgædʒɪt/ *n.* small mechanical device or tool. □ **gadgetry** *n.* [origin unknown]

gadolinium /ˌgædəˈlɪnɪəm/ *n.* metallic element of the lanthanide series. [*Gadolin*, name of a mineralogist]

gadwall /ˈgædwɔːl/ *n.* brownish-grey freshwater duck. [origin unknown]

Gael /geɪl/ *n.* **1** Scottish Celt. **2** Gaelic-speaking Celt. [Gaelic *Gaidheal*]

Gaelic /ˈgeɪlɪk, ˈgæ-/ *–n.* Celtic language of Ireland and Scotland. *–adj.* of the Celts or the Celtic languages.

gaff[1] *–n.* **1 a** stick with an iron hook for landing large fish. **b** barbed fishing-spear. **2** spar to which the head of a fore-and-aft sail is bent. *–v.* seize (a fish) with a gaff. [Provençal *gaf* hook]

gaff[2] *n. slang* □ **blow the gaff** reveal a plot or secret. [origin unknown]

gaffe /gæf/ *n.* blunder; indiscreet act or remark. [French]

gaffer /ˈgæfə(r)/ *n.* **1** old fellow. **2** *colloq.* foreman, boss. **3** chief electrician in a film or television production unit. [probably from GODFATHER]

Gafsa /ˈgæfsə/ industrial town in central Tunisia; phosphates are exported; pop. (1984) 61 000.

gag *–n.* **1** thing thrust into or tied across the mouth, esp. to prevent speaking or crying out. **2** joke or comic scene. **3** parliamentary closure. **4** thing restricting free speech. *–v.* (**-gg-**) **1** apply a gag to. **2** silence; deprive of free speech. **3** choke, retch. **4** make gags as a comedian etc. [origin uncertain]

gaga /ˈgɑːgɑː/ *adj. slang* **1** senile. **2** slightly crazy. [French]

gage[1] *n.* **1** pledge; thing deposited as security. **2** symbol of a challenge to fight, esp. a glove thrown down. [Germanic: related to WED, WAGE]

gage[2] *US* var. of GAUGE.

gaggle /ˈgæg(ə)l/ *n.* **1** flock of geese. **2** *colloq.* disorganized group of people. [imitative]

gaiety /ˈgeɪətɪ/ *n.* (*US* **gayety**) **1** being gay; mirth. **2** merrymaking. **3** bright appearance. [French: related to GAY]

gaily *adv.* in a gay or careless manner (*gaily decorated*; *gaily announced their departure*).

gain *–v.* **1** obtain or win (*gain advantage*; *gain recognition*). **2** acquire as profits etc., earn. **3** (often foll. by *in*) get more of, improve (*gain momentum*; *gain in experience*). **4** benefit, profit. **5** (of a clock etc.) become fast; become fast by (a specified amount of time). **6** (often foll. by *on*, *upon*) come closer to a person or thing pursued. **7 a** reclaim (land from the sea). **b** win (a battle). **8** reach (a desired place). *–n.* **1** increase of wealth etc.; profit, improvement. **2** (in *pl.*) sums of money got by trade etc. **3** increase in amount. □ **gain ground 1** advance. **2** (foll. by *on*) catch up (a person pursued). [French from Germanic]

Gabon /gəˈbɒn/ republic in W Africa, on the Gulf of Guinea. Rich mineral resources form the basis of Gabon's economy; oil is a major source of income, while uranium and manganese are also exported. There are also large timber reserves, esp. of the hardwood okoumé, which contribute to export revenue. The trans-Gabon railway, opened in 1986, has eased transport problems. Farming is mostly at subsistence level: chief crops include cassava, sugar cane, bananas, and maize. The economy is healthy, with increased profits expected from oil; IMF debt rescheduling will supplement income. Gabon became fully independent from France in 1960. Opposition to the one-party system, established in 1967, led to multi-party elections in 1990 but the ruling party retained control of the government. President, Omar Bongo; capital, Libreville.

languages	French (official), Bantu
currency	CFA franc (CFAF) of 100 centimes
pop. (est. 1996)	1 173 000
GNP (1994)	US$3.6B
literacy	73% (m); 53% (f)
life expectancy	51 (m); 55 (f)

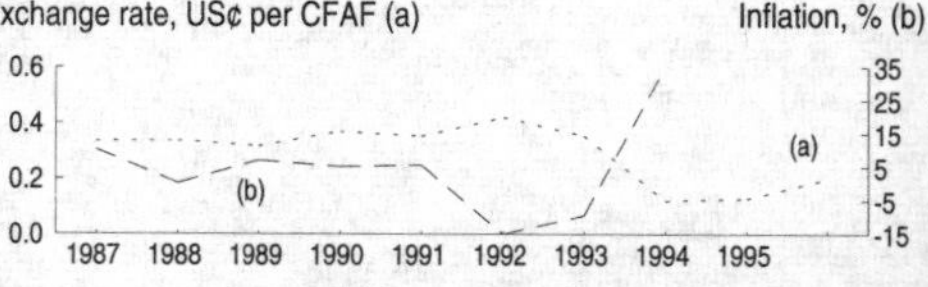

gainful *adj.* **1** (of employment) paid. **2** lucrative. □ **gainfully** *adv.*

gainsay /geɪn'seɪ/ *v.* deny, contradict. [Old Norse: related to AGAINST, SAY]

gait *n.* manner of walking or forward motion. [Old Norse]

gaiter *n.* covering of cloth, leather, etc., for the lower leg. [French *guêtre*]

gal *n. slang* girl. [representing a variant pronunciation]

gal. *abbr.* (also **gall.**) gallon(s).

gala /'gɑːlə/ *n.* festive occasion or gathering (*swimming gala*). [ultimately from French *gale* rejoicing from Germanic]

galactic /gə'læktɪk/ *adj.* of a galaxy or galaxies.

galantine /'gælən,tiːn/ *n.* white meat boned, stuffed, spiced, etc. and served cold. [French from Latin]

Galapagos Islands /gə'læpəgəs/ archipelago in the Pacific, W of Ecuador, to which it belongs; pop. (est. 1996) 13 976.

Galatz /gæ'læts/ port in E Romania, on the lower Danube; industries include shipbuilding, textiles, and iron and steel; pop. (est. 1993) 324 234.

galaxy /'gæləksɪ/ *n.* (*pl.* **-ies**) **1** independent system of stars, gas, dust, etc., in space. **2** (**the Galaxy**) Milky Way. **3** (foll. by *of*) brilliant company (*galaxy of talent*). [Greek *gala* milk]

gale *n.* **1** very strong wind or storm. **2** outburst, esp. of laughter. [origin unknown]

Galicia /gə'lɪsɪə/ autonomous region of NW Spain; tin and tungsten are mined; pop. (est. 1994) 2 720 761; capital, Santiago de Compostella. □ **Galician** *adj.* & *n.*

gall[1] /gɔːl/ *n.* **1** *slang* impudence. **2** rancour. **3** bitterness. **4** bile. [Old Norse]

gall[2] /gɔːl/ *–n.* **1** sore made by chafing. **2** mental soreness or its cause. **3** place rubbed bare. *–v.* **1** rub sore. **2** vex, humiliate. [Low German or Dutch *galle*]

gall[3] /gɔːl/ *n.* growth produced by insects etc. on plants and trees, esp. on oak. [Latin *galla*]

gall. *abbr.* var. of GAL.

gallant *–adj.* /'gælənt/ **1** brave. **2** fine, stately. **3** /gə'lænt/ very attentive to women. *–n.* /gə'lænt/ ladies' man. □ **gallantly** /'gæləntlɪ/ *adv.* [French *galer* make merry]

gallantry /'gæləntrɪ/ *n.* (*pl.* **-ies**) **1** bravery. **2** devotion to women. **3** polite act or speech.

gall-bladder *n.* organ storing bile.

Galle /gɑːlə/ seaport on the SW coast of Sri Lanka; cement is produced; pop. (est. 1990) 84 000.

galleon /'gælɪən/ *n. hist.* warship (usu. Spanish). [French or Spanish: related to GALLEY]

galleria /,gælə'riːə/ *n.* collection of small shops under a single roof. [Italian]

gallery /'gælərɪ/ *n.* (*pl.* **-ies**) **1** room or building for showing works of art. **2** balcony, esp. in a church, hall, etc. (*minstrels' gallery*). **3** highest balcony in a theatre. **4 a** covered walk partly open at the side; colonnade. **b** narrow passage in the thickness of a wall or on corbels, open towards the interior of the building. **5** long narrow room or passage (*shooting-gallery*). **6** horizontal underground passage in a mine etc. **7** group of spectators at a golf-match etc. □ **play to the gallery** seek to win approval by appealing to popular taste. [French *galerie*]

galley /'gælɪ/ *n.* (*pl.* **-s**) **1** *hist.* **a** long flat single-decked vessel usu. rowed by slaves or criminals. **b** ancient Greek or Roman warship. **2** ship's or aircraft's kitchen. **3** *Printing* (in full **galley proof**) proof in continuous form before division into pages. [Latin *galea*]

galley-slave *n.* drudge.

Gallic /'gælɪk/ *adj.* **1** French or typically French. **2** of Gaul or the Gauls. [Latin *Gallicus*]

Gallicism /'gælɪ,sɪz(ə)m/ *n.* French idiom. [related to GALLIC]

gallinaceous /,gælɪ'neɪʃəs/ *adj.* of the order including domestic poultry, pheasants, etc. [Latin *gallina* hen]

gallium /'gælɪəm/ *n.* soft bluish-white metallic element. [Latin *Gallia* France: so named patriotically by its discoverer Lecoq]

gallivant /'gælɪ,vænt/ *v. colloq.* gad about. [origin uncertain]

Gallo- *comb. form* French. [Latin]

gallon /'gælən/ *n.* **1** measure of capacity equal to eight pints (4.5 litres; for wine, or *US*, 3.8 litres). **2** (in *pl.*) *colloq.* large amount. [French]

gallop /'gæləp/ *–n.* **1** fastest pace of a horse etc., with all the feet off the ground together in each stride. **2** ride at this pace. *–v.* (**-p-**) **1 a** (of a horse etc. or its rider) go at a gallop. **b** make (a horse etc.) gallop. **2** read, talk, etc., fast. **3** progress rapidly (*galloping consumption*). [French: related to WALLOP]

♦ **galloping inflation** *n.* = HYPERINFLATION.

---

gallows /'gæləʊz/ *n.pl.* (usu. treated as *sing.*) structure, usu. of two uprights and a crosspiece, for hanging criminals. [Old Norse]

gallstone *n.* small hard mass forming in the gall-bladder.

Gallup poll /'gæləp/ *n.* = OPINION POLL. [*Gallup*, name of a statistician]

galore /gə'lɔː(r)/ *adv.* in plenty (*whisky galore*). [Irish *go leor* enough]

galosh /gə'lɒʃ/ *n.* (also **golosh**) (usu. in *pl.*) overshoe, usu. of rubber. [French]

galumph /gə'lʌmf/ *–v.* (esp. as **galumphing** *adj.*) *colloq.* move noisily or clumsily. [coined by Lewis Carroll, perhaps from GALLOP, TRIUMPH]

galvanic /gæl'vænɪk/ *adj.* **1 a** producing an electric current by chemical action. **b** (of electricity) produced by chemical action. **2 a** sudden and remarkable (*had a gal-*

Gambia /'gæmbɪə/, **Republic of The** country in W Africa, consisting of a narrow strip on either side of the River Gambia upstream from its mouth, forming an enclave in Senegal. Agriculture is the mainstay of the economy, peanuts and peanut products being the most important exports; fish and fish products also contribute to export revenue and rice, millet, sorghum, and cotton are grown as food crops. Tourism is an increasing source of income, and revenue is also generated by entrepôt trade with neighbouring countries. The economy is stable, and a new treaty with Senegal (signed 1991) should increase trade. A former British colony, The Gambia became independent in 1965, and a republic within the Commonwealth in 1970. A coup in 1994 ousted the president and installed a military council. The leader of the coup, Yayah Jammeh assumed the presidency and suspended the constitution. A new constitution was approved in 1996 and Jammeh was elected president. President, Captain Yayah Jammeh; capital, Banjul. □ **Gambian** *adj.* & *n.*

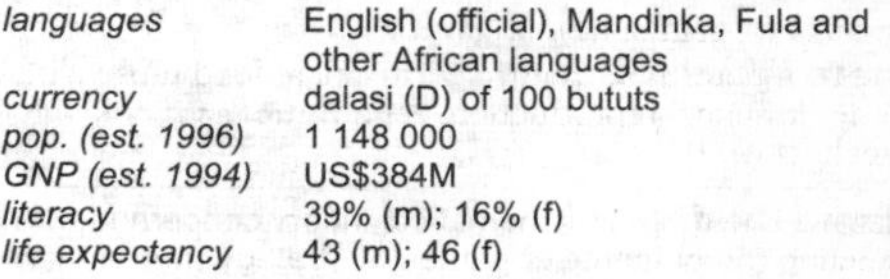

languages	English (official), Mandinka, Fula and other African languages
currency	dalasi (D) of 100 bututs
pop. (est. 1996)	1 148 000
GNP (est. 1994)	US$384M
literacy	39% (m); 16% (f)
life expectancy	43 (m); 46 (f)

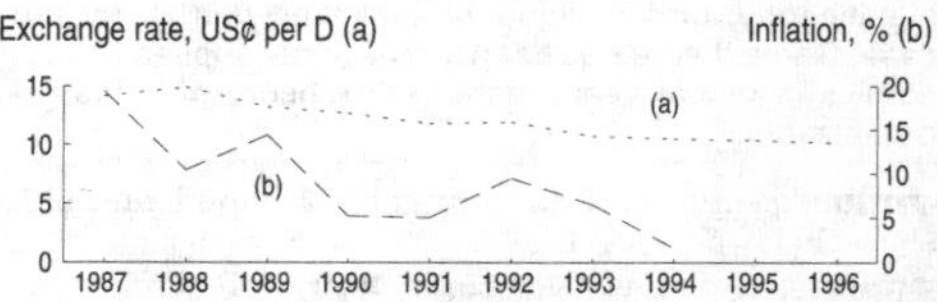

vanic effect). **b** stimulating; full of energy. □ **galvanically** *adv.*

galvanize /ˈgælvəˌnaɪz/ *v.* (also **-ise**) (**-zing** or **-sing**) **1** (often foll. by *into*) rouse forcefully, esp. by shock or excitement (*was galvanized into action*). **2** stimulate by or as by electricity. **3** coat (iron) with zinc to protect against rust. □ **galvanization** /-ˈzeɪʃ(ə)n/ *n.* [*Galvani*, name of a physiologist]

galvanometer /ˌgælvəˈnɒmɪtə(r)/ *n.* instrument for detecting and measuring small electric currents. □ **galvanometric** /-nəˈmetrɪk/ *adj.*

Galway /ˈgɔːlweɪ/ **1** county on the W coast of the Republic of Ireland, in the province of Connaught; pop. (1991) 180 364. Dairy and sheep farming and fishing are the main occupations. **2** its capital city, a seaport; pop. (1991) 50 853.

Gambier Islands /ˈgæmbɪə(r)/ group of coral islands in the Tuamotu Archipelago in French Polynesia; pop. (1986) 582.

gambit /ˈgæmbɪt/ *n.* **1** chess opening in which a player sacrifices a piece or pawn to secure an advantage. **2** opening move in a discussion etc. **3** trick or device. [Italian *gambetto* tripping up]

gamble /ˈgæmb(ə)l/ *–v.* (**-ling**) **1** play games of chance for money. **2 a** bet (a sum of money) in gambling. **b** (often foll. by *away*) lose by gambling. **3** risk much in the hope of great gain. **4** (foll. by *on*) act in the hope of. *–n.* **1** risky undertaking. **2** spell of gambling. □ **gambler** *n.*

gamboge /gæmˈbəʊdʒ/ *n.* gum resin used as a yellow pigment and as a purgative. [*Cambodia* in SE Asia]

gambol /ˈgæmb(ə)l/ *–v.* (**-ll-**; *US* **-l-**) skip or jump about playfully. *–n.* frolic, caper. [French *gambade* leap, from Italian *gamba* leg]

game[1] *–n.* **1** form of play or sport, esp. a competitive one with rules. **2** portion of play forming a scoring unit, e.g. in bridge or tennis. **3** (in *pl.*) series of athletic etc. contests (*Olympic Games*). **4 a** piece of fun, jest (*didn't mean to upset you; it was only a game*). **b** (in *pl.*) dodges, tricks (*none of your games!*). **5** *colloq.* **a** scheme (*so that's your game*). **b** type of activity or business (*have been in the antiques game a long time*). **6 a** wild animals or birds hunted for sport or food. **b** their flesh as food. *–adj.* spirited; eager and willing (*are you game for a walk?*). *–v.* (**-ming**) gamble for money stakes. □ **the game is up** scheme is revealed or foiled. **on the game** *slang* working as a prostitute. □ **gamely** *adv.* [Old English]

game[2] *adj. colloq.* (of a leg, arm, etc.) crippled. [origin unknown]

gamecock *n.* cock bred and trained for cock-fighting.

gamekeeper *n.* person employed to breed and protect game.

gamelan /ˈgæməˌlæn/ *n.* **1** SE Asian orchestra mainly of percussion instruments. **2** type of xylophone used in this. [Javanese]

gamesmanship *n.* art of winning games by gaining psychological advantage.

gamester /ˈgeɪmstə(r)/ *n.* gambler.

gamete /ˈgæmiːt/ *n.* mature germ cell able to unite with another in sexual reproduction. □ **gametic** /gəˈmetɪk/ *adj.* [Greek, = wife]

♦ **game theory** *n.* mathematical theory concerned with predicting the outcome of games of strategy (rather than games of chance) in which the participants have incomplete information about the others' intentions. Under perfect competition there is no scope for game theory, as individual actions are assumed not to influence others significantly; under oligopoly, however, this is not the case. Game theory has been increasingly applied to economics in recent years, esp. in the theory of industrial organizations.

---

gamin /ˈgæmɪn/ *n.* **1** street urchin. **2** impudent child. [French]

gamine /gæˈmiːn/ *n.* **1** girl gamin. **2** girl with mischievous charm. [French]

♦ **gaming contract** *n.* contract involving the playing of a game of chance by any number of people for money (a **wagering contract** involving only two people), and usu. no action can be brought to recover money paid or won under them.

---

gamma /ˈgæmə/ *n.* **1** third letter of the Greek alphabet (Γ, γ). **2** third-class mark for a piece of work etc. [Greek]

gamma radiation *n.* (also **gamma rays**) electromagnetic radiation of shorter wavelength than X-rays.

♦ **gamma stocks** *n.pl.* one of four categories of shares used as a measure of market liquidity between 1986 and 1991 on the London Stock Exchange. See NORMAL MARKET SIZE.

---

gammon /ˈgæmən/ *n.* **1** bottom piece of a flitch of bacon including a hind leg. **2** ham of a pig cured like bacon. [French: related to JAMB]

gammy /ˈgæmɪ/ *adj.* (**-ier, -iest**) *slang* = GAME[2]. [dial. form of GAME[2]]

gamut /ˈgæmət/ *n.* entire range or scope. □ **run the gamut of** experience or perform the complete range of. [Latin *gamma ut*, words arbitrarily taken as names of notes]

gamy *adj.* (**-ier, -iest**) smelling or tasting like high game.

Gand see GHENT.

gander *n.* **1** male goose. **2** *slang* look, glance (*take a gander*). [Old English]

Gandzha /ˈgɑːndʒə/ (formerly **Elizavetpol, Kirovabad**) industrial city in Azerbaijan; products include textiles, building materials, and wine; pop. (est. 1991) 282 200.

gang *n.* **1** band of persons associating for some (usu. antisocial or criminal) purpose. **2** set of workers, slaves, or prisoners. □ **gang up** *colloq.* **1** (often foll. by *with*) act together. **2** (foll. by *on*) combine against. [Old Norse]

Ganga see GANGES.

ganger *n.* foreman of a gang of workers.

Ganges /ˈgændʒiːz/ (Hindi **Ganga** /ˈgʌŋgə/) river in N India, flowing SE from the Himalayas to Bangladesh, where it reaches the Bay of Bengal in the world's largest delta.

gangling /ˈgæŋglɪŋ/ *adj.* (of a person) loosely built; lanky. [frequentative of Old English *gang* go]

ganglion /ˈgæŋglɪən/ *n.* (*pl.* **-lia** or **-s**) structure containing an assemblage of nerve cells. □ **ganglionic** /-ˈɒnɪk/ *adj.* [Greek]

gangly /ˈgæŋglɪ/ *adj.* (**-ier, -iest**) = GANGLING.

gangplank *n.* movable plank for boarding or disembarking from a ship etc.

gangrene /ˈgæŋgriːn/ *n.* death of body tissue, usu. resulting from obstructed circulation. □ **gangrenous** /-grɪnəs/ *adj.* [Greek *gaggraina*]

gangster *n.* member of a gang of violent criminals.

gangue /gæŋ/ *n.* valueless earth etc. in which ore is found. [German: related to GANG]

gangway *n.* **1** passage, esp. between rows of seats. **2 a** opening in a ship's bulwarks. **b** bridge from ship to shore.

gannet /ˈgænɪt/ *n.* **1** large diving sea bird. **2** *slang* greedy person. [Old English]

Gansu /gænˈsuː/ (also **Kansu**) province in N central China; coal and oil are produced; pop. (est. 1995) 23 780 000; capital, Lanzhou (Lanchow).

gantry /ˈgæntrɪ/ *n.* (*pl.* **-ies**) structure supporting a travelling crane, railway or road signals, rocket-launching equipment, etc. [probably *gawn*, a dial. form of GALLON, + TREE]

Gantt chart /gænt/ *n.* chart showing, in horizontal lines, activity planned to occur in specified periods, indicated by vertical bands. [Gantt, name of a management consultant]

GAO *abbr.* (in the US) General Accounting Office.

gaol var. of JAIL.

gaolbird var. of JAILBIRD.

gaolbreak var. of JAILBREAK.

gaoler var. of JAILER.

gap *n.* **1** empty space, interval; deficiency. **2** breach in a hedge, fence, etc. **3** wide divergence in views etc. □ **gappy** *adj.* [Old Norse]

♦ **gap analysis** *n. Commerce* methodical tabulation of all the known requirements of consumers in a particular category of products, together with a cross-listing of all the features provided by existing products to satisfy these requirements, which exposes any gaps that exist and therefore provides a pointer to any new products that could supply an unfulfilled demand.

gape –*v.* (**-ping**) **1 a** open one's mouth wide. **b** be or become wide open; split. **2** (foll. by *at*) stare at. –*n.* **1** open-mouthed stare; open mouth. **2** rent, opening. [Old Norse]

garage /'gærɑːʒ, -rɪdʒ/ –*n.* **1** building for housing a vehicle. **2** establishment selling petrol etc., or repairing and selling vehicles. –*v.* (**-ging**) put or keep in a garage. [French]

garb –*n.* clothing, esp. of a distinctive kind. –*v.* (usu. in *passive* or *refl.*) dress. [Germanic: related to GEAR]

garbage /'gɑːbɪdʒ/ *n.* **1** esp. *US* refuse. **2** *colloq.* nonsense. **3** stored computer data that is no longer valid or no longer wanted. See also GIGO. [Anglo-French]

garble /'gɑːb(ə)l/ *v.* (**-ling**) **1** (esp. as **garbled** *adj.*) unintentionally distort or confuse (facts, messages, etc.). **2** make a (usu. unfair) selection from (facts, statements, etc.). [Italian from Arabic]

garbology /gɑː'bɒlədʒɪ/ *n.* study of the contents of domestic dustbins to analyse the consumption patterns of householders. □ **garbologist** *n.*

garden /'gɑːd(ə)n/ –*n.* **1** piece of ground for growing flowers, fruit, or vegetables, and as a place of recreation. **2** (esp. in *pl.*) grounds laid out for public enjoyment. **3** (*attrib.*) cultivated (*garden plants*). –*v.* cultivate or tend a garden. □ **gardening** *n.* [Germanic: related to YARD[2]]

garden centre *n.* place where plants and garden equipment are sold.

garden city *n.* town spaciously laid out with parks etc.

gardener *n.* person who gardens, esp. for a living.

gardenia /gɑː'diːnɪə/ *n.* tree or shrub with large fragrant flowers. [*Garden*, name of a naturalist]

garden party *n.* party held on a lawn or in a garden.

garfish /'gɑːfɪʃ/ *n.* (*pl.* same or **-es**) fish with a long spearlike snout. [Old English, = spear-fish]

gargantuan /gɑː'gæntjʊən/ *adj.* gigantic. [from the name *Gargantua*, a giant in Rabelais]

gargle /'gɑːg(ə)l/ –*v.* (**-ling**) wash (the throat) with a liquid kept in motion by breathing through it. –*n.* liquid for gargling. [French: related to GARGOYLE]

gargoyle /'gɑːgɔɪl/ *n.* grotesque carved face or figure, esp. as a spout from the gutter of a building. [French, = throat]

garibaldi /ˌgærɪ'bɔːldɪ/ *n.* (*pl.* **-s**) biscuit containing a layer of currants. [*Garibaldi*, name of an Italian patriot]

garish /'geərɪʃ/ *adj.* obtrusively bright; showy; gaudy. □ **garishly** *adv.* **garishness** *n.* [obsolete *gaure* stare]

garland /'gɑːlənd/ –*n.* wreath of flowers etc., worn on the head or hung as a decoration. –*v.* adorn or crown with a garland or garlands. [French]

garlic /'gɑːlɪk/ *n.* plant of the onion family with a pungent bulb used in cookery. □ **garlicky** *adj.* [Old English, = spear-leek]

garment /'gɑːmənt/ *n.* **1** article of dress. **2** outward covering. [French: related to GARNISH]

garner /'gɑːnə(r)/ –*v.* **1** collect. **2** store. –*n. literary* storehouse or granary. [Latin: related to GRANARY]

garnet /'gɑːnɪt/ *n.* glassy silicate mineral, esp. a red kind used as a gem. [medieval Latin *granatum* POMEGRANATE]

garnish /'gɑːnɪʃ/ –*v.* decorate (esp. food). –*n.* decoration, esp. to food. [French *garnir* from Germanic]

♦ **garnishee order** /ˌgɑːnɪ'ʃiː/ *n. Law* order made by a judge on behalf of a judgement creditor restraining a third party (often a bank), called a **garnishee**, from paying money to the judgement debtor until sanctioned to do so by the court. The order may also specify that the garnishee must pay a stated sum to the judgement creditor, or to the court, from the funds belonging to the judgement debtor.

garotte var. of GARROTTE.

garret /'gærɪt/ *n.* attic or room in a roof. [French, = watch-tower: related to GARRISON]

garrison /'gærɪs(ə)n/ –*n.* troops stationed in a town etc. to defend it. –*v.* (**-n-**) **1** provide with or occupy as a garrison. **2** place on garrison duty. [French *garir* defend, from Germanic]

garrotte /gə'rɒt/ (also **garotte**; *US* **garrote**) –*v.* (**-ting**) execute or kill by strangulation, esp. with a wire collar. –*n.* device used for this. [French or Spanish]

garrulous /'gærʊləs/ *adj.* talkative. □ **garrulity** /gə'ruːlɪtɪ/ *n.* **garrulousness** *n.* [Latin]

garter *n.* **1** band worn to keep a sock or stocking up. **2** (**the Garter**) **a** highest order of English knighthood. **b** badge or membership of this. [French]

garter stitch *n.* plain knitting stitch.

gas –*n.* (*pl.* **-es**) **1** any airlike substance (i.e. not solid or liquid) moving freely to fill any space available. **2** such a substance (esp. found naturally or extracted from coal) used as fuel (also *attrib.*: *gas cooker*; *gas industry*). **3** nitrous oxide or other gas as an anaesthetic. **4** poisonous gas used in war. **5** *US colloq.* petrol, gasoline. **6** *slang* idle talk; boasting. **7** *slang* enjoyable or amusing thing or person. –*v.* (**gases, gassed, gassing**) **1** expose to gas, esp. to kill. **2** *colloq.* talk idly or boastfully. [Dutch invented word based on Greek *khaos* = CHAOS]

gasbag *n. slang* idle talker.

gas chamber *n.* room filled with poisonous gas to kill people or animals.

gaseous /'gæsɪəs/ *adj.* of or like gas.

gas fire *n.* domestic heater burning gas.

gas-fired *adj.* using gas as fuel.

gash –*n.* long deep slash, cut, or wound. –*v.* make a gash in; cut. [French]

gasholder *n.* large receptacle for storing gas; gasometer.

gasify /'gæsɪˌfaɪ/ *v.* (**-ies, -ied**) convert into gas. □ **gasification** /-fɪ'keɪʃ(ə)n/ *n.*

gasket /'gæskɪt/ *n.* sheet or ring of rubber etc., shaped to seal the junction of metal surfaces. [French *garcette*]

gaslight *n.* light from burning gas.

gasman *n.* man who installs or services gas appliances, or reads gas meters.

gas mask *n.* respirator as a protection against poison gas.

gasoline /'gæsəˌliːn/ *n.* (also **gasolene**) *US* petrol.

gasometer /gæ'sɒmɪtə(r)/ *n.* large tank from which gas is distributed by pipes. [French *gazomètre*: related to GAS, -METER]

gasp /gɑːsp/ –*v.* **1** catch one's breath with an open mouth as in exhaustion or astonishment. **2** utter with gasps. –*n.* convulsive catching of breath. [Old Norse]

gas panel display *n.* = PLASMA DISPLAY.

gas ring *n.* hollow ring perforated with gas jets, for cooking etc.

gassy *adj.* (**-ier, -iest**) **1 a** of or like gas. **b** full of gas. **2** *colloq.* verbose.

gasteropod var. of GASTROPOD.

gastric /'gæstrɪk/ *adj.* of the stomach. [French: related to GASTRO-]

gastric flu *n. colloq.* intestinal disorder of unknown cause.

gastric juice *n.* digestive fluid secreted by the stomach glands.

gastritis /gæ'straɪtɪs/ *n.* inflammation of the stomach.

gastro- *comb. form* stomach. [Greek *gastēr* stomach]

gastro-enteritis /ˌgæstrəʊˌentəˈraɪtɪs/ *n.* inflammation of the stomach and intestines.

gastronome /ˈgæstrəˌnəʊm/ *n.* gourmet. [Greek *gastēr* stomach, *nomos* law]

gastronomy /gæˈstrɒnəmɪ/ *n.* science or art of good eating and drinking. □ **gastronomic** /ˌgæstrəˈnɒmɪk/ *adj.* **gastronomical** /ˌgæstrəˈnɒmɪk(ə)l/ *adj.* **gastronomically** /ˌgæstrəˈnɒmɪkəlɪ/ *adv.*

gastropod /ˈgæstrəˌpɒd/ *n.* (also **gasteropod**) mollusc that moves by means of a ventral muscular organ, e.g. a snail. [from GASTRO-, Greek *pous pod-* foot]

gasworks *n.* place where gas is manufactured for lighting and heating.

gate –*n.* **1** barrier, usu. hinged, used to close an opening made for entrance and exit through a wall, fence, etc. **2** such an opening. **3** means of entrance or exit. **4** numbered place of access to aircraft at an airport. **5** device regulating the passage of water in a lock etc. **6 a** number of people entering by payment at the gates of a sports ground etc. **b** amount of money taken thus. **7 a** electrical signal that causes or controls the passage of other signals. **b** electrical circuit with an output that depends on the combination of several inputs. See LOGIC GATE. –*v.* (**-ting**) confine to college or school as a punishment. □ **gated** *adj.* [Old English]

gateau /ˈgætəʊ/ *n.* (*pl.* **-s** or **-x** /-təʊz/) large rich cake filled with cream etc. [French]

gatecrasher *n.* uninvited guest at a party etc. □ **gatecrash** *v.*

gatehouse *n.* house standing by or over a gateway, esp. to a large house or park.

◆ **gatekeeper** *n.* **1** person who controls entry through a gate. **2** manager in a large company who controls the flow of information and decides what information shall be passed upwards to a parent company and downwards to a subsidiary.

---

gateleg *n.* (in full **gateleg table**) table with folding flaps supported by legs swung open like a gate. □ **gatelegged** *adj.*

gatepost *n.* post at either side of a gate.

◆ **Gates** /geɪts/, **William Henry (Bill)** (1955–) US computer software executive, founder (1976) and chairman of Microsoft Corporation, of which he is now chief executive officer. Gates built Microsoft on a disk operating system and windows system, the phenomenal success of which gave Microsoft a near monopoly. He is now investing in delivering the Internet to households via television. In 1997 Microsoft bought Web TV and an 11.5% share in Comcast, the fourth-largest cable company in the US. Gates's personal net worth was put at $36.4 billion, making him one of the richest men in the US.

---

gateway *n.* **1** opening which can be closed with a gate. **2** means of access (*gateway to the South*; *gateway to success*).

gather /ˈgæðə(r)/ –*v.* **1** bring or come together; accumulate. **2** pick or collect as harvest. **3** infer or deduce. **4 a** increase (*gather speed*). **b** collect (*gather dust*). **5** summon up (energy etc.). **6** draw together in folds or wrinkles. **7** (often as **gathering** *adj.*) come to a head (*gathering storm*). **8** develop a purulent swelling. –*n.* fold or pleat. □ **gather up** bring together; pick up from the ground; draw into a small compass. [Old English]

gathering *n.* **1** assembly. **2** purulent swelling. **3** group of leaves taken together in bookbinding.

GATT /gæt/ *abbr.* = GENERAL AGREEMENT ON TARIFFS AND TRADE.

gauche /gəʊʃ/ *adj.* **1** socially awkward. **2** tactless. □ **gauchely** *adv.* **gaucheness** *n.* [French]

gaucherie /ˈgəʊʃəˌriː/ *n.* gauche manners or act. [French: related to GAUCHE]

gaucho /ˈgaʊtʃəʊ/ *n.* (*pl.* **-s**) cowboy from the South American pampas. [Spanish from Quechua]

gaudy /ˈgɔːdɪ/ *adj.* (**-ier, -iest**) tastelessly showy. □ **gaudily** *adv.* **gaudiness** *n.* [obsolete *gaud* ornament, from Latin *gaudeo* rejoice]

gauge /geɪdʒ/ (*US* **gage**: see also sense 6) –*n.* **1** standard measure, esp. of the capacity or contents of a barrel, fineness of a textile, diameter of a bullet, or thickness of sheet metal. **2** instrument for measuring pressure, width, length, thickness, etc. **3** distance between rails or opposite wheels. **4** capacity, extent. **5** criterion, test. **6** (usu. **gage**) *Naut.* position relative to the wind. –*v.* (**-ging**) **1** measure exactly. **2** measure the capacity or content of. **3** estimate (a person, situation, etc.). [French]

Gaul /gɔːl/ *n.* inhabitant of ancient Gaul. [French from Germanic]

Gaulish –*adj.* of the Gauls. –*n.* their language.

gaunt /gɔːnt/ *adj.* **1** lean, haggard. **2** grim, desolate. □ **gauntness** *n.* [origin unknown]

gauntlet[1] /ˈgɔːntlɪt/ *n.* **1** stout glove with a long loose wrist. **2** *hist.* armoured glove. □ **pick up** (or **take up**) **the gauntlet** accept a challenge. **throw down the gauntlet** issue a challenge. [French diminutive of *gant* glove]

gauntlet[2] /ˈgɔːntlɪt/ *n.* □ **run the gauntlet 1** undergo harsh criticism. **2** pass between two rows of people and receive blows from them, as a punishment or ordeal. [Swedish *gatlopp* from *gata* lane, *lopp* course]

gauss /gaʊs/ *n.* (*pl.* same) unit of magnetic flux density. [*Gauss*, name of a mathematician]

gauze /gɔːz/ *n.* **1** thin transparent fabric of silk, cotton, etc. **2** fine mesh of wire etc. □ **gauzy** *adj.* (**-ier, -iest**). [French from *Gaza* in Palestine]

GAV *abbr. Accounting* gross annual value.

gave *past* of GIVE.

gavel /ˈgæv(ə)l/ *n.* hammer used for calling attention by an auctioneer, chairman, or judge. [origin unknown]

gavotte /gəˈvɒt/ *n.* **1** old French dance. **2** music for this. [French from Provençal]

gawk –*v. colloq.* gawp. –*n.* awkward or bashful person. [obsolete *gaw* GAZE]

gawky *adj.* (**-ier, -iest**) awkward or ungainly. □ **gawkily** *adv.* **gawkiness** *n.*

gawp *v. colloq.* stare stupidly or obtrusively. [related to YELP]

gay –*adj.* **1** light-hearted, cheerful. **2** brightly coloured. **3** *colloq.* homosexual. **4** *colloq.* careless, thoughtless (*gay abandon*). –*n. colloq.* (esp. male) homosexual. □ **gayness** *n.* [French]

■ **Usage** Sense 3 is generally informal in tone, but is favoured by homosexual groups.

gayety *US* var. of GAIETY.

Gazankulu /ˌgæzənˈkuːluː/ former Bantu homeland in South Africa, in the former province of Transvaal.

Gaza Strip /ˈgɑːzə/ strip of coastal territory in the SE Mediterranean, formerly part of Palestine held by Egypt, occupied by Israel since 1967; in 1994–5 administration was passed to the new Palestinian National Authority; pop. (1993) 748 400.

gaze –*v.* (**-zing**) (foll. by *at*, *into*, *on*, etc.) look fixedly. –*n.* intent look. [origin unknown]

gazebo /gəˈziːbəʊ/ *n.* (*pl.* **-s**) summer-house, turret, etc., with a wide view. [perhaps a fanciful formation from GAZE]

gazelle /gəˈzel/ *n.* (*pl.* same or **-s**) small graceful antelope. [Arabic *ġazāl*]

gazette /gəˈzet/ –*n.* **1** newspaper (used in the title). **2** official publication with announcements etc. –*v.* (**-tting**) announce or name in an official gazette. [French from Italian]

gazetteer /ˌgæzɪˈtɪə(r)/ *n.* geographical index. [Italian: related to GAZETTE]

gazpacho /gæˈspætʃəʊ/ *n.* (*pl.* **-s**) cold Spanish soup. [Spanish]

gazump /gəˈzʌmp/ *v. colloq.* **1** raise the price of, or accept a higher offer for, a property after accepting a verbal offer from (a buyer) but before the exchange of contracts has taken place. The intending purchaser has no remedy, even though expenditure may have been incurred on legal fees, surveys, etc. **2** swindle. [origin unknown]

gazunder /gə'zʌndə(r)/ *v. colloq.* lower an offer made to (a seller) for a property just before the exchange of contracts. [from GAZUMP, UNDER]

GB *abbr. & international vehicle registration* Great Britain.

GBA *international vehicle registration* Alderney.

GBG *international vehicle registration* Guernsey.

GBH *abbr.* grievous bodily harm.

GBJ *international vehicle registration* Jersey.

GBM *international vehicle registration* Isle of Man.

g.b.o. *abbr.* goods in bad order.

GBTA *abbr.* Guild of Business Travel Agents.

GBZ *international vehicle registration* Gibraltar.

GC *abbr.* George Cross.

GCA *international vehicle registration* Guatemala.

GCBS *abbr.* General Council of British Shipping.

GCE *abbr.* General Certificate of Education.

GCHQ *abbr.* Government Communications Headquarters.

GCSE *abbr.* General Certificate of Secondary Education.

Gd *symb.* gadolinium.

Gdańsk /gdænsk/ (German **Danzig** /'dæntsɪg/) industrial port and shipbuilding centre in N Poland, on an inlet of the Baltic Sea; pop. (est. 1995) 463 100.

GDP *abbr.* = GROSS DOMESTIC PRODUCT.

♦ **GDP deflator** *n.* factor by which the value of gross domestic product at current prices must be reduced (deflated) to express GDP in terms of the prices of some base year (e.g. 1990). It is thus a measure of inflation.

GDR *abbr. hist.* German Democratic Republic.

Ge *symb.* germanium.

gear *–n.* **1** (often in *pl.*) **a** set of toothed wheels that work together, esp. those connecting the engine of a vehicle to the road wheels. **b** particular setting of these (*first gear*). **2** equipment, apparatus, or tackle. **3** *colloq.* clothing. *–v.* **1** (foll. by *to*) adjust or adapt to. **2** (often foll. by *up*) equip with gears. **3** (foll. by *up*) make ready or prepared. **4** put in gear. □ **in gear** with a gear engaged. **out of gear** with no gear engaged. [Old Norse]

gearbox *n.* **1** set of gears with its casing, esp. in a vehicle. **2** the casing itself.

gearing *n.* **1** set or arrangement of gears. **2** see CAPITAL GEARING.

♦ **gearing adjustment** *n.* adjustment in current-cost accounting to allow for the fact that in inflationary times profits may accrue to a company from its fixed-interest capital, so that the whole cost of capital maintenance need not fall on the profits available to the ordinary shareholders.

♦ **gearing effect** *n.* way in which the capital gearing of a company affects its shareholders' dividends.

♦ **gearing ratio** *n.* ratio of a company's debt to its equity or of its debt to its debt plus equity, usu. expressed as a percentage.

---

gear lever *n.* (also **gear shift**) lever used to engage or change gear.

gearwheel *n.* toothed wheel in a set of gears.

GEC *abbr.* General Electric Company.

gecko /'gekəʊ/ *n.* (*pl.* **-s**) tropical house-lizard. [Malay]

gee[1] *int.* (also **gee whiz** /wɪz/) esp. *US colloq.* expression of surprise etc. [perhaps an abbreviation of JESUS]

gee[2] /dʒiː/ *int.* (usu. foll. by *up*) command to a horse etc. to start or go faster. [origin unknown]

gee-gee /'dʒiːdʒiː/ *n. colloq.* (a child's word for) a horse.

Geelong /dʒiː'lɒŋ/ port and oil-refining centre on the S coast of Australia, in the state of Victoria; pop. (est. 1995) 152 600.

geese *pl.* of GOOSE.

geezer /'giːzə(r)/ *n. slang* person, esp. an old man. [dial. *guiser* mummer]

Geiger counter /'gaɪgə(r)/ *n.* device for detecting and measuring radioactivity. [*Geiger*, name of a physicist]

geisha /'geɪʃə/ *n.* (*pl.* same or **-s**) Japanese woman trained to entertain men. [Japanese]

gel *–n.* **1** semi-solid jelly-like colloid. **2** jelly-like substance used for setting the hair. *–v.* (**-ll-**) **1** form a gel. **2** = JELL 2. [from GELATIN]

gelatin /'dʒelətɪn/ *n.* (also **gelatine** /-ˌtiːn/) transparent tasteless substance from skin, tendons, etc., used in cookery, photography, etc. □ **gelatinize** /dʒɪ'lætɪˌnaɪz/ *v.* (also **-ise**) (**-zing** or **-sing**). [Italian: related to JELLY]

gelatinous /dʒɪ'lætɪnəs/ *adj.* of a jelly-like consistency.

geld /geld/ *v.* castrate. [Old Norse]

gelding *n.* gelded animal, esp. a horse.

gelignite /'dʒelɪgˌnaɪt/ *n.* explosive made from nitroglycerine. [from GELATIN, IGNEOUS]

gem *–n.* **1** precious stone, esp. cut and polished or engraved. **2** thing of great beauty or worth. *–v.* (**-mm-**) adorn with or as with gems. [Latin *gemma* bud, jewel]

geminate *–adj.* /'dʒemɪnət/ combined in pairs. *–v.* /'dʒemɪˌneɪt/ (**-ting**) **1** double, repeat. **2** arrange in pairs. □ **gemination** /-'neɪʃ(ə)n/ *n.* [Latin: related to GEMINI]

Gemini /'dʒemɪˌnaɪ/ *n.* (*pl.* **-s**) **1** constellation and third sign of the zodiac (the Twins). **2** person born when the sun is in this sign. [Latin, = twins]

gemma *n.* (*pl.* **gemmae** /-miː/) small cellular body in plants such as mosses, that separates from the mother-plant and starts a new one. □ **gemmation** /-'meɪʃ(ə)n/ *n.* [Latin, see GEM]

gemstone *n.* precious stone used as a gem.

Gen. *abbr.* General.

gen *slang –n.* information. *–v.* (**-nn-**) (foll. by *up*) gain or give information. [probably *gen*eral information]

-gen *comb. form Chem.* that which produces (*hydrogen; antigen*). [Greek *-genes* born]

gendarme /'ʒɒndɑːm/ *n.* (in French-speaking countries) police officer. [French *gens d'armes* men of arms]

gender *n.* **1 a** classification roughly corresponding to the two sexes and sexlessness. **b** class of noun according to this classification (see MASCULINE, FEMININE, NEUTER). **2** *colloq.* sex. [Latin GENUS]

gene /dʒiːn/ *n.* unit in a chromosome determining heredity. [German]

genealogy /ˌdʒiːnɪ'ælədʒɪ/ *n.* (*pl.* **-ies**) **1** descent traced continuously from an ancestor, pedigree. **2** study of pedigrees. **3** organism's line of development from earlier forms. □ **genealogical** /-ə'lɒdʒɪk(ə)l/ *adj.* **genealogically** /-ə'lɒdʒɪkəlɪ/ *adv.* **genealogist** *n.* [Greek *genea* race]

genera *pl.* of GENUS.

general /'dʒenər(ə)l/ *–adj.* **1** including or affecting all or most parts or cases of things. **2** prevalent, usual (*the general feeling*). **3** not partial or particular or local. **4** not limited in application, true of all or nearly all cases (*as a general rule*). **5** not restricted or specialized (*general knowledge; general hospital*). **6** not detailed (*general idea*). **7** vague (*spoke only in general terms*). **8** chief, head; having overall authority (*general manager; Secretary-General*). *–n.* **1 a** army officer next below Field Marshal. **b** = *lieutenant-general* (see LIEUTENANT COLONEL), MAJOR-GENERAL. **2** commander of an army. **3** strategist (*a great general*). **4** head of a religious order, e.g. of Jesuits etc. □ **in general 1** as a normal rule; usually. **2** for the most part. [Latin *generalis*]

♦ **general agent** see AGENT 1.

♦ **General Agreement on Tariffs and Trade** *n.* (also **GATT**) trade treaty in operation since 1948, to which 95 nations are party and a further 28 nations apply its rules de facto; thus some 90% of world trade is governed by GATT regulations. Its objectives are to expand world trade and to provide a permanent forum for international trade problems. Special attention is given to the trade problems of developing countries. The **Tokyo round**, concluded in 1979, agreed many tariff reductions, non-tariff measures, and a revised anti-dumping code. The **Uruguay round**, concluded in 1994, established the WORLD TRADE ORGANIZATION (WTO) as a successor to GATT to come into operation in 1996. The further tariff reductions agreed in the Uruguay round will be implemented by the WTO by 2002.

general anaesthetic *n.* anaesthetic affecting the whole body, usu. with loss of consciousness.

♦ **general average** see AVERAGE *n.* 4.

General Certificate of Education *n.* (also **GCE**) examination set esp. for secondary-school pupils at advanced level (and, formerly, ordinary level) in England, Wales and Northern Ireland.

General Certificate of Secondary Education *n.* (also **GCSE**) examination replacing and combining the GCE ordinary level and CSE examinations.

♦ **General Commissioners** *n.pl.* body of local businessmen appointed by the Lord Chancellor to hear appeals against assessments to income tax, corporation tax, and capital-gains tax. They sit with a clerk to give them guidance on legal and technical matters. Cf. SPECIAL COMMISSIONERS.

♦ **general crossing** see CHEQUE.

♦ **general damages** see DAMAGES.

general election *n.* national parliamentary election.

♦ **general equilibrium analysis** *n.* simultaneous analysis of the behaviour of all agents in an economy, including all possible feedback effects. The best-known result proved that under certain conditions a perfectly competitive economy will produce a Pareto-optimal outcome (see PARETO OPTIMALITY). This result has been used by neoclassical economists to advocate the extension of competition within and between economies. Extending this work has been very difficult because of the complexity of the analysis. Thus, while a partial equilibrium analysis is less rigorous, it has often been more productive.

generalissimo /ˌdʒenərəˈlɪsɪˌməʊ/ *n.* (*pl.* **-s**) commander of a combined military and naval and air force, or of combined armies. [Italian superlative]

generality /ˌdʒenəˈrælɪtɪ/ *n.* (*pl.* **-ies**) **1** general statement or rule. **2** general applicability. **3** lack of detail. **4** (foll. by *of*) main body or majority.

generalize /ˈdʒenərəˌlaɪz/ *v.* (also **-ise**) (**-zing** or **-sing**) **1 a** speak in general or indefinite terms. **b** form general notions. **2** reduce to a general statement. **3** infer (a rule etc.) from particular cases. **4** bring into general use. □ **generalization** /-ˈzeɪʃ(ə)n/ *n.*

generally *adv.* **1** usually; in most respects or cases (*generally get up early*; *was generally well-behaved*). **2** in a general sense; without regard to particulars or exceptions (*generally speaking*). **3** for the most part (*not generally known*).

general meeting *n.* meeting open to all the members of a society etc.

♦ **general offer** *n.* offer of sale made to the general public rather than to a restricted number of people. For example, an object displayed in a shop window with a price tag is a general offer; the shopkeeper must sell to anyone willing to pay the price.

♦ **general partner** see PARTNERSHIP 3.

general practice *n.* work of a general practitioner.

general practitioner *n.* community doctor treating cases of all kinds in the first instance.

general-purpose computer *n.* computer that can be used for any function for which it can be conveniently programmed and can thus perform a series of unrelated tasks.

general staff *n.* staff assisting a military commander at headquarters.

general strike *n.* simultaneous strike of workers in all or most trades.

♦ **general theory** *n. Econ.* general theory of employment, interest, and money put forward by J. M. Keynes, which represents the first attempt to distinguish macroeconomics from microeconomics. In it, Keynes attempted to synthesize the behaviour of consumption, investment, and the money markets and to provide a rationale for involuntary unemployment. Published in 1936, during the Depression, the theory offered prescriptions for eliminating unemployment, which were widely accepted and pursued by economists and governments after the Second World War. However, since the 1970s the new classical macroeconomists have successfully challenged many of Keynes' assumptions, although debate still continues as to what Keynes really meant.

♦ **general union** see TRADE UNION.

generate /ˈdʒenəˌreɪt/ *v.* (**-ting**) bring into existence; produce. [Latin: related to GENUS]

generation /ˌdʒenəˈreɪʃ(ə)n/ *n.* **1** all the people born at about the same time. **2** single stage in a family history (*three generations were present in the photograph*). **3** stage in (esp. technological) development (*fourth-generation computers*). **4** average time in which children are ready to take the place of their parents (about 30 years). **5** production, esp. of electricity. **6** procreation. [Latin: related to GENERATE]

generation gap *n.* differences of outlook or opinion between different generations.

generative /ˈdʒenərətɪv/ *adj.* **1** of procreation. **2** productive.

generator *n.* **1** machine for converting mechanical into electrical energy. **2** apparatus for producing gas, steam, etc. **3** *Computing* see REPORT PROGRAM GENERATOR.

generic /dʒɪˈnerɪk/ *–adj.* **1** characteristic of or relating to a class; general, not specific or special. **2** *Biol.* characteristic of or belonging to a genus. *–n.* product, e.g. a drug or food product, that is not branded (see BRAND *n.* 1b; OWN BRAND). It is packaged more simply than its identical branded equivalent and is not promoted by the manufacturer; it is therefore cheaper. □ **generically** *adv.* [Latin: related to GENUS]

♦ **generic advertising** *n.* advertising a type of product or service (e.g. wool or fabric conditioners) rather than a branded product or service.

♦ **generic name** *n.* **1** name of a genus. **2** name of a class or category of products, e.g. videos or pens, as opposed to the name of a particular product in a class. Cf. BRAND *n.* 1b.

generous /ˈdʒenərəs/ *adj.* **1** giving or given freely. **2** magnanimous, unprejudiced. **3** abundant, copious. □ **generosity** /-ˈrɒsɪtɪ/ *n.* **generously** *adv.* [Latin: related to GENUS]

genesis /ˈdʒenɪsɪs/ *n.* **1** origin; mode of formation or generation. **2** (**Genesis**) first book of the Old Testament, with an account of the Creation. [Greek *gen-* be produced]

gene therapy *n.* introduction of normal genes into cells in place of defective or missing ones in order to correct genetic disorders.

genetic /dʒɪˈnetɪk/ *adj.* **1** of genetics or genes. **2** of or in origin. □ **genetically** *adv.* [from GENESIS]

genetic code *n.* arrangement of genetic information in chromosomes.

genetic engineering *n.* manipulation of DNA to modify hereditary features.

genetic fingerprinting *n.* (also **genetic profiling**) identifying individuals by DNA patterns.

genetics *n.pl.* (treated as *sing.*) the study of heredity and the variation of inherited characteristics. □ **geneticist** /-tɪsɪst/ *n.*

Geneva /dʒɪˈniːvə/ city in SW Switzerland, a banking and financial centre; pop. (1995) 172 737. Manufactures include watches, precision instruments, and chemicals.

genial /ˈdʒiːnɪəl/ *adj.* **1** jovial, sociable, kindly. **2** (of the climate) mild and warm; conducive to growth. **3** cheering. □ **geniality** /-ˈælɪtɪ/ *n.* **genially** *adv.* [Latin: related to GENIUS]

genie /ˈdʒiːnɪ/ *n.* (*pl.* **genii** /-nɪˌaɪ/) (in Arabian tales) spirit or goblin with magical powers. [French *génie* GENIUS: cf. JINNEE]

genital /ˈdʒenɪt(ə)l/ –*adj.* of animal reproduction or the reproductive organs. –*n.* (in *pl.*) external reproductive organs. [Latin *gigno genit-* beget]

genitalia /ˌdʒenɪˈteɪlɪə/ *n.pl.* genitals. [Latin, neuter pl. of *genitalis*: see GENITAL]

genitive /ˈdʒenɪtɪv/ *Gram.* –*n.* case expressing possession or close association, corresponding to *of*, *from*, etc. –*adj.* of or in this case. [Latin: related to GENITAL]

genius /ˈdʒiːnɪəs/ *n.* (*pl.* **geniuses**) **1 a** exceptional intellectual or creative power or other natural ability or tendency. **b** person with this. **2** tutelary spirit of a person, place, etc. **3** person or spirit powerfully influencing a person for good or evil. **4** prevalent feeling or association etc. of a people or place. [Latin]

Genoa /ˈdʒenəʊə/ (Italian **Genova** /ˈdʒenəvə/) city and seaport in NW Italy, capital of Liguria; industries include engineering and oil refining; pop. (1994) 659 754.

genocide /ˈdʒenəˌsaɪd/ *n.* deliberate extermination of a people or nation. □ **genocidal** /-ˈsaɪd(ə)l/ *adj.* [Greek *genos* race, -CIDE]

genome /ˈdʒiːnəʊm/ *n.* **1** the haploid set of chromosomes of an organism. **2** the genetic material of an organism.

-genous *comb. form* forming adjectives meaning 'produced' (*endogenous*).

genre /ˈʒɑ̃rə/ *n.* **1** kind or style of art etc. **2** painting of scenes from ordinary life. [French: related to GENDER]

Gent see GHENT.

gent *n. colloq.* **1** gentleman. **2** (**the Gents**) *colloq.* men's public lavatory. [shortening of GENTLEMAN]

genteel /dʒenˈtiːl/ *adj.* **1** affectedly refined or stylish. **2** upper-class. □ **genteelly** *adv.* [French *gentil*: related to GENTLE]

gentian /ˈdʒenʃ(ə)n/ *n.* mountain plant usu. with blue flowers. [Latin *gentiana* from *Gentius*, king of Illyria]

Gentile /ˈdʒentaɪl/ –*adj.* not Jewish; heathen. –*n.* person who is not Jewish. [Latin *gentilis* from *gens* family]

gentility /dʒenˈtɪlɪtɪ/ *n.* **1** social superiority. **2** genteel manners or behaviour. [French: related to GENTLE]

gentle /ˈdʒent(ə)l/ *adj.* (**gentler, gentlest**) **1** not rough or severe; mild, kind (*a gentle nature*). **2** moderate (*gentle breeze*). **3** (of birth, pursuits, etc.) honourable, of or fit for gentlefolk. **4** quiet; requiring patience (*gentle art*). □ **gentleness** *n.* **gently** *adv.* [Latin: related to GENTILE]

gentlefolk *n.pl.* people of good family.

gentleman *n.* **1** man (in polite or formal use). **2** chivalrous well-bred man. **3** man of good social position (*country gentleman*). **4** man of gentle birth attached to a royal household (*gentleman in waiting*). **5** (in *pl.*) (as a form of address) male audience or part of this.

gentlemanly *adj.* like or befitting a gentleman.

gentleman's agreement *n.* (also **gentlemen's agreement**) agreement binding in honour but not enforceable.

gentlewoman *n. archaic* woman of good birth or breeding.

gentrification /ˌdʒentrɪfɪˈkeɪʃ(ə)n/ *n.* upgrading of a working-class urban area by the arrival of more affluent residents. □ **gentrify** /-ˌfaɪ/ *v.* (**-ies, -ied**).

gentry /ˈdʒentrɪ/ *n.pl.* **1** people next below the nobility. **2** *derog.* people (*these gentry*). [French: related to GENTLE]

genuflect /ˈdʒenjuːˌflekt/ *v.* bend one's knee, esp. in worship. □ **genuflection** /-ˈflekʃ(ə)n/ *n.* (also **genuflexion**). [Latin *genu* knee, *flecto* bend]

genuine /ˈdʒenjuːɪn/ *adj.* **1** really coming from its reputed source etc. **2** properly so called; not sham; sincere. □ **genuinely** *adv.* **genuineness** *n.* [Latin]

genus /ˈdʒiːnəs/ *n.* (*pl.* **genera** /ˈdʒenərə/) **1** taxonomic category of animals or plants with common structural characteristics, usu. containing several species. **2** (in logic) kind of things including subordinate kinds or species. **3** *colloq.* kind, class. [Latin *genus -eris*]

geo- *comb. form* earth. [Greek *gē*]

geocentric /ˌdʒiːəʊˈsentrɪk/ *adj.* **1** considered as viewed from the earth's centre. **2** having the earth as the centre. □ **geocentrically** *adv.*

geode /ˈdʒiːəʊd/ *n.* **1** cavity lined with crystals. **2** rock containing this. [Greek *geōdēs* earthy]

◆ **geodemographic segmentation** see MARKET SEGMENTATION.

---

geodesic /ˌdʒiːəʊˈdiːzɪk/ *adj.* (also **geodetic** /-ˈdetɪk/) of geodesy.

geodesic line *n.* shortest possible line between two points on a curved surface.

geodesy /dʒiːˈɒdɪsɪ/ *n.* the study of the shape and area of the earth. [Greek *geōdaisia*]

geographical /ˌdʒiːəˈgræfɪk(ə)l/ *adj.* (also **geographic**) of geography. □ **geographically** *adv.*

geographical mile *n.* distance of one minute of longitude or latitude at the equator (about 1.85 km).

geography /dʒɪˈɒgrəfɪ/ *n.* **1** science of the earth's physical features, resources, climate, population, etc. **2** features or arrangement of an area, rooms, etc. □ **geographer** *n.* [Latin from Greek]

geology /dʒɪˈɒlədʒɪ/ *n.* **1** science of the earth's crust, strata, origin of its rocks, etc. **2** geological features of a district. □ **geological** /ˌdʒiːəˈlɒdʒɪk(ə)l/ *adj.* **geologically** /ˌdʒiːəˈlɒdʒɪkəlɪ/ *adv.* **geologist** *n.*

geometric /ˌdʒiːəˈmetrɪk/ *adj.* (also **geometrical**) **1** of

---

Georgia /ˈdʒɔːdʒɪə/, **Republic of** country in central Asia, formerly a constituent republic of the Soviet Union. There are rich mineral resources, esp. manganese and coal, and industries include metallurgy, machine-building, construction, and food processing; hydroelectricity is produced. Agriculture is important; crops include tea, grapes (for wine), tobacco, and citrus fruits. The economy is weak and unlikely to recover until regional disputes have been settled and violent conflict ceases within the country. Food products and ferrous metals are among the major exports. Under Russian rule in the 19th century, Georgia became part of the Transcaucasian Soviet Federated Republic in 1922 and a separate Soviet republic in 1936. Its independence, declared unilaterally in 1990, was internationally recognized in 1992. Since then, the republic has been plagued by civil war between government forces and separatists in the autonomous region of Abkhazia. However, following the re-election of Shevardnadze in 1995 some measure of political and economic stability was introduced, with a decrease in terrorism and an economic upswing. The situation in Abkhazia and South Ossetia remains unresolved. Head of state, Eduard Shevardnadze; capital, Tbilisi.

languages	Georgian (official), Russian
currency	lari of 100 tetri
pop. (est. 1996)	5 360 000
GNP (1994)	US$3B
literacy	99% (m); 99% (f)
life expectancy	69 (m); 76 (f)

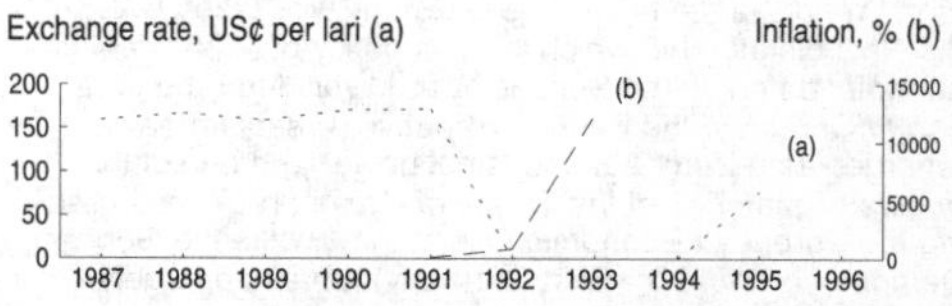

geometry. **2** (of a design etc.) with regular lines and shapes. □ **geometrically** *adv.*

♦ **geometric mean** *n.* mathematical average obtained by calculating the *n*th root of the product of a set of *n* numbers. For example the geometric mean of 7, 100, and 107 is $\sqrt[3]{74\,900} = 42.15$.

---

geometric progression *n.* progression with a constant ratio between successive quantities (as 1, 3, 9, 27).

geometry /dʒɪ'ɒmətrɪ/ *n.* science of the properties and relations of lines, surfaces, and solids. □ **geometrician** /-'trɪʃ(ə)n/ *n.* [from GEO-, -METRY]

geophysics /ˌdʒiːəʊ'fɪzɪks/ *n.pl.* (treated as *sing.*) physics of the earth.

Geordie /'dʒɔːdɪ/ *n.* native of Tyneside. [name *George*]

George Cross /dʒɔːdʒ/ *n.* decoration for bravery awarded esp. to civilians. [King *George* VI]

George Town 1 capital of the Cayman Islands, on the island of Grand Cayman; pop. (est. 1989) 12 921. **2** (also **Penang**) chief port of Malaysia and capital of the state of Penang, on Penang Island; pop. (1991) 219 376.

Georgetown /'dʒɔːdʒtaʊn/ capital and chief port of Guyana; pop. (est. 1992) 248 500.

georgette /dʒɔː'dʒet/ *n.* thin dress-material similar to crêpe. [*Georgette* de la Plante, name of a dressmaker]

Georgia /'dʒɔːdʒɪə/ state in the SE US, bordering on the Atlantic; pop. (est. 1996) 7 353 225; capital, Atlanta. It has textile, manufacturing, chemical, and food-processing industries, and agriculture is important; crops include peanuts, tobacco, and fruit.

Georgian[1] /'dʒɔːdʒ(ə)n/ *adj.* of the time of Kings George I–IV or of George V and VI.

Georgian[2] /'dʒɔːdʒ(ə)n/ *–adj.* of Georgia in central Asia or the US. *–n.* **1** native or language of Georgia in central Asia. **2** native of Georgia in the US.

Ger. *abbr.* German(y).

Geraldton /'dʒerəldt(ə)n/ seaport and resort in W Western Australia; pop. (1991) 24 360.

geranium /dʒə'reɪnɪəm/ *n.* (*pl.* **-s**) **1** (in general use) cultivated pelargonium. **2** herb or shrub bearing fruit shaped like a crane's bill. [Greek *geranos* crane]

gerbil /'dʒɜːbɪl/ *n.* (also **jerbil**) mouselike desert rodent with long hind legs. [French: related to JERBOA]

geriatric /ˌdʒerɪ'ætrɪk/ *–adj.* **1** of old people. **2** *colloq.* old, outdated. *–n.* old person. [Greek *gēras* old age, *iatros* doctor]

geriatrics *n.pl.* (usu. treated as *sing.*) branch of medicine or social science dealing with the health and care of old people. □ **geriatrician** /-ə'trɪʃ(ə)n/ *n.*

germ *n.* **1** micro-organism, esp. one causing disease. **2** portion of an organism capable of developing into a new one; rudiment of an animal or plant in seed (*wheat germ*). **3** thing that may develop; elementary principle. □ **germy** *adj.* (**-ier, -iest**). [Latin *germen* sprout]

German /'dʒɜːmən/ *–n.* **1 a** native or national of Germany. **b** person of German descent. **2** language of Germany. *–adj.* of Germany or its people or language. [Latin *Germanus*]

german /'dʒɜːmən/ *adj.* (placed after *brother, sister,* or *cousin*) having both parents the same, or both grandparents the same on one side (*brother german; cousin german*). [Latin *germanus*]

germander /dʒɜː'mændə(r)/ *n.* plant of the mint family. [Greek, = ground-oak]

germane /dʒɜː'meɪn/ *adj.* (usu. foll. by *to*) relevant (to a subject). [var. of GERMAN]

Germanic /dʒɜː'mænɪk/ *–adj.* **1** having German characteristics. **2** *hist.* of the Germans. **3** of the Scandinavians, Anglo-Saxons, or Germans. *–n.* **1** the branch of Indo-European languages which includes English, German, Dutch, and the Scandinavian languages. **2** the primitive language of Germanic peoples.

germanium /dʒɜː'meɪnɪəm/ *n.* brittle greyish-white semi-metallic element. [related to GERMAN]

German measles *n.pl.* disease like mild measles; rubella.

Germano- *comb. form* German.

German shepherd *n.* (also **German shepherd dog**) = ALSATIAN.

German silver *n.* white alloy of nickel, zinc, and copper.

germicide /'dʒɜːmɪˌsaɪd/ *n.* substance that destroys germs. □ **germicidal** /-'saɪd(ə)l/ *adj.*

germinal /'dʒɜːmɪn(ə)l/ *adj.* **1** of germs. **2** in the earliest stage of development. **3** productive of new ideas. □ **germinally** *adv.* [related to GERM]

germinate /'dʒɜːmɪˌneɪt/ *v.* (**-ting**) **1** sprout, bud, or develop. **2** cause to do this. □ **germination** /-'neɪʃ(ə)n/ *n.* **germinative** *adj.* [Latin: related to GERM]

germ warfare *n.* use of germs to spread disease in war.

gerontology /ˌdʒerɒn'tɒlədʒɪ/ *n.* the study of old age and the process of ageing. [Greek *gerōn geront-* old man]

Germany /'dʒɜːmənɪ/, **Federal Republic of** country in central Europe. Germany is heavily industrialized, with electronics, engineering, iron and steel, coalmining, chemicals, and textiles among its main industries. Exports include motor vehicles, scientific instruments, photographic products, machinery, chemicals, and pharmaceutical products. Some 37% of electric power is generated by the nuclear industry. Agriculture is declining in importance, but the wine and brewing industries are well established and forestry continues to generate income. The reunification of Germany in 1990 entailed the transformation of the former East German economy, a process that has proved costly to the former West Germany. The public sector deficit increased, and inflation and unemployment have risen considerably. However, the Deutschmark has remained strong.
History. Loosely unified under the Holy Roman Empire during the Middle Ages, the multiplicity of small German states became unified with the rise of Prussia and the formation of the German empire in the mid-19th century. Defeated in the First World War, in the 1930s Germany was taken over by the Nazi dictatorship which led to a policy of expansionism and total defeat in the Second World War. After the partition of Germany, the Federal Republic (West Germany) emerged as a European industrial power and one of the original signatories of the Treaty of Rome (1957) establishing the European Economic Community, while the German Democratic Republic (East Germany) remained largely under Soviet domination. After the general collapse of Communism in E Europe towards the end of 1989, East and West Germany reunited in 1990. Following reunification Germany experienced a number of economic problems and entered into its worst post-war recession, with high rates of unemployment in the mid-to-late 1990s. A number of largely unpopular austerity measures have been introduced, many tampering with social welfare schemes. President, Roman Herzog; chancellor, Helmut Kohl; capital, Berlin; provisional seat of government, Bonn.

language	German
currency	Deutschmark (DM) of 100 pfennige
pop. (est. 1996)	81 891 000
GNP (est. 1994)	US$2075B
literacy	99%
life expectancy	73 (m); 79 (f)

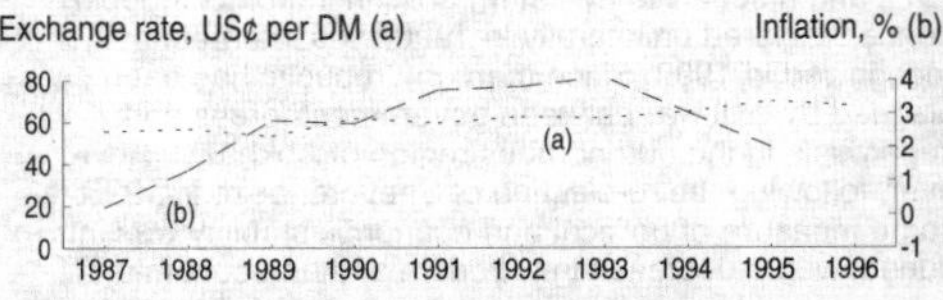

gerrymander /ˈdʒerɪˌmændə(r)/ *–v.* manipulate the boundaries of (a constituency etc.) so as to give undue influence to some party or class. *–n.* this practice. [Governor *Gerry* of Massachusetts]

gerund /ˈdʒerənd/ *n.* verbal noun, in English ending in *-ing* (e.g. *do you mind my asking you?*). [Latin]

Ges. *abbr.* (German) Gesellschaft (= limited company).

gesso /ˈdʒesəʊ/ *n.* (*pl.* **-es**) gypsum as used in painting or sculpture. [Italian: related to GYPSUM]

Gestapo /geˈstɑːpəʊ/ *n. hist.* Nazi secret police. [German, from *Ge*heime *Sta*ats*po*lizei]

gestation /dʒeˈsteɪʃ(ə)n/ *n.* **1 a** process of carrying or being carried in the uterus between conception and birth. **b** this period. **2** development of a plan, idea, etc. □ **gestate** *v.* (**-ting**). [Latin *gesto* carry]

gesticulate /dʒeˈstɪkjʊˌleɪt/ *v.* (**-ting**) **1** use gestures instead of, or to reinforce, speech. **2** express thus. □ **gesticulation** /-ˈleɪʃ(ə)n/ *n.* [Latin: related to GESTURE]

gesture /ˈdʒestʃə(r)/ *–n.* **1** significant movement of a limb or the body. **2** use of such movements, esp. as a rhetorical device. **3** action to evoke a response or convey intention, usu. friendly. *–v.* (**-ring**) gesticulate. [Latin *gestura* from *gero* wield]

get /get/ *v.* (**getting**; *past* **got**; *past part.* **got** or *US* **gotten**) (and in *comb.*) **1** come into possession of; receive or earn (*get a job; got £200 a week; got first prize*). **2** fetch or procure (*get my book for me; got a new car*). **3** go to reach or catch (a bus, train, etc.). **4** prepare (a meal etc.). **5** (cause to) reach some state or become (*get rich; get married; get to be famous; got them ready; got him into trouble*). **6** obtain as a result of calculation. **7** contract (a disease etc.). **8** establish communication by telephone etc. with; receive (a broadcast signal). **9** experience or suffer; have inflicted on one; receive as one's lot or penalty (*got four years in prison*). **10 a** succeed in bringing, placing, etc. (*get it round the corner; get it on to the agenda*). **b** (cause to) succeed in coming or going (*will get you there somehow; got absolutely nowhere; got home*). **11** (prec. by *have*) **a** possess (*have not got a penny*). **b** (foll. by *to* + infin.) be bound or obliged (*have got to see you*). **12** (foll. by *to* + infin.) induce; prevail upon (*got them to help me*). **13** *colloq.* understand (a person or an argument) (*have you got that?; I get your point; do you get me?*). **14** *colloq.* harm, injure, kill, esp. in retaliation (*I'll get you for that*). **15** *colloq.* **a** annoy. **b** affect emotionally. **c** attract. **16** (foll. by *to* + infin.) develop an inclination (*am getting to like it*). **17** (foll. by verbal noun) begin (*get going*). **18** establish (an idea etc.) in one's mind. **19** *archaic* beget. □ **get about 1** travel extensively or fast; go from place to place. **2** begin walking etc. (esp. after illness). **get across 1** communicate (an idea etc.). **2** (of an idea etc.) be communicated. **get ahead** make progress (esp. in a career etc.). **get along** (or **on**) (foll. by *together, with*) live harmoniously. **get around** = *get about.* **get at 1** reach; get hold of. **2** *colloq.* imply. **3** *colloq.* nag, criticize. **get away 1** escape, start. **2** (as *int.*) *colloq.* expressing disbelief or scepticism. **3** (foll. by *with*) escape blame or punishment for. **get back at** *colloq.* retaliate against. **get by** *colloq.* manage, even if with difficulty. **get cracking** see CRACK. **get down 1** alight, descend (from a vehicle, ladder, etc.). **2** record in writing. **get a person down** depress or deject him or her. **get down to** begin working on. **get hold of** grasp, secure, acquire, obtain; make contact with (a person). **get in 1** arrive, obtain a place in a college etc. **2** be elected. **get it** *slang* be punished. **get off 1** *colloq.* (cause to) be acquitted; escape with little or no punishment. **2** start. **3** alight from (a bus etc.). **4** (foll. by *with, together*) *colloq.* form an amorous or sexual relationship, esp. quickly. **get on 1** make progress; manage. **2** enter (a bus etc.). **3** = *get along.* **4** (usu. as **getting on** adj.) grow old. **get on to** *colloq.* **1** make contact with. **2** understand; become aware of. **get out 1** leave or escape or help to do this. **2** manage to go outdoors. **3** alight from a vehicle. **4** transpire; become known. **get out of** avoid or escape (a duty etc.). **get over 1** recover from (an illness, upset, etc.). **2** overcome (a difficulty). **3** = *get across.* **get a thing over** (or **over with**) complete (a tedious task) quickly. **get one's own back** *colloq.* have one's revenge. **get rid of** see RID. **get round 1** coax or cajole (a person) esp. to secure a favour. **2** evade (a law etc.). **get round to** deal with (a task etc.) in due course. **get somewhere** make progress; be initially successful. **get there** *colloq.* **1** succeed. **2** understand what is meant. **get through 1** pass (an examination etc.). **2** finish or use up (esp. resources). **3** make contact by telephone. **4** (foll. by *to*) succeed in making (a person) understand. **get together** gather, assemble. **get up 1** rise from sitting etc., or from bed after sleeping etc. **2** (of wind etc.) begin to be strong. **3** prepare or organize. **4** produce or stimulate (*get up steam*). **5** (often *refl.*) dress or arrange elaborately; arrange the appearance of. **6** (foll. by *to*) *colloq.* indulge or be involved in (*always getting up to mischief*). [Old Norse]

get-at-able /getˈætəb(ə)l/ *adj. colloq.* accessible.

getaway *n.* escape, esp. after a crime.

get-out *n.* means of avoiding something.

get-together *n. colloq.* social gathering.

get-up *n. colloq.* style or arrangement of dress etc.

get-up-and-go *n. colloq.* energy, enthusiasm.

geyser /ˈgiːzə(r)/ *n.* **1** intermittent hot spring. **2** apparatus for heating water. [Icelandic *Geysir* from *geysa* to gush]

GF *–symb.* Guinean franc. *–airline flight code* Gulf Air.

GFTU *abbr.* (in the US) General Federation of Trade Unions.

Ghana /ˈgɑːnə/, **Republic of** (formerly **Gold Coast**) country in W Africa, with its S coastline on the Gulf of Guinea. The country's principal crop is cocoa, of which it is one of the world's chief producers. Agricultural diversification is encouraged by the government, in order to increase exports and provide raw materials, esp. cotton and rubber, for developing light industries. There has been considerable investment (both domestic and foreign) in mining, gold and diamonds being important sources of export revenue; manganese and bauxite are also exported. Hydroelectricity is generated by the Volta Dam. Forestry and fishing provide employment and timber is exported. The economy relies heavily on aid, but gold production is rising steadily, and export revenues should help to counteract the adverse effects of drought on the cocoa crop.
History. In 1957 Ghana gained independence as a member state of the Commonwealth, the first British colony to do so, and in 1960 became a republic. Since then it has been mostly under military rule. In 1992 a referendum supported the establishment of a multi-party democracy, banned since 1981, and presidential and parliamentary elections were held at the end of the year. Rawlings was re-elected in 1992, though many opposition parties and a large proportion of the electorate boycotted the elections. However, Rawlings was re-elected again in 1996 despite facing a unified opposition. President, Flight Lieutenant Jerry Rawlings; capital, Accra. □ **Ghanaian** /gɑːˈneɪən/ *adj. & n.*

languages	English (official), Twi, Fanti and other African languages
currency	cedi of 100 pesewas
pop. (est. 1996)	16 904 000
GNP (est. 1994)	US$7.3B
literacy	70% (m); 50% (f)
life expectancy	53 (m); 57 (f)

Exchange rate, US¢ per cedi (a) Inflation, % (b)

GH *–international vehicle registration* Ghana. *–airline flight code* Ghana Airways.

ghastly /ˈgɑːstlɪ/ *adj.* (**-ier, -iest**) **1** horrible, frightful. **2** *colloq.* unpleasant. **3** deathlike, pallid. □ **ghastliness** *n.* [obsolete *gast* terrify]

ghee /giː/ *n.* Indian clarified butter. [Hindi from Sanskrit]

Ghent /gent/ (Flemish **Gent**, French **Gand** /gɑ̃/) Belgian city and port, the capital of East Flanders; industries include textiles, metallurgy, chemicals, and electronics; pop. (1995) 227 072.

gherkin /ˈgɜːkɪn/ *n.* small pickled cucumber. [Dutch]

ghetto /ˈgetəʊ/ *n.* (*pl.* **-s**) **1** part of a city occupied by a minority group. **2** *hist.* Jewish quarter in a city. **3** segregated group or area. [Italian]

ghetto-blaster *n. slang* large portable radio, esp. for playing loud pop music.

ghillie var. of GILLIE.

ghost /gəʊst/ *–n.* **1** supposed apparition of a dead person or animal; disembodied spirit. **2** shadow or semblance (*not a ghost of a chance*). **3** secondary image in a defective telescope or television picture. *–v.* (often foll. by *for*) act as ghost-writer of (a work). □ **ghostliness** *n.* **ghostly** *adj.* (**-ier, -iest**). [Old English]

ghosting *n.* appearance of a 'ghost' image in a television picture.

ghost town *n.* town with few or no remaining inhabitants.

ghost train *n.* (at a funfair) open-topped miniature railway in which the rider experiences ghoulish sights, sounds, etc.

ghost-writer *n.* person who writes on behalf of the credited author.

ghoul /guːl/ *n.* **1** person morbidly interested in death etc. **2** evil spirit or phantom. **3** spirit in Muslim folklore preying on corpses. □ **ghoulish** *adj.* **ghoulishly** *adv.* [Arabic]

GHQ *abbr.* General Headquarters.

ghyll var. of GILL^3.

GI /dʒiːˈaɪ/ *n.* (often *attrib.*) soldier in the US army. [abbreviation of *g*overnment (or *g*eneral) *i*ssue]

giant /ˈdʒaɪənt/ *–n.* **1** (*fem.* **giantess**) imaginary or mythical being of human form but superhuman size. **2** person or thing of great size, ability, courage, etc. *–attrib. adj.* **1** gigantic. **2** of a very large kind. [Greek *gigas gigant-*]

Gib. *abbr.* Gibraltar.

gibber *v.* jabber inarticulately. [imitative]

gibberish *n.* unintelligible or meaningless speech; nonsense.

gibbet /ˈdʒɪbɪt/ *–n. hist.* **1 a** gallows. **b** post with an arm on which an executed criminal was hung. **2** (prec. by *the*) death by hanging. *–v.* (**-t-**) **1** put to death by hanging. **2** expose or hang up on a gibbet. [French *gibet*]

gibbon /ˈgɪbən/ *n.* long-armed SE Asian anthropoid ape. [French]

gibbous /ˈgɪbəs/ *adj.* **1** convex. **2** (of a moon or planet) having the bright part greater than a semicircle and less than a circle. **3** humpbacked. [Latin *gibbus* hump]

gibe (also **jibe**) *–v.* (**-bing**) (often foll. by *at*) jeer, mock. *–n.* jeering remark, taunt. [perhaps from French *giber* handle roughly]

giblets /ˈdʒɪblɪts/ *n.pl.* edible organs etc. of a bird, removed and usu. cooked separately. [French *gibelet* game stew]

Gibraltar /dʒɪˈbrɔːltə(r)/ British Crown Colony comprising a fortified town and rocky headland (the Rock of Gibraltar) at the S tip of the Iberian peninsula on the Strait of Gibraltar (the only outlet of the Mediterranean Sea to the Atlantic); pop. (est. 1990) 31 265. Tourism, offshore banking and finance, and services for shipping are the main industries. Gibraltar is a strategically important British naval base, and British defence expenditure is a source of income. It was formally ceded to Britain in 1713; since the Second World War Spain has forcefully urged her claim to the territory. □ **Gibraltarian** /ˌdʒɪbrɔːlˈteərɪən/ *adj.* & *n.*

giddy /ˈgɪdɪ/ *adj.* (**-ier, -iest**) **1** dizzy, tending to fall or stagger. **2 a** mentally intoxicated (*giddy with success*). **b** excitable, frivolous, flighty. **3** making dizzy (*giddy heights*). □ **giddily** *adv.* **giddiness** *n.* [Old English]

◆ **Giffen good** /ˈgɪf(ə)n/ *n. Econ.* a good for which demand falls at the same time as its price falls (and vice versa), upsetting the usual relationship between price and demand (see DEMAND THEORY). The usual example is that of potatoes during the Irish potato famine in the 19th century: as the price of potatoes rose, the demand also rose because no close substitutes were available. [*Giffen*, name of an economist]

---

gift /gɪft/ *n.* **1** thing given; present. **2** natural ability or talent. **3** the power to give (*in his gift*). **4** giving. **5** *Law* transfer of an asset from one person to another for no consideration. See also INHERITANCE TAX; INTER VIVOS GIFT; LIFETIME TRANSFER. **6** *colloq.* easy task. [Old Norse: related to GIVE]

gifted *adj.* talented; intelligent.

gift of the gab *n. colloq.* eloquence, loquacity.

gift token *n.* (also **gift voucher**) voucher used as a gift and exchangeable for goods.

◆ **gift with reservation** *n. Law* gift in which the donor retains some benefit (e.g. the gift of a house in which the donor continues to reside). In general, the donor is treated as not having parted with the asset until he or she releases the reservation.

---

gift-wrap *v.* wrap attractively as a gift.

gig^1 /gɪg/ *n.* **1** light two-wheeled one-horse carriage. **2** light ship's boat for rowing or sailing. **3** rowing-boat esp. for racing. [probably imitative]

gig^2 /gɪg/ *colloq. –n.* engagement to play music etc., usu. for one night. *–v.* (**-gg-**) perform a gig. [origin unknown]

giga- *comb. form* **1** one thousand million (10^9). **2** *Computing* power of 2 nearest to 10^9 (2^{30}). [Greek: related to GIANT]

gigantic /dʒaɪˈgæntɪk/ *adj.* huge, giant-like. □ **gigantically** *adv.* [Latin: related to GIANT]

giggle /ˈgɪg(ə)l/ *–v.* (**-ling**) laugh in half-suppressed spasms. *–n.* **1** such a laugh. **2** *colloq.* amusing person or thing; joke (*did it for a giggle*). □ **giggly** *adj.* (**-ier, -iest**). [imitative]

GIGO /ˈgaɪgəʊ/ *abbr.* (also **gigo**) *Computing* garbage in garbage out, signifying that a program working on incorrect data produces incorrect results.

gigolo /ˈdʒɪgəˌləʊ/ *n.* (*pl.* **-s**) young man paid by an older woman to be her escort or lover. [French]

Gijón /hiːˈhəʊn/ port and industrial city in N Spain, on the Bay of Biscay; products include iron, steel, oil, and chemicals; pop. (est. 1994) 269 644.

Gilbert Islands /ˈgɪlbət/ group of islands in the central Pacific, forming part of Kiribati.

gild^1 /gɪld/ *v.* (*past part.* **gilded** or as adj. in sense 1 **gilt**) **1** cover thinly with gold. **2** tinge with a golden colour. **3** give a false brilliance to. □ **gild the lily** try to improve what is already satisfactory. [Old English: related to GOLD]

gild^2 var. of GUILD.

gill^1 /gɪl/ *n.* (usu. in *pl.*) **1** respiratory organ in a fish etc. **2** vertical radial plate on the underside of a mushroom etc. **3** flesh below a person's jaws and ears. [Old Norse]

gill^2 /dʒɪl/ *n.* unit of liquid measure equal to $^1/_4$ pint. [French]

gill^3 /gɪl/ *n.* (also **ghyll**) **1** deep usu. wooded ravine. **2** narrow mountain torrent. [Old Norse]

gillie /ˈgɪlɪ/ *n.* (also **ghillie**) *Scot.* man or boy attending a person hunting or fishing. [Gaelic]

gillyflower /ˈdʒɪlɪˌflaʊə(r)/ *n.* clove-scented flower, e.g. a wallflower or the clove-scented pink. [French *gilofre*]

gilt^1 /gɪlt/ *–adj.* **1** thinly covered with gold. **2** gold-coloured. *–n.* **1** gilding. **2** = GILT-EDGED SECURITY. [from GILD^1]

gilt[2] /gɪlt/ *n.* young sow. [Old Norse]

gilt-edged *adj.* (of securities, stocks, etc.) having a high degree of reliability.

◆ **gilt-edged market makers** *n.pl.* = GILTS PRIMARY DEALERS.

◆ **gilt-edged security** *n.* (also **gilt**) fixed-interest security or stock issued by the British government in the form of **exchequer stocks** or **Treasury stocks**. Gilts are among the safest of all investments, as the government is unlikely to default on interest or on principal repayments. They may be irredeemable (see CONSOLS) or redeemable. **Redeemable gilts** are classified as: **long-dated gilts** or **longs** (not redeemable for 15 years or more), **medium-dated gilts** or **mediums** (redeemable in five to 15 years), or **short-dated gilts** or **shorts** (redeemable in less than five years). Like most fixed-interest securities, gilts are sensitive not only to interest rates but also to inflation rates. This led the government to introduce **index-linked gilts** in the 1970s, with interest payments moving in a specified way relative to inflation.

◆ **gilts primary dealers** *n.pl.* (also **gilt-edged market makers**) market makers approved and supervised by the Bank of England for dealing directly with the Bank of England in gilt-edged securities. They have to some extent taken over the role of the government broker.

---

gimbals /ˈdʒɪmb(ə)lz/ *n.pl.* contrivance of rings and pivots for keeping instruments horizontal in ships, aircraft, etc. [var. of *gimmal* from French *gemel* double finger-ring]

gimcrack /ˈdʒɪmkræk/ *–adj.* showy but flimsy and worthless. *–n.* showy ornament; knick-knack. [origin unknown]

gimlet /ˈgɪmlɪt/ *n.* small tool with a screw-tip for boring holes. [French]

gimlet eye *n.* eye with a piercing glance.

gimmick /ˈgɪmɪk/ *n.* trick or device, esp. to attract attention or publicity. □ **gimmickry** *n.* **gimmicky** *adj.* [origin unknown]

gimp /gɪmp/ *n.* (also **gymp**) **1** twist of silk etc. with cord or wire running through it. **2** fishing-line of silk etc. bound with wire. [Dutch]

gin[1] *n.* spirit made from grain or malt and flavoured with juniper berries. [Dutch *geneva*: related to JUNIPER]

gin[2] *–n.* **1** snare, trap. **2** machine separating cotton from its seeds. **3** a kind of crane and windlass. *–v.* **(-nn-) 1** treat (cotton) in a gin. **2** trap. [French: related to ENGINE]

ginger /ˈdʒɪndʒə(r)/ *–n.* **1 a** hot spicy root usu. powdered for use in cooking, or preserved in syrup, or candied. **b** plant having this root. **2** light reddish-yellow. **3** spirit, mettle. *–adj.* of a ginger colour. *–v.* **1** flavour with ginger. **2** (foll. by *up*) enliven. □ **gingery** *adj.* [Old English and French, ultimately from Sanskrit]

ginger ale *n.* ginger-flavoured non-alcoholic drink.

ginger beer *n.* mildly alcoholic or non-alcoholic cloudy drink made from fermented ginger and syrup.

gingerbread *–n.* ginger-flavoured treacle cake. *–attrib. adj.* gaudy, tawdry.

ginger group *n.* group urging a party or movement to stronger policy or action.

gingerly *–adv.* in a careful or cautious manner. *–adj.* showing great care or caution. [perhaps from French *gensor* delicate]

ginger-nut *n.* ginger-flavoured biscuit.

gingham /ˈgɪŋəm/ *n.* plain-woven cotton cloth, esp. striped or checked. [Dutch from Malay]

gingivitis /ˌdʒɪndʒɪˈvaɪtɪs/ *n.* inflammation of the gums. [Latin *gingiva* GUM[1], -ITIS]

◆ **Gini coefficient** /ˈdʒiːniː/ see LORENZ CURVE. [*Gini*, name of a statistician]

---

ginkgo /ˈgɪŋkgəʊ/ *n.* (*pl.* **-s**) tree with fan-shaped leaves and yellow flowers. [Chinese, = silver apricot]

GINO /ˈdʒiːnəʊ/ *abbr. Computing* graphical input output.

ginormous /dʒaɪˈnɔːməs/ *adj. slang* enormous. [from GIANT, ENORMOUS]

gin rummy *n.* a form of the card-game rummy.

ginseng /ˈdʒɪnseŋ/ *n.* **1** plant found in E Asia and North America. **2** root of this used as a medicinal tonic. [Chinese]

gippy tummy /ˈdʒɪpɪ/ *n. colloq.* diarrhoea affecting visitors to hot countries. [from EGYPTIAN]

Gipsy var. of GYPSY.

giraffe /dʒɪˈrɑːf/ *n.* (*pl.* same or **-s**) large four-legged African animal with a long neck and forelegs. [French, ultimately from Arabic]

gird /gɜːd/ *v.* (*past* and *past part.* **girded** or **girt**) **1** encircle, attach, or secure, with a belt or band. **2** enclose or encircle. **3** (foll. by *round*) place (a cord etc.) round. □ **gird** (or **gird up**) **one's loins** prepare for action. [Old English]

girder *n.* iron or steel beam or compound structure for bridge-building etc.

girdle[1] /ˈgɜːd(ə)l/ *–n.* **1** belt or cord worn round the waist. **2** corset. **3** thing that surrounds. **4** bony support for the limbs (*pelvic girdle*). *–v.* **(-ling)** surround with a girdle. [Old English]

girdle[2] /ˈgɜːd(ə)l/ *n. Scot.* & *N.Engl.* var. of GRIDDLE.

girl /gɜːl/ *n.* **1** female child, daughter. **2** *colloq.* young woman. **3** *colloq.* girlfriend. **4** female servant. □ **girlhood** *n.* **girlish** *adj.* **girly** *adj.* [origin uncertain]

girl Friday *n.* female helper or follower.

girlfriend *n.* **1** person's regular female companion or lover. **2** female friend.

girlie *adj. colloq.* (of a magazine etc.) depicting young women in erotic poses.

girl scout *n.* = SCOUT *n.* 4.

giro /ˈdʒaɪrəʊ/ *–n.* (*pl.* **-s**) **1 a** banking arrangement for settling debts that has been used in Europe for many years. In 1968 the Post Office set up the UK **National Girobank** (now **Girobank plc**) based on a central office in Bootle, Merseyside. Originally a system for settling debts between people who did not have bank accounts, it now offers many of the services provided by commercial banks, with the advantage that there are many more post offices, at which Girobank services are provided, than there are bank branches. Also the post offices are open for longer hours than banks. Girobank also offers banking services to businesses, including an **automatic debit transfer** system, enabling businesses to collect money from a large number of customers at regular intervals for a small charge. **b** (also **Bank Giro**) banking system operated in the UK, independently of Girobank, by the clearing banks. It has no central organization, being run by bank branches. The service enables customers to make payments from their accounts by credit transfer to others who may or may not have bank accounts. **c** (also **Bancogiro**) banking system in operation in Europe, enabling customers of the same bank to make payments to each other by immediate book entry. **2** cheque or payment by giro. *–v.* **(-es, -ed)** pay by giro. [German from Italian]

girt see GIRD.

girth /gɜːθ/ *n.* **1** distance round a thing. **2** band round the body of a horse to secure the saddle etc. [Old Norse: related to GIRD]

Gisborne /ˈgɪzbɔːn/ seaport and resort in New Zealand, on the East Cape of North Island; wool, meat, and dairy produce are exported; pop. (1994) 31 700.

gismo /ˈgɪzməʊ/ *n.* (also **gizmo**) (*pl.* **-s**) *slang* gadget. [origin unknown]

gist *n.* substance or essence of a matter. [Latin *jaceo* LIE[1]]

git /gɪt/ *n. slang* silly or contemptible person. [*get* (n.), = fool]

gîte /ʒiːt/ *n.* furnished holiday house in the French countryside. [French]

give /gɪv/ *–v.* **(-ving;** *past* **gave;** *past part.* **given** /ˈgɪv(ə)n/) **1** transfer the possession of freely; hand over as a present; donate. **2 a** transfer temporarily; provide with (*gave him* *the dog to hold; gave her a new hip*). **b** administer (medicine). **c** deliver (a message). **3** (usu. foll. by *for*) make over in exchange or payment. **4 a** confer; grant (a benefit, honour, etc.). **b** accord; bestow (love, time, etc.). **c** pledge (*gave his word*). **5 a** perform (an action etc.) (*gave a jump; gave a performance; gave an interview*). **b** utter; declare (*gave a shriek; gave the batsman out*). **6** (in *passive*; foll. by *to*) be inclined to or fond of (*is given to boasting; is given to strong drink*). **7** yield to pressure; collapse. **8** yield as a product or result (*gives an average of 7*). **9 a** consign, put (*gave him into custody*). **b** sanction the marriage of (a daughter etc.). **10** devote; dedicate (*gave his life to the cause*). **11** present; offer; show; hold out (*gives no sign of life; gave her his arm; give me an example*). **12** impart; be a source of; cause (*gave me a cold; gave me trouble; gave much pain*). **13** concede (*I give you the benefit of the doubt*). **14** deliver (a judgement etc.) authoritatively. **15** provide (a party, meal, etc.) as host. **16** (in past part.) assume or grant or specify (*given the circumstances; in a given situation; given that we earn so little*). **17** (*absol.*) *colloq.* tell what one knows. *–n.* capacity to yield or comply; elasticity. □ **give and take 1** exchange of words, ideas, blows, etc. **2** ability to compromise. **give away 1** transfer as a gift. **2** hand over (a bride) to a bridegroom. **3** reveal (a secret etc.). **give the game** (or **show**) **away** reveal a secret or intention. **give in 1** yield; acknowledge defeat. **2** hand in (a document etc.) to an official etc. **give it to a person** *colloq.* scold or punish. **give me** I prefer (*give me Greece any day*). **give off** emit (fumes etc.). **give oneself up to 1** abandon oneself to (despair etc.). **2** addict oneself to. **give on to** (or **into**) (of a window, corridor, etc.) overlook or lead into. **give or take** *colloq.* accepting as a margin of error in estimating. **give out 1** announce; emit; distribute. **2** be exhausted. **3** run short. **give over 1** *colloq.* stop or desist. **2** hand over. **3** devote. **give rise to** cause. **give a person to understand** inform or assure. **give up 1** resign; surrender. **2** part with. **3** deliver (a wanted person etc.). **4** pronounce incurable or insoluble; renounce hope of. **5** renounce or cease (an activity). **give way** yield under pressure, give precedence. **not give a damn** (or **monkey's** or **toss** etc.) *colloq.* not care at all. □ **giver** *n.* [Old English]

give-away *n. colloq.* **1** unintentional revelation. **2** thing given as a gift or at a low price.

Giza /'gi:zə/, **El** city in N Egypt; pop. (est. 1992) 2 144 000. Tourism is important (it is the site of famous pyramids and the great Sphinx); it also has textile and film industries.

gizmo var. of GISMO.

gizzard /'gɪzəd/ *n.* **1** second part of a bird's stomach, for grinding food. **2** muscular stomach of some fish etc. [French]

GKS *abbr. Computing* graphics kernel system.

GL *–abbr. Shipping* (in Germany) Germanischer Lloyd (classification society). *–postcode* Gloucester.

4GL *abbr. Computing* fourth-generation language.

glacé /'glæseɪ/ *adj.* **1** (of fruit, esp. cherries) preserved in sugar. **2** (of cloth etc.) smooth; polished. [French]

glacé icing *n.* icing made with icing sugar and water.

glacial /'gleɪʃ(ə)l/ *adj.* **1** of ice. **2** *Geol.* characterized or produced by ice. [Latin *glacies* ice]

glacial period *n.* period when an exceptionally large area was covered by ice.

glaciated /'gleɪsɪˌeɪtɪd/ *adj.* **1** marked or polished by the action of ice. **2** covered by glaciers or ice sheets. □ **glaciation** /-'eɪʃ(ə)n/ *n.* [*glaciate* freeze, from Latin: related to GLACIAL]

glacier /'glæsɪə(r)/ *n.* mass of land ice formed by the accumulation of snow on high ground. [French: related to GLACIAL]

glad *adj.* (**gladder, gladdest**) **1** (*predic.*) pleased. **2** expressing or causing pleasure (*glad cry; glad news*). **3** ready and willing (*am glad to help*). □ **be glad of** find useful. □ **gladly** *adv.* **gladness** *n.* [Old English]

gladden /'glæd(ə)n/ *v.* make or become glad.

glade *n.* open space in a forest. [origin unknown]

glad eye *n.* (prec. by *the*) *colloq.* amorous glance.

glad hand *n. colloq.* hearty welcome.

gladiator /'glædɪˌeɪtə(r)/ *n. hist.* trained fighter in ancient Roman shows. □ **gladiatorial** /-ɪə'tɔ:rɪəl/ *adj.* [Latin *gladius* sword]

gladiolus /ˌglædɪ'əʊləs/ *n.* (*pl.* **-li** /-laɪ/) plant of the lily family with sword-shaped leaves and flower-spikes. [Latin, diminutive of *gladius* sword]

glad rags *n.pl. colloq.* best clothes.

gladsome *adj. poet.* cheerful, joyous.

Gladstone bag /'glædst(ə)n/ *n.* bag with two compartments joined by a hinge. [*Gladstone*, name of a statesman]

glair *n.* **1** white of egg. **2** adhesive preparation made from this. [French]

Glam. *abbr.* Glamorgan.

glam *adj. colloq.* glamorous. [abbreviation]

Glamorgan see MID GLAMORGAN; SOUTH GLAMORGAN; WEST GLAMORGAN.

glamorize /'glæməˌraɪz/ *v.* (also **-ise**) (**-zing** or **-sing**) make glamorous or attractive.

glamour /'glæmə(r)/ *n.* (*US* **glamor**) **1** physical, esp. cosmetic, attractiveness. **2** alluring or exciting beauty or charm. □ **glamorous** *adj.* **glamorously** *adv.* [var. of GRAMMAR in obsolete sense 'magic']

glance /glɑ:ns/ *–v.* (**-cing**) **1** (often foll. by *down, up, over,* etc.) look briefly, direct one's eye. **2** strike at an angle and glide off an object (*glancing blow; ball glanced off his bat*). **3** (usu. foll. by *over*) refer briefly or indirectly to a subject or subjects. **4** (of light etc.) flash or dart. *–n.* **1** brief look. **2** flash or gleam. **3** glancing stroke in cricket. □ **at a glance** immediately upon looking. [origin uncertain]

gland *n.* **1** organ or similar structure secreting substances for use in the body or for ejection. **2** *Bot.* similar organ in a plant. [Latin *glandulae* pl.]

glanders /'glændəz/ *n.pl.* contagious disease of horses. [French *glandre*: related to GLAND]

glandular /'glændjʊlə(r)/ *adj.* of a gland or glands.

glandular fever *n.* infectious disease with swelling of the lymph glands.

glare *–v.* (**-ring**) **1** look fiercely or fixedly. **2** shine dazzlingly or oppressively. *–n.* **1 a** strong fierce light, esp. sunshine. **b** oppressive public attention (*glare of publicity*). **2** fierce or fixed look. **3** tawdry brilliance. [Low German or Dutch]

glaring *adj.* **1** obvious, conspicuous (*glaring error*). **2** shining oppressively. □ **glaringly** *adv.*

Glasgow /'glæzgəʊ/ city in Scotland, in Strathclyde region; pop. (est. 1995) 674 800. The city owes its growth successively to the tobacco, cotton, iron and steel, and shipbuilding industries. Although these industries are no longer of major significance, Glasgow has remained an important commercial centre.

glasnost /'glæznɒst/ *n.* (in the former Soviet Union) policy of more open government and access to information. [Russian, = openness]

glass /glɑ:s/ *–n.* **1 a** (often *attrib.*) hard, brittle, usu. transparent substance, made by fusing sand with soda and lime etc. **b** substance of similar properties. **2** glass objects collectively. **3 a** glass drinking vessel. **b** its contents. **4** mirror. **5** glazed frame for plants. **6** barometer. **7** covering of a watch-face. **8** lens. **9** (in *pl.*) **a** spectacles. **b** binoculars. *–v.* (usu. as **glassed** *adj.*) fit with glass. □ **glassful** *n.* (*pl.* **-s**). [Old English]

glass-blowing *n.* blowing semi-molten glass to make glassware.

♦ **glass ceiling** *n. colloq.* notional barrier limiting the career advancement of employees, esp. of women and minority groups.

---

glass fibre *n.* filaments of glass made into fabric or embedded in plastic as reinforcement.

glasshouse *n.* **1** greenhouse. **2** *slang* military prison.

glass-paper *n.* paper coated with glass particles, for smoothing and polishing.

glassware *n.* articles made of glass.

glass wool *n.* mass of fine glass fibres for packing and insulation.

glassy *adj.* (**-ier, -iest**) **1** like glass. **2** (of the eye, expression, etc.) abstracted; dull; fixed.

Glaswegian /glæz'wiːdʒ(ə)n/ *–adj.* of Glasgow. *–n.* native of Glasgow. [after *Norwegian*]

glaucoma /glɔː'kəʊmə/ *n.* eye-condition with increased pressure in the eyeball and gradual loss of sight. □ **glaucomatous** *adj.* [Greek *glaukos* greyish blue]

glaze *–v.* (**-zing**) **1** fit (a window etc.) with glass or (a building) with windows. **2 a** cover (pottery etc.) with a glaze. **b** fix (paint) on pottery thus. **3** cover (pastry, cloth, etc.) with a glaze. **4** (often foll. by *over*) (of the eyes) become glassy. **5** give a glassy surface to. *–n.* **1** vitreous substance for glazing pottery. **2** smooth shiny coating on food etc. **3** thin coat of transparent paint to modify underlying tone. **4** surface formed by glazing. [from GLASS]

glazier /'gleɪzjə(r)/ *n.* person whose trade is glazing windows etc.

gleam *–n.* faint or brief light or show. *–v.* emit gleams, shine. [Old English]

glean *v.* **1** acquire (facts etc.) in small amounts. **2** gather (corn left by reapers). [French]

gleanings *n.pl.* things gleaned, esp. facts.

glebe *n.* piece of land as part of a clergyman's benefice and providing income. [Latin *gl(a)eba* clod, soil]

glee *n.* **1** mirth; delight. **2** part-song for three or more (esp. male) voices. [Old English]

gleeful *adj.* joyful. □ **gleefully** *adv.* **gleefulness** *n.*

glen *n.* narrow valley. [Gaelic]

glengarry /glen'gærɪ/ *n.* (*pl.* **-ies**) brimless Scottish hat cleft down the centre and with ribbons at the back. [*Glengarry* in Scotland]

glib *adj.* (**glibber, glibbest**) speaking or spoken quickly or fluently but without sincerity. □ **glibly** *adv.* **glibness** *n.* [obsolete *glibbery* slippery, perhaps imitative]

glide *–v.* (**-ding**) **1** move smoothly and continuously. **2** (of an aircraft or pilot) fly without engine-power. **3** pass gradually or imperceptibly. **4** go stealthily. **5** cause to glide. *–n.* gliding movement. [Old English]

glide path *n.* aircraft's line of descent to land.

glider *n.* light aircraft without an engine.

glimmer *–v.* shine faintly or intermittently. *–n.* **1** feeble or wavering light. **2** (also **glimmering**) (usu. foll. by *of*) small sign (of hope etc.). [probably Scandinavian]

glimpse *–n.* (often foll. by *of, at*) **1** brief view or look. **2** faint transient appearance (*glimpses of the truth*). *–v.* (**-sing**) have a brief view of (*glimpsed his face in the crowd*). [related to GLIMMER]

glint *–v.* flash, glitter. *–n.* flash, sparkle. [probably Scandinavian]

glissade /glɪ'sɑːd/ *–n.* **1** controlled slide down a snow slope in mountaineering. **2** gliding step in ballet. *–v.* (**-ding**) perform a glissade. [French]

glissando /glɪ'sændəʊ/ *n.* (*pl.* **-di** /-dɪ/ or **-s**) *Mus.* continuous slide of adjacent notes. [French *glissant* sliding: related to GLISSADE]

glisten /'glɪs(ə)n/ *–v.* shine like a wet or polished surface. *–n.* glitter; sparkle. [Old English]

glitch *n. colloq.* sudden irregularity or malfunction (of equipment etc.). [origin unknown]

glitter *–v.* **1** shine with a bright reflected light; sparkle. **2** (usu. foll. by *with*) be showy or splendid. *–n.* **1** sparkle. **2** showiness. **3** tiny pieces of sparkling material as decoration etc. □ **glittery** *adj.* [Old Norse]

glitterati /ˌglɪtə'rɑːtɪ/ *n.pl. slang* rich fashionable people. [from GLITTER, LITERATI]

glitz *n. slang* showy glamour. □ **glitzy** *adj.* (**-ier, -iest**). [from GLITTER, RITZY]

gloaming /'gləʊmɪŋ/ *n. Scot.* or *poet.* twilight. [Old English]

gloat *–v.* (often foll. by *over* etc.) look or consider with greed, malice, etc. *–n.* act of gloating. [origin unknown]

glob *n. colloq.* mass or lump of semi-liquid substance, e.g. mud. [perhaps from BLOB, GOB[2]]

global /'gləʊb(ə)l/ *adj.* **1** worldwide (*global conflict*). **2** all-embracing. □ **globally** *adv.* [French: related to GLOBE]

◆ **globalization** /ˌgləʊb(ə)laɪ'zeɪʃ(ə)n/ *n.* (also **-isation**) **1** process enabling investment in financial markets to be carried out on an international basis, largely as a result of deregulation and improvements in technology. See also DISINTERMEDIATION. **2** process by which a company etc. expands to operate internationally.

◆ **global product** *n.* product marketed throughout the world with the same brand name, e.g. Coca Cola, Guinness, Levi, and McDonald's, usu. enabling an advertisement or image to be used worldwide.

◆ **global search** *n.* word-processing operation in which a complete document is searched by the computer, in order to locate every occurrence of a particular word or phrase. In **global search and replace**, the word or phrase is replaced automatically by some other designated word or phrase.

---

global warming *n.* increase in the temperature of the earth's atmosphere caused by the greenhouse effect.

globe *n.* **1 a** (prec. by *the*) the earth. **b** spherical representation of it with a map on the surface. **2** spherical object, e.g. a fish-bowl, lamp, etc. [Latin *globus*]

globe artichoke *n.* the partly edible head of the artichoke plant.

globe-trotter *n. colloq.* person who travels widely. □ **globe-trotting** *n.* & *attrib. adj.*

globular /'glɒbjʊlə(r)/ *adj.* **1** globe-shaped. **2** composed of globules.

globule /'glɒbjuːl/ *n.* small globe or round particle or drop. [Latin *globulus*]

globulin /'glɒbjʊlɪn/ *n.* molecule-transporting protein in plant and animal tissues.

glockenspiel /'glɒkənˌspiːl/ *n.* musical instrument with bells or metal bars or tubes struck by hammers. [German, = bell-play]

gloom *n.* **1** darkness; obscurity. **2** melancholy; despondency. [origin unknown]

gloomy *adj.* (**-ier, -iest**) **1** dark; unlit. **2** depressed or depressing. □ **gloomily** *adv.* **gloominess** *n.*

glorify /'glɔːrɪˌfaɪ/ *v.* (**-ies, -ied**) **1** make glorious. **2** make seem better or more splendid than it is. **3** (as **glorified** *adj.*) invested with more attractiveness, importance, etc. than it has in reality (*glorified waitress*). **4** extol. □ **glorification** /-fɪ'keɪʃ(ə)n/ *n.* [Latin: related to GLORY]

glorious /'glɔːrɪəs/ *adj.* **1** possessing or conferring glory; illustrious. **2** *colloq.* often *iron.* splendid, excellent (*glorious day; glorious muddle*). □ **gloriously** *adv.*

glory /'glɔːrɪ/ *–n.* (*pl.* **-ies**) **1** renown, fame; honour. **2** adoring praise. **3** resplendent majesty, beauty, etc. **4** thing that brings renown, distinction, or pride. **5** heavenly bliss and splendour. **6** *colloq.* state of exaltation, prosperity, etc. **7** halo of a saint etc. *–v.* (**-ies, -ied**) (often foll. by *in*) pride oneself. [Latin *gloria*]

glory-hole *n. colloq.* untidy room, cupboard, etc.

Glos. /glɒs/ *abbr.* Gloucestershire.

gloss[1] *–n.* **1** surface shine or lustre. **2** deceptively attractive appearance. **3** (in full **gloss paint**) paint giving a glossy finish. *–v.* make glossy. □ **gloss over** seek to conceal, esp. by mentioning only briefly. [origin unknown]

gloss[2] *–n.* **1** explanatory comment added to a text, e.g. in the margin. **2** interpretation or paraphrase. *–v.* add a gloss to (a text, word, etc.). [Latin *glossa* tongue]

glossary /'glɒsərɪ/ *n.* (*pl.* **-ies**) **1** list or dictionary of technical or special words. **2** collection of glosses. [Latin: related to GLOSS[2]]

glossy *–adj.* (**-ier, -iest**) **1** smooth and shiny (*glossy paper*). **2** printed on such paper. *–n.* (*pl.* **-ies**) *colloq.* glossy magazine or photograph. □ **glossily** *adv.* **glossiness** *n.*

glottal /ˈglɒt(ə)l/ *adj.* of the glottis.
glottal stop *n.* sound produced by the sudden opening or shutting of the glottis.
glottis /ˈglɒtɪs/ *n.* opening at the upper end of the wind-pipe and between the vocal cords. [Greek]
Gloucester /ˈglɒstə(r)/ town in W England, county town of Gloucestershire; manufactures include aircraft components, agricultural machinery, and matches; pop. (est. 1994) 104 800. –*n.* (usu. **double Gloucester**, orig. a richer kind) cheese made in Gloucestershire.
Gloucestershire /ˈglɒstə,ʃɪə(r)/ county in SW England; pop. (est. 1994) 549 500; county town, Gloucester. It is mainly agricultural, but there is some engineering.
glove /glʌv/ –*n.* **1** hand-covering for protection, warmth, etc., usu. with separate fingers. **2** boxing glove. –*v.* (**-ving**) cover or provide with gloves. [Old English]
glove compartment *n.* recess for small articles in the dashboard of a car etc.
glove puppet *n.* small puppet fitted on the hand and worked by the fingers.
glover *n.* glove-maker.
glow /gləʊ/ –*v.* **1 a** emit light and heat without flame. **b** shine as if heated in this way. **2** (often foll. by *with*) **a** (of the body) be heated. **b** show or feel strong emotion (*glowed with pride*). **3** show a warm colour. **4** (as **glowing** *adj.*) expressing pride or satisfaction (*glowing report*). –*n.* **1** glowing state. **2** bright warm colour. **3** feeling of satisfaction or well-being. [Old English]
glower /ˈglaʊə(r)/ –*v.* **1** (often foll. by *at*) look angrily. **2** look dark or threatening. –*n.* glowering look. [origin uncertain]
glow-worm *n.* beetle whose wingless female emits light from the end of the abdomen.
gloxinia /glɒkˈsɪnɪə/ *n.* American tropical plant with large bell-shaped flowers. [*Gloxin*, name of a botanist]
glucose /ˈgluːkəʊz/ *n.* sugar found in the blood or in fruit juice etc., and as a constituent of starch, cellulose, etc. [Greek *gleukos* sweet wine]
glue /gluː/ –*n.* adhesive substance. –*v.* (**glues, glued, gluing** or **glueing**) **1** fasten or join with glue. **2** keep or put very close (*eye glued to the keyhole*). □ **gluey** /ˈgluːɪ/ *adj.* (**gluier, gluiest**). [Latin *glus*: related to GLUTEN]
glue ear *n.* blocking of the Eustachian tube, esp. in children.
glue-sniffing *n.* inhalation of fumes from adhesives as an intoxicant. □ **glue-sniffer** *n.*
glum *adj.* (**glummer, glummest**) dejected; sullen. □ **glumly** *adv.* **glumness** *n.* [var. of GLOOM]
glut –*v.* (**-tt-**) **1** feed (a person, one's stomach, etc.) or indulge (a desire etc.) to the full; satiate. **2** fill to excess. **3** overstock (a market). –*n.* **1** supply exceeding demand. **2** full indulgence; surfeit. [French *gloutir* swallow: related to GLUTTON]
glutamate /ˈgluːtə,meɪt/ *n.* salt or ester of glutamic acid, esp. a sodium salt used to enhance the flavour of food.
glutamic acid /gluːˈtæmɪk/ *n.* amino acid normally found in proteins. [from GLUTEN, AMINE]
gluten /ˈgluːt(ə)n/ *n.* mixture of proteins present in cereal grains; sticky protein substance left when starch is washed out of flour. [Latin *gluten -tin-* glue]
glutinous /ˈgluːtɪnəs/ *adj.* sticky; like glue. [Latin: related to GLUTEN]
glutton /ˈglʌt(ə)n/ *n.* **1** greedy eater. **2** (often foll. by *for*) *colloq.* person insatiably eager (*glutton for work*). **3** voracious animal of the weasel family. □ **gluttonous** *adj.* **gluttonously** *adv.* [Latin *gluttio* SWALLOW[1]]
glutton for punishment *n.* person eager to take on hard or unpleasant tasks.
gluttony /ˈglʌtənɪ/ *n.* greed or excess in eating. [French: related to GLUTTON]
glycerine /ˈglɪsə,riːn/ *n.* (also **glycerol**, *US* **glycerin** /-rɪn/) thick sweet colourless liquid used as medicine, ointment, etc., and in explosives. [Greek *glukeros* sweet]
glycerol /ˈglɪsə,rɒl/ *n.* = GLYCERINE.
glycogen /ˈglaɪkədʒ(ə)n/ *n.* polysaccharide serving as a store of carbohydrates, esp. in animal tissues.
glycolysis /glaɪˈkɒlɪsɪs/ *n.* breakdown of glucose by enzymes with the release of energy.
GM *abbr.* **1** general manager. **2** geometric mean. **3** George Medal.
gm *abbr.* gram(s).
G-man /ˈdʒiːmæn/ *n. US colloq.* federal criminal-investigation officer. [from Government]
GMB *abbr.* General, Municipal, Boilermakers (trade union).
g.m.b. *abbr.* good merchantable brand.
GmbH *abbr.* (German) Gesellschaft mit beschränkter Haftung (= private limited company).
g.m.q. *abbr.* good merchantable quality.
GMS *abbr.* grant-maintained status.
GMT *abbr.* Greenwich Mean Time.
gnarled /nɑːld/ *adj.* (of a tree, hands, etc.) knobbly, twisted, rugged. [var. of *knarled*: related to KNURL]
gnash /næʃ/ *v.* **1** grind (the teeth). **2** (of the teeth) strike together. [Old Norse]
gnat /næt/ *n.* small two-winged biting fly. [Old English]
gnaw /nɔː/ *v.* **1 a** (usu. foll. by *away* etc.) wear away by biting. **b** (often foll. by *at, into*) bite persistently. **2 a** corrode; wear away. **b** (of pain, fear, etc.) torment. [Old English]
gneiss /naɪs/ *n.* coarse-grained metamorphic rock of feldspar, quartz, and mica. [German]
GNMA *abbr.* (in the US) Government National Mortgage Association.
gnome /nəʊm/ *n.* **1 a** dwarfish legendary spirit or goblin living underground. **b** figure of this as a garden ornament. **2** (esp. in *pl.*) *colloq.* person with sinister influence, esp. financial (*gnomes of Zurich*). □ **gnomish** *adj.* [French]
gnomic /ˈnəʊmɪk/ *adj.* of aphorisms; sententious. [Greek *gnōmē* opinion]
gnomon /ˈnəʊmɒn/ *n.* rod or pin etc. on a sundial, showing the time by its shadow. [Greek, = indicator]
gnostic /ˈnɒstɪk/ –*adj.* **1** of knowledge; having special mystical knowledge. **2** (**Gnostic**) concerning the Gnostics. –*n.* (**Gnostic**) (usu. in *pl.*) early Christian heretic claiming mystical knowledge. □ **Gnosticism** /-,sɪz(ə)m/ *n.* [Greek *gnōsis* knowledge]
GNP *abbr.* = GROSS NATIONAL PRODUCT.
gnu /nuː/ *n.* (*pl.* same or **-s**) oxlike antelope. [Bushman *nqu*]
GNVQ *abbr.* General National Vocational Qualification. See VOCATIONAL TRAINING.
go[1] /gəʊ/ –*v.* (*3rd sing. present* **goes** /gəʊz/; *past* **went**; *past part.* **gone** /gɒn/) **1 a** start moving or be moving from one place or point in time to another; travel, proceed. **b** (foll. by *and* + verb) *colloq.* expressing annoyance (*you went and told him*). **2** (foll. by verbal noun) make a special trip for; participate in (*went skiing*; *goes running*). **3** lie or extend in a certain direction (*the road goes to London*). **4** leave; depart (*they had to go*). **5** move, act, work, etc. (*clock doesn't go*). **6 a** make a specified movement (*go like this with your foot*). **b** make a sound (often of a specified kind) (*gun went bang*; *door bell went*). **c** (of an animal) make (its characteristic cry) (*the cow went 'moo'*). **d** *colloq.* say (*so he goes to me 'Why didn't you like it?'*). **7** be in a specified state (*go hungry*; *went in fear of his life*). **8 a** pass into a specified condition (*gone bad*; *went to sleep*). **b** *colloq.* die. **c** proceed or escape in a specified condition (*poet went unrecognized*). **9** (of time or distance) pass, elapse; be traversed (*ten days to go before Easter*; *the last mile went quickly*). **10 a** (of a document, verse, song, etc.) have a specified content or wording (*the tune goes like this*). **b** be current or accepted (*so the story goes*). **c** be suitable; fit; match (*the shoes don't go with the hat*; *those pinks don't go*). **d** be regularly kept or put (*the forks go here*). **e** find room; fit (*this won't go into the cupboard*). **11 a** turn out, proceed; take a course or view (*things went well*; *Liverpool went Labour*). **b** be successful (*make the party go*). **12 a** be sold (*went for £1*; *went cheap*). **b** (of money) be spent. **13**

a be relinquished or abolished (*the car will have to go*). **b** fail, decline; give way, collapse (*his sight is going*; *the bulb has gone*). **14** be acceptable or permitted; be accepted without question (*anything goes*; *what I say goes*). **15** (often foll. by *by*, *with*, *on*, *upon*) be guided by; judge or act on or in harmony with (*have nothing to go on*; *a good rule to go by*). **16** attend regularly (*goes to school*). **17** (foll. by pres. part.) *colloq.* proceed (often foolishly) to do (*went running to the police*; *don't go making him angry*). **18** act or proceed to a certain point (*will go so far and no further*; *went as high as £100*). **19** (of a number) be capable of being contained in another (*6 into 5 won't go*). **20** (usu. foll. by *to*) be allotted or awarded; pass (*first prize went to the girl*). **21** (foll. by *to*, *towards*) amount to; contribute to (*12 inches go to make a foot*; *this will go towards your holiday*). **22** (in *imper.*) begin motion (a starter's order in a race) (*ready, steady, go!*). **23** (usu. foll. by *by*, *under*) be known or called (*goes by the name of Droopy*). **24** *colloq.* proceed to (*go jump in the lake*). **25** (foll. by *for*) apply to (*that goes for me too*). –*n.* (*pl.* **goes**) **1** mettle; animation (*has a lot of go in her*). **2** vigorous activity (*it's all go*). **3** *colloq.* success (*made a go of it*). **4** *colloq.* attempt; turn (*I'll have a go*; *it's my go*). –*adj. colloq.* functioning properly (*all systems are go*). □ **go about 1** set to work at. **2** be socially active. **3** (foll. by pres. part.) make a habit of doing. **go ahead** proceed without hesitation. **go along with** agree to or with. **go back on** fail to keep (a promise etc.). **go begging** see BEG. **go down 1 a** (of an amount) become less through use (*coffee has gone down*). **b** subside (*the flood went down*). **c** decrease in price. **2 a** (of a ship) sink. **b** (of the sun) set. **c** (of a curtain) fall. **3** deteriorate; (of a computer system etc.) cease to function. **4** be recorded in writing. **5** be swallowed. **6** (often foll. by *with*) find acceptance. **7** *colloq.* leave university. **8** *colloq.* be sent to prison. **go down with** become ill with (a disease). **go far** see FAR. **go for 1** go to fetch. **2** pass or be accounted as (*went for nothing*). **3** prefer; choose. **4** *colloq.* strive to attain (*go for it!*). **5** *colloq.* attack (*the dog went for him*). **go halves** (often foll. by *with*) share equally. **go in 1** enter a room, house, etc. **2** (of the sun etc.) become obscured by cloud. **go in for 1** enter as a competitor. **2** take as one's style, pursuit, etc. **go into 1** enter (a profession, hospital, etc.). **2** investigate. **go a long way 1** (often foll. by *towards*) have a great effect. **2** (of food, money, etc.) last a long time, buy much. **3** = *go far*. **go off 1** explode. **2** leave the stage. **3** wear off. **4** (esp. of foodstuffs) deteriorate. **5** go to sleep. **6** *colloq.* begin to dislike (*I've gone off him*). **go off well** (or **badly** etc.) (of an enterprise etc.) be received or accomplished well (or badly etc.). **go on 1** (often foll. by pres. part.) continue, persevere (*decided to go on with it*; *went on trying*). **2** *colloq.* **a** talk at great length. **b** (foll. by *at*) nag. **3** (foll. by *to* + infin.) proceed (*went on to become a star*). **4** (also **go upon**) *colloq.* use as evidence. **go out 1** leave a room, house, etc. **2** be extinguished. **3** be broadcast. **4** (often foll. by *with*) be courting. **5** cease to be fashionable. **6** *colloq.* lose consciousness. **7** (usu. foll. by *to*) (of the heart etc.) expand with sympathy etc. towards (*my heart goes out to them*). **8** (of a tide) ebb to low tide. **go over 1** inspect the details of; rehearse; retouch. **2** (of a play etc.) be received, esp. favourably. **go public** apply to a stock exchange to become a public limited company. **go round 1** spin, revolve. **2** (of food etc.) suffice for everybody. **3** (usu. foll. by *to*) visit informally. **go slow** work slowly, as a form of industrial action. **go through 1** be dealt with or completed. **2** discuss or scrutinize in detail. **3** perform. **4** undergo. **5** *colloq.* use up; spend (money etc.). **go through with** complete. **go to blazes** (or **hell**) *slang* exclamation of dismissal, contempt, etc. **go too far** see FAR. **go under** sink; fail; succumb. **go up 1** rise in price. **2** *colloq.* enter university. **3** be consumed (in flames etc.); explode. **go with 1** be harmonious with; match. **2** be courting. **go without** manage without; forgo (also *absol.*). **have a go at 1** attack. **2** attempt. **on the go** *colloq.* **1** in constant motion. **2** constantly working. [Old English: *went* is originally a past of WEND]

go[2] /gəʊ/ *n.* Japanese board-game. [Japanese]

Goa /ˈgəʊə/ state (since 1987) on the W coast of India; pop. (1991) 1 169 753; capital, Panaji. It is mainly agricultural, but there is some mining and tourism is important. □ **Goan** *adj.* & *n.* **Goanese** /ˌgəʊəˈniːz/ *adj.* & *n.*

goad –*v.* **1** urge on with a goad. **2** (usu. foll. by *on*, *into*) irritate; stimulate. –*n.* **1** spiked stick used for urging cattle forward. **2** anything that torments or incites. [Old English]

go-ahead –*n.* permission to proceed. –*adj.* enterprising.

goal *n.* **1** object of ambition or effort; destination. **2 a** structure into or through which the ball has to be sent to score in certain games. **b** point won. **3** point marking the finish of a race. [origin unknown]

goalie *n. colloq.* = GOALKEEPER.

goalkeeper *n.* player defending a goal.

goalpost *n.* either of the two upright posts of a goal.

goat *n.* **1** hardy domesticated mammal, with horns and (in the male) a beard. **2** lecherous man. **3** *colloq.* foolish person. **4** (**the Goat**) zodiacal sign or constellation Capricorn. □ **get a person's goat** *colloq.* irritate a person. [Old English]

goatee /gəʊˈtiː/ *n.* small pointed beard.

goatherd *n.* person who tends goats.

goatskin *n.* **1** skin of a goat. **2** garment or bottle made of goatskin.

gob[1] *n. slang* mouth. [origin unknown]

gob[2] *slang* –*n.* clot of slimy matter. –*v.* (**-bb-**) spit. [French *go(u)be* mouthful]

g.o.b. *abbr.* good ordinary brand.

gobbet /ˈgɒbɪt/ *n.* **1** piece or lump of flesh, food, etc. **2** extract from a text, esp. one set for translation or comment. [French diminutive of *gobe* GOB[2]]

gobble[1] /ˈgɒb(ə)l/ *v.* (**-ling**) eat hurriedly and noisily. [from GOB[2]]

gobble[2] /ˈgɒb(ə)l/ *v.* (**-ling**) **1** (of a turkeycock) make a characteristic guttural sound. **2** make such a sound when speaking. [imitative]

gobbledegook /ˈgɒb(ə)ldɪˌguːk/ *n.* (also **gobbledygook**) *colloq.* pompous or unintelligible jargon. [probably imitative of a turkeycock]

go-between *n.* intermediary.

goblet /ˈgɒblɪt/ *n.* drinking-vessel with a foot and stem. [French diminutive of *gobel* cup]

goblin /ˈgɒblɪn/ *n.* mischievous ugly dwarflike creature of folklore. [Anglo-French]

gobsmacked *adj. slang* astounded, flabbergasted.

gob-stopper *n.* large hard sweet.

go-cart *n.* var. of GO-KART.

GOCO *abbr.* government-owned, contractor-operated.

god *n.* **1 a** (in many religions) superhuman being or spirit worshipped as having power over nature, human fortunes, etc. **b** image, idol, etc., symbolizing a god. **2** (**God**) (in Christian and other monotheistic religions) creator and ruler of the universe. **3** adored or greatly admired person. **4** (in *pl.*) *Theatr.* gallery. □ **God forbid** may it not happen! **God knows 1** it is beyond all knowledge. **2** I call God to witness that. **God willing** if Providence allows. [Old English]

godchild *n.* person in relation to his or her godparent.

god-daughter *n.* female godchild.

goddess /ˈgɒdɪs/ *n.* **1** female deity. **2** adored woman.

godfather *n.* **1** male godparent. **2** esp. *US* person directing an illegal organization, esp. the Mafia.

♦ **godfather offer** *n. colloq.* tender offer pitched so high that the management of the target company is unable to discourage shareholders from accepting it.

God-fearing *adj.* earnestly religious.

God-forsaken *adj.* dismal.

godhead *n.* (also **Godhead**) **1 a** state of being God or a god. **b** divine nature. **2** deity. **3** (**the Godhead**) God.

godless *adj.* **1** impious; wicked. **2** without a god. **3** not recognizing God. □ **godlessness** *n.*

godlike *adj.* resembling God or a god.

godly *adj.* (**-ier, -iest**) pious, devout. □ **godliness** *n.*
godmother *n.* female godparent.
godparent *n.* person who presents a child at baptism and responds on the child's behalf.
godsend *n.* unexpected but welcome event or acquisition.
godson *n.* male godchild.
Godspeed /gɒd'spiːd/ *int.* expression of good wishes to a person starting a journey.
Godthåb /'gɒthɔːb/ (Eskimo **Nuuk** /nuːk/) former name for Nuuk, capital of Greenland.
goer *n.* **1** person or thing that goes (*slow goer*). **2** (often in *comb.*) person who attends, esp. regularly (*churchgoer*). **3** *colloq.* **a** lively or persevering person. **b** sexually promiscuous person.
go-getter *n. colloq.* aggressively enterprising person.
goggle /'gɒg(ə)l/ –*v.* (**-ling**) **1 a** (often foll. by *at*) look with wide-open eyes. **b** (of the eyes) be rolled about; protrude. **2** roll (the eyes). –*adj.* (usu. *attrib.*) (of the eyes) protuberant or rolling. –*n.* (in *pl.*) spectacles for protecting the eyes. [probably imitative]
goggle-box *n. colloq.* television set.
go-go *adj. colloq.* (of a dancer, music, etc.) in modern style; lively, erotic, and rhythmic.
going /'gəʊɪŋ/ –*n.* **1** act or process of going. **2 a** condition of the ground for walking, riding, etc. **b** progress affected by this. –*adj.* **1** in or into action (*set the clock going*). **2** existing, available (*there's cold beef going*). **3** current, prevalent (*the going rate*). □ **get going** start steadily talking, working, etc. **going on fifteen** etc. esp. *US* approaching one's fifteenth etc. birthday. **going on for** approaching (a time, age, etc.). **going strong** continuing vigorously. **going to** intending to; about to. **to be going on with** to start with; for the time being. **while the going is good** while conditions are favourable.
going concern *n.* thriving business.

♦ **going-concern concept** *n.* principle of accounting practice that assumes businesses to be going concerns, unless circumstances indicate otherwise. It assumes that an enterprise will continue in operation for the foreseeable future, so that the accounts assume no intention or necessity to liquidate or significantly curtail the scale of the enterprise's operation. The implications of this principle are that assets are shown at cost, or at cost less depreciation, and not at their breakup values; it also assumes that liabilities applicable only on liquidation are not shown.

going-over *n.* (*pl.* **goings-over**) **1** *colloq.* inspection or overhaul. **2** *slang* thrashing.
goings-on *n.pl.* (esp. morally suspect) behaviour.
goitre /'gɔɪtə(r)/ *n.* (*US* **goiter**) morbid enlargement of the thyroid gland. [Latin *guttur* throat]
go-kart *n.* (also **go-cart**) miniature racing car with a skeleton body.
gold /gəʊld/ –*n.* **1** precious yellow metallic element. **2** colour of gold. **3 a** coins or articles made of gold. **b** wealth. **4** something precious or beautiful. **5** = GOLD MEDAL. –*adj.* **1** made wholly or chiefly of gold. **2** coloured like gold. [Old English]

♦ **gold card** *n.* credit card that entitles its holder to various benefits (e.g. an unsecured overdraft, some insurance cover, a higher limit) in addition to those offered to standard card holders.
♦ **gold clause** *n.* clause in a loan agreement between governments stipulating that repayments must be made in the gold equivalent of the currency involved at the time either the agreement or the loan was made. The purpose is to protect the lender against a fall in the borrower's currency, esp. in countries suffering high rates of inflation.

Gold Coast 1 see GHANA. **2** resort city in Australia, on the E coast of Queensland; pop. (est. 1991) 139 899.

♦ **gold coins** *n.pl.* coins made of gold, which ceased to circulate after the First World War. There have been various restrictions on dealing in and exporting gold coins at various times. Since 1979 gold coins may be imported and exported without restriction, except that gold coins more than 50 years old with a value in excess of £8000 cannot be exported without authorization from the Department of Trade and Industry. See also BRITANNIA COINS; KRUGERRAND.

goldcrest *n.* tiny bird with a golden crest.
gold-digger *n. slang* woman who cultivates men to obtain money from them.
gold-dust *n.* gold in fine particles as often found naturally.
golden *adj.* **1 a** made or consisting of gold. **b** yielding gold. **2** coloured or shining like gold (*golden hair*). **3** precious; excellent.
golden age *n.* period of a nation's greatest prosperity, cultural merit, etc.
golden eagle *n.* large eagle with yellow-tipped head-feathers.

♦ **golden handcuffs** see GOLDEN HELLO.
♦ **golden handshake** *n. colloq.* payment, usu. large, given on redundancy or early retirement. See COMPENSATION FOR LOSS OF OFFICE.
♦ **golden hello** *n. colloq.* financial incentive paid by a firm to a newly employed specialist, who leaves another firm. **Golden handcuffs** are financial inducements used to persuade specialists to stay in a particular firm. Golden hellos and golden handcuffs became popular at the time of the Big Bang, when the major stockbroking firms were attempting to gain a large share of the market by employing the leading investment analysts, dealers, etc.

golden jubilee *n.* fiftieth anniversary.
golden mean *n.* the principle of moderation.

♦ **golden parachute** *n. colloq.* clause in the employment contract of a senior executive in a company that provides for financial and other benefits if the executive is sacked or decides to leave as the result of a take-over or change of ownership.

golden retriever *n.* retriever with a thick golden-coloured coat.
golden rod *n.* plant with a spike of yellow flowers.
golden rule *n.* basic principle of action, esp. 'do as you would be done by'.

♦ **golden share** *n.* share in a company that controls at least 51% of the voting rights. A golden share has been retained by the UK government in some privatization issues to ensure that the company does not fall into foreign or other unacceptable hands.

golden wedding *n.* fiftieth anniversary of a wedding.
gold-field *n.* district in which gold occurs naturally.
goldfinch *n.* songbird with a yellow band across each wing.
goldfish *n.* (*pl.* same or **-es**) small reddish-golden Chinese carp.
gold foil *n.* gold beaten into a thin sheet.
gold leaf *n.* gold beaten into a very thin sheet.

♦ **gold market** see BULLION.

gold medal *n.* medal of gold, usu. awarded as first prize.
gold-mine *n.* **1** place where gold is mined. **2** *colloq.* source of great wealth.
gold plate *n.* **1** vessels made of gold. **2** material plated with gold.
gold-plate *v.* plate with gold.

♦ **gold pool** *n. hist.* organization of eight countries (Belgium, France, Italy, Netherlands, Switzerland, UK, US, and West Germany) that between 1961 and 1968 joined together in an attempt to stabilize the price of gold.

gold-rush *n.* rush to a newly-discovered gold-field.

♦ **Goldsmith** /'gəʊld,smɪθ/, **Sir James Michael** (1933–97) Franco-British industrialist, founder of a number of industrial commercial and financial companies, including Mothercare (co-founder), Cavenham Ltd., and Générale Occidentale (chairman 1969–87). Establishing the Goldsmith Foundation, of which he was chief executive, and retiring from active participation in business in 1991, he turned his attention to politics. A member for France of the European Parliament from 1994, in 1995 he founded the Referendum Party, UK. Opposing further UK integration with the European Union and campaigning for a referendum, Goldsmith's single-issue party failed to gain any seats in the 1997 general election.

goldsmith *n.* worker in gold.

♦ **gold standard** *n. hist.* monetary system in which a country's currency unit was fixed in terms of gold; currency was freely convertible into gold and free import and export of gold was permitted. The UK was on the gold standard from the early 19th century until it finally withdrew in 1931. Most other countries withdrew soon after. See also INTERNATIONAL MONETARY FUND.

♦ **gold tranche** see RESERVE TRANCHE.

golf *–n.* game in which a small hard ball is driven with clubs into a series of 18 or 9 holes with the fewest possible strokes. *–v.* play golf. □ **golfer** *n.* [origin unknown]

golf ball *n.* **1** ball used in golf. **2** *colloq.* small ball used in some electric typewriters and computer printers to carry the type.

golf club *n.* **1** club used in golf. **2** association for playing golf. **3** premises of this.

golf-course *n.* (also **golf-links**) course on which golf is played.

golliwog /'gɒlɪ,wɒg/ *n.* black-faced soft doll with fuzzy hair. [origin uncertain]

golly[1] /'gɒlɪ/ *int.* expressing surprise. [euphemism for GOD]

golly[2] /'gɒlɪ/ *n.* (*pl.* **-ies**) *colloq.* = GOLLIWOG. [abbreviation]

golosh var. of GALOSH.

gonad /'gəʊnæd/ *n.* animal organ producing gametes, esp. the testis or ovary. [Greek *gonē* seed]

gondola /'gɒndələ/ *n.* **1** light flat-bottomed boat used on Venetian canals. **2** car suspended from an airship or balloon, or attached to a ski-lift. [Italian]

gondolier /,gɒndə'lɪə(r)/ *n.* oarsman on a gondola. [Italian: related to GONDOLA]

gone /gɒn/ *adj.* **1** (of time) past (*not until gone nine*). **2 a** lost; hopeless. **b** dead. **3** *colloq.* pregnant for a specified time (*already three months gone*). **4** *slang* completely enthralled or entranced, esp. by rhythmic music, drugs, etc. □ **be gone** depart; leave temporarily (cf. BEGONE). **gone on** *slang* infatuated with. [past part. of GO[1]]

goner /'gɒnə(r)/ *n. slang* person or thing that is doomed or irrevocably lost.

gong *n.* **1** metal disc with a turned rim, giving a resonant note when struck. **2** saucer-shaped bell. **3** *slang* medal. [Malay]

gonorrhoea /,gɒnə'rɪə/ *n.* (*US* **gonorrhea**) venereal disease with inflammatory discharge from the urethra or vagina. [Greek, = semen-flux]

goo *n. colloq.* **1** sticky or slimy substance. **2** sickly sentiment. [origin unknown]

good /gʊd/ *–adj.* (**better**, **best**) **1** having the right or desired qualities; adequate. **2 a** (of a person) efficient, competent (*good at French*; *good driver*). **b** effective, reliable (*good brakes*). **3 a** kind. **b** morally excellent; virtuous (*good deed*). **c** well-behaved (*good child*). **4** enjoyable, agreeable (*good party*; *good news*). **5** thorough, considerable (*a good wash*). **6 a** not less than (*waited a good hour*). **b** considerable in number, quality, etc. (*a good many people*). **7** beneficial (*milk is good for you*). **8 a** valid, sound (*good reason*). **b** financially sound (*his credit is good*). **9** in exclamations of surprise (*good heavens!*). **10** (sometimes patronizing) commendable, worthy (*good old George*; *my good man*). **11** in courteous greetings and farewells (*good morning*). *–n.* **1** (only in *sing.*) that which is good; what is beneficial or morally right (*only good can come of it*; *what good will it do?*). **2** (in *pl.*) **a** movable property or merchandise. **b** things to be transported. **c** (prec. by *the*) *colloq.* what one has undertaken to supply (esp. *deliver the goods*). **3** *Econ.* commodity or service regarded as satisfying a human need. An **economic good** is one that is both needed and sufficiently scarce to command a price. A **free good** is needed but is in abundant supply and therefore does not need to be purchased (e.g. air). However, a commodity or service that is free but has required an effort to produce or obtain is not a free good in this sense. See also CAPITAL GOODS; CONSUMER GOODS. *–adv. US colloq.* well (*doing pretty good*). □ **as good as** practically. **be (a certain amount) to the good** have as net profit or advantage. **for good (and all)** finally, permanently. **good for 1** beneficial to; having a good effect on. **2** able to perform. **3** able to be trusted to pay. **good riddance** see RIDDANCE. **have the goods on a person** *slang* have information about a person giving one an advantage over him or her. **in good faith** with honest or sincere intentions. **in good time 1** with no risk of being late. **2** (also **all in good time**) in due course but without haste. **to the good** having as profit or benefit. [Old English]

good Book *n.* (prec. by *the*) the Bible.

goodbye /gʊd'baɪ/ (*US* **goodby**) *–int.* expressing good wishes on parting, ending a telephone conversation, etc. *–n.* (*pl.* **-byes** or *US* **-bys**) parting; farewell. [from *God be with you!*]

good faith *n.* sincerity of intention.

good-for-nothing *–adj.* worthless. *–n.* worthless person.

Good Friday *n.* Friday before Easter Sunday, commemorating the Crucifixion.

♦ **Goodhart's law** /'gʊd,hɑ:ts/ *n.* law in economics that any attempt by a government to control an economic variable will distort that variable so as to render the government's control ineffective, largely because the public will attempt to evade the control. The law was first applied to measures of the money supply, e.g. M0, M1, that monetarist governments attempted to control in order to reduce inflation. [*Goodhart*, name of an economist]

good-hearted *adj.* kindly, well-meaning.

good humour *n.* genial mood.

good-humoured *adj.* cheerful, amiable. □ **good-humouredly** *adv.*

goodie var. of GOODY *n.*

good job *n.* fortunate state of affairs.

good-looking *adj.* handsome.

goodly /'gʊdlɪ/ *adj.* (**-ier**, **-iest**) **1** handsome. **2** of imposing size etc. □ **goodliness** *n.* [Old English]

good nature *n.* friendly disposition.

good-natured *adj.* kind, patient; easygoing. □ **good-naturedly** *adv.*

goodness *–n.* **1** virtue; excellence. **2** kindness (*had the goodness to wait*). **3** what is beneficial in a thing. *–int.* (esp. as a substitution for 'God') expressing surprise, anger, etc. (*goodness me!*; *goodness knows*). [Old English]

♦ **goods-in-transit insurance** *n.* insurance covering property against loss or damage while it is in transit from one place to another or being stored during a journey. Such policies often specify the means of transport to be used, which may include the postal service. Goods shipped solely by sea are not covered by this type of policy. See also MARINE INSURANCE.

good-tempered *adj.* having a good temper; not easily annoyed.

goodwill *n.* **1** kindly feeling. **2** established reputation of a business etc. as enhancing its value. **3** *Finance* intangible asset that normally represents the excess of the value of a business over the value of its tangible assets. This excess value is largely attributable to the fact that the business generates profits in excess of the return to be expected from investing a sum equivalent to the value of the tangible assets alone. The goodwill is a saleable asset when a business is sold and is sometimes shown as such in the balance sheet. However, for limited companies, the Companies Act (1981) stipulates that goodwill purchased in this way must be written off by charges to the profit and loss account over a period not exceeding its economic life. See AMORTIZE 2b.

good will *n.* intention that good will result (see also GOODWILL).

good works *n.pl.* charitable acts.

goody –*n.* (also **goodie**) (*pl.* **-ies**) **1** *colloq.* good or favoured person. **2** (usu. in *pl.*) something good or attractive, esp. to eat. –*int.* expressing childish delight.

goody-goody *colloq.* –*n.* (*pl.* **-ies**) smug or obtrusively virtuous person. –*adj.* obtrusively or smugly virtuous.

gooey *adj.* (**gooier, gooiest**) *slang* **1** viscous, sticky. **2** sentimental. [from GOO]

goof *slang* –*n.* **1** foolish or stupid person. **2** mistake. –*v.* **1** bungle. **2** blunder. [Latin *gufus* coarse]

goofy *adj.* (**-ier, -iest**) *slang* **1** stupid. **2** having protruding or crooked front teeth.

googly /ˈguːglɪ/ *n.* (*pl.* **-ies**) *Cricket* ball bowled so as to bounce in an unexpected direction. [origin unknown]

goon *n. slang* **1** stupid person. **2** esp. *US* ruffian hired by racketeers etc. [origin uncertain]

goose *n.* (*pl.* **geese**) **1 a** large water-bird with webbed feet and a broad bill. **b** female of this (opp. GANDER 1). **c** flesh of a goose as food. **2** *colloq.* simpleton. [Old English]

gooseberry /ˈgʊzbərɪ/ *n.* (*pl.* **-ies**) **1** yellowish-green berry with juicy flesh. **2** thorny shrub bearing this. □ **play gooseberry** *colloq.* be an unwanted extra person. [origin uncertain]

goose-flesh *n.* (also **goose-pimples**; *US* **goose-bumps**) bristling state of the skin produced by cold, fright, etc.

goose-step *n.* military marching step in which the knees are kept stiff.

gopher /ˈgəʊfə(r)/ *n.* American burrowing rodent, ground-squirrel, or burrowing tortoise. [origin uncertain]

Gordian /ˈgɔːdɪən/ *adj.* □ **cut the Gordian knot** solve a problem by force or by evasion. [*Gordius* king of Phrygia, who tied a knot later cut by Alexander the Great]

gore[1] *n.* blood shed and clotted. [Old English, = dirt]

gore[2] *v.* (**-ring**) pierce with a horn, tusk, etc. [origin unknown]

gore[3] –*n.* **1** wedge-shaped piece in a garment. **2** triangular or tapering piece in an umbrella etc. –*v.* (**-ring**) shape (a garment) with a gore. [Old English, = triangle of land]

gorge –*n.* **1** narrow opening between hills. **2** act of gorging. **3** contents of the stomach. –*v.* (**-ging**) **1** feed greedily. **2 a** (often *refl.*) satiate. **b** devour greedily. □ **one's gorge rises at** one is sickened by. [French, = throat]

gorgeous /ˈgɔːdʒəs/ *adj.* **1** richly coloured, sumptuous. **2** *colloq.* very pleasant, splendid (*gorgeous weather*). **3** *colloq.* strikingly beautiful. □ **gorgeously** *adv.* [French]

gorgon /ˈgɔːgən/ *n.* **1** (in Greek mythology) each of three snake-haired sisters (esp. Medusa) with the power to turn anyone who looked at them to stone. **2** frightening or repulsive woman. [Greek *gorgos* terrible]

Gorgonzola /ˌgɔːgənˈzəʊlə/ *n.* type of rich cheese with bluish-green veins. [*Gorgonzola* in Italy]

gorilla /gəˈrɪlə/ *n.* largest anthropoid ape, native to Africa. [Greek, perhaps from African = wild man]

Gorky /ˈgɔːkɪ/ see NIZHNY NOVGOROD.

gormless /ˈgɔːmlɪs/ *adj. colloq.* foolish, lacking sense. □ **gormlessly** *adv.* [originally *gaumless* from dial. *gaum* understanding]

gorse *n.* spiny yellow-flowered shrub; furze. □ **gorsy** *adj.* [Old English]

Gorsedd /ˈgɔːseð/ *n.* Druidic order, meeting before the eisteddfod. [Welsh, literally 'throne']

gory *adj.* (**-ier, -iest**) **1** involving bloodshed; bloodthirsty. **2** covered in gore. □ **gorily** *adv.* **goriness** *n.*

gosh *int.* expressing surprise. [euphemism for GOD]

goshawk /ˈgɒshɔːk/ *n.* large short-winged hawk. [Old English: related to GOOSE, HAWK[1]]

gosling /ˈgɒzlɪŋ/ *n.* young goose. [Old Norse: related to GOOSE]

go-slow *n.* working slowly, as a form of industrial action. See also WORK-TO-RULE.

gospel /ˈgɒsp(ə)l/ *n.* **1** teaching or revelation of Christ. **2** (**Gospel**) **a** record of Christ's life in the first four books of the New Testament. **b** each of these books. **c** portion from one of them read at a service. **3** (also **gospel truth**) thing regarded as absolutely true. **4** (in full **gospel music**) Black American religious singing. [Old English: related to GOOD, SPELL[1] = news]

gossamer /ˈgɒsəmə(r)/ –*n.* **1** filmy substance of small spiders' webs. **2** delicate filmy material. –*adj.* light and flimsy as gossamer. [origin uncertain]

gossip /ˈgɒsɪp/ –*n.* **1 a** unconstrained talk or writing, esp. about persons or social incidents. **b** idle talk. **2** person who indulges in gossip. –*v.* (**-p-**) talk or write gossip. □ **gossipy** *adj.* [Old English, originally 'godparent', hence 'familiar acquaintance']

gossip column *n.* section of a newspaper devoted to gossip about well-known people. □ **gossip columnist** *n.*

got *past* and *past part.* of GET.

Göteborg see GOTHENBURG.

Goth *n.* **1** member of a Germanic tribe that invaded the Roman Empire in the 3rd–5th centuries. **2** uncivilized or ignorant person. [Old English *Gota* and Greek *Gothoi*]

goth *n.* **1** style of rock music with an intense or droning blend of guitars, bass, and drums, often with apocalyptic or mystical lyrics. **2** performer or devotee of this music, or member of the subculture favouring black clothing and white-painted faces with black make-up.

Gothenburg /ˈgɒθənˌbɜːg/ (Swedish **Göteborg** /ˈjɜːtəˌbɔːr/) seaport in SW Sweden; industries include oil refining, shipbuilding, and manufacturing; pop. (est. 1996) 449 189.

Gothic –*adj.* **1** of the Goths. **2** in the style of architecture prevalent in W Europe in the 12th–16th centuries, characterized by pointed arches. **3** (of a novel etc.) in a style popular in the 18th–19th centuries, with supernatural or horrifying events. **4** barbarous, uncouth. –*n.* **1** Gothic language. **2** Gothic architecture. [Latin: related to GOTH]

Gotland /ˈgɒtlənd/ Swedish island in the Baltic Sea; pop. (est. 1996) 58 120; capital, Visby. Cattle- and sheep-raising are the main occupations, but tourism is also important.

gotten *US past part.* of GET.

gouache /gʊˈɑːʃ/ *n.* **1** method of painting in opaque pigments ground in water and thickened with a gluelike substance. **2** these pigments. [French from Italian]

Gouda /ˈgaʊdə/ *n.* flat round usu. Dutch cheese. [*Gouda* in Holland]

gouge /gaʊdʒ/ –*n.* chisel with a concave blade. –*v.* (**-ging**) **1** cut with or as with a gouge. **2** (foll. by *out*) force out (esp. an eye with the thumb) with or as with a gouge. [Latin *gubia*]

goulash /ˈguːlæʃ/ *n.* highly-seasoned Hungarian stew of meat and vegetables. [Magyar *gulyás-hús*, = herdsman's meat]

gourd /gʊəd/ *n.* **1 a** fleshy usu. large fruit with a hard skin. **b** climbing or trailing plant of the cucumber family bearing this. **2** dried skin of the gourd-fruit, used as a drinking-vessel etc. [Latin *cucurbita*]

gourde /gʊəd/ *n.* standard monetary unit of Haiti. [from French *gourd* heavy]

gourmand /ˈgʊəmənd/ *n.* **1** glutton. **2** gourmet. [French]

■ **Usage** The use of *gourmand* in sense 2 is considered incorrect by some people.

gourmandise /ˈgʊəmɑ̃ˌdiːz/ *n.* gluttony.

gourmet /ˈɡʊəmeɪ/ *n.* connoisseur of good food. [French]

gout *n.* disease with inflammation of the smaller joints, esp. of the toe. □ **gouty** *adj.* [Latin *gutta* drop]

govern /ˈɡʌv(ə)n/ *v.* **1** rule or control with authority; conduct the policy and affairs of. **2** influence or determine (a person or course of action). **3** be a standard or principle for. **4** check or control (esp. passions). **5** *Gram.* (esp. of a verb or preposition) have (a noun or pronoun or its case) depending on it. [Greek *kubernaō* steer]

governance /ˈɡʌvənəns/ *n.* **1** act or manner of governing. **2** function of governing. [French: related to GOVERN]

governess /ˈɡʌvənɪs/ *n.* woman employed to teach children in a private household.

government /ˈɡʌvənmənt/ *n.* **1** act or manner of governing. **2** system by which a state is governed. **3 a** body of persons governing a state. **b** (usu. **Government**) particular ministry in office. **4** the state as an agent. □ **governmental** /-ˈment(ə)l/ *adj.*

◆ **government actuary** *n.* government officer with a small team of actuaries, with the responsibility of estimating future expenditure on the basis of observed population trends. The government actuary provides a consulting service to government departments and to Commonwealth governments, advising on social security schemes and superannuation arrangements and on government supervision of insurance companies and Friendly Societies.

◆ **government broker** *n.* stockbroker appointed by the government to sell government securities on the London Stock Exchange, under the instructions of the Bank of England, and to act as broker to the National Debt Commissioners. Until October 1986 (see BIG BANG) the government broker was traditionally the senior partner of Mullins & Co. Since then, when the Bank of England started its own gilt-edged dealing room, the government broker has been appointed from the gilt-edged division of the Bank of England, although some of the broker's functions are now undertaken by the gilts primary dealers.

◆ **government security** *n.* (also **government stock**) = GILT-EDGED SECURITY.

◆ **Government Statistical Service** *n.* (also **GSS**) service of statistical information and advice provided to the UK government by specialist staffs employed in the statistics divisions of individual government departments. The statistics collected are made generally available through such publications as *Social Trends*, published for the Central Statistical Office by HM Stationery Office.

governor *n.* **1** ruler. **2 a** official governing a province, town, etc. **b** representative of the Crown in a colony. **3** executive head of each state of the US. **4** officer commanding a fortress etc. **5** head or member of the governing body of an institution. **6** official in charge of a prison. **7 a** *slang* one's employer. **b** *slang* one's father. **8** *Mech.* automatic regulator controlling the speed of an engine etc. □ **governorship** *n.*

Governor-General *n.* representative of the Crown in a Commonwealth country that regards the Queen as head of state.

gown *n.* **1** loose flowing garment, esp. a woman's long dress. **2** official robe of an alderman, judge, cleric, academic, etc. **3** surgeon's overall. [Latin *gunna* fur]

goy *n.* (*pl.* **-im** or **-s**) Jewish name for a non-Jew. [Hebrew, = people]

Gozo /ˈɡəʊzəʊ/ one of the three main islands of Malta.

GP *abbr.* general practitioner.

GPIB *abbr. Computing* general-purpose interface bus.

GPM *abbr. US* graduated payment mortgage.

GPMU *abbr.* Graphical, Paper, and Media Union.

GPO *abbr.* General Post Office.

GPS *abbr.* Graduated Pension Scheme.

GR *international vehicle registration* Greece.

gr *abbr.* (also **gr.**) **1** gram(s). **2** grains. **3** gross.

grab *–v.* (**-bb-**) **1** seize suddenly. **2** take greedily or unfairly. **3** *slang* attract the attention of, impress. **4** (foll. by *at*) snatch at. **5** (of brakes) act harshly or jerkily. *–n.* **1** sudden clutch or attempt to seize. **2** mechanical device for clutching. [Low German or Dutch]

grace *–n.* **1** attractiveness, esp. in elegance of proportion or manner or movement. **2** courteous good will (*had the grace to apologize*). **3** attractive feature; accomplishment (*social graces*). **4 a** (in Christian belief) the unmerited favour of God. **b** state of receiving this. **5** goodwill, favour. **6** delay granted as a favour (*a year's grace*). **7** short thanksgiving before or after a meal. **8** (**Grace**) (in Greek mythology) each of three beautiful sister goddesses, bestowers of beauty and charm. **9** (**Grace**) (prec. by *His*, *Her*, *Your*) forms of description or address for a duke, duchess, or archbishop. *–v.* (**-cing**) (often foll. by *with*) add grace to; confer honour on (*graced us with his presence*). □ **with good** (or **bad**) **grace** as if willingly (or reluctantly). [Latin *gratia*]

graceful *adj.* having or showing grace or elegance. □ **gracefully** *adv.* **gracefulness** *n.*

graceless *adj.* lacking grace, elegance, or charm.

grace-note *n. Mus.* extra note as an embellishment.

gracious /ˈɡreɪʃəs/ *–adj.* **1** kind; indulgent and beneficent to inferiors. **2** (of God) merciful, benign. *–int.* expressing surprise. □ **graciously** *adv.* **graciousness** *n.* [Latin: related to GRACE]

gracious living *n.* elegant way of life.

gradate /ɡrəˈdeɪt/ *v.* (**-ting**) **1** (cause to) pass gradually from one shade to another. **2** arrange in steps or grades of size etc.

gradation /ɡrəˈdeɪʃ(ə)n/ *n.* (usu. in *pl.*) **1** stage of transition or advance. **2 a** certain degree in rank, intensity, etc. **b** arrangement in such degrees. □ **gradational** *adj.* [Latin: related to GRADE]

grade *–n.* **1 a** certain degree in rank, merit, proficiency, etc. **b** class of persons or things of the same grade. **2** mark indicating the quality of a student's work. **3** *US* class in school. **4** gradient, slope. *–v.* (**-ding**) **1** arrange in grades. **2** (foll. by *up*, *down*, *off*, *into*, etc.) pass gradually between grades, or into a grade. **3** give a grade to (a student). **4** reduce (a road etc.) to easy gradients. [Latin *gradus* step]

gradient /ˈɡreɪdɪənt/ *n.* **1** stretch of road, railway, etc., that slopes. **2** amount of such a slope. [probably from GRADE after *salient*]

Grad.IPM *abbr.* Graduate of the Institute of Personnel Management.

gradual /ˈɡrædʒʊəl/ *adj.* **1** progressing by degrees. **2** not rapid, steep, or abrupt. □ **gradually** *adv.* [Latin: related to GRADE]

gradualism /ˈɡrædʒʊəˌlɪz(ə)m/ *n.* policy of gradual reform.

graduate *–n.* /ˈɡrædʒʊət/ person holding an academic degree. *–v.* /ˈɡrædʒʊˌeɪt/ (**-ting**) **1** obtain an academic degree. **2** (foll. by *to*) move up to (a higher grade of activity etc.). **3** mark out in degrees or parts. **4** arrange in gradations; apportion (e.g. tax) according to a scale. □ **graduation** /ˌɡrædʒʊˈeɪʃ(ə)n/ *n.* [medieval Latin *graduor* take a degree: related to GRADE]

Graeco-Roman /ˌɡriːkəʊˈrəʊmən/ *adj.* of the Greeks and Romans.

graffiti /ɡrəˈfiːtɪ/ *n.pl.* (*sing.* **graffito**) writing or drawing scribbled, scratched, or sprayed on a surface. [Italian *graffio* a scratch]

■ **Usage** The singular or collective use of the form *graffiti* is considered incorrect by some people, but it is frequently found, e.g. *graffiti has appeared.*

graft[1] /ɡrɑːft/ *–n.* **1** *Bot.* **a** shoot or scion inserted into a slit of stock, from which it receives sap. **b** place where a graft is inserted. **2** *Surgery* piece of living tissue, organ, etc., transplanted surgically. **3** *slang* hard work. *–v.* **1** (often foll. by *into*, *on*, *together*, etc.) insert (a scion) as a graft. **2** transplant (living tissue). **3** (foll. by *in*, *on*) insert or fix (a thing) permanently to another. **4** *slang* work hard. [Greek *graphion* stylus]

graft[2] /ɡrɑːft/ *colloq.* *–n.* **1** practices, esp. bribery, used to secure illicit gains in politics or business. **2** such gains. *–v.* seek or make such gains. [origin unknown]

Grail *n.* (in full **Holy Grail**) (in medieval legend) cup or platter used by Christ at the Last Supper. [medieval Latin *gradalis* dish]

grain *–n.* **1** fruit or seed of a cereal. **2** (*collect.*) wheat or any allied grass used as food; corn. **3** small hard particle of salt, sand, etc. **4** unit of weight, 0.0648 gram. **5** smallest possible quantity (*not a grain of truth in it*). **6** roughness of surface. **7** texture of skin, wood, stone, etc. **8 a** pattern of lines of fibre in wood or paper. **b** lamination in stone etc. *–v.* **1** paint in imitation of the grain of wood etc. **2** give a granular surface to. **3** form into grains. □ **against the grain** contrary to one's natural inclination or feeling. □ **grainy** *adj.* (**-ier**, **-iest**). [Latin *granum*]

gram *n.* (also **gramme**) metric unit of mass equal to one-thousandth of a kilogram. [Greek *gramma* small weight]

-gram *comb. form* forming nouns denoting a thing written or recorded (often in a certain way) (*anagram*; *epigram*; *telegram*). [Greek *gramma* thing written]

graminaceous /ˌgræmɪˈneɪʃəs/ *adj.* of or like grass. [Latin *gramen* grass]

graminivorous /ˌgræmɪˈnɪvərəs/ *adj.* feeding on grass, cereals, etc.

grammar /ˈgræmə(r)/ *n.* **1** the study or rules of a language's inflections or other means of showing the relation between words. **2** observance or application of the rules of grammar (*bad grammar*). **3** book on grammar. [Greek *gramma* letter]

grammarian /grəˈmeərɪən/ *n.* expert in grammar or linguistics.

grammar school *n.* esp. *hist.* selective state secondary school with a mainly academic curriculum.

grammatical /grəˈmætɪk(ə)l/ *adj.* of or conforming to the rules of grammar. □ **grammatically** *adv.*

gramme var. of GRAM.

gramophone /ˈgræməˌfəʊn/ *n.* = RECORD-PLAYER. [inversion of *phonogram*: as PHONO-, GRAM]

gramophone record = RECORD *n.* 3.

Grampian /ˈgræmpɪən/ former local government region in NE Scotland; its capital was Aberdeen. The region's economy was associated with the production of North Sea oil.

grampus /ˈgræmpəs/ *n.* (*pl.* **-puses**) a kind of dolphin with a blunt snout. [Latin *crassus piscis* fat fish]

gran *n. colloq.* grandmother. [abbreviation]

Granada /grəˈnɑːdə/ **1** city in S Spain, in Andalusia; manufactures include textiles, soap, and paper; pop. (est. 1994) 271 180. **2** city in Nicaragua, centre of an agricultural region; manufactures include soap and furniture; pop. (est. 1995) 74 396.

granadilla /ˌgrænəˈdɪlə/ *n.* passion-fruit. [Spanish, diminutive of *granada* pomegranate]

granary /ˈgrænərɪ/ *n.* (*pl.* **-ies**) **1** storehouse for threshed grain. **2** region producing, and esp. exporting, much corn. [Latin: related to GRAIN]

grand *–adj.* **1** splendid, magnificent, imposing, dignified. **2** main; of chief importance. **3** (**Grand**) of the highest rank (*Grand Duke*). **4** *colloq.* excellent, enjoyable. **5** belonging to high society. **6** (in *comb.*) (in names of family relationships) denoting the second degree of ascent or descent (*granddaughter*). *–n.* **1** = GRAND PIANO. **2** (*pl.* same) (usu. in *pl.*) esp. *US slang* a thousand dollars or pounds. □ **grandly** *adv.* **grandness** *n.* [Latin *grandis* full-grown]

grandad *n.* (also **grand-dad**) *colloq.* **1** grandfather. **2** elderly man.

grandchild *n.* child of one's son or daughter.

granddaughter *n.* female grandchild.

grandee /grænˈdiː/ *n.* **1** Spanish or Portuguese nobleman of the highest rank. **2** person of high rank. [Spanish and Portuguese *grande*: related to GRAND]

grandeur /ˈgrændʒə(r)/ *n.* **1** majesty, splendour; dignity of appearance or bearing. **2** high rank, eminence. **3** nobility of character. [French: related to GRAND]

grandfather *n.* male grandparent.

grandfather clock *n.* clock in a tall wooden case, driven by weights.

grandfather file *Computing* see MASTER FILE.

grandiloquent /grænˈdɪləkwənt/ *adj.* pompous or inflated in language. □ **grandiloquence** *n.* [Latin: related to GRAND, *-loquus* from *loquor* speak]

grandiose /ˈgrændɪˌəʊs/ *adj.* **1** producing or meant to produce an imposing effect. **2** planned on an ambitious scale. □ **grandiosity** /-ˈɒsɪtɪ/ *n.* [Italian: related to GRAND]

grand jury *n.* esp. *US* jury selected to examine the validity of an accusation prior to trial.

grandma /ˈgrænmɑː/ *n. colloq.* grandmother.

grand mal /grɑ̃ ˈmæl/ *n.* serious form of epilepsy with loss of consciousness. [French, = great sickness]

grand master *n.* chess-player of the highest class.

grandmother *n.* female grandparent.

Grand National *n.* steeplechase held annually at Aintree, Liverpool.

grand opera *n.* opera on a serious theme, or in which the entire libretto (including dialogue) is sung.

grandpa /ˈgrænpɑː/ *n. colloq.* grandfather.

grandparent *n.* parent of one's father or mother.

grand piano *n.* large full-toned piano with horizontal strings.

Grand Prix /grɑ̃ ˈpriː/ *n.* any of several important international motor or motor-cycle racing events. [French, = great or chief prize]

grandsire *n. archaic* grandfather.

grand slam *n.* **1** *Sport* winning of all of a group of matches etc. **2** *Bridge* winning of 13 tricks.

grandson *n.* male grandchild.

grandstand *n.* main stand for spectators at a racecourse etc.

grand total *n.* sum of other totals.

grand tour *n. hist.* cultural tour of Europe.

grange /greɪndʒ/ *n.* country house with farm-buildings. [Latin *granica*: related to GRAIN]

graniferous /grəˈnɪfərəs/ *adj.* producing grain or a grain-like seed. [Latin: related to GRAIN]

granite /ˈgrænɪt/ *n.* granular crystalline rock of quartz, mica, etc., used for building. [Italian *granito*: related to GRAIN]

granivorous /grəˈnɪvərəs/ *adj.* feeding on grain. [Latin: related to GRAIN]

granny /ˈgrænɪ/ *n.* (also **grannie**) (*pl.* **-ies**) *colloq.* grandmother. [diminutive of *grannam* from archaic *grandam*: related to GRAND, DAME]

◆ **granny bond** *n. colloq.* index-linked savings certificate (see NATIONAL SAVINGS) formerly only available to persons over retirement age.

---

granny flat *n.* part of a house made into self-contained accommodation for an elderly relative.

granny knot *n.* reef-knot crossed the wrong way and therefore insecure.

grant /grɑːnt/ *–v.* **1 a** consent to fulfil (a request etc.). **b** allow (a person) to have (a thing). **2** give formally; transfer legally. **3** (often foll. by *that*) admit as true; concede. *–n.* **1** process of granting. **2** sum of money given by the state. **3** legal conveyance by written instrument. □ **take for granted 1** assume something to be true or valid. **2** cease to appreciate through familiarity. □ **grantor** /-ˈtɔː(r)/ *n.* (esp. in sense 2 of *v.*). [French *gr(e)anter* var. of *creanter* from Latin *credo* entrust]

◆ **granter** *n.* **1** the seller of a traded option. **2** one who grants.

◆ **grant-in-aid** *n.* grant from central government to a local authority for particular services.

---

grant-maintained *adj.* (of a school) funded by central rather than local government.

◆ **grant of probate** *n.* order from the High Court in the UK authorizing the executors of a will to deal with and distribute the property of the deceased person. If the person died intestate or did not appoint executors, the administrator of the estate has to obtain letters of administration.

granular /'grænjʊlə(r)/ *adj.* of or like grains or granules. □ **granularity** /-'lærɪtɪ/ *n.* [Latin: related to GRANULE]

granulate /'grænjʊˌleɪt/ *v.* (**-ting**) **1** form into grains. **2** roughen the surface of. □ **granulation** /-'leɪʃ(ə)n/ *n.*

granule /'grænju:l/ *n.* small grain. [Latin diminutive of *granum*: related to GRAIN]

grape *n.* berry (usu. green, purple, or black) growing in clusters on a vine, used as fruit and in making wine. [French, probably from *grappe* hook]

grapefruit *n.* (*pl.* same) large round usu. yellow citrus fruit.

grape hyacinth *n.* plant of the lily family with clusters of usu. blue flowers.

grapeshot *n. hist.* small balls used as charge in a cannon and scattering when fired.

grapevine *n.* **1** vine. **2** *colloq.* the means of transmission of a rumour.

graph /grɑ:f/ *–n.* diagram showing the relation between variable quantities, usu. of two variables, each measured along one of a pair of axes. *–v.* plot or trace on a graph. [abbreviation of *graphic formula*]

-graph *comb. form* forming nouns and verbs meaning: **1** thing written or drawn etc. in a specified way (*photograph*). **2** instrument that records (*seismograph*).

-grapher *comb. form* forming nouns denoting a person concerned with a subject (*geographer*; *radiographer*). [Greek *-graphō* write]

graphic /'græfɪk/ *adj.* **1** of or relating to the visual or descriptive arts, esp. writing and drawing. **2** vividly descriptive. □ **graphically** *adv.* [Greek *graphē* writing]

-graphic *comb. form* (also **-graphical**) forming adjectives corresponding to nouns in *-graphy*.

graphic arts *n.pl.* visual and technical arts involving design or the use of lettering.

graphic novel *n.* novel in comic-strip format.

graphics *n.pl.* (usu. treated as *sing.*) **1** products of the graphic arts. **2** use of diagrams in calculation and design. **3** see COMPUTER GRAPHICS.

graphics adapter *n.* electronic device added to a personal computer to allow it to drive a VDU capable of displaying computer graphics, or to produce higher resolution or colour.

graphics card (also **graphics board**) *Computing* see EXPANSION CARD.

graphics display *n. Computing* visual display unit that can display pictures, graphs, and charts as well as text.

graphite /'græfaɪt/ *n.* crystalline allotropic form of carbon used as a lubricant, in pencils, etc. □ **graphitic** /-'fɪtɪk/ *adj.* [German *Graphit* from Greek *graphō* write]

graphology /grə'fɒlədʒɪ/ *n.* the study of handwriting, esp. as a supposed guide to character. □ **graphologist** *n.* [Greek: related to GRAPHIC]

graph paper *n.* paper printed with a network of lines as a basis for drawing graphs.

-graphy *comb. form* forming nouns denoting: **1** descriptive science (*geography*). **2** technique of producing images (*photography*). **3** style or method of writing etc. (*calligraphy*).

grapnel /'græpn(ə)l/ *n.* **1** device with iron claws, for dragging or grasping. **2** small anchor with several flukes. [French *grapon*: related to GRAPE]

grapple /'græp(ə)l/ *–v.* (**-ling**) **1** (often foll. by *with*) fight in close combat. **2** (foll. by *with*) try to manage (a difficult problem etc.). **3 a** grip with the hands; come to close quarters with. **b** seize with or as with a grapnel. *–n.* **1 a** hold or grip in or as in wrestling. **b** contest at close quarters. **2** clutching-instrument; grapnel. [French *grapil*: related to GRAPNEL]

grappling-iron *n.* (also **grappling-hook**) = GRAPNEL.

grasp /grɑ:sp/ *–v.* **1 a** clutch at; seize greedily. **b** hold firmly. **2** (foll. by *at*) try to seize; accept avidly. **3** understand or realize (a fact or meaning). *–n.* **1** firm hold; grip. **2** (foll. by *of*) **a** mastery (*a grasp of the situation*). **b** mental hold. □ **grasp the nettle** tackle a difficulty boldly. [earlier *grapse*: related to GROPE]

grasping *adj.* avaricious.

grass /grɑ:s/ *–n.* **1 a** any of a group of wild plants with green blades that are eaten by ruminants. **b** plant of the family which includes cereals, reeds, and bamboos. **2** pasture land. **3** grass-covered ground, lawn. **4** grazing (*out to grass*). **5** *slang* marijuana. **6** *slang* informer. *–v.* **1** cover with turf. **2** *US* provide with pasture. **3** *slang* **a** betray, esp. to the police. **b** inform the police. □ **grassy** *adj.* (**-ier, -iest**). [Old English]

Grasse /grɑ:s/ town in SE France, near Cannes, centre of the French perfume-making industry; pop. (1990) 42 080.

grasshopper *n.* jumping and chirping insect.

grassland *n.* large open area covered with grass, esp. used for grazing.

grass roots *n.pl.* **1** fundamental level or source. **2** ordinary people; rank and file of an organization, esp. a political party.

grass snake *n.* common harmless European snake.

grass widow *n.* (also **grass widower**) person whose husband (or wife) is away for a prolonged period.

grate[1] *v.* (**-ting**) **1** reduce to small particles by rubbing on a serrated surface. **2** (often foll. by *against*, *on*) rub with a harsh scraping sound. **3** utter in a harsh tone. **4** (often foll. by *on*) **a** sound harshly. **b** have an irritating effect. **5** grind (one's teeth). **6** creak. □ **grater** *n.* [French from Germanic]

grate[2] *n.* **1** fireplace or furnace. **2** metal frame confining fuel in this. [Latin *cratis* hurdle]

grateful /'greɪtfʊl/ *adj.* **1** thankful; feeling or showing gratitude. **2** pleasant, acceptable. □ **gratefully** *adv.* [obsolete *grate* from Latin *gratus*]

gratify /'grætɪˌfaɪ/ *v.* (**-ies, -ied**) **1 a** please, delight. **b** please by compliance. **2** yield to (a feeling or desire). □ **gratification** /-fɪ'keɪʃ(ə)n/ *n.* [Latin: related to GRATEFUL]

grating *n.* **1** framework of parallel or crossed metal bars. **2** *Optics* set of parallel wires, lines ruled on glass, etc.

gratis /'grɑ:tɪs/ *adv.* & *adj.* free; without charge. [Latin]

gratitude /'grætɪˌtju:d/ *n.* being thankful; readiness to return kindness. [Latin: related to GRATEFUL]

gratuitous /grə'tju:ɪtəs/ *adj.* **1** given or done free of charge. **2** uncalled-for; lacking good reason. □ **gratuitously** *adv.* **gratuitousness** *n.* [Latin, = spontaneous]

gratuity /grə'tju:ɪtɪ/ *n.* (*pl.* **-ies**) = TIP[3] *n.* 1. [Latin: related to GRATEFUL]

grave[1] *n.* **1** trench dug in the ground for the burial of a corpse; mound or memorial stone placed over this. **2** (prec. by *the*) death. [Old English]

grave[2] *–adj.* **1 a** serious, weighty, important. **b** dignified, solemn, sombre. **2** extremely serious or threatening. *–n.* /grɑ:v/ = GRAVE ACCENT. □ **gravely** *adv.* [Latin *gravis* heavy]

grave[3] *v.* (**-ving**; *past part.* **graven** or **graved**) **1** (foll. by *in*, *on*) fix indelibly (on one's memory). **2** *archaic* engrave, carve. [Old English]

grave accent /grɑ:v/ *n.* a mark (`) placed over a vowel to denote pronunciation, length, etc.

gravedigger *n.* person who digs graves.

gravel /'græv(ə)l/ *–n.* **1** mixture of coarse sand and small stones, used for paths etc. **2** *Med.* aggregations of crystals formed in the urinary tract. *–v.* (**-ll-**; *US* **-l-**) lay or strew with gravel. [French diminutive, perhaps of *grave* shore]

gravelly *adj.* **1** of or like gravel. **2** (of a voice) deep and rough-sounding.

graven *past part.* of GRAVE[3].

graven image *n.* idol.

Graves /grɑːv/ *n.* light usu. white wine from Graves in France.

gravestone *n.* stone (usu. inscribed) marking a grave.

graveyard *n.* burial-ground.

gravid /'grævɪd/ *adj.* pregnant. [Latin *gravidus*: related to GRAVE[2]]

gravimeter /grə'vɪmɪtə(r)/ *n.* instrument measuring the difference in the force of gravity between two places. [Latin: related to GRAVE[2]]

gravimetry /grə'vɪmɪtrɪ/ *n.* measurement of weight. □ **gravimetric** /ˌgrævɪ'metrɪk/ *adj.*

gravitate /'grævɪˌteɪt/ *v.* (**-ting**) **1** (foll. by *to*, *towards*) move or be attracted to. **2 a** move or tend by force of gravity towards. **b** sink by or as if by gravity. [related to GRAVE[2]]

gravitation /ˌgrævɪ'teɪʃ(ə)n/ *n. Physics* **1** force of attraction between any particle of matter in the universe and any other. **2** effect of this, esp. the falling of bodies to the earth. □ **gravitational** *adj.*

gravity /'grævɪtɪ/ *n.* **1 a** force that attracts a body to the centre of the earth etc. **b** degree of intensity of this. **c** gravitational force. **2** property of having weight. **3 a** importance, seriousness. **b** solemnity. [Latin: related to GRAVE[2]]

gravy /'greɪvɪ/ *n.* (*pl.* **-ies**) **1** juices exuding from meat during and after cooking. **2** sauce for food, made from these etc. [perhaps from a misreading of French *grané* from *grain* spice, GRAIN]

gravy-boat *n.* boat-shaped vessel for serving gravy.

gravy train *n. slang* source of easy financial benefit.

gray *US* var. of GREY.

grayling *n.* (*pl.* same) silver-grey freshwater fish. [from GREY, -LING]

Graz /grɑːts/ second-largest city of Austria, the industrial capital of Styria province; manufactures include textiles, chemicals, and iron and steel; pop. (1991) 237 810.

graze[1] *v.* (**-zing**) **1** (of cattle, sheep, etc.) eat growing grass. **2 a** feed (cattle etc.) on growing grass. **b** feed on (grass). **3** pasture cattle. [Old English: related to GRASS]

graze[2] *–v.* (**-zing**) **1** rub or scrape (part of the body, esp. the skin). **2 a** touch lightly in passing. **b** (foll. by *against*, *along*, etc.) move with a light passing contact. *–n.* abrasion. [perhaps from GRAZE[1], as if 'take off the grass close to the ground']

grazier /'greɪzɪə(r)/ *n.* **1** person who feeds cattle for market. **2** *Austral.* large-scale sheep-farmer etc. [from GRASS]

grazing *n.* grassland suitable for pasturage.

GRE *abbr.* Guardian Royal Exchange.

grease /griːs/ *–n.* **1** oily or fatty matter, esp. as a lubricant. **2** melted fat of a dead animal. *–v.* (**-sing**) smear or lubricate with grease. □ **grease the palm of** *colloq.* bribe. [Latin *crassus* (adj.) fat]

greasepaint *n.* make-up used by actors.

greaseproof *adj.* impervious to grease.

greaser *n. slang* member of a gang of youths with long hair and motor cycles.

greasy *adj.* (**-ier**, **-iest**) **1 a** of or like grease. **b** smeared or covered with grease. **c** containing or having too much grease. **2 a** slippery. **b** (of a person or manner) unpleasantly unctuous. □ **greasily** *adv.* **greasiness** *n.*

great /greɪt/ *–adj.* **1 a** of a size, amount, extent, or intensity considerably above the normal or average (*a great hole*; *great care*). **b** also with implied admiration, contempt, etc., esp. in exclamations (*you great idiot!*; *great stuff!*). **c** reinforcing other words denoting size, quantity, etc. (*great big hole*). **2** important, pre-eminent (*the great thing is not to get caught*). **3** grand, imposing (*great occasion*). **4** distinguished. **5** remarkable in ability, character, etc. (*great men*; *great thinker*). **6** (foll. by *at*, *on*) competent, well-informed. **7** fully deserving the name of; doing a thing extensively (*great reader*; *great believer in tolerance*). **8** (also **greater**) the larger of the name, species, etc. (*great auk*; *greater celandine*). **9** *colloq.* very enjoyable or satisfactory (*had a great time*). **10** (in *comb.*) (in names of family relationships) denoting one degree further removed upwards or downwards (*great-uncle*; *great-great-grandmother*). *–n.* **1** great or outstanding person or thing. **2** (in *pl.*) (**Greats**) *colloq.* (at Oxford University) honours course or final examinations in classics and philosophy. □ **greatness** *n.* [Old English]

Great Bear see BEAR[2].

Great Britain England, Wales, and Scotland considered as a unit. Wales was politically incorporated with England in the 16th century, and the Act of Union formally united Scotland with England in 1707. Together with Northern Ireland, it constitutes the United Kingdom of Great Britain and Northern Ireland. See UNITED KINGDOM.

great circle *n.* circle on the surface of a sphere whose plane passes through the sphere's centre.

greatcoat *n.* heavy overcoat.

Great Dane *n.* dog of a large short-haired breed.

great deal *n.* = DEAL[1] *n.* 1.

Greater Manchester metropolitan county of NW England; pop. (est. 1994) 2 578 000; the county council was abolished in 1986, when administration passed to a number of unitary authorities.

Great Lakes five large interconnected lakes (Superior, Michigan, Huron, Erie, and Ontario) in North America. Except for Lake Michigan, which is wholly within the US, they lie on the Canada–US border. They are connected to the Atlantic Ocean by the St Lawrence Seaway and form an important commercial waterway.

greatly *adv.* by a considerable amount; much (*greatly admired*; *greatly superior*).

great tit *n.* Eurasian songbird with black and white head markings.

Great War *n.* world war of 1914–18.

greave *n.* (usu. in *pl.*) armour for the shin. [French, = shin]

grebe *n.* a kind of diving bird. [French]

Grecian /'griːʃ(ə)n/ *adj.* (of architecture or facial outline) Greek. [Latin *Graecia* Greece]

Grecian nose *n.* straight nose that continues the line of the forehead without a dip.

greed *n.* excessive desire, esp. for food or wealth. [from GREEDY]

greedy *adj.* (**-ier**, **-iest**) **1** having or showing greed. **2** (foll. by *for*, or *to* + infin.) very eager. □ **greedily** *adv.* **greediness** *n.* [Old English]

Greek *–n.* **1 a** native or national of Greece. **b** person of Greek descent. **2** language of Greece. *–adj.* of Greece or its people or language; Hellenic. □ **Greek to me** *colloq.* incomprehensible to me. [Old English ultimately from Greek *Graikoi*]

Greek cross *n.* cross with four equal arms.

green *–adj.* **1** of the colour between blue and yellow in the spectrum; coloured like grass. **2** covered with leaves or grass. **3** (of fruit etc. or wood) unripe or unseasoned. **4** not dried, smoked, or tanned. **5** inexperienced, gullible. **6 a** (of the complexion) pale, sickly-hued. **b** jealous, envious. **7** young, flourishing. **8** not withered or worn out (*a green old age*). **9** (also **Green**) concerned with protection of the environment as a political principle; not harmful to the environment. *–n.* **1** green colour or pigment. **2** green clothes or material. **3 a** piece of public grassy land (*village green*). **b** grassy area used for a special purpose (*putting-green*). **4** (in *pl.*) green vegetables. **5** (also **Green**) supporter of an environmentalist group or party. *–v.* make or become green. □ **greenish** *adj.* **greenly** *adv.* **greenness** *n.* [Old English]

green belt *n.* area of open land round a city, designated for preservation.

♦ **Green Book** *n. colloq.* publication, entitled *Unlisted Securities Market*, issued by the London Stock Exchange. It sets out the terms and conditions for admission to the USM and the subsequent obligations of the companies involved.

---

green card *n.* international insurance document for motorists, which provides proof that a motor insurance policy issued in one country satisfies the insurance regulations of another. The card contains details of the policy cover in the language of every country subscribing to the system. Although the first European Community directive on motor insurance means that green cards are not essential, they are the easiest and most convenient method of proving adequate insurance cover is held. Holding a green card, however, does not automatically imply that the full cover of the policy operates in other countries.

◆ **green currencies** *n.pl.* currencies of members of the European Community using artificial rates of exchange for the purposes of the Common Agricultural Policy (CAP). Their object is to protect farm prices in the member countries from the wide variations due to fluctuations in the real rates of exchange. Green currencies use as their base the European Currency Unit (or ecu). The **green pound** is the British pound sterling used as a green currency. It is used to calculate payments due by or to the UK to or from the fund of the CAP, i.e. when the value of the pound sterling differs from the value of the green pound.

greenery *n.* green foliage or growing plants.

green-eyed *adj. colloq.* jealous.

◆ **green-field project** *n.* project that starts from scratch, e.g. building a factory on a virgin site in the country.

greenfinch *n.* finch with green and yellow plumage.

green fingers *n. colloq.* skill in growing plants.

greenfly *n.* **1** green aphid. **2** these collectively.

greengage *n.* roundish green variety of plum. [Sir W. *Gage*, name of a botanist]

greengrocer *n.* retailer of fruit and vegetables.

greengrocery *n.* (*pl.* **-ies**) **1** greengrocer's business. **2** goods sold by a greengrocer.

greenhorn *n.* inexperienced person; new recruit.

greenhouse *n.* light structure with the sides and roof mainly of glass, for rearing plants.

greenhouse effect *n.* trapping of the sun's warmth in the lower atmosphere of the earth, caused by an increase in carbon dioxide, methane, etc.

greenhouse gas *n.* any of the gases, esp. carbon dioxide and methane, that contribute to the greenhouse effect.

Greenland /'griːnlənd/ largest island in the world, lying to the NE of North America and mostly within the Arctic Circle; fishing and fish processing are the main sources of income and mineral resources (including lead, zinc, iron ore, and oil) are being exploited; pop. (1992) 55 385; capital, Nuuk. Greenland became part of Denmark in 1953, with internal autonomy from 1979; it withdrew from the EC in 1985. □ **Greenlander** *n.*

green light *n.* **1** signal to proceed on a road, railway, etc. **2** *colloq.* permission to proceed with a project.

◆ **greenmail** *n.* (esp. in the US) purchase of a large block of shares in a company, which are then sold back to the company at a premium over the market price in return for a promise not to launch a bid for the company.

Greenock /'griːnək, 'gre-/ port in W Scotland; industries include chemicals and engineering; pop. (1981) 57 300.

Green Paper *n.* preliminary report of government proposals, for discussion.

◆ **green pound** see GREEN CURRENCIES.

◆ **green product** *n.* product that its manufacturers claim will not cause damage to the environment, esp. a new product or formulation that is being launched to replace one that is said to cause environmental damage.

green revolution *n.* greatly increased crop production in underdeveloped countries.

green-room *n.* room in a theatre for actors and actresses who are off stage.

green-stick fracture *n.* bone-fracture, esp. in children, in which one side of the bone is broken and one only bent.

greenstuff *n.* vegetation; green vegetables.

greensward *n.* expanse of grassy turf.

green tea *n.* tea made from steam-dried leaves.

Greenwich /'grenɪtʃ, 'grɪnɪdʒ/ London borough, former site of the Royal Observatory; pop. (1991) 211 141.

Greenwich Mean Time *n.* (also **GMT**) local time on the meridian of Greenwich, used as an international basis of time-reckoning until 1972.

greenwood *n.* a wood in summer.

greeny *adj.* greenish.

greet[1] *v.* **1** address politely or welcomingly on meeting or arrival. **2** receive or acknowledge in a specified way. **3** (of a sight, sound, etc.) become apparent to or noticed by. [Old English]

greet[2] *v. Scot.* weep. [Old English]

greeting *n.* **1** act or instance of welcoming etc. **2** words, gestures, etc., used to greet a person. **3** (often in *pl.*) expression of goodwill.

greetings card *n.* decorative card sent to convey greetings.

Greece /griːs/ country in SE Europe comprising a peninsula bounded by the Ionian, Mediterranean, and Aegean Seas, and numerous outlying islands. Agriculture remains important to the economy, though there has been a substantial increase in industrialization; tobacco, cereals, olives and olive oil, fresh fruit (including peaches and grapes), and currants are among the main exports. The chief industries include food processing, textiles, chemicals, metallurgy, rubber, plastics, and electrical equipment. Natural gas and oil have been discovered, and electricity production has increased. Nickel, bauxite, iron ore, and other minerals are mined and processed. Tourism, popular since Roman times, is an important source of income. High inflation and rising unemployment continue to be a problem. Greece became a member of the European Community in 1981. Austerity measures were introduced in 1996 in an attempt to reduce public debt in accordance with EU criteria for economic and monetary union.
History. From about 1200 BC village settlements developed into city-states, of which the most prominent were Athens and Sparta, and rising populations and expanding trade led to overseas colonization; by the 8th century BC Greece had become a centre of culture. In 146 BC Greece was made a Roman province then, after the Roman Empire was divided in AD 395, it became part of the Eastern Empire, centred on Constantinople. Conquered by the Ottoman Turks in 1466, Greece remained under Turkish rule until the successful war of independence (1821–30), after which it became a monarchy and then in 1973 a republic. President, Constantine Stephanopoulos; prime minister, Costas Simitis; capital, Athens.

language	Greek
currency	drachma (Dr) of 100 lepta
pop. (1996)	10 493 000
GNP (est. 1994)	US$80B
literacy	98% (m); 93% (f)
life expectancy	74 (m); 79 (f)

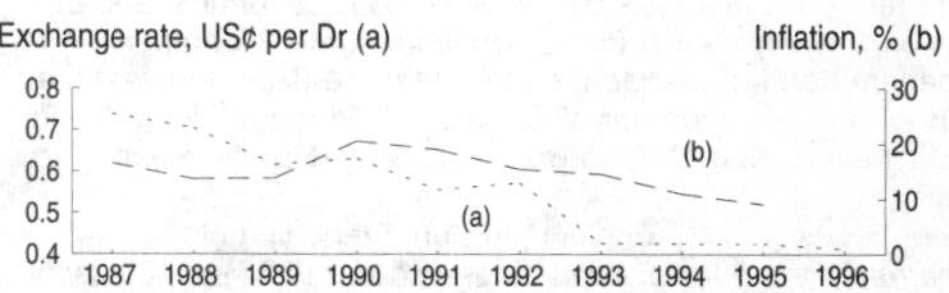

gregarious /grɪˈgeərɪəs/ *adj.* **1** fond of company. **2** living in flocks or communities. □ **gregariousness** *n.* [Latin *grex gregis* flock]

Gregorian calendar /grɪˈgɔːrɪən/ *n.* calendar introduced in 1582 by Pope Gregory XIII.

Gregorian chant /grɪˈgɔːrɪən/ *n.* plainsong ritual music, named after Pope Gregory I.

gremlin /ˈgremlɪn/ *n. colloq.* imaginary mischievous sprite regarded as responsible for mechanical faults etc. [origin unknown]

grenade /grɪˈneɪd/ *n.* small bomb thrown by hand (**hand-grenade**) or shot from a rifle. [French: related to POMEGRANATE]

grenadier /ˌgrenəˈdɪə(r)/ *n.* **1** (**Grenadiers** or **Grenadier Guards**) first regiment of the royal household infantry. **2** *hist.* soldier armed with grenades.

Grenadine Islands /ˈgrenəˌdiːn/ (also **Grenadines**) chain of small islands in the West Indies, divided between St Vincent and Grenada.

Grenoble /grəˈnəʊbl/ city in SE France, having metallurgical, textile, paper, and engineering industries; pop. (1990) 153 973.

♦ **Gresham's law** /ˈgreʃəmz/ *n.* hypothesis that bad money will drive out good. For example, if there are gold coins in circulation and the government tries to save money by lowering the gold content of a new coinage, the old coins will fall out of circulation, as no one will exchange the good (old) for the bad (new). Instead the good coins will be melted down and sold for their gold value. [*Gresham*, name of a financier]

---

grew *past* of GROW.

grey /greɪ/ (*US* **gray**) *–adj.* **1** of a colour intermediate between black and white. **2** dull, dismal. **3 a** (of hair) turning white with age etc. **b** having grey hair. **4** anonymous, unidentifiable. *–n.* **1 a** grey colour or pigment. **b** grey clothes or material (*dressed in grey*). **2** grey or white horse. *–v.* make or become grey. □ **greyish** *adj.* **greyness** *n.* [Old English]

grey area *n.* situation or topic not clearly defined.

Grey Friar *n.* Franciscan friar.

greyhound *n.* dog of a tall slender breed capable of high speed. [Old English, = bitch-hound]

♦ **grey knight** *n.* counter-bidder in a take-over battle whose ultimate intentions are undeclared. The original unwelcome bidder is the black knight, the welcome counter-bidder for the target company is the white knight. The grey knight is an ambiguous intervener whose appearance is unwelcome to all.

---

greylag *n.* (in full **greylag goose**) European wild goose. [from GREY]

♦ **grey market** *n.* **1** any legal market for goods that are in short supply (cf. BLACK MARKET). **2** market in shares that have not been issued, although they are due to be issued in a short time. Market makers will often deal with investors or speculators who are willing to trade in anticipation of receiving an allotment of these shares or are willing to cover their deals after flotation. A grey market provides an indication of the market price (and premium, if any) after flotation.

---

grey matter *n.* **1** the darker tissues of the brain and spinal cord. **2** *colloq.* intelligence.

grey squirrel *n.* American squirrel brought to Europe in the 19th century.

♦ **grey wave** *n. colloq.* company that is thought to be potentially profitable and ultimately a good investment, but that is unlikely to fulfil expectations in the near future. The fruits of an investment in the present should be available when the investor has grey hair.

GRI *abbr. NZ* guaranteed retirement income.

grid *n.* **1** grating. **2** system of numbered squares printed on a map and forming the basis of map references. **3** network of lines, electric-power connections, gas-supply lines, etc. **4** pattern of lines marking the starting-places on a motor-racing track. **5** perforated electrode controlling the flow of electrons in a thermionic valve etc. **6** arrangement of town streets in a rectangular pattern. [from GRIDIRON]

griddle /ˈgrɪd(ə)l/ *n.* circular iron plate placed over a source of heat for baking etc. [Latin *cratis* hurdle]

gridiron /ˈgrɪdˌaɪən/ *n.* cooking utensil of metal bars for broiling or grilling. [related to GRIDDLE]

grief *n.* **1** intense sorrow. **2** cause of this. □ **come to grief** meet with disaster. [French: related to GRIEVE]

grievance /ˈgriːv(ə)ns/ *n.* real or fancied cause for complaint. [French: related to GRIEF]

grieve *v.* (**-ving**) **1** cause grief to. **2** suffer grief. [Latin: related to GRAVE[2]]

grievous *adj.* **1** (of pain etc.) severe. **2** causing grief. **3** injurious. **4** flagrant, heinous. □ **grievously** *adv.* [French: related to GRIEVE]

grievous bodily harm *n. Law* serious injury inflicted intentionally.

griffin /ˈgrɪfɪn/ *n.* (also **gryphon** /-f(ə)n/) fabulous creature with an eagle's head and wings and a lion's body. [Latin *gryphus* from Greek]

griffon /ˈgrɪf(ə)n/ *n.* **1** dog of a small terrier-like breed. **2** large vulture. **3** = GRIFFIN. [French, = GRIFFIN]

grill *–n.* **1 a** device on a cooker for radiating heat downwards. **b** = GRIDIRON. **2** food cooked on a grill. **3** (in full **grill room**) restaurant specializing in grilled food. *–v.* **1** cook or be cooked under a grill or on a gridiron. **2** subject or be subjected to extreme heat. **3** subject to severe questioning. [French: related to GRIDDLE]

grille *n.* (also **grill**) **1** grating or latticed screen, used as a partition etc. **2** metal grid protecting the radiator of a vehicle.

grilse *n.* (*pl.* same or **-s**) young salmon that has returned to fresh water from the sea for the first time. [origin unknown]

grim *adj.* (**grimmer, grimmest**) **1** of stern or forbidding appearance. **2** harsh, merciless. **3** ghastly, joyless (*has a grim truth in it*). **4** unpleasant, unattractive. □ **grimly** *adv.* **grimness** *n.* [Old English]

Grenada /grəˈneɪdə/ country in the West Indies, consisting of the island of Grenada (in the Windward Islands) and the S Grenadines. With an economy based on agriculture, the most important exports are fish, nutmeg, mace, bananas, cocoa, sugar, and citrus fruits. Tourism has grown since the 1980s but the increasing revenue that this generates is insufficient to lessen the fiscal deficit, and the economy is weak. A former British colony, Grenada became an independent state within the Commonwealth in 1974 and is a member of CARICOM. Prime minister, Keith Mitchell; capital, St George's. □ **Grenadian** *adj.* & *n.*

languages	English (official), French patois
currency	East Caribbean dollar (EC$) of 100 cents
pop. (est. 1996)	97 900
GNP (1994)	US$241M
literacy	85%
life expectancy	68 (m); 73 (f)

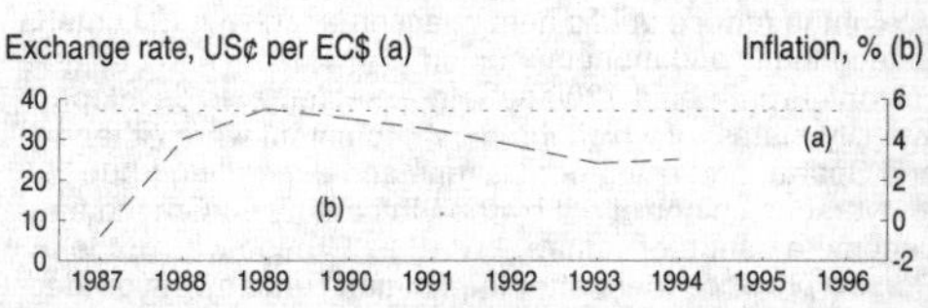

grimace /'grɪməs, -'meɪs/ *–n.* distortion of the face made in disgust etc. or to amuse. *–v.* (**-cing**) make a grimace. [French from Spanish]

grime *–n.* soot or dirt ingrained in a surface. *–v.* (**-ming**) blacken with grime; befoul. □ **griminess** *n.* **grimy** *adj.* (**-ier, -iest**). [Low German or Dutch]

grin *–v.* (**-nn-**) **1 a** smile broadly, showing the teeth. **b** make a forced, unrestrained, or stupid smile. **2** express by grinning. *–n.* act of grinning. □ **grin and bear it** take pain etc. stoically. [Old English]

grind /graɪnd/ *–v.* (*past* and *past part.* **ground**) **1** reduce to small particles or powder by crushing. **2 a** sharpen or smooth by friction. **b** rub or rub together gratingly. **3** (often foll. by *down*) oppress; harass with exactions. **4 a** (often foll. by *away*) work or study hard. **b** (foll. by *out*) produce with effort. *–n.* **1** act or instance of grinding. **2** *colloq.* hard dull work (*the daily grind*). **3** size of ground particles. □ **grind to a halt** stop laboriously. [Old English]

grinder *n.* **1** person or thing that grinds, esp. a machine. **2** molar tooth.

grindstone *n.* **1** thick revolving disc used for grinding, sharpening, and polishing. **2** a kind of stone used for this. □ **keep one's nose to the grindstone** work hard and continuously.

grip *–v.* (**-pp-**) **1 a** grasp tightly. **b** take a firm hold, esp. by friction. **2** compel the attention of. *–n.* **1 a** firm hold; tight grasp. **b** manner of grasping or holding. **2** power of holding attention. **3 a** intellectual mastery. **b** effective control of one's behaviour etc. (*lose one's grip*). **4 a** part of a machine that grips. **b** part by which a weapon etc. is held. **5** = HAIRGRIP. **6** travelling bag. □ **come** (or **get**) **to grips with** approach purposefully; begin to deal with. [Old English]

gripe *–v.* (**-ping**) **1** *colloq.* complain. **2** affect with gastric pain. *–n.* **1** (usu. in *pl.*) colic. **2** *colloq.* complaint. **3** grip, clutch. [Old English]

Gripe Water *n. propr.* preparation to relieve colic in infants.

grisly /'grɪzlɪ/ *adj.* (**-ier, -iest**) causing horror, disgust, or fear. □ **grisliness** *n.* [Old English]

grist *n.* corn to grind. □ **grist to the** (or **a person's**) **mill** source of profit or advantage. [Old English: related to GRIND]

gristle /'grɪs(ə)l/ *n.* tough flexible animal tissue; cartilage. □ **gristly** /-slɪ/ *adj.* [Old English]

grit *–n.* **1** particles of stone or sand, esp. as irritating or hindering. **2** coarse sandstone. **3** *colloq.* pluck, endurance. *–v.* (**-tt-**) **1** spread grit on (icy roads etc.). **2** clench (the teeth). **3** make a grating sound. □ **gritter** *n.* **gritty** *adj.* (**-ier, -iest**). [Old English]

grits *n.pl.* **1** coarsely ground grain, esp. oatmeal. **2** oats that have been husked but not ground. [Old English]

grizzle /'grɪz(ə)l/ *v.* (**-ling**) *colloq.* **1** (esp. of a child) cry fretfully. **2** complain whiningly. □ **grizzly** *adj.* [origin unknown]

grizzled /'grɪz(ə)ld/ *adj.* **1** (of hair) grey or streaked with grey. **2** having grizzled hair. [*grizzle* grey from French *grisel*]

grizzly /'grɪzlɪ/ *–adj.* (**-ier, -iest**) grey, grey-haired. *–n.* (*pl.* **-ies**) (in full **grizzly bear**) large variety of brown bear, found in North America.

groan *–v.* **1 a** make a deep sound expressing pain, grief, or disapproval. **b** utter with groans. **2** (usu. foll. by *under, beneath, with*) be loaded or oppressed. *–n.* sound made in groaning. [Old English]

groat *n. hist.* silver coin worth four old pence. [Low German or Dutch: related to GREAT]

groats *n.pl.* hulled or crushed grain, esp. oats. [Old English]

grocer *n.* dealer in food and household provisions. [Anglo-French *grosser* from Latin *grossus* GROSS]

grocery *n.* (*pl.* **-ies**) **1** grocer's trade or shop. **2** (in *pl.*) goods, esp. food, sold by a grocer.

grog *n.* drink of spirit (orig. rum) and water. [origin uncertain]

groggy *adj.* (**-ier, -iest**) incapable or unsteady. □ **groggily** *adv.* **grogginess** *n.*

groin[1] *–n.* **1** depression between the belly and the thigh. **2** *Archit.* **a** edge formed by intersecting vaults. **b** arch supporting a vault. *–v. Archit.* build with groins. [origin uncertain]

groin[2] *US* var. of GROYNE.

grommet /'grɒmɪt/ *n.* (also **grummet** /'grʌmɪt/) **1** metal, plastic, or rubber eyelet placed in a hole to protect or insulate a rope or cable etc. passed through it. **2** tube passed through the eardrum to make a communication with the middle ear. [French]

Groningen /'grəʊnɪŋən/ **1** agricultural province in NE Netherlands; pop. (est. 1995) 557 995. **2** its capital city; industries include textiles, clothing, and sugar refining; pop. (est. 1995) 170 748.

groom *–n.* **1** person employed to take care of horses. **2** = BRIDEGROOM. **3** *Mil.* any of certain officers of the Royal Household. *–v.* **1 a** curry or tend (a horse). **b** give a neat appearance to (a person etc.). **2** (of an ape etc.) clean and comb the fur of (its fellow). **3** prepare or train (a person) for a particular purpose or job. [origin unknown]

groove *–n.* **1** channel or elongated hollow, esp. one made to guide motion or receive a corresponding ridge. **2** spiral track cut in a gramophone record. *–v.* (**-ving**) **1** make a groove or grooves in. **2** *slang* enjoy oneself. [Dutch]

groovy *adj.* (**-ier, -iest**) **1** *slang* excellent. **2** of or like a groove.

grope *–v.* (**-ping**) **1** (usu. foll. by *for*) feel about or search blindly. **2** (foll. by *for, after*) search mentally. **3** feel (one's way) towards something. **4** *slang* fondle clumsily for sexual pleasure. *–n.* act of groping. [Old English]

grosgrain /'grəʊgreɪn/ *n.* corded fabric of silk etc. [French, = coarse grain: related to GROSS, GRAIN]

gros point /grəʊ 'pwæ̃/ *n.* cross-stitch embroidery on canvas. [French: related to GROSS, POINT]

gross /grəʊs/ *–adj.* **1** overfed, bloated. **2** (of a person, manners, or morals) coarse, unrefined, or indecent. **3** flagrant (*gross negligence*). **4** total; not net (*gross tonnage*). **5** (of the senses etc.) dull. *–v.* produce as gross profit. *–n.* (*pl.* same) amount equal to twelve dozen. □ **gross up** convert (a net return) into the equivalent gross amount. For example, if a net dividend (d) has been paid after deduction of r% tax, the gross equivalent (g) is given by: $g = 100d/(100 - r)$. □ **grossly** *adv.* **grossness** *n.* [Latin *grossus*]

♦ **gross domestic product** *n.* (also **GDP**) total monetary value of the goods produced and services provided by an economy over a specified period. It is measured in three ways:

(1) on the basis of expenditure, i.e. the value of all goods and services bought, including consumption, capital expenditure, increase in the value of stocks, government expenditure, and exports less imports;

(2) on the basis of income, i.e. income arising from employment, self-employment, rent, company profits (public and private), and stock appreciation;

(3) on the basis of the value added by industry, i.e. the value of sales less the costs of raw materials.

In the UK, statistics for GDP are published monthly by the government on all three bases, although there are large discrepancies between each measure. Economists are usu. interested in the real rate of change of GDP to measure the performance of an economy, rather than the absolute level of GDP. See also GDP DEFLATOR; GROSS NATIONAL PRODUCT; NET NATIONAL PRODUCT.

♦ **gross income** *n.* **1** income of a person or organization before the deduction of the expenses incurred in earning it. **2** income that is liable to tax but from which the tax has not been deducted. For many types of income, tax may be deducted at source leaving the taxpayer with a net amount.

♦ **gross interest** *n.* amount of interest applicable to a particular loan or deposit before tax is deducted. Interest rates may be quoted gross (as they are on government securities) or net (as in most building society deposits or bank deposits). The gross interest less the tax deducted at the basic rate of income tax gives the **net interest**. Any tax suffered is usu. available as a credit against tax liabilities. Since 1991 those with a low income and non-tax-payers have been able to apply to have interest on bank and building-society accounts paid gross.

♦ **gross investment** see NET INVESTMENT.

♦ **gross margin** *n.* (for a retailer) difference between the retail price of goods offered for sale and the wholesale price at which they are purchased. This is often expressed as a percentage of the retail price, whereas the **mark-up** is often expressed as a fraction of the wholesale (purchase) price. For example, a mark-up of ⅓ on a price of £75, will give a retail price of £100, which is a 25% gross margin.

♦ **gross national product** *n.* (also **GNP**) gross domestic product (GDP) with the addition of interest, profits, and dividends received from abroad. The GNP better reflects the welfare of the population in monetary terms, although it is not as accurate a guide as to the productive performance of the economy as the GDP. See also NET NATIONAL PRODUCT.

♦ **gross profit** *n.* total sales revenue of an organization, less the cost of the goods sold. The cost of the goods sold includes their purchase price and costs of bringing them to a state to be sold but not the costs of distribution, general administration, or finance costs.

♦ **gross receipts** *n.pl.* total amount of money received by a business in a specified period before any deductions for costs, raw materials, taxation, etc. Cf. NET RECEIPTS.

♦ **gross register tonnage** see TONNAGE 1.

♦ **gross weight** *n.* **1** total weight of a package including its contents and the packing. The **net weight** is the weight of the contents only, i.e. after deducting the weight of the packing (called the **tare**). **2** total weight of a vehicle (road or rail) and the goods it is carrying, as shown by a weighbridge. The weight of the goods alone (i.e. the **net weight**) is obtained by deducting the weight of the unloaded vehicle (called the **tare**).

♦ **gross yield** *n.* yield on a security calculated before tax is deducted. It is often quoted for the purpose of comparison even on ordinary shares, where dividends have tax deducted before they are paid. The yield after tax is called the **net yield**.

---

gro. t. *abbr.* gross tons (or tonnage).

grotesque /grəʊ'tesk/ *–adj.* **1** comically or repulsively distorted. **2** incongruous, absurd. *–n.* **1** decorative form interweaving human and animal features. **2** comically distorted figure or design. □ **grotesquely** *adv.* **grotesqueness** *n.* [Italian: related to GROTTO]

grotto /'grɒtəʊ/ *n.* (*pl.* **-es** or **-s**) **1** picturesque cave. **2** artificial ornamental cave. [Italian *grotta* from Greek *kruptē* CRYPT]

grotty /'grɒtɪ/ *adj.* (**-ier**, **-iest**) *slang* unpleasant, dirty, shabby, unattractive. [shortening of GROTESQUE]

grouch *colloq. –v.* grumble. *–n.* **1** discontented person. **2** fit of grumbling or the sulks. □ **grouchy** *adj.* (**-ier**, **-iest**). [related to GRUDGE]

ground[1] *–n.* **1 a** surface of the earth, esp. as contrasted with the air around it. **b** part of this specified in some way (*low ground*). **2 a** position, area, or distance on the earth's surface. **b** extent of a subject dealt with (*the book covers a lot of ground*). **3** (often in *pl.*) reason, justification. **4** area of a special kind or use (often in *comb.*: *cricket-ground*; *fishing-grounds*). **5** (in *pl.*) enclosed land attached to a house etc. **6** area or basis for agreement etc. (*common ground*). **7** (in painting etc.) the surface giving the predominant colour. **8** (in *pl.*) solid particles, esp. of coffee, forming a residue. **9** *US Electr.* = EARTH *n.* 4. **10** bottom of the sea. **11** floor of a room etc. **12** (in full **ground bass**) *Mus.* short theme in the bass constantly repeated with the upper parts of the music varied. **13** (*attrib.*) (of animals) living on or in the ground; (of plants) dwarfish or trailing. *–v.* **1** refuse authority for (a pilot or an aircraft) to fly. **2 a** run (a ship) aground; strand. **b** (of a ship) run aground. **3** (foll. by *in*) instruct thoroughly (in a subject). **4** (often as **grounded** *adj.*) (foll. by *on*) base (a principle, conclusion, etc.) on. **5** *US Electr.* = EARTH *v.* □ **break new** (or **fresh) ground** treat a subject previously not dealt with. **get off the ground** *colloq.* make a successful start. **give** (or **lose) ground** retreat, decline. **go to ground 1** (of a fox etc.) enter its earth etc. **2** (of a person) become inaccessible for a prolonged period. **hold one's ground** not retreat. **on the grounds of** because of. [Old English]

ground[2] *past* and *past part.* of GRIND.

ground control *n.* personnel directing the landing etc. of aircraft etc.

ground cover *n.* low-growing plants covering the surface of the earth.

ground elder *n.* garden weed spreading by means of underground stems.

ground floor *n.* floor of a building at ground level.

ground frost *n.* frost on the surface of the ground or in the top layer of soil.

ground glass *n.* **1** glass made non-transparent by grinding etc. **2** glass ground to a powder.

grounding *n.* basic training or instruction.

groundless *adj.* without motive or foundation.

groundnut *n.* = PEANUT 1, 2.

ground-plan *n.* **1** plan of a building at ground level. **2** general outline of a scheme.

ground-rent *n.* rent payable under a lease that has been granted or assigned for a capital sum (premium). Normally, long leases on offices, flats, etc. are granted for such a premium, payable when the lease is first granted; in addition the leaseholder pays the landlord a relatively small annual ground-rent.

groundsel /'graʊns(ə)l/ *n.* wild plant with small yellow flowers, used as a food for cage-birds etc. [Old English]

groundsheet *n.* waterproof sheet for spreading on the ground.

groundsman *n.* person who maintains a sports ground.

ground speed *n.* aircraft's speed relative to the ground.

ground swell *n.* heavy sea caused by a distant or past storm or an earthquake.

groundwater *n.* water found in soil or in pores, crevices, etc., in rock.

groundwork *n.* preliminary or basic work.

group /gru:p/ *–n.* **1** number of persons or things located close together, or considered or classed together. **2** number of people working together etc. **3** = GROUP OF COMPANIES. **4** ensemble playing popular music. **5** division of an air force etc. *–v.* **1** form or be formed into a group. **2** (often foll. by *with*) place in a group or groups. [Italian *gruppo*]

♦ **group accounts** see GROUP OF COMPANIES.

---

group captain *n.* RAF officer next below air commodore.

♦ **group discussion** *n.* marketing research technique that brings between six and eight respondents together for at least an hour to discuss a marketing issue in a relaxed manner under the guidance of an interviewer. The interviewer, who is a specialist acting on behalf of a client, first draws up a **topic guide** that identifies the points to be explored. A sample of respondents, who must not know one another, is recruited to match certain criteria (e.g. if the problem concerned tea all respondents would be tea drinkers). The group meets in the interviewer's home or in a hotel; with the discussion being tape-recorded, the interviewer describes the problem and then adopts a passive role, allowing the group to discuss their views and interjecting further questions only if some aspect of the problem is not being explored adequately. After a minimum of four group discussions, the interviewer will have sufficient material to write a report and recommend a particular action. Group discussions are a qualitative procedure (see QUALITATIVE MARKETING RESEARCH) frequently used to determine attitudes to particular products or advertisements.

groupie *n. slang* ardent follower of touring pop groups, esp. a young woman seeking sexual relations with their members.

♦ **group income** *n.* dividends and other payments made between members of groups of companies in specified circumstances that obviate the need for accounting for advance corporation tax. Like franked investment income group income is not liable to corporation tax in the recipient company.

♦ **group life assurance** *n.* life assurance that covers a number of people, usu. a group of employees or the members of a particular club or association. Often a single policy is issued and premiums are deducted from salaries or club-membership fees. In return for an agreement that all employees or members join the scheme, insurers are prepared to ask only a few basic questions about the health of a person joining. However, with the advent of Aids insurers are no longer prepared to waive all health enquiries.

♦ **group of companies** *n.* a holding (or parent) company together with its subsidiaries. A company is a **subsidiary** of another company if the parent company holds more than half of the nominal value of its equity capital or holds some shares in it and controls the composition of its board of directors. If one company has subsidiaries, which themselves have subsidiaries, all the companies involved are members of the same group. Groups of companies are required by the UK Companies Act (1985) to file **group accounts**, which usu. consist of a consolidated balance sheet and a consolidated profit and loss account for the whole group. In certain circumstances the Department of Trade and Industry will permit groups to publish separate accounts for each subsidiary without consolidation or to omit certain subsidiaries from group accounts. The reasons for doing so, however, have to be bona fide.

♦ **Group of Five** *n.* (also **G5**) five countries, France, Japan, UK, US, and Germany, who have agreed to stabilize their exchange rates by acting together to overcome adverse market forces.

♦ **Group of Seven** *n.* (also **G7, G-7**) the seven leading industrial nations: US, Japan, Germany, France, UK, Italy, and Canada. This group evolved from the first economic summit held in 1976 and now holds an annual meeting attended by heads of state. The original aim was to discuss economic coordination but the agenda has since broadened to include political issues. However, increasing enthusiasm for international economic cooperation in the 1980s led to collective action, for example on exchange rates as a result of meetings of G7 finance ministers.

♦ **Group of Seventy Seven** *n.* (also **G77**) the developing countries of the world.

♦ **Group of Ten** *n.* (also **G10, Paris Club**) ten relatively prosperous industrial nations that agreed in 1962 to lend money to the International Monetary Fund (IMF): Belgium, Canada, France, Italy, Japan, Netherlands, Sweden, West Germany (now unified Germany), UK, and US. They inaugurated special drawing rights.

♦ **Group of Three** *n.* (also **G3**) the three largest industrialized economies: US, Germany, and Japan.

♦ **group relief** *n.* means of enabling a company within a group of companies to transfer to another company in the same group the benefit of its own tax losses or certain other payments for which it is unable to obtain tax relief in its own right. This relief is not available for all losses and the requirements for group status are rigidly defined. There are other possible tax reliefs available within groups, e.g. surrender of advance corporation tax, group roll-overs, and group income, although none of these qualify as group relief.

group therapy *n.* therapy in which people are brought together to assist one another psychologically.

grouse[1] *n.* (*pl.* same) **1** game-bird with a plump body and feathered legs. **2** its flesh as food. [origin uncertain]

grouse[2] *colloq.* –*v.* (**-sing**) grumble or complain. –*n.* complaint. [origin unknown]

grout –*n.* thin fluid mortar. –*v.* provide or fill with grout. [origin uncertain]

grove *n.* small wood or group of trees. [Old English]

grovel /ˈgrɒv(ə)l/ *v.* (**-ll-**; *US* **-l-**) **1** behave obsequiously. **2** lie prone in abject humility. □ **grovelling** *adj.* [obsolete *grovelling* (adv.) from Old Norse *á grúfu* face down]

grow /grəʊ/ *v.* (*past* **grew**; *past part.* **grown**) **1** increase in size, height, quantity, degree, etc. **2** develop or exist as a living plant or natural product. **3 a** produce (plants etc.) by cultivation. **b** allow (a beard etc.) to develop. **4** become gradually (*grow rich*). **5** (foll. by *on*) become gradually more favoured by. **6** (in *passive*; foll. by *over* etc.) be covered with a growth. □ **grow out of 1** become too large to wear. **2** become too mature to retain (a habit etc.). **3** develop from. **grow up 1** advance to maturity. **2** (of a custom) arise. [Old English]

grower *n.* **1** (often in *comb.*) person growing produce (*fruit-grower*). **2** plant that grows in a specified way (*fast grower*).

growing pains *n.pl.* **1** early difficulties in the development of a project etc. **2** neuralgic pain in children's legs due to fatigue etc.

growl –*v.* **1 a** (often foll. by *at*) make a low guttural sound, usu. of anger. **b** murmur angrily. **2** rumble. **3** (often foll. by *out*) utter with a growl. –*n.* **1** growling sound. **2** angry murmur. **3** rumble. [probably imitative]

grown *past part.* of GROW.

grown-up –*adj.* adult. –*n.* adult person.

growth /grəʊθ/ *n.* **1** act or process of growing. **2** increase in size or value. See CAPITAL GROWTH; GROWTH STOCK. **3** something that has grown or is growing. **4** *Med.* morbid formation.

♦ **growth curve** *n.* curve on a graph in which a variable (such as a population, the sales of a product, or the price of a security) is plotted as a function of time, thus illustrating the growth of the variable.

♦ **growth industry** *n.* any industry expected to grow faster than others.

♦ **growth recession** see RECESSION 1.

♦ **growth stock** *n.* stock or share that is expected to offer the investor sustained capital growth and to provide capital gain (cf. INCOME STOCK). The investor will usu. expect a growth stock to be an ordinary share in a company whose products are selling well and whose sales are expected to expand, whose capital expenditure on new plant and equipment is high, whose earnings are growing, and whose management is strong, resourceful, and investing in product development and long-term research.

groyne *n.* (*US* **groin**) timber, stone, or concrete wall built at right angles to the coast to check beach erosion. [dial. *groin* snout, from French]

GRT *abbr.* gross registered tonnage. See TONNAGE 1.

gr. t. *abbr.* gross ton.

grub –*n.* **1** larva of an insect. **2** *colloq.* food. –*v.* (**-bb-**) **1** dig superficially. **2** (foll. by *up*, *out*) **a** extract by digging. **b** extract (information etc.) by searching in books etc. **3** rummage. [Old English]

grubby *adj.* (**-ier, -iest**) **1** dirty. **2** of or infested with grubs. □ **grubbily** *adv.* **grubbiness** *n.*

grudge –*n.* persistent feeling of ill will or resentment. –*v.* (**-ging**) **1** be resentfully unwilling to give or allow. **2** (foll. by verbal noun or *to* + infin.) be reluctant to do. [French]

gruel /ˈgruːəl/ *n.* liquid food of oatmeal etc. boiled in milk or water. [French from Germanic]

gruelling *adj.* (*US* **grueling**) extremely demanding or tiring.

gruesome /'gruːsəm/ *adj.* horrible, grisly, disgusting. □ **gruesomely** *adv.* [Scandinavian]

gruff *adj.* **1 a** (of a voice) low and harsh. **b** (of a person) having a gruff voice. **2** surly. □ **gruffly** *adv.* **gruffness** *n.* [Low German or Dutch *grof* coarse]

grumble /'grʌmb(ə)l/ *–v.* (**-ling**) **1** complain peevishly. **2** rumble. *–n.* **1** complaint. **2** rumble. □ **grumbler** *n.* [obsolete *grumme*]

grummet var. of GROMMET.

grumpy /'grʌmpɪ/ *adj.* (**-ier, -iest**) morosely irritable. □ **grumpily** *adv.* **grumpiness** *n.* [imitative]

grunt *–n.* **1** low guttural sound made by a pig. **2** similar sound. *–v.* **1** make a grunt. **2** make a similar sound, esp. to express discontent. **3** utter with a grunt. [Old English, imitative]

Gruyère /'gruːjeə(r)/ *n.* a firm pale cheese. [*Gruyère* in Switzerland]

gr. wt. *abbr.* gross weight.

gryphon var. of GRIFFIN.

GSM *abbr.* general sales manager.

g.s.m. *abbr. Commerce* good sound merchantable (quality).

GSP *abbr. Econ.* gross social product.

♦ **GSS** *abbr.* = GOVERNMENT STATISTICAL SERVICE.

GST *abbr. NZ & Canadian* goods and services tax.

G-string /'dʒiːstrɪŋ/ *n.* **1** *Mus.* string sounding the note G. **2** narrow strip of cloth etc. covering only the genitals and attached to a string round the waist.

G-suit /'dʒiːsuːt, -sjuːt/ *n.* garment with inflatable pressurized pouches, worn by pilots and astronauts to enable them to withstand high acceleration. [*g* = gravity, SUIT]

GSVQ *abbr.* General Scottish Vocational Qualification.

GT[1] *n.* high-performance saloon car. [Italian *gran turismo* great touring]

GT[2] *airline flight code* GB Airways.

g.t. *abbr.* gross tonnage.

GTC *abbr.* (also **g.t.c.**) *Commerce* good till cancelled (or countermanded).

gtd. *abbr.* guaranteed.

GU *–postcode* Guildford. *–US postcode* Guam.

Guadalajara /ˌgwædələ'hɑːrə/ second-largest city in Mexico, an important communications centre with handicraft industries; pop. (1990) 2 846 000.

Guadalcanal /ˌgwædəlkə'næl/ largest of the Solomon Islands, containing the capital, Honiara; products include copra and rubber; pop. (est. 1996) 59 064.

Guadeloupe /ˌgwɑːdə'luːp/ group of islands in the Lesser Antilles, an overseas department of France; pop. (est. 1996) 427 000; capital, Basse-Terre. The main industries are rum distilling and sugar refining; bananas and sugar form the chief exports. □ **Guadeloupian** *adj.* & *n.*

Guam /gwɑːm/ largest of the Mariana Islands, in the W Pacific, an unincorporated territory of the US; pop. (1990) 133 152; capital, Agaña. It is a US military and naval base with a ship-repairing industry.

Guanajuato /ˌgwænə'hwɑːtəʊ/ **1** state of central Mexico; pop. (est. 1995) 4 393 160. **2** its capital city, a resort; pop. (1990) 113 580.

Guangdong /gwæŋ'dʊŋ/ (also **Kwangtung** /kwæŋ'tʊŋ/) province of S China; pop. (est. 1995) 66 890 000; capital, Canton. Its products include silk, sugar, tobacco, and minerals.

Guangxi Zhuang /'gwæŋʃiː 'dʒwæŋ/ (also **Kwangsi Chuang** /'kwæŋsiː 'tʃwæŋ/) autonomous region and province of S China, producing sugar cane, timber, manganese, and tin; pop. (est. 1995) 44 930 000; capital, Nanning.

guano /'gwɑːnəʊ/ *n.* (*pl.* **-s**) **1** excrement of sea birds, used as manure. **2** artificial manure, esp. that made from fish. [Spanish from Quechua]

guar. *abbr.* guarantee(d).

guaraní /ˌgwɑːrə'niː/ *n.* standard monetary unit of Paraguay. [Spanish]

guarantee /ˌgærən'tiː/ *–n.* **1 a** formal promise or assurance, esp. that something is of a specified quality and durability (see WARRANTY 3). **b** document giving such an undertaking. **2** = GUARANTY. **3** person making a guaranty or giving a security. *–v.* (**-tees, -teed**) **1 a** give or serve as a guarantee for. **b** provide with a guarantee. **2** give a promise or assurance. **3** (foll. by *to*) secure the possession of (a thing) for a person. [related to WARRANT]

♦ **guaranteed-income bond** *n.* bond issued by a life-assurance company that guarantees the purchaser a fixed income as well as a guaranteed return of capital at the end of the term. See also SINGLE-PREMIUM ASSURANCE.

♦ **guaranteed minimum pension** *n.* earnings-related component of a state pension that a person would have been entitled to as an employee of a company, had he or she not contracted out of the state earnings-related pension scheme (SERPS). Any private pension contract must pay at least the guaranteed minimum pension if it is to be an acceptable replacement of a SERPS pension.

♦ **guaranteed stocks** *n.pl.* stocks issued by UK nationalized industries on which the income is guaranteed by the government.

---

guarantor /ˌgærən'tɔː(r)/ *n.* person who gives a guarantee or guaranty.

♦ **guaranty** /'gærəntɪ/ *n.* (*pl.* **-ies**) (also **guarantee**) **1** written or other undertaking made by a person (**guarantor**), who is not a party to a contract between two others,

---

Guatemala /ˌgwætɪ'mɑːlə/, **Republic of** country in N Central America, bordering on the Pacific Ocean and with a short coastline on the Caribbean Sea. The land is fertile, but subject to frequent earthquakes. The principal exports are coffee, sugar, bananas, and cotton. Oil was discovered in the 1970s and production continues to increase. Rubber, essential oils, and forest products, including chicle gum and timber, are also produced. Industrial diversification is being promoted; the plastics industry in particular is expanding. Inflation has been cut, and investment encouraged by low interest rates.

History. Guatemala was conquered by the Spanish in 1523–4. After independence it formed the core of the short-lived Central American Federation (1828–38) before becoming an independent republic in its own right. Its history since then has frequently been characterized by military dictatorship and political unrest; the country returned to civilian rule in 1982. In 1992 it gave up its claims on Belize. Since 1960 there has been an ongoing civil war with left-wing, predominantly Mayan Indian, guerillas. Various accords have been signed in the mid 1990s, including recognition of the rights of indigenous peoples. President, Alvaro Arzú Irigoyen; capital, Guatemala City. □ **Guatemalan** *adj.* & *n.*

languages	Spanish (official), Indian languages
currency	quetzal (Q) of 100 centavos
pop. (est. 1996)	10 928 000
GNP (1994)	US$12B
literacy	71% (m); 57% (f)
life expectancy	62 (m); 67 (f)

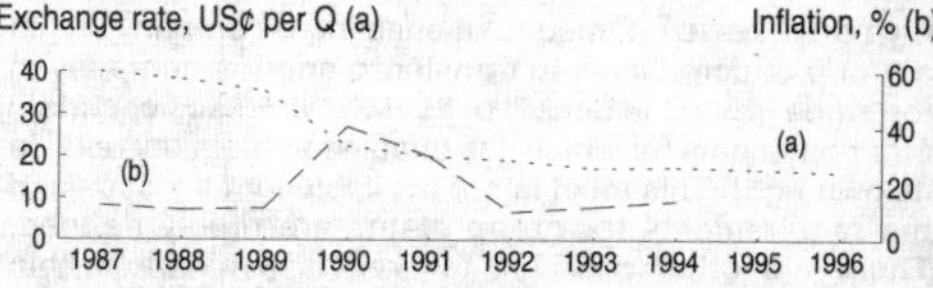

that the guarantor will be liable if one of the parties fails to fulfil the contractual obligations. For example, a bank may make a loan to a person, provided that a guarantor is prepared to repay the loan if the borrower fails to do so. The banker may require the guarantor to provide some security to support the guaranty. **2** thing serving as security.

---

guard /gɑːd/ *–v.* **1** (often foll. by *from, against*) watch over and defend or protect. **2** keep watch by (a door etc.) to control entry or exit. **3** supervise (prisoners etc.) and prevent from escaping. **4** keep (thoughts or speech) in check. **5** (foll. by *against*) take precautions. *–n.* **1** state of vigilance. **2** person who protects or keeps watch. **3** soldiers etc. protecting a place or person; escort. **4** official in general charge of a train. **5** part of an army detached for some purpose (*advance guard*). **6** (in *pl.*) (usu. **Guards**) body of troops nominally employed to guard a monarch. **7** thing that protects (*fire-guard*). **8** *US* prison warder. **9** defensive posture or motion in boxing etc. □ **be on** (or **keep** or **stand**) **guard** keep watch. **off** (or **off one's**) **guard** unprepared for some surprise or difficulty. **on** (or **on one's**) **guard** prepared for all contingencies. [Germanic: related to WARD (n.)]

guarded *adj.* (of a remark etc.) cautious. □ **guardedly** *adv.*

guardhouse *n.* building used to accommodate a military guard or to detain prisoners.

guardian /'gɑːdɪən/ *n.* **1** protector, keeper. **2** person having legal custody of another, esp. a minor. □ **guardianship** *n.* [French: related to WARD, WARDEN]

guardroom *n.* room serving the same purpose as a guardhouse.

guardsman *n.* soldier belonging to a body of guards or regiment of Guards.

Guatemala City capital of Guatemala, in the S of the country; pop. (est. 1995) 1 675 495.

guava /'gwɑːvə/ *n.* **1** edible pale orange fruit with pink flesh. **2** tree bearing this. [Spanish]

Guayaquil /ˌgwɑːjə'kiːl/ chief port and largest city of Ecuador; industries include tanning, textiles, and food processing; pop. (est. 1995) 1 877 031.

gubernatorial /ˌgjuːbənə'tɔːrɪəl/ *adj.* esp. *US* of or relating to a governor. [Latin *gubernator* governor]

gudgeon[1] /'gʌdʒ(ə)n/ *n.* small freshwater fish often used as bait. [Latin *gobio* goby]

gudgeon[2] /'gʌdʒ(ə)n/ *n.* **1** a kind of pivot. **2** tubular part of a hinge. **3** socket for a rudder. **4** pin holding two blocks of stone etc. together. [French diminutive: related to GOUGE]

guelder rose /'geldə(r)/ *n.* shrub with round bunches of creamy-white flowers. [Dutch from *Gelderland* in the Netherlands]

Guernsey /'gɜːnzɪ/ second-largest of the Channel Islands; pop. (1991) 58 867; capital, St Peter Port. Agriculture (esp. dairy farming), horticulture, financial services, and tourism are the main sources of income. *–n.* (*pl.* **-eys**) **1** one of a breed of dairy cattle from Guernsey. **2** (**guernsey**) type of thick woollen sweater.

Guerrero /ge'reəˌrəʊ/ state of SW central Mexico, on the Pacific Coast; pop. (est. 1995) 2 915 497; capital, Chilpancingo.

guerrilla /gə'rɪlə/ *n.* (also **guerilla**) member of a small independently acting (usu. political) group taking part in irregular fighting. [Spanish diminutive: related to WAR]

guess /ges/ *–v.* **1** (often *absol.*) estimate without calculation or measurement. **2** form a hypothesis or opinion about; conjecture; think likely. **3** conjecture or estimate correctly. **4** (foll. by *at*) make a conjecture about. *–n.* estimate, conjecture. □ **I guess** *colloq.* I think it likely; I suppose. [origin uncertain]

guesswork *n.* process of or results got by guessing.

guest /gest/ *n.* **1** person invited to visit another's house or to have a meal etc. at another's expense. **2** person lodging at a hotel etc. **3** outside performer invited to take part with a regular body of performers. [Old Norse]

guest-house *n.* private house offering paid accommodation.

guestimate /'gestɪmət/ *n.* (also **guesstimate**) *colloq.* estimate based on a mixture of guesswork and calculation. [from GUESS, ESTIMATE]

guff *n. slang* empty talk. [imitative]

guffaw /gʌ'fɔː/ *–n.* boisterous laugh. *–v.* utter a guffaw. [imitative]

GUI /'guːɪ/ *abbr. Computing* graphic user interface. See USER INTERFACE.

Guiana /giː'ɑːnə/ region in N South America now comprising Suriname, Guyana, French Guiana, and part of Venezuela and of Brazil.

guidance /'gaɪd(ə)ns/ *n.* **1** advice or direction for solving a problem etc. **2** guiding or being guided.

guide /gaɪd/ *–n.* **1** person who leads or shows the way. **2** person who conducts tours. **3** adviser. **4** directing principle. **5** book with essential information on a subject, esp. = GUIDEBOOK. **6** thing marking a position or guiding the eye. **7** bar etc. directing the motion of something. **8** (**Guide**) member of a girls' organization similar to the Scouts. *–v.* (**-ding**) **1** act as guide to. **2** be the principle or motive of. [French from Germanic]

guidebook *n.* book of information about a place for tourists etc.

guided missile *n.* missile under remote control or directed by equipment within itself.

guide-dog *n.* dog trained to guide a blind person.

guideline *n.* principle directing action.

Guider *n.* adult leader of Guides.

guild /gɪld/ *n.* (also **gild**) **1** association of people for mutual aid or the pursuit of a common goal. **2** medieval association of craftsmen or merchants. [Low German or Dutch *gilde*]

guilder /'gɪldə(r)/ *n.* standard monetary unit of the Netherlands, Netherlands Antilles, and Suriname. [alteration of Dutch *gulden* golden]

Guinea /'gɪnɪ/, **Republic of** country on the W coast of Africa. Agriculture is important in the economy, palm kernels, pineapples, bananas, and coffee being the main cash crops; cassava and other root crops, maize, and millet are among the food crops. However, most export revenue is generated by products of the mining industry, esp. bauxite, alumina, and diamonds. The majority of industry and trade has been nationalized. The weak economy is hindered by uncertainty resulting from the proposed political transition to a multi-party democracy. Formerly part of French West Africa, Guinea became an independent republic in 1958. The military controls the government but tentative steps have been taken to establish a multi-party democracy. A multiparty system was introduced in 1992 and opposition parties were legalized. Conté was re-elected in 1993 amid allegations of electoral fraud. A mutiny in 1996 was quickly subdued. President, Lansana Conté; capital, Conakry.

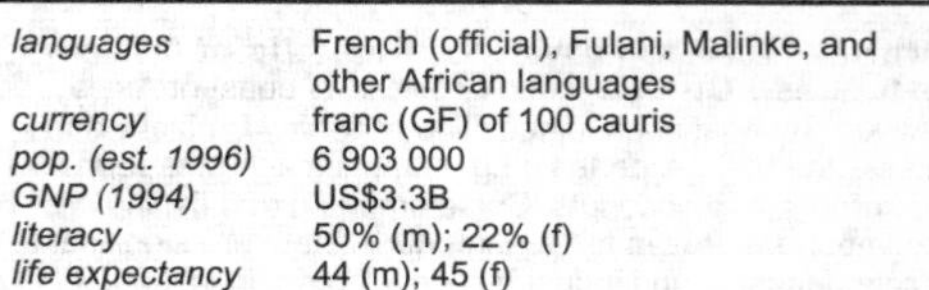

languages	French (official), Fulani, Malinke, and other African languages
currency	franc (GF) of 100 cauris
pop. (est. 1996)	6 903 000
GNP (1994)	US$3.3B
literacy	50% (m); 22% (f)
life expectancy	44 (m); 45 (f)

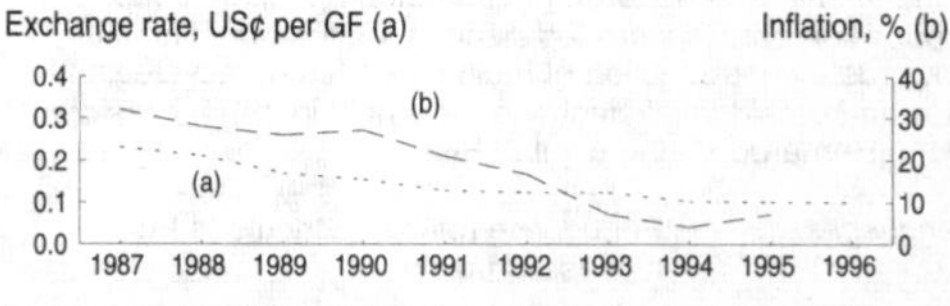

---

guildhall *n.* meeting-place of a medieval guild; town hall.

guile /gaɪl/ *n.* cunning or sly behaviour; treachery, deceit. □ **guileful** *adj.* **guileless** *adj.* [French from Scandinavian]

Guilin /gweɪˈlɪn/ (also **Kweilin** /kweɪˈlɪn/) city in S China, in Guangxi Zhuang; pop. (est. 1990) 364 130. The surrounding limestone hills are a tourist attraction.

guillemot /ˈgɪlɪˌmɒt/ *n.* fast-flying sea bird nesting on cliffs etc. [French]

guillotine /ˈgɪləˌtiːn/ –*n.* **1** machine with a blade sliding vertically in grooves, used for beheading. **2** device for cutting paper etc. **3** method of preventing delay in the discussion of a legislative bill by fixing times at which various parts of it must be voted on. –*v.* (**-ning**) use a guillotine on. [*Guillotin*, name of a physician]

guilt /gɪlt/ *n.* **1** fact of having committed a specified or implied offence. **2** feeling of having done wrong. [Old English]

guiltless *adj.* (often foll. by *of* an offence) innocent.

guilty *adj.* (**-ier**, **-iest**) **1** culpable of or responsible for a wrong. **2** conscious of or affected by guilt. **3** causing a feeling of guilt (*a guilty secret*). **4** (often foll. by *of*) having committed a (specified) offence. □ **guiltily** *adv.* **guiltiness** *n.* [Old English: related to GUILT]

Guinea, Gulf of large inlet of the Atlantic Ocean bordering the south-facing coast of W Africa from Gambia to Gabon.

guinea /ˈgɪnɪ/ *n.* **1** *hist.* sum of 21 shillings (£1.05). **2** *hist.* former British gold coin first coined for the African trade. [GUINEA]

guinea-fowl *n.* African fowl with slate-coloured white-spotted plumage.

guinea-pig *n.* **1** domesticated South American cavy. **2** person used in an experiment.

guipure /ˈgiːpjʊə(r)/ *n.* heavy lace of linen pieces joined by embroidery. [French]

guise /gaɪz/ *n.* **1** assumed appearance; pretence. **2** external appearance. [Germanic: related to WISE[2]]

guitar /gɪˈtɑː(r)/ *n.* usu. six-stringed musical instrument played with the fingers or a plectrum. □ **guitarist** *n.* [Greek *kithara* harp]

Guiyang /gweɪˈjæŋ/ (also **Kweiyang** /kweɪˈjæŋ/) city in S China, capital of Guizhou province; products include steel, aluminium, and machinery; pop. (est. 1991) 1 530 000.

Guizhou /gweɪˈdʒəʊ/ (also **Kweichow** /kweɪˈdʒəʊ/) province of S China; pop. (est. 1995) 34 580 000; capital, Guiyang. Silk, tobacco, and minerals are produced.

Gujarat /ˌguːdʒəˈrɑːt/ **1** state in W India; pop. (1991) 41 309 582; capital, Gandhinagar. It is heavily industrialized, producing machinery, chemicals, and textiles. **2** see GUJRAT.

Gujarati /ˌgʊdʒəˈrɑːtɪ/ (also **Gujerati**) –*n.* (*pl.* **-s**) **1** native of Gujarat. **2** language of Gujarat. –*adj.* of Gujarat, its people, or language.

Gujranwala /ˌgʊdʒrənˈwɑːlə/ city in Pakistan, in Punjab province; manufactures include ceramics, textiles, and leather goods; pop. (1981) 597 000.

Gujrat /ˈguːdʒrɑːt/ (also **Gujarat**) city in Pakistan, in Punjab province; manufactures include cotton goods, furniture, pottery, and carpets; pop. (1981) 154 000.

gulch *n. US* ravine, esp. one in which a torrent flows. [origin uncertain]

gulf *n.* **1** stretch of sea consisting of a deep inlet with a narrow mouth. **2** deep hollow; chasm. **3** wide difference of feelings, opinion, etc. [Greek *kolpos*]

Gulf States states with a coastline on the Persian Gulf, esp. Bahrain, Kuwait, Oman, Qatar, Saudi Arabia, and the United Arab Emirates (and often including Iran and Iraq), comprising the world's chief oil-producing region.

Gulf Stream *n.* warm current flowing from the Gulf of Mexico to Newfoundland where it is deflected across the Atlantic Ocean.

gull[1] *n.* long-winged web-footed sea bird. [probably Welsh *gwylan*]

gull[2] *v.* dupe, fool. [perhaps from obsolete *gull* yellow from Old Norse]

gullet /ˈgʌlɪt/ *n.* food-passage extending from the mouth to the stomach. [Latin *gula* throat]

gullible *adj.* easily persuaded or deceived. □ **gullibility** /-ˈbɪlɪtɪ/ *n.* [from GULL[2]]

gully /ˈgʌlɪ/ *n.* (*pl.* **-ies**) **1** water-worn ravine. **2** gutter or drain. **3** *Cricket* fielding position between point and slips. [French *goulet*: related to GULLET]

gulp –*v.* **1** (often foll. by *down*) swallow hastily, greedily, or with effort. **2** swallow gaspingly or with difficulty; choke. **3** (foll. by *down, back*) suppress (esp. tears). –*n.* **1** act of gulping. **2** large mouthful of a drink. [Dutch *gulpen*, imitative]

gum[1] –*n.* **1 a** viscous secretion of some trees and shrubs. **b** adhesive substance made from this. **2** *US* chewing gum. **3** = GUMDROP. **4** = GUM ARABIC. **5** = GUM-TREE. –*v.* (**-mm-**) **1** (usu. foll. by *down, together*, etc.) fasten with gum. **2** apply gum to. □ **gum up** *colloq.* interfere with the smooth running of. [Greek *kommi* from Egyptian *kemai*]

gum[2] *n.* (usu. in *pl.*) firm flesh around the roots of the teeth. [Old English]

gum[3] *n.* □ **by gum!** *colloq.* by God! [corruption of *God*]

gum arabic *n.* gum exuded by some kinds of acacia.

gumboil *n.* small abscess on the gum.

gumboot *n.* rubber boot.

gumdrop *n.* hard translucent sweet made with gelatin etc.

gummy[1] *adj.* (**-ier**, **-iest**) **1** sticky. **2** exuding gum.

gummy[2] *adj.* (**-ier**, **-iest**) toothless.

gumption /ˈgʌmpʃ(ə)n/ *n. colloq.* **1** resourcefulness, initiative. **2** common sense. [origin unknown]

gum-tree *n.* tree exuding gum, esp. a eucalyptus. □ **up a gum-tree** *colloq.* in great difficulties.

gun –*n.* **1** weapon consisting of a metal tube from which

Guinea-Bissau /ˌgɪnɪbɪˈsaʊ/, **Republic of** (formerly **Portuguese Guinea**) country on the W coast of Africa, between Senegal and Guinea. The economy is chiefly agricultural, the main exports being peanuts, cashews, palm oil and kernels, and coconuts. Cattle breeding and fishing are also important; frozen fish is exported. There are significant bauxite deposits, and industry is developing. Inflation continues to cause economic problems. The country gained independence from Portugal, as a republic, in 1974. Constitutional rule was restored in 1984 after a military coup; opposition parties were legalized in 1991 as the first step towards the introduction of multi-party democracy; legislative and presidential elections were held in 1994. President, João Bernardo Vieira; capital, Bissau.

languages	Portuguese (official), Crioulo (a Portuguese Creole)
currency	peso (PG) of 100 centavos
pop. (1996)	1 096 000
GNP (1994)	US$253M
literacy	68% (m); 42% (f)
life expectancy	42 (m); 45 (f)

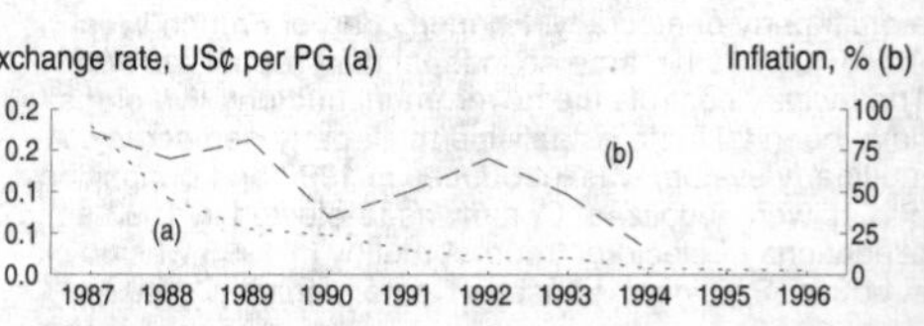

---

bullets or other missiles are propelled with great force, esp. by a contained explosion. **2** starting pistol. **3** device for discharging insecticide, grease etc., in the required direction. **4** member of a shooting-party. **5** *US* gunman. –*v.* (**-nn-**) **1 a** (usu. foll. by *down*) shoot (a person) with a gun. **b** shoot at with a gun. **2** go shooting. **3** (foll. by *for*) seek out determinedly to attack or rebuke. □ **go great guns** *colloq.* proceed vigorously or successfully. **stick to one's guns** *colloq.* maintain one's position under attack. [perhaps an abbreviation of the Scandinavian woman's name *Gunnhildr*, applied to cannon etc.]

gunboat *n.* small vessel with heavy guns.

gunboat diplomacy *n.* political negotiation backed by the threat of force.

gun-carriage *n.* wheeled support for a gun.

gun-cotton *n.* explosive made by steeping cotton in acids.

gun dog *n.* dog trained to retrieve game shot by sportsmen.

gunfight *n.* *US* fight with firearms. □ **gunfighter** *n.*

gunfire *n.* firing of a gun or guns.

gunge /gʌndʒ/ *colloq.* –*n.* sticky or viscous matter. –*v.* (**-ging**) (usu. foll. by *up*) clog with gunge. □ **gungy** *adj.* [origin uncertain]

gung-ho /gʌŋˈhəʊ/ *adj.* zealous, arrogantly eager. [Chinese *gonghe* work together]

gunman *n.* man armed with a gun, esp. when committing a crime.

gun-metal *n.* **1** a dull bluish-grey colour. **2** alloy formerly used for guns.

gunnel var. of GUNWALE.

gunner *n.* **1** artillery soldier (esp. as an official term for a private). **2** *Naut.* warrant-officer in charge of a battery, magazine, etc. **3** member of an aircraft crew who operates a gun.

gunnery *n.* **1** construction and management of large guns. **2** firing of guns.

gunny /ˈgʌnɪ/ *n.* (*pl.* **-ies**) **1** coarse sacking, usu. of jute fibre. **2** sack made of this. [Hindi and Marathi]

gunpoint *n.* □ **at gunpoint** threatened with a gun or an ultimatum etc.

gunpowder *n.* explosive made of saltpetre, sulphur, and charcoal.

gunrunner *n.* person engaged in the illegal sale or importing of firearms. □ **gunrunning** *n.*

gunshot *n.* **1** shot fired from a gun. **2** range of a gun (*within gunshot*).

gunslinger *n.* esp. *US slang* gunman.

gunsmith *n.* maker and repairer of small firearms.

gunwale /ˈgʌn(ə)l/ *n.* (also **gunnel**) upper edge of the side of a boat or ship. [from GUN, WALE, because it was formerly used to support guns]

guppy /ˈgʌpɪ/ *n.* (*pl.* **-ies**) freshwater fish of the West Indies and South America frequently kept in aquariums. [*Guppy*, name of a clergyman]

gurgle /ˈgɜːg(ə)l/ –*v.* (**-ling**) **1** make a bubbling sound as of water from a bottle. **2** utter with such a sound. –*n.* gurgling sound. [probably imitative]

Gurkha /ˈgɜːkə/ *n.* **1** member of the dominant Hindu race in Nepal. **2** Nepalese soldier serving in the British army. [Sanskrit]

gurnard /ˈgɜːnəd/ *n.* (*pl.* same or **-s**) marine fish with a large spiny head and finger-like pectoral rays. [French]

guru /ˈgʊruː/ *n.* (*pl.* **-s**) **1** Hindu spiritual teacher or head of a religious sect. **2** influential or revered teacher. [Hindi]

gush –*v.* **1** emit or flow in a sudden and copious stream. **2** speak or behave effusively. –*n.* **1** sudden or copious stream. **2** effusive manner. [probably imitative]

gusher *n.* **1** oil well from which oil flows without being pumped. **2** effusive person.

gusset /ˈgʌsɪt/ *n.* **1** piece let into a garment etc. to strengthen or enlarge it. **2** bracket strengthening an angle of a structure. [French]

gust –*n.* **1** sudden strong rush of wind. **2** burst of rain, smoke, emotion, etc. –*v.* blow in gusts. □ **gusty** *adj.* (**-ier, -iest**). [Old Norse]

gusto /ˈgʌstəʊ/ *n.* zest; enjoyment. [Latin *gustus* taste]

gut –*n.* **1** the intestine. **2** (in *pl.*) the bowel or entrails. **3** (in *pl.*) *colloq.* personal courage and determination; perseverance. **4** *slang* stomach, belly. **5** (in *pl.*) **a** contents. **b** essence. **6 a** material for violin strings etc. **b** material for fishing-lines made from the silk-glands of silkworms. **7** (*attrib.*) **a** instinctive (*a gut reaction*). **b** fundamental (*a gut issue*). –*v.* (**-tt-**) **1** remove or destroy the internal fittings of (a house etc.). **2** remove the guts of (a fish). □ **hate a person's guts** *colloq.* dislike a person intensely. [Old English]

gutless *adj. colloq.* lacking courage or energy.

gutsy *adj.* (**-ier, -iest**) *colloq.* **1** courageous. **2** greedy.

gutta-percha /ˌgʌtəˈpɜːtʃə/ *n.* tough rubbery substance obtained from latex. [Malay]

gutted *adj. slang* utterly exhausted or fed-up.

gutter –*n.* **1** shallow trough below the eaves of a house, or a channel at the side of a street, to carry off rainwater. **2** (prec. by *the*) poor or degraded background or environment. **3** open conduit. **4** groove. –*v.* (of a candle) burn unsteadily and melt away rapidly. [Latin *gutta* drop]

guttering *n.* **1** gutters of a building etc. **2** material for gutters.

gutter press *n.* sensational newspapers.

guttersnipe *n.* street urchin.

guttural /ˈgʌtər(ə)l/ –*adj.* **1** throaty, harsh-sounding. **2** *Phonet.* (of a consonant) produced in the throat or by the back of the tongue and palate. **3** of the throat. –*n.* *Phonet.* guttural consonant (e.g. *k*, *g*). □ **gutturally** *adv.* [Latin *guttur* throat]

guv *n. slang* = GOVERNOR 7. [abbreviation]

GUY *international vehicle registration* Guyana.

guy[1] /gaɪ/ –*n.* **1** *colloq.* man; fellow. **2** effigy of Guy Fawkes burnt on 5 Nov. –*v.* ridicule. [*Guy* Fawkes, name of a conspirator]

guy[2] /gaɪ/ –*n.* rope or chain to secure a tent or steady a

---

Guyana /gaɪˈænə/, **Cooperative Republic of** country on the NE coast of South America. The economy is mainly agricultural; sugar and rice are the main cash crops. Livestock farming and cotton growing are expanding, and fishing (esp. for shrimps) has become an important export industry. Mining is a major industry: bauxite, gold, and diamonds are all exported; timber also contributes to export revenue. Privatization of state-run industries has started to attract foreign investment. Guyana is a member of CARICOM. Established, with adjacent areas, as the colony of British Guiana in 1831, it gained independence as Guyana in 1966 and became a republic within the Commonwealth in 1970. The first free elections for 28 years were held in 1992. President, Sam Hinds; prime minister, Janet Jagan; capital, Georgetown. □ **Guyanese** /ˌgaɪəˈniːz/ *adj.* & *n.*

languages	English (official), Hindi, Urdu, Amerindian dialects
currency	dollar (G$) of 100 cents
pop. (est. 1996)	712 000
GNP (1994)	US$434M
literacy	98% (m); 97% (f)
life expectancy	58 (m); 63 (f)

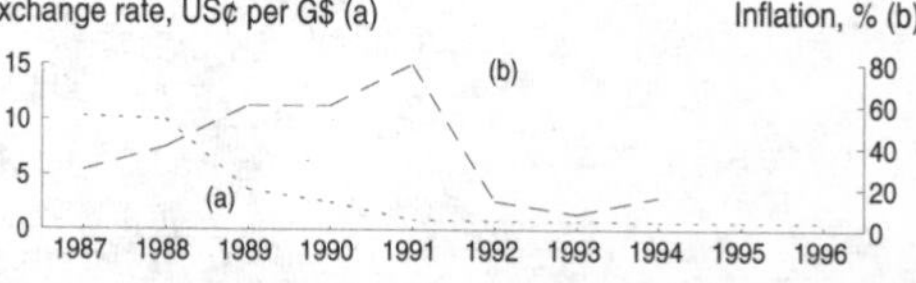

crane-load etc. –*v.* secure with a guy or guys. [probably Low German]

guzzle /'gʌz(ə)l/ *v.* (**-ling**) eat or drink greedily. [probably French *gosiller* from *gosier* throat]

GVW *abbr.* gross vehicle weight.

Gwalior /'gwɑːlɪ,ɔː(r)/ city in central India; manufactures include pottery, footwear, biscuits, and cigarettes; pop. (1991) 690 765.

Gwent /gwent/ former county of SE Wales; its county town was Newport.

GWP *abbr.* gross world product.

Gwynedd /'gwɪneð/ county of NW Wales; pop. (est. 1994) 240 300; county town, Caernarfon. Slate-quarrying no longer provides much employment, but there are textile and electronics industries, and tourism is important. In 1996 it became a unitary authority.

gybe /dʒaɪb/ *v.* (*US* **jibe**) (**-bing**) **1** (of a fore-and-aft sail or boom) swing across. **2** cause (a sail) to do this. **3** (of a ship or its crew) change course so that this happens. [Dutch]

gym /dʒɪm/ *n. colloq.* **1** gymnasium. **2** gymnastics. [abbreviation]

gymkhana /dʒɪm'kɑːnə/ *n.* horse-riding competition. [Hindustani *gendkhāna* ball-house, assimilated to GYMNASIUM]

gymnasium /dʒɪm'neɪzɪəm/ *n.* (*pl.* **-s** or **-sia**) room or building equipped for gymnastics. [Greek *gumnos* naked]

gymnast /'dʒɪmnæst/ *n.* person who does gymnastics, esp. an expert.

gymnastic /dʒɪm'næstɪk/ *adj.* of or involving gymnastics. □ **gymnastically** *adv.*

gymnastics *n.pl.* (also treated as *sing.*) **1** exercises performed in order to develop or display physical agility. **2** other forms of physical or mental agility.

gymnosperm /'dʒɪmnəʊ,spɜːm/ *n.* any of a group of plants having seeds unprotected by an ovary, including conifers, cycads, and ginkgos. [Greek *gumnos* naked]

gymp var. of GIMP.

gymslip *n.* sleeveless tunic worn by schoolgirls.

gynaecology /,gaɪnɪ'kɒlədʒɪ/ *n.* (*US* **gynecology**) science of the physiological functions and diseases of women. □ **gynaecological** /-kə'lɒdʒɪk(ə)l/ *adj.* **gynaecologist** *n.* [Greek *gunē gunaik-* woman, -LOGY]

gypsum /'dʒɪpsəm/ *n.* mineral used esp. to make plaster of Paris. [Greek *gupsos*]

Gypsy *n.* (also **Gipsy**) (*pl.* **-ies**) **1** member of a nomadic people of Europe and North America, of Hindu origin with dark skin and hair. **2** (**gypsy**) person resembling or living like a Gypsy. [from EGYPTIAN]

gyrate /,dʒaɪə'reɪt/ *v.* (**-ting**) move in a circle or spiral; revolve, whirl. □ **gyration** /-'reɪʃ(ə)n/ *n.* **gyratory** *adj.* [Greek: related to GYRO-]

gyrfalcon /'dʒɜː,fɔːlkən/ *n.* large falcon of the northern hemisphere. [French from Old Norse]

gyro /'dʒaɪərəʊ/ *n.* (*pl.* **-s**) *colloq.* = GYROSCOPE. [abbreviation]

gyro- *comb. form* rotation. [Greek *guros* ring]

gyrocompass /'dʒaɪərəʊ,kʌmpəs/ *n.* compass giving true north and bearings from it by means of a gyroscope.

gyroscope /'dʒaɪərə,skəʊp/ *n.* rotating wheel whose axis is free to turn but maintains a fixed direction unless perturbed, esp. used for stabilization or with the compass in an aircraft, ship, etc.

H[1] /eɪtʃ/ *n.* (also **h**) (*pl.* **Hs** or **H's**) **1** eighth letter of the alphabet (see AITCH). **2** anything having the form of an H (esp. in *comb.*: *H-girder*).

H[2] *abbr.* (also **H.**) **1** (of a pencil-lead) hard. **2** *Advertising* half-page. **3** henry(s). **4** *slang* heroin. **5** (water) hydrant.

H[3] *–symb.* hydrogen. *–international vehicle registration* Hungary.

h. *abbr.* (also **h**) **1** hecto-. **2** height. **3** hot. **4** hour(s).

H4 *international civil aircraft marking* Solomon Islands.

HA *–international civil aircraft marking* Hungary. *–postcode* Harrow. *–airline flight code* Hawaiian Air.

Ha *symb.* hahnium.

ha[1] /hɑː/ (also **hah**) *–int.* expressing surprise, derision, triumph, etc. (cf. HA HA). *–v.* in **hum and ha**: see HUM. [imitative]

ha[2] *symb.* hectare(s).

Haarlem /ˈhɑːləm/ city in the Netherlands, capital of the province of North Holland and commercial centre of the Dutch bulb industry; pop. (est. 1995) 148 947.

♦ **Haas** /hɑːs/, **Peter E.** (1918–) US businessman, president (1970–81), chief executive officer (1976–81), chairman (1981–89), and chairman of the executive committee (from 1989) of Levi Strauss & Co., the market-leading jeansmaker. He and his relative **Robert Douglas Haas** (1942–) – president and chief executive officer (1984–89) and chairman (from 1989), both heirs of Levi Strauss, led a leverage buyout of the company.

---

habeas corpus /ˌheɪbɪəs ˈkɔːpəs/ *n.* writ requiring a person to be brought before a judge or into court, esp. to investigate the lawfulness of his or her detention. [Latin, = you must have the body]

haberdasher /ˈhæbəˌdæʃə(r)/ *n.* dealer in dress accessories and sewing-goods. □ **haberdashery** *n.* (*pl.* **-ies**). [probably Anglo-French]

habiliment /həˈbɪlɪmənt/ *n.* (usu. in *pl.*) *archaic* clothes. [French from *habiller* fit out]

habit /ˈhæbɪt/ *n.* **1** settled or regular tendency or practice (often foll. by *of* + verbal noun: *has a habit of ignoring me*). **2** practice that is hard to give up. **3** mental constitution or attitude. **4** dress, esp. of a religious order. [Latin *habeo habit-* have]

habitable *adj.* suitable for living in. □ **habitability** /-ˈbɪlɪtɪ/ *n.* [Latin *habito* inhabit]

habitat /ˈhæbɪˌtæt/ *n.* natural home of an animal or plant. [Latin, = it dwells]

habitation /ˌhæbɪˈteɪʃ(ə)n/ *n.* **1** inhabiting (*fit for habitation*). **2** house or home.

habit-forming *adj.* causing addiction.

habitual /həˈbɪtʃʊəl/ *adj.* **1** done constantly or as a habit. **2** regular, usual. **3** given to a (specified) habit (*habitual smoker*). □ **habitually** *adv.*

habituate /həˈbɪtʃʊˌeɪt/ *v.* (**-ting**) (often foll. by *to*) accustom. □ **habituation** /-ˈeɪʃ(ə)n/ *n.* [Latin: related to HABIT]

habitué /həˈbɪtʃʊˌeɪ/ *n.* habitual visitor or resident. [French]

háček /ˈhætʃek/ *n.* diacritic (ˇ) placed over a letter to modify its sound in some languages. [Czech, diminutive of *hák* hook]

hachures /hæˈʃjʊə(r)/ *n.pl.* parallel lines on a map indicating the degree of steepness of hills. [French: related to HATCH[3]]

hacienda /ˌhæsɪˈendə/ *n.* (in Spanish-speaking countries) estate with a dwelling-house. [Spanish, from Latin *facienda* things to be done]

hack[1] *–v.* **1** cut or chop roughly. **2** *Football etc.* kick the shin of (an opponent). **3** (often foll. by *at*) deliver cutting blows. **4** cut (one's way) through foliage etc. **5** *colloq.* gain unauthorized access to (data in a computer). **6** *slang* manage, cope with; tolerate. **7** (as **hacking** *adj.*) (of a cough) short, dry, and frequent. *–n.* **1** kick with the toe of a boot. **2** gash or wound, esp. from a kick. **3 a** mattock. **b** miner's pick. [Old English]

hack[2] *–n.* **1 a** = HACKNEY. **b** horse let out for hire. **2** person hired to do dull routine work, esp. writing. *–attrib. adj.* **1** used as a hack. **2** typical of a hack; commonplace (*hack work*). *–v.* ride on horseback on a road at an ordinary pace. [abbreviation of HACKNEY]

hacker *n.* **1** person or thing that hacks or cuts roughly. **2** *colloq.* **a** person who uses a computer to gain unauthorized access to a computer network. **b** person whose hobby is computing or computer programming.

hackle /ˈhæk(ə)l/ *n.* **1 a** (in *pl.*) erectile hairs on an animal's neck, rising when it is angry or alarmed. **b** feather(s) on the neck of a domestic cock etc. **2** steel comb for dressing flax. □ **make one's hackles rise** cause one to be angry or indignant. [Old English]

hackney /ˈhæknɪ/ *n.* (*pl.* **-s**) horse for ordinary riding. [*Hackney* in London]

hackney carriage *n.* taxi.

hackneyed /ˈhæknɪd/ *adj.* (of a phrase etc.) made trite by overuse.

hacksaw *n.* saw with a narrow blade set in a frame, for cutting metal.

had *past* and *past part.* of HAVE.

haddock /ˈhædək/ *n.* (*pl.* same) N Atlantic marine fish used as food. [probably French]

Hades /ˈheɪdiːz/ *n.* (in Greek mythology) the underworld. [Greek, originally a name of Pluto]

hadj var. of HAJJ.

hadji var. of HAJJI.

hadn't /ˈhæd(ə)nt/ *contr.* had not.

haemal /ˈhiːm(ə)l/ *adj.* (*US* **hem-**) of the blood. [Greek *haima* blood]

haematite /ˈhiːməˌtaɪt/ *n.* (*US* **hem-**) a ferric oxide ore. [Latin: related to HAEMAL]

haematology /ˌhiːməˈtɒlədʒɪ/ *n.* (*US* **hem-**) the study of the blood. □ **haematologist** *n.*

haemoglobin /ˌhiːməˈgləʊbɪn/ *n.* (*US* **hem-**) oxygen-carrying substance in the red blood cells of vertebrates. [from GLOBULIN]

haemophilia /ˌhiːməˈfɪlɪə/ *n.* (*US* **hem-**) hereditary failure of the blood to clot normally with the tendency to bleed severely from even a slight injury. [Greek *haima* blood, *philia* loving]

haemophiliac *n.* (*US* **hem-**) person with haemophilia.

haemorrhage /ˈhemərɪdʒ/ (*US* **hem-**) *–n.* **1** profuse loss of blood from a ruptured blood-vessel. **2** damaging loss, esp. of people or assets. *–v.* (**-ging**) suffer a haemorrhage. [Greek *haima* blood, *rhēgnumi* burst]

haemorrhoids /ˈheməˌrɔɪdz/ *n.pl.* (*US* **hem-**) swollen veins in the wall of the anus; piles. [Greek *haima* blood, *-rhoos* -flowing]

hafnium /ˈhæfnɪəm/ *n.* silvery lustrous metallic element. [Latin *Hafnia* Copenhagen]

haft /hɑːft/ *n.* handle of a dagger, knife, etc. [Old English]

hag *n.* **1** ugly old woman. **2** witch. [Old English]

haggard /ˈhægəd/ *adj.* looking exhausted and distraught. [French *hagard*]

haggis /ˈhægɪs/ *n.* Scottish dish of offal boiled in a sheep's stomach with suet, oatmeal, etc. [origin unknown]

haggle /ˈhæg(ə)l/ *–v.* (**-ling**) (often foll. by *about*, *over*) bargain persistently. *–n.* haggling. [Old Norse]

hagio- *comb. form* of saints. [Greek *hagios* holy]

hagiography /ˌhægɪˈɒgrəfɪ/ *n.* writing about saints' lives. □ **hagiographer** *n.*

hagiology /ˌhægɪˈɒlədʒɪ/ *n.* literature dealing with the lives and legends of saints.

hagridden *adj.* afflicted by nightmares or anxieties.

Hague /heɪg/, **The** (Dutch **'s-Gravenhage** /ˈsxrɑːvən͵hɑxə/ or **Den Haag** /den ˈhɑːg/) seat of government and administrative centre of the Netherlands, on the North Sea coast in South Holland; pop. (est. 1995) 442 105.

hah var. of HA[1].

ha ha /hɑːˈhɑː/ *int.* representing laughter (*iron.* when spoken). [Old English]

ha-ha /ˈhɑːhɑː/ *n.* ditch with a wall in it, forming a boundary or fence without interrupting the view. [French]

hahnium /ˈhɑːnɪəm/ *n.* artificially produced radioactive element. [*Hahn*, name of a chemist]

Haifa /ˈhaɪfə/ chief seaport of Israel, in the NW of the country; industries include oil and petrol refining; pop. (est. 1996) 252 300.

haiku /ˈhaɪkuː/ *n.* (*pl.* same) very short Japanese three-part poem of usu. 17 syllables. [Japanese]

hail[1] *–n.* **1** pellets of frozen rain. **2** (foll. by *of*) barrage or onslaught. *–v.* **1 a** (prec. by *it* as subject) hail falls. **b** come down forcefully. **2** pour down (blows, words, etc.). [Old English]

hail[2] *–v.* **1** signal to (a taxi etc.) to stop. **2** greet enthusiastically. **3** acclaim (*hailed him king*). **4** (foll. by *from*) originate or come (*hails from Leeds*). *–int. archaic* or *joc.* expressing greeting. *–n.* act of hailing. [Old Norse *heill*: related to WASSAIL]

hail-fellow-well-met *adj.* friendly, esp. too friendly towards strangers.

Hail Mary *n.* the Ave Maria (see AVE).

hailstone *n.* pellet of hail.

hailstorm *n.* period of heavy hail.

Hainan /haɪˈnæn/ island in the South China Sea forming an autonomous region of China; pop. (est. 1995) 7 110 000; capital, Haikou. Iron ore and other minerals are mined, and rubber and timber are produced.

Haiphong /haɪˈfɒŋ/ port in N Vietnam; manufactures include cement, plastics, and textiles; pop. (est. 1992) 783 134.

hair *n.* **1 a** any of the fine threadlike strands growing from the skin of mammals, esp. from the human head. **b** these collectively (*has long hair*). **2** thing resembling a hair. elongated cell growing from a plant. **4** very small quan tity or extent (also *attrib.*: *hair crack*). □ **get in a person' hair** *colloq.* annoy a person. **keep one's hair on** *colloq* keep calm; not get angry. **let one's hair down** *collo* enjoy oneself by abandoning restraint. **make one's hai stand on end** *colloq.* horrify one. **not turn a hair** remai unmoved or unaffected. □ **hairless** *adj.* [Old English]

hairbrush *n.* brush for tidying the hair.

haircloth *n.* stiff cloth woven from hair.

haircut *n.* **1** act of cutting the hair (*needs a haircut*). style in which the hair is cut. **3** *colloq.* difference betwee prices at which a market maker or broker will buy an sell.

hairdo *n.* (*pl.* **-s**) style of or act of styling the hair.

hairdresser *n.* **1** person who cuts and styles the hair esp. for a living. **2** hairdresser's shop. □ **hairdressing** *n*

hair-drier *n.* (also **hair-dryer**) device for drying the hai with warm air.

hairgrip *n.* flat hairpin with the ends close together.

hairline *n.* **1** edge of a person's hair, esp. on the forehead **2** very narrow line, crack (usu. **hairline crack**), etc.

hairnet *n.* piece of netting for confining the hair.

hair of the dog *n.* further alcoholic drink taken to cur the effects of drink.

hairpiece *n.* quantity of hair augmenting a person' natural hair.

hairpin *n.* U-shaped pin for fastening the hair.

hairpin bend *n.* sharp U-shaped bend in a road.

hair-raising *adj.* terrifying.

hair's breadth *n.* a tiny amount or margin.

hair shirt *n.* shirt of haircloth, worn formerly by peni tents and ascetics.

hair-slide *n.* clip for keeping the hair in place.

hair-splitting *adj.* & *n.* quibbling.

hairspray *n.* liquid sprayed on the hair to keep it in place.

hairspring *n.* fine spring regulating the balance-wheel in a watch.

hairstyle *n.* particular way of arranging the hair. □ **hair-stylist** *n.*

hair-trigger *n.* trigger of a firearm set for release at the slightest pressure.

hairy *adj.* (**-ier, -iest**) **1** covered with hair. **2** *slang* frightening, dangerous. □ **hairiness** *n.*

hajj /hædʒ/ *n.* (also **hadj**) Islamic pilgrimage to Mecca. [Arabic]

hajji /ˈhædʒɪ/ *n.* (also **hadji**) (*pl.* **-s**) Muslim who has made the pilgrimage to Mecca. [Persian from Arabic]

haka /ˈhɑːkə/ *n. NZ* **1** Maori ceremonial war dance with

Haiti /ˈheɪtɪ/, **Republic of** country in the Caribbean, occupying the W portion of the island of Hispaniola. The economy is based on agriculture, the main cash crops being coffee, sugar, and sisal; sorghum, rice, bananas, and sweet potatoes are also grown and cattle, goats, and pigs are raised. Some bauxite and copper is mined, but mineral resources remain largely untapped. Hydroelectricity is a significant source of power, and there is some light manufacturing industry, assembling goods for re-export. The military coup in 1991 provoked international condemnation and led to the imposition of a trade embargo, which is unlikely to be lifted until democracy is restored, and the suspension of foreign aid. This has severely damaged the economy, which will continue to contract while inflation rises. Sanctions were lifted in 1995. In 1996 some foreign aid, previously suspended, was released.

History. A French colony from 1697, Haiti was proclaimed an independent state in 1804, after the rebellion of its Black slave population. The country's recent history has been dominated by the repressive dictatorship (1957–71) of François Duvalier and a subsequent succession of military coups, the latest of which (in 1991) forced Jean-Bertrand Aristide, the democratically elected president, into exile and installed a provisional government. In 1993, threatened by the UN with further economic sanctions, the government took steps towards reinstating Aristide. Aristide returned to Haiti in 1994 and appointed a new government. Democratic elections were held in 1995. Prime minister, Rony Smarth; capital, Port-au-Prince. □ **Haitian** *adj.* & *n.*

languages	French, Haitian Creole
currency	gourde (G) of 100 centimes
pop. (est. 1996)	6 732 000
GNP (1994)	US$1.5B
literacy	48% (m); 42% (f)
life expectancy	47 (m); 51 (f)

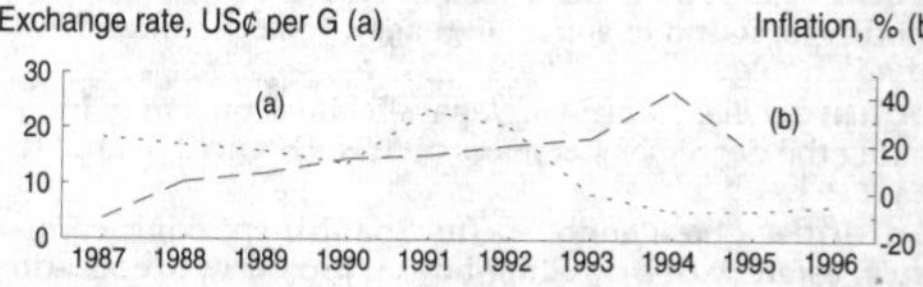

chanting. **2** imitation of this by a sports team before a match. [Maori]

hake *n.* (*pl.* same) marine fish resembling the cod, used as food. [origin uncertain]

halal /hɑːˈlɑːl/ *n.* (also **hallal**) (often *attrib.*) meat from an animal killed according to Muslim law. [Arabic]

halberd /ˈhælbəd/ *n. hist.* combined spear and battleaxe. [French from German]

halcyon /ˈhælsɪən/ *adj.* calm, peaceful, happy (*halcyon days*). [Greek, = kingfisher, because it was reputed to calm the sea at midwinter]

hale *adj.* strong and healthy (esp. in **hale and hearty**). [var. of WHOLE]

half /hɑːf/ *–n.* (*pl.* **halves** /hɑːvz/) **1** either of two (esp. equal) parts into which a thing is divided. **2** *colloq.* half a pint, esp. of beer. **3** *Sport* either of two equal periods of play. **4** *colloq.* half-price fare or ticket, esp. for a child. **5** *colloq.* = HALF-BACK. *–adj.* **1** amounting to half (*half the men*). **2** forming a half (*a half share*). *–adv.* **1** (often in *comb.*) to the extent of half; partly (*half cooked*). **2** to some extent (esp. in idiomatic phrases: *half dead*; *am half convinced*). **3** (in reckoning time) by the amount of half (an hour etc.) (*half past two*). □ **at half cock** see COCK[1]. **by half** (prec. by *too* + adj.) excessively (*too clever by half*). **by halves** imperfectly or incompletely (*does nothing by halves*). **half a mind** see MIND. **half the time** see TIME. **not half 1** *slang* extremely, violently (*he didn't half swear*). **2** not nearly (*not half long enough*). **3** *colloq.* not at all (*not half bad*). [Old English]

■ **Usage** In sense 3 of the adverb, the word 'past' is often omitted in colloquial usage, e.g. *came at half two*. In some parts of Scotland and Ireland this means 'half past one'.

half-and-half *adj.* being half one thing and half another.

half-back *n. Sport* player between the forwards and full backs.

half-baked *adj. colloq.* **1** not thoroughly thought out; foolish. **2** (of enthusiasm etc.) only partly committed.

half board *n.* provision of bed, breakfast, and one main meal at a hotel etc.

half-breed *n. offens.* = HALF-CASTE.

half-brother *n.* brother with whom one has only one parent in common.

half-caste *n. offens.* person of mixed race.

◆ **half-commission man** *n.* person who is not a member of a stock exchange but works for a stockbroker, introducing clients in return for half, or some other agreed share, of the commission.

---

half-crown *n.* (also **half a crown**) former coin and monetary unit worth 2s. 6d. ($12^1/_2$p).

half-cut *adj. sl.* fairly drunk.

half-dozen *n.* (also **half a dozen**) *colloq.* six, or about six.

half-duplex *adj.* (also **HDX**) *Computing* (of a circuit) allowing the two-way transmission of signals but not simultaneously.

half-hardy *adj.* (of a plant) able to grow in the open except in severe frost.

half-hearted *adj.* lacking enthusiasm. □ **half-heartedly** *adv.* **half-heartedness** *n.*

half hitch *n.* knot formed by passing the end of a rope round its standing part and then through the loop.

half holiday *n.* half a day as holiday.

half-hour *n.* **1** (also **half an hour**) period of 30 minutes. **2** point of time 30 minutes after any hour o'clock. □ **half-hourly** *adj.* & *adv.*

half-life *n.* time taken for radioactivity etc. to fall to half its original value.

half-light *n.* dim imperfect light.

half-mast *n.* position of a flag halfway down a mast, as a mark of respect for a deceased person.

half measures *n.pl.* unsatisfactory compromise or inadequate policy.

half moon *n.* **1** moon when only half its surface is illuminated. **2** time when this occurs. **3** semicircular object.

half nelson see NELSON.

halfpenny /ˈheɪpnɪ/ *n.* (*pl.* **-pennies** or **-pence** /ˈheɪpəns/) former coin worth half a penny.

■ **Usage** The halfpenny was withdrawn from circulation in 1984.

half-sister *n.* sister with whom one has only one parent in common.

half-term *n.* short holiday halfway through a school term.

half-timbered *adj.* having walls with a timber frame and a brick or plaster filling.

half-time *n.* **1** mid-point of a game or contest. **2** short break occurring at this time.

half-title *n.* title or short title of a book printed on the front of the leaf preceding the title-page.

half-tone *n.* photographic illustration in which various tones of grey are produced from small and large black dots.

half-truth *n.* statement that (esp. deliberately) conveys only part of the truth.

half-volley *n.* (in ball games) playing of the ball as soon as it bounces off the ground.

halfway *–adv.* **1** at a point midway between two others (*halfway to Rome*). **2** to some extent, more or less (*is halfway acceptable*). *–adj.* situated halfway (*reached a halfway point*).

halfway house *n.* **1** compromise. **2** halfway point in a progression. **3** centre for rehabilitating ex-prisoners etc. **4** inn midway between two towns.

halfwit *n.* foolish or stupid person. □ **halfwitted** *adj.*

halibut /ˈhælɪbət/ *n.* (*pl.* same) large marine flat-fish used as food. [from HOLY (perhaps because eaten on holy days), *butt* flat-fish]

Halifax /ˈhælɪˌfæks/ major port in Canada, on the E seaboard, capital of Nova Scotia; city pop. (est. 1992) 182 253; metropolitan area pop. (1991) 320 501. It has steel and oil-refining industries.

halitosis /ˌhælɪˈtəʊsɪs/ *n.* = BAD BREATH. [Latin *halitus* breath]

hall /hɔːl/ *n.* **1** area into which the front entrance of a house etc. opens. **2** large room or building for meetings, concerts, etc. **3** large country house or estate. **4** (in full **hall of residence**) residence for students. **5** (in a college etc.) dining-room. **6** premises of a guild (*Fishmongers' Hall*). **7** large public room in a palace etc. [Old English]

hallal var. of HALAL.

Halle /ˈhælə/ city in central Germany, on the River Saale; industries include sugar refining and coalmining; pop. (est. 1995) 290 054.

hallelujah var. of ALLELUIA.

halliard var. of HALYARD.

hallmark *–n.* **1** series of marks stamped on articles made of gold, silver, or platinum in the UK to indicate the maker, the hall or assay office making the mark, the quality of the metal, and the date of assay. Each of the halls (there are currently four: London, Birmingham, Sheffield, and Edinburgh) has a distinguishing mark (e.g. a leopard for London, an anchor for Birmingham). The quality of gold is indicated by a carat mark (22, 18, 14, and 9 carats) before 1975 and as the number of parts per 1000 thereafter. The quality mark for silver in England is a lion (passant) and in Scotland a thistle or lion (rampant). The date is indicated by a letter in a specifically shaped shield. Hallmarks on precious metals are accepted internationally and there are heavy penalties for forging them or selling articles made of these metals (except those exempt) without them. **2** distinctive feature. *–v.* stamp with a hallmark.

hallo var. of HELLO.

halloo /həˈluː/ *int.* inciting dogs to the chase or calling attention. [perhaps from *hallow* pursue with shouts]

hallow /ˈhæləʊ/ *v.* **1** make holy, consecrate. **2** honour as holy. [Old English: related to HOLY]

Hallowe'en /ˌhæləʊ'iːn/ *n.* eve of All Saints' Day, 31 Oct.

♦ **hall test** *n.* marketing research test conducted in a room or hall close to a shopping centre. Consumers, selected at random, are invited to come to the hall to participate in the test, which involves answering questions about their buying habits, purchases, etc.

hallucinate /hə'luːsɪˌneɪt/ *v.* (**-ting**) experience hallucinations. □ **hallucinant** *adj.* & *n.* [Greek *alussō* be uneasy]

hallucination /həˌluːsɪ'neɪʃ(ə)n/ *n.* illusion of seeing or hearing something not actually present. □ **hallucinatory** /hə'luːsɪnətərɪ/ *adj.*

hallucinogen /hə'luːsɪnədʒ(ə)n/ *n.* drug causing hallucinations. □ **hallucinogenic** /-'dʒenɪk/ *adj.*

hallway *n.* entrance-hall or corridor.

halm var. of HAULM.

Halmahera /ˌhælmə'hɜːrə/ largest of the Molucca Islands; there is some fishing and small-scale farming; pop. (1990) 138 000.

halo /'heɪləʊ/ *–n.* (*pl.* **-es**) **1** disc or circle of light shown surrounding the head of a sacred person. **2** glory associated with an idealized person etc. **3** circle of white or coloured light round a luminous body, esp. the sun or moon. *–v.* (**-es, -ed**) surround with a halo. [Greek *halōs* threshing-floor, disc of the sun or moon]

halogen /'hælədʒ(ə)n/ *n.* any of the non-metallic elements (fluorine, chlorine, bromine, iodine, and astatine) which form a salt (e.g. sodium chloride) when combined with a metal. [Greek *hals halos* salt, -GEN]

halon /'heɪlɒn/ *n.* any of various gaseous compounds of carbon, bromine, and other halogens, used to extinguish fires. [related to HALOGEN]

halt[1] /hɔːlt/ *–n.* **1** stop (usu. temporary) (*come to a halt*). **2** minor stopping-place on a local railway line. *–v.* stop; come or bring to a halt. □ **call a halt (to)** decide to stop. [German: related to HOLD]

halt[2] /hɔːlt/ *–v.* (esp. as **halting** *adj.*) proceed hesitantly. *–adj. archaic* lame. □ **haltingly** *adv.* [Old English]

halter /'hɔːltə(r)/ *n.* **1** headstall and rope for leading or tying up a horse etc. **2 a** strap round the neck holding a dress etc. up and leaving the shoulders and back bare. **b** (also **halterneck**) dress etc. held by this. [Old English]

halva /'hælvə/ *n.* confection of sesame flour and honey etc. [Yiddish from Turkish *helva* from Arabic *ḥalwa*]

halve /hɑːv/ *v.* (**-ving**) **1** divide into two halves or parts; share equally between two. **2** reduce by half. **3** *Golf* use the same number of strokes as one's opponent in (a hole or match).

halves *pl.* of HALF.

halyard /'hæljəd/ *n.* (also **halliard**) rope or tackle for raising or lowering a sail, yard, etc. [archaic *hale* drag forcibly]

ham *–n.* **1 a** upper part of a pig's leg salted and dried or smoked for food. **b** meat from this. **2** back of the thigh; thigh and buttock. **3** *colloq.* (often *attrib.*) inexpert or unsubtle actor or piece of acting. **4** *colloq.* operator of an amateur radio station. *–v.* (**-mm-**) (usu. in **ham it up**) *colloq.* overact. [Old English]

♦ **Hambro** /'hæmbrəʊ/, **Charles Eric Alexander** (1930–) British banker, chairman of the banking group Hambros plc (since 1983) and of Guardian Royal Exchange (since 1988). Hambros bank was founded by the Danish Baron Hambro in 1839. Charles Hambro's cousin Jocelyn Olaf Hambro (1919–94) was active in the bank, and Jocelyn's son Rupert Nicholas Hambro (1943–), chairman (since 1994) of J. O. Hambro & Co., was also chairman (1983–86) of the bank.

Hamburg /'hæmbɜːg/ **1** city and major port in N Germany, on the River Elbe; industries include shipbuilding, engineering, and food processing; pop. (est. 1995) 1 705 874. **2** small state (*Land*) comprising the city of Hamburg and the surrounding area; pop. (est. 1990) 1 626 000.

hamburger /'hæmˌbɜːgə(r)/ *n.* cake of minced beef, usu. eaten in a soft bread roll. [HAMBURG]

ham-fisted *adj.* (also **ham-handed**) *colloq.* clumsy.

Hamilton /'hæmɪlt(ə)n/ **1** capital of Bermuda; pop. (est. 1994) 1100. **2** port and industrial city in Canada, in S Ontario, with iron and steel, machinery, and other important heavy industries; city pop. (1991) 318 499; metropolitan area pop. 599 760. **3** city in New Zealand, in Waikato region, North Island, major centre of a lumbering and agricultural region; pop. (1996) 106 700.

Hamitic /hə'mɪtɪk/ *–n.* group of African languages including ancient Egyptian and Berber. *–adj.* of this group. [from the name *Ham* (Gen. 10:6 ff.)]

hamlet /'hæmlɪt/ *n.* small village, esp. without a church. [French *hamelet* diminutive]

♦ **Hamlyn** /'hæmlɪn/, **Paul** (1926–) British publisher, chairman of Reed International Books. Hamlyn founded his first publishing company, Hamlyn Publishing, in 1950 and sold it 15 years later for £2.3 million. He repurchased this company in 1986. In 1971 he founded the Octopus Publishing Group, selling it to Reed International in 1987 for some £214 million. From the sale of his Octopus company he gave £50 million to charity and £100,000 to the Labour Party.

Hammamet /'hæməˌmet/ fishing-port and resort town in NE Tunisia; pop. (1984) 30 441.

hammer *–n.* **1 a** tool with a heavy metal head at right angles to its handle, used for driving nails etc. **b** similar device, as for exploding the charge in a gun, striking the strings of a piano, etc. **2** auctioneer's mallet. **3** metal ball attached to a wire for throwing in an athletic contest. *–v.* **1 a** hit or beat with or as with a hammer. **b** strike loudly. **2 a** drive in (nails) with a hammer. **b** fasten or secure by hammering (*hammered the lid down*). **3** (usu. foll. by *in*) inculcate (ideas, knowledge, etc.) forcefully or repeatedly. **4** *colloq.* defeat utterly; beat up. **5** (foll. by *at*, *away at*) work hard or persistently at. □ **come under the hammer** be sold at auction. **hammer out 1** make flat or smooth by hammering. **2** work out details of (a plan etc.) laboriously. **3** play (a tune, esp. on the piano) loudly or clumsily. [Old English]

hammer and sickle *n.* symbols of the industrial worker and peasant used as an emblem of international communism and formerly of the USSR.

hammer and tongs *adv. colloq.* with great vigour and commotion.

Hammerfest /'hæməˌfest/ fishing-port in NW Norway, on the island of Kvaløya; pop. (est. 1991) 6900. It is the northernmost town of Europe.

hammerhead *n.* shark with a flattened head and with eyes in lateral extensions of it.

♦ **hammering** *n.* **1** *colloq.* total defeat; beating. **2** announcement on the London Stock Exchange that a broker is unable to meet his obligations, formerly (until 1970) introduced by three blows of a hammer by a waiter and followed by the broker's name.

hammerlock *n. Wrestling* hold in which the arm is twisted and bent behind the back.

hammer-toe *n.* toe bent permanently downwards.

hammock /'hæmək/ *n.* bed of canvas or rope network suspended by cords at the ends. [Spanish from Carib]

hammy *adj.* (**-ier, -iest**) *colloq.* over-theatrical.

hamper[1] *n.* large basket, usu. with a hinged lid and containing food. [French *hanap* goblet]

hamper[2] *v.* prevent the free movement of; hinder. [origin unknown]

Hampshire /'hæmpʃɪə(r)/ county in S England; pop. (est. 1994) 1 605 700; county town, Winchester. Primarily agricultural, it has oil-refining, chemical, and pharmaceutical industries.

hamster *n.* mouselike rodent with a short tail and large cheek-pouches for storing food. [German]

hamstring *–n.* **1** each of five tendons at the back of the knee. **2** great tendon at the back of the hock in quadrupeds. *–v.* (*past* and *past part.* **-strung** or **-stringed**)

1 cripple by cutting the hamstrings of (a person or animal). **2** impair the activity or efficiency of.

hand *–n.* **1 a** end part of the human arm beyond the wrist. **b** (in other primates) end part of a forelimb. **2 a** (often in *pl.*) control, management, custody, disposal (*is in good hands*). **b** agency or influence (*suffered at their hands*). **c** share in an action; active support (*had a hand in it; give me a hand*). **3** thing like a hand, esp. the pointer of a clock. **4** right or left side or direction relative to a person or thing. **5 a** skill (*has a hand for making pastry*). **b** person skilful in some respect. **6** person who does or makes something, esp. distinctively (*picture by the same hand*). **7** person's writing or its style. **8** person etc. as a source (*at first hand*). **9** pledge of marriage. **10** manual worker, esp. at a factory or farm; member of a ship's crew. **11 a** playing-cards dealt to a player. **b** round of play. **12** *colloq.* burst of applause. **13** unit of measure of a horse's height, 4 inches (10.16 cm). **14** forehock of pork. **15** (*attrib.*) **a** operated by or held in the hand (*hand-drill*). **b** done by hand, not machine (*hand-knitted*). *–v.* **1** (foll. by *in, to, over*, etc.) deliver; transfer by hand or otherwise. **2** *colloq.* give away too readily (*handed them the advantage*). □ **all hands** entire crew or workforce. **at hand 1** close by. **2** about to happen. **by hand 1** by a person, not a machine. **2** delivered privately, not by post. **from hand to mouth** satisfying only one's immediate needs. **get** (or **have** or **keep) one's hand in** become (or be or remain) in practice. **hand down 1** pass ownership or use of to a later generation etc. **2 a** transmit (a decision) from a higher court etc. **b** *US* express (an opinion or verdict). **hand it to** *colloq.* award deserved praise to. **hand on** pass (a thing) to the next in a series. **hand out 1** serve, distribute. **2** award, allocate (*handed out stiff penalties*). **hand round** serve, distribute. **hands down** with no difficulty; completely. **in hand 1** receiving attention. **2** in reserve. **3** under control. **on hand** available. **on the one** (or **the other) hand** from one (or another) point of view. **out of hand 1** out of control. **2** peremptorily (*refused out of hand*). **put** (or **set) one's hand to** start work on; engage in. **to hand** within easy reach; available. **turn one's hand to** undertake (as a new activity). □ **-handed** *adj.* (in *comb.*). [Old English]

handbag *n.* small bag carried esp. by a woman.

handball *n.* **1** game with a ball thrown by hand among players or against a wall. **2** *Football* intentional touching of the ball, constituting a foul.

handbell *n.* small bell for ringing by hand, esp. one of a set.

handbill *n.* printed notice distributed by hand.

handbook *n.* short manual or guidebook.

handbrake *n.* brake operated by hand.

h. & c. *abbr.* hot and cold (water).

handcart *n.* small cart pushed or drawn by hand.

handclap *n.* clapping of the hands.

handcraft *–n.* = HANDICRAFT. *–v.* make by handicraft.

handcuff *–n.* each of a pair of linked metal rings for securing a prisoner's wrist(s). *–v.* put handcuffs on.

handful *n.* (*pl.* **-s**) **1** quantity that fills the hand. **2** small number or amount. **3** *colloq.* troublesome person or task.

hand-grenade see GRENADE.

handgun *n.* small firearm held in and fired with one hand.

handhold *n.* something for the hand to grip on (in climbing etc.).

handicap /'hændɪ,kæp/ *–n.* **1** physical or mental disability. **2** thing that makes progress or success difficult. **3 a** disadvantage imposed on a superior competitor to make chances more equal. **b** race etc. in which this is imposed. **4** number of strokes by which a golfer normally exceeds par for a course. *–v.* (**-pp-**) **1** impose a handicap on. **2** place at a disadvantage. [*hand i'* (= in) *cap* describing a kind of sporting lottery]

handicapped *adj.* suffering from a physical or mental disability.

handicraft /'hændɪ,krɑːft/ *n.* work requiring manual and artistic skill. [from earlier HANDCRAFT]

hand in glove *adj.* in collusion or association.

hand in hand *adv.* **1** in close association (*power and money go hand in hand*). **2** (**hand-in-hand**) holding hands.

handiwork /'hændɪ,wɜːk/ *n.* work done or a thing made by hand, or by a particular person. [Old English]

handkerchief /'hæŋkətʃɪf/ *n.* (*pl.* **-s** or **-chieves** /-,tʃiːvz/) square of cloth for wiping one's nose etc.

handle /'hænd(ə)l/ *–n.* **1** part by which a thing is held, carried, or controlled. **2** fact that may be taken advantage of (*gave a handle to his critics*). **3** *colloq.* personal title. *–v.* (**-ling**) **1** touch, feel, operate, or move with the hands. **2** manage, deal with (*can handle people*). **3** deal in (goods). **4** treat (a subject). [Old English: related to HAND]

handlebar *n.* (usu. in *pl.*) steering-bar of a bicycle etc.

handlebar moustache *n.* thick moustache with curved ends.

handler *n.* **1** person who handles or deals in something. **2** person who trains and looks after an animal (esp. a police dog).

handmade *adj.* made by hand as opposed to machine.

handmaid *n.* (also **handmaiden**) *archaic* female servant.

hand-me-down *n.* article of clothing etc. passed on from another person.

hand-out *n.* **1** thing given free to a needy person. **2** statement given to the press etc.; notes given out in a class etc.

hand-over *n.* handing over.

hand-over-fist *adv. colloq.* with rapid progress.

hand-pick *v.* choose carefully or personally.

handrail *n.* narrow rail for holding as a support.

handsaw *n.* saw worked by one hand.

handset *n.* telephone mouthpiece and earpiece as one unit.

handshake *n.* **1** clasping of a person's hand as a greeting etc. **2** *Computing* exchange of signals that establishes communication between two or more devices (by synchronizing them) and allows data to be transferred.

hands off *–int.* warning not to touch or interfere with something. *–adj.* & *adv.* (also **hands-off**) not requiring the manual use of controls.

handsome /'hænsəm/ *adj.* (**handsomer, handsomest**) **1** (usu. of a man) good-looking. **2** (of an object) imposing, attractive. **3 a** generous, liberal (*handsome present*). **b** (of a price, fortune, etc.) considerable. □ **handsomely** *adv.*

hands on (also **hands-on**) *–adj.* & *adv.* of or requiring personal operation at a keyboard. *–attrib. adj.* practical rather than theoretical (*lacks hands-on experience*).

handspring *n.* gymnastic feat consisting of a handstand, somersaulting, and landing in a standing position.

handstand *n.* supporting oneself on one's hands with one's feet in the air.

hand-to-hand *adj.* (of fighting) at close quarters.

handwork *n.* work done with the hands. □ **handworked** *adj.*

handwriting *n.* **1** writing done with a pen, pencil, etc. **2** person's particular style of this. □ **handwritten** *adj.*

handy *adj.* (**-ier, -iest**) **1** convenient to handle or use; useful. **2** ready to hand. **3** clever with the hands. □ **handily** *adv.* **handiness** *n.*

handyman *n.* person able to do occasional repairs etc.; odd-job man.

hang *–v.* (*past* and *past part.* **hung** except in sense 7) **1 a** secure or cause to be supported from above, esp. with the lower part free. **b** (foll. by *up, on, on to*, etc.) attach by suspending from the top. **2** set up (a door etc.) on hinges. **3** place (a picture) on a wall or in an exhibition. **4** attach (wallpaper) to a wall. **5** (foll. by *on*) *colloq.* blame (a thing) on (a person) (*can't hang that on me*). **6** (foll. by *with*) decorate by suspending pictures etc. (*hall hung with tapestries*). **7** (*past* and *past part.* **hanged**) **a** suspend or be suspended by the neck with a noosed rope until dead, esp. as a form of capital punishment. **b** as a mild oath (*hang the expense*). **8** let droop (*hang one's head*). **9** suspend (meat or game) from a hook and leave until dry, tender, or high. **10** be or remain hung (in various senses). **11** remain static in the air. **12** (often foll. by *over*) be present or imminent, esp. oppressively or threateningly (*a hush hung over the room*). **13** (foll. by *on*) **a** be contingent or dependent on (*everything hangs on his reply*). **b** listen closely to (*hangs on my every word*). –*n.* way a thing hangs or falls. □ **get the hang of** *colloq.* understand the technique or meaning of. **hang about** (or **around**) **1 a** stand about or spend time aimlessly; not move away. **b** linger near (a person or place). **2** (often foll. by *with*) *colloq.* associate with. **hang back** show reluctance to act or move. **hang fire** be slow in taking action or in progressing. **hang heavily** (or **heavy**) (of time) seem to pass slowly. **hang in** *US colloq.* **1** persist, persevere. **2** linger. **hang on 1** (often foll. by *to*) continue to hold or grasp. **2** (foll. by *to*) retain; fail to give back. **3** *colloq.* **a** wait for a short time. **b** (in telephoning) not ring off during a pause in the conversation. **4** *colloq.* continue; persevere. **hang out 1** suspend from a window, clothes-line, etc. **2 a** protrude downwards (*shirt hanging out*). **b** (foll. by *of*) lean out of (a window etc.). **3** *slang* frequent or live in a place. **hang together 1** make sense. **2** remain associated. **hang up 1** hang from a hook etc. **2** (often foll. by *on*) end a telephone conversation by replacing the receiver (*he hung up on me*). **3** (usu. in *passive*, foll. by *on*) *slang* be a psychological problem or obsession for (*is hung up on her father*). **not care** (or **give) a hang** *colloq.* not care at all. [Old English]

hangar /'hæŋə(r)/ *n.* building for housing aircraft etc. [French]

hangdog *adj.* shamefaced.

hanger *n.* **1** person or thing that hangs. **2** (in full **coat-hanger**) shaped piece of wood etc. for hanging clothes on.

hanger-on *n.* (*pl.* **hangers-on**) follower or dependant, esp. an unwelcome one.

hang-glider *n.* glider with a fabric wing on a light frame, from which the operator is suspended. □ **hang-glide** *v.* **hang-gliding** *n.*

hanging *n.* **1** execution by suspending by the neck. **2** (usu. in *pl.*) draperies hung on a wall etc.

hangman *n.* **1** executioner who hangs condemned persons. **2** word-game for two players, with failed guesses recorded by drawing a representation of a gallows.

hangnail *n.* = AGNAIL.

hang-out *n.* *slang* place frequented by a person; haunt.

hangover *n.* **1** severe headache etc. from drinking too much alcohol. **2** survival from the past.

♦ **Hang Seng Index** /hæŋ seŋ/ *n.* arithmetically weighted index based on the capital value of 33 stocks on the Hong Kong Stock Exchange. [*Hang Seng*, name of a bank]

---

hang-up *n.* *slang* emotional problem or inhibition.

Hangzhou /hæŋ'dʒəʊ/ (also **Hangchow** /hæŋ'ʃaʊ/) city in E China, capital of Zhejiang province; products include jute, silk, tea, and chemicals; pop. (est. 1995) 1 340 000.

hank *n.* coil or skein of wool or thread etc. [Old Norse]

hanker *v.* (foll. by *for*, *after*, or *to* + infin.) long for; crave. □ **hankering** *n.* [from obsolete *hank*]

hanky /'hæŋkɪ/ *n.* (also **hankie**) (*pl.* **-ies**) *colloq.* handkerchief. [abbreviation]

hanky-panky /ˌhæŋkɪ'pæŋkɪ/ *n.* *slang* **1** naughtiness, esp. sexual. **2** double-dealing; trickery. [origin unknown]

Hannover see HANOVER.

Hanoi /hæ'nɔɪ/ capital of Vietnam, and formerly of North Vietnam before the reunification of the country; industries include paper, textiles, and engineering; pop. (est. 1992) 2 154 900.

Hanover /'hænəvə(r)/ (German **Hannover**) city in N Germany, capital of Lower Saxony; pop. (est. 1995) 525 764. A major industrial centre and the site of an annual international industrial fair, it manufacture machinery, motor vehicles, and textiles.

Hanoverian /ˌhænə'vɪərɪən/ *adj.* of British sovereign from George I to Victoria. [HANOVER]

Hansard /'hænsɑːd/ *n.* official verbatim record of debate in the British Parliament. [*Hansard*, name of its firs printer]

Hansen's disease /'hæns(ə)nz/ *n.* leprosy. [*Hansen* name of a physician]

hansom /'hænsəm/ *n.* (in full **hansom cab**) *hist.* two wheeled horse-drawn cab. [*Hansom*, name of an archi tect]

♦ **Hanson** /'hæns(ə)n/, **James Edward, Baron Hanso** (1922–) British businessman, co-founder and chairma (since 1965) of Hanson plc, a group that has specialize in acquiring large companies and selling the component at a profit. In May 1992 Hanson bought a 2.8% stake in IC

Hants /hænts/ *abbr.* Hampshire. [Old English *Hantescire*

Hanukkah /'hɑːnəkə/ *n.* Jewish festival of lights, com memorating the purification of the Temple in 165 BC [Hebrew *ḥănukkāh* consecration]

haphazard /hæp'hæzəd/ *adj.* done etc. by chance; ran dom. □ **haphazardly** *adv.* [archaic *hap* chance, luck from Old Norse *happ*]

hapless *adj.* unlucky.

haploid /'hæplɔɪd/ *adj.* (of an organism or cell) with a single set of chromosomes. [Greek *haplous* single, *eidos* form]

happen /'hæpən/ *v.* **1** occur (by chance or otherwise). **2** (foll. by *to* + infin.) have the (good or bad) fortune to (*I happened to meet her*). **3** (foll. by *to*) be the (esp. unwelcome) fate or experience of (*what happened to you?*). **4** (foll. by *on*) encounter or discover by chance. □ **as it happens** in fact; in reality. [related to HAPHAZARD]

happening *n.* **1** event. **2** improvised or spontaneous theatrical etc. performance.

happy /'hæpɪ/ *adj.* (**-ier**, **-iest**) **1** feeling or showing pleasure or contentment. **2 a** fortunate; characterized by happiness. **b** (of words, behaviour, etc.) apt, pleasing. □ **happily** *adv.* **happiness** *n.*

happy-go-lucky *adj.* cheerfully casual.

happy hour *n.* time of the day when goods, esp. drinks, are sold at reduced prices.

happy medium *n.* compromise; avoidance of extremes.

hara-kiri /ˌhærə'kɪrɪ/ *n.* ritual suicide by disembowelment with a sword, formerly practised by samurai to avoid dishonour. [Japanese *hara* belly, *kiri* cutting]

♦ **hara-kiri swap** *n.* financial swap made with no profit margin.

---

harangue /hə'ræŋ/ –*n.* lengthy and earnest speech. –*v.* (**-guing**) make a harangue to; lecture. [French *arenge* from medieval Latin]

Harare /hə'rɑːrɪ/ (formerly **Salisbury**) capital of Zimbabwe; pop. (1992) 1 184 169. The industrial and commercial centre of a tobacco-growing region, it also has metallurgical, textile, and food-processing industries.

harass /'hærəs, hə'ræs/ *v.* **1** trouble and annoy continually. **2** make repeated attacks on. □ **harassment** *n.* [French]

■ **Usage** The second pronunciation given, with the stress on the second syllable, is common, but is considered incorrect by some people.

Harbin /'hɑːbɪn/ (also **Haerhpin**) city in NE China, capital of Heilongjiang province and an industrial and commercial centre; pop. (est. 1991) 2 830 000.

harbinger /'hɑːbɪndʒə(r)/ *n.* **1** person or thing that announces or signals the approach of another. **2** forerunner. [Germanic: related to HARBOUR]

harbour /'hɑːbə(r)/ (*US* **harbor**) –*n.* **1** place of shelter for ships. **2** shelter; refuge. –*v.* **1** give shelter to (esp. a criminal). **2** keep in one's mind (esp. resentment etc.). [Old English, = army shelter]

harbour-master *n.* official in charge of a harbour.

hard *–adj.* **1** (of a substance etc.) firm and solid. **2 a** difficult to understand, explain, or accomplish. **b** (foll. by *to* + infin.) not easy to (*hard to please*). **3** difficult to bear (*a hard life*). **4** unfeeling; severely critical. **5** (of a season or the weather) severe. **6** unpleasant to the senses, harsh (*hard colours*). **7 a** strenuous, enthusiastic, intense (*a hard worker*). **b** severe, uncompromising (*a hard bargain*). **c** *Polit.* extreme; most radical (*the hard right*). **8 a** (of liquor) strongly alcoholic. **b** (of drugs) potent and addictive. **c** (of pornography) highly obscene. **9** (of water) containing mineral salts that make lathering difficult. **10** established; not disputable (*hard facts*). **11** (of currency, prices, etc.) high; not likely to fall in value. **12** (of a consonant) guttural (as *c* in *cat*, *g* in *go*). *–adv.* strenuously, intensely, copiously (*try hard*; *raining hard*). □ **be hard on 1** be difficult for. **2** be severe in one's treatment or criticism of. **3** be unpleasant to (the senses). **be hard put to it** (usu. foll. by *to* + infin.) find it difficult. **hard by** close by. **hard on** (or **upon**) close to in pursuit etc. □ **hardish** *adj.* **hardness** *n.* [Old English]

hard and fast *adj.* (of a rule or distinction) definite, unalterable, strict.

hardback *–adj.* bound in boards covered with cloth etc. *–n.* hardback book.

hardbitten *adj. colloq.* tough and cynical; hard-headed.

hardboard *n.* stiff board made of compressed and treated wood pulp.

hard-boiled *adj.* **1** (of an egg) boiled until the white and yolk are solid. **2** *colloq.* (of a person) tough, shrewd.

hard cash *n.* negotiable coins and banknotes.

♦ **hard commodities** *n.pl.* metals and other solid raw materials.

---

hard copy *n.* material printed by a computer on paper; permanent copy.

hardcore *n.* solid material, esp. rubble, as road-foundation.

hard core *n.* **1** irreducible nucleus. **2** *colloq.* **a** the most committed members of a society etc. **b** conservative or reactionary minority (see also HARDCORE).

hard-core *adj.* **1** forming a nucleus. **2** blatant, uncompromising. **3** (of pornography) explicit, obscene.

♦ **hard currency** *n.* currency commonly accepted throughout the world, usu. a currency of a Western industrialized country although other currencies have achieved this status, esp. within regional trading blocs. Holdings of hard currency are valued because of their universal purchasing power. Countries with soft currencies go to great lengths to obtain and maintain stocks of hard currencies, often imposing strict restrictions on their use by the private citizen.

♦ **hard disk** *n. Computing* rigid magnetic disk enclosed in a sealed container, used to store information. Almost always non-removable, hard disks are used in various sizes, ranging from packs containing a stack of disks in a plastic hood to Winchester disks. Hard disks can hold more information than floppy disks, are more reliable, and operate more quickly. See also MAGNETIC DISK.

---

hard-done-by *adj.* unfairly treated.

harden *v.* **1** make or become hard or harder. **2** become, or make (one's attitude etc.), less sympathetic. **3** (of prices etc.) cease to fall or fluctuate. □ **harden off** inure (a plant) to the cold by gradually increasing its exposure.

hardening of the arteries *n.* = ARTERIOSCLEROSIS.

hard-headed *adj.* practical; not sentimental. □ **hard-headedness** *n.*

hard-hearted *adj.* unfeeling. □ **hard-heartedness** *n.*

hardihood /ˈhɑːdɪˌhʊd/ *n.* boldness, daring.

hard labour *n.* heavy manual work as a punishment, esp. in a prison.

hard line *n.* unyielding adherence to a policy. □ **hard-liner** *n.*

hard luck *n.* worse fortune than one deserves.

hardly *adv.* **1** scarcely; only just (*hardly knew me*). **2** only with difficulty (*can hardly see*). **3** surely not (*can hardly have realised*). □ **hardly any** almost no; almost none. **hardly ever** very seldom.

hard-nosed *adj. colloq.* realistic, uncompromising.

hard of hearing *adj.* somewhat deaf.

hard-on *n. coarse slang* erection of the penis.

hard pad *n.* form of distemper in dogs etc.

hard palate *n.* front part of the palate.

hard-pressed *adj.* **1** closely pursued. **2** burdened with urgent business.

hard roe see ROE[1].

hard sell *n.* aggressive salesmanship.

hardship *n.* **1** severe suffering or privation. **2** circumstance causing this.

hard shoulder *n.* hard surface alongside a motorway for stopping on in an emergency.

hard tack *n. Naut.* ship's biscuit.

hardtop *n.* car with a rigid (usu. detachable) roof.

hard up *adj.* short of money.

hardware *n.* **1** tools and household articles of metal etc. **2** heavy machinery or armaments. **3** mechanical and electronic components of a computer, including the central processing unit, disk drive, and printer. Cf. SOFTWARE.

hard-wearing *adj.* able to stand much wear.

hard-wired *adj.* (of circuitry) permanently interconnected so that its function cannot be changed.

hardwood *n.* wood from a deciduous broad-leaved tree.

hard-working *adj.* diligent.

hardy /ˈhɑːdɪ/ *adj.* (**-ier, -iest**) **1** robust; capable of enduring difficult conditions. **2** (of a plant) able to grow in the open air all year. □ **hardiness** *n.* [French *hardi* made bold]

hardy annual *n.* annual plant that may be sown in the open.

hare *–n.* mammal like a large rabbit, with long ears, short tail, and long hind legs. *–v.* (**-ring**) run rapidly. [Old English]

harebell *n.* plant with pale-blue bell-shaped flowers.

hare-brained *adj.* rash, wild.

harelip *n.* often *offens.* = CLEFT LIP.

harem /ˈhɑːriːm/ *n.* **1** women of a Muslim household. **2** their quarters. [Arabic, = sanctuary]

Hargeisa /hɑːˈgeɪsə/ city and trading centre in NW Somalia, capital of the former British Somaliland; pop. (1988) 400 000.

haricot /ˈhærɪˌkəʊ/ *n.* (in full **haricot bean**) variety of French bean with small white seeds dried and used as a vegetable. [French]

hark *v.* (usu. in *imper.*) *archaic* listen attentively. □ **hark back** revert to earlier topic. [Old English]

harlequin /ˈhɑːlɪkwɪn/ *–n.* (**Harlequin**) name of a mute character in pantomime, usu. masked and dressed in a diamond-patterned costume. *–attrib. adj.* in varied colours. [French]

harlequinade /ˌhɑːlɪkwɪˈneɪd/ *n.* **1** part of a pantomime featuring Harlequin. **2** piece of buffoonery.

harlot /ˈhɑːlət/ *n. archaic* prostitute. □ **harlotry** *n.* [French, = knave]

harm *–n.* hurt, damage. *–v.* cause harm to. □ **out of harm's way** in safety. [Old English]

harmful *adj.* causing or likely to cause harm. □ **harmfully** *adv.* **harmfulness** *n.*

harmless *adj.* **1** not able or likely to cause harm. **2** inoffensive. □ **harmlessly** *adv.* **harmlessness** *n.*

harmonic /hɑːˈmɒnɪk/ *–adj.* of or relating to harmony; harmonious. *–n. Mus.* overtone accompanying (and forming a note with) a fundamental at a fixed interval. □ **harmonically** *adv.*

harmonica *n.* small rectangular musical instrument played by blowing and sucking air through it.

harmonious /hɑːˈməʊnɪəs/ *adj.* **1** sweet-sounding; tuneful. **2** forming a pleasing or consistent whole. **3** free from disagreement or dissent. □ **harmoniously** *adv.*

harmonium /hɑːˈməʊnɪəm/ *n.* keyboard instrument in which the notes are produced by air driven through metal reeds by foot-operated bellows. [Latin: related to HARMONY]

harmonize /ˈhɑːməˌnaɪz/ *v.* (also **-ise**) (**-zing** or **-sing**) **1** add notes to (a melody) to produce harmony. **2** bring into or be in harmony. **3** make or form a pleasing or consistent whole. □ **harmonization** /-ˈzeɪʃ(ə)n/ *n.*

harmony /ˈhɑːmənɪ/ *n.* (*pl.* **-ies**) **1** combination of simultaneously sounded musical notes to produce chords and chord progressions, esp. as creating a pleasing effect. **2 a** apt or aesthetic arrangement of parts. **b** pleasing effect of this. **3** agreement, concord. □ **in harmony 1** in agreement. **2** (of singing etc.) producing chords; not discordant. [Greek *harmonia* joining]

harness /ˈhɑːnɪs/ –*n.* **1** equipment of straps etc. by which a horse is fastened to a cart etc. and controlled. **2** similar arrangement for fastening a thing to a person's body. –*v.* **1 a** put a harness on. **b** (foll. by *to*) attach by harness to. **2** make use of (natural resources), esp. to produce energy. □ **in harness** in the routine of daily work. [French *harneis* military equipment]

harp –*n.* large upright stringed instrument plucked with the fingers. –*v.* (foll. by *on, on about*) talk repeatedly and tediously about. □ **harpist** *n.* [Old English]

harpoon /hɑːˈpuːn/ –*n.* barbed spearlike missile with a rope attached, for catching whales etc. –*v.* spear with a harpoon. [Greek *harpē* sickle]

harpsichord /ˈhɑːpsɪˌkɔːd/ *n.* keyboard instrument with horizontal strings plucked mechanically. □ **harpsichordist** *n.* [Latin *harpa* harp, *chorda* string]

harpy /ˈhɑːpɪ/ *n.* (*pl.* **-ies**) **1** mythological monster with a woman's head and body and a bird's wings and claws. **2** grasping unscrupulous person. [Greek *harpuiai* snatchers]

harridan /ˈhærɪd(ə)n/ *n.* bad-tempered old woman. [origin uncertain]

harrier /ˈhærɪə(r)/ *n.* **1** hound used for hunting hares. **2** group of cross-country runners. **3** hawklike bird of prey. [from HARE, HARRY]

Harrisburg /ˈhærɪsˌbɜːg/ city in the US, capital of Pennsylvania; manufactures include bricks, steel, and clothing; pop. (est. 1992) 53 430.

harrow /ˈhærəʊ/ –*n.* heavy frame with iron teeth dragged over ploughed land to break up clods etc. –*v.* **1** draw a harrow over (land). **2** (usu. as **harrowing** *adj.*) distress greatly. [Old Norse *hervi*]

harry /ˈhærɪ/ *v.* (**-ies, -ied**) **1** ravage or despoil. **2** harass. [Old English]

harsh *adj.* **1** unpleasantly rough or sharp, esp. to the senses. **2** severe, cruel. □ **harshen** *v.* **harshly** *adv.* **harshness** *n.* [Low German]

hart *n.* (*pl.* same or **-s**) male of the (esp. red) deer, esp. after its 5th year. [Old English]

hartebeest /ˈhɑːtɪˌbiːst/ *n.* large African antelope with curving horns. [Afrikaans]

Hartford /ˈhɑːtfəd/ city in the US, capital of Connecticut; pop. (est. 1994) 124 196. It is a centre for the US insurance industry.

harum-scarum /ˌheərəmˈskeərəm/ *colloq.* –*adj.* wild and reckless. –*n.* such a person. [rhyming formation on HARE, SCARE]

harvest /ˈhɑːvɪst/ –*n.* **1 a** process of gathering in crops etc. **b** season of this. **2** season's yield. **3** product of any action. –*v.* gather as harvest, reap. [Old English]

harvester *n.* **1** reaper. **2** reaping-machine, esp. with sheaf-binding.

harvest festival *n.* Christian thanksgiving service for the harvest.

♦ **harvesting strategy** *n.* strategy whereby a short-term profit is made from a particular product shortly before withdrawing it from the market, often achieved by reducing the marketing support it enjoys, e.g. advertising, on the assumption that the effects of earlier advertising will still be felt and the product will continue to sell.

harvest moon *n.* full moon nearest to the autumn equinox (22 or 23 Sept.).

harvest mouse *n.* small mouse nesting in the stalks of growing grain.

♦ **Harvey-Jones** /ˈhɑːvɪ ˈdʒəʊnz/, **Sir John** (1924–) British businessman, chairman of ICI (1982–7) and deputy chairman of Grand Metropolitan plc (1987–91). He became widely known through his BBC TV *Troubleshooter* series (1990, 1991, 1992, 1995), in which he gave advice to ailing companies.

Haryana /hʌrɪˈɑːnə/ state of N India; pop. (1991) 16 463 648; capital, Chandigarh. It is mainly agricultural, producing grain, sugar cane, and cotton, but has some light industry.

has *3rd sing. present* of HAVE.

has-been *n. colloq.* person or thing of declined importance.

hash[1] –*n.* **1** dish of cooked meat cut into small pieces and reheated. **2 a** mixture; jumble. **b** mess. **3** recycled material. –*v.* (often foll. by *up*) recycle (old material). □ **make a hash of** *colloq.* make a mess of; bungle. **settle a person's hash** *colloq.* deal with and subdue a person. [French *hacher* cut up]

hash[2] *n. colloq.* hashish. [abbreviation]

hashish /ˈhæʃɪʃ/ *n.* resinous product of hemp, smoked or chewed as a narcotic. [Arabic]

haslet /ˈhæzlɪt/ *n.* pieces of (esp. pig's) offal cooked together, usu. as a meat loaf. [French *hastelet*]

hasn't /ˈhæz(ə)nt/ *contr.* has not.

hasp /hɑːsp/ *n.* hinged metal clasp fitting over a staple and secured by a padlock. [Old English]

Hasselt /ˈhæselt/ city in NE Belgium, capital of Limbourg province; industries include brewing and distilling; pop. (est. 1995) 67 486.

hassle /ˈhæs(ə)l/ *colloq.* –*n.* trouble; problem; argument. –*v.* (**-ling**) harass, annoy. [originally a dial. word]

hassock /ˈhæsək/ *n.* thick firm cushion for kneeling on. [Old English]

haste /heɪst/ –*n.* urgency of movement or action; excessive hurry. –*v.* (**-ting**) *archaic* = HASTEN 1. □ **in haste** quickly, hurriedly. **make haste** hurry; be quick. [French from Germanic]

hasten /ˈheɪs(ə)n/ *v.* **1** make haste; hurry. **2** cause to occur or be ready or be done sooner.

hasty /ˈheɪstɪ/ *adj.* (**-ier, -iest**) **1** hurried; acting too quickly. **2** said, made, or done too quickly or too soon; rash. □ **hastily** *adv.* **hastiness** *n.*

hat *n.* **1** (esp. outdoor) covering for the head. **2** *colloq.* person's present capacity (*wearing his managerial hat*). □ **keep it under one's hat** *colloq.* keep it secret. **pass the hat round** collect contributions of money. **take one's hat off to** *colloq.* acknowledge admiration for. [Old English]

hatband *n.* band of ribbon etc. round a hat above the brim.

hatbox *n.* box to hold a hat, esp. for travelling.

hatch[1] *n.* **1** opening in a wall between a kitchen and dining-room for serving food. **2** opening or door in an aircraft etc. **3 a** = HATCHWAY. **b** cover for this. [Old English]

hatch[2] –*v.* **1 a** (often foll. by *out*) (of a young bird or fish etc.) emerge from the egg. **b** (of an egg) produce a young animal. **2** incubate (an egg). **3** (also foll. by *up*) devise (a plot etc.). –*n.* **1** act of hatching. **2** brood hatched. [earlier *hacche*, from Germanic]

hatch[3] *v.* mark with close parallel lines. □ **hatching** *n.* [French *hacher*: related to HASH[1]]

hatchback *n.* car with a sloping back hinged at the top to form a door.

hatchet /ˈhætʃɪt/ *n.* light short-handled axe. [French *hachette*]

hatchet man *n. colloq.* person hired to kill, dismiss, or otherwise harm another.

hatchway *n.* opening in a ship's deck for raising and lowering cargo.

hate *–v.* **(-ting) 1** dislike intensely. **2** *colloq.* **a** dislike. **b** be reluctant (to do something) (*I hate to disturb you; I hate fighting*). *–n.* **1** hatred. **2** *colloq.* hated person or thing. [Old English]

hateful *adj.* arousing hatred.

hatpin *n.* long pin for securing a hat to the hair.

hatred /'heɪtrɪd/ *n.* extreme dislike or ill will.

hatstand *n.* stand with hooks for hanging hats etc. on.

hatter *n.* maker or seller of hats.

hat trick *n.* **1** *Cricket* taking of three wickets by the same bowler with three successive balls. **2** three consecutive successes etc.

haughty /'hɔːtɪ/ *adj.* **(-ier, -iest)** arrogant and disdainful. □ **haughtily** *adv.* **haughtiness** *n.* [*haught, haut* from French, = high]

haul /hɔːl/ *–v.* **1** pull or drag forcibly. **2** transport by lorry, cart, etc. **3** turn a ship's course. **4** *colloq.* (usu. foll. by *up*) bring for reprimand or trial. *–n.* **1** hauling. **2** amount gained or acquired. **3** distance to be traversed (*a short haul*). □ **haul over the coals** see COAL. [French *haler* from Old Norse *hala*]

haulage *n.* **1** commercial transport of goods, esp. by road. **2** charge for this.

haulier /'hɔːlɪə(r)/ *n.* person or firm engaged in the transport of goods; haulage contractor.

haulm /hɔːm/ *n.* (also **halm**) **1** stalk or stem. **2** stalks or stems of peas, beans, etc., collectively. [Old English]

haunch /hɔːntʃ/ *n.* **1** fleshy part of the buttock with the thigh. **2** leg and loin of a deer etc. as food. [French from Germanic]

haunt /hɔːnt/ *–v.* **1** (of a ghost) visit (a place) regularly. **2** frequent (a place). **3** linger in the mind of. *–n.* place frequented by a person or animal. [French from Germanic]

haunting *adj.* (of a memory, melody, etc.) tending to linger in the mind; poignant, evocative.

haute couture /ˌəʊt kuː'tjʊə(r)/ *n.* high fashion; leading fashion houses or their products. [French]

haute cuisine /ˌəʊt kwɪ'ziːn/ *n.* high-class cookery. [French]

hauteur /əʊ'tɜː(r)/ *n.* haughtiness. [French]

Havana /hə'vænə/ capital of Cuba and chief port of the West Indies, famous for its cigars; pop. (est. 1994) 2 241 000. *–n.* cigar made at Havana or elsewhere in Cuba.

have /hæv, həv/ *–v.* **(-ving;** *3rd sing. present* **has** /hæz/; *past* and *past part.* **had) 1** as an auxiliary verb with *past part.* or *ellipt.*, to form the perfect, pluperfect, and future perfect tenses, and the conditional mood (*has, had, will have, seen; had I known, I would have gone; yes, I have*). **2** own or be able to use; be provided with (*has a car; had no time*). **3** hold in a certain relationship (*has a sister; had no equals*). **4** contain as a part or quality (*box has a lid; has big eyes*). **5 a** experience (*had a good time, a shock, a pain*). **b** be subjected to a specified state (*had my car stolen; book has a page missing*). **c** cause (a person or thing) to be in a particular state or take particular action (*had him sacked; had us worried; had my hair cut; had a copy made; had them to stay*). **6 a** engage in (an activity) (*have an argument, sex*). **b** hold (a meeting, party, etc.). **7** eat or drink (*had a beer*). **8** (usu. in *neg.*) accept or tolerate; permit to (*I won't have it; won't have you say that*). **9 a** feel (*have no doubt; has nothing against me*). **b** show (mercy, pity, etc.). **c** (foll. by *to* + infin.) show by action that one is influenced by (a feeling, quality, etc.) (*have the sense to stop*). **10 a** give birth to (offspring). **b** conceive mentally (an idea etc.). **11** receive, obtain (*had a letter from him; not a ticket to be had*). **12** be burdened with or committed to (*has a job to do*). **13 a** have obtained (a qualification) (*has six O levels*). **b** know (a language) (*has no Latin*). **14** *slang* **a** get the better of (*I had him there*). **b** (usu. in *passive*) cheat, deceive (*you were had*). **15** *coarse slang* have sexual intercourse with. *–n.* **1** (usu. in *pl.*) *colloq.* person with wealth or resources. **2** *slang* swindle. □ **had best** see BEST. **had better** see BETTER. **have got to** *colloq.* = have *to*. **have had it** *colloq.* **1** have missed one's chance. **2** have passed one's prime. **3** have been killed, defeated, etc. **have it 1** (foll. by *that*) maintain that. **2** win a decision in a vote etc. **3** *colloq.* have found the answer etc. **have it away** (or **off**) *coarse slang* have sexual intercourse. **have it in for** *colloq.* be hostile or ill-disposed towards. **have it out** (often foll. by *with*) *colloq.* attempt to settle a dispute by argument. **have on 1** wear (clothes). **2** have (an engagement). **3** *colloq.* tease, hoax. **have to** be obliged to, must. **have up** *colloq.* bring (a person) before a judge, interviewer, etc. [Old English]

haven /'heɪv(ə)n/ *n.* **1** refuge. **2** harbour, port. [Old English]

have-not *n.* (usu. in *pl.*) *colloq.* person lacking wealth or resources.

haven't /'hæv(ə)nt/ *contr.* have not.

haver /'heɪvə(r)/ *v.* **1** vacillate, hesitate. **2** *dial.* talk foolishly. [origin unknown]

haversack /'hævəˌsæk/ *n.* stout canvas bag carried on the back or over the shoulder. [German *Habersack*, = oats-sack]

havoc /'hævək/ *n.* widespread destruction; great disorder. [French *havo(t)*]

haw[1] *n.* hawthorn berry. [Old English]

haw[2] see HUM.

Hawaii /hə'waɪɪ/ state of the US comprising a chain of islands (including Hawaii) in the N Pacific; pop. (est. 1996) 1 183 723; capital, Honolulu. Tourism is the main industry, but chemicals, steel, and textiles are produced and agriculture, producing sugar and pineapples, is important. □ **Hawaiian** *adj.* & *n.*

hawfinch *n.* large finch with a thick beak for cracking seeds. [from HAW[1], FINCH]

hawk[1] *–n.* **1** bird of prey with a curved beak, rounded short wings, and a long tail. **2** *Polit.* person who advocates aggressive policies. *–v.* hunt with a hawk. □ **hawkish** *adj.* [Old English]

hawk[2] *v.* carry about or offer (goods) for sale. [back-formation from HAWKER]

hawk[3] *v.* **1** clear the throat noisily. **2** (foll. by *up*) bring (phlegm etc.) up from the throat. [imitative]

hawker *n.* person who travels about selling goods. [Low German or Dutch]

hawk-eyed *adj.* keen-sighted.

hawser /'hɔːzə(r)/ *n.* thick rope or cable for mooring or towing a ship. [French, *haucier* hoist, from Latin *altus* high]

hawthorn *n.* thorny shrub with small dark-red berries. [related to HAW[1]]

hay *n.* grass mown and dried for fodder. □ **make hay (while the sun shines)** seize opportunities. [Old English]

haycock *n.* conical heap of hay.

hay fever *n.* allergy with asthmatic symptoms etc., caused by pollen or dust.

haymaking *n.* mowing grass and spreading it to dry. □ **haymaker** *n.*

haystack *n.* (also **hayrick**) packed pile of hay with a pointed or ridged top.

haywire *adj. colloq.* badly disorganized, out of control.

hazard /'hæzəd/ *–n.* **1** danger or risk. **2** source of this. **3** *Golf* obstacle, e.g. a bunker. *–v.* **1** venture (*hazard a guess*). **2** risk. [Arabic *az-zahr* chance, luck]

hazardous *adj.* risky.

haze *n.* **1** thin atmospheric vapour. **2** mental obscurity or confusion. [back-formation from HAZY]

hazel /'heɪz(ə)l/ *n.* **1** hedgerow shrub bearing round brown edible nuts. **2** greenish-brown. [Old English]

hazelnut *n.* nut of the hazel.

hazy *adj.* **(-ier, -iest) 1** misty. **2** vague, indistinct. **3** confused, uncertain. □ **hazily** *adv.* **haziness** *n.* [origin unknown]

HB *–abbr.* (of pencil-lead) hard black. *–international civil aircraft marking* Switzerland and Liechtenstein.

H-bomb /ˈeɪtʃbɒm/ *n.* = HYDROGEN BOMB. [from H^3]

HC *international civil aircraft marking* Ecuador.

H/C *abbr.* (also **h/c**) *Insurance* held covered.

HCF *abbr.* highest common factor.

HCI *abbr.* human–computer interface (or interaction). See USER INTERFACE.

HCIMA *abbr.* Hotel Catering and Institutional Management Association.

HD *postcode* Huddersfield.

HDD *abbr. Computing* head-down display.

HDLC *abbr. Computing* high-level data link control (communications protocol).

HDX *abbr.* = HALF-DUPLEX.

HE *abbr.* **1** His or Her Excellency. **2** His Eminence. **3** high explosive.

He *symb.* helium.

he /hiː/ *–pron.* (*obj.* **him**; *poss.* **his**; *pl.* **they**) **1** the man, boy, or male animal previously named or in question. **2** person etc. of unspecified sex (*if anyone comes he will have to wait, he who hesitates*). *–n.* **1** male; man. **2** (in *comb.*) male (*he-goat*). [Old English]

head /hed/ *–n.* **1** upper part of the human body, or foremost or upper part of an animal's body, containing the brain, mouth, and sense-organs. **2 a** seat of intellect (*use your head*). **b** mental aptitude or tolerance (*a good head for business; no head for heights*). **3** thing like a head in form or position, esp.: **a** the operative part of a tool. **b** the top of a nail. **c** the leaves or flowers at the top of a stem. **d** foam on the top of a glass of beer etc. **4 a** person in charge, esp. the principal teacher of a school. **b** position of command. **5** front part of a queue etc. **6** upper end of a table or bed etc. **7** top or highest part of a page, stairs, etc. **8 a** individual person as a unit (*£10 per head*). **b** (*pl.* same) individual animal as a unit (*20 head*). **9 a** side of a coin bearing the image of a head. **b** (usu. in *pl.*) this as a choice when tossing a coin. **10 a** source of a river etc. **b** end of a lake at which a river enters it. **11** height or length of a head as a measure. **12** part of a machine in contact with or very close to what is being worked on, esp.: **a** the part of a tape recorder that touches the moving tape and converts signals. **b** the part of a record-player that holds the playing cartridge and stylus. **13** (usu. in phr. **come to a head**) climax, crisis. **14 a** confined body of water or steam in an engine etc. **b** pressure exerted by this. **15** promontory (esp. in place-names) (*Beachy Head*). **16** heading or headline. **17** fully developed top of a boil etc. **18** *colloq.* headache. **19** (*attrib.*) chief, principal. *–v.* **1** be at the head or front of. **2** be in charge of. **3** provide with a head or heading. **4** (often foll. by *for*) face, move, or direct in a specified direction (*is heading for trouble*). **5** hit (a ball etc.) with the head. □ **above** (or **over**) **one's head** beyond one's understanding. **come to a head** reach a crisis. **get it into one's head** (foll. by *that*) **1** adopt a mistaken idea. **2** form a definite plan. **give a person his** (or **her**) **head** allow a person to act freely. **go to one's head 1** make one slightly drunk. **2** make one conceited. **head off 1** get ahead of so as to intercept and turn aside. **2** forestall. **keep** (or **lose**) **one's head** remain (or fail to remain) calm. **off one's head** *slang* crazy. **off the top of one's head** *colloq.* impromptu. **on one's** (or **one's own**) **head** as one's own responsibility. **out of one's head** *slang* crazy. **over one's head 1** beyond one's understanding. **2** without one's rightful knowledge or involvement, esp. of action taken by a subordinate consulting one's own superior. **3** with disregard for one's own (stronger) claim (*was promoted over my head*). **put heads together** consult together. **take it into one's head** (foll. by *that* + clause or *to* + infin.) decide, esp. impetuously. **turn a person's head** make a person conceited. [Old English]

headache *n.* **1** continuous pain in the head. **2** *colloq.* worrying problem. □ **headachy** *adj.*

headband *n.* band worn round the head as decoration or to confine the hair.

head-banger *n. slang* **1** person who shakes his or her head violently to the rhythm of music. **2** crazy or eccentric person.

headboard *n.* upright panel at the head of a bed.

head-butt *–n.* thrust with the head into the chin or body of another person. *–v.* attack with a head-butt.

headcount *n.* **1** counting of individual people. **2** total number of people, esp. employees.

head crash *n.* (also **disk crash**) *Computing* accidental and disastrous contact of a read/write head with the surface of a hard disk as it rotates in a disk drive. (The head should fly just above the surface.) The contact destroys several tracks of data and the damaged disk has to be thrown away. Disks should be backed up at regular intervals so that in the event of a crash a duplicate is available.

headdress *n.* covering for the head.

header *n.* **1** *Football* shot or pass made with the head. **2** *colloq.* headlong fall or dive. **3** brick etc. laid at right angles to the face of a wall. **4** (in full **header-tank**) tank of water etc. maintaining pressure in a plumbing system.

head first *adv.* **1** with the head foremost. **2** precipitately.

headgear *n.* hat or headdress.

head-hunting *n.* **1** collecting of the heads of dead enemies as trophies. **2** seeking of (esp. senior) staff by approaching people employed elsewhere. See EMPLOYMENT AGENCY. □ **head-hunt** *v.* **head-hunter** *n.*

heading *n.* **1 a** title at the head of a page or section of a book etc. **b** section of a subject of discourse etc. **2** horizontal passage made in preparation for building a tunnel, or in a mine.

head in the sand *n.* refusal to acknowledge danger or difficulty.

headlamp *n.* = HEADLIGHT.

headland *n.* promontory.

♦ **head lease** n. main or first lease, out of which subleases may be created.

---

headlight *n.* **1** strong light at the front of a vehicle. **2** beam from this.

headline *n.* **1** heading at the top of an article or page, esp. in a newspaper. **2** (in *pl.*) summary of the most important items in a news bulletin.

headlock *n. Wrestling* hold with an arm round the opponent's head.

headlong *adv.* & *adj.* **1** with the head foremost. **2** in a rush.

headman *n.* chief man of a tribe etc.

headmaster *n.* (*fem.* **headmistress**) = HEAD TEACHER.

head-on *adj.* & *adv.* **1** with the front foremost (*head-on crash*). **2** in direct confrontation.

head over heels *–n.* turning over completely in forward motion as in a somersault etc. *–adv.* utterly (*head over heels in love*).

headphones *n.pl.* set of earphones fitting over the head, for listening to audio equipment etc.

headquarters *n.* (as *sing.* or *pl.*) administrative centre of an organization.

headrest *n.* support for the head, esp. on a seat.

headroom *n.* space or clearance above a vehicle, person's head, etc.

headscarf *n.* scarf worn round the head and tied under the chin.

headset *n.* headphones, often with a microphone attached.

headship *n.* position of head or chief, esp. in a school.

headshrinker *n. slang* psychiatrist.

headstall *n.* part of a halter or bridle fitting round a horse's head.

head start *n.* advantage granted or gained at an early stage.

headstone *n.* stone set up at the head of a grave.

headstrong *adj.* self-willed.

head teacher *n.* teacher in charge of a school.

headwaters *n.pl.* streams flowing from the sources of a river.

headway *n.* **1** progress. **2** ship's rate of progress. **3** headroom.

head wind *n.* wind blowing from directly in front.

headword *n.* word forming a heading.

heady *adj.* (**-ier, -iest**) **1** (of liquor) potent. **2** intoxicating, exciting. **3** impulsive, rash. **4** headachy. □ **headily** *adv.* **headiness** *n.*

heal *v.* **1** (often foll. by *up*) become sound or healthy again. **2** cause to heal. **3** put right (differences etc.). **4** alleviate (sorrow etc.). □ **healer** *n.* [Old English: related to WHOLE]

health /helθ/ *n.* **1** state of being well in body or mind. **2** person's mental or physical condition. **3** soundness, esp. financial or moral. [Old English: related to WHOLE]

♦ **Health and Safety Commission** *n.* (also **HSC**) commission appointed by the Secretary of State for Employment to look after the health, safety, and welfare of people at work, to protect the public from risks arising from work activities, and to control the use and storage of explosives and other dangerous substances. It is composed of representatives from trade unions, employers, and local authorities with a full-time chairman. The **Health and Safety Executive** is a statutory body that advises the Commission and carries out its policies through 20 area offices. It includes HM Factory Inspectorate and a Medical Division, which itself includes the Employment Medical Advisory Service.

---

health centre *n.* building containing various local medical services and doctors' practices.

health farm *n.* establishment offering improved health by a regime of dieting, exercise, etc.

health food *n.* natural food, thought to promote good health.

healthful *adj.* conducive to good health; beneficial.

health service *n.* public service providing medical care.

health visitor *n.* trained nurse who visits mothers and babies, or the sick or elderly, at home.

healthy *adj.* (**-ier, -iest**) **1** having, showing, or promoting good health. **2** indicative of (esp. moral or financial) health (*a healthy sign*). **3** substantial (*won by a healthy 40 seconds*). □ **healthily** *adv.* **healthiness** *n.*

heap –*n.* **1** disorderly pile. **2** (esp. in *pl.*) *colloq.* large number or amount. **3** *slang* dilapidated vehicle. –*v.* **1** (foll. by *up*, *together*, etc.) collect or be collected in a heap. **2** (foll. by *with*) load copiously with. **3** (foll. by *on*, *upon*) give or offer copiously (*heaped insults on them*). [Old English]

hear *v.* (*past* and *past part.* **heard** /hɜːd/) **1** (also *absol.*) perceive with the ear. **2** listen to (*heard them on the radio*). **3** listen judicially to (a case etc.). **4** be told or informed. **5** (foll. by *from*) be contacted by, esp. by letter or telephone. **6** be ready to obey (an order). **7** grant (a prayer). □ **have heard of** be aware of the existence of. **hear! hear!** *int.* expressing agreement. **hear a person out** listen to all a person says. **will not hear of** will not allow. □ **hearer** *n.* [Old English]

hearing *n.* **1** faculty of perceiving sounds. **2** range within which sounds may be heard (*within hearing*). **3** opportunity to state one's case (*a fair hearing*). **4** trial of a case before a court.

hearing-aid *n.* small device to amplify sound, worn by a partially deaf person.

hearken /'hɑːkən/ *v. archaic* (often foll. by *to*) listen. [Old English: related to HARK]

hearsay *n.* rumour, gossip.

hearse /hɜːs/ *n.* vehicle for conveying the coffin at a funeral. [French *herse* harrow, from Latin *hirpex* large rake]

heart /hɑːt/ *n.* **1** hollow muscular organ maintaining the circulation of blood by rhythmic contraction and dilation. **2** region of the heart; the breast. **3 a** centre of thought, feeling, and emotion (esp. love). **b** capacity for feeling emotion (*has no heart*). **4 a** courage or enthusiasm (*take heart*). **b** mood or feeling (*change of heart*). **5 a** central or innermost part of something. **b** essence (*heart of the matter*). **6** compact tender inner part of a cabbage etc. **7 a** heart-shaped thing. **b** conventional representation of a heart with two equal curves meeting at a point at the bottom and a cusp at the top. **8 a** playing-card of the suit denoted by a red figure of a heart. **b** (in *pl.*) this suit. □ **at heart 1** in one's inmost feelings. **2** basically. **break a person's heart** overwhelm a person with sorrow. **by heart** from memory. **give** (or **lose) one's heart** (often foll. by *to*) fall in love (with). **have the heart** (usu. with *neg.*; foll. by *to* + infin.) be insensitive or hard-hearted enough (*didn't have the heart to ask him*). **take to heart** be much affected by. **to one's heart's content** see CONTENT[1]. **with all one's heart** sincerely; with all goodwill. [Old English]

heartache *n.* mental anguish.

heart attack *n.* sudden occurrence of coronary thrombosis.

heartbeat *n.* pulsation of the heart.

heartbreak *n.* overwhelming distress. □ **heartbreaking** *adj.* **heartbroken** *adj.*

heartburn *n.* burning sensation in the chest from indigestion.

hearten *v.* make or become more cheerful. □ **heartening** *adj.*

heart failure *n.* failure of the heart to function properly, esp. as a cause of death.

heartfelt *adj.* sincere; deeply felt.

hearth /hɑːθ/ *n.* **1** floor of a fireplace. **2** the home. [Old English]

hearthrug *n.* rug laid before a fireplace.

heartily *adv.* **1** in a hearty manner. **2** very (*am heartily sick of it*).

heartland *n.* central part of an area.

heartless *adj.* unfeeling, pitiless. □ **heartlessly** *adv.*

heart-lung machine *n.* machine that temporarily takes over the functions of the heart and lungs.

heart-rending *adj.* very distressing.

heart-searching *n.* examination of one's own feelings and motives.

heartsick *adj.* despondent.

heartstrings *n.pl.* one's deepest feelings.

heartthrob *n. colloq.* person for whom one has (esp. immature) romantic feelings.

heart-to-heart –*attrib. adj.* (of a conversation etc.) candid, intimate. –*n.* candid or personal conversation.

heart-warming *adj.* emotionally rewarding or uplifting.

heartwood *n.* dense inner part of a tree-trunk, yielding the hardest timber.

hearty *adj.* (**-ier, -iest**) **1** strong, vigorous. **2** (of a meal or appetite) large. **3** warm, friendly. □ **heartiness** *n.*

heat –*n.* **1** condition of being hot. **2** *Physics* form of energy arising from the motion of bodies' molecules. **3** hot weather. **4** warmth of feeling; anger or excitement. **5** (foll. by *of*) most intense part or period of activity (*heat of battle*). **6** (usu. preliminary or trial) round in a race etc. –*v.* **1** make or become hot or warm. **2** inflame. □ **on heat** (of mammals, esp. females) sexually receptive. [Old English]

heated *adj.* angry; impassioned. □ **heatedly** *adv.*

heater *n.* stove or other heating device.

heath *n.* **1** area of flattish uncultivated land with low shrubs. **2** plant growing on a heath, esp. heather. [Old English]

heathen /'hiːð(ə)n/ –*n.* **1** person not belonging to a predominant religion, esp. not a Christian, Jew, or Muslim. **2** person regarded as lacking culture or moral principles. –*adj.* **1** of heathens. **2** having no religion. [Old English]

heather /'heðə(r)/ *n.* any of various shrubs growing esp. on moors and heaths. [origin unknown]

Heath Robinson /hiːθ ˈrɒbɪns(ə)n/ *adj.* absurdly ingenious and impracticable. [name of a cartoonist]

heating *n.* **1** imparting or generation of heat. **2** equipment used to heat a building etc.

heatproof *–adj.* able to resist great heat. *–v.* make heatproof.

heat shield *n.* device to protect (esp. a spacecraft) from excessive heat.

heatwave *n.* period of unusually hot weather.

heave *–v.* (**-ving**; *past* and *past part.* **heaved** or esp. *Naut.* **hove** /həʊv/) **1** lift or haul with great effort. **2** utter with effort (*heaved a sigh*). **3** *colloq.* throw. **4** rise and fall rhythmically or spasmodically. **5** *Naut.* haul by rope. **6** retch. *–n.* heaving. □ **heave in sight** come into view. **heave to** esp. *Naut.* bring or be brought to a standstill. [Old English]

heaven /ˈhev(ə)n/ *n.* **1** place regarded in some religions as the abode of God and the angels, and of the blessed after death. **2** place or state of supreme bliss. **3** *colloq.* delightful thing. **4** (usu. **Heaven**) God, Providence (often as an exclam. or mild oath: *Heavens*). **5** (**the heavens**) esp. *poet.* the sky as seen from the earth, in which the sun, moon, and stars appear. □ **heavenward** *adv.* (also **heavenwards**). [Old English]

heavenly *adj.* **1** of heaven; divine. **2** of the heavens or sky. **3** *colloq.* very pleasing; wonderful.

heavenly bodies *n.pl.* the sun, stars, planets, etc.

heaven-sent *adj.* providential.

heavier-than-air *attrib. adj.* (of an aircraft) weighing more than the air it displaces.

heavy /ˈhevɪ/ *–adj.* (**-ier, -iest**) **1** of great or unusually high weight; difficult to lift. **2** of great density (*heavy metal*). **3** abundant, considerable (*heavy crop*; *heavy traffic*). **4** severe, intense, extensive (*heavy fighting*; *a heavy sleep*). **5** doing a thing to excess (*heavy drinker*). **6** striking or falling with force; causing strong impact (*heavy blows*; *heavy rain*; *heavy sea*; *a heavy fall*). **7** (of machinery, artillery, etc.) very large of its kind; large in calibre etc. **8** needing much physical effort (*heavy work*). **9** carrying heavy weapons (*the heavy brigade*). **10** serious or sombre in tone or attitude; dull, tedious. **11 a** hard to digest. **b** hard to read or understand. **12** (of bread etc.) too dense from not having risen. **13** (of ground) difficult to traverse or work. **14** oppressive; hard to endure (*heavy demands*). **15 a** coarse, ungraceful (*heavy features*). **b** unwieldy. *–n.* (*pl.* **-ies**) **1** *colloq.* large violent person; thug (esp. hired). **2** villainous or tragic role or. **3** (usu. in *pl.*) *colloq.* serious newspaper. **4** anything large or heavy of its kind, e.g. a vehicle. *–adv.* heavily (esp. in *comb.*: *heavy-laden*). □ **heavy on** using a lot of (*heavy on petrol*). **make heavy weather of** see WEATHER. □ **heavily** *adv.* **heaviness** *n.* **heavyish** *adj.* [Old English]

heavy-duty *adj.* intended to withstand hard use.

heavy going *n.* slow or difficult progress.

heavy-handed *adj.* **1** clumsy. **2** overbearing, oppressive. □ **heavy-handedly** *adv.* **heavy-handedness** *n.*

heavy-hearted *adj.* sad, doleful.

heavy hydrogen *n.* = DEUTERIUM.

heavy industry *n.* industry producing metal, machinery, etc.

heavy metal *n.* **1** heavy guns. **2** metal of high density. **3** *colloq.* loud kind of rock music with a pounding rhythm.

heavy petting *n.* erotic fondling that stops short of intercourse.

♦ **heavy share** *n. Finance* share that has a high price relative to the average price of shares on the market. Heavy shares are often split, i.e. the par value is divided by two, three, or four, which has the same effect on the market price.

---

heavy water *n.* water composed of deuterium and oxygen.

heavyweight *n.* **1 a** weight in certain sports, in amateur boxing over 81 kg. **b** sportsman of this weight. **2** person etc. of above average weight. **3** *colloq.* person of influence or importance.

hebdomadal /hebˈdɒməd(ə)l/ *adj. formal* weekly, esp. meeting weekly. [Greek *hepta* seven]

hebe /ˈhiːbɪ/ *n.* evergreen flowering shrub from New Zealand. [Greek goddess *Hēbē*]

Hebei /həˈbeɪ/ (also **Hopeh** /həˈpeɪ/) province of NE China; pop. (est. 1995) 63 880 000; capital, Shijiazhuang. Coal, cotton, cereals, textiles, and iron are produced.

Hebraic /hiːˈbreɪɪk/ *adj.* of Hebrew or the Hebrews.

Hebrew /ˈhiːbruː/ *–n.* **1** member of a Semitic people orig. centred in ancient Palestine. **2 a** their language. **b** modern form of this, used esp. in Israel. *–adj.* **1** of or in Hebrew. **2** of the Hebrews or the Jews. [Hebrew, = one from the other side of the river]

Hebrides /ˈhebrɪˌdiːz/ group of about 500 islands off the NW coast of Scotland. The Inner Hebrides (including Skye) are divided between Highland and Strathclyde regions; the Outer Hebrides (including Lewis with Harris) form the Western Isles area. The main occupations are farming, fishing, and the manufacture of textiles and woollens. □ **Hebridean** /-ˈdiːən/ *adj.* & *n.*

heck *int. colloq.* mild exclamation of surprise or dismay. [a form of HELL]

heckle /ˈhek(ə)l/ *v.* (**-ling**) interrupt and harass (a public speaker). □ **heckler** *n.* [var. of HACKLE]

hectare /ˈhekteə(r)/ *n.* metric unit of square measure, 100 ares (2.471 acres or 10 000 square metres). [French: related to HECTO-, ARE[2]]

hectic /ˈhektɪk/ *adj.* **1** busy and confused; excited. **2** feverish. □ **hectically** *adv.* [Greek *hektikos* habitual]

hecto- *comb. form* hundred. [Greek *hekaton*]

hectogram /ˈhektəˌgræm/ *n.* (also **hectogramme**) metric unit of mass equal to 100 grams.

hector /ˈhektə(r)/ *–v.* bully, intimidate. *–n.* bully. [from the name *Hector* in the *Iliad*]

he'd /hiːd/ *contr.* **1** he had. **2** he would.

♦ **hedge** *–n.* **1** fence or boundary of dense bushes or shrubs. **2** protection against possible loss. *–v.* (**-ging**) **1** surround or bound with a hedge. **2** (foll. by *in*) enclose. **3 a** reduce one's risk of loss on (a bet) by compensating transactions on the other side. **b** avoid committing oneself. **4** *Finance* **a** (of a trader or dealer) protect an open position, esp. a sale or a purchase of a commodity, currency, security, etc. that is likely to fluctuate in price over the period that the position remains open (see OPEN POSITION). For example, a manufacturer may contract to sell all that can be produced of a product for the next six months. If the product depends on a raw material that fluctuates in price, and if there is insufficient raw material in stock, the manufacturer will have an open position. This can be hedged by buying the raw material required on a futures contract; if it has to be paid for in a foreign currency the manufacturer may also hedge the currency needs by buying that foreign currency forward. Operations of this type do not offer total protection because the prices of spot goods and futures do not always move together, but it is possible to reduce the vulnerability of an open position substantially by hedging. See also OPTION 3. **b** protect one's capital against the ravages of inflation by buying equities or making other investments that are likely to rise with the general level of prices. [Old English]

---

hedgehog *n.* small insect-eating mammal with a piglike snout and a coat of spines, rolling itself up into a ball when attacked.

hedge-hop *v.* fly at a very low altitude.

hedgerow *n.* row of bushes etc. forming a hedge.

hedge sparrow *n.* common grey and brown bird; the dunnock.

♦ **hedonic demand theory** *n. Econ.* theory that the price an individual will pay for a good reflects the sum of the characteristics of that good (implying that demand for the characteristics is the true object of demand theory, not

the goods themselves). It is, however, very difficult to enumerate all the characteristics of goods in practice.

hedonism /'hiːdə,nɪz(ə)m/ *n.* **1** belief in pleasure as mankind's proper aim. **2** behaviour based on this. □ **hedonist** *n.* **hedonistic** /-'nɪstɪk/ *adj.* (also **hedonic** /-'dɒnɪk/) [Greek *hēdonē* pleasure]

heebie-jeebies /,hiːbɪ'jiːbɪz/ *n.pl.* (prec. by *the*) *slang* nervous anxiety, tension. [origin unknown]

heed –*v.* attend to; take notice of. –*n.* careful attention. □ **heedful** *adj.* **heedless** *adj.* **heedlessly** *adv.* [Old English]

hee-haw /'hiːhɔː/ –*n.* bray of a donkey. –*v.* make a braying sound. [imitative]

heel[1] –*n.* **1** back of the foot below the ankle. **2 a** part of a sock etc. covering this. **b** part of a shoe etc. supporting this. **3** thing like a heel in form or position. **4** crust end of a loaf of bread. **5** *colloq.* scoundrel. **6** (as *int.*) command to a dog to walk close to its owner's heel. –*v.* **1** fit or renew a heel on (a shoe etc.). **2** touch the ground with the heel as in dancing. **3** (foll. by *out*) *Rugby* pass the ball with the heel. □ **at heel 1** (of a dog) close behind. **2** (of a person etc.) under control. **at** (or **on) the heels of** following closely after (a person or event). **cool** (or **kick) one's heels** be kept waiting. **down at heel 1** (of a shoe) with the heel worn down. **2** (of a person) shabby. **take to one's heels** run away. **to heel 1** (of a dog) close behind. **2** (of a person etc.) under control. **turn on one's heel** turn sharply round. [Old English]

heel[2] –*v.* (often foll. by *over*) **1** (of a ship etc.) lean over. **2** cause (a ship etc.) to do this. –*n.* act or amount of heeling. [obsolete *heeld*, from Germanic]

heel[3] var. of HELE.

heelball *n.* **1** mixture of hard wax and lampblack used by shoemakers for polishing. **2** this or a similar mixture used in brass-rubbing.

hefty /'heftɪ/ *adj.* (**-ier, -iest**) **1** (of a person) big and strong. **2** (of a thing) large, heavy, powerful. □ **heftily** *adv.* **heftiness** *n.* [*heft* weight: related to HEAVE]

hegemony /hɪ'gemənɪ/ *n.* leadership, esp. by one state of a confederacy. [Greek *hēgemōn* leader]

Hegira /'hedʒɪrə/ *n.* (also **Hejira**) **1** Muhammad's flight from Mecca in AD 622. **2** Muslim era reckoned from this date. [Arabic *hijra* departure]

Heidelberg /'haɪd(ə)l,bɜːg/ city in SW Germany; manufactures include printing presses, cigars, and electrical goods; pop. (est. 1995) 138 964.

heifer /'hefə(r)/ *n.* young cow, esp. one that has not had more than one calf. [Old English]

height /haɪt/ *n.* **1** measurement from base to top or head to foot. **2** elevation above the ground or a recognized level. **3** considerable elevation (*situated at a height*). **4** high place or area. **5** top. **6 a** most intense part or period (*battle was at its height*). **b** extreme example (*the height of fashion*). [Old English]

heighten *v.* make or become higher or more intense.

Heilongjiang /,heɪlʊŋdʒɪ'æŋ/ (also **Heilungkiang** /-kɪ'æŋ/) province of NE China; pop. (est. 1995) 36 720 000; capital, Harbin. Timber, wheat, oil, coal, and gold are produced.

heinous /'heɪnəs/ *adj.* utterly odious or wicked. [French *haïr* hate]

heir /eə(r)/ *n.* (*fem.* **heiress**) person entitled to property or rank as the legal successor of its former holder. [Latin *heres hered-*]

heir apparent *n.* heir whose claim cannot be set aside by the birth of another heir.

heirloom *n.* **1** piece of personal property that has been in a family for several generations. **2** piece of property as part of an inheritance.

heir presumptive *n.* heir whose claim may be set aside by the birth of another heir.

Hejaz /hɪ'dʒæz/ (also **Hijaz, Western Province**) coastal region of W Saudi Arabia, extending along the Red Sea; there is some light industry.

Hejira var. of HEGIRA.

held *past* and *past part.* of HOLD[1].

hele /hiːl/ *v.* (**-ling**) (also **heel**) (foll. by *in*) set (a plant) in the ground temporarily and cover its roots. [Old English]

Helena /'helɪnə/ city in the US, capital of Montana, the commercial centre of a mining and agricultural region; pop. (1990) 24 569.

Helgoland see HELIGOLAND.

helical /'hiːlɪk(ə)l/ *adj.* having the form of a helix.

helices *pl.* of HELIX.

helicopter /'helɪ,kɒptə(r)/ *n.* wingless aircraft obtaining lift and propulsion from horizontally revolving overhead blades. [Greek: related to HELIX, *pteron* wing]

Heligoland /'helɪgə,lænd/ (German **Helgoland** /'helgə,lɑːnt/) small island in the North Sea, off the coast of Germany. Formerly belonging to Denmark and then to Britain, in 1890 it was given to Germany.

helio- *comb. form* sun. [Greek *hēlios* sun]

heliocentric /,hiːlɪə'sentrɪk/ *adj.* **1** regarding the sun as centre. **2** considered as viewed from the sun's centre.

heliograph /'hiːlɪə,grɑːf/ –*n.* **1** signalling apparatus reflecting sunlight in flashes. **2** message sent by means of this. –*v.* send (a message) by heliograph.

heliotrope /'hiːlɪə,trəʊp/ *n.* plant with fragrant purple flowers. [Greek: related to HELIO-, *trepō* turn]

heliport /'helɪ,pɔːt/ *n.* place where helicopters take off and land.

helium /'hiːlɪəm/ *n.* light inert gaseous element used in airships and as a refrigerant. [related to HELIO-]

helix /'hiːlɪks/ *n.* (*pl.* **helices** /'hiːlɪ,siːz/) spiral curve (like a corkscrew) or coiled curve (like a watch spring). [Latin from Greek]

hell –*n.* **1** place regarded in some religions as the abode of the dead, or of devils and condemned sinners. **2** place or state of misery or wickedness. –*int.* expressing anger, surprise, etc. □ **the hell** (usu. prec. by *what, where, who*, etc.) expressing anger, disbelief, etc. (*who the hell is this?; the hell you are!*). **beat** etc. **the hell out of** *colloq.* beat etc. without restraint. **come hell or high water** no matter what the difficulties. **for the hell of it** *colloq.* just for fun. **get hell** *colloq.* be severely scolded or punished. **give a person hell** *colloq.* scold or punish a person. **a** (or **one) hell of a** *colloq.* outstanding example of (*a hell of a mess; one hell of a party*). **like hell** *colloq.* **1** not at all. **2** recklessly, exceedingly. [Old English]

he'll /hiːl/ *contr.* he will; he shall.

hell-bent *adj.* (foll. by *on*) recklessly determined.

hellebore /'helɪ,bɔː(r)/ *n.* evergreen plant with usu. white, purple, or green flowers, e.g. the Christmas rose. [Greek *(h)elleborus*]

Hellene /'heliːn/ *n.* **1** native of modern Greece. **2** ancient Greek. □ **Hellenic** /he'lenɪk, -'liːnɪk/ *adj.* [Greek]

Hellenism /'helɪ,nɪz(ə)m/ *n.* (esp. ancient) Greek character or culture. □ **Hellenist** *n.*

Hellenistic /,helɪ'nɪstɪk/ *adj.* of Greek history, language, and culture of the late 4th to the late 1st century BC.

hell-fire *n.* fire(s) regarded as existing in hell.

hell for leather *adv.* at full speed.

hell-hole *n.* oppressive or unbearable place.

hellish –*adj.* **1** of or like hell. **2** *colloq.* extremely difficult or unpleasant. –*adv. colloq.* extremely (*hellish expensive*). □ **hellishly** *adv.*

hello /hə'ləʊ/ (also **hallo, hullo**) –*int.* expression of informal greeting, or of surprise, or to call attention. –*n.* (*pl.* **-s**) cry of 'hello'. [var. of earlier *hollo*]

Hell's Angel *n.* member of a gang of male motor-cycle enthusiasts notorious for outrageous and violent behaviour.

helm *n.* tiller or wheel for controlling a ship's rudder. □ **at the helm** in control; at the head of an organization etc. [Old English]

helmet /'helmɪt/ *n.* protective head-covering worn by a policeman, motor cyclist, etc. [French from Germanic]

helmsman /'helmzmən/ *n.* person who steers a ship.

helot /ˈhelət/ *n.* serf, esp. (**Helot**) of a class in ancient Sparta. [Latin from Greek]

help –*v.* **1** provide with the means towards what is needed or sought (*helped me with my work*; *helped me (to) pay my debts*; *helped him on with his coat*). **2** (often *absol.*) be of use or service to (*does that help?*). **3** contribute to alleviating (a pain or difficulty). **4** prevent or remedy (*it can't be helped*). **5** (usu. with *neg.*) **a** refrain from (*can't help it*; *could not help laughing*). **b** *refl.* refrain from acting (*couldn't help himself*). **6** (often foll. by *to*) serve (a person with food). –*n.* **1** helping or being helped (*need your help*; *came to our help*). **2** person or thing that helps. **3** *colloq.* domestic assistant or assistance. **4** remedy or escape (*there is no help for it*). □ **help oneself** (often foll. by *to*) **1** serve oneself (with food etc.). **2** take without permission. **help a person out** give a person help, esp. in difficulty. □ **helper** *n.* [Old English]

helpful *adj.* giving help; useful. □ **helpfully** *adv.* **helpfulness** *n.*

helping *n.* portion of food at a meal.

helpless *adj.* **1** lacking help or protection; defenceless. **2** unable to act without help. □ **helplessly** *adv.* **helplessness** *n.*

helpline *n.* telephone service providing help with problems.

helpmate *n.* helpful companion or partner.

Helsingborg /ˈhelsɪŋˌbɔːg/ (Swedish **Hälsingborg**) port in S Sweden, situated on the Øresund (Sound) opposite Elsinore (Helsingør) in Denmark; industries include copper smelting, chemicals, and sugar refining; pop. (est. 1996) 114 339.

Helsingør see ELSINORE.

Helsinki /ˈhelsɪŋkɪ, -ˈsɪŋkɪ/ (Swedish **Helsingfors** /ˈhelsɪŋˌfɔːʃ/) capital of Finland; industries include textiles, metals, food processing, and paper; pop. (est. 1996) 525 031.

helter-skelter /ˌheltəˈskeltə(r)/ –*adv.* & *adj.* in disorderly haste. –*n.* (at a fairground) external spiral slide round a tower. [imitative]

hem[1] –*n.* border of cloth where the edge is turned under and sewn down. –*v.* (**-mm-**) turn down and sew in the edge of (cloth etc.). □ **hem in** confine; restrict the movement of. [Old English]

hem[2] –*int.* calling attention or expressing hesitation by a slight cough. –*n.* utterance of this. –*v.* (**-mm-**) say *hem*; hesitate in speech. □ **hem and haw** = *hum and haw* (see HUM[1]). [imitative]

hemal etc. *US* var. of HAEMAL etc.

he-man *n.* masterful or virile man.

hemi- *comb. form* half. [Greek, = Latin *semi-*]

hemipterous /heˈmɪptərəs/ *adj.* of the insect order including aphids, bugs, and cicadas, with piercing or sucking mouthparts. [Greek *pteron* wing]

hemisphere /ˈhemɪˌsfɪə(r)/ *n.* **1** half a sphere. **2** half of the earth, esp. as divided by the equator (into *northern* and *southern hemisphere*) or by a line passing through the poles (into *eastern* and *western hemisphere*). □ **hemispherical** /-ˈsferɪk(ə)l/ *adj.* [Greek: related to HEMI-, SPHERE]

hemline *n.* lower edge of a skirt etc.

hemlock /ˈhemlɒk/ *n.* **1** poisonous plant with fernlike leaves and small white flowers. **2** poison made from this. [Old English]

hemp *n.* **1** (in full **Indian hemp**) Asian herbaceous plant. **2** its fibre used to make rope and stout fabrics. **3** narcotic drug made from the hemp plant. [Old English]

hempen *adj.* made of hemp.

hemstitch –*n.* decorative stitch. –*v.* hem with this stitch.

hen *n.* female bird, esp. of a domestic fowl. [Old English]

Henan /həˈnæn/ (also **Honan**) province of NE central China; pop. (est. 1995) 90 270 000; capital, Zhengzhou. Cotton, silk, cereals, and coal are produced.

henbane *n.* poisonous hairy plant with an unpleasant smell.

hence *adv.* **1** from this time (*two years hence*). **2** for this reason (*hence we seem to be wrong*). **3** *archaic* from here. [Old English]

henceforth *adv.* (also **henceforward**) from this time onwards.

henchman *n.* usu. *derog.* trusted supporter. [Old English *hengst* horse, MAN]

henge /hendʒ/ *n.* prehistoric monument consisting of a circle of stone or wood uprights. [*Stonehenge* in S England]

henna /ˈhenə/ –*n.* **1** tropical shrub. **2** reddish dye made from it and used to colour hair. –*v.* (**hennaed, hennaing**) dye with henna. [Arabic]

hen-party *n. colloq.* social gathering of women only.

henpeck *v.* (usu. in *passive*) (of a wife) constantly nag her husband.

henry /ˈhenrɪ/ *n.* (*pl.* **-s** or **-ies**) *Electr.* SI unit of inductance. [*Henry*, name of a physicist]

hep var. of HIP[4].

hepatic /hɪˈpætɪk/ *adj.* of the liver. [Greek *hēpar -atos* liver]

hepatitis /ˌhepəˈtaɪtɪs/ *n.* inflammation of the liver. [related to HEPATIC]

hepta- *comb. form* seven. [Greek]

heptagon /ˈheptəgən/ *n.* plane figure with seven sides and angles. □ **heptagonal** /-ˈtægən(ə)l/ *adj.* [Greek: related to HEPTA-, *-gōnos* angled]

her –*pron.* **1** *objective case* of SHE (*I like her*). **2** *colloq.* she (*it's her all right*; *am older than her*). –*poss. pron.* (*attrib.*) of or belonging to her or herself (*her house*; *her own business*). [Old English dative and genitive of SHE]

Heraklion /hɪˈræklɪən/ (Greek **Iráklion** /ɪˈræklɪən/) seaport and the administrative centre of the Greek island of Crete, on the N coast; pop. (1991) 117 167. A tourist centre, it also exports raisins, grapes, and olive oil.

herald /ˈher(ə)ld/ –*n.* **1** official messenger bringing news. **2** forerunner, harbinger. **3 a** *hist.* officer responsible for state ceremonial and etiquette. **b** official concerned with pedigrees and coats of arms. –*v.* proclaim the approach of; usher in. □ **heraldic** /-ˈrældɪk/ *adj.* [French from Germanic]

heraldry *n.* **1** art or knowledge of a herald. **2** coats of arms.

Herat /həˈræt/ city in W Afghanistan; industries include flour milling and textiles; pop. (est. 1992) 186 800.

herb *n.* **1** any non-woody seed-bearing plant. **2** plant with leaves, seeds, or flowers used for flavouring, food, medicine, scent, etc. □ **herby** *adj.* (**-ier, -iest**). [Latin *herba*]

herbaceous /hɜːˈbeɪʃəs/ *adj.* of or like herbs.

herbaceous border *n.* garden border containing esp. perennial flowering plants.

herbage *n.* vegetation collectively, esp. as pasture.

herbal –*adj.* of herbs in medicinal and culinary use. –*n.* book describing the medicinal and culinary uses of herbs.

herbalist *n.* **1** dealer in medicinal herbs. **2** writer on herbs.

herbarium /hɜːˈbeərɪəm/ *n.* (*pl.* **-ria**) **1** systematically arranged collection of dried plants. **2** book, room, etc. for these.

herbicide /ˈhɜːbɪˌsaɪd/ *n.* poison used to destroy unwanted vegetation.

herbivore /ˈhɜːbɪˌvɔː(r)/ *n.* animal that feeds on plants. □ **herbivorous** /-ˈbɪvərəs/ *adj.* [Latin *voro* devour]

Herculean /ˌhɜːkjʊˈliːən/ *adj.* having or requiring great strength or effort. [from the name *Hercules*, Latin alteration of Greek *Hēraklēs*]

herd –*n.* **1** a number of animals, esp. cattle, feeding or travelling or kept together. **2** (prec. by *the*) *derog.* large number of people; mob (*tends to follow the herd*). –*v.* **1** (cause to) go in a herd (*herded together for warmth*; *herded the cattle into the field*). **2** look after (sheep, cattle, etc.). [Old English]

herd instinct *n.* (prec. by *the*) tendency to think and act as a crowd.

herdsman *n.* man who owns or tends a herd.

here *–adv.* **1** in or at or to this place or position (*come here; sit here*). **2** indicating a person's presence or a thing offered (*my son here will show you; here is your coat*). **3** at this point in the argument, situation, etc. (*here I have a question*). *–n.* this place (*get out of here; lives near here; fill it up to here*). *–int.* **1** calling attention: short for *come here, look here,* etc. (*here, where are you going with that?*). **2** indicating one's presence in a roll-call: short for *I am here.* □ **here goes!** *colloq.* expression indicating the start of a bold act. **here's to** I drink to the health of. **here we are** *colloq.* said on arrival at one's destination. **here we go again** *colloq.* the same, usu. undesirable, events are recurring. **here you are** said on handing something to somebody. **neither here nor there** of no importance. [Old English]

hereabouts /ˌhɪərəˈbaʊts/ *adv.* (also **hereabout**) near this place.

hereafter /hɪərˈɑːftə(r)/ *–adv.* from now on; in the future. *–n.* **1** the future. **2** life after death.

here and now *adv.* at this very moment; immediately.

here and there *adv.* in various places.

hereby /hɪəˈbaɪ/ *adv.* by this means; as a result of this.

hereditable /hɪˈredɪtəb(ə)l/ *adj.* that can be inherited. [Latin: related to HEIR]

◆ **hereditament** /ˌherɪˈdɪtəmənt/ *n.* real property, originally property that would be inherited by the heir on intestacy. **Corporeal hereditaments** are physical real property, e.g. land, buildings, trees, and minerals. **Incorporeal hereditaments** are intangible rights, e.g. easements or profits à prendre, attached to land. [Latin: related to HEIR]

---

hereditary /hɪˈredɪtərɪ/ *adj.* **1** (of a disease, instinct, etc.) able to be passed down genetically from one generation to another. **2 a** descending by inheritance. **b** holding a position by inheritance. [Latin: related to HEIR]

heredity /hɪˈredɪtɪ/ *n.* **1 a** passing on of physical or mental characteristics genetically. **b** these characteristics. **2** genetic constitution.

Hereford /ˈherɪfəd/ city in W England, in Hereford and Worcester; pop. (1991) 54 326. The centre of an agricultural region, it produces cider, beer, leather goods, and chemicals. *–n.* animal of a breed of red and white beef cattle.

Hereford and Worcester county in W central England, bordering on Wales; pop. (est. 1994) 699 900; county town, Worcester. Mainly agricultural, producing fruit, vegetables, and cattle, it also has chemical and engineering industries.

herein /hɪəˈrɪn/ *adv. formal* in this matter, book, etc.

hereinafter /ˌhɪərɪnˈɑːftə(r)/ *adv.* esp. *Law formal* **1** from this point on. **2** in a later part of this document etc.

hereof /hɪərˈɒv/ *adv. formal* of this.

heresy /ˈherəsɪ/ *n.* (*pl.* **-ies**) **1** esp. *RC Ch.* religious belief or practice contrary to orthodox doctrine. **2** opinion contrary to what is normally accepted or maintained. [Greek *hairesis* choice]

heretic /ˈherətɪk/ *n.* **1** person believing in or practising religious heresy. **2** holder of an unorthodox opinion. □ **heretical** /hɪˈretɪk(ə)l/ *adj.*

hereto /hɪəˈtuː/ *adv. formal* to this matter.

heretofore /ˌhɪətʊˈfɔː(r)/ *adv. formal* before this time.

hereupon /ˌhɪərəˈpɒn/ *adv.* after this; in consequence of this.

herewith /hɪəˈwɪð/ *adv.* with this (esp. of an enclosure in a letter etc.).

heritable /ˈherɪtəb(ə)l/ *adj.* **1** *Law* capable of being inherited or of inheriting. **2** *Biol.* genetically transmissible from parent to offspring. [French: related to HEIR]

heritage /ˈherɪtɪdʒ/ *n.* **1** what is or may be inherited. **2** inherited circumstances, benefits, etc. **3** a nation's historic buildings, monuments, countryside, etc., esp. when regarded as worthy of preservation.

hermaphrodite /hɜːˈmæfrəˌdaɪt/ *–n.* person, animal, or plant having both male and female reproductive organs. *–adj.* combining both sexes. □ **hermaphroditic** /-ˈdɪtɪk/ *adj.* [from *Hermaphroditus,* son of *Hermes* and *Aphrodite,* who became joined in one body to a nymph]

hermetic /hɜːˈmetɪk/ *adj.* with an airtight closure. □ **hermetically** *adv.* [from the Greek god *Hermes,* regarded as the founder of alchemy]

hermit /ˈhɜːmɪt/ *n.* person (esp. an early Christian) living in solitude and austerity. □ **hermitic** /-ˈmɪtɪk/ *adj.* [Greek *erēmos* solitary]

hermitage *n.* **1** hermit's dwelling. **2** secluded dwelling.

hermit-crab *n.* crab that lives in a mollusc's cast-off shell.

hernia /ˈhɜːnɪə/ *n.* protrusion of part of an organ through the wall of the body cavity containing it. [Latin]

Herning /ˈhɜːnɪŋ/ city in Denmark, in central Jutland; manufactures include textiles and machinery; pop. (1995) 57 751.

hero /ˈhɪərəʊ/ *n.* (*pl.* **-es**) **1** person noted or admired for nobility, courage, outstanding achievements, etc. **2** chief male character in a play, story, etc. [Greek *hērōs*]

heroic /hɪˈrəʊɪk/ *–adj.* of, fit for, or like a hero; very brave. *–n.* (in *pl.*) **1** high-flown language or sentiments. **2** unduly bold behaviour. □ **heroically** *adv.*

heroin /ˈherəʊɪn/ *n.* addictive analgesic drug derived from morphine, often used as a narcotic. [German: related to HERO, from the effect on the user's self-esteem]

heroine /ˈherəʊɪn/ *n.* **1** woman noted or admired for nobility, courage, outstanding achievements, etc. **2** chief female character in a play, story, etc. [Greek: related to HERO]

heroism /ˈherəʊˌɪz(ə)m/ *n.* heroic conduct or qualities. [French *héroïsme*: related to HERO]

heron /ˈherən/ *n.* long-legged wading bird with a long S-shaped neck. [French from Germanic]

hero-worship *–n.* idealization of an admired person. *–v.* idolize.

herpes /ˈhɜːpiːz/ *n.* virus disease causing skin blisters. [Greek *herpō* creep]

Herr /heə(r)/ *n.* (*pl.* **Herren** /ˈherən/) **1** title of a German man; Mr. **2** German man. [German]

herring /ˈherɪŋ/ *n.* (*pl.* same or **-s**) N Atlantic fish used as food. [Old English]

herring-bone *n.* stitch or weave consisting of a series of small 'V' shapes making a zigzag pattern.

herring-gull *n.* large gull with dark wing-tips.

hers /hɜːz/ *poss. pron.* the one or ones belonging to or associated with her (*it is hers; hers are over there*). □ **of hers** of or belonging to her (*friend of hers*).

herself /həˈself/ *pron.* **1 a** *emphat. form* of SHE OR HER (*she herself will do it*). **b** *refl. form* of HER (*she has hurt herself*). **2** in her normal state of body or mind (*does not feel quite herself today*). □ **be herself** see ONESELF. **by herself** see *by oneself.* [Old English: related to HER, SELF]

Hertfordshire /ˈhɑːfədʃɪə(r)/ county in SE England; pop. (est. 1994) 1 005 400; county town, Hertford. Arable farming is important and it has tanning and printing industries.

Herts. /hɑːts/ *abbr.* Hertfordshire.

hertz *n.* (*pl.* same) SI unit of frequency, equal to one cycle per second. [*Hertz,* name of a physicist]

he's /hiːz, hɪz/ *contr.* **1** he is. **2** he has.

hesitant /ˈhezɪt(ə)nt/ *adj.* hesitating; irresolute. □ **hesitance** *n.* **hesitancy** *n.* **hesitantly** *adv.*

hesitate /ˈhezɪˌteɪt/ *v.* (**-ting**) **1** show or feel indecision or uncertainty; pause in doubt (*hesitated over her choice*). **2** be reluctant (*I hesitate to say so*). □ **hesitation** /-ˈteɪʃ(ə)n/ *n.* [Latin *haereo haes-* stick fast]

Hesse /ˈhesə/ (German **Hessen** /ˈhes(ə)n/) state (*Land*) of W Germany; pop. (est. 1995) 5 980 700; capital, Wiesbaden. Potatoes, sugar beet, and wheat are grown; industries include publishing and the manufacture of machinery and chemicals.

hessian /ˈhesɪən/ *n.* strong coarse sacking made of hemp or jute. [HESSE]

hetero- *comb. form* other, different. [Greek *heteros* other]

heterodox /ˈhetərəʊˌdɒks/ *adj.* not orthodox. □ **heterodoxy** *n.* [from HETERO-, Greek *doxa* opinion]

heterodyne /ˈhetərəʊˌdaɪn/ *adj. Radio* relating to the production of a lower frequency from the combination of two almost equal high frequencies. [from HETERO-, Greek *dunamis* force]

heterogeneous /ˌhetərəʊˈdʒiːnɪəs/ *adj.* **1** diverse in character. **2** varied in content. □ **heterogeneity** /-dʒɪˈniːɪtɪ/ *n.* [Latin from Greek *genos* kind]

heteromorphic /ˌhetərəʊˈmɔːfɪk/ *adj.* (also **heteromorphous** /-ˈmɔːfəs/) *Biol.* of dissimilar forms. □ **heteromorphism** *n.*

heterosexual /ˌhetərəʊˈsekʃʊəl/ –*adj.* feeling or involving sexual attraction to the opposite sex. –*n.* heterosexual person. □ **heterosexuality** /-ˈælɪtɪ/ *n.*

het up *predic. adj. colloq.* excited, overwrought. [*het*, a dial. word = heated]

heuristic /hjʊəˈrɪstɪk/ *adj.* **1** allowing or assisting to discover. **2** proceeding to a solution by trial and error. [Greek *heuriskō* find]

hew *v.* (*past part.* **hewn** /hjuːn/ or **hewed**) **1** chop or cut with an axe, sword, etc. **2** cut into shape. [Old English]

hex[1] –*v.* **1** practise witchcraft. **2** bewitch. –*n.* magic spell. [German]

hex[2] *n.* = HEXADECIMAL NOTATION. [abbreviation]

hexa- *comb. form* six. [Greek]

◆ **hexadecimal notation** /ˌheksəˈdesɪm(ə)l/ *n.* (also **hex**) number system that uses 16 symbols, the ten digits 0–9 and the letters A–F, to represent numbers, and thus has 16 as a base. For example, the decimal number 26 is written as 1A in hex. Hexadecimal numbers are widely used in computer programming as they are easier to follow than binary notation, yet are easy to convert to binary if required.

hexagon /ˈheksəgən/ *n.* plane figure with six sides and angles. □ **hexagonal** /-ˈsægən(ə)l/ *adj.* [Greek: related to HEXA-, *-gōnos* angled]

hexagram /ˈheksəˌgræm/ *n.* figure formed by two intersecting equilateral triangles.

hexameter /hekˈsæmɪtə(r)/ *n.* line of verse with six metrical feet.

hey /heɪ/ *int.* calling attention or expressing joy, surprise, inquiry, etc. [imitative]

heyday /ˈheɪdeɪ/ *n.* time of greatest success or prosperity. [Low German]

hey presto! *int.* conjuror's phrase on completing a trick.

HF *abbr.* high frequency.

Hf *symb.* hafnium.

HG *postcode* Harrogate.

Hg *symb.* mercury. [Latin *hydrargyrom]*

hg *symb.* hectogram(s).

HGV *abbr.* heavy goods vehicle.

HH –*abbr.* **1** Her or His Highness. **2** His Holiness. **3** (of pencil-lead) double-hard. –*international civil aircraft marking* Haiti.

HI –*abbr.* Hawaiian Islands. –*international civil aircraft marking* Dominican Republic. –*US postcode* Hawaii.

hi /haɪ/ *int.* calling attention or as a greeting.

hiatus /haɪˈeɪtəs/ *n.* (*pl.* **-tuses**) **1** break or gap in a series or sequence. **2** break between two vowels coming together but not in the same syllable, as in *though oft the ear.* [Latin *hio* gape]

hibernate /ˈhaɪbəˌneɪt/ *v.* (**-ting**) (of an animal) spend the winter in a dormant state. □ **hibernation** /-ˈneɪʃ(ə)n/ *n.* [Latin *hibernus* wintry]

Hibernian /haɪˈbɜːnɪən/ *archaic poet.* –*adj.* of Ireland. –*n.* native of Ireland. [Latin *Hibernia* Ireland]

hibiscus /hɪˈbɪskəs/ *n.* (*pl.* **-cuses**) cultivated shrub with large bright-coloured flowers. [Greek *hibiskos* marsh mallow]

hiccup /ˈhɪkʌp/ (also **hiccough**) –*n.* **1** involuntary spasm of the diaphragm causing a characteristic sound 'hic'. **2** temporary or minor stoppage or difficulty. –*v.* (**-p-**) make a hiccup. [imitative]

hick *n.* (often *attrib.*) esp. *US colloq.* country bumpkin, provincial. [familiar form of *Richard*]

hickory /ˈhɪkərɪ/ *n.* (*pl.* **-ies**) **1** North American tree yielding wood and nutlike edible fruits. **2** the tough heavy wood of this. [Virginian *pohickery*]

◆ **Hicksian demand function** /ˈhɪksɪən/ *n.* (also **compensated demand function**) *Econ.* function that expresses an individual's demand for goods by means of prices at a particular level of utility. Unlike the Marshallian demand function, a change in the price of a good will have only one effect on the Hicksian demand function; as the level of utility is held constant, this is the substitution effect. [*Hicks*, name of an economist]

hid *past* of HIDE[1].

Hidalgo /hɪˈdælgəʊ/ state of central Mexico; pop. (est. 1995) 2 111 782; capital, Pachuca de Soto. Opals and metals are mined and there are metalworking, textile, and cement-manufacturing industries.

HIDB *abbr.* Highlands and Islands Development Board.

hidden *past part.* of HIDE[1].

hidden agenda *n.* secret motivation behind a policy, statement, etc.; ulterior motive.

◆ **hidden reserve** *n.* (also **off-balance-sheet reserve, secret reserve**) funds held in reserve but not disclosed on the balance sheet, arising when an asset is deliberately either undisclosed or undervalued. Such reserves are permitted for some banking institutions but are not permitted for limited companies as they reduce profits and therefore the corporation tax liability of the company.

◆ **hidden tax** *n.* tax, the incidence of which may be hidden from the person who is suffering it (see INCIDENCE OF TAXATION). An example could be a tax levied on goods at the wholesale level, which increases the retail price in such a way that the final customer cannot detect either that it has happened or the amount of the extra cost. Again, a government might introduce a hidden tax by artificially causing the price of a certain utility to be raised above its usual commercial value.

◆ **hidden unemployment** *n.* (also **concealed unemployment**) unemployment that does not appear in government statistics, which are usu. based on figures for those drawing unemployment benefit. In addition to these people there will be some who are doing very little productive work, although they are not claiming benefit. These include workers on short time for whom their employers are expecting to be able to provide work shortly; workers who are not usefully employed, although their employers think they are; and others not claiming benefit for a variety of reasons.

hide[1] –*v.* (**-ding**; *past* **hid**; *past part.* **hidden**) **1** put or keep out of sight. **2** conceal oneself. **3** (usu. foll. by *from*) keep (a fact) secret. **4** conceal. –*n.* camouflaged shelter used for observing wildlife. □ **hider** *n.* [Old English]

hide[2] *n.* **1** animal's skin, esp. when tanned or dressed. **2** *colloq.* the human skin, esp. the backside. [Old English]

hide-and-seek *n.* game in which players hide and another searches for them.

hideaway *n.* hiding-place or place of retreat.

hidebound *adj.* **1** narrow-minded. **2** constricted by tradition.

hideous /ˈhɪdɪəs/ *adj.* **1** very ugly, revolting. **2** *colloq.* unpleasant. □ **hideosity** /-ˈɒsɪtɪ/ *n.* (*pl.* **-ies**). **hideously** *adv.* [Anglo-French *hidous*]

hide-out *n. colloq.* hiding-place.

hiding[1] *n. colloq.* a thrashing. □ **on a hiding to nothing** with no chance of succeeding. [from HIDE[2]]

hiding[2] *n.* **1** act of hiding. **2** state of remaining hidden (*go into hiding*). [from HIDE[1]]

hiding-place *n.* place of concealment.

hierarchy /ˈhaɪəˌrɑːkɪ/ *n.* (*pl.* **-ies**) system of grades of status or authority ranked one above the other. □ **hierarchical** /-ˈrɑːkɪk(ə)l/ *adj.* [Greek *hieros* sacred, *arkhō* rule]

♦ **hierarchy of effects** *n.* steps in the persuasion process that lead a consumer to purchase a particular product, namely awareness, knowledge, liking, preference, conviction, and finally a decision to purchase.

hieratic /ˌhaɪəˈrætɪk/ *adj.* **1** of priests. **2** of the ancient Egyptian hieroglyphic writing as used by priests. [Greek *hiereus* priest]

hieroglyph /ˈhaɪərəglɪf/ *n.* picture representing a word, syllable, or sound, as used in ancient Egyptian etc. [Greek *hieros* sacred, *gluphō* carve]

hieroglyphic /ˌhaɪərəˈglɪfɪk/ *–adj.* of or written in hieroglyphs. *–n.* (in *pl.*) hieroglyphs; hieroglyphic writing.

hi-fi /ˈhaɪfaɪ/ *colloq. –adj.* of high fidelity. *–n.* (*pl.* **-s**) set of high-fidelity equipment. [abbreviation]

higgledy-piggledy /ˌhɪgəldɪˈpɪgəldɪ/ *adv.* & *adj.* in confusion or disorder. [origin uncertain]

high /haɪ/ *–adj.* **1 a** of great vertical extent (*high building*). **b** (*predic.*; often in *comb.*) of a specified height (*one inch high*; *waist-high*). **2 a** far above ground or sea level etc. (*high altitude*). **b** inland, esp. when raised (*High Asia*). **3** extending above the normal level (*jersey with a high neck*). **4 a** of exalted quality (*high minds*). **b** lavish; superior (*high living*; *high fashion*). **5** of exalted rank (*high society*; *is high in the government*). **6 a** great; intense; extreme; powerful (*high praise*; *high temperature*). **b** greater than normal (*high prices*). **c** extreme or very traditional in religious or political opinion (*high Tory*). **7** performed at, to, or from a considerable height (*high diving*; *high flying*). **8** (often foll. by *on*) *colloq.* intoxicated by alcohol or esp. drugs. **9** (of a sound etc.) of high frequency; shrill. **10** (of a period, age, time, etc.) at its peak (*high noon*; *high summer*; *High Renaissance*). **11 a** (of meat etc.) beginning to go bad; off. **b** (of game) well-hung and slightly decomposed. *–n.* **1** high, or the highest, level or figure. **2** area of high pressure; anticyclone. **3** *slang* euphoric state, esp. drug-induced (*am on a high*). *–adv.* **1** far up; aloft (*flew the flag high*). **2** in or to a high degree. **3** at a high price. **4** (of a sound) at or to a high pitch. □ **high opinion of** favourable opinion of. **on high** in or to heaven or a high place. **on one's high horse** *colloq.* acting arrogantly. [Old English]

high altar *n.* chief altar in a church.

high and dry *adj.* stranded; aground.

high and low *adv.* everywhere (*searched high and low*).

high and mighty *adj. colloq.* arrogant.

highball *n. US* drink of spirits and soda etc., served with ice in a tall glass.

highbrow *colloq. –adj.* intellectual; cultural. *–n.* intellectual or cultured person.

high chair *n.* infant's chair with long legs and a tray for meals.

High Church *n.* section of the Church of England emphasizing ritual, priestly authority, and sacraments.

high-class *adj.* of high quality.

high colour *n.* flushed complexion.

high command *n.* army commander-in-chief and associated staff.

High Commission *n.* embassy from one Commonwealth country to another. □ **High Commissioner** *n.*

High Court *n.* (also in England **High Court of Justice**) supreme court of justice for civil cases.

high day *n.* festal day.

higher animal *n.* (also **higher plant**) animal or plant evolved to a high degree.

higher education *n.* education at university etc.

♦ **higher rate** *n.* rate above the standard (or basic) rate in the UK income tax schedule of rates. The higher rate may apply to all income above a specified figure or there may be a series of higher-rate bands, the tax rate in each band being higher than its predecessor. See also PROGRESSIVE TAX.

high explosive *n.* extremely explosive substance used in shells, bombs, etc.

highfalutin /ˌhaɪfəˈluːtɪn/ *adj.* (also **highfaluting** /-tɪŋ/) *colloq.* pompous, pretentious. [origin unknown]

high fidelity *n.* high-quality sound reproduction with little distortion.

high-flown *adj.* (of language etc.) extravagant, bombastic.

high-flyer *n.* (also **high-flier**) **1** ambitious person. **2** person or thing of great potential. □ **high-flying** *adj.*

high frequency *n.* frequency, esp. in radio, of 3–30 megahertz.

high gear *n.* gear such that the driven end of a transmission revolves faster than the driving end.

high-handed *adj.* disregarding others' feelings; overbearing. □ **high-handedly** *adv.* **high-handedness** *n.*

high heels *n.pl.* women's shoes with high heels.

♦ **high-involvement product** *n.* product, e.g. a car, house, or hi-fi equipment, that involves the consumer in taking time and trouble before deciding on a purchase. This will include looking in several catalogues, shops, etc. to compare prices and the products themselves. Cf. LOW-INVOLVEMENT PRODUCT.

high jinks *n.pl.* boisterous fun.

high jump *n.* **1** athletic event consisting of jumping over a high bar. **2** *colloq.* drastic punishment (*he's for the high jump*).

Highland /ˈhaɪlənd/ local government region in N Scotland; pop. (est. 1994) 207 500; capital, Inverness. Industries include tourism and service industries for North Sea oil production.

highland *–n.* (usu. in *pl.*) **1** area of high land. **2** (**the Highlands**) mountainous part of Scotland. *–adj.* of or in a highland or the Highlands. □ **highlander** *n.* (also **Highlander**). [Old English, = promontory: related to HIGH]

Highland cattle *n.* cattle of a shaggy-haired breed with long curved horns.

Highland fling see FLING *n.* 3.

high-level *adj.* (of negotiations etc.) conducted by high-ranking people.

high-level language *n.* (also **HLL**) kind of programming language whose features reflect the requirements of the programmer, being designed for the solution of problems in one or more areas of application. HLLs are usu. at a level of abstraction close to natural language (cf. LOW-LEVEL LANGUAGE). Before being run on a particular computer, programs written in a high-level language must be translated into a form that can be accepted by that computer (see MACHINE CODE). This is achieved by means of a special program (see COMPILER 2; INTERPRETER 2). Each statement in the original program (called the **source program**) is translated into many machine instructions. A source program can be translated into different machine codes using different compilers or interpreters. As a result, programs written in high-level languages can be moved from, say, one microcomputer to another. The number and variety of HLLs now available is large and still growing. Examples include BASIC, COBOL, Fortran, C, Pascal, Ada, and Prolog.

highlight *–n.* **1** moment or detail of vivid interest; outstanding feature. **2** (in a painting etc.) bright area. **3** (usu. in *pl.*) light streak in the hair produced by bleaching. *–v.* **1** bring into prominence; draw attention to. **2** mark with a highlighter.

highlighter *n.* marker pen for emphasizing a printed word etc. by overlaying it with colour.

highly /ˈhaɪlɪ/ *adv.* **1** in a high degree (*highly amusing*; *commend it highly*). **2** favourably (*think highly of him*).

highly-strung *adj.* very sensitive or nervous.

high-minded *adj.* having high moral principles. □ **high-mindedly** *adv.* **high-mindedness** *n.*

highness *n.* **1** state of being high (*highness of taxation*). **2** (**Highness**) title used when addressing or referring to a prince or princess (*Her Highness*; *Your Royal Highness*).

high-octane *adj.* (of fuel used in internal-combustion engines) not detonating readily during the power stroke.

high-pitched *adj.* **1** (of a sound) high. **2** (of a roof) steep.

high point *n.* the maximum or best state reached.

high-powered *adj.* **1** having great power or energy. **2** important or influential.

high pressure *n.* **1** high degree of activity or exertion. **2** atmospheric condition with the pressure above average.

high priest *n.* (*fem.* **high priestess**) **1** chief priest, esp. Jewish. **2** head of a cult.

high-ranking *adj.* of high rank, senior.

high-rise *–attrib. adj.* (of a building) having many storeys. *–n.* such a building.

high-risk *attrib. adj.* involving or exposed to danger (*high-risk sports*).

high road *n.* main road.

high school *n.* **1** grammar school. **2** *US* & *Scot.* secondary school.

high sea *n.* (also **high seas**) open seas not under any country's jurisdiction.

high season *n.* busiest period at a resort etc.

high-speed *attrib. adj.* operating at great speed.

high-spirited *adj.* vivacious; cheerful; lively.

high spot *n.* important place or feature.

high street *n.* principal shopping street of a town.

high table *n.* dining-table for the most important guests or members.

high tea *n.* evening meal usu. consisting of a cooked dish, bread and butter, tea, etc.

high-tech *adj.* **1** employing, requiring, or involved in high technology. **2** imitating styles more usual in industry etc.

high technology *n.* advanced technological development, esp. in electronics.

high tension *n.* = HIGH VOLTAGE.

high tide *n.* time or level of the tide at its peak.

high time *n.* time that is overdue (*it is high time they arrived*).

high treason *n.* = TREASON.

high-up *n. colloq.* person of high rank.

high voltage *n.* electrical potential large enough to injure or damage.

high water *n.* = HIGH TIDE.

high-water mark *n.* level reached at high water.

highway *n.* **1 a** public road. **b** main route. **2** direct course of action (*on the highway to success*).

Highway Code *n.* official booklet of guidance for road-users.

highwayman *n. hist.* robber of travellers etc., usu. mounted.

high wire *n.* high tightrope.

♦ **high yielder** *n.* stock or share that gives a high yield but is more speculative than most, i.e. its price may fluctuate.

---

hijack /ˈhaɪdʒæk/ *–v.* **1** seize control of (a vehicle etc.), esp. to force it to a different destination. **2** seize (goods) in transit. **3** take control of (talks etc.) by force or subterfuge. *–n.* a hijacking. □ **hijacker** *n.* [origin unknown]

hike *–n.* **1** long walk, esp. in the country for pleasure. **2** rise in prices etc. *–v.* (**-king**) **1** go for a hike. **2** walk laboriously. **3** (usu. foll. by *up*) hitch up (clothing etc.); become hitched up. **4** (usu. foll. by *up*) raise (prices etc.). □ **hiker** *n.* [origin unknown]

hilarious /hɪˈleərɪəs/ *adj.* **1** exceedingly funny. **2** boisterously merry. □ **hilariously** *adv.* **hilarity** /-ˈlærɪtɪ/ *n.* [Greek *hilaros* cheerful]

hill *n.* **1** naturally raised area of land, lower than a mountain. **2** (often in *comb.*) heap, mound (*anthill*). **3** sloping piece of road. □ **over the hill** *colloq.* past the prime of life. [Old English]

hill-billy *n. US colloq.*, often *derog.* person from a remote rural area in a southern state.

hillock /ˈhɪlək/ *n.* small hill, mound.

hillside *n.* sloping side of a hill.

hilltop *n.* top of a hill.

hillwalking *n.* hiking in hilly country. □ **hillwalker** *n.*

hilly *adj.* (**-ier, -iest**) having many hills. □ **hilliness** *n.*

hilt *n.* handle of a sword, dagger, etc. □ **up to the hilt** completely. [Old English]

Hilversum /ˈhɪlvəˌsʊm/ town in the Netherlands, in North Holland province; pop. (1991) 84 600. It is the centre of the Dutch radio and television network.

him *pron.* **1** *objective case* of HE (*I saw him*). **2** *colloq.* he (*it's him again*; *taller than him*). [Old English, dative of HE]

Himachal Pradesh /hɪˌmɑːtʃ(ə)l prəˈdeʃ/ state in N India; pop. (1991) 5 170 877; capital, Simla. Forestry and farming are the main activities, but hydroelectricity production is a developing industry.

Himalayas /ˌhɪməˈleɪəz/ system of high mountains forming the NE boundary of the Indian subcontinent. □ **Himalayan** *adj.*

himself /hɪmˈself/ *pron.* **1 a** *emphat. form* of HE or HIM (*he himself will do it*). **b** *refl. form* of HIM (*he has hurt himself*). **2** in his normal state of body or mind (*does not feel quite himself today*). □ **be himself** see ONESELF. **by himself** see *by oneself*. [Old English: related to HIM, SELF]

hind[1] /haɪnd/ *adj.* at the back (*hind leg*). [Old English *hindan* from behind]

hind[2] /haɪnd/ *n.* female (esp. red) deer, esp. in and after the third year. [Old English]

hinder[1] /ˈhɪndə(r)/ *v.* impede; delay. [Old English]

hinder[2] /ˈhaɪndə(r)/ *adj.* rear, hind (*the hinder part*). [Old English]

Hindi /ˈhɪndɪ/ *n.* **1** group of spoken dialects of N India. **2** literary form of Hindustani, an official language of India. [Urdu *Hind* India]

hindmost *adj.* furthest behind.

hindquarters *n.pl.* hind legs and rump of a quadruped.

hindrance /ˈhɪndrəns/ *n.* **1** hindering; being hindered. **2** thing that hinders.

hindsight *n.* wisdom after the event.

Hindu /ˈhɪnduː/ *–n.* (*pl.* **-s**) follower of Hinduism. *–adj.* of Hindus or Hinduism. [Urdu *Hind* India]

Hinduism /ˈhɪnduːˌɪz(ə)m/ *n.* main religious and social system of India, including the belief in reincarnation, several gods, and a caste system.

Hindustani /ˌhɪndʊˈstɑːnɪ/ *n.* language based on Hindi, used as a lingua franca in much of India. [from HINDU, *stān* country]

hinge /hɪndʒ/ *–n.* **1** movable joint on which a door, lid, etc., turns or swings. **2** principle on which all depends. *–v.* (**-ging**) **1** (foll. by *on*) depend (on a principle, an event, etc.). **2** attach or be attached by a hinge. [related to HANG]

hinny /ˈhɪnɪ/ *n.* (*pl.* **-ies**) offspring of a female donkey and a male horse. [Greek *hinnos*]

hint *–n.* **1** slight or indirect indication or suggestion. **2** small piece of practical information. **3** very small trace; suggestion (*a hint of perfume*). *–v.* suggest slightly or indirectly. □ **hint at** give a hint of; refer indirectly to. **take a hint** heed a hint. [obsolete *hent* grasp]

hinterland /ˈhɪntəˌlænd/ *n.* **1** district beyond a coast or river's banks. **2** area served by a port or other centre. [German]

hip[1] *n.* projection of the pelvis and the upper part of the thigh-bone. [Old English]

hip[2] *n.* fruit of a rose, esp. wild. [Old English]

hip[3] *int.* introducing a united cheer (*hip, hip, hooray*). [origin unknown]

hip[4] *adj.* (also **hep**) (**-pper, -ppest**) *slang* trendy, stylish. [origin unknown]

hip-bath *n.* portable bath in which one sits immersed to the hips.

hip-bone *n.* bone forming the hip.

hip-flask *n.* flask for spirits etc., carried in a hip-pocket.

hippie /ˈhɪpɪ/ *n.* (also **hippy**) (*pl.* **-ies**) *colloq.* (esp. in the 1960s) person rejecting convention, typically with long hair, jeans, beads, etc., and taking hallucinogenic drugs. [from HIP[4]]

hippo /ˈhɪpəʊ/ *n.* (*pl.* **-s**) *colloq.* hippopotamus. [abbreviation]

hip-pocket *n.* trouser-pocket just behind the hip.

Hippocratic oath /ˌhɪpəˈkrætɪk/ *n.* statement of ethics of the medical profession. [*Hippocrates*, name of a Greek physician]

hippodrome /ˈhɪpəˌdrəʊm/ *n.* **1** music-hall or dancehall. **2** (in classical antiquity) course for chariot races etc. [Greek *hippos* horse, *dromos* race]

hippopotamus /ˌhɪpəˈpɒtəməs/ *n.* (*pl.* **-muses** or **-mi** /-ˌmaɪ/) large African mammal with short legs and thick skin, inhabiting rivers, lakes, etc. [Greek *hippos* horse, *potamos* river]

hippy[1] var. of HIPPIE.

hippy[2] *adj.* having large hips.

hipster[1] *–adj.* (of a garment) hanging from the hips rather than the waist. *–n.* (in *pl.*) such trousers.

hipster[2] *n. slang* hip person.

hire *–v.* (**-ring**) **1** purchase the temporary use of (a thing) (*hired a van from them*). **2** esp. *US* employ (a person). *–n.* **1** hiring or being hired. **2** payment for this. □ **for** (or **on**) **hire** ready to be hired. **hire out** grant the temporary use of (a thing) for payment. □ **hireable** *adj.* **hirer** *n.* [Old English]

hireling *n.* usu. *derog.* person who works (only) for money.

♦ **hire purchase** *n.* (also **HP**) method of buying goods in which the purchaser takes possession of them as soon as an initial instalment of the price (a deposit) is paid, and obtains ownership of the goods when all the agreed number of subsequent instalments have been paid. A **hire-purchase agreement** differs from a **credit-sale agreement** and **sale by instalments** (or a **deferred payment agreement**) because in these transactions ownership passes when the contract is signed. It also differs from a contract of hire, because in this case ownership never passes. Hire-purchase agreements were formerly controlled by government regulations stipulating the minimum deposit and the length of the repayment period. These controls were removed in 1982. Hire-purchase agreements were also formerly controlled by the Hire Purchase Act (1965), but most are now regulated by the Consumer Credit Act (1974). In this act a hire-purchase agreement is regarded as one in which goods are bailed in return for periodical payments by the bailee; ownership passes to the bailee if the terms of the agreement are complied with and the bailee exercises the option to purchase. A hire-purchase agreement often involves a finance company as a third party. The seller of the goods sells them outright to the finance company, which enters into a hire-purchase agreement with the hirer.

---

hi-res /ˈhaɪˈrez/ *n.* & *adj. colloq.* high resolution. [abbreviation]

Hiroshima /hɪˈrɒʃɪmə/ city in Japan, capital of Chugoku region on the island of Honshu; pop. (1995) 1 108 868. Largely destroyed in 1945 by the first atomic bomb, which led to Japan's surrender in the Second World War, the city was rebuilt and is now a centre of the Japanese car industry.

hirsute /ˈhɜːsjuːt/ *adj.* hairy, shaggy. [Latin]

his /hɪz/ *poss. pron.* **1** (*attrib.*) of or belonging to him or himself (*his house*; *his own business*). **2** the one or ones belonging to or associated with him (*it is his*; *his are over there*). □ **of his** of or belonging to him (*friend of his*). [Old English, genitive of HE]

Hispanic /hɪˈspænɪk/ *–adj.* **1** of Spain or Spain and Portugal. **2** of Spain and other Spanish-speaking countries. *–n.* Spanish-speaking person living in the US. [Latin *Hispania* Spain]

Hispaniola /ˌhɪspænˈjəʊlə/ island of the Greater Antilles in the West Indies, divided between the Republic of Haiti and the Dominican Republic.

hiss *–v.* **1** make a sharp sibilant sound, as of the letter *s*. **2** express disapproval of by hisses. **3** whisper urgently or angrily. *–n.* **1** sharp sibilant sound as of the letter *s*. **2** *Electronics* interference at audio frequencies. [imitative]

histamine /ˈhɪstəˌmiːn/ *n.* chemical compound in body tissues etc., associated with allergic reactions. [from HISTOLOGY, AMINE]

histogram /ˈhɪstəˌgræm/ *n.* statistical diagram of rectangles with areas proportional to the value of a number of variables. [Greek *histos* mast]

histology /hɪˈstɒlədʒɪ/ *n.* the study of tissue structure. [Greek *histos* web]

historian /hɪˈstɔːrɪən/ *n.* **1** writer of history. **2** person learned in history.

historic /hɪˈstɒrɪk/ *adj.* **1** famous or important in history or potentially so (*historic moment*). **2** *Gram.* (of a tense) used to narrate past events.

historical *adj.* **1** of or concerning history (*historical evidence*). **2** (of the study of a subject) showing its development over a period. **3** factual, not fictional or legendary. **4** belonging to the past, not the present. **5** (of a novel etc.) dealing with historical events. □ **historically** *adv.*

♦ **historical-cost accounting** *n.* traditional form of accounting, in which assets are shown in balance sheets at their cost to the organization (historical cost), less any appropriate depreciation. In times of high inflation this method tends to overstate profits. Cf. CURRENT-COST ACCOUNTING; CURRENT PURCHASING POWER ACCOUNTING.

---

historicism /hɪˈstɒrɪˌsɪz(ə)m/ *n.* **1** theory that social and cultural phenomena are determined by history. **2** belief that historical events are governed by laws.

historicity /ˌhɪstəˈrɪsɪtɪ/ *n.* historical truth or authenticity.

historiography /hɪˌstɔːrɪˈɒgrəfɪ/ *n.* **1** the writing of history. **2** the study of this. □ **historiographer** *n.*

history /ˈhɪstərɪ/ *n.* (*pl.* **-ies**) **1** continuous record of (esp. public) events. **2 a** the study of past events, esp. human affairs. **b** total accumulation of past events, esp. relating to human affairs or a particular nation, person, thing, etc. **3** eventful past (*this house has a history*). **4** (foll. by *of*) past record (*had a history of illness*). **5 a** systematic or critical account of or research into past events etc. **b** similar record or account of natural phenomena. **6** historical play. □ **make history** do something memorable. [Greek *historia* inquiry]

histrionic /ˌhɪstrɪˈɒnɪk/ *–adj.* (of behaviour) theatrical, dramatic. *–n.* (in *pl.*) insincere and dramatic behaviour designed to impress. [Latin *histrio* actor]

hit *–v.* (**-tt-**; *past* and *past part.* **hit**) **1 a** strike with a blow or missile. **b** (of a moving body) strike with force (*the plane hit the ground*). **c** reach (a target etc.) with a directed missile (*hit the wicket*). **2** cause to suffer; affect adversely. **3** (often foll. by *at*, *against*) direct a blow. **4** (often foll. by *against*, *on*) knock (a part of the body) (*hit his head*). **5** achieve, reach (*hit the right tone*; *can't hit the high notes*). **6** *colloq.* **a** encounter (*hit a snag*). **b** arrive at (*hit town*). **c** indulge heavily in, esp. liquor etc. (*hit the bottle*). **7** esp. *US slang* rob or kill. **8** occur forcefully to (*it only hit him later*). **9 a** propel (a ball etc.) with a bat etc. to score runs or points. **b** score in this way (*hit a six*). *–n.* **1 a** blow, stroke. **b** collision. **2** shot etc. that hits its target. **3** *colloq.* popular success. □ **hit back** retaliate. **hit below the belt 1** esp. *Boxing* give a foul blow. **2** treat or behave unfairly. **hit the hay** (or **sack**) *colloq.* go to bed. **hit it off** (often foll. by *with*, *together*) *colloq.* get on well (with a person). **hit the nail on the head** state the truth exactly. **hit on** (or **upon**) find by chance. **hit out** deal vigorous physical or verbal blows. **hit the road** *slang* depart. **hit the roof** see ROOF. [Old English from Old Norse]

hit-and-run *attrib. adj.* **1** (of a driver, raider, etc.) causing damage or injury and leaving the scene immediately. **2** (of an accident, attack, etc.) perpetrated by such a person or people.

hitch *–v.* **1** fasten or be fastened with a loop, hook, etc.; tether. **2** move (a thing) slightly or with a jerk. **3** *colloq.* **a** = HITCHHIKE. **b** obtain (a lift) by hitchhiking. *–n.* **1** temporary obstacle or snag. **2** abrupt pull or push. **3** noose or knot of various kinds. **4** *colloq.* free ride in a vehicle. □ **get hitched** *colloq.* marry. **hitch up** lift (esp. clothing) with a jerk. [origin uncertain]

hitchhike *v.* (**-king**) travel by seeking free lifts in passing vehicles. □ **hitchhiker** *n.*

hi-tech /'haɪtek/ *adj.* = HIGH-TECH. [abbreviation]

hither /'hɪðə(r)/ *adv. formal* to or towards this place. [Old English]

hither and thither *adv.* to and fro.

hitherto /ˌhɪðə'tuː/ *adv.* until this time, up to now.

hit list *n. slang* list of prospective victims.

hit man *n. slang* hired assassin.

hit-or-miss *adj.* liable to error, random.

hit parade *n. colloq.* list of the current best-selling pop records.

Hittite /'hɪtaɪt/ *–n.* member or language of an ancient people of Asia Minor and Syria. *–adj.* of the Hittites. [Hebrew]

HIV *abbr.* human immunodeficiency virus, either of two viruses causing Aids.

hive *n.* beehive. □ **hive off** (**-ving**) separate from a larger group. [Old English]

hives *n.pl.* skin-eruption, esp. nettle-rash. [origin unknown]

HK *–abbr. & international vehicle registration* Hong Kong. *–international civil aircraft marking* Colombia.

HKJ *international vehicle registration* Jordan.

HL *international civil aircraft marking* South Korea.

HLL *abbr.* = HIGH-LEVEL LANGUAGE.

HM *–abbr.* Her (or His) Majesty('s). *–airline flight code* Air Seychelles.

HMC *abbr.* Household Mortgage Corporation.

HMFI *abbr.* Her (*or* His) Majesty's Factory Inspectorate.

HMG *abbr.* Her (or His) Majesty's Government.

HMI *abbr.* **1** Her (or His) Majesty's Inspector (of Schools). **2** *Computing* human–machine interface.

HMIT *abbr.* Her (or His) Majesty's Inspector of Taxes.

HMLR *abbr.* Her (or His) Majesty's Land Registry.

HMS *abbr.* Her (or His) Majesty's Ship.

HMSO *abbr.* Her (or His) Majesty's Stationery Office. See STATIONERY OFFICE.

HNC *abbr.* Higher National Certificate.

HND *abbr.* Higher National Diploma.

Ho *symb.* holmium.

ho /həʊ/ *int.* expressing triumph, derision, etc., or calling attention. [natural exclamation]

hoard *–n.* stock or store (esp. of money or food). *–v.* amass and store. □ **hoarder** *n.* [Old English]

hoarding *n.* **1** large, usu. wooden, structure used to carry advertisements etc. **2** temporary fence round a building site etc. [obsolete *hoard* from French: *hourd*]

hoar-frost *n.* frozen water vapour on vegetation etc. [Old English]

hoarse *adj.* **1** (of the voice) rough and deep; husky, croaking. **2** having such a voice. □ **hoarsely** *adv.* **hoarseness** *n.* [Old Norse]

hoary *adj.* (**-ier, -iest**) **1 a** (of hair) grey or white with age. **b** having such hair; aged. **2** old and trite (*hoary joke*). [Old English]

hoax *–n.* humorous or malicious deception. *–v.* deceive (a person) with a hoax. [probably a shortening of *hocus* in HOCUS-POCUS]

hob *n.* **1** flat heating surface with hotplates or burners, on a cooker or as a separate unit. **2** flat metal shelf at the side of a fireplace for heating a pan etc. [perhaps var. of HUB]

Hobart /'həʊbaːt/ capital and chief port of Tasmania, Australia; industries include zinc refining and food processing; pop. (est. 1995) 194 700.

hobble /'hɒb(ə)l/ *–v.* (**-ling**) **1** walk lamely; limp. **2** tie together the legs of (a horse etc.) to prevent it from straying. *–n.* **1** uneven or infirm gait. **2** rope etc. for hobbling a horse etc. [probably Low German]

hobby /'hɒbɪ/ *n.* (*pl.* **-ies**) leisure-time activity pursued for pleasure. [from the name *Robin*]

hobby-horse *n.* **1** child's toy consisting of a stick with a horse's head. **2** favourite subject or idea.

hobgoblin /'hɒbˌgɒblɪn/ *n.* mischievous imp; bogy. [from HOBBY, GOBLIN]

hobnail *n.* heavy-headed nail for boot-soles. [from HOB]

hobnob /'hɒbnɒb/ *v.* (**-bb-**) (usu. foll. by *with*) mix socially or informally. [*hab nab* have or not have]

hobo /'həʊbəʊ/ *n.* (*pl.* **-es** or **-s**) *US* wandering worker; tramp. [origin unknown]

Hobson's choice /'hɒbs(ə)nz/ *n.* choice of taking the thing offered or nothing. [*Hobson*, name of a carrier who let out horses thus]

Ho Chi Minh City /həʊ tʃɪ 'mɪn/ (formerly **Saigon**) city in S Vietnam; industries include metalworking, chemicals, and textiles; pop. (est. 1992) 4 322 300.

hock[1] *n.* joint of a quadruped's hind leg between the knee and the fetlock. [Old English]

hock[2] *n.* German white wine from the Rhineland. [*Hochheim* in Germany]

hock[3] *v.* esp. *US colloq.* pawn; pledge. □ **in hock 1** in pawn. **2** in debt. **3** in prison. [Dutch]

hockey /'hɒkɪ/ *n.* team game with hooked sticks and a small hard ball. [origin unknown]

hocus-pocus /ˌhəʊkəs'pəʊkəs/ *n.* deception; trickery. [sham Latin]

hod *n.* **1** V-shaped trough on a pole used for carrying bricks etc. **2** portable receptacle for coal. [French *hotte* pannier]

Hodeida /həʊ'deɪdə/ chief port of Yemen, in the W of the country on the Red Sea; exports include cotton and coffee; pop. (1986) 155 100.

hodgepodge var. of HOTCHPOTCH.

Hodgkin's disease /'hɒdʒkɪnz/ *n.* malignant disease of lymphatic tissues, usu. characterized by enlargement of the lymph nodes. [*Hodgkin*, name of a physician]

hoe *–n.* long-handled tool with a blade, used for weeding etc. *–v.* (**hoes, hoed, hoeing**) weed (crops); loosen (earth); dig up with a hoe. [French from Germanic]

Hoek van Holland see HOOK OF HOLLAND.

hog *–n.* **1** castrated male pig. **2** *colloq.* greedy person. *–v.* (**-gg-**) *colloq.* take greedily; hoard selfishly; monopolize. □ **go the whole hog** *colloq.* do something completely or thoroughly. □ **hoggish** *adj.* [Old English]

hogmanay /'hɒgməˌneɪ/ *n. Scot.* New Year's Eve. [probably French]

hogshead *n.* **1** large cask. **2** liquid or dry measure (about 50 gallons). [from HOG: the reason for the name is unknown]

hogwash *n. colloq.* nonsense, rubbish.

ho-ho /həʊ'həʊ/ *int.* **1** representing a deep jolly laugh. **2** expressing surprise, triumph, or derision. [reduplication of HO]

hoick *v. colloq.* (often foll. by *out*) lift or pull, esp. with a jerk. [perhaps var. of HIKE]

hoi polloi /ˌhɔɪ pə'lɔɪ/ *n.* the masses; the common people. [Greek, = the many]

■ **Usage** This phrase is often preceded by *the*, which is, strictly speaking, unnecessary since *hoi* means 'the'.

hoist *–v.* **1** raise or haul up. **2** raise by means of ropes and pulleys etc. *–n.* **1** act of hoisting, lift. **2** apparatus for hoisting. □ **hoist with one's own petard** caught by one's own trick etc. [earlier *hoise*, probably from Low German]

hoity-toity /ˌhɔɪtɪ'tɔɪtɪ/ *adj.* haughty. [obsolete *hoit* romp]

Hokkaido /hɒ'kaɪdəʊ/ most northerly of the four main

islands of Japan; pop. (1995) 5 692 217; capital, Sapporo. Coalmining is the main industry.

hokum /'həʊkəm/ *n.* esp. *US slang* **1** sentimental, sensational, or unreal material in a film or play etc. **2** bunkum; rubbish. [origin unknown]

hold[1] /həʊld/ *–v.* (*past* and *past part.* **held**) **1 a** keep fast; grasp (esp. in the hands or arms). **b** (also *refl.*) keep or sustain (a thing, oneself, one's head, etc.) in a particular position. **c** grip so as to control (*hold the reins*). **2** have the capacity for, contain (*holds two pints*). **3** possess, gain, or have, esp.: **a** be the owner or tenant of (land, property, stocks, etc.). **b** gain or have gained (a qualification, record, etc.). **c** have the position of (a job or office). **d** keep possession of (a place etc.), esp. against attack. **4** remain unbroken; not give way (*roof held under the storm*). **5** celebrate or conduct (a meeting, festival, conversation, etc.). **6 a** keep (a person etc.) in a place or condition (*held him in suspense*). **b** detain, esp. in custody. **7 a** engross (*book held him for hours*). **b** dominate (*held the stage*). **8** (foll. by *to*) keep (a person etc.) to (a promise etc.). **9** (of weather) continue fine. **10** think, believe; assert (*held it to be plain; held that the earth was flat*). **11** regard with a specified feeling (*held him in contempt*). **12** cease; restrain (*hold your fire*). **13** keep or reserve (*please hold our seats*). **14** be able to drink (alcohol) without effect (*can't hold his drink*). **15** (of a court etc.) lay down; decide. **16** *Mus.* sustain (a note). **17** = *hold the line*. *–n.* **1** (foll. by *on, over*) influence or power over (*has a strange hold over me*). **2** manner of holding in wrestling etc. **3** grasp (*take hold of him*). **4** (often in *comb.*) thing to hold by (*seized the handhold*). □ **hold (a thing) against (a person)** resent or regard it as discreditable to (a person). **hold back 1** impede the progress of; restrain. **2** keep for oneself. **3** (often foll. by *from*) hesitate; refrain. **hold one's breath** see BREATH. **hold down 1** repress. **2** *colloq.* be competent enough to keep (one's job etc.). **hold the fort 1** act as a temporary substitute. **2** cope in an emergency. **hold forth** speak at length or tediously. **hold one's ground** see GROUND[1]. **hold hands** grasp one another by the hand as a sign of affection or for support or guidance. **hold it** cease action or movement. **hold the line** not ring off (in a telephone connection). **hold one's nose** compress the nostrils to avoid a bad smell. **hold off 1** delay, not begin. **2** keep one's distance. **hold on 1** keep one's grasp on something. **2** wait a moment. **3** = *hold the line*. **hold out 1** stretch forth (a hand etc.). **2** offer (an inducement etc.). **3** maintain resistance. **4** persist or last. **hold out for** continue to demand. **hold out on** *colloq.* refuse something to (a person). **hold over** postpone. **hold one's own** maintain one's position; not be beaten. **hold one's tongue** *colloq.* remain silent. **hold to ransom 1** keep prisoner until a ransom is paid. **2** demand concessions from by threats. **hold up 1** support, sustain. **2** exhibit, display. **3** hinder, obstruct. **4** stop and rob by force. **hold water** (of reasoning) be sound, bear examination. **hold with** (usu. with *neg.*) *colloq.* approve of. **on hold** holding the telephone line. **take hold** (of a custom or habit) become established. **with no holds barred** with no restrictions of method. [Old English]

hold[2] /həʊld/ *n.* cavity in the lower part of a ship or aircraft for cargo. [Old English: related to HOLLOW]

holdall *n.* large soft travelling bag.

♦ **holder** *n.* **1** person or thing that holds. **2** person possessing or controlling something. **3** *Law* person in possession of a bill of exchange or promissory note, who may be the payee, the endorsee, or the bearer. When value (which includes a past debt or liability) has at any time been given for a bill, the holder is a **holder for value**, as regards the acceptor and all who were parties to the bill before value was given. A **holder in due course** has taken a bill of exchange in good faith and for value, before it was overdue, and without notice of previous dishonour or of any defect in the title of the person who negotiated or transferred the bill. He or she holds the bill free from any defect of title of prior parties and may enforce payment against all parties liable on the bill.

---

holding *n.* **1** tenure of land. **2** stocks, property, etc. held.

holding company *n.* (also **parent company**) company that holds the shares of other companies, which it then controls. See also GROUP OF COMPANIES.

hold-up *n.* **1** stoppage or delay. **2** robbery by force.

hole *n.* **1 a** empty space in a solid body. **b** opening in or through something. **2** animal's burrow. **3** (in games) cavity or receptacle for a ball. **4** *colloq.* small or dingy place. **5** *colloq.* awkward situation. **6** *Golf* **a** point scored by a player who gets the ball from tee to hole with the fewest strokes. **b** terrain or distance from tee to hole. □ **hole up** *US colloq.* hide oneself. **make a hole in** use a large amount of. □ **holey** *adj.* [Old English]

hole-and-corner *adj.* secret; underhand.

hole in the heart *n. colloq.* congenital defect in the heart membrane.

holiday /'hɒlɪˌdeɪ/ *–n.* **1** (often in *pl.*) extended period of recreation, esp. spent away from home or travelling; break from work. **2** day of festivity or recreation when no work is done, esp. a religious festival etc. *–v.* spend a holiday. [Old English: related to HOLY, DAY]

♦ **holiday and travel insurance** *n.* insurance against a variety of risks for the duration of a person's holiday. Although policies vary, an average policy covers the policyholder's baggage and personal effects for all risks (see ALL-RISKS POLICY); compensation for delays while travelling to or from the holiday; refund of deposits lost if the holiday has to be cancelled for any of a number of specific causes; theft or loss of money, traveller's cheques, or credit cards; payment of medical expenses or costs of flying home in the event of illness or injury; and payment of legal compensation for injuring other people or damaging their property because of negligence.

---

holiday camp *n.* place for holiday-makers with facilities on site.

holiday-maker *n.* person on holiday.

holier-than-thou *adj. colloq.* self-righteous.

holiness /'həʊlɪnɪs/ *n.* **1** being holy or sacred. **2** (**Holiness**) title used when addressing or referring to the Pope. [Old English: related to HOLY]

holism /'həʊlɪz(ə)m/ *n.* (also **wholism**) **1** *Philos.* theory that certain wholes are greater than the sum of their parts. **2** *Med.* treating of the whole person rather than the symptoms of a disease. □ **holistic** /-'lɪstɪk/ *adj.* [Greek *holos* whole]

♦ **holistic evaluation** *n.* evaluation of an advertising or marketing campaign as a whole, as distinct from an analysis of the results of its constituent parts.

Holland /'hɒlənd/ former province of the Netherlands, now divided into the provinces of North and South Holland. Its name is often used interchangeably with the Netherlands as the name of the country.

hollandaise sauce /ˌhɒlən'deɪz/ *n.* creamy sauce of melted butter, egg-yolks, vinegar, etc. [French]

holler *v.* & *n. US colloq.* shout. [French *holà* hello!]

hollow /'hɒləʊ/ *–adj.* **1 a** having a cavity; not solid. **b** sunken (*hollow cheeks*). **2** (of a sound) echoing. **3** empty; hungry. **4** meaningless (*hollow victory*). **5** insincere (*hollow laugh*). *–n.* **1** hollow place; hole. **2** valley; basin. *–v.* (often foll. by *out*) make hollow; excavate. *–adv. colloq.* completely (*beaten hollow*). □ **hollowly** *adv.* **hollowness** *n.* [Old English]

holly /'hɒlɪ/ *n.* (*pl.* **-ies**) evergreen shrub with prickly leaves and red berries. [Old English]

hollyhock /'hɒlɪˌhɒk/ *n.* tall plant with showy flowers. [from HOLY, obsolete *hock* mallow]

Hollywood /'hɒlɪˌwʊd/ district of Los Angeles, California, centre of the US film industry since 1911; pop. (1985) 250 000.

holm /həʊm/ *n.* (in full **holm-oak**) evergreen oak with holly-like young leaves. [dial. *holm* holly]

holmium /'həʊlmɪəm/ *n.* metallic element of the lanthanide series. [Latin *Holmia* Stockholm]

holocaust /ˈhɒləˌkɔːst/ *n.* **1** large-scale destruction, esp. by fire or nuclear war. **2** (**the Holocaust**) mass murder of the Jews by the Nazis 1939–45. [Greek *holos* whole, *kaustos* burnt]

hologram /ˈhɒləˌgræm/ *n.* photographic pattern that gives a three-dimensional image when illuminated by coherent light. [Greek *holos* whole, -GRAM]

holograph /ˈhɒləˌgrɑːf/ *–adj.* wholly written by hand by the person named as the author. *–n.* holograph document. [Greek *holos* whole, -GRAPH]

holography /həˈlɒgrəfi/ *n.* the study or production of holograms.

hols /hɒlz/ *n.pl. colloq.* holidays. [abbreviation]

holster /ˈhəʊlstə(r)/ *n.* leather case for a pistol or revolver, worn on a belt etc. [Dutch]

holy /ˈhəʊlɪ/ *adj.* (**-ier**, **-iest**) **1** morally and spiritually excellent or perfect, and to be revered. **2** belonging to or devoted to God. **3** consecrated, sacred. [Old English: related to WHOLE]

Holy Communion see COMMUNION.

Holy Ghost *n.* = HOLY SPIRIT.

Holy Grail see GRAIL.

Holyhead /ˌhɒlɪˈhed/ port and resort on Holyhead Island, off the coast of Anglesey, N Wales; pop. (est. 1990) 11 796.

Holy Land *n.* area between the River Jordan and the Mediterranean Sea.

holy of holies *n.* **1** sacred inner chamber of the Jewish temple. **2** thing regarded as most sacred.

holy orders *n.pl.* the status of a bishop, priest, or deacon.

Holy Roman Empire *n. hist.* western part of the Roman Empire as revived by Charlemagne in 800 AD.

Holy See *n.* papacy or papal court.

Holy Spirit *n.* Third Person of the Trinity, God as spiritually acting.

Holy Week *n.* week before Easter.

Holy Writ *n.* holy writings, esp. the Bible.

homage /ˈhɒmɪdʒ/ *n.* tribute, expression of reverence (*pay homage to*). [Latin *homo* man]

Homburg /ˈhɒmbɜːg/ *n.* man's felt hat with a narrow curled brim and a lengthwise dent in the crown. [*Homburg* in Germany]

home *–n.* **1 a** place where one lives; fixed residence. **b** dwelling-house. **2** family circumstances (*comes from a good home*). **3** native land. **4** institution caring for people or animals. **5** place where a thing originates, is kept, or is native or most common. **6 a** finishing-point in a race. **b** (in games) place where one is safe; goal. **7** *Sport* home match or win. *–attrib. adj.* **1 a** of or connected with one's home. **b** carried on, done, or made, at home. **2** in one's own country (*home industries; the home market*). **3** *Sport* played on one's own ground etc. (*home match*). *–adv.* **1** to, at, or in one's home or country (*go home; is he home yet?*). **2** to the point aimed at; completely (*drove the nail home*). *–v.* (**-ming**) **1** (esp. of a trained pigeon) return home. **2** (often foll. by *on*, *in on*) (of a vessel, missile, etc.) be guided towards a destination or target. **3** send or guide homewards. □ **at home 1** in one's house or native land. **2** at ease (*make yourself at home*). **3** (usu. foll. by *in*, *on*, *with*) familiar or well informed. **4** available to callers. [Old English]

home and dry *predic. adj.* having achieved one's aim.

♦ **home audit** *n.* marketing research conducted in the home by means of panels of householders who keep a diary on a regular basis recording the products they buy and when they buy them.

♦ **home banking** *n.* system enabling normal banking transactions to be carried out from a home or office by means of a computer linked to a bank's computer.

---

home-brew *n.* beer or other alcoholic drink brewed at home.

home-coming *n.* arrival at home.

Home Counties *n.pl.* the counties closest to London.

home economics *n.pl.* the study of household management.

home farm *n.* principal farm on an estate, providing produce for the owner.

home-grown *adj.* grown or produced at home.

Home Guard *n. hist.* British citizen army organized for defence in 1940.

home help *n.* person helping with housework etc., esp. one provided by a local authority.

homeland *n.* **1** one's native land. **2** formerly any of several partially self-governing areas in South Africa reserved for Black South Africans (the official name for a Bantustan). Transkei, Bophuthatswana, Venda, and Ciskei were given the nominal status of independent republics, but this was not recognized outside South Africa; these homelands were reincorporated into South Africa in 1994.

homeless *adj.* lacking a home. □ **homelessness** *n.*

homely *adj.* (**-ier**, **-iest**) **1** simple, plain, unpretentious. **2** *US* (of facial appearance) plain, unattractive. **3** comfortable, cosy. □ **homeliness** *n.*

home-made *adj.* made at home.

Home Office *n.* British government department dealing with law and order, immigration, etc., in England and Wales.

homeopathy *US* var. of HOMOEOPATHY.

Homeric /həʊˈmerɪk/ *adj.* **1** of, or in the style of, Homer. **2** of Bronze Age Greece as described in Homer's poems.

home rule *n.* government of a country or region by its own citizens.

Home Secretary *n.* Secretary of State in charge of the Home Office.

♦ **home service assurance** *n.* (also **industrial life assurance**) life assurance, usu. for a small amount, the premiums for which are paid on a regular basis (weekly or monthly) and collected by an agent of the assurance company, who calls at the policyholder's home. Records of the premium payments are kept in a book, which (together with the policy document) has to be produced to make a claim. This type of assurance began in industrial areas, where small weekly policies were purchased to help pay the funeral expenses of the policyholder.

♦ **home shopping** *n.* direct marketing by television, in which programmes or entire channels are dedicated to selling goods or services.

---

homesick *adj.* depressed by absence from home. □ **homesickness** *n.*

homespun *–adj.* **1** made of yarn spun at home. **2** plain, simple. *–n.* homespun cloth.

homestead /ˈhəʊmsted/ *n.* house, esp. a farmhouse, and outbuildings.

home truth *n.* basic but unwelcome information about oneself.

homeward /ˈhəʊmwəd/ *–adv.* (also **homewards**) towards home. *–adj.* going towards home.

homework *n.* **1** work to be done at home, esp. by a school pupil. **2** preparatory work or study.

homey *adj.* (also **homy**) (**-mier**, **-miest**) suggesting home; cosy.

homicide /ˈhɒmɪˌsaɪd/ *n.* **1** killing of a human being by another. **2** person who kills a human being. □ **homicidal** /-ˈsaɪd(ə)l/ *adj.* [Latin *homo* man]

homily /ˈhɒmɪlɪ/ *n.* (*pl.* **-ies**) **1** sermon. **2** tedious moralizing discourse. □ **homiletic** /-ˈletɪk/ *adj.* [Greek *homilia*]

homing *attrib. adj.* **1** (of a pigeon) trained to fly home. **2** (of a device) for guiding to a target etc.

hominid /ˈhɒmɪnɪd/ *–adj.* of the primate family including humans and their fossil ancestors. *–n.* member of this family. [Latin *homo homin-* man]

hominoid /ˈhɒmɪˌnɔɪd/ *–adj.* like a human. *–n.* animal resembling a human.

homo /ˈhəʊməʊ/ *n.* (*pl.* **-s**) *colloq. offens.* homosexual. [abbreviation]

homo- *comb. form* same. [Greek *homos* same]

homoeopathy /ˌhəʊmɪˈɒpəθɪ/ *n.* (*US* **homeopathy**) treatment of disease by minute doses of drugs that in a healthy person would produce symptoms of the disease. □ **homoeopath** /ˈhəʊmɪəʊˌpæθ/ *n.* **homoeopathic** /-ˈpæθɪk/ *adj.* [Greek *homoios* like: related to PATHOS]

homogeneous /ˌhəʊməʊˈdʒiːnɪəs/ *adj.* **1** of the same kind. **2** consisting of parts all of the same kind; uniform. □ **homogeneity** /-dʒɪˈniːɪtɪ/ *n.* **homogeneously** *adv.* [from HOMO-, Greek *genos* kind]

■ **Usage** *Homogeneous* is often confused with *homogenous* which is a term in biology meaning 'similar owing to common descent'.

homogenize /həˈmɒdʒɪˌnaɪz/ *v.* (also **-ise**) (**-zing** or **-sing**) **1** make homogeneous. **2** treat (milk) so that the fat droplets are emulsified and the cream does not separate.

homograph /ˈhɒməˌgrɑːf/ *n.* word spelt like another but of different meaning or origin (e.g. POLE[1], POLE[2]).

homologous /həˈmɒləgəs/ *adj.* **1 a** having the same relation, relative position, etc. **b** corresponding. **2** *Biol.* (of organs etc.) similar in position and structure but not necessarily in function. [from HOMO-, Greek *logos* ratio]

homology /həˈmɒlədʒɪ/ *n.* homologous state or relation; correspondence.

homonym /ˈhɒmənɪm/ *n.* **1** word spelt or pronounced like another but of different meaning; homograph or homophone. **2** namesake. [from HOMO-, *onoma* name]

homophobia /ˌhəʊməˈfəʊbɪə/ *n.* hatred or fear of homosexuals. □ **homophobe** /ˈhəʊm-/ *n.* **homophobic** *adj.*

homophone /ˈhɒməˌfəʊn/ *n.* word pronounced like another but of different meaning or origin (e.g. *pair, pear*). [from HOMO-, Greek *phōnē* sound]

Homo sapiens /ˌhəʊməʊ ˈsæpɪenz/ *n.* modern humans regarded as a species. [Latin, = wise man]

homosexual /ˌhəʊməʊˈsekʃʊəl/ *–adj.* feeling or involving sexual attraction only to people of the same sex. *–n.* homosexual person. □ **homosexuality** /-ˈælɪtɪ/ *n.* [from HOMO-, SEXUAL]

homy var. of HOMEY.

Hon. *abbr.* **1** Honorary. **2** Honourable.

Honan see HENAN.

hone *–n.* whetstone, esp. for razors. *–v.* (**-ning**) sharpen on or as on a hone. [Old English]

honest /ˈɒnɪst/ *–adj.* **1** fair and just; not cheating or stealing. **2** free of deceit and untruthfulness; sincere. **3** fairly earned (*an honest living*). **4** blameless but undistinguished. *–adv. colloq.* genuinely, really. [Latin *honestus*]

honestly *adv.* **1** in an honest way. **2** really (*I don't honestly know*).

honesty *n.* **1** being honest. **2** truthfulness. **3** plant with purple or white flowers and flat round semi-transparent seed-pods.

honey /ˈhʌnɪ/ *n.* (*pl.* **-s**) **1** sweet sticky yellowish fluid made by bees from nectar. **2** colour of this. **3 a** sweetness. **b** sweet thing. **4** esp. *US* (usu. as a form of address) darling. [Old English]

honey-bee *n.* common hive-bee.

honeycomb *–n.* **1** bees' wax structure of hexagonal cells for honey and eggs. **2** pattern arranged hexagonally. *–v.* **1** fill with cavities or tunnels, undermine. **2** mark with a honeycomb pattern. [Old English]

honeydew *n.* **1** sweet sticky substance excreted by aphids on leaves and stems. **2** variety of melon.

honeyed *adj.* (of words, flattery, etc.) sweet, sweet-sounding.

honeymoon *–n.* **1** holiday taken by a newly married couple. **2** initial period of enthusiasm or goodwill. *–v.* spend a honeymoon. □ **honeymooner** *n.*

honeysuckle *n.* climbing shrub with fragrant yellow or pink flowers.

Hong Kong /hɒŋ ˈkɒŋ/ Special Administrative Region of China, formerly a British Crown Colony. Hong Kong, on the SE coast of China, comprises Hong Kong island, the Kowloon peninsula, and the New Territories (on the mainland). Hong Kong is a major financial and manufacturing centre, exporting textiles, clothing, and electronic and plastic products. Its container port is the third largest in the world and there are shipbuilding and ship-repairing industries. By an agreement between the British and Chinese governments (signed in 1984), in 1997 China resumed sovereignty over Hong Kong, which became a Special Administrative Region whose basic law guarantees present systems and life-styles until 2047. In October 1997 the Hong Kong stock exchange suffered a record crash.

Honiara /ˌhəʊnɪˈɑːrə/ capital of the Solomon Islands, on the NW coast of the island of Guadalcanal; exports include coconuts and timber; pop. (1989) 33 749.

honk *–n.* **1** sound of a car horn. **2** cry of a wild goose. *–v.* (cause to) make a honk. [imitative]

honky-tonk /ˈhɒŋkɪˌtɒŋk/ *n. colloq.* **1** ragtime piano music. **2** cheap or disreputable nightclub etc. [origin unknown]

Honolulu /ˌhɒnəˈluːluː/ capital and principal port of Hawaii, situated on the SE coast of the island of Oahu; pop. (est. 1994) 385 881. A tourist and economic centre, it is a stop on trans-Pacific ocean crossings and has a major US naval base at Pearl Harbor.

honor *US* var. of HONOUR.

honorable *US* var. of HONOURABLE.

honorarium /ˌɒnəˈreərɪəm/ *n.* (*pl.* **-s** or **-ria**) fee, esp. a voluntary payment for professional services rendered without the normal fee. [Latin: related to HONOUR]

honorary /ˈɒnərərɪ/ *adj.* **1** conferred as an honour (*honorary degree*). **2** (of an office or its holder) unpaid.

honorific /ˌɒnəˈrɪfɪk/ *adj.* **1** conferring honour. **2** implying respect.

honour /ˈɒnə(r)/ (*US* **honor**) *–n.* **1** high respect, public regard. **2** adherence to what is right or an accepted standard of conduct. **3** nobleness of mind, magnanimity (*honour among thieves*). **4** thing conferred as a distinction, esp. an official award for bravery or achievement. **5** priv-

---

Honduras /hɒnˈdjuːrəs/, **Republic of** country in Central America, between Guatemala and Nicaragua. Agriculture, forestry, and fishing are the principal economic activities; the main exports are coffee, bananas, timber (esp. pine, mahogany, and cedar), shrimps and lobsters, and frozen meat. Hydroelectricity is an increasing source of power. There is some mining (esp. of zinc and lead) and light manufacturing industry. The IMF is closely monitoring the weak economy, and tax reforms have improved the fiscal position. Honduras was a dependency of Spain until the proclamation of independence in 1821; since 1982, after a period of military rule, the country has stabilized as a democracy. In 1996 economic problems were causing internal tensions, notably among the military. President, Carlos Roberto Reina; capital, Tegucigalpa. □ **Honduran** *adj.* & *n.*

language	Spanish
currency	lempira (L) of 100 centavos
pop. (est. 1996)	5 666 000
GNP (1994)	US$3.1B
literacy	75% (m); 70% (f)
life expectancy	64 (m); 69 (f)

Exchange rate, US¢ per L (a) Inflation, % (b)

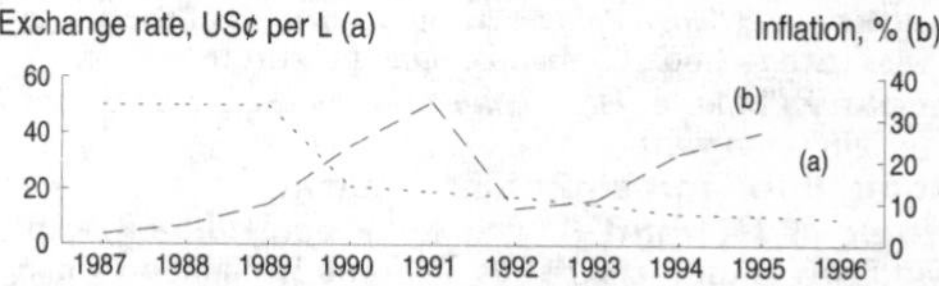

---

ilege, special right (*had the honour of being invited*). **6 a** exalted position. **b** (**Honour**) (prec. by *your*, *his*, etc.) title of a circuit judge etc. **7** (foll. by *to*) person or thing that brings honour (*an honour to her profession*). **8 a** chastity (of a woman). **b** reputation for this. **9** (in *pl.*) specialized degree course or special distinction in an examination. **10** (in card-games) the four or five highest-ranking cards. **11** *Golf* the right of driving off first. –*v.* **1** respect highly. **2** confer honour on. **3** accept or pay (a bill or cheque) when due. □ **do the honours** perform the duties of a host to guests etc. **in honour of** as a celebration of. **on one's honour** (usu. foll. by *to* + infin.) under a moral obligation. [Latin *honor* repute]

honourable *adj.* (*US* **honorable**) **1** deserving, bringing, or showing honour. **2** (**Honourable**) title indicating distinction, given to certain high officials, the children of certain ranks of the nobility, and (in the House of Commons) to MPs. □ **honourably** *adv.*

Honshu /hɒn'ʃuː/ largest of the four main islands of Japan; pop. (1995) 100 995 000. Traditionally a centre of the silk industry, it now also has engineering, iron and steel, chemical, and textile industries.

hooch *n. US colloq.* alcoholic liquor, esp. inferior or illicit whisky. [Alaskan]

HOOD /hʊd/ *abbr. Computing* hierarchical object-oriented design.

hood[1] /hʊd/ –*n.* **1 a** covering for the head and neck, esp. as part of a garment. **b** separate hoodlike garment. **2** folding top of a car etc. **3** *US* bonnet of a car etc. **4** protective cover. –*v.* cover with or as with a hood. [Old English]

hood[2] /hʊd/ *n. US slang* gangster, gunman. [abbreviation of HOODLUM]

-hood *suffix* forming nouns: **1** of condition or state (*childhood*; *falsehood*). **2** designating a group (*sisterhood*; *neighbourhood*). [Old English]

hooded *adj.* **1** having a hood. **2** (of an animal) having a hoodlike part (*hooded crow*).

hoodlum /'huːdləm/ *n.* **1** street hooligan, young thug. **2** gangster. [origin unknown]

hoodoo /'huːduː/ *n.* esp. *US* **1 a** bad luck. **b** thing or person that brings this. **2** voodoo. [alteration of VOODOO]

hoodwink *v.* deceive, delude. [from HOOD[1]: originally = 'blindfold']

hoof /huːf/ *n.* (*pl.* **-s** or **hooves** /-vz/) horny part of the foot of a horse etc. □ **hoof it** *slang* go on foot. [Old English]

hoo-ha /'huːhɑː/ *n. slang* commotion. [origin unknown]

hook /hʊk/ –*n.* **1 a** bent or curved piece of metal etc. for catching hold or for hanging things on. **b** (in full **fish-hook**) bent piece of wire for catching fish. **2** curved cutting instrument (*reaping-hook*). **3** bend in a river, curved strip of land, etc. **4 a** hooking stroke. **b** *Boxing* short swinging blow. –*v.* **1** grasp or secure with hook(s). **2** catch with or as with a hook. **3** *slang* steal. **4** (in sports) send (the ball) in a curve or deviating path. **5** *Rugby* secure (the ball) and pass it backward with the foot in the scrum. □ **by hook or by crook** by one means or another. **off the hook 1** *colloq.* out of difficulty or trouble. **2** (of a telephone receiver) not on its rest. [Old English]

hookah /'hʊkə/ *n.* oriental tobacco-pipe with a long tube passing through water for cooling the smoke as it is drawn through. [Urdu from Arabic, = casket]

hook and eye *n.* small metal hook and loop as a fastener on a garment.

hooked *adj.* **1** hook-shaped. **2** (often foll. by *on*) *slang* addicted or captivated.

hooker *n.* **1** *Rugby* player in the front row of the scrum who tries to hook the ball. **2** *slang* prostitute.

hookey /'hʊkɪ/ *n. US* □ **play hookey** *slang* play truant. [origin unknown]

hook, line, and sinker *adv.* entirely.

Hook of Holland (Dutch **Hoek van Holland**) cape and port of the Netherlands, in South Holland province, linked by ferry to Harwich, Hull, and Dublin.

hook-up *n.* connection, esp. of broadcasting equipment.

hookworm *n.* worm with hooklike mouthparts, infesting humans and animals.

hooligan /'huːlɪgən/ *n.* young ruffian. □ **hooliganism** *n.* [origin unknown]

hoop –*n.* **1** circular band of metal, wood, etc., esp. as part of a framework. **2** ring bowled along by a child, or for circus performers to jump through. **3** arch through which balls are hit in croquet. –*v.* bind or encircle with hoop(s). □ **be put** (or **go**) **through the hoop** (or **hoops**) undergo rigorous testing. [Old English]

hoop-la *n.* fairground game with rings thrown to encircle a prize.

hoopoe /'huːpuː/ *n.* salmon-pink bird with black and white wings and a large erectile crest. [Latin *upupa* (imitative of its cry)]

hooray /hʊ'reɪ/ *int.* = HURRAH.

Hooray Henry /'huːreɪ/ *n. slang* loud upper-class young man.

hoot –*n.* **1** owl's cry. **2** sound made by a car's horn etc. **3** shout expressing scorn or disapproval. **4** *colloq.* **a** laughter. **b** cause of this. **5** (also **two hoots**) *slang* anything at all, in the slightest degree (*don't care a hoot*; *doesn't matter two hoots*). –*v.* **1** utter or make hoot(s). **2** greet or drive away with scornful hoots. **3** sound (a car horn etc.). [imitative]

hooter *n.* **1** thing that hoots, esp. a car's horn or a siren. **2** *slang* nose.

Hoover –*n. propr.* vacuum cleaner. –*v.* (**hoover**) **1** (also *absol.*) clean with a vacuum cleaner. **2** (foll. by *up*) **a** suck up with a vacuum cleaner. **b** clean a room etc. with a vacuum cleaner. [name of the manufacturer]

hooves *pl.* of HOOF.

hop[1] –*v.* (**-pp-**) **1** (of a bird, frog, etc.) spring with two or all feet at once. **2** (of a person) jump on one foot. **3** move or go quickly (*hopped over the fence*). **4** cross (a ditch etc.) by hopping. –*n.* **1** hopping movement. **2** *colloq.* informal dance. **3** short journey, esp. a flight. □ **hop in** (or **out**) *colloq.* get into (or out of) a car etc. **hop it** *slang* go away. **on the hop** *colloq.* unprepared (*caught on the hop*). [Old English]

hop[2] *n.* **1** climbing plant bearing cones. **2** (in *pl.*) its ripe cones, used to flavour beer. [Low German or Dutch]

hope –*n.* **1** expectation and desire for a thing. **2** person or thing giving cause for hope. **3** what is hoped for. –*v.* (**-ping**) **1** feel hope. **2** expect and desire. **3** feel fairly confident. □ **hope against hope** cling to a mere possibility. [Old English]

hopeful –*adj.* **1** feeling hope. **2** causing or inspiring hope. **3** likely to succeed, promising. –*n.* person likely to succeed.

hopefully *adv.* **1** in a hopeful manner. **2** it is to be hoped (*hopefully, we will succeed*).

■ **Usage** The use of *hopefully* in sense 2 is common but is considered incorrect by some people.

Hopeh see HEBEI.

hopeless *adj.* **1** feeling no hope. **2** admitting no hope (*hopeless case*). **3** incompetent. □ **hopelessly** *adv.* **hopelessness** *n.*

hopper[1] *n.* **1** container tapering downward to an opening for discharging its contents. **2** hopping insect.

hopper[2] *n.* hop-picker.

hopping mad *predic. adj. colloq.* very angry.

hopscotch *n.* children's game of hopping over squares marked on the ground to retrieve a stone etc. [from HOP[1], SCOTCH]

horde *n.* usu. *derog.* large group, gang. [Turkish *ordū* camp]

horehound /'hɔːhaʊnd/ *n.* herbaceous plant yielding a bitter aromatic juice used against coughs etc. [Old English, = hoary herb]

horizon /hə'raɪz(ə)n/ *n.* **1** line at which the earth and sky appear to meet. **2** limit of mental perception, experience, interest, etc. □ **on the horizon** (of an event) just imminent or becoming apparent. [Greek *horizō* bound]

horizontal /ˌhɒrɪ'zɒnt(ə)l/ *–adj.* **1** parallel to the plane of the horizon, at right angles to the vertical. **2** of or concerned with the same work, status, etc. (*it was a horizontal move rather than promotion*). *–n.* horizontal line, plane, etc. □ **horizontality** /-'tælɪtɪ/ *n.* **horizontally** *adv.*

♦ **horizontal integration** see INTEGRATION 3.
♦ **horizontal mobility** see MOBILITY OF LABOUR.

hormone /'hɔːməʊn/ *n.* **1** regulatory substance produced in an organism and transported in tissue fluids to stimulate cells or tissues into action. **2** similar synthetic substance. □ **hormonal** /-'məʊn(ə)l/ *adj.* [Greek *hormaō* impel]

hormone replacement therapy *n.* treatment to relieve menopausal symptoms by boosting a woman's oestrogen levels.

Hormuz /'hɔːmʊz/, **Strait of** strait separating Iran from the Arabian peninsula and linking the Persian Gulf with the Gulf of Oman, which leads to the Arabian Sea. It is of strategic and economic importance as a waterway through which sea traffic to and from the oil-rich Gulf States must pass.

horn *n.* **1 a** hard outgrowth, often curved and pointed, on the head of esp. hoofed animals. **b** each of two branched appendages on the head of (esp. male) deer. **c** hornlike projection on animals, e.g. a snail's tentacle. **2** substance of which horns are made. **3** *Mus.* **a** = FRENCH HORN. **b** wind instrument played by lip vibration, orig. made of horn, now usu. of brass. **4** instrument sounding a warning. **5** receptacle or instrument made of horn. **6** horn-shaped projection. **7** extremity of the moon or other crescent. **8** arm of a river etc. □ **horn in** *slang* intrude, interfere. □ **horned** *adj.* **hornist** *n.* (in sense 3 of *n.*). [Old English]

hornbeam *n.* tree with a hard tough wood.

hornbill *n.* bird with a hornlike excrescence on its large curved bill.

hornblende /'hɔːnblend/ *n.* dark-brown, black, or green mineral occurring in many rocks. [German]

hornet /'hɔːnɪt/ *n.* large wasp capable of inflicting a serious sting. [Low German or Dutch]

horn of plenty *n.* a cornucopia.

hornpipe *n.* **1** lively dance (esp. associated with sailors). **2** music for this.

horn-rimmed *adj.* (esp. of spectacles) having rims made of horn or a similar substance.

♦ **horns and halo effect** *n.* tendency to permit judgement of another person, esp. in a job interview, to be unduly influenced by unfavourable (horns) or favourable (halo) first impressions based on appearances.

horny *adj.* (**-ier, -iest**) **1** of or like horn. **2** hard like horn. **3** *slang* sexually excited. □ **horniness** *n.*

horology /hə'rɒlədʒɪ/ *n.* art of measuring time or making clocks, watches, etc. □ **horological** /ˌhɒrə'lɒdʒɪk(ə)l/ *adj.* [Greek *hōra* time]

horoscope /'hɒrəˌskəʊp/ *n.* **1** forecast of a person's future from a diagram showing the relative positions of the stars and planets at his or her birth. **2** such a diagram. [Greek *hōra* time, *skopos* observer]

horrendous /hə'rendəs/ *adj.* horrifying. □ **horrendously** *adv.* [Latin: related to HORRIBLE]

horrible /'hɒrɪb(ə)l/ *adj.* **1** causing or likely to cause horror. **2** *colloq.* unpleasant. □ **horribly** *adv.* [Latin *horreo* bristle, shudder at]

horrid /'hɒrɪd/ *adj.* **1** horrible, revolting. **2** *colloq.* unpleasant (*horrid weather*).

horrific /hə'rɪfɪk/ *adj.* horrifying. □ **horrifically** *adv.*

horrify /'hɒrɪˌfaɪ/ *v.* (**-ies, -ied**) arouse horror in; shock. □ **horrifying** *adj.*

horror /'hɒrə(r)/ *–n.* **1** painful feeling of loathing and fear. **2 a** (often foll. by *of*) intense dislike. **b** (often foll. by *at*) *colloq.* intense dismay. **3 a** person or thing causing horror. **b** *colloq.* bad or mischievous person etc. **4** (in *pl.*; prec. by *the*) fit of depression, nervousness, etc. *–attrib. adj.* (of films etc.) designed to interest by arousing feelings of horror.

hors-d'œuvre /ɔː'dɜːvr/ *n.* food served as an appetizer at the start of a meal. [French, = outside the work]

horse *–n.* **1 a** large four-legged mammal with flowing mane and tail, used for riding and to carry and pull loads. **b** adult male horse; stallion or gelding. **c** (*collect.*; as *sing.*) cavalry. **2** vaulting-block. **3** supporting frame (*clothes-horse*). *–v.* (**-sing**) (foll. by *around*) fool about. □ **from the horse's mouth** *colloq.* (of information etc.) from the original or an authoritative source. [Old English]

horseback *n.* □ **on horseback** mounted on a horse.

horsebox *n.* closed vehicle for transporting horse(s).

horse-brass *n.* brass ornament orig. for a horse's harness.

horse chestnut *n.* **1** large tree with upright conical clusters of flowers. **2** dark brown fruit of this.

horse-drawn *adj.* (of a vehicle) pulled by a horse or horses.

horseflesh *n.* **1** flesh of a horse, esp. as food. **2** horses collectively.

horsefly *n.* any of various biting insects troublesome esp. to horses.

Horse Guards *n.pl.* cavalry brigade of the household troops.

horsehair *n.* hair from the mane or tail of a horse, used for padding etc.

horseman *n.* **1** rider on horseback. **2** skilled rider. □ **horsemanship** *n.*

Horsens /'hɔːsənz/ port in E Denmark; pop. (1995) 55 252.

horseplay *n.* boisterous play.

horsepower *n.* (*pl.* same) imperial unit of power (about 750 watts), esp. for measuring the power of an engine.

horse-race *n.* race between horses with riders. □ **horse-racing** *n.*

horseradish *n.* plant with a pungent root used to make a sauce.

horse sense *n. colloq.* plain common sense.

horseshoe *n.* **1** U-shaped iron shoe for a horse. **2** thing of this shape.

horsetail *n.* **1** horse's tail. **2** plant resembling it.

horsewhip *–n.* whip for driving horses. *–v.* (**-pp-**) beat with a horsewhip.

horsewoman *n.* **1** woman who rides on horseback. **2** skilled woman rider.

horsy *adj.* (**-ier, -iest**) **1** of or like a horse. **2** concerned with or devoted to horses.

horticulture /'hɔːtɪˌkʌltʃə(r)/ *n.* art of garden cultivation. □ **horticultural** /-'kʌltʃər(ə)l/ *adj.* **horticulturist** /-'kʌltʃərɪst/ *n.* [Latin *hortus* garden, CULTURE]

hosanna /həʊ'zænə/ *n.* & *int.* shout of adoration (Matt. 21:9, 15, etc.). [Hebrew]

hose /həʊz/ *–n.* **1** (also **hose-pipe**) flexible tube for conveying water. **2 a** (*collect.*; as *pl.*) stockings and socks. **b** *hist.* breeches (*doublet and hose*). *–v.* (**-sing**) (often foll. by *down*) water, spray, or drench with a hose. [Old English]

hosier /'həʊzɪə(r)/ *n.* dealer in hosiery.

hosiery *n.* stockings and socks.

hospice /'hɒspɪs/ *n.* **1** home for people who are ill (esp. terminally) or destitute. **2** lodging for travellers, esp. one kept by a religious order. [Latin: related to HOST²]

hospitable /hɒ'spɪtəb(ə)l/ *adj.* giving hospitality. □ **hospitably** *adv.* [Latin *hospito* entertain: related to HOST²]

hospital /'hɒspɪt(ə)l/ *n.* **1** institution providing medical and surgical treatment and nursing care for ill and injured people. **2** *hist.* hospice. [Latin: related to HOST²]

hospitality /ˌhɒspɪ'tælɪtɪ/ *n.* friendly and generous reception and entertainment of guests or strangers.

hospitalize /'hɒspɪtəˌlaɪz/ *v.* (also **-ise**) (**-zing** or **-sing**) send or admit (a patient) to hospital. □ **hospitalization** /-'zeɪʃ(ə)n/ *n.*

host[1] /həʊst/ *n.* (usu. foll. by *of*) large number of people or things. [Latin *hostis* enemy, army]

host[2] /həʊst/ *–n.* **1** person who receives or entertains another as a guest. **2** compère. **3** *Biol.* animal or plant having a parasite. **4** recipient of a transplanted organ etc. **5** landlord of an inn. *–v.* be host to (a person) or of (an event). [Latin *hospes hospitis* host, guest]

host[3] /həʊst/ *n.* (usu. prec. by *the*; often **Host**) bread consecrated in the Eucharist. [Latin *hostia* victim]

hostage /'hɒstɪdʒ/ *n.* person seized or held as security for the fulfilment of a condition. [Latin *obses obsidis* hostage]

host computer *n.* computer attached to a network, mainly in order to provide services to the network users rather than to function in the operation of the network. Hosts can range from small microcomputers to mainframes. The latter may provide powerful computation facilities, a large filestore, special programs or programming languages, and access to one or more databases.

hostel /'hɒst(ə)l/ *n.* **1** house of residence or lodging for students, nurses, etc. **2** = YOUTH HOSTEL. [medieval Latin: related to HOSPITAL]

hostelling *n.* (*US* **hosteling**) practice of staying in youth hostels. □ **hosteller** *n.*

hostelry *n.* (*pl.* **-ies**) *archaic* inn.

hostess /'həʊstɪs/ *n.* **1** woman who receives or entertains a guest. **2** woman employed to entertain customers at a nightclub etc. **3** stewardess on an aircraft etc. [related to HOST[2]]

hostile /'hɒstaɪl/ *adj.* **1** of an enemy. **2** (often foll. by *to*) unfriendly, opposed. □ **hostilely** *adv.* [Latin: related to HOST[1]]

♦ **hostile take-over** *n.* (also **hostile bid**) take-over bid that is opposed by the directors or shareholders of the target company.

---

hostility /hɒ'stɪlɪtɪ/ *n.* (*pl.* **-ies**) **1** being hostile, enmity. **2** state of warfare. **3** (in *pl.*) acts of warfare.

hot *–adj.* (**hotter, hottest**) **1** having a high temperature. **2** causing a sensation of heat (*hot flush*). **3** (of pepper, spices, etc.) pungent. **4** (of a person) feeling heat. **5 a** ardent, passionate, excited. **b** (often foll. by *for, on*) eager, keen (*in hot pursuit*). **c** angry or upset. **6** (of news etc.) fresh, recent. **7** *Hunting* (of the scent) fresh, recent. **8 a** (of a player, competitor, or feat) very skilful, formidable. **b** (foll. by *on*) knowledgeable about. **9** (esp. of jazz) strongly rhythmical. **10** *slang* (of stolen goods) difficult to dispose of because identifiable. **11** *slang* radioactive. *–v.* (**-tt-**) (usu. foll. by *up*) *colloq.* **1** make or become hot. **2** make or become more active, exciting, or dangerous. □ **have the hots for** *slang* be sexually attracted to. **hot under the collar** angry, resentful, embarrassed. **like hot cakes** see CAKE. **make it** (or **things) hot for a person** persecute a person. □ **hotly** *adv.* **hotness** *n.* **hottish** *adj.* [Old English]

hot air *n. slang* empty or boastful talk.

hot-air balloon *n.* balloon containing air heated by burners below it, causing it to rise.

hotbed *n.* **1** (foll. by *of*) environment conducive to (vice, intrigue, etc.). **2** bed of earth heated by fermenting manure.

hot-blooded *adj.* ardent, passionate.

hotchpotch /'hɒtʃpɒtʃ/ *n.* (also **hodgepodge** /'hɒdʒpɒdʒ/) confused mixture or jumble, esp. of ideas. [French *hochepot* shake pot]

hot cross bun *n.* bun marked with a cross and traditionally eaten on Good Friday.

hot dog *n. colloq.* hot sausage in a soft roll.

hotel /həʊ'tel/ *n.* (usu. licensed) establishment providing accommodation and meals for payment. [French: related to HOSTEL]

hotelier /həʊ'telɪə(r)/ *n.* hotel-keeper.

hot flush see FLUSH[1].

hotfoot *–adv.* in eager haste. *–v.* hurry eagerly (esp. *hotfoot it*).

hot gospeller *n. colloq.* eager preacher of the gospel.

hothead *n.* impetuous person. □ **hotheaded** *adj.* **hotheadedness** *n.*

hothouse *n.* **1** heated (mainly glass) building for rearing tender plants. **2** environment conducive to the rapid growth or development of something.

hot line *n.* direct exclusive telephone etc. line, esp. for emergencies.

♦ **hot money** *n.* **1** money that moves at short notice from one financial centre to another in search of the highest short-term interest rates, for the purposes of arbitrage, or because its owners are apprehensive of some political intervention in the money market, e.g. a devaluation. Hot money can influence a country's balance of payments. **2** *slang* money that has been acquired dishonestly and must therefore be untraceable.

---

hotplate *n.* heated metal plate etc. (or a set of these) for cooking food or keeping it hot.

hotpot *n.* casserole of meat and vegetables topped with potato.

hot potato *n. colloq.* contentious matter.

hot rod *n.* vehicle modified to have extra power and speed.

hot seat *n. slang* **1** position of difficult responsibility. **2** electric chair.

hot spot *n.* **1** small region that is relatively hot. **2** lively or dangerous place.

hot stuff *n. colloq.* **1** formidably capable or important person or thing. **2** sexually attractive person. **3** erotic book, film, etc.

hot-tempered *adj.* impulsively angry.

Hottentot /'hɒtən,tɒt/ *n.* **1** member of a SW African Negroid people. **2** their language. [Afrikaans]

hot water *n. colloq.* difficulty or trouble.

hot-water bottle *n.* (usu. rubber) container filled with hot water to warm a bed.

houmous var. of HUMMUS.

hound *–n.* **1** dog used in hunting. **2** *colloq.* despicable man. *–v.* harass or pursue. [Old English]

hour /aʊə(r)/ *n.* **1** twenty-fourth part of a day and night, 60 minutes. **2** time of day, point in time (*a late hour*; *what is the hour?*). **3** (in *pl.* with preceding numerals in form 18.00, 20.30, etc.) this number of hours and minutes past midnight on the 24-hour clock (*will assemble at 20.00 hours*). **4 a** period for a specific purpose (*lunch hour*; *keep regular hours*). **b** (in *pl.*) fixed working or open period (*office hours*; *opening hours*). **5** short period of time (*an idle hour*). **6** present time (*question of the hour*). **7** time for action etc. (*the hour has come*). **8** expressing distance by travelling time (*we are an hour from London*). **9** *RC Ch.* prayers to be said at one of seven fixed times of day (*book of hours*). **10** (prec. by *the*) each time o'clock of a whole number of hours (*buses leave on the hour*; *on the half hour*; *at a quarter past the hour*). □ **after hours** after closing-time. [Greek *hōra*]

hourglass *n.* two vertically connected glass bulbs containing sand taking an hour to pass from upper to lower bulb.

houri /'hʊərɪ/ *n.* (*pl.* **-s**) beautiful young woman of the Muslim Paradise. [Persian from Arabic, = dark-eyed]

hourly *–adj.* **1** done or occurring every hour. **2** frequent. **3** per hour (*hourly wage*). *–adv.* **1** every hour. **2** frequently.

house *–n.* /haʊs/ (*pl.* /'haʊzɪz/) **1** building for human habitation. **2** building for a special purpose or for animals or goods (*opera-house*; *summer-house*; *hen-house*). **3 a** religious community. **b** its buildings. **4 a** body of pupils living in the same building at a boarding-school. **b** such a building. **c** division of a day-school for games, competitions, etc. **5** royal family or dynasty (*House of York*). **6 a** firm or institution. **b** its premises. **7 a** legislative or deliberative assembly. **b** building for this. **8** audience or performance in a theatre etc. **9** *Astrol.* twelfth part of the heavens. *–v.* /haʊz/ (**-sing**) **1** provide with a house or other accommodation. **2** store (goods etc.). **3** enclose or encase (a part or fitting). **4** fix in a socket, mortise, etc. □ **keep house** provide for or manage a household. **like a house on fire 1** vigorously, fast. **2** successfully, excellently. **on the house** free. **put** (or **set**) **one's house in order** make necessary reforms. [Old English]

house-agent *n.* agent for the sale and letting of houses.

house arrest *n.* detention in one's own house, not in prison.

houseboat *n.* boat equipped for living in.

housebound *adj.* confined to one's house through illness etc.

♦ **house brand** *n.* = OWN BRAND.

---

housebreaking /ˈhaʊsˌbreɪkɪŋ/ *n.* act of breaking into a building, esp. in daytime, to commit a crime. □ **housebreaker** *n.*

■ **Usage** In 1968 housebreaking was replaced as a statutory crime in English law by *burglary*.

housecoat *n.* woman's informal indoor coat or gown.

housefly *n.* common fly often entering houses.

household *n.* **1** occupants of a house as a unit. **2** house and its affairs.

householder *n.* **1** person who owns or rents a house. **2** head of a household.

♦ **household insurance** *n.* insurance that covers the structure of a home (often called **buildings insurance**) or the personal goods and effects kept inside a home under a **contents policy**. A **comprehensive householder's policy** will cover both the buildings and the contents.

---

household troops *n.pl.* troops nominally guarding the sovereign.

household word *n.* (also **household name**) **1** familiar name or saying. **2** familiar person or thing.

house-hunting *n.* seeking a house to buy or rent.

house-husband *n.* man who does a wife's traditional household duties.

♦ **house journal** *n.* journal produced by a large organization for the benefit of its employees, usu. to keep all levels of employees informed of the general policy of the company, to function as a forum for employees, and often to provide social news. It often helps to create a corporate identity, esp. if employees are widely distributed geographically.

---

housekeeper *n.* person, esp. a woman, employed to manage a household.

housekeeping *n.* **1** management of household affairs. **2** money allowed for this. **3** operations of maintenance, record-keeping, etc. in an organization. **4** actions performed within a computer program or within a computer system in order to maintain internal orderliness. In the case of a computer system, housekeeping involves backing up the filestore, deleting files that are no longer required or whose expiry dates have passed, and many other mundane but essential tasks.

house lights *n.pl.* lights in a theatre auditorium.

housemaid *n.* female servant in a house.

housemaid's knee *n.* inflammation of the kneecap.

houseman *n.* resident junior doctor at a hospital etc.

house-martin *n.* black and white bird nesting on house walls etc.

housemaster *n.* (*fem.* **housemistress**) teacher in charge of a house, esp. at a boarding-school.

house music *n.* style of pop music, typically using drum machines and synthesized bass lines with sparse repetitive vocals and a fast beat.

house of cards *n.* insecure scheme etc.

House of Commons *n.* elected chamber of Parliament.

House of Keys *n.* (in the Isle of Man) elected chamber of the Tynwald.

House of Lords *n.* chamber of Parliament that is mainly hereditary.

house party *n.* group of guests staying at a country house etc.

house-plant *n.* plant grown indoors.

house-proud *adj.* attentive to the care and appearance of the home.

houseroom *n.* space or accommodation in one's house. □ **not give houseroom to** not have in any circumstances.

housetop *n.* roof of a house. □ **shout** etc. **from the housetops** announce publicly.

house-trained *adj.* **1** (of animals) trained to be clean in the house. **2** *colloq.* well-mannered.

house-warming *n.* party celebrating a move to a new home.

housewife *n.* **1** woman who manages a household and usu. does not have a full-time paid job. **2** /ˈhʌzɪf/ case for needles, thread, etc. □ **housewifely** *adj.* [from HOUSE, WIFE = woman]

housework *n.* regular housekeeping work, e.g. cleaning and cooking.

housey-housey /ˌhaʊzɪˈhaʊzɪ/ *n.* (also **housie-housie**) *slang* gambling form of lotto.

housing /ˈhaʊzɪŋ/ *n.* **1 a** dwelling-houses collectively. **b** provision of these. **2** shelter, lodging. **3** rigid casing for machinery etc. **4** hole or niche cut in one piece of wood for another to fit into.

housing estate *n.* residential area planned as a unit.

Houston /ˈhjuːst(ə)n/ city in the US, an inland port of Texas, linked to the Gulf of Mexico by the Houston Ship Canal; pop. (1994) 1 702 086. It has important oil and petrochemical industries, and is a centre for space research.

hove *past* of HEAVE.

hovel /ˈhɒv(ə)l/ *n.* small miserable dwelling. [origin unknown]

hover /ˈhɒvə(r)/ *–v.* **1** (of a bird etc.) remain in one place in the air. **2** (often foll. by *about, round*) wait close at hand, linger. *–n.* **1** hovering. **2** state of suspense. [obsolete *hove* hover]

hovercraft *n.* (*pl.* same) vehicle travelling on a cushion of air provided by a downward blast.

hoverport *n.* terminal for hovercraft.

how *–interrog. adv.* **1** by what means, in what way (*how do you do it?*; *tell me how you do it*; *how could you?*). **2** in what condition, esp. of health (*how are you?*; *how do things stand?*). **3 a** to what extent (*how far is it?*; *how would you like to take my place?*; *how we laughed!*). **b** to what extent good or well, what … like (*how was the film?*; *how did they play?*). *–rel. adv.* in whatever way, as (*do it how you can*). *–conj. colloq.* that (*told us how he'd been in India*). □ **how about** *colloq.* would you like (*how about a quick swim?*). **how do you do?** a formal greeting. **how many** what number. **how much 1** what amount. **2** what price. **how's that? 1** what is your opinion or explanation of that? **2** *Cricket* (said to an umpire) is the batsman out or not? [Old English]

howbeit /haʊˈbiːɪt/ *adv. archaic* nevertheless.

howdah /ˈhaʊdə/ *n.* (usu. canopied) seat for riding on an elephant or camel. [Urdu *hawda*]

however /haʊˈevə(r)/ *adv.* **1 a** in whatever way (*do it however you want*). **b** to whatever extent (*must go however inconvenient*). **2** nevertheless.

howitzer /ˈhaʊɪtsə(r)/ *n.* short gun for the high-angle firing of shells. [Czech *houfnice* catapult]

howl *–n.* **1** long loud doleful cry of a dog etc. **2** prolonged wailing noise. **3** loud cry of pain, rage, derision, or laughter. *–v.* **1** make a howl. **2** weep loudly. **3** utter with a howl. □ **howl down** prevent (a speaker) from being heard by howls of derision. [imitative]

howler *n. colloq.* glaring mistake.

howsoever /ˌhaʊsəʊˈevə(r)/ *adv. formal* **1** in whatsoever way. **2** to whatsoever extent.

hoy *int.* used to call attention. [natural cry]

hoyden /ˈhɔɪd(ə)n/ *n.* boisterous girl. [Dutch *heiden*: related to HEATHEN]

HP *–abbr.* **1** Hewlett–Packard (US electronics and computing manufacturer). **2** = HIRE PURCHASE. *–international civil aircraft marking* Panama. *–postcode* Hemel Hempstead.

h.p. 1 half pay. **2** hire purchase. **3** (also **hp**) horsepower.

HQ *abbr.* headquarters.

HR *–postcode* Hereford. *–international civil aircraft marking* Honduras.

Hr *abbr.* = HERR.

hr. *abbr.* hour.

HRH *abbr.* Her or His Royal Highness.

HRM *abbr.* = HUMAN-RESOURCE MANAGEMENT.

hrs. *abbr.* hours.

HRT *abbr.* hormone replacement therapy.

hryvna /hrʌvnə/ *n.* (*pl.* **hryvny**) standard monetary unit of Ukraine.

HS *international civil aircraft marking* Thailand.

HSC *abbr.* = HEALTH AND SAFETY COMMISSION.

HSE *abbr.* Health and Safety Executive.

HSI *abbr.* human–system interface (or interaction). See USER INTERFACE.

HT *abbr.* high tension.

HU *postcode* Hull.

Huambo /ˈwæmbəʊ/ (formerly **Nova Lisboa**) city in W Angola; railway industries and agriculture are important; pop. (1995) 400 000.

Huang Ho see YELLOW RIVER.

hub *n.* **1** central part of a wheel, rotating on or with the axle. **2** centre of interest, activity, etc. [origin uncertain]

hubble-bubble /ˈhʌb(ə)lˌbʌb(ə)l/ *n.* **1** simple hookah. **2** bubbling sound. **3** confused talk. [imitative]

hubbub /ˈhʌbʌb/ *n.* **1** confused noise of talking. **2** disturbance. [perhaps of Irish origin]

hubby /ˈhʌbɪ/ *n.* (*pl.* **-ies**) *colloq.* husband. [abbreviation]

Hubei /huːˈbeɪ/ (also **Hupeh**) province of E central China; pop. (est. 1995) 57 190 000; capital, Wuhan. It is mainly agricultural, producing wheat, rice, and cotton, but some gypsum, iron ore, and phosphorus are mined.

hubris /ˈhjuːbrɪs/ *n.* arrogant pride or presumption. □ **hubristic** /-ˈbrɪstɪk/ *adj.* [Greek]

huckleberry /ˈhʌkəlbərɪ/ *n.* **1** low-growing North American shrub. **2** blue or black fruit of this. [probably an alteration of *hurtleberry*, WHORTLEBERRY]

huckster *–n.* aggressive salesman; hawker. *–v.* **1** haggle. **2** hawk (goods). [Low German]

huddle /ˈhʌd(ə)l/ *–v.* (**-ling**) **1** (often foll. by *up*) crowd together; nestle closely. **2** (often foll. by *up*) curl one's body into a small space. **3** heap together in a muddle. *–n.* **1** confused or crowded mass. **2** *colloq.* close or secret conference (esp. in **go into a huddle**). [perhaps from Low German]

Hué /hweɪ/ city in central Vietnam, a commercial centre with textile, chemical, and cement industries; pop. (est. 1992) 219 149.

hue *n.* **1** colour, tint. **2** variety or shade of colour. [Old English]

hue and cry *n.* loud outcry. [French *huer* shout]

huff *–n. colloq.* fit of petty annoyance. *–v.* **1** blow air, steam, etc. **2** (esp. **huff and puff**) bluster self-importantly but ineffectually. **3** *Draughts* remove (an opponent's piece) as a forfeit. □ **in a huff** *colloq.* annoyed and offended. [imitative of blowing]

huffy *adj.* (**-ier, -iest**) *colloq.* **1** apt to take offence. **2** offended. □ **huffily** *adv.* **huffiness** *n.*

hug *–v.* (**-gg-**) **1** squeeze tightly in one's arms, esp. with affection. **2** (of a bear) squeeze (a person) between its forelegs. **3** keep close to; fit tightly around. *–n.* **1** strong clasp with the arms. **2** squeezing grip in wrestling. [probably Scandinavian]

huge *adj.* **1** extremely large; enormous. **2** (of an abstract thing) very great. □ **hugeness** *n.* [French *ahuge*]

hugely *adv.* **1** extremely (*hugely successful*). **2** very much (*enjoyed it hugely*).

hugger-mugger /ˈhʌgəˌmʌgə(r)/ *–adj.* & *adv.* **1** in secret. **2** confused; in confusion. *–n.* **1** secrecy. **2** confusion. [origin uncertain]

Huguenot /ˈhjuːgəˌnəʊ/ *n. hist.* French Protestant. [French]

huh /hə/ *int.* expressing disgust, surprise, etc. [imitative]

hula /ˈhuːlə/ *n.* (also **hula-hula**) Polynesian dance performed by women, with flowing arm movements. [Hawaiian]

hula hoop *n.* large hoop spun round the body.

hulk *n.* **1** body of a dismantled ship. **2** *colloq.* large clumsy-looking person or thing. [Old English]

hulking *adj. colloq.* bulky; clumsy.

Hull /hʌl/ (also **Kingston-upon-Hull**) city and port in NE England, in Humberside; industries include fish-processing, electrical goods, paint, pharmaceuticals, and textiles; pop. (est. 1994) 269 100.

hull[1] *n.* body of a ship, airship, etc. [perhaps related to HOLD[2]]

hull[2] *–n.* outer covering of a fruit, esp. the pod of peas and beans, the husk of grain, or the green calyx of a strawberry. *–v.* remove the hulls from (fruit etc.). [Old English]

hullabaloo /ˌhʌləbəˈluː/ *n.* uproar. [reduplication of *hallo, hullo*, etc.]

♦ **hull insurance** *n.* marine or aircraft insurance covering the structure of a ship, boat, hovercraft, or aeroplane and the equipment maintained permanently on board.

---

hullo var. of HELLO.

hum *–v.* (**-mm-**) **1** make a low steady continuous sound like a bee. **2** sing with closed lips. **3** utter a slight inarticulate sound. **4** *colloq.* be active (*really made things hum*). **5** *colloq.* smell unpleasantly. *–n.* **1** humming sound. **2** *colloq.* bad smell. □ **hum and haw** (or **ha**) hesitate; be indecisive. [imitative]

human /ˈhjuːmən/ *–adj.* **1** of or belonging to the species *Homo sapiens*. **2** consisting of human beings (*the human race*). **3** of or characteristic of humankind, esp. as being weak, fallible, etc. (*is only human*). **4** showing warmth, sympathy, etc. (*is very human*). *–n.* human being. [Latin *humanus*]

human being *n.* man, woman, or child.

♦ **human capital** *n.* skills, general or specific, acquired by an individual in the course of training and work experience. Wages reflect in part a return on human capital, which may explain large variations in wages for apparently similar jobs and why even in a recession a firm may retain its workers on relatively high wages, in spite of involuntary unemployment. See also EFFICIENCY WAGE THEORY; IMPLICIT CONTRACT THEORY. Cf. PHYSICAL CAPITAL.

---

human chain *n.* line of people formed for passing things along, as a protest, etc.

human–computer interface *n.* (also **HCI**) former name for USER INTERFACE.

humane /hjuːˈmeɪn/ *adj.* **1** benevolent, compassionate. **2** inflicting the minimum of pain. **3** (of learning) tending to civilize. □ **humanely** *adv.* **humaneness** *n.*

humane killer *n.* instrument for the painless slaughter of animals.

humanism /ˈhjuːməˌnɪz(ə)m/ *n.* **1** non-religious philosophy based on liberal human values. **2** (often **Humanism**) literary culture, esp. that of the Renaissance. □ **humanist** *n.* **humanistic** /-ˈnɪstɪk/ *adj.*

humanitarian /hjuːˌmænɪˈteərɪən/ *–n.* person who seeks to promote human welfare. *–adj.* of humanitarians. □ **humanitarianism** *n.*

humanity /hjuːˈmænɪtɪ/ *n.* (*pl.* **-ies**) **1 a** the human race. **b** human beings collectively. **c** being human. **2** humaneness, benevolence. **3** (in *pl.*) subjects concerned with human culture, e.g. language, literature, and history.

humanize *v.* (also **-ise**) (**-zing** or **-sing**) make human or humane. □ **humanization** /-ˈzeɪʃ(ə)n/ *n.* [French: related to HUMAN]

humankind *n.* human beings collectively.

humanly *adv.* **1** by human means (*if it is humanly possible*). **2** in a human manner.

human nature *n.* general characteristics and feelings of mankind.

♦ **human-resource management (HRM)** *n.* management of the people in an organization, esp. by encouraging individuals to set personal goals and rewards in accordance with the organization's objectives. It also includes all the functions of traditional personnel management.

---

human rights *n.pl.* rights held to be common to all.

human shield *n.* person(s) placed in the line of fire in order to discourage attack.

human–system interface *n.* (also **HSI**) former name for USER INTERFACE.

Humberside /ˈhʌmbəˌsaɪd/ former county in NE England; its county town was Beverley. In 1996 it was replaced by four unitary authorities. Industries included iron and steel, petrochemicals, and fish-processing and agriculture.

humble /ˈhʌmb(ə)l/ *–adj.* **1** having or showing low self-esteem. **2** of low social or political rank. **3** modest in size, pretensions, etc. *–v.* (**-ling**) **1** make humble; abase. **2** lower the rank or status of. □ **eat humble pie** apologize humbly; accept humiliation. □ **humbleness** *n.* **humbly** *adv.* [Latin *humilis*: related to HUMUS]

humbug /ˈhʌmbʌg/ *–n.* **1** lying or deception; hypocrisy. **2** impostor. **3** hard boiled striped peppermint sweet. *–v.* (**-gg-**) **1** be or behave like an impostor. **2** deceive, hoax. [origin unknown]

humdinger /ˈhʌmˌdɪŋə(r)/ *n. slang* excellent or remarkable person or thing. [origin unknown]

humdrum /ˈhʌmdrʌm/ *adj.* commonplace, dull, monotonous. [a reduplication of HUM]

humerus /ˈhjuːmərəs/ *n.* (*pl.* **-ri** /-ˌraɪ/) the bone of the upper arm. □ **humeral** *adj.* [Latin, = shoulder]

humid /ˈhjuːmɪd/ *adj.* (of the air or climate) warm and damp. [Latin *humidus*]

humidifier /hjuːˈmɪdɪˌfaɪə(r)/ *n.* device for keeping the atmosphere moist in a room etc.

humidify /hjuːˈmɪdɪˌfaɪ/ *v.* (**-ies, -ied**) make (air etc.) humid.

humidity /hjuːˈmɪdɪtɪ/ *n.* (*pl.* **-ies**) **1** dampness. **2** degree of moisture, esp. in the atmosphere.

humiliate /hjuːˈmɪlɪˌeɪt/ *v.* (**-ting**) injure the dignity or self-respect of. □ **humiliating** *adj.* **humiliation** /-ˈeɪʃ(ə)n/ *n.* [Latin: related to HUMBLE]

humility /hjuːˈmɪlɪtɪ/ *n.* **1** humbleness, meekness. **2** humble condition. [French: related to HUMILIATE]

hummingbird *n.* small tropical bird that makes a humming sound with its wings when it hovers.

hummock /ˈhʌmək/ *n.* hillock or hump. [origin unknown]

hummus /ˈhʊmʊs/ *n.* (also **houmous**) dip or appetizer made from ground chick-peas, sesame oil, lemon, and garlic. [Turkish]

humor *US* var. of HUMOUR.

humoresque /ˌhjuːməˈresk/ *n.* short lively piece of music. [German *Humoreske*]

humorist *n.* humorous writer, talker, or actor.

humorous /ˈhjuːmərəs/ *adj.* showing humour or a sense of humour. □ **humorously** *adv.*

humour /ˈhjuːmə(r)/ (*US* **humor**) *–n.* **1 a** quality of being amusing or comic. **b** the expression of humour in literature, speech, etc. **2** (in full *sense of humour*) ability to perceive or express humour. **3** state of mind; inclination (*bad humour*). **4** (in full **cardinal humour**) *hist.* each of the four fluids (blood, phlegm, choler, melancholy), thought to determine a person's physical and mental qualities. *–v.* gratify or indulge (a person or taste etc.). □ **out of humour** displeased. □ **humourless** *adj.* [Latin *humor* moisture]

hump *–n.* **1** rounded protuberance on a camel's back, or as an abnormality on a person's back. **2** rounded raised mass of earth etc. **3** critical point in an undertaking. **4** (prec. by *the*) *slang* fit of depression or vexation (*gave me the hump*). *–v.* **1** (often foll. by *about*) *colloq.* lift or carry (heavy objects etc.) with difficulty. **2** make hump-shaped. [probably Low German or Dutch]

humpback *n.* **1 a** deformed back with a hump. **b** person with this. **2** whale with a dorsal fin forming a hump. □ **humpbacked** *adj.*

humpback bridge *n.* small bridge with a steep ascent and descent.

humph /həmf/ *int.* & *n.* inarticulate sound of doubt or dissatisfaction. [imitative]

humus /ˈhjuːməs/ *n.* organic constituent of soil formed by the decomposition of vegetation. [Latin, = soil]

Hun *n.* **1** *offens.* German (esp. in military contexts). **2** member of a warlike Asiatic nomadic people who ravaged Europe in the 4th–5th centuries. **3** vandal. □ **Hunnish** *adj.* [Old English]

Hunan /huːˈnæn/ province of S central China; pop. (est. 1995) 63 550 000; capital, Changsha. Its economy is based on farming, forestry, and mining.

Hungary /ˈhʌŋgərɪ/, **Republic of** country in central Europe, bordering on Slovakia in the N and Austria in the W. Industry is varied, but manufacturing predominates; exports include machinery, transport equipment, chemicals, and textiles. Reserves of brown coal, bauxite, gas, and oil are exploited. Agriculture produces wheat, maize, sugar beet, grain, and livestock (esp. cattle), and the wine industry is expanding. Hungary has been practising market-oriented economic reforms for many years and is therefore managing economic transition better than some other formerly Communist states. Although implementation of these reforms (which include privatization of state industries), together with loss of trade with the former Soviet Union, have led to a deep recession, confidence in Hungarian business is increasing and direct investment from abroad is speeding recovery. A trade agreement with the EC was signed in 1991, and Hungary has since been invited to join the EU early in the next century. Economic problems have persisted, despite wide-scale privatization; austerity measures were introduced in 1996.

History. Following the collapse of the Austro-Hungarian Empire in 1918, Hungary became a republic and then a constitutional monarchy. After participation in the Second World War on the Axis side, Hungary was occupied by the Soviets and became a Communist state in 1949. The Communist system was abandoned towards the end of 1989 and a democratic constitution established. The 1994 general elections were won by the former ruling communist party. President, Árpád Göncz; prime minister, Gyula Horn; capital, Budapest.

language	Hungarian
currency	forint (Ft) of 100 fillér
pop. (est. 1996)	10 201 000
GNP (1994)	US$39B
literacy	99.3% (m); 98.5% (f)
life expectancy	64 (m); 74 (f)

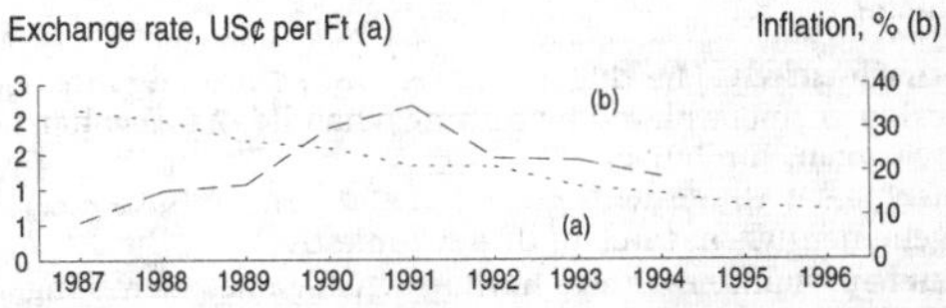

hunch –*v.* bend or arch into a hump. –*n.* **1** intuitive feeling or idea. **2** hump. [origin unknown]

hunchback *n.* = HUMPBACK 1. □ **hunchbacked** *adj.*

hundred /ˈhʌndrəd/ *adj.* & *n.* (*pl.* **hundreds** or (in sense 1) **hundred**) (in *sing.*, prec. by *a* or *one*) **1** ten times ten. **2** symbol for this (100, c, C). **3** (in *sing.* or *pl.*) *colloq.* a large number. **4** (in *pl.*) the years of a specified century (*the seventeen hundreds*). **5** *hist.* subdivision of a county or shire, having its own court. □ **hundredfold** *adj.* & *adv.* **hundredth** *adj.* & *n.* [Old English]

hundreds and thousands *n.pl.* tiny coloured sweets for decorating cakes etc.

hundredweight *n.* (*pl.* same or **-s**) **1** unit of weight equal to 112 lb., or *US* equal to 100 lb. In the UK it is no longer legal to use the hundredweight in trade. **2** weight equal to 50 kg (110.2 lb.).

hung *past* and *past part.* of HANG.

Hungarian /hʌŋˈgeərɪən/ –*n.* **1 a** native or national of Hungary. **b** person of Hungarian descent. **2** language of Hungary. –*adj.* of Hungary or its people or language. [medieval Latin]

hunger /ˈhʌŋgə(r)/ –*n.* **1 a** lack of food. **b** feeling of discomfort or exhaustion caused by this. **2** (often foll. by *for*, *after*) strong desire. –*v.* **1** (often foll. by *for*, *after*) crave or desire. **2** feel hunger. [Old English]

hunger strike *n.* refusal of food as a protest.

hung-over *adj. colloq.* suffering from a hangover.

hung parliament *n.* parliament in which no party has a clear majority.

hungry /ˈhʌŋgrɪ/ *adj.* (**-ier, -iest**) **1** feeling or showing hunger; needing food. **2** inducing hunger (*hungry work*). **3** craving (*hungry for news*). □ **hungrily** *adv.* [Old English]

hunk *n.* **1** large piece cut off (*hunk of bread*). **2** *colloq.* sexually attractive man. □ **hunky** *adj.* (**-ier, -iest**). [probably Dutch]

hunky-dory /ˌhʌŋkɪˈdɔːrɪ/ *adj.* esp. *US colloq.* excellent. [origin unknown]

hunt –*v.* **1** (also *absol.*) **a** pursue and kill (wild animals, esp. foxes, or game) for sport or food. **b** use (a horse or hounds) for hunting. **c** (of an animal) chase (its prey). **2** (foll. by *after*, *for*) seek, search. **3** (of an engine etc.) run alternately too fast and too slow. **4** scour (a district) for game. **5** (as **hunted** *adj.*) (of a look etc.) terrified as if being hunted. –*n.* **1** practice or instance of hunting. **2 a** association of people hunting with hounds. **b** area for hunting. □ **hunt down** pursue and capture. □ **hunting** *n.* [Old English]

hunter *n.* **1 a** (*fem.* **huntress**) person or animal that hunts. **b** horse used in hunting. **2** person who seeks something. **3** pocket-watch with a hinged cover protecting the glass.

hunter's moon *n.* next full moon after the harvest moon.

huntsman *n.* **1** hunter. **2** hunt official in charge of hounds.

Hupeh see HUBEI.

hurdle /ˈhɜːd(ə)l/ –*n.* **1 a** each of a series of light frames to be cleared by athletes in a race. **b** (in *pl.*) hurdle-race. **2** obstacle or difficulty. **3** portable rectangular frame used as a temporary fence etc. –*v.* (**-ling**) **1** run in a hurdle-race. **2** fence off etc. with hurdles. [Old English]

hurdler /ˈhɜːdlə(r)/ *n.* **1** athlete who runs in hurdle-races. **2** maker of hurdles.

♦ **hurdle rate** *n.* rate of return that a proposed project must achieve if it is to be worth considering. It is often based on the cost of the capital involved adjusted by a risk factor.

---

hurdy-gurdy /ˌhɜːdɪˈgɜːdɪ/ *n.* (*pl.* **-ies**) **1** droning musical instrument played by turning a handle. **2** *colloq.* barrel-organ. [imitative]

hurl –*v.* **1** throw with great force. **2** utter (abuse etc.) vehemently. –*n.* forceful throw. [imitative]

hurley /ˈhɜːlɪ/ *n.* **1** (also **hurling**) Irish game resembling hockey. **2** stick used in this.

hurly-burly /ˌhɜːlɪˈbɜːlɪ/ *n.* boisterous activity; commotion. [a reduplication of HURL]

Huron see GREAT LAKES.

hurrah /hʊˈrɑː/ *int.* & *n.* (also **hurray** /hʊˈreɪ/) exclamation of joy or approval. [earlier *huzza*, origin uncertain]

hurricane /ˈhʌrɪkən/ *n.* **1** storm with a violent wind, esp. a West Indian cyclone. **2** *Meteorol.* wind of 65 knots (75 m.p.h.) or more, force 12 on the Beaufort scale. [Spanish and Portuguese from Carib]

hurricane-lamp *n.* oil-lamp designed to resist a high wind.

hurry /ˈhʌrɪ/ –*n.* **1** great or eager haste. **2** (with *neg.* or *interrog.*) need for haste (*there is no hurry*; *what's the hurry?*). –*v.* (**-ies, -ied**) **1** move or act hastily. **2** cause to hurry. **3** (as **hurried** *adj.*) hasty; done rapidly. □ **hurry along** (or **up**) (cause to) make haste. **in a hurry 1** hurrying. **2** *colloq.* easily or readily (*you will not beat that in a hurry*). □ **hurriedly** *adv.* [imitative]

hurt –*v.* (*past* and *past part.* **hurt**) **1** (also *absol.*) cause pain or injury to. **2** cause mental pain or distress to. **3** suffer pain (*my arm hurts*). –*n.* **1** injury. **2** harm, wrong. [French *hurter* knock]

hurtful *adj.* causing (esp. mental) hurt. □ **hurtfully** *adv.*

hurtle /ˈhɜːt(ə)l/ *v.* (**-ling**) **1** move or hurl rapidly or noisily. **2** come with a crash. [from HURT in the obsolete sense 'strike hard']

husband /ˈhʌzbənd/ –*n.* married man, esp. in relation to his wife. –*v.* use (resources) economically; eke out. [Old English, = house-dweller]

husbandry *n.* **1** farming. **2** management of resources.

hush –*v.* make or become silent or quiet. –*int.* calling for silence. –*n.* expectant stillness or silence. □ **hush up** suppress public mention of (an affair). [*husht*, an obsolete exclamation, taken as a past part.]

hush-hush *adj. colloq.* highly secret, confidential.

hush money *n. slang* money paid to ensure discretion.

husk –*n.* **1** dry outer covering of some fruits or seeds. **2** worthless outside part of a thing. –*v.* remove husk(s) from. [probably Low German]

husky[1] /ˈhʌskɪ/ *adj.* (**-ier, -iest**) **1** (of a person or voice) dry in the throat; hoarse. **2** of or full of husks. **3** dry as a husk. **4** tough, strong, hefty. □ **huskily** *adv.* **huskiness** *n.*

husky[2] /ˈhʌskɪ/ *n.* (*pl.* **-ies**) dog of a powerful breed used in the Arctic for pulling sledges. [perhaps from corruption of ESKIMO]

huss *n.* dogfish as food. [origin unknown]

hussar /hʊˈzɑː(r)/ *n.* soldier of a light cavalry regiment. [Magyar *huszár*]

hussy /ˈhʌsɪ/ *n.* (*pl.* **-ies**) *derog.* impudent or promiscuous girl or woman. [contraction of HOUSEWIFE]

hustings /ˈhʌstɪŋz/ *n.* election campaign or proceedings. [Old English, = house of assembly, from Old Norse]

hustle /ˈhʌs(ə)l/ –*v.* (**-ling**) **1** jostle, bustle. **2** (foll. by *into*, *out of*, etc.) force, coerce, or hurry (*hustled them out of the room*; *was hustled into agreeing*). **3** *slang* **a** solicit business. **b** engage in prostitution. **4** *slang* obtain by energetic activity. –*n.* act or instance of hustling. □ **hustler** *n.* [Dutch]

hut *n.* small simple or crude house or shelter. [French *hutte* from Germanic]

hutch *n.* box or cage for rabbits etc. [French *huche*]

HV –*international civil aircraft marking* the Vatican. –*airline flight code* Transavia.

Hwange /ˈwæŋgiː, ˈhw-/ (formerly **Wankie**) town in W Zimbabwe, centre of the country's coalmining industry; pop. (1989) 40 000.

HWM *abbr.* high-water mark.

HX *postcode* Halifax.

hyacinth /ˈhaɪəsɪnθ/ *n.* **1** bulbous plant with racemes of bell-shaped (esp. purplish-blue) fragrant flowers. **2** purplish-blue. [Greek *huakinthos*]

hyaena var. of HYENA.

♦ **Hyams** /ˈhaɪəmz/, **Henry** (1928–) British property developer, whose Oldham Estates was sold over his head

in 1988, earning him £150 million. Centre Point, an office block in London, remained unoccupied for 13 years causing considerable controversy.

---

hybrid /'haɪbrɪd/ *–n.* **1** offspring of two plants or animals of different species or varieties. **2** thing composed of diverse elements, e.g. a word with parts taken from different languages. *–adj.* **1** bred as a hybrid. **2** heterogeneous. □ **hybridism** *n.* [Latin]

hybrid computer see ANALOG COMPUTER.

hybridize *v.* (also **-ise**) (**-zing** or **-sing**) **1** subject (a species etc.) to cross-breeding. **2 a** produce hybrids. **b** (of an animal or plant) interbreed. □ **hybridization** /-'zeɪʃ(ə)n/ *n.*

Hyderabad /'haɪdərə,bæd/ **1** city in S India, capital of Andhra Pradesh; manufactures include carpets, railway equipment, and pharmaceuticals; pop. (1995) 5 343 000. **2** city in SE Pakistan, in the province of Sind; light industry produces pottery, glass, and furniture; pop. (1991) 1 000 000.

hydra /'haɪdrə/ *n.* **1** freshwater polyp with a tubular body and tentacles. **2** something hard to destroy. [Greek, a mythical snake with many heads that grew again when cut off]

hydrangea /haɪ'dreɪndʒə/ *n.* shrub with globular clusters of white, pink, or blue flowers. [Greek *hudōr* water, *aggos* vessel]

hydrant /'haɪdrənt/ *n.* outlet (esp. in a street) with a nozzle for a hose, for drawing water from the main. [as HYDRO-]

hydrate /'haɪdreɪt/ *–n.* compound in which water is chemically combined with another compound or an element. *–v.* (**-ting**) **1** combine chemically with water. **2** cause to absorb water. □ **hydration** /-'dreɪʃ(ə)n/ *n.* [French: related to HYDRO-]

hydraulic /haɪ'drɔːlɪk/ *adj.* **1** (of water, oil, etc.) conveyed through pipes or channels. **2** (of a mechanism etc.) operated by liquid moving in this way (*hydraulic brakes*). □ **hydraulically** *adv.* [Greek *hudōr* water, *aulos* pipe]

hydraulics *n.pl.* (usu. treated as *sing.*) science of the conveyance of liquids through pipes etc., esp. as motive power.

hydride /'haɪdraɪd/ *n.* compound of hydrogen with an element.

hydro /'haɪdrəʊ/ *n.* (*pl.* **-s**) *colloq.* **1** hotel or clinic etc., orig. providing hydropathic treatment. **2** hydroelectric power plant. [abbreviation]

hydro- *comb. form* **1** having to do with water (*hydroelectric*). **2** combined with hydrogen (*hydrochloric*). [Greek *hudro-* from *hudōr* water]

hydrocarbon /,haɪdrəʊ'kɑːbən/ *n.* compound of hydrogen and carbon.

hydrocephalus /,haɪdrə'sefələs/ *n.* accumulated fluid in the brain, esp. in young children. □ **hydrocephalic** /-sɪ'fælɪk/ *adj.* [Greek *kephalē* head]

hydrochloric acid /,haɪdrə'klɒrɪk/ *n.* solution of the colourless gas hydrogen chloride in water.

hydrocyanic acid /,haɪdrəsaɪ'ænɪk/ *n.* highly poisonous liquid smelling of bitter almonds; prussic acid.

hydrodynamics /,haɪdrəʊdaɪ'næmɪks/ *n.pl.* (usu. treated as *sing.*) science of forces acting on or exerted by fluids (esp. liquids). □ **hydrodynamic** *adj.*

hydroelectric /,haɪdrəʊɪ'lektrɪk/ *adj.* **1** generating electricity by water-power. **2** (of electricity) so generated. □ **hydroelectricity** /-'trɪsɪtɪ/ *n.*

hydrofoil /'haɪdrə,fɔɪl/ *n.* **1** boat equipped with planes for lifting its hull out of the water to increase its speed. **2** such a plane.

hydrogen /'haɪdrədʒ(ə)n/ *n.* tasteless odourless gas, the lightest element, occurring in water and all organic compounds. □ **hydrogenous** /-'drɒdʒɪnəs/ *adj.* [French: related to HYDRO-, -GEN]

hydrogenate /haɪ'drɒdʒɪ,neɪt/ *v.* (**-ting**) charge with or cause to combine with hydrogen. □ **hydrogenation** /-'neɪʃ(ə)n/ *n.*

hydrogen bomb *n.* immensely powerful bomb utilizing the explosive fusion of hydrogen nuclei.

hydrogen peroxide *n.* viscous unstable liquid with strong oxidizing properties.

hydrogen sulphide *n.* poisonous unpleasant-smelling gas formed by rotting animal matter.

hydrography /haɪ'drɒgrəfɪ/ *n.* science of surveying and charting seas, lakes, rivers, etc. □ **hydrographer** *n.* **hydrographic** /-drə'græfɪk/ *adj.*

hydrology /haɪ'drɒlədʒɪ/ *n.* science of the properties of water, esp. of its movement in relation to land. □ **hydrologist** *n.*

hydrolyse /'haɪdrə,laɪz/ *v.* (*US* **-lyze**) (**-sing** or **-zing**) decompose by hydrolysis.

hydrolysis /haɪ'drɒlɪsɪs/ *n.* chemical reaction of a substance with water, usu. resulting in decomposition. [Greek *lusis* dissolving]

hydrometer /haɪ'drɒmɪtə(r)/ *n.* instrument for measuring the density of liquids.

hydropathy /haɪ'drɒpəθɪ/ *n.* (medically unorthodox) treatment of disease by water. □ **hydropathic** /,haɪdrə'pæθɪk/ *adj.* [related to PATHOS]

hydrophilic /,haɪdrə'fɪlɪk/ *adj.* **1** having an affinity for water. **2** wettable by water. [Greek *philos* loving]

hydrophobia /,haɪdrə'fəʊbɪə/ *n.* **1** aversion to water, esp. as a symptom of rabies in humans. **2** rabies, esp. in humans. □ **hydrophobic** *adj.*

hydroplane /'haɪdrə,pleɪn/ *n.* **1** light fast motor boat that skims over water. **2** finlike attachment enabling a submarine to rise and descend.

hydroponics /,haɪdrə'pɒnɪks/ *n.* growing plants without soil, in sand, gravel, or liquid, with added nutrients. [Greek *ponos* labour]

hydrosphere /'haɪdrə,sfɪə(r)/ *n.* waters of the earth's surface.

hydrostatic /,haɪdrə'stætɪk/ *adj.* of the equilibrium of liquids and the pressure exerted by liquid at rest. [related to STATIC]

hydrostatics *n.pl.* (usu. treated as *sing.*) mechanics of the hydrostatic properties of liquids.

hydrotherapy /,haɪdrə'θerəpɪ/ *n.* use of water, esp. swimming, in the treatment of arthritis, paralysis, etc.

hydrous /'haɪdrəs/ *adj.* containing water. [related to HYDRO-]

hydroxide /haɪ'drɒksaɪd/ *n.* compound containing oxygen and hydrogen as either a hydroxide ion or a hydroxyl group.

hydroxyl /haɪ'drɒksɪl/ *n.* (*attrib.*) univalent group containing hydrogen and oxygen.

hyena /haɪ'iːnə/ *n.* (also **hyaena**) doglike flesh-eating mammal. [Latin from Greek]

hygiene /'haɪdʒiːn/ *n.* **1** conditions or practices, esp. cleanliness, conducive to maintaining health. **2** science of maintaining health. □ **hygienic** /-'dʒiːnɪk/ *adj.* **hygienically** /-'dʒiːnɪkəlɪ/ *adv.* **hygienist** *n.* [Greek *hugiēs* healthy]

hygrometer /haɪ'grɒmɪtə(r)/ *n.* instrument for measuring the humidity of the air or a gas. [Greek *hugros* wet]

hygroscope /'haɪgrə,skəʊp/ *n.* instrument indicating but not measuring the humidity of the air.

hygroscopic /,haɪgrə'skɒpɪk/ *adj.* **1** of the hygroscope. **2** (of a substance) tending to absorb moisture from the air.

hymen /'haɪmen/ *n.* membrane at the opening of the vagina, usu. broken at the first occurrence of sexual intercourse. [Greek *humēn* membrane]

hymenopterous /,haɪmə'nɒptərəs/ *adj.* of an order of insects having four transparent wings, including bees, wasps, and ants. [Greek, = membrane-winged]

hymn /hɪm/ *–n.* **1** song of esp. Christian praise. **2** crusading theme (*hymn of freedom*). *–v.* praise or celebrate in hymns. [Greek *humnos*]

hymnal /'hɪmn(ə)l/ *n.* book of hymns. [medieval Latin: related to HYMN]

hymnology /hɪm'nɒlədʒɪ/ *n.* (*pl.* **-ies**) **1** the composition or study of hymns. **2** hymns collectively. □ **hymnologist** *n.*

hyoscine /'haɪə,si:n/ *n.* poisonous alkaloid found in plants of the nightshade family, used to prevent motion sickness etc. [Greek *huoskuamos* henbane from *hus huos* pig, *kuamos* bean]

hype /haɪp/ *slang* –*n.* extravagant or intensive promotion of a product etc. –*v.* (**-ping**) promote with hype. [origin unknown]

hyped up *adj. slang* nervously excited or stimulated. [shortening of HYPODERMIC]

hyper /'haɪpə(r)/ *adj. slang* hyperactive, highly-strung. [abbreviation of HYPERACTIVE]

hyper- *prefix* meaning: **1** over, beyond, above (*hypersonic*). **2** too (*hypersensitive*). [Greek *huper* over]

hyperactive /,haɪpə'ræktɪv/ *adj.* (of a person) abnormally active.

hyperbola /haɪ'pɜ:bələ/ *n.* (*pl.* **-s** or **-lae** /-,li:/) plane curve produced when a cone is cut by a plane that makes a larger angle with the base than the side of the cone makes. □ **hyperbolic** /,haɪpə'bɒlɪk/ *adj.* [Greek *hyperbolē*, = excess: related to HYPER-, *ballō* throw]

hyperbole /haɪ'pɜ:bəlɪ/ *n.* exaggeration, esp. for effect. □ **hyperbolical** /-'bɒlɪk(ə)l/ *adj.*

hyperbolic function *n.* function related to a rectangular hyperbola, e.g. a hyperbolic cosine or sine.

hypercritical /,haɪpə'krɪtɪk(ə)l/ *adj.* excessively critical. □ **hypercritically** *adv.*

hyperglycaemia /,haɪpəglaɪ'si:mɪə/ *n.* (*US* **hyperglycemia**) excess of glucose in the bloodstream. [from HYPER-, Greek *glukus* sweet, *haima* blood]

♦ **hyperinflation** /,haɪpərɪn'fleɪʃ(ə)n/ *n.* (also **galloping inflation**) extremely high inflation, usu. associated with inflation rates of some 50% per month, within a period of only a few months, and with social disorder.

---

hypermarket /'haɪpə,mɑ:kɪt/ *n.* very large supermarket or DIY store. Able to buy in bulk, hypermarkets base their attraction on low prices for a wide range of products; they are often located adjacent to towns to attract car-owning consumers, who can make many of their purchases in one place where parking facilities are provided.

hypermedia /'haɪpə,mi:dɪə/ *n.* provision of several media (e.g. audio, video, and graphics) on one computer system, with cross-references from one to another (often *attrib.*: *hypermedia database*).

hypersensitive /,haɪpə'sensɪtɪv/ *adj.* excessively sensitive. □ **hypersensitivity** /-'tɪvɪtɪ/ *n.*

hypersonic /,haɪpə'sɒnɪk/ *adj.* **1** of speeds of more than five times that of sound. **2** of sound-frequencies above about a thousand million hertz.

hypertension /,haɪpə'tenʃ(ə)n/ *n.* **1** abnormally high blood pressure. **2** great emotional tension.

hypertext /'haɪpə,tekst/ *n.* provision of several texts on one computer system, with cross-references from one to another. As with an encyclopedia, the texts may be entered at many points and may be read in any order by the choice of words or key phrases as search parameters for the next section of text to be viewed. There are facilities for windowing viewed text, selecting next view by marking text fragments using mouse or keyboard, searching the text database or indexes, and displaying the new text.

hyperthermia /,haɪpə'θɜ:mɪə/ *n.* abnormally high body-temperature. [from HYPER-, Greek *thermē* heat]

hyperthyroidism /,haɪpə'θaɪrɔɪ,dɪz(ə)m/ *n.* overactivity of the thyroid gland, resulting in an increased rate of metabolism.

hyperventilation /,haɪpə,ventɪ'leɪʃ(ə)n/ *n.* abnormally rapid breathing. □ **hyperventilate** *v.* (**-ting**).

hyphen /'haɪf(ə)n/ –*n.* sign (-) used to join words semantically or syntactically (e.g. *fruit-tree, pick-me-up, rock-forming*), to indicate the division of a word at the end of a line, or to indicate a missing or implied element (as in *man- and womankind*). –*v.* = HYPHENATE. [Greek *huphen* together]

hyphenate /'haɪfə,neɪt/ *v.* (**-ting**) **1** write (a compound word) with a hyphen. **2** join (words) with a hyphen. □ **hyphenation** /-'neɪʃ(ə)n/ *n.*

hypnosis /hɪp'nəʊsɪs/ *n.* **1** state like sleep in which the subject acts only on external suggestion. **2** artificially produced sleep. [Greek *hupnos* sleep]

hypnotherapy /,hɪpnəʊ'θerəpɪ/ *n.* treatment of mental disorders by hypnosis.

hypnotic /hɪp'nɒtɪk/ –*adj.* **1** of or producing hypnosis. **2** inducing sleep. –*n.* hypnotic drug or influence. □ **hypnotically** *adv.* [Greek: related to HYPNOSIS]

hypnotism /'hɪpnə,tɪz(ə)m/ *n.* the study or practice of hypnosis. □ **hypnotist** *n.*

hypnotize /'hɪpnə,taɪz/ *v.* (also **-ise**) (**-zing** or **-sing**) **1** produce hypnosis in. **2** fascinate; capture the mind of.

hypo[1] /'haɪpəʊ/ *n.* sodium thiosulphate (incorrectly called hyposulphite) used as a photographic fixer. [abbreviation]

hypo[2] /'haɪpəʊ/ *n.* (*pl.* **-s**) *slang* = HYPODERMIC *n.* [abbreviation]

hypo- *prefix* **1** under (*hypodermic*). **2** below normal (*hypotension*). **3** slightly. [Greek *hupo* under]

hypocaust /'haɪpə,kɔ:st/ *n.* space for underfloor hot-air heating in ancient Roman houses. [from HYPO-, *kaustos* burnt]

hypochondria /,haɪpə'kɒndrɪə/ *n.* abnormal and ill-founded anxiety about one's health. [Latin from Greek, = soft parts of the body below the ribs, where melancholy was thought to arise]

hypochondriac /,haɪpə'kɒndrɪ,æk/ –*n.* person given to hypochondria. –*adj.* of or affected by hypochondria.

hypocrisy /hɪ'pɒkrɪsɪ/ *n.* (*pl.* **-ies**) **1** false claim to virtue; insincerity, pretence. **2** instance of this. [Greek, = acting, feigning]

hypocrite /'hɪpəkrɪt/ *n.* person given to hypocrisy. □ **hypocritical** /-'krɪtɪk(ə)l/ *adj.* **hypocritically** /-'krɪtɪkəlɪ/ *adv.*

hypodermic /,haɪpə'dɜ:mɪk/ –*adj.* **1** of the area beneath the skin. **2 a** injected beneath the skin. **b** (of a syringe, etc.) used to do this. –*n.* hypodermic injection or syringe. [from HYPO-, Greek *derma* skin]

hypotension /,haɪpəʊ'tenʃ(ə)n/ *n.* abnormally low blood pressure.

hypotenuse /haɪ'pɒtə,nju:z/ *n.* side opposite the right angle of a right-angled triangle. [Greek, = subtending line]

hypothalamus /,haɪpə'θæləməs/ *n.* (*pl.* **-mi** /-,maɪ/) region of the brain controlling body-temperature, thirst, hunger, etc. □ **hypothalamic** *adj.* [Latin: related to HYPO-, Greek *thalamos* inner room]

♦ **hypothecation** /haɪ,pɒθɪ'keɪʃ(ə)n/ *n.* **1** authority given to a banker, usu. as a **letter of hypothecation**, to enable the banker to sell goods pledged as security for a loan. The goods have often been pledged as security in relation to a documentary bill, the banker being entitled to sell the goods if the bill is dishonoured by non-acceptance or non-payment. **2** mortgage granted by a ship's master to secure the repayment with interest, on the safe arrival of the ship at its destination, of money borrowed during a voyage as a matter of necessity (e.g. to pay for urgent repairs). The hypothecation of a ship itself, with or without cargo, is called **bottomry** and is effected by a **bottomry bond**; that of its cargo alone is **respondentia** and requires a **respondentia bond**. The bondholder is entitled to a maritime lien. [Latin from Greek *hupothēkē* deposit]

---

hypothermia /,haɪpəʊ'θɜ:mɪə/ *n.* abnormally low body-temperature. [from HYPO-, Greek *thermē* heat]

hypothesis /haɪ'pɒθɪsɪs/ *n.* (*pl.* **-theses** /-,si:z/) proposition or supposition made as the basis for reasoning or investigation. [Greek, = foundation]

hypothesize /haɪ'pɒθɪ,saɪz/ *v.* (also **-ise**) (**-zing** or **-sing**) form or assume a hypothesis.

hypothetical /ˌhaɪpəˈθetɪk(ə)l/ *adj.* **1** of, based on, or serving as a hypothesis. **2** supposed; not necessarily true. □ **hypothetically** *adv.*

hypothyroidism /ˌhaɪpəʊˈθaɪrɔɪˌdɪz(ə)m/ *n.* subnormal activity of the thyroid gland, resulting in cretinism. □ **hypothyroid** *n.* & *adj.*

hypoventilation /ˌhaɪpəʊˌventɪˈleɪʃ(ə)n/ *n.* abnormally slow breathing.

hyssop /ˈhɪsəp/ *n.* **1** small bushy aromatic herb, formerly used medicinally. **2** *Bibl.* plant whose twigs were used for sprinkling in Jewish rites. [ultimately from Greek *hyssōpos*, of Semitic origin]

hysterectomy /ˌhɪstəˈrektəmɪ/ *n.* (*pl.* **-ies**) surgical removal of the womb. [Greek *hustera* womb, -ECTOMY]

hysteresis /ˌhɪstəˈriːsɪs/ *n.* phenomenon whereby changes in an effect lag behind changes in its cause. In economics, it refers to the assumption that the present level of an economic variable depends on past levels. For example, when unemployment rises wages might be expected to fall and the demand for labour to rise, so that unemployment would quickly disappear. If there is hysteresis, however, this may not occur since workers, once excluded from the labour market, may lose skills and therefore be unable to compete with employed workers to push down wages. [Greek *husteros* coming after]

hysteria /hɪˈstɪərɪə/ *n.* **1** wild uncontrollable emotion or excitement. **2** functional disturbance of the nervous system, of psychoneurotic origin. [Greek *hustera* womb]

hysteric /hɪˈsterɪk/ *n.* **1** (in *pl.*) **a** fit of hysteria. **b** *colloq.* overwhelming laughter (*we were in hysterics*). **2** hysterical person.

hysterical *adj.* **1** of or affected with hysteria. **2** uncontrollably emotional. **3** *colloq.* extremely funny. □ **hysterically** *adv.*

HZ *international civil aircraft marking* Saudi Arabia.

Hz *symb.* hertz.

Ii

I[1] /aɪ/ *n.* (also **i**) (*pl.* **Is** or **I's**) **1** ninth letter of the alphabet. **2** (as a roman numeral) 1.

I[2] /aɪ/ *pron.* (*obj.* **me**; *poss.* **my, mine**; *pl.* **we**) used by a speaker or writer to refer to himself or herself. [Old English]

I[3] *–symb.* iodine. *–international vehicle registration & international civil aircraft marking* Italy.

I[4] *abbr.* (also **I.**) **1** Island(s). **2** Isle(s). **3** Ireland, Irish. **4** single column inch (of advertisements).

IA *–abbr.* = INSTITUTE OF ACTUARIES. *–US postcode* Iowa. *–airline flight code* Iraqi Airways.

Ia. *abbr.* Iowa.

IAA *abbr.* International Advertising Association.

IAB *abbr.* Industrial Advisory Board.

IADB *abbr.* Inter-American Development Bank.

IAEE *abbr.* International Association of Energy Economists.

-ial var. of -AL.

IAM *abbr.* Institute of Administrative Management.

IAMA *abbr.* Incorporated Advertising Managers' Association.

iambic /aɪˈæmbɪk/ *Prosody –adj.* of or using iambuses. *–n.* (usu. in *pl.*) iambic verse.

iambus /aɪˈæmbəs/ *n.* (*pl.* **-buses** or **-bi** /-baɪ/) metrical foot consisting of one short followed by one long syllable (⏑–). [Greek, = lampoon]

-ian var. of -AN.

IAP *abbr.* Internet access provider.

IAS *abbr. Computing* immediate access store.

IASA *abbr.* International Air Safety Association.

Iaşi /ˈjæʃɪ/ (German **Jassy**) city in E Romania; there are chemical, textile, and electronics industries; pop. (est. 1993) 337 643.

IATA /aɪˈɑːtə, iːˈɑːtə/ *abbr.* International Air Transport Association.

IB *–abbr.* **1** in bond. **2** industrial business. **3** International Bank (for Reconstruction and Development). **4** invoice book. *–airline flight code* Iberia International Airlines of Spain.

IBA *abbr.* = INDEPENDENT BROADCASTING AUTHORITY.

Ibadan /ˌɪbəˈdɑːn, ɪˈbæd(ə)n/ city in SW Nigeria; manufactures include vehicles, plastics, and chemicals; pop. (est. 1995) 1 365 000.

IBB *abbr.* Invest in Britain Bureau.

IBBR *abbr. Finance* interbank bid rate.

IBEL *abbr. Finance* interest-bearing eligible liability.

Iberia /aɪˈbɪərɪə/ region forming the extreme SW peninsula of Europe, occupied by Spain and Portugal. □ **Iberian** *adj.* & *n.* [Latin from Greek *Ibēres* Spaniards]

ibex /ˈaɪbeks/ *n.* (*pl.* **-es**) wild mountain goat with thick curved ridged horns. [Latin]

IBG *abbr. Computing* interblock gap.

IBI *abbr.* (also **i.b.i.**) *Bookkeeping* invoice book inwards.

ibid. /ˈɪbɪd/ *abbr.* in the same book or passage etc. [Latin *ibidem* in the same place]

-ibility *suffix* forming nouns from, or corresponding to, adjectives in *-ible.*

ibis /ˈaɪbɪs/ *n.* (*pl.* **-es**) wading bird with a curved bill, long neck, and long legs. [Greek, from Egyptian]

Ibiza /ɪˈbiːθə/ **1** Spanish island, westernmost of the Balearic Islands; tourism is the most important industry; pop. (1986) 45 000. **2** its capital city, a port.

-ible *suffix* forming adjectives meaning 'that may or may be' (*forcible*; *possible*). [Latin]

-ibly *suffix* forming adverbs corresponding to adjectives in *-ible.*

IBM *abbr.* International Business Machines Corporation (computer manufacturer).

IBMBR *abbr. Finance* interbank market bid rate.

IBO *abbr.* (also **i.b.o.**) *Bookkeeping* invoice book outwards.

Ibo /ˈiːbəʊ/ *n.* (also **Igbo**) (*pl.* same or **-s**) **1** member of a Black people of SE Nigeria. **2** their language. [native name]

IBRD *abbr.* = INTERNATIONAL BANK FOR RECONSTRUCTION AND DEVELOPMENT.

IBRO *abbr.* International Bank Research Organization.

IBS *abbr.* (also **IB(Scot.)**) Institute of Bankers in Scotland.

-ic *suffix* **1** forming adjectives (*Arabic*; *classic*; *public*) and nouns (*critic*; *epic*; *mechanic*; *music*). **2** combined in higher valence or degree of oxidation (*ferric*; *sulphuric*). [Latin *-icus*, Greek *-ikos*]

ICA *abbr.* **1** (also **ICAEW**) Institute of Chartered Accountants in England and Wales. See INSTITUTE OF CHARTERED ACCOUNTANTS. **2** International Coffee Agreement. **3** International Commodity Agreement.

ICAI *abbr.* Institute of Chartered Accountants in Ireland. See INSTITUTE OF CHARTERED ACCOUNTANTS.

-ical *suffix* forming adjectives corresponding to nouns or adjectives in *-ic* or *-y* (*classical*; *historical*).

ICAO *abbr.* International Civil Aviation Organization.

ICAS *abbr.* Institute of Chartered Accountants of Scotland. See INSTITUTE OF CHARTERED ACCOUNTANTS.

ICC *abbr.* **1** = INTERNATIONAL CHAMBER OF COMMERCE. **2** International Convention Centre (Birmingham). **3** (in the US) Interstate Commerce Commission.

ICCA *abbr.* International Cocoa Agreement.

ICD *abbr.* Institute of Cooperative Directors.

ice *–n.* **1 a** frozen water. **b** sheet of this on water. **2** ice-cream or water-ice (*ate an ice*). *–v.* (**icing**) **1** mix with or cool in ice (*iced drinks*). **2** (often foll. by *over*, *up*) **a** cover or become covered with ice. **b** freeze. **3** cover (a cake etc.) with icing. □ **on ice 1** performed by skaters. **2** *colloq.* in reserve. **on thin ice** in a risky situation. [Old English]

ice age *n.* glacial period.

ice-axe *n.* cutting tool used by mountaineers.

iceberg *n.* large floating mass of ice. □ **the tip of the iceberg** small perceptible part of something very large or complex. [Dutch]

iceberg lettuce *n.* crisp type of round lettuce.

ice blue *adj.* & *n.* (as adj. often hyphenated) very pale blue.

icebox *n.* **1** compartment in a refrigerator for making or storing ice. **2** *US* refrigerator.

ice-breaker *n.* **1** ship designed to break through ice. **2** joke, incident, etc. that breaks the ice.

ice bucket *n.* bucket holding ice, used to chill wine.

ice-cap *n.* permanent covering of ice, esp. in polar regions.

ice-cream *n.* sweet creamy frozen food, usu. flavoured.

ice-cube *n.* small block of ice for drinks etc.

ice-field *n.* expanse of ice, esp. in polar regions.

ice hockey *n.* form of hockey played on ice.

Icelander /ˈaɪsləndə(r)/ *n.* **1** native or national of Iceland. **2** person of Icelandic descent.

Icelandic /aɪs'lændɪk/ *–adj.* of Iceland. *–n.* language of Iceland.

ice lolly *n.* (also **iced lolly**) flavoured ice on a stick.

ice-pack *n.* **1** = PACK ICE. **2** ice applied to the body for medical purposes.

ice-pick *n.* tool with a spike for splitting up ice.

ice-plant *n.* plant with speckled leaves.

ice-rink *n.* = RINK *n.* 1.

ice-skate *–n.* boot with a blade beneath, for skating on ice. *–v.* skate on ice. □ **ice-skater** *n.*

ICFTU *abbr.* International Confederation of Free Trade Unions.

ICGS *abbr.* interactive computer-graphics system.

ICHCA *abbr.* International Cargo Handling Co-ordination Association.

ichneumon /ɪk'njuːmən/ *n.* **1** (in full **ichneumon fly**) small wasp depositing eggs in or on the larva of another as food for its own larva. **2** mongoose noted for destroying crocodile eggs. [Greek from *ikhnos* footstep]

ichthyology /ˌɪkθɪ'ɒlədʒɪ/ *n.* the study of fishes. □ **ichthyological** /-ə'lɒdʒɪk(ə)l/ *adj.* **ichthyologist** *n.* [Greek *ikhthus* fish]

ichthyosaurus /ˌɪkθɪə'sɔːrəs/ *n.* (also **ichthyosaur** /'ɪkθɪəˌsɔːr/) (*pl.* **sauruses** or **-saurs**) extinct marine reptile with four flippers and usu. a large tail. [Greek *ikhthus* fish, *sauros* lizard]

ICI *abbr.* Imperial Chemical Industries.

-ician *suffix* forming nouns denoting persons skilled in subjects having nouns usu. ending in *-ic* or *-ics* (*magician*; *politician*). [French *-icien*]

icicle /'aɪsɪk(ə)l/ *n.* hanging tapering piece of ice, formed from dripping water. [from ICE, obsolete *ickle* icicle]

icing *n.* **1** coating of sugar etc. on a cake or biscuit. **2** formation of ice on a ship or aircraft. □ **icing on the cake** inessential though attractive addition or enhancement.

icing sugar *n.* finely powdered sugar.

ICJ *abbr.* International Court of Justice.

ICL *abbr.* International Computers Ltd.

ICM *abbr.* Institute of Credit Management.

icon /'aɪkɒn/ *n.* (also **ikon**) **1** painting of Christ etc., esp. in the Eastern Church. **2** image or statue. **3** pictorial symbol on a VDU screen of a program, option, etc., esp. for selection. □ **iconic** /aɪ'kɒnɪk/ *adj.* [Greek *eikōn* image]

iconoclast /aɪ'kɒnəˌklæst/ *n.* **1** person who attacks cherished beliefs. **2** *hist.* person destroying religious images. □ **iconoclasm** *n.* **iconoclastic** /-'klæstɪk/ *adj.* [Greek: related to ICON, *klaō* break]

iconography /ˌaɪkə'nɒgrəfɪ/ *n.* **1** the illustration of a subject by drawings or figures. **2** the study of portraits, esp. of an individual, or of artistic images or symbols. [Greek: related to ICON]

iconostasis /ˌaɪkə'nɒstəsɪs/ *n.* (*pl.* **-stases** /-ˌsiːz/) (in the Eastern Church) screen bearing icons. [Greek: related to ICON]

icosahedron /ˌaɪkəsə'hiːdrən/ *n.* solid figure with twenty faces. [Greek *eikosi* twenty, *hedra* base]

ICR *abbr.* *Computing* intelligent character recognition.

ICRP *abbr.* International Commission on Radiological Protection.

ICS *abbr.* Institute of Chartered Shipbrokers. **2** International Chamber of Shipping. **3** *Finance* investors' compensation scheme.

-ics *suffix* (treated as *sing.* or *pl.*) forming nouns denoting arts, sciences, etc. (*athletics*; *politics*).

ICSA *abbr.* = INSTITUTE OF CHARTERED SECRETARIES AND ADMINISTRATORS.

ICWA *abbr.* Institute of Cost and Works Accountants.

icy /'aɪsɪ/ *adj.* (**-ier, -iest**) **1** very cold. **2** covered with or abounding in ice. **3** (of a tone or manner) unfriendly, hostile. □ **icily** *adv.* **iciness** *n.*

ID *–abbr.* identification, identity (*ID card*). *–symb.* Iraqi dinar. *–US postcode* Idaho.

Id. *abbr.* Idaho.

id *n.* person's inherited unconscious psychological impulses. [Latin, = that]

I'd /aɪd/ *contr.* **1** I had. **2** I should; I would.

IDA *abbr.* = INTERNATIONAL DEVELOPMENT ASSOCIATION.

Idaho /'aɪdəˌhəʊ/ state in the NW US; pop. (est. 1996) 1 189 251; capital, Boise. Silver, antimony, coal, and gas are mined and there is a timber industry.

IDB *abbr.* **1** illicit diamond buying (or buyer). **2** Industrial Development Bank.

IDC *abbr.* = INDUSTRIAL DEVELOPMENT CERTIFICATE.

IDD *abbr.* international direct dialling.

IDDD *abbr.* international direct distance dialling.

-ide *suffix Chem.* forming nouns denoting binary compounds of an element (*sodium chloride*; *lead sulphide*; *calcium carbide*). [extended from OXIDE]

idea /aɪ'dɪə/ *n.* **1** plan etc. formed by mental effort (*an idea for a book*). **2 a** mental impression or concept. **b** vague belief or fancy (*had an idea you were married*). **3** intention or purpose (*the idea is to make money*). **4** archetype or pattern. **5** ambition or aspiration (*have ideas*; *put ideas into a person's head*). □ **have no idea** *colloq.* **1** not know at all. **2** be completely incompetent. **not one's idea of** *colloq.* not what one regards as (*not my idea of a holiday*). [Greek, = form, kind]

ideal /aɪ'diːəl/ *–adj.* **1** answering to one's highest conception; perfect. **2** existing only in idea; visionary. *–n.* perfect type, thing, concept, principle, etc., esp. as a standard to emulate. [French: related to IDEA]

idealism *n.* **1** forming or pursuing ideals, esp. unrealistically. **2** representation of things in ideal form. **3** system of thought in which objects are held to be in some way dependent on the mind. □ **idealist** *n.* **idealistic** /-'lɪstɪk/ *adj.* **idealistically** /-'lɪstɪkəlɪ/ *adv.*

idealize *v.* (also **-ise**) (**-zing** or **-sing**) regard or represent as ideal or perfect. □ **idealization** /-'zeɪʃ(ə)n/ *n.*

ideally *adv.* **1** in ideal circumstances. **2** according to an ideal.

idée fixe /ˌiːdeɪ 'fiːks/ *n.* (*pl.* ***idées fixes*** pronunc. same) dominating idea; obsession. [French, = fixed idea]

identical /aɪ'dentɪk(ə)l/ *adj.* **1** (often foll. by *with*) (of dif-

---

Iceland /'aɪslənd/, **Republic of** volcanic island country in the N Atlantic, just S of the Arctic Circle. The Icelandic economy is dominated by fishing, and fish and fish products are the chief exports. Other industries include aluminium smelting and fertilizer production: aluminium, ferro-silicon, and diatomite are exported. The country is potentially rich in hydroelectric and geothermal power. Iceland was under Norwegian rule from 1262 to 1380, when it passed to Denmark. Granted internal self-government in 1874, it became an independent republic in 1944. Iceland is a member of Efta, and the proposed formation of a European Economic Area comprising Efta and EC members should result in opening up of the Icelandic economy. President, Olafur Ragnar Grimsson; prime minister, David Oddsson; capital, Reykjavik.

language	Icelandic
currency	króna (ISk) of 100 aurar
pop. (est. 1996)	270 000
GNP (1995)	US$6.8B
literacy	99.9%
life expectancy	77 (m); 81 (f)

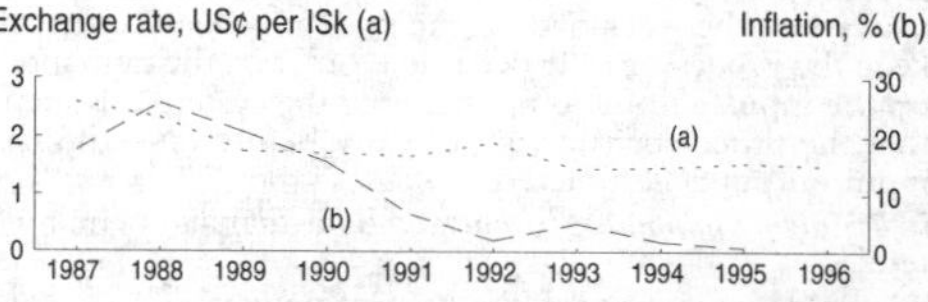

ferent things) absolutely alike. **2** one and the same. **3** (of twins) developed from a single ovum. □ **identically** *adv.* [Latin *identicus*: related to IDENTITY]

identification /aɪˌdentɪfɪ'keɪʃ(ə)n/ *n.* **1** identifying. **2** means of identifying (also *attrib.*: *identification card*).

identification parade *n.* group of people from whom a suspect is to be identified.

identify /aɪ'dentɪˌfaɪ/ *v.* (**-ies, -ied**) **1** establish the identity of; recognize. **2** select or discover (*identify the best solution*). **3** (also *refl.*; foll. by *with*) associate inseparably or very closely (with a party, policy, etc.). **4** (often foll. by *with*) treat as identical. **5** (foll. by *with*) put oneself in the place of (another person). □ **identifiable** *adj.* **identifier** *n.* [medieval Latin *identifico*: related to IDENTITY]

Identikit /aɪ'dentɪkɪt/ *n.* (often *attrib.*) *propr.* picture of esp. a wanted suspect assembled from standard components using witnesses' descriptions. [from IDENTITY, KIT]

identity /aɪ'dentɪtɪ/ *n.* (*pl.* **-ies**) **1 a** condition of being a specified person or thing. **b** individuality, personality (*felt he had lost his identity*). **2** identification or the result of it (*mistaken identity*; *identity card*). **3** absolute sameness (*identity of interests*). **4** *Algebra* **a** equality of two expressions for all values of the quantities. **b** equation expressing this. [Latin *identitas* from *idem* same]

ideogram /'ɪdɪəˌgræm/ *n.* character symbolizing a thing without indicating the sounds in its name (e.g. a numeral, Chinese characters). [Greek *idea* form, -GRAM]

ideograph /'ɪdɪəˌgrɑːf/ *n.* = IDEOGRAM. □ **ideographic** /-'græfɪk/ *adj.* **ideography** /ˌɪdɪ'ɒgrəfɪ/ *n.*

ideologue /'aɪdɪəˌlɒg/ *n.* often *derog.* adherent of an ideology. [French: related to IDEA]

ideology /ˌaɪdɪ'ɒlədʒɪ/ *n.* (*pl.* **-ies**) **1** ideas at the basis of an economic or political theory (*Marxist ideology*). **2** characteristic thinking of a class etc. (*bourgeois ideology*). □ **ideological** /-ə'lɒdʒɪk(ə)l/ *adj.* **ideologically** /-ə'lɒdʒɪkəlɪ/ *adv.* **ideologist** *n.* [French: related to IDEA, -LOGY]

ides /aɪdz/ *n.pl.* day of the ancient Roman month (the 15th day of March, May, July, and October, the 13th of other months). [Latin *idus*]

idiocy /'ɪdɪəsɪ/ *n.* (*pl.* **-ies**) **1** foolishness; foolish act. **2** extreme mental imbecility.

idiom /'ɪdɪəm/ *n.* **1** phrase etc. established by usage and not immediately comprehensible from the words used (e.g. *over the moon*, *see the light*). **2** form of expression peculiar to a language etc. **3** language of a people or country. **4** characteristic mode of expression in art etc. [Greek *idios* own]

idiomatic /ˌɪdɪə'mætɪk/ *adj.* **1** relating or conforming to idiom. **2** characteristic of a particular language. □ **idiomatically** *adv.*

idiosyncrasy /ˌɪdɪəʊ'sɪŋkrəsɪ/ *n.* (*pl.* **-ies**) attitude, behaviour, or opinion peculiar to a person; anything highly individual or eccentric. □ **idiosyncratic** /-'krætɪk/ *adj.* **idiosyncratically** /-'krætɪkəlɪ/ *adv.* [Greek *idios* private, *sun* with, *krasis* mixture]

idiot /'ɪdɪət/ *n.* **1** stupid person. **2** mentally deficient person incapable of rational conduct. □ **idiotic** /-'ɒtɪk/ *adj.* **idiotically** /-'ɒtɪkəlɪ/ *adv.* [Greek *idiōtēs*, = private citizen, ignorant person]

idle /'aɪd(ə)l/ –*adj.* (**idler, idlest**) **1** lazy, indolent. **2** not in use; not working. **3** (of time etc.) unoccupied. **4** purposeless; groundless (*idle rumour*). **5** useless, ineffective (*idle protest*). –*v.* (**-ling**) **1** be idle. **2** run (an engine) or (of an engine) be run slowly without doing any work. **3** (foll. by *away*) pass (time etc.) in idleness. □ **idleness** *n.* **idler** *n.* **idly** *adv.* [Old English]

idle time *n.* time during which the central processor of a computer system is performing no useful function, usu. when the workload on the system is insufficient to keep the processor fully occupied, or when the demands on the input/output components of the system are such that the processor runs out of work before outstanding input/output is completed.

IDMS *abbr. Computing* integrated data-management system.

IDN *abbr. Computing* integrated data network.

idol /'aɪd(ə)l/ *n.* **1** image of a deity etc. as an object of worship. **2** object of excessive or supreme adulation. [Greek *eidōlon* image, phantom]

idolater /aɪ'dɒlətə(r)/ *n.* **1** worshipper of idols. **2** devoted admirer. □ **idolatrous** *adj.* **idolatry** *n.* [related to IDOL, Greek *latreuō* worship]

idolize *v.* (also **-ise**) (**-zing** or **-sing**) **1** venerate or love excessively. **2** make an idol of. □ **idolization** /-'zeɪʃ(ə)n/ *n.*

IDP *abbr.* **1** Institute of Data Processing. **2** integrated data processing.

IDPM *abbr.* Institute of Data Processing Management.

IDS *abbr.* **1** Income Data Services. **2** Industry Department for Scotland. **3** Institute of Development Studies.

IDT *abbr.* industrial design technology.

idyll /'ɪdɪl/ *n.* **1** short description, esp. in verse, of a peaceful or romantic, esp. rural, scene or incident. **2** such a scene or incident. [Greek *eidullion*]

idyllic /ɪ'dɪlɪk/ *adj.* **1** blissfully peaceful and happy. **2** of or like an idyll. □ **idyllically** *adv.*

i.e. *abbr.* that is to say. [Latin *id est*]

-ie see -Y².

IEA *abbr.* **1** Institute of Economic Affairs. **2** International Energy Agency.

IEC *abbr.* industrial energy conservation.

IET *abbr.* interest equalization tax.

I/F *abbr.* insufficient funds (written on a dishonoured cheque).

if –*conj.* **1** introducing a conditional clause: **a** on the condition or supposition that; in the event that (*if he comes I will tell him*; *if you are tired we can rest*). **b** (with past tense) implying that the condition is not fulfilled (*if I knew I would say*). **2** even though (*I'll finish it, if it takes me all day*). **3** whenever (*if I am not sure I ask*). **4** whether (*see if you can find it*). **5** expressing a wish, surprise, or request (*if I could just try!*; *if it isn't my old hat!*; *if you wouldn't mind?*). –*n.* condition, supposition (*too many ifs about it*). □ **if only 1** even if for no other reason than (*I'll come if only to see her*). **2** (often *ellipt.*) expression of regret; I wish that (*if only I had thought of it*). [Old English]

IFA *abbr.* **1** = INDEPENDENT FINANCIAL ADVISER. **2** International Fiscal Association.

IFBPW *abbr.* International Federation of Business and Professional Women.

◆ **IFC** *abbr.* = INTERNATIONAL FINANCE CORPORATION.

IFE *abbr. Computing* intelligent front end.

IFF *abbr.* Institute of Freight Forwarders.

iffy *adj.* (**-ier, -iest**) *colloq.* uncertain; dubious.

IFIP *abbr.* International Federation for Information Processing.

IFPW *abbr.* International Federation of Petroleum (and Chemical) Workers.

Igbo var. of IBO.

igloo /'ɪgluː/ *n.* Eskimo dome-shaped dwelling, esp. of snow. [Eskimo, = house]

igneous /'ɪgnɪəs/ *adj.* **1** of fire; fiery. **2** (esp. of rocks) volcanic. [Latin *ignis* fire]

ignite /ɪg'naɪt/ *v.* (**-ting**) **1** set fire to. **2** catch fire. **3** provoke or excite (feelings etc.). [Latin *ignio ignit-* set on fire]

ignition /ɪg'nɪʃ(ə)n/ *n.* **1** mechanism for, or the action of, starting combustion in an internal-combustion engine. **2** igniting or being ignited.

ignoble /ɪg'nəʊb(ə)l/ *adj.* (**-bler, -blest**) **1** dishonourable. **2** of low birth, position, or reputation. □ **ignobly** *adv.* [Latin: related to IN-¹, NOBLE]

ignominious /ˌɪgnə'mɪnɪəs/ *adj.* shameful, humiliating. □ **ignominiously** *adv.* [Latin: related to IGNOMINY]

ignominy /'ɪgnəmɪnɪ/ *n.* dishonour, infamy. [Latin: related to IN-¹, Latin *(g)nomen* name]

ignoramus /ˌɪgnə'reɪməs/ *n.* (*pl.* **-muses**) ignorant person. [Latin, = we do not know: related to IGNORE]

ignorance /'ɪgnərəns/ *n.* lack of knowledge. [French from Latin: related to IGNORE]

ignorant *adj.* **1** (often foll. by *of, in*) lacking knowledge (esp. of a fact or subject). **2** *colloq.* uncouth. □ **ignorantly** *adv.*

ignore /ɪg'nɔː(r)/ *v.* (**-ring**) refuse to take notice of; intentionally disregard. [Latin *ignoro* not know]

IGO *abbr.* inter-governmental organization.

iguana /ɪg'wɑːnə/ *n.* large American, West Indian, or Pacific lizard with a dorsal crest. [Spanish from Carib *iwana*]

iguanodon /ɪ'gwɑːnəˌdɒn/ *n.* large plant-eating dinosaur with small forelimbs. [from IGUANA, which it resembles, after *mastodon* etc.]

IIB *abbr.* International Patent Institute. [French *Institut international des brevets*]

IIM *abbr.* Institution of Industrial Managers.

IIRS *abbr.* (in the Irish Republic) Institute for Industrial Research and Standards.

IKBS *abbr. Computing* intelligent knowledge-based system.

ikebana /ˌɪkɪ'bɑːnə/ *n.* art of Japanese flower arrangement. [Japanese, = living flowers]

ikon var. of ICON.

IL *–US postcode* Illinois. *–international vehicle registration* Israel.

I/L *abbr.* import licence.

il- *prefix* assim. form of IN-[1], IN-[2] before *l.*

Île-de-France /ˌiːldə'frɑ̃s/ region of N central France, incorporating the city of Paris; pop. (est. 1994) 10 954 623.

ileum /'ɪlɪəm/ *n.* (*pl.* **ilea**) third and last portion of the small intestine. [Latin *ilium*]

ilex /'aɪleks/ *n.* **1** tree or shrub of the genus including the common holly. **2** holm-oak. [Latin]

iliac /'ɪlɪˌæk/ *adj.* of the lower body (*iliac artery*). [Latin *ilia* flanks]

ilk *n.* **1** *colloq.*, usu. *derog.* sort, family, class, etc. **2** (in **of that ilk**) *Scot.* of the ancestral estate with the same name as the family (*Guthrie of that ilk*). [Old English]

Ill. *abbr.* Illinois.

ill *–adj.* (*attrib.* except in sense 1) **1** (usu. *predic.*) not in good health; unwell. **2** wretched, unfavourable (*ill fortune; ill luck*). **3** harmful (*ill effects*). **4** hostile, unkind (*ill feeling*). **5** faulty, unskilful (*ill management*). **6** (of manners or conduct) improper. *–adv.* **1** badly, wrongly, imperfectly (*ill-matched; ill-provided*). **2** scarcely (*can ill afford it*). **3** unfavourably (*spoke ill of them*). *–n.* **1** injury, harm. **2** evil. □ **ill at ease** embarrassed, uneasy. [Old Norse]

I'll /aɪl/ *contr.* I shall; I will.

ill-advised *adj.* foolish; imprudent.

ill-assorted *adj.* badly matched; mixed.

ill-bred *adj.* badly brought up; rude.

ill-defined *adj.* not clearly defined.

ill-disposed *adj.* **1** (often foll. by *towards*) unfavourably disposed. **2** malevolent.

illegal /ɪ'liːg(ə)l/ *adj.* **1** not legal. **2** criminal. **3 a** unauthorized; prohibited. **b** *Computing* not recognized; not accepted. □ **illegality** /-'gælɪtɪ/ *n.* (*pl.* **-ies**). **illegally** *adv.*

♦ **illegal contract** *n.* contract prohibited by statute (e.g. one between traders providing for minimum resale prices) or illegal at common law on the grounds of public policy. An illegal contract is totally void, but neither party (unless innocent of the illegality) can recover any money paid or property transferred under it. Related transactions may also be affected.

♦ **illegal partnership** *n.* partnership formed for an illegal purpose and therefore disallowed by law. A partnership of more than 20 partners is illegal, except in the case of certain professionals, e.g. accountants, solicitors, and stockbrokers.

---

illegible /ɪ'ledʒɪb(ə)l/ *adj.* not legible. □ **illegibility** /-'bɪlɪtɪ/ *n.* **illegibly** *adv.*

illegitimate /ˌɪlɪ'dʒɪtɪmət/ *adj.* **1** born of parents not married to each other. **2** unlawful. **3** improper. **4** wrongly inferred. □ **illegitimacy** *n.* **illegitimately** *adv.*

ill-fated *adj.* destined to or bringing bad fortune.

ill-favoured *adj.* unattractive.

ill-founded *adj.* (of an idea etc.) baseless.

ill-gotten *adj.* gained unlawfully or wickedly.

ill health *n.* poor physical or mental condition.

ill humour *n.* irritability.

illiberal /ɪ'lɪbər(ə)l/ *adj.* **1** intolerant, narrow-minded. **2** without liberal culture; vulgar. **3** stingy; mean. □ **illiberality** /-'rælɪtɪ/ *n.* **illiberally** *adv.*

illicit /ɪ'lɪsɪt/ *adj.* unlawful, forbidden. □ **illicitly** *adv.*

Illinois /ɪlɪ'nɔɪ/ state in the Midwest of the US; pop. (est. 1996) 11 846 544; capital, Springfield. Primarily agricultural, the state is a major producer of soya beans; coalmining is also important, and machinery, electrical goods, and electronic equipment are among the principal manufactures.

illiterate /ɪ'lɪtərət/ *–adj.* **1** unable to read. **2** uneducated. *–n.* illiterate person. □ **illiteracy** *n.* **illiterately** *adv.*

ill-mannered *adj.* having bad manners; rude.

ill-natured *adj.* churlish, unkind.

illness *n.* **1** disease. **2** being ill.

illogical /ɪ'lɒdʒɪk(ə)l/ *adj.* devoid of or contrary to logic. □ **illogicality** /-'kælɪtɪ/ *n.* (*pl.* **-ies**). **illogically** *adv.*

ill-omened *adj.* doomed.

ill-tempered *adj.* morose, irritable.

ill-timed *adj.* done or occurring at an inappropriate time.

ill-treat *v.* treat badly; abuse.

illuminate /ɪ'luːmɪˌneɪt/ *v.* (**-ting**) **1** light up; make bright. **2** decorate (buildings etc.) with lights. **3** decorate (a manuscript etc.) with gold, colour, etc. **4** help to explain (a subject etc.). **5** enlighten spiritually or intellectually. **6** shed lustre on. □ **illuminating** *adj.* **illumination** /-'neɪʃ(ə)n/ *n.* **illuminative** *adj.* [Latin *lumen* light]

illumine /ɪ'ljuːmɪn/ *v.* (**-ning**) *literary* **1** light up; make bright. **2** enlighten.

ill-use *v.* = ILL-TREAT.

illusion /ɪ'luːʒ(ə)n/ *n.* **1** false impression or belief. **2** state of being deceived by appearances. **3** figment of the imagination. □ **be under the illusion** (foll. by *that*) believe mistakenly. □ **illusive** *adj.* **illusory** *adj.* [Latin *illudo* mock]

illusionist *n.* conjuror.

illustrate /'ɪləˌstreɪt/ *v.* (**-ting**) **1 a** provide (a book etc.) with pictures. **b** elucidate by drawings, pictures, examples, etc. **2** serve as an example of. □ **illustrator** *n.* [Latin *lustro* light up]

illustration /ˌɪlə'streɪʃ(ə)n/ *n.* **1** drawing or picture in a book, magazine, etc. **2** explanatory example. **3** illustrating.

illustrative /'ɪləstrətɪv/ *adj.* (often foll. by *of*) explanatory; exemplary.

illustrious /ɪ'lʌstrɪəs/ *adj.* distinguished, renowned. [Latin *illustris*: related to ILLUSTRATE]

ill will *n.* bad feeling; animosity.

ILO *abbr.* = INTERNATIONAL LABOUR ORGANIZATION.

Iloilo /ˌiːlə'wiːləʊ/ port in the Philippines, on the S coast of the island of Panay; exports include fabrics, sugar, and rice; pop. (est. 1994) 302 200.

ILU *abbr.* = INSTITUTE OF LONDON UNDERWRITERS.

im- *prefix* assim. form of IN-[1], IN-[2] before *b, m,* or *p.*

I'm /aɪm/ *contr.* I am.

image /'ɪmɪdʒ/ *–n.* **1** representation of an object, e.g. a statue. **2** reputation or persona of a person, company, etc. **3** appearance as seen in a mirror or through a lens. **4** mental picture or idea. **5** simile or metaphor. *–v.* (**-ging**) **1** make an image of; portray. **2** reflect, mirror. **3** describe or imagine vividly. □ **be the image of** be or look exactly like. [Latin *imago imagin-*]

imagery *n.* **1** figurative illustration, esp. in literature. **2** images; statuary, carving. **3** mental images collectively.

imaginary /ɪ'mædʒɪnərɪ/ *adj.* **1** existing only in the imagination. **2** *Math.* being the square root of a negative quantity. [Latin: related to IMAGE]

imagination /ɪˌmædʒɪˈneɪʃ(ə)n/ *n.* **1** mental faculty of forming images or concepts of objects or situations not existent or not directly experienced. **2** mental creativity or resourcefulness.

imaginative /ɪˈmædʒɪnətɪv/ *adj.* having or showing imagination. □ **imaginatively** *adv.* **imaginativeness** *n.*

imagine /ɪˈmædʒɪn/ *v.* (**-ning**) **1 a** form a mental image or concept of. **b** picture to oneself. **2** think of as probable (*can't imagine he'd be so stupid*). **3** guess (*can't imagine what he is doing*). **4** suppose (*I imagine you'll need help*). □ **imaginable** *adj.* [Latin *imaginor*]

imago /ɪˈmeɪgəʊ/ *n.* (*pl.* **-s** or **imagines** /ɪˈmædʒɪˌniːz/) fully developed stage of an insect, e.g. a butterfly. [Latin: see IMAGE]

imam /ɪˈmɑːm/ *n.* **1** leader of prayers in a mosque. **2** title of various Muslim leaders. [Arabic]

imbalance /ɪmˈbæləns/ *n.* **1** lack of balance. **2** disproportion.

imbecile /ˈɪmbɪˌsiːl/ *–n.* **1** *colloq.* stupid person. **2** person with a mental age of about five. *–adj.* mentally weak; stupid, idiotic. □ **imbecilic** /-ˈsɪlɪk/ *adj.* **imbecility** /-ˈsɪlɪtɪ/ *n.* (*pl.* **-ies**). [French from Latin]

imbibe /ɪmˈbaɪb/ *v.* (**-bing**) **1** drink (esp. alcohol). **2 a** assimilate (ideas etc.). **b** absorb (moisture etc.). **3** inhale (air etc.). [Latin *bibo* drink]

imbroglio /ɪmˈbrəʊlɪəʊ/ *n.* (*pl.* **-s**) **1** confused or complicated situation. **2** confused heap. [Italian: related to IN-[2], BROIL]

Imbros /ˈɪmbrɒs/ (Turkish **Imroz** /ˈɪmrɒz/) Turkish island in the NE Aegean Sea, near the entrance to the Dardanelles; pop. (1980) 4802.

imbue /ɪmˈbjuː/ *v.* (**-bues, -bued, -buing**) (often foll. by *with*) **1** inspire or permeate (with feelings, opinions, or qualities). **2** saturate. **3** dye. [Latin *imbuo*]

IMC *abbr.* Institute of Management Consultants.

IMCO *abbr.* Inter-governmental Maritime Consultative Organization (of the UN).

IMF *abbr.* = INTERNATIONAL MONETARY FUND.

imitate /ˈɪmɪˌteɪt/ *v.* (**-ting**) **1** follow the example of; copy. **2** mimic. **3** make a copy of. **4** be like. □ **imitable** *adj.* **imitator** *n.* [Latin *imitor -tat-*]

imitation /ˌɪmɪˈteɪʃ(ə)n/ *n.* **1** imitating or being imitated. **2** copy. **3** counterfeit (often *attrib.*: *imitation leather*).

imitative /ˈɪmɪtətɪv/ *adj.* **1** (often foll. by *of*) imitating; following a model or example. **2** (of a word) reproducing a natural sound (e.g. *fizz*), or otherwise suggestive (e.g. *blob*).

IMM *abbr.* **1** International Mercantile Marine. **2** International Monetary Market.

immaculate /ɪˈmækjʊlət/ *adj.* **1** perfectly clean and tidy. **2** perfect (*immaculate timing*). **3** innocent, faultless. □ **immaculately** *adv.* **immaculateness** *n.* [Latin: related to IN-[1], *macula* spot]

Immaculate Conception *n. RC Ch.* doctrine that the Virgin Mary was without original sin from conception.

immanent /ˈɪmənənt/ *adj.* **1** (often foll. by *in*) indwelling, inherent. **2** (of God) omnipresent. □ **immanence** *n.* [Latin: related to IN-[2], *maneo* remain]

immaterial /ˌɪməˈtɪərɪəl/ *adj.* **1** unimportant; irrelevant. **2** not material; incorporeal. □ **immateriality** /-ˈælɪtɪ/ *n.*

immature /ˌɪməˈtjʊə(r)/ *adj.* **1** not mature. **2** undeveloped, esp. emotionally. **3** unripe. □ **immaturely** *adv.* **immaturity** *n.*

immeasurable /ɪˈmeʒərəb(ə)l/ *adj.* not measurable; immense. □ **immeasurably** *adv.*

immediate /ɪˈmiːdɪət/ *adj.* **1** occurring or done at once (*immediate reply*). **2** nearest, next; direct (*immediate vicinity*; *immediate future*; *immediate cause of death*). **3** most pressing or urgent (*our immediate concern*). □ **immediacy** *n.* **immediateness** *n.* [Latin: related to IN-[1], MEDIATE]

immediate-access store *n.* (also **IAS**) *Computing* = MAIN STORE.

◆ **immediate annuity** *n.* annuity contract that begins to make payments as soon as the contract has come into force.

◆ **immediate holding company** *n.* company that has a controlling interest in another company, even though it is itself controlled by a third company, which is the holding company of both companies.

---

immediately *–adv.* **1** without pause or delay. **2** without intermediary. *–conj.* as soon as.

immemorial /ˌɪmɪˈmɔːrɪəl/ *adj.* ancient beyond memory or record (*from time immemorial*).

immense /ɪˈmens/ *adj.* **1** extremely large; huge. **2** considerable (*immense difference*). □ **immenseness** *n.* **immensity** *n.* [Latin *metior mens-* measure]

immensely *adv.* **1** *colloq.* very much (*enjoyed myself immensely*). **2** to an immense degree (*immensely rich*).

immerse /ɪˈmɜːs/ *v.* (**-sing**) **1 a** (often foll. by *in*) dip, plunge. **b** submerge (a person). **2** (often *refl.* or in *passive*; often foll. by *in*) absorb or involve deeply. **3** (often foll. by *in*) bury, embed. [Latin *mergo mers-* dip]

immersion /ɪˈmɜːʃ(ə)n/ *n.* **1** immersing or being immersed. **2** baptism by total bodily immersion. **3** mental absorption.

immersion heater *n.* electric device immersed in a liquid to heat it, esp. in a hot-water tank.

immigrant /ˈɪmɪgrənt/ *–n.* person who immigrates. *–adj.* **1** immigrating. **2** of immigrants.

◆ **immigrant remittances** *n.pl.* money sent by immigrants from the country in which they work to their families in their native countries. These sums can be a valuable source of foreign exchange for the native countries.

---

immigrate /ˈɪmɪˌgreɪt/ *v.* come into a country and settle. □ **immigration** /-ˈgreɪʃ(ə)n/ *n.* [related to IN-[2], MIGRATE]

imminent /ˈɪmɪnənt/ *adj.* impending; about to happen (*war is imminent*). □ **imminence** *n.* **imminently** *adv.* [Latin *immineo* be impending]

immiscible /ɪˈmɪsɪb(ə)l/ *adj.* (often foll. by *with*) not able to be mixed. □ **immiscibility** /-ˈbɪlɪtɪ/ *n.*

immobile /ɪˈməʊbaɪl/ *adj.* **1** not moving. **2** unable to move or be moved. □ **immobility** /-ˈbɪlɪtɪ/ *n.*

immobilize /ɪˈməʊbɪˌlaɪz/ *v.* (also **-ise**) (**-zing** or **-sing**) **1** make or keep immobile. **2** keep (a limb or patient) still for healing purposes. □ **immobilization** /-ˈzeɪʃ(ə)n/ *n.*

immoderate /ɪˈmɒdərət/ *adj.* excessive; lacking moderation. □ **immoderately** *adv.*

immodest /ɪˈmɒdɪst/ *adj.* **1** lacking modesty; conceited. **2** shameless, indecent. □ **immodestly** *adv.* **immodesty** *n.*

immolate /ˈɪməˌleɪt/ *v.* (**-ting**) kill or offer as a sacrifice. □ **immolation** /-ˈleɪʃ(ə)n/ *n.* [Latin, = sprinkle with meal]

immoral /ɪˈmɒr(ə)l/ *adj.* **1** not conforming to accepted morality; morally wrong. **2** sexually promiscuous or deviant. □ **immorality** /ˌɪməˈrælɪtɪ/ *n.* (*pl.* **-ies**). **immorally** *adv.*

immortal /ɪˈmɔːt(ə)l/ *–adj.* **1 a** living for ever; not mortal. **b** divine. **2** unfading. **3** famous for all time. *–n.* **1 a** immortal being. **b** (in *pl.*) gods of antiquity. **2** person, esp. an author, remembered long after death. □ **immortality** /ˌɪmɔːˈtælɪtɪ/ *n.* **immortalize** *v.* (also **-ise**) (**-zing** or **-sing**). **immortally** *adv.*

immovable /ɪˈmuːvəb(ə)l/ *adj.* (also **immoveable**) **1** not able to be moved. **2** steadfast, unyielding. **3** emotionless. **4** not subject to change (*immovable law*). **5** motionless. **6** (of property) consisting of land, houses, etc. □ **immovability** /-ˈbɪlɪtɪ/ *n.* **immovably** *adv.*

immune /ɪˈmjuːn/ *adj.* **1 a** (often foll. by *against, from, to*) protected against infection through inoculation etc. **b** relating to immunity (*immune system*). **2** (foll. by *from, to*) exempt from or proof against a charge, duty, criticism, etc. [Latin *immunis* exempt]

immunity *n.* (*pl.* **-ies**) **1** ability of an organism to resist infection by means of antibodies and white blood cells. **2** (often foll. by *from*) freedom or exemption.

immunize /ˈɪmjuːˌnaɪz/ *v.* (also **-ise**) (**-zing** or **-sing**) make immune, usu. by inoculation. □ **immunization** /-ˈzeɪʃ(ə)n/ *n.*

immunodeficiency /ˌɪmjuːˌnəʊdɪˈfɪʃənsɪ/ *n.* reduction in normal immune defences.

immunoglobulin /ˌɪmjuːnəʊˈglɒbjʊlɪn/ *n.* any of a group of related proteins functioning as antibodies.

immunology /ˌɪmjuːˈnɒlədʒɪ/ *n.* the study of immunity. □ **immunological** /-nəˈlɒdʒɪk(ə)l/ *adj.* **immunologist** *n.*

immunotherapy /ˌɪmjuːnəʊˈθerəpɪ/ *n.* prevention or treatment of disease with substances that stimulate the immune response.

immure /ɪˈmjʊə(r)/ *v.* (**-ring**) **1** imprison. **2** *refl.* shut oneself away. [Latin *murus* wall]

immutable /ɪˈmjuːtəb(ə)l/ *adj.* unchangeable. □ **immutability** /-ˈbɪlɪtɪ/ *n.* **immutably** *adv.*

imp *n.* **1** mischievous child. **2** small devil or sprite. [Old English, = young shoot]

impact –*n.* /ˈɪmpækt/ **1** effect of sudden forcible contact between two solid bodies etc.; collision. **2** strong effect or impression. –*v.* /ɪmˈpækt/ **1** press or fix firmly. **2** (as **impacted** *adj.*) (of a tooth) wedged between another tooth and the jaw. **3** (often foll. by *on*) have an impact on. □ **impaction** /ɪmˈpækʃ(ə)n/ *n.* [Latin: related to IMPINGE]

◆ **impact day** *n.* day on which the terms of a new issue of shares are made public.

---

impact printer see PRINTER 3.

impair /ɪmˈpeə(r)/ *v.* damage, weaken. □ **impairment** *n.* [Latin, = make worse, from *pejor*]

impala /ɪmˈpɑːlə/ *n.* (*pl.* same or **-s**) small African antelope. [Zulu]

impale /ɪmˈpeɪl/ *v.* (**-ling**) transfix or pierce with a sharp stake etc. □ **impalement** *n.* [Latin *palus* PALE[2]]

impalpable /ɪmˈpælpəb(ə)l/ *adj.* **1** not easily grasped by the mind; intangible. **2** imperceptible to the touch. **3** (of powder) very fine. □ **impalpability** /-ˈbɪlɪtɪ/ *n.* **impalpably** *adv.*

impart /ɪmˈpɑːt/ *v.* (often foll. by *to*) **1** communicate (news etc.). **2** give a share of (a thing). [Latin: related to PART]

impartial /ɪmˈpɑːʃ(ə)l/ *adj.* treating all alike; unprejudiced, fair. □ **impartiality** /-ʃɪˈælɪtɪ/ *n.* **impartially** *adv.*

impassable /ɪmˈpɑːsəb(ə)l/ *adj.* not able to be traversed. □ **impassability** /-ˈbɪlɪtɪ/ *n.* **impassableness** *n.* **impassably** *adv.*

impasse /ˈæmpæs, ˈɪm-/ *n.* deadlock. [French: related to PASS[1]]

impassible /ɪmˈpæsɪb(ə)l/ *adj.* **1** impassive. **2** incapable of feeling, emotion, or injury. □ **impassibility** /-ˈbɪlɪtɪ/ *n.* **impassibly** *adv.* [Latin *patior pass-* suffer]

impassioned /ɪmˈpæʃ(ə)nd/ *adj.* filled with passion; ardent. [Italian *impassionato*: related to PASSION]

impassive /ɪmˈpæsɪv/ *adj.* incapable of or not showing emotion; serene. □ **impassively** *adv.* **impassiveness** *n.* **impassivity** /-ˈsɪvɪtɪ/ *n.*

impasto /ɪmˈpæstəʊ/ *n.* *Art* technique of laying on paint thickly. [Italian]

impatiens /ɪmˈpeɪʃɪˌenz/ *n.* any of several plants including the busy Lizzie. [Latin: related to IMPATIENT]

impatient /ɪmˈpeɪʃ(ə)nt/ *adj.* **1** lacking, or showing a lack of, patience or tolerance. **2** restlessly eager. **3** (foll. by *of*) intolerant of. □ **impatience** *n.* **impatiently** *adv.*

impeach /ɪmˈpiːtʃ/ *v.* **1** charge with a crime against the state, esp. treason. **2** *US* charge (a public official) with misconduct. **3** call in question, disparage. □ **impeachable** *adj.* **impeachment** *n.* [French *empecher* from Latin *pedica* fetter]

impeccable /ɪmˈpekəb(ə)l/ *adj.* faultless, exemplary. □ **impeccability** /-ˈbɪlɪtɪ/ *n.* **impeccably** *adv.* [related to IN-[1], Latin *pecco* sin]

impecunious /ˌɪmpɪˈkjuːnɪəs/ *adj.* having little or no money. □ **impecuniosity** /-ˈɒsɪtɪ/ *n.* **impecuniousness** *n.* [related to PECUNIARY]

impedance /ɪmˈpiːd(ə)ns/ *n.* total effective resistance of an electric circuit etc. to an alternating current. [from IMPEDE]

■ **Usage** *Impedance* is sometimes confused with *impediment*, which means 'a hindrance' or 'a speech defect'.

impede /ɪmˈpiːd/ *v.* (**-ding**) obstruct; hinder. [Latin *impedio* from *pes ped-* foot]

impediment /ɪmˈpedɪmənt/ *n.* **1** hindrance or obstruction. **2** speech defect, e.g. a stammer. [Latin: related to IMPEDE]

■ **Usage** See note at *impedance*.

impedimenta /ɪmˌpedɪˈmentə/ *n.pl.* **1** encumbrances. **2** baggage, esp. of an army.

impel /ɪmˈpel/ *v.* (**-ll-**) **1** drive, force, or urge. **2** propel. [Latin *pello* drive]

impend /ɪmˈpend/ *v.* (often foll. by *over*) **1** (of a danger, event, etc.) be threatening or imminent. **2** hang. □ **impending** *adj.* [Latin *pendeo* hang]

impenetrable /ɪmˈpenɪtrəb(ə)l/ *adj.* **1** not able to be penetrated. **2** inscrutable. **3** inaccessible to ideas, influences, etc. □ **impenetrability** /-ˈbɪlɪtɪ/ *n.* **impenetrableness** *n.* **impenetrably** *adv.*

impenitent /ɪmˈpenɪt(ə)nt/ *adj.* not sorry, unrepentant. □ **impenitence** *n.*

imperative /ɪmˈperətɪv/ –*adj.* **1** urgent; obligatory. **2** commanding, peremptory. **3** *Gram.* (of a mood) expressing a command (e.g. *come here!*). –*n.* **1** *Gram.* imperative mood. **2** command. **3** essential or urgent thing. [Latin *impero* command]

imperceptible /ˌɪmpəˈseptɪb(ə)l/ *adj.* **1** not perceptible. **2** very slight, gradual, or subtle. □ **imperceptibility** /-ˈbɪlɪtɪ/ *n.* **imperceptibly** *adv.*

imperfect /ɪmˈpɜːfɪkt/ –*adj.* **1** not perfect; faulty, incomplete. **2** *Gram.* (of a tense) denoting action in progress but not completed (e.g. *they were singing*). –*n.* imperfect tense. □ **imperfectly** *adv.*

◆ **imperfect competition** *n.* (also **imperfect market**) *Econ.* market in which some of the assumptions of perfect competition do not apply. For example, there may be incomplete information about the market or firms may be able to influence the prices of goods sold by their output decisions. Using perfect competiton as a benchmark, economists are interested in analysing specific forms of imperfect competition in order to understand inefficiencies in the real world, such as large-scale unemployment and excessive volatility in financial markets.

---

imperfection /ˌɪmpəˈfekʃ(ə)n/ *n.* **1** state of being imperfect. **2** fault, blemish.

imperial /ɪmˈpɪərɪəl/ *adj.* **1** of or characteristic of an empire or similar sovereign state. **2 a** of an emperor. **b** majestic, august; authoritative. **3** (of non-metric weights and measures) statutory in the UK, esp. formerly (*imperial gallon*; *imperial units*). □ **imperially** *adv.* [Latin *imperium* dominion]

imperialism *n.* **1** imperial rule or system. **2** usu. *derog.* policy of dominating other nations by acquiring dependencies etc. □ **imperialist** *n.* & *adj.* **imperialistic** /-ˈlɪstɪk/ *adj.*

◆ **imperial preference** see PREFERENTIAL DUTY.

---

imperil /ɪmˈperɪl/ *v.* (**-ll-**; *US* **-l-**) endanger.

imperious /ɪmˈpɪərɪəs/ *adj.* overbearing, domineering. □ **imperiously** *adv.* **imperiousness** *n.*

imperishable /ɪmˈperɪʃəb(ə)l/ *adj.* not able to perish, indestructible.

impermanent /ɪmˈpɜːmənənt/ *adj.* not permanent. □ **impermanence** *n.* **impermanency** *n.*

impermeable /ɪmˈpɜːmɪəb(ə)l/ *adj.* not permeable, not allowing fluids to pass through. □ **impermeability** /-ˈbɪlɪtɪ/ *n.*

impermissible /ˌɪmpəˈmɪsɪb(ə)l/ *adj.* not allowable.

impersonal /ɪm'pɜːsən(ə)l/ *adj.* **1** without personal reference; objective, impartial. **2** without human attributes; cold, unfeeling. **3** *Gram.* **a** (of a verb) used esp. with *it* as a subject (e.g. *it is snowing*). **b** (of a pronoun) = INDEFINITE 3. □ **impersonality** /-'nælɪtɪ/ *n.* **impersonally** *adv.*

♦ **impersonal account** *n.* ledger account that does not bear the name of a person. These accounts usu. comprise the nominal accounts, having such names as motor vehicles, heat and light, and stock in trade.

impersonate /ɪm'pɜːsə,neɪt/ *v.* (**-ting**) **1** pretend to be (another person), esp. as entertainment or fraud. **2** act (a character). □ **impersonation** /-'neɪʃ(ə)n/ *n.* **impersonator** *n.* [from IN-[2], Latin PERSONA]

impertinent /ɪm'pɜːtɪnənt/ *adj.* **1** insolent, disrespectful. **2** esp. *Law* irrelevant. □ **impertinence** *n.* **impertinently** *adv.*

imperturbable /,ɪmpə'tɜːbəb(ə)l/ *adj.* not excitable; calm. □ **imperturbability** /-'bɪlɪtɪ/ *n.* **imperturbably** *adv.*

impervious /ɪm'pɜːvɪəs/ *adj.* (usu. foll. by *to*) **1** impermeable. **2** not responsive (to argument etc.).

impetigo /,ɪmpɪ'taɪgəʊ/ *n.* contagious skin infection forming pimples and sores. [Latin *impeto* assail]

impetuous /ɪm'petjʊəs/ *adj.* **1** acting or done rashly or with sudden energy. **2** moving forcefully or rapidly. □ **impetuosity** /-'ɒsɪtɪ/ *n.* **impetuously** *adv.* **impetuousness** *n.* [Latin: related to IMPETUS]

impetus /'ɪmpɪtəs/ *n.* **1** force with which a body moves. **2** driving force or impulse. [Latin *impeto* assail]

impiety /ɪm'paɪətɪ/ *n.* (*pl.* **-ies**) **1** lack of piety or reverence. **2** act etc. showing this.

impinge /ɪm'pɪndʒ/ *v.* (**-ging**) (usu. foll. by *on, upon*) **1** make an impact or effect. **2** encroach. □ **impingement** *n.* [Latin *pango pact-* fix]

impious /'ɪmpɪəs/ *adj.* **1** not pious. **2** wicked, profane.

impish *adj.* of or like an imp; mischievous. □ **impishly** *adv.* **impishness** *n.*

implacable /ɪm'plækəb(ə)l/ *adj.* unable to be appeased. □ **implacability** /-'bɪlɪtɪ/ *n.* **implacably** *adv.*

implant –*v.* /ɪm'plɑːnt/ **1** (often foll. by *in*) insert or fix. **2** (often foll. by *in*) instil (an idea etc.) in a person's mind. **3** plant. **4** **a** insert (tissue etc.) in a living body. **b** (in *passive*) (of a fertilized ovum) become attached to the wall of the womb. –*n.* /'ɪmplɑːnt/ thing implanted, esp. a piece of tissue. □ **implantation** /-'teɪʃ(ə)n/ *n.* [Latin: related to PLANT]

implausible /ɪm'plɔːzɪb(ə)l/ *adj.* not plausible. □ **implausibility** /-'bɪlɪtɪ/ *n.* **implausibly** *adv.*

implement –*n.* /'ɪmplɪmənt/ tool, instrument, utensil. –*v.* /'ɪmplɪ,ment/ put (a decision, plan, contract, etc.) into effect. [Latin *impleo* fulfil]

implementation /,ɪmplɪmen'teɪʃ(ə)n/ *n.* **1** carrying out. **2** working version of a given design of a system. **3** processes involved in developing a working version of a system from a given design. **4** way in which some part of a system is made to fulfil its function.

implicate /'ɪmplɪ,keɪt/ *v.* (**-ting**) **1** (often foll. by *in*) show (a person) to be involved (in a crime etc.). **2** imply. [Latin *plico* fold]

implication /,ɪmplɪ'keɪʃ(ə)n/ *n.* **1** thing implied. **2** implicating or implying.

implicit /ɪm'plɪsɪt/ *adj.* **1** implied though not plainly expressed. **2** absolute, unquestioning (*implicit belief*). □ **implicitly** *adv.* [Latin: related to IMPLICATE]

♦ **implicit contract theory** *n. Econ.* theory, introduced in the 1970s, that wage contracts contain an element of insurance for workers. Thus firms provide an implicit contract guaranteeing stable wages and employment in return for lower average pay, much as an insurance company charges a premium. This theory explains why, even in a recession, employers are reluctant to reduce wages and thus create the possibility of involuntary unemployment. Unfortunately it has subsequently been shown that overemployment is just as likely an outcome as underemployment as a result of implicit contracts. However, the theory has provided many new insights into the operation of labour markets.

♦ **implied term** *n.* provision of a contract not agreed to by the parties in words but either regarded by the courts as necessary to give effect to their presumed intentions or introduced into the contract by statute (as in the case of contracts for the sale of goods). An implied term may constitute either a condition of the contract or a warranty; if it is introduced by statute it often cannot be expressly excluded.

implode /ɪm'pləʊd/ *v.* (**-ding**) (cause to) burst inwards. □ **implosion** /ɪm'pləʊʒ(ə)n/ *n.* [from IN-[2]: cf. EXPLODE]

implore /ɪm'plɔː(r)/ *v.* (**-ring**) **1** (often foll. by *to* + infin.) entreat (a person). **2** beg earnestly for. [Latin *ploro* weep]

imply /ɪm'plaɪ/ *v.* (**-ies, -ied**) **1** (often foll. by *that*) strongly suggest or insinuate without directly stating (*what are you implying?*). **2** signify, esp. as a consequence (*silence implies guilt*). [Latin: related to IMPLICATE]

impolite /,ɪmpə'laɪt/ *adj.* (**impolitest**) ill-mannered, uncivil, rude. □ **impolitely** *adv.* **impoliteness** *n.*

impolitic /ɪm'pɒlɪtɪk/ *adj.* inexpedient, unwise. □ **impoliticly** *adv.*

imponderable /ɪm'pɒndərəb(ə)l/ –*adj.* **1** not able to be estimated. **2** very light; weightless. –*n.* (usu. in *pl.*) imponderable thing. □ **imponderability** /-'bɪlɪtɪ/ *n.* **imponderably** *adv.*

import –*v.* /ɪm'pɔːt, 'ɪm-/ **1** bring in (esp. foreign goods or services) to a country. **2** imply, indicate, signify. –*n.* /'ɪmpɔːt/ **1** (esp. in *pl.*) imported article or service. **2** importing. **3** what is implied; meaning. **4** importance. □ **importation** /,ɪmpɔː'teɪʃ(ə)n/ *n.* **importer** /ɪm'pɔːtə(r)/ *n.* [Latin *importo* carry in]

important /ɪm'pɔːt(ə)nt/ *adj.* **1** (often foll. by *to*) of great effect or consequence; momentous. **2** (of a person) having high rank or authority. **3** pompous. □ **importance** *n.* **importantly** *adv.* [Latin *importo* carry in, signify]

♦ **import deposit** *n.* sum of money deposited by an importer with the Customs and Excise authorities when goods are imported. As a means of restricting importation to a country, it was used by the UK in 1968–70, as an alternative to raising import duties when it had an agreement with GATT not to do so.

♦ **import duty** *n.* tax or tariff on imported goods, either a fixed amount or a percentage of the value of the goods. Import duties have been a major type of barrier used to protect domestic production against foreign competition and they have also been an important source of government revenue, esp. in developing countries.

♦ **import entry form** *n.* form completed by a UK importer of goods and submitted to the Customs and Excise for assessment of the import duty, if any. When passed by the Customs the form functions as a warrant to permit the goods to be removed from the port of entry.

♦ **import licence** *n.* permit allowing an importer to bring a stated quantity of certain goods into a country. Import licences are needed when import restrictions include import quotas, currency restrictions, and prohibition. They also function as a means of exchange control, the licence both permitting importation and allowing the importer to purchase the required foreign currency.

♦ **import quota** *n.* import restriction imposed on imported goods, to reduce the quantity of certain goods allowed into a country from a particular exporting country, in a stated period. The purpose may be to conserve foreign currency, if there is an unfavourable balance of payments, or to protect the home market against foreign competition (see PROTECTIONISM). Quotas are usu. enforced by means of import licences.

♦ **import restrictions** *n.pl.* restrictions imposed on goods and services imported into a country, which usu. need to be paid for in the currency of the exporting country. This can cause a serious problem to the importing country's balance of payments, hence the need for restrictions, which include tariffs, import quotas, currency restrictions, and prohibition. The restrictions may also be imposed to protect the home industry against foreign competition (see PROTECTIONISM) or during the course of political bargaining.

♦ **import surcharge** *n.* extra tax applied by a government on certain imports in addition to the normal tariff, usu. as a temporary measure by a government that is in difficulty with its balance of payments, but does not wish to violate its international tariff agreements.

---

importunate /ɪm'pɔːtjʊnət/ *adj.* making persistent or pressing requests. □ **importunity** /ˌɪmpɔː'tjuːnɪtɪ/ *n.* [Latin *importunus* inconvenient]

importune /ˌɪmpə'tjuːn/ *v.* (**-ning**) **1** pester (a person) with requests. **2** solicit as a prostitute.

impose /ɪm'pəʊz/ *v.* (**-sing**) **1** (often foll. by *on, upon*) lay (a tax, duty, charge, or obligation) on. **2** enforce compliance with. **3** also *refl.* (foll. by *on, upon*, or *absol.*) take advantage of (*will not impose on you any longer*). **4** (often foll. by *on, upon*) inflict (a thing) on. [Latin *impono*]

imposing *adj.* impressive, formidable, esp. in appearance.

imposition /ˌɪmpə'zɪʃ(ə)n/ *n.* **1** imposing or being imposed. **2** unfair demand or burden. **3** tax, duty.

impossible /ɪm'pɒsɪb(ə)l/ *adj.* **1** not possible. **2** *colloq.* not easy, convenient, or believable. **3** *colloq.* (esp. of a person) outrageous, intolerable. □ **impossibility** /-'bɪlɪtɪ/ *n.* (*pl.* **-ies**). **impossibly** *adv.*

impost[1] /'ɪmpəʊst/ *n.* tax, duty, or tribute. [Latin *impono impost-* impose]

impost[2] /'ɪmpəʊst/ *n.* upper course of a pillar, carrying an arch.

impostor /ɪm'pɒstə(r)/ *n.* (also **imposter**) **1** person who assumes a false character or pretends to be someone else. **2** swindler.

imposture /ɪm'pɒstʃə(r)/ *n.* fraudulent deception.

impotent /'ɪmpət(ə)nt/ *adj.* **1** powerless, ineffective. **2** (of a male) unable to achieve an erection or orgasm. □ **impotence** *n.*

impound /ɪm'paʊnd/ *v.* **1** confiscate. **2** take legal possession of. **3** shut up (animals) in a pound.

impoverish /ɪm'pɒvərɪʃ/ *v.* make poor. □ **impoverishment** *n.* [French: related to POVERTY]

impracticable /ɪm'præktɪkəb(ə)l/ *adj.* not practicable. □ **impracticability** /-'bɪlɪtɪ/ *n.* **impracticably** *adv.*

impractical /ɪm'præktɪk(ə)l/ *adj.* **1** not practical. **2** esp. *US* not practicable. □ **impracticality** /-'kælɪtɪ/ *n.*

imprecation /ˌɪmprɪ'keɪʃ(ə)n/ *n. formal* oath, curse. [Latin *precor* pray]

imprecise /ˌɪmprɪ'saɪs/ *adj.* not precise. □ **imprecisely** *adv.* **impreciseness** *n.* **imprecision** /-'sɪʒ(ə)n/ *n.*

impregnable /ɪm'pregnəb(ə)l/ *adj.* strong enough to be secure against attack. □ **impregnability** /-'bɪlɪtɪ/ *n.* **impregnably** *adv.* [French: related to IN-[1], Latin *prehendo* take]

impregnate /'ɪmpregˌneɪt/ *v.* (**-ting**) **1** (often foll. by *with*) fill or saturate. **2** (often foll. by *with*) imbue (with feelings etc.). **3 a** make (a female) pregnant. **b** fertilize (an ovum). □ **impregnation** /-'neɪʃ(ə)n/ *n.* [Latin: related to PREGNANT]

impresario /ˌɪmprɪ'sɑːrɪəʊ/ *n.* (*pl.* **-s**) organizer of public entertainment, esp. a theatrical etc. manager. [Italian]

impress –*v.* /ɪm'pres/ **1** (often foll. by *with*) **a** affect or influence deeply. **b** affect (a person) favourably (*was most impressed*). **2** (often foll. by *on*) emphasize (an idea etc.) (*must impress on you the need to be prompt*). **3 a** (often foll. by *on*) imprint or make (a mark). **b** mark (a thing) with a stamp, seal, etc. –*n.* /'ɪmpres/ **1** mark made by a seal, stamp, etc. **2** characteristic mark or quality. □ **impressible** /ɪm'presɪb(ə)l/ *adj.* [French: related to PRESS[1]]

impression /ɪm'preʃ(ə)n/ *n.* **1** effect (esp. on the mind or feelings). **2** notion or belief (esp. vague or mistaken). **3** imitation of a person or sound, esp. as entertainment. **4 a** impressing. **b** mark impressed. **5** unaltered reprint from standing type or plates. **6** number of copies of a book etc. issued at one time. **7** print taken from a wood or copper engraving.

impressionable *adj.* easily influenced. □ **impressionability** /-'bɪlɪtɪ/ *n.* **impressionably** *adv.*

impressionism /ɪm'preʃəˌnɪz(ə)m/ *n.* **1** style or movement in art concerned with conveying the effect of natural light on objects. **2** style of music or writing seeking to convey esp. fleeting feelings or experience. □ **impressionist** *n.* **impressionistic** /-'nɪstɪk/ *adj.*

impressive /ɪm'presɪv/ *adj.* causing respect, approval, or admiration. □ **impressively** *adv.* **impressiveness** *n.*

♦ **imprest account** /ɪm'prest/ *n.* means of controlling petty-cash expenditure in which a person is given a certain sum of money (a float or imprest). On providing appropriate vouchers for the amounts spent, the person is reimbursed so that the float is restored. Thus at any given time the person should have either vouchers or cash amounting to the float. [orig. *in prest*: related to PRESS[2]]

---

imprimatur /ˌɪmprɪ'mɑːtə(r)/ *n.* **1** *RC Ch.* licence to print (a religious book etc.). **2** official approval. [Latin, = let it be printed]

■ **Usage** *Imprimatur* is sometimes confused with sense 2 of *imprint*.

imprint –*v.* /ɪm'prɪnt/ **1** (often foll. by *on*) impress firmly, esp. on the mind. **2 a** (often foll. by *on*) make a stamp or impression of (a figure etc.) on a thing. **b** make an impression on (a thing) with a stamp etc. –*n.* /'ɪmprɪnt/ **1** impression, stamp. **2** printer's or publisher's name etc. printed in a book.

■ **Usage** See note at *imprimatur*.

imprison /ɪm'prɪz(ə)n/ *v.* **1** put in prison. **2** confine. □ **imprisonment** *n.*

improbable /ɪm'prɒbəb(ə)l/ *adj.* **1** unlikely. **2** difficult to believe. □ **improbability** /-'bɪlɪtɪ/ *n.* **improbably** *adv.*

improbity /ɪm'prəʊbɪtɪ/ *n.* (*pl.* **-ies**) **1** wickedness; dishonesty. **2** wicked or dishonest act.

impromptu /ɪm'prɒmptjuː/ –*adj.* & *adv.* extempore, unrehearsed. –*n.* (*pl.* **-s**) **1** extempore performance or speech. **2** short, usu. solo, instrumental composition, often improvisatory in style. [French from Latin *in promptu* in readiness]

improper /ɪm'prɒpə(r)/ *adj.* **1** unseemly; indecent. **2** inaccurate, wrong. □ **improperly** *adv.*

improper fraction *n.* fraction in which the numerator is greater than or equal to the denominator.

impropriety /ˌɪmprə'praɪətɪ/ *n.* (*pl.* **-ies**) **1** lack of propriety; indecency. **2** instance of this. **3** incorrectness.

improve /ɪm'pruːv/ *v.* (**-ving**) **1 a** make or become better. **b** (foll. by *on, upon*) produce something better than. **2** (as **improving** *adj.*) giving moral benefit (*improving literature*). □ **improvable** *adj.* **improvement** *n.* [Anglo-French *emprower* from French *prou* profit]

improvident /ɪm'prɒvɪd(ə)nt/ *adj.* **1** lacking foresight. **2** profligate; wasteful. **3** incautious. □ **improvidence** *n.* **improvidently** *adv.*

improvise /'ɪmprəˌvaɪz/ *v.* (**-sing**) (also *absol.*) **1** compose or perform (music, verse, etc.) extempore. **2** provide or construct from materials not intended for the purpose. □ **improvisation** /-'zeɪʃ(ə)n/ *n.* **improvisational** /-'zeɪʃən(ə)l/ *adj.* **improvisatory** /-'zeɪtərɪ/ *adj.* [Latin *improvisus* unforeseen]

imprudent /ɪm'pruːd(ə)nt/ *adj.* unwise, indiscreet. □ **imprudence** *n.* **imprudently** *adv.*

impudent /'ɪmpjʊd(ə)nt/ *adj.* impertinent. □ **impudence** *n.* **impudently** *adv.* [Latin *pudeo* be ashamed]

impugn /ɪm'pjuːn/ *v.* challenge or call in question. □ **impugnment** *n.* [Latin *pugno* fight]

impulse /'ɪmpʌls/ *n.* **1** sudden urge (*felt an impulse to laugh*). **2** tendency to follow such urges (*man of impulse*). **3** impelling; a push. **4** impetus. **5** *Physics* **a** large temporary force producing a change of momentum (e.g. a hammer-blow). **b** change of momentum so produced. **6** wave of excitation in a nerve. [Latin: related to PULSE[1]]

impulse buying *n.* purchasing goods on impulse, usu. encouraged by such factors as prominent shelf position.

impulsion /ɪm'pʌlʃ(ə)n/ *n.* **1** impelling. **2** mental impulse. **3** impetus.

impulsive /ɪm'pʌlsɪv/ *adj.* **1** tending to act on impulse. **2** done on impulse. **3** tending to impel. □ **impulsively** *adv.* **impulsiveness** *n.*

impunity /ɪm'pjuːnɪtɪ/ *n.* exemption from punishment, bad consequences, etc. □ **with impunity** without punishment etc. [Latin *poena* penalty]

impure /ɪm'pjʊə(r)/ *adj.* **1** adulterated. **2** dirty. **3** unchaste.

impurity *n.* (*pl.* **-ies**) **1** being impure. **2** impure thing or part.

♦ **imputation system of taxation** *n.* system of corporation tax in which some, or all, of the corporation tax is treated as a tax credit on account of the income tax payable by the shareholders on their dividends. Such a system was used in the UK between 1972 and 1999, when it was abolished; the imputation works through the system of advance corporation tax.

---

impute /ɪm'pjuːt/ *v.* (**-ting**) (foll. by *to*) attribute (a fault etc.) to. □ **imputation** /-'teɪʃ(ə)n/ *n.* [Latin *puto* reckon]

♦ **imputed cost** *n.* estimate of the opportunity cost of making use of a resource that is already owned and so has no formal price. In arriving at the true cost of a process, the imputed cost must be added to the actual outlay.

IMRA *abbr.* Industrial Marketing Research Association.

♦ **IMRO** /'ɪmrəʊ/ *abbr.* Investment Management Regulatory Organization. See SELF-REGULATING ORGANIZATION.

Imroz see IMBROS.

IMS *abbr.* **1** *propr.* Information Management System, a database management system. **2** Institute of Management Services.

IMSM *abbr.* Institute of Marketing and Sales Management.

IN *US postcode* Indiana.

In *symb.* indium.

in *–prep.* **1** expressing inclusion or position within limits of space, time, circumstance, etc. (*in England*; *in bed*; *in 1989*; *in the rain*). **2 a** within (a certain time) (*finished it in two hours*). **b** after (a certain time) (*will be leaving in an hour*). **3** with respect to (*blind in one eye*; *good in parts*). **4** as a proportionate part of (*one in three failed*; *gradient of one in six*). **5** with the form or arrangement of (*packed in tens*; *falling in folds*). **6** as a member of (*in the army*). **7** involved with (*is in banking*). **8** as the content of (*there is something in what you say*). **9** within the ability of (*does he have it in him?*). **10** having the condition of; affected by (*in bad health*; *in danger*). **11** having as a purpose (*in search of*; *in reply to*). **12** by means of or using as material (*drawn in pencil*; *modelled in bronze*). **13 a** using as the language of expression (*written in French*). **b** (of music) having as its key (*symphony in C*). **14** (of a word) having as a beginning or ending (*words in un-*). **15** wearing (*in blue*; *in a suit*). **16** with the identity of (*found a friend in Mary*). **17** (of an animal) pregnant with (*in calf*). **18** into (with a verb of motion or change: *put it in the box*; *cut it in two*). **19** introducing an indirect object after a verb (*believe in*; *engage in*; *share in*). **20** forming adverbial phrases (*in any case*; *in reality*; *in short*). *–adv.* expressing position within limits, or motion to such a position: **1** into a room, house, etc. (*come in*). **2** at home, in one's office, etc. (*is not in*). **3** so as to be enclosed (*locked in*). **4** in a publication (*is the advert in?*). **5** in or to the inward side (*rub it in*). **6 a** in fashion or season (*long skirts are in*). **b** elected or in office (*Democrat got in*). **7** favourable (*their luck was in*). **8** *Cricket* (of a player or side) batting. **9** (of transport) at the platform etc. (*the train is in*). **10** (of a season, order, etc.) having arrived or been received. **11** (of a fire) continuing to burn. **12** denoting effective action (*join in*). **13** (of the tide) at the highest point. **14** (in *comb.*) *colloq.* denoting prolonged concerted action, esp. by large numbers (*sit-in*; *teach-in*). *–adj.* **1** internal; living in; inside (*in-patient*). **2** fashionable (*the in thing to do*). **3** confined to a small group (*in-joke*). □ **in all** see ALL. **in between** see BETWEEN *adv.* **in for 1** about to undergo or get. **2** competing in or for. **in on** sharing in; privy to. **ins and outs** (often foll. by *of*) all the details. **in so far as** see FAR. **in that** because; in so far as. **in with** on good terms with; favourably placed for (*in with a chance*). [Old English]

in. *abbr.* inch(es).

in-[1] *prefix* (also **il-, im-, ir-**) added to: **1** adjectives, meaning 'not' (*inedible*; *insane*). **2** nouns, meaning 'without, lacking' (*inaction*). [Latin]

in-[2] *prefix* (also **il-, im-, ir-**) in, on, into, towards, within (*induce*; *influx*; *insight*; *intrude*). [from IN, or from Latin *in* (prep.)]

inability /ˌɪnə'bɪlɪtɪ/ *n.* **1** being unable. **2** lack of power or means.

in absentia /ˌɪn æb'sentɪə/ *adv.* in (his, her, or their) absence. [Latin]

inaccessible /ˌɪnək'sesɪb(ə)l/ *adj.* **1** not accessible. **2** (of a person) unapproachable. □ **inaccessibility** /-'bɪlɪtɪ/ *n.*

inaccurate /ɪn'ækjʊrət/ *adj.* not accurate. □ **inaccuracy** *n.* (*pl.* **-ies**). **inaccurately** *adv.*

inaction /ɪn'ækʃ(ə)n/ *n.* lack of action.

inactive /ɪn'æktɪv/ *adj.* **1** not active. **2** not operating. **3** indolent. □ **inactivity** /-'tɪvɪtɪ/ *n.*

inadequate /ɪn'ædɪkwət/ *adj.* **1** not adequate; insufficient. **2** (of a person) incompetent; weak. □ **inadequacy** *n.* (*pl.* **-ies**). **inadequately** *adv.*

inadmissible /ˌɪnəd'mɪsɪb(ə)l/ *adj.* that cannot be admitted or allowed. □ **inadmissibility** /-'bɪlɪtɪ/ *n.* **inadmissibly** *adv.*

inadvertent /ˌɪnəd'vɜːt(ə)nt/ *adj.* **1** unintentional. **2** negligent, inattentive. □ **inadvertence** *n.* **inadvertently** *adv.* [from IN-[1], *advert* refer (to)]

inadvisable /ˌɪnəd'vaɪzəb(ə)l/ *adj.* not advisable. □ **inadvisability** /-'bɪlɪtɪ/ *n.*

inalienable /ɪn'eɪlɪənəb(ə)l/ *adj.* that cannot be transferred to another or taken away (*inalienable rights*).

inamorato /ɪnˌæmə'rɑːtəʊ/ *n.* (*fem.* **inamorata**) (*pl.* **-s**) *literary* lover. [Italian *inamorato*: related to IN-[2], Latin *amor* love]

inane /ɪ'neɪn/ *adj.* **1** silly, senseless. **2** empty, void. □ **inanely** *adv.* **inanity** /-'ænɪtɪ/ *n.* (*pl.* **-ies**). [Latin *inanis*]

inanimate /ɪn'ænɪmət/ *adj.* **1** not endowed with, or deprived of, animal life (*an inanimate object*). **2** spiritless, dull.

inapplicable /ˌɪnə'plɪkəb(ə)l/ *adj.* (often foll. by *to*) not applicable or relevant. □ **inapplicability** /-'bɪlɪtɪ/ *n.*

inapposite /ɪn'æpəzɪt/ *adj.* not apposite.

inappropriate /ˌɪnə'prəʊprɪət/ *adj.* not appropriate. □ **inappropriately** *adv.* **inappropriateness** *n.*

inapt /ɪn'æpt/ *adj.* **1** not apt or suitable. **2** unskilful. □ **inaptitude** *n.*

inarticulate /ˌɪnɑː'tɪkjʊlət/ *adj.* **1** unable to express oneself clearly. **2** (of speech) not articulate; indistinct. **3** dumb. **4** esp. *Anat.* not jointed. □ **inarticulately** *adv.*

inasmuch /ˌɪnəz'mʌtʃ/ *adv.* (foll. by *as*) **1** since, because. **2** to the extent that. [from *in as much*]

inattentive /ˌɪnə'tentɪv/ *adj.* **1** not paying attention. **2** neglecting to show courtesy. □ **inattention** *n.* **inattentively** *adv.*

inaudible /ɪn'ɔːdɪb(ə)l/ *adj.* unable to be heard. □ **inaudibly** *adv.*

inaugural /ɪ'nɔːgjʊr(ə)l/ *–adj.* of or for an inauguration. *–n.* inaugural speech, lecture, etc. [French from Latin *auguro* take omens: related to AUGUR]

inaugurate /ɪ'nɔːgjʊˌreɪt/ *v.* (**-ting**) **1** admit formally to office. **2** begin (an undertaking) or initiate the public use of (a building etc.), with a ceremony. **3** begin, introduce. □ **inauguration** /-'reɪʃ(ə)n/ *n.* **inaugurator** *n.*

inauspicious /ˌɪnɔː'spɪʃəs/ *adj.* **1** ill-omened, not favourable. **2** unlucky. □ **inauspiciously** *adv.* **inauspiciousness** *n.*

in-between *attrib. adj. colloq.* intermediate.

inboard /'ɪnbɔːd/ *–adv.* within the sides or towards the centre of a ship, aircraft, or vehicle. *–adj.* situated inboard.

inborn /'ɪnbɔːn, ɪn'bɔːn/ *adj.* existing from birth; natural, innate.

inbred /ɪn'bred/ *adj.* **1** inborn. **2** produced by inbreeding.

inbreeding /ɪn'briːdɪŋ/ *n.* breeding from closely related animals or persons. □ **inbreed** *v.* (*past* and *past part.* **-bred**).

Inbucon /'ɪnbjuːˌkɒn/ *n.* International Business Consultants (organization). [abbreviation]

inbuilt /ɪn'bɪlt/ *adj.* built-in.

Inc. *abbr. US* Incorporated (after the names of corporations, usu. those with limited liability).

Inca /'ɪŋkə/ *n.* member of a people of Peru before the Spanish conquest. [Quechua, = lord]

incalculable /ɪn'kælkjʊləb(ə)l/ *adj.* **1** too great for calculation. **2** not calculable beforehand. **3** uncertain, unpredictable. □ **incalculability** /-'bɪlɪtɪ/ *n.* **incalculably** *adv.*

incandesce /ˌɪnkæn'des/ *v.* (**-cing**) (cause to) glow with heat.

incandescent *adj.* **1** glowing with heat. **2** shining. **3** (of artificial light) produced by a glowing filament etc. □ **incandescence** *n.* [Latin *candeo* be white]

incantation /ˌɪnkæn'teɪʃ(ə)n/ *n.* magical formula; spell, charm. □ **incantational** *adj.* [Latin *canto* sing]

incapable /ɪn'keɪpəb(ə)l/ *adj.* **1 a** not capable. **b** too honest, kind, etc., to do something (*incapable of hurting anyone*). **2** not capable of rational conduct (*drunk and incapable*). □ **incapability** /-'bɪlɪtɪ/ *n.* **incapably** *adv.*

incapacitate /ˌɪnkə'pæsɪˌteɪt/ *v.* (**-ting**) make incapable or unfit.

incapacity /ˌɪnkə'pæsɪtɪ/ *n.* **1** inability; lack of power. **2** legal disqualification.

incarcerate /ɪn'kɑːsəˌreɪt/ *v.* (**-ting**) imprison. □ **incarceration** /-'reɪʃ(ə)n/ *n.* [medieval Latin *carcer* prison]

incarnate *–adj.* /ɪn'kɑːnət/ embodied in flesh, esp. in human form (*is the devil incarnate*). *–v.* /'ɪnkɑːˌneɪt, -'kɑːneɪt/ (**-ting**) **1** embody in flesh. **2** put (an idea etc.) into concrete form. **3** be the living embodiment of (a quality). [Latin *incarnor* be made flesh: related to CARNAGE]

incarnation /ˌɪnkɑː'neɪʃ(ə)n/ *n.* **1 a** embodiment in (esp. human) flesh. **b** (**the Incarnation**) the embodiment of God in Christ. **2** (often foll. by *of*) living type (of a quality etc.).

incautious /ɪn'kɔːʃəs/ *adj.* heedless, rash. □ **incautiously** *adv.*

incendiary /ɪn'sendɪərɪ/ *–adj.* **1** (of a bomb) designed to cause fires. **2 a** of arson. **b** guilty of arson. **3** inflammatory. *–n.* (*pl.* **-ies**) **1** incendiary bomb. **2** arsonist. □ **incendiarism** *n.* [Latin *incendo -cens-* set fire to]

incense[1] /'ɪnsens/ *n.* **1** gum or spice producing a sweet smell when burned. **2** smoke of this, esp. in religious ceremonial. [Church Latin *incensum*]

incense[2] /ɪn'sens/ *v.* (**-sing**) make angry. [Latin: related to INCENDIARY]

incentive /ɪn'sentɪv/ *–n.* **1** motive or incitement. **2** payment or concession encouraging effort in work. *–attrib. adj.* serving to motivate or incite (*incentive scheme*). [Latin *incentivus* that sets the tune]

♦ **incentive compatibility** *n. Econ.* compatibility of an economic rule or mechanism with the incentives of the individuals concerned. Non-incentive compatible rules are usu. of limited use with regard to government policy. For example, it is of little use for the government to ask individuals how much they value a good provided by the state (e.g. roads), and use this response as a basis for deciding how much to spend on roads, as all road users have an incentive to overstate their needs. Such a mechanism for determining expenditure on roads is not incentive compatible.

---

inception /ɪn'sepʃ(ə)n/ *n.* beginning. [Latin *incipio -cept-* begin]

inceptive /ɪn'septɪv/ *adj.* **1 a** beginning. **b** initial. **2** (of a verb) denoting the beginning of an action.

incessant /ɪn'ses(ə)nt/ *adj.* unceasing, continual, repeated. □ **incessantly** *adv.* [Latin *cesso* cease]

incest /'ɪnsest/ *n.* sexual intercourse between persons too closely related to marry. [Latin *castus* chaste]

incestuous /ɪn'sestjʊəs/ *adj.* **1** of or guilty of incest. **2** having relationships restricted to a particular group or organization. □ **incestuously** *adv.*

♦ **incestuous share dealing** *n.* buying and selling of shares in companies that belong to the same group, in order to obtain an advantage of some kind, usu. a tax advantage. The legality of the transaction will depend on its nature.

---

inch *–n.* **1** linear measure of $^1/_{12}$ of a foot (2.54 cm). **2** (as a unit of rainfall) 1 inch depth of water. **3** (as a unit of map-scale) so many inches representing 1 mile. **4** small amount (usu. with *neg.*: *would not yield an inch*). *–v.* move gradually. □ **every inch** entirely (*looked every inch a queen*). **within an inch of** almost to the point of. [Old English from Latin *uncia* OUNCE]

inchoate /ɪn'kəʊeɪt/ *adj.* **1** just begun. **2** undeveloped. □ **inchoation** /-'eɪʃ(ə)n/ *n.* [Latin *inchoo, incoho* begin]

■ **Usage** *Inchoate* is sometimes used incorrectly to mean 'chaotic' or 'incoherent'.

♦ **inchoate instrument** *n. Finance* negotiable instrument in which not all the necessary particulars are given.

Inchon /ɪn'tʃɒn/ port in South Korea, on the Yellow Sea W of Seoul; pop. (1987) 1 526 435.

incidence /'ɪnsɪd(ə)ns/ *n.* **1** (often foll. by *of*) range, scope, extent, or rate of occurrence or influence (of disease, tax, etc.). **2** falling of a line, ray, particles, etc., on a surface. **3** coming into contact with a thing. [Latin *cado* fall]

♦ **incidence of taxation** *n.* impact of a tax on those who bear its burden, rather than those who pay it. For example, VAT is paid by traders, but the ultimate burden of it falls on the consumer of the trader's goods or services. Again, a company may pay corporation tax but if it then raises its prices or reduces its employees' wages to recoup the tax it may be said to have shifted the incidence.

---

incident *–n.* **1** occurrence, esp. a minor one. **2** public disturbance (*the march took place without incident*). **3** clash of armed forces (*frontier incident*). **4** distinct piece of action in a play, film, etc. *–adj.* **1** (often foll. by *to*) apt to occur; naturally attaching. **2** (often foll. by *on, upon*) (of light etc.) falling. [Latin *cado* fall]

incidental /ˌɪnsɪ'dent(ə)l/ *–adj.* (often foll. by *to*) **1** small and relatively unimportant, minor; supplementary. **2** not essential. *–n.* (usu. in *pl.*) minor detail, expense, event, etc.

incidentally *adv.* **1** by the way. **2** in an incidental way.

incidental music *n.* background music in a film, broadcast, etc.

incinerate /ɪn'sɪnəˌreɪt/ *v.* (**-ting**) burn to ashes. □ **incineration** /-'reɪʃ(ə)n/ *n.* [medieval Latin *cinis ciner-* ashes]

incinerator *n.* furnace or device for incineration.

incipient /ɪn'sɪpɪənt/ *adj.* **1** beginning. **2** in an early stage. [Latin *incipio* begin]

incise /ɪn'saɪz/ *v.* (**-sing**) **1** make a cut in. **2** engrave. [Latin *caedo* cut]

incision /ɪn'sɪʒ(ə)n/ *n.* **1** cutting, esp. by a surgeon. **2** cut made in this way.

incisive /ɪn'saɪsɪv/ *adj.* **1** sharp. **2** clear and effective.

incisor /ɪn'saɪzə(r)/ *n.* cutting-tooth, esp. at the front of the mouth.

incite /ɪn'saɪt/ *v.* (**-ting**) (often foll. by *to*) urge or stir up. □ **incitement** *n.* [Latin *cito* rouse]

incivility /ˌɪnsɪ'vɪlɪtɪ/ *n.* (*pl.* **-ies**) **1** rudeness. **2** impolite act.

inclement /ɪn'klemənt/ *adj.* (of the weather) severe or stormy. □ **inclemency** *n.*

inclination /ˌɪnklɪ'neɪʃ(ə)n/ *n.* **1** disposition or propensity. **2** liking, affection. **3** slope, slant. **4** angle between lines. **5** dip of a magnetic needle. **6** slow nod of the head. [Latin: related to INCLINE]

incline –*v.* /ɪn'klaɪn/ (**-ning**) **1** (usu. in *passive*) **a** dispose or influence (*am inclined to think so*; *does not incline me to agree*; *don't feel inclined*). **b** have a specified tendency (*the door is inclined to bang*). **2 a** be disposed (*I incline to think so*). **b** (often foll. by *to*, *towards*) tend. **3** (cause to) lean, usu. from the vertical; slope. **4** bend forward or downward. –*n.* /'ɪnklaɪn/ slope. □ **incline one's ear** listen favourably. [Latin *clino* bend]

inclined plane *n.* sloping plane used e.g. to reduce work in raising a load.

include /ɪn'kluːd/ *v.* (**-ding**) **1** comprise or reckon in as part of a whole. **2** (as **including** *prep.*) if we include (*six, including me*). **3** put in a certain category etc. □ **inclusion** /-ʒ(ə)n/ *n.* [Latin *includo -clus-* enclose, from *claudo* shut]

inclusive /ɪn'kluːsɪv/ *adj.* **1** (often foll. by *of*) including. **2** including the limits stated (*pages 7 to 26 inclusive*). **3** including all or much (*inclusive terms*). □ **inclusively** *adv.* **inclusiveness** *n.*

incognito /ˌɪnkɒg'niːtəʊ/ –*predic. adj.* & *adv.* with one's name or identity kept secret. –*n.* (*pl.* **-s**) **1** person who is incognito. **2** pretended identity. [Italian, = unknown: related to IN-[1], COGNITION]

incognizant /ɪn'kɒgnɪz(ə)nt/ *adj. formal* unaware. □ **incognizance** *n.*

incoherent /ˌɪnkəʊ'hɪərənt/ *adj.* **1** unintelligible. **2** lacking logic or consistency; not clear. □ **incoherence** *n.* **incoherently** *adv.*

incombustible /ˌɪnkəm'bʌstɪb(ə)l/ *adj.* that cannot be burnt.

income /'ɪnkʌm/ *n.* **1** money received by a person or organization, esp. periodically or in a year, from work, investments, etc. From the point of view of taxation, income has to be distinguished from capital. **2** *Econ.* flow of economic value attributed to an individual or group of individuals over a particular period (see VALUE *n.* 1). The total of income throughout an individual's life, minus expenditure, is equal to that person's wealth. Both income and wealth are usu. considered to include more than simply money; for example, benefits in kind, services rendered by governments, and human capital should all be included. [from IN, COME]

♦ **income and expenditure account** *n.* account, similar to a profit and loss account, prepared by an organization whose main purpose is not the generation of profit (e.g. a charity). It records the income and expenditure of the organization and results in either a surplus of income over expenditure or of expenditure over income.

♦ **income bond** *n.* **1** (in full **National Savings Income Bond**) bond introduced by the Department for National Savings in 1982, offering monthly interest payments on investments between £2000 and £100,000. Interest is taxable but not deducted at source. The bonds have a guaranteed life of 10 years. Indexed income bonds were withdrawn in 1987. **2** = GUARANTEED-INCOME BOND.

♦ **income distribution** *n.* payment by a unit trust of its half-yearly income to unit holders, in proportion to their holdings. The income distributed is the total income less the manager's service charge and income tax at the standard rate.

♦ **income effect** *n.* change in the overall purchasing power of an individual as the price of a good changes (cf. SUBSTITUTION EFFECT). For example, if the price of butter falls, a consumer will be able to purchase the same quantity as before and still have some income remaining to spend on other goods. The income effect is usu. thought to be negative with respect to the good whose price has changed, implying in the above example that expenditure on butter would rise.

♦ **income in kind** *n.* = BENEFITS IN KIND.

♦ **income profit** *n.* any sum accruing to a person or organization that represents pure income and is not partly a payment of capital. If annual payments are pure income profit they are assessable to Schedule D Case III for income tax purposes; if not there may be a capital element to be disentangled.

♦ **income redistribution** *n.* use of taxation to ensure that the incomes of the richer members of the community are reduced and those of the poorer members are increased. Tax theorists tend to favour ability-to-pay taxation and progressive taxes for this purpose, combined with various forms of income support for the poorer members of the community.

♦ **incomes policy** *n.* government policy aimed at controlling inflation and maintaining full employment by holding down increases in wages and prices by statutory or other means. In the 1960s and 1970s, when Keynesianism, demand-pull, and cost-push theories of inflation were popular, incomes policies were widely pursued in the developed world. This reflected the strong belief that inflation and unemployment were closely connected (see PHILLIPS CURVE), although incomes policies were unpopular with workers, whose wages were held down, often to an extent that caused a fall in the purchasing power of their incomes, as a result of inflation. However, the emergence of stagflation cast doubts on the benefits of these policies; with the rise of monetarism and the increasing popularity of laissez-faire government in the 1980s, incomes policies became much less attractive.

♦ **income stock** *n.* stock or share bought primarily for the steady and relatively high income it can be expected to produce, usu. a fixed-interest gilt or an ordinary share with a good yield record. Cf. GROWTH STOCK.

♦ **income support** *n.* government benefit for those with low incomes in the UK, esp. those who are unemployed, over 60, bringing up children alone, or unable to work through disability or through caring for relatives. Those with capital or savings in excess of £8000 are not eligible.

♦ **income tax** *n.* tax levied on income. The principal direct tax in most countries, it is levied on the incomes of either individual taxpayers or households. It lends itself particularly well to ability-to-pay taxation and progressive taxation, although it may discourage work and risk-bearing investment. In the UK, the tax is calculated on the taxpayer's taxable income, i.e. gross income less income-tax allowances. In the tax year 1998–9 the rate of income tax on taxable earnings up to £4,300 is 20%. On earnings from £4,301 to £27,100 the basic rate of 23% applies. For earnings over £27,100 the higher rate of tax is 40%. See also PAYE.

♦ **income-tax allowances** *n.pl.* statutory sums that may be deducted from gross income in calculating income tax before the scale of rates is applied. These allowances are primarily concerned with the individual circumstances of the taxpayer (see PERSONAL ALLOWANCES).

♦ **income tax year** *n.* = FISCAL YEAR.

♦ **income velocity of circulation** see VELOCITY OF CIRCULATION.

---

incoming –*adj.* **1** coming in (*incoming telephone calls*). **2** succeeding another (*incoming tenant*). –*n.* (usu. in *pl.*) revenue, income.

incommensurable /ˌɪnkə'menʃərəb(ə)l/ *adj.* (often foll. by *with*) **1** not commensurable. **2** having no common factor, integral or fractional. □ **incommensurability** /-'bɪlɪtɪ/ *n.*

incommensurate /ˌɪnkə'menʃərət/ *adj.* **1** (often foll. by *with*, *to*) out of proportion; inadequate. **2** = INCOMMENSURABLE.

incommode /ˌɪnkə'məʊd/ *v.* (**-ding**) *formal* **1** inconvenience. **2** trouble, annoy.

incommodious *adj. formal* too small for comfort; inconvenient.

incommunicable /ˌɪnkəˈmjuːnɪkəb(ə)l/ *adj.* that cannot be communicated.

incommunicado /ˌɪnkəˌmjuːnɪˈkɑːdəʊ/ *adj.* **1** without means of communication. **2** (of a prisoner) in solitary confinement. [Spanish *incomunicado*]

incommunicative /ˌɪnkəˈmjuːnɪkətɪv/ *adj.* uncommunicative.

incomparable /ɪnˈkɒmpərəb(ə)l/ *adj.* without an equal; matchless. □ **incomparability** /-ˈbɪlɪtɪ/ *n.* **incomparably** *adv.*

incompatible /ˌɪnkəmˈpætɪb(ə)l/ *adj.* not compatible. □ **incompatibility** /-ˈbɪlɪtɪ/ *n.*

incompetent /ɪnˈkɒmpɪt(ə)nt/ *–adj.* lacking the necessary skill. *–n.* incompetent person. □ **incompetence** *n.*

incomplete /ˌɪnkəmˈpliːt/ *adj.* not complete.

incomprehensible /ɪnˌkɒmprɪˈhensɪb(ə)l/ *adj.* that cannot be understood.

incomprehension /ɪnˌkɒmprɪˈhenʃ(ə)n/ *n.* failure to understand.

inconceivable /ˌɪnkənˈsiːvəb(ə)l/ *adj.* **1** that cannot be imagined. **2** *colloq.* most unlikely. □ **inconceivably** *adv.*

inconclusive /ˌɪnkənˈkluːsɪv/ *adj.* (of an argument, evidence, or action) not decisive or convincing.

incongruous /ɪnˈkɒŋgrʊəs/ *adj.* **1** out of place; absurd. **2** (often foll. by *with*) out of keeping. □ **incongruity** /-ˈgruːɪtɪ/ *n.* (*pl.* **-ies**). **incongruously** *adv.*

inconsequent /ɪnˈkɒnsɪkwənt/ *adj.* **1** irrelevant. **2** lacking logical sequence. **3** disconnected. □ **inconsequence** *n.*

inconsequential /ɪnˌkɒnsɪˈkwenʃ(ə)l/ *adj.* **1** unimportant. **2** = INCONSEQUENT. □ **inconsequentially** *adv.*

inconsiderable /ˌɪnkənˈsɪdərəb(ə)l/ *adj.* **1** of small size, value, etc. **2** not worth considering. □ **inconsiderably** *adv.*

inconsiderate /ˌɪnkənˈsɪdərət/ *adj.* (of a person or action) lacking regard for others; thoughtless. □ **inconsiderately** *adv.* **inconsiderateness** *n.*

inconsistent /ˌɪnkənˈsɪst(ə)nt/ *adj.* not consistent. □ **inconsistency** *n.* (*pl.* **-ies**). **inconsistently** *adv.*

inconsolable /ˌɪnkənˈsəʊləb(ə)l/ *adj.* (of a person, grief, etc.) that cannot be consoled. □ **inconsolably** *adv.*

inconspicuous /ˌɪnkənˈspɪkjʊəs/ *adj.* not conspicuous; not easily noticed. □ **inconspicuously** *adv.* **inconspicuousness** *n.*

inconstant /ɪnˈkɒnst(ə)nt/ *adj.* **1** fickle, changeable. **2** variable, not fixed. □ **inconstancy** *n.* (*pl.* **-ies**).

incontestable /ˌɪnkənˈtestəb(ə)l/ *adj.* that cannot be disputed. □ **incontestably** *adv.*

incontinent /ɪnˈkɒntɪnənt/ *adj.* **1** unable to control the bowels or bladder. **2** lacking self-restraint (esp. in sexual matters). □ **incontinence** *n.*

incontrovertible /ˌɪnkɒntrəˈvɜːtɪb(ə)l/ *adj.* indisputable, undeniable. □ **incontrovertibly** *adv.*

inconvenience /ˌɪnkənˈviːnɪəns/ *–n.* **1** lack of ease or comfort; trouble. **2** cause or instance of this. *–v.* (**-cing**) cause inconvenience to.

inconvenient *adj.* causing trouble, difficulty, or discomfort; awkward. □ **inconveniently** *adv.*

♦ **inconvertible** /ˌɪnkənˈvɜːtɪb(ə)l/ *adj.* **1** not convertible. **2** (of currency) unable to be freely exchanged for another. **3** (of paper money) not convertible into gold. Most paper money is now inconvertible, but until 1931, in the UK, the Bank of England had an obligation to supply any holder of a banknote with the appropriate quantity of gold. □ **inconvertibility** /-ˈbɪlɪtɪ/ *n.*

---

incorporate *–v.* /ɪnˈkɔːpəˌreɪt/ (**-ting**) **1** include as a part or ingredient (*incorporated all the latest features*). **2** (often foll. by *in, with*) unite (in one body). **3** admit as a member of a company etc. **4** (esp. as **incorporated** *adj.*) form into a legal corporation. *–adj.* /ɪnˈkɔːpərət/ incorporated. □ **incorporation** /-ˈreɪʃ(ə)n/ *n.* [Latin *corpus* body]

♦ **incorporated company** see COMPANY 3.

♦ **Incorporated Society of British Advertisers Ltd.** *n.* (also **ISBA**) society founded in 1900 as the Advertisers Protection Society. It is open to any advertising company and is concerned with all matters relating to advertising.

---

incorporeal /ˌɪnkɔːˈpɔːrɪəl/ *adj.* without physical or material existence. □ **incorporeally** *adv.* **incorporeity** /-pəˈriːɪtɪ/ *n.*

incorrect /ˌɪnkəˈrekt/ *adj.* **1** not correct or true. **2** improper, unsuitable. □ **incorrectly** *adv.*

incorrigible /ɪnˈkɒrɪdʒɪb(ə)l/ *adj.* (of a person or habit) that cannot be corrected or improved. □ **incorrigibility** /-ˈbɪlɪtɪ/ *n.* **incorrigibly** *adv.*

incorruptible /ˌɪnkəˈrʌptɪb(ə)l/ *adj.* **1** that cannot be corrupted, esp. by bribery. **2** that cannot decay. □ **incorruptibility** /-ˈbɪlɪtɪ/ *n.* **incorruptibly** *adv.*

♦ **Incoterms** /ˈɪnkəʊˌtɜːmz/ *n.* glossary of terms used in international trade published by the International Chamber of Commerce in Paris. It gives precise definitions to eliminate misunderstandings between traders in different countries. [from INTERNATIONAL CHAMBER OF COMMERCE, TERM]

---

increase *–v.* /ɪŋˈkriːs/ (**-sing**) make or become greater or more numerous. *–n.* /ˈɪnkriːs/ **1** growth, enlargement. **2** (of people, animals, or plants) multiplication. **3** amount or extent of an increase. □ **on the increase** increasing. [Latin *cresco* grow]

♦ **increasing capital** *n.* increasing the number or value of the shares in a company to augment its authorized share capital. A company cannot increase its share capital unless authorized to do so by its articles of association.

---

increasingly /ɪŋˈkriːsɪŋglɪ/ *adv.* more and more.

♦ **increasing returns to scale** see RETURNS TO SCALE.

---

incredible /ɪnˈkredɪb(ə)l/ *adj.* **1** that cannot be believed. **2** *colloq.* amazing, extremely good. □ **incredibility** /-ˈbɪlɪtɪ/ *n.* **incredibly** *adv.*

incredulous /ɪnˈkredjʊləs/ *adj.* unwilling to believe; showing disbelief. □ **incredulity** /ˌɪnkrɪˈdjuːlɪtɪ/ *n.* **incredulously** *adv.*

increment /ˈɪŋkrɪmənt/ *n.* increase or added amount, esp. on a fixed salary scale. □ **incremental** /-ˈment(ə)l/ *adj.* [Latin *cresco* grow]

♦ **incremental cost** *n. Econ.* cost incurred purely because of the occurrence of a specific event. An incremental cost is similar to a marginal cost; it tends to be used when the principal significance is the exclusion of all costs except those that would not have been incurred but for the specific project in view.

---

incriminate /ɪnˈkrɪmɪˌneɪt/ *v.* (**-ting**) **1** make (a person) appear to be guilty. **2** charge with a crime. □ **incrimination** /-ˈneɪʃ(ə)n/ *n.* **incriminatory** *adj.* [Latin: related to CRIME]

incrustation /ˌɪnkrʌˈsteɪʃ(ə)n/ *n.* **1** encrusting. **2** crust or hard coating. **3** deposit on a surface. [Latin: related to CRUST]

incubate /ˈɪŋkjʊˌbeɪt/ *v.* (**-ting**) **1** hatch (eggs) by sitting on them or by artificial heat. **2** cause (micro-organisms) to develop. **3** develop slowly. [Latin *cubo* lie]

incubation /ˌɪŋkjʊˈbeɪʃ(ə)n/ *n.* **1** incubating. **2** period between infection and the appearance of the first symptoms.

incubator *n.* apparatus providing artificial warmth for hatching eggs, rearing premature babies, or developing micro-organisms.

incubus /ˈɪŋkjʊbəs/ *n.* (*pl.* **-buses** or **-bi** /-ˌbaɪ/) **1** demon formerly believed to have sexual intercourse with sleeping women. **2** nightmare. **3** oppressive person or thing. [Latin: as INCUBATE]

inculcate /'ɪnkʌl,keɪt/ *v.* (**-ting**) (often foll. by *upon, in*) urge or impress (a habit or idea) persistently. □ **inculcation** /-'keɪʃ(ə)n/ *n.* [Latin *calco* tread]

incumbency /ɪn'kʌmbənsɪ/ *n.* (*pl.* **-ies**) office or tenure of an incumbent.

incumbent *–adj.* **1** resting as a duty (*it is incumbent on you to do it*). **2** (often foll. by *on*) lying, pressing. **3** currently holding office (*the incumbent president*). *–n.* holder of an office or post, esp. a benefice. [Latin *incumbo* lie upon]

incunabulum /,ɪnkju:'næbjʊləm/ *n.* (*pl.* **-la**) **1** early printed book, esp. from before 1501. **2** (in *pl.*) early stages of a thing. [Latin, (in *pl.*) = swaddling-clothes]

incur /ɪn'kɜ:(r)/ *v.* (**-rr-**) bring on oneself (danger, blame, loss, etc.). [Latin *curro* run]

incurable /ɪn'kjʊərəb(ə)l/ *–adj.* that cannot be cured. *–n.* incurable person. □ **incurability** /-'bɪlɪtɪ/ *n.* **incurably** *adv.*

incurious /ɪn'kjʊərɪəs/ *adj.* lacking curiosity.

incursion /ɪn'kɜ:ʃ(ə)n/ *n.* invasion or attack, esp. sudden or brief. □ **incursive** *adj.* [Latin: related to INCUR]

incurve /ɪn'kɜ:v/ *v.* (**-ving**) **1** bend into a curve. **2** (as **incurved** *adj.*) curved inwards. □ **incurvation** /-'veɪʃ(ə)n/ *n.*

IND *international vehicle registration* India.

Ind. *abbr.* Indiana.

indebted /ɪn'detɪd/ *adj.* (usu. foll. by *to*) owing gratitude or money. □ **indebtedness** *n.* [French *endetté*: related to DEBT]

indecent /ɪn'di:s(ə)nt/ *adj.* **1** offending against decency. **2** unbecoming; unsuitable (*indecent haste*). □ **indecency** *n.* (*pl.* **-ies**). **indecently** *adv.*

indecent assault *n.* sexual attack not involving rape.

indecent exposure *n.* exposing one's genitals in public.

indecipherable /,ɪndɪ'saɪfərəb(ə)l/ *adj.* that cannot be deciphered.

indecision /,ɪndɪ'sɪʒ(ə)n/ *n.* inability to decide; hesitation.

indecisive /,ɪndɪ'saɪsɪv/ *adj.* **1** (of a person) not decisive; hesitating. **2** not conclusive (*an indecisive battle*). □ **indecisively** *adv.* **indecisiveness** *n.*

indeclinable /,ɪndɪ'klaɪnəb(ə)l/ *adj. Gram.* that cannot be declined; having no inflections.

indecorous /ɪn'dekərəs/ *adj.* **1** improper, undignified. **2** in bad taste. □ **indecorously** *adv.*

indeed /ɪn'di:d/ *–adv.* **1** in truth; really. **2** admittedly. *–int.* expressing irony, incredulity, etc.

indefatigable /,ɪndɪ'fætɪgəb(ə)l/ *adj.* unwearying, unremitting. □ **indefatigably** *adv.*

indefeasible /,ɪndɪ'fi:zɪb(ə)l/ *adj. literary* (esp. of a claim, rights, etc.) that cannot be forfeited or annulled. □ **indefeasibly** *adv.*

indefensible /,ɪndɪ'fensɪb(ə)l/ *adj.* that cannot be defended or justified. □ **indefensibility** /-'bɪlɪtɪ/ *n.* **indefensibly** *adv.*

indefinable /,ɪndɪ'faɪnəb(ə)l/ *adj.* that cannot be defined; mysterious. □ **indefinably** *adv.*

indefinite /ɪn'definɪt/ *adj.* **1** vague, undefined. **2** unlimited. **3** (of adjectives, adverbs, and pronouns) not determining the person etc. referred to (e.g. *some, someone, anyhow*).

indefinite article *n.* word (e.g. *a, an* in English) preceding a noun and implying 'any of several'.

indefinitely *adv.* **1** for an unlimited time (*was postponed indefinitely*). **2** in an indefinite manner.

indelible /ɪn'delɪb(ə)l/ *adj.* that cannot be rubbed out or removed. □ **indelibly** *adv.* [Latin *deleo* efface]

indelicate /ɪn'delɪkət/ *adj.* **1** coarse, unrefined. **2** tactless. □ **indelicacy** *n.* (*pl.* **-ies**). **indelicately** *adv.*

indemnify /ɪn'demnɪ,faɪ/ *v.* (**-ies, -ied**) **1** (often foll. by *from, against*) secure (a person) in respect of harm, a loss, etc. **2** (often foll. by *for*) exempt from a penalty. **3** compensate. □ **indemnification** /-fɪ'keɪʃ(ə)n/ *n.* [Latin *indemnis* free from loss]

indemnity /ɪn'demnɪtɪ/ *n.* (*pl.* **-ies**) **1 a** compensation for damage. **b** sum exacted by a victor in war. **2** agreement by one party to make good the losses suffered by another, usu. by payment of money, repair, replacement, or reinstatement (see also INDEMNITY INSURANCE). **3** exemption from penalties. **4** undertaking by a bank's client who has lost a document (e.g. a share certificate or bill of lading) that the bank will be held harmless against any consequences of the document's absence if it proceeds to service the documents that have not been mislaid. The bank usu. requires a letter of indemnity to make sure that it suffers no loss (see LETTER OF INDEMNITY).

◆ **indemnity insurance** *n.* insurance designed to compensate a policyholder for a loss suffered, by the payment of money, repair, replacement, or reinstatement. In every case the policyholder is entitled to be restored to the same financial position as existed immediately before the relevant event. There must be no element of profit to the policyholder nor any element of loss. Most (but not all) insurance policies are indemnity contracts; personal accident and life-assurance policies are not contracts of indemnity as it is impossible to calculate the value of a lost life or limb.

---

indent *–v.* /ɪn'dent/ **1** make or impress marks, notches, dents, etc. in. **2** start (a line of print or writing) further from the margin than others. **3** draw up (a legal document) in duplicate. **4 a** (often foll. by *on, upon* a person, *for* a thing) make a requisition. **b** order (goods) by requisition. *–n.* /'ɪndent/ **1 a** order (esp. from abroad) for goods. **b** official requisition for stores. **2** indented line. **3** indentation. **4** indenture. [Latin *dens dentis* tooth]

indentation /,ɪnden'teɪʃ(ə)n/ *n.* **1** indenting or being indented. **2** notch.

indention /ɪn'denʃ(ə)n/ *n.* **1** indenting, esp. in printing. **2** notch.

indenture /ɪn'dentʃə(r)/ *–n.* **1** (usu. in *pl.*) sealed agreement or contract (see APPRENTICE *n.* 1). **2** formal list, certificate, etc. **3** any deed, esp. one creating or transferring an estate in land. *–v.* (**-ring**) *hist.* bind by indentures, esp. as an apprentice. [Anglo-French: related to INDENT]

independent /,ɪndɪ'pend(ə)nt/ *–adj.* **1 a** (often foll. by *of*) not depending on authority or control. **b** self-governing. **2 a** not depending on another person for one's opinions or livelihood. **b** (of income or resources) making it unnecessary to earn one's living. **3** unwilling to be under an obligation to others. **4** acting independently of any political party. **5** not depending on something else for its validity etc. (*independent proof*). **6** (of broadcasting, a school, etc.) not supported by public funds. *–n.* person who is politically independent. □ **independence** *n.* **independently** *adv.*

◆ **Independent Broadcasting Authority** *n.* (also **IBA**) organization formed in 1972 from the Independent Television Authority, itself set up in 1954 to provide television services in addition to those of the BBC. The IBA appoints local radio and ITV programme companies, owns transmitters, supervises the programmes broadcast, and controls advertising on radio and television. Both ITV and local radio are financed mainly by the sale of advertising time.

◆ **independent financial adviser** *n.* (also **IFA**) person defined under the Financial Services Act (1986) as an adviser who is not committed to the products of any one company or organization. Such a person is licensed to operate by one of the Self-Regulating Organizations or Recognized Professional Bodies. With no loyalties except to the customer, the IFA must offer best advice from the whole market place. Eight categories of IFA exist, grouped into four main areas: advising on investments; arranging and transacting life assurance, pensions, and unit trusts; arranging and transacting other types of investments; and management of investments. All licensed independent financial advisers contribute to a compensation fund for the protection of their customers.

♦ **independent intermediary** *n.* person who acts as a representative of a prospective policyholder in the arrangement of an insurance or assurance policy. In life assurance and pensions the person can represent more than one insurer and is legally bound to offer advice to clients on the type of assurance or investment contracts best suited to their needs. In general insurance the independent intermediary can represent more than six insurers and is responsible for advising clients on policies that best suit their needs. Intermediaries must, themselves, have professional-indemnity insurance to cover any errors that they may make. Although, in both cases, intermediaries are the servants of the policyholder (and the insurer is therefore not responsible for their errors), they are paid by the insurer in the form of a commission, being an agreed percentage of the first or renewal premium paid by the policyholder.

♦ **independent retailer** *n.* small retailer, usu. owning between one and nine shops.

---

in-depth *adj.* thorough.

indescribable /ˌɪndɪˈskraɪbəb(ə)l/ *adj.* **1** too good or bad etc. to be described. **2** that cannot be described. □ **indescribably** *adv.*

indestructible /ˌɪndɪˈstrʌktɪb(ə)l/ *adj.* that cannot be destroyed. □ **indestructibility** /-ˈbɪlɪtɪ/ *n.* **indestructibly** *adv.*

indeterminable /ˌɪndɪˈtɜːmɪnəb(ə)l/ *adj.* that cannot be ascertained or settled. □ **indeterminably** *adv.*

indeterminate /ˌɪndɪˈtɜːmɪnət/ *adj.* **1** not fixed in extent, character, etc. **2** left doubtful; vague. **3** *Math.* of no fixed value. □ **indeterminacy** *n.*

indeterminate vowel *n.* vowel /ə/ heard in '*a* mom*e*nt *a*go'.

index /ˈɪndeks/ –*n.* (*pl.* **indexes** or **indices** /ˈɪndɪˌsiːz/) **1** alphabetical list of subjects etc. with references, usu. at the end of a book. **2** = CARD INDEX. **3** measure of prices or wages compared with a previous month, year, etc. See RETAIL PRICE INDEX. **4** *Math.* exponent of a number. **5** pointer, sign, or indicator. –*v.* **1** provide (a book etc.) with an index. **2** enter in an index. **3** relate (wages etc.) to a price index. [Latin]

♦ **indexation** /ˌɪndekˈseɪʃ(ə)n/ *n.* policy of connecting such economic variables as wages, taxes, social security payments, or pensions to rises in the general price level, often advocated by economists in the belief that it mitigates the effects of inflation. In practice, complete indexation is rarely possible, so that inflation usu. leaves somebody worse off (e.g. lenders, savers) and somebody better off (borrowers). See RETAIL PRICE INDEX.

♦ **indexation allowance** *n.* amount that can be deducted from capital gains in the UK since 1982 to offset the effects of inflation for capital-gains tax purposes. It involves indexing items of allowable expenditure by reference to the retail price index. The rules for indexation are contained in the Finance Acts (1982 and 1985).

---

index finger *n.* forefinger.

♦ **index futures** *n.pl.* futures contract on a financial futures market, such as the London International Financial Futures and Options Exchange, which offers facilities for trading in futures and options on the FT-SE 100 Index and the FT-SE Eurotrack 100 Index (see FINANCIAL TIMES SHARE INDEXES). On the FT-SE 100 Index the trading unit is £25 per index point; thus if a futures contract is purchased when the index stands at 2400, say, the buyer is covering an equivalent purchase of equities of £60,000 (£25 × 2400). If the index rises 100 points the purchaser can sell a matching futures contract at this level, making a profit of £2500 (£25 × 100). On the FT-SE Eurotrack 100 Index the trading unit is DM100 per index point. See also PORTFOLIO INSURANCE.

♦ **index-linked** *adj.* related to the value of a price index. See INDEXATION; GILT-EDGED SECURITY; NATIONAL SAVINGS.

♦ **index number** *n.* number used to represent the changes in a set of values between a base year and the present. See FINANCIAL TIMES SHARE INDEXES; RETAIL PRICE INDEX.

♦ **Index of Industrial Production** *n.* UK index produced by the Central Statistical Office to show changes in the volume of production of the main British industries and of the economy as a whole.

Indiaman /ˈɪndɪəmən/ *n.* (*pl.* **-men**) *hist.* ship engaged in trade with India or the East Indies.

Indian /ˈɪndɪən/ –*n.* **1 a** native or national of India. **b** person of Indian descent. **2** (in full **American Indian**) **a** original inhabitant of America. **b** any of the languages of the American Indians. –*adj.* **1** of India or the subconti-

---

India /ˈɪndɪə/, **Republic of** country in S Asia, a member state of the Commonwealth, occupying the greater part of the Indian subcontinent, a peninsula bounded by the Arabian Sea and the Bay of Bengal and on the N by the Himalayas. The second most populous country in the world, India faces serious problems arising from poverty and the high rate of illiteracy. The economy is heavily dependent on agriculture, which contributes nearly 40% of the GDP and employs about two-thirds of the labour force. Food crops include rice, cereals, and pulses; the chief cash crops are tea, cotton, rice, sugar, spices, jute, and coffee. Fish constitute an important export. The major industries are based on the extraction and processing of mineral resources, esp. coal, iron ore, gemstones (esp. diamonds), and oil; limestone, zinc, and lead are also mined. Industrial production is increasing; manufactured exports include engineering products, transport equipment, jewellery and gems, iron and steel, electric components, textiles and garments, and jute and leather goods. Privatization of state corporations has recently been introduced and foreign companies encouraged. In the mid 1990s financial reforms were successfully undertaken to encourage foreign investment.

History. European penetration of the Indian subcontinent began in the 17th century, with Britain eventually triumphing over her colonial rivals. In 1765 the British East India Company acquired the right to administer Bengal and afterwards other parts; in 1858, after the Indian Mutiny, the Crown took over the Company's authority, and in 1877 Queen Victoria was proclaimed Empress of India. Rising nationalism during the early part of the 20th century resulted in independence and partition in 1947, but the new states of India (with a Hindu majority) and Pakistan (largely Muslim) did not prove good neighbours, going to war several times over the disputed territory of Kashmir and the Pakistani enclave (now Bangladesh) in the NE. India itself has continued to be plagued by conflict between Hindus and Muslims. President, Kocheril Raman Narayanan; prime minister, Atal Behari Vajpayee; capital, Delhi.

languages	Hindi & English (official), many Indian languages
currency	rupee (Re; *pl.* Rs) of 100 paisa
pop. (1996)	952 969 000
GNP (1994)	US$278B
literacy	65% (m); 37% (f)
life expectancy	58 (m); 59 (f)

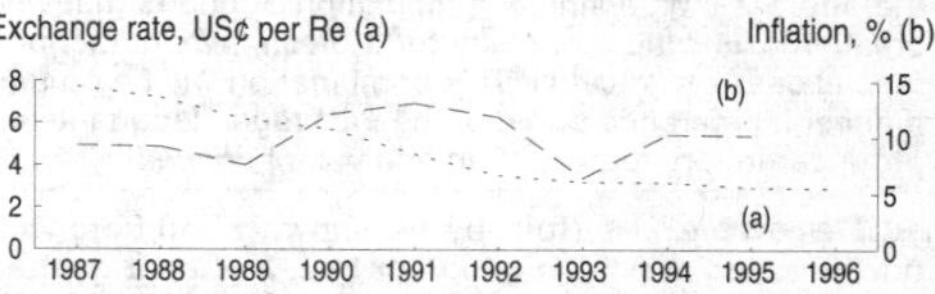

nent comprising India, Pakistan, and Bangladesh. **2** of the original peoples of America.

Indiana /ˌɪndɪ'ænə/ state in the Midwest of the US; pop. (est. 1996) 5 840 528; capital, Indianapolis. Agriculture produces soya beans, maize, vegetables (esp. tomatoes), and pigs; manufactures include machinery, electrical goods, motor vehicles, and chemicals.

Indianapolis /ˌɪndɪə'næpəlɪs/ city in the US, the capital of Indiana; pop. (1994) 752 279. Manufacturing industries produce esp. car and aircraft parts and chemicals; the city also hosts an annual 500-mile (804.5 km) motor race.

Indian corn *n.* maize.

Indian elephant *n.* the elephant of India, smaller than the African elephant.

Indian file *n.* = SINGLE FILE.

Indian hemp see HEMP 1.

Indian ink *n.* **1** black pigment. **2** ink made from this.

Indian Ocean ocean S of India, extending from the E coast of Africa to the East Indies and Australia.

Indian summer *n.* **1** dry warm weather in late autumn. **2** late tranquil period of life.

indiarubber *n.* rubber for erasing pencil marks etc.

indicate /'ɪndɪˌkeɪt/ *v.* (**-ting**) (often foll. by *that*) **1** point out; make known. **2** be a sign of; show the presence of. **3** call for; require (*stronger measures are indicated*). **4** state briefly. **5** give as a reading or measurement. **6** point by hand; use a vehicle's indicator (*failed to indicate*). □ **indication** /-'keɪʃ(ə)n/ *n.* [Latin *dico* make known]

indicative /ɪn'dɪkətɪv/ *–adj.* **1** (foll. by *of*) suggestive; serving as an indication. **2** *Gram.* (of a mood) stating a fact. *–n. Gram.* **1** indicative mood. **2** verb in this mood.

indicator *n.* **1** flashing light on a vehicle showing the direction in which it is about to turn. **2** person or thing that indicates. **3** device indicating the condition of a machine etc. **4** recording instrument. **5** board giving information, esp. times of trains etc. **6** *Econ.* statistical measure representing an economic variable. For example, M3 is one measure of the money supply. Indicators are useful both in the formulation of economic theory and in assessing the effectiveness of economic policy. However, an indicator is not the same as the underlying variable itself. For example, the retail price index is a sample of the prices of goods and therefore only approximates to the actual level of prices.

indicatory /ɪn'dɪkətərɪ/ *adj.* (often foll. by *of*) indicative.

indices *pl.* of INDEX.

indict /ɪn'daɪt/ *v.* accuse formally by legal process. [Anglo-French: related to IN-[2], DICTATE]

indictable *adj.* **1** (of an offence) making the doer liable to be charged with a crime. **2** (of a person) so liable.

indictment *n.* **1 a** indicting, accusation. **b** document containing this. **2** thing that serves to condemn or censure (*an indictment of society*).

indie /'ɪndɪ/ *colloq. –adj.* (of a pop group or record label) independent, not belonging to one of the major companies. *–n.* such a group or label. [abbreviation of INDEPENDENT]

indifference /ɪn'dɪfrəns/ *n.* **1** lack of interest or attention. **2** unimportance.

◆ **indifference curve** *n. Econ.* curve on a graph representing the amounts of different goods that will yield the same level of utility to an individual. Each indifference curve represents a different level of utility. In consumer theory, assuming that individuals are rational, it follows that there will be a single combination of goods that will create maximization of utility for a given level of income (see BUDGET CONSTRAINT). This combination will be on the highest indifference curve of the individual. Isoquants in producer theory represent an equivalent concept.

---

indifferent *adj.* **1** (foll. by *to*) showing indifference; unconcerned. **2** neither good nor bad. **3** of poor quality or ability. □ **indifferently** *adv.*

indigenous /ɪn'dɪdʒɪnəs/ *adj.* (often foll. by *to*) native or belonging naturally to a place. [Latin: from a root *gen-* be born]

indigent /'ɪndɪdʒ(ə)nt/ *adj. formal* needy, poor. □ **indigence** *n.* [Latin *egeo* need]

indigestible /ˌɪndɪ'dʒestɪb(ə)l/ *adj.* **1** difficult or impossible to digest. **2** too complex to read or understand. □ **indigestibility** /-'bɪlɪtɪ/ *n.*

indigestion /ˌɪndɪ'dʒestʃ(ə)n/ *n.* **1** difficulty in digesting food. **2** pain caused by this.

indignant /ɪn'dɪgnənt/ *adj.* feeling or showing indignation. □ **indignantly** *adv.* [Latin *dignus* worthy]

indignation /ˌɪndɪg'neɪʃ(ə)n/ *n.* anger at supposed injustice etc.

indignity /ɪn'dɪgnɪtɪ/ *n.* (*pl.* **-ies**) **1** humiliating treatment or quality. **2** insult.

indigo /'ɪndɪˌgəʊ/ *n.* (*pl.* **-s**) **1** colour between blue and violet in the spectrum. **2** dye of this colour. [Greek *indikon* Indian dye]

indirect /ˌɪndaɪ'rekt/ *adj.* **1** not going straight to the point. **2** (of a route etc.) not straight. **3 a** not directly sought (*indirect result*). **b** not primary (*indirect cause*). □ **indirectly** *adv.*

◆ **indirect costs** *n.pl.* = OVERHEAD COSTS.

◆ **indirect labour** *n.* **1** employees of a contractor who carry out work for another organization. This organization employs the contractor to supply the labour for a particular task. For example, some councils use a contractor, and indirect labour, to collect refuse. **2** part of a workforce in an organization (e.g. office staff, cleaners, canteen workers, etc.) that does not directly produce goods or provide the service that the organization sells.

---

indirect object *n. Gram.* person or thing affected by a verbal action but not primarily acted on (e.g. *him* in *give him the book*).

indirect question *n. Gram.* question in indirect speech.

indirect speech *n.* = REPORTED SPEECH.

◆ **indirect taxation** *n.* taxation that is intended to be borne by persons or organizations other than those who pay the tax (cf. DIRECT TAXATION). The principal **indirect tax** in the UK is VAT, which is paid by traders as goods or services enter into the chain of production, but is ultimately borne by the consumer of the goods or services. One of the advantages of indirect taxes is that they can be collected from comparatively few sources while their economic effects can be widespread.

◆ **indirect utility function** *n. Econ.* utility function that expresses the preferences of individuals in terms of the prices of goods and services and the individual's income.

---

indiscernible /ˌɪndɪ'sɜːnɪb(ə)l/ *adj.* that cannot be discerned.

indiscipline /ɪn'dɪsɪplɪn/ *n.* lack of discipline.

indiscreet /ˌɪndɪ'skriːt/ *adj.* **1** not discreet. **2** injudicious, unwary. □ **indiscreetly** *adv.*

indiscretion /ˌɪndɪ'skreʃ(ə)n/ *n.* indiscreet conduct or action.

indiscriminate /ˌɪndɪ'skrɪmɪnət/ *adj.* making no distinctions; done or acting at random (*indiscriminate shooting*). □ **indiscriminately** *adv.*

indispensable /ˌɪndɪ'spensəb(ə)l/ *adj.* that cannot be dispensed with; necessary. □ **indispensability** /-'bɪlɪtɪ/ *n.* **indispensably** *adv.*

indisposed /ˌɪndɪ'spəʊzd/ *adj.* **1** slightly unwell. **2** averse or unwilling. □ **indisposition** /-spə'zɪʃ(ə)n/ *n.*

indisputable /ˌɪndɪ'spjuːtəb(ə)l/ *adj.* that cannot be disputed. □ **indisputably** *adv.*

indissoluble /ˌɪndɪ'sɒljʊb(ə)l/ *adj.* **1** that cannot be dissolved or broken up. **2** firm and lasting. □ **indissolubly** *adv.*

indistinct /ˌɪndɪ'stɪŋkt/ *adj.* **1** not distinct. **2** confused, obscure. □ **indistinctly** *adv.*

indistinguishable /ˌɪndɪˈstɪŋgwɪʃəb(ə)l/ *adj.* (often foll. by *from*) not distinguishable.

indite /ɪnˈdaɪt/ *v.* (**-ting**) *formal* or *joc.* **1** put (a speech etc.) into words. **2** write (a letter etc.). [French: related to INDICT]

indium /ˈɪndɪəm/ *n.* soft silvery-white metallic element occurring in zinc blende etc. [Latin *indicum* INDIGO]

individual /ˌɪndɪˈvɪdʒʊəl/ *–adj.* **1** of, for, or characteristic of, a single person etc. **2 a** single (*individual words*). **b** particular; not general. **3** having a distinct character. **4** designed for use by one person. *–n.* **1** single member of a class. **2** single human being. **3** *colloq.* person (*a tiresome individual*). **4** distinctive person. [medieval Latin: related to DIVIDE]

individualism *n.* **1** social theory favouring free action by individuals. **2** being independent or different. □ **individualist** *n.* **individualistic** /-ˈlɪstɪk/ *adj.*

individuality /ˌɪndɪvɪdʒʊˈælɪtɪ/ *n.* **1** individual character, esp. when strongly marked. **2** separate existence.

individualize *v.* (also **-ise**) (**-zing** or **-sing**) **1** give an individual character to. **2** (esp. as **individualized** *adj.*) personalize (*individualized notepaper*).

individually *adv.* **1** one by one. **2** personally. **3** distinctively.

indivisible /ˌɪndɪˈvɪzɪb(ə)l/ *adj.* not divisible.

Indo- *comb. form* Indian; Indian and.

Indo-China /ˌɪndəʊˈtʃaɪnə/ peninsula of SE Asia containing Burma, Thailand, peninsular Malayasia, Laos, Cambodia, and Vietnam. □ **Indo-Chinese** *adj.* & *n.*

indoctrinate /ɪnˈdɒktrɪˌneɪt/ *v.* (**-ting**) teach to accept a particular belief uncritically. □ **indoctrination** /-ˈneɪʃ(ə)n/ *n.*

Indo-European /ˌɪndəʊˌjʊərəˈpɪən/ *–adj.* **1** of the family of languages spoken over most of Europe and Asia as far as N India. **2** of the hypothetical parent language of this family. *–n.* **1** Indo-European family of languages. **2** hypothetical parent language of these.

indolent /ˈɪndələnt/ *adj.* lazy; averse to exertion. □ **indolence** *n.* **indolently** *adv.* [Latin *doleo* suffer pain]

indomitable /ɪnˈdɒmɪtəb(ə)l/ *adj.* **1** unconquerable. **2** unyielding. □ **indomitably** *adv.* [Latin: related to IN-[1], *domito* tame]

indoor *adj.* of, done, or for use in a building or under cover.

indoors /ɪnˈdɔːz/ *adv.* into or in a building.

Indore /ɪnˈdɔː(r)/ city and trading centre in central India, in Madhya Pradesh; industries include engineering and cotton milling; pop. (1991) 1 091 674.

indorse var. of ENDORSE.

♦ **indorsement** var. of ENDORSEMENT.

indrawn /ˈɪndrɔːn/ *adj.* (of breath etc.) drawn in.

indubitable /ɪnˈdjuːbɪtəb(ə)l/ *adj.* that cannot be doubted. □ **indubitably** *adv.* [Latin *dubito* doubt]

induce /ɪnˈdjuːs/ *v.* (**-cing**) **1** prevail on; persuade. **2** bring about. **3 a** bring on (labour) artificially. **b** bring on labour in (a mother). **c** speed up the birth of (a baby). **4** produce (a current) by induction. **5** infer; deduce. □ **inducible** *adj.* [Latin *duco duct-* lead]

inducement *n.* attractive offer; incentive; bribe.

induct /ɪnˈdʌkt/ *v.* (often foll. by *to, into*) **1** introduce into office, install (into a benefice etc.). **2** *archaic* lead (to a seat, into a room, etc.); install. [related to INDUCE]

inductance *n.* property of an electric circuit generating an electromotive force by virtue of the current flowing through it.

induction /ɪnˈdʌkʃ(ə)n/ *n.* **1** act of inducting or inducing. **2** act of bringing on (esp. labour) by artificial means. **3** inference of a general law from particular instances. **4** (often *attrib.*) formal introduction to a new job etc. (*induction course*). **5** *Electr.* **a** production of an electric or magnetic state by the proximity (without contact) of an electrified or magnetized body. **b** production of an electric current by a change of magnetic field. **6** drawing of the fuel mixture into the cylinders of an internal-combustion engine.

inductive /ɪnˈdʌktɪv/ *adj.* **1** (of reasoning etc.) based on induction. **2** of electric or magnetic induction.

inductor *n.* component (in an electric circuit) having inductance.

indue var. of ENDUE.

indulge /ɪnˈdʌldʒ/ *v.* (**-ging**) **1** (often foll. by *in*) take pleasure freely. **2** yield freely to (a desire etc.). **3** (also *refl.*) gratify the wishes of. **4** *colloq.* take alcoholic liquor. [Latin *indulgeo* give free rein to]

indulgence *n.* **1** indulging or being indulgent. **2** thing indulged in. **3** *RC Ch.* remission of punishment still due after absolution. **4** privilege granted.

indulgent *adj.* **1** lenient; ready to overlook faults etc. **2** indulging. □ **indulgently** *adv.*

Indus /ˈɪndəs/ river in S Asia, flowing from Tibet through Kashmir and Pakistan to the Arabian Sea.

industrial /ɪnˈdʌstrɪəl/ *adj.* **1** of, engaged in, or for use in or serving the needs of industries. **2** (of a nation etc.) having developed industries. □ **industrially** *adv.*

♦ **industrial action** *n.* coordinated disruptive action in a trade dispute by employees, with or without the support of a trade union, who seek to force employers to agree to their demands relating to wages, terms of employment,

Indonesia /ˌɪndəˈniːzjə, -ʒə, -ʃə/, **Republic of** (formerly **Dutch East Indies**) country in SE Asia, composed of the islands of Java, Sumatra, S Borneo, the W part of New Guinea (Irian Jaya), the Moluccas, Sulawesi, and a host of minor islands. The economy expanded considerably from the mid-1980s until the mid-1990s, esp. under Western and Japanese influence, but in terms of per capita income Indonesia remains one of the world's poorest countries. Agriculture contributes about a quarter of the GDP and, together with its associated industries, employs nearly 70% of the population. Principal cash crops include palm oil, coffee, tea, sugar cane, tobacco, coconuts, and spices; the staple crop is rice. Indonesia is rich in mineral resources and its principal export-earners are oil and liquefied natural gas; attempts have been made to diversify and reduce dependence on these. Other minerals extracted include tin, bauxite, coal, nickel, gold, and copper. Tropical rain forests provide another important export, timber, and Indonesia is a major producer of natural rubber. Tourism is increasingly important. In early 1998 the economy suffered a serious collapse, provoking food riots and civil disorder. The IMF and the US government stepped in with a series of emergency measures. *History.* Colonized, largely by the Dutch, in the early 17th century, the area was conquered by the Japanese in 1942 and upon liberation was proclaimed a republic by local nationalists. Sovereignty passed formally to the new Indonesian government in 1949 and the last Dutch enclave in the area was finally handed over in 1963. The country has been under military dictatorship since 1967 and Indonesia's annexation of East Timor in 1976 was widely condemned. In 1996 two Timorese activists were awarded the Nobel Prize for peace. President, General Suharto; capital, Jakarta (on Java). □ **Indonesian** *adj.* & *n.*

languages	Bahasa Indonesia (official), Javanese
currency	rupiah (Rp) of 100 sen
pop. (est. 1996)	198 189 000
GNP (1994)	US$167B
literacy	84% (m); 69% (f)
life expectancy	63 (m); 66(f)

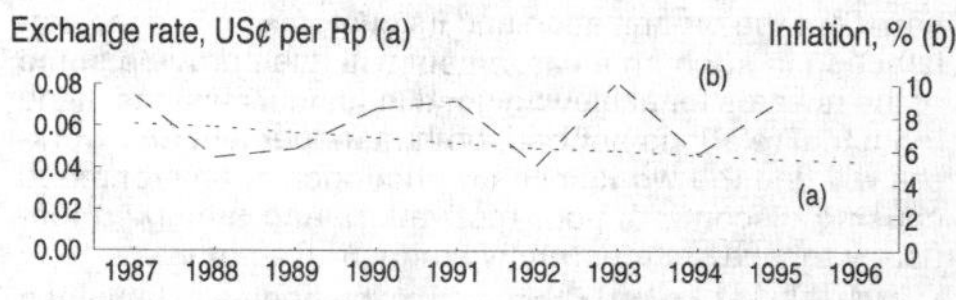

working conditions, etc. It may take the form of a go-slow, overtime ban, work-to-rule, sit-down strike, or strike.

♦ **industrial bank** *n.* relatively small finance house that specializes in hire purchase, obtaining its own funds by accepting long-term deposits, largely from the general public.

♦ **industrial democracy** *n.* system in which workers participate in the management of an organization or in sharing its profits. Workers' participation in making decisions can improve industrial relations and add to workers' job satisfaction and motivation. Various schemes have been tried; for example, including worker directors on the boards of some nationalized industries, workers' councils, and profit-sharing schemes.

♦ **industrial development certificate** *n.* (also **IDC**) certificate required by an industrial organization wishing to build a new factory in the UK or to extend an existing one. An IDC has to accompany any application for planning permission for industrial property. The certificate is issued by the Department of the Environment.

♦ **industrial disability benefit** *n.* benefit paid by the Department of Social Security in the UK to compensate for disablement resulting from an industrial accident or from certain diseases due to the nature of a person's employment. A weekly payment is made on a scale of disablement ranging from 14% to 100%. No benefit is paid for less than 14% disablement. Claimants have to submit to a medical examination. The payment is made if the claimant is still suffering disability 15 weeks or more after the accident or onset of the disease.

♦ **industrial dispute** *n.* = TRADE DISPUTE.

♦ **industrial espionage** *n.* spying on a competitor to obtain trade secrets by dishonest means. The information sought often refers to the development of new products, innovative manufacturing techniques, commissioned market surveys, forthcoming advertising campaigns, research plans, etc. The means used include a wide range of telephone- and computer-tapping devices, infiltration of the competitor's workforce, etc.

♦ **industrial estate** *n.* = TRADING ESTATE.

---

industrialism *n.* system in which manufacturing industries are prevalent.

industrialist *n.* owner or manager in industry.

industrialize *v.* (also **-ise**) (**-zing** or **-sing**) make (a nation etc.) industrial. □ **industrialization** /-'zeɪʃ(ə)n/ *n.*

♦ **industrial life assurance** *n.* = HOME SERVICE ASSURANCE.

♦ **industrial marketing research** *n.* (also **business marketing research**) marketing research undertaken among organizations that buy and add value to products and services but are not the final consumers. Cf. CONSUMER RESEARCH.

♦ **industrial medicine** *n.* health care provided by employers for their employees. Apart from the provision of first aid and nursing care in larger organizations, its main aims are prophylactic: the prevention of accidents by providing adequate guards for machinery, the prevention of disease by controlling noxious fumes, dusts, etc., and the prevention of stress by providing the best possible working environment. In addition, regular check-ups are often provided to monitor the health of members of staff.

♦ **industrial psychology** *n.* study of behaviour at work and of the best ways of minimizing stress in an industrial setting and improving industrial relations.

♦ **industrial relations** *n.pl.* relations between management and workers. If industrial relations are good, the whole workforce will be well motivated to work hard for the benefit of the organization and its customers. The job satisfaction in such an environment will itself provide some of the rewards for achieving good industrial relations. If the industrial relations are bad, both management and workers will find the workplace an uncongenial environment, causing discontent, poor motivation, and a marked tendency to take self-destructive industrial action.

♦ **industrial tribunal** *n.* any of the bodies established under the UK employment protection legislation to hear disputes between employers and employees or trade unions relating to statutory terms and conditions of employment. For example, the tribunals hear complaints concerning unfair dismissal, redundancy, equal pay, and maternity rights. Tribunals may also hear complaints from members of trade unions concerning unjustifiable disciplining by their union. The tribunal usu. consists of a legally qualified chairman and two independent laymen. It differs from a civil court in that it cannot enforce its awards (this must be done by separate application to a court) and it can conduct its proceedings informally. Strict rules of evidence need not apply and the parties can present their own case or be represented by anyone they wish at their own expense; legal aid is not available. The tribunal has wide powers to declare a party in breach of a contract of employment, to award compensation, and to order the reinstatement or re-engagement of a dismissed employee.

♦ **industrial union** see TRADE UNION.

---

industrious /ɪn'dʌstrɪəs/ *adj.* hard-working. □ **industriously** *adv.*

industry /'ɪndəstrɪ/ *n.* (*pl.* **-ies**) **1 a** organized activity in which capital and labour are utilized to produce goods; commercial enterprise. **b** sector of an economy that is concerned with manufacture. **2** concerted activity (*a hive of industry*). **3** diligence. [Latin *industria*]

-ine *suffix* **1** forming adjectives, meaning 'belonging to, of the nature of' (*Alpine*; *asinine*). **2** forming feminine nouns (*heroine*). [Latin *-inus*]

inebriate –*v.* /ɪ'niːbrɪˌeɪt/ (**-ting**) **1** make drunk. **2** excite. –*adj.* /ɪ'niːbrɪət/ drunken. –*n.* /ɪ'niːbrɪət/ drunkard. □ **inebriation** /-'eɪʃ(ə)n/ *n.* **inebriety** /-'braɪətɪ/ *n.* [Latin *ebrius* drunk]

inedible /ɪn'edɪb(ə)l/ *adj.* not suitable for eating.

ineducable /ɪn'edjʊkəb(ə)l/ *adj.* incapable of being educated.

ineffable /ɪn'efəb(ə)l/ *adj.* **1** too great for description in words. **2** that must not be uttered. □ **ineffability** /-'bɪlɪtɪ/ *n.* **ineffably** *adv.* [Latin *effor* speak out]

ineffective /ˌɪnɪ'fektɪv/ *adj.* not achieving the desired effect or results. □ **ineffectively** *adv.* **ineffectiveness** *n.*

ineffectual /ˌɪnɪ'fektʃʊəl/ *adj.* ineffective, feeble. □ **ineffectually** *adv.* **ineffectualness** *n.*

inefficient /ˌɪnɪ'fɪʃ(ə)nt/ *adj.* **1** not efficient or fully capable. **2** (of a machine etc.) wasteful. □ **inefficiency** *n.* **inefficiently** *adv.*

inelegant /ɪn'elɪgənt/ *adj.* **1** ungraceful. **2** unrefined. □ **inelegance** *n.* **inelegantly** *adv.*

ineligible /ɪn'elɪdʒɪb(ə)l/ *adj.* not eligible or qualified. □ **ineligibility** /-'bɪlɪtɪ/ *n.*

ineluctable /ˌɪnɪ'lʌktəb(ə)l/ *adj.* inescapable, unavoidable. [Latin *luctor* strive]

inept /ɪ'nept/ *adj.* **1** unskilful. **2** absurd, silly. **3** out of place. □ **ineptitude** *n.* **ineptly** *adv.* [Latin: related to APT]

inequable /ɪn'ekwəb(ə)l/ *adj.* **1** unfair. **2** not uniform.

inequality /ˌɪnɪ'kwɒlɪtɪ/ *n.* (*pl.* **-ies**) **1** lack of equality. **2** variability. **3** unevenness.

inequitable /ɪn'ekwɪtəb(ə)l/ *adj.* unfair, unjust.

inequity /ɪn'ekwɪtɪ/ *n.* (*pl.* **-ies**) unfairness, injustice.

ineradicable /ˌɪnɪ'rædɪkəb(ə)l/ *adj.* that cannot be rooted out.

inert /ɪ'nɜːt/ *adj.* **1** without inherent power of action, motion, or resistance. **2** not reacting chemically with other substances (*inert gas*). **3** sluggish, slow; lifeless. [Latin *iners -ert-*: related to ART]

inertia /ɪ'nɜːʃə/ *n.* **1** *Physics* property of matter by which it continues in its existing state of rest or motion unless an external force is applied. **2 a** inertness, lethargy. **b** tendency to remain unchanged (*inertia of the system*). □ **inertial** *adj.* [Latin: related to INERT]

inertia reel *n.* reel allowing a seat-belt to unwind freely but locking on impact etc.

inertia selling *n.* sending of unsolicited goods to a

person, on a sale-or-return basis, in the hope of making a sale.

inescapable /ˌɪnɪˈskeɪpəb(ə)l/ *adj.* that cannot be escaped or avoided.

inessential /ˌɪnɪˈsenʃ(ə)l/ *–adj.* not necessary; dispensable. *–n.* inessential thing.

inestimable /ɪnˈestɪməb(ə)l/ *adj.* too great, precious, etc., to be estimated. □ **inestimably** *adv.*

inevitable /ɪnˈevɪtəb(ə)l/ *–adj.* **1** unavoidable; sure to happen. **2** *colloq.* tiresomely familiar. *–n.* (prec. by *the*) inevitable fact, event, etc. □ **inevitability** /-ˈbɪlɪtɪ/ *n.* **inevitably** *adv.* [Latin *evito* avoid]

inexact /ˌɪnɪgˈzækt/ *adj.* not exact. □ **inexactitude** *n.* **inexactly** *adv.*

inexcusable /ˌɪnɪkˈskjuːzəb(ə)l/ *adj.* that cannot be excused or justified. □ **inexcusably** *adv.*

inexhaustible /ˌɪnɪgˈzɔːstɪb(ə)l/ *adj.* that cannot be used up, endless.

inexorable /ɪnˈeksərəb(ə)l/ *adj.* relentless; unstoppable. □ **inexorably** *adv.* [Latin *exoro* entreat]

inexpedient /ˌɪnɪkˈspiːdɪənt/ *adj.* not expedient.

inexpensive /ˌɪnɪkˈspensɪv/ *adj.* not expensive.

inexperience /ˌɪnɪkˈspɪərɪəns/ *n.* lack of experience, knowledge, or skill. □ **inexperienced** *adj.*

inexpert /ɪnˈekspɜːt/ *adj.* unskilful; lacking expertise.

inexpiable /ɪnˈekspɪəb(ə)l/ *adj.* that cannot be expiated or appeased.

inexplicable /ˌɪnɪkˈsplɪkəb(ə)l/ *adj.* that cannot be explained. □ **inexplicably** *adv.*

inexpressible /ˌɪnɪkˈspresɪb(ə)l/ *adj.* that cannot be expressed. □ **inexpressibly** *adv.*

inextinguishable /ˌɪnɪkˈstɪŋgwɪʃəb(ə)l/ *adj.* that cannot be extinguished or destroyed.

in extremis /ˌɪn ɪkˈstriːmɪs/ *adj.* **1** at the point of death. **2** in great difficulties; in an emergency. [Latin]

inextricable /ˌɪnɪkˈstrɪkəb(ə)l/ *adj.* **1** inescapable. **2** that cannot be separated, loosened, or solved. □ **inextricably** *adv.*

infallible /ɪnˈfælɪb(ə)l/ *adj.* **1** incapable of error. **2** unfailing; sure to succeed. **3** (of the Pope) incapable of doctrinal error. □ **infallibility** /-ˈbɪlɪtɪ/ *n.* **infallibly** *adv.*

infamous /ˈɪnfəməs/ *adj.* notoriously bad. □ **infamously** *adv.* **infamy** /ˈɪnfəmɪ/ *n.* (*pl.* **-ies**).

infant /ˈɪnf(ə)nt/ *n.* **1 a** child during the earliest period of its life. **b** schoolchild below the age of seven years. **2** (esp. *attrib.*) thing in an early stage of its development. **3** *Law* person under 18. □ **infancy** *n.* [Latin *infans* unable to speak]

infanta /ɪnˈfæntə/ *n. hist.* daughter of a Spanish or Portuguese king. [Spanish and Portuguese: related to INFANT]

infanticide /ɪnˈfæntɪˌsaɪd/ *n.* **1** killing of an infant, esp. soon after birth. **2** person who kills an infant.

infantile /ˈɪnfənˌtaɪl/ *adj.* **1** of or like infants. **2** childish, immature. □ **infantilism** /ɪnˈfæntɪˌlɪz(ə)m/ *n.*

infantile paralysis *n.* poliomyelitis.

◆ **infant industry** *n.* new industry that may merit some protection against foreign competition in the short term. The argument in favour of providing protection, say in the form of a tariff on imported competitors' goods, is that it would provide a period during which the new industry could streamline its process and make the necessary economies in order for it to become truly competitive with all market producers.

---

infantry /ˈɪnfəntrɪ/ *n.* (*pl.* **-ies**) body of foot-soldiers; foot-soldiers collectively. [Italian *infante* youth, foot-soldier]

infantryman *n.* soldier of an infantry regiment.

infarct /ˈɪnfɑːkt/ *n.* small area of dead tissue caused by an inadequate blood supply. □ **infarction** /ɪnˈfɑːkʃ(ə)n/ *n.* [Latin *farcio farct-* stuff]

infatuate /ɪnˈfætjʊˌeɪt/ *v.* (**-ting**) (usu. as **infatuated** *adj.*) **1** inspire with intense usu. transitory fondness or admiration. **2** affect with extreme folly. □ **infatuation** /-ˈeɪʃ(ə)n/ *n.* [Latin: related to FATUOUS]

infect /ɪnˈfekt/ *v.* **1** affect or contaminate with a germ, virus, or disease. **2** imbue, taint. [Latin *inficio -fect-* taint]

infection /ɪnˈfekʃ(ə)n/ *n.* **1 a** infecting or being infected. **b** instance of this; disease. **2** communication of disease, esp. by air, water, etc.

infectious *adj.* **1** infecting. **2** (of a disease) transmissible by infection. **3** (of emotions etc.) quickly affecting or spreading to others. □ **infectiously** *adv.* **infectiousness** *n.*

infelicity /ˌɪnfɪˈlɪsɪtɪ/ *n.* (*pl.* **-ies**) **1** inapt expression etc. **2** unhappiness. □ **infelicitous** *adj.*

infer /ɪnˈfɜː(r)/ *v.* (**-rr-**) **1** deduce or conclude. **2** imply. □ **inferable** *adj.* [Latin *fero* bring]

■ **Usage** The use of *infer* in sense 2 is considered incorrect by some people.

inference /ˈɪnfərəns/ *n.* **1** inferring. **2** thing inferred. □ **inferential** /-ˈrenʃ(ə)l/ *adj.*

inferior /ɪnˈfɪərɪə(r)/ *–adj.* **1** (often foll. by *to*) lower in rank, quality, etc. **2** of poor quality. **3** situated below. **4** written or printed below the line. *–n.* person inferior to another, esp. in rank. [Latin, comparative of *inferus*]

◆ **inferior good** *n. Econ.* good for which demand falls in absolute terms as income rises. It is a good for which the income elasticity of demand is less than zero. See also ENGEL CURVE; LUXURY GOOD; NECESSARY GOOD; NORMAL GOOD.

---

inferiority /ɪnˌfɪərɪˈɒrɪtɪ/ *n.* being inferior.

inferiority complex *n.* feeling of inadequacy, sometimes marked by compensating aggressive behaviour.

infernal /ɪnˈfɜːn(ə)l/ *adj.* **1** of hell; hellish. **2** *colloq.* detestable, tiresome. □ **infernally** *adv.* [Latin *infernus* low]

inferno /ɪnˈfɜːnəʊ/ *n.* (*pl.* **-s**) **1** raging fire. **2** scene of horror or distress. **3** hell. [Italian: related to INFERNAL]

infertile /ɪnˈfɜːtaɪl/ *adj.* **1** not fertile. **2** unable to have offspring. □ **infertility** /-fəˈtɪlɪtɪ/ *n.*

infest /ɪnˈfest/ *v.* (esp. of vermin) overrun (a place). □ **infestation** /-ˈsteɪʃ(ə)n/ *n.* [Latin *infestus* hostile]

infidel /ˈɪnfɪd(ə)l/ *–n.* unbeliever in esp. the supposed true religion. *–adj.* **1** of infidels. **2** unbelieving. [Latin *fides* faith]

infidelity /ˌɪnfɪˈdelɪtɪ/ *n.* (*pl.* **-ies**) unfaithfulness, esp. adultery. [Latin: related to INFIDEL]

infield *n. Cricket* the part of the ground near the wicket.

infighting *n.* **1** conflict or competitiveness between colleagues. **2** boxing within arm's length.

infill /ˈɪnfɪl/ *–n.* **1** material used to fill a hole, gap, etc. **2** filling gaps (esp. in row of buildings). *–v.* fill in (a cavity etc.).

infilling *n.* = INFILL *n.*

infiltrate /ˈɪnfɪlˌtreɪt/ *v.* (**-ting**) **1 a** enter (a territory, political party, etc.) gradually and imperceptibly. **b** cause to do this. **2** permeate by filtration. **3** (often foll. by *into, through*) introduce (fluid) by filtration. □ **infiltration** /-ˈtreɪʃ(ə)n/ *n.* **infiltrator** *n.* [from IN-[2], FILTRATE]

infinite /ˈɪnfɪnɪt/ *–adj.* **1** boundless, endless. **2** very great or many. *–n.* **1** (**the Infinite**) God. **2** (**the infinite**) infinite space. □ **infinitely** *adv.* [Latin: related to IN-[1], FINITE]

infinitesimal /ˌɪnfɪnɪˈtesɪm(ə)l/ *–adj.* infinitely or very small. *–n.* infinitesimal amount. □ **infinitesimally** *adv.*

infinitive /ɪnˈfɪnɪtɪv/ *–n.* form of a verb expressing the verbal notion without a particular subject, tense, etc. (e.g. *see* in *we came to see, let him see*). *–adj.* having this form.

infinitude /ɪnˈfɪnɪˌtjuːd/ *n. literary* = INFINITY 1, 2.

infinity /ɪnˈfɪnɪtɪ/ *n.* (*pl.* **-ies**) **1** being infinite; boundlessness. **2** infinite number or extent. **3** infinite distance (*gaze into infinity*). **4** *Math.* infinite quantity.

infirm /ɪnˈfɜːm/ *adj.* physically weak, esp. through age.

infirmary *n.* (*pl.* **-ies**) **1** hospital. **2** sick-quarters in a school etc.

infirmity *n.* (*pl.* **-ies**) **1** being infirm. **2** particular physical weakness.

infix /ɪn'fɪks/ *v.* fasten or fix in.

in flagrante delicto /ˌɪn fləˌgræntɪ dɪ'lɪktəʊ/ *adv.* in the very act of committing an offence. [Latin, = in blazing crime]

inflame /ɪn'fleɪm/ *v.* (**-ming**) **1** provoke to strong feeling, esp. anger. **2** cause inflammation in; make hot. **3** aggravate. **4** catch or set on fire. **5** light up with or as with flames.

inflammable /ɪn'flæməb(ə)l/ *adj.* easily set on fire or excited. □ **inflammability** /-'bɪlɪtɪ/ *n.*

■ **Usage** Where there is a danger of *inflammable* being understood to mean the opposite, i.e. 'not easily set on fire', *flammable* can be used to avoid confusion.

inflammation /ˌɪnflə'meɪʃ(ə)n/ *n.* **1** inflaming. **2** bodily condition with heat, swelling, redness, and usu. pain.

inflammatory /ɪn'flæmətərɪ/ *adj.* **1** tending to cause anger etc. **2** of inflammation.

inflatable /ɪn'fleɪtəb(ə)l/ *–adj.* that can be inflated. *–n.* inflatable object.

inflate /ɪn'fleɪt/ *v.* (**-ting**) **1** distend with air or gas. **2** (usu. foll. by *with*; usu. in *passive*) puff up (with pride etc.). **3 a** cause inflation of (the currency). **b** raise (prices) artificially. **4** (as **inflated** *adj.*) (esp. of language, opinions, etc.) bombastic, overblown, exaggerated. [Latin *inflo -flat-*]

♦ **inflation** /ɪn'fleɪʃ(ə)n/ *n.* **1** inflating. **2** *Econ.* persistent rise in the level of prices and wages throughout an economy. If the rises in wages are sufficient to raise production costs, further rises in prices inevitably occur, creating an **inflationary spiral** in which the rate of inflation increases continuously and in some cases alarmingly (see HYPERINFLATION). The causes of inflation are not simple and probably cannot be ascribed to any single factor, although according to monetarism it is an inevitable consequence of too rapid an increase in the money supply. Monetarists therefore believe that inflation can be restricted by judicious control of the money supply. They also tend to support the view that high unemployment is a deterrent to persistent wage claims and therefore provides a curb on the inflationary spiral. It also reduces the total demand in the economy. Keynesians believe that factors other than the money supply create inflation. According to this theory, low inflation and low unemployment can both be maintained by a rigidly enforced incomes policy. The rate of inflation in an economy is usu. measured by means of price indexes, notably the retail price index. See also COST-PUSH INFLATION; DEMAND-PULL INFLATION. □ **inflationary** *adj.*

♦ **inflation accounting** *n.* method of accounting that, unlike historical-cost accounting, attempts to take account of the fact that a monetary unit (e.g. the pound sterling) does not have a constant value; because of the effects of inflation, successive accounts expressed in that unit do not necessarily give a fair view of the trend of profits. The principal methods of dealing with inflation have been current-cost accounting and current purchasing power accounting.

♦ **inflationary gap** *n.* **1** difference between the total spending in an economy (both private and public) and the total spending that would be needed to maintain full employment. **2** government expenditure in excess of taxation income and borrowing from the public. This excess will be financed by increasing the money supply, by printing paper money, or by borrowing from banks.

♦ **inflationary spiral** see INFLATION 2.

♦ **inflation tax** *n.* tax levied to deprive traders of some of the benefit they obtain by raising prices excessively or agreeing to excessive wage demands in a time of inflation. Such a tax does not exist in the UK, although it has been proposed.

inflect /ɪn'flekt/ *v.* **1** change the pitch of (the voice). **2 a** change the form of (a word) to express grammatical relation. **b** undergo such a change. **3** bend, curve. □ **inflective** *adj.* [Latin *flecto flex-* bend]

inflection /ɪn'flekʃ(ə)n/ *n.* (also **inflexion**) **1** inflecting or being inflected. **2 a** inflected word. **b** suffix etc. used to inflect. **3** modulation of the voice. □ **inflectional** *adj.* [Latin: related to INFLECT]

inflexible /ɪn'fleksɪb(ə)l/ *adj.* **1** unbendable. **2** unbending. □ **inflexibility** /-'bɪlɪtɪ/ *n.* **inflexibly** *adv.*

inflexion var. of INFLECTION.

inflict /ɪn'flɪkt/ *v.* (usu. foll. by *on*) **1** deal (a blow etc.). **2** often *joc.* impose (suffering, oneself, etc.) on (*shall not inflict myself on you any longer*). □ **infliction** *n.* **inflictor** *n.* [Latin *fligo flict-* strike]

inflight *attrib. adj.* occurring or provided during a flight.

inflorescence /ˌɪnflə'res(ə)ns/ *n.* **1 a** complete flower-head of a plant. **b** arrangement of this. **2** flowering. [Latin: related to IN-^{2}, FLOURISH]

inflow *n.* **1** flowing in. **2** something that flows in.

influence /'ɪnflʊəns/ *–n.* **1** (usu. foll. by *on*) effect a person or thing has on another. **2** (usu. foll. by *over*, *with*) moral ascendancy or power. **3** thing or person exercising this. *–v.* (**-cing**) exert influence on; affect. □ **under the influence** *colloq.* drunk. [Latin *influo* flow in]

influential /ˌɪnflʊ'enʃ(ə)l/ *adj.* having great influence. □ **influentially** *adv.*

influenza /ˌɪnflʊ'enzə/ *n.* virus infection causing fever, aches, and catarrh. [Italian: related to INFLUENCE]

influx /'ɪnflʌks/ *n.* flowing in, esp. of people or things into a place. [Latin: related to FLUX]

info /'ɪnfəʊ/ *n. colloq.* information. [abbreviation]

♦ **infopreneurial industry** /ˌɪnfəʊprə'nɜːrɪəl/ *n.* manufacture and sale of electronic office and factory equipment for the distribution of information. See INFORMATION TECHNOLOGY. [from INFORMATION, ENTREPRENEUR, -IAL]

inform /ɪn'fɔːm/ *v.* **1** tell (*informed them of their rights*). **2** (usu. foll. by *against*, *on*) give incriminating information about a person to the authorities. [Latin: related to FORM]

informal /ɪn'fɔːm(ə)l/ *adj.* **1** without formality. **2** not formal. □ **informality** /-'mælɪtɪ/ *n.* (*pl.* **-ies**). **informally** *adv.*

informant *n.* giver of information.

information /ˌɪnfə'meɪʃ(ə)n/ *n.* **1 a** something told; knowledge. **b** items of knowledge; news. **2** charge or complaint lodged with a court etc. **3** *Computing* data that has been processed into a more useful or intelligible form. See also DATA 2. **4** *Econ.* data that determines the expectation and choices of individuals. Techniques for analysing economic problems involving incomplete information have been developed. Some examples of information problems are the measurement of risk in financial markets, the study of incentives in labour and other markets (see MORAL HAZARD), and the study of rational expectations.

information processing *n.* organization and manipulation of pieces of information in order to derive additional information. The computer is an information-processing machine.

♦ **information retrieval** *n.* the tracing of information stored in books, computers, etc.

information storage *n.* recording of information, usu. on magnetic tape or disk, so that it may be used at some later time, the information being organized and labelled so that it may be readily accessed.

♦ **information technology** *n.* (also **IT**) study or use of processes for handling, storing, retrieving, and distributing information. It thus incorporates the technology of both computing and of telephony, television, and other means of telecommunication. Information can be transferred between computers using cables, satellite links, or telephone lines. Networks of connected computers can be used, for example, to send electronic mail or to interrogate databases. These systems also enable electronic transfer of funds to be made between banks, as well as telebanking and teleshopping from the home. The same technology is used in the entertainment industry to provide cable and satellite television and videotape and laser disk films.

---

informative /ɪn'fɔːmətɪv/ *adj.* giving information; instructive.

informed *adj.* **1** knowing the facts. **2** having some knowledge.

informer *n.* person who informs, esp. against others.

infra /'ɪnfrə/ *adv.* below, further on (in a book etc.). [Latin, = below]

infra- *comb. form* below.

infraction /ɪn'frækʃ(ə)n/ *n.* infringement. [Latin: related to INFRINGE]

infra dig /ˌɪnfrə 'dɪg/ *predic. adj. colloq.* beneath one's dignity. [Latin *infra dignitatem*]

infrared /ˌɪnfrə'red/ *adj.* of or using rays with a wavelength just longer than the red end of the visible spectrum.

infrastructure /'ɪnfrəˌstrʌktʃə(r)/ *n.* **1 a** basic structural foundations of a society or enterprise. **b** (also **social overhead capital**) essential goods and services, e.g. electricity supply, roads, bridges, and sewers, regarded as a country's economic foundation and usu. requiring substantial investment. **2** permanent installations as a basis for military etc. operations.

infrequent /ɪn'friːkwənt/ *adj.* not frequent. □ **infrequently** *adv.*

infringe /ɪn'frɪndʒ/ *v.* **(-ging) 1** break or violate (a law, another's rights, etc.). **2** (usu. foll. by *on*) encroach; trespass. □ **infringement** *n.* [Latin *frango fract-* break]

infuriate /ɪn'fjʊərɪˌeɪt/ *v.* make furious; irritate greatly. □ **infuriating** *adj.* **infuriatingly** *adv.* [medieval Latin: related to FURY]

infuse /ɪn'fjuːz/ *v.* **(-sing) 1** (usu. foll. by *with*) fill (with a quality). **2** steep (tea leaves etc.) in liquid to extract the content; be steeped thus. **3** (usu. foll. by *into*) instil (life etc.). [Latin *infundo -fus-*: related to FOUND[3]]

infusible /ɪn'fjuːzɪb(ə)l/ *adj.* that cannot be melted. □ **infusibility** /-'bɪlɪtɪ/ *n.*

infusion /ɪn'fjuːʒ(ə)n/ *n.* **1 a** infusing. **b** liquid extract obtained thus. **2** infused element.

-ing[1] *suffix* forming nouns from verbs denoting: **1** verbal action or its result (*asking*). **2** material associated with a process etc. (*piping*; *washing*). **3** occupation or event (*banking*; *wedding*). [Old English]

-ing[2] *suffix* **1** forming the present participle of verbs (*asking*; *fighting*), often as adjectives (*charming*; *strapping*). **2** forming adjectives from nouns (*hulking*) and verbs (*balding*). [Old English]

ingenious /ɪn'dʒiːnɪəs/ *adj.* **1** clever at inventing, organizing, etc. **2** cleverly contrived. □ **ingeniously** *adv.* [Latin *ingenium* cleverness]

■ **Usage** *Ingenious* is sometimes confused with *ingenuous*.

ingénue /ˌæʒeɪ'njuː/ *n.* **1** unsophisticated young woman. **2** such a part in a play. [French: related to INGENUOUS]

ingenuity /ˌɪndʒɪ'njuːɪtɪ/ *n.* inventiveness, cleverness.

ingenuous /ɪn'dʒenjʊəs/ *adj.* **1** artless. **2** frank. □ **ingenuously** *adv.* [Latin *ingenuus* free-born, frank]

■ **Usage** *Ingenuous* is sometimes confused with *ingenious*.

ingest /ɪn'dʒest/ *v.* **1** take in (food etc.). **2** absorb (knowledge etc.). □ **ingestion** /ɪn'dʒestʃ(ə)n/ *n.* [Latin *gero* carry]

inglenook /'ɪŋg(ə)lˌnʊk/ *n.* space within the opening on either side of a large fireplace. [perhaps Gaelic *aingeal* fire, light]

inglorious /ɪn'glɔːrɪəs/ *adj.* **1** shameful. **2** not famous.

ingoing *adj.* going in.

ingot /'ɪŋgət/ *n.* (usu. oblong) piece of cast metal, esp. gold. [origin uncertain]

ingraft var. of ENGRAFT.

ingrained /ɪn'greɪnd/ *adj.* **1** deeply rooted; inveterate. **2** (of dirt etc.) deeply embedded.

ingratiate /ɪn'greɪʃɪˌeɪt/ *v.refl.* **(-ting)** (usu. foll. by *with*) bring oneself into favour. □ **ingratiating** *adj.* **ingratiatingly** *adv.* [Latin *in gratiam* into favour]

ingratitude /ɪn'grætɪˌtjuːd/ *n.* lack of due gratitude.

ingredient /ɪn'griːdɪənt/ *n.* component part in a mixture. [Latin *ingredior* enter into]

ingress /'ɪngres/ *n.* act or right of going in. [Latin *ingressus*: related to INGREDIENT]

ingrowing *adj.* (esp. of a toenail) growing into the flesh. □ **ingrown** *adj.*

inguinal /'ɪŋgwɪn(ə)l/ *adj.* of the groin. [Latin *inguen* groin]

inhabit /ɪn'hæbɪt/ *v.* **(-t-)** dwell in; occupy. □ **inhabitable** *adj.* [Latin: related to HABIT]

inhabitant *n.* person etc. who inhabits a place.

inhalant /ɪn'heɪlənt/ *n.* medicinal substance for inhaling.

inhale /ɪn'heɪl/ *v.* **(-ling)** (often *absol.*) breathe in (air, gas, smoke, etc.). □ **inhalation** /-hə'leɪʃ(ə)n/ *n.* [Latin *halo* breathe]

inhaler *n.* device for administering an inhalant, esp. to relieve asthma.

inhere /ɪn'hɪə(r)/ *v.* **(-ring)** be inherent. [Latin *haereo haes-* stick]

inherent /ɪn'herənt/ *adj.* (often foll. by *in*) existing in something as an essential or permanent attribute. □ **inherence** *n.* **inherently** *adv.*

♦ **inherent vice** *n.* defect or weakness of an item, esp. of a cargo, that causes it to suffer some form of damage or destruction without the intervention of an outside cause. For example, certain substances, e.g. jute, when shipped in bales, can warm up spontaneously, causing damage to the fibre. Damage by this cause is excluded from most cargo insurance policies as an excepted peril.

---

inherit /ɪn'herɪt/ *v.* **(-t-) 1** receive (property, rank, title, etc.) by legal succession. **2** derive (a characteristic) from one's ancestors. **3** derive (a situation etc.) from a predecessor. □ **inheritable** *adj.* **inheritor** *n.* [Latin *heres* heir]

inheritance *n.* **1** thing that is inherited. **2** inheriting.

♦ **inheritance tax** *n.* tax levied on amounts inherited, usu. in excess of a specified amount that is free of tax (£223,000 in the UK, from the tax year 1998–9). A true inheritance tax would be based on the amounts inherited by an individual or possibly by a household. The inheritance tax introduced in 1986 in the UK is not strictly such a tax since it taxes the total estate left by a deceased person together with a tapered charge on gifts made by that person up to seven years before his or her death. This charge is added to the cumulative total used to calculate the amount of inheritance tax due. For the purposes of working out any inheritance tax due, the estate is said to be comprised of chargeable assets only, e.g. houses and stocks and shares.

---

inhibit /ɪn'hɪbɪt/ *v.* **(-t-) 1** hinder, restrain, or prevent (action or progress). **2** (as **inhibited** *adj.*) suffering from inhibition. **3** (usu. foll. by *from* + verbal noun) prohibit (a person etc.). □ **inhibitory** *adj.* [Latin *inhibeo -hibit-* hinder]

inhibition /ˌɪnhɪ'bɪʃ(ə)n/ *n.* **1** *Psychol.* restraint on the direct expression of an instinct. **2** *colloq.* emotional resistance to a thought, action, etc. **3** inhibiting or being inhibited.

inhospitable /ˌɪnhɒ'spɪtəb(ə)l/ *adj.* **1** not hospitable. **2** (of a region etc.) not affording shelter, favourable conditions, etc. □ **inhospitably** *adv.*

in-house *adj.* & *adv.* within an institution, company, etc.

inhuman /ɪn'hjuːmən/ *adj.* brutal; unfeeling; barbarous. □ **inhumanity** *n.* (*pl.* **-ies**). **inhumanly** *adv.*

inhumane /ˌɪnhjuː'meɪn/ *adj.* = INHUMAN. □ **inhumanely** *adv.*

inimical /ɪ'nɪmɪk(ə)l/ *adj.* **1** hostile. **2** harmful. □ **inimically** *adv.* [Latin *inimicus* enemy]

inimitable /ɪ'nɪmɪtəb(ə)l/ *adj.* impossible to imitate. □ **inimitably** *adv.*

iniquity /ɪ'nɪkwɪtɪ/ *n.* (*pl.* **-ies**) **1** wickedness. **2** gross injustice. □ **iniquitous** *adj.* [French from Latin *aequus* just]

initial /ɪ'nɪʃ(ə)l/ *–adj.* of or at the beginning. *–n.* initial letter, esp. (in *pl.*) those of a person's names. *–v.* (**-ll-**; *US* **-l-**) mark or sign with one's initials. □ **initially** *adv.* [Latin *initium* beginning]

♦ **initial charge** *n.* charge paid to the managers of a unit trust by an investor when the units are first purchased, usu. 5% or 6% of the invested amount.

---

initial letter *n.* first letter of a word.

♦ **initial public offering** *n.* (also **IPO**) *US* = FLOTATION.

---

initiate *–v.* /ɪ'nɪʃɪˌeɪt/ (**-ting**) **1** begin; set going; originate. **2 a** admit (a person) into a society, office, etc., esp. with a ritual. **b** instruct (a person) in a subject. *–n.* /ɪ'nɪʃɪət/ (esp. newly) initiated person. □ **initiation** /-'eɪʃ(ə)n/ *n.* **initiator** *n.* **initiatory** /ɪ'nɪʃjətərɪ/ *adj.* [Latin *initium* beginning]

initiative /ɪ'nɪʃətɪv/ *n.* **1** ability to initiate things; enterprise (*lacks initiative*). **2** first step. **3** (prec. by *the*) power or right to begin. □ **have the initiative** esp. *Mil.* be able to control the enemy's movements. [French: related to INITIATE]

inject /ɪn'dʒekt/ *v.* **1 a** (usu. foll. by *into*) drive (a solution, medicine, etc.) by or as if by a syringe. **b** (usu. foll. by *with*) fill (a cavity etc.) by injecting. **c** administer medicine etc. to (a person) by injection. **2** place (a quality, money, etc.) into something. □ **injection** *n.* **injector** *n.* [Latin *injicere -ject-* from *jacio* throw]

injudicious /ˌɪndʒuː'dɪʃəs/ *adj.* unwise; ill-judged.

injunction /ɪn'dʒʌŋkʃ(ə)n/ *n.* **1** authoritative order. **2** judicial order restraining a person or body from an act, or compelling redress to an injured party. This is an equitable remedy granted usu. by the High Court. An **interlocutory injunction** lasts only until the main action is heard. **Interim injunctions**, lasting a short time only, may be granted on the application of one party without the other being present (an **ex parte interim injunction**) if there is great urgency. **Prohibitory injunctions** forbid the doing of a particular act; **mandatory injunctions** order a person to do some act. Failure to obey an injunction is contempt of court and punishable by a fine or imprisonment. [Latin: related to ENJOIN]

injure /'ɪndʒə(r)/ *v.* (**-ring**) **1** harm or damage. **2** do wrong to. [back-formation from INJURY]

injured *adj.* **1** harmed or hurt. **2** offended.

injurious /ɪn'dʒʊərɪəs/ *adj.* **1** hurtful. **2** (of language) insulting. **3** wrongful.

injury /'ɪndʒərɪ/ *n.* (*pl.* **-ies**) **1** physical harm or damage. **2** offence to feelings etc. **3** esp. *Law* wrongful action or treatment. [Latin *injuria*]

injury time *n.* extra playing-time at a football etc. match to compensate for time lost in dealing with injuries.

injustice /ɪn'dʒʌstɪs/ *n.* **1** lack of fairness. **2** unjust act. □ **do a person an injustice** judge a person unfairly. [French from Latin: related to IN-[1]]

ink *–n.* **1** coloured fluid or paste used for writing, printing, etc. **2** black liquid ejected by a cuttlefish etc. *–v.* **1** (usu. foll. by *in*, *over*, etc.) mark with ink. **2** cover (type etc.) with ink. [Greek *egkauston* purple ink used by Roman emperors]

ink-jet printer *n.* printer, used for example in computing, in which fine drops of quick-drying ink are projected on to the paper to form the characters. It is much quieter in operation than an impact printer. In one design, employed for instance in the **bubble-jet printer**, the print head contains a column of nozzles, each nozzle being capable of ejecting a single drop of ink at a time. As the head moves along the line to be printed, the appropriate characters are built up.

inkling /'ɪŋklɪŋ/ *n.* (often foll. by *of*) slight knowledge or suspicion; hint. [origin unknown]

inkstand *n.* stand for one or more ink bottles.

ink-well *n.* pot for ink, usu. housed in a hole in a desk.

inky *adj.* (**-ier**, **-iest**) of, as black as, or stained with ink. □ **inkiness** *n.*

inland *–adj.* /'ɪnlənd/ **1** in the interior of a country. **2** carried on within a country. *–adv.* /ɪn'lænd/ in or towards the interior of a country.

♦ **inland bill** *n.* bill of exchange that is both drawn and payable in the UK. Any other bill is classed as a **foreign bill**.

♦ **Inland Revenue** *n.* government department assessing and collecting taxes. See BOARD OF INLAND REVENUE.

♦ **inland waterways** see BRITISH WATERWAYS BOARD.

---

in-law *n.* (often in *pl.*) relative by marriage.

inlay *–v.* /ɪn'leɪ/ (*past* and *past part.* **inlaid** /ɪn'leɪd/) **1** embed (a thing in another) so that the surfaces are even. **2** decorate (a thing with inlaid work). *–n.* /'ɪnleɪ/ **1** inlaid work. **2** material inlaid. **3** filling shaped to fit a tooth-cavity. [from IN-[2], LAY[1]]

inlet /'ɪnlət/ *n.* **1** small arm of the sea, a lake, or a river. **2** piece inserted. **3** way of entry. [from IN, LET[1]]

in loco parentis /ɪn ˌləʊkəʊ pə'rentɪs/ *adv.* (acting) for or instead of a parent. [Latin]

inmate *n.* occupant of a hospital, prison, institution, etc. [probably from INN, MATE[1]]

in memoriam /ˌɪn mɪ'mɔːrɪˌæm/ *prep.* in memory of (a dead person). [Latin]

inmost *adj.* most inward. [Old English]

inn *n.* **1** pub, sometimes with accommodation. **2** *hist.* house providing accommodation, esp. for travellers. [Old English: related to IN]

innards /'ɪnədz/ *n.pl. colloq.* entrails. [special pronunciation of INWARD]

innate /ɪ'neɪt/ *adj.* inborn; natural. □ **innately** *adv.* [Latin *natus* born]

inner *–adj.* (usu. *attrib.*) **1** inside; interior. **2** (of thoughts, feelings, etc.) deeper. *–n. Archery* **1** division of the target next to the bull's-eye. **2** shot striking this. □ **innermost** *adj.* [Old English, comparative of IN]

inner city *n.* central area of a city, esp. regarded as having particular problems (also (with hyphen) *attrib.*: *inner-city housing*).

inner man *n.* (also **inner woman**) **1** soul or mind. **2** *joc.* stomach.

Inner Mongolia autonomous region of N China; pop. (est. 1995) 22 600 000; capital, Hohhot. There is some mining, but agriculture (producing wheat) is the main occupation.

inner tube *n.* separate inflatable tube inside a pneumatic tyre.

innings *n.* (*pl.* same) **1** esp. *Cricket* part of a game during which a side is batting. **2** period during which a government, party, person, etc. is in office or can achieve something. [obsolete *in* (verb) = go in]

innkeeper *n.* person who keeps an inn.

innocent /'ɪnəs(ə)nt/ *–adj.* **1** free from moral wrong. **2** (usu. foll. by *of*) not guilty (of a crime etc.). **3** simple; guileless. **4** harmless. *–n.* innocent person, esp. a young child. □ **innocence** *n.* **innocently** *adv.* [Latin *noceo* hurt]

innocuous /ɪ'nɒkjʊəs/ *adj.* harmless. [Latin *innocuus*: related to INNOCENT]

Inn of Court *n.* each of the four legal societies admitting people to the English bar.

innovate /'ɪnəˌveɪt/ *v.* (**-ting**) bring in new methods, ideas, products, etc.; make changes. See also PATENT *n.* 1. □ **innovation** /-'veɪʃ(ə)n/ *n.* **innovative** *adj.* **innovator** *n.* **innovatory** *adj.* [Latin *novus* new]

Innsbruck /'ɪnzbrʊk/ city in W Austria, a winter sports

centre and capital of Tyrol; glass and textiles are manufactured; pop. (1991) 118 112.

innuendo /ˌɪnjʊˈendəʊ/ *n.* (*pl.* **-es** or **-s**) allusive remark or hint, usu. disparaging or with a double meaning. [Latin, = by nodding at: related to IN-[2], *nuo* nod]

Innuit var. of INUIT.

innumerable /ɪˈnjuːmərəb(ə)l/ *adj.* too many to be counted. □ **innumerably** *adv.*

innumerate /ɪˈnjuːmərət/ *adj.* having no knowledge of basic mathematics. □ **innumeracy** *n.*

inoculate /ɪˈnɒkjʊˌleɪt/ *v.* (**-ting**) treat (a person or animal) with vaccine or serum to promote immunity against a disease. □ **inoculation** /-ˈleɪʃ(ə)n/ *n.* [Latin *oculus* eye, bud]

inoffensive /ˌɪnəˈfensɪv/ *adj.* not objectionable; harmless.

inoperable /ɪnˈɒpərəb(ə)l/ *adj. Surgery* that cannot successfully be operated on.

inoperative /ɪnˈɒpərətɪv/ *adj.* not working or taking effect.

inopportune /ɪnˈɒpəˌtjuːn/ *adj.* not appropriate, esp. not timely.

inordinate /ɪnˈɔːdɪnət/ *adj.* excessive. □ **inordinately** *adv.* [Latin: related to ORDAIN]

inorganic /ˌɪnɔːˈgænɪk/ *adj.* **1** *Chem.* (of a compound) not organic, usu. of mineral origin. **2** without organized physical structure. **3** extraneous.

in-patient *n.* patient who lives in hospital while under treatment.

input /ˈɪnpʊt/ *–n.* **1 a** what is put in or taken in. **b** data or programs entered into a computer using a keyboard, mouse, etc. **c** (in *pl.*) resources (land, labour, capital, and entrepreneurial ability) required by an organization to enable it to provide its outputs (goods or services). **2** place where energy, information, etc. enters a system. **3** action of putting in or feeding in. **4** contribution of information etc. *–v.* (**inputting**; *past* and *past part.* **input** or **inputted**) (often foll. by *into*) **1** put in. **2** supply (data, programs, etc. to a computer etc.).

input device *n.* device, e.g. a keyboard, mouse, voice input device, or bar-code reader, that transfers data, programs, or signals into a computer. An input device need not be operated by a person; it could for example be a temperature sensor. There may be many input devices in a computer system, each device providing some means of communication with the computer. See also USER INTERFACE.

input/output *n.* (also **I/O**) **1** components or processes in a computer system that are concerned with the passing of information into and out of the system, and thus link the system with the outside world. **2** (*attrib.*) concerned with the passage of such information (*input/output device*).

♦ **input tax** *n.* VAT included in the price a trader pays for the goods and services acquired for use in the trader's business. This tax can be deducted from the trader's output tax in arriving at the amount that must be accounted for to the Customs and Excise.

---

inquest /ˈɪŋkwest/ *n.* **1** *Law* inquiry by a coroner's court into the cause of a death. **2** *colloq.* discussion analysing the outcome of a game, election, etc. [Romanic: related to INQUIRE]

inquietude /ɪnˈkwaɪɪˌtjuːd/ *n.* uneasiness. [Latin: related to QUIET]

inquire /ɪnˈkwaɪə(r)/ *v.* (**-ring**) **1** seek information formally; make a formal investigation. **2** = ENQUIRE. [Latin *quaero quisit-* seek]

inquiry *n.* (*pl.* **-ies**) **1** investigation, esp. an official one. **2** = ENQUIRY.

♦ **inquiry test** *n.* method of testing the response to an advertisement or a particular medium by comparing the number of inquiries received as a result of it.

---

inquisition /ˌɪnkwɪˈzɪʃ(ə)n/ *n.* **1** intensive search or investigation. **2** judicial or official inquiry. **3** (**the Inquisition**) *RC Ch. hist.* ecclesiastical tribunal for the violent suppression of heresy, esp. in Spain. □ **inquisitional** *adj.* [Latin: related to INQUIRE]

inquisitive /ɪnˈkwɪzɪtɪv/ *adj.* **1** unduly curious; prying. **2** seeking knowledge. □ **inquisitively** *adv.* **inquisitiveness** *n.*

inquisitor /ɪnˈkwɪzɪtə(r)/ *n.* **1** official investigator. **2** *hist.* officer of the Inquisition.

inquisitorial /ɪnˌkwɪzɪˈtɔːrɪəl/ *adj.* **1** of or like an inquisitor. **2** prying. □ **inquisitorially** *adv.*

inquorate /ɪnˈkwɔːreɪt/ *adj.* not constituting a quorum.

in re /ɪn ˈriː/ *prep.* = RE[1]. [Latin]

INRI *abbr.* Jesus of Nazareth, King of the Jews. [Latin *Iesus Nazarenus Rex Iudaeorum*]

inroad *n.* **1** (often in *pl.*) encroachment; using up of resources etc. **2** hostile attack.

inrush *n.* rapid influx.

ins. *abbr.* **1** inches. **2** insurance.

insalubrious /ˌɪnsəˈluːbrɪəs/ *adj.* (of a climate or place) unhealthy.

insane *adj.* **1** mad. **2** *colloq.* extremely foolish. □ **insanely** *adv.* **insanity** /-ˈsænɪtɪ/ *n.* (*pl.* **-ies**).

insanitary /ɪnˈsænɪtərɪ/ *adj.* not sanitary; dirty.

insatiable /ɪnˈseɪʃəb(ə)l/ *adj.* **1** unable to be satisfied. **2** extremely greedy. □ **insatiability** /-ˈbɪlɪtɪ/ *n.* **insatiably** *adv.*

insatiate /ɪnˈseɪʃɪət/ *adj.* never satisfied.

inscribe /ɪnˈskraɪb/ *v.* (**-bing**) **1 a** (usu. foll. by *in, on*) write or carve (words etc.) on a surface, page, etc. **b** (usu. foll. by *with*) mark (a surface) with characters. **2** (usu. foll. by *to*) write an informal dedication in or on (a book etc.). **3** enter the name of (a person) on a list or in a book. **4** *Geom.* draw (a figure) within another so that points of it lie on the boundary of the other. [Latin *scribo* write]

♦ **inscribed stock** *n.* (also **registered stock**) shares in loan stock, for which the names of the holders are kept in a register rather than by the issue of a certificate of ownership. On a transfer, a new name has to be registered, which makes them cumbersome and unpopular in practice.

---

inscription /ɪnˈskrɪpʃ(ə)n/ *n.* **1** words inscribed. **2** inscribing. □ **inscriptional** *adj.* [Latin: related to INSCRIBE]

inscrutable /ɪnˈskruːtəb(ə)l/ *adj.* mysterious, impenetrable. □ **inscrutability** /-ˈbɪlɪtɪ/ *n.* **inscrutably** *adv.* [Latin *scrutor* search]

INSEAD /ˈɪnsɪæd/ *n.* (also **Insead**) European Institute of Administrative Affairs. [French, abbreviation of *Institut européen d'administration des affaires*]

insect /ˈɪnsekt/ *n.* small invertebrate of a class characteristically having a head, thorax, abdomen, two antennae, three pairs of thoracic legs, and usu. one or two pairs of thoracic wings. [Latin: related to SECTION]

insecticide /ɪnˈsektɪˌsaɪd/ *n.* substance for killing insects.

insectivore /ɪnˈsektɪˌvɔː(r)/ *n.* **1** animal that feeds on insects. **2** plant which captures and absorbs insects. □ **insectivorous** /-ˈtɪvərəs/ *adj.* [from INSECT, Latin *voro* devour]

insecure /ˌɪnsɪˈkjʊə(r)/ *adj.* **1 a** unsafe; not firm. **b** (of a surface etc.) liable to give way. **2** uncertain; lacking confidence. □ **insecurity** /-ˈkjʊrɪtɪ/ *n.*

inseminate /ɪnˈsemɪˌneɪt/ *v.* (**-ting**) **1** introduce semen into. **2** sow (seed etc.). □ **insemination** /-ˈneɪʃ(ə)n/ *n.* [Latin: related to SEMEN]

insensate /ɪnˈsenseɪt/ *adj.* **1** without physical sensation. **2** without sensibility. **3** stupid. [Latin: related to SENSE]

insensible /ɪnˈsensɪb(ə)l/ *adj.* **1** unconscious. **2** (usu. foll. by *of, to*) unaware (*insensible of her needs*). **3** callous. **4** too small or gradual to be perceived. □ **insensibility** /-ˈbɪlɪtɪ/ *n.* **insensibly** *adv.*

insensitive /ɪnˈsensɪtɪv/ *adj.* (often foll. by *to*) **1** unfeeling; boorish; crass. **2** not sensitive to physical stimuli. □

insensitively *adv.* **insensitiveness** *n.* **insensitivity** /-ˈtɪvɪtɪ/ *n.*

insentient /ɪnˈsenʃ(ə)nt/ *adj.* not sentient; inanimate.

inseparable /ɪnˈsepərəb(ə)l/ *adj.* (esp. of friends) unable or unwilling to be separated. □ **inseparability** /-ˈbɪlɪtɪ/ *n.* **inseparably** *adv.*

insert *–v.* /ɪnˈsɜːt/ place or put (a thing) into another. *–n.* /ˈɪnsɜːt/ something (esp. pages) inserted. [Latin *sero sert-* join]

insertion /ɪnˈsɜːʃ(ə)n/ *n.* **1** inserting. **2** thing inserted.

in-service *attrib. adj.* (of training) for those actively engaged in the profession or activity concerned.

inset *–n.* /ˈɪnset/ **1 a** extra section inserted in a book etc. **b** small map etc. within the border of a larger one. **2** piece let into a dress etc. *–v.* /ɪnˈset/ (**insetting**; *past* and *past part.* **inset** or **insetted**) **1** put in as an inset. **2** decorate with an inset.

inshore *adv.* & *adj.* at sea but close to the shore.

inside *–n.* /ɪnˈsaɪd/ **1 a** inner side. **b** inner part; interior. **2** side away from the road. **3** (usu. in *pl.*) *colloq.* stomach and bowels. *–adj.* /ˈɪnsaɪd/ **1** situated on or in the inside. **2** *Football* & *Hockey* nearer to the centre of the field. *–adv.* /ɪnˈsaɪd/ **1** on, in, or to the inside. **2** *slang* in prison. *–prep.* /ɪnˈsaɪd/ **1** on the inner side of; within. **2** in less than (*inside an hour*). □ **inside out 1** with the inner surface turned outwards. **2** thoroughly (*knew his subject inside out*).

inside information *n.* information not normally accessible to outsiders.

inside job *n. colloq.* crime committed by a person living or working on the premises burgled etc.

♦ **inside money** *n.* bank deposits held by individuals that are offset by loans to other individuals. Inside money is the basis of the neutrality of money proposition. Cf. OUTSIDE MONEY.

insider /ɪnˈsaɪdə(r)/ *n.* **1** person who is within an organization etc. **2** person privy to a secret.

♦ **insider dealing** *n.* (also **insider trading**) *Stock Exch.* dealing in company securities with a view to making a profit or avoiding a loss while in possession of information that, if generally known, would affect their price. Under the Companies Securities (Insider Dealing) Act (1985) those who are or have been connected with a company (e.g. the directors, the company secretary, employees, and professional advisers) are prohibited from such dealing on or, in certain circumstances, off the stock exchange if they acquired the information by virtue of their connection and in confidence. The prohibition extends to certain unconnected persons to whom the information has been conveyed.

♦ **insider-outsider theory** *n. Econ.* theory that employed workers (insiders) may be able to maintain high wages even in periods of high unemployment, as they can prevent outsiders from competing for jobs. This may result from the power of unions or from the level of skills and training required before workers become effective. This theory has been used to explain the persistence of high unemployment in the Western economies in the 1970s and 1980s (see also HYSTERESIS).

insidious /ɪnˈsɪdɪəs/ *adj.* **1** proceeding inconspicuously but harmfully. **2** crafty. □ **insidiously** *adv.* **insidiousness** *n.* [Latin *insidiae* ambush]

insight *n.* (usu. foll. by *into*) **1** capacity of understanding hidden truths etc. **2** instance of this.

insignia /ɪnˈsɪgnɪə/ *n.* (treated as *sing.* or *pl.*) badge. [Latin *signum* sign]

insignificant /ˌɪnsɪgˈnɪfɪkənt/ *adj.* **1** unimportant. **2** meaningless. □ **insignificance** *n.*

insincere /ˌɪnsɪnˈsɪə(r)/ *adj.* not sincere. □ **insincerely** *adv.* **insincerity** /-ˈserɪtɪ/ *n.* (*pl.* **-ies**).

insinuate /ɪnˈsɪnjʊˌeɪt/ *v.* (**-ting**) **1** hint obliquely, esp. unpleasantly. **2** (often *refl.*; usu. foll. by *into*) **a** introduce (a person etc.) into favour etc., by subtle manipulation. **b** introduce (a thing, oneself, etc.) deviously into a place. □ **insinuation** /-ˈeɪʃ(ə)n/ *n.* [Latin *sinuo* curve]

insipid /ɪnˈsɪpɪd/ *adj.* **1** lacking vigour or character; dull. **2** tasteless. □ **insipidity** /-ˈpɪdɪtɪ/ *n.* **insipidly** *adv.* [Latin *sapio* have savour]

insist /ɪnˈsɪst/ *v.* (usu. foll. by *on* or *that*; also *absol.*) maintain or demand assertively (*insisted on my going*; *insisted that he was innocent*). [Latin *sisto* stand]

insistent *adj.* **1** (often foll. by *on*) insisting. **2** forcing itself on the attention. □ **insistence** *n.* **insistently** *adv.*

in situ /ɪn ˈsɪtjuː/ *adv.* in its proper or original place. [Latin]

insobriety /ˌɪnsəˈbraɪətɪ/ *n.* intemperance, esp. in drinking.

insofar /ˌɪnsəʊˈfɑː(r)/ *adv.* = *in so far* (see FAR).

insole *n.* fixed or removable inner sole of a boot or shoe.

insolent /ˈɪnsələnt/ *adj.* impertinently insulting. □ **insolence** *n.* **insolently** *adv.* [Latin *soleo* be accustomed]

insoluble /ɪnˈsɒljʊb(ə)l/ *adj.* **1** incapable of being solved. **2** incapable of being dissolved. □ **insolubility** /-ˈbɪlɪtɪ/ *n.* **insolubly** *adv.*

♦ **insolvency** /ɪnˈsɒlv(ə)nsɪ/ *n.* inability to pay one's debts when they fall due, which may often lead to bankruptcy or (for companies) liquidation. In both of these cases the normal procedure is for a specialist, a trustee in bankruptcy or a liquidator, to be appointed to gather and dispose of the assets of the insolvent and to pay the creditors. An insolvent person may have valuable assets that are not immediately realizable.

♦ **insolvency practitioner** *n.* person appointed to officiate in the liquidation of a company or in bankruptcy proceedings as a liquidator, a provisional liquidator, an administrative receiver, the supervisor of a voluntary arrangement, or a trustee in bankruptcy. Under the Insolvency Act (1986), insolvency practitioners must meet certain statutory requirements, including membership of an approved professional body (e.g. the Institute of Chartered Accountants or the Insolvency Practitioners' Association).

insolvent /ɪnˈsɒlv(ə)nt/ *–adj.* unable to pay one's debts; bankrupt. *–n.* insolvent person.

insomnia /ɪnˈsɒmnɪə/ *n.* sleeplessness, esp. habitual. [Latin *somnus* sleep]

insomniac /ɪnˈsɒmnɪˌæk/ *n.* person suffering from insomnia.

insomuch /ˌɪnsəʊˈmʌtʃ/ *adv.* **1** (foll. by *that*) to such an extent. **2** (foll. by *as*) inasmuch. [originally *in so much*]

insouciant /ɪnˈsuːsɪənt/ *adj.* carefree; unconcerned. □ **insouciance** *n.* [French *souci* care]

inspect /ɪnˈspekt/ *v.* **1** look closely at. **2** examine officially. □ **inspection** *n.* [Latin *specio spect-* look]

♦ **inspection and investigation of a company** *n.* inquiry into the running of a company made by inspectors appointed by the Department of Trade and Industry. It may be held to supply company members with information or to investigate fraud, unfair prejudice, nominee shareholdings, or insider dealing. The inspectors' report is usu. published.

inspector *n.* **1** person who inspects. **2** official employed to supervise. **3** police officer next above sergeant in rank. □ **inspectorate** *n.*

♦ **inspector of taxes** *n.* civil servant responsible to the Board of Inland Revenue for issuing tax returns and assessments, the conduct of appeals, and agreeing tax liabilities with taxpayers.

inspiration /ˌɪnspəˈreɪʃ(ə)n/ *n.* **1 a** creative force or influence. **b** person etc. stimulating creativity etc. **c** divine influence, esp. on the writing of Scripture etc. **2** sudden brilliant idea. □ **inspirational** *adj.*

inspire /ɪnˈspaɪə(r)/ *v.* (**-ring**) **1** stimulate (a person) to esp. creative activity. **2 a** (usu. foll. by *with*) animate (a person) with a feeling. **b** create (a feeling) in a person (*inspires confidence*). **3** prompt; give rise to (*a poem inspired by love*). **4** (as **inspired** *adj.*) characterized by inspiration. □ **inspiring** *adj.* [Latin *spiro* breathe]

inspirit /ɪn'spɪrɪt/ *v.* (**-t-**) **1** put life into; animate. **2** encourage.

inst. *abbr.* **1** = INSTANT *adj.* 4 (*the 6th inst.*). **2** (often **Inst.**) **a** institute. **b** institution.

instability /ˌɪnstə'bɪlɪtɪ/ *n.* **1** lack of stability. **2** unpredictability in behaviour etc.

install /ɪn'stɔːl/ *v.* (also **instal**) (**-ll-**) **1** place (equipment etc.) in position ready for use. **2** place (a person) in an office or rank with ceremony. **3** establish (oneself, a person, etc.). □ **installation** /ˌɪnstə'leɪʃ(ə)n/ *n.* [Latin: related to STALL[1]]

instalment *n.* (*US* **installment**) **1** any of several usu. equal payments for something, esp. when buying goods on hire purchase, settling a debt, or buying a new issue of shares. **2** any of several parts, esp. of a broadcast or published story. [Anglo-French *estaler* fix]

instance /'ɪnst(ə)ns/ *–n.* **1** example or illustration of. **2** particular case (*that's not true in this instance*). *–v.* (**-cing**) cite as an instance. □ **for instance** as an example. **in the first** (or **second** etc.) **instance** in the first (or second etc.) place; at the first (or second etc.) stage (of a proceeding). [French from Latin *instantia* contrary example]

instant *–adj.* **1** occurring immediately. **2** (of food etc.) processed for quick preparation. **3** urgent; pressing. **4** *Commerce* of the current month (*the 6th instant*). *–n.* **1** precise moment (*come here this instant*). **2** short space of time (*in an instant*). [Latin *insto* be urgent]

instantaneous /ˌɪnstən'teɪnɪəs/ *adj.* occurring or done in an instant. □ **instantaneously** *adv.*

instantly *adv.* immediately; at once.

instead /ɪn'sted/ *adv.* **1** (foll. by *of*) in place of. **2** as an alternative.

instep *n.* **1** inner arch of the foot between the toes and the ankle. **2** part of a shoe etc. over or under this. [ultimately from IN-[2], STEP]

instigate /'ɪnstɪˌgeɪt/ *v.* (**-ting**) **1** bring about by incitement or persuasion. **2** urge on, incite. □ **instigation** /-'geɪʃ(ə)n/ *n.* **instigator** *n.* [Latin *stigo* prick]

instil /ɪn'stɪl/ *v.* (*US* **instill**) (**-ll-**) (often foll. by *into*) **1** introduce (a feeling, idea, etc.) into a person's mind etc. gradually. **2** put (a liquid) into something in drops. □ **instillation** /-'leɪʃ(ə)n/ *n.* **instilment** *n.* [Latin *stillo* drop]

instinct *–n.* /'ɪnstɪŋkt/ **1 a** innate pattern of behaviour, esp. in animals. **b** innate impulse. **2** intuition. *–predic. adj.* /ɪn'stɪŋkt/ (foll. by *with*) imbued, filled (with life, beauty, etc.). □ **instinctive** /-'stɪŋktɪv/ *adj.* **instinctively** /-'stɪŋktɪvlɪ/ *adv.* **instinctual** /-'stɪŋktjʊəl/ *adj.* [Latin *stinguo* prick]

institute /'ɪnstɪˌtjuːt/ *–n.* **1** society or organization for the promotion of science, education, etc. **2** its premises. *–v.* (**-ting**) **1** establish; found. **2** initiate (an inquiry etc.). **3** (usu. foll. by *to*, *into*) appoint (a person) as a cleric in a church etc. [Latin *statuo* set up]

♦ **Institute cargo clauses** *n.pl.* clauses issued by the Institute of London Underwriters that are added to standard marine insurance policies for cargo to widen or restrict the cover given. Each clause has a wording agreed by a committee of insurance companies and Lloyd's underwriters. By attaching particular clauses to the policy the insurers are able to create an individual policy to suit the clients' requirements.

♦ **Institute of Actuaries** *n.* one of the two professional bodies in the UK to which actuaries belong. To become an actuary it is necessary to qualify as a fellow of one or the other. The Institute is in London; the other organization, the **Faculty of Actuaries**, is based in Edinburgh.

♦ **Institute of Chartered Accountants** *n.* any of the three professional accountancy bodies in the UK, the **Institute of Chartered Accountants in England and Wales**, the **Institute of Chartered Accountants of Scotland**, and the **Institute of Chartered Accountants in Ireland**. The institutes are separate but recognize similar codes of practice. The largest is the England and Wales institute, with some 90 000 members, who are identified by the letters ACA or FCA (as are members of the Ireland institute; in Scotland members use the letters CA). The institutes ensure high standards of education and training in accountancy, provide qualification by examination, and supervise professional conduct in the service of clients and of the public. They are members of the Consultative Committee of Accountancy Bodies, whose Accounting Standards Committee is responsible for drafting accounting standards.

♦ **Institute of Chartered Secretaries and Administrators** *n.* (also **ICSA**) professional body for secretaries and administrators in the UK. Founded in 1891 and granted a Royal Charter in 1902, the institute represents members' interests to government bodies on such matters as company law; publishes journals, reports, pamphlets, and papers; promotes the professional standing of members; and conducts the education and examination of members.

♦ **Institute of Directors** *n.* (also **IoD**) institution, founded in 1903 and granted a Royal Charter in 1906, which any director of a UK company can apply to join. A non-political organization, it aims to further the cause of free enterprise and to assist its members in the functions of leadership throughout industry and commerce.

♦ **Institute of London Underwriters** *n.* (also **ILU**) association of UK insurance companies that cooperate with each other in providing a market for marine insurance and aviation insurance. Although Lloyd's underwriters are not members of the institute, the two organizations work closely with each other. The ILU appoints agents to settle claims, provides certificates of insurance for cargo shippers insured by members, and is responsible for drawing up its own insurance contracts for the use of members. See also INSTITUTE CARGO CLAUSES.

♦ **Institute of Management Services** *n.* (also **IMS**) institution, founded in 1941, that is the professional and qualifying body for people in management services. Its main aims are to create and maintain professional standards for the practice of management services; to provide a system of qualifying examinations; and to encourage research and development in management services.

♦ **Institute of Marketing** *n.* association founded in 1911 to develop knowledge about marketing, to provide services for members and registered students in the field of marketing, and to promote the principles and practices of marketing throughout industry.

♦ **Institute of Personnel Management** *n.* (also **IPM**) professional organization for personnel managers in the UK, founded in 1913. The Institute, an independent and non-political body, aims to encourage and assist the development of personnel management by promoting investigation and research and establishing standards of qualification and performance.

♦ **Institute of Practitioners in Advertising** *n.* (also **IPA**) professional organization, established in 1917, for UK advertising agencies. Its members handle some 95% of all UK advertising.

♦ **Institute of Public Relations** *n.* (also **IPR**) professional organization, established in 1948, for UK public relations consultancies. It is the largest in Europe.

♦ **Institute of Sales Promotion** *n.* (also **ISP**) professional organization for UK sales-promotion agencies. Its purpose is to raise the status of the role of sales promotion in the UK. The Institute was formed in 1978, following the reorganization of the Sales Promotion Executives Association, itself founded in 1969.

---

institution /ˌɪnstɪ'tjuːʃ(ə)n/ *n.* **1 a** organization or society founded for a particular purpose. **b** = INSTITUTIONAL INVESTOR. **2** established law, practice, or custom. **3** *colloq.* (of a person etc.) familiar object. **4** instituting or being instituted.

institutional *adj.* **1** of or like an institution. **2** typical of institutions. □ **institutionally** *adv.*

♦ **institutional investor** *n.* (also **institution**) large organization, e.g. an insurance company, unit trust, bank, trade union, or a pension fund of a large company, that has substantial sums of money to invest on a stock exchange, usu. in the UK, in both gilts and equities. Institutions usu. employ their own investment analysts and advisers; they are usu. able to influence stock exchange sentiment more profoundly than private investors and their policies can often affect share prices. Because institutions can build up significant holdings in companies, they can also influence company policy, usu. by making their opinions known at shareholders' meetings, esp. during take-over negotiations.

institutionalize *v.* (also **-ise**) (**-zing** or **-sing**) **1** (as **institutionalized** *adj.*) made dependent after a long period in an institution. **2** place or keep (a person) in an institution. **3** make institutional.

instruct /ɪn'strʌkt/ *v.* **1** teach (a person) a subject etc.; train. **2** (usu. foll. by *to* + infin.) direct; command. **3** *Law* **a** employ (a lawyer). **b** inform. □ **instructor** *n.* [Latin *instruo -struct-* build, teach]

instruction /ɪn'strʌkʃ(ə)n/ *n.* **1** (often in *pl.*) **a** order. **b** direction (as to how a thing works etc.). **2** teaching (*course of instruction*). **3** see MACHINE INSTRUCTION. □ **instructional** *adj.*

instruction set *n.* all the instructions that a particular computer is capable of performing. See MACHINE INSTRUCTION.

instructive /ɪn'strʌktɪv/ *adj.* tending to instruct; enlightening.

instrument /'ɪnstrəmənt/ *n.* **1** tool or implement, esp. for delicate or scientific work. **2** (in full **musical instrument**) device for producing musical sounds. **3 a** thing used in performing an action. **b** person made use of. **4** measuring-device, esp. in an aeroplane. **5** *Econ.* tool used by a government in achieving its macroeconomic targets. For example, interest rates and the money supply may be considered instruments in the pursuit of stable prices, while government expenditure and taxation may be considered instruments in the pursuit of full employment. **6** formal, esp. legal, document. See also NEGOTIABLE INSTRUMENT. [Latin *instrumentum*: related to INSTRUCT]

instrumental /,ɪnstrə'ment(ə)l/ *adj.* **1** serving as an instrument or means. **2** (of music) performed on instruments. **3** of, or arising from, an instrument (*instrumental error*).

instrumentalist *n.* performer on a musical instrument.

instrumentality /,ɪnstrəmen'tælɪtɪ/ *n.* agency or means.

instrumentation /,ɪnstrəmen'teɪʃ(ə)n/ *n.* **1 a** provision or use of instruments. **b** instruments collectively. **2 a** arrangement of music for instruments. **b** the particular instruments used in a piece.

Inst.SMM *abbr.* Institute of Sales and Marketing Management.

insubordinate /,ɪnsə'bɔːdɪnət/ *adj.* disobedient; rebellious. □ **insubordination** /-'neɪʃ(ə)n/ *n.*

insubstantial /,ɪnsəb'stænʃ(ə)l/ *adj.* **1** lacking solidity or substance. **2** not real.

insufferable /ɪn'sʌfərəb(ə)l/ *adj.* **1** intolerable. **2** unbearably conceited etc. □ **insufferably** *adv.*

insufficient /,ɪnsə'fɪʃ(ə)nt/ *adj.* not sufficient; inadequate. □ **insufficiency** *n.* **insufficiently** *adv.*

insular /'ɪnsjʊlə(r)/ *adj.* **1 a** of or like an island. **b** separated or remote. **2** narrow-minded. □ **insularity** /-'lærɪtɪ/ *n.* [Latin *insula* island]

insulate /'ɪnsjʊ,leɪt/ *v.* (**-ting**) **1** prevent the passage of electricity, heat, or sound from (a thing, room, etc.) by interposing non-conductors. **2** isolate. □ **insulation** /-'leɪʃ(ə)n/ *n.* **insulator** *n.* [Latin *insula* island]

insulin /'ɪnsjʊlɪn/ *n.* hormone regulating the amount of glucose in the blood, the lack of which causes diabetes. [Latin *insula* island]

insult –*v.* /ɪn'sʌlt/ **1** speak to or treat with scornful abuse. **2** offend the self-respect or modesty of. –*n.* /'ɪnsʌlt/ insulting remark or action. □ **insulting** *adj.* **insultingly** *adv.* [Latin *insulto* leap on, assail]

insuperable /ɪn'suːpərəb(ə)l/ *adj.* **1** (of a barrier) impossible to surmount. **2** (of a difficulty etc.) impossible to overcome. □ **insuperability** /-'bɪlɪtɪ/ *n.* **insuperably** *adv.* [Latin *supero* overcome]

insupportable /,ɪnsə'pɔːtəb(ə)l/ *adj.* **1** unable to be endured. **2** unjustifiable.

♦ **insurable interest** *n.* legal right to enter into an insurance contract. A person is said to have an insurable interest if the event insured against could cause that person a financial loss. For example, anyone may insure their own property as they would incur a loss if an item was lost, destroyed, or damaged. If no financial loss would occur, no insurance can be arranged. The limit of an insurable interest is the value of the item concerned, although there is no limit on the amount of life assurance because the financial effects of death cannot be accurately measured. Insurable interest was made a condition of all insurance by the Life Assurance Act (1774). Without an insurable interest, an insured person is unable to enforce an insurance contract (or life-assurance contract) as it is the insurable interest that distinguishes insurance from a bet or wager.

♦ **insurable risk** see RISK *n.* 1.

♦ **insurance** /ɪn'ʃʊərəns/ *n.* **1 a** provision of financial protection in the event of specified happenings. In an insurance contract an insurer promises to pay a specified amount to another party, the insured, if a particular event (known as the peril) happens and the insured suffers a financial loss as a result. The insured's part of the contract is to promise to pay an amount of money (the **insurance premium**), either once or at regular intervals. In order for an insurance contract to be valid, the insured must have an insurable interest. It is usual to use the word 'insurance' to cover events (e.g. a fire) that may or may not happen, whereas 'assurance' refers to an event (e.g. death) that must occur at some time. See ACCIDENT INSURANCE; FIRE INSURANCE; HOLIDAY AND TRAVEL INSURANCE; HOUSEHOLD INSURANCE; LIABILITY INSURANCE; LIFE ASSURANCE; LIVESTOCK AND BLOODSTOCK INSURANCE; MARINE INSURANCE; MOTOR INSURANCE; PLUVIAL INSURANCE; PRIVATE HEALTH INSURANCE; PROPERTY INSURANCE. **b** = INSURANCE POLICY. **2 a** insurance premium. **b** sum paid out as compensation for theft, damage, etc. [French: related to ENSURE]

♦ **insurance broker** *n.* person who is registered with the Insurance Brokers Registration Council to offer advice on all insurance matters and arrange cover, on behalf of the client, with an insurer. An insurance broker's income comes from commission paid by insurers, usu. in the form of an agreed percentage of the first premium or on subsequent premiums. See also LLOYD'S.

♦ **Insurance Brokers Registration Council** *n.* statutory body established under the Insurance Brokers Registration Act (1977). It is responsible for the registration and training of insurance brokers and for laying down rules relating to such matters as accounting practice, staff qualifications, advertising, and the orderly conduct and discipline of broking businesses.

♦ **Insurance Ombudsman** *n.* = FINANCIAL OMBUDSMAN 3.

♦ **insurance policy** *n.* document that sets out the terms and conditions of an insurance contract, stating the benefits payable and the premium required. See INSURANCE 1a; LIFE ASSURANCE.

♦ **insurance premium** see INSURANCE 1a.

♦ **insurance tied agent** *n.* agent who represents a particular insurance company or companies. In life and pensions insurance, a tied agent represents only one insurer and is only able to advise the public on the policies offered by that one company. In general insurance (motor, household, holiday, etc.), a tied agent represents no more than six insurers, who are jointly responsible for the financial consequences of any failure or mistake the agent makes. In both cases the agent receives a commission for each policy that is sold and a further commission on each subsequent renewal of the policy. The commission is calculated as an agreed percentage of the total premium paid by the policyholder. The distinction between the two forms of insurance tied agent was a consequence of the Financial Services Act (1987) and the General Insurance Selling Code (1989) of the Association of British Insurers.

insure /ɪn'ʃʊə(r)/ *v.* (**-ring**) (often foll. by *against*; also *absol.*) secure compensation in the event of loss or damage to (property, life, a person, etc.) by advance regular payments. [var. of ENSURE]

◆ **insured** *n.* (usu. prec. by *the*) person or company covered by an insurance policy. See also ASSURED *n.*

insurer *n.* person, company, or syndicate that underwrites an insurance risk.

insurgent /ɪn'sɜːdʒ(ə)nt/ *–adj.* in active revolt. *–n.* rebel. □ **insurgence** *n.* [Latin *surgo surrect-* rise]

insurmountable /ˌɪnsə'maʊntəb(ə)l/ *adj.* unable to be surmounted or overcome.

insurrection /ˌɪnsə'rekʃ(ə)n/ *n.* rebellion. □ **insurrectionist** *n.* [Latin: related to INSURGENT]

insusceptible /ˌɪnsə'septɪb(ə)l/ *adj.* not susceptible.

intact /ɪn'tækt/ *adj.* **1** undamaged; entire. **2** untouched. □ **intactness** *n.* [Latin *tango tact-* touch]

intaglio /ɪn'tɑːlɪəʊ/ *n.* (*pl.* **-s**) **1** gem with an incised design. **2** engraved design. [Italian: related to IN-², TAIL²]

intake *n.* **1** action of taking in. **2 a** number (of people etc.), or amount, taken in or received. **b** such people etc. (*this year's intake*). **3** place where water is taken into a pipe, or fuel or air enters an engine etc.

intangible /ɪn'tændʒɪb(ə)l/ *–adj.* **1** unable to be touched. **2** unable to be grasped mentally. *–n.* thing that cannot be precisely assessed or defined. □ **intangibility** /-'bɪlɪtɪ/ *n.* **intangibly** *adv.* [Latin: related to INTACT]

◆ **intangible asset** *n.* (also **invisible asset**) asset that can neither be seen nor touched and whose value cannot be precisely assessed. The most common of these are goodwill, patents, trade marks, and copyrights. While goodwill is called either an intangible asset or an invisible asset, such assets as insurance policies and less tangible overseas investments are usu. described as invisible.

integer /'ɪntɪdʒə(r)/ *n.* whole number, possibly with a negative value, or zero. [Latin, = untouched, whole]

integral /'ɪntɪgr(ə)l/ *–adj.* also /-'teg-/ **1 a** of or necessary to a whole. **b** forming a whole. **c** complete. **2** of or denoted by an integer. *–n. Math.* quantity of which a given function is the derivative. □ **integrally** *adv.* [Latin: related to INTEGER]

■ **Usage** The alternative pronunciation given for the adjective, stressed on the second syllable, is considered incorrect by some people.

integral calculus *n.* mathematics concerned with finding integrals, their properties and application, etc.

integrate /'ɪntɪˌgreɪt/ *v.* (**-ting**) **1 a** combine (parts) into a whole. **b** complete by the addition of parts. **2** bring or come into equal membership of society, a school, etc. **3** desegregate, esp. racially (a school etc.). **4** *Math.* calculate the integral of.

integrated circuit *n.* (also **IC**) complete electronic circuit that is manufactured as a single package: all the individual devices (mainly transistors and diodes) required to realize the function of the circuit are fabricated on a single chip of semiconductor, usu. silicon. As the fabrication technologies have advanced, ICs have become cheaper, with improved performance and reliability. In addition, the number of components that can be fabricated on a single chip is continuously and rapidly increasing.

◆ **integrated software** *n.* group of computer programs that are coordinated into a compatible interrelated whole, usu. one in which word-processing, database, spreadsheet, graphics, and communications programs are integrated into one package. It is possible to transfer data between the programs. For example, data produced by the spreadsheet can be transferred to the graphics program and output as a chart, and data from the database can be incorporated into a letter produced using the word processor.

◆ **integration** /ɪntɪ'greɪʃ(ə)n/ *n.* **1** bringing or coming together. **2** combination; amalgamation. **3** combination of two or more companies under the same control for their mutual benefit, by reducing competition, saving costs by reducing overheads, capturing a larger market share, pooling technical or financial resources, cooperating on research and development, etc. In **horizontal** (or **lateral**) **integration** the businesses carry out the same stage in the production process or produce similar products or services; they are therefore competitors. In a monopoly, horizontal integration is complete, while in an oligopoly there is considerable horizontal integration. In **vertical integration** a company obtains control of its suppliers (sometimes called **backward integration**) or of the concerns that buy its products or services (**forward integration**). **4** *Math.* process of integrating.

integrity /ɪn'tegrɪtɪ/ *n.* **1** moral excellence; honesty. **2** wholeness; soundness. **3** (of computer data) measure of the correctness of data following processing. For data to have integrity, it should not have been accidentally altered or destroyed during processing by errors arising in the hardware or software of the system. (Neither should it have been deliberately altered or destroyed by an unauthorized person.) To protect against such errors, copies of the data are usu. organized on a regular basis. [Latin: related to INTEGER]

integument /ɪn'tegjʊmənt/ *n.* natural outer covering, as a skin, husk, rind, etc. [Latin *tego* cover]

intellect /'ɪntəˌlekt/ *n.* **1 a** faculty of reasoning, knowing, and thinking. **b** understanding. **2** clever or knowledgeable person. [Latin: related to INTELLIGENT]

intellectual /ˌɪntə'lektʃʊəl/ *–adj.* **1** of or appealing to the intellect. **2** possessing a highly developed intellect. **3** requiring the intellect. *–n.* intellectual person. □ **intellectuality** /-'ælɪtɪ/ *n.* **intellectualize** *v.* (also **-ise**) (**-zing** or **-sing**). **intellectually** *adv.*

◆ **intellectual property** *n.* intangible asset, such as a copyright, patent, or trade mark. See also ROYALTY 3.

intelligence /ɪn'telɪdʒ(ə)ns/ *n.* **1 a** intellect; understanding. **b** quickness of understanding. **2 a** the collecting of information, esp. of military or political value. **b** information so collected. **c** people employed in this.

intelligence quotient *n.* number denoting the ratio of a person's intelligence to the average.

intelligent *adj.* **1** having or showing intelligence, esp. of a high level. **2** clever. **3** *Computing* **a** having a built-in capability to store and manipulate data. **b** able to modify action in the light of ongoing events. □ **intelligently** *adv.* [Latin *intelligo -lect-* understand]

◆ **intelligent knowledge-based system** *n.* = EXPERT SYSTEM.

intelligentsia /ˌɪntelɪ'dʒentsɪə/ *n.* class of intellectuals regarded as possessing culture and political initiative. [Russian *intelligentsiya*]

intelligent terminal see TERMINAL *n.* 5.

intelligible /ɪn'telɪdʒɪb(ə)l/ *adj.* able to be understood. □ **intelligibility** /-'bɪlɪtɪ/ *n.* **intelligibly** *adv.*

intemperate /ɪn'tempərət/ *adj.* **1** immoderate. **2 a** given to excessive drinking of alcohol. **b** excessively indulgent in one's appetites. □ **intemperance** *n.*

intend /ɪn'tend/ *v.* **1** have as one's purpose (*we intend to go*; *we intend going*). **2** (usu. foll. by *for, as*) design or destine (a person or a thing) (*I intend him to go*; *I intend it as a warning*). [Latin *tendo* stretch]

intended –*adj.* done on purpose. –*n. colloq.* one's fiancé or fiancée.

intense /ɪn'tens/ *adj.* (**intenser, intensest**) **1** existing in a high degree; violent; forceful; extreme (*intense joy*; *intense cold*). **2** very emotional. □ **intensely** *adv.* **intenseness** *n.* [Latin *intensus* stretched]

■ **Usage** *Intense* is sometimes confused with *intensive*, and wrongly used to describe a course of study etc.

intensifier /ɪn'tensɪˌfaɪə(r)/ *n.* **1** thing that makes something more intense. **2** word or prefix used to give force or emphasis, e.g. *thundering* in *a thundering nuisance*.

intensify *v.* (**-ies, -ied**) make or become intense or more intense. □ **intensification** /-fɪ'keɪʃ(ə)n/ *n.*

intensity *n.* (*pl.* **-ies**) **1** intenseness. **2** amount of some quality, e.g. force, brightness, etc.

intensive *adj.* **1** thorough, vigorous; directed to a single point, area, or subject (*intensive study*; *intensive bombardment*). **2** of or relating to intensity. **3** serving to increase production in relation to costs (*intensive farming*). **4** (usu. in *comb.*) *Econ.* making much use of (*labour-intensive*). **5** (of an adjective, adverb, etc.) expressing intensity, as *really* in *my feet are really cold.* □ **intensively** *adv.* **intensiveness** *n.*

■ **Usage** See note at *intense.*

intensive care *n.* **1** constant monitoring etc. of a seriously ill patient. **2** part of a hospital devoted to this.

♦ **intensive distribution** *n.* distribution-of-products strategy in which the maximum number of wholesale and retail outlets are encouraged to stock such products as sweets, soft drinks, and camera films, to provide maximum brand exposure and convenience for consumers.

intent /ɪn'tent/ –*n.* intention; purpose (*with intent to defraud*). –*adj.* **1** (usu. foll. by *on*) **a** resolved, determined. **b** attentively occupied. **2** (esp. of a look) earnest; eager. □ **to all intents and purposes** practically; virtually. □ **intently** *adv.* **intentness** *n.* [Latin *intentus*]

intention /ɪn'tenʃ(ə)n/ *n.* **1** thing intended; aim, purpose. **2** intending (*done without intention*).

intentional *adj.* done on purpose. □ **intentionally** *adv.*

inter /ɪn'tɜː(r)/ *v.* (**-rr-**) bury (a corpse etc.). [Latin *terra* earth]

inter- *comb. form* **1** between, among (*intercontinental*). **2** mutually, reciprocally (*interbreed*). [Latin *inter* between, among]

♦ **inter-account dealing** *n.* speculative transactions on the London Stock Exchange in which all individual purchases and sales within an account cancel each other out, so that only differences have to be settled. See also CASH AND NEW.

interact /ˌɪntər'ækt/ *v.* act on each other. □ **interaction** *n.*

interactive *adj.* **1** reciprocally active. **2** (of a computer or other electronic device) allowing a two-way flow of information between it and a user. The response by a computer to a user's instructions (fed in using a keyboard, mouse, etc.) usu. occurs sufficiently rapidly that the user can work almost continuously. □ **interactively** *adv.*

inter alia /ˌɪntər 'eɪlɪə/ *adv.* among other things. [Latin]

♦ **interbank market** *n.* **1** part of the London money market in which banks lend to each other and to other large financial institutions. The London Inter Bank Offered Rate (LIBOR) is the rate of interest charged on interbank loans. **2** market between banks in foreign currencies, including spot currencies and forward options.

interbreed /ˌɪntə'briːd/ *v.* (*past* and *past part.* **-bred**) **1** (cause to) breed with members of a different race or species to produce a hybrid. **2** breed within one family etc.

intercalary /ɪn'tɜːkələrɪ/ *attrib. adj.* **1 a** (of a day or a month) inserted in the calendar to harmonize it with the solar year. **b** (of a year) having such an addition. **2** interpolated. [Latin *calo* proclaim]

intercede /ˌɪntə'siːd/ *v.* (**-ding**) (usu. foll. by *with*) intervene on behalf of another; plead. [Latin: related to CEDE]

intercept /ˌɪntə'sept/ *v.* **1** seize, catch, or stop (a person or thing) going from one place to another. **2** (usu. foll. by *from*) cut off (light etc.). □ **interception** *n.* **interceptive** *adj.* **interceptor** *n.* [Latin *intercipio -cept-* from *capio* take]

intercession /ˌɪntə'seʃ(ə)n/ *n.* interceding. □ **intercessor** *n.* [Latin: related to INTERCEDE]

interchange –*v.* /ˌɪntə'tʃeɪndʒ/ (**-ging**) **1** (of two people) exchange (things) with each other. **2** put each of (two things) in the other's place; alternate. –*n.* /'ɪntəˌtʃeɪndʒ/ **1** (often foll. by *of*) exchange between two people etc. **2** alternation. **3** road junction where traffic streams do not cross.

interchangeable *adj.* that can be interchanged, esp. without affecting the way a thing works. □ **interchangeably** *adv.*

inter-city /ˌɪntə'sɪtɪ/ *adj.* existing or travelling between cities.

intercom /'ɪntəˌkɒm/ *n. colloq.* **1** system of intercommunication by radio or telephone. **2** instrument used in this. [abbreviation]

intercommunicate /ˌɪntəkə'mjuːnɪˌkeɪt/ *v.* (**-ting**) **1** communicate reciprocally. **2** (of rooms etc.) open into each other. □ **intercommunication** /-'keɪʃ(ə)n/ *n.*

intercommunion /ˌɪntəkə'mjuːnɪən/ *n.* **1** mutual communion. **2** mutual action or relationship, esp. between Christian denominations.

interconnect /ˌɪntəkə'nekt/ *v.* connect with each other. □ **interconnection** /-'nekʃ(ə)n/ *n.*

intercontinental /ˌɪntəˌkɒntɪ'nent(ə)l/ *adj.* connecting or travelling between continents.

intercourse /'ɪntəˌkɔːs/ *n.* **1** communication or dealings between individuals, nations, etc. **2** = SEXUAL INTERCOURSE. [Latin: related to COURSE]

♦ **inter-dealer broker** *n.* member of the London Stock Exchange who is only permitted to deal with market makers, rather than the public.

interdenominational /ˌɪntədɪˌnɒmɪ'neɪʃən(ə)l/ *adj.* concerning more than one (religious) denomination.

interdepartmental /ˌɪntəˌdiːpɑːt'ment(ə)l/ *adj.* concerning more than one department.

interdependent /ˌɪntədɪ'pend(ə)nt/ *adj.* dependent on each other. □ **interdependence** *n.*

interdict –*n.* /'ɪntədɪkt/ **1 a** authoritative prohibition. **b** *Sc. Law* = INJUNCTION 2. **2** *RC Ch.* sentence debarring a person, or esp. a place, from ecclesiastical functions and privileges. –*v.* /ˌɪntə'dɪkt/ **1** prohibit (an action). **2** forbid the use of. **3** (usu. foll. by *from* + verbal noun) restrain (a person). **4** (usu. foll. by *to*) forbid (a thing) to a person. □ **interdiction** /-'dɪkʃ(ə)n/ *n.* **interdictory** /-'dɪktərɪ/ *adj.* [Latin *dico* say]

interdisciplinary /ˌɪntəˌdɪsɪ'plɪnərɪ/ *adj.* of or between more than one branch of learning.

interest /'ɪntrəst/ –*n.* **1 a** concern; curiosity (*have no interest in fishing*). **b** quality exciting curiosity etc. (*this book lacks interest*). **2** subject, hobby, etc., in which one is concerned. **3** advantage or profit (*it is in my interest to go*). **4 a** charge made for borrowing a sum of money. **b** money so paid. See also INTEREST RATE. **5 a** thing in which one has a stake or concern (*business interests*). **b** financial stake (in an undertaking etc.). **c** legal concern, title, or right (in property). **6 a** party or group with a common interest (*the brewing interest*). **b** principle or cause with which this is concerned. –*v.* **1** excite the curiosity or attention of. **2** (usu. foll. by *in*) cause (a person) to take a personal interest. **3** (as **interested** *adj.*) having a private interest; not impartial or disinterested. [Latin, = it matters]

♦ **interest arbitrage** *n.* transactions between financial centres in foreign currencies that take advantage of differentials in interest rates between the two centres and the difference between the forward and spot exchange rates. In some circumstances it is possible to make a profit by buying a foreign currency, changing it into the currency of the home market, lending it for a fixed period, and buying back the foreign currency on a forward basis.

♦ **interest cover** *n.* extent to which a company's earnings cover interest paid on its loan capital, usu. expressed as profits before tax divided by the interest due.

---

interesting *adj.* causing curiosity; holding the attention. □ **interestingly** *adv.*

♦ **interest-only mortgage** *n.* mortgage for those who have an asset that can be used to repay the capital at the end of the loan period. During the loan period the borrower pays only the interest on the mortgage.

♦ **interest rate** *n.* charge made for borrowing a sum of money, expressed as a percentage of the total sum loaned, for a stated period of time (usu. one year). Thus, an interest rate of 15% per annum means that for every £100 borrowed for one year, the borrower has to pay a charge of £15, or a charge in proportion for longer or shorter periods. In **simple interest**, the charge is calculated on the sum loaned only, thus $I = Prt$, where I is the interest, P is the principal sum, r is the interest rate, and t is the period. In **compound interest**, the charge is calculated on the sum loaned plus any interest that has accrued in previous periods. In this case $I = P[(1 + r)^n - 1]$, where n is the number of periods for which interest is separately calculated. Thus, if £500 is loaned for 2 years at a rate of 12% per annum, compounded quarterly, the value of n will be $4 \times 2 = 8$ and the value of r will be 12/4 = 3%. Thus, $I = 500[(1.03)^8 - 1]$ = £133.38, whereas on a simple-interest basis it would be only £120. In general, interest rates depend on the money supply, the demand for loans, government policy, the risk of nonrepayment as assessed by the lender, and the period of the loan. In economics, interest has two functions to perform: (i) to make the amount saved by households equal the amount that firms wish to borrow for investment; (ii) to make the amount of credit demanded equal the supply of credit. The interest rate that achieves this equilibrium is known as the **natural rate of interest**. It implies that an actual interest rate below the natural rate will cause a rise in the prices of consumer goods (see TIME PREFERENCE), which will fuel inflation and lead to an inadequate rate of savings. See also INTEREST-RATE POLICY; LOANABLE-FUNDS THEORY; TERM STRUCTURE.

♦ **interest-rate futures** *n.pl.* form of financial futures that enables investors, portfolio managers, borrowers, etc. to obtain protection against future movements in interest rates. Interest-rate futures also enable dealers to speculate on these movements. In the UK, interest-rate futures are dealt in on the London International Financial Futures and Options Exchange, using contracts for three-month sterling, Eurodollars, ecus, etc. in the short term and long gilts, US Treasury bonds, ecu bonds, etc. in the long term.

♦ **interest-rate margin** *n.* **1** amount charged to borrowers over and above the base rate. This margin is the bank's profit on the transaction but has to take account of risk of loss or default by the borrower. **2** difference between the rate at which banks lend and the rate they pay for deposits. It may be a major indicator of banks' profitability.

♦ **interest-rate option** *n.* form of option enabling traders and speculators to hedge themselves against future changes in interest rates.

♦ **interest-rate policy** *n.* policy by which governments influence interest rates through the supply of bonds. Higher rates of interest will discourage investment and reduce the demand for money, giving a downward impetus to both employment and prices. Lower interest rates will have the opposite effect.

♦ **interest-rate swap** *n.* form of dealing between banks, security houses, and companies in which borrowers exchange fixed-interest rates for floating-interest rates, or vice versa. Swaps can be in the same currency or cross-currency.

♦ **interest-sensitive** *adj.* denoting an activity that is sensitive to changes in the general level of interest rates, e.g. consumer goods usu. bought on some form of hire-purchase basis are interest-sensitive because they cost more as interest rates rise.

♦ **interest yield** see YIELD *n.* 2.

---

interface –*n.* **1** surface forming a boundary between two regions. **2** means or place of interaction between two systems etc.; interaction (*the interface between psychology and education*). **3** esp. *Computing* apparatus for connecting two pieces of equipment so that they can be operated jointly, despite differences in the speed of working etc. Several interfaces are classified as **standard interfaces**; these may be developed by, say, a national electronics association or an international body, or they may be industry standards. All the characteristics of a standard interface are in accordance with a set of predetermined values. Use of a standard interface allows computer systems and components from different manufacturers to be interconnected. –*v.* (**-cing**) (often foll. by *with*) **1** connect with (another piece of equipment etc.) by an interface. **2** interact.

■ **Usage** The use of the noun and verb in sense 2 is deplored by some people.

interfacing *n.* stiffish material between two layers of fabric in collars etc.

interfere /ˌɪntəˈfɪə(r)/ *v.* (**-ring**) **1** (usu. foll. by *with*) **a** (of a person) meddle; obstruct a process etc. **b** (of a thing) be a hindrance. **2** (usu. foll. by *in*) intervene, esp. without invitation or necessity. **3** (foll. by *with*) *euphem.* molest or assault sexually. **4** (of light or other waves) combine so as to cause interference. [Latin *ferio* strike]

interference *n.* **1** act of interfering. **2** fading or disturbance of received radio signals. **3** *Physics* combination of two or more wave motions to form a resultant wave in which the displacement is reinforced or cancelled.

interferon /ˌɪntəˈfɪərɒn/ *n.* any of various proteins inhibiting the development of a virus in a cell etc.

interfuse /ˌɪntəˈfjuːz/ *v.* (**-sing**) **1 a** (usu. foll. by *with*) mix (a thing) with; intersperse. **b** blend (things). **2** (of two things) blend with each other. □ **interfusion** /-ˈfjuːʒ(ə)n/ *n.* [Latin: related to FUSE[1]]

intergalactic /ˌɪntəgəˈlæktɪk/ *adj.* of or situated between galaxies.

interim /ˈɪntərɪm/ –*n.* intervening time. –*adj.* provisional, temporary. [Latin, = in the interim]

♦ **interim accounts** see FINAL ACCOUNTS.

♦ **interim dividend** see DIVIDEND 1.

♦ **interim report** *n.* **1** any report other than a final report. **2** *Commerce* report that a company makes halfway through its financial year, setting out the state of its profits for the first half year and in some cases justifying its interim dividend. An interim report is a requirement for a company seeking a quotation on the London Stock Exchange.

---

interior /ɪnˈtɪərɪə(r)/ –*adj.* **1** inner. **2** inland. **3** internal; domestic. **4** (usu. foll. by *to*) situated further in or within. **5** existing in the mind. **6** coming from inside. –*n.* **1** interior part; inside. **2** interior part of a region. **3** home affairs of a country (*Minister of the Interior*). **4** representation of the inside of a room etc. [Latin]

interior decoration *n.* decoration of the interior of a building etc. □ **interior decorator** *n.*

interior design *n.* design of the interior of a building. □ **interior designer** *n.*

interject /ˌɪntəˈdʒekt/ *v.* **1** utter (words) abruptly or parenthetically. **2** interrupt. [Latin *jacio* throw]

interjection /ˌɪntəˈdʒekʃ(ə)n/ *n.* exclamation, esp. as a part of speech (e.g. *ah!*, *dear me!*).

interlace /ˌɪntəˈleɪs/ *v.* (**-cing**) **1** bind intricately together; interweave. **2** cross each other intricately. □ **interlacement** *n.*

Interlaken /ˈɪntəˌlɑːkən/ tourist resort in central Switzerland, chief town of the Bernese Alps; pop. (1980) 4852.

interlard /ˌɪntəˈlɑːd/ *v.* (usu. foll. by *with*) mix (writing or speech) with unusual words or phrases. [French]

interleave /ˌɪntəˈliːv/ *v.* (**-ving**) insert (usu. blank) leaves between the leaves of (a book etc.).

interline /ˌɪntəˈlaɪn/ *v.* (**-ning**) put an extra layer of material between the fabric of (a garment) and its lining.

interlink /ˌɪntəˈlɪŋk/ *v.* link or be linked together.

interlock /ˌɪntəˈlɒk/ *–v.* **1** engage with each other by overlapping. **2** lock or clasp within each other. *–n.* **1** machine-knitted fabric with fine stitches. **2** mechanism for preventing a set of operations from being performed in any but the prescribed sequence.

interlocutor /ˌɪntəˈlɒkjʊtə(r)/ *n. formal* person who takes part in a conversation. [Latin *loquor* speak]

interlocutory *adj. formal* **1** of dialogue. **2** (of a decree etc.) given provisionally in a legal action.

interloper /ˈɪntəˌləʊpə(r)/ *n.* **1** intruder. **2** person who interferes in others' affairs, esp. for profit. [after *landloper* vagabond, from Dutch *loopen* run]

interlude /ˈɪntəˌluːd/ *n.* **1 a** pause between the acts of a play. **b** something performed during this pause. **2** contrasting event, time, etc. in the middle of something (*comic interlude*). **3** piece of music played between other pieces etc. [medieval Latin *ludus* play]

intermarry /ˌɪntəˈmærɪ/ *v.* (**-ies, -ied**) (foll. by *with*) (of races, castes, families, etc.) become connected by marriage. □ **intermarriage** /-rɪdʒ/ *n.*

intermediary /ˌɪntəˈmiːdɪərɪ/ *–n.* (*pl.* **-ies**) **1** intermediate person or thing, esp. a mediator. **2** person or organization that acts as an agent or broker between the parties to a transaction. *–adj.* acting as mediator; intermediate.

intermediate /ˌɪntəˈmiːdɪət/ *–adj.* coming between two things in time, place, order, character, etc. *–n.* **1** intermediate thing. **2** chemical compound formed by one reaction and then used in another. [Latin *intermedius*]

♦ **intermediate good** *n. Econ.* a good in the course of production, therefore neither a raw material nor a finished product.

♦ **intermediation** /ˌɪntəˌmiːdɪˈeɪʃ(ə)n/ *n.* **1** (in the money markets) process of borrowing money at one rate of interest and lending it at a higher rate. **2** activity of a bank or similar financial institution in being an intermediary between two parties to a contract, in which the intermediary accepts all or part of the credit risk or other commercial risks. See also DISINTERMEDIATION.

---

interment /ɪnˈtɜːmənt/ *n.* burial.

■ **Usage** *Interment* is sometimes confused with *internment*, which means 'confinement'.

intermezzo /ˌɪntəˈmetsəʊ/ *n.* (*pl.* **-mezzi** /-tsɪ/ or **-s**) **1 a** short connecting instrumental movement in a musical work. **b** similar independent piece. **2** short light dramatic or other performance inserted between the acts of a play. [Italian]

interminable /ɪnˈtɜːmɪnəb(ə)l/ *adj.* **1** endless. **2** tediously long. □ **interminably** *adv.*

intermingle /ˌɪntəˈmɪŋg(ə)l/ *v.* (**-ling**) mix together; mingle.

intermission /ˌɪntəˈmɪʃ(ə)n/ *n.* **1** pause or cessation. **2** interval in a cinema etc. [Latin: related to INTERMITTENT]

intermittent /ˌɪntəˈmɪt(ə)nt/ *adj.* occurring at intervals; not continuous. □ **intermittently** *adv.* [Latin *mitto miss-* let go]

intermix /ˌɪntəˈmɪks/ *v.* mix together.

intern *–n.* /ˈɪntɜːn/ (also **interne**) *US* = HOUSEMAN. *–v.* /ɪnˈtɜːn/ oblige (a prisoner, alien, etc.) to reside within prescribed limits. □ **internment** *n.* [French: related to INTERNAL]

■ **Usage** *Internment* is sometimes confused with *interment*, which means 'burial'.

internal /ɪnˈtɜːn(ə)l/ *adj.* **1** of or situated in the inside or invisible part. **2** of the inside of the body (*internal injuries*). **3** of a nation's domestic affairs. **4** (of a student) attending a university etc. as well as taking its examinations. **5** used or applying within an organization. **6 a** intrinsic. **b** of the mind or soul. □ **internality** /-ˈnælɪtɪ/ *n.* **internally** *adv.* [medieval Latin *internus* internal]

♦ **internal audit** *n.* audit that an organization carries out on its own behalf, usu. to ensure that its own internal controls are operating satisfactorily. Whereas an external audit is almost always concerned with financial matters, an internal audit may also be concerned with such matters as the observation of the safety and health at work regulations or of the equal opportunities legislation. It may also be used to detect any theft or fraud. See also INTERNAL CONTROL.

---

internal-combustion engine *n.* engine with its motive power generated by the explosion of gases or vapour with air in a cylinder.

♦ **internal control** *n.* **a** any of the measures an organization employs to ensure that opportunities for fraud or misfeasance are minimized. Examples include the requirement of more than one signature on certain documents, security arrangements for stock-handling, division of tasks, keeping of control accounts, use of special passwords for handling computer files, etc. It is one of the principal concerns of an internal audit to ensure that internal controls are working properly so that the external auditors can have faith in the accounts produced by the organization. This should also reassure management of the integrity of its operations. **b** effect of these measures collectively.

---

internal evidence *n.* evidence derived from the contents of the thing discussed.

internalize *v.* (also **-ise**) (**-zing** or **-sing**) *Psychol.* make (attitudes, behaviour, etc.) part of one's nature by learning or by unconscious assimilation. □ **internalization** /-ˈzeɪʃ(ə)n/ *n.*

♦ **internal rate of return** *n.* (also **IRR**) *Econ.* rate of return that discounts the net present value of a project to zero. This is a method used in conjunction with discounted cash flow in order to discover what rate of return on the outlay is represented by the cash flows from the project. If the IRR exceeds the market rate of interest then the project is profitable. The IRR is usu. considered less reliable than the actual net present value as a means of appraising a project. First, if returns in different periods fluctuate from positive to negative, a unique IRR will not exist. Secondly, the IRR tends to favour projects with large returns early on, even if they have a low net present value. See also NET PRESENT VALUE; PAYBACK PERIOD.

♦ **Internal Revenue Service** *n.* (also **IRS**) US federal organization that assesses and collects all personal and business federal taxes.

---

international /ˌɪntəˈnæʃən(ə)l/ *–adj.* **1** existing or carried on between nations. **2** agreed on or used by all or many nations. *–n.* **1 a** contest, esp. in sport, between teams representing different countries. **b** member of such a team. **2** (**International**) any of four successive associations for socialist or Communist action. □ **internationality** /-ˈnælɪtɪ/ *n.* **internationally** *adv.*

♦ **International Bank for Reconstruction and Development** *n.* (also **IBRD**) specialized agency working in coordination with the United Nations, established in 1945 to help finance postwar reconstruction and to help raise standards of living in developing countries, by making loans to governments or guaranteeing outside loans. It lends on broadly commercial terms, either for specific projects or for more general social purposes; funds are raised on the international capital markets. The Bank and its affiliates, the International Development Association and the International Finance Corporation, are often known as the **World Bank**; it is owned by the governments of 151 countries. Members must also be members of the International Monetary Fund. The headquarters of the Bank are in Washington, with offices in Paris and Tokyo.

♦ **International Chamber of Commerce** *n.* (also **ICC**) international business organization that represents business interests in international affairs. Its office is in Paris. See also INCOTERMS.

♦ **International Development Association** *n.* (also **IDA**) affiliate of the International Bank for Reconstruction and Development (IBRD) established in 1960 to provide assistance for poorer developing countries (those with a GNP of less than $835 per head). With the IBRD it is known as the **World Bank**. It is funded by subscription and transfers from the net earnings of IBRD. The headquarters of the IDA are in Washington, with offices in Paris and Tokyo, administered by IBRD staff.

♦ **International Finance Corporation** *n.* (also **IFC**) affiliate of the International Bank for Reconstruction and Development (IBRD) established in 1956 to provide assistance for private investment projects. Although the IFC and IBRD are separate entities, both legally and financially, the IFC is able to borrow from the IBRD and reloan to private investors. The headquarters of the IFC are in Washington. Its importance increased in the 1980s after the emergence of the debt crisis and the subsequent reliance on the private sector.

♦ **International Fund for Agricultural Development** *n.* (also **IFAD**) fund, proposed by the 1974 World Food Conference, that began operations in 1977 with the purpose of providing additional funds for agricultural and rural development in developing countries. The headquarters of the IFAD are in Rome.

---

internationalism *n.* advocacy of a community of interests among nations. □ **internationalist** *n.*

internationalize *v.* (also **-ise**) (**-zing** or **-sing**) **1** make international. **2** bring under the protection or control of two or more nations.

♦ **International Labour Organization** *n.* (also **ILO**) special agency of the United Nations, established under the Treaty of Versailles in 1919, with the aim of promoting lasting peace through social justice. The ILO establishes international labour standards, runs a programme of technical assistance to developing countries, and attacks unemployment through its World Employment Programme. The ILO is financed by contributions from its member states. Its headquarters, the International Labour Office, is in Geneva.

♦ **International Monetary Fund** *n.* (also **IMF**) special agency of the United Nations established in 1945 to promote international monetary cooperation and expand international trade, stabilize exchange rates, and help countries experiencing short-term balance of payments difficulties to maintain their exchange rates. The IMF assists a member by supplying the amount of foreign currency it wishes to purchase in exchange for the equivalent amount of its own currency. The member repays this amount by buying back its own currency in a currency acceptable to the IMF, usu. within three to five years (see also SPECIAL DRAWING RIGHTS). The IMF is financed by subscriptions from its members, the amount determined by an estimate of their means. Voting power is related to the amount of the subscription: the higher the contribution the higher the voting rights. The head office of the IMF is in Washington. See also CONDITIONALITY.

♦ **International Petroleum Exchange** *n.* (also **IPE**) financial exchange, founded in London in 1980, that deals in futures contracts and options (including traded options) in oil (gas oil, Brent crude oil, and heavy fuel oil) with facilities for making an exchange of futures for actuals. It is located in St Katharine Dock and shared with the LONDON COMMODITY EXCHANGE.

♦ **International Standards Organization** *n.* (also **ISO**) organization founded in 1946 to standardize measurements and other standards for industrial, commercial, and scientific purposes. The British Standards Institution is a member.

♦ **International Stock Exchange of the UK and Republic of Ireland Ltd.** (also **ISE**) see LONDON STOCK EXCHANGE.

♦ **International Telecommunication Union** *n.* (also **ITU**) special agency of the United Nations founded in Paris in 1865 as the International Telegraph Union. It sets up international regulations for telegraph, telephone, and radio services; promotes international cooperation for the improvement of telecommunications; and is concerned with the development of technical facilities. It is responsible for the allocation and registration of radio frequencies for communications. Its headquarters are in Geneva.

♦ **International Union of Credit and Investment Insurers** *n.* = BERNE UNION.

---

interne var. of INTERN *n.*

internecine /ˌɪntəˈniːsaɪn/ *adj.* mutually destructive. [Latin *internecinus* deadly]

internee /ˌɪntɜːˈniː/ *n.* person interned.

Internet *n.* international network of computers connected by modems, dedicated lines, telephone cables, satellite links, etc., with associated software controlling the movement of data. It offers facilities for accessing remote databases, transfer of data between computers, ELECTRONIC MAIL, and FAX services. The Internet has been widely exploited for commercial purposes, including electronic shopping, advertising, and marketing research.

interpenetrate /ˌɪntəˈpenɪˌtreɪt/ *v.* (**-ting**) **1** penetrate each other. **2** pervade. □ **interpenetration** /-ˈtreɪʃ(ə)n/ *n.*

interpersonal /ˌɪntəˈpɜːsən(ə)l/ *adj.* between persons, social (*interpersonal skills*).

interplanetary /ˌɪntəˈplænɪtərɪ/ *adj.* **1** between planets. **2** of travel between planets.

interplay /ˈɪntəˌpleɪ/ *n.* reciprocal action.

Interpol /ˈɪntəˌpɒl/ *n.* International Criminal Police Organization. [abbreviation]

interpolate /ɪnˈtɜːpəˌleɪt/ *v.* (**-ting**) **1 a** insert (words) in a book etc., esp. misleadingly. **b** make such insertions in (a book etc.). **2** interject (a remark) in a conversation. **3** estimate (values) between known ones in the same range, usu. on a graph. Cf. EXTRAPOLATE. □ **interpolation** /-ˈleɪʃ(ə)n/ *n.* **interpolator** *n.* [Latin *interpolo* furbish]

interpose /ˌɪntəˈpəʊz/ *v.* (**-sing**) **1** (often foll. by *between*) insert (a thing) between others. **2** say (words) as an interruption; interrupt. **3** exercise or advance (a veto or objection) so as to interfere. **4** (foll. by *between*) intervene (between parties). □ **interposition** /-pəˈzɪʃ(ə)n/ *n.* [Latin *pono* put]

interpret /ɪnˈtɜːprɪt/ *v.* (**-t-**) **1** explain the meaning of (words, a dream, etc.). **2** make out or bring out the meaning of (creative work). **3** act as an interpreter. **4** explain or understand (behaviour etc.) in a specified manner. □ **interpretation** /-ˈteɪʃ(ə)n/ *n.* **interpretative** *adj.* **interpretive** *adj.* [Latin *interpres -pretis* explainer]

interpreter *n.* **1** person who interprets, esp. one who translates foreign speech orally. **2** computer program that converts a program written in a high-level language into a form that can be accepted and executed by a computer; it analyses each line of code in the high-level language program and then carries out the specified actions. In contrast to a compiler, an interpreter does not translate the whole program prior to execution. Program run times are much slower than when a compiler is used.

interracial /ˌɪntəˈreɪʃ(ə)l/ *adj.* between or affecting different races.

interregnum /ˌɪntəˈregnəm/ *n.* (*pl.* **-s**) **1** interval when the normal government or leadership is suspended, esp. between successive reigns or regimes. **2** interval, pause. [Latin *regnum* reign]

interrelate /ˌɪntərɪˈleɪt/ *v.* (**-ting**) **1** relate (two or more things) to each other. **2** (of two or more things) relate to each other. □ **interrelation** *n.* **interrelationship** *n.*

interrogate /ɪnˈterəˌgeɪt/ *v.* (**-ting**) question (a person), esp. closely or formally. □ **interrogation** /-'geɪʃ(ə)n/ *n.* **interrogator** *n.* [Latin *rogo* ask]

interrogative /ˌɪntə'rɒgətɪv/ *–adj.* of, like, or used in a question. *–n.* interrogative word (e.g. *what?*).

interrogatory /ˌɪntə'rɒgətərɪ/ *–adj.* questioning (*interrogatory tone*). *–n.* (*pl.* **-ies**) formal set of questions.

interrupt /ˌɪntə'rʌpt/ *–v.* **1** break the continuous progress of (an action, speech, person speaking, etc.). **2** obstruct (a person's view etc.). *–n. Computing* signal that is sent to a processor, making it suspend its current task and start another. □ **interruption** *n.* [Latin: related to RUPTURE]

interrupter *n.* (also **interruptor**) **1** person or thing that interrupts. **2** device for interrupting, esp. an electric circuit.

intersect /ˌɪntə'sekt/ *v.* **1** divide (a thing) by crossing it. **2** (of lines, roads, etc.) cross each other. [Latin: related to SECTION]

intersection /ˌɪntə'sekʃ(ə)n/ *n.* **1** intersecting. **2** place where two roads intersect. **3** point or line common to lines or planes that intersect.

intersperse /ˌɪntə'spɜːs/ *v.* (**-sing**) **1** (often foll. by *between, among*) scatter. **2** (foll. by *with*) vary (a thing) by scattering other things among it. □ **interspersion** *n.* [Latin: related to SPARSE]

interstate /'ɪntəˌsteɪt/ *adj.* existing or carried on between states, esp. those of the US.

interstellar /ˌɪntə'stelə(r)/ *adj.* between stars.

interstice /ɪn'tɜːstɪs/ *n.* **1** intervening space. **2** chink or crevice. [Latin *interstitium* from *sisto* stand]

interstitial /ˌɪntə'stɪʃ(ə)l/ *adj.* of, forming, or occupying interstices. □ **interstitially** *adv.*

intertwine /ˌɪntə'twaɪn/ *v.* (**-ning**) (often foll. by *with*) entwine (together).

interval /'ɪntəv(ə)l/ *n.* **1** intervening time or space. **2** pause or break, esp. between the parts of a performance. **3** difference in pitch between two sounds. □ **at intervals** here and there; now and then. [Latin *intervallum* space between ramparts]

intervene /ˌɪntə'viːn/ *v.* (**-ning**) **1** occur in time between events. **2** interfere; prevent or modify events. **3** be situated between things. **4** come in as an extraneous factor. [Latin *venio vent-* come]

intervention /ˌɪntə'venʃ(ə)n/ *n.* **1** intervening. **2** interference, esp. by a state. **3** mediation.

interventionist *n.* person who favours intervention.

♦ **intervention price** see COMMON AGRICULTURAL POLICY.

---

interview /'ɪntəˌvjuː/ *–n.* **1** oral examination of an applicant. **2** conversation with a reporter, for a broadcast or publication. **3** meeting face to face, esp. for consultation. *–v.* hold an interview with. □ **interviewee** /-vjuː'iː/ *n.* **interviewer** *n.* [French *entrevue*: related to INTER-, *vue* sight]

♦ ***inter vivos* gift** /'ɪntə 'viːvɒs/ *n.* gift made between living people, which was subject to the former capital-transfer tax. See LIFETIME TRANSFER. [Latin]

---

interwar /ˌɪntə'wɔː(r)/ *attrib. adj.* existing in the period between two wars.

interweave /ˌɪntə'wiːv/ *v.* (**-ving**; *past* **-wove**; *past part.* **-woven**) **1** weave together. **2** blend intimately.

♦ **intestacy** /ɪn'testəsɪ/ *n.* state of a person who has died without having left a will. Intestacy can be either total (if no will is left at all) or partial (if not all the deceased's property is left by will). The Administration of Estates Act contains a table showing the destination of the property in an intestacy. If the intestate has no close relatives but a spouse survives, then the spouse takes everything. If children or grandchildren survive, the spouse takes £40,000 plus a life interest in half of the remaining estate. The children or grandchildren take the rest. If the intestate is survived by a spouse and other close relatives but not by children or grandchildren, the spouse receives £85,000 plus half the rest of the estate, and the remainder goes to the nearest of the surviving relatives. If there are no relatives, the estate goes to the Crown as *bona vacantia*.

---

intestate /ɪn'testeɪt/ *–adj.* not having left a will before death. *–n.* person who has died intestate. [Latin: related to TESTAMENT]

intestine /ɪn'testɪn/ *n.* (in *sing.* or *pl.*) lower part of the alimentary canal. □ **intestinal** *adj.* [Latin *intus* within]

♦ **in-the-money option** see INTRINSIC VALUE 2.

---

intifada /ˌɪntɪ'fɑːdə/ *n.* Arab uprising. [Arabic]

intimacy /'ɪntɪməsɪ/ *n.* (*pl.* **-ies**) **1** state of being intimate. **2** intimate remark or act; sexual intercourse.

intimate[1] /'ɪntɪmət/ *–adj.* **1** closely acquainted; familiar (*intimate friend*). **2** private and personal. **3** (usu. foll. by *with*) having sexual relations. **4** (of knowledge) detailed, thorough. **5** (of a relationship between things) close. *–n.* close friend. □ **intimately** *adv.* [Latin *intimus* inmost]

intimate[2] /'ɪntɪˌmeɪt/ *v.* (**-ting**) **1** (often foll. by *that*) state or make known. **2** imply, hint. □ **intimation** /-'meɪʃ(ə)n/ *n.* [Latin *intimo* announce: related to INTIMATE[1]]

intimidate /ɪn'tɪmɪˌdeɪt/ *v.* (**-ting**) frighten or overawe, esp. to subdue or influence. □ **intimidation** /-'deɪʃ(ə)n/ *n.* [medieval Latin: related to TIMID]

into /'ɪntʊ, 'ɪntə/ *prep.* **1** expressing motion or direction to a point on or within (*walked into a tree*; *ran into the house*). **2** expressing direction of attention etc. (*will look into it*). **3** expressing a change of state (*turned into a dragon*; *separated into groups*). **4** after the beginning of (*five minutes into the game*). **5** *colloq.* interested in. [Old English: related to IN, TO]

intolerable /ɪn'tɒlərəb(ə)l/ *adj.* that cannot be endured. □ **intolerably** *adv.*

intolerant /ɪn'tɒlərənt/ *adj.* not tolerant, esp. of others' beliefs or behaviour. □ **intolerance** *n.*

intonation /ˌɪntə'neɪʃ(ə)n/ *n.* **1** modulation of the voice; accent. **2** intoning. **3** accuracy of musical pitch. [medieval Latin: related to INTONE]

intone /ɪn'təʊn/ *v.* (**-ning**) **1** recite (prayers etc.) with prolonged sounds, esp. in a monotone. **2** utter with a particular tone. [medieval Latin: related to IN-[2]]

in toto /ɪn 'təʊtəʊ/ *adv.* completely. [Latin]

intoxicant /ɪn'tɒksɪkənt/ *–adj.* intoxicating. *–n.* intoxicating substance.

intoxicate /ɪn'tɒksɪˌkeɪt/ *v.* (**-ting**) **1** make drunk. **2** excite or elate beyond self-control. □ **intoxication** /-'keɪʃ(ə)n/ *n.* [medieval Latin: related to TOXIC]

intra- *prefix* on the inside, within. [Latin *intra* inside]

intractable /ɪn'træktəb(ə)l/ *adj.* **1** hard to control or deal with. **2** difficult, stubborn. □ **intractability** /-'bɪlɪtɪ/ *n.* **intractably** *adv.*

intramural /ˌɪntrə'mjʊər(ə)l/ *adj.* **1** situated or done within the walls of an institution etc. **2** forming part of normal university etc. studies. □ **intramurally** *adv.* [Latin *murus* wall]

intramuscular /ˌɪntrə'mʌskjʊlə(r)/ *adj.* in or into muscle tissue.

intransigent /ɪn'trænsɪdʒ(ə)nt/ *–adj.* uncompromising, stubborn. *–n.* intransigent person. □ **intransigence** *n.* [Spanish *los intransigentes* extremists]

intransitive /ɪn'trænsɪtɪv/ *adj.* (of a verb) not taking a direct object.

♦ **intrapreneur** /ˌɪntrəprə'nɜː/ *n.* executive within a large organization who uses the entrepreneurial approach to management by risk-taking, building up separate profit centres, intra-group trading, etc.

---

intra-uterine /ˌɪntrə'juːtəˌraɪn/ *adj.* within the womb.

intravenous /ˌɪntrə'viːnəs/ *adj.* in or into a vein or veins. □ **intravenously** *adv.*

in-tray *n.* tray for incoming documents.

intrepid /ɪn'trepɪd/ *adj.* fearless; very brave. □ **intrepidity** /-trɪ'pɪdɪtɪ/ *n.* **intrepidly** *adv.* [Latin *trepidus* alarmed]

intricate /ˈɪntrɪkət/ *adj.* very complicated; perplexingly detailed. □ **intricacy** /-kəsɪ/ *n.* (*pl.* **-ies**). **intricately** *adv.* [Latin: related to IN-[2], *tricae* tricks]

intrigue –*v.* /ɪnˈtriːg/ (**-gues, -gued, -guing**) **1** (foll. by *with*) **a** carry on an underhand plot. **b** use secret influence. **2** arouse the curiosity of. –*n.* /ˈɪntriːg/ **1** underhand plot or plotting. **2** secret arrangement (*amorous intrigues*). □ **intriguing** *adj.* esp. in sense 2 of *v.* **intriguingly** *adv.* [French from Italian *intrigo*]

intrinsic /ɪnˈtrɪnzɪk/ *adj.* inherent, essential (*intrinsic power*). □ **intrinsically** *adv.* [Latin *intrinsecus* inwardly]

♦ **intrinsic value** *n.* **1** value something has because of its nature, before it has been processed in any way. **2** difference between the market value of the underlying security in a traded option and the exercise price. An option with an intrinsic value is said to be **in the money**; an option with zero intrinsic value is **at the money**; one with less intrinsic value than zero is **out of the money**. See also TIME VALUE.

---

intro /ˈɪntrəʊ/ *n.* (*pl.* **-s**) *colloq.* introduction. [abbreviation]

intro- *comb. form* into. [Latin]

introduce /ˌɪntrəˈdjuːs/ *v.* (**-cing**) **1** (foll. by *to*) make (a person or oneself) known by name to another, esp. formally. **2** announce or present to an audience. **3** bring (a custom etc.) into use. **4** bring (legislation) before Parliament etc. **5** (foll. by *to*) initiate (a person) in a subject. **6** insert. **7** bring in; usher in; bring forward. **8** occur just before the start of. **9** put on sale for the first time. □ **introducible** *adj.* [Latin *duco* lead]

introduction /ˌɪntrəˈdʌkʃ(ə)n/ *n.* **1** introducing or being introduced. **2** formal presentation of one person to another. **3** explanatory section at the beginning of a book etc. **4** introductory treatise. **5** method of issuing shares on the London Stock Exchange in which a broker or issuing house takes small quantities of the company's shares and issues them to clients at opportune moments. It is also used by existing public companies that wish to issue additional shares. Cf. ISSUE BY TENDER; OFFER FOR SALE; PLACING; PUBLIC ISSUE. **6** thing introduced.

introductory /ˌɪntrəˈdʌktərɪ/ *adj.* serving as an introduction; preliminary.

introit /ˈɪntrɔɪt/ *n.* psalm or antiphon sung or said as the priest approaches the altar for the Eucharist. [Latin *introitus* entrance]

introspection /ˌɪntrəˈspekʃ(ə)n/ *n.* examination of one's own thoughts. □ **introspective** *adj.* [Latin *specio spect-* look]

introvert /ˈɪntrəˌvɜːt/ –*n.* **1** person predominantly concerned with his or her own thoughts. **2** shy thoughtful person. –*adj.* (also **introverted**) characteristic of an introvert. □ **introversion** /-ˈvɜːʃ(ə)n/ *n.*

intrude /ɪnˈtruːd/ *v.* (**-ding**) (foll. by *on, upon, into*) **1** come uninvited or unwanted. **2** force on a person. [Latin *trudo trus-* thrust]

intruder *n.* person who intrudes, esp. a trespasser.

intrusion /ɪnˈtruːʒ(ə)n/ *n.* **1** intruding. **2** influx of molten rock between existing strata etc. □ **intrusive** *adj.*

intrust var. of ENTRUST.

intuition /ˌɪntjuːˈɪʃ(ə)n/ *n.* immediate insight or understanding without conscious reasoning. □ **intuit** /ɪnˈtjuːɪt/ *v.* **intuitional** *adj.* [Latin *tueor tuit-* look]

intuitive /ɪnˈtjuːɪtɪv/ *adj.* of, possessing, or perceived by intuition. □ **intuitively** *adv.* **intuitiveness** *n.* [medieval Latin: related to INTUITION]

Inuit /ˈɪnʊɪt/ *n.* (also **Innuit**) (*pl.* same or **-s**) North American Eskimo. [Eskimo *inuit* people]

inundate /ˈɪnʌnˌdeɪt/ *v.* (**-ting**) (often foll. by *with*) **1** flood. **2** overwhelm. □ **inundation** /-ˈdeɪʃ(ə)n/ *n.* [Latin *unda* wave]

inure /ɪˈnjʊə(r)/ *v.* (**-ring**) **1** (often in *passive*; foll. by *to*) accustom (a person) to an esp. unpleasant thing. **2** *Law* take effect. □ **inurement** *n.* [Anglo-French: related to IN, *eure* work, from Latin *opera*]

inv. *abbr.* invoice.

invade /ɪnˈveɪd/ *v.* (**-ding**) (often *absol.*) **1** enter (a country etc.) under arms to control or subdue it. **2** swarm into. **3** (of a disease) attack. **4** encroach upon (a person's rights, esp. privacy). □ **invader** *n.* [Latin *vado vas-* go]

invalid[1] /ˈɪnvəlɪd, -ˌliːd/ –*n.* person enfeebled or disabled by illness or injury. –*attrib. adj.* **1** of or for invalids. **2** sick, disabled. –*v.* (**-d-**) **1** (often foll. by *out* etc.) remove (an invalid) from active service. **2** (usu. in *passive*) disable (a person) by illness. □ **invalidism** *n.* **invalidity** /ˌɪnvəˈlɪdɪtɪ/*n.* [Latin: related to IN-[1]]

invalid[2] /ɪnˈvælɪd/ *adj.* not valid. □ **invalidity** /ˌɪnvəˈlɪdɪtɪ/ *n.*

invalidate /ɪnˈvælɪˌdeɪt/ *v.* (**-ting**) make (a claim etc.) invalid. □ **invalidation** /-ˈdeɪʃ(ə)n/ *n.*

invaluable /ɪnˈvæljʊəb(ə)l/ *adj.* above valuation; very valuable. □ **invaluably** *adv.*

invariable /ɪnˈveərɪəb(ə)l/ *adj.* **1** unchangeable. **2** always the same. **3** *Math.* constant. □ **invariably** *adv.*

invasion /ɪnˈveɪʒ(ə)n/ *n.* invading or being invaded.

invasive /ɪnˈveɪsɪv/ *adj.* **1** (of weeds, cancer cells, etc.) tending to spread. **2** (of surgery) involving large incisions etc. **3** tending to encroach.

invective /ɪnˈvektɪv/ *n.* strong verbal attack. [Latin: related to INVEIGH]

inveigh /ɪnˈveɪ/ *v.* (foll. by *against*) speak or write with strong hostility. [Latin *invehor -vect-* assail]

inveigle /ɪnˈveɪg(ə)l/ *v.* (**-ling**) (foll. by *into*, or *to* + infin.) entice; persuade by guile. □ **inveiglement** *n.* [Anglo-French from French *aveugler* to blind]

invent /ɪnˈvent/ *v.* **1** create by thought, originate (a method, device, etc.). **2** concoct (a false story etc.). □ **inventor** *n.* [Latin *invenio -vent-* find]

invention /ɪnˈvenʃ(ə)n/ *n.* **1** inventing or being invented. **2** thing invented. **3** fictitious story. **4** inventiveness.

inventive *adj.* able to invent; imaginative. □ **inventively** *adv.* **inventiveness** *n.*

♦ **inventoriable cost** /ˌɪnvənˈtʊərɪəb(ə)l/ *n.* any cost that can be included in the valuation of stocks, work in progress, or inventories, according to accepted accounting standards.

---

inventory /ˈɪnvəntərɪ/ –*n.* (*pl.* **-ies**) **1** complete list of goods, household items, personal possessions, etc. **2** goods listed in this. **3** *US* = STOCK-IN-TRADE 1. –*v.* (**-ies, -ied**) **1** make an inventory of. **2** enter (goods) in an inventory. [medieval Latin: related to INVENT]

♦ **inventory and valuation policy** *n.* insurance policy, usu. on household goods and personal effects, that is based on a written schedule of every item in the premises. This schedule, which is prepared by professional valuers, shows the value of each item. In such policies, insurers agree that in the event of a claim they will not require any further proof of value, which they would require without a valued schedule. Inventory and valuation policies are rare because of the time and expense involved in obtaining a valuation and the problems of having to add to the cover any new items purchased and of inflationary rises in the value of objects.

Invercargill /ˌɪnvəˈkɑːgɪl/ city in New Zealand, capital of Southland region, South Island; industries include meat packing and aluminium smelting; pop. (1991) 51 980.

Inverness /ˌɪnvəˈnes/ city in Scotland, in Highland region; tourism, tanning, distilling, and engineering are important industries; pop. (1985) 58 000.

inverse /ɪnˈvɜːs/ –*adj.* inverted in position, order, or relation. –*n.* **1** inverted state. **2** (often foll. by *of*) the direct opposite. [Latin: related to INVERT]

inverse proportion *n.* (also **inverse ratio**) relation between two quantities such that one increases in proportion as the other decreases.

inversion /ɪnˈvɜːʃ(ə)n/ *n.* **1** turning upside down. **2** reversal of a normal order, position, or relation.

invert /ɪn'vɜːt/ *v.* **1** turn upside down. **2** reverse the position, order, or relation of. [Latin *verto vers-* turn]

invertebrate /ɪn'vɜːtɪbrət/ *–adj.* (of an animal) not having a backbone. *–n.* invertebrate animal.

inverted commas *n.pl.* = QUOTATION MARKS.

invest /ɪn'vest/ *v.* **1 a** (often foll. by *in*) apply or use (money), esp. for profit. **b** (foll. by *in*) put money for profit into (stocks etc.). **2** (often foll. by *in*) devote (time etc.) to an enterprise. **3** (foll. by *in*) *colloq.* buy (something useful). **4 a** (foll. by *with*) provide or credit (a person etc. with qualities) (*invested her with magical importance*; *invested his tone with irony*). **b** (foll. by *in*) attribute or entrust (qualities or feelings) to (a person etc.) (*power invested in the doctor*). **5** (often foll. by *with, in*) clothe with the insignia of office; install in an office. □ **investor** *n.* [Latin *vestis* clothing]

investigate /ɪn'vestɪ,geɪt/ *v.* (**-ting**) **1** inquire into; examine. **2** make a systematic inquiry. □ **investigation** /-'geɪʃ(ə)n/ *n.* **investigative** /-gətɪv/ *adj.* **investigator** *n.* **investigatory** /-gətərɪ/ *adj.* [Latin *vestigo* track]

investiture /ɪn'vestɪ,tʃə(r)/ *n.* formal investing of a person with honours or rank. [medieval Latin: related to INVEST]

investment *n.* **1** investing. **2** (also **financial investment**) purchase of assets (securities, works of art, bank and building-society deposits, etc.) with a primary view to their financial return, either as income or capital gain. This represents a means of saving. The level of financial investment in an economy will be related to such factors as the interest rate, the extent to which investments are likely to prove profitable, and the general climate of business confidence. **3** (also **capital investment**) purchase of capital goods, e.g. plant and machinery in a factory, in order to produce goods for future consumption. The higher the level of capital investment in an economy, the faster it will grow. **4** money invested. **5** property etc. in which money is invested.

♦ **investment analyst** *n.* person employed by stockbrokers, banks, insurance companies, unit trusts, pension funds, etc. to give advice on the making of investments. Many pay special attention to the study of equities in the hope of being able to advise their employers to make profitable purchases of ordinary shares. To do this they use a variety of techniques, including a comparison of a company's present profits with its future trading prospects; this enables the analyst to single out the companies likely to outperform the general level of the market.

♦ **investment bank** *n.* US bank that fulfils many of the functions of a UK merchant bank. It is usu. one that advises on mergers and acquisitions and provides finance for industrial corporations by buying shares in a company and selling them in relatively small lots to investors.

♦ **investment bond** *n.* single-premium life-assurance policy in which an investment of a fixed amount is made (usu. over £1000) in an asset-backed fund. Interest is paid at an agreed rate and at the end of the period the investment is returned with any growth. Investment bonds confer attractive tax benefits in some circumstances. See also SINGLE-PREMIUM ASSURANCE; TOP SLICING.

♦ **investment club** *n.* group of investors who, by pooling their resources, are able to make more frequent and larger investments on a stock exchange, often being able to reduce brokerage and to spread the risk of serious loss. In comparison, unit trusts and investment trusts have the advantage of professional management.

♦ **investment company** *n.* = INVESTMENT TRUST.

♦ **investment grant** *n.* (also **investment incentive**) grant made to a company by a government to encourage investment in plant, machinery, buildings, etc. The incentives may take various forms, some being treated as a deduction for tax purposes, others being paid whether or not the company makes a profit.

♦ **investment income** *n.* **1** person's income derived from investments. **2** income of a business derived from its outside investments rather than from its trading activities.

♦ **Investment Management Regulatory Organization** (also **IMRO**) see SELF-REGULATING ORGANIZATION.

♦ **investment manager** *n.* = FUND MANAGER.

♦ **Investment Ombudsman** *n.* = FINANCIAL OMBUDSMAN 4.

♦ **investment portfolio** *n.* = PORTFOLIO 2.

♦ **investment trust** *n.* (also **investment company**) company that invests the funds provided by shareholders in a wide variety of securities, its profits being made from the income and capital gains provided by these securities. (It is not usu. a trust in the normal sense.) The investments made are usu. restricted to securities quoted on a stock exchange. Like unit trusts, investment trusts spread the risk of investment and make use of professional managers but differ in that the investors are shareholders. See also ACCUMULATION UNIT.

♦ **Investors Compensation Scheme** *n.* scheme set up in the UK in 1988 under the Financial Services Act (1986) to compensate private investors who lose money as a result of a default or failure of an investment firm authorized by the Securities and Investment Board.

---

inveterate /ɪn'vetərət/ *adj.* **1** (of a person) confirmed in a habit etc. **2** (of a habit etc.) long-established. □ **inveteracy** *n.* [Latin *vetus* old]

invidious /ɪn'vɪdɪəs/ *adj.* likely to cause resentment or anger (*invidious position*; *invidious task*). [Latin *invidiosus*: related to ENVY]

invigilate /ɪn'vɪdʒɪ,leɪt/ *v.* (**-ting**) supervise people taking an exam. □ **invigilation** /-'leɪʃ(ə)n/ *n.* **invigilator** *n.* [Latin: related to VIGIL]

invigorate /ɪn'vɪgə,reɪt/ *v.* (**-ting**) give vigour or strength to. □ **invigorating** *adj.* [medieval Latin: related to VIGOUR]

invincible /ɪn'vɪnsɪb(ə)l/ *adj.* unconquerable. □ **invincibility** /-'bɪlɪtɪ/ *n.* **invincibly** *adv.* [Latin *vinco* conquer]

inviolable /ɪn'vaɪələb(ə)l/ *adj.* not to be violated or dishonoured. □ **inviolability** /-'bɪlɪtɪ/ *n.* **inviolably** *adv.*

inviolate /ɪn'vaɪələt/ *adj.* **1** not violated. **2** safe (from violation or harm). □ **inviolacy** *n.*

invisible /ɪn'vɪzɪb(ə)l/ *–adj.* not visible to the eye. *–n.* (in *pl.*) = INVISIBLE EXPORTS. See also INVISIBLE BALANCE. □ **invisibility** /-'bɪlɪtɪ/ *n.* **invisibly** *adv.*

♦ **invisible asset** *n.* = INTANGIBLE ASSET.

♦ **invisible balance** *n.* balance of payments between countries that arises as a result of transactions involving services, such as insurance, banking, shipping, and tourism (often known as **invisibles**), rather than the sale and purchase of goods. Invisibles can play an important part in a nation's current account, although they are often difficult to quantify. The UK relies on a substantial invisible balance in its balance of payments.

♦ **invisible exports** *n.pl.* (also **invisible imports** etc.) intangible commodities, esp. services, involving payment between countries; invisibles.

♦ **invisible hand** *n. Econ.* unseen forces by which the pursuit of rational self-interest (see RATIONALITY 3) achieves a socially desirable outcome. Conceived by Adam Smith (1723–90) to describe the operation of a market economy, the idea forms the basis of neoclassical theories about general equilibrium and Pareto optimality.

---

invitation /,ɪnvɪ'teɪʃ(ə)n/ *n.* **1** inviting or being invited. **2** letter or card etc. used to invite.

♦ **invitation to treat** see OFFER *n.* 2.

---

invite *–v.* /ɪn'vaɪt/ (**-ting**) **1** (often foll. by *to*, or *to* + infin.) ask (a person) courteously to come, or to do something. **2** make a formal courteous request for. **3** tend to call forth unintentionally. **4 a** attract. **b** be attractive. *–n.* /'ɪnvaɪt/ *colloq.* invitation. [Latin *invito*]

inviting *adj.* **1** attractive. **2** tempting. □ **invitingly** *adv.*

in vitro /ɪn 'viːtrəʊ/ *adv.* (of biological processes) taking place in a test-tube or other laboratory environment. [Latin, = in glass]

invocation /ˌɪnvə'keɪʃ(ə)n/ *n.* **1** invoking or being invoked, esp. in prayer. **2** summoning of supernatural beings, e.g. the Muses, for inspiration. **3** *Eccl.* the words 'In the name of the Father' etc. used to preface a sermon etc. □ **invocatory** /ɪn'vɒkətərɪ/ *adj.* [Latin: related to INVOKE]

♦ **invoice** /'ɪnvɔɪs/ –*n.* bill for usu. itemized goods or services. A **commercial invoice** will usu. give a description of the goods and state how and when the goods were dispatched by the seller, who is responsible for insuring them in transit, and the payment terms. –*v.* **(-cing) 1** send an invoice to. **2** make an invoice of. [earlier *invoyes* pl. of *invoy*: related to ENVOY]

---

invoke /ɪn'vəʊk/ *v.* **(-king) 1** call on (a deity etc.) in prayer or as a witness. **2** appeal to (the law, a person's authority, etc.). **3** summon (a spirit) by charms etc. **4** ask earnestly for (vengeance etc.). [Latin *voco* call]

involuntary /ɪn'vɒləntərɪ/ *adj.* **1** done without exercising the will; unintentional. **2** (of a muscle) not under the control of the will. □ **involuntarily** *adv.* **involuntariness** *n.*

♦ **involuntary unemployment** *n.* unemployment in which workers who would be willing to work for lower wages than those in employment are still unable to find work. J. M. Keynes argued that recessions are characterized by involuntary unemployment because firms may be unwilling or unable to cut the wages of workers they employ. Although neoclassical economists have found difficulty accepting this concept in recent years, a number of theories (including the implicit contract theory and the efficiency wage theory) have been suggested to explain it.

---

involute /'ɪnvəˌluːt/ *adj.* **1** involved, intricate. **2** curled spirally. [Latin: related to INVOLVE]

involuted *adj.* complicated, abstruse.

involution /ˌɪnvə'luːʃ(ə)n/ *n.* **1** involving. **2** intricacy. **3** curling inwards. **4** part that curls inwards.

involve /ɪn'vɒlv/ *v.* **(-ving) 1** (often foll. by *in*) cause (a person or thing) to share the experience or effect (of a situation, activity, etc.). **2** imply, entail, make necessary. **3** (often foll. by *in*) implicate (a person) in a charge, crime, etc. **4** include or affect in its operations. **5** (as **involved** *adj.*) **a** (often foll. by *in*) concerned. **b** complicated in thought or form. **c** amorously associated. □ **involvement** *n.* [Latin *volvo* roll]

invulnerable /ɪn'vʌlnərəb(ə)l/ *adj.* that cannot be wounded, damaged, or hurt, physically or mentally. □ **invulnerability** /-'bɪlɪtɪ/ *n.* **invulnerably** *adv.*

inward /'ɪnwəd/ –*adj.* **1** directed towards the inside; going in. **2** situated within. **3** mental, spiritual. –*adv.* (also **inwards**) **1** towards the inside. **2** in the mind or soul. [Old English: related to IN, -WARD]

inwardly *adv.* **1** on the inside. **2** in the mind or soul. **3** not aloud.

inwrought /ɪn'rɔːt/ *adj.* **1** (often foll. by *with*) (of a fabric) decorated (with a pattern). **2** (often foll. by *in, on*) (of a pattern) wrought (in or on a fabric).

I/O *abbr. Computing* = INPUT/OUTPUT.

IOCU *abbr.* International Organization of Consumers' Unions.

IoD *abbr.* = INSTITUTE OF DIRECTORS.

iodide /'aɪəˌdaɪd/ *n.* any compound of iodine with another element or group.

iodine /'aɪəˌdiːn/ *n.* **1** black crystalline element forming a violet vapour. **2** solution of this as an antiseptic. [French *iode* from Greek *iōdēs* violet-like]

IOM *abbr.* Isle of Man.

ion /'aɪən/ *n.* atom or group of atoms that has lost one or more electrons (= CATION), or gained one or more electrons (= ANION). [Greek, = going]

-ion *suffix* (usu. as **-sion, -tion, -xion**) forming nouns denoting: **1** verbal action (*excision*). **2** instance of this (*a suggestion*). **3** resulting state or product (*vexation; concoction*). [Latin *-io*]

Ionian Islands /aɪ'əʊnɪən/ chain of islands in the Ionian Sea, including Corfu and Cephalonia, forming a region of Greece; tourism is the main industry; pop. (1991) 193 734.

Ionian Sea part of the Mediterranean Sea between W Greece and S Italy, at the mouth of the Adriatic.

Ionic /aɪ'ɒnɪk/ *adj.* of the order of Greek architecture characterized by a column with scroll-shapes on either side of the capital. [from *Ionia* in Greek Asia Minor]

ionic /aɪ'ɒnɪk/ *adj.* of or using ions. □ **ionically** *adv.*

ionize *v.* (also **-ise**) **(-zing** or **-sing)** convert or be converted into an ion or ions. □ **ionization** /-'zeɪʃ(ə)n/ *n.*

ionizer *n.* device producing ions to improve the quality of the air.

ionosphere /aɪ'ɒnəˌsfɪə(r)/ *n.* ionized region of the atmosphere above the stratosphere, reflecting radio waves. □ **ionospheric** /-'sferɪk/ *adj.*

IOP *abbr. Computing* input/output processor.

IOS *abbr. Computing* integrated office system.

IOSCO /aɪ'ɒskəʊ/ *abbr.* (also **Iosco**) International Organization of Securities Commissions.

iota /aɪ'əʊtə/ *n.* **1** ninth letter of the Greek alphabet (Ι, ι). **2** (usu. with *neg.*) a jot. [Greek *iōta*]

IOU /ˌaɪəʊ'juː/ *n.* signed document acknowledging a debt. It can be used as legal evidence of a debt, but is not a negotiable instrument or a promissory note and requires no stamp (unless it includes a promise to pay). [from *I owe you*]

IOW *abbr.* Isle of Wight.

Iran /ɪ'rɑːn/, **Islamic Republic of** (former name, until 1935, **Persia**) country in the Middle East, lying between the Caspian Sea and the Persian Gulf. Industrial production in Iran was disrupted by the 1979 revolution and by the Iran-Iraq War but is now recovering and private industry is being encouraged. Oil production is a major industry and the country has the second largest natural gas reserves in the world; together petroleum and gas account for 75% of Iran's export earnings. Metal ores, coal, magnesite, and gypsum are also extracted. There are various manufacturing industries, including textiles and food processing; manufactured exports include carpets, dried fruit and nuts (esp. pistachios), and caviare. In 1995 the USA imposed a trade and investment embargo on Iran.

History. From earliest times the country was ruled by various Persian dynasties, interspersed by periods under Arab, Turkish, Tartar, and Mongol rule; Islam was established in the 7th century. A coup in 1925 brought the Pahlavi family to the throne, but following the overthrow of the Shah in 1979 Iran became an Islamic fundamentalist state. From 1980 to 1988 Iran was involved in war with Iraq. Leader of the Islamic Republic, Ayatollah Seyed Ali Khameni; president, Seyed Mohammad Khatami; capital, Tehran.

languages	Farsi (official), Kurdish, Turkish, Arabic
currency	rial (Rls)
pop. (1996)	62 231 000
GNP (1994)	US$161B
literacy	73% (m); 55% (f)
life expectancy	65 (m); 68 (f)

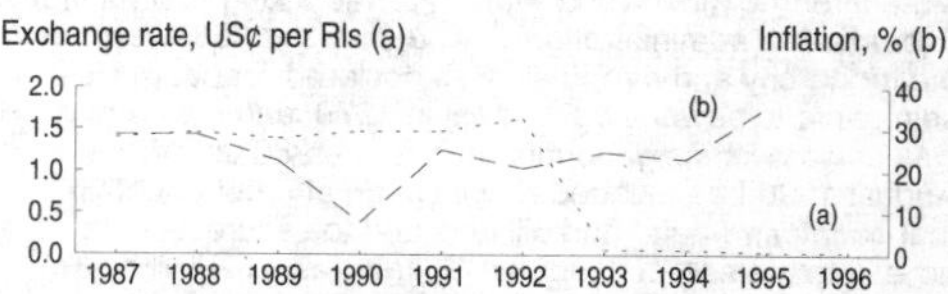

Iowa /ˈaɪəwə/ state in the Midwest of the US; pop. (est. 1996) 2 851 792; capital, Des Moines. Agriculture and its associated industries are important, producing livestock (esp. pigs), corn, and fodder crops.

IP *–abbr.* **1** image processing. **2** imperial preference. *–postcode* Ipswich.

IPA *abbr.* **1** Insolvency Practitioners' Association. **2** = INSTITUTE OF PRACTITIONERS IN ADVERTISING. **3** International Phonetic Alphabet. **4** International Publishers' Association.

IPCS *abbr. Computing* intelligent process-control system.

IPE *abbr.* = INTERNATIONAL PETROLEUM EXCHANGE.

ipecacuanha /ˌɪpɪˌkækjʊˈɑːnə/ *n.* root of a South American shrub, used as an emetic and purgative. [Portuguese from South American Indian, = emetic creeper]

IPFA *abbr.* (Member or Associate of the Chartered) Institute of Public Finance and Accountancy.

IPI *abbr.* Institute of Patentees and Inventors.

Ipiros see EPIRUS.

♦ **IPM** *abbr.* = INSTITUTE OF PERSONNEL MANAGEMENT.

♦ **IPO** *abbr. US* initial public offering (a flotation).

Ipoh /iːˈpəʊ/ city in Malaysia, capital of the state of Perak; tin-mining is the main industry; pop. (1991) 382 633.

IPR *abbr.* = INSTITUTE OF PUBLIC RELATIONS.

IPS *abbr.* **1** Institute of Purchasing and Supply. **2** *Computing* interpretative programming system.

IPSE /ˈɪpsɪ/ *abbr. Computing* integrated project support environment.

ipso facto /ˌɪpsəʊ ˈfæktəʊ/ *adv.* by that very fact. [Latin]

IQ *abbr.* intelligence quotient.

IQA *abbr.* Institute of Quality Assurance.

IQS *abbr.* Institute of Quantity Surveyors.

Iquitos /ɪˈkiːtɒs/ river port and oil exploration centre in E Peru, on the River Amazon; pop. (est. 1993) 274 759.

IR *–abbr.* **1** information retrieval. **2** Inland Revenue. *–international vehicle registration* Iran. *–airline flight code* Iran Air.

Ir *symb* iridium.

Ir. *abbr.* Ireland, Irish.

ir- *prefix* assim. form of IN-[1], IN-[2] before *r*.

IRA *abbr.* Irish Republican Army.

Iráklion see HERAKLION.

Iranian /ɪˈreɪnɪən/ *–adj.* **1** of Iran. **2** of the group of languages including Persian. *–n.* **1** native or national of Iran. **2** person of Iranian descent.

Iraqi /ɪˈrɑːkɪ/ *–adj.* of Iraq. *–n.* (*pl.* **-s**) **1 a** native or national of Iraq. **b** person of Iraqi descent. **2** the form of Arabic spoken in Iraq.

irascible /ɪˈræsɪb(ə)l/ *adj.* irritable; hot-tempered. □ **irascibility** /-ˈbɪlɪtɪ/ *n.* **irascibly** *adv.* [Latin *irascor* grow angry, from *ira* anger]

irate /aɪˈreɪt/ *adj.* angry, enraged. □ **irately** *adv.* **irateness** *n.* [Latin *iratus* from *ira* anger]

IRC *abbr.* **1** Industrial Reorganization Corporation. **2** International Red Cross. **3** International Research Council.

IRCert. *abbr.* Industrial Relations Certificate.

Ire. *abbr.* Ireland.

ire /ˈaɪə(r)/ *n. literary* anger. [Latin *ira*]

Ireland /ˈaɪələnd/ island of the British Isles, lying W of Great Britain, divided between the Republic of Ireland and Northern Ireland. English invasions began in the 12th century and by the 17th century English authority was extended over the whole of the island. Revolts against English rule, and against the imposition of Protestantism, continued until the end of the 18th century, when British political and economic supremacy was finally established with the union of Britain and Ireland in 1801. During the 19th century Ireland sank deeper into destitution; its agricultural produce and assets dropped in value and the failure of the potato crop (Ireland's staple) in the 1840s caused widespread famine. The Home Rule movement failed to achieve its aims and implementation of the Home Rule bill passed in 1914 was delayed by the outbreak of the First World War. An act of 1920 divided Ireland into two parts: Southern Ireland, later recognized as an independent state (see IRELAND, REPUBLIC OF), and Northern Ireland (see separate entry).

Irian Jaya /ˌɪrɪən ˈdʒaɪə/ (formerly **West Irian**) province of E Indonesia comprising the W half of the island of New Guinea together with the adjacent small islands; pop. (est. 1995) 1 956 300; capital, Jayapura. The islands have important deposits of nickel, copper, and oil.

iridaceous /ˌɪrɪˈdeɪʃəs/ *adj.* of the iris family of plants.

iridescent /ˌɪrɪˈdes(ə)nt/ *adj.* **1** showing rainbow-like luminous colours. **2** changing colour with position. □ **iridescence** *n.*

iridium /ɪˈrɪdɪəm/ *n.* hard white metallic element of the platinum group.

IRIS *abbr.* International Research and Information Service.

iris /ˈaɪərɪs/ *n.* **1** circular coloured membrane behind the cornea of the eye, with a circular opening (pupil) in the

Iraq /ɪˈrɑːk/, **Republic of** country in the Middle East bordering on the Persian Gulf. Iraq's economy has been disrupted in recent years through the lengthy Iran-Iraq War (1980–8) and the Gulf War (1990–1). The country's industrial plants and communications network sustained heavy damage during the Gulf War and its major oil-production industry, which accounted formerly for 45% of the GDP, was considerably disrupted. The UN imposed mandatory economic sanctions on Iraq in August 1990 with a worldwide ban on its oil exports; these sanctions, which were modified in 1991 to allow 20% of pre-war production, have had a devastating effect on the country's economy. Agriculture makes a contribution to the economy with dates being the principal cash crop; other crops include wheat, barley, rice, and cotton.
History. Site of ancient Mesopotamia, the region was conquered by Arabia in the 7th century and from 1534 formed part of the Ottoman empire. It became an independent state after the First World War. Iraq was a kingdom (at first under British administration) until a coup in 1958 overthrew the monarchy and a republic was declared. Saddam Hussein came to power as president in 1979, and the country was at war with neighbouring Iran from 1980 until 1988. In August 1990 Iraq invaded Kuwait in an attempt to obtain that country's wealth and oilfields and to secure its own access to the sea-outlet of the Gulf; it was expelled by an international coalition of forces in February 1991. Following a revolt in 1991, Kurds in the N of the country made moves towards establishing autonomous government in that region; persecution of Kurds and of Shiites in the S continues. Since 1990 UN sanctions have been in place and there has been a world-wide ban on Iraqi oil exports. However, in 1996, an agreement was reached allowing Iraq to sell a certain amount of oil to enable the purchase of food and medicine. A proportion of this revenue will pay for reparations for Gulf War victims and provide aid for the Kurds. President, Saddam Hussein; capital, Baghdad.

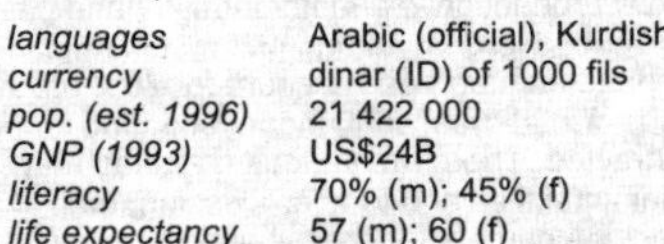

languages	Arabic (official), Kurdish
currency	dinar (ID) of 1000 fils
pop. (est. 1996)	21 422 000
GNP (1993)	US$24B
literacy	70% (m); 45% (f)
life expectancy	57 (m); 60 (f)

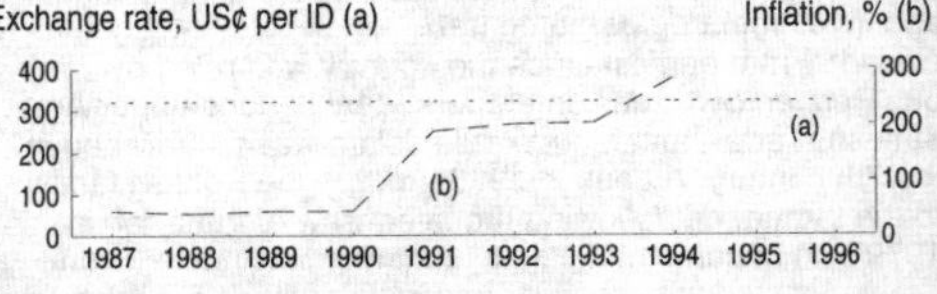

centre. **2** plant of a family with bulbs or tuberous roots, sword-shaped leaves, and showy flowers. **3** adjustable diaphragm for regulating the size of a central hole, esp. for the admission of light to a lens. [Greek *iris iridos* rainbow]

Irish /ˈaɪərɪʃ/ *–adj.* of Ireland or its people. *–n.* **1** Celtic language of Ireland. **2** (prec. by *the*; treated as *pl.*) the people of Ireland. [Old English]

Irish bull *n.* = BULL³.

Irish coffee *n.* coffee with a dash of whiskey and a little sugar, topped with cream.

Irishman *n.* man who is Irish by birth or descent.

Irish Sea sea separating Ireland from England and Wales.

Irish stew *n.* stew of mutton, potato, and onion.

Irishwoman *n.* woman who is Irish by birth or descent.

irk *v.* irritate, bore, annoy. [origin unknown]

irksome *adj.* annoying, tiresome. □ **irksomely** *adv.*

Irkutsk /ɪəˈkʊtsk/ city in S Russia, industrial centre of E Siberia; pop. (est. 1995) 585 000. On a major railway junction, it manufactures ships, aircraft, machinery, textiles, and chemicals.

IRL *international vehicle registration* Republic of Ireland.

IRO *abbr.* **1** industrial relations officer. **2** Inland Revenue Office.

iron /ˈaɪən/ *–n.* **1** grey metallic element used for tools and constructions and found in some foods, e.g. spinach. **2** this as a symbol of strength or firmness (*man of iron*; *iron will*). **3** tool made of iron. **4** implement with a flat base which is heated to smooth clothes etc. **5** golf club with an iron or steel sloping face. **6** (usu. in *pl.*) fetter. **7** (usu. in *pl.*) stirrup. **8** (often in *pl.*) iron support for a malformed leg. *–adj.* **1** made of iron. **2** very robust. **3** unyielding, merciless. *–v.* smooth (clothes etc.) with an iron. □ **iron out** remove (difficulties etc.). [Old English]

Iron Age *n.* period when iron replaced bronze in the making of tools and weapons.

ironclad *–adj.* **1** clad or protected with iron. **2** impregnable. *–n. hist.* warship protected by iron plates.

Iron Cross *n.* German military decoration.

Iron Curtain *n. hist.* former notional barrier to the passage of people and information between the Soviet bloc and the West.

ironic /aɪˈrɒnɪk/ *adj.* (also **ironical**) using or displaying irony. □ **ironically** *adv.*

ironing *n.* clothes etc. for ironing or just ironed.

ironing-board *n.* narrow folding table on which clothes etc. are ironed.

iron in the fire *n.* undertaking, opportunity (usu. in *pl.*: *too many irons in the fire*).

iron lung *n.* rigid case fitted over a patient's body for administering prolonged artificial respiration.

ironmaster *n.* manufacturer of iron.

ironmonger *n.* dealer in hardware etc. □ **ironmongery** *n.* (*pl.* **-ies**).

iron rations *n.pl.* small emergency supply of food.

ironstone *n.* **1** rock containing much iron. **2** a kind of hard white pottery.

ironware *n.* articles made of iron.

ironwork *n.* **1** articles made of iron. **2** work in iron.

ironworks *n.* (as *sing.* or *pl.*) factory where iron is smelted or iron goods are made.

irony /ˈaɪrənɪ/ *n.* (*pl.* **-ies**) **1** expression of meaning, often humorous or sarcastic, using language of a different or opposite tendency. **2** apparent perversity of an event or circumstance in reversing human intentions. **3** *Theatr.* use of language with one meaning for a privileged audience and another for those addressed or concerned. [Greek *eirōneia* pretended ignorance]

IRQ *international vehicle registration* Iraq.

◆ **IRR** *abbr.* = INTERNAL RATE OF RETURN.

irradiate /ɪˈreɪdɪˌeɪt/ *v.* (**-ting**) **1** subject to radiation. **2** shine upon; light up. **3** throw light on (a subject). □ **irradiation** /ɪˌreɪdɪˈeɪʃ(ə)n/ *n.* [Latin *irradio* shine on, from *radius* ray]

irrational /ɪˈræʃən(ə)l/ *adj.* **1** illogical; unreasonable. **2** not endowed with reason. **3** *Math.* not commensurate with the natural numbers. □ **irrationality** /-ˈnælɪtɪ/ *n.* **irrationally** *adv.*

Irrawaddy /ˌɪrəˈwɒdɪ/ principal river of Burma, flowing SW across the country in a large delta into the Bay of Bengal.

irreconcilable /ɪˈrekənˌsaɪləb(ə)l/ *adj.* **1** implacably hostile. **2** (of ideas etc.) incompatible. □ **irreconcilability** /-ˈbɪlɪtɪ/ *n.* **irreconcilably** *adv.*

irrecoverable /ˌɪrɪˈkʌvərəb(ə)l/ *adj.* not able to be recovered or remedied. □ **irrecoverably** *adv.*

irredeemable /ˌɪrɪˈdiːməb(ə)l/ *–adj.* **1** not able to be redeemed. **2** hopeless. **3** (of securities) having no date for the redemption of the capital sum. *–n.* (in *pl.*) irredeemable securities, e.g. Consols and some debentures. The price of fixed-interest irredeemables on the open market varies inversely with the level of interest rates. □ **irredeemably** *adv.*

irredentist /ˌɪrɪˈdentɪst/ *n.* person advocating the restoration to his or her country of any territory formerly belonging to it. □ **irredentism** *n.* [Italian *irredenta* unredeemed]

irreducible /ˌɪrɪˈdjuːsɪb(ə)l/ *adj.* not able to be reduced or simplified. □ **irreducibility** /-ˈbɪlɪtɪ/ *n.* **irreducibly** *adv.*

irrefutable /ˌɪrɪˈfjuːtəb(ə)l/ *adj.* that cannot be refuted. □ **irrefutably** *adv.*

irregular /ɪˈregjʊlə(r)/ *–adj.* **1** not regular; unsymmetrical, uneven; varying in form. **2** not occurring at regular intervals. **3** contrary to a rule, principle, or custom; abnormal. **4** (of troops) not belonging to the regular

Ireland, Republic of country in W Europe, occupying four-fifths of the island of Ireland. Agriculture is important, yielding dairy produce and livestock (esp. beef cattle) for export; crops include barley, wheat, sugar beet, and potatoes. Reserves of zinc and lead are mined, and peat is extensively cut for use as a fuel. Manufacturing industries are expanding and produce foods, beverages, transport equipment, chemicals, office machinery, and textiles for export; tourism is also an important source of revenue. Ireland joined the EC (now EU) in 1973 and has benefited considerably by membership, which has provided both increased trading outlets and development funds. During the mid-1990s Ireland had the fastest growing economy in the developed world. Inflation is low, but unemployment is a continuing problem.
History. Following partition of the island, Southern Ireland was recognized as a dominion, the Irish Free State, in 1921. The name was changed to Eire in 1937 and assumed its present form in 1949, when the republic left the Commonwealth. President, Mary McAleese; prime minister, Bertie Ahern; capital, Dublin.

languages	Irish, English
currency	punt (Irish pound; I£) of 100 pence
pop. (est. 1996)	3 599 000
GNP (1994)	US$48B
literacy	99%
life expectancy	72 (m); 77 (f)

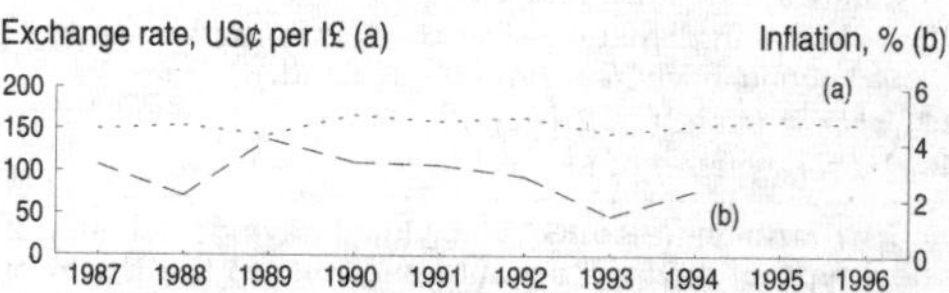

army. **5** (of a verb, noun, etc.) not inflected according to the usual rules. **6** disorderly. *–n.* (in *pl.*) irregular troops. □ **irregularity** /-'lærɪtɪ/ *n.* (*pl.* **-ies**). **irregularly** *adv.*

irrelevant /ɪ'relɪv(ə)nt/ *adj.* (often foll. by *to*) not relevant. □ **irrelevance** *n.* **irrelevancy** *n.* (*pl.* **-ies**).

irreligious /ˌɪrɪ'lɪdʒəs/ *adj.* lacking or hostile to religion; irreverent.

irremediable /ˌɪrɪ'miːdɪəb(ə)l/ *adj.* that cannot be remedied. □ **irremediably** *adv.*

irremovable /ˌɪrɪ'muːvəb(ə)l/ *adj.* that cannot be removed. □ **irremovably** *adv.*

irreparable /ɪ'repərəb(ə)l/ *adj.* (of an injury, loss, etc.) that cannot be rectified or made good. □ **irreparably** *adv.*

irreplaceable /ˌɪrɪ'pleɪsəb(ə)l/ *adj.* that cannot be replaced.

irrepressible /ˌɪrɪ'presɪb(ə)l/ *adj.* that cannot be repressed or restrained. □ **irrepressibly** *adv.*

irreproachable /ˌɪrɪ'prəʊtʃəb(ə)l/ *adj.* faultless, blameless. □ **irreproachably** *adv.*

irresistible /ˌɪrɪ'zɪstɪb(ə)l/ *adj.* too strong, delightful, or convincing to be resisted. □ **irresistibly** *adv.*

irresolute /ɪ'rezəˌluːt/ *adj.* **1** hesitant. **2** lacking in resoluteness. □ **irresolutely** *adv.* **irresoluteness** *n.* **irresolution** /-'luːʃ(ə)n, -'ljuːʃ(ə)n/ *n.*

irrespective /ˌɪrɪ'spektɪv/ *adj.* (foll. by *of*) not taking into account; regardless of.

irresponsible /ˌɪrɪ'spɒnsɪb(ə)l/ *adj.* **1** acting or done without due sense of responsibility. **2** not responsible for one's conduct. □ **irresponsibility** /-'bɪlɪtɪ/ *n.* **irresponsibly** *adv.*

irretrievable /ˌɪrɪ'triːvəb(ə)l/ *adj.* that cannot be retrieved or restored. □ **irretrievably** *adv.*

irreverent /ɪ'revərənt/ *adj.* lacking reverence. □ **irreverence** *n.* **irreverently** *adv.*

irreversible /ˌɪrɪ'vɜːsɪb(ə)l/ *adj.* not reversible or alterable. □ **irreversibly** *adv.*

irrevocable /ɪ'revəkəb(ə)l/ *adj.* **1** unalterable. **2** gone beyond recall. □ **irrevocably** *adv.*

♦ **irrevocable documentary acceptance credit** *n.* form of irrevocable confirmed letter of credit in which a foreign importer of UK goods opens a credit with a UK bank or the UK office of a local bank. The bank then issues an irrevocable letter of credit to the exporter, guaranteeing to accept bills of exchange drawn on it on presentation of the shipping documents.

♦ **irrevocable letter of credit** see LETTER OF CREDIT.

---

irrigate /'ɪrɪˌgeɪt/ *v.* (**-ting**) **1 a** water (land) by means of channels etc. **b** (of a stream etc.) supply (land) with water. **2** supply (a wound etc.) with a constant flow of liquid. □ **irrigable** *adj.* **irrigation** /-'geɪʃ(ə)n/ *n.* **irrigator** *n.* [Latin *rigo* moisten]

irritable /'ɪrɪtəb(ə)l/ *adj.* **1** easily annoyed. **2** (of an organ etc.) very sensitive to contact. □ **irritability** /-'bɪlɪtɪ/ *n.* **irritably** *adv.* [Latin: related to IRRITATE]

irritant /'ɪrɪt(ə)nt/ *–adj.* causing irritation. *–n.* irritant substance.

irritate /'ɪrɪˌteɪt/ *v.* (**-ting**) **1** excite to anger; annoy. **2** stimulate discomfort in (a part of the body). **3** *Biol.* stimulate (an organ) to action. □ **irritating** *adj.* **irritation** /-'teɪʃ(ə)n/ *n.* **irritative** *adj.* [Latin *irrito*]

irrupt /ɪ'rʌpt/ *v.* (foll. by *into*) enter forcibly or violently. □ **irruption** *n.* [Latin: related to RUPTURE]

IRRV *abbr.* Institute of Revenues, Rating, and Valuation.

IRS *abbr.* **1** *Computing* information retrieval system. **2** = INTERNAL REVENUE SERVICE.

IS *–abbr.* **1** information science. **2** information service. *–international vehicle registration* Iceland.

Is. *abbr.* **1** Island(s). **2** Isle(s).

is *3rd sing. present* of BE.

♦ **Isa** /aɪsə/ *n.* (also **ISA**) individual savings account, a new type of savings account available in the UK from April 1999 to replace PEPs and TESSAs. Individuals will be entitled to save up to £5000 per annum tax free (£7000 in the first year, of which £3000 can be in cash). [abbreviation]

ISAC *abbr.* Industrial Safety Advisory Council.

ISBA *abbr.* = INCORPORATED SOCIETY OF BRITISH ADVERTISERS LTD.

ISBN *abbr.* international standard book number.

Ischia /'ɪskɪə/ Italian island and tourist resort W of the mainland, in the Tyrrhenian Sea; pop. (1985) 26 000.

ISD *abbr.* international subscriber dialling.

ISDN *abbr. Computing* Integrated Services Digital Network.

ISE *abbr.* International Stock Exchange of the UK and the Republic of Ireland Ltd. (see LONDON STOCK EXCHANGE).

-ise var. of -IZE.

■ **Usage** See note at *-ize*.

ISF *abbr.* International Shipping Federation.

Isfahan /ˌɪsfə'hɑːn/ (also **Esfahan, Ispahan**) industrial city in W central Iran; manufactures include steel, textiles, and carpets; pop. (1991) 1 127 030.

-ish *suffix* forming adjectives: **1** from nouns, meaning: **a** having the qualities of (*boyish*). **b** of the nationality of (*Danish*). **2** from adjectives, meaning 'somewhat' (*thickish*). **3** *colloq.* denoting an approximate age or time of day (*fortyish*; *six-thirtyish*). [Old English]

isinglass /'aɪzɪŋˌglɑːs/ *n.* **1** gelatin obtained from fish, esp. sturgeon, and used in making jellies, glue, etc. **2** mica. [Dutch *huisenblas* sturgeon's bladder]

ISk *symb.* króna.

Iskenderun /ɪs'kendəˌruːn/ (formerly **Alexandretta**) port and naval base in S Turkey, on the NE coast of the Mediterranean Sea; pop. (est. 1994) 156 800.

isl. *abbr.* (also **Isl.**) **1** island. **2** isle.

Islam /'ɪzlɑːm/ *n.* **1** the religion of the Muslims, proclaimed by Muhammad. **2** the Muslim world. □ **Islamic** /ɪz'læmɪk/ *adj.* [Arabic, = submission (to God)]

Islamabad /ɪz'lɑːməˌbɑːd/ capital, since 1967, of Pakistan, replacing Rawalpindi; pop. (est. 1990) 350 000.

island /'aɪlənd/ *n.* **1** piece of land surrounded by water. **2** = TRAFFIC ISLAND. **3** detached or isolated thing. [Old English *īgland*; first syllable influenced by ISLE]

islander *n.* native or inhabitant of an island.

isle /aɪl/ *n. poet.* (and in place-names) island, esp. a small one. [French *ile* from Latin *insula*]

Isle of Man island in the Irish Sea, a self-governing British Crown dependency with its own legislature (the Tynwald) and judicial system; pop. (1991) 69 788; capital, Douglas. The island is a tax haven and has banking and insurance industries; tourism is an important source of revenue.

Isle of Wight /waɪt/ island off the S coast of England, a county since 1974; tourism and yachting are important; pop. (1991) 124 577.

islet /'aɪlɪt/ *n.* **1** small island. **2** *Anat.* structurally distinct portion of tissue. [French diminutive of ISLE]

♦ **ISLM model** *n. Econ.* model that shows how the equilibrium levels of interest and national output are determined. It involves manipulation of the IS (investment-savings) curve and the LM (liquidity-money) curve, and finds simultaneously the equilibrium values of these variables in the money market and the savings-investment market. The aim of the model was to provide a framework for contrasting Keynes' general theory with the standard neoclassical (later monetarist) theory and a basis for policy analysis. Although the ISLM model has been the standard textbook analysis for some fifty years, it lacks proper microfoundations and has failed to resolve the major issues in macroeconomics.

---

ism /'ɪz(ə)m/ *n. colloq.* usu. *derog.* any distinctive doctrine or practice. [from -ISM]

-ism *suffix* forming nouns, esp. denoting: **1** action or its result (*baptism*; *organism*). **2** system or principle (*Conser-*

vatism; jingoism). **3** state or quality (*heroism; barbarism*). **4** basis of prejudice or discrimination (*racism; sexism*). **5** peculiarity in language (*Americanism*). [Greek *-ismos*]

isn't /'ɪz(ə)nt/ *contr.* is not.

ISO *abbr.* **1** industrial safety officer. **2** = INTERNATIONAL STANDARDS ORGANIZATION.

iso- *comb. form* equal. [Greek *isos* equal]

isobar /'aɪsəʊ,bɑː(r)/ *n.* line on a map connecting places with the same atmospheric pressure. □ **isobaric** /-'bærɪk/ *adj.* [Greek *baros* weight]

isochronous /aɪ'sɒkrənəs/ *adj.* **1** occurring at the same time. **2** occupying equal time.

♦ **isocost** /'aɪsəʊ,kɒst/ *n. Econ.* set of combinations of goods that have the same total cost; this can be represented by a curve on a graph. In producer theory isocosts refer to inputs and, making certain assumptions, there will be a unique minimum cost of producing a given level of output, which can be represented as the point at which a particular isoquant curve touches the lowest possible isocost curve.

isolate /'aɪsə,leɪt/ *v.* (**-ting**) **1 a** place apart or alone. **b** place (a contagious or infectious patient etc.) in quarantine. **2** separate (a substance) from a mixture. **3** insulate (electrical apparatus), esp. by a physical gap; disconnect. □ **isolation** /-'leɪʃ(ə)n/ *n.* [Latin *insulatus* made into an island]

isolationism *n.* policy of holding aloof from the affairs of other countries or groups. □ **isolationist** *n.*

isomer /'aɪsəmə(r)/ *n.* one of two or more compounds with the same molecular formula but a different arrangement of atoms. □ **isomeric** /-'merɪk/ *adj.* **isomerism** /aɪ'sɒmə,rɪz(ə)m/ *n.* [Greek ISO-, *meros* share]

isometric /,aɪsəʊ'metrɪk/ *adj.* **1** of equal measure. **2** (of muscle action) developing tension while the muscle is prevented from contracting. **3** (of a drawing etc.) with the plane of projection at equal angles to the three principal axes of the object shown. [Greek *isometria* equality of measure]

isomorphic /,aɪsəʊ'mɔːfɪk/ *adj.* (also **isomorphous** /-fəs/) exactly corresponding in form and relations. [from ISO-, Greek *morphē* form]

♦ **isoquant** /'aɪsəʊ,kwɒnt/ *n. Econ.* combinations of inputs that can be used to produce a given level of output; this can be represented as a curve on a graph. The concept is analogous to that of an indifference curve in consumer theory. Given the prices of inputs faced by a firm, by making certain additional assumptions, the firm or entrepreneur will be able to choose a single combination of inputs that minimizes costs for a given level of output (i.e. on a particular isoquant); this combination will also maximize profits. [from ISO-, QUANTUM]

isosceles /aɪ'sɒsɪ,liːz/ *adj.* (of a triangle) having two sides equal. [from ISO-, Greek *skelos* leg]

isotherm /'aɪsəʊ,θɜːm/ *n.* line on a map connecting places with the same temperature. □ **isothermal** /-'θɜːm(ə)l/ *adj.* [from ISO-, Greek *thermē* heat]

isotope /'aɪsə,təʊp/ *n.* one of two or more forms of an element differing from each other in relative atomic mass, and in nuclear but not chemical properties. □ **isotopic** /-'tɒpɪk/ *adj.* [from ISO-, Greek *topos* place]

isotropic /,aɪsəʊ'trɒpɪk/ *adj.* having the same physical properties in all directions. □ **isotropy** /aɪ'sɒtrəpɪ/ *n.* [from ISO-, Greek *tropos* turn]

♦ **ISP** *abbr.* = INSTITUTE OF SALES PROMOTION.

Ispahan see ISFAHAN.

ISPEMA *abbr.* Industrial Safety (Personal Equipment) Manufacturers' Association.

ISR *abbr.* information storage and retrieval.

Israeli /ɪz'reɪlɪ/ *–adj.* of the modern State of Israel. *–n.* (*pl.* **-s**) **1** native or national of Israel. **2** person of Israeli descent. [Hebrew]

Israelite /'ɪzrɪə,laɪt/ *n. hist.* native of ancient Israel; Jew. [Hebrew]

ISRO *abbr.* International Securities Regulatory Organization.

ISSN *abbr.* International Standard Serial Number.

issue /'ɪʃuː/ *–n.* **1 a** act of giving out or circulating shares, notes, stamps, etc. **b** quantity of coins, banknotes, copies of a newspaper, etc. circulated at one time. **c** number of shares or amount of stock on offer to the public at a particular time. See also NEW ISSUE; RIGHTS ISSUE; SCRIP ISSUE. **d** each of a regular series of a magazine etc. (*the May issue*). **2 a** outgoing, outflow. **b** way out, outlet, esp. the place of the emergence of a stream etc. **3** point in question; important subject of debate or litigation. **4** result; outcome. **5** *Law* children, progeny (*without male*

Israel /'ɪzreɪl/, **State of** country in SW Asia, bordering on the Mediterranean, with the River Jordan forming part of its E border. Since 1948 industrial and agricultural production in Israel have increased rapidly. Much of the country is very fertile and large areas of former desert have been brought under cultivation through massive irrigation programmes. A large variety of crops can be grown and citrus and other fruit, vegetables, and flowers are exported. Israel is a centre for diamond cutting and polishing and these contribute to the country's exports in value. The aircraft and military industries are important; other manufactures include machinery, plastics, rubber, textiles, cement, glass, and paper. The tourist industry is showing signs of recovery following the Gulf War (1990–1). Israel is now the most industrialized country and one of the strongest military powers in the Middle East. Future economic development will depend on the progress of the Middle East peace talks and the rate of immigration from the former Soviet Union, both of which will influence investment in the country.

History. Although Israel is the ancient and traditional home of the Jewish people, for most of its history it was controlled by other nations until, following the surrender of the British mandate at the end of the Second World War, the independent Jewish State of Israel was proclaimed in 1948. Conflict with the surrounding Arab states led to wars in 1948, 1956, 1967, and 1973, and resulted in Israel's expansion to her present boundaries. In the late 1980s and early 1990s the uprising of Palestinians in the occupied West Bank and Gaza Strip and (in 1990–1) Palestinian support for Saddam Hussein of Iraq in the Gulf War, produced dangerous tensions. Following elections in 1992 the extreme right-wing government was replaced by a Labour-dominated coalition and prospects for progress in the Arab–Israeli peace negotiations improved. In 1993 Israel and the Palestinian Liberation Organization (PLO) signed a peace agreement. In 1994–5 Israel granted autonomous status to Jericho and the Gaza Strip, with a Palestinian National Authority assuming control. In 1995 Israeli prime minister Yitzhak Rabin was assassinated by a Jewish extremist opposed to the peace process. Subsequently, the peace process has stalled. President, Ezer Weizmann; prime minister, Binyamin Netanyahu; capital, Jerusalem.

languages	Hebrew, Arabic
currency	shekel (NIS) of 100 agorot
pop. (est. 1996)	5 481 000
GNP (1994)	US$78B
literacy	97% (m); 93% (f)
life expectancy	75 (m); 79 (f)

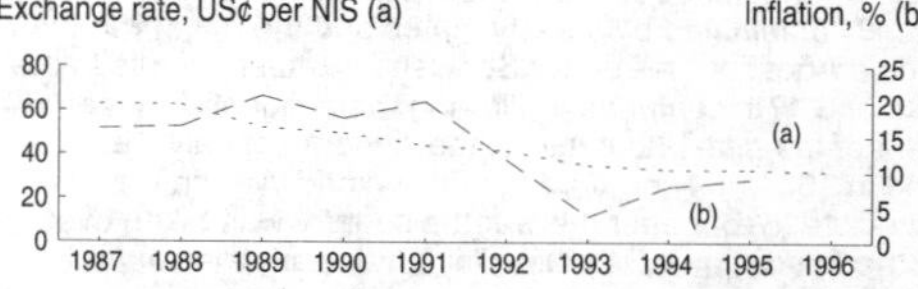

issue). –*v*. (**issues, issued, issuing**) **1** *literary* go or come out. **2 a** send forth; publish; put into circulation. **b** supply, esp. officially or authoritatively (foll. by *to, with*: *issued passports to them; issued them with passports*). **3 a** (often foll. by *from*) be derived or result. **b** (foll. by *in*) end, result. **4** (foll. by *from*) emerge from a condition. □ **at issue** under discussion; in dispute. **join** (or **take**) **issue** (foll. by *with* a person etc., *about, on, over* a subject) disagree or argue. [Latin *exitus*: related to EXIT]

♦ **issue by tender** *n.* method of issuing shares on the London Stock Exchange in which an issuing house asks investors to tender for them. The stocks or shares are then allocated to the highest bidders. It is usual for the tender documents to state the lowest price acceptable. This method may be used for a new issue or for loan stock, but is not frequently employed. Cf. INTRODUCTIONS; OFFER FOR SALE; PLACING; PUBLIC ISSUE.

♦ **issued share capital** see SHARE CAPITAL.

♦ **issue price** *n.* price at which a new issue of shares is sold to the public (see NEW ISSUE). Once the issue has been made the securities will have a market price, which may be above (at a premium on) or below (at a discount on) the issue price (see also STAG 2). In an introduction, offer for sale, or public issue, the issue price is fixed by the company on the advice of its stockbrokers and bankers; in an issue by tender the issue price is fixed by the highest bidder; in a placing the issue price is negotiated by the issuing house or broker involved.

♦ **issuing house** *n.* financial institution, usu. a merchant bank, that specializes in the flotation of private companies on a stock exchange. In some cases the issuing house will itself purchase the whole issue (see UNDERWRITER), thus ensuring that there is no uncertainty in the amount of money the company will raise by flotation. It will then sell the shares to the public, usu. by an offer for sale, introduction, issue by tender, or placing.

-ist *suffix* forming personal nouns denoting: **1** adherent of a system etc. in *-ism*: (*Marxist; fatalist*). **2** person pursuing, using, or concerned with something as an interest or profession (*balloonist; tobacconist*). **3** person who does something expressed by a verb in *-ize* (*plagiarist*). **4** person who subscribes to a prejudice or practises discrimination (*racist; sexist*). [Greek *-istēs*]

Istanbul /ˌɪstænˈbʊl/ (formerly **Constantinople, Byzantium**) port and the former capital (until 1923) of Turkey; pop. (1994) 7 615 400. Tourist and manufacturing industries are important, products including textiles, leather, cement, glass, and tobacco.

ISTC *abbr.* Iron and Steel Trades' Confederation (trade union).

ISTEA *abbr.* Iron and Steel Trades Employers' Association.

isthmus /ˈɪsməs/ *n.* (*pl.* **-es**) narrow piece of land connecting two larger bodies of land. [Greek *isthmos*]

ISV *abbr.* independent software vendor.

ISVA *abbr.* Incorporated Society of Valuers and Auctioneers.

IT *abbr.* **1** income tax. **2** industrial tribunal. **3** = INFORMATION TECHNOLOGY.

it *pron.* (*poss.* **its**; *pl.* **they**) **1** thing (or occasionally an animal or child) previously named or in question (*took a stone and threw it*). **2** person in question (*Who is it? It is I*). **3** as the subject of an impersonal verb (*it is raining; it is winter; it is two miles to Bath*). **4** as a substitute for a deferred subject or object (*it is silly to talk like that; I take it that you agree*). **5** as a substitute for a vague object (*brazen it out*). **6** as the antecedent to a relative word or clause (*it was an owl that I heard*). **7** exactly what is needed. **8** extreme limit of achievement. **9** *colloq.* **a** sexual intercourse. **b** sex appeal. **10** (in children's games) player who has to perform a required feat. □ **that's it** *colloq.* that is: **1** what is required. **2** the difficulty. **3** the end, enough. [Old English]

Itaipu /iːˈtaɪpuː/ dam on the Paraná River in SW Brazil, one of the world's largest hydroelectric installations, formally opened in 1982.

Italian /ɪˈtæljən/ –*n.* **1 a** native or national of Italy. **b** person of Italian descent. **2** Romance language of Italy. –*adj.* of or relating to Italy.

Italianate /ɪˈtæljəˌneɪt/ *adj.* of Italian style or appearance.

Italian vermouth *n.* sweet kind of vermouth.

italic /ɪˈtælɪk/ –*adj.* **1 a** of the sloping kind of letters now used esp. for emphasis and in foreign words. **b** (of handwriting) compact and pointed like early Italian handwriting. **2** (**Italic**) of ancient Italy. –*n.* **1** letter in italic type. **2** this type. [Latin *italicus* related to ITALIAN]

italicize /ɪˈtælɪˌsaɪz/ *v.* (also **-ise**) (**-zing** or **-sing**) print in italics.

ITB *abbr.* Industry Training Board.

ITC *abbr.* **1** Imperial Tobacco Company. **2** Independent Television Commission. **3** Industrial Training Council. **4** International Tin Council. **5** International Trade Centre. **6** *US* investment tax credit.

itch –*n.* **1** irritation in the skin. **2** impatient desire. **3** (prec. by *the*) (in general use) scabies. –*v.* **1** feel an irri-

Italy /ˈɪtəlɪ/, **Republic of** country in S Europe comprising a peninsula that juts S into the Mediterranean Sea and a number of offshore islands of which the largest are Sicily and Sardinia. Italy is divided between the industrialized N and the poorer agricultural S. Industry is the dominant sector of the economy with manufactures including textiles and clothing, machinery, motor vehicles, and chemicals. The country is poor in mineral resources but deposits of oil and natural gas discovered since 1947 have been exploited; marble is extracted and other minerals include iron ores and pyrites, mercury, lead, zinc, and aluminium. Agricultural produce includes wheat, maize, grapes, and olives and there is an important wine industry. Tourism is also a major source of revenue. A founder member of the European Community, Italy left the ERM in 1992 as a consequence of its poor economic performance, compared to stronger EC countries, largely as a result of rising wages. *History*. The centre of the Roman Empire, Italy was subsequently dominated by the city-states and the papacy in the Middle Ages, but fell under Spanish and Austrian rule in the 16th and 17th centuries. Following the nationalist movement of the mid-19th century, the kingdom of Italy was created in 1861. Italy entered the First World War on the Allied side in 1915, but after the war the country was taken over by the Fascist dictator Mussolini; participation in support of Germany during the Second World War resulted in defeat and much devastation. A republic was established by popular vote in 1946. Since 1947 the country has experienced a considerable degree of political instability with frequent changes of government, culminating (1993) in a major political crisis with the discovery of widespread corruption in government and state-run industry. President, Oscar Luigi Scalfaro; prime minister, Romano Prodi; capital, Rome.

language	Italian (official), German
currency	lira (L) of 100 centesimi
pop. (est. 1996)	57 500 000
GNP (1994)	US$1101B
literacy	97% (m); 96% (f)
life expectancy	73 (m); 80 (f)

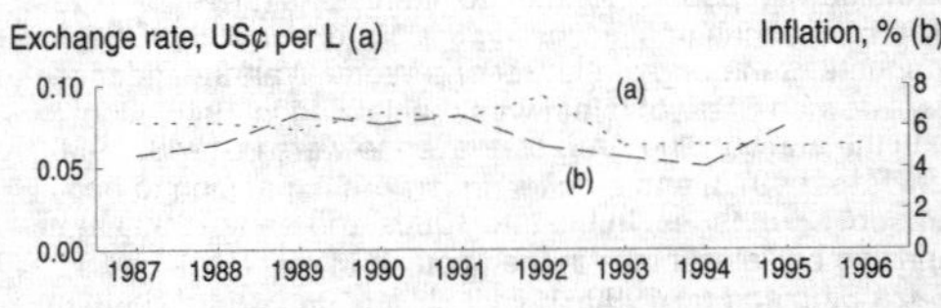

tation in the skin. **2** feel a desire to do something (*itching to tell you*). [Old English]

itching palm *n.* avarice.

itchy *adj.* (**-ier, -iest**) having or causing an itch. □ **have itchy feet** *colloq.* **1** be restless. **2** have a strong urge to travel. □ **itchiness** *n.*

it'd /ˈɪtəd/ *contr. colloq.* **1** it had. **2** it would.

-ite *suffix* forming nouns meaning 'a person or thing connected with' (*Israelite*; *Trotskyite*; *graphite*; *dynamite*). [Greek *-itēs*]

item /ˈaɪtəm/ *n.* **1** any of a number of enumerated things. **2** separate or distinct piece of news etc. [Latin, = in like manner]

itemize *v.* (also **-ise**) (**-zing** or **-sing**) state item by item. □ **itemization** /-ˈzeɪʃ(ə)n/ *n.*

iterate /ˈɪtəˌreɪt/ *v.* (**-ting**) repeat; state repeatedly. □ **iteration** /-ˈreɪʃ(ə)n/ *n.* **iterative** /-rətɪv/ *adj.* [Latin *iterum* again]

ITF *abbr.* **1** International Trade Federations. **2** International Transport Workers' Federation.

-itic *suffix* forming adjectives and nouns corresponding to nouns in *-ite*, *-itis*, etc. (*Semitic*; *arthritic*). [Latin *-iticus*, Greek *-itikos*]

itinerant /aɪˈtɪnərənt/ *–adj.* travelling from place to place. *–n.* itinerant person. [Latin *iter itiner-* journey]

itinerary /aɪˈtɪnərərɪ/ *n.* (*pl.* **-ies**) **1** detailed route. **2** record of travel. **3** guidebook.

-itis *suffix* forming nouns, esp.: **1** names of inflammatory diseases (*appendicitis*). **2** *colloq.* with ref. to conditions compared to diseases (*electionitis*). [Greek]

it'll /ˈɪt(ə)l/ *contr. colloq.* it will; it shall.

ITMA *abbr.* Institute of Trade Mark Agents.

ITO *abbr.* International Trade Organization.

ITS *abbr.* **1** Industrial Training Service. **2** (in the US) Intermarket Trading System. **3** International Trade Secretariat.

its *poss. pron.* of it; of itself.

it's *contr.* **1** it is. **2** it has.

itself /ɪtˈself/ *pron.* emphatic and refl. form of IT. □ **be itself** see ONESELF. **by itself** see *by oneself*. **in itself** viewed in its essential qualities (*not in itself a bad thing*). [Old English: related to IT, SELF]

ITT *abbr.* International Telephone and Telegraph Corporation.

ITU *abbr.* = INTERNATIONAL TELECOMMUNICATION UNION.

ITV *abbr.* Independent Television.

-ity *suffix* forming nouns denoting: **1** quality or condition (*humility*; *purity*). **2** instance of this (*monstrosity*). [Latin *-itas*]

IUAI *abbr.* International Union of Aviation Insurers.

IUD *abbr.* intra-uterine (contraceptive) device.

IUMI *abbr.* International Union of Marine Insurance.

IV *–abbr.* (also **i.v.**) invoice value. *–airline flight code* Air Gambia. *–postcode* Inverness.

IVA *abbr.* individual voluntary arrangement (in bankruptcy proceedings).

I've /aɪv/ *contr.* I have.

-ive *suffix* forming adjectives meaning 'tending to', and corresponding nouns (*suggestive*; *corrosive*; *palliative*). [Latin *-ivus*]

IVF *abbr. in vitro* fertilization.

ivory /ˈaɪvərɪ/ *n.* (*pl.* **-ies**) **1** hard substance of the tusks of an elephant etc. **2** creamy-white colour of this. **3** (usu. in *pl.*) **a** article made of ivory. **b** *slang* thing made of or resembling ivory, esp. a piano key or a tooth. [Latin *ebur*]

Ivory Coast see CÔTE D'IVOIRE.

ivory tower *n.* seclusion or withdrawal from the harsh realities of life (often *attrib.*: *ivory tower professors*).

ivy /ˈaɪvɪ/ *n.* (*pl.* **-ies**) climbing evergreen shrub with shiny five-angled leaves. [Old English]

IWW *abbr.* **1** Industrial Workers of the World. **2** International Workers of the World.

IY *airline flight code* Yemen Airways.

-ize *suffix* (also **-ise**) forming verbs, meaning: **1** make or become such (*Americanize*; *realize*). **2** treat in such a way (*monopolize*; *pasteurize*). **3 a** follow a special practice (*economize*). **b** have a specified feeling (*sympathize*). □ **-ization** /-ˈzeɪʃ(ə)n/ *suffix* forming nouns. [Greek *-izō*]

■ **Usage** The form *-ize* has been in use in English since the 16th century; it is widely used in American English, but is not an Americanism. The alternative spelling *-ise* (reflecting a French influence) is in common use, esp. in British English, and is obligatory in certain cases: (*a*) where it forms part of a larger word-element, such as *-mise* (= sending) in *compromise*, and *-prise* (= taking) in *surprise*; and (*b*) in verbs corresponding to nouns with *-s-* in the stem, such as *advertise* and *televise*.

Izmir /ɪzˈmɪə(r)/ (formerly **Smyrna** /ˈsmɜːnə/) seaport and naval base in W Turkey, on an inlet of the Aegean Sea; manufactures include steel, electronics, and plastics; pop. (est. 1994) 1 985 300.

Izmit /ɪzˈmɪt/ city in NW Turkey, on an inlet of the Sea of Marmara; industries include oil refining, paper, and petrochemicals; pop. (est. 1994) 275 800.

Iznik /ɪzˈnɪk/ town in NW Turkey, a noted centre for the production of coloured tiles since the 16th century; pop. (1990) 19 230.

J[1] /dʒeɪ/ *n.* (also **j**) (*pl.* **Js** or **J's**) tenth letter of the alphabet.

J[2] *–symb.* joule(s). *–international vehicle registration* Japan.

J2 *international civil aircraft marking* Djibouti.

J3 *international civil aircraft marking* Grenada.

J5 *international civil aircraft marking* Guinea-Bissau.

J6 *international civil aircraft marking* St Lucia.

J7 *international civil aircraft marking* Dominica.

J8 *international civil aircraft marking* St Vincent.

JA *–abbr.* (also **J/A**) joint account. *–international vehicle registration* Jamaica. *–international civil aircraft marking* Japan.

jab *–v.* (**-bb-**) **1 a** poke roughly. **b** stab. **2** (foll. by *into*) thrust (a thing) hard or abruptly. *–n.* **1** abrupt blow, thrust, or stab. **2** *colloq.* hypodermic injection. [var. of *job* = prod]

Jabalpur /ˌdʒʌbəl'pʊə(r)/ industrial city and military post in central India, in Madhya Pradesh; manufactures include textiles, oil, and armaments; pop. (1991) 741 927.

jabber *–v.* **1** chatter volubly. **2** utter (words) in this way. *–n.* chatter; gabble. [imitative]

jabot /'ʒæbəʊ/ *n.* ornamental frill etc. on the front of a shirt or blouse. [French]

JAC *abbr.* (in the US) Junior Association of Commerce.

jacaranda /ˌdʒækə'rændə/ *n.* tropical American tree with trumpet-shaped blue flowers or hard scented wood. [Tupi]

jacinth /'dʒæsɪnθ/ *n.* reddish-orange zircon used as a gem. [Latin: related to HYACINTH]

jack *–n.* **1** device for raising heavy objects, esp. vehicles. **2** court-card with a picture of a soldier, page, etc. **3** ship's flag, esp. showing nationality. **4** device using a single-pronged plug to connect an electrical circuit. **5** small white target ball in bowls. **6 a** = JACKSTONE. **b** (in *pl.*) game of jackstones. **7** (**Jack**) familiar form of *John*, esp. typifying the common man, male animal, etc. (*I'm all right, Jack*). *–v.* (usu. foll. by *up*) **1** raise with or as with a jack (in sense 1). **2** *colloq.* raise (e.g. prices). □ **every man jack** every person. **jack in** *slang* abandon (an attempt etc.). [familiar form of the name *John*]

jackal /'dʒæk(ə)l/ *n.* **1** African or Asian wild animal of the dog family, scavenging in packs for food. **2** *colloq.* menial. [Persian]

jackanapes /'dʒækəˌneɪps/ *n. archaic* rascal. [earlier *Jack Napes*, supposed to refer to the Duke of Suffolk]

jackass *n.* **1** male ass. **2** stupid person.

jackboot *n.* **1** military boot reaching above the knee. **2** this as a militaristic or fascist symbol.

jackdaw *n.* grey-headed bird of the crow family.

jacket /'dʒækɪt/ *n.* **1 a** short coat with sleeves. **b** protective or supporting garment (*life-jacket*). **2** casing or covering round a boiler etc. **3** = DUST-JACKET. **4** skin of a potato. **5** animal's coat. [French]

jacket potato *n.* potato baked in its skin.

Jack Frost *n.* frost personified.

jack-in-the-box *n.* toy figure that springs out of a box.

jackknife *–n.* **1** large clasp-knife. **2** dive in which the body is bent and then straightened. *–v.* (**-fing**) (of an articulated vehicle) fold against itself in an accident.

jack of all trades *n.* multi-skilled person.

jack-o'-lantern *n.* **1** will-o'-the wisp. **2** pumpkin lantern.

jack plane *n.* medium-sized joinery plane.

jack plug *n.* plug for use with a jack (see JACK *n.* 4).

jackpot *n.* large prize, esp. accumulated in a game, lottery, etc. □ **hit the jackpot** *colloq.* **1** win a large prize. **2** have remarkable luck or success.

jackrabbit *n. US* large prairie hare.

Jack Russell /dʒæk 'rʌs(ə)l/ *n.* short-legged breed of terrier.

Jacksonville /'dʒæksənˌvɪl/ city in the US, in Florida; pop. (est. 1994) 665 070. Industries include paper and chemicals, and there is a naval base.

jackstone *n.* **1** metal etc. piece used in tossing-games. **2** (in *pl.*) game with a ball and jackstones.

Jack tar *n.* sailor.

Jacobean /ˌdʒækə'biːən/ *–adj.* **1** of the reign of James I. **2** (of furniture) heavy and dark in style. *–n.* Jacobean person. [Latin *Jacobus* James]

Jacobite /'dʒækəˌbaɪt/ *n. hist.* supporter of James II after his flight, or of the Stuarts.

Jacquard /'dʒækɑːd/ *n.* **1** apparatus with perforated cards, for weaving figured fabrics. **2** (in full **Jacquard loom**) loom with this. **3** fabric or article so made. [name of its inventor]

Jacuzzi /dʒə'kuːzɪ/ *n.* (*pl.* **-s**) *propr.* large bath with massaging underwater jets of water. [name of its inventor and manufacturers]

Jamaica /dʒə'meɪkə/ island country in the Caribbean Sea SE of Cuba. The economy is based traditionally on mineral production and agriculture, the main exports being alumina, sugar, bauxite, bananas, coffee, and rum; tourism is also an important source of revenue. A fall in world aluminium prices in the late 1980s resulted in depletion of Jamaican foreign reserves and widening of the trade deficit. Continuing pressure on the exchange rate forced the government to float the dollar in 1991, bringing about devaluation in an attempt to boost non-traditional exports and encourage tourism, which has been adversely affected by domestic unrest caused by high unemployment. Formerly a Spanish and then a British colony, Jamaica became self-governing in 1944 and an independent Commonwealth state in 1962; it is a member of CARICOM. Prime minister, Percival J. Patterson; capital, Kingston. □ **Jamaican** *adj.* & *n.*

languages	English (official), Creole
currency	dollar (J$) of 100 cents
pop. (est. 1996)	2 505 000
GNP (1994)	US$3.5B
literacy	80% (m); 89% (f)
life expectancy	71 (m); 75 (f)

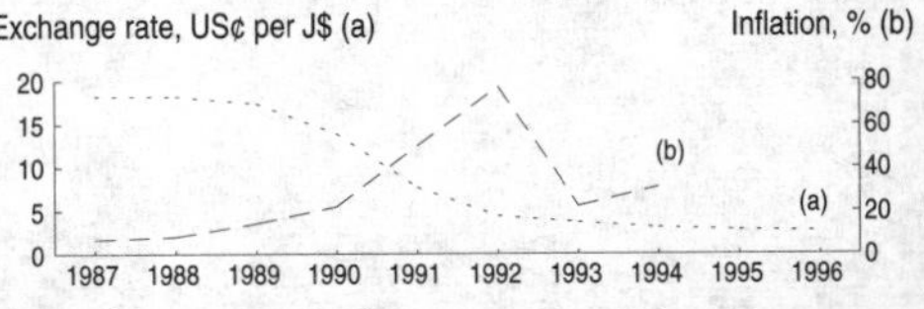

jade[1] *n.* **1** hard usu. green stone used for ornaments etc. **2** green colour of jade. [Spanish *ijada* from Latin *ilia* flanks (named as a cure for colic)]

jade[2] *n.* **1** inferior or worn-out horse. **2** *derog.* disreputable woman. [origin unknown]

jaded *adj.* tired out; surfeited.

j'adoube /ʒɑːˈduːb/ *int. Chess* declaration of the intention to adjust a piece without moving it. [French, = I adjust]

Jaffna /ˈdʒæfnə/ **1** district in N Sri Lanka; fishing is an important source of income; pop. (est. 1993) 879 000. **2** its capital city; pop. (est. 1990) 129 100.

jag[1] *–n.* sharp projection of rock etc. *–v.* (**-gg-**) **1** cut or tear unevenly. **2** make indentations in. [imitative]

jag[2] *n. slang* **1** drinking bout. **2** period of indulgence in an activity, emotion, etc. [originally dial., = load]

jagged /ˈdʒægɪd/ *adj.* **1** unevenly cut or torn. **2** deeply indented. □ **jaggedly** *adv.* **jaggedness** *n.*

jaguar /ˈdʒægjʊə(r)/ *n.* large American flesh-eating spotted animal of the cat family. [Tupi]

jail (also **gaol**) *–n.* **1** place for the detention of prisoners. **2** confinement in a jail. *–v.* put in jail. [French *jaiole*, ultimately from Latin *cavea* cage]

jailbird *n.* (also **gaolbird**) prisoner or habitual criminal.

jailbreak *n.* (also **gaolbreak**) escape from jail.

jailer *n.* (also **gaoler**) person in charge of a jail or prisoners.

Jaipur /dʒaɪˈpʊə(r)/ city in NW India, capital of Rajasthan; jewellery, enamelware, carved stone, and textiles are produced; pop. (1991) 1 458 183.

Jakarta /dʒəˈɑːtə/ (also **Djakarta**, formerly **Batavia**) capital of Indonesia, in NW Java; pop. (1990) 8 259 266. It has textile, chemical, and plastics industries; exports include tea and coffee.

Jalalabad /dʒəˈlæləˌbæd/ city in E Afghanistan; products include refined sugar and handicrafts; pop. (est. 1990) 55 000.

jalap /ˈdʒæləp/ *n.* purgative drug from the tuberous roots of a Mexican climbing plant. [Spanish *Xalapa*, name of a Mexican city, from Aztec]

Jalisco /hæˈliːskəʊ/ state in W central Mexico; pop. (est. 1995) 5 990 054; capital, Guadalajara. There are textile mills, electricity-generating plants, mines, and cement works.

jalopy /dʒəˈlɒpɪ/ *n.* (*pl.* **-ies**) *colloq.* dilapidated old vehicle. [origin unknown]

jalousie /ˈʒælʊˌziː/ *n.* slatted blind or shutter to keep out rain etc. and control light. [French: related to JEALOUSY]

jam[1] *–v.* (**-mm-**) **1 a** (usu. foll. by *into*, *together*, etc.) squeeze, cram, or wedge into a space. **b** become wedged. **2** cause (machinery etc.) to become wedged or (of machinery etc.) become wedged and unworkable. **3 a** block (a passage, road, etc.) by crowding etc. **b** (foll. by *in*) obstruct the exit of (*was jammed in*). **4** (usu. foll. by *on*) apply (brakes etc.) forcefully or abruptly. **5** make (a radio transmission) unintelligible by interference. **6** *colloq.* (in jazz etc.) improvise with other musicians. *–n.* **1** squeeze, crush. **2** crowded mass (*traffic jam*). **3** *colloq.* predicament. **4** stoppage (of a machine etc.) due to jamming. **5** (in full *jam session*) *colloq.* (in jazz etc.) improvised ensemble playing. [imitative]

jam[2] *n.* **1** conserve of boiled fruit and sugar. **2** *colloq.* easy or pleasant thing (*money for jam*). □ **jam tomorrow** promise of future treats etc. that never materialize. [perhaps from JAM[1]]

jamb /dʒæm/ *n.* side post or side face of a doorway, window, or fireplace. [French *jambe* leg, from Latin]

jamboree /ˌdʒæmbəˈriː/ *n.* **1** celebration. **2** large rally of Scouts. [origin unknown]

Jamestown /ˈdʒeɪmztaʊn/ capital and chief port of the island of St Helena, in the S Atlantic; pop. (1992) 1500.

jamjar *n.* glass jar for jam.

Jammu and Kashmir /ˈdʒʌmuː, kæʃˈmɪə(r)/ state in NW India; pop. (1991) 7 718 700; capitals, Srinagar (in summer) and Jammu (in winter). The region produces timber, silk, and carpets. See also KASHMIR.

jammy *adj.* (**-ier, -iest**) **1** covered with jam. **2** *colloq.* **a** lucky. **b** profitable.

jam-packed *adj. colloq.* full to capacity.

Jan. *abbr.* January.

j. & w.o. *abbr. Insurance* jettisoning and washing overboard.

JANET /ˈdʒænɪt/ *abbr. Computing* Joint Academic Network.

jangle /ˈdʒæŋg(ə)l/ *–v.* (**-ling**) **1** (cause to) make a (esp. harsh) metallic sound. **2** irritate (the nerves etc.) by discord etc. *–n.* harsh metallic sound. [French]

janitor /ˈdʒænɪtə(r)/ *n.* **1** doorkeeper. **2** caretaker. [Latin *janua* door]

January /ˈdʒænjʊərɪ/ *n.* (*pl.* **-ies**) first month of the year. [Latin *Janus*, guardian god of doors]

Jap *n.* & *adj. colloq.* often *offens.* = JAPANESE. [abbreviation]

Japan, Sea of sea between Japan and the mainland of Asia.

japan /dʒəˈpæn/ *–n.* hard usu. black varnish, orig. from Japan. *–v.* (**-nn-**) **1** varnish with japan. **2** make black and glossy. [JAPAN]

Japanese /ˌdʒæpəˈniːz/ *–n.* (*pl.* same) **1 a** native or

Japan /dʒəˈpæn/ country in E Asia, occupying a series of islands in the Pacific roughly parallel with the E coast of the Asiatic mainland. Japan is now the leading economic power in SE Asia and the most highly industrialized country in that region, with a range of manufacturing industries that produce electrical and electronic goods, machinery, motor vehicles, chemicals, shipping, and textiles, all of which are major exports. Agriculture is intensive, rice being the main crop; timber production is important and the country is one of the world's leading fishing nations. Tokyo has become one of the main financial centres of the world. In 1997 the Japanese stock exchange and several leading finance houses endured a dramatic crash precipitated by a financial crisis in southeast Asia, centred on Thailand and Indonesia. *History*. According to Japanese tradition, the empire was founded in 660 BC by the emperor Jimmu. From the 12th century onwards the country was dominated by succeeding clans of military warriors, but with the restoration of direct Imperial rule in 1868 it entered the modernizing process, which was accelerated by successful wars against China (1894–5) and Russia (1904–5), and by the 1930s had occupied parts of China. Japan fought against the Allies in the Second World War, surrendering in 1945 after the dropping of atomic bombs on Hiroshima and Nagasaki; a constitutional monarchy was established in 1947. The conservative Liberal Democratic Party held power continuously from 1955 until 1993: it has since (1996) returned as a minority government. Head of state, Emperor Akihito; prime minister, Ryutaro Hashimoto; capital, Tokyo.

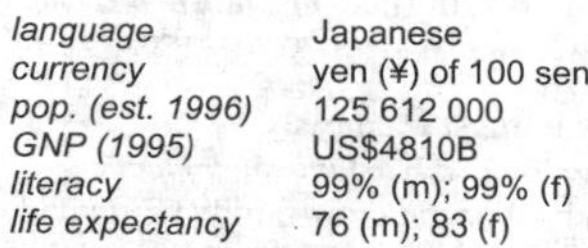

language	Japanese
currency	yen (¥) of 100 sen
pop. (est. 1996)	125 612 000
GNP (1995)	US$4810B
literacy	99% (m); 99% (f)
life expectancy	76 (m); 83 (f)

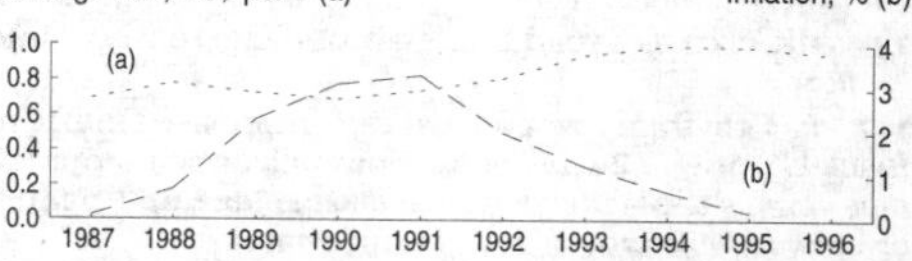

national of Japan. **b** person of Japanese descent. **2** language of Japan. *–adj.* of Japan, its people, or its language.

jape *–n.* practical joke. *–v.* (**-ping**) play a joke. [origin unknown]

japonica /dʒəˈpɒnɪkə/ *n.* flowering shrub with bright red flowers and round edible fruits. [Latinized name for *Japanese*]

jar[1] *n.* **1 a** container, usu. of glass and cylindrical. **b** contents of this. **2** *colloq.* glass of beer. [French from Arabic]

jar[2] *–v.* (**-rr-**) **1** (often foll. by *on*) (of sound, manner, etc.) sound discordant, grate (on the nerves etc.). **2 a** (often foll. by *against, on*) (cause to) strike (esp. part of the body) with vibration or shock (*jarred his neck*). **b** vibrate with shock etc. **3** (often foll. by *with*) be at variance or in conflict. *–n.* **1** jarring sound or sensation. **2** physical shock or jolt. [imitative]

jar[3] *n.* □ **on the jar** ajar. [obsolete *char* turn: see AJAR, CHAR[2]]

jardinière /ˌʒɑːdɪˈnjeə(r)/ *n.* **1** ornamental pot or stand for plants. **2** dish of mixed vegetables. [French]

jargon /ˈdʒɑːgən/ *n.* **1** words or expressions used by a particular group or profession (*medical jargon*). **2** debased or pretentious language. [French]

Jarrow /ˈdʒærəʊ/ town in NE England, in Tyne and Wear, having oil installations, ship-repair yards, and chemical works; pop. (1991) 29 325. Its name is associated with the hunger-marches to London during the Great Depression of the 1930s.

jasmine /ˈdʒæzmɪn/ *n.* ornamental shrub with white or yellow flowers. [French from Arabic from Persian]

jasper /ˈdʒæspə(r)/ *n.* opaque quartz, usu. red, yellow, or brown. [French from Latin from Greek *iaspis*]

Jassy see IAŞI.

jaundice /ˈdʒɔːndɪs/ *–n.* **1** yellowing of the skin etc. caused by liver disease, bile disorder, etc. **2** disordered (esp. mental) vision. **3** envy. *–v.* (**-cing**) **1** affect with jaundice. **2** (esp. as **jaundiced** *adj.*) affect (a person) with envy, resentment, etc. [French *jaune* yellow]

jaunt /dʒɔːnt/ *–n.* short pleasure trip. *–v.* take a jaunt. [origin unknown]

jaunting car *n.* light horse-drawn vehicle formerly used in Ireland.

jaunty /ˈdʒɔːntɪ/ *adj.* (**-ier, -iest**) **1** cheerful and self-confident. **2** sprightly. □ **jauntily** *adv.* **jauntiness** *n.* [French: related to GENTLE]

Java /ˈdʒɑːvə/ Indonesian island in the Malay Archipelago; pop. (est. 1995) 102 910 500 (with Madura); capital, Jakarta. Rice, sugar cane, kapok, and teak are produced and industries include synthetic textiles.

Javanese /ˌdʒɑːvəˈniːz/ *–n.* (*pl.* same) **1 a** native of Java. **b** person of Javanese descent. **2** language of Java. *–adj.* (also **Javan**) of Java, its people, or its language.

javelin /ˈdʒævəlɪn/ *n.* light spear thrown in sport or, formerly, as a weapon. [French]

jaw *–n.* **1 a** upper or lower bony structure in vertebrates containing the teeth. **b** corresponding parts of certain invertebrates. **2 a** (in *pl.*) the mouth with its bones and teeth. **b** narrow mouth of a valley, channel, etc. **c** gripping parts of a tool etc. **d** grip (*jaws of death*). **3** *colloq.* tedious talk (*hold your jaw*). *–v. colloq.* speak, esp. at tedious length. [French]

jawbone *n.* lower jaw in most mammals.

jaw-breaker *n. colloq.* long or hard word.

jay *n.* noisy European bird of the crow family with vivid plumage. [Latin *gaius, gaia*, perhaps from the name *Gaius*: cf. *jackdaw, robin*]

jaywalk *v.* cross a road carelessly or dangerously. □ **jaywalker** *n.*

jazz *–n.* **1** rhythmic syncopated esp. improvised music of Black US origin. **2** *slang* pretentious talk or behaviour (*all that jazz*). *–v.* play or dance to jazz. □ **jazz up** brighten or enliven. □ **jazzer** *n.* [origin uncertain]

jazzman *n.* jazz-player.

jazzy *adj.* (**-ier, -iest**) **1** of or like jazz. **2** vivid, showy.

JCB /ˌdʒeɪsiːˈbiː/ *n. propr.* mechanical excavator with a shovel and a digging arm. [*J. C.* BAMFORD]

JCC *abbr.* Junior Chamber of Commerce.

JCI *abbr.* Junior Chamber International.

JCL *abbr. Computing* job-control language.

JCR *abbr.* Junior Common (or Combination) Room.

◆ **J-curve effect** *n. Econ.* increase in the value of imports or a fall in the value of exports caused by a depreciation of a domestic currency. In the long term, it is expected that the falling value of the currency will make exports more competitive, causing them to increase, and imports more expensive, causing demand for them to fall. However, in the short term import and export volumes will usu. be slow to adjust, so that imports will cost more in the depreciated currency and exports will earn less; the resulting decline in the balance of payments is represented by the hook of the J. The subsequent fall in imports and rise in exports causing the balance of payments to rise sharply is represented by the upstroke of the J.

JD *symb.* Jordanian dinar.

JDB *abbr.* Japan Development Bank.

J.Dip.MA *abbr.* Joint Diploma in Management Accounting Services.

JE *airline flight code* Manx Airlines.

jealous /ˈdʒeləs/ *adj.* **1** resentful of rivalry in love. **2** (often foll. by *of*) envious (of a person etc.). **3** (often foll. by *of*) fiercely protective (of rights etc.). **4** (of God) intolerant of disloyalty. **5** (of inquiry, supervision, etc.) vigilant. □ **jealously** *adv.* [medieval Latin *zelosus*: related to ZEAL]

jealousy *n.* (*pl.* **-ies**) **1** jealous state or feeling. **2** instance of this. [French: related to JEALOUS]

jeans /dʒiːnz/ *n.pl.* casual esp. denim trousers. [earlier *geane fustian*, = material from Genoa]

JEC *abbr.* Joint Economic Committee (of US Congress).

Jeddah /ˈdʒedə/ (also **Jiddah** /ˈdʒɪdə/) seaport in Saudi Arabia, on the Red Sea coast; industries include cement, steel, and oil refining; pop. (est. 1991) 1 500 000.

Jeep *n. propr.* small sturdy esp. military vehicle with four-wheel drive. [originally US, from the initials of *general purposes*]

jeepers /ˈdʒiːpəz/ *int. US slang* expressing surprise etc. [corruption of *Jesus*]

jeer *–v.* (often foll. by *at*) scoff derisively; deride. *–n.* taunt. □ **jeeringly** *adv.* [origin unknown]

Jefferson City /ˈdʒefəs(ə)n/ city in the US, capital of Missouri; primarily an administrative centre, it also manufactures electrical appliances and cosmetics; pop. (1990) 35 481.

jehad var. of JIHAD.

Jehovah /dʒəˈhəʊvə/ *n.* Hebrew name of God in the Old Testament. [Hebrew *yahveh*]

Jehovah's Witness *n.* member of a millenarian Christian sect rejecting the supremacy of the state and religious institutions over personal conscience, faith, etc.

jejune /dʒɪˈdʒuːn/ *adj.* **1** intellectually unsatisfying; shallow, meagre, scanty, dry. **2** puerile. **3** (of land) barren. [Latin *jejunus*]

jejunum /dʒɪˈdʒuːnəm/ *n.* small intestine between the duodenum and ileum. [Latin: related to JEJUNE]

Jekyll and Hyde /ˌdʒekɪl ənd ˈhaɪd/ *n.* person having opposing good and evil personalities. [names of a character in a story by R. L. Stevenson]

jell *v. colloq.* **1** set as jelly. **2** (of ideas etc.) take a definite form; cohere. [back-formation from JELLY]

jellaba var. of DJELLABA.

jellify /ˈdʒelɪˌfaɪ/ *v.* (**-ies, -ied**) turn into jelly; make or become like jelly. □ **jellification** /-fɪˈkeɪʃ(ə)n/ *n.*

jelly /ˈdʒelɪ/ *–n.* (*pl.* **-ies**) **1 a** (usu. fruit-flavoured) translucent dessert set with gelatin. **b** similar preparation as a jam, condiment, or sweet (*redcurrant jelly*). **c** similar preparation from meat, bones, etc., and gelatin (*marrowbone jelly*). **2** any similar substance. **3** *slang* gelignite.

–*v.* (**-ies, -ied**) (cause to) set as or in a jelly, congeal (*jellied eels*). □ **jelly-like** *adj.* [French *gelée* from Latin *gelo* freeze]

jelly baby *n.* jelly-like baby-shaped sweet.

jellyfish *n.* (*pl.* same or **-es**) marine animal with a jelly-like body and stinging tentacles.

jemmy /'dʒemɪ/ *n.* (*pl.* **-ies**) burglar's short crowbar. [from the name *James*]

Jena /'jeɪnə/ town in central Germany; industries include chemicals, engineering, and manufacture of optical instruments at the Zeiss works; pop. (est. 1995) 102 204.

jenny /'dʒenɪ/ *n.* (*pl.* **-ies**) **1** *hist.* = SPINNING-JENNY. **2** female donkey. [from the name *Janet*]

jenny-wren *n.* female wren.

jeopardize /'dʒepə,daɪz/ *v.* (also **-ise**) (**-zing** or **-sing**) endanger.

jeopardy /'dʒepədɪ/ *n.* danger, esp. severe. [obsolete French *iu parti* divided play]

jerbil var. of GERBIL.

jerboa /dʒɜː'bəʊə/ *n.* small jumping desert rodent. [Arabic]

jeremiad /,dʒerɪ'maɪæd/ *n.* doleful complaint or lamentation. [Church Latin: related to JEREMIAH]

Jeremiah /,dʒerɪ'maɪə/ *n.* dismal prophet, denouncer of the times. [Lamentations of *Jeremiah*, in the Old Testament]

Jerez /'hereθ/ (also **Jerez de la Frontera**) town in Spain, in Andalusia, centre of the sherry-making industry; pop. (est. 1994) 190 400.

jerk[1] –*n.* **1** sharp sudden pull, twist, twitch, start, etc. **2** spasmodic muscular twitch. **3** (in *pl.*) *colloq.* exercises (*physical jerks*). **4** *slang* fool. –*v.* move, pull, thrust, twist, throw, etc., with a jerk. □ **jerk off** *coarse slang* masturbate. [imitative]

jerk[2] *v.* cure (beef) by cutting it in long slices and drying it in the sun. [Quechua *echarqui* dried fish in strips]

jerkin /'dʒɜːkɪn/ *n.* **1** sleeveless jacket. **2** *hist.* man's close-fitting, esp. leather, jacket. [origin unknown]

jerky *adj.* (**-ier, -iest**) **1** moving suddenly or abruptly. **2** spasmodic. □ **jerkily** *adv.* **jerkiness** *n.*

jeroboam /,dʒerə'bəʊəm/ *n.* wine bottle of 4–12 times the ordinary size. [*Jeroboam* in the Old Testament]

♦ **jerque note** /dʒɜːk/ *n.* certificate issued by a UK customs officer to the master of a ship, stating satisfaction that the cargo on the ship has been correctly entered on the manifest and that no unentered cargo has been found after searching the ship. [perhaps from Italian *cercare* search]

Jerry /'dʒerɪ/ *n.* (*pl.* **-ies**) *slang* **1** German (esp. soldier). **2** Germans collectively. [probably an alteration of *German*]

jerry /'dʒerɪ/ *n.* (*pl.* **-ies**) *slang* chamber-pot. [probably an abbreviation of JEROBOAM]

jerry-builder *n.* incompetent builder using cheap materials. □ **jerry-building** *n.* **jerry-built** *adj.* [origin uncertain]

jerrycan *n.* (also **jerrican**) a kind of (orig. German) petrol- or water-can. [from JERRY]

Jersey /'dʒɜːzɪ/ largest of the Channel Islands; pop. (1991) 84 082; capital, St Helier. Dairy farming (esp. of cattle for export), finance, and tourism are important sources of revenue. –*n.* light-brown dairy cattle from Jersey.

jersey /'dʒɜːzɪ/ *n.* (*pl.* **-s**) **1** knitted usu. woollen pullover. **2** plain-knitted (orig. woollen) fabric. [JERSEY]

Jerusalem /dʒə'ruːsələm/ capital of Israel, holy city of the Jews, Christians, and Muslims; tourism is a major industry; pop. (est. 1996) 591 400. Divided between Israel and Jordan in 1949, the entire city was taken over by Israel in 1967.

Jerusalem artichoke *n.* **1** a kind of sunflower with edible tubers. **2** this as a vegetable. [corruption of Italian *girasole* sunflower]

jest –*n.* **1** joke; fun. **2 a** raillery, banter. **b** object of derision. –*v.* joke; fool about. □ **in jest** in fun. [Latin *gesta* exploits]

jester *n. hist.* professional clown at a medieval court etc.

Jesuit /'dʒezjʊɪt/ *n.* member of the Society of Jesus, a Roman Catholic order. [Latin *Jesus*, founder of the Christian religion]

Jesuitical /,dʒezjʊ'ɪtɪk(ə)l/ *adj.* **1** of the Jesuits. **2** often *offens.* equivocating, casuistic.

Jesus /'dʒiːzəs/ *int. colloq.* exclamation of surprise, dismay, etc. [name of the founder of the Christian religion]

jet[1] –*n.* **1** stream of water, gas, flame, etc., shot esp. from a small opening. **2** spout or nozzle for this purpose. **3** jet engine or jet plane. –*v.* (**-tt-**) **1** spurt out in jets. **2** *colloq.* send or travel by jet plane. [French *jeter* throw from Latin *jacto*]

jet[2] *n.* (often *attrib.*) hard black lignite often carved and highly polished. [French *jaiet* from *Gagai* in Asia Minor]

jet black *adj.* & *n.* (as adj. often hyphenated) deep glossy black.

JETCO /'dʒet,kəʊ/ *abbr.* Japan Export Trading Company.

jet engine *n.* engine using jet propulsion, esp. of an aircraft.

jet lag *n.* exhaustion etc. felt after a long flight across time zones.

jet plane *n.* plane with a jet engine.

jet-propelled *adj.* **1** having jet propulsion. **2** very fast.

jet propulsion *n.* propulsion by the backward ejection of a high-speed jet of gas etc.

JETRO /'dʒetrəʊ/ *abbr.* Japan External Trade Organization.

jetsam /'dʒetsəm/ *n.* **1** objects washed ashore, esp. jettisoned from a ship. **2** items of a ship's cargo that have been thrown overboard and sink below the surface of the water. Cf. FLOTSAM. [contraction of JETTISON]

jet set *n.* wealthy people who travel widely, esp. for pleasure. □ **jet-setter** *n.* **jet-setting** *n.* & *attrib. adj.*

jettison /'dʒetɪs(ə)n/ –*v.* **1 a** throw (esp. heavy material) overboard to lighten a ship etc. **b** drop (goods) from an aircraft. **2** abandon; get rid of. –*n.* **1** jettisoning. **2** (in *pl.*) items of a ship's cargo that have been thrown overboard to lighten the ship in dangerous circumstances. If the items are insured they constitute a general average loss (see AVERAGE *n.* 4). [Anglo-French *getteson*: related to JET[1]]

jetty /'dʒetɪ/ *n.* (*pl.* **-ies**) **1** pier or breakwater to protect or defend a harbour, coast, etc. **2** landing-pier. [French *jetee*: related to JET[1]]

Jew /dʒuː/ *n.* **1** person of Hebrew descent or whose religion is Judaism. **2** *slang offens.* miserly person. [Greek *ioudaios*]

■ **Usage** The stereotype conveyed in sense 2 is deeply offensive. It arose from historical associations of Jews as moneylenders in medieval England.

jewel /'dʒuːəl/ –*n.* **1 a** precious stone. **b** this used in watchmaking. **2** jewelled personal ornament. **3** precious person or thing. –*v.* (**-ll-**; *US* **-l-**) (esp. as **jewelled** *adj.*) adorn or set with jewels. [French]

jeweller *n.* (*US* **jeweler**) maker of or dealer in jewels or jewellery.

jewellery /'dʒuːəlrɪ/ *n.* (also **jewelry**) rings, brooches, necklaces, etc., regarded collectively.

Jewess /'dʒuːes/ *n.* often *offens.* woman or girl of Hebrew descent or whose religion is Judaism.

Jewish *adj.* **1** of Jews. **2** of Judaism. □ **Jewishness** *n.*

Jewry /'dʒʊərɪ/ *n.* Jews collectively.

jew's harp *n.* small musical instrument held between the teeth.

Jezebel /'dʒezə,bel/ *n.* shameless or immoral woman. [*Jezebel* in the Old Testament]

Jiangsu /dʒɪæŋ'suː/ (also **Kiangsu**) province in E China; pop. (est. 1995) 70 210 000; capital, Nanjing. It produces wheat, rice, cotton, tea, silk, ceramics, and copper.

Jiangxi /dʒıæŋ'ʃi:/ (also **Kiangsi**) province in SE China; pop. (est. 1995) 40 150 000; capital, Nanchang. An important rice-growing region, it has resources of coal, uranium, and other minerals and manufactures porcelain.

jib[1] *n.* **1** triangular staysail. **2** projecting arm of a crane. [origin unknown]

jib[2] *v.* (**-bb-**) **1** (esp. of a horse) stop and refuse to go on. **2** (foll. by *at*) show aversion to. □ **jibber** *n.* [origin unknown]

jibe[1] var. of GIBE.

jibe[2] *US* var. of GYBE.

Jibuti see DJIBOUTI.

JICNAR /'dʒıknɑ:/ *abbr.* = JOINT INDUSTRY COMMITTEE FOR NATIONAL READERSHIP.

JICRAR /'dʒıkrɑ:/ *abbr.* = JOINT INDUSTRY COMMITTEE FOR RADIO AUDIENCE RESEARCH.

JICTAR /'dʒıktɑ:/ *abbr.* Joint Industry Committee for Television Advertising Research.

jiff *n.* (also **jiffy,** *pl.* **-ies**) *colloq.* short time; moment (*in a jiffy*). [origin unknown]

Jiffy bag /'dʒıfı/ *n. propr.* padded envelope.

jig *–n.* **1 a** lively leaping dance. **b** music for this. **2** device that holds a piece of work and guides the tools operating on it. *–v.* (**-gg-**) **1** dance a jig. **2** (often foll. by *about*) move quickly and jerkily up and down; fidget. **3** work on or equip with a jig or jigs. [origin unknown]

jigger /'dʒıgə(r)/ *n.* **1** *Billiards colloq.* cue-rest. **2 a** measure of spirits etc. **b** small glass holding this. [partly from JIG]

jiggered /'dʒıgəd/ *adj. colloq.* (as a mild oath) confounded (*I'll be jiggered*). [euphemism]

jiggery-pokery /ˌdʒıgərı'pəʊkərı/ *n. colloq.* trickery; swindling. [origin uncertain]

jiggle /'dʒıg(ə)l/ *–v.* (**-ling**) (often foll. by *about* etc.) shake or jerk lightly; fidget. *–n.* light shake. [from JIG]

jigsaw *n.* **1 a** (in full **jigsaw puzzle**) picture on board or wood etc. cut into irregular interlocking pieces to be reassembled as a pastime. **b** problem consisting of various pieces of information. **2** mechanical fretsaw with a fine blade.

jihad /dʒı'hæd/ *n.* (also **jehad**) Muslim holy war against unbelievers. [Arabic *jihād*]

Jilin /dʒi:'lın/ (also **Kirin**) province in NE China; pop. (est. 1995) 25 740 000; capital, Changchun. Agriculture and forestry are important, and there is some mining.

jilt *v.* abruptly reject or abandon (esp. a lover). [origin unknown]

Jim Crow /'krəʊ/ *n. US colloq.* **1** segregation of Blacks. **2** *offens.* a Black. [nickname]

jim-jams /'dʒımdʒæmz/ *n.pl.* **1** *slang* = DELIRIUM TREMENS. **2** *colloq.* nervousness; depression. [fanciful reduplication]

Jinan /dʒi:'næn/ (also **Tsinan**) city in E China, capital of Shandong province; industries include textiles and food processing; pop. (1990) 1 480 915.

jingle /'dʒıŋg(ə)l/ *–n.* **1** mixed ringing or clinking noise. **2 a** repetition of sounds in a phrase etc. **b** short catchy verse or song in advertising etc. *–v.* (**-ling**) **1** (cause to) make a jingling sound. **2** (of writing) be full of alliteration, rhymes, etc. [imitative]

jingo /'dʒıŋgəʊ/ *n.* (*pl.* **-es**) supporter of war; blustering patriot. □ **by jingo!** mild oath. □ **jingoism** *n.* **jingoist** *n.* **jingoistic** /-'ıstık/ *adj.* [conjuror's word]

jink *–v.* **1** move elusively; dodge. **2** elude by dodging. *–n.* dodging or eluding. [originally Scots: imitative]

jinnee /dʒı'ni:/ *n.* (also **jinn, djinn** /dʒın/) (*pl.* **jinn** or **djinn**) (in Muslim mythology) spirit in human or animal form having power over people. [Arabic]

jinx *colloq. –n.* person or thing that seems to cause bad luck. *–v.* (esp. as **jinxed** *adj.*) subject to bad luck. [perhaps var. of *jynx* wryneck, charm]

JIT *abbr.* (also **j.i.t.**) just-in-time, denoting a method of reducing wastage in industry by manufacturing or ordering items as they are required.

jitter *colloq. –n.* (**the jitters**) extreme nervousness. *–v.* be nervous; act nervously. □ **jittery** *adj.* **jitteriness** *n.* [origin unknown]

jitterbug *–n.* **1** nervous person. **2** *hist.* fast popular dance. *–v.* (**-gg-**) *hist.* dance the jitterbug.

jiu-jitsu var. of JU-JITSU.

jive *–n.* **1** lively dance popular esp. in the 1950s. **2** music for this. *–v.* (**-ving**) dance to or play jive music. □ **jiver** *n.* [origin uncertain]

JL *airline flight code* Japan Airlines.

JM *airline flight code* Air Jamaica.

Jnr. *abbr.* Junior.

JO *abbr.* job order.

job *–n.* **1** piece of work to be done; task. **2** position in, or piece of, paid employment. **3** *colloq.* difficult task (*had a job to find it*). **4** *slang* crime, esp. a robbery. **5** state of affairs etc. (*bad job*). *–v.* (**-bb-**) **1** do jobs; do piece-work. **2** deal in stocks; buy and sell (stocks or goods). **3** deal corruptly with (a matter). □ **job backwards** look back on a transaction or event, esp. financial, and think about how one might have acted differently in retrospect. **just the job** *colloq.* exactly what is wanted. **make a job** (or **good job) of** do well. **on the job** *colloq.* **1** at work. **2** engaged in sexual intercourse. **out of a job** unemployed. [origin unknown]

♦ **job analysis** *n.* detailed study of a particular job, the tools and equipment needed to do it, and its relation to other jobs in an organization. The analysis should also provide the information needed to say how the job should best be done and the qualifications, experience, or aptitudes of the person best suited to doing it.

---

jobber *n.* **1** person who jobs. **2** *hist.* = STOCKJOBBER. **3** dealer who buys and sells commodities etc. for his or her own account.

jobbery *n.* corrupt dealing.

jobbing *attrib. adj.* freelance; pieceworking (*jobbing gardener*).

jobcentre *n.* local government office that advertises available jobs, assists employers to find suitable employees, and provides training facilities for trades in which there are shortages of skilled workers. Most centres also offer occupational advice on retraining.

♦ **job costing** *n.* attribution of separate costs to each job undertaken, a method of costing used, esp. in engineering, when a variety of different jobs are undertaken and there is no homogeneous product.

♦ **job description** see PERSONNEL SELECTION.

♦ **job enrichment** *n.* approach to job design that enhances staff motivation by increasing the tasks required of an employee, esp. those requiring autonomous decisions and personal control.

♦ **job evaluation** *n.* assessment of the work involved in a particular job, the responsibilities borne by the person who does it, and the skills, experience, or qualifications required, all with a view to evaluating the appropriate remuneration for the job and the differentials between it and other work in the same organization.

---

job-hunt *v. colloq.* seek employment.

jobless *adj.* unemployed. □ **joblessness** *n.*

job lot *n.* mixed lot bought at auction etc.

♦ **job satisfaction** *n.* sense of fulfilment felt by employees who enjoy their work and do it well. Its absence leads to absenteeism, accident proneness, and a demotivated workforce producing shoddy work.

Job's comforter /dʒəʊbz/ *n.* person who intends to comfort but increases distress. [*Job* in the Old Testament]

jobs for the boys *n.pl. colloq.* appointments for members of one's own group etc.

job-sharing *n.* sharing of a full-time job by two or more part-time employees.

jobsheet *n.* sheet for recording details of jobs done.

◆ **job specification** see PERSONNEL SELECTION.

Jock *n. slang* Scotsman. [Scots form of the name *Jack*]

jockey /'dʒɒkɪ/ *–n.* (*pl.* **-s**) rider in horse-races, esp. professional. *–v.* (**-eys, -eyed**) **1** trick, cheat, or outwit. **2** (foll. by *away, out, into*, etc.) manoeuvre (a person). □ **jockey for position** manoeuvre for advantage. [diminutive of JOCK]

jockstrap *n.* support or protection for the male genitals, worn esp. in sport. [slang *jock* genitals]

jocose /dʒə'kəʊs/ *adj.* playful; jocular. □ **jocosely** *adv.* **jocosity** /-'kɒsɪtɪ/ *n.* (*pl.* **-ies**). [Latin *jocus* jest]

jocular /'dʒɒkjʊlə(r)/ *adj.* **1** fond of joking. **2** humorous. □ **jocularity** /-'lærɪtɪ/ *n.* (*pl.* **-ies**). **jocularly** *adv.*

jocund /'dʒɒkənd/ *adj. literary* merry, cheerful. □ **jocundity** /dʒə'kʌndɪtɪ/ *n.* (*pl.* **-ies**). **jocundly** *adv.* [French from Latin *jucundus* pleasant]

Jodhpur /'dʒɒdpʊə(r)/ city in W India, in Rajasthan state; handicraft industries are important; pop. (1991) 666 279.

jodhpurs /'dʒɒdpəz/ *n.pl.* riding breeches tight below the knee. [JODHPUR]

Joe Bloggs *n. colloq.* hypothetical average man.

jog *–v.* (**-gg-**) **1** run slowly, esp. as exercise. **2** push or jerk, esp. unsteadily. **3** nudge, esp. to alert. **4** stimulate (the memory). **5** (often foll. by *on, along*) trudge; proceed ploddingly (*must jog on somehow*). **6** (of a horse) trot. *–n.* **1** spell of jogging; slow walk or trot. **2** push, jerk, or nudge. [probably imitative]

jogger *n.* person who jogs, esp. for exercise.

joggle /'dʒɒg(ə)l/ *–v.* (**-ling**) move in jerks. *–n.* slight shake.

Jogjakarta /ˌjɒgjə'kɑːtə/ city on the island of Java, capital of Indonesia 1945–9; pop. (1990) 412 392.

jogtrot *n.* slow regular trot.

Johannesburg /dʒəʊ'hænɪsˌbɜːg/ largest city of the Republic of South Africa in Gauteng, and the centre of the country's gold-mining industry; other industries include diamond cutting, chemicals, textiles, and engineering; pop. (1991) 1 916 063.

john /dʒɒn/ *n. US slang* lavatory. [from the name *John*]

John Bull /dʒɒn/ *n.* England or the typical Englishman. [name of a character in an 18th-century satire]

John Dory /dʒɒn 'dɔːrɪ/ *n.* (*pl.* same or **-ies**) edible marine fish. [see DORY]

johnny /'dʒɒnɪ/ *n.* (*pl.* **-ies**) **1** *slang* condom. **2** *colloq.* fellow; man. [diminutive of *John*]

johnny-come-lately *n. colloq.* newcomer; upstart.

Johor /dʒə'hɔː(r)/ (also **Johore**) state of Malaysia, joined by a causeway to Singapore, on which it depends for trading facilities; pop. (1991) 2 074 297; capital, Johor Baharu, pop. (1980) 249 880. Products include rubber, tin, and bauxite.

joie de vivre /ˌʒwɑː də 'viːvrə/ *n.* exuberance; high spirits. [French, = joy of living]

join *–v.* **1** (often foll. by *to, together*) put together; fasten, unite (with one or several things or people). **2** connect (points) by a line etc. **3** become a member of (a club, organization, etc.). **4 a** take one's place with (a person, group, etc.). **b** (foll. by *in, for*, etc.) take part with (others) in an activity etc. (*joined them in prayer*). **5** (often foll. by *with, to*) come together; be united. **6** (of a river etc.) be or become connected or continuous with. *–n.* point, line, or surface at which things are joined. □ **join battle** begin fighting. **join forces** combine efforts. **join hands** **1** clasp hands. **2** combine in an action etc. **join in** (also *absol.*) take part in (an activity). **join up 1** enlist for military service. **2** (often foll. by *with*) unite, connect. [Latin *jungo junct-*]

joiner *n.* **1** maker of finished wood fittings. **2** *colloq.* person who joins an organization or who readily joins societies etc. □ **joinery** *n.* (in sense 1).

joint *–n.* **1** place at which two or more things or parts of a structure are joined; device for joining these. **2** point at which two bones fit together. **3** division of an animal carcass as meat. **4** *slang* restaurant, bar, etc. **5** *slang* marijuana cigarette. **6** *Geol.* crack in rock. *–adj.* **1** held, done by, or belonging to, two or more persons etc. (*joint mortgage; joint action*). **2** sharing with another (*joint author; joint favourite*). *–v.* **1** connect by joint(s). **2** divide at a joint or into joints. □ **out of joint 1** (of a bone) dislocated. **2** out of order. □ **jointly** *adv.* [French: related to JOIN]

◆ **joint account** *n.* bank account or a building-society account held in the names of two or more people, often husband and wife. On the death of one party the balance in the account goes to the survivor(s), except in the case of partnerships, executors' accounts, or trustees' accounts. It is usual for any of the holders of a joint account to operate it alone.

◆ **joint and several liability** *n.* liability that is entered into as a group, on the understanding that if any of the group fail in their undertaking the liability must be shared by the remainder. Thus if two people enter into a joint and several guarantee for a bank loan, if one becomes bankrupt the other is liable for repayment of the whole loan.

◆ **Joint Industry Committee for National Readership** *n.* (also **JICNAR**) committee formed in 1968 to provide readership surveys, although continuous research and surveys have been undertaken since 1956. The committee comprises members of the Institute of Practitioners in Advertising, the Incorporated Society of British Advertisers Ltd., and the Newspaper and Periodical Contributors Committee. The committee reports twice yearly on the reading habits of 28 000 individuals, covering 200 titles. It also includes television viewing, commercial radio audiences, and special interests.

◆ **Joint Industry Committee for Radio Audience Research** *n.* (also **JICRAR**) committee composed of representatives of the Institute of Practitioners in Advertising, the Incorporated Society of British Advertisers Ltd., and independent radio companies. The committee provides information on the listening habits of radio audiences.

◆ **joint investment** *n.* security purchased by more than one person. The certificate will bear the names of all the parties, but only the first named will receive notices. To dispose of the holding all the parties must sign the transfer deed.

◆ **joint-life annuity** *n.* annuity that involves two people (usu. husband and wife), beginning payment on a specified date and continuing until both persons have died. A **last-survivor annuity** also involves two people but only begins payment on the death of one of the two people and pays until the death of the other. Cf. SINGLE-LIFE PENSION.

---

joint stock *n.* capital held jointly; common fund.

◆ **joint-stock bank** *n.* (also **JSB**) UK bank that is a public limited company rather than a private bank (which is a partnership). During the 19th century many private banks failed; the joint-stock banks became stronger, however, largely as a result of amalgamations and careful investment. In the present century, they became known as the commercial banks or high-street banks.

◆ **joint-stock company** *n.* company in which the members pool their stock and trade on the basis of their joint stock. This differs from the earliest type of company, the merchant corporations or regulated companies of the 14th century, in which members traded with their own stock, subject to the rules of the company. Joint-stock companies originated in the 17th century and some still exist, although they are now rare.

◆ **joint supply** *n.* (also **complementary supply**) supply of two or more separate commodities that are produced by the same process; examples include milk and butter, wool and mutton, and petrol and heavy oil. If the demand for one increases, the supply of the other will also increase, but its price will fall unless its demand also increases.

♦ **joint tenants** *n.pl.* two or more persons who jointly own an interest in land. When one dies, that person's share is taken by the other(s) by right of survivorship. No one tenant has rights to any particular part of the property and no tenant may exclude another.

---

jointure /'dʒɔɪntʃə(r)/ *–n.* estate settled on a wife by her husband for use after his death. *–v.* provide with a jointure. [Latin: related to JOIN]

joist *n.* supporting beam in a floor, ceiling, etc. [French *giste* from Latin *jaceo* lie]

jojoba /həʊ'həʊbə/ *n.* plant with seeds yielding an oily extract used in cosmetics etc. [Mexican Spanish]

joke *–n.* **1** thing said or done to cause laughter; witticism. **2** ridiculous person or thing. *–v.* (**-king**) make jokes; tease (*only joking*). □ **no joke** *colloq.* serious matter. □ **jokingly** *adv.* **joky** *adj.* (also **jokey**). **jokily** *adv.* **jokiness** *n.* [probably Latin *jocus* jest]

joker *n.* **1** person who jokes. **2** *slang* person. **3** playing-card used in some games.

jollify /'dʒɒlɪˌfaɪ/ *v.* (**-ies, -ied**) make merry. □ **jollification** /-fɪ'keɪʃ(ə)n/ *n.*

jollity /'dʒɒlɪtɪ/ *n.* (*pl.* **-ies**) merrymaking; festivity. [French *joliveté*: related to JOLLY[1]]

jolly[1] /'dʒɒlɪ/ *–adj.* (**-ier, -iest**) **1** cheerful; merry. **2** festive, jovial. **3** *colloq.* pleasant, delightful. *–adv. colloq.* very. *–v.* (**-ies, -ied**) (usu. foll. by *along*) *colloq.* coax or humour in a friendly way. *–n.* (*pl.* **-ies**) *colloq.* party or celebration. □ **jollily** *adv.* **jolliness** *n.* [French *jolif* gay, pretty: perhaps related to YULE]

jolly[2] /'dʒɒlɪ/ *n.* (*pl.* **-ies**) (in full **jolly boat**) clinker-built ship's boat smaller than a cutter. [origin unknown: perhaps related to YAWL]

Jolly Roger *n.* pirates' black flag, usu. with skull and crossbones.

jolt /dʒəʊlt/ *–v.* **1** disturb or shake (esp. in a moving vehicle) with a jerk. **2** shock; perturb. **3** move along jerkily. *–n.* **1** jerk. **2** surprise or shock. □ **jolty** *adj.* (**-ier, -iest**). [origin unknown]

Jonah /'dʒəʊnə/ *n.* person who seems to bring bad luck. [*Jonah* in the Old Testament]

Jönköping /jɜ:n'tʃɜ:pɪŋ/ industrial city in S Sweden; manufactures include matches, paper, footwear, and machinery; pop. (est. 1996) 196 429.

jonquil /'dʒɒŋkwɪl/ *n.* narcissus with small fragrant yellow or white flowers. [ultimately from Latin *juncus* rush plant]

Jordan, River river rising in Syria and Lebanon and flowing S to the Dead Sea, forming part of the border between Jordan and Israel.

josh *slang –v.* **1** tease, banter. **2** indulge in ridicule. *–n.* good-natured or teasing joke. [origin unknown]

joss *n.* Chinese idol. [ultimately from Latin *deus* god]

joss-stick *n.* incense-stick for burning.

jostle /'dʒɒs(ə)l/ *–v.* (**-ling**) **1** (often foll. by *away, from, against,* etc.) push against; elbow, esp. roughly or in a crowd. **2** (foll. by *with*) struggle roughly. *–n.* jostling. [from JOUST]

jot *–v.* (**-tt-**) (usu. foll. by *down*) write briefly or hastily. *–n.* very small amount (*not one jot*). [Greek IOTA]

jotter *n.* small pad or notebook.

jotting *n.* (usu. in *pl.*) jotted note.

joule /dʒu:l/ *n.* SI unit of work or energy. [*Joule*, name of a physicist]

journal /'dʒɜ:n(ə)l/ *n.* **1** newspaper or periodical. **2** daily record of events; diary. **3** book of prime entry in which transfers to be made from one account to another are recorded. It is used for transfers not recorded in any other of the books of prime entry, e.g. the sales day book or the cash-book. **4** part of a shaft or axle that rests on bearings. [Latin *diurnalis* DIURNAL]

journalese /ˌdʒɜ:nə'li:z/ *n.* hackneyed writing characteristic of newspapers.

journalism *n.* profession of writing for or editing newspapers etc.

journalist *n.* person writing for or editing newspapers etc. □ **journalistic** /-'lɪstɪk/ *adj.*

journey /'dʒɜ:nɪ/ *–n.* (*pl.* **-s**) **1** act of going from one place to another, esp. at a long distance. **2** time taken for this (*a day's journey*). *–v.* (**-s, -ed**) make a journey. [French *jornee* day, day's work or travel, from Latin *diurnus* daily]

journeyman *n.* **1** qualified mechanic or artisan who works for another. **2** *derog.* reliable but not outstanding worker.

joust /dʒaʊst/ *hist. –n.* combat between two knights on horseback with lances. *–v.* engage in a joust. □ **jouster** *n.* [French *jouste* from Latin *juxta* near]

Jove *n.* (in Roman mythology) Jupiter. □ **by Jove!** exclamation of surprise etc. [Latin *Jupiter Jov-*]

jovial /'dʒəʊvɪəl/ *adj.* merry, convivial, hearty. □ **joviality** /-'ælɪtɪ/ *n.* **jovially** *adv.* [Latin *jovialis*: related to JOVE]

jowl[1] *n.* **1** jaw or jawbone. **2** cheek (*cheek by jowl*). [Old English]

Jordan /'dʒɔ:d(ə)n/, **Hashemite Kingdom of** Arab state E of the River Jordan, bordered by Syria, Israel, Saudi Arabia, and Iraq; its only outlet to the sea is the port of Aqaba at the NE end of the Red Sea. Much of Jordan's industrial activities are concentrated on the mining of phosphates and potash (both exported); there are enough reserves of gas to provide a power source but the country is dependent for oil on Saudi Arabia and Iraq. The region is largely desert, agriculture being concentrated in the Jordan valley; crops include cereals, olives, grapes, and citrus fruits (fruits and vegetables are exported). Tourism is a developing industry. The economy was severely affected by Jordan's support for Iraq during the Gulf War (1990–1), but recovered in 1992 as money brought in by Jordanians expelled from Kuwait boosted investment and foreign-exchange reserves. However, the long-term economic future of Jordan rests largely on a successful outcome to the Middle East peace process and continuing improvement of relations with Saudi Arabia.

History. Under Turkish rule from the 16th century, in 1916 the region was made a British protectorate, the Amirate of Transjordan; this became independent in 1946 and assumed its present name in 1949. During the Arab-Israeli war of 1948–9 the Jordanians overran the West Bank, but were driven from this by Israel in the Six-Day War of 1967. In 1994 Jordan and Israel concluded a peace agreement that ended the state of war, which had existed since 1948. Also, in 1994 a border crossing between the two countries was established. In 1995 Israeli forces withdrew from land in the Arava valley, which was returned to Jordan. Head of state, King Hussein II; prime minister, Abdel Salam Majali; capital, Amman. □ **Jordanian** /-'deɪnɪən/ *adj.* & *n.*

languages	Arabic (official), English
currency	dinar (JD) of 1000 fils
pop. (est. 1996)	4 333 000
GNP (1994)	US$5.8B
literacy	91% (m); 79% (f)
life expectancy	64 (m); 69 (f)

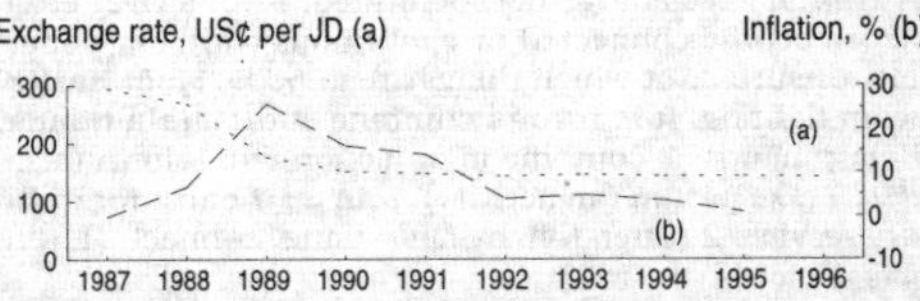

jowl[2] *n.* loose hanging skin on the throat or neck. □ **jowly** *adj.* [Old English]

joy *n.* **1** (often foll. by *at, in*) pleasure; extreme gladness. **2** thing causing joy. **3** *colloq.* satisfaction, success (*got no joy*). □ **joyful** *adj.* **joyfully** *adv.* **joyfulness** *n.* **joyless** *adj.* **joyous** *adj.* **joyously** *adv.* [French *joie* from Latin *gaudium*]

joyride *colloq.* –*n.* pleasure ride in esp. a stolen car. –*v.* (-**ding**; *past* **-rode**; *past part* **-ridden**) go for a joyride. □ **joyrider** *n.*

joystick *n.* **1** *colloq.* control column of an aircraft. **2** lever controlling movement of the cursor or some other symbol on a VDU screen etc., used with computer games and some computer-aided design programs.

JP –*abbr.* Justice of the Peace. –*airline flight code* Adria Airways.

Jr. *abbr.* Junior.

JSB *abbr.* = JOINT-STOCK BANK.

JTS *abbr.* job training standards.

JU *airline flight code* JAT Yugoslav Airlines.

Juba /'ʒuːbə/ city in S Sudan, a communications and trade centre; pop. (1993) 114 980.

jubilant /'dʒuːbɪlənt/ *adj.* exultant, rejoicing. □ **jubilance** *n.* **jubilantly** *adv.* **jubilation** /-'leɪʃ(ə)n/ *n.* [Latin *jubilo* shout]

jubilee /'dʒuːbɪˌliː/ *n.* **1** anniversary, esp. the 25th or 50th. **2** time of rejoicing. [Hebrew, ultimately, = ram's-horn trumpet]

Judaic /dʒuː'deɪɪk/ *adj.* of or characteristic of the Jews. [Greek: related to JEW]

Judaism /'dʒuːdeɪˌɪz(ə)m/ *n.* religion of the Jews.

Judas /'dʒuːdəs/ *n.* traitor. [*Judas* Iscariot who betrayed Christ]

judder –*v.* shake noisily or violently. –*n.* juddering. [imitative: cf. *shudder*]

judge /dʒʌdʒ/ –*n.* **1** public official appointed to hear and try legal cases. **2** person appointed to decide in a contest, dispute, etc. **3 a** person who decides a question. **b** person regarded as having judgement of a specified type (*am no judge; good judge of art*). –*v.* (**-ging**) **1** form an opinion or judgement (about); estimate, appraise. **2** act as a judge (of). **3 a** try (a case) at law. **b** pronounce sentence on. **4** (often foll. by *to* + infin. or *that* + clause) conclude, consider. [Latin *judex judic-*]

judgement *n.* (also **judgment**) **1** critical faculty; discernment (*error of judgement*). **2** good sense. **3** opinion or estimate (*in my judgement*). **4** sentence of a court of justice. **5** often *joc.* deserved misfortune. □ **against one's better judgement** contrary to what one really feels to be advisable.

judgemental /dʒʌdʒ'ment(ə)l/ *adj.* (also **judgmental**) **1** of or by way of judgement. **2** condemning, critical. □ **judgementally** *adv.*

♦ **judgement creditor** *n.* person in whose favour a court decides, ordering the judgement debtor to pay the sum owed. If the judgement debtor fails to pay, the judgement creditor must return to the court asking for the judgement to be enforced.

Judgement Day *n.* (in Judaism, Christianity, and Islam) day on which mankind will be judged by God.

♦ **judgement debtor** *n.* person against whom a court judgement has been entered ordering the payment of a debt. See JUDGEMENT CREDITOR.

---

judicature /'dʒuːdɪkətʃə(r)/ *n.* **1** administration of justice. **2** judge's position. **3** judges collectively. [medieval Latin *judico* judge]

judicial /dʒuː'dɪʃ(ə)l/ *adj.* **1** of, done by, or proper to a court of law. **2** having the function of judgement (*judicial assembly*). **3** of or proper to a judge. **4** impartial. □ **judicially** *adv.* [Latin *judicium* judgement]

judiciary /dʒuː'dɪʃərɪ/ *n.* (*pl.* **-ies**) judges of a state collectively.

judicious /dʒuː'dɪʃəs/ *adj.* sensible, prudent. □ **judiciously** *adv.*

judo /'dʒuːdəʊ/ *n.* sport derived from ju-jitsu. [Japanese, = gentle way]

jug –*n.* **1** deep vessel for liquids, with a handle and a lip for pouring. **2** contents of this. **3** *slang* prison. –*v.* (**-gg-**) (usu. as **jugged** *adj.*) stew or boil (esp. hare) in a casserole etc. □ **jugful** *n.* (*pl.* **-s**). [origin uncertain]

juggernaut /'dʒʌgəˌnɔːt/ *n.* **1** large heavy lorry etc. **2** overwhelming force or object. [Hindi *Jagannath*, = lord of the world]

juggle /'dʒʌg(ə)l/ –*v.* (**-ling**) **1 a** (often foll. by *with*) keep several objects in the air at once by throwing and catching. **b** perform such feats with (balls etc.). **2** deal with (several activities) at once. **3** (often foll. by *with*) misrepresent or rearrange (facts) adroitly. –*n.* **1** juggling. **2** fraud. □ **juggler** *n.* [French from Latin *jocus* jest]

jugular /'dʒʌgjʊlə(r)/ –*adj.* of the neck or throat. –*n.* = JUGULAR VEIN. [Latin *jugulum* collar-bone]

jugular vein *n.* any of several large veins in the neck carrying blood from the head.

juice /dʒuːs/ *n.* **1** liquid part of vegetables or fruits. **2** animal fluid, esp. a secretion (*gastric juice*). **3** *colloq.* petrol; electricity. [French from Latin]

juicy *adj.* (**-ier, -iest**) **1** full of juice; succulent. **2** *colloq.* interesting; racy, scandalous. **3** *colloq.* profitable. □ **juicily** *adv.* **juiciness** *n.*

ju-jitsu /dʒuː'dʒɪtsuː/ *n.* (also **jiu-jitsu, ju-jutsu**) Japanese system of unarmed combat and physical training. [Japanese *jūjutsu* gentle skill]

ju-ju /'dʒuːdʒuː/ *n.* **1** charm or fetish of some W African peoples. **2** supernatural power attributed to this. [perhaps French *joujou* toy]

jujube /'dʒuːdʒuːb/ *n.* small flavoured jelly-like lozenge. [Greek *zizuphon*]

ju-jutsu var. of JU-JITSU.

jukebox /'dʒuːkbɒks/ *n.* coin-operated record-playing machine. [Black *juke* disorderly]

Jul. *abbr.* July.

julep /'dʒuːlep/ *n.* **1 a** sweet drink, esp. as a vehicle for medicine. **b** medicated drink as a mild stimulant etc. **2** *US* iced and flavoured spirits and water (*mint julep*). [Persian *gulāb* rose-water]

Julian /'dʒuːlɪən/ *adj.* of Julius Caesar. [Latin *Julius*]

Julian calendar *n.* calendar introduced by Julius Caesar, with a year of 365 days, every fourth year having 366.

julienne /ˌdʒuːlɪ'en/ –*n.* vegetables cut into short thin strips. –*adj.* cut into thin strips. [French from name *Jules* or *Julien*]

Juliet cap /'dʒuːlɪət/ *n.* small net skullcap worn by brides etc. [*Juliet* in Shakespeare's *Romeo & Juliet*]

July /dʒuː'laɪ/ *n.* (*pl.* **Julys**) seventh month of the year. [Latin *Julius* Caesar]

jumble /'dʒʌmb(ə)l/ –*v.* (**-ling**) (often foll. by *up*) confuse; mix up; muddle. –*n.* **1** confused state or heap; muddle. **2** articles in a jumble sale. [probably imitative]

jumble sale *n.* sale of second-hand articles, esp. for charity.

jumbo /'dʒʌmbəʊ/ *n.* (*pl.* **-s**) *colloq.* **1** (*often attrib.*) large animal (esp. an elephant), person, or thing (*jumbo packet*). **2** (in full **jumbo jet**) large airliner for several hundred passengers. [probably from MUMBO-JUMBO]

■ **Usage** In sense 2, *jumbo* is usu. applied specifically to the Boeing 747.

jump –*v.* **1** rise off the ground etc. by sudden muscular effort in the legs. **2** (often foll. by *up, from, in, out,* etc.) move suddenly or hastily (*jumped into the car*). **3** jerk or twitch from shock or excitement etc. **4 a** change, esp. advance in status or rise, rapidly (*prices jumped*). **b** cause to do this. **5** (often foll. by *about*) change the subject etc. rapidly. **6** pass over (an obstacle etc.) by jumping. **7** skip (a passage in a book etc.). **8** cause (a horse etc.) to jump. **9** (foll. by *to, at*) reach (a conclusion) hastily. **10** (of a train) leave (the rails). **11** pass (a red traffic-light etc.). **12** get on or off (a train etc.) quickly, esp. illegally or dangerously. **13** attack (a person) unexpectedly. *–n.* **1** act of jumping. **2** sudden jerk caused by shock or excitement. **3** abrupt rise in amount, value, status, etc. **4** obstacle to be jumped. **5 a** sudden transition. **b** gap in a series, logical sequence, etc. □ **jump at** accept eagerly. **jump bail** fail to appear for trial having been released on bail. **jump down a person's throat** *colloq.* reprimand or contradict a person fiercely. **jump the gun** *colloq.* begin prematurely. **jump on** *colloq.* attack or criticize severely. **jump out of one's skin** *colloq.* be extremely startled. **jump the queue** take unfair precedence. **jump ship** (of a seaman) desert. **jump to it** *colloq.* act promptly. **one jump ahead** one stage further on than a rival etc. [imitative]

jumped-up *adj. colloq.* upstart.

jumper[1] *n.* **1** knitted pullover. **2** loose outer jacket worn by sailors. **3** *US* pinafore dress. [probably *jump* short coat]

jumper[2] *n.* **1** person or animal that jumps. **2** short wire used to make or break an electrical circuit.

jumping bean *n.* seed of a Mexican plant that jumps with the movement of a larva inside.

jump-jet *n.* vertical take-off jet aircraft.

jump-lead *n.* cable for conveying current from the battery of one vehicle to that of another.

jump-off *n.* deciding round in showjumping.

jump-start *–v.* start (a vehicle) by pushing it or with jump-leads. *–n.* act of jump-starting.

jump suit *n.* one-piece garment for the whole body.

jumpy *adj.* (**-ier, -iest**) **1** nervous; easily startled. **2** making sudden movements. □ **jumpiness** *n.*

Jun. *abbr.* **1** June. **2** Junior.

junction /'dʒʌŋkʃ(ə)n/ *n.* **1** joint; joining-point. **2** place where railway lines or roads meet. **3** joining. [Latin: related to JOIN]

junction box *n.* box containing a junction of electric cables etc.

juncture /'dʒʌŋktʃə(r)/ *n.* **1** critical convergence of events; point of time (*at this juncture*). **2** joining-point. **3** joining.

June *n.* sixth month of the year. [Latin *Junius* from *Juno*, name of a goddess]

Juneau /'dʒuːnəʊ/ seaport in the US, capital of Alaska; exports include gold and furs; pop. (1990) 26 751.

Jungian /'jʊŋɪən/ *–adj.* of the Swiss psychologist Carl Jung or his theories. *–n.* supporter of Jung or of his theories.

jungle /'dʒʌŋg(ə)l/ *n.* **1 a** land overgrown with tangled vegetation, esp. in the tropics. **b** an area of this. **2** wild tangled mass. **3** place of bewildering complexity, confusion, or struggle. □ **law of the jungle** state of ruthless competition. □ **jungly** *adj.* [Hindi from Sanskrit]

junior /'dʒuːnɪə(r)/ *–adj.* **1** (often foll. by *to*) inferior in age, standing, or position. **2** the younger (esp. appended to the name of a son for distinction from his father). **3** of the lower or lowest position (*junior partner*). **4** (of a school) for younger pupils, usu. aged 7–11. *–n.* **1** junior person. **2** person at the lowest level (in an office etc.). [Latin, comparative of *juvenis* young]

junior common room *n.* (also **junior combination room**) **1** common-room for undergraduates in a college. **2** undergraduates of a college collectively.

juniper /'dʒuːnɪpə(r)/ *n.* evergreen shrub or tree with prickly leaves and dark-purple berry-like cones. [Latin *juniperus*]

junk[1] *–n.* **1** discarded articles; rubbish. **2** anything regarded as of little value. **3** *slang* narcotic drug, esp. heroin. *–v.* discard as junk. [origin unknown]

junk[2] *n.* flat-bottomed sailing-vessel in the China seas. [Javanese *djong*]

junk bond *n.* bond bearing high interest but deemed to be a risky investment. The issuing of junk bonds to finance the take-over of large companies in the US is a practice that has developed rapidly over recent years and has spread elsewhere. See LEVERAGED BUYOUT.

junket /'dʒʌŋkɪt/ *–n.* **1** pleasure outing. **2** official's tour at public expense. **3** sweetened and flavoured milk curds. **4** feast. *–v.* (**-t-**) feast, picnic. [French *jonquette* rush-basket (used for junket 3 and 4), from Latin *juncus* rush]

junk food *n.* food, such as sweets and crisps, with low nutritional value.

junkie *n. slang* drug addict.

junk mail *n.* unsolicited advertising matter sent by post.

junk shop *n.* second-hand or cheap antiques shop.

junta /'dʒʌntə/ *n.* (usu. military) clique taking power in a *coup d'état*. [Spanish: related to JOIN]

jural /'dʒʊər(ə)l/ *adj.* **1** of law. **2** of rights and obligations. [Latin *jus jur-* law, right]

Jurassic /dʒʊə'ræsɪk/ *Geol. –adj.* of the second period of the Mesozoic era. *–n.* this era or system. [French from *Jura* mountains]

juridical /dʒʊə'rɪdɪk(ə)l/ *adj.* **1** of judicial proceedings. **2** relating to the law. [Latin *jus jur-* law, *dico* say]

jurisdiction /ˌdʒʊərɪs'dɪkʃ(ə)n/ *n.* **1** (often foll. by *over*, *of*) administration of justice. **2 a** legal or other authority. **b** extent of this; territory it extends over. □ **jurisdictional** *adj.*

jurisprudence /ˌdʒʊərɪs'pruːd(ə)ns/ *n.* science or philosophy of law. □ **jurisprudential** /-'denʃ(ə)l/ *adj.*

jurist /'dʒʊərɪst/ *n.* expert in law. □ **juristic** /-'rɪstɪk/ *adj.*

juror /'dʒʊərə(r)/ *n.* **1** member of a jury. **2** person taking an oath.

jury /'dʒʊərɪ/ *n.* (*pl.* **-ies**) **1** body of usu. twelve people giving a verdict in a court of justice. **2** body of people awarding prizes in a competition.

jury-box *n.* enclosure for the jury in a lawcourt.

jury-rigged /'dʒʊərɪrɪgd/ *adj. Naut.* having temporary makeshift rigging. [origin uncertain]

just *–adj.* **1** morally right or fair. **2** (of treatment etc.) deserved (*just reward*). **3** well-grounded; justified (*just anger*). **4** right in amount etc.; proper. *–adv.* **1** exactly (*just what I need*). **2** a little time ago; very recently (*has just seen them*). **3** *colloq.* simply, merely (*just good friends*; *just doesn't make sense*). **4** barely; no more than (*just managed it*). **5** *colloq.* positively; indeed (*just splendid*; *won't I just tell him!*). **6** quite (*not just yet*). □ **just about** *colloq.* almost exactly; almost completely. **just in case** as a precaution. **just now 1** at this moment. **2** a little time ago. **just the same** = *all the same*. **just so 1** exactly arranged (*everything just so*). **2** it is exactly as you say. □ **justly** *adv.* **justness** *n.* [Latin *justus* from *jus* right]

justice /'dʒʌstɪs/ *n.* **1** justness, fairness. **2** authority exercised in the maintenance of right. **3** judicial proceedings (*brought to justice*; *Court of Justice*). **4** magistrate; judge. □ **do justice to 1** treat fairly. **2** appreciate properly. **do oneself justice** perform at one's best. **with justice** reasonably. [Latin *justitia*]

Justice of the Peace *n.* (also **JP**) unpaid lay magistrate appointed to hear minor cases.

justifiable /'dʒʌstɪˌfaɪəb(ə)l/ *adj.* able to be justified. □ **justifiably** *adv.*

justify /'dʒʌstɪˌfaɪ/ *v.* (**-ies, -ied**) **1** show the justice or correctness of (a person, act, assertion, etc.). **2** (esp. in *passive*) cite or constitute adequate grounds for (conduct, a claim, etc.); vindicate. **3** (as **justified** *adj.*) just, right (*justified in assuming*). **4** *Printing* & *Computing* adjust (a line of printed or typed characters) to give even margins. The lines are **left-justified** when only the left-hand margin is regular or **right-justified** when only the right-hand margin is regular. Word-processing systems usu. allow the user to specify both the right and the left margin, between which text is automatically justified as it is typed in; hyphenation is usu. offered as an option. □ **justification** /-fɪ'keɪʃ(ə)n/ *n.* **justificatory** /-fɪˌkeɪtərɪ/ *adj.*

jut *–v.* (**-tt-**) (often foll. by *out*, *forth*) protrude, project. *–n.* projection. [var. of JET[1]]

jute *n.* **1** fibre from the bark of an E Indian plant, used esp. for sacking, mats, etc. **2** plant yielding this. [Bengali]

Jutland /'dʒʌtlənd/ (Danish **Jylland** /'juːlæn/) peninsula in NW Europe stretching N from Germany to form part of Denmark.

juvenile /ˈdʒuːvəˌnaɪl/ *–adj.* **1 a** youthful. **b** of or for young people. **2** often *derog.* immature (*juvenile behaviour*). *–n.* **1** young person. **2** actor playing a juvenile part. [Latin *juvenis* young]

juvenile court *n.* court for children under 17.

juvenile delinquency *n.* offences committed by people below the age of legal responsibility. □ **juvenile delinquent** *n.*

juvenilia /ˌdʒuːvəˈnɪlɪə/ *n.pl.* author's or artist's youthful works.

juxtapose /ˌdʒʌkstəˈpəʊz/ *v.* **(-sing) 1** place (things) side by side. **2** (foll. by *to*, *with*) place (a thing) beside another. □ **juxtaposition** /-pəˈzɪʃ(ə)n/ *n.* **juxtapositional** /-pəˈzɪʃən(ə)l/ *adj.* [Latin *juxta* next, *pono* put]

JV *abbr. Commerce* joint venture.

j.w.o. *abbr. Insurance* jettisoning and washing overboard.

JY *–airline flight code* Jersey European Airways. *–international civil aircraft marking* Jordan.

Jylland see JUTLAND.

Jyväskylä /juːˈvɑːskjʊlə/ city in central Finland, capital of Keski-Suomi province; paper, pharmaceuticals, and munitions are manufactured; pop. (1994) 73 083.

K[1] /keɪ/ *n.* (also **k**) (*pl.* **Ks** or **K's**) eleventh letter of the alphabet.

K[2] *abbr.* (also **K.**) **1** King, King's. **2** Köchel (catalogue of Mozart's works). **3** (also **k**) (prec. by a numeral) *Computing* **a** = KILOBYTE. **b** kilobit (see KILO- 2). **4** thousand. [sense 4 as abbreviation of KILO-]

K[3] *–symb.* **1** potassium. **2** kelvin(s). *–international vehicle registration* Cambodia. [sense 1 Latin *kalium*]

k *–abbr.* **1** kilo-. **2** knot(s). *–symb. Currency* **a** kina. **b** kwacha (of Zambia). **c** kyat.

KA *postcode* Kilmarnock.

Kabul /'kɑːbʊl/ capital of Afghanistan; products include textiles, plastics, and glass; pop. (est. 1988) 1 424 400.

Kabwe /'kæbwɪ/ (formerly **Broken Hill**) town in central Zambia; copper, cadmium, lead, and zinc are mined; pop. (1990) 166 519.

Kaffir /'kæfə(r)/ *n.* **1** *hist.* member or language of a S African people of the Bantu family. **2** *S.Afr. offens.* any Black African. **3** (in *pl.*) *colloq.* shares in South African gold-mining companies on the London Stock Exchange. [Arabic, = infidel]

Kafkaesque /ˌkæfkə'resk/ *adj.* impenetrably oppressive or nightmarish, as in the fiction of Franz Kafka.

kaftan var. of CAFTAN.

Kagoshima /ˌkægɒ'ʃiːmə/ city and port in Japan, on Kyushu island; manufactures include porcelain and textiles; pop. (1995) 546 300.

Kairouan /ˌkaɪruː'ɑːn/ Muslim holy city in N Tunisia; carpets and craft goods are manufactured; pop. (1994) 102 600.

kaiser /'kaɪzə(r)/ *n. hist.* emperor, esp. of Germany, Austria, or the Holy Roman Empire. [Latin CAESAR]

◆ ***kaizen*** /kaɪ'ʒen/ *n.* philosophy of continuous improvement of working practices underlying TOTAL QUALITY MANAGEMENT and JIT techniques. [Japanese]

---

kalashnikov /kə'læʃnɪˌkɒf/ *n.* type of Soviet rifle or sub-machine-gun. [Russian]

kale *n.* variety of cabbage, esp. with wrinkled leaves and no heart. [northern English var. of COLE]

kaleidoscope /kə'laɪdəˌskəʊp/ *n.* **1** tube containing mirrors and pieces of coloured glass etc. producing changing reflected patterns when shaken. **2** constantly changing pattern, group, etc. □ **kaleidoscopic** /-'skɒpɪk/ *adj.* [Greek *kalos* beautiful, *eidos* form, -SCOPE]

kalends var. of CALENDS.

kaleyard *n. Scot.* kitchen garden.

Kalgoorlie /kæl'gʊəlɪ/ gold-mining town in S central Western Australia; pop. (est. 1991) 26 079.

Kalimantan /ˌkælɪ'mæntæn/ SE part of the island of Borneo, belonging to Indonesia; timber, oil, and coal are produced; pop. (est. 1995) 10 520 500.

Kalinin /kə'liːnɪn/ see TVER.

Kaliningrad /kə'liːnɪnˌgræd/ (formerly **Königsberg**) ice-free Baltic seaport in W Russia; industries include shipbuilding, engineering, and food processing; pop. (est. 1995) 419 000.

Kalmar /'kælmɑː(r)/ city in SE Sweden, opposite the island of Öland; pop. (1994) 58 070. It manufactures matches, paper, and glassware.

Kamchatka /kæm'tʃætkə/ peninsula in E Russia, separating the Sea of Okhotsk from the Bering Sea. Its chief port is Petropavlovsk-Kamchatskiy.

kamikaze /ˌkæmɪ'kɑːzɪ/ *–n. hist.* **1** explosive-laden Japanese aircraft deliberately crashed on a ship etc. during the war of 1939–45. **2** pilot of this. *–attrib. adj.* **1** of a kamikaze. **2** reckless, esp. suicidal. [Japanese, = divine wind]

◆ **kamikaze pricing** *n.* practice of offering loans at exceptionally low interest rates to capture a large share of the corporate banking market.

Kampala /kæm'pɑːlə/ capital of Uganda, an administrative centre with food-processing, textile, and other light industries; pop. (est. 1991) 773 463.

Kampuchea /ˌkæmpʊ'tʃɪə/ see CAMBODIA.

Kan. *abbr.* Kansas.

◆ ***kanban*** /'kænbæn/ *n.* **1** JIT manufacturing process in which the movements of materials through a process are recorded on specially designed cards. **2** any of the cards used for ordering materials in such a system. [Japanese]

Kandahar /ˌkændə'hɑː(r)/ city and commercial centre in S Afghanistan; wool and cotton are processed; pop. (est. 1988) 225 500.

Kandy /'kændɪ/ city in central Sri Lanka, a commercial centre for the tea industry; pop. (est. 1990) 104 000.

kangaroo /ˌkæŋgə'ruː/ *n.* (*pl.* **-s**) **1** Australian marsupial with strong hind legs for jumping. **2** (in *pl.*) *colloq.* Australian shares, esp. in mining, land, and tobacco companies, on the London Stock Exchange. [Aboriginal]

kangaroo court *n.* illegal court, e.g. held by strikers or mutineers.

KaNgwane /ˌkɑː'ngwɑːneɪ/ former Bantu homeland in South Africa. It was abolished following democratic elections held in 1994.

Kano /'kɑːnəʊ/ city in N Nigeria, a trading centre (esp. for peanuts and livestock) with various light manufacturing and heavy industries; pop. (est. 1995) 657 300.

Kanpur /kɑːn'pʊə(r)/ (formerly **Cawnpore** /kɔːn'pɔː(r)/) city in India, on the River Ganges in Uttar Pradesh, a major communications and industrial centre whose manufactures include leather goods, plastics, and chemicals; pop. (1991) 1 874 400.

Kans. *abbr.* Kansas.

Kansas /'kænsəs/ state in the Midwest of the US; pop. (est. 1996) 2 572 150; capital, Topeka. Agricultural produce includes wheat, sorghum, and cattle and there are various manufacturing and food-processing industries; mining, esp. of petroleum and gas, is important.

Kansas City 1 industrial city in the US, in NE Kansas; manufactures include chemicals, motor vehicles, and paper goods; pop. (est. 1994) 142 630. **2** city in the US, in NW Missouri, adjacent to Kansas City, Kans.; pop. (est. 1994) 443 878. A marketing and distribution centre for a large agricultural region, it has food-processing and various other manufacturing industries.

Kansu see GANSU.

Kanto /kæn'təʊ/ region of Japan, on the island of Honshu; pop. (1995) 39 518 468; capital, Tokyo.

Kaohsiung /ˌkaʊʃɪ'ʊŋ/ main seaport of Taiwan, situated on the W coast of the island; industries include oil refining and food processing; pop. (est. 1996) 1 196 459.

kaolin /'keɪəlɪn/ *n.* fine soft white clay used esp. for porcelain and in medicines. [Chinese *kao-ling* high hill]

kapok /'keɪpɒk/ *n.* fine fibrous cotton-like substance from a tropical tree, used for padding. [Malay]

kappa /ˈkæpə/ *n.* tenth letter of the Greek alphabet (Κ, κ). [Greek]

kaput /kəˈpʊt/ *predic. adj. slang* broken, ruined. [German]

karabiner /ˌkærəˈbiːnə(r)/ *n.* coupling link used by mountaineers. [German, literally 'carbine']

Karachi /kəˈrɑːtʃɪ/ largest city and seaport of Pakistan, capital of Sind province; manufactures include textiles, machinery, chemicals, and plastics; pop. (est. 1995) 9 863 000.

karakul /ˈkærəˌkʊl/ *n.* (also **caracul**) **1** Asian sheep with a dark curled fleece when young. **2** fur of or like this. [Russian]

karaoke /ˌkærɪˈəʊkɪ/ *n.* entertainment in nightclubs etc. with customers singing to a backing track. [Japanese, = empty orchestra]

Kara Sea /ˈkɑːrə/ arm of the Arctic Ocean E of the island of Novaya Zemlaya and N of Russia.

karate /kəˈrɑːtɪ/ *n.* Japanese system of unarmed combat using the hands and feet as weapons. [Japanese, = empty hand]

Karelia /kəˈriːlɪə/ autonomous republic of NW Russia; there are timber, chemical, and mining industries, and fishing is important; pop. (est. 1995) 788 000. □ **Karelian** *adj.* & *n.*

Kariba /kəˈriːbə/, **Lake** artificial lake on the Zambia–Zimbabwe frontier, which was created by building the Kariba Dam across the Zambezi River and provides hydroelectric power for a wide area in both countries.

Karl-Marx-Stadt see CHEMNITZ.

Karlovy Vary /ˌkɑːləvɪ ˈvɑːrɪ/ (German **Carlsbad** /ˈkɑːlzbæd/) spa town in the Czech Republic, famous for its alkaline thermal springs; pop. (1991) 56 290.

Karlsruhe /ˈkɑːlzruːə/ industrial city in W Germany, a port on the Rhine; industries include oil refining, engineering, and nuclear research; pop. (est. 1995) 277 011.

karma /ˈkɑːmə/ *n. Buddhism* & *Hinduism* person's actions in previous lives, believed to decide his or her fate in future existences. [Sanskrit, = action, fate]

Karnataka /kəˈnɑːtəkə/ (formerly **Mysore**) state in S India; pop. (1991) 44 817 398; capital, Bangalore. Rice, sugar cane, tea, coffee, and cotton are grown, and forests provide teak and sandalwood; iron ore, gold, and other minerals are mined.

Kärnten see CARINTHIA.

Kars /kɑːs/ city in NE Turkey, noted for its cheese, woollen textiles, felt, and carpet-weaving; pop. (1990) 79 496.

Kashmir /kæʃˈmɪə(r)/ northernmost region of the Indian subcontinent. It was partitioned in 1949, the NW area being controlled by Pakistan, and the remainder becoming a state of India (see JAMMU AND KASHMIR).

Kasur /kəˈsʊə(r)/ city in NE Pakistan, in Punjab province; industries include tanning and weaving; pop. (1981) 155 000.

Kathmandu /ˌkætmænˈduː/ capital of Nepal, a communications and trade centre; pop. (est. 1993) 535 000.

Katowice /ˌkætəˈviːtseɪ/ city in S Poland, industrial centre of the Upper Silesian coalmining region; pop. (est. 1995) 355 100.

Kattegat /ˈkætɪˌgæt/ sea-channel separating Sweden and Denmark.

kauri /ˈkaʊrɪ/ *n.* (*pl.* **-s**) coniferous New Zealand tree yielding timber and resin. [Maori]

Kaválla /kəˈvælə/ port in NE Greece, on the Aegean coast of the province of Macedonia; pop. (est. 1991) 58 576.

Kawasaki /ˌkæwəˈsɑːkɪ/ industrial city in Japan, on Honshu Island; manufactures include vehicles, machine tools, chemicals, and textiles; pop. (1995) 1 202 811.

kayak /ˈkaɪæk/ *n.* **1** Eskimo one-man canoe of wood and sealskins. **2** small covered canoe. [Eskimo]

Kazakh /ˈkæzɑːk/ *–n.* **1** native of Kazakhstan. **2** language of Kazakhstan. *–adj.* of the people or language of Kazakhstan.

Kazan /kəˈzæn, -ˈzænjə/ city and port in W Russia; industries include oil refining, electrical engineering, and food processing; pop. (est. 1993) 1 085 000.

kazoo /kəˈzuː/ *n.* toy musical instrument into which the player sings or hums. [origin uncertain]

KB *abbr. Computing* **1** kilobyte. **2** knowledge base.

KBE *abbr.* Knight Commander of the Order of the British Empire.

KBES *abbr. Computing* knowledge-based expert system.

KBS *abbr. Computing* knowledge-based system.

k byte *n.* (also **K byte**) *Computing* = KILOBYTE. [contraction]

KC *abbr.* King's Counsel.

Kčs *symb.* koruna.

KD *–abbr.* (also **k.d.**) knocked (or knock) down (of goods). *–symb.* Kuwaiti dinar.

KDC *abbr.* (also **k.d.c.**) knocked-down condition (of goods).

KE *airline flight code* Korean Air.

kea /ˈkiːə, ˈkeɪə/ *n.* New Zealand parrot with brownish-green and red plumage. [Maori, imitative]

kebab /kɪˈbæb/ *n.* pieces of meat, vegetables, etc. cooked on a skewer (cf. DONER KEBAB, SHISH KEBAB). [Urdu from Arabic]

Kedah /ˈkedə/ state of Malaysia, in the NW of the Malay peninsula; products include rubber, iron, and tungsten; pop. (est. 1993) 1 412 000; capital, Alor Setar.

kedge *–v.* (**-ging**) **1** move (a ship) with a hawser attached to a small anchor. **2** (of a ship) move in this way. *–n.* (in full **kedge-anchor**) small anchor for this purpose. [origin uncertain]

kedgeree /ˌkedʒəˈriː/ *n.* dish of fish, rice, hard-boiled eggs, etc. [Hindi]

keel *–n.* main lengthwise member of the base of a ship etc. *–v.* **1** (often foll. by *over*) (cause to) fall down or over. **2** turn keel upwards. □ **on an even keel** steady; balanced. [Old Norse]

♦ **keelage** *n.* fee paid by the owners of a ship for being permitted to dock in certain ports and harbours.

Kazakhstan /ˌkæzɑːkˈstɑːn/, **Republic of** country in central Asia, extending from the Caspian Sea E to China. The country's economy relies heavily on its rich mineral resources, including oil, gas, copper, lead, zinc, iron ore, and coal. Agriculture is also important, with both stock-rearing and arable farming (esp. of cereals and cotton); textiles are exported. Until 1991 Kazakhstan was a constituent republic of the Soviet Union. The Socialist (formerly Communist) government, which remained in power after independence was declared, has shown a cautious approach to market reforms but initiated a privatization programme in 1992. President, Nursultan Nazarbaev; capital, Akmola.

languages	Kazakh (official), Russian
currency	tenge of 100 tiyn
pop. (1996)	16 677 000
GNP (1994)	US$18.8B
literacy	99% (m); 96% (f)
life expectancy	64 (m); 73 (f)

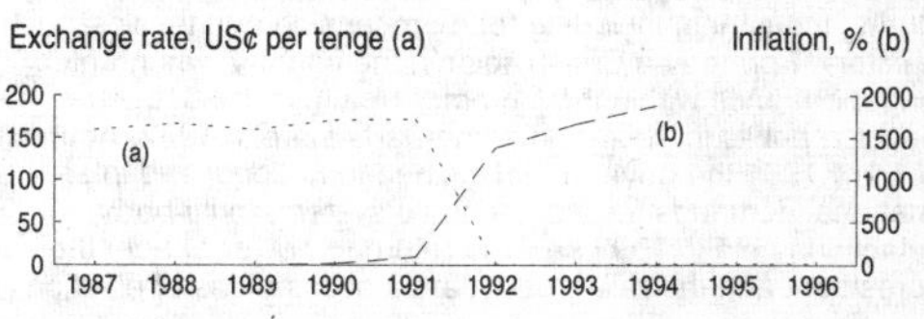

keelhaul *v.* **1** drag (a person) under the keel of a ship as a punishment. **2** scold or rebuke severely.

Keeling Islands see COCOS ISLANDS.

keelson /ˈkiːls(ə)n/ *n.* (also **kelson** /ˈkels(ə)n/) line of timber fastening a ship's floor-timbers to its keel. [origin uncertain]

keen[1] *adj.* **1** enthusiastic, eager. **2** (foll. by *on*) enthusiastic about, fond of. **3** (of the senses) sharp. **4** intellectually acute. **5** (of a knife etc.) sharp. **6** (of a sound, light, etc.) penetrating, vivid. **7** (of a wind etc.) piercingly cold. **8** (of a pain etc.) acute. **9** (of a price) competitive. □ **keenly** *adv.* **keenness** *n.* [Old English]

keen[2] *–n.* Irish wailing funeral song. *–v.* (often foll. by *over, for*) wail mournfully, esp. at a funeral. [Irish *caoine* from *caoinim* wail]

keep *–v.* (*past* and *past part.* **kept**) **1** have continuous charge of; retain possession of. **2** (foll. by *for*) retain or reserve for (a future time) (*kept it for later*). **3** retain or remain in a specified condition, position, place, etc. (*keep cool; keep out; keep them happy; knives are kept here*). **4** (foll. by *from*) restrain, hold back. **5** detain (*what kept you?*). **6** observe, honour, or respect (a law, custom, commitment, secret, etc.) (*keep one's word; keep the sabbath*). **7** own and look after (animals). **8 a** clothe, feed, maintain, etc. (a person, oneself, etc.). **b** (foll. by *in*) maintain (a person) with a supply of. **9** carry on; manage (a business etc.). **10** maintain (a diary, house, accounts, etc.) regularly and in proper order. **11** normally have on sale (*do you keep buttons?*). **12** guard or protect (a person or place). **13** preserve (*keep order*). **14** (foll. by verbal noun) continue; repeat habitually (*keeps telling me*). **15** continue to follow (a way or course). **16 a** (esp. of food) remain in good condition. **b** (of news etc.) not suffer from delay in telling. **17** (often foll. by *to*) remain in (one's bed, room, etc.). **18** maintain (a person) as one's mistress etc. (*kept woman*). *–n.* **1** maintenance, food, etc. (*hardly earn your keep*). **2** *hist.* tower, esp. the central stronghold of a castle. □ **for keeps** *colloq.* permanently, indefinitely. **how are you keeping?** how are you? **keep at** (cause to) persist with. **keep away** (often foll. by *from*) avoid, prevent from being near. **keep back 1** remain or keep at a distance. **2** retard the progress of. **3** conceal. **4** withhold (*kept back £50*). **keep down 1** hold in subjection. **2** keep low in amount. **3** stay hidden. **4** not vomit (food eaten). **keep one's hair on** see HAIR. **keep one's hand in** see HAND. **keep in with** remain on good terms with. **keep off 1** (cause to) stay away from. **2** ward off. **3** abstain from. **4** avoid (a subject) (*let's keep off religion*). **keep on 1** continue; do continually (*kept on laughing*). **2** continue to employ. **3** (foll. by *at*) nag. **keep out 1** keep or remain outside. **2** exclude. **keep to 1** adhere to (a course, promise, etc.). **2** confine oneself to. **keep to oneself 1** avoid contact with others. **2** keep secret. **keep track of** see TRACK. **keep under** repress. **keep up 1** maintain (progress, morale, etc.). **2** keep in repair etc. **3** carry on (a correspondence etc.). **4** prevent from going to bed. **5** (often foll. by *with*) not fall behind. **keep up with the Joneses** compete socially with one's neighbours. [Old English]

keeper *n.* **1** person who looks after or is in charge of animals, people, or a thing. **2** custodian of a museum, forest, etc. **3 a** = WICKET-KEEPER. **b** = GOALKEEPER. **4 a** sleeper in a pierced ear. **b** ring that keeps another on the finger.

keep-fit *n.* regular physical exercises.

keeping *n.* **1** custody, charge (*in safe keeping*). **2** agreement, harmony (esp. *in* or *out of keeping (with)*).

keepsake *n.* souvenir, esp. of a person.

Kefallinia see CEPHALONIA.

Keflavik /ˈkefləˌviːk/ fishing-port in SW Iceland; pop. (1994) 7627. Iceland's international airport is located nearby, and there is a NATO air base.

keg *n.* small barrel. [Old Norse]

keg beer *n.* beer kept in a metal keg under pressure.

Kelantan /keˈlænt(ə)n/ state of Malaysia, in the N of the Malay peninsula; pop. (1991) 1 181 680; capital, Kota Baharu. Tin, manganese, and gold are mined; other products include rubber and copra.

kelp *n.* **1** large brown seaweed suitable for manure. **2** its calcined ashes, formerly a source of sodium, potassium, etc. [origin unknown]

kelpie /ˈkelpɪ/ *n. Scot.* **1** malevolent water-spirit, usu. in the form of a horse. **2** Australian sheepdog. [origin unknown]

kelson var. of KEELSON.

Kelt var. of CELT.

kelt *n.* salmon or sea trout after spawning. [origin unknown]

kelter var. of KILTER.

kelvin /ˈkelvɪn/ *n.* SI unit of thermodynamic temperature. [*Kelvin* name of a physicist]

Kelvin scale *n.* scale of temperature with zero at absolute zero.

Kemerovo /ˈkemərəvə/ industrial city in S Russia; coalmining and chemical production are important; pop. (est. 1995) 503 000.

ken *–n.* range of knowledge or sight (*beyond my ken*). *–v.* (**-nn-**; *past* and *past part.* **kenned** or **kent**) *Scot.* & *N.Engl.* **1** recognize at sight. **2** know. [Old English, = make known: related to CAN[1]]

Ken. *abbr.* Kentucky.

kendo /ˈkendəʊ/ *n.* Japanese fencing with two-handed bamboo swords. [Japanese, = sword-way]

kennel /ˈken(ə)l/ *–n.* **1** small shelter for a dog. **2** (in *pl.*) breeding or boarding place for dogs. *–v.* (**-ll-**; *US* **-l-**) put into or keep in a kennel. [French *chenil* from Latin *canis* dog]

Kent /kent/ county in SE England; pop. (est. 1994) 1 546 300; county town, Maidstone. Market gardening

---

Kenya /ˈkenjə/, **Republic of** country in E Africa, bisected by the equator and with a coastline on the Indian Ocean. The economy is based on agriculture, the main exports being tea, coffee, fruit, and vegetables; hides and skins are also exported. Exploited mineral resources include soda ash, salt, and limestone, and hydroelectricity has been developed as a power source. Oil refining is an important industry, making a significant contribution to export revenue. There are also steel and textile industries. Tourism is also a source of income, the main attraction being the wildlife reserves, and there are growing manufacturing industries, including food processing and textiles. *History.* Formerly a British colony, the country was granted independence within the Commonwealth in 1963, becoming a republic in 1964 and a one-party state in 1982. At the end of 1991 the government yielded to national and international demands for a democratic system; multi-party elections held in 1992 saw the return to power of both the president and the ruling party, amid accusations of election rigging that were supported by Commonwealth observers. Daniel arap Moi was re-elected president in January 1998, again amidst allegations of election rigging. President, Daniel arap Moi; capital, Nairobi. □ **Kenyan** *adj.* & *n.*

languages	Swahili, English
currency	shilling (KSh) of 100 cents
pop. (1996)	29 137 000
GNP (1994)	US$6.6B
literacy	86 % (m); 70% (f)
life expectancy	57 (m); 57 (f)

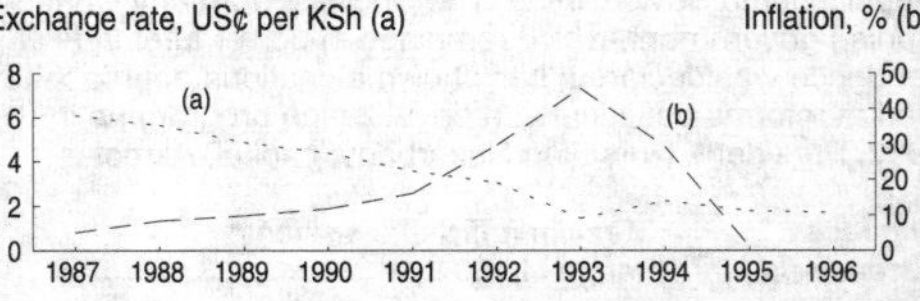

and agriculture are major activities; industries include paper manufacture and oil refining.

kent *past* and *past part.* of KEN.

Kentucky /ken'tʌkɪ/ state in the central SE US; pop. (est. 1996) 3 883 723; capital, Frankfort. Tobacco-, cattle-, and dairy-farming are traditional occupations, and the state is known for its thoroughbred horses. Coalmining is important; manufacturing industries produce machinery, paints, and textiles.

kepi /'keɪpɪ/ *n.* (*pl.* **-s**) French military cap with a horizontal peak. [French *képi*]

kept *past* and *past part.* of KEEP.

Kerala /'kerələ/ state in SW India; pop. (est. 1994) 30 555 000; capital, Trivandrum. Crops include rice, tea, coffee, and nuts; fishing is also important. □ **Keralite** /-laɪt/ *adj.* & *n.*

keratin /'kerətɪn/ *n.* fibrous protein in hair, feathers, hooves, claws, horns, etc. [Greek *keras kerat-* horn]

kerb *n.* stone edging to a pavement or raised path. [var. of CURB]

kerb-crawling *n. colloq.* driving slowly in order to engage a prostitute.

kerb drill *n.* precautions before crossing a road.

♦ **kerb market** *n.* **1** *hist.* trading on the street after the formal close of business of the London Stock Exchange. **2** dealing on the London Metal Exchange in any metal, after the formal ring trading in specified metals. **3** any informal financial market, e.g. one for dealing in securities not listed on a stock exchange.

kerbstone *n.* stone forming part of a kerb.

kerchief /'kɜːtʃɪf/ *n.* **1** headscarf, neckerchief. **2** *poet.* handkerchief. [Anglo-French *courchef*: related to COVER, CHIEF]

kerfuffle /kə'fʌf(ə)l/ *n. colloq.* fuss, commotion. [originally Scots]

Kérkira see CORFU.

♦ **Kerkorian** /kɜː'kɔːrɪən/, **Kirk** (1917–) US businessman, chief executive officer (1973–74), vice-chairman (1974–79) and controlling stockholder of film company MGM. He has bought the company three times and sold it twice.

Kerkrade /'kɜːkrɑːdə/ mining town in the Netherlands; pop. (1994) 52 848.

kermes /'kɜːmɪz/ *n.* **1** female of an insect with a berry-like appearance. **2** (in full **kermes oak**) evergreen oak on which this feeds. **3** red dye made from these insects dried. [Arabic]

kernel /'kɜːn(ə)l/ *n.* **1** (usu. soft) edible centre within the hard shell of a nut, fruit stone, seed, etc. **2** whole seed of a cereal. **3** essence of anything. [Old English: related to CORN[1]]

kerosene /'kerə,siːn/ *n.* (also **kerosine**) esp. *US* fuel oil for use in jet engines, boilers, etc.; paraffin oil. [Greek *kēros* wax]

Kerry /'kerɪ/ county in the SW Republic of Ireland, in the province of Munster; pop. (est. 1991) 121 719; capital, Tralee. The main occupations are fishing and farming; tourism is the principal industry.

kestrel /'kestr(ə)l/ *n.* small hovering falcon. [origin uncertain]

♦ **Keswick** /'kezɪk/, **Simon Lindley** (1942–) British businessman, director (since 1972) and formerly chairman (1983–9) of Jardine Matheson Holdings Ltd., the powerful Hong Kong trading group with whose success in the last decade he is widely credited. He is also a director (since 1991) of Hanson plc. He works closely with his brother, **Henry Neville Lindley Keswick** (1938–), the current chairman (since 1989) of Jardine Matheson Holdings Ltd. and deputy chairman (since 1993) of Sun Alliance plc.

ketch *n.* small two-masted sailing-boat. [probably from CATCH]

ketchup /'ketʃʌp/ *n.* (*US* **catsup** /'kætsəp/) spicy esp. tomato sauce used as a condiment. [Chinese]

ketone /'kiːtəʊn/ *n.* any of a class of organic compounds including propanone (acetone). [German *Keton*, alteration of *Aketon* ACETONE]

kettle /'ket(ə)l/ *n.* vessel for boiling water in. □ **a different kettle of fish** a different matter altogether. **a fine** (or **pretty) kettle of fish** *iron.* an awkward state of affairs. [Old Norse]

kettledrum *n.* large bowl-shaped drum.

key[1] /kiː/ *–n.* (*pl.* **-s**) **1** (usu. metal) instrument for moving the bolt of a lock. **2** similar implement for operating a switch. **3** instrument for grasping screws, nuts, etc., or for winding a clock etc. **4** (often in *pl.*) finger-operated button or lever on a typewriter, piano, computer keyboard, etc. **5** means of advance, access, etc. (*key to success*). **6** (*attrib.*) essential (*key element*). **7 a** solution or explanation. **b** word or system for solving a cipher or code. **c** explanatory list of symbols used in a map, table, etc. **d** *Computing* value held in one of the fields of a record and used to identify that record in a file or other collection of records. **8** *Mus.* system of notes related to each other and based on a particular note (*key of C major*). **9** tone or style of thought or expression. **10** piece of wood or metal inserted between and securing others. **11** coat of wall plaster between the laths securing other coats. **12** roughness of a surface helping the adhesion of plaster etc. **13** winged fruit of the sycamore etc. **14** device for making or breaking an electric circuit. *–v.* (**keys, keyed**) **1** (foll. by *in*, *on*, etc.) fasten with a pin, wedge, bolt, etc. **2** (often foll. by *in*) enter (data) by means of a keyboard. **3** roughen (a surface) to help the adhesion of plaster etc. **4** (foll. by *to*) align or link (one thing to another). □ **keyed up** tense, nervous, excited. [Old English]

key[2] /kiː/ *n.* low-lying island or reef, esp. in the West Indies. [Spanish *cayo*]

keyboard *–n.* **1** set of keys on a typewriter, computer, piano, etc. A computer keyboard consists of the standard typewriter layout (the QWERTY keyboard) plus some additional keys, which usu. include a **control key, function keys, cursor keys**, and a **numerical keypad**. The control key operates in the same way as a shift key but allows non-character information to be sent to the computer, e.g. 'carriage return' or 'clear screen'; the function keys send not one but a whole sequence of characters to the computer at a time, and can often be programmed by the user to send commonly used sequences; the cursor keys are used to move the screen cursor to a new position; the numerical keypad duplicates the normal typewriter number keys and speeds up the entry of numerical data by allowing one-handed operation. **2** electronic musical instrument with keys arranged as on a piano. *–v.* enter (data) by means of a keyboard. □ **keyboarder** *n.* (in sense 1 of *n.*). **keyboardist** *n.* (in sense 2 of *n.*).

♦ **keyed advertisement** *n.* advertisement designed to enable the advertiser to know where a respondent saw it, for instance by including a code number of a particular department in the return address.

keyhole *n.* hole in a door etc. for a key.

keyhole surgery *n. colloq.* minimally invasive surgery carried out through a very small incision.

Keynesian /'keɪnzɪən/ *–adj.* of the economic theories of J. M. Keynes, esp. regarding state intervention in the economy. See also GENERAL THEORY; KEYNESIANISM. *–n.* proponent of Keynes's theories.

♦ **Keynesianism** *n.* approach to macroeconomics based on the work of J. M. Keynes. Failures of coordination between markets, even if these are internally efficient, may generate recession and mass unemployment. For example, unemployed workers may be unable to find jobs because there is no demand for the goods they produce although these same workers would demand the goods if they were employed and earned wages. In this view, governments have a role to play by putting money into workers' pockets through public works, i.e. creating the demand and raising the level of production through the multiplier process (see MULTIPLIER 2). This view of the economy was widely accepted between the late 1940s and the 1960s, when it came under attack first by the monetarists and more recently by the new classical macroeconomists.

keynote *n.* **1** (esp. *attrib.*) prevailing tone or idea, esp. in a speech, conference, etc. **2** *Mus.* note on which a key is based.

keypad *n.* **1** small keyboard etc. for a portable electronic device, telephone, etc. **2** *Computing* small keyboard with only a few keys, usu. used for encoding a particular sort of information. For example, a **numerical keypad** is used to feed numerical data into a computer, and can be operated much quicker than an all-purpose keyboard (of which it may be part).

♦ **key-person assurance** *n.* insurance on the life of a key employee (male or female) of a company, esp. the life of a senior executive in a small company, whose death would be a serious loss to the company. In the event of the key person dying, the benefit is paid to the company. In order that there should be an insurable interest, a loss of profit must be the direct result of the death of the key person.

keypunch –*n.* keyboard-operated device for recording data by means of punched holes or notches on cards or paper tape. –*v.* record (data) thus.

key-ring *n.* ring for keeping keys on.

key signature *n. Mus.* any of several combinations of sharps or flats indicating the key of a composition.

keystone *n.* **1** central principle of a system, policy, etc. **2** central locking stone in an arch.

keystroke *n.* single depression of a key on a keyboard, esp. as a measure of work.

key to disk *n.* system of data entry in which the data entered by a number of keyboard operators is recorded on a magnetic disk under the control of a small computer. The data from each keyboard is routed by the computer to the appropriate file on the disk. The data encoded on the disk is verified, often by comparing it with data entered by a second operator working from the same source. The disk can then be transferred to the computer on which the data is to be processed. Alternatively the data can be transferred to a magnetic tape.

key to tape *n.* system of data entry in which the data entered by a keyboard operator is recorded on a magnetic tape. The data encoded on the tape is then verified, often by comparing it with data entered by a second operator working from the same document. The tape can then be transferred to a computer so that the data can be processed. When there are a number of keyboards available, associated data on individual tapes can be merged on to one tape before input to the computer.

keyword *n.* **1** key to a cipher etc. **2 a** word of great significance. **b** significant word used in indexing.

KFAED *abbr.* Kuwait Fund for Arab Economic Development.

KG *abbr.* **1** Knight of the Order of the Garter. **2** (German) Kommanditgesellschaft (= limited partnership).

kg *abbr.* kilogram(s).

KGB *n.* state security police of the former USSR. [Russian abbreviation, = committee of state security]

Khabarovsk /ˌkæbəˈrɒfsk/ city in E Russia, a major transport centre with engineering and oil-refining industries; pop. (est. 1995) 618 000.

khaki /ˈkɑːkɪ/ –*adj.* dull brownish-yellow. –*n.* (*pl.* **-s**) **1** khaki fabric or uniform. **2** dull brownish-yellow colour. [Urdu, = dusty]

Khalkís see CHALCIS.

khan /kɑːn/ *n.* title of rulers and officials in Central Asia, Afghanistan, etc. □ **khanate** *n.* [Turki, = lord]

Khaniá see CANEA.

Kharg Island /kɑːg/ small island at the head of the Persian Gulf, site of Iran's principal deep-water oil terminal.

Kharkov /ˈkɑːkɒf/ industrial city in Ukraine, in the Donets Basin coalmining region; pop. (est. 1996) 1 555 000.

Khartoum /kɑːˈtuːm/ capital of Sudan; manufactures include textiles and glass; pop. (1993) 924 505.

Khios see CHIOS.

Khulna /ˈkuːlnə/ city and trading centre in Bangladesh, on the Ganges delta; industries include shipbuilding and textiles; pop. (1991) 877 388.

kHz *abbr.* kilohertz.

Kiangsu see JIANGSU.

kibbutz /kɪˈbʊts/ *n.* (*pl.* **kibbutzim** /-ˈtsiːm/) communal esp. farming settlement in Israel. [Hebrew, = gathering]

kibosh /ˈkaɪbɒʃ/ *n. slang* nonsense. □ **put the kibosh on** put an end to. [origin unknown]

kick –*v.* **1** strike, strike out, or propel forcibly, with the foot or hoof. **2** (often foll. by *at, against*) protest at; rebel against. **3** *slang* give up (a habit). **4** (often foll. by *out* etc.) expel or dismiss forcibly. **5** *refl.* be annoyed with oneself. **6** *Football* score (a goal) by a kick. –*n.* **1** kicking action or blow. **2** *colloq.* **a** sharp stimulant effect, esp. of alcohol. **b** (often in *pl.*) thrill (*did it for kicks*). **3** strength, resilience (*no kick left*). **4** *colloq.* specified temporary interest (*on a jogging kick*). **5** recoil of a gun when fired. □ **kick about** (or **around**) *colloq.* **1 a** drift idly from place to place. **b** be unused or unwanted. **2 a** treat roughly. **b** discuss unsystematically. **kick the bucket** *slang* die. **kick one's heels** see HEEL. **kick off 1 a** *Football* start or resume a match. **b** *colloq.* begin. **2** remove (shoes etc.) by kicking. **kick over the traces** see TRACE[2]. **kick up** (or **kick up a fuss, dust**, etc.) *colloq.* create a disturbance; object. **kick a person upstairs** dispose of a person by promotion etc. [origin unknown]

kickback *n. colloq.* **1** recoil. **2** (usu. illegal) payment for help or favours, esp. in business.

kick-off *n. Football* start or resumption of a match.

kickstand *n.* rod for supporting a bicycle or motor cycle when stationary.

kick-start –*n.* (also **kick-starter**) device to start the engine of a motor cycle etc. by the downward thrust of a pedal. –*v.* start (a motor cycle etc.) in this way.

kid[1] –*n.* **1** young goat. **2** leather from this. **3** *colloq.* child. –*v.* (**-dd-**) (of a goat) give birth. □ **handle with kid gloves** treat carefully. [Old Norse]

kid[2] *v.* (also *refl.*) (**-dd-**) *colloq.* deceive, trick, tease (*don't kid yourself; only kidding*). □ **no kidding** *slang* that is the truth. [origin uncertain]

kiddie /ˈkɪdɪ/ *n.* (also **kiddy**) (*pl.* **-ies**) *slang* = KID[1] *n.* 3.

kiddo /ˈkɪdəʊ/ *n.* (*pl.* **-s**) *slang* = KID[1] *n.* 3.

kidnap *v.* (**-pp-**; *US* **-p-**) **1** abduct (a person etc.), esp. to obtain a ransom. **2** steal (a child). □ **kidnapper** *n.* [from KID[1], *nap* = NAB]

kidney /ˈkɪdnɪ/ *n.* (*pl.* **-s**) **1** either of two organs in the abdominal cavity of vertebrates which remove nitrogenous wastes from the blood and excrete urine. **2** animal's kidney as food. [origin unknown]

kidney bean *n.* red-skinned dried bean.

kidney machine *n.* machine able to take over the function of a damaged kidney.

kidney-shaped *adj.* having one side concave and the other convex.

Kiel /kiːl/ naval port in N Germany, capital of Schleswig-Holstein; industries include engineering and shipbuilding; pop. (est. 1995) 246 586.

Kiev /ˈkiːef/ capital of Ukraine; industries include metallurgy, chemicals, textiles, and manufacture of machinery; pop. (est. 1996) 2 630 000.

Kigali /kɪˈgɑːlɪ/ capital of Rwanda, a centre of the mining industry and coffee trade; pop. (est. 1991) 232 700.

Kikládhes see CYCLADES.

Kildare /kɪlˈdeə(r)/ county in the E Republic of Ireland, in the province of Leinster; pop. (est. 1991) 122 516;

capital, Naas. It is an agricultural region, noted for its racehorse breeding.

Kilkenny /kɪl'kenɪ/ **1** county in the S Republic of Ireland, in the province of Leinster; cattle- and dairy-farming are the main occupations; pop. (est. 1991) 73 613. **2** its county town; pop. (1981) 16 900.

kill *–v.* **1** (also *absol.*) deprive of life or vitality; cause death or the death of. **2** destroy (feelings etc.). **3** *refl. colloq.* **a** overexert oneself (*don't kill yourself trying*). **b** laugh heartily. **4** *colloq.* overwhelm with amusement. **5** switch off (a light, engine, etc.). **6** *Computing colloq.* delete. **7** *colloq.* cause pain or discomfort to (*my feet are killing me*). **8** pass (time, or a specified period) usu. while waiting (*an hour to kill before the interview*). **9** defeat (a bill in Parliament). **10 a** *Tennis* etc. hit (the ball) so that it cannot be returned. **b** stop (the ball) dead. **11** make ineffective (taste, sound, pain, etc.) (*carpet killed the sound*). *–n.* **1** act of killing (esp. in hunting). **2** animal(s) killed, esp. by a hunter. **3** *colloq.* destruction or disablement of an enemy aircraft etc. □ **dressed to kill** dressed showily or alluringly. **in at the kill** present at a successful conclusion. **kill off 1** destroy completely. **2** (of an author) bring about the death of (a fictional character). **kill or cure** (usu. *attrib.*) (of a remedy etc.) drastic, extreme. **kill two birds with one stone** achieve two aims at once. **kill with kindness** spoil with overindulgence. [perhaps related to QUELL]

Killarney /kɪ'lɑːnɪ/ market town in the SW Republic of Ireland, in Co. Kerry; the beauty of the nearby lakes and mountains attracts many tourists; pop. (1991) 7250.

killer *n.* **1 a** person, animal, or thing that kills. **b** murderer. **2** *colloq.* **a** impressive, formidable, or excellent thing. **b** hilarious joke.

killer instinct *n.* **1** innate tendency to kill. **2** ruthless streak.

killer whale *n.* dolphin with a prominent dorsal fin.

killing *–n.* **1 a** causing of death. **b** instance of this. **2** *colloq.* great (esp. financial) success (*make a killing*). *–adj. colloq.* **1** very funny. **2** exhausting.

killjoy *n.* gloomy or censorious person, esp. at a party etc.

kiln *n.* furnace or oven for burning, baking, or drying, esp. for calcining lime or firing pottery etc. [Old English from Latin *culina* kitchen]

kilo /'kiːləʊ/ *n.* (*pl.* **-s**) kilogram. [French, abbreviation]

kilo- *comb. form* **1** 1000 (*kilometre, kilovolt*). **2** *Computing* power of 2 nearest to 1000 (2^{10}, i.e. 1024), most frequently encountered in the context of storage capacity. With magnetic disks, magnetic tape, and main store, the capacity is normally reckoned in terms of the number of bytes that can be stored (see KILOBYTE). Semiconductor memory (RAM or ROM) is sometimes considered in terms of the number of bits that can be stored in the device (1 **kilobit** = 2^{10} bits). See also MEGA- 2. [Greek *khilioi*]

kilobyte /'kɪlə,baɪt/ *n.* (also **K, K byte, k byte**) *Computing* 1024 (i.e. 2^{10}) bytes as a measure of memory capacity etc. See also KILO- 2; BYTE.

kilocalorie /'kɪlə,kælərɪ/ *n.* = CALORIE.

kilocycle /'kɪlə,saɪk(ə)l/ *n. hist.* kilohertz.

kilogram /'kɪlə,græm/ *n.* (also **-gramme**) SI unit of mass, approx. 2.205 lb.

kilohertz /'kɪlə,hɜːts/ *n.* 1000 hertz.

kilojoule /'kɪlə,dʒuːl/ *n.* 1000 joules, esp. as a measure of the energy value of foods.

kilolitre /'kɪlə,liːtə(r)/ *n.* (*US* **-liter**) 1000 litres (220 imperial gallons).

kilometre /'kɪlə,miːtə(r), kɪ'lɒmɪtə(r)/ *n.* (*US* **-meter**) 1000 metres (approx. 0.62 miles). □ **kilometric** /,kɪlə'metrɪk/ *adj.*

■ **Usage** The second pronunciation given, with the stress on the second syllable, is considered incorrect by some people.

kiloton /'kɪlə,tʌn/ *n.* (also **kilotonne**) unit of explosive power equivalent to 1000 tons of TNT.

kilovolt /'kɪlə,vɒlt/ *n.* 1000 volts.

kilowatt /'kɪlə,wɒt/ *n.* 1000 watts.

kilowatt-hour *n.* electrical energy equal to a power consumption of 1000 watts for one hour.

kilt *–n.* pleated knee-length usu. tartan skirt, traditionally worn by Highland men. *–v.* **1** tuck up (the skirts) round the body. **2** (esp. as **kilted** *adj.*) gather in vertical pleats. [Scandinavian]

kilter /'kɪltə(r)/ *n.* (also **kelter** /'kel-/) good working order (esp. *out of kilter*). [origin unknown]

Kimberley /'kɪmbəlɪ/ city in Northern Cape, South Africa, a diamond-mining centre with engineering and textile industries; pop. (1991) 167 060.

kimono /kɪ'məʊnəʊ/ *n.* (*pl.* **-s**) **1** long sashed Japanese robe. **2** similar dressing-gown. [Japanese]

kin *–n.* one's relatives or family. *–predic. adj.* related. [Old English]

-kin *suffix* forming diminutive nouns (*catkin*; *manikin*). [Dutch]

kina /'kiːnə/ *n.* standard monetary unit of Papua New Guinea. [Papuan]

kind /kaɪnd/ *–n.* **1** race, species, or natural group of animals, plants, etc. (*human kind*). **2** class, type, sort, variety. **3** natural way, fashion, etc. (*true to kind*). *–adj.* (often foll. by *to*) friendly, generous, or benevolent. □ **in kind 1** in the same form, likewise (*was insulted and replied in kind*). **2** (of payment) in goods or labour, not money. **3** character, quality (*differ in degree but not in kind*). **kind of** *colloq.* to some extent (*I kind of expected it*). **a kind of** loosely resembling (*he's a kind of doctor*). [Old English]

■ **Usage** In sense 2 of the noun, *these kinds of* is usu. preferred to *these kind of*.

kindergarten /'kɪndə,gɑːt(ə)n/ *n.* class or school for very young children. [German, = children's garden]

kind-hearted *adj.* of a kind disposition. □ **kind-heartedly** *adv.* **kind-heartedness** *n.*

kindle /'kɪnd(ə)l/ *v.* (**-ling**) **1** light, catch, or set on fire. **2** arouse or inspire. **3** become aroused or animated. [Old Norse]

kindling *n.* small sticks etc. for lighting fires.

kindly[1] *adv.* **1** in a kind manner (*spoke kindly*). **2** often *iron.* please (*kindly go away*). □ **look kindly upon** regard sympathetically. **take kindly to** be pleased by; like.

kindly[2] *adj.* (**-ier, -iest**) **1** kind, kind-hearted. **2** (of a climate etc.) pleasant, mild. □ **kindlily** *adv.* **kindliness** *n.*

kindness *n.* **1** being kind. **2** kind act.

kindred /'kɪndrɪd/ *–adj.* related, allied, or similar. *–n.* **1** one's relations collectively. **2** blood relationship. **3** resemblance in character. [Old English, = kinship]

kindred spirit *n.* person like or in sympathy with oneself.

kinematics /,kɪnɪ'mætɪks/ *n.pl.* (usu. treated as *sing.*) branch of mechanics concerned with the motion of objects without reference to cause. □ **kinematic** *adj.* [Greek *kinēma -matos* motion]

kinetic /kɪ'netɪk/ *adj.* of or due to motion. □ **kinetically** *adv.* [Greek *kineo* move]

kinetic art *n.* sculpture etc. designed to move.

kinetic energy *n.* energy of motion.

kinetics *n.pl.* **1** = DYNAMICS 1a. **2** (usu. treated as *sing.*) branch of physical chemistry measuring and studying the rates of chemical reactions.

◆ **King, John Leonard, Baron King of Wartnaby** (1918–) British businessman, chairman (1981–93) and president (from 1993) of British Airways, which he transformed from a public-sector national airline into a profitable private-sector airline with global interests. The final months of his chairmanship were clouded by BA's unethical conduct towards a rival airline. Lord King has held many other directorships and chairmanships (including the Olympic Appeals Committee).

---

king *n.* **1** (as a title usu. **King**) male sovereign, esp. a hereditary ruler. **2** pre-eminent person or thing (*oil king*). **3** (*attrib.*) large (or the largest) kind of plant, animal, etc. (*king penguin*). **4** *Chess* piece which must be checkmated for a win. **5** crowned piece in draughts. **6** court-card depicting a king. **7** (**the King**) national anthem when the sovereign is male. □ **kingly** *adj.* **kingship** *n.* [Old English]

King Charles spaniel *n.* small black and tan spaniel.

kingcup *n.* marsh marigold.

kingdom *n.* **1** territory or state ruled by a king or queen. **2** spiritual reign or sphere of God. **3** domain. **4** division of the natural world (*plant kingdom*). **5** specified sphere (*kingdom of the heart*). [Old English]

kingdom come *n. colloq.* the next world.

kingfisher *n.* small bird with brightly coloured plumage, diving for fish etc.

King of Arms *n.* a chief herald.

king of beasts *n.* lion.

king of birds *n.* eagle.

kingpin *n.* **1** main, large, or vertical bolt, esp. as a pivot. **2** essential person or thing.

king-post *n.* upright post from the tie-beam of a roof to the apex of a truss.

King's Counsel *n.* = QUEEN'S COUNSEL.

King's English *n.* = QUEEN'S ENGLISH.

King's evidence see EVIDENCE.

King's Guide *n.* = QUEEN'S GUIDE.

King's highway *n.* = QUEEN'S HIGHWAY.

king-size *adj.* (also **-sized**) very large.

King's Proctor *n.* = QUEEN'S PROCTOR.

King's Scout *n.* = QUEEN'S SCOUT.

Kingston /ˈkɪŋst(ə)n/ capital and chief port of Jamaica; city pop. (1991) 103 771; metropolitan area pop. 643 801.

Kingston-upon-Hull see HULL.

Kingstown /ˈkɪŋstaʊn/ capital of St Vincent; exports include bananas and cotton; pop. (est. 1994) 27 049.

kink –*n.* **1 a** twist or bend in wire etc. **b** tight wave in hair. **2** mental twist or quirk, esp. when perverse. –*v.* (cause to) form a kink. [Low German or Dutch]

Kinki /ˈkiːnkiː/ region of Japan, in S Honshu; pop. (1995) 22 468 188; capital, Osaka. Much of Japan's industrial activity is concentrated here, esp. in Osaka and Kobe.

kinky *adj.* (**-ier, -iest**) **1** *colloq.* **a** sexually perverted or unconventional. **b** (of clothing etc.) bizarre and sexually provocative. **2** having kinks. □ **kinkily** *adv.* **kinkiness** *n.*

kinsfolk *n.pl.* one's blood relations.

Kinshasa /kɪnˈʃɑːsə/ (formerly **Léopoldville**) capital of Democratic Republic of Congo; industries include food processing, textiles, and chemicals; pop. (est. 1994) 4 655 313.

kinship *n.* **1** blood relationship. **2** likeness; sympathy.

kinsman *n.* (*fem.* **kinswoman**) **1** blood relation. **2** relation by marriage.

■ **Usage** Use of *kinsman* in sense 2 is considered incorrect by some people.

kiosk /ˈkiːɒsk/ *n.* **1** light open-fronted booth selling food, newspapers, tickets, etc. **2** telephone box. [Turkish from Persian]

kip[1] *slang* –*n.* **1** sleep; nap. **2** bed or cheap lodgings. –*v.* (**-pp-**) (often foll. by *down*) sleep. [cf. Danish *kippe* mean hut]

kip[2] *n.* standard monetary unit of Laos. [Thai]

kipper /ˈkɪpə(r)/ –*n.* fish, esp. a herring, split, salted, dried, and usu. smoked. –*v.* cure (a herring etc.) thus. [origin uncertain]

kir /kɜː(r)/ *n.* dry white wine with *crème de cassis*.

kirby-grip /ˈkɜːbɪgrɪp/ *n.* (also **Kirbigrip** *propr.*) type of sprung hairgrip. [*Kirby*, name of the manufacturer]

Kirghiz var. of KYRGYZ.

Kirghizia /kɜːˈgiːzɪə/ see KYRGYZSTAN.

Kirin see JILIN.

Kiritimati /ˌkɪrɪtɪˈmɑːtɪ/ (formerly **Christmas Island**) largest atoll in the world, one of the Line Islands of Kiribati in the Pacific Ocean; pop. (1990) 2537.

kirk *n. Scot.* & *N.Engl.* **1** church. **2** (**the Kirk** or **the Kirk of Scotland**) Church of Scotland. [Old Norse *kirkja* = CHURCH]

Kirkcaldy /kɜːˈkɔːdɪ/ industrial town and port in E Scotland; manufactures include linoleum, canvas, and paper; pop. (1981) 46 500.

Kirk-session *n.* lowest court in the Church of Scotland.

Kirkuk /kəˈkʊk/ industrial city in N Iraq, regional centre of the oil industry; pop. (est. 1987) 418 624.

Kirov /ˈkɪərɒf/ (formerly **Vyatka**) industrial town and port in NW Russia; manufactures include rolling stock, tyres, and machine tools; pop. (est. 1995) 464 000.

kirsch /kɪəʃ/ *n.* brandy distilled from cherries. [German, = cherry]

Kiruna /kɪˈruːnə/ town in N Sweden, at the centre of the Lapland iron-mining region; pop. (1990) 26 150.

Kishinev /ˌkɪʃɪˈnjɒf/ capital of Moldova; food processing is the main industry; pop. (est. 1994) 662 000.

kismet /ˈkɪzmet/ *n.* destiny, fate. [Turkish from Arabic]

kiss –*v.* **1** touch with the lips, esp. as a sign of love, affection, greeting, or reverence. **2** (of two people) touch each others' lips in this way. **3** lightly touch. –*n.* **1** touch with the lips. **2** light touch. □ **kiss and tell** recount one's sexual exploits. **kiss a person's arse** *coarse slang* toady to. **kiss the dust** submit abjectly. [Old English]

kiss-curl *n.* small curl of hair on the forehead, nape, etc.

kisser *n.* **1** person who kisses. **2** *slang* mouth; face.

kiss of death *n.* apparent good luck etc. which causes ruin.

kiss of life *n.* mouth-to-mouth resuscitation.

kissogram /ˈkɪsəˌgræm/ *n.* (also **Kissagram** *propr.*) novelty telegram or greeting delivered with a kiss.

kit –*n.* **1** articles, equipment, etc. for a specific purpose (*first-aid kit*). **2** specialized, esp. sports, clothing or uniform (*football kit*). **3** set of parts needed to assemble furniture, a model, etc. –*v.* (**-tt-**) (often foll. by *out*, *up*) equip with kit. [Dutch]

Kitakyushu /ˌkiːtəˈkjuːʃuː/ industrial city and port in S Japan, on Kyushu island; pop. (1995) 1 019 562.

kitbag *n.* large usu. cylindrical bag used for a soldier's or traveller's kit.

Kiribati /ˈkɪrɪˌbæs/, **Republic of** small country in the SW Pacific, consisting of groups of islands including the Gilbert Islands, the Line Islands, and the Phoenix Islands. The phosphate deposits that were formerly a main source of revenue are almost exhausted, and the principal exports are now copra and fish; budgetary assistance is provided by aid from the UK.

History. The country was formerly part of the British protectorate of the Gilbert and Ellice Islands, which became a colony in 1915. Links with the Ellice Islands (now Tuvalu) ended in 1975, and in 1979 Kiribati became an independent republic within the Commonwealth. President, Teatao Teannaki; capital, Tarawa.

languages	English (official), Gilbertese
currency	Australian dollar ($A) of 100 cents
pop. (1996)	81 800
GNP (1994)	US$56M
literacy	90%
life expectancy	62 (m); 67 (f)

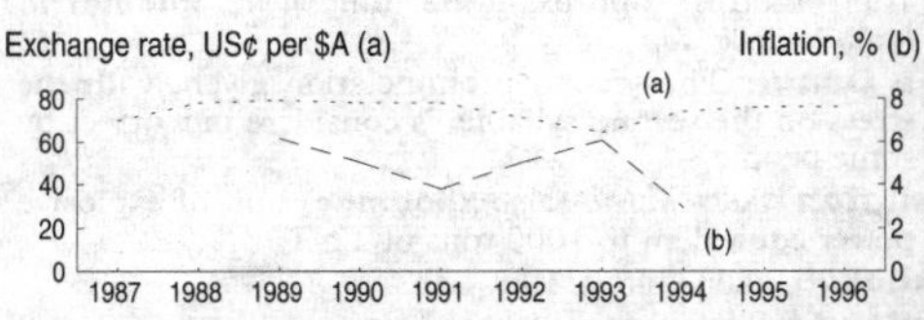

kitchen /ˈkɪtʃɪn/ *n.* **1** place where food is prepared and cooked. **2** kitchen fitments (*half-price kitchens*). [Latin *coquina*]

Kitchener /ˈkɪtʃɪnə(r)/ city in Canada, in SE Ontario; a financial centre, it also manufactures furniture, foods, and leather and rubber goods; city pop. (1991) 168 282; metropolitan area pop. 356 421.

kitchenette /ˌkɪtʃɪˈnet/ *n.* small kitchen or cooking area.

kitchen garden *n.* garden with vegetables, fruit, herbs, etc.

kitchenware *n.* cooking utensils.

kite *n.* **1** light framework with a thin covering flown on a string in the wind. **2** soaring bird of prey. **3** *colloq.* = ACCOMMODATION BILL. [Old English]

♦ **kite-flying** *n.* (also **kiting**) *colloq.* discounting of an accommodation bill at a bank, knowing that the person on whom it is drawn will dishonour it.

Kitemark *n.* official kite-shaped mark on goods approved by the British Standards Institution.

kith *n.* □ **kith and kin** friends and relations. [Old English, originally 'knowledge': related to CAN[1]]

kitsch /kɪtʃ/ *n.* (often *attrib.*) vulgar, pretentious, or worthless art. □ **kitschy** *adj.* (**-ier, -iest**). [German]

kitten /ˈkɪt(ə)n/ –*n.* young cat, ferret, etc. –*v.* (of a cat etc.) give birth (to). □ **have kittens** *colloq.* be very upset or anxious. [Anglo-French diminutive of *chat* CAT]

kittenish *adj.* playful, lively, or flirtatious.

kittiwake /ˈkɪtɪˌweɪk/ *n.* a kind of small seagull. [imitative of its cry]

kitty[1] /ˈkɪtɪ/ *n.* (*pl.* **-ies**) **1** fund of money for communal use. **2** pool in some card-games. [origin unknown]

kitty[2] /ˈkɪtɪ/ *n.* (*pl.* **-ies**) childish name for a kitten or cat.

Kitwe /ˈkiːtweɪ/ city in Zambia, commercial and industrial centre of the Copperbelt mining region; pop. (1990) 338 207.

kiwi /ˈkiːwiː/ *n.* (*pl.* **-s**) **1** flightless long-billed New Zealand bird. **2** (**Kiwi**) *colloq.* New Zealander. [Maori]

kiwi fruit *n.* green-fleshed fruit of a climbing plant.

kJ *abbr.* kilojoule(s).

KK *abbr.* (Japanese) kabushiki kaisha (= joint-stock company).

KL –*abbr.* Kuala Lumpur. –*airline flight code* KLM – Royal Dutch Airlines.

kl *abbr.* kilolitre(s).

Klaxon /ˈklæks(ə)n/ *n. propr.* horn or warning hooter. [name of the manufacturer]

Kleenex /ˈkliːneks/ *n.* (*pl.* same or **-es**) *propr.* disposable paper handkerchief.

kleptomania /ˌkleptəˈmeɪnɪə/ *n.* obsessive apparently motiveless urge to steal. □ **kleptomaniac** /-nɪˌæk/ *n.* & *adj.* [Greek *kleptēs* thief]

♦ **Kluge** /kluːgə/, **John Werner** (1914–) US businessman, born in Germany, founder and chairman of Metromedia. After buying the WGAY radio station in 1946, he acquired in 1959 Metropolitan Broadcasting, including television stations in New York and Washington. Kluge uses the renamed Metromedia as a vehicle for an assortment of enterprises, including new wireless telecommunications interests in Eastern Europe, Russia, and China.

km *abbr.* kilometre(s).

KN *symb. Currency* kip.

kn *abbr.* knot(s).

knack *n.* **1** acquired faculty or trick of doing a thing. **2** habit (*a knack of offending people*). [origin unknown]

knacker –*n.* buyer of useless horses etc. for slaughter, or of old houses, ships, etc. for the materials. –*v. slang* (esp. as **knackered** *adj.*) exhaust, wear out. [origin unknown]

knapsack /ˈnæpsæk/ *n.* soldier's or hiker's usu. canvas bag carried on the back. [German *knappen* bite, SACK[1]]

knapweed /ˈnæpwiːd/ *n.* plant with thistle-like purple flowers. [from *knop* ornamental knob or tuft]

knave *n.* **1** rogue, scoundrel. **2** = JACK *n.* 2. □ **knavery** *n.* (*pl.* **-ies**). **knavish** *adj.* [Old English, originally = boy, servant]

knead *v.* **1 a** work into a dough, paste, etc. by pummelling. **b** make (bread, pottery, etc.) thus. **2** massage (muscles etc.) as if kneading. [Old English]

knee –*n.* **1 a** (often *attrib.*) joint between the thigh and the lower leg in humans. **b** corresponding joint in other animals. **c** area around this. **d** lap (*sat on his knee*). **2** part of a garment covering the knee. –*v.* (**knees, kneed, kneeing**) **1** touch or strike with the knee (*kneed him in the groin*). **2** *colloq.* make (trousers) bulge at the knee. □ **bring a person** (or **thing**) **to his** (or **her** or **its**) **knees** reduce to submission or a state of weakness. [Old English]

knee-bend *n.* bending of the knee, esp. as a physical exercise.

knee-breeches *n.pl.* close-fitting trousers to the knee or just below.

kneecap –*n.* **1** convex bone in front of the knee. **2** protective covering for the knee. –*v.* (**-pp-**) *slang* (of a terrorist) shoot (a person) in the knee or leg as a punishment.

knee-deep *adj.* **1** (usu. foll. by *in*) **a** immersed up to the knees. **b** deeply involved. **2** so deep as to reach the knees.

knee-high *adj.* so high as to reach the knees.

knee-jerk *n.* **1** sudden involuntary kick caused by a blow on the tendon just below the knee. **2** (*attrib.*) predictable, automatic, stereotyped.

kneel *v.* (*past* and *past part.* **knelt** /nelt/ or esp. *US* **kneeled**) fall or rest on the knees or a knee. [Old English: related to KNEE]

knee-length *adj.* reaching the knees.

kneeler *n.* **1** cushion for kneeling on. **2** person who kneels.

knees-up *n. colloq.* lively party or gathering.

knell –*n.* **1** sound of a bell, esp. for a death or funeral. **2** announcement, event, etc., regarded as an ill omen. –*v.* **1** ring a knell. **2** proclaim by or as by a knell. [Old English]

knelt *past* and *past part.* of KNEEL.

knew *past* of KNOW.

knickerbocker /ˈnɪkəˌbɒkə(r)/ *n.* (in *pl.*) loose-fitting breeches gathered at the knee or calf. [the pseudonym of W. Irving, author of *History of New York*]

Knickerbocker Glory *n.* ice-cream served with fruit etc. in a tall glass.

knickers *n.pl.* woman's or girl's undergarment for the lower torso. [abbreviation of KNICKERBOCKER]

knick-knack /ˈnɪknæk/ *n.* (also **nick-nack**) trinket or small dainty ornament etc. [from KNACK in the obsolete sense 'trinket']

knife –*n.* (*pl.* **knives**) **1** metal blade for cutting or as a weapon, with usu. one long sharp edge fixed in a handle. **2** cutting-blade in a machine. **3** (as **the knife**) surgical operation. –*v.* (**-fing**) cut or stab with a knife. □ **at knife-point** threatened with a knife or an ultimatum etc. **get** (or **have got) one's knife into** treat maliciously, persecute. [Old English]

knife-edge *n.* **1** edge of a knife. **2** position of extreme danger or uncertainty.

knife-pleat *n.* narrow flat usu. overlapping pleat on a skirt etc.

knight /naɪt/ –*n.* **1** man awarded a non-hereditary title (*Sir*) by a sovereign. **2** *hist.* **a** man, usu. noble, raised to honourable military rank after service as a page and squire. **b** military follower, attendant, or lady's champion in a war or tournament. **3** man devoted to a cause, woman, etc. **4** *Chess* piece usu. shaped like a horse's head. –*v.* confer a knighthood on. □ **knighthood** *n.* **knightly** *adj. poet.* [Old English, originally = boy]

knight commander see COMMANDER.

knight errant *n.* **1** medieval knight in search of chivalrous adventures. **2** chivalrous or quixotic man. □ **knight-errantry** *n.*

knit *v.* (**-tt-**; *past* and *past part.* **knitted** or (esp. in senses 2–4) **knit**) **1** (also *absol.*) **a** make (a garment etc.) by interlocking loops of esp. wool with knitting-needles or a knitting-machine. **b** make (a plain stitch) in knitting (*knit one, purl one*). **2** momentarily wrinkle (the forehead) or (of the forehead) become momentarily wrinkled. **3** (often foll. by *together*) make or become close or compact. **4** (often foll. by *together*) (of a broken bone) become joined; heal. □ **knit up** make or repair by knitting. □ **knitter** *n.* [Old English]

knitting *n.* work being knitted.

knitting-machine *n.* machine for knitting.

knitting-needle *n.* thin pointed rod used esp. in pairs for knitting by hand.

knitwear *n.* knitted garments.

knives *pl.* of KNIFE.

knob *n.* **1** rounded protuberance, esp. at the end or on the surface of a thing, e.g. the handle of a door, drawer, a radio control, etc. **2** small piece (of butter etc.). □ **with knobs on** *slang* that and more (*same to you with knobs on*). □ **knobby** *adj.* **knoblike** *adj.* [Low German *knobbe* knot, knob]

knobbly /'nɒblɪ/ *adj.* (**-ier, -iest**) hard and lumpy. [*knobble*, diminutive of KNOB]

knock –*v.* **1 a** strike with an audible sharp blow. **b** (often foll. by *at*) strike (a door etc.) to gain admittance. **2** make (a hole etc.) by knocking. **3** (usu. foll. by *in, out, off,* etc.) drive (a thing, person, etc.) by striking (*knocked the ball into the hole*; *knocked those ideas out of him*). **4** *slang* criticize. **5 a** (of an engine) make a thumping or rattling noise. **b** = PINK[3]. **6** *coarse slang offens.* = *knock off* 6. –*n.* **1** act or sound of knocking. **2** knocking sound in esp. an engine. □ **knock about** (or **around**) *colloq.* **1** strike repeatedly; treat roughly. **2 a** wander aimlessly or adventurously. **b** be present, esp. by chance (*a cup knocking about somewhere*). **c** (usu. foll. by *with*) be associated socially. **knock back 1** *slang* eat or drink, esp. quickly. **2** *slang* disconcert. **knock down 1** strike (esp. a person) to the ground. **2** demolish. **3** (usu. foll. by *to*) (at an auction) sell (an article) to a bidder by a knock with a hammer. **4** *colloq.* lower the price of (an article). **5** *US slang* steal. **knock off 1** strike off with a blow. **2** *colloq.* finish (work) (*knocked off at 5.30*; *knocked off work early*). **3** *colloq.* produce (a work of art etc.) or do (a task) rapidly. **4** (often foll. by *from*) deduct (a sum) from a price etc. **5** *slang* steal. **6** *coarse slang offens.* have sexual intercourse with (a woman). **7** *slang* kill. **knock on the head** *colloq.* put an end to (a scheme etc.). **knock on** (or **knock) wood** *US* = *touch wood.* **knock out 1** make unconscious by a blow on the head. **2** defeat (a boxer) by knocking him or her down for a count of 10. **3** defeat, esp. in a knockout competition. **4** *slang* astonish. **5** (often *refl.*) *colloq.* exhaust. **knock sideways** *colloq.* astonish, shock. **knock spots off** defeat easily. **knock together** assemble hastily or roughly. **knock up 1** make hastily. **2** waken by a knock at the door. **3** esp. *US slang* make pregnant. **4** practise tennis etc. before formal play begins. [Old English]

knockabout *attrib. adj.* **1** (of comedy) boisterous; slapstick. **2** (of clothes) hard-wearing.

knock-down *attrib. adj.* **1** overwhelming. **2** (of a price) very low. **3** (of a price at auction) reserve. **4** (of furniture etc.) easily dismantled and reassembled.

knocker *n.* **1** hinged esp. metal instrument on a door for knocking with. **2** (in *pl.*) *coarse slang* woman's breasts.

◆ **knock-for-knock agreement** *n.* agreement between motor insurers that they will pay for their own policyholders' accident damage without seeking any contribution from the other insurers, irrespective of blame but provided that the relevant policies cover the risk involved. The agreement has cut down the expensive administration of claim and counterclaim, which has helped to reduce the cost of premiums.

◆ **knocking copy** *n.* advertising or publicity material that attacks a rival product.

---

knocking-shop *n. slang* brothel.

knock knees *n.pl.* abnormal curvature of the legs inwards at the knee. □ **knock-kneed** *adj.*

knock-on effect *n.* secondary, indirect, or cumulative effect.

knockout *n.* **1** act of making unconscious by a blow. **2** (usu. *attrib.*) *Boxing* etc. such a blow. **3** competition in which the loser in each round is eliminated (also *attrib.*: *knockout round*). **4** *colloq.* outstanding or irresistible person or thing.

knock-up *n.* practice at tennis etc.

knoll /nəʊl/ *n.* hillock, mound. [Old English]

knot[1] –*n.* **1 a** intertwining of rope, string, hair, etc., so as to fasten. **b** set method of this (*reef knot*). **c** knotted ribbon etc. as an ornament. **d** tangle in hair, knitting, etc. **2** unit of a ship's or aircraft's speed, equivalent to one nautical mile per hour. **3** (usu. foll. by *of*) cluster (*knot of journalists*). **4** bond, esp. of marriage. **5** hard lump of organic tissue. **6 a** hard mass in a tree-trunk where a branch grows out. **b** round cross-grained piece in timber marking this. **7** central point in a problem etc. –*v.* (**-tt-**) **1** tie in a knot. **2** entangle. **3** unite closely. □ **at a rate of knots** *colloq.* very fast. **tie in knots** *colloq.* baffle or confuse completely. [Old English]

knot[2] *n.* small sandpiper. [origin unknown]

knotgrass *n.* wild plant with creeping stems and small pink flowers.

knot-hole *n.* hole in timber where a knot has fallen out.

knotty *adj.* (**-ier, -iest**) **1** full of knots. **2** puzzling (*knotty problem*).

know /nəʊ/ *v.* (*past* **knew**; *past part.* **known** /nəʊn/) **1** (often foll. by *that, how, what,* etc.) **a** have in the mind; have learnt; be able to recall (*knows a lot about cars*). **b** (also *absol.*) be aware of (a fact) (*I think he knows*). **c** have a good command of (*knew German*; *knows his tables*). **2** be acquainted or friendly with. **3 a** (often foll. by *to* + infin.) recognize; identify (*I knew him at once*; *knew them to be rogues*). **b** (foll. by *from*) be able to distinguish (*did*

Korea, Democratic People's Republic of (also **North Korea**) country in E Asia, occupying the N part of the Korean peninsula (see KOREA). It is rich in minerals, including coal, iron ore, copper, zinc, and lead, and industrially developed, manufacturing machinery, metal goods, chemicals, and textiles; all industry is nationalized and agriculture is organized on a collective basis, rice and maize being the main crops. The collapse of the Soviet Union, North Korea's principal market for exports and source of financial aid, contributed to the deepening economic crisis of the 1990s. In 1994 Kim Il Sung, head of state since 1948, died and was succeeded as president by his son. The economic situation was made worse by severe floods in 1995, which left half a million people homeless. Widespread starvation ensued and in 1998 the World Food Programme launched a massive aid operation. In 1998 the economy was thought to be on the brink of total collapse. Any recovery will depend on improved relations with South Korea and Japan. President, Kim Jong-il; capital, Pyongyang.

language	Korean
currency	won (w) of 100 chon
pop. (1996)	23 904 000
GNP (1994)	US$21.3B
literacy	95% (m); 95% (f)
life expectancy	68 (m); 75 (f)

Exchange rate, US¢ per w

not know him from Adam). **4** be subject to (*joy knew no bounds*). **5** have personal experience of (fear etc.). **6** (as **known** *adj.*) **a** publicly acknowledged (*known fact*). **b** *Math.* (of a quantity etc.) having a value that can be stated. **7** have understanding or knowledge. □ **in the know** *colloq.* knowing inside information. **know of** be aware of; have heard of (*not that I know of*). **know one's own mind** be decisive, not vacillate. **know what's what** have knowledge of the world, life, etc. **you know** *colloq.* **1** implying something generally known etc. (*you know, the pub on the corner*). **2** expression used as a gap-filler in conversation. **you never know** it is possible. □ **knowable** *adj.* [Old English]

know-all *n. colloq.* person who claims or seems to know everything.

know-how *n.* practical knowledge; natural skill.

knowing *adj.* **1** suggesting that one has inside information (*a knowing look*). **2** showing knowledge; shrewd.

knowingly *adv.* **1** consciously; intentionally (*wouldn't knowingly hurt him*). **2** in a knowing manner (*smiled knowingly*).

knowledge /'nɒlɪdʒ/ *n.* **1 a** (usu. foll. by *of*) awareness or familiarity (of or with a person or thing) (*have no knowledge of that*). **b** person's range of information. **2 a** (usu. foll. by *of*) understanding of a subject etc. (*good knowledge of Greek*). **b** sum of what is known (*every branch of knowledge*). □ **to my knowledge** as far as I know.

knowledgeable *adj.* (also **knowledgable**) well-informed; intelligent. □ **knowledgeability** /-'bɪlɪtɪ/ *n.* **knowledgeably** *adv.*

known *past part.* of KNOW.

KNPC *abbr.* Kuwait National Petroleum Company.

knuckle /'nʌk(ə)l/ –*n.* **1** bone at a finger-joint, esp. that connecting the finger to the hand. **2 a** knee- or ankle-joint of a quadruped. **b** this as a joint of meat, esp. of bacon or pork. –*v.* (**-ling**) strike, press, or rub with the knuckles. □ **knuckle down** (often foll. by *to*) **1** apply oneself seriously (to a task etc.). **2** (also **knuckle under**) give in; submit. [Low German or Dutch diminutive of *knoke* bone]

knuckleduster *n.* metal guard worn over the knuckles in fighting, esp. in order to inflict greater damage.

knuckle sandwich *n. slang* punch in the mouth.

knurl *n.* small projecting knob, ridge, etc. [Low German or Dutch]

KO *abbr.* knockout.

koala /kəʊ'ɑːlə/ *n.* (in full **koala bear**) small Australian bearlike marsupial with thick grey fur. [Aboriginal]

Kobe /'kəʊbeɪ/ seaport in Japan, on Honshu island; industries include shipbuilding, engineering, and steel; pop. (1995) 1 423 830.

København see COPENHAGEN.

KOC *abbr.* Kuwait Oil Company.

kohl /kəʊl/ *n.* black powder used as eye make-up, esp. in Eastern countries. [Arabic]

kohlrabi /kəʊl'rɑːbɪ/ *n.* (*pl.* **-bies**) cabbage with an edible turnip-like swollen stem. [German, from Italian *cavolo rapa*]

kola var. of COLA.

Kola Peninsula /'kəʊlə/ peninsula on the NW coast of Russia, separating the White Sea from the Barents Sea. The port of Murmansk lies on its N coast.

kolkhoz /kʌl'xɔːz/ *n.* collective farm in the former USSR. [Russian]

♦ **Kondratieff waves** /kən'drɑːtɪˌef/ *n.pl.* long cycles in economic activity, thought to last about 40 years, the last downswing having been the depression of the 1930s. There is little supporting evidence of these cycles. [*Kondratieff*, name of a Russian economist]

Königsberg /'kɜːnɪgzˌbeəg/ see KALININGRAD.

Konya /'kɒnjə/ city in SW central Turkey; manufactures include carpets and silks; pop. (1990) 1 750 303.

koodoo var. of KUDU.

kook *n. US slang* crazy or eccentric person. □ **kooky** *adj.* (**-ier, -iest**). [probably from CUCKOO]

kookaburra /'kʊkəˌbʌrə/ *n.* Australian kingfisher with a strange laughing cry. [Aboriginal]

kopek (also **kopeck**) var. of COPECK.

koppie /'kɒpɪ/ *n.* (also **kopje**) *S.Afr.* small hill. [Afrikaans *koppie* little head]

Koran /kɔː'rɑːn/ *n.* Islamic sacred book. [Arabic, = recitation]

Kordofan /ˌkɔːdə'fɑːn/ region of central Sudan; products include gum arabic; pop. (1983) 3 093 300.

Korea /kə'riːə/ former country in E Asia, situated on a peninsula between the Sea of Japan and the Yellow Sea. Ruled from the 14th century by a Korean dynasty, and maintaining close ties with China, Korea suffered as a result of its position between Chinese and Japanese spheres of influence. In 1910 it was annexed by Japan, remaining part of the Japanese Empire until that country's surrender at the end of the Second World War. The N half of the country was then occupied by the Soviets and the S half by the Americans: separate republics were created in 1948, divided by the 38th parallel (see KOREA, DEMOCRATIC PEOPLE'S REPUBLIC OF; KOREA, REPUBLIC OF), and two years later the Northern invasion of the South resulted in the Korean War (1950–3). The borders were restored at the end of the war.

Korean /kə'rɪən/ –*n.* **1** native or national of North or South Korea. **2** language of Korea. –*adj.* of Korea, its people, or language.

Kortrijk /'kɔːtraɪk/ (French **Courtrai**) textile manufacturing city in Belgium, in the province of West Flanders; pop. (1993) 76 264.

koruna /kɒ'ruːnə/ *n.* standard monetary unit of the Czech Republic and Slovakia (formerly of Czechoslovakia). [Czech, = CROWN]

kosher /'kəʊʃə(r)/ –*adj.* **1** (of food or a food-shop) ful-

---

Korea, Republic of (also **South Korea**) country in E Asia, occupying the S part of the Korean peninsula. Agriculture produces rice, barley and other cereals, tobacco, hemp, and fruit. The fishing industry is important and contributes to export revenue, but most exports derive from the highly developed manufacturing sector, including ships, iron and steel products, cars, electrical and electronic goods, clothing, and textiles. The recent rapid rise in domestic consumption has resulted in a high rate of inflation and a decrease in the economic growth rate.
History. After years of repressive rule following the Korean War, in 1987 a new and more democratic constitution was adopted; elections in 1993 resulted in victory for a civilian president, who promised economic reform and moves towards unification with North Korea (see also KOREA). During 1995–96 former president Roh Tae Woo was imprisoned for corruption, while former president Chun Doo Hwan was tried for his part in a coup in 1979. Chun Doo Hwan was sentenced to death but this was later commuted. President, Kim Young Sam; capital, Seoul.

language	Korean
currency	won (w) of 100 chon
pop. (1996)	45 232 000
GNP (1994)	US$366B
literacy	99% (m); 93% (f)
life expectancy	68 (m); 76 (f)

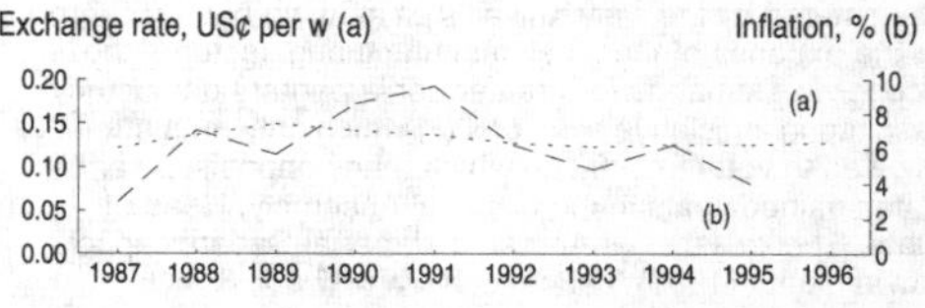

filling the requirements of Jewish law. **2** *colloq.* correct, genuine, legitimate. *–n.* kosher food or shop. [Hebrew, = proper]

Kosovo-Metohija /ˈkɒsəˌvəʊ/ province of SW Serbia, bordering on Albania and Macedonia; pop. (est. 1995) 1 989 000; capital, Priština. Formerly self-governing, the province, which has a large Albanian majority, was stripped of its autonomy in 1990, after voting for full independent status; civil unrest continues.

Kota Baharu /ˌkəʊtə ˈbɑːruː/ town in NE peninsular Malaysia, capital of Kelantan state; pop. (1991) 219 713. It has a major power station.

Kota Kinabalu /ˈkəʊtə ˌkɪnəbəˈluː/ seaport in Malaysia, on the N coast of Borneo, capital of the state of Sabah; industries include rice milling and fishing; pop. (1991) 208 484.

Kotka /ˈkɒtkə/ seaport in SE Finland; industries include sugar refining and flour milling; pop. (1992) 56 462.

Kourou /kʊˈruː/ town in French Guiana; pop. (1990) 11 208. A satellite-launching station was established near Kourou in 1967.

Kowloon /kaʊˈluːn/ peninsula at the S tip of mainland China, opposite Hong Kong island and forming part of the former British colony of Hong Kong.

kowtow /kaʊˈtaʊ/ *–n. hist.* Chinese custom of kneeling with the forehead touching the ground, esp. in submission. *–v.* **1** (usu. foll. by *to*) act obsequiously. **2** *hist.* perform the kowtow. [Chinese, = knock the head]

Kozhikode /ˌkəʊʒɪˈkəʊd/ (formerly **Calicut**) port in SW India, in W Kerala, an important trading centre on the Malabar coast; pop. (est. 1991) 420 000.

k.p.h. *abbr.* kilometres per hour.

KQ *airline flight code* Kenya Airways.

Kr *symb.* krypton.

kraal /krɑːl/ *n. S.Afr.* **1** village of huts enclosed by a fence. **2** enclosure for cattle or sheep. [Afrikaans from Portuguese *curral*, of Hottentot origin]

Kraków see CRACOW.

Krasnodar /ˈkræsnəˌdɑː(r)/ city in SW Russia; industries include food processing; pop. (est. 1995) 646 000.

Krasnoyarsk /ˌkræsnəˈjɑːsk/ city in SW Russia; hydroelectricity and aluminium are produced; pop. (est. 1995) 869 000.

Kraut /kraʊt/ *n. slang offens.* German. [shortening of SAUERKRAUT]

Krefeld /ˈkreɪfelt/ industrial town and port in NW Germany, on the Rhine, known for its silk and velvet industries; pop. (est. 1995) 249 662.

kremlin /ˈkremlɪn/ *n.* **1** (**the Kremlin**) **a** citadel in Moscow. **b** Russian government housed within it. **2** citadel within a Russian town. [Russian]

krill *n.* tiny planktonic crustaceans. [Norwegian *kril* tiny fish]

Kristiansand /ˌkriːstjənˈsɑːn/ ferry port and industrial centre in S Norway, having shipyards, textile mills, and metal- and food-processing plants; pop. (1990) 65 543.

♦ **Kristiansen** /ˌkriːstjənˈsen/, **Kjeld Kirk** (1947–) Danish businessman, head of Lego Group, the world's fifth-largest toy company, formed in 1997 by consolidating most of the family's 50 Lego companies. Lego has opened new theme parks to succeed the original Legoland and is now targetting the CD-ROM market.

Kríti see CRETE.

Krivoy Rog /krɪˈvɔɪ rɒg/ industrial city in SE Ukraine, at the centre of an iron-ore basin; pop. (est. 1996) 720 000.

KRL *abbr. Computing* knowledge representation language (in artificial intelligence).

krona /ˈkrəʊnə/ *n.* (*pl.* **kronor**) standard monetary unit of Sweden. [Swedish, = CROWN]

króna /ˈkrəʊnə/ *n.* (*pl.* **krónur**) standard monetary unit of Iceland. [Icelandic, = CROWN]

krone /ˈkrəʊnə/ *n.* (*pl.* **kroner**) standard monetary unit of Denmark and Norway. [Danish and Norwegian, = CROWN]

kroon /kruːn/ *n.* standard monetary unit of Estonia.

krugerrand /ˈkruːgəˌrɑːnt/ *n.* South African coin containing 1 troy ounce of gold. Minted since 1967 for investment purposes, it enables investors to evade restrictions on holding gold. Since 1975 an import licence has been required to bring them into the UK. See also BRITANNIA COINS. [*Kruger*, name of a South African statesman]

krummhorn /ˈkrʌmhɔːn/ *n.* (also **crumhorn**) medieval wind instrument. [German]

krypton /ˈkrɪptɒn/ *n.* inert gaseous element used in fluorescent lamps etc. [Greek *kruptō* hide]

KS *US postcode* Kansas.

KSh *symb.* Kenya shilling.

KT *postcode* Kingston-upon-Thames.

Kt. *abbr.* Knight.

kt. *abbr.* knot.

KU *airline flight code* Kuwait Airways.

Ku *symb.* kurchatovium.

Kuala Lumpur /ˈkwɑːlə ˈlʊmpʊə(r)/ capital of Malaysia, the commercial centre of a tin-mining and rubber-producing region; pop. (1991) 1 145 075.

Kuching /ˈkuːtʃɪŋ/ port in Malaysia, capital of the state of Sarawak; pop. (1991) 147 729.

kudos /ˈkjuːdɒs/ *n. colloq.* glory; renown. [Greek]

kudu /ˈkuːduː/ *n.* (also **koodoo**) (*pl.* same or **-s**) African antelope with white stripes and corkscrew-shaped ridged horns. [Xhosa]

Kufic /ˈkjuːfɪk/ (also **Cufic**) *–n.* early angular form of the Arabic alphabet used esp. in decorative inscriptions. *–adj.* of or in this script. [from *Kufa*, city in Iraq]

Kuibishev /ˈkuːɪbɪˌʃef/ see SAMARA.

Ku Klux Klan /ˌkuːklʌksˈklæn/ *n.* secret White racist society in the southern US. [origin uncertain]

Kumayri /ˌkʊmaɪˈrɪ/ (formerly **Aleksandropol**, **Leninakan**) city in NW Armenia; the city was devastated by an earthquake in 1988; pop. (1991) 120 000.

Kuwait /kuːˈweɪt/, **State of** Arab sheikdom on the NW coast of the Persian Gulf. Kuwait is one of the world's leading oil-producing countries and oil is the principal export. An autonomous sheikdom from the 18th century, the country came under British protection in 1899, becoming fully independent again in 1961. In August 1990 it was invaded and occupied by Iraq, being liberated in February 1991 after Iraq's defeat by US-led multinational forces in the Gulf War. Devastated by the war, Kuwait's oil industry has recovered, at the expense of the small manufacturing sector of the economy. Demands for greater parliamentary democracy resulted in legislative elections (in which only men are allowed to vote) in 1992, in which many opposition candidates gained seats in the National Assembly. Head of state, Sheikh Jaber al-Ahmad al-Jabar al-Sabah; capital, Kuwait, pop. (1993) 31 241. □ **Kuwaiti** *adj.* & *n.*

languages	Arabic (official), English
currency	dinar (KD) of 1000 fils
pop. (1996)	2 070 000
GNP (1994)	US$31.4B
literacy	83% (m); 74% (f)
life expectancy	74 (m); 79 (f)

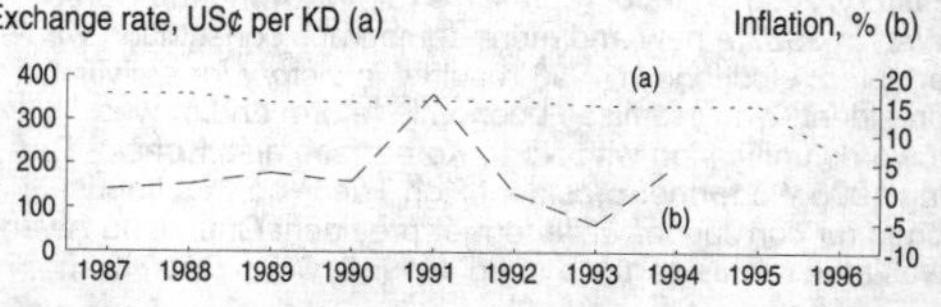

kümmel /ˈkʊm(ə)l/ *n.* sweet liqueur flavoured with caraway and cumin seeds. [German: related to CUMIN]

kumquat /ˈkʌmkwɒt/ *n.* (also **cumquat**) **1** small orange-like fruit. **2** shrub or small tree yielding this. [Chinese *kin kü* gold orange]

kuna /kuːna/ *n.* standard monetary unit of Croatia.

kung fu /kʌŋ ˈfuː/ *n.* Chinese form of karate. [Chinese]

Kunming /kʊnˈmɪŋ/ city in S China, capital of Yunnan province; industries include iron and steel, copper-smelting, and chemicals; pop. (est. 1991) 1 520 000.

♦ **Kuok** /kwɒk/, **Robert** (1923–) Malaysian businessman, founder and chairman of Shangri-La, Asia's largest luxury hotel group, and Coca-Cola bottler in China. Kuok made his fortune in the Malaysian sugar and rice industries and in commodity trading. In 1993 Coca-Cola sold 87.5% of the Chinese bottling venture to Kerry Group, Kuok's Hong Kong-based conglomerate. His other investments include the China World Trade Centre and the *South China Morning Post*, the world's most profitable newspaper.

Kuopio /ˈkwəʊpɪˌəʊ/ city in central Finland; industries include timber- and flour-processing; pop. (1992) 82 340.

kurchatovium /ˌkɜːtʃəˈtəʊvɪəm/ *n.* = RUTHERFORDIUM. [*Kurchatov*, name of a Russian physicist]

Kurd *n.* member of an Aryan Islamic people living in Kurdistan. [Kurdish]

Kurdish /ˈkɜːdɪʃ/ *–adj.* of or relating to the Kurds or their language. *–n.* Iranian language of the Kurds.

Kurdistan /ˌkɜːdɪˈstɑːn/ region inhabited by the Kurds, covering parts of Turkey, Iraq, Iran, and Syria.

Kuria Muria Islands /ˌkʊərɪə ˈmʊərɪə/ group of five islands in the Arabian Sea, belonging to Oman.

Kuril Islands /ˈkjʊəriːl/ (also **Kurile Islands, Kurils**) group of 56 Russian islands between the Sea of Okhotsk and the N Pacific Ocean, stretching from the S tip of Kamchatka to the NE corner of the island of Hokkaido. They formerly (until 1945) belonged to Japan, who continues to demand their return.

Kuznetz Basin /kʊzˈnjets/ (also **Kuznetsk, Kuzbas** /kʊzˈbæs/) industrial region in Russia, between Tomsk and Novokuznetsk. The region is rich in iron and coal deposits.

kV *abbr.* kilovolt(s).

KW *postcode* Kirkwall, Orkney.

kW *abbr.* kilowatt(s).

kwacha /ˈkwɑːtʃə/ *n.* standard monetary unit of Malawi and Zambia. [native word, = dawn]

KwaNdebele /ˌkwɑːəndəˈbiːlɪ/ former Bantu homeland in South Africa. It was abolished following democratic elections held in 1994.

Kwangsi Chuang see GUANGXI ZHUANG.

Kwangtung see GUANGDONG.

kwanza /ˈkwænzə/ *n.* standard monetary unit of Angola. [Bantu word]

KwaZulu /kwɑːˈzuːluː/ (formerly **Zululand**) former Bantu homeland of the Zulu people in South Africa. It was abolished following democratic elections held in 1994 and, together with the former province of Natal, became KwaZulu-Natal.

KwaZulu-Natal /kwɑːˈzuluː-nəˈtɒl/ province of the Republic of South Africa, on the E coast; pop. (est. 1995) 8 713 000; capital, Pietermaritzburg. KwaZulu-Natal was formed in 1994 from the province of Natal and the Zulu homeland of Kwazulu. Products include sugar cane, maize, and tropical fruits; forestry is also important. There are also paper, chemical, oil-refining, and food-processing industries.

Kweichow see GUIZHOU.

Kweilin see GUILIN.

Kweiyang see GUIYANG.

kWh *abbr.* kilowatt-hour(s).

KWIC /kwɪk/ *abbr.* key word in context (*KWIC index*).

KWOC /kwɒk/ *abbr.* key word out of context (*KWOC index*).

KWT *international vehicle registration* Kuwait.

KX *airline flight code* Cayman Airways.

KY *–postcode* Kirkcaldy. *–US postcode* Kentucky.

Ky. *abbr.* Kentucky.

kyat /kɪˈɑːt/ *n.* standard monetary unit of Burma (Myanmar). [Burmese]

kyle /kaɪl/ *n.* (in Scotland) narrow channel, strait. [Gaelic *caol* strait]

Kyoto /kɪˈəʊtəʊ/ city in Japan, on Honshu island; manufactures include silk, porcelain, and lacquerware; pop. (1995) 1 463 600.

Kyrenia /kaɪˈriːnɪə/ market town and resort on the N coast of Cyprus; pop. (1985) 7000.

Kyrgyz /ˈkɜːgiːz/ (also **Kirghiz, Kirgiz**) *–n.* **1** native of Kyrgyzstan. **2** language of Kyrgyzstan. *–adj.* of the people or language of Kyrgyzstan.

Kyushu /kɪˈuːʃuː/ southernmost of the four main islands of Japan; pop. (1995) 13 424 000; capital, Fukuoka. Coalmining is important; other products include rice, silk, timber, and tea.

Kyrgyzstan /ˌkɜːgɪˈstɑːn/, **Republic of** (formerly **Kirghizia**) country in central Asia, bordered by Kazakhstan, China, Tajikistan, and Uzbekistan, formerly (until 1991) a Soviet republic. Agriculture is important to the economy, producing both livestock (esp. sheep and cattle) and crops (esp. sugar beet, cotton, and wheat). Minerals, including coal, oil, and gas, are mined; other industrial activities include food processing and textiles. The most democratic of the former Soviet central Asian republics, Kyrgyzstan has initiated market reforms, backed by the IMF, to improve its struggling economy, and is seeking trading partners outside the former Soviet Union. A new constitution came into effect in 1994. President, Askar Akaev; capital, Pishpek.

languages	Kyrgyz, Russian (both official)
currency	som of 100 tyiyn
pop. (1996)	4 521 000
GNP (1994)	US$2.8B
literacy	98% (m); 95% (f)
life expectancy	64 (m); 72 (f)

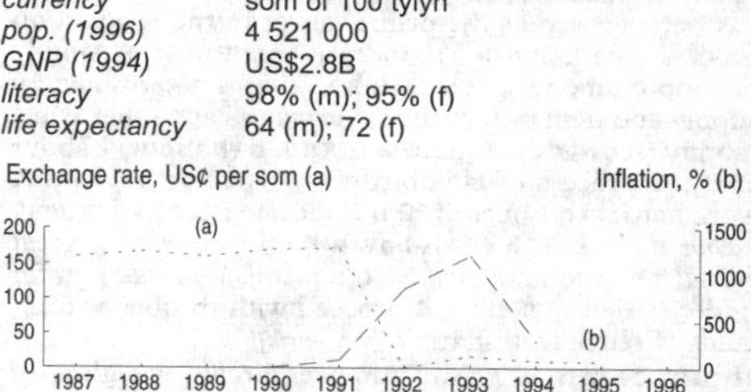

Ll

L[1] /el/ *n.* (also **l**) (*pl.* **Ls** or **L's**) **1** twelfth letter of the alphabet. **2** (as a roman numeral) 50.

L[2] *abbr.* (also **L.**) **1** learner driver. **2** Lake.

L[3] *–symb. Currency* **1** lempira. **2** Italian lira (or lire). *–international vehicle registration* Luxembourg. *–postcode* Liverpool.

l *abbr.* **1** (also **l.**) left. **2** (also **l.**) length. **3** (also **l.**) line. **4** litre(s).

£ *symb.* pound(s) (money). [Latin *libra*]

LA *–abbr.* **1** Latin America(n). **2** Los Angeles. *–postcode* Lancaster. *–US postcode* Louisiana. *–airline flight code* Lan Chile.

La *symb.* lanthanum.

La. *abbr.* Louisiana.

la var. of LAH.

Lab. *abbr.* **1** Labour. **2** Labrador.

lab *n. colloq.* laboratory. [abbreviation]

label /'leɪb(ə)l/ *–n.* **1** piece of paper etc. attached to an object to give information about it. **2** short classifying phrase applied to a person etc. **3** logo, title, or trade mark of a company. *–v.* (**-ll-**; *US* **-l-**) **1** attach a label to. **2** (usu. foll. by *as*) assign to a category. **3** replace (an atom) by an atom of a usu. radioactive isotope as a means of identification. [French]

labial /'leɪbɪəl/ *–adj.* **1 a** of the lips. **b** of, like, or serving as a lip. **2** (of a sound) requiring partial or complete closure of the lips. *–n.* labial sound (e.g. *p, m, v*). [Latin *labia* lips]

labium /'leɪbɪəm/ *n.* (*pl.* **labia**) (usu. in *pl.*) each fold of skin of the two pairs enclosing the vulva. [Latin, = lip]

labor etc. *US* & *Austral.* var. of LABOUR etc.

laboratory /lə'bɒrətərɪ/ *n.* (*pl.* **-ies**) room, building, or establishment for scientific experiments, research, chemical manufacture, etc. [Latin: related to LABORIOUS]

laborious /lə'bɔːrɪəs/ *adj.* **1** needing hard work or toil. **2** (esp. of literary style) showing signs of toil. □ **laboriously** *adv.* [Latin: related to LABOUR]

labour /'leɪbə(r)/ (*US* & *Austral.* **labor**) *–n.* **1** physical or mental work; exertion. **2 a** workers, esp. manual, considered as a political and economic force. In economics, labour is regarded as a factor of production usu. combined with land and capital to produce outputs. Labour has been viewed as the prime mover of the production process (see LABOUR THEORY OF VALUE), or as simply one input among several, whose value is determined by supply and demand, in the same way as any other commodity (see NEOCLASSICAL SCHOOL). **b** (**Labour**) Labour Party. **3** process of childbirth. **4** particular task. *–v.* **1** work hard; exert oneself. **2 a** elaborate needlessly (*don't labour the point*). **b** (as **laboured** *adj.*) done with great effort; not spontaneous. **3** (often foll. by *under*) suffer under (a delusion etc.). **4** proceed with trouble or difficulty. [French from Latin *labor, -oris*]

labour camp *n.* prison camp enforcing a regime of hard labour.

Labour Day *n.* May 1 (or in the US and Canada the first Monday in September), celebrated in honour of working people.

labourer *n.* (*US* **laborer**) person doing unskilled, usu. manual, work for wages.

Labour Exchange *n. colloq.* or *hist.* employment exchange.

◆ **labour-intensive** *adj.* denoting an industry, firm, job, etc. in which the remuneration paid to employees represents a higher proportion of the costs of production than the cost of raw materials or capital equipment. In the reverse case the industry, firm, etc. is said to be **capital-intensive**. For example, publishing is a labour-intensive industry, printing is capital-intensive.

◆ **labour market** *n. Econ.* market that determines who has jobs and the rate of pay for a particular job.

Labour Party *n.* political party formed to represent the interests of working people.

◆ **labour-rate variance** *n. Econ.* variance arising when the rate at which labour is paid differs from the standard rate (see VARIANCE 3).

---

labour-saving *adj.* designed to reduce or eliminate work.

◆ **labour theory of value** *n. Econ.* theory that the value of an item is dependent on the quantity of labour that is required to make it. First developed by Adam Smith, it was at the core of the Classical school of economics and subsequently of Marxist economic theory. In practice, the theory has few useful applications and was superseded by the Marginalist theory of value, which associates the value of a good with its utility and its scarcity.

◆ **labour turnover rate** *n.* ratio, usu. expressed as a percentage, of the number of employees leaving an organization or industry in a stated period to the average number of employees working in that organization or industry during the period.

◆ **labor union** *n. US* = TRADE UNION.

Labrador[1] /'læbrəˌdɔː(r)/ **1** (also **Labrador-Ungava**) NE peninsula of Canada, from Hudson Bay to the mouth of the St Lawrence River, most of which constitutes part of Quebec. **2** the E section of this peninsula which forms the mainland section of the province of Newfoundland and Labrador; chief town, Battle Harbour. There are important fisheries and hydroelectric power stations; iron ore is mined.

Labrador[2] /'læbrəˌdɔː(r)/ *n.* retriever of a breed with a black or golden coat. [LABRADOR[1]]

Labuan /lə'buːən/ island off the N coast of Borneo, forming a Federal Territory of Malaysia; products include rubber, sago, and copra; pop. (1991) 54 307; capital, Victoria.

laburnum /lə'bɜːnəm/ *n.* tree with drooping golden flowers yielding poisonous seeds. [Latin]

labyrinth /'læbərɪnθ/ *n.* **1** complicated network of passages etc. **2** intricate or tangled arrangement. **3** the complex structure of the inner ear. □ **labyrinthine** /-'rɪnθaɪn/ *adj.* [Latin from Greek]

lac *n.* resinous substance secreted as a protective covering by a SE Asian insect. [Hindustani]

Laccadive Islands /'lækədɪv/ see LAKSHADWEEP.

lace *–n.* **1** fine open fabric or trimming, made by weaving thread in patterns. **2** cord etc. passed through holes or hooks for fastening shoes etc. *–v.* (**-cing**) **1** (usu. foll. by *up*) fasten or tighten with a lace or laces. **2** add spirits to (a drink). **3** (often foll. by *through*) pass (a shoelace etc.) through. [Latin *laqueus* noose]

La Ceiba /lɑː 'seɪbə/ seaport on the Caribbean coast of Honduras; exports include coconuts, abaca fibre, and oranges; pop. (1994) 86 000.

lacerate /'læsəˌreɪt/ *v.* (**-ting**) **1** mangle or tear (esp.

flesh etc.). **2** cause pain to (the feelings etc.). □ **laceration** /-'reɪʃ(ə)n/ *n.* [Latin *lacer* torn]

lace-up –*n.* shoe fastened with a lace. –*attrib. adj.* (of a shoe etc.) fastened by a lace or laces.

◆ **laches** /'lætʃɪz/ *n. Law* neglect and unreasonable delay in enforcing an equitable right. If a plaintiff with full knowledge of the facts takes an unnecessarily long time to bring an action (e.g. to set aside a contract obtained by fraud) the court will not assist the plaintiff. No set period is given but if the action is covered by limitation-of-actions legislation, the period given will not be shortened. Otherwise the time allowed depends on the circumstances. [French *lasche* slack: related to LAX]

lachrymal /'lækrɪm(ə)l/ *adj.* (also **lacrimal**) of or for tears (*lacrimal duct*). [Latin *lacrima* tear]

lachrymose /'lækrɪ,məʊs/ *adj. formal* given to weeping; tearful.

lack –*n.* (usu. foll. by *of*) want, deficiency. –*v.* be without or deficient in. [Low German or Dutch]

lackadaisical /,lækə'deɪzɪk(ə)l/ *adj.* unenthusiastic; listless; idle. □ **lackadaisically** *adv.* [from archaic *lackaday*]

lackey /'lækɪ/ *n.* (*pl.* **-s**) **1** servile follower; toady. **2** footman, manservant. [Catalan *alacay*]

lacking *adj.* absent or deficient (*money was lacking*; *is lacking in determination*).

lacklustre *adj.* (*US* **lackluster**) **1** lacking in vitality etc. **2** dull.

Laconia /lə'kəʊnɪə/ department of SW Greece, an important territory in ancient times; pop. (1991) 95 696; administrative centre, Sparta. □ **Laconian** *adj.* & *n.*

laconic /lə'kɒnɪk/ *adj.* terse, using few words. □ **laconically** *adv.* [Greek *Lakōn* Spartan]

lacquer /'lækə(r)/ –*n.* **1** varnish made of shellac or a synthetic substance. **2** substance sprayed on the hair to keep it in place. –*v.* coat with lacquer. [French *lacre* = LAC]

lacrimal var. of LACHRYMAL.

lacrosse /lə'krɒs/ *n.* game like hockey, but with the ball carried in a crosse. [French *la* the, CROSSE]

lactate[1] /læk'teɪt/ *v.* (**-ting**) (of mammals) secrete milk. [as LACTATION]

lactate[2] /'lækteɪt/ *n.* salt or ester of lactic acid.

lactation /læk'teɪʃ(ə)n/ *n.* **1** secretion of milk. **2** suckling. [Latin: related to LACTIC]

lacteal /'læktɪəl/ –*adj.* **1** of milk. **2** conveying chyle etc. –*n.* (in *pl.*) *Anat.* vessels which absorb fats. [Latin *lacteus*: related to LACTIC]

lactic /'læktɪk/ *adj.* of milk. [Latin *lac lactis* milk]

lactic acid *n.* acid formed esp. in sour milk.

lactose /'læktəʊs/ *n.* sugar that occurs in milk.

lacuna /lə'kju:nə/ *n.* (*pl.* **lacunae** /-ni:/ or **-s**) **1** gap. **2** missing portion etc., esp. in an ancient MS etc. [Latin: related to LAKE[1]]

lacy /'leɪsɪ/ *adj.* (**-ier, -iest**) of or resembling lace fabric.

lad *n.* **1** boy, youth. **2** *colloq.* man. [origin unknown]

Ladakh /lə'dɑ:k/ region of E Kashmir in NW India, in Jammu and Kashmir state, manufacturing woollen cloth; chief town, Leh.

ladder –*n.* **1** set of horizontal bars fixed between two uprights and used for climbing up or down. **2** vertical strip of unravelled stitching in a stocking etc. **3** hierarchical structure, esp. as a means of career advancement. –*v.* **1** cause a ladder in (a stocking etc.). **2** develop a ladder. [Old English]

ladder-back *n.* upright chair with a back resembling a ladder.

lade *v.* (**-ding**; *past part.* **laden**) **1 a** load (a ship). **b** ship (goods). **2** (as **laden** *adj.*) (usu. foll. by *with*) loaded, burdened. [Old English]

la-di-da /,lɑ:dɪ'dɑ:/ *adj. colloq.* pretentious or snobbish, esp. in manner or speech. [imitative]

ladies' man *n.* (also **lady's man**) man fond of female company.

ladle /'leɪd(ə)l/ –*n.* deep long-handled spoon used for serving liquids. –*v.* (**-ling**) (often foll. by *out*) transfer (liquid) with a ladle. [Old English]

lady /'leɪdɪ/ *n.* (*pl.* **-ies**) **1 a** woman regarded as being of superior social status or as having refined manners. **b** (**Lady**) title of peeresses, female relatives of peers, the wives and widows of knights, etc. **2** (often *attrib.*) woman; female (*ask that lady*; *lady butcher*). **3** *colloq.* wife, girlfriend. **4** ruling woman (*lady of the house*). **5** (**the Ladies** or **Ladies'**) women's public lavatory. [Old English, = loaf-kneader]

ladybird *n.* small beetle, usu. red with black spots.

Lady chapel *n.* chapel dedicated to the Virgin Mary.

Lady Day *n.* Feast of the Annunciation, 25 Mar.

lady-in-waiting *n.* lady attending a queen or princess.

lady-killer *n.* habitual seducer of women.

ladylike *adj.* like or befitting a lady.

◆ **Lady Macbeth strategy** /mək'beθ/ *n.* strategy used in take-over battles in which a third party makes a bid that the target company would favour, appearing to act as a white knight, but subsequently changes allegiance and joins the original bidder. [*Lady Macbeth*, name of a character in Shakespeare's *Macbeth*]

ladyship *n.* □ **her** (or **your**) **ladyship** respectful form of reference or address to a Lady.

lady's slipper *n.* plant of the orchid family with a slipper-shaped lip on its flowers.

lady's man var. of LADIES' MAN.

◆ **Laffer curve** /'læfə(r)/ *n. Econ.* curve on a graph showing government tax revenue plotted against the percentage rate of taxation. Supply-side economists believe that this curve is hill-shaped, so that at very high rates of taxation a cut in percentage rates will actually increase government tax revenues. This belief is based on the view that lower tax rates will induce individuals to work harder and earn more income, enabling more tax to be raised at the lower rate. [*Laffer*, name of an economist]

LAFTA /'læftə/ *abbr. hist.* Latin American Free Trade Area. See LATIN AMERICAN INTEGRATION ASSOCIATION.

lag[1] –*v.* (**-gg-**) fall behind; not keep pace. –*n.* delay. [origin uncertain]

lag[2] –*v.* (**-gg-**) enclose in heat-insulating material. –*n.* insulating cover. [Old Norse]

lag[3] *n. slang* habitual convict. [origin unknown]

lager /'lɑ:gə(r)/ *n.* a kind of light effervescent beer. [German, = store]

lager lout *n. colloq.* youth behaving violently etc. as a result of excessive drinking.

laggard /'lægəd/ *n.* person who lags behind.

lagging *n.* material used to lag a boiler etc. against loss of heat.

lagoon /lə'gu:n/ *n.* stretch of salt water separated from the sea by a sandbank, reef, etc. [Latin LACUNA pool]

Lagos /'leɪgɒs/ chief port and former capital of Nigeria; an important industrial and commercial centre, it exports palm oil, palm kernels, and peanuts; pop. (est. 1995) 1 484 000.

lah /lɑ:/ *n.* (also **la**) *Mus.* sixth note of a major scale. [Latin *labii*, word arbitrarily taken]

Lahore /lə'hɔ:(r)/ city in Pakistan, capital of Punjab province; industries include engineering, chemicals, and textiles; pop. (est. 1990) 3 500 000.

◆ **LAIA** *abbr.* = LATIN AMERICAN INTEGRATION ASSOCIATION.

laid *past* and *past part.* of LAY[1].

laid paper *n.* paper with the surface marked in fine ribs.

laid up *adj.* **1** confined to bed or the house. **2** (of a ship) out of service.

lain *past part.* of LIE[1].

◆ **Laing** /læŋ/, **Sir (John) Maurice** (1918–) British

businessman, life-president (from 1982) and former chairman (1976–82) of John Laing plc, the construction company founded by his father, Sir John Laing. He is also a former director of the Bank of England (1963–80). His elder brother, Sir (William) Kirby Laing (1916–), is a former chairman (1978–87) and president (1987–90) of Laing Properties plc.

---

lair *n.* **1** wild animal's resting-place. **2** person's hiding-place. [Old English]

laird *n. Scot.* landed proprietor. [from LORD]

laissez-faire /ˌleseɪ'feə(r)/ *n.* (also ***laisser-faire***) policy of non-interference. [French, = let act]

◆ ***laissez-faire* economy** *n.* economy in which government intervention is kept to a minimum and market forces are allowed to rule. Such policies were popular with Western governments until the time of Keynes, when mass unemployment caused them to become discredited. During the stagflation of the late 1960s and 1970s they became, once again, fashionable.

---

laity /'leɪɪtɪ/ *n.* lay people, as distinct from the clergy. [from LAY[2]]

lake[1] *n.* large body of water surrounded by land. [Latin *lacus*]

lake[2] *n.* **1** reddish pigment orig. made from lac. **2** pigment obtained by combining an organic colouring matter with a metallic oxide, hydroxide, or salt. [var. of LAC]

Lake District *n.* (also **the Lakes**) region of lakes in Cumbria.

lakh /læk/ *n.* (in India, Pakistan, and Bangladesh; usu. foll. by *of*) hundred thousand (rupees etc.). See also CRORE. [Hindi *lākh*]

Lakshadweep /ˌlækʃæ'dwiːp/ (formerly **Laccadive, Minicoy, and Amindivi Islands**) Union Territory of India, off the coast of Malabar; products include coir, copra, and fish; pop. (est. 1994) 56 000; capital, Kavaratti.

La Louvière /lɑː luːvɪ'eə(r)/ industrial city in Belgium, in the province of Hainaut; industries include coal, steel, and ceramics; pop. (est. 1995) 76 879.

lam *v.* **(-mm-)** *slang* thrash; hit. [perhaps Scandinavian]

lama /'lɑːmə/ *n.* Tibetan or Mongolian Buddhist monk. [Tibetan]

lamasery /'lɑːməsərɪ/ *n.* (*pl.* **-ies**) monastery of lamas. [French]

lamb /læm/ *–n.* **1** young sheep. **2** its flesh as food. **3** mild, gentle, or kind person. *–v.* give birth to lambs. □ **The Lamb** (or **Lamb of God**) name for Christ. [Old English]

lambada /læm'bɑːdə/ *n.* fast erotic Brazilian dance in which couples dance with their stomachs touching each other. [Portuguese, = a beating]

lambaste /læm'beɪst/ *v.* **(-ting)** (also **lambast** /-'bæst/) *colloq.* thrash, beat. [from LAM, BASTE[1]]

lambda /'læmdə/ *n.* eleventh letter of the Greek alphabet (Λ, λ). [Greek]

lambent /'læmbənt/ *adj.* **1** (of a flame or a light) playing on a surface. **2** (of the eyes, sky, wit, etc.) lightly brilliant. □ **lambency** *n.* [Latin *lambo* lick]

lambswool *n.* soft fine wool from a young sheep.

lame *–adj.* **1** disabled in the foot or leg. **2 a** (of an argument, excuse, etc.) unconvincing. **b** (of verse etc.) halting. *–v.* **(-ming)** make lame; disable. □ **lamely** *adv.* **lameness** *n.* [Old English]

lamé /'lɑːmeɪ/ *n.* fabric with gold or silver threads interwoven. [French]

lame duck *n.* **1** helpless person. **2** company with high prestige and a large workforce that is unable to meet foreign competition without government support.

lament /lə'ment/ *–n.* **1** passionate expression of grief. **2** song etc. of mourning etc. *–v.* (also *absol.*) **1** express or feel grief for or about. **2** (as **lamented** *adj.*) used to refer to a recently dead person. □ **lament for** (or **over**) mourn or regret. [Latin *lamentor*]

lamentable /'læməntəb(ə)l/ *adj.* deplorable, regrettable. □ **lamentably** *adv.*

lamentation /ˌlæmən'teɪʃ(ə)n/ *n.* **1** lamenting. **2** lament.

lamina /'læmɪnə/ *n.* (*pl.* **-nae** /-ˌniː/) thin plate or scale. □ **laminar** *adj.* [Latin]

laminate *–v.* /'læmɪˌneɪt/ **(-ting) 1** beat or roll into thin plates. **2** overlay with metal plates, a plastic layer, etc. **3** split into layers. *–n.* /'læmɪnət/ laminated structure, esp. of layers fixed together. *–adj.* /'læmɪnət/ in the form of thin plates. □ **lamination** /-'neɪʃ(ə)n/ *n.*

Lammas /'læməs/ *n.* (in full **Lammas Day**) first day of August, formerly kept as harvest festival. [Old English: related to LOAF[1], MASS[2]]

lamp *n.* **1** device for producing a steady light, esp.: **a** an electric bulb, and usu. its holder. **b** an oil-lamp. **c** a gas-jet and mantle. **2** device producing esp. ultraviolet or infrared radiation. [Greek *lampas* torch]

lampblack *n.* pigment made from soot.

lamplight *n.* light from a lamp.

lamplighter *n. hist.* person who lit street lamps.

lampoon /læm'puːn/ *–n.* satirical attack on a person etc. *–v.* satirize. □ **lampoonist** *n.* [French *lampon*]

lamppost *n.* tall post supporting a street-light.

lamprey /'læmprɪ/ *n.* (*pl.* **-s**) eel-like aquatic animal with a sucker mouth. [Latin *lampreda*]

lampshade *n.* translucent cover for a lamp.

LAMSAC *abbr.* Local Authorities' Management Services and Computer Committee.

LAN /læn/ *abbr.* = LOCAL AREA NETWORK.

Lancashire /'læŋkəʃɪə(r)/ county in NW England; pop. (est. 1994) 1 424 000; county town, Preston. The former mining and textile industries have declined, and attempts have been made to encourage light manufacturing.

Lancaster /'læŋkæstə(r)/ city in NW England, formerly the county town of Lancashire; manufactures include plastics and floor coverings; pop. (1991) 44 497.

Lancastrian /læŋ'kæstrɪən/ *–n.* **1** native of Lancashire or Lancaster. **2** *hist.* member or supporter of the House of Lancaster in the Wars of the Roses. *–adj.* of or concerning Lancashire or Lancaster, or the House of Lancaster. [LANCASTER]

lance /lɑːns/ *–n.* long spear, esp. one used by a horseman. *–v.* **(-cing) 1** prick or cut open with a lancet. **2** pierce with a lance. [French from Latin]

lance-corporal *n.* lowest rank of NCO in the Army.

lanceolate /'lɑːnsɪələt/ *adj.* shaped like a lance-head, tapering at each end.

lancer *n.* **1** *hist.* soldier of a cavalry regiment armed with lances. **2** (in *pl.*) **a** quadrille. **b** music for this.

lancet /'lɑːnsɪt/ *n.* small broad two-edged surgical knife with a sharp point.

lancet arch *n.* (also **lancet light** or **window**) narrow arch or window with a pointed head.

Lanchow see LANZHOU.

Lancs. *abbr.* Lancashire.

land *–n.* **1** solid part of the earth's surface. **2 a** expanse of country; ground, soil. **b** this in relation to its use, quality, etc., or as a basis for agriculture. **3** country, nation, state. **4 a** any part of the earth's surface that can be owned, including all buildings, trees, minerals, etc. attached to or forming part of it. It also includes the airspace above the land necessary for its reasonable enjoyment. In law, a first-floor flat can constitute a separate piece of land, although it has no contact with the soil, just as a cellar may be a separate estate in land. **b** (in *pl.*) estates. **5** *Econ.* factor of production usu. combined with labour and capital to produce outputs. It includes air, sea, minerals, etc., as well as land for building on. Although it costs nothing to produce and is in fixed supply, the application of capital to land (as in irrigation) can considerably alter its characteristics and value. *–v.* **1 a** set or go ashore. **b** (often foll. by *at*) disembark. **2** bring (an aircraft) to the ground or another surface. **3** alight on the ground etc. **4** bring (a fish) to land. **5** (also *refl.*; often foll. by *up*) *colloq.* bring to, reach, or find oneself in a certain situation or place. **6** *colloq.* **a** deal (a person etc. a blow etc.). **b** (foll. by *with*) present (a person) with (a problem, job, etc.). **7** *colloq.* win or obtain (a prize, job, etc.). □ **how the land lies** what is the state of affairs. **land on one's feet** attain a good position, job, etc., by luck. □ **landless** *adj.* [Old English]

land-agent *n.* **1** steward of an estate. **2** agent for the sale of estates.

landau /'lændɔː/ *n.* four-wheeled enclosed carriage with a divided top. [*Landau* in Germany]

◆ **land bank** *n.* **1** amount of land a developer owns that is awaiting development. **2** (**Land Bank**) = AGRICULTURAL BANK.

◆ **land certificate** *n.* document that takes the place of a title deed for registered land. It is granted to the registered proprietor of the land and indicates ownership. It will usu. be kept in the Land Registry if the land is subject to a mortgage.

◆ **land charges** *n.pl. Law* contracts, payments, or other matters to which land is subject; they must either be dealt with before the land is sold or they will bind the purchaser. Formerly, they bound a purchaser who had notice of them. Now most of them must be registered if they are to remain effective, either under the Land Charges Act (1972; applicable to unregistered land) or under the Land Registration Act (1925; applicable to registered land).

◆ **Land Charges Register** *n.* **1** register of land charges on unregistered land, kept at the Land Registry. Charges are registered against the name of the estate owner. The kinds of charges that must be registered are set out in the Land Charges Act (1972) and include estate contracts, equitable easements, restrictive covenants, and Inland Revenue charges. Registration constitutes actual notice to any person of the existence of the charge. If the purchaser of the land is unable to discover the charge (e.g. because it is registered against the name of an estate owner that does not appear on the title-deeds available to the purchaser), compensation may be payable to the purchaser at public expense. If a charge is not registered it will not bind a purchaser for money or money's worth of a legal estate in the land, even if the person had notice of the charge. Some charges, if not registered, will not bind the purchaser for value of any interest (whether legal or equitable) in the land. **2** (also **Local Land Charges Register**) register kept by each London borough, the City of London, and each district council. Public authorities may register statutory restrictions on land, e.g. under town and country planning legislation. These are registered against the land itself, not the estate owner. If restrictions are not registered, the purchaser is still bound by them, but will be entitled to compensation.

L & D *abbr.* **1** loans and discounts. **2** loss and damage.

landed *adj.* **1** owning land. **2** consisting of land. **3** denoting an export price in which the exporter pays all the charges to the port of destination and also pays the landing charges but not any dock dues or onward carriage charges to the importer's factory or warehouse. Cf. C.I.F.; FRANCO.

landfall *n.* approach to land, esp. after a sea or air journey.

landfill *n.* **1** waste material etc. used to landscape or reclaim land. **2** process of disposing of rubbish in this way.

land-girl *n.* woman doing farm work, esp. in wartime.

landing *n.* **1** platform at the top of or part way up a flight of stairs. **2** coming to land **3** place where ships etc. land.

◆ **landing account** *n.* account prepared by a public warehousing company to the owner of goods that have recently been landed from a ship and taken into the warehouse. It states the date on which the warehouse rent begins and also the quantity of goods and their condition (from the external appearance of the packages).

◆ **landing charges** *n.pl.* charges incurred in disembarking a cargo, or part of it, from a ship at the port of destination.

landing-craft *n.* craft designed for putting troops and equipment ashore.

landing-gear *n.* undercarriage of an aircraft.

◆ **landing order** *n.* document given to an importer by the UK Customs and Excise, enabling newly imported goods to be removed from a ship or quay to a bonded warehouse, pending payment of duty or their re-export.

landing-stage *n.* platform for disembarking goods and passengers.

landlady *n.* **1** woman who lets land or premises, granting a lease to a tenant. She may or may not be the freehold owner. See also LANDLORD AND TENANT. **2** woman who keeps a public house, boarding-house, etc.

land-line *n.* means of telecommunication over land.

landlocked *adj.* almost or entirely enclosed by land.

landlord *n.* **1** person who lets land or premises, granting a lease to a tenant. The landlord may or may not be the freehold owner. See also LANDLORD AND TENANT. **2** man who keeps a public house, boarding-house, etc.

◆ **landlord and tenant** *n.pl. Law* the parties to a lease. The law of landlord and tenant is that governing the creation, termination, and regulation of leases. Many leases, both business and residential, are subject to statutory control. This means that the right of the landlord to end a lease and evict tenants may be restricted and the rent may be controlled. It is therefore essential to consider statutory rights when considering the relation between the parties, as well as those given by the lease.

landlubber *n.* person unfamiliar with the sea.

landmark *n.* **1** conspicuous object in a district, landscape, etc. **2** prominent and critical event etc.

land mass *n.* large area of land.

land-mine *n.* explosive mine laid in or on the ground.

landowner *n.* owner of (esp. much) land. □ **landowning** *adj.* & *n.*

◆ **land registration** *n.* system of registration of title introduced by the Land Registration Act (1925). Land is registered by reference to a map rather than against the name of any estate owner. Three registers are kept: the **property register** records the land and estate, referring to a map and mentioning any interests benefiting the land (e.g. easements and restrictive covenants); the **proprietorship register** sets out the name of the owner, the nature of the title (freehold, leasehold, etc.), and any restrictions on the way the land may be dealt with (whether subject to a trust etc.); the **charges register** contains notice of rights adverse to the land, e.g. mortgages and land charges as defined in the Land Charges Act (1972). The owner's title is guaranteed by registration in most circumstances. Rights in registered land may be a registered interest, which amounts to ownership of the freehold or leasehold estate; an overriding interest, which binds a purchaser without needing to be registered; or a minor interest, which needs to be protected by an entry on the register (e.g. interest under a trust or restrictive covenant). The purpose of land registration was to simplify conveyancing, so that instead of checking title-deeds, a search of the register would reveal all relevant matters. Unfortunately the simplicity of the system is breached by the difficulties arising from overriding interests. Eventually, all land in England and Wales will be registered, enabling unregistered conveyancing to disappear. See also RECTIFICATION OF REGISTER 1; REGISTERED LAND CERTIFICATE.

◆ **Land Registry** *n.* official body that keeps the various land registers (see LAND REGISTRATION) and is responsible for implementing the policy of registering title to all land in England and Wales. The main registry is in Lincoln's Inn Fields in London, but there are also regional registries.

landscape /'lændskeɪp/ *–n.* **1** scenery as seen in a broad view. **2** (often *attrib.*) picture representing this; this genre of painting. –*v.* (**-ping**) improve (a piece of land) by landscape gardening. [Dutch *landscap*]

landscape gardening *n.* laying out of grounds to resemble natural scenery.

landslide *n.* **1** sliding down of a mass of land from a mountain, cliff, etc. **2** overwhelming victory in an election.

landslip *n.* = LANDSLIDE 1.

♦ **land waiter** *n.* UK customs officer who examines goods at the ports for export or import and ensures that the correct taxes or duties are levied.

---

lane *n.* **1** narrow road. **2** division of a road for a stream of traffic. **3** strip of track etc. for a competitor in a race. **4** path regularly followed by a ship, aircraft, etc. **5** gangway between crowds of people. [Old English]

language /'læŋgwɪdʒ/ *n.* **1** use of words in an agreed way as a method of human communication. **2** system of words of a particular community or country etc. **3 a** faculty of speech. **b** style of expression; use of words, etc. (*poetic language*). **4** see PROGRAMMING LANGUAGE. **5** any method of communication. **6** professional or specialized vocabulary. [Latin *lingua* tongue]

language laboratory *n.* room equipped with tape recorders etc. for learning a foreign language.

Languedoc /lɑ̃g'dɒk/ former province of S France. Lower Languedoc was united with the former province of Roussillon to form Languedoc-Roussillon.

Languedoc-Roussillon /lɑ̃g'dɒk-ruːsɪ'ɒn/ region of S France; pop. (est. 1994) 2 212 025; chief town Montpellier. It is a major wine-producing region and tourism is important.

languid /'læŋgwɪd/ *adj.* lacking vigour; idle; inert. □ **languidly** *adv.* [related to LANGUISH]

languish /'læŋgwɪʃ/ *v.* lose or lack vitality. □ **languish for** droop or pine for. **languish under** suffer under (depression, confinement, etc.). [Latin *langueo*]

languor /'læŋgə(r)/ *n.* **1** lack of energy; idleness. **2** soft or tender mood or effect. **3** oppressive stillness. □ **languorous** *adj.*

lank *adj.* **1** (of hair, grass, etc.) long and limp. **2** thin and tall. [Old English]

lanky *adj.* (**-ier**, **-iest**) ungracefully thin and long or tall. □ **lankiness** *n.*

lanolin /'lænəlɪn/ *n.* fat found on sheep's wool and used in cosmetics etc. [Latin *lana* wool, *oleum* OIL]

Lansing /'lænsɪŋ/ city in the US, capital of Michigan; car components are manufactured; pop. (est. 1994) 119 590.

lantern /'lænt(ə)n/ *n.* **1** lamp with a transparent case protecting a flame etc. **2** raised structure on a dome, room, etc., glazed to admit light. **3** light-chamber of a lighthouse. [Greek *lamptēr* torch]

lantern jaws *n.pl.* long thin jaws and chin.

lanthanide /'lænθəˌnaɪd/ *n.* any element of the lanthanide series. [German: related to LANTHANUM]

lanthanide series *n. Chem.* series of 15 metallic elements from lanthanum to lutetium in the periodic table, having similar chemical properties.

lanthanum /'lænθənəm/ *n.* metallic element, first of the lanthanide series. [Greek *lanthanō* escape notice]

lanyard /'lænjəd/ *n.* **1** cord worn round the neck or the shoulder, to which a knife etc. may be attached. **2** *Naut.* short rope or line used for securing, tightening, etc. [French *laniere*, assimilated to YARD[1]]

Lanzhou /læn'dʒəʊ/ (also **Lanchow** /læn'tʃaʊ/) city in N China, capital of Gansu province; industries include oil refining and plutonium processing; pop. (est. 1991) 1 510 000.

LAO *international vehicle registration* Laos.

Lao /laʊ/ (also **Laotian** /'laʊʃɪən, lɑː'əʊʃɪən/ –*n.* **1** native or national of Laos. **2** language of Laos. –*adj.* of Laos or its people or language.

Laodicean /ˌleɪəʊdɪ'siːən/ *adj.* half-hearted, esp. in religion or politics. [*Laodicea* in Asia Minor (Rev. 3:16)]

Laoighis /'leɪɪʃ/ (also **Laois** or **Leix**; formerly **Queen's County**) county in the central Republic of Ireland, in the province of Leinster; pop. (1991) 52 314; capital, Portlaoise. Cattle- and dairy-farming are important; manufactures include textiles and machinery.

lap[1] *n.* **1** front of the body from the waist to the knees of a sitting person. **2** clothing covering this. □ **in the lap of the gods** beyond human control. **in the lap of luxury** in extremely luxurious surroundings. [Old English]

lap[2] –*n.* **1 a** one circuit of a racetrack etc. **b** section of a journey etc. **2 a** amount of overlapping. **b** overlapping part. **3** single turn of thread etc. round a reel etc. –*v.* (**-pp-**) **1** lead or overtake (a competitor in a race) by one or more laps. **2** (often foll. by *about, round*) fold or wrap (a garment etc.) round. **3** (usu. foll. by *in*) enfold in wraps etc. **4** (as **lapped** *adj.*) (usu. foll. by *in*) enfolded caressingly. **5** cause to overlap. [probably from LAP[1]]

lap[3] –*v.* (**-pp-**) **1 a** (esp. of an animal) drink with the tongue. **b** (usu. foll. by *up, down*) consume (liquid) greedily. **c** (usu. foll. by *up*) consume (gossip, praise, etc.) greedily. **2** (of waves etc.) ripple; make a lapping sound against (the shore). –*n.* **1 a** act of lapping. **b** amount of liquid taken up. **2** sound of wavelets. [Old English]

La Paz /lɑː 'pæz/ administrative capital (seat of government) of Bolivia, in the W of the country; pop. (1992) 711 036.

lap-dog *n.* small pet dog.

lapel /lə'pel/ *n.* part of either side of a coat-front etc., folded back against itself. [from LAP[1]]

lapidary /'læpɪdərɪ/ –*adj.* **1** concerned with stone or stones. **2** engraved upon stone. **3** concise, well-expressed, epigrammatic. –*n.* (*pl.* **-ies**) cutter, polisher, or engraver, of gems. [Latin *lapis lapid-* stone]

Laos /'lɑːɒs/ (officially **Lao People's Democratic Republic**) small landlocked country in SE Asia. Political upheavals have hindered the development of the Laotian economy but programmes have been initiated to expand the private sector and reverse the policy of enforced collectivization of agriculture. Most of the population are engaged in agriculture, esp. production of the staple crop, rice. The few manufacturing industries are concentrated on the processing of raw materials, esp. sawmilling and handicrafts. Valuable mineral resources (tin, iron ore, gold, and gypsum) are yet to be fully exploited. A major export is hydroelectric power, to Thailand; other exports include logs, wood products, garments, and coffee.

History. Formerly part of French Indochina, Laos became independent as a constitutional monarchy in 1949, but for most of the next 25 years was torn by civil war between the Communist Pathet Lao movement (latterly aided by North Vietnam) and government supporters (aided by the US and Thai mercenaries). In 1975 the Pathet Lao achieved total control of the country, the king abdicated, and Laos became a Communist state. President, Nouhak Phoumsavan; prime minister, Gen. Khamtai Siphandon; capital, Vientiane.

languages	Lao (official), French
currency	kip (KN) of 100 at
pop. (1996)	5 023 000
GNP (1994)	US$1.4B
literacy	92% (m); 75% (f)
life expectancy	51 (m); 54 (f)

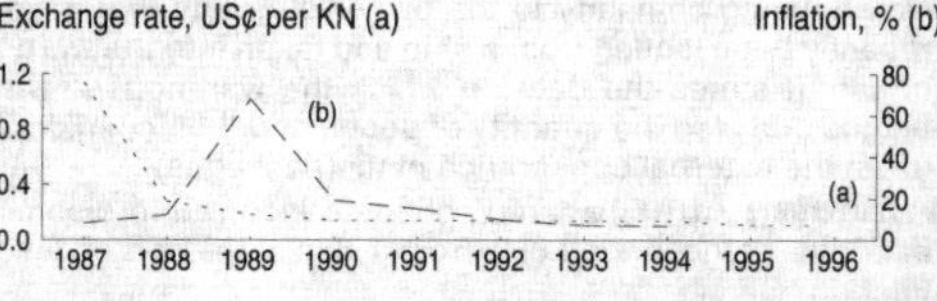

lapis lazuli /ˌlæpɪs 'læzjʊlɪ/ *n.* **1** blue mineral used as a gemstone. **2** bright blue pigment. **3** its colour. [related to LAPIDARY, AZURE]

Lapland /'læplænd/ region of N Europe inhabited by Lapps, extending from the Norwegian coast to NW Russia; reindeer farming, fishing, trapping, and hunting are the main sources of income. □ **Laplander** *n.*

lap of honour *n.* ceremonial circuit of a racetrack etc. by a winner.

Lapp *n.* **1** member of a Mongol people of N Scandinavia and NW Russia. **2** their language. [Swedish]

lappet /'læpɪt/ *n.* **1** small flap or fold of a garment etc. **2** hanging piece of flesh. [from LAP[1]]

lapse –*n.* **1** slight error; slip of memory etc. **2** weak or careless decline into an inferior state. **3** (foll. by *of*) passage of time. –*v.* (**-sing**) **1** fail to maintain a position or standard. **2** (foll. by *into*) fall back into an inferior or previous state. **3** (of a right or privilege etc.) become invalid through disuse, failure to renew, etc. **4** (as **lapsed** *adj.*) that has lapsed. [Latin *lapsus* from *labor laps-* slip]

Laptev Sea /'læptef/ arm of the Arctic Ocean lying to the N of mainland Russia, between the Taimyr peninsula and the New Siberian Islands.

laptop *n.* (often *attrib.*) portable microcomputer suitable for use while travelling.

lapwing /'læpwɪŋ/ *n.* plover with a shrill cry. [Old English: related to LEAP, WINK: from its mode of flight]

LAR *international vehicle registration* Libya.

larboard /'lɑːbəd/ *n.* & *adj. archaic* = PORT[3]. [originally *ladboard*, perhaps 'side on which cargo was taken in': related to LADE]

larceny /'lɑːsənɪ/ *n.* (*pl.* **-ies**) theft of personal property. □ **larcenous** *adj.* [Anglo-French from Latin *latrocinium*]
■ **Usage** In 1968 *larceny* was replaced as a statutory crime in English law by *theft*.

larch *n.* **1** deciduous coniferous tree with bright foliage. **2** its wood. [Latin *larix -icis*]

lard –*n.* pig fat used in cooking etc. –*v.* **1** insert strips of fat or bacon in (meat etc.) before cooking. **2** (foll. by *with*) garnish (talk etc.) with strange terms. [French = bacon, from Latin *lardum*]

larder *n.* room or large cupboard for storing food.

lardy *adj.* like lard.

lardy-cake *n.* cake made with lard, currants, etc.

large *adj.* **1** of relatively great size or extent. **2** of the larger kind (*large intestine*). **3** comprehensive. **4** pursuing an activity on a large scale (*large farmer*). □ **at large 1** at liberty. **2** as a body or whole. **3** at full length, with all details. □ **largeness** *n.* **largish** *adj.* [Latin *largus* copious]

large as life *adj. colloq.* in person, esp. prominently.

largely *adv.* to a great extent (*largely my own fault*).

large-scale *adj.* made or occurring on a large scale.

largesse /lɑː'ʒes/ *n.* (also **largess**) money or gifts freely given. [Latin *largus*: related to LARGE]

largo /'lɑːgəʊ/ *Mus.* –*adv.* & *adj.* in a slow tempo and dignified style. –*n.* (*pl.* **-s**) largo passage or movement. [Italian, = broad]

lari /læri/ *n.* standard monetary unit of Georgia.

lariat /'lærɪət/ *n.* **1** lasso. **2** tethering-rope. [Spanish *la reata*]

Larissa /lə'rɪsə/ (Greek **Lárisa**) city in NE Greece, capital of Thessaly; products include silk and other textiles and tobacco; pop. (1991) 112 777.

lark[1] *n.* small bird with a tuneful song, esp. the skylark. [Old English]

lark[2] *colloq.* –*n.* **1** frolic; amusing incident. **2** type of activity (*fed up with this digging lark*). –*v.* (foll. by *about*) play tricks. [origin uncertain]

larkspur *n.* plant with a spur-shaped calyx.

larva /'lɑːvə/ *n.* (*pl.* **-vae** /-viː/) stage of an insect's development between egg and pupa. □ **larval** *adj.* [Latin, = ghost]

laryngeal /lə'rɪndʒɪəl/ *adj.* of the larynx.

laryngitis /ˌlærɪn'dʒaɪtɪs/ *n.* inflammation of the larynx.

larynx /'lærɪŋks/ *n.* (*pl.* **larynges** /lə'rɪndʒiːz/) hollow organ in the throat holding the vocal cords. [Latin from Greek]

lasagne /lə'sænjə/ *n.* pasta in the form of sheets. [Italian pl., from Latin *lasanum* cooking-pot]

lascivious /lə'sɪvɪəs/ *adj.* **1** lustful. **2** inciting to lust. □ **lasciviously** *adv.* [Latin]

laser /'leɪzə(r)/ *n.* device that generates an intense beam of coherent light, or other electromagnetic radiation, in one direction. [*l*ight *a*mplification by *s*timulated *e*mission of *r*adiation]

♦ **laser disk** *n.* disk with a silvery surface, on which information is stored and read by a laser. Compact discs and videodiscs are common examples. Laser disks are also used to store computer data (when they are usu. called **optical disks**) and for the publication of large information databases. The disk surface is covered by circular tracks made up of tiny pits that hold the information; the pits are burnt into the disk by a laser beam when recording the information. The information is read by means of a low-power laser beam directed onto the relevant track as the disk rotates. Some laser disks are read-only or write-once disks; however, erasable disks are available.

---

laser printer *n.* high-speed printer, used in computing, desktop publishing, etc., in which the image is produced in the form of a pattern of very fine dots by the action of a laser beam. The beam writes the image on the surface of a drum or band in the form of a pattern of electric charge. This charge pattern is transferred to paper and a permanent visible image is produced. Laser printers generate high-quality print (in a wide variety of type styles) and graphics.

♦ **LASH** *n.* method of cargo handling in which cargo-carrying barges (lighters) are lifted on and off ocean-going ships by the ship's own crane, thus reducing to a minimum the need for port facilities. [*l*ighter *a*board *sh*ip]

---

lash –*v.* **1** make a sudden whiplike movement. **2** beat with a whip etc. **3** (often foll. by *against*, *down*, etc.) (of rain etc.) beat, strike. **4** criticize harshly. **5** rouse, incite. **6** (foll. by *down*, *together*, etc.) fasten with a cord etc. –*n.* **1** sharp blow made by a whip etc. **2** flexible end of a whip. **3** eyelash. □ **lash out 1** speak or hit out angrily. **2** *colloq.* spend money extravagantly. [imitative]

lashings *n.pl. colloq.* (foll. by *of*) plenty.

Las Palmas /lɑːs 'pælmɑːs/ resort in the Canary Islands, on the NW coast of Gran Canaria; pop. (est. 1994) 371 787.

lass *n.* esp. *Scot.* & *N.Engl.* or *poet.* girl. [Old Norse]

Lassa fever /'læsə/ *n.* acute febrile viral disease of tropical Africa. [*Lassa* in Nigeria]

lassitude /'læsɪˌtjuːd/ *n.* **1** languor. **2** disinclination to exert oneself. [Latin *lassus* tired]

lasso /læ'suː/ –*n.* (*pl.* **-s** or **-es**) rope with a noose at one end, esp. for catching cattle. –*v.* (**-es, -ed**) catch with a lasso. [Spanish *lazo*: related to LACE]

last[1] /lɑːst/ –*adj.* **1** after all others; coming at or belonging to the end. **2** most recent; next before a specified time (*last Christmas*). **3** only remaining (*last chance*). **4** (prec. by *the*) least likely or suitable (*the last person I'd want*). **5** lowest in rank (*last place*). –*adv.* **1** after all others (esp. in *comb.*: *last-mentioned*). **2** on the most recent occasion (*when did you last see him?*). **3** lastly. –*n.* **1** person or thing that is last, last-mentioned, most recent, etc. **2** (prec. by *the*) last mention or sight etc. (*shall never hear the last of it*). **3** last performance of certain acts (*breathed his last*). **4** (prec. by *the*) the end; death (*fighting to the last*). □ **at last** (or **long last**) in the end; after much delay. [Old English, = latest]

last[2] /lɑːst/ *v.* **1** remain unexhausted or alive for a specified or considerable time (*food to last a week*). **2** continue for a specified time (*match lasts an hour*). □ **last out** be strong enough or sufficient for the whole of a given period. [Old English]

last[3] /lɑːst/ *n.* shoemaker's model for shaping a shoe etc.

□ **stick to one's last** not meddle in what one does not understand. [Old English]

last-ditch *attrib. adj.* (of an attempt etc.) final, desperate.

♦ **last in, first out** *n.* (also **LIFO**) *Accounting* method of charging homogeneous items of stock to production when the cost of the items has changed. It is assumed, both for costing and stock valuation purposes, that the latest items taken into stock are those used in production although this may not necessarily correspond with the physical movement of the goods. The LIFO method is not acceptable to the Inland Revenue in the UK. Cf. FIRST IN, FIRST OUT 1.

lasting *adj.* permanent; durable.

lastly *adv.* finally; in the last place.

last minute *n.* (also **last moment**) the time just before an important event (often (with hyphen) *attrib.*: *last-minute panic*).

last name *n.* surname.

last post *n.* bugle-call at military funerals or as a signal to retire for the night.

last rites *n.pl.* rites for a person about to die.

last straw *n.* (prec. by *the*) slight addition to a burden that makes it finally unbearable.

♦ **last-survivor policy** *n.* **1** assurance policy on the lives of two people, the sum assured being paid on the death of the last to die (see also JOINT-LIFE ANNUITY). **2** contract in which assurance is arranged by a group of people, who all pay premiums into a fund while they are alive. No payment is made until only one person from the group is left alive. At that point the survivor receives all the policy proceeds. Contracts of this kind are not available in the UK.

♦ **last trading day** *n.* last day on which commodity trading for a particular delivery period can be transacted.

last trump *n.* (prec. by *the*) trumpet-blast to wake the dead on Judgement Day.

last word *n.* (prec. by *the*) **1** final or definitive statement. **2** (often foll. by *in*) latest fashion.

Las Vegas /læs 'veɪgəs/ city in the US, in S Nevada, noted for its casinos and nightclubs; pop. (est. 1994) 327 878.

lat. *abbr.* latitude.

Latakia /ˌlætə'kiːə/ seaport on the coast of Syria, opposite the NE tip of Cyprus; pop. (est. 1994) 306 535. It is famous for its tobacco.

latch *–n.* **1** bar with a catch and lever as a fastening for a gate etc. **2** spring-lock preventing a door from being opened from the outside without a key. *–v.* fasten with a latch. □ **latch on** (often foll. by *to*) *colloq.* **1** attach oneself (to). **2** understand. **on the latch** fastened by the latch (sense 1) only. [Old English]

latchkey *n.* (*pl.* **-s**) key of an outer door.

late *–adj.* **1** after the due or usual time; occurring or done after the proper time. **2 a** far on in the day or night or in a specified period. **b** far on in development. **3** flowering or ripening towards the end of the season. **4** no longer alive; no longer having the specified status, former (*my late husband*; *the late prime minister*). **5** of recent date. *–adv.* **1** after the due or usual time. **2** far on in time. **3** at or till a late hour. **4** at a late stage of development. **5** formerly but not now (*late of the Scillies*). □ **late in the day** *colloq.* at a late stage in the proceedings. □ **lateness** *n.* [Old English]

latecomer *n.* person who arrives late.

lateen /lə'tiːn/ *adj.* (of a ship) rigged with a lateen sail. [French *voile latine* Latin sail]

lateen sail *n.* triangular sail on a long yard at an angle of 45° to the mast.

lately *adv.* not long ago; recently. [Old English: related to LATE]

latent /'leɪt(ə)nt/ *adj.* existing but not developed or manifest; concealed, dormant. □ **latency** *n.* [Latin *lateo* be hidden]

latent heat *n. Physics* heat required to convert a solid into a liquid or vapour, or a liquid into a vapour, without change of temperature.

lateral /'lætər(ə)l/ *–adj.* **1** of, at, towards, or from the side or sides. **2** descended from the sibling of a person in direct line. *–n.* lateral shoot or branch. □ **laterally** *adv.* [Latin *latus later-* side]

♦ **lateral integration** see INTEGRATION 3.

lateral thinking *n.* method of solving problems other than by using conventional logic.

latex /'leɪteks/ *n.* (*pl.* **-xes**) **1** milky fluid of esp. the rubber tree. **2** synthetic product resembling this. [Latin, = liquid]

lath /lɑːθ/ *n.* (*pl.* **laths** /lɑːθs, lɑːðz/) thin flat strip of wood. [Old English]

lathe /leɪð/ *n.* machine for shaping wood, metal, etc., by rotating the article against cutting tools. [origin uncertain]

lather /'lɑːðə(r)/ *–n.* **1** froth produced by agitating soap etc. and water. **2** frothy sweat. **3** state of agitation. *–v.* **1** (of soap etc.) form a lather. **2** cover with lather. **3** *colloq.* thrash. [Old English]

Latin /'lætɪn/ *–n.* language of ancient Rome and its empire. *–adj.* **1** of or in Latin. **2** of the countries or peoples using languages descended from Latin. **3** of the Roman Catholic Church. [Latin *Latium* district around Rome]

Latin America parts of Central and South America where Spanish or Portuguese is the main language. □ **Latin American** *adj.* & *n.*

♦ **Latin American Integration Association** *n.* (also **LAIA**) economic grouping of South American countries with headquarters in Montevideo. It took over the Latin American Free Trade Area (LAFTA) in 1981. Its members are Argentina, Bolivia, Brazil, Chile, Colombia, Ecuador, Mexico, Paraguay, Peru, Uruguay, and Venezuela.

Latinate /'lætɪˌneɪt/ *adj.* having the character of Latin.

Latinize /'lætɪˌnaɪz/ *v.* (also **-ise**) (**-zing** or **-sing**) give a Latin form to. □ **Latinization** /-'zeɪʃ(ə)n/ *n.*

latish *adj.* & *adv.* fairly late.

latitude /'lætɪˌtjuːd/ *n.* **1 a** angular distance on a meridian north or south of the equator. **b** (usu. in *pl.*) regions or climes. **2** tolerated variety of action or opinion. □ **latitudinal** /-'tjuːdɪn(ə)l/ *adj.* [Latin *latus* broad]

latitudinarian /ˌlætɪˌtjuːdɪ'neərɪən/ *–adj.* liberal, esp. in religion. *–n.* latitudinarian person.

Latium /'leɪʃɪəm/ (Italian **Lazio** /'lætsɪˌəʊ/) region of W central Italy; pop. (est. 1994) 5 185 316; capital, Rome. Agriculture is important, producing esp. olives and other fruits, wine, and cereals; there are also food-processing, textile, chemical, and service industries.

latrine /lə'triːn/ *n.* communal lavatory, esp. in a camp. [Latin *latrina*]

lats /lætz/ *n.* (*pl.* **lati** /lætɪ/) standard monetary unit of Latvia.

latter *adj.* **1 a** second-mentioned of two, or last-mentioned of three or more. **b** (prec. by *the*; usu. *absol.*) the second- or last-mentioned person or thing. **2** nearer the end (*latter part of the year*). **3** recent. **4** of the end of a period, the world, etc. [Old English, = later]

■ **Usage** The use of *latter* to mean 'last mentioned of three or more' is considered incorrect by some people.

latter-day *attrib. adj.* modern, contemporary.

Latter-day Saints *n.pl.* Mormons' name for themselves.

latterly *adv.* **1** recently. **2** in the latter part of life or a period.

lattice /'lætɪs/ *n.* **1** structure of crossed laths or bars with spaces between, used as a screen, fence, etc. **2** regular periodic arrangement of atoms, ions, or molecules. □ **latticed** *adj.* [French *lattis* from *latte* LATH]

lattice window *n.* window with small panes set in diagonally crossing strips of lead.

Latvian /'lætvɪən/ *–n.* **1 a** native or national of Latvia. **b** person of Latvian descent. **2** language of Latvia. *–adj.* of Latvia, its people, or language.

laud /lɔːd/ *–v.* praise or extol. *–n.* **1** praise; hymn of praise. **2** (in *pl.*) the first morning prayer of the Roman Catholic Church. [Latin *laus laud-*]

laudable *adj.* commendable. □ **laudability** /-'bɪlɪtɪ/ *n.* **laudably** *adv.*

■ **Usage** *Laudable* is sometimes confused with *laudatory.*

laudanum /'lɔːdnəm/ *n.* solution prepared from opium. [perhaps from medieval Latin]

laudatory /'lɔːdətərɪ/ *adj.* praising.

■ **Usage** *Laudatory* is sometimes confused with *laudable.*

♦ **Lauder** /'lɔːdə(r)/, **Estée** (1908–) US business executive, chairman and founder of Estée Lauder Inc., the cosmetic manufacturer. Lauder began her career in cosmetics by selling skin-care products formulated by her uncle in the 1930s, setting up her first office in New York in 1944 with the help of her husband, Joseph Lauder. The Estée Lauder group is now run by Lauder's son, **Leonard Alan Lauder** (1933–), and includes cosmetics sold under the Aramis, Clinique, and Prescriptives labels.

---

laugh /lɑːf/ *–v.* **1** make the sounds and movements usual in expressing lively amusement, scorn, etc. **2** express by laughing. **3** (foll. by *at*) ridicule, make fun of. *–n.* **1** sound, act, or manner of laughing. **2** *colloq.* comical thing. □ **laugh off** get rid of (embarrassment or humiliation) by joking. **laugh up one's sleeve** laugh secretly. [Old English]

laughable *adj.* ludicrous; amusing. □ **laughably** *adv.*

laughing *n.* laughter. □ **no laughing matter** serious matter. □ **laughingly** *adv.*

laughing-gas *n.* nitrous oxide as an anaesthetic.

laughing jackass *n.* = KOOKABURRA.

laughing stock *n.* person or thing open to general ridicule.

laughter /'lɑːftə(r)/ *n.* act or sound of laughing. [Old English]

Launceston /'lɔːnsəst(ə)n/ city and port in Australia, in N Tasmania; industries include engineering, aluminium smelting, and sawmilling; pop. (1991) 93 520.

launch[1] /lɔːntʃ/ *–v.* **1** set (a vessel) afloat. **2** hurl or send forth (a weapon, rocket, etc.). **3** start or set in motion (an enterprise, person, etc.). **4** formally introduce (a new product) with publicity etc. **5** (foll. by *out*, *into*, etc.) **a** make a start on (an enterprise etc.). **b** burst into (strong language etc.). *–n.* act of launching. [Anglo-Norman *launcher*: related to LANCE]

launch[2] /lɔːntʃ/ *n.* **1** large motor boat. **2** man-of-war's largest boat. [Spanish *lancha*]

launcher *n.* structure to hold a rocket during launching.

launch pad *n.* (also **launching pad**) platform with a supporting structure, for launching rockets from.

launder /'lɔːndə(r)/ *v.* **1** wash and iron (clothes etc.). **2** *colloq.* process (money acquired illegally, by theft, drug dealing, etc.) so that it appears to have come from a legitimate source, often by paying the illegal cash into a foreign bank and transferring its equivalent to a UK bank. [French: related to LAVE]

launderette /lɔːn'dret/ *n.* (also **laundrette**) establishment with coin-operated washing-machines and driers for public use.

laundress /'lɔːndrɪs/ *n.* woman who launders, esp. professionally.

laundry /'lɔːndrɪ/ *n.* (*pl.* **-ies**) **1 a** place for washing clothes etc. **b** firm washing clothes etc. commercially. **2** clothes or linen for laundering or newly laundered.

laureate /'lɒrɪət, 'lɔː-/ *–adj.* wreathed with laurel as a mark of honour. *–n.* = POET LAUREATE. □ **laureateship** *n.* [related to LAUREL]

laurel /'lɒr(ə)l/ *n.* **1** = BAY². **2** (in *sing.* or *pl.*) wreath of bay-leaves as an emblem of victory or poetic merit. **3** any of various plants with dark-green glossy leaves. □ **look to one's laurels** beware of losing one's pre-eminence. **rest on one's laurels** see REST. [Latin *laurus* bay]

Lausanne /ləʊ'zæn/ town in W Switzerland, on the N shore of Lake Geneva; manufactures include precision instruments and leather goods; pop. (est. 1995) 116 795.

LAUTRO /'lɔːtrəʊ/ *abbr.* (also **Lautro**) Life Assurance and Unit Trust Regulatory Organization. Its functions were taken over in 1993 by the PERSONAL INVESTMENT AUTHORITY.

lav *n. colloq.* lavatory. [abbreviation]

lava /'lɑːvə/ *n.* matter flowing from a volcano and solidifying as it cools. [Latin *lavo* wash]

lavatorial /ˌlævə'tɔːrɪəl/ *adj.* of or like lavatories; (esp. of humour) relating to excretion.

lavatory /'lævətərɪ/ *n.* (*pl.* **-ies**) **1** receptacle for urine and faeces, usu. with a means of disposal. **2** room or compartment containing this. [Latin: related to LAVA]

lavatory paper *n.* = TOILET PAPER.

lave *v.* (**-ving**) *literary* **1** wash, bathe. **2** (of water) wash against; flow along. [Latin *lavo* wash]

lavender /'lævɪndə(r)/ *n.* **1 a** evergreen shrub with purple aromatic flowers. **b** its flowers and stalks dried and used to scent linen etc. **2** pale mauve colour. [Latin *lavandula*]

lavender-water *n.* light perfume made with distilled lavender.

laver /'leɪvə(r), 'lɑː-/ *n.* edible seaweed. [Latin]

lavish /'lævɪʃ/ *–adj.* **1** giving or producing in large quantities; profuse. **2** generous. *–v.* (often foll. by *on*) bestow

---

Latvia /'lætvɪə/, **Republic of** country in NE Europe, on the Baltic Sea, formerly a constituent republic of the Soviet Union. Since the Second World War Latvia has been increasingly industrialized and is no longer a predominantly agricultural country. It is in transition from a command economy to a market economy and is striving to lessen its dependence on other former Soviet states, although Russia remains its chief trading partner. Privatization programmes have been undertaken. Manufactures include railway locomotives, telephone equipment, agricultural machinery, and timber products. Textiles are a major export. Agriculture is still important, esp. cattle-, pig-, and dairy-farming, and contributes to exports; large state and collective farms are being converted to shareholding enterprises. Under Russian control from 1795, Latvia became an independent state in 1918 but was annexed by the Soviet Union in 1940, being occupied by Germany during the Second World War. It regained its independence in 1991: in 1994 the last Russian troops left the country. President, Guntis Ulmanis; prime minister, Andris Skele; capital, Riga.

languages	Latvian (official), Russian
currency	lats of 100 santimes
pop. (1996)	2 516 843
GNP (1994)	US$5.9B
literacy	99% (m); 99% (f)
life expectancy	60 (m); 70 (f)

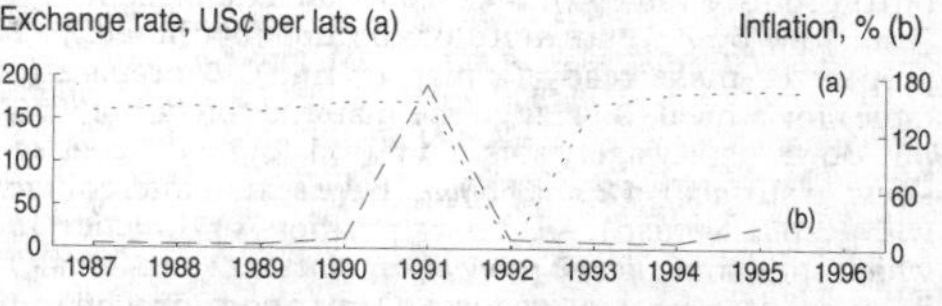

or spend (money, effort, praise, etc.) abundantly. □ **lavishly** *adv.* [French *lavasse* deluge: related to LAVE]

law *n.* **1 a** rule enacted or customary in a community and recognized as commanding or forbidding certain actions. **b** body of such rules. **2** controlling influence of laws; respect for laws. **3** laws collectively as a social system or subject of study. **4** binding force (*her word is law*). **5** (prec. by *the*) **a** the legal profession. **b** *colloq.* the police. **6** (in *pl.*) jurisprudence. **7 a** the judicial remedy. **b** the lawcourts as providing this (*go to law*). **8** rule of action or procedure. **9** regularity in natural occurrences (*laws of nature*; *law of gravity*). **10** divine commandments. □ **be a law unto oneself** do what one considers right; disregard custom. **lay down the law** be dogmatic or authoritarian. **take the law into one's own hands** redress a grievance by one's own means, esp. by force. [Old English from Old Norse, = thing laid down]

law-abiding *adj.* obedient to the laws.

lawbreaker *n.* person who breaks the law. □ **law-breaking** *n.* & *adj.*

lawcourt *n.* court of law.

lawful *adj.* conforming with or recognized by law; not illegal. □ **lawfully** *adv.* **lawfulness** *n.*

lawgiver *n.* person who formulates laws; legislator.

lawless *adj.* **1** having no laws or law enforcement. **2** disregarding laws. □ **lawlessness** *n.*

Law Lord *n.* member of the House of Lords qualified to perform its legal work.

lawmaker *n.* legislator.

lawn[1] *n.* piece of closely-mown grass in a garden etc. [French *launde* glade]

lawn[2] *n.* fine linen or cotton. [probably from *Laon* in France]

lawnmower *n.* machine for cutting lawns.

lawn tennis *n.* tennis played with a soft ball on outdoor grass or a hard court.

◆ **law of one price** *n. Econ.* rule that, in the absence of trade barriers or transport costs, competition will ensure that a particular good will sell at the same price in all countries. The theory of purchasing-power parity is based on this law.

◆ **law of statistical regularity** *n.* basic assumption in statistics that a random sample taken from a larger group will reflect the characteristics of the larger group. The larger the size of the sample in relation to the whole group, the more accurately it will reflect the group.

---

lawrencium /lə'rensɪəm/ *n.* artificially made transuranic metallic element. [*Lawrence*, name of a physicist]

◆ **Law Society** *n.* professional body for solicitors in England and Wales, incorporated by royal charter in 1831. It controls the education and examination of articled clerks and the admission of solicitors. It also regulates their professional standards and conduct.

---

lawsuit *n.* bringing of a dispute, claim, etc. before a lawcourt.

lawyer /'lɔːjə(r)/ *n.* legal practitioner, esp. a solicitor.

lax *adj.* **1** lacking care or precision. **2** not strict. □ **laxity** *n.* **laxly** *adv.* **laxness** *n.* [Latin *laxus* loose]

laxative /'læksətɪv/ *–adj.* facilitating evacuation of the bowels. *–n.* laxative medicine. [Latin: related to LAX]

lay[1] *–v.* (*past* and *past part.* **laid**) **1** place on a surface, esp. horizontally or in the proper or specified place. **2** put or bring into the required position or state (*lay carpet*). **3** make by laying (*lay foundations*). **4** (often *absol.*) (of a hen bird) produce (an egg). **5** cause to subside or lie flat. **6** (usu. foll. by *on*); attribute or impute (blame etc.). **7** prepare or make ready (a plan or trap). **8** prepare (a table) for a meal. **9** arrange the material for (a fire). **10** put down as a wager; stake. **11** (foll. by *with*) coat or strew (a surface). **12** *slang offens.* have sexual intercourse with (esp. a woman). *–n.* **1** way, position, or direction in which something lies. **2** *slang offens.* partner (esp. female) in, or act of, sexual intercourse. □ **lay about one** hit out on all sides. **lay aside 1** put to one side. **2** cease to consider. **lay at the door of** impute to. **lay bare** expose, reveal. **lay claim to** claim as one's own. **lay down 1** put on a flat surface. **2** give up (an office). **3** formulate (a rule). **4** store (wine) for maturing. **5** sacrifice (one's life). **lay (one's) hands on** obtain, locate. **lay hands on** seize or attack. **lay hold of** seize. **lay in** provide oneself with a stock of. **lay into** *colloq.* punish or scold harshly. **lay it on thick** (or **with a trowel**) *colloq.* flatter or exaggerate grossly. **lay low** overthrow or humble. **lay off 1** discharge (unneeded workers), esp. temporarily. **2** *colloq.* desist. **lay on 1** provide. **2** impose. **3** inflict (blows). **4** spread on (paint etc.). **lay open 1** break the skin of. **2** (foll. by *to*) expose (to criticism etc.). **lay out 1** spread out, expose to view. **2** prepare (a corpse) for burial. **3** *colloq.* knock unconscious. **4** arrange (grounds etc.) according to a design. **5** expend (money). **lay to rest** bury in a grave. **lay up** store, save. **lay waste** ravage, destroy. [Old English]

■ **Usage** The intransitive use of *lay*, meaning *lie*, as in *she was laying on the floor*, is incorrect in standard English.

lay[2] *adj.* **1 a** non-clerical. **b** not ordained into the clergy. **2 a** not professionally qualified. **b** of or done by such persons. [Greek *laos* people]

lay[3] *n.* **1** short poem meant to be sung. **2** song. [French]

lay[4] *past* of LIE[1].

layabout *n.* habitual loafer or idler.

lay-by *n.* (*pl.* **-bys**) area at the side of a road where vehicles may stop.

◆ **lay days** *n.pl.* number of days allowed to a ship to load or unload without incurring demurrage. **Reversible lay days** permit the shipper to add to the days allowed for unloading any days saved while loading. Lay days may be calculated as running days (all consecutive days), working days (excluding Sundays and public holidays), or weather working days (working days on which the weather allows work to be carried out).

---

layer *–n.* **1** thickness of matter, esp. one of several, covering a surface. **2** person or thing that lays. **3** hen that lays eggs. **4** shoot fastened down to take root while attached to the parent plant. *–v.* **1** arrange in layers. **2** cut (hair) in layers. **3** propagate (a plant) by a layer.

layette /leɪ'et/ *n.* set of clothing etc. for a newborn child. [French from Dutch]

lay figure *n.* **1** jointed figure of a human body used by artists for arranging drapery on etc. **2** unrealistic character in a novel etc. [Dutch *led* joint]

layman *n.* (*fem.* **laywoman**) **1** non-ordained member of a Church. **2** person without professional or specialized knowledge.

lay-off *n.* discharge, usu. temporary, of workers.

◆ **lay-off pay** *n. US* See REDUNDANCY 1.

La'youn /lɑː'juːn/ (Arabic **El Aaiún** /el aɪ'uːn/) city in Morocco, capital of Western Sahara and distribution centre of a phosphate-mining region; pop. (1982) 96 800.

layout *n.* **1** way in which land, a building, printed matter, etc., is arranged or set out. **2** something arranged in a particular way; display.

lay reader *n.* lay person licensed to conduct some religious services.

laze *–v.* (**-zing**) **1** spend time idly. **2** (foll. by *away*) pass (time) idly. *–n.* spell of lazing. [back-formation from LAZY]

Lazio see LATIUM.

lazy *adj.* (**-ier, -iest**) **1** disinclined to work, doing little work. **2** of or inducing idleness. □ **lazily** *adv.* **laziness** *n.* [perhaps from Low German]

lazybones *n.* (*pl.* same) *colloq.* lazy person.

LB *–international vehicle registration* Liberia. *–airline flight code* Lloyd Aereo Boliviano.

lb. *abbr.* pound(s) (weight). [Latin *libra*]

LBC *abbr.* **1** Land Bank Commission. **2** London Broadcasting Company.

LBCH *abbr.* = LONDON BANKERS' CLEARING HOUSE.
LBO *abbr.* = LEVERAGED BUYOUT.
LBS *abbr.* London Business School.
l.b.w. *abbr.* leg before wicket.
LC –*abbr.* (also **L/C**) letter of credit. –*airline flight code* Loganair.
l.c. *abbr.* **1** (also **lc**, **l/c**) letter of credit. **2** = LOC. CIT. **3** lower case.
LCC *abbr.* **1** *Accounting & Computing* life-cycle cost(ing). **2** = LONDON CHAMBER OF COMMERCE AND INDUSTRY.
LCD *abbr.* **1** = LIQUID CRYSTAL DISPLAY. **2** lowest (or least) common denominator.
LCE *abbr.* = LONDON COMMODITY EXCHANGE.
LCH *abbr.* = LONDON CLEARING HOUSE.
LCL *abbr. Commerce* **1** *US* less-than-carload lot. **2** less-than-container load.
LCM *abbr.* **1** *Computing* life-cycle management. **2** lowest (or least) common multiple.
L/Cpl *abbr.* Lance-Corporal.
LD –*symb.* Libyan dinar. –*postcode* Llandrindod Wells.
Ld. *abbr.* Lord.
LDC *abbr.* **1** less-developed country. **2** local distribution company.
LDN *abbr.* less-developed nation.
LDP *abbr. Finance* London daily price.
LDX *abbr.* long-distance xerography.
LE *postcode* Leicester.
Le *symb.* leone.
£E *symb.* Egyptian pound.
LEA *abbr.* Local Education Authority.
lea *n. poet.* meadow, field. [Old English]
leach *v.* **1** make (a liquid) percolate through some material. **2** subject (bark, ore, ash, or soil) to the action of percolating fluid. **3** (foll. by *away*, *out*) remove (soluble matter) or be removed in this way. [Old English]
lead[1] /liːd/ –*v.* (*past* and *past part.* **led**) **1** cause to go with one, esp. by guiding or going in front. **2 a** direct the actions or opinions of. **b** (often foll. by *to*, or *to* + infin.) guide by persuasion or example (*what led you to think that*). **3** (also *absol.*) provide access to; bring to a certain position (*gate leads you into a field*; *road leads to Lincoln*). **4** pass or go through (a life etc. of a specified kind). **5 a** have the first place in. **b** (*absol.*) go first; be ahead in a race etc. **c** (*absol.*) be pre-eminent in some field. **6** be in charge of (*leads a team*). **7** (also *absol.*) play (a card) or a card of (a particular suit) as first player in a round. **8** (foll. by *to*) result in. **9** (foll. by *with*) (of a newspaper or news broadcast) have as its main story (*led with the royal wedding*). **10** (foll. by *through*) make (a liquid, strip of material, etc.) pass through a certain course. –*n.* **1** guidance given by going in front; example. **2 a** leading place (*take the lead*). **b** amount by which a competitor is ahead of the others. **3** clue. **4** strap etc. for leading a dog etc. **5** conductor (usu. a wire) conveying electric current to an appliance. **6 a** chief part in a play etc. **b** person playing this. **c** (*attrib.*) chief performer or instrument of a specified type (*lead guitar*). **7** *Cards* **a** act or right of playing first. **b** card led. **8** *Insurance* first named underwriting syndicate on a Lloyd's insurance policy. When a broker seeks to cover a risk a large syndicate is approached to act as lead, which encourages smaller syndicates to cover a share of the risk. The premium rate is calculated by the lead; if others wish to join in the risk they have to insure at that rate. □ **lead by the nose** cajole into compliance. **lead off** begin. **lead on** entice dishonestly. **lead up the garden path** *colloq.* mislead. **lead up to** form a preparation for; direct conversation towards. [Old English]
lead[2] /led/ –*n.* **1** heavy bluish-grey soft metallic element. **2 a** graphite. **b** thin length of this in a pencil. **3** lump of lead used in sounding water. **4** (in *pl.*) **a** strips of lead covering a roof. **b** piece of lead-covered roof. **5** (in *pl.*) lead frames holding the glass of a lattice etc. **6** blank space between lines of print. –*v.* **1** cover, weight, or frame with lead. **2** space (printed matter) with leads. [Old English]
leaden /'led(ə)n/ *adj.* **1** of or like lead. **2** heavy or slow. **3** lead-coloured.
leader *n.* **1 a** person or thing that leads. **b** person followed by others. **2** principal player in a music group or of the first violins in an orchestra. **3** = LEADING ARTICLE. **4** shoot of a plant at the apex of a stem or of the main branch. □ **leadership** *n.*
lead-free *adj.* (of petrol) without added lead compounds.
lead-in *n.* introduction, opening, etc.
leading[1] *adj.* chief; most important.
leading[2] /'ledɪŋ/ *n. Printing* = LEAD[2] *n.* 6.
leading aircraftman *n.* rank above aircraftman in the RAF.
leading article *n.* newspaper article giving editorial opinion.
leading light *n.* prominent and influential person.
leading note *n. Mus.* seventh note of a diatonic scale.
leading question *n.* question prompting the answer wanted.

■ **Usage** *Leading question* does not mean a 'principal' or 'loaded' or 'searching' question.

lead pencil *n.* pencil of graphite in wood.
lead-poisoning *n.* poisoning by absorption of lead into the body.
leaf –*n.* (*pl.* **leaves**) **1** each of several flattened usu. green structures of a plant, growing usu. on the side of a stem. **2 a** foliage regarded collectively. **b** state of bearing leaves (*tree in leaf*). **3** single thickness of paper. **4** very thin sheet of metal etc. **5** hinged part, extra section, or flap of a table etc. –*v.* **1** put forth leaves. **2** (foll. by *through*) turn over the pages of (a book etc.). □ **leafage** *n.* **leafy** *adj.* (**-ier**, **-iest**). [Old English]
leaflet /'liːflɪt/ –*n.* **1** sheet of paper, pamphlet, etc. giving information. **2** young leaf. **3** *Bot.* division of a compound leaf. –*v.* (**-t-**) distribute leaflets (to).
leaf-mould *n.* soil or compost consisting chiefly of decayed leaves.
leaf-stalk *n.* stalk joining a leaf to a stem.
league[1] /liːg/ –*n.* **1** people, countries, groups, etc., combining for a particular purpose. **2** agreement to combine in this way. **3** group of sports clubs which compete for a championship. **4** class of contestants etc. –*v.* (**-gues**, **-gued**, **-guing**) (often foll. by *together*) join in a league. □ **in league** allied, conspiring. [Latin *ligo* bind]
league[2] /liːg/ *n. hist.* varying measure of distance, usu. about three miles. [Latin from Celtic]
league table *n.* list in ranked order of success etc.
leak –*n.* **1 a** hole through which matter passes accidentally in or out. **b** matter passing through thus. **c** act of passing through thus. **2 a** similar escape of electrical charge. **b** charge that escapes. **3** disclosure of secret information. –*v.* **1 a** pass through a leak. **b** lose or admit through a leak. **2** disclose (secret information). **3** (often foll. by *out*) become known. □ **have** (or **take**) **a leak** *slang* urinate. □ **leaky** *adj.* (**-ier**, **-iest**). [Low German or Dutch]
leakage *n.* **1** action or result of leaking. **2** allowance for loss of a liquid in transit, due to evaporation or other causes.
lean[1] –*v.* (*past* and *past part.* **leaned** or **leant** /lent/) **1** (often foll. by *across*, *back*, *over*, etc.) be or place in a sloping position; incline from the perpendicular. **2** (foll. by *against*, *on*, *upon*) (cause to) rest for support against etc. **3** (foll. by *on*, *upon*) rely on. **4** (foll. by *to*, *towards*) be inclined or partial to. –*n.* deviation from the perpendicular; inclination. □ **lean on** *colloq.* put pressure on (a person) to act in a certain way. **lean over backwards** see BACKWARDS. [Old English]
lean[2] –*adj.* **1** (of a person or animal) thin; having no superfluous fat. **2** (of meat) containing little fat. **3** meagre. –*n.* lean part of meat. □ **leanness** *n.* [Old English]

◆ **lean-back** *n.* period of cautious inaction by a government agency before intervening in a market. For example, a central bank might allow a lean-back period to elapse to allow exchange rates to stabilize, before intervening in the foreign exchange market.

---

leaning *n.* tendency or partiality.

lean-to *n.* (*pl.* **-tos**) building with its roof leaning against a larger building or a wall.

lean years *n.pl.* years of scarcity.

leap *–v.* (*past* and *past part.* **leaped** or **leapt** /lept/) jump or spring forcefully. *–n.* forceful jump. □ **by leaps and bounds** with startlingly rapid progress. **leap in the dark** daring step or enterprise. [Old English]

leap-frog *–n.* game in which players vault with parted legs over others bending down. *–v.* (**-gg-**) **1** perform such a vault (over). **2** overtake alternately.

leap year *n.* year with 366 days (including 29th Feb. as an intercalary day).

learn /lɜːn/ *v.* (*past* and *past part.* **learned** /lɜːnt, lɜːnd/ or **learnt**) **1** gain knowledge of or skill in. **2** commit to memory. **3** (foll. by *of*) be told about. **4** (foll. by *that, how,* etc.) become aware of. **5** receive instruction. **6** *archaic* or *dial.* teach. [Old English]

learned /'lɜːnɪd/ *adj.* **1** having much knowledge acquired by study. **2** showing or requiring learning (*a learned work*). **3** (of a publication) academic.

learner *n.* **1** person who is learning a subject or skill. **2** (in full **learner driver**) person who is learning to drive but has not yet passed a driving test.

learning *n.* knowledge acquired by study.

♦ **learning curve** *n.* graphical representation of a trainee's progress in learning a task. Typically the curve will climb sharply to a plateau, while learning is consolidated, before rising to the final level, representing the output of the skilled worker. In complicated tasks more sophisticated means have to be used to measure progress.

---

lease *–n.* contract by which the owner of property allows another to use it for a specified time, usu. in return for payment. To be a **legal lease** it must be created by deed (unless it is for less than three years), take effect on possession (i.e. start immediately), and be for the best rent obtainable without taking a premium. A lease that is not a legal lease may, however, be valid in equity as an agreement for a lease. This must be registered or any rights under it may be lost on the sale of the freehold or of a superior lease. A lease usu. constitutes a bargain between the parties (see LANDLORD AND TENANT), containing rights and obligations on both sides. It may come to an end on the expiry of the term; alternatively it may be ended earlier, by the tenant surrendering it to the landlord or by the landlord ending it for the breach of some condition (e.g. failure to pay the rent or leaving the premises in disrepair). A lease may be assigned to someone else (e.g. a leasehold flat may be sold for a capital sum); the new tenant will then take over the responsibilities under the lease (see also HEAD LEASE). A **repairing lease** is one in which the tenant is obliged to pay for all repairs and is usu. bound to leave the property at the end of the lease in the same condition that it was at the start of the lease. *–v.* (**-sing**) **1** grant or take on lease. **2** hire (equipment, e.g. a car or a piece of machinery) to avoid the capital cost involved in owning it or to avoid purchasing equipment that quickly becomes obsolete. □ **new lease of** (*US* **on) life** improved prospect of living, or of use after repair. [Anglo-French *lesser* let, from Latin *laxo* loosen]

♦ **lease-back** *n.* (also **renting back**) method of raising finance in which an organization sells its land or buildings to an investor (usu. an insurance company) on condition that the investor will lease the property back to the organization for a fixed term at an agreed rental. This releases capital for the organization.

---

leasehold *–n.* **1** holding of property or land by lease. This is the most common way for blocks of offices to be owned, with separate leases for each office. **2** property or land held by lease. It will eventually revert to the freehold owner, although there has been some statutory modification of this right to repossession (e.g. in the Rent Acts). *–attrib. adj.* held by lease (*leasehold land*). □ **leaseholder** *n.*

leash *–n.* strap for holding a dog etc.; lead. *–v.* **1** put a leash on. **2** restrain. □ **straining at the leash** eager to begin. [French *lesse*: related to LEASE]

least *–adj.* **1** smallest, slightest. **2** (of a species etc.) very small. *–n.* the least amount. *–adv.* in the least degree. □ **at least 1** at any rate. **2** (also **at the least**) not less than. **in the least** (or **the least**) (usu. with *neg.*) at all (*not in the least offended*). **to say the least** putting the case moderately. [Old English, superlative of LESS]

least common denominator *n.* = LOWEST COMMON DENOMINATOR.

least common multiple *n.* = LOWEST COMMON MULTIPLE.

leather /'leðə(r)/ *–n.* **1** material made from the skin of an animal by tanning etc. **2** piece of leather for polishing with. **3** leather part(s) of a thing. **4** *slang* cricket-ball or football. **5** (in *pl.*) leather clothes. *–v.* **1** beat, thrash. **2** cover with leather. **3** polish or wipe with a leather. [Old English]

leatherback *n.* large marine turtle with a leathery shell.

leather-bound *adj.* bound in leather.

Leatherette /ˌleðə'ret/ *n. propr.* imitation leather.

leather-jacket *n.* crane-fly grub with a tough skin.

leathery *adj.* **1** like leather. **2** tough.

leave[1] *v.* (**-ving**; *past* and *past part.* **left**) **1 a** go away from. **b** (often foll. by *for*) depart. **2** cause to or let remain; depart without taking. **3** (also *absol.*) cease to reside at or belong to or work for. **4** abandon; cease to live with (one's family etc.). **5** have remaining after one's death. **6** bequeath. **7** (foll. by *to* + infin.) allow (a person or thing) to do something independently. **8** (foll. by *to*) commit to another person etc. (*leave that to me*). **9 a** abstain from consuming or dealing with. **b** (in *passive*; often foll. by *over*) remain over. **10 a** deposit or entrust (a thing) to be attended to in one's absence (*left a message with his secretary*). **b** depute (a person) to perform a function in one's absence. **11** allow to remain or cause to be in a specified state or position (*left the door open*; *left me exhausted*). □ **leave alone** refrain from disturbing, not interfere with. **leave a person cold** not impress or excite a person. **leave off 1** come to or make an end. **2** discontinue. **leave out** omit; exclude. [Old English]

leave[2] *n.* **1** (often foll. by *to* + infin.) permission. **2 a** (in full **leave of absence**) permission to be absent from duty. **b** period for which this lasts. □ **on leave** legitimately absent from duty. **take one's leave (of)** bid farewell (to). **take leave of one's senses** go mad. [Old English]

leaved *adj.* having a leaf or leaves, esp. (in *comb.*) of a specified kind or number (*four-leaved clover*).

leaven /'lev(ə)n/ *–n.* **1** substance causing dough to ferment and rise. **2** pervasive transforming influence; admixture. *–v.* **1** ferment (dough) with leaven. **2** permeate and transform; modify with a tempering element. [Latin *levo* lift]

leaves *pl.* of LEAF.

leave-taking *n.* act of taking one's leave.

leavings *n.pl.* things left over.

Lebanese /ˌlebə'niːz/ *–adj.* of Lebanon. *–n.* (*pl.* same) **1** native or national of Lebanon. **2** person of Lebanese descent.

Lebowa /lə'bəʊə/ former Bantu homeland in South Africa. It was abolished following democratic elections held in 1994.

LEC *abbr.* (in Scotland) Local Enterprise Company.

lech *colloq. –v.* (often foll. by *after*) lust. *–n.* **1** lecherous man. **2** lust. [back-formation from LECHER]

lecher *n.* lecherous man. [French *lechier* live in debauchery]

lecherous *adj.* lustful, having excessive sexual desire. □ **lecherously** *adv.*

lechery *n.* excessive sexual desire.

lectern /'lekt(ə)n/ *n.* **1** stand for holding a book in a church etc. **2** similar stand for a lecturer etc. [Latin *lectrum* from *lego* read]

lecture /'lektʃə(r)/ *–n.* **1** talk giving specified information to a class etc. **2** long serious speech, esp. as a reprimand. *–v.* (**-ring**) **1** (often foll. by *on*) deliver lecture(s). **2** talk seriously or reprovingly to. □ **lectureship** *n.* [Latin: related to LECTERN]

lecturer *n.* person who lectures, esp. as a teacher in higher education.

LED *abbr.* light-emitting diode, used in self-luminous displays in digital clocks etc.

led *past* and *past part.* of LEAD[1].

lederhosen /'leɪdəˌhəʊz(ə)n/ *n.pl.* leather shorts as worn by some men in Bavaria etc. [German, = leather trousers]

ledge *n.* narrow horizontal or shelflike projection. [origin uncertain]

ledger *n.* main record of the accounts of a business. Traditionally, a ledger was a large book with separate pages for each account. In modern systems, ledgers may consist of separate cards or computer records. The most common ledgers are the **nominal ledger** containing the impersonal accounts, the **sales** (or **debtors'**) **ledger** containing the accounts of an organization's customers, and the **purchase** (or **creditors'**) **ledger** containing the accounts of an organization's suppliers. [Dutch]

lee *n.* **1** shelter given by a close object (*under the lee of*). **2** (in full **lee side**) side away from the wind. [Old English]

leech *n.* **1** bloodsucking worm formerly much used medically. **2** person who sponges on others. [Old English]

Leeds /liːdz/ industrial city in N England, in West Yorkshire; industries include textiles, printing, and engineering; pop. (est. 1994) 724 400.

leek *n.* **1** plant of the onion family with flat leaves forming a cylindrical bulb, used as food. **2** this as a Welsh national emblem. [Old English]

leer *–v.* look slyly, lasciviously, or maliciously. *–n.* leering look. [perhaps from obsolete *leer* cheek]

leery *adj.* (**-ier, -iest**) *slang* **1** knowing, sly. **2** (foll. by *of*) wary.

lees /liːz/ *n.pl.* **1** sediment of wine etc. **2** dregs. [French]

leeward /'liːwəd, *Naut.* 'luːəd/ *–adj.* & *adv.* on or towards the side sheltered from the wind. *–n.* leeward region or side.

Leeward Islands /'liːwəd/ **1** group of islands in the E Caribbean that constitute the N part of the Lesser Antilles and include Antigua, St Kitts, Montserrat, and the islands of Guadeloupe. **2** group of islands in the S Pacific Ocean, in French Polynesia.

leeway *n.* **1** allowable scope of action. **2** sideways drift of a ship to leeward of the desired course.

left[1] *–adj.* **1** on or towards the west side of the human body, or of any object, when facing north. **2** (also **Left**) *Polit.* of the Left. *–adv.* on or to the left side. *–n.* **1** left-hand part, region, or direction. **2** *Boxing* **a** left hand. **b** blow with this. **3** (often **Left**) group or section favouring socialism; socialists collectively. [Old English, originally = 'weak, worthless']

left[2] *past* and *past part.* of LEAVE[1].

left bank *n.* bank of a river on the left facing downstream.

left-hand *attrib. adj.* **1** on or towards the left side of a person or thing. **2** done with the left hand. **3** (of a screw) = LEFT-HANDED 4b.

left-handed *adj.* **1** naturally using the left hand for writing etc. **2** (of a tool etc.) for use by the left hand. **3** (of a blow) struck with the left hand. **4 a** turning to the left. **b** (of a screw) turned anticlockwise to tighten. **5** awkward, clumsy. **6 a** (of a compliment) ambiguous. **b** of doubtful sincerity. □ **left-handedly** *adv.* **left-handedness** *n.*

left-hander *n.* **1** left-handed person. **2** left-handed blow.

leftism *n.* socialist political principles. □ **leftist** *n.* & *adj.*

left-justified see JUSTIFY 4.

left luggage *n.* luggage deposited for later retrieval.

leftmost *adj.* furthest to the left.

leftover *–n.* (usu. in *pl.*) surplus items (esp. of food). *–attrib. adj.* remaining over, surplus.

leftward /'leftwəd/ *–adv.* (also **leftwards**) towards the left. *–adj.* going towards or facing the left.

left wing *–n.* **1** more socialist section of a political party or system. **2** left side of a football etc. team on the field. *–adj.* (**left-wing**) socialist, radical. □ **left-winger** *n.*

lefty /'leftɪ/ *n.* (*pl.* **-ies**) *colloq.* **1** *Polit.* often *derog.* left-winger. **2** left-handed person.

leg *n.* **1** each of the limbs on which a person or animal walks and stands. **2** leg of an animal or bird as food. **3** part of a garment covering a leg. **4** support of a chair,

---

Lebanon /'lebənən/, **Republic of** country in the Middle East, with a coastline on the Mediterranean Sea. Until the mid-1970s the service industries (banking, international trade, and insurance) were the major sources of income and Beirut the commercial centre of the Middle East. Since 1975, however, the country's economy has been severely disrupted by civil war, and by the early 1990s nearly half the population was unemployed; economic revival will depend on maintaining and strengthening the political stability that had begun to be achieved in 1991. Manufacturing industries include food processing, textiles, machinery, metal products, and traditional handicrafts but production has been interrupted by the troubles. Fruits, esp. citrus fruit, apples, grapes, bananas, and olives, are the most important agricultural products. Lebanon was once heavily forested but little remains of the famous cedars of Lebanon and the land has been converted to arable production.
History. Lebanon became a French mandate after the First World War and achieved independence in 1944. For a generation the Christian community dominated the country, but friction between Christians and Muslims (later supported by Palestinian guerrillas) led to the outbreak of civil war in 1975. This resulted in military intervention by Syria, who imposed a ceasefire and remained to control inter-faction fighting, and by Israel, to force expulsion of the Palestinians. By 1992 the government had extended its authority over areas of the country not under Syrian and Israeli control and government forces had succeeded in disbanding most of the opposing Lebanese militias but unrest continues; parliamentary elections in 1992 were widely boycotted by Christians because of the continued military presence of Syria. In 1993 the Lebanese government initiated a ten-year reconstruction plan; the plan was impeded by Israeli bombing of Hezbollah targets in Beirut in 1996, but continues with aid from the World Bank. President, Elias Hrawi; prime minister, Rafiq al-Hariri; capital, Beirut.

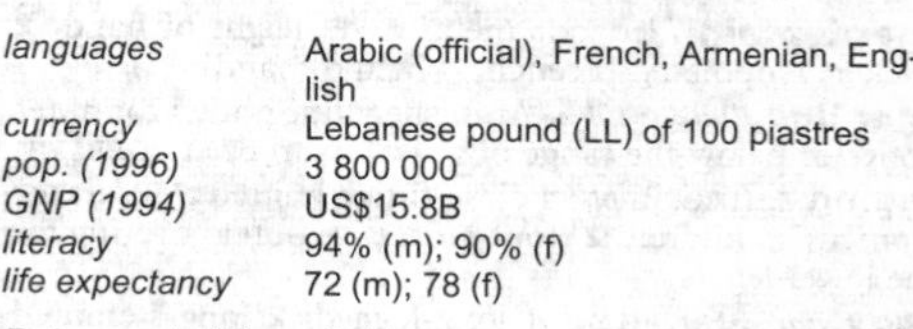

languages	Arabic (official), French, Armenian, English
currency	Lebanese pound (LL) of 100 piastres
pop. (1996)	3 800 000
GNP (1994)	US$15.8B
literacy	94% (m); 90% (f)
life expectancy	72 (m); 78 (f)

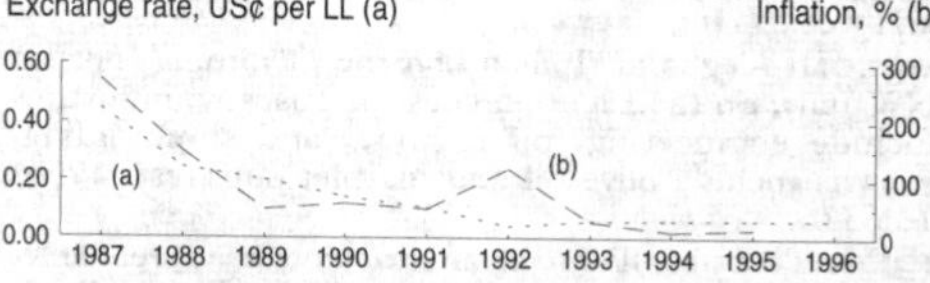

table, etc. **5** *Cricket* the half of the field (divided lengthways) in which the batsman's feet are placed. **6 a** section of a journey. **b** section of a relay race. **c** stage in a competition. □ **leg it** (**-gg-**) *colloq.* walk or run hard. **not have a leg to stand on** be unable to support one's argument by facts or sound reasons. **on one's last legs** near death or the end of usefulness etc. □ **legged** /legd, 'legɪd/ *adj.* (also in *comb.*). [Old Norse]

legacy /'legəsɪ/ *n.* (*pl.* **-ies**) **1** gift left in a will. **2** thing handed down by a predecessor. [Latin *lego* bequeath]

legal /'liːg(ə)l/ *adj.* **1** of or based on law; concerned with law. **2** appointed or required by law. **3** permitted by law. □ **legally** *adv.* [Latin *lex leg-* law]

legal aid *n.* state assistance for legal advice or action.

legalese /ˌliːgə'liːz/ *n. colloq.* technical language of legal documents.

legalistic /ˌliːgə'lɪstɪk/ *adj.* adhering excessively to a law or formula. □ **legalism** /'liːgəˌlɪz(ə)m/ *n.* **legalist** /'liːgəlɪst/ *n.*

legality /lɪ'gælɪtɪ/ *n.* (*pl.* **-ies**) **1** lawfulness. **2** (in *pl.*) obligations imposed by law.

legalize /'liːgəˌlaɪz/ *v.* (also **-ise**) (**-zing** or **-sing**) **1** make lawful. **2** bring into harmony with the law. □ **legalization** /-'zeɪʃ(ə)n/ *n.*

♦ **legal reserve** *n.* minimum amount of money that building societies, insurance companies, etc. are bound by law to hold as security for the benefit of their customers.

---

legal separation see SEPARATION 2.

♦ **legal tender** *n.* money that must be accepted in discharge of a debt. It may be **limited legal tender**, which must be accepted but only up to specified limits of payment, or **unlimited legal tender**, which is acceptable in settlement of debts of any amount. Bank of England notes and the £2 and £1 coins are unlimited legal tender in the UK. Other Royal Mint coins are limited legal tender.

---

legate /'legət/ *n.* ambassador of the Pope. [Latin *lego* depute]

legatee /ˌlegə'tiː/ *n.* recipient of a legacy. [Latin *lego* bequeath]

legation /lɪ'geɪʃ(ə)n/ *n.* **1** diplomatic minister and his or her staff. **2** this minister's official residence. [Latin: related to LEGATE]

legato /lɪ'gɑːtəʊ/ *Mus. –adv.* & *adj.* in a smooth flowing manner. *–n.* (*pl.* **-s**) **1** legato passage. **2** legato playing. [Italian, = bound, from *ligo* bind]

leg before *–adj.* & *adv.* (in full **leg before wicket**) *Cricket* (of a batsman) out because of stopping the ball, other than with the bat or hand, which would otherwise have hit the wicket. *–n.* such a dismissal.

leg-bye *n. Cricket* run scored from a ball that touches the batsman.

legend /'ledʒ(ə)nd/ *n.* **1 a** traditional story; myth. **b** these collectively. **2** *colloq.* famous or remarkable event or person. **3** inscription. **4** explanation on a map etc. of symbols used. [Latin *legenda* what is to be read]

legendary *adj.* **1** of, based on, or described in a legend. **2** *colloq.* remarkable.

legerdemain /ˌledʒədə'meɪn/ *n.* **1** sleight of hand. **2** trickery, sophistry. [French, = light of hand]

leger line /'ledʒə(r)/ *n. Mus.* short line added for notes above or below the range of a staff. [var. of LEDGER]

legging *n.* (usu. in *pl.*) **1** close-fitting knitted trousers for women or children. **2** stout protective outer covering for the lower leg.

leggy *adj.* (**-ier**, **-iest**) **1** long-legged. **2** long-stemmed and weak. □ **legginess** *n.*

Leghorn /'leghɔːn/ (Italian **Livorno** /lɪ'vɔːnəʊ/) port in NW Italy, on the Ligurian coast of Tuscany; industries include engineering, oil refining, and shipbuilding; exports include olive oil and marble; pop. (est. 1994) 165 536.

legible /'ledʒɪb(ə)l/ *adj.* clear enough to read; readable. □ **legibility** /-'bɪlɪtɪ/ *n.* **legibly** *adv.* [Latin *lego* read]

legion /'liːdʒ(ə)n/ *–n.* **1** division of 3000–6000 men in the ancient Roman army. **2** large organized body. *–predic. adj.* great in number (*his good works were legion*). [Latin *legio -onis*]

legionary *–adj.* of a legion or legions. *–n.* (*pl.* **-ies**) member of a legion.

legionnaire /ˌliːdʒə'neə(r)/ *n.* member of a legion. [French: related to LEGION]

legionnaires' disease *n.* form of bacterial pneumonia.

legislate /'ledʒɪsˌleɪt/ *v.* (**-ting**) make laws. □ **legislator** *n.* [from LEGISLATION]

legislation /ˌledʒɪs'leɪʃ(ə)n/ *n.* **1** law-making. **2** laws collectively. [Latin *lex legis* law, *latus* past part. of *fero* carry]

legislative /'ledʒɪslətɪv/ *adj.* of or empowered to make legislation.

legislature /'ledʒɪsˌleɪtʃə(r), -lətʃə(r)/ *n.* legislative body of a state.

legit /lɪ'dʒɪt/ *adj. colloq.* legitimate (in sense 2). [abbreviation]

legitimate /lɪ'dʒɪtəmət/ *adj.* **1** (of a child) born of parents married to each other. **2** lawful, proper, regular. **3** logically acceptable. □ **legitimacy** *n.* **legitimately** *adv.* [Latin *legitimo* legitimize, from *lex legis* law]

legitimatize /lɪ'dʒɪtəməˌtaɪz/ *v.* (also **-ise**) (**-zing** or **-sing**) legitimize.

legitimize /lɪ'dʒɪtəˌmaɪz/ *v.* (also **-ise**) (**-zing** or **-sing**) **1** make legitimate. **2** serve as a justification for. □ **legitimization** /-'zeɪʃ(ə)n/ *n.*

legless *adj.* **1** having no legs. **2** *slang* very drunk.

Lego /'legəʊ/ *n. propr.* toy consisting of interlocking plastic building blocks. [Danish *leg godt* play well]

leg-of-mutton sleeve *n.* sleeve which is full and loose on the upper arm but close-fitting on the forearm.

leg-pull *n. colloq.* hoax.

leg-room *n.* space for the legs of a seated person.

legume /'legjuːm/ *n.* **1** leguminous plant. **2** edible part of a leguminous plant. [Latin *legumen -minis* from *lego* pick, because pickable by hand]

leguminous /lɪ'gjuːmɪnəs/ *adj.* of the family of plants with seeds in pods (e.g. peas and beans).

leg up *n.* help given to mount a horse etc., or to overcome an obstacle or problem; boost.

leg warmer *n.* either of a pair of tubular knitted garments covering the leg from ankle to knee or thigh.

Leh /leɪ/ trading town in N India, in E Jammu and Kashmir, chief town of Ladakh region; pop. (1981) 8718.

Le Havre /lə 'hɑːvr/ port in NW France, on the English Channel, at the mouth of the Seine, important for transatlantic cargo and a ferry service to England; pop. (1990) 197 219.

lei[1] /'leɪiː/ *n.* Polynesian garland of flowers. [Hawaiian]

lei[2] *pl.* of LEU.

Leicester /'lestə(r)/ town in central England, in Leicestershire; industries include hosiery, knitwear, footwear, and engineering; pop. (est. 1994) 293 400.

Leicestershire /'lestəˌʃɪə(r)/ county in central England; pop. (est. 1994) 916 900; county town, Leicester. Dairy, livestock, and arable farming are important; products include cheese, coal, hosiery, and footwear.

Leics. *abbr.* Leicestershire.

Leiden /'laɪd(ə)n/ (formerly **Leyden**) industrial city in the Netherlands, in the province of South Holland; industries include textiles and metallurgy; pop. (est. 1995) 115 473.

Leinster /'lenstə(r)/ province in the SE Republic of Ireland; pop. (1991) 1 860 949; capital, Dublin.

Leipzig /'laɪpzɪg/ city in E central Germany; a centre of the publishing and music trade, it also has iron and steel, chemical, and textile industries; pop. (est. 1995) 481 121. Trade fairs have been held here since the 12th century.

leisure /'leʒə(r)/ *n.* **1** free time. **2** enjoyment of free time. □ **at leisure 1** not occupied. **2** in an unhurried manner.

at one's leisure when one has time. [Anglo-French *leisour* from Latin *licet* it is allowed]

leisure centre *n.* public building with sports facilities etc.

leisured *adj.* having ample leisure.

leisurely /'leʒəlɪ/ *–adj.* unhurried, relaxed. *–adv.* without hurry. □ **leisureliness** *n.*

leisurewear *n.* informal clothes, esp. sportswear.

leitmotif /'laɪtməʊ,tiːf/ *n.* (also **leitmotiv**) recurrent theme in a musical etc. composition representing a particular person, idea, etc. [German: related to LEAD[1], MOTIVE]

Leitrim /'liːtrɪm/ county in the W Republic of Ireland, in the province of Connaught; pop. (1991) 25 301; capital, Carrick-on-Shannon. Sheep- and cattle-farming are important; there are also various textile industries.

lek /lek/ *n.* standard monetary unit of Albania. [Albanian]

Le Mans /lə 'mɑ̃/ industrial and commercial town in NW France; pop. (1990) 148 465. It is the site of an annual 24-hour sports-car race.

lemming /'lemɪŋ/ *n.* small Arctic rodent reputed to rush into the sea and drown during migration. [Norwegian]

Lemnos /'lemnɒs/ (Greek **Límnos** /'liːmnɒs/) Greek island in the N Aegean Sea; fruit and tobacco are exported. The chief town is Kástron.

lemon /'lemən/ *n.* **1 a** yellow oval citrus fruit with acidic juice. **b** tree bearing it. **2** pale yellow colour. **3** *colloq.* person or thing regarded as a failure. □ **lemony** *adj.* [Arabic *laimūn*]

lemonade /,lemə'neɪd/ *n.* **1** drink made from lemon juice. **2** synthetic substitute for this.

lemon balm *n.* bushy plant smelling and tasting of lemon.

lemon curd *n.* (also **lemon cheese**) creamy conserve made from lemons.

lemon geranium *n.* lemon-scented pelargonium.

lemon sole /'lemən/ *n.* (*pl.* same or **-s**) flat-fish of the plaice family. [French *limande*]

lempira /lem'pɪərə/ *n.* standard monetary unit of Honduras. [from *Lempira*, name of an American Indian chief]

lemur /'liːmə(r)/ *n.* tree-dwelling primate of Madagascar. [Latin *lemures* ghosts]

lend *v.* (*past* and *past part.* **lent**) **1** (usu. foll. by *to*) grant (to a person) the use of (a thing) on the understanding that it or its equivalent shall be returned. **2** allow the use of (money) at interest. **3** bestow or contribute (*lends a certain charm*). □ **lend an ear** listen. **lend a hand** help. **lend itself to** (of a thing) be suitable for. □ **lender** *n.* [Old English: related to LOAN]

♦ **lender of last resort** *n.* country's central bank with responsibility for controlling its banking system. In the UK, the Bank of England fulfils this role, lending to discount houses, either by repurchasing treasury bills, lending on other paper assets, or granting direct loans, charging the base rate of interest. Commercial banks do not go directly to the Bank of England; they borrow from the discount houses.

---

length *n.* **1** measurement or extent from end to end. **2** extent in or of time. **3** distance a thing extends. **4** length of a horse, boat, etc., as a measure of the lead in a race. **5** long stretch or extent. **6** degree of thoroughness in action (*went to great lengths*). **7** piece of a certain length (*length of cloth*). **8** *Prosody* quantity of a vowel or syllable. **9** *Cricket* **a** distance from the batsman at which the ball pitches. **b** proper amount of this. **10** length of a swimming-pool as a measure of distance swum. □ **at length** **1** in detail. **2** after a long time. [Old English: related to LONG[1]]

lengthen *v.* make or become longer.

lengthways *adv.* in a direction parallel with a thing's length.

lengthwise *–adv.* lengthways. *–adj.* lying or moving lengthways.

lengthy *adj.* (**-ier, -iest**) of unusual or tedious length. □ **lengthily** *adv.* **lengthiness** *n.*

lenient /'liːnɪənt/ *adj.* merciful, not severe. □ **lenience** *n.* **leniency** *n.* **leniently** *adv.* [Latin *lenis* gentle]

Leninakan /,lenɪnə'kɑːn/ see KUMAYRI.

Leningrad /'lenɪn,græd/ see ST PETERSBURG.

lens /lenz/ *n.* **1** piece of a transparent substance with one or (usu.) both sides curved for concentrating or dispersing light-rays esp. in optical instruments. **2** combination of lenses used in photography. **3** transparent substance behind the iris of the eye. **4** = CONTACT LENS. [Latin *lens lent-* lentil (from the similarity of shape)]

Lent *n. Eccl.* period of fasting and penitence from Ash Wednesday to Holy Saturday. □ **Lenten** *adj.* [Old English, = spring]

lent *past* and *past part.* of LEND.

lentil /'lentɪl/ *n.* **1** pea-like plant. **2** its seed, esp. used as food. [Latin *lens*]

lento /'lentəʊ/ *Mus. –adj.* slow. *–adv.* slowly. [Italian]

Leo /'liːəʊ/ *n.* (*pl.* **-s**) **1** constellation and fifth sign of the zodiac (the Lion). **2** person born when the sun is in this sign. [Latin]

León /leɪ'ɒn/ **1** city in W Nicaragua; there are distilleries, tanneries, and food-processing plants; pop. (est. 1994) 171 375. **2** city in central Mexico, a commercial and distribution centre; manufactures include footwear and leather goods; pop. (1990) 867 920.

leone /liː'əʊnɪ/ *n.* standard monetary unit of Sierra Leone. [from SIERRA LEONE]

leonine /'liːə,naɪn/ *adj.* **1** like a lion. **2** of or relating to lions. [Latin: related to LEO]

leopard /'lepəd/ *n.* large African or Asian animal of the cat family with a black-spotted yellowish or all black coat, panther. [Greek *leōn* lion, *pardos* panther]

Léopoldville /'liːə,pəʊldvɪl/ see KINSHASA.

leotard /'liːə,tɑːd/ *n.* close-fitting one-piece garment worn by dancers etc. [*Léotard*, name of a trapeze artist]

leper /'lepə(r)/ *n.* **1** person with leprosy. **2** person who is shunned. [Greek *lepros* scaly]

lepidopterous /,lepɪ'dɒptərəs/ *adj.* of the order of insects with four scale-covered wings, including butterflies and moths. □ **lepidopterist** *n.* [Greek *lepis -idos* scale, *pteron* wing]

leprechaun /'leprə,kɔːn/ *n.* small mischievous sprite in Irish folklore. [Irish *lu* small, *corp* body]

leprosy /'leprəsɪ/ *n.* contagious disease that damages the skin and nerves. □ **leprous** *adj.* [related to LEPER]

lesbian /'lezbɪən/ *–n.* homosexual woman. *–adj.* of female homosexuality. □ **lesbianism** *n.* [LESBOS]

Lesbos /'lezbɒs/ (Greek **Lésvos** /'lezvɒs/) largest of the Greek islands, in the Aegean Sea off the W coast of Turkey; industries include tourism and sardine fishing; pop. (1991) 105 082; chief town, Mytilene.

lese-majesty /liːz 'mædʒɪstɪ/ *n.* **1** treason. **2** insult to a sovereign or ruler. **3** presumptuous conduct. [French *lèse-majesté* injured sovereignty]

lesion /'liːʒ(ə)n/ *n.* **1** damage. **2** injury. **3** morbid change in the functioning or texture of an organ etc. [Latin *laedo laes-* injure]

LESS *abbr.* least-cost estimating and scheduling.

less *–adj.* **1** smaller in extent, degree, duration, number, etc. **2** of smaller quantity, not so much (*less meat*). **3** *colloq.* fewer (*less biscuits*). *–adv.* to a smaller extent, in a lower degree. *–n.* smaller amount, quantity, or number (*will take less; for less than £10*). *–prep.* minus (*made £1000 less tax*). [Old English]

■ **Usage** The use of *less* to mean 'fewer', as in sense 3, is regarded as incorrect in standard English.

-less *suffix* forming adjectives and adverbs: **1** from nouns, meaning 'not having, without, free from' (*powerless*). **2** from verbs, meaning 'not accessible to, affected by, or performing the action of the verb' (*fathomless; ceaseless*). [Old English]

lessee /le'siː/ *n.* (often foll. by *of*) person who is granted a lease; tenant. See LANDLORD AND TENANT. [French: related to LEASE]

lessen /ˈles(ə)n/ *v.* make or become less, diminish.

lesser *adj.* (usu. *attrib.*) not so great as the other(s) (*lesser evil*; *lesser mortals*).

lesson /ˈles(ə)n/ *n.* **1** spell of teaching. **2** (in *pl.*; foll. by *in*) systematic instruction. **3** thing learnt by a pupil. **4** experience that serves to warn or encourage (*let that be a lesson*). **5** passage from the Bible read aloud during a church service. [French *leçon* from Latin *lego lect-*]

lessor /leˈsɔː(r)/ *n.* person granting a lease; landlord. See LANDLORD AND TENANT. [Anglo-French: related to LEASE]

lest *conj. formal* **1** in order that not, for fear that (*lest he forget*). **2** that (*afraid lest we should be late*). [Old English: related to LESS]

■ **Usage** *Lest* is followed by *should* or the subjunctive (see examples above).

Lésvos see LESBOS.

let¹ –*v.* (**-tt-**; *past* and *past part.* **let**) **1 a** allow to, not prevent or forbid. **b** cause to (*let me know*). **2** (foll. by *into*) allow to enter. **3** grant the use of (rooms, land, etc.) for rent or hire. **4** allow or cause (liquid or air) to escape (*let blood*). **5** *aux.* supplying the first and third persons of the imperative in exhortations (*let us pray*), commands (*let it be done at once*; *let there be light*), assumptions, etc. (*let AB equal CD*). –*n.* act of letting a house, room, etc. □ **let alone 1** not to mention, far less or more (*hasn't got a television, let alone a video*). **2** = *let be*. **let be** not interfere with, attend to, or do. **let down 1** lower. **2** fail to support or satisfy, disappoint. **3** lengthen (a garment). **4** deflate (a tyre). **let down gently** reject or disappoint without humiliating. **let drop** (or **fall**) drop (esp. a word or hint) intentionally or by accident. **let go 1** release. **2 a** (often foll. by *of*) lose one's hold. **b** lose hold of. **let oneself go 1** act spontaneously. **2** neglect one's appearance or habits. **let in 1** allow to enter (*let the dog in*; *let in a flood of light*). **2** (foll. by *for*) involve (a person, often oneself) in loss or difficulty. **3** (foll. by *on*) allow (a person) to share a secret, privileges, etc. **let loose** release, unchain. **let off 1 a** fire (a gun). **b** explode (a bomb). **2** allow or cause (steam etc.) to escape. **3 a** not punish or compel. **b** (foll. by *with*) punish lightly. **let off steam** release pent-up energy or feeling. **let on** *colloq.* **1** reveal a secret. **2** pretend. **let out 1** release. **2** reveal (a secret etc.). **3** make (a garment) looser. **4** put out to rent or to contract. **let rip 1** act without restraint. **2** speak violently. **let up** *colloq.* **1** become less intense or severe. **2** relax one's efforts. **to let** available for rent. [Old English]

let² –*n.* obstruction of a ball or player in tennis etc., requiring the ball to be served again. –*v.* (**-tt-**; *past* and *past part.* **letted** or **let**) *archaic* hinder, obstruct. □ **without let or hindrance** unimpeded. [Old English: related to LATE]

-let *suffix* forming nouns, usu. diminutive (*flatlet*) or denoting articles of ornament or dress (*anklet*). [French]

let-down *n.* disappointment.

lethal /ˈliːθ(ə)l/ *adj.* causing or sufficient to cause death. □ **lethally** *adv.* [Latin *letum* death]

lethargy /ˈleθədʒɪ/ *n.* **1** lack of energy. **2** morbid drowsiness. □ **lethargic** /lɪˈθɑːdʒɪk/ *adj.* **lethargically** /lɪˈθɑːdʒɪkəlɪ/ *adv.* [Greek *lēthargos* forgetful]

Leticia /ləˈtiːsɪə/ town and river port in SE Colombia, on the Amazon; pop. (1992) 32 694.

let-out *n. colloq.* opportunity to escape a commitment etc.

LETS *abbr.* Local Employment and Trade System.

letter –*n.* **1** character representing one or more of the sounds used in speech. **2 a** written or printed message, usu. sent in an envelope by post. **b** (in *pl.*) addressed legal or formal document. **3** precise terms of a statement, the strict verbal interpretation (*letter of the law*). **4** (in *pl.*) **a** literature. **b** acquaintance with books, erudition. –*v.* **1** inscribe letters on. **2** classify with letters. □ **to the letter** with adherence to every detail. [French from Latin *littera*]

letter-bomb *n.* terrorist explosive device in the form of a postal packet.

letter-box *n.* box or slot into which letters are posted or delivered.

lettered *adj.* well-read or educated.

letterhead *n.* **1** printed heading on stationery. **2** stationery with this.

◆ **letter of allotment** see ALLOTMENT 4.

◆ **letter of credit** *n.* letter from one banker to another authorizing the payment of a specified sum to the person named in the letter on certain specified conditions (see LETTER OF INDICATION). Commercially, letters of credit are widely used in the international import and export trade as a means of payment. In an export contract, the exporter may require the foreign importer to open a letter of credit at the importer's local bank (the issuing bank) for the amount of the goods. This will state that it is to be negotiable at a bank (the negotiating bank) in the exporter's country in favour of the exporter; often, the exporter (who is called the beneficiary of the credit) will give the name of the negotiating bank. On presentation of the shipping documents (which are listed in the letter of credit) the beneficiary will receive payment from the negotiating bank. An **irrevocable letter of credit** cannot be cancelled by the person who opens it or by the issuing bank without the beneficiary's consent, whereas a **revocable letter of credit** can. In a **confirmed letter of credit** the negotiating bank guarantees to pay the beneficiary, even if the issuing bank fails to honour its commitments; in an **unconfirmed letter of credit** this guarantee is not given. A confirmed irrevocable letter of credit therefore provides the most reliable means of being paid for exported goods. However, all letters of credit have an expiry date, after which they can only be negotiated by the consent of all the

---

Lesotho /ləˈsuːtuː/, **Kingdom of** (formerly **Basutoland**) landlocked mountainous country forming an enclave in the Republic of South Africa. The economy is based on agriculture, esp. livestock farming, but soil erosion through overgrazing and recent droughts have affected production. Some small-scale industries have been developed but Lesotho has few natural resources, with the exception of some diamonds, and is dependent on South Africa (around half the adult male labour force is employed in that country). Work has begun on the Highlands Water Scheme, which is aimed to provide water for an industrial zone of South Africa and hydroelectric power for Lesotho (most of the country's electricity is currently supplied by South Africa). Tourism is another source of foreign exchange.

History. Formerly under British protection, Lesotho became an independent kingdom within the Commonwealth in 1966. The country was effectively under military control from 1986 until 1993, when civilian rule was restored after multi-party elections. Head of state, King Letsie III; prime minister, Ntsu Mokhehle; capital, Maseru.

languages	Sesotho, English
currency	loti (*pl.* maloti, Ml) of 100 lisente
pop. (1996)	1 971 000
GNP (1994)	US$1.3B
literacy	81% (m); 62% (f)
life expectancy	58 (m); 63 (f)

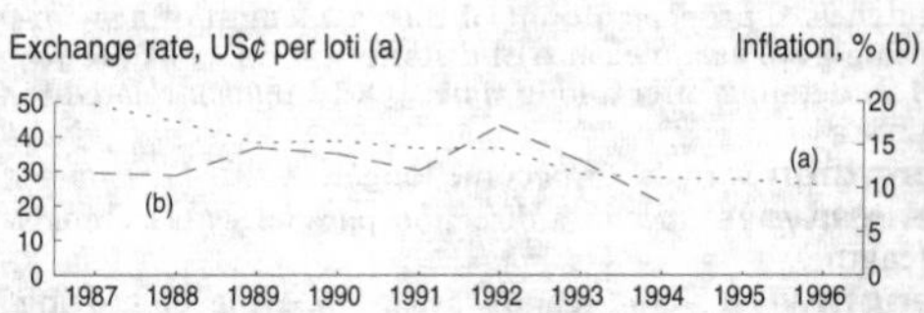

parties. In 1983 the International Chamber of Commerce recommended that the term 'letter of credit' should be replaced by 'documentary credit'.

◆ **letter of hypothecation** see HYPOTHECATION 1.

◆ **letter of indemnity** *n.* **1** letter stating that the organization issuing it will compensate the person to whom it is addressed for a specified loss. See also INDEMNITY 4. **2** letter written to a company registrar asking for a replacement for a lost share certificate and indemnifying the company against any loss that it might incur in so doing. It may be required to be countersigned by a bank. **3** letter written by an exporter accepting responsibility for any losses arising from faulty packing, short weight, etc. at the time of shipment. If this letter accompanies the shipping documents, the shipping company will issue a clean bill of lading, even if the packages are damaged, enabling the exporter to negotiate the documents and receive payment without trouble.

◆ **letter of indication** *n.* (also **letter of identification**) letter issued by a bank to a customer to whom a letter of credit has been supplied. The letter has to be produced with the letter of credit at the negotiating bank; it provides evidence of the bearer's identity and a specimen of his or her signature. It is used esp. with a circular letter of credit carried by travellers, although traveller's cheques are now more widely used.

◆ **letter of intent** *n.* letter in which a person formally sets out his or her intentions to do something (e.g. signing a contract) in certain circumstances, which are often specified in detail in the letter. The letter does not constitute either a contract or a promise to do anything, but it does indicate the writer's serious wish to pursue the course set out.

◆ **letter of licence** *n.* letter from a creditor to a debtor who is having trouble raising the money to settle the debt. The letter states that the creditor will allow the debtor a stated time to pay and will not initiate proceedings against the debtor before that time. See also ARRANGEMENT 6.

◆ **letter of regret** *n.* letter from a company, or its bankers, stating that an application for an allotment from a new issue of shares has been unsuccessful.

◆ **letter of renunciation** *n.* **1** form, often attached to an allotment letter, on which a person who has been allotted shares in a new issue renounces his or her rights to them, either absolutely or in favour of someone else (during the **renunciation period**). **2** form on the reverse of some unit-trust certificates, which the holder completes when wishing to dispose of the holding. The completed certificate is sent to the trust managers.

◆ **letter of set-off** see SET-OFF 2.

---

letterpress *n.* **1** printed words of an illustrated book. **2** printing from raised type.

◆ **letter-quality** *adj.* (also **LQ**) *Computing* producing or denoting printed output of a quality that is adequate for business correspondence; **near letter-quality (NLQ)** is slightly inferior to letter-quality.

◆ **letters of administration** *n.pl.* order authorizing the person named (the administrator) to distribute the property of a deceased person, who has not appointed anyone else to do so. The distribution must be in accordance with the deceased's will, or the rules of intestacy if no will was left.

---

lettuce /ˈletɪs/ *n.* plant with crisp leaves used in salads. [Latin *lactuca* from *lac lact-* milk]

let-up *n. colloq.* **1** reduction in intensity. **2** relaxation of effort.

leu /ˈleɪuː/ *n.* (*pl.* **lei** /leɪ/) standard monetary unit of Romania. [Romanian, = lion]

leuco- *comb. form* white. [Greek *leukos* white]

leucocyte /ˈluːkəˌsaɪt/ *n.* white blood cell.

leukaemia /luːˈkiːmɪə/ *n.* (*US* **leukemia**) malignant disease in which the bone-marrow etc. produces too many leucocytes. [Greek *leukos* white, *haima* blood]

Leuven /ˈlɜːv(ə)n/ (French **Louvain** /ˈluːvæ̃/) town in Belgium, in Flemish Brabant; manufactures include chemicals and leather goods; pop. (est. 1995) 87 165.

lev /lef/ *n.* standard monetary unit of Bulgaria and Moldova. [Bulgarian, = lion]

Levant /lɪˈvænt/ *n.* (prec. by *the*) *archaic* eastern Mediterranean countries. [French, = point of sunrise, from Latin *levo* lift]

Levantine /ˈlevənˌtaɪn/ *–adj.* of or trading to the Levant. *–n.* native or inhabitant of the Levant.

levee /ˈlevɪ/ *n. US* **1** embankment against river floods. **2** natural embankment built up by a river. **3** landing-place. [French *levée* past part. of *lever* raise: related to LEVY]

level /ˈlev(ə)l/ *–n.* **1** horizontal line or plane. **2** height or value reached; position on a real or imaginary scale (*eye level*; *sugar level*; *danger level*). **3** social, moral, or intellectual standard. **4** plane of rank or authority (*talks at Cabinet level*). **5** instrument giving a line parallel to the plane of the horizon. **6** level surface. **7** flat tract of land. *–adj.* **1** flat and even; not bumpy. **2** horizontal. **3** (often foll. by *with*) **a** on the same horizontal plane as something else. **b** having equality with something else. **4** even, uniform, equable, or well-balanced. *–v.* (**-ll-**; *US* **-l-**) **1** make level. **2** raze. **3** (also *absol.*) aim (a missile or gun). **4** (also *absol.*; foll. by *at*, *against*) direct (an accusation etc.). □ **do one's level best** *colloq.* do one's utmost. **find one's level** reach the right social, intellectual, etc. position. **level down** bring down to a standard. **level off** make or become level. **level out** make or become level. **level up** bring up to a standard. **on the level 1** honestly, without deception. **2** honest, truthful. **on a level with 1** in the same horizontal plane as. **2** equal with. [Latin diminutive of *libra* balance]

level crossing *n.* crossing of a railway and a road, or two railways, at the same level.

level-headed *adj.* mentally well-balanced, sensible. □ **level-headedness** *n.*

leveller *n.* (*US* **leveler**) **1** person who advocates the abolition of social distinctions. **2** person or thing that levels.

level pegging *n.* equality of scores etc.

lever /ˈliːvə(r)/ *–n.* **1** bar resting on a pivot, used to prise. **2** bar pivoted about a fulcrum (fixed point) which can be acted upon by a force (effort) in order to move a load. **3** projecting handle moved to operate a mechanism. **4** means of exerting moral pressure. *–v.* **1** use a lever. **2** (often foll. by *away*, *out*, *up*, etc.) lift, move, etc. with a lever. [Latin *levo* raise]

leverage *n.* **1** action or power of a lever. **2** power to accomplish a purpose. **3** use by a company of its limited assets to guarantee substantial loans to finance its business. **4** *US* = CAPITAL GEARING.

◆ **leveraged buyout** /ˈlevərɪdʒd/ *n.* (also **LBO**) esp. *US* take-over ploy in which a small company, whose assets are limited, borrows heavily on these assets and the assets of the target company in order to finance a take-over of a larger company, often making use of junk bonds.

---

leveret /ˈlevərɪt/ *n.* young hare, esp. one in its first year. [Latin *lepus lepor-* hare]

leviathan /lɪˈvaɪəθ(ə)n/ *n.* **1** *Bibl.* sea-monster. **2** very large or powerful thing. [Latin from Hebrew]

Levis /ˈliːvaɪz/ *n.pl.* (also **Levi's** *propr.*) type of (orig. blue) denim jeans or overalls reinforced with rivets. [*Levi* Strauss, name of the manufacturer]

levitate /ˈlevɪˌteɪt/ *v.* (**-ting**) **1** rise and float in the air (esp. with reference to spiritualism). **2** cause to do this. □ **levitation** /-ˈteɪʃ(ə)n/ *n.* [Latin *levis* light, after GRAVITATE]

levity /ˈlevɪtɪ/ *n.* lack of serious thought, frivolity. [Latin *levis* light]

levy /ˈlevɪ/ *–v.* (**-ies, -ied**) **1** impose or collect compulsorily (payment etc.). **2** enrol (troops etc.). **3** wage (war). *–n.* (*pl.* **-ies**) **1 a** collecting of a contribution, tax, etc. **b** contribution etc. levied. **2 a** act of enrolling troops etc. **b** (in *pl.*) troops enrolled. [Latin *levo* raise]

lewd /ljuːd/ *adj.* **1** lascivious. **2** obscene. [Old English, originally = lay, vulgar]

lexical /'leksɪk(ə)l/ *adj.* **1** of the words of a language. **2** of or as of a lexicon. [Greek *lexikos, lexikon*: see LEXICON]

lexicography /ˌleksɪ'kɒgrəfɪ/ *n.* compiling of dictionaries. □ **lexicographer** *n.* [from LEXICON, -GRAPHY]

lexicon /'leksɪkən/ *n.* **1** dictionary, esp. of Greek, Hebrew, Syriac, or Arabic. **2** vocabulary of a person etc. [Greek *lexis* word]

Lexington /'leksɪŋt(ə)n/ city in the US, in Kentucky, a centre for horse breeding and the distribution of agricultural produce and coal; pop. (1990) 225 366.

Leyden /'laɪd(ə)n/ see LEIDEN.

Leyden jar *n.* early capacitor consisting of a glass jar with layers of metal foil on the outside and inside. [LEIDEN]

Leyte /'leɪtɪ/ island in the central Philippines; pop. (1990) 1 806 000; chief towns, Tacloban and Ormoc. Farming and fishing are the main occupations.

LF *–abbr.* low frequency. *–symb.* Luxembourg franc.

LG *airline flight code* Luxair.

LGTB *abbr.* Local Government Training Board.

LH *airline flight code* Lufthansa.

Lhasa /'lɑːsə/ capital of Tibet; manufactures include handicrafts, carpets, electric motors, pharmaceuticals, and cement; pop. (1992) 124 000.

Li *symb.* lithium.

LIAB *abbr.* Licentiate of the International Association of Book-Keepers.

liability /ˌlaɪə'bɪlɪtɪ/ *n.* (*pl.* **-ies**) **1** being liable. **2** troublesome responsibility; handicap. **3** financial obligation. See CONTINGENT LIABILITY; CURRENT LIABILITIES; DEFERRED LIABILITY; LIMITED COMPANY; LONG-TERM LIABILITY; SECURED LIABILITY. **4** (in *pl.*) debts etc. for which one is liable.

♦ **liability insurance** *n.* insurance that provides for the payment of any compensation and court costs the policyholder becomes legally liable to pay because of claims for injury to other people or damage to their property as a result of the policyholder's negligence. Policies often define the areas in which they will deal with liability, e.g. personal liability or employers' liability.

---

liable /'laɪəb(ə)l/ *predic. adj.* **1** legally bound. **2** (foll. by *to*) subject to. **3** (foll. by *to* + infin.) under an obligation. **4** (foll. by *to*) exposed or open to (something undesirable). **5** (foll. by *to* + infin.) apt, likely (*it is liable to rain*). **6** (foll. by *for*) answerable. [French *lier* bind, from Latin *ligo*]

■ **Usage** Use of *liable* in sense 5, though common, is considered incorrect by some people.

liaise /lɪ'eɪz/ *v.* (**-sing**) (foll. by *with, between*) *colloq.* establish cooperation, act as a link. [back-formation from LIAISON]

liaison /lɪ'eɪzɒn/ *n.* **1** communication or cooperation. **2** illicit sexual relationship. [French *lier* bind: see LIABLE]

liana /lɪ'ɑːnə/ *n.* climbing plant of tropical forests. [French]

Liaoning /ˌliːaʊ'nɪŋ/ province of NE China; pop. (est. 1995) 40 670 000; capital, Shenyang. The province has rich deposits of coal and iron and produces steel, petroleum, cement, machinery, and electricity.

liar /'laɪə(r)/ *n.* person who tells a lie or lies.

Lib. *abbr.* Liberal.

lib *n. colloq.* (in names of political movements) liberation. [abbreviation]

LIBA *abbr.* Lloyd's Insurance Brokers' Association.

libation /laɪ'beɪʃ(ə)n/ *n.* **1** pouring out of a drink-offering to a god. **2** such a drink-offering. [Latin]

libel /'laɪb(ə)l/ *–n.* **1** *Law* **a** published false statement that is damaging to a person's reputation. **b** act of publishing this. **2** false and defamatory misrepresentation or statement. *–v.* (**-ll-**; *US* **-l-**) **1** defame by libellous statements. **2** *Law* publish a libel against. □ **libellous** *adj.* [Latin *libellus* diminutive of *liber* book]

liberal /'lɪbər(ə)l/ *–adj.* **1** abundant, ample. **2** giving freely, generous. **3** open-minded. **4** not strict or rigorous. **5** for the general broadening of the mind (*liberal studies*). **6 a** favouring moderate political and social reform. **b** (**Liberal**) of or characteristic of Liberals. *–n.* **1** person of liberal views. **2** (**Liberal**) supporter or member of a Liberal Party. □ **liberalism** *n.* **liberality** /-'rælɪtɪ/ *n.* **liberally** *adv.* [Latin *liber* free]

■ **Usage** In the UK the name *Liberal* was discontinued in official political use in 1988 when the party regrouped to form the *Social and Liberal Democrats*. In 1989 this name was officially replaced by *Liberal Democratic Party*.

Liberal Democrat *n.* member of the party formed from the Liberal Party and the Social Democratic Party.

■ **Usage** See note at *liberal*.

liberalize /'lɪbərəˌlaɪz/ *v.* (also **-ise**) (**-zing** or **-sing**) make or become more liberal or less strict. □ **liberalization** /-'zeɪʃ(ə)n/ *n.*

liberate /'lɪbəˌreɪt/ *v.* (**-ting**) **1** (often foll. by *from*) set free. **2** free (a country etc.) from an oppressor or enemy. **3** (often as **liberated** *adj.*) free (a person) from rigid social conventions. □ **liberation** /-'reɪʃ(ə)n/ *n.* **liberator** *n.* [Latin *liberare liberat-* from *liber* free]

libertine /'lɪbəˌtiːn/ *–n.* licentious person, rake. *–adj.* licentious. [Latin, = freedman, from *liber* free]

liberty /'lɪbətɪ/ *n.* (*pl.* **-ies**) **1** freedom from captivity etc. **2** right or power to do as one pleases. **3** (usu. in *pl.*) right or privilege granted by authority. □ **at liberty 1** free. **2** (foll. by *to* + infin.) permitted. **take liberties** (often foll.

Liberia /laɪ'bɪərɪə/, **Republic of** country in W Africa, bordering on the Atlantic, between Côte d'Ivoire and Sierra Leone. Civil war in 1990–6 resulted in suspension of most economic activity although slow reconstruction is now taking place. The economy is largely dependent on the export of primary products, esp. iron ore and concentrates, crude rubber, uncut diamonds, coffee, timber, and palm kernels. The agricultural sector employed about two-thirds of the labour force, rice and cassava being the chief food crops. Disruption of agricultural production during the fighting led to famine and many of the population fled as refugees to neighbouring countries. Liberia's large open-registry (flag of convenience) merchant shipping fleet has been a significant source of foreign exchange.
History. Liberia was founded in 1822 as a settlement for freed Black slaves from the US. It was proclaimed independent in 1847 with a constitution based on that of the US. Rebellion against the government in 1989 resulted in civil war during which the president was killed; although a ceasefire, monitored by ECOWAS forces, was negotiated in 1990 and an interim government established, the civil war continued. A transitional government was formed in 1994, though fighting continued between the various factions. A ceasefire in 1996 allowed presidential and legislative elections to be held in 1997. President, Charles Taylor; capital, Monrovia. □ **Liberian** *adj.* & *n.*

languages	English (official), African languages
currency	dollar (L$) of 100 cents
pop. (1996)	2 111 000
GNP (1994)	US$973M
literacy	54% (m); 22% (f)
life expectancy	55 (m); 60 (f)

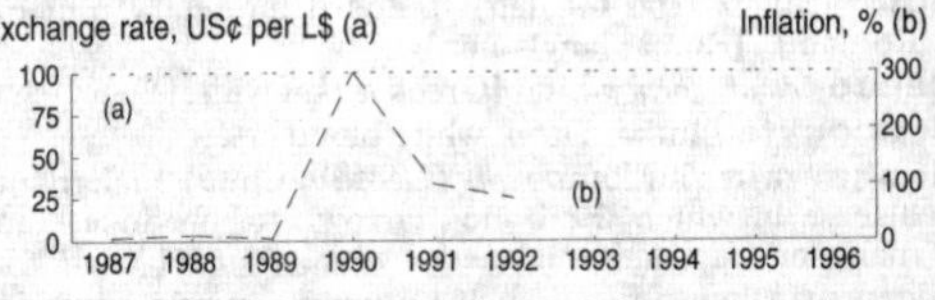

by *with*) behave in an unduly familiar manner. [Latin: related to LIBERAL]

LIBID /'li:bɪd/ *abbr.* London Inter-Bank Bid Rate.

libidinous /lɪ'bɪdɪnəs/ *adj.* lustful. [Latin: related to LIBIDO]

libido /lɪ'bi:ˌdəʊ/ *n.* (*pl.* **-s**) psychic drive or energy, esp. that associated with sexual desire. □ **libidinal** /lɪ'bɪdɪn(ə)l/ *adj.* [Latin, = lust]

♦ **LIBOR** /'li:bɔ:(r)/ *abbr.* = LONDON INTER-BANK OFFERED RATE.

Libra /'li:brə/ *n.* **1** constellation and seventh sign of the zodiac (the Scales). **2** person born when the sun is in this sign. [Latin, = pound weight]

librarian /laɪ'breərɪən/ *n.* person in charge of or assisting in a library. □ **librarianship** *n.*

library /'laɪbrərɪ/ *n.* (*pl.* **-ies**) **1** collection of books. **2** room or building where these are kept. **3 a** similar collection of films, records, computer programs or subroutines, etc. **b** place where these are kept. **4** set of books issued in similar bindings. [Latin *liber* book]

libretto /lɪ'bretəʊ/ *n.* (*pl.* **-ti** /-tɪ/ or **-s**) text of an opera etc. □ **librettist** *n.* [Italian, = little book]

Libreville /'li:brəˌvi:l/ capital of Gabon; industries include sawmilling, cloth printing, brewing, and flour milling; pop. (est. 1993) 362 386.

Lic. *abbr.* Licentiate.

lice *pl.* of LOUSE.

licence /'laɪs(ə)ns/ *n.* (*US* **license**) **1** official permit to own or use something, do something, or carry on a trade. Licences may be required for social reasons or simply to enable revenue to be collected. Since the Consumer Credit Act (1974) all businesses involved with giving credit to purchasers of goods must be licensed by the Office of Fair Trading. See also FRANCHISE *n.* 3; CARRIER 2. **2 a** permission. **b** formal permission to enter or occupy land. The simplest kind gives the licensee the permission of the landowner to be on land (e.g. the right of a visitor to enter a house). **Contractual licences** are permissions to be on land in the furtherance of some contractual right (e.g. the right of the holder of a cinema ticket to be in the cinema). This type of licence has been used to get round the Rent Acts (which apply to leases only). **3** liberty of action, esp. when excessive. **4** writer's or artist's deliberate deviation from fact, correct grammar, etc. (*poetic licence*). [Latin *licet* it is allowed]

license /'laɪs(ə)ns/ *–v.* (**-sing**) **1** grant a licence to. **2** authorize the use of (premises) for a certain purpose. *–n.* *US* var. of LICENCE.

♦ **licensed dealer** *n.* dealer licensed by the Department of Trade and Industry to provide investment advice and deal in securities, either as an agent or principal. Licensed dealers are not members of the London Stock Exchange and are not covered by its compensation fund.

♦ **licensed deposit taker** *n. hist.* category of financial institutions as defined by the Banking Act (1979), which divided banking into recognized banks, licensed deposit takers, and exempt institutions. The licensed deposit taker had to satisfy the Bank of England that it conducted its business in a prudent manner. The Banking Act (1987), however, established a single category of authorized institutions eligible to carry out banking business.

licensee /ˌlaɪsən'si:/ *n.* holder of a licence, esp. to sell alcoholic liquor.

licentiate /laɪ'senʃɪət/ *n.* holder of a certificate of professional competence. [medieval Latin: related to LICENCE]

licentious /laɪ'senʃəs/ *adj.* sexually promiscuous. [Latin: related to LICENCE]

lichee var. of LYCHEE.

lichen /'laɪkən, 'lɪtʃ(ə)n/ *n.* plant composed of a fungus and an alga in association, growing on and colouring rocks, tree-trunks, etc. [Greek *leikhēn*]

lich-gate *n.* (also **lych-gate**) roofed gateway to a churchyard where a coffin awaits the clergyman's arrival. [from *lich* = corpse]

licit /'lɪsɪt/ *adj. formal* permitted, lawful. [Latin: related to LICENCE]

lick *–v.* **1** pass the tongue over. **2** bring into a specified condition by licking (*licked it all up*; *licked it clean*). **3** (of a flame etc.) play lightly over. **4** *colloq.* defeat. **5** *colloq.* thrash. *–n.* **1** act of licking with the tongue. **2** *colloq.* fast pace (*at a lick*). **3** smart blow. □ **lick a person's boots** be servile. **lick into shape** make presentable or efficient. **lick one's lips** (or **chops**) look forward with relish. **lick one's wounds** be in retirement regaining strength etc. after defeat. [Old English]

lick and a promise *n. colloq.* hasty performance of a task, esp. washing oneself.

licorice var. of LIQUORICE.

lid *n.* **1** hinged or removable cover, esp. for a container. **2** = EYELID. □ **put the lid on** *colloq.* **1** be the culmination of. **2** put a stop to. □ **lidded** *adj.* (also in *comb.*). [Old English]

lido /'li:dəʊ/ *n.* (*pl.* **-s**) public open-air swimming-pool or bathing-beach. [*Lido*, name of a beach near Venice]

lie[1] /laɪ/ *–v.* (**lies**; **lying**; *past* **lay**; *past part.* **lain**) **1** be in

Libya /'lɪbɪə/ country in N Africa consisting chiefly of desert, with a narrow coastal plain bordering on the Mediterranean Sea. Libya is one of the world's leading oil producers and oil and natural gas production are the main industries. Dependence on the export of crude oil, which constitutes over 95% of exports in value, is being offset by attempts to develop the oil-refining sector; liquefied natural gas is also an important export. Other manufacturing industries include processing of agricultural produce and traditional handicrafts. Subsistence agriculture is important, esp. livestock farming (sheep, goats, and cattle); crop production (mainly barley, wheat, olives, citrus fruits, and almonds) is restricted to the narrow coastal areas and oases. The country's economy was adversely affected by sanctions imposed by the UN in 1992, in response to Libya's refusal to allow the extradition of two Libyans suspected of being responsible for the Lockerbie air disaster (1988).

History. Under Turkish domination from the 16th century, the country was annexed by Italy in 1912 and remained under Italian rule until after the Second World War. After a brief period of French and British administration, it achieved full independence as a kingdom in 1951. The monarchy was overthrown in a revolution in 1969 and in 1977 the country was officially named the Socialist People's Libyan Arab Jamahiriya, with a radical revolutionary leadership. Relations with both neighbouring Arab countries and Western states are very difficult. Since 1992, when Libya refused to extradite two suspects in the bombing of a plane over Lockerbie, Scotland, economic sanctions have been in place. Head of state ('Leader of the Revolution'), Col. Muammar al-Gadaffi; capital, Tripoli. □ **Libyan** *adj.* & *n.*

languages	Arabic (official), Italian, English
currency	dinar (LD) of 1000 dirhams
pop. (1996)	5 445 000
GDP (1994)	US$32.9B
literacy	87% (m); 63% (f)
life expectancy	62 (m); 66 (f)

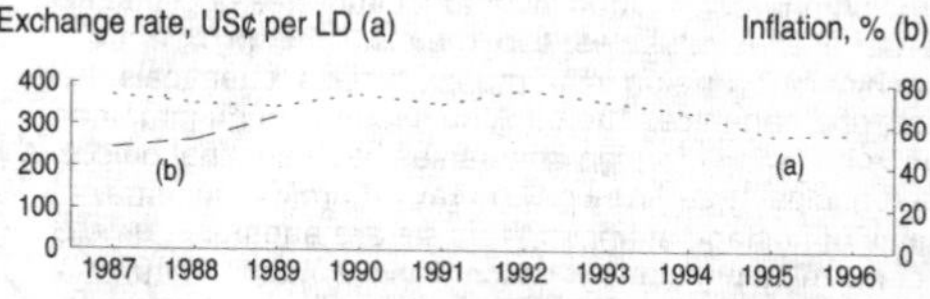

or assume a horizontal position on a surface; be at rest on something. **2** (of a thing) rest flat on a surface. **3** remain undisturbed or undiscussed etc. (*let matters lie*). **4 a** be kept, remain, or be in a specified state or place (*lie hidden*; *lie in wait*; *books lay unread*). **b** (of abstract things) exist; be in a certain position or relation (*answer lies in education*). **5 a** be situated (*village lay to the east*). **b** be spread out to view. –*n.* way, direction, or position in which a thing lies. □ **lie down** assume a lying position; have a short rest. **lie down under** accept (an insult etc.) without protest. **lie in** stay in bed late in the morning. **lie low 1** keep quiet or unseen. **2** be discreet about one's intentions. **lie with** be the responsibility of (a person) (*decision lies with you*). **take lying down** (usu. with *neg.*) accept (an insult etc.) without protest. [Old English]

■ **Usage** The transitive use of *lie*, meaning *lay*, as in *lie her on the bed*, is incorrect in standard English.

lie² /laɪ/ –*n.* **1** intentionally false statement (*tell a lie*). **2** something that deceives. –*v.* (**lies, lied, lying**) **1** tell a lie or lies. **2** (of a thing) be deceptive. □ **give the lie to** show the falsity of (a supposition etc.). [Old English]

lied /liːd/ *n.* (*pl.* **lieder**) German song, esp. of the Romantic period. [German]

lie-detector *n.* instrument supposedly determining whether a person is lying, by testing for certain physiological changes.

lie-down *n.* short rest.

Liège /lɪˈeɪʒ/ (Flemish **Luik** /laɪk/) **1** province of E Belgium; pop. (est. 1995) 1 015 007. **2** its capital city; manufactures include armaments, textiles, and paper; pop. (est. 1995) 192 393.

liege usu. *hist.* –*adj.* entitled to receive, or bound to give, feudal service or allegiance. –*n.* **1** (in full **liege lord**) feudal superior or sovereign. **2** (usu. in *pl.*) vassal, subject. [medieval Latin *laeticus*, probably from Germanic]

lie-in *n.* prolonged stay in bed in the morning.

◆ **lien** /ˈliːən/ *n. Law* right of one person to retain possession of goods owned by another until the possessor's claims against the owner have been satisfied. In a **general lien**, the goods are held as security for all the outstanding debts of the owner, whereas in a **particular lien** only the claims of the possessor in respect of the goods held must be satisfied. Thus an unpaid seller may in some contracts be entitled to retain the goods until the price is received, a carrier may have a lien over goods being transported, and a repairer over goods being repaired. Whether a lien arises or not depends on the terms of the contract and usual trade practice. This type of lien is a **possessory lien**, but sometimes actual possession of the goods is not necessary. In an **equitable lien**, for example, the claim exists independently of possession. A purchaser of the property involved who is given notice of the lien will be bound by it. Similarly a **maritime lien**, which binds a ship or cargo in connection with some maritime liability, does not depend on possession and can be enforced by arrest and sale (unless security is given). Examples of maritime liens are the lien of a salvor and the liens of seamen for their wages and of masters for their wages and outgoings. [Latin *ligo* bind]

lie of the land *n.* state of affairs.

lieu /ljuː/ *n.* □ **in lieu 1** instead. **2** (foll. by *of*) in the place of. [Latin *locus* place]

Lieut. *abbr.* Lieutenant.

lieutenant /lefˈtenənt/ *n.* **1 a** army officer next in rank below captain. **b** naval officer next in rank below lieutenant commander. **2** deputy. □ **lieutenancy** *n.* (*pl.* **-ies**). [French: related to LIEU place, TENANT holder]

lieutenant colonel *n.* (also **lieutenant commander** or **general**) officers ranking next below colonel, commander, or general.

life *n.* (*pl.* **lives**) **1** capacity for growth, functional activity, and continual change until death. **2** living things and their activity (*insect life*; *is there life on Mars?*). **3 a** period during which life lasts, or the period from birth to the present time or from the present time to death (*have done it all my life*; *will regret it all my life*). **b** duration of a thing's existence or ability to function. **4 a** person's state of existence as a living individual (*sacrificed their lives*). **b** living person (*many lives were lost*). **5 a** individual's actions or fortunes; manner of existence (*start a new life*). **b** particular aspect of this (*private life*). **6** business and pleasures of the world (*in Paris you really see life*). **7** energy, liveliness (*full of life*). **8** biography. **9** *colloq.* = LIFE SENTENCE. □ **for dear** (or **one's) life** as if or in order to escape death. **for life** for the rest of one's life. **not on your life** *colloq.* most certainly not. [Old English]

◆ **life annuity** *n.* annuity that ceases to be paid on the death of a specified person, who may or may not be the annuitant.

◆ **life assurance** *n.* (also **life insurance**) insurance that pays a specified amount of money on the death of the life assured or, in the case of an endowment assurance policy, on the death of the life assured or at the end of an agreed period, whichever is the earlier. See also WHOLE (OF) LIFE POLICY; QUALIFYING POLICY.

◆ **Life Assurance and Unit Trust Regulatory Organization** (also **LAUTRO**, **Lautro**) see SELF-REGULATING ORGANIZATION.

◆ **life assured** *n.* person upon whose death an agreed payment is made under a life-assurance policy. The life assured need not be the owner of the policy.

lifebelt *n.* buoyant belt for keeping a person afloat.

lifeblood *n.* **1** blood, as being necessary to life. **2** vital factor or influence.

lifeboat *n.* **1** special boat for rescuing those in distress at sea. **2** ship's small boat for use in emergency. **3** fund set up to rescue dealers on an exchange in the event of a market collapse and the ensuing insolvencies.

lifebuoy *n.* buoyant support for keeping a person afloat.

life cycle *n.* **1** series of changes in the life of an organism, including reproduction. **2** series of phases in the duration of a computer system, computer program, etc., including design, production, testing, and operation. **3** see FAMILY LIFE CYCLE. **4** see PRODUCT LIFE CYCLE.

◆ **life-cycle hypothesis** *n. Econ.* hypothesis that an individual's consumption over any period is proportional to expected wealth. For example, an individual with a strong expectation of success in later life will borrow to finance consumption in early life. This hypothesis is now considered more acceptable than either Keynesian theo-

Liechtenstein /ˈlɪktən͵staɪn/, **Principality of** small country in central Europe, in the Rhine valley between Switzerland and Austria. In terms of GNP per capita, Liechtenstein is one of the richest nations in the world. Since the Second World War agriculture has declined in favour of light industries, esp. metals, light engineering, machinery, precision instruments, textiles, chemicals, furniture, and ceramics. The banking sector is of major importance and many foreign companies have nominal offices in the principality as firms pay no tax on profit or income. Sales of postage stamps to tourists are another source of income. The principality, which was created in 1719, became a member of Efta in 1991 and joined the European Economic Area in 1995. Head of state, Prince Hans Adam II; prime minister, Mario Frick; capital, Vaduz. □ **Liechtensteiner** *n.*

language	German
currency	Swiss franc (SwF) of 100 centimes (or rappen)
pop. (1990)	31 400
GNP (1991)	US$978M
literacy	100%
life expectancy	66 (m); 77 (f)

ries of consumption or the permanent income hypothesis, which are both based on current income rather than wealth.

lifeguard *n.* expert swimmer employed to rescue bathers from drowning.

Life Guards *n.pl.* regiment of the royal household cavalry.

life insurance *n.* = LIFE ASSURANCE.

life-jacket *n.* buoyant jacket for keeping a person afloat.

lifeless *adj.* **1** dead. **2** unconscious. **3** lacking movement or vitality. □ **lifelessly** *adv.* [Old English]

lifelike *adj.* closely resembling life or the person or thing represented.

lifeline *n.* **1** rope etc. used for life-saving. **2** sole means of communication or transport.

lifelong *adj.* lasting a lifetime.

♦ **life office** *n.* company that provides life assurance.

life peer *n.* peer whose title lapses on death.

life-preserver *n.* **1** short stick with a heavily loaded end. **2** life-jacket etc.

lifer *n. slang* person serving a life sentence.

life sciences *n.pl.* biology and related subjects.

life sentence *n.* sentence of imprisonment for an indefinite period.

life-size *adj.* (also **-sized**) of the same size as the person or thing represented.

lifestyle *n.* way of life of a person or group.

♦ **lifestyle business** *n.* small business in which the owners are more anxious to pursue the interests that reflect their lifestyle than to make more than a comfortable living.

life-support machine *n.* respirator.

lifetime *n.* **1** duration of a person's life. **2** time during which something functions, is useful, etc.

♦ **lifetime transfer** *n.* gift made between living people, which may have to be taken into account for inheritance tax. Certain transfers are exempt, e.g. transfers between spouses, certain marriage, charitable, or political gifts, and annual gifts of less than a specified sum. A tapering relief is given for lifetime transfers made over the seven years prior to the donor's death, while gifts made seven years before death escape tax.

♦ **LIFFE** /laɪf/ *abbr.* = LONDON INTERNATIONAL FINANCIAL FUTURES AND OPTIONS EXCHANGE.

LIFO /ˈlaɪfəʊ/ *abbr.* = LAST IN, FIRST OUT.

lift –*v.* **1** (often foll. by *up*, *off*, *out*, etc.) raise or remove to a higher position. **2** go up; be raised; yield to an upward force. **3** give an upward direction to (the eyes or face). **4** elevate to a higher plane of thought or feeling. **5** (of fog etc.) rise, disperse. **6** remove (a barrier or restriction). **7** transport (supplies, troops, etc.) by air. **8** *colloq.* **a** steal. **b** plagiarize (a passage of writing etc.). **9** dig up (esp. potatoes etc.). –*n.* **1** lifting or being lifted. **2** ride in another person's vehicle (*gave them a lift*). **3 a** apparatus for raising and lowering persons or things to different floors of a building etc. **b** apparatus for carrying persons up or down a mountain etc. **4 a** transport by air. **b** quantity of goods transported by air. **5** upward pressure which air exerts on an aerofoil. **6** supporting or elevating influence; feeling of elation. □ **lift down** pick up and bring to a lower position. [Old Norse: related to LOFT]

lift-off *n.* vertical take-off of a spacecraft or rocket.

ligament /ˈlɪgəmənt/ *n.* band of tough fibrous tissue linking bones. [Latin *ligo* bind]

ligature /ˈlɪgətʃə(r)/ –*n.* **1** tie or bandage. **2** *Mus.* slur, tie. **3** two or more letters joined, e.g. æ. **4** bond; thing that unites. –*v.* (**-ring**) bind or connect with a ligature. [Latin *ligo* bind]

■ **Usage** Sense 3 of this word is sometimes confused with *digraph*, which means 'two separate letters together representing one sound'.

light[1] /laɪt/ –*n.* **1** the natural agent (electromagnetic radiation) that stimulates sight and makes things visible. **2** the medium or condition of the space in which this is present (*just enough light to see*). **3** appearance of brightness (*saw a distant light*). **4** source of light, e.g. the sun, a lamp, fire, etc. **5** (often in *pl.*) traffic-light. **6 a** flame or spark serving to ignite. **b** device producing this. **7** aspect in which a thing is regarded (*appeared in a new light*). **8 a** mental illumination. **b** spiritual illumination by divine truth. **9** vivacity etc. in a person's face, esp. in the eyes. **10** eminent person (*leading light*). **11** bright parts of a picture etc. **12** window or opening in a wall to let light in. –*v.* (*past* **lit**; *past part.* **lit** or **lighted**) (*attrib.*) **1** set burning; begin to burn. **2** (often foll. by *up*) provide with light or lighting; make prominent by means of light. **3** show (a person) the way or surroundings with a light. **4** (usu. foll. by *up*) (of the face or eyes) brighten with animation, pleasure, etc. –*adj.* **1** well provided with light; not dark. **2** (of a colour) pale (*light blue*; *light-blue ribbon*). □ **bring** (or **come) to light** reveal or be revealed. **in a good** (or **bad) light** giving a favourable (or unfavourable) impression. **in the light of** taking account of. **light up 1** *colloq.* begin to smoke a cigarette etc. **2** = sense 2 of *v.* **3** = sense 4 of *v.* □ **lightish** *adj.* [Old English]

light[2] /laɪt/ –*adj.* **1** not heavy. **2 a** relatively low in weight, amount, density, intensity, etc. (*light arms, traffic, metal, rain*). **b** deficient in weight (*light coin*). **3 a** carrying or suitable for small loads (*light railway*). **b** (of a ship) unladen. **c** carrying only light arms, armaments, etc. **4** (of food) easy to digest. **5** (of entertainment, music, etc.) intended for amusement only; not profound. **6** (of sleep or a sleeper) easily disturbed. **7** easily borne or done (*light duties*). **8** nimble; quick-moving (*light step*; *light rhythm*). **9** (of a building etc.) graceful, elegant. **10 a** free from sorrow; cheerful (*light heart*). **b** giddy (*light in the head*). –*adv.* **1** in a light manner (*tread light*; *sleep light*). **2** with a minimum load (*travel light*). –*v.* (*past* and *past part.* **lit** or **lighted**) (foll. by *on*, *upon*) come upon or find by chance. □ **make light of** treat as unimportant. □ **lightish** *adj.* **lightly** *adv.* **lightness** *n.* [Old English]

light-bulb *n.* glass bulb containing an inert gas and a metal filament, providing light when an electric current is passed through it.

♦ **light dues** *n.pl.* levy on shipowners for maintaining lighthouses, beacons, buoys, etc., collected in the UK by HM Customs and Excise on behalf of Trinity House.

lighten[1] *v.* **1 a** make or become lighter in weight. **b** reduce the weight or load of. **2** bring relief to (the mind etc.). **3** mitigate (a penalty).

lighten[2] *v.* **1** shed light on. **2** make or grow bright.

lighter[1] *n.* device for lighting cigarettes etc.

lighter[2] *n.* boat, usu. flat-bottomed and without its own means of propulsion, for transferring goods, e.g. from a ship to a wharf or another ship. The charge for transporting goods by lighter is the **lighterage**. See also LASH. [Dutch: related to LIGHT[2] in the sense 'unload']

lighter-than-air *attrib. adj.* (of an aircraft) weighing less than the air it displaces.

light-fingered *adj.* given to stealing.

light flyweight *n.* **1** amateur boxing weight up to 48 kg. **2** amateur boxer of this weight.

light-footed *adj.* nimble.

light-headed *adj.* giddy, delirious. □ **light-headedness** *n.*

light-hearted *adj.* **1** cheerful. **2** (unduly) casual. □ **light-heartedly** *adv.*

light heavyweight *n.* (also **cruiserweight**) **1** weight in certain sports between middleweight and heavyweight, in amateur boxing 75–81 kg. **2** sportsman of this weight.

lighthouse *n.* tower etc. containing a beacon light to warn or guide ships at sea.

light industry *n.* manufacture of small or light articles.

lighting *n.* **1** equipment in a room or street etc. for producing light. **2** arrangement or effect of lights.

lighting-up time *n.* time after which vehicles must show the prescribed lights.

light meter *n.* instrument for measuring the intensity of the light, esp. to show the correct photographic exposure.

light middleweight *n.* **1** weight in amateur boxing of 67–71 kg. **2** amateur boxer of this weight.

lightning *–n.* flash of bright light produced by an electric discharge between clouds or between clouds and the ground. *–attrib. adj.* very quick. [from LIGHTEN[2]]

lightning-conductor *n.* (also **lightning-rod**) metal rod or wire fixed to an exposed part of a building or to a mast to divert lightning into the earth or sea.

light pen *n.* hand-held penlike instrument used together with a computer display device for the input of data to a computer graphics system. Its main function is to point to small areas of the screen, e.g. a single character or a small graphical object; it can also be used to draw shapes on the screen.

lights *n.pl.* lungs of sheep, pigs, etc., used as a food esp. for pets. [from LIGHT[2]: cf. LUNG]

lightship *n.* moored or anchored ship with a beacon light.

lightweight *–adj.* **1** of below average weight. **2** of little importance or influence. *–n.* **1** lightweight person, animal, or thing. **2 a** weight in certain sports between featherweight and welterweight, in amateur boxing 57–60 kg. **b** sportsman of this weight.

light welterweight *n.* **1** weight in amateur boxing of 60–63.5 kg. **2** amateur boxer of this weight.

light-year *n.* distance light travels in one year, nearly 6 million million miles.

ligneous /'lɪgnɪəs/ *adj.* **1** (of a plant) woody. **2** of the nature of wood. [Latin *lignum* wood]

lignite /'lɪgnaɪt/ *n.* brown coal of woody texture.

lignum vitae /ˌlɪgnəm 'vaɪtɪ/ *n.* a hard-wooded tree. [Latin, = wood of life]

Liguria /laɪ'dʒʊərɪə/ region of N Italy; industries include tourism, engineering, and petrochemicals; pop. (est. 1994) 1 662 658; capital, Genoa.

likable var. of LIKEABLE.

♦ **Li Ka-Shing** /liː 'kɑː'ʃɪŋ/ (1928–) Hong Kong industrialist, financier, and property developer. In 1979 his company, Cheung Kong Holdings, bought a large stake in the first company to be registered in Hong Kong, Huchinson Whampoa Ltd. In 1997 the market value of his holdings was $70 billion – some 13% of the Hong Kong stock market.

---

like[1] *–adj.* (**more like, most like**) **1 a** having some or all of the qualities of another, each other, or an original. **b** resembling in some way, such as (*good writers like Dickens*). **2** characteristic of (*not like them to be late*). **3** in a suitable state or mood for (*felt like working*; *felt like a cup of tea*). *–prep.* in the manner of; to the same degree as (*drink like a fish*; *acted like an idiot*). *–adv.* **1** *slang* so to speak (*did a quick getaway, like*). **2** *colloq.* likely, probably (*as like as not*). *–conj. colloq.* **1** as (*cannot do it like you do*). **2** as if (*ate like they were starving*). *–n.* **1** counterpart; equal; similar person or thing. **2** (prec. by *the*) thing or things of the same kind (*will never do the like again*). □ **and the like** and similar things. **like anything** *colloq.* very much, vigorously. **the likes of** *colloq.* a person such as. **more like it** *colloq.* nearer what is required. **what is he** (or **it** etc.) **like?** what sort of person is he (or thing is it etc.)? [Old English]

■ **Usage** The use of *like* as a conjunction is considered incorrect by some people.

like[2] *–v.* (**-king**) **1** find agreeable or enjoyable. **2 a** choose to have; prefer (*like my tea weak*). **b** wish for or be inclined to (*would like a nap*; *should like to come*). *–n.* (in *pl.*) things one likes or prefers. [Old English]

-like *comb. form* forming adjectives from nouns, meaning 'similar to, characteristic of' (*doglike*; *shell-like*; *tortoise-like*).

■ **Usage** In formations not generally current the hyphen should be used. It may be omitted when the first element is of one syllable, unless it ends in *-l*.

likeable *adj.* (also **likable**) pleasant; easy to like. □ **likeably** *adv.*

likelihood /'laɪklɪˌhʊd/ *n.* probability. □ **in all likelihood** very probably.

likely /'laɪklɪ/ *–adj.* (**-ier, -iest**) **1** probable; such as may well happen or be true. **2** to be reasonably expected (*not likely to come now*). **3** promising; apparently suitable (*a likely spot*). *–adv.* probably. □ **not likely!** *colloq.* certainly not, I refuse. [Old Norse: related to LIKE[1]]

like-minded *adj.* having the same tastes, opinions, etc.

liken *v.* (foll. by *to*) point out the resemblance of (a person or thing to another). [from LIKE[1]]

likeness *n.* **1** (usu. foll. by *between*, *to*) resemblance. **2** (foll. by *of*) semblance or guise (*in the likeness of a ghost*). **3** portrait, representation.

likewise *adv.* **1** also, moreover. **2** similarly (*do likewise*).

liking *n.* **1** what one likes; one's taste (*is it to your liking?*). **2** (foll. by *for*) regard or fondness; taste or fancy.

lilac /'laɪlək/ *–n.* **1** shrub with fragrant pinkish-violet or white blossoms. **2** pale pinkish-violet colour. *–adj.* of this colour. [Persian]

lilangeni /lɪlən'geɪniː/ *n.* (*pl.* **emalangeni** /ˌemələn-/) standard monetary unit of Swaziland. [African language]

liliaceous /ˌlɪlɪ'eɪʃəs/ *adj.* of the lily family. [related to LILY]

Lille /liːl/ city in NW France, capital of Nord-Pas-de-Calais region; industries include chemicals, machinery, textiles, and brewing; pop. (1990) 178 301.

lilliputian /ˌlɪlɪ'pjuːʃ(ə)n/ *–n.* diminutive person or thing. *–adj.* diminutive. [*Lilliput* in Swift's *Gulliver's Travels*]

Lilo /'laɪləʊ/ *n.* (*pl.* **-s**) (also **Li-Lo** *propr.*) type of inflatable mattress. [from *lie low*]

Lilongwe /lɪ'lɒŋweɪ/ capital of Malawi; products include tobacco and textiles; pop. (est. 1994) 395 500.

lilt *–n.* **1** light springing rhythm. **2** tune with this. *–v.* (esp. as **lilting** *adj.*) speak etc. with a lilt; have a lilt. [origin unknown]

lily /'lɪlɪ/ *n.* (*pl.* **-ies**) **1** bulbous plant with large trumpet-shaped flowers on a tall stem. **2** heraldic fleur-de-lis. [Latin *lilium*]

lily-livered *adj.* cowardly.

lily of the valley *n.* plant with white bell-shaped fragrant flowers.

lily white *adj.* & *n.* (as adj. often hyphenated) pure white.

Lima /'liːmə/ capital of Peru; manufactures include textiles, plastics, chemicals, machinery, and synthetic fibres; pop. (1993) 421 570.

Limassol /'lɪməˌsɒl/ port on the S coast of Cyprus; exports include wine and fruit; pop. (est. 1994) 143 400.

limb[1] /lɪm/ *n.* **1** arm, leg, or wing. **2** large branch of a tree. **3** branch of a cross. □ **out on a limb** isolated. [Old English]

limb[2] /lɪm/ *n.* specified edge of the sun, moon, etc. [Latin *limbus* hem, border]

limber[1] *–adj.* **1** lithe. **2** flexible. *–v.* (usu. foll. by *up*) **1** make (oneself or a part of the body etc.) supple. **2** warm up in preparation for athletic etc. activity. [origin uncertain]

limber[2] *–n.* detachable front part of a gun-carriage. *–v.* attach a limber to. [perhaps from Latin *limo -onis* shaft]

limbo[1] /'lɪmbəʊ/ *n.* (*pl.* **-s**) **1** (in some Christian beliefs) supposed abode of the souls of unbaptized infants, and of the just who died before Christ. **2** intermediate state or condition of awaiting a decision etc. [Latin *in limbo*: related to LIMB[2]]

limbo[2] /'lɪmbəʊ/ *n.* (*pl.* **-s**) West Indian dance in which the dancer bends backwards to pass under a horizontal bar which is progressively lowered. [West Indian word, perhaps = LIMBER[1]]

Limburg /'lɪmbɜːg/ **1** (French **Limbourg** /læ̃bʊəg/) province of NE Belgium; coalmining and dairy farming are important; pop. (1995) 771 613; capital, Hasselt. **2** mainly agricultural province of the SE Netherlands; pop. (est. 1995) 1 130 050; capital, Maastricht.

lime[1] *–n.* **1** (in full **quicklime**) white substance (calcium oxide) obtained by heating limestone. **2** (in full **slaked lime**) calcium hydroxide obtained by reacting quicklime with water, used as a fertilizer and in making mortar. *–v.* (**-ming**) treat with lime. □ **limy** *adj.* (**-ier, -iest**). [Old English]

lime[2] *n.* **1 a** fruit like a lemon but green, rounder, smaller, and more acid. **b** tree which produces this fruit. **2** (in full **lime-green**) yellowish-green colour. [French from Arabic]

lime[3] *n.* (in full **lime-tree**) tree with heart-shaped leaves and fragrant creamy blossom. [alteration of *line* = Old English *lind* = LINDEN]

LIMEAN /'li:mi:n/ *abbr.* London Inter-Bank Mean Rate.

limekiln *n.* kiln for heating limestone.

limelight *n.* **1** intense white light used formerly in theatres. **2** (prec. by *the*) the glare of publicity.

Limerick /'lɪmərɪk/ **1** county in the SW Republic of Ireland, in the province of Munster; dairy farming is the main activity; pop. (est. 1991) 161 856. **2** its capital city, a port on the River Shannon with flour-milling, tanning, and brewing industries; pop. (est. 1991) 52 040.

limerick /'lɪmərɪk/ *n.* humorous five-line verse with a rhyme-scheme *aabba*. [origin uncertain]

limestone *n.* rock composed mainly of calcium carbonate.

Limey /'laɪmɪ/ *n.* (*pl.* **-s**) *US slang offens.* British person (orig. a sailor) or ship. [from LIME[2], because of the former enforced consumption of lime juice in the British Navy]

limit /'lɪmɪt/ *–n.* **1** point, line, or level beyond which something does not or may not extend or pass. **2** greatest or smallest amount permissible. **3** *Finance* **a** (also **limit order**) order given by an investor to a stockbroker or commodity broker restricting a particular purchase to a stated maximum price or a particular sale to a stated minimum price. The order will also be restricted as to time; it may be given firm for a stated period or firm until cancelled. **b** maximum fluctuation (up or down) allowed in certain markets over a stated period (usu. one day's trading). In some volatile circumstances the market moves the limit up (or down). *–v.* (**-t-**) **1** set or serve as a limit to. **2** (foll. by *to*) restrict. □ **at limit** *Finance* at a stated limiting price (i.e. not above a stated price if buying or not below a stated price if selling): an instruction to a broker to buy or sell shares, stocks, commodities, currencies, etc. as specified. When issuing such an instruction the principal should also state for how long the instruction stands. Cf. *at best* (see BEST). **be the limit** *colloq.* be intolerable. **within limits** with some degree of freedom. □ **limitless** *adj.* [Latin *limes limit-* boundary, frontier]

limitation /,lɪmɪ'teɪʃ(ə)n/ *n.* **1** limiting or being limited. **2** limit (of ability etc.) (often in *pl.*: *know one's limitations*). **3** limiting circumstance.

◆ **limitation of actions** *n. Law* legally specified period beyond which civil actions cannot be brought. Actions in simple contract and tort must be brought within six years of the cause of action. There are several special rules, including that for strict liability actions for defective products, in which case the period is three years from the accrual of the cause of action or (if later) the date on which the plaintiff knew, or should have known, the material facts, but not later than ten years from the date on which the product was first put into circulation. The present UK law is contained in the Limitations Act (1980), the Latent Damage Act (1986), and the Consumer Protection Act (1987).

limited *adj.* **1** confined within limits. **2** not great in scope or talents. **3** restricted to a few examples (*limited edition*). **4** (after a company name) being a limited company.

◆ **limited carrier** see CARRIER 2.

limited company *n.* (also **limited liability company**) company whose members are legally responsible only to a specified amount for its debts. The liability may be **limited by shares**, in which case the liability of the members on a winding-up is limited to the amount (if any) unpaid on their shares. This is by far the most common type of registered company. The liability of the members may alternatively be **limited by guarantee**; in this case the liability of members is limited by the company memorandum to a certain amount, which the members undertake to contribute on winding-up. These are usu. societies, clubs, or trade associations. Since 1980 it has not been possible for such a company to be formed with a share capital, or converted to a company limited by guarantee with a share capital. See also PUBLIC LIMITED COMPANY.

◆ **limited liability** see LIMITED COMPANY.

◆ **limited market** *n.* financial market for a particular security in which buying and selling is difficult, usu. because a large part of the issue is held by very few people or institutions.

◆ **limited partner** see PARTNERSHIP 3.

◆ **limited recourse finance** *n.* loan made to a company established by a property developer to manage a specific project, in which the lender has no recourse to the developer's other assets.

◆ **limit order** *n.* = LIMIT *n.* 3a.

◆ **limit price** *n.* highest price that established sellers in a market can charge for a product, without inducing a new seller to enter the market. The limit price is usu. lower than the monopoly price but higher than the competitive price. It enables established sellers to make higher profits than they would if they sold at the competitive price and it also ensures that new firms will not enter the market and drive the prices down to competitive levels.

limn /lɪm/ *v. archaic* paint. [French *luminer* from Latin *lumino* ILLUMINATE]

Límnos see LEMNOS.

limo /'lɪməʊ/ *n.* (*pl.* **-s**) *US colloq.* limousine. [abbreviation]

Limoges /lɪ'məʊʒ/ city in W central France, capital of Limousin region, centre of French porcelain production; pop. (1990) 175 646.

Limón /lɪ'məʊn/ (also **Puerto Limón** /'pwɜ:təʊ/) chief Caribbean port of Costa Rica; pop. (1995) 56 525.

Limousin /,lɪmu:'sæ̃/ region of central France; pop. (est. 1994) 719 347; capital, Limoges.

limousine /,lɪmʊ'zi:n/ *n.* large luxurious car. [French]

limp[1] *–v.* walk or proceed lamely or awkwardly. *–n.* lame walk. [perhaps from obsolete *limphalt*: related to HALT[2]]

limp[2] *adj.* **1** not stiff or firm. **2** without energy or will. □ **limply** *adv.* **limpness** *n.* [perhaps from LIMP[1]]

limpet /'lɪmpɪt/ *n.* marine gastropod with a conical shell, sticking tightly to rocks. [Old English]

limpet mine *n.* delayed-action mine attached to a ship's hull.

limpid /'lɪmpɪd/ *adj.* clear, transparent. □ **limpidity** /-'pɪdɪtɪ/ *n.* [Latin]

linage /'laɪnɪdʒ/ *n.* **1** number of lines in printed or written matter. **2** payment by the line.

linchpin *n.* **1** pin passed through an axle-end to keep a wheel in position. **2** person or thing vital to an organization etc. [Old English *lynis* = axle-tree]

Lincoln /'lɪŋkən/ **1** city in the US, capital of Nebraska; industries include engineering, oil refining, and food processing; pop. (est. 1994) 203 076. **2** city in E England, county town of Lincolnshire; manufactures include machinery, radios, and metal goods; pop. (1991) 80 281.

Lincolnshire /'lɪŋkən,ʃɪə(r)/ county in E England; pop. (est. 1994) 605 600; county town, Lincoln. It is mainly an agricultural and horticultural region.

Lincs. *abbr.* Lincolnshire.

linctus /ˈlɪŋktəs/ *n.* syrupy medicine, esp. a soothing cough mixture. [Latin *lingo* lick]

linden /ˈlɪnd(ə)n/ *n.* lime-tree. [Old English *lind(e)*]

line[1] –*n.* **1** continuous mark made on a surface. **2** similar mark, esp. a furrow or wrinkle. **3** use of lines in art. **4 a** straight or curved continuous extent of length without breadth. **b** track of a moving point. **5** contour or outline (*has a slimming line*). **6 a** curve connecting all points having a specified common property. **b** (**the Line**) the Equator. **7 a** limit or boundary. **b** mark limiting the area of play, the starting or finishing point in a race, etc. **8 a** row of persons or things. **b** direction as indicated by them. **c** *US* queue. **9 a** row of printed or written words. **b** portion of verse written in one line. **10** (in *pl.*) **a** piece of poetry. **b** words of an actor's part. **c** specified amount of text etc. to be written out as a school punishment. **11** short letter or note (*drop me a line*). **12** length of cord, rope, etc., usu. serving a specified purpose. **13 a** wire or cable for a telephone or telegraph. **b** connection by means of this. **14 a** single track of a railway. **b** one branch or route of a railway system, or the whole system under one management. **15 a** regular succession of buses, ships, aircraft, etc., plying between certain places. **b** company conducting this. **16** connected series of persons following one another in time (esp. several generations of a family); stock. **17** course or manner of procedure, conduct, thought, etc. (*along these lines*; *don't take that line*). **18** direction, course, or channel (*lines of communication*). **19** department of activity; branch of business. **20** type of product (*new line in hats*). **21 a** connected series of military fieldworks. **b** arrangement of soldiers or ships side by side. **22** each of the very narrow horizontal sections forming a television picture. **23** level of the base of most letters in printing and writing. –*v.* (**-ning**) **1** mark with lines. **2** cover with lines. **3** position or stand at intervals along (*crowds lined the route*). □ **all along the line** at every point. **bring into line** make conform. **come into line** conform. **get a line on** *colloq.* get information about. **in line for** likely to receive. **in** (or **out of) line with** in (or not in) accordance with. **lay** (or **put) it on the line** *colloq.* speak frankly. **line up 1** arrange or be arranged in a line or lines. **2** have ready. **out of line** not in alignment; inappropriate. [Latin *linea* from *linum* flax]

line[2] *v.* (**-ning**) **1** cover the inside surface of (a garment, box, etc.) with a layer of usu. different material. **2** serve as a lining for. **3** *colloq.* fill, esp. plentifully. [obsolete *line* linen used for linings]

lineage /ˈlɪnɪɪdʒ/ *n.* lineal descent; ancestry. [Latin: related to LINE[1]]

lineal /ˈlɪnɪəl/ *adj.* **1** in the direct line of descent or ancestry. **2** linear. □ **lineally** *adv.*

lineament /ˈlɪnɪəmənt/ *n.* (usu. in *pl.*) distinctive feature or characteristic, esp. of the face. [Latin: related to LINE[1]]

♦ **line and staff management** *n.* system of management used in large organizations in which there are two separate hierarchies: the **line management** side consists of **line managers** with responsibility for deciding the policy of and running the organization's main activities (manufacturing, sales, etc.), while the **staff management**, and its separate **staff managers**, are responsible for providing such supporting services as warehousing, accounting, transport, personnel management, and plant maintenance.

---

linear /ˈlɪnɪə(r)/ *adj.* **1** of or in lines. **2** long and narrow and of uniform breadth. □ **linearity** /-ˈærɪtɪ/ *n.* **linearly** *adv.*

Linear B *n.* form of Bronze Age writing found in Greece: an earlier undeciphered form (**Linear A**) also exists.

♦ **linear depreciation** *n.* depreciation charges that when plotted on a graph against time yield a straight line, as a constant amount is written off the asset each accounting period.

---

lineation /ˌlɪnɪˈeɪʃ(ə)n/ *n.* marking with or drawing of lines.

line-drawing *n.* drawing in which images are produced with lines.

♦ **line extending** *n.* increasing a line of products by adding variations of an existing brand. For example, Coca Cola extended its line with Diet Coke. Line extending runs the risk of weakening the brand name. Cf. LINE FILLING.

---

line feed *n. Computing* **1** means by which the paper in a printer is moved up a specified number of lines until the printing mechanism is opposite the next line to be printed. **2** means by which the cursor on a screen is moved down one line.

♦ **line filling** *n.* adding products to an existing line of products in order to leave no opportunities for competitors. In **horizontal line filling**, a video manufacturer may produce machines with a variety of features (half-speed copying, multi-recording memory, etc.) at the top end of the price range, and relatively cheap cost-effective machines at the opposite end; a competitor can therefore only compete on price. In **vertical line-filling** a manufacturer may produce a wide variety of brand names within a single product line; some detergent manufacturers do this. Cf. LINE EXTENDING.

Line Islands group of eleven islands in the central Pacific Ocean, eight of which are part of the Republic of Kiribati; the remaining three are uninhabited dependencies of the US.

♦ **line management** see LINE AND STAFF MANAGEMENT.

---

linen /ˈlɪnɪn/ –*n.* **1** cloth woven from flax. **2** (*collect.*) articles made or orig. made of linen, as sheets, shirts, underwear, etc. –*adj.* made of linen. [Old English: related to Latin *linum* flax]

linen basket *n.* basket for dirty washing.

line of fire *n.* expected path of gunfire etc.

line of vision *n.* straight line along which an observer looks.

line-out *n.* (in Rugby) parallel lines of opposing forwards at right angles to the touchline for the throwing in of the ball.

line printer *n.* machine that prints output from a computer a line at a time, at a rate of up to several thousand lines per minute. Line printers may be impact or non-impact printers (see PRINTER 3).

liner[1] *n.* ship or aircraft etc. carrying passengers on a regular line. See also SHIPPING CONFERENCE.

liner[2] *n.* removable lining.

linesman *n.* umpire's or referee's assistant who decides whether a ball has fallen within the playing area or not.

line-up *n.* **1** line of people for inspection. **2** arrangement of persons in a team, band, etc.

ling[1] *n.* (*pl.* same) long slender marine fish. [probably Dutch]

ling[2] *n.* any of various heathers. [Old Norse]

-ling *suffix* **1** denoting a person or thing: **a** connected with (*hireling*). **b** having the property of being (*weakling*) or undergoing (*starveling*). **2** denoting a diminutive (*duckling*), often derogatory (*lordling*). [Old English]

linger /ˈlɪŋgə(r)/ *v.* **1** stay about. **2** (foll. by *over*, *on*, etc.) dally (*linger over dinner*; *lingered on the final note*). **3** (esp. of an illness) be protracted. **4** (often foll. by *on*) be slow in dying. [Old English *lengan*: related to LONG[1]]

lingerie /ˈlæ̃ʒərɪ/ *n.* women's underwear and nightclothes. [French *linge* linen]

lingo /ˈlɪŋgəʊ/ *n.* (*pl.* **-s** or **-es**) *colloq.* **1** foreign language. **2** vocabulary of a special subject or group. [probably from Portuguese *lingoa* from Latin *lingua* tongue]

lingua franca /ˌlɪŋgwə ˈfræŋkə/ *n.* (*pl.* **lingua francas**) **1** language used in common by speakers with different native languages. **2** system for mutual understanding. [Italian, = Frankish tongue]

lingual /ˈlɪŋgw(ə)l/ *adj.* **1** of or formed by the tongue. **2**

of speech or languages. □ **lingually** *adv.* [Latin *lingua* tongue, language]

linguist /ˈlɪŋɡwɪst/ *n.* person skilled in languages or linguistics.

linguistic /lɪŋˈɡwɪstɪk/ *adj.* of language or the study of languages. □ **linguistically** *adv.*

linguistics *n.* the study of language and its structure.

liniment /ˈlɪnɪmənt/ *n.* embrocation. [Latin *linio* smear]

lining *n.* material which lines a surface etc.

link –*n.* **1** one loop or ring of a chain etc. **2 a** connecting part; one in a series. **b** state or means of connection. **3** cuff-link. –*v.* **1** (foll. by *together*, *to*, *with*) connect or join (two things or one to another). **2** clasp or intertwine (hands or arms). **3** (foll. by *on*, *to*, *in to*) be joined; attach oneself to (a system, company, etc.). □ **link up** (foll. by *with*) connect or combine. □ **linker** *n.* [Old Norse]

linkage *n.* **1** linking or being linked, esp. the linking of quite different political issues in negotiations. **2** link or system of links.

link editor *n.* (also **linkage editor**, **linker**) *Computing* utility program that combines a number of user-written or library routines, which have already been compiled or assembled but are individually incomplete, into a single executable program. This program is then either stored on disk or placed in main store for immediate execution.

◆ **Linkline** *n. propr.* telephone service provided by British Telecom for advertisers of a wide variety of goods and services. Customers call Linkline, either free or at a local charge, and the rest of the charge is paid by the advertiser.

linkman *n.* person providing continuity in a broadcast programme.

Linköping /lɪnˈkɜːpɪŋ/ industrial town in SE Sweden; manufactures include cars and textiles; pop. (est. 1996) 131 370.

links *n.pl.* (treated as *sing.* or *pl.*) golf-course. [Old English, = rising ground]

link-up *n.* act or result of linking up.

Linnaean *adj.* of Linnaeus or his system of classifying plants and animals.

■ **Usage** This word is spelt *Linnean* in *Linnean Society*.

linnet /ˈlɪnɪt/ *n.* brown-grey finch. [French *linnette* from *lin* flax, because it eats flax-seed]

lino /ˈlaɪnəʊ/ *n.* (*pl.* **-s**) linoleum. [abbreviation]

linocut *n.* **1** design carved in relief on a block of linoleum. **2** print made from this.

linoleum /lɪˈnəʊlɪəm/ *n.* canvas-backed material thickly coated with a preparation of linseed oil and powdered cork etc., esp. as a floor covering. [Latin *linum* flax, *oleum* oil]

linseed /ˈlɪnsiːd/ *n.* seed of flax. [Old English: related to LINE[1]]

linseed oil *n.* oil extracted from linseed and used in paint and varnish.

linsey-woolsey /ˌlɪnzɪˈwʊlzɪ/ *n.* fabric of coarse wool woven on a cotton warp. [probably from *Lindsey* in Suffolk + WOOL]

lint *n.* **1** linen or cotton with a raised nap on one side, used for dressing wounds. **2** fluff. [perhaps from French *linette* from *lin* flax]

lintel /ˈlɪnt(ə)l/ *n.* horizontal timber, stone, etc., across the top of a door or window. [French: related to LIMIT]

Linz /lɪnts/ industrial city in N Austria, a port on the River Danube; iron and steel are processed; pop. (est. 1991) 202 855.

lion /ˈlaɪən/ *n.* **1** (*fem.* **lioness**) large tawny flesh-eating wild cat of Africa and S Asia. **2** (**the Lion**) zodiacal sign or constellation Leo. **3** brave or celebrated person. [Latin *leo*]

lion-heart *n.* courageous person. □ **lion-hearted** *adj.*

lionize *v.* (also **-ise**) (**-zing** or **-sing**) treat as a celebrity.

lion's share *n.* largest or best part.

LIP *abbr.* life insurance policy.

lip –*n.* **1** either of the two fleshy parts forming the edges of the mouth-opening. **2** edge of a cup, vessel, etc., esp. the part shaped for pouring from. **3** *colloq.* impudent talk. –*v.* (**-pp-**) **1** touch with the lips; apply the lips to. **2** touch lightly. □ **lipped** *adj.* (also in *comb.*). [Old English]

Lipari Islands /ˈlɪpərɪ/ (also **Aeolian Islands**) group of seven Italian volcanic islands in the Mediterranean Sea, N of Sicily; exports include pumice stone and fruit; pop. (est. 1987) 10 300; chief town, Lipari (on Lipari).

lipid /ˈlɪpɪd/ *n.* any of a group of fatlike substances that are insoluble in water but soluble in organic solvents, including fatty acids, oils, waxes, and steroids. [Greek *lipos* fat]

liposuction /ˈlaɪpəʊˌsʌkʃ(ə)n/ *n.* technique in cosmetic surgery for removing excess fat from under the skin by suction.

lip-read *v.* understand (speech) from observing a speaker's lip-movements.

lip-service *n.* insincere expression of support etc.

lipstick *n.* stick of cosmetic for colouring the lips.

liquefy /ˈlɪkwɪˌfaɪ/ *v.* (**-ies, -ied**) make or become liquid. □ **liquefaction** /-ˈfækʃ(ə)n/ *n.* [Latin: related to LIQUID]

liqueur /lɪˈkjʊə(r)/ *n.* any of several strong sweet alcoholic spirits. [French]

liquid /ˈlɪkwɪd/ –*adj.* **1** having a consistency like that of water or oil, flowing freely but of constant volume. **2** having the qualities of water in appearance. **3** (of sounds) clear and pure. –*n.* **1** liquid substance. **2** *Phonet.* sound of *l* or *r*. [Latin *liqueo* be liquid]

◆ **liquid assets** *n.pl.* (also **liquid capital**, **quick assets**, **realizable assets**) assets held in cash or in something that can be readily turned into cash (e.g. deposits in a bank current account, trade debts, marketable investments). See also LIQUID RATIO.

liquidate /ˈlɪkwɪˌdeɪt/ *v.* (**-ting**) **1** wind up the affairs of (a company) by ascertaining liabilities and apportioning assets (see also LIQUIDATION; LIQUIDATOR). **2** pay off (a debt). **3** wipe out, kill. [medieval Latin: related to LIQUID]

◆ **liquidated damages** see DAMAGES.

liquidation /ˌlɪkwɪˈdeɪʃ(ə)n/ *n.* **1** (also **winding-up**) distribution of a company's assets among its creditors and members prior to its dissolution, so bringing the life of the company to an end. See also CREDITORS' VOLUNTARY LIQUIDATION; MEMBERS' VOLUNTARY LIQUIDATION; COMPULSORY LIQUIDATION. **2** elimination; destruction. □ **go into liquidation** (of a company etc.) be wound up and have its assets apportioned.

◆ **liquidation committee** *n.* committee set up by creditors of a company being wound up in order to consent to the liquidator exercising certain powers. When the company is unable to pay its debts, the committee is usu. composed of creditors only; otherwise it consists of creditors and contributories.

◆ **liquidator** *n.* person appointed by a court, or by the members of a company or its creditors, to regularize the company's affairs on a liquidation. In the case of a members' voluntary liquidation, it is the members of the company who appoint the liquidator. In a creditors' voluntary liquidation, the liquidator may be appointed by company members before the **meeting of creditors** or by the creditors themselves at the meeting; in the former case the liquidator can only exercise his powers with the consent of the court. If two liquidators are appointed, the court resolves which one is to act. In a compulsory liquidation, the court appoints a provisional liquidator after the winding-up petition has been presented; after the order has been granted, the court appoints the official receiver as liquidator, until or unless another officer is appointed.

The liquidator is in a relationship of trust with the company and the creditors as a body; if appointed in a compulsory liquidation, he or she is an officer of the court, is under statutory obligations, and may not profit from the position. A liquidator must be a qualified insolvency practitioner. On appointment, the liquidator assumes control of the company, collects the assets, pays the debts, and distributes any surplus to company members according to their rights. In the case of a compulsory liquidation, the liquidator is supervised by the court, the liquidation committee, and the Department of Trade and Industry. He or she receives a statement of affairs from the company officers and must report on these to the court.

♦ **liquid capital** *n.* = LIQUID ASSETS.

liquid crystal *n.* turbid liquid with some order in its molecular arrangement.

liquid crystal display *n.* (also **LCD**) visual display in electronic devices, in which the reflectivity of a matrix of liquid crystals changes as a signal is applied. LCDs are used in digital watches and calculators as well as some small televisions and computers.

liquidity /lɪˈkwɪdɪtɪ/ *n.* (*pl.* **-ies**) **1** state of being liquid. **2** availability of liquid assets, enabling a person or organization to pay debts when they fall due and also to move into new investment opportunities.

♦ **liquidity-preference theory** *n. Econ.* theory associating the desire that people have to hold money with various motives, esp. transactions demand, precautionary demand, and speculative demand. First introduced by J. M. Keynes, this theory supplied a basis for many conclusions concerning the tendency of economies to suffer recession and depression, characterized by involuntary unemployment. Liquidity-preference theory rejects the loanable-funds theory and the natural rate of interest. It also underplays the role of the interest rate in ensuring that plans for present and future consumption are balanced (see TIME PREFERENCE), now seen as a fundamental weakness in the theory.

♦ **liquidity ratio** *n.* = CASH RATIO.

♦ **liquidity trap** *n.* situation that could arise in an economy in which interest rates have fallen so low that investors allow their preference for liquidity to prevent them from investing in bonds. The liquidity trap was described by J. M. Keynes in his general theory to point out that traditional views (now associated with monetarism) were inconsistent. As a result of the liquidity trap, falling investment could lead to falling aggregate demand as well as falling prices and wages, but with no tendency to restore equilibrium between aggregate supply and demand. Neoclassical economists were quick to point out that falling prices would increase the real value of consumers' wealth, thus increasing the demand for goods, which would lead to the restoration of (full-employment) equilibrium. The liquidity trap is now considered to have little practical relevance.

liquidize /ˈlɪkwɪˌdaɪz/ *v.* (also **-ise**) (**-zing** or **-sing**) reduce to a liquid state.

liquidizer *n.* (also **-iser**) machine for liquidizing foods.

♦ **liquid ratio** *n.* (also **acid-test ratio**) ratio of the liquid assets of an organization to its current liabilities. The liquid assets are usu. taken to be trade debt and cash and any other assets that are readily marketable. The ratio gives an indication of the organization's ability to pay its debts without needing to make further sales. It therefore provides the ultimate (acid-test) proof of its solvency.

liquor /ˈlɪkə(r)/ *n.* **1** alcoholic (esp. distilled) drink. **2** other liquid, esp. that produced in cooking. [Latin: related to LIQUID]

liquorice /ˈlɪkərɪs, -rɪʃ/ *n.* (also **licorice**) **1** black root extract used as a sweet and in medicine. **2** plant from which it is obtained. [Greek *glukus* sweet, *rhiza* root]

lira /ˈlɪərə/ *n.* (*pl.* **lire** pronunc. same or /-reɪ/) standard monetary unit of Italy, Malta, San Marino, Turkey, and Vatican City State. [Latin *libra* pound]

Lisbon /ˈlɪzbən/ (Portuguese **Lisboa** /liːʒˈbəʊə/) capital and chief port of Portugal; products include steel, textiles, chemicals, and pottery; pop. (1991) 681 063.

lisle /laɪl/ *n.* fine cotton thread for stockings etc. [LILLE]

lisp –*n.* speech defect in which *s* is pronounced like *th* in *thick* and *z* is pronounced like *th* in *this*. –*v.* speak or utter with a lisp. [Old English]

lissom /ˈlɪsəm/ *adj.* lithe, agile. [ultimately from LITHE]

list[1] –*n.* **1** number of items, names, etc., written or printed together as a record or aid to memory. **2** (in *pl.*) **a** palisades enclosing an area for a tournament. **b** scene of a contest. –*v.* **1** make a list of. **2** enter in a list. **3** (as **listed** *adj.*) **a** (of a building) of historical importance and officially protected. **b** see LISTED SECURITY. **c** see LISTED COMPANY. □ **enter the lists** issue or accept a challenge. [Old English]

list[2] –*v.* (of a ship etc.) lean over to one side. –*n.* process or instance of listing. [origin unknown]

♦ **listed company** *n.* company that has a listing agreement with the London Stock Exchange and whose shares therefore have a quotation on the main market. See LISTING REQUIREMENTS.

♦ **listed security** *n.* security that has a quotation on a recognized stock exchange. On the London Stock Exchange, it is a security that has a quotation in the Official List of Securities of the main market. See also FLOTATION; LISTING REQUIREMENTS.

listen /ˈlɪs(ə)n/ *v.* **1 a** make an effort to hear something. **b** attentively hear a person speaking. **2** (foll. by *to*) **a** give attention with the ear. **b** take notice of; heed. **3** (also **listen out**) (often foll. by *for*) seek to hear by waiting alertly. □ **listen in 1** tap a telephonic communication. **2** use a radio receiving set. [Old English]

listener *n.* **1** person who listens. **2** person who listens to the radio.

listeria /lɪˈstɪərɪə/ *n.* any of several bacteria infecting humans and animals eating contaminated food. [*Lister*, name of a surgeon]

listing *n.* **1 a** list. **b** entry on a list. **2** output from a printer of a computer system (*program listing*, *error listing*).

♦ **listing requirements** *n.pl.* conditions that must be satisifed before a security can be traded on a stock exchange. To achieve a quotation in the Official List of Securities of the main market of the London Stock Exchange, the requirements contained in a **listing agreement** must be signed by the company seeking quotation. The two main requirements are usu. that the value of the company's assets should exceed a certain value, and that the company publish specific financial information, both at the time of flotation and regularly thereafter. Listing requirements are generally more stringent the larger the market. See also YELLOW BOOK.

listless *adj.* lacking energy or enthusiasm. □ **listlessly** *adv.* **listlessness** *n.* [from obsolete *list* inclination]

list price *n.* price of something as shown in a published list. It may be the retail price of a consumer good as recommended by the manufacturer and shown on the manufacturer's price list; if no price-maintenance agreements apply, a discount on the list price may be offered by the retailer to attract trade. A supplier's price is shown on an invoice to a retailer or wholesaler, before deduction of any discounts.

♦ **list renting** *n.* practice of renting a list of potential customers to an organization involved in direct-mail selling or to a charity raising funds. When use of the list is restricted to one mailshot, the owner of the list usu. carries out the mailing, so that the hirer cannot copy it for subsequent use.

Lit *symb.* Italian lira.

lit *past* and *past part.* of LIGHT[1], LIGHT[2].

litany /ˈlɪtənɪ/ *n.* (*pl.* **-ies**) **1 a** series of supplications to God recited by a priest etc. with set responses by the congregation. **b** (**the Litany**) that in the Book of Common Prayer. **2** tedious recital (*litany of woes*). [Greek *litaneia* prayer]

litas /ˈliːtɑːs/ *n.* (*pl.* **litai** /ˈliːteɪ/ or **litu** /ˈliːtuː/) standard monetary unit of Lithuania.

litchi var. of LYCHEE.

liter *US* var. of LITRE.

literacy /'lɪtərəsɪ/ *n.* ability to read and write. [Latin *litera* letter]

literal /'lɪtər(ə)l/ *–adj.* **1** taking words in their basic sense without metaphor or allegory. **2** corresponding exactly to the original words (*literal translation*). **3** prosaic; matter-of-fact. **4** so called without exaggeration (*literal bankruptcy*). **5** of a letter or the letters of the alphabet. *–n.* misprint. □ **literally** *adv.* [Latin *littera* letter]

literalism *n.* insistence on a literal interpretation; adherence to the letter. □ **literalist** *n.*

literary /'lɪtərərɪ/ *adj.* **1** of or concerned with books or literature etc. **2** (of a word or idiom) used chiefly by writers; formal. □ **literariness** *n.* [Latin: related to LETTER]

literate /'lɪtərət/ *–adj.* able to read and write; educated. *–n.* literate person.

literati /ˌlɪtə'rɑːtɪ/ *n.pl.* the class of learned people.

literature /'lɪtərətʃə(r)/ *n.* **1** written works, esp. those valued for form and style. **2** writings of a country or period or on a particular subject. **3** literary production. **4** *colloq.* printed matter, leaflets, etc.

lithe /laɪð/ *adj.* flexible, supple. [Old English]

lithium /'lɪθɪəm/ *n.* soft silver-white metallic element. [Greek *lithion* from *lithos* stone]

litho /'laɪθəʊ/ *colloq. –n.* = LITHOGRAPHY. *–v.* **(-oes, -oed)** lithograph. [abbreviation]

lithograph /'lɪθəˌgrɑːf/ *–n.* lithographic print. *–v.* print by lithography. [Greek *lithos* stone]

lithography /lɪ'θɒgrəfɪ/ *n.* process of printing from a plate so treated that ink adheres only to the design to be printed. □ **lithographer** *n.* **lithographic** /ˌlɪθə'græfɪk/ *adj.* **lithographically** /ˌlɪθə'græfɪkəlɪ/ *adv.*

Lithuanian /ˌlɪθjuː'eɪnɪən/ *–n.* **1 a** native or national of Lithuania. **b** person of Lithuanian descent. **2** language of Lithuania. *–adj.* of Lithuania, its people, or language.

litigant /'lɪtɪgənt/ *–n.* party to a lawsuit. *–adj.* engaged in a lawsuit. [related to LITIGATE]

litigate /'lɪtɪˌgeɪt/ *v.* **(-ting) 1** take legal action. **2** contest (a point) at law. □ **litigation** /-'geɪʃ(ə)n/ *n.* **litigator** *n.* [Latin *lis lit-* lawsuit]

litigious /lɪ'tɪdʒəs/ *adj.* **1** fond of litigation. **2** contentious. [Latin: related to LITIGATE]

litmus /'lɪtməs/ *n.* dye from lichens, turned red by acid and blue by alkali. [Old Norse, = dye-moss]

litmus paper *n.* paper stained with litmus, used to test for acids or alkalis.

litmus test *n. colloq.* real or ultimate test.

litotes /laɪ'təʊtiːz/ *n.* (*pl.* same) ironic understatement, esp. using the negative (e.g. *I shan't be sorry* for *I shall be glad*). [Greek *litos* plain, meagre]

litre /'liːtə(r)/ *n.* (*US* **liter**) metric unit of capacity equal to 1 cubic decimetre (1.76 pints). [Greek *litra*]

Litt.D. *abbr.* Doctor of Letters. [Latin *Litterarum Doctor*]

litter *–n.* **1 a** refuse, esp. paper, discarded in a public place. **b** odds and ends lying about. **2** young animals brought forth at one birth. **3** vehicle containing a couch and carried on men's shoulders or by animals. **4** a kind of stretcher for the sick and wounded. **5** straw etc., as bedding for animals. **6** granulated material for use as an animal's, esp. a cat's, toilet indoors. *–v.* **1** make (a place) untidy with refuse. **2** give birth to (whelps etc.). **3 a** provide (a horse etc.) with litter as bedding. **b** spread straw etc. on (a stable-floor etc.). [Latin *lectus* bed]

litterbug *n. colloq.* person who drops litter in the street etc.

litter-lout *n. colloq.* = LITTERBUG.

little /'lɪt(ə)l/ *–adj.* **(littler, littlest; less** or **lesser, least) 1** small in size, amount, degree, etc.; often used affectionately or condescendingly (*friendly little chap; silly little fool*). **2 a** short in stature. **b** of short distance or duration. **3** (prec. by *a*) a certain though small amount of (*give me a little butter*). **4** trivial (*questions every little thing*). **5** only a small amount (*had little sleep*). **6** operating on a small scale; humble, ordinary (*the little shopkeeper; the little man*). **7** smaller or the smallest of the name (*little hand of a clock; little auk*). **8** young or younger (*little boy; my little sister*). *–n.* **1** not much; only a small amount (*got little out of it; did what little I could*). **2** (usu. prec. by *a*) **a** a certain but no great amount (*knows a little of everything*). **b** short time or distance (*after a little*). *–adv.* **(less, least) 1** to a small extent only (*little-known author; little more than speculation*). **2** not at all; hardly (*they little thought*). **3** (prec. by *a*) somewhat (*is a little deaf*). [Old English]

Little Bear see BEAR².

little by little *adv.* by degrees; gradually.

little end *n.* the smaller end of a connecting-rod, attached to the piston.

little grebe *n.* small water-bird of the grebe family.

little people *n.pl.* (prec. by *the*) fairies.

Little Rock city in the US, capital of Arkansas and a commercial centre for the surrounding region; pop. (est. 1994) 178 136.

little woman *n.* (prec. by *the*) *colloq.* often *derog.* one's wife.

littoral /'lɪtər(ə)l/ *–adj.* of or on the shore. *–n.* region lying along a shore. [Latin *litus litor-* shore]

liturgy /'lɪtədʒɪ/ *n.* (*pl.* **-ies**) **1** prescribed form of public worship. **2** (**the Liturgy**) the Book of Common Prayer. □ **liturgical** /-'tɜːdʒɪk(ə)l/ *adj.* **liturgically** /-'tɜːdʒɪkəlɪ/ *adv.* [Greek *leitourgia* public worship]

livable var. of LIVEABLE.

live¹ /lɪv/ *v.* **(-ving) 1** have life; be or remain alive. **2** have

---

Lithuania /ˌlɪθjuː'eɪnɪə/, **Republic of** country in NE Europe, on the E coast of the Baltic Sea, formerly (1940–91) a constituent Soviet republic. Lithuania's predominantly agricultural economy was rapidly industrialized by the Soviet Union following the Second World War; manufacturing industry now produces mainly machinery, textiles, chemicals, metalworking equipment, processed foods, and paper and pulp products. In the agricultural sector, milk and meat production are important; crops include rye, oats, flax, sugar beet, and potatoes; live animals are exported. Limestone and dolomite are mined for the construction industry and tourism is being developed. Formerly dependent on the Soviet Union, Lithuania's economy is suffering from the effects of conversion to a market system. The unpopularity of recent market reforms was reflected in the results of the 1992 parliamentary elections, in which the ruling coalition was defeated by the Democratic Labour (formerly Communist) Party; however, they were defeated in legislative elections held in 1996. In 1995 Lithuania applied for membership of the EU; the following year the country entered into a treaty of association with the EU. In 1997 Lithuania began the privatization of energy, transport and communication sectors. President, Valdas Adamkus; prime minister, Gediminas Vagnorius; capital, Vilnius.

languages	Lithuanian (official), Russian, Polish
currency	litas of 100 centai
pop. (1996)	3 707 000
GNP (1994)	US$4.9B
literacy	99% (m); 97% (f)
life expectancy	63 (m); 75 (f)

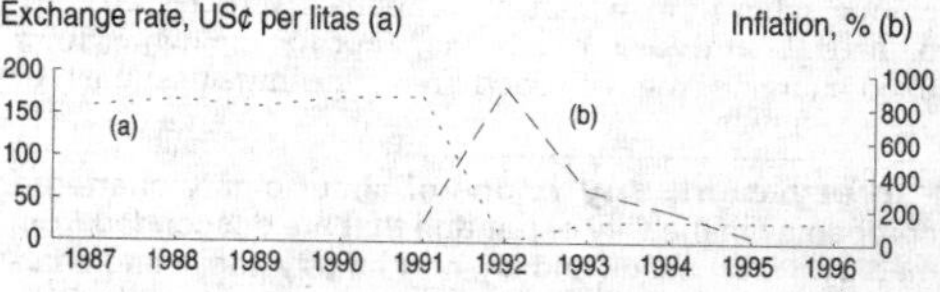

one's home (*lives up the road*). **3** (foll. by *on*) subsist or feed (*lives on fruit*). **4** (foll. by *on, off*) depend for subsistence (*lives off the state; lives on a pension*). **5** (foll. by *on, by*) sustain one's position (*live on their reputation; lives by his wits*). **6 a** spend or pass (*lived a full life*). **b** express in one's life (*lives his faith*). **7** conduct oneself, arrange one's habits, etc., in a specified way (*live quietly*). **8** (often foll. by *on*) (of a person or thing) survive; remain (*memory lived on*). **9** enjoy life to the full (*not really living*). □ **live and let live** condone others' failings so as to be similarly tolerated. **live down** cause (past guilt, a scandal, etc.) to be forgotten by blameless conduct thereafter. **live for** regard as one's life's purpose (*lives for her music*). **live in** (or **out**) reside on (or off) the premises of one's work. **live it up** *colloq.* live gaily and extravagantly. **live a lie** keep up a pretence. **live together** (esp. of a couple not married to each other) share a home and have a sexual relationship. **live up to** fulfil. **live with 1** share a home with. **2** tolerate. [Old English]

live[2] /laɪv/ *–adj.* **1** (*attrib.*) that is alive; living. **2** (of a broadcast, performance, etc.) heard or seen at the time of its performance or with an audience present. **3** of current interest or importance (*a live issue*). **4** glowing, burning (*live coals*). **5** (of a match, bomb, etc.) not yet kindled or exploded. **6** (of a wire etc.) charged with or carrying electricity. *–adv.* **1** in order to make a live broadcast (*going live now to the House of Commons*). **2** as a live performance etc. (*show went out live*). [from ALIVE]

liveable /'lɪvəb(ə)l/ *adj.* (also **livable**) **1** *colloq.* (usu. **liveable-in**) (of a house etc.) fit to live in. **2** (of a life) worth living. **3** *colloq.* (usu. **liveable-with**) (of a person) easy to live with.

lived-in *adj.* **1** (of a room etc.) showing signs of habitation. **2** *colloq.* (of a face) marked by experience.

live-in *attrib. adj.* (of a sexual partner, employee, etc.) cohabiting; resident.

livelihood /'laɪvlɪˌhʊd/ *n.* means of living; job, income. [Old English: related to LIFE]

livelong /'lɪvlɒŋ/ *adj.* in its entire length (*the livelong day*). [from obsolete *lief*, assimilated to LIVE[1]]

lively /'laɪvlɪ/ *adj.* (**-ier, -iest**) **1** full of life; vigorous, energetic. **2** vivid (*lively imagination*). **3** cheerful. **4** *joc.* exciting, dangerous (*made things lively for him*). □ **liveliness** *n.* [Old English]

liven /'laɪv(ə)n/ *v.* (often foll. by *up*) *colloq.* make or become lively, cheer up.

liver[1] /'lɪvə(r)/ *n.* **1** large glandular organ in the abdomen of vertebrates. **2** liver of some animals as food. [Old English]

liver[2] /'lɪvə(r)/ *n.* person who lives in a specified way (*a fast liver*).

liveried /'lɪvərɪd/ *adj.* wearing livery.

liverish /'lɪvərɪʃ/ *adj.* **1** suffering from a liver disorder. **2** peevish, glum.

Liverpool /'lɪvəˌpuːl/ city and seaport in NW England; pop. (est. 1994) 474 000. Liverpool's traditional industries of shipbuilding and engineering have declined, but it remains the UK's chief Atlantic port, with food-processing and other manufacturing industries.

Liverpudlian /ˌlɪvə'pʌdlɪən/ *–n.* native of Liverpool. *–adj.* of Liverpool. [LIVERPOOL]

liver sausage *n.* sausage of cooked liver etc.

liverwort *n.* small mosslike or leafless plant sometimes lobed like a liver.

livery /'lɪvərɪ/ *n.* (*pl.* **-ies**) **1** distinctive uniform of a member of a livery company or of a servant. **2** distinctive guise or marking (*birds in their winter livery*). **3** distinctive colour scheme in which a company's vehicles etc. are painted. □ **at livery** (of a horse) kept for the owner for a fixed charge. [Anglo-French *liveré*, feminine past part. of *livrer* DELIVER]

♦ **livery company** *n.* one of about eighty chartered companies in the City of London that are descended from medieval craft guilds and are now largely social and charitable institutions. Several support public schools (e.g. Merchant Taylors, Haberdashers, Mercers) and although none are now trading companies, some still have some involvement in their trades (e.g. Fishmongers). In 1878 they joined together to form the City and Guilds of London Institute, which founded the City and Guilds College of the Imperial College of Science and Technology and has been involved in other forms of technical education.

---

livery stable *n.* stable where horses are kept at livery or let out for hire.

lives *pl.* of LIFE.

livestock *n.* (usu. treated as *pl.*) animals on a farm, kept for use or profit.

♦ **livestock and bloodstock insurance** *n.* insurance covering livestock and bloodstock owners against financial losses caused by the death of an animal. Policies may be widened to include cover for treatment fees for certain specified diseases or lost profits for stud animals. Insurances can be arranged to cover single animals or for whole herds.

---

live wire *n.* spirited person.

livid /'lɪvɪd/ *adj.* **1** *colloq.* furious. **2** of a bluish leaden colour (*livid bruise*). [Latin]

living /'lɪvɪŋ/ *–n.* **1** being alive (*that's what living is all about*). **2** livelihood. **3** position held by a clergyman, providing an income. *–adj.* **1** contemporary; now alive. **2** (of a likeness) exact, lifelike. **3** (of a language) still in vernacular use. □ **within living memory** within the memory of people still alive.

living-room *n.* room for general day use.

Livingstone /'lɪvɪŋstən/ see MARAMBA.

living wage *n.* wage on which one can live without privation.

Livorno see LEGHORN.

lizard /'lɪzəd/ *n.* reptile with usu. a long body and tail, four legs, and a rough or scaly hide. [Latin *lacertus*]

LJ *abbr.* (*pl.* **L JJ**) Lord Justice.

Ljubljana /luːb'ljɑːnə/ capital of Slovenia; manufactures include textiles, chemicals, and paper; pop. (est. 1995) 276 119.

LK *symb.* lek.

LL *–symb.* (also **£L, £Leb.**) Lebanese pound. *–postcode* Llandudno.

'll *v.* (usu. after pronouns) shall, will (*I'll; that'll*). [abbreviation]

llama /'lɑːmə/ *n.* South American ruminant kept as a beast of burden and for its soft woolly fleece. [Spanish from Quechua]

LL B *abbr.* Bachelor of Laws. [Latin *legum baccalaureus*]

LL D *abbr.* Doctor of Laws. [Latin *legum doctor*]

Llds. *abbr.* Lloyd's.

LL M *abbr.* Master of Laws. [Latin *legum magister*]

♦ **Lloyd's** /lɔɪdz/ *n.* corporation of underwriters (**Lloyd's underwriters**) and insurance brokers (**Lloyd's brokers**). Originating around 1689, it was established in the Royal Exchange by 1774 and in 1871 was incorporated by act of parliament. It now occupies a building in Lime Street. As a corporation, Lloyd's itself does not underwrite insurance business; all its business comes through Lloyd's brokers, who are in touch with the public, and is underwritten by syndicates of Lloyd's underwriters, who do not, themselves, contact the public. Lloyd's underwriters must each deposit a substantial sum of money with the corporation and accept unlimited liability. They are grouped into syndicates, run by a syndicate manager or agent, but most of the members of syndicates are **names**, underwriting members of Lloyd's who take no part in organizing the underwriting business, but who share in the profits or losses of the syndicate and provide the risk capital. In the late 1980s and early 1990s some syndicates made enormous losses and many names were ruined financially. In order to replace them, Lloyd's had to admit limited companies as names in 1993, thus breaking their tradition of unlimited liability. [*Lloyd*, proprietor of the coffee-house where the society originally met]

♦ **Lloyd's agent** *n.* person situated in a port to manage the business of Lloyd's members, keeping the corporation informed of shipping movements and accidents, arranging surveys, helping in the settlement of marine insurance claims, and assisting masters of ships.

♦ **Lloyd's broker** see LLOYD'S.

♦ **Lloyd's List and Shipping Gazette** *n.* (formerly **Lloyd's List**) daily newspaper published by Lloyd's. Founded in 1734, it gives details of the movements of ships and aircraft, accidents, etc. **Lloyd's Loading List**, published weekly by Lloyd's, lists ships loading in British and continental ports, with their closing dates for accepting cargo. It also gives general news on the insurance market.

♦ **Lloyd's Register of Shipping** *n.* society formed by Lloyd's in 1760 to inspect and classify all ocean-going vessels in excess of 100 tonnes. Ships are periodically surveyed by **Lloyd's surveyors** and classified according to the condition of their hulls, engines, and trappings. The society also provides a technical advice service. Its annual publication, **Lloyd's Register of British and Foreign Shipping** (or simply **Lloyd's Register**), enables underwriters to have instant access to the information they need to underwrite marine risks.

♦ **Lloyd's underwriter** see LLOYD'S.

Lm *symb.* Maltese lira.

LME *abbr.* = LONDON METAL EXCHANGE.

LMX *abbr.* London Market Excess of Loss (at Lloyd's).

LN *–international civil aircraft marking* Norway. *–postcode* Lincoln. *–airline flight code* Libyan Arab Airlines.

ln *abbr.* natural logarithm.

LO *airline flight code* Lot Polish Airlines.

lo /ləʊ/ *int. archaic* look. □ **lo and behold** *joc.* formula introducing mention of a surprising fact. [Old English]

loach *n.* (*pl.* same or **-es**) small freshwater fish. [French]

load *–n.* **1 a** what is carried or to be carried. **b** amount usu. or actually carried (often in *comb.*: *lorry-load of bricks*). **2** burden or commitment of work, responsibility, care, etc. **3** *colloq.* **a** (in *pl.*; often foll. by *of*) plenty, a lot (*loads of money, people*). **b** (**a load of**) a quantity (*a load of nonsense*). **4** amount of power carried by an electric circuit or supplied by a generating station. *–v.* **1 a** put a load on or aboard. **b** place (a load) aboard a ship, on a vehicle, etc. **2** (often foll. by *up*) (of a vehicle or person) take a load aboard. **3** (often foll. by *with*) burden, strain (*loaded with food*). **4** (also **load up**) (foll. by *with*) overburden, overwhelm (*loaded us with work, with abuse*). **5 a** put ammunition in (a gun), film in (a camera), a cassette in (a tape recorder), etc. **b** put (a film, cassette, etc.) into a device. **c** copy (a computer program) from backing store into main store so that it may be executed. **6** give a bias to. □ **get a load of** *slang* take note of. [Old English, = way]

loaded *adj.* **1** *slang* **a** rich. **b** drunk. **c** *US* drugged. **2** (of dice etc.) weighted. **3** (of a question or statement) carrying some hidden implication.

loader *n.* **1** loading-machine. **2** (in *comb.*) gun, machine, lorry, etc., loaded in a specified way (*breech-loader*; *front-loader*). □ **-loading** *adj.* (in *comb.*) (in sense 2).

♦ **load line** *n.* (also **Plimsoll line**) one of a series of lines marked on the hull of a ship to show the extent to which the hull may be safely immersed in the water. The original line ran right round the hull. The modern markings, usu. painted on the hull amidships, apply to different conditions. The line marked TF applies to tropical fresh water, F fresh water, T tropical sea water, S summer sea water, W winter sea water and WNA winter in the North Atlantic. Shipowners and masters who allow vessels to be overloaded face heavy penalties.

---

loadstone var. of LODESTONE.

loaf[1] *n.* (*pl.* **loaves**) **1** unit of baked bread, usu. of a standard size or shape. **2** other food made in the shape of a loaf and cooked. **3** *slang* head as the seat of common sense. [Old English]

loaf[2] *v.* (often foll. by *about, around*) spend time idly; hang about. [back-formation from LOAFER]

loafer *n.* **1** idle person. **2** (**Loafer**) *propr.* flat soft-soled leather shoe. [origin uncertain]

loam *n.* rich soil of clay, sand, and humus. □ **loamy** *adj.* [Old English]

loan *–n.* **1** thing lent, esp. a sum of money lent for an agreed period of time and often at an agreed rate of interest (unless it is an **interest-free loan**). See also BANK LOAN; BRIDGING LOAN; PERSONAL LOAN. **2** lending or being lent. *–v.* lend (money, works of art, etc.). □ **on loan** being lent. [Old English]

♦ **loanable-funds theory** *n. Econ.* theory that interest rates must rise or fall until the amount that borrowers wish to raise in loans is exactly matched by the amount of funds lenders wish to lend in that period. It is based on the theory of the natural rate of interest (see INTEREST RATE).

♦ **loan account** *n.* account opened by a bank in the name of a customer to whom it has granted a loan, rather than an overdraft facility. The amount of the loan is debited to this account and any repayments are credited; interest is charged on the full amount of the loan less any repayments. The customer's current account is credited with the amount of the loan. With an overdraft facility, interest is only charged on the amount of the overdraft, which may be less than the full amount of the loan.

♦ **loanback** *n.* arrangement in which an individual can borrow from the accumulated funds of his or her pension scheme. Usu. a commercial rate of interest has to be credited to fund for the use of the capital. Some life assurance companies offer loan facilities on this basis of up to fifteen times the annual pension premium.

♦ **loan capital** *n.* money required to finance the activities of an organization that is raised by loans (see DEBENTURE 1; cf. SHARE CAPITAL). The principal advantages of loan capital over share capital are that it can be readily repaid when the company has funds, interest charges are deductible for tax purposes, and there is no capital duty on the issue of loan stock. Unlike share capital, loan capital is a fixed-interest return.

♦ **Loan Guarantee Scheme** *n.* UK government scheme that guarantees 70% of a company's overdraft for a 3% premium. The bank must accept the risk for the balance of 30%. Its purpose is to support small businesses.

♦ **loan note** *n.* form of loan stock in which an investor takes a note rather than cash as the result of a share offer to defer tax liability. The yield is often variable and may be linked to the London Inter-Bank Offered Rate. Loan notes are usu. not marketable but are usu. repayable on demand.

---

loan shark *n. colloq.* person who lends money at exorbitant rates of interest.

♦ **loan stock** see DEBENTURE 1.

---

loath *predic. adj.* (also **loth**) disinclined, reluctant (*loath to admit it*). [Old English]

loathe /ləʊð/ *v.* (**-thing**) detest, hate. □ **loathing** *n.* [Old English]

loathsome /'ləʊðsəm/ *adj.* arousing hatred or disgust; repulsive.

loaves *pl.* of LOAF[1].

LOB *abbr.* Location of Offices Bureau.

lob *–v.* (**-bb-**) hit or throw (a ball etc.) slowly or in a high arc. *–n.* such a ball. [probably Low German or Dutch]

lobar /'ləʊbə(r)/ *adj.* of a lobe, esp. of the lung (*lobar pneumonia*).

lobate /'ləʊbeɪt/ *adj.* having a lobe or lobes.

lobby /'lɒbɪ/ *–n.* (*pl.* **-ies**) **1** porch, ante-room, entrance-hall, or corridor. **2 a** (in the House of Commons) large hall used esp. for interviews between MPs and the public. **b** (also **division lobby**) each of two corridors to which MPs retire to vote. **3 a** body of lobbyists (*anti-abor-*

tion lobby). **b** organized rally of lobbying members of the public. **4** (prec. by *the*) group of journalists who receive unattributable briefings from the government (*lobby correspondent*). *–v.* (**-ies**, **-ied**) **1** solicit the support of (an influential person). **2** (of members of the public) inform in order to influence (legislators, an MP, etc.). **3** frequent a parliamentary lobby. [Latin *lobia* lodge]

lobbyist *n.* person who lobbies an MP etc., esp. professionally.

lobe *n.* **1** lower soft pendulous part of the outer ear. **2** similar part of other organs, esp. the brain, liver, and lung. □ **lobed** *adj.* [Greek *lobos* lobe, pod]

lobelia /lə'biːlɪə/ *n.* plant with bright, esp. blue, flowers. [*Lobel*, name of a botanist]

Lobito /lʊ'biːtəʊ/ seaport on the Atlantic coast of Angola; pop. (latest est.) 150 000. Linked by rail to Democratic Republic of Congo, Zambia, and the Mozambique port of Beira, Lobito is one of the best natural harbours on the W coast of Africa.

lobotomy /lə'bɒtəmɪ/ *n.* (*pl.* **-ies**) incision into the frontal lobe of the brain, formerly used in some cases of mental disorder. [from LOBE]

lobscouse /'lɒbskaʊs/ *n.* sailor's dish of meat stewed with vegetables and ship's biscuit. [origin unknown]

lobster *n.* **1** marine crustacean with two pincer-like claws. **2** its flesh as food. [Latin *locusta* lobster, LOCUST]

lobster-pot *n.* basket for trapping lobsters.

lobworm *n.* large earthworm used as fishing-bait. [from LOB in obsolete sense 'pendulous object']

local /'ləʊk(ə)l/ *–adj.* **1** belonging to, existing in, or peculiar to a particular place (*local history*). **2** of the neighbourhood (*local paper*). **3** of or affecting a part and not the whole (*local anaesthetic*). **4** (of a telephone call) to a nearby place and charged at a lower rate. *–n.* **1** inhabitant of a particular place. **2** (often prec. by *the*) *colloq.* local public house. **3** local anaesthetic. **4** person who has a seat on a commodity futures market and who deals for him- or herself. □ **locally** *adv.* [Latin *locus* place]

♦ **local area network** *n.* (also **LAN**) collection of linked computer stations (usu. microcomputers) restricted to a small local area, e.g. an office building or a university campus. Stations in the network are able to communicate both with a central computer and with each other. The network is used as a communications system as well as providing wide access to central computing facilities.

---

local authority *n.* administrative body in local government.

local colour *n.* touches of detail in a story etc. designed to provide a realistic background.

locale /ləʊ'kɑːl/ *n.* scene or locality of an event or occurrence. [French *local*]

local government *n.* system of administration of a county, district, parish, etc., by the elected representatives of those who live there.

locality /ləʊ'kælɪtɪ/ *n.* (*pl.* **-ies**) **1** district. **2** site or scene of a thing. **3** thing's position. [Latin: related to LOCAL]

localize /'ləʊkəˌlaɪz/ *v.* (also **-ise**) (**-zing** or **-sing**) **1** restrict or assign to a particular place. **2** invest with the characteristics of a particular place. **3** decentralize.

♦ **local loan** *n.* loan issued by a local government authority for financing capital expenditure.

---

local time *n.* time in a particular place.

local train *n.* train stopping at all the stations on its route.

Locarno /lə'kɑːnəʊ/ resort in S Switzerland, on Lake Maggiore; pop. (1990) 14 150.

locate /ləʊ'keɪt/ *v.* (**-ting**) **1** discover the exact place of. **2** establish in a place; situate. **3** state the locality of. [Latin: related to LOCAL]

■ **Usage** *Locate* should not be used to mean merely 'find' as in *can't locate my key*.

location /ləʊ'keɪʃ(ə)n/ *n.* **1** particular place. **2** locating. **3** natural, not studio, setting for a film etc. (*filmed on location*). **4** (also **storage location**) **a** place in which information can be stored in a computer, in main store or backing store. **b** area within a computer memory capable of storing a single unit of information in binary form. Each location can be identified by an address, allowing an item of information to be stored or retrieved from there. Locations on disk tend to hold a number of bytes and are addressed by track and sector. Main store is divided into either bytes or words, each location being individually addressed.

loc. cit. *abbr.* in the passage cited. [Latin *loco citato*]

loch /lɒk, lɒx/ *n. Scot.* lake or narrow inlet of the sea. [Gaelic]

loci *pl.* of LOCUS.

lock[1] *–n.* **1** mechanism for fastening a door etc., with a bolt that requires a key of a particular shape to work it. **2** confined section of a canal or river within sluice-gates, for moving boats from one level to another. **3 a** turning of a vehicle's front wheels. **b** (in full **full lock**) maximum extent of this. **4** interlocked or jammed state. **5** wrestling-hold that keeps an opponent's limb fixed. **6** (in full **lock forward**) player in the second row of a Rugby scrum. **7** mechanism for exploding the charge of a gun. *–v.* **1 a** fasten with a lock. **b** (foll. by *up*) shut (a house etc.) thus. **c** (of a door etc.) be lockable. **2 a** (foll. by *up, in, into*) enclose (a person or thing) by locking. **b** (foll. by *up*) *colloq.* imprison (a person). **3** (often foll. by *up, away*) store inaccessibly (*capital locked up in land*). **4** (foll. by *in*) hold fast (in sleep, an embrace, a struggle, etc.). **5** (usu. in *passive*) (of land, hills, etc.) enclose. **6** make or become rigidly fixed. **7** (cause to) jam or catch. □ **lock on to** (of a missile etc.) automatically find and then track (a target). **lock out 1** keep out by locking the door. **2** (of an employer) subject (employees) to a lock-out. **under lock and key** locked up. □ **lockable** *adj.* [Old English]

lock[2] *n.* **1** portion of hair that hangs together. **2** (in *pl.*) the hair of the head (*golden locks*). [Old English]

locker *n.* (usu. lockable) cupboard or compartment, esp. for public use.

locket /'lɒkɪt/ *n.* small ornamental case for a portrait or lock of hair, worn on a chain round the neck. [French diminutive of *loc* latch, LOCK[1]]

lockjaw *n.* form of tetanus in which the jaws become rigidly closed.

lock-keeper *n.* person in charge of a river or canal lock.

lockout *n.* employer's exclusion of employees from the workplace until certain terms are agreed to.

locksmith *n.* maker and mender of locks.

lock, stock, and barrel *adv.* completely.

lock-up *–n.* **1** house or room for the temporary detention of prisoners. **2** premises that can be locked up, esp. a small shop. **3** investment in assets that are not readily realizable, esp. one that is specifically intended to be held for a long period. *–attrib. adj.* that can be locked up (*lock-up garage*).

loco[1] /'ləʊkəʊ/ *n.* (*pl.* **-s**) *colloq.* locomotive engine. [abbreviation]

loco[2] /'ləʊkəʊ/ *predic. adj. slang* crazy. [Spanish]

♦ **loco**[3] /'ləʊkəʊ/ *adj.* denoting a price for goods that are located in a specified place, usu. the seller's warehouse or factory, and for which the buyer has to pay all charges involved in loading, transporting, or shipping them to their destination (*a loco price*; *£100 per tonne, loco Islington factory*). [Latin, = from a place]

---

locomotion /ˌləʊkə'məʊʃ(ə)n/ *n.* motion or the power of motion from place to place. [Latin LOCUS, MOTION]

locomotive /ˌləʊkə'məʊtɪv/ *–n.* engine for pulling trains. *–adj.* of, having, or effecting locomotion.

locum tenens /ˌləʊkəm 'tiːnenz, 'te-/ *n.* (*pl.* **locum tenentes** /tɪ'nentiːz/) (also *colloq.* **locum**) deputy acting esp. for a doctor or clergyman. [Latin, = (one) holding a place]

locus /'ləʊkəs/ *n.* (*pl.* **loci** /-saɪ/) **1** position or locality. **2**

line or curve etc. formed by all the points satisfying certain conditions, or by the defined motion of a point or line or surface. [Latin, = place]

locus classicus /ˌləʊkəs ˈklæsɪkəs/ *n.* (*pl.* ***loci classici*** /ˌləʊsaɪ ˈklæsɪˌsaɪ/) best known or most authoritative passage on a subject. [Latin: related to LOCUS]

♦ ***locus poenitentiae*** /ˌləʊkəs piːnɪˈtenʃɪiː/ *n. Law* opportunity for the parties to an illegal contract to reconsider their positions, decide not to carry out the illegal act, and so save the contract from being void. Once the illegal purpose has been carried out, no action in law is possible. [Latin, = opportunity to repent]

locust /ˈləʊkəst/ *n.* African or Asian grasshopper migrating in swarms and consuming all vegetation. [Latin *locusta* locust, LOBSTER]

locution /ləˈkjuːʃ(ə)n/ *n.* **1** word, phrase, or idiom. **2** style of speech. [Latin *loquor locut-* speak]

lode *n.* vein of metal ore. [var. of LOAD]

lodestar *n.* **1** star used as a guide in navigation, esp. the pole star. **2 a** guiding principle. **b** object of pursuit. [from LODE in obsolete sense 'way, journey']

lodestone *n.* (also **loadstone**) **1** magnetic oxide of iron. **2 a** piece of this used as a magnet. **b** thing that attracts.

lodge *–n.* **1** small house at the entrance to a park or grounds of a large house, occupied by a gatekeeper etc. **2** small house used in the sporting seasons (*hunting lodge*). **3** porter's room at the gate of a college, factory, etc. **4** members or meeting-place of a branch of a society such as the Freemasons. **5** beaver's or otter's lair. *–v.* (**-ging**) **1 a** reside or live, esp. as a lodger. **b** provide with temporary accommodation. **2** submit or present (a complaint etc.) for attention. **3** become fixed or caught; stick. **4** deposit (money etc.) for security. **5** (foll. by *in, with*) place (power etc.) in a person. [French *loge*: related to LEAF]

lodger *n.* person paying for accommodation in another's house.

lodging *n.* **1** temporary accommodation (*a lodging for the night*). **2** (in *pl.*) room or rooms rented for lodging in.

Lodz /wʊtʃ/ (Polish **Łódź**) city in Poland; manufactures include textiles, chemicals, and electrical goods; pop. (est. 1995) 828 500.

loess /ˈləʊɪs/ *n.* deposit of fine wind-blown soil, esp. in the basins of large rivers. [Swiss German, = loose]

Lofoten Islands /ləˈfəʊt(ə)n/ group of Norwegian islands off the NW coast of Norway, in rich fishing waters; pop. (est. 1985) with Vesterålen Islands 66 600.

loft *–n.* **1** attic. **2** room over a stable. **3** gallery in a church or hall. **4** pigeon-house. **5** backward slope on the face of a golf-club. **6** lofting stroke. *–v.* send (a ball etc.) high up. [Old English, = air, upper room]

lofty *adj.* (**-ier, -iest**) **1** (of things) of imposing height. **2** haughty, aloof. **3** exalted, noble (*lofty ideals*). □ **loftily** *adv.* **loftiness** *n.*

log[1] *–n.* **1** unhewn piece of a felled tree; any large rough piece of wood, esp. cut for firewood. **2** *hist.* floating device for gauging a ship's speed. **3** record of events occurring during the voyage of a ship or aircraft. **4** any systematic record of deeds, experiences, etc. **5** = LOGBOOK. *–v.* (**-gg-**) **1 a** enter (a ship's speed, or other transport details) in a logbook. **b** enter (data etc.) in a regular record. **2** attain (a distance, speed, etc., thus recorded) (*had logged over 600 miles*). **3** cut into logs. □ **log in** (or **on**) identify oneself when entering a multi-access computer system, giving name (or account number) and password. **log off** (or **out**) close one's on-line access to a computer system. **sleep like a log** sleep soundly. [origin unknown]

log[2] *n.* logarithm. [abbreviation]

logan /ˈləʊgən/ *n.* (in full **logan-stone**) poised heavy stone rocking at a touch. [= (dial.) *logging*, = rocking]

loganberry /ˈləʊgənbərɪ/ *n.* (*pl.* **-ies**) dark red fruit, hybrid of a blackberry and a raspberry. [*Logan*, name of a horticulturalist]

logarithm /ˈlɒgəˌrɪð(ə)m/ *n.* one of a series of arithmetic exponents tabulated to simplify computation by making it possible to use addition and subtraction instead of multiplication and division. □ **logarithmic** /-ˈrɪðmɪk/ *adj.* **logarithmically** /-ˈrɪðmɪkəlɪ/ *adv.* [Greek *logos* reckoning, *arithmos* number]

logbook *n.* **1** book containing a detailed record or log. **2** vehicle registration document.

log cabin *n.* hut built of logs.

logger *n. US* lumberjack.

loggerhead /ˈlɒgəˌhed/ *n.* □ **at loggerheads** (often foll. by *with*) disagreeing or disputing. [probably dial. from *logger* wooden block]

loggia /ˈləʊdʒə, ˈlɒ-/ *n.* open-sided gallery or arcade. [Italian, = LODGE]

logging *n.* work of cutting and preparing forest timber.

logic /ˈlɒdʒɪk/ *–n.* **1 a** science of reasoning. **b** particular system or method of reasoning. **2 a** chain of reasoning (regarded as sound or unsound). **b** use of or ability in argument. **3** inexorable force, compulsion, or consequence (*the logic of events*). **4 a** principles used in designing a computer etc. **b** circuits using this (*digital logic*). *–attrib. adj.* (also **logical**) *Computing* denoting or involving electronic digital circuits (*logic gate; logic operation*). □ **logician** /ləˈdʒɪʃ(ə)n/ *n.* [related to -LOGIC]

-logic *comb. form* (also **-logical**) forming adjectives corresponding esp. to nouns in *-logy* (*pathological; zoological*). [Greek *-logikos*]

logical *adj.* **1** of or according to logic (*the logical conclusion*). **2** correctly reasoned. **3** defensible or explicable on the ground of consistency. **4** capable of correct reasoning. □ **logicality** /-ˈkælɪtɪ/ *n.* **logically** *adv.* [Greek *logos* word, reason]

logic circuit *n. Computing* electronic circuit consisting of interconnected logic gates and possibly other components. Logic circuits are found in all types of computer devices, including the central processor where they perform various arithmetic, logic, and control operations, and in memory devices (e.g. ROM and RAM) and counters.

logic gate *n.* electronic device used to control the flow of signals in a computer. It does this by performing a particular logic operation on its inputs (see LOGIC OPERATION). There are usu. between two and eight inputs to a gate and one output. An input signal is either at a high voltage or at a low voltage, the level changing with time. The signal thus has a binary nature. As the input signals switch between their high and low levels, the output voltage changes, the value depending on the logic operation performed by the gate. For example, an AND gate has a high output only when all its inputs are high at the same time. The output of an OR gate is low only when all inputs are low at the same time. In any logic gate the output changes extremely rapidly in response to a change in input.

logic instruction *n.* (also **logical instruction**) *Computing* machine instruction specifying a logic operation and the operand or operands on which the logic operation is to be performed.

logic operation *n.* (also **logical operation**) operation performed on quantities (operands) that can be assigned a truth value; this value is either 'true' or 'false'. The result of the operation is in accordance with the rules of Boolean algebra, and again has a value 'true' or 'false'. The operands may be statements or formulae. In computing, electronic circuits (see LOGIC GATE) are constructed so as to perform logic operations on their input signals.

-logist *comb. form* forming nouns meaning 'person skilled in *-logy*' (*geologist*).

logistics /ləˈdʒɪstɪks/ *n.pl.* **1** organization of (orig. military) services and supplies. **2** control of the movement of materials in a factory, from the arrival of raw materials to the packaging of the product, known as **materials management**, together with **distribution management** (or **marketing logistics**), which includes the storage of goods and their distribution to distributors and consumers. **3** organization of any complex operation. □ **logistic** *adj.* **logistical** *adj.* **logistically** *adv.* [French *loger* lodge]

log-jam *n.* deadlock.

logo /ˈləʊgəʊ/ *n.* (*pl.* **-s**) emblem of an organization used in its display material etc. [abbreviation of *logotype* from Greek *logos* word]

-logy *comb. form* forming nouns denoting: **1** a subject of study (*biology*). **2** speech or discourse or a characteristic of this (*trilogy*; *tautology*; *phraseology*). [Greek *-logia* from *logos* word]

loin *n.* **1** (in *pl.*) side and back of the body between the ribs and the hip-bones. **2** joint of meat from this part of an animal. [French *loigne* from Latin *lumbus*]

loincloth *n.* cloth worn round the hips, esp. as a sole garment.

Loire /ləˈwɑː(r)/ longest river in France, flowing N and W to the Atlantic Ocean at St Nazaire. The Loire valley is particularly noted for its vineyards.

loiter *v.* **1** stand about idly; linger. **2** go slowly with frequent stops. □ **loiter with intent** linger in order to commit a felony. □ **loiterer** *n.* [Dutch]

loll *v.* **1** stand, sit, or recline in a lazy attitude. **2** hang loosely. [imitative]

Lolland /ˈlɒlɑːn/ Danish island in the Baltic Sea to the S of Zealand; it produces cereals, fruit, and sugar beet; pop. (est. 1988) 80 500.

lollipop /ˈlɒlɪˌpɒp/ *n.* hard sweet on a stick. [origin uncertain]

lollipop man *n.* (also **lollipop lady**) *colloq.* warden using a circular sign on a pole to stop traffic for children to cross the road.

lollop /ˈlɒləp/ *v.* (**-p-**) *colloq.* **1** flop about. **2** move in ungainly bounds. [probably from LOLL, TROLLOP]

lolly /ˈlɒlɪ/ *n.* (*pl.* **-ies**) **1** *colloq.* lollipop. **2** = ICE LOLLY. **3** *slang* money. [abbreviation]

Lombard /ˈlɒmbɑːd/ *–n.* native or inhabitant of Lombardy. *–adj.* of or relating to Lombards or Lombardy.

♦ **Lombard rate** *n.* **1** rate of interest at which the German central bank, the Bundesbank, lends to German commercial banks, usu. ½% above the discount rate. **2** interest rate charged by a German commercial bank lending against security. See also SPECIAL LOMBARD RATE.

♦ **Lombard Street** *n.* street in the City of London, formerly occupied by Lombard bankers, that is the centre of the UK money market. It contains the offices of many commercial banks, bill brokers, and discount houses, and the Bank of England is round the corner.

Lombardy /ˈlɒmbədɪ/ (Italian **Lombardia**) region of central N Italy; pop. (est. 1994) 8 901 023; capital, Milan. It is the country's most industrialized region, with many commercial and banking services; manufactures include steel, machine tools, motor cars, textiles, and chemicals.

Lombok /ˈlɒmbɒk/ Indonesian island, one of the Lesser Sundas, between Bali and Sumbawa; rice, coffee, and tobacco are grown; pop. (1991) 2 500 000.

Lomé /ˈləʊmeɪ/ capital and chief port of Togo; pop. (est. 1990) 450 000.

Lomé Convention *n.* trade agreement of 1975, signed in Lomé, between the EC and various African, Caribbean, and Pacific Ocean states, for technical cooperation and development aid. It was renewed in 1979 and 1985.

London /ˈlʌnd(ə)n/ **1** capital of the United Kingdom, a port on the River Thames; the City of London is the commercial, banking, and insurance centre (see CITY 2); pop. (1994) 6 967 500. **2** industrial city in Canada, in SE Ontario, the manufacturing and financial centre of the province; city pop. (1991) 303 165; metropolitan area pop. (1991) 381 522.

♦ **London acceptance credit** *n.* method of providing immediate cash for a UK exporter of goods. On shipment of the goods the exporter draws a bill of exchange on the foreign buyer. The accepted bill is then pledged to a merchant bank in London, which accepts an accommodation bill drawn by the exporter. The acceptance can be discounted on the bank's reputation, to provide the exporter with immediate finance, whereas the foreign buyer's acceptance would be difficult, or impossible, to discount in London.

♦ **London Bankers' Clearing House** *n.* organization in Lombard Street that daily sets off all cheques drawn for and against the clearing banks in the UK. See also ASSOCIATION FOR PAYMENT CLEARING SERVICES.

♦ **London Chamber of Commerce and Industry** *n.* (also **LCC**) largest chamber of commerce in the UK, providing the normal services of a chamber of commerce and in addition running courses and examinations in business subjects.

♦ **London Clearing House** *n.* (also **LCH**) clearing house established in 1888 (known before 1991 as the International Commodities Clearing House and originally as the London Produce Clearing House). LCH is an independent body, owned by six major UK commercial banks. It provides futures and options markets with netting and settlement services as well as becoming a counter-party to every transaction between its members. In this capacity LCH takes the risk of its members defaulting, which it covers by collecting margins from members; it also provides an independent guarantee of £200 million from its shareholders and from the insurance market. Exchanges making use of LCH facilities include the London International Financial Futures and Options Exchange, London Commodity Exchange, the London Metal Exchange, and the International Petroleum Exchange.

♦ **London Commodity Exchange (LCE)** *n.* commodity exchange, which emerged in 1954 as a successor to the London Commercial Sale Rooms. It merged with the Soft Commodity Futures Trade Association to form a single Recognized Investment Exchange under the Financial Services Act (1986). The LCE is Europe's leading market for trading in futures and options in cocoa, coffee, sugar, wheat, barley, and potatoes. The market also includes the Baltic International Freight Futures Exchange (BIFFEX), on which futures in dry cargo freight are traded. LCE makes use of the services provided by the London Clearing House.

Londonderry /ˈlʌndənˌderɪ/ (also **Derry**) **1** county in Northern Ireland; agriculture and fishing are important and industries include textiles, light engineering, and chemicals. **2** its county town, a port with light industries; pop. (1981) 62 697. See also DERRY 1.

Londoner *n.* native or inhabitant of London.

♦ **London Inter-Bank Offered Rate** *n.* (also **LIBOR**) rate of interest in the short-term wholesale market (see INTERBANK MARKET 1) in which banks lend to each other. The loans are for a minimum of £250,000 for periods from overnight up to five years. The importance of the market is that it allows individual banks to adjust their liquidity positions quickly, covering shortages by borrowing from banks with surpluses. This reduces the need for each bank to hold large quantities of liquid assets, thus releasing funds for more profitable lending transactions.

♦ **London International Financial Futures and Options Exchange** *n.* (also **LIFFE**) market in financial futures that opened in 1982, in London's Royal Exchange, to provide facilities within the European time zone for dealing in options and futures contracts, including those in government bonds, stock-and-share indexes, foreign currencies, and interest rates. The bargain details are passed to the London Clearing House. Automated (electronic) pit trading was introduced in 1989.

♦ **London Metal Exchange** *n.* (also **LME**) central market for non-ferrous metals, established in London in 1877 to supply a central market for the import of large quantities of metal from abroad. The Exchange deals in copper, lead, zinc, aluminium (all in minimum lots of 25 tonnes), tin (minimum 5 tonnes), and nickel (minimum 6 tonnes). The official prices of the LME are used by producers and consumers worldwide for their long-term contracts. Dealings on the LME include futures and options contracts. Bargains are transmitted to the London Clearing House.

London pride *n.* pink-flowered saxifrage.

♦ **London Stock Exchange** *n.* financial market in London that deals in securities. Dealings in securities began in London in the 17th century. The development of the industrial revolution encouraged many other share markets to flourish throughout the UK, all the remnants of which amalgamated in 1973 to form The Stock Exchange of Great Britain and Ireland. In 1986 (see BIG BANG) this organization became the **International Stock Exchange of the UK and Republic of Ireland Ltd.** Its major reforms included:

(i) allowing banks, insurance companies, and overseas securities houses to become members and to buy existing member firms;

(ii) abolishing scales of commissions, allowing commissions to be negotiated;

(iii) abolishing the division of members into jobbers and brokers, enabling a member firm to deal with the public, to buy and sell shares for their own account, and to act as market makers;

(iv) the introduction of SEAQ, a computerized dealing system that has virtually abolished face-to-face dealing on the floor of exchange.

In merging with members of the international broking community in London, the International Stock Exchange became a registered investment exchange and The Securities Association Ltd. became a Self-Regulating Organization (SRO) complying with the Financial Services Act (1986). In 1991 the Securities Association Ltd. merged with the Association of Futures Brokers and Dealers Ltd. to form the Securities and Futures Authority (SFA), which is now the SRO responsible for the Stock Exchange. The market in traded options in equities, currencies, and indexes has moved to LIFFE. See MAIN MARKET; ALTERNATIVE INVESTMENT MARKET.

---

lone *attrib. adj.* **1** solitary; without companions. **2** isolated. **3** unmarried, single (*lone parent*). [from ALONE]

lone hand *n.* **1** hand played or player playing against the rest at cards. **2** person or action without allies.

lonely /'ləʊnlɪ/ *adj.* (**-ier, -iest**) **1** without companions (*lonely existence*). **2** sad because of this. **3** unfrequented, isolated, uninhabited. □ **loneliness** *n.*

lonely hearts *n.pl.* people seeking friendship or marriage through a newspaper column, club, etc.

loner *n.* person or animal that prefers to be alone.

lonesome /'ləʊnsəm/ *adj.* esp. *US* **1** lonely. **2** making one feel forlorn (*a lonesome song*).

lone wolf *n.* loner.

long[1] *–adj.* (**longer** /'lɒŋgə(r)/; **longest** /'lɒŋgɪst/) **1** measuring much from end to end in space or time. **2** (following a measurement) in length or duration (*2 metres long; two months long*). **3 a** consisting of many items (*a long list*). **b** seemingly more than the stated amount; tedious (*ten long miles*). **4** of elongated shape. **5** lasting or reaching far back or forward in time (*long friendship*). **6** far-reaching; acting at a distance; involving a great interval or difference. **7** (of a vowel or syllable) having the greater of the two recognized durations. **8** (of odds or a chance) reflecting a low level of probability. **9** (of stocks) bought in large quantities in advance, with the expectation of a rise in price. **10** (foll. by *on*) *colloq.* well supplied with. *–n.* **1** long interval or period (*will not take long; won't be long*). **2** (in *pl.*) **a** long-dated gilt-edged securities. **b** securities, commodities, currencies, etc. held in a long position. *–adv.* (**longer** /'lɒŋgə(r)/; **longest** /'lɒŋgɪst/) **1** by or for a long time (*long before; long ago*). **2** (following nouns of duration) throughout a specified time (*all day long*). **3** (in *compar.*) after an implied point of time (*shall not wait any longer*). □ **as** (or **so) long as** provided that. **before long** soon. **in the long run** (or **term**) eventually, ultimately. **the long and the short of it 1** all that need be said. **2** the eventual outcome. **not by a long shot** (or **chalk**) by no means. □ **longish** *adj.* [Old English]

long[2] *v.* (foll. by *for* or *to* + infin.) have a strong wish or desire for. [Old English, = seem LONG[1] to]

long. *abbr.* longitude.

Long Beach resort city in the US, in California; industries include aircraft manufacture and oil refining; pop. (est. 1994) 433 852.

longboat *n.* sailing-ship's largest boat.

longbow *n.* bow drawn by hand and shooting a long feathered arrow.

♦ **long-dated gilt** see GILT-EDGED SECURITY.

---

long-distance *–attrib. adj.* travelling or operating between distant places. *–adv.* between distant places (*phone long-distance*).

long division *n.* division of numbers with details of the calculations written down.

long-drawn *adj.* (also **long-drawn-out**) prolonged.

longeron /'lɒndʒərən/ *n.* longitudinal member of a plane's fuselage. [French]

longevity /lɒn'dʒevɪtɪ/ *n. formal* long life. [Latin *longus* long, *aevum* age]

long face *n.* dismal expression.

Longford /'lɒŋfəd/ **1** county in the central Republic of Ireland, in the province of Leinster; it is mainly agricultural; pop. (est. 1991) 30 293. **2** its capital city; pop. (est. 1995) 6800.

longhand *n.* ordinary handwriting.

long haul *n.* **1** transport over a long distance. **2** prolonged effort or task.

longing /'lɒŋɪŋ/ *–n.* intense desire. *–adj.* having or showing this. □ **longingly** *adv.*

long in the tooth *predic. adj. colloq.* old.

longitude /'lɒŋgɪˌtjuːd, 'lɒndʒ-/ *n.* **1** angular distance east or west from a standard meridian such as Greenwich to the meridian of any place. **2** angular distance of a celestial body, esp. along the ecliptic. [Latin *longitudo* length, from *longus* long]

longitudinal /ˌlɒŋgɪ'tjuːdɪn(ə)l, ˌlɒndʒ-/ *adj.* **1** of or in length. **2** running lengthwise. **3** of longitude. □ **longitudinally** *adv.*

long johns *n.pl. colloq.* long underpants.

long jump *n.* athletic contest of jumping as far as possible along the ground in one leap.

long-life *adj.* (of milk etc.) treated to prolong its period of usability.

long-lived *adj.* having a long life; durable.

long-lost *attrib. adj.* that has been lost for a long time.

long-playing *adj.* (of a gramophone record) playing for about 20–30 minutes on each side.

♦ **long position** *n.* position held by a dealer in securities, commodities, currencies, etc. in which holdings exceed sales, because the dealer expects prices to rise enabling a profit to be made by selling at the higher levels. Cf. SHORT POSITION.

---

long-range *adj.* **1** having a long range. **2** relating to a period of time far into the future (*long-range weather forecast*).

♦ **long run** *n.* period of time that is sufficiently long for all the economic factors of production to be varied by a firm to enable it to obtain the most efficient combination. Cf. SHORT RUN.

---

long-running *adj.* continuing for a long time (*a long-running musical*).

longshore *attrib. adj.* **1** existing on or frequenting the shore. **2** directed along the shore. [from *along shore*]

longshoreman *n. US* docker.

long shot *n.* **1** wild guess or venture. **2** bet at long odds.

long sight *n.* ability to see clearly only what is comparatively distant.

long-sighted *adj.* **1** having long sight. **2** far-sighted. □ **long-sightedness** *n.*

long-standing *adj.* that has long existed.

long-suffering *adj.* bearing provocation patiently.

long-term *adj.* of or for a long period of time (*long-term plans*).

♦ **long-term debt** *n.* loans and debentures that are not due for repayment for at least ten years.

♦ **long-term liability** *n.* sum owed that does not have to be repaid within the next accounting period of a business. In some contexts it may be regarded as one not due for repayment within the next three, or possibly ten, years.

---

long ton *n.* mass of 2240 pounds. See TON 1.

long wave *n.* radio wave of frequency less than 300 kHz.

longways *adv.* (also **longwise**) = LENGTHWAYS.

long-winded *adj.* (of a speech or writing) tediously lengthy.

loo *n. colloq.* lavatory. [origin uncertain]

loofah /'luːfə/ *n.* rough bath-sponge made from the dried pod of a type of gourd. [Arabic]

look /lʊk/ *–v.* **1 a** (often foll. by *at, down, up,* etc.) use one's sight; turn one's eyes in some direction. **b** turn one's eyes on; examine (*looked me in the eyes; looked us up and down*). **2 a** make a visual or mental search (*I'll look in the morning*). **b** (foll. by *at*) consider, examine (*must look at the facts*). **3** (foll. by *for*) search for, seek, be on the watch for. **4** inquire (*when one looks deeper*). **5** have a specified appearance; seem (*look a fool; future looks bleak*). **6** (foll. by *to*) **a** consider; be concerned about (*look to the future*). **b** rely on (*look to me for support*). **7** (foll. by *into*) investigate. **8** (foll. by *what, where, whether,* etc.) ascertain or observe by sight. **9** (of a thing) face some direction. **10** indicate (emotion etc.) by one's looks. **11** (foll. by *that*) take care; make sure. **12** (foll. by *to* + infin.) aim (*am looking to finish it soon*). *–n.* **1** act of looking; gaze, glance. **2** (in *sing.* or *pl.*) appearance of a face; expression. **3** appearance of a thing (*by the look of it*). **4** style, fashion (*this year's look; the wet look*). *–int.* (also **look here!**) calling attention, expressing a protest, etc. □ **look after** attend to; take care of. **look one's age** appear as old as one really is. **look back 1** (foll. by *on, to*) turn one's thoughts to (something past). **2** (usu. with *neg.*) cease to progress (*he's never looked back*). **look down on** (or **look down one's nose at**) regard with contempt or superiority. **look forward to** await (an expected event) eagerly or with specified feelings. **look in** make a short visit or call. **look on 1** (often foll. by *as*) regard. **2** be a spectator. **look oneself** appear well (esp. after illness etc.). **look out 1** direct one's sight or put one's head out of a window etc. **2** (often foll. by *for*) be vigilant or prepared. **3** (foll. by *on, over,* etc.) have or afford an outlook. **4** search for and produce. **5** (as *imper.*) warning of immediate danger etc. **look over** inspect. **look smart** make haste. **look up 1** search for (esp. information in a book). **2** *colloq.* visit (a person). **3** improve in prospect. **look up to** respect or admire. **not like the look of** find alarming or suspicious. [Old English]

look-alike *n.* person or thing closely resembling another.

looker *n.* **1** person of a specified appearance (*good-looker*). **2** *colloq.* attractive woman.

looker-on *n.* (*pl.* **lookers-on**) spectator.

look-in *n. colloq.* chance of participation or success (*never gets a look-in*).

looking-glass *n.* mirror.

lookout *n.* **1** watch or looking out (*on the lookout*). **2 a** observation-post. **b** person etc. stationed to keep watch. **3** prospect (*it's a bad lookout*). **4** *colloq.* person's own concern (*that's your lookout*).

loom[1] *n.* apparatus for weaving. [Old English]

loom[2] *v.* **1** appear dimly, esp. as a vague and often threatening shape. **2** (of an event) be ominously close. [probably Low German or Dutch]

loon *n.* **1** a kind of diving bird. **2** *colloq.* crazy person (cf. LOONY). [Old Norse]

loony *slang –n.* (*pl.* **-ies**) lunatic. *–adj.* (**-ier, -iest**) crazy. □ **looniness** *n.* [abbreviation]

loony-bin *n. slang offens.* mental home or hospital.

loop *–n.* **1 a** figure produced by a curve, or a doubled thread etc., that crosses itself. **b** thing, path, etc., forming this figure. **2** similarly shaped attachment used as a fastening. **3** ring etc. as a handle etc. **4** contraceptive coil. **5** (in full **loop-line**) railway or telegraph line that diverges from a main line and joins it again. **6** skating or aerobatic manoeuvre describing a loop. **7** complete circuit for an electric current. **8** endless band of tape or film allowing continuous repetition. **9** sequence of computer operations repeated until some condition is satisfied. *–v.* **1** form or bend into a loop. **2** fasten with a loop or loops. **3** form a loop. **4** (also **loop the loop**) fly in a circle vertically. [origin unknown]

loophole *n.* **1** means of evading a rule etc. without infringing it. **2** narrow vertical slit in the wall of a fort etc.

loopy *adj.* (**-ier, -iest**) *slang* crazy, daft.

loose *–adj.* **1** not tightly held, fixed, etc. (*loose handle; loose stones*). **2** free from bonds or restraint. **3** not held together (*loose papers*). **4** not compact or dense (*loose soil*). **5** inexact (*loose translation*). **6** morally lax. **7** (of the tongue) indiscreet. **8** tending to diarrhoea. **9** (in *comb.*) loosely (*loose-fitting*). *–v.* (**-sing**) **1** free; untie or detach; release. **2** relax (*loosed my hold*). **3** discharge (a missile). □ **at a loose end** unoccupied. **on the loose 1** escaped from captivity. **2** enjoying oneself freely. □ **loosely** *adv.* **looseness** *n.* **loosish** *adj.* [Old Norse]

loose cover *n.* removable cover for an armchair etc.

♦ **loose insert** *n.* advertising leaflet distributed with another publication and usu. inserted loosely within its pages.

---

loose-leaf *adj.* (of a notebook etc.) with pages that can be removed and replaced.

loosen *v.* make or become loose or looser. □ **loosen a person's tongue** make a person talk freely. **loosen up 1** relax. **2** limber up.

loot *–n.* **1** spoil, booty. **2** *slang* money. *–v.* **1** rob or steal, esp. after rioting etc. **2** plunder. □ **looter** *n.* [Hindi]

lop *v.* (**-pp-**) **1 a** (often foll. by *off, away*) cut or remove (a part or parts) from a whole, esp. branches from a tree. **b** remove branches from (a tree). **2** (often foll. by *off*) remove (items) as superfluous. [Old English]

lope *–v.* (**-ping**) run with a long bounding stride. *–n.* long bounding stride. [Old Norse: related to LEAP]

lop-eared *adj.* having drooping ears. [related to LOB]

lopsided *adj.* unevenly balanced. □ **lopsidedness** *n.* [related to LOB]

loquacious /lə'kweɪʃəs/ *adj.* talkative. □ **loquacity** /-'kwæsɪtɪ/ *n.* [Latin *loquor* speak]

loquat /'ləʊkwɒt/ *n.* **1** small yellow egg-shaped fruit. **2** tree bearing it. [Chinese]

lord *–n.* **1** master or ruler. **2** *hist.* feudal superior, esp. of a manor. **3** peer of the realm or person with the title *Lord.* **4** (**Lord**) (often prec. by *the*) God or Christ. **5** (**Lord**) **a** prefixed as the designation of a marquis, earl, viscount, or baron, or (to the Christian name) of the younger son of a duke or marquis. **b** (**the Lords**) = HOUSE OF LORDS. *–int.* (**Lord, good Lord,** etc.) expressing surprise, dismay, etc. □ **lord it over** domineer. [Old English, = bread-keeper: related to LOAF[1], WARD]

Lord Chamberlain *n.* official in charge of the Royal Household.

Lord Chancellor *n.* (also **Lord High Chancellor**) highest officer of the Crown, presiding in the House of Lords etc.

Lord Chief Justice *n.* president of the Queen's Bench Division.

Lord Lieutenant *n.* **1** chief executive authority and head of magistrates in each county. **2** *hist.* viceroy of Ireland.

lordly *adj.* (**-ier, -iest**) **1** haughty, imperious. **2** suitable for a lord. □ **lordliness** *n.*

Lord Mayor *n.* title of the mayor in some large cities.

Lord Privy Seal *n.* senior cabinet minister without official duties.

lords and ladies *n.* wild arum.

Lord's Day *n.* Sunday.

lordship *n.* **1** (usu. **Lordship**) title used in addressing or referring to a man with the rank of Lord (*Your Lordship; His Lordship*). **2** (foll. by *over*) dominion, rule.

Lord's Prayer *n.* the Our Father.

Lords spiritual *n.pl.* bishops in the House of Lords.

Lord's Supper *n.* Eucharist.

Lords temporal *n.pl.* members of the House of Lords other than bishops.

lore *n.* body of traditions and knowledge on a subject or held by a particular group (*bird lore; gypsy lore*). [Old English: related to LEARN]

♦ **Lorenz curve** /lə'rents/ *n. Econ.* curve on a graph showing the degree of equality in the distribution among a population of some variable, usu. income or wealth. It is drawn by plotting the cumulative percentage of the population (e.g. households) against the cumulative percentage of, say, income, starting from the lowest income and ending with the highest. Complete equality would be represented by a 45° line between the axes. The degree of curvature away from the 45° line represents the degree of inequality. The **Gini coefficient** is a measure of this degree of inequality, being the ratio of the area between the actual curve and the 45° line to the area under the 45° line. [*Lorenz*, name of an economist]

---

lorgnette /lɔː'njet/ *n.* pair of eyeglasses or opera-glasses on a long handle. [French *lorgner* to squint]

lorn *adj. archaic* desolate, forlorn. [Old English, past part. of LOSE]

Lorraine /lə'reɪn/ region and former province of NE France,bordering on Germany, Belgium, and Luxembourg; pop. (est. 1990) 2 305 700; capital, Nancy. It has important deposits of iron ore.

lorry /'lɒrɪ/ *n.* (*pl.* **-ies**) large vehicle for transporting goods etc. [origin uncertain]

Los Alamos /lɒs 'ælə,mɒs/ city in the US, in N New Mexico, developed as a centre for atomic research in the 1940s; pop. (1990) 11 455. The first atomic bomb and hydrogen bomb were developed here.

Los Angeles /lɒs 'ændʒɪ,liːz/ city in the US, in California; pop. (est. 1994) 3 448 613. Centre of the US film industry and a tourist attraction, it is also important for aircraft manufacture and oil refining.

lose /luːz/ *v.* (**-sing**; *past* and *past part.* **lost**) **1** be deprived of or cease to have, esp. by negligence. **2** be deprived of (a person) by death. **3** become unable to find, follow, or understand (*lose one's way*). **4** let or have pass from one's control or reach (*lost my chance; lost his composure*). **5** be defeated in (a game, lawsuit, battle, etc.). **6** get rid of (*lost our pursuers; lose weight*). **7** forfeit (a right to a thing). **8** spend (time, efforts, etc.) to no purpose. **9 a** suffer loss or detriment. **b** be worse off. **10** cause (a person) the loss of (*will lose you your job*). **11** (of a clock etc.) become slow; become slow by (a specified time). **12** (in *passive*) disappear, perish; be dead (*lost at sea; is a lost art*). □ **be lost** (or **lose oneself) in** be engrossed in. **be lost on** be wasted on, or not noticed or appreciated by. **be lost to** be no longer affected by or accessible to (*is lost to pity; is lost to the world*). **be lost without** be dependent on (*am lost without my diary*). **get lost** *slang* (usu. in *imper.*) go away. **lose face** see FACE. **lose out 1** (often foll. by *on*) *colloq.* be unsuccessful; not get a full chance or advantage (in). **2** (foll. by *to*) be beaten in competition or replaced by. [Old English]

loser *n.* **1** person or thing that loses, esp. a contest (*is a bad loser*). **2** *colloq.* person who regularly fails.

loss *n.* **1** losing or being lost. **2** thing or amount lost. **3** detriment resulting from losing. □ **at a loss** (sold etc.) for less than was paid for it. **be at a loss** be puzzled or uncertain. [probably back-formation from LOST]

♦ **loss adjuster** *n.* person appointed by an insurer to negotiate an insurance claim. The loss adjuster, who is independent of the insurer, discusses the claim with both the insurer and the policyholder, producing a report recommending the basis on which the claim should be settled. The insurer pays a fee for this service based on the amount of work involved for the loss adjuster, not on the size of the settlement.

♦ **loss assessor** *n.* person who acts on behalf of the policyholder in handling a claim. A fee is charged for this service, usu. a percentage of the amount received by the policyholder.

♦ **loss-leader** *n.* product or service offered for sale by an organization at a loss in order to attract customers. This practice was curbed in the UK by the Resale Prices Act (1976), although it still continues, esp. in supermarkets.

♦ **loss-of-profits policy** *n.* = BUSINESS-INTERRUPTION POLICY.

♦ **loss ratio** *n.* total of the claims paid out by an insurance company, underwriting syndicate, etc., expressed as a percentage of the amount of premiums coming in in the same period. Insurers use this figure as a guide to the profitability of their business when they are reconsidering premium rates for a particular risk.

---

lost *past* and *past part.* of LOSE.

lost cause *n.* hopeless undertaking.

lot *n.* **1** *colloq.* (prec. by *a* or in *pl.*) **a** a large number or amount (*a lot of people; lots of milk*). **b** *colloq.* much (*a lot warmer; smiles a lot*). **2 a** each of a set of objects used to make a chance selection. **b** this method of deciding (*chosen by lot*). **3** share or responsibility resulting from it. **4** person's destiny, fortune, or condition. **5** (esp. *US*) plot; allotment of land (*parking lot*). **6** article or set of articles for sale at an auction etc. **7** group of associated persons or things. □ **cast** (or **draw) lots** decide by lots. **throw in one's lot with** decide to share the fortunes of. **the** (or **the whole) lot** the total number or quantity. **a whole lot** *colloq.* very much (*is a whole lot better*). [Old English]

■ **Usage** In sense 1a, *a lot of* is somewhat informal, but acceptable in serious writing, whereas *lots of* is not acceptable.

loth var. of LOATH.

Lothario /lə'θɑːrɪəʊ, -'θeərɪəʊ/ *n.* (*pl.* **-s**) libertine. [name of a character in a play]

Lothian /'ləʊðɪən/ former local government region in SE central Scotland; industries included electronics, distilling, and engineering. In 1996 Lothian was abolished and the council areas of West Lothian, Midlothian, and Edinburgh were formed.

loti /'lɒtiː/ *n.* (*pl.* **maloti** /mə'lɒtiː/) standard monetary unit of Lesotho. [Sesotho]

lotion /'ləʊʃ(ə)n/ *n.* medicinal or cosmetic liquid preparation applied externally. [Latin *lavo lot-* wash]

lottery /'lɒtərɪ/ *n.* (*pl.* **-ies**) **1** means of raising money by selling numbered tickets and giving prizes to the holders of numbers drawn at random. **2** thing whose success is governed by chance. [Dutch: related to LOT]

lotto /'lɒtəʊ/ *n.* game of chance like bingo, but with numbers drawn by players instead of called. [Italian]

lotus /'ləʊtəs/ *n.* **1** legendary plant inducing luxurious languor when eaten. **2** a kind of water lily etc., esp. used symbolically in Hinduism and Buddhism. [Greek *lōtos*]

lotus-eater *n.* person given to indolent enjoyment.

lotus position *n.* cross-legged position of meditation with the feet resting on the thighs.

Louangphrabang see LUANG PRABANG.

loud *–adj.* **1** strongly audible, noisy. **2** (of colours etc.) gaudy, obtrusive. *–adv.* loudly. □ **out loud** aloud. □ **loudish** *adj.* **loudly** *adv.* **loudness** *n.* [Old English]

loud hailer *n.* electronic device for amplifying the voice.

loudspeaker *n.* apparatus that converts electrical signals into sound.

lough /lɒk, lɒx/ *n. Ir.* lake, arm of the sea. [Irish: related to LOCH]

◆ Louis-Dreyfus /ˈluːɪs ˈdrɛfys/, **Gérard** (1932–) French businessman, head of Louis-Dreyfus & Company, one of the world's most successful commodity traders, which is wholly made by the Louis-Dreyfus family. The family also runs the world's third-largest orange juice processor and holds the European licence for Ralph Lauren, as well as commanding a fleet of cargo ships.

Louisiana /luːˌiːzɪˈænə/ state in the SW US, bordering on the Gulf of Mexico; pop. (est. 1996) 4 350 579; capital, Baton Rouge. It is important agriculturally, producing beef cattle, dairy produce, soya beans, rice, and cotton; there are deposits of coal, oil, and gas.

Louisville /ˈluːɪˌvɪl/ port and industrial city in the US, in NW Kentucky; products include tobacco, whiskey, and chemicals; pop. (est. 1994) 270 308.

lounge *–v.* (**-ging**) **1** recline comfortably; loll. **2** stand or move about idly. *–n.* **1** place for lounging, esp.: **a** a sitting-room in a house. **b** a public room (e.g. in a hotel). **c** a place in an airport etc. with seats for waiting passengers. **2** spell of lounging. [origin uncertain]

lounge bar *n.* more comfortable bar in a pub etc.

lounge suit *n.* man's suit for ordinary day (esp. business) wear.

lour *v.* (also **lower**) **1** frown; look sullen. **2** (of the sky etc.) look dark and threatening. [origin unknown]

louse *–n.* **1** (*pl.* **lice**) parasitic insect. **2** (*pl.* **louses**) *slang* contemptible person. *–v.* (**-sing**) delouse. □ **louse up** *slang* make a mess of. [Old English]

lousy /ˈlaʊzɪ/ *adj.* (**-ier, -iest**) **1** *colloq.* very bad; disgusting; ill (*feel lousy*). **2** (often foll. by *with*) *colloq.* well supplied, teeming. **3** infested with lice. □ **lousily** *adv.* **lousiness** *n.*

lout *n.* rough-mannered person. □ **loutish** *adj.* [origin uncertain]

Louth /laʊθ/ county in the Republic of Ireland, in the province of Leinster; agriculture produces cattle, oats, and potatoes; pop. (est. 1991) 90 707; capital, Dundalk.

Louvain see LEUVEN.

louvre /ˈluːvə(r)/ *n.* (also **louver**) **1** each of a set of overlapping slats designed to admit air and some light and exclude rain. **2** domed structure on a roof with side openings for ventilation etc. □ **louvred** *adj.* [French *lover* skylight]

lovable /ˈlʌvəb(ə)l/ *adj.* (also **loveable**) inspiring love or affection.

lovage /ˈlʌvɪdʒ/ *n.* herb used for flavouring etc. [French *levesche* from Latin *ligusticum* Ligurian]

lovat /ˈlʌvət/ *n.* & *adj.* muted green. [*Lovat* in Scotland]

love /lʌv/ *–n.* **1** deep affection or fondness. **2** sexual passion. **3** sexual relations. **4 a** beloved one; sweetheart (often as a form of address). **b** *colloq.* form of address regardless of affection. **5** *colloq.* person of whom one is fond. **6** affectionate greetings (*give him my love*). **7** (in games) no score; nil. *–v.* (**-ving**) **1** feel love or a deep fondness for. **2** delight in; admire; greatly cherish. **3** *colloq.* like very much (*loves books*). **4** (foll. by verbal noun, or *to* + infin.) be inclined, esp. as a habit; greatly enjoy (*children love dressing up*; *loves to run*). □ **fall in love** (often foll. by *with*) suddenly begin to love. **for love** for pleasure not profit. **for the love of** for the sake of. **in love** (often foll. by *with*) enamoured (of). **make love** (often foll. by *to*) **1** have sexual intercourse (with). **2** *archaic* pay amorous attention (to). **not for love or money** *colloq.* not in any circumstances. [Old English]

loveable var. of LOVABLE.

love affair *n.* romantic or sexual relationship between two people.

love-bird *n.* parrot, esp. one seeming to show great affection for its mate.

love bite *n.* bruise made by a partner's biting etc. during lovemaking.

love-child *n.* child of unmarried parents.

love-hate relationship *n.* intense relationship involving ambivalent emotions.

love-in-a-mist *n.* blue-flowered cultivated plant.

loveless *adj.* unloving or unloved or both.

love-lies-bleeding *n.* cultivated plant with drooping spikes of purple-red blooms.

lovelorn *adj.* pining from unrequited love.

lovely *–adj.* (**-ier, -iest**) **1** *colloq.* pleasing, delightful. **2** beautiful. *–n.* (*pl.* **-ies**) *colloq.* pretty woman. □ **lovely and** *colloq.* delightfully (*lovely and warm*). □ **loveliness** *n.* [Old English]

lovemaking *n.* **1** sexual play, esp. intercourse. **2** *archaic* courtship.

love-nest *n. colloq.* secluded retreat for (esp. illicit) lovers.

lover *n.* **1** person in love with another. **2** person with whom another is having sexual relations. **3** (in *pl.*) unmarried couple in love or having sexual relations. **4** person who likes or enjoys a specified thing (*music lover*).

love-seat *n.* small sofa in the shape of an S, with two seats facing in opposite directions.

lovesick *adj.* languishing with love.

lovey-dovey /ˌlʌvɪˈdʌvɪ/ *adj. colloq.* fondly affectionate, sentimental.

loving *–adj.* feeling or showing love; affectionate. *–n.* affection; love. □ **lovingly** *adv.*

loving-cup *n.* two-handled drinking-cup.

low[1] /ləʊ/ *–adj.* **1** not high or tall (*low wall*). **2 a** not elevated in position (*low altitude*). **b** (of the sun) near the horizon. **3** of or in humble rank or position (*of low birth*). **4** of small or less than normal amount, extent, or intensity (*low temperature*; *low in calories*). **5** small or reduced in quantity (*stocks are low*). **6** coming below the normal level (*low neck*). **7** dejected; lacking vigour (*feeling low*). **8** (of a sound) not shrill or loud. **9** not exalted or sublime; commonplace. **10** unfavourable (*low opinion*). **11** abject, mean, vulgar (*low cunning*; *low slang*). **12** (of a geological period) earlier. *–n.* **1** low or the lowest level or number (*pound reached a new low*). **2** area of low pressure. *–adv.* **1** in or to a low position or state. **2** in a low tone (*speak low*). **3** (of a sound) at or to a low pitch. □ **lowish** *adj.* **lowness** *n.* [Old Norse]

low[2] /ləʊ/ *–n.* sound made by cattle; moo. *–v.* make this sound. [Old English]

low-born *adj.* of humble birth.

lowbrow *–adj.* not intellectual or cultured. *–n.* lowbrow person.

Low Church *n.* section of the Church of England attaching little importance to ritual, priestly authority, and the sacraments.

low-class *adj.* of low quality or social class.

low comedy *n.* comedy bordering on farce.

Low Countries area comprising the Netherlands, Belgium, and Luxembourg.

low-down *–adj.* mean, dishonourable. *–n. colloq.* (prec. by *the*; usu. foll. by *on*) relevant information.

lower[1] *–adj.* (*compar.* of LOW[1]). **1** less high in position or status. **2** situated below another part (*lower lip*). **3 a** situated on less high land (*Lower Egypt*). **b** situated to the South (*Lower California*). **4** (of a mammal, plant, etc.) evolved to only a slight degree. *–adv.* in or to a lower position, status, etc. □ **lowermost** *adj.*

lower[2] *v.* **1** let or haul down. **2** make or become lower. **3** degrade.

lower[3] var. of LOUR.

Lower California see BAJA CALIFORNIA.

lower case *n.* small letters.

lower class *n.* working class.

Lower House *n.* larger and usu. elected body in a legislature, esp. the House of Commons.

Lower Saxony state (*Land*) in NW Germany; pop. (est. 1995) 7 715 400; capital, Hanover. Mainly agricultural, it also has some mining of coal, iron ore, and other minerals.

lowest *adj.* (*superl.* of LOW[1]) least high in position or status.

lowest common denominator *n.* **1** *Math.* lowest common multiple of the denominators of several fractions. **2** the worst or most vulgar common feature of members of a group.

lowest common multiple *n. Math.* least quantity that is a multiple of two or more given quantities.

low frequency *n.* frequency, esp. in radio, 30 to 300 kilohertz.

low gear *n.* gear such that the driven end of a transmission revolves slower than the driving end.

low-grade *adj.* of low quality.

♦ **low-involvement product** *n.* cheap product that involves the consumer in little or no trouble or deliberation when making a purchase. Advertising is often used to develop brand loyalty for such products. Cf. HIGH-INVOLVEMENT PRODUCT.

---

low-key *adj.* lacking intensity, restrained.

lowland –*n.* (usu. in *pl.*) low-lying country. –*adj.* of or in lowland. □ **lowlander** *n.*

low-level language *n.* type of computer programming language whose features directly reflect the facilities provided by a particular computer or class of computers. It is usu. an assembly language. Cf. HIGH-LEVEL LANGUAGE.

lowly *adj.* (**-ier, -iest**) humble; unpretentious. □ **lowliness** *n.*

low-lying *adj.* near to the ground or sea level.

low-pitched *adj.* **1** (of a sound) low. **2** (of a roof) having only a slight slope.

low pressure *n.* **1** low degree of activity or exertion. **2** atmospheric condition with the pressure below average.

low-rise –*adj.* (of a building) having few storeys. –*n.* such a building.

low season *n.* period of fewest visitors at a resort etc.

Low Sunday *n.* Sunday after Easter.

low tide *n.* (also **low water**) time or level of the tide at its ebb.

loyal /ˈlɔɪəl/ *adj.* **1** (often foll. by *to*) faithful. **2** steadfast in allegiance etc. □ **loyally** *adv.* **loyalty** *n.* (*pl.* **-ies**). [Latin: related to LEGAL]

loyalist *n.* **1** person who remains loyal to the legitimate sovereign etc. **2** (**Loyalist**) (esp. extremist) supporter of union between Great Britain and Northern Ireland. □ **loyalism** *n.*

loyal toast *n.* toast to the sovereign.

♦ **loyalty bonus** *n.* bonus paid to someone for being loyal in specific circumstances, esp. the cash or free shares given to a subscriber to a privatization share issue, who retains the shares for which they have subscribed beyond a specified date.

Loyalty Islands group of islands in the SW Pacific forming part of the French overseas territory of New Caledonia; pop. (1989) 17 912. Copra is the main export.

lozenge /ˈlɒzɪndʒ/ *n.* **1** rhombus. **2** small sweet or medicinal tablet to be dissolved in the mouth. **3** lozenge-shaped object. [French]

LP *abbr.* **1** Limited Partnership. **2** *Computing* linear programming. **3** long-playing (record).

L-plate *n.* sign bearing the letter L, attached to a vehicle to show that it is being driven by a learner. [from PLATE]

lpm *abbr.* lines per minute.

LPO *abbr.* London Philharmonic Orchestra.

L'pool *abbr.* Liverpool.

LPSO *abbr.* Lloyd's Policy Signing Office.

LQ *abbr.* = LETTER-QUALITY.

LR *abbr.* **1** Law Report. **2** Lloyd's Register (see LLOYD'S REGISTER OF SHIPPING).

Lr *symb.* lawrencium.

LS –*abbr.* (also **l.s.**) (Latin, on a document) locus sigilli (= the place of the seal). –*symb.* (also **S£**) Syrian pound. –*international vehicle registration* Lesotho. –*postcode* Leeds.

LSD *abbr.* lysergic acid diethylamide, a powerful hallucinogenic drug.

LSd *symb.* (also **£Sd**) Sudanese pound.

l.s.d. /ˌelesˈdiː/ *n.* (also **£.s.d.**) **1** *hist.* pounds, shillings, and pence (in former British currency). **2** money, riches. [Latin *librae, solidi, denarii*]

LSE *abbr.* **1** London School of Economics and Political Science. **2** = LONDON STOCK EXCHANGE.

LSI *abbr. Electronics* large-scale integration (of integrated circuits).

LSO *abbr.* London Symphony Orchestra.

l.s.t. *abbr.* (also **LST**) local standard time.

LT *international vehicle registration* Lithuania.

Lt. *abbr.* **1** Lieutenant. **2** light.

LT *symb.* Turkish lira.

l.t. *abbr.* **1** local time. **2** long ton.

Ltd. *abbr.* Limited. This (or the Welsh equivalent) must appear in the name of a private limited company in the UK. Cf. PUBLIC LIMITED COMPANY.

LU *postcode* Luton.

Lu *symb.* lutetium.

l/u *abbr. Shipping* laid (or lying) up.

Luanda /luːˈændə/ capital of Angola, a port in the NW of the country; pop. (est. 1993) 2 000 000. Oil is refined, and diamonds, iron, coffee, timber, and tobacco are exported.

Luang Prabang /luːˌæŋ prəˈbæŋ/ (also **Louangphrabang**) town in N Laos, a port and trading centre on the Mekong River; pop. (1985) 68 399.

lubber *n.* clumsy fellow, lout. [origin uncertain]

Lübeck /ˈluːbek/ city and port in N Germany, on the Baltic coast; industries include shipbuilding and metal founding; pop. (est. 1995) 216 854.

Lublin /ˈlʊblɪn/ industrial and commercial city in E Poland; manufactures include agricultural machinery, beer, and textiles; pop. (est. 1995) 352 500.

lubricant /ˈluːbrɪkənt/ *n.* substance used to reduce friction.

lubricate /ˈluːbrɪˌkeɪt/ *v.* (**-ting**) **1** apply oil or grease etc. to. **2** make slippery. □ **lubrication** /-ˈkeɪʃ(ə)n/ *n.* **lubricator** *n.* [Latin *lubricus* slippery]

lubricious /luːˈbrɪʃəs/ *adj.* **1** slippery, evasive. **2** lewd. □ **lubricity** *n.* [Latin: related to LUBRICATE]

Lubumbashi /ˌluːbʊmˈbæʃɪ/ (formerly **Elisabethville**) city in SE Democratic Republic of Congo, capital of the Shaba copper-mining region; pop. (est. 1994) 851 381.

LUC *abbr.* London Underwriters Centre.

♦ **Lucas critique** /ˈluːkəs/ *n.* view that government policies based on a particular model of the economy must take account of the way in which individuals change their behaviour if they become aware that the government is using that model. The critique suggests that relationships between economic variables based on individual choices may not remain stable, making policy formulation difficult if not impossible. See also RATIONAL EXPECTATIONS. [*Lucas*, name of an economist]

Lucerne /luːˈsɜːn/ (German **Luzern**) resort on the W shore of Lake Lucerne, in central Switzerland; pop. (1994) 61 656.

lucerne /luːˈsɜːn/ *n.* = ALFALFA. [Provençal, = glow-worm, referring to its shiny seeds]

lucid /ˈluːsɪd/ *adj.* **1** expressing or expressed clearly. **2** sane. □ **lucidity** /-ˈsɪdɪtɪ/ *n.* **lucidly** *adv.* **lucidness** *n.* [Latin *lux luc-* light]

Lucifer /ˈluːsɪfə(r)/ *n.* Satan. [Latin: related to LUCID, *fero* bring]

luck *n.* **1** good or bad fortune. **2** circumstances of life (beneficial or not) brought by this. **3** good fortune; success due to chance (*in luck*; *out of luck*). □ **no such luck** *colloq.* unfortunately not. [Low German or Dutch]

luckless *adj.* unlucky; ending in failure.

Lucknow /ˈlʌknaʊ/ city in India, capital of Uttar Pradesh; an agricultural trading centre with food-processing industries, it also manufactures railway equipment, chemicals, textiles, and handicrafts; pop. (1991) 1 619 115.

lucky *adj.* (**-ier**, **-iest**) **1** having or resulting from good luck. **2** bringing good luck (*lucky charm*). □ **luckily** *adv.*

lucky dip *n.* tub containing articles varying in value and chosen at random.

lucrative /ˈluːkrətɪv/ *adj.* profitable. □ **lucratively** *adv.* **lucrativeness** *n.* [Latin: related to LUCRE]

lucre /ˈluːkə(r)/ *n. derog.* financial gain. [Latin *lucrum* gain]

Lüda /luːˈdɑː/ city and port complex in NE China, in Liaoning province, comprising the cities of Lüshun and Dalian; industries include railway engineering and shipbuilding; pop. (est. 1990) 1 723 000.

Luddite /ˈlʌdaɪt/ *–n.* **1** person opposed to industrial progress or new technology. **2** *hist.* member of a band of English artisans who destroyed machinery (1811–6). *–adj.* of the Luddites. □ **Ludditism** *n.* [Ned *Lud*, name of a destroyer of machinery]

ludicrous /ˈluːdɪkrəs/ *adj.* absurd, ridiculous, laughable. □ **ludicrously** *adv.* **ludicrousness** *n.* [Latin *ludicrum* stage play]

ludo /ˈluːdəʊ/ *n.* simple board-game played with dice and counters. [Latin, = I play]

luff *v.* (also *absol.*) **1** steer (a ship) nearer the wind. **2** raise or lower (a crane's jib). [French, probably from Low German]

LUG *abbr. Computing* local users group.

lug *–v.* (**-gg-**) **1** drag or carry with effort. **2** pull hard. *–n.* **1** hard or rough pull. **2** *colloq.* ear. **3** projection on an object by which it may be carried, fixed in place, etc. [probably Scandinavian]

Lugano /luːˈgɑːnəʊ/ resort and financial centre in S Switzerland; pop. (est. 1995) 26 800.

Lugansk /luːˈgænsk/ (formerly (1935–91) **Voroshilovgrad**) industrial city in E Ukraine, in the Donets Basin; manufactures include machinery, steel, and chemicals; pop. (est. 1996) 487 000.

luggage /ˈlʌgɪdʒ/ *n.* suitcases, bags, etc., for a traveller's belongings. [from LUG]

lugger /ˈlʌgə(r)/ *n.* small ship with four-cornered sails. [from LUGSAIL]

lughole *n. slang* ear.

lugsail *n.* four-cornered sail on a yard. [probably from LUG]

lugubrious /luːˈguːbrɪəs/ *adj.* doleful. □ **lugubriously** *adv.* **lugubriousness** *n.* [Latin *lugeo* mourn]

lugworm *n.* large marine worm used as bait. [origin unknown]

Luik see LIÈGE.

lukewarm *adj.* **1** moderately warm; tepid. **2** unenthusiastic, indifferent. [Old English (now dial.) *luke* warm, WARM]

lull *–v.* **1** soothe or send to sleep. **2** (usu. foll. by *into*) deceive (a person) into undue confidence (*lulled into a false sense of security*). **3** allay (suspicions etc.), usu. by deception. **4** (of noise, a storm, etc.) abate or fall quiet. *–n.* temporary quiet period. [imitative]

lullaby /ˈlʌləˌbaɪ/ *n.* (*pl.* **-ies**) soothing song to send a child to sleep. [related to LULL]

lumbago /lʌmˈbeɪgəʊ/ *n.* rheumatic pain in the muscles of the lower back. [Latin *lumbus* loin]

lumbar /ˈlʌmbə(r)/ *adj.* of the lower back area. [as LUMBAGO]

lumbar puncture *n.* withdrawal of spinal fluid from the lower back for diagnosis.

lumber /ˈlʌmbə(r)/ *–n.* **1** disused and cumbersome articles. **2** partly prepared timber. *–v.* **1** (usu. foll. by *with*) leave (a person etc.) with something unwanted or unpleasant. **2** (usu. foll. by *up*) obstruct, fill inconveniently. **3** cut and prepare forest timber. **4** move in a slow clumsy way. [origin uncertain]

lumberjack *n.* person who fells and transports lumber.

lumber-jacket *n.* jacket of the kind worn by lumberjacks.

lumber-room *n.* room where disused things are kept.

luminary /ˈluːmɪnərɪ/ *n.* (*pl.* **-ies**) **1** *literary* natural light-giving body. **2** wise or inspiring person. **3** celebrated member of a group (*show-business luminaries*). [Latin *lumen lumin-* light]

luminescence /ˌluːmɪˈnes(ə)ns/ *n.* emission of light without heat. □ **luminescent** *adj.*

luminous /ˈluːmɪnəs/ *adj.* **1** shedding light. **2** phosphorescent, visible in darkness (*luminous paint*). □ **luminosity** /-ˈnɒsɪtɪ/ *n.*

lump[1] *–n.* **1** compact shapeless mass. **2** tumour; swelling, bruise. **3** heavy, dull, or ungainly person. **4** (prec. by *the*) *slang* casual workers in the building trade. See LUMP SYSTEM. *–v.* **1** (usu. foll. by *together* etc.) treat as all alike; put together in a lump. **2** (of sauce etc.) become lumpy. □ **lump in the throat** feeling of pressure there, caused by emotion. [Scandinavian]

lump[2] *v. colloq.* put up with ungraciously (*like it or lump it*). [imitative]

lumpectomy /lʌmˈpektəmɪ/ *n.* (*pl.* **-ies**) surgical removal of a lump from the breast.

lumpish *adj.* **1** heavy and clumsy. **2** stupid, lethargic.

lump sugar *n.* sugar in cubes.

◆ **lump sum** *n.* **1** sum of money paid all at once, rather than in instalments. **2** sum of money paid for freight, irrespective of the size of the cargo. **3** insurance benefit, e.g. a sum of money paid on retirement or redundancy or to the beneficiaries on the death of an insured person. Retirement pensions can consist of a lump sum plus a reduced pension. **4** form of damages given in tort cases.

◆ **lump-sum tax** *n.* tax that calls on the taxpayer to pay a fixed amount, which is unrelated to any factor and which cannot be avoided by any action. Lump-sum taxes are said to be Pareto-efficient (see PARETO OPTIMALITY), as they do not cause individuals to alter their pattern of consumption or employment, as most other taxes do. There are few examples of genuine lump-sum taxes, although a poll tax is often described as one.

◆ **lump system** *n.* system of employment used in the building trade in which workers are self-employed and paid lump sums for an agreed amount of work. This formerly enabled workers to avoid paying tax and insurance on their earnings; this kind of tax evasion has now been greatly reduced as employers now have to give to the Inland Revenue the details (including names and addresses) of all payments to self-employed workers.

---

lumpy *adj.* (**-ier**, **-iest**) full of or covered with lumps. □ **lumpily** *adv.* **lumpiness** *n.*

lunacy /ˈluːnəsɪ/ *n.* (*pl.* **-ies**) **1** insanity. **2** mental unsoundness. **3** great folly. [Latin: related to LUNAR]

lunar /ˈluːnə(r)/ *adj.* of, like, concerned with, or determined by the moon. [Latin *luna* moon]

lunar module *n.* small craft for travelling between the moon and a spacecraft in orbit around it.

lunar month *n.* **1** period of the moon's revolution, esp. the interval between new moons (about $29^1/_2$ days). **2** (in general use) four weeks.

lunate /ˈluːneɪt/ *adj.* crescent-shaped.

lunatic /ˈluːnətɪk/ *–n.* **1** insane person. **2** wildly foolish person. *–adj.* insane; extremely reckless or foolish. [related to LUNACY]

lunatic asylum *n. hist.* mental home or hospital.

lunatic fringe *n.* extreme or eccentric minority group.

lunation /luːˈneɪʃ(ə)n/ *n.* interval between new moons, about $29^1/_2$ days. [medieval Latin: related to LUNAR]

lunch –*n.* midday meal. –*v.* **1** take lunch. **2** entertain to lunch. [shortening of LUNCHEON]

luncheon /ˈlʌntʃ(ə)n/ *n. formal* lunch. [origin unknown]

luncheon meat *n.* tinned meat loaf of pork etc.

luncheon voucher *n.* (also **LV**) voucher issued to employees and exchangeable for food at many restaurants and shops. LVs are tax-free up to a fixed daily value and can be used as a fringe benefit. They are sold to employers by luncheon-voucher firms, who pay the restaurants the face value of the tickets, making a commission on the transaction.

LUNCO *abbr.* Lloyd's Underwriters Non-Marine Claims Office.

Lund /lʊnd/ city in SW Sweden; industries include printing, publishing, and sugar refining; pop. (1994) 95 895.

lung *n.* either of the pair of respiratory organs in humans and many other vertebrates. [Old English: related to LIGHT[2]]

lunge –*n.* **1** sudden movement forward. **2** the basic attacking move in fencing. **3** long rope on which a horse is held and made to circle round its trainer. –*v.* (**-ging**) (usu. foll. by *at, out*) deliver or make a lunge. [French *allonger* from *long* LONG[1]]

lupin /ˈluːpɪn/ *n.* cultivated plant with long tapering spikes of flowers. [related to LUPINE]

lupine /ˈluːpaɪn/ *adj.* of or like wolves. [Latin *lupinus* from *lupus* wolf]

lupus /ˈluːpəs/ *n.* autoimmune inflammatory skin disease. [Latin, = wolf]

lurch[1] –*n.* stagger; sudden unsteady movement or leaning. –*v.* stagger; move or progress unsteadily. [originally Naut., of uncertain origin]

lurch[2] *n.* □ **leave in the lurch** desert (a friend etc.) in difficulties. [obsolete French *lourche* a kind of backgammon]

lurcher /ˈlɜːtʃə(r)/ *n.* cross-bred dog, usu. a working dog crossed with a greyhound. [related to LURK]

lure –*v.* (**-ring**) **1** (usu. foll. by *away, into*) entice. **2** recall with a lure. –*n.* **1** thing used to entice. **2** (usu. foll. by *of*) enticing quality (of a pursuit etc.). **3** falconer's apparatus for recalling a hawk. [French from Germanic]

Lurex /ˈljʊəreks/ *n. propr.* **1** type of yarn incorporating a glittering metallic thread. **2** fabric made from this.

lurid /ˈljʊərɪd/ *adj.* **1** bright and glaring in colour. **2** sensational, shocking (*lurid details*). **3** ghastly, wan (*lurid complexion*). □ **luridly** *adv.* [Latin]

lurk *v.* **1** linger furtively. **2 a** lie in ambush. **b** (usu. foll. by *in, under, about*, etc.) hide, esp. for sinister purposes. **3** (as **lurking** *adj.*) dormant (*a lurking suspicion*). [perhaps from LOUR]

Lusaka /luːˈsɑːkə/ capital of Zambia, the centre of an agricultural region, with food-processing, paint, plastics, and clothing industries; pop. (1990) 982 362.

luscious /ˈlʌʃəs/ *adj.* **1** richly sweet in taste or smell. **2** (of style) over-rich. **3** voluptuously attractive. [perhaps related to DELICIOUS]

lush[1] *adj.* **1** (of vegetation) luxuriant and succulent. **2** luxurious. **3** *slang* excellent. [origin uncertain]

lush[2] *n. slang* alcoholic, drunkard. [origin uncertain]

Lüshun /luːˈʃuːn/ see LÜDA.

lust –*n.* **1** strong sexual desire. **2** (usu. foll. by *for, of*) passionate desire for or enjoyment of (*lust for power; lust of battle*). **3** sensuous appetite regarded as sinful (*lusts of the flesh*). –*v.* (usu. foll. by *after, for*) have a strong or excessive (esp. sexual) desire. □ **lustful** *adj.* **lustfully** *adv.* [Old English]

lustre /ˈlʌstə(r)/ *n.* (*US* **luster**) **1** gloss, shining surface. **2** brilliance, splendour. **3** iridescent glaze on pottery and porcelain. □ **lustrous** *adj.* [Latin *lustro* illumine]

lusty *adj.* (**-ier, -iest**) **1** healthy and strong. **2** vigorous, lively. □ **lustily** *adv.* **lustiness** *n.* [from LUST]

LUT *abbr. Computing* look-up table.

lutanist var. of LUTENIST.

lute[1] /luːt/ *n.* guitar-like instrument with a long neck and a pear-shaped body. [Arabic]

lute[2] /luːt/ –*n.* clay or cement for making joints airtight etc. –*v.* (**-ting**) apply lute to. [Latin *lutum* mud]

lutenist /ˈluːtənɪst/ *n.* (also **lutanist**) lute-player. [related to LUTE[1]]

lutetium /luːˈtiːʃəm/ *n.* silvery metallic element, the heaviest of the lanthanide series. [*Lutetia*, ancient name of Paris]

Lutheran /ˈluːθərən/ –*n.* **1** follower of Luther. **2** member of the Lutheran Church. –*adj.* of Luther, or the Protestant Reformation and the doctrines associated with him. □ **Lutheranism** *n.* [Martin *Luther*, religious reformer]

♦ **Lutine Bell** /ˈluːtiːn/ *n.* bell that hangs in the underwriting room at Lloyd's and is rung for ceremonial occasions and to draw the attention of underwriters to an important announcement. It was formerly rung once if a ship sank and twice for good news. [*Lutine*, name of the ship, insured by Lloyd's and lost at sea with most of its cargo of bullion, from which the bell was recovered]

lux *n.* (*pl.* same) the SI unit of illumination. [Latin]

Luxor /ˈlʌksə(r)/ city in Egypt, a tourist centre containing monuments of ancient Thebes; pop. (est. 1992) 155 000.

luxuriant /lʌgˈzjʊərɪənt/ *adj.* **1** growing profusely. **2** exuberant. **3** florid. □ **luxuriance** *n.* **luxuriantly** *adv.* [Latin: related to LUXURY]

■ **Usage** *Luxuriant* is sometimes confused with *luxurious*.

luxuriate /lʌgˈzjʊərɪˌeɪt/ *v.* (**-ting**) **1** (foll. by *in*) take

---

Luxembourg /ˈlʌksəmˌbɜːg/, **Grand Duchy of** country in W Europe, situated between Belgium, Germany, and France. Luxembourg is an important international and financial centre, containing the headquarters of the European Investment Bank, the European Monetary Cooperation Fund, the European Court of Justice, and the Secretariat of the European Parliament. The iron and steel industry remains a major sector of the economy; other manufactures include metal products, machinery, and food products. Agriculture includes livestock raising and wine production; the principal crops are cereals, potatoes, and wine grapes. Exports include base metals and manufactures, plastics, rubber products, transport equipment, and machinery.
History. Luxembourg became a grand duchy under Dutch sovereignty in 1815, losing its W province to Belgium in 1839; the E part became independent in 1867. Occupied by Germany during both World Wars, Luxembourg formed a customs union with Belgium in 1922 (see also BENELUX) and was a founder member of the EC. Head of state, Grand Duke Jean; prime minister, Jean-Claude Juncher; capital, Luxembourg, pop. (1991) 75 377. □ **Luxembourger** *n.*

languages	French, German, Letzeburgesch (national language)
currency	franc (LF) of 100 centimes
pop. (1996)	415 000
GNP (1994)	US$15.9B
literacy	100%
life expectancy	72 (m); 79 (f)

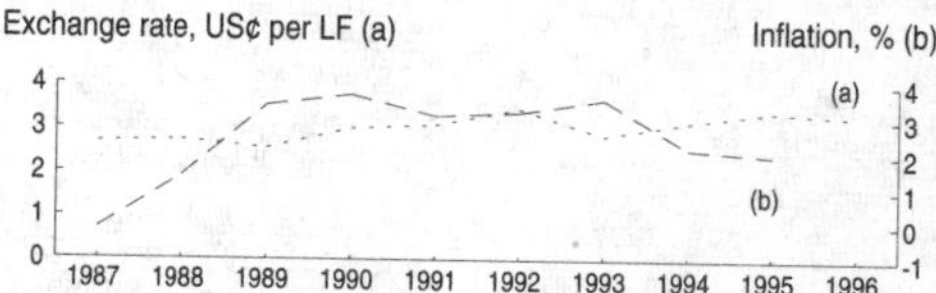

---

self-indulgent delight in, enjoy as a luxury. **2** relax in comfort.

luxurious /lʌɡˈzjʊərɪəs/ *adj.* **1** supplied with luxuries. **2** extremely comfortable. **3** fond of luxury. □ **luxuriously** *adv.* [Latin: related to LUXURY]

■ **Usage** *Luxurious* is sometimes confused with *luxuriant*.

luxury /ˈlʌkʃərɪ/ *n.* (*pl.* **-ies**) **1** choice or costly surroundings, possessions, etc. **2** thing giving comfort or enjoyment but not essential. **3** (*attrib.*) comfortable and expensive (*luxury flat*). [Latin *luxus* abundance]

♦ **luxury good** *n. Econ.* good for which demand increases more than proportionately as income rises; the income elasticity of demand is thus greater than unity. See also ENGEL CURVE; INFERIOR GOOD; NECESSARY GOOD; NORMAL GOOD.

Luzon /luːˈzɒn/ largest island of the Philippines, containing the capital (Manila); pop. (est. 1995) 32 558 000. It has important deposits, esp. chromite, and produces rice, grain, sugar cane, timber, and hemp.

LV *–abbr.* luncheon voucher. *–international vehicle registration* Latvia. *–international civil aircraft marking* Argentina.

LVA *abbr.* Licensed Victuallers' Association.

Lvov /ləˈvɒf/ industrial city in W Ukraine, near the Polish frontier; industries include engineering, food processing, chemicals, and textiles; pop. (est. 1996) 802 000.

Lw *symb. hist.* lawrencium.

■ **Usage** The symbol *Lw* has been replaced by *Lr*.

LWL *abbr.* **1** (also **l.w.l.**) length (at) water-line (of a ship). **2** *Shipping* load water-line.

LX *international civil aircraft marking* Luxembourg.

LY *–international civil aircraft marking* Lithuania. *–airline flight code* El Al Israel Airlines.

-ly[1] *suffix* forming adjectives, esp. from nouns, meaning: **1** having the qualities of (*princely*). **2** recurring at intervals of (*daily*). [Old English]

-ly[2] *suffix* forming adverbs from adjectives (*boldly*; *happily*). [Old English]

lychee /ˈlaɪtʃɪ, ˈlɪ-/ *n.* (also **litchi, lichee**) **1** sweet white juicy fruit in a brown skin. **2** tree, orig. from China, bearing this. [Chinese]

lych-gate var. of LICH-GATE.

Lycra /ˈlaɪkrə/ *n. propr.* elastic polyurethane fabric used esp. for sportswear.

lye /laɪ/ *n.* **1** water made alkaline with wood ashes. **2** any alkaline solution for washing. [Old English]

lying *pres. part.* of LIE[1], LIE[2].

lymph /lɪmf/ *n.* **1** colourless fluid from the tissues of the body, containing white blood cells. **2** this fluid used as a vaccine. [Latin *lympha*]

lymphatic /lɪmˈfætɪk/ *adj.* **1** of, secreting, or conveying lymph. **2** (of a person) pale, flabby, or sluggish.

lymphatic system *n.* network of vessels conveying lymph.

lymph gland *n.* (also **lymph node**) small mass of tissue in the lymphatic system.

lymphoma /lɪmˈfəʊmə/ *n.* (*pl.* **-s** or **-mata**) tumour of the lymph nodes.

lynch /lɪntʃ/ *v.* (of a mob) put (a person) to death without a legal trial. □ **lynching** *n.* [originally *US*, after *Lynch*, 18th-century. Justice of the Peace in Virginia]

lynch law *n.* procedure followed when a person is lynched.

lynx /lɪŋks/ *n.* (*pl.* same or **-es**) wild cat with a short tail and spotted fur. [Greek *lugx*]

lynx-eyed *adj.* keen-sighted.

Lyons /ˈliːɔ̃/ (French **Lyon**) city in SE France, capital of the Rhône-Alpes region; a major financial and textile centre, it also manufactures cars and chemicals; pop. (1990) 424 444.

lyre /ˈlaɪə(r)/ *n.* ancient U-shaped stringed instrument. [Greek *lura*]

lyre-bird *n.* Australian bird, the male of which has a lyre-shaped tail display.

lyric /ˈlɪrɪk/ *–adj.* **1** (of poetry) expressing the writer's emotions, usu. briefly and in stanzas. **2** (of a poet) writing in this manner. **3** meant or fit to be sung, songlike. *–n.* **1** lyric poem. **2** (in *pl.*) words of a song. [Latin: related to LYRE]

lyrical *adj.* **1** = LYRIC. **2** resembling, or using language appropriate to, lyric poetry. **3** *colloq.* highly enthusiastic (*wax lyrical about*). □ **lyrically** *adv.*

lyricism /ˈlɪrɪˌsɪz(ə)m/ *n.* quality of being lyric.

lyricist /ˈlɪrɪsɪst/ *n.* writer of (esp. popular) lyrics.

lysergic acid diethylamide /laɪˈsɜːdʒɪk, ˌdaɪəˈθaɪləˌmaɪd/ *n.* = LSD. [from hydro*lys*is, *erg*ot, -IC]

-lysis *comb. form* forming nouns denoting disintegration or decomposition (*electrolysis*). [Greek *lusis* loosening]

-lyte *suffix* forming nouns denoting substances that can be decomposed (*electrolyte*). [Greek *lutos* loosened]

LZ *international civil aircraft marking* Bulgaria.

M[1] /em/ *n.* (*pl.* **Ms** or **M's**) **1** thirteenth letter of the alphabet. **2** (as a roman numeral) 1000.

M[2] *abbr.* **1** (also **M.**) Master. **2** mega-. **3** = MEGABYTE. **4** (also **M.**) million. **5** (also **M.**) Monsieur. **6** motorway.

M[3] *–international vehicle registration* Malta. *–postcode* Manchester.

m *abbr.* **1** (also **m.**) male. **2** (also **m.**) masculine. **3** (also **m.**) married. **4** (also **m.**) mile(s). **5** metre(s). **6** milli-. **7** (also **m.**) million(s). **8** (also **m.**) minute(s).

♦ **M0, M1, M2, M3, M4, M5** see MONEY SUPPLY.

MA *–abbr.* Master of Arts. *–US postcode* Massachusetts. *–international vehicle registration* Morocco. *–airline flight code* Malev Hungarian Airlines.

ma /mɑː/ *n. colloq.* mother. [abbreviation of MAMMA]

m/a *abbr. Bookkeeping* my account.

MAA *abbr.* Manufacturers' Agents Association of Great Britain.

ma'am /mæm, mɑːm, məm/ *n.* madam (used esp. in addressing a royal lady). [contraction]

Maastricht /ˈmɑːstrɪxt/ industrial city in the Netherlands, capital of the province of Limburg; pop. (est. 1995) 118 341.

Maastricht Treaty *n.* legislation, signed in 1992, creating the EUROPEAN UNION (EU) from the existing 12 member countries of the European Economic Community (EEC). The 12 states agreed to European Monetary Union (EMU; see EUROPEAN MONETARY SYSTEM) leading to eventual political union. The Treaty, named after the Dutch town in which it was agreed, commits member states, inter alia, to a single currency – the EURO. It also committed members to a EUROPEAN CENTRAL BANK (ECB). The Treaty came into force in 1993. European Monetary Union was designed to be achieved in three stages, starting with participation in the Exchange Rate Mechanism (ERM). The second stage creates the EUROPEAN MONETARY INSTITUTE (EMI) to set qualifying conditions for a move towards the establishment of a single currency. The third stage, to be achieved by January 1999, locks participating states into a fixed exchange rate and activates the European Central Bank as the governor of economic and monetary policy throughout the European Union. The current timetable envisages a single currency by the year 2002.

The UK government, together with Italy and Spain, withdrew from the Exchange Rate Mechanism in September 1992, exercising opt-outs on the Maastricht Treaty. The UK government has promised a referendum of the British people before the government decides at what point to rejoin the ERM and the move towards the single currency. An **Inter-Government Conference (IGC)** began work in 1996 to set the framework of conditions and the timetable for EMU and the move to a single currency.

MAAT *abbr.* Member of the Association of Accounting Technicians.

M.Ac. *abbr.* Master of Accountancy.

mac *n.* (also **mack**) *colloq.* mackintosh. [abbreviation]

macabre /məˈkɑːbr/ *adj.* grim, gruesome. [French]

macadam /məˈkædəm/ *n.* **1** broken stone as material for road-making. **2** = TARMACADAM. □ **macadamize** *v.* (also **-ise**) (**-zing** or **-sing**). [*McAdam*, name of a surveyor]

macadamia /ˌmækəˈdeɪmɪə/ *n.* edible seed of an Australian tree. [*Macadam*, name of a chemist]

♦ **McAlpine** /məˈkælpaɪn/, **Sir Robin (1906–93)** British businessman, former chairman (1967–77) of the family construction business Sir Robert McAlpine & Sons Ltd. and former president (1966–71) of the Federation of Civil Engineering Contractors.

Macao /məˈkaʊ/ (Portuguese **Macáu**) **1** peninsula in SE China, forming (with the nearby islands of Taipa and Colôane) an overseas province of Portugal; pop. (est. 1990) 479 000. Textile manufacturing is the main industry. **2** its capital, a free port and tourist centre which occupies most of the peninsula; pop. (est. 1994) 395 304.

macaque /məˈkæk/ *n.* a kind of monkey, e.g. the rhesus monkey and Barbary ape, with prominent cheek-pouches. [Portuguese, = monkey]

macaroni /ˌmækəˈrəʊnɪ/ *n.* small pasta tubes. [Italian from Greek]

macaroon /ˌmækəˈruːn/ *n.* small almond cake or biscuit. [Italian: related to MACARONI]

Macassar /məˈkæsə(r)/ see UJUNG PADANG.

Macáu see MACAO.

macaw /məˈkɔː/ *n.* long-tailed brightly coloured American parrot. [Portuguese *macao*]

McCarthyism /məˈkɑːθɪˌɪz(ə)m/ *n. hist.* hunting out and sacking of Communists in the US. [*McCarthy*, name of a senator]

McCoy /məˈkɔɪ/ *n.* □ **the real McCoy** *colloq.* the real thing; the genuine article. [origin uncertain]

mace[1] *n.* **1** staff of office, esp. symbol of the Speaker's authority in the House of Commons. **2** person bearing this. [French from Romanic]

mace[2] *n.* dried outer covering of the nutmeg as a spice. [Latin *macir*]

macédoine /ˈmæsɪˌdwɑːn/ *n.* mixed vegetables or fruit, esp. diced or jellied. [French]

Macedonia /ˌmæsɪˈdəʊnɪə/ **1** region of SE Europe originally comprising an ancient kingdom that in modern times was divided between Yugoslavia and Greece. The Yugoslav republic of Macedonia became an independent state in 1993 (see separate entry). **2** area of NE Greece comprising three local government regions: Macedonia Central, Macedonia East and Thrace, and Macedonia West; pop. (1991) 2 574 024. □ **Macedonian** *adj.* & *n.*

macerate /ˈmæsəˌreɪt/ *v.* (**-ting**) **1** soften by soaking. **2** waste away by fasting. □ **maceration** /-ˈreɪʃ(ə)n/ *n.* [Latin]

Mach /mɑːk/ *n.* (in full **Mach number**) ratio of the speed of a body to the speed of sound in the surrounding medium. [*Mach*, name of a physicist]

machete /məˈʃetɪ/ *n.* broad heavy knife, esp. of Central America. [Spanish from Latin]

machiavellian /ˌmækɪəˈvelɪən/ *adj.* elaborately cunning; scheming, unscrupulous. □ **machiavellianism** *n.* [*Machiavelli*, name of a political writer]

machination /ˌmækɪˈneɪʃ(ə)n/ *n.* (usu. in *pl.*) plot, intrigue. □ **machinate** /ˈmæk-/ *v.* (**-ting**). [Latin: related to MACHINE]

machine /məˈʃiːn/ *–n.* **1** apparatus for applying mechanical power, having several interrelated parts. **2** particular machine, esp. a vehicle or an electrical or electronic apparatus, e.g. a computer. **3** controlling system of an organization etc. (*party machine*). **4** person who acts mechanically. **5** (esp. in *comb.*) mechanical dispenser with slots for coins (*cigarette machine*). *–v.* (**-ning**) make or operate on with a machine. [Greek *mēkhanē*]

♦ **machine code** *n.* (also **machine language**) code used to represent the instructions that a particular computer is capable of performing, and therefore specific to a particular computer. It is the form in which programs must be recorded on magnetic disk etc. and entered into main storage, and is the form subsequently used for processing (see also MACHINE INSTRUCTION). In order for the computer hardware to handle it, machine code is expressed in binary form: every operation, item of data, etc. consists of a particular sequence of bits. Computer programs are usu. written in a high-level language (e.g. COBOL), which is translated into machine code by a program (see COMPILER 2; INTERPRETER 2). A large number of machine code instructions are required for each high-level language statement. A program written in assembly language (a 'readable' form of machine code) is converted into machine code by a program known as an assembler.

♦ **machine-down time** *n.* period during which a machine cannot be used, usu. because of breakdown. If a machine is 'down', clearly production is not taking place, but it is customary in costing to attribute costs to the down time.

machine-gun –*n.* automatic gun giving continuous fire. –*v.* (**-nn-**) shoot at with a machine-gun.

♦ **machine-idle time** *n.* period during which a machine is not being used. This is similar in effect to machine-down time though it may be caused by lack of work rather than by a fault in the machine.

machine instruction *n.* (also **computer instruction**) instruction that can be recognized by the processing unit of a computer. It is written in the machine code designed for that particular computer, and can be interpreted and executed directly by the control unit and the arithmetic and logic unit of that computer. A machine instruction consists of a statement of the operation to be performed (arithmetic, logical, etc.), and some method of specifying the object(s) upon which the operation is to be performed together with an indication of where the result is to go.

machine-readable *adj.* in a form that a computer can process.

machinery *n.* (*pl.* **-ies**) **1** machines. **2** mechanism. **3** (usu. foll. by *of*) organized system. **4** (usu. foll. by *for*) means devised.

machine tool *n.* mechanically operated tool.

machinist *n.* **1** person who operates a machine, esp. a sewing-machine or a machine tool. **2** person who makes machinery.

machismo /mə'kɪzməʊ, -'tʃɪzməʊ/ *n.* being macho; masculine pride. [Spanish]

macho /'mætʃəʊ/ *adj.* aggressively masculine. [from MACHISMO]

Mach one *n.* (also **Mach two** etc.) the speed (or twice etc. the speed) of sound.

macintosh var. of MACKINTOSH.

mack var. of MAC.

Mackay /mə'kaɪ/ port in NE Australia, on the coast of Queensland, the centre of Australia's sugar industry; pop. (1993) 55 772.

mackerel /'mækr(ə)l/ *n.* (*pl.* same or **-s**) marine fish used as food. [Anglo-French]

mackerel sky *n.* sky dappled with rows of small white fleecy clouds.

mackintosh /'mækɪn,tɒʃ/ *n.* (also **macintosh**) **1** waterproof coat or cloak. **2** cloth waterproofed with rubber. [*Macintosh*, name of its inventor]

macramé /mə'krɑːmɪ/ *n.* **1** art of knotting cord or string in patterns to make decorative articles. **2** work so made. [Arabic, = bedspread]

♦ **macro** /'mækrəʊ/ *n.* (in full **macro-instruction**) sequence of computer instructions generated by a special piece of software called a **macrogenerator**. Instead of writing the same sequence of instructions every time it is needed, the programmer defines a macro by giving the sequence a symbolic name, which is used in the program. The macrogenerator (which may be part of a larger piece of software, such as an assembler) automatically substitutes the sequence for all occurrences of the name.

macro- *comb. form* **1** long. **2** large, large-scale. [Greek *makros* long]

macrobiotic /,mækrəʊbaɪ'ɒtɪk/ –*adj.* of a diet intended to prolong life, esp. consisting of wholefoods. –*n.* (in *pl.*; treated as *sing.*) theory of such a diet. [Greek *bios* life]

macrocarpa /,mækrəʊ'kɑːpə/ *n.* evergreen tree, often cultivated for hedges or wind-breaks. [Greek MACRO-, *karpos* fruit]

macrocosm /'mækrəʊ,kɒz(ə)m/ *n.* **1** universe. **2** the whole of a complex structure. [from MACRO-, COSMOS]

♦ **macroeconomic model** *n.* model of a country's economy based on macroeconomic theory and econometric analysis. These models make use of past data on such variables as output, employment, and consumption to forecast future values. In the UK, many such models are constructed by various groups of economists; the most influential is the model constructed by the Treasury. However, the quality and usefulness of the forecasts so obtained are still widely debated.

♦ **macroeconomics** /,mækrəʊ,iːkə'nɒmɪks/ *n.* the study of the economy as a whole. It considers economic aggregates and their relationships to, for example, money, employment, interest rates, government spending, investment, and consumption; it also seeks to establish what role, if any, the government should play in the economy. J. M. Keynes is widely credited with the foundation of macroeconomics since he sought to explain that even if

Macedonia, Former Yugoslav Republic of country in SE Europe, bordered by Serbia, Bulgaria, Greece, and Albania. Agriculture is important; crops include wheat, maize, grapes, and plums, and livestock (esp. sheep) are raised. Copper ore and iron ore are mined and manufacturing industry produces clothing and footwear, textiles, machinery and transport equipment, chemicals, and food products for export. Macedonia's economy has been severely disrupted by the war in Yugoslavia, which has deprived it of its major trading partners, and by lack of foreign aid due to delay in international recognition of its independence. The latter has been caused mainly by Greece, which objected to the territorial claims implied by the name 'Macedonia' (the republic borders on a Greek province of the same name); the current name, under which the country was admitted to the UN in April 1993, is a provisional one. Greece imposed an economic blockade in 1994 following the establishment of diplomatic relations between a number of EU countries and the Former Yugoslav Republic of Macedonia. The blockade was lifted the next year following alterations to the Macedonia flag. President, Kiro Gligorov; capital, Skopje.

language	Macedonian
currency	denar
pop. (1996)	1 968 000
GNP (1994)	US$1.6B
literacy	94% (m); 84% (f)
life expectancy	70 (m); 74 (f)

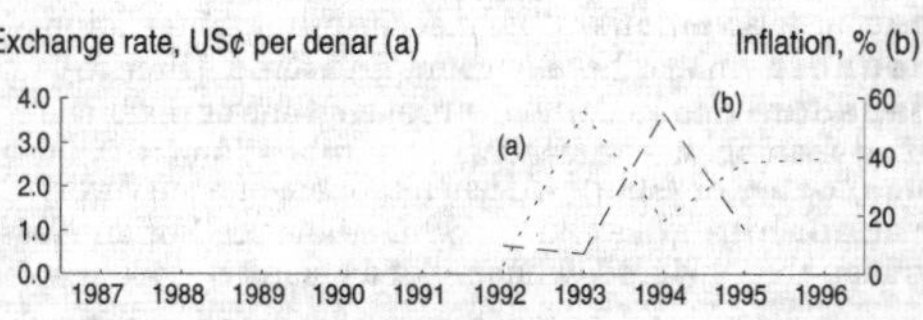

the economy is operating efficiently at the microeconomic level, unemployment and recession may still occur at the macroeconomic level, because of the lack of coordination between markets. See also KEYNESIANISM; MONETARISM. □ **macroeconomic** *adj.*

◆ **macroenvironment** /ˌmækrəʊɪnˈvaɪərənmənt/ *n.* wider environment over which businesses have no control but which determine business strategy and success, it includes the physical environment, economic climate, legal infrastructure, demographic make-up of its markets, and prevailing social and cultural issues.

---

macron /ˈmækrɒn/ *n.* mark (¯) over a long or stressed vowel. [Greek, neuter of *makros* long]

macroscopic /ˌmækrəʊˈskɒpɪk/ *adj.* **1** visible to the naked eye. **2** regarded in terms of large units.

macula /ˈmækjʊlə/ *n.* (*pl.* **-lae** /-ˌliː/) dark, esp. permanent, spot in the skin. □ **maculation** /-ˈleɪʃ(ə)n/ *n.* [Latin, = spot, mesh]

mad *adj.* (**madder, maddest**) **1** insane; frenzied. **2** wildly foolish. **3** (often foll. by *about, on*) *colloq.* wildly excited or infatuated. **4** *colloq.* angry. **5** (of an animal) rabid. **6** wildly light-hearted. □ **like mad** *colloq.* with great energy or enthusiasm. □ **madness** *n.* [Old English]

madam /ˈmædəm/ *n.* **1** polite or respectful form of address or mode of reference to a woman. **2** *colloq.* conceited or precocious girl or young woman. **3** woman brothel-keeper. [related to MADAME]

Madame /məˈdɑːm, ˈmædəm/ *n.* **1** (*pl.* **Mesdames** /meɪˈdɑːm, -ˈdæm/) Mrs or madam (used of or to a French-speaking woman). **2** (**madame**) = MADAM 1. [French *ma dame* my lady]

madcap *–adj.* wildly impulsive. *–n.* wildly impulsive person.

mad cow disease *n. colloq.* = BSE.

madden *v.* **1** make or become mad. **2** irritate. □ **maddening** *adj.* **maddeningly** *adv.*

madder /ˈmædə(r)/ *n.* **1** herbaceous plant with yellowish flowers. **2 a** red dye from its root. **b** its synthetic substitute. [Old English]

◆ **mad dog** *n. colloq.* company with potential for rapid growth provided it can raise sufficient risk capital.

---

made 1 *past* and *past part.* of MAKE. **2** *adj.* **a** built or formed (*well-made*). **b** successful (*self-made man; be made*). □ **have** (or **have got) it made** *colloq.* be sure of success. **made for** ideally suited to. **made of** consisting of. **made of money** *colloq.* very rich.

Madeira /məˈdɪərə/ (also **Madeira Islands** or **Madeiras**) group of islands in the Atlantic Ocean off NW Africa, which are in Portuguese possession but partially autonomous; pop. (est. 1993) 253 800; capital, Funchal (on Madeira, the largest island). Madeira wine is the principal export and tourism is important. *–n.* **1** fortified white wine from Madeira. **2** (in full **Madeira cake**) kind of sponge cake.

Mademoiselle /ˌmædəmwəˈzel/ *n.* (*pl.* **Mesdemoiselles**) /ˌmeɪdm-/ **1** Miss or madam (used of or to an unmarried French-speaking woman). **2** (**mademoiselle**) **a** young Frenchwoman. **b** French governess. [French *ma* my, *demoiselle* DAMSEL]

made to measure *adj.* tailor-made.

madhouse *n.* **1** *colloq.* scene of confused uproar. **2** *archaic* mental home or hospital.

Madhya Pradesh /ˌmɑːdɪə prəˈdeʃ/ state in central India; pop. (est. 1994) 71 950 000; capital, Bhopal. It is mainly agricultural, but coal, iron ore, aluminium, and other minerals are mined and industries, powered by hydroelectricity, include mineral processing.

Madison /ˈmædɪs(ə)n/ city in the US, capital of Wisconsin and the commercial and industrial centre of an agricultural region; manufactures include agricultural machinery and medical equipment; pop. (est. 1994) 194 586.

madly *adv.* **1** in a mad manner. **2** *colloq.* **a** passionately. **b** extremely.

madman *n.* man who is mad.

Madonna /məˈdɒnə/ *n.* **1** (prec. by *the*) the Virgin Mary. **2** (**madonna**) picture or statue of her. [Italian, = my lady]

Madras /məˈdrɑːs, -æs/ **1** seaport on the E coast of India, capital of Tamil Nadu state; name formally changed to Chennai in 1995; manufactures include vehicles, textiles, and fertilizers; pop. (1991) 5 421 985. **2** see TAMIL NADU.

Madrid /məˈdrɪd/ capital of Spain; manufactures include glassware, porcelain, textiles, chemicals, and leather goods; pop. (est. 1994) 3 041 101.

madrigal /ˈmædrɪg(ə)l/ *n.* part-song, usu. unaccompanied, for several voices. [Italian]

Madura /məˈdʊərə/ Indonesian island off the NE coast of Java; cattle raising and fish farming are the main activities; chief town, Pamekasan.

Madurai /ˌmɑːdʊˈraɪ/ city in S India, in Tamil Nadu state; manufactures include brassware and textiles; pop. (1991) 940 989.

madwoman *n.* woman who is mad.

MA(Econ.) *abbr.* Master of Arts in Economics.

maelstrom /ˈmeɪlstrəm/ *n.* **1** great whirlpool. **2** state of confusion. [Dutch]

maenad /ˈmiːnæd/ *n.* **1** bacchante. **2** frenzied woman. □ **maenadic** /-ˈnædɪk/ *adj.* [Greek *mainomai* rave]

maestro /ˈmaɪstrəʊ/ *n.* (*pl.* **maestri** /-strɪ/ or **-s**) **1** distinguished musician, esp. a conductor, composer, or teacher. **2** great performer in any sphere. [Italian]

Madagascar /ˌmædəˈgæskə(r)/, **Democratic Republic of** (former name (1958–75) **Malagasy Republic**) island country in the Indian Ocean, off the E coast of Africa. The economy is mainly agricultural; the staple crop is rice and cattle farming is important. Cash crops include coffee (the chief export), vanilla, cloves and clove oil, sugar cane, shrimps, and tropical fruit; agricultural produce constitutes about three-quarters of exports. Minerals include chromite, graphite, and mica, and offshore reserves of oil and natural gas were discovered in the late 1980s. A range of economic reforms are being implemented to increase agricultural production, improve communications, create more small industries, and increase exploitation of mineral resources.

History. Madagascar remained independent, despite rival French and British attempts at domination, until colonized by the French in 1896. It regained full independence (as the Malagasy Republic) in 1960 and in 1975 a new socialist constitution was adopted. In 1991, after socialist policies had led to poor economic performance and considerable social unrest, a transitional administration was formed, and in 1993 the multi-party presidential election was won by the opposition candidate. In 1995 President Zafy stepped down following the legislature's announcement that it intended to begin impeachment proceedings. A former military ruler, Didier Ratsiraka was the subsequent election. President, Didier Ratsiraka; capital, Antananarivo.

languages	Malagasy, French, English
currency	franc (FMG) of 100 centimes
pop. (1996)	13 671 000
GNP (1994)	US$3B
literacy	87% (m); 73% (f)
life expectancy	55 (m); 58 (f)

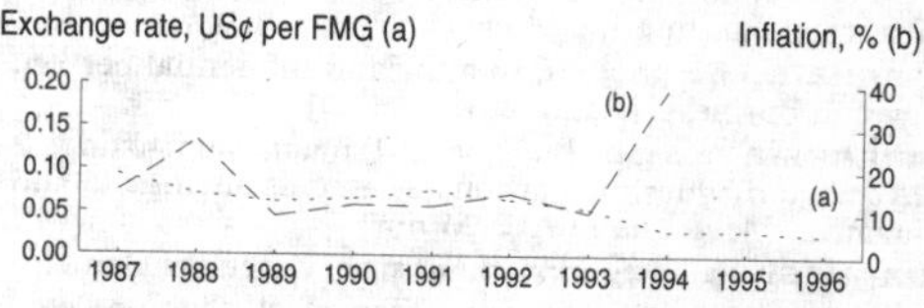

Mae West /meɪ 'west/ *n. slang* inflatable life-jacket. [name of a film actress]

MAFF /mæf/ *abbr.* Ministry of Agriculture, Fisheries, and Food.

Mafia /'mæfɪə/ *n.* **1** organized body of criminals, orig. in Sicily, now also in Italy and the US. **2** (**mafia**) group regarded as exerting an intimidating and corrupt power. [Italian dial., = bragging]

Mafioso /ˌmæfɪ'əʊsəʊ/ *n.* (*pl.* **Mafiosi** /-sɪ/) member of the Mafia. [Italian: related to MAFIA]

mag *n. colloq.* = MAGAZINE 1. [abbreviation]

magazine /ˌmægə'ziːn/ *n.* **1** illustrated periodical publication containing articles, stories, etc. **2** chamber holding cartridges to be fed automatically to the breech of a gun. **3** similar device in a slide projector etc. **4** military store for arms etc. **5** store for explosives. [Arabic *makẖāzin*]

Magdeburg /'mægdɪˌbɜːg/ industrial city in E Germany, the capital of Saxony-Anhalt; industries include oil refining, chemicals, and textiles; pop. (est. 1995) 265 379.

Magellan /mə'gelən/, **Strait of** channel separating the S tip of mainland South America from Tierra del Fuego and providing a passage between the S Atlantic and S Pacific Oceans.

magenta /mə'dʒentə/ –*n.* **1** shade of crimson. **2** aniline crimson dye. –*adj.* of or coloured with magenta. [*Magenta* in N Italy]

maggot /'mægət/ *n.* larva, esp. of the housefly or bluebottle. □ **maggoty** *adj.* [perhaps an alteration of *maddock*, from Old Norse]

Maghrib /'mægrɪb/ (also **Maghreb**) region of N and NW Africa, between the Atlantic Ocean and Egypt, occupied by Algeria, Tunisia, and parts of Morocco and Libya.

magi *pl.* of MAGUS.

magic /'mædʒɪk/ –*n.* **1 a** supposed art of influencing or controlling events supernaturally. **b** witchcraft. **2** conjuring tricks. **3** inexplicable influence. **4** enchanting quality or phenomenon. –*adj.* **1** of magic. **2** producing surprising results. **3** *colloq.* wonderful, exciting. –*v.* (**-ck-**) change or create by or as if by magic. □ **like magic** very rapidly. **magic away** cause to disappear as if by magic. [Greek *magikos*: related to MAGUS]

magical *adj.* **1** of magic. **2** resembling, or produced as if by, magic. **3** wonderful, enchanting. □ **magically** *adv.*

magic eye *n.* photoelectric device used for detection, automatic control, etc.

magician /mə'dʒɪʃ(ə)n/ *n.* **1** person skilled in magic. **2** conjuror.

magic lantern *n.* primitive form of slide projector.

magisterial /ˌmædʒɪ'stɪərɪəl/ *adj.* **1** imperious. **2** authoritative. **3** of a magistrate. □ **magisterially** *adv.* [medieval Latin: related to MASTER]

magistracy /'mædʒɪstrəsɪ/ *n.* (*pl.* **-ies**) **1** magisterial office. **2** magistrates collectively.

magistrate /'mædʒɪˌstreɪt/ *n.* **1** civil officer administering the law. **2** official conducting a court for minor cases and preliminary hearings. [Latin: related to MASTER]

magma /'mægmə/ *n.* (*pl.* **magmata** or **-s**) molten rock under the earth's crust, from which igneous rock is formed by cooling. [Greek *massō* knead]

Magna Carta /ˌmægnə 'kɑːtə/ *n.* (also **Magna Charta**) charter of liberty obtained from King John in 1215. [medieval Latin, = great charter]

magnanimous /mæg'nænɪməs/ *adj.* nobly generous; not petty in feelings or conduct. □ **magnanimity** /ˌmægnə'nɪmɪtɪ/ *n.* **magnanimously** *adv.* [Latin *magnus* great, *animus* mind]

magnate /'mægneɪt/ *n.* wealthy and influential person, usu. in business. [Latin *magnus* great]

magnesia /mæg'niːʃə, -ʒə/ *n.* **1** magnesium oxide. **2** hydrated magnesium carbonate, used as an antacid and laxative. [*Magnesia* in Asia Minor]

magnesium /mæg'niːzɪəm/ *n.* silvery metallic element.

magnet /'mægnɪt/ *n.* **1** piece of iron, steel, alloy, ore, etc., having the properties of attracting iron and of pointing approximately north and south when suspended. **2** lodestone. **3** person or thing that attracts. [Greek *magnēs -ētos* of Magnesia: related to MAGNESIA]

magnetic /mæg'netɪk/ *adj.* **1 a** having the properties of a magnet. **b** produced or acting by magnetism. **2** capable of being attracted by or acquiring the properties of a magnet. **3** strongly attractive (*magnetic personality*). □ **magnetically** *adv.*

♦ **magnetic disk** *n.* flat circular disk coated with a magnetic material, used to store data in a computer system. The data is recorded, in the magnetic coating, in circular tracks around the centre of the disk; it is stored as a pattern of magnetized spots. The tracks are divided into sectors (see SECTOR 4). The disk is rotated in a disk drive, under a read/write head, which can both read the pattern of magnetized spots on the disk and write a pattern onto the disk (see DISK DRIVE). Items of data can be located directly, within a very short period of time, as there is random access to a magnetic disk. It follows that files of data can be stored on disk either in an ordered sequence or in a random manner. In addition, data within a file can be accessed either in sequential order or randomly. Disks are used as backing store in large and small computers, the access time being brief enough for on-line processing. Disks can be either rigid or flexible (see HARD DISK; FLOPPY DISK). Some hard disks (fixed disks) are permanently fixed inside the disk drive. Others, e.g. floppy disks, can be removed from the disk drive. Large computers also use cartridge disks (in which the disks are held in a plastic cover) and disk packs (a stack of disks in a plastic hood). The storage capacity depends on a number of factors including type and size of disk, the number of tracks per disk, and the recording density along the tracks.

---

magnetic field *n.* area of force around a magnet.

♦ **magnetic ink character recognition** *n.* (also **MICR**) process in which letters, numbers, and other characters, printed in magnetic ink, are read and encoded by electronic means. The ink is used on cheques and other documents to enable them to be automatically sorted and the characters to be read and fed into a computer.

---

magnetic mine *n.* underwater mine detonated by the approach of a large mass of metal, e.g. a ship.

magnetic needle *n.* piece of magnetized steel used as an indicator on the dial of a compass etc.

magnetic north *n.* point indicated by the north end of a magnetic needle.

magnetic pole *n.* point near the north or south pole where a magnetic needle dips vertically.

magnetic storm *n.* disturbance of the earth's magnetic field by charged particles from the sun etc.

magnetic strip *n.* strip of magnetic film on a credit card etc. on which machine-readable data is encoded, esp. for identification and security purposes.

♦ **magnetic tape** *n.* **1** plastic strip coated with magnetic material for recording sound or pictures. **2** similar material for storing computer data in the form of a series of magnetized spots, which run lengthwise along the tape. The data is read by moving the tape past a read/write head (see TAPE UNIT; SERIAL ACCESS). Magnetic tape is used as off-line backing store in large computers. See also BACKING STORE; MAGNETIC DISK.

---

magnetism /'mægnɪˌtɪz(ə)m/ *n.* **1 a** magnetic phenomena and their science. **b** property of producing these. **2** attraction; personal charm.

magnetize /'mægnɪˌtaɪz/ *v.* (also **-ise**) (**-zing** or **-sing**) **1** give magnetic properties to. **2** make into a magnet. **3** attract as a magnet does. □ **magnetizable** *adj.* **magnetization** /-'zeɪʃ(ə)n/ *n.*

magneto /mæg'niːtəʊ/ *n.* (*pl.* **-s**) electric generator using permanent magnets (esp. for the ignition of an internal-combustion engine). [abbreviation of *magneto-electric*]

Magnificat /mæg'nɪfɪ,kæt/ *n.* hymn of the Virgin Mary used as a canticle. [from its opening word]

magnification /,mægnɪfɪ'keɪʃ(ə)n/ *n.* **1** magnifying or being magnified. **2** degree of this.

magnificent /mæg'nɪfɪs(ə)nt/ *adj.* **1** splendid, stately. **2** *colloq.* fine, excellent. □ **magnificence** *n.* **magnificently** *adv.* [Latin *magnificus* from *magnus* great]

magnify /'mægnɪ,faɪ/ *v.* (**-ies**, **-ied**) **1** make (a thing) appear larger than it is, as with a lens. **2** exaggerate. **3** intensify. **4** *archaic* extol. □ **magnifiable** *adj.* **magnifier** *n.* [Latin: related to MAGNIFICENT]

magnifying glass *n.* lens used to magnify.

magnitude /'mægnɪ,tju:d/ *n.* **1** largeness. **2** size. **3** importance. **4 a** degree of brightness of a star. **b** class of stars arranged according to this (*of the third magnitude*). □ **of the first magnitude** very important. [Latin *magnus* great]

magnolia /mæg'nəʊlɪə/ *n.* **1** tree with dark-green foliage and waxy flowers. **2** creamy-pink colour. [*Magnol*, name of a botanist]

magnox /'mægnɒks/ *n.* magnesium-based alloy used to enclose uranium fuel elements in some nuclear reactors. [*mag*nesium *no ox*idation]

magnum /'mægnəm/ *n.* (*pl.* **-s**) wine bottle twice the normal size. [Latin, neuter of *magnus* great]

magnum opus /,mægnəm 'əʊpəs/ *n.* great work of art, literature, etc., esp. an artist's most important work. [Latin]

magpie /'mægpaɪ/ *n.* **1** a kind of crow with a long tail and black and white plumage. **2** chatterer. **3** indiscriminate collector. [from *Mag*, abbreviation of *Margaret*, PIE[2]]

magus /'meɪgəs/ *n.* (*pl.* **magi** /'meɪdʒaɪ/) **1** priest of ancient Persia. **2** sorcerer. **3** (**the Magi**) the 'wise men' from the East (Matt. 2:1–12). [Persian *magus*]

Magyar /'mægjɑ:(r)/ *–n.* **1** member of the chief ethnic group in Hungary. **2** their language. *–adj.* of this people. [native name]

maharaja /,mɑ:hə'rɑ:dʒə/ *n.* (also **maharajah**) *hist.* title of some Indian princes. [Hindi, = great rajah]

maharanee /,mɑ:hə'rɑ:nɪ/ *n.* (also **maharani**) (*pl.* **-s**) *hist.* maharaja's wife or widow. [Hindi, = great ranee]

Maharashtra /,mɑ:hə'ræʃtrə/ state in W India bordering on the Arabian Sea; pop. (est. 1994) 85 565 000; capital, Bombay. Minerals, including bauxite and iron ore, are mined and there is considerable industrialization, manufactures including cotton textiles, chemicals, machinery, and oil products. □ **Maharashtrian** *adj.* & *n.*

maharishi /,mɑ:hə'rɪʃɪ/ *n.* (*pl.* **-s**) great Hindu sage. [Hindi]

mahatma /mə'hætmə/ *n.* **1** (in India etc.) revered person. **2** one of a class of persons supposed by some Buddhists to have preternatural powers. [Sanskrit, = great soul]

mah-jong /mɑ:'dʒɒŋ/ *n.* (also **mah-jongg**) game played with 136 or 144 pieces called tiles. [Chinese dial. *ma-tsiang* sparrows]

mahlstick var. of MAULSTICK.

mahogany /mə'hɒgənɪ/ *n.* (*pl.* **-ies**) **1** reddish-brown tropical wood used for furniture. **2** its colour. [origin unknown]

mahonia /mə'həʊnɪə/ *n.* evergreen shrub with yellow bell-shaped flowers. [French or Spanish]

Mahore /mə'hɔ:(r)/ see MAYOTTE.

mahout /mə'haʊt/ *n.* (in India etc.) elephant-driver. [Hindi from Sanskrit]

maid *n.* **1** female servant. **2** *archaic* or *poet.* girl, young woman. [abbreviation of MAIDEN]

maiden /'meɪd(ə)n/ *n.* **1 a** *archaic* or *poet.* girl; young unmarried woman. **b** (*attrib.*) unmarried (*maiden aunt*). **2** = MAIDEN OVER. **3** (*attrib.*) (of a female animal) unmated. **4** (often *attrib.*) **a** horse that has never won a race. **b** race open only to such horses. **5** (*attrib.*) first (*maiden speech*; *maiden voyage*). □ **maidenhood** *n.* **maidenly** *adj.* [Old English]

maidenhair *n.* fern with hairlike stalks and delicate fronds.

maidenhead *n.* **1** virginity. **2** hymen.

maiden name *n.* woman's surname before marriage.

maiden over *n.* over in cricket in which no runs are scored.

maid of honour *n.* **1** unmarried lady attending a queen or princess. **2** esp. *US* principal bridesmaid.

maidservant *n.* female servant.

mail[1] *–n.* **1 a** letters and parcels etc. carried by post. **b** postal system. **c** one complete delivery or collection of mail. **2** see ELECTRONIC MAIL. **3** vehicle carrying mail. *–v.* send by post or electronic mail. [French *male* wallet]

mail[2] *n.* armour of metal rings or plates. [French *maille* from Latin *macula*]

mailbag *n.* large sack for carrying mail.

mailbox *n.* *US* letter-box.

mailing list *n.* list of people to whom advertising matter etc. is posted. See also DIRECT-MAIL SELLING; LIST RENTING.

♦ **mail merge** see WORD PROCESSOR.

---

mail order *n.* purchase of goods by post.

♦ **mail-order house** *n.* firm that specializes in selling goods direct to customers by post. Orders are obtained from an illustrated catalogue supplied by the firm or by agents, who introduce the catalogue. The low costs of selling, esp. the absence of retail premises, enable the mail-order houses to offer goods at competitive prices. See also DIRECT-MAIL SELLING.

---

mailshot *n.* advertising, selling, or fund-raising material sent to potential customers or donors.

♦ **mail survey** *n.* market research conducted by mail. As respondents have time to consider their answers, this form of research has advantages over both telephone surveys and face-to-face surveys, although it does suffer from low returns.

---

maim *v.* cripple, disable, mutilate. [French *mahaignier*]

main *–adj.* **1** chief, principal. **2** exerted to the full (*by main force*). *–n.* **1** principal duct etc. for water, sewage, etc. **2** (usu. in *pl.*; prec. by *the*) **a** central distribution network for electricity, gas, water, etc. **b** domestic electricity supply as distinct from batteries. **3** *poet.* high seas (*Spanish Main*). □ **in the main** mostly. [Old English]

main brace *n.* brace attached to the main yard.

main chance *n.* (prec. by *the*) one's own interests.

Maine /meɪn/ state in the NE US, on the Atlantic coast; pop. (est. 1996) 1 243 316; capital, Augusta. Extensive forests provide timber for manufacturing industries and quarrying of building stone, sand, and gravel is important.

♦ **mainframe** *n.* (often *attrib.*) large general-purpose computer system, requiring an air-conditioned room and special staff, including operators, programmers, and system analysts, to run it. Used by large organizations, e.g. banks, mainframes can handle vast amounts of information with ease and calculate at high speed. They can also handle many users simultaneously (see TIME-SHARING 2). Cf. MICROCOMPUTER; MINICOMPUTER.

Mainland /'meɪnlənd/ **1** largest island in Orkney; pop. (1991) 15 128; chief town, Kirkwall. **2** largest island in Shetland; pop. (1991) 17 596; chief town, Lerwick.

mainland *n.* large continuous extent of land, excluding neighbouring islands.

mainline *v.* (**-ning**) *slang* **1** take drugs intravenously. **2** inject (drugs) intravenously. □ **mainliner** *n.*

main line *n.* railway line linking large cities.

mainly /'meɪnlɪ/ *adv.* mostly; chiefly.

♦ **main market** *n.* premier market for the trading of equities on the London Stock Exchange. For this market the listing requirements are the most stringent and the liquidity of the market is greater than in the ALTERNATIVE INVESTMENT MARKET. A company wishing to enter this market must have audited trading figures covering at least five years and must place 25% of its shares in public hands. The main market currently deals in 2600 securities. Cf. OVER-THE-COUNTER MARKET; UNLISTED SECURITIES MARKET.

---

mainmast *n.* principal mast of a ship.

main memory *n.* = MAIN STORE.

mainsail /'meɪnseɪl, -s(ə)l/ *n.* **1** (in a square-rigged vessel) lowest sail on the mainmast. **2** (in a fore-and-aft rigged vessel) sail set on the after part of the mainmast.

mainspring *n.* **1** principal spring of a watch, clock, etc. **2** chief motivating force; incentive.

mainstay *n.* **1** chief support. **2** stay from the maintop to the foot of the foremast.

main store *n.* (also **main storage, main memory, immediate-access store**) computer memory closely associated with the processor of a computer (see PROCESSOR 3), from which program instructions and data can be retrieved extremely rapidly for handling by the computer and in which the resulting data is stored prior to being transferred to backing store or output device. Programs can only be executed when they are in main store. Programs and associated data are not, however, retained permanently there but are kept in backing store until required by the processor. The backing store in a particular computer (large or small) has a larger storage capacity than the main store in that computer. Main store consists of semiconductor memory to which there is random access. It is very reliable and is becoming highly miniaturized.

mainstream *n.* **1** (often *attrib.*) ultimately prevailing trend in opinion, fashion, etc. **2** type of swing jazz, esp. with solo improvisation. **3** principal current of a river etc.

♦ **mainstream corporation tax** *n.* (also **MCT**) the corporation tax for which a company is liable for an accounting period after the relevant advance corporation tax (ACT) has been deducted. In the imputation system of corporation tax in the UK, payments on account of ACT are paid when dividends are paid to shareholders. Mainstream corporation tax is the balance remaining to be paid.

---

maintain /meɪn'teɪn/ *v.* **1** cause to continue; keep up (an activity etc.). **2** support by work, expenditure, etc. **3** assert as true. **4** preserve (a house, machine, etc.) in good repair. **5** provide means for. [Latin *manus* hand, *teneo* hold]

maintained school *n.* school supported from public funds, state school.

maintenance /'meɪntənəns/ *n.* **1** maintaining or being maintained. **2 a** provision of the means to support life. **b** alimony. **3** activity, including tests, measurements, modifications, replacements, and upgrading, that aims to prevent the occurrence of faults in machinery, computers, computer programs, etc. (**preventive maintenance**) or corrects an existing fault (**corrective maintenance**). [French: related to MAINTAIN]

maintop *n.* platform above the head of the lower mainmast.

maintopmast *n.* mast above the head of the lower mainmast.

main yard *n.* yard on which the mainsail is extended.

maiolica /mə'jɒlɪkə/ *n.* (also **majolica**) white tin-glazed earthenware decorated with metallic colours or enamelled. [Italian, from the former name of Majorca]

maisonette /ˌmeɪzə'net/ *n.* **1** flat on more than one floor. **2** small house. [French *maisonnette* diminutive of *maison* house]

maize *n.* **1** cereal plant of North America. **2** cobs or grain of this. [French or Spanish]

Maj. *abbr.* Major.

majestic /mə'dʒestɪk/ *adj.* stately and dignified; imposing. □ **majestically** *adv.*

majesty /'mædʒɪstɪ/ *n.* (*pl.* **-ies**) **1** stateliness, dignity, or authority, esp. of bearing, language, etc. **2 a** royal power. **b** (**Majesty**) (prec. by *His, Her, Your*) forms of description or address for a sovereign or a sovereign's wife or widow (*Your Majesty*; *Her Majesty the Queen Mother*). [Latin *majestas*: related to MAJOR]

majolica var. of MAIOLICA.

major /'meɪdʒə(r)/ *–adj.* **1** relatively great in size, intensity, scope, or importance. **2** (of surgery) serious. **3** *Mus.* **a** (of a scale) having intervals of a semitone above its third and seventh notes. **b** (of an interval) greater by a semitone than a minor interval (*major third*). **c** (of a key) based on a major scale. **4** of full legal age. *–n.* **1 a** army officer next below lieutenant-colonel. **b** officer in charge of a band section (*drum major*). **2** person of full legal age. **3** *US* **a** student's main subject or course. **b** student of this. *–v.* (foll. by *in*) *US* study or qualify in (a subject) as one's main subject. [Latin, comparative of *magnus* great]

Majorca /mə'jɔːkə/ (Spanish **Mallorca** /mæl'jɔːkə/) Spanish island, largest of the Balearic Islands; pop. (est. 1987) 605 512; capital, Palma. Tourism is important, and there is some marble quarrying.

major-domo /ˌmeɪdʒə'dəʊməʊ/ *n.* (*pl.* **-s**) chief steward of a great household. [medieval Latin *major domus* highest official of the household]

majorette /ˌmeɪdʒə'ret/ *n.* = DRUM MAJORETTE. [abbreviation]

Malawi /mə'lɑːwɪ/, **Republic of** (former name, until 1963, **Nyasaland**) landlocked country in S central Africa, almost totally dependent on Mozambique for access to the sea. Much of its E border is formed by Lake Malawi (formerly Lake Nyasa). The economy is predominantly agricultural; maize is the main subsistence crop and tobacco, sugar, tea, peanuts, and cotton the principal exports. There are light manufacturing industries, including food processing, textiles and clothing, and building materials, and small-scale enterprises are being developed. Mineral resources are sparse but some coal, limestone, and gemstones are mined. Hydroelectricity is the main power source. Malawi's economy is recovering from the disruption of its traditional transport routes caused by the civil war in Mozambique. *History.* A British protectorate (Nyasaland) from 1891, becoming part of the Federation of Rhodesia and Nyasaland in 1953, it achieved independence within the Commonwealth in 1964 and became a republic in 1966 and a one-party state. Malawi has recently come under increasing pressure to adopt a more democratic system of government and in 1993, after a referendum endorsing multi-party democracy, the government agreed to prepare for multi-party elections. Presidential and legislative elections took place in 1994. After three decades in power Hastings Banda was defeated and Bakili Muluzi became president. Following the elections much foreign aid was restored. President, Bakili Muluzi; capital, Lilongwe. □ **Malawian** *adj.* & *n.*

languages	English, Chichewa
currency	kwacha (MK) of 100 tambala
pop. (1996)	9 453 000
GNP (1994)	US$1.5B
literacy	71% (m); 41% (f)
life expectancy	37 (m); 37 (f)

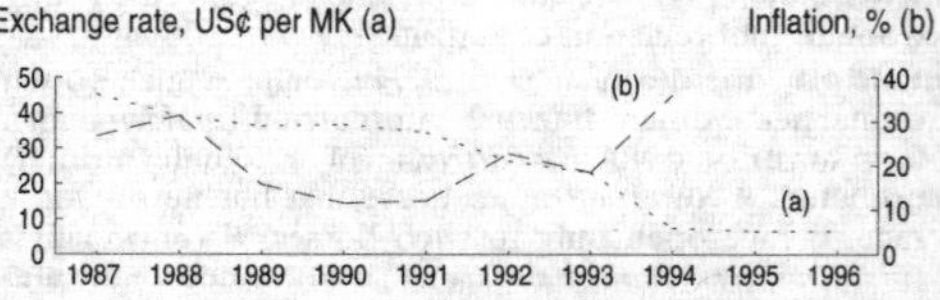

major-general *n.* officer next below a lieutenant-general.

majority /mə'dʒɒrɪtɪ/ *n.* (*pl.* **-ies**) **1** (usu. foll. by *of*) greater number or part. **2 a** number of votes by which a candidate wins. **b** party etc. receiving the greater number of votes. **3** full legal age. **4** rank of major. [medieval Latin: related to MAJOR]

■ **Usage** In sense 1, *majority* is strictly used only with countable nouns, as in *the majority of people*, and not (e.g.) *the majority of the work*.

majority rule *n.* principle that the greater number should exercise the greater power.

Makassar /mə'kæsə(r)/ see UJUNG PADANG.

make *–v.* (**-king**; *past* and *past part.* **made**) **1** construct; create; form from parts or other substances. **2** cause or compel (*made me do it*). **3 a** cause to exist; bring about (*made a noise*). **b** cause to become or seem (*made him angry*; *made a fool of me*; *made him a knight*). **4** compose; prepare; write (*made her will*; *made a film*). **5** constitute; amount to; be reckoned as (*2 and 2 make 4*). **6 a** undertake (*made a promise*; *make an effort*). **b** perform (an action etc.) (*made a face*; *made a bow*). **7** gain, acquire, procure (money, a living, a profit, etc.). **8** prepare (tea, coffee, a meal, etc.). **9 a** arrange (a bed) for use. **b** arrange and light materials for (a fire). **10 a** proceed (*made towards the river*). **b** (foll. by *to* + infin.) act as if with the intention to (*he made to go*). **11** *colloq.* **a** arrive at (a place) or in time for (a train etc.). **b** manage to attend; manage to attend on (a certain day) or at (a certain time) (*couldn't make the meeting last week*; *can make any day except Friday*). **c** achieve a place in (*made the first eleven*). **12** establish or enact (a distinction, rule, law, etc.). **13** consider to be; estimate as (*what do you make the total?*). **14** secure the success or advancement of (*his second novel made him*; *it made my day*). **15** accomplish (a distance, speed, score, etc.). **16 a** become by development (*made a great leader*). **b** serve as (*makes a useful seat*). **17** (usu. foll. by *out*) represent as (*makes him out a liar*). **18** form in the mind (*make a judgement*). **19** (foll. by *it* + compl.) **a** determine, establish, or choose (*let's make it Tuesday*). **b** bring to (a chosen value etc.) (*make it a dozen*). *–n.* **1** type or brand of manufacture. **2** way a thing is made. □ **make away with 1** = *make off with*. **2** = *do away with*. **make believe** pretend. **make the best of** see BEST. **make a clean breast** see BREAST. **make a clean sweep** see SWEEP. **make a day** (or **night** etc.) **of it** devote a whole day (or night etc.) to an activity. **make do 1** manage with the inadequate means available. **2** (foll. by *with*) manage with (something) as an inferior substitute. **make for 1** tend to result in. **2** proceed towards (a place). **3** attack. **make good 1** repay, repair, or compensate for. **2** achieve (a purpose); be successful. **make the grade** succeed. **make it** *colloq.* **1** succeed in reaching, esp. in time. **2** succeed. **make it up 1** be reconciled. **2** remedy a deficit. **make it up to** remedy negligence, an injury, etc. to (a person). **make love** see LOVE. **make a meal of** see MEAL[1]. **make merry** see MERRY. **make money** acquire wealth. **make the most of** see MOST. **make much** (or **little**) **of** treat as important (or unimportant). **make a name for oneself** see NAME. **make no bones about** see BONE. **make nothing of 1** treat as trifling. **2** be unable to understand, use, or deal with. **make of 1** construct from. **2** conclude from or about (*can you make anything of it?*). **make off** depart hastily. **make off with** carry away; steal. **make or break** cause the success or ruin of. **make out 1** discern or understand. **2** assert; pretend. **3** *colloq.* progress; fare. **4** write out (a cheque etc.) or fill in (a form). **make over 1** transfer the possession of. **2** refashion. **make a price** *Stock Exch.* (of a market maker) quote a selling price and a buying price for a security, which are binding, without knowing whether the enquirer wishes to buy or sell. **make up 1** act to overcome (a deficiency). **2** complete (an amount etc.). **3** (foll. by *for*) compensate for. **4** be reconciled. **5** put together; prepare (*made up the medicine*). **6** concoct (a story). **7** apply cosmetics (to). **8** prepare (a bed) with fresh linen. **make up one's mind** decide. **make up to** curry favour with. **make water** urinate. **make way 1** (often foll. by *for*) allow room to pass. **2** (foll. by *for*) be superseded by. **make one's way** go; prosper. **on the make** *colloq.* intent on gain. [Old English]

make-believe *–n.* pretence. *–attrib. adj.* pretended.

maker *n.* **1** person who makes. **2** (**Maker**) God.

makeshift *–adj.* temporary. *–n.* temporary substitute or device.

make-up *n.* **1** cosmetics, as used generally or by actors. **2** character, temperament, etc. **3** composition (of a thing).

makeweight *n.* **1** small quantity added to make up the weight. **2** person or thing supplying a deficiency.

making *n.* (in *pl.*) **1** earnings; profit. **2** essential qualities or ingredients (*has the makings of a pilot*). □ **be the making of** ensure the success of. **in the making** in the course of being made or formed. [Old English: related to MAKE]

making a book *n.* speculative buying of shares, commodities, financial futures, etc., without having sold them, or selling shares, commodities, etc., without having bought them.

MAL *international vehicle registration* Malaysia.

mal- *comb. form* **1 a** bad, badly (*malpractice*; *maltreat*). **b** faulty (*malfunction*). **2** not (*maladroit*). [French *mal* badly, from Latin *male*]

Malaysia /mə'leɪʒə/ country in SE Asia, a federation composed of peninsular Malaysia (the Malay Peninsula S of Thailand) and the N part of Borneo, comprising the states of Sarawak and Sabah. Agriculture is an important occupation; rice, the staple food, is produced throughout the country and rubber, palm oil, pepper, and tea are exported. Dense forest provides considerable quantities of tropical hardwoods for export, although some limited conservation measures have been introduced. Manufacturing has overtaken agriculture as the largest single contributor to the economy; manufactured exports include electronic goods, thermionic valves, food products, electrical machinery and transport equipment, chemical products, mineral fuels, and rubber goods. Malaysia is a major exporter of tin; other minerals exploited include iron ore, bauxite, ilmenite, and gold. The tourist industry is expanding and makes a significant contribution to the economy.

History. Opened up by the Portuguese and Dutch in the 16th and 17th centuries, the area came under British protection in the early 19th century. The Federation of Malaya, comprising the peninsular states, was formed in 1948, becoming independent within the Commonwealth in 1957. In 1963 the Federation was enlarged to include Sarawak, Sabah, and Singapore (seceded in 1965) and adopted its present name. In 1997 Malaysia experienced dramatic currency and stock market crashes that caused financial problems throughout the Far East. Head of state, Tuanka Jaafar Ibni Al-Marhum Tuanka Abdul Rahman; prime minister, Datuk Seri Mahathir Muhammad; capital, Kuala Lumpur. □ **Malaysian** *adj.* & *n.*

languages	Malay (official), English, Chinese, Indian languages
currency	ringgit (M$) of 100 sen
pop. (1996)	20 359 000
GNP (1994)	US$68B
literacy	89% (m); 78% (f)
life expectancy	70 (m); 74 (f)

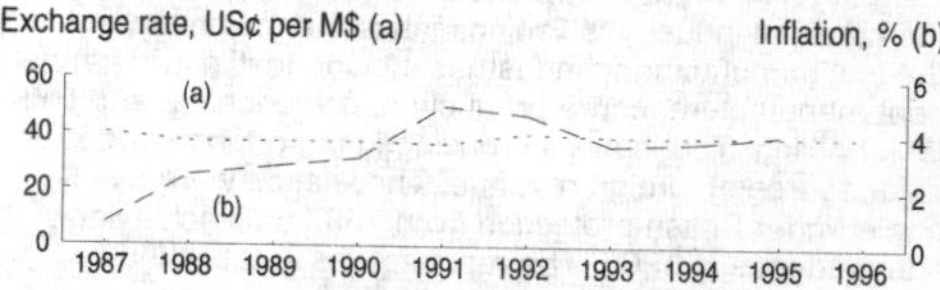

Malabo /mə'lɑːbəʊ/ capital of Equatorial Guinea, a port on the island of Bioko; pop. (est. 1991) 58 040.

Malacca /mə'lækə/ see MELAKA.

Malacca, Strait of channel between the Malay Peninsula and the Indonesian island of Sumatra, an important sea-passage linking the Indian Ocean to the South China Sea. The port of Singapore lies on this strait.

malachite /'mælə,kaɪt/ *n.* green mineral used for ornament. [Greek *molokhitis*]

maladjusted /,mælə'dʒʌstɪd/ *adj.* (of a person) unable to adapt to or cope with the demands of a social environment. □ **maladjustment** *n.*

maladminister /,mæləd'mɪnɪstə(r)/ *v.* manage badly or improperly. □ **maladministration** /-'streɪʃ(ə)n/ *n.*

maladroit /,mælə'drɔɪt/ *adj.* clumsy; bungling. [French: related to MAL-]

malady /'mælədɪ/ *n.* (*pl.* **-ies**) ailment, disease. [French *malade* sick]

Málaga /'mæləgə/ resort and seaport in S Spain, on the Andalusian coast; pop. (est. 1994) 531 433. *–n.* sweet fortified wine from Málaga.

Malagasy /,mælə'gæsɪ/ *–adj.* of or relating to Madagascar. *–n.* language of Madagascar.

malaise /mə'leɪz/ *n.* **1** general bodily discomfort or lassitude. **2** feeling of unease or demoralization. [French: related to EASE]

malapropism /'mæləprɒ,pɪz(ə)m/ *n.* comical misuse of a word in mistake for one sounding similar, e.g. *alligator* for *allegory*. [Mrs *Malaprop*, name of a character in Sheridan's *The Rivals*]

malaria /mə'leərɪə/ *n.* recurrent fever caused by a parasite transmitted by a mosquito bite. □ **malarial** *adj.* [Italian, = bad air]

malarkey /mə'lɑːkɪ/ *n. colloq.* humbug; nonsense. [origin unknown]

Malay /mə'leɪ/ *–n.* **1** member of a people predominating in Malaysia and Indonesia. **2** their language. *–adj.* of this people or language. [Malay *malāyu*]

Malaya /mə'leɪə/ see MALAYSIA. □ **Malayan** *n.* & *adj.*

Malay Archipelago very large group of islands, including Sumatra, Java, Borneo, the Philippines, and New Guinea, lying SE of Asia and NE of Australia.

Malay Peninsula narrow peninsula in SE Asia occupied by SW Thailand and peninsular Malaysia.

malcontent /'mælkən,tent/ *–n.* discontented person. *–adj.* discontented. [French: related to MAL-]

Malé /'mɑːleɪ/ capital of the Maldives; shipping and tourism are important sources of income; pop. (1995) 62 973.

male *–adj.* **1** of the sex that can beget offspring by fertilization. **2** of men or male animals, plants, etc.; masculine. **3** (of plants or flowers) containing stamens but no pistil. **4** (of parts of machinery etc.) designed to enter or fill the corresponding hollow part (*male screw*). *–n.* male person or animal. □ **maleness** *n.* [Latin *masculus* from *mas* a male]

male chauvinist *n.* = CHAUVINIST 2.

malediction /,mælɪ'dɪkʃ(ə)n/ *n.* **1** curse. **2** utterance of a curse. □ **maledictory** *adj.* [Latin *maledictio*: related to MAL-]

malefactor /'mælɪ,fæktə(r)/ *n.* criminal; evil-doer. □ **malefaction** /-'fækʃ(ə)n/ *n.* [Latin *male* badly, *facio fact-* do]

male menopause *n. colloq.* crisis of potency, confidence, etc., supposed to afflict some men in middle life.

malevolent /mə'levələnt/ *adj.* wishing evil to others. □ **malevolence** *n.* **malevolently** *adv.* [Latin *volo* wish]

malfeasance /mæl'fiːz(ə)ns/ *n. formal* misconduct, esp. in an official capacity. [French: related to MAL-]

malformation /,mælfɔː'meɪʃ(ə)n/ *n.* faulty formation. □ **malformed** /-'fɔːmd/ *adj.*

malfunction /mæl'fʌŋkʃ(ə)n/ *–n.* failure to function normally. *–v.* fail to function normally.

malice /'mælɪs/ *n.* **1** desire to harm or cause difficulty to others; ill-will. **2** *Law* harmful intent. [Latin *malus* bad]

malice aforethought *n. Law* intention to commit a crime, esp. murder.

malicious /mə'lɪʃəs/ *adj.* given to or arising from malice. □ **maliciously** *adv.*

malign /mə'laɪn/ *–adj.* **1** (of a thing) injurious. **2** (of a disease) malignant. **3** malevolent. *–v.* speak ill of; slander. □ **malignity** /mə'lɪgnɪtɪ/ *n.* [Latin *malus* bad]

malignant /mə'lɪgnənt/ *adj.* **1 a** (of a disease) very virulent or infectious. **b** (of a tumour) spreading or recurring; cancerous. **2** harmful; feeling or showing intense ill-will. □ **malignancy** *n.* **malignantly** *adv.* [Latin: related to MALIGN]

Malines see MECHELEN.

malinger /mə'lɪŋgə(r)/ *v.* pretend to be ill, esp. to escape work. □ **malingerer** *n.* [French *malingre* sickly]

mall /mæl, mɔːl/ *n.* **1** sheltered walk or promenade. **2** shopping precinct. [*The Mall*, street in London]

mallard /'mælɑːd/ *n.* (*pl.* same) a kind of wild duck. [French]

malleable /'mælɪəb(ə)l/ *adj.* **1** (of metal etc.) that can be shaped by hammering. **2** easily influenced; pliable. □ **malleability** /-'bɪlɪtɪ/ *n.* **malleably** *adv.* [medieval Latin: related to MALLET]

mallet /'mælɪt/ *n.* **1** hammer, usu. of wood. **2** implement for striking a croquet or polo ball. [Latin *malleus* hammer]

Mallorca see MAJORCA.

mallow /'mæləʊ/ *n.* plant with hairy stems and leaves and pink or purple flowers. [Latin *malva*]

Malmö /'mælmɜː/ port in SW Sweden, on the Øresund opposite Copenhagen; industries include textiles, shipbuilding, and food processing; pop. (est. 1996) 245 699.

malmsey /'mɑːmzɪ/ *n.* a strong sweet wine. [Low German or Dutch from *Monemvasia* in Greece]

malnourished /mæl'nʌrɪʃt/ *adj.* suffering from malnutrition. □ **malnourishment** *n.*

malnutrition /,mælnjuː'trɪʃ(ə)n/ *n.* condition resulting from the lack of foods necessary for health.

malodorous /mæl'əʊdərəs/ *adj.* evil-smelling.

maloti *pl.* of LOTI.

malpractice /mæl'præktɪs/ *n.* improper, negligent, or criminal professional conduct.

malt /mɔːlt/ *–n.* **1** barley, or other grain, steeped, germinated, and dried, for brewing etc. **2** *colloq.* malt whisky; malt liquor. *–v.* convert (grain) into malt. □ **malty** *adj.* (**-ier, -iest**). [Old English]

malted milk *n.* drink made from dried milk and extract of malt.

Maldives /'mɔːldaɪvz/, **Republic of** (former name, until 1969, **Maldive Islands**) country consisting of a chain of coral islands in the Indian Ocean SW of Sri Lanka. The principal industry is fishing; fish is the major export. The few manufacturing industries include textile and garment manufacture, copra production, fish canning, and soft-drink bottling. Tourism is increasing in importance and is a major source of foreign revenue. The islands were a sultanate under British protection from 1887 until achieving independence in 1965. The republic was established in 1968 and became a full member of the Commonwealth in 1985. President, Maumoon Abdul Gayoom; capital, Malé. □ **Maldivian** /-'dɪvɪən/ *adj.* & *n.*

languages	Divehi (a form of Sinhalese), English
currency	rufiyaa (Rf) of 100 laari
pop. (1996)	266 000
GNP (1994)	US$221M
literacy	90% (m); 90% (f)
life expectancy	65 (m); 63 (f)

Maltese /mɔːlˈtiːz/ –*n.* (*pl.* same) native or language of Malta. –*adj.* of Malta.

Maltese cross *n.* cross with the arms broadening outwards, often indented at the ends.

Malthusian /mælˈθjuːzɪən/ *adj.* of Malthus's doctrine that the population should be restricted so as to prevent an increase beyond its means of subsistence. □ **Malthusianism** *n.* [*Malthus*, name of a clergyman]

maltose /ˈmɔːltəʊz/ *n.* sugar made from starch by enzymes in malt, saliva, etc. [French: related to MALT]

maltreat /mælˈtriːt/ *v.* ill-treat. □ **maltreatment** *n.* [French: related to MAL-]

malt whisky *n.* whisky made solely from malted barley.

Maluku see MOLUCCA ISLANDS.

Malvinas /mælˈviːnəs/, **Islas** see FALKLAND ISLANDS.

mama /məˈmɑː/ *n.* (also **mamma**) *archaic* mother. [imitative of child's *ma, ma*]

mamba /ˈmæmbə/ *n.* venomous African snake. [Zulu *imamba*]

mambo /ˈmæmbəʊ/ *n.* (*pl.* **-s**) Latin American dance like the rumba. [American Spanish]

mamma var. of MAMA.

mammal /ˈmæm(ə)l/ *n.* warm-blooded vertebrate of the class secreting milk to feed its young. □ **mammalian** /-ˈmeɪlɪən/ *adj.* & *n.* [Latin *mamma* breast]

mammary /ˈmæmərɪ/ *adj.* of the breasts.

mammogram /ˈmæməˌgræm/ *n.* image obtained by mammography. [Latin *mamma* milk-secreting organ]

mammography /mæˈmɒgrəfɪ/ *n.* X-ray technique for screening the breasts for tumours etc.

Mammon /ˈmæmən/ *n.* wealth regarded as a god or evil influence. [Aramaic *māmōn*]

mammoth /ˈmæməθ/ –*n.* large extinct elephant with a hairy coat and curved tusks. –*adj.* huge. [Russian]

Man. *abbr.* Manitoba.

man –*n.* (*pl.* **men**) **1** adult human male. **2 a** human being; person. **b** the human race. **3 a** workman (*the manager spoke to the men*). **b** manservant, valet. **4** (usu. in *pl.*) soldiers, sailors, etc., esp. non-officers. **5** suitable or appropriate person; expert (*he is your man*; *the man for the job*). **6 a** husband (*man and wife*). **b** *colloq.* boyfriend, lover. **7** human being of a specified type or historical period (*Renaissance man*; *Peking man*). **8** piece in chess, draughts, etc. **9** *colloq.* as a form of address. **10** person pursued; opponent (*police caught their man*). –*v.* (**-nn-**) **1** supply with a person or people for work or defence. **2** work, service, or defend (*man the pumps*). **3** fill (a post). □ **as one man** in unison. **be one's own man** be independent. **to a man** without exception. □ **manlike** *adj.* [Old English]

man about town *n.* fashionable socializer.

manacle /ˈmænək(ə)l/ –*n.* (usu. in *pl.*) **1** fetter for the hand; handcuff. **2** restraint. –*v.* (**-ling**) fetter with manacles. [Latin *manus* hand]

manage /ˈmænɪdʒ/ *v.* (**-ging**) **1** organize; regulate; be in charge of. **2** succeed in achieving; contrive (*managed to come*; *managed a smile*; *managed to ruin the day*). **3** (often foll. by *with*) succeed with limited resources etc.; be able to cope. **4** succeed in controlling. **5** (often prec. by *can* etc.) **a** cope with (*couldn't manage another bite*). **b** be free to attend on or at (*can manage Monday*). **6** use or wield (a tool etc.). □ **manageable** *adj.* [Latin *manus* hand]

◆ **managed currency** *n.* currency in which the government controls, or at least influences, the exchange rate. This control (known as **managed floating**) is usu. exerted by the central bank buying and selling in the foreign-exchange market. See also CLEAN FLOATING.

◆ **managed fund** *n.* fund, made up of investments in a wide range of securities, that is managed by a life-assurance company to provide low-risk investments for the smaller investor, usu. in the form of investment bonds, unit trusts, or unit-linked saving plans. The fund managers will have a stated investment policy favouring a specific category of investments.

◆ **management** *n.* **1** managing or being managed. **2** administration of business or public undertakings, comprising both an organizational skill, including the ability to delegate, and an entrepreneurial sense. The latter involves recognizing and making use of opportunities, predicting market needs and trends, and achieving goals by sustained drive, skilful negotiation, and articulate advocacy. **3** people engaged in management. **Top management** includes the chief executive (see also MANAGING DIRECTOR) of an organization, his or her deputy or deputies, the board of directors, and the managers in charge of the divisions or departments of the organization. **Middle management** consists largely of the managers to whom top management delegates the day-to-day running of the organization. The management in large organizations is usu. divided into two categories: line managers and staff managers (see LINE AND STAFF MANAGEMENT). See also BRITISH INSTITUTE OF MANAGEMENT.

◆ **management accountant** *n.* accountant whose primary role is to advise the management of a company on the consequences of their activities. A management accountant is likely to be involved in the organization's budgetary procedures and will be responsible for producing monthly management figures; he or she will also be involved in advising on new developments, pricing, cash-flow requirements, and the financial consequences of various projects. The professional organization of management accountants in the UK is the Chartered Institute of Management Accountants (see CHARTERED ACCOUNTANT).

◆ **management agreement** *n.* formal agreement setting out the objectives and services provided by an investment adviser or stockbroker in managing a client's portfolio and the costs of this service.

◆ **management audit** *n.* independent review of the management of an organization, carried out by a firm of

---

Mali /ˈmɑːlɪ/, **Republic of** (former name, until 1959, **French Sudan**) inland country in W Africa, S of Algeria. The economy is based mainly on agriculture (chiefly subsistence), which contributes about half of the GDP; livestock farming and river fishing are also important. The chief exports are cotton and cotton products, livestock, meat, and dried fish. Manufacturing industries are mainly based on processing agricultural produce. Gold, which is exported, and salt are exploited and Mali also possesses some reserves of bauxite, uranium, and oil. The tourist industry is being developed.

History. Colonized by the French in the late 19th century, Mali briefly associated with Senegal as the Federation of Mali in 1959 and gained full independence as a republic in 1960. After considerable civil unrest, the president was overthrown in 1991 and a new constitution, providing for a multi-party political system, was adopted the following year. President, Alpha Oumar Konare; prime minister, Ibrahim Boubacar Keita; capital, Bamako. □ **Malian** *adj.* & *n.*

languages	French (official), Bambara (an African language)
currency	CFA franc (CFAF) of 100 centimes
pop. (1996)	9 204 000
GNP (1994)	US$2.4B
literacy	26% (m); 11% (f)
life expectancy	44 (m); 48 (f)

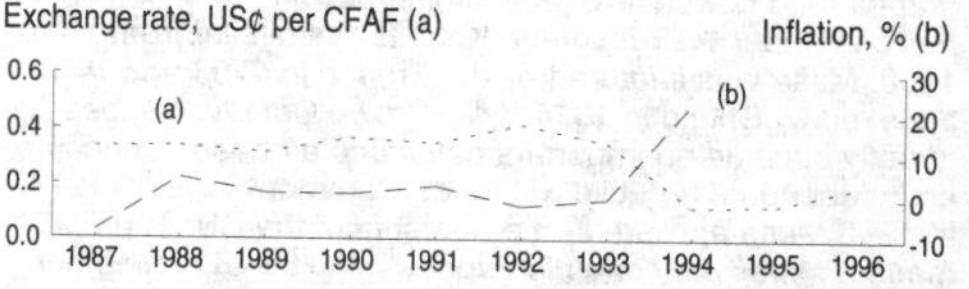

management consultants specializing in this type of review. The review will cover all aspects of running the organization, including the control of production, marketing, sales, finance, personnel, warehousing, etc.

◆ **management buy-in** *n.* acquisition of a company by a team of managers, usu. specially formed for the purpose, often backed by a venture-capital organization. Their normal target is the small family-owned company, which the owners wish to sell, or occasionally an unwanted subsidiary of a public company.

◆ **management buyout** *n.* (also **MBO**) acquisition of a company by its managers, often in the face of closure, after the acquisition of the company by another group that wishes to dispose of it, or occasionally as a result of its owners wishing to dispose of the business through a trade sale. In some cases a management buyout occurs when a large corporate group of companies wishes to divest itself of an operating division. Financial backers tend to like managers who know the company's business intimately, staking their own assets and taking full control of the company with the aim of boosting its profitability. Popularized in the early 1980s, management buyouts have occasionally failed, but many have continued to profit and a few have been sold on to major groups.

◆ **management by exception** *n.* management technique that seeks to highlight differences between actual and budgeted costs or any abnormal feature in the running of an organization in order that managerial time should be devoted to those exceptional items. Smoothly running operations and accurately budgeted costs thus receive less attention than the problem areas.

◆ **management company** *n.* company that manages unit trusts. Its fees, known as **management charges**, are usu. stated in the agreement setting up the trust and are paid by the unit holders.

◆ **management consultant** *n.* professional adviser who specializes in giving advice to organizations on ways for improving their efficiency and hence their profitability. They come into an organization as total outsiders, uninfluenced by either internal politics or personal relationships, and analyse the way the business is run. At the end of a period, during which two or more members of the consultant firm have spent a considerable time in the organization, they provide a detailed report, giving their suggestions for improving efficiency. Their advice usu. spans board-level policy-making and planning, the use of available resources (department by department), the best use of manpower, and a critical assessment of industrial relations, production, marketing, and sales. See MANAGEMENT CONSULTANTS' ASSOCIATION; INSTITUTE OF MANAGEMENT SERVICES.

◆ **Management Consultants' Association** *n.* (also **MCA**) association founded in 1956 to establish and maintain the professional standards of the management consultancy profession in the UK.

◆ **management information system** *n.* (also **MIS**) computer database held within a company, to which only management has access. It enables all the managers in the organization to have the same basic data on which to formulate their decisions.

manager *n.* **1** person controlling or administering a business or part of a business. **2** person controlling the affairs, training, etc. of a person or team in sports, entertainment, etc. **3** person of a specified level of skill in household or financial affairs etc. (*a good manager*). □ **managerial** /ˌmænɪˈdʒɪərɪəl/ *adj.*

manageress /ˌmænɪdʒəˈres/ *n.* woman manager, esp. of a shop, hotel, etc.

◆ **managerial theory of the firm** *n. Econ.* theory that the managers of a firm make choices on behalf of their firm on the basis of their own utility rather than of profit maximization. Factors determining the managerial utility function include salary, prestige, market share, and job security. Although this assumption may be more realistic than those based on profit maximization, predictions about the behaviour of firms and markets are much more difficult. See also SATISFICING BEHAVIOUR.

◆ **managing director** *n.* (also **MD**) company director responsible for the day-to-day running of a company. Second in the hierarchy only to the chairman, if there is one, the managing director is the company's chief executive, a title that is becoming increasingly popular in the UK.

Managua /məˈnɑːgwə/ capital of Nicaragua; industries include meat processing, textiles, and oil refining; pop. (est. 1995) 819 731.

Manama /məˈnɑːmə/ capital of Bahrain; pop. (1992) 140 401. It is a free port, its economy being based on the oil industry.

mañana /mænˈjɑːnə/ *–adv.* tomorrow (esp. to indicate procrastination). *–n.* indefinite future. [Spanish]

manat /ˈmænæt/ *n.* standard monetary unit of Azerbaijan.

man-at-arms *n.* (*pl.* **men-at-arms**) *archaic* soldier.

manatee /ˌmænəˈtiː/ *n.* large aquatic plant-eating mammal. [Spanish from Carib]

Manaus /məˈnaʊs/ city in NW Brazil, an important inland port and principal commercial centre of the upper Amazon region; pop. (1991) 1 005 634.

Manawatu-Wanganui /ˌmænəˈwɑːtuː/ administrative region of North Island, New Zealand, and a productive agricultural area; pop. (est. 1994) 232 500; chief town, Palmerston North.

Manchester /ˈmæntʃestə(r)/ industrial and commercial city in NW England, in Greater Manchester, a port linked to the sea by the Manchester Ship Canal; pop. (est. 1994) 431 100. Industries include engineering, chemicals, food processing, textiles, banking, and insurance.

Manchuria /mænˈtʃʊərɪə/ region of NE China; coal, iron, and other minerals are mined and timber is exploited.

Malta /ˈmɔːltə, ˈmɒ-/, **Republic of** island country in the central Mediterranean, S of Sicily. The economy has diversified since the closure of the foreign naval and military bases on which it was formerly dependent. The naval dockyards have been converted to commercial use and the island's leading industry is now the state-owned Malta Drydocks. Manufactured exports include electrical equipment, machinery, processed foods, textiles and clothing, plastics, and chemicals. Tourism is very important to the economy. Agriculture produces mainly vegetables and fruit (esp. grapes) and flowers are grown for export.

History. Under the rule of the Knights Hospitaller from 1530, Malta was captured by the French in 1798 and annexed by Britain in 1814. As a Crown Colony, it subsequently became an important naval and air base. It became an independent republic within the Commonwealth in 1974. In 1993 Malta applied for membership of the EU. The EU made a series of economic reforms conditional to membership and, in 1996, Malta withdrew its application. President, Dr Ugo Misfud Bonnici; prime minister, Dr Alfred Sant; capital, Valletta.

languages	Maltese, English
currency	lira (Lm) of 100 cents
pop. (1996)	372 000
GNP (1992)	US$2.6B
literacy	96% (m); 95% (f)
life expectancy	74 (m); 79 (f)

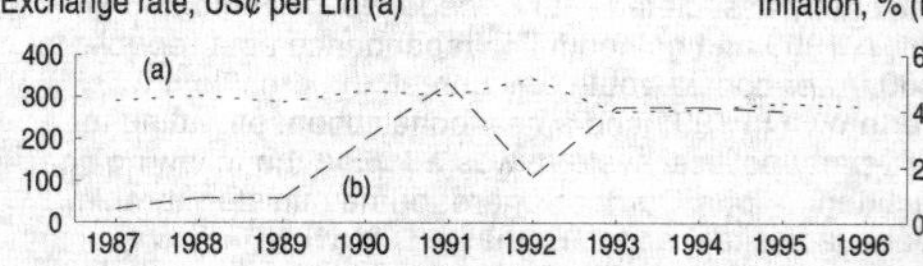

Mancunian /mæŋ'kju:nɪən/ *–n.* native of Manchester. *–adj.* of Manchester. [Latin *Mancunium*]

mandala /'mændələ/ *n.* circular figure as a religious symbol of the universe. [Sanskrit]

Mandalay /,mændə'leɪ/ city in central Burma, on the Irrawaddy River, commercial centre of upper Burma; pop. (est. 1995) 677 000.

mandamus /mæn'deɪməs/ *n.* judicial writ issued as a command to an inferior court, or ordering a person to perform a public or statutory duty. [Latin, = we command]

mandarin /'mændərɪn/ *n.* **1** (**Mandarin**) official language of China. **2** *hist.* Chinese official. **3** powerful person, esp. a top civil servant. **4** (in full **mandarin orange**) = TANGERINE 1. [Hindi *mantrī*]

mandate /'mændeɪt/ *–n.* **1** official command or instruction. **2** authority given by electors to a government, trade union, etc. **3** written authority given by one person (the mandator) to another (the mandatory) giving the mandatory the power to act on behalf of the mandator. It comes to an end on the death, mental illness, or bankruptcy of the mandator. See also DIVIDEND MANDATE. *–v.* (**-ting**) instruct (a delegate) how to act or vote. □ **mandator** *n.* [Latin *mandatum*, past part. of *mando* command]

mandatory /'mændətərɪ/ *–adj.* **1** compulsory. **2** of or conveying a command. *–n.* person to whom a mandate is given. □ **mandatorily** *adv.* [Latin: related to MANDATE]

mandible /'mændɪb(ə)l/ *n.* **1** jaw, esp. the lower jaw in mammals and fishes. **2** upper or lower part of a bird's beak. **3** either half of the crushing organ in the mouth-parts of an insect etc. [Latin *mando* chew]

Man. Dir. *abbr.* Managing Director.

mandolin /,mændə'lɪn/ *n.* a kind of lute with paired metal strings plucked with a plectrum. □ **mandolinist** *n.* [French from Italian]

mandrake /'mændreɪk/ *n.* poisonous narcotic plant with large yellow fruit. [Greek *mandragoras*]

mandrel /'mændr(ə)l/ *n.* **1** lathe-shaft to which work is fixed while being turned. **2** cylindrical rod round which metal or other material is forged or shaped. [origin unknown]

mandrill /'mændrɪl/ *n.* large W African baboon. [probably from MAN, DRILL[4]]

M&S *abbr.* Marks & Spencer plc.

mane *n.* **1** long hair on the neck of a horse, lion, etc. **2** *colloq.* person's long hair. [Old English]

manège /mæ'neɪʒ/ *n.* (also **manege**) **1** riding-school. **2** movements of a trained horse. **3** horsemanship. [Italian: related to MANAGE]

maneuver *US* var. of MANOEUVRE.

man Friday *n.* male helper or follower.

manful *adj.* brave; resolute. □ **manfully** *adv.*

manganese /'mæŋgə,ni:z/ *n.* **1** grey brittle metallic element. **2** black mineral oxide of this used in glass-making etc. [Italian: related to MAGNESIA]

mange /meɪndʒ/ *n.* skin disease in hairy and woolly animals. [French *mangeue* itch, from Latin *manduco* chew]

mangel-wurzel /'mæŋg(ə)l,wɜ:z(ə)l/ *n.* (also **mangold-** /'mæŋg(ə)ld-/) large beet used as cattle food. [German *Mangold* beet, *Wurzel* root]

manger /'meɪndʒə(r)/ *n.* box or trough for horses or cattle to feed from. [Latin: related to MANGE]

mange-tout /mɑ̃ʒ'tu:/ *n.* a kind of pea eaten in the pod. [French, = eat-all]

mangle[1] /'mæŋg(ə)l/ *–n.* machine of two or more cylinders for squeezing water from and pressing wet clothes. *–v.* (**-ling**) press (clothes etc.) in a mangle. [Dutch *mangel*]

mangle[2] /'mæŋg(ə)l/ *v.* (**-ling**) **1** hack or mutilate by blows. **2** spoil (a text etc.) by gross blunders. **3** cut roughly so as to disfigure. [Anglo-French *ma(ha)ngler*: probably related to MAIM]

mango /'mæŋgəʊ/ *n.* (*pl.* **-es** or **-s**) **1** tropical fruit with yellowish flesh. **2** tree bearing this. [Tamil *mānkāy*]

mangold-wurzel var. of MANGEL-WURZEL.

mangrove /'mæŋgrəʊv/ *n.* tropical tree or shrub growing in shore-mud with many tangled roots above ground. [origin unknown]

mangy /'meɪndʒɪ/ *adj.* (**-ier**, **-iest**) **1** having mange. **2** squalid; shabby.

manhandle *v.* (**-ling**) **1** *colloq.* handle (a person) roughly. **2** move by human effort.

Manhattan /mæn'hæt(ə)n/ island in the US, at the mouth of the Hudson River, a borough of New York containing the commercial and cultural centre of the city; pop. (1990) 1 487 536.

manhole *n.* covered opening in a pavement, sewer, etc. for workmen to gain access.

manhood *n.* **1** state of being a man. **2 a** manliness; courage. **b** a man's sexual potency. **3** men of a country etc.

man-hour *n.* work done by one person in one hour, estimates of which are used in costing jobs etc.

manhunt *n.* organized search for a person, esp. a criminal.

mania /'meɪnɪə/ *n.* **1** mental illness marked by excitement and violence. **2** (often foll. by *for*) excessive enthusiasm; obsession. [Greek *mainomai* be mad]

-mania *comb. form* **1** denoting a special type of mental disorder (*megalomania*). **2** denoting enthusiasm or admiration (*Beatlemania*).

maniac /'meɪnɪ,æk/ *–n.* **1** *colloq.* person behaving wildly (*too many maniacs on the road*). **2** *colloq.* obsessive enthusiast. **3** person suffering from mania. *–adj.* of or behaving like a maniac. □ **maniacal** /mə'naɪək(ə)l/ *adj.* **maniacally** /mə'naɪəkəlɪ/ *adv.*

-maniac *comb. form* forming adjectives and nouns meaning 'affected with -mania' or 'a person affected with -mania' (*nymphomaniac*).

manic /'mænɪk/ *adj.* **1** of or affected by mania. **2** *colloq.* wildly excited; frenzied; excitable. □ **manically** *adv.*

Manicaland /mə'ni:kə,lænd/ gold-mining province of E Zimbabwe; pop. (1992) 1 537 676; capital, Mutare.

manic-depressive *–adj.* relating to a mental disorder with alternating periods of elation and depression. *–n.* person with such a disorder.

manicure /'mænɪ,kjʊə(r)/ *–n.* cosmetic treatment of the hands and fingernails. *–v.* (**-ring**) give a manicure to (the hands or a person). □ **manicurist** *n.* [Latin *manus* hand, *cura* care]

manifest /'mænɪ,fest/ *–adj.* clear or obvious to the eye or mind. *–v.* **1** show (a quality or feeling) by one's acts etc. **2** show plainly to the eye or mind. **3** be evidence of; prove. **4** *refl.* (of a thing) reveal itself. **5** (of a ghost) appear. *–n.* cargo or passenger list carried by a ship or aircraft. The cargo list has to be signed by the captain (or first officer) before being handed to the customs on leaving and arriving at a port or airport. □ **manifestation** /-'steɪʃ(ə)n/ *n.* **manifestly** *adv.* [Latin *manifestus*]

manifesto /,mænɪ'festəʊ/ *n.* (*pl.* **-s**) declaration of policies, esp. by a political party. [Italian: related to MANIFEST]

manifold /'mænɪ,fəʊld/ *–adj.* **1** many and various. **2** having various forms, parts, applications, etc. *–n.* **1** manifold thing. **2** pipe or chamber branching into several openings. [Old English: related to MANY, -FOLD]

manikin /'mænɪkɪn/ *n.* little man; dwarf. [Dutch]

Manila /mə'nɪlə/ capital and chief port of the Philippines; industries include textiles, food processing, and pharmaceuticals; city pop. (est. 1994) 1 894 667; metropolitan area pop. 8 594 150. *–n.* (also **Manilla**) **1** cigar or cheroot made in Manila. **2** (in full **Manila hemp**) strong fibre of a Philippine tree, used for rope etc. **3** (also **manila**) strong brown paper made from Manila hemp or other material.

man in the street *n.* ordinary person.

manipulate /mə'nɪpjʊ,leɪt/ *v.* (**-ting**) **1** handle, esp. with skill. **2** manage (a person, situation, etc.) to one's own advantage, esp. unfairly. **3** move (part of a patient's body) by hand in order to increase flexion etc. **4** *Computing* edit or move (text, data, etc.). □ **manipulable** /-ləb(ə)l/ *adj.* **manipulation** /-'leɪʃ(ə)n/ *n.* **manipulator** *n.* [Latin *manus* hand]

manipulative /mə'nɪpjʊlətɪv/ *adj.* tending to exploit a situation, person, etc., for one's own ends. □ **manipulatively** *adv.*

Manipur /ˌmænɪ'pʊə(r)/ state of NE India; products include silk and hardwoods; pop. (est. 1994) 2 010 000; capital, Imphal. □ **Manipuri** *adj.* & *n.*

Manit. *abbr.* Manitoba.

Manitoba /ˌmænɪ'təʊbə/ province of central Canada; pop. (est. 1995) 1 137 500; capital, Winnipeg. Arable and livestock farming are important; the chief manufacturing industries produce foods and beverages, machinery, and metal products.

mankind *n.* **1** human species. **2** male people.

manky /'mæŋkɪ/ *adj.* (**-ier, -iest**) *colloq.* **1** bad, inferior, defective. **2** dirty. [obsolete *mank* defective]

manly *adj.* (**-ier, -iest**) **1** having qualities associated with a man (e.g. strength and courage). **2** befitting a man. □ **manliness** *n.*

man–machine interface *n.* (also **MMI**) former name for USER INTERFACE.

man-made *adj.* (of textiles) artificial, synthetic.

manna /'mænə/ *n.* **1** substance miraculously supplied as food to the Israelites in the wilderness (Exod. 16). **2** unexpected benefit (esp. *manna from heaven*). [Old English ultimately from Hebrew]

Mannar /mə'nɑː(r)/ **1** island off the NW coast of Sri Lanka; coconuts are produced; pop. (est. 1993) 137 000. **2** town and port on this island; pop. (1981) 14 000.

manned *adj.* (of a spacecraft etc.) having a human crew.

mannequin /'mænɪkɪn/ *n.* **1** fashion model. **2** window dummy. [French, = MANIKIN]

manner /'mænə(r)/ *n.* **1** way a thing is done or happens. **2** (in *pl.*) **a** social behaviour (*good manners*). **b** polite behaviour (*has no manners*). **c** modes of life; social conditions. **3** outward bearing, way of speaking, etc. **4** style (*in the manner of Rembrandt*). **5** kind, sort (*not by any manner of means*). □ **in a manner of speaking** in a way; so to speak. **to the manner born** *colloq.* naturally at ease in a particular situation etc. [Latin *manus* hand]

mannered *adj.* **1** (in *comb.*) having specified manners (*ill-mannered*). **2** esp. *Art* full of mannerisms.

mannerism *n.* **1** habitual gesture or way of speaking etc. **2 a** stylistic trick in art etc. **b** excessive use of these. □ **mannerist** *n.*

mannerly *adj.* well-mannered, polite.

Mannheim /'mænhaɪm/ industrial port in SW Germany, on the Rhine; manufactures include heavy machinery, motor vehicles, glass, and chemicals; pop. (est. 1995) 316 223.

mannish *adj.* **1** (of a woman) masculine in appearance or manner. **2** characteristic of a man. □ **mannishly** *adv.*

manoeuvre /mə'nuːvə(r)/ (*US* **maneuver**) *–n.* **1** planned and controlled movement of a vehicle or body of troops etc. **2** (in *pl.*) large-scale exercise of troops, ships, etc. **3** agile or skilful movement. **4** artful plan. *–v.* (**-ring**) **1** move (a thing, esp. a vehicle) carefully. **2** perform or cause (troops etc.) to perform manoeuvres. **3 a** (usu. foll. by *into*, *out of*, etc.) manipulate (a person, thing, etc.) by scheming or adroitness. **b** use artifice. □ **manoeuvrable** *adj.* **manoeuvrability** /-vrə'bɪlɪtɪ/ *n.* [medieval Latin *manu operor* work with the hand]

man of letters *n.* scholar or author.

man of the world see WORLD.

man-of-war *n.* (*pl.* **men-of-war**) warship.

manor /'mænə(r)/ *n.* **1** (also **manor-house**) large country house with lands. **2** *hist.* feudal lordship over lands. **3** *slang* district covered by a police station. □ **manorial** /mə'nɔːrɪəl/ *adj.* [Latin *maneo* remain]

manpower *n.* number of people available for work, service, etc.

manqué /'mɒŋkeɪ/ *adj.* (placed after noun) that might have been but is not (*an actor manqué*). [French]

mansard /'mænsɑːd/ *n.* roof with four sloping sides, each of which becomes steeper halfway down. [*Mansart*, name of an architect]

manse /mæns/ *n.* ecclesiastical residence, esp. a Scottish Presbyterian minister's house. [medieval Latin: related to MANOR]

manservant *n.* (*pl.* **menservants**) male servant.

mansion /'mænʃ(ə)n/ *n.* **1** large grand house. **2** (in *pl.*) large building divided into flats. [Latin: related to MANOR]

manslaughter *n.* unintentional but not accidental unlawful killing of a human being.

mantel /'mænt(ə)l/ *n.* mantelpiece or mantelshelf. [var. of MANTLE]

mantelpiece *n.* **1** structure of wood, marble, etc. above and around a fireplace. **2** = MANTELSHELF.

mantelshelf *n.* shelf above a fireplace.

mantilla /mæn'tɪlə/ *n.* lace scarf worn by Spanish women over the hair and shoulders. [Spanish: related to MANTLE]

mantis /'mæntɪs/ *n.* (*pl.* same or **mantises**) (in full **praying mantis**) predacious insect that holds its forelegs like hands folded in prayer. [Greek, = prophet]

mantissa /mæn'tɪsə/ *n.* part of a logarithm after the decimal point. [Latin, = makeweight]

mantle /'mænt(ə)l/ *–n.* **1** loose sleeveless cloak. **2** covering (*mantle of snow*). **3** fragile lacelike tube fixed round a gas-jet to give an incandescent light. **4** region between the crust and the core of the earth. *–v.* (**-ling**) clothe; conceal, envelop. [Latin *mantellum* cloak]

man to man *adv.* candidly.

mantra /'mæntrə/ *n.* **1** Hindu or Buddhist devotional incantation. **2** Vedic hymn. [Sanskrit, = instrument of thought]

mantrap *n.* trap for catching trespassers etc.

manual /'mænjʊəl/ *–adj.* **1** of or done with the hands (*manual labour*). **2 a** worked by hand, not automatically (*manual gear-change*). **b** (of a vehicle) worked by manual gear-change. *–n.* **1** reference book. **2** organ keyboard played with the hands, not the feet. **3** *colloq.* vehicle with manual transmission. □ **manually** *adv.* [Latin *manus* hand]

manufacture /ˌmænjʊ'fæktʃə(r)/ *–n.* **1** making of articles, esp. in a factory etc. **2** branch of industry (*woollen manufacture*). *–v.* (**-ring**) **1** make (articles), esp. on an industrial scale. **2** invent or fabricate (evidence, a story, etc.). □ **manufacturer** *n.* [Latin *manufactum* made by hand]

♦ **manufacturer brand** *n.* brand name created by a manufacturer. Polaroid is an example.

♦ **manufacturer's agent** *n.* commission agent usu. having a franchise to sell a particular manufacturer's products in a particular country or region for a given period. See also COMMISSION *n.* 4.

♦ **manufacturer's recommended price** *n.* (also **MRP**) = RECOMMENDED RETAIL PRICE.

♦ **manufacturing account** *n.* part of a profit-and-loss account in which the manufactured cost of goods sold is calculated by taking direct costs, factory overheads, etc. and adjusting for changes in stocks of raw material and work in progress.

---

manure /mə'njʊə(r)/ *–n.* fertilizer, esp. dung. *–v.* (**-ring**) apply manure to (land etc.). [Anglo-French *mainoverer* = MANOEUVRE]

manuscript /'mænjʊskrɪpt/ *–n.* **1** text written by hand. **2** author's handwritten or typed text. **3** handwritten form (*produced in manuscript*). *–adj.* written by hand. [medieval Latin *manuscriptus* written by hand]

Manx /mæŋks/ *–adj.* of the Isle of Man. *–n.* **1** former Celtic language of the Isle of Man. **2** (prec. by *the*; treated as *pl.*) Manx people. [Old Norse]

Manx cat *n.* tailless variety of cat.

many /'menɪ/ *–adj.* (**more**; **most**) great in number;

numerous (*many people*). –*n.* (as *pl.*) **1** many people or things. **2** (prec. by *the*) the majority of people. □ **a good** (or **great) many** a large number. **many's the time** often. **many a time** many times. [Old English]

Maoism /'maʊɪz(ə)m/ *n.* Communist doctrines of Mao Zedong. □ **Maoist** *n.* & *adj.* [*Mao* Zedong, name of a Chinese statesman]

Maori /'maʊrɪ/ –*n.* (*pl.* same or **-s**) **1** member of the aboriginal people of New Zealand. **2** their language. –*adj.* of this people. [native name]

MAP *abbr.* **1** *Computing* Manufacturing Automation Protocol, agreement facilitating the exchange of data relating to design and manufacture of mechanical-engineering products. **2** modified American plan (payment system in US hotels).

map –*n.* **1 a** flat representation of the earth's surface, or part of it. **b** diagram of a route etc. **2** similar representation of the stars, sky, moon, etc. **3** diagram showing the arrangement or components of a thing. –*v.* **(-pp-) 1** represent on a map. **2** *Math.* associate each element of (a set) with one element of another set. □ **map out** plan in detail. [Latin *mappa* napkin]

maple /'meɪp(ə)l/ *n.* **1** any of various trees or shrubs grown for shade, ornament, wood, or sugar. **2** its wood. [Old English]

maple-leaf *n.* emblem of Canada.

maple sugar *n.* sugar produced by evaporating the sap of some kinds of maple.

maple syrup *n.* syrup made by evaporating maple sap or dissolving maple sugar.

Maputo /mə'puːtəʊ/ (formerly **Lourenço Marques**) capital and chief port of Mozambique; industries include brewing, ship repairing, and fish canning; pop. (est. 1991) 931 531.

maquette /mə'ket/ *n.* preliminary model or sketch. [Italian *macchia* spot]

Maquis /mæ'kiː, 'mæ-/ *n.* (*pl.* same) **1** French resistance movement during the German occupation (1940–5). **2** member of this. [French, = brushwood]

Mar. *abbr.* March.

mar *v.* **(-rr-)** spoil; disfigure. [Old English]

marabou /'mærə,buː/ *n.* **1** large W African stork. **2** its down as trimming etc. [French from Arabic]

maraca /mə'rækə/ *n.* clublike bean-filled gourd etc., shaken rhythmically in pairs in Latin American music. [Portuguese]

Maracaibo /,mærə'kaɪbəʊ/ **1** lake in NW Venezuela, developed as a major oil-producing region. **2** city and port on the NW shore of this lake, a centre of oil and petrochemical production; pop. (est. 1990) 1 364 000.

Maramba /mə'ræmbə/ (formerly **Livingstone**) city in Zambia, capital of Southern province; industries include car assembly and tourism; pop. (est. 1989) 102 000.

maraschino /,mærə'skiːnəʊ/ *n.* (*pl.* **-s**) sweet liqueur made from black cherries. [Italian]

maraschino cherry *n.* cherry preserved in maraschino and used in cocktails etc.

marathon /'mærəθ(ə)n/ *n.* **1** long-distance running race, usu. of 26 miles 385 yards (42.195 km). **2** long-lasting or difficult undertaking etc. [*Marathon* in Greece, scene of a decisive battle in 490 BC: a messenger supposedly ran with news of the outcome to Athens]

maraud /mə'rɔːd/ *v.* **1** make a plundering raid (on). **2** pilfer systematically. □ **marauder** *n.* [French *maraud* rogue]

marble /'mɑːb(ə)l/ –*n.* **1** crystalline limestone capable of taking a polish, used in sculpture and architecture. **2** (often *attrib.*) **a** anything of marble (*marble clock*). **b** anything like marble in hardness, coldness, etc. (*her features were marble*). **3 a** small, esp. glass, ball as a toy. **b** (in *pl.*; treated as *sing.*) game using these. **4** (in *pl.*) *slang* one's mental faculties (*he's lost his marbles*). **5** (in *pl.*) collection of sculptures (*Elgin Marbles*). –*v.* **(-ling) 1** (esp. as **marbled** *adj.*) stain or colour (paper, soap, etc.) to look like variegated marble. **2** (as **marbled** *adj.*) (of meat) striped with fat and lean. [Latin *marmor* from Greek]

marble cake *n.* mottled cake of light and dark sponge.

marbling *n.* **1** colouring or marking like marble. **2** streaks of fat in lean meat.

marcasite /'mɑːkə,saɪt/ *n.* **1** yellowish crystalline iron sulphide. **2** crystals of this used in jewellery. [Arabic *markashita*]

March *n.* third month of the year. [Latin *Martius* of Mars]

march[1] –*v.* **1** (cause to) walk in a military manner with a regular tread (*army marched past*; *marched him away*). **2 a** walk purposefully. **b** (often foll. by *on*) (of events etc.) continue unrelentingly (*time marches on*). **3** (foll. by *on*) advance towards (a military objective). –*n.* **1 a** act of marching. **b** uniform military step (*slow march*). **2** long difficult walk. **3** procession as a demonstration. **4** (usu. foll. by *of*) progress or continuity (*march of events*). **5 a** music to accompany a march. **b** similar musical piece. □ **marcher** *n.* [French *marcher*]

march[2] –*n. hist.* **1** (usu. in *pl.*) boundary, frontier (esp. between England and Scotland or Wales). **2** tract of land between two countries, esp. disputed. –*v.* (foll. by *upon*, *with*) (of a country, an estate, etc.) border on. [French *marche* from medieval Latin *marca*]

Marche /'mɑːkeɪ/ (English **the Marches**) agricultural region of E central Italy, producing cereals, fruit, wine, vegetables, and cattle; pop. (est. 1994) 1 438 223; capital, Ancona.

March hare *n.* hare exuberant in the breeding season (*mad as a March hare*).

marching orders *n.pl.* **1** order for troops to mobilize etc. **2** dismissal (*gave him his marching orders*).

marchioness /,mɑːʃə'nes/ *n.* **1** wife or widow of a marquess. **2** woman holding the rank of marquess. [medieval Latin: related to MARCH[2]]

march past –*n.* marching of troops past a saluting-point at a review. –*v.* (of troops) carry out a march past.

Mar del Plata /mɑː del 'plɑːtə/ popular resort and fishing centre in central Argentina, on the Atlantic coast; pop. (1991) 512 880.

Mardi Gras /,mɑːdɪ 'grɑː/ *n.* **1 a** Shrove Tuesday in some Catholic countries. **b** merrymaking on this day. **2** last day of a carnival etc. [French, = fat Tuesday]

mare[1] *n.* female equine animal, esp. a horse. [Old English]

mare[2] /'mɑːreɪ/ *n.* (*pl.* **maria** /'mɑːrɪə/ or **-s**) **1** large dark flat area on the moon, once thought to be sea. **2** similar area on Mars. [Latin, = sea]

mare's nest *n.* illusory discovery.

mare's tail *n.* **1** tall slender marsh plant. **2** (in *pl.*) long straight streaks of cirrus cloud.

♦ **Mareva injunction** /mə'riːvə/ *n. Law* court order preventing the defendant from dealing with specified assets. It is granted in cases in which the plaintiff can show that any judgement obtained against the defendant will be worthless, because the defendant will dissipate assets to avoid paying. [*Mareva Compania Naviera SA*, name of plaintiff in such a case]

---

margarine /,mɑːdʒə'riːn/ *n.* butter-substitute made from vegetable oils or animal fats with milk etc. [Greek *margaron* pearl]

Margarita /,mɑːgə'riːtə/ Venezuelan island in the Caribbean Sea; pearl fishing is important.

marge *n. colloq.* margarine. [abbreviation]

margin /'mɑːdʒɪn/ –*n.* **1** edge or border of a surface. **2** blank border flanking print etc. **3** amount by which a thing exceeds, falls short, etc. (*won by a narrow margin*). **4** percentage of the cost of goods that has to be added to the cost to arrive at the selling price. See also GROSS MARGIN. **5** *Finance* **a** difference between the prices at which a market maker or commodity dealer will buy and sell. **b** (in commodity and currency dealing) amount advanced by a speculator or investor to a broker or dealer, when buying futures. **c** money or securities deposited with a stockbroker to cover any possible losses a client may make. See also MARGIN CALL. **6** lower limit (*his effort fell below the margin*). –*v.* (**-n-**) provide with a margin or marginal notes. [Latin *margo -ginis*]

marginal *adj.* **1** of or written in a margin. **2 a** of or at the edge. **b** insignificant (*of merely marginal interest*). **3** (of a parliamentary seat etc.) held by a small majority. **4** close to the limit, esp. of profitability. **5** (of land) difficult to cultivate; unprofitable. **6** barely adequate. □ **marginally** *adv.* [medieval Latin: related to MARGIN]

◆ **marginal analysis** see MARGINALISTS.

◆ **marginal cost** *n.* additional cost of producing an additional unit of output. In conditions of perfect competition, marginal cost would be equal to the market price.

◆ **marginal costing** *n.* process of costing products or activities by taking account only of the direct costs of the product or activity. The direct costs are usu. compared with the selling price of the product or service in order to see what contribution the item makes towards fixed overheads and profit. Cf. ABSORPTION COSTING.

---

marginalia /ˌmɑːdʒɪˈneɪlɪə/ *n.pl.* marginal notes.

◆ **Marginalists** *n.pl.* followers of a school of thought dating from the 1870s, on which modern neoclassical economics is based. They argue that economic value is determined by the rate of exchange (or price) of the last unit of a good supplied in the market. This broke with the Classical school's view of value, which was defined as the quantity of labour embodied in a unit of output. **Marginal analysis** was then applied to the behaviour of consumers (see MARGINAL UTILITY) and the behaviour of the firm. When applied to a particular firm or to households, this analysis yields a partial equilibrium explanation of choice; applied to the economy as a whole it provides a general equilibrium solution, describing the efficient allocation of all resources.

---

marginalize /ˈmɑːdʒɪnəˌlaɪz/ *v.* (also **-ise**) (**-zing** or **-sing**) make or treat as insignificant. □ **marginalization** /-ˈzeɪʃ(ə)n/ *n.*

◆ **marginal productivity** *n.* additional output that a producer will achieve by the addition of one unit of a factor of production (e.g. an additional employee).

◆ **marginal propensity to consume** *n.* additional consumption generated by a unit increase in income. Coined by Keynes, the phrase features in his general theory in association with the multiplier.

◆ **marginal relief** *n.* relief given by a tax authority if a marginal increase in a person's earnings brings that person's income into a higher tax bracket and results in an unfair tax burden. One option for the taxpayer would be to pay tax at the lower rate, adding to the tax the amount by which the increased income exceeds the limit for this lower rate.

◆ **marginal revenue** *n.* additional revenue that a producer will achieve by selling one additional unit of production.

◆ **marginal tax rate** *n.* additional tax paid for each unit increase in income. In the UK, for example, a taxpayer paying tax at the higher rate will pay tax at this rate on all additional earnings and also on all taxable capital gains. Under a progressive tax system there is a tendency for the marginal tax rates of the poor and the rich to be very high, giving rise to the poverty trap for the poor and, it is claimed, work disincentives for the rich.

◆ **marginal utility** *n. Econ.* additional utility derived by an individual from the consumption of an additional unit of a good or service (see UTILITY 4). One condition for the Pareto economic efficiency (see PARETO OPTIMALITY) of an economy is that for all goods the ratios of marginal utilities to their prices should be equal. If this were not the case some individuals could switch from consumption of one good at the margin to another and retain the same utility at a lower cost; this would be a Pareto improvement.

◆ **margin call** *n.* call to a client from a commodity broker or stockbroker to increase the amount of money or securities deposited with the broker as a safeguard. This usu. happens if the client has an open position in a market that is moving adversely for this position.

---

margin of error *n.* allowance for miscalculation etc.

marguerite /ˌmɑːɡəˈriːt/ *n.* ox-eye daisy. [Latin *margarita* pearl]

maria *pl.* of MARE².

Mariana Islands /ˌmærɪˈɑːnə/ (also **Marianas**) group of islands in the NW Pacific, formerly part of the Trust Territory of the Pacific Islands, administered by the US. They comprise Guam (now a US unincorporated territory) and the islands and atolls of the **Northern Marianas**, which in 1975 became a commonwealth (self-governing since 1978) in union with the US. Products include sugar cane, coffee, and coconuts.

marigold /ˈmærɪˌɡəʊld/ *n.* plant with golden or bright yellow flowers. [*Mary* (probably the Virgin), *gold* (dial.) marigold]

marijuana /ˌmærɪˈhwɑːnə/ *n.* (also **marihuana**) dried leaves etc. of hemp, smoked in cigarettes as a drug. [American Spanish]

marimba /məˈrɪmbə/ *n.* **1** xylophone played by natives of Africa and Central America. **2** modern orchestral instrument derived from this. [Congolese]

marina /məˈriːnə/ *n.* harbour for pleasure-yachts etc. [Latin: related to MARINE]

marinade /ˌmærɪˈneɪd, ˈmæ-/ –*n.* **1** mixture of wine, vinegar, oil, spices, etc., for soaking meat, fish, etc. before cooking. **2** meat, fish, etc., so soaked. –*v.* (**-ding**) soak in a marinade. [Spanish *marinar* pickle in brine: related to MARINE]

marinate /ˈmærɪˌneɪt/ *v.* (**-ting**) = MARINADE. □ **marination** /-ˈneɪʃ(ə)n/ *n.* [French: related to MARINE]

marine /məˈriːn/ –*adj.* **1** of, found in, or produced by the sea. **2 a** of shipping or naval matters (*marine insurance*). **b** for use at sea. –*n.* **1** soldier trained to serve on land or sea. **2** country's shipping, fleet, or navy (*merchant marine*). [Latin *mare* sea]

◆ **marine insurance** *n.* insurance of ships or their cargo against specified causes of loss or damage that might be encountered at sea. It also covers cargo in transit over land at each end of the voyage, ships under construction or repair, and drilling rigs.

---

mariner /ˈmærɪnə(r)/ *n.* seaman.

marionette /ˌmærɪəˈnet/ *n.* puppet worked by strings. [French: related to *Mary*]

marital /ˈmærɪt(ə)l/ *adj.* of marriage or marriage relations. [Latin *maritus* husband]

maritime /ˈmærɪˌtaɪm/ *adj.* **1** connected with the sea or seafaring (*maritime insurance*). **2** living or found near the sea. [Latin: related to MARINE]

Mariupol /ˌmærɪˈuːpɒl/ (formerly **Zhdanov**) industrial port in SE Ukraine; pop. (est. 1996) 510 000.

marjoram /ˈmɑːdʒərəm/ *n.* aromatic herb used in cookery. [French from medieval Latin]

mark¹ –*n.* **1** spot, sign, stain, scar, etc., on a surface etc. **2** (esp. in *comb.*) **a** written or printed symbol (*question mark*). **b** number or letter denoting proficiency, conduct, etc. (*black mark*; *46 marks out of 50*). **3** (usu. foll. by *of*) sign of quality, character, feeling, etc. (*mark of respect*). **4 a** sign, seal, etc., of identification. **b** cross etc. made as a signature by an illiterate person. **5** lasting effect (*war left its mark*). **6 a** target etc. (*missed the mark*). **b** standard, norm (*his work falls below the mark*). **7** line etc. indicating a position. **8** (usu. **Mark**) (followed by a numeral) particular design, model, etc., of a car, aircraft, etc. (*Mark 2 Ford Granada*). **9** runner's starting-point in a race. –*v.* **1 a** make a mark on. **b** mark with initials, name, etc. to identify etc. **2** correct and assess (a student's work etc.). **3** attach a price to (*marked the doll at £5*). **4** notice or observe (*marked his agitation*). **5 a** characterize (*day was marked by storms*). **b** acknowledge, celebrate (*marked the occasion with a toast*). **6** name or indicate on a map etc. (*the pub isn't marked*). **7** keep close to (an opponent in sport) to hinder him. **8** (as **marked** *adj.*) have natural marks (*is marked with dark spots*). □ **beside** (or **off** or **wide of**) **the mark 1** irrelevant. **2** not accurate. **make one's mark** attain distinction; make an impression. **one's mark** *colloq.* opponent, object, etc., of one's own size etc. (*the little one's more my mark*). **mark down 1** reduce the price of (goods etc.). **2** make a written note of. **3** reduce the examination marks of. **mark off** separate by a boundary etc. **mark out 1** plan (a course of action etc.). **2** destine (*marked out for success*). **3** trace out (boundaries etc.). **mark time 1** march on the spot without moving forward. **2** act routinely while awaiting an opportunity to advance. **mark up 1 a** add a proportion to the price of (goods etc.) for profit. **b** *Stock Exch.* raise (the price of a particular security) in anticipation of an increased demand. **2** mark or correct (text etc.). **off the mark 1** having made a start. **2** = *beside the mark.* **on the mark** ready to start. **on your mark** (or **marks**) get ready to start (esp. a race). **up to the mark** normal (esp. of health). [Old English]

mark[2] *n.* = DEUTSCHMARK. [German]

mark-down *n.* reduction in price.

marked *adj.* **1** having a visible mark. **2** clearly noticeable (*marked difference*). **3** (of playing-cards) marked on their backs to assist cheating. □ **markedly** /-kɪdlɪ/ *adv.*

♦ **marked cheque** *n.* cheque that the bank on which it is drawn has marked 'good for payment'. This practice has been replaced in the UK by the use of bank drafts, although it is still used in the US, where such cheques are called **certified checks.**

---

marked man *n.* person singled out, esp. for attack.

marker *n.* **1** thing marking a position etc. **2** person or thing that marks. **3** broad-tipped felt-tipped pen. **4** scorer in a game.

♦ **marker barrel** *n.* standard oil price based on one barrel of Saudi Arabian oil or some other internationally recognized oil (e.g. North Sea Brent crude). It sets standard prices for oil in the rest of the world.

---

market /'mɑːkɪt/ –*n.* **1** gathering of buyers and sellers of provisions, livestock, and other items of value. A physical market in which traders haggle for the best price is one of the basic concepts of trade and a considerable part of economics concerns the operation of such markets. The absence of a physical market for some goods is usu. seen as one of the major sources of economic inefficiency. **2** space for this. **3** (often foll. by *for*) demand for a commodity etc., often measured by sales during a specified period (*no market for sheds*). **4** place or group providing such a demand. **5** conditions etc. for buying or selling; rate of purchase and sale (*market is sluggish*). **6** organized gathering in which trading in securities (see STOCK EXCHANGE), commodities (see COMMODITY MARKET), currencies, etc. takes place. –*v.* (**-t-**) **1** offer for sale, esp. by advertising etc. **2** *archaic* buy or sell goods in a market. □ **be in the market for** wish to buy. **be on the market** be offered for sale. **put on the market** offer for sale. □ **marketer** *n.* [Latin *mercor* buy]

marketable *adj.* able or fit to be sold. □ **marketability** /-'bɪlɪtɪ/ *n.*

♦ **marketable security** *n.* stock, share, bond, etc. that can be bought or sold on a stock exchange. Cf. NON-MARKETABLE SECURITY.

♦ **Market and Opinion Research International** *n.* (also **MORI**) market research organization engaged in a wide variety of research activities, best known for its social and political research and its MORI opinion polls.

♦ **market assessment** *n.* identification and evaluation of a market for a particular good or service to ascertain its size and to estimate the price that the product or service would command. See also MARKETING RESEARCH.

♦ **market capitalization** *n.* (also **market valuation**) value of a company obtained by multiplying the number of its issued shares by their market price.

♦ **market-clearing assumption** *n. Econ.* assumption that the interaction of choices made by utility-maximizing individuals ensures that the quantity of goods supplied equals the quantity demanded in any particular market. If this were not the case, a mutually advantageous trade could take place, to provide a Pareto improvement (see PARETO OPTIMALITY). Market clearing is an important assumption in, for example, new classical macroeconomics, which denies the possibility of an effective government monetary policy or fiscal policy. Keynesians, however, argue that market clearing may not occur due to inefficiencies inherent in the economy (see EFFICIENCY WAGE THEORY; HYSTERESIS; INSIDER-OUTSIDER THEORY), which could provide a possible justification for monetary policy or fiscal policy.

---

market-day *n.* day on which a market is regularly held.

marketeer /,mɑːkɪ'tɪə(r)/ *n.* **1** supporter of the EC and British membership of it. **2** marketer.

♦ **market forces** *n.pl.* forces of supply and demand that in a free market determine the quantity available of a particular product or service and the price at which it is offered. In general, a rise in demand will cause both supply and price to increase, while a rise in supply will cause both a fall in price and a drop in demand, although many markets have individual features that modify this simple analysis. In practice, most markets are not free, being influenced either by restrictions on supply or by government intervention that can affect demand, supply, or price.

---

market garden *n.* farm where vegetables and fruit are grown for sale in markets.

♦ **market imperfection** see IMPERFECT COMPETITION.

♦ **marketing** *n.* **1** offering goods or services for sale. **2** trade done at a market. **3** identifying, maximizing, and satisfying consumer demand for a company's products. Marketing a product involves such tasks as anticipating changes in demand (usu. on the basis of marketing research), promotion of the product, ensuring that its quality, availability, and price meet the needs of the market, and providing after-sales service. See also DIRECT MARKETING; SALES PROMOTION.

♦ **marketing audit** *n.* review of an organization's marketing capabilities based on a structured appraisal of a marketing department's internal strengths and weaknesses, which helps the company decide how best to respond to external opportunities and threats. Sales are analysed, the effectiveness of the marketing mix is assessed, and, externally, the marketing environment is monitored. When the marketing audit has been completed, a marketing plan is drawn up based on its results.

♦ **Marketing Board** *n.* organization established in the UK under the provisions of the Marketing Acts by producers, with government support, in order to achieve orderly supply and marketing of products when differentiation between the products of individual producers is difficult. Such boards have been set up to market milk, eggs, potatoes, wool, etc.

♦ **marketing environment** *n.* combined influence of all the factors external to a company that could affect its sales. These factors include cultural traditions, technological developments, competitors' activity, government policies, and changes in distribution channels. The marketing environment cannot be controlled by the company and, because it may change frequently, requires constant monitoring.

♦ **marketing intelligence** *n.* information gathered by a company to form a picture of its competitors' activities, capabilities, and intentions in the marketing of a product.

♦ **marketing logistics** see LOGISTICS 2.

♦ **marketing mix** *n.* factors controlled by a company that can influence consumer buying of its products. The four components of a marketing mix (often called the **four Ps**) are the product (quality, branding, packaging, and other features), pricing (recommended retail price, discounts for large orders, and credit terms), promotion (see SALES PROMOTION), and place (where to sell the product, which distributors and transport services to use, and desirable stock levels). The potential profitability of a particular marketing mix and its acceptability to its market are assessed by marketing research.

◆ **marketing plan** *n.* detailed statement (usu. prepared annually) of how a company's marketing mix will be used to achieve its market objectives. See also MARKETING AUDIT.

◆ **marketing research** *n.* systematic collection and analysis of data to resolve problems concerning marketing, undertaken to reduce the risk of inappropriate marketing activity. Data is almost always collected from a sample of the target market, by such methods as observation, interviews, and audit of shop sales. Interviews are the most common technique, and can be carried out face-to-face, by telephone, or by post (see also STRUCTURED INTERVIEW). When the results have been analysed (usu. by computer), recommendations regarding the original problem can be made. See also QUALITATIVE MARKETING RESEARCH; QUANTITATIVE MARKETING RESEARCH. Cf. MARKET RESEARCH.

◆ **market instrument** *n.* negotiable instrument used for short-term debt.

◆ **Market Intelligence Reports** *n.pl.* (also **MINTEL**) market research reports published by Mintel Publications Ltd., which provide an important source of information on consumer markets in the UK. The company also reports on developments in retailing and on the leisure sector of the market.

◆ **market leader** *n.* company that has the largest market share for a particular product or service in an area or country.

◆ **market maker** *n.* dealer in securities on the London Stock Exchange who undertakes to buy and sell securities as a principal and is therefore obliged to announce buying and selling prices for a particular security at a particular time. Before October 1986 (see BIG BANG) this function was performed by a stockjobber, who was then obliged to deal with the public through a stockbroker. However since October 1986, when the rules changed, market makers attempt to make a profit by dealing in securities as principals (selling at a higher price than that at which they buy) as well as acting as agents, working for a commission. While this dual role may create a conflict of interest for market makers (see CHINESE WALL; FRONT RUNNING), it avoids the restrictive trade practice of the former system and reduces the cost of dealing in the market.

◆ **market objectives** *n.pl.* objectives to be fulfilled by a marketing plan. They are determined by interpreting the relevant parts of a corporate plan in the light of a marketing audit.

◆ **market order** *n.* order given to a stockbroker, commodity broker, dealer, etc. to buy or sell specified securities or commodities immediately at the prevailing market price.

◆ **market orientation** see PRODUCT ORIENTATION.

◆ **market penetration** *n.* **1** process of entering a market to establish a new brand or product, which may be achieved by offering the brand or product at a low initial price to familiarize the public with its name. **2** measure of the extent to which a market has been penetrated, equal to the ratio of all the owners of that brand or product to the total number of potential owners, usu. expressed as a percentage. Cf. MARKET SHARE.

market-place *n.* **1** open space for a market. **2** commercial world.

◆ **market price** *n.* **1** price of a raw material, product, service, security, etc. in an open market. In a formal market (e.g. a stock exchange, commodity market, or foreign-exchange market) there is often a margin between the buying and selling price; there are, therefore, two market prices and the average of the buying and selling price is then often quoted. **2** *Econ.* price at which commodities are exchanged in a market, either for money or for each other (see BARTER *n.* 1).

◆ **market rate of discount** *n.* = BILL RATE.

market research *n.* surveying of consumers' needs and preferences to discover the size of the market for a particular brand or product. The techniques of marketing research are used but the objective is more restricted.

◆ **Market Research Society** *n.* (also **MRS**) professional association in the UK for those who use survey techniques for marketing, social, and economic research. The MRS aims to maintain professional standards, to provide its members with training programmes and information about new techniques, and to represent the interests of its members to government and commerce.

◆ **market segmentation** *n.* division of a market into homogeneous groups of consumers, each of which can be expected to respond to a different marketing mix. There are numerous ways of segmenting markets, the more traditional being by age, sex, family size, income, occupation, and social class; the more recent **geodemographic segmentation** identifies housing areas in which people share a common lifestyle and will be more likely to buy certain types of products. Another frequently used method is **benefit segmentation**; for example, the toothpaste market can be segmented into those primarily concerned with dental protection and those concerned with a fresh taste. Once a segment has been identified, the marketer can then develop a unique marketing mix to reach it, for example by advertising only in the newspapers read by that market segment. Therefore, to be of practical value, a market segment must be large enough to warrant the development costs. See also SAGACITY; SEGMENTATION.

◆ **market share** *n.* share of the total sales of all brands or products competing in the same market that is captured by one particular brand or product, usu. expressed as a percentage.

◆ **market skimming** *n.* marketing tactic in which a new brand or product is launched at a high price to sell to the small market segment that is indifferent to price or is attracted by the prestige value of paying premium prices. If necessary, the price can be reduced later.

◆ **market testing** *n.* = TEST MARKETING.

market town *n.* town where a market is held.

◆ **market valuation** *n.* = MARKET CAPITALIZATION.

◆ **market value** *n.* value of an asset if it were to be sold on the open market at its current market price. When land is involved it may be necessary to distinguish between the market value in its present use and that in some alternative use.

marking *n.* (usu. in *pl.*) **1** identification mark. **2** colouring of an animal's fur etc. **3** (in *pl.*) official number of bargains that have taken place during a working day on the London Stock Exchange.

markka /ˈmɑːkə/ *n.* standard monetary unit of Finland. [Finnish, = mark (currency)]

mark reading see OPTICAL MARK READING.

marksman *n.* skilled shot, esp. with a pistol or rifle. □ **marksmanship** *n.*

mark-up *n.* **1** amount added to a price by the retailer for profit. See also GROSS MARGIN. **2** corrections in a text.

marl –*n.* soil of clay and lime, used as fertilizer. –*v.* apply marl to. □ **marly** *adj.* [medieval Latin *margila*]

Marlborough /ˈmɔːlbərə/ administrative region of South Island, New Zealand; pop. (1996) 40 464; chief town, Blenheim. Sheep farming is important, and there are engineering, textile, and food-processing industries.

marlin /ˈmɑːlɪn/ *n.* (*pl.* same or **-s**) *US* long-nosed marine fish. [from MARLINSPIKE]

marlinspike *n.* pointed iron tool used to separate strands of rope etc. [*marling* from Dutch *marlen* from *marren* bind]

marmalade /'mɑːmə,leɪd/ *n.* bitter preserve of citrus fruit, usu. oranges. [Portuguese *marmelo* quince]

Marmite /'mɑːmaɪt/ *n. propr.* thick brown spread made from yeast and vegetable extract. [French, = cooking-pot]

marmoreal /mɑː'mɔːrɪəl/ *adj.* of or like marble. [Latin: related to MARBLE]

marmoset /'mɑːmə,zet/ *n.* small monkey with a long bushy tail. [French]

marmot /'mɑːmət/ *n.* heavy-set burrowing rodent with a short bushy tail. [Latin *mus* mouse, *mons* mountain]

marocain /'mærə,keɪn/ *n.* fabric of ribbed crêpe. [French, = Moroccan]

maroon[1] /mə'ruːn/ *adj.* & *n.* brownish-crimson. [French *marron* chestnut]

maroon[2] /mə'ruːn/ *v.* **1** leave (a person) isolated, esp. on an island. **2** (of weather etc.) cause (a person) to be forcibly detained. [French *marron* wild person, from Spanish *cimarrón*]

marque /mɑːk/ *n.* make of car, as distinct from a specific model (*the Jaguar marque*). [French, = MARK[1]]

marquee /mɑː'kiː/ *n.* large tent for social functions etc. [French *marquise*]

Marquesas Islands /mɑː'keɪsəs/ group of volcanic islands in the S Pacific, forming part of the overseas territory of French Polynesia; pop. (1988) 7538. Copra, cotton, and vanilla are exported.

marquess /'mɑːkwɪs/ *n.* British nobleman ranking between duke and earl. [var. of MARQUIS]

marquetry /'mɑːkɪtrɪ/ *n.* inlaid work in wood, ivory, etc. [French: related to MARQUE]

marquis /'mɑːkwɪs/ *n.* (*pl.* **-quises**) foreign nobleman ranking between duke and count. [French: related to MARCH[2]]

marquise /mɑː'kiːz/ *n.* **1** wife or widow of a marquis. **2** woman holding the rank of marquis.

Marrakesh /,mærə'keʃ/ city in Morocco, a centre for commerce (producing carpets and leather goods) and tourism; pop. (est. 1993) 602 000.

marram /'mærəm/ *n.* shore grass that binds sand. [Old Norse, = sea-haulm]

marriage /'mærɪdʒ/ *n.* **1** legal union of a man and a woman for cohabitation and often procreation. **2** act or ceremony marking this. **3** particular such union (*a happy marriage*). **4** intimate union, combination. [French *marier* MARRY]

marriageable *adj.* free, ready, or fit for marriage. □ **marriageability** /-'bɪlɪtɪ/ *n.*

marriage bureau *n.* company arranging introductions with a view to marriage.

marriage certificate *n.* certificate verifying a legal marriage.

marriage guidance *n.* counselling of couples with marital problems.

marriage licence *n.* licence to marry.

marriage lines *n.pl.* marriage certificate.

marriage of convenience *n.* loveless marriage for gain.

marriage settlement *n.* legal property arrangement between spouses.

married *–adj.* **1** united in marriage. **2** of marriage (*married name*; *married life*). *–n.* (usu. in *pl.*) married person (*young marrieds*).

marron glacé /,mærɒn 'glæseɪ/ *n.* (*pl.* **marrons glacés** pronunc. same) chestnut preserved in syrup. [French]

marrow /'mærəʊ/ *n.* **1** large fleshy usu. striped gourd eaten as a vegetable. **2** soft fatty substance in the cavities of bones. **3** essential part. □ **to the marrow** right through. [Old English]

marrowbone *n.* bone containing edible marrow.

marrowfat *n.* a kind of large pea.

marry /'mærɪ/ *v.* (**-ies**, **-ied**) **1** take, join, or give in marriage. **2 a** enter into marriage. **b** (foll. by *into*) become a member of (a family) by marriage. **3 a** unite intimately, combine. **b** pair (socks etc.). □ **marry off** find a spouse for. **marry up** link, join. [Latin *maritus* husband]

♦ **Mars** /mɑːz/, **Forest, Jr.** (1929–) US businessman, chairman of Mars Inc., the world's second largest confectioner, which was founded by his grandfather. The UK Mars company was founded by his father, Forest Mars Sr.

Marsala /mɑː'sɑːlə/ *n.* a dark sweet fortified dessert wine. [*Marsala* in Sicily]

Marseillaise /,mɑːseɪ'jeɪz/ *n.* French national anthem. [French, = of MARSEILLES]

Marseilles /mɑː'seɪ, -'seɪlz/ (French **Marseille**) French seaport on the Mediterranean coast; industries include oil refining, chemicals, and metallurgy; pop. (est. 1990) 1 087 000.

marsh *n.* (often *attrib.*) low watery land. □ **marshy** *adj.* (**-ier**, **-iest**). **marshiness** *n.* [Old English]

marshal /'mɑːʃ(ə)l/ *–n.* **1** (**Marshal**) high-ranking officer of state or in the armed forces (*Earl Marshal*; *Field Marshal*). **2** officer arranging ceremonies, controlling racecourses, crowds, etc. *–v.* (**-ll-**) **1** arrange (soldiers, one's thoughts, etc.) in due order. **2** conduct (a person) ceremoniously. [French *mareschal*]

♦ **Marshallian demand function** /mɑː'ʃeɪlɪən/ *n.* (also **uncompensated demand function**) *Econ.* function that expresses the quantities of goods demanded by an individual in terms of the price of a good and the income of the individual. The sum of Marshallian demands represents the indirect utility function. An increase in the price of a good will affect Marshallian demands in two ways: through the price change itself (the substitution effect) and through the effective change in the value of the individual's income (the income effect). Cf. HICKSIAN DEMAND FUNCTION. [*Marshall*, name of an economist]

---

marshalling yard *n.* yard for assembling goods trains etc.

Marshal of the Royal Air Force *n.* highest rank in the RAF.

marsh gas *n.* methane.

marshland *n.* land consisting of marshes.

marshmallow /mɑːʃ'mæləʊ/ *n.* soft sticky sweet made of sugar, albumen, gelatin, etc. [MARSH MALLOW]

marsh mallow *n.* shrubby herbaceous plant.

marsh marigold *n.* golden-flowered plant.

marsupial /mɑː'suːpɪəl/ *–n.* mammal giving birth to underdeveloped young subsequently carried in a pouch. *–adj.* of or like a marsupial. [Greek *marsupion* pouch]

Marshall Islands /'mɑːʃ(ə)l/, **Republic of the** country consisting of a group of islands in the NW Pacific, administered by the US as part of the Pacific Islands Trust Territory from 1947 until 1986, when they became a republic in free association with the US; the independence of the republic was recognized internationally in 1990. The islands' economy is based on agriculture and fishing, coconut oil and copra being major exports, together with the service industries, including banking, insurance, and tourism. President, Amata Kabua; capital, Majuro, pop. (1990) 20 000. □ **Marshallese** *adj.* & *n.*

languages	English (official), Marshallese (Micronesian language)
currency	US dollar (US$) of 100 cents
pop. (1996)	58 500
GNP (1994)	US$105M
literacy	92% (m); 90% (f)
life expectancy	62 (m); 65 (f)

mart *n.* **1** trade centre. **2** auction-room. **3** market. [Dutch: related to MARKET]

Martello /mɑːˈteləʊ/ *n.* (*pl.* **-s**) (in full **Martello tower**) small circular coastal fort. [Cape *Mortella* in Corsica]

marten /ˈmɑːtɪn/ *n.* weasel-like carnivore with valuable fur. [Dutch from French]

martial /ˈmɑːʃ(ə)l/ *adj.* **1** of warfare. **2** warlike. [Latin *martialis* of Mars]

martial arts *n.pl.* oriental fighting sports such as judo and karate.

martial law *n.* military government with ordinary law suspended.

Martian /ˈmɑːʃ(ə)n/ *–adj.* of the planet Mars. *–n.* hypothetical inhabitant of Mars. [Latin]

martin /ˈmɑːtɪn/ *n.* a kind of swallow, esp. the house-martin and sand-martin. [probably St *Martin*, name of a 4th-century bishop]

martinet /ˌmɑːtɪˈnet/ *n.* strict disciplinarian. [*Martinet*, name of a drill-master]

martingale /ˈmɑːtɪŋˌgeɪl/ *n.* strap(s) preventing a horse from rearing etc. [French, origin uncertain]

Martini /mɑːˈtiːnɪ/ *n.* (*pl.* **-s**) **1** *propr.* type of vermouth. **2** cocktail of gin and French vermouth. [*Martini* and Rossi, name of a firm selling vermouth]

Martinique /ˌmɑːtɪˈniːk/ West Indian island, one of the Lesser Antilles, forming an overseas department of France; pop. (1996) 394 000; capital, Fort de France. Rum, sugar, and bananas are exported, and tourism is a developing industry.

Martinmas /ˈmɑːtɪnməs/ *n.* St Martin's day, 11 Nov. [from MASS²]

martyr /ˈmɑːtə(r)/ *–n.* **1 a** person killed for persisting in a belief. **b** person who suffers for a cause etc. **c** person who suffers or pretends to suffer to get pity etc. **2** (foll. by *to*) *colloq.* constant sufferer from (an ailment). *–v.* **1** put to death as a martyr. **2** torment. □ **martyrdom** *n.* [Greek *martur* witness]

marvel /ˈmɑːv(ə)l/ *–n.* **1** wonderful thing. **2** (foll. by *of*) wonderful example of (a quality). *–v.* (**-ll-**; *US* **-l-**) (foll. by *at* or *that*) feel surprise or wonder. [Latin *miror* wonder at]

marvellous /ˈmɑːvələs/ *adj.* (*US* **marvelous**) **1** astonishing. **2** excellent. □ **marvellously** *adv.* [French: related to MARVEL]

Marxism /ˈmɑːksɪz(ə)m/ *n.* political and economic theories of Marx, predicting the overthrow of capitalism and common ownership of the means of production in a classless society. □ **Marxist** *n.* & *adj.*

Marxism-Leninism *n.* Marxism as developed by Lenin. □ **Marxist-Leninist** *n.* & *adj.*

♦ **Marxist economics** *n.pl.* (as *sing.*) branch of Classical economics developed by Marx. Developing Adam Smith's concept of labour as the source of economic value (see LABOUR THEORY OF VALUE), Marx argued that capitalists extract surplus value from workers by means of the production process, leaving them only a subsistence wage. In Marx's view, capitalist economies would be subject to ever deepening crises, which would eventually destroy capitalism, leaving the state open to control by the workers. Marx's predictions have largely proved inaccurate; although crises have continued to occur, living standards in capitalist countries have risen, enabling capitalism to enjoy the support of many workers.

Maryland /ˈmeərɪˌlænd/ state in the US, on the Atlantic coast; pop. (est. 1996) 5 071 604; capital, Annapolis; chief port, Baltimore. There are printing and publishing industries, and manufacturing of metal products, textiles, and electrical equipment.

marzipan /ˈmɑːzɪˌpæn/ *–n.* paste of ground almonds, sugar, etc., used in confectionery. *–v.* (**-nn-**) cover with marzipan. [German from Italian]

Masbate /mæsˈbɑːtɪ/ **1** island in the central Philippines; agriculture is the main economic activity; pop. (1990) 599 355. **2** its chief town and trading centre; pop. (latest est.) 55 000.

mascara /mæˈskɑːrə/ *n.* cosmetic for darkening the eyelashes. [Italian, = mask]

mascot /ˈmæskɒt/ *n.* person, animal, or thing supposed to bring luck. [Provençal *masco* witch]

masculine /ˈmæskjʊlɪn/ *–adj.* **1** of men. **2** having qualities considered appropriate to a man. **3** *Gram.* of or denoting the male gender. *–n. Gram.* masculine gender or word. □ **masculinity** /-ˈlɪnɪtɪ/ *n.* [Latin: related to MALE]

maser /ˈmeɪzə(r)/ *n.* device used to amplify or generate coherent electromagnetic radiation in the microwave range. [*m*icrowave *a*mplification by *s*timulated *e*mission of *r*adiation]

Maseru /ˌmæsəˈruː/ capital of Lesotho, centre of road, rail, and air networks; industries include diamond processing; pop. (1990) 170 000.

mash *–n.* **1** soft or confused mixture. **2** mixture of boiled grain, bran, etc., fed to horses etc. **3** *colloq.* mashed potatoes. **4** mixture of malt and hot water used in brewing. **5** soft pulp made by crushing, mixing with water, etc. *–v.* **1** crush (potatoes etc.) to a pulp. **2** *dial.* **a** infuse (tea). **b** (of tea) draw. □ **masher** *n.* [Old English]

Mashhad /mæʃˈhæd/ city in NE Iran, a centre of Shiite pilgrimage; products include carpets and turquoise; pop. (1991) 1 759 155.

mask /mɑːsk/ *–n.* **1** covering for all or part of the face as a disguise or for protection against infection etc. **2** respirator. **3** likeness of a person's face, esp. one from a mould (*death-mask*). **4** disguise, pretence (*throw off the mask*). *–v.* **1** cover with a mask. **2** conceal. **3** protect. [Arabic *maskara* buffoon]

masking tape *n.* adhesive tape used in decorating to protect areas where paint is not wanted.

masochism /ˈmæsəˌkɪz(ə)m/ *n.* **1** sexual perversion involving one's own pain or humiliation. **2** *colloq.* enjoyment of what appears to be painful or tiresome. □ **masochist** *n.* **masochistic** /-ˈkɪstɪk/ *adj.* **masochistically** /-ˈkɪstɪkəlɪ/ *adv.* [von Sacher-*Masoch*, name of a novelist]

mason /ˈmeɪs(ə)n/ *n.* **1** person who builds with stone. **2** (**Mason**) Freemason. [French]

Masonic /məˈsɒnɪk/ *adj.* of Freemasons.

masonry *n.* **1 a** stonework. **b** work of a mason. **2** (**Masonry**) Freemasonry.

masque /mɑːsk/ *n.* musical drama with mime, esp. in the 16th and 17th centuries. [var. of MASK]

masquerade /ˌmæskəˈreɪd/ *–n.* **1** false show, pretence. **2** masked ball. *–v.* (**-ding**) (often foll. by *as*) appear falsely or in disguise. [Spanish *máscara* mask]

Mass. *abbr.* Massachusetts.

mass¹ *–n.* **1** shapeless body of matter. **2** dense aggregation of objects (*mass of fibres*). **3** (in *sing.* or *pl.*; usu. foll. by *of*) large number or amount. **4** (usu. foll. by *of*) unbroken expanse (of colour etc.). **5** (prec. by *the*) **a** the majority. **b** (in *pl.*) ordinary people. **6** *Physics* quantity of matter a body contains. **7** (*attrib.*) on a large scale (*mass hysteria*; *mass audience*). *–v.* assemble into a mass or as one body. [Latin *massa* from Greek]

mass² *n.* (often **Mass**) **1** Eucharist, esp. in the Roman Catholic Church. **2** celebration of this. **3** liturgy used in this. **4** musical setting of parts of this. [Latin *missa* dismissal]

Massachusetts /ˌmæsəˈtʃuːsɪts/ state in the NE US, bordering on the Atlantic; pop. (est. 1996) 6 092 352; capital, Boston. The manufacturing industries are important, producing electrical equipment, precision instruments, textiles, chemicals, and food products.

massacre /ˈmæsəkə(r)/ *–n.* **1** mass killing. **2** utter defeat or destruction. *–v.* (**-ring**) **1** kill (esp. many people) cruelly or violently. **2** *colloq.* defeat heavily. [French]

massage /ˈmæsɑːʒ/ *–n.* rubbing and kneading of the muscles and joints with the hands, to relieve stiffness, cure strains, stimulate, etc. *–v.* (**-ging**) **1** apply massage to. **2** manipulate (statistics etc.) to give an acceptable result. **3** flatter (a person's ego etc.). [French]

massage parlour *n.* **1** establishment providing massage. **2** *euphem.* brothel.

Massawa /mə'sɑːwə/ port in N Ethiopia, in Eritrea on the Red Sea; it is an important outlet for the country's exports; pop. (1992) 40 000.

masseur /mæ'sɜː(r)/ *n.* (*fem.* **masseuse** /mæ'sɜːz/) person who gives massage for a living. [French: related to MASSAGE]

massif /'mæsiːf/ *n.* compact group of mountain heights. [French: related to MASSIVE]

massive /'mæsɪv/ *adj.* **1** large and heavy or solid. **2** (of the features, head, etc.) relatively large or solid. **3** exceptionally large or severe (*massive heart attack*). **4** substantial, impressive. □ **massively** *adv.* **massiveness** *n.* [Latin: related to MASS[1]]

mass media *n.pl.* = MEDIA 2.

mass noun *n. Gram.* noun that is not normally countable and cannot be used with the indefinite article (e.g. *bread*).

♦ **mass production** *n.* manufacture of large quantities of a standardized article, possibly of high quality but not involving individual craftsmanship. Generally making use of continuous automated processes in which high-speed machines are operated by relatively small numbers of relatively unskilled employees. □ **mass-produce** *v.*

---

mast[1] /mɑːst/ *n.* **1** long upright post of timber etc. on a ship's keel to support sails. **2** post etc. for supporting a radio or television aerial. **3** flag-pole (*half-mast*). □ **before the mast** as an ordinary seaman. □ **masted** *adj.* (also in *comb.*). **master** *n.* (also in *comb.*). [Old English]

mast[2] /mɑːst/ *n.* fruit of the beech, oak, etc., esp. as food for pigs. [Old English]

mastectomy /mæs'tektəmɪ/ *n.* (*pl.* **-ies**) surgical removal of a breast. [Greek *mastos* breast]

master /'mɑːstə(r)/ *–n.* **1** person having control or ownership (*master of the house; dog obeyed his master; master of the hunt*). **2** captain of a merchant ship. **3** male teacher. **4** prevailing person. **5 a** skilled tradesman able to teach others (often *attrib.*: *master carpenter*). **b** skilled practitioner (*master of innuendo*). **6** holder of a usu. post-graduate university degree (*Master of Arts*). **7** revered teacher in philosophy etc. **8** great artist. **9** *Chess* etc. player at international level. **10** original copy of a film, recording, etc., from which others can be made. **11** (**Master**) title for a boy not old enough to be called *Mr.* **12** *archaic* employer. *–attrib. adj.* **1** commanding, superior (*master hand*). **2** main, principal (*master bedroom*). **3** controlling others (*master plan*). *–v.* **1** overcome, defeat. **2** gain full knowledge of or skill in. [Latin *magister*]

master-class *n.* class given by a famous musician etc.

master file *n. Computing* data file that is subject to frequent requests for data and frequent updating of the values stored, and thus considered an authoritative source of information. A master file can be updated by being completely rewritten by the system. The version prior to a particular update is called the **father file**, while the one before that is the **grandfather file**. The father file, and often the grandfather file, are retained as backup copies of the master file.

masterful *adj.* **1** imperious, domineering. **2** masterly. □ **masterfully** *adv.*

■ **Usage** *Masterful* is normally used of a person, whereas *masterly* is used of achievements, abilities, etc.

master-key *n.* key that opens several different locks.

masterly *adj.* very skilful.

■ **Usage** See note at *masterful.*

mastermind *–n.* **1** person with an outstanding intellect. **2** person directing a scheme etc. *–v.* plan and direct (a scheme etc.).

Master of Ceremonies *n.* **1** person introducing speakers at a banquet or entertainers in a variety show. **2** person in charge of a ceremonial or social occasion.

Master of the Rolls *n.* judge who presides over the Court of Appeal.

masterpiece *n.* **1** outstanding piece of artistry or workmanship. **2** person's best work.

master-stroke *n.* skilful tactic etc.

master-switch *n.* switch controlling the supply of electricity etc. to an entire system.

mastery *n.* **1** control, dominance. **2** (often foll. by *of*) comprehensive knowledge or skill.

masthead *n.* **1** top of a ship's mast, esp. as a place of observation or punishment. **2** title of a newspaper etc. at the head of the front page or editorial page.

mastic /'mæstɪk/ *n.* **1** gum or resin from the mastic tree, used in making varnish. **2** (in full **mastic tree**) evergreen tree yielding this. **3** waterproof filler and sealant. [Greek *mastikhē*]

masticate /'mæstɪˌkeɪt/ *v.* (**-ting**) grind or chew (food) with one's teeth. □ **mastication** /-'keɪʃ(ə)n/ *n.* **masticatory** *adj.* [Latin from Greek]

mastiff /'mæstɪf/ *n.* dog of a large strong breed with drooping ears. [Latin *mansuetus* tame]

mastitis /mæ'staɪtɪs/ *n.* inflammation of the breast or udder. [Greek *mastos* breast]

mastodon /'mæstəˌdɒn/ *n.* (*pl.* same or **-s**) large extinct mammal resembling the elephant. [Greek *mastos* breast, *odous* tooth]

mastoid /'mæstɔɪd/ *–adj.* shaped like a breast. *–n.* **1** = MASTOID PROCESS. **2** (usu. in *pl.*) *colloq.* inflammation of the mastoid process. [Greek *mastos* breast]

mastoid process *n.* conical prominence on the temporal bone behind the ear.

masturbate /'mæstəˌbeɪt/ *v.* (**-ting**) (usu. *absol.*) sexually arouse (oneself or another) by manual stimulation of the genitals. □ **masturbation** /-'beɪʃ(ə)n/ *n.* [Latin]

MAT *abbr. Insurance* marine, aviation, and transport.

mat[1] *–n.* **1** small piece of coarse material on a floor, esp. for wiping one's shoes on. **2** piece of cork, rubber, etc., to protect a surface from a hot dish etc. placed on it. **3** padded floor covering in gymnastics, wrestling, etc. *–v.* (**-tt-**) (esp. as **matted** *adj.*) entangle or become entangled in a thick mass (*matted hair*). □ **on the mat** *slang* being reprimanded. [Old English]

mat[2] var. of MATT.

Matabeleland /ˌmætə'biːlɪˌlænd/ region in S Zimbabwe, divided into the provinces of Matabeleland North and Matabeleland South, having important deposits of gold.

Matadi /mə'tɑːdɪ/ chief port of Democratic Republic of Congo, on the Congo River; pop. (est. 1991) 172 926.

matador /'mætəˌdɔː(r)/ *n.* bullfighter whose task is to kill the bull. [Spanish from *matar* kill: related to *mate* in CHECKMATE]

match[1] *–n.* **1** contest or game in which players or teams compete. **2 a** person as an equal contender (*meet one's match*). **b** person or thing exactly like or corresponding to another. **3** marriage. **4** person viewed as a marriage prospect. *–v.* **1** correspond (to); harmonize (with) (*his socks do not match; curtains match the wallpaper*). **2** equal. **3** (foll. by *against, with*) place in conflict or competition with. **4** find material etc. that matches (another) (*can you match this silk?*). **5** find a person or thing suitable for another. □ **match up** (often foll. by *with*) fit to form a whole; tally. **match up to** be as good as or equal to. [Old English]

match[2] *n.* **1** short thin piece of wood etc. with a combustible tip. **2** wick or cord etc. for firing a cannon etc. [French *mesche*]

matchboard *n.* tongued and grooved board fitting with similar boards.

matchbox *n.* box for holding matches.

♦ **matched bargain** *n.* transaction in which a sale of a particular quantity of stock is matched with a purchase of the same quantity of the same stock. Transactions of this kind are carried out on the London Stock Exchange by **matching brokers**.

---

matchless *adj.* incomparable.

matchmaker *n.* person who arranges marriages or schemes to bring couples together. □ **matchmaking** *n.*

match point *n. Tennis* etc. **1** position when one side needs only one more point to win the match. **2** this point.

matchstick *n.* stem of a match.

matchwood *n.* **1** wood suitable for matches. **2** minute splinters.

mate[1] *–n.* **1** friend or fellow worker. **2** *colloq.* form of address, esp. to another man. **3 a** each of a breeding pair, esp. of birds. **b** *colloq.* partner in marriage. **c** (in *comb.*) fellow member or joint occupant of (*team-mate*; *room-mate*). **4** officer on a merchant ship. **5** assistant to a skilled worker (*plumber's mate*). *–v.* (**-ting**) (often foll. by *with*) **1** come or bring together for breeding. **2** *Mech.* fit well. [Low German]

mate[2] *n.* & *v.* (**-ting**) *Chess* = CHECKMATE.

mater /ˈmeɪtə(r)/ *n. slang* mother. [Latin]

■ **Usage** *Mater* is now only found in jocular or affected use.

material /məˈtɪərɪəl/ *–n.* **1** matter from which a thing is made. **2** cloth, fabric. **3** (in *pl.*) things needed for an activity (*building materials*). **4** person or thing of a specified kind or suitable for a purpose (*officer material*). **5** (in *sing.* or *pl.*) information etc. for a book etc. **6** (in *sing.* or *pl.*, often foll. by *of*) elements, constituent parts, or substance. *–adj.* **1** of matter; corporeal; not spiritual. **2** of bodily comfort etc. (*material well-being*). **3** (often foll. by *to*) important, significant, relevant. [Latin *materia* MATTER]

◆ **material fact** *n.* **1** information that could be provided by a witness in court proceedings and could influence the decision of the court. **2** any important piece of information that a person seeking insurance must disclose to enable the insurer to decide whether or not to accept the insurance and to calculate the premium. While a person cannot be penalized for not revealing facts that he or she does not know or cannot reasonably be expected to know, the insurance contract can become void if facts that are deliberately concealed might influence whether or not the insurer accepts the risk, the premium charged, or the exceptions that are made. **3** relevant information about a company that must be made public in its prospectus if it is seeking a flotation on a stock exchange.

materialism *n.* **1** greater interest in material possessions and comfort than in spiritual values. **2** *Philos.* theory that nothing exists but matter. □ **materialist** *n.* **materialistic** /-ˈlɪstɪk/ *adj.* **materialistically** /-ˈlɪstɪkəlɪ/ *adv.*

◆ **materiality** /məˌtɪərɪˈælɪtɪ/ *n. Accounting* state of having sufficient significance to require separate disclosure. A statement issued by the Institute of Chartered Accountants in England and Wales says "a matter is material if its nondisclosure, misstatement, or omission would be likely to distort the view given by the accounts or other statement under consideration".

materialize *v.* (also **-ise**) (**-zing** or **-sing**) **1** become actual fact; happen. **2** *colloq.* appear or be present. **3** represent in or assume bodily form. □ **materialization** /-ˈzeɪʃ(ə)n/ *n.*

materially *adv.* substantially, significantly.

◆ **materials management** see LOGISTICS 2.

matériel /məˌtɪərɪˈel/ *n.* means, esp. materials and equipment in warfare. [French]

maternal /məˈtɜːn(ə)l/ *adj.* **1** of or like a mother; motherly. **2** related through the mother (*maternal uncle*). **3** of the mother in pregnancy and childbirth. □ **maternally** *adv.* [Latin *mater* mother]

maternity /məˈtɜːnɪtɪ/ *n.* **1** motherhood. **2** motherliness. **3** (*attrib.*) for women during pregnancy and childbirth (*maternity leave*; *maternity dress*). [French from medieval Latin: related to MATERNAL]

◆ **maternity rights** *n.pl.* rights a woman has from her employer when she is absent from work wholly or partly because of her pregnancy or confinement. In the UK an employee is entitled to statutory maternity pay if she has been working for the same employer continuously for at least six months ending in the 15th week before the baby is due, pays National Insurance, and leaves work between the 11th and 6th week before the expected date of confinement. Women who have worked more than 16 hours a week for two years, or more than eight hours a week for five years, are entitled to a higher statutory rate (nine-tenths of their normal average weekly pay) for the first six weeks of their absence in addition to the lower rate for a further 12 weeks. Employers recover the amount of the payments by setting the amount against their National Insurance payments. The employee is also entitled to return to her former job at any time within 29 weeks after the beginning of the week of the baby's birth provided she notifies her employer in writing three weeks before she leaves work.

◆ **mate's receipt** *n.* document signed by the mate of a ship as proof that the goods specified in the document have been loaded onto the ship, esp. if they have been delivered direct to the ship, rather than from a quayside warehouse. The mate's receipt functions as a document of title, which may be required as proof of loading in an f.o.b. contract, pending the issue of the bill of lading.

matey (also **maty**) *–adj.* (**-tier, -tiest**) sociable; familiar, friendly. *–n.* (*pl.* **-s**) *colloq.* (as a form of address) mate. □ **mateyness** *n.* (also **matiness**). **matily** *adv.*

math *n. US colloq.* mathematics. [abbreviation]

mathematical /ˌmæθəˈmætɪk(ə)l/ *adj.* **1** of mathematics. **2** rigorously precise. □ **mathematically** *adv.*

mathematical tables *n.pl.* tables of logarithms and trigonometric values etc.

mathematics /ˌmæθəˈmætɪks/ *n.pl.* **1** (also treated as

Mauritania /ˌmɒrɪˈteɪnɪə/, **Islamic Republic of** country in W Africa with a coastline on the Atlantic Ocean. The economy is predominantly agricultural: livestock, esp. cattle, are important and crops include millet, sorghum, beans, and rice. The fishing industry is a major source of revenue and fish processing is the chief manufacturing activity. Potentially rich deposits of iron ore are exploited, forming, with dried and salt fish, the chief exports. Gold is also exported.

History. A French protectorate from 1902 and a colony from 1920, Mauritania achieved full independence in 1960. It relinquished its claims to territory in Western Sahara in 1979 (see WESTERN SAHARA). The country came under military rule in 1978; multi-party elections were held in 1996 but unrest continues between Arabs, who still dominate the government, and Black Africans. President, Col. Maaouya Ould Sidi Ahmed Taya; prime minister, Cheikh Afia Ould Mohamed Khouna; capital, Nouakchott. □ **Mauritanian** *adj.* & *n.*

languages	Arabic
currency	ouguiya (UM) of 5 khoums
pop. (1996)	2 333 000
GNP (1994)	US$1.06B
literacy	49% (m); 26% (f)
life expectancy	45 (m); 51 (f)

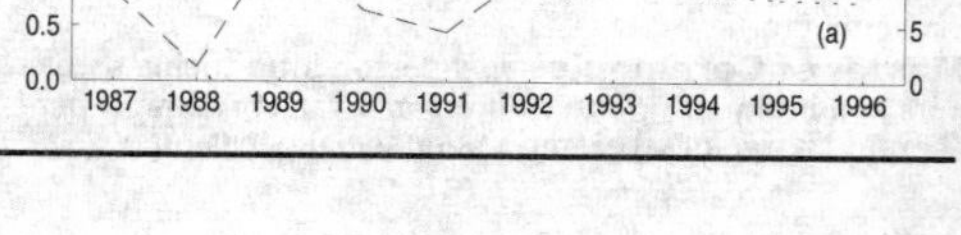

Exchange rate, US¢ per UM (a) Inflation, % (b)

1.5 1.0 0.5 0.0 | 15 10 5 0 | (a) (b)

1987 1988 1989 1990 1991 1992 1993 1994 1995 1996

sing.) abstract science of number, quantity, and space. **2** (as *pl.*) use of this in calculation etc. □ **mathematician** /-mə'tɪʃ(ə)n/ *n.* [Greek *manthanō* learn]

maths *n. colloq.* mathematics. [abbreviation]

MATIF /'mætiːf/ *abbr.* French international financial futures exchange. [French *Marché à Terme des Instruments Financiers*]

matinée /'mætɪˌneɪ/ *n.* (*US* **matinee**) afternoon performance in the theatre, cinema, etc. [French from *matin* morning: related to MATINS]

matinée coat *n.* (also **matinée jacket**) baby's short knitted coat.

matinée idol *n.* handsome actor.

matins /'mætɪnz/ *n.* (also **mattins**) (as *sing.* or *pl.*) morning prayer, esp. in the Church of England. [Latin *matutinus* of the morning]

Mato Grosso /ˌmætəʊ 'grɒsəʊ/ area of SW Brazil divided into two states, Mato Grosso and Goiás. Formerly densely forested, the area is now important agriculturally and has diamond and silver mines.

matriarch /'meɪtrɪˌɑːk/ *n.* female head of a family or tribe. □ **matriarchal** /-'ɑːk(ə)l/ *adj.* [Latin *mater* mother]

matriarchy /'meɪtrɪˌɑːkɪ/ *n.* (*pl.* **-ies**) female-dominated system of society, with descent through the female line.

matrices *pl.* of MATRIX.

matricide /'meɪtrɪˌsaɪd, 'mæ-/ *n.* **1** killing of one's mother. **2** person who does this. [Latin: related to MATER, -CIDE]

matriculate /mə'trɪkjʊˌleɪt/ *v.* (**-ting**) enrol at a college or university. □ **matriculation** /-'leɪʃ(ə)n/ *n.* [medieval Latin: related to MATRIX]

matrimony /'mætrɪmənɪ/ *n.* rite or state of marriage. □ **matrimonial** /-'məʊnɪəl/ *adj.* [Latin *matrimonium*: related to MATER]

matrix /'meɪtrɪks/ *n.* (*pl.* **matrices** /-ˌsiːz/ or **-es**) **1** mould in which a thing is cast or shaped. **2** place etc. in which a thing is developed. **3** rock in which gems, fossils, etc., are embedded. **4 a** *Math.* rectangular array of elements treated as a single element. **b** *Computing* see ARRAY *n.* 3. [Latin, = womb]

◆ **matrix printer** *n.* computer printer that produces characters as a pattern of dots. See DOT MATRIX PRINTER; LASER PRINTER.

matron /'meɪtrən/ *n.* **1** woman in charge of nursing in a hospital. **2** married, esp. staid, woman. **3** woman housekeeper at a school etc. [Latin *matrona*: related to MATER]

■ **Usage** In sense 1, *senior nursing officer* is now the official term.

matronly *adj.* like a matron, esp. portly or staid.

matron of honour *n.* married woman attending the bride at a wedding.

MATSA *abbr.* Managerial Administrative Technical Staff Association.

Matsuyama /ˌmætsuː'jɑːmə/ city and port in Japan, capital of Shikoku island; manufactures include machinery, chemicals, and textiles; pop. (1995) 460 870.

matt (also **mat**) *–adj.* not shiny or glossy; dull. *–n.* (in full **matt paint**) paint giving a dull flat finish. [French: related to MATE[2]]

matter *–n.* **1** physical substance having mass and occupying space, as distinct from mind and spirit. **2** specified substance (*colouring matter; reading matter*). **3** (prec. by *the*; often foll. by *with*) (thing) amiss (*something the matter with him*). **4** content as distinct from style, form, etc. **5** (often foll. by *of, for*) situation etc. under consideration or as an occasion for (regret etc.) (*matter for concern; matter of discipline*). **6** pus or a similar substance discharged from the body. *–v.* (often foll. by *to*) be of importance; have significance. □ **as a matter of fact** in reality; actually. **for that matter 1** as far as that is concerned. **2** and indeed also. **a matter of** approximately; amounting to (*a matter of 40 years*). **no matter 1** (foll. by *when, how*, etc.) regardless of. **2** it is of no importance. [Latin *materia* timber, substance]

matter of course *n.* natural or expected thing.

matter-of-fact *adj.* **1** unimaginative, prosaic. **2** unemotional. □ **matter-of-factly** *adv.* **matter-of-factness** *n.*

matter of life and death *n.* matter of vital importance.

matting *n.* fabric for mats.

mattins var. of MATINS.

mattock /'mætək/ *n.* agricultural tool like a pickaxe, with an adze and a chisel edge. [Old English]

mattress /'mætrɪs/ *n.* stuffed, or air- or water-filled cushion the size of a bed. [Arabic *almaṭraḥ*]

maturate /'mætjʊˌreɪt/ *v.* (**-ting**) (of a boil etc.) come to maturation. [Latin: related to MATURE]

maturation /ˌmætjʊ'reɪʃ(ə)n/ *n.* **1** maturing or being matured. **2** formation of pus. [French or medieval Latin: related to MATURE]

mature /mə'tʃʊə(r)/ *–adj.* (**maturer, maturest**) **1 a** fully developed, adult. **b** sensible, wise. **2** ripe; seasoned. **3** (of thought etc.) careful, considered. **4** (of a bill, insurance policy, etc.) due, payable. *–v.* (**-ring**) **1** develop fully; ripen. **2** perfect (a plan etc.). **3** (of a bill, insurance policy, etc.) become due or payable. □ **maturely** *adv.* **matureness** *n.* **maturity** *n.* [Latin *maturus* timely]

mature student *n.* adult student.

◆ **maturity date** *n.* date on which a document (e.g. a bond, bill of exchange, or insurance policy) becomes due for payment. In some cases, esp. for redeemable government stocks, the maturity date is known as the **redemption date**.

matutinal /ˌmætjuː'taɪn(ə)l, mə'tjuːtɪn(ə)l/ *adj.* of the morning; early. [Latin: related to MATINS]

maty var. of MATEY.

maudlin /'mɔːdlɪn/ *adj.* weakly or tearfully sentimental, esp. from drunkenness. [French *Madeleine*, referring to pictures of Mary Magdalen weeping]

maul /mɔːl/ *–v.* **1** tear the flesh of; claw. **2** handle roughly.

Mauritius /mə'rɪʃəs/, **Republic of** island country in the Indian Ocean, E of Madagascar. The economy has traditionally been dependent on sugar production, over half of which is grown on plantations; tea and tobacco are also grown commercially. Since the 1980s the government has pursued a policy of diversification to encourage labour-intensive manufacturing, esp. of clothing and textiles, for export; manufacturing now provides over half of total exports in value. The third main source of revenue is the tourist industry.

History. Mauritius was ceded by France to Britain in 1810 and, after 158 years as a Crown Colony, became independent as a member of the Commonwealth in 1968. It became a republic in 1992. President, Cassam Uteem; prime minister, Dr Navinchandra Ramgoolam; capital, Port Louis. □ **Mauritian** *adj.* & *n.*

languages	English (official), French, Creole
currency	rupee (Mau Re, *pl.* Mau Rs) of 100 cents
pop. (1996)	1 141 000
GNP (1994)	US$3.5B
literacy	85% (m); 74% (f)
life expectancy	66 (m); 73 (f)

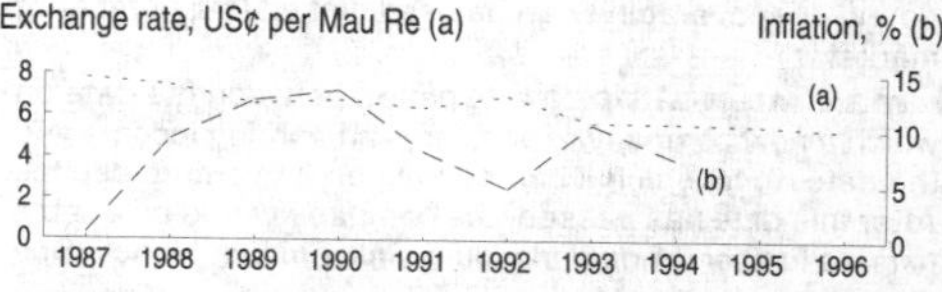

3 damage by criticism. *–n.* **1** *Rugby* loose scrum. **2** brawl. **3** heavy hammer. [Latin *malleus* hammer]

maulstick /ˈmɔːlstɪk/ *n.* (also **mahlstick**) stick held to support the hand in painting. [Dutch *malen* paint]

maunder /ˈmɔːndə(r)/ *v.* **1** talk ramblingly. **2** move or act listlessly or idly. [origin unknown]

Maundy /ˈmɔːndɪ/ *n.* distribution of Maundy money. [French *mandé* from Latin *mandatum* command]

Maundy money *n.* specially minted silver coins distributed by the British sovereign on Maundy Thursday.

Maundy Thursday *n.* Thursday before Easter.

Mau Re *symb.* (*pl.* **Mau Rs**) Mauritian rupee.

mausoleum /ˌmɔːsəˈliːəm/ *n.* magnificent tomb. [from *Mausōlos*, king of Caria, whose tomb had this name]

mauve /məʊv/ *–adj.* pale purple. *–n.* this colour. □ **mauvish** *adj.* [Latin: related to MALLOW]

maverick /ˈmævərɪk/ *n.* **1** unorthodox or independent-minded person. **2** *US* unbranded calf or yearling. [*Maverick*, name of an owner of unbranded cattle]

maw *n.* **1** stomach of an animal or *colloq.* greedy person. **2** jaws or throat of a voracious animal. [Old English]

mawkish /ˈmɔːkɪʃ/ *adj.* feebly sentimental; sickly. □ **mawkishly** *adv.* **mawkishness** *n.* [obsolete *mawk* MAGGOT]

max. *abbr.* maximum.

maxi /ˈmæksɪ/ *n.* (*pl.* **-s**) *colloq.* maxi-coat, -skirt, etc. [abbreviation]

maxi- *comb. form* very large or long. [abbreviation of MAXIMUM; cf. MINI-]

maxilla /mækˈsɪlə/ *n.* (*pl.* **-llae** /-liː/) jaw or jawbone, esp. (in vertebrates) the upper jaw. □ **maxillary** *adj.* [Latin]

maxim /ˈmæksɪm/ *n.* general truth or rule of conduct briefly expressed. [French or medieval Latin: related to MAXIMUM]

maxima *pl.* of MAXIMUM.

maximal /ˈmæksɪm(ə)l/ *adj.* of or being a maximum.

♦ **maximization of utility** *n.* assumption in neoclassical economics that individuals and firms maximize both utility and profits in the light of available information. Although maximization depends on the concept of rationality, which has been frequently subject to question, the maximizing assumption has been extremely helpful in practice; in particular it has enabled economists to introduce mathematical calculus into economics, from which general theories and predictions have been developed.

---

maximize /ˈmæksɪˌmaɪz/ *v.* (also **-ise**) (**-zing** or **-sing**) make as large or great as possible. □ **maximization** /-ˈzeɪʃ(ə)n/ *n.* [Latin: related to MAXIMUM]

■ **Usage** *Maximize* should not be used to mean 'to make as good as possible' or 'to make the most of'.

maximum /ˈmæksɪməm/ *–n.* (*pl.* **-ma**) highest possible amount, size, etc. *–adj.* greatest in amount, size, etc. [Latin *maximus* greatest]

♦ **maximum fluctuation** *n.* maximum daily price fluctuation that is permitted in some markets. See LIMIT *n.* 3.

♦ **maximum investment plan** *n.* (also **MIP**) unit-linked endowment policy marketed by a life-assurance company that is designed to produce maximum profit rather than life-assurance protection. It calls for regular premiums, usu. over ten years, with options to continue. These policies normally enable a tax-free fund to be built up over ten years and, because of the regular premiums, pound cost averaging can be used, linked to a number of markets.

♦ **maximum slippage** *n.* period between the date on which a new company expects to start earning income and the date up to which it can survive on its venture capital. After this date has passed, the company would be unable to raise further funds and would sink into insolvency. See also DEATH-VALLEY CURVE.

May *n.* **1** fifth month of the year. **2** (**may**) hawthorn, esp. in blossom. [Latin *Maius* of the goddess Maia]

may *v.aux.* (*3rd sing. present* **may**; *past* **might** /maɪt/) **1** expressing: **a** (often foll. by *well* for emphasis) possibility (*it may be true*; *you may well lose your way*). **b** permission (*may I come in?*). **c** a wish (*may he live to regret it*). **d** uncertainty or irony (*who may you be?*; *who are you, may I ask?*). **2** in purpose clauses and after *wish*, *fear*, etc. (*hope he may succeed*). □ **be that as it may** (or **that is as may be**) it is possible (but) (*be that as it may, I still want to go*). **may as well** = *might as well* (see MIGHT[1]). [Old English]

■ **Usage** In sense 1b, both *can* and *may* are used to express permission; in more formal contexts *may* is preferred since *can* also denotes capability (*can I move?* = am I physically able to move?; *may I move?* = am I allowed to move?).

Maya /ˈmɑːjə/ *n.* **1** (*pl.* same or **-s**) member of an ancient Indian people of Central America. **2** their language. □ **Mayan** *adj.* & *n.* [native name]

maybe /ˈmeɪbiː/ *adv.* perhaps. [from *it may be*]

May Day *n.* 1 May as a Spring festival or international holiday in honour of workers.

mayday /ˈmeɪdeɪ/ *n.* international radio distress-signal. [representing pronunciation of French *m'aidez* help me]

mayflower *n.* any of various flowers that bloom in May.

mayfly *n.* a kind of insect living briefly in spring.

mayhem /ˈmeɪhem/ *n.* destruction; havoc. [Anglo-French *mahem*: related to MAIM]

mayn't /ˈmeɪənt/ *contr.* may not.

Mayo /ˈmeɪəʊ/ agricultural county in the W Republic of Ireland, in the province of Connaught; pop. (1991) 110 713; capital, Castlebar.

mayonnaise /ˌmeɪəˈneɪz/ *n.* **1** thick creamy dressing of egg-yolks, oil, vinegar, etc. **2** dish dressed with this (*egg mayonnaise*). [French]

mayor /meə(r)/ *n.* **1** head of the corporation of a city or borough. **2** head of a district council with the status of a borough. □ **mayoral** *adj.* [Latin: related to MAJOR]

mayoralty /ˈmeərəltɪ/ *n.* (*pl.* **-ies**) **1** office of mayor. **2** period of this.

mayoress /ˈmeərɪs/ *n.* **1** woman mayor. **2** wife or official consort of a mayor.

Mayotte /mæˈjɒt/ (also **Mahore**) island in the Indian Ocean, NW of Madagascar, part of the Comoros Islands group; products include vanilla, essence of ylang-ylang, and coffee; pop. (est. 1994) 109 600; chief town, Mamoudzou, pop. (latest est.) 10 000. Mayotte also includes the smaller island of Pomanzi, where the former capital, Dzaoudzi, is located. When the Comoros elected to become independent in 1974, Mayotte decided to remain a French territory, becoming a Territorial Collectivity of France in 1976 following a referendum.

maypole *n.* decorated pole for dancing round on May Day.

May queen *n.* girl chosen to preside over May Day festivities.

Mazar-e-Sharif /mæˌzɑːriːʃəˈriːf/ city in N Afghanistan; industries include flour milling and textile production; pop. (est. 1988) 130 600.

maze *n.* **1** network of paths and hedges designed as a puzzle for those who enter it. **2** labyrinth. **3** confused network, mass, etc. [related to AMAZE]

mazurka /məˈzɜːkə/ *n.* **1** lively Polish dance in triple time. **2** music for this. [French or German from Polish]

MB *abbr.* **1** Bachelor of Medicine. **2** *Computing* **a** megabyte. **b** megabit. [sense 1 from Latin *Medicinae Baccalaureus*]

MBA *abbr.* Master of Business Administration.

Mbabane /ˌəmbɑːˈbɑːnɪ/ capital of Swaziland; pop. (1986) 38 300. Tourism is important.

MBC *abbr.* **1** metropolitan borough council. **2** municipal borough council.

MBCS *abbr.* Member of the British Computer Society.

MBE *abbr.* Member of the Order of the British Empire.

MBM *abbr.* Master of Business Management.

MBO *abbr.* **1** = MANAGEMENT BUYOUT. **2** management by objectives.

MBS *abbr.* Manchester Business School.

M.B.Sc. *abbr.* Master of Business Science.

Mbyte *abbr.* (also **M byte**) = MEGABYTE.

MC *–abbr.* **1** Master of Ceremonies. **2** Military Cross. **3** Member of Congress. *–international vehicle registration* Monaco.

M/C *abbr.* Manchester.

MCA *abbr.* **1** = MANAGEMENT CONSULTANTS' ASSOCIATION. **2** *propr. Computing* micro channel architecture. **3** = MONETARY COMPENSATORY AMOUNT.

MCAM *abbr.* Member of the CAM Foundation.

MCBSI *abbr.* Member of the Chartered Building Societies Institute.

MCC *abbr.* **1** Marylebone Cricket Club. **2** metropolitan county council.

McCarthyism, McCoy see at MACC-.

MCGA *abbr. Computing* multicolour graphics array.

MCIM *abbr.* Member of the Chartered Institute of Marketing.

MCIOB *abbr.* Member of the Chartered Institute of Building.

MCIS *abbr.* Member of the Institute of Chartered Secretaries and Administrators. [formerly *M*ember of the *C*hartered *I*nstitute of *S*ecretaries]

M.Com. *abbr.* Master of Commerce.

MCT *abbr.* **1** = MAINSTREAM CORPORATION TAX. **2** Member of the Association of Corporate Treasurers.

MD *–abbr.* **1** Doctor of Medicine. **2** = MANAGING DIRECTOR. **3** (also **M/D**) *Banking* memorandum of deposit. *–US postcode* Maryland. [sense 1 from Latin *Medicinae Doctor*]

Md *symb.* mendelevium.

Md. *abbr.* Maryland.

M/d *abbr. Commerce* months after date.

MDA *abbr. Computing* monochrome display adaptor.

MDC *abbr.* **1** metropolitan district council. **2** modification and design control. **3** more developed country.

MDR *abbr. Computing* memory data register.

MDT *abbr. Computing* mean downtime.

ME *–abbr.* myalgic encephalomyelitis, a condition with prolonged flu-like symptoms and depression. *–postcode* Medway. *–US postcode* Maine. *–airline flight code* Middle East Airlines.

Me. *abbr.* Maine.

me[1] /miː/ *pron.* **1** *objective case* of I[2] (*he saw me*). **2** *colloq.* = I[2] (*it's me all right; is taller than me*). [Old English accusative and dative of I[2]]

me[2] /miː/ *n.* (also **mi**) *Mus.* third note of a major scale. [Latin *mira*, word arbitrarily taken]

mea culpa /ˌmeɪə 'kʊlpə/ *–n.* acknowledgement of error. *–int.* expressing this. [Latin, = by my fault]

mead *n.* alcoholic drink of fermented honey and water. [Old English]

meadow /'medəʊ/ *n.* **1** piece of grassland, esp. one used for hay. **2** low marshy ground, esp. near a river. □ **meadowy** *adj.* [Old English]

meadowsweet *n.* fragrant meadow and marsh plant with creamy-white flowers.

meagre /'miːgə(r)/ *adj.* (*US* **meager**) **1** scant in amount or quality. **2** lean, thin. [Anglo-French *megre* from Latin *macer*]

meal[1] *n.* **1** occasion when food is eaten. **2** the food eaten at a meal. □ **make a meal of** *colloq.* treat (a task etc.) too laboriously or fussily. [Old English]

meal[2] *n.* **1** grain or pulse ground to powder. **2** *Scot.* oatmeal. **3** *US* maize flour. [Old English]

meals on wheels *n.pl.* (usu. treated as *sing.*) regular voluntary esp. lunch deliveries to old people, invalids, etc.

meal-ticket *n. colloq.* person or thing that is a source of maintenance or income.

mealtime *n.* usual time of eating.

mealy *adj.* (**-ier, -iest**) **1** of, like, or containing meal. **2** (of a complexion) pale. □ **mealiness** *n.*

mealy-mouthed *adj.* afraid to speak plainly.

mean[1] *v.* (*past* and *past part.* **meant** /ment/) **1** have as one's purpose or intention (*meant no harm by it; I didn't mean to break it*). **2** design or destine for a purpose (*meant to be used*). **3** intend to convey or refer to (*I mean Richmond in Surrey*). **4** (often foll. by *that*) entail, involve, portend, signify (*this means war; means that he is dead*). **5** (of a word) have as its equivalent in the same or another language. **6** (foll. by *to*) be of specified importance to (*that means a lot to me*). □ **mean business** *colloq.* be in earnest. **mean it** not be joking or exaggerating. **mean well** have good intentions. [Old English]

mean[2] *adj.* **1** niggardly; not generous. **2** ignoble, small-minded. **3** (of capacity, understanding, etc.) inferior, poor. **4** shabby; inadequate (*mean hovel*). **5 a** malicious, ill-tempered. **b** *US* vicious or aggressive in behaviour. **6** *US colloq.* skilful, formidable (*a mean fighter*). □ **no mean** a very good (*no mean feat*). □ **meanly** *adv.* **meanness** *n.* [Old English]

mean[3] *–n.* **1** median point (*mean between modesty and pride*). **2 a** term midway between the first and last terms of an arithmetical etc. progression. **b** quotient of the sum of several quantities and their number; average; arithmetic mean. *–adj.* **1** (of a quantity) equally far from two extremes. **2** calculated as a mean. [Latin *medianus* MEDIAN]

meander /mɪ'ændə(r)/ *–v.* **1** wander at random. **2** (of a stream) wind about. *–n.* **1** (in *pl.*) sinuous windings of a river, path, etc. **2** circuitous journey. [Greek *Maiandros*, a winding river in ancient Phrygia]

♦ **mean deviation** *n.* arithmetic mean of the deviations (all taken as positive numbers) of all the numbers in a set of numbers from their arithmetic mean. For example, the arithmetic mean of 5, 8, 9, and 10 is 8, and therefore the deviations from this mean are 3, 0, 1, and 2, giving a mean deviation of 1.5.

---

meanie /'miːnɪ/ *n.* (also **meany**) (*pl.* **-ies**) *colloq.* niggardly or small-minded person.

meaning *–n.* **1** what is meant. **2** significance. **3** importance. *–adj.* expressive, significant (*meaning glance*). □ **meaningly** *adv.*

meaningful *adj.* **1** full of meaning; significant. **2** *Logic* able to be interpreted. □ **meaningfully** *adv.* **meaningfulness** *n.*

meaningless *adj.* having no meaning or significance. □ **meaninglessly** *adv.* **meaninglessness** *n.*

♦ **mean price** *n.* = MIDDLE PRICE.

---

means *n.pl.* **1** (often treated as *sing.*) action, agent, device, or method producing a result (*means of quick travel*). **2 a** money resources (*live beyond one's means*). **b** wealth (*man of means*). □ **by all means** certainly. **by means of** by the agency etc. of. **by no means** certainly not. [from MEAN[3]]

mean sea level *n.* level halfway between high and low water.

means test *–n.* assessment of the income and capital of a person or family to determine eligibility for benefits provided by the state or a charity. *–v.* (**means-test**) subject to or base on a means test.

meant *past* and *past part.* of MEAN[1].

meantime *–adv.* = MEANWHILE. *–n.* intervening period (esp. *in the meantime*).

■ **Usage** As an adverb, *meantime* is less common than *meanwhile*.

meanwhile *–adv.* **1** in the intervening period of time. **2** at the same time. *–n.* intervening period (esp. *in the meanwhile*).

meany var. of MEANIE.

measles /'miːz(ə)lz/ *n.pl.* (also treated as *sing.*) infectious viral disease marked by a red rash. [Low German *masele* or Dutch *masel*]

measly /ˈmiːzlɪ/ *adj.* (**-ier**, **-iest**) *colloq.* meagre, contemptible.

measure /ˈmeʒə(r)/ *–n.* **1** size or quantity found by measuring. **2** system or unit of measuring (*liquid measure; 20 measures of wheat*). **3** rod, tape, vessel, etc. for measuring. **4** (often foll. by *of*) degree, extent, or amount (*a measure of wit*). **5** factor determining evaluation etc. (*sales are the measure of popularity*). **6** (usu. in *pl.*) suitable action to achieve some end. **7** legislative bill, act, etc. **8** prescribed extent or quantity. **9** poetic metre. **10** mineral stratum (*coal measures*). *–v.* (**-ring**) **1** ascertain the extent or quantity of (a thing) by comparison with a known standard. **2** be of a specified size. **3** ascertain the size of (a person) for clothes. **4** estimate (a quality etc.) by some criterion. **5** (often foll. by *off*) mark (a line etc. of a given length). **6** (foll. by *out*) distribute in measured quantities. **7** (foll. by *with, against*) bring (oneself or one's strength etc.) into competition with. □ **beyond measure** excessively. **for good measure** as a finishing touch. **in some measure** partly. **measure up 1** take the measurements (of). **2** (often foll. by *to*) have the qualifications (for). □ **measurable** *adj.* [Latin *mensura* from *metior* measure]

measured *adj.* **1** rhythmical; regular (*measured tread*). **2** (of language) carefully considered.

♦ **measured daywork** *n.* work for which a daily production target is set and a daily wage agreed on this basis. If the target is reached the worker receives the agreed daily wage; if it is not reached (or is exceeded) the worker is paid pro rata.

measureless *adj.* not measurable; infinite.

measurement *n.* **1** measuring. **2** amount measured. **3** (in *pl.*) detailed dimensions.

meat *n.* **1** animal flesh as food. **2** (often foll. by *of*) substance; chief part. □ **meatless** *adj.* [Old English]

meatball *n.* small round ball of minced meat.

Meath /miːθ/ agricultural county in the E Republic of Ireland, in the province of Leinster; pop. (est. 1991) 105 540; capital, Trim.

meat loaf *n.* minced meat etc. moulded and baked.

meat safe *n.* ventilated cupboard for storing meat.

meaty *adj.* (**-ier**, **-iest**) **1** full of meat; fleshy. **2** of or like meat. **3** substantial, full of interest, satisfying. □ **meatiness** *n.*

M.Ec. *abbr.* Master of Economics.

Mecca /ˈmekə/ city in W Saudi Arabia, the holiest city of the Islamic faith; pop. (1991) 630 000. The pilgrims who visit the city have traditionally provided most of its income, but the manufacturing industries, producing furniture, pottery, and textiles, are becoming increasingly important. *–n.* place one aspires to visit.

mechanic /mɪˈkænɪk/ *n.* person skilled in using or repairing machinery. [Latin: related to MACHINE]

mechanical *adj.* **1** of machines or mechanisms. **2** working or produced by machinery. **3** (of an action etc.) automatic; repetitive. **4** (of an agency, principle, etc.) belonging to mechanics. **5** of mechanics as a science. □ **mechanically** *adv.* [Latin: related to MECHANIC]

mechanical engineer *n.* person qualified in the design, construction, etc. of machines.

mechanics *n.pl.* (usu. treated as *sing.*) **1** branch of applied mathematics dealing with motion etc. **2** science of machinery. **3** routine technical aspects of a thing (*mechanics of local government*).

mechanism /ˈmekəˌnɪz(ə)m/ *n.* **1** structure or parts of a machine. **2** system of parts working together. **3** process; method (*defence mechanism; no mechanism for complaints*). □ **mechanistic** /-ˈnɪstɪk/ *adj.* [Greek: related to MACHINE]

mechanize /ˈmekəˌnaɪz/ *v.* (also **-ise**) (**-zing** or **-sing**) **1** introduce machines in (a factory etc.). **2** make mechanical. **3** equip with tanks, armoured cars, etc. □ **mechanization** /-ˈzeɪʃ(ə)n/ *n.*

Mechelen /ˈmexələn/ (French **Malines** /mæˈliːn/) city in N Belgium; manufactures include textiles, esp. lace; pop. (est. 1995) 75 718.

MECI *abbr.* Member of the Institute of Employment Consultants.

Mecklenburg-West Pomerania /ˈmeklənˌbɜːg/ state (*Land*) of Germany, on the Baltic coastal plain; pop. (est. 1995) 1 832 300; capital, Schwerin.

M.Econ. *abbr.* Master of Economics.

Med *n. colloq.* Mediterranean Sea. [abbreviation]

medal /ˈmed(ə)l/ *n.* commemorative metal disc etc., esp. awarded for military or sporting prowess. [Latin: related to METAL]

medallion /mɪˈdæljən/ *n.* **1** large medal. **2** thing so shaped, e.g. a decorative panel etc. [Italian: related to MEDAL]

medallist /ˈmedəlɪst/ *n.* (*US* **medalist**) winner of a (specified) medal (*gold medallist*).

Medan /məˈdɑːn/ city in Indonesia, in NE Sumatra, capital of North Sumatra province; pop. (1990) 1 685 972. It is the commercial centre of a tobacco-growing region.

meddle /ˈmed(ə)l/ *v.* (**-ling**) (often foll. by *with, in*) interfere in others' concerns. □ **meddler** *n.* [Latin: related to MIX]

meddlesome *adj.* interfering.

Medellín /ˌmedeɪˈiːn/ city in Colombia, notorious as a major centre of Colombia's drug trade; pop. (est. 1995) 1 621 356. Its industries include steel processing, engineering, and textiles.

media /ˈmiːdɪə/ *n.pl.* **1** *pl.* of MEDIUM. **2** (usu. prec. by *the*) mass communications (esp. newspapers and broadcasting) regarded collectively.

■ **Usage** *Media* is commonly used with a singular verb (e.g. *the media is biased*), but this is not generally accepted (cf. DATA).

♦ **media analysis** *n.* (also **media research, media planning**) investigation into the relative effectiveness and the relative costs of using the various advertising media in an advertising campaign. Before committing an advertising budget it is necessary to carry out market research on potential customers, their reading habits, television-watching habits, how many times the advertisers wish the potential customers to see an advertisement, how great a percentage of the market they wish to reach, etc. These elements all need to be considered and balanced to plan a campaign that will effectively reach its target audience at a reasonable cost.

mediaeval var. of MEDIEVAL.

medial /ˈmiːdɪəl/ *adj.* = MEDIAN. □ **medially** *adv.* [Latin *medius* middle]

median /ˈmiːdɪən/ *–adj.* situated in the middle. *–n.* **1** straight line drawn from any vertex of a triangle to the middle of the opposite side. **2** middle value, or average of the two middle values, in an ordered sequence of numbers. [Latin: related to MEDIAL]

mediate /ˈmiːdɪˌeɪt/ *v.* (**-ting**) **1** (often foll. by *between*) intervene (between disputants) to settle a quarrel etc. **2** bring about (a result) thus. □ **mediator** *n.* [Latin *medius* middle]

♦ **mediation** /ˌmiːdɪˈeɪʃ(ə)n/ *n.* **1** mediating; intercession. **2** intervention of a neutral third party in an industrial dispute to enable the two sides to reach a compromise solution to their differences, usu. by a mediator seeing representatives of each side separately and then together. If the mediator has power to make binding awards the process is known as arbitration; if the mediator can only suggest means of settling the dispute it is known as **conciliation**. See ADVISORY, CONCILIATION, AND ARBITRATION SERVICE; ARBITRATION.

medic /ˈmedɪk/ *n. colloq.* medical practitioner or student. [Latin *medicus* physician]

medical /ˈmedɪk(ə)l/ *–adj.* of medicine in general or as distinct from surgery (*medical ward*). *–n. colloq.* medical examination. □ **medically** *adv.*

medical certificate *n.* certificate of fitness or unfitness for work etc.

medical examination *n.* examination to determine a person's physical fitness.

♦ **medical insurance** *n.* = PRIVATE HEALTH INSURANCE.

---

medical officer *n.* person in charge of the health services of a local authority etc.

medical practitioner *n.* physician or surgeon.

medicament /mɪˈdɪkəmənt/ *n.* = MEDICINE 2.

Medicare /ˈmedɪˌkeə(r)/ *n.* US federally funded health insurance scheme for the elderly. [from MEDICAL, CARE]

medicate /ˈmedɪˌkeɪt/ *v.* (**-ting**) **1** treat medically. **2** impregnate with medicine etc. □ **medicative** /-kətɪv/ *adj.* [Latin *medicare medicat-*]

medication /ˌmedɪˈkeɪʃ(ə)n/ *n.* **1** = MEDICINE 2. **2** treatment using drugs.

medicinal /mɪˈdɪsɪn(ə)l/ *adj.* (of a substance) healing. □ **medicinally** *adv.*

medicine /ˈmeds(ə)n/ *n.* **1** science or practice of the diagnosis, treatment, and prevention of disease, esp. as distinct from surgery. **2** drug etc. for the treatment or prevention of disease, esp. taken by mouth. □ **take one's medicine** submit to something disagreeable. [Latin *medicina*]

Medicine Hat city in Canada, an agricultural centre in SE Alberta; pop. (1991) 43 625.

medicine man *n.* tribal, esp. North American Indian, witch-doctor.

medieval /ˌmedɪˈiːv(ə)l/ *adj.* (also **mediaeval**) **1** of the Middle Ages. **2** *colloq.* old-fashioned. [Latin *medium aevum* middle age]

medieval history *n.* history of the 5th–15th centuries.

medieval Latin *n.* Latin of about AD 600–1500.

Medina /meˈdiːnə/ oasis city in W Saudi Arabia; pop. (est. 1991) 400 000. As the second-holiest city of the Islamic faith, Medina derives much of its income from pilgrims.

mediocre /ˌmiːdɪˈəʊkə(r)/ *adj.* **1** indifferent in quality. **2** second-rate. [Latin *mediocris*]

mediocrity /ˌmiːdɪˈɒkrɪtɪ/ *n.* (*pl.* **-ies**) **1** being mediocre. **2** mediocre person.

meditate /ˈmedɪˌteɪt/ *v.* (**-ting**) **1** (often foll. by *on*, *upon*) engage in (esp. religious) contemplation. **2** plan mentally. □ **meditation** /-ˈteɪʃ(ə)n/ *n.* **meditator** *n.* [Latin *meditor*]

meditative /ˈmedɪtətɪv/ *adj.* **1** inclined to meditate. **2** indicative of meditation, thoughtful. □ **meditatively** *adv.* **meditativeness** *n.*

Mediterranean /ˌmedɪtəˈreɪnɪən/ *adj.* of the Mediterranean Sea or its surrounding region (*Mediterranean cookery*). [Latin *mediterraneus* inland]

Mediterranean Sea almost landlocked sea between S Europe and Africa; connected with the Atlantic Ocean by the Strait of Gibraltar and with the Red Sea by the Suez Canal.

medium /ˈmiːdɪəm/ *–n.* (*pl.* **media** or **-s**) **1** middle quality, degree, etc. between extremes (*find a happy medium*). **2** means of communication (*medium of television*). **3** substance, e.g. air, through which sense-impressions are conveyed. **4** physical environment etc. of a living organism. **5** means. **6 a** material or form used by an artist, composer, etc. **b** material used in computing for the input, output, or storage of data. **7** liquid (e.g. oil or gel) used for diluting paints. **8** (*pl.* **-s**) person claiming to communicate with the dead. **9** (in *pl.*) medium-dated gilts. *–adj.* **1** between two qualities, degrees, etc. **2** average (*of medium height*). [Latin *medius* middle]

♦ **medium-dated gilt** see GILT-EDGED SECURITY.

♦ **medium of exchange** *n.* substance or article of little intrinsic value that is used to pay for goods or services. In primitive economies various articles (e.g. sea shells) have been used for this purpose but money is now used universally.

---

medium-range *adj.* (of an aircraft, missile, etc.) able to travel a medium distance.

♦ **medium-sized company** *n.* company, as defined by the UK Companies Act (1981), that falls below any two of the following three size criteria: gross assets £2,800,000; turnover £5,750,000; average number of employees 250. If these companies are not public limited companies or banking, insurance, or shipping companies, they may file abbreviated profit and loss accounts with the Registrar of Companies (see MODIFIED ACCOUNTS), although they must provide their own shareholders with the full statutory information. Cf. SMALL COMPANY.

♦ **medium-term financial assistance** *n.* (also **MTFA**) loan available to member states of the European Community experiencing monetary difficulties due to adverse balance of payments. The donor countries may attach conditions on granting these loans, which usu. have a term of two to five years.

♦ **medium-term liabilities** *n.pl.* liabilities falling due in, say, more than one but less than ten years.

♦ **medium-term note** *n.* unsecured note issued in a Eurocurrency with a maturity of about three to six years.

---

medium wave *n.* radio wave of frequency between 300 kHz and 3 MHz.

medlar /ˈmedlə(r)/ *n.* **1** tree bearing small brown apple-like fruits, eaten when decayed. **2** such a fruit. [French *medler* from Greek *mespilē*]

medley /ˈmedlɪ/ *n.* (*pl.* **-s**) **1** varied mixture. **2** collection of tunes etc. played as one piece. [French *medlee*]

Médoc /meɪˈdɒk, ˈmedɒk/ wine-producing region of SW France; chief town, Lesparre. *–n.* red claret from this region.

medulla /mɪˈdʌlə/ *n.* **1** inner part of certain organs etc., e.g. the kidney. **2** soft internal tissue of plants. □ **medullary** *adj.* [Latin]

medulla oblongata /ˌɒblɒŋˈgɑːtə/ *n.* hindmost part of the brain, formed from a continuation of the spinal cord.

medusa /mɪˈdjuːsə/ *n.* (*pl.* **medusae** /-siː/ or **-s**) jellyfish. [Greek *Medousa*, name of a Gorgon]

meek *adj.* humble and submissive or gentle. □ **meekly** *adv.* **meekness** *n.* [Old Norse]

meerkat /ˈmɪəkæt/ *n.* S African mongoose. [Dutch, = sea-cat]

meerschaum /ˈmɪəʃəm/ *n.* **1** soft white clay-like substance. **2** tobacco-pipe with its bowl made from this. [German, = sea-foam]

Meerut /ˈmɪərət/ industrial city in N India, in Uttar Pradesh; pop. (1991) 753 778.

meet[1] *–v.* (*past* and *past part.* **met**) **1** encounter (a person etc.) or (of two or more people) come together by accident or design; come face to face (with) (*met on the bridge*). **2** be present by design at the arrival of (a person, train, etc.). **3** come or seem to come together or into contact (with); join (*where the sea and the sky meet; jacket won't meet*). **4** make the acquaintance of (*delighted to meet you; all met at Oxford*). **5** come together for business, worship, etc. (*union met management*). **6 a** deal with or answer (a demand, objection, etc.) (*met the proposal with hostility*). **b** satisfy or conform with (*agreed to meet the new terms*). **7** pay (a bill etc.); honour (a cheque) (*meet the cost*). **8** (often foll. by *with*) experience, encounter, or receive (*met their death; met with hostility*). **9** confront in battle etc. *–n.* **1** assembly for a hunt. **2** assembly for sport, esp. athletics. □ **make ends meet** see END. **meet the case** be adequate. **meet the eye** be visible or evident. **meet a person half way** compromise with. **meet up** *colloq.* (often foll. by *with*) = sense 1 of *v.* **meet with 1** see sense 8 of *v.* **2** receive (a reaction) (*met with her approval*). **3** esp. *US* = sense 1 of *v.* [Old English]

meet[2] *adj. archaic* fitting, proper. [related to METE]

meeting *n.* **1** coming together. **2** assembly of esp. a society, committee, etc. **3** = RACE MEETING.

♦ **meeting of creditors** see BANKRUPTCY; CREDITORS' VOLUNTARY LIQUIDATION; LIQUIDATOR.

---

meg *n.* megabyte. [abbreviation]

mega /ˈmegə/ *slang –adj.* **1** excellent. **2** enormous. *–adv.* extremely.

mega- *comb. form* **1** large. **2 a** one million (10^6) in the metric system of measurement. **b** *Computing* power of 2 nearest to 10^6 (i.e. 2^{20}), most frequently encountered in terms of storage capacity. See MEGABYTE. **3** *slang* extremely; very big (*mega-stupid*; *mega-project*). [Greek *megas* great]

megabuck /ˈmegəˌbʌk/ *n. US slang* million dollars.

megabyte /ˈmegəˌbaɪt/ *n.* (also **M, Mbyte, M byte**) *Computing* 1 048 576 (i.e. 2^{20}) bytes as a measure of storage capacity of magnetic disks, magnetic tape, and main memory.

megadeath /ˈmegəˌdeθ/ *n.* death of one million people (in war).

megahertz /ˈmegəˌhɜːts/ *n.* (*pl.* same) one million hertz, esp. as a measure of radio frequency.

megalith /ˈmegəlɪθ/ *n.* large stone, esp. as a prehistoric monument or part of one. □ **megalithic** /-ˈlɪθɪk/ *adj.* [Greek *lithos* stone]

megalomania /ˌmegələˈmeɪnɪə/ *n.* **1** mental disorder producing delusions of grandeur. **2** passion for grandiose schemes. □ **megalomaniac** *adj.* & *n.* [Greek *megas* great, MANIA]

megalosaurus /ˌmegələˈsɔːrəs/ *n.* (*pl.* **-ruses**) large flesh-eating dinosaur with stout hind legs and small forelimbs. [Greek *megas* great, *sauros* lizard]

megaphone /ˈmegəˌfəʊn/ *n.* large funnel-shaped device for amplifying the voice. [Greek *megas* great, *phōnē* sound]

megastar /ˈmegəˌstɑː(r)/ *n. colloq.* very famous entertainer etc.

megaton /ˈmegəˌtʌn/ *n.* unit of explosive power equal to one million tons of TNT.

megavolt /ˈmegəˌvəʊlt/ *n.* one million volts, esp. as a unit of electromotive force.

megawatt /ˈmegəˌwɒt/ *n.* one million watts, esp. as a measure of electrical power.

Meghalaya /ˌmegəˈleɪə/ state of NE India; pop. (est. 1994) 1 960 000; capital, Shillong. It is an agricultural region, producing rice, potatoes, cotton, and fruit.

megohm /ˈmegəʊm/ *n.* one million ohms.

meiosis /maɪˈəʊsɪs/ *n.* (*pl.* **meioses** /-siːz/) **1** cell division that results in gametes with half the normal chromosome number. **2** = LITOTES. [Greek *meiōn* less]

Mekele /mɪˈkeɪlɪ/ city in N Ethiopia, capital of Tigray province; products include salt, incense, and resin; pop. (est. 1994) 119 779.

Meknès /mekˈnes/ city in N Morocco, a centre for trade in wine and carpets; pop. (est. 1993) 401 000.

Mekong /miːˈkɒŋ/ river in SE Asia, rising in Tibet and flowing SE and S to its extensive delta on the South China Sea.

Melaka /məˈlækə/ (formerly **Malacca**) **1** state in SW Malaysia, on the W coast of the Strait of Malacca; products include rice, tin, rubber, and copra; pop. (est. 1993) 583 400. **2** its capital and chief port, an important trading centre; pop. (1980) 88 073.

melamine /ˈmeləˌmiːn/ *n.* **1** white crystalline compound producing resins. **2** (in full **melamine resin**) plastic made from this and used esp. for laminated coatings. [from arbitrary *melam*, AMINE]

melancholia /ˌmelənˈkəʊlɪə/ *n.* depression and anxiety. [Latin: related to MELANCHOLY]

melancholy /ˈmelənkəlɪ/ *–n.* **1** pensive sadness. **2 a** mental depression. **b** tendency to this. *–adj.* sad; saddening, depressing; expressing sadness. □ **melancholic** /-ˈkɒlɪk/ *adj.* [Greek *melas* black, *kholē* bile]

Melanesia /ˌmeləˈniːʃə/ island-group in the SW Pacific containing the Bismarck Archipelago, the Solomon Islands, Santa Cruz, Vanuatu, New Caledonia, Fiji, and the intervening islands. □ **Melanesian** *adj.* & *n.*

mélange /meɪˈlɑ̃ʒ/ *n.* mixture, medley. [French *mêler* mix]

melanin /ˈmelənɪn/ *n.* dark pigment in the hair, skin, etc., causing tanning in sunlight. [Greek *melas* black]

melanoma /ˌmeləˈnəʊmə/ *n.* malignant skin tumour.

Melba toast /ˈmelbə/ *n.* very thin crisp toast. [*Melba*, name of a soprano]

Melbourne /ˈmelbən, -bɔːn/ city in Australia, capital of Victoria and a major commercial centre; industries include heavy engineering, food processing, and textiles; pop. (est. 1995) 3 218 100.

meld *v.* merge, blend. [origin uncertain]

mêlée /ˈmeleɪ/ *n.* (*US* **melee**) **1** confused fight, skirmish, or scuffle. **2** muddle. [French: related to MEDLEY]

Melilla /meˈlɪljə/ Spanish port, an enclave on the Mediterranean coast of Morocco; iron ore is its chief export; pop. (est. 1994) 58 052.

mellifluous /mɪˈlɪfluəs/ *adj.* (of a voice etc.) pleasing, musical, flowing. □ **mellifluously** *adv.* **mellifluousness** *n.* [Latin *mel* honey, *fluo* flow]

mellow /ˈmeləʊ/ *–adj.* **1** (of sound, colour, light) soft and rich, free from harshness. **2** (of character) gentle; mature. **3** genial, jovial. **4** *euphem.* partly intoxicated. **5** (of fruit) soft, sweet, and juicy. **6** (of wine) well-matured, smooth. **7** (of earth) rich, loamy. *–v.* make or become mellow. □ **mellowly** *adv.* **mellowness** *n.* [origin unknown]

melodeon /mɪˈləʊdɪən/ *n.* (also **melodion**) **1** small organ similar to the harmonium. **2** small German accordion. [from MELODY, HARMONIUM]

melodic /mɪˈlɒdɪk/ *adj.* of melody; melodious. □ **melodically** *adv.* [Greek: related to MELODY]

melodious /mɪˈləʊdɪəs/ *adj.* **1** of, producing, or having melody. **2** sweet-sounding. □ **melodiously** *adv.* **melodiousness** *n.* [French: related to MELODY]

melodrama /ˈmeləˌdrɑːmə/ *n.* **1** sensational play etc. appealing blatantly to the emotions. **2** this type of drama. **3** theatrical language, behaviour, etc. □ **melodramatic** /-drəˈmætɪk/ *adj.* **melodramatically** /-drəˈmætɪkəlɪ/ *adv.* [Greek *melos* music, DRAMA]

melody /ˈmelədɪ/ *n.* (*pl.* **-ies**) **1** single notes arranged to make a distinctive recognizable pattern; tune. **2** principal part in harmonized music. **3** musical arrangement of words. **4** sweet music, tunefulness. [Greek *melos* song: related to ODE]

melon /ˈmelən/ *n.* **1** sweet fleshy fruit of various climbing plants of the gourd family. **2** such a gourd. [Greek *mēlon* apple]

melt *v.* **1** become liquefied or change to liquid by the action of heat; dissolve. **2** (as **molten** *adj.*) (esp. of metals etc.) liquefied by heat (*molten lava*; *molten lead*). **3** (of food) be delicious, seeming to dissolve in the mouth. **4** soften, or (of a person, the heart, etc.) be softened, by pity, love, etc. (*a melting look*). **5** (usu. foll. by *into*) merge imperceptibly; change into (*night melted into dawn*). **6** (often foll. by *away*) (of a person) leave or disappear unobtrusively (*melted into the background*). □ **melt away** disappear by or as if by liquefaction. **melt down 1** melt (esp. metal) for reuse. **2** become liquid and lose structure. [Old English]

meltdown *n.* **1** melting of a structure, esp. the overheated core of a nuclear reactor. **2** disastrous event, esp. a rapid fall in share values.

melting-point *n.* temperature at which a solid melts.

melting-pot *n.* place for mixing races, theories, etc.

member /ˈmembə(r)/ *n.* **1** person etc. belonging to a society, team, group, etc. **2** (**Member**) person elected to certain assemblies etc. **3** part of a larger structure, e.g. of a group of figures or mathematical set. **4 a** part or organ of the body, esp. a limb. **b** = PENIS. [Latin *membrum* limb]

♦ **member bank** *n.* bank that belongs to a central banking or clearing system. In the UK it is a commercial bank that is a member of the Association for Payment Clearing Services; in the US it is a commercial bank that is a member of the Federal Reserve System.

♦ **member firm** *n.* firm of brokers or market makers that is a member of the London Stock Exchange (International

Stock Exchange). There are some 395 member firms. Banks, insurance companies, and overseas securities houses can now become corporate members.

◆ **member of a company** *n.* shareholder of a company whose name is entered in the register of members. Founder members are those who sign the memorandum of association; anyone subsequently coming into possession of the company's shares becomes a member.

---

membership *n.* **1** being a member. **2** number or body of members.

◆ **members' voluntary liquidation** *n.* (also **members' voluntary winding-up**) winding-up of a company by a special resolution of the members in circumstances in which the company is solvent. Before making the winding-up resolution, the directors must make a declaration of solvency. It is a criminal offence to make such a declaration without reasonable grounds for believing that it is true. When the resolution has been passed, a liquidator is appointed; if, during the course of the winding-up, the liquidator believes that the company will not be able to pay its debts, a meeting of creditors must be called and the winding-up is treated as a members' compulsory liquidation.

---

membrane /'membreɪn/ *n.* **1** pliable sheetlike tissue connecting or lining organs in plants and animals. **2** thin pliable sheet or skin. □ **membranous** /'membrənəs/ *adj.* [Latin *membrana* skin, parchment: related to MEMBER]

memento /mɪ'mentəʊ/ *n.* (*pl.* **-es** or **-s**) souvenir of a person or event. [Latin, imperative of *memini* remember]

memento mori /mɪˌmentəʊ 'mɔːrɪ/ *n.* skull etc. as a reminder of death. [Latin, = remember you must die]

memo /'meməʊ/ *n.* (*pl.* **-s**) *colloq.* memorandum. [abbreviation]

memoir /'memwɑː(r)/ *n.* **1** historical account etc. written from personal knowledge or special sources. **2** (in *pl.*) autobiography, esp. partial or dealing with specific events or people. **3** essay on a learned subject. [French *mémoire*: related to MEMORY]

memorabilia /ˌmemərə'bɪlɪə/ *n.pl.* souvenirs of memorable events. [Latin: related to MEMORABLE]

memorable /'memərəb(ə)l/ *adj.* **1** worth remembering. **2** easily remembered. □ **memorably** *adv.* [Latin *memor* mindful]

memorandum /ˌmemə'rændəm/ *n.* (*pl.* **-da** or **-s**) **1** note or record for future use. **2** informal written message, esp. in business, diplomacy, etc. [see MEMORABLE]

◆ **memorandum of association** *n.* official document setting out the details of a company's existence. It must be signed by the first subscribers and must contain the following information (as it applies to the company in question): the company name, a statement that the company is a public company, the address of the registered office, the objects of the company (called the **objects clause**), a statement of limited liability, the amount of the guarantee, and the amount of authorized share capital and its division.

◆ **memorandum of satisfaction** *n.* document stating that a mortgage or charge on property has been repaid. It has to be signed by all the parties concerned and a copy sent to the Registrar of Companies if the mortgage or charge was made by a company.

---

memorial /mɪ'mɔːrɪəl/ *–n.* object etc. established in memory of a person or event. *–attrib. adj.* commemorating (*memorial service*). [Latin: related to MEMORY]

memorize /'meməˌraɪz/ *v.* (also **-ise**) (**-zing** or **-sing**) commit to memory.

memory /'memərɪ/ *n.* (*pl.* **-ies**) **1** faculty by which things are recalled to or kept in the mind. **2 a** this in an individual (*my memory is failing*). **b** store of things remembered (*deep in my memory*). **3** recollection; remembrance, esp. of a person etc.; person or thing remembered (*memory of better times; his mother's memory*). **4 a** device or medium in which data or program instructions can be held for subsequent use by a computer. The word 'memory' is synonymous with 'store' and 'storage' but is most frequently used in the terms random-access memory (see RAM) and read-only memory (see ROM), which are forms of semiconductor memory used for main store. See also STORAGE DEVICE. **b** = MAIN STORE. **c** storage capacity of a computer etc. **5** posthumous reputation (*his memory lives on; of blessed memory*). **6** length of remembered time of a specific person, group, etc. (*within living memory*). **7** remembering (*deed worthy of memory*). □ **from memory** as remembered (without checking). **in memory of** to keep alive the remembrance of. [Latin *memoria* from *memor* mindful]

memory card (also **memory board**) see EXPANSION CARD.

memory lane *n.* (usu. prec. by *down, along*) *joc.* sentimental remembering.

Memphis /'memfɪs/ city and river port in the US, on the Mississippi in SW Tennessee; pop. (est. 1994) 614 289. Trading in cotton, timber, and livestock, it also manufactures textiles and chemicals.

memsahib /'memsɑːb/ *n. Anglo-Ind. hist.* Indian name for a European married woman in India. [from MA'AM, SAHIB]

men *pl.* of MAN.

menace /'menɪs/ *–n.* **1** threat. **2** dangerous thing or person. **3** *joc.* pest, nuisance. *–v.* (**-cing**) threaten. □ **menacingly** *adv.* [Latin *minax* from *minor* threaten]

ménage /meɪ'nɑːʒ/ *n.* household. [Latin: related to MANOR]

ménage à trois /meɪˌnɑːʒ ɑː 'trwɑː/ *n.* (*pl.* ***ménages à trois***) household of three, usu. a married couple and a lover. [French, = household of three]

menagerie /mɪ'nædʒərɪ/ *n.* small zoo. [French: related to MÉNAGE]

Menai Strait /'menaɪ/ channel separating Anglesey from NW Wales.

mend *–v.* **1** restore to good condition; repair. **2** regain health. **3** improve (*mend matters*). *–n.* darn or repair in material etc. □ **mend one's ways** reform oneself. **on the mend** recovering, esp. in health. [Anglo-French: related to AMEND]

mendacious /men'deɪʃəs/ *adj.* lying, untruthful. □ **mendacity** /-'dæsɪtɪ/ *n.* (*pl.* **-ies**). [Latin *mendax*]

mendelevium /ˌmendə'liːvɪəm/ *n.* artificially made transuranic radioactive metallic element. [*Mendeleev*, name of a chemist]

Mendelian /men'diːlɪən/ *adj.* of Mendel's theory of heredity by genes. [*Mendel*, name of a botanist]

mendicant /'mendɪkənt/ *–adj.* **1** begging. **2** (of a friar) living solely on alms. *–n.* **1** beggar. **2** mendicant friar. [Latin *mendicus* beggar]

mending *n.* **1** action of repairing. **2** things, esp. clothes, to be mended.

Mendoza /men'dəʊsə/ **1** province of W Argentina; pop. (est. 1995) 1 500 818. **2** its capital city, commercial centre of an important wine-producing region; pop. (1991) 773 113.

menfolk *n.pl.* men, esp. the men of a family.

menhir /'menhɪə(r)/ *n.* usu. prehistoric monument of a tall upright stone. [Breton *men* stone, *hir* long]

menial /'miːnɪəl/ *–adj.* (of esp. work) degrading, servile. *–n.* domestic servant. [Anglo-French *meinie* retinue]

meninges /mɪ'nɪndʒiːz/ *n.pl.* three membranes enclosing the brain and spinal cord. [Greek *mēnigx* membrane]

meningitis /ˌmenɪn'dʒaɪtɪs/ *n.* (esp. viral) infection and inflammation of the meninges.

meniscus /mɪ'nɪskəs/ *n.* (*pl.* **menisci** /-saɪ/) **1** curved upper surface of liquid in a tube. **2** lens convex on one side and concave on the other. [Greek *mēniskos* crescent, from *mēnē* moon]

menopause /'menəˌpɔːz/ *n.* **1** ceasing of menstruation. **2** period in a woman's life (usu. 45–55) when this occurs. □ **menopausal** /-'pɔːz(ə)l/ *adj.* [Greek *mēn* month, PAUSE]

menorah /mɪ'nɔːrə/ *n.* seven-branched Jewish candelabrum. [Hebrew, = candlestick]

Menorca see MINORCA.

menses /'mensiːz/ *n.pl.* flow of menstrual blood etc. [Latin, pl. of *mensis* month]

mens rea /menz 'riːə/ *n. Law* criminal intent. [Latin, = guilty mind]

menstrual /'menstrʊəl/ *adj.* of menstruation. [Latin *menstruus* monthly]

menstrual cycle *n.* process of ovulation and menstruation.

menstruate /'menstrʊˌeɪt/ *v.* (**-ting**) undergo menstruation.

menstruation /ˌmenstrʊ'eɪʃ(ə)n/ *n.* process of discharging blood etc. from the uterus, usu. at monthly intervals from puberty to menopause.

mensuration /ˌmensjʊə'reɪʃ(ə)n/ *n.* **1** measuring. **2** measuring of lengths, areas, and volumes. [Latin: related to MEASURE]

menswear *n.* clothes for men.

-ment *suffix* **1** forming nouns expressing the means or result of verbal action (*abridgement*; *embankment*). **2** forming nouns from adjectives (*merriment*; *oddment*). [Latin *-mentum*]

mental /'ment(ə)l/ *adj.* **1** of, in, or done by the mind. **2** caring for mental patients. **3** *colloq.* insane. □ **mentally** *adv.* [Latin *mens ment-* mind]

mental age *n.* degree of mental development in terms of the average age at which such development is attained.

mental block *n.* inability due to subconscious mental factors.

mental deficiency *n.* abnormally low intelligence.

mentality /men'tælɪtɪ/ *n.* (*pl.* **-ies**) mental character or disposition; kind or degree of intelligence.

mental patient *n.* sufferer from mental illness.

mental reservation *n.* silent qualification made while seeming to agree.

menthol /'menθɒl/ *n.* mint-tasting organic alcohol found in oil of peppermint etc., used as a flavouring and to relieve local pain. [Latin: related to MINT[1]]

mentholated /'menθəˌleɪtɪd/ *adj.* treated with or containing menthol.

mention /'menʃ(ə)n/ *–v.* **1** refer to briefly or by name. **2** reveal or disclose (*do not mention this to anyone*). **3** (usu. as **mention in dispatches**) award a minor military honour to in war. *–n.* **1** reference, esp. by name. **2** minor military or other honour. □ **don't mention it** polite reply to an apology or thanks. **not to mention** and also. [Latin *mentio*]

mentor /'mentɔː(r)/ *n.* experienced and trusted adviser. [*Mentor* in Homer's *Odyssey*]

menu /'menjuː/ *n.* **1** list of dishes available in a restaurant etc., or to be served at a meal. **2** *Computing* list of options displayed on a VDU. The user typically makes a selection by positioning the cursor on the selected option using a mouse or by touching a selected area of a touch-sensitive screen. When many options are available the user may be presented first with a main menu, from which more detailed menus can be selected. Any program that obtains input from a user by means of a menu is said to be **menu-driven**. A well-designed menu system can make a complicated program simple to use. [Latin: related to MINUTE[2]]

MEP *abbr.* Member of the European Parliament.

Mephistophelean /ˌmefɪstə'fiːlɪən/ *adj.* fiendish. [*Mephistopheles*, evil spirit to whom Faust sold his soul in German legend]

mercantile /'mɜːkənˌtaɪl/ *adj.* **1** of trade, trading. **2** commercial. [Latin: related to MERCHANT]

♦ **mercantile agent** see FACTOR 3a.

♦ **mercantile law** *n.* commercial law, which includes those aspects of a country's legal code that apply to banking, companies, contracts, copyrights, insolvency, insurance, patents, the sale of goods, shipping, trade marks, transport, and warehousing.

mercantile marine *n.* merchant shipping.

♦ **mercantilism** *n. Econ.* theory prevalent between 1500 and 1800, mainly in England and France. Its main characteristics were a belief that exports created wealth for a nation, while imports diminished wealth; that gold and silver bullion (specie) should be accumulated by a country in order to encourage trade internally; and that to achieve these ends governments should encourage exports of manufactured goods and imports of bullion while restricting exports of bullion and imports of manufactured goods. The theory became discredited when it was shown that trade need not benefit only one country. See also COMPARATIVE ADVANTAGE.

Mercator projection /mɜː'keɪtə/ *n.* (also **Mercator's projection**) map of the world projected on to a cylinder so that all the parallels of latitude have the same length as the equator. [*Mercator*, name of a geographer]

mercenary /'mɜːsɪnərɪ/ *–adj.* primarily concerned with or working for money etc. *–n.* (*pl.* **-ies**) hired soldier in foreign service. □ **mercenariness** *n.* [Latin from *merces* reward]

mercer *n.* dealer in textile fabrics. [Latin *merx merc-* goods]

mercerize /'mɜːsəˌraɪz/ *v.* (also **-ise**) (**-zing** or **-sing**) treat (cotton) with caustic alkali to strengthen and make lustrous. [*Mercer*, name of its alleged inventor]

merchandise /'mɜːtʃənˌdaɪz/ *–n.* goods for sale. *–v.* (**-sing**) **1** trade, traffic (in). **2** advertise or promote (goods, an idea, or a person). [French: related to MERCHANT]

♦ **merchandising** *n.* promotion in a retail outlet of selected products using displays to encourage impulse buying, free samples and gifts, temporary price reductions, etc. Merchandising policy is usu. designed to influence the retailer's sales pattern and is influenced by such factors as the firm's market, the speed at which different products sell, margins, and service considerations. Sometimes merchandising is used to attract customers into the shop.

merchant /'mɜːtʃ(ə)nt/ *n.* **1** trader who buys goods for resale, acting as a principal and usu. holding stocks. Typically a merchant sells goods in smaller lots than those bought and often exports goods or is involved in entrepôt trade. **2** esp. *US* & *Scot.* retail trader. **3** *colloq.* usu. *derog.* person devoted to a specified activity etc. (*speed merchant*). [Latin *mercor* trade (v.)]

merchantable *adj.* saleable, marketable.

♦ **merchantable quality** *n.* implied condition respecting the state of goods sold in the course of business. Such goods should be as fit for their ordinary purpose as it is reasonable to expect, taking into account any description applied to them, the price (if relevant), and all the other relevant circumstances. The condition does not apply with regard to defects specifically drawn to the buyer's attention or defects that the buyer should have noticed if the goods were examined before the contract is made.

♦ **merchant bank** *n.* bank dealing in commercial loans and finance. Merchant banks, many long-established, formerly specialized in financing foreign trade and also functioned as accepting houses. More recently they have tended to diversify into the field of hire-purchase finance, the granting of long-term loans (esp. to companies), advising companies on flotations and take-over bids, underwriting new issues, and managing investment portfolios and unit trusts. Some offer a limited banking service. Their knowledge of international trade makes them specialists in dealing with the large multinational companies.

merchantman *n.* (*pl.* **-men**) merchant ship.

merchant navy *n.* nation's commercial shipping.

merchant ship *n.* ship carrying merchandise.

merciful /ˈmɜːsɪˌfʊl/ *adj.* showing mercy. □ **mercifulness** *n.*

mercifully *adv.* **1** in a merciful manner. **2** fortunately (*mercifully, the sun came out*).

merciless /ˈmɜːsɪləs/ *adj.* showing no mercy. □ **mercilessly** *adv.*

mercurial /mɜːˈkjʊərɪəl/ *adj.* **1** (of a person) volatile. **2** of or containing mercury. [Latin: related to MERCURY]

mercury /ˈmɜːkjʊrɪ/ *n.* **1** silvery heavy liquid metallic element used in barometers, thermometers, etc. **2** (**Mercury**) planet nearest to the sun. □ **mercuric** /-ˈkjʊərɪk/ *adj.* **mercurous** *adj.* [Latin *Mercurius*, Roman messenger-god]

mercy /ˈmɜːsɪ/ *–n.* (*pl.* **-ies**) **1** compassion or forbearance towards defeated enemies or offenders or as a quality. **2** act of mercy. **3** (*attrib.*) done out of compassion (*mercy killing*). **4** thing to be thankful for (*small mercies*). *–int.* expressing surprise or fear. □ **at the mercy of 1** in the power of. **2** liable to danger or harm from. **have mercy on** (or **upon**) show mercy to. [Latin *merces* reward, pity]

mere[1] /mɪə(r)/ *attrib. adj.* (**merest**) being solely or only what is specified (*a mere boy*; *no mere theory*). □ **merely** *adv.* [Latin *merus* unmixed]

mere[2] /mɪə(r)/ *n. dial.* or *poet.* lake. [Old English]

meretricious /ˌmerəˈtrɪʃəs/ *adj.* showily but falsely attractive. [Latin *meretrix* prostitute]

merganser /mɜːˈgænsə(r)/ *n.* (*pl.* same or **-s**) a diving duck. [Latin *mergus* diver, *anser* goose]

merge *v.* (**-ging**) **1** (often foll. by *with*) **a** combine. **b** join or blend gradually. **2** combine items from (two or more computer files). For example, there are programs that merge names and addresses held on a mailing list file with a word-processing file to produce a mailshot. **3** (foll. by *in*) (cause to) lose character and identity in (something else). [Latin *mergo* dip]

♦ **merger** *n.* combining, esp. of two or more commercial organizations into one in order to increase efficiency and sometimes to avoid competition. Approval of the Monopolies and Mergers Commission may be required and the merger must be conducted on lines sanctioned by the City Code on Take-overs and Mergers. Mergers are usu. amicably arranged by all the parties concerned, unlike some take-overs.

♦ **merger accounting** *n.* method of accounting in which the assets of a merged subsidiary company are shown in the accounts of the parent company using the historical-cost accounting principle. This is based on their value at the time of acquisition, which may be less than their present value.

Mérida /ˈmeɪriːðə/ city in SE Mexico, the capital of Yucatán state and industrial and commercial centre of a region producing henequen fibre; pop. (1990) 556 819.

meridian /məˈrɪdɪən/ *n.* **1 a** circle of constant longitude, passing through a given place and the terrestrial poles. **b** corresponding line on a map. **2** (often *attrib.*) prime; full splendour. [Latin *meridies* midday]

meridional *adj.* **1** of or in the south (esp. of Europe). **2** of a meridian.

meringue /məˈræŋ/ *n.* **1** sugar, whipped egg-whites, etc., baked crisp. **2** small cake of this, esp. filled with whipped cream. [French]

merino /məˈriːnəʊ/ *n.* (*pl.* **-s**) **1** (in full **merino sheep**) variety of sheep with long fine wool. **2** soft cashmere-like material, orig. of merino wool. **3** fine woollen yarn. [Spanish]

merit /ˈmerɪt/ *–n.* **1** quality of deserving well. **2** excellence, worth. **3** (usu. in *pl.*) **a** thing that entitles one to reward or gratitude. **b** intrinsic rights and wrongs (*merits of a case*). *–v.* (**-t-**) deserve. [Latin *meritum* value, from *mereor* deserve]

♦ **merit bonus** *n.* bonus granted to an employee as a reward for good work.

♦ **merit good** *n.* commodity, e.g. education, regarded (usu. by a government) as intrinsically good. Conversely, a commodity generally regarded as intrinsically bad (e.g. cigarettes) is known as a **merit bad**.

---

meritocracy /ˌmerɪˈtɒkrəsɪ/ *n.* (*pl.* **-ies**) **1** government by those selected for merit. **2** group selected in this way. **3** society governed thus.

meritorious /ˌmerɪˈtɔːrɪəs/ *adj.* praiseworthy.

merlin /ˈmɜːlɪn/ *n.* small falcon. [Anglo-French]

mermaid *n.* legendary creature with a woman's head and trunk and a fish's tail. [from MERE[2] 'sea', MAID]

merry /ˈmerɪ/ *adj.* (**-ier**, **-iest**) **1 a** joyous. **b** full of laughter or gaiety. **2** *colloq.* slightly drunk. □ **make merry** be festive. □ **merrily** *adv.* **merriment** *n.* **merriness** *n.* [Old English]

merry-go-round *n.* **1 a** fairground ride with revolving model horses or cars. **b** = ROUNDABOUT 2a. **2** cycle of bustling activity.

merrymaking *n.* festivity, fun. □ **merrymaker** *n.*

Mersa Matruh /ˌmɜːsə məˈtruː/ port, resort, and market town in NW Egypt, on the Mediterranean coast; pop. (est. 1984) 40 470.

Merseyside /ˈmɜːzɪˌsaɪd/ metropolitan county of NW England; pop. (est. 1994) 1 434 400. In 1986 its administrative powers were devolved to a number of district councils.

mésalliance /meɪˈzælɪˌɑ̃s/ *n.* marriage with a social inferior. [French]

mescal /ˈmeskæl/ *n.* peyote cactus. [Spanish from Nahuatl]

mescal buttons *n.pl.* disc-shaped dried tops from the mescal, esp. as an intoxicant.

mescaline /ˈmeskəˌlɪn/ *n.* (also **mescalin**) hallucinogenic alkaloid present in mescal buttons.

Mesdames *pl.* of MADAME.

Mesdemoiselles *pl.* of MADEMOISELLE.

mesembryanthemum /mɪˌzembrɪˈænθɪməm/ *n.* S African fleshy-leaved plant with bright daisy-like flowers that open fully in sunlight. [Greek, = noon flower]

mesh *–n.* **1** network fabric or structure. **2** each of the open spaces in a net or sieve etc. **3** (in *pl.*) **a** network. **b** snare. *–v.* **1** (often foll. by *with*) (of the teeth of a wheel) be engaged. **2** be harmonious. **3** catch in a net. □ **in mesh** (of the teeth of wheels) engaged. [Dutch]

mesmerize /ˈmezməˌraɪz/ *v.* (also **-ise**) (**-zing** or **-sing**) **1** hypnotize. **2** fascinate, spellbind. □ **mesmerism** *n.* **mesmerizingly** *adv.* [*Mesmer*, name of a physician]

meso- *comb. form* middle, intermediate. [Greek *mesos* middle]

mesolithic /ˌmezəʊˈlɪθɪk/ *adj.* of the part of the Stone Age between the palaeolithic and neolithic periods. [Greek *lithos* stone]

mesomorph /ˈmesəʊˌmɔːf/ *n.* person with a compact muscular body. [Greek *morphē* form]

meson /ˈmiːzɒn/ *n.* elementary particle believed to help hold nucleons together in the atomic nucleus. [from MESO-]

Mesopotamia /ˌmesəpəˈteɪmɪə/ region of SW Asia between the rivers Tigris and Euphrates. The site of several ancient civilizations, it now lies within Iraq. □ **Mesopotamian** *adj.* & *n.*

mesosphere /ˈmesəʊˌsfɪə(r)/ *n.* region of the atmosphere from the top of the stratosphere to an altitude of about 80 km.

Mesozoic /ˌmesəʊˈzəʊɪk/ *–adj.* of the geological era marked by the development of dinosaurs, and the first mammals, birds, and flowering plants. *–n.* this era. [Greek *zōion* animal]

mess *–n.* **1** dirty or untidy state of things. **2** state of confusion, embarrassment, or trouble. **3** something spilt etc. **4** disagreeable concoction. **5 a** soldiers etc. dining together. **b** army dining-hall. **c** meal taken there. **6** domestic animal's excreta. **7** *archaic* portion of liquid or pulpy food. *–v.* **1** (often foll. by *up*) make a mess of; dirty; muddle. **2** *US* (foll. by *with*) interfere with. **3** take one's meals. **4** *colloq.* defecate. □ **make a mess of** bungle. **mess about** (or **around**) **1** potter; fiddle. **2** *colloq.* make things awkward or inconvenient for (a person). [Latin *missus* course of a meal: related to MESSAGE]

message /ˈmesɪdʒ/ *n.* **1** communication sent by one person to another. **2** exalted or spiritual communication. **3** (in *pl.*) *Scot.*, *Ir.*, & *N.Engl.* shopping. □ **get the message** *colloq.* understand (a hint etc.). [Latin *mitto miss-* send]

Messeigneurs *pl.* of MONSEIGNEUR.

messenger /ˈmesɪndʒə(r)/ *n.* person who carries a message.

Messiah /mɪˈsaɪə/ *n.* **1 a** promised deliverer of the Jews. **b** Christ regarded as this. **2** liberator of an oppressed people. [Hebrew, = anointed]

Messianic /ˌmesɪˈænɪk/ *adj.* **1** of the Messiah. **2** inspired by hope or belief in a Messiah. [French: related to MESSIAH]

Messieurs *pl.* of MONSIEUR.

Messina /meˈsiːnə/ city and port in Italy, in NE Sicily, on the **Strait of Messina** separating Sicily from the mainland; manufactures include pasta, chemicals, and soap; pop. (est. 1994) 233 845.

mess kit *n.* soldier's cooking and eating utensils.

Messrs /ˈmesəz/ *pl.* of MR. [abbreviation of MESSIEURS]

messy *adj.* (**-ier, -iest**) **1** untidy or dirty. **2** causing or accompanied by a mess. **3** difficult to deal with; awkward. □ **messily** *adv.* **messiness** *n.*

met[1] *past* and *past part.* of MEET[1].

met[2] *adj. colloq.* **1** meteorological. **2** metropolitan. **3** (**the Met**) **a** (in full **the Met Office**) Meteorological Office. **b** Metropolitan Police in London. [abbreviation]

meta- *comb. form* **1** denoting change of position or condition (*metabolism*). **2** denoting position: **a** behind, after, or beyond (*metaphysics*). **b** of a higher or second-order kind (*metalanguage*). [Greek *meta* with, after]

metabolism /mɪˈtæbəˌlɪz(ə)m/ *n.* all the chemical processes in a living organism producing energy and growth. □ **metabolic** /ˌmetəˈbɒlɪk/ *adj.* [Greek *metabolē* change: related to META-, Greek *ballō* throw]

metabolite /mɪˈtæbəˌlaɪt/ *n.* substance formed in or necessary for metabolism.

metabolize /mɪˈtæbəˌlaɪz/ *v.* (also **-ise**) (**-zing** or **-sing**) process or be processed by metabolism.

metacarpus /ˌmetəˈkɑːpəs/ *n.* (*pl.* **-carpi** /-paɪ/) **1** part of the hand between the wrist and the fingers. **2** set of five bones in this. □ **metacarpal** *adj.* [related to META-, CARPUS]

metal /ˈmet(ə)l/ *–n.* **1 a** any of a class of workable elements such as gold, silver, iron, or tin, usu. good conductors of heat and electricity and forming basic oxides. **b** alloy of any of these. **2** molten material for making glass. **3** (in *pl.*) rails of a railway line. **4** = ROAD-METAL. *–adj.* made of metal. *–v.* (**-ll-**; *US* **-l-**) **1** make or mend (a road) with road-metal. **2** cover or fit with metal. [Greek *metallon* mine]

metalanguage /ˈmetəˌlæŋgwɪdʒ/ *n.* **1** form of language used to discuss language. **2** system of propositions about propositions.

metal detector *n.* electronic device for locating esp. buried metal.

metallic /mɪˈtælɪk/ *adj.* **1** of or like metal or metals (*metallic taste*). **2** sounding like struck metal. **3** shiny (*metallic blue*). □ **metallically** *adv.*

metalliferous /ˌmetəˈlɪfərəs/ *adj.* (of rocks) containing metal.

metallize /ˈmetəˌlaɪz/ *v.* (also **-ise**; *US* **metalize**) (**-zing** or **-sing**) **1** render metallic. **2** coat with a thin layer of metal.

metallography /ˌmetəˈlɒgrəfɪ/ *n.* descriptive science of metals.

metalloid /ˈmetəˌlɔɪd/ *n.* element intermediate in properties between metals and non-metals, e.g. boron, silicon, and germanium.

metallurgy /mɪˈtælədʒɪ, ˈmetəˌlɜːdʒɪ/ *n.* **1** science of metals and their application. **2** extraction and purification of metals. □ **metallurgic** /ˌmetəˈlɜːdʒɪk/ *adj.* **metallurgical** /ˌmetəˈlɜːdʒɪk(ə)l/ *adj.* **metallurgist** *n.* [Greek *metallon* METAL, *-ourgia* working]

metalwork *n.* **1** art of working in metal. **2** metal objects collectively. □ **metalworker** *n.*

metamorphic /ˌmetəˈmɔːfɪk/ *adj.* **1** of metamorphosis. **2** (of rock) transformed naturally, e.g. by heat or pressure. □ **metamorphism** *n.* [from META-, Greek *morphē* form]

metamorphose /ˌmetəˈmɔːfəʊz/ *v.* (**-sing**) (often foll. by *to*, *into*) change in form or nature.

metamorphosis /ˌmetəˈmɔːfəsɪs, -ˈfəʊsɪs/ *n.* (*pl.* **-phoses** /-ˌsiːz/) **1** change of form, esp. from a pupa to an insect etc. **2** change of character, conditions, etc. [Greek *morphē* form]

metaphor /ˈmetəˌfɔː(r)/ *n.* **1** application of a name or description to something to which it is not literally applicable (e.g. *a glaring error*). **2** instance of this. □ **metaphoric** /-ˈfɒrɪk/ *adj.* **metaphorical** /-ˈfɒrɪk(ə)l/ *adj.* **metaphorically** /-ˈfɒrɪkəlɪ/ *adv.* [Latin from Greek]

metaphysic /ˌmetəˈfɪzɪk/ *n.* system of metaphysics.

metaphysical *adj.* **1** of metaphysics. **2** *colloq.* excessively abstract or theoretical. **3** (of esp. 17th-century English poetry) subtle and complex in imagery.

metaphysics /ˌmetəˈfɪzɪks/ *n.pl.* (usu. treated as *sing.*) **1** branch of philosophy dealing with the nature of existence, truth, and knowledge. **2** *colloq.* abstract talk; mere theory. [Greek, as having followed physics in Aristotle's works]

metastasis /meˈtæstəsɪs/ *n.* (*pl.* **-stases** /-ˌsiːz/) transference of a bodily function, disease, etc., from one part or organ to another. [Greek, = removal]

metatarsus /ˌmetəˈtɑːsəs/ *n.* (*pl.* **-tarsi** /-saɪ/) **1** part of the foot between the ankle and the toes. **2** set of five bones in this. □ **metatarsal** *adj.* [related to META-, TARSUS]

mete *v.* (**-ting**) (usu. foll. by *out*) *literary* apportion or allot (punishment or reward). [Old English]

meteor /ˈmiːtɪə(r)/ *n.* **1** small solid body from outer space that becomes incandescent when entering the earth's atmosphere. **2** streak of light from a meteor. [Greek *meteōros* lofty]

meteoric /ˌmiːtɪˈɒrɪk/ *adj.* **1** rapid; dazzling (*meteoric rise to fame*). **2** of meteors. □ **meteorically** *adv.*

meteorite /ˈmiːtɪəˌraɪt/ *n.* fallen meteor, or fragment of natural rock or metal from outer space.

meteoroid /ˈmiːtɪəˌrɔɪd/ *n.* small body that becomes visible as it passes through the earth's atmosphere as a meteor.

meteorology /ˌmiːtɪəˈrɒlədʒɪ/ *n.* the study of atmospheric phenomena, esp. for forecasting the weather. □ **meteorological** /-rəˈlɒdʒɪk(ə)l/ *adj.* **meteorologist** *n.* [Greek *meteōrologia*: related to METEOR]

meter[1] /ˈmiːtə(r)/ *–n.* **1** instrument that measures or records, esp. gas, electricity, etc. used, distance travelled, etc. **2** = PARKING-METER. *–v.* measure or record by meter. [from METE]

meter[2] *US* var. of METRE[1],[2].

-meter *comb. form* **1** forming nouns denoting measuring instruments (*barometer*). **2** forming nouns denoting lines of poetry with a specified number of measures (*pentameter*). [Greek *metron* measure]

methadone /ˈmeθəˌdəʊn/ *n.* narcotic analgesic drug used esp. as a substitute for morphine or heroin. [6-di*methyl*amino-4,4-*d*iphenyl-3-heptan*one*]

methanal /ˈmeθəˌnæl/ *n.* = FORMALDEHYDE. [from METHANE, ALDEHYDE]

methane /ˈmiːθeɪn/ *n.* colourless odourless inflammable gaseous hydrocarbon, the main constituent of natural gas. [from METHYL]

methanoic acid /ˌmeθəˈnəʊɪk/ *n.* = FORMIC ACID. [related to METHANE]

methanol /ˈmeθəˌnɒl/ *n.* colourless volatile inflammable liquid hydrocarbon, used as a solvent. [from METHANE, ALCOHOL]

methinks /mɪˈθɪŋks/ *v.* (*past* **methought** /mɪˈθɔːt/)

archaic it seems to me. [Old English: related to ME[1], THINK]

method /ˈmeθəd/ *n.* **1** way of doing something; systematic procedure. **2** orderliness; regular habits. □ **method in one's madness** sense in apparently foolish or strange behaviour. [Greek: related to META-, *hodos* way]

methodical /mɪˈθɒdɪk(ə)l/ *adj.* characterized by method or order. □ **methodically** *adv.*

Methodist /ˈmeθədɪst/ *–n.* member of a Protestant denomination originating in the 18th-century Wesleyan evangelistic movement. *–adj.* of Methodists or Methodism. □ **Methodism** *n.*

methodology /ˌmeθəˈdɒlədʒɪ/ *n.* (*pl.* **-ies**) **1** body of methods used in a particular activity. **2** science of method. □ **methodological** /-dəˈlɒdʒɪk(ə)l/ *adj.* **methodologically** /-dəˈlɒdʒɪkəlɪ/ *adv.*

♦ **method study** see WORK STUDY.

methought *past* of METHINKS.

meths *n. colloq.* methylated spirit. [abbreviation]

methyl /ˈmeθɪl, ˈmiːθaɪl/ *n.* univalent hydrocarbon radical CH_3, present in many organic compounds. [Greek *methu* wine, *hulē* wood]

methyl alcohol *n.* = METHANOL.

methylate /ˈmeθɪˌleɪt/ *v.* (**-ting**) **1** mix or impregnate with methanol. **2** introduce a methyl group into (a molecule or compound).

methylated spirit *n.* (also **methylated spirits** *n.pl.*) alcohol treated to make it unfit for drinking and exempt from duty.

metical /ˈmetɪˌkæl/ *n.* (*pl.* **-cais**) standard monetary unit of Mozambique. [Portuguese]

meticulous /məˈtɪkjʊləs/ *adj.* **1** giving great attention to detail. **2** very careful and precise. □ **meticulously** *adv.* **meticulousness** *n.* [Latin *metus* fear]

métier /ˈmetjeɪ/ *n.* **1** one's trade, profession, or field of activity. **2** one's forte. [Latin: related to MINISTER]

metonymy /mɪˈtɒnɪmɪ/ *n.* substitution of the name of an attribute or adjunct for that of the thing meant (e.g. *Crown* for *king, the turf* for *horse-racing*). [Greek: related to META-, *onuma* name]

metre[1] /ˈmiːtə(r)/ *n.* (*US* **meter**) metric unit and the base SI unit of linear measure, equal to about 39.4 inches. □ **metreage** /ˈmiːtərɪdʒ/ *n.* [Greek *metron* measure]

metre[2] /ˈmiːtə(r)/ *n.* (*US* **meter**) **1 a** poetic rhythm, esp. as determined by the number and length of feet in a line. **b** metrical group or measure. **2** basic rhythm of music. [related to METRE[1]]

metre-kilogram-second *n.* denoting a system of measure using the metre, kilogram, and second.

metric /ˈmetrɪk/ *adj.* of or based on the metre. [French: related to METRE[1]]

-metric *comb. form* (also **-metrical**) forming adjectives corresponding to nouns in *-meter* and *-metry* (*thermometric; geometric*).

metrical *adj.* **1** of or composed in metre (*metrical psalms*). **2** of or involving measurement (*metrical geometry*). □ **metrically** *adv.* [Greek: related to METRE[2]]

metricate *v.* (**-ting**) convert to a metric system. □ **metrication** /-ˈkeɪʃ(ə)n/ *n.*

♦ **metric system** *n.* decimal measuring system with the metre and gram (or kilogram) as units of length and mass. It was first formalized in France at the end of the 18th century and by the 1830s was being widely adopted in Europe. In the UK, imperial units remained supreme until 1963, when the yard was redefined as 0.9144 metre and the pound as 0.453 592 37 kilogram. The Metrication Board set up in 1969 failed to achieve its target of the metrication of British industry by 1975 and metrication now proceeds on a voluntary basis, in which it is envisaged that pints of beer, miles per hour, yards, and feet will persist until the end of the century. However, the Weights and Measures Act (1985) lists certain units that may no longer be used for trade: these include the hundredweight, ton, bushel, square mile, cubic yard, and cubic foot. It is hoped that before the end of the century such units as the therm and British thermal unit will have been abandoned. For all scientific purposes and many trade and industrial purposes the form of the metric system known as SI units is now in use. In the US metrication has been even slower than in the UK.

metric ton *n.* = TONNE.

metro /ˈmetrəʊ/ *n.* (*pl.* **-s**) underground railway system, esp. in Paris. [French shortened from *métropolitain* metropolitan]

♦ **metrology** /mɪtˈrɒlədʒɪ/ *n.* scientific study of weights and measures. The subject has long been closely associated with trade and commerce, which is based on the exchange of measured quantities of goods or services for money or measured quantities of other goods or services. See METRIC SYSTEM; SI UNITS.

metronome /ˈmetrəˌnəʊm/ *n.* device ticking at a selected

Mexico /ˈmeksɪˌkəʊ/, **United States of** country in Central America with extensive coastlines on the Atlantic and Pacific Oceans, bordered by the US to the N. Since the mid-1970s the expansion of the oil industry has provided the main stimulus to economic development, and Mexico is now a leading oil producer. There are also large reserves of natural gas; other important minerals are gold, silver, copper, lead, zinc, mercury, iron, sulphur, uranium, fluorite, and graphite. The chief manufacturing industries are based on this mineral wealth and include motor vehicles, iron and steel, oil refining, and chemicals. Agriculture is relatively undeveloped, but production is improving. Exports, mainly to the US, include oil, cars and engines, fruits and vegetables, coffee, and shrimps. There is also an important tourist industry. Mexico is a member of LAIA, and in 1992 concluded a free-trade agreement with the US and Canada (NAFTA: see NORTH AMERICAN FREE TRADE AGREEMENT).
History. Formerly the centre of Aztec and Mayan civilization, Mexico was conquered and colonized by the Spanish in the early 16th century, achieving independence in 1821. Territory was lost to the US in the Mexican War of 1846–8. The long dictatorship of Porfirio Díaz, in which economic development benefited conservative landowners and foreign investors, came to an end with the Mexican Revolution, which began in 1910 and culminated in the constitution of 1917. This brought about social and political reform and established the present form of government, which is dominated by the Party of Institutionalized Revolution (PRI). In recent years the PRI has faced increased opposition and charges of corruption and fraud. In 1995 there was an armed revolt in Chiapas. In the 1997 elections the PRI lost control of the Chamber of Deputies for the first time in nearly 70 years. Austerity measures were introduced in 1995 at the behest of the IMF. President, Ernesto Zedillo Ponce de León; capital, Mexico City. □ **Mexican** *adj.* & *n.*

languages	Spanish (official), Indian languages
currency	peso (Mex$) of 100 centavos
pop. (1996)	92 711 000
GNP (1994)	US$368B
literacy	88% (m); 83% (f)
life expectancy	69 (m); 75 (f)

Exchange rate, US¢ per Mex$ (a) (log scale) — Inflation, % (b)

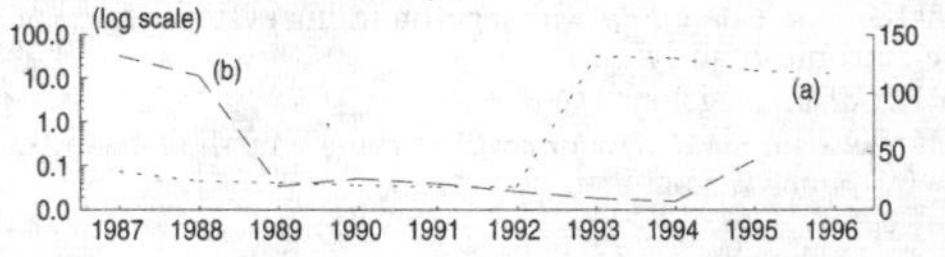

rate to mark time for musicians. [Greek *metron* measure, *nomos* law]

metropolis /mɪ'trɒpəlɪs/ *n.* chief city, capital. [Greek *mētēr* mother, *polis* city]

metropolitan /ˌmetrə'pɒlɪt(ə)n/ *–adj.* **1** of a metropolis. **2** of or forming a mother country as distinct from its colonies etc. (*metropolitan France*). *–n.* **1** bishop having authority over the bishops of a province. **2** inhabitant of a metropolis.

-metry *comb. form* forming nouns denoting procedures and systems involving measurement (*geometry*).

mettle /'met(ə)l/ *n.* **1** quality or strength of character. **2** spirit, courage. □ **on one's mettle** keen to do one's best. □ **mettlesome** *adj.* [from METAL *n.*]

Metz /mets/ industrial city in NE France, centre of the Lorraine coal- and iron-producing region; it has varied manufacturing industries; pop. (1990) 123 920.

MeV *abbr.* mega-electronvolt(s).

mew[1] *–n.* characteristic cry of a cat, gull, etc. *–v.* utter this sound. [imitative]

mew[2] *n.* gull, esp. the common gull. [Old English]

mewl *v.* **1** whimper. **2** mew like a cat. [imitative]

mews /mju:z/ *n.* (treated as *sing.*) stabling round a yard etc., now used esp. for housing. [originally sing. *mew* 'cage for hawks': French from Latin *muto* change]

MEX *international vehicle registration* Mexico.

Mexicali /ˌmeksɪ'kɑ:lɪ/ city in NW Mexico, capital of Baja California state, on the US border; pop. (1990) 438 377. It is the commercial and processing centre of a productive agricultural region.

Mexico City capital of Mexico; pop. (1990) 15 047 685 (metropolitan area). It is heavily industrialized, its products including iron, steel, chemicals, and textiles.

MEZ *abbr.* (German) Mitteleuropäische Zeit (= Central European Time).

mezzanine /'metsəˌni:n, 'mez-/ *n.* **1** storey between two others (usu. between the ground and first floors). **2** (*attrib.*) intermediate stage in a financial process. **Mezzanine funding** is an intermediate stage in the funding of a new company, lying between the provision of a loan and the taking of a share in its equity. [Italian: related to MEDIAN]

mezzo /'metsəʊ/ *Mus. –adv.* half, moderately. *–n.* (in full **mezzo-soprano**) (*pl.* **-s**) **1** female singing-voice between soprano and contralto. **2** singer with this voice. [Latin *medius* middle]

mezzo forte *adj.* & *adv.* fairly loud(ly).

mezzo piano *adj.* & *adv.* fairly soft(ly).

mezzotint /'metsəʊtɪnt/ *n.* **1** method of printing or engraving in which a plate is roughened by scraping to produce tones and half-tones. **2** print so produced. [Italian: related to MEZZO, TINT]

mf *abbr.* mezzo forte.

MFLOPS /'emˌflɒps/ *abbr.* (also **Mflops**) *Computing* million floating-point operations per second.

MFM *abbr. Computing* modified frequency modulation (in disk formatting).

MFN *abbr.* most favoured nation (in trade agreements).

Mg *symb.* magnesium.

mg *abbr.* milligram(s).

MGI *abbr.* Member of the Institute of Certificated Grocers.

M. Glam. *abbr.* Mid Glamorgan.

Mgr. *abbr.* **1** Manager. **2** *Monseigneur*. **3** *Monsignor.*

MH *airline flight code* Malaysia Airlines.

MHCIMA *abbr.* Member of the Hotel Catering and Institutional Management Association.

MHS *abbr. Computing* message-handling system (form of electronic-mail system).

MHz *abbr.* megahertz.

MI *–international civil aircraft marking* Marshall Islands. *–US postcode* Michigan.

mi var. of ME[2].

mi. *abbr.* mile(s).

M.I.5 *abbr.* UK department of Military Intelligence concerned with state security.

■ **Usage** This term is not in official use.

M.I.6 *abbr.* UK department of Military Intelligence concerned with espionage.

■ **Usage** This term is not in official use.

MIAM *abbr.* Member of the Institute of Administrative Management.

Miami /maɪ'æmɪ/ city and port in the US, on the E coast of Florida; pop. (est. 1994) 373 024. It is an important financial and trading centre, as well as a year-round holiday resort.

miaow /mɪ'aʊ/ *–n.* characteristic cry of a cat. *–v.* make this cry. [imitative]

miasma /mɪ'æzmə/ *n.* (*pl.* **-mata** or **-s**) *archaic* infectious or noxious vapour. [Greek, = defilement]

MIB(Scot.) *abbr.* Member of the Institute of Bankers in Scotland.

mica /'maɪkə/ *n.* silicate mineral found as glittering scales in granite etc. or in crystals separable into thin transparent plates. [Latin, = crumb]

mice *pl.* of MOUSE.

Mich. *abbr.* **1** Michaelmas. **2** Michigan.

Michaelmas /'mɪkəlməs/ *n.* feast of St Michael, 29 September. [related to MASS[2]]

Michaelmas daisy *n.* autumn-flowering aster.

Michigan /'mɪʃɪgən/ state in the NW US; pop. (est. 1996) 9 594 350; capital, Lansing. The manufacturing industries are important, producing motor vehicles, machinery, iron and steel, and chemicals; tourism is also a source of revenue.

Michoacán /ˌmi:tʃwɑ:'kɑ:n/ state of W Mexico; pop. (est. 1995) 3 896 133; capital, Morelia. Forestry and agriculture are important.

mick *n. slang offens.* Irishman. [pet form of *Michael*]

mickey /'mɪkɪ/ *n.* (also **micky**) □ **take the mickey** (often foll. by *out of*) *slang* tease, mock, ridicule. [origin uncertain]

Mickey Finn /ˌmɪkɪ 'fɪn/ *n. slang* drugged drink intended to make the victim unconscious. [origin uncertain]

mickle /'mɪk(ə)l/ *n.* (also **muckle** /'mʌk(ə)l/) *archaic* or *Scot.* large amount. □ **many a little makes a mickle** (also *erron.* **many a mickle makes a muckle**) small amounts accumulate. [Old Norse]

micky var. of MICKEY.

MICR *abbr.* = MAGNETIC-INK CHARACTER RECOGNITION.

micro /'maɪkrəʊ/ *n.* (*pl.* **-s**) *colloq.* **1** = MICROCOMPUTER. **2** = MICROPROCESSOR.

micro- *comb. form* **1** small (*microchip*). **2** concerned with small objects etc. (*microscope*). **3** denoting a factor of one millionth (10^{-6}) (*microgram*). [Greek *mikros* small]

microbe /'maɪkrəʊb/ *n.* micro-organism (esp. a bacterium causing disease or fermentation). □ **microbial** /-'krəʊbɪəl/ *adj.* **microbic** /-'krəʊbɪk/ *adj.* [Greek *mikros* small, *bios* life]

microbiology /ˌmaɪkrəʊbaɪ'ɒlədʒɪ/ *n.* the study of micro-organisms. □ **microbiologist** *n.*

microchip /'maɪkrəʊtʃɪp/ *n.* small piece of semiconductor (usu. silicon) used to carry integrated circuits.

microcircuit /'maɪkrəʊˌsɜ:kɪt/ *n.* integrated circuit on a microchip.

microclimate /'maɪkrəʊˌklaɪmɪt/ *n.* small localized climate, e.g. inside a greenhouse.

◆ **microcomputer** /'maɪkrəʊkəmˌpju:tə(r)/ *n.* small computer with a microprocessor as its central processor plus storage and input/output facilities for data and programs. Although microcomputers have limited abilities compared with the larger mainframes and minicomputers, they are sufficiently powerful to meet the needs of many small businesses, their uses including producing payrolls, word processing, invoicing, and compiling mailing lists. The storage capacity of main store in a microcomputer is many tens or hundreds of times lower than that of mainframe computers (although it has a similar access time). Backing store consists mainly of a combination of floppy disks, hard disks, and optical disks (see MAIN STORE; BACKING STORE). Data and programs are entered on a keyboard or read from floppy disk; data can also be captured from scanners and network connections as well as mice, light pens, joysticks, and other pointing devices. Information is displayed on a VDU, which is an integral part of the microcomputer (rather than remote from it as in larger computer systems). A printer can usu. be connected for a more permanent form of output.

---

microcosm /ˈmaɪkrəˌkɒz(ə)m/ *n.* (often foll. by *of*) miniature representation, e.g. mankind or a community seen as a small-scale model of the universe; epitome. □ **microcosmic** /-ˈkɒzmɪk/ *adj.* [from MICRO-, COSMOS]

microdot /ˈmaɪkrəʊˌdɒt/ *n.* microphotograph of a document etc. reduced to the size of a dot.

♦ **microeconomics** /ˌmaɪkrəʊˌiːkəˈnɒmɪks/ *n.* analysis of economic behaviour at the level of the firm or the individual (cf. MACROECONOMICS). For the individual or household it is concerned with the optimal allocation of a given budget, the labour supply choice, and the effects of taxation. For the firm it is largely concerned with the production process, costs, and the marketing of output, dependent on the type of competition faced (see IMPERFECT COMPETITION; MONOPOLY 1; OLIGOPOLY; PERFECT COMPETITION).

---

micro-electronics /ˌmaɪkrəʊɪlekˈtrɒnɪks/ *n.* design, manufacture, and use of microchips and microcircuits.

microfiche /ˈmaɪkrəʊˌfiːʃ/ *n.* (*pl.* same or **-s**) small flat piece of film bearing microphotographs of documents etc. See also COMPUTER OUTPUT MICROFILM. [from MICRO-, French *fiche* slip of paper]

microfilm /ˈmaɪkrəʊfɪlm/ *–n.* length of film bearing microphotographs of documents etc. See also COMPUTER OUTPUT MICROFILM. *–v.* photograph on microfilm.

♦ **microfoundations** *n.pl. Econ.* basis for a macroeconomic model in which economic events are controlled by the rational utility-maximizing behaviour of individuals. It was realized in the late 1960s that traditional macroeconomic models, such as the ISLM model, had no such basis; much of macroeconomics since then has therefore focused on establishing these foundations. This has polarized the debate between monetarists and Keynesians of the 1950s and 1960s much more sharply: traditional monetarists emphasize the market-clearing assumption, Pareto optimality, and rational expectations (see NEW CLASSICAL MACROECONOMICS; MARKET-CLEARING ASSUMPTION) as a basis of analysis, while traditional Keynesians now emphasize the possibility of market failures (see EFFICIENCY WAGE THEORY; HYSTERESIS; INSIDER-OUTSIDER THEORY).

---

microlight /ˈmaɪkrəʊˌlaɪt/ *n.* a kind of motorized hang-glider.

micromesh /ˈmaɪkrəʊˌmeʃ/ *n.* (often *attrib.*) fine-meshed material, esp. nylon.

micrometer /maɪˈkrɒmɪtə(r)/ *n.* gauge for accurate small-scale measurement.

micron /ˈmaɪkrɒn/ *n.* one-millionth of a metre. [Greek *mikros* small]

Micronesia /ˌmaɪkrəʊˈniːʒə/ island-group in the W Pacific Ocean, including the Mariana, Caroline, and Marshall Islands and Kiribati. □ **Micronesian** *adj.* & *n.*

micro-organism /ˌmaɪkrəʊˈɔːgəˌnɪz(ə)m/ *n.* microscopic organism, e.g. bacteria, protozoa, and viruses.

microphone /ˈmaɪkrəˌfəʊn/ *n.* instrument for converting sound waves into electrical energy for reconversion into sound after transmission or recording. [from MICRO-, Greek *phōnē* sound]

microphotograph /ˌmaɪkrəʊˈfəʊtəˌgrɑːf/ *n.* photograph reduced to a very small size. [from MICRO-]

♦ **microprocessor** /ˌmaɪkrəʊˈprəʊsesə(r)/ *n.* integrated circuit implementing all the arithmetic, logical, and control functions of a computer's central processing unit. It forms the basis of the microcomputer. Microprocessors are characterized by a combination of their speed of operation, their word length (16-bit, 32-bit, etc.), their instruction set (i.e. the set of instructions that the computer is capable of performing), and their architecture (i.e. storage organization and addressing methods, I/O operation, etc.). They are used in many devices, including photosetting machines, car electronics, and cameras, as well as computers.

---

microprogram /ˌmaɪkrəʊˈprəʊgræm/ *–n.* sequence of fundamental instructions that describe all the steps involved in a particular computer operation. It is the means by which an operation is accomplished, and is set into action once a machine instruction is loaded into a computer. Almost all processors in both large and small computers are now controlled by microprograms, which are usu. stored in the processor's control unit. *–v.* (**-mm-**) control by microprogram.

microscope /ˈmaɪkrəˌskəʊp/ *n.* instrument with lenses for magnifying objects or details invisible to the naked eye. [from MICRO-, -SCOPE]

microscopic /ˌmaɪkrəˈskɒpɪk/ *adj.* **1** visible only with a microscope. **2** extremely small. **3** of or by means of a microscope. □ **microscopically** *adv.*

microscopy /maɪˈkrɒskəpɪ/ *n.* use of microscopes.

microsecond /ˈmaɪkrəʊˌsekənd/ *n.* one-millionth of a second.

microsurgery /ˈmaɪkrəʊˌsɜːdʒərɪ/ *n.* intricate surgery using microscopes.

microwave /ˈmaɪkrəʊˌweɪv/ *–n.* **1** electromagnetic wave with a wavelength in the range 0.001–0.3m. **2** (in full **microwave oven**) oven using microwaves to cook or heat food quickly. *–v.* (**-ving**) cook in a microwave oven.

MICS *abbr.* Member of the Institute of Chartered Shipbrokers.

micturition /ˌmɪktjʊəˈrɪʃ(ə)n/ *n. formal* urination. [Latin]

mid *attrib. adj.* (usu. in *comb.*) the middle of (*mid-air*; *mid-June*). [Old English]

midday *n.* (often *attrib.*) middle of the day; noon. [Old English: related to MID, DAY]

midden /ˈmɪd(ə)n/ *n.* **1** dunghill. **2** refuse heap. [Scandinavian: related to MUCK]

middle /ˈmɪd(ə)l/ *–attrib. adj.* **1** at an equal distance, time, or number from extremities; central. **2** intermediate in rank, quality, etc. **3** average (*of middle height*). *–n.* **1** (often foll. by *of*) middle point, position, or part. **2** waist. □ **in the middle of 1** in the process of. **2** during. [Old English]

middle age *n.* period between youth and old age. □ **middle-aged** *adj.*

Middle Ages *n.* (prec. by *the*) period of European history from *c.*1000 to 1453.

middle-age spread *n.* (also **middle-aged spread**) increased bodily girth at middle age.

middlebrow *colloq. –adj.* having or appealing to non-intellectual or conventional tastes. *–n.* middlebrow person.

Micronesia, Federated States of country in the W Pacific Ocean comprising the island states of Yap, Kosrae, Chuuk (formerly Truk), and Pohnpei. The economy is dependent on subsistence agriculture, government spending, and tourism; copra and fish are the main exports. The states were administered by the US as part of the Pacific Islands Trust Territory from 1947 until 1986, when they entered into free association with the US as an independent state; independence was finally recognized by the UN in 1990. Head of state, Jacob Nena; capital, Palikir (on Pohnpei).

languages	English, Micronesian languages
currency	US dollar (US$) of 100 cents
pop. (1996)	106 000
GNP (1984)	US$202M
literacy	67% (m); 87% (f)
life expectancy	70 (m); 77 (f)

middle C *n.* C near the middle of the piano keyboard, (in notation) the note between the treble and bass staves.

middle class *n.* social class between the upper and the lower, including professional and business workers. □ **middle-class** *adj.*

middle distance *n.* **1** (in a landscape) part between the foreground and the background. **2** *Athletics* race distance of esp. 400 or 800 metres.

middle ear *n.* cavity behind the eardrum.

Middle East (prec. by *the*) area covered by countries from Egypt to Iran inclusive. □ **Middle Eastern** *adj.*

Middle English *n.* English language from *c.*1150 to 1500.

middle game *n.* central phase of a chess game.

♦ **middleman** *n.* **1** person or organization making a profit by trading in goods as an intermediary between the producer and the consumer. Middlemen include agents, brokers, dealers, merchants, factors, wholesalers, distributors, and retailers. They earn their profit by providing a variety of different services, including finance, bulk buying, holding stocks, breaking bulk, risk sharing, making a market and stabilizing prices, providing information about products (to consumers) and about markets (to producers), providing a distribution network, and introducing buyers to sellers. **2** intermediary.

♦ **middle management** see MANAGEMENT 3.

---

middle name *n.* **1** name between first name and surname. **2** *colloq.* person's most characteristic quality (*tact is my middle name*).

middle-of-the-road *adj.* **1** moderate; avoiding extremes. **2** of general appeal.

♦ **middle price** *n.* (also **mean price**) average of the offer price of a security, commodity, currency, etc. and the bid price. It is the middle price that is often quoted in the financial press.

Middlesbrough /'mɪdəlzbrə/ town in NE England; it was the county town of the former county of Cleveland; industries include iron and steel, engineering, and chemicals; pop. (est. 1993) 144 800.

middle school *n.* school for children from about 9 to 13 years.

middle-sized *adj.* of medium size.

middleweight *n.* **1** weight in certain sports between welterweight and light heavyweight, in amateur boxing 71-5 kg. **2** sportsman of this weight.

middling *–adj.* moderately good. *–adv.* fairly, moderately.

Middx. *abbr.* Middlesex.

midfield *n. Football* central part of the pitch, away from the goals. □ **midfielder** *n.*

midge *n.* gnatlike insect. [Old English]

midget /'mɪdʒɪt/ *n.* **1** extremely small person or thing. **2** (*attrib.*) very small.

Mid Glamorgan /glə'mɔːgən/ former county in SE Wales its county town was Cardiff. There were light industries and sheep farming.

MIDI /'mɪdɪ/ *n.* (also **midi**) an interface allowing electronic musical instruments, synthesizers, and computers to be interconnected and used simultaneously. [abbreviation of *m*usical *i*nstrument *d*igital *i*nterface]

midi system *n.* set of compact stacking components of hi-fi equipment.

midland *–n.* **1** (**the Midlands**) inland counties of central England. **2** middle part of a country. *–adj.* of or in the midland or Midlands.

mid-life *n.* middle age.

mid-life crisis *n.* crisis of self-confidence in early middle age.

midnight *n.* middle of the night; 12 o'clock at night. [Old English]

midnight blue *adj.* & *n.* (as adj. often hyphenated) very dark blue.

midnight sun *n.* sun visible at midnight during the summer in polar regions.

mid-off *n. Cricket* position of the fielder near the bowler on the off side.

mid-on *n. Cricket* position of the fielder near the bowler on the on side.

MIDPM *abbr.* Member of the Institute of Data Processing Management.

midriff *n.* front of the body just above the waist. [Old English, = mid-belly]

midshipman *n.* naval officer ranking next above a cadet.

midships *adv.* = AMIDSHIPS.

midst *–prep. poet.* amidst. *–n.* middle. □ **in the midst of** among; in the middle of. **in our** (or **your** or **their) midst** among us (or you or them). [related to MID]

midstream *–n.* middle of a stream etc. *–adv.* (also **in midstream**) in the middle of an action etc. (*abandoned the project midstream*).

midsummer *n.* period of or near the summer solstice, about 21 June. [Old English]

Midsummer Day *n.* (also **Midsummer's Day**) 24 June.

midsummer madness *n.* extreme folly.

midway *adv.* in or towards the middle of the distance between two points.

Midwest /mɪd'west/ part of the US occupying the N half of the Mississippi River basin, including the states of Ohio, Indiana, Illinois, Michigan, Wisconsin, Iowa, and Minnesota.

midwicket *n. Cricket* position of a fielder on the leg side opposite the middle of the pitch.

midwife *n.* person trained to assist at childbirth. □ **midwifery** /-ˌwɪfrɪ, -'wɪfərɪ/ *n.* [originally = with-woman]

midwinter *n.* period of or near the winter solstice, about 22 Dec. [Old English]

mien *n. literary* person's look or bearing. [probably obsolete *demean*]

M.I.Ex. *abbr.* Member of the Institute of Export.

MIFF *abbr.* Member of the Institute of Freight Forwarders.

miff *v. colloq.* (usu. as **miffed** *adj.*) offend. [origin uncertain]

might[1] /maɪt/ *past* of MAY, used esp.: **1** in reported speech, expressing possibility (*said he might come*) or permission (*asked if I might leave*) (cf. MAY 1, 2). **2** (foll. by perfect infin.) expressing a possibility based on a condition not fulfilled (*if you'd looked you might have found it*). **3** (foll. by present infin. or perfect infin.) expressing complaint that an obligation or expectation is not or has not been fulfilled (*they might have asked*). **4** expressing a request (*you might call in at the butcher's*). **5** *colloq.* **a** = MAY 1 (*it might be true*). **b** (in tentative questions) = MAY 2 (*might I have the pleasure of this dance?*). **c** = MAY 4 (*who might you be?*). □ **might as well** expressing lukewarm acquiescence (*might as well try*).

might[2] /maɪt/ *n.* strength, power. □ **with might and main** with all one's power. [Old English: related to MAY]

might-have-been *n. colloq.* **1** past possibility that no longer applies. **2** person of unfulfilled promise.

mightn't /'maɪt(ə)nt/ *contr.* might not.

mighty *–adj.* (**-ier, -iest**) **1** powerful, strong. **2** massive, bulky. **3** *colloq.* great, considerable. *–adv. colloq.* very (*mighty difficult*). □ **mightily** *adv.* **mightiness** *n.* [Old English: related to MIGHT[2]]

mignonette /ˌmɪnjə'net/ *n.* plant with fragrant grey-green flowers. [French, diminutive of *mignon* small]

migraine /'miːgreɪn, 'maɪ-/ *n.* recurrent throbbing headache often with nausea and visual disturbance. [Greek *hēmikrania*: related to HEMI-, CRANIUM]

migrant /'maɪgrənt/ *–adj.* migrating. *–n.* migrant person or animal, esp. a bird.

♦ **migrant worker** *n.* person who has migrated to a country or region to work, attracted by better wages. A substantial proportion of the worker's earnings is often sent back to any family remaining in the worker's native country. This can have an adverse effect on the balance of payments of countries that attract substantial numbers of migrant workers and conversely can be advantageous to countries from which many workers migrate. Migrant workers can also cause problems with the trade unions in the countries to which they migrate.

---

migrate /maɪ'greɪt/ *v.* (**-ting**) **1** move from one place and settle in another, esp. abroad. **2** (of a bird or fish) change its habitation seasonally. **3** move under natural forces. □ **migration** /-'greɪʃ(ə)n/ *n.* **migrator** *n.* **migratory** /'maɪgrətərɪ/ *adj.* [Latin *migro*]

MIIM *abbr.* Member of the Institute of Industrial Managers.

M.I.Inf.Sc. *abbr.* Member of the Institute of Information Sciences.

mikado /mɪ'kɑːdəʊ/ *n.* (*pl.* **-s**) *hist.* emperor of Japan. [Japanese, = august door]

mike *n. colloq.* microphone. [abbreviation]

Míkonos see MYKONOS.

mil *n.* one-thousandth of an inch, as a unit of measure for the diameter of wire etc. [Latin *mille* thousand]

milady /mɪ'leɪdɪ/ *n.* (*pl.* **-ies**) (esp. as a form of address) English noblewoman. [French from *my Lady*]

milage var. of MILEAGE.

Milan /mɪ'læn/ (Italian **Milano** /mɪ'lɑːnəʊ/) commercial and industrial city in NW Italy, capital of Lombardy region; manufactures include motor vehicles, aircraft, chemicals, and textiles, and the publishing industry is important; pop. (est. 1994) 1 334 171.

milch *adj.* giving milk. [Old English: related to MILK]

milch cow *n.* source of easy profit.

mild /maɪld/ *–adj.* **1** (esp. of a person) gentle and conciliatory. **2** not severe or harsh. **3** (of the weather) moderately warm. **4** (of flavour etc.) not sharp or strong. **5** tame, feeble; lacking vivacity. *–n.* dark mild draught beer (cf. BITTER). □ **mildish** *adj.* **mildness** *n.* [Old English]

mildew /'mɪldjuː/ *–n.* **1** destructive growth of minute fungi on plants. **2** similar growth on damp paper, leather, etc. *–v.* taint or be tainted with mildew. □ **mildewy** *adj.* [Old English]

mildly *adv.* in a mild fashion. □ **to put it mildly** as an understatement.

mild-mannered *adj.* = MILD 1.

mild steel *n.* strong and tough steel not readily tempered.

mile *n.* **1** (also **statute mile**) unit of linear measure equal to 1760 yards (approx. 1.6 kilometres). **2** (in *pl.*) *colloq.* great distance or amount (*miles better*). **3** race extending over a mile. [Latin *mille* thousand]

mileage *n.* (also **milage**) **1** number of miles travelled, esp. by a vehicle per unit of fuel. **2** *colloq.* profit, advantage.

miler *n. colloq.* person or horse specializing in races of one mile.

milestone *n.* **1** stone beside a road marking a distance in miles. **2** significant event or point in a life, history, project, etc.

milfoil /'mɪlfɔɪl/ *n.* common yarrow with small white flowers. [Latin: related to MILE, FOIL[2]]

MILGA *abbr.* Member of the Institute of Local Government Administrators.

milieu /mɪ'ljɜː, 'miː-/ *n.* (*pl.* **milieux** or **-s** /-ljɜːz/) person's environment or social surroundings. [French]

militant /'mɪlɪt(ə)nt/ *–adj.* **1** combative; aggressively active in support of a cause. **2** engaged in warfare. *–n.* militant person. □ **militancy** *n.* **militantly** *adv.* [Latin: related to MILITATE]

militarism /'mɪlɪtə,rɪz(ə)m/ *n.* **1** aggressively military policy etc. **2** military spirit. □ **militarist** *n.* **militaristic** /-'rɪstɪk/ *adj.*

militarize /'mɪlɪtə,raɪz/ *v.* (also **-ise**) (**-zing** or **-sing**) **1** equip with military resources. **2** make military or warlike. **3** imbue with militarism. □ **militarization** /-'zeɪʃ(ə)n/ *n.*

military /'mɪlɪtərɪ/ *–adj.* of or characteristic of soldiers or armed forces. *–n.* (as *sing.* or *pl.*; prec. by *the*) the army. □ **militarily** *adv.* [Latin *miles milit-* soldier]

military honours *n.pl.* burial rites of a soldier, royalty, etc., performed by the military.

military police *n.* (as *pl.*) army police force disciplining soldiers.

militate /'mɪlɪ,teɪt/ *v.* (**-ting**) (usu. foll. by *against*) have force or effect; tell. [Latin: related to MILITARY]

■ **Usage** *Militate* is often confused with *mitigate*.

militia /mɪ'lɪʃə/ *n.* military force, esp. one conscripted in an emergency. □ **militiaman** *n.* [Latin, = military service]

milk *–n.* **1** opaque white fluid secreted by female mammals for the nourishment of their young. **2** milk of cows, goats, or sheep as food. **3** milklike juice of the coconut etc. *–v.* **1** draw milk from (a cow etc.). **2** exploit (a person or situation) to the utmost. [Old English]

milk and honey *n.* abundance; prosperity.

milk and water *n.* feeble or insipid writing, speech, etc.

milk chocolate *n.* chocolate made with milk.

milk float *n.* small usu. electric vehicle used in delivering milk.

milkmaid *n.* girl or woman who milks cows or works in a dairy.

milkman *n.* person who sells or delivers milk.

Milk of Magnesia *n. propr.* white suspension of magnesium hydroxide usu. in water, taken as an antacid or laxative.

milk-powder *n.* dehydrated milk.

milk pudding *n.* pudding, esp. of rice, baked with milk.

milk round *n.* **1** fixed route for milk delivery. **2** regular trip with calls at several places. **3** annual visit to universities by the personnel managers of large companies seeking graduates to join their organizations.

milk run *n.* routine expedition etc.

milk shake *n.* drink of whisked milk, flavouring, etc.

milksop *n.* weak or timid man or youth.

milk tooth *n.* temporary tooth in young mammals.

milky *adj.* (**-ier, -iest**) **1** of, like, or mixed with milk. **2** (of a gem or liquid) cloudy; not clear. □ **milkiness** *n.*

Milky Way *n.* **1** luminous band of stars. **2** = GALAXY.

mill *–n.* **1 a** building fitted with a mechanical device for grinding corn. **b** such a device. **2** device for grinding any solid to powder etc. (*pepper-mill*). **3 a** building fitted with machinery for manufacturing processes etc. (*cotton-mill*). **b** such machinery. *–v.* **1** grind (corn), produce (flour), or hull (seeds) in a mill. **2** (esp. as **milled** *adj.*) produce a ribbed edge on (a coin). **3** cut or shape (metal) with a rotating tool. **4** (often foll. by *about, around*) move aimlessly, esp. in a confused mass. □ **go** (or **put**) **through the mill** undergo (or cause to undergo) intensive work, pain, training, etc. [Latin *molo* grind]

millefeuille /miːl'fɜːj/ *n.* rich cake of puff pastry split and filled with jam, cream, etc. [French, = thousand-leaf]

millennium /mɪ'lenɪəm/ *n.* (*pl.* **-s** or **millennia**) **1** period of 1000 years, esp. that of Christ's prophesied reign on earth (Rev. 20:1–5). **2** (esp. future) period of happiness and prosperity. □ **millennial** *adj.* [Latin *mille* thousand]

millepede var. of MILLIPEDE.

miller *n.* **1** proprietor or tenant of a mill, esp. a corn-mill. **2** person operating a milling machine. [related to MILL]

miller's thumb *n.* small spiny freshwater fish.

millesimal /mɪ'lesɪm(ə)l/ *–adj.* **1** thousandth. **2** of, belonging to, or dealing with, a thousandth or thousandths. *–n.* thousandth part. [Latin *mille* thousand]

millet /'mɪlɪt/ *n.* **1** cereal plant bearing small nutritious seeds. **2** seed of this. [Latin *milium*]

millet-grass *n.* tall woodland grass.

milli- *comb. form* thousand, esp. denoting a factor of one thousandth. [Latin *mille* thousand]

milliard /'mɪljəd/ *n.* one thousand million. [French *mille* thousand]

■ **Usage** *Milliard* is now largely superseded by *billion*.

millibar /'mɪlɪ,bɑː(r)/ *n.* unit of atmospheric pressure equivalent to 100 pascals.

milligram /ˈmɪlɪˌgræm/ *n.* (also **-gramme**) one-thousandth of a gram.

millilitre /ˈmɪlɪˌliːtə(r)/ *n.* (*US* **-liter**) one-thousandth of a litre (0.002 pint).

millimetre /ˈmɪlɪˌmiːtə(r)/ *n.* (*US* **-meter**) one-thousandth of a metre (0.039 in.).

milliner /ˈmɪlɪnə(r)/ *n.* person who makes or sells women's hats. □ **millinery** *n.* [*Milan* in Italy]

million /ˈmɪljən/ *n.* & *adj.* (*pl.* same or (in sense 2) **-s**) (in *sing.* prec. by *a* or *one*) **1** thousand thousand. **2** (in *pl.*) *colloq.* very large number. **3** million pounds or dollars. □ **millionth** *adj.* & *n.* [French, probably from Italian *mille* thousand]

millionaire /ˌmɪljəˈneə(r)/ *n.* (*fem.* **millionairess**) person who has over a million pounds, dollars, etc. [French *millionnaire*: related to MILLION]

millipede /ˈmɪlɪˌpiːd/ *n.* (also **millepede**) small crawling invertebrate with a long segmented body with two pairs of legs on each segment. [Latin *mille* thousand, *pes ped-* foot]

millisecond /ˈmɪlɪˌsekənd/ *n.* one-thousandth of a second.

millpond *n.* pool of water retained by a dam for operating a mill-wheel. □ **like a millpond** (of water) very calm.

mill-race *n.* current of water that drives a mill-wheel.

millstone *n.* **1** each of two circular stones for grinding corn. **2** heavy burden or responsibility.

mill-wheel *n.* wheel used to drive a water-mill.

millworker *n.* factory worker.

millwright *n.* person who designs or builds mills.

milometer /maɪˈlɒmɪtə(r)/ *n.* instrument for measuring the number of miles travelled by a vehicle.

milord /mɪˈlɔːd/ *n.* (esp. as a form of address) English nobleman. [French from *my lord*]

milt *n.* **1** spleen in mammals. **2** sperm-filled reproductive gland or the sperm of a male fish. [Old English]

Milwaukee /mɪlˈwɔːkiː/ industrial port and city in SE Wisconsin, on Lake Michigan; pop. (est. 1994) 617 044. Manufactures include heavy machinery, engines, and electrical equipment and brewing is important.

MIMC *abbr.* Member of the Institute of Management Consultants.

mime *–n.* **1** acting without words, using only gestures. **2** performance using mime. **3** (also **mime artist**) mime actor. *–v.* (**-ming**) **1** (also *absol.*) convey by mime. **2** (often foll. by *to*) mouth words etc. in time with a soundtrack (*mime to a record*). [Greek *mimos*]

mimeograph /ˈmɪmɪəˌgrɑːf/ *–n.* **1** machine which duplicates from a stencil. **2** copy so produced. *–v.* reproduce by this process. [Greek *mimeomai* imitate]

mimetic /mɪˈmetɪk/ *adj.* of or practising imitation or mimicry. [Greek *mimētikos*: see MIMEOGRAPH]

MIMI *abbr.* Member of the Institute of the Motor Industry.

mimic /ˈmɪmɪk/ *–v.* (**-ck-**) **1** imitate (a person, gesture, etc.) esp. to entertain or ridicule. **2** copy minutely or servilely. **3** resemble closely. *–n.* person skilled in imitation. □ **mimicry** *n.* [Greek *mimikos*: related to MIME]

mimosa /mɪˈməʊzə/ *n.* **1** shrub with globular usu. yellow flowers. **2** acacia plant with showy yellow flowers. [Latin: related to MIME]

Min. *abbr.* **1** Minister. **2** Ministry.

min. *abbr.* **1** minute(s). **2** minimum. **3** minim (fluid measure).

mina var. of MYNA.

minaret /ˌmɪnəˈret/ *n.* slender turret next to a mosque, from which the muezzin calls at hours of prayer. [French or Spanish from Turkish from Arabic]

Minas Gerais /ˌmiːnæs ʒeˈræiːs/ state of SE Brazil, a major source of iron ore, gold, and diamonds; pop. (est. 1995) 16 505 300; capital, Belo Horizonte.

minatory /ˈmɪnətərɪ/ *adj. formal* threatening, menacing. [Latin *minor* threaten]

mince *–v.* (**-cing**) **1** cut up or grind (esp. meat) finely. **2** (usu. as **mincing** *adj.*) speak or esp. walk effeminately or affectedly. *–n.* minced meat. □ **mince matters** (or **one's words**) (usu. with *neg.*) speak evasively or unduly mildly. □ **mincer** *n.* [Latin *minutia* something small]

mincemeat *n.* mixture of currants, sugar, spices, suet, etc. □ **make mincemeat of** utterly defeat.

mince pie *n.* pie containing mincemeat.

mind /maɪnd/ *–n.* **1 a** seat of consciousness, thought, volition, and feeling. **b** attention, concentration (*mind keeps wandering*). **2** intellect. **3** memory (*can't call it to mind*). **4** opinion (*of the same mind*). **5** way of thinking or feeling (*the Victorian mind*). **6** focussed will (*put one's mind to it*). **7** sanity (*lose one's mind*). **8** person in regard to mental faculties (*a great mind*). *–v.* **1** object; be upset (*do you mind if I smoke?*; *minded terribly when she left*). **2** (often foll. by *out*) heed; take care (to) (*mind you come on time*; *mind the step*; *mind how you go*; *mind out!*). **3** look after (*mind the house*). **4** apply oneself to, concern oneself with (*mind my own business*). □ **be in two minds** be undecided. **do you mind!** *iron.* expression of annoyance. **have a good** (or **half a) mind to** feel inclined to (*I've a good mind to report you*). **have (it) in mind** intend. **in one's mind's eye** in one's imagination. **mind one's Ps & Qs** be careful in one's behaviour. **mind you** used to qualify a statement (*mind you, it wasn't easy*). **never mind 1** let alone; not to mention. **2** used to comfort or console. **3** (also **never you mind**) used to evade a question. **to my mind** in my opinion. [Old English]

Mindanao /ˌmɪndəˈnaʊ/ second-largest island of the Philippines; hemp and timber are exported; pop. (1990) 14 298 000; chief city, Davao.

mind-blowing *adj. slang* **1** mind-boggling; overwhelming. **2** (esp. of drugs etc.) inducing hallucinations.

mind-boggling *adj. colloq.* unbelievable, startling.

minded *adj.* **1** (in *comb.*) **a** inclined to think in some specified way, or with a specified interest (*mathematically minded*; *fair-minded*; *car-minded*). **b** having a specified kind of mind (*high-minded*). **2** (usu. foll. by *to* + infin.) disposed or inclined.

minder *n.* **1** (often in *comb.*) person employed to look after a person or thing (*child minder*). **2** *slang* bodyguard.

mindful *adj.* (often foll. by *of*) taking heed or care; giving thought (to). □ **mindfully** *adv.*

mindless *adj.* **1** lacking intelligence; brutish (*mindless violence*). **2** not requiring thought or skill (*mindless work*). **3** (usu. foll. by *of*) heedless of (advice etc.). □ **mindlessly** *adv.* **mindlessness** *n.*

Mindoro /mɪnˈdɔːrəʊ/ island in the NW central Philippines; products include timber and coal; pop. (est. 1995) 912 000; chief town, Calapan.

mind-read *v.* discern the thoughts of (another person). □ **mind-reader** *n.*

mine[1] *poss. pron.* the one(s) of or belonging to me (*it is mine*; *mine are over there*). □ **of mine** of or belonging to me (*a friend of mine*). [Old English]

mine[2] *–n.* **1** excavation to extract metal, coal, salt, etc. **2** abundant source (of information etc.). **3** military explosive device placed in the ground or in the water. *–v.* (**-ning**) **1** obtain (metal, coal, etc.) from a mine. **2** (also *absol.*, often foll. by *for*) dig in (the earth etc.) for ore etc. or to tunnel. **3** lay explosive mines under or in. □ **mining** *n.* [French]

minefield *n.* **1** area planted with explosive mines. **2** *colloq.* hazardous subject or situation.

minelayer *n.* ship or aircraft for laying explosive mines.

miner *n.* person who works in a mine. [French: related to MINE[2]]

mineral /ˈmɪnər(ə)l/ *n.* (often *attrib.*) **1** inorganic substance. **2** substance obtained by mining. **3** (often in *pl.*) artificial mineral water or similar carbonated drink. [French or medieval Latin: related to MINE[2]]

mineralize /ˈmɪnərəˌlaɪz/ *v.* (also **-ise**) (**-zing** or **-sing**) impregnate (water etc.) with a mineral substance.

mineralogy /ˌmɪnəˈrælədʒɪ/ *n.* the study of minerals. □ **mineralogical** /-rəˈlɒdʒɪk(ə)l/ *adj.* **mineralogist** *n.*

mineral water *n.* **1** natural water often containing dissolved salts. **2** artificial imitation of this, esp. soda water.

minestrone /ˌmɪnɪˈstrəʊnɪ/ *n.* soup containing vegetables and pasta, beans, or rice. [Italian]

minesweeper *n.* ship for clearing explosive mines from the sea.

mineworker *n.* miner.

Ming *n.* (often *attrib.*) Chinese porcelain made during the Ming dynasty (1368–1644).

mingle /ˈmɪŋg(ə)l/ *v.* (**-ling**) **1** mix, blend. **2** (often foll. by *with*) mix socially. [Old English]

mingy /ˈmɪndʒɪ/ *adj.* (**-ier, -iest**) *colloq.* mean, stingy. □ **mingily** *adv.* [probably from MEAN², STINGY]

mini /ˈmɪnɪ/ *n.* (*pl.* **-s**) **1** *colloq.* miniskirt. **2** minicomputer. **3** (**Mini**) *propr.* make of small car. [abbreviation]

mini- *comb. form* miniature; small of its kind (*minibus*).

miniature /ˈmɪnɪtʃə(r)/ *–adj.* **1** much smaller than normal. **2** represented on a small scale. *–n.* **1** any miniature object. **2** detailed small-scale portrait. **3** this genre. □ **in miniature** on a small scale. □ **miniaturist** *n.* (in senses 2 and 3 of *n.*). [Latin *minium* red lead]

miniaturize *v.* (also **-ise**) (**-zing** or **-sing**) produce in a smaller version; make small. □ **miniaturization** /-ˈzeɪʃ(ə)n/ *n.*

minibus /ˈmɪnɪˌbʌs/ *n.* small bus for about twelve passengers.

minicab /ˈmɪnɪˌkæb/ *n.* car used as a taxi, hireable only by telephone.

♦ **minicomputer** /ˈmɪnɪkəmˌpjuːtə(r)/ *n.* computer of medium power, usu. smaller and less capable in terms of performance than a contemporary mainframe computer, and hence cheaper. A minicomputer might also be outperformed by a sophisticated microcomputer. Minicomputers are often used to control industrial processes, and also for small multi-user systems where personal computers would be inappropriate because of the need to share data or programs. Mainframe computers often have a number of minicomputers to perform such tasks as input/output or communications, thus freeing the power of the mainframe processor for more demanding tasks.

minim /ˈmɪnɪm/ *n.* **1** *Mus.* note equal to two crotchets or half a semibreve. **2** one-sixtieth of a fluid drachm, about a drop. [Latin *minimus* least]

minima *pl.* of MINIMUM.

minimal /ˈmɪnɪm(ə)l/ *adj.* **1** very minute or slight. **2** being a minimum. □ **minimally** *adv.*

minimalism /ˈmɪnɪməˌlɪz(ə)m/ *n.* **1** *Art* use of simple or primary forms, often geometric and massive. **2** *Mus.* repetition of short phrases incorporating changes very gradually. □ **minimalist** *n.* & *adj.*

minimize /ˈmɪnɪˌmaɪz/ *v.* (also **-ise**) (**-zing** or **-sing**) **1** reduce to, or estimate at, the smallest possible amount or degree. **2** estimate or represent at less than true value or importance. □ **minimization** /-ˈzeɪʃ(ə)n/ *n.*

minimum /ˈmɪnɪməm/ (*pl.* **minima**) *–n.* least possible or attainable amount (*reduced to a minimum*). *–adj.* that is a minimum. [Latin: related to MINIM]

♦ **minimum lending rate** *n.* (also **MLR**) *hist.* minimum rate at which the Bank of England would lend to the discount houses. It was introduced in 1971, as the successor to the bank rate, and suspended in 1981; the government reserved the right to reintroduce MLR at any time, which it did for one day in January 1985. See also BASE RATE 2.

♦ **minimum subscription** *n.* minimum sum of money, stated in the prospectus of a new company, that the directors consider must be raised if the company is to be viable.

♦ **minimum wage** *n.* lowest wage permitted by law or agreement. In the UK there is no national statutory minimum (although in certain industries wages councils formerly prescribed minimum rates of pay). In some other countries there are national minimum wages.

minion /ˈmɪnjən/ *n. derog.* servile subordinate. [French *mignon*]

minipill /ˈmɪnɪpɪl/ *n.* contraceptive pill containing a progestogen only (not oestrogen).

miniseries /ˈmɪnɪˌsɪərɪz/ *n.* (*pl.* same) short series of related television programmes.

miniskirt /ˈmɪnɪˌskɜːt/ *n.* very short skirt.

minister /ˈmɪnɪstə(r)/ *–n.* **1** head of a government department. **2** clergyman, esp. in the Presbyterian and Nonconformist Churches. **3** diplomat, usu. ranking below an ambassador. *–v.* (usu. foll. by *to*) help, serve, look after (a person, cause, etc.). □ **ministerial** /-ˈstɪərɪəl/ *adj.* [Latin, = servant]

Minister of State *n.* government minister, esp. holding a rank below that of Head of Department.

Minister of the Crown *n. Parl.* member of the Cabinet.

Minister without Portfolio *n.* government minister not in charge of a specific department of state.

ministration /ˌmɪnɪˈstreɪʃ(ə)n/ *n.* **1** (usu. in *pl.*) help or service (*kind ministrations*). **2** ministering, esp. in religious matters. **3** (usu. foll. by *of*) supplying of help, justice, etc. □ **ministrant** /ˈmɪnɪstrənt/ *adj.* & *n.* [Latin: related to MINISTER]

ministry /ˈmɪnɪstrɪ/ *n.* (*pl.* **-ies**) **1 a** government department headed by a minister. **b** building for this. **2 a** (prec. by *the*) vocation, office, or profession of a religious minister. **b** period of tenure of this. **3** (prec. by *the*) body of ministers of a government or religion. **4** period of government under one prime minister. **5** ministering, ministration. [Latin: related to MINISTER]

mink *n.* (*pl.* same or **-s**) **1** small semi-aquatic stoatlike animal bred for its thick brown fur. **2** this fur. **3** coat of this. [Swedish]

Minn. *abbr.* Minnesota.

Minneapolis /ˌmɪnɪˈæpəlɪs/ industrial city and port in the US, on the Mississippi River in SE Minnesota; as the centre of a grain-producing region, flour milling is an important industry; pop. (est. 1994) 354 590.

Minnesota /ˌmɪnɪˈsəʊtə/ state in the N central US on the Canadian border; pop. (est. 1996) 4 657 758; capital, St Paul. Manufacturing industries (esp. food processing), copper mining, and tourism are important.

minnow /ˈmɪnəʊ/ *n.* small freshwater carp. [Old English]

Minoan /mɪˈnəʊən/ *–adj.* of the Bronze Age civilization centred on Crete (*c.*3000–1100 BC). *–n.* person of this civilization. [*Minos*, legendary king of Crete]

minor /ˈmaɪnə(r)/ *–adj.* **1** lesser or comparatively small in size or importance (*minor poet*). **2** *Mus.* **a** (of a scale) having intervals of a semitone above its second, fifth, and seventh notes. **b** (of an interval) less by a semitone than a major interval. **c** (of a key) based on a minor scale. *–n.* **1** person under full legal age. **2** *US* student's subsidiary subject or course. *–v.* (foll. by *in*) *US* study (a subject) as a subsidiary. [Latin, = less]

Minorca /mɪˈnɔːkə/ (Spanish **Menorca**) second-largest of the Balearic Islands; pop. (est. 1995) 62 550; capital and chief port, Mahon. Tourism and shoe manufacture are major sources of income.

minority /maɪˈnɒrɪtɪ/ *n.* (*pl.* **-ies**) **1** (often foll. by *of*) smaller number or part, esp. in politics. **2** state of having less than half the votes or support (*in the minority*). **3** small group of people differing from others in race, religion, language, etc. **4** (*attrib.*) of or done by the minority (*minority interests*). **5 a** being under full legal age. **b** period of this. [French or medieval Latin: related to MINOR]

♦ **minority interest** *n.* **1** interest of a minority. **2** share or claim of individual shareholders in a company more than 50% of which is owned by a holding company. These shareholders will receive their full share of profits in the form of dividends although they will be unable to influence company policy as they will always be outvoted by the majority interest held by the holding company.

♦ **minority protection** *n.* remedies evolved to safe-

guard a minority of company members from the abuse of majority rule. They include just and equitable winding-up, applying for relief on the basis of unfair prejudice, bringing a derivative or representative action, and seeking an inspection and investigation of the company.

Minsk /mɪnsk/ capital of Belarus; manufactures include vehicles, machinery, and textiles; pop. (est. 1987) 1 543 000.

M.Inst.A.M. *abbr.* Member of the Institute of Administrative Management.

M.Inst.D. *abbr.* Member of the Institute of Directors.

minster *n.* **1** large or important church. **2** church of a monastery. [Old English: related to MONASTERY]

M.Inst.P.I. *abbr.* Member of the Institute of Patentees and Inventors.

minstrel /'mɪnstr(ə)l/ *n.* **1** medieval singer or musician. **2** (usu. in *pl.*) entertainer with a blacked face singing ostensibly Black songs in a group. [related to MINISTER]

M.Inst.T.M. *abbr.* Member of the Institute of Travel Managers in Industry and Commerce.

mint[1] *n.* **1** aromatic herb used in cooking. **2** peppermint. **3** peppermint sweet. □ **minty** *adj.* (**-ier**, **-iest**). [Latin *menta* from Greek]

mint[2] *–n.* **1** factory, owned by a government or a bank, in which coins and banknotes are manufactured. See ROYAL MINT. **2** *colloq.* vast sum (*making a mint*). *–v.* **1** make (a coin) by stamping metal. **2** invent, coin (a word, phrase, etc.). □ **in mint condition** as new. [Latin *moneta*]

♦ **MINTEL** /'mɪntel/ *n.* = MARKET INTELLIGENCE REPORTS. [contraction]

♦ **mint par of exchange** *n. hist.* rate of exchange between two currencies on the gold standard, which was determined by the gold content of the basic coin.

---

minuet /ˌmɪnjʊ'et/ *–n.* **1** slow stately dance for two in triple time. **2** music for this, often as a movement in a suite etc. *–v.* (**-t-**) dance a minuet. [French diminutive]

minus /'maɪnəs/ *–prep.* **1** with the subtraction of (*7 minus 4 equals 3*). **2** below zero (*minus 2°*). **3** *colloq.* lacking (*returned minus their dog*). *–adj.* **1** *Math.* negative. **2** *Electronics* having a negative charge. *–n.* **1** = MINUS SIGN. **2** *Math.* negative quantity. **3** *colloq.* disadvantage. [Latin, neuter of MINOR]

minuscule /'mɪnəˌskjuːl/ *adj. colloq.* extremely small or unimportant. [Latin diminutive: related to MINUS]

minus sign *n.* the symbol –, indicating subtraction or a negative value.

minute[1] /'mɪnɪt/ *–n.* **1** sixtieth part of an hour. **2** distance covered in one minute (*ten minutes from the shops*). **3 a** moment (*expecting her any minute*). **b** (prec. by *the*) *colloq.* present time (*not here at the minute*). **c** (prec. by *the*, foll. by a clause) as soon as (*the minute you get back*). **4** sixtieth part of an angular degree. **5** (in *pl.*) summary of the proceedings of a meeting. **6** official memorandum authorizing or recommending a course of action. *–v.* (**-ting**) **1** record in minutes. **2** send the minutes of a meeting to. □ **up to the minute** completely up to date. [Latin *minuo* lessen]

minute[2] /maɪ'njuːt/ *adj.* (**-est**) **1** very small. **2** accurate, detailed. □ **minutely** *adv.* [Latin *minutus*: related to MINUTE[1]]

minute steak *n.* thin quickly-cooked slice of steak.

minutiae /maɪ'njuːʃiː/ *n.pl.* very small, precise, or minor details. [Latin: related to MINUTE[1]]

minx /mɪŋks/ *n.* pert, sly, or playful girl. [origin unknown]

Miocene /'mɪəˌsiːn/ *Geol. –adj.* of the fourth epoch of the Tertiary period. *–n.* this epoch. [Greek *meiōn* less, *kainos* new]

MIP *abbr.* **1** = MARINE INSURANCE POLICY. **2** = MAXIMUM INVESTMENT PLAN. **3** monthly investment plan.

MIPA *abbr.* Member of the Institute of Practitioners in Advertising.

MIPM *abbr.* Member of the Institute of Personnel Management.

MIPR *abbr.* Member of the Institute of Public Relations.

MIPS *abbr.* (also **mips**) *Computing* million instructions per second (measure of processing speed).

Miquelon see ST PIERRE AND MIQUELON.

miracle /'mɪrək(ə)l/ *n.* **1** extraordinary, supposedly supernatural, event. **2** remarkable occurrence or development (*economic miracle*). **3** (usu. foll. by *of*) remarkable specimen (*a miracle of ingenuity*). [Latin *mirus* wonderful]

miracle play *n.* medieval play on biblical themes.

miraculous /mɪ'rækjʊləs/ *adj.* **1** being a miracle. **2** supernatural. **3** remarkable, surprising. □ **miraculously** *adv.* [French or medieval Latin: related to MIRACLE]

mirage /'mɪrɑːʒ/ *n.* **1** optical illusion caused by atmospheric conditions, esp. the appearance of a pool of water in a desert etc. from the reflection of light. **2** illusory thing. [Latin *miro* look at]

MIRAS /'maɪræs/ *abbr.* mortgage interest relief at source. See MORTGAGE INTEREST RELIEF.

mire *–n.* **1** area of swampy ground. **2** mud, dirt. *–v.* (**-ring**) **1** plunge or sink in a mire. **2** involve in difficulties. **3** bespatter; besmirch. □ **miry** *adj.* [Old Norse]

mirror /'mɪrə(r)/ *–n.* **1** polished surface, usu. of coated glass, reflecting an image. **2** anything reflecting or illuminating a state of affairs etc. *–v.* reflect in or as in a mirror. [Latin *miro* look at]

mirror image *n.* identical image or reflection with left and right reversed.

mirth *n.* merriment, laughter. □ **mirthful** *adj.* [Old English: related to MERRY]

MIS *abbr.* **1** = MANAGEMENT INFORMATION SYSTEM. **2** Member of the Institute of Statisticians.

mis-[1] *prefix* added to verbs and verbal derivatives: meaning 'amiss', 'badly', 'wrongly', 'unfavourably' (*mislead; misshapen; mistrust*). [Old English]

mis-[2] *prefix* occurring in some verbs, nouns, and adjectives meaning 'badly', 'wrongly', 'amiss', 'ill-', or having a negative force (*misadventure; mischief*). [Latin *minus*]

misadventure /ˌmɪsəd'ventʃə(r)/ *n.* **1** *Law* accident without crime or negligence (*death by misadventure*). **2** bad luck. **3** a misfortune.

misalliance /ˌmɪsə'laɪəns/ *n.* unsuitable alliance, esp. a marriage.

misanthrope /'mɪsənˌθrəʊp/ *n.* (also **misanthropist** /mɪ'sænθrəpɪst/) **1** person who hates mankind. **2** person who avoids human society. □ **misanthropic** /-'θrɒpɪk/ *adj.* **misanthropically** /-'θrɒpɪkəlɪ/ *adv.* [Greek *misos* hatred, *anthrōpos* man]

misanthropy /mɪ'sænθrəpɪ/ *n.* condition or habits of a misanthrope.

misapply /ˌmɪsə'plaɪ/ *v.* (**-ies**, **-ied**) apply (esp. funds) wrongly. □ **misapplication** /mɪsˌæplɪ'keɪʃ(ə)n/ *n.*

misapprehend /ˌmɪsæprɪ'hend/ *v.* misunderstand (words, a person). □ **misapprehension** /-'henʃ(ə)n/ *n.*

misappropriate /ˌmɪsə'prəʊprɪˌeɪt/ *v.* (**-ting**) take (another's money etc.) for one's own use; embezzle. □ **misappropriation** /-'eɪʃ(ə)n/ *n.*

misbegotten /ˌmɪsbɪ'gɒt(ə)n/ *adj.* **1** illegitimate, bastard. **2** contemptible, disreputable.

misbehave /ˌmɪsbɪ'heɪv/ *v.* & *refl.* (**-ving**) behave badly. □ **misbehaviour** *n.*

misc. *abbr.* miscellaneous.

miscalculate /ˌmɪs'kælkjʊˌleɪt/ *v.* (**-ting**) calculate wrongly. □ **miscalculation** /-'leɪʃ(ə)n/ *n.*

miscarriage /'mɪsˌkærɪdʒ/ *n.* spontaneous premature expulsion of a foetus from the womb.

miscarriage of justice *n.* failure of the judicial system to attain justice.

miscarry /mɪs'kærɪ/ *v.* (**-ies**, **-ied**) **1** (of a woman) have a miscarriage. **2** (of a plan etc.) fail.

miscast /mɪs'kɑːst/ *v.* (*past* and *past part.* **-cast**) allot an unsuitable part to (an actor) or unsuitable actors to (a play etc.).

miscegenation /ˌmɪsɪdʒɪ'neɪʃ(ə)n/ *n.* interbreeding of

races, esp. of Whites and non-Whites. [related to MIX, GENUS]

miscellaneous /ˌmɪsəˈleɪnɪəs/ *adj.* **1** of mixed composition or character. **2** (foll. by a plural noun) of various kinds. □ **miscellaneously** *adv.* [Latin *misceo* mix]

miscellany /mɪˈselənɪ/ *n.* (*pl.* **-ies**) **1** mixture, medley. **2** book containing various literary compositions. [Latin: related to MISCELLANEOUS]

mischance /mɪsˈtʃɑːns/ *n.* **1** bad luck. **2** instance of this. [French: related to MIS-[2]]

mischief /ˈmɪstʃɪf/ *n.* **1** troublesome, but not malicious, conduct, esp. of children (*get into mischief*). **2** playfulness; malice (*eyes full of mischief*). **3** harm, injury (*do someone a mischief*). □ **make mischief** create discord. [French: related to MIS-[2], *chever* happen]

mischievous /ˈmɪstʃɪvəs/ *adj.* **1** (of a person) disposed to mischief. **2** (of conduct) playful; malicious. **3** harmful. □ **mischievously** *adv.* **mischievousness** *n.*

miscible /ˈmɪsɪb(ə)l/ *adj.* capable of being mixed. □ **miscibility** /-ˈbɪlɪtɪ/ *n.* [medieval Latin: related to MIX]

misconceive /ˌmɪskənˈsiːv/ *v.* (**-ving**) **1** (often foll. by *of*) have a wrong idea or conception. **2** (as **misconceived** *adj.*) badly planned, organized, etc. □ **misconception** /-ˈsepʃ(ə)n/ *n.* [from MIS-[1]]

misconduct /mɪsˈkɒndʌkt/ *n.* improper or unprofessional behaviour.

misconstrue /ˌmɪskənˈstruː/ *v.* (**-strues, -strued, -struing**) interpret wrongly. □ **misconstruction** /-ˈstrʌkʃ(ə)n/ *n.*

miscopy /mɪsˈkɒpɪ/ *v.* (**-ies, -ied**) copy inaccurately.

miscount /mɪsˈkaʊnt/ *–v.* (also *absol.*) count inaccurately. *–n.* inaccurate count.

miscreant /ˈmɪskrɪənt/ *n.* vile wretch, villain. [French: related to MIS-[2], *creant* believer]

misdeed /mɪsˈdiːd/ *n.* evil deed, wrongdoing, crime. [Old English]

misdemeanour /ˌmɪsdɪˈmiːnə(r)/ *n.* (*US* **misdemeanor**) **1** misdeed. **2** *hist* indictable offence less serious than a felony. [from MIS-[1]]

misdiagnose /ˌmɪsˈdaɪəgˌnəʊz/ *v.* (**-sing**) diagnose incorrectly. □ **misdiagnosis** /-ˈnəʊsɪs/ *n.*

misdial /mɪsˈdaɪəl/ *v.* (also *absol.*) (**-ll-**; *US* **-l-**) dial (a telephone number etc.) incorrectly.

misdirect /ˌmɪsdaɪˈrekt/ *v.* direct wrongly. □ **misdirection** *n.*

misdoing /mɪsˈduːɪŋ/ *n.* misdeed.

miser /ˈmaɪzə(r)/ *n.* **1** person who hoards wealth and lives miserably. **2** avaricious person. □ **miserly** *adj.* [Latin, = wretched]

miserable /ˈmɪzərəb(ə)l/ *adj.* **1** wretchedly unhappy or uncomfortable. **2** contemptible, mean. **3** causing wretchedness or discomfort (*miserable weather*). □ **miserableness** *n.* **miserably** *adv.* [Latin: related to MISER]

misericord /mɪˈzerɪˌkɔːd/ *n.* projection under a choir stall seat serving (when the seat is turned up) to support a person standing. [Latin *misericordia* pity]

misery /ˈmɪzərɪ/ *n.* (*pl.* **-ies**) **1** condition or feeling of wretchedness. **2** cause of this. **3** *colloq.* constantly depressed or discontented person. [Latin: related to MISER]

♦ **misfeasance** /mɪsˈfiːz(ə)ns/ *n.* **1** negligent or otherwise improper performance of a lawful act. **2** act by an officer of a company in the nature of a breach of trust or breach of duty, esp. one relating to the company's assets. [French: related to MIS-[2]]

♦ **misfeasance summons** *n.* application to the court by a creditor, contributory, liquidator, or the official receiver during the course of winding up a company. The court is asked to examine the conduct of a company officer who is suspected of a breach of trust or duty and it can order the person to make restitution to the company.

---

misfield /mɪsˈfiːld/ *–v.* (also *absol.*) (in cricket, baseball, etc.) field (the ball) badly. *–n.* instance of this. [from MIS-[1]]

misfire /mɪsˈfaɪə(r)/ *–v.* (**-ring**) **1** (of a gun, motor engine, etc.) fail to go off or start or function smoothly. **2** (of a plan etc.) fail to have the intended effect. *–n.* such failure.

misfit *n.* **1** person unsuited to an environment, occupation, etc. **2** garment etc. that does not fit.

misfortune /mɪsˈfɔːtʃ(ə)n/ *n.* **1** bad luck. **2** instance of this.

misgive /mɪsˈgɪv/ *v.* (**-ving**; *past* **-gave**; *past part.* **-given** /-ˈgɪv(ə)n/) (of a person's mind, heart, etc.) fill (a person) with suspicion or foreboding.

misgiving /mɪsˈgɪvɪŋ/ *n.* (usu. in *pl.*) feeling of mistrust or apprehension.

misgovern /mɪsˈgʌv(ə)n/ *v.* govern badly. □ **misgovernment** *n.*

misguided /mɪsˈgaɪdɪd/ *adj.* mistaken in thought or action. □ **misguidedly** *adv.* **misguidedness** *n.*

mishandle /mɪsˈhænd(ə)l/ *v.* (**-ling**) **1** deal with incorrectly or inefficiently. **2** handle roughly or rudely.

mishap /ˈmɪshæp/ *n.* unlucky accident.

mishear /mɪsˈhɪə(r)/ *v.* (*past* and *past part.* **-heard** /-ˈhɜːd/) hear incorrectly or imperfectly.

mishit *–v.* /mɪsˈhɪt/ (**-tt-**; *past* and *past part.* **-hit**) hit (a ball etc.) badly. *–n.* /ˈmɪshɪt/ faulty or bad hit.

mishmash *n.* confused mixture. [reduplication of MASH]

misinform /ˌmɪsɪnˈfɔːm/ *v.* give wrong information to, mislead. □ **misinformation** /-fəˈmeɪʃ(ə)n/ *n.* [from MIS-[1]]

misinterpret /ˌmɪsɪnˈtɜːprɪt/ *v.* (**-t-**) **1** interpret wrongly. **2** draw a wrong inference from. □ **misinterpretation** /-ˈteɪʃ(ə)n/ *n.*

misjudge /mɪsˈdʒʌdʒ/ *v.* (**-ging**) (also *absol.*) **1** judge wrongly. **2** have a wrong opinion of. □ **misjudgement** *n.* (also **-judgment**).

miskey /mɪsˈkiː/ *v.* (**-keys, -keyed**) key (data) wrongly.

Miskolc /ˈmiːʃkɒlts/ industrial city in Hungary, manufacturing iron, steel, and chemicals; pop. (est. 1996) 180 000.

mislay /mɪsˈleɪ/ *v.* (*past* and *past part.* **-laid**) accidentally put (a thing) where it cannot readily be found.

mislead /mɪsˈliːd/ *v.* (*past* and *past part.* **-led**) cause to infer what is not true; deceive.□ **misleading** *adj.* [Old English]

mismanage /mɪsˈmænɪdʒ/ *v.* (**-ging**) manage badly or wrongly. □ **mismanagement** *n.* [from MIS-[1]]

mismatch *–v.* /mɪsˈmætʃ/ match unsuitably or incorrectly. *–n.* /ˈmɪsmætʃ/ **1** bad match. **2** *Finance* floating-rate note with a monthly interest coupon in which the interest rate is that applicable to a note of longer maturity.

misnomer /mɪsˈnəʊmə(r)/ *n.* **1** name or term used wrongly. **2** wrong use of a name or term. [Anglo-French: related to MIS-[2], *nommer* to name]

misogyny /mɪˈsɒdʒɪnɪ/ *n.* hatred of women. □ **misogynist** *n.* **misogynistic** /-ˈnɪstɪk/ *adj.* [Greek *misos* hatred, *gunē* woman]

misplace /mɪsˈpleɪs/ *v.* (**-cing**) **1** put in the wrong place. **2** bestow (affections, confidence, etc.) on an inappropriate object. □ **misplacement** *n.*

misprint *–n.* /ˈmɪsprɪnt/ printing error. *–v.* /mɪsˈprɪnt/ print wrongly.

misprision /mɪsˈprɪʒ(ə)n/ *n.* *Law* **1** (in full **misprision of a felony** or **of treason**) deliberate concealment of one's knowledge of a crime or treason. **2** wrong action or omission. [Anglo-French: related to MIS-[2], *prendre* take]

mispronounce /ˌmɪsprəˈnaʊns/ *v.* (**-cing**) pronounce (a word etc.) wrongly. □ **mispronunciation** /-ˌnʌnsɪˈeɪʃ(ə)n/ *n.* [from MIS-[1]]

misquote /mɪsˈkwəʊt/ *v.* (**-ting**) quote inaccurately. □ **misquotation** /-ˈteɪʃ(ə)n/ *n.*

misread /mɪsˈriːd/ *v.* (*past* and *past part.* **-read** /-ˈred/) read or interpret wrongly.

misrepresent /ˌmɪsreprɪˈzent/ *v.* represent wrongly; give a false account or idea of.

◆ **misrepresentation** /ˌmɪsreprɪzenˈteɪʃ(ə)n/ *n.* **1** inaccurate or false account or idea. **2** *Law* untrue statement of fact, made by one party to the other in the course of negotiating a contract, that induces the other party to enter into the contract. The person making the misrepresentation is called the **representor**, and the person to whom it is made is the **representee**. A false statement of law, opinion, or intention does not constitute a misrepresentation; nor does a statement of fact known by the representee to be untrue. Moreover, unless the representee relies on the statement so that it becomes an inducement (though not necessarily the only inducement) to enter into the contract, it is not a misrepresentation. The remedies for misrepresentation vary according to the degree of culpability of the representor. If the representor is guilty of **fraudulent misrepresentation** (i.e. not honestly believing in the truth of the statement made) the representee may, subject to certain limitations, set the contract aside and may also sue for damages. If the representor is guilty of **negligent misrepresentation** (i.e. believing the statement without reasonable grounds) the representee may also rescind the contract and sue for damages. If the representor has committed merely an **innocent misrepresentation** (reasonably believing a statement to be true) the representee is restricted to rescinding the contract.

misrule /mɪsˈruːl/ *–n.* bad government; disorder. *–v.* (**-ling**) govern badly.

miss[1] *–v.* **1** (also *absol.*) fail to hit, reach, find, catch, etc. (an object or goal). **2** fail to catch (a bus, train, etc.) or see (an event) or meet (a person). **3** fail to seize (an opportunity etc.) (*missed my chance*). **4** fail to hear or understand (*missed what you said*). **5 a** regret the loss or absence of (*did you miss me?*). **b** notice the loss or absence of (*won't be missed until evening*). **6** avoid (*go early to miss the traffic*). **7** (of an engine etc.) fail, misfire. *–n.* failure to hit, reach, attain, connect, etc. □ **be missing** not have (*am missing a page*) (see also MISSING). **give (a thing) a miss** *colloq.* not attend or partake of (*gave the party a miss*). **miss out 1** omit, leave out. **2** (usu. foll. by *on*) *colloq.* fail to get or experience. [Old English]

miss[2] *n.* **1** (**Miss**) **a** title of an unmarried woman or girl. **b** title of a beauty queen (*Miss World*). **2** title used to address a female schoolteacher, shop assistant, etc. **3** girl or unmarried woman. [from MISTRESS]

Miss. *abbr.* Mississippi.

missal /ˈmɪs(ə)l/ *n. RC Ch.* **1** book containing the texts for the Mass throughout the year. **2** book of prayers. [Latin *missa* MASS[2]]

missel thrush var. of MISTLE THRUSH.

misshapen /mɪsˈʃeɪpən/ *adj.* ill-shaped, deformed, distorted. [from MIS-[1], *shapen* (archaic) = *shaped*]

missile /ˈmɪsaɪl/ *n.* **1** object or weapon suitable for throwing at a target or for discharge from a machine. **2** weapon directed by remote control or automatically. [Latin *mitto miss-* send]

missing *adj.* **1** not in its place; lost. **2** (of a person) not yet traced or confirmed as alive but not known to be dead. **3** not present.

missing link *n.* **1** thing lacking to complete a series. **2** hypothetical intermediate type, esp. between humans and apes.

mission /ˈmɪʃ(ə)n/ *n.* **1 a** task or goal assigned to a person or group. **b** journey undertaken as part of this. **c** person's vocation. **2** military or scientific operation or expedition. **3** body of persons sent to conduct negotiations or propagate a religious faith. **4** missionary post. [Latin: related to MISSILE]

missionary /ˈmɪʃənərɪ/ *–adj.* of or concerned with religious missions. *–n.* (*pl.* **-ies**) person doing missionary work. [Latin: related to MISSION]

missionary position *n. colloq.* position for sexual intercourse with the woman lying on her back and the man lying on top and facing her.

missionary salesperson *n.* employee of the sales department of an organization who visits prospective customers to distribute information, answer questions, deal with complaints, etc., but not to take orders.

missis /ˈmɪsɪz/ *n.* (also **missus** /-səz/) *colloq.* or *joc.* **1** form of address to a woman. **2** wife. □ **the missis** my or your wife. [from MISTRESS]

Mississippi /ˌmɪsɪˈsɪpɪ/ **1** river in the US, rising near the Canadian border in Minnesota and flowing S to the Gulf of Mexico, providing a major commercial waterway. **2** state of the US, E of the lower Mississippi River; pop. (est. 1996) 2 716 115; capital, Jackson. Shipbuilding is the main industry; cotton, textiles, and paper are also important products.

missive /ˈmɪsɪv/ *n.* **1** *joc.* letter. **2** official letter. [Latin: related to MISSILE]

Missouri /mɪˈzʊərɪ/ **1** river in the US, one of the main tributaries of the Mississippi, rising in the Rocky Mountains in Montana and flowing into it from the W. **2** state of the US lying W of the Mississippi River; pop. (est, 1996) 5 358 692; capital, Jefferson City. Manufacturing industries are important, including transport and aerospace equipment, printing and publishing, and food processing, and the state is a leading producer of lead.

misspell /mɪsˈspel/ *v.* (*past* and *past part.* **-spelt** or **-spelled**) spell wrongly.

misspend /mɪsˈspend/ *v.* (*past* and *past part.* **-spent**) (esp. as **misspent** *adj.*) spend amiss or wastefully.

misstate /mɪsˈsteɪt/ *v.* (**-ting**) state wrongly or inaccurately. □ **misstatement** *n.*

missus var. of MISSIS.

mist *–n.* **1 a** diffuse cloud of minute water droplets near the ground. **b** condensed vapour obscuring glass etc. **2** dimness or blurring of the sight caused by tears etc. **3** cloud of particles resembling mist. *–v.* (usu. foll. by *up*, *over*) cover or become covered with mist or as with mist. [Old English]

mistake /mɪˈsteɪk/ *–n.* **1** incorrect idea or opinion; thing incorrectly done or thought. **2** error of judgement. **3** *Law* misunderstanding or erroneous belief about a matter of fact (**mistake of fact**) or a matter of law (**mistake of law**). In civil cases, mistake is particularly important in the law of contract. Mistakes of law have no effect on the validity of agreements, and neither do many mistakes of fact. When a mistake of fact does do so, it may render the agreement void under common-law rules (in which case it is referred to as an **operative mistake**) or it may make it voidable, i.e. liable, subject to certain limitations, to be set aside under the more lenient rules of equity. When both parties to an agreement are under a misunderstanding, the mistake may be classified as either a **common mistake** (i.e. a single mistake shared by both) or a **mutual mistake** (i.e. each misunderstanding the other). In the case of common mistake, the mistake renders the contract void only if it robs it of all substance. The principal (and almost the only) example is when the subject matter of the contract has, unknown to both parties, ceased to exist. A common mistake about some particular attribute of the subject matter (e.g. that it is an original, not a copy) is not an operative mistake. However, a common mistake relating to any really fundamental matter will render a contract voidable. In the case of mutual mistake, the contract is valid if only one interpretation of what was agreed can be deduced from the parties' words and conduct. Otherwise, the mistake is operative and the contract void. When only one party to a contract is under a misunderstanding, that person's mistake may be called a **unilateral mistake** and it makes the contract void if it relates to the fundamental nature of the offer and the other party knew or ought to have known of it. Otherwise, the contract is valid so far as the law of mistake is concerned, though the circumstances may be such as to make it voidable for misrepresentation. A deed or other signed document (whether or not constituting a contract) that does not correctly record what both parties intended may be rectified by the courts. When one signatory to a document was fundamentally mistaken as to the character or effect of the transaction it embodies, that person may (unless he or she was careless) plead this mistake as a defence to any action based on the document. –*v.* (**-king**; *past* **mistook** /-ˈstʊk/; *past part.* **mistaken**) **1** misunderstand the meaning of. **2** (foll. by *for*) wrongly take or identify (*mistook me for you*). **3** choose wrongly (*mistake one's vocation*). [Old Norse: related to MIS-[1], TAKE]

mistaken /mɪˈsteɪkən/ *adj.* **1** wrong in opinion or judgement. **2** based on or resulting from this (*mistaken loyalty; mistaken identity*). □ **mistakenly** *adv.*

mister /ˈmɪstə(r)/ *n. colloq.* or *joc.* form of address to a man. [from MASTER; cf. MR]

mistime /mɪsˈtaɪm/ *v.* (**-ming**) say or do at the wrong time. [related to MIS-[1]]

mistle thrush /ˈmɪs(ə)l/ *n.* (also **missel thrush**) large thrush with a spotted breast, feeding on mistletoe berries. [Old English]

mistletoe /ˈmɪs(ə)lˌtəʊ/ *n.* parasitic plant with white berries growing on apple and other trees. [Old English]

mistook *past* of MISTAKE.

mistral /ˈmɪstr(ə)l/ *n.* cold N or NW wind in S France. [Latin: related to MASTER]

mistreat /mɪsˈtriːt/ *v.* treat badly. □ **mistreatment** *n.*

mistress /ˈmɪstrɪs/ *n.* **1** female head of a household. **2 a** woman in authority. **b** female owner of a pet. **3** female teacher. **4** woman having an illicit sexual relationship with a (usu. married) man. [French *maistre* MASTER, -ESS]

mistrial /mɪsˈtraɪəl/ *n.* trial rendered invalid by error.

mistrust /mɪsˈtrʌst/ –*v.* **1** be suspicious of. **2** feel no confidence in. –*n.* **1** suspicion. **2** lack of confidence. □ **mistrustful** *adj.* **mistrustfully** *adv.*

misty *adj.* (**-ier, -iest**) **1** of or covered with mist. **2** dim in outline. **3** obscure, vague (*misty idea*). □ **mistily** *adv.* **mistiness** *n.* [Old English: related to MIST]

misunderstand /ˌmɪsʌndəˈstænd/ *v.* (*past* and *past part.* **-understood** /-ˈstʊd/) **1** understand incorrectly. **2** misinterpret the words or actions of (a person).

misunderstanding *n.* **1** failure to understand correctly. **2** slight disagreement or quarrel.

misusage /mɪsˈjuːsɪdʒ/ *n.* **1** wrong or improper usage. **2** ill-treatment.

misuse –*v.* /mɪsˈjuːz/ (**-sing**) **1** use wrongly; apply to the wrong purpose. **2** ill-treat. –*n.* /mɪsˈjuːs/ wrong or improper use or application.

MIT *abbr.* Massachusetts Institute of Technology.

MITD *abbr.* Member of the Institute of Training and Development.

mite[1] *n.* small arachnid, esp. of a kind found in cheese etc. [Old English]

mite[2] *n.* **1** any small monetary unit. **2** small object or person, esp. a child. **3** modest contribution. [probably the same as MITE[1]]

miter *US* var. of MITRE.

MITI *abbr.* (in Japan) Ministry of International Trade and Industry.

mitigate /ˈmɪtɪˌgeɪt/ *v.* (**-ting**) make less intense or severe. □ **mitigation** /-ˈgeɪʃ(ə)n/ *n.* [Latin *mitis* mild]

mitigating circumstances *n.pl.* circumstances permitting greater leniency.

♦ **mitigation of damage** *n.* minimizing the loss incurred by the person who suffered the loss and is claiming damages as a result of it. The injured party has a duty to take all reasonable steps to mitigate any loss and the courts will not, therefore, award damages to compensate for a loss that could have been avoided by reasonable action.

Mitilíni see MYTILENE.

mitosis /maɪˈtəʊsɪs/ *n. Biol.* type of cell division that results in two nuclei each having the same number and kind of chromosomes as the parent nucleus. □ **mitotic** /-ˈtɒtɪk/ *adj.* [Greek *mitos* thread]

mitre /ˈmaɪtə(r)/ (*US* **miter**) –*n.* **1** tall deeply-cleft head-dress worn by bishops and abbots, esp. as a symbol of office. **2** joint of two pieces of wood etc. at an angle of 90°, such that the line of junction bisects this angle. –*v.* (**-ring**) **1** bestow a mitre on. **2** join with a mitre. [Greek *mitra* turban]

MITT *abbr.* Member of the Institute of Travel and Tourism.

mitt *n.* **1** (also **mitten**) glove with only two compartments, one for the thumb and the other for all four fingers. **2** glove leaving the fingers and thumb-tip exposed. **3** *slang* hand or fist. **4** baseball glove. [Latin: related to MOIETY]

mix –*v.* **1** combine or put together (two or more substances or things) so that the constituents of each are diffused among those of the other(s). **2** prepare (a compound, cocktail, etc.) by combining the ingredients. **3** combine (activities etc.) (*mix business and pleasure*). **4 a** join, be mixed, or combine, esp. readily (*oil and water will not mix*). **b** be compatible. **c** be sociable (*must learn to mix*). **5 a** (foll. by *with*) (of a person) be harmonious or sociable with; have regular dealings with. **b** (foll. by *in*) participate in. **6** drink different kinds of (alcoholic liquor) in close succession. **7** combine (two or more sound signals) into one. –*n.* **1 a** mixing; mixture. **b** proportion of materials in a mixture. **2** ingredients prepared commercially for making a cake, concrete, etc. □ **be mixed up in** (or **with**) be involved in or with (esp. something undesirable). **mix it** *colloq.* start fighting. **mix up 1** mix thoroughly. **2** confuse. [back-formation from MIXED]

mixed /mɪkst/ *adj.* **1** of diverse qualities or elements. **2** containing persons from various backgrounds etc. **3** for persons of both sexes (*mixed school*). [Latin *misceo* mix]

mixed bag *n.* diverse assortment.

mixed blessing *n.* thing having advantages and disadvantages.

mixed doubles *n.pl. Tennis* doubles game with a man and a woman on each side.

♦ **mixed economy** *n.* economic system in which some goods and services are produced by the government and some by private enterprise. It lies between a command economy and a complete laissez-faire economy. In practice, however, most economies are mixed; the significant feature is whether an economy is moving towards or away from a more laissez-faire situation.

---

mixed farming *n.* farming of both crops and livestock.

mixed feelings *n.pl.* mixture of pleasure and dismay about something.

mixed grill *n.* dish of various grilled meats and vegetables etc.

mixed marriage *n.* marriage between persons of different race or religion.

mixed metaphor *n.* combination of inconsistent metaphors (e.g. *this tower of strength will forge ahead*).

mixed-up *adj. colloq.* mentally or emotionally confused; socially ill-adjusted.

mixer *n.* **1** machine for mixing foods etc. **2** person who manages socially in a specified way (*a good mixer*). **3** (usu. soft) drink to be mixed with another. **4** device that receives two or more separate signals from microphones etc. and combines them in a single output.

mixer tap *n.* tap through which both hot and cold water can be drawn together.

mixture /ˈmɪkstʃə(r)/ *n.* **1** process or result of mixing. **2** combination of ingredients, qualities, characteristics, etc. [Latin: related to MIXED]

mix-up *n.* confusion, misunderstanding.

♦ **mix variance** *n. Econ.* variance arising because the mix of goods actually sold or produced differs from that budgeted for.

---

mizen /ˈmɪz(ə)n/ *n.* (also **mizzen**) (in full **mizen-sail**) lowest fore-and-aft sail of a fully rigged ship's mizen-mast. [Italian: related to MEZZANINE]

mizen-mast *n.* (also **mizzen-mast**) mast next aft of the mainmast.

Mizoram /mɪˈzɔːrəm/ state of NE India; pop. (est. 1994)

775 000; capital, Aizawl. Farming and weaving support the population.

MK –*symb.* Malawi kwacha. –*postcode* Milton Keynes. –*airline flight code* Air Mauritius.

mkt *abbr.* market.

ML *postcode* Motherwell.

Ml *symb.* maloti (see LOTI).

ml *abbr.* **1** millilitre(s). **2** mile(s).

M.Litt. *abbr.* Master of Letters. [Latin *Magister Litterarum*]

Mlle *abbr.* (*pl.* **-s**) Mademoiselle.

♦ **MLR** *abbr.* = MINIMUM LENDING RATE.

MM –*abbr.* **1** mercantile marine. **2** Messieurs. **3** Military Medal. –*airline flight code* SAM Colombia.

mm *abbr.* millimetre(s).

m.m. *abbr.* (also **M/m**) made merchantable.

Mmabatho /mə'bɑːtəʊ/ city in North-West Province, South Africa, capital of the former independent homeland of Bophuthatswana, which was abolished in 1994; pop. (1985) 28 000.

MMB *abbr.* Milk Marketing Board.

♦ **MMC** *abbr.* = MONOPOLIES AND MERGERS COMMISSION.

MMDA *abbr. US* money market deposit account.

Mme *abbr.* (*pl.* **-s**) Madame.

MMI *abbr.* man–machine interface (or interaction). See USER INTERFACE.

MMS *abbr.* Member of the Institute of Management Services.

MMU *abbr. Computing* memory management unit.

MN –*abbr.* Merchant Navy. –*US postcode* Minnesota.

Mn *symb.* manganese.

MNC *abbr.* multinational company.

MNE *abbr.* multinational enterprise.

mnemonic /nɪ'mɒnɪk/ –*adj.* of or designed to aid the memory. –*n.* mnemonic word, verse, etc. □ **mnemonically** *adv.* [Greek *mnēmōn* mindful]

MO –*abbr.* **1** (also **m.o.**) mail order. **2** manually operated. **3** Medical Officer. **4** money order. –*US postcode* Missouri.

Mo *symb.* molybdenum.

Mo. *abbr.* Missouri.

mo /məʊ/ *n.* (*pl.* **-s**) *colloq.* moment. [abbreviation]

moa /'məʊə/ *n.* (*pl.* **-s**) extinct flightless New Zealand bird resembling the ostrich. [Maori]

moan –*n.* **1** long murmur expressing physical or mental suffering. **2** low plaintive sound of wind etc. **3** *colloq.* complaint; grievance. –*v.* **1** make a moan or moans. **2** *colloq.* complain, grumble. **3** utter with moans. □ **moaner** *n.* [Old English]

moat *n.* defensive ditch round a castle etc., usu. filled with water. [French *mote* mound]

mob –*n.* **1** disorderly crowd; rabble. **2** (prec. by *the*) usu. *derog.* the populace. **3** *colloq.* gang; group. –*v.* (**-bb-**) crowd round in order to attack or admire. [Latin *mobile vulgus* excitable crowd]

mob-cap *n. hist.* woman's large indoor cap covering all the hair. [obsolete *mob*, originally = slut]

mobile /'məʊbaɪl/ –*adj.* **1** movable; able to move easily or get out and about. **2** (of the face etc.) readily changing its expression. **3** (of a shop etc.) accommodated in a vehicle so as to serve various places. **4** (of a person) able to change his or her social status. –*n.* decoration that may be hung so as to turn freely. □ **mobility** /mə'bɪlɪtɪ/ *n.* [Latin *moveo* move]

mobile home *n.* large caravan usu. permanently parked and used as a residence.

♦ **mobility of labour** *n.* extent to which workers are willing to move from one region or country to another (**geographical mobility**) or to change from one occupation to another (**occupational mobility**). In **horizontal mobility** there is no change of status, whereas in **vertical mobility** there is. An upward change in status will increase a worker's mobility, whereas a downward change will reduce it. The more highly skilled a worker, the less the occupational mobility will be, but such workers will often be highly geographically mobile. An unskilled worker will often be both occupationally and geographically mobile. In the UK, many government retraining schemes aim to increase occupational mobility; at the same time considerable effort goes into encouraging new industries into areas of high unemployment to reduce the need for geographical mobility.

---

mobilize /'məʊbɪˌlaɪz/ *v.* (also **-ise**) (**-zing** or **-sing**) esp. *Mil.* make or become ready for service or action. □ **mobilization** /-'zeɪʃ(ə)n/ *n.*

Möbius strip /'mɜːbɪəs/ *n. Math.* one-sided surface formed by joining the ends of a narrow rectangle after twisting one end through 180°. [*Möbius*, name of a mathematician]

mobster *n. slang* gangster.

MOC *abbr.* management and operating contractor.

moccasin /'mɒkəsɪn/ *n.* soft flat-soled shoe orig. worn by North American Indians. [American Indian]

mocha /'mɒkə/ *n.* **1** coffee of fine quality. **2** flavouring made with this. [*Mocha*, port on the Red Sea]

mock –*v.* **1** (often foll. by *at*) ridicule; scoff (at); act with scorn or contempt for. **2** mimic contemptuously. **3** defy or delude contemptuously. –*attrib. adj.* **1** sham, imitation. **2** as a trial run (*mock exam*). –*n.* (in *pl.*) *colloq.* mock examinations. □ **mockingly** *adv.* [French *moquer*]

♦ **mock auction** *n.* auction during which a lot is sold to someone at a price lower than that person's highest bid, part of the price is repaid or credited to the bidder, the right to bid is restricted to those who have bought or agreed to buy one or more articles, or articles are given away or offered as gifts. Under the Mock Auction Act (1961) it is an offence to promote or conduct a mock auction.

---

mocker *n.* person who mocks. □ **put the mockers on** *slang* **1** bring bad luck to. **2** put a stop to.

mockery *n.* (*pl.* **-ies**) **1** derision, ridicule. **2** counterfeit or absurdly inadequate representation. **3** ludicrously or insultingly futile action etc.

mockingbird *n.* bird that mimics the notes of other birds.

mock orange *n.* white-flowered heavy-scented shrub.

mock turtle soup *n.* soup made from a calf's head etc. to resemble turtle soup.

mock-up *n.* experimental model or replica of a proposed structure etc.

MOD *abbr.* **1** mail-order department. **2** Ministry of Defence.

mod *colloq.* –*adj.* modern. –*n.* young person (esp. in the 1960s) of a group known for its smart modern dress. [abbreviation]

modal /'məʊd(ə)l/ *adj.* **1** of mode or form, not of substance. **2** *Gram.* **a** of the mood of a verb. **b** (of an auxiliary verb, e.g. *would*) used to express the mood of another verb. **3** *Mus.* denoting a style of music using a particular mode. [Latin: related to MODE]

mod cons *n.pl.* modern conveniences.

mode *n.* **1** way in which a thing is done. **2** prevailing fashion or custom. **3** *Mus.* any of several types of scale. [French and Latin *modus* measure]

model /'mɒd(ə)l/ –*n.* **1** representation in three dimensions of an existing person or thing or of a proposed structure, esp. on a smaller scale (often *attrib.*: *model train*). **2** simplified description of a system etc., to assist calculations and predictions. **3** figure in clay, wax, etc., to be reproduced in another material. **4** particular design or style, esp. of a car. **5 a** exemplary person or thing. **b** (*attrib.*) ideal, exemplary. **6** person employed to pose for an artist or photographer or to wear clothes etc. for display. **7** garment etc. by a well-known designer, or a copy of this. –*v.* (**-ll-**; *US* **-l-**) **1 a** fashion or shape (a figure) in clay, wax, etc. **b** (foll. by *after*, *on*, etc.) form (a thing in imitation of). **2 a** act or pose as a model. **b** (of a person acting as a model) display (a garment). [Latin: related to MODE]

♦ **modem** /'məʊdem/ *n.* combined device for modulation and demodulation, e.g. between a computer and a telephone line. It converts the digital signal of the computer into a suitable form for transmission, and any incoming telephone signal into a digital form that can be fed to the computer. A pair of modems can thus be used to connect two units (e.g. two computers, or a computer and a terminal) across a telephone line. [portmanteau word]

moderate *–adj.* /'mɒdərət/ **1** avoiding extremes; temperate in conduct or expression. **2** fairly large or good. **3** (of the wind) of medium strength. **4** (of prices) fairly low. *–n.* /'mɒdərət/ person who holds moderate views, esp. in politics. *–v.* /'mɒdə,reɪt/ (**-ting**) **1** make or become less violent, intense, rigorous, etc. **2** (also *absol.*) act as moderator of or to. □ **moderately** /-rətlɪ/ *adv.* **moderateness** /-rətnəs/ *n.* [Latin]

moderation /,mɒdə'reɪʃ(ə)n/ *n.* **1** moderateness. **2** moderating. □ **in moderation** in a moderate manner or degree.

moderato /,mɒdə'rɑːtəʊ/ *adj.* & *adv. Mus.* at a moderate pace. [Italian]

moderator *n.* **1** arbitrator, mediator. **2** presiding officer. **3** Presbyterian minister presiding over an ecclesiastical body. **4** *Physics* substance used in a nuclear reactor to retard neutrons.

modern /'mɒd(ə)n/ *–adj.* **1** of present and recent times. **2** in current fashion; not antiquated. *–n.* person living in modern times. □ **modernity** /-'dɜːnɪtɪ/ *n.* [Latin *modo* just now]

modern English *n.* English from about 1500 onwards.

modernism *n.* modern ideas or methods, esp. in art. □ **modernist** *n.* & *adj.*

modernize *v.* (also **-ise**) (**-zing** or **-sing**) **1** make modern; adapt to modern needs or habits. **2** adopt modern ways or views. □ **modernization** /-'zeɪʃ(ə)n/ *n.*

modest /'mɒdɪst/ *adj.* **1** having or expressing a humble or moderate estimate of one's own merits. **2** diffident, bashful. **3** decorous. **4** moderate or restrained in amount, extent, severity, etc. **5** unpretentious, not extravagant. □ **modestly** *adv.* **modesty** *n.* [French from Latin]

modicum /'mɒdɪkəm/ *n.* (foll. by *of*) small quantity. [Latin: related to MODE]

modification /,mɒdɪfɪ'keɪʃ(ə)n/ *n.* **1** modifying or being modified. **2** change made. □ **modificatory** /'mɒd-/ *adj.* [Latin: related to MODIFY]

♦ **modified accounts** *n.pl.* form of statutory annual accounts for small companies and medium-sized companies in the UK. Currently all companies have to submit full accounts to their shareholders, although consideration is being given to shortened accounts even for large companies. However, the small and medium-sized companies need file only modified accounts with the Registrar of Companies. For small companies, modified accounts consist only of a balance sheet, certain specified notes, and a copy of the auditors' report. In the case of medium-sized companies the profit and loss account may omit some information but otherwise full information must be filed.

modify /'mɒdɪ,faɪ/ *v.* (**-ies, -ied**) **1** make less severe or extreme. **2** make partial changes in. **3** *Gram.* qualify or expand the sense of (a word etc.). [Latin: related to MODE]

modish /'məʊdɪʃ/ *adj.* fashionable. □ **modishly** *adv.*

modiste /mɒ'diːst/ *n.* milliner; dressmaker. [French: related to MODE]

modular program /'mɒdjʊlə(r)/ *n.* computer program that is broken down into a set of components (modules) of manageable size, each with a well-defined purpose and boundary. The basis on which a program is broken down could be that each module involves one specific task to be performed by the computer. Alternatively each module could involve a single design decision. It should be possible for the modules to be developed, tested, and debugged independently. Modules can then be brought together and tested to see if they operate together correctly. Finally the whole program can be tested to ensure that it is performing in the desired way. A modular program is easy to amend or update, in many cases the modifications being necessary in just one module.

modulate /'mɒdjʊ,leɪt/ *v.* (**-ting**) **1 a** regulate or adjust. **b** moderate. **2** adjust or vary the tone or pitch of (the speaking voice). **3** cause (a wave or signal) to vary in order to convey a signal. **4** *Mus.* (cause to) change from one key to another. □ **modulation** /-'leɪʃ(ə)n/ *n.* **modulator** *n.* [Latin: related to MODULE]

module /'mɒdjuːl/ *n.* **1** standardized part or independent unit in construction, esp. of furniture, a building, or an electronic system. **2** independent self-contained unit or component, as of a computer program (see MODULAR PROGRAM). **3** unit or period of training or education. □ **modular** *adj.* [Latin: related to MODULUS]

modulus /'mɒdjʊləs/ *n.* (*pl.* **moduli** /-,laɪ/) *Math.* constant factor or ratio. [Latin, = measure: related to MODE]

modus operandi /,məʊdəs ,ɒpə'rændɪ/ *n.* (*pl.* ***modi operandi*** /,məʊdɪ/) method of working. [Latin, = way of operating]

modus vivendi /,məʊdəs vɪ'vendɪ/ *n.* (*pl.* ***modi vivendi*** /,məʊdɪ/) **1** way of living or coping. **2** arrangement between people who agree to differ. [Latin, = way of living]

mog *n.* (also **moggie**) *slang* cat. [originally a dial. word]

Mogadishu /,mɒgə'dɪʃuː/ capital and chief port of Somalia; pop. (est. 1990) 900 000.

Mogadon /'mɒgə,dɒn/ *n. propr.* hypnotic drug used to treat insomnia.

mogul /'məʊg(ə)l/ *n.* **1** *colloq.* important or influential person. **2** (**Mogul**) *hist.* **a** Mongolian. **b** (often **the Great Mogul**) emperor of Delhi in the 16th–19th centuries. [Persian and Arabic: related to MONGOL]

mohair /'məʊheə(r)/ *n.* **1** hair of the angora goat. **2** yarn or fabric from this. [ultimately from Arabic, = choice]

Mohammedan var. of MUHAMMADAN.

Mohican /məʊ'hiːkən/ *–adj.* (of a hairstyle) with the head shaved except for a strip of hair from the middle of the forehead to the back of the neck, often worn in long spikes. *–n.* such a hairstyle. [*Mohicans*, North American Indian people]

♦ **Mohn** /məʊn/, **Reinhard** (1921–) German publisher, chairman of the world's largest media company, Bertelsmann AG Reinhard. On returning to Germany after spending most of World War II in a US POW camp, Mohn discovered that the publishing company founded in 1835 by a member of his family had been destroyed; he rebuilt the plant and started to publish again in 1948. During the 1980s he acquired a number of international publishing companies (including Transworld Publishing, owners of the US Bantam and UK Corgi imprints) and for a while owned the New York Mets baseball team. In 1997 the Mohn family owned 20% of Bertelsman, and Reinhard Mohn controlled the trust that held 69% of the remainder. In 1998 Bertelsmann AG Reinhard acquired another major international publisher, Random Century.

moiety /'mɔɪətɪ/ *n.* (*pl.* **-ies**) *Law* or *literary* **1** half. **2** each of the two parts of a thing. [Latin *medietas* from *medius* middle]

moire /mwɑː(r)/ *n.* (in full **moire antique**) watered fabric, usu. silk. [French: related to MOHAIR]

moiré /'mwɑːreɪ/ *adj.* **1** (of silk) watered. **2** (of metal) having a clouded appearance. [French: related to MOIRE]

moiré pattern *n.* pattern observed when one pattern of lines etc. is superimposed on another.

moist *adj.* slightly wet; damp. [French]

moisten /'mɔɪs(ə)n/ *v.* make or become moist.

moisture /'mɔɪstʃə(r)/ *n.* water or other liquid diffused in a small quantity as vapour, or within a solid, or condensed on a surface.

moisturize *v.* (also **-ise**) (**-zing** or **-sing**) make less dry (esp. the skin by use of a cosmetic). □ **moisturizer** *n.*

molar /'məʊlə(r)/ *–adj.* (usu. of a mammal's back teeth) serving to grind. *–n.* molar tooth. [Latin *mola* millstone]

molasses /mə'læsɪz/ *n.pl.* (treated as *sing.*) **1** uncrystallized syrup extracted from raw sugar. **2** *US* treacle. [Portuguese from Latin *mel* honey]

mold *US* var. of MOULD[1], MOULD[2], MOULD[3].

Moldavia /mɒl'deɪvɪə/ *hist.* **1** principality in SE Europe from which, together with Wallachia, the kingdom of Romania was formed in 1859. **2** (also **Moldavian Soviet Socialist Republic**) Soviet republic formed from territory ceded by Romania in 1940 (see MOLDOVA). □ **Moldavian** *adj.* & *n.*

molder *US* var. of MOULDER.

molding *US* var. of MOULDING.

moldy *US* var. of MOULDY.

mole[1] *n.* **1** small burrowing mammal with dark velvety fur and very small eyes. **2** *slang* spy established in a position of trust in an organization. [Low German or Dutch]

mole[2] *n.* small permanent dark spot on the skin. [Old English]

mole[3] *n.* **1** massive structure serving as a pier, breakwater, or causeway. **2** artificial harbour. [Latin *moles* mass]

mole[4] *n. Chem.* the SI unit of amount of a substance equal to the quantity containing as many elementary units as there are atoms in 0.012 kg of carbon-12. [German *Mol* from *Molekül* MOLECULE]

molecular /mə'lekjʊlə(r)/ *adj.* of, relating to, or consisting of molecules. □ **molecularity** /-'lærɪtɪ/ *n.*

molecular weight *n.* = RELATIVE MOLECULAR MASS.

molecule /'mɒlɪˌkjuːl/ *n.* **1** smallest fundamental unit (usu. a group of atoms) of a chemical compound that can take part in a chemical reaction. **2** (in general use) small particle. [Latin diminutive: related to MOLE[3]]

molehill *n.* small mound thrown up by a mole in burrowing. □ **make a mountain out of a molehill** overreact to a minor difficulty.

molest /mə'lest/ *v.* **1** annoy or pester (a person). **2** attack or interfere with (a person), esp. sexually. □ **molestation** /-'steɪʃ(ə)n/ *n.* **molester** *n.* [Latin *molestus* troublesome]

Molise /mɒ'liːzɪ/ agricultural region of E Italy, on the Adriatic coast; pop. (est. 1994) 331 990; capital, Campobasso.

moll *n. slang* **1** gangster's female companion. **2** prostitute. [pet form of *Mary*]

mollify /'mɒlɪˌfaɪ/ *v.* (**-ies, -ied**) appease. □ **mollification** /-fɪ'keɪʃ(ə)n/ *n.* [Latin *mollis* soft]

mollusc /'mɒləsk/ *n.* (*US* **mollusk**) invertebrate with a soft body and usu. a hard shell, e.g. snails and oysters. [Latin *molluscus* soft]

mollycoddle /'mɒlɪˌkɒd(ə)l/ *v.* (**-ling**) coddle, pamper. [related to MOLL, CODDLE]

Molotov cocktail /'mɒləˌtɒf/ *n.* crude incendiary device, usu. a bottle filled with inflammable liquid. [*Molotov*, name of a Russian statesman]

molt *US* var. of MOULT.

molten /'məʊlt(ə)n/ *adj.* melted, esp. made liquid by heat. [from MELT]

molto /'mɒltəʊ/ *adv. Mus.* very. [Latin *multus* much]

Molucca Islands /mə'lʌkə/ (also **Moluccas** or **Maluku** /mə'luːkuː/; formerly **Spice Islands**) group of Indonesian islands, SE of the Philippines; spices, copra, and timber are exported; pop. (est. 1995) 2 094 700; capital, Ambon (Amboina), pop. (1990) 206 260.

molybdenum /mə'lɪbdɪnəm/ *n.* silver-white metallic element added to steel to give strength and resistance to corrosion. [Greek *molubdos* lead]

mom *n. US colloq.* mother. [abbreviation of MOMMA]

Mombasa /mɒm'bæsə/ seaport and industrial city in SE Kenya, on the Indian Ocean; industries include oil refining; pop. (est. 1991) 600 000.

moment /'məʊmənt/ *n.* **1** very brief portion of time. **2** an exact point of time (*I came the moment you called*). **3** importance (*of no great moment*). **4** product of a force and the distance from its line of action to a point. □ **at the moment** now. **in a moment** very soon. **man** (or **woman** etc.) **of the moment** the one of importance at the time in question. [Latin: related to MOMENTUM]

momentary *adj.* lasting only a moment; transitory. □ **momentarily** *adv.* [Latin: related to MOMENT]

moment of truth *n.* time of crisis or test.

momentous /mə'mentəs/ *adj.* very important. □ **momentously** *adv.* **momentousness** *n.*

momentum /mə'mentəm/ *n.* (*pl.* **momenta**) **1** quantity of motion of a moving body, the product of its mass and velocity. **2** impetus gained by movement. **3** strength or continuity derived from an initial effort. [Latin *moveo* move]

momma /'mɒmə/ *n. US colloq.* mother. [var. of MAMA]

mommy /'mɒmɪ/ *n.* (*pl.* **-ies**) esp. *US colloq.* = MUMMY[1].

Mon. *abbr.* Monday.

monad /'mɒnæd, 'məʊ-/ *n.* **1** the number one; unit. **2** *Philos.* ultimate unit of being (e.g. a soul, an atom, a person, God). □ **monadic** /mə'nædɪk/ *adj.* [Greek *monas -ados* unit]

♦ **monadic testing** *n.* technique used in marketing research in which consumers are presented with a product to test on its own, rather than being asked to compare it with a competing product (see PAIRED COMPARISON).

Monaghan /'mɒnəhən/ **1** county in the N Republic of Ireland, in the province of Ulster; mainly agricultural, it also has a textile industry; pop. (est. 1991) 51 262. **2** its capital city; pop. (est. 1995) 6200.

Moldova /mɒl'dəʊvə/, **Republic of** country in SE Europe, bordered by Ukraine to the N and E and by Romania to the W, formerly (1940–92) a Soviet republic (see MOLDAVIA). Moldova declared its independence from the Soviet Union in 1991. Following independence ethnic Russians and Ukrainians declared independence from Moldova as the Transdniester republic; Moldova refused to recognize an independent Transdniester and war followed. In 1992 a cease-fire was declared; in the 1994 constitution Transdniester was recognized as an autonomous region. A 1995 referendum in Transdniester approved independence. Agriculture is the mainstay of the economy, the fertile land producing grapes and other fruit, vegetables, tobacco, wheat, and maize; there are wine-making and food-processing industries. Machinery is exported, although the industrial sector has been badly affected by civil war (which has continued since the republic became independent) between government forces, representing the majority ethnic Romanian population, and the Ukrainian and Russian minorities, who have declared independence as the Transdniester Republic. Parliamentary elections in 1998 resulted in the formation of a Communist-led coalition. President, Petru Lucinschi; capital, Kishinev. □ **Moldovan** *adj.* & *n.*

languages	Romanian (official), Russian
currency	leu (Moldovan) of 100 bani
pop. (1996)	4 372 000
GNP (1994)	US$3.8B
literacy	98% (m); 94% (f)
life expectancy	64 (m); 71 (f)

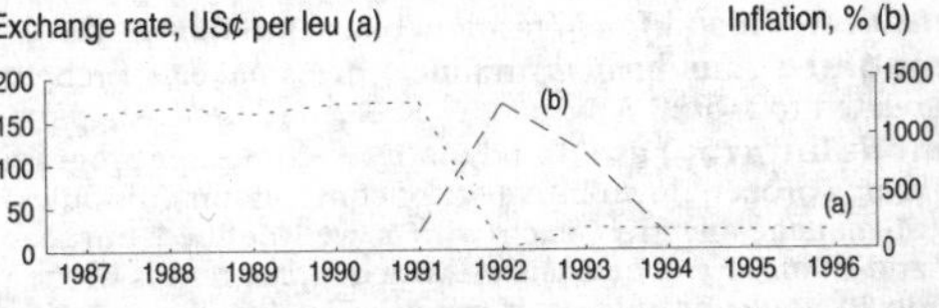

monarch /'mɒnək/ *n.* sovereign with the title of king, queen, emperor, empress, or equivalent. □ **monarchic** /mə'nɑːkɪk/ *adj.* **monarchical** /mə'nɑːkɪk(ə)l/ *adj.* [Greek: related to MONO-, *arkhō* rule]

monarchism *n.* advocacy of monarchy. □ **monarchist** *n.* [French: related to MONARCH]

monarchy *n.* (*pl.* **-ies**) **1** form of government with a monarch at the head. **2** state with this. □ **monarchial** /mə'nɑːkɪəl/ *adj.* [Greek: related to MONARCH]

monastery /'mɒnəstrɪ/ *n.* (*pl.* **-ies**) residence of a community of monks. [Latin *monasterium* from Greek *monazō* alone]

monastic /mə'næstɪk/ *adj.* of or like monasteries or monks, nuns, etc. □ **monastically** *adv.* **monasticism** /-ˌsɪz(ə)m/ *n.* [Greek: related to MONASTERY]

Monastir /ˌmɒnə'stɪə(r)/ resort town in E Tunisia; manufactures include textiles.

Mönchengladbach /ˌmʊnxən'glædbæx/ city in NW Germany; pop. (est. 1995) 266 073. Centre of the German textile industry, it is also the site of the NATO headquarters for N Europe.

Monday /'mʌndeɪ/ *–n.* day of the week following Sunday. *–adv. colloq.* **1** on Monday. **2** (**Mondays**) on Mondays; each Monday. [Old English]

MONEP /'mɒnep/ *abbr.* French traded options market. [French *Marché des Options Négotiables de Paris*]

♦ **monetarism** /'mʌnɪtəˌrɪz(ə)m/ *n.* **1** control of the supply of money as the chief method of stabilizing the economy. **2** school of thought advocating this. Based on the quantity theory of money, it relates the price level to the quantity of money in the economy. Latterly, monetarism has been the main opponent to Keynesianism, claiming that monetary factors are a major influence on the economy and that, in particular, government expansion of the money supply will tend to generate inflation rather than employment. Pure monetarism has, however, become confused with more general criticisms of Keynesianism by economic theorists and the crude distinction between monetarism and Keynesianism is misleading (see NEW CLASSICAL MACROECONOMICS). □ **monetarist** *n.* & *adj.*

monetary /'mʌnɪtərɪ/ *adj.* **1** of the currency in use. **2** of or consisting of money. [Latin: related to MONEY]

♦ **monetary aggregate** *n.* any of several measures of the money supply from the narrow M0 to the broad M5. See MONEY SUPPLY.

♦ **monetary assets and liabilities** *n.pl.* amounts receivable (assets) or payable (liabilities) that appear in a company's accounts as specific sums of money, e.g. cash and bank balances, loans, debtors and creditors. These are to be distinguished from such non-monetary items as plant and machinery, stock-in-trade, or equity investments, which although they are also expressed in accounts at a value (frequently cost) are not necessarily realizable at that value.

♦ **monetary compensatory amount** *n.* (also **MCA**) subsidies and taxes on farm products produced within the EC that form part of the Common Agricultural Policy. They are used to bridge the gap between the green pound and foreign exchange rates to prevent fluctuation in these rates from altering the farm prices. The object is to enable agricultural products to cost the same in all member countries and to prevent trading between countries in these products purely to make a profit as a result of changes in the exchange rate.

♦ **monetary economy** *n.* economy in which money is the medium of exchange. An economy based on barter is now extremely rare.

♦ **monetary inflation** *n.* **1** inflation related to the expansion of the money supply. **2** theory proposing this. See MONETARY POLICY; QUANTITY THEORY OF MONEY.

♦ **monetary policy** *n.* means by which governments try to affect macroeconomic conditions by increasing or decreasing the supply of money. Three main options are available: printing more money (now rarely used in practice); direct controls over money held by the monetary sector; open-market operations. The traditional Keynesian view has been that monetary policy is at best a blunt instrument (money does not matter), while monetarists have held the opposite view. The new classical macroeconomists, using the theory of rational expectations, have argued that monetary policy is ineffective if it is anticipated. In practice, governments have tended to employ 'tight' monetary policies, in the belief that this restrains inflation. Cf. FISCAL POLICY.

♦ **monetary reform** *n.* revision of a country's currency by the introduction of a new currency unit or a substantial change to an existing system. Examples include decimalization of the UK currency (1971) and the change from the austral to the peso in Argentina (1992).

♦ **monetary system** *n.* **1** system used by a country to provide the public with money for internal use and to control the exchange of its own currency with those of foreign countries. **2** system used by a country for implementing its monetary policy. **3** system used to control the exchange rate of a group of countries. See EUROPEAN MONETARY SYSTEM.

♦ **monetary theory** *n.* any theory concerned with the influence of the quantity of money in an economic system. See MONETARY POLICY; QUANTITY THEORY OF MONEY.

♦ **monetary unit** *n.* standard unit of currency in a country, related to monetary units of other countries by a foreign exchange rate.

♦ **monetization** /ˌmʌnɪtaɪ'zeɪʃ(ə)n/ *n.* sale of treasury bills to banks by the UK government to finance a budgetary deficit.

money /'mʌnɪ/ *n.* **1** coins and banknotes as a medium of exchange. Money functions as a unit of account and a store of value. Originally it enhanced economic development by enabling goods to be bought and sold without the need for barter. However, throughout history money has been beset by the problem of its debasement as a store of value as a result of inflation. Now that the supply of money is a monopoly of the state, most governments are committed in principle to stable prices. The central debate in economics over the past 50 years has been whether fiscal policy and monetary policy can have any effect other than to create inflation. **2** (*pl.* **-eys** or **-ies**) (in *pl.*) sums of money. **3 a** wealth. **b** wealth as power (*money talks*). **c** rich person or family (*married into money*). □ **for my money** in my opinion; for my preference. **in the money** *colloq.* having or winning a lot of money. **money for jam** (or **old rope**) *colloq.* profit for little or no trouble. [Latin *moneta*]

♦ **money at call and short notice** *n.* asset appearing in the balance sheet of a bank. It includes funds lent

---

Monaco /'mɒnəˌkəʊ/, **Principality of** country in S Europe on the Mediterranean coast, a small enclave within French territory near the Italian frontier. With no land available for agriculture, the service industries of banking, finance, and tourism are important to the economy. Manufacturing industries are mainly light, producing chemicals, pharmaceuticals, plastics, and micro-electronics. Monaco is largely dependent on imports from France, with which it maintains a customs union. It became a constitutional monarchy in 1911, although the constitution was briefly suspended in 1959–62. Head of state, Prince Rainier III; capital, Monaco-Ville, pop. (1982) 1234. □ **Monacan** *adj.* & *n.*

languages	French (official), English, Italian
currency	French franc (F) of 100 centimes
pop. (est. 1995)	30 600
GDP (1992)	US$596M
literacy	99% (m); 99% (f)
life expectancy	72 (m); 80 (f)

to discount houses, money brokers, the stock exchange, bullion brokers, corporate customers, and increasingly to other banks. 'At call' money is repayable on demand, whereas 'short notice' money implies that notice of repayment of up to 14 days will be given. After cash, money at call and short notice are the banks' most liquid assets. They are usu. interest-earning secured loans but their importance lies in providing the banks with an opportunity to use their surplus funds and to adjust their cash and liquidity requirements.

moneybags *n.pl.* (treated as *sing.*) *colloq.* usu. *derog.* wealthy person.

◆ **money broker** *n.* broker who arranges short-term loans in the money market, i.e. between banks, discount houses, and dealers in government securities. Money brokers do not themselves lend or borrow money; they work for a commission arranging loans on a day-to-day and overnight basis.

moneyed /'mʌnɪd/ *adj.* wealthy.

money-grubber *n. colloq.* person greedily intent on amassing money. □ **money-grubbing** *n.* & *adj.*

◆ **money illusion** *n. Econ.* belief that an increase in wages is of benefit to wage-earners, even if prices have increased by the same percentage. Keynesian theory concerning the role of the Phillips curve in reducing unemployment implicitly relied on the existence of the money illusion, which was one of the main reasons for the fall of Keynesianism.

◆ **moneylender** *n.* person whose business is to lend money at interest. The Consumer Credit Act (1974), which replaced the earlier Moneylenders Acts, excludes pawnbrokers, friendly and building societies, corporate bodies with special powers to lend money, banks, and insurance companies from this definition. The act requires all moneylenders to be registered, to obtain an annual licence to lend money, and to state the true annual percentage rate of interest at which a loan is made.

moneymaker *n.* **1** person who earns much money. **2** thing, idea, etc. that produces much money. □ **moneymaking** *n.* & *adj.*

◆ **money market** *n.* **1** trade in short-term stocks, loans, etc. In the UK, money brokers arrange for loans between the banks, the government, the discount houses and the accepting houses, with the Bank of England acting as lender of last resort. The main items of exchange are bills of exchange, treasury bills, and trade bills. The market takes place in and around Lombard Street in the City of London. Private investors, through their banks, can place deposits in the money market at a higher rate of interest than bank deposit accounts, for sums usu. in excess of £10,000. **2** the foreign-exchange market and the bullion market in addition to the short-term loan market.

money-market instrument *n.* financial instrument traded on a money market, usu. with a short-term life, such as a certificate of deposit.

money order *n.* order for payment of a specified sum, issued by a bank or Post Office.

money-spinner *n.* thing that brings in a profit.

◆ **money supply** *n.* quantity of money issued by a country's monetary authorities (usu. the central bank). If the demand for money is stable, the widely accepted quantity theory of money implies that increases in the money supply will lead directly to an increase in the price level, i.e. to inflation. Since the 1970s most Western governments have attempted to reduce inflation by controlling the money supply. This raises the issues of how to measure the money supply and how to control it (see INTEREST-RATE POLICY). In the UK various measures of the money supply have been used, from the very narrow M0 to the very broad M5:

M0 — notes and coins in circulation plus the banks' till money and the banks' balances with the Bank of England;

M1 — notes and coins in circulation plus private-sector current accounts and deposit accounts that can be transferred by cheque;

M2 — notes and coins in circulation plus non-interest-bearing bank deposits plus building society deposits plus National Savings accounts;

M3 — M1 plus all other private-sector bank deposits plus certificates of deposit;

M3c — M3 plus foreign currency bank deposits;

M4 — M1 plus most private-sector bank deposits plus holdings of money-market instruments (e.g. treasury bills);

M5 — M4 plus building society deposits.

◆ **money-supply rule** *n.* policy proposed by the new classical macroeconomists in which a government states in advance the extent to which it intends to expand the money supply. It is based on the belief that fiscal policy and monetary policy cannot affect the real variables in an economic situation but that uncertainty concerning government intentions can destabilize markets. In these circumstances a stable-policy rule is the best a government can achieve.

◆ **money wages** *n.pl.* wages expressed in money terms only, without taking inflation into account. Cf. REAL WAGES.

monger /'mʌŋgə(r)/ *n.* (usu. in *comb.*) **1** dealer, trader (*fishmonger*). **2** usu. *derog.* promoter, spreader (*warmonger*; *scaremonger*). [Latin *mango* dealer]

Mongol /'mɒŋg(ə)l/ *–adj.* **1** of the Asian people. **2** resembling this people. **3** (**mongol**) *offens.* suffering from

Mongolia /mɒŋ'gəʊlɪə/, **Republic of** large and sparsely populated country in NE Asia, bordered by Russia and China. The Mongolians are traditionally nomadic herders of sheep, goats, horses, cattle, and camels. Animal herding remains the major source of employment; wool, hides, and other animal products are exported. After the adoption of Communist policies the land was collectivized into huge cooperatives and state farms in the 1950s. With aid from other socialist states, esp. the former Soviet Union, industrialization developed but this aid has now ceased. The chief manufactures are food products, beverages, tobacco, textiles, leather goods, and wood products. Copper and molybdenum, mined in N Mongolia, provide a large proportion of export revenue; other minerals include coal, oil, gold, tungsten, lead, and uranium.
History. The centre of the medieval Mongol empire, Mongolia subsequently became a Chinese province, achieving de facto independence in 1911. In 1924 it became a Communist state, the Mongolian People's Republic, after the Soviet model. Free elections were held in 1990 and a new constitution, adopted in 1992, introduced a free-market economy. In 1996 the former communists suffered electoral defeat, ending 75 years of communist rule. President, Natsagiin Bagabandi; prime minister, Mendsaihany Enkhsahan; capital, Ulan Bator.

languages	Mongolian (official), Chinese, Russian
currency	tugrik of 100 möngö
pop. (1996)	2 334 000
GNP (1994)	US$801M
literacy	88% (m); 77% (f)
life expectancy	64 (m); 67 (f)

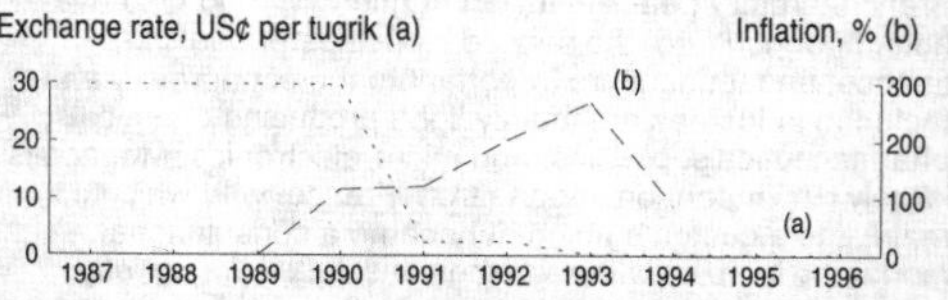

Down's syndrome. *–n.* **1** Mongolian. **2** (**mongol**) *offens.* person suffering from Down's syndrome. [native name: perhaps from *mong* brave]

Mongolian /mɒŋ'gəʊlɪən/ *–n.* **1** native or inhabitant of Mongolia. **2** language of Mongolia. *–adj.* of or relating to Mongolia or its people or language.

mongolism /'mɒŋgə,lɪz(ə)m/ *n.* = DOWN'S SYNDROME.

■ **Usage** The term *Down's syndrome* is now preferred.

Mongoloid /'mɒŋgə,lɔɪd/ *–adj.* **1** characteristic of the Mongolians, esp. in having a broad flat yellowish face. **2** (**mongoloid**) *offens.* having the characteristic symptoms of Down's syndrome. *–n.* Mongoloid or mongoloid person.

mongoose /'mɒŋguːs/ *n.* (*pl.* **-s**) small flesh-eating civet-like mammal. [Marathi]

mongrel /'mʌŋgr(ə)l/ *–n.* **1** dog of no definable type or breed. **2** other animal or plant resulting from the crossing of different breeds or types. *–adj.* of mixed origin, nature, or character. [related to MINGLE]

monies see MONEY 2.

monism /'mɒnɪz(ə)m/ *n.* **1** doctrine that only one ultimate principle or being exists. **2** theory denying the duality of matter and mind. □ **monist** *n.* **monistic** /-'nɪstɪk/ *adj.* [Greek *monos* single]

monitor /'mɒnɪt(ə)r/ *–n.* **1** person or device for checking or warning. **2** school pupil with disciplinary or other special duties. **3 a** television receiver used in a studio to select or verify the picture being broadcast. **b** simple television receiver that can be used as one of the components of a microcomputer system. **4** person who listens to and reports on foreign broadcasts etc. **5** detector of radioactive contamination. *–v.* **1** act as a monitor of. **2** maintain regular surveillance over. **3** regulate the strength of (a recorded or transmitted signal). [Latin *moneo* warn]

monitory /'mɒnɪtərɪ/ *adj. literary* giving or serving as a warning. [Latin *monitorius*: related to MONITOR]

monk /mʌŋk/ *n.* member of a religious community of men living under vows. □ **monkish** *adj.* [Greek *monakhos* from *monos* alone]

monkey /'mʌŋkɪ/ *–n.* (*pl.* **-eys**) **1** any of various primates, including marmosets, baboons etc., esp. a small long-tailed kind. **2** mischievous person, esp. a child. *–v.* (**-eys, -eyed**) **1** (often foll. by *with*) tamper or play mischievous tricks. **2** (foll. by *around, about*) fool around. [origin unknown]

monkey business *n. colloq.* mischief.

monkey-nut *n.* peanut.

monkey-puzzle *n.* tree with hanging prickly branches.

monkey tricks *n.pl. colloq.* mischief.

monkey wrench *n.* wrench with an adjustable jaw.

monkshood /'mʌŋkshʊd/ *n.* poisonous plant with hood-shaped flowers.

mono /'mɒnəʊ/ *colloq. –adj.* monophonic. *–n.* monophonic reproduction. [abbreviation]

mono- *comb. form* (usu. **mon-** before a vowel) one, alone, single. [Greek *monos* alone]

monochromatic /,mɒnəkrə'mætɪk/ *adj.* **1** (of light or other radiation) of a single colour or wavelength. **2** containing only one colour. □ **monochromatically** *adv.*

monochrome /'mɒnə,krəʊm/ *–n.* photograph or picture done in one colour or different tones of this, or in black and white only. *–adj.* having or using only one colour or in black and white only. [from MONO-, Greek *khrōma* colour]

monocle /'mɒnək(ə)l/ *n.* single eyeglass. □ **monocled** *adj.* [Latin: related to MONO-, *oculus* eye]

monocotyledon /,mɒnə,kɒtɪ'liːd(ə)n/ *n.* flowering plant with one cotyledon. □ **monocotyledonous** *adj.*

monocular /mə'nɒkjʊlə(r)/ *adj.* with or for one eye. [related to MONOCLE]

monody /'mɒnədɪ/ *n.* (*pl.* **-ies**) **1** ode sung by a single actor in a Greek tragedy. **2** poem lamenting a person's death. □ **monodist** *n.* [Greek: related to MONO-, ODE]

monogamy /mə'nɒgəmɪ/ *n.* practice or state of being married to one person at a time. □ **monogamous** *adj.* [Greek *gamos* marriage]

monogram /'mɒnə,græm/ *n.* two or more letters, esp. a person's initials, interwoven as a device.

monograph /'mɒnə,grɑːf/ *n.* treatise on a single subject.

monolingual /,mɒnəʊ'lɪŋgw(ə)l/ *adj.* speaking or using only one language.

monolith /'mɒnəlɪθ/ *n.* **1** single block of stone, esp. shaped into a pillar etc. **2** person or thing like a monolith in being massive, immovable, or solidly uniform. □ **monolithic** /-'lɪθɪk/ *adj.* [Greek *lithos* stone]

monologue /'mɒnə,lɒg/ *n.* **1 a** scene in a drama in which a person speaks alone. **b** dramatic composition for one performer. **2** long speech by one person in a conversation etc. [French from Greek *monologos* speaking alone]

monomania /,mɒnə'meɪnɪə/ *n.* obsession by a single idea or interest. □ **monomaniac** *n.* & *adj.*

monophonic /,mɒnə'fɒnɪk/ *adj.* (of sound-reproduction) using only one channel of transmission. [Greek *phōnē* sound]

monoplane /'mɒnə,pleɪn/ *n.* aeroplane with one set of wings.

♦ **Monopolies and Mergers Commission** *n.* (also **MMC**) commission established in the UK in 1948 as the Monopolies and Restrictive Practices Commission and reconstructed under its present title by the Fair Trading Act (1973). It investigates questions referred to it on unregistered monopolies relating to the supply of goods in the UK, the transfer of newspapers, mergers qualifying for investigation under the Fair Trading Act, and uncompetitive practices and restrictive labour practices, including public-sector monopolies as laid down in the provisions of the Competition Act (1980).

---

monopolist /mə'nɒpəlɪst/ *n.* person who has or advocates a monopoly. □ **monopolistic** /-'lɪstɪk/ *adj.*

monopolize /mə'nɒpə,laɪz/ *v.* (also **-ise**) (**-zing** or **-sing**) **1** obtain exclusive possession or control of (a trade or commodity etc.). **2** dominate or prevent others from sharing in (a conversation etc.). □ **monopolization** /-'zeɪʃ(ə)n/ *n.* **monopolizer** *n.*

♦ **monopoly** /mə'nɒpəlɪ/ *n.* (*pl.* **-ies**) **1 a** possession or control of the trade in a commodity or service by a single seller or producer. **b** market in which this operates. A monopoly in which there are many buyers (consumers) is usu. considered inefficient, since self-interest will lead the monopolist to produce less than is Pareto-optimal and at a higher price (cf. MONOPSONY). In the process the monopolist will earn pure economic profits, reflecting this privileged position. Governments usu. try to eliminate, regulate, or nationalize monopolies. See also PRICE DISCRIMINATION. **2** (foll. by *of*, *US on*) exclusive possession, control, or exercise. [Greek *pōleō* sell]

♦ **monopsony** /mə'nɒpsənɪ/ *n.* market in which there is only a single buyer. The combination of monopsony and monopoly is a **bilateral monopoly**. If there are many sellers, the buyer may be able to exploit this market position, a situation in which governments frequently find themselves. However, the buyer will not be able to drive prices below those necessary to achieve normal economic profits (in the same way that a monopolist drives prices higher), since in this case an entrepreneur would either become bankrupt or leave the market. □ **monopsonist** *n.* [Greek *opsōnia* purchase]

---

monorail /'mɒnəʊ,reɪl/ *n.* railway with a single-rail track.

monosodium glutamate /,mɒnəʊ'səʊdɪəm 'gluːtə,meɪt/ *n.* sodium salt of glutamic acid used to enhance the flavour of food. [Latin *gluten* glue]

monosyllable /'mɒnə,sɪləb(ə)l/ *n.* word of one syllable. □ **monosyllabic** /-'læbɪk/ *adj.*

monotheism /'mɒnə,θiːɪz(ə)m/ *n.* doctrine that there is only one god. □ **monotheist** *n.* **monotheistic** /-'ɪstɪk/ *adj.*

monotone /'mɒnə,təʊn/ *–n.* **1** sound or utterance continuing or repeated on one note without change of pitch. **2** sameness of style in writing. *–adj.* without change of pitch.

monotonous /mə'nɒtənəs/ *adj.* lacking in variety; tedious through sameness. □ **monotonously** *adv.* **monotony** *n.*

monovalent /ˌmɒnə'veɪlənt/ *adj.* univalent.

monoxide /mə'nɒksaɪd/ *n.* oxide containing one oxygen atom.

Monrovia /mɒn'rəʊvɪə/ capital and chief port of Liberia; pop. (est. 1990) 668 000.

Mons /mɒnz/ (Flemish **Bergen** /'beəxən/) city in Belgium; industries include oil processing, textiles, tobacco, and porcelain; pop. (est. 1995) 92 666.

Monseigneur /ˌmɒnsen'jɜː(r)/ *n.* (*pl.* ***Messeigneurs*** /ˌmesen'jɜː(r)/) title given to an eminent French person, esp. a prince, cardinal, archbishop, or bishop. [French *mon* my, SEIGNEUR]

Monsieur /mə'sjɜː(r)/ *n.* (*pl.* **Messieurs** /me'sjɜː(r)/) title used of or to a French-speaking man, corresponding to Mr or sir. [French *mon* my, *sieur* lord]

Monsignor /mɒn'siːnjə(r)/ *n.* (*pl.* ***-nori*** /-'njɔːrɪ/) title of various Roman Catholic priests and officials. [Italian: related to MONSEIGNEUR]

monsoon /mɒn'suːn/ *n.* **1** wind in S Asia, esp. in the Indian Ocean. **2** rainy season accompanying the summer monsoon. [Arabic *mawsim*]

monster *n.* **1** imaginary creature, usu. large and frightening, made up of incongruous elements. **2** inhumanly cruel or wicked person. **3** misshapen animal or plant. **4** large, usu. ugly, animal or thing. **5** (*attrib.*) huge. [Latin *monstrum* from *moneo* warn]

monstrance *n. RC Ch.* vessel in which the host is exposed for veneration. [Latin *monstro* show]

monstrosity /mɒn'strɒsɪtɪ/ *n.* (*pl.* **-ies**) **1** huge or outrageous thing. **2** monstrousness. **3** = MONSTER 3. [Latin: related to MONSTROUS]

monstrous *adj.* **1** like a monster; abnormally formed. **2** huge. **3 a** outrageously wrong or absurd. **b** atrocious. □ **monstrously** *adv.* **monstrousness** *n.* [Latin: related to MONSTER]

Mont. *abbr.* Montana.

montage /mɒn'tɑːʒ/ *n.* **1** selection, cutting, and piecing together as a consecutive whole, of separate sections of cinema or television film. **2 a** composite whole made from juxtaposed photographs etc. **b** production of this. [French: related to MOUNT[1]]

Montana /mɒn'tænə/ state in the N US, bordering on Canada; pop. (est. 1996) 879 372; capital, Helena. Agriculture, esp. cattle ranching and wheat farming, is important; there is also mining of copper and other minerals.

Monte Carlo /ˌmɒntɪ 'kɑːləʊ/ one of the four communes of Monaco, famous as a gambling resort and as the terminus of a car rally; pop. (1985) 12 000.

Montego Bay /mɒn'teɪgəʊ/ free port and tourist resort in Jamaica, on the N coast; pop. (1991) 83 446.

Montenegro /ˌmɒntɪ'niːgrəʊ/ constituent republic of the Federal Republic of Yugoslavia, allied with Serbia (see YUGOSLAVIA); raising of livestock, esp. sheep, goats, and cattle, is important; pop. (est. 1995) 635 000; capital, Podgorica. □ **Montenegrin** *adj.* & *n.*

Monterrey /ˌmɒnte'reɪ/ city in NE Mexico, capital of Nueva León state; industries include metallurgy, chemicals, and textiles; pop. (1990) 2 251 697.

Montevideo /ˌmɒntɪvɪ'deɪəʊ/ capital and chief port of Uruguay; industries include meat packing, wool processing, and textiles; pop. (1996) 1 378 707.

Montgomery /mɒnt'gʌmerɪ, -'gɒmərɪ/ industrial city and agricultural trading centre in the US, capital of Alabama; manufactures include fertilizers and furniture; pop. (est. 1994) 195 471.

month /mʌnθ/ *n.* **1** (in full **calendar month**) **a** each of twelve periods into which a year is divided. **b** period of time between the same dates in successive calendar months. **2** period of 28 days. [Old English]

monthly *–adj.* done, produced, or occurring once every month. *–adv.* every month. *–n.* (*pl.* **-ies**) monthly periodical.

♦ *Monthly Digest of Statistics* *n.* monthly publication of the UK Central Statistical Office providing statistical information on industry, national income, and the UK population.

---

month of Sundays *n. colloq.* very long period.

Montpelier /mɒnt'peljə(r)/ city in the US, capital of Vermont; pop. (1990) 8247.

Montpellier /mɔ̃'pelɪeɪ/ city in S France; pop. (1990) 210 866. A centre for trade in wine and brandy, it has various manufacturing industries.

Montreal /ˌmɒntrɪ'ɔːl/ city in Canada, a port on the St Lawrence River and commercial centre of Quebec; city pop. (1995) 1 017 666; metropolitan area pop. (1995) 3 328 300. Its many industries include oil refining, aircraft manufacture, brewing, and meat packing.

Montreux /mɔ̃'trɜː/ resort town in Switzerland, on Lake Geneva; pop. (est. 1990) 19 850. An annual television festival (first held in 1961) takes place here in the spring.

Montserrat /ˌmɒntsə'ræt/ British Crown Colony comprising one of the Leeward Islands in the West Indies. In 1997 a massive volcanic eruption rendered some two-thirds of the island (including the capital, Plymouth) uninhabitable and caused about half the population (previously some 12,000) to leave. Its economy was based on tourism and related industries and agriculture.

monument /'mɒnjʊmənt/ *n.* **1** anything enduring that serves to commemorate or celebrate, esp. a structure or building. **2** stone etc. placed over a grave or in a church etc. in memory of the dead. **3** ancient building or site etc. that has been preserved. **4** lasting reminder. [Latin *moneo* remind]

monumental /ˌmɒnjʊ'ment(ə)l/ *adj.* **1 a** extremely great; stupendous (*monumental effort*). **b** (of a work of art etc.) massive and permanent. **2** of or serving as a monument. □ **monumentally** *adv.*

monumental mason *n.* maker of tombstones etc.

moo *–n.* (*pl.* **-s**) cry of cattle. *–v.* (**moos, mooed**) make this sound. [imitative]

mooch *v. colloq.* **1** (usu. foll. by *about, around*) wander aimlessly around. **2** esp. *US* cadge; steal. [probably from French *muchier* skulk]

mood[1] *n.* **1** state of mind or feeling. **2** fit of bad temper or depression. □ **in the mood** (usu. foll. by *for*, or *to* + infin.) inclined. [Old English]

mood[2] *n.* **1** *Gram.* form or set of forms of a verb indicating whether it expresses a fact, command, wish, etc. (*subjunctive mood*). **2** distinction of meaning expressed by different moods. [alteration of MODE]

moody *–adj.* (**-ier, -iest**) given to changes of mood; gloomy, sullen. *–n.* (*pl.* **-ies**) *colloq.* bad mood; tantrum. □ **moodily** *adv.* **moodiness** *n.* [related to MOOD[1]]

moon *–n.* **1 a** natural satellite of the earth, orbiting it monthly, illuminated by the sun and reflecting some light to the earth. **b** this regarded in terms of its waxing and waning in a particular month (*new moon*). **c** the moon when visible (*there is no moon tonight*). **2** satellite of any planet. **3** (prec. by *the*) *colloq.* something desirable but unattainable (*promised them the moon*). *–v.* **1** wander about aimlessly or listlessly. **2** *slang* expose one's buttocks. □ **many moons ago** a long time ago. **moon over** act dreamily thinking about (a loved one). **over the moon** *colloq.* extremely happy. □ **moonless** *adj.* [Old English]

moonbeam *n.* ray of moonlight.

moon boot *n.* thickly-padded boot for low temperatures.

moon-face *n.* round face.

Moonie /'muːnɪ/ *n. colloq.* member of the Unification Church. [Sun Myung *Moon*, name of its founder]

moonlight *–n.* **1** light of the moon. **2** (*attrib.*) lit by the moon. *–v.* (**-lighted**) *colloq.* have two paid occupations, esp. a full-time daytime job and a part-time evening job. □ **moonlighter** *n.*

moonlight flit *n.* hurried departure by night, esp. to avoid paying a debt.

moonlit *adj.* lit by the moon.

moonscape *n.* **1** surface or landscape of the moon. **2** area resembling this; wasteland.

moonshine *n.* **1** foolish or unrealistic talk or ideas. **2** *slang* illicitly distilled or smuggled alcohol.

moonshot *n.* launching of a spacecraft to the moon.

moonstone *n.* feldspar of pearly appearance.

moonstruck *adj.* slightly mad.

moony *adj.* (**-ier, -iest**) listless; stupidly dreamy.

Moor /mʊə(r), mɔː(r)/ *n.* member of a Muslim people of NW Africa. □ **Moorish** *adj.* [Greek *Mauros*]

moor[1] /mʊə(r), mɔː(r)/ *n.* **1** open uncultivated upland, esp. when covered with heather. **2** tract of ground preserved for shooting. [Old English]

moor[2] /mʊə(r), mɔː(r)/ *v.* attach (a boat etc.) to a fixed object. □ **moorage** *n.* [probably Low German]

moorhen *n.* small waterfowl.

mooring *n.* **1** (often in *pl.*) place where a boat etc. is moored. **2** (in *pl.*) set of permanent anchors and chains.

moorland *n.* extensive area of moor.

moose *n.* (*pl.* same) North American deer; elk. [Narragansett]

Moose Jaw industrial town in Canada, in S central Saskatchewan; industries include oil refining and food processing; pop. (est. 1991) 33 593.

moot *–adj.* debatable, undecided (*moot point*). *–v.* raise (a question) for discussion. *–n. hist.* assembly. [Old English]

mop *–n.* **1** bundle of yarn or cloth or a sponge on the end of a stick, for cleaning floors etc. **2** similarly-shaped implement for various purposes. **3** thick mass of hair. **4** mopping or being mopped (*gave it a mop*). *–v.* (**-pp-**) **1** wipe or clean with or as with a mop. **2 a** wipe tears or sweat etc. from (one's face etc.). **b** wipe away (tears etc.). □ **mop up 1** wipe up with or as with a mop. **2** *colloq.* absorb. **3** dispatch; make an end of. **4 a** complete the occupation of (a district etc.) by capturing or killing enemy troops left there. **b** capture or kill (stragglers). [origin uncertain]

mope *–v.* (**-ping**) **1** be depressed or listless. **2** wander about listlessly. *–n.* person who mopes. □ **mopy** *adj.* (**-ier, -iest**). [origin unknown]

moped /ˈməʊped/ *n.* two-wheeled low-powered motor vehicle with pedals. [Swedish: related to MOTOR, PEDAL]

Mopti /ˈmɒptɪ/ city in central Mali, at the junction of the Niger and Bani rivers; pop. (1987) 73 979. It is the commercial centre of an agricultural region.

moquette /mɒˈket/ *n.* thick pile or looped material used for upholstery etc. [French]

moraine /məˈreɪn/ *n.* area of debris carried down and deposited by a glacier. [French]

moral /ˈmɒr(ə)l/ *–adj.* **1 a** concerned with goodness or badness of human character or behaviour, or with the distinction between right and wrong. **b** concerned with accepted rules and standards of human behaviour. **2 a** virtuous in general conduct. **b** capable of moral action. **3** (of rights or duties etc.) founded on moral not actual law. **4** associated with the psychological rather than the physical (*moral courage*; *moral support*). *–n.* **1** moral lesson of a fable, story, event, etc. **2** (in *pl.*) moral behaviour, e.g. in sexual conduct. □ **morally** *adv.* [Latin *mos mor-* custom]

morale /məˈrɑːl/ *n.* confidence, determination, etc. of a person or group. [French *moral*: related to MORAL]

♦ **moral hazard** *n. Insurance* incentive to cheat in the absence of penalties for cheating. This is often associated with **adverse selection**, the incentive to conceal information about one's true nature. A typical example of a person exposed to moral hazard is the owner of an insured car, who has little or no incentive to guard against theft; an example of adverse selection occurs when a person purchasing health insurance has no incentive to reveal health problems that might require treatment. The effect is to make health insurance more expensive for everyone else.

---

moralist /ˈmɒrəlɪst/ *n.* **1** person who practises or teaches morality. **2** person who follows a natural system of ethics. □ **moralistic** /-ˈlɪstɪk/ *adj.*

morality /məˈrælɪtɪ/ *n.* (*pl.* **-ies**) **1** degree of conformity to moral principles. **2** right moral conduct. **3** science of morals. **4** particular system of morals (*commercial morality*).

morality play *n. hist.* drama with personified abstract qualities and including a moral lesson.

moralize /ˈmɒrə,laɪz/ *v.* (also **-ise**) (**-zing** or **-sing**) **1** (often foll. by *on*) indulge in moral reflection or talk. **2** make moral or more moral. □ **moralization** /-ˈzeɪʃ(ə)n/ *n.*

moral law *n.* the conditions to be satisfied by any right course of action.

moral philosophy *n.* branch of philosophy concerned with ethics.

moral victory *n.* defeat that has some of the satisfactory elements of victory.

morass /məˈræs/ *n.* **1** entanglement; confusion. **2** *literary* bog. [French *marais* related to MARSH]

♦ **moratorium** /,mɒrəˈtɔːrɪəm/ *n.* (*pl.* **-s** or **-ria**) **1** (often foll. by *on*) temporary prohibition or suspension (of an activity). **2 a** agreement between a creditor and a debtor to postpone payment of the debt. For example, repayment of all the trading debts in a particular market might be suspended as a result of some exceptional crisis in the market. In these circumstances, not to call a moratorium would probably lead to more insolvencies than the market could stand. The intention is to give firms time to find out exactly what their liabilities are and make the necessary financial arrangements to settle these liabilities. **b** period of this postponement. [Latin *moror* delay]

---

morbid *adj.* **1 a** (of the mind, ideas, etc.) unwholesome. **b** given to morbid feelings. **2** *colloq.* melancholy. **3** *Med.* of the nature of or indicative of disease. □ **morbidity** /-ˈbɪdɪtɪ/ *n.* **morbidly** *adv.* [Latin *morbus* disease]

mordant /ˈmɔːd(ə)nt/ *–adj.* **1** (of sarcasm etc.) caustic, biting. **2** pungent, smarting. **3** corrosive or cleansing. **4** serving to fix dye. *–n.* mordant substance. [Latin *mordeo* bite]

more /mɔː(r)/ *–adj.* greater in quantity or degree; additional (*more problems than last time*; *bring some more water*). *–n.* greater quantity, number, or amount (*more than three people*; *more to it than meets the eye*). *–adv.* **1** to a greater degree or extent. **2** forming the comparative of adjectives and adverbs, esp. those of more than one syllable (*more absurd*; *more easily*). □ **more and more** to an increasing degree. **more of** to a greater extent. **more or less** approximately; effectively; nearly. **what is more** as an additional point. [Old English]

moreish /ˈmɔːrɪʃ/ *adj.* (also **morish**) *colloq.* (of food) causing a desire for more.

morello /məˈreləʊ/ *n.* (*pl.* **-s**) sour kind of dark cherry. [Italian, = blackish]

Morelos /məˈreɪlɒs/ state of central Mexico; the economy is based on agriculture; pop. (est. 1995) 1 442 587; capital, Cuernavaca.

moreover /mɔːˈrəʊvə(r)/ *adv.* besides, in addition to what has been said.

mores /ˈmɔːreɪz/ *n.pl.* customs or conventions of a community. [Latin, pl. of *mos* custom]

morganatic /,mɔːgəˈnætɪk/ *adj.* **1** (of a marriage) between a person of high rank and one of lower rank, the spouse and children having no claim to the possessions or title of the person of higher rank. **2** (of a spouse) married in this way. [Latin *morganaticus* from Germanic, = 'morning gift', from a husband to his wife on the morning after consummation of a marriage]

morgue /mɔːg/ *n.* **1** mortuary. **2** (in a newspaper office) room or file of miscellaneous information. [French, originally the name of a Paris mortuary]

♦ **MORI** /ˈmɔːrɪ/ *abbr.* (also **Mori**) = MARKET AND OPINION RESEARCH INTERNATIONAL.

moribund /ˈmɒrɪˌbʌnd/ *adj.* **1** at the point of death. **2** lacking vitality. [Latin *morior* die]

morish var. of MOREISH.

♦ **Morita** /mɒˈriːtə/, **Akio** (1921–) Japanese business executive, co-founder and chairman (since 1976) of the Sony Corporation. Sony bought up many firms in the 1980s, including CBS records and Columbia pictures. In 1989 Akio tarnished his image in the US when he contributed to an anti-American book.

Mormon /ˈmɔːmən/ *n.* member of the Church of Jesus Christ of Latter-Day Saints. □ **Mormonism** *n.* [*Mormon*, name of the supposed author of the book on which Mormonism is founded]

morn *n. poet.* morning. [Old English]

mornay /ˈmɔːneɪ/ *n.* cheese-flavoured white sauce. [origin uncertain]

morning *n.* **1** early part of the day, ending at noon or lunch-time (*this morning*; *during the morning*). **2** *attrib.* taken, occurring, or appearing during the morning (*morning coffee*). □ **in the morning** *colloq.* tomorrow morning. [from MORN]

morning after *n. colloq.* = HANGOVER 1.

morning-after pill *n.* contraceptive pill taken some hours after intercourse.

morning coat *n.* coat with tails, and with the front cut away.

morning dress *n.* man's morning coat and striped trousers.

morning glory *n.* twining plant with trumpet-shaped flowers.

morning sickness *n.* nausea felt in the morning in esp. early pregnancy.

morning star *n.* planet, usu. Venus, seen in the east before sunrise.

morocco /məˈrɒkəʊ/ *n.* (*pl.* **-s**) fine flexible leather of goatskin tanned with sumac. [MOROCCO]

moron /ˈmɔːrɒn/ *n.* **1** *colloq.* very stupid person. **2** adult with a mental age of 8–12. □ **moronic** /məˈrɒnɪk/ *adj.* [Greek *mōros* foolish]

Moroni /məˈrəʊnɪ/ capital of the Comoros, on the island of Great Comoro; manufactures include soft drinks, cement, metal products, and processed essential oils; pop. (1991) 30 000.

morose /məˈrəʊs/ *adj.* sullen, gloomy. □ **morosely** *adv.* **moroseness** *n.* [Latin *mos mor-* manner]

morpheme /ˈmɔːfiːm/ *n. Linguistics* meaningful unit of a language that cannot be further divided (e.g. *in*, *come*, *-ing*, forming *incoming*). [Greek *morphē* form]

morphia /ˈmɔːfɪə/ *n.* (in general use) = MORPHINE.

morphine /ˈmɔːfiːn/ *n.* narcotic drug from opium, used to relieve pain. [Latin *Morpheus* god of sleep]

morphology /mɔːˈfɒlədʒɪ/ *n.* the study of the forms of things, esp. of animals and plants and of words and their structure. □ **morphological** /-fəˈlɒdʒɪk(ə)l/ *adj.* [Greek *morphē* form]

morris dance /ˈmɒrɪs/ *n.* traditional English dance in fancy costume, with ribbons and bells. □ **morris dancer** *n.* **morris dancing** *n.* [*morys*, var. of *Moorish*: related to MOOR]

morrow *n.* (usu. prec. by *the*) *literary* the following day. [related to MORN]

Morse /mɔːs/ *–n.* (in full **Morse code**) code in which letters are represented by combinations of long and short light or sound signals. *–v.* (**-sing**) signal by Morse code. [*Morse*, name of an electrician]

morsel /ˈmɔːs(ə)l/ *n.* mouthful; small piece (esp. of food). [Latin *morsus* bite]

mortal *–adj.* **1** subject to death. **2** causing death; fatal. **3** (of combat) fought to the death. **4** associated with death (*mortal agony*). **5** (of an enemy) implacable. **6** (of pain, fear, an affront, etc.) intense, very serious. **7** *colloq.* long and tedious (*for two mortal hours*). **8** *colloq.* conceivable, imaginable (*every mortal thing*; *of no mortal use*). *–n.* human being. □ **mortally** *adv.* [Latin *mors mort-* death]

mortality /mɔːˈtælɪtɪ/ *n.* (*pl.* **-ies**) **1** being subject to death. **2** loss of life on a large scale. **3 a** number of deaths in a given period etc. **b** MORTALITY RATE.

♦ **mortality rate** *n.* (also **death rate**) number of deaths per 1000 of the average population in a given year. It can be subdivided into different rates for different age groups of the population and for different regions.

♦ **mortality table** *n.* (also **life table**) actuarial table prepared on the basis of mortality rates for people in different occupations in different regions of a country. It provides life-assurance companies with the information they require to quote for life-assurance policies, annuities, etc.

mortal sin *n.* sin that deprives the soul of divine grace.

mortar /ˈmɔːtə(r)/ *–n.* **1** mixture of lime or cement, sand, and water, for bonding bricks or stones. **2** short large-bore cannon for firing shells at high angles. **3** vessel in which ingredients are pounded with a pestle. *–v.* **1** plaster or join with mortar. **2** bombard with mortar shells. [Latin *mortarium*]

Morocco /məˈrɒkəʊ/, **Kingdom of** country in the NW corner of Africa, with coastlines on the Mediterranean Sea and Atlantic Ocean. The economy is sustained by a well-developed mining industry, the country being one of the leading exporters of phosphates; other mineral exports include fluorite, barytes, manganese, iron ore, lead, and zinc. Agriculture, however, remains the main occupation of the population. Crops include cereals, citrus fruit, olives, beans, and chick-peas; fruit and vegetables are the main agricultural exports. The industrial sector includes the manufacture of phosphate products (esp. fertilizers and phosphoric acid), oil refining, cement production, and food processing. There is a fishing industry, canned sardines being exported, and tourism is important, though adversely affected by the Gulf War.

History. Morocco was penetrated by the Portuguese in the 15th century and later fell under French and Spanish influence, each country establishing protectorates in the early 20th century. It became an independent state after the withdrawal of the colonial powers in 1956. The entire territory of Western Sahara came under Moroccan control in 1979 (see WESTERN SAHARA); a referendum on the future of the region, in which there are demands for independence, has been expected since 1992 but has not taken place as agreement on voter eligibility cannot be agreed. Head of state, King Hassan II; prime minister, Abdellatif Filal; capital, Rabat. □ **Moroccan** *adj.* & *n.*

languages	Arabic (official), Berber, French
currency	dirham (DH) of 100 centimes
pop. (1996)	26 736 000
GNP (1994)	US$30B
literacy	56% (m); 31% (f)
life expectancy	67 (m); 71 (f)

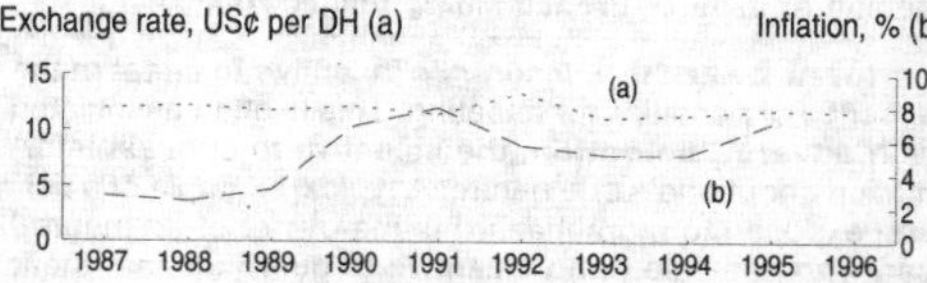

mortarboard *n.* **1** academic cap with a stiff flat square top. **2** flat board for holding mortar.

♦ **mortgage** /'mɔːgɪdʒ/ *–n.* **1** right in property created as security for a loan (usu. for the purchase of the property) or payment of a debt and terminated on payment of the loan or debt. The borrower (mortgager), who offers the security, is usu. a house purchaser; the lender (mortgagee), who provides the money, is usu. a building society or bank. In theory, the mortgagee always has the right to take possession of mortgaged property even if there has been no default. This right is usu. excluded by building-society mortgages until default. Where residential property is concerned, the court has power to delay the recovery of possession if there is a realistic possibility that the default will be remedied in a reasonable time. In case of default, the mortgagee has a statutory right to sell the property, but this will usu. be exercised after obtaining possession first. Any surplus after the debt and the mortgagee's expenses have been met must be paid to the mortgager. The mortgagee also has a statutory right to appoint a receiver to manage mortgaged property in the event of default; this power is useful where business property is concerned. As a final resort, a mortgage may be brought to an end by foreclosure, in which the court orders the transfer of the property to the mortgagee. The court will not order foreclosure where a sale would be more appropriate. **2** sum of money lent in this transaction. A building-society or bank mortgage is repaid over a fixed period (often 25 years) by instalments, either of capital and interest (**repayment mortgage**) or of interest only, with other arrangements being made to repay the capital, e.g. by means of an endowment assurance policy (this is known as an **endowment mortgage**). See also MORTGAGE INTEREST RELIEF. **3** deed effecting this transaction. See also SECOND MORTGAGE. *–v.* (**-ging**) convey (a property) by mortgage. □ **mortgageable** *adj.* [French, = dead pledge: related to GAGE[1]]

♦ **mortgage-backed security** *n.* bond or note in which collateral is provided by a mortgage or a portfolio of mortgages, usu. insured to cover any defaults.

♦ **mortgage debenture** *n.* loan made to a company by an investor, secured on the real property of the company. See DEBENTURE.

♦ **mortgagee** /ˌmɔːgɪ'dʒiː/ *n.* creditor in a mortgage.

♦ **mortgagee in possession** *n.* mortgagee who has exercised the right to take possession of the mortgaged property; this may happen at any time, even if there has been no default by the mortgager. However, the mortgage deed may contain an agreement not to do this unless there is default and a court order will be needed to obtain possession in the case of a dwelling house. The court may adjourn the hearing to allow the mortgager time to pay. The mortgagee will either receive the rents and profits if the property has been let or be empowered to manage the property. The mortgagee is not entitled to reap any personal benefit beyond repayment of the interest and the principal debt, must carry out reasonable repairs, and must not damage the property.

♦ **mortgage interest relief** *n.* income-tax allowance on the value of the interest paid on mortgages up to a specified figure (currently £30,000) to which a mortgager is entitled if the mortgaged property is his or her main residence. For mortgages made on or after 1 August 1988, the limit of mortgage relief applies to the property rather than to the borrower. Thus when two or more people share a residence, the relief is allocated between them in equal shares. Previously, they were each entitled to the full relief. Under the **MIRAS** (mortgage interest relief at source) scheme, interest payments made to a bank, building society, etc. are made after deduction of an amount equivalent to the relief of due income tax at the basic rate, and therefore no other relief is necessary, unless the person paying the mortgage pays tax at a higher rate. From April 1998 the relief was cut from 15% to 10%.

♦ **mortgager** /'mɔːgɪdʒə(r)/ *n.* (also **mortgagor** /-'dʒɔː(r)/) debtor in a mortgage.

---

mortgage rate *n.* rate of interest charged by a mortgagee.

mortice var. of MORTISE.

mortician /mɔː'tɪʃ(ə)n/ *n. US* undertaker. [Latin *mors mort-* death]

mortify /'mɔːtɪˌfaɪ/ *v.* (**-ies, -ied**) **1 a** cause (a person) to feel shamed, humiliated, or sorry. **b** wound (a person's feelings). **2** bring (the body, the flesh, the passions, etc.) into subjection by self-denial or discipline. **3** (of flesh) be affected by gangrene or necrosis. □ **mortification** /-fɪ'keɪʃ(ə)n/ *n.* **mortifying** *adj.* [Latin: related to MORTICIAN]

mortise /'mɔːtɪs/ (also **mortice**) *–n.* hole in a framework designed to receive the end of another part, esp. a tenon. *–v.* (**-sing**) **1** join securely, esp. by mortise and tenon. **2** cut a mortise in. [French from Arabic]

mortise lock *n.* lock recessed in the frame of a door etc.

mortuary /'mɔːtjʊərɪ/ *–n.* (*pl.* **-ies**) room or building in which dead bodies are kept until burial or cremation. *–attrib. adj.* of death or burial. [medieval Latin *mortuus* dead]

MOS *abbr.* metal oxide semiconductor (or silicon), an integrated circuit technology.

Mosaic /məʊ'zeɪɪk/ *adj.* of Moses. [French from *Moses* in the Old Testament]

mosaic /məʊ'zeɪɪk/ *n.* **1 a** picture or pattern produced by arranging small variously coloured pieces of glass or stone etc. **b** this as an art form. **2** diversified thing. **3** (*attrib.*) of or like a mosaic. [Greek: ultimately related to MUSE[2]]

Mosaic Law *n.* the laws attributed to Moses and listed in the Pentateuch.

Moscow /'mɒskəʊ/ capital of Russia, the country's political and economic centre; pop. (est. 1995) 8 717 000. Heavy engineering, textiles, chemicals, printing, publishing, and electronics are among its industries.

moselle /məʊ'zel/ *n.* dry white wine from the Moselle valley in Germany.

mosey /'məʊzɪ/ *v.* (**-eys, -eyed**) (often foll. by *along*) *slang* go in a leisurely manner. [origin unknown]

Moslem var. of MUSLIM.

mosque /mɒsk/ *n.* Muslim place of worship. [Arabic *masgid*]

mosquito /mɒs'kiːtəʊ/ *n.* (*pl.* **-es**) biting insect, esp. one of which the female punctures the skin with a long proboscis to suck blood. [Spanish and Portuguese, diminutive of *mosca* fly]

mosquito-net *n.* net to keep off mosquitoes.

moss *n.* **1** small flowerless plant growing in dense clusters in bogs, on the ground, trees, stones, etc. **2** *Scot.* & *N.Engl.* bog, esp. a peatbog. □ **mossy** *adj.* (**-ier, -iest**). [Old English]

most /məʊst/ *–adj.* **1** greatest in quantity or degree. **2** the majority of (*most people think so*). *–n.* **1** greatest quantity or number (*this is the most I can do*). **2** the majority (*most of them are missing*). *–adv.* **1** in the highest degree. **2** forming the superlative of adjectives and adverbs, esp. those of more than one syllable (*most absurd*; *most easily*). **3** *US colloq.* almost. □ **at most** no more or better than (*this is at most a makeshift*). **at the most 1** as the greatest amount. **2** not more than. **for the most part 1** mainly. **2** usually. **make the most of** employ to the best advantage. [Old English]

-most *suffix* forming superlative adjectives and adverbs from prepositions and other words indicating relative position (*foremost*; *uttermost*). [Old English]

♦ **most-favoured-nation clause** *n.* clause in a trade agreement between two countries stating that each will accord to the other the same treatment as regards tariffs and quotas as they extend to the most favoured nation with which each trades.

---

mostly *adv.* **1** mainly. **2** usually.

Most Reverend *n.* title of archbishops.

Mosul /'məʊsʊl/ city in NW Iraq; pop. (1987) 664 221.

Now a centre of Iraq's oil industry, it formerly produced fine cotton goods, giving its name to 'muslin'.

MOT *abbr.* (in full **MOT test**) compulsory annual test of vehicles of more than a specified age. [*M*inistry *o*f *T*ransport]

mot /məʊ/ *n.* (*pl.* ***mots*** pronunc. same) = BON MOT. [French, = word]

mote *n.* speck of dust. [Old English]

motel /məʊ'tel/ *n.* roadside hotel for motorists. [from *mo*tor ho*tel*]

motet /məʊ'tet/ *n. Mus.* short religious choral work. [French: related to MOT]

moth *n.* **1** nocturnal insect like a butterfly but without clubbed antennae. **2** insect of this type breeding in cloth etc., on which its larva feeds. [Old English]

mothball *n.* ball of naphthalene etc. placed in stored clothes to deter moths. □ **in mothballs** stored unused for a considerable time.

moth-eaten *adj.* **1** damaged by moths. **2** time-worn.

mother /'mʌðə(r)/ *–n.* **1** female parent. **2** woman, quality, or condition etc. that gives rise to something else (*necessity is the mother of invention*). **3** (in full **Mother Superior**) head of a female religious community. *–v.* **1** treat as a mother does. **2** give birth to; be the mother or origin of. □ **motherhood** *n.* **motherless** *adj.* [Old English]

Mother Carey's chicken *n.* = STORM PETREL 1.

mother country *n.* country in relation to its colonies.

mother earth *n.* the earth as mother of its inhabitants.

Mothering Sunday *n.* = MOTHER'S DAY.

mother-in-law *n.* (*pl.* **mothers-in-law**) husband's or wife's mother.

motherland *n.* one's native country.

motherly *adj.* kind or tender like a mother. □ **motherliness** *n.*

mother-of-pearl *n.* smooth iridescent substance forming the inner layer of the shell of oysters etc.

Mother's Day *n.* day when mothers are honoured with presents, (in the UK) the fourth Sunday in Lent, (in the US) the second Sunday in May.

mother tongue *n.* native language.

mothproof *–adj.* (of clothes) treated so as to repel moths. *–v.* treat (clothes) in this way.

motif /məʊ'tiːf/ *n.* **1** theme that is repeated and developed in an artistic work. **2** decorative design or pattern. **3** ornament sewn separately on a garment. [French: related to MOTIVE]

motion /'məʊʃ(ə)n/ *–n.* **1** moving; changing position. **2** gesture. **3** formal proposal put to a meeting of a company, committee, legislature, etc. A motion passed by a majority becomes a resolution. If there is a decision to amend the motion, the amended motion, known as the **substantive motion**, is then discussed and voted upon. **4** application to a court for an order. **5 a** an evacuation of the bowels. **b** (in *sing.* or *pl.*) faeces. *–v.* (often foll. by *to* + infin.) **1** direct (a person) by a gesture. **2** (often foll. by *to* a person) make a gesture directing (*motioned to me to leave*). □ **go through the motions** do something perfunctorily or superficially. **in motion** moving; not at rest. **put** (or **set) in motion** set going or working. □ **motionless** *adj.* [Latin: related to MOVE]

motion picture *n.* (esp. US) cinema film.

motivate /'məʊtɪˌveɪt/ *v.* (**-ting**) **1** supply a motive to; be the motive of. **2** cause (a person) to act in a particular way. **3** stimulate the interest of (a person in an activity). □ **motivation** /-'veɪʃ(ə)n/ *n.* **motivational** /-'veɪʃən(ə)l/ *adj.*

♦ **motivational research** *n.* (also **MR**) form of marketing research in which the motivations for consumers preferring one product rather than another are studied. It may form the basis of a plan to launch a competitive product or of a campaign to boost sales of an existing product.

---

motive /'məʊtɪv/ *–n.* **1** what induces a person to act in a particular way. **2** = MOTIF. *–adj.* **1** tending to initiate movement. **2** concerned with movement. [Latin *motivus*: related to MOVE]

motive power *n.* moving or impelling power, esp. a source of energy used to drive machinery.

mot juste /məʊ'ʒuːst/ *n.* (*pl.* ***mots justes*** pronunc. same) most appropriate expression.

motley /'mɒtlɪ/ *–adj.* (**-lier, -liest**) **1** diversified in colour. **2** of varied character (*a motley crew*). *–n. hist.* jester's particoloured costume. [origin unknown]

moto-cross /'məʊtəʊˌkrɒs/ *n.* cross-country racing on motor cycles. [from MOTOR, CROSS]

motor /'məʊtə(r)/ *–n.* **1** thing that imparts motion. **2** machine (esp. one using electricity or internal combustion) supplying motive power for a vehicle or other machine. **3** = CAR 1. **4** (*attrib.*) **a** giving, imparting, or producing motion. **b** driven by a motor (*motor-mower*). **c** of or for motor vehicles. **d** *Anat.* relating to muscular movement or the nerves activating it. *–v.* go or convey in a motor vehicle. [Latin: related to MOVE]

motor bike *n. colloq.* = MOTOR CYCLE.

motor boat *n.* motor-driven boat.

motorcade /'məʊtəˌkeɪd/ *n.* procession of motor vehicles. [from MOTOR, after *cavalcade*]

motor car *n.* = CAR 1.

motor cycle *n.* two-wheeled motor vehicle without pedal propulsion. □ **motor cyclist** *n.*

♦ **motor insurance** *n.* form of insurance covering loss or damage to motor vehicles and any legal liabilities for bodily injury or damage to other people's property. Drivers have a legal obligation to be covered against third-party claims (see THIRD-PARTY INSURANCE), but most drivers or owners of vehicles have a **comprehensive insurance**, providing wide coverage of all the risks involved in owning a motor vehicle. An intermediate cover, known as **third-party, fire, and theft**, leaves the owner of a vehicle uninsured for damage to his or her vehicle in the case of an accident. See also NO-CLAIM BONUS.

♦ **Motor Insurers Bureau** *n.* body, formed in 1946, to which all motor insurers in the UK must belong. Its primary function is to deal with domestic claims for bodily injury or damage to third-party property caused by uninsured or untraced drivers. As all drivers must have third-party insurance cover by law, it would be unfair for victims to suffer if the driver could not be traced or was uninsured. When such a claim is submitted to the Motor Insurers Bureau, it selects, on a rota basis, an insurance company to deal with the claim as if it had insured the driver. The second function of the Bureau is to issue international motor-insurance certificates (see GREEN CARD) to UK drivers and to administer the international agreements that form the basis of the green-card system. It also acts as a paying bureau for claims arising in other countries caused by UK green-card holders and as a handling bureau for claims arising from accidents caused by foreign drivers visiting the UK.

---

motorist *n.* driver of a car.

motorize *v.* (also **-ise**) (**-zing** or **-sing**) **1** equip with motor transport. **2** provide with a motor.

motorman *n.* driver of an underground train, tram, etc.

motor scooter see SCOOTER.

motor vehicle *n.* road vehicle powered by an internal-combustion engine.

motorway *n.* road for fast travel, with separate carriageways and limited access.

Motown /'məʊtaʊn/ *n. propr.* music with elements of rhythm and blues, associated with Detroit. [*Mo*tor *Town*, = DETROIT]

mottle *v.* (**-ling**) (esp. as **mottled** *adj.*) mark with spots or smears of colour. [back-formation from MOTLEY]

motto /'mɒtəʊ/ *n.* (*pl.* **-es**) **1** maxim adopted as a rule of conduct. **2** phrase or sentence accompanying a coat of arms. **3** appropriate inscription. **4** joke, maxim, etc. in a paper cracker. [Italian: related to MOT]

mould[1] /məʊld/ (*US* **mold**) *–n.* **1** hollow container into which a substance is poured or pressed to harden into a required shape. **2 a** vessel for shaping puddings etc. **b** pudding etc. made in this way. **3** form or shape. **4** frame or template for producing mouldings. **5** character or type (*in heroic mould*). *–v.* **1** make (an object) in a required shape or from certain ingredients (*moulded out of clay*). **2** give shape to. **3** influence the development of. [French *modle* from Latin MODULUS]

mould[2] /məʊld/ *n.* (*US* **mold**) furry growth of fungi occurring esp. in moist warm conditions. [Old Norse]

mould[3] /məʊld/ *n.* (*US* **mold**) **1** loose earth. **2** upper soil of cultivated land, esp. when rich in organic matter. [Old English]

moulder *v.* (*US* **molder**) **1** decay to dust. **2** (foll. by *away*) rot or crumble. **3** deteriorate. [from MOULD[3]]

moulding *n.* (*US* **molding**) **1** ornamentally shaped outline of plaster etc. as an architectural feature, esp. in a cornice. **2** similar feature in woodwork etc.

mouldy *adj.* (*US* **moldy**) (**-ier, -iest**) **1** covered with mould. **2** stale; out of date. **3** *colloq.* dull, miserable. □ **mouldiness** *n.*

Moulmein /muːl'meɪn/ port in SE Burma, trading esp. in teak and rice; pop. (1983) 219 991.

moult /məʊlt/ (*US* **molt**) *–v.* (also *absol.*) shed (feathers, hair, a shell etc.) in the process of renewing plumage, a coat, etc. *–n.* moulting. [Latin *muto* change]

mound *n.* **1** raised mass of earth, stones, etc. **2** heap or pile; large quantity. **3** hillock. [origin unknown]

mount[1] *–v.* **1** ascend; climb on to. **2 a** get up on (a horse etc.) to ride it. **b** set on horseback. **c** (as **mounted** *adj.*) serving on horseback (*mounted police*). **3 a** (often foll. by *up*) accumulate. **b** (of a feeling) increase. **4** (often foll. by *on, in*) set (an object) on a support or in a backing, frame, etc., esp. for viewing. **5** organize, arrange, set in motion (a play, exhibition, attack, guard, etc.). **6** (of a male animal) get on to (a female) to copulate. *–n.* **1** backing, etc. on which a picture etc. is set for display. **2** horse for riding. **3** setting for a gem etc. [Latin: related to MOUNT[2]]

mount[2] *n. archaic* (except before a name): mountain, hill (*Mount Everest*). [Latin *mons mont-*]

mountain /'maʊntɪn/ *n.* **1** large abrupt natural elevation of the ground. **2** large heap or pile; huge quantity. **3** large surplus stock, esp. of agricultural produce (e.g. butter). According to the Common Agricultural Policy, farmers in the European Community are guaranteed a minimum price for their produce, which the EC has to buy. Unable to sell the mountain within its member countries, which would depress prices, the EC has to dispose of mountains to charitable causes or sell them outside the EC at very low prices. □ **make a mountain out of a molehill** see MOLEHILL. [Latin: related to MOUNT[2]]

mountain ash *n.* tree with scarlet berries; rowan.

mountain bike *n.* sturdy bike with many gears for riding over rough terrain.

mountaineer /ˌmaʊntɪ'nɪə(r)/ *–n.* person who practises mountain-climbing. *–v.* climb mountains as a sport. □ **mountaineering** *n.*

mountain lion *n.* puma.

mountainous *adj.* **1** having many mountains. **2** huge.

mountain range *n.* continuous line of mountains.

mountain sickness *n.* sickness caused by thin air at great heights.

mountainside *n.* sloping side of a mountain.

mountebank /'maʊntɪˌbæŋk/ *n.* **1** swindler; charlatan. **2** *hist.* itinerant quack. [Italian, = mount on bench]

Mountie *n. colloq.* member of the Royal Canadian Mounted Police. [abbreviation]

mounting *n.* **1** = MOUNT[1] *n.* 1. **2** in senses of MOUNT[1] *v.*

Mount Isa /'aɪzə/ lead- and silver-mining town in Queensland, Australia; pop. (est. 1987) 24 200.

mourn /mɔːn/ *v.* (often foll. by *for, over*) feel or show deep sorrow or regret for (a dead person, a lost thing, a past event, etc.). [Old English]

mourner *n.* person who mourns, esp. at a funeral.

mournful *adj.* doleful, sad, expressing mourning. □ **mournfully** *adv.* **mournfulness** *n.*

mourning *n.* **1** expressing of sorrow for a dead person, esp. by wearing black clothes. **2** such clothes.

mouse *–n.* (*pl.* **mice**) **1** small rodent, esp. of a kind infesting houses. **2** timid or feeble person. **3** (*pl.* **-s** or **mice**) *Computing* small hand-held device that is moved around a flat surface, causing corresponding movements of the cursor on a VDU screen. The mouse has one or more buttons, which are pressed to indicate to the computer that the cursor has reached a desired position. *–v.* /also maʊz/ (**-sing**) (of a cat, owl, etc.) hunt mice. □ **mouser** *n.* [Old English]

mousetrap *n.* **1** trap for catching mice. **2** (often *attrib.*) *colloq.* poor quality cheese.

moussaka /mʊ'sɑːkə/ *n.* (also **mousaka**) Greek dish of minced meat, aubergine, etc. [Greek or Turkish]

mousse /muːs/ *n.* **1 a** dessert of whipped cream, eggs, etc., usu. flavoured with fruit or chocolate. **b** meat or fish purée made with whipped cream etc. **2** foamy substance applied to the hair to enable styling. [French, = froth]

moustache /mə'stɑːʃ/ *n.* (*US* **mustache**) hair left to grow on a man's upper lip. [Greek *mustax*]

mousy /'maʊsɪ/ *adj.* (**-ier, -iest**) **1** of or like a mouse. **2** (of a person) timid, feeble. **3** nondescript light brown.

mouth /maʊθ/ *–n.* (*pl.* **mouths** /maʊðz/) **1 a** external opening in the head, through which most animals take in food and emit communicative sounds. **b** (in humans and some animals) cavity behind it containing the means of biting and chewing and the vocal organs. **2** opening of a container, cave, trumpet, etc. **3** place where a river enters the sea. **4** an individual as needing sustenance (*an extra mouth to feed*). **5** *colloq.* **a** meaningless or ineffectual talk. **b** impudent talk; cheek. *–v.* /maʊð/ (**-thing**) **1** say or speak by moving the lips but with no sound. **2** utter or speak insincerely or without understanding (*mouthing platitudes*). □ **put words into a person's mouth** represent a person as having said something. **take the words out of a person's mouth** say what another was about to say. [Old English]

mouthful *n.* (*pl.* **-s**) **1** quantity of food etc. that fills the mouth. **2** small quantity. **3** *colloq.* long or complicated word or phrase.

mouth-organ *n.* = HARMONICA.

mouthpiece *n.* **1** part of a musical instrument, telephone, etc., placed next to the lips. **2** *colloq.* person who speaks for another or others.

mouth-to-mouth *adj.* (of resuscitation) in which a person breathes into a subject's lungs through the mouth.

mouthwash *n.* liquid antiseptic etc. for rinsing the mouth or gargling.

mouth-watering *adj.* (of food etc.) having a delicious smell or appearance.

movable /'muːvəb(ə)l/ *adj.* (also **moveable**) **1** that can be moved. **2** variable in date from year to year (*movable feast*). [related to MOVE]

move /muːv/ *–v.* (**-ving**) **1** (cause to) change position or posture. **2** put or keep in motion; rouse, stir. **3 a** take a turn in a board-game. **b** change the position of (a piece) in a board-game. **4** (often foll. by *about, away, off,* etc.) go or proceed. **5** take action, esp. promptly (*moved to reduce crime*). **6** make progress (*project is moving fast*). **7** (also *absol.*) change (one's home or place of work). **8** (foll. by *in*) be socially active in (a specified group etc.) (*moves in the best circles*). **9** affect (a person) with (usu. tender) emotion. **10** (foll. by *to*) provoke (a person to laughter etc.) (*was moved to tears*). **11** (foll. by *to*, or *to* + infin.) prompt or incline (a person to a feeling or action). **12** (cause to) change one's attitude (*nothing can move me on this issue*). **13 a** cause (the bowels) to be evacuated. **b** (of the bowels) be evacuated. **14** (often foll. by *that*) propose in a meeting, etc. **15** (foll. by *for*) make a formal request or application. **16** sell; be sold. *–n.* **1** act or process of moving. **2** change of house, premises, etc. **3** step taken to secure an object. **4 a** changing of the position of a piece in a board-game. **b** player's turn to do this. □ **get a move on** *colloq.* hurry up. **make a move** take action. **move along** (or **on**) advance, progress, esp. to avoid crowding etc. **move away** go to live in another area. **move heaven and earth** (foll. by *to* + infin.) make extraordinary efforts. **move in 1** take up residence in a new home. **2** get into a position of readiness or proximity (for an offensive action etc.). **move in with** start to share accommodation with (an existing resident). **move out** leave one's home. **move over** (or **up**) adjust one's position to make room for another. **on the move** moving. [Latin *moveo*]

moveable var. of MOVABLE.

movement *n.* **1 a** moving or being moved. **b** instance of this (*watched his every movement*). **2** moving parts of a mechanism (esp. a clock or watch). **3 a** body of persons with a common object (*peace movement*). **b** campaign undertaken by them. **4** (in *pl.*) person's activities and whereabouts. **5** *Mus.* principal division of a longer musical work. **6** motion of the bowels. **7** rise or fall in price(s) on the stock market. **8** progress.

mover *n.* **1** person, animal, or thing that moves or dances, esp. in a specified way. **2** person who moves a proposition. **3** (also **prime mover**) originator.

movie *n.* esp. *US colloq.* cinema film.

moving *adj.* emotionally affecting. □ **movingly** *adv.*

♦ **moving average** *n.* series of averages calculated from data in a time series, which reduces the effects of temporary seasonal variations. For example, a moving average of the monthly sales figures for an organization might be calculated by averaging the 12 months from January to December for the December figure, the 12 months from February to January for the January figure, and so on.

---

moving staircase *n.* escalator.

mow /məʊ/ *v.* (*past part.* **mowed** or **mown**) **1** (also *absol.*) cut (grass, hay, etc.) with a scythe or machine. **2** cut down the produce of (a field) or the grass etc. of (a lawn) by mowing. □ **mow down** kill or destroy randomly or in great numbers. □ **mower** *n.* [Old English]

mozzarella /ˌmɒtsəˈrelə/ *n.* Italian curd cheese, orig. of buffalo milk. [Italian]

MP *abbr.* Member of Parliament.

mp *abbr.* mezzo piano.

MPA *abbr.* **1** Master of Professional Accounting. **2** Master of Public Administration.

m.p.g. *abbr.* miles per gallon.

m.p.h. *abbr.* miles per hour.

M.Phil. *abbr.* Master of Philosophy.

MPO *abbr.* management and personnel office.

MPU *abbr. Computing* microprocessor unit.

Mpy *abbr.* (Dutch) Maatschappij (= Company).

MR *abbr.* **1** (also **M/R**) *Commerce* mate's receipt. **2** = MOTIVATIONAL RESEARCH.

Mr /ˈmɪstə(r)/ *n.* (*pl.* **Messrs**) **1** title of a man without a higher title (*Mr Jones*). **2** title prefixed to a designation of office etc. (*Mr President*; *Mr Speaker*). [abbreviation of MISTER]

♦ **MRP** *abbr.* manufacturer's recommended price. See RECOMMENDED RETAIL PRICE.

MRS *abbr.* **1** = MARKET RESEARCH SOCIETY. **2** *Computing* monitored retrievable storage.

Mrs /ˈmɪsɪz/ *n.* (*pl.* same) title of a married woman without a higher title (*Mrs Jones*). [abbreviation of MISTRESS]

MRVA *abbr.* Member of the Rating and Valuation Association.

MS *–abbr.* **1** (*pl.* **MSS** /emˈesɪz/) manuscript. **2** (also **M/S**) **a** mail steamer. **b** *US* motor ship. **3** multiple sclerosis. *–international vehicle registration* Mauritius. *–airline flight code* Egyptair. *–US postcode* Mississippi.

Ms /mɪz, məz/ *n.* title of a married or unmarried woman without a higher title. [combination of MRS, MISS[2]]

m/s *abbr.* (also **M/s**) *Finance* months after sight.

MSBA *abbr.* Master of Science in Business Administration.

M.S.Bus. *abbr.* Master of Science in Business.

M.Sc. *abbr.* Master of Science.

MSCI Index *abbr. Finance* Morgan Stanley Capital International World Index.

♦ **MS-DOS** /ˌemesˈdɒs/ *abbr. propr. Computing* Microsoft disk operating system, for use on microcomputers that are based on the Intel 16-bit and 32-bit family of microprocessors and support a single user at any one time. Designed originally for the IBM Personal Computer (on which it is known as **PC-DOS** or, in IBM literature, **DOS**), it is one of the most popular operating systems for larger microcomputers.

MSF *abbr.* Manufacturing, Science, and Finance (trade union).

MSI *abbr.* medium-scale integration (on integrated circuits).

MSQ *abbr.* managing service quality.

MST *abbr. US* Mountain Standard Time.

Mozambique /ˌməʊzæmˈbiːk/, **Republic of** (Portuguese **Moçambique**) country on the E coast of Africa, bordered by the Republic of South Africa in the S and W. Subsistence agriculture forms the basis of the economy, the staple food crops being maize and rice. Cashew nuts, of which Mozambique is the world's largest producer, are the chief cash crop; other agricultural exports include tea, sugar cane, and cotton. Prawns are also a major export. Food processing is the chief manufacturing industry, predominantly sugar refining and cashew-nut processing; other manufactures include textiles, cement, fertilizers, agricultural implements, tyres, and railway carriages. Coal and bauxite are mined. Since the 1980s economic development has been severely hindered by the effects of civil war, a shortage of skilled workers, and severe drought.

History. Colonized by the Portuguese in the early 16th century, the country gained full independence in 1975 as the People's Republic of Mozambique, a socialist one-party state; civil war subsequently broke out between government (Frelimo) forces and rebel guerrillas of a national resistance movement (Renamo). In 1990 a new constitution, ensuring multi-party democracy and market reform, was adopted and the country assumed its present name; a ceasefire between the government and Renamo leaders was agreed in 1992, together with the promise of multiparty elections, which were held in 1994 and won by Frelimo. Mozambique became a member of the Commonwealth in 1996. President, Joaquim Alberto Chissano; prime minister, Pascoal Mocumbi; capital, Maputo. □ **Mozambican** *adj.* & *n.*

languages	Portuguese (official), African languages
currency	metical (Mt) of 100 centavos
pop. (1996)	17 887 000
GNP (1994)	US$1.3B
literacy	57% (m); 23% (f)
life expectancy	46 (m); 49 (f)

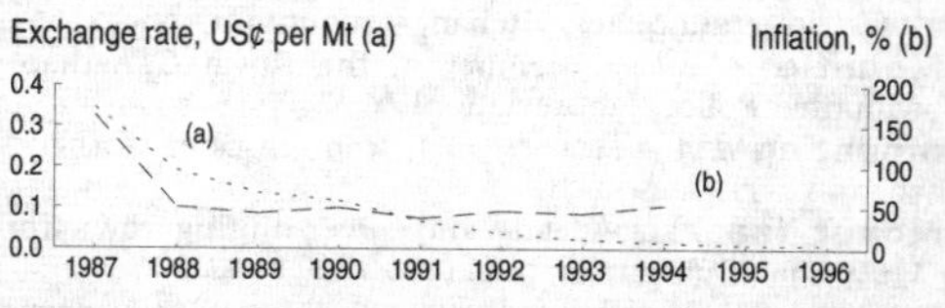

MT –*abbr.* **1** (also **M/T**) mail transfer. **2** mean time. –*US postcode* Montana.

Mt *symb.* metical.

Mt. *abbr.* Mount.

m.t. *abbr.* metric ton(s).

MTAI *abbr.* Member of the Institute of Travel Agents.

MTBF *abbr.* mean time between failures (figure of merit for computer reliability).

MTFA *abbr.* = MEDIUM-TERM FINANCIAL ASSISTANCE.

MTO *abbr.* made to order.

MTU *abbr.* magnetic tape unit. See TAPE UNIT.

mu /mjuː/ *n.* **1** twelfth Greek letter (Μ, μ). **2** (μ, as a symbol) = MICRO- 2. [Greek]

much –*adj.* **1** existing or occurring in a great quantity (*much trouble*; *too much noise*). **2** (prec. by *as, how, that,* etc.) with relative sense (*I don't know how much money you want*). –*n.* **1** a great quantity (*much of that is true*). **2** (prec. by *as, how, that,* etc.) with relative sense (*we do not need that much*). **3** (usu. in *neg.*) noteworthy or outstanding example (*not much to look at*). –*adv.* **1** in a great degree (*much to my surprise*; *is much the same*; *I much regret it*; *much annoyed*; *much better*; *much the best*). **2** for a large part of one's time; often (*he is not here much*). □ **as much** so (*I thought as much*). **a bit much** *colloq.* excessive, immoderate. **much as** even though (*cannot come, much as I would like to*). **much of a muchness** very nearly the same. **not much of a** *colloq.* a rather poor. [from MICKLE]

mucilage /ˈmjuːsɪlɪdʒ/ *n.* **1** viscous substance obtained from plants. **2** adhesive gum. [Latin: related to MUCUS]

muck –*n.* **1** *colloq.* dirt or filth; anything disgusting. **2** farmyard manure. **3** *colloq.* mess. –*v.* **1** (usu. foll. by *up*) *colloq.* **a** bungle (a job). **b** make dirty or untidy. **2** (foll. by *out*) remove manure from. □ **make a muck of** *colloq.* bungle. **muck about** (or **around**) *colloq.* **1** potter or fool about. **2** (foll. by *with*) fool or interfere with. **muck in** (often foll. by *with*) *colloq.* share tasks etc. equally. [Scandinavian]

mucker *n. slang* friend, mate. [probably from *muck in*: related to MUCK]

muckle var. of MICKLE.

muckrake *v.* (**-king**) search out and reveal scandal. □ **muckraker** *n.* **muckraking** *n.*

muck-spreader *n.* machine for spreading dung. □ **muck-spreading** *n.*

mucky *adj.* (**-ier, -iest**) covered with muck, dirty.

mucous /ˈmjuːkəs/ *adj.* of or covered with mucus. □ **mucosity** /-ˈkɒsɪtɪ/ *n.* [Latin *mucosus*: related to MUCUS]

mucous membrane *n.* mucus-secreting tissue lining body cavities etc.

mucus /ˈmjuːkəs/ *n.* slimy substance secreted by a mucous membrane. [Latin]

mud *n.* soft wet earth. □ **fling** (or **sling** or **throw) mud** speak disparagingly or slanderously. **one's name is mud** one is in disgrace. [German]

muddle –*v.* (**-ling**) (often foll. by *up*) **1** bring into disorder. **2** bewilder, confuse. –*n.* **1** disorder. **2** confusion. □ **muddle along** (or **on**) progress in a haphazard way. **muddle through** succeed despite one's inefficiency. [perhaps Dutch, related to MUD]

muddle-headed *adj.* mentally disorganized, confused.

muddy –*adj.* (**-ier, -iest**) **1** like mud. **2** covered in or full of mud. **3** (of liquid, colour, or sound) not clear, impure. **4** vague, confused. –*v.* (**-ies, -ied**) make muddy. □ **muddiness** *n.*

mudflap *n.* flap hanging behind the wheel of a vehicle, to prevent splashes.

mud-flat *n.* stretch of muddy land uncovered at low tide.

mudguard *n.* curved strip over a bicycle wheel etc. to protect the rider from splashes.

mud pack *n.* cosmetic paste applied thickly to the face.

mud-slinger *n. colloq.* person given to making abusive or disparaging remarks. □ **mud-slinging** *n.*

muesli /ˈmuːzlɪ, ˈmjuː-/ *n.* breakfast food of crushed cereals, dried fruits, nuts, etc., eaten with milk. [Swiss German]

muezzin /muːˈezɪn/ *n.* Muslim crier who proclaims the hours of prayer. [Arabic]

muff[1] *n.* covering, esp. of fur, for keeping the hands or ears warm. [Dutch *mof*]

muff[2] *v. colloq.* **1** bungle. **2** miss (a catch, ball, etc.). [origin unknown]

muffin /ˈmʌfɪn/ *n.* **1** light flat round spongy cake, eaten toasted and buttered. **2** *US* similar round cake made from batter or dough. [origin unknown]

muffle *v.* (**-ling**) **1** (often foll. by *up*) wrap or cover for warmth, or to deaden sound. **2** (usu. as **muffled** *adj.*) stifle (an utterance). [perhaps French *moufle* thick glove, MUFF[1]]

muffler *n.* **1** wrap or scarf worn for warmth. **2** thing used to deaden sound. **3** *US* silencer of a vehicle.

mufti /ˈmʌftɪ/ *n.* civilian clothes (*in mufti*). [Arabic]

mug[1] –*n.* **1 a** drinking-vessel, usu. cylindrical with a handle and no saucer. **b** its contents. **2** *slang* gullible person. **3** *slang* face or mouth. –*v.* (**-gg-**) attack and rob, esp. in public. □ **a mug's game** *colloq.* foolish or unprofitable activity. □ **mugger** *n.* **mugful** *n.* (*pl.* **-s**). **mugging** *n.* [Scandinavian]

mug[2] *v.* (**-gg-**) (usu. foll. by *up*) *slang* learn (a subject) by concentrated study. [origin unknown]

muggins /ˈmʌgɪnz/ *n.* (*pl.* same or **mugginses**) *colloq.* gullible person (often meaning oneself: *so muggins had to pay*). [perhaps from the surname]

muggy *adj.* (**-ier, -iest**) (of weather etc.) oppressively humid. □ **mugginess** *n.* [Old Norse]

mug shot *n. slang* photograph of a face, esp. for police records.

Muhammadan /məˈhæməd(ə)n/ *n.* & *adj.* (also **Mohammedan**) = MUSLIM. [*Muhammad*, name of a prophet]

■ **Usage** The term *Muhammadan* is not used by Muslims, and is often regarded as offensive.

mujahidin /ˌmʊdʒəhəˈdiːn/ *n.pl.* (also **mujahedin, -deen**) guerrilla fighters in Islamic countries, esp. Muslim fundamentalists. [Persian and Arabic: related to JIHAD]

Mukalla /mʊˈkælə/ port in Yemen, on the Gulf of Aden; fish canning and boat building are the main industries; pop. (est. 1995) 154 360.

Mukden see SHENYANG.

mulatto /mjuːˈlætəʊ/ *n.* (*pl.* **-s** or **-es**) person of mixed White and Black parentage. [Spanish *mulato* young mule]

mulberry /ˈmʌlbərɪ/ *n.* (*pl.* **-ies**) **1** tree bearing edible purple or white berries, and leaves used to feed silkworms. **2** its fruit. **3** dark-red or purple. [Latin *morum* mulberry, BERRY]

mulch –*n.* layer of wet straw, leaves, or plastic, etc., spread around or over a plant to enrich or insulate the soil. –*v.* treat with mulch. [Old English, = soft]

mule[1] *n.* **1** offspring of a male donkey and a female horse, or (in general use) of a female donkey and a male horse (cf. HINNY). **2** stupid or obstinate person. **3** (in full **spinning mule**) a kind of spinning-machine. [Latin *mulus*]

mule[2] *n.* backless slipper. [French]

muleteer /ˌmjuːləˈtɪə(r)/ *n.* mule-driver. [French *muletier*: related to MULE[1]]

Mulhouse /mʊˈluːz/ industrial city in NE France; manufactures include textiles and electrical goods; pop. (1990) 109 905.

mulish *adj.* stubborn.

mull[1] *v.* (often foll. by *over*) ponder, consider. [probably Dutch]

mull[2] *v.* warm (wine or beer) with added sugar, spices, etc. [origin unknown]

mull[3] *n. Scot.* promontory. [origin uncertain]

mullah /ˈmʌlə/ *n.* Muslim learned in theology and sacred law. [ultimately Arabic *mawlā*]

mullet *n.* (*pl.* same) any of several kinds of marine fish valued for food. [Greek *mullos*]

mulligatawny /ˌmʌlɪgəˈtɔːnɪ/ *n.* highly seasoned soup orig. from India. [Tamil, = pepper-water]

mullion /ˈmʌljən/ *n.* vertical bar dividing the lights in a window. □ **mullioned** *adj.* [probably French *moinel* middle: related to MEAN[3]]

Multan /mʊlˈtɑːn/ commercial city in central Pakistan, in Punjab province; manufactures include textiles, jewellery, and precision instruments; pop. (est. 1995) 1 075 000.

multi- *comb. form* many. [Latin *multus* much, many]

♦ **multi-access** /ˌmʌltɪˈækses/ *adj.* (of a computer system) allowing apparently simultaneous access to the computer from several terminals. A multi-access system is thus a multi-user system. It is based on the technique of time sharing and is used mainly for interactive working. The operating system of the computer is responsible for sharing main store, processor, and other resources among the terminals in use.

---

multicoloured /ˈmʌltɪˌkʌləd/ *adj.* of many colours.

multicultural /ˌmʌltɪˈkʌltʃər(ə)l/ *adj.* of several cultural groups. □ **multiculturalism** *n.*

multidirectional /ˌmʌltɪdaɪˈrekʃən(ə)l/ *adj.* of, involving, or operating in several directions.

multifarious /ˌmʌltɪˈfeərɪəs/ *adj.* **1** many and various. **2** of great variety. □ **multifariousness** *n.* [Latin *multifarius*]

multiform /ˈmʌltɪˌfɔːm/ *adj.* **1** having many forms. **2** of many kinds.

multifunction card *n.* **1** (also **multifunctional card**) plastic card issued by a bank or building society to its customers to function as a cheque card, debit card, and cashcard. Multifunction cards operate in conjunction with a personal identification number. **2** (also **multifunction board**) *Computing* see EXPANSION CARD.

multilateral /ˌmʌltɪˈlætər(ə)l/ *adj.* **1** (of an agreement etc.) in which three or more parties participate. **2** having many sides. □ **multilaterally** *adv.*

♦ **multilateral trade agreement** *n.* trading arrangement between a number of nations in which there is agreement to abolish quotas and tariffs or to accept that there will be a surplus or deficit on the balance of payments.

---

multilingual /ˌmʌltɪˈlɪŋgw(ə)l/ *adj.* in, speaking, or using several languages.

multimedia –*attrib. adj.* using more than one medium of communication. –*n.* = HYPERMEDIA.

multimillion /ˈmʌltɪˌmɪljən/ *attrib. adj.* costing or involving several million (pounds, dollars, etc.) (*multimillion dollar fraud*).

multimillionaire /ˌmʌltɪˌmɪljəˈneə(r)/ *n.* person with a fortune of several millions.

multinational /ˌmʌltɪˈnæʃən(ə)l/ –*adj.* **1** operating in several countries. **2** of several nationalities. –*n.* corporation that has production operations in more than one country for various reasons, including securing supplies of raw materials, utilizing cheap labour sources, and bypassing protectionist barriers. Multinationals may be seen as an efficient form of organization, making effective use of the world's resources and transferring technology between countries. On the other hand, some have excessive power, are beyond the control of governments, and are able to exploit host countries, esp. in the Third World.

multiple /ˈmʌltɪp(ə)l/ –*adj.* **1** having several parts, elements, or components. **2** many and various. –*n.* **1** number that contains another without a remainder (*56 is a multiple of 7*). **2** see PRICE-EARNINGS RATIO. [Latin *multiplus*: related to MULTIPLEX]

♦ **multiple application** *n.* submission of more than one application form for a new issue of shares that is likely to be oversubscribed (see ALLOTMENT 4). In many countries it is illegal to do so either if the applications are made in the same name or if false names are used.

---

multiple-choice *adj.* (of an examination question) accompanied by several possible answers from which the correct one has to be chosen.

♦ **multiple exchange rate** *n.* exchange rate quoted by a country that has more than one value, depending on the use to which the currency is put. For example, some countries have quoted a specially favourable rate for tourists or for importers of desirable goods.

---

multiple sclerosis see SCLEROSIS.

♦ **multiple shop** *n.* (also **multiple store**) = CHAIN STORE.

♦ **multiple taxation** *n.* taxation of the same income by more than two countries. Cf. DOUBLE TAXATION.

---

multiplex /ˈmʌltɪˌpleks/ –*adj.* **1** manifold; of many elements. **2** using or involving a multiplexer. –*v.* merge information using a multiplexer. [Latin: related to MULTI-, *-plex -plicis* -fold]

multiplexer *n.* (also **MUX, mux**) device that merges information from several input channels so that it can be transmitted on a single output channel. One transmission channel can thus be shared among multiple sources of information or multiple users. This can be achieved by allocating to each source or user a specific time slot in which to use the transmission channel; this is known as **time division multiplexing** (**TDM**). Alternatively the transmission channel can be divided into channels of smaller bandwidth (frequency range) and each source or user is given exclusive use of one of these channels; this is known as **frequency division multiplexing** (**FDM**). Multiplexers are often used in pairs, connected by a single transmission channel and allowing contact to be made between any of a large choice of points at each end.

multiplicand /ˌmʌltɪplɪˈkænd/ *n.* quantity to be multiplied by another.

multiplication /ˌmʌltɪplɪˈkeɪʃ(ə)n/ *n.* multiplying.

multiplication sign *n.* sign (×) to indicate that one quantity is to be multiplied by another.

multiplication table *n.* list of multiples of a particular number, usu. from 1 to 12.

multiplicity /ˌmʌltɪˈplɪsɪtɪ/ *n.* (*pl.* **-ies**) **1** manifold variety. **2** (foll. by *of*) great number.

♦ **multiplier** /ˈmʌltɪˌplaɪə(r)/ *n.* **1** quantity by which a given number is multiplied. **2** *Econ.* feedback effect generated by a change in an economic variable. For example, an increase in total investment will raise national income by an amount equal to its monetary value, but in addition it will have a wider positive feedback effect by stimulating other parts of the economy, thus creating new jobs and additional demand for goods. When applied to government expenditure and aggregate demand, the multiplier has a much broader connotation, applying to any situation in which there are feedback effects. Multipliers may be negative as well as positive.

---

multiply /ˈmʌltɪˌplaɪ/ *v.* (**-ies, -ied**) **1** (also *absol.*) obtain from (a number) another that is a specified number of times its value (*multiply 6 by 4 and you get 24*). **2** increase in number, esp. by procreation. **3** produce a large number of (instances etc.). **4 a** breed (animals). **b** propagate (plants). [Latin *multiplico*: related to MULTIPLEX]

multiprocessing system *n.* (also **multiprocessor**) computer system in which two or more processors may be active at any particular time. Two or more programs can therefore be executed at the same time (see MULTIPROGRAMMING SYSTEM). The processors share some or all of main store and other resources, e.g. input/output devices and parts of the system software. The allocation and release of resources is under the control of the operating system.

multiprogramming system *n.* computer system in which several individual programs may be executed at the same time. A multiprocessing system is a multiprogramming system. It is also feasible for a multiprogramming system to be operated with only one processor. On any processor only one processing task can take place at a particular time. In a multiprogramming system there is rapid switching between the tasks to be performed for each of the programs running. For example, while one program is waiting for an input or output operation to be completed, another program can be allocated use of the processor. This switching procedure is under the control of the operating system, which also controls the allocation and release of other resources in the system. Multiprogramming enables optimum use to be made of the computer resources as a whole: a processor operates very much faster than its peripheral devices, and valuable processor time is wasted if the processor remains idle while a program uses a peripheral.

multi-purpose /ˌmʌltɪˈpɜːpəs/ *attrib. adj.* having several purposes.

multiracial /ˌmʌltɪˈreɪʃ(ə)l/ *adj.* of several races.

multi-storey /ˌmʌltɪˈstɔːrɪ/ *attrib. adj.* having several storeys.

♦ **multi-tasking** *adj.* (of a computer system) capable of running more than one processing task at the same time.

---

multitude *n.* **1** (often foll. by *of*) great number. **2** large gathering of people; crowd. **3** (**the multitude**) the common people. [French from Latin]

multitudinous /ˌmʌltɪˈtjuːdɪnəs/ *adj.* **1** very numerous. **2** consisting of many individuals. [Latin: related to MULTITUDE]

♦ **multi-user** /ˌmʌltɪˈjuːzə(r)/ *attrib. adj.* (of a computer system) apparently serving more than one user simultaneously. Multi-user systems are usu. multi-tasking, and are essential for all large-scale computer applications. For example, they allow large databases to be accessed and manipulated by many users at the same time.

---

mum[1] *n. colloq.* = MUMMY[1].

mum[2] *adj. colloq.* silent (*keep mum*). □ **mum's the word** say nothing. [imitative]

mumble –*v.* (**-ling**) speak or utter indistinctly. –*n.* indistinct utterance or sound. [related to MUM[2]]

mumbo-jumbo /ˌmʌmbəʊˈdʒʌmbəʊ/ *n.* (*pl.* **-s**) **1** meaningless or ignorant ritual. **2** meaningless or unnecessarily complicated language; nonsense. [*Mumbo Jumbo*, name of a supposed African idol]

mummer *n.* actor in a traditional mime. [French *momeur*: cf. MUM[2]]

mummery *n.* (*pl.* **-ies**) **1** ridiculous (esp. religious) ceremonial. **2** performance by mummers. [French *momerie*: related to MUMMER]

mummify /ˈmʌmɪˌfaɪ/ *v.* (**-ies, -ied**) preserve (a body) as a mummy. □ **mummification** /-fɪˈkeɪʃ(ə)n/ *n.*

mummy[1] /ˈmʌmɪ/ *n.* (*pl.* **-ies**) *colloq.* mother. [imitative of a child's pronunciation]

mummy[2] /ˈmʌmɪ/ *n.* (*pl.* **-ies**) body of a human being or animal embalmed for burial, esp. in ancient Egypt. [Persian *mūm* wax]

mumps *n.pl.* (treated as *sing.*) infectious disease with swelling of the neck and face. [imitative of mouth-shape]

munch *v.* eat steadily with a marked action of the jaws. [imitative]

München see MUNICH.

mundane /mʌnˈdeɪn/ *adj.* **1** dull, routine. **2** of this world. □ **mundanely** *adv.* **mundanity** /-ˈdænɪtɪ/ *n.* [Latin *mundus* world]

mung *n.* (in full **mung bean**) leguminous Indian plant used as food. [Hindi *mūng*]

Munich /ˈmjuːnɪk/ (German **München** /ˈmʊnxən/) commercial and industrial city in SW Germany, capital of Bavaria; manufactures include electrical goods, chemicals, and beer, and tourism is important; pop. (est. 1995) 1 224 676.

municipal /mjuːˈnɪsɪp(ə)l/ *adj.* of a municipality or its self-government. □ **municipalize** *v.* (also **-ise**) (**-zing** or **-sing**). **municipally** *adv.* [Latin *municipium* free city]

♦ **municipal bond** *n.* esp. *US* bond issued by a local government authority.

---

municipality /mjuːˌnɪsɪˈpælɪtɪ/ *n.* (*pl.* **-ies**) **1** town or district having local self-government. **2** governing body of this area.

munificent /mjuːˈnɪfɪs(ə)nt/ *adj.* (of a giver or a gift) splendidly generous. □ **munificence** *n.* [Latin *munus* gift: related to -FIC]

muniment /ˈmjuːnɪm(ə)nt/ *n.* (usu. in *pl.*) document kept as evidence of rights or privileges etc. [Latin *munio* fortify]

munition /mjuːˈnɪʃ(ə)n/ *n.* (usu. in *pl.*) military weapons, ammunition etc. [Latin, = fortification: related to MUNIMENT]

Munster /ˈmʌnstə(r)/ province of the S Republic of Ireland; pop. (1991) 1 009 533.

Münster /ˈmʊnstə(r)/ city in NW Germany, a port on the Dortmund–Ems Canal (see DORTMUND); pop. (est. 1995) 264 887. The service industries provide most employment in the city.

muon /ˈmjuːɒn/ *n. Physics* unstable elementary particle like an electron, but with a much greater mass. [μ (MU), the symbol for it]

mural /ˈmjʊər(ə)l/ –*n.* painting executed directly on a wall. –*adj.* of, on, or like a wall. [Latin *murus* wall]

Murcia /ˈmɜːʃə, Spanish ˈmʊəθɪə/ **1** autonomous region in SE Spain; pop. (est. 1994) 1 070 401. **2** its capital city; industries include textiles, esp. silk; pop. (est. 1994) 341 531.

murder –*n.* **1** intentional unlawful killing of a human being by another. **2** *colloq.* unpleasant, troublesome, or dangerous state of affairs. –*v.* **1** kill (a human being) intentionally and unlawfully. **2** *colloq.* **a** utterly defeat. **b** spoil by a bad performance, mispronunciation, etc. □ **cry blue murder** *colloq.* make an extravagant outcry. **get away with murder** *colloq.* do whatever one wishes and escape punishment. □ **murderer** *n.* **murderess** *n.* [Old English]

murderous *adj.* **1** (of a person, weapon, action, etc.) capable of, intending, or involving murder or great harm. **2** *colloq.* extremely arduous or unpleasant.

♦ **Murdoch** /ˈmɜːdɒk/, **(Keith) Rupert** (1931–) Australian-born publisher and media entrepreneur. Chairman of News International plc since 1969, and director (since 1981) and chairman (1982–90; 1994–) of the Times Newspapers Holdings Ltd., he is also president of News America Publishing Inc. Murdoch's interests include television companies and the HarperCollins publishing group.

---

murk *n.* darkness, poor visibility. [probably Scandinavian]

murky *adj.* (**-ier, -iest**) **1** dark, gloomy. **2** (of darkness, liquid, etc.) thick, dirty. **3** suspiciously obscure (*murky past*). □ **murkily** *adv.* **murkiness** *n.*

Murmansk /mʊəˈmænsk/ fishing-port in NW Russia, on the Kola Bay, an inlet of the Barents Sea; pop. (est. 1995) 407 000. The harbour is ice-free throughout the year.

murmur /ˈmɜːmə(r)/ –*n.* **1** subdued continuous sound, as made by waves, a brook, etc. **2** softly spoken or nearly inarticulate utterance. **3** subdued expression of discontent. –*v.* **1** make a murmur. **2** utter (words) in a low voice. **3** (usu. foll. by *at, against*) complain in low tones, grumble. [Latin]

Murphy's Law /ˈmɜːfɪz/ *n. joc.* any of various maxims about the perverseness of things. [*Murphy*, Irish surname]

murrain /ˈmʌrɪn/ *n.* infectious disease of cattle. [Anglo-French *moryn*]

Murray /ˈmʌrɪ/ principal river of Australia, rising in New South Wales and flowing W to the Indian Ocean.

Mus.B. *abbr.* (also **Mus. Bac.**) Bachelor of Music. [Latin *Musicae Baccalaureus*]

Muscadet /ˈmʌskəˌdeɪ/ *n.* **1** a dry white wine from the Loire region of France. **2** variety of grape used for this. [*Muscadet* grape]

Muscat /ˈmʌskæt/ capital of Oman, a port on the Gulf of Oman; pop. (1993) 51 969.

muscat /ˈmʌskət/ *n.* **1** sweet usu. fortified white wine made from musk-flavoured grapes. **2** this grape. [Provençal: related to MUSK]

muscatel /ˌmʌskəˈtel/ *n.* **1** = MUSCAT. **2** raisin from a muscat grape.

muscle /ˈmʌs(ə)l/ *–n.* **1** fibrous tissue producing movement in or maintaining the position of an animal body. **2** part of an animal body that is composed of muscles. **3** strength, power. *–v.* (**-ling**) (foll. by *in, in on*) *colloq.* force oneself on others; intrude by forceful means. □ **not move a muscle** be completely motionless. [Latin diminutive of *mus* mouse]

muscle-bound *adj.* with muscles stiff and inelastic through excessive exercise.

muscle-man *n.* man with highly developed muscles.

Muscovite /ˈmʌskəˌvaɪt/ *–n.* native or citizen of Moscow. *–adj.* of Moscow. [from *Muscovy*, principality of Moscow]

Muscovy duck /ˈmʌskəvɪ/ *n.* crested duck with red markings on its head. [*Muscovy*, principality of Moscow]

muscular /ˈmʌskjʊlə(r)/ *adj.* **1** of or affecting the muscles. **2** having well-developed muscles. **3** robust. □ **muscularity** /-ˈlærɪtɪ/ *n.*

muscular Christianity *n.* Christian life of cheerful physical activity as described in the writings of Charles Kingsley.

muscular dystrophy *n.* hereditary progressive wasting of the muscles.

musculature /ˈmʌskjʊlətʃə(r)/ *n.* muscular system of a body or organ.

Mus.D. *abbr.* (also **Mus. Doc.**) Doctor of Music. [Latin *Musicae Doctor*]

muse[1] /mjuːz/ *v.* (**-sing**) **1** (usu. foll. by *on, upon*) ponder, reflect. **2** say meditatively. [French]

muse[2] /mjuːz/ *n.* **1** (in Greek and Roman mythology) any of the nine goddesses who inspire poetry, music, etc. **2** (usu. prec. by *the*) poet's inspiration. [Greek *Mousa*]

museum /mjuːˈzɪəm/ *n.* building used for storing and exhibiting objects of historical, scientific, or cultural interest. [Greek: related to MUSE[2]]

museum piece *n.* **1** specimen of art etc. fit for a museum. **2** *derog.* old-fashioned or quaint person or object.

mush *n.* **1** soft pulp. **2** feeble sentimentality. **3** *US* maize porridge. [apparently var. of MASH]

mushroom *–n.* **1** edible fungus with a stem and domed cap. **2** pinkish-brown colour of this. *–v.* appear or develop rapidly. [French *mousseron* from Latin]

mushroom cloud *n.* mushroom-shaped cloud from a nuclear explosion.

mushy *adj.* (**-ier, -iest**) **1** like mush; soft. **2** feebly sentimental. □ **mushiness** *n.*

music /ˈmjuːzɪk/ *n.* **1** art of combining vocal or instrumental sounds in a harmonious or expressive way. **2** sounds so produced. **3** musical composition. **4** written or printed score of this. **5** pleasant natural sound. □ **music to one's ears** something one is pleased to hear. [Greek: related to MUSE[2]]

musical *–adj.* **1** of music. **2** (of sounds etc.) melodious, harmonious. **3** fond of, sensitive to, or skilled in music. **4** set to or accompanied by music. *–n.* musical film or play. □ **musicality** /-ˈkælɪtɪ/ *n.* **musically** *adv.*

musical box *n.* box containing a mechanism which plays a tune.

musical chairs *n.pl.* **1** party game in which the players compete in successive rounds for a decreasing number of chairs. **2** series of changes or political manoeuvring etc.

music centre *n.* equipment combining radio, record-player, tape recorder, etc.

music-hall *n.* **1** variety entertainment with singing, dancing, etc. **2** theatre for this.

musician /mjuːˈzɪʃ(ə)n/ *n.* person who plays a musical instrument, esp. professionally. □ **musicianly** *adj.* **musicianship** *n.* [French: related to MUSIC]

musicology /ˌmjuːzɪˈkɒlədʒɪ/ *n.* the academic study of music. □ **musicologist** *n.* **musicological** /-kəˈlɒdʒɪk(ə)l/ *adj.*

music stand *n.* support for sheet music.

music stool *n.* piano stool.

musk *n.* **1** substance secreted by the male musk deer and used in perfumes. **2** plant which orig. had a smell of musk. □ **musky** *adj.* (**-ier, -iest**). **muskiness** *n.* [Latin *muscus* from Persian]

musk deer *n.* small hornless Asian deer.

musket *n. hist.* infantryman's (esp. smooth-bored) light gun. [Italian *moschetto* crossbow bolt]

musketeer /ˌmʌskəˈtɪə(r)/ *n. hist.* soldier armed with a musket.

musketry /ˈmʌskɪtrɪ/ *n.* **1** muskets; soldiers armed with muskets. **2** knowledge of handling small arms.

musk ox *n.* shaggy North American ruminant with curved horns.

muskrat *n.* **1** large North American aquatic rodent with a musky smell. **2** its fur.

musk-rose *n.* rambling rose smelling of musk.

Muslim /ˈmʊzlɪm, ˈmʌ-/ (also **Moslem** /ˈmɒzləm/) *–n.* follower of the Islamic religion. *–adj.* of the Muslims or their religion. [Arabic: related to ISLAM]

muslin /ˈmʌzlɪn/ *n.* fine delicately woven cotton fabric. [Italian *Mussolo* MOSUL]

musquash /ˈmʌskwɒʃ/ *n.* = MUSKRAT. [Algonquian]

mussel /ˈmʌs(ə)l/ *n.* bivalve mollusc, esp. of the kind used for food. [Old English: related to MUSCLE]

must[1] *–v.aux.* (*present* **must**; *past* **had to** or in indirect speech **must**) (foll. by infin., or *absol.*) **1 a** be obliged to (*you must go to school*). **b** in ironic questions (*must you slam the door?*). **2** be certainly (*you must be her sister*). **3** ought to (*must see what can be done*). **4** expressing insistence (*must ask you to leave*). **5** (foll. by *not* + infin.) **a** not be permitted to, be forbidden to (*must not smoke*). **b** ought not; need not (*mustn't think he's angry; must not worry*). **c** expressing insistence that something should not be done (*they must not be told*). *–n. colloq.* thing that should not be missed (*this exhibition is a must*). □ **I must say** often *iron.* I cannot refrain from saying (*I must say he tries hard; a fine way to behave, I must say*). **must needs** see NEEDS. [Old English]

■ **Usage** In sense 1a, the negative (i.e. lack of obligation) is expressed by *not have to* or *need not*; *must not* denotes positive forbidding, as in *you must not smoke*.

must[2] *n.* grape juice before fermentation is complete. [Old English from Latin]

mustache *US* var. of MOUSTACHE.

mustang *n.* small wild horse of Mexico and California. [Spanish]

mustard /ˈmʌstəd/ *n.* **1 a** plant with slender pods and yellow flowers. **b** seeds of this crushed into a paste and used as a spicy condiment. **2** plant eaten at the seedling stage, often with cress. **3** brownish-yellow colour. [Romanic: related to MUST[2]]

mustard gas *n.* colourless oily liquid, whose vapour is a powerful irritant.

muster *–v.* **1** collect (orig. soldiers) for inspection, to check numbers, etc. **2** collect, gather together. **3** summon (courage etc.). *–n.* assembly of persons for inspection. □ **pass muster** be accepted as adequate. [Latin *monstro* show]

Mustique /mʊˈstiːk/ small Caribbean island in the N Grenadines, part of the territory of St Vincent and the Grenadines.

mustn't /ˈmʌs(ə)nt/ *contr.* must not.

musty *adj.* (**-ier, -iest**) **1** mouldy, stale. **2** dull, antiquated. □ **mustily** *adv.* **mustiness** *n.* [perhaps an alteration of *moisty*: related to MOIST]

mutable /ˈmjuːtəb(ə)l/ *adj. literary* liable to change. □ **mutability** /-ˈbɪlɪtɪ/ *n.* [Latin *muto* change]

mutagen /ˈmjuːtədʒ(ə)n/ *n.* agent promoting genetic mutation. □ **mutagenic** /-ˈdʒenɪk/ *adj.* **mutagenesis** /-ˈdʒenɪsɪs/ *n.* [from MUTATION, -GEN]

mutant /ˈmjuːt(ə)nt/ *–adj.* resulting from mutation. *–n.* mutant organism or gene.

Mutare /muːˈtɑːrɪ/ (formerly, until 1982, **Umtali** /ʊmˈtɑːlɪ/) town in E Zimbabwe, trading centre for a fruit- and timber-producing region; industries include paper milling and food canning; pop. (1992) 131 808.

mutate /mjuːˈteɪt/ *v.* (**-ting**) (cause to) undergo mutation.

mutation /mjuːˈteɪʃ(ə)n/ *n.* **1** change, alteration. **2** genetic change which, when transmitted to offspring, gives rise to heritable variations. **3** mutant. [Latin *muto* change]

mutatis mutandis /muːˌtɑːtis muːˈtændis/ *adv.* (in comparing cases) making the necessary alterations. [Latin]

mute /mjuːt/ *–adj.* **1** silent, refraining from or temporarily bereft of speech. **2** (of a person or animal) dumb. **3** not expressed in speech (*mute protest*). **4** (of a letter) not pronounced. *–n.* **1** dumb person. **2** device for damping the sound of a musical instrument. **3** unsounded consonant. *–v.* (**-ting**) **1** deaden or soften the sound of (esp. a musical instrument). **2 a** tone down, make less intense. **b** (as **muted** *adj.*) (of colours etc.) subdued. □ **mutely** *adv.* **muteness** *n.* [Latin *mutus*]

mute button *n.* device on a telephone to temporarily prevent the caller from hearing what is being said at the receiver's end, or on a television etc. to temporarily turn off the sound.

mute swan *n.* common white swan.

mutilate /ˈmjuːtɪˌleɪt/ *v.* (**-ting**) **1 a** deprive (a person or animal) of a limb or organ. **b** destroy the use of (a limb or organ). **2** excise or damage part of (a book etc.). □ **mutilation** /-ˈleɪʃ(ə)n/ *n.* [Latin *mutilus* maimed]

mutineer /ˌmjuːtɪˈnɪə(r)/ *n.* person who mutinies. [Romanic: related to MOVE]

mutinous /ˈmjuːtɪnəs/ *adj.* rebellious; ready to mutiny. □ **mutinously** *adv.*

mutiny /ˈmjuːtɪnɪ/ *–n.* (*pl.* **-ies**) open revolt, esp. by soldiers or sailors against their officers. *–v.* (**-ies, -ied**) (often foll. by *against*) revolt; engage in mutiny.

mutt *n.* **1** *slang* ignorant or stupid person. **2** *derog.* dog. [abbreviation of MUTTON-HEAD]

mutter *–v.* **1** (also *absol.*) utter (words) in a barely audible manner. **2** (often foll. by *against, at*) murmur or grumble. *–n.* **1** muttered words or sounds. **2** muttering. [related to MUTE]

mutton *n.* flesh of sheep as food. [medieval Latin *multo* sheep]

mutton dressed as lamb *n. colloq.* middle-aged or elderly woman dressed to appear younger.

mutton-head *n. colloq.* stupid person.

mutual /ˈmjuːtʃʊəl/ *adj.* **1** (of feelings, actions, etc.) experienced or done by each of two or more parties to or towards the other(s) (*mutual affection*). **2** *colloq.* common to two or more persons (*a mutual friend*). **3** having the same (specified) relationship to each other (*mutual well-wishers*). □ **mutuality** /-ˈælɪtɪ/ *n.* **mutually** *adv.* [Latin *mutuus* borrowed]

■ **Usage** The use of *mutual* in sense 2, although often found, is considered incorrect by some people, for whom *common* is preferable.

♦ **mutual fund** *n. US* = UNIT TRUST.

♦ **mutual life-assurance company** *n.* type of life-assurance company that grew out of the Friendly Societies. There are no shareholders and apart from benefits and running expenses there are no other withdrawals from the fund; thus any profits are distributed to policy-holders.

♦ **mutual mistake** see MISTAKE *n.* 3.

MUX *n.* (also **mux**) = MULTIPLEXER.

Muzak /ˈmjuːzæk/ *n.* **1** *propr.* system of piped music used in public places. **2** (**muzak**) recorded light background music. [fanciful var. of MUSIC]

muzzle *–n.* **1** projecting part of an animal's face, including the nose and mouth. **2** guard, usu. of straps or wire, put over an animal's nose and mouth to stop it biting or feeding. **3** open end of a firearm. *–v.* (**-ling**) **1** put a muzzle on. **2** impose silence on. [medieval Latin *musum*]

muzzy *adj.* (**-ier, -iest**) **1** mentally hazy. **2** blurred, indistinct. □ **muzzily** *adv.* **muzziness** *n.* [origin unknown]

MV *abbr.* **1** merchant vessel. **2** (also **M/V**) motor vessel.

m.v. *abbr.* **1** market value. **2** mean variation. **3** motor vessel.

MVL *abbr.* motor-vehicle licence.

MW *–abbr.* **1** medium wave. **2** megawatt(s). *–international vehicle registration* Malawi.

MX *airline flight code* Mexicana.

my /maɪ/ *poss. pron.* (*attrib.*) **1** of or belonging to me. **2** affectionate, patronizing, etc. form of address (*my dear boy*). **3** in expressions of surprise (*my God!*; *oh my!*). **4** *colloq.* indicating a close relative etc. of the speaker (*my Johnny's ill again*). □ **my Lady** (or **Lord**) form of address to certain titled persons. [from MINE[1]]

myalgia /maɪˈældʒə/ *n.* muscular pain. □ **myalgic** *adj.* [Greek *mus* muscle]

Myanmar /ˌmiːænˈmɑː(r)/, **Union of** see BURMA.

mycelium /maɪˈsiːlɪəm/ *n.* (*pl.* **-lia**) microscopic thread-like parts of a fungus. [Greek *mukēs* mushroom]

Mycenaean /ˌmaɪsɪˈniːən/ *–adj.* of the late Bronze Age civilization in Greece (*c.*1580–1100 BC), depicted in the Homeric poems. *–n.* person of this civilization. [Latin *Mycenaeus*]

mycology /maɪˈkɒlədʒɪ/ *n.* **1** the study of fungi. **2** fungi of a particular region. □ **mycologist** *n.* [Greek *mukēs* mushroom]

Mykonos /ˈmɪkəˌnɒs/ (Greek **Míkonos** /ˈmiːkəˌnɒs/) Greek island of the Cyclades in the Aegean Sea, popular with tourists; pop. (est. 1994) 5700.

Mymensingh /ˌmaɪmənˈsɪŋ/ port in central Bangladesh, on the Brahmaputra River; industries include textiles and sugar refining; pop. (1991) 202 000.

myna /ˈmaɪnə/ *n.* (also **mynah, mina**) talking bird of the starling family. [Hindi]

myopia /maɪˈəʊpɪə/ *n.* **1** short-sightedness. **2** lack of imagination or insight. □ **myopic** /-ˈɒpɪk/ *adj.* **myopically** /-ˈɒpɪkəlɪ/ *adv.* [Greek *muō* shut, *ōps* eye]

MYRA /ˈmaɪrə/ *abbr. Finance* multi-year rescheduling agreement.

myriad /ˈmɪrɪəd/ *literary –n.* an indefinitely great number. *–adj.* innumerable. [Greek *murioi* 10 000]

myrrh /mɜː(r)/ *n.* gum resin used in perfume, medicine, incense, etc. [Latin *myrrha* from Greek]

myrtle /ˈmɜːt(ə)l/ *n.* evergreen shrub with shiny leaves and white scented flowers. [Greek *murtos*]

myself /maɪˈself/ *pron.* **1** *emphat. form* of I[2] or ME[1] (*I saw it myself*). **2** *refl. form* of ME[1] (*I was angry with myself*). □ **be myself** see ONESELF. **I myself** I for my part (*I myself am doubtful*). [Old English: related to ME[1], SELF]

Mysore /maɪˈsɔː(r)/ see KARNATAKA.

mysterious /mɪˈstɪərɪəs/ *adj.* full of or wrapped in mystery. □ **mysteriously** *adv.* [French: related to MYSTERY]

mystery /ˈmɪstərɪ/ *n.* (*pl.* **-ies**) **1** secret, hidden, or inexplicable matter. **2** secrecy or obscurity. **3** (*attrib.*) secret, undisclosed (*mystery guest*). **4** practice of making a secret of things (*engaged in mystery and intrigue*). **5** (in full **mystery story**) fictional work dealing with a puzzling event, esp. a murder. **6** a religious truth divinely revealed. **7** (in *pl.*) **a** secret religious rites of the ancient Greeks, Romans, etc. **b** *archaic* Eucharist. [Greek *mustērion*: related to MYSTIC]

mystery play *n.* miracle play.

mystery tour *n.* pleasure trip to an unspecified destination.

mystic /ˈmɪstɪk/ *–n.* person who seeks by contemplation etc. to achieve unity with the Deity, or who believes in the spiritual apprehension of truths that are beyond the understanding. –*adj.* = MYSTICAL. □ **mysticism** /-ˌsɪz(ə)m/ *n.* [Greek *mustēs* initiated person]

mystical *adj.* **1** of mystics or mysticism. **2** mysterious; occult; of hidden meaning. **3** spiritually allegorical or symbolic. □ **mystically** *adv.*

mystify /ˈmɪstɪˌfaɪ/ *v.* (**-ies**, **-ied**) **1** bewilder, confuse. **2** wrap in mystery. □ **mystification** /-fɪˈkeɪʃ(ə)n/ *n.* [French: related to MYSTIC or MYSTERY]

mystique /mɪˈstiːk/ *n.* atmosphere of mystery and veneration attending some activity, person, profession, etc. [French: related to MYSTIC]

myth /mɪθ/ *n.* **1** traditional story usu. involving supernatural or imaginary persons and embodying popular ideas on natural or social phenomena etc. **2** such narratives collectively. **3** widely held but false notion. **4** fictitious person, thing, or idea. **5** allegory (*Platonic myth*). □ **mythical** *adj.* **mythically** *adv.* [Greek *muthos*]

mythology /mɪˈθɒlədʒɪ/ *n.* (*pl.* **-ies**) **1** body of myths. **2** the study of myths. □ **mythological** /-θəˈlɒdʒɪk(ə)l/ *adj.* **mythologize** *v.* (also **-ise**) (**-zing** or **-sing**). [Greek: related to MYTH]

Mytilene /ˌmɪtɪˈliːnɪ/ (Greek **Mitilíni**) chief town of the Greek island of Lesbos, in the Aegean Sea, a port trading esp. in olive oil and citrus fruits; pop. (est. 1991) 25 440.

myxomatosis /ˌmɪksəməˈtəʊsɪs/ *n.* viral disease of rabbits. [Greek *muxa* mucus]

Nn

N[1] /en/ *n.* (also **n**) (*pl.* **Ns** or **N's**) **1** fourteenth letter of the alphabet. **2** (usu. **n**) indefinite number. □ **to the nth degree** to the utmost.

N[2] *abbr.* (also **N.**) **1** North; Northern. **2** New.

N[3] *–symb.* nitrogen. *–international vehicle registration* Norway. *–international civil aircraft marking* United States. *–postcode* North London.

n *abbr.* (also **n.**) **1** name. **2** *Commerce* net. **3** neuter.

NA *–abbr.* **1** *Banking* new account. **2** North America. *–international vehicle registration* Netherlands Antilles.

N/A *abbr.* **1** (also **N/a**) *Banking* new account. **2** (also **N/a**) *Banking* no account. **3** (also **N/a**) *Banking* no advice. **4** *Banking & Commerce* non-acceptance. **5** (also **n/a**) not applicable. **6** (also **n/a**) not available.

Na *symb.* sodium. [Latin *natrium*]

n.a.a. *abbr. Shipping* not always afloat.

NAAFI /ˈnæfɪ/ *abbr.* **1** Navy, Army, and Air Force Institutes. **2** canteen for servicemen run by the NAAFI.

NAB *abbr.* National Australia Bank.

nab *v.* (**-bb-**) *slang* **1** arrest; catch in wrongdoing. **2** grab. [origin unknown]

Nabeul /næˈbɜːl/ resort city in NE Tunisia; pop. (1984) 39 500.

Nablus /ˈnæbləs/ town in the West Bank area; pop. (est. 1989) 98 000.

NAC *abbr.* National Advisory Council.

Nacala /nəˈkɑːlə/ deep-water port in Mozambique, on the NE coast, linked by rail with landlocked Malawi.

nacho /ˈnætʃəʊ, ˈnɑː-/ *n.* (*pl.* **-s**) tortilla chip, usu. topped with melted cheese and spices etc. [origin uncertain]

NACODS /ˈneɪkɒdz/ *abbr.* National Association of Colliery Overmen, Deputies, and Shotfirers (trade union).

nacre /ˈneɪkə(r)/ *n.* mother-of-pearl from any shelled mollusc. □ **nacreous** /ˈneɪkrɪəs/ *adj.* [French]

nadir /ˈneɪdɪə(r)/ *n.* **1** part of the celestial sphere directly below an observer. **2** lowest point; time of deep despair. [Arabic, = opposite]

naevus /ˈniːvəs/ *n.* (*US* **nevus**) (*pl.* **naevi** /-vaɪ/) **1** raised red birthmark. **2** = MOLE[2]. [Latin]

NAf *symb.* Netherlands Antilles guilder.

naff *adj. slang* **1** unfashionable. **2** rubbishy. [origin unknown]

NAFTA /ˈnæftə/ *abbr.* **1** New Zealand–Australia Free Trade Agreement. **2** = NORTH AMERICAN FREE TRADE AGREEMENT.

nag[1] *v.* (**-gg-**) **1 a** persistently criticize or scold. **b** (often foll. by *at*) find fault or urge, esp. persistently. **2** (of a pain) be persistent. [originally a dial. word]

nag[2] *n. colloq.* horse. [origin unknown]

Nagaland /ˈnɑːgəˌlænd/ state in NE India; pop. (est. 1994) 1 410 000; capital, Kohima. Rice, sugar cane, and vegetables are produced; forest products (esp. mahogany) are also important. A resistance movement for independence has been active since the state was formed in 1963.

Nagar Haveli see DADRA AND NAGAR HAVELI.

Nagasaki /ˌnægəˈsɑːkɪ/ city in Japan, on the island of Kyushu, a port on the East China Sea; pop. (1995) 438 724. Target of the second atomic bomb attack in 1945 (see HIROSHIMA), the city was rebuilt and is now a centre of the shipbuilding industry.

Nagorno-Karabakh /nəˈgɔːnəʊˌkærəˈbæx/ autonomous region in Azerbaijan; pop. (est. 1991) 193 300; capital, Stepanakert. Primarily agricultural, producing cotton, grapes, and wheat, it also has deposits of metal and minerals. Armenian claims to the region, supported by the largely Armenian population, led to riots in 1988 and the conflict has continued since the breakup of the Soviet Union in 1992.

Nagoya /nəˈgɔɪə/ city and port in Japan, capital of Chubu region on the island of Honshu; industries include steel and textiles; pop. (1995) 2 152 258.

Nagpur /ˈnɑːgpʊə(r)/ city in central India, in the state of Maharashtra; industries include metallurgy, transport equipment, and cotton; pop. (1991) 1 624 752.

naiad /ˈnaɪæd/ *n.* water-nymph. [Latin from Greek]

nail *–n.* **1** small metal spike hammered in to join things together or as a peg or decoration. **2** horny covering on the upper surface of the tip of the human finger or toe. *–v.* **1** fasten with a nail or nails. **2** secure or get hold of (a person or thing). **3** keep (attention etc.) fixed. **4** expose or discover (a lie or liar). □ **nail down 1** bind (a person) to a promise etc. **2** define precisely. **3** fasten (a thing) with nails. **nail in a person's coffin** something thought to increase the risk of death. **on the nail** (esp. of payment) without delay. [Old English]

nail-file *n.* roughened metal or emery strip used for smoothing the nails.

nail polish *n.* (also **nail varnish**) varnish, usu. coloured, applied to the nails.

naira /ˈnaɪrə/ *n.* standard monetary unit of Nigeria. [contraction of NIGERIA]

Nairobi /naɪˈrəʊbɪ/ capital of Kenya; manufactures include textiles, chemicals, glass, and furniture; pop. (est. 1991) 2 000 000.

♦ **NAIRU** /ˈneɪruː/ *abbr. Econ.* non-accelerating inflation rate of unemployment, a modification of the natural rate of unemployment that represents inverse relationships between unemployment and the rate of increase in inflation, rather than inflation itself. Historically, increases in the rate of inflation have been associated with falls in unemployment and it may be that governments can exploit this relationship to reduce unemployment. This possibility, and the reasons for its existence, remains a central issue in macroeconomics.

---

naïve /naɪˈiːv/ *adj.* (also **naive**) **1** innocent; unaffected. **2** foolishly credulous. **3** (of art) produced in a sophisticated society but lacking conventional expertise. □ **naïvely** *adv.* **naïvety** *n.* (also ***naïveté***). [Latin *nativus* NATIVE]

Najaf /ˈnædʒæf/ holy city of the Shiite Muslims, in S Iraq; pop. (1987) 309 010.

NAK *abbr.* (also **nak**) *Telecom.* negative acknowledgement.

naked /ˈneɪkɪd/ *adj.* **1** without clothes; nude. **2** without its usual covering. **3** undisguised (*the naked truth*). **4** (of a light, flame, sword, etc.) unprotected or unsheathed. □ **nakedly** *adv.* **nakedness** *n.* [Old English]

♦ **naked call writing** *n.* selling (writing) a call option on equities that one does not own. A person may do this if he or she expects the price of a particular share to fall or remain unchanged. It is, however, a dangerous strategy because if the price rises the shares will have to be purchased at the market price in order to deliver them, thus involving an unlimited risk.

♦ **naked debenture** *n.* unsecured debenture.

---

naked eye *n.* (prec. by *the*) unassisted vision, e.g. without a telescope etc.

nakfa /ˈnækfɑ/ *n.* standard monetary unit of Eritrea.

Nakhichevan /ˌnɑːxɪtʃəˈvɑːn/ autonomous republic of Azerbaijan, forming an enclave in Armenia; pop. (1994) 315 000; capital, Nakhichevan; pop. (1994) 66 800. It is mainly agricultural, producing cereals, cotton, and tobacco; it also has textile and food-processing industries.

Nakhon Sawan /nɑːˌkɒn səˈwɑːn/ river port in central Thailand; pop. (est. 1991) 108 569.

Nakuru /næˈkuːruː/ industrial city in W Kenya, the trading centre of an agricultural region; pop. (est. 1991) 124 200.

NALGO /ˈnælgəʊ/ *abbr.* National and Local Government Officers' Association (trade union).

N. Am. *abbr.* North America(n).

Namaqualand /nəˈmɑːkwəˌlænd/ region in SW Africa divided into Little Namaqualand, in South Africa, which has important reserves of diamonds and copper, and Great Namaqualand, in Namibia.

NAMAS *abbr.* National Measurement and Accreditation Service.

namby-pamby /ˌnæmbɪˈpæmbɪ/ *–adj.* insipidly pretty or sentimental; weak. *–n.* (*pl.* **-ies**) namby-pamby person. [fanciful formulation on the name of the writer *Ambrose* Philips]

name *–n.* **1** word by which an individual person, family, animal, place, or thing is spoken of etc. **2 a** usu. abusive term used of a person etc. (*called him names*). **b** word denoting an object or esp. a class of objects etc. (*what is the name of those flowers?*). **3** famous person. **4** reputation, esp. a good one. **5** see LLOYD'S; SYNDICATE *n.* 2. **6** means of referring to or identifying some element in a computer program, computer network, or some other system. *–v.* (**-ming**) **1** give a name to. **2** state the name of. **3** mention; specify; cite. **4** nominate. □ **have to one's name** possess. **in name only** not in reality. **in the name of** as representing; by virtue of (*in the name of the law*). **make a name for oneself** become famous. □ **nameable** *adj.* [Old English]

name-day *n.* feast-day of the saint after whom a person is named.

name-dropping *n.* familiar mention of famous people as a form of boasting.

nameless *adj.* **1** having or showing no name. **2** unnamed (*our informant, who shall be nameless*). **3** too horrific to be named (*nameless vices*).

namely *adv.* that is to say; in other words.

Namen see NAMUR.

name-plate *n.* plate or panel bearing the name of an occupant of a room etc.

namesake *n.* person or thing having the same name as another. [probably from *for the name's sake*]

Namur /nəˈmʊə(r)/ (Flemish **Namen** /ˈnɑːmən/) **1** province in central Belgium; pop. (est. 1995) 434 446. **2** its capital city; manufactures include glass, paper, and leather goods; pop. (est. 1995) 105 014.

nan *n.* (also **nana, nanna** /ˈnænə/) *colloq.* grandmother. [childish pronunciation]

Nanaimo /næˈnaɪməʊ/ port in Canada, in British Columbia on the E coast of Vancouver Island; pop. (1991) 60 129.

Nanchang /nænˈtʃæŋ/ city in SE China, capital of Jiangxi province; pop. (est. 1991) 1 350 000.

Nancy /ˈnɑ̃sɪ/ town in NE France, capital of Lorraine; industries include iron, salt, machinery, and textiles; pop. (1990) 102 410.

nancy /ˈnænsɪ/ *n.* (*pl.* **-ies**) (in full **nancy boy**) *slang offens.* effeminate man, esp. a homosexual. [pet form of *Ann*]

Nanjing /nænˈdʒɪŋ/ (also **Nanking** /nænˈkɪŋ/) industrial city and port in E China, capital of Jiangsu province; pop. (est. 1991) 2 500 000.

Nanning /nænˈnɪŋ/ city in S China, capital of Guangxi Zhuang; pop. (est. 1991) 1 070 000. It is the commercial centre of an agricultural region and has food-processing and other industries; manufactures include paper and agricultural machinery.

nanny /ˈnænɪ/ *n.* (*pl.* **-ies**) **1** child's nurse. **2** *colloq.* grandmother. **3** (in full **nanny-goat**) female goat. [related to NANCY]

nano- *comb. form* denoting a factor of 10^{-9} (*nanosecond*). [Greek *nanos* dwarf]

Nantes /nɑ̃t/ city and major port in W France, on the River Loire, capital of Pays de la Loire region; industries include shipbuilding and oil refining; pop. (1990) 252 029.

NAO *abbr.* National Audit Office.

nap[1] *–v.* (**-pp-**) sleep lightly or briefly. *–n.* short sleep or doze, esp. by day. □ **catch a person napping** detect in negligence etc; catch off guard. [Old English]

nap[2] *n.* raised pile on textiles, esp. velvet. [Low German or Dutch]

nap[3] *–n.* **1** form of whist in which players declare the number of tricks they expect to take. **2** racing tip claimed to be almost a certainty. *–v.* (**-pp-**) name (a horse etc.) as a probable winner. □ **go nap 1** attempt to take all five tricks in nap. **2** risk everything. [*Napoleon*]

napalm /ˈneɪpɑːm/ *–n.* thick jellied hydrocarbon mixture used in bombs. *–v.* attack with napalm bombs. [from NAPHTHALENE, PALM[1]]

nape *n.* back of the neck. [origin unknown]

NAPF *abbr.* National Association of Pension Funds.

naphtha /ˈnæfθə/ *n.* inflammable hydrocarbon distilled from coal etc. [Latin from Greek]

naphthalene /ˈnæfθəˌliːn/ *n.* white crystalline substance produced by distilling coal tar.

Napier /ˈneɪpɪə(r)/ seaport in New Zealand, on North

Namibia /nəˈmɪbɪə/, **Republic of** (former name, until 1968, **South West Africa**) country in SW Africa, between Angola and South Africa. Subsistence agriculture employs much of the labour force. Livestock rearing is important, cattle being exported, although agricultural production was affected by drought in the early 1990s. Namibia has a potentially rich fishery (esp. of pilchards) and the expanding fishing industry is a major source of prospective growth. Mining, however, still makes a large contribution to exports by value, including diamonds, uranium, and copper. Manufacturing industries, including mineral, fish, and meat processing, are relatively underdeveloped.
History. A German protectorate from 1884 until 1915, the territory was thereafter administered by South Africa, to which it was mandated by the League of Nations in 1919. Despite increasing international insistence, after 1946, that this mandate had ended, South Africa continued to administer the country for many years. Namibia finally became independent, and a member of the Commonwealth, in 1990 after free elections had been held towards the end of 1989. The enclave of Walvis Bay was returned in 1994. President, Dr Sam Nujoma; prime minister, Hage Geingob; capital, Windhoek. □ **Namibian** *adj.* & *n.*

languages	English (official), Afrikaans, German
currency	dollar (N$) of 100 cents
pop. (1996)	1 709 000
GNP (1994)	US$3B
literacy	77% (m); 73% (f)
life expectancy	57 (m); 60 (f)

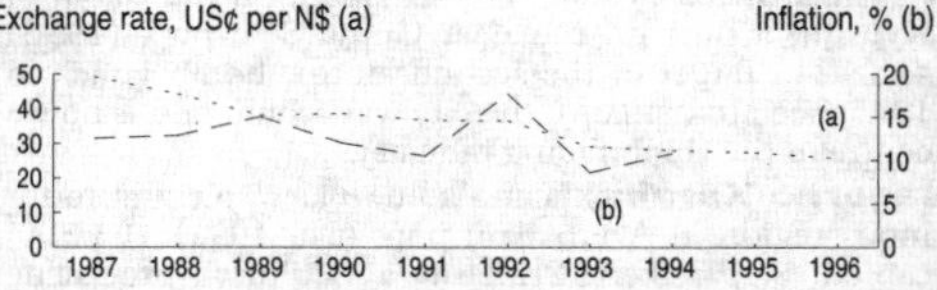

Island, major centre of the country's wool trade; pop. (1994) 111 700.

napkin /'næpkɪn/ *n.* **1** piece of linen etc. for wiping the lips, fingers, etc. at meals. **2** baby's nappy. [French *nappe* from Latin *mappa* MAP]

Naples /'neɪpəlz/ (Italian **Napoli** /'næpəlɪ/) city and port on the W coast of Italy, capital of Campania; pop. (est. 1994) 1 061 583. A commercial and tourist centre, it has textile, oil-refining, food-processing, and car-manufacturing industries.

NAPO /'næpəʊ/ *abbr.* National Association of Probation Officers (trade union).

nappy /'næpɪ/ *n.* (*pl.* **-ies**) piece of towelling etc. wrapped round a baby to absorb or retain urine and faeces. [from NAPKIN]

Nara /'nɑːrə/ city in Japan, on the island of Honshu; pop. (1995) 359 234.

narcissism /'nɑːsɪ,sɪz(ə)m/ *n.* excessive or erotic interest in oneself. □ **narcissistic** /-'sɪstɪk/ *adj.* [*Narkissos*, name of a youth in Greek myth who fell in love with his reflection]

narcissus /nɑː'sɪsəs/ *n.* (*pl.* **-cissi** /-saɪ/) any of several flowering bulbs, including the daffodil. [Latin from Greek]

narcosis /nɑː'kəʊsɪs/ *n.* **1** state of insensibility. **2** induction of this. [Greek *narkē* numbness]

narcotic /nɑː'kɒtɪk/ *–adj.* **1** (of a substance) inducing drowsiness etc. **2** (of a drug) affecting the mind. *–n.* narcotic substance, drug, or influence. [Greek *narkōtikos*]

nark *slang –n.* police informer or decoy. *–v.* annoy. [Romany *nāk* nose]

narrate /nə'reɪt/ *v.* (**-ting**) **1** give a continuous story or account of. **2** provide a spoken accompaniment for (a film etc.). □ **narration** /nə'reɪʃ(ə)n/ *n.* **narrator** *n.* [Latin *narro*]

narrative /'nærətɪv/ *–n.* ordered account of connected events. *–adj.* of or by narration.

narrow /'nærəʊ/ *–adj.* (**-er, -est**) **1 a** of small width. **b** confined or confining (*within narrow bounds*). **2** of limited scope (*in the narrowest sense*). **3** with little margin (*narrow escape*). **4** precise; exact. **5** = NARROW-MINDED. *–n.* (usu. in *pl.*) narrow part of a strait, river, pass, street, etc. *–v.* become or make narrow; contract; lessen. □ **narrowly** *adv.* **narrowness** *n.* [Old English]

narrow boat *n.* canal boat.

narrow-minded *adj.* rigid or restricted in one's views, intolerant. □ **narrow-mindedness** *n.*

♦ **narrow money** *n. colloq.* M0, or sometimes M1: the part of the money supply that can directly perform the function of a medium of exchange. See MONEY SUPPLY.

♦ **narrow-range securities** *n.pl.* see TRUSTEE INVESTMENTS.

Narvik /'nɑːvɪk/ ice-free port in Norway, on the NW coast opposite the Lofoten Islands, linked by rail to the iron-ore mines of N Sweden; pop. (1990) 18 500.

narwhal /'nɑːw(ə)l/ *n.* Arctic white whale, the male of which has a long tusk. [Dutch from Danish]

NASA /'næsə/ *abbr.* (in the US) National Aeronautics and Space Administration.

nasal /'neɪz(ə)l/ *–adj.* **1** of the nose. **2** (of a letter or a sound) pronounced with the breath passing through the nose, e.g. *m*, *n*, *ng*. **3** (of the voice or speech) having many nasal sounds. *–n.* nasal letter or sound. □ **nasalize** *v.* (also **-ise**) (**-zing** or **-sing**). **nasally** *adv.* [Latin *nasus* nose]

nascent /'næs(ə)nt/ *adj.* **1** in the act of being born. **2** just beginning to be; not yet mature. □ **nascency** /'næsənsɪ/ *n.* [Latin: related to NATAL]

NASD *abbr.* (in the US) National Association of Securities Dealers Inc.

NASDAQ /'næs,dæk/ *abbr.* = NATIONAL ASSOCIATION OF SECURITIES DEALERS AUTOMATED QUOTATION SYSTEM.

♦ **NASDAQ index** *n.* price index of the National Association of Securities Dealers Automated Quotation System for over-the-counter trading. The index is market-value-weighted. There are six indexes covering different sectors of the market, all of which were based on 5 Feb. 1971. Two newer indexes are the NASDAQ-100 and the NASDAQ-Financial, operating from 1 Feb. 1985, valued at 250.

♦ **NASDAQ International** *n.* international service based on NASDAQ that came into operation in January 1992. It provides a screen-based quotation system to support market-making in US registered equities from 8.30 a.m. until 2 p.m. London time (i.e. between 3.30 a.m. and 9 a.m. Eastern Standard Time) on US business days. Most US and Canadian equity securities are available on the system.

♦ **Nash equilibrium** *n.* equilibrium in an economy in which every individual is maximizing his or her utility, taking into account the actions of all other individuals. It is a central concept in game theory (which permits the solution of problems in bargaining theory). [*Nash*, name of an economist]

Nashville /'næʃvɪl/ city in the US, capital of Tennessee; pop. (est. 1994) 504 505. A centre of the country-and-western music industry, it also has railway engineering, printing and publishing, glass, and clothing industries.

Nassau /'næsɔː/ capital of the Bahamas, a port and tourist centre on New Providence Island; pop. (1990) 172 196.

nasturtium /nə'stɜːʃəm/ *n.* trailing plant with edible leaves and bright orange, yellow, or red flowers. [Latin]

nasty /'nɑːstɪ/ *–adj.* (**-ier, -iest**) **1** highly unpleasant. **2** difficult to negotiate. **3** (of a person or animal) ill-natured. *–n.* (*pl.* **-ies**) *colloq.* horror film, esp. one on video and depicting cruelty or killing. □ **nastily** *adv.* **nastiness** *n.* [origin unknown]

nasty piece of work *n. colloq.* unpleasant or contemptible person.

NAS/UWT *abbr.* National Association of Schoolmasters/Union of Women Teachers.

Nat. *abbr.* **1** National. **2** Nationalist. **3** Natural.

Natal see KWAZULU-NATAL.

natal /'neɪt(ə)l/ *adj.* of or from one's birth. [Latin *natalis* from *nascor nat-* be born]

NATFHE *abbr.* National Association of Teachers in Further and Higher Education (trade union).

nation /'neɪʃ(ə)n/ *n.* community of people of mainly common descent, history, language, etc., forming a state or inhabiting a territory. [Latin: related to NATAL]

national /'næʃən(ə)l/ *–adj.* **1** of a, or the, nation. **2** characteristic of a particular nation. *–n.* **1** citizen of a specified country. **2** fellow-countryman. **3** (**the National**) = GRAND NATIONAL. □ **nationally** *adv.*

national anthem *n.* song adopted by a nation, intended to inspire patriotism.

♦ **National Association of Securities Dealers Automated Quotation System** *n.* (also **NASDAQ**) US computer system for trading in over-the-counter securities that began operations on 8 Feb. 1971, when it was the first screen-based trading system with no market floor. It is now the second largest stock market in the US, share traded in 1991 being worth $694,000 million. In 1991 NASDAQ had 425 active market makers, with an average of 10.5 market makers per security; it had 179 939 terminals in the US and some 25 453 terminals operating in Canada, Switzerland, the UK, Germany, and France (see also NASDAQ INTERNATIONAL). NASDAQ provided the basis for the SEAQ system on the London Stock Exchange.

♦ **national bank** *n.* US commercial bank established by federal charter and required to be a member of the Federal Reserve System. National banks were created by the National Bank Act (1863) and formerly issued their own banknotes. Cf. STATE BANK.

♦ **National Chamber of Trade** *n.* (also **NCT**) non-profit-making organization founded in 1897, with headquarters in Henley-on-Thames, that links and represents local chambers of trade and commerce, national trade associations, and individual businesses in the UK. It maintains lobbies scrutinizing legislation in both Westminster and Brussels and provides expert advice for affiliated chambers and members.

◆ **National Coal Board** (also **NCB**) see BRITISH COAL CORPORATION.

◆ **National Consumer Council** *n.* (also **NCC**) organization set up by the UK government in 1975 to watch over consumer interests and speak for the consumer to the government, nationalized industries, and independent industry and commerce. It deals only with issues of policy.

---

national curriculum *n.* common programme of study for pupils in the maintained schools of England and Wales, with tests at specified ages.

◆ **national debt** *n.* money owed by a central government, including both internal and overseas debts. Net government borrowing each year is added to the national debt. By the end of the financial year 1990, the UK national debt amounted to £192.6 billion, of which £6.7 billion was non-sterling and £185.9 billion was in sterling. The non-sterling debt is important because interest on it adversely affects the balance of payments. Management of the national debt, which can be an important aspect of government monetary policy, is in the hands of the **National Debt Commissioners** of the Bank of England.

◆ **National Economic Development Office** *n. hist.* UK government organization whose council, the National Economic Development Council (**NEDC** or **Neddy**), of which the Chancellor of the Exchequer was chairman, brought together members of the government (including the secretaries of state for Education and Science, Employment, Energy, Environment, and Trade and Industry), management, and the unions to consider issues concerning employment and economic growth.

◆ **National Enterprise Board** (also **NEB**) see BRITISH TECHNOLOGY GROUP.

National Front *n.* UK political party with extreme reactionary views on immigration etc.

◆ **National Girobank** see GIRO *n.* 1a.

---

national grid *n.* **1** network of high-voltage electric power lines between major power stations. **2** metric system of geographical coordinates used in maps of the British Isles.

National Health *n.* (also **National Health Service**, **NHS**) system of national medical care paid for mainly by taxation.

◆ **national income** *n.* total annual money value of the goods and services produced by a country. See GROSS NATIONAL PRODUCT; NATIONAL INCOME ACCOUNTS; NET NATIONAL PRODUCT.

◆ **national income accounts** *n.pl.* accounts that provide figures for the main macroeconomic variables, such as gross national product, consumption, and investment. Almost all countries produce national income accounts, which are widely used for evaluating national economic performances. Although the UN provides a standard system for measurement of national income accounts, many countries do not follow these and many disagreements remain as to how they should be measured. See also CIRCULAR FLOW OF INCOME.

◆ **National Institute of Economic and Social Research** *n.* (also **NIESR**) organization founded in 1938 with the aim of increasing knowledge of the social and economic conditions of contemporary society. It conducts research by its own staff and in cooperation with the universities and other academic bodies. The Institute publishes a quarterly analysis of the economic situation and prospects in the *National Institute Economic Review*.

◆ **National Insurance** *n.* (also **NI**) levy in the UK for social security purposes, notionally intended to fund sickness and unemployment benefits and national retirement pensions. There are four classes of payment: Class 1 primary and secondary, paid by employees and employers respectively, based on the wages and salaries of employees; Class 2, a weekly sum paid by the self-employed; Class 3, voluntary contributions to keep up contribution requirements; Class 4, a further levy on the self-employed based on levels of profit. See also STATE EARNINGS-RELATED PENSION SCHEME.

---

nationalism *n.* **1** patriotic feeling, principles, etc. **2** policy of national independence. □ **nationalist** *n.* & *adj.* **nationalistic** /-ˈlɪstɪk/ *adj.*

nationality /ˌnæʃəˈnælɪtɪ/ *n.* (*pl.* **-ies**) **1** status of belonging to a particular nation (*has British nationality*). **2** condition of being national; distinctive national qualities. **3** ethnic group forming a part of one or more political nations.

◆ **nationalization** /ˌnæʃənəlaɪˈzeɪʃ(ə)n/ *n.* (also **-isation**) **1** process of nationalizing an industry etc. Historically, nationalization has been achieved through compulsory purchase, although this need not necessarily be the case. Nationalization has often been pursued as much for political as economic ends and the economic justifications themselves are varied. One strong argument for nationalization is that if a company possesses a natural monopoly, the pure economic profits it earns should be shared by the whole population through state ownership. Another argument might be that particular industries are strategically important for the nation and therefore cannot be entrusted to private enterprise. In the 1980s and 1990s Conservative governments in the UK have tended to reverse Labour's nationalization of the 1950s, 1960s, and 1970s with a series of privatization measures (see PRIVATIZATION). **2** making national.

---

nationalize /ˈnæʃənəˌlaɪz/ *v.* (also **-ise**) (**-zing** or **-sing**) **1** take (an industry, land, resources, etc.) into state ownership (see NATIONALIZATION 1). **2** make national.

national park *n.* area of natural beauty protected by the state for the use of the public.

◆ **national plan** *n.* economic plan formulated by a government as a blueprint for its economic development over a stated period, usu. five or ten years.

◆ **National Research and Development Corporation** (also **NRDC**) see BRITISH TECHNOLOGY GROUP.

◆ **National Savings** *n.* (in full **Department for National Savings**) UK government department established in 1969, before which it was known as the Post Office Savings Department. It is responsible for administering a wide range of schemes for personal savers, including Premium Bonds, income bonds, and yearly savings plans. In addition the department has offered a range of **National Savings Certificates** costing either £10 (up to 1985) or £25 (from 1985), some of which have been index-linked. The income they pay is income-tax free and the element of capital gain is free of capital-gains tax. See also NATIONAL SAVINGS BANK; NATIONAL SAVINGS STOCK REGISTER.

◆ **National Savings Bank** *n.* (also **NSB**) savings bank operated by the Department for National Savings through the agency of the Post Office. It offers ordinary accounts with a minimum deposit of £5 and a maximum of £10,000, and investment accounts paying a higher rate of interest for deposits of between £5 and £25,000.

◆ **National Savings Stock Register** *n.* organization run by the Department for National Savings to enable members of the public to purchase certain Treasury stock and other gilts as an alternative to the main Bank of England Stock Register. Purchases and sales are made by post and income is taxable, but is paid before deduction of tax (unlike the Bank of England Register). Because transactions are carried out by post, this method does not provide the maximum flexibility for dealing in a moving market.

---

national service *n. hist.* conscripted peacetime military service.

nationwide *adj.* & *adv.* extending over the whole nation.

native /ˈneɪtɪv/ *–n.* **1 a** (usu. foll. by *of*) person born in a specified place. **b** local inhabitant. **2** often *offens.* member of a non-White indigenous people, as regarded by colonial settlers. **3** (usu. foll. by *of*) indigenous animal or plant. *–adj.* **1** inherent; innate. **2** of one's birth (*native country*). **3** (usu. foll. by *to*) belonging to a specified place. **4** (esp. of a non-European) indigenous; born in a place. **5** (of metal etc.) found in a pure or uncombined state. [Latin: related to NATAL]

nativity /nəˈtɪvɪtɪ/ *n.* (*pl.* **-ies**) **1** (esp. **the Nativity**) **a** Christ's birth. **b** festival of Christ's birth. **2** birth. [Latin: related to NATIVE]

NATLAS /ˈnætlæs/ *abbr.* National Testing Laboratory Accreditation Scheme.

NATO /ˈneɪtəʊ/ *abbr.* (also **Nato**) North Atlantic Treaty Organization.

NATS /næts/ *abbr.* National Air Traffic Services.

natter *colloq. –v.* chatter idly. *–n.* aimless chatter. [imitative, originally dial.]

natterjack /ˈnætəˌdʒæk/ *n.* a kind of small toad. [perhaps from NATTER]

natty /ˈnætɪ/ *adj.* (**-ier**, **-iest**) *colloq.* trim; smart. □ **nattily** *adv.* [cf. NEAT]

natural /ˈnætʃər(ə)l/ *–adj.* **1 a** existing in or caused by nature (*natural landscape*). **b** uncultivated (*in its natural state*). **2** in the course of nature (*died of natural causes*). **3** not surprising; to be expected (*natural for her to be upset*). **4** unaffected, spontaneous. **5** innate (*natural talent for music*). **6** not disguised or altered (as by make-up etc.). **7** likely or suited by its or their nature to be such (*natural enemies; natural leader*). **8** physically existing (*the natural world*). **9** illegitimate. **10** *Mus.* (of a note) not sharpened or flattened (*B natural*). *–n.* **1** *colloq.* (usu. foll. by *for*) person or thing naturally suitable, adept, etc. **2** *Mus.* **a** sign (♮) denoting a return to natural pitch. **b** natural note. □ **naturalness** *n.* [Latin: related to NATURE]

natural gas *n.* gas found in the earth's crust, not manufactured.

natural history *n.* the study of animals or plants.

♦ **natural increase** *n.* difference between the number of births and the number of deaths in a particular population over a particular period. To find out whether a population is increasing or decreasing it is also necessary to know the net migration rate (the difference between emigration and immigration).

naturalism *n.* **1** theory or practice in art and literature of realistic representation. **2 a** theory of the world that excludes the supernatural or spiritual. **b** moral or religious system based on this. □ **naturalistic** /-ˈlɪstɪk/ *adj.*

naturalist *n.* **1** person who studies natural history. **2** adherent of naturalism.

naturalize *v.* (also **-ise**) (**-zing** or **-sing**) **1** admit (a foreigner) to citizenship. **2** successfully introduce (an animal, plant, etc.) into another region. **3** adopt (a foreign word, custom, etc.). □ **naturalization** /-ˈzeɪʃ(ə)n/ *n.*

♦ **natural justice** *n.* minimum standard of fairness to be applied when resolving a dispute. The main rules of natural justice include the right to be heard, whereby each party to the dispute should be given an opportunity to answer any allegations made by the other party, and the rule against bias, whereby the person involved in settling the dispute should act impartially, esp. by disclosing any interest in the outcome of the dispute. The rules of natural justice apply equally in judicial as well as in administrative proceedings. Alleging a breach of natural justice is the method commonly used to challenge an administrative decision before the courts.

natural law *n.* **1** unchanging moral principles common to all human beings. **2** correct statement of an invariable sequence between specified conditions and a specified phenomenon.

naturally *adv.* **1** in a natural manner. **2** (qualifying a whole sentence) as might be expected; of course.

♦ **natural monopoly** *n.* monopoly in which the minimum efficient scale of production is greater than or equal to the total demand, as, for example, in electricity distribution. More generally, monopolies may exist as a result of barriers to entry, government privilege, or limited information. It is important that legislators know which type of monopoly they are confronting, since enforcing competition in markets in which there are barriers to entry is likely to increase efficiency, while the same policy directed at a natural monopoly can be expected to reduce efficiency. Natural monopolies are usu. considered best harnessed for the benefit of the public by regulation, taxation, or nationalization.

natural number *n.* whole number greater than 0.

♦ **natural rate of interest** see INTEREST RATE.

♦ **natural rate of unemployment** *n.* rate of unemployment consistent with the productive potential of an economy. The concept was introduced by Milton Friedman, who argued that any attempts by governments to reduce unemployment below the natural rate would necessarily fail. In the context of the Phillips curve, this means that there is no long-term inverse relationship between inflation and unemployment. More recently it has been argued that there is not even a short-term inverse relationship (see NEW CLASSICAL MACROECONOMICS). Econometric attempts to estimate the natural rate of unemployment have proved inconclusive. See also NAIRU.

natural resources *n.pl.* materials or conditions occurring in nature and capable of economic exploitation.

natural science *n.* **1** the study of the natural or physical world. **2** (in *pl.*) sciences used for this.

natural selection *n.* Darwinian theory of the survival and propagation of organisms best adapted to their environment.

♦ **natural wastage** *n.* method by which an organization can contract without making people redundant, relying on resignations, retirements, or deaths. If the time is available, this method of reducing a workforce causes the least tension. See also REDUNDANCY 1.

nature /ˈneɪtʃə(r)/ *n.* **1** thing's or person's innate or essential qualities or character. **2** (often **Nature**) **a** physical power causing all material phenomena. **b** these phenomena. **3** kind or class (*things of this nature*). **4** inherent impulses determining character or action. □ **by nature** innately. **in** (or **by) the nature of things 1** inevitable. **2** inevitably. [Latin *natura*: related to NATAL]

Nauru /naʊˈruː/, **Republic of** small island country in the SW Pacific, lying near the Equator. Nauru has little fertile land and most food products, including drinking water, have to be imported. Phosphate rock constitutes much of the island's surface area and the economy is almost totally dependent on the extraction of phosphates, the sole export. The island is being developed as a transport centre and tax haven to maintain the economy once phosphate deposits run out.
History. Annexed by Germany in 1888, Nauru became a British mandate, administered by Australia, after the First World War; in 1947 the mandate was replaced by a trusteeship under which Nauru continued to be administered by Australia. Since 1968 it has been an independent republic with a limited form of membership of the Commonwealth. President, Kinza Clodumar; capital, Yaren. □ **Nauruan** *adj.* & *n.*

languages	Nauruan (official), English
currency	Australian dollar ($A) of 100 cents
pop. (est. 1996)	10 600
GNP (est. 1989)	$A111M
literacy	99% (m); 99% (f)

natured *adj.* (in *comb.*) having a specified disposition (*good-natured*).

nature reserve *n.* tract of land managed so as to preserve its flora, fauna, physical features, etc.

nature trail *n.* signposted path through the countryside designed to draw attention to natural phenomena.

naturism *n.* nudism. □ **naturist** *n.*

naught /nɔːt/ *archaic* or *literary* –*n.* nothing, nought. –*adj.* (usu. *predic.*) worthless; useless. □ **come to naught** come to nothing, fail. **set at naught** despise. [Old English: related to NO², WIGHT]

naughty /'nɔːtɪ/ *adj.* (**-ier, -iest**) **1** (esp. of children) disobedient; badly behaved. **2** *colloq. joc.* indecent. □ **naughtily** *adv.* **naughtiness** *n.* [from NAUGHT]

nausea /'nɔːsɪə/ *n.* **1** inclination to vomit. **2** revulsion. [Greek *naus* ship]

nauseate /'nɔːsɪˌeɪt/ *v.* (**-ting**) affect with nausea. □ **nauseating** *adj.* **nauseatingly** *adv.*

nauseous /'nɔːsɪəs/ *adj.* **1** causing nausea. **2** inclined to vomit (*feel nauseous*). **3** disgusting; loathsome.

nautical /'nɔːtɪk(ə)l/ *adj.* of sailors or navigation. [Greek *nautēs* sailor]

nautical mile *n.* unit of approx. 2025 yards (1852 metres).

nautilus /'nɔːtɪləs/ *n.* (*pl.* **nautiluses** or **nautili** /-ˌlaɪ/) cephalopod mollusc with a spiral shell, esp. (**pearly nautilus**) one having a chambered shell. [Greek *nautilos*: related to NAUTICAL]

♦ **NAV** *abbr.* = NET ASSET VALUE.

---

naval /'neɪv(ə)l/ *adj.* **1** of the or a navy. **2** of ships. [Latin *navis* ship]

Navarre /nə'vɑː(r)/ (Spanish **Navarra**) autonomous region of N Spain; pop. (est. 1994) 523 614; capital Pamplona.

nave¹ *n.* central part of a church, usu. from the west door to the chancel excluding the side aisles. [Latin *navis* ship]

nave² *n.* hub of a wheel. [Old English]

navel /'neɪv(ə)l/ *n.* depression in the centre of the belly marking the site of attachment of the umbilical cord. [Old English]

navel orange *n.* orange with a navel-like formation at the top.

navigable /'nævɪgəb(ə)l/ *adj.* **1** (of a river etc.) suitable for ships to pass through. **2** seaworthy. **3** steerable. □ **navigability** /-'bɪlɪtɪ/ *n.* [Latin: related to NAVIGATE]

navigate /'nævɪˌgeɪt/ *v.* (**-ting**) **1** manage or direct the course of (a ship or aircraft) using maps and instruments. **2 a** sail on (a sea, river, etc.). **b** fly through (the air). **3** (in a car etc.) assist the driver by map-reading etc. **4** sail a ship; sail in a ship. □ **navigator** *n.* [Latin *navigo* from *navis*]

navigation /ˌnævɪ'geɪʃ(ə)n/ *n.* **1** act or process of navigating. **2** art or science of navigating. □ **navigational** *adj.*

navvy /'nævɪ/ –*n.* (*pl.* **-ies**) labourer employed in building or excavating roads, canals, etc. –*v.* (**-ies, -ied**) work as a navvy. [abbreviation of *navigator*]

navy /'neɪvɪ/ *n.* (*pl.* **-ies**) **1** (often **the Navy**) **a** whole body of a state's ships of war, including crews, maintenance systems, etc. **b** officers and men of a navy. **2** (in full **navy blue**) dark-blue colour as of naval uniforms. **3** *poet.* fleet of ships. [Romanic *navia* ship: related to NAVAL]

Naxos /'næksɒs/ Greek island in the S Aegean, the largest of the Cyclades; pop. (est. 1994) 14 900.

nay –*adv.* **1** or rather; and even; and more than that (*large, nay, huge*). **2** *archaic* = NO² *adv.* 1. –*n.* utterance of 'nay'; 'no' vote. [Old Norse, = not ever]

Nayarit /ˌnaɪɑː'riːt/ state in W Mexico; pop. (est. 1995) 895 975; capital, Tepic.

Nazarene /ˌnæzə'riːn/ –*n.* **1 a** (prec. by *the*) Christ. **b** (esp. in Jewish or Muslim use) Christian. **2** native or inhabitant of Nazareth. –*adj.* of Nazareth. [Latin from Greek]

Nazi /'nɑːtsɪ/ –*n.* (*pl.* **-s**) *hist.* member of the German National Socialist party. –*adj.* of the Nazis or Nazism. □ **Nazism** *n.* [representing pronunciation of *Nati-* in German *Nationalsozialist*]

NB *abbr.* **1** note well. **2** New Brunswick. [sense 1 from Latin *nota bene*]

Nb *symb.* niobium.

NBC *abbr.* (in the US) National Broadcasting Company.

NBK *abbr.* National Bank of Kuwait.

NBL *abbr.* National Book League.

NBS *abbr.* **1** (in the US) National Bureau of Standards. **2** Newcastle Business School.

NBV *abbr.* = NET BOOK VALUE.

NC *abbr.* **1** National Curriculum. **2** North Carolina. **3** numerical control or numerically controlled (*NC machine*).

N/C *abbr.* (also **n/c**) **1** new charter. **2** no charge.

NCB *abbr.* **1** *hist.* National Coal Board (see BRITISH COAL CORPORATION). **2** no-claim bonus.

NCBAE *abbr.* no-claim bonus as earned.

NCC *abbr.* **1** National Computing Centre. **2** = NATIONAL CONSUMER COUNCIL. **3** National Curriculum Council.

NCET *abbr.* National Council for Educational Technology.

NCI *abbr. Finance* = NEW COMMUNITY INSTRUMENT.

NCO *abbr.* non-commissioned officer.

NCP *abbr.* National Car Parks.

NCPS *abbr.* non-contributory pension scheme.

NCR *abbr.* no carbon required (of paper).

NCSC *abbr.* **1** (in Australia) National Companies and Securities Commission. **2** (in the US) National Computer Security Center.

♦ **NCT** *abbr.* = NATIONAL CHAMBER OF TRADE.

NCU *abbr.* National Communications Union.

NCV *abbr.* (also **n.c.v.**) no commercial value.

NCVO *abbr.* National Council for Voluntary Organizations.

NCVQ *abbr.* National Council for Vocational Qualifications.

NCW *abbr.* National Council of Women of Great Britain.

ND –*abbr.* **1** national debt. **2** National Diploma. **3** no date. **4** non-delivery. –*US postcode* North Dakota.

Nd *symb.* neodymium.

n.d. *abbr.* **1** *US Stock Exch.* next day (delivery). **2** no date (or not dated). **3** non-delivery. **4** *Banking* not drawn.

N.Dak. *abbr.* North Dakota.

NDIC *abbr.* National Defence Industries Council.

N'Djamena /ˌəndʒæ'meɪnə/ (formerly, until 1973, **Fort Lamy** /læ'miː/) capital of Chad, a port in the SW of the country; pop. (1993) 530 965.

Ndola /ən'dəʊlə/ city in Zambia, capital of the Copperbelt mining province; pop. (1990) 376 311.

♦ **NDP** *abbr.* = NET DOMESTIC PRODUCT.

NDPS *abbr.* National Data Processing Service.

NDR *abbr.* non-domestic rates.

NE –*abbr.* **1** north-east. **2** north-eastern. –*postcode* Newcastle. –*US postcode* Nebraska.

N/E *abbr.* **1** (also **n/e, NE**) *Banking* no effects (i.e. no funds). **2** *Accounting* not entered.

Ne *symb.* neon.

Neanderthal /nɪ'ændəˌtɑːl/ *adj.* of the type of human widely distributed in palaeolithic Europe, with a retreating forehead and massive brow-ridges. [region in W Germany]

neap *n.* (in full **neap tide**) tide at the times of the month when there is least difference between high and low water. [Old English]

Neapolitan /nɪə'pɒlɪt(ə)n/ –*n.* native or citizen of Naples. –*adj.* of Naples. [Greek *Neapolis* Naples]

near –*adv.* **1** (often foll. by *to*) to or at a short distance in space or time. **2** closely (*as near as one can guess*). *–prep.* **1** to or at a short distance from (in space, time, condition, or resemblance). **2** (in *comb.*) almost (*near-hysterical*). *–adj.* **1** close (to), not far (in place or time) (*my flat's very near; the man nearest you; in the near future*). **2 a** closely related. **b** intimate. **3** (of a part of a vehicle, animal, or road) on the left side. **4** close; narrow (*near escape*). **5** similar (to) (*is nearer the original*). **6** *colloq.* niggardly. *–v.* approach; draw near to. □ **come** (or **go**) **near** (foll. by verbal noun, or *to* + verbal noun) be on the point of, almost succeed in. **near at hand** within easy reach. **near the knuckle** *colloq.* verging on the indecent. □ **nearish** *adj.* **nearness** *n.* [Old Norse, originally = nigher: related to NIGH]

nearby *–adj.* near in position. *–adv.* close; not far away.

Near East *n.* (prec. by *the*) region comprising the countries of the E Mediterranean. □ **Near Eastern** *adj.*

♦ **near letter-quality** *adj.* (also **NLQ**) see LETTER-QUALITY.

---

nearly *adv.* **1** almost. **2** closely. □ **not nearly** nothing like.

near miss *n.* **1** bomb etc. falling close to the target. **2** narrowly avoided collision. **3** not quite successful attempt.

♦ **near money** *n.* asset, e.g. a bill of exchange, that is immediately transferable and may be used to settle some but not all debts, although it is not as liquid as banknotes and coins. Near money is not included in the money supply indicators.

---

nearside *n.* (often *attrib.*) left side of a vehicle, animal, etc.

near-sighted *adj.* = SHORT-SIGHTED.

near thing *n.* narrow escape.

neat *adj.* **1** tidy and methodical. **2** elegantly simple. **3** brief, clear, and pointed. **4 a** cleverly executed. **b** dextrous. **5** (of esp. alcoholic liquor) undiluted. □ **neatly** *adv.* **neatness** *n.* [French *net* from Latin *nitidus* shining]

neaten *v.* make neat.

neath *prep. poet.* beneath. [from BENEATH]

♦ **NEB** *abbr.* National Enterprise Board. See BRITISH TECHNOLOGY GROUP.

Neb. *abbr.* (also **Nebr.**) Nebraska.

Nebraska /nɪ'bræskə/ state in the central US; pop. (est. 1996) 1 652 093; capital, Lincoln. It is mainly agricultural, producing corn, wheat, and cattle; industries include food processing, machinery, chemicals, and printing and publishing.

nebula /'nebjʊlə/ *n.* (*pl.* **nebulae** /-ˌliː/) cloud of gas and dust seen in the night sky, sometimes glowing and sometimes appearing as a dark silhouette. □ **nebular** *adj.* [Latin, = mist]

nebulous *adj.* **1** cloudlike. **2** indistinct, vague. [Latin: related to NEBULA]

NEC *abbr.* **1** National Executive Committee. **2** National Exhibition Centre (Birmingham).

n.e.c. *abbr.* not elsewhere classified.

necessary /'nesəsərɪ/ *–adj.* **1** requiring to be done; requisite, essential. **2** determined, existing, or happening by natural laws etc., not by free will; inevitable. *–n.* (*pl.* **-ies**) (usu. in *pl.*) any of the basic requirements of life. □ **the necessary** *colloq.* **1** money. **2** an action etc. needed for a purpose. □ **necessarily** /'nes-, -'serɪlɪ/ *adv.* [Latin *necesse* needful]

♦ **necessary good** *n. Econ.* good for which demand increases as income rises but less than proportionately. It is a good for which the income elasticity of demand lies between one and zero. See also ENGEL CURVE; INFERIOR GOOD; LUXURY GOOD; NORMAL GOOD.

---

necessitarian /nɪˌsesɪ'teərɪən/ *–n.* person who holds that all action is predetermined and free will is impossible. *–adj.* of such a person or theory. □ **necessitarianism** *n.*

necessitate /nɪ'sesɪˌteɪt/ *v.* (**-ting**) make necessary (esp. as a result) (*will necessitate some sacrifice*).

necessitous /nɪ'sesɪtəs/ *adj.* poor; needy.

necessity /nɪ'sesɪtɪ/ *n.* (*pl.* **-ies**) **1** indispensable thing. **2** pressure of circumstances. **3** imperative need. **4** want; poverty. **5** constraint or compulsion regarded as a natural law governing all human action. □ **of necessity** unavoidably.

neck *–n.* **1 a** part of the body connecting the head to the shoulders. **b** part of a garment round the neck. **2** something resembling a neck; narrow part of a cavity, vessel, or object such as a bottle or violin. **3** length of a horse's head and neck as a measure of its lead in a race. **4** flesh of an animal's neck as food. **5** *slang* impudence. *–v. colloq.* kiss and caress amorously. □ **get it in the neck** *colloq.* **1** be severely reprimanded or punished. **2** suffer a severe blow. **up to one's neck** (often foll. by *in*) *colloq.* very deeply involved; very busy. [Old English]

neck and neck *adj.* & *adv.* (running) level in a race etc.

neckband *n.* strip of material round the neck of a garment.

neckerchief *n.* square of cloth worn round the neck. [from KERCHIEF]

necklace /'nekləs/ *n.* **1** chain or string of beads, precious stones, etc., worn round the neck. **2** *S.Afr.* tyre soaked or filled with petrol, placed round a victim's neck, and set alight.

neckline *n.* edge or shape of a garment-opening at the neck.

necktie *n.* esp. *US* = TIE *n.* 2.

necro- *comb. form* corpse. [Greek *nekros* corpse]

necromancy /'nekrəʊˌmænsɪ/ *n.* **1** divination by supposed communication with the dead. **2** magic. □ **necromancer** *n.* [from NECRO-, *mantis* seer]

necrophilia /ˌnekrə'fɪlɪə/ *n.* morbid and esp. sexual attraction to corpses.

necropolis /ne'krɒpəlɪs/ *n.* ancient cemetery or burial place. [Greek: related to NECRO-, *polis* city]

necrosis /ne'krəʊsɪs/ *n.* death of tissue. □ **necrotic** /-'krɒtɪk/ *adj.* [Greek *nekroō* kill]

nectar /'nektə(r)/ *n.* **1** sugary substance produced by plants and made into honey by bees. **2** (in Greek and Roman mythology) the drink of the gods. **3** drink compared to this. □ **nectarous** *adj.* [Latin from Greek]

nectarine /'nektərɪn/ *n.* smooth-skinned variety of peach. [from NECTAR]

♦ **NEDC** *abbr.* **1** (also **Neddy**) National Economic Development Council (see NATIONAL ECONOMIC DEVELOPMENT OFFICE). **2** North East Development Council.

---

neddy /'nedɪ/ *n.* (*pl.* **-ies**) *colloq.* **1** donkey. **2** (**Neddy**) = NEDC 1. [pet form of *Edward*]

née /neɪ/ *adj.* (*US* **nee**) (used in adding a married woman's maiden name after her surname) born (*Mrs Ann Hall, née Browne*). [French, feminine past part. of *naître* be born]

need *–v.* **1** stand in want of; require. **2** (foll. by *to* + infin.; *3rd sing. present neg. or interrog.* **need** without *to*) be under the necessity or obligation (*needs to be done well; he need not come; need you ask?*). *–n.* **1** requirement (*my needs are few*). **2** circumstances requiring some course of action (*no need to worry; if need be*). **3** destitution; poverty. **4** crisis; emergency (*failed them in their need*). □ **have need of** require. **need not have** did not need to (but did). [Old English]

needful *adj.* requisite. □ **needfully** *adv.*

needle /'niːd(ə)l/ *–n.* **1 a** very thin pointed rod of smooth steel etc. with a slit (eye) for thread at the blunt end, used in sewing. **b** larger plastic, wooden, etc. slender rod without an eye, used in knitting etc. **2** pointer on a dial. **3** any of several small thin pointed instruments, esp.: **a** the end of a hypodermic syringe. **b** = STYLUS 1. **4 a** obelisk (*Cleopatra's Needle*). **b** pointed rock or peak. **5** leaf of a fir or pine tree. **6** (**the needle**) *slang* fit of bad temper or nervousness. *–v.* (**-ling**) *colloq.* irritate; provoke. [Old English]

needlecord *n.* fine-ribbed corduroy fabric.

needle-point *n.* **1** lace made with needles, not bobbins. **2** = GROS OR PETIT POINT.

needless *adj.* **1** unnecessary. **2** uncalled for. □ **needlessly** *adv.*

needlewoman *n.* **1** seamstress. **2** woman or girl with specified sewing skill.

needlework *n.* sewing or embroidery.

needs *adv. archaic* (usu. prec. or foll. by *must*) of necessity.

needy *adj.* (**-ier, -iest**) poor; destitute. □ **neediness** *n.*

ne'er /neə(r)/ *adv. poet.* = NEVER. [contraction]

ne'er-do-well *–n.* good-for-nothing person. *–adj.* good-for-nothing.

nefarious /nɪ'feərɪəs/ *adj.* wicked. [Latin *nefas* wrong *n.*]

neg. *abbr.* **1** esp. *Photog.* negative. **2** negligence.

negate /nɪ'geɪt/ *v.* (**-ting**) **1** nullify. **2** assert or imply the non-existence of. [Latin *nego* deny]

negation /nɪ'geɪʃ(ə)n/ *n.* **1** absence or opposite of something actual or positive. **2** act of denying. **3** negative statement. **4** negative or unreal thing.

negative /'negətɪv/ *–adj.* **1** expressing or implying denial, prohibition, or refusal (*negative answer*). **2** (of a person or attitude) lacking positive attributes. **3** marked by the absence of qualities (*negative reaction*). **4** of the opposite nature to a thing regarded as positive. **5** (of a quantity) less than zero, to be subtracted from others or from zero. **6** *Electr.* **a** of the kind of charge carried by electrons. **b** containing or producing such a charge. *–n.* **1** negative statement or word. **2** *Photog.* **a** image with black and white reversed or colours replaced by complementary ones, from which positive pictures are obtained. **b** developed film or plate bearing such an image. *–v.* (**-ving**) **1** refuse to accept or countenance; veto. **2** disprove. **3** contradict (a statement). **4** neutralize (an effect). □ **in the negative** with negative effect. □ **negatively** *adv.* **negativity** /-'tɪvɪtɪ/ *n.*

negative acknowledgement *Computing* see ACKNOWLEDGEMENT 4.

♦ **negative cash flow** *n.* cash flow in which the outflows exceed the inflows.

♦ **negative equity** *n.* asset that has a market value below the sum of money borrowed to purchase it. It may refer to a house, bought at a time of high prices on a mortgage, which now has a current market value below the sum still outstanding on the mortgage.

♦ **negative income tax** *n.* (also **NIT**) means of targeting social security benefits to those most in need. The payments would be made through the income-tax system by granting personal allowances to taxpayers so that the standard rate of income tax on these allowances would constitute a minimum amount required for living. Those with high incomes would obtain that amount as an income-tax relief, while those with incomes lower than the allowance would have a negative income-tax liability and be paid the appropriate sums. The principal objection to the system is that to cover the needs of the disadvantaged the wealthier would obtain excessively high allowances.

♦ **negative net worth** *n.* value of an organization that has liabilities in excess of its assets.

---

negativism *n.* negative attitude; extreme scepticism.

neglect /nɪ'glekt/ *–v.* **1** fail to care for or to do; be remiss about. **2** (foll. by *to* + infin.) fail; overlook the need to. **3** not pay attention to; disregard. *–n.* **1** negligence. **2** neglecting or being neglected. **3** (usu. foll. by *of*) disregard. □ **neglectful** *adj.* **neglectfully** *adv.* [Latin *neglego neglect-*]

negligée /'neglɪ,ʒeɪ/ *n.* (also **negligee, néglilgé**) woman's flimsy dressing-gown. [French, past part. of *négliger* NEGLECT]

negligence /'neglɪdʒ(ə)ns/ *n.* **1** lack of proper care and attention. **2** culpable carelessness. **3** *Law* tort in which a breach of a **duty of care** results in damage to the person to whom the duty is owed. Such a duty is owed by manufacturers to the consumers who buy their products, by professional persons to their clients, by a director of a company to its shareholders, etc. A person who has suffered loss or injury as a result of a breach of the duty of care can claim damages in tort. □ **negligent** *adj.* **negligently** *adv.* [Latin: related to NEGLECT]

negligible /'neglɪdʒɪb(ə)l/ *adj.* not worth considering; insignificant. □ **negligibly** *adv.* [French: related to NEGLECT]

Negombo /nɪ'gɒmbəʊ/ seaport in Sri Lanka, on the W coast; pop. (1981) 60 700.

♦ **negotiability** /nɪ,gəʊʃə'bɪlɪtɪ/ *n. Law* ability of a document to change hands, thereby entitling its owner to some benefit, so that legal ownership of the benefit passes by delivery or endorsement of the document. For a document to be negotiable it must also entitle the holder to bring an action in law if necessary. See NEGOTIABLE INSTRUMENT.

---

negotiable /nɪ'gəʊʃəb(ə)l/ *adj.* **1** open to discussion. **2** able to be negotiated. □ **not negotiable** words marked on a cheque etc. indicating that it ceases to be a negotiable instrument, thus providing a safeguard against theft.

♦ **negotiable instrument** *n.* document of title that can be freely negotiated (see NEGOTIABILITY). Such documents are cheques and bills of exchange, in which the stated payee of the instrument can negotiate the instrument by either inserting the name of a different payee or by making the document 'open' by endorsing it (signing one's name), usu. on the reverse. Holders of negotiable instruments cannot pass on a better title than they possess. Bills of exchange, including cheques, in which the payee is named or that bear a restrictive endorsement (e.g. 'not negotiable') are **non-negotiable instruments**.

---

negotiate /nɪ'gəʊʃɪ,eɪt/ *v.* (**-ting**) **1** (usu. foll. by *with*) confer in order to reach mutually acceptable terms for an agreement, contract, etc. **2** arrange (an affair) or bring about (a result) by negotiating. **3** find a way over, through, etc. (an obstacle, difficulty, etc.). **4** transfer (a bill of exchange or cheque) for consideration (see NEGOTIABILITY). □ **negotiation** /-ʃɪ'eɪʃ(ə)n/ *n.* **negotiator** *n.* [Latin *negotium* business]

Negress /'ni:grɪs/ *n.* female Negro.

■ **Usage** The term *Negress* is often considered offensive; *Black* is usu. preferred.

Negri Sembilan /nə,gri: səm'bi:lən/ state in Malaysia, on the Malay Peninsula; pop. (est. 1993) 723 900; capital, Seremban. Rubber, coconuts, rice, and tin are produced.

Negritude /'negrɪ,tju:d/ *n.* **1** state of being Black. **2** affirmation of Black culture. [French]

Negro /'ni:grəʊ/ *–n.* (*pl.* **-es**) member of a dark-skinned race orig. native to Africa. *–adj.* **1** of Negroes. **2** (as **negro**) *Zool.* black or dark. [Latin *niger nigri* black]

■ **Usage** The term *Negro* is often considered offensive; *Black* is usu. preferred.

Negroid /'ni:grɔɪd/ *–adj.* (of physical features etc.) characteristic of Black people. *–n.* Negro.

Negros /'neɪgrɒs/ fourth-largest island of the Philippines; sugar production is important; pop. (est. 1990) 3 168 000; chief city, Bacolod.

neigh /neɪ/ *–n.* cry of a horse. *–v.* make a neigh. [Old English]

neighbour /'neɪbə(r)/ (*US* **neighbor**) *–n.* **1** person living next door to or near or nearest another. **2** fellow human being. **3** person or thing near or next to another. *–v.* border on; adjoin. [Old English: related to NIGH, BOOR]

neighbourhood *n.* (*US* **neighborhood**) **1** district; vicinity. **2** people of a district. □ **in the neighbourhood of** roughly; about.

neighbourhood watch *n.* organized local vigilance by householders to discourage crime.

neighbourly *adj.* (*US* **neighborly**) like a good neighbour; friendly; kind. □ **neighbourliness** *n.*

neither /'naɪðə(r), 'niːð-/ *–adj. & pron.* (foll. by sing. verb) not the one nor the other (of two things); not either (*neither of the accusations is true; neither of them knows; neither wish was granted; neither went to the fair*). *–adv.* **1** not either; not on the one hand (foll. by *nor*; introducing the first of two or more things in the negative: *neither knowing nor caring; neither the teachers nor the parents nor the children*). **2** also not (*if you do not, neither shall I*). *–conj. archaic* nor yet; nor (*I know not, neither can I guess*). [Old English: related to NO², WHETHER]

Nejd /nedʒd/ (also **Najd**, **Central Province**) region of Saudi Arabia, in the centre of the country, consisting chiefly of desert; pop. (est. 1985) 3 632 092.

Nelson /'nels(ə)n/ port and resort in New Zealand, on the N coast of South Island; pop. (1994) 50 200.

nelson /'nels(ə)n/ *n.* wrestling-hold in which one arm is passed under the opponent's arm from behind and the hand is applied to the neck (**half nelson**), or both arms and hands are applied (**full nelson**). [apparently from the name *Nelson*]

nematode /'nemə,təʊd/ *n.* worm with a slender unsegmented cylindrical shape. [Greek *nēma* thread]

nem. con. *abbr.* with no one dissenting. [Latin *nemine contradicente*]

nemesis /'neməsɪs/ *n.* (*pl.* **nemeses** /-,siːz/) **1** retributive justice. **2** downfall caused by this. [Greek, = retribution]

neo- *comb. form* **1** new, modern. **2** new form of. [Greek *neos* new]

♦ **neoclassical school** *n. Econ.* mainstream school of thought deriving from the work of the Marginalists, who defined value in relation to scarcity (see LABOUR THEORY OF VALUE) and regarded the balance of supply and demand as determining equilibrium prices. This method was first applied in microeconomics and used to describe the utility and profit-maximizing behaviour of individuals and firms. The application of neoclassical principles to macroeconomics has been somewhat slower, since it was not immediately accepted that economic aggregates reflect the sum of individual choices. However, the development of general equilibrium theory has enabled **neoclassical macroeconomists** to conform to a similar pattern to that earlier established in microeconomics (see NEW CLASSICAL MACROECONOMICS).

neoclassicism /,niːəʊ'klæsɪ,sɪz(ə)m/ *n.* revival of classical style or treatment in the arts. □ **neoclassical** /-k(ə)l/ *adj.*

neodymium /,niːə'dɪmɪəm/ *n.* metallic element of the lanthanide series. [from NEO-, Greek *didumos* twin]

neolithic /,niːə'lɪθɪk/ *adj.* of the later part of the Stone Age. [Greek *lithos* stone]

neologism /niː'ɒlə,dʒɪz(ə)m/ *n.* **1** new word. **2** coining of new words. [Greek *logos* word]

neon /'niːɒn/ *n.* inert gaseous element giving an orange glow when electricity is passed through it. [Greek, = new]

neophyte /'niːə,faɪt/ *n.* **1** new convert. **2** *RC Ch.* novice of a religious order. **3** beginner. [Greek *phuton* plant]

Nepali /nɪ'pɔːlɪ/ *–n.* (*pl.* same or **-is**) **1 a** native or national of Nepal. **b** person of Nepali descent. **2** language of Nepal. *–adj.* of or relating to Nepal or its language or people.

nephew /'nefjuː/ *n.* son of one's brother or sister or of one's spouse's brother or sister. [Latin *nepos*]

nephritic /nɪ'frɪtɪk/ *adj.* **1** of or in the kidneys. **2** of nephritis. [Greek *nephros* kidney]

nephritis /nɪ'fraɪtɪs/ *n.* inflammation of the kidneys.

ne plus ultra /,neɪ plʊs 'ʊltrɑː/ *n.* **1** furthest attainable point. **2** acme, perfection. [Latin, = not further beyond]

nepotism /'nepə,tɪz(ə)m/ *n.* favouritism shown to relatives in conferring offices. [Italian *nepote* nephew]

neptunium /nep'tjuːnɪəm/ *n.* transuranic metallic element produced when uranium atoms absorb bombarding neutrons. [*Neptune*, name of a planet]

nerd *n.* (also **nurd**) esp. *US slang* foolish, feeble, or uninteresting person. [origin uncertain]

nereid /'nɪərɪɪd/ *n.* sea-nymph. [Latin from Greek]

nerve *–n.* **1 a** fibre or bundle of fibres that transmits impulses of sensation or motion between the brain or spinal cord and other parts of the body. **b** material constituting these. **2 a** coolness in danger; bravery. **b** *colloq.* impudence. **3** (in *pl.*) nervousness; mental or physical stress. *–v.* (**-ving**) **1** (usu. *refl.*) brace (oneself) to face danger etc. **2** give strength, vigour, or courage to. □ **get on a person's nerves** irritate a person. [Latin *nervus* sinew, bowstring]

nerve cell *n.* cell transmitting impulses in nerve tissue.

nerve-centre *n.* **1** group of closely connected nerve-cells. **2** centre of control.

nerve gas *n.* poisonous gas affecting the nervous system.

nerveless *adj.* **1** lacking vigour. **2** (of style) diffuse.

nerve-racking *adj.* causing mental strain.

nervous *adj.* **1** easily upset, timid, highly strung. **2** anxious. **3** affecting the nerves. **4** (foll. by *of* + verbal noun) afraid (*am nervous of meeting them*). □ **nervously** *adv.* **nervousness** *n.*

nervous breakdown *n.* period of mental illness, usu. resulting from severe stress.

nervous system *n.* body's network of nerve cells.

Nepal /nə'pɔːl/, **Kingdom of** country in S Asia, bordered by China (Tibet) to the N and India to the S, dominated by the Himalayas. A remote landlocked and mountainous country, Nepal is among the least developed nations in the world. The economy is predominantly agricultural; 80% of the labour force were employed in this sector in 1997. The main cash crops are jute, rice, grains, pulses, and sugar cane; medicinal herbs and timber are also exported. Nepal has few mineral resources but mica is mined E of Kathmandu. Much of the country's manufacturing sector is based on traditional cottage industries, carpets and handicrafts being exported; other manufactures include bricks and tiles, textiles, and paper. Tourism is a major source of foreign revenue.

History. The country was conquered by the Gurkhas in the 18th century and despite defeats by the British in the early 19th century has maintained its independence. After 28 years of absolute monarchy, mass agitation for political reform resulted in the introduction in 1990 of a new constitution establishing a constitutional monarchy and multi-party democracy; parliamentary elections were held the following year. Head of state, King Birendra Bir Bikram Shah Dev; prime minister, Lokendra Bahadur Chand; capital, Kathmandu. □ **Nepalese** /,nepə'liːz/ *adj.* & *n.*

language	Nepali
currency	rupee (NRe; *pl.* NRs) of 100 paisa
pop. (1996)	20 892 000
GNP (1994)	US$4.1B
literacy	51% (m); 23% (f)
life expectancy	55 (m); 53 (f)

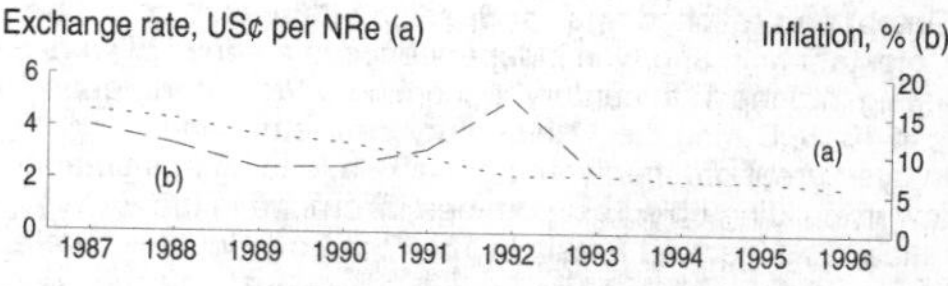

nervy *adj.* (**-ier, -iest**) *colloq.* nervous; easily excited.

nescient /ˈnesɪənt/ *adj. literary* (foll. by *of*) lacking knowledge. □ **nescience** *n.* [Latin *ne-* not, *scio* know]

-ness *suffix* forming nouns from adjectives, expressing: **1** state or condition, or an instance of this (*happiness*; *a kindness*). **2** something in a certain state (*wilderness*). [Old English]

nest –*n.* **1** structure or place where a bird lays eggs and shelters its young. **2** any creature's breeding-place or lair. **3** snug retreat or shelter. **4** brood or swarm. **5** group or set of similar objects, often of different sizes and fitting one inside the other (*nest of tables*). –*v.* **1** use or build a nest. **2** take wild birds' nests or eggs. **3** (of objects) fit together or one inside another. [Old English]

nest egg *n.* sum of money saved for the future.

nestle /ˈnes(ə)l/ *v.* (**-ling**) **1** (often foll. by *down, in*, etc.) settle oneself comfortably. **2** press oneself against another in affection etc. **3** (foll. by *in, into*, etc.) push (a head or shoulder etc.) affectionately or snugly. **4** lie half hidden or embedded. [Old English]

nestling /ˈnestlɪŋ/ *n.* bird too young to leave its nest.

net[1] –*n.* **1** open-meshed fabric of cord, rope, etc. **2** piece of net used esp. to restrain, contain, or delimit, or to catch fish etc. **3** structure with a net used in various games. –*v.* (**-tt-**) **1 a** cover, confine, or catch with a net. **b** procure as with a net. **2** hit (a ball) into the net, esp. of a goal. [Old English]

net[2] (also **nett**) –*adj.* **1** (esp. of money) remaining after all necessary deductions. **2** (of a weight) excluding that of the packaging etc. See also GROSS WEIGHT. **3** (of an effect, result, etc.) ultimate, actual. –*v.* (**-tt-**) gain or yield (a sum) as net profit. [French: related to NEAT]

◆ **net assets** *n.pl.* assets of an organization less its current liabilities. The resultant figure is equal to the capital of the organization. Opinion varies as to whether long-term liabilities should be treated as part of the capital and are therefore not deductible in arriving at net assets, or whether they are part of the liabilities and therefore deductible. The latter view is probably technically preferable. See also NET CURRENT ASSETS; NET WORTH.

◆ **net asset value** *n.* (also **NAV**) total assets of an organization less all liabilities and all capital charges (including debentures, loan stocks, and preference shares). The **net asset value per share** is the NAV divided by the total number of ordinary shares issued.

netball *n.* team game in which goals are scored by throwing a ball through a high horizontal ring from which a net hangs.

◆ **net book value** *n.* (also **NBV**) *Accounting* value at which an asset appears in the books of an organization (usu. as at the date of the last balance sheet) less any depreciation that has been applied since its purchase or its last revaluation.

◆ **net current assets** *n.pl.* current assets less current liabilities. The resultant figure is also known as working or circulating capital, as it represents the amount of the organization's capital that is constantly being turned over in the course of its trade. See also NET ASSETS.

◆ **net domestic product** *n.* (also **NDP**) gross domestic product of a country less capital consumption (i.e. depreciation).

Neth. *abbr.* Netherlands.

nether /ˈneðə(r)/ *adj. archaic* = LOWER[1]. [Old English]

Netherlands Antilles two groups of Dutch islands in the West Indies. One group, lying N of Venezuela, comprises the islands of Bonaire and Curaçao; the other group, situated at the N end of the Lesser Antilles, includes the islands of St Eustatius, St Martin, and Saba; pop. (est. 1994) 202 244; capital, Willemstad. Oil refining (centred on Curaçao) is an important source of revenue; there are also various small manufacturing industries. See also ARUBA.

nether regions *n.pl.* (also **nether world**) hell; the underworld.

◆ **net income** *n.* **1** income of a person or organization after the deduction of the appropriate expenses incurred in earning it. **2** gross income from which tax has been deducted.

◆ **net interest** see GROSS INTEREST.

◆ **net investment** *n.* addition to the stock of capital goods in an economy during a particular period (the **gross investment**) less capital consumption (i.e. depreciation).

◆ **net national product** *n.* (also **NNP**) gross national product less capital consumption (i.e. depreciation) during the period. NNP is therefore equal to the national income, i.e. the amount of money available in the economy for expenditure on goods and services. NNP cannot be considered a very accurate measure, however, as it is difficult to calculate depreciation reliably.

◆ **net present value** *n.* (also **NPV**) economic value of a project calculated by summing its costs and revenues over its full life and deducting the former from the latter; a positive NPV indicates the project should be profitable. Future costs and revenues should be discounted by the relevant interest rate, e.g. the organization's cost of capital (see DISCOUNTED CASH FLOW). Calculating NPVs can be

Netherlands /ˈneðələndz/, **Kingdom of the** (Dutch **Nederland**) country in W Europe, bordering on the North Sea. Since the Second World War the Netherlands has emerged as an industrial power. Industries contributing to exports include oil and gas, engineering, electronics, aircraft and defence equipment, petrochemicals, rubber, plastics, printing, metals, textiles and clothing, and food processing. Natural gas reserves now provide about half of the country's energy requirements. The Netherlands is traditionally a trading nation and entrepôt trade, banking, and shipping are important to the economy. Agriculture and horticulture are highly developed and mechanized; the chief agricultural exports are dairy products and livestock, vegetables, and flower bulbs. The fishing industry (esp. oysters) and tourism are also important sources of revenue. *History.* In the 16th century the territory occupied by the present-day Netherlands, Belgium, and Luxembourg (the Low Countries) formed part of the Hapsburg empire. The N (Dutch) part revolted against Spanish attempts to crush the Protestant faith and won independence in a series of wars lasting into the 17th century, becoming a Protestant republic in 1648. During the 17th century the Netherlands enjoyed great prosperity and became a leading maritime power, building up a vast commercial empire in the East Indies, S Africa, and Brazil. In 1814 the Low Countries were united under a monarchy, but Belgium became an independent kingdom in 1839 and Luxembourg gained its independence in 1867. The Netherlands maintained its neutrality in the First World War but was occupied by the Germans in the Second. In 1947 the country joined with Belgium and Luxembourg to form an economic union (see BENELUX) and it was a founder member of the EC. Head of state, Queen Beatrix; prime minister, Wim Kok; capital, Amsterdam; seat of government, The Hague. □ **Netherlander** *n.*

language	Dutch
currency	guilder (f) of 100 cents
pop. (1996)	15 589 000
GNP (1994)	US$338B
literacy	99% (m); 99% (f)
life expectancy	74 (m); 80 (f)

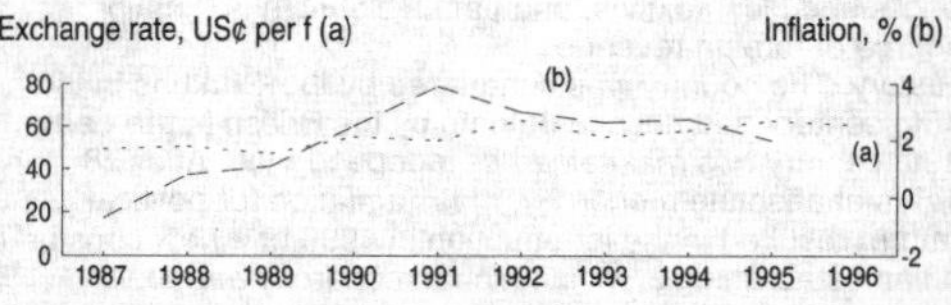

difficult and often involves highly subjective judgements (e.g. estimating future interest rates). Frequently, therefore, simpler calculations are used (see PAYBACK PERIOD). See also INTERNAL RATE OF RETURN. Cf. ACCOUNTING RATE OF RETURN.

♦ **net price** *n.* price a buyer pays for goods or services after all discounts have been deducted.

♦ **net profit** *n.* **1** (also **net profit before taxation**) profit of an organization when all receipts and expenses have been taken into account. In trading organizations, net profit is arrived at by deducting from the gross profit all the expenses not already taken into account in arriving at the gross profit. **2** (also **net profit after taxation**) final profit of an organization, after all appropriate taxes have been deducted from the net profit before taxation. See also PROFIT AND LOSS ACCOUNT 2.

♦ **net-profit ratio** *n.* ratio of net profit to the total sales of an organization. It is used in analysing the profitability of organizations and is an indicator of the extent to which sales have been profitable.

♦ **net realizable value** *n.* (also **NRV**) net value of an asset if it were to be sold, equal to the sum received for it less the costs of the sale and of bringing it into a saleable condition.

♦ **net receipts** *n.pl.* total amount of money received by a business in a specified period after deducting costs, raw materials, taxation, etc. Cf. GROSS RECEIPTS.

♦ **net register tonnage** see TONNAGE 1.

♦ **net relevant earnings** *n.pl.* person's non-pensionable earned income before personal allowances have been deducted but after deduction of expenses, capital allowances, losses, or any stock relief agreed with the Inland Revenue.

♦ **net reproduction rate** *n.* (also **NRR**) number of female children in a population divided by the number of female adults in the previous generation. This figure gives a good guide to population trends: if it exceeds unity the population is expanding.

♦ **net return** *n.* profit made on an investment after the deduction of all expenses, either before or after deduction of capital-gains tax.

---

nett var. of NET[2].

♦ **net tangible assets** *n.pl.* (also **NTA**) tangible assets of an organization less its current liabilities. In analysing the affairs of an organization the NTA indicate its financial strength in terms of being solvent, without having to resort to such nebulous (and less easy to value) assets as goodwill. See also PRICE–NET TANGIBLE ASSETS RATIO.

---

netting *n.* **1** netted fabric. **2** piece of this. **3** process of setting off matching sales and purchases against each other, usu. by a clearing-house, esp. of futures, options, and transactions in forward foreign currencies.

nettle /ˈnet(ə)l/ –*n.* **1** plant with jagged leaves covered with stinging hairs. **2** plant resembling this. –*v.* (**-ling**) irritate, provoke. [Old English]

nettle-rash *n.* skin eruption like nettle stings.

network –*n.* **1** arrangement of intersecting horizontal and vertical lines. **2** complex system of railways etc. **3** people connected by the exchange of information etc., professionally or socially. **4** system of connected electrical conductors. **5** group of broadcasting stations connected for the simultaneous broadcast of a programme. **6** number of computers connected together so that by following agreed procedures, or **protocols**, information can be exchanged. The computers, called **nodes**, are dispersed throughout an organization, a region, or even across a continent (see LOCAL AREA NETWORK; WIDE AREA NETWORK 1). They communicate with each other using communications links, e.g. high-speed telephone and satellite links, electric cables, or optical fibres. Networks allow the computers to share each other's facilities. Often, one node is a large central computer, which may, for example, have fast printers or hold a large database of information. Networks also allow the computers to communicate with each other, so that memos and other messages can be sent electronically. Nodes may be at a junction of two or more communication lines or may be at an end-point of a line. A particular piece of information has to be routed along a set of lines to reach its specified destination, being **switched** at the nodes from one line to another, often by a computer. A particular destination is specified by its address, which forms part of the transmitted signal. In a **broadcast network**, all nodes are attached to a single communications line and messages appear at all nodes, only the addressed node taking action. –*v.* broadcast on a network.

♦ **net worth** *n.* value of an organization when its liabilities have been deducted from the value of its assets. To equate it with net asset value can be misleading, since balance sheets rarely show the real value of assets; in order to arrive at the true net worth it would normally be necessary to assess the true market values of the assets rather than their book values. It would also be necessary to value goodwill, which may not even appear in the balance sheet.

♦ **net yield** see GROSS YIELD.

---

neural /ˈnjʊər(ə)l/ *adj.* of a nerve or the central nervous system. [Greek *neuron* nerve]

neuralgia /njʊəˈrældʒə/ *n.* intense pain along a nerve, esp. in the head or face. □ **neuralgic** *adj.*

neuritis /njʊəˈraɪtɪs/ *n.* inflammation of a nerve or nerves.

neuro- *comb. form* nerve or nerves. [Greek *neuron* nerve]

neurology /njʊəˈrɒlədʒɪ/ *n.* the study of nerve systems. □ **neurological** /-rəˈlɒdʒɪk(ə)l/ *adj.* **neurologist** *n.*

neuron /ˈnjʊərɒn/ *n.* (also **neurone** /-rəʊn/) nerve cell.

neurosis /njʊəˈrəʊsɪs/ *n.* (*pl.* **neuroses** /-siːz/) irrational or disturbed behaviour pattern, associated with nervous distress.

neurosurgery /ˌnjʊərəʊˈsɜːdʒərɪ/ *n.* surgery on the nervous system, esp. the brain or spinal cord. □ **neurosurgeon** *n.* **neurosurgical** *adj.*

neurotic /njʊəˈrɒtɪk/ –*adj.* **1** caused by or relating to neurosis. **2** suffering from neurosis. **3** *colloq.* abnormally sensitive or obsessive. –*n.* neurotic person. □ **neurotically** *adv.*

neuter /ˈnjuːtə(r)/ –*adj.* **1** *Gram.* neither masculine nor feminine. **2** (of a plant) having neither pistils nor stamen. **3** (of an insect) sexually undeveloped. –*n.* **1** *Gram.* neuter gender or word. **2 a** non-fertile insect, esp. a worker bee or ant. **b** castrated animal. –*v.* castrate or spay. [Latin]

neutral /ˈnjuːtr(ə)l/ –*adj.* **1** not supporting either of two opposing sides, impartial. **2** belonging to a neutral State etc. (*neutral ships*). **3** indistinct, vague, indeterminate. **4** (of a gear) in which the engine is disconnected from the driven parts. **5** (of colours) not strong or positive; grey or beige. **6** *Chem.* neither acid nor alkaline. **7** *Electr.* neither positive nor negative. **8** *Biol.* sexually undeveloped; asexual. –*n.* **1 a** neutral state or person. **b** citizen of a neutral state. **2** neutral gear. □ **neutrality** /-ˈtrælɪtɪ/ *n.* [Latin *neutralis* of neuter gender]

♦ **neutrality of money** *n. Econ.* belief, originating from the theories of new classical macroeconomics, that the quantity of money in the economy can only affect prices (i.e. inflation), rather than such real variables as investment or the level of employment. As the economy will always operate at the natural rate of unemployment and government policies will be fully anticipated by individuals with rational expectations, choices will be adjusted to counter the effects of government policy. For example, if a government tries to raise investment, the price of investment goods will rise; this will discourage previously planned purchases, which will no longer be made, so all that will have changed will be prices, which will have increased.

---

neutralize *v.* (also **-ise**) (**-zing** or **-sing**) **1** make neutral. **2** make ineffective by an opposite force or effect. **3** exempt or exclude (a place) from the sphere of hostilities. □ **neutralization** /-ˈzeɪʃ(ə)n/ *n.*

neutrino /njuːˈtriːnəʊ/ *n.* (*pl.* **-s**) elementary particle with zero electric charge and probably zero mass. [Italian, diminutive of *neutro* neutral: related to NEUTER]

neutron /ˈnjuːtrɒn/ *n.* elementary particle of about the same mass as a proton but without an electric charge. [from NEUTRAL]

neutron bomb *n.* bomb producing neutrons and little blast, destroying life but not property.

Nev. *abbr.* Nevada.

Nevada /nɪˈvɑːdə/ state in the W US; pop. (est. 1996) 1 603 163; capital, Carson City. Industries include copper smelting, cement, food processing, and electronics; tourism is also important, and metallic ores and other minerals are produced.

never /ˈnevə(r)/ *adv.* **1 a** at no time; on no occasion; not ever. **b** *colloq.* as an emphatic negative (*I never heard you come in*). **2** not at all (*never fear*). **3** *colloq.* (expressing surprise) surely not (*you never left the door open!*). □ **well I never!** expressing great surprise. [Old English, = not ever]

nevermore *adv.* at no future time.

never-never *n.* (often prec. by *the*) *colloq.* hire purchase.

nevertheless /ˌnevəðəˈles/ *adv.* in spite of that; notwithstanding.

Nevis /ˈniːvɪs/ one of the Leeward Islands, forming part of the state of St Kitts and Nevis; pop. (1991) 8794; capital, Charlestown.

nevus *US* var. of NAEVUS.

NEW *abbr. US* net economic welfare.

new –*adj.* **1 a** of recent origin or arrival. **b** made, discovered, acquired, or experienced recently or now for the first time. **2** in original condition; not worn or used. **3 a** renewed; reformed (*new life*; *the new order*). **b** reinvigorated (*felt like a new person*). **4** different from a recent previous one (*has a new job*). **5** (often foll. by *to*) unfamiliar or strange (*all new to me*). **6** (usu. prec. by *the*) often *derog.* **a** later, modern. **b** newfangled. **c** given to new or modern ideas. **d** recently affected by social change (*the new rich*). **7** (often prec. by *the*) advanced in method or theory. **8** (in place-names) discovered or founded later than and named after (*New York*). –*adv.* (usu. in *comb.*) newly, recently (*new-found*; *new-baked*). □ **newish** *adj.* **newness** *n.* [Old English]

New Age *n.* set of beliefs replacing traditional Western culture, with alternative approaches to religion, medicine, the environment, etc.

Newark /ˈnjuːək/ industrial city in the US, in New Jersey; jewellery, cutlery, and chemicals are produced; pop. (est. 1994) 258 751.

new arrival *n. colloq.* newborn child.

newborn *adj.* recently born.

New Britain island of Papua New Guinea, lying between the islands of New Guinea and New Ireland; pop. (1990) 312 955; capital, Rabaul. Exports include copra and minerals.

new broom *n.* new employee etc. eager to make changes.

New Brunswick /ˈbrʌnzwɪk/ maritime province of SE Canada; pop. (est. 1995) 760 100; capital, Fredericton. Fishing is important; there is also some farming and mining of lead, zinc, and copper, but the forestry industry has declined.

New Caledonia island in the SW Pacific Ocean, forming, with its dependencies, a French Overseas Territory; pop. (est. 1994) 183 200; capital, Nouméa. Nickel is mined and exported; the meat-preserving industry is also important, and other exports include copra and coffee.

Newcastle /ˈnjuːkɑːs(ə)l/ industrial port and city in Australia, on the coast of New South Wales; iron and steel are the main industries; pop. (est. 1995) 466 000.

Newcastle upon Tyne city and chief port of NE England, county town of Tyne and Wear; pop. (est. 1994) 283 600. It is a commercial centre with shipbuilding, marine engineering, electrical engineering, and chemical industries.

♦ **new classical macroeconomics** *n. Econ.* school of thought that developed in the 1970s by applying the concept of rational expectations to macroeconomic theory. Keynesians and monetarists argued that fiscal or monetary policy could be used to raise the level of output and employment in the economy at least in the short term; the new classicists disagreed, claiming that any reflation of the economy will be fully anticipated by individuals and firms, who will adjust their behaviour in such a way that the economy will remain unchanged in real terms. For example, if the government increased public expenditure to create jobs, taxpayers – realizing that this would have to be paid for through higher taxes in the future – would reduce their present expenditure by an equal amount in order to save money to pay future tax bills. Nevertheless, the extra money injected into the economy would raise prices and cause inflation. See also REAL TERMS; NOMINAL TERMS.

---

newcomer *n.* **1** person recently arrived. **2** beginner in some activity.

♦ **New Community Instrument** *n.* (also **NCI**) loan organized on the international money market by the European Investment Bank.

New Delhi see DELHI.

newel /ˈnjuːəl/ *n.* **1** supporting central post of winding stairs. **2** (also **newel post**) top or bottom supporting post of a stair-rail. [Latin *nodus* knot]

♦ **new entrants** *n.pl.* **1** people looking for work for the first time, mainly school-leavers but also housewives, esp. with the recent opportunities for job sharing. **2** firms entering an industry for the first time, either new organizations or established organizations entering a new field.

---

newfangled /njuːˈfæŋg(ə)ld/ *adj. derog.* different from what one is used to; objectionably new. [= new taken]

♦ **new for old** *n.* basis for household insurance policies in which payments of claims are not subject to a deduction for wear and tear, a claim being met by the payment of the price of a new item of a similar type.

Newfoundland /ˈnjuːfəndlənd, -ˈfaʊndlənd/ (in full **Newfoundland and Labrador**) province of Canada, comprising the island of Newfoundland, at the mouth of the St Lawrence River, and the E coast of Labrador; pop. (est. 1995) 575 400; capital, St John's. Forestry, mining, and fishing are important industries; products include pulp and paper, iron, zinc, copper, and offshore oil. –*n.* (in full **Newfoundland dog**) dog of a very large breed with a thick coarse coat. □ **Newfoundlander** *n.*

New Guinea island in the SW Pacific Ocean, N of Australia, consisting of Papua New Guinea in the E and the Indonesian province of Irian Jaya in the W.

New Hampshire state in the NE US, bordering on the Atlantic; pop. (est. 1996) 1 162 481; capital, Concord. Manufacturing and tourism are important sources of revenue; products include electrical machinery, paper, and wood.

New Hebrides see VANUATU.

New Ireland island of Papua New Guinea, lying to the N of New Britain; pop. (1990) 87 194; capital, Kavieng.

♦ **new issue** *n.* issue of shares being offered on a stock exchange for the first time. See FLOTATION.

New Jersey state in the NE US, bordering on the Atlantic; pop. (est. 1996) 7 987 933; capital, Trenton. Industries include chemicals, textiles, electrical machinery, and tourism; it is also a copper-smelting and -refining centre. Agricultural produce includes tomatoes, peppers, potatoes, and peaches.

newly *adv.* **1** recently. **2** afresh, anew.

newly-wed *n.* recently married person.

Newmarket /ˈnjuːˌmɑːkɪt/ town in E England, in Suffolk, noted as a horse-racing centre; pop. (est. 1988) 16 830.

new mathematics *n.pl.* (also **new maths**) (also treated as *sing.*) system of elementary maths teaching with an emphasis on investigation and set theory.

New Mexico state in the SW US; pop. (est. 1996) 1 713 407; capital, Santa Fé. It has significant deposits of oil and natural gas; uranium and manganese ore and potash are also produced. Forestry and tourism are important.

new moon *n.* **1** moon when first seen as a crescent after conjunction with the sun. **2** time of its appearance.

New Orleans /ɔːˈlɪənz/ industrial port and commercial city in the US, in Louisiana on the Gulf of Mexico; industries include food processing, chemicals, oil, and shipbuilding; pop. (est. 1994) 484 149.

New Plymouth seaport in New Zealand, on the W coast of North Island; cheese is exported; pop. (1994) 49 500.

new potatoes *n.pl.* earliest potatoes of a new crop.

♦ **new product development** *n.* (also **NPD**) marketing procedure in which new ideas are developed into viable new products or extensions to existing products or product ranges. New ideas, which are generated either internally (e.g. by scientific research) or by feedback from consumers, are first screened for prima facie viability; the few that remain are further reduced by concept tests and detailed analysis of their potential profitability. Any ideas that survive these obstacles are subjected to extensive product development. Prototypes are made and tested within the company and among consumers, and improvements made. This cycle is repeated until satisfactory marketing research results are obtained, when the new product will be launched, possibly at first in a restricted area (see TEST MARKETING).

Newry /ˈnjuːrɪ/ port in SE Northern Ireland, in County Down; pop. (1981) 19 400.

news /njuːz/ *n.pl.* (usu. treated as *sing.*) **1** information about important or interesting recent events, esp. when published or broadcast. **2** (prec. by *the*) broadcast report of news. **3** newly received or noteworthy information. [from NEW]

newsagent *n.* seller of or shop selling newspapers etc.

newscast *n.* radio or television broadcast of news reports.

newscaster *n.* = NEWSREADER.

news conference *n.* press conference.

newsflash *n.* single item of important news broadcast urgently and often interrupting other programmes.

newsletter *n.* informal printed report issued periodically to members of a club etc.

New South Wales state in SE Australia; pop. (est. 1996) 6 173 000; capital, Sydney. Agriculture is important, producing cereals (esp. wheat), fruit and vegetables, beef cattle, and dairy products. Coal, silver, lead, zinc, and copper are mined. Industrial activity (including iron and steel, textiles, and chemicals) is centred on Sydney.

newspaper *n.* **1** printed publication of loose folded sheets containing news, advertisements, correspondence, etc. **2** paper forming this (*wrapped in newspaper*).

Newspeak *n.* ambiguous euphemistic language used esp. in political propaganda. [an artificial official language in Orwell's *Nineteen Eighty-Four*]

newsprint *n.* low-quality paper on which newspapers are printed.

newsreader *n.* person who reads out broadcast news bulletins.

newsreel *n.* short cinema film of recent events.

news room *n.* room in a newspaper or broadcasting office where news is processed.

news-sheet *n.* simple form of newspaper; newsletter.

news-stand *n.* stall for the sale of newspapers.

new star *n.* nova.

new style *n.* dating reckoned by the Gregorian Calendar.

news-vendor *n.* newspaper-seller.

newsworthy *adj.* topical; noteworthy as news.

newsy *adj.* (**-ier**, **-iest**) *colloq.* full of news.

newt *n.* small amphibian with a well-developed tail. [*ewt*, with *n* from *an*: var. of *evet* EFT]

New Territories part of the territory of Hong Kong lying N of the Kowloon peninsula and including the islands of Lantau, Tsing Yi, and Lamma.

New Testament *n.* part of the Bible concerned with the life and teachings of Christ and his earliest followers.

♦ **new time** *n.* next accounting period on the London Stock Exchange. A purchase or sale of securities during the last two dealing days of an account may be made for settlement during the next account.

---

newton /ˈnjuːt(ə)n/ *n.* SI unit of force that, acting on a mass of one kilogram, increases its velocity by one metre per second every second. [*Newton*, name of a scientist]

new town *n.* town planned and built all at once with government funds.

New Wave *n.* a style of rock music.

New World *n.* North and South America.

new year *n.* year just begun or about to begin; first few days of a year.

New Year's Day *n.* 1 January.

New Zealand /ˈziːlənd/ country in the S Pacific, a member state of the Commonwealth, about 1900 km (1200 miles) E of Australia, consisting of two major islands (North and South Islands) and several smaller islands. The economy was predominantly agricultural: livestock rearing, esp. of sheep, is important and New Zealand is a major producer of wool, which with meat and dairy produce form the chief exports. Horticulture and forestry are also major industries, fruit (esp. kiwi fruit), timber, and timber products being exported. Coal, oil, natural gas, gold, silver, iron ore, and limestone are all exploited. Manufactures include textiles and clothing, chemicals, plastics, electronic goods, and metal products. Tourism is a major source of foreign exchange. Hydroelectricity supplies almost all domestic demand. During the 1980s New Zealand suffered severe economic problems including slow growth, increasing unemployment, and high inflation. New measures introduced in the late 1980s and early 1990s succeeded in reducing inflation levels.
History. The islands came under British sovereignty in 1840; colonization led to a series of wars with the native Maoris in the 1860s and 1870s. Full dominion status was granted in 1907, and independence in 1931. The conservative National Party has held power since 1990. Prime minister, Jenny Shipley; capital, Wellington. □ **New Zealander** *n.*

languages	English, Maori
currency	dollar ($NZ) of 100 cents
pop. (1996)	3 619 000
GNP (1994)	US$46.5B
literacy	99% (m); 99% (f)
life expectancy	74 (m); 80 (f)

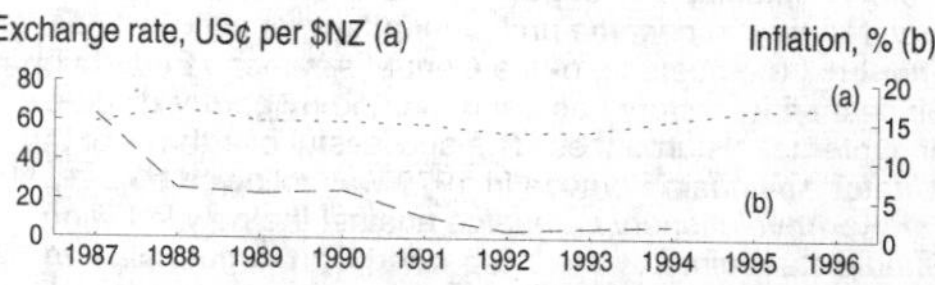

New Year's Eve *n.* 31 December.

New York 1 state in the NE US, bordering on the Atlantic; pop. (est. 1996) 18 184 774; capital, Albany. Industries include food processing, printing and publishing, and the manufacture of clothing and electrical machinery. **2** largest city and greatest port of the US, in the state of New York; pop. (est. 1994) 7 323 253. A leading commercial and cultural centre, it contains the financial district of Wall Street and is the site of the headquarters of the United Nations.

♦ **New York Stock Exchange** *n.* (also **NYSE**) main US stock exchange, situated on New York City's Wall Street. Founded in 1792, it is an unincorporated organization with over 1500 members. See DOW JONES INDUSTRIAL AVERAGE; STANDARD AND POOR'S 500 STOCK INDEX.

next *–adj.* **1** (often foll. by *to*) being, positioned, or living nearest. **2** nearest in order of time; soonest encountered (*next Friday*; *ask the next person you see*). *–adv.* **1** (often foll. by *to*) in the nearest place or degree (*put it next to mine*). **2** on the first or soonest occasion (*when we next meet*). *–n.* next person or thing. *–prep. colloq.* next to. □ **next to** almost (*next to nothing left*). [Old English, superlative of NIGH]

next-best *adj.* the next in order of preference.

next door *adj.* & *adv.* (as *adj.* often hyphenated) in the next house or room.

next of kin *n.sing.* & *pl.* closest living relative(s).

next world *n.* (prec. by *the*) life after death.

nexus /'neksəs/ *n.* (*pl.* same) connected group or series. [Latin *necto nex-* bind]

NF *abbr.* **1** Newfoundland. **2** (also **N/F**) *Banking* no funds.

NFBTE *abbr.* National Federation of Building Trades Employers.

NFC *abbr.* National Freight Consortium.

NFFE *abbr.* (in the US) National Federation of Federal Employees.

NFFPT *abbr.* National Federation of Fruit and Potato Trades.

NFHA *abbr.* National Federation of Housing Associations.

Nfld *abbr.* Newfoundland.

NFS *abbr.* **1** *Computing* network file service (or system). **2** not for sale.

NFSE *abbr.* National Federation of Self-Employed (and Small Businesses).

NFU *abbr.* National Farmers' Union.

NG *postcode* Nottingham.

NGNP *abbr.* nominal gross national product.

NGO *abbr.* non-governmental organization.

ngultrum /ŋ'guːltrəm/ *n.* standard monetary unit of Bhutan. [Bhutanese]

NH *–airline flight code* All Nippon Airways. *–abbr.* & *US postcode* New Hampshire.

NHBC *abbr.* National House-Building Council.

NHI *abbr.* National Health Insurance.

NHS *abbr.* National Health Service.

Nhulunbuy /ˌnjuːlən'baɪ/ bauxite-mining centre in Australia, on the Gove Peninsula of Arnhem Land in Northern Territory; pop. (1986) 3800.

NI *abbr.* **1** = NATIONAL INSURANCE. **2** Northern Ireland. **3** North Island (New Zealand).

Ni *symb.* nickel.

niacin /'naɪəsɪn/ *n.* = NICOTINIC ACID. [shortening]

Niagara /naɪ'ægərə/ river forming the US–Canada border, famous for its spectacular waterfalls which are a major source of hydroelectric power.

Niamey /'njɑːmeɪ/ capital of Niger, the administrative and commercial centre of the country; pop. (est. 1995) 495 000.

nib *n.* **1** pen-point. **2** (in *pl.*) shelled and crushed coffee or cocoa beans. [Low German or Dutch]

nibble /'nɪb(ə)l/ *–v.* (**-ling**) **1** (foll. by *at*) **a** take small bites at. **b** take cautious interest in. **2** eat in small amounts. **3** bite at gently, cautiously, or playfully. *–n.* **1** act of nibbling. **2** very small amount of food. [Low German or Dutch]

nibs *n.* □ **his nibs** *joc. colloq.* mock title used with reference to an important or self-important person. [origin unknown]

NIC *–abbr.* **1** (also **nic**) National Insurance contribution. **2** newly industrialized country. *–international vehicle registration* Nicaragua.

Nice /niːs/ city in SE France, a resort on the French Riviera; pop. (1990) 345 674.

nice *adj.* **1** pleasant, satisfactory. **2** (of a person) kind, good-natured. **3** *iron.* bad or awkward (*nice mess*). **4** fine or subtle (*nice distinction*). **5** fastidious; delicately sensitive. **6** (foll. by an adj., often with *and*) satisfactory in terms of the quality described (*a nice long time*; *nice and warm*). □ **nicely** *adv.* **niceness** *n.* **nicish** *adj.* (also **niceish**). [originally = foolish, from Latin *nescius* ignorant]

NICEC *abbr.* National Institute for Careers Education and Counselling.

nicety /'naɪsɪtɪ/ *n.* (*pl.* **-ies**) **1** subtle distinction or detail. **2** precision. □ **to a nicety** with exactness.

niche /niːʃ/ *n.* **1** shallow recess, esp. in a wall. **2** comfortable or apt position in life or employment. **3** position from which an entrepreneur exploits a gap in the market; profitable corner of the market. See CONCENTRATED SEGMENTATION. [Latin *nidus* nest]

nick *–n.* **1** small cut or notch. **2** *slang* **a** prison. **b** police station. **3** *colloq.* condition (*in good nick*). *–v.* **1** make a nick or nicks in. **2** *slang* **a** steal. **b** arrest, catch. □ **in the nick of time** only just in time. [origin uncertain]

Nicaragua /ˌnɪkə'rægjʊə/, **Republic of** largest country in Central America, with a coastline on both the Atlantic and Pacific Oceans. The economy is predominantly agricultural, Nicaragua's chief exports being coffee, beef, cotton, sugar, and bananas. Forestry and fishing (esp. of shellfish) are also important. Minerals include gold, silver, lead, and zinc. Manufacturing industries, on a small scale, include food processing, oil refining, chemicals, and textiles. The economy, severely disrupted by the effects of civil war and a US trade embargo imposed 1985–90, is starting to show signs of recovery.

History. Colonized by the Spaniards in the early 16th century, Nicaragua became an independent republic in 1838 after brief membership of the Central American Federation. Since then its history has been marked by border disputes and internal disturbances. The successful overthrow of the dictator Anastasio Somoza in 1979 was followed by a counter-revolutionary campaign against the new left-wing Sandinista regime by the US-backed Contra guerrillas. In the 1990 election the Sandinistas were defeated by a coalition of opposition parties. President, Arnoldo Alemán Lacayo; capital, Managua. □ **Nicaraguan** *adj.* & *n.*

language	Spanish
currency	córdoba oro (C$) of 100 centavos
pop. (1996)	4 272 000
GNP (1994)	US$1.3B
literacy	64% (m); 66% (f)
life expectancy	63 (m); 67 (f)

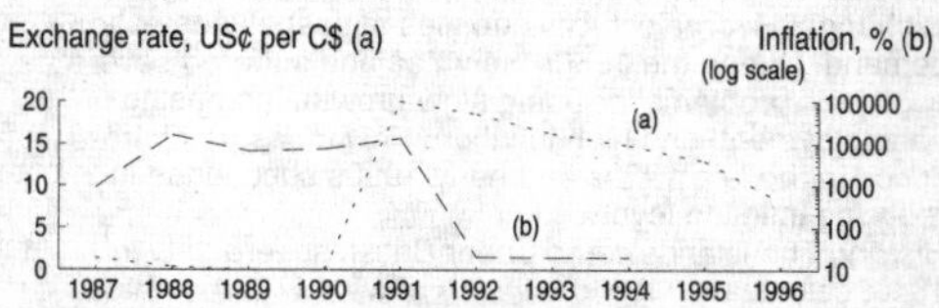

nickel /'nɪk(ə)l/ *n.* **1** silver-white metallic element, used esp. in magnetic alloys. **2** *colloq.* US five-cent coin. [German]

nickel silver *n.* = GERMAN SILVER.

nickel steel *n.* type of stainless steel with chromium and nickel.

nicker *n.* (*pl.* same) *slang* pound sterling. [origin unknown]

nick-nack var. of KNICK-KNACK.

nickname /'nɪkneɪm/ –*n.* familiar or humorous name given to a person or thing instead of or as well as the real name. –*v.* (**-ming**) **1** give a nickname to. **2** call by a nickname. [earlier *eke-name*, with *n* from *an*: *eke* = addition, from Old English: related to EKE]

Nicobar Islands see ANDAMAN AND NICOBAR ISLANDS.

Nicosia /,nɪkə'siːə/ capital of Cyprus, divided since 1974 into Greek and Turkish sectors; industries include food processing, textiles, and cigarettes; pop. (est. 1994) 186 400 (excluding Turkish sector).

nicotine /'nɪkə,tiːn/ *n.* poisonous alkaloid present in tobacco. [French from *Nicot*, introducer of tobacco into France]

nicotinic acid /,nɪkə'tɪnɪk/ *n.* vitamin of the B complex.

nictitate /'nɪktɪ,teɪt/ *v.* (**-ting**) blink or wink. □ **nictitation** /-'teɪʃ(ə)n/ *n.* [Latin]

nictitating membrane *n.* transparent third eyelid in amphibians, birds, and some other animals.

niece *n.* daughter of one's brother or sister or of one's spouse's brother or sister. [Latin *neptis* granddaughter]

NIESR *abbr.* = NATIONAL INSTITUTE OF ECONOMIC AND SOCIAL RESEARCH.

NIF *abbr.* = NOTE ISSUANCE FACILITY.

niff *n.* & *v. colloq.* smell, stink. □ **niffy** *adj.* (**-ier**, **-iest**). [originally a dial. word]

nifty /'nɪftɪ/ *adj.* (**-ier**, **-iest**) *colloq.* **1** clever, adroit. **2** smart, stylish. [origin uncertain]

Niger, River river in W Africa, rising in Guinea near the frontier of Sierra Leone and flowing through Mali, Niger, and Nigeria to the Gulf of Guinea; a source of hydroelectric power.

niggard /'nɪgəd/ *n.* stingy person. [probably of Scandinavian origin]

niggardly *adj.* stingy. □ **niggardliness** *n.*

nigger *n. offens.* Black or dark-skinned person. [Spanish NEGRO]

niggle /'nɪg(ə)l/ *v.* (**-ling**) **1** be over-attentive to details. **2** find fault in a petty way. **3** *colloq.* irritate; nag pettily. □ **niggling** *adj.* [origin unknown]

nigh /naɪ/ *adv., prep.,* & *adj. archaic* or *dial.* near. [Old English]

night /naɪt/ *n.* **1** period of darkness between one day and the next; time from sunset to sunrise. **2** nightfall. **3** darkness of night. **4** night or evening appointed for some activity regarded in a certain way (*last night of the Proms*). [Old English]

nightbird *n.* person who is most active at night.

nightcap *n.* **1** *hist.* cap worn in bed. **2** hot or alcoholic drink taken at bedtime.

nightclub *n.* club providing refreshment and entertainment late at night.

nightdress *n.* woman's or child's loose garment worn in bed.

nightfall *n.* end of daylight.

nightgown *n.* = NIGHTDRESS.

nightie *n. colloq.* nightdress.

nightingale /'naɪtɪŋ,geɪl/ *n.* small reddish-brown bird, of which the male sings melodiously, esp. at night. [Old English, = night-singer]

nightjar *n.* nocturnal bird with a characteristic harsh cry.

night-life *n.* entertainment available at night in a town.

night-light *n.* dim light kept burning in a bedroom at night.

night-long *adj.* & *adv.* throughout the night.

nightly –*adj.* **1** happening, done, or existing in the night. **2** recurring every night. –*adv.* every night.

nightmare *n.* **1** frightening dream. **2** *colloq.* frightening or unpleasant experience or situation. **3** haunting fear. □ **nightmarish** *adj.* [evil spirit (incubus) once thought to lie on and suffocate sleepers: Old English *mære* incubus]

night safe *n.* safe with access from the outer wall of a commercial bank for the deposit of money etc. when the bank is closed. By using this service shopkeepers etc. can avoid keeping large sums overnight.

night school *n.* institution providing classes in the evening.

nightshade *n.* any of various plants with poisonous berries. [Old English]

nightshirt *n.* long shirt worn in bed.

nightspot *n.* nightclub.

night-time *n.* time of darkness.

night-watchman *n.* **1** person employed to keep watch at night. **2** *Cricket* inferior batsman sent in near the close of a day's play.

NIHCA *abbr.* Northern Ireland Hotels and Caterers Association.

nihilism /'naɪɪ,lɪz(ə)m/ *n.* **1** rejection of all religious and moral principles. **2** belief that nothing really exists. □ **nihilist** *n.* **nihilistic** /-'lɪstɪk/ *adj.* [Latin *nihil* nothing]

Nijmegen /'naɪmeɪgən/ industrial city in the E Netherlands; engineering is important; pop. (1994) 147 018.

-nik *suffix* forming nouns denoting a person associated with a specified thing or quality (*beatnik*). [Russian (as SPUTNIK) and Yiddish]

Niger /'naɪdʒə(r)/, **Republic of** landlocked country in W Africa, lying mainly in the Sahara, bounded in the W and N by Mali, Algeria, and Libya and in the S and E by Burkina Faso, Nigeria, and Chad. Agriculture is important to the economy; cowpeas and livestock are major exports and millet, sorghum, cassava, and rice are the principal subsistence crops. During the 1980s major anti-desertification and reafforestation programmes were implemented to offset the effects of earlier droughts. Niger possesses important deposits of uranium, which is the major export; cassiterite, gypsum, coal, salt, and gold are also exploited. *History.* A French colony (part of French West Africa) from 1922, Niger became an autonomous republic within the French Community in 1958 and fully independent in 1960. In 1974 the country came under military rule that lasted until 1987. A new democratic constitution was adopted in 1991 and the country's first multi-party elections held in 1993. In 1994 a peace agreement was signed by the government and Tuareg guerrillas, who had been fighting since 1991. In January 1996 a military coup, headed by Colonel Ibrahim Barre Mainassara overthrew the government and suspended the constitution. A new constitution was adopted in May 1996 and Mainassara was subsequently elected president. President, General Ibrahim Barre Mainassara; capital, Niamey.

languages	French (official), African languages
currency	CFA franc (CFAF) of 100 centimes
pop. (1996)	9 465 000
GNP (1994)	US$2B
literacy	20% (m); 6% (f)
life expectancy	40 (m); 39 (f)

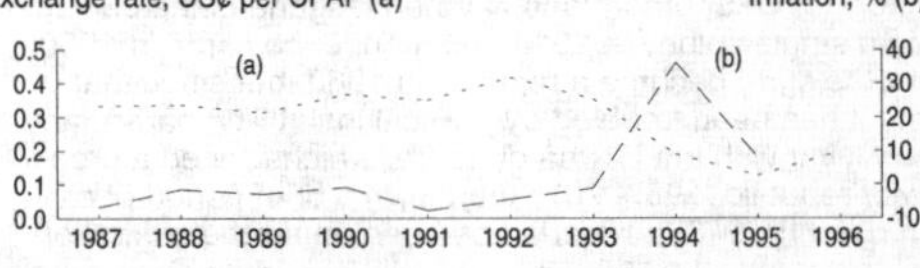

◆ **Nikkei Stock Average** /ˈnɪkeɪ/ *n.* (formerly **Nikkei Dow Index**, **Nikkei Dow Jones Index**) index of 225 Japanese industrial shares that gives an indication of the movement of share prices at the Tokyo Stock Exchange; it was reconstructed in 1991. [Japanese, from *Nikon Keizai* Shimbun, name of newspaper group that administers the index]

nil *n.* nothing; no number or amount (esp. as a score in games). [Latin]

Nile /naɪl/ river flowing from E central Africa through Egypt to the Mediterranean Sea; the high dam at Aswan provides irrigation and hydroelectric power.

nimble /ˈnɪmb(ə)l/ *adj.* (**-bler, -blest**) quick and light in movement or function; agile. □ **nimbly** *adv.* [Old English, = quick to seize]

nimbus /ˈnɪmbəs/ *n.* (*pl.* **nimbi** /-baɪ/ or **nimbuses**) **1** halo. **2** rain-cloud. [Latin, = cloud]

Nimby /ˈnɪmbɪ/ *–adj.* objecting to the siting of unpleasant developments in one's own locality. *–n.* (*pl.* **-ies**) person who so objects. [*n*ot *i*n *m*y *b*ack *y*ard]

nincompoop /ˈnɪŋkəm,puːp/ *n.* foolish person. [origin unknown]

nine *adj.* & *n.* **1** one more than eight. **2** symbol for this (9, ix, IX). **3** size etc. denoted by nine. [Old English]

nine days' wonder *n.* person or thing that is briefly famous.

ninefold *adj.* & *adv.* **1** nine times as much or as many. **2** consisting of nine parts.

ninepin *n.* **1** (in *pl.*; usu. treated as *sing.*) game in which nine pins are bowled at. **2** pin used in this game.

nineteen /naɪnˈtiːn/ *adj.* & *n.* **1** one more than eighteen. **2** symbol for this (19, xix, XIX). **3** size etc. denoted by nineteen. □ **talk nineteen to the dozen** see DOZEN. □ **nineteenth** *adj.* & *n.* [Old English]

ninety /ˈnaɪntɪ/ *adj.* & *n.* (*pl.* **-ies**) **1** product of nine and ten. **2** symbol for this (90, xc, XC). **3** (in *pl.*) numbers from 90 to 99, esp. the years of a century or of a person's life. □ **ninetieth** *adj.* & *n.* [Old English]

Ningxia /ˈnɪŋʃɪ,ɑː/ (also **Ningsia**) autonomous region in N China; pop. (est. 1995) 5 040 000; capital, Yinchuan.

ninny /ˈnɪnɪ/ *n.* (*pl.* **-ies**) foolish person. [origin uncertain]

NINO /ˈniːnəʊ/ *abbr.* no inspector, no operator (system).

ninth /naɪnθ/ *adj.* & *n.* **1** next after eighth. **2** any of nine equal parts of a thing. □ **ninthly** *adv.*

niobium /naɪˈəʊbɪəm/ *n.* rare metallic element occurring naturally. [*Niobe* in Greek legend]

Nip *n. slang offens.* Japanese person. [abbreviation of *Nipponese* from Japanese *Nippon* Japan]

nip[1] *–v.* (**-pp-**) **1** pinch, squeeze, or bite sharply. **2** (often foll. by *off*) remove by pinching etc. **3** (of the cold etc.) cause pain or harm to. **4** (foll. by *in*, *out*, etc.) *colloq.* go nimbly or quickly. *–n.* **1 a** pinch, sharp squeeze. **b** bite. **2** biting cold. □ **nip in the bud** suppress or destroy (esp. an idea) at an early stage. [Low German or Dutch]

nip[2] *n.* small quantity of spirits. [from *nipperkin* small measure]

nipper *n.* **1** person or thing that nips. **2** claw of a crab etc. **3** *colloq.* young child. **4** (in *pl.*) any tool for gripping or cutting.

nipple /ˈnɪp(ə)l/ *n.* **1** small projection in which the mammary ducts of either sex of mammals terminate and from which in females milk is secreted for the young. **2** teat of a feeding-bottle. **3** device like a nipple in function. **4** nipple-like protuberance. [perhaps from *neb* tip]

nippy *adj.* (**-ier, -iest**) *colloq.* **1** quick, nimble. **2** chilly. [from NIP[1]]

NIRC *abbr.* National Industrial Relations Court.

NIREX /ˈnaɪreks/ *abbr.* Nuclear Industry Radioactive Waste Executive.

nirvana /nɪəˈvɑːnə, nɜː-/ *n.* (in Buddhism) perfect bliss attained by the extinction of individuality. [Sanskrit, = extinction]

NIS *symb.* shekel.

NISC *abbr.* National Industrial Safety Committee.

Nissen hut /ˈnɪs(ə)n/ *n.* tunnel-shaped hut of corrugated iron with a cement floor. [*Nissen*, name of an engineer]

NIST *abbr.* (in the US) National Institute of Standards and Technology.

NIT *abbr.* = NEGATIVE INCOME TAX.

nit *n.* **1** egg or young form of a louse or other parasitic insect. **2** *slang* stupid person. [Old English]

nit-picking *n.* & *adj. colloq.* fault-finding in a petty manner.

nitrate *–n.* /ˈnaɪtreɪt/ **1** any salt or ester of nitric acid. **2** potassium or sodium nitrate as a fertilizer. *–v.* /naɪˈtreɪt/ (**-ting**) treat, combine, or impregnate with nitric acid. □ **nitration** /-ˈtreɪʃ(ə)n/ *n.* [French: related to NITRE]

nitre /ˈnaɪtə(r)/ *n.* (*US* **niter**) saltpetre. [Greek *nitron*]

nitric /ˈnaɪtrɪk/ *adj.* of or containing nitrogen.

nitric acid *n.* colourless corrosive poisonous liquid.

nitride /ˈnaɪtraɪd/ *n.* binary compound of nitrogen. [from NITRE]

nitrify /ˈnaɪtrɪ,faɪ/ *v.* (**-ies, -ied**) **1** impregnate with nitro-

---

Nigeria /naɪˈdʒɪərɪə/, **Federal Republic of** country on the W coast of Africa, a member state of the Commonwealth, bordered by the River Niger to the N. Oil reserves, discovered in the 1960s and 1970s, are the largest in Africa and oil production now provides almost all of Nigeria's export revenue. Nigeria is a member of OPEC. Other mineral reserves include natural gas, tin, coal, iron ore, and columbite. The construction, manufacturing, and service industries are being encouraged to counteract the effects of fluctuating oil prices; manufactures include fertilizers, petrochemicals, steel, and textiles. Agriculture, on which the economy was formerly based, still employs much of the working population although production has been affected by drought; the principal agricultural exports are cocoa, peanuts, cashews, palm oil, and rubber. Timber production and fishing are also important.

History. The territory came under British influence in the 18th and 19th centuries, the colony of Lagos and the protectorates of Southern and Northern Nigeria being unified into a single colony in 1914. Independence came in 1960 and the state became a republic in 1963, but since that time it has been troubled by political instability, particularly a civil war with the E area of Biafra, which formed a breakaway republic (1967–70). Apart from a brief period of civilian rule (1979–83), Nigeria has been under the control of the military since 1966; a return to civilian rule is scheduled for 1993. Democratic elections were held in 1993, but were annulled by President Babangida, who had come to power in a military coup in 1985. In 1995 Babangida was ousted in a coup that brough Abacha to power. Later in 1995 Nigeria was suspended from the Commonwealth following the execution of writer Ken Saro-Wiwa and other political activists. President, General Sanni Abacha; capital, Abuja. □ **Nigerian** *adj.* & *n.*

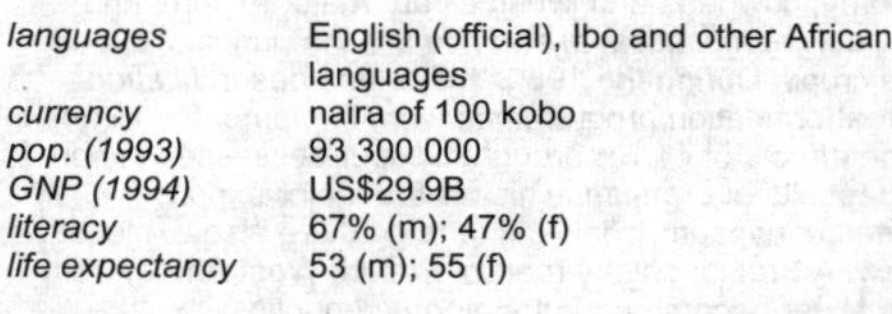

languages	English (official), Ibo and other African languages
currency	naira of 100 kobo
pop. (1993)	93 300 000
GNP (1994)	US$29.9B
literacy	67% (m); 47% (f)
life expectancy	53 (m); 55 (f)

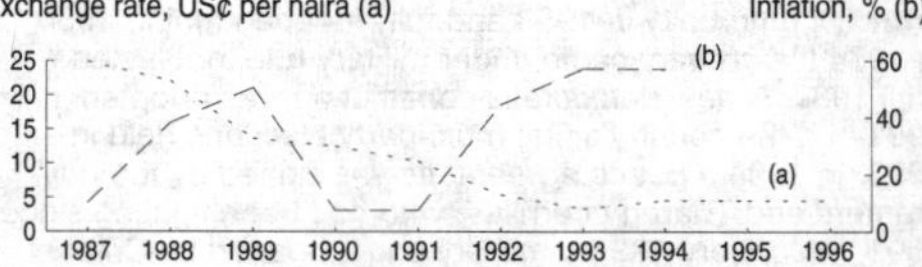

gen. **2** convert into nitrites or nitrates. □ **nitrification** /-fɪˈkeɪʃ(ə)n/ *n.* [French: related to NITRE]

nitrite /ˈnaɪtraɪt/ *n.* any salt or ester of nitrous acid. [from NITRE]

nitro- *comb. form* of or containing nitric acid, nitre, or nitrogen. [Greek: related to NITRE]

nitrogen /ˈnaɪtrədʒ(ə)n/ *n.* gaseous element that forms four-fifths of the atmosphere. □ **nitrogenous** /-ˈtrɒdʒɪnəs/ *adj.* [French]

nitroglycerine /ˌnaɪtrəʊˈglɪsərɪn/ *n.* (*US* **nitroglycerin**) explosive yellow liquid made by reacting glycerol with a mixture of concentrated sulphuric and nitric acids.

nitrous oxide /ˈnaɪtrəs/ *n.* colourless gas used as an anaesthetic. [Latin: related to NITRE]

nitty-gritty /ˌnɪtɪˈgrɪtɪ/ *n. slang* realities or practical details of a matter. [origin uncertain]

nitwit *n. colloq.* stupid person. [perhaps from NIT, WIT]

Niue /ˈnjuːeɪ/ coral island belonging to New Zealand, in the S Pacific E of the islands of Tonga; copra and bananas are exported; pop. (est. 1993) 1977. Niue is self-governing in free association with New Zealand.

Nizhny Novgorod /ˌnɪʒnɪ ˈnɒvgərɒd/ (formerly (1932–91) **Gorky**) city in Russia, a port on the River Volga; industries include chemicals, textiles, and the manufacture of machinery; pop. (est. 1995) 1 383 000.

NJ *abbr.* & *US postcode* New Jersey.

Nkr *symb.* Norwegian krone.

Nkz *symb.* kwanza.

NL *–abbr.* (in Australia) no liability (after the name of a public limited company). *–international vehicle registration* Netherlands.

NLP *abbr.* **1** *Computing* natural language processing. **2** *US* neighborhood loan program.

◆ **NLQ** *abbr.* near letter-quality. See LETTER-QUALITY.

NLRB *abbr.* (in the US) National Labor Relations Board.

NM *abbr.* & *US postcode* New Mexico.

N/m *abbr.* no mark(s) (on a bill of lading).

N.Mex. *abbr.* New Mexico.

NMP *abbr. Econ.* net material product.

NMS *abbr.* **1** = NORMAL MARKET SIZE. **2** *Stock Exch.* (in the US) National Market System.

NMW *abbr.* national minimum wage.

NN *postcode* Northampton.

NNE *abbr.* north-north-east.

◆ **NNP** *abbr.* = NET NATIONAL PRODUCT.

NNW *abbr.* north-north-west.

N/O *abbr.* (also **N/o**) no orders.

No[1] *symb.* nobelium.

No[2] var. of NOH.

No. *abbr.* number. [Latin *numero*, ablative of *numerus* number]

no[1] /nəʊ/ *adj.* **1** not any (*there is no excuse*). **2** not a, quite other than (*is no fool*). **3** hardly any (*did it in no time*). **4** used elliptically in a notice etc., to forbid etc. the thing specified (*no parking*). □ **no way** *colloq.* **1** it is impossible. **2** I will not agree etc. **no wonder** see WONDER. [related to NONE]

no[2] /nəʊ/ *–adv.* **1** indicating that the answer to the question is negative, the statement etc. made or course of action intended or conclusion arrived at is not correct or satisfactory, the request or command will not be complied with, or the negative statement made is correct. **2** (foll. by *compar.*) by no amount; not at all (*no better than before*). *–n.* (*pl.* **noes**) **1** utterance of the word *no*. **2** denial or refusal. **3** 'no' vote. □ **no longer** not now or henceforth as formerly. **or no** or not (*pleasant or no, it is true*). [Old English]

nob[1] *n. slang* person of wealth or high social position. [origin unknown]

nob[2] *n. slang* head. [from KNOB]

no-ball *n. Cricket* unlawfully delivered ball.

nobble /ˈnɒb(ə)l/ *v.* (**-ling**) *slang* **1** try to influence (e.g. a judge), esp. unfairly. **2** tamper with (a racehorse) to prevent its winning. **3** steal. **4** seize, catch. [dial. *knobble* beat]

nobelium /nəʊˈbiːlɪəm/ *n.* artificially produced radioactive transuranic metallic element. [from *Nobel*: see NOBEL PRIZE]

Nobel prize /nəʊˈbel/ *n.* any of six international prizes awarded annually for physics, chemistry, physiology or medicine, literature, economics, and the promotion of peace. [from *Nobel*, Swedish chemist and engineer, who endowed them]

nobility /nəʊˈbɪlɪtɪ/ *n.* (*pl.* **-ies**) **1** nobleness of character, mind, birth, or rank. **2** class of nobles, highest social class.

noble /ˈnəʊb(ə)l/ *–adj.* (**nobler, noblest**) **1** belonging to the aristocracy. **2** of excellent character; magnanimous. **3** of imposing appearance. *–n.* nobleman, noblewoman. □ **nobleness** *n.* **nobly** *adv.* [Latin *(g)nobilis*]

noble gas *n.* any of a group of gaseous elements that almost never combine with other elements.

nobleman *n.* peer.

noblesse oblige /nəʊˌbles ɒˈbliːʒ/ *n.* privilege entails responsibility. [French]

noblewoman *n.* peeress.

nobody /ˈnəʊbədɪ/ *–pron.* no person. *–n.* (*pl.* **-ies**) person of no importance.

no-claim bonus *n.* (also **no-claims bonus**) reduction of an insurance premium after an agreed period without a claim. The system is mostly used in motor insurance, in which discounts of 33% for one claim-free year can rise to 60% of a premium for four successive years. The bonus is lost or reduced if a claim is made, whether the insured is at fault or not.

nocturnal /nɒkˈtɜːn(ə)l/ *adj.* of or in the night; done or active by night. [Latin *nox noct-* night]

nocturne /ˈnɒktɜːn/ *n.* **1** *Mus.* short romantic composition, usu. for piano. **2** picture of a night scene. [French]

nod *–v.* (**-dd-**) **1** incline one's head slightly and briefly in assent, greeting, or command. **2** let one's head fall forward in drowsiness; be drowsy. **3** incline (one's head). **4** signify (assent etc.) by a nod. **5** (of flowers, plumes, etc.) bend downwards and sway. **6** make a mistake due to a momentary lack of alertness or attention. *–n.* nodding of the head. □ **nod off** *colloq.* fall asleep. [origin unknown]

NODC *abbr.* non-OPEC developing country.

noddle /ˈnɒd(ə)l/ *n. colloq.* head. [origin unknown]

noddy *n.* (*pl.* **-ies**) **1** simpleton. **2** tropical sea bird. [origin unknown]

node *n.* **1 a** part of a plant stem from which leaves emerge. **b** knob on a root or branch. **2** natural swelling. **3** either of two points at which a planet's orbit intersects the plane of the ecliptic or the celestial equator. **4** point of minimum disturbance in a standing wave system. **5** point at which a curve intersects itself. **6 a** point in a computer network where communication lines are interconnected. **b** computer or other device used to make the connection or connections (see NETWORK *n.* 6). □ **nodal** *adj.* [Latin *nodus* knot]

nodule /ˈnɒdjuːl/ *n.* **1** small rounded lump of anything. **2** small tumour, node, or ganglion, or a swelling on the root of a legume containing bacteria etc. □ **nodular** *adj.* [Latin diminutive: related to NODE]

Noel /nəʊˈel/ *n.* Christmas. [Latin: related to NATAL]

noggin /ˈnɒgɪn/ *n.* **1** small mug. **2** small measure, usu. $^1/_4$ pint, of spirits. **3** *slang* head. [origin unknown]

no go *adj.* (usu. hyphenated when *attrib.*) *colloq.* impossible, hopeless, forbidden (*tried to get him to agree, but it was clearly no go; no-go area*).

Noh /nəʊ/ *n.* (also **No**) traditional Japanese drama. [Japanese]

noise /nɔɪz/ *–n.* **1** sound, esp. a loud or unpleasant one. **2** series or confusion of loud sounds. **3** unwanted electrical signals producing disturbances in the output of a system. **4** (in *pl.*) conventional remarks, or speechlike sounds without actual words (*made sympathetic noises*). –*v.* (**-sing**) (usu. in *passive*) make public; spread abroad (a person's fame or a fact). [Latin NAUSEA]

noiseless *adj.* making little or no noise. □ **noiselessly** *adv.*

noisome /'nɔɪsəm/ *adj. literary* **1** harmful, noxious. **2** evil-smelling. [from ANNOY]

noisy *adj.* (**-ier, -iest**) **1** making much noise. **2** full of noise. □ **noisily** *adv.* **noisiness** *n.*

nomad /'nəʊmæd/ *n.* **1** member of a tribe roaming from place to place for pasture. **2** wanderer. □ **nomadic** /-'mædɪk/ *adj.* [Greek *nomas nomad-* from *nemō* to pasture]

no man's land *n.* **1** space between two opposing armies. **2** area not assigned to any owner.

nom de plume /ˌnɒm də 'pluːm/ *n.* (*pl.* ***noms de plume*** pronunc. same) writer's assumed name. [sham French, = pen-name]

nomen /'nəʊmen/ *n.* ancient Roman's second or family name, as in Marcus *Tullius* Cicero. [Latin, = name]

nomenclature /nəʊ'menklətʃə(r)/ *n.* **1** person's or community's system of names for things. **2** terminology of a science etc. [Latin *nomen* name, *calo* call]

nominal /'nɒmɪn(ə)l/ *adj.* **1** existing in name only; not real or actual. **2** (of a sum of money etc.) very small. **3** of or in names (*nominal and essential distinctions*). **4** of, as, or like a noun. □ **nominally** *adv.* [Latin *nomen* name]

♦ **nominal account** *n.* ledger account that is not a personal account in that it bears the name of a concept, e.g. light and heat, bad debts, investments, etc., rather than the name of a person. See also NOMINAL LEDGER.

♦ **nominal capital** see SHARE CAPITAL.

♦ **nominal damages** see DAMAGES.

nominalism *n.* doctrine that universals or general ideas are mere names. □ **nominalist** *n.* **nominalistic** /-'lɪstɪk/ *adj.*

♦ **nominal ledger** *n.* ledger containing the nominal accounts and real accounts necessary to prepare the accounts of an organization. This ledger is distinguished from the personal ledgers, e.g. the sales and purchases ledgers, which contain the accounts of customers and suppliers respectively.

♦ **nominal partner** see PARTNERSHIP 3.

♦ **nominal price** *n.* **1** minimal price fixed for the sake of having some consideration for a transaction. It need bear no relation to the market value of the item. **2** = PAR VALUE.

♦ **nominal terms** *n.pl. Econ.* representation of the value of a good in money terms, rather than in terms of the quantity of another good for which it can be exchanged. Because the overall price level tends to change from year to year, and because different countries have different currencies, it is usu. necessary to convert values from nominal terms to real terms by applying some factor (e.g. a rate of exchange or a price index). Macroeconomists are particularly interested in separating the effects of government policy into real effects and nominal effects.

♦ **nominal value** *n.* = PAR VALUE.

♦ **nominal yield** *n.* = YIELD *n.* 2.

nominate /'nɒmɪˌneɪt/ *v.* (**-ting**) **1** propose (a candidate) for election. **2** appoint to an office. **3** name or appoint (a date or place). □ **nominator** *n.* [Latin: related to NOMINAL]

♦ **nomination** /ˌnɒmɪ'neɪʃ(ə)n/ *n.* **1** nominating. **2** person proposed for election. **3** person to whom the proceeds of a life-assurance policy should be paid as specified by the policyholder.

nominative /'nɒmɪnətɪv/ *Gram.* –*n.* case expressing the subject of a verb. –*adj.* of or in this case.

nominee /ˌnɒmɪ'niː/ *n.* **1.** person who is nominated. **2** person named by another (the **nominator**) to act on the nominator's behalf, often to conceal the identity of the nominator (see NOMINEE SHAREHOLDING).

♦ **nominee shareholding** *n.* shareholding held in the name of a bank, stockbroker, company, individual, etc. that is not the name of the beneficial owner of the shares. A shareholding may be in the name of nominees to facilitate dealing or to conceal the identity of the true owner. Although this cover was formerly used in the early stages of a take-over, to enable the bidder clandestinely to build up a substantial holding in the target company, this is now prevented by the Companies Act (1981), which makes it mandatory for anyone holding 5% or more of the shares in a public company to declare that interest to the company. The earlier Companies Act (1967) made it mandatory for directors to openly declare their holdings, and those of their families, in the companies of which they are directors.

non- *prefix* giving the negative sense of words with which it is combined. [Latin *non* not]

■ **Usage** The number of words that can be formed from the suffix *non-* is unlimited; consequently, only the most current and noteworthy can be given here.

♦ **non-accelerating inflation rate of unemployment** /ˌnɒnək'seləˌreɪtɪŋ/ see NAIRU.

♦ **non-acceptance** /ˌnɒnək'septəns/ *n.* failure by the person on whom a bill of exchange is drawn to accept it on presentation.

nonagenarian /ˌnəʊnədʒɪ'neərɪən/ *n.* person from 90 to 99 years old. [Latin *nonageni* ninety each]

non-aggression /ˌnɒnə'greʃ(ə)n/ *n.* lack of or restraint from aggression (often *attrib.*: *non-aggression pact*).

nonagon /'nɒnəgən/ *n.* plane figure with nine sides and angles. [Latin *nonus* ninth, after HEXAGON]

non-alcoholic /ˌnɒnælkə'hɒlɪk/ *adj.* containing no alcohol.

non-aligned /ˌnɒnə'laɪnd/ *adj.* (of a state) not aligned with a major power. □ **non-alignment** *n.*

♦ **non-assented stock** /ˌnɒnə'sentɪd/ see ASSENTED STOCK.

non-belligerent /ˌnɒnbə'lɪdʒərənt/ –*adj.* not engaged in hostilities. –*n.* non-belligerent state etc.

nonce *n.* □ **for the nonce** for the time being; for the present occasion. [from *for than anes* = for the one]

nonce-word *n.* word coined for one occasion.

nonchalant /'nɒnʃələnt/ *adj.* calm and casual. □ **nonchalance** *n.* **nonchalantly** *adv.* [French *chaloir* be concerned]

non-com /'nɒnkɒm/ *n. colloq.* non-commissioned officer. [abbreviation]

non-combatant /nɒn'kɒmbət(ə)nt/ *n.* person not fighting in a war, esp. a civilian, army chaplain, etc.

non-commissioned /ˌnɒnkə'mɪʃ(ə)nd/ *adj.* (of an officer) not holding a commission.

noncommittal /ˌnɒnkə'mɪt(ə)l/ *adj.* avoiding commitment to a definite opinion or course of action.

non compos mentis /ˌnɒn kɒmpɒs 'mentɪs/ *adj.* (also ***non compos***) not in one's right mind. [Latin, = not having control of one's mind]

non-conductor /ˌnɒnkən'dʌktə(r)/ *n.* substance that does not conduct heat or electricity.

nonconformist /ˌnɒnkən'fɔːmɪst/ *n.* **1** person who does not conform to the doctrine or discipline of an established Church, esp. (**Nonconformist**) member of a (usu. Protestant) sect dissenting from the Anglican Church. **2** person who does not conform to a prevailing principle.

nonconformity /ˌnɒnkən'fɔːmɪtɪ/ *n.* **1** nonconformists as a body, or their principles. **2** (usu. foll. by *to*) failure to conform. **3** lack of correspondence between things.

non-contributory /ˌnɒnkən'trɪbjʊtərɪ/ *adj.* not involving contributions.

♦ **non-contributory pension** *n.* pension in which the full premium is paid by an employer or the state and the pensioner makes no contribution.

non-cooperation /ˌnɒnkəʊˌɒpəˈreɪʃ(ə)n/ *n.* failure to cooperate.

nondescript /ˈnɒndɪskrɪpt/ *–adj.* lacking distinctive characteristics, not easily classified. *–n.* nondescript person or thing. [related to DESCRIBE]

non-domiciled /nɒnˈdɒmɪˌsaɪld/ *adj.* not domiciled in one's country of origin but residing permanently abroad.

non-drinker /nɒnˈdrɪŋkə(r)/ *n.* person who does not drink alcoholic liquor.

non-driver /nɒnˈdraɪvə(r)/ *n.* person who does not drive a motor vehicle.

♦ **non-durables** /nɒnˈdjʊərəb(ə)lz/ *n.pl.* consumer goods used up within a short period of time.

none /nʌn/ *–pron.* **1** (foll. by *of*) **a** not any of (*none of this concerns me; none of them have found it*). **b** not any one of (*none of them has come*). **2 a** no persons (*none but fools believe it*). **b** no person (*none but a fool believes it*). **3** (usu. with the preceding noun implied) not any (*you have money and I have none*). *–adv.* (foll. by *the* + compar., or *so, too*) by no amount; not at all (*am none the wiser*). [Old English, = not one]

■ **Usage** In sense 1b, the verb following *none* can be singular or plural according to meaning.

nonentity /nɒˈnentɪtɪ/ *n.* (*pl.* **-ies**) **1** person or thing of no importance. **2 a** non-existence. **b** non-existent thing. [medieval Latin]

nones /nəʊnz/ *n.pl.* day of the ancient Roman month (the 7th day of March, May, July, and October, the 5th of other months). [Latin *nonus* ninth]

non-essential /ˌnɒnɪˈsenʃ(ə)l/ *–adj.* not essential. *–n.* non-essential thing.

nonetheless /ˌnʌnðəˈles/ *adv.* (also **none the less**) nevertheless.

non-event /ˌnɒnɪˈvent/ *n.* insignificant event, esp. contrary to hopes or expectations.

♦ **non-executive director** /ˌnɒnɪgˈzekjʊtɪv/ *n.* member of a board of directors who is involved in planning and policy-making, but not in the day-to-day management of the company. A non-executive director is often employed for prestige (if well known), for experience or contacts, or for specialist knowledge, which may only be required occasionally. Cf. EXECUTIVE DIRECTOR.

non-existent /ˌnɒnɪgˈzɪst(ə)nt/ *adj.* not existing.

non-fattening /nɒnˈfætənɪŋ/ *adj.* (of food) not containing many calories.

non-ferrous /nɒnˈferəs/ *adj.* (of a metal) other than iron or steel.

non-fiction /nɒnˈfɪkʃ(ə)n/ *n.* literary work other than fiction.

non-flammable /nɒnˈflæməb(ə)l/ *adj.* not inflammable.

♦ **non-impact printer** /nɒnˈɪmpækt/ see PRINTER 3.

non-interference /ˌnɒnɪntəˈfɪərəns/ *n.* = NON-INTERVENTION.

non-intervention /ˌnɒnɪntəˈvenʃ(ə)n/ *n.* (esp. political) principle or practice of not becoming involved in others' affairs.

♦ **non-marketable security** /nɒnˈmɑːkɪtəb(ə)l/ *n.* UK government security that cannot be bought and sold on a stock exchange (cf. MARKETABLE SECURITY). Non-marketable securities include savings bonds and National Savings Certificates, tax-reserve certificates, etc., all of which form part of the national debt.

non-member *n.* person who is not a member.

♦ **non-monetary advantages and disadvantages** /nɒnˈmʌnɪtərɪ/ *n.pl.* aspects of an employment that are not connected with its financial remuneration. They include the employee's subjective opinion of the working environment, the stimulation or boredom of the work itself, the companionship or isolation experienced at work, the distance travelled to reach work, etc. These aspects of an employment, together with the salary, bonuses, commission, and fringe benefits, make a person decide either to stay in a job or seek another.

♦ **non-negotiable instrument** /nɒnnɪˈgəʊʃəb(ə)l/ see NEGOTIABLE INSTRUMENT.

non-nuclear /nɒnˈnjuːklɪə(r)/ *adj.* **1** not involving nuclei or nuclear energy. **2** (of a state etc.) not having nuclear weapons.

non-observance /ˌnɒnəbˈzɜːv(ə)ns/ *n.* failure to observe (an agreement, requirement, etc.).

non-operational /ˌnɒnɒpəˈreɪʃən(ə)l/ *adj.* **1** that does not operate. **2** out of order.

nonpareil /ˈnɒnpər(ə)l, ˌnɒnpəˈreɪl/ *–adj.* unrivalled or unique. *–n.* such a person or thing. [French *pareil*]

non-partisan /ˌnɒnpɑːtɪˈzæn/ *adj.* not partisan.

non-party /nɒnˈpɑːtɪ/ *adj.* independent of political parties.

non-payment /nɒnˈpeɪmənt/ *n.* failure to pay; lack of payment.

♦ **non-performing loan** /ˌnɒnˈpəfɔːmɪŋ/ *n.* **1** loan in which the interest payments are overdue. **2** loan by a bank to a developing country, on which interest payments ceased in the 1980s.

nonplus /nɒnˈplʌs/ *v.* (**-ss-**) completely perplex. [Latin *non plus* not more]

♦ **non-price competition** /nɒnˈpraɪs/ *n.* form of competition in which two or more producers sell goods or services at the same price but compete to increase their share of the market by such measures as advertising, sales promotion campaigns, improving the quality of the product or service, and (for goods) improving the packaging, offering free servicing and installation, or giving free gifts of unrelated products or services.

♦ **non-profitability sampling** /nɒnˈprɒfɪtəbɪlɪtɪ/ *n.* technique in marketing research in which the researcher makes personal judgements, instead of random selection, in choosing a representative sample of people to interview. This reduces the statistical validity of the results, which are then not sufficiently reliable to use as a basis for estimating profits.

non-profit-making /nɒnˈprɒfɪtˌmeɪkɪŋ/ *adj.* (of an enterprise) not conducted primarily to make a profit.

♦ **non-profit marketing** *n.* applying marketing concepts to organizations, e.g. symphony orchestras, museums, and charities, that are not profit-orientated.

non-proliferation /ˌnɒnprəˌlɪfəˈreɪʃ(ə)n/ *n.* prevention of an increase in something, esp. possession of nuclear weapons.

♦ **non-qualifying policy** /nɒnˈkwɒlɪfaɪɪŋ/ *n.* life-assurance policy that does not satisfy the qualification rules contained in Schedule 15 of the Income and Corporation Taxes Act (1988): no tax relief can be obtained on the premium payments of such a policy.

non-resident /nɒnˈrezɪd(ə)nt/ *–adj.* **1** not residing in a particular place. **2** (of a post) not requiring the holder to reside at the place of work. *–n.* status of an individual who formerly lived in one country for fiscal purposes but who has moved to another country, either for employment or permanently. This person's liability to tax in the first country is restricted to income from sources within that country. □ **non-residential** /-ˈdenʃ(ə)l/ *adj.*

non-resistance /ˌnɒnrɪˈzɪst(ə)ns/ *n.* practice or principle of not resisting authority.

non-returnable /ˌnɒnrɪ'tɜːnəb(ə)l/ *adj.* that is not to be returned.

non-sectarian /ˌnɒnsek'teərɪən/ *adj.* not sectarian.

nonsense /'nɒns(ə)ns/ *n.* **1** (often as *int.*) absurd or meaningless words or ideas. **2** foolish or extravagant conduct. □ **nonsensical** /-'sensɪk(ə)l/ *adj.* **nonsensically** /-'sensɪkəlɪ/ *adv.*

non sequitur /nɒn 'sekwɪtə(r)/ *n.* conclusion that does not logically follow from the premisses. [Latin, = it does not follow]

non-slip /nɒn'slɪp/ *adj.* **1** that does not slip. **2** that inhibits slipping.

non-smoker /nɒn'sməʊkə(r)/ *n.* **1** person who does not smoke. **2** train compartment etc. where smoking is forbidden. □ **non-smoking** *adj.*

non-specialist /nɒn'speʃəlɪst/ *n.* person who is not a specialist (in a particular subject).

non-specific /ˌnɒnspɪ'sɪfɪk/ *adj.* that cannot be specified.

non-standard /nɒn'stændəd/ *adj.* not standard.

non-starter /nɒn'stɑːtə(r)/ *n. colloq.* person or scheme that is unlikely to succeed.

non-stick /nɒn'stɪk/ *adj.* that does not allow things to stick to it.

non-stop /nɒn'stɒp/ *–adj.* **1** (of a train etc.) not stopping at intermediate places. **2** done without a stop or intermission. *–adv.* without stopping.

non-swimmer /nɒn'swɪmə(r)/ *n.* person who cannot swim.

♦ **non-tariff barrier** /nɒn'tærɪf/ *n.* (also **NTB**) see TOKYO ROUND.

♦ **non-tariff office** see TARIFF OFFICE.

♦ **non-taxable income** /nɒn'tæksəb(ə)l/ *n.* income that is not taxed, e.g. (in the UK) interest on National Savings Certificates, a personal equity plan, or a TESSA.

---

non-toxic /nɒn'tɒksɪk/ *adj.* not toxic.

non-transferable /ˌnɒntræns'fɜːrəb(ə)l/ *adj.* that may not be transferred.

non-U /nɒn'juː/ *adj. colloq.* not characteristic of the upper class. [from U[2]]

non-union /nɒn'juːnɪən/ *adj.* **1** not belonging to a trade union. **2** not done or made by trade-union members.

non-verbal /nɒn'vɜːb(ə)l/ *adj.* not involving words or speech.

non-violence /nɒn'vaɪələns/ *n.* avoidance of violence, esp. as a principle. □ **non-violent** *adj.*

non-voting /nɒn'vəʊtɪŋ/ *adj.* **1** not having or using a vote. **2** (of shares) not entitling the holder to vote. See A SHARES.

non-White /nɒn'waɪt/ *–adj.* not White. *–n.* non-White person.

noodle[1] /'nuːd(ə)l/ *n.* strip or ring of pasta. [German]

noodle[2] /'nuːd(ə)l/ *n.* **1** simpleton. **2** *slang* head. [origin unknown]

nook /nʊk/ *n.* corner or recess; secluded place. [origin unknown]

noon *n.* twelve o'clock in the day, midday. [Latin *nona* (*hora*) ninth (hour): originally = 3 p.m.]

noonday *n.* midday.

no one *n.* no person; nobody.

noose *–n.* **1** loop with a running knot. **2** snare, bond. *–v.* **(-sing)** catch with or enclose in a noose. [French *no(u)s* from Latin *nodus* NODE]

♦ **no-par-value** *adj.* (also **NPV**) denoting a share issued without a par value. Dividends on such shares are quoted as an amount of money per share rather than as a percentage of the nominal price. NPV shares are not allowed by UK law but they are issued by some US and Canadian companies.

---

nor *conj.* and not; and not either (*neither one thing nor the other; can neither read nor write*). [contraction of obsolete *nother*: related to NO[2], WHETHER]

nor' /nɔː(r)/ *n., adj., & adv.* (esp. in compounds) = NORTH (*nor'wester*). [abbreviation]

Nordic /'nɔːdɪk/ *–adj.* of the tall blond long-headed Germanic people of Scandinavia. *–n.* Nordic person. [French *nord* north]

Norf. *abbr.* Norfolk.

Norfolk /'nɔːfək/ county in E England; pop. (est. 1994) 768 500; county town, Norwich. Arable farming and turkey rearing are the chief agricultural activities; there is also some fishing and tourism.

Norfolk Island Australian island in the Pacific Ocean, E of Australia and N of New Zealand; pop. (1993) 2665; chief town, Kingston.

Norfolk jacket *n.* man's loose belted jacket with box pleats. [NORFOLK]

norm *n.* **1** standard, pattern, or type. **2** standard amount of work etc. **3** customary behaviour etc. [Latin *norma* carpenter's square]

normal /'nɔːm(ə)l/ *–adj.* **1** conforming to a standard; regular, usual, typical. **2** free from mental or emotional disorder. **3** *Geom.* (of a line) at right angles, perpendicular. *–n.* **1 a** normal value of a temperature etc. **b** usual state, level, etc. **2** line at right angles. □ **normalcy** *n.* esp. *US.* **normality** /-'mælɪtɪ/ *n.* [Latin *normalis*: related to NORM]

normal distribution *n.* function that represents the distribution of many random variables as a symmetrical bell-shaped graph.

♦ **normal economic profit** *n.* theoretical minimum profit required to keep an entrepreneur in a particular business. It must be at least as much as could be earned by investing the capital in some other business. If the entrepreneur was to earn abnormally high profits, new firms would enter the industry and the entrepreneur's profits would fall; if the profit was too low the entrepreneur would leave the industry, allowing others to make better profits. Thus in perfect competition only normal profits can be made. In a monopoly, abnormally high profits can be earned as a result of barriers to entry.

♦ **normal good** *n. Econ.* good for which the absolute level of demand increases as income expands. This does not necessarily mean that a consumer will spend the same proportion of income on a normal good as his or her income expands, but it does mean that more will be spent in absolute terms: the income elasticity of demand is thus greater than zero. The assumption that goods are normal is usu. made in economic analysis for the purposes of simplification. See also ENGEL CURVE; GIFFEN GOOD; INFERIOR GOOD; LUXURY GOOD; NECESSARY GOOD.

---

normalize *v.* (also **-ise**) **(-zing** or **-sing)** **1** make or become normal. **2** cause to conform. □ **normalization** /-'zeɪʃ(ə)n/ *n.*

normally *adv.* **1** in a normal manner. **2** usually.

♦ **Normal Market Size** *n.* (also **NMS**) classification system for trading in securities, which replaced the alpha, beta, gamma, and delta classification used on the London Stock Exchange in January 1991. NMS is the minimum size of the package of shares in a company traded in normal-sized market transactions; there are 12 categories. The main purpose of the system is to fix the size of transactions in which market makers are obliged to deal, and to set a basis on which the bargains should be published.

♦ **normal price** *n. Econ.* theoretical price of a good or service when there is equilibrium between supply and demand. Although the actual price will be influenced by a number of short-term factors, in the long term it will tend to move towards the normal price.

♦ **normal retirement age** *n.* age of an individual when he or she retires. This is normally 65 for a man and 60 for a woman in the UK. It is at these ages that state pensions begin. However, other policies can nominate other pre-agreed dates, which the Inland Revenue will accept in certain cases.

Norman /'nɔːmən/ *–n.* **1** native or inhabitant of medieval

Normandy. **2** descendant of the people of mixed Scandinavian and Frankish origin established there in the 10th century. **3** Norman French. **4** style of architecture found in Britain under the Normans. –*adj.* **1** of the Normans. **2** of the Norman style of architecture. [Old Norse, = NORTHMAN]

Norman Conquest *n.* conquest of England by William of Normandy in 1066.

Normandy /ˈnɔːməndɪ/ former province of NW France, on the English Channel, now divided into the two regions of Upper Normandy (Haute-Normandie) and Lower Normandy (Basse-Normandie). Dairy farming, sheep rearing, and horticulture (producing esp. apples) are important.

Norman French *n.* French as spoken by the Normans or (after 1066) in English lawcourts.

normative /ˈnɔːmətɪv/ *adj.* of or establishing a norm. [Latin: related to NORM]

♦ **normative economics** *n.* economic analysis that includes judgements about what ought to be done, rather than simply theorizing (cf. POSITIVE ECONOMICS). For example, Keynesian analysis contains both positive elements (the study of involuntary unemployment) and normative elements (the recommendation that fiscal policy should be used to reduce unemployment). It is usu. difficult to separate the positive from the normative in an economic theory.

Norn *n.* any of three goddesses of destiny in Scandinavian mythology. [Old Norse]

Norrköping /ˈnɔːkəpɪŋ/ seaport in SE Sweden, on an inlet of the Baltic Sea, having shipbuilding and engineering industries; pop. (est. 1996) 123 795.

Norse –*n.* **1** Norwegian language. **2** Scandinavian language-group. –*adj.* of ancient Scandinavia, esp. Norway. □ **Norseman** *n.* [Dutch *noor(d)sch* northern]

north –*n.* **1 a** point of the horizon 90° anticlockwise from east. **b** compass point corresponding to this. **c** direction in which this lies. **2** (usu. **the North**) **a** part of a country or town lying to the north. **b** the industrialized nations. –*adj.* **1** towards, at, near, or facing the north. **2** from the north (*north wind*). –*adv.* **1** towards, at, or near the north. **2** (foll. by *of*) further north than. □ **to the north** (often foll. by *of*) in a northerly direction. [Old English]

North America the N half of the American land mass, connected to South America by the Isthmus of Panama, bordered by the Atlantic Ocean to the E and the Pacific Ocean to the W. It includes Canada, the United States of America, and Mexico; the US has progressively dominated the continent, both economically and politically. □ **North American** *adj.* & *n.*

♦ **North American Free Trade Agreement** *n.* (also **NAFTA**) agreement between the US, Canada, and Mexico, entered into in 1992, in which US and Canadian capital, expertise, and technology is to be combined with Mexican resources and cheap labour to create a free trade area over a ten-year period.

Northamptonshire /nɔːˈθæmptənʃə(r)/ county in England, in the E Midlands; pop. (est. 1994) 594 800; county town, Northampton. Mainly agricultural, it produces cereals, potatoes, sugar beet, and livestock; there are also shoemaking, food-processing, engineering, and printing industries.

Northants /nɔːˈθænts/ *abbr.* Northamptonshire.

northbound *adj.* travelling or leading northwards.

North Brabant province in the S Netherlands; agricultural produce includes wheat and sugar beet; pop. (1995) 2 276 207; capital, 's-Hertogenbosch.

North Carolina /ˌkærəˈlaɪnə/ state in the US, on the Atlantic coast; pop. (est. 1996) 7 322 870; capital, Raleigh. Industries include textiles, furniture, food processing, and tobacco.

north country *n.* northern England.

North Dakota /dəˈkəʊtə/ state in the N central US, bordering on Canada; pop. (est. 1996) 643 539; capital, Bismarck. Agriculture (esp. wheat) and mining (coal and oil) are the chief sources of revenue; manufacturing industry is increasing.

North-East *n.* part of a country or town to the north-east.

north-east –*n.* **1** point of the horizon midway between north and east. **2** direction in which this lies. –*adj.* of, towards, or coming from the north-east. –*adv.* towards, at, or near the north-east.

northeaster /nɔːθˈiːstə(r)/ *n.* north-east wind.

north-easterly *adj.* & *adv.* = NORTH-EAST.

north-eastern *adj.* on the north-east side.

northerly /ˈnɔːðəlɪ/ –*adj.* & *adv.* **1** in a northern position or direction. **2** (of wind) from the north. –*n.* (*pl.* **-ies**) such a wind.

northern /ˈnɔːð(ə)n/ *adj.* of or in the north. □ **northernmost** *adj.* [Old English]

northerner *n.* native or inhabitant of the north.

Northern hemisphere *n.* the half of the earth north of the equator.

Northern Ireland unit of the UK comprising the six NE counties of Ireland; pop. (1991) 1 573 282; capital, Belfast. It was established in 1920 as a self-governing province, but its history has been marked by violent conflicts between the Protestant majority and the Roman Catholic minority favouring union with the Irish Republic. The presence of British army units (from 1969) failed to keep the peace, and continuing terrorist activities resulted in the imposition of direct rule from Westminster (1972). Talks involving most of Northern Ireland's political parties began in 1994, with the aim of agreeing on a system of government; despite setbacks, a compromise document was accepted by most parties in 1998 as the basis for establishing new institutions. See also IRELAND; UNITED KINGDOM.

northern lights *n.pl.* aurora borealis.

Northern Rhodesia see ZAMBIA.

Northern Territory state in central N Australia; pop. (est. 1996) 177 500; capital, Darwin. There are important deposits of iron ore, manganese, copper, gold, uranium, and other minerals; beef cattle are reared.

Northman *n.* native of Scandinavia, esp. Norway. [Old English]

north-north-east *n.* point or direction midway between north and north-east.

north-north-west *n.* point or direction midway between north and north-west.

North Pole *n.* northernmost point of the earth's axis of rotation.

North Rhine-Westphalia (German **Nordrhein-Westfalen** /nɔːtˌraɪnvestˈfɑːlən/) state (*Land*) in W Germany; pop. (est. 1995) 17 816 100; capital, Düsseldorf. It is a major industrial area and is rich in coal and other minerals.

North Sea part of the Atlantic Ocean between the mainland of Europe and the E coast of Britain; important for the exploitation of oil and gas deposits under the sea-bed.

North Star *n.* pole star.

Northumb. *abbr.* Northumberland.

Northumberland /nɔːˈθʌmbələnd/ county in the extreme NE of England; pop. (est. 1994) 307 700; county town, Morpeth. Sheep farming is important.

northward /ˈnɔːθwəd/ –*adj.* & *adv.* (also **northwards**) towards the north. –*n.* northward direction or region.

North-West *n.* part of a country or town to the north-west.

north-west –*n.* **1** point of the horizon midway between north and west. **2** direction in which this lies. –*adj.* of, towards, or coming from the north-west. –*adv.* towards, at, or near the north-west.

northwester /nɔːθˈwestə(r)/ *n.* north-west wind.

north-westerly *adj.* & *adv.* = NORTH-WEST.

north-western *adj.* on the north-west side.

North-West Frontier Province province in NW Pakistan; pop. (est. 1985) 12 287 000; capital, Peshawar. Fruit, sugar cane, and tobacco are grown.

Northwest Territories the part of Canada lying N of the provinces and E of Yukon Territory; pop. (est. 1995) 65 800; capital, Yellowknife. Mining is the most important economic activity: there are deposits of silver, gold, zinc, lead, pitchblende, tungsten, and oil. In 1993 legislation was passed, following a number of referendums, to establish Nunavut, an Inuit territory, in 1999. The new territory will comprise 844 960 square miles of the eastern part of Northwest Territories.

North Yorkshire county in NE England; pop. (est. 1994) 726 100; county town, Northallerton. Mainly agricultural, it produces cereals and has dairy and sheep farming; there is also some coalmining and tourism.

Norw. *abbr.* **1** Norway. **2** Norwegian.

Norwegian /nɔːˈwiːdʒ(ə)n/ *–n.* **1 a** native or national of Norway. **b** person of Norwegian descent. **2** language of Norway. *–adj.* of or relating to Norway. [medieval Latin *Norvegia* from Old Norse, = northway]

nor'wester /nɔːˈwestə(r)/ *n.* northwester.

Norwich /ˈnɒrɪdʒ, -ɪtʃ/ city in E England, county town of Norfolk; pop. (est. 1993) 128 100. Financial services are important; it also has shoemaking, electrical engineering, printing, food-processing, and chemical industries.

Nos. *pl.* of No.

nose /nəʊz/ *–n.* **1** organ above the mouth of a human or animal, used for smelling and breathing. **2 a** sense of smell. **b** ability to detect a particular thing (*a nose for scandal*). **3** odour or perfume of wine etc. **4** front end or projecting part of a thing, e.g. of a car or aircraft. *–v.* **(-sing) 1** (usu. foll. by *about, around*, etc.) pry or search. **2** (often foll. by *out*) **a** perceive the smell of, discover by smell. **b** detect. **3** thrust one's nose against or into. **4** make one's way cautiously forward. □ **by a nose** by a very narrow margin. **get up a person's nose** *slang* annoy a person. **keep one's nose clean** *slang* stay out of trouble. **put a person's nose out of joint** *colloq.* annoy; make envious. **turn up one's nose** (usu. foll. by *at*) *colloq.* show disdain. **under a person's nose** *colloq.* right before a person. **with one's nose in the air** haughtily. [Old English]

nosebag *n.* bag containing fodder, hung on a horse's head.

noseband *n.* lower band of a bridle, passing over the horse's nose.

nosebleed *n.* bleeding from the nose.

nosedive *–n.* **1** steep downward plunge by an aeroplane. **2** sudden plunge or drop. *–v.* **(-ving)** make a nosedive.

nosegay *n.* small bunch of flowers.

nose-to-tail *adj.* & *adv.* (of vehicles) one close behind another.

nosh *slang –v.* eat. *–n.* **1** food or drink. **2** *US* snack. [Yiddish]

nosh-up *n.* large meal.

nostalgia /nɒˈstældʒə/ *n.* **1** (often foll. by *for*) yearning for a past period. **2** severe homesickness. □ **nostalgic** *adj.* **nostalgically** *adv.* [Greek *nostos* return home]

nostril /ˈnɒstr(ə)l/ *n.* either of the two openings in the nose. [Old English, = nose-hole]

♦ **nostro account** /ˈnɒstrəʊ/ *n.* bank account conducted by a UK bank with a bank in another country, usu. in the currency of that country. Cf. VOSTRO ACCOUNT. [Italian *nostro* our]

---

nostrum /ˈnɒstrəm/ *n.* **1** quack remedy, patent medicine. **2** pet scheme, esp. for political or social reform. [Latin, = 'of our own make']

nosy *adj.* **(-ier, -iest)** *colloq.* inquisitive, prying. □ **nosily** *adv.* **nosiness** *n.*

Nosy Parker *n. colloq.* busybody.

not *adv.* expressing negation, esp.: **1** (also **n't** joined to a preceding verb) following an auxiliary verb or *be* or (in a question) the subject of such a verb (*I cannot say; she isn't there; am I not right?*). **2** used elliptically for a negative phrase etc. (*Is she coming? — I hope not; Do you want it? — Certainly not!*). □ **not at all** (in polite reply to thanks) there is no need for thanks. **not half** see HALF. **not quite 1** almost. **2** noticeably not (*not quite proper*). [contraction of NOUGHT]

■ **Usage** The use of *not* with verbs other than auxiliaries or *be* is now *archaic* except with participles and infinitives (*not knowing, I cannot say; we asked them not to come*).

notable /ˈnəʊtəb(ə)l/ *–adj.* worthy of note; remarkable, eminent. *–n.* eminent person. □ **notability** /-ˈbɪlɪtɪ/ *n.* **notably** *adv.* [Latin *noto* NOTE]

notary /ˈnəʊtərɪ/ *n.* (*pl.* **-ies**) (in full **notary public**) solicitor etc. who attests or certifies deeds and other documents and notes (see NOTING) dishonoured bills of exchange. □ **notarial** /nəʊˈteərɪəl/ *adj.* [Latin *notarius* secretary]

notation /nəʊˈteɪʃ(ə)n/ *n.* **1** representation of numbers, quantities, the pitch and duration of musical notes, etc., by symbols. **2** any set of such symbols. [Latin: related to NOTE]

notch *–n.* V-shaped indentation on an edge or surface. *–v.* **1** make notches in. **2** (usu. foll. by *up*) record or score with or as with notches. [Anglo-French]

note *–n.* **1** brief written record as an aid to memory (often in *pl.*: *make notes*). **2** observation, usu. unwritten, of experiences etc. (*compare notes*). **3** short or informal letter. **4** formal diplomatic communication. **5** short annotation or additional explanation in a book etc. **6** *Finance*

Norway /ˈnɔːweɪ/, **Kingdom of** country occupying the N and W part of the Scandinavian peninsula. Offshore oil and natural gas, first exploited in significant quantities in 1975, now contribute heavily to the economy and, with petrochemicals, form a major source of export revenue. Abundant hydroelectric power resources have enabled the expansion of manufacturing and other industries in a policy to reduce dependence on oil and gas. Manufacturing industries include food processing, engineering, paper production, and metal processing. Other important industries are shipping, mining, fishing (esp. for herring and cod), and forestry. The principal non-hydrocarbon exports are machinery and transport equipment, fish and fish products, manufactured goods, paper and pulp, iron ore and pyrites, ferro-alloys, and zinc.

History. An independent kingdom in Viking and early medieval times, Norway was united with Denmark and Sweden in 1397, becoming, after the latter's departure in 1523, little more than a Danish territory. Ceded to Sweden in 1814, it regained its independence in 1905; the country was under German occupation from 1940 to 1945. Norway has been a member of Efta since 1960. In a referendum held in 1994 a majority of the population voted against becoming a member of the EU. Head of state, King Harald V; prime minister, Kjell Magne Bondevik; capital, Oslo.

languages	Norwegian (official), Lapp
currency	krone (Nkr) of 100 øre
pop. (1996)	4 382 000
GNP (1994)	US$114B
literacy	100%
life expectancy	74 (m); 80 (f)

Exchange rate, US¢ per Nkr (a) Inflation, % (b)

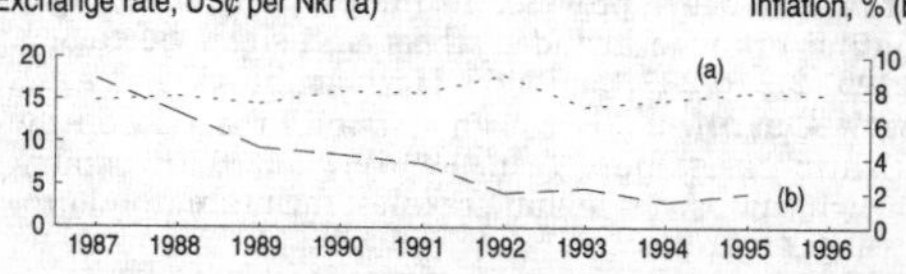

---

a = BANKNOTE. **b** negotiable record of an unsecured loan, esp. one in which the capital is repayable in less than five years. **7 a** notice, attention (*worthy of note*). **b** eminence (*person of note*). **8 a** single musical tone of definite pitch. **b** written sign representing its pitch and duration. **c** key of a piano etc. **9** quality or tone of speaking, expressing mood or attitude etc. (*note of optimism*). *–v.* (**-ting**) **1** observe, notice; give attention to. **2 a** (often foll. by *down*) record as a thing to be remembered or observed. **b** *Banking & Law* see NOTING. **3** (in *passive*; often foll. by *for*) be well known. □ **hit** (or **strike) the right note** speak or act in exactly the right manner. [Latin *nota* mark (n.), *noto* mark (v.)]

notebook *n.* **1** small book for making notes. **2** small personal computer with a liquid-crystal display screen that folds down over the keyboard.

notecase *n.* wallet for holding banknotes.

♦ **note issuance facility** *n.* (also **NIF**) means of enabling short-term borrowers in the Eurocurrency markets to issue Euronotes, with maturities of less than one year, when the need arises rather than having to arrange a separate issue of Euronotes each time they need to borrow. A **revolving underwriting facility (RUF)** achieves the same objective.

---

notelet /ˈnəʊtlɪt/ *n.* small folded usu. decorated sheet of paper for an informal letter.

notepaper *n.* paper for writing letters.

noteworthy *adj.* worthy of attention; remarkable.

nothing /ˈnʌθɪŋ/ *–n.* **1** not anything (*nothing has been done*). **2** no thing (often foll. by compl.: *I see nothing that I want*). **3** person or thing of no importance. **4** non-existence; what does not exist. **5** no amount; nought. *–adv.* not at all, in no way. □ **be** (or **have) nothing to do with 1** have no connection with. **2** not be involved or associated with. **for nothing 1** at no cost. **2** to no purpose. **have nothing on 1** be naked. **2** have no engagements. **nothing doing** *colloq.* **1** no prospect of success or agreement. **2** I refuse. [Old English: related to NO[1], THING]

nothingness *n.* **1** non-existence. **2** worthlessness, triviality.

notice /ˈnəʊtɪs/ *–n.* **1** attention, observation (*escaped my notice*). **2** displayed sheet etc. bearing an announcement. **3 a** intimation or warning, esp. a formal one. **b** formal announcement or declaration of intention to end an agreement or leave employment at a specified time. **4** short published review of a new play, book, etc. *–v.* (**-cing**) (often foll. by *that, how*, etc.) perceive, observe. □ **at short** (or **a moment's) notice** with little warning. **take notice** (or **no notice**) show signs (or no signs) of interest. **take notice of 1** observe. **2** act upon. [Latin *notus* known]

noticeable *adj.* perceptible; noteworthy. □ **noticeably** *adv.*

notice-board *n.* board for displaying notices.

notifiable /ˈnəʊtɪˌfaɪəb(ə)l/ *adj.* (of a disease etc.) that must be notified to the health authorities.

notify /ˈnəʊtɪˌfaɪ/ *v.* (**-ies, -ied**) **1** (often foll. by *of* or *that*) inform or give formal notice to (a person). **2** make known. □ **notification** /-fɪˈkeɪʃ(ə)n/ *n.* [Latin *notus* known]

♦ **noting** *n.* procedure adopted if a bill of exchange has been dishonoured by non-acceptance or by non-payment. Not later than the next business day after the day on which it was dishonoured, the holder has to hand it to a notary, who re-presents the bill; if it is still unaccepted or unpaid, the notary notes the circumstances in a register and also on a **notarial ticket**, which is attached to the bill. The noting can then, if necessary, be extended to a protest.

♦ **noting score** *n.* average number of readers noticing a particular advertisement or editorial item on first reading a newspaper or magazine, expressed as a percentage of the total readership.

---

notion /ˈnəʊʃ(ə)n/ *n.* **1 a** concept or idea; conception. **b** opinion. **c** vague view or understanding. **2** inclination or intention. [Latin *notio*: related to NOTIFY]

notional *adj.* hypothetical, imaginary. □ **notionally** *adv.*

♦ **notional income** *n.* income that is not received although it might be deemed to be properly chargeable to income tax. An example is the rental income one could receive from one's own home, if one were not living in it. This was formerly taxed under Schedule A. A further example might be interest foregone on the grant of an interest-free loan.

---

notorious /nəʊˈtɔːrɪəs/ *adj.* well-known, esp. unfavourably. □ **notoriety** /-təˈraɪətɪ/ *n.* **notoriously** *adv.* [Latin *notus* known]

Nottingham /ˈnɒtɪŋəm/ city in N central England, county town of Nottinghamshire; pop. (est. 1994) 282 400. Industries include textiles, pharmaceuticals, food processing, engineering, and telecommunications.

Nottinghamshire /ˈnɒtɪŋəmˌʃɪə(r)/ county in England, in the E Midlands; pop. (est. 1994) 1 030 900; county town, Nottingham. Agricultural activities include dairy and arable farming and market gardening; there is also some coalmining. Most of the industry is centred on Nottingham.

Notts. /nɒts/ *abbr.* Nottinghamshire.

notwithstanding /ˌnɒtwɪðˈstændɪŋ/ *–prep.* in spite of; without prevention by. *–adv.* nevertheless. [from NOT, WITHSTAND]

Nouadhibou /ˌnwædɪˈbuː/ principal port of Mauritania, linked by rail to the iron-ore mines of Zouérate on the W edge of the Sahara; pop. (est. 1992) 72 305.

Nouakchott /ˈnwækʃɒt/ capital of Mauritania; pop. (est. 1992) 480 395.

nougat /ˈnuːgɑː/ *n.* sweet made from sugar or honey, nuts, and egg-white. [French from Provençal]

nought /nɔːt/ *n.* **1** digit 0; cipher. **2** *poet.* or *archaic* nothing. [Old English: related to NOT, AUGHT]

noughts and crosses *n.pl.* pencil-and-paper game in which players seek to complete a row of three noughts or three crosses.

Nouméa /nuːˈmeɪə/ capital and chief port of New Caledonia; nickel, chrome, iron, and manganese are exported; pop. (1989) 65 110.

noun *n.* word used to name a person, place, or thing. [Latin *nomen* name]

nourish /ˈnʌrɪʃ/ *v.* **1** sustain with food. **2** foster or cherish (a feeling etc.). □ **nourishing** *adj.* [Latin *nutrio* to feed]

nourishment *n.* sustenance, food.

nous /naʊs/ *n.* **1** *colloq.* common sense; gumption. **2** *Philos.* mind, intellect. [Greek]

nouveau riche /ˌnuːvəʊ ˈriːʃ/ *n.* (*pl.* ***nouveaux riches*** pronunc. same) person who has recently acquired (usu. ostentatious) wealth. [French, = new rich]

nouvelle cuisine /ˌnuːvel kwɪˈziːn/ *n.* modern style of cookery avoiding heaviness and emphasizing presentation. [French, = new cookery]

Nov. *abbr.* November.

nova /ˈnəʊvə/ *n.* (*pl.* **novae** /-viː/ or **-s**) star showing a sudden burst of brightness and then subsiding. [Latin, = new]

Nova Lisboa see HUAMBO.

Nova Scotia /ˌnəʊvə ˈskəʊʃə/ province of SE Canada, comprising a peninsula projecting into the Atlantic and the adjoining Cape Breton Island; pop. (est. 1995) 937 800; capital, Halifax. Copper, gypsum, and salt are mined and there are iron and steel and pulp and paper industries; other sources of revenue include fishing and tourism. □ **Nova Scotian** *adj.* & *n.*

♦ **novation** /nəʊˈveɪʃ(ə)n/ *n.* replacement of one legal agreement by a new obligation, with the agreement of all the parties. For example, on exchanges using the London Clearing House (LCH), transactions between members are novated by the LCH, so that one contract is created between the buyer and LCH while a matching contact is created between the seller and LCH. □ **novate** *v.* [from Latin *novāre* renew]

novel[1] /'nɒv(ə)l/ *n.* fictitious prose story of book length. [Latin *novus* new]

novel[2] /'nɒv(ə)l/ *adj.* of a new kind or nature. [Latin *novus* new]

novelette /ˌnɒvə'let/ *n.* short novel.

novelist /'nɒvəlɪst/ *n.* writer of novels.

novella /nə'velə/ *n.* (*pl.* **-s**) short novel or narrative story. [Italian: related to NOVEL[1]]

novelty /'nɒvəltɪ/ *n.* (*pl.* **-ies**) **1** newness. **2** new or unusual thing or occurrence. **3** small toy or trinket. [related to NOVEL[2]]

November /nəʊ'vembə(r)/ *n.* eleventh month of the year. [Latin *novem* nine, originally the 9th month of the Roman year]

novena /nə'viːnə/ *n. RC Ch.* devotion consisting of special prayers or services on nine successive days. [Latin *novem* nine]

novice /'nɒvɪs/ *n.* **1 a** probationary member of a religious order. **b** new convert. **2** beginner. [Latin *novicius*, from *novus* new]

noviciate /nə'vɪʃɪət/ *n.* (also **novitiate**) **1** period of being a novice. **2** religious novice. **3** novices' quarters. [medieval Latin: related to NOVICE]

Novi Sad /ˌnɒvɪ 'sɑːt/ industrial city in N Serbia, NE Yugoslavia, capital of the province of Vojvodina; pop. (1991) 179 626.

Novokuznetsk /ˌnɒvəkuz'netsk/ industrial city in Russia, in central Siberia; machinery, iron, steel, and aluminium are produced; pop. (est. 1995) 572 000.

Novosibirsk /ˌnɒvəsɪ'bɪəsk/ city in W central Russia; industries include textiles, chemicals, and machinery; pop. (est. 1995) 1 369 000.

NOW *abbr. US Banking* negotiable order of withdrawal.

now *–adv.* **1** at the present or mentioned time. **2** immediately (*I must go now*). **3** by this time. **4** under the present circumstances (*I cannot now agree*). **5** on this further occasion (*what do you want now?*). **6** in the immediate past (*just now*). **7** (esp. in a narrative) then, next (*the police now arrived*). **8** (without reference to time, giving various tones to a sentence) surely, I insist, I wonder, etc. (*now what do you mean by that?*; *oh come now!*). *–conj.* (often foll. by *that*) as a consequence of the fact (*now that I am older*). *–n.* this time; the present. □ **for now** until a later time (*goodbye for now*). **now and again** (or **then**) from time to time; intermittently. [Old English]

nowadays /'naʊəˌdeɪz/ *–adv.* at the present time or age; in these times. *–n.* the present time.

nowhere /'nəʊweə(r)/ *–adv.* in or to no place. *–pron.* no place. □ **get nowhere** make no progress. **nowhere near** not nearly. [Old English]

no-win *attrib. adj.* of or designating a situation in which success is impossible.

nowt *n. colloq.* or *dial.* nothing. [from NOUGHT]

noxious /'nɒkʃəs/ *adj.* harmful, unwholesome. [Latin *noxa* harm]

nozzle /'nɒz(ə)l/ *n.* spout on a hose etc. from which a jet issues. [diminutive of NOSE]

NP *–abbr.* **1** National Power plc. **2** notary public. *–postcode* Newport.

Np *symb.* neptunium.

n/p *abbr.* (also **n.p.**) net proceeds.

NPA *abbr.* Newspaper Publishers' Association.

♦ **NPD** *abbr.* = NEW PRODUCT DEVELOPMENT.

n.p.f. *abbr.* not provided for.

NPV *abbr.* **1** = NET PRESENT VALUE. **2** = NO-PAR-VALUE.

NR *–abbr.* (also **n.r.**) *Insurance* no risk. *–postcode* Norwich.

nr. *abbr.* near.

NRA *abbr.* National Rivers Authority.

NRDC *abbr.* National Research and Development Corporation. See BRITISH TECHNOLOGY GROUP.

NRPB *abbr.* National Radiological Protection Board.

NRR *abbr.* net reproduction rate (of populations).

NRs *symb.* Nepalese rupees.

NRT *abbr.* net register tonnage. See TONNAGE 1.

♦ **NRV** *abbr.* = NET REALIZABLE VALUE.

NS *abbr.* **1** new style. **2** new series. **3** Nova Scotia.

n.s. *abbr.* **1** not specified. **2** *Banking* not sufficient (funds).

NSA *abbr.* **1** (in the US) National Shipping Authority. **2** (in the US) National Standards Association. **3** non-sterling area.

NSB *abbr.* = NATIONAL SAVINGS BANK.

NSC *abbr.* **1** National Safety Council. **2** National Savings Certificate.

n.s.f. *abbr. Banking* not sufficient funds.

NSCC *abbr.* National Securities Clearing Corporation.

NSPCC *abbr.* National Society for the Prevention of Cruelty to Children.

NSW *abbr.* New South Wales.

NT *abbr.* **1** New Testament. **2** Northern Territory (of Australia). **3** National Trust.

n.t. *abbr.* **1** net terms. **2** net tonnage.

n't see NOT.

NTA *abbr.* = NET TANGIBLE ASSETS.

♦ **NTB** *abbr.* non-tariff barrier. See TOKYO ROUND.

NTDA *abbr.* National Trade Development Association.

nth see N[1].

NTM *abbr.* non-tariff measure.

nt. wt. *abbr.* net weight.

Nu *symb. Currency* ngultrum.

nu /njuː/ *n.* thirteenth letter of the Greek alphabet (Ν, ν). [Greek]

nuance /'njuːɑ̃s/ *n.* subtle shade of meaning, feeling, colour, etc. [Latin *nubes* cloud]

nub *n.* **1** point or gist (of a matter or story). **2** (also **nubble**) small lump, esp. of coal. □ **nubbly** *adj.* [related to KNOB]

nubile /'njuːbaɪl/ *adj.* (of a woman) marriageable or sexually attractive. □ **nubility** /-'bɪlɪtɪ/ *n.* [Latin *nubo* become the wife of]

nuclear /'njuːklɪə(r)/ *adj.* **1** of, relating to, or constituting a nucleus. **2** using nuclear energy.

nuclear bomb *n.* bomb using the release of energy by nuclear fission or fusion or both.

nuclear energy *n.* energy obtained by nuclear fission or fusion.

nuclear family *n.* a couple and their child or children.

nuclear fission *n.* nuclear reaction in which a heavy nucleus splits spontaneously or on impact with another particle, with the release of energy.

nuclear fuel *n.* source of nuclear energy.

nuclear fusion *n.* nuclear reaction in which atomic nuclei of low atomic number fuse to form a heavier nucleus with the release of energy.

nuclear physics *n.pl.* (treated as *sing.*) physics of atomic nuclei.

nuclear power *n.* **1** power generated by a nuclear reactor. **2** country that has nuclear weapons.

nuclear reactor *n.* device in which a nuclear fission chain reaction is used to produce energy.

nuclear weapon *n.* weapon using the release of energy by nuclear fission or fusion or both.

nucleate /'njuːklɪˌeɪt/ *–adj.* having a nucleus. *–v.* (**-ting**) form or form into a nucleus. [Latin: related to NUCLEUS]

nucleic acid /njuː'kliːɪk/ *n.* either of two complex organic molecules (DNA and RNA), present in all living cells.

nucleon /'njuːklɪˌɒn/ *n.* proton or neutron.

nucleus /'njuːklɪəs/ *n.* (*pl.* **nuclei** /-lɪˌaɪ/) **1 a** central part or thing round which others are collected. **b** kernel of an aggregate or mass. **2** initial part meant to receive additions. **3** central core of an atom. **4** large dense part of a cell, containing the genetic material. [Latin, = kernel, diminutive of *nux nuc-* nut]

NUCPS *abbr.* National Union of Civil and Public Servants.

nude *–adj.* naked, bare, unclothed. *–n.* **1** painting, sculpture, etc. of a nude human figure. **2** nude person. □ **in the nude** naked. □ **nudity** *n.* [Latin *nudus*]

nudge *–v.* **(-ging) 1** prod gently with the elbow to attract attention. **2** push gradually. *–n.* prod; gentle push. [origin unknown]

nudist /'nju:dɪst/ *n.* person who advocates or practises going unclothed. □ **nudism** *n.*

◆ ***nudum pactum*** /'nju:dʊm 'pæktʊm/ *n. Law* agreement that is unenforceable because no consideration is mentioned. See also CONTRACT *n.* 1. [Latin, = nude contract]

Nuevo León /ˌnweɪvəʊ leɪ'əʊn/ state in NE Mexico; pop. (est. 1995) 3 549 273; capital, Monterrey.

nugatory /'nju:gətərɪ/ *adj.* **1** futile, trifling. **2** inoperative; not valid. [Latin *nugae* jests]

nugget /'nʌgɪt/ *n.* **1** lump of gold etc., as found in the earth. **2** lump of anything. **3** something valuable. [apparently from dial. *nug* lump]

nuisance /'nju:s(ə)ns/ *n.* person, thing, or circumstance causing trouble or annoyance. [French, = hurt, from *nuire nuis-* injure from Latin *noceo* to hurt]

NUIW *abbr.* National Union of Insurance Workers.

NUJ *abbr.* National Union of Journalists.

nuke *colloq. –n.* nuclear weapon. *–v.* **(-king)** attack with nuclear weapons. [abbreviation]

Nuku'alofa /ˌnu:ku:ə'ləʊfə/ capital of Tonga, situated on the island of Tongatapu; exports include copra and bananas; pop. (est. 1990) 34 000.

null *adj.* **1** (esp. **null and void**) invalid. **2** non-existent. **3** without character or expression. □ **nullity** *n.* [Latin *nullus* none]

nullify /'nʌlɪˌfaɪ/ *v.* **(-ies, -ied)** neutralize, invalidate. □ **nullification** /-fɪ'keɪʃ(ə)n/ *n.*

NUM *abbr.* National Union of Mineworkers.

NUMAST /'nju:mæst/ *abbr.* National Union of Marine, Aviation, and Shipping Transport Officers.

numb /nʌm/ *–adj.* (often foll. by *with*) deprived of feeling; paralysed. *–v.* **1** make numb. **2** stupefy, paralyse. □ **numbness** *n.* [obsolete *nome* past part. of *nim* take: related to NIMBLE]

number *–n.* **1 a** arithmetical value representing a particular quantity. **b** word, symbol, or figure representing this. **c** arithmetical value showing position in a series (*registration number*). **2** (often foll. by *of*) total count or aggregate (*the number of accidents has decreased*). **3** numerical reckoning (*the laws of number*). **4 a** (in *sing.* or *pl.*) quantity, amount (*a large number of people*; *only in small numbers*). **b** (**a number of**) several (of). **c** (in *pl.*) numerical preponderance (*force of numbers*). **5** person or thing having a place in a series, esp. a single issue of a magazine, an item in a programme, etc. **6** company, collection, group (*among our number*). **7** *Gram.* **a** classification of words by their singular or plural forms. **b** such a form. *–v.* **1** include (*I number you among my friends*). **2** assign a number or numbers to. **3** amount to (a specified number). **4** count. □ **one's days are numbered** one does not have long to live. **have a person's number** *colloq.* understand a person's real motives, character, etc. **one's number is up** *colloq.* one is doomed to die soon. **without number** innumerable. [Latin *numerus*]

■ **Usage** In sense 4b, *a number of* is normally used with a plural verb: *a number of problems remain.*

number cruncher *n. colloq.* powerful computer designed or used mainly for numerical and mathematical work, usu. of a scientific or technical nature. See also SUPERCOMPUTER.

number crunching *n. colloq.* process of making complex calculations.

◆ **numbered account** *n.* bank account identified only by a number. This service, offered by some Swiss banks, encourages funds that have been obtained illegally to find their way to Switzerland.

---

numberless *adj.* innumerable.

number one *–n. colloq.* oneself. *–adj.* most important (*the number one priority*).

number-plate *n.* plate on a vehicle showing its registration number.

numerable /'nju:mərəb(ə)l/ *adj.* that can be counted. [Latin: related to NUMBER]

numeral /'nju:mər(ə)l/ *–n.* symbol or group of symbols denoting a number. *–adj.* of or denoting a number. [Latin: related to NUMBER]

numerate /'nju:mərət/ *adj.* acquainted with the basic principles of mathematics. □ **numeracy** *n.* [Latin *numerus* number, after *literate*]

numeration /ˌnju:mə'reɪʃ(ə)n/ *n.* **1** method or process of numbering. **2** calculation. [Latin: related to NUMBER]

numerator /'nju:məˌreɪtə(r)/ *n.* number above the line in a vulgar fraction showing how many of the parts indicated by the denominator are taken (e.g. 2 in $^2/_3$). [Latin: related to NUMBER]

numerical /nju:'merɪk(ə)l/ *adj.* of or relating to a number or numbers. □ **numerically** *adv.* [medieval Latin: related to NUMBER]

numerical keypad see KEYPAD 2.

numerology /ˌnju:mə'rɒlədʒɪ/ *n.* the study of the supposed occult significance of numbers.

numerous /'nju:mərəs/ *adj.* **1** many. **2** consisting of many. [Latin: related to NUMBER]

numinous /'nju:mɪnəs/ *adj.* **1** indicating the presence of a divinity. **2** spiritual, awe-inspiring. [Latin *numen* deity]

numismatic /ˌnju:mɪz'mætɪk/ *adj.* of or relating to coins or medals. [Greek *nomisma* coin]

numismatics *n.pl.* (usu. treated as *sing.*) the study of coins or medals. □ **numismatist** /-'mɪzmətɪst/ *n.*

numskull *n.* stupid person. [from NUMB]

nun *n.* member of a religious community of women living under certain vows. [Latin *nonna*]

nuncio /'nʌnsɪəʊ/ *n.* (*pl.* **-s**) papal ambassador. [Latin *nuntius* messenger]

nunnery *n.* (*pl.* **-ies**) religious house of nuns.

NUPE /'nju:pɪ/ *abbr.* National Union of Public Employees.

nuptial /'nʌpʃ(ə)l/ *–adj.* of marriage or weddings. *–n.* (usu. in *pl.*) wedding. [Latin *nubo nupt-* wed]

nurd var. of NERD.

Nuremberg /'njʊərəmˌbɜ:g/ (German **Nürnberg** /'nʊənˌbeəg/) city in Germany, in Bavaria; it has important metalworking and electrical industries; pop. (est. 1995) 495 845.

nurse /nɜ:s/ *–n.* **1** person trained to care for the sick or infirm or provide medical advice and treat minor medical problems. **2** = NURSEMAID. *–v.* **(-sing) 1 a** work as a nurse. **b** attend to (a sick person). **2** feed or be fed at the breast. **3** hold or treat carefully. **4 a** foster; promote the development of. **b** harbour (a grievance etc.). [Latin: related to NOURISH]

nurseling var. of NURSLING.

nursemaid *n.* woman in charge of a child or children.

nursery /'nɜ:sərɪ/ *n.* (*pl.* **-ies**) **1 a** a room or place equipped for young children. **b** = DAY NURSERY. **2** place where plants are reared for sale. [probably Anglo-French: related to NURSE]

nurseryman *n.* owner of or worker in a plant nursery.

nursery rhyme *n.* simple traditional song or rhyme for children.

nursery school *n.* school for children between three and five.

nursery slopes *n.pl.* gentle slopes for novice skiers.

nursing home *n.* privately run hospital or home for invalids, old people, etc.

nursling /ˈnɜːslɪŋ/ *n.* (also **nurseling**) infant that is being suckled.

nurture /ˈnɜːtʃə(r)/ –*n.* **1** bringing up, fostering care. **2** nourishment. –*v.* (**-ring**) bring up; rear. [French: related to NOURISH]

Nusa Tenggara /ˈnuːsə teŋˈɡɑːrə/ see SUNDA ISLANDS.

NUT *abbr.* National Union of Teachers.

nut *n.* **1 a** fruit consisting of a hard or tough shell around an edible kernel. **b** this kernel. **2** pod containing hard seeds. **3** small usu. hexagonal flat piece of metal etc. with a threaded hole through it for screwing on the end of a bolt to secure it. **4** *slang* person's head. **5** *slang* crazy or eccentric person. **6** small lump (of coal etc.). **7** (in *pl.*) *coarse slang* testicles.□ **do one's nut** *slang* be extremely angry. [Old English]

nutcase *n. slang* crazy person.

nutcracker *n.* (usu. in *pl.*) device for cracking nuts.

nuthatch *n.* small bird which climbs up and down tree-trunks.

nutmeg *n.* **1** hard aromatic seed used as a spice and in medicine. **2** East Indian tree bearing this. [French *nois* nut, *mugue* MUSK]

nutria /ˈnjuːtrɪə/ *n.* coypu fur. [Spanish, = otter]

nutrient /ˈnjuːtrɪənt/ –*n.* substance that provides essential nourishment. –*adj.* serving as or providing nourishment. [Latin *nutrio* nourish]

nutriment /ˈnjuːtrɪmənt/ *n.* **1** nourishing food. **2** intellectual or artistic etc. nourishment.

nutrition /njuːˈtrɪʃ(ə)n/ *n.* food, nourishment. □ **nutritional** *adj.* **nutritionist** *n.*

nutritious /njuːˈtrɪʃəs/ *adj.* efficient as food.

nutritive /ˈnjuːtrɪtɪv/ *adj.* **1** of nutrition. **2** nutritious.

nuts *predic. adj. slang* crazy, mad.□ **be nuts about** (or **on**) *colloq.* be very fond of. [pl. of NUT]

nuts and bolts *n.pl. colloq.* practical details.

nutshell *n.* hard exterior covering of a nut. □ **in a nutshell** in a few words.

nutter *n. slang* crazy person.

nutty *adj.* (**-ier, -iest**) **1 a** full of nuts. **b** tasting like nuts. **2** *slang* crazy. □ **nuttiness** *n.*

Nuuk /nʊk/ the capital of Greenland, a port on the Davis Strait; pop. (1993) 12 181. It was known by the Danish name Godthåb until 1979 and is the oldest Danish settlement. It has fish canning and freezing plants.

nux vomica /nʌks ˈvɒmɪkə/ *n.* **1** E Indian tree. **2** seeds of this tree, containing strychnine. [Latin, = abscess nut]

nuzzle /ˈnʌz(ə)l/ *v.* (**-ling**) **1** prod or rub gently with the nose. **2** (foll. by *into, against, up to*) press the nose gently. **3** (also *refl.*) nestle; lie snug. [from NOSE]

NV –*abbr.* **1** (Dutch) Naamloze Vennootschap (= public limited company). **2** (also **n.v.**) *Finance* non-voting (shares). **3** (Norwegian) Norske Veritas (ship-classification society). –*US postcode* Nevada.

N/V *abbr. Banking* no value.

NVI *abbr.* non-value indicator (type of postage stamp).

◆ **NVQ** *abbr.* National Vocational Qualification. See VOCATIONAL TRAINING.

NW –*abbr.* **1** north-west. **2** north-western. –*postcode* north-west London. –*airline flight code* Northwest Airlines.

n.w. *abbr.* net weight.

NWT *abbr.* Northwest Territories.

n. wt. *abbr.* net weight.

NY *abbr.* & *US postcode* New York.

Nyasaland /naɪˈæsə,lænd/ see MALAWI.

NYC *abbr.* New York City.

nylon /ˈnaɪlɒn/ *n.* **1** tough light elastic synthetic fibre. **2** nylon fabric. **3** (in *pl.*) stockings of nylon. [invented word]

NYMEX /ˈnaɪmeks/ *abbr.* New York Mercantile Exchange.

nymph /nɪmf/ *n.* **1** mythological semi-divine spirit regarded as a maiden and associated with an aspect of nature, esp. rivers and woods. **2** *poet.* beautiful young woman. **3** immature form of some insects. [Greek *numphē* nymph, bride]

nympho /ˈnɪmfəʊ/ *n.* (*pl.* **-s**) *colloq.* nymphomaniac. [abbreviation]

nymphomania /,nɪmfəˈmeɪnɪə/ *n.* excessive sexual desire in a woman. □ **nymphomaniac** *n.* & *adj.* [from NYMPH, -MANIA]

NYS *abbr.* New York State.

NYSE *abbr.* = NEW YORK STOCK EXCHANGE.

Nyslott see SAVONLINNA.

NZ *abbr.* & *international vehicle registration* New Zealand.

NZEF *abbr.* New Zealand Employers' Federation.

NZFL *abbr.* New Zealand Federation of Labor.

O[1] /əʊ/ *n.* (also **o**) (*pl.* **Os** or **O's**) **1** fifteenth letter of the alphabet. **2** (**0**) nought, zero.

O[2] *abbr.* (also **O.**) Old.

O[3] *symb.* oxygen.

O[4] /əʊ/ *int.* **1** var. of OH. **2** prefixed to a name in the vocative (*O God*). [natural exclamation]

o' /ə/ *prep.* of, on (esp. in phrases: *o'clock*; *will-o'-the-wisp*). [abbreviation]

-o *suffix* forming usu. *slang* or *colloq.* variants or derivatives (*beano*; *wino*). [perhaps from OH]

-o- *suffix* terminal vowel of comb. forms (*neur-*; *Franco-*). [originally Greek]

■ **Usage** This suffix is often elided before a vowel, as in *neuralgia*.

OA *–abbr.* **1** objective analysis. **2** (also **o.a.**) office automation. **3** operational analysis. **4** (also **o.a.**) overall. *–airline flight code* Olympic Airways.

oaf *n.* (*pl.* **-s**) **1** awkward lout. **2** stupid person. □ **oafish** *adj.* **oafishly** *adv.* **oafishness** *n.* [Old Norse: related to ELF]

oak *n.* **1** acorn-bearing tree with lobed leaves. **2** its durable wood. **3** (*attrib.*) of oak. **4** (**the Oaks**) (treated as *sing.*) annual race at Epsom for fillies. [Old English]

oak-apple *n.* (also **oak-gall**) a kind of growth formed on oak trees by the larvae of certain wasps.

Oakland /'əʊklənd/ industrial port in the US, in W California on the E side of San Francisco Bay; pop. (est. 1994) 366 926.

oakum /'əʊkəm/ *n.* loose fibre obtained by picking old rope to pieces and used esp. in caulking. [Old English, = off-comb]

♦ **O. & M.** *abbr.* = ORGANIZATION AND METHODS.

OAP *abbr.* old-age pensioner.

OAPEC /əʊ'eɪpek/ *abbr.* Organization of Arab Petroleum Exporting Countries.

oar /ɔː(r)/ *n.* **1** pole with a blade used to propel a boat by leverage against the water. **2** rower. □ **put one's oar in** interfere. [Old English]

oarsman *n.* (*fem.* **oarswoman**) rower. □ **oarsmanship** *n.*

OAS *abbr.* Organization of American States.

oasis /əʊ'eɪsɪs/ *n.* (*pl.* **oases** /-siːz/) **1** fertile place in a desert. **2** area or period of calm in the midst of turbulence. [Latin from Greek]

oast *n.* kiln for drying hops. [Old English]

oast-house *n.* building containing an oast.

oat *n.* **1 a** hardy cereal plant grown as food. **b** (in *pl.*) grain yielded by this. **2** oat plant or a variety of it. **3** (in *pl.*) *slang* sexual gratification. □ **off one's oats** *colloq.* not hungry. □ **oaten** *adj.* [Old English]

oatcake *n.* thin oatmeal biscuit.

oath *n.* (*pl.* **-s** /əʊðz/) **1** solemn declaration naming God etc. as witness. **2** profanity, curse. □ **on** (or **under**) **oath** having sworn a solemn oath. [Old English]

oatmeal *n.* **1** meal ground from oats. **2** greyish-fawn colour flecked with brown.

OAU *abbr.* Organization of African Unity.

Oaxaca /wə'hɑːkə/ **1** state in S Mexico; pop. (est. 1995) 3 224 270. **2** (in full **Oaxaca de Juárez**) its capital city; industries include flour-milling, textiles, and handicrafts; pop. (1990) 212 818.

OB *–abbr.* **1** (in life-assurance policies) ordinary business. **2** outside broadcast. *–international civil aircraft marking* Peru.

ob. *abbr.* he or she died. [Latin *obiit*]

ob- *prefix* (also **oc-** before *c*, **of-** before *f*, **op-** before *p*) esp. in words from Latin, meaning: **1** exposure. **2** meeting or facing. **3** direction. **4** resistance. **5** hindrance or concealment. **6** finality or completeness. [Latin *ob* towards, against, in the way of]

o/b *abbr.* on or before (preceding a date).

obbligato /ˌɒblɪ'gɑːtəʊ/ *n.* (*pl.* **-s**) *Mus.* accompaniment forming an integral part of a composition. [Italian, = obligatory]

obdurate /'ɒbdjʊrət/ *adj.* **1** stubborn. **2** hardened. □ **obduracy** *n.* [Latin *duro* harden]

OBE *abbr.* Officer of the Order of the British Empire.

obedient /əʊ'biːdɪənt/ *adj.* **1** obeying or ready to obey. **2** submissive to another's will. □ **obedience** *n.* **obediently** *adv.* [Latin: related to OBEY]

obeisance /əʊ'beɪs(ə)ns/ *n.* **1** bow, curtsey, or other respectful gesture. **2** homage. □ **obeisant** *adj.* [French: related to OBEY]

obelisk /'ɒbəlɪsk/ *n.* tapering usu. four-sided stone pillar as a monument or landmark. [Greek diminutive: related to OBELUS]

obelus /'ɒbələs/ *n.* (*pl.* **obeli** /-ˌlaɪ/) dagger-shaped reference mark (†). [Greek, = pointed pillar, SPIT[2]]

obese /əʊ'biːs/ *adj.* very fat. □ **obesity** *n.* [Latin *edo* eat]

obey /əʊ'beɪ/ *v.* **1 a** carry out the command of. **b** carry out (a command). **2** do what one is told to do. **3** be actuated by (a force or impulse). [Latin *obedio* from *audio* hear]

obfuscate /'ɒbfʌˌskeɪt/ *v.* (**-ting**) **1** obscure or confuse (a mind, topic, etc.). **2** stupefy, bewilder. □ **obfuscation** /-'keɪʃ(ə)n/ *n.* [Latin *fuscus* dark]

obituary /ə'bɪtjʊərɪ/ *n.* (*pl.* **-ies**) **1** notice of a death or deaths. **2** account of the life of a deceased person. **3** (*attrib.*) of or serving as an obituary. [Latin *obitus* death]

object *–n.* /'ɒbdʒɪkt/ **1** material thing that can be seen or touched. **2** person or thing to which action or feeling is directed (*object of attention*). **3** thing sought or aimed at. **4** *Gram.* noun or its equivalent governed by an active transitive verb or by a preposition. **5** *Philos.* thing external to the thinking mind or subject. **6** see OBJECT-ORIENTED PROGRAMMING. *–v.* /əb'dʒekt/ (often foll. by *to*, *against*) **1** express opposition, disapproval, or reluctance. **2** protest. □ **no object** not forming an important or restricting factor (*money no object*). □ **objector** /əb'dʒektə(r)/ *n.* [Latin *jacio ject-* throw]

objectify /əb'dʒektɪˌfaɪ/ *v.* (**-ies**, **-ied**) present as an object; express in concrete form.

objection /əb'dʒekʃ(ə)n/ *n.* **1** expression or feeling of opposition or disapproval. **2** objecting. **3** adverse reason or statement. [Latin: related to OBJECT]

objectionable *adj.* **1** unpleasant, offensive. **2** open to objection. □ **objectionably** *adv.*

objective /əb'dʒektɪv/ *–adj.* **1** external to the mind; actually existing. **2** dealing with outward things or exhibiting facts uncoloured by feelings or opinions. **3** esp. *Accounting* capable of being independently verified. **4** *Gram.* (of a case or word) in the form appropriate to the object. *–n.* **1** something sought or aimed at. **2** *Gram.* objective case. □ **objectively** *adv.* **objectivity** /ˌɒbdʒek'tɪvɪtɪ/ *n.* [medieval Latin: related to OBJECT]

object-lesson *n.* striking practical example of some principle.

object-oriented programming *n.* (also **OOP**) system of computer programming in which the central feature is the **object**, a package of information together with a description of its manipulation. In such a program, written in an **object-oriented language** (**OOL**), the real-world objects of a problem and the processing requirements of these objects are identified, and 'messages' are passed between the objects to initiate actions.

♦ **objects clause** see MEMORANDUM OF ASSOCIATION.

objet d'art /ˌɒbʒeɪ 'dɑː/ *n.* (*pl.* ***objets d'art*** pronunc. same) small decorative object. [French, = object of art]

oblate /'ɒbleɪt/ *adj. Geom.* (of a spheroid) flattened at the poles. [Latin: related to OB-, cf. PROLATE]

oblation /əʊ'bleɪʃ(ə)n/ *n.* thing offered to a divine being. [Latin: related to OFFER]

obligate /'ɒblɪˌgeɪt/ *v.* (**-ting**) bind (a person) legally or morally (*was obligated to attend*). [Latin: related to OBLIGE]

obligation /ˌɒblɪ'geɪʃ(ə)n/ *n.* **1** constraining power of a law, duty, contract, etc. **2** duty, task. **3** binding agreement. **4** indebtedness for a service or benefit (*be under an obligation*). [Latin: related to OBLIGE]

obligatory /ə'blɪgətərɪ/ *adj.* **1** binding. **2** compulsory. □ **obligatorily** *adv.* [Latin: related to OBLIGE]

♦ **obligatory expenditure** *n.* European Union spending governed by treaties, such as the Common Agricultural Policy, which can be increased by the European Parliament but which it cannot reduce without the agreement of the Council of Ministers.

oblige /ə'blaɪdʒ/ *v.* (**-ging**) **1** constrain, compel. **2** be binding on. **3** do (a person) a small favour, help. **4** (as **obliged** *adj.*) indebted, grateful. □ **much obliged** thank you. [Latin *obligo* bind]

obliging *adj.* accommodating, helpful. □ **obligingly** *adv.*

oblique /ə'bliːk/ *–adj.* **1** slanting; at an angle. **2** not going straight to the point; indirect. **3** *Gram.* (of a case) other than nominative or vocative. *–n.* oblique stroke (/). □ **obliquely** *adv.* **obliqueness** *n.* **obliquity** /ə'blɪkwɪtɪ/ *n.* [French from Latin]

obliterate /ə'blɪtəˌreɪt/ *v.* (**-ting**) blot out, destroy, leave no clear traces of. □ **obliteration** /-'reɪʃ(ə)n/ *n.* [Latin *oblitero* erase, from *litera* letter]

oblivion /ə'blɪvɪən/ *n.* state of having or being forgotten. [Latin *obliviscor* forget]

oblivious /ə'blɪvɪəs/ *adj.* unaware or unconscious. □ **obliviously** *adv.* **obliviousness** *n.*

oblong /'ɒblɒŋ/ *–adj.* rectangular with adjacent sides unequal. *–n.* oblong figure or object. [Latin *oblongus* longish]

obloquy /'ɒbləkwɪ/ *n.* **1** being generally ill spoken of. **2** abuse. [Latin *obloquium* contradiction, from *loquor* speak]

obnoxious /əb'nɒkʃəs/ *adj.* offensive, objectionable. □ **obnoxiously** *adv.* **obnoxiousness** *n.* [Latin *noxa* injury]

OBO *abbr.* ore-bulk-oil (ship).

oboe /'əʊbəʊ/ *n.* woodwind double-reed instrument with a piercing plaintive tone. □ **oboist** /'əʊbəʊɪst/ *n.* [French *hautbois* from *haut* high, *bois* wood]

obscene /əb'siːn/ *adj.* **1** offensively indecent. **2** *colloq.* highly offensive. **3** *Law* (of a publication) tending to deprave or corrupt. □ **obscenely** *adv.* **obscenity** /-'senɪtɪ/ *n.* (pl. **-ies**). [Latin *obsc(a)enus* abominable]

obscurantism /ˌɒbskjʊə'ræntɪz(ə)m/ *n.* opposition to knowledge and enlightenment. □ **obscurantist** *n.* & *adj.* [Latin *obscurus* dark]

obscure /əb'skjʊə(r)/ *–adj.* **1** not clearly expressed or easily understood. **2** unexplained. **3** dark. **4** indistinct. **5** hidden; unnoticed. **6** (of a person) undistinguished, hardly known. *–v.* (**-ring**) **1** make obscure or unintelligible. **2** conceal. □ **obscurity** *n.* [French from Latin]

obsequies /'ɒbsɪkwɪz/ *n.pl.* funeral rites. [Latin *obsequiae*]

obsequious /əb'siːkwɪəs/ *adj.* servile, fawning. □ **obsequiously** *adv.* **obsequiousness** *n.* [Latin *obsequor* comply with]

observance /əb'zɜːv(ə)ns/ *n.* **1** keeping or performing of a law, duty, etc. **2** rite or ceremony.

observant *adj.* **1** acute in taking notice. **2** attentive in observance. □ **observantly** *adv.*

observation /ˌɒbzə'veɪʃ(ə)n/ *n.* **1** observing or being observed. **2** power of perception. **3** remark, comment. **4** thing observed by esp. scientific study. □ **observational** *adj.*

observatory /əb'zɜːvətərɪ/ *n.* (*pl.* **-ies**) building for astronomical or other observation.

observe /əb'zɜːv/ *v.* (**-ving**) **1** perceive, become aware of. **2** watch carefully. **3 a** follow or keep (rules etc.). **b** celebrate or perform (an occasion, rite, etc.). **4** remark. **5** take note of scientifically. □ **observable** *adj.* [Latin *servo* watch, keep]

observer *n.* **1** person who observes. **2** interested spectator. **3** person who attends a meeting etc. to note the proceedings but does not participate.

obsess /əb'ses/ *v.* fill the mind of (a person) continually; preoccupy. □ **obsessive** *adj.* & *n.* **obsessively** *adv.* **obsessiveness** *n.* [Latin *obsideo obsess-* besiege]

obsession /əb'seʃ(ə)n/ *n.* **1** obsessing or being obsessed. **2** persistent idea dominating a person's mind. □ **obsessional** *adj.* **obsessionally** *adv.*

obsidian /əb'sɪdɪən/ *n.* dark glassy rock formed from lava. [Latin from *Obsius*, discoverer of a similar stone]

♦ **obsolescence** /ˌɒbsə'les(ə)ns/ *n.* **1** condition of becoming obsolete. **2** depreciation of an item that may not have actually worn out but has become out of date because a more efficient or more fashionable model has become available. **Built-in obsolescence** or **planned obsolescence** is a deliberate policy adopted by a manufacturer to limit the durability of a product in order to encourage the consumer to buy a replacement more quickly than might otherwise be necessary. The morality of this technique is usu. defended on the grounds that many Western economies depend on strong consumer demand; if such consumer durables as cars and washing machines were built to last for their purchaser's lifetime, consumer demand would be reduced to a level that would create enormous unemployment. [Latin *soleo* be accustomed]

obsolescent /ˌɒbsə'les(ə)nt/ *adj.* **1** becoming obsolete. **2** becoming outdated or outmoded. See OBSOLESCENCE 2.

obsolete /'ɒbsəˌliːt/ *adj.* no longer used, antiquated.

obstacle /'ɒbstək(ə)l/ *n.* thing that obstructs progress. [Latin *obsto* stand in the way]

obstetrician /ˌɒbstə'trɪʃ(ə)n/ *n.* specialist in obstetrics.

obstetrics /əb'stetrɪks/ *n.pl.* (treated as *sing.*) branch of medicine and surgery dealing with childbirth. □ **obstetric** *adj.* [Latin *obstetrix* midwife, from *obsto* be present]

obstinate /'ɒbstɪnət/ *adj.* **1** stubborn, intractable. **2** firmly continuing in one's action or opinion despite advice. □ **obstinacy** *n.* **obstinately** *adv.* [Latin *obstino* persist]

obstreperous /əb'strepərəs/ *adj.* **1** turbulent, unruly. **2** noisy. □ **obstreperously** *adv.* **obstreperousness** *n.* [Latin *obstrepo* shout at]

obstruct /əb'strʌkt/ *v.* **1** block up; make hard or impossible to pass along or through. **2** prevent or retard the progress of. [Latin *obstruo obstruct-* block up]

obstruction /əb'strʌkʃ(ə)n/ *n.* **1** obstructing or being obstructive. **2** thing that obstructs, blockage. **3** *Sport* act of unlawfully obstructing another player.

obstructive *adj.* causing or intended to cause an obstruction. □ **obstructively** *adv.* **obstructiveness** *n.*

obtain /əb'teɪn/ *v.* **1** acquire, secure; have granted to one, get. **2** be in vogue, prevail. □ **obtainable** *adj.* [Latin *teneo* hold]

obtrude /əb'truːd/ *v.* (**-ding**) **1** be or become obtrusive. **2** (often foll. by *on*, *upon*) thrust (oneself, a matter, etc.)

importunately forward. □ **obtrusion** *n.* [Latin *obtrudo* thrust against]

obtrusive /əb'tru:sɪv/ *adj.* **1** unpleasantly noticeable. **2** obtruding oneself. □ **obtrusively** *adv.* **obtrusiveness** *n.*

obtuse /əb'tju:s/ *adj.* **1** dull-witted. **2** (of an angle) between 90° and 180°. **3** of blunt form; not sharp-pointed or sharp-edged. □ **obtuseness** *n.* [Latin *obtundo obtus-* beat against, blunt]

obverse /'ɒbvɜ:s/ *n.* **1** counterpart, opposite. **2** side of a coin or medal etc. bearing the head or principal design. **3** front, proper, or top side of a thing. [Latin *obverto obvers-* turn towards]

obviate /'ɒbvɪ,eɪt/ *v.* (**-ting**) get round or do away with (a need, inconvenience, etc.). [Latin *obvio* prevent]

obvious /'ɒbvɪəs/ *adj.* easily seen, recognized, or understood. □ **obviously** *adv.* **obviousness** *n.* [Latin *ob viam* in the way]

OC *abbr.* **1** Officer Commanding. **2** overseas country.

o.c. *abbr.* **1** office copy. **2** = OPEN CHARTER. **3** = OPEN COVER.

oc- see OB-.

o/c *abbr.* overcharge.

OCAM *abbr.* (also **OCAMM**) African and Malagasy (or African, Malagasy, and Mauritian) Common Organization. [French *Organisation commune africaine et malgache* (or *africaine, malgache, et mauritienne*)]

ocarina /,ɒkə'ri:nə/ *n.* small egg-shaped musical wind instrument. [Italian *oca* goose]

OCAS *abbr.* Organization of Central American States.

Oc.B/L *abbr. Shipping* ocean bill of lading.

occasion /ə'keɪʒ(ə)n/ *–n.* **1 a** special event or happening. **b** time of this. **2** reason, need. **3** suitable juncture, opportunity. **4** immediate but subordinate cause. *–v.* cause, esp. incidentally. □ **on occasion** now and then; when the need arises. [Latin *occido occas-* go down]

occasional *adj.* **1** happening irregularly and infrequently. **2** made or meant for, or acting on, a special occasion. □ **occasionally** *adv.*

occasional table *n.* small table for use as required.

Occident /'ɒksɪd(ə)nt/ *n. poet.* or *rhet.* **1** (prec. by *the*) West. **2** western Europe. **3** Europe and America as distinct from the Orient. [Latin *occidens -entis* setting, sunset, west]

occidental /,ɒksɪ'dent(ə)l/ *–adj.* **1** of the Occident. **2** western. *–n.* native of the Occident.

occiput /'ɒksɪ,pʌt/ *n.* back of the head. □ **occipital** /-'sɪpɪt(ə)l/ *adj.* [Latin *caput* head]

occlude /ə'klu:d/ *v.* (**-ding**) **1** stop up or close. **2** *Chem.* absorb and retain (gases). **3** (as **occluded** *adj.*) *Meteorol.* (of a frontal system) formed when a cold front overtakes a warm front, raising warm air from ground level. □ **occlusion** *n.* [Latin *occludo occlus-* close up]

occult /ɒ'kʌlt, 'ɒ-/ *adj.* **1** involving the supernatural; mystical. **2** esoteric. □ **the occult** occult phenomena generally. [Latin *occulo occult-* hide]

occupant /'ɒkjʊpənt/ *n.* person who occupies, esp. lives in, a place etc. □ **occupancy** *n.* (*pl.* **-ies**). [Latin: related to OCCUPY]

occupation /,ɒkjʊ'peɪʃ(ə)n/ *n.* **1** person's employment or profession. **2** pastime. **3** occupying or being occupied. **4** taking or holding of a country etc. by force.

occupational *adj.* of or connected with one's occupation.

♦ **occupational hazard** *n.* risk of accident or illness at one's place of work. Dangerous jobs usu. command higher salaries than those involving no risks, the increase being known as **danger money**. See also HEALTH AND SAFETY COMMISSION.

♦ **occupational pension scheme** *n.* pension scheme open to employees within a certain trade or profession or working for a particular firm. In an insured scheme, an insurance company pays the benefits under the scheme in return for having the premiums to invest. In a self-administered scheme, the pension-fund trustees are responsible for investing the contributions themselves. In order to run an occupational pension scheme, an organization must satisfy the Occupational Pension Board that the scheme complies with the conditions allowing employers to contract out of the state earnings-related pension scheme. After 1988 certain regulations relating to occupational pensions schemes were introduced. See also PERSONAL PENSION SCHEME.

---

occupational therapy *n.* programme of mental or physical activity to assist recovery from disease or injury.

occupier /'ɒkjʊ,paɪə(r)/ *n.* person living in a house etc. as its owner or tenant.

occupy /'ɒkjʊ,paɪ/ *v.* (**-ies, -ied**) **1** live in; be the tenant of. **2** take up or fill (space, time, or a place). **3** hold (a position or office). **4** take military possession of. **5** place oneself in (a building etc.) forcibly or without authority as a protest. **6** keep busy or engaged. [Latin *occupo* seize]

occur /ə'kɜ:(r)/ *v.* (**-rr-**) **1** come into being as an event or process. **2** exist or be encountered in some place or conditions. **3** (foll. by *to*) come into the mind of. [Latin *occurro* befall]

occurrence /ə'kʌrəns/ *n.* **1** occurring. **2** incident or event.

ocean /'əʊʃ(ə)n/ *n.* **1** large expanse of sea, esp. each of the main areas called the Atlantic, Pacific, Indian, Arctic, and Antarctic Oceans. **2** (often in *pl.*) *colloq.* very large expanse or quantity. □ **oceanic** /,əʊʃɪ'ænɪk/ *adj.* [Greek *ōkeanos*]

ocean-going *adj.* (of a ship) able to cross oceans.

oceanography /,əʊʃə'nɒgrəfɪ/ *n.* the study of the oceans. □ **oceanographer** *n.*

ocelot /'ɒsɪ,lɒt/ *n.* leopard-like cat of South and Central America. [French from Nahuatl]

ochre /'əʊkə(r)/ *n.* (*US* **ocher**) **1** earth used as yellow, brown, or red pigment. **2** pale brownish-yellow colour. □ **ochreous** /'əʊkrɪəs/ *adj.* [Greek *ōkhra*]

o'clock /ə'klɒk/ *adv.* of the clock (used to specify the hour) (*6 o'clock*).

♦ **OCR** *abbr.* = OPTICAL CHARACTER RECOGNITION.

Oct. *abbr.* October.

octa- *comb. form* (also **oct-** before a vowel) eight. [Latin *octo*, Greek *oktō* eight]

octagon /'ɒktəgən/ *n.* plane figure with eight sides and angles. □ **octagonal** /-'tægən(ə)l/ *adj.* [Greek: related to OCTA-, *-gōnos* -angled]

octahedron /,ɒktə'hi:drən/ *n.* (*pl.* **-s**) solid figure contained by eight (esp. triangular) plane faces. □ **octahedral** *adj.* [Greek]

♦ **octal notation** /'ɒkt(ə)l/ *n.* number system that uses eight digits, 0–7, to represent numbers. For example, the decimal number 26 is written as 32 in octal notation. Although less popular than hexadecimal notation, octal notation is used in computer programming as it is easier to follow than binary notation, yet is easy to convert to binary if required.

---

octane /'ɒkteɪn/ *n.* colourless inflammable hydrocarbon occurring in petrol. [from OCTA-]

octane number *n.* (also **octane rating**) figure indicating the antiknock properties of a fuel.

octave /'ɒktɪv/ *n.* **1** *Mus.* **a** interval between (and including) two notes, one having twice or half the frequency of vibration of the other. **b** eight notes occupying this interval. **c** each of the two notes at the extremes of this interval. **2** eight-line stanza. [Latin *octavus* eighth]

octavo /ɒk'teɪvəʊ/ *n.* (*pl.* **-s**) **1** size of a book or page given by folding a sheet of standard size three times to form eight leaves. **2** book or sheet of this size. [Latin: related to OCTAVE]

octet /ɒk'tet/ *n.* (also **octette**) **1 a** musical composition for eight performers. **b** the performers. **2** group of eight. [Italian or German: related to OCTA-]

octo- *comb. form* eight. [see OCTA-]

October /ɒk'təʊbə(r)/ *n.* tenth month of the year. [Latin *octo* eight, originally the 8th month of the Roman year]

octogenarian /ˌɒktəʊdʒɪ'neərɪən/ *n.* person from 80 to 89 years old. [Latin *octogeni* 80 each]

octopus /'ɒktəpəs/ *n.* (*pl.* **-puses**) sea mollusc with eight suckered tentacles. [Greek: related to OCTO-, *pous* foot]

ocular /'ɒkjʊlə(r)/ *adj.* of or connected with the eyes or sight; visual. [Latin *oculus* eye]

oculist /'ɒkjʊlɪst/ *n.* specialist in the treatment of the eyes.

OD[1] /əʊ'di:/ *slang –n.* drug overdose. *–v.* (**OD's, OD'd, OD'ing**) take an overdose. [abbreviation]

OD[2] *–abbr.* organization development. *–international civil aircraft marking* Lebanon.

O/D *abbr.* (also **O/d, o/d**) **1** on demand. **2** overdraft (or overdrawn).

ODA *abbr.* **1** *Computing* open document architecture. **2** = OVERSEAS DEVELOPMENT ADMINISTRATION.

odd *adj.* **1** strange, remarkable, eccentric. **2** casual, occasional (*odd jobs; odd moments*). **3** not normally considered; unconnected (*in some odd corner; picks up odd bargains*). **4 a** (of numbers) not integrally divisible by two, e.g. 1, 3, 5. **b** bearing such a number (*no parking on odd dates*). **5** left over when the rest have been distributed or divided into pairs (*odd sock*). **6** detached from a set or series (*odd volumes*). **7** (appended to a number, sum, weight, etc.) somewhat more than (*forty odd; forty-odd people*). **8** by which a round number, given sum, etc., is exceeded (*we have 102 – do you want the odd 2?*). □ **oddly** *adv.* **oddness** *n.* [Old Norse *oddi* angle, point, third or odd number]

oddball *n. colloq.* eccentric person.

◆ **odd-even pricing** *n.* pricing of a product so that the price ends in an odd number of pence, which is not far below the next number of pounds (e.g. £4.99 in preference to £5.00), in order to make the product appear cheaper.

---

oddity /'ɒdɪtɪ/ *n.* (*pl.* **-ies**) **1** strange person, thing, or occurrence. **2** peculiar trait. **3** strangeness.

◆ **odd lot** see ROUND LOT.

---

odd man out *n.* person or thing differing from the others in a group in some respect.

oddment *n.* **1** odd article; something left over. **2** (in *pl.*) miscellaneous articles.

odds *n.pl.* **1** ratio between the amounts staked by the parties to a bet, based on the expected probability either way. **2** balance of probability or advantage (*the odds are against it; the odds are in your favour*). **3** difference giving an advantage (*it makes no odds*). □ **at odds** (often foll. by *with*) in conflict or at variance. **over the odds** above the normal price etc. [apparently from ODD]

odds and ends *n.pl.* miscellaneous articles or remnants.

odds-on *–n.* state when success is more likely than failure. *–adj.* (of a chance) better than even; likely.

ode *n.* lyric poem of exalted style and tone. [Greek *ōidē* song]

Odense /'əʊdənsə/ port in Denmark, on the island of Fünen (Fyn); it exports dairy produce and also has shipbuilding, sugar-refining, and textile industries; pop. (est. 1995) 182 617.

Oder /'əʊdə(r)/ (Czech and Polish **Odra** /'əʊdrə/) river in central Europe, rising in the mountains of the Czech Republic and flowing N through W Poland to the Baltic Sea. Forming part of the border between Poland and Germany, it is of great commercial importance.

Odessa /əʊ'desə/ city and seaport in Ukraine, on the NW coast of the Black Sea; there are ship-repairing, engineering, and chemical industries, and fishing and whaling are important; pop. (est. 1996) 1 046 000.

ODI *abbr.* Overseas Development Institute.

odious /'əʊdɪəs/ *adj.* hateful, repulsive. □ **odiously** *adv.* **odiousness** *n.* [related to ODIUM]

odium /'əʊdɪəm/ *n.* widespread dislike or disapproval of a person or action. [Latin, = hatred]

odometer /əʊ'dɒmɪtə(r), ɒ-/ *n. US* = MILOMETER. [Greek *hodos* way]

odoriferous /ˌəʊdə'rɪfərəs/ *adj.* diffusing a (usu. agreeable) odour. [Latin: related to ODOUR]

odour /'əʊdə(r)/ *n.* (*US* **odor**) **1** smell or fragrance. **2** quality or trace (*an odour of intolerance*). **3** regard, repute (*in bad odour*). □ **odorous** *adj.* **odourless** *adj.* [Latin *odor*]

ODP *abbr.* **1** official (or overall) development planning. **2** open-door policy.

odyssey /'ɒdɪsɪ/ *n.* (*pl.* **-s**) long adventurous journey. [title of the Homeric epic poem on the adventures of Odysseus]

OE *international civil aircraft marking* Austria.

OECD *abbr.* = ORGANIZATION FOR ECONOMIC COOPERATION AND DEVELOPMENT.

OECS *abbr.* Organization of Eastern Caribbean States.

oedema /ɪ'di:mə/ *n.* (*US* **edema**) accumulation of excess fluid in body tissues, causing swelling. [Greek *oideō* swell]

Oedipus complex /'i:dɪpəs/ *n.* child's, esp. a boy's, subconscious sexual desire for the parent of the opposite sex. □ **Oedipal** *adj.* [Greek *Oidipous*, who unknowingly married his mother]

OEEC *abbr. hist.* Organization for European Economic Cooperation. See ORGANIZATION FOR ECONOMIC COOPERATION AND DEVELOPMENT.

OEM *abbr.* original equipment manufacturer, usu. an organization that purchases equipment (e.g. electronic circuitry) that is to be built into one of its products.

OEO *abbr.* (in the US) Office of Economic Opportunity.

OEP *abbr.* (in the US) Office of Economic Preparedness.

o'er /'əʊə(r)/ *adv.* & *prep. poet.* = OVER. [contraction]

OES *abbr.* (in the US) Office of Economic Stabilization.

oesophagus /i:'sɒfəgəs/ *n.* (*US* **esophagus**) (*pl.* **-gi** /-ˌdʒaɪ/ or **-guses**) passage from the mouth to the stomach; gullet. [Greek]

oestrogen /'i:strədʒ(ə)n/ *n.* (*US* **estrogen**) **1** sex hormone developing and maintaining female characteristics of the body. **2** this produced artificially for use in medicine. [Greek *oistros* frenzy, -GEN]

oestrus /'i:strəs/ *n.* (also **oestrum**, *US* **estrus**) recurring period of sexual receptivity in many female mammals. □ **oestrous** *adj.* [Greek *oistros* frenzy]

œuvre /'ɜ:vr/ *n.* works of a creative artist regarded collectively. [French, = work, from Latin *opera*]

of /ɒv, əv/ *prep.* expressing: **1** origin or cause (*paintings of Turner; died of cancer*). **2** material or substance (*house of cards; built of bricks*). **3** belonging or connection (*thing of the past; articles of clothing; head of the business*). **4** identity or close relation (*city of Rome; a pound of apples; a fool of a man*). **5** removal or separation (*north of the city; got rid of them; robbed us of £1000*). **6** reference or direction (*beware of the dog; suspected of lying; very good of you; short of money*). **7** objective relation (*love of music; in search of peace*). **8** partition, classification, or inclusion (*no more of that; part of the story; this sort of book*). **9** description, quality, or condition (*the hour of prayer; person of tact; girl of ten; on the point of leaving*). **10** *US* time in relation to the following hour (*a quarter of three*). □ **be of** possess, give rise to (*is of great interest*). **of an evening** (or **morning** etc.) *colloq.* **1** on most evenings (or mornings etc.). **2** at some time in the evenings (or mornings etc.). **of late** recently. **of old** formerly. [Old English]

of- see OB-.

Off. *abbr.* **1** Office. **2** Officer.

off *–adv.* **1** away; at or to a distance (*drove off; 3 miles off*). **2** out of position; not on, touching, or attached; loose, separate, gone (*has come off; take your coat off*). **3** so as to be rid of (*sleep it off*). **4** so as to break continuity or continuance; discontinued, stopped (*turn off the radio; take a day off; the game is off*). **5** not available on a menu etc. (*chips are off*). **6** to the end; entirely; so as to be clear (*clear off; finish off; pay off*). **7** situated as regards money, supplies, etc. (*well off*). **8** off stage (*noises off*). **9** (of food etc.) beginning to decay. *–prep.* **1 a** from; away, down, or up from (*fell off the chair; took something off the price*). **b** not on (*off the pitch*). **2 a** temporarily relieved of or abstaining from (*off duty*). **b** temporarily not attracted by (*off his food*). **c** not achieving (*off form*). **3** using as a source or means of support (*live off the land*). **4** leading from; not far from (*a street off the Strand*). **5** at a short distance to sea from (*sank off Cape Horn*). *–adj.* **1** far, further (*off side of the wall*). **2** (of a part of a vehicle, animal, or road) right (*the off front wheel*). **3** *Cricket* designating the half of the field (as divided lengthways through the pitch) to which the striker's feet are pointed. **4** *colloq.* **a** annoying, unfair (*that's really off*). **b** somewhat unwell (*feeling a bit off*). *–n.* **1** the off side in cricket. **2** start of a race. □ **off and on** intermittently; now and then. **off the cuff** see CUFF[1]. **off the peg** see PEG. [var. of OF]

■ **Usage** The use of *off of* for the preposition *off* (sense 1a), e.g. *picked it up off of the floor,* is non-standard and should be avoided.

offal /ˈɒf(ə)l/ *n.* **1** less valuable edible parts of a carcass, esp. the heart, liver, etc. **2** refuse, scraps. [Dutch *afval*: related to OFF, FALL]

Offaly /ˈɒfəlɪ/ county in the Republic of Ireland, in the province of Leinster; pop. (1991) 58 494; capital, Tullamore. It is mainly agricultural, producing wheat, oats, barley, and cattle.

◆ **off-balance-sheet finance** *n.* use of company funds to hire or lease an expensive piece of equipment rather than purchasing it, enabling a company to make use of the equipment without having to invest capital. The item does not appear on the balance sheet as an asset and therefore the capital employed will be understated.

◆ **off-balance-sheet reserve** *n.* = HIDDEN RESERVE.

offbeat *–adj.* **1** not coinciding with the beat. **2** eccentric, unconventional. *–n.* any of the unaccented beats in a bar.

◆ **off-card rate** *n.* advertising charging rate that is different from that shown on the rate card, having been separately negotiated.

off-centre *adj.* & *adv.* not quite centrally placed.

off chance *n.* (prec. by *the*) remote possibility.

off colour *predic. adj.* **1** unwell. **2** *US* somewhat indecent.

offcut *n.* remnant of timber, paper, etc., after cutting.

off-day *n. colloq.* day when one is not at one's best.

offence /əˈfens/ *n.* (*US* **offense**) **1** illegal act; transgression. **2** upsetting of feelings, insult; umbrage (*give offence; take offence*). **3** aggressive action. [related to OFFEND]

offend /əˈfend/ *v.* **1** cause offence to, upset. **2** displease, anger. **3** (often foll. by *against*) do wrong; transgress. □ **offender** *n.* **offending** *adj.* [Latin *offendo offens-* strike against, displease]

offense *US* var. of OFFENCE.

offensive /əˈfensɪv/ *–adj.* **1** causing offence; insulting. **2** disgusting. **3 a** aggressive, attacking. **b** (of a weapon) for attacking. *–n.* aggressive action, attitude, or campaign. □ **offensively** *adv.* **offensiveness** *n.*

offer *–v.* **1** present for acceptance, refusal, or consideration. **2** (foll. by *to* + infin.) express readiness or show intention. **3** provide; give an opportunity for. **4** make available for sale. **5** present to the attention. **6** present (a sacrifice etc.). **7** present itself; occur (*as opportunity offers*). **8** attempt (violence, resistance, etc.). *–n.* **1** expression of readiness to do or give if desired, or to buy or sell. **2** price at which a seller is willing to sell something. If there is an acceptance of the offer a legally binding contract has been entered into. In law, an offer is distinguished from an **invitation to treat**, which is an invitation by one person or firm to others to make an offer (for example by displaying goods in a shop window). See also FIRM OFFER 2; OFFER PRICE; QUOTATION 4. **3** proposal (esp. of marriage). **4** bid. □ **on offer** for sale at a certain (esp. reduced) price. [Latin *offero oblat-*]

◆ **offer by prospectus** *n.* offer to the public of a new issue of shares or debentures made directly by means of a prospectus, a document giving a detailed account of the aims, objects, and capital structure of the company, as well as its past history. The prospectus must conform to the provisions of the Companies Act (1985). Cf. OFFER FOR SALE.

◆ **offer document** *n.* document sent to the shareholders of a company that is the subject of a take-over bid. It gives details of the offer being made and usu. provides shareholders with reasons for accepting the terms of the offer.

◆ **offer for sale** *n.* invitation to the general public to purchase the stock of a company through an intermediary, e.g. an issuing house or merchant bank (cf. OFFER BY PROSPECTUS); it is one of the most frequently used means of flotation. An offer for sale is usu. at a fixed price, which requires some form of balloting or rationing if the demand for the shares exceeds supply, but may be an issue by tender, in which case individuals offer to purchase a fixed quantity of stock at or above some minimum price and the stock is allocated to the highest bidders.

offering *n.* **1** contribution or gift, esp. of money. **2** thing offered as a sacrifice etc.

◆ **offer price** *n.* price at which a security is offered for sale by a market maker or units in a unit trust are sold by an institution. Cf. BID PRICE.

◆ **offer to purchase** *n.* = TAKE-OVER BID.

offertory /ˈɒfətərɪ/ *n.* (*pl.* **-ies**) **1** offering of the bread and wine at the Eucharist. **2** collection of money at a religious service. [Church Latin: related to OFFER]

offhand *–adj.* curt or casual in manner. *–adv.* without preparation or thought (*can't say offhand*). □ **offhanded** *adj.* **offhandedly** *adv.* **offhandedness** *n.*

office /ˈɒfɪs/ *n.* **1** room or building used as a place of business, esp. for clerical or administrative work. **2** room or area for a particular business (*ticket office*). **3** local centre of a large business (*our London office*). **4** position with duties attached to it. **5** tenure of an official position (*hold office*). **6** (**Office**) quarters, staff, or collective authority of a government department etc. (*Foreign Office*). **7** duty, task, function. **8** (usu. in *pl.*) piece of kindness; service (esp. *through the good offices of*). **9** authorized form of worship. [Latin *officium* from *opus* work, *facio fic-* do]

◆ **Office of Fair Trading** *n.* (also **OFT**) government department that, under the Director General of Fair Trading, reviews commercial activities in the UK and aims to protect the consumer against unfair practices. Established in 1973, it is responsible for the administration of the Fair Trading Act (1973), the Consumer Credit Act (1974), the Restrictive Trade Practices Act (1976), the Estate Agents Act (1979), the Competition Act (1980), and the Control of Misleading Advertisements Regulations (1988). Its five main areas of activity are consumer affairs, consumer credit, monopolies and mergers, restrictive trade practices, and anti-competitive practices.

◆ **Office of Telecommunications** *n.* (also **OFTEL**) government body set up in 1984 to supervise the telecommunications industry. It is responsible for issuing licences, regulating competition in the industry, and protecting the interests of the consumer.

officer /ˈɒfɪsə(r)/ *n.* **1** person holding a position of authority or trust, esp. one with a commission in the army, navy, air force, etc. **2** policeman or policewoman. **3** holder of a post in a society (e.g. the president or secretary). **4** (also **company officer**) person who acts in an official capacity in a company. Company officers include the directors, managers, the company secretary, and in some circumstances the company's auditors and solicitors. The Companies Act (1985) empowers a court dealing with a liquidation to investigate the conduct of the company's officers with a view to recovering any money they may have obtained illegally or incorrectly.

official /ə'fɪʃ(ə)l/ *–adj.* **1** of an office or its tenure. **2** characteristic of officials and bureaucracy. **3** properly authorized. *–n.* person holding office or engaged in official duties. □ **officialdom** *n.* **officially** *adv.*

officialese /əˌfɪʃə'li:z/ *n. derog.* language characteristic of official documents.

♦ **Official List** *n.* **1** list of all the securities traded on the main market of the London Stock Exchange. See LISTED SECURITY; LISTING REQUIREMENTS; YELLOW BOOK. **2** (in full **Stock Exchange Daily Official List**) list prepared daily by the London Stock Exchange, recording all the bargains that have been transacted in listed securities during the day. It also gives dividend dates, rights issues, prices, and other information.

♦ **official rate** *n.* rate of exchange given to a currency by a government. If the official rate differs from the market rate, the government must be prepared to support its official rate by buying or selling in the open market to make the two rates coincide.

♦ **official receiver** *n.* person appointed by the Secretary of State for Trade and Industry to act as a receiver in bankruptcy and winding-up cases. The High Court and each county court that has jurisdiction over insolvency matters has an official receiver, who is an officer of the court. Deputy official receivers may also be appointed. The official receiver commonly acts as the liquidator of a company being wound up by the court.

official secrets *n.pl.* confidential information involving national security.

♦ **official strike** see STRIKE *n.* 2.

officiate /ə'fɪʃɪˌeɪt/ *v.* (**-ting**) **1** act in an official capacity. **2** conduct a religious service. □ **officiation** /-'eɪʃ(ə)n/ *n.* **officiator** *n.*

officious /ə'fɪʃəs/ *adj.* **1** domineering. **2** intrusive in correcting etc. □ **officiously** *adv.* **officiousness** *n.*

offing *n.* more distant part of the sea in view. □ **in the offing** not far away; likely to appear or happen soon. [probably from OFF]

off-key *adj.* & *adv.* **1** out of tune. **2** not quite fitting.

off-licence *n.* **1** shop selling alcoholic drink. **2** licence for this.

off-line *Computing –adj.* (of equipment) not usable, either because it is not connected to a computer or because the system has been forbidden to use it (*off-line printer; off-line file*). Cf. ON-LINE. *–adv.* with a delay between the production of data and its processing; not under direct computer control.

offload *v.* get rid of (esp. something unpleasant) by passing it to someone else.

off-peak *adj.* used or for use at times other than those of greatest demand.

off-piste *adj.* (of skiing) away from prepared ski runs.

offprint *n.* printed copy of an article etc. originally forming part of a larger publication.

offscreen *adj.* & *adv.* beyond the range of a film camera etc.; when not being filmed.

off-season *n.* time of the year when business etc. is slack.

offset *–n.* **1** side-shoot from a plant serving for propagation. **2** compensation, consideration or amount diminishing or neutralizing the effect of a contrary one. **3** sloping ledge in a wall etc. **4** bend in a pipe etc. to carry it past an obstacle. **5** (often *attrib.*) method of printing in which ink is transferred from a plate or stone to a rubber surface and from there to paper etc. (*offset litho*). *–v.* (**-setting**; *past* and *past part.* **-set**) **1** counterbalance, compensate. **2** print by the offset process.

offshoot *n.* **1** side-shoot or branch. **2** derivative.

offshore *adj.* **1** at sea some distance from the shore. **2** (of the wind) blowing seawards. **3** outside a particular country, esp. for taxation purposes.

♦ **offshore banking** *n.* practice of offering financial services in locations that have attractive tax advantages to non-residents. Offshore banking centres are based in many European countries, e.g. France, Switzerland, the Isle of Man, and Jersey, as well as the Middle East, the Caribbean, and Asia. These locations are often described as tax havens because they can legally reduce customers' tax liabilities.

♦ **offshore financial centre** *n.* centre that provides advantageous deposit and lending rates to non-residents because of low taxation, liberal exchange controls, and low reserve requirements for banks. Some countries have made a lucrative business out of offshore banking; the Cayman Islands is currently one of the world's largest offshore centres. In Europe, the Channel Islands and the Isle of Man are very popular. The US and, more recently, Japan have both established domestic offshore facilities that enable non-residents to conduct their business under more liberal regulations than domestic transactions. Their objective is to stop funds moving outside the country.

♦ **offshore fund** *n.* **1** fund that is based in a tax haven outside the UK to avoid UK taxation. Offshore funds operate in the same way as unit trusts but are not supervised by the Department of Trade and Industry. **2** fund held outside the country of residence of the holder. See OFFSHORE BANKING; OFFSHORE FINANCIAL CENTRE.

♦ **Offshore Supplies Office** *n.* department of the UK Department of Trade and Industry set up in Glasgow in 1973, now with offices also in London. It encourages, monitors, advises, and assists the offshore oil and gas industries, providing finance and research and development.

offside *–adj.* (of a player in a field game) in a position where he or she may not play the ball. *–n.* (often *attrib.*) right side of a vehicle, animal, etc.

offspring *n.* (*pl.* same) **1** person's child, children, or descendants. **2** animal's young or descendants. **3** result. [Old English: see OFF, SPRING]

off-stage *adj.* & *adv.* not on the stage; not visible to the audience.

off-street *adj.* (esp. of parking) other than on a street.

♦ **off-the-peg research** *n.* marketing research that uses existing data, rather than a fresh investigation of a market. See also DESK RESEARCH.

♦ **off-the-shelf company** *n.* company that is registered with the Registrar of Companies although it does not trade and has no directors. It can, however, be sold and reformed into a new company with the minimum of formality and expense. Such companies are easily purchased from specialist brokers.

off-the-wall *adj.* esp. *US slang* crazy, absurd, outlandish.

off white *adj.* & *n.* (as adj. often hyphenated) white with a grey or yellowish tinge.

OFGAS /'ɒfˌgæs/ *abbr.* (also **Ofgas**) Office of Gas Supply.

OFT *abbr.* = OFFICE OF FAIR TRADING.

oft *adv. archaic* often. [Old English]

♦ **OFTEL** /'ɒfˌtel/ *abbr.* (also **Oftel**) = OFFICE OF TELECOMMUNICATIONS.

often /'ɒf(ə)n/ *adv.* (**oftener**, **oftenest**) **1 a** frequently; many times. **b** at short intervals. **2** in many instances.

oft-times *adv.* often.

OFWAT /'ɒfˌwɒt/ *abbr.* (also **Ofwat**) Office of Water Services.

Ogaden /ˌɒgə'den, 'ɒg-/ desert region in SE Ethiopia, largely inhabited by Somali nomads. Successive governments of neighbouring Somalia have laid claim to this territory, which they call Western Somalia.

ogee /'əʊdʒi:/ *n.* S-shaped line or moulding. [apparently from OGIVE]

ogive /'əʊdʒaɪv/ *n.* **1** pointed arch. **2** diagonal rib of a vault. [French]

OGL *abbr. Commerce* open general licence.

ogle /ˈəʊg(ə)l/ *–v.* (**-ling**) look amorously or lecherously (at). *–n.* amorous or lecherous look. [probably Low German or Dutch]

OGM *abbr.* ordinary general meeting.

ogre /ˈəʊgə(r)/ *n.* (*fem.* **ogress** /-grɪs/) **1** man-eating giant in folklore. **2** terrifying person. □ **ogreish** /ˈəʊgərɪʃ/ *adj.* (also **ogrish**). [French]

OH *–international civil aircraft marking* Finland. *US postcode* Ohio.

oh /əʊ/ *int.* (also **O**) expressing surprise, pain, entreaty, etc. □ **oh** (or **o) for** I wish I had. [var. of O[4]]

o.h. *abbr.* office hours.

OHG *abbr.* (German) Offene Handelsgesellschaft (= partnership).

Ohio /əʊˈhaɪəʊ/ state in the NE US; pop. (est. 1996) 11 172 782; capital, Columbus. It is an important industrial region; metals are processed and there is mining of coal, gas, oil, and other mineral deposits.

ohm /əʊm/ *n.* SI unit of electrical resistance. [*Ohm*, name of a physicist]

OHMS *abbr.* on Her (or His) Majesty's Service.

oho /əʊˈhəʊ/ *int.* expressing surprise or exultation. [from O[4], HO]

OHP *abbr.* overhead projector.

oi *int.* calling attention or expressing alarm etc. [var. of HOY]

-oid *suffix* forming adjectives and nouns, denoting form or resemblance (*asteroid*; *rhomboid*; *thyroid*). [Greek *eidos* form]

oil *–n.* **1** any of various viscous, usu. inflammable liquids insoluble in water (*cooking oil*; *drill for oil*). **2** *US* petroleum. **3** (in *comb.*) using oil as fuel (*oil-heater*). **4 a** (usu. in *pl.*) = OIL-PAINT. **b** picture painted in oil-paints. *–v.* **1** apply oil to; lubricate. **2** impregnate or treat with oil (*oiled silk*). □ **oil the wheels** help make things go smoothly. [Latin *oleum* olive oil]

oilcake *n.* compressed linseed from which the oil has been extracted, used as fodder or manure.

oilcan *n.* can with a long nozzle for oiling machinery.

oilcloth *n.* fabric, esp. canvas, waterproofed with oil or another substance.

oil-colour var. of OIL-PAINT.

oiled *adj. slang* drunk.

oilfield *n.* area yielding mineral oil.

oil-fired *adj.* using oil as fuel.

oil of turpentine *n.* volatile pungent oil distilled from turpentine, used as a solvent in mixing paints and varnishes, and in medicine.

oil-paint *n.* (also **oil-colour**) paint made by mixing powdered pigment in oil. □ **oil-painting** *n.*

oil rig *n.* structure with equipment for drilling an oil well.

oilskin *n.* **1** cloth waterproofed with oil. **2 a** garment of this. **b** (in *pl.*) suit of this.

oil-slick *n.* patch of oil, esp. on the sea.

oilstone *n.* fine-grained flat stone used with oil for sharpening flat tools, e.g. chisels, planes, etc.

oil well *n.* well from which mineral oil is drawn.

oily *adj.* (**-ier, -iest**) **1** of or like oil. **2** covered or soaked with oil. **3** (of a manner etc.) fawning, unctuous, ingratiating. □ **oiliness** *n.*

ointment /ˈɔɪntmənt/ *n.* smooth greasy healing or cosmetic preparation for the skin. [Latin *unguo* anoint]

OJT *abbr.* on-the-job training.

OK[1] /əʊˈkeɪ/ (also **okay**) *colloq. –adj.* (often as *int.*) all right; satisfactory. *–adv.* well, satisfactorily. *–n.* (*pl.* **OKs**) approval, sanction. *–v.* (**OK's, OK'd, OK'ing**) approve, sanction. [originally US: probably abbreviation of *orl* (or *oll*) *korrect*, jocular form of 'all correct']

OK[2] *–US postcode* Oklahoma. *–international civil aircraft marking* Czech Republic and Slovakia.

okapi /əʊˈkɑːpɪ/ *n.* (*pl.* same or **-s**) African giraffe-like mammal but with a shorter neck and striped body. [Mbuba]

Okara /əʊˈkɑːrə/ commercial city in NE Pakistan, in Punjab province; pop. (1981) 154 000.

okay var. of OK[1].

Okhotsk /əʊˈxɒtsk/, **Sea of** inlet of the N Pacific Ocean off the E coast of Russia, bounded to the E by the Kamchatka peninsula and to the SE by the Kuril Islands.

Okinawa /ˌɒkɪˈnɑːwə/ Japanese island, the largest of the Ryukyu Islands; pop. (1995) 1 274 000; capital, Naha, pop. 304 000. Rice, sugar cane, and sweet potatoes are grown; fishing is also important.

Okla. *abbr.* Oklahoma.

Oklahoma /ˌəʊkləˈhəʊmə/ state in the S central US; pop. (est. 1996) 3 300 902; capital, Oklahoma City. It has rich oil reserves, and agriculture (esp. cattle) is also important; manufactures include processed food, machinery, and electrical equipment.

Oklahoma City city in the US, capital of Oklahoma and a major industrial, commercial, and distribution centre for the surrounding region; pop. (est. 1994) 463 201.

okra /ˈəʊkrə/ *n.* tall, orig. African plant with long ridged seed-pods used for food. [West African native name]

OL *–abbr.* **1** *Computing* on-line. **2** operating licence. *–postcode* Oldham.

-ol *suffix* in the names of alcohols or analogous compounds. [from ALCOHOL and Latin *oleum* oil]

Öland /ˈɜːlænd/ Swedish island in the Baltic Sea, off the SE coast of Sweden; pop. (est. 1988) 24 100; chief town, Borgholm.

old /əʊld/ *adj.* (**older, oldest**) **1 a** advanced in age; far on in the natural period of existence. **b** not young or near its beginning. **2** made long ago. **3** long in use. **4** worn, dilapidated, or shabby from the passage of time. **5** having the characteristics of age (*child has an old face*). **6** practised, inveterate (*old offender*). **7** belonging to the past; lingering on; former (*old times*; *old memories*; *our old house*). **8** dating from far back; long established or known; ancient, primeval (*an old family*; *old friends*; *old as the hills*). **9** (appended to a period of time) of age (*is four years old*; *four-year-old boy*; *a four-year-old*). **10** (of a language) as used in former or earliest times. **11** *colloq.* as a term of affection or casual reference (*good old Charlie*; *old thing*). □ **oldish** *adj.* **oldness** *n.* [Old English]

old age *n.* later part of normal life.

old-age pension see PENSION[1] *n.* 1. □ **old-age pensioner** *n.*

Old Bill *n. slang* **1** the police. **2** a policeman.

old boy *n.* **1** former male pupil of a school. **2** *colloq.* **a** elderly man. **b** (as a form of address) = OLD MAN.

old boy network *n. colloq.* preferment in employment, esp. of fellow ex-pupils of public schools.

old country *n.* (prec. by *the*) native country of colonists etc.

olden *attrib. adj. archaic* old; of old.

old-fashioned *adj.* showing or favouring the tastes of former times.

old girl *n.* **1** former female pupil of a school. **2** *colloq.* **a** elderly woman. **b** affectionate term of address to a girl or woman.

Old Glory *n. US* US national flag.

old gold *adj.* & *n.* (as adj. often hyphenated) dull brownish-gold colour.

old guard *n.* original, past, or conservative members of a group.

old hand *n.* person with much experience.

old hat *adj. colloq.* hackneyed.

oldie *n. colloq.* old person or thing.

old lady *n. colloq.* one's mother or wife.

♦ **Old Lady of Threadneedle Street** *n. colloq.* = BANK OF ENGLAND. [after the name of the London street in which the Bank stands]

---

old maid *n.* **1** *derog.* elderly unmarried woman. **2** prim and fussy person.

old man *n. colloq.* **1** one's husband or father. **2** affectionate form of address to a boy or man.

old man's beard *n.* wild clematis, with grey fluffy hairs round the seeds.

old master *n.* **1** great artist of former times, esp. of the 13th–17th centuries in Europe. **2** painting by such a painter.

Old Nick *n. colloq.* the Devil.

Old Norse *n.* **1** Germanic language from which the Scandinavian languages are derived. **2** language of Norway and its colonies until the 14th century.

old school *n.* traditional attitudes or people having them.

old school tie *n.* excessive loyalty to traditional values and to former pupils of one's own, esp. public, school.

old soldier *n.* (also **old stager** or **timer**) experienced person.

old style *n.* dating reckoned by the Julian calendar.

Old Testament *n.* part of the Bible containing the scriptures of the Hebrews.

old-time *attrib. adj.* belonging to former times (*old-time dancing*).

old wives' tale *n.* unscientific belief.

old woman *n. colloq.* **1** one's wife or mother. **2** fussy or timid man.

Old World *n.* Europe, Asia, and Africa.

old year *n.* year just ended or ending.

♦ **Old Years** *n.pl.* business years up to 1985 at Lloyd's during which very heavy losses were made.

oleaginous /ˌəʊlɪˈædʒɪnəs/ *adj.* **1** like or producing oil. **2** oily. [Latin: related to OIL]

oleander /ˌəʊlɪˈændə(r)/ *n.* evergreen flowering Mediterranean shrub. [Latin]

O level *n. hist.* = ORDINARY LEVEL. [abbreviation]

olfactory /ɒlˈfæktərɪ/ *adj.* of the sense of smell (*olfactory nerves*). [Latin *oleo* smell, *facio* make]

oligarch /ˈɒlɪˌgɑːk/ *n.* member of an oligarchy. [Greek *oligoi* few]

oligarchy *n.* (*pl.* **-ies**) **1** government, or state governed, by a small group of people. **2** members of such a government. □ **oligarchic** /-ˈgɑːkɪk/ *adj.* **oligarchical** /-ˈgɑːkɪk(ə)l/ *adj.*

Oligocene /ˈɒlɪgəˌsiːn/ *–adj.* of the third geological epoch of the Tertiary period. *–n.* this epoch. [Greek *oligos* little, *kainos* new]

♦ **oligopoly** /ˌɒlɪˈgɒpəlɪ/ *n.* (*pl.* **-ies**) *Econ.* market in which relatively few sellers supply many buyers, each seller being able to control his or her prices to a certain extent while recognizing that competitors' actions will influence profits. This is a departure from the assumption, in perfect competition, that there are a large number of firms in any particular market. If there are only a few firms, each one may be able to influence the market price by controlling the amount they produce, thus earning higher profits. Oligopoly is a common feature of the real world; studies have shown that in developed countries markets tend to become more oligopolistic. There is some doubt, however, as to whether prices really are higher under oligopoly. See also CONTESTABLE MARKETS THEORY. □ **oligopolistic** /-ˈlɪstɪk/ *adj.* [Greek *oligos* little, *polein* sell]

olive /ˈɒlɪv/ *–n.* **1** small oval hard-stoned fruit, green when unripe and bluish-black when ripe. **2** tree bearing this. **3** its wood. **4** olive green. *–adj.* **1** olive-green. **2** (of the complexion) yellowish-brown. [Latin *oliva* from Greek]

olive branch *n.* gesture of reconciliation or peace.

olive green *adj.* & *n.* (as adj. often hyphenated) dull yellowish green.

olive oil *n.* cooking-oil extracted from olives.

olivine /ˈɒlɪˌviːn/ *n.* mineral (usu. olive-green) composed of magnesium-iron silicate.

Olomouc /ˌɒlɒˈmaʊts/ industrial city in the E Czech Republic; pop. (est. 1995) 106 278.

Olympia /əˈlɪmpɪə/ seaport in the US, capital of Washington state; there are fishing, mining, and timber industries; pop. (1990) 33 840.

Olympiad /əˈlɪmpɪˌæd/ *n.* **1 a** period of four years between Olympic games, used by the ancient Greeks in dating events. **b** four-yearly celebration of the ancient Olympic Games. **2** celebration of the modern Olympic Games. **3** regular international competition in chess etc. [Greek *Olumpias Olumpiad-*: related to OLYMPIC]

Olympian /əˈlɪmpɪən/ *–adj.* **1 a** of Olympus. **b** celestial. **2** (of manners etc.) magnificent, condescending, superior. **3** = OLYMPIC *adj.*. *–n.* **1** Greek god dwelling on Olympus. **2** person of superhuman ability or calm. **3** competitor in the Olympic games. [from Mt. *Olympus* in Greece, or as OLYMPIC]

Olympic /əˈlɪmpɪk/ *–adj.* of the Olympic games. *–n.pl.* (**the Olympics**) Olympic games. [Greek from *Olympia* in S Greece]

Olympic games *n.pl.* **1** ancient Greek athletic festival held at Olympia every four years. **2** modern international revival of this.

OM *abbr.* Order of Merit.

OMA /ˈəʊmə/ *abbr. US Finance* orderly marketing agreement.

Omagh /əʊˈmɑː/ **1** district in Northern Ireland, in county Tyrone; pop. (1991) 45 809. **2** town in Northern Ireland, county town of Tyrone; manufactures include dairy products; pop. (1991) 17 280.

Omaha /ˈəʊməˌhɑː/ city in the US, in E Nebraska on the Missouri River; it has meat-processing and other industries; pop. (est. 1994) 345 033.

Oman, Gulf of inlet of the Arabian Sea, connected by the Strait of Hormuz to the Persian Gulf.

OMB *abbr.* (in the US) Office of Management and Budget.

Oman /əʊˈmɑːn/, **Sultanate of** (former name, until 1970, **Muscat and Oman**) country in SW Asia at the E corner of the Arabian peninsula. The economy is based on the production and export of oil, which provides most of Oman's export earnings. Since the first oil was exported in 1967 Oman has seen rapid development, although the collapse in international oil prices in 1986 led to some economic uncertainty. Copper, chromite, marble, gypsum, and limestone are also extracted and manufacturing industries include oil refining, cement production, and copper smelting. Agriculture is mainly at subsistence level but beef production and the cultivation of fruits (esp. dates), cereals, and tobacco are important. Oman relies on immigrant labour to supplement its own small working population. In the mid-1990s Oman embarked on a policy of economic diversification to lessen its dependence on the oil industry. The sultanate became a British protectorate in 1891 and, despite achieving full independence in 1952, still retains links with the UK. Head of state, Sultan Qaboos ibn Sa'id; capital, Muscat. □ **Omani** *adj.* & *n.*

languages	Arabic (official), English, Urdu
currency	rial (RO) of 1000 baizas
pop. (1996)	2 251 000
GNP (1994)	US$10.7B
literacy	20%
life expectancy	67 (m); 71 (f)

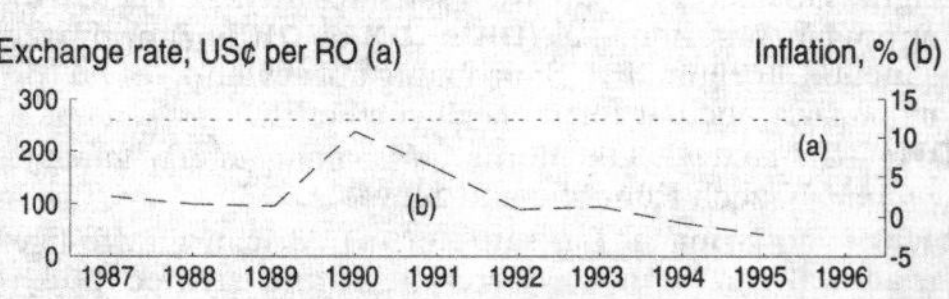

ombudsman /ˈɒmbʊdzmən/ *n.* (*pl.* **-men**) official appointed to investigate complaints against public authorities. See COMMISSIONER FOR LOCAL ADMINISTRATION; FINANCIAL OMBUDSMAN; PARLIAMENTARY COMMISSIONER FOR ADMINISTRATION. [Swedish, = legal representative]

OMC *abbr.* operation and maintenance costs.

Omdurman /ˈɒmdɜːmən/ city in the Sudan; products include textiles, handicrafts, and agricultural produce; pop. (1993) 1 267 077.

omega /ˈəʊmɪgə/ *n.* **1** last (24th) letter of the Greek alphabet (Ω, ω). **2** last of a series; final development. [Greek *ō mega* = great O]

omelette /ˈɒmlɪt/ *n.* beaten eggs fried and often folded round a savoury filling. [French]

omen /ˈəʊmən/ *–n.* **1** event or object portending good or evil. **2** prophetic significance (*of good omen*). *–v.* (usu. in *passive*) portend. [Latin]

omicron /əˈmaɪkrən, ˈɒmɪ-/ *n.* fifteenth letter of the Greek alphabet (O, o). [Greek *o mikron* = small o]

ominous /ˈɒmɪnəs/ *adj.* **1** threatening. **2** of evil omen; inauspicious. □ **ominously** *adv.* [Latin: related to OMEN]

omission /əʊˈmɪʃ(ə)n/ *n.* **1** omitting or being omitted. **2** thing omitted.

omit /əʊˈmɪt/ *v.* (**-tt-**) **1** leave out; not insert or include. **2** leave undone. **3** (foll. by verbal noun or *to* + infin.) fail or neglect. [Latin *omitto omiss-*]

omni- *comb. form* all. [Latin *omnis* all]

omnibus /ˈɒmnɪbəs/ *–n.* **1** *formal* bus. **2** volume containing several literary works previously published separately. *–adj.* **1** serving several purposes at once. **2** comprising several items. [Latin, = for all]

◆ **omnibus research** *n.* marketing research surveys based on multipart questionnaires sent out regularly to a panel of respondents. Space on the questionnaire is available to companies that have specific marketing research needs, esp. those having a limited number of questions to ask, which would not alone justify setting up a separate research study.

omnipotent /ɒmˈnɪpət(ə)nt/ *adj.* having great or absolute power. □ **omnipotence** *n.* [Latin: related to POTENT]

omnipresent /ˌɒmnɪˈprez(ə)nt/ *adj.* present everywhere. □ **omnipresence** *n.* [Latin: related to PRESENT[1]]

omniscient /ɒmˈnɪsɪənt/ *adj.* knowing everything or much. □ **omniscience** *n.* [Latin *scio* know]

omnivorous /ɒmˈnɪvərəs/ *adj.* **1** feeding on both plant and animal material. **2** reading, observing, etc. everything that comes one's way. □ **omnivore** /ˈɒmnɪˌvɔː(r)/ *n.* **omnivorousness** *n.* [Latin *voro* devour]

OMR *abbr.* = OPTICAL MARK READING.

Omsk /ɒmsk/ city and river port in Russia, in central Siberia; industries include engineering and oil refining; pop. (est. 1995) 1 163 000.

ON *abbr.* Ontario.

on *–prep.* **1** (so as to be) supported by, attached to, covering, or enclosing (*sat on a chair; stuck on the wall; rings on her fingers; leaned on his elbow*). **2** carried with; about the person of (*have you a pen on you?*). **3** (of time) exactly at; during (*on 29 May; on the hour; on schedule; closed on Tuesday*). **4** immediately after or before (*I saw them on my return*). **5** as a result of (*on further examination*). **6** (so as to be) having membership etc. of or residence at or in (*is on the board of directors; lives on the continent*). **7** supported, succoured, or fuelled by (*lives on a grant; lives on sandwiches; runs on diesel*). **8** close to; just by (*house on the sea; lives on the main road*). **9** in the direction of; against. **10** so as to threaten; touching or striking (*advanced on Rome; pulled a knife on me; a punch on the nose*). **11** having as an axis or pivot (*turned on his heels*). **12** having as a basis or motive (*works on a ratchet; arrested on suspicion*). **13** having as a standard, confirmation, or guarantee (*had it on good authority; did it on purpose; I promise on my word*). **14** concerning or about (*writes on frogs*). **15** using or engaged with (*is on the pill; here on business*). **16** so as to affect (*walked out on her*). **17** at the expense of (*the drinks are on me; the joke is on him*). **18** added to (*disaster on disaster; ten pence on a pint of beer*). **19** in a specified manner or state (*on the cheap; on the run*). *–adv.* **1** (so as to be) covering or in contact (*put your boots on*). **2** in the appropriate direction; towards something (*look on*). **3** further forward; in an advanced position or state (*time is getting on*). **4** with continued movement or action (*play on*). **5** in operation or activity (*light is on; chase was on*). **6** due to take place as planned (*is the party still on?*). **7** *colloq.* **a** willing to participate or approve, make a bet, etc. (*you're on*). **b** practicable or acceptable (*that's just not on*). **8** being shown or performed (*a good film on tonight*). **9** on stage. **10** on duty. **11** forward (*head on*). *–adj. Cricket* designating the part of the field on the striker's side and in front of the wicket. *–n. Cricket* the on side. □ **be on about** *colloq.* discuss, esp. tediously. **be on at** *colloq.* nag or grumble at. **be on to** *colloq.* realize the significance or intentions of. **on and off** intermittently; now and then. **on and on** continually; at tedious length. **on time** punctual, punctually. **on to** to a position on. [Old English]

onanism /ˈəʊnəˌnɪz(ə)m/ *n. literary* masturbation. [*Onan*, biblical person]

ONC *abbr.* Ordinary National Certificate.

once /wʌns/ *–adv.* **1** on one occasion only. **2** at some point or period in the past. **3** ever or at all (*if you once forget it*). **4** multiplied by one. *–conj.* as soon as. *–n.* one time or occasion (*just the once*). □ **all at once 1** suddenly. **2** all together. **at once 1** immediately. **2** simultaneously. **for once** on this (or that) occasion, even if at no other. **once again** (or **more**) another time. **once and for all** (or **once for all**) in a final manner, esp. after much hesitation. **once** (or **every once) in a while** from time to time. **once or twice** a few times. **once upon a time** at some unspecified time in the past. [originally genitive of ONE]

once-over *n. colloq.* rapid inspection.

oncogene /ˈɒŋkəˌdʒiːn/ *n.* gene which can transform a cell into a cancer cell. [Greek *ogkos* mass]

oncology /ɒŋˈkɒlədʒɪ/ *n.* the study of tumours. [Greek *ogkos* mass]

oncoming *adj.* approaching from the front.

◆ **oncosts** *n.pl.* costs of a product or service over and above the direct costs; overhead costs.

OND *abbr.* Ordinary National Diploma.

one /wʌn/ *–adj.* **1** single and integral in number. **2** (with a noun implied) a single person or thing of the kind expressed or implied (*one of the best; a nasty one*). **3** particular but undefined, esp. as contrasted with another (*that is one view; one night last week*). **4** only such (*the one man who can do it*). **5** forming a unity (*one and undivided*). **6** identical; the same (*of one opinion*). *–n.* **1 a** lowest cardinal number. **b** thing numbered with it. **2** unity; a unit (*one is half of two; came in ones and twos*). **3** single thing, person, or example (often referring to a noun previously expressed or implied: *the big dog and the small one*). **4** *colloq.* drink (*a quick one; have one on me*). **5** story or joke (*the one about the parrot*). *–pron.* **1** person of a specified kind (*loved ones; like one possessed*). **2** any person, as representing people in general (*one is bound to lose in the end*). **3** I, me. □ **all one** (often foll. by *to*) a matter of indifference. **at one** in agreement. **one and all** everyone. **one by one** singly, successively. **one day 1** on an unspecified day. **2** at some unspecified future date. **one or two** *colloq.* a few. [Old English]

■ **Usage** The use of the pronoun *one* to mean 'I' or 'me' (e.g. *one would like to help*) is often regarded as an affectation.

one another *pron.* each the other or others (as a formula of reciprocity: *love one another*).

one-armed bandit *n. colloq.* fruit machine with a long handle.

one-horse *attrib. adj.* **1** using a single horse. **2** *colloq.* small, poorly equipped.

one-horse race *n.* contest in which one competitor is far superior to all the others.

one-liner *n.* short joke or remark in a play, comedy routine, etc.

one-man *attrib. adj.* involving or operated by only one man.

oneness *n.* **1** singleness. **2** uniqueness. **3** agreement. **4** sameness.

one-night stand *n.* **1** single performance of a play etc. in a place. **2** *colloq.* sexual liaison lasting only one night.

one-off *–attrib. adj.* made or done as the only one; not repeated. *–n.* one-off occurrence, achievement, etc.

onerous /ˈəʊnərəs/ *adj.* burdensome. □ **onerousness** *n.* [Latin: related to ONUS]

oneself *pron.* reflexive and emphatic form of *one* (*kill oneself; do it oneself*). □ **be oneself** act in one's normal unconstrained manner.

one-sided *adj.* unfair, partial. □ **one-sidedly** *adv.* **one-sidedness** *n.*

one's money's-worth *n.* good value for one's money.

one-time *attrib. adj.* former.

one-to-one *adj.* & *adv.* **1** involving or between only two people. **2** with one member of one group corresponding to one of another.

one-track mind *n.* mind preoccupied with one subject.

one-up *adj. colloq.* having a particular advantage. □ **one-upmanship** *n.*

one-way *adj.* allowing movement, travel, etc. in one direction only.

ongoing *adj.* **1** continuing. **2** in progress.

onion /ˈʌnjən/ *n.* vegetable with an edible bulb of a pungent smell and flavour. □ **oniony** *adj.* [Latin *unio -onis*]

on-line *Computing –adj.* directly connected, so that a computer immediately receives an input from or sends an output to a peripheral process etc.; carried out while so connected or under direct computer control. *–adv.* with the processing of data carried out simultaneously with its production; while connected to a computer; under direct computer control. Cf. OFF-LINE.

onlooker *n.* spectator. □ **onlooking** *adj.*

only /ˈəʊnlɪ/ *–adv.* **1** solely, merely, exclusively; and no one or nothing more besides (*needed six only; is only a child*). **2** no longer ago than (*saw them only yesterday*). **3** not until (*arrives only on Tuesday*). **4** with no better result than (*hurried home only to find her gone*). *–attrib. adj.* **1** existing alone of its or their kind (*their only son*). **2** best or alone worth considering (*the only place to eat*). *–conj. colloq.* except that; but (*I would go, only I feel ill*). [Old English: related to ONE]

■ **Usage** In informal English *only* is usu. placed between the subject and verb regardless of what it refers to (e.g. *I only want to talk to you*); in more formal English it is often placed more exactly, esp. to avoid ambiguity (e.g. *I want to talk only to you*). In speech, intonation usu. serves to clarify the sense.

only too *adv.* extremely.

o.n.o. *abbr.* or near offer.

onomatopoeia /ˌɒnəˌmætəˈpiːə/ *n.* formation of a word from a sound associated with what is named (e.g. *cuckoo, sizzle*). □ **onomatopoeic** *adj.* [Greek *onoma* name, *poieō* make]

onrush *n.* onward rush.

onscreen *adj.* & *adv.* within the range of a film camera etc; when being filmed.

onset *n.* **1** attack. **2** impetuous beginning.

onshore *adj.* **1** on the shore. **2** (of the wind) blowing landwards from the sea.

onside *adj.* (of a player in a field game) not offside.

onslaught /ˈɒnslɔːt/ *n.* fierce attack. [Dutch: related to ON, *slag* blow]

♦ **on-stream** *adj.* (of an investment or asset) bringing in the income expected of it.

---

on-street *adj.* (esp. of parking) along a street.

Ont. *abbr.* Ontario.

Ontario /ɒnˈteərɪˌəʊ/ province in SE Canada; pop. (est. 1995) 11 100 300; capital, Toronto. Nickel, coal, zinc, and iron are mined, and there are also important steel, pulp and paper, textile, motor-vehicle, and petrochemical industries; Ontario is the most agriculturally productive Canadian province.

onto *prep.* = *on to.*

■ **Usage** The form *onto* is still not fully accepted in the way that *into* is, although it is in wide use. It is however useful in distinguishing sense as between *we drove on to the beach* (i.e. in that direction) and *we drove onto the beach* (i.e. in contact with it).

ontology /ɒnˈtɒlədʒɪ/ *n.* branch of metaphysics dealing with the nature of being. □ **ontological** /-təˈlɒdʒɪk(ə)l/ *adj.* **ontologically** /-təˈlɒdʒɪkəlɪ/ *adv.* **ontologist** *n.* [Greek *ont-* being]

onus /ˈəʊnəs/ *n.* (*pl.* **onuses**) burden, duty, responsibility. [Latin]

onward /ˈɒnwəd/ *–adv.* (also **onwards**) **1** forward, advancing. **2** into the future (*from 1985 onwards*). *–adj.* forward, advancing.

onyx /ˈɒnɪks/ *n.* semiprecious variety of agate with coloured layers. [Greek *onnx*]

OO *international civil aircraft marking* Belgium.

o/o *abbr.* (also **o.o.**) on order.

OOD *abbr. Computing* object-oriented design.

oodles /ˈuːd(ə)lz/ *n.pl. colloq.* very great amount. [origin unknown]

ooh /uː/ *int.* expressing surprise, delight, pain, etc. [natural exclamation]

OOL *abbr.* object-oriented language. See OBJECT-ORIENTED PROGRAMMING.

oolite /ˈəʊəˌlaɪt/ *n.* granular limestone. □ **oolitic** /-ˈlɪtɪk/ *adj.* [Greek *ōion* egg]

oompah /ˈʊmpɑː/ *n. colloq.* rhythmical sound of deep brass instruments. [imitative]

oomph /ʊmf/ *n. slang* **1** energy, enthusiasm. **2** attractiveness, esp. sex appeal. [origin uncertain]

OOP *abbr.* = OBJECT-ORIENTED PROGRAMMING.

oops /ʊps/ *int. colloq.* on making an obvious mistake. [natural exclamation]

Oostende see OSTEND.

ooze[1] *–v.* (**-zing**) **1** trickle or leak slowly out. **2** (of a substance) exude fluid. **3** (often foll. by *with*) exude (a feeling) freely (*oozed (with) charm*). *–n.* sluggish flow. □ **oozy** *adj.* [Old English]

ooze[2] *n.* wet mud. □ **oozy** *adj.* [Old English]

OP *abbr. Insurance* open policy.

op *n. colloq.* operation. [abbreviation]

op. *abbr.* opus.

op- see OB-.

opacity /əʊˈpæsɪtɪ/ *n.* opaqueness. [Latin: related to OPAQUE]

opal /ˈəʊp(ə)l/ *n.* semiprecious stone usu. of a milky or bluish colour and sometimes showing changing colours. [Latin]

opalescent /ˌəʊpəˈles(ə)nt/ *adj.* iridescent. □ **opalescence** *n.*

opaline /ˈəʊpəˌlaɪn/ *adj.* opal-like, opalescent.

opaque /əʊˈpeɪk/ *adj.* (**opaquer, opaquest**) **1** not transmitting light. **2** impenetrable to sight. **3** unintelligible. **4** unintelligent, stupid. □ **opaquely** *adv.* **opaqueness** *n.* [Latin *opacus* shaded]

op art *n. colloq.* = OPTICAL ART. [abbreviation]

OPAS *abbr.* Occupational Pensions Advisory Service.

OPB *abbr.* Occupational Pensions Board.

op. cit. *abbr.* in the work already quoted. [Latin *opere citato*]

OPCS *abbr.* Office of Population Censuses and Surveys.

OPEC /ˈəʊpek/ *abbr.* = ORGANIZATION OF PETROLEUM EXPORTING COUNTRIES.

open /ˈəʊpən/ *–adj.* **1** not closed, locked, or blocked up;

allowing access. **2** unenclosed, unconfined, unobstructed (*the open road; open views*). **3 a** uncovered, bare, exposed (*open drain; open wound*). **b** (of a goal etc.) unprotected, undefended. **4** undisguised, public, manifest (*open hostilities*). **5** expanded, unfolded, or spread out (*had the map open on the table*). **6** (of a fabric) not close; with gaps. **7 a** frank and communicative. **b** open-minded. **8 a** accessible to visitors or customers; ready for business. **b** (of a meeting) admitting all, not restricted to members etc. **9** (of a race, competition, scholarship, etc.) unrestricted as to who may compete. **10** (foll. by *to*) **a** willing to receive (*is open to offers*). **b** (of a choice, offer, or opportunity) available (*three courses open to us*). **c** vulnerable to, allowing of (*open to abuse; open to doubt*). **11** (of a return ticket) not restricted as to the day of travel. *–v.* **1** make or become open or more open. **2** (foll. by *into, on to*, etc.) (of a door, room, etc.) give access as specified (*opened on to a patio*). **3 a** start, establish, or set going (a business, activity, etc.) (*opened a new shop; opened fire*). **b** start (*conference opens today*). **4** (often foll. by *with*) start; begin speaking, writing, etc. (*show opens with a song; he opened with a joke*). **5** ceremonially declare (a building etc.) in use. *–n.* **1** (prec. by *the*) **a** open space, country, or air. **b** public notice; general attention (esp. *into the open*). **2** open championship or competition etc. □ **open a person's eyes** enlighten a person. **open out 1** unfold. **2** develop, expand. **3** become communicative. **open up 1** unlock (premises). **2** make accessible. **3** reveal; bring to notice. **4** accelerate. **5** begin shooting or sounding. □ **openness** *n.* [Old English]

open air *n.* outdoors. □ **open-air** *attrib. adj.*

open-and-shut *adj.* straightforward.

open book *n.* person who is easily understood.

opencast *adj.* (of a mine or mining) with removal of the surface layers and working from above, not from shafts.

♦ **open charter** *n.* hire of a ship or aircraft enabling the charterer to use the vessel to carry any cargo to any port.

♦ **open cheque** see CHEQUE.

Open College *n.* college offering training and vocational courses mainly by correspondence.

♦ **open cover** *n.* (also **open policy**) marine cargo insurance policy in which the insurer agrees to cover any voyage undertaken by the policyholder's vessel(s) or any cargo shipped by a particular shipper. A policy condition requires a declaration to be completed on a weekly, monthly, or quarterly basis indicating the vessels involved, the commodities carried, and the voyages undertaken. Insurers use the declaration to calculate the premium. The main advantage of a policy of this kind is that the insurer can be confident that all cargos have insurance cover without the need to notify insurers of the details before the voyage. In some cases there may be a policy limit above which the insurance ceases. On such policies it is necessary to keep a running total of the sums insured to make sure that the policy limit is not exceeded.

♦ **open credit** *n.* **1** unlimited credit offered by a supplier to a trusted client. **2** arrangement between a bank and a customer enabling the customer to cash cheques up to a specified amount at a bank or branches other than his or her own. This practice is less used since credit cards and cashcards were introduced.

open day *n.* day when the public may visit a place normally closed to them.

open-door *attrib. adj.* open, accessible.

♦ **open-door policy** *n.* import policy of a country in which all goods from all sources are imported on the same terms, usu. free of import duties.

♦ **open economy** *n.* economy in which a significant percentage of goods and services are traded internationally. The degree of openness of an economy usu. depends on the amount of overseas trade in which the country is involved or the political policies of its government. Thus the UK economy is relatively open, as the economy is significantly dependent on foreign trade; the US economy is relatively closed as overseas trade is not very important to its economy.

open-ended *adj.* having no predetermined limit.

♦ **open-ended question** *n.* question used in marketing research that has to be answered in the respondent's own words rather than by 'yes', 'no', or 'don't know'.

♦ **open-end trust** *n.* esp. *US* unit trust in which the managers of the trust may vary the investments held without notifying the unit holders.

opener *n.* **1** device for opening tins, bottles, etc. **2** *colloq.* first item on a programme etc.

♦ **open general licence** *n.* import licence for goods on which there are no import restrictions.

open-handed *adj.* generous.

open-hearted *adj.* frank and kindly.

open-heart surgery *n.* surgery with the heart exposed and the blood made to bypass it.

open house *n.* hospitality for all visitors.

♦ **open indent** *n.* order to an overseas purchasing agent to buy certain goods, without specifying the manufacturer. If the manufacturer is specified this is a **closed indent**.

opening *–n.* **1** aperture or gap. **2** opportunity. **3** beginning; initial part. *–attrib. adj.* initial, first (*opening remarks*).

♦ **opening prices** *n.pl.* bid prices and offer prices made at the opening of a day's trading on any security or commodity market. They may not always be identical to the previous evening's closing prices, esp. if any significant events have taken place during the intervening period.

opening-time *n.* time at which public houses may legally open for custom.

open letter *n.* letter of protest etc. addressed to an individual and published in a newspaper etc.

openly *adv.* **1** frankly. **2** publicly.

open market *n.* unrestricted market in which prices are determined by supply and demand; free market.

♦ **open-market operations** *n.pl.* purchase and sale by a government of bonds (gilt-edged securities) in exchange for money. This is the main mechanism by which monetary policy in developed economies operates. To buy (or sell) more bonds the government must raise (or lower) their price and hence reduce (or increase) interest rates. In Keynesian theory, lower interest rates will stimulate investment and so raise national output. However, in such theories as those of new classical macroeconomics, this will only have the effect of raising the level of prices (i.e. fuelling inflation).

open-minded *adj.* accessible to new ideas; unprejudiced.

open-mouthed *adj.* aghast with surprise.

♦ **open outcry** *n.* = CALL-OVER.

open-plan *adj.* (of a house, office, etc.) having large undivided rooms.

♦ **open policy** *n.* = OPEN COVER.

♦ **open position** *n.* trading position in which a dealer has commodities, securities, or currencies bought but unsold or unhedged (see HEDGE *v.* 4), or sales that are neither covered nor hedged. In the former position the dealer has a **bull position** and in the latter, a **bear position**. In either case the dealer is vulnerable to market fluctuations until the position is closed or hedged. See also OPTION 3.

♦ **open-pricing agreement** *n.* agreement between firms operating in an oligopolistic market in which prices and intended price changes are circulated to those taking part in the agreement in order to avoid a price war.

open prison *n.* prison with few restraints on prisoners' movements.

open question *n.* matter on which different views are legitimate.

open sandwich *n.* sandwich without a top slice of bread.

open sea *n.* expanse of sea away from land.

open secret *n.* supposed secret known to many.

♦ **open shop** see CLOSED SHOP.

open society *n.* society with freedom of belief.

open system *n. Computing* system in which components conform to non-proprietary standards rather than to standards laid down by a specific producer of hardware or software. There is an international effort to achieve **open systems interconnection** (**OSI**) between computer and data communication systems without regard to manufacturer or the proprietary standards to which the equipment conforms.

Open University *n.* university teaching mainly by broadcasting and correspondence, and open to those without academic qualifications.

open verdict *n.* verdict affirming that a crime has been committed but not specifying the criminal or (in case of violent death) the cause.

openwork *n.* pattern with intervening spaces in metal, leather, lace, etc.

opera[1] /'ɒpərə/ *n.* **1 a** drama set to music for singers and instrumentalists. **b** this as a genre. **2** opera-house. [Latin, = labour, work]

opera[2] *pl.* of OPUS.

operable /'ɒpərəb(ə)l/ *adj.* **1** that can be operated. **2** suitable for treatment by surgical operation. [Latin: related to OPERATE]

opera-glasses *n.pl.* small binoculars for use at the opera or theatre.

opera-house *n.* theatre for operas.

operand /'ɒpə,rænd/ *n.* quantity or function upon which an arithmetic or logic operation is performed.

operate /'ɒpə,reɪt/ *v.* (**-ting**) **1** work, control. **2** be in action; function. **3 a** perform a surgical operation. **b** conduct a military etc. action. **c** be active in business etc. **4** bring about. [Latin *operor* work: related to OPUS]

operatic /,ɒpə'rætɪk/ *adj.* of or like an opera or opera singer (*an operatic voice*). □ **operatically** *adv.*

operatics /,ɒpə'rætɪks/ *n.pl.* production and performance of operas.

♦ **operating budget** *n.* forecast of the financial requirements for the future trading of an organization, including its planned sales, production, cash flow, etc. An operating budget is normally designed for a fixed period, usu. one year, and forms the plan for that period's trading activities. Any divergences from it are usu. monitored and, if appropriate, changes can then be made to it as the period progresses.

♦ **operating costs** *n.pl.* = OVERHEAD COSTS.

♦ **operating profit (**or **loss)** *n.* profit (or loss) made by a company as a result of its principal trading activity. This is arrived at by deducting its **operating expenses** from its trading profit, or adding its operating expenses to its trading loss; in either case this is before taking into account any extraordinary items.

♦ **operating system** *n.* collection of programs that controls the basic operation of a computer, including such tasks as start-up routines, input and output, and memory allocation. It is also responsible for loading and executing programs. In small systems, the operating system loads a program and then gives it control of the machine. In larger multi-tasking systems, the operating system always retains control of the machine, ensuring that the separate programs do not interfere with each other and controlling the amount of processing time each receives. See also CP/M; MS-DOS.

operating theatre *n.* room for surgical operations.

operation /,ɒpə'reɪʃ(ə)n/ *n.* **1** action, scope, or method of working or operating. **2** active process. **3** piece of work, esp. one in a series (*begin operations*). **4** act of surgery on a patient. **5** military manoeuvre. **6** financial transaction. **7** state of functioning (*in operation*). **8** subjection of a number etc. to a process affecting its value or form, e.g. multiplication. [Latin: related to OPERATE]

operational *adj.* **1** of or engaged in or used for operations. **2** able or ready to function. □ **operationally** *adv.*

♦ **operational research** *n.* (also **operations research**, **OR**) application of scientific principles to industrial and commercial problems in order to arrive at the most efficient and economic method of achieving the desired objective. It basically consists of making a clear statement of the problem, designing a model to represent the possible solutions using different strategies, and applying the solutions obtained from the analysis of the model to the real problem. It makes use of game theory, critical-path analysis, simulation techniques, etc.

♦ **operation job card** *n.* card or form on which an employee writes up the details of a particular task and the length of time it took to complete. It is used in work studies.

operations research *n.* = OPERATIONAL RESEARCH.

operative /'ɒpərətɪv/ *–adj.* **1** in operation; having effect. **2** having the main relevance (*'may' is the operative word*). **3** of or by surgery. *–n.* worker, esp. a skilled one. [Latin: related to OPERATE]

operator *n.* **1** person operating a machine etc., esp. connecting lines in a telephone exchange. **2** person engaging in business. **3** *colloq.* person acting in a specified way (*smooth operator*). **4** symbol or function denoting an operation in mathematics, computing, etc.

operculum /ə'pɜːkjʊləm/ *n.* (*pl.* **-cula**) **1** fish's gill-cover. **2** any of various other parts covering or closing an aperture in an animal or plant. [Latin *operio* cover (v.)]

operetta /,ɒpə'retə/ *n.* **1** light opera. **2** one-act or short opera. [Italian, diminutive of OPERA[1]]

ophidian /əʊ'fɪdɪən/ *–n.* member of a suborder of reptiles including snakes. *–adj.* **1** of this order. **2** snakelike. [Greek *ophis* snake]

ophthalmia /ɒf'θælmɪə/ *n.* inflammation of the eye. [Greek *ophthalmos* eye]

ophthalmic /ɒf'θælmɪk/ *adj.* of or relating to the eye and its diseases.

ophthalmic optician *n.* optician qualified to prescribe as well as dispense spectacles etc.

ophthalmology /,ɒfθæl'mɒlədʒɪ/ *n.* the study of the eye. □ **ophthalmologist** *n.*

ophthalmoscope /ɒf'θælmə,skəʊp/ *n.* instrument for examining the eye.

opiate /'əʊpɪət/ *–adj.* **1** containing opium. **2** narcotic, soporific. *–n.* **1** drug containing opium, usu. to ease pain or induce sleep. **2** soothing influence. [Latin: related to OPIUM]

opine /əʊ'paɪn/ *v.* (**-ning**) (often foll. by *that*) *literary* hold or express as an opinion. [Latin *opinor* believe]

opinion /ə'pɪnjən/ *n.* **1** unproven belief. **2** view held as probable. **3** what one thinks about something. **4** piece of professional advice (*a second opinion*). **5** estimation (*low opinion of*). [Latin: related to OPINE]

opinionated /ə'pɪnjə,neɪtɪd/ *adj.* dogmatic in one's opinions.

opinion poll *n.* assessment of public opinion by questioning a representative sample.

opium /'əʊpɪəm/ *n.* drug made from the juice of a certain poppy, used esp. as an analgesic and narcotic. [Latin from Greek *opion*]

OPM *abbr.* **1** (in the US) Office of Personnel Management. **2** output per man.

Oporto /əʊ'pɔːtəʊ/ (Portuguese **Porto**) port and principal city of N Portugal; port wine is the chief export; pop. (1991) 309 485.

opossum /ə'pɒsəm/ *n.* **1** tree-living American marsupial. **2** *Austral.* & *NZ* = POSSUM 2. [Virginian Indian]

opp. *abbr.* opposite.

◆ **Oppenheimer** /'ɒpən,haɪmə(r)/, **Harry Frederick** (1908–) South African industrialist, chairman (1957–82) of the Anglo-American Coporation of South Africa and chairman (1957–84) and a director (1934–94) of De Beers Consolidated Mines, he made his fortune from gold, mineral, and diamond extraction. His son, **Nicholas Frank Oppenheimer** (1945–), succeeded him as chairman (1984–85) of De Beers and is now deputy chairman of both De Beers and Anglo-American.

opponent /ə'pəʊnənt/ *n.* person who opposes. [Latin *oppono opposit-* set against]

opportune /'ɒpə,tjuːn/ *adj.* **1** well-chosen or esp. favourable (*opportune moment*). **2** (of an action or event) well-timed. [Latin *opportunus* (of the wind) driving towards the PORT[1]]

opportunism /,ɒpə'tjuːnɪz(ə)m, 'ɒp-/ *n.* adaptation of one's policy or judgement to circumstances or opportunity, esp. regardless of principle. □ **opportunist** *n.* **opportunistic** /-'nɪstɪk/ *adj.* **opportunistically** /-'nɪstɪkəlɪ/ *adv.*

◆ **opportunities to see** *n.pl.* (also **OTS**) number of times a member of the public (or an audience) may, on average, be expected to see a particular advertisement.

opportunity /,ɒpə'tjuːnɪtɪ/ *n.* (*pl.* **-ies**) favourable chance or opening offered by circumstances.

◆ **opportunity cost** *n.* benefit lost by not employing an economic resource in the most profitable alternative activity. For example, the opportunity cost to a self-employed person is the highest salary he or she could earn elsewhere. Economists use the concept of opportunity cost to decide whether or not the allocation of resources is efficient. In the example above, if efficiency is judged by income alone, self-employment is efficient only if the income earned exceeds the best alternative salary, i.e. the opportunity cost. Opportunity cost is a much broader concept than accounting cost, and therefore the former is generally preferred when weighing up the costs and benefits of investment decisions (see also COST-BENEFIT ANALYSIS). For example, in a situation in which investment in competing and mutually exclusive projects is being considered, the opportunity cost of selecting one project is the revenue obtainable from the next best option.

opposable /ə'pəʊzəb(ə)l/ *adj. Zool.* (of the thumb in primates) capable of facing and touching the other digits on the same hand.

oppose /ə'pəʊz/ *v.* (**-sing**) **1** set oneself against; resist; argue or compete against. **2** (foll. by *to*) place in opposition or contrast. □ **as opposed to** in contrast with. □ **opposer** *n.* [Latin: related to OPPONENT]

opposite /'ɒpəzɪt/ *–adj.* **1** facing, on the other side (*opposite page*; *the house opposite*). **2** (often foll. by *to*, *from*) contrary; diametrically different (*opposite opinion*). *–n.* opposite thing, person, or term. *–adv.* facing, on the other side (*lives opposite*). *–prep.* **1** facing (*sat opposite me*). **2** in a complementary role to (another actor etc.).

opposite number *n.* person holding an equivalent position in another group etc.

opposite sex *n.* (prec. by *the*) either sex in relation to the other.

opposition /,ɒpə'zɪʃ(ə)n/ *n.* **1** resistance, antagonism. **2** being hostile or in conflict or disagreement. **3** contrast, antithesis. **4 a** group or party of opponents or competitors. **b** (**the Opposition**) chief parliamentary party opposed to that in office. **5** act of placing opposite. **6** diametrically opposite position of two celestial bodies. [Latin: related to POSITION]

oppress /ə'pres/ *v.* **1** keep in subservience. **2** govern or treat cruelly. **3** weigh down (with cares or unhappiness). □ **oppression** *n.* **oppressor** *n.* [Latin: related to PRESS[1]]

oppressive *adj.* **1** oppressing. **2** (of weather) close and sultry. □ **oppressively** *adv.* **oppressiveness** *n.*

opprobrious /ə'prəʊbrɪəs/ *adj.* (of language) very scornful; abusive.

opprobrium /ə'prəʊbrɪəm/ *n.* **1** disgrace. **2** cause of this. [Latin, = infamy, reproach]

oppugn /ə'pjuːn/ *v. literary* controvert, call in question. [Latin *oppugno* fight against]

OPQ *abbr.* occupational personality questionnaire.

opt *v.* (usu. foll. by *for*) make a choice, decide. □ **opt out** (often foll. by *of*) choose not to participate (in). [Latin *opto* choose, wish]

optative /'ɒptətɪv, ɒp'teɪtɪv/ *Gram. –adj.* (esp. of a mood in Greek) expressing a wish. *–n.* optative mood or form. [Latin: related to OPT]

optic /'ɒptɪk/ *adj.* of the eye or sight (*optic nerve*). [Greek *optos* seen]

optical *adj.* **1** of sight; visual. **2** of or according to optics. **3** aiding sight. □ **optically** *adv.*

optical art *n.* art using contrasting colours to create the illusion of movement.

◆ **optical character recognition** *n.* (also **OCR**) recognition of printed characters by light-sensitive optical scanners. The scanner recognizes the shape of a letter by scanning it with a very fine point of light. It then uses a computer to compare the pattern of reflected light with the patterns of the letters of the alphabet stored in its memory. Easily recognizable characters are usu. necessary but some scanners will read typewritten characters. OCR is used by banks to read the information printed on cheques.

optical disk *n. Computing* storage device in the form of a disk covered with a special layer on which data or images can be stored and retrieved by optical means. It is a type of laser disk and its storage capacity can be extremely high. There are three broad classes: **read-only** disks, to which information is added at the time of manufacture and cannot subsequently be changed; **write-once** disks, where information is added by the customer but once written cannot be erased; **erasable** disks, where recorded data or images can be erased and rewritten. The information is retrieved from an optical disk (and in some cases written to it) by an **optical disk drive**, which is similar in operation to a magnetic disk drive.

optical fibre *n.* thin glass fibre through which light can be transmitted to carry signals.

optical illusion *n.* **1** image which deceives the eye. **2** mental misapprehension caused by this.

optical mark reading *n.* (also **OMR**) process of data entry to a computer in which an optical device detects marks made by a person in a choice of positions indicated on a document.

optician /ɒp'tɪʃ(ə)n/ *n.* **1** maker, seller, or prescriber of spectacles and contact lenses etc. **2** person trained in the detection and correction of poor eyesight. [medieval Latin: related to OPTIC]

optics *n.pl.* (treated as *sing.*) science of light and vision.

optimal /'ɒptɪm(ə)l/ *adj.* best or most favourable. [Latin *optimus* best]

optimism /'ɒptɪ,mɪz(ə)m/ *n.* **1** inclination to hopefulness and confidence. **2** *Philos.* belief that this world is as good as it could be or that good must ultimately prevail over evil. □ **optimist** *n.* **optimistic** /-'mɪstɪk/ *adj.* **optimistically** /-'mɪstɪkəlɪ/ *adv.* [Latin *optimus* best]

optimize /'ɒptɪ,maɪz/ *v.* (also **-ise**) (**-zing** or **-sing**) make the best or most effective use of. □ **optimization** /-'zeɪʃ(ə)n/ *n.*

optimum /'ɒptɪməm/ *–n.* (*pl.* **optima**) **1** most favourable conditions (for growth etc.). **2** best practical solution. *–adj.* = OPTIMAL. [Latin, neuter of *optimus* best]

◆ **optimum population** *n.* population of an economic community in which the income per head is a maximum, i.e. in which there are sufficient people to provide an adequate labour force but not so many that there is high unemployment.

---

option /ˈɒpʃ(ə)n/ *n.* **1 a** choosing; choice. **b** thing that is or may be chosen. **2** liberty to choose. **3** right to buy or sell a fixed quantity of a commodity, currency, or security at a particular date at a particular price (the exercise price). The purchaser of an option is not obliged to buy or sell at the exercise price and will only do so if it is profitable (cf. FUTURES CONTRACT); the purchaser may allow the option to lapse, in which case only the initial purchase price of the option (the option money) is lost. In London, options in commodity futures are bought and sold on London FOX, and options on share indexes, foreign currencies, and interest rates are dealt with through the London International Financial Futures and Options Exchange (LIFFE). An option to buy is known as a **call option** and is usu. purchased in the expectation of a rising price; an option to sell is called a **put option** and is bought in the expectation of a falling price or to protect a profit on an investment. Options, like futures, allow individuals and firms to hedge against the risk of wide fluctuations in prices; they also allow speculators to gamble for large profits with limited liability. Professional traders in options make use of a large range of potential strategies, often purchasing combinations of options that reflect particular expectations or cover several contingencies (see BUTTERFLY 3; STRADDLE *n.*). **Traded options** can be bought and sold on an exchange at all times, i.e. there is a trade in the options themselves. **Traditional options**, however, once purchased, cannot be resold. Traditional options in equities are dealt in on the London Stock Exchange, but traded options in equities are now dealt in on LIFFE. In a **European option** the buyer can only exercise the right to take up the option or let it lapse on the expiry date, whereas with an **American option** this right can be exercised at any time up to the expiry date. European options are therefore cheaper than American options. See also EXERCISE NOTICE; EXPIRY DATE 2; HEDGE *v.* 4; INTRINSIC VALUE 2; OPTION TO DOUBLE; TIME VALUE. □ **keep** (or **leave**) **one's options open** not commit oneself. [Latin: related to OPT]

optional *adj.* not obligatory. □ **optionally** *adv.*

optional extra *n.* item costing extra if one chooses to have it.

♦ **option dealer** *n.* dealer who buys and sells either traded options or traditional options on a stock exchange, commodity exchange, or currency exchange. See OPTION 3.

♦ **option money** *n.* price paid for an option. The cost of a call option is often known as the **call money** and that for a put option as the **put money** (see OPTION 3).

♦ **option to double** *n.* **1** option by a seller to sell double the quantity of securities for which he or she has sold an option, if so desired. In some markets this is called a **put-of-more option**. **2** option by a buyer to buy double the quantity of securities for which he or she has bought an option, if so desired. In some markets this is called a **call-of-more option**.

♦ **option to purchase** *n.* **1** right given to shareholders to buy shares in certain companies in certain circumstances at a reduced price. **2** right purchased or given to a person to buy something at a specified price on or before a specified date. Until the specified date has passed, the seller undertakes not to sell the property to anyone else and not to withdraw it from sale.

---

opulent /ˈɒpjʊlənt/ *adj.* **1** wealthy. **2** luxurious. **3** abundant. □ **opulence** *n.* [Latin *opes* wealth]

opus /ˈəʊpəs/ *n.* (*pl.* **opuses** or **opera** /ˈɒpərə/) **1** musical composition numbered as one of a composer's works (*Beethoven, opus 15*). **2** any artistic work (cf. MAGNUM OPUS). [Latin, = work]

OR *–abbr.* **1** official receiver. **2** operational (or operations) requirement. **3** = OPERATIONAL RESEARCH. **4** *Insurance* owner's risk. *–US postcode* Oregon.

or[1] *conj.* **1** introducing an alternative (*white or black*; *take it or leave it*; *whether or not*). **2** introducing an alternative name (*the lapwing or peewit*). **3** introducing an afterthought (*came in laughing – or was it crying?*). **4** = *or else* 1 (*run or you'll be late*). □ **or else 1** otherwise (*run, or else you will be late*). **2** *colloq.* expressing a warning or threat (*be good or else*). [Old English]

or[2] *n. Heraldry* gold. [Latin *aurum* gold]

-or *suffix* forming nouns denoting esp. an agent (*actor*; *escalator*) or condition (*error*; *horror*). [Latin]

oracle /ˈɒrək(ə)l/ *n.* **1 a** place at which divine advice or prophecy was sought in classical antiquity. **b** response given. **c** prophet or prophetess at an oracle. **2** person or thing regarded as a source of wisdom etc. □ **oracular** /ɒˈrækjʊlə(r)/ *adj.* [Latin *oraculum* from *oro* speak]

Oradea /ɒˈrɑːdɪə/ industrial city in W Romania; products include machine tools and chemicals; pop. (est. 1993) 221 559.

oral /ˈɔːr(ə)l/ *–adj.* **1** by word of mouth; spoken; not written (*oral examination*). **2** done or taken by the mouth (*oral sex*; *oral contraceptive*). *–n. colloq.* spoken examination. □ **orally** *adv.* [Latin *os oris* mouth]

Oran /ɔːˈrɑːn/ (Arabic **Wahran** /wɑːˈrɑːn/) seaport in Algeria, on the Mediterranean coast; cereals, wine, and wool are exported; pop. (1987) 609 823.

orange /ˈɒrɪndʒ/ *–n.* **1 a** roundish reddish-yellow juicy citrus fruit. **b** tree bearing this. **2** its colour. *–adj.* orange-coloured. [Arabic *nāranj*]

orangeade /ˌɒrɪndʒˈeɪd/ *n.* orange-flavoured, usu. fizzy, drink.

Orange Free State /ˈɒrɪndʒ/ former inland province of the Republic of South Africa. In 1994, as part of the administrative reorganization of South Africa, it became Free State; pop. (est. 1995) 2 782 000; capital, Bloemfontein. Mainly agricultural, it produces wheat, maize, and livestock; there is also some mining of diamonds, uranium, gold, and coal.

Orangeman *n.* member of a political society formed in 1795 to support Protestantism in Ireland. [William of *Orange*]

orangery /ˈɒrɪndʒərɪ/ *n.* (*pl.* **-ies**) place, esp. a building, where orange-trees are cultivated.

orang-utan /ɔːˌræŋuːˈtæn/ *n.* (also **orang-outang** /-uːˈtæŋ/) large reddish-haired long-armed anthropoid ape of the East Indies. [Malay, = wild man]

Oranjestad /ɒˈrænjəˌstɑːt/ capital of the island of Aruba in the West Indies; pop. (1991) 20 046.

oration /ɔːˈreɪʃ(ə)n/ *n.* formal or ceremonial speech. [Latin *oratio* discourse, prayer, from *oro* speak, pray]

orator /ˈɒrətə(r)/ *n.* **1** person making a formal speech. **2** eloquent public speaker. [Latin: related to ORATION]

oratorio /ˌɒrəˈtɔːrɪəʊ/ *n.* (*pl.* **-s**) semi-dramatic work for orchestra and voices esp. on a sacred theme. [Church Latin]

oratory /ˈɒrətərɪ/ *n.* (*pl.* **-ies**) **1** art of or skill in public speaking. **2** small private chapel. □ **oratorical** /-ˈtɒrɪk(ə)l/ *adj.* [French and Latin *oro* speak, pray]

orb *n.* **1** globe surmounted by a cross as part of coronation regalia. **2** sphere, globe. **3** *poet.* celestial body. **4** *poet.* eye. [Latin *orbis* ring]

orbicular /ɔːˈbɪkjʊlə(r)/ *adj. formal* circular or spherical. [Latin *orbiculus* diminutive of *orbis* ring]

orbit /ˈɔːbɪt/ *–n.* **1 a** curved course of a planet, satellite, etc. **b** one complete passage around a body. **2** range or sphere of action. **3** eye socket. *–v.* (**-t-**) **1** move in orbit round. **2** put into orbit. □ **orbiter** *n.* [Latin *orbitus* circular]

orbital *adj.* **1** of an orbit or orbits. **2** (of a road) passing round the outside of a town.

orca /ˈɔːkə/ *n.* any of various cetaceans, esp. the killer whale. [Latin]

Orcadian /ɔːˈkeɪdɪən/ *–adj.* of the Orkney Islands. *–n.* native of the Orkney Islands. [Latin *Orcades* ORKNEY ISLANDS]

orch. *abbr.* **1** orchestrated by. **2** orchestra.

orchard /ˈɔːtʃəd/ *n.* piece of enclosed land with fruit-trees. [Latin *hortus* garden]

orchestra /ˈɔːkɪstrə/ *n.* **1** large group of instrumentalists combining strings, woodwinds, brass, and percussion. **2** (in full **orchestra pit**) part of a theatre etc. where the orchestra plays, usu. in front of the stage and on a lower level. □ **orchestral** /-ˈkestr(ə)l/ *adj.* [Greek, = area for the chorus in drama]

orchestrate /ˈɔːkɪˌstreɪt/ *v.* (**-ting**) **1** arrange or compose for orchestral performance. **2** arrange (elements) to achieve a desired result. □ **orchestration** /-ˈstreɪʃ(ə)n/ *n.*

orchid /ˈɔːkɪd/ *n.* any of various plants with brilliant flowers. [Greek *orkhis*, originally = testicle]

ordain /ɔːˈdeɪn/ *v.* **1** confer holy orders on. **2** decree, order. [Latin *ordino*: related to ORDER]

ordeal /ɔːˈdiːl/ *n.* **1** painful or horrific experience; severe trial. **2** *hist.* test of an accused person by subjection to severe pain, with survival taken as proof of innocence. [Old English]

order –*n.* **1 a** condition in which every part, unit, etc. is in its right place; tidiness. **b** specified sequence, succession, etc. (*alphabetical order; the order of events*). **2** authoritative command, direction, instruction, etc. **3** state of obedience to law, authority, etc. **4 a** direction to supply or pay something. **b** goods etc. to be supplied. **5** social class; its members (*the lower orders*). **6** kind; sort (*talents of a high order*). **7** constitution or nature of the world, society, etc. (*the moral order; the order of things*). **8** taxonomic rank below a class and above a family. **9** religious fraternity with a common rule of life. **10** grade of the Christian ministry. **11** any of the five classical styles of architecture (*Doric order*). **12 a** company of persons distinguished by a particular honour (*Order of the Garter*). **b** insignia worn by its members. **13** *Eccl.* the stated form of divine service (*the order of confirmation*). **14** system of rules or procedure (at meetings etc.) (*point of order*). –*v.* **1** command; bid; prescribe. **2** command or direct (a person) to a specified destination (*ordered them home*). **3** direct a waiter, tradesman, etc. to supply (*ordered dinner; ordered a new suit*). **4** (often as **ordered** *adj.*) put in order; regulate (*an ordered life*). **5** (of God, fate, etc.) ordain. □ **in** (or **out of**) **order 1** in the correct (or incorrect) sequence or position. **2** fit (or not fit) for use. **3** according (or not according) to the rules at a meeting etc. **in order that** with the intention; so that. **in order to** with the purpose of doing; with a view to **of** (or **in**) **the order of** approximately. **on order** ordered but not yet received. **order about** command officiously. **to order** as specified by the customer. [Latin *ordo ordin-* row, command, etc.]

♦ **order cheque** see CHEQUE.

♦ **order-driven** *adj.* denoting an electronic market system, esp. for a stock exchange (see SETS), in which prices are determined by the publication of orders to buy or sell. Cf. QUOTE-DRIVEN.

Order in Council *n.* executive order, often approved by Parliament but not debated.

orderly –*adj.* **1** methodically arranged or inclined, tidy. **2** well-behaved. –*n.* (*pl.* **-ies**) **1** male cleaner in a hospital. **2** soldier who carries orders for an officer etc. □ **orderliness** *n.*

orderly room *n.* room in a barracks used for company business.

♦ **order of business** *n.* sequence of the items on the agenda of a business meeting. It is usual to adopt the following order: apologies for absence; reading and signing of the minutes of the last meeting; matters arising from these minutes; new correspondence received; reading and adoption of reports, accounts, etc.; election of officers and auditors; any special motions; any other business; date of next meeting. See also ANNUAL GENERAL MEETING; EXTRAORDINARY GENERAL MEETING.

---

order of the day *n.* **1** prevailing state of things. **2** principal action, procedure, or programme.

order-paper *n.* written or printed order of the day's proceedings, esp. in Parliament.

ordinal /ˈɔːdɪn(ə)l/ *n.* (in full **ordinal number**) number defining position in a series, e.g. 'first', 'second', 'third', etc. [Latin: related to ORDER]

ordinance /ˈɔːdɪnəns/ *n.* **1** decree. **2** religious rite. [Latin: related to ORDAIN]

ordinand /ˈɔːdɪnənd/ *n.* candidate for ordination. [Latin: related to ORDAIN]

ordinary /ˈɔːdɪnərɪ/ –*adj.* **1** normal, usual. **2** commonplace, unexceptional. –*n.* (*pl.* **-ies**) *RC Ch.* **1** parts of a service that do not vary from day to day. **2** rule or book laying down the order of service. □ **in the ordinary way** in normal circumstances. **out of the ordinary** unusual. □ **ordinarily** *adv.* **ordinariness** *n.* [Latin: related to ORDER]

ordinary level *n. hist.* lowest level of the GCE examination.

♦ **ordinary resolution** see RESOLUTION 3.

---

ordinary seaman *n.* sailor of the lowest rank.

♦ **ordinary share** *n.* fixed unit of the share capital of a company. Shares in publicly owned quoted companies are usu. traded on stock exchanges and represent one of the most important types of security for investors. Shares yield dividends, representing a proportion of the profits of a company (cf. FIXED-INTEREST SECURITY; PREFERENCE SHARE). In the long term, ordinary shares, by means of capital growth, yield higher rewards, on average, than most alternative forms of securities, which compensates for the greater element of risk they entail. See also CONVERTIBLE *n.* 2; GROWTH STOCK.

---

ordinate /ˈɔːdɪnət/ *n. Math.* coordinate measured usu. vertically. [Latin: related to ORDAIN]

ordination /ˌɔːdɪˈneɪʃ(ə)n/ *n.* conferring of holy orders, ordaining.

ordnance /ˈɔːdnəns/ *n.* **1** artillery; military supplies. **2** government service dealing with these. [contraction of ORDINANCE]

Ordnance Survey *n.* official survey of the UK producing detailed maps.

Ordovician /ˌɔːdəˈvɪʃɪən/ –*adj.* of the second period in the Palaeozoic era. –*n.* this period. [Latin *Ordovices*, an ancient British tribe in N Wales]

ordure /ˈɔːdjʊə(r)/ *n.* dung. [Latin *horridus*: related to HORRID]

Ore. *abbr.* (also **Oreg.**) Oregon.

ore /ɔː(r)/ *n.* solid rock or mineral from which metal or other valuable minerals may be extracted. [Old English]

Örebro /ˈɜːrəˌbruː/ industrial city in S central Sweden; machinery, chemicals, and footwear are produced; pop. (est. 1996) 119 635.

oregano /ˌɒrɪˈgɑːnəʊ/ *n.* dried wild marjoram as seasoning. [Spanish, = ORIGAN]

Oregon /ˈɒrɪgən/ state in the US, on the Pacific coast; pop. (est. 1996) 3 203 735; capital, Salem. Forestry and agriculture are the main sources of revenue; there are also metal-processing industries.

♦ **O'Reilly** /ˌəʊˈraɪlɪ/, **Anthony John Francis** (1936–) Irish businessman, president (1979–96), chief executive officer (from 1979), and chairman (from 1987) of the food giant H. J. Heinz, in which he holds a 1.6% share. He is also chairman of Independent Newspapers (from 1980), which dominates the Irish and South African newspaper markets, and of the Irish crystal- and china maker Waterford Wedgwood (from 1993). His net worth was $1.2 billion in 1997.

Orenburg /ˈɒrənˌbɜːg/ city in W Russia; it has engineering industries and also manufactures consumer goods; pop. (est. 1995) 532 000.

Øresund /ˈɜːrəˌsʊnd/ (English **the Sound**) narrow channel between Sweden and the Danish island of Zealand.

organ /ˈɔːgən/ *n.* **1 a** musical instrument having pipes supplied with air from bellows and operated by keyboards and pedals. **b** instrument producing similar sounds electronically. **c** harmonium. **2 a** part of an animal or plant body serving a particular function (*vocal organs*; *digestive organs*). **b** esp. *joc.* penis. **3** medium of communication, esp. a newspaper representing a party or interest. [Greek *organon* tool]

organdie /ˈɔːgəndɪ/ *n.* fine translucent muslin, usu. stiffened. [French]

organ-grinder *n.* player of a barrel-organ.

organic /ɔːˈgænɪk/ *adj.* **1** of or affecting a bodily organ or organs. **2** (of a plant or animal) having organs or an organized physical structure. **3** produced without the use of artificial fertilizers, pesticides, etc. **4** (of a chemical compound etc.) containing carbon. **5 a** structural, inherent. **b** constitutional. **6** organized or systematic (*an organic whole*). □ **organically** *adv.* [Greek: related to ORGAN]

organic chemistry *n.* chemistry of carbon compounds.

organism /ˈɔːgəˌnɪz(ə)m/ *n.* **1** individual plant or animal. **2** living being with interdependent parts. **3** system made up of interdependent parts. [French: related to ORGANIZE]

organist /ˈɔːgənɪst/ *n.* organ-player.

organization /ˌɔːgənaɪˈzeɪʃ(ə)n/ *n.* (also **-isation**) **1** organizing or being organized. **2** organized body, system, or society. □ **organizational** *adj.*

♦ **organizational buying** *n.* way in which an organization (as opposed to an individual consumer) identifies, evaluates, and chooses the products it buys. See DECISION-MAKING UNIT.

♦ **organization and methods** *n.pl.* (usu. treated as *sing.*) (also **O. & M.**) form of work study involving the organization of procedures and controls in a business and the methods of implementing them in management terms. It is usu. applied to office procedures rather than factory production.

♦ **Organization for Economic Cooperation and Development** *n.* (also **OECD**) organization formed in 1961, replacing the Organization for European Economic Cooperation (OEEC), to promote cooperation among industrialized member countries on economic and social policies. Its objectives are to assist member countries in formulating policies designed to achieve high economic growth while maintaining financial stability, contributing to world trade on a multilateral basis, and stimulating members' aid to developing countries. Members are Australia, Austria, Belgium, Canada, Denmark, Finland, France, Germany, Greece, Iceland, Ireland, Italy, Japan, Luxembourg, the Netherlands, New Zealand, Norway, Portugal, Spain, Sweden, Switzerland, Turkey, UK, and US.

♦ **Organization of Petroleum Exporting Countries** *n.* (also **OPEC**) organization created in 1960 to unify and coordinate the petroleum policies of member countries and to protect their interests, individually and collectively. Present members are Algeria, Gabon, Indonesia, Iran, Iraq, Kuwait, Libya, Nigeria, Qatar, Saudi Arabia, UAE, and Venezuela; Ecuador withdrew from OPEC in 1993.

---

organize /ˈɔːgəˌnaɪz/ *v.* (also **-ise**) (**-zing** or **-sing**) **1 a** give an orderly structure to, systematize. **b** make arrangements for (a person or oneself). **2** initiate, arrange for. **3** (often *absol.*) **a** enlist (a person or group) in a trade union, political party, etc. **b** form (a trade union etc.). **4** (esp. as **organized** *adj.*) make organic; make into living tissue. □ **organizer** *n.* [Latin: related to ORGAN]

♦ **organized market** *n.* formal market in a specific place in which buyers and sellers meet to trade according to agreed rules and procedures. Stock exchanges and commodity markets are examples of organized markets.

---

organ-loft *n.* gallery for an organ.

organza /ɔːˈgænzə/ *n.* thin stiff transparent silk or synthetic dress fabric. [origin uncertain]

orgasm /ˈɔːgæz(ə)m/ *–n.* climax of sexual excitement. *–v.* have a sexual orgasm. □ **orgasmic** /-ˈgæzmɪk/ *adj.* [Greek, = excitement]

orgy /ˈɔːdʒɪ/ *n.* (*pl.* **-ies**) **1** wild party with indiscriminate sexual activity. **2** excessive indulgence in an activity. □ **orgiastic** /-ˈæstɪk/ *adj.* [Greek *orgia* pl.]

oriel /ˈɔːrɪəl/ *n.* (in full **oriel window**) projecting window of an upper storey. [French]

orient /ˈɔːrɪənt/ *–n.* (**the Orient**) countries east of the Mediterranean, esp. E Asia. *–v.* **1 a** place or determine the position of with the aid of a compass; find the bearings of. **b** (often foll. by *towards*) direct. **2** place (a building etc.) to face east. **3** turn eastward or in a specified direction. □ **orient oneself** determine how one stands in relation to one's surroundings. [Latin *oriens -entis* rising, sunrise, east]

oriental /ˌɔːrɪˈent(ə)l/ (often **Oriental**) *–adj.* of the East, esp. E Asia; of the Orient. *–n.* native of the Orient.

orientate /ˈɔːrɪənˌteɪt/ *v.* (**-ting**) = ORIENT *v.* [apparently from ORIENT]

orientation /ˌɔːrɪənˈteɪʃ(ə)n/ *n.* **1** orienting or being oriented. **2 a** relative position. **b** person's attitude or adjustment in relation to circumstances. **3** introduction to a subject or situation; briefing. □ **orientational** *adj.*

orienteering /ˌɔːrɪənˈtɪərɪŋ/ *n.* competitive sport in which runners cross open country with a map, compass, etc. [Swedish]

orifice /ˈɒrɪfɪs/ *n.* opening, esp. the mouth of a cavity. [Latin *os or-* mouth, *facio* make]

origami /ˌɒrɪˈgɑːmɪ/ *n.* art of folding paper into decorative shapes. [Japanese]

origan /ˈɒrɪgən/ *n.* (also **origanum** /əˈrɪgənəm/) wild marjoram. [Latin from Greek]

origin /ˈɒrɪdʒɪn/ *n.* **1** starting-point; source. **2 a** (often in *pl.*) ancestry, parentage. **b** birth, extraction (*country of origin*). **3** *Math.* point from which coordinates are measured. **4** country from which a commodity originates (*shipment from origin*). [Latin *origo origin-* from *orior* rise]

original /əˈrɪdʒɪn(ə)l/ *–adj.* **1** existing from the beginning; earliest; innate. **2** inventive; creative; not derivative or imitative. **3** not copied or translated; by the artist etc. himself (*in the original Greek*; *has an original Rembrandt*). *–n.* original model, pattern, picture, etc. from which another is copied or translated. □ **originality** /-ˈnælɪtɪ/ *n.* **originally** *adv.*

♦ **original goods** *n.pl.* natural products that have no economic value until factors of production are applied to them. They include virgin land, wild fruit, natural waterways, etc.

---

original sin *n.* innate human sinfulness held to be a result of the Fall.

originate /əˈrɪdʒɪˌneɪt/ *v.* (**-ting**) **1** cause to begin; initiate. **2** have as an origin; begin. □ **origination** /-ˈneɪʃ(ə)n/ *n.* **originator** *n.*

oriole /ˈɔːrɪəʊl/ *n.* (in full **golden oriole**) bird with black and yellow plumage in the male. [Latin *aurum* gold]

Orissa /əˈrɪsə/ state in E India; pop. (est. 1994) 33 795 000; capital, Bhubaneswar. Rice and sugar cane are grown, and iron ore, manganese, and coal are mined; other sources of revenue include fishing, forestry, and heavy industry.

Orkney Islands /ˈɔːknɪ/ (also **Orkneys**) group of islands off the NE tip of Scotland, constituting an island area (Orkney) of Scotland; pop. (est. 1996) 19 800; chief town, Kirkwall. Agriculture (esp. beef-cattle farming) is a major source of revenue; industrial activities include fish curing and the exploitation of North Sea oil.

Orleans /ɔːˈliːənz/ (French **Orléans**) city in France, on the River Loire; the wine and brandy trade is important, and machinery, textiles, and electrical goods are produced; pop. (est. 1990) 107 965.

ormolu /ˈɔːməˌluː/ *n.* **1** (often *attrib.*) gilded bronze or gold-coloured alloy. **2** articles made of or decorated with these. [French *or moulu* powdered gold]

Ormuz /ˈɔːmuːz/ var. of HORMUZ.

ornament /ˈɔːnəmənt/ *–n.* **1 a** thing used to adorn or decorate. **b** quality or person bringing honour or distinction. **2** decoration, esp. on a building (*tower rich in ornament*). **3** musical embellishment. *–v.* /ˈɔːnəˌment/ adorn; beautify. □ **ornamental** /-ˈment(ə)l/ *adj.* **ornamentation** /-menˈteɪʃ(ə)n/ *n.* [Latin *orno* adorn]

ornate /ɔːˈneɪt/ *adj.* **1** elaborately adorned. **2** (of literary style) convoluted; flowery. □ **ornately** *adv.* **ornateness** *n.* [Latin: related to ORNAMENT]

ornithology /ˌɔːnɪˈθɒlədʒɪ/ *n.* the study of birds. □ **ornithological** /-θəˈlɒdʒɪk(ə)l/ *adj.* **ornithologist** *n.* [Greek *ornis ornith-* bird]

OROM *abbr. Computing* optical read-only memory.

orotund /ˈɒrəˌtʌnd/ *adj.* **1** (of the voice) full, round; imposing. **2** (of writing, style, etc.) pompous; pretentious. [Latin *ore rotundo* with rounded mouth]

orphan /ˈɔːf(ə)n/ *–n.* child whose parents are dead. *–v.* bereave (a child) of its parents. [Latin from Greek, = bereaved]

orphanage *n.* home for orphans.

orrery /ˈɒrərɪ/ *n.* (*pl.* **-ies**) clockwork model of the solar system. [Earl of *Orrery*]

orris /ˈɒrɪs/ *n.* **1** a kind of iris. **2** = ORRISROOT. [alteration of IRIS]

orrisroot *n.* fragrant iris root used in perfumery etc.

ORS *abbr.* Operational Research Society.

ortho- *comb. form* **1** straight. **2** right, correct. [Greek *orthos* straight]

orthodontics /ˌɔːθəˈdɒntɪks/ *n.pl.* (treated as *sing.*) correction of irregularities in the teeth and jaws. □ **orthodontic** *adj.* **orthodontist** *n.* [Greek *odous odont-* tooth]

orthodox /ˈɔːθəˌdɒks/ *adj.* **1** holding usual or accepted opinions, esp. on religion, morals, etc. **2** generally approved, conventional (*orthodox medicine*). **3** (also **Orthodox**) (of Judaism) strictly traditional. □ **orthodoxy** *n.* [Greek *doxa* opinion]

Orthodox Church *n.* Eastern Church with the Patriarch of Constantinople as its head, and including the national Churches of Russia, Romania, Greece, etc.

orthography /ɔːˈθɒgrəfɪ/ *n.* (*pl.* **-ies**) spelling (esp. with reference to its correctness). □ **orthographic** /-ˈgræfɪk/ *adj.* [Greek *orthographia*]

orthopaedics /ˌɔːθəˈpiːdɪks/ *n.pl.* (treated as *sing.*) (*US* **-pedics**) branch of medicine dealing with the correction of diseased, deformed, or injured bones or muscles. □ **orthopaedic** *adj.* **orthopaedist** *n.* [Greek *pais paid-* child]

ortolan /ˈɔːtələn/ *n.* European bunting, eaten as a delicacy. [Latin *hortus* garden]

Oruro /əˈrʊərəʊ/ mining city in W Bolivia, producing tin, silver, and copper; pop. (est. 1993) 201 831.

Orvieto /ˌɔːvɪˈeɪtəʊ/ town in Italy, in Umbria, centre of a wine-producing area; tourism is also important; pop. (1990) 21 575.

-ory *suffix* **1** forming nouns denoting a place (*dormitory*; *refectory*). **2** forming adjectives and nouns relating to or involving a verbal action (*accessory*; *compulsory*). [Latin *-orius*, *-orium*]

OS *abbr.* **1** old style. **2** *Computing* operating system. **3** ordinary seaman. **4** Ordnance Survey. **5** out of stock. **6** outsize.

Os *symb.* osmium.

o/s *abbr.* **1** (also **O/s**) out of stock. **2** outsize. **3** (also **O/s**) *Banking* outstanding.

OS/2 *abbr. Computing* Operating System/2 (produced by IBM and Microsoft).

Osaka /əʊˈsɑːkə/ port and commercial city in Japan, capital of Kinki region on Honshu island; manufactures include textiles, chemicals, and electrical equipment; pop. (1995) 2 602 352.

Oscar /ˈɒskə(r)/ *n.* any of the statuettes awarded by the US Academy of Motion Picture Arts and Sciences for excellence in film acting, directing, etc. [man's name]

oscillate /ˈɒsɪˌleɪt/ *v.* (**-ting**) **1** (cause to) swing to and fro. **2** vacillate; vary between extremes. **3** (of an electric current) undergo high-frequency alternations. □ **oscillation** /-ˈleɪʃ(ə)n/ *n.* **oscillator** *n.* [Latin *oscillo* swing]

oscillo- *comb. form* oscillation, esp. of an electric current.

oscilloscope /əˈsɪləˌskəʊp/ *n.* device for viewing oscillations by a display on the screen of a cathode-ray tube.

-ose *suffix* forming adjectives denoting possession of a quality (*grandiose*; *verbose*). [Latin *-osus*]

OSHA /ˈəʊʃə/ *abbr.* (in the US) Occupational Safety and Health Administration.

OSI *abbr.* **1** on-site inspection. **2** open systems interconnection. See OPEN SYSTEM.

osier /ˈəʊzɪə(r)/ *n.* **1** willow used in basketwork. **2** shoot of this. [French]

-osis *suffix* denoting a process or condition (*apotheosis*; *metamorphosis*), esp. a pathological state (*neurosis*; *thrombosis*). [Latin or Greek]

-osity *suffix* forming nouns from adjectives in *-ose* and *-ous* (*verbosity*; *curiosity*). [Latin *-ositas*]

Oslo /ˈɒzləʊ/ capital and chief port of Norway; a financial centre, it also has an important shipbuilding industry and manufactures consumer goods; pop. (est. 1996) 487 908.

osmium /ˈɒzmɪəm/ *n.* heavy hard bluish-white metallic element. [Greek *osmē* smell]

osmosis /ɒzˈməʊsɪs/ *n.* **1** passage of a solvent through a semi-permeable membrane into a more concentrated solution. **2** process by which something is acquired by absorption. □ **osmotic** /-ˈmɒtɪk/ *adj.* [Greek *ōsmos* push]

Osnabrück /ˈɒznəˌbrʊk/ textile-manufacturing city in NW Germany; other industries include iron, steel, and motor vehicles; pop. (est. 1995) 168 050.

osprey /ˈɒspreɪ/ *n.* (*pl.* **-s**) large bird of prey feeding on fish. [Latin *ossifraga* from *os* bone, *frango* break]

osseous /ˈɒsɪəs/ *adj.* **1** of bone. **2** bony. [Latin *os oss-* bone]

ossicle /ˈɒsɪk(ə)l/ *n.* small bone or piece of bonelike substance. [Latin diminutive: related to OSSEOUS]

ossify /ˈɒsɪˌfaɪ/ *v.* (**-ies, -ied**) **1** turn into bone; harden. **2** make or become rigid, callous, or unprogressive. □ **ossification** /-fɪˈkeɪʃ(ə)n/ *n.* [Latin: related to OSSEOUS]

Ostend /ɒˈstend/ (Flemish **Oostende** /əʊˈstendə/, French **Ostende** /ɒˈstɑ̃d/) seaport and resort in Belgium, on the North Sea, with ferry links to Dover; there are shipbuilding and fish-processing industries; pop. (est. 1995) 68 858.

ostensible /ɒˈstensɪb(ə)l/ *adj.* concealing the real; professed. □ **ostensibly** *adv.* [Latin *ostendo ostens-* show]

ostensive /ɒˈstensɪv/ *adj.* directly showing.

ostentation /ˌɒstenˈteɪʃ(ə)n/ *n.* **1** pretentious display of wealth etc. **2** showing off. □ **ostentatious** *adj.* **ostentatiously** *adv.*

osteo- *comb. form* bone. [Greek *osteon*]

osteoarthritis /ˌɒstɪəʊɑːˈθraɪtɪs/ *n.* degenerative disease of joint cartilage. □ **osteoarthritic** /-ˈθrɪtɪk/ *adj.*

osteopathy /ˌɒstɪˈɒpəθɪ/ *n.* treatment of disease through the manipulation of bones. □ **osteopath** /ˈɒstɪəˌpæθ/ *n.*

osteoporosis /ˌɒstɪəʊpəˈrəʊsɪs/ *n.* condition of brittle bones caused esp. by hormonal changes or deficiency of calcium or vitamin D.

Österreich see AUSTRIA.

ostler /ˈɒslə(r)/ *n. hist.* stableman at an inn. [related to HOSTEL]

ostracize /ˈɒstrəˌsaɪz/ *v.* (also **-ise**) (**-zing** or **-sing**) exclude from society; refuse to associate with. □ **ostracism** /-ˌsɪz(ə)m/ *n.* [Greek (*ostrakon* potsherd, on which a vote was recorded in ancient Athens to expel a powerful or unpopular citizen)]

Ostrava /ˈɒstrəvə/ industrial and coalmining city in the E Czech Republic; pop. (est. 1995) 325 827.

ostrich /ˈɒstrɪtʃ/ *n.* **1** large African swift-running flightless bird. **2** person who refuses to acknowledge an awkward truth. [Latin *avis* bird, *struthio* (from Greek) ostrich]

OT *abbr.* **1** Old Testament. **2** overtime.

OTC *abbr.* **1** Organization for Trade Cooperation. **2** over the counter (see OVER-THE-COUNTER MARKET).

◆ **OTE** *abbr.* on-target earnings, the salary and commission a salesperson should be able to earn.

---

other /ˈʌðə(r)/ *–adj.* **1** not the same as one or some already mentioned or implied; separate in identity or distinct in kind (*other people; use other means*). **2 a** further; additional (*a few other examples*). **b** second of two (*open your other eye*). **3** (prec. by *the*) only remaining. (*must be in the other pocket; where are the other two?*). **4** (foll. by *than*) apart from. *–n.* or *pron.* other person or thing. (*some others have come; give me one other; where are the others?*). □ **other than 1** except (*never speaks to me other than to insult me; has no friends other than me*). **2** differently; not (*cannot do other than laugh; never appears other than happy*). [Old English]

■ **Usage** In sense 2 of *other than, otherwise* is standard except in less formal use.

other day *n.* (also **other night**) (prec. by *the*) a few days (or nights) ago.

other half *n. colloq.* one's wife or husband.

otherwise *–adv.* **1** or else; in different circumstances (*hurry, otherwise we'll be late*). **2** in other respects (*is otherwise very suitable*). **3** in a different way (*could not have acted otherwise*). **4** as an alternative (*otherwise known as Jack*). *–adj.* (*predic.*) different (*the matter is quite otherwise*). [Old English: related to WISE[2]]

■ **Usage** See note at *other*.

other woman *n.* (prec. by *the*) married man's mistress.

other-worldly *adj.* **1** of another world. **2** dreamily distracted from mundane life.

otiose /ˈəʊtɪəʊs/ *adj.* serving no practical purpose; not required. [Latin *otium* leisure]

Otranto /ɒˈtræntəʊ/, **Strait of** channel linking the Adriatic Sea with the Ionian Sea and separating the 'heel' of Italy from Albania.

OTS *abbr.* = OPPORTUNITIES TO SEE.

OTT *abbr. colloq.* over-the-top.

Ottawa /ˈɒtəwə/ capital of Canada, in Ontario; city pop. (1991) 313 987; metropolitan area pop. 920 857. Engineering, food-processing, publishing, and timber-related industries are important.

otter /ˈɒtə(r)/ *n.* **1** aquatic fish-eating mammal with webbed feet and thick brown fur. **2** its fur. [Old English]

Ottoman /ˈɒtəmən/ *–adj.* **1** of the dynasty of Osman (or Othman) I or the empire ruled by his descendants. **2** Turkish. *–n.* (*pl.* **-s**) **1** Turk of the Ottoman period. **2** (**ottoman**) upholstered seat without back or arms, sometimes a box with a padded top. [French from Arabic]

OU *abbr.* **1** Open University. **2** Oxford University.

Ouagadougou /ˌwɑːgəˈduːguː/ capital of Burkina Faso, a major centre of communications; pop. (est. 1993) 690 000.

oubliette /ˌuːblɪˈet/ *n.* secret dungeon with a trapdoor entrance. [French *oublier* forget]

ouch *int.* expressing sharp or sudden pain. [imitative]

ought /ɔːt/ *v.aux.* (as present and past, the only form now in use) **1** expressing duty or rightness (*we ought to be thankful; it ought to have been done long ago*). **2** advisability (*you ought to see a dentist*). **3** probability (*it ought to rain soon*). □ **ought not** negative form of *ought* (*he ought not to have stolen it*). [Old English, past of OWE]

oughtn't /ˈɔːt(ə)nt/ *contr.* ought not.

ouguiya /uːˈgiːə/ *n.* standard monetary unit of Mauritania. [French from Arabic]

Ouija /ˈwiːdʒə/ *n.* (in full **Ouija board**) *propr.* board marked with letters or signs and used with a movable pointer to try to obtain messages at a seance. [French *oui*, German *ja*, yes]

Oulu /ˈaʊluː/ (Swedish **Uleåborg** /ˈuːlɪɔːˌbɔː(r)/) **1** province in central Finland; pop. (est. 1995) 449 709. **2** its capital city, a port on the Gulf of Bothnia; there are shipbuilding and saw-milling industries; pop. (est. 1996) 109 094.

ounce *n.* **1** unit of weight, $^1/_{16}$ lb. or approx. 28 g. **2** very small quantity. [Latin *uncia* twelfth part of a pound or a foot]

our *poss. pron.* **1** of or belonging to us or society (*our children's future*). **2** *colloq.* indicating a relative, friend, etc. of the speaker (*our Barry works there; our friend here*). [Old English]

Our Father *n.* prayer beginning with these words (Matt. 6:9-13).

Our Lady *n.* Virgin Mary.

Our Lord *n.* Christ.

ours *poss. pron.* the one or ones belonging to or associated with us (*it is ours; ours are best; a friend of ours*).

ourself *pron. archaic* = MYSELF as used by a sovereign etc.

ourselves *pron.* **1 a** *emphat. form* of WE or US (*we did it ourselves*). **b** *refl. form* of US (*we are pleased with ourselves*). **2** in our normal state of body or mind (*not quite ourselves today*). □ **be ourselves** see ONESELF. **by ourselves** see *by oneself*.

-ous *suffix* **1** forming adjectives meaning 'abounding in, characterized by, of the nature of' (*envious; glorious; mountainous; poisonous*). **2** *Chem.* denoting a state of lower valence than *-ic* (*ferrous; sulphurous*). [Anglo-French *-ous*, from Latin *asus*]

ousel var. of OUZEL.

oust *v.* drive out or expel, esp. by seizing the place of. [Latin *obsto* oppose]

out *–adv.* **1** away from or not in or at a place etc. (*keep him out; get out; tide is out*). **2** indicating: **a** dispersal away from a centre etc. (*share out*). **b** coming or bringing into the open (*call out; will look it out for you*). **c** need for attentiveness (*watch out; listen out*). **3** not in one's house, office, etc. (*tell them I'm out*). **4** to or at an end; completely (*tired out; die out; fight it out; my luck was out; typed it out*). **5** (of a fire, candle, etc.) not burning. **6** in error (*was 3% out*). **7** *colloq.* unconscious (*is out cold*). **8** (of a limb etc.) dislocated (*put his arm out*). **9** (of a political party etc.) not in office. **10** (of a jury) considering its verdict. **11** (of workers) on strike. **12** (of a secret) revealed. **13** (of a flower) open. **14** (of a book, record, etc.) published, on sale. **15** (of a star) visible after dark. **16** no longer in fashion (*turn-ups are out*). **17** (of a batsman etc.) dismissed from batting. **18** not worth considering (*that idea is out*). **19** (prec. by *superl.*) *colloq.* known to exist (*the best game out*). **20** (of a mark etc.) removed (*washed the stain out*). *–prep.* out of (*looked out the window*). *–n.* way of escape. *–v.* come or go out; emerge (*murder will out*). □ **out for** intent on, determined to get. **out of 1** from within. **2** not within. **3** from among. **4** beyond the range of (*out of reach*). **5** so as to be without, lacking (*was swindled out of his money; out of sugar*). **6** from (*get money out of him*). **7** because of (*asked out of curiosity*). **8** by the use of (*what did you make it out of?*). **out of bounds** see BOUND[2]. **out of date** see DATE[1]. **out of order** see ORDER. **out of pocket** see POCKET. **out of the question** see QUESTION. **out of sorts** see SORT. **out of this world** see WORLD. **out of the way** see WAY. **out to** determined to. [Old English]

■ **Usage** The use of *out* as a preposition, e.g. *he walked out the room*, is non-standard. *Out of* should be used.

out- *prefix* in senses **1** so as to surpass or exceed (*outdo*). **2** external, separate (*outline*). **3** out of; away from; outward (*outgrowth*).

outage /ˈaʊtɪdʒ/ *n.* period during which a power-supply etc. is not operating.

out and about *adj.* active outdoors (esp. after an illness etc.).

out and out *–adj.* thorough; complete. *–adv.* thoroughly.

outback *n.* remote inland areas of Australia.

outbalance /aʊtˈbæləns/ *v.* (**-cing**) outweigh.

outbid /aʊtˈbɪd/ *v.* (**-bidding**; *past* and *past part.* **-bid**) bid higher than.

outboard motor *n.* portable engine attached to the outside of a boat.

outbreak *n.* sudden eruption of anger, war, disease, fire, etc.

outbuilding *n.* shed, barn, etc. detached from a main building.

outburst *n.* **1** verbal explosion of anger etc. **2** bursting out (*outburst of steam*).

outcast –*n.* person rejected by family or society. –*adj.* rejected; homeless.

outclass /aʊt'klɑːs/ *v.* surpass in quality.

outcome *n.* result.

outcrop *n.* **1 a** emergence of a stratum etc. at a surface. **b** stratum etc. emerging. **2** noticeable manifestation.

outcry *n.* (*pl.* **-ies**) **1** strong public protest. **2** *Stock Exch.* see CALL-OVER.

outdated /aʊt'deɪtɪd/ *adj.* out of date; obsolete.

outdistance /aʊt'dɪst(ə)ns/ *v.* (**-cing**) leave (a competitor) behind completely.

outdo /aʊt'duː/ *v.* (**-doing**; *3rd sing. present* **-does**; *past* **-did**; *past part.* **-done**) exceed, excel, surpass.

outdoor *attrib. adj.* **1** done, existing, or used out of doors. **2** fond of the open air (*an outdoor type*).

outdoors /aʊt'dɔːz/ –*adv.* in or into the open air. –*n.* the open air.

outer *adj.* **1** outside; external (*pierced the outer layer*). **2** farther from the centre or the inside. □ **outermost** *adj.*

outer space *n.* universe beyond the earth's atmosphere.

outface /aʊt'feɪs/ *v.* (**-cing**) disconcert by staring or by a display of confidence.

outfall *n.* outlet of a river, drain, etc.

outfield *n.* outer part of a cricket or baseball pitch. □ **outfielder** *n.*

outfit *n.* **1** set of clothes or equipment. **2** *colloq.* group of people regarded as an organization.

outfitter *n.* supplier of clothing.

outflank /aʊt'flæŋk/ *v.* **1** extend beyond the flank of (an enemy). **2** outmanoeuvre, outwit.

outflow *n.* **1** outward flow. **2** amount that flows out.

outfox /aʊt'fɒks/ *v.* outwit.

outgoing –*adj.* **1** friendly. **2** retiring from office. **3** going out. –*n.* (in *pl.*) expenditure.

outgrow /aʊt'grəʊ/ *v.* (*past* **-grew**; *past part.* **-grown**) **1** grow too big for. **2** leave behind (a childish habit etc.). **3** grow faster or taller than.

outgrowth *n.* **1** offshoot. **2** natural product or development.

outhouse *n.* small building adjoining or apart from a house.

outing *n.* pleasure trip, excursion.

outlandish /aʊt'lændɪʃ/ *adj.* bizarre, strange. □ **outlandishly** *adv.* **outlandishness** *n.* [Old English, from *outland* foreign country]

outlast /aʊt'lɑːst/ *v.* last longer than.

outlaw –*n.* **1** fugitive from the law. **2** *hist.* person deprived of the protection of the law. –*v.* **1** declare (a person) an outlaw. **2** make illegal; proscribe.

outlay *n.* expenditure.

◆ **outlay tax** *n.* = EXPENDITURE TAX.

---

outlet *n.* **1** means of exit or escape. **2** means of expressing feelings. **3 a** market for goods. **b** shop (*retail outlet*).

outline –*n.* **1** rough draft. **2** summary. **3** sketch consisting of only contour lines. **4** (in *sing.* or *pl.*) **a** lines enclosing or indicating an object. **b** contour. **c** external boundary. **5** (in *pl.*) main features or principles. –*v.* (**-ning**) **1** draw or describe in outline. **2** mark the outline of.

outlive /aʊt'lɪv/ *v.* (**-ving**) **1** live longer than (a person). **2** live beyond (a period or date).

outlook *n.* **1** prospect, view. **2** mental attitude.

outlying *adj.* far from a centre; remote.

outmanoeuvre /ˌaʊtmə'nuːvə(r)/ *v.* (**-ring**) (*US* **-maneuver**) secure an advantage over by skilful manoeuvring.

outmatch /aʊt'mætʃ/ *v.* be more than a match for.

outmoded /aʊt'məʊdɪd/ *adj.* **1** outdated. **2** out of fashion.

outnumber /aʊt'nʌmbə(r)/ *v.* exceed in number.

out of doors *adj.* & *adv.* in or into the open air.

out of it *predic. adj.* **1** (of a person) not included; forlorn. **2** *colloq.* unconscious, dazed.

◆ **out-of-the-money option** see INTRINSIC VALUE 2.

---

outpace /aʊt'peɪs/ *v.* (**-cing**) **1** go faster than. **2** outdo in a contest.

outpatient *n.* non-resident hospital patient.

outplacement *n.* assistance in finding a new job after redundancy.

outpost *n.* **1** detachment posted at a distance from an army. **2** distant branch or settlement (*outpost of empire*).

outpouring *n.* (usu. in *pl.*) copious expression of emotion.

output –*n.* **1** amount produced (by a machine, worker, etc.). **2** electrical power etc. delivered by an apparatus. **3** printout, results, etc. from a computer. **4** place where energy, information, etc. leaves a system. –*v.* (**-tt**; *past* and *past part.* **-put** or **-putted**) (of a computer) supply (results etc.).

output device *n.* device that converts the information held within a computer system into a form that can be understood and used by people, or is suitable for input to another machine. The visual display unit (VDU) and the printer are the most common output devices. Other output systems include speech synthesis and computer output microfilm.

◆ **output tax** *n.* VAT that a trader adds to the price of the goods or services supplied. The trader must account for output tax to HM Customs and Excise, having first deducted the input tax.

---

outrage –*n.* **1** extreme violation of others' rights, sentiments, etc. **2** gross offence or indignity. **3** fierce resentment. –*v.* (**-ging**) **1** subject to outrage. **2** commit an outrage against. **3** shock and anger. [French *outrer* exceed, from Latin *ultra* beyond]

outrageous /aʊt'reɪdʒəs/ *adj.* **1** immoderate. **2** shocking. **3** immoral, offensive. □ **outrageously** *adv.*

outrank /aʊt'ræŋk/ *v.* be superior in rank to.

outré /'uːtreɪ/ *adj.* eccentric, unconventional. [French, past part. of *outrer*: see OUTRAGE]

outrider *n.* mounted guard or motor cyclist riding ahead of a procession etc.

outrigger *n.* **1** spar or framework projecting over the side of a ship, racing boat, or canoe to give stability. **2** boat fitted with this.

outright –*adv.* **1** altogether, entirely. **2** not gradually. **3** without reservation, openly. –*adj.* **1** downright, complete. **2** undisputed (*outright winner*).

outrun /aʊt'rʌn/ *v.* (**-nn-**; *past* **-ran**; *past part.* **-run**) **1** run faster or farther than. **2** go beyond (a point or limit).

outsell /aʊt'sel/ *v.* (*past* and *past part.* **-sold**) **1** sell more than. **2** be sold in greater quantities than.

outset *n.* □ **at** (or **from**) **the outset** from the beginning.

outshine /aʊt'ʃaɪn/ *v.* (**-ning**; *past* and *past part.* **-shone**) **1** shine brighter than. **2** surpass in excellence etc.

outside –*n.* /aʊt'saɪd, 'aʊtsaɪd/ **1** external side or surface; outer parts. **2** external appearance; outward aspect. **3** position on the outer side (*gate opens from the outside*). –*adj.* /'aʊtsaɪd/ **1 a** of, on, or nearer the outside; outer. **b** not in the main building (*outside toilet*). **2** not belonging to a particular group or organization (*outside help*). **3** (of a chance etc.) remote; very unlikely. **4** (of an estimate etc.) the greatest or highest possible (*the outside price*). **5** (of a player in football etc.) positioned nearest to the edge of the field (*outside left*). –*adv.* /aʊt'saɪd/ **1** on or to the outside. **2** in or to the open air. **3** not within, enclosed, or included. **4** *slang* not in prison. –*prep.* /aʊt'saɪd/ **1** not in; to or at the exterior of. **2** external to, not included in, beyond the limits of. □ **at the outside**

(of an estimate etc.) at the most. **from the outside** from an objective or impartial standpoint.

outside broadcast *n.* one not made in a studio.

◆ **outside broker** *n.* stockbroker who is not a member of a stock exchange but acts as an intermediary between the public and a stockbroker who is a member.

◆ **outside director** *n.* member of the board of directors of a company who is not employed directly by that company, but may be employed by a holding company or associated company. Outside directors are usu. non-executive directors.

outside interest *n.* hobby etc. not connected with one's work.

◆ **outside money** *n.* money issued from outside an economic system, usu. either by a government or by other countries (i.e. foreign currency). It has been argued that a fall in the level of prices may increase the value of outside money in an economy, creating a positive wealth effect (cf. INSIDE MONEY). However, even outside money issued by a government may have no wealth effect (see RICARDIAN EQUIVALENCE THEOREM).

outsider /aʊt'saɪdə(r)/ *n.* **1** non-member of some group, organization, profession, etc. **2** competitor thought to have little chance.

outside world *n.* society outside the confines of an institution etc.

outsize *adj.* unusually large.

outskirts *n.pl.* outer area of a town etc.

outsmart /aʊt'smɑːt/ *v.* outwit, be cleverer than.

◆ **outsourcing** /'aut,sɔːsɪŋ/ *n.* buying components, subassemblies, finished products, or services from outside suppliers rather than providing them internally.

outspoken /aʊt'spəʊkən/ *adj.* saying openly what one thinks; frank. □ **outspokenly** *adv.* **outspokenness** *n.*

outspread /aʊt'spred/ *–adj.* spread out; expanded. *–v.* spread out; expand.

outstanding /aʊt'stændɪŋ/ *adj.* **1** conspicuous because of excellence. **2 a** (of a debt) not yet settled. **b** still to be dealt with (*work outstanding*). □ **outstandingly** *adv.*

outstation *n.* remote branch or outpost.

outstay /aʊt'steɪ/ *v.* stay longer than (one's welcome etc.).

outstretched /aʊt'stretʃt/ *adj.* stretched out.

outstrip /aʊt'strɪp/ *v.* **(-pp-) 1** go faster than. **2** surpass, esp. competitively.

out-take *n.* film or tape sequence rejected in editing.

out-tray *n.* tray for outgoing documents etc.

outvote /aʊt'vəʊt/ *v.* **(-ting)** defeat by a majority of votes.

outward /'aʊtwəd/ *–adj.* **1** situated on or directed towards the outside. **2** going out. **3** bodily, external, apparent. *–adv.* (also **outwards**) in an outward direction; towards the outside. □ **outwardly** *adv.* [Old English: related to OUT-, -WARD]

outward bound *adj.* going away from home.

outwardness *n.* external existence; objectivity.

outwards var. of OUTWARD *adv.*

outweigh /aʊt'weɪ/ *v.* exceed in weight, value, importance, or influence.

outwit /aʊt'wɪt/ *v.* **(-tt-)** be too clever for; overcome by greater ingenuity.

outwork *n.* **1** advanced or detached part of a fortification. **2** work done off the premises of the firm etc. which supplies it. □ **outworker** *n.* (in sense 2).

ouzel /'uːz(ə)l/ *n.* (also **ousel**) **1** (in full **ring ouzel**) white-breasted thrush. **2** (in full **water ouzel**) diving bird; dipper. [Old English, = blackbird]

ouzo /'uːzəʊ/ *n.* (*pl.* **-s**) Greek aniseed-flavoured spirit. [Greek]

ova *pl.* of OVUM.

oval /'əʊv(ə)l/ *–adj.* **1** egg-shaped, ellipsoidal. **2** having the outline of an egg, elliptical. *–n.* **1** egg-shaped or elliptical closed curve. **2** thing with an oval outline. [Latin: related to OVUM]

ovary /'əʊvərɪ/ *n.* (*pl.* **-ies**) **1** each of the female reproductive organs in which ova are produced. **2** hollow base of the carpel of a flower. □ **ovarian** /ə'veərɪən/ *adj.*

ovation /əʊ'veɪʃ(ə)n/ *n.* enthusiastic reception, esp. applause. [Latin *ovo* exult]

oven /'ʌv(ə)n/ *n.* enclosed compartment for heating or cooking food etc. [Old English]

ovenproof *adj.* suitable for use in an oven; heat-resistant.

oven-ready *adj.* (of food) prepared before sale for immediate cooking in the oven.

ovenware *n.* dishes for cooking food in the oven.

over *–adv.* expressing movement, position, or state above or beyond something stated or implied: **1** outward and downward from a brink or from any erect position (*knocked me over*). **2** so as to cover or touch a whole surface (*paint it over*). **3** so as to produce a fold or reverse position (*bend it over; turn it over*). **4 a** across a street or other space (*cross over; came over from France*). **b** for a visit etc. (*invited them over*). **5** with transference or change from one hand, part, etc., to another (*went over to the enemy; swapped them over*). **6** with motion above something; so as to pass across something (*climb over; fly over; boil over*). **7** from beginning to end with repetition or detailed consideration (*think it over; did it six times over*). **8** in excess; in addition, besides (*left over*). **9** for or until a later time (*hold it over*). **10** at an end; settled; completely finished (*crisis is over; it's over between us; get it over with*). **11** (in full **over to you**) (as *int.*) (in radio conversations etc.) it is your turn to speak. **12** umpire's call to change ends in cricket. *–prep.* **1** above, in, or to a position higher than. **2** out and down from; down from the edge of (*fell over the cliff*). **3** so as to cover (*hat over his eyes*). **4** above and across; so as to clear, on or to the other side of (*flew over Scotland; bridge over the Avon; look over the wall*). **5** concerning; while occupied with (*laughed over it; fell asleep over a book*). **6 a** in superiority of; superior to; in charge of (*victory over them; reign over two kingdoms*). **b** in preference to. **7 a** throughout (*travelled over most of Africa*). **b** so as to deal with completely (*went over the plans*). **8 a** for or through the duration of (*stay over Monday night; over the years*). **b** during the course of (*did it over the weekend*). **9** beyond; more than (*bids of over £50; is he over 18?*). **10** transmitted by (*heard it over the radio*). **11** in comparison with (*gained 20% over last year*). **12** recovered from (*am over my cold; got over it in time*). *–n.* **1** sequence of six balls in cricket bowled from one end of the pitch. **2** play resulting from this. *–adj.* (see also OVER-). **1** upper, outer. **2** superior. **3** extra. □ **over again** once again, again from the beginning. **over against** in contrast with. **over all** taken as a whole. **over and above** in addition to; not to mention. **over and over** repeatedly. **over one's head** see HEAD. **over the hill** see HILL. **over the moon** see MOON. **over the way** (in a street etc.) facing or opposite. [Old English]

over- *prefix* **1** excessively. **2** upper, outer. **3** = OVER in various senses (*overshadow*). **4** completely (*overawe; overjoyed*).

over-abundance /,əʊvərə'bʌnd(ə)ns/ *n.* excessive quantity. □ **over-abundant** *adj.*

overact /,əʊvər'ækt/ *v.* act (a role) in an exaggerated manner.

over-active /,əʊvər'æktɪv/ *adj.* excessively active.

overall *–attrib. adj.* /'əʊvər,ɔːl/ **1** total, inclusive of all (*overall cost*). **2** taking everything into account, general (*overall improvement*). *–adv.* /,əʊvər'ɔːl/ **1** including everything (*cost £50 overall*). **2** on the whole, generally (*did well overall*). *–n.* /'əʊvər,ɔːl/ **1** protective outer garment. **2** (in *pl.*) protective outer trousers or suit.

overambitious /,əʊvəræm'bɪʃəs/ *adj.* excessively ambitious.

over-anxious /,əʊvər'æŋkʃəs/ *adj.* excessively anxious.

overarm *adj.* & *adv.* with the hand above the shoulder (*bowl overarm; overarm service*).

overate *past* of OVEREAT.

overawe /ˌəʊvərˈɔː/ *v.* (**-wing**) overcome with awe.

overbalance /ˌəʊvəˈbæləns/ *v.* (**-cing**) **1** lose balance and fall. **2** cause to do this.

overbear /ˌəʊvəˈbeə(r)/ *v.* (*past* **-bore**; *past part.* **-borne**) **1** (as **overbearing** *adj.*) **a** domineering, bullying. **b** overpowering. **2** bear down by weight, force, or emotion. **3** repress by power or authority.

overbid *–v.* /ˌəʊvəˈbɪd/ (**-dd-**; *past* and *past part.* **-bid**) make a higher bid than. *–n.* /ˈəʊvəbɪd/ bid that is higher than another, or higher than is justified.

overblown /ˌəʊvəˈbləʊn/ *adj.* **1** inflated or pretentious. **2** (of a flower) past its prime.

overboard *adv.* from a ship into the water (*fall overboard*). □ **go overboard** *colloq.* **1** be highly enthusiastic. **2** behave immoderately.

overbook /ˌəʊvəˈbʊk/ *v.* (also *absol.*) make too many bookings for (an aircraft, hotel, etc.).

overbore *past* of OVERBEAR.

overborne *past part.* of OVERBEAR.

overburden /ˌəʊvəˈbɜːd(ə)n/ *v.* burden (a person, thing, etc.) to excess.

♦ **overbuy** /ˌəʊvəˈbaɪ/ *v.* (*past* and *past part.* **-bought**) **1** purchase more of a good than one needs or has orders for. **2** purchase more securities or commodities than are covered by margins deposited with a broker or dealer. In a falling market a bull speculator can become overbought without having made a fresh purchase. **3** (as **overbought** *adj.*) (of a market) having risen too rapidly as a result of excessive buying and therefore unstable and likely to fall if unsupported.

overcame *past* of OVERCOME.

♦ **overcapitalization** /ˌəʊvəˌkæpɪtəlaɪˈzeɪʃ(ə)n/ *n.* (also **-isation**) state in which an organization has too much capital for the needs of its business. If a business has more capital than it needs it is likely to be overburdened by interest charges or by the need to spread profits too thinly by way of dividends to shareholders. Businesses can now reduce overcapitalization by repaying long-term debts or by buying their own shares. □ **overcapitalize** *v.*

overcast /ˈəʊvəˌkɑːst/ *adj.* **1** (of the sky) covered with cloud. **2** (in sewing) edged with stitching to prevent fraying.

overcautious /ˌəʊvəˈkɔːʃəs/ *adj.* excessively cautious.

overcharge /ˌəʊvəˈtʃɑːdʒ/ *v.* (**-ging**) **1** charge too high a price to (a person). **2** put too much charge into (a battery, gun, etc.). **3** put excessive detail into (a description, picture, etc.).

overcoat *n.* warm outdoor coat.

overcome /ˌəʊvəˈkʌm/ *v.* (**-ming**; *past* **-came**; *past part.* **-come**) **1** prevail over, master, be victorious. **2** (usu. as **overcome** *adj.*) **a** make faint (*overcome by smoke*). **b** (usu. foll. by *with*, *by*) make weak or helpless (*overcome with grief*).

overcompensate /ˌəʊvəˈkɒmpenˌseɪt/ *v.* (**-ting**) **1** (usu. foll. by *for*) compensate excessively. **2** strive exaggeratedly to make amends etc.

overconfident /ˌəʊvəˈkɒnfɪd(ə)nt/ *adj.* excessively confident.

overcook /ˌəʊvəˈkʊk/ *v.* cook too much or for too long.

overcrowd /ˌəʊvəˈkraʊd/ *v.* (usu. as **overcrowded** *adj.*) fill beyond what is usual or comfortable. □ **overcrowding** *n.*

overdevelop /ˌəʊvədɪˈveləp/ *v.* (**-p-**) **1** develop too much. **2** *Photog.* treat with developer for too long.

overdo /ˌəʊvəˈduː/ *v.* (**-doing**; *3rd sing. present* **-does**; *past* **-did**; *past part.* **-done**) **1** carry to excess, go too far. **2** (esp. as **overdone** *adj.*) overcook. □ **overdo it** (or **things**) *colloq.* exhaust oneself.

overdose *n.* excessive dose of a drug etc.

♦ **overdraft** *n.* **1** loan made to a customer with a cheque account at a bank or building society, in which the account is allowed to go into debit, usu. up to a specified limit (the **overdraft limit**). Interest is charged on the daily debit balance. This is a less costly way of borrowing than taking a bank loan (providing the interest rates are the same) as, with an overdraft, credits are taken into account. **2** overdrawing of a bank or building society cheque account.

overdraw /ˌəʊvəˈdrɔː/ *v.* (*past* **-drew**; *past part.* **-drawn**) **1** draw more from (a bank or building society cheque account) than the amount credited. **2** (as **overdrawn** *adj.*) having overdrawn one's account.

overdress /ˌəʊvəˈdres/ *v.* dress with too much formality.

overdrive *n.* **1** mechanism in a vehicle providing a gear above top gear for economy at high speeds. **2** state of high activity.

overdue /ˌəʊvəˈdjuː/ *adj.* past the due time for payment, arrival, return, etc.

overeager /ˌəʊvərˈiːgə(r)/ *adj.* excessively eager.

overeat /ˌəʊvərˈiːt/ *v.* (*past* **-ate**; *past part.* **-eaten**) eat too much.

overemphasize /ˌəʊvərˈemfəˌsaɪz/ *v.* (also **-ise**) (**-zing** or **-sing**) give too much emphasis to.

overenthusiasm /ˌəʊvərɪnˈθjuːzɪˌæz(ə)m/ *n.* excessive enthusiasm. □ **overenthusiastic** /-ˈæstɪk/ *adj.* **overenthusiastically** /-ˈæstɪkəlɪ/ *adv.*

♦ **over-entry certificate** *n.* document issued by HM Customs and Excise stating that imported goods have paid excessive duty on entry into the country, which may be reclaimed. If too little duty has been paid, **post-entry duty** is claimed.

overestimate *–v.* /ˌəʊvərˈestɪˌmeɪt/ (**-ting**) form too high an estimate of. *–n.* /ˌəʊvərˈestɪmət/ too high an estimate. □ **overestimation** /-ˈmeɪʃ(ə)n/ *n.*

overexcite /ˌəʊvərɪkˈsaɪt/ *v.* (**-ting**) excite excessively. □ **overexcitement** *n.*

overexert /ˌəʊvərɪgˈzɜːt/ *v.* exert too much. □ **overexertion** /-ɪgˈzɜːʃ(ə)n/ *n.*

overexpose /ˌəʊvərɪkˈspəʊz/ *v.* (**-sing**) **1** expose too much to the public. **2** expose (film) too long. □ **overexposure** *n.*

overfeed /ˌəʊvəˈfiːd/ *v.* (*past* and *past part.* **-fed**) feed excessively.

overfill /ˌəʊvəˈfɪl/ *v.* fill to excess or to overflowing.

overfish /ˌəʊvəˈfɪʃ/ *v.* deplete (a stream etc.) by too much fishing.

overflow *–v.* /ˌəʊvəˈfləʊ/ **1** flow over (the brim etc.). **2 a** (of a receptacle etc.) be so full that the contents overflow. **b** (of contents) overflow a container. **3** (of a crowd etc.) extend beyond the limits of (a room etc.). **4** flood (a surface or area). **5** (of kindness, a harvest, etc.) be very abundant. *–n.* /ˈəʊvəˌfləʊ/ **1** what overflows or is superfluous. **2** outlet for excess water etc.

overfly /ˌəʊvəˈflaɪ/ *v.* (**-flies**; *past* **-flew**; *past part.* **-flown**) fly over or beyond (a place or territory).

overfond /ˌəʊvəˈfɒnd/ *adj.* (often foll. by *of*) having too great an affection or liking for (*overfond of chocolate*; *overfond parent*).

overfull /ˌəʊvəˈfʊl/ *adj.* filled excessively.

♦ **over-full employment** *n.* situation in which there are more jobs than people seeking work. It tends to be inflationary as employers increase the wages offered, to attract employees, and in addition employers have to resort to less well-qualified employees, which lowers the efficiency of industry.

♦ **overfunding** /ˌəʊvəˈfʌndɪŋ/ *n.* policy available to the UK government in which it sells more government securities than it needs to pay for public spending. The objective of the policy is to absorb surplus money and so curb inflation.

♦ **overgear** /ˌəʊvəˈgɪə/ *v.* cause (a company) to have too high a proportion of loan stock and preference shares in comparison to its equity capital.

overground *adj.* **1** raised above the ground. **2** not underground.

overgrown /ˌəʊvəˈgrəʊn/ *adj.* **1** grown too big. **2** wild; covered with weeds etc. □ **overgrowth** *n.*

overhang –*v.* /ˌəʊvəˈhæŋ/ (*past* and *past part.* **-hung**) project or hang over. –*n.* /ˈəʊvəˌhæŋ/ **1** overhanging. **2** overhanging part or amount. **3** shares that underwriters have to buy when a new issue has not been fully taken up by the market.

overhaul –*v.* /ˌəʊvəˈhɔːl/ **1** thoroughly examine the condition of and repair if necessary. **2** overtake. –*n.* /ˈəʊvəˌhɔːl/ thorough examination, with repairs if necessary.

overhead –*adv.* /ˌəʊvəˈhed/ **1** above head height. **2** in the sky. –*adj.* /ˈəʊvəˌhed/ placed overhead. –*n.* /ˈəʊvəˌhed/ (in *pl.*) = OVERHEAD COSTS.

♦ **overhead costs** *n.pl.* (also **indirect costs, operating costs**) costs of production of goods or services that are not direct costs, i.e. costs over and above those for materials and labour employed in producing the goods or services. These are divided into **fixed costs** and **variable costs**, the former being those that do not change over broad levels of activity (e.g. factory rent, depreciation of plant and machinery) and the latter being those costs that do vary with levels of production (e.g. fuel and power).

overhead projector *n.* projector for producing an enlarged image of a transparency.

♦ **overhead variance** *n.* variance arising because overhead costs differ from those budgeted for.

overhear /ˌəʊvəˈhɪə(r)/ *v.* (*past* and *past part.* **-heard**) (also *absol.*) hear unintentionally or as an eavesdropper.

overheat /ˌəʊvəˈhiːt/ *v.* **1** make or become too hot. **2** cause inflation (in) by placing excessive pressure on resources at a time of expanding demand. The overheating of an economy during a boom reflects the inability of some firms to increase output as fast as demand; they therefore choose to profit from the excess demand by raising prices. **3** (as **overheated** *adj.*) overexcited.

Overijssel /ˌəʊvərˈaɪs(ə)l/ province in the E central Netherlands; pop. (1995) 1 050 389; capital, Zwolle. Agriculture (esp. dairy farming and fodder crops) is important, and textiles and machinery are produced.

overindulge /ˌəʊvərɪnˈdʌldʒ/ *v.* (**-ging**) indulge to excess. □ **overindulgence** *n.* **overindulgent** *adj.*

♦ **overinsure** /ˌəʊvərɪnˈʃʊə(r)/ *v.* insure (an item) for more than its full value, even though insurers are only obliged to pay the full value (usu. the replacement value) of an insured item and no more. If insurers find a policyholder has overinsured an item, the premium for the cover above the true value is returned. □ **overinsurance** *n.*

♦ **overinvestment** /ˌəʊvərɪnˈvestmənt/ *n.* excessive investment of capital, esp. in the manufacturing industry towards the end of a boom as a result of over-optimistic expectations of future demand. When the boom begins to fade, the manufacturer is left with surplus capacity and therefore makes no further capital investments, which itself creates unemployment and fuels the imminent recession.

overjoyed /ˌəʊvəˈdʒɔɪd/ *adj.* filled with great joy.

overkill *n.* **1** excess of capacity to kill or destroy. **2** excess.

overland /ˈəʊvəˌlænd, -ˈlænd/ *adj.* & *adv.* **1** by land. **2** not by sea.

overlap –*v.* /ˌəʊvəˈlæp/ (**-pp-**) **1** (cause to) partly cover and extend beyond (*don't overlap them*). **2** (of two things) be placed so that one overlaps the other (*overlapping tiles*). **3** partly coincide. –*n.* /ˈəʊvəˌlæp/ **1** overlapping. **2** overlapping part or amount.

over-large /ˌəʊvəˈlɑːdʒ/ *adj.* too large.

overlay –*v.* /ˌəʊvəˈleɪ/ (*past* and *past part.* **-laid**) **1** lay over. **2** (foll. by *with*) cover (a thing) with (a coating etc.). –*n.* /ˈəʊvəˌleɪ/ **1** thing laid over another. **2** piece of card or plastic placed over or around a computer keyboard to indicate what special functions have been assigned to particular keys.

overleaf /ˌəʊvəˈliːf/ *adv.* on the other side of the leaf of a book.

overlie /ˌəʊvəˈlaɪ/ *v.* (**-lying**; *past* **-lay**; *past part.* **-lain**) **1** lie on top of. **2** smother (a child etc.) thus.

overload –*v.* /ˌəʊvəˈləʊd/ **1** load excessively (with baggage, work, etc.). **2** put too great a demand on (an electrical circuit etc.). –*n.* /ˈəʊvəˌləʊd/ excessive quantity or demand.

over-long /ˌəʊvəˈlɒŋ/ *adj.* & *adv.* too long.

overlook /ˌəʊvəˈlʊk/ *v.* **1** fail to notice; tolerate. **2** have a view of from above. **3** supervise.

overlord *n.* supreme lord.

overly *adv.* excessively; too.

overman /ˌəʊvəˈmæn/ *v.* (**-nn-**) provide with too large a crew, staff, etc.

over-much /ˌəʊvəˈmʌtʃ/ –*adv.* to too great an extent. –*adj.* excessive.

overnight /ˌəʊvəˈnaɪt/ –*adv.* **1** for a night. **2** during the night. **3** instantly, suddenly. –*adj.* **1** done or for use etc. overnight. **2** instant (*overnight success*).

♦ **overnight loan** *n.* loan made by a bank to a bill broker to enable the broker to take up bills of exchange. Initially the loan will be repayable the following day but it is usu. renewable. If it is not, the broker must turn to the lender of last resort, i.e. the Bank of England in the UK.

over-particular /ˌəʊvəpəˈtɪkjʊlə(r)/ *adj.* excessively particular or fussy.

overpass *n.* road or railway line that passes over another by means of a bridge.

overpay /ˌəʊvəˈpeɪ/ *v.* (*past* and *past part.* **-paid**) pay too highly or too much. □ **overpayment** *n.*

overplay /ˌəʊvəˈpleɪ/ *v.* give undue importance to; overemphasize. □ **overplay one's hand** act on an unduly optimistic estimation of one's chances.

overpopulated /ˌəʊvəˈpɒpjʊˌleɪtɪd/ *adj.* having too large a population. □ **overpopulation** /-ˈleɪʃ(ə)n/ *n.*

overpower /ˌəʊvəˈpaʊə(r)/ *v.* **1** subdue, conquer. **2** (esp. as **overpowering** *adj.*) be too intense or overwhelming for (*overpowering smell*). □ **overpoweringly** *adv.*

overprice /ˌəʊvəˈpraɪs/ *v.* (**-cing**) price too highly.

overprint –*v.* /ˌəʊvəˈprɪnt/ print over (a surface already printed). –*n.* /ˈəʊvəprɪnt/ words etc. overprinted.

overproduce /ˌəʊvəprəˈdjuːs/ *v.* (**-cing**) **1** (often *absol.*) produce more of (a commodity) than is wanted. **2** produce (a play, recording, etc.) to an excessive degree. □ **overproduction** /-ˈdʌkʃ(ə)n/ *n.*

overprotective /ˌəʊvəprəˈtektɪv/ *adj.* excessively protective.

overqualified /ˌəʊvəˈkwɒlɪˌfaɪd/ *adj.* too highly qualified for a particular job etc.

overrate /ˌəʊvəˈreɪt/ *v.* (**-ting**) **1** assess or value too highly. **2** (as **overrated** *adj.*) not as good as it is said to be.

overreach /ˌəʊvəˈriːtʃ/ *v.* outwit, cheat. □ **overreach oneself** fail by attempting too much.

overreact /ˌəʊvərɪˈækt/ *v.* respond more forcibly than is justified. □ **overreaction** *n.*

override –*v.* /ˌəʊvəˈraɪd/ (**-ding**; *past* **-rode**; *past part.* **-ridden**) **1** (often as **overriding** *adj.*) have priority over (*overriding consideration*). **2 a** intervene and make ineffective. **b** interrupt the action of (an automatic device), esp. to take manual control. –*n.* /ˈəʊvəˌraɪd/ **1** suspension of an automatic function. **2** device for this.

overrider *n.* each of a pair of projecting pieces on the bumper of a car.

overripe /ˌəʊvəˈraɪp/ *adj.* excessively ripe.

overrule /ˌəʊvəˈruːl/ *v.* (**-ling**) **1** set aside (a decision etc.) by superior authority. **2** reject a proposal of (a person) in this way.

overrun /ˌəʊvəˈrʌn/ *v.* (**-nn-**; *past* **-ran**; *past part.* **-run**) **1**

swarm or spread over. **2** conquer (a territory) by force. **3** (usu. *absol.*) exceed (an allotted time).

overseas –*adv.* /ˌəʊvəˈsiːz/ across the sea; abroad. –*attrib. adj.* /ˈəʊvəˌsiːz/ of places across the sea; foreign.

◆ **overseas company** *n.* company incorporated outside the UK that has a branch or a subsidiary company in the UK. Overseas companies with a place of business in the UK have to make a return to the Registrar of Companies, giving particulars of their memorandum of association, directors, and secretary as well as providing an annual balance sheet and profit-and-loss account.

◆ **Overseas Development Administration** *n.* (also **ODA**) UK government department dealing with the administration of aid to overseas countries, including both financial and technical assistance. Previously the Ministry for Overseas Development, the ODA is now part of the Foreign and Commonwealth Office, with a minister solely responsible for it.

◆ **overseas-income taxation** *n.* taxation of income arising outside the national boundaries of the taxing authority. Most countries tax the worldwide income of their permanent residents, as well as the incomes arising in the country to outsiders. This can involve double (or multiple) taxation, for which reliefs are often provided by double-taxation treaties.

◆ **overseas investment** *n.* investment by the government, industry, or members of the public of a country in the industry of another country. For members of the public this is often most easily achieved by investing through foreign stock exchanges.

oversee /ˌəʊvəˈsiː/ *v.* (**-sees**; *past* **-saw**; *past part.* **-seen**) officially supervise (workers etc.); superintend. □ **overseer** *n.*

◆ **oversell** /ˌəʊvəˈsel/ *v.* (*past* and *past part.* **-sold**) **1** sell more of (a product or service) than can be supplied. **2** use aggressive methods to sell (a product). **3** (as **oversold** *adj.*) (of a market) having fallen too fast as a result of excessive selling and therefore expected to have an upward reaction.

over-sensitive /ˌəʊvəˈsensɪtɪv/ *adj.* excessively sensitive; easily hurt or quick to react. □ **over-sensitiveness** *n.* **over-sensitivity** /-ˈtɪvɪtɪ/ *n.*

oversew *v.* (*past part.* **-sewn** or **-sewed**) sew (two edges) with stitches passing over the join.

oversexed /ˌəʊvəˈsekst/ *adj.* having unusually strong sexual desires.

overshadow /ˌəʊvəˈʃædəʊ/ *v.* **1** appear much more prominent or important than. **2** cast into the shade.

overshoe *n.* outer protective shoe worn over an ordinary one.

overshoot /ˌəʊvəˈʃuːt/ *v.* (*past* and *past part.* **-shot**) **1** pass or send beyond (a target or limit). **2** fly beyond or taxi too far along (the runway) when landing or taking off. □ **overshoot the mark** go beyond what is intended or proper.

◆ **overshooting** *n.* situation in which there is a sharp increase in the value of an asset followed by a slow adjustment to equilibrium, caused by a change in expectations. It is usu. applied to an analysis of the real exchange rates and has been used to explain the extreme volatility of exchange rates in the 1970s and 1980s (for example, between 1980 and 1984 the US dollar rose by around 70% against foreign currencies and between 1985 and 1987 fell by 40%). Overshooting provides an argument for more government intervention in the determination of exchange rates.

◆ **overside delivery** *n.* unloading of a cargo over the side of a ship into lighters.

oversight *n.* **1** failure to do or notice something. **2** inadvertent mistake. **3** supervision.

oversimplify /ˌəʊvəˈsɪmplɪˌfaɪ/ *v.* (**-ies, -ied**) (also *absol.*) distort (a problem etc.) by stating it in too simple terms. □ **oversimplification** /-fɪˈkeɪʃ(ə)n/ *n.*

oversize *adj.* (also **-sized**) of greater than the usual size.

oversleep /ˌəʊvəˈsliːp/ *v.* (*past* and *past part.* **-slept**) sleep beyond the intended time of waking.

oversold /ˌəʊvəˈsəʊld/ *past* and *past part.* of OVERSELL.

overspecialize /ˌəʊvəˈspeʃəˌlaɪz/ *v.* (also **-ise**) (**-zing** or **-sing**) concentrate too much on one aspect or area. □ **overspecialization** /-ˈzeɪʃ(ə)n/ *n.*

overspend /ˌəʊvəˈspend/ *v.* (*past* and *past part.* **-spent**) spend too much or beyond one's means.

overspill *n.* **1** what is spilt over or overflows. **2** surplus population moving to a new area.

overspread /ˌəʊvəˈspred/ *v.* (*past* and *past part.* **-spread**) **1** cover the surface of. **2** (as **overspread** *adj.*) (usu. foll. by *with*) covered.

overstate /ˌəʊvəˈsteɪt/ *v.* (**-ting**) **1** state too strongly. **2** exaggerate. □ **overstatement** *n.*

overstay /ˌəʊvəˈsteɪ/ *v.* stay longer than (one's welcome etc.).

oversteer –*n.* /ˈəʊvəˌstɪə(r)/ tendency of a vehicle to turn more sharply than was intended. –*v.* /ˌəʊvəˈstɪə(r)/ (of a vehicle) exhibit oversteer.

overstep /ˌəʊvəˈstep/ *v.* (**-pp-**) pass beyond (a permitted or acceptable limit). □ **overstep the mark** violate conventional behaviour etc.

overstock /ˌəʊvəˈstɒk/ *v.* stock excessively.

overstrain /ˌəʊvəˈstreɪn/ *v.* strain too much.

overstretch /ˌəʊvəˈstretʃ/ *v.* **1** stretch too much. **2** (esp. as **overstretched** *adj.*) make excessive demands on (resources, a person, etc.).

overstrung *adj.* **1** /ˌəʊvəˈstrʌŋ/ (of a person, nerves, etc.) too highly strung. **2** /ˈəʊvəˌstrʌŋ/ (of a piano) with strings in sets crossing each other obliquely.

overstuffed /ˌəʊvəˈstʌft/ *adj.* **1** (of furniture) made soft and comfortable by thick upholstery. **2** stuffed too full.

◆ **oversubscribe** /ˌəʊvəsəbˈskraɪb/ *v.* (**-bing**) (usu. as **oversubscribed** *adj.*) apply for more than the amount available of (a new issue of shares etc.). Applications for oversubscribed shares must be scaled down according to a set of rules devised by the company issuing the shares or their advisers. Alternatively some companies prefer to allocate the shares by ballot (see ALLOTMENT 4). New issues are usu. oversubscribed because of difficulty in arriving at an issue price that will be low enough to attract sufficient investors to take up the whole issue and yet will give the company the maximum capital. Speculative purchases by stags also make it difficult to price a new issue. Cf. UNDERSUBSCRIBED. □ **oversubscription** /-ˈskrɪpʃ(ə)n/ *n.*

overt /əʊˈvɜːt/ *adj.* done openly; unconcealed. □ **overtly** *adv.* [French, past part. of *ouvrir* open]

overtake /ˌəʊvəˈteɪk/ *v.* (**-king**; *past* **-took**; *past part.* **-taken**) **1** (also *absol.*) catch up with and pass while travelling in the same direction. **2** (of misfortune etc.) come suddenly upon.

overtax /ˌəʊvəˈtæks/ *v.* **1** make excessive demands on. **2** tax too heavily.

◆ **over-the-counter market** *n.* (also **OTC market**) market in which shares are traded outside the jurisdiction of a recognized stock exchange. OTC markets tend to deal in smaller quantities of stocks (and bonds), they tend to be less liquid, and they provide less investor protection. The world's largest OTC market is NASDAQ in the US. In the UK, OTC markets have generally been considered less respectable and were abolished in 1987.

over-the-top *adj. colloq.* excessive.

overthrow –*v.* /ˌəʊvəˈθrəʊ/ (*past* **-threw**; *past part.* **-thrown**) **1** remove forcibly from power. **2** conquer, overcome. –*n.* /ˈəʊvəˌθrəʊ/ defeat, downfall.

overtime –*n.* **1** time worked in addition to regular hours. **2** payment for this, which is usu. higher than the basic rate of pay. –*adv.* in addition to regular hours.

♦ **overtime ban** *n.* form of industrial action in which employees refuse to work overtime, thus causing considerable dislocation to normal working but clearly less than would occur in a total strike.

overtone *n.* **1** *Mus.* any of the tones above the lowest in a harmonic series. **2** subtle extra quality or implication.

♦ **overtrading** /ˌəʊvəˈtreɪdɪŋ/ *n.* trading by an organization beyond the resources provided by its existing capital. Overtrading tends to lead to liquidity problems as too much stock is bought on credit and too much credit is extended to customers, so that ultimately there is not sufficient cash available to pay the debts as they arise. The solution is either to cut back on trading or to raise further permanent capital.

overture /ˈəʊvəˌtjʊə(r)/ *n.* **1** orchestral piece opening an opera etc. **2** composition in this style. **3** (usu. in *pl.*) **a** opening of negotiations. **b** formal proposal or offer. [French: related to OVERT]

overturn /ˌəʊvəˈtɜːn/ *v.* **1** (cause to) fall down or over. **2** reverse; overthrow.

overuse –*v.* /ˌəʊvəˈjuːz/ (**-sing**) use too much. –*n.* /ˌəʊvəˈjuːs/ excessive use.

overview *n.* general survey.

overweening /ˌəʊvəˈwiːnɪŋ/ *adj.* arrogant, presumptuous.

overweight –*adj.* /ˌəʊvəˈweɪt/ above an allowed or suitable weight. –*n.* /ˈəʊvəˌweɪt/ excess weight; preponderance.

overwhelm /ˌəʊvəˈwelm/ *v.* **1** overpower with emotion or a burden. **2** overcome by force of numbers. **3** bury or drown beneath a huge mass.

overwhelming *adj.* **1** too great to resist or overcome (*an overwhelming desire to laugh*). **2** by a great number (*the overwhelming majority*). □ **overwhelmingly** *adv.*

overwind /ˌəʊvəˈwaɪnd/ *v.* (*past* and *past part.* **-wound**) wind (a watch etc.) beyond the proper stopping point.

overwork /ˌəʊvəˈwɜːk/ –*v.* **1** (cause to) work too hard. **2** weary or exhaust with too much work. **3** (esp. as **overworked** *adj.*) make excessive use of (*an overworked phrase*). **4** (as **overworked** *adj.*) = OVERWROUGHT 2. –*n.* excessive work.

overwrite /ˌəʊvəˈraɪt/ *v.* (**-ting**; *past* and *past part.* **-written**) *Computing* **1** destroy the contents of a storage location by writing a new item of data to that location. **2** write a new version of a file on backing store on top of the existing version.

overwrought /ˌəʊvəˈrɔːt/ *adj.* **1** overexcited, nervous, distraught. **2** too elaborate.

ovi- *comb. form* egg, ovum. [from OVUM]

oviduct /ˈəʊvɪˌdʌkt/ *n.* tube through which an ovum passes from the ovary.

Oviedo /ˌɒvɪˈeɪdəʊ/ city in NW Spain, capital of Asturias region, having mining and food-processing industries; pop. (est. 1994) 201 712.

oviform /ˈəʊvɪˌfɔːm/ *adj.* egg-shaped.

ovine /ˈəʊvaɪn/ *adj.* of or like sheep. [Latin *ovis* sheep]

oviparous /əʊˈvɪpərəs/ *adj.* producing young from eggs hatching after leaving the body. [from OVUM, Latin *-parus* bearing]

ovoid /ˈəʊvɔɪd/ *adj.* (of a solid) egg-shaped. [related to OVUM]

ovulate /ˈɒvjʊˌleɪt/ *v.* (**-ting**) produce ova or ovules, or discharge them from the ovary. □ **ovulation** /-ˈleɪʃ(ə)n/ *n.* [related to OVUM]

ovule /ˈɒvjuːl/ *n.* structure that contains the germ cell in a female plant. [related to OVUM]

ovum /ˈəʊvəm/ *n.* (*pl.* **ova**) female egg-cell from which young develop after fertilization. [Latin, = egg]

ow *int.* expressing sudden pain. [natural exclamation]

owe /əʊ/ *v.* (**-wing**) **1 a** be under obligation (to a person etc.) to pay or repay (money, gratitude, etc.). **b** (usu. foll. by *for*) be in debt. **2** have a duty to render (*owe allegiance*). **3** (usu. foll. by *to*) be indebted to a person or thing for (*we owe our success to the weather*). [Old English]

owing /ˈəʊɪŋ/ *predic. adj.* **1** owed; yet to be paid. **2** (foll. by *to*) **a** caused by. **b** (as *prep.*) because of.

■ **Usage** The use of *owing to* as a preposition meaning 'because of' is entirely acceptable (e.g. *couldn't come owing to the snow*), unlike this use of *due to*.

owl *n.* **1** nocturnal bird of prey with large eyes and a hooked beak. **2** solemn or wise-looking person. □ **owlish** *adj.* [Old English]

owlet *n.* small or young owl.

own /əʊn/ –*adj.* (prec. by possessive) **1 a** belonging to oneself or itself; not another's (*saw it with my own eyes*). **b** individual, peculiar, particular (*has its own charm*). **2** used to emphasize identity rather than possession (*cooks his own meals*). **3** (*absol.*) private property (*is it your own?*). –*v.* **1** have as property; possess. **2** admit as valid, true, etc. **3** acknowledge paternity, authorship, or possession of. □ **come into one's own 1** receive one's due. **2** achieve recognition. **get one's own back** get revenge. **hold one's own** maintain one's position. **of one's own** belonging to oneself. **on one's own 1** alone, independent. **2** independently, without help. **own up** (often foll. by *to*) confess frankly. □ **-owned** *adj.* (in *comb.*). [Old English]

♦ **own brand** *n.* (also **own label**, **private brand**, **house brand**) (often *attrib.*) product sold under a distributor's own name or trade mark through its own outlets. These items are either made specially for the distributor or are versions of the manufacturer's equivalent brand. Own-brand goods are promoted by the distributor rather than the manufacturer and are typically 10–20% cheaper to the distributor than an equivalent brand. Own brands are sold principally by chain stores.

owner *n.* person who owns something.

owner-occupier *n.* person who owns and occupies a house.

♦ **ownership** *n.* **1** state or fact of being an owner. **2** rights over property, including rights of possession, exclusive enjoyment, destruction, etc. In UK common law, land cannot be owned outright, as all land belongs to the Crown and is held in tenure by the 'owner'. However, an owner of an estate in land in fee simple is to all intents and purposes an outright owner. In general, ownership can be split between different persons. For example, a trustee has the legal ownership of trust property but the beneficiary has the equitable or beneficial ownership. If goods are stolen, the owner still has ownership but not possession. Similarly, if goods are hired or pledged to someone, the owner has ownership but no immediate right to possession.

own goal *n.* **1** goal scored by mistake against the scorer's own side. **2** act etc. that has the unintended effect of harming one's own interests.

owt *n. colloq.* or *dial.* anything. [var. of AUGHT]

OX *postcode* Oxford.

ox *n.* (*pl.* **oxen**) **1** large usu. horned ruminant used for draught, milk, and meat. **2** castrated male of a domesticated species of cattle. [Old English]

oxalic acid /ɒkˈsælɪk/ *n.* very poisonous and sour acid found in sorrel and rhubarb leaves. [Greek *oxalis* wood sorrel]

oxbow *n.* loop formed by a horseshoe bend in a river.

Oxbridge *n.* (also *attrib.*) Oxford and Cambridge universities regarded together, esp. in contrast to newer ones. [portmanteau word]

oxen *pl.* of OX.

ox-eye daisy *n.* daisy with white petals and a yellow centre.

Oxf. *abbr.* Oxford.

Oxfam /ˈɒksfæm/ *abbr.* Oxford Committee for Famine Relief.

Oxford /ˈɒksfəd/ city in S central England, county town

of Oxfordshire and the seat of a major English university; industries include car manufacture, tourism, and publishing; pop. (est. 1993) 132 000.

Oxford blue *adj.* & *n.* (as adj. often hyphenated) a dark blue, often with a purple tinge.

Oxfordshire /ˈɒksfəd,ʃɪə(r)/ county in the SE Midlands of England; pop. (est. 1994) 590 200; county town, Oxford. Agricultural activities include arable farming; motor vehicles are manufactured near Oxford.

oxhide *n.* **1** hide of an ox. **2** leather from this.

oxidation /,ɒksɪˈdeɪʃ(ə)n/ *n.* process of oxidizing. [French: related to OXIDE]

oxide /ˈɒksaɪd/ *n.* binary compound of oxygen. [French: related to OXYGEN]

oxidize /ˈɒksɪ,daɪz/ *v.* (also **-ise**) (**-zing** or **-sing**) **1** combine with oxygen. **2** make or become rusty. **3** coat (metal) with oxide. □ **oxidization** /-ˈzeɪʃ(ə)n/ *n.*

Oxon. *abbr.* **1** Oxfordshire. **2** (esp. in degree titles) of Oxford University. [Latin *Oxonia* (sense 1), *Oxoniensis* (sense 2): related to OXONIAN]

Oxonian /ɒkˈsəʊnɪən/ *–adj.* of Oxford or Oxford University. *–n.* **1** member of Oxford University. **2** native or inhabitant of Oxford. [*Oxonia* Latinized name of *Ox(en)ford*]

oxtail *n.* tail of an ox, often used in making soup.

oxyacetylene /,ɒksɪəˈsetɪ,liːn/ *adj.* of or using a mixture of oxygen and acetylene, esp. in cutting or welding metals.

oxygen /ˈɒksɪdʒ(ə)n/ *n.* tasteless odourless gaseous element essential to plant and animal life. [Greek *oxus* sharp, -GEN (because it was thought to be present in all acids)]

oxygenate /ˈɒksɪdʒə,neɪt/ *v.* (**-ting**) supply, treat, or mix with oxygen; oxidize.

oxygen tent *n.* tentlike enclosure supplying a patient with air rich in oxygen.

oxymoron /,ɒksɪˈmɔːrɒn/ *n.* figure of speech in which apparently contradictory terms appear in conjunction (e.g. *faith unfaithful kept him falsely true*). [Greek, = pointedly foolish, from *oxus* sharp, *mōros* dull]

OY *international civil aircraft marking* Denmark.

oyez /əʊˈjes/ *int.* (also **oyes**) uttered, usu. three times, by a public crier or a court officer to command attention. [Anglo-French, = hear!, from Latin *audio*]

oyster *–n.* **1** bivalve mollusc, esp. an edible kind, sometimes producing a pearl. **2** symbol of all one desires (*the world is my oyster*). **3** oyster white. *–adj.* oyster white. [Greek *ostreon*]

oyster-catcher *n.* wading sea bird.

oyster white *adj.* & *n.* (as adj. often hyphenated) greyish white.

oz. *abbr.* ounce(s). [Italian *onza* ounce]

ozone /ˈəʊzəʊn/ *n.* **1** *Chem.* unstable form of oxygen with three atoms in a molecule, having a pungent odour. **2** *colloq.* **a** invigorating air at the seaside etc. **b** exhilarating influence. [Greek *ozō* smell (v.)]

ozone-friendly *adj.* not containing chemicals destructive to the ozone layer.

ozone layer *n.* layer of ozone in the stratosphere that absorbs most of the sun's ultraviolet radiation.

Pp

P[1] /piː/ *n.* (also **p**) (*pl.* **Ps** or **P's**) sixteenth letter of the alphabet.

P[2] *abbr.* (also **P.**) **1** (on road signs) parking. **2** *Chess* pawn. **3** (also P) proprietary.

P[3] *–symb.* **1** phosphorus. **2** *Currency* pula. *–international vehicle registration* Portugal. *–international civil aircraft marking* North Korea.

p *abbr.* (also **p.**) **1** penny, pence. **2** page. **3** piano (softly).

P2 *international civil aircraft marking* Papua New Guinea.

P4 *international civil aircraft marking* Aruba.

P45 *n.* form relating to unemployment benefit issued by the DSS.

PA *–abbr.* **1** (also **P/A**) particular average (see AVERAGE *n.* 4). **2** personal account, denoting a transaction made by a professional investment adviser for his or her own account rather than for the firm for which the adviser works. **3** *Taxation* personal allowance. **4** = PERSONAL ASSISTANT. **5** (also **P/A**) = POWER OF ATTORNEY. **6** (also **P/A**) *Banking* & *Bookkeeping* private account. **7** *US* public accountant. **8** public address (system). *–postcode* Paisley. *–US postcode* Pennsylvania. *–international vehicle registration* Panama. *–airline flight code* Pan American World Airways.

Pa *symb.* protactinium.

Pa. *abbr.* Pennsylvania.

pa /pɑː/ *n. colloq.* father. [abbreviation of PAPA]

p.a. *abbr.* per annum.

pa'anga /pæ'æŋgə/ *n.* standard monetary unit of Tonga. [Tongan]

pabulum /'pæbjʊləm/ *n.* food, esp. for the mind. [Latin]

♦ **PABX** *abbr.* private automatic branch exchange. See PRIVATE BRANCH EXCHANGE.

PAC *abbr.* **1** Public Accounts Committee. **2** *Stock Exch.* put-and-call (option).

PACE /peɪs/ *abbr.* **1** performance and cost evaluation. **2** precision analog computing equipment. **3** Police and Criminal Evidence Act (1984).

pace[1] *–n.* **1 a** single step in walking or running. **b** distance covered in this. **2** speed in walking or running. **3** rate of movement or progression. **4** way of walking or running; gait (*ambling pace*). *–v.* (**-cing**) **1 a** walk slowly and evenly (*pace up and down*). **b** (of a horse) amble. **2** traverse by pacing. **3** set the pace for (a rider, runner, etc.). **4** (foll. by *out*) measure by pacing. □ **keep pace** (often foll. by *with*) advance at an equal rate (to). **put a person** etc. **through his** (or **her**) **paces** test a person's qualities in action etc. **set the pace** determine the speed; lead. [French *pas* from Latin *passus*]

pace[2] /'pɑːtʃeɪ, 'peɪsɪ/ *prep.* (in stating a contrary opinion) with due respect to (the person named). [Latin, ablative of *pax* peace]

pace bowler *n. Cricket* fast bowler.

pacemaker *n.* **1** competitor who sets the pace in a race. **2** natural or artificial device for stimulating the heart muscle.

pace-setter *n.* **1** leader. **2** = PACEMAKER 1.

pachyderm /'pækɪ,dɜːm/ *n.* thick-skinned mammal, esp. an elephant or rhinoceros. □ **pachydermatous** /-'dɜːmətəs/ *adj.* [Greek *pakhus* thick, *derma* skin]

pacific /pə'sɪfɪk/ *–adj.* **1** peaceful; tranquil. **2** (**Pacific**) of or adjoining the Pacific Ocean. *–n.* (**the Pacific**) the Pacific Ocean. [Latin *pax pacis* peace]

Pacific Ocean world's largest ocean, covering one-third of the earth's surface, separating Asia and Australia from North and South America and extending from Antarctica in the S to the Bering Strait (which links it to the Arctic Ocean) in the N.

Pacific rim *n.* regions, countries, etc. lying on the western shores of the Pacific Ocean, esp. in the context of their developing manufacturing capacity and consumer markets.

Pacific Time *n.* standard time used in the Pacific region of Canada and the US.

pacifier /'pæsɪ,faɪə(r)/ *n.* **1** person or thing that pacifies. **2** *US* baby's dummy.

pacifism /'pæsɪ,fɪz(ə)m/ *n.* belief that war and violence are morally unjustifiable. □ **pacifist** *n.* & *adj.*

pacify /'pæsɪ,faɪ/ *v.* (**-ies, -ied**) **1** appease (a person, anger, etc.). **2** bring (a country etc.) to a state of peace. □ **pacification** /-fɪ'keɪʃ(ə)n/ *n.* **pacificatory** /pə'sɪfɪkətərɪ/ *adj.*

pack[1] *–n.* **1 a** collection of things wrapped up or tied together for carrying. **b** = BACKPACK. **2** set of packaged items. **3** usu. *derog.* lot or set (*pack of lies*; *pack of thieves*). **4** set of playing-cards. **5** group of hounds, wild animals, etc. **6** organized group of Cub Scouts or Brownies. **7** *Rugby* team's forwards. **8** = FACE-PACK. **9** = PACK ICE. *–v.* **1** (often foll. by *up*) **a** fill (a suitcase, bag, etc.) with clothes etc. **b** put (things) in a bag or suitcase, esp. for travelling. **2** (often foll. by *in, into*) crowd or cram (*packed a lot into a few hours*; *packed in like sardines*). **3** (esp. in *passive*; often foll. by *with*) fill (*restaurant was packed*; *fans packed the stadium*; *packed with information*). **4** cover (a thing) with packaging. **5** be suitable for packing. **6** *colloq.* **a** carry (a gun etc.). **b** be capable of delivering (a forceful punch). **7** (of animals or Rugby forwards) form a pack. □ **pack in** *colloq.* stop, give up (*packed in his job*). **pack it in** (or **up**) *colloq.* end or stop it. **pack off** send (a person) away, esp. summarily. **pack them in** fill a theatre etc. with a capacity audience. **pack up** *colloq.* **1** stop functioning; break down. **2** retire from an activity, contest, etc. **send packing** *colloq.* dismiss summarily. [Low German or Dutch]

pack[2] *v.* select (a jury etc.) or fill (a meeting) so as to secure a decision in one's favour. [probably from PACT]

package *–n.* **1 a** bundle of things packed. **b** parcel, box, etc., in which things are packed. **2** (in full **package deal**) set of proposals or items offered or agreed to as a whole. **3** *Computing* set of programs designed to be sold to a number of users and used in computerized accounting systems for purchase and sales ledgers, stock control, payroll records, etc. **4** *colloq.* = PACKAGE HOLIDAY. *–v.* (**-ging**) make up into or enclose in a package. □ **packager** *n.*

package holiday *n.* (also **package tour**) holiday (or tour) with travel, hotels, etc. at an inclusive price.

packaging *n.* **1 a** wrapping or container for goods. **b** design of such. **2** process of packing goods. **3** activity that combines several operations and enables the packager to deliver a finished or near-finished product to a selling organization. For example, many non-fiction books are produced by **book packagers**, who write, illustrate, typeset, and print books, which they deliver to publishers, who sell them to the public under their own imprint.

packed lunch *n.* lunch of sandwiches etc. prepared and packed to be eaten away from home.

packed out *adj.* full, crowded.

packer *n.* person or thing that packs, esp. a dealer who prepares and packs food.

packet /ˈpækɪt/ *n.* **1** small package. **2** *colloq.* large sum of money won, lost, or spent. **3** see PACKET SWITCHING. **4** (in full **packet-boat**) *hist.* mail-boat or passenger ship.

packet switching *n.* process enabling information (in digital form) to be sent automatically from one computer on a network to any other, the information being switched from one communication line to another until it reaches its specified destination. The information is transmitted in units known as **packets**. At each switching point along its route the packet is checked for errors, stored temporarily, and forwarded to the next point when the necessary resources become available. The packets of a partitioned message, document, etc. are reassembled when they reach their final destination. The device that assembles the packets for transmission and then reassembles them is called a **PAD** (packet assembler/disassembler). National and international packet-switching services have been set up by many bodies that provide communication services; British Telecom's packet-switching service is called **PSS** (packet switch stream). These services allow data to be transmitted at very high speeds (up to about two million bits per second).

packhorse *n.* horse for carrying loads.

pack ice *n.* crowded floating ice in the sea.

packing *n.* material used to pack esp. fragile articles.

packthread *n.* stout thread for sewing or tying up packs.

pact *n.* agreement; treaty. [Latin *pactum*]

PAD *abbr.* packet assembler/disassembler (see PACKET SWITCHING).

pad[1] *–n.* **1** thick piece of soft material used to protect, fill out hollows, hold or absorb liquid, etc. **2** sheets of blank paper fastened together at one edge, for writing or drawing on. **3** fleshy underpart of an animal's foot or of a human finger. **4** guard for the leg and ankle in sports. **5** flat surface for helicopter take-off or rocket-launching. **6** *slang* lodgings, flat, etc. **7** floating leaf of a water lily. *–v.* (**-dd-**) **1** provide with a pad or padding; stuff. **2** (foll. by *out*) lengthen or fill out (a book etc.) with unnecessary material. [probably Low German or Dutch]

pad[2] *–v.* (**-dd-**) **1** walk with a soft dull steady step. **2** travel, or tramp along (a road etc.), on foot. *–n.* sound of soft steady steps. [Low German *pad* PATH]

Padang /pæˈdæŋ/ seaport in Indonesia, capital of West Sumatra province; exports include coal, coffee, rubber, and copra; pop. (1990) 477 344.

padded cell *n.* room with padded walls in a mental hospital.

padding *n.* soft material used to pad or stuff.

paddle[1] /ˈpæd(ə)l/ *–n.* **1** short broad-bladed oar used without a rowlock. **2** paddle-shaped instrument. **3** fin, flipper. **4** board on a paddle-wheel or mill-wheel. **5** action or spell of paddling. *–v.* (**-ling**) **1** move on water or propel a boat by paddles. **2** row gently. [origin unknown]

paddle[2] /ˈpæd(ə)l/ *–v.* (**-ling**) walk barefoot, or dabble the feet or hands, in shallow water. *–n.* act of paddling. [probably Low German or Dutch]

paddle-boat *n.* (also **paddle-steamer**) boat (or steamer) propelled by a paddle-wheel.

paddle-wheel *n.* wheel for propelling a ship, with boards round the circumference.

paddock /ˈpædək/ *n.* **1** small field, esp. for keeping horses in. **2** turf enclosure at a racecourse for horses or cars. [*parrock*, var. of PARK]

Paddy /ˈpædɪ/ *n.* (*pl.* **-ies**) *colloq.* often *offens.* Irishman. [Irish *Padraig* Patrick]

paddy[1] /ˈpædɪ/ *n.* (*pl.* **-ies**) **1** (in full **paddy-field**) field where rice is grown. **2** rice before threshing or in the husk. [Malay]

paddy[2] /ˈpædɪ/ *n.* (*pl.* **-ies**) *colloq.* rage; fit of temper. [from PADDY]

padlock /ˈpædlɒk/ *–n.* detachable lock hanging by a pivoted hook on the object fastened. *–v.* secure with a padlock. [origin unknown]

padre /ˈpɑːdrɪ/ *n.* chaplain in the army etc. [Italian, Spanish, and Portuguese, = father, priest]

Padua /ˈpædjuːə/ (Italian **Padova** /ˈpædəvə/) city in NE Italy; industries include machinery and textile manufacture; pop. (est. 1994) 212 589.

paean /ˈpiːən/ *n.* (*US* **pean**) song of praise or triumph. [Latin from Greek]

paederast var. of PEDERAST.

paederasty var. of PEDERASTY.

paediatrics /ˌpiːdɪˈætrɪks/ *n.pl.* (treated as *sing.*) (*US* **pediatrics**) branch of medicine dealing with children and their diseases. □ **paediatric** *adj.* **paediatrician** /-əˈtrɪʃ(ə)n/ *n.* [from PAEDO-, Greek *iatros* physician]

paedo- *comb. form* (*US* **pedo-**) child. [Greek *pais paid-* child]

paedophile /ˈpiːdəˌfaɪl/ *n.* (*US* **pedophile**) person who displays paedophilia.

paedophilia /ˌpiːdəˈfɪlɪə/ *n.* (*US* **pedophilia**) sexual attraction felt towards children.

paella /paɪˈelə/ *n.* Spanish dish of rice, saffron, chicken, seafood, etc., cooked and served in a large shallow pan. [Latin PATELLA]

paeony var. of PEONY.

pagan /ˈpeɪgən/ *–n.* non-religious person, pantheist, or heathen, esp. in pre-Christian times. *–adj.* **1 a** of pagans. **b** irreligious. **2** pantheistic. □ **paganism** *n.* [Latin *paganus* from *pagus* country district]

page[1] *–n.* **1 a** leaf of a book, periodical, etc. **b** each side of this. **c** what is written or printed on this. **2** episode; memorable event. *–v.* (**-ging**) paginate. [Latin *pagina*]

page[2] *–n.* **1** liveried boy or man employed to run errands, attend to a door, etc. **2** boy as a personal attendant of a bride etc. *–v.* (**-ging**) **1** (in hotels, airports, etc.) summon by esp. making an announcement. **2** summon by pager. [French]

pageant /ˈpædʒ(ə)nt/ *n.* **1 a** brilliant spectacle, esp. an elaborate parade. **b** spectacular procession or play illustrating historical events. **c** tableau etc. on a fixed stage or moving vehicle. **2** empty or specious show. [origin unknown]

pageantry *n.* (esp. on state occasions) spectacular show; pomp.

page-boy *n.* **1** = PAGE[2] *n.* 2. **2** woman's hairstyle with the hair bobbed and rolled under.

page printer *n.* *Computing* printer (e.g. a laser printer) that produces a complete page at a time.

pager *n.* (in full **radio pager**) bleeping radio device, calling its wearer to the telephone etc. See RADIO PAGING.

paginate /ˈpædʒɪˌneɪt/ *v.* (**-ting**) assign numbers to the pages of (a book etc.). □ **pagination** /-ˈneɪʃ(ə)n/ *n.* [Latin: related to PAGE[1]]

pagoda /pəˈgəʊdə/ *n.* **1** Hindu or Buddhist temple etc., esp. a many-tiered tower, in India and the Far East. **2** ornamental imitation of this. [Portuguese]

pah /pɑː/ *int.* expressing disgust or contempt. [natural exclamation]

Pahang /pəˈhæŋ/ state of Malaysia, in the SE of the Malay Peninsula; pop. (est. 1993) 1 056 100; capital, Kuantan. Gold and tin are mined; other products include rice, coconuts, and rubber.

paid *past* and *past part.* of PAY[1].

paid-up *adj.* having paid one's subscription to a trade-union, club, etc., or having done what is required to be considered a full member of a particular group (*paid-up feminist*).

♦ **paid-up capital** *n.* (also **fully paid capital**) total amount of money that shareholders have paid to a company for their shares. See SHARE CAPITAL.

♦ **paid-up policy** *n.* endowment assurance policy in which the assured has decided to stop paying premiums before the end of the policy term. This results in a surrender value, which instead of being returned in cash to the assured is used to purchase a single-premium whole-of-life assurance. In this way the life assurance protection continues (for a reduced amount), while the policyholder is relieved of the need to pay further premiums. If the original policy was a with-profits policy, the bonuses paid up to the time the premiums ceased would be included in the surrender value. If it is a unit-linked policy, capital units actually allocated would be allowed to appreciate to the end of the term.

♦ **paid-up share** *n.* share the par value of which has been paid in full. See SHARE CAPITAL.

pail *n.* **1** bucket. **2** amount contained in this. □ **pailful** *n.* (*pl.* **-s**). [Old English]

pain *–n.* **1** any unpleasant bodily sensation produced by illness, accident, etc. **2** mental suffering. **3** (also **pain in the neck** or **arse**) *colloq.* troublesome person or thing; nuisance. *–v.* **1** cause pain to. **2** (as **pained** *adj.*) expressing pain (*pained expression*). □ **be at** (or **take) pains** take great care. **in pain** suffering pain. **on** (or **under) pain of** with (death etc.) as the penalty. [Latin *poena* penalty]

painful *adj.* **1** causing bodily or mental pain. **2** (esp. of part of the body) suffering pain. **3** causing trouble or difficulty; laborious (*painful climb*). □ **painfully** *adv.*

painkiller *n.* drug for alleviating pain. □ **painkilling** *adj.*

painless *adj.* not causing pain. □ **painlessly** *adv.*

painstaking /'peɪnz,teɪkɪŋ/ *adj.* careful, industrious, thorough. □ **painstakingly** *adv.*

paint *–n.* **1** pigment, esp. in liquid form, for colouring a surface. **2** this as a dried film or coating (*paint peeled off*). *–v.* **1 a** cover (a wall, object, etc.) with paint. **b** apply paint of a specified colour to (*paint the door green*). **2** depict (an object, scene, etc.) in paint; produce (a picture) thus. **3** describe vividly (*painted a gloomy picture*). **4** *joc.* or *archaic* **a** apply make-up to (the face, skin, etc.). **b** apply (a liquid to the skin etc.). □ **paint out** efface with paint. **paint the town red** *colloq.* enjoy oneself flamboyantly. [Latin *pingo pict-*]

paintbox *n.* box holding dry paints for painting pictures.

paintbrush *n.* brush for applying paint.

painted lady *n.* orange-red spotted butterfly.

painter[1] *n.* person who paints; artist or decorator.

painter[2] *n.* rope attached to the bow of a boat for tying it to a quay etc. [origin unknown]

painterly *adj.* **1** characteristic of a painter or paintings; artistic. **2** (of a painting) lacking clearly defined outlines.

painting *n.* **1** process or art of using paint. **2** painted picture.

paint shop *n.* part of a factory where cars etc. are sprayed or painted.

paintwork *n.* painted, esp. wooden, surface or area in a building etc.

painty *adj.* of or covered in paint (*painty smell*).

pair *–n.* **1** set of two people or things used together or regarded as a unit. **2** article (e.g. scissors, trousers, or pyjamas) consisting of two joined or corresponding parts. **3 a** engaged or married couple. **b** mated couple of animals. **4** two horses harnessed side by side (*coach and pair*). **5** member of a pair in relation to the other (*cannot find its pair*). **6** two playing-cards of the same denomination. **7** either or both of two MPs etc. on opposite sides agreeing not to vote on certain occasions. *–v.* **1** (often foll. by *off*) arrange or be arranged in couples. **2 a** join or be joined in marriage. **b** (of animals) mate. [Latin *paria*: related to PAR]

♦ **paired comparison** *n.* technique used in marketing research in which consumers are presented with pairs of competing products and asked to choose the one they prefer. The number of times each brand of the product is selected as a preference in a large number of such tests will reveal an order of brand preference. Cf. MONADIC TESTING.

pair of scales *n.* simple balance.

Paisley /'peɪzlɪ/ town in central Scotland, in Strathclyde region; noted for its colourful distinctively patterned shawls, it has textile and engineering industries and produces starch and cornflour; pop. (1981) 84 800. *–n.* (*pl.* **-s**) (often *attrib.*) **1** pattern of curved feather-shaped figures. **2** soft woollen shawl etc. having this pattern.

pajamas *US* var. of PYJAMAS.

Paki /'pækɪ/ *n.* (*pl.* **-s**) *slang offens.* Pakistani. [abbreviation]

Pakistani /,pɑːkɪ'stɑːnɪ/ *–n.* (*pl.* **-s**) **1** native or national of Pakistan. **2** person of Pakistani descent. *–adj.* of Pakistan.

PAL *abbr. Computing* & *Electronics* programmable array logic.

pal *–n. colloq.* friend, mate, comrade. *–v.* (**-ll-**) (usu. foll. by *up*) associate; form a friendship. [Romany]

palace /'pælɪs/ *n.* **1** official residence of a sovereign, president, archbishop, or bishop. **2** splendid or spacious building. [Latin *palatium*]

palace revolution *n.* (also **palace coup**) (usu. non-violent) overthrow of a sovereign, government, etc. by a bureaucracy.

Pakistan /,pɑːkɪ'stɑːn, ,pæk-/ **Islamic Republic of** country in S Asia, bordered by Afghanistan to the N and India to the E. The economy is predominantly agricultural; raw cotton, cotton textiles and yarn, and rice are major exports and wheat, sugar cane, maize, and tobacco are also grown. There are deposits of coal, oil, natural gas, iron ore, copper, limestone, and rock salt. There is some manufacturing and engineering industry, producing textiles, clothing, carpets, and leather (all exported), chemical fertilizers, cement, paints and varnishes, paper, and sugar. Fishing is also important, and there is a developing steel industry.

History. Part of the Indian subcontinent, Pakistan was created as a separate country, comprising the territories of East Pakistan and West Pakistan to the NE and NW of India respectively in which the population was predominantly Muslim, following the British withdrawal in 1947. Pakistan's history since independence has been characterized by border disputes with India over Kashmir, military involvement in politics, and regional unrest. In 1972, after several months of fighting, East Pakistan became the independent state of Bangladesh; Pakistan withdrew from the Commonwealth as a protest against the decision of Britain, Australia, and New Zealand to recognize Bangladesh, but rejoined in 1989. Violent unrest followed allegations of ballot-rigging in the general election of 1977; Gen. Zia-ul-Haq took power after a military coup, and in 1979 Zulfikar Ali Bhutto, the former prime minister, was executed. His daughter Benazir Bhutto became prime minister in 1988, following the death of Zia in an air crash; she was dismissed from office in 1990. Following the dismissal of her successor, Bhutto was re-elected in 1993; however she was dismissed again in 1996 following allegations of mismanagement and corruption. President, Muhammad Rafiq Tarar; prime minister, Mian Muhammad Nawaz Sharif; capital, Islamabad.

languages	Urdu (official), Punjabi, Sindhi, Pashto, English
currency	rupee (PRe; *pl.* PRs) of 100 paisa
pop. (1996)	133 500 000
GNP (1994)	US$55.5B
literacy	47% (m); 22% (f)
life expectancy	62 (m); 64 (f)

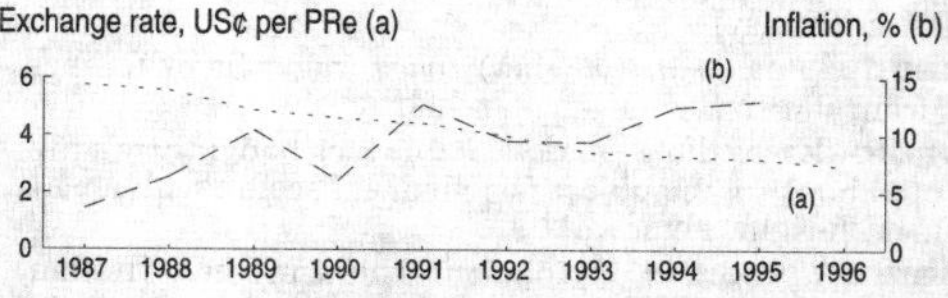

palaeo- *comb. form* (*US* **paleo-**) ancient; prehistoric. [Greek *palaios*]

Palaeocene /ˈpælɪəˌsiːn/ (*US* **Paleocene**) *Geol. –adj.* of the earliest epoch of the Tertiary period. *–n.* this epoch or system. [from PALAEO-, Greek *kainos* new]

palaeography /ˌpælɪˈɒgrəfɪ/ *n.* (*US* **paleography**) the study of ancient writing and documents. □ **palaeographer** *n.* [French: related to PALAEO-]

palaeolithic /ˌpælɪəʊˈlɪθɪk/ *adj.* (*US* **paleolithic**) of the early part of the Stone Age. [Greek *lithos* stone]

palaeontology /ˌpælɪɒnˈtɒlədʒɪ/ *n.* (*US* **paleontology**) the study of life in the geological past. □ **palaeontologist** *n.* [Greek *ōn, ont-* being]

Palaeozoic /ˌpælɪəʊˈzəʊɪk/ (*US* **Paleozoic**) *–adj.* of an era of geological time marked by the appearance of plants and animals, esp. invertebrates. *–n.* this era. [Greek *zōion* animal]

palais /ˈpæleɪ/ *n. colloq.* public dancehall. [French, = hall]

palanquin /ˌpælənˈkiːn/ *n.* (also **palankeen**) (in India and the East) covered litter for one. [Portuguese]

palatable /ˈpælətəb(ə)l/ *adj.* **1** pleasant to taste. **2** (of an idea etc.) acceptable, satisfactory.

palatal /ˈpælət(ə)l/ *–adj.* **1** of the palate. **2** (of a sound) made by placing the tongue against the hard palate (e.g. *y* in *yes*). *–n.* palatal sound.

palate /ˈpælət/ *n.* **1** structure closing the upper part of the mouth cavity in vertebrates. **2** sense of taste. **3** mental taste; liking. [Latin *palatum*]

palatial /pəˈleɪʃ(ə)l/ *adj.* (of a building) like a palace; spacious and splendid. □ **palatially** *adv.* [Latin: related to PALACE]

palatinate /pəˈlætɪˌneɪt/ *n.* territory under the jurisdiction of a Count Palatine.

palatine /ˈpæləˌtaɪn/ *adj.* (also **Palatine**) *hist.* **1** (of an official etc.) having local authority that elsewhere belongs only to a sovereign (*Count Palatine*). **2** (of a territory) subject to this authority. [Latin: related to PALACE]

Palau /pəˈlaʊ/ (also **Belau** /bəˈlaʊ/) group of islands in the W Pacific Ocean, part of the US Trust Territory of the Pacific Islands from 1947. The islands became an autonomous republic in 1981; in 1993 Palau entered into a Compact of Free Association with the US; pop. (est. 1994) 18 000; capital and main island, Koror, pop. (1990) 10 493.

palaver /pəˈlɑːvə(r)/ *n. colloq.* tedious fuss and bother. [Latin: related to PARABLE]

Palawan /pəˈlɑːwən/ island in the W Philippines, separating the Sulu Sea from the South China Sea; activities include fishing, forestry, and the production of mercury and chromite; pop. (est. 1994) 424 800.

pale[1] *–adj.* **1** (of a person, colour, or complexion) light or faint; whitish, ashen. **2** of faint lustre; dim. *–v.* (**-ling**) **1** grow or make pale. **2** (often foll. by *before, beside*) seem feeble in comparison (with). □ **palely** *adv.* **paleness** *n.* **palish** *adj.* [Latin *pallidus*]

pale[2] *n.* **1** pointed piece of wood for fencing etc.; stake. **2** boundary. □ **beyond the pale** outside the bounds of acceptable behaviour. [Latin *palus*]

paleface *n.* name supposedly used by North American Indians for the White man.

Palembang /pɑːˈlembɑːŋ, ˌpɑːləmˈbɑːŋ/ deepwater port in Indonesia, capital of South Sumatra province; locally produced oil is refined and exported; pop. (1990) 1 084 483.

paleo- *comb. form US* var. of PALAEO-.

Paleocene *US* var. of PALAEOCENE.

paleography *US* var. of PALAEOGRAPHY.

paleolithic *US* var. of PALAEOLITHIC.

paleontology *US* var. of PALAEONTOLOGY.

Paleozoic *US* var. of PALAEOZOIC.

Palermo /pəˈlɜːməʊ/ seaport in Italy, the capital of Sicily, on the N coast of the island; industries include shipbuilding and textiles; pop. (est. 1994) 694 749.

Palestine /ˈpælɪˌstaɪn/ territory in SW Asia on the E coast of the Mediterranean Sea, which in biblical times comprised a Hebrew kingdom. Conquered by the Arabs in AD 634, it formed part of the Ottoman empire from 1516 to 1917. The name 'Palestine' was revived as an official political title for the land W of the River Jordan mandated to Britain in 1920. Increased Jewish immigration led to revolts by the Arab population, and Palestine was partitioned into Jewish and Arab states in 1947. The following year the State of Israel was established, and subsequent Arab-Israeli wars resulted in the loss of the Arab state; its territories not under Israeli control now form parts of Jordan and Egypt (see also WEST BANK; GAZA STRIP). Many thousands of Palestinians were displaced when the State of Israel was established and in subsequent struggles, leading to persistent violence and unrest. In 1993 an accord was signed between Israel and the Palestine Liberation Organization (PLO), under which administration of the West Bank and Gaza Strip was handed to a new Palestinian National Authority (from 1994). Yasser Arafat became president of the Palestine National Assembly in 1996. □ **Palestinian** /ˌpælɪˈstɪnɪən/ *adj.* & *n.*

palette /ˈpælɪt/ *n.* **1** artist's thin board or slab for laying and mixing colours on. **2** range of colours used by an artist. [French from Latin *pala* spade]

palette-knife *n.* **1** thin flexible steel blade with a handle for mixing colours or applying or removing paint. **2** blunt round-ended flexible kitchen knife.

palimony /ˈpælɪmənɪ/ *n.* esp. *US colloq.* allowance paid by either partner of a separated unmarried couple to the other. [from PAL, ALIMONY]

palimpsest /ˈpælɪmpˌsest/ *n.* **1** writing-material or manuscript on which the original writing has been effaced for re-use. **2** monumental brass turned and re-engraved on the reverse side. [Greek *palin* again, *psēstos* rubbed]

palindrome /ˈpælɪnˌdrəʊm/ *n.* word or phrase reading the same backwards as forwards (e.g. *nurses run*). □ **palindromic** /-ˈdrɒmɪk/ *adj.* [Greek *palindromos* running back: related to PALIMPSEST, *drom-* run]

paling *n.* **1** fence of pales. **2** pale.

palisade /ˌpælɪˈseɪd/ *–n.* **1** fence of pales or iron railings. **2** strong pointed wooden stake. *–v.* (**-ding**) enclose or provide with a palisade. [French: related to PALE[2]]

pall[1] /pɔːl/ *n.* **1** cloth spread over a coffin etc. **2** shoulder-band with pendants, worn as an ecclesiastical vestment and sign of authority. **3** dark covering (*pall of darkness*). [Latin *pallium* cloak]

pall[2] /pɔːl/ *v.* (often foll. by *on*) become uninteresting (to). [from APPAL]

palladium /pəˈleɪdɪəm/ *n.* rare white metallic element used as a catalyst and in jewellery. [*Pallas*, name of an asteroid]

pallbearer *n.* person helping to carry or escort a coffin at a funeral.

pallet[1] /ˈpælɪt/ *n.* **1** straw mattress. **2** mean or makeshift bed. [Latin *palea* straw]

pallet[2] /ˈpælɪt/ *n.* portable platform for transporting and storing loads, designed to be lifted by a fork-lift truck or pallet truck. [French: related to PALETTE]

palliasse /ˈpælɪˌæs/ *n.* straw mattress. [Latin: related to PALLET[1]]

palliate /ˈpælɪˌeɪt/ *v.* (**-ting**) **1** alleviate (disease) without curing it. **2** excuse, extenuate. □ **palliative** /-ətɪv/ *n.* & *adj.* [Latin *pallio* cloak: related to PALL[1]]

pallid /ˈpælɪd/ *adj.* pale, esp. from illness. [Latin: related to PALE[1]]

pallor /ˈpælə(r)/ *n.* paleness. [Latin *palleo* be pale]

pally *adj.* (**-ier, -iest**) *colloq.* friendly.

palm[1] /pɑːm/ *n.* **1** (usu. tropical) tree-like plant with no branches and a mass of large leaves at the top. **2** leaf of this as a symbol of victory. [Latin *palma*]

palm[2] /pɑːm/ *–n.* **1** inner surface of the hand between the wrist and fingers. **2** part of a glove that covers this. *–v.* conceal in the hand. □ **palm off 1** (often foll. by *on*) impose fraudulently (on a person) (*palmed my old car off on him*). **2** (often foll. by *with*) cause (a person) to accept unwillingly or unknowingly (*palmed him off with my old car*). [Latin *palma*]

Palma /'pælmə/ (in full **Palma de Mallorca**) industrial port, resort, and capital of the Balearic Islands, chief town of the island of Majorca; textiles, shoes, and craft goods are produced; pop. (est. 1994) 322 008.

palmate /'pælmeɪt/ *adj.* **1** shaped like an open hand. **2** having lobes etc. like spread fingers. [Latin *palmatus*: related to PALM[2]]

Palmerston North /'pɑːməst(ə)n/ city and agricultural centre in New Zealand, on North Island; pop. (1994) 75 200.

palmetto /pæl'metəʊ/ *n.* (*pl.* **-s**) small palm tree. [Spanish *palmito* diminutive of *palma* PALM[1]]

palmistry /'pɑːmɪstrɪ/ *n.* fortune-telling from lines etc. on the palm of the hand. □ **palmist** *n.*

palm oil *n.* oil from various palms.

Palm Springs resort city in the US, in SE California, a fashionable desert oasis with hot springs; pop. (1990) 40 181.

Palm Sunday *n.* Sunday before Easter, celebrating Christ's entry into Jerusalem.

palmtop computer *n.* very small hand-held computer with a small screen and compressed keyboard, used as a personal organizer, etc.

palmy /'pɑːmɪ/ *adj.* (**-ier**, **-iest**) **1** of, like, or abounding in palms. **2** triumphant, flourishing (*palmy days*).

palomino /,pælə'miːnəʊ/ *n.* (*pl.* **-s**) golden or cream-coloured horse with light-coloured mane and tail. [Latin *palumba* dove]

palpable /'pælpəb(ə)l/ *adj.* **1** able to be touched or felt. **2** readily perceived. □ **palpably** *adv.* [Latin *palpo* caress]

palpate /'pælpeɪt/ *v.* (**-ting**) examine (esp. medically) by touch. □ **palpation** /-'peɪʃ(ə)n/ *n.*

palpitate /'pælpɪ,teɪt/ *v.* (**-ting**) pulsate, throb, tremble. [Latin *palpito* frequentative of *palpo* touch gently]

palpitation /,pælpɪ'teɪʃ(ə)n/ *n.* **1** throbbing, trembling. **2** (often in *pl.*) increased rate of heartbeat due to exertion, agitation, or disease.

palsy /'pɔːlzɪ/ *–n.* (*pl.* **-ies**) paralysis, esp. with involuntary tremors. *–v.* (**-ies**, **-ied**) affect with palsy. [French: related to PARALYSIS]

paltry /'pɔːltrɪ/ *adj.* (**-ier**, **-iest**) worthless, contemptible, trifling. □ **paltriness** *n.* [from *palt* rubbish]

♦ **Palumbo** /pə'lʌmbəʊ/, **Peter Garth, Baron Palumbo** (1935–) British property developer and philanthropist. His property business was founded by his father, an Italian immigrant. His plans (1991) to demolish listed Victorian City buildings and replace them with modern buildings were accepted by the House of Lords. Lord Palumbo is chancellor of Portsmouth University (since 1992) and has served as chairman of the Arts Council (1989–94).

---

pampas /'pæmpəs/ *n.pl.* large treeless plains in South America. [Spanish from Quechua]

pampas-grass *n.* tall South American ornamental grass.

pamper *v.* overindulge (a person, taste, etc.); spoil. [obsolete *pamp* cram]

pamphlet /'pæmflɪt/ *–n.* small usu. unbound booklet or leaflet. *–v.* (**-t-**) distribute pamphlets to. [*Pamphilus*, name of medieval poem]

pamphleteer /,pæmflɪ'tɪə(r)/ *n.* writer of (esp. political) pamphlets.

Pamplona /pæm'pləʊnə/ city in N Spain, capital of Navarre; centre of an agricultural region, it produces wine, textiles, leather, crafts, and chemicals; pop. (est. 1994) 182 465.

Pan. *abbr.* Panama.

pan[1] *–n.* **1 a** broad usu. metal vessel used for cooking etc. **b** contents of this. **2** panlike vessel in which substances are heated etc. **3** similar shallow container, e.g. the bowl of a pair of scales. **4** lavatory bowl. **5** part of the lock in old guns. **6** hollow in the ground (*salt-pan*). *–v.* (**-nn-**) **1** *colloq.* criticize severely. **2 a** (foll. by *off*, *out*) wash (gold-bearing gravel) in a pan. **b** search for gold thus. □ **pan out 1** (of an action etc.) turn out; work out well or in a specified way. **2** (of gravel) yield gold. □ **panful** *n.* (*pl.* **-s**). **panlike** *adj.* [Old English]

pan[2] *–v.* (**-nn-**) **1** swing (a film camera) horizontally to give a panoramic effect or to follow a moving object. **2** (of a camera) be moved thus. *–n.* panning movement. [from PANORAMA]

pan- *comb. form* **1** all; the whole of. **2** relating to the whole of a continent, racial group, religion, etc. (*pan-American*). [Greek *pan*, neuter. of *pas pantos* all]

panacea /,pænə'siːə/ *n.* universal remedy. [Greek: related to PAN-, *akos* remedy]

panache /pə'næʃ/ *n.* assertive flamboyance; confidence of style or manner. [French, = plume]

Panaji /pæ'nɑːdʒɪ/ city in W India, capital of the state of Goa; pop. (1991) 85 515.

panama /'pænə,mɑː/ *n.* straw hat with a brim and indented crown. [PANAMA]

Panama Canal canal across the isthmus of Panama, connecting the Atlantic and Pacific Oceans. It was built by the US in 1904–14 in territory (the **Panama Canal Zone**) that was ceded in perpetuity from the Republic of Panama; this territory reverted to Panamanian jurisdiction in 1979. Control of the canal itself remains with the US until 1999, after which it will be ceded to Panama.

Panama City capital of Panama; pop. (est. 1994) 445 902.

panatella /,pænə'telə/ *n.* long thin cigar. [American Spanish, = long thin biscuit]

Panama /,pænə'mɑː/, **Republic of** country in Central America, situated on the isthmus that connects North and South America. The economy is largely agricultural; bananas, sugar, and coffee are exported and coconuts, rice, maize, and cacao are also grown. Fishing (esp. of shrimps for export) and shipping registration are other important sources of revenue, and tourism is increasing. Other exports include petroleum products (from the oil-refining industry) and clothing; there are also food-processing and construction industries.

History. Colonized by Spain in the early 16th century, Panama formed part of the Republic of Great Colombia in 1821 and later became a Colombian province. It gained full independence in 1903. From the early 1980s Gen. Manuel Noriega had effective control of the country; his attempt to assume official power in 1989, coupled with accusations of corruption and drug trafficking, led to his deposition by a US task force. The US invasion caused political and economic instability. Noriega was subsequently taken to the US, where, in 1992, he was convicted on drugs charges. The 1991 constitution abolished the armed forces. President, Ernesto Pérez Balladares; capital, Panama City. □ **Panamanian** /-'meɪnɪən/ *adj.* & *n.*

languages	Spanish (official), English
currency	balboa (B) of 100 centésimos
pop (1996)	2 674 000
GNP (1994)	US$6.9B
literacy	88% (m); 88% (f)
life expectancy	71 (m); 76 (f)

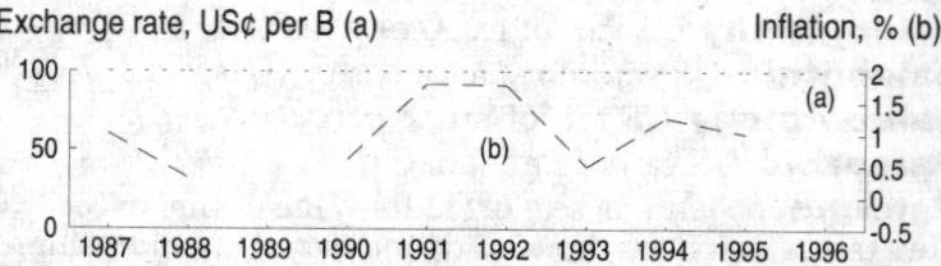

Panay /pæ'naɪ/ island in the central Philippines; pop. (1980) 2 595 300; chief city, Iloilo. Rice, maize, and sugar are grown, and coal and copper are mined; other activities include fishing and forestry.

pancake *n.* **1** thin flat cake of fried batter usu. rolled up with a filling. **2** flat cake of make-up etc.

Pancake Day *n.* Shrove Tuesday (when pancakes are traditionally eaten).

pancake landing *n. colloq.* emergency aircraft landing with the undercarriage still retracted.

panchromatic /ˌpænkrəʊ'mætɪk/ *adj.* (of a film etc.) sensitive to all visible colours of the spectrum.

pancreas /'pæŋkrɪəs/ *n.* gland near the stomach supplying digestive fluid and secreting insulin. □ **pancreatic** /-'ætɪk/ *adj.* [Greek *kreas* flesh]

panda /'pændə/ *n.* **1** (also **giant panda**) large bearlike black and white mammal native to China and Tibet. **2** (also **red panda**) reddish-brown Himalayan racoon-like mammal. [Nepali]

panda car *n.* police patrol car.

pandemic /pæn'demɪk/ *adj.* (of a disease etc.) widespread; universal. [Greek *dēmos* people]

pandemonium /ˌpændɪ'məʊnɪəm/ *n.* **1** uproar; utter confusion. **2** scene of this. [place in hell in Milton's *Paradise Lost*: related to PAN-, DEMON]

pander /'pændə(r)/ *–v.* (foll. by *to*) gratify or indulge (a person or weakness etc.). *–n.* **1** procurer; pimp. **2** person who encourages coarse desires. [*Pandare*, name of a character in the story of Troilus and Cressida]

pandit var. of PUNDIT 1.

P. & L. *abbr.* profit and loss.

P. & O. *abbr.* Peninsular and Oriental Shipping Company.

Pandora's box /pæn'dɔːrəz/ *n.* process that once begun will generate many unmanageable problems. [a box in Greek mythology from which many ills were released on mankind]

p. & p. *abbr.* postage and packing.

pane *n.* single sheet of glass in a window or door. [Latin *pannus* a cloth]

panegyric /ˌpænɪ'dʒɪrɪk/ *n.* eulogy; speech or essay of praise. [Greek *agora* assembly]

panel /'pæn(ə)l/ *–n.* **1** distinct, usu. rectangular, section of a surface (e.g. of a wall, door, or vehicle). **2** strip of material in a garment. **3** team in a broadcast game, discussion, etc. **4 a** list of available jurors. **b** jury. *–v.* (**-ll-**; *US* **-l-**) fit, cover, or decorate with panels. [Latin diminutive of *pannus*: related to PANE]

panel-beater *n.* person who beats out the metal panels of vehicles.

panel game *n.* broadcast quiz etc. played by a panel.

panelling *n.* (*US* **paneling**) **1** panelled work. **2** wood for making panels.

panellist *n.* (*US* **panelist**) member of a panel.

pang *n.* (often in *pl.*) sudden sharp pain or painful emotion. [obsolete *pronge*]

pangolin /pæŋ'gəʊlɪn/ *n.* scaly Asian and African anteater. [Malay]

panic /'pænɪk/ *–n.* **1** sudden uncontrollable fear. **2** infectious fright, esp. in commercial dealings. *–v.* (**-ck-**) (often foll. by *into*) affect or be affected with panic (*was panicked into buying*). □ **panicky** *adj.* [Greek *Pan*, rural god]

panicle /'pænɪk(ə)l/ *n.* loose branching cluster of flowers, as in oats. [Latin *paniculum* diminutive of *panus* thread]

panic stations *n.pl. colloq.* state of emergency.

panic-stricken *adj.* (also **panic-struck**) affected with panic.

panjandrum /pæn'dʒændrəm/ *n.* **1** mock title for an important person. **2** pompous official etc. [invented word]

pannier /'pænɪə(r)/ *n.* basket, bag, or box, esp. one of a pair carried by a donkey etc., bicycle, or motor cycle. [Latin *panis* bread]

panoply /'pænəplɪ/ *n.* (*pl.* **-ies**) **1** complete or splendid array. **2** complete suit of armour. [Greek *hopla* arms]

panorama /ˌpænə'rɑːmə/ *n.* **1** unbroken view of a surrounding region. **2** complete survey of a subject, series of events, etc. **3** picture or photograph containing a wide view. **4** continuous passing scene. □ **panoramic** /-'ræmɪk/ *adj.* [Greek *horama* view]

pan-pipes *n.pl.* musical instrument made of a series of short graduated pipes fixed together. [from *Pan*, Greek rural god]

pansy /'pænzɪ/ *n.* (*pl.* **-ies**) **1** cultivated plant with flowers of various rich colours. **2** *colloq. offens.* **a** effeminate man. **b** male homosexual. [French *pensée* thought, pansy]

pant *–v.* **1** breathe with short quick breaths. **2** (often foll. by *out*) utter breathlessly. **3** (usu. foll. by *for*) yearn, crave. **4** (of the heart etc.) throb violently. *–n.* **1** panting breath. **2** throb. [Greek: related to FANTASY]

pantaloons /ˌpæntə'luːnz/ *n.pl.* (esp. women's) baggy trousers gathered at the ankles. [French from Italian]

pantechnicon /pæn'teknɪkən/ *n.* large furniture removal van. [from TECHNIC: originally as the name of a bazaar]

pantheism /'pænθɪˌɪz(ə)m/ *n.* **1** belief that God is in all nature. **2** worship that admits or tolerates all gods. □ **pantheist** *n.* **pantheistic** /-'ɪstɪk/ *adj.* [Greek *theos* god]

pantheon /'pænθɪən/ *n.* **1** building in which illustrious dead are buried or have memorials. **2** the deities of a people collectively. **3** temple dedicated to all the gods. [Greek *theion* divine]

panther *n.* **1** leopard, esp. with black fur. **2** *US* puma. [Greek *panthēr*]

pantie-girdle *n.* woman's girdle with a crotch shaped like pants.

panties /'pæntɪz/ *n.pl. colloq.* short-legged or legless underpants worn by women and girls. [diminutive of PANTS]

pantihose /'pæntɪˌhəʊz/ *n.* (usu. treated as *pl.*) *US* women's tights.

pantile /'pæntaɪl/ *n.* curved roof-tile. [from PAN[1]]

panto /'pæntəʊ/ *n.* (*pl.* **-s**) *colloq.* = PANTOMIME. [abbreviation]

pantograph /'pæntəˌgrɑːf/ *n.* **1** instrument with jointed rods for copying a plan or drawing etc. on a different scale. **2** jointed framework conveying a current to an electric vehicle from overhead wires. [from PAN-, -GRAPH]

pantomime /'pæntəˌmaɪm/ *n.* **1** Christmas theatrical entertainment based on a fairy tale. **2** gestures and facial expression conveying meaning, esp. in drama and dance. **3** *colloq.* absurd or outrageous piece of behaviour. [Greek: related to PAN-, MIME]

pantry /'pæntrɪ/ *n.* (*pl.* **-ies**) **1** small room or cupboard in which crockery, cutlery, table linen, etc., are kept. **2** larder. [Latin *panis* bread]

pants *n.pl.* **1** underpants or knickers. **2** *US* trousers. □ **bore** (or **scare** etc.) **the pants off** *colloq.* bore, scare, etc., greatly. **with one's pants down** *colloq.* in an embarrassingly unprepared state. [abbreviation of PANTALOONS]

pap[1] *n.* **1** soft or semi-liquid food for infants or invalids. **2** light or trivial reading matter. [Low German or Dutch]

pap[2] *n. archaic* or *dial.* nipple. [Scandinavian]

papa /pə'pɑː/ *n. archaic* father (esp. as a child's word). [Greek *papas*]

papacy /'peɪpəsɪ/ *n.* (*pl.* **-ies**) **1** pope's office or tenure. **2** papal system. [medieval Latin *papatia*: related to POPE]

papal /'peɪp(ə)l/ *adj.* of a pope or the papacy. [medieval Latin: related to POPE]

paparazzo /ˌpæpə'rætsəʊ/ *n.* (*pl.* **-zzi** /-tsɪ/) freelance photographer who pursues celebrities to photograph them. [Italian]

papaw var. of PAWPAW.

papaya var. of PAWPAW. [earlier form of PAWPAW]

Papeete /ˌpɑːpɪ'eɪtɪ, -'iːtɪ/ capital of French Polynesia, on the NW coast of Tahiti; tourism is important; pop. (1988) 78 814.

paper *–n.* **1** material made in thin sheets from the pulp of wood etc., used for writing, drawing, or printing on, or as wrapping material etc. **2** (*attrib.*) **a** made of or using paper. **b** flimsy like paper. **3** = NEWSPAPER. **4 a** printed document. **b** (in *pl.*) identification etc. documents. **c** (in *pl.*) documents of a specified kind (*divorce papers*). **5** *Commerce* **a** negotiable documents, e.g. bills of exchange. **b** (*attrib.*) not actual; theoretical (*paper profits*). **6 a** set of printed questions in an examination. **b** written answers to these. **7** = WALLPAPER. **8** essay or dissertation. **9** piece of paper, esp. as a wrapper etc. –*v.* **1** decorate (a wall etc.) with wallpaper. **2** (foll. by *over*) **a** cover (a hole or blemish) with paper. **b** disguise or try to hide (a fault etc.). □ **on paper 1** in writing. **2** in theory; from written or printed evidence. [Latin PAPYRUS]

paperback *n.* (often *attrib.*) book bound in paper or card, not boards.

paper-boy *n.* (also **paper-girl**) boy or girl who delivers or sells newspapers.

paper-chase *n.* cross-country run following a trail of torn-up paper.

paper-clip *n.* clip of bent wire or plastic for fastening papers together.

paper-hanger *n.* person who hangs wallpaper, esp. for a living.

paper-knife *n.* blunt knife for opening letters etc.

paper-mill *n.* mill in which paper is made.

♦ **paper money** *n.* **1** legal tender in the form of banknotes. **2** banknotes and any form of paper that can be used as money, e.g. cheques, bills of exchange, promissory notes, etc., even though they are not legal tender.

♦ **paper profit** *n.* profit shown by the books or accounts of an organization, which may not be a realized profit because the value of an asset has fallen below its book value, because the asset, although nominally showing a profit, has not actually been sold, or because some technicality of bookkeeping might show an activity to be profitable when it is not. For example, a share that has risen in value since its purchase might show a paper profit but this would not be a real profit since the value of the share might fall again before it is sold.

paper round *n.* **1** job of regularly delivering newspapers. **2** route for this.

paper tape *n.* continuous strip of paper of uniform width and thickness on which data can be encoded by punching patterns of holes. Materials of greater strength, e.g. laminates of paper and polyester, are also used; all these forms can be referred to as **punched tape**. Punched tape was once widely used for the input, output, and storage of data, esp. in scientific and engineering applications.

paper tiger *n.* apparently threatening, but ineffectual, person or thing.

paperweight *n.* small heavy object for keeping loose papers in place.

paperwork *n.* routine clerical or administrative work.

papery *adj.* like paper in thinness or texture.

papier mâché /ˌpæpɪeɪ ˈmæʃeɪ/ *n.* paper pulp moulded into boxes, trays, etc. [French, = chewed paper]

papilla /pəˈpɪlə/ *n.* (*pl.* **papillae** /-liː/) small nipple-like protuberance in or on the body, as that at the base of a hair, feather, etc. □ **papillary** *adj.* [Latin]

papist /ˈpeɪpɪst/ *n.* often *derog.* **1** (often *attrib.*) Roman Catholic. **2** *hist.* advocate of papal supremacy. [related to POPE]

papoose /pəˈpuːs/ *n.* North American Indian young child. [Algonquian]

paprika /ˈpæprɪkə/ *n.* **1** red pepper. **2** condiment made from this. [Magyar]

pap test *n.* cervical smear test. [*Papanicolaou*, name of a US scientist]

papyrus /pəˈpaɪərəs/ *n.* (*pl.* **papyri** /-raɪ/) **1** aquatic plant of N Africa. **2 a** writing-material made in ancient Egypt from the pithy stem of this. **b** text written on this. [Latin from Greek]

PAR /pɑː/ *abbr.* **1** *Computing* positive acknowledgement and retransmission. **2** programme analysis review.

Par. *abbr.* Paraguay.

par *n.* **1** average or normal amount, degree, condition, etc. (*feel below par*). **2** equality; equal status or footing (*on a par with*). **3** *Golf* number of strokes a first-class player should normally require for a hole or course. **4** = PAR VALUE. **5** (in full **par of exchange**) recognized value of one country's currency in terms of another's. □ **par for the course** *colloq.* what is normal or to be expected. [Latin, = equal]

par- var. of PARA-[1] before a vowel or *h* (*parody*).

Pará see BELÉM.

para /ˈpærə/ *n. colloq.* **1** paratrooper. **2** paragraph. [abbreviation]

para-[1] *prefix* (also **par-**) **1** beside (*paramilitary*). **2** beyond (*paranormal*). [Greek]

para-[2] *comb. form* protect, ward off (*parachute*; *parasol*). [Latin *paro* defend]

parable /ˈpærəb(ə)l/ *n.* **1** story used to illustrate a moral or spiritual lesson. **2** allegory. [Greek *parabolē* comparison]

parabola /pəˈræbələ/ *n.* open plane curve formed by the intersection of a cone with a plane parallel to its side. □ **parabolic** /ˌpærəˈbɒlɪk/ *adj.* [Greek *parabolē* placing side by side: related to PARABLE]

Paracel Islands /ˌpærəˈsel/ (also **Paracels**) group of

Papua New Guinea /ˈpæpʊə, ˈgɪnɪ/, **State of** country in the Pacific Ocean, off the NE coast of Australia, comprising the E part of the island of New Guinea and adjacent islands (including the Admiralty Islands, New Britain, New Ireland, and the N Solomon Islands). Agriculture is the main occupation and provides copra, coconut oil, coffee, cocoa, tea, and palm oil for export. The chief sources of export revenue, however, are the country's rich mineral resources, esp. copper, gold, and silver (see also BOUGAINVILLE); there are also deposits of nickel, chromite, and bauxite. Forestry is also important, providing timber for both export and local consumption. Industry is centred on the processing of the country's natural products.
History. Papua New Guinea was formed from the administrative union of Papua (SE New Guinea with adjacent islands), an Australian Territory since 1906, and the Trust Territory of New Guinea (NE New Guinea), an Australian trusteeship since 1921. Self-government was achieved in 1973, and in 1975 the combined territories became an independent state within the Commonwealth. Secessionist rebels on the island of Bougainville declared independence in 1990. In 1997 the prime minister resigned following a dispute with the army concerning the employment of mercenaries to suppress the rebels on Bougainville. Governor-general, Sir Wiwa Korowi; prime minister, Bill Skate; capital, Port Moresby. □ **Papua New Guinean** *adj.* & *n.*

languages	English (official), 715 local languages
currency	kina (k) of 100 toea
pop. (1996)	4 400 000
GNP (1994)	US$4.8B
literacy	64% (m); 37% (f)
life expectancy	57 (m); 58 (f)

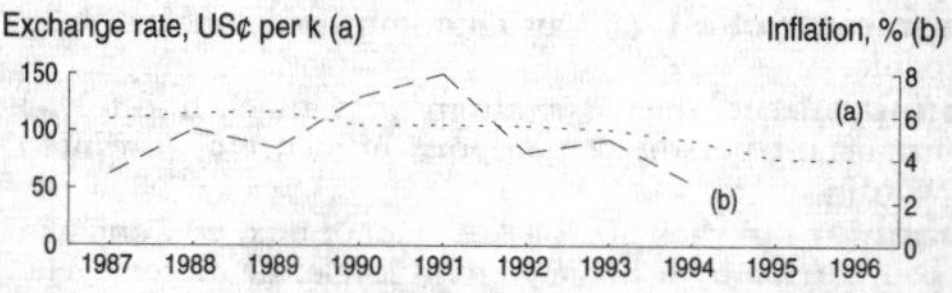

about 130 small barren coral islands and reefs in the South China Sea to the SE of the Chinese island of Hainan. They lie close to deposits of oil and are claimed by both China and Vietnam.

paracetamol /ˌpærəˈsiːtəˌmɒl/ *n.* **1** drug used to relieve pain and reduce fever. **2** tablet of this. [from *para-acetylaminophenol*]

parachute /ˈpærəˌʃuːt/ *–n.* rectangular or umbrella-shaped apparatus allowing a slow and safe descent esp. from an aircraft, or used to retard forward motion etc. (often *attrib.*: *parachute troops*). *–v.* (**-ting**) convey or descend by parachute. □ **parachutist** *n.* [French: related to PARA-², CHUTE¹]

parade /pəˈreɪd/ *–n.* **1** public procession. **2 a** ceremonial muster of troops for inspection. **b** = PARADE-GROUND. **3** ostentatious display (*made a parade of their wealth*). **4** public square, promenade, or row of shops. *–v.* (**-ding**) **1** march ceremonially. **2** assemble for parade. **3** display ostentatiously. **4** march through (streets etc.) in procession. □ **on parade 1** taking part in a parade. **2** on display. [Latin *paro* prepare]

parade-ground *n.* place for the muster and drilling of troops.

paradiddle /ˈpærəˌdɪd(ə)l/ *n.* drum roll with alternate beating of sticks. [imitative]

paradigm /ˈpærəˌdaɪm/ *n.* example or pattern, esp. a set of noun or verb inflections. □ **paradigmatic** /-dɪgˈmætɪk/ *adj.* [Latin from Greek]

paradise /ˈpærəˌdaɪs/ *n.* **1** (in some religions) heaven. **2** place or state of complete happiness. **3** (in full **earthly paradise**) abode of Adam and Eve; garden of Eden. □ **paradisaical** /-dɪˈseɪɪk(ə)l/ *adj.* **paradisal** /ˈpærəˌdaɪs(ə)l/ *adj.* **paradisiacal** /-dɪˈsaɪək(ə)l/ *adj.* **paradisical** /-ˈdɪsɪk(ə)l/ *adj.* [Greek *paradeisos*]

paradox /ˈpærəˌdɒks/ *n.* **1 a** seemingly absurd or contradictory though often true statement. **b** self-contradictory or absurd statement. **2** person or thing having contradictory qualities etc. **3** paradoxical quality. □ **paradoxical** /-ˈdɒksɪk(ə)l/ *adj.* **paradoxically** /-ˈdɒksɪkəlɪ/ *adv.* [Greek: related to PARA-¹, *doxa* opinion]

♦ **paradox of thrift** *n. Econ.* paradoxical fall in the actual amount of money saved in an economy as a result of an increase in the desire to save. The paradox arises because thrift leads to a fall in consumption, causing goods to remain unsold; this leads firms to invest less and employ fewer people, causing incomes to fall; ultimately, although the percentage of incomes saved may have risen, incomes themselves will have fallen by so much that the actual amount saved is reduced. Neoclassical economists argue that movements in interest rates can usu. pre-empt this chain of events.

paraffin /ˈpærəfɪn/ *n.* **1** inflammable waxy or oily hydrocarbon distilled from petroleum or shale, used in liquid form (also **paraffin oil**) esp. as a fuel. **2** *Chem.* = ALKANE. [Latin, = having little affinity]

paraffin wax *n.* paraffin in its solid form.

paragon /ˈpærəgən/ *n.* (often foll. by *of*) model of excellence etc. [Greek *parakonē*]

paragraph /ˈpærəˌgrɑːf/ *–n.* **1** distinct section of a piece of writing, beginning on a new often indented line. **2** symbol (usu. ¶) used to mark a new paragraph, or as a reference mark. **3** short item in a newspaper. *–v.* arrange (a piece of writing) in paragraphs. [Greek: related to PARA-¹, -GRAPH]

parakeet /ˈpærəˌkiːt/ *n.* small usu. long-tailed parrot. [French: related to PARROT]

parallax /ˈpærəˌlæks/ *n.* **1** apparent difference in the position or direction of an object caused when the observer's position is changed. **2** angular amount of this. [Greek, = change]

parallel /ˈpærəˌlel/ *–adj.* **1 a** (of lines or planes) continuously side by side and equidistant. **b** (foll. by *to*, *with*) (of a line or plane) having this relation (to or with another). **2** (of circumstances etc.) precisely similar, analogous, or corresponding. **3 a** (of processes etc.) occurring or performed simultaneously. **b** *Computing* involving the simultaneous transfer or processing of the individual parts of a whole (*parallel transmission of data*). *–n.* **1** person or thing precisely analogous to another. **2** comparison (*drew a parallel between them*). **3** (in full **parallel of latitude**) **a** each of the imaginary parallel circles of constant latitude on the earth's surface. **b** corresponding line on a map (*49th parallel*). **4** *Printing* two parallel lines (‖) as a reference mark. *–v.* (**-l-**) **1** be parallel, or correspond, to. **2** represent as similar; compare. **3** cite as a parallel instance. □ **in parallel** (of electric circuits) arranged so as to join at common points at each end. □ **parallelism** *n.* [Greek, = alongside one another]

parallel bars *n.pl.* pair of parallel rails on posts for gymnastics.

parallelepiped /ˌpærəleˈlepɪˌped, -ləˈpaɪpɪd/ *n.* solid body of which each face is a parallelogram. [Greek: related to PARALLEL, *epipedon* plane surface]

parallelogram /ˌpærəˈleləˌgræm/ *n.* four-sided plane rectilinear figure with opposite sides parallel.

parallel processing *n. Computing* **1** method of computing that involves the execution of two or more processes at the same time in a single computer system; this implies that two or more processors are in operation at the same time. **2** situation in which a number of processes are potentially active, but only one is actually being run at any particular instant. See also MULTIPROCESSING SYSTEM.

paralyse /ˈpærəˌlaɪz/ *v.* (*US* **paralyze**) (**-sing** or **-zing**) **1** affect with paralysis. **2** render powerless; cripple. [Greek: related to PARA-¹, *luō* loosen]

paralysis /pəˈrælɪsɪs/ *n.* **1** impairment or loss of esp. the motor function of the nerves, causing immobility. **2** powerlessness.

paralytic /ˌpærəˈlɪtɪk/ *–adj.* **1** affected by paralysis. **2** *slang* very drunk. *–n.* person affected by paralysis.

Paraguay /ˈpærəˌgwaɪ/, **Republic of** inland country in South America, situated between Argentina, Bolivia, and Brazil. The economy is based on agriculture, esp. livestock rearing and the cultivation of cotton, soya beans, oil-seeds, and coffee for export; the export of meat has declined, but remains important. Forestry is a major industry, producing timber for export. Hydroelectricity is a developing source of power.

History. Once part of the Spanish viceroyalties of Peru and La Plata, Paraguay achieved its independence in 1811. It lost much territory and over half of its population in war against Brazil, Argentina, and Uruguay in 1865–70, but gained land to the W as a result of the Chaco War with Bolivia in 1932–5. In 1954, after a period of political instability, the country came under military dictatorship that lasted until 1989. The first free elections, held in 1991, were followed by further constitutional reforms; in 1993 the country's first civilian president was democratically elected. Paraguay is a member of LAIA. President, Juan Carlos Wasmosy; capital, Asuncíon. □ **Paraguayan** *adj.* & *n.*

languages	Spanish, Guaraní
currency	guaraní of 100 céntimos
pop. (1996)	4 964 000
GNP (1994)	US$7.6B
literacy	93% (m); 90% (f)
life expectancy	64 (m); 69 (f)

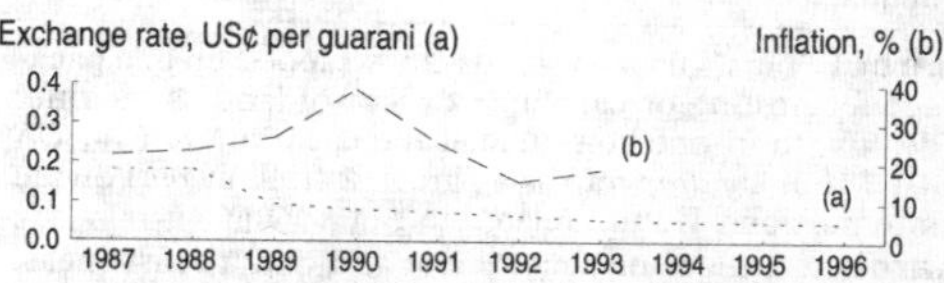

Paramaribo /ˌpærəˈmærɪbəʊ/ capital and chief port of Suriname; pop. (est. 1993) 200 970.

paramedic /ˌpærəˈmedɪk/ *n.* paramedical worker.

paramedical *adj.* (of services etc.) supplementing and assisting medical work.

parameter /pəˈræmɪtə(r)/ *n.* **1** *Math.* quantity constant in the case considered but varying in different cases. **2 a** (esp. measurable or quantifiable) characteristic or feature. **b** (loosely) limit or boundary, esp. of a subject for discussion. [Greek PARA-[1], -METER]

paramilitary /ˌpærəˈmɪlɪtərɪ/ *–adj.* (of forces) organized on military lines. *–n.* (*pl.* **-ies**) member of an unofficial paramilitary organization, esp. in Northern Ireland.

paramount /ˈpærəˌmaʊnt/ *adj.* **1** supreme; most important. **2** in supreme authority. [Anglo-French *par* by, *amont* above: see AMOUNT]

paramour /ˈpærəˌmʊə(r)/ *n. archaic* or *derog.* illicit lover of a married person. [French *par amour* by love]

paranoia /ˌpærəˈnɔɪə/ *n.* **1** mental disorder with delusions of persecution and self-importance. **2** abnormal suspicion and mistrust. □ **paranoiac** *adj.* & *n.* **paranoiacally** *adv.* **paranoic** /-ˈnəʊɪk, -ˈnɔɪɪk/ *adj.* **paranoically** /-ˈnəʊɪkəlɪ, -ˈnɔɪɪkəlɪ/ *adv.* **paranoid** /ˈpærəˌnɔɪd/ *adj.* & *n.* [Greek: related to NOUS]

paranormal /ˌpærəˈnɔːm(ə)l/ *adj.* beyond the scope of normal scientific investigation or explanation.

parapet /ˈpærəpɪt/ *n.* **1** low wall at the edge of a roof, balcony, bridge, etc. **2** defence of earth or stone. [French or Italian: related to PARA-[2], *petto* breast]

paraphernalia /ˌpærəfəˈneɪlɪə/ *n.pl.* (also treated as *sing.*) miscellaneous belongings, equipment, accessories, etc. [Greek: related to PARA-[1], *phernē* dower]

paraphrase /ˈpærəˌfreɪz/ *–n.* expression of a passage in other words. *–v.* (**-sing**) express the meaning of (a passage) thus. [Greek: related to PARA-[1]]

paraplegia /ˌpærəˈpliːdʒə/ *n.* paralysis below the waist. □ **paraplegic** *adj.* & *n.* [Greek: related to PARA-[1], *plēssō* strike]

parapsychology /ˌpærəsaɪˈkɒlədʒɪ/ *n.* the study of mental phenomena outside the sphere of ordinary psychology (hypnosis, telepathy, etc.).

paraquat /ˈpærəˌkwɒt/ *n.* a quick-acting highly toxic herbicide. [from PARA-[1], QUATERNARY]

parascending /ˈpærəˌsendɪŋ/ *n.* sport in which participants wearing open parachutes are towed behind a vehicle or motor boat to gain height before release for a conventional descent.

parasite /ˈpærəˌsaɪt/ *n.* **1** organism living in or on another and feeding on it. **2** person exploiting another or others. □ **parasitic** /-ˈsɪtɪk/ *adj.* **parasitically** /-ˈsɪtɪkəlɪ/ *adv.* **parasitism** *n.* [Greek: related to PARA-[1], *sitos* food]

parasol /ˈpærəˌsɒl/ *n.* light umbrella giving shade from the sun. [Italian: related to PARA-[2], *sole* sun]

paratrooper /ˈpærəˌtruːpə(r)/ *n.* member of a body of paratroops.

paratroops /ˈpærəˌtruːps/ *n.pl.* parachute troops. [contraction]

paratyphoid /ˌpærəˈtaɪfɔɪd/ *n.* (often *attrib.*) fever resembling typhoid.

par avion /ˌpɑːr æˈvjɔ̃/ *adv.* by airmail. [French, = by aeroplane]

parboil /ˈpɑːbɔɪl/ *v.* boil until partly cooked. [Latin *par-* = PER-, confused with PART]

♦ **par bond** *n.* financial instrument or security bought and sold at its face value, rather than at a discount or premium.

parcel /ˈpɑːs(ə)l/ *–n.* **1** goods etc. wrapped up in a package for posting or carrying. **2** piece of land. **3** quantity dealt with in one commercial transaction. *–v.* (**-ll-**; *US* **-l-**) **1** (foll. by *up*) wrap as a parcel. **2** (foll. by *out*) divide into portions. [Latin: related to PARTICLE]

parch *v.* **1** make or become hot and dry. **2** roast (peas, corn, etc.) slightly. [origin unknown]

parchment /ˈpɑːtʃmənt/ *n.* **1 a** skin, esp. of sheep or goat, prepared for writing or painting on. **b** manuscript written on this. **2** high-grade paper resembling parchment. [Latin *Pergamum*, now *Bergama* in Turkey]

pardon /ˈpɑːd(ə)n/ *–n.* **1** forgiveness for an offence, error, etc. **2** (in full **free pardon**) remission of the legal consequences of a crime or conviction. *–v.* **1** forgive or excuse. **2** release from the legal consequences of an offence, error, etc. *–int.* (also **pardon me** or **I beg your pardon**) **1** formula of apology or disagreement. **2** request to repeat something said. □ **pardonable** *adj.* [Latin *perdono*: related to PER-, *dono* give]

pare /peə(r)/ *v.* (**-ring**) **1 a** trim or shave by cutting away the surface or edge. **b** (often foll. by *off, away*) cut off (the surface or edge). **2** (often foll. by *away, down*) diminish little by little. [Latin *paro* prepare]

parent /ˈpeərənt/ *–n.* **1** person who has or adopts a child; father or mother. **2** animal or plant from which others are derived. **3** (often *attrib.*) source, origin, etc. *–v.* (also *absol.*) be the parent of. □ **parental** /pəˈrent(ə)l/ *adj.* **parenthood** *n.* [Latin *pario* bring forth]

parentage *n.* lineage; descent from or through parents.

♦ **parent company** *n.* = HOLDING COMPANY.

parenthesis /pəˈrenθəsɪs/ *n.* (*pl.* **parentheses** /-ˌsiːz/) **1 a** explanatory or qualifying word, clause, or sentence inserted into a sentence etc., and usu. marked off by brackets, dashes, or commas. **b** (in *pl.*) round brackets ( ) used for this. **2** interlude or interval. □ **parenthetic** /ˌpærənˈθetɪk/ *adj.* **parenthetically** /ˌpærənˈθetɪkəlɪ/ *adv.* [Greek: related to PARA-[1], EN-[2], THESIS]

parenting *n.* (skill of) bringing up children.

parent-teacher association *n.* social and fund-raising organization of a school's parents and teachers.

♦ **Pareto optimality** /pæˈreɪtəʊ/ *n.* condition of efficiency that has been very useful for analysing the efficiency of economic systems and for formulating economic policies. An allocation or distribution of goods and services in an economy is said to show Pareto optimality if no alternative allocation could make at least one individual better off, without making anyone worse off. See also GENERAL EQUILIBRIUM ANALYSIS. □ **Pareto optimal** *adj.* [*Pareto*, name of an economist]

♦ **Pareto's Rule** *n.* rule originally stating that 80% of a nation's income will only benefit 20% of the population. This ratio of 80:20 can be widely extended, e.g. 80% of the value of an inventory is locked up in 20% of the items; 80% of a company's profits come from 20% of its products; and 80% of car breakdowns require only 20% of the spare-part range.

par excellence /ˌpɑːr eksəˈlɑ̃s/ *adv.* being the supreme example of its kind (*the short story par excellence*). [French]

parfait /ˈpɑːfeɪ/ *n.* **1** rich iced pudding of whipped cream, eggs, etc. **2** layers of ice-cream, meringue, etc., served in a tall glass. [French *parfait* PERFECT]

pariah /pəˈraɪə/ *n.* **1** social outcast. **2** *hist.* member of a low caste or of no caste in S India. [Tamil]

parietal /pəˈraɪət(ə)l/ *adj.* of the wall of the body or any of its cavities. [Latin *paries* wall]

parietal bone *n.* either of a pair of bones in the skull.

paring *n.* strip or piece cut off.

♦ ***pari passu*** /ˌpærɪ ˈpæsuː/ *adv.* with equal progress, pace, or speed. When a new issue of shares is said to rank *pari passu* with existing shares, the new shares carry the same dividend rights and winding-up rights as the existing shares. [Latin]

Paris /ˈpærɪs/ capital and political, commercial, and cultural centre of France, situated on the River Seine; city pop. (est. 1990) 2 175 110; metropolitan area pop. 9 063 384.

♦ **Paris Bourse** *n.* since 1991, the only stock exchange in France.

♦ **Paris Club** *n.* = GROUP OF TEN.

parish /'pærɪʃ/ *n.* **1** area having its own church and clergyman. **2** (in full **civil parish**) local government district. **3** inhabitants of a parish. [Latin *parochia* from Greek *oikos* dwelling]

parish clerk *n.* official performing various duties for a church.

parish council *n.* administrative body in a civil parish.

parishioner /pə'rɪʃənə(r)/ *n.* inhabitant of a parish. [obsolete *parishen*: related to PARISH]

parish register *n.* book recording christenings, marriages, and burials, at a parish church.

parity /'pærɪtɪ/ *n.* **1** equality, equal status or pay. **2** parallelism or analogy (*parity of reasoning*). **3** equivalence of one currency with another; being at par. [Latin *paritas*: related to PAR]

♦ **parity grid** see EUROPEAN MONETARY SYSTEM.

park –*n.* **1** large public garden in a town, for recreation. **2** land attached to a country house etc. **3 a** large area of uncultivated land for public recreational use. **b** large enclosed area where wild animals are kept in captivity (*wildlife park*). **4** area for parking vehicles etc. (*car park*). **5** area for a specified purpose (*business park*). **6 a** *US* sports ground. **b** (usu. prec. by *the*) football pitch. –*v.* **1** (also *absol.*) leave (a vehicle) temporarily. **2** *colloq.* deposit and leave, usu. temporarily. **3** *Finance* put (one's shares in a company) in the name of someone else or of nominees in order to hide their real ownership. □ **park oneself** *colloq.* sit down. [French from Germanic]

parka /'pɑːkə/ *n.* **1** long usu. green anorak with fur round the hood. **2** hooded skin jacket worn by Eskimos. [Aleutian]

parkin /'pɑːkɪn/ *n.* cake of ginger, oatmeal, treacle, etc. [origin uncertain]

parking-lot *n.* *US* outdoor car park.

parking-meter *n.* coin-operated meter allocating a length of time for which a vehicle may be parked in a street.

parking-ticket *n.* notice of a penalty imposed for parking illegally.

Parkinson's disease /'pɑːkɪns(ə)nz/ *n.* (also **Parkinsonism**) progressive disease of the nervous system with tremor, muscular rigidity, and emaciation. [*Parkinson*, name of a surgeon]

♦ **Parkinson's law** *n.* any of several aphorisms said to apply to large organizations. They include: work expands to fill the time available for it; expenditure rises to meet income; and subordinates multiply at a fixed rate that is independent of the amount of work produced. [*Parkinson*, name of a writer]

parkland *n.* open grassland with trees etc.

parky /'pɑːkɪ/ *adj.* (**-ier, -iest**) *colloq.* or *dial.* chilly. [origin unknown]

parlance /'pɑːləns/ *n.* vocabulary or idiom of a particular subject, group, etc. [French from *parler* speak]

parley /'pɑːlɪ/ –*n.* (*pl.* **-s**) conference of disputants, esp. to discuss peace terms etc. –*v.* (**-leys, -leyed**) (often foll. by *with*) hold a parley. [French *parler*: related to PARLANCE]

parliament /'pɑːləmənt/ *n.* **1** (**Parliament**) **a** (in the UK) highest legislature, consisting of the Sovereign, the House of Lords, and the House of Commons. **b** members of this for a particular period, esp. between elections. **2** similar legislature in other states. [French: related to PARLANCE]

parliamentarian /ˌpɑːləmen'teərɪən/ *n.* member of a parliament, esp. an expert in its procedures.

parliamentary /ˌpɑːlə'mentərɪ/ *adj.* **1** of a parliament. **2** enacted or established by a parliament. **3** (of language, behaviour, etc.) polite.

♦ **Parliamentary Commissioner for Administration** *n.* (also **PCA**) ombudsman responsible for investigating complaints referred to him or her by an MP from members of the public against maladministration by government departments and certain public bodies. The **Health Service Commissioners** are responsible for investigating complaints against the National Health Service. Cf. COMMISSIONER FOR LOCAL ADMINISTRATION; FINANCIAL OMBUDSMAN.

parlour /'pɑːlə(r)/ *n.* (*US* **parlor**) **1** *archaic* sitting-room in a private house. **2** esp. *US* shop providing specified goods or services (*beauty parlour*; *ice-cream parlour*). [Anglo-French: related to PARLEY]

parlour game *n.* indoor game, esp. a word-game.

parlous /'pɑːləs/ *adj.* *archaic* or *joc.* dangerous or difficult. [from *perilous*: see PERIL]

PARM *abbr.* programme analysis for resource management.

Parma /'pɑːmə/ city and agricultural centre in N Italy; Parmesan cheese and other foods are produced; pop. (est. 1994) 169 299.

Parmesan /ˌpɑːmɪ'zæn/ *n.* hard dry cheese made orig. at Parma and usu. used grated. [Italian *parmegiano* of Parma]

parochial /pə'rəʊkɪəl/ *adj.* **1** of a parish. **2** (of affairs, views, etc.) merely local, narrow, or provincial. □ **parochialism** *n.* **parochially** *adv.* [Latin: related to PARISH]

parody /'pærədɪ/ –*n.* (*pl.* **-ies**) **1** humorous exaggerated imitation of an author, literary work, style, etc. **2** feeble imitation; travesty. –*v.* (**-ies, -ied**) **1** compose a parody of. **2** mimic humorously. □ **parodist** *n.* [Latin or Greek: related to PARA-[1], ODE]

♦ **par of exchange** *n.* theoretical rate of exchange between two currencies in which there is equilibrium between the supply and demand for each currency. The par value lies between the market buying and selling rates. See also MINT PAR OF EXCHANGE.

parole /pə'rəʊl/ –*n.* **1** temporary or permanent release of a prisoner before the expiry of a sentence, on the promise of good behaviour. **2** such a promise. –*v.* (**-ling**) put (a prisoner) on parole. [French, = word: related to PARLANCE]

Paros /'peərɒs/ Greek island of the Cyclades, in the S Aegean, noted for its fine white marble (Parian marble) used for sculpture since ancient times; pop. (est. 1981) 7881.

parotid /pə'rɒtɪd/ –*adj.* situated near the ear. –*n.* (in full **parotid gland**) salivary gland in front of the ear. [Greek: related to PARA-[1], *ous ōt-* ear]

paroxysm /'pærəkˌsɪz(ə)m/ *n.* **1** (often foll. *by of*) sudden attack or outburst (of rage, coughing, etc.). **2** fit of disease. □ **paroxysmal** /-'sɪzm(ə)l/ *adj.* [Greek *oxus* sharp]

parquet /'pɑːkeɪ/ –*n.* **1** flooring of wooden blocks arranged in a pattern. **2** *US* stalls of a theatre. –*v.* (**-eted** /-eɪd/; **-eting** /-eɪɪŋ/) floor (a room) thus. [French, diminutive of *parc* PARK]

parquetry /'pɑːkɪtrɪ/ *n.* use of wooden blocks to make floors or inlay for furniture.

parr /pɑː(r)/ *n.* young salmon. [origin unknown]

parricide /'pærɪˌsaɪd/ *n.* **1** murder of a near relative, esp. of a parent. **2** person who commits parricide. □ **parricidal** /-'saɪd(ə)l/ *adj.* [Latin: see PARENT, PATER, -CIDE]

parrot /'pærət/ –*n.* **1** mainly tropical bird with a short hooked bill, often vivid plumage, and the ability to mimic the human voice. **2** person who mechanically repeats another's words or actions. –*v.* (**-t-**) repeat mechanically. [French, diminutive of *Pierre* Peter]

parrot-fashion *adv.* (learning or repeating) mechanically, by rote.

parry /'pærɪ/ –*v.* (**-ies, -ied**) **1** avert or ward off (a weapon or attack), esp. with a countermove. **2** deal skilfully with (an awkward question etc.). –*n.* (*pl.* **-ies**) act of parrying. [Italian *parare* ward off]

parse /pɑːz/ *v.* (**-sing**) **1** describe (a word in context) grammatically, stating its inflection, relation to the sentence, etc. **2** resolve (a sentence) into its component parts and describe them grammatically. [perhaps from French *pars* parts: related to PART]

parsec /ˈpɑːsek/ *n.* unit of stellar distance, equal to about 3.25 light-years. [from PARALLAX, SECOND^2]

parsimony /ˈpɑːsɪmənɪ/ *n.* carefulness in the use of money etc.; stinginess. □ **parsimonious** /-ˈməʊnɪəs/ *adj.* [Latin *parco pars-* spare]

parsley /ˈpɑːslɪ/ *n.* herb with crinkly aromatic leaves, used to season and garnish food. [Greek *petra* rock, *selinon* parsley]

parsnip /ˈpɑːsnɪp/ *n.* **1** plant with a pale-yellow tapering root. **2** this root eaten as a vegetable. [Latin *pastinaca*]

parson /ˈpɑːs(ə)n/ *n.* **1** rector. **2** vicar; clergyman. [Latin: related to PERSON]

parsonage *n.* church house provided for a parson.

parson's nose *n.* fatty flesh at the rump of a cooked fowl.

part *–n.* **1** some but not all of a thing or group of things. **2** essential member, constituent, or component (*part of the family*; *spare parts*). **3** portion of a human or animal body. **4** division of a book, broadcast serial, etc., esp. issued or broadcast at one time. **5** each of several equal portions of a whole (*3 parts sugar to 2 parts flour*). **6 a** allotted share. **b** person's share in an action etc. (*had no part in it*). **c** duty (*not my part to interfere*). **7 a** character assigned to, or words spoken by, an actor on stage. **b** melody etc. assigned to a particular voice or instrument. **c** printed or written copy of an actor's or musicians's part. **8** side in an agreement or dispute. **9** (in *pl.*) region or district (*am not from these parts*). **10** (in *pl.*) abilities (*man of many parts*). *–v.* **1** divide or separate into parts (*crowd parted*). **2 a** leave one another's company (*parted the best of friends*). **b** (foll. by *from*) say goodbye to. **3** (foll. by *with*) give up; hand over. **4** separate (hair of the head) to make a parting. *–adv.* in part; partly (*part iron and part wood*). □ **for the most part** see MOST. **for one's part** as far as one is concerned. **in part** (or **parts**) partly. **on the part of** made or done by (*no objection on my part*). **part and parcel** (usu. foll. by *of*) an essential part. **part company** see COMPANY. **play a part 1** be significant or contributory. **2** act deceitfully. **3** perform a theatrical role. **take in good part** not be offended by. **take part** (often foll. by *in*) assist or have a share (in). **take the part of** support; side with. [Latin *pars part-*]

partake /pɑːˈteɪk/ *v.* (**-king**; *past* **partook**; *past part.* **partaken**) **1** (foll. by *of, in*) take a share or part. **2** (foll. by *of*) eat or drink some or *colloq.* all (of a thing). [back-formation from *partaker* = *part-taker*]

parterre /pɑːˈteə(r)/ *n.* **1** level space in a formal garden occupied by flower-beds. **2** *US* pit of a theatre. [French, = on the ground]

part-exchange *–n.* transaction in which goods are given as part of the payment. *–v.* give (goods) thus.

parthenogenesis /ˌpɑːθənəʊˈdʒenɪsɪs/ *n.* reproduction without fertilization, esp. in invertebrates and lower plants. [Greek *parthenos* virgin]

Parthian shot /ˈpɑːθɪən/ *n.* remark or glance etc. on leaving. [*Parthia*, ancient kingdom in W Asia: from the custom of a retreating Parthian horseman firing a shot at the enemy]

partial /ˈpɑːʃ(ə)l/ *adj.* **1** not complete; forming only part. **2** biased. **3** (foll. by *to*) having a liking for. □ **partiality** /-ʃɪˈælɪtɪ/ *n.* **partially** *adv.* **partialness** *n.* [Latin: related to PART]

partial eclipse *n.* eclipse in which only part of the luminary is covered.

♦ **partial equilibrium analysis** *n.* analysis of the behaviour of a particular individual, firm, household, or industry in isolation from the rest of the economy. In order to simplify the analysis, it is unrealistically assumed that the choices of the agents studied have no effects on the rest of the economy. This often produces some of the most interesting results in economics, but these results must be treated with caution. Cf. GENERAL EQUILIBRIUM ANALYSIS.

♦ **partial loss** *n. Marine insurance* = AVERAGE *n.* 4.

---

participant /pɑːˈtɪsɪpənt/ *n.* participator.

participate /pɑːˈtɪsɪˌpeɪt/ *v.* (**-ting**) (often foll. by *in*) take part or a share (in). □ **participation** /-ˈpeɪʃ(ə)n/ *n.* **participator** *n.* **participatory** *adj.* [Latin *particeps -cip-* taking PART]

♦ **participating preference share** see PREFERENCE SHARE.

♦ **participation rate** *n.* percentage of a population that is available for employment. The rate for women tends to vary greatly from year to year, whereas the rate for men tends to remain constant. Supply-side economists sometimes claim that cuts in taxation would raise participation rates and therefore raise national income.

---

participle /ˈpɑːtɪˌsɪp(ə)l/ *n.* word formed from a verb (e.g. *going, gone, being, been*) and used in compound verb-forms (e.g. *is going, has been*) or as an adjective (e.g. *working woman, burnt toast*). □ **participial** /-ˈsɪpɪəl/ *adj.* [Latin: related to PARTICIPATE]

particle /ˈpɑːtɪk(ə)l/ *n.* **1** minute portion of matter. **2** smallest possible amount (*particle of sense*). **3 a** minor part of speech, esp. a short undeclinable one. **b** common prefix or suffix such as *in-*, *-ness*. [Latin *particula* diminutive of *pars* PART]

particoloured /ˈpɑːtɪˌkʌləd/ *adj.* (*US* **-colored**) of more than one colour. [related to PART, COLOUR]

particular /pəˈtɪkjʊlə(r)/ *–adj.* **1** relating to or considered as one thing or person as distinct from others; individual (*in this particular case*). **2** more than is usual; special (*took particular care*). **3** scrupulously exact; fastidious. **4** detailed (*full and particular account*). *–n.* **1** detail; item. **2** (in *pl.*) information; detailed account. □ **in particular** especially, specifically. [Latin: related to PARTICLE]

♦ **particular average** *n.* (also **PA**) see AVERAGE *n.* 4.

---

particularity /pəˌtɪkjʊˈlærɪtɪ/ *n.* **1** quality of being individual or particular. **2** fullness or minuteness of detail.

particularize /pəˈtɪkjʊləˌraɪz/ *v.* (also **-ise**) (**-zing** or **-sing**) (also *absol.*) **1** name specially or one by one. **2** specify (items). □ **particularization** /-ˈzeɪʃ(ə)n/ *n.*

particularly /pəˈtɪkjʊləlɪ/ *adv.* **1** especially, very. **2** specifically (*particularly asked for you*). **3** in a particular or fastidious manner.

parting *n.* **1** leave-taking or departure (often *attrib.*: *parting words*). **2** dividing line of combed hair. **3** division; separating.

parting shot *n.* = PARTHIAN SHOT.

partisan /ˌpɑːtɪˈzæn/ (also **partizan**) *–n.* **1** strong, esp. unreasoning, supporter of a party, cause, etc. **2** guerrilla. *–adj.* **1** of partisans. **2** biased. □ **partisanship** *n.* [Italian: related to PART]

partition /pɑːˈtɪʃ(ə)n/ *–n.* **1** structure dividing a space, esp. a light interior wall. **2** division into parts, esp. *Polit.* of a country. *–v.* **1** divide into parts. **2** (foll. by *off*) separate (part of a room etc.) with a partition. [Latin *partior* divide]

partitive /ˈpɑːtɪtɪv/ *–adj.* (of a word, form, etc.) denoting part of a collective group or quantity. *–n.* partitive word (e.g. *some, any*) or form. [French or medieval Latin: related to PARTITION]

partizan var. of PARTISAN.

partly *adv.* **1** with respect to a part or parts. **2** to some extent.

♦ **partly paid shares** *n.pl.* shares on which the full nominal (par) value has not been paid. Formerly, partly paid shares were issued by some banks and insurance companies to inspire confidence: they could always call on their shareholders for further funds if necessary. Shareholders, however, did not like the liability of being called upon to pay out further sums for their shares and the practice largely died out. It has been revived for large new share issues, esp. in privatizations, in which shareholders pay an initial sum for their shares and subsequently pay one or more calls (demands) on specified dates. See also SHARE CAPITAL.

partner /'pɑːtnə(r)/ *–n.* **1** person who shares or takes part with another or others, esp. in a business (see PARTNERSHIP 3). **2** companion in dancing. **3** player (esp. one of two) on the same side in a game. **4** either member of a married or unmarried couple. *–v.* be the partner of. [alteration of *parcener* joint heir]

partnership *n.* **1** state of being a partner or partners. **2** pair or group of partners. **3** association of two or more people formed for the purpose of carrying on a business. Partnerships are governed by the Partnership Act (1890). Unlike an incorporated company, a partnership does not have a legal personality of its own and therefore partners are liable for the debts of the firm. **General partners** are fully liable for these debts, **limited partners** only to the extent of their investment. A **limited partnership** is one consisting of both general and limited partners and is governed by the Limited Partnership Act (1907). A **partnership-at-will** is one for which no term has been agreed: any partner may end the partnership at any time provided that notice of this intention is given to all the other partners. A **nominal partner** is one who allows his or her name to be used for the benefit of the partnership, usu. for a reward but not for a share of the profits, and is not a legal partner. Partnerships are usu. governed by a **partnership agreement** that lays down the way in which profits are to be shared, the procedure to be adopted on the death, retirement, or bankruptcy of a partner, and the rules for withdrawing capital from the partnership. Partners do not draw salaries and are not paid interest on their capital.

♦ **partnership-at-will** see PARTNERSHIP 3.

part of speech *n.* grammatical class of words (in English noun, pronoun, adjective, adverb, verb, etc.).

partook *past* of PARTAKE.

partridge /'pɑːtrɪdʒ/ *n.* (*pl.* same or **-s**) game-bird, esp. European or Asian. [Greek *perdix*]

part-song *n.* song with three or more voice-parts, often unaccompanied.

part-time *–adj.* (esp. of a job) occupying less than the normal working week etc. *–adv.* (also **part time**) as a part-time activity (*works part time*).

part-timer *n.* person employed in part-time work.

parturient /pɑː'tjʊərɪənt/ *adj. formal* about to give birth. [Latin *pario part-* bring forth]

parturition /ˌpɑːtjʊ'rɪʃ(ə)n/ *n. formal* giving birth.

party /'pɑːtɪ/ *–n.* (*pl.* **-ies**) **1** social gathering, usu. of invited guests. **2** people working or travelling together (*search party*). **3** political group putting forward candidates in elections and usu. organized on a national basis. **4** each side in an agreement or dispute. **5** (foll. by *to*) *Law* accessory (to an action). **6** *colloq.* person. *–v.* (**-ies, -ied**) attend a party; celebrate. [Romanic: related to PART]

party line *n.* **1** policy adopted by a political party etc. **2** shared telephone line.

party-wall *n.* wall common to adjoining buildings or rooms.

♦ **par value** *n.* (also **face value, nominal value, nominal price**) price given to a share or other security when it is issued. If the market value of a security exceeds the par value it is said to be **above par**; if it falls below the par value it is **below par**. Gilt-edged securities are always repayed **at par** (usu. £100), i.e. at the par value.

parvenu /'pɑːvəˌnjuː/ *n.* (*pl.* **-s**; *fem.* **parvenue**) (often *attrib.*) newly rich social climber; upstart. [Latin: related to PER-, *venio* come]

pas /pɑː/ *n.* (*pl.* same) step in esp. ballet. [French, = step]

pascal /'pæsk(ə)l/ *n.* **1** SI unit of pressure. **2** (**Pascal**) programming language intended for teaching the principles and practice of programming, and now popular for applications programming, esp. on microcomputers. [*Pascal*, name of a mathematician]

paschal /'pæsk(ə)l/ *adj.* **1** of the Jewish Passover. **2** of Easter. [Hebrew *pesah*]

pas de deux /ˌpɑː də 'dɜː/ *n.* dance for two. [French, = step for two]

pash *n. slang* brief infatuation. [abbreviation of PASSION]

pasha /'pɑːʃə/ *n. hist.* title (placed after the name) of a Turkish military commander, governor, etc. [Turkish]

Pashto /'pʌʃtəʊ/ *–n.* language of Afghanistan, parts of Pakistan, etc. *–adj.* of or in this language. [Pashto]

paso doble /ˌpæsəʊ 'dəʊbleɪ/ *n.* Latin American ballroom dance. [Spanish, = double step]

pasque-flower /'pæsk/ *n.* a kind of anemone with bell-shaped purple flowers. [French *passe-fleur*]

pass[1] /pɑːs/ *–v.* **1** (often foll. by *along, by, down, on*, etc.) move onward, esp. past something. **2 a** go past; leave on one side or behind. **b** overtake, esp. in a vehicle. **3** (cause to) be transferred from one person or place to another (*title passes to his son; pass the butter*). **4** surpass; exceed (*passes all understanding*). **5** get through. **6 a** go unremarked or uncensured (*let the matter pass*). **b** (foll. by *as, for*) be accepted or known as. **7** move; cause to go (*passed her hand over her face*). **8 a** be successful or adequate, esp. in an examination. **b** be successful in (an examination). **c** (of an examiner) judge (a candidate) to be satisfactory. **9 a** (of a bill) be approved by (Parliament etc.). **b** cause or allow (a bill) to proceed. **c** (of a bill or proposal) be approved. **10** occur, elapse; happen (*time passes slowly; heard what passed*). **11** (cause to) circulate; be current. **12** spend (time or a period) (*passed the afternoon reading*). **13** (also *absol.*) (in field games) send (the ball) to a team-mate. **14 a** forgo one's turn or chance. **b** leave a quiz question etc. unanswered. **15** (foll. by *to, into, from*) change (from one form or state to another). **16** come to an end. **17** discharge (esp. faeces or urine) from the body. **18** (foll. by *on, upon*) utter (legal sentence, criticism) upon; adjudicate. *–n.* **1** act of passing. **2 a** success in an examination. **b** university degree without honours. **3 a** permit, esp. for admission, leave, etc. **b** ticket or permit giving free entry, access, travel, etc. **4** (in field games) transference of the ball to a team-mate. **5** desperate position (*come to a fine pass*). □ **in passing** in the course of conversation etc. **make a pass at** *colloq.* make sexual advances to. **pass away 1** *euphem.* die. **2** cease to exist. **pass by 1** go past. **2** disregard, omit. **pass muster** see MUSTER. **pass a name** (of a broker) disclose the name of a principal for whom he or she is acting. In some commodity trades a broker who passes a name usu. does not guarantee the buyer's solvency. If the broker does not pass the principal's name, he or she usu. guarantees the solvency of the principal, who therefore may have to pay an additional brokerage to remain anonymous. **pass off 1** (of feelings etc.) disappear gradually. **2** (of proceedings) be carried through (in a specified way). **3** (foll. by *as*) **a** misrepresent or disguise (a person or thing) as something else. **b** market (goods) with a design, packaging, or trade name that is very similar to that of another organization. Buyers will thereby think that the goods are those of the other organization, which will be entitled to bring an action against the seller. **4** evade or lightly dismiss (an awkward remark etc.). **pass on 1** proceed. **2** *euphem.* die. **3** transmit to the next person in a series. **pass out 1** become unconscious. **2** complete military training. **pass over 1** omit, ignore, or disregard. **2** ignore the claims of (a person) to promotion etc. **3** *euphem.* die. **pass round 1** distribute. **2** give to one person after another. **pass the time of day** see TIME. **pass up** *colloq.* refuse or neglect (an opportunity etc.). **pass water** urinate. [Latin *passus* PACE[1]]

pass[2] /pɑːs/ *n.* narrow way through mountains. [var. of PACE[1]]

passable *adj.* **1** barely satisfactory; adequate. **2** (of a road, pass, etc.) that can be traversed. □ **passably** *adv.*

passage /'pæsɪdʒ/ *n.* **1** process or means of passing;

transit. **2** = PASSAGEWAY. **3** liberty or right to pass through. **4** journey by sea or air. **5** transition from one state to another. **6** short extract from a book, piece of music, etc. **7** passing of a bill etc. into law. **8** duct etc. in the body. [French: related to PASS[1]]

passageway *n.* narrow path or way; corridor.

passbook *n.* book issued to an account-holder recording deposits and withdrawals.

passé /'pæseɪ/ *adj.* (*fem.* ***passée***) **1** old-fashioned. **2** past its prime. [French]

passenger /'pæsɪndʒə(r)/ *n.* **1** (often *attrib.*) traveller in or on a vehicle (other than the driver, pilot, crew, etc.) (*passenger seat*). **2** *colloq.* idle member of a team, crew, etc. [French *passager*: related to PASSAGE]

passer-by *n.* (*pl.* **passers-by**) person who goes past, esp. by chance.

passerine /'pæsə,ri:n/ *–n.* perching bird such as the sparrow and most land birds. *–adj.* of passerines. [Latin *passer* sparrow]

passim /'pæsɪm/ *adv.* throughout; at several points in a book, article, etc. [Latin]

passion /'pæʃ(ə)n/ *n.* **1** strong emotion. **2** outburst of anger (*flew into a passion*). **3** intense sexual love. **4 a** strong enthusiasm (*passion for football*). **b** object arousing this. **5** (**the Passion**) **a** suffering of Christ during his last days. **b** Gospel account of this. **c** musical setting of this. □ **passionless** *adj.* [Latin *patior pass-* suffer]

passionate /'pæʃənət/ *adj.* dominated, displaying, or caused by strong emotion. □ **passionately** *adv.*

passion-flower *n.* climbing plant with a flower supposedly suggestive of the instruments of the Crucifixion.

passion-fruit *n.* edible fruit of some species of passion-flower.

passion-play *n.* miracle play representing the Passion.

Passion Sunday *n.* fifth Sunday in Lent.

passive /'pæsɪv/ *adj.* **1** acted upon, not acting. **2** showing no interest or initiative; submissive. **3** *Chem.* not active; inert. **4** *Gram.* indicating that the subject undergoes the action of the verb (e.g. in *they were seen*). □ **passively** *adv.* **passivity** /-'sɪvɪtɪ/ *n.* [Latin: related to PASSION]

passive resistance *n.* non-violent refusal to cooperate.

passive smoking *n.* involuntary inhalation of others' cigarette smoke.

passkey *n.* **1** private key to a gate etc. **2** master-key.

passmark *n.* minimum mark needed to pass an examination.

Passover /'pɑ:s,əʊvə(r)/ *n.* Jewish spring festival commemorating the Exodus from Egypt. [from PASS[1], OVER]

passport *n.* **1** official document certifying the holder's identity and citizenship, and authorizing travel abroad. **2** (foll. by *to*) thing that ensures admission or attainment (*passport to success*). [French *passeport*: related to PASS[1], PORT[1]]

password *n.* **1** prearranged selected word or phrase securing recognition, admission, etc. **2** particular sequence of letters, numbers, etc. used to verify the identity of someone wishing to gain access to a computer system or to certain parts of a system. The password is fed into the computer and checked against the stored version of the password: only if the two sequences agree will the user be granted access. Passwords form part of the log on sequence in most modern computer systems. They are used, for example, in systems that hold sensitive data (i.e. for security reasons) or when charges are made for use of system resources. Passwords can also be granted to programs in order to control access to data.

past /pɑ:st/ *–adj.* **1** gone by in time (*in past years*; *the time is past*). **2** recently gone by (*the past month*). **3** of a former time (*past president*). **4** *Gram.* expressing a past action or state. *–n.* **1** (prec. by *the*) **a** past time. **b** past events (*cannot undo the past*). **2** person's past life, esp. if discreditable (*man with a past*). **3** past tense or form. *–prep.* **1** beyond in time or place (*is past two o'clock*; *lives just past the pub*). **2** beyond the range, duration, or compass of (*past endurance*). *–adv.* so as to pass by (*ran past*). □ **not put it past** believe it possible of (a person). **past it** *colloq.* old and useless. [from PASS[1]]

pasta /'pæstə/ *n.* dried flour paste in various shapes (e.g. lasagne or spaghetti). [Italian: related to PASTE]

paste /peɪst/ *–n.* **1** any moist fairly stiff mixture, esp. of powder and liquid. **2** dough of flour with fat, water, etc. **3** liquid adhesive used for sticking paper etc. **4** meat or fish spread (*anchovy paste*). **5** hard glasslike composition used for imitation gems. *–v.* (**-ting**) **1** fasten or coat with paste. **2** *slang* **a** beat or thrash. **b** bomb or bombard heavily. □ **pasting** *n.* (esp. in sense 2 of *v.*). [Latin *pasta* lozenge, from Greek]

pasteboard *n.* **1** stiff material made by pasting together sheets of paper. **2** (*attrib.*) flimsy, unsubstantial.

pastel /'pæst(ə)l/ *n.* **1** (often *attrib.*) light shade of a colour (*pastel blue*). **2** crayon of powdered pigments bound with a gum solution. **3** drawing in pastel. [French *pastel*, or Italian *pastello* diminutive of PASTA]

pastern /'pæst(ə)n/ *n.* part of a horse's foot between fetlock and hoof. [French from Latin]

paste-up *n.* document prepared for copying etc. by pasting sections on to a backing.

pasteurize /'pɑ:stʃə,raɪz/ *v.* (also **-ise**) (**-zing** or **-sing**) partially sterilize (milk etc.) by heating. □ **pasteurization** /-'zeɪʃ(ə)n/ *n.* [*Pasteur*, name of a chemist]

pastiche /pæ'sti:ʃ/ *n.* **1** picture or musical composition from or imitating various sources. **2** literary or other work composed in the style of a well-known author etc. [Latin *pasta* PASTE]

pastille /'pæstɪl/ *n.* small sweet or lozenge. [French from Latin]

pastime /'pɑ:staɪm/ *n.* recreation, hobby. [from PASS[1], TIME]

past master *n.* expert.

pastor /'pɑ:stə(r)/ *n.* minister, esp. of a Nonconformist church. [Latin *pasco past-* feed]

pastoral /'pɑ:stər(ə)l/ *–adj.* **1** of shepherds, flocks, or herds. **2** (of land) used for pasture. **3** (of a poem, picture, etc.) portraying (esp. romanticized) country life. **4** of a pastor. *–n.* **1** pastoral poem, play, picture, etc. **2** letter from a pastor (esp. a bishop) to the clergy or people. [Latin *pastoralis*: related to PASTOR]

pastorale /,pæstə'rɑ:l/ *n.* (*pl.* **-s** or **-li** /-li:/) musical work with a rustic theme or atmosphere. [Italian: related to PASTORAL]

pastorate /'pɑ:stərət/ *n.* **1** office or tenure of a pastor. **2** body of pastors.

pastrami /pæ'strɑ:mɪ/ *n.* seasoned smoked beef. [Yiddish]

pastry /'peɪstrɪ/ *n.* (*pl.* **-ies**) **1** dough of flour, fat, and water used as a base and covering for pies etc. **2** cake etc. made wholly or partly of this. [from PASTE]

pastry-cook *n.* cook who specializes in pastry.

pasturage /'pɑ:stʃərɪdʒ/ *n.* **1** land for pasture. **2** pasturing of cattle etc.

pasture /'pɑ:stʃə(r)/ *–n.* **1** grassland suitable for grazing. **2** herbage for animals. *–v.* (**-ring**) **1** put (animals) to pasture. **2** (of animals) graze. [Latin: related to PASTOR]

pasty[1] /'pæstɪ/ *n.* (*pl.* **-ies**) pastry shaped around esp. a meat and vegetable filling. [Latin: related to PASTE]

pasty[2] /'peɪstɪ/ *adj.* (**-ier, -iest**) unhealthily pale (*pasty-faced*). □ **pastiness** *n.*

pat[1] *–v.* (**-tt-**) **1** strike gently with a flat palm, esp. in affection, sympathy, etc. **2** flatten or mould by patting. *–n.* **1** light stroke or tap, esp. with the hand in affection etc. **2** sound made by this. **3** small mass (esp. of butter) formed by patting. □ **pat on the back** congratulatory gesture. [probably imitative]

pat[2] *–adj.* **1** prepared or known thoroughly. **2** apposite or opportune, esp. glibly so (*a pat answer*). *–adv.* **1** in a pat manner. **2** appositely. □ **have off pat** know or have memorized perfectly. [related to PAT[1]]

pataca /pəˈtɑːkə/ *n.* standard monetary unit of Macao. [Portuguese from Arabic]

Patagonia /ˌpætəˈɡəʊnɪə/ southernmost region of South America, chiefly a dry barren plateau in S Argentina and Chile. Sheep-farming is the main occupation; there are also important oil- and coalfields. □ **Patagonian** *adj.* & *n.*

patch –*n.* **1** material used to mend a hole or as reinforcement. **2** shield protecting an injured eye. **3** large or irregular distinguishable area. **4** *colloq.* period of a specified, esp. unpleasant, kind (*went through a bad patch*). **5** piece of ground. **6** *colloq.* area assigned to, or patrolled by, esp. a police officer. **7** plants growing in one place (*cabbage patch*). **8** scrap, remnant. **9** *Computing* small section of code, often provided by a software supplier, that allows a user to correct or modify a program. –*v.* **1** (often foll. by *up*) repair with a patch or patches. **2** (of material) serve as a patch to. **3** (often foll. by *up*) put together, esp. hastily. **4** (foll. by *up*) settle (a quarrel etc.), esp. hastily or temporarily. □ **not a patch on** *colloq.* greatly inferior to. [perhaps French, var. of PIECE]

patchboard *n.* board with electrical sockets linked by movable leads to enable changeable permutations of connection.

patchouli /pəˈtʃuːlɪ/ *n.* **1** strongly scented East Indian plant. **2** perfume from this. [native name in Madras]

patch pocket *n.* piece of cloth sewn on a garment as a pocket.

patch test *n.* test for allergy by applying patches of allergenic substances to the skin.

patchwork *n.* **1** (often. *attrib.*) stitching together of small pieces of variegated cloth to form a pattern (*patchwork quilt*). **2** thing composed of fragments etc.

patchy *adj.* (**-ier, -iest**) **1** uneven in quality. **2** having or existing in patches. □ **patchily** *adv.* **patchiness** *n.*

pate *n. archaic* or *colloq.* head. [origin unknown]

pâté /ˈpæteɪ/ *n.* paste of mashed and spiced meat or fish etc. [French, = PASTY[1]]

pâté de foie gras /ˌpæteɪ də fwɑː ˈɡrɑː/ *n.* fatted goose liver pâté. [French]

patella /pəˈtelə/ *n.* (*pl.* **patellae** /-liː/) kneecap. □ **patellar** *adj.* [Latin, = pan, diminutive of *patina*: related to PATEN]

paten /ˈpæt(ə)n/ *n.* shallow dish for bread at the Eucharist. [Latin *patina*]

patent /ˈpeɪt(ə)nt, ˈpæt-/ –*n.* **1** official document conferring a right or title, esp. the sole right to make, use, or sell a specified invention. In the UK patents are granted by the Crown through the Patent Office. An applicant for a patent (usu. the inventor or the inventor's employer) must show that the invention is new, is not obvious, and is capable of industrial application. A patent remains valid for 20 years from the date of application (the **priority date**) provided that the patentee continues to pay the appropriate fees. During this time, the patentee may assign the patent or grant licences to use it. Such transactions are registered in a public register at the Patent Office. If anyone infringes the monopoly, the patentee may sue for an injunction and damages or an account of profits. However, a patent from the Patent Office gives exclusive rights in the UK only: the inventor must obtain a patent from the European Patent Office in Munich and patents in other foreign countries for protection of the invention elsewhere. **2** invention or process so protected. –*adj.* **1** /ˈpeɪt(ə)nt/ obvious, plain. **2** conferred or protected by patent. **3 a** proprietary. **b** to which one has a proprietary claim. –*v.* obtain a patent for (an invention). □ **patently** /ˈpeɪtəntlɪ/ *adv.* (in sense 1 of *adj.*). [Latin *pateo* lie open]

♦ **patent agent** *n.* member of the Chartered Institute of Patent Agents, who gives advice on obtaining patents and prepares patent applications.

---

patentee /ˌpeɪtənˈtiː/ *n.* **1** person who takes out or holds a patent. **2** person entitled temporarily to the benefit of a patent.

patent leather *n.* glossy leather.

patent medicine *n.* proprietary medicine available without prescription.

patent office *n.* **1** office issuing patents. **2** (**Patent Office**) UK government office, part of the Department of Trade and Industry, that administers the Patent Acts, the Registered Designs Act, and the Trade Marks Act. It also deals with questions relating to the Copyright Acts, and provides an information service about patent specifications.

pater /ˈpeɪtə(r)/ *n. colloq.* father. [Latin]

■ **Usage** *Pater* is now only found in jocular or affected use.

paterfamilias /ˌpeɪtəfəˈmɪlɪˌæs/ *n.* male head of a family or household. [Latin, = father of the family]

paternal /pəˈtɜːn(ə)l/ *adj.* **1** of, like, or appropriate to a father; fatherly. **2** related through the father. **3** (of a government etc.) limiting freedom and responsibility by well-meant regulations. □ **paternally** *adv.* [Latin: related to PATER]

paternalism *n.* policy of governing or behaving in a paternal way. □ **paternalistic** /-ˈlɪstɪk/ *adj.*

paternity /pəˈtɜːnɪtɪ/ *n.* **1** fatherhood. **2** one's paternal origin.

paternity suit *n.* lawsuit held to determine if a certain man is the father of a certain child.

paternoster /ˌpætəˈnɒstə(r)/ *n.* Lord's Prayer, esp. in Latin. [Latin *pater noster* our father]

path /pɑːθ/ *n.* (*pl.* **paths** /pɑːðz/) **1** way or track made for or by walking. **2** line along which a person or thing moves (*flight path*). **3** course of action. [Old English]

pathetic /pəˈθetɪk/ *adj.* **1** arousing pity, sadness, or contempt. **2** *colloq.* miserably inadequate. □ **pathetically** *adv.* [Greek *pathos* from *paskhō* suffer]

pathetic fallacy *n.* attribution of human emotions to inanimate things, esp. in literature.

pathfinder *n.* explorer; pioneer.

pathogen /ˈpæθədʒ(ə)n/ *n.* agent causing disease. □ **pathogenic** /-ˈdʒenɪk/ *adj.* [Greek *pathos* suffering, -GEN]

pathological /ˌpæθəˈlɒdʒɪk(ə)l/ *adj.* **1** of pathology. **2** of or caused by physical or mental disorder (*pathological fear of spiders*). □ **pathologically** *adv.*

pathology /pəˈθɒlədʒɪ/ *n.* the study or symptoms of disease. □ **pathologist** *n.* [Greek *pathos*: related to PATHETIC]

pathos /ˈpeɪθɒs/ *n.* evocation of pity or sadness in speech, writing, etc. [Greek: related to PATHETIC]

pathway *n.* path or its course.

patience /ˈpeɪʃ(ə)ns/ *n.* **1** ability to endure delay, hardship, provocation, etc. **2** perseverance or forbearance. **3** solo card-game. [Latin: related to PASSION]

patient –*adj.* having or showing patience. –*n.* person receiving or registered to receive medical treatment. □ **patiently** *adv.*

patina /ˈpætɪnə/ *n.* (*pl.* **-s**) **1** film, usu. green, formed on old bronze. **2** similar film on other surfaces. **3** gloss produced by age on woodwork. [Latin: related to PATEN]

patio /ˈpætɪəʊ/ *n.* (*pl.* **-s**) **1** paved usu. roofless area adjoining a house. **2** inner roofless court in a Spanish or Spanish-American house. [Spanish]

patisserie /pəˈtiːsərɪ/ *n.* **1** shop where pastries are made and sold. **2** pastries collectively. [Latin: related to PASTE]

Patna /ˈpætnə/ city in India, capital of the state of Bihar; pop. (1991) 917 243.

Patna rice *n.* rice with long firm grains. [from PATNA]

patois /ˈpætwɑː/ *n.* (*pl.* same /-wɑːz/) regional dialect, differing from the literary language. [French]

Patras /ˈpætrəs/ (Greek **Pátrai** /ˈpætraɪ/) industrial port in Greece, in the NW Peloponnese; tobacco, currants, and olive oil are exported; pop. (1991) 155 180.

patriarch /ˈpeɪtrɪˌɑːk/ *n.* **1** male head of a family or tribe. **2** (often in *pl.*) any of those regarded as fathers of the human race, esp. the sons of Jacob, or Abraham, Isaac, and Jacob, and their forefathers. **3** *Eccl.* **a** chief bishop in the Orthodox Church. **b** *RC Ch.* bishop ranking immediately below the pope. **4** venerable old man. □ **patriarchal** /-'ɑːk(ə)l/ *adj.* [Greek *patria* family, *arkhēs* ruler]

patriarchate /'peɪtrɪˌɑːkət/ *n.* **1** office, see, or residence of a Church patriarch. **2** rank of a tribal patriarch.

patriarchy /'peɪtrɪˌɑːkɪ/ *n.* (*pl.* **-ies**) male-dominated social system, with descent through the male line.

patrician /pə'trɪʃ(ə)n/ *–n. hist.* member of the nobility in ancient Rome. *–adj.* **1** aristocratic. **2** *hist.* of the ancient Roman nobility. [Latin *patricius*: related to PATER]

patricide /'pætrɪˌsaɪd/ *n.* = PARRICIDE (esp. with reference to the killing of one's father). □ **patricidal** /-'saɪd(ə)l/ *adj.* [Latin, alteration of *parricida*]

patrimony /'pætrɪmənɪ/ *n.* (*pl.* **-ies**) **1** property inherited from one's father or ancestor. **2** heritage. □ **patrimonial** /-'məʊnɪəl/ *adj.* [Latin: related to PATER]

patriot /'peɪtrɪət, 'pæt-/ *n.* person devoted to and ready to defend his or her country. □ **patriotic** /-'ɒtɪk/ *adj.* **patriotically** /-'ɒtɪklɪ/ *adv.* **patriotism** *n.* [Greek *patris* fatherland]

patristic /pə'trɪstɪk/ *adj.* of the early Christian writers or their work. [Latin: related to PATER]

patrol /pə'trəʊl/ *–n.* **1** act of walking or travelling around an area, esp. regularly, for security or supervision. **2** guards, police, etc. sent out on patrol. **3 a** troops sent out to reconnoitre. **b** such reconnaissance. **4** unit of six to eight Scouts or Guides. *–v.* (**-ll-**) **1** carry out a patrol of. **2** act as a patrol. [German *Patrolle* from French]

patrol car *n.* police car used for patrols.

patron /'peɪtrən/ *n.* (*fem.* **patroness**) **1** person financially supporting a person, cause, etc. **2** customer of a shop etc. [Latin *patronus*: related to PATER]

patronage /'pætrənɪdʒ/ *n.* **1** patron's or customer's support. **2** right or control of appointments to office, privileges, etc. **3** condescending manner.

patronize /'pætrəˌnaɪz/ *v.* (also **-ise**) (**-zing** or **-sing**) **1** treat condescendingly. **2** be a patron or customer of. □ **patronizing** *adj.* **patronizingly** *adv.*

patron saint *n.* saint regarded as protecting a person, place, activity, etc.

patronymic /ˌpætrə'nɪmɪk/ *n.* name derived from the name of a father or ancestor, e.g. *Johnson*, *O'Brien*, *Ivanovich*. [Greek *patēr* father, *onoma* name]

patten /'pæt(ə)n/ *n. hist.* shoe or clog with a raised sole or set on an iron ring, for walking in mud etc. [French *patin*]

patter[1] *–n.* sound of quick light steps or taps. *–v.* make this sound (*rain pattering on the window-panes*). [from PAT[1]]

patter[2] *–n.* **1** rapid speech used by a comedian. **2** salesman's persuasive talk. *–v.* talk or say glibly or mechanically. [originally *pater*, = PATERNOSTER]

pattern /'pæt(ə)n/ *–n.* **1** repeated decorative design on wallpaper, cloth, etc. **2** regular or logical form, order, etc. (*behaviour pattern*). **3** model, design, or instructions for making something (*knitting pattern*). **4** excellent example, model (*pattern of elegance*). **5** wooden or metal shape from which a mould is made for a casting. **6** random combination of shapes or colours. *–v.* **1** (usu. foll. by *after*, *on*) model (a thing) on a design etc. **2** decorate with a pattern. [from PATRON]

patty /'pætɪ/ *n.* (*pl.* **-ies**) little pie or pasty. [French PÂTÉ, after PASTY[1]]

PAU *abbr.* Pan American Union.

paucity /'pɔːsɪtɪ/ *n.* smallness of number or quantity. [Latin *paucus* few]

paunch /pɔːntʃ/ *n.* belly, stomach, esp. when protruding. □ **paunchy** *adj.* (**-ier, -iest**). [Anglo-French *pa(u)nche* from Latin *pantices* bowels]

pauper /'pɔːpə(r)/ *n.* poor person. □ **pauperism** *n.* [Latin, = poor]

pause /pɔːz/ *–n.* **1** temporary stop or silence. **2** *Mus.* mark (⌒) over a note or rest that is to be lengthened. *–v.* (**-sing**) make a pause; wait. □ **give pause to** cause to hesitate. [Greek *pauō* stop]

pavane /pə'vɑːn/ *n.* (also **pavan** /'pæv(ə)n/) *hist.* **1** a kind of stately dance. **2** music for this. [French from Spanish]

pave *v.* (**-ving**) cover (a street, floor, etc.) with a durable surface. □ **pave the way** (usu. foll. by *for*) make preparations. □ **paving** *n.* [Latin *pavio* ram (v.)]

pavement *n.* **1** paved path for pedestrians beside a road. **2** covering of a street, floor, etc., made of usu. rectangular stones. [Latin *pavimentum*: related to PAVE]

pavement artist *n.* artist who draws in chalk on paving-stones for tips.

pavilion /pə'vɪljən/ *n.* **1** building at a sports ground for changing, refreshments, etc. **2** summerhouse or decorative shelter in a park. **3** large tent at a show, fair, etc. **4** building or stand for entertainments, at an exhibition, etc. [Latin *papilio* butterfly]

paving-stone *n.* large flat stone for paving.

pavlova /pæv'ləʊvə/ *n.* meringue cake with cream and fruit. [*Pavlova*, name of a ballerina]

Pavlovian /pæv'ləʊvɪən/ *adj.* **1** reacting predictably to a stimulus. **2** of such a stimulus or response. [*Pavlov*, name of a physiologist]

paw *–n.* **1** foot of an animal having claws or nails. **2** *colloq.* person's hand. *–v.* **1** strike or scrape with a paw or foot. **2** *colloq.* fondle awkwardly or indecently. [French *poue* from Germanic]

pawl *n.* **1** lever with a catch for the teeth of a wheel or bar. **2** *Naut.* short bar used to lock a capstan, windlass, etc. [Low German or Dutch]

pawn[1] *n.* **1** *Chess* piece of the smallest size and value. **2** person used by others for their own purposes. [French *poun* from Latin *pedo -onis* foot-soldier]

pawn[2] *–v.* **1** deposit (a thing) with a pawnbroker as security for money lent. **2** pledge or wager (one's life, honour, etc.). *–n.* object left in pawn. □ **in pawn** held as security. [French *pan* from Germanic]

pawnbroker *n.* person who lends money at interest on the security of personal property. Borrowers can reclaim their goods by repaying the loan and interest within a stated period. However, if the borrower defaults the pawnbroker is free to sell the goods. The operation of pawnbrokers is governed by the Consumer Credit Act (1974).

pawnshop *n.* pawnbroker's shop.

pawpaw /'pɔːpɔː/ *n.* (also **papaw** /pə'pɔː/, **papaya** /pə'paɪə/) **1** elongated melon-shaped fruit with orange flesh. **2** tropical tree bearing this. [Spanish and Portuguese *papaya*]

PAX *abbr. Telephony* private automatic exchange.

pax *n.* **1** kiss of peace. **2** (as *int.*) *slang* call for a truce (used esp. by schoolchildren). [Latin, = peace]

pay *–v.* (*past* and *past part.* **paid**) **1** (also *absol.*) give (a person etc.) what is due for services done, goods received, debts incurred, etc. (*paid him in full*). **2 a** give (a usu. specified amount) for work done, a debt, etc. (*they pay £6 an hour*). **b** (foll. by *to*) hand over the amount of (a debt, wages, etc.) to (*paid the money to the assistant*). **3 a** give, bestow, or express (attention, a compliment, etc.) (*paid them no heed*). **b** make (a visit) (*paid a call on their uncle*). **4** (also *absol.*) (of a business, attitude, etc.) be profitable or advantageous to (a person etc.). **5** reward or punish (*shall pay you for that*). **6** (usu. as **paid** *adj.*) recompense (work, time, etc.) (*paid holiday*). **7** (usu. foll. by *out*, *away*) let out (a rope) by slackening it. *–n.* wages. □ **in the pay of** employed by. **pay back 1** repay. **2** punish or have revenge on. **pay for 1** hand over the money for. **2** bear the cost of. **3** suffer or be punished for (a fault etc.). **pay in** pay (money) into a bank etc. account. **pay its** (or **one's**) **way** cover costs. **pay one's last respects** attend a funeral to show respect. **pay off 1** dismiss (workers) with a final payment. **2** *colloq.* yield good results; succeed. **3** pay (a debt) in full. **pay one's respects** make a polite visit. **pay through the nose** *colloq.* pay much more than a fair price. **pay up** pay the full amount (of). **put paid to**

colloq. **1** deal effectively with (a person). **2** terminate (hopes etc.). [Latin *paco* appease: related to PEACE]

payable *adj.* that must or may be paid; due (*payable in April*). □ **payable to bearer** (of a bill of exchange) having neither the payee nor endorsee named, so that the holder, by adding his or her name, can make the bill payable to order. **payable to order** (of a bill of exchange) having the payee named and with no restrictions or endorsements, so that it can be paid to the endorsee.

◆ **pay and file** *n.* administrative system for UK corporation tax, in which from October 1993 companies will be required to pay their corporation tax nine months after the end of their accounting period.

◆ **pay-as-you-earn** see PAYE.

◆ **payback period** *n.* length of time that a project will take to recover the initial outlay it requires, used as a criterion for accepting capital projects. The assumption is that any further recoveries are then pure profit. This is a relatively unsophisticated method of appraising a capital project (cf. DISCOUNTED CASH FLOW; NET PRESENT VALUE), although it is frequently used in industry. See also INTERNAL RATE OF RETURN.

---

pay-bed *n.* private hospital bed.

pay-claim *n.* (esp. a trade union's) demand for a pay increase.

pay-day *n.* day on which wages are paid.

◆ **PAYE** *abbr.* pay-as-you-earn, a means of collecting income tax by deducting it from wages and salaries at source. Because it is often difficult to collect tax at the end of the year from wage- and salary-earners, the onus is placed on employers to collect the tax from their employees as payments are made to them. There is an elaborate system of administration to ensure that broadly the correct amount of tax is deducted week by week or month by month and that the employer remits the tax collected to the Inland Revenue very quickly.

◆ **payee** /peɪˈiː/ *n.* person or organization to be paid, esp. the person or organization to whom a cheque is made payable.

◆ **paying banker** *n.* bank on which a bill of exchange (including a cheque) has been drawn and which is responsible for paying it if it is correctly drawn and correctly endorsed (if necessary).

---

paying guest *n.* boarder.

◆ **paying-in book** *n.* book of slips used to pay cash, cheques, etc. into a bank account. The counterfoil of the slip is stamped by the bank if the money is paid in over the counter.

---

payload *n.* **1** part of an aircraft's load yielding revenue. **2** explosive warhead carried by a rocket etc. **3** goods carried by a road vehicle.

paymaster *n.* **1** official who pays troops, workmen, etc. **2** usu. *derog.* person, organization, etc., to whom another owes loyalty because of payment given. **3** (in full **Paymaster General**) Treasury minister responsible for payment of public-service pensions and also acting as paying agent for certain government departments.

payment *n.* **1** paying. **2** amount paid. **3** reward, recompense.

◆ **payment by results** *n.* (also **PBR**) system of payment in which an employee's pay is directly linked to his or her performance. It is usu. a premium bonus scheme. See also PIECE RATE; LUMP SYSTEM.

◆ **payment for honour** *n.* = ACCEPTANCE SUPRA PROTEST.

◆ **payment in advance** *n.* (also **prepayment**) payment for goods or services before they have been received. In company accounts, this often refers to rates or rents paid for periods that carry over into the next accounting period.

◆ **payment in due course** *n.* payment of a bill of exchange when it matures (becomes due).

◆ **payment in kind** *n.* payment that is not made in cash but in goods or services. It is often in the form of a discount or an allowance (e.g. cheap fares for British Airways employees, staff prices for food at supermarkets, etc.) and is regarded as a bonus or fringe benefit.

◆ **payment on account** *n.* **1** payment made for goods or services before the goods or services are finally billed. **2** payment towards meeting a liability that is not the full amount of the liability. The sum paid will be credited to the account of the payer in the books of the payee as a part-payment of the ultimate liability.

◆ **payment supra protest** *n.* = ACCEPTANCE SUPRA PROTEST.

◆ **payment terms** *n.pl.* agreed way in which a buyer pays the seller for goods. The commonest are cash with order or cash on delivery, prompt cash (i.e. within 14 days of delivery), cash in 30, 60, or 90 days from date of invoice, letter of credit, cash against documents, documents against acceptance, or acceptance credit.

---

pay-off *n. slang* **1** payment. **2** climax. **3** final reckoning.

payola /peɪˈəʊlə/ *n.* esp. *US slang* bribe offered for unofficial promotion of a product etc. in the media.

pay-packet *n.* envelope etc. containing an employee's wages.

pay phone *n.* telephone, provided for public use, requiring cash or a phonecard to be used to pay for the call. Some pay phones will accept standard credit cards. Mobile radio pay phones are available on some mainline rail routes, ferry routes, and long-distance coach routes.

payroll *n.* list of employees receiving regular pay.

◆ **payroll tax** *n.* tax based on the total of an organization's payroll. The main function of such a tax would be to discourage high wages or over-employment. The current employers' Class 1 National Insurance contributions constitute such a tax.

PB *abbr.* **1** pass book. **2** Premium Bond.

Pb *symb.* lead. [Latin *plumbum*]

PBR *abbr.* = PAYMENT BY RESULTS.

◆ **PBX** *abbr.* = PRIVATE BRANCH EXCHANGE.

PC *abbr.* **1** = PERSONAL COMPUTER. **2** police constable. **3** *colloq.* politically correct (or political correctness). **4** Privy Counsellor. **5** process control. **6** (in the US) professional corporation.

P/C *abbr.* (also **p/c**) **1** petty cash. **2** price(s) current.

pc. *abbr.* **1** percentage. **2** price.

p.c. *abbr.* **1** per cent. **2** postcard.

PCA *abbr.* = PARLIAMENTARY COMMISSIONER FOR ADMINISTRATION.

PCB *abbr.* **1** petty-cash book. **2** polychlorinated biphenyl, any of several toxic aromatic compounds formed as waste in industrial processes. **3** printed circuit board (see PRINTED CIRCUIT).

p.c.m. *abbr.* per calendar month.

PCN *abbr. Computing* personal communications network.

PCTE *abbr. Computing* portable common tool environment.

PD *abbr.* **1** port dues. **2** postal district. **3** (also **P/D**) price dividend (see PRICE–DIVIDEND RATIO). **4** *Insurance* property damage. **5** *Computing* public domain (software).

Pd *symb.* palladium.

pd. *abbr.* **1** paid. **2** passed.

p.d. *abbr.* **1** = PER DIEM. **2** postage due. **3** (also **p/d**) post-dated.

PDL *abbr.* **1** *Computing* page description language. **2** poverty datum line. **3** *Computing* program design language.

PDM *abbr.* physical distribution management.

PDN *abbr.* public data network.

PDP *abbr. Computing* parallel distributed processing.

p.d.q. *abbr. colloq.* pretty damn quick.

PDR *abbr.* (also **P/D ratio**) = PRICE–DIVIDEND RATIO.

PDS *abbr. Computing* programming documentation standards.

PE *–abbr.* **1** *Insurance* personal effects. **2** physical education. **3** (also **P/E**) price earnings (see PRICE–EARNINGS RATIO). **4** *Statistics* probable error. **5** *Computing* processing element. **6** procurement executive. *–international vehicle registration* Peru. *–postcode* Peterborough.

pea *n.* **1 a** hardy climbing plant with edible seeds growing in pods. **b** its seed. **2** similar plant (*sweet pea*; *chickpea*). [from PEASE taken as a plural]

peace *n.* **1 a** quiet; tranquillity. **b** mental calm; serenity. **2 a** (often *attrib.*) freedom from or the cessation of war (*peace talks*). **b** (esp. **Peace**) treaty of peace between states etc. at war. **3** freedom from civil disorder. □ **at peace 1** in a state of friendliness. **2** serene. **3** *euphem.* dead. **hold one's peace** keep silent. **keep the peace** prevent, or refrain from, strife. **make one's peace** (often foll. by *with*) re-establish friendly relations. **make peace** agree to end a war or quarrel. [Latin *pax pac-*]

peaceable *adj.* **1** disposed to peace. **2** peaceful; tranquil. [Latin *placibilis* pleasing: related to PLEASE]

peace dividend *n.* public money which becomes available when defence spending is reduced.

peaceful *adj.* **1** characterized by peace; tranquil. **2** not infringing peace (*peaceful coexistence*). □ **peacefully** *adv.* **peacefulness** *n.*

♦ **peaceful picketing** see PICKETING.

---

peacemaker *n.* person who brings about peace. □ **peacemaking** *n.* & *adj.*

peace-offering *n.* propitiatory or conciliatory gift.

peace-pipe *n.* tobacco-pipe as a token of peace among North American Indians.

peacetime *n.* period when a country is not at war.

peach[1] *n.* **1 a** round juicy fruit with downy yellow or pink skin. **b** tree bearing this. **2** yellowish-pink colour. **3** *colloq.* **a** person or thing of superlative quality. **b** attractive young woman. □ **peachy** *adj.* (**-ier**, **-iest**). [Latin *persica* Persian (apple)]

peach[2] *v.* (usu. foll. by *against, on*) *colloq.* turn informer; inform. [from obsolete *appeach*: related to IMPEACH]

peach Melba *n.* dish of peaches, ice-cream, and raspberry sauce.

peacock *n.* (*pl.* same or **-s**) male peafowl, with brilliant plumage and an erectile fanlike tail with eyelike markings. [from Latin *pavo* peacock, COCK[1]]

peacock blue *adj.* & *n.* (as adj. often hyphenated) lustrous greenish blue of a peacock's neck.

peacock butterfly *n.* butterfly with eyelike wing markings.

peafowl *n.* a kind of pheasant; peacock, peahen.

pea green *adj.* & *n.* (as adj. often hyphenated) bright green.

peahen *n.* female peafowl.

peak[1] *–n.* **1** projecting usu. pointed part, esp.: **a** the pointed top of a mountain. **b** a mountain with a peak. **c** a stiff brim at the front of a cap. **2 a** highest point of a curve, graph, etc. (*peak of the wave*). **b** time of greatest success, fitness, etc. **3** *attrib.* maximum, busiest (*peak viewing*; *peak hours*). *–v.* reach its highest value, quality, etc. (*output peaked*). □ **peaked** *adj.* [related to PICK[2]]

peak[2] *v.* **1** waste away. **2** (as **peaked** *adj.*) sharp-featured; pinched. [origin unknown]

peak-load *n.* maximum of electric power demand etc.

♦ **peak time** *n.* period of television airtime, usu. the middle part of the evening, when the highest number of people are viewing and for which the highest advertising rate is charged.

---

peaky *adj.* (**-ier**, **-iest**) **1** sickly; puny. **2** white-faced.

peal *–n.* **1 a** loud ringing of a bell or bells, esp. a series of changes. **b** set of bells. **2** loud repeated sound, esp. of thunder, laughter, etc. *–v.* **1** (cause to) sound in a peal. **2** utter sonorously. [from APPEAL]

pean *US* var. of PAEAN.

peanut *n.* **1** plant of the pea family bearing pods underground that contain seeds used for food and oil. **2** seed of this. **3** (in *pl.*) *colloq.* paltry thing or amount, esp. of money.

peanut butter *n.* paste of ground roasted peanuts.

pear /peə(r)/ *n.* **1** yellowish or greenish fleshy fruit, tapering towards the stalk. **2** tree bearing this. [Latin *pirum*]

pearl /pɜːl/ *–n.* **1 a** (often *attrib.*) rounded usu. white or bluish-grey lustrous solid formed within the shell of certain oysters, highly prized as a gem. **b** imitation of this. **c** (in *pl.*) necklace of pearls. **2** precious thing; finest example. **3** thing like a pearl, e.g. a dewdrop or tear. *–v.* **1** *poet.* form or sprinkle with pearly drops. **2** reduce (barley etc.) to small rounded grains. **3** fish for pearls. [Italian *perla*, from Latin *perna* leg]

pearl barley *n.* barley ground to small rounded grains.

pearl bulb *n.* translucent electric light bulb.

pearl button *n.* mother-of-pearl button, or an imitation of it.

pearl-diver *n.* person who dives for pearl-oysters.

pearlite var. of PERLITE.

pearly *–adj.* (**-ier**, **-iest**) like, containing, or adorned with pearls; lustrous. *–n.* (*pl.* **-ies**) **1** pearly king or queen. **2** (in *pl.*) pearly king's or queen's clothes.

Pearly Gates *n.pl. colloq.* gates of Heaven.

pearly king *n.* (also **pearly queen**) London costermonger (or his wife) wearing clothes covered with pearl buttons.

pearly nautilus see NAUTILUS.

peasant /ˈpez(ə)nt/ *n.* **1** (in some rural agricultural countries) small farmer, agricultural worker. **2** *derog.* lout; boor. □ **peasantry** *n.* (*pl.* **-ies**). [Anglo-French *paisant* from *paìs* country]

pease /piːz/ *n.pl. archaic* peas. [Latin *pisa*]

pease-pudding *n.* boiled split peas (served esp. with boiled beef or ham).

peashooter *n.* small tube for blowing dried peas through as a toy.

pea-souper *n. colloq.* thick yellowish fog.

peat *n.* **1** partly carbonized vegetable matter used for fuel, in horticulture, etc. **2** cut piece of this. □ **peaty** *adj.* [perhaps Celtic: related to PIECE]

peatbog *n.* bog composed of peat.

pebble /ˈpeb(ə)l/ *n.* small stone worn smooth esp. by the action of water. □ **pebbly** *adj.* [Old English]

pebble-dash *n.* mortar with stone chippings in it as a coating for external walls.

pecan /ˈpiːkən/ *n.* **1** pinkish-brown smooth nut with an edible kernel. **2** type of hickory producing this. [Algonquian]

peccadillo /ˌpekəˈdɪləʊ/ *n.* (*pl.* **-es** or **-s**) trifling offence; venial sin. [Spanish *pecadillo*, from Latin *pecco* to sin (v.)]

peck[1] *–v.* **1** strike or bite with a beak. **2** kiss hastily or perfunctorily. **3 a** make (a hole) by pecking. **b** (foll. by *out, off*) remove or pluck out by pecking. **4** (also *absol.*) *colloq.* eat listlessly; nibble at. *–n.* **1** stroke, mark, or bite made by a beak. **2** hasty or perfunctory kiss. □ **peck at 1** eat (food) listlessly; nibble. **2** carp at; nag. **3** strike repeatedly with a beak. [probably Low German]

peck[2] *n.* measure of capacity for dry goods, equal to 2 gallons or 8 quarts. □ **a peck of** large number or amount of. [Anglo-French]

pecker *n. US coarse slang* penis. □ **keep your pecker up** *colloq.* remain cheerful.

pecking order *n.* social hierarchy, orig. as observed among hens.

peckish *adj. colloq.* hungry.

Pécs /peɪtʃ/ industrial city in SW Hungary, at the centre of a noted wine-producing region; pop. (1996) 163 000.

pectin /ˈpektɪn/ *n.* soluble gelatinous carbohydrate found in ripe fruits etc. and used as a setting agent in jams and jellies. □ **pectic** *adj.* [Greek *pēgnumi* make solid]

pectoral /ˈpektər(ə)l/ *–adj.* of or worn on the breast or chest (*pectoral fin*; *pectoral muscle*; *pectoral cross*). –*n.* pectoral muscle or fin. [Latin *pectus -tor-* chest]

peculate /ˈpekjʊˌleɪt/ *v.* (**-ting**) embezzle (money). □ **peculation** /-ˈleɪʃ(ə)n/ *n.* **peculator** *n.* [Latin: related to PECULIAR]

peculiar /pɪˈkjuːlɪə(r)/ *adj.* **1** strange; odd; unusual. **2 a** (usu. foll. by *to*) belonging exclusively (*peculiar to the time*). **b** belonging to the individual (*in their own peculiar way*). **3** particular; special (*point of peculiar interest*). [Latin *peculium* private property, from *pecu* cattle]

peculiarity /pɪˌkjuːlɪˈærɪtɪ/ *n.* (*pl.* **-ies**) **1** idiosyncrasy; oddity. **2** characteristic. **3** being peculiar.

peculiarly /pɪˈkjuːlɪəlɪ/ *adv.* **1** more than usually, especially (*peculiarly annoying*). **2** oddly.

pecuniary /pɪˈkjuːnɪərɪ/ *adj.* **1** of or concerning money. **2** (of an offence) entailing a money penalty. [Latin *pecunia* money, from *pecu* cattle]

pedagogue /ˈpedəˌgɒg/ *n. archaic* or *derog.* schoolmaster; teacher. □ **pedagogic** /-ˈgɒgɪk, -ˈgɒdʒɪk/ *adj.* **pedagogical** /-ˈgɒgɪk(ə)l, -ˈgɒdʒɪk(ə)l/ *adj.* [Greek *pais paid-* child, *agō* lead]

pedagogy /ˈpedəˌgɒdʒɪ, -ˌgɒgɪ/ *n.* science of teaching.

pedal –*n.* /ˈped(ə)l/ lever or key operated by foot, esp. in a vehicle, on a bicycle, or on some musical instruments (e.g. the organ). –*v.* /ˈped(ə)l/ (**-ll-**; *US* **-l-**) **1** operate the pedals of a bicycle, organ, etc. **2** propel (a bicycle etc.) with the pedals. –*adj.* /ˈpiːd(ə)l/ of the foot or feet. [Latin *pes ped-* foot]

pedalo /ˈpedəˌləʊ/ *n.* (*pl.* **-s**) pedal-operated pleasure-boat.

pedant /ˈped(ə)nt/ *n. derog.* person who insists on adherence to formal rules or literal meaning. □ **pedantic** /pɪˈdæntɪk/ *adj.* **pedantically** /pɪˈdæntɪkəlɪ/ *adv.* **pedantry** *n.* [French from Italian]

peddle /ˈped(ə)l/ *v.* (**-ling**) **1 a** sell (goods) as a pedlar. **b** advocate or promote. **2** sell (drugs) illegally. **3** engage in selling, esp. as a pedlar. [back-formation from PEDLAR]

peddler *n.* **1** person who sells drugs illegally. **2** *US* var. of PEDLAR.

pederast /ˈpedəˌræst/ *n.* (also **paederast**) man who engages in pederasty.

pederasty /ˈpedəˌræstɪ/ *n.* (also **paederasty**) anal intercourse between a man and a boy. [Greek *pais paid-* boy, *erastēs* lover]

pedestal /ˈpedɪst(ə)l/ *n.* **1** base supporting a column or pillar. **2** stone etc. base of a statue etc. □ **put on a pedestal** admire disproportionately, idolize. [Italian *piedestallo*, = foot of stall]

pedestrian /pɪˈdestrɪən/ –*n.* (often *attrib.*) person who is walking, esp. in a town. –*adj.* prosaic; dull; uninspired. □ **pedestrianize** *v.* (also **-ise**) (**-zing** or **-sing**). [Latin: related to PEDAL]

pedestrian crossing *n.* part of a road where crossing pedestrians have right of way.

pediatrics *US* var. of PAEDIATRICS.

pedicure /ˈpedɪˌkjʊə(r)/ *n.* **1** care or treatment of the feet, esp. the toenails. **2** person practising this for a living. [Latin *pes ped-* foot, *cura* care]

pedigree /ˈpedɪˌgriː/ *n.* **1** (often *attrib.*) recorded line of descent (esp. a distinguished one) of a person or pure-bred animal. **2** genealogical table. **3** *colloq.* 'life history' of a person, thing, idea, etc. □ **pedigreed** *adj.* [*pedegru* from French *pie de grue* (unrecorded) crane's foot, a mark denoting succession in pedigrees]

pediment /ˈpedɪmənt/ *n.* triangular part crowning the front of a building, esp. over a portico. [from *periment*, perhaps a corruption of PYRAMID]

pedlar /ˈpedlə(r)/ *n.* (*US* **peddler**) **1** travelling seller of small items. **2** (usu. foll. by *of*) retailer (of gossip etc.). [alteration of *pedder* from *ped* pannier]

pedo- *US* var. of PAEDO-.

pedometer /pɪˈdɒmɪtə(r)/ *n.* instrument for estimating distance walked by recording the number of steps taken. [Latin *pes ped-* foot: related to -METER]

pedophile *US* var. of PAEDOPHILE.

pedophilia *US* var. of PAEDOPHILIA.

peduncle /pɪˈdʌŋk(ə)l/ *n.* stalk of a flower, fruit, or cluster, esp. a main stalk bearing a solitary flower or subordinate stalks. □ **peduncular** /-kjʊlə(r)/ *adj.* [related to PEDOMETER, -UNCLE]

pee *colloq.* –*v.* (**pees, peed**) urinate. –*n.* **1** act of urinating. **2** urine. [from PISS]

peek –*v.* (usu. foll. by *in, out, at*) peep slyly, glance. –*n.* quick or sly look. [origin unknown]

peel –*v.* **1 a** strip the skin, rind, wrapping, etc. from. **b** (usu. foll. by *off*) strip (skin, peel, wrapping, etc.). **2 a** become bare of skin, paint, etc. **b** (often foll. by *off*) (of skin, paint, etc.) flake off. **3** (often foll. by *off*) *colloq.* (of a person) strip ready for exercise etc. –*n.* outer covering of a fruit, vegetable, etc.; rind. □ **peel off** veer away and detach oneself from a group etc. [Old English from Latin *pilo* strip of hair]

peeling *n.* (usu. in *pl.*) stripped-off piece of peel.

peen *n.* wedge-shaped or thin or curved end of a hammer-head. [Latin *pinna* point]

peep[1] –*v.* **1** (usu. foll. by *at, in, out, into*) look through a narrow opening; look furtively. **2** (usu. foll. by *out*) come slowly into view; emerge. –*n.* **1** furtive or peering glance. **2** first appearance (*peep of day*). [origin unknown]

peep[2] –*v.* make a shrill feeble sound as of young birds, mice, etc. –*n.* **1** such a sound. **2** slight sound, utterance, or complaint (*not a peep out of them*). [imitative]

peep-hole *n.* small hole for peeping through.

peeping Tom *n.* furtive voyeur.

peep-show *n.* small exhibition of pictures etc. viewed through a lens or hole set into a box etc.

peer[1] *v.* (usu. foll. by *into, at*, etc.) look closely or with difficulty. [origin unknown]

peer[2] *n.* **1 a** (*fem.* **peeress**) member of one of the degrees of the nobility in Britain or Ireland, i.e. a duke, marquis, earl, viscount, or baron. **b** noble of any country. **2** person who is equal in ability, standing, rank, or value. [Latin *par* equal]

peerage *n.* **1** peers as a class; the nobility. **2** rank of peer or peeress.

peer group *n.* group of people of the same age, status, etc.

peerless *adj.* unequalled, superb.

peer of the realm *n.* peer entitled to sit in the House of Lords.

peeve *colloq.* –*v.* (**-ving**) (usu. as **peeved** *adj.*) irritate, annoy. –*n.* cause or state of irritation. [back-formation from PEEVISH]

peevish *adj.* irritable. □ **peevishly** *adv.* [origin unknown]

peewit /ˈpiːwɪt/ *n.* (also **pewit**) lapwing. [a sound imitative of its cry]

peg –*n.* **1** pin or bolt of wood, metal, etc., for holding things together, hanging garments on, holding up a tent, etc. **2** each of the pins used to tighten or loosen the strings of a violin etc. **3** pin for marking position, e.g. on a cribbage-board. **4** = CLOTHES-PEG. **5** occasion or pretext (*peg to hang an argument on*). **6** drink, esp. of spirits. –*v.* (**-gg-**) **1** (usu. foll. by *down, in, out*, etc.) fix (a thing) with a peg. **2** fix or stabilize (prices, wages, etc.) at existing levels by government order to control inflation. **3** fix (a country's exchange rate) on foreign exchange markets. See CRAWLING PEG; FIXED EXCHANGE RATE. **4** mark (the score) with pegs on a cribbage-board. □ **off the peg** (of clothes) ready-made. **peg away** (often foll. by *at*) work consistently. **peg out 1** *slang* die. **2** mark the boundaries of. **square peg in a round hole** misfit. **take a person down a peg or two** humble a person. [probably Low German or Dutch]

pegboard *n.* board with small holes for pegs, used for displays, games, etc.

peg-leg *n. colloq.* **1** artificial leg. **2** person with this.

Pegu /peˈguː/ city and port in S Burma; pop. (latest est.) 150 400.

PEI *abbr.* Prince Edward Island.

pejorative /pɪ'dʒɒrətɪv/ *–adj.* derogatory. *–n.* derogatory word. [Latin *pejor* worse]

peke *n. colloq.* Pekingese. [abbreviation]

Peking /piː'kɪŋ/ (now transliterated as **Beijing**) capital of China; there are iron and steel, textile, and other industries; pop. (est. 1991) 7 000 000.

Pekingese /ˌpiːkɪ'niːz/ *n.* (also **Pekinese**) (*pl.* same) lap-dog of a short-legged breed with long hair and a snub nose. [from PEKING]

pelargonium /ˌpelə'gəʊnɪəm/ *n.* plant with red, pink, or white flowers and, often, fragrant leaves; geranium. [Greek *pelargos* stork]

pelf *n. derog.* or *joc.* money; wealth. [French: related to PILFER]

pelican /'pelɪkən/ *n.* large water-bird with a large bill and a pouch in its throat for storing fish. [Greek *pelekan*]

pelican crossing *n.* pedestrian crossing with traffic lights operated by pedestrians.

pelisse /pɪ'liːs/ *n. hist.* **1** woman's long cloak with armholes or sleeves. **2** fur-lined cloak as part of a hussar's uniform. [Latin *pellicia* (garment) of fur, from *pellis* skin]

pellagra /pə'lægrə/ *n.* disease with cracking of the skin and often ending in insanity. [Italian *pelle* skin]

pellet /'pelɪt/ *n.* **1** small compressed ball of paper, bread, etc. **2** pill. **3** piece of small shot. [French *pelote* from Latin *pila* ball]

pellicle /'pelɪk(ə)l/ *n.* thin skin, membrane, or film. [Latin diminutive of *pellis* skin]

pell-mell /pel'mel/ *adv.* **1** headlong, recklessly. **2** in disorder or confusion. [French *pêle-mêle*]

pellucid /pɪ'luːsɪd/ *adj.* **1** transparent. **2** (of style, speech, etc.) clear. [Latin: related to PER-]

pelmet /'pelmɪt/ *n.* narrow border of cloth, wood, etc. fitted esp. above a window to conceal the curtain rail. [probably French]

Peloponnese /'peləpəˌniːs/ (Greek **Pelopónnisos** /ˌpelə'pɒnɪˌsɒs/) mountainous S peninsula of Greece, connected to the mainland by the Isthmus of Corinth; pop. (1991) 607 428.

pelt[1] *–v.* **1** (usu. foll. by *with*) strike repeatedly with thrown objects. **2** (usu. foll. by *down*) (of rain etc.) fall quickly and torrentially. **3** run fast. *–n.* pelting. □ **at full pelt** as fast as possible. [origin unknown]

pelt[2] *n.* undressed skin, usu. of a fur-bearing mammal. [French, ultimately from Latin *pellis* skin]

pelvis /'pelvɪs/ *n.* basin-shaped cavity in most vertebrates, formed from the hip-bone with the sacrum and other vertebrae. □ **pelvic** *adj.* [Latin, = basin]

Pemba /'pembə/ **1** seaport in NE Mozambique; pop. (1980) 41 200. **2** Tanzanian island, off the E coast of the mainland, a major producer of cloves; pop. (1988) 265 039.

pen[1] *–n.* **1** instrument for writing etc. with ink. **2** (**the pen**) occupation of writing. *–v.* (**-nn-**) write. [Latin *penna* feather]

pen[2] *–n.* small enclosure for cows, sheep, poultry, etc. *–v.* (**-nn-**) (often foll. by *in*, *up*) enclose or shut up, esp. in a pen. [Old English]

pen[3] *n.* female swan. [origin unknown]

penal /'piːn(ə)l/ *adj.* **1** of or concerning punishment or its infliction. **2** (of an offence) punishable, esp. by law. □ **penally** *adv.* [Latin *poena* PAIN]

penalize /'piːnəˌlaɪz/ *v.* (**-ise**) (**-zing** or **-sing**) **1** subject (a person) to a penalty or disadvantage. **2** make or declare (an action) penal.

penalty /'penəltɪ/ *n.* (*pl.* **-ies**) **1** punishment for breaking a law, rule, etc. **2** arbitrary pre-arranged sum that becomes payable if one party breaches a contract or undertaking, usu. expressly stated in a **penalty clause** of the contract. Unlike liquidated damages, a penalty will be disregarded by the courts and treated as being void. Liquidated damages will generally be treated as a penalty if the amount payable is extravagant and unconscionable compared with the maximum loss that could result from the breach. However, use of the words 'penalty' or 'liquidated damages' is inconclusive as the legal position depends on the interpretation by the courts of the clause in which they appear. **3** disadvantage, loss, etc., esp. as a result of one's own actions. **4** *Sport* disadvantage imposed for a breach of the rules etc. [medieval Latin: related to PENAL]

penalty area *n. Football* ground in front of the goal in which a foul by defenders involves the award of a penalty kick.

penalty kick *n. Football* free kick at the goal resulting from a foul in the penalty area.

penance /'penəns/ *n.* **1** act of self-punishment as reparation for guilt. **2 a** (in the Roman Catholic and Orthodox Church) sacrament including confession of and absolution for sins. **b** penalty imposed, esp. by a priest, for a sin. □ **do penance** perform a penance. [related to PENITENT]

Penang /pɪ'næŋ/ (also **Pinang**) **1** Malaysian island off the coast of the Malay Peninsula. **2** state of Malaysia consisting of this island and a coastal strip on the mainland; pop. (est. 1993) 1 141 500; capital, George Town (on Penang island). Rice is grown; tin-mining and rubber production are also important.

pence *pl.* of PENNY.

penchant /'pɑ̃ʃɑ̃/ *n.* (followed by *for*) inclination or liking. [French]

pencil /'pens(ə)l/ *–n.* **1** instrument for writing or drawing, usu. a thin rod of graphite etc. enclosed in a wooden cylinder or metal case. **2** (*attrib.*) resembling a pencil in shape (*pencil skirt*). *–v.* (**-ll-**; *US* **-l-**) **1** write, draw, or mark with a pencil. **2** (usu. foll. by *in*) write, note, or arrange provisionally. [Latin *penicillum* paintbrush]

pendant /'pend(ə)nt/ *n.* hanging jewel etc., esp. one attached to a necklace, bracelet, etc. [French *pendre* hang]

pendent /'pend(ə)nt/ *adj. formal* **1 a** hanging. **b** overhanging. **2** undecided, pending. □ **pendency** *n.*

pending *–predic. adj.* **1** awaiting decision or settlement, undecided. **2** about to come into existence (*patent pending*). *–prep.* **1** during (*pending further inquiries*). **2** until (*bailed pending trial*). [after French: see PENDANT]

pendulous /'pendjʊləs/ *adj.* hanging down; drooping and swinging. [Latin *pendulus* from *pendeo* hang]

pendulum /'pendjʊləm/ *n.* (*pl.* **-s**) weight suspended so as to swing freely, esp. a rod with a weighted end regulating a clock. [Latin neuter adjective: related to PENDULOUS]

penetrate /'penɪˌtreɪt/ *v.* (**-ting**) **1 a** find access into or through. **b** (usu. foll. by *with*) imbue with; permeate. **2** see into, find out, or discern. **3** see through (darkness, fog, etc.). **4** be absorbed by the mind. **5** (as **penetrating** *adj.*) **a** having or suggesting sensitivity or insight. **b** (of a voice etc.) easily heard through or above other sounds; piercing. **6** enter (a market) to establish a new brand, product, etc. See MARKET PENETRATION. □ **penetrable** /-trəb(ə)l/ *adj.* **penetrability** /-trə'bɪlɪtɪ/ *n.* **penetration** /-'treɪʃ(ə)n/ *n.* **penetrative** /-trətɪv/ *adj.* [Latin]

♦ **penetration strategy** *n.* marketing strategy based on low prices and extensive advertising to increase a product's market share. For penetration strategy to be effective the market will have to be large enough for the seller to be able to sustain low profit margins. See also MARKET PENETRATION.

---

pen-friend *n.* friend communicated with by letter only.

penguin /'peŋgwɪn/ *n.* flightless black and white sea bird of the southern hemisphere, with wings developed into flippers for swimming underwater. [origin unknown]

penicillin /ˌpenɪ'sɪlɪn/ *n.* antibiotic, produced naturally by mould or synthetically. [Latin *penicillum*: related to PENCIL]

peninsula /pɪ'nɪnsjʊlə/ *n.* piece of land almost surrounded by water or projecting far into a sea etc. □ **peninsular** *adj.* [Latin *paene* almost, *insula* island]

penis /'piːnɪs/ *n.* male organ of copulation and (in mammals) urination. [Latin]

penitent /ˈpenɪt(ə)nt/ *–adj.* repentant. *–n.* **1** repentant sinner. **2** person doing penance under the direction of a confessor. □ **penitence** *n.* **penitently** *adv.* [Latin *paeniteo* repent]

penitential /ˌpenɪˈtenʃ(ə)l/ *adj.* of penitence or penance.

penitentiary /ˌpenɪˈtenʃərɪ/ *–n.* (*pl.* **-ies**) *US* federal or state prison. *–adj.* **1** of penance. **2** of reformatory treatment. [Latin: related to PENITENT]

penknife *n.* small folding knife.

Penn. *abbr.* (also **Penna.**) Pennsylvania.

pen-name *n.* literary pseudonym.

pennant /ˈpenənt/ *n.* **1** tapering flag, esp. that flown at the masthead of a vessel in commission. **2** = PENNON. [blend of PENDANT and PENNON]

penniless /ˈpenɪlɪs/ *adj.* having no money; destitute.

pennon /ˈpenən/ *n.* **1** long narrow flag, triangular or swallow-tailed. **2** long pointed streamer on a ship. [Latin *penna* feather]

Pennsylvania /ˌpensɪlˈveɪnɪə/ state of the NE US; pop. (est. 1996) 12 056 112; capital, Harrisburg. It is a major producer of coal, oil, and iron and steel; agricultural activities include dairy farming and the cultivation of cereals, fruit, and vegetables.

penny /ˈpenɪ/ *n.* (*pl.* for separate coins **-ies**, for a sum of money **pence** /pens/) **1 a** British coin and monetary unit worth one-hundredth of a pound. **b** coin and monetary unit of the Republic of Ireland worth one-hundredth of a punt. **2** *hist.* British bronze coin and monetary unit equal to one-two-hundred-and-fortieth of a pound. □ **in for a penny, in for a pound** exhortation to total commitment to an undertaking. **pennies from heaven** unexpected benefits. **the penny drops** *colloq.* one understands at last. **penny wise and pound foolish** mean in small expenditures but wasteful of large amounts. **a pretty penny** a large sum of money. **two a penny** easily obtained and so almost worthless. [Old English]

penny black *n.* first adhesive postage stamp (1840, price one penny).

penny farthing *n.* early type of bicycle with a large front and small rear wheel.

penny-pinching *–n.* meanness. *–adj.* mean. □ **penny-pincher** *n.*

pennyroyal /ˌpenɪˈrɔɪəl/ *n.* creeping kind of mint. [Anglo-French *puliol real* royal thyme]

♦ **penny shares** *n.pl.* securities with a very low market price traded on a stock exchange. They are popular with small investors, who can acquire a significant holding in a company for a very low cost. Moreover, a rise of a few pence in a low-priced share can represent a high percentage profit. However, they are usu. shares in companies that have fallen on hard times and may, indeed, be close to bankruptcy. The investor in this type of share is hoping for a rapid recovery or a take-over.

---

penny whistle *n.* tin pipe with six finger holes.

pennywort *n.* wild plant with rounded leaves, growing esp. in marshy places.

pennyworth *n.* as much as can be bought for a penny.

penology /piːˈnɒlədʒɪ/ *n.* the study of the punishment of crime and prison management. □ **penologist** *n.* [Latin *poena* penalty]

pen-pal *n. colloq.* = PEN-FRIEND.

pen-pushing *n. colloq. derog.* clerical work. □ **pen-pusher** *n.*

pension[1] /ˈpenʃ(ə)n/ *–n.* **1** regular payment made by a government to people above a specified age, to widows, or to the disabled. In the UK, contributory **retirement pensions** are usu. paid by the state from the age of 65 for men or 60 for women, irrespective of whether or not the pensioners have retired from full-time employment. A non-working wife or widow also receives a state pension based on her husband's contributions. Self-employed people are also required to contribute towards their pensions. The state pays non-contributory **old-age pensions** to people over 80 if they are not already receiving a retirement pension. Since 1978 state pensions have been augmented by SERPS (see STATE EARNINGS-RELATED PENSION SCHEME) to relate pensions to inflation and to ensure that men and women are treated equally. **2** similar payments made by an employer, private pension fund, etc. on the retirement of an employee. See ANNUITY 2; ENDOWMENT ASSURANCE; EXECUTIVE PENSION PLAN; OCCUPATIONAL PENSION SCHEME; PERSONAL PENSION SCHEME; SINGLE-LIFE PENSION. *–v.* grant a pension to. □ **pension off 1** dismiss with a pension. **2** cease to employ or use. [Latin *pendo pens-* pay]

pension[2] /pɑ̃ˈsjɔ̃/ *n.* European, esp. French, boarding-house. [French: related to PENSION[1]]

pensionable *adj.* **1** entitled to a pension. **2** (of a service, job, etc.) entitling an employee to a pension.

♦ **pensionable earnings** *n.pl.* part of an employee's salary that is used to calculate the final pension entitlement. Unless otherwise stated, overtime, commission, and bonuses are normally excluded.

♦ **pensioneer trustee** /ˌpenʃəˈnɪə/ *n.* person authorized by the Superannuation Funds Office of the Inland Revenue to oversee the management of a pension fund in accordance with the provisions of the Pension Trust Deed.

---

pensioner *n.* recipient of a pension, esp. the retirement pension. [French: related to PENSION[1]]

♦ **pension fund** *n.* sum of money, derived from state or private pension contributions, invested to give as high a return as possible to provide the funds from which pensions are paid. In the UK, pension funds managed by individual organizations work closely with insurance companies and investment trusts, being together the institutional investors that have a dominant influence on many securities traded on the London Stock Exchange. The enormous amount of money accumulated by these pension funds, which grows by weekly and monthly contributions, needs prudent management; real estate and works of art are often purchased for investment by pension funds in addition to stock-exchange securities. See also PENSIONEER TRUSTEE; SUPERANNUATION FUNDS OFFICE.

♦ **pension mortgage** *n.* mortgage in which the borrower repays interest only and also contributes to a pension plan designed to provide an eventual tax-free lump sum, part of which is used to pay off the capital at the end of the mortgage term and the rest to provide a pension for the borrower's retirement. This type of mortgage is particularly suitable for the self-employed or those without a company pension.

♦ **pension scheme** *n.* arrangement the main purpose of which is to provide a defined class of individuals (called members of the scheme) with pensions. A pension scheme may include benefits other than a pension and may provide a pension for dependants of deceased members. See also OCCUPATIONAL PENSION SCHEME; PERSONAL ANNUITY SCHEME; PERSONAL PENSION SCHEME.

♦ **Pensions Ombudsman** *n.* = FINANCIAL OMBUDSMAN 5.

---

pensive /ˈpensɪv/ *adj.* deep in thought. □ **pensively** *adv.* [French *penser* think]

pent *adj.* (often foll. by *in, up*) closely confined; shut in (*pent-up feelings*). [from PEN[2]]

penta- *comb. form* five. [Greek *pente* five]

pentacle /ˈpentək(ə)l/ *n.* figure used as a symbol, esp. in magic, e.g. a pentagram. [medieval Latin *pentaculum*: related to PENTA-]

pentagon /ˈpentəgən/ *n.* **1** plane figure with five sides and angles. **2** (**the Pentagon**) **a** pentagonal Washington headquarters of the US forces. **b** leaders of the US forces. □ **pentagonal** /-ˈtægən(ə)l/ *adj.* [Greek *pentagōnon*: related to PENTA-]

pentagram /ˈpentəˌgræm/ *n.* five-pointed star. [Greek: see PENTA-, -GRAM]

pentameter /penˈtæmɪtə(r)/ *n.* line of verse with five metrical feet. [Greek: see PENTA-, -METER]

Pentateuch /ˈpentəˌtjuːk/ *n.* first five books of the Old Testament. [Greek *teukhos* book]

pentathlon /penˈtæθlən/ *n.* athletic event comprising five different events for each competitor. □ **pentathlete** /-ˈtæθliːt/ *n.* [Greek: see PENTA-, *athlon* contest]

pentatonic /ˌpentəˈtɒnɪk/ *adj.* consisting of five musical notes.

Pentecost /ˈpentɪˌkɒst/ *n.* **1** Whit Sunday. **2** Jewish harvest festival, on the fiftieth day after the second day of Passover. [Greek *pentēkostē* fiftieth (day)]

pentecostal /ˌpentɪˈkɒst(ə)l/ *adj.* (of a religious group) emphasizing the divine gifts, esp. the power to heal the sick, and often fundamentalist.

penthouse /ˈpenthaʊs/ *n.* (esp. luxurious) flat on the roof or top floor of a tall building. [Latin: related to APPEND]

penultimate /pɪˈnʌltɪmət/ *adj.* & *n.* last but one. [Latin *paenultimus* from *paene* almost, *ultimus* last]

penumbra /pɪˈnʌmbrə/ *n.* (*pl.* **-brae** /-briː/ or **-s**) **1** partly shaded region around the shadow of an opaque body, esp. that around the shadow of the moon or earth in an eclipse. **2** partial shadow. □ **penumbral** *adj.* [Latin *paene* almost, UMBRA]

penurious /pɪˈnjʊərɪəs/ *adj.* **1** poor. **2** stingy; grudging. **3** scanty. [medieval Latin: related to PENURY]

penury /ˈpenjʊrɪ/ *n.* (*pl.* **-ies**) **1** destitution; poverty. **2** lack; scarcity. [Latin]

Penza /ˈpjenzə/ city in W Russia; it has food-processing and various other manufacturing industries; pop. (est. 1995) 534 000.

peon /ˈpiːən/ *n.* Spanish American day-labourer. [Portuguese and Spanish: related to PAWN[1]]

peony /ˈpiːənɪ/ *n.* (also **paeony**) (*pl.* **-ies**) plant with large globular red, pink, or white flowers. [Greek *paiōnia*]

people /ˈpiːp(ə)l/ *–n.pl.* except in sense 2. **1** persons in general or of a specified kind (*people don't like rudeness*; *famous people*). **2** persons composing a community, tribe, race, nation, etc. (*a warlike people*; *peoples of the Commonwealth*). **3** (**the people**) **a** the mass of people in a country etc. not having special rank or position. **b** these as an electorate. **4** parents or other relatives (*my people disapprove*). **5 a** subjects, armed followers, etc. **b** congregation of a parish priest etc. *–v.* (**-ling**) (usu. foll. by *with*) **1** fill with people, animals, etc.; populate. **2** (esp. as **peopled** *adj.*) inhabit. [Latin *populus*]

PEP *abbr.* **1** /pep/ = PERSONAL EQUITY PLAN. **2** political and economic planning.

pep *colloq.* *–n.* vigour; spirit. *–v.* (**-pp-**) (usu. foll. by *up*) fill with vigour. [abbreviation of PEPPER]

◆ **PEP mortgage** *n.* mortgage in which the borrower repays only the interest on the loan to the lender, but at the same time puts regular sums into a personal equity plan (PEP). When the PEPs mature they are used to repay the capital. The PEP mortgage is similar to an endowment mortgage, except that the PEP mortgage does not provide any life-assurance cover. The advantages are that PEP funds are untaxed, unlike endowments, and that the borrower has the flexibility of being able to change the PEP provider each year.

---

pepper *–n.* **1** hot aromatic condiment from the dried berries of certain plants. **2** anything pungent. **3 a** capsicum plant, grown as a vegetable. **b** its fruit. *–v.* **1** sprinkle or treat with or as if with pepper. **2** pelt with missiles. [Sanskrit *pippalī*]

pepper-and-salt *adj.* with small patches of dark and light colour intermingled.

peppercorn *n.* **1** dried pepper berry. **2** (in full **peppercorn rent**) nominal rent. In theory one peppercorn (or some other nominal sum) is payable as a rent to indicate that a property is leasehold and not freehold, the peppercorn representing the consideration. In practice it amounts to a rent-free lease.

pepper-mill *n.* device for grinding pepper by hand.

peppermint *n.* **1 a** mint plant grown for its strong-flavoured oil. **b** this oil. **2** sweet flavoured with peppermint.

pepperoni /ˌpepəˈrəʊnɪ/ *n.* beef and pork sausage seasoned with pepper. [Italian *peperone* chilli]

pepper-pot *n.* small container with a perforated lid for sprinkling pepper.

peppery *adj.* **1** of, like, or containing pepper. **2** hot-tempered. **3** pungent.

pep pill *n.* pill containing a stimulant drug.

peppy *adj.* (**-ier, -iest**) *colloq.* vigorous, energetic, bouncy.

pepsin /ˈpepsɪn/ *n.* enzyme contained in the gastric juice. [Greek *pepsis* digestion]

pep talk *n.* (usu. short) talk intended to enthuse, encourage, etc.

peptic /ˈpeptɪk/ *adj.* concerning or promoting digestion. [Greek *peptikos* able to digest]

peptic ulcer *n.* ulcer in the stomach or duodenum.

peptide /ˈpeptaɪd/ *n.* *Biochem.* compound consisting of two or more amino acids bonded in sequence. [Greek *peptos* cooked]

PER *abbr.* **1** = PRICE–EARNINGS RATIO. **2** Professional and Executive Recruitment. **3** Professional Employment Register.

per *prep.* **1** for each (*two sweets per child*; *five miles per hour*). **2** by means of; by; through (*per post*). **3** (in full **as per**) in accordance with (*as per instructions*). □ **as per advice** words written on a bill of exchange to indicate that the drawee has been informed that the bill is being drawn on him or her. **as per usual** *colloq.* as usual. [Latin]

per- *prefix* **1** through; all over (*pervade*). **2** completely; very (*perturb*). **3** to destruction; to the bad (*perdition*; *pervert*). [Latin *per-*: related to PER]

peradventure /pərədˈventʃə(r)/ *adv.* *archaic* or *joc.* perhaps. [French: related to PER, ADVENTURE]

Perak /ˈpeərə, peˈræk/ state of Malaysia, on the W side of the Malay Peninsula, a major tin-mining centre; pop. (1991) 1 880 016; capital, Ipoh.

perambulate /pəˈræmbjʊˌleɪt/ *v.* (**-ting**) **1** walk through, over, or about (streets, the country, etc.). **2** walk from place to place. □ **perambulation** /-ˈleɪʃ(ə)n/ *n.* [Latin *perambulo*: related to AMBLE]

perambulator *n.* *formal* = PRAM.

per an. *abbr.* (also **per ann.**) per annum.

per annum /pər ˈænəm/ *adv.* for each year. [Latin]

P/E ratio *abbr.* = PRICE–EARNINGS RATIO.

percale /pəˈkeɪl/ *n.* closely woven cotton fabric. [French]

per capita /pə ˈkæpɪtə/ *adv.* & *adj.* (also **per caput** /ˈkæpʊt/) for each person. [Latin, = by heads]

◆ **per capita income** *n.* average income of a group, obtained by dividing the group's total income by its number of members. The **national per capita income** is the ratio of the national income to the population.

---

perceive /pəˈsiːv/ *v.* (**-ving**) **1** apprehend, esp. through the sight; observe. **2** (usu. foll. by *that*, *how*, etc.) apprehend with the mind; understand; see or regard. □ **perceivable** *adj.* [Latin *percipio -cept-* seize, understand]

per cent /pə ˈsent/ (*US* **percent**) *–adv.* in every hundred. *–n.* **1** percentage. **2** one part in every hundred (*half a per cent*).

percentage *n.* **1** rate or proportion per cent. **2** proportion.

percentile /pəˈsentaɪl/ *n.* *Statistics* **1** each of 99 points at which a range of data is divided to make 100 groups of equal size. **2** each of these groups.

perceptible /pəˈseptɪb(ə)l/ *adj.* capable of being perceived by the senses or intellect. □ **perceptibility** /-ˈbɪlɪtɪ/ *n.* **perceptibly** *adv.* [Latin: related to PERCEIVE]

perception /pəˈsepʃ(ə)n/ *n.* **1** act or faculty of perceiving. **2** (often foll. by *of*) intuitive recognition of a truth, aesthetic quality, etc.; way of seeing, understanding. □ **perceptual** /pəˈseptʃʊəl/ *adj.*

perceptive /pəˈseptɪv/ *adj.* **1** sensitive; discerning. **2**

capable of perceiving.□ **perceptively** *adv.* **perceptiveness** *n.* **perceptivity** /-ˈtɪvɪtɪ/ *n.*

♦ **perceptual mapping** *n. Econ.* use of mathematical psychology to understand the structure of a market. Consumer images of different brands of a product are plotted on a graph or map; the closer two brands are on the map, the closer they are as competitors. Perceptual mapping is also used in the development of a new product; the closer a new product appears on a map to an ideal product, the more likely the new product is to succeed.

perch[1] –*n.* **1** bar, branch, etc. used by a bird to rest on. **2** high place for a person or thing to rest on. **3** *hist.* measure of length, esp. for land, of $5^1/_2$ yards. –*v.* (usu. foll. by *on*) settle or rest on or as on a perch etc. [Latin *pertica* pole]

perch[2] *n.* (*pl.* same or **-es**) edible European spiny-finned freshwater fish. [Latin *perca* from Greek]

perchance /pəˈtʃɑːns/ *adv. archaic* or *poet.* **1** by chance. **2** maybe. [Anglo-French *par* by]

percipient /pəˈsɪpɪənt/ *adj.* able to perceive; conscious. □ **percipience** *n.* [Latin: related to PERCEIVE]

percolate /ˈpɜːkəˌleɪt/ *v.* (**-ting**) **1** (often foll. by *through*) **a** (of liquid etc.) filter or ooze gradually. **b** (of an idea etc.) permeate gradually. **2** prepare (coffee) in a percolator. **3** strain (a liquid, powder, etc.) through a fine mesh etc. □ **percolation** /-ˈleɪʃ(ə)n/ *n.* [Latin *colum* strainer]

percolator *n.* machine making coffee by circulating boiling water through ground beans.

♦ **per contra** /pɜː ˈkɒntrə/ –*adv.* on the opposite side (of an account, assessment, etc.). –*adj.* denoting a bookkeeping entry on this side, when two entries, a debit and a credit, are on opposite sides of the same page. [Italian]

percussion /pəˈkʌʃ(ə)n/ *n.* **1 a** (often *attrib.*) playing of music by striking instruments with sticks etc. (*percussion instrument*). **b** such instruments collectively. **2** gentle tapping of the body in medical diagnosis. **3** forcible striking of one esp. solid body against another. □ **percussionist** *n.* **percussive** *adj.* [Latin *percutio -cuss-* strike]

percussion cap *n.* small amount of explosive powder contained in metal or paper and exploded by striking.

♦ **per diem** /pɜː ˈdiːem, ˈdaɪem/ –*adv.* & *adj.* for each day. –*n.* fee charged by a professional person who is paid a specified fee for each day that he or she is employed. [Latin]

perdition /pəˈdɪʃ(ə)n/ *n.* eternal death; damnation. [Latin *perdo -dit-* destroy]

peregrine /ˈperɪgrɪn/ *n.* (in full **peregrine falcon**) a kind of falcon much used for hawking. [Latin *peregrinus* foreign]

peremptory /pəˈremptərɪ/ *adj.* **1** (of a statement or command) admitting no denial or refusal. **2** (of a person, manner, etc.) imperious; dictatorial. □ **peremptorily** *adv.* **peremptoriness** *n.* [Latin *peremptorius* deadly, decisive]

perennial /pəˈrenɪəl/ –*adj.* **1** lasting through a year or several years. **2** (of a plant) lasting several years. **3** lasting a long time or for ever. –*n.* perennial plant. □ **perennially** *adv.* [Latin *perennis* from *annus* year]

perestroika /ˌpereˈstrɔɪkə/ *n.* (in the former USSR) reform of the economic and political system. [Russian, = restructuring]

perfect /ˈpɜːfɪkt/ –*adj.* **1** complete; not deficient. **2** faultless. **3** very enjoyable, excellent (*perfect evening*). **4** exact, precise (*perfect circle*). **5** entire, unqualified (*perfect stranger*). **6** *Gram.* (of a tense) denoting a completed action or event (e.g. *he has gone*). –*v.* /pəˈfekt/ **1** make perfect. **2** complete. –*n. Gram.* the perfect tense. □ **perfect the sight** see BILL OF SIGHT. □ **perfectible** /pəˈfektɪb(ə)l/ *adj.* **perfectibility** /pəˌfektɪˈbɪlɪtɪ/ *n.* [Latin *perficere -fect-* complete (v.)]

♦ **perfect competition** *n. Econ.* market situation in which there are sufficiently large numbers of buyers and sellers for no individual to be able to influence the market price. Perfect competition assumes that sellers (if they are firms) pursue profit maximization, all agents have perfect knowledge of the market, all the factors of production are perfectly mobile, there are no government regulations interfering with the market, the products of each firm are identical, and there is free entry into or exit from the market. On these assumptions perfect competition will ensure that in the long run the market price is equal to the average and marginal cost of production, that output is equal to the economically efficient level, and that economic welfare will be maximized. However, if any of the assumptions are unjustified the market cannot be guaranteed to be efficient. Although few markets in the real world satisfy these conditions, many come quite close to doing so, e.g. commodity markets and the stock market. Economists usu. make use of the idea of a perfectly competitive market as a benchmark in discussing economic policy, rather than believing that such markets actually exist.

perfection /pəˈfekʃ(ə)n/ *n.* **1** making, becoming, or being perfect. **2** faultlessness. **3** perfect person, thing, or example. □ **to perfection** exactly; completely. [Latin: related to PERFECT]

perfectionism *n.* uncompromising pursuit of excellence. □ **perfectionist** *n.* & *adj.*

perfectly *adv.* **1** completely; quite. **2** in a perfect way.

♦ **perfect market** *n.* market in which there is perfect competition.

perfect pitch *n.* = ABSOLUTE PITCH.

perfidy /ˈpɜːfɪdɪ/ *n.* breach of faith; treachery. □ **perfidious** /-ˈfɪdɪəs/ *adj.* [Latin *perfidia* from *fides* faith]

perforate /ˈpɜːfəˌreɪt/ *v.* (**-ting**) **1** make a hole or holes through; pierce. **2** make a row of small holes in (paper etc.) so that a part may be torn off easily. □ **perforation** /-ˈreɪʃ(ə)n/ *n.* [Latin *perforo* pierce through]

perforce /pəˈfɔːs/ *adv. archaic* unavoidably; necessarily. [French *par force* by FORCE[1]]

perform /pəˈfɔːm/ *v.* **1** (also *absol.*) carry into effect; do. **2** execute (a function, play, piece of music, etc.). **3** act in a play; play music, sing, etc.; execute tricks. **4** function. □ **performer** *n.* [Anglo-French: related to PER-, FURNISH]

performance /pəˈfɔːməns/ *n.* **1** (usu. foll. by *of*) **a** act, process, or manner of performing or functioning. **b** execution (of a duty etc.). **2** performing of a play, music, etc.; instance of this. **3** *colloq.* fuss; emotional scene.

♦ **performance bond** *n.* bond given by a bank to a third party guaranteeing that if a specified customer fails to fulfil all the terms of a specified contract, the bank will be responsible for any loan sustained by the third party.

♦ **performance indicators** *n.pl.* indicators that measure a company's performance, often divided into strategic, operational, behavioural, and ethical.

performing arts *n.pl.* drama, music, dance, etc.

perfume /ˈpɜːfjuːm/ –*n.* **1** sweet smell. **2** fluid containing the essence of flowers etc.; scent. –*v.* /also pəˈfjuːm/ (**-ming**) impart a sweet scent to. [Italian *parfumare* smoke through]

perfumer /pəˈfjuːmə(r)/ *n.* maker or seller of perfumes. □ **perfumery** *n.* (*pl.* **-ies**).

perfunctory /pəˈfʌŋktərɪ/ *adj.* done merely out of duty; superficial, careless. □ **perfunctorily** *adv.* **perfunctoriness** *n.* [Latin: related to FUNCTION]

pergola /ˈpɜːgələ/ *n.* arbour or covered walk formed of growing plants trained over trellis-work. [Italian]

perhaps /pəˈhæps/ *adv.* it may be; possibly.

peri- *prefix* round, about. [Greek]

perianth /ˈperɪˌænθ/ *n.* outer part of a flower. [Greek *anthos* flower]

pericardium /ˌperɪˈkɑːdɪəm/ *n.* (*pl.* **-dia**) membranous sac enclosing the heart. [Greek *kardia* heart]

perigee /ˈperɪˌdʒiː/ *n.* point of a planet's or comet's orbit where it is nearest the earth. [Greek *perigeion*]

perihelion /ˌperɪˈhiːlɪən/ *n.* (*pl.* **-lia**) point of a planet's or comet's orbit where it is nearest the sun's centre. [related to PERI-, Greek *hēlios* sun]

peril /ˈperɪl/ *n.* **1** serious and immediate danger. **2** event that can cause a financial loss, against which an insurance contract provides cover (see also RISK *n.* 1). An **excepted peril** is one that is not usu. covered by an insurance policy. Excepted perils in the carriage of goods include acts of God, inherent vice, negligence, and loss resulting from enemy action (**Queen's enemies**). □ **perilous** *adj.* **perilously** *adv.* [Latin *peric(u)lum*]

perimeter /pəˈrɪmɪtə(r)/ *n.* **1 a** circumference or outline of a closed figure. **b** length of this. **2** outer boundary of an enclosed area. [Greek: related to -METER]

perineum /ˌperɪˈniːəm/ *n.* (*pl.* **-nea**) region of the body between the anus and the scrotum or vulva. □ **perineal** *adj.* [Latin from Greek]

period /ˈpɪərɪəd/ *–n.* **1** length or portion of time. **2** distinct portion of history, a person's life, etc. **3** time forming part of a geological era. **4** interval between recurrences of an astronomical or other phenomenon. **5** time allowed for a lesson in school. **6** occurrence of menstruation (often *attrib.*: *period pains*). **7** complete sentence, esp. one consisting of several clauses. **8** esp. *US* **a** = FULL STOP. **b** *colloq.* used at the end of a statement to indicate finality (*I'm not going, period*). *–adj.* characteristic of some past period (*period furniture*). [Greek *hodos* way]

◆ **period bill** *n.* (also **term bill**) bill of exchange payable on a specific date rather than on demand.

periodic /ˌpɪərɪˈɒdɪk/ *adj.* appearing or occurring at intervals. □ **periodicity** /-rɪəˈdɪsɪtɪ/ *n.*

periodical *–n.* newspaper, magazine, etc. issued at regular intervals. *–adj.* periodic. □ **periodically** *adv.*

periodic table *n.* arrangement of elements in order of increasing atomic number and in which elements of similar chemical properties appear at regular intervals.

◆ **period of grace** *n.* time, usu. three days, allowed for payment of a bill of exchange (except those payable at sight or on demand) after it matures.

periodontics /ˌperɪəˈdɒntɪks/ *n.pl.* (treated as *sing.*) branch of dentistry concerned with the structures surrounding and supporting the teeth. [Greek *odous* tooth]

peripatetic /ˌperɪpəˈtetɪk/ *–adj.* **1** (of a teacher) working in more than one school or college etc. **2** going from place to place; itinerant. *–n.* peripatetic person, esp. a teacher. [Greek *pateō* walk]

peripheral /pəˈrɪfər(ə)l/ *–adj.* **1** of minor importance; marginal. **2** of the periphery. *–n.* (also **peripheral device**) any input, output, or storage device that can be controlled by a computer's central processing unit, e.g. a floppy disk or printer.

peripheral nervous system *n.* nervous system outside the brain and spinal cord.

periphery /pəˈrɪfərɪ/ *n.* (*pl.* **-ies**) **1** boundary of an area or surface. **2** outer or surrounding region. [Greek *pherō* bear]

periphrasis /pəˈrɪfrəsɪs/ *n.* (*pl.* **-phrases** /-ˌsiːz/) **1** roundabout way of speaking; circumlocution. **2** roundabout phrase. □ **periphrastic** /ˌperɪˈfræstɪk/ *adj.* [Greek: related to PHRASE]

periscope /ˈperɪˌskəʊp/ *n.* apparatus with a tube and mirrors or prisms, by which an observer in a trench, submerged submarine, or at the back of a crowd etc., can see things otherwise out of sight. □ **periscopic** /-ˈskɒpɪk/ *adj.*

perish /ˈperɪʃ/ *v.* **1** be destroyed; suffer death or ruin. **2 a** (esp. of rubber) lose its normal qualities; deteriorate, rot. **b** cause to rot or deteriorate. **3** (in *passive*) suffer from cold. [Latin *pereo*]

perishable *–adj.* liable to perish; subject to decay. *–n.* thing, esp. a foodstuff, subject to rapid decay.

perisher *n. slang* annoying person.

perishing *colloq. –adj.* **1** confounded. **2** freezing cold. *–adv.* confoundedly.

peristalsis /ˌperɪˈstælsɪs/ *n.* involuntary muscular wave-like movement by which the contents of the digestive tract are propelled along it. [Greek *peristellō* wrap around]

peritoneum /ˌperɪtəˈniːəm/ *n.* (*pl.* **-s** or **-nea**) membrane lining the cavity of the abdomen. □ **peritoneal** *adj.* [Greek *peritonos* stretched around]

peritonitis /ˌperɪtəˈnaɪtɪs/ *n.* inflammatory disease of the peritoneum.

periwig /ˈperɪwɪg/ *n.* esp. *hist.* wig. [alteration of PERUKE]

periwinkle[1] /ˈperɪˌwɪŋk(ə)l/ *n.* evergreen trailing plant with blue, purple, or white flowers. [Latin *pervinca*]

periwinkle[2] /ˈperɪˌwɪŋk(ə)l/ *n.* = WINKLE *n.* [origin unknown]

perjure /ˈpɜːdʒə(r)/ *v.refl.* (**-ring**) *Law* **1** wilfully tell a lie when on oath. **2** (as **perjured** *adj.*) guilty of or involving perjury. □ **perjurer** *n.* [French from Latin *juro* swear]

perjury *n.* (*pl.* **-ies**) *Law* act of wilfully telling a lie when on oath.

perk[1] *v.* □ **perk up 1** recover confidence, courage, life, or zest. **2** restore confidence, courage, or liveliness in. **3** smarten up. **4** raise (one's head etc.) briskly. [origin unknown]

perk[2] *n. colloq.* perquisite. [abbreviation]

perky *adj.* (**-ier, -iest**) lively; cheerful. □ **perkily** *adv.* **perkiness** *n.*

Perlis /ˈpɜːlɪs/ smallest state of Malaysia, the most northerly state on the Malay Peninsula; pop. (1991) 184 070; capital, Kangar. Rice and coconuts are grown; other products include rubber and tin.

perlite /ˈpɜːlaɪt/ *n.* (also **pearlite**) glassy type of vermiculite used for insulation etc. [French *perle* pearl]

Perm /pɜːm/ industrial city and port in W Russia; industries include engineering, oil refining, and the manufacture of chemicals and footwear; pop. (est. 1995) 1 032 000.

perm[1] *–n.* permanent wave. *–v.* give a permanent wave to. [abbreviation]

perm[2] *colloq. –n.* permutation. *–v.* make a permutation of. [abbreviation]

permafrost /ˈpɜːməˌfrɒst/ *n.* subsoil which remains frozen all year, as in polar regions. [from PERMANENT, FROST]

permanent /ˈpɜːmənənt/ *adj.* lasting, or intended to last or function, indefinitely. □ **permanence** *n.* **permanency** *n.* **permanently** *adv.* [Latin *permaneo* remain to the end]

◆ **permanent establishment** *n.* fixed place of business that a trader of one country has in another country, thus rendering the person liable to that second country's taxation. It includes a place of management, branch, office, factory, or workshop, but it may exclude some sales offices and storage depots. The concept is important in double-taxation treaties.

◆ **permanent health insurance** *n.* (also **PHI**) form of health insurance that provides an income (maximum 75% of salary) up to normal retirement age (or pension age) to replace an income lost by prolonged illness or disability in which the insured is unable to perform any part of his or her normal duties. Premiums are related to age and occupation and normally are fixed; benefits, which are not paid for the first 4–13 weeks of disability, are tax-free for one year and thereafter are taxed. Cf. SICKNESS AND ACCIDENT INSURANCE.

◆ **permanent income hypothesis** *n. Econ.* hypothesis that individuals base their consumption decisions on the value of their expected average income, ignoring any windfall gains or losses in any particular year. This hypothesis was proposed by Milton Friedman as an alternative to the Keynesian view, in which a temporary rise in income engineered by a government tends to raise consumption and output by means of the multiplier process. According to the permanent income hypothesis, consumers will ignore any temporary rise in income created by government action, consumption will be unchanged, and therefore the multiplier process will not operate. Cf. LIFE-CYCLE HYPOTHESIS.

♦ **permanent interest bearing share** *n.* (also **PIBS**) fixed-interest non-redeemable security paying a high rate of interest but carrying the risk that with other fixed-interest loans it will be the last to be paid out in the event of a liquidation.

---

permanent wave *n.* long-lasting artificial wave in the hair.

permeable /ˈpɜːmɪəb(ə)l/ *adj.* capable of being permeated. □ **permeability** /-ˈbɪlɪtɪ/ *n.* [related to PERMEATE]

permeate /ˈpɜːmɪˌeɪt/ *v.* (**-ting**) **1** penetrate throughout; pervade; saturate. **2** (usu. foll. by *through, among*, etc.) diffuse itself. □ **permeation** /-ˈeɪʃ(ə)n/ *n.* [Latin *permeo* pass through]

Permian /ˈpɜːmɪən/ *–adj.* of the last period of the Palaeozoic era. *–n.* this period. [*Perm* in Russia]

♦ **per mille** /pəˈmɪl/ (also **per mil**) *adv.* in every thousand. In insurance it denotes that the premium is the stated figure for each £1000 of insured value. [Latin]

---

permissible /pəˈmɪsɪb(ə)l/ *adj.* allowable. □ **permissibility** /-ˈbɪlɪtɪ/ *n.* [French or medieval Latin: related to PERMIT]

permission /pəˈmɪʃ(ə)n/ *n.* (often foll. by *to* + infin.) consent; authorization. □ **permission to deal** permission by the London Stock Exchange to deal in the shares of a newly floated company. It must be sought three days after the issue of a prospectus. [Latin *permissio*: related to PERMIT]

permissive /pəˈmɪsɪv/ *adj.* **1** tolerant or liberal, esp. in sexual matters. **2** giving permission. □ **permissiveness** *n.* [French or medieval Latin: related to PERMIT]

permit *–v.* /pəˈmɪt/ (**-tt-**) **1** give permission or consent to; authorize. **2 a** allow; give an opportunity to. **b** give an opportunity (*circumstances permitting*). **3** (foll. by *of*) admit. *–n.* /ˈpɜːmɪt/ **1 a** document giving permission to act. **b** document etc. which allows entry. **2** *formal* permission. [Latin *permitto -miss-* allow]

permutation /ˌpɜːmjʊˈteɪʃ(ə)n/ *n.* **1** one of the possible ordered arrangements or groupings of a set of things. **2** combination or selection of a specified number of things from a larger group, esp. matches in a football pool. [Latin *permuto* change thoroughly]

Pernambuco see RECIFE.

pernicious /pəˈnɪʃəs/ *adj.* very harmful or destructive; deadly. [Latin *pernicies* ruin]

pernicious anaemia *n.* defective formation of red blood cells through lack of vitamin B.

pernickety /pəˈnɪkɪtɪ/ *adj. colloq.* fastidious; over-precise. [origin unknown]

peroration /ˌperəˈreɪʃ(ə)n/ *n.* concluding part of a speech. [Latin *oro* speak]

♦ **Perot** /pəˈrəʊ/, **Ross** (1930–) US industrialist and philanthropist. He founded the Electronic Data Systems Corporation in Dallas in 1962, remaining chairman until 1986. In 1988 he founded Perot Systems Corporation, of which he is still chairman. In 1992 Perot was an unsuccessful independent candidate in the presidential election.

---

peroxide /pəˈrɒksaɪd/ *–n.* **1 a** = HYDROGEN PEROXIDE. **b** (often *attrib.*) solution of hydrogen peroxide used esp. to bleach the hair. **2** compound of oxygen with another element containing the greatest possible proportion of oxygen. *–v.* (**-ding**) bleach (the hair) with peroxide. [from PER-, OXIDE]

perpendicular /ˌpɜːpənˈdɪkjʊlə(r)/ *–adj.* **1 a** (usu. foll. by *to*) at right angles (to a given line, plane, or surface). **b** at right angles to the plane of the horizon. **2** upright, vertical. **3** (of a slope etc.) very steep. **4** (**Perpendicular**) *Archit.* of the third stage of English Gothic (15th–16th centuries) with vertical tracery in large windows. *–n.* **1** perpendicular line. **2** (prec. by *the*) perpendicular line or direction (*is out of the perpendicular*). □ **perpendicularity** /-ˈlærɪtɪ/ *n.* [Latin *perpendiculum* plumb-line]

perpetrate /ˈpɜːpɪˌtreɪt/ *v.* (**-ting**) commit (a crime, blunder, or anything outrageous). □ **perpetration** /-ˈtreɪʃ(ə)n/ *n.* **perpetrator** *n.* [Latin *perpetro* perform]

perpetual /pəˈpetʃʊəl/ *adj.* **1** lasting for ever or indefinitely. **2** continuous, uninterrupted. **3** *colloq.* frequent (*perpetual interruptions*). □ **perpetually** *adv.* [Latin *perpetuus* continuous]

♦ **perpetual debenture** *n.* **1** bond or debenture that can never be redeemed. See IRREDEEMABLE *n.* **2** bond or debenture that cannot be redeemed on demand.

♦ **perpetual inventory** *n.* method of continuous stock control in which an account is kept for each item of stock; one side of the account records the deliveries of that type of stock and the other side records the issues from the stock. Thus, the balance of the account at any time provides a record of either the number of items in stock or their values, or both. This method is used in large organizations in which it is important to control the amount of capital tied up in the running of the business. It also provides a means of checking pilferage. Less sophisticated organizations rely on annual stocktaking to discover how much stock they have.

---

perpetual motion *n.* motion of a hypothetical machine which once set in motion would run for ever unless subject to an external force or to wear.

♦ **perpetual succession** *n.* continued existence of a corporation until it is legally dissolved. A corporation, being a separate legal person, is unaffected by the death or other departure of any member but continues in existence no matter how many changes in membership occur.

---

perpetuate /pəˈpetʃʊˌeɪt/ *v.* (**-ting**) **1** make perpetual. **2** preserve from oblivion. □ **perpetuation** /-ˈeɪʃ(ə)n/ *n.* **perpetuator** *n.* [Latin *perpetuo*]

♦ **Perpetuities and Accumulations Act (1964)** *n.* act reforming the **rule against perpetuities**. This rule exists to prevent a donor of a gift from directing its destination too far into the future and thus creating uncertainty as to the ultimate ownership of the property. Under the old law, the ownership had to become certain within the period of an existing lifetime (i.e. the lifetime of a person living at the date of the gift) plus 21 years. If there was any possibility, however remote, that this would not happen, the gift was void. Under the Perpetuities and Accumulations Act, a 'wait and see' period allows a gift to remain valid until it becomes clear that it will in fact offend against the rule against perpetuities, and the donor may choose a perpetuity period of 80 years instead of the uncertain 'life in being plus 21 years'. The act also allows the age at which a person is to benefit from a gift to be reduced, if this will save the gift from infringing the rule against perpetuities.

---

perpetuity /ˌpɜːpɪˈtjuːɪtɪ/ *n.* (*pl.* **-ies**) **1** state or quality of being perpetual. **2** perpetual annuity. **3** perpetual possession or position. □ **in perpetuity** for ever. [Latin: related to PERPETUAL]

Perpignan /ˌpɜːpiːnˈjɑ̃/ city in S France, in the NE foothills of the Pyrenees, a centre of tourism and of the wine trade; pop. (est. 1990) 108 049.

perplex /pəˈpleks/ *v.* **1** puzzle, bewilder, or disconcert. **2** complicate or confuse (a matter). □ **perplexedly** /-ɪdlɪ/ *adv.* **perplexing** *adj.* [Latin *perplexus* involved]

perplexity /pəˈpleksɪtɪ/ *n.* (*pl.* **-ies**) **1** state of being perplexed. **2** thing that perplexes.

per pro. /pɜː ˈprəʊ/ *abbr.* (also **p.p., pp**) through the agency of (used in signatures made on behalf of, and authorized by, a person or firm who accepts responsibility for the documents so signed). [Latin *per procurationem*]

■ **Usage** The correct sequence is A *per pro.* B, where B is signing on behalf of A.

perquisite /ˈpɜːkwɪzɪt/ *n.* **1** extra benefit or allowance additional to a main income etc. **2** customary extra right or privilege. [Latin *perquiro -quisit-* search diligently for]

■ **Usage** *Perquisite* is sometimes confused with *prerequisite*, which means 'thing required as a precondition'.

perry /ˈperɪ/ *n.* (*pl.* **-ies**) drink made from fermented pear juice. [French *peré*: related to PEAR]

per se /pɜː ˈseɪ/ *adv.* by or in itself; intrinsically. [Latin]

persecute /ˈpɜːsɪˌkjuːt/ *v.* (**-ting**) **1** subject (a person etc.) to hostility or ill-treatment, esp. on grounds of political or religious belief. **2** harass, worry. □ **persecution** /-ˈkjuːʃ(ə)n/ *n.* **persecutor** *n.* [Latin *persequor -secut-* pursue]

persevere /ˌpɜːsɪˈvɪə(r)/ *v.* (**-ring**) (often foll. by *in*, *with*) continue steadfastly or determinedly; persist. □ **perseverance** *n.* [Latin: related to SEVERE]

Persia /ˈpɜːʃə/ see IRAN.

Persian /ˈpɜːʃ(ə)n/ *-n.* **1** native or inhabitant of ancient or modern Persia (now Iran); person of Persian descent. **2** language of ancient Persia or modern Iran. **3** (in full **Persian cat**) cat of a breed with long silky hair. *-adj.* of or relating to Persia or its people or language.

■ **Usage** The preferred terms for the language (see sense 2 of the noun) are *Iranian* and *Farsi* respectively.

Persian Gulf (also **Arabian Gulf**) arm of the Arabian Sea, to which it is connected by the Strait of Hormuz and the Gulf of Oman, separating the Arabian peninsula from mainland Asia.

Persian lamb *n.* silky tightly curled fur of a young karakul, used in clothing.

persiflage /ˈpɜːsɪˌflɑːʒ/ *n.* light raillery, banter. [French]

persimmon /pɜːˈsɪmən/ *n.* **1** tropical evergreen tree. **2** its edible tomato-like fruit. [Algonquian]

persist /pəˈsɪst/ *v.* **1** (often foll. by *in*) continue firmly or obstinately (in an opinion or action) esp. despite obstacles, remonstrance, etc. **2** (of a phenomenon etc.) continue in existence; survive. □ **persistence** *n.* **persistent** *adj.* **persistently** *adv.* [Latin *sisto* stand]

person /ˈpɜːs(ə)n/ *n.* **1** individual human being. **2** living body of a human being (*found on my person*). **3** *Gram.* any of three classes of personal pronouns, verb-forms, etc.: the person speaking (**first person**); the person spoken to (**second person**); the person spoken of (**third person**). **4** (in *comb.*) used to replace *-man* in offices open to either sex (*salesperson*). **5** (in Christianity) God as Father, Son, or Holy Ghost. □ **in person** physically present. [Latin: related to PERSONA]

persona /pəˈsəʊnə/ *n.* (*pl.* **-nae** /-niː/) aspect of the personality as shown to or perceived by others. [Latin, = actor's mask]

personable *adj.* pleasing in appearance and behaviour.

personage *n.* person, esp. of rank or importance.

persona grata /pəˌsəʊnə ˈgrɑːtə/ *n.* (*pl.* ***personae gratae*** /-niː, -tiː/) person acceptable to certain others.

personal /ˈpɜːsən(ə)l/ *adj.* **1** one's own; individual; private. **2** done or made in person (*my personal attention*). **3** directed to or concerning an individual (*personal letter*). **4** referring (esp. in a hostile way) to an individual's private life or concerns (*personal remarks*; *no need to be personal*). **5** of the body and clothing (*personal hygiene*). **6** existing as a person (*a personal God*). **7** *Gram.* of or denoting one of the three persons (*personal pronoun*).

♦ **personal accident and sickness insurance** see SICKNESS AND ACCIDENT INSURANCE.

♦ **personal account** *n.* **1** account in a ledger that bears the name of an individual or of an organization; it records the state of indebtedness of the named person to the organization keeping the account or vice versa. Personal accounts are normally kept in the sales (or total debtors) ledger and the purchases (or total creditors) ledger. **2** see PA 2.

♦ **personal allowances** *n.pl.* sums deductible from taxable income under an income-tax system to allow for personal circumstances. The principal allowances in the UK system are a personal allowance to which all taxpayers are entitled, a married couple's allowance, a single parent's allowance, and age relief. See also ADDITIONAL PERSONAL ALLOWANCE.

♦ **personal annuity scheme** *n.* contributory pension for the self-employed or those not covered by an occupational pension.

♦ **personal assistant** *n.* (also **PA**) person who is appointed to help a manager or director and who has wider responsibilities than a secretary.

---

personal column *n.* part of a newspaper devoted to private advertisements and messages.

personal computer *n.* (also **PC**) general-purpose computer designed for operation and use by one person at a time. All personal computers are microcomputers, but microcomputers are not necessarily personal computers. Personal computers range from cheap domestic machines of limited capability to expensive and highly sophisticated systems. The ratio of computing power to cost is sufficiently high, however, for PCs not to have to be used continuously to be cost-effective.

personal data see DATA PROTECTION.

♦ **personal equity plan** *n.* (also **PEP**) government scheme to encourage individuals to invest directly in UK quoted companies, offering investors certain tax benefits. The investment is administered by an authorized plan manager. Plans are either discretionary (in which the plan manager makes the investment decisions) or non-discretionary (in which the investor makes the decisions). Investors may put in a lump sum or regular monthly amounts. Re-invested dividends are free of income tax and capital gains tax is not incurred, as long as the investment is retained in the plan for at least a complete calendar year. There is a limit on the amount an individual can invest in a plan in any year, depending upon whether it is a general PEP (£6000 maximum p.a.) or a single-company PEP (an additional £3000 p.a.). In 1997 it was announced that PEPs will be replaced by ISAS in April 1999.

---

personal identification device *n.* (also **PID**) card or badge issued to an authorized user of a computer system and containing a machine-readable sequence of characters that identifies that person. The PID must be inserted into a terminal of the computer system before access to the system is granted. In many cases a person must use a PID in conjunction with a personal identification number (PIN) to gain access.

♦ **personal identification number** *n.* (also **PIN**) number allocated to the holder of a cashcard or a credit card and used in electronic funds transfer at point of sale to identify the card owner. The number is given to the card holder in secret and is memorized so that if the card is stolen it cannot be used.

♦ **Personal Investment Authority** see SELF-REGULATING ORGANIZATION.

---

personality /ˌpɜːsəˈnælɪtɪ/ *n.* (*pl.* **-ies**) **1 a** person's distinctive character or qualities (*has a strong personality*). **b** socially attractive qualities (*was clever but had no personality*). **2** famous person (*TV personality*). **3** (in *pl.*) personal remarks.

personalize *v.* (also **-ise**) (**-zing** or **-sing**) **1** make personal, esp. by marking with one's name etc. **2** personify.

♦ **personal loan** *n.* loan to a private person by a bank or building society for domestic purposes, buying a car, etc. There is usu. no security required and consequently a high rate of interest is charged. Repayment is usu. by monthly instalments over a fixed period. This is a more expensive way of borrowing from a bank than by means of an overdraft.

---

personally *adv.* **1** in person (*see to it personally*). **2** for one's own part (*speaking personally*). **3** in a personal manner (*took the criticism personally*).

personal organizer *n.* means of keeping track of personal affairs, esp. a loose-leaf notebook divided into sections or a hand-held computer that is programmed to serve the same purpose.

♦ **personal pension scheme** *n.* (also **PPS**, **personal pension plan**, **PPP**) pension scheme entered into by an employee who wishes to contract out of the state earnings-related pension scheme (SERPS). An employee may start his or her own pension scheme, whether or not the employer has an occupational pension scheme. Personal pension schemes must provide a half-rate widower's benefit. They must be approved by the Occupational Pension Board before a person can contract out of SERPS. An employee with a personal pension in place of SERPS or an occupational pension scheme pays National Insurance contributions at the full ordinary rate. The Department of Social Security pays the difference between the lower contracted-out rate and the full ordinary rate for the personal pension scheme. The self-employed may also enter into a PPS. Under the Pension's Act 1993, the Pensions Ombudsman was appointed to deal with complaints relating to personal pension schemes.

personal pronoun *n.* pronoun replacing the subject, object, etc., of a clause etc., e.g. *I, we, you, them, us.*

personal property *n.* (also **personalty**) *Law* all one's property except land and those interests in land that pass to one's heirs, i.e. any property other than real property (realty). This distinction is used esp. in distinguishing property for inheritance tax. Personal property includes money, shares, chattels, etc.

♦ **personal representative** *n.* person whose duty is to gather in the assets of the estate of a deceased person, to pay any liabilities, and to distribute the residue. Personal representatives of a person dying testate are known as executors; those of a person dying intestate are known as administrators.

personal stereo *n.* small portable cassette player, often with radio or CD player, used with lightweight headphones.

♦ **personalty** /'pɜːsənəltɪ/ *n.* (*pl.* **-ties**) = PERSONAL PROPERTY.

persona non grata /pə,səʊnə nɒn (or nəʊn) 'grɑːtə/ *n.* (*pl.* ***personae non gratae*** /-niː, -tiː/) person not acceptable.

personify /pə'sɒnɪ,faɪ/ *v.* (**-ies**, **-ied**) **1** represent (an abstraction or thing) as having human characteristics. **2** symbolize (a quality etc.) by a figure in human form. **3** (usu. as **personified** *adj.*) be a typical example of; embody (*she personifies youthful arrogance*; *he was niceness personified*). □ **personification** /-fɪ'keɪʃ(ə)n/ *n.*

personnel /,pɜːsə'nel/ *n.* staff of an organization, the armed forces, a public service, etc. [French, = personal]

personnel department *n.* part of an organization concerned with the appointment, training, and welfare of employees.

♦ **personnel management** *n.* management of people in relation to their work and within an organization as a whole, both for the benefit of the organization and the employees. During the inflationary period of 1960–80, high employment and the trend towards computerization gave rise to new needs for employers; this, coupled with an increase in legislation relating to employment, made the **personnel officer's** role of particular importance. Although all managers are to a greater or lesser extent concerned with personnel management, in this period many large organizations appointed specialist personnel managers to centralize manpower planning policies, recruitment and selection, education and training of staff, and the terms and conditions of employment, with special reference to industrial relations, health and safety at work, and the legal aspects of employers and employees. With the rise in unemployment in the 1980s, the emphasis shifted from personnel management to personnel selection. Changing technology and the need for higher efficiency and greater flexibility to meet the needs of increased international competition meant more and more time spent on manpower planning, training, and a general restructuring of organizations to encourage growth without an expansion in personnel. The current trend is to place greater emphasis on personnel morale and ways of achieving consistent job satisfaction through variation, esp. by training employees to do more than one job. See also HUMAN-RESOURCE MANAGEMENT; INSTITUTE OF PERSONNEL MANAGEMENT.

♦ **personnel selection** *n.* method of choosing the most suitable applicant for a vacancy within an organization. Ideally, a **job description** is written, detailing the essential qualifications and experience required for the job together with any other relevant information. The job description enables a **job specification** to be created, showing how the vacancy would fit in the structure of the organization, the salary level, and any fringe benefits. A search for the right person then begins, using advertisements in newspapers, trade papers, or employment agencies; if the vacancy is sufficiently senior a head hunter may be employed. Initial selection is then made by inviting letters of application (or using application forms) supported by a curriculum vitae and listing the applicants that most closely match the job specification. Screening interviews may then be held, which may include practical tests so that a short list of final candidates can be drawn up. Second interviews are sometimes required and, when appropriate, psychological tests are used. The number of interviews and the extent of testing depend on the level of the position within the organization. Interviews may be conducted by a single person or by a panel; applicants may be seen singly or in groups. Moreover the extent to which the personnel department is involved in the selection will depend on the particular organization.

perspective /pə'spektɪv/ *–n.* **1 a** art of drawing solid objects on a two-dimensional surface so as to give the right impression of relative positions, size, etc. **b** picture so drawn. **2** apparent relation between visible objects as to position, distance, etc. **3** mental view of the relative importance of things. **4** view, esp. stretching into the distance. *–adj.* of or in perspective. □ **in** (or **out of**) **perspective 1** drawn or viewed according (or not according) to the rules of perspective. **2** correctly (or incorrectly) regarded in terms of relative importance. [Latin *perspicio -spect-* look at]

Perspex /'pɜːspeks/ *n. propr.* tough light transparent thermoplastic. [related to PERSPECTIVE]

perspicacious /,pɜːspɪ'keɪʃəs/ *adj.* having mental penetration or discernment. □ **perspicacity** /-'kæsɪtɪ/ *n.* [Latin *perspicax*: related to PERSPECTIVE]

■ **Usage** *Perspicacious* is sometimes confused with *perspicuous*.

perspicuous /pə'spɪkjʊəs/ *adj.* **1** easily understood; clearly expressed. **2** expressing things clearly. □ **perspicuity** /-'kjuːɪtɪ/ *n.* [Latin: related to PERSPECTIVE]

■ **Usage** *Perspicuous* is sometimes confused with *perspicacious*.

perspiration /,pɜːspɪ'reɪʃ(ə)n/ *n.* **1** sweat. **2** sweating. [French: related to PERSPIRE]

perspire /pə'spaɪə(r)/ *v.* (**-ring**) sweat. [Latin *spiro* breathe]

persuade /pə'sweɪd/ *v.* (**-ding**) **1** (often foll. by *of* or *that*) cause (another person or oneself) to believe. **2** (often foll. by *to* + infin.) induce. □ **persuadable** *adj.* **persuasible** *adj.* [Latin *persuadeo -suas-* induce]

persuasion /pə'sweɪʒ(ə)n/ *n.* **1** persuading. **2** persuasiveness. **3** belief or conviction. **4** religious belief, or the group or sect holding it. [Latin: related to PERSUADE]

persuasive /pə'sweɪsɪv/ *adj.* good at persuading. □ **persuasively** *adv.* **persuasiveness** *n.* [French or medieval Latin: related to PERSUADE]

PERT /pɜːt/ *abbr.* project (or programme, performance) evaluation and review technique, for planning, scheduling, and controlling projects. Dependencies of distinct activities are expressed in the form of a **PERT chart** that forms the logical sequence of activities that must occur before a project can be completed.

pert *adj.* **1** saucy, impudent. **2** jaunty. □ **pertly** *adv.* **pertness** *n.* [Latin *apertus* open]

pertain /pə'teɪn/ *v.* **1** (foll. by *to*) **a** relate or have reference to. **b** belong to as a part, appendage, or accessory. **2** (usu. foll. by *to*) be appropriate to. [Latin *pertineo* belong to]

Perth /pɜːθ/ **1** capital and commercial centre of the state of Western Australia, on the estuary of the River Swan; pop. (est. 1995) 1 262 600 (including its port, Fremantle). **2** city in E Scotland, in Tayside region; industries include textiles, whisky distilling, and tourism; pop. (est. 1989) 44 000.

pertinacious /ˌpɜːtɪ'neɪʃəs/ *adj.* stubborn; persistent (in a course of action etc.). □ **pertinacity** /-'næsɪtɪ/ *n.* [Latin *pertinax*: related to PERTAIN]

pertinent /'pɜːtɪnənt/ *adj.* (often foll. by *to*) relevant. □ **pertinence** *n.* **pertinency** *n.* [Latin: related to PERTAIN]

perturb /pə'tɜːb/ *v.* **1** disturb mentally; agitate. **2** throw into confusion or disorder. □ **perturbation** /-'beɪʃ(ə)n/ *n.* [French from Latin]

peruke /pə'ruːk/ *n. hist.* wig. [French from Italian]

peruse /pə'ruːz/ *v.* (**-sing**) **1** read or study carefully. **2** *joc.* read or look at desultorily.□ **perusal** *n.* [originally = 'use up']

pervade /pə'veɪd/ *v.* (**-ding**) **1** spread throughout, permeate. **2** be rife among or through. □ **pervasion** *n.* **pervasive** *adj.* [Latin *pervado* penetrate]

perverse /pə'vɜːs/ *adj.* **1** deliberately or stubbornly departing from what is reasonable or required. **2** intractable. □ **perversely** *adv.* **perversity** *n.* (*pl.* **-ies**). [Latin: related to PERVERT]

perversion /pə'vɜːʃ(ə)n/ *n.* **1** perverting or being perverted. **2** preference for an abnormal form of sexual activity. [Latin: related to PERVERT]

pervert *–v.* /pə'vɜːt/ **1** turn (a person or thing) aside from its proper use or nature. **2** misapply (words etc.). **3** lead astray from right conduct or (esp. religious) beliefs; corrupt. **4** (as **perverted** *adj.*) showing perversion. *–n.* /'pɜːvɜːt/ perverted person, esp. sexually. [Latin *verto vers-* turn]

pervious /'pɜːvɪəs/ *adj.* **1** permeable. **2** (usu. foll. by *to*) **a** affording passage. **b** accessible (to reason etc.). [Latin *via* road]

PESC *abbr.* Public Expenditure Survey Committee.

peseta /pə'seɪtə/ *n.* standard monetary unit of Spain and Andorra. [Spanish]

Peshawar /pə'ʃɑːwə(r)/ city in Pakistan, capital of North-West Frontier Province, a trading centre with textile and footwear industries; pop. (est. 1995) 1 676 000.

pesky /'peskɪ/ *adj.* (**-ier, -iest**) esp. *US colloq.* troublesome; annoying. [origin unknown]

peso /'peɪsəʊ/ *n.* (*pl.* **-s**) standard monetary unit of Argentina, Chile, Colombia, Cuba, Dominican Republic, Guinea-Bissau, Mexico, the Philippines, and Uruguay. [Spanish]

pessary /'pesərɪ/ *n.* (*pl.* **-ies**) **1** device worn in the vagina to support the uterus or as a contraceptive. **2** vaginal suppository. [Latin from Greek]

pessimism /'pesɪˌmɪz(ə)m/ *n.* **1** tendency to be gloomy or expect the worst. **2** *Philos.* belief that this world is as bad as it could be or that all things tend to evil. □ **pessimist** *n.* **pessimistic** /-'mɪstɪk/ *adj.* **pessimistically** /-'mɪstɪkəlɪ/ *adv.* [Latin *pessimus* worst]

pest *n.* **1** troublesome or annoying person or thing. **2** destructive animal, esp. one which attacks food sources. [Latin *pestis* plague]

pester *v.* trouble or annoy, esp. with frequent or persistent requests. [probably French *empestrer* encumber: influenced by PEST]

pesticide /'pestɪˌsaɪd/ *n.* substance for destroying pests, esp. insects.

pestilence /'pestɪləns/ *n.* fatal epidemic disease, esp. bubonic plague. [Latin *pestis* plague]

pestilent *adj.* **1** deadly. **2** harmful or morally destructive. **3** *colloq.* troublesome, annoying.

pestilential /ˌpestɪ'lenʃ(ə)l/ *adj.* **1** of or relating to pestilence. **2** pestilent.

PESTL /pestl/ *abbr.* political, environmental, social, technological, and legal issues that could affect the strategic development of a business.

pestle /'pes(ə)l/ *n.* club-shaped instrument for pounding substances in a mortar. [Latin *pistillum* from *pinso* pound]

◆ **PET** *abbr.* = POTENTIALLY EXEMPT TRANSFER.

pet[1] *–n.* **1** domestic or tamed animal kept for pleasure or companionship. **2** darling, favourite. *–attrib. adj.* **1** kept as a pet (*pet lamb*). **2** of or for pet animals (*pet food*). **3** often *joc.* favourite or particular (*pet hate*). **4** expressing fondness or familiarity (*pet name*). *–v.* (**-tt-**) **1** fondle erotically. **2** treat as a pet; stroke, pat. [origin unknown]

pet[2] *n.* fit of ill-humour. [origin unknown]

petal /'pet(ə)l/ *n.* each of the parts of the corolla of a flower. □ **petalled** *adj.* [Greek *petalon* leaf]

petard /pɪ'tɑːd/ *n. hist.* small bomb used to blast down a door etc. [French]

Peru /pə'ruː/, **Republic of** country in South America, on the Pacific coast. Agriculture is a major source of employment; cash crops include cotton, sugar cane, and coffee, and llamas, alpacas, and vicuñas bred in the mountain districts provide wool for export. Fishing and mining are the main sources of foreign-exchange revenue, producing fishmeal, copper, lead, zinc, and gold for export. There are deposits of oil in the jungle and offshore, and petroleum products are exported.

History. The former centre of the Inca empire, Peru had been under Spanish control for nearly three centuries when it declared its independence in 1821; a democratic republic was subsequently established. It lost territory in the S in war with Chile (1879–83) and had border disputes with Colombia and Ecuador to the N in the 1930s and 1940s. In recent years Peru has suffered from severe economic difficulties, with rampant inflation, and terrorist activity by left-wing guerrilla groups. In an attempt to counter these, the president, Alberto Fujimori, has introduced radical market-oriented economic reforms and enlisted military support in suppressing terrorism, suspending the constitution in 1992. A new constitution was introduced in 1993. Fujimori was re-elected to a second term in 1995. In late 1996 and early 1997 the left-wing Tupac Amaru overran the Japanese ambassadors residence, taking a number of hostages and demanding the release of political prisoners. The seige ended following Peruvian forces storming the ambassador's residence. Peru is a member of LAIA. President, Alberto Fujimori; prime minister, Dr Oscar de la Puente Raygada; capital, Lima. □ **Peruvian** *adj.* & *n.*

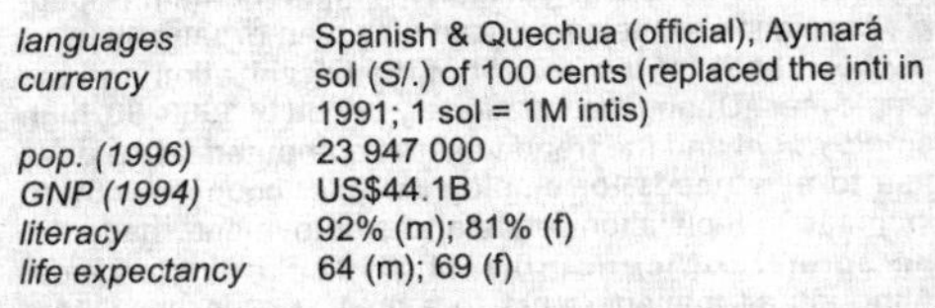

languages	Spanish & Quechua (official), Aymará
currency	sol (S/.) of 100 cents (replaced the inti in 1991; 1 sol = 1M intis)
pop. (1996)	23 947 000
GNP (1994)	US$44.1B
literacy	92% (m); 81% (f)
life expectancy	64 (m); 69 (f)

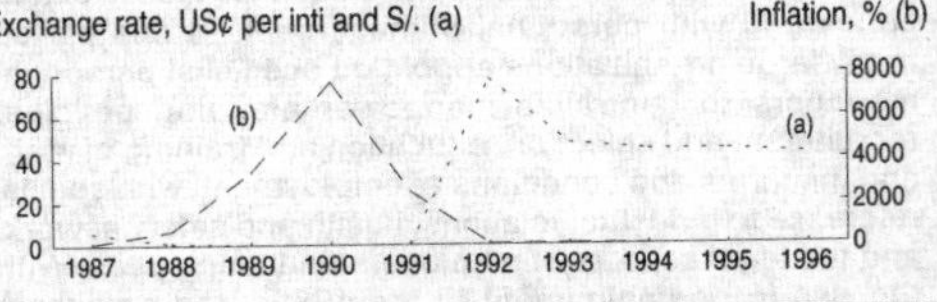

peter /ˈpiːtə(r)/ *v.* □ **peter out** diminish, come to an end. [origin unknown]

Peter Pan *n.* person who remains youthful or is immature. [hero of J. M. Barrie's play (1904)]

petersham /ˈpiːtəʃəm/ *n.* thick corded silk ribbon. [Lord *Petersham*, name of an army officer]

pethidine /ˈpeθɪˌdiːn/ *n.* synthetic soluble analgesic used esp. in childbirth. [perhaps from the chemical *piperidine*]

petiole /ˈpetɪˌəʊl/ *n.* slender stalk joining a leaf to a stem. [French from Latin]

petit bourgeois /ˌpetɪ ˈbʊəʒwɑː/ *n.* (*pl.* **petits bourgeois** pronunc. same) member of the lower middle classes. [French]

petite /pəˈtiːt/ *adj.* (of a woman) of small and dainty build. [French, = little]

petit four /ˌpetɪ ˈfɔː(r)/ *n.* (*pl.* **petits fours** /ˈfɔːz/) very small fancy cake. [French, = small oven]

petition /pəˈtɪʃ(ə)n/ –*n.* **1** supplication, request. **2** formal written request, esp. one signed by many people, appealing to an authority. **3** *Law* application to a court for a writ etc. –*v.* **1** make or address a petition to. **2** (often foll. by *for, to*) appeal earnestly or humbly. [Latin *peto petit-* ask]

petit mal /ˌpetɪ ˈmæl/ *n.* mild form of epilepsy. [French, = little sickness]

petit point /ˌpetɪ ˈpwæ̃/ *n.* embroidery on canvas using small stitches. [French, = little point]

petrel /ˈpetr(ə)l/ *n.* sea bird, usu. flying far from land. [origin unknown]

Petri dish /ˈpiːtrɪ/ *n.* shallow covered dish used for the culture of bacteria etc. [*Petri*, name of a bacteriologist]

petrify /ˈpetrɪˌfaɪ/ *v.* (**-ies, -ied**) **1** paralyse with fear, astonishment, etc. **2** change (organic matter) into a stony substance. **3** become like stone. □ **petrifaction** /-ˈfækʃ(ə)n/ *n.* [Latin *petra* rock, from Greek]

petrochemical /ˌpetrəʊˈkemɪk(ə)l/ *n.* substance industrially obtained from petroleum or natural gas.

petrodollar /ˈpetrəʊˌdɒlə(r)/ *n.* US dollar regarded as a notional unit of currency earned by a petroleum-exporting country. Reserves of US dollars were deposited with banks as a result of the steep rises in the price of oil in the 1970s. The export revenues of the oil-exporting nations increased rapidly in this period, leading to large current-account surpluses, which had an important impact on the world's financial system.

petrol /ˈpetr(ə)l/ *n.* **1** refined petroleum used as a fuel in motor vehicles, aircraft, etc. **2** (*attrib.*) concerned with the supply of petrol (*petrol pump*). [Latin: related to PETROLEUM]

petroleum /pɪˈtrəʊlɪəm/ *n.* hydrocarbon oil found in the upper strata of the earth, refined for use as fuel etc. [Latin *petra* rock, *oleum* oil]

petroleum jelly *n.* translucent solid mixture of hydrocarbons used as a lubricant, ointment, etc.

♦ **petroleum revenue tax** *n.* (also **PRT**) tax on the profits from oil exploration and mining occurring under the authority of licences granted in accordance with the Petroleum (Production) Act (1934) or the Petroleum (Production) Act (Northern Ireland) (1964). This tax was the principal means enabling the UK government to obtain a share in the profits made from oil in the North Sea.

Petropavlovsk-Kamchatski /ˈpetrəpævˌlɒfskæmˌtʃætskɪ/ fishing-port and naval base in E Russia, on the E coast of the Kamchatka peninsula; industries include fish processing and ship repairing; pop. (est. 1995) 239 000.

pet shop *n.* shop selling animals to be kept as pets.

petticoat /ˈpetɪˌkəʊt/ *n.* **1** woman's or girl's undergarment hanging from the waist or shoulders. **2** (*attrib.*) often *derog.* feminine. [*petty coat*]

pettifog /ˈpetɪˌfɒg/ *v.* (**-gg-**) **1** practise legal trickery. **2** quibble or wrangle about trivial points. [origin unknown]

pettish *adj.* peevish, petulant; easily put out. [from PET²]

petty *adj.* (**-ier, -iest**) **1** unimportant; trivial. **2** small-minded. **3** minor, inferior, on a small scale. **4** *Law* (of a crime) of lesser importance. □ **pettily** *adv.* **pettiness** *n.* [French *petit* small]

♦ **petty cash** *n.* amount of cash that an organization keeps in notes or coins on its premises to pay small items of expense. This is to be distinguished from cash, which normally refers to amounts held at banks. Petty-cash transactions are normally recorded in a petty-cash book, the balance of which should agree with the amounts of petty cash held at any given time.

---

petty officer *n.* naval NCO.

petulant /ˈpetjʊlənt/ *adj.* peevishly impatient or irritable. □ **petulance** *n.* **petulantly** *adv.* [Latin *peto* seek]

petunia /pɪˈtjuːnɪə/ *n.* cultivated plant with white, purple, red, etc., funnel-shaped flowers. [French *petun* tobacco]

pew *n.* **1** (in a church) long bench with a back; enclosed compartment. **2** *colloq.* seat (esp. *take a pew*). [Latin PODIUM]

pewit var. of PEEWIT.

pewter /ˈpjuːtə(r)/ *n.* **1** grey alloy of tin, antimony, and copper. **2** utensils made of this. [French *peutre*]

PEX *n.* discounted airline fare. [probably from APEX]

peyote /peɪˈəʊtɪ/ *n.* **1** Mexican cactus. **2** hallucinogenic drug prepared from this. [American Spanish from Nahuatl]

pf *abbr.* pfennig.

pfennig /ˈfenɪg/ *n.* one-hundredth of a Deutschmark. [German]

PFP *abbr.* personal financial planning.

PG *abbr.* (of a film) classified as suitable for children subject to parental guidance.

Pg. *abbr.* **1** Portugal. **2** Portuguese.

PGA *abbr. Computing* programmable gate array.

PH –*international civil aircraft marking* Netherlands. –*postcode* Perth. –*airline flight code* Polynesian Airlines.

pH /piːˈeɪtʃ/ *n.* measure of the acidity or alkalinity of a solution. [German *Potenz* power, *H* (symbol for hydrogen)]

phagocyte /ˈfægəˌsaɪt/ *n.* leucocyte capable of engulfing and absorbing foreign matter. [Greek *phag-* eat, *kutos* cell]

phalanx /ˈfælæŋks/ *n.* (*pl.* **phalanxes** or **phalanges** /fəˈlændʒiːz/) **1** *Gk Antiq.* line of battle, esp. a body of infantry drawn up in close order. **2** set of people etc. forming a compact mass, or banded for a common purpose. [Latin from Greek]

phallus /ˈfæləs/ *n.* (*pl.* **phalli** /-laɪ/ or **phalluses**) **1** (esp. erect) penis. **2** image of this as a symbol of natural generative power. □ **phallic** *adj.* [Latin from Greek]

phantasm /ˈfænˌtæz(ə)m/ *n.* illusion, phantom. □ **phantasmal** /-ˈtæzm(ə)l/ *adj.* [Latin: related to PHANTOM]

phantasmagoria /ˌfæntæzməˈgɔːrɪə/ *n.* shifting series of real or imaginary figures as seen in a dream. □ **phantasmagoric** /-ˈgɒrɪk/ *adj.* [probably from French *fantasmagorie*: related to PHANTASM]

phantom /ˈfæntəm/ –*n.* **1** ghost, apparition, spectre. **2** mental illusion. –*attrib. adj.* illusory. [Greek *phantasma*]

♦ **phantom withdrawal** *n.* removal of funds from a bank account through an automated teller machine by unauthorized means and without the consent of the account holder.

Pharaoh /ˈfeərəʊ/ *n.* **1** ruler of ancient Egypt. **2** title of this ruler. [Old English from Church Latin *Pharao*, ultimately from Egyptian]

Pharisee /ˈfærɪˌsiː/ *n.* **1** member of an ancient Jewish sect, distinguished by strict observance of the traditional and written law. **2** self-righteous person; hypocrite. □ **Pharisaic** /-ˈseɪɪk/ *adj.* [Hebrew *pārûš*]

pharmaceutical /ˌfɑːməˈsjuːtɪk(ə)l/ *adj.* **1** of or engaged in pharmacy. **2** of the use or sale of medicinal drugs. [Latin from Greek *pharmakon* drug]

pharmaceutics *n.pl.* (usu. treated as *sing.*) = PHARMACY 1.

pharmacist /'fɑːməsɪst/ *n.* person qualified to prepare and dispense drugs.

pharmacology /ˌfɑːmə'kɒlədʒɪ/ *n.* the study of the action of drugs on the body. □ **pharmacological** /-kə'lɒdʒɪk(ə)l/ *adj.* **pharmacologist** *n.*

pharmacopoeia /ˌfɑːməkə'piːə/ *n.* **1** book, esp. one officially published, containing a list of drugs with directions for use. **2** stock of drugs. [Greek *pharmakopoios* drug-maker]

pharmacy /'fɑːməsɪ/ *n.* (*pl.* **-ies**) **1** preparation and (esp. medicinal) dispensing of drugs. **2** pharmacist's shop, dispensary.

pharynx /'færɪŋks/ *n.* (*pl.* **pharynges** /-rɪnˌdʒiːz/ or **-xes**) cavity behind the nose and mouth. □ **pharyngeal** /-rɪn'dʒiːəl/ *adj.* **pharyngitis** /-rɪn'dʒaɪtɪs/ *n.* [Latin from Greek]

phase /feɪz/ –*n.* **1** stage in a process of change or development. **2** each of the aspects of the moon or a planet, according to the amount of its illumination. **3** *Physics* stage in a periodically recurring sequence, esp. the waveform of alternating electric currents or light. –*v.* (**-sing**) carry out (a programme etc.) in phases or stages. □ **phase in** (or **out**) bring gradually into (or out of) use. [Greek *phasis* appearance]

Ph.D. *abbr.* Doctor of Philosophy. [Latin *philosophiae doctor*]

pheasant /'fez(ə)nt/ *n.* long-tailed game-bird. [Greek *Phasianos* of Phasis, name of a river associated with the bird]

phenobarbitone /ˌfiːnəʊ'bɑːbɪˌtəʊn/ *n.* narcotic and sedative barbiturate drug used esp. to treat epilepsy. [from PHENOL, BARBITURATE]

phenol /'fiːnɒl/ *n.* **1** hydroxyl derivative of benzene. **2** any hydroxyl derivative of an aromatic hydrocarbon. [French]

phenomenal /fɪ'nɒmɪn(ə)l/ *adj.* **1** extraordinary, remarkable. **2** of the nature of a phenomenon. □ **phenomenally** *adv.*

phenomenon /fɪ'nɒmɪnən/ *n.* (*pl.* **-mena**) **1** fact or occurrence that appears or is perceived, esp. one of which the cause is in question. **2** remarkable person or thing. [Greek *phainō* show]

■ **Usage** The plural form of this word, *phenomena*, is often used mistakenly for the singular. This should be avoided.

pheromone /'ferəˌməʊn/ *n.* substance secreted and released by an animal for detection and response by another usu. of the same species. [Greek *pherō* convey, HORMONE]

phew /fjuː/ *int.* expression of relief, astonishment, weariness, etc. [imitative]

◆ **PHI** *abbr.* = PERMANENT HEALTH INSURANCE.

phi /faɪ/ *n.* twenty-first letter of the Greek alphabet (Φ, ϕ). [Greek]

phial /'faɪəl/ *n.* small glass bottle, esp. for liquid medicine. [Greek *phiale* broad flat dish]

PHIGS /fɪgs/ *abbr. Computing* programmers' hierarchical interactive graphics standard.

Phil. *abbr.* Philadelphia.

phil- var. of PHILO-.

-phil var. of -PHILE.

Philadelphia /ˌfɪlə'delfɪə/ city in the US, in Pennsylvania; it has manufacturing, oil-refining, and shipbuilding industries and the largest freshwater port in the world; pop. (est. 1994) 1 524 249.

philadelphus /ˌfɪlə'delfəs/ *n.* flowering shrub, esp. the mock orange. [Latin from Greek]

philander /fɪ'lændə(r)/ *v.* flirt or have casual affairs with women. □ **philanderer** *n.* [Greek *anēr andr-* male person]

philanthropy /fɪ'lænθrəpɪ/ *n.* **1** love of mankind. **2** practical benevolence. □ **philanthropic** /-'θrɒpɪk/ *adj.* **philanthropist** *n.* [Greek *anthrōpos* human being]

philately /fɪ'lætəlɪ/ *n.* the study and collecting of postage stamps. □ **philatelist** *n.* [Greek *atelēs* tax-free]

-phile *comb. form* (also **-phil**) forming nouns and adjectives denoting fondness for what is specified (*bibliophile*). [Greek *philos* loving]

philharmonic /ˌfɪlhɑː'mɒnɪk/ *adj.* fond of music (usu. in the names of orchestras etc.). [Italian: related to HARMONIC]

philippic /fɪ'lɪpɪk/ *n.* bitter verbal attack. [Greek from *Philip* II of Macedon]

Philistine /'fɪlɪˌstaɪn/ –*n.* **1** member of a people of ancient Palestine. **2** (usu. **philistine**) person who is hostile or indifferent to culture. –*adj.* (usu. **philistine**) hostile or indifferent to culture. □ **philistinism** /-stɪˌnɪz(ə)m/ *n.* [Hebrew *pᵉlištī*]

Phillips /'fɪlɪps/ *n.* (usu. *attrib.*) *propr.* denoting a screw with a cross-shaped slot, or a corresponding screwdriver. [name of the US manufacturer]

◆ **Phillips curve** *n.* curve on a graph plotting the rate of inflation against unemployment; it is based on empirical evidence produced by the economist A. W. H. Phillips for the UK between 1880 and 1950. It showed that when the rate of inflation was high, unemployment tended to be low, and vice versa. A theoretical interpretation of this

Philippines /'fɪlɪˌpiːnz/, **Republic of the** country in SE Asia consisting of a chain of over 7000 islands of the Malay Archipelago, the chief of which are Luzon in the N and Mindanao in the S, all separated from the Asian mainland by the South China Sea. The incompetance of the Marcos regime meant that the country did not experience the rapid economic growth of many of its southeast Asian neighbours; however, since the deposition of Marcos economic growth has been restored. Agriculture is the major source of employment: copra, coconut oil, bananas, and sugar are exported and rice, maize, and tobacco are also grown. Forestry is important, providing hardwood timber, bamboo, and gums and resins. The mining industry is one of the fastest-growing sectors of the economy, producing copper, iron ore, gold, silver, lead, zinc, manganese, and other minerals, some of which are exported. Other industries include oil refining, food processing, and textiles; manufacturing industry is increasing in accordance with the government policy of diversification; clothing and electronic goods are among the main exports. Tourism is also a source of revenue.
History. Conquered by Spain in 1565, the islands were ceded to the US following the Spanish-American War in 1898. The Philippines achieved full independence as a republic in 1946, but continued to maintain close links with the US. The country prospered during the early presidency of Ferdinand Marcos, who came to power in 1965, but his leadership became increasingly corrupt and authoritarian, with the suppression of opposition parties, and he was deposed in 1986. A new and democratic constitution was introduced in 1987. In 1996 a peace agreement was signed with Muslim rebels in Mindanao. President, Fidel V. Ramos; capital, Manila.

languages	Filipino & English (official), Spanish
currency	peso of 100 centavos
pop. (1996)	71 750 000
GNP (1994)	US$63.3B
literacy	94% (m); 93% (f)
life expectancy	66 (m); 70 (f)

Exchange rate, US¢ per peso (a) Inflation, % (b)

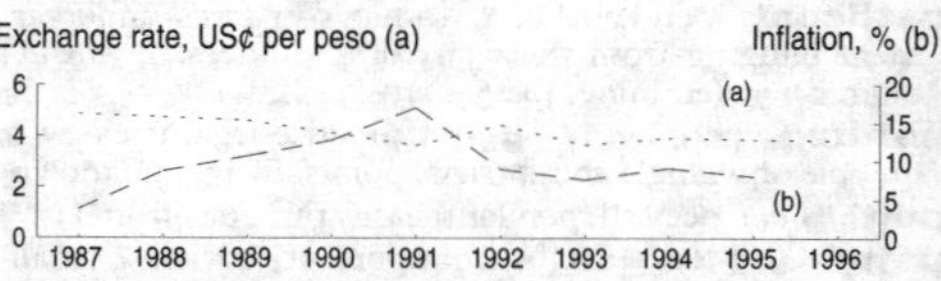

result was then spuriously added to Keynesianism, suggesting that governments could achieve fine tuning of the economy by changes in fiscal and monetary policy to obtain acceptable rates of inflation and unemployment. The stagflation of the 1970s showed that this was not, in fact, possible; this led to the view that, in the long run, there is a natural rate of unemployment from which the economy cannot deviate, irrespective of government policy. Monetarists, such as Milton Friedman, believed that in the short run government policy could regulate inflation and unemployment, although more recently the new classical macroeconomists have argued that even this is not possible.

---

philo- *comb. form* (also **phil-** before a vowel or *h*) denoting a liking for what is specified. [Greek *philos* friend]

philodendron /ˌfɪlə'dendrən/ *n.* (*pl.* **-s** or **-dra**) tropical evergreen climber cultivated as a house-plant. [Greek *dendron* tree]

philology /fɪ'lɒlədʒɪ/ *n.* the study of language, esp. in its historical and comparative aspects. □ **philological** /-lə'lɒdʒɪk(ə)l/ *adj.* **philologist** *n.* [French from Latin from Greek: related to PHILO-, -LOGY]

philosopher /fɪ'lɒsəfə(r)/ *n.* **1** expert in or student of philosophy. **2** person who lives by a philosophy or is wise.

philosophers' stone *n.* (also **philosopher's stone**) supreme object of alchemy, a substance supposed to change other metals into gold or silver.

philosophical /ˌfɪlə'sɒfɪk(ə)l/ *adj.* (also **philosophic**) **1** of or according to philosophy. **2** skilled in or devoted to philosophy. **3** calm in adversity. □ **philosophically** *adv.*

philosophize /fɪ'lɒsəˌfaɪz/ *v.* (also **-ise**) (**-zing** or **-sing**) **1** reason like a philosopher. **2** speculate; theorize. □ **philosophizer** *n.*

philosophy /fɪ'lɒsəfɪ/ *n.* (*pl.* **-ies**) **1** use of reason and argument in seeking truth and knowledge of reality, esp. knowledge of the causes and nature of things and of the principles governing existence. **2 a** particular system or set of beliefs reached by this. **b** personal rule of life. [Greek: related to PHILO-, *sophia* wisdom]

philtre /'fɪltə(r)/ *n.* (*US* **philter**) love-potion. [Greek *phileō* to love]

phlebitis /flɪ'baɪtɪs/ *n.* inflammation of a vein. □ **phlebitic** /-'bɪtɪk/ *adj.* [Greek *phleps phleb-* vein]

phlegm /flem/ *n.* **1** thick viscous substance secreted by the mucous membranes of the respiratory passages, discharged by coughing. **2 a** calmness. **b** sluggishness. **3** *hist.* phlegm regarded as one of the four bodily humours. [Greek *phlegma*]

phlegmatic /fleg'mætɪk/ *adj.* calm, unexcitable. □ **phlegmatically** *adv.*

phloem /'fləʊem/ *n.* tissue conducting sap in plants. [Greek *phloos* bark]

phlox /flɒks/ *n.* (*pl.* same or **-es**) plant with scented clusters of esp. white, blue, or red flowers. [Greek *phlox*, name of a plant (literally 'flame')]

Phnom Penh /nɒm 'pen/ capital of Cambodia, a centre of commerce with textile and food-processing industries; pop. (est. 1994) 920 000.

-phobe *comb. form* forming nouns denoting a person with a specified fear or aversion (*xenophobe*). [Greek *phobos* fear]

phobia /'fəʊbɪə/ *n.* abnormal or morbid fear or aversion. □ **phobic** *adj.* & *n.* [from -PHOBIA]

-phobia *comb. form* forming nouns denoting a specified fear or aversion (*agoraphobia*). □ **-phobic** *comb. form* forming adjectives.

Phoenix /'fi:nɪks/ city in the US, capital of Arizona; centre of the local cotton trade, it has textile and aircraft industries; pop. (est. 1994) 1 048 949.

phoenix /'fi:nɪks/ *n.* mythical bird, the only one of its kind, that burnt itself on a pyre and rose from the ashes to live again. [Greek *phoinix*]

Phoenix Islands group of eight islands forming part of the Republic of Kiribati in the SW Pacific.

phone *n.* & *v.* (**-ning**) *colloq.* = TELEPHONE. [abbreviation]

phone book *n.* = TELEPHONE DIRECTORY.

phonecard *n.* card containing prepaid units for use with a cardphone.

phone-in *n.* broadcast programme during which listeners or viewers telephone the studio and participate.

phoneme /'fəʊni:m/ *n.* unit of sound in a specified language that distinguishes one word from another (e.g. *p*, *b*, *d*, *t* as in pad, pat, bad, bat, in English). □ **phonemic** /-'ni:mɪk/ *adj.* [Greek *phōneō* speak]

phonetic /fə'netɪk/ *adj.* **1** representing vocal sounds. **2** (of spelling etc.) corresponding to pronunciation. □ **phonetically** *adv.* [Greek: related to PHONEME]

phonetics *n.pl.* (usu. treated as *sing.*) **1** vocal sounds. **2** the study of these. □ **phonetician** /ˌfəʊnɪ'tɪʃ(ə)n/ *n.*

phoney /'fəʊnɪ/ (also **phony**) *colloq.* –*adj.* (**-ier, -iest**) **1** sham; counterfeit. **2** fictitious. –*n.* (*pl.* **-eys** or **-ies**) phoney person or thing. □ **phoniness** *n.* [origin unknown]

phonic /'fɒnɪk/ *adj.* of sound; of vocal sounds. [Greek *phōnē* voice]

phono- *comb. form* sound. [Greek *phōnē* voice, sound]

phonograph /'fəʊnəˌgrɑ:f/ *n.* **1** early form of gramophone. **2** *US* gramophone.

phonology /fə'nɒlədʒɪ/ *n.* the study of sounds in language or a particular language; a language's sound system. □ **phonological** /ˌfəʊnə'lɒdʒɪk(ə)l, ˌfɒn-/ *adj.*

phony var. of PHONEY.

phosphate /'fɒsfeɪt/ *n.* salt or ester of phosphoric acid, esp. used as a fertilizer. [French: related to PHOSPHORUS]

phosphor /'fɒsfə(r)/ *n.* synthetic fluorescent or phosphorescent substance. [Latin PHOSPHORUS]

phosphorescence /ˌfɒsfə'res(ə)ns/ *n.* **1** radiation similar to fluorescence but detectable after excitation ceases. **2** emission of light without combustion or perceptible heat. □ **phosphoresce** *v.* (**-cing**). **phosphorescent** *adj.*

phosphorus /'fɒsfərəs/ *n. Chem.* non-metallic element existing in allotropic forms, esp. as a whitish waxy substance burning slowly at ordinary temperatures and so luminous in the dark. □ **phosphoric** /-'fɒrɪk/ *adj.* **phosphorous** *adj.* [Greek *phōs* light, *-phoros* -bringing]

photo /'fəʊtəʊ/ *n.* (*pl.* **-s**) = PHOTOGRAPH *n.* [abbreviation]

photo- *comb. form* denoting: **1** light. **2** photography. [Greek *phōs phōt-* light]

photochemistry /ˌfəʊtəʊ'kemɪstrɪ/ *n.* the study of the chemical effects of light.

photocopier /'fəʊtəʊˌkɒpɪə(r)/ *n.* machine for producing photocopies.

photocopy –*n.* (*pl.* **-ies**) photographic copy of printed or written material. –*v.* (**-ies, -ied**) make a photocopy of.

photoelectric /ˌfəʊtəʊɪ'lektrɪk/ *adj.* marked by or using emissions of electrons from substances exposed to light. □ **photoelectricity** /-'trɪsɪtɪ/ *n.*

photoelectric cell *n.* device using the effect of light to generate current.

photo finish *n.* close finish of a race or contest, where the winner is distinguishable only on a photograph.

photofit *n.* reconstructed picture of a suspect made from composite photographs.

photogenic /ˌfəʊtəʊ'dʒenɪk/ *adj.* **1** looking attractive in photographs. **2** *Biol.* producing or emitting light.

photograph /'fəʊtəˌgrɑ:f/ –*n.* picture formed by means of the chemical action of light or other radiation on sensitive film. –*v.* (also *absol.*) take a photograph of (a person etc.). □ **photographer** /fə'tɒgrəfə(r)/ *n.* **photographic** /-'græfɪk/ *adj.* **photographically** /-'græfɪkəlɪ/ *adv.*

photography /fə'tɒgrəfɪ/ *n.* the taking and processing of photographs.

photogravure /ˌfəʊtəʊgrə'vjʊə(r)/ *n.* **1** image produced from a photographic negative transferred to a metal plate and etched in. **2** this process. [French *gravure* engraving]

photojournalism /ˌfəʊtəʊ'dʒɜ:nəˌlɪz(ə)m/ *n.* the relating of news by photographs, esp. in magazines etc. □ **photojournalist** *n.*

photolithography /ˌfəʊtəʊlɪˈθɒgrəfɪ/ *n.* lithography using plates made photographically.

photometer /fəʊˈtɒmɪtə(r)/ *n.* instrument for measuring light. □ **photometric** /ˌfəʊtəʊˈmetrɪk/ *adj.* **photometry** /-ˈtɒmɪtrɪ/ *n.*

photon /ˈfəʊtɒn/ *n.* quantum of electromagnetic radiation energy, proportional to the frequency of radiation. [after *electron*]

photo opportunity *n.* organized opportunity for the press etc. to photograph a celebrity.

photosensitive /ˌfəʊtəʊˈsensɪtɪv/ *adj.* reacting to light.

Photostat /ˈfəʊtəʊˌstæt/ *–n. propr.* **1** type of photocopier. **2** copy made by it. *–v.* (**photostat**) (**-tt-**) make a Photostat of.

photosynthesis /ˌfəʊtəʊˈsɪnθɪsɪs/ *n.* process in which the energy of sunlight is used by organisms, esp. green plants, to synthesize carbohydrates from carbon dioxide and water. □ **photosynthesize** *v.* (also **-ise**) (**-zing** or **-sing**). **photosynthetic** /-ˈθetɪk/ *adj.*

♦ **phototypesetting** /ˌfəʊtəʊˈtaɪpˌsetɪŋ/ *n.* = FILMSETTING.

phrase /freɪz/ *–n.* **1** group of words forming a conceptual unit, but not a sentence. **2** idiomatic or short pithy expression. **3** mode of expression. **4** *Mus.* group of notes forming a distinct unit within a melody. *–v.* (**-sing**) **1** express in words. **2** *Mus.* divide (music) into phrases, esp. in performance. □ **phrasal** *adj.* [Greek *phrasis* from *phrazō* tell]

phrase book *n.* book for travellers, listing useful expressions with their foreign equivalents.

phraseology /ˌfreɪzɪˈɒlədʒɪ/ *n.* (*pl.* **-ies**) **1** choice or arrangement of words. **2** mode of expression. □ **phraseological** /-zɪəˈlɒdʒɪk(ə)l/ *adj.*

phrenetic var. of FRENETIC.

phrenology /frɪˈnɒlədʒɪ/ *n. hist.* the study of the shape and size of the cranium as a supposed indication of character and mental faculties. □ **phrenological** /-nəˈlɒdʒɪk(ə)l/ *adj.* **phrenologist** *n.* [Greek *phrēn* mind]

Phuket /puːˈket/ **1** largest island of Thailand, situated at the head of the Strait of Malacca off the W coast of the Malay Peninsula. **2** port at the S end of this island, a major resort centre and outlet to the Indian Ocean.

phut /fʌt/ *n.* dull abrupt sound as of impact or an explosion. □ **go phut** *colloq.* (esp. of a plan) collapse, break down. [perhaps from Hindi *phaṭnā* to burst]

phylactery /fɪˈlæktərɪ/ *n.* (*pl.* **-ies**) small leather box containing Hebrew texts, worn by Jewish men at prayer. [Greek *phulassō* guard]

phyllo pastry var. of FILO PASTRY.

phylum /ˈfaɪləm/ *n.* (*pl.* **phyla**) *Biol.* taxonomic rank below a kingdom, comprising a class or classes and subordinate taxa. [Greek *phulon* race]

physic /ˈfɪzɪk/ *n.* esp. *archaic.* **1** medicine. **2** art of healing. **3** medical profession. [Greek *phusikē* of nature]

physical /ˈfɪzɪk(ə)l/ *–adj.* **1** of the body (*physical exercise*). **2** of matter; material. **3 a** of, or according to, the laws of nature. **b** of physics. *–n.* **1** *US* medical examination. **2** (in *pl.*) actuals (see ACTUAL *n.*). □ **physically** *adv.*

♦ **physical capital** *n.* items such as plant and machinery, buildings, and land that can be used to produce goods and services. It is compared to financial capital, i.e. money, and human capital.

physical chemistry *n.* application of physics to the study of chemical behaviour.

♦ **physical controls** *n.pl.* direct measures used by a government to regulate an economy, compared to indirect controls, which influence the price mechanism. For example, the imposition of a quota on a specific import would be a physical control, whereas a surcharge on that import would be an indirect control.

♦ **physical distribution management** see LOGISTICS 2.

physical geography *n.* branch of geography dealing with natural features.

physical jerks *n.pl. colloq.* physical exercises.

physical science *n.* sciences used in the study of inanimate natural objects.

physician /fɪˈzɪʃ(ə)n/ *n.* doctor, esp. a specialist in medical diagnosis and treatment.

physicist /ˈfɪzɪsɪst/ *n.* person skilled in physics.

physics /ˈfɪzɪks/ *n.pl.* (treated as *sing.*) branch of science dealing with the properties and interactions of matter and energy. [Latin *physica* (pl.) from Greek: related to PHYSIC]

♦ **physiocrat** /ˈfɪzɪəʊˌkræt/ *n.* member of a group of 18th-century French economists who believed that agriculture was the only source of wealth, as trade and manufacture were seen to be merely the exchange of goods of equal value (cf. MERCANTILISM). While most of their doctrines, such as the proposal that taxes should be imposed on land alone, are now generally ignored, they are credited with being the earliest advocates of free trade and with laying down the foundations of the work of Adam Smith. [French: related to PHYSIC, -CRAT]

physiognomy /ˌfɪzɪˈɒnəmɪ/ *n.* (*pl.* **-ies**) **1 a** cast or form of a person's features, expression, etc. **b** supposed art of judging character from facial characteristics etc. **2** external features of a landscape etc. [Greek: related to PHYSIC, GNOMON]

physiology /ˌfɪzɪˈɒlədʒɪ/ *n.* **1** science of the functions of living organisms and their parts. **2** these functions. □ **physiological** /-zɪəˈlɒdʒɪk(ə)l/ *adj.* **physiologist** *n.* [Latin: related to PHYSIC, -LOGY]

physiotherapy /ˌfɪzɪəʊˈθerəpɪ/ *n.* treatment of disease, injury, deformity, etc., by physical methods including massage, heat treatment, remedial exercise, etc. □ **physiotherapist** *n.* [related to PHYSIC, THERAPY]

physique /fɪˈziːk/ *n.* bodily structure and development. [French: related to PHYSIC]

pi /paɪ/ *n.* **1** sixteenth letter of the Greek alphabet (Π, π). **2** (as π) the symbol of the ratio of the circumference of a circle to its diameter (approx. 3.14). [Greek]

p.i. *abbr. Insurance* professional indemnity (policy).

PIA *abbr.* **1** Pakistan International Airlines Corporation. **2** *Computing* peripheral interface adaptor. **3** Personal Investment Authority (see SELF-REGULATING ORGANIZATION).

pia mater /ˌpaɪə ˈmeɪtə(r)/ *n.* delicate innermost membrane enveloping the brain and spinal cord. [Latin, = tender mother]

pianissimo /ˌpɪəˈnɪsɪˌməʊ/ *Mus. –adj.* very soft. *–adv.* very softly. *–n.* (*pl.* **-s** or **-mi** /-mɪ/) very soft playing or passage. [Italian, superlative of PIANO²]

pianist /ˈpɪənɪst/ *n.* piano-player.

piano¹ /pɪˈænəʊ/ *n.* (*pl.* **-s**) keyboard instrument with metal strings struck by hammers. [Italian, abbreviation of PIANOFORTE]

piano² /ˈpjɑːnəʊ/ *Mus. –adj.* soft. *–adv.* softly. *–n.* (*pl.* **-s** or **-ni** /-nɪ/) soft playing or passage. [Latin *planus* flat, (of sound) soft]

piano-accordion *n.* accordion with a small keyboard like that of a piano.

pianoforte /ˌpɪænəʊˈfɔːtɪ/ *n. formal* or *archaic* = PIANO¹. [Italian, earlier *piano e forte* soft and loud]

Pianola /pɪəˈnəʊlə/ *n. propr.* a kind of automatic piano. [diminutive]

piazza /pɪˈætsə/ *n.* public square or market-place. [Italian: related to PLACE]

PIBOR /ˈpiːbɔː(r)/ *abbr.* Paris interbank offered rate.

pibroch /ˈpiːbrɒk/ *n.* martial or funerary bagpipe music. [Gaelic]

♦ **PIBS** *abbr.* = PERMANENT INTEREST BEARING SHARE.

pica /ˈpaɪkə/ *n.* **1** unit of type-size (1/6 inch). **2** size of letters in typewriting (10 per inch). [Latin: related to PIE²]

picador /ˈpɪkə,dɔː(r)/ *n.* mounted man with a lance in a bullfight. [Spanish]

Picardy /ˈpɪkədɪ/ (French **Picardie**) region in N France; pop. (est. 1994) 1 851 565; capital, Amiens.

picaresque /,pɪkəˈresk/ *adj.* (of a style of fiction) dealing with the episodic adventures of rogues etc. [Spanish *picaro* rogue]

■ **Usage** *Picaresque* is sometimes used to mean 'transitory' or 'roaming', but this is considered incorrect in standard English.

picayune /,pɪkəˈjuːn/ *US colloq. –n.* **1** small coin. **2** insignificant person or thing. *–adj.* mean; contemptible; petty. [French *picaillon*]

piccalilli /,pɪkəˈlɪlɪ/ *n.* (*pl.* **-s**) pickle of chopped vegetables, mustard, and hot spices. [origin unknown]

piccaninny /,pɪkəˈnɪnɪ/ *n.* (*US* **pickaninny**) (*pl.* **-ies**) often *offens.* small Black or Australian Aboriginal child. [West Indian Negro from Spanish *pequeño* or Portuguese *pequeno* little]

piccolo /ˈpɪkə,ləʊ/ *n.* (*pl.* **-s**) small flute sounding an octave higher than the ordinary one. [Italian, = small]

pick¹ *–v.* **1** (also *absol.*) choose carefully. **2** detach or pluck (a flower, fruit, etc.) from a stem, tree, etc. **3 a** probe with the finger, an instrument, etc. to remove unwanted matter. **b** clear (a bone, carcass, etc.) of scraps of meat etc. **4** (also *absol.*) (of a person) eat (food, a meal, etc.) in small bits. *–n.* **1** act of picking. **2 a** selection, choice. **b** right to select (*had first pick of the prizes*). **3** (usu. foll. by *of*) best (*the pick of the bunch*). □ **pick and choose** select fastidiously. **pick at 1** eat (food) without interest. **2** find fault with. **pick a person's brains** extract ideas, information, etc., from a person for one's own use. **pick holes in** find fault with (an idea etc.). **pick a lock** open a lock with an instrument other than the proper key, esp. with criminal intent. **pick off 1** pluck (leaves etc.) off. **2** shoot (people etc.) one by one without haste. **pick on 1** find fault with; nag at. **2** select. **pick out 1** take from a larger number. **2** distinguish from surrounding objects; identify. **3** play (a tune) by ear on the piano etc. **4** (often foll. by *in, with*) accentuate (decoration, a painting, etc.) with a contrasting colour. **pick over** select the best from. **pick a person's pockets** steal from a person's pockets. **pick a quarrel** start an argument deliberately. **pick to pieces** = *take to pieces* (see PIECE). **pick up 1** grasp and raise. **2 a** acquire by chance or without effort. **b** learn effortlessly. **3** stop for and take along with one. **4** become acquainted with (a person) casually, esp for sexual purposes. **5** (of one's health, the weather, share prices, etc.) recover, improve, etc. **6** (of an engine etc.) recover speed. **7** (of the police etc.) arrest. **8** detect by scrutiny or with a telescope, radio, etc. **9** accept the responsibility of paying (a bill etc.). **10** resume, take up anew (*picked up where we left off*). □ **picker** *n.* [from PIKE]

pick² *n.* **1** long-handled tool with a usu. curved iron bar pointed at one or both ends, used for breaking up hard ground etc. **2** *colloq.* plectrum. **3** any instrument for picking. [from PIKE]

pickaback var. of PIGGYBACK.

pickaninny *US* var. of PICCANINNY.

pickaxe /ˈpɪkæks/ *n.* (*US* **pickax**) = PICK² 1. [French: related to PIKE]

picket /ˈpɪkɪt/ *–n.* **1** one or more persons stationed outside a place of work to persuade others not to enter during a strike etc. **2** pointed stake driven into the ground. **3 a** small body of troops sent out to watch for the enemy. **b** group of sentries. *–v.* (**-t-**) **1 a** station or act as a picket. **b** beset or guard with a picket or pickets. **2** secure (a place) with stakes. **3** tether (an animal). [French *piquer* prick]

◆ **picketing** *n.* form of industrial action involving pickets and often a picket line. The right to **peaceful picketing** at one's own place of work was established by the Trade Union Act (1975). It is not lawful if it has not first been authorized by a ballot of the union involved and if the reason for the action is because the employer involved is employing a non-union employee. **Secondary picketing**, picketing other people's place of work (i.e. picketing employers not otherwise involved in the dispute), is a civil offence under the Employment Acts (1980; 1982). **Flying pickets**, pickets who join a picket line although they are neither employees of the organization being picketed nor union representatives of employees, have no immunity from civil action.

---

picket line *n.* boundary established by workers on strike, esp. at the entrance to the place of work, which other workers, delivery lorries, and customers' collection lorries are asked not to cross.

pickings *n.pl.* **1** profits or gains acquired easily or dishonestly. **2** leftovers.

pickle /ˈpɪk(ə)l/ *–n.* **1 a** (often in *pl.*) food, esp. vegetables, preserved in brine, vinegar, mustard, etc. **b** the liquid used for this. **2** *colloq.* plight (*in a pickle*). *–v.* (**-ling**) **1** preserve in or treat with pickle. **2** (as **pickled** *adj.*) *slang* drunk. [Low German or Dutch *pekel*]

pick-me-up *n.* **1** tonic for the nerves etc. **2** a good experience that cheers.

pickpocket *n.* person who steals from people's pockets.

pick-up *n.* **1** *slang* person met casually, esp. for sexual purposes. **2** small open motor truck. **3** part of a record-player carrying the stylus. **4** device on an electric guitar etc. that converts string vibrations into electrical signals. **5** act of picking up.

picky *adj.* (**-ier, -iest**) *colloq.* excessively fastidious.

pick-your-own *adj.* (usu. *attrib.*) (of fruit and vegetables) dug or picked by the customer at the farm etc.

picnic /ˈpɪknɪk/ *–n.* **1** outing including an outdoor meal. **2** meal eaten out of doors. **3** (usu. with *neg.*) *colloq.* something agreeable or easily accomplished etc. *–v.* (**-ck-**) take part in a picnic. [French *pique-nique*]

pico- *comb. form* denoting a factor of 10^{-12} (*picometre*). [Spanish *pico* beak, peak, little bit]

Pict *n.* member of an ancient people of N Britain. □ **Pictish** *adj.* [Latin]

pictograph /ˈpɪktə,grɑːf/ *n.* (also **pictogram** /-,græm/) **1** pictorial symbol for a word or phrase. **2** pictorial representation of statistics etc. □ **pictographic** /-ˈgræfɪk/ *adj.* [Latin *pingo pict-* paint]

pictorial /pɪkˈtɔːrɪəl/ *–adj.* **1** of or expressed in a picture or pictures. **2** illustrated. *–n.* periodical with pictures as the main feature. □ **pictorially** *adv.* [Latin *pictor* painter: related to PICTURE]

picture /ˈpɪktʃə(r)/ *–n.* **1 a** (often *attrib.*) painting, drawing, photograph, etc., esp. as a work of art. **b** portrait. **c** beautiful object. **2** total mental or visual impression produced; scene. **3 a** film. **b** (**the pictures**) cinema; cinema performance. *–v.* (**-ring**) **1** (also *refl.*; often foll. by *to*) imagine (*pictured it to herself*). **2** represent in a picture. **3** describe graphically. □ **get the picture** *colloq.* grasp the drift of information etc. **in the picture** *colloq.* fully informed. [Latin *pingo pict-* paint]

picture postcard *n.* postcard with a picture on one side.

picturesque /,pɪktʃəˈresk/ *adj.* **1** beautiful or striking to look at. **2** (of language etc.) strikingly graphic. [Italian *pittoresco*, assimilated to PICTURE]

picture window *n.* large window of one pane of glass.

PID *abbr.* = PERSONAL IDENTIFICATION DEVICE.

piddle /ˈpɪd(ə)l/ *v.* (**-ling**) **1** *colloq.* urinate. **2** (as **piddling** *adj.*) *colloq.* trivial; trifling. **3** (foll. by *about, around*) work or act in a trifling way. [origin unknown]

pidgin /ˈpɪdʒɪn/ *n.* simplified language used between people not having a common language. [corruption of *business*]

pidgin English *n.* pidgin in which the chief language is English, used orig. between Chinese and Europeans.

pie¹ /paɪ/ *n.* **1** baked dish of meat, fish, fruit, etc., usu. with a top and base of pastry. **2** thing resembling a pie (*mud pie*). □ **easy as pie** very easy. [origin uncertain]

pie[2] /paɪ/ *n. archaic* magpie. [Latin *pica*]

piebald /ˈpaɪbɔːld/ *–adj.* (esp. of a horse) having irregular patches of two colours, esp. black and white. *–n.* piebald animal. [from PIE[2], BALD]

piece /piːs/ *–n.* **1 a** (often foll. by *of*) distinct portion forming part of or broken off from a larger object. **b** each of the parts of which a set or category is composed (*five-piece band*). **2** coin. **3** (usu. short) literary or musical composition; picture; play. **4** item or instance (*piece of news*; *piece of impudence*). **5 a** object used to make moves in a board-game. **b** chessman (strictly, other than a pawn). **6** definite quantity in which a thing is sold. **7** (often foll. by *of*) enclosed portion (of land etc.). **8** *slang derog.* woman. *–v.* (**-cing**) (usu. foll. by *together*) form into a whole; put together; join. □ **go to pieces** collapse emotionally. **in** (or **all in) one piece 1** unbroken. **2** unharmed. **of a piece** (often foll. by *with*) uniform, consistent. **a piece of cake** see CAKE. **a piece of one's mind** sharp rebuke or lecture. **say one's piece** give one's opinion or make a prepared statement. **take to pieces 1** break up or dismantle. **2** criticize harshly. [Anglo-French, probably from Celtic]

pièce de résistance /ˌpjes də reɪˈziːstɑ̃s/ *n.* (*pl.* ***pièces de résistance*** pronunc. same) most important or remarkable item, esp. a dish at a meal. [French]

piecemeal *–adv.* piece by piece; gradually. *–adj.* gradual; unsystematic. [from PIECE, MEAL[1]]

♦ **piece rate** *n.* rate of pay that is directly related to output and not to time (cf. TIME RATE). Employees are paid a specific price for each unit made, often combined with a basic salary. In modern factories, many tasks have been mechanized, making this method of payment less common, although it is simple to operate and popular with employees. Piece rate, to be attractive to workers, depends on speed of production, therefore the standard of quality and safety may suffer if adequate precautions are not taken. See also PAYMENT BY RESULTS; PREMIUM BONUS.

piece-work *n.* work paid for according to the amount produced.

♦ **Piëch** /piːex/, **Ferdinand** (1937–) German businessman and engineer, chairman (from 1993) of Volkswagen AG. A grandson of Ferdinand Porsche, designer of the VW "Beetle" and the first Porsche sports car, his family owns 76% of the publicly traded Porsche, where he worked as an engineer from 1963 to 1971.

pie chart *n.* circle divided into sectors to represent relative quantities.

piecrust *n.* baked pastry crust of a pie.

pied /paɪd/ *adj.* particoloured. [from PIE[2]]

pied-à-terre /ˌpjeɪdɑːˈteə(r)/ *n.* (*pl.* ***pieds-à-terre*** pronunc. same) (usu. small) flat, house, etc. kept for occasional use. [French, literally 'foot to earth']

Piedmont /ˈpiːdmɒnt/ (Italian **Piemonte** /pjeɪˈmɒnteɪ/) region in NW Italy; pop. (est. 1994) 4 306 565; capital, Turin. Industries include engineering (mainly in Turin), textiles, chemicals, and food processing; cereals, rice, and wine are among the agricultural products of the region.

pie-eyed *adj. slang* drunk.

pie in the sky *n.* (used without an article) unrealistic prospect of future happiness.

pier *n.* **1 a** structure built out into the sea, a lake, etc., as a promenade and landing-stage. **b** breakwater. **2 a** support of an arch or of the span of a bridge; pillar. **b** solid masonry between windows etc. [Latin *pera*]

pierce *v.* (**-cing**) **1 a** (of a sharp instrument etc.) penetrate. **b** (often foll. by *with*) make a hole in or through with a sharp-pointed instrument. **c** make (a hole etc.). **2** (as **piercing** *adj.*) (of a glance, sound, light, pain, cold, etc.) keen, sharp, or unpleasantly penetrating. **3** (often foll. by *through*, *into*) force a way through or into, penetrate. [French *percer* from Latin *pertundo* bore through]

pier-glass *n.* large mirror, used orig. to fill wall-space between windows.

Pierre /ˈpɪə(r)/ city in the US, capital of South Dakota, on the Missouri River; pop. (1990) 12 906.

pierrot /ˈpɪərəʊ/ *n.* (*fem.* **pierrette** /pɪəˈret/) **1** white-faced entertainer in pier shows etc. with a loose white clown's costume. **2** French pantomime character so dressed. [French, diminutive of *Pierre* Peter]

pietà /ˌpɪeˈtɑː/ *n.* representation of the Virgin Mary holding the dead body of Christ on her lap. [Italian, = PIETY]

pietism /ˈpaɪəˌtɪz(ə)m/ *n.* **1** pious sentiment. **2** exaggerated or affected piety. [German: related to PIETY]

piety /ˈpaɪətɪ/ *n.* (*pl.* **-ies**) **1** quality of being pious. **2** pious act. [Latin: related to PIOUS]

piffle /ˈpɪf(ə)l/ *colloq. –n.* nonsense; empty speech. *–v.* (**-ling**) talk or act feebly; trifle. [imitative]

piffling *adj. colloq.* trivial; worthless.

pig *–n.* **1** omnivorous hoofed bristly broad-snouted mammal, esp. a domesticated kind. **2** its flesh as food. **3** *colloq.* greedy, dirty, or unpleasant person. **4** oblong mass of metal (esp. iron or lead) from a smelting-furnace. **5** *slang derog.* police officer. *–v.* (**-gg-**) *colloq.* eat (food) greedily. □ **buy a pig in a poke** acquire something without previous sight or knowledge of it. **pig it** *colloq.* live in a disorderly or filthy fashion. **pig out** (often foll. by *on*) esp. *US slang* eat gluttonously. [Old English]

pigeon /ˈpɪdʒ(ə)n/ *n.* bird of the dove family. [Latin *pipio -onis*]

pigeon-hole *–n.* each of a set of compartments on a wall etc. for papers, letters, etc. *–v.* **1** assign to a preconceived category. **2** deposit in a pigeon-hole. **3** put aside for future consideration.

pigeon-toed *adj.* having the toes turned inwards.

piggery *n.* (*pl.* **-ies**) **1** pig farm. **2** = PIGSTY.

piggish *adj.* greedy; dirty; mean.

piggy *–n.* (*pl.* **-ies**) *colloq.* little pig. *–adj.* (**-ier, -iest**) **1** like a pig. **2** (of features etc.) like those of a pig.

piggyback (also **pickaback** /ˈpɪkəˌbæk/) *–n.* ride on the back and shoulders of another person. *–adv.* on the back and shoulders of another person. [origin unknown]

piggy bank *n.* pig-shaped money box.

pigheaded *adj.* obstinate. □ **pigheadedness** *n.*

pig-iron *n.* crude iron from a smelting-furnace.

piglet /ˈpɪglɪt/ *n.* young pig.

pigment /ˈpɪgmənt/ *–n.* **1** colouring-matter used as paint or dye. **2** natural colouring-matter of animal or plant tissue. *–v.* colour with or as if with pigment. □ **pigmentary** *adj.* [Latin *pingo* paint]

pigmentation /ˌpɪgmənˈteɪʃ(ə)n/ *n.* **1** natural colouring of plants, animals, etc. **2** excessive colouring of tissue by the deposition of pigment.

pigmy var. of PYGMY.

♦ **Pigou effect** /ˈpiːʒuː/ *n.* = WEALTH EFFECT. [*Pigou*, name of an economist]

pigskin *n.* **1** hide of a pig. **2** leather made from this.

pigsty *n.* (*pl.* **-ies**) **1** pen for pigs. **2** filthy house, room, etc.

pigswill *n.* kitchen refuse and scraps fed to pigs.

pigtail *n.* plait of hair hanging from the back of the head.

PIK *abbr.* payment in kind.

pike *n.* (*pl.* same or **-s**) **1** large voracious freshwater fish with a long narrow snout. **2** *hist.* weapon with a pointed metal head on a long wooden shaft. [Old English]

pikestaff *n.* wooden shaft of a pike. □ **plain as a pikestaff** quite plain or obvious.

PIL *abbr.* payment in lieu.

pilaster /pɪˈlæstə(r)/ *n.* rectangular column projecting slightly from a wall. □ **pilastered** *adj.* [Latin *pila* pillar]

pilau /pɪˈlaʊ/ *n.* (also **pilaff, pilaf** /pɪˈlæf/) Middle Eastern or Indian dish of rice boiled with meat, vegetables, spices, etc. [Turkish]

pilchard /'pɪltʃəd/ *n.* small marine fish of the herring family. [origin unknown]

pile[1] *–n.* **1** heap of things laid upon one another. **2** large imposing building. **3** *colloq.* **a** large quantity. **b** large amount of money. **4 a** series of plates of dissimilar metals laid one on another alternately to produce an electric current. **b** = NUCLEAR REACTOR. **5** funeral pyre. *–v.* (**-ling**) **1 a** (often foll. by *up, on*) heap up. **b** (foll. by *with*) load. **2** (usu. foll. by *in, into, on, out of,* etc.) crowd hurriedly or tightly. □ **pile it on** *colloq.* exaggerate. **pile up 1** accumulate; heap up. **2** *colloq.* cause (a vehicle etc.) to crash. [Latin *pila*]

pile[2] *n.* **1** heavy beam driven vertically into the ground to support a bridge, the foundations of a house, etc. **2** pointed stake or post. [Latin *pilum* javelin]

pile[3] *n.* soft projecting surface on a carpet, velvet, etc. [Latin *pilus* hair]

pile-driver *n.* machine for driving piles into the ground.

piles *n.pl. colloq.* haemorrhoids. [Latin *pila* ball]

pile-up *n. colloq.* multiple crash of road vehicles.

pilfer /'pɪlfə(r)/ *v.* (also *absol.*) steal (objects), esp. in small quantities. [French *pelfre*]

pilgrim /'pɪlgrɪm/ *n.* **1** person who journeys to a sacred place for religious reasons. **2** traveller. [Latin: related to PEREGRINE]

pilgrimage *n.* **1** pilgrim's journey. **2** any journey taken for sentimental reasons.

Pilgrim Fathers *n.pl.* English Puritans who founded the colony of Plymouth, Massachusetts, in 1620.

◆ **Pilkington** /'pɪlkɪŋt(ə)n/, **Sir Anthony (Richard)** (1935–) British businessman, formerly chairman (1980–95) of Pilkington plc, the glass-making company, and a director (1984–94) of the National Westminster Bank. He has been a director of ICI since 1991.

PILL /pɪl/ *abbr. Computing* programmed instruction language learning.

pill *n.* **1 a** ball or a flat disc of solid medicine for swallowing whole. **b** (usu. prec. by *the*) *colloq.* contraceptive pill. **2** unpleasant or painful necessity. [Latin *pila* ball]

pillage /'pɪlɪdʒ/ *–v.* (**-ging**) (also *absol.*) plunder, sack. *–n.* pillaging, esp. in war. [French *piller* plunder]

pillar /'pɪlə(r)/ *n.* **1** slender vertical structure of stone etc. used as a support or for ornament. **2** person regarded as a mainstay (*pillar of the faith*). **3** upright mass of air, water, rock, etc. □ **from pillar to post** (rushing etc.) from one place to another. [Latin *pila* pillar]

pillar-box *n.* public postbox shaped like a pillar.

pillar-box red *adj.* & *n.* bright red.

pillbox *n.* **1** shallow cylindrical box for holding pills. **2** hat of a similar shape. **3** *Mil.* small partly underground enclosed concrete fort.

pillion /'pɪljən/ *n.* seating for a passenger behind a motor cyclist. □ **ride pillion** travel seated behind a motor cyclist. [Gaelic *pillean* small cushion]

pillory /'pɪlərɪ/ *–n.* (*pl.* **-ies**) *hist.* wooden framework with holes for the head and hands, imprisoning a person and allowing him or her to be publicly ridiculed. *–v.* (**-ies, -ied**) **1** expose to ridicule. **2** *hist.* put in the pillory. [French]

pillow /'pɪləʊ/ *–n.* **1** soft support for the head, esp. in bed. **2** pillow-shaped block or support. *–v.* rest on or as if on a pillow. [Latin *pulvinus* cushion]

pillowcase *n.* (also **pillowslip**) washable cover for a pillow.

PILOT /'paɪlət/ *abbr. Computing* programmed inquiry, learning, or teaching.

pilot /'paɪlət/ *–n.* **1** person who operates the controls of an aircraft. **2** person qualified to take charge of a ship entering or leaving harbour. **3** (usu. *attrib.*) experimental undertaking or test (*pilot scheme*). **4** guide. *–v.* (**-t-**) **1** act as a pilot of. **2** conduct or initiate as a pilot. [Greek *pēdon*]

pilot-light *n.* **1** small gas burner kept alight to light another. **2** electric indicator light or control light.

pilot officer *n.* lowest commissioned rank in the RAF.

◆ **pilot production** *n.* small-scale production of a new product in order to check and, if necessary, improve the production method. The product itself is often used in a marketing exercise to monitor its reception by the market and, in some cases, to improve it.

◆ **pilot study** *n.* small-scale marketing research study conducted as a trial so that any problems can be eliminated before a full study is undertaken. For example, a pilot study might show that changes are needed in a questionnaire because questions are ambiguous, miss the point, etc.

Pilsen /'pɪls(ə)n/ (Czech **Plzeň**) industrial city in the W Czech Republic, noted for its lager beer; there are also engineering, chemical, and other industries; pop. (est. 1995) 171 908.

PIM *abbr. Computing* personal information manager.

pimento /pɪ'mentəʊ/ *n.* (*pl.* **-s**) **1** tree native to Jamaica. **2** berries of this, usu. crushed for culinary use; allspice. **3** = PIMIENTO. [Latin: related to PIGMENT]

pi meson var. of PION.

pimiento /,pɪmɪ'entəʊ/ *n.* (*pl.* **-s**) = SWEET PEPPER. [see PIMENTO]

pimp *–n.* man who lives off the earnings of a prostitute or a brothel. *–v.* act as a pimp. [origin unknown]

pimpernel /'pɪmpə,nel/ *n.* = SCARLET PIMPERNEL. [Latin *piper* PEPPER]

pimple /'pɪmp(ə)l/ *n.* **1** small hard inflamed spot on the skin. **2** anything resembling a pimple. □ **pimply** *adj.* [Old English]

PIMS *abbr.* = PROFIT IMPACT OF MARKET STRATEGY.

PIN /pɪn/ *abbr.* = PERSONAL IDENTIFICATION NUMBER.

pin *–n.* **1** small thin pointed piece of metal with a round or flattened head used (esp. in sewing) for holding things in place, attaching one thing to another, etc. **2** peg of wood or metal for various purposes. **3** (in idioms) something of small value (*not worth a pin*). **4** (in *pl.*) *colloq.* legs. *–v.* (**-nn-**) **1 a** (often foll. by *to, up, together*) fasten with a pin or pins. **b** transfix with a pin, lance, etc. **2** (usu. foll. by *on*) put (blame, responsibility, etc.) on (a person etc.). **3** (often foll. by *against, on,* etc.) seize and hold fast. □ **pin down 1** (often foll. by *to*) bind (a person etc.) to a promise, arrangement, etc. **2** force (a person) to declare his or her intentions. **3** restrict the actions of (an enemy etc.). **4** specify (a thing) precisely. **pin one's faith** (or **hopes** etc.) **on** rely implicitly on. [Latin *pinna* point etc.]

pina colada /,piːnə kə'lɑːdə/ *n.* cocktail of pineapple juice, rum, and coconut. [Spanish]

pinafore /'pɪnə,fɔː(r)/ *n.* **1** apron, esp. with a bib. **2** (in full **pinafore dress**) collarless sleeveless dress worn over a blouse or jumper. [from PIN, AFORE]

Pinang see PENANG.

pinball *n.* game in which small metal balls are shot across a board to strike pins.

PINC *abbr.* = PROPERTY INCOME CERTIFICATE.

pince-nez /pæns'neɪ/ *n.* (*pl.* same) pair of eyeglasses with a nose-clip. [French, = pinch-nose]

pincer movement *n.* movement by two wings of an army converging to surround an enemy.

pincers /'pɪnsəz/ *n.pl.* **1** (also **pair of pincers**) gripping-tool resembling scissors but with blunt jaws. **2** front claws of lobsters and some other crustaceans. [related to PINCH]

pinch *–v.* **1 a** squeeze tightly, esp. between finger and thumb. **b** (often *absol.*) (of a shoe etc.) constrict painfully. **2** (of cold, hunger, etc.) affect painfully. **3** *slang* **a** steal. **b** arrest. **4** (as **pinched** *adj.*) (of the features) drawn. **5 a** (usu. foll. by *in, of, for,* etc.) stint. **b** be niggardly. **6** (usu. foll. by *out, back, down*) remove (leaves, buds, etc.) to encourage bushy growth. *–n.* **1** act of pinching. **2** amount that can be taken up with fingers and thumb (*pinch of snuff*). **3** the stress caused by poverty etc. □ **at** (or **in**) **a pinch** in an emergency. [French *pincer*]

pinchbeck *–n.* goldlike alloy of copper and zinc used in cheap jewellery etc. *–adj.* counterfeit, sham. [*Pinchbeck*, name of a watchmaker]

pincushion *n.* small pad for holding pins.

pine[1] *n.* **1** evergreen coniferous tree with needle-shaped leaves growing in clusters. **2** its wood. **3** (*attrib.*) made of pine. [Latin *pinus*]

pine[2] *v.* (**-ning**) **1** (often foll. by *away*) decline or waste away from grief etc. **2** long eagerly. [Old English]

pineal /'pɪnɪəl/ *adj.* shaped like a pine cone. [Latin *pinea*: related to PINE[1]]

pineal body *n.* (also **pineal gland**) conical gland in the brain, secreting a hormone-like substance.

pineapple /'paɪn,æp(ə)l/ *n.* **1** large juicy tropical fruit with yellow flesh and tough segmented skin. **2** plant bearing this. [from PINE[1], APPLE]

pine cone *n.* fruit of the pine.

pine nut *n.* edible seed of various pines.

ping *–n.* single short high ringing sound. *–v.* (cause to) make a ping. [imitative]

ping-pong *n. colloq.* = TABLE TENNIS. [imitative]

pinhead *n.* **1** head of a pin. **2** very small thing or spot. **3** *colloq.* stupid person.

pinhole *n.* **1** hole made by a pin. **2** hole into which a peg fits.

pinhole camera *n.* camera with a pinhole aperture and no lens.

pinion[1] /'pɪnjən/ *–n.* **1** outer part of a bird's wing. **2** *poet.* wing; flight-feather. *–v.* **1** cut off the pinion of (a wing or bird) to prevent flight. **2 a** bind the arms of (a person). **b** (often foll. by *to*) bind (the arms, a person, etc.) fast to a thing. [Latin *pinna*]

pinion[2] /'pɪnjən/ *n.* **1** small cog-wheel engaging with a larger one. **2** cogged spindle engaging with a wheel. [Latin *pinea* pine-cone: related to PINE[1]]

pink[1] *–n.* **1** pale red colour. **2** cultivated plant with fragrant flowers. **3** (prec. by *the*) the most perfect condition, the peak (*the pink of health*). **4** person with socialist tendencies. *–adj.* **1** of a pale red colour. **2** tending to socialism. □ **in the pink** *colloq.* in very good health. □ **pinkish** *adj.* **pinkness** *n.* **pinky** *adj.* [origin unknown]

pink[2] *v.* **1** pierce slightly. **2** cut a scalloped or zigzag edge on. [perhaps from Low German or Dutch]

pink[3] *v.* (of a vehicle engine) emit high-pitched explosive sounds caused by faulty combustion. [imitative]

♦ **Pink Book** *n.* = UK BALANCE OF PAYMENTS.

♦ **pink form** *n.* application form in a flotation that is printed on pink paper and usu. distributed to employees of the company to give them preference in the allocation of shares.

---

pink gin *n.* gin flavoured with angostura bitters.

pinking shears *n.pl.* dressmaker's serrated shears for cutting a zigzag edge.

pinko /'pɪŋkəʊ/ *adj.* (*pl.* **-s**) esp. *US slang* socialist.

pin-money *n.* **1** *hist.* allowance to a woman from her husband. **2** very small sum of money.

pinnace /'pɪnɪs/ *n.* ship's small boat. [French]

pinnacle /'pɪnək(ə)l/ *n.* **1** culmination or climax. **2** natural peak. **3** small ornamental turret crowning a buttress, roof, etc. [Latin *pinna* PIN]

pinnate /'pɪneɪt/ *adj.* (of a compound leaf) having leaflets on either side of the leaf-stalk. [Latin *pinnatus* feathered: related to PINNACLE]

pinny /'pɪnɪ/ *n.* (*pl.* **-ies**) *colloq.* pinafore. [abbreviation]

pinpoint *–n.* **1** point of a pin. **2** something very small or sharp. **3** (*attrib.*) precise, accurate. *–v.* locate with precision.

pinprick *n.* trifling irritation.

pins and needles *n.pl.* tingling sensation in a limb recovering from numbness.

pinstripe *n.* **1** (often *attrib.*) narrow stripe in cloth (*pinstripe suit*). **2** (in *sing.* or *pl.*) pinstripe suit (*came wearing his pinstripes*). □ **pinstriped** *adj.*

pint /paɪnt/ *n.* **1** measure of capacity for liquids etc., $^1/_8$ gal. (0.568 litre). **2 a** *colloq.* pint of beer. **b** pint of a liquid, esp. milk. **3** measure of shellfish containable in a pint mug (*pint of whelks*). [French]

pinta /'paɪntə/ *n. colloq.* pint of milk. [corruption of *pint of*]

pin-table *n.* table used in playing pinball.

pintail *n.* duck or grouse with a pointed tail.

pintle /'pɪnt(ə)l/ *n.* pin or bolt, esp. one on which some other part turns. [Old English]

pint-sized *adj. colloq.* very small.

pin-tuck *n.* very narrow ornamental tuck.

pin-up *n.* **1** photograph of a popular or sexually attractive person, hung on the wall. **2** person in such a photograph.

pin-wheel *n.* small Catherine wheel.

Pinyin /pɪn'jɪn/ *n.* system of romanized spelling for transliterating Chinese. [Chinese]

PIO *abbr. Computing* parallel input/output.

pion /'paɪɒn/ *n.* (also **pi meson**) subatomic particle having a mass many times greater than that of an electron. [from PI]

pioneer /,paɪə'nɪə(r)/ *–n.* **1** initiator of an enterprise; investigator of a subject etc. **2** explorer or settler; colonist. *–v.* **1** initiate (an enterprise etc.) for others to follow. **2** be a pioneer. [French *pionnier*: related to PAWN[1]]

pious /'paɪəs/ *adj.* **1** devout; religious. **2** sanctimonious. **3** dutiful. □ **piously** *adv.* **piousness** *n.* [Latin]

pip[1] *–n.* seed of an apple, pear, orange, grape, etc. *–v.* (**-pp-**) remove the pips from (fruit etc.). □ **pipless** *adj.* [abbreviation of PIPPIN]

pip[2] *n.* short high-pitched sound, usu. electronically produced, esp. as a time signal. [imitative]

pip[3] *v.* (**-pp-**) *colloq.* **1** hit with a shot. **2** (also **pip at the post**) defeat narrowly or at the last moment. [origin unknown]

pip[4] *n.* **1** any of the spots on a playing-card, dice, or domino. **2** star (1–3 according to rank) on the shoulder of an army officer's uniform. [origin unknown]

pip[5] *n.* **1** disease of poultry etc. **2** *colloq.* fit of disgust or bad temper (esp. *give one the pip*). [Low German or Dutch]

pipe *–n.* **1** tube of metal, plastic, etc., used to convey water, gas, etc. **2 a** narrow tube with a bowl at one end containing tobacco for smoking. **b** quantity of tobacco held by this. **3 a** wind instrument of a single tube. **b** any of the tubes by which sound is produced in an organ. **c** (in *pl.*) = BAGPIPE. **4** tubular organ, vessel, etc. in an animal's body. **5** high note or song, esp. of a bird. **6 a** boatswain's whistle. **b** sounding of this. **7** cask for wine, esp. as a measure, usu. = 105 gal. (about 477 litres). *–v.* (**-ping**) **1 a** convey (oil, water, gas, etc.) by pipes. **b** provide with pipes. **2** play (a tune etc.) on a pipe or pipes. **3** (esp. as **piped** *adj.*) transmit (recorded music etc.) by wire or cable. **4** (usu. foll. by *up*, *on*, *to*, etc.) *Naut.* **a** summon (a crew). **b** signal the arrival of (an officer etc.) on board. **5** utter in a shrill voice. **6** decorate or trim with piping. **7** lead or bring (a person etc.) by the sound of a pipe or pipes. □ **pipe down** *colloq.* be quiet or less insistent. **pipe up** begin to play, sing, speak, etc. □ **pipeful** *n.* (*pl.* **-s**). [Latin *pipo* chirp]

pipeclay *n.* fine white clay used for tobacco-pipes, whitening leather, etc.

pipe-cleaner *n.* piece of flexible tufted wire for cleaning a tobacco-pipe.

pipedream *n.* unattainable or fanciful hope or scheme. [originally as experienced when smoking an opium pipe]

pipeline *n.* **1** long, usu. underground, pipe for conveying esp. oil. **2** channel supplying goods, information, etc. □ **in the pipeline** being dealt with or prepared; under discussion, on the way.

piper *n.* person who plays a pipe, esp. the bagpipes.

pipette /pɪ'pet/ *n. Chem.* slender tube for transferring or measuring small quantities of liquids. [French diminutive: related to PIPE]

piping *n.* **1** pipelike fold or cord for edging or decorating clothing, upholstery, etc. **2** ornamental lines of icing, cream, potato, etc. on a cake etc. **3** lengths of pipe, system of pipes. □ **piping hot** (of food, water, etc.) very hot.

pipit /'pɪpɪt/ *n.* small bird resembling a lark. [imitative]

pippin /'pɪpɪn/ *n.* **1** apple grown from seed. **2** red and yellow eating apple. [French]

pipsqueak *n. colloq.* insignificant or contemptible person or thing. [imitative]

piquant /'pi:kənt, -kɑ:nt/ *adj.* **1** agreeably pungent, sharp, or appetizing. **2** pleasantly stimulating to the mind. □ **piquancy** *n.* [French *piquer* prick]

pique /pi:k/ *–v.* (**piques, piqued, piquing**) **1** wound the pride of, irritate. **2** arouse (curiosity, interest, etc.). *–n.* resentment; hurt pride. [French: related to PIQUANT]

piquet /pɪ'ket/ *n.* card-game for two players with a pack of 32 cards. [French]

♦ **piracy** /'paɪrəsɪ/ *n.* (*pl.* **-ies**) **1** illegal act of robbery, detention, or violence committed on a ship or aircraft, excluding acts committed for political purposes and during a war. In marine insurance it extends to include any form of plundering at sea. **2** infringement of copyright. The usual remedy is for the copyright holder to obtain an injunction to end the infringement. This may not be possible in a foreign country and many British and American books etc. are pirated in foreign countries by copying them photographically and printing them cheaply. [related to PIRATE]

Piraeus /paɪ'rɪəs/ chief port of Greece, SW of Athens; wine and olive oil are exported and there are shipbuilding, chemical, and oil-refining industries; pop. (1991) 169 622.

piranha /pɪ'rɑ:nə/ *n.* voracious South American freshwater fish. [Portuguese]

pirate /'paɪərət/ *–n.* **1 a** seafaring robber attacking ships. **b** ship used by pirates. **2** (often *attrib.*) person who infringes another's copyright or business rights or who broadcasts without official authorization (*pirate radio station*). *–v.* (**-ting**) reproduce (a book etc.) or trade (goods) without permission. □ **piratical** /-'rætɪk(ə)l/ *adj.* [Latin *pirata* from Greek]

pirouette /,pɪrʊ'et/ *–n.* dancer's spin on one foot or the point of the toe. *–v.* (**-tting**) perform a pirouette. [French, = spinning-top]

Pisa /'pi:zə/ city in N Italy; manufactures include textiles, machinery, and glass; pop. (1990) 101 500. A centre of tourism, it is noted for its 'Leaning Tower' and other buildings.

piscatorial /,pɪskə'tɔ:rɪəl/ *adj.* of fishermen or fishing. □ **piscatorially** *adv.* [Latin *piscator* angler, from *piscis* fish]

Pisces /'paɪsi:z/ *n.* (*pl.* same) **1** constellation and twelfth sign of the zodiac (the Fish or Fishes). **2** person born when the sun is in this sign. [Latin, pl. of *piscis* fish]

piscina /pɪ'si:nə/ *n.* (*pl.* **-nae** /-ni:/ or **-s**) **1** stone basin near the altar in a church for draining water used in rinsing the chalice etc. **2** fish-pond. [Latin, from *piscis* fish]

Pishpek /pɪʃ'pek/ (also **Bishkek**, formerly (1925–91) **Frunze** /'fru:nzjə/) capital of Kyrgyzstan; there are textile, food, and tobacco industries and agricultural machinery is manufactured; pop. (est. 1994) 597 000.

piss *coarse slang –v.* **1** urinate. **2** discharge (blood etc.) with urine. **3** (as **pissed** *adj.*) drunk. *–n.* **1** urine. **2** act of urinating. □ **piss about** fool or mess about. **piss down** rain heavily. **piss off 1** go away. **2** (often as **pissed off** *adj.*) annoy; depress. **piss on** show utter contempt for (a person or thing). **take the piss** (often foll. by *out of*) mock; make fun of. [French, imitative]

piss artist *n.* **1** drunkard. **2** person who fools about.

piss-taking *n.* mockery. □ **piss-taker** *n.*

piss-up *n.* drinking spree.

pistachio /pɪ'stɑ:ʃɪəʊ/ *n.* (*pl.* **-s**) **1** edible pale-green nut. **2** tree yielding this. [Persian *pistah*]

piste /pi:st/ *n.* ski-run of compacted snow. [French, = racetrack]

pistil /'pɪstɪl/ *n.* female organs of a flower, comprising the stigma, style, and ovary. □ **pistillate** *adj.* [Latin: related to PESTLE]

pistol /'pɪst(ə)l/ *n.* small handgun. [Czech *pišt'al*]

piston /'pɪst(ə)n/ *n.* **1** sliding cylinder fitting closely in a tube in which it moves up and down, used in an internal-combustion engine to impart motion, or in a pump to receive motion. **2** sliding valve in a trumpet etc. [Italian: related to PESTLE]

piston-ring *n.* ring on a piston sealing the gap between piston and cylinder wall.

piston-rod *n.* rod or crankshaft by which a piston imparts motion.

pit[1] *–n.* **1 a** deep hole in the ground, usu. large. **b** coalmine. **c** covered hole as a trap for animals. **2** hollow on a surface, esp. an indentation of the skin. **3 a** = *orchestra pit* (see ORCHESTRA 2). **b** usu. *hist.* seating at the back of the stalls. **4** (**the pits**) *slang* worst imaginable place, situation, person, etc. **5 a** area at the side of a track where racing cars are serviced and refuelled. **b** sunken area in a workshop floor for access to a car's underside. **6** area of a stock market or commodity exchange in which a particular stock or commodity is traded, esp. one in which dealings in certain commodities take place by open outcry (see LONDON INTERNATIONAL FINANCIAL FUTURES AND OPTIONS EXCHANGE; CALL-OVER). A member who is allowed to trade on the floor but wishes to conceal his or her identity may use a **pit broker** to carry out the transactions. *–v.* (**-tt-**) **1** (usu. foll. by *against*) set (one's wits, strength, etc.) in competition. **2** (usu. as **pitted** *adj.*) make pits, scars, craters, etc. in. **3** put into a pit. [Old English from Latin *puteus* well]

pit[2] *v.* (**-tt-**) (usu. as **pitted** *adj.*) remove stones from (fruit). [origin uncertain]

pita var. of PITTA.

pit-a-pat /'pɪtə,pæt/ (also **pitter-patter**) *–adv.* **1** with a sound like quick light steps. **2** falteringly (*heart went pit-a-pat*). *–n.* such a sound. [imitative]

pit bull terrier *n.* small American dog noted for ferocity.

Pitcairn Islands /'pɪtkeən/ British dependency comprising a group of islands in the S Pacific, NE of New Zealand; pop. (1995) 54. Pitcairn Island, the chief of the group and the only inhabited island, was settled in 1790 by mutineers from HMS *Bounty*. Its economy is based on subsistence fishing and agriculture and handicraft manufacture.

pitch[1] *–v.* **1** erect and fix (a tent, camp, etc.). **2** throw. **3** fix in a definite position. **4** express in a particular style or at a particular level. **5** (often foll. by *against, into*, etc.) fall heavily, esp. headlong. **6** (of a ship etc.) plunge backwards and forwards in a lengthwise direction. **7** *Mus.* set at a particular pitch. **8** *Cricket* **a** cause (a bowled ball) to strike the ground at a specified point etc. **b** (of a ball) strike the ground thus. *–n.* **1** area of play in a field-game. **2** height, degree, intensity, etc. (*excitement had reached such a pitch*). **3** degree of slope, esp. of a roof. **4** *Mus.* quality of a sound governed by the rate of vibrations producing it; highness or lowness of a note. **5** act of throwing. **6** pitching motion of a ship etc. **7** *colloq.* salesman's persuasive talk. **8** place where a street vendor is stationed. **9** distance between successive points, lines, etc. (e.g. character spacing on a typewriter). □ **pitch in** *colloq.* set to work vigorously. **pitch into** *colloq.* **1** attack forcibly. **2** assail (food, work, etc.) vigorously. [origin uncertain]

pitch[2] *–n.* dark resinous substance from the distillation of tar or turpentine, used for making ships watertight etc. *–v.* coat with pitch. □ **pitchy** *adj.* (**-ier, -iest**). [Latin *pix pic-*]

pitch-black *adj.* (also **pitch-dark**) very or completely dark.

pitchblende /'pɪtʃblend/ *n.* uranium oxide occurring in pitchlike masses and yielding radium. [German: related to PITCH[2]]

pitched battle *n.* **1** vigorous argument etc. **2** planned battle between sides in prepared positions and on chosen ground.

pitched roof *n.* sloping roof.

pitcher[1] *n.* large jug with a lip and a handle. [related to BEAKER]

pitcher[2] *n.* player who delivers the ball in baseball.

pitchfork *–n.* long-handled two-pronged fork for pitching hay etc. *–v.* **1** throw with or as if with a pitchfork. **2** (usu. foll. by *into*) thrust (a person) forcibly into a position, office, etc.

pitch-pine *n.* pine-tree yielding much resin.

piteous /'pɪtɪəs/ *adj.* deserving or arousing pity; wretched. □ **piteously** *adv.* **piteousness** *n.* [Romanic: related to PITY]

pitfall *n.* **1** unsuspected danger or drawback. **2** covered pit for trapping animals.

pith *n.* **1** spongy white tissue lining the rind of an orange etc. **2** essential part. **3** spongy tissue in the stems and branches of plants. **4** strength; vigour; energy. [Old English]

pit-head *n.* **1** top of a mineshaft. **2** area surrounding this (also *attrib.*: *pit-head ballot*).

pith helmet *n.* protective sun-helmet made of dried pith from plants.

pithy *adj.* (**-ier, -iest**) **1** (of style, speech, etc.) terse and forcible. **2** of or like pith. □ **pithily** *adv.* **pithiness** *n.*

pitiable /'pɪtɪəb(ə)l/ *adj.* deserving or arousing pity or contempt. □ **pitiably** *adv.* [French: related to PITY]

pitiful /'pɪtɪˌfʊl/ *adj.* **1** causing pity. **2** contemptible. □ **pitifully** *adv.*

pitiless /'pɪtɪlɪs/ *adj.* showing no pity (*pitiless heat*). □ **pitilessly** *adv.*

pit of the stomach *n.* depression below the breastbone.

piton /'piːtɒn/ *n.* peg driven into rock or a crack to support a climber or rope. [French]

pitta /'pɪtə/ *n.* (also **pita**) flat hollow unleavened bread which can be split and filled. [modern Greek, = a kind of cake]

pittance /'pɪt(ə)ns/ *n.* very small allowance or remuneration. [Romanic: related to PITY]

pitter-patter var. of PIT-A-PAT.

Pittsburgh /'pɪtsbɜːg/ industrial city in the US, in SW Pennsylvania; pop. (est. 1994) 358 883. Formerly a steel-producing city, Pittsburgh is now a major centre of high technology; machinery, coal, glass, and chemicals are produced.

pituitary /pɪ'tjuːɪtərɪ/ *n.* (*pl.* **-ies**) (also **pituitary gland**) small ductless gland at the base of the brain. [Latin *pituita* phlegm]

pity /'pɪtɪ/ *–n.* **1** sorrow and compassion for another's suffering. **2** cause for regret (*what a pity!*). *–v.* (**-ies, -ied**) feel (often contemptuous) pity for. □ **take pity on** help out of pity for. □ **pitying** *adj.* **pityingly** *adv.* [Latin: related to PIETY]

pivot /'pɪvət/ *–n.* **1** shaft or pin on which something turns or oscillates. **2** crucial or essential person, point, etc. *–v.* (**-t-**) **1** turn on or as on a pivot. **2** provide with a pivot. □ **pivotal** *adj.* [French]

pixel /'pɪks(ə)l/ *n. Computing* **1** any of the minute areas of uniform illumination of which a pictorial image on a display screen is composed (see VISUAL DISPLAY UNIT). The resolution of a graphics display is measured in terms of how many pixels there are across and down the screen. **2** element in a large array that is holding pictorial information (see ARRAY *n.* 3). It contains data representing the brightness, the colour, or some other property of a small region of an image. [abbreviation of *picture element*]

pixie /'pɪksɪ/ *n.* (also **pixy**) (*pl.* **-ies**) fairy-like being. [origin unknown]

pizza /'piːtsə/ *n.* Italian dish of a layer of dough baked with a topping of tomatoes, cheese, etc. [Italian, = pie]

pizzeria /ˌpiːtsə'riːə/ *n.* pizza restaurant.

pizzicato /ˌpɪtsɪ'kɑːtəʊ/ *Mus. –adv.* plucking. *–adj.* (of a note, passage, etc.) performed pizzicato. *–n.* (*pl.* **-s** or **-ti** /-tɪ/) note, passage, etc. played pizzicato. [Italian]

PJ *international civil aircraft marking* Netherlands Antilles.

PK *–international vehicle registration* Pakistan. *–international civil aircraft marking* Indonesia and West Irian. *–airline flight code* Pakistan International Airlines.

PL *–abbr.* **1** (also **P/L**) *Marine insurance* partial loss. **2** (also **P/L**) *Law* product liability. **3** programmed learning. **4** programming language. *–postcode* Plymouth. *–international vehicle registration* Poland.

pl. *abbr.* **1** plural. **2** (usu. **Pl.**) place. **3** plate.

PLA *abbr.* **1** Port of London Authority. **2** *Computing* programmed (or programmable) logic array.

placable /'plækəb(ə)l/ *adj.* easily placated; mild; forgiving. □ **placability** /-'bɪlɪtɪ/ *n.* [Latin *placo* appease]

placard /'plækɑːd/ *–n.* large notice for public display. *–v.* set up placards on (a wall etc.). [French from Dutch *placken* glue (v.)]

placate /plə'keɪt/ *v.* (**-ting**) pacify; conciliate. □ **placatory** /plə'keɪtərɪ/ *adj.* [Latin *placo* appease]

place *–n.* **1 a** particular portion of space. **b** portion of space occupied by a person or thing. **c** proper or natural position. **2** city, town, village, etc. **3** residence, home. **4** group of houses in a town etc., esp. a square. **5** (esp. large) country house. **6** rank or status. **7** space, esp. a seat, for a person. **8** building or area for a specific purpose (*place of work*). **9** point reached in a book etc. (*lost my place*). **10** particular spot on a surface, esp. of the skin (*sore place*). **11 a** employment or office. **b** duties or entitlements of office etc. (*not my place to criticize*). **12** position as a member of a team, student in a college, etc. **13** any of the first three (or four) positions in a race, esp. other than the winner. **14** position of a digit in a series indicated in decimal or similar notation. *–v.* (**-cing**) **1** put in a particular or proper place or state or order; arrange. **2** identify, classify, or remember correctly. **3** assign to a particular place, class, or rank; locate. **4** find employment or a living etc. for. **5** make or state (an order or bet etc.). **6** (often foll. by *in, on,* etc.) have (confidence etc.). **7** state the position of (any of the first three or four runners) in a race. **8** (as **placed** *adj.*) among the first three (or four) in a race. □ **give place to 1** make room for. **2** yield precedence to. **3** be succeeded by. **go places** *colloq.* be successful. **in place** in the right position; suitable. **in place of** in exchange for; instead of. **in places** at only some places or parts. **out of place 1** in the wrong position. **2** unsuitable. **put a person in his** (or **her) place** deflate a person. **take place** occur. **take the place of** be substituted for. □ **placement** *n.* [Latin *platea* broad way]

placebo /plə'siːbəʊ/ *n.* (*pl.* **-s**) **1** medicine with no physiological effect prescribed for psychological reasons. **2** dummy pill etc. used in a controlled trial. [Latin, = I shall be acceptable]

place-kick *n.* kick in football with the ball placed on the ground.

place-mat *n.* small table-mat for a person's plate.

place-name *n.* name of a town, village, etc.

placenta /plə'sentə/ *n.* (*pl.* **-tae** /-tiː/ or **-s**) organ in the uterus of pregnant mammals nourishing the foetus through the umbilical cord and expelled after birth. □ **placental** *adj.* [Greek, = flat cake]

placer /'pleɪsə(r)/ *n.* deposit of sand, gravel, etc. containing valuable minerals in particles. [American Spanish]

place-setting *n.* set of cutlery etc. for one person at a table.

placid /'plæsɪd/ *adj.* **1** calm; not easily excited or irritated. **2** tranquil, serene. □ **placidity** /plə'sɪdɪtɪ/ *n.* **placidly** *adv.* **placidness** *n.* [Latin *placeo* please]

◆ **placing** *n.* sale of shares by a company to a selected group of individuals or institutions. Placings can be used either as a means of flotation or to raise additional capital for a quoted company (see also PRE-EMPTION RIGHTS; RIGHTS ISSUE). Placings are usu. the cheapest way of raising capital on a stock exchange and they also allow the directors of a company to influence the selection of shareholders. The success of a placing usu. depends on the placing power of the company's stockbroker. Cf. INTRODUCTION 5; ISSUE BY TENDER; OFFER FOR SALE; PUBLIC ISSUE.

---

placket /'plækɪt/ *n.* **1** opening or slit in a garment, for fastenings or access to a pocket. **2** flap of fabric under this. [var. of PLACARD]

plagiarize /'pleɪdʒə,raɪz/ *v.* (also **-ise**) (**-zing** or **-sing**) **1** (also *absol.*) take and pass off (another's thoughts, writings, etc.) as one's own. **2** pass off the thoughts etc. of (another person) as one's own. □ **plagiarism** *n.* **plagiarist** *n.* **plagiarizer** *n.* [Latin *plagiarius* kidnapper]

plague /pleɪg/ *–n.* **1** deadly contagious disease. **2** (foll. by *of*) *colloq.* infestation of a pest etc. **3** great trouble or affliction. **4** *colloq.* nuisance. *–v.* (**plagues, plagued, plaguing**) **1** *colloq.* pester, annoy. **2** afflict, hinder (*plagued by back pain*). **3** affect with plague. [Latin *plaga* stroke, infection]

plaice /pleɪs/ *n.* (*pl.* same) marine flat-fish used as food. [Latin *platessa*]

plaid /plæd/ *n.* **1** (often *attrib.*) chequered or tartan, esp. woollen, twilled cloth (*plaid skirt*). **2** long piece of this worn over the shoulder in Highland Scottish costume. [Gaelic]

plain *–adj.* **1** clear, evident. **2** readily understood, simple. **3** (of food, decoration, etc.) simple. **4** not beautiful or distinguished-looking. **5** outspoken; straightforward. **6** unsophisticated; not luxurious (*a plain man*; *plain living*). *–adv.* **1** clearly. **2** simply. *–n.* **1** level tract of country. **2** basic knitting stitch. □ **plainly** *adv.* **plainness** *n.* [Latin *planus*]

plainchant *n.* = PLAINSONG.

plain chocolate *n.* dark chocolate without added milk.

plain clothes *n.pl.* ordinary clothes, not uniform (*plain-clothes police*).

plain dealing *n.* candour; straightforwardness.

plain flour *n.* flour containing no raising agent.

plain sailing *n.* uncomplicated situation or course of action.

plainsong *n.* unaccompanied church music sung in unison in medieval modes and in free rhythm corresponding to the accentuation of the words.

plain-spoken *adj.* frank.

plaint *n.* **1** *Law* accusation; charge. **2** *literary* complaint, lamentation. [French *plainte* from Latin *plango* lament]

plaintiff /'pleɪntɪf/ *n.* person who brings a case against another into court. [French *plaintif*: related to PLAINTIVE]

plaintive /'pleɪntɪv/ *adj.* expressing sorrow; mournful-sounding. □ **plaintively** *adv.* [French: related to PLAINT]

plait /plæt/ *–n.* length of hair, straw, etc., in three or more interlaced strands. *–v.* **1** weave (hair etc.) into a plait. **2** make by interlacing strands (*plaited belt*). [French *pleit* from Latin *plico* fold]

plan *–n.* **1** method or procedure for doing something; design, scheme, or intention. See also BUSINESS PLAN. **2** drawing etc. of a building or structure, made by projection on to a horizontal plane. **3** map of a town or district. **4** scheme of an arrangement (*seating plan*). *–v.* (**-nn-**) **1** arrange (a procedure etc.) beforehand; form a plan; intend. **2** make a plan of or design for. **3** (as **planned** *adj.*) in accordance with a plan (*planned parenthood*). **4** make plans. □ **plan on** (often foll. by *pres. part.*) *colloq.* aim at; intend. □ **planning** *n.* [French]

planchette /plɑːn'ʃet/ *n.* small board on castors with a pencil, said to write spirit messages when a person's fingers rest lightly on it. [French diminutive: related to PLANK]

plane[1] *–n.* **1** flat surface such that a straight line joining any two points on it lies wholly in it. **2** level surface. **3** *colloq.* = AEROPLANE. **4** flat surface producing lift by the action of air or water over and under it (usu. in *comb.*: *hydroplane*). **5** (often foll. by *of*) level of attainment, knowledge, etc. *–adj.* **1** (of a surface etc.) perfectly level. **2** (of an angle, figure, etc.) lying in a plane. *–v.* (**-ning**) glide. [Latin *planus* PLAIN]

plane[2] *–n.* tool for smoothing a usu. wooden surface by paring shavings from it. *–v.* (**-ning**) **1** smooth with a plane. **2** (often foll. by *away, down*) pare with a plane. [Latin: related to PLANE[1]]

plane[3] *n.* tall tree with maple-like leaves and bark which peels in uneven patches. [Greek *platanos*]

planet /'plænɪt/ *n.* celestial body orbiting round a star. □ **planetary** *adj.* [Greek, = wanderer]

planetarium /,plænɪ'teərɪəm/ *n.* (*pl.* **-s** or **-ria**) **1** domed building in which images of stars, planets, constellations, etc. are projected. **2** device for such projection.

plangent /'plændʒ(ə)nt/ *adj. literary* **1** loud and reverberating. **2** plaintive. [Latin: related to PLAINT]

plank *–n.* **1** long flat piece of timber. **2** item in a political or other programme. *–v.* **1** provide or cover with planks. **2** (usu. foll. by *down*) *colloq.* **a** put down or deposit roughly or violently. **b** pay (money) on the spot. □ **walk the plank** *hist.* be made to walk blindfold along a plank over the side of a ship to one's death in the sea. [Latin *planca*]

planking *n.* planks as flooring etc.

plankton /'plæŋkt(ə)n/ *n.* chiefly microscopic organisms drifting in the sea or fresh water. [Greek, = wandering]

◆ **planned economy** *n.* = COMMAND ECONOMY.

◆ **planned location of industry** *n.* government intervention in the location of new industries in an area or country. As old industries in a region gradually decrease, new industries are required to take their place to avoid high unemployment and skilled workers moving away. Most governments provide assistance to those wishing to set up new industries in these areas.

◆ **planned obsolescence** see OBSOLESCENCE 2.

◆ **planned shopping centre** *n.* group of businesses, primarily retailers, sharing a single building or a related set of buildings and usu. controlled by a management belonging to the developer of the centre. Planned shopping centres are common in the US and some are opening in the UK.

---

planner *n.* **1** person who plans new towns etc. **2** person who makes plans. **3** list, table, etc., with information helpful in planning.

◆ **planning blight** *n.* difficulty in selling or developing a site, building, etc. because it is affected by a government or local-authority development plan. Planning blight may be ended by a compulsory purchase by the government or local authority, but it may continue indefinitely if the government plans fail to mature or if the site itself is not required by the development but is rendered unsaleable or less valuable by its proximity to a development.

◆ **planning permission** *n.* permission that must be obtained from a local authority in the UK before building on or developing a site or before changing the use of an existing site or building, in accordance with the Town and Country Planning Act (1971).

---

plant /plɑːnt/ *–n.* **1 a** organism usu. containing chlorophyll enabling it to live wholly on inorganic substances, and lacking the power of voluntary movement. **b** small organism of this kind, as distinguished from a shrub or tree. **2 a** area of an organization in which production or some other technological process takes place. **b** (also **plant and machinery**) assets used by a business for the purpose of carrying on its activities. In the UK, for tax purposes, a distinction is made between those assets that businesses use in carrying on their trade, which are accepted as plant and for which capital allowances can be obtained, and the setting in which the trade is carried on (for which capital allowances are normally denied). **3** *colloq.* something deliberately placed so as to incriminate another. *–v.* **1** place (seeds, plants, etc.) in soil for growing. **2** (often foll. by *in, on*, etc.) put or fix in position. **3** (often *refl.*) station (a person etc.), esp. as a spy. **4** cause (an idea etc.) to be established, esp. in another person's mind. **5** deliver (a blow, kiss, etc.) with a deliberate aim. **6** *colloq.* place (something incriminating) for later discovery. □ **plant out** transfer from a pot or frame to the open ground; set out (seedlings) at intervals. □ **plantlike** *adj.* [Latin *planta*]

plantain[1] /ˈplæntɪn/ *n.* plant with broad flat leaves spread close to the ground and seeds used as food for birds. [Latin *plantago*]

plantain[2] /ˈplæntɪn/ *n.* **1** a kind of banana plant, grown for its fruit. **2** banana-like fruit of this. [Spanish]

♦ **plant and machinery register** *n.* record kept by an organization of the various items of plant and machinery it owns. The record will normally show dates and costs of purchase, the location of the assets, amounts provided for depreciation, dates of disposal, selling or scrap values, etc.

---

plantation /plɑːnˈteɪʃ(ə)n, plæn-/ *n.* **1** estate on which cotton, tobacco, etc. is cultivated. **2** area planted with trees etc. **3** *hist.* colony. [Latin: related to PLANT]

planter *n.* **1** manager or owner of a plantation. **2** container for house-plants.

plaque /plæk, plɑːk/ *n.* **1** commemorative tablet, esp. fixed to a building. **2** deposit on teeth where bacteria proliferate. [Dutch *plak* tablet: related to PLACARD]

plasma /ˈplæzmə/ *n.* (also **plasm** /ˈplæz(ə)m/) **1 a** colourless fluid part of blood, lymph, or milk, in which corpuscles or fat-globules are suspended. **b** this taken from blood for transfusions. **2** = PROTOPLASM. **3** gas of positive ions and free electrons in about equal numbers. □ **plasmic** *adj.* [Greek *plassō* shape (v.)]

plasma display *n.* (also **plasma panel display**) display device with a flat screen, used in computing etc., the characters or pictorial information being produced by electrical discharge through a gas.

plaster /ˈplɑːstə(r)/ *–n.* **1** soft mixture of lime, sand, and water etc. applied to walls, ceilings, etc., to dry into a smooth hard surface. **2** = STICKING-PLASTER. **3** = PLASTER OF PARIS. *–v.* **1** cover (a wall etc.) with plaster. **2** coat, daub, cover thickly. **3** stick or apply (a thing) thickly like plaster. **4** (often foll. by *down*) smooth (esp. hair) with water etc. **5** (as **plastered** *adj.*) *slang* drunk. □ **plasterer** *n.* [Greek *emplastron*]

plasterboard *n.* two boards with a filling of plaster for partitions, walls, etc.

plaster cast *n.* **1** bandage stiffened with plaster of Paris and applied to a broken limb etc. **2** statue or mould made of plaster.

plaster of Paris *n.* fine white gypsum plaster for plaster casts etc.

plastic /ˈplæstɪk/ *–n.* **1** synthetic resinous substance that can be given any shape. **2** (in full **plastic money**) *colloq.* credit card(s). *–adj.* **1** made of plastic. **2** capable of being moulded; pliant, supple. **3** giving form to clay, wax, etc. □ **plasticity** /-ˈtɪsɪtɪ/ *n.* **plasticize** /-ˌsaɪz/ *v.* (also **-ise**) (**-zing** or **-sing**). **plasticizer** /-ˌsaɪzə(r)/ *n.* (also **-iser**). **plasticky** *adj.* [Greek: related to PLASMA]

plastic arts *n.pl.* arts involving modelling or the representation of solid objects.

plastic bomb *n.* bomb containing plastic explosive.

plastic explosive *n.* putty-like explosive.

Plasticine /ˈplæstəˌsiːn/ *n. propr.* pliant material used for modelling.

plastic surgery *n.* reconstruction or repair of damaged or unsightly skin, muscle, etc., esp. by the transfer of tissue. □ **plastic surgeon** *n.*

plate *–n.* **1 a** shallow usu. circular vessel from which food is eaten or served. **b** contents of this. **2** similar vessel used for a collection in church etc. **3** (*collect.*) **a** utensils of silver, gold, or other metal. **b** objects of plated metal. **4** piece of metal with a name or inscription for affixing to a door etc. **5** illustration on special paper in a book. **6** thin sheet of metal, glass, etc., coated with a sensitive film for photography. **7** flat thin usu. rigid sheet of metal etc., often as part of a mechanism. **8 a** smooth piece of metal etc. for engraving. **b** impression from this. **9 a** silver or gold cup as a prize for a horse-race etc. **b** race with this as a prize. **10 a** thin piece of plastic material, moulded to the shape of the mouth, on which artificial teeth are mounted. **b** *colloq.* denture. **11** each of several rigid sheets of rock thought to form the earth's outer crust. **12** thin flat organic structure or formation. *–v.* (**-ting**) **1** apply a thin coat esp. of silver, gold, or tin to (another metal). **2** cover (esp. a ship) with plates of metal, for protection. □ **on a plate** *colloq.* available with little trouble to the recipient. **on one's plate** *colloq.* for one to deal with. □ **plateful** *n.* (*pl.* **-s**). [Latin *platta* from *plattus* flat]

plateau /ˈplætəʊ/ *–n.* (*pl.* **-x** or **-s** /-təʊz/) **1** area of fairly level high ground. **2** state of little variation after an increase. *–v.* (**plateauing, plateaus, plateaued**) (often foll. by *out*) reach a level or static state after an increase. [French: related to PLATE]

plate glass *n.* thick fine-quality glass for shop windows etc.

platelayer *n.* person employed in fixing and repairing railway rails.

platelet /ˈpleɪtlɪt/ *n.* small colourless disc of protoplasm found in blood and involved in clotting.

platen /ˈplæt(ə)n/ *n.* **1** plate in a printing-press which presses the paper against the type. **2** cylindrical roller in a typewriter etc. against which the paper is held. [French *platine*: related to PLATE]

plate-rack *n.* rack in which plates are placed to drain.

plate tectonics *n.pl.* (usu. treated as *sing.*) the study of the earth's surface based on the concept of moving 'plates' (see PLATE *n.* 11) forming its structure.

platform /ˈplætfɔːm/ *n.* **1** raised level surface, esp. one from which a speaker addresses an audience or one alongside the line at a railway station. **2** floor area at the entrance to a bus etc. **3** thick sole of a shoe. **4** declared policy of a political party. [French: related to PLATE, FORM]

platinum /ˈplætɪnəm/ *n. Chem.* white heavy precious metallic element that does not tarnish. [earlier *platina* from Spanish, diminutive from *plata* silver]

platinum blonde (also **platinum blond**) *–adj.* silvery-blond. *–n.* person with such hair.

platitude /ˈplætɪˌtjuːd/ *n.* commonplace remark, esp. one solemnly delivered. □ **platitudinous** /-ˈtjuːdɪnəs/ *adj.* [French: related to PLATE]

Platonic /pləˈtɒnɪk/ *adj.* **1** of Plato or his ideas. **2** (**platonic**) (of love or friendship) not sexual. [Greek *Platōn* (5th-4th centuries BC), name of a Greek philosopher]

Platonism /ˈpleɪtəˌnɪz(ə)m/ *n.* philosophy of Plato or his followers. □ **Platonist** *n.*

platoon /pləˈtuːn/ *n.* **1** subdivision of a military company. **2** group of persons acting together. [French *peloton* diminutive of *pelote* PELLET]

platter *n.* large flat dish or plate. [Anglo-French *plater*: related to PLATE]

platypus /ˈplætɪpəs/ *n.* (*pl.* **-puses**) Australian aquatic egg-laying mammal, with a ducklike bill and flat tail. [Greek, = flat foot]

plaudit /ˈplɔːdɪt/ *n.* (usu. in *pl.*) **1** round of applause. **2** expression of approval. [Latin *plaudite*, imperative of *plaudo plaus-* clap]

plausible /ˈplɔːzɪb(ə)l/ *adj.* **1** (of a statement etc.) reasonable or probable. **2** (of a person) persuasive but deceptive. □ **plausibility** /-ˈbɪlɪtɪ/ *n.* **plausibly** *adv.* [Latin: related to PLAUDIT]

play *–v.* **1** (often foll. by *with*) occupy or amuse oneself pleasantly. **2** (foll. by *with*) act light-heartedly or flippantly with (a person's feelings etc.). **3 a** perform on or be able to perform on (a musical instrument). **b** perform (a piece of music etc.). **c** cause (a record, record-player, etc.) to produce sounds. **4 a** (foll. by *in*) perform a role in (a drama etc.). **b** perform (a drama or role) on stage etc. **c** give a dramatic performance at (a particular theatre or place). **5** act in real life the part of (*play truant*; *play the fool*). **6** (foll. by *on*) perform (a trick or joke etc.) on (a person). **7** *colloq.* cooperate; do what is wanted (*they* *won't play*). **8** gamble, gamble on. **9 a** take part in (a game or recreation). **b** compete with (another player or team) in a game. **c** occupy (a specified position) in a team for a game. **d** assign (a player) to a position. **10** move (a piece) or display (a playing-card) in one's turn in a game. **11** (also *absol.*) strike (a ball etc.) or execute (a stroke) in a game. **12** move about in a lively manner; flit, dart. **13** (often foll. by *on*) **a** touch gently. **b** emit light, water, etc. (*fountains gently playing*). **14** allow (a fish) to exhaust itself pulling against a line. **15** (often foll. by *at*) **a** engage half-heartedly (in an activity). **b** pretend to be. *–n.* **1** recreation, amusement, esp. as the spontaneous activity of children. **2 a** playing of a game. **b** action or manner of this. **3** dramatic piece for the stage etc. **4** activity or operation (*the play of fancy*). **5 a** freedom of movement. **b** space or scope for this. **6** brisk, light, or fitful movement. **7** gambling. □ **in** (or **out of) play** *Sport* (of the ball etc.) in (or not in) a position to be played according to the rules. **make a play for** *colloq.* make a conspicuous attempt to acquire. **make play with** use ostentatiously. **play about** (or **around**) behave irresponsibly. **play along** pretend to cooperate. **play back** play (sounds recently recorded). **play ball** *colloq.* cooperate. **play by ear 1** perform (music) without having seen it written down. **2** (also **play it by ear**) *colloq.* proceed step by step according to results. **play one's cards right** (or **well**) *colloq.* make good use of opportunities; act shrewdly. **play down** minimize the importance of. **played out** exhausted of energy or usefulness. **play fast and loose** act unreliably. **play the field** see FIELD. **play for time** seek to gain time by delaying. **play the game** observe the rules; behave honourably. **play havoc** (or **hell) with** *colloq.* cause great confusion or difficulty to; disrupt. **play into a person's hands** act so as unwittingly to give a person an advantage. **play it cool** *colloq.* be relaxed or apparently indifferent. **play the market** speculate in stocks etc. **play off** (usu. foll. by *against*) **1** oppose (one person against another), esp. for one's own advantage. **2** play an extra match to decide a draw or tie. **play on 1** continue to play. **2** take advantage of (a person's feelings etc.). **play safe** (or **for safety**) avoid risks. **play up 1** behave mischievously. **2** annoy in this way. **3** cause trouble; be irritating. **play up to** flatter, esp. to win favour. **play with fire** take foolish risks. [Old English]

play-act *v.* **1** act in a play. **2** pretend; behave insincerely. □ **play-acting** *n.*

play-back *n.* playing back of a sound.

playbill *n.* poster advertising a play.

playboy *n.* wealthy pleasure-seeking man.

player *n.* **1** participant in a game. **2** person playing a musical instrument. **3** actor.

playfellow *n.* playmate.

playful *adj.* **1** fond of or inclined to play. **2** done in fun. □ **playfully** *adv.* **playfulness** *n.*

playgoer *n.* person who goes often to the theatre.

playground *n.* outdoor area for children to play in.

playgroup *n.* organized regular meeting of preschool children for supervised play.

playhouse *n.* theatre.

playing-card *n.* one of a set of usu. 52 oblong cards, divided into four suits and used in games.

playing-field *n.* field for outdoor games.

playlet *n.* short play.

playmate *n.* child's companion in play.

play-off *n.* match played to decide a draw or tie.

play on words *n.* pun.

play-pen *n.* portable enclosure for a young child to play in.

play school *n.* nursery school or kindergarten.

plaything *n.* **1** toy or other thing to play with. **2** person used merely as an object of amusement or pleasure.

playtime *n.* time for play or recreation.

playwright *n.* person who writes plays.

PLC *abbr.* **1** = PRODUCT LIFE CYCLE. **2** = PUBLIC LIMITED COMPANY.

plc *abbr.* = PUBLIC LIMITED COMPANY.

PLD *abbr. Computing* programmable logic device.

plea *n.* **1** appeal, entreaty. **2** *Law* formal statement by or on behalf of a defendant. **3** excuse. [Latin *placitum* decree: related to PLEASE]

pleach *v.* entwine or interlace (esp. branches to form a hedge). [Latin: related to PLEXUS]

plead *v.* **1** (foll. by *with*) make an earnest appeal to. **2** (of an advocate) address a lawcourt. **3** maintain (a cause) in a lawcourt. **4** (foll. by *guilty* or *not guilty*) declare oneself to be guilty or not guilty of a charge. **5** allege as an excuse (*plead insanity*). **6** (often as **pleading** *adj.*) make an appeal or entreaty (*in a pleading voice*). [Anglo-French *pleder*: related to PLEA]

pleading *n.* (usu. in *pl.*) formal statement of the cause of an action or defence.

pleasant /ˈplez(ə)nt/ *adj.* (**-er, -est**) pleasing to the mind, feelings, or senses. □ **pleasantly** *adv.* [French: related to PLEASE]

pleasantry *n.* (*pl.* **-ies**) **1** amusing or polite remark. **2** humorous speech. **3** jocularity.

please /pliːz/ *v.* (**-sing**) **1** be agreeable to; make glad; give pleasure. **2** (in *passive*) **a** (foll. by *to* + infin.) be glad or willing to (*am pleased to help*). **b** (often foll. by *about, at, with*) derive pleasure or satisfaction (from). **3** (with *it* as subject) be the inclination or wish of (*it did not please him to attend*). **4** think fit (*take as many as you please*). **5** used in polite requests (*come in, please*). □ **if you please** if you are willing, esp. *iron.* to indicate unreasonableness (*then, if you please, we had to pay*). **please oneself** do as one likes. □ **pleased** *adj.* **pleasing** *adj.* [French *plaisir* from Latin *placeo*]

pleasurable /ˈpleʒərəb(ə)l/ *adj.* causing pleasure. □ **pleasurably** *adv.*

pleasure /ˈpleʒə(r)/ *n.* **1** feeling of satisfaction or joy. **2** enjoyment. **3** source of pleasure or gratification. **4** one's will or desire (*what is your pleasure?*). **5** sensual gratification. **6** (*attrib.*) done or used for pleasure. [French: related to PLEASE]

pleat *–n.* fold or crease, esp. a flattened fold in cloth doubled upon itself. *–v.* make a pleat or pleats in. [from PLAIT]

pleb *n. colloq.* usu. *derog.* = PLEBEIAN *n.* 2. □ **plebby** *adj.* [abbreviation of PLEBEIAN]

plebeian /plɪˈbiːən/ *–n.* **1** commoner, esp. in ancient Rome. **2** working-class person, esp. an uncultured one. *–adj.* **1** of the common people. **2** uncultured, coarse. [Latin *plebs plebis* common people]

plebiscite /ˈplebɪˌsaɪt/ *n.* referendum. [Latin *plebiscitum*: related to PLEBEIAN]

plectrum /ˈplektrəm/ *n.* (*pl.* **-s** or **-tra**) thin flat piece of plastic etc. for plucking the strings of a guitar etc. [Greek *plēssō* strike]

pledge *–n.* **1** solemn promise. **2** article given by a borrower (**pledgor**) to a lender (**pledgee**) as a security for a debt etc., remaining in the ownership of the pledgor although in the possession of the pledgee until the debt is repaid. See also PAWNBROKER. **3** thing put in pawn. **4** thing given as a token of favour etc., or of something to come. **5** drinking of a person's health, toast. **6** solemn promise to abstain from alcohol (*sign the pledge*). *–v.* (**-ging**) **1 a** deposit as security. **b** pawn. **2** promise solemnly by the pledge of (one's honour, word, etc.). **3** bind by a solemn promise. **4** drink to the health of. □ **pledge one's troth** see TROTH. [French *plege*]

Pleiades /ˈplaɪəˌdiːz/ *n.pl.* cluster of seven stars in the constellation Taurus. [Latin from Greek]

Pleistocene /ˈplaɪstəˌsiːn/ *Geol. –adj.* of the first epoch of the Quaternary period. *–n.* this epoch. [Greek *pleistos* most, *kainos* new]

plenary /ˈpliːnərɪ/ *adj.* **1** (of an assembly) to be attended by all members. **2** entire, unqualified (*plenary indulgence*). [Latin *plenus* full]

plenipotentiary /ˌplenɪpəˈtenʃərɪ/ *–n.* (*pl.* **-ies**) person (esp. a diplomat) invested with full authority to act. *–adj.* having this power. [Latin: related to PLENARY, POTENT]

plenitude /ˈplenɪˌtjuːd/ *n. literary* **1** fullness, completeness. **2** abundance. [Latin: related to PLENARY]

plenteous /ˈplentɪəs/ *adj. literary* plentiful. [French *plentivous*: related to PLENTY]

plentiful /ˈplentɪˌfʊl/ *adj.* abundant, copious. □ **plentifully** *adv.*

plenty /ˈplentɪ/ *–n.* (often foll. by *of*) abundance, sufficient quantity or number (*we have plenty; plenty of time; a time of plenty*). *–adj. colloq.* plentiful. *–adv. colloq.* fully, quite. [Latin *plenitas*: related to PLENARY]

plenum /ˈpliːnəm/ *n.* full assembly of people or a committee etc. [Latin, neuter of *plenus* full]

pleonasm /ˈpliːəˌnæz(ə)m/ *n.* use of more words than are needed (e.g. *see with one's eyes*). □ **pleonastic** /-ˈnæstɪk/ *adj.* [Greek *pleon* more]

plethora /ˈpleθərə/ *n.* over-abundance. [Greek, = fullness]

pleura /ˈplʊərə/ *n.* (*pl.* **-rae** /-riː/) membrane enveloping the lungs. □ **pleural** *adj.* [Greek *pleura* rib]

pleurisy /ˈplʊərəsɪ/ *n.* inflammation of the pleura. □ **pleuritic** /-ˈrɪtɪk/ *adj.* [Greek: related to PLEURA]

Pleven /ˈplev(ə)n/ industrial town in N Bulgaria; pop. (est. 1996) 125 029.

plexus /ˈpleksəs/ *n.* (*pl.* same or **plexuses**) *Anat.* network of nerves or vessels (*solar plexus*). [Latin *plecto plex-* plait]

PL/I *n. Computing* high-level programming language developed by IBM in the late 1960s to combine what were considered the best features of Fortran, Algol-60, and COBOL, and intended to replace all three. PL/I is a very large comprehensive language, and although it is used fairly widely in IBM installations it was never taken up to any large extent by other manufacturers. [*P*rogramming *L*anguage *I*]

pliable /ˈplaɪəb(ə)l/ *adj.* **1** bending easily; supple. **2** yielding, compliant. □ **pliability** /-ˈbɪlɪtɪ/ *n.* [French: related to PLY[1]]

pliant /ˈplaɪənt/ *adj.* = PLIABLE 1. □ **pliancy** *n.*

pliers /ˈplaɪəz/ *n.pl.* pincers with parallel flat surfaces for holding small objects, bending wire, etc. [from dial. *ply* bend: related to PLIABLE]

plight[1] /plaɪt/ *n.* unfortunate condition or state. [Anglo-French *plit* PLAIT]

plight[2] /plaɪt/ *v. archaic* **1** pledge. **2** (foll. by *to*) engage (oneself) in marriage. □ **plight one's troth** see TROTH. [Old English]

plimsoll /ˈplɪms(ə)l/ *n.* (also **plimsole**) rubber-soled canvas sports shoe. [from PLIMSOLL LINE]

Plimsoll line /ˈplɪms(ə)l/ *n.* (also **Plimsoll mark**) = LOAD LINE. [*Plimsoll*, name of a politician]

plinth *n.* **1** lower square slab at the base of a column. **2** base supporting a vase or statue etc. [Greek, = tile]

Pliocene /ˈplaɪəˌsiːn/ *Geol. –adj.* of the last epoch of the Tertiary period. *–n.* this epoch. [Greek *pleiōn* more, *kainos* new]

PL/M *abbr.* Programming Language for Microcomputers.

PLO *abbr.* Palestine Liberation Organization.

plod *–v.* (**-dd-**) **1** walk doggedly or laboriously; trudge. **2** work slowly and steadily. *–n.* spell of plodding. □ **plodder** *n.* [probably imitative]

Ploieşti /plɔɪˈeʃt/ oil-refining city in central Romania; pop. (est. 1993) 254 304.

plonk[1] *–v.* **1** set down hurriedly or clumsily. **2** (usu. foll. by *down*) set down firmly. *–n.* heavy thud. [imitative]

plonk[2] *n. colloq.* cheap or inferior wine. [origin unknown]

plonker *n. coarse slang* **1** fool. **2** penis.

plop *–n.* sound as of a smooth object dropping into water without a splash. *–v.* (**-pp-**) fall or drop with a plop. *–adv.* with a plop. [imitative]

plosive /ˈpləʊsɪv/ *–adj.* pronounced with a sudden release of breath. *–n.* plosive sound. [from EXPLOSIVE]

plot *–n.* **1** defined and usu. small piece of land. **2** interrelationship of the main events in a play, novel, film, etc. **3** conspiracy or secret plan. *–v.* (**-tt-**) **1** make a plan or map of. **2** (also *absol.*) plan or contrive secretly (a crime etc.). **3** mark on a chart or diagram. **4** make (a curve etc.) by marking out a number of points. **5** provide (a play, novel, film, etc.) with a plot. [Old English and French *complot*]

plotter *n.* **1** person who plots. **2** device that converts coded information from a computer into graphs or pictures drawn on paper or transparent film by means of one or more pens.

plough /plaʊ/ (*US* **plow**) *–n.* **1** implement for cutting furrows in the soil and turning it up. **2** implement resembling this (*snowplough*). **3** (**the Plough**) the Great Bear (see BEAR[2]) or its seven bright stars. *–v.* **1** (also *absol.*) turn up (the earth) with a plough. **2** (foll. by *out, up,* etc.) turn or extract with a plough. **3** furrow or scratch (a surface) as with a plough. **4** produce (a furrow or line) thus. **5** (foll. by *through*) advance laboriously, esp. through work, a book, etc. **6** (foll. by *through, into*) move violently like a plough. **7** *colloq.* fail in an examination. □ **plough back 1** plough (grass etc.) into the soil to enrich it. **2** reinvest (profits) in the business producing them. See RETAINED PROFITS. [Old English]

ploughman *n.* (*US* **plowman**) person who uses a plough.

ploughman's lunch *n.* meal of bread and cheese with pickle and salad.

ploughshare *n.* (*US* **plowshare**) cutting blade of a plough.

Plovdiv /ˈplɒvdɪf/ second-largest city in Bulgaria; manufactures include carpets and food products; pop. (est. 1996) 344 326.

plover /ˈplʌvə(r)/ *n.* plump-breasted wading bird, e.g. the lapwing. [Latin *pluvia* rain]

plow *US* var. of PLOUGH.

plowman *US* var. of PLOUGHMAN.

plowshare *US* var. of PLOUGHSHARE.

ploy *n.* cunning manoeuvre to gain advantage. [origin unknown]

◆ **PLR** *abbr.* = PUBLIC LENDING RIGHT.

---

pluck *–v.* **1** pick or pull out or away. **2** strip (a bird) of feathers. **3** pull at, twitch. **4** (foll. by *at*) tug or snatch at. **5** sound (the string of a musical instrument) with a finger or plectrum. **6** plunder. *–n.* **1** courage, spirit. **2** plucking; twitch. **3** animal's heart, liver, and lungs as food. □ **pluck up** summon up (one's courage etc.). [Old English]

plucky *adj.* (**-ier, -iest**) brave, spirited. □ **pluckily** *adv.* **pluckiness** *n.*

plug *–n.* **1** piece of solid material fitting tightly into a hole, used to fill a gap or cavity or act as a wedge or stopper. **2 a** device of metal pins in an insulated casing, fitting into holes in a socket for making an electrical connection. **b** *colloq.* electric socket. **3** = SPARK-PLUG. **4** *colloq.* piece of free publicity for an idea, product, etc. **5** cake or stick of tobacco; piece of this for chewing. *–v.* (**-gg-**) **1** (often foll. by *up*) stop (a hole etc.) with a plug. **2** *slang* shoot or hit (a person etc.). **3** *colloq.* seek to popularize (an idea, product, etc.) by constant recommendation. **4** *colloq.* (foll. by *away (at)*) work steadily (at). □ **plug in** connect electrically by inserting a plug into a socket. [Low German or Dutch]

plug-compatible see COMPATIBILITY 3.

plug-hole *n.* hole, esp. in a sink or bath, which can be closed by a plug.

plug-in *attrib. adj.* designed to be plugged into a socket.

plum *n.* **1 a** small sweet oval fleshy fruit with a flattish pointed stone. **b** tree bearing this. **2** reddish-purple colour. **3** raisin used in cooking. **4** *colloq.* something prized (often *attrib.*: *plum job*). □ **have a plum in one's mouth** have an affectedly rich voice. [Latin: related to PRUNE[1]]

plumage /ˈpluːmɪdʒ/ *n.* bird's feathers. [French: related to PLUME]

plumb /plʌm/ *–n.* lead ball, esp. attached to the end of a line for finding the depth of water or testing whether a wall etc. is vertical. *–adv.* **1** exactly (*plumb in the centre*). **2** vertically. **3** *US slang* quite, utterly (*plumb crazy*). *–adj.*

vertical. –*v.* **1 a** provide with plumbing. **b** (often foll. by *in*) fit as part of a plumbing system. **c** work as a plumber. **2** sound or test with a plumb. **3** reach or experience (an extreme feeling) (*plumb the depths of fear*). **4** learn in detail the facts about (a matter). □ **out of plumb** not vertical. [Latin *plumbum* lead]

plumber *n.* person who fits and repairs the apparatus of a water-supply, heating, etc.

plumbing *n.* **1** system or apparatus of water-supply etc. **2** work of a plumber. **3** *colloq.* lavatory installations.

plumb-line *n.* line with a plumb attached.

plume /pluːm/ –*n.* **1** feather, esp. a large one used for ornament. **2** ornament of feathers etc. worn on a helmet or hat or in the hair. **3** something resembling this (*plume of smoke*). –*v.* (**-ming**) **1** decorate or provide with a plume or plumes. **2** *refl.* (foll. by *on, upon*) pride (oneself on esp. something trivial). **3** (of a bird) preen (itself or its feathers). [Latin *pluma*]

plummet /'plʌmɪt/ –*n.* **1** plumb, plumb-line. **2** sounding-line. **3** weight attached to a fishing-line to keep the float upright. –*v.* (**-t-**) fall or plunge rapidly. [French: related to PLUMB]

plummy *adj.* (**-ier, -iest**) **1** abounding or rich in plums. **2** *colloq.* (of a voice) sounding affectedly rich in tone. **3** *colloq.* good, desirable.

plump[1] –*adj.* full or rounded in shape; fleshy. –*v.* (often foll. by *up, out*) make or become plump (*plumped up the cushion*). □ **plumpness** *n.* [Low German or Dutch *plomp* blunt]

plump[2] –*v.* **1** (foll. by *for*) decide on, choose. **2** (often foll. by *down*) drop or fall abruptly. –*n.* abrupt or heavy fall. –*adv. colloq.* with a plump. [Low German or Dutch *plompen*, imitative]

plum pudding *n.* = CHRISTMAS PUDDING.

plumy /'pluːmɪ/ *adj.* (**-ier, -iest**) **1** plumelike, feathery. **2** adorned with plumes.

plunder /'plʌndə(r)/ –*v.* **1** rob or steal, esp. in wartime; loot. **2** exploit (another person's or common property) for one's own profit. –*n.* **1** activity of plundering. **2** property so acquired. [German *plündern*]

plunge –*v.* (**-ging**) **1** (usu. foll. by *in, into*) **a** thrust forcefully or abruptly. **b** dive. **c** (cause to) enter a condition or embark on a course impetuously (*they plunged into marriage; the room was plunged into darkness*). **2** immerse completely. **3 a** move suddenly and dramatically downward. **b** (foll. by *down, into*, etc.) move with a rush (*plunged down the stairs*). **4** *colloq.* run up gambling debts. –*n.* plunging action or movement; dive. □ **take the plunge** *colloq.* take a decisive step. [Romanic: related to PLUMB]

plunger *n.* **1** part of a mechanism that works with a plunging or thrusting movement. **2** rubber cup on a handle for clearing blocked pipes by a plunging and sucking action.

pluperfect /pluː'pɜːfɪkt/ *Gram.* –*adj.* (of a tense) denoting an action completed prior to some past point of time as: *he had gone by then*. –*n.* pluperfect tense. [Latin *plus quam perfectum* more than perfect]

plural /'plʊər(ə)l/ –*adj.* **1** more than one in number. **2** *Gram.* (of a word or form) denoting more than one. –*n. Gram.* **1** plural word or form. **2** plural number. [Latin: related to PLUS]

pluralism *n.* **1** form of society embracing many minority groups and cultural traditions. **2** the holding of more than one office at a time, esp. in the Church. □ **pluralist** *n.* **pluralistic** /-'lɪstɪk/ *adj.*

plurality /plʊə'rælɪtɪ/ *n.* (*pl.* **-ies**) **1** state of being plural. **2** = PLURALISM 2. **3** large number. **4** *US* majority that is not absolute.

pluralize /'plʊərə,laɪz/ *v.* (also **-ise**) (**-zing** or **-sing**) make plural, express in the plural.

plus –*prep.* **1** with the addition of (symbol +). **2** (of temperature) above zero (*plus 2°*). **3** *colloq.* with; having gained; newly possessing. –*adj.* **1** (after a number) at least (*fifteen plus*). **2** (after a grade etc.) rather better than (*beta plus*). **3** *Math.* positive. **4** having a positive electrical charge. **5** (*attrib.*) additional, extra. –*n.* **1** the symbol +. **2** additional or positive quantity. **3** advantage. –*conj. colloq.* also; and furthermore. [Latin, = more]

■ **Usage** The use of *plus* as a conjunction, as in *they arrived late, plus they wanted a meal*, is considered incorrect by some people.

plus-fours *n.pl.* men's long wide knickerbockers. [the length was increased by 4 inches to create an overhang]

plush –*n.* cloth of silk or cotton etc., with a long soft nap. –*adj.* **1** made of plush. **2** *colloq.* = PLUSHY. □ **plushly** *adv.* **plushness** *n.* [Latin: related to PILE[3]]

plushy *adj.* (**-ier, -iest**) *colloq.* stylish, luxurious. □ **plushiness** *n.*

Pluto /'pluːtəʊ/ *n.* outermost known planet of the solar system. [Greek *Ploutōn* god of the underworld]

plutocracy /pluː'tɒkrəsɪ/ *n.* (*pl.* **-ies**) **1 a** government in which power is in the hands of the wealthy, i.e. landowners, industrialists, and bankers. **b** state so governed. **2** wealthy élite. □ **plutocratic** /-ə'krætɪk/ *adj.* [Greek *ploutos* wealth]

plutocrat /'pluːtə,kræt/ *n.* **1** member of a plutocracy. **2** wealthy person.

plutonic /pluː'tɒnɪk/ *adj.* formed as igneous rock by solidification below the surface of the earth. [Latin *Pluto*, god of the underworld]

plutonium /pluː'təʊnɪəm/ *n.* radioactive metallic element. [*Pluto*, name of a planet]

pluvial /'pluːvɪəl/ *adj.* **1** of rain; rainy. **2** *Geol.* caused by rain. [Latin *pluvia* rain]

♦ **pluvial insurance** *n.* (also **pluvius insurance**) insurance against loss of income or profits caused by rain or other weather conditions. The main demand comes from the organizers of outdoor summer events, who could suffer financially if rain caused the event to be curtailed or abandoned. For events in which any profits would be uncertain, e.g. a summer fete, the policy specifies that claims are to be based on the number of millimetres of rain that fall in an agreed period at an agreed weather station near to the site of the event. If the amount of lost revenue can be easily calculated from ticket sales at an event (e.g. a cricket test match or tennis match), a policy paying for lost profit can be arranged.

---

ply[1] /plaɪ/ *n.* (*pl.* **-ies**) **1** thickness or layer of cloth or wood etc. **2** strand of yarn or rope etc. [French *pli*: related to PLAIT]

ply[2] /plaɪ/ *v.* (**-ies, -ied**) **1** use or wield (a tool, weapon, etc.). **2** work steadily at (*ply one's trade*). **3** (foll. by *with*) **a** supply continuously (with food, drink, etc.). **b** approach repeatedly (with questions, etc.). **4 a** (often foll. by *between*) (of a vehicle etc.) travel regularly to and fro. **b** work (a route) thus. **5** (of a taxi-driver etc.) attend regularly for custom (*ply for hire*). [from APPLY]

Plymouth /'plɪməθ/ **1** port and naval base in SW England, on the Devon coast; clothing and processed foods are manufactured; pop. (est. 1994) 255 800. **2** capital and chief port of the island of Montserrat in the West Indies; pop. (1991) 3500.

Plymouth Brethren *n.pl.* Calvinistic religious body with no formal creed and no official order of ministers. [PLYMOUTH 1]

plywood *n.* strong thin board made by gluing layers of wood with the direction of the grain alternating.

PL/Z *abbr.* Programming Language Zilog.

Plzeň see PILSEN.

PM *abbr.* **1** prime minister. **2** post-mortem. **3** preventive (or predictive) maintenance (esp. of computers).

Pm *symb.* promethium.

pm. *abbr.* premium.

p.m. *abbr.* after noon. [Latin *post meridiem*]

PMBX *abbr. Telephony* private manual branch exchange.

PMC *abbr.* Personnel Management Centre.

PMD *abbr.* (in the US) Program for Management Development.

PMG *abbr.* Paymaster General.

p.m.h. *abbr.* per man-hour.

PML *abbr. Insurance* probable maximum loss.

PMS *abbr.* **1** premenstrual syndrome. **2** project management system.

PMT *abbr.* **1** premenstrual tension. **2** project management team. **3** post-market trading.

P/N *abbr.* (also **PN, p.n.**) promissory note.

pneumatic /njuːˈmætɪk/ *adj.* **1** filled with air or wind (*pneumatic tyre*). **2** operated by compressed air (*pneumatic drill*). [Greek *pneuma* wind]

pneumoconiosis /ˌnjuːməʊˌkɒnɪˈəʊsɪs/ *n.* lung disease caused by the inhalation of dust or small particles. [Greek *pneumōn* lung, *konis* dust]

pneumonia /njuːˈməʊnɪə/ *n.* inflammation of one or both lungs. [Greek *pneumōn* lung]

PNG *abbr.* & *international vehicle registration* Papua New Guinea.

PNYA *abbr.* Port of New York Authority.

PO *–abbr.* **1** Patent Office. **2** personnel officer. **3** Petty Officer. **4** Pilot Officer. **5** postal order. **6** Post Office. *–postcode* Portsmouth.

Po *symb.* polonium.

po /pəʊ/ *n.* (*pl.* **-s**) *colloq.* chamber-pot. [from POT[1]]

POA *abbr.* Prison Officers' Association (trade union).

poach[1] *v.* **1** cook (an egg) without its shell in or over boiling water. **2** cook (fish etc.) by simmering in a small amount of liquid. □ **poacher** *n.* [French *pochier*: related to POKE[2]]

poach[2] *v.* **1** (also *absol.*) catch (game or fish) illegally. **2** (often foll. by *on*) trespass or encroach on (another's property, territory, etc.). **3** appropriate (another's ideas, staff, etc.). □ **poacher** *n.* [earlier *poche*: related to POACH[1]]

pock *n.* (also **pock-mark**) small pus-filled spot on the skin, esp. caused by chickenpox or smallpox. □ **pock-marked** *adj.* [Old English]

pocket /ˈpɒkɪt/ *–n.* **1** small bag sewn into or on clothing, for carrying small articles. **2** pouchlike compartment in a suitcase, car door, etc. **3** one's financial resources (*beyond my pocket*). **4** isolated group or area (*pockets of resistance*). **5** cavity in the earth containing ore, esp. gold. **6** pouch at the corner or on the side of a billiard- or snooker-table into which balls are driven. **7** = AIR POCKET. **8** (*attrib.*) **a** small enough or intended for carrying in a pocket. **b** smaller than the usual size. *–v.* (**-t-**) **1** put into one's pocket. **2** appropriate, esp. dishonestly. **3** confine as in a pocket. **4** submit to (an injury or affront). **5** conceal or suppress (one's feelings). **6** *Billiards* etc. drive (a ball) into a pocket. □ **in pocket** having gained in a transaction. **in a person's pocket 1** under a person's control. **2** close to or intimate with a person. **out of pocket** having lost in a transaction. [Anglo-French diminutive: related to POKE[2]]

pocketbook *n.* **1** notebook. **2** folding case for papers or money carried in a pocket.

pocketful *n.* (*pl.* **-s**) as much as a pocket will hold.

pocket knife *n.* = PENKNIFE.

pocket money *n.* money for minor expenses, esp. given to children.

POD *abbr.* **1** pay(ment) on delivery. **2** port of debarkation.

pod *–n.* long seed-vessel, esp. of a pea or bean. *–v.* (**-dd-**) **1** bear or form pods. **2** remove (peas etc.) from pods. [origin unknown]

Podgorica /ˈpɒdgɒˌriːtsə/ (formerly (1948–92) **Titograd**) city in the Federal Republic of Yugoslavia, capital of Montenegro; pop. (1991) 117 875.

podgy /ˈpɒdʒɪ/ *adj.* (**-ier, -iest**) **1** short and fat. **2** plump, fleshy. □ **podginess** *n.* [*podge* short fat person]

podium /ˈpəʊdɪəm/ *n.* (*pl.* **-s** or **podia**) rostrum. [Greek *podion* diminutive of *pous pod-* foot]

POE *abbr.* **1** port of embarkation. **2** port of entry.

poem /ˈpəʊɪm/ *n.* **1** metrical composition, usu. concerned with feeling or imaginative description. **2** elevated composition in verse or prose. **3** something with poetic qualities (*a poem in stone*). [Greek *poieō* make]

poesy /ˈpəʊəzɪ/ *n. archaic* poetry. [French, ultimately as POEM]

poet /ˈpəʊɪt/ *n.* (*fem.* **poetess**) **1** writer of poems. **2** highly imaginative or expressive person. [Greek *poiētēs*: related to POEM]

poetaster /ˌpəʊɪˈtæstə(r)/ *n.* inferior poet. [from POET, Latin *-aster* derogatory suffix]

poetic /pəʊˈetɪk/ *adj.* (also **poetical**) of or like poetry or poets. □ **poetically** *adv.*

poetic justice *n.* very appropriate punishment or reward.

poetic licence *n.* writer's or artist's transgression of established rules for effect.

Poet Laureate *n.* (*pl.* **Poets Laureate**) poet appointed to write poems for state occasions.

poetry /ˈpəʊɪtrɪ/ *n.* **1** art or work of a poet. **2** poems collectively. **3** poetic or tenderly pleasing quality. [medieval Latin: related to POET]

po-faced *adj.* **1** solemn-faced, humourless. **2** smug. [perhaps from PO, influenced by *poker-faced*]

pogo /ˈpəʊgəʊ/ *n.* (*pl.* **-s**) (also **pogo stick**) stiltlike toy with a spring, used for jumping about on. [origin uncertain]

pogrom /ˈpɒgrəm/ *n.* organized massacre (orig. of Jews in Russia). [Russian]

poignant /ˈpɔɪnjənt/ *adj.* **1** painfully sharp to the emotions or senses; deeply moving. **2** arousing sympathy. **3** sharp or pungent in taste or smell. **4** pleasantly piquant. □ **poignance** *n.* **poignancy** *n.* **poignantly** *adv.* [Latin: related to POINT]

poinsettia /pɔɪnˈsetɪə/ *n.* plant with large scarlet bracts surrounding small yellow flowers. [*Poinsett*, name of a diplomat]

point *–n.* **1** sharp or tapered end of a tool, weapon, pencil, etc. **2** tip or extreme end. **3** that which in geometry has position but not magnitude. **4** particular place or position. **5** precise or critical moment (*when it came to the point, he refused*). **6** very small mark on a surface. **7** dot or other punctuation mark. **8** = DECIMAL POINT. **9** stage or degree in progress or increase (*abrupt to the point of rudeness*). **10** temperature at which a change of state occurs (*freezing-point*). **11** single item or particular (*explained it point by point*). **12** unit of scoring in games or of measuring value etc. **13** significant or essential thing; what is intended or under discussion (*the point of my question; get to the point*). **14** sense, purpose; advantage, value (*saw no point in staying*). **15** characteristic (*tact is not his strong point*). **16 a** each of 32 directions marked at equal distances round a compass. **b** corresponding direction towards the horizon. **17** (usu. in *pl.*) pair of movable tapering rails that allow a train to pass from one line to another. **18** = POWER POINT. **19** (usu. in *pl.*) electrical contact in the distributor of a vehicle. **20** *Cricket* **a** fielder on the off side near the batsman. **b** this position. **21** tip of the toe in ballet. **22** promontory. **23** (usu. in *pl.*) extremities of a dog, horse, etc. **24** unit of measurement (1/12 pica or 1/72 inch) used in printing and typography. **25** *Finance* = TICK[1] *n.* 4. *–v.* **1** (usu. foll. by *to, at*) **a** direct or aim (a finger, weapon, etc.). **b** direct attention. **2** (foll. by *at, towards*) aim or be directed to. **3** (foll. by *to*) indicate; be evidence of (*it all points to murder*). **4** give force to (words or actions). **5** fill the joints of (brickwork) with smoothed mortar or cement. **6** (also *absol.*) (of a dog) indicate the presence of (game) by acting as pointer. □ **at** (or **on**) **the point of** on the verge of. **beside the point** irrelevant. **in point** relevant (*the case in point*). **in point of fact** see FACT. **make a point of** insist on (doing etc.); treat or regard as essential; call particular attention to (an action). **point out** indicate; draw attention to. **point up** emphasize. **to the point** relevant; relevantly. **up to a point** to some extent but not completely. [Latin *pungo punct-* prick]

point-blank *–adj.* **1 a** (of a shot) aimed or fired at very close range. **b** (of a range) very close. **2** (of a remark etc.) blunt, direct. *–adv.* **1** at very close range. **2** directly, bluntly.

point-duty *n.* traffic control by a police officer, esp. at a road junction.

Pointe-à-Pitre /ˌpwætɑːˈpiːtr/ largest town in Guadeloupe, the chief port and commercial centre of the islands; pop. (1990) 26 029.

pointed *adj.* **1** sharpened or tapering to a point. **2** (of a remark etc.) having point; cutting. **3** emphasized. □ **pointedly** *adv.*

Pointe-Noire /ˌpwætˈnwɑː(r)/ chief seaport and oil terminal of the Republic of Congo; pop. (est. 1995) 576 206.

pointer *n.* **1** thing that points or indicates, e.g. the index hand of a gauge. See also POINTING DEVICE. **2** rod for pointing to features on a chart etc. **3** *colloq.* hint. **4** dog of a breed that on scenting game stands rigid looking towards it. **5** (in *pl.*) two stars in the Great Bear in line with the pole star.

pointillism /ˈpwæntɪˌlɪz(ə)m/ *n.* technique of impressionist painting using tiny dots of pure colour which become blended in the viewer's eye. □ **pointillist** *n.* & *adj.* [French *pointiller* mark with dots]

pointing *n.* **1** cement filling the joints of brickwork. **2** facing produced by this.

pointing device *n.* device, e.g. a mouse, light pen, or cursor key, that identifies a point on a display screen and transmits its location to a computer.

pointless *adj.* lacking purpose or meaning; ineffective, fruitless. □ **pointlessly** *adv.* **pointlessness** *n.*

point of honour *n.* thing of great importance to one's reputation or conscience.

point of no return *n.* point in a journey or enterprise at which it becomes essential or more practical to continue to the end.

point of order *n.* query in a debate etc. as to whether correct procedure is being followed.

♦ **point of sale** *n.* (also **POS**) place at which a consumer makes a purchase, usu. a retail shop. It may, however, also be a doorstep (in door-to-door selling), a market stall, or a mail-order house. See also ELECTRONIC POINT OF SALE.

---

point of view *n.* **1** position from which a thing is viewed. **2** way of considering a matter.

point-to-point *n.* steeplechase for hunting horses.

poise /pɔɪz/ *–n.* **1** composure, self-possession. **2** equilibrium. **3** carriage (of the head etc.). *–v.* (**-sing**) **1** balance; hold suspended or supported. **2** be balanced or suspended. [Latin *pendo pens-* weigh]

poised *adj.* **1 a** composed, self-assured. **b** carrying oneself gracefully or with dignity. **2** (often foll. by *for*, or *to* + infin.) ready for action.

poison /ˈpɔɪz(ə)n/ *–n.* **1** substance that when introduced into or absorbed by a living organism causes death or injury, esp. one that kills by rapid action even in a small quantity. **2** *colloq.* harmful influence. *–v.* **1** administer poison to. **2** kill, injure, or infect with poison. **3** treat (a weapon) with poison. **4** corrupt or pervert (a person or mind). **5** spoil or destroy (a person's pleasure etc.). □ **poisoner** *n.* **poisonous** *adj.* [Latin: related to POTION]

poison ivy *n.* North American climbing plant secreting an irritant oil from its leaves.

poison-pen letter *n.* malicious anonymous letter.

♦ **poison pill** *n.* tactic that is used by a company fearing an unwanted take-over to ensure that a successful take-over bid will trigger some event that substantially reduces the value of the company. Examples of such tactics include the sale of some prized asset to a friendly company or bank or the issue of securities with a conversion option enabling the bidder's shares to be bought at a reduced price if the bid is successful. See also PORCUPINE PROVISIONS; STAGGERED DIRECTORSHIPS.

Poitiers /ˈpwætɪˌeɪ/ city in W central France, the capital of Poitou-Charentes region; there are metallurgical, textile, and other industries; pop. (1990) 78 894.

Poitou /pwæˈtuː/ former province of W central France now united with Charentes to form Poitou-Charentes region.

poke[1] *–v.* (**-king**) **1 a** thrust or push with the hand, a stick, etc. **b** (foll. by *out, up*, etc.) be thrust forward, protrude. **2** (foll. by *at* etc.) make thrusts. **3** thrust the end of a finger etc. against. **4** (foll. by *in*) produce (a hole etc. in a thing) by poking. **5** stir (a fire) with a poker. **6 a** (often foll. by *about, around*) potter. **b** (foll. by *about, into*) pry; search. **7** *coarse slang* have sexual intercourse with. *–n.* **1** act of poking. **2** thrust, nudge. □ **poke fun at** ridicule. **poke one's nose into** *colloq.* pry or intrude into. [German or Dutch]

poke[2] *n. dial.* bag, sack. □ **buy a pig in a poke** see PIG. [French dial.]

poker[1] *n.* metal rod for stirring a fire.

poker[2] *n.* card-game in which bluff is used as players bet on the value of their hands. [origin unknown]

Poland /ˈpəʊlənd/, **Republic of** country in NE Europe, with a coastline on the Baltic Sea, bordered by Germany, the Czech Republic, Slovakia, Ukraine, Belarus, and Lithuania. Despite rapid advances in urbanization and industrialization, Poland is still affected by severe economic problems. Agriculture and forestry are important sectors of the economy, producing timber, livestock, rye, oats, wheat, potatoes, sugar beet, and other crops. There are deposits of copper, iron, sulphur, and natural gas, and some of the largest coalfields in the world; copper and coal are exported. Industries include shipbuilding, engineering, textiles, chemicals, and food processing; manufactured exports include machinery, transport equipment, iron and steel, chemicals, light industrial products, and foodstuffs. Implementation of market reforms and restructuring of the formerly state-run industry (over half of output now comes from the private sector) has resulted in increased productivity; exports to Western markets have increased and Poland is seeking entry into the European Community.
History. The dominant E European power in the 16th century, Poland suffered severely from the rise of Russian, Swedish, Prussian, and Austrian power, losing territory and eventually its independent identity by 1795; the country did not regain full independence (as a republic) until after the First World War. Its invasion by German forces in 1939 precipitated the Second World War, and after 1945 it was dominated by the USSR until the late 1980s, when the rise of the independent trade union movement Solidarity, led by Lech Walesa, brought about democratic reforms. Multiparty elections held in 1989 resulted in the first non-Communist government for nearly 45 years; this was followed by a succession of coalition governments. In 1997 a new constitution was approved and Poland was invited to join NATO. Polish membership of the EU has been approved. President, Lech Walesa; prime minister, Jerzy Buzek; capital, Warsaw.

language	Polish
currency	zloty (Zl) of 100 groszy
pop. (1996)	38 731 000
GNP (1994)	US$94.6B
literacy	99% (m); 99% (f)
life expectancy	67 (m); 76 (f)

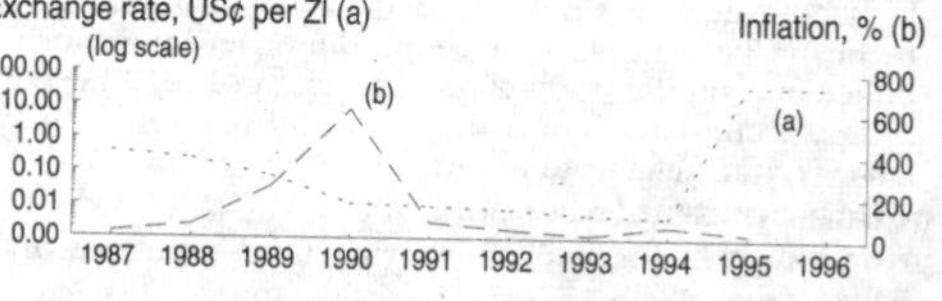

poker-face *n.* impassive countenance assumed by a poker-player. □ **poker-faced** *adj.*

poky /ˈpəʊkɪ/ *adj.* (**-ier**, **-iest**) (of a room etc.) small and cramped. □ **pokiness** *n.* [from POKE[1]]

polar /ˈpəʊlə(r)/ **1** *adj.* of or near a pole of the earth or of the celestial sphere. **2** having magnetic or electric polarity. **3** directly opposite in character. [Latin: related to POLE[2]]

polar bear *n.* large white bear living in the Arctic regions.

polar circle *n.* each of the circles parallel to the equator at 23° 27′ from either pole.

polarity /pəˈlærɪtɪ/ *n.* (*pl.* **-ies**) **1** tendency of a magnet etc. to point with its extremities to the magnetic poles of the earth or of a body to lie with its axis in a particular direction. **2** state of having two poles with contrary qualities. **3** state of having two opposite tendencies, opinions, etc. **4** electrical condition of a body (positive or negative). **5** attraction towards an object.

polarize /ˈpəʊləˌraɪz/ *v.* (also **-ise**) (**-zing** or **-sing**) **1** restrict the vibrations of (light-waves etc.) to one direction. **2** give magnetic or electric polarity to. **3** divide into two opposing groups. □ **polarization** /-ˈzeɪʃ(ə)n/ *n.*

Polaroid /ˈpəʊləˌrɔɪd/ *n. propr.* **1** material in thin sheets polarizing light passing through it. **2** camera with internal processing that produces a print rapidly after each exposure. **3** (in *pl.*) sunglasses with Polaroid lenses.

polder /ˈpəʊldə(r)/ *n.* piece of land reclaimed from the sea or a river, esp. in the Netherlands. [Dutch]

Pole *n.* **1** native or national of Poland. **2** person of Polish descent. [German from Polish]

pole[1] *n.* **1** long slender rounded piece of wood, metal, etc., esp. with the end placed in the ground as a support etc. **2** = PERCH[1] 3. □ **up the pole** *slang* **1** crazy. **2** in difficulty. [Latin *palus* stake]

pole[2] *n.* **1** (in full **north pole, south pole**) **a** each of the two points in the celestial sphere about which the stars appear to revolve. **b** each of the ends of the axis of rotation of the earth (*North Pole*; *South Pole*). **2** each of the two opposite points on the surface of a magnet at which magnetic forces are strongest. **3** each of two terminals (positive and negative) of an electric cell or battery etc. **4** each of two opposed principles. □ **be poles apart** differ greatly. [Greek, = axis]

■ **Usage** The spelling is *North Pole* and *South Pole* when used as geographical designations.

poleaxe /ˈpəʊlæks/ (*US* **-ax**) *–n.* **1** *hist.* = BATTLEAXE 1. **2** butcher's axe. *–v.* (**-xing**) **1** hit or kill with a poleaxe. **2** (esp. as **poleaxed** *adj.*) *colloq.* dumbfound, overwhelm. [Low German or Dutch: related to POLL, AXE]

polecat /ˈpəʊlkæt/ *n.* **1** small brownish-black mammal of the weasel family. **2** *US* skunk. [origin unknown]

pole-jump var. of POLE-VAULT.

polemic /pəˈlemɪk/ *–n.* **1** forceful verbal or written controversy or argument. **2** (in *pl.*) art or practice of controversial discussion. *–adj.* (also **polemical**) involving dispute; controversial. □ **polemicist** /-sɪst/ *n.* [Greek *polemos* war]

pole star *n.* **1** star in the Little Bear, near the North Pole in the sky. **2** thing serving as a guide.

pole-vault (also **pole-jump**) *–n.* vault, or sport of vaulting, over a high bar with the aid of a pole held in the hands. *–v.* perform this. □ **pole-vaulter** *n.*

police /pəˈliːs/ *–n.* (as *pl.*) **1** (usu. prec. by *the*) the civil force responsible for maintaining public order. **2** its members. **3** force with similar functions (*military police*). *–v.* (**-cing**) **1** keep (a place or people) in order by means of police or a similar body. **2** provide with police. **3** keep in order, administer, control (*problem of policing the new law*). [Latin: related to POLICY[1]]

police constable see CONSTABLE.

police dog *n.* dog, esp. an Alsatian, used in police work.

police force *n.* body of police of a country, district, or town.

policeman *n.* (*fem.* **policewoman**) member of a police force.

police officer *n.* member of a police force.

police state *n.* totalitarian state controlled by political police.

police station *n.* office of a local police force.

policy[1] /ˈpɒlɪsɪ/ *n.* (*pl.* **-ies**) **1** course of action adopted by a government, business, individual, etc. **2** prudent conduct; sagacity. [Latin *politia* POLITY]

■ **Usage** See note at *polity*.

policy[2] /ˈpɒlɪsɪ/ *n.* (*pl.* **-ies**) **1** contract of insurance. **2** document containing this. See INSURANCE POLICY. [French *police*, ultimately from Greek *apodeixis* proof]

policyholder *n.* person or body holding an insurance policy.

♦ **policy mix** *n.* combination of fiscal, monetary, and other policies employed by a government to achieve an economic objective.

♦ **policy proof of interest** *n.* (also **PPI**) insurance policy (usu. marine insurance) in which the insurers agree that they will not insist on the usual requirement that the insured must prove an insurable interest existed in the subject matter before a claim is paid. The possession of the policy is all that is required. These policies are a matter of trust between insurer and insured as they are not legally enforceable. They are issued for convenience in cases in which an insurable interest exists but is extremely difficult to prove or in which an insurable interest might come into existence later in the voyage.

---

polio /ˈpəʊlɪəʊ/ *n.* = POLIOMYELITIS. [abbreviation]

poliomyelitis /ˌpəʊlɪəʊˌmaɪəˈlaɪtɪs/ *n.* infectious viral disease of the grey matter of the central nervous system with temporary or permanent paralysis. [Greek *polios* grey, *muelos* marrow]

Polish /ˈpəʊlɪʃ/ *–adj.* **1** of Poland. **2** of the Poles or their language. *–n.* language of Poland.

polish /ˈpɒlɪʃ/ *–v.* (often foll. by *up*) **1** make or become smooth or glossy by rubbing. **2** (esp. as **polished** *adj.*) refine or improve; add the finishing touches to. *–n.* **1** substance used for polishing. **2** smoothness or glossiness produced by friction. **3** refinement, elegance. □ **polish off** finish (esp. food) quickly. [Latin *polio*]

polite /pəˈlaɪt/ *adj.* (**politer**, **politest**) **1** having good manners; courteous. **2** cultivated, refined. □ **politely** *adv.* **politeness** *n.* [Latin *politus*: related to POLISH]

politic /ˈpɒlɪtɪk/ *–adj.* **1** (of an action) judicious, expedient. **2** (of a person) prudent, sagacious. **3** political (now only in *body politic*). *–v.* (**-ck-**) engage in politics. [Greek: related to POLITY]

political /pəˈlɪtɪk(ə)l/ *adj.* **1 a** of or concerning the state or its government, or public affairs generally. **b** of or engaged in politics. **2** taking or belonging to a side in politics. **3** concerned with seeking power, status, etc. (*political decision*). □ **politically** *adv.* [Latin: related to POLITIC]

political asylum *n.* state protection given to a political refugee from another country.

political economy *n.* study of the economic aspects of government.

political geography *n.* geography dealing with boundaries and the possessions of states.

political prisoner *n.* person imprisoned for political reasons.

political science *n.* study of political activity and systems of government.

politician /ˌpɒlɪˈtɪʃ(ə)n/ *n.* **1** person involved in politics, esp. professionally as an MP. **2** esp. *US derog.* person who manoeuvres; schemer, time-server.

politicize /pəˈlɪtɪˌsaɪz/ *v.* (also **-ise**) (**-zing** or **-sing**) **1 a** give a political character to. **b** make politically aware. **2** engage in or talk politics. □ **politicization** /-ˈzeɪʃ(ə)n/ *n.*

politico /pəˈlɪtɪˌkəʊ/ *n.* (*pl.* **-s**) *colloq.* politician or political enthusiast. [Spanish]

politics /ˈpɒlɪtɪks/ *n.pl.* **1** (treated as *sing.* or *pl.*) **a** art and science of government. **b** public life and affairs. **2** (usu.

treated as *pl.*) political principles or practice (*what are his politics?*). **3** activities concerned with seeking power, status, etc.

polity /ˈpɒlɪtɪ/ *n.* (*pl.* **-ies**) **1** form or process of civil government. **2** organized society; state. [Greek *politēs* citizen from *polis* city]

■ **Usage** This word is sometimes confused with *policy*.

polka /ˈpɒlkə/ *–n.* **1** lively dance of Bohemian origin. **2** music for this. *–v.* (**-kas, -kaed** /-kəd/ or **-ka'd, -kaing** /-kəɪŋ/) dance the polka. [Czech *půlka*]

polka dot *n.* round dot as one of many forming a regular pattern on a textile fabric etc.

poll /pəʊl/ *–n.* **1 a** (often in *pl.*) voting or the counting of votes at an election (*go to the polls*). **b** result of voting or number of votes recorded. **2** = OPINION POLL. **3** human head. *–v.* **1 a** take the vote or votes of. **b** receive (so many votes). **c** give (a vote). **2** record the opinion of (a person or group) in an opinion poll. **3** cut off the top of (a tree or plant), esp. make a pollard of. **4** (esp. as **polled** *adj.*) cut the horns off (cattle). [perhaps from Low German or Dutch]

pollack /ˈpɒlək/ *n.* (also **pollock**) (*pl.* same or **-s**) edible marine fish related to the cod. [origin unknown]

pollard /ˈpɒləd/ *–n.* **1** animal that has lost or cast its horns; ox, sheep, or goat of a hornless breed. **2** tree whose branches have been cut back to encourage the dense growth of young branches. *–v.* make (a tree) a pollard. [from POLL]

pollen /ˈpɒlən/ *n.* fine dustlike grains discharged from the male part of a flower, each containing the fertilizing element. [Latin]

pollen count *n.* index of the amount of pollen in the air, published as a warning to hay fever sufferers.

pollinate /ˈpɒlɪˌneɪt/ *v.* (**-ting**) (also *absol.*) convey pollen to or sprinkle (a stigma) with pollen. □ **pollination** /-ˈneɪʃ(ə)n/ *n.* **pollinator** *n.*

polling *n.* registering or casting of votes.

polling-booth *n.* compartment in which a voter stands to mark the ballot-paper.

polling-day *n.* election day.

polling-station *n.* building, often a school, used for voting at an election.

pollock var. of POLLACK.

pollster *n.* person who organizes an opinion poll.

poll tax *n. hist.* **1** *informal* = COMMUNITY CHARGE. **2** tax levied on every adult, being an equal levy from everyone's resources whatever their circumstances. Poll taxes do not take account of persons' ability to pay or the marginal utility of income.

pollute /pəˈluːt/ *v.* (**-ting**) **1** contaminate (the environment). **2** make foul or impure. □ **pollutant** *adj.* & *n.* **polluter** *n.* **pollution** *n.* [Latin *polluo -lut-*]

polo /ˈpəʊləʊ/ *n.* game like hockey played on horseback with a long-handled mallet. [Balti, = ball]

polonaise /ˌpɒləˈneɪz/ *n.* **1** slow dance of Polish origin. **2** music for this. [French: related to POLE]

polo-neck *n.* **1** high round turned-over collar. **2** sweater with this.

polonium /pəˈləʊnɪəm/ *n.* radioactive metallic element, occurring naturally in uranium ores. [medieval Latin *Polonia* Poland]

poltergeist /ˈpɒltəˌgaɪst/ *n.* noisy mischievous ghost, esp. one causing physical damage. [German]

poltroon /pɒlˈtruːn/ *n.* spiritless coward. □ **poltroonery** *n.* [Italian *poltro* sluggard]

poly /ˈpɒlɪ/ *n.* (*pl.* **-s**) *colloq.* polytechnic. [abbreviation]

poly- *comb. form* **1** many (*polygamy*). **2** polymerized (*polyunsaturated*; *polyester*). [Greek *polus* many]

polyandry /ˈpɒlɪˌændrɪ/ *n.* polygamy in which a woman has more than one husband. □ **polyandrous** /-ˈændrəs/ *adj.* [Greek *anēr andr-* male]

polyanthus /ˌpɒlɪˈænθəs/ *n.* (*pl.* **-thuses**) flowering plant cultivated from hybridized primulas. [Greek *anthos* flower]

polychromatic /ˌpɒlɪkrəʊˈmætɪk/ *adj.* **1** many-coloured. **2** (of radiation) containing more than one wavelength. □ **polychromatism** /-ˈkrəʊməˌtɪz(ə)m/ *n.*

polychrome /ˈpɒlɪˌkrəʊm/ *–adj.* in many colours. *–n.* polychrome work of art. [Greek: related to POLY-, CHROME]

polyester /ˌpɒlɪˈestə(r)/ *n.* synthetic fibre or resin.

polyethene /ˈpɒlɪˌeθiːn/ *n.* = POLYTHENE.

polyethylene /ˌpɒlɪˈeθɪˌliːn/ *n.* = POLYTHENE.

polygamy /pəˈlɪgəmɪ/ *n.* practice of having more than one wife or (less usu.) husband at once. □ **polygamist** *n.* **polygamous** *adj.* [Greek *gamos* marriage]

polyglot /ˈpɒlɪˌglɒt/ *–adj.* knowing, using, or written in several languages. *–n.* polyglot person. [Greek *glōtta* tongue]

polygon /ˈpɒlɪgən, -ˌgɒn/ *n.* figure with many (usu. five or more) sides and angles. □ **polygonal** /pəˈlɪgən(ə)l/ *adj.* [Greek *-gōnos* angled]

polygraph /ˈpɒlɪˌgrɑːf/ *n.* machine for reading physiological characteristics (e.g. pulse-rate); lie-detector.

polygyny /pəˈlɪdʒɪnɪ/ *n.* polygamy in which a man has more than one wife. □ **polygynous** /pəˈlɪdʒɪnəs/ *adj.* [Greek *gunē* woman]

polyhedron /ˌpɒlɪˈhiːdrən/ *n.* (*pl.* **-dra**) solid figure with many (usu. more than six) faces. □ **polyhedral** *adj.* [Greek *hedra* base]

polymath /ˈpɒlɪˌmæθ/ *n.* person of great or varied learning. [Greek *manthanō math-* learn]

polymer /ˈpɒlɪmə(r)/ *n.* compound of one or more large molecules formed from repeated units of smaller molecules. □ **polymeric** /-ˈmerɪk/ *adj.* **polymerize** *v.* (also **-ise**) (**-zing** or **-sing**). **polymerization** /-ˈzeɪʃ(ə)n/ *n.* [Greek *polumeros* having many parts]

polymorphous /ˌpɒlɪˈmɔːfəs/ *adj.* (also **polymorphic**) passing through various forms in successive stages of development.

Polynesia /ˌpɒlɪˈniːʒə/ the islands of the central and W Pacific, including those of French Polynesia, Hawaii, Samoa (see also SAMOA), Tonga, Tuvalu, and Kiribati. □ **Polynesian** *adj.* & *n.*

polynomial /ˌpɒlɪˈnəʊmɪəl/ *–n.* expression of more than two algebraic terms. *–adj.* of or being a polynomial. [from POLY-, BINOMIAL]

polyp /ˈpɒlɪp/ *n.* **1** simple organism with a tube-shaped body. **2** small usu. benign growth on a mucous membrane. [Greek *pous* foot]

polyphony /pəˈlɪfənɪ/ *n.* (*pl.* **-ies**) *Mus.* contrapuntal music. □ **polyphonic** /ˌpɒlɪˈfɒnɪk/ *adj.* [Greek *phōnē* sound]

polypropene /ˌpɒlɪˈprəʊpiːn/ *n.* = POLYPROPYLENE.

polypropylene /ˌpɒlɪˈprəʊpɪˌliːn/ *n.* any polymer of propylene, including thermoplastic materials used for films, fibres, or moulding materials.

polysaccharide /ˌpɒlɪˈsækəˌraɪd/ *n.* any of a group of complex carbohydrates, e.g. starch. [see SACCHARIN]

polystyrene /ˌpɒlɪˈstaɪəˌriːn/ *n.* a polymer of styrene, a kind of hard plastic, often foamed for packaging. [*styrene* from Greek *sturax* a resin]

polysyllabic /ˌpɒlɪsɪˈlæbɪk/ *adj.* **1** having many syllables. **2** using words of many syllables. [medieval Latin from Greek]

polysyllable /ˈpɒlɪˌsɪləb(ə)l/ *n.* polysyllabic word.

polytechnic /ˌpɒlɪˈteknɪk/ *–n.* college offering courses in many (esp. vocational) subjects up to degree level. The UK polytechnics have become universities, awarding their own degrees. *–adj.* giving instruction in various vocational or technical subjects. [Greek *tekhnē* art]

polytheism /ˈpɒlɪθiːˌɪz(ə)m/ *n.* belief in or worship of more than one god. □ **polytheist** *n.* **polytheistic** /-ˈɪstɪk/ *adj.* [Greek *theos* god]

polythene /ˈpɒlɪˌθiːn/ *n.* a tough light plastic. [from POLYETHYLENE]

polyunsaturated /ˌpɒlɪʌnˈsætʃəˌreɪtɪd/ *adj.* (of a fat or oil) having a chemical structure capable of further reaction and not contributing to the accumulation of cholesterol in the blood.

polyurethane /ˌpɒlɪˈjʊərəˌθeɪn/ *n.* synthetic resin or plastic used esp. in paints or foam. [related to UREA, ETHANE]

polyvinyl chloride /ˌpɒlɪˈvaɪnɪl/ *n.* a vinyl plastic used for electrical insulation or as a fabric etc.; PVC.

Pom *n. Austral. & NZ slang offens.* = POMMY. [abbreviation]

pomace /ˈpʌmɪs/ *n.* crushed apples in cider-making. [Latin *pomum* apple]

pomade /pəˈmɑːd/ *n.* scented ointment for the hair and head. [Italian: related to POMACE]

pomander /pəˈmændə(r)/ *n.* **1** ball of mixed aromatic substances. **2** container for this. [Anglo-French from medieval Latin]

pomegranate /ˈpɒmɪˌgrænɪt/ *n.* **1** tropical fruit with a tough rind, reddish pulp, and many seeds. **2** tree bearing this. [French *pome grenate* from Romanic, = many-seeded apple]

pomelo /ˈpʌməˌləʊ/ *n.* (*pl.* **-s**) **1** = SHADDOCK. **2** *US* = GRAPEFRUIT. [origin unknown]

pommel /ˈpʌm(ə)l/ *–n.* **1** knob, esp. at the end of a sword-hilt. **2** upward projecting front of a saddle. *–v.* (**-ll-**; *US* **-l-**) = PUMMEL. [Latin *pomum* apple]

Pommy /ˈpɒmɪ/ *n.* (also **pommie**) (*pl.* **-ies**) *Austral. & NZ slang offens.* British person, esp. a recent immigrant. [origin uncertain]

pomp *n.* **1** splendid display; splendour. **2** specious glory. [Latin from Greek *pompe*]

pom-pom /ˈpɒmpɒm/ *n.* automatic quick-firing gun. [imitative]

pompon /ˈpɒmpɒn/ *n.* (also **pompom**) **1** ornamental tuft or bobble on a hat, shoes, etc. **2** (often *attrib.*) dahlia etc. with small tightly-clustered petals. [French]

pompous /ˈpɒmpəs/ *n.* self-important, affectedly grand or solemn. □ **pomposity** /pɒmˈpɒsɪtɪ/ *n.* (*pl.* **-ies**). **pompously** *adv.* **pompousness** *n.* [Latin: related to POMP]

ponce *slang –n.* **1** man who lives off a prostitute's earnings; pimp. **2** *offens.* homosexual or effeminate man. *–v.* (**-cing**) act as a ponce. □ **ponce about** move about effeminately or ineffectually. [origin unknown]

poncho /ˈpɒntʃəʊ/ *n.* (*pl.* **-s**) cloak of a usu. blanket-like piece of cloth with a slit in the middle for the head. [South American Spanish]

pond *n.* small body of still water. [var. of POUND[3]]

ponder *v.* **1** think over; consider. **2** muse, be deep in thought. [Latin *pondero* weigh]

ponderable *adj. literary* having appreciable weight or significance. [Latin: related to PONDER]

ponderous /ˈpɒndərəs/ *adj.* **1** slow and awkward, esp. because of great weight. **2** (of style etc.) laborious; dull. □ **ponderously** *adv.* **ponderousness** *n.* [Latin *pondus -der-* weight]

Pondicherry /ˌpɒndɪˈtʃerɪ/ **1** Union Territory in SE India; rice and millet are grown; pop. (est. 1994) 894 000. **2** its capital city; pop. (1991) 203 065.

pondweed *n.* aquatic plant growing in still water.

pong *v. colloq.* stink. □ **pongy** *adj.* (**-ier, -iest**). [origin unknown]

poniard /ˈpɒnjəd/ *n.* dagger. [French *poignard* from Latin *pugnus* fist]

Pontianak /ˌpɒntɪˈɑːnæk/ seaport in Indonesia, capital of the province of West Kalimantan, on the W coast of Borneo; pop. (1990) 387 112. Rubber, sugar, and palm oil are produced, and there are also shipbuilding and timber industries.

pontiff /ˈpɒntɪf/ *n.* Pope. [Latin *pontifex -fic-* priest]

pontifical /pɒnˈtɪfɪk(ə)l/ *adj.* **1** papal. **2** pompously dogmatic. □ **pontifically** *adv.*

pontificate *–v.* /pɒnˈtɪfɪˌkeɪt/ (**-ting**) **1** be pompously dogmatic. **2** play the pontiff. *–n.* /pɒnˈtɪfɪkət/ **1** office of a bishop or pope. **2** period of this.

pontoon[1] /pɒnˈtuːn/ *n.* card-game in which players try to acquire cards with a face value totalling 21. [probably a corruption of VINGT-ET-UN]

pontoon[2] /pɒnˈtuːn/ *n.* **1** flat-bottomed boat. **2** each of several boats etc. used to support a temporary bridge. [Latin *ponto -on-* punt]

pony /ˈpəʊnɪ/ *n.* (*pl.* **-ies**) horse of any small breed. [perhaps from French *poulenet* foal]

pony-tail *n.* hair drawn back, tied, and hanging down behind the head.

pony-trekking *n.* travelling across country on ponies for pleasure.

poodle /ˈpuːd(ə)l/ *n.* dog of a breed with a curly coat that is usu. clipped. [German *Pudel*]

poof /pʊf/ *n.* (also **poofter**) *slang offens.* effeminate or homosexual man. [origin unknown]

pooh /puː/ *int.* expressing impatience, contempt, or disgust at a bad smell. [imitative]

pooh-pooh /puːˈpuː/ *v.* express contempt for, ridicule. [reduplication of POOH]

pool[1] *n.* **1** small body of still water. **2** small shallow body of any liquid. **3** swimming-pool. **4** deep place in a river. [Old English]

pool[2] *–n.* **1 a** common supply of persons, vehicles, commodities, etc. for sharing by a group of people. **b** group of persons sharing duties etc. **2** common fund, e.g. of profits of separate firms or of players' stakes in gambling. **3** arrangement between competing parties to fix prices and share business. **4** *US* **a** game on a billiard-table with usu. 16 balls. **b** game on a billiard-table in which each player has a ball of a different colour with which he or she tries to pocket the others in fixed order, the winner taking all of the stakes. *–v.* **1** put into a common fund. **2** share in common. [French *poule*]

pools *n.pl.* (prec. by *the*) = FOOTBALL POOL.

Poona see PUNE.

poop *n.* stern of a ship; the aftermost and highest deck. [Latin *puppis*]

poor *adj.* **1** without enough money to live comfortably. **2** (foll. by *in*) deficient in (a possession or quality). **3 a** scanty, inadequate. **b** less good than is usual or expected (*poor visibility; is a poor driver*). **c** paltry; inferior (*came a poor third*). **4** deserving pity or sympathy; unfortunate (*you poor thing*). **5** spiritless, despicable. □ **poor man's** inferior or cheaper substitute for. [Latin *pauper*]

poorhouse *n. hist.* = WORKHOUSE.

poor law *n. hist.* law concerning public support of the poor.

poorly *–adv.* in a poor manner, badly. *–predic. adj.* unwell.

poor relation *n.* inferior or subordinate member of a family etc.

POP *abbr.* **1** (also **p.o.p.**) point of purchase. **2** Post Office preferred (size of envelopes etc.). **3** proof of purchase.

pop[1] *–n.* **1** sudden sharp explosive sound as of a cork when drawn. **2** *colloq.* effervescent drink. *–v.* (**-pp-**) **1** (cause to) make a pop. **2** (foll. by *in, out, up*, etc.) go, move, come, or put unexpectedly or abruptly (*pop out to the shop*). **3** *slang* pawn. *–adv.* with the sound of a pop (*go pop*). □ **pop off** *colloq.* die. **pop the question** *colloq.* propose marriage. [imitative]

pop[2] *n. colloq.* **1** (in full **pop music**) highly successful commercial music, esp. since the 1950s. **2** (*attrib.*) of or relating to pop music (*pop concert, group, song*). **3** pop record or song (*top of the pops*). [abbreviation]

pop[3] *n.* esp. *US colloq.* father. [from PAPA]

pop. *abbr.* population.

popadam var. of POPPADAM.

pop art *n.* art based on modern popular culture and the mass media.

popcorn *n.* Indian corn which bursts open when heated.

pop culture *n.* commercial culture based on popular taste.

pope *n.* head of the Roman Catholic Church (*the Pope; we have a new pope*). [Greek *papas* patriarch]

popery /ˈpəʊpərɪ/ *n. derog.* papal system; Roman Catholicism.

pop-eyed *adj. colloq.* **1** having bulging eyes. **2** wide-eyed (with surprise etc.).

popgun *n.* child's toy gun shooting pellets etc. by the compression of air.

popinjay /ˈpɒpɪnˌdʒeɪ/ *n.* fop, conceited person. [Arabic *babagha* parrot]

popish /ˈpəʊpɪʃ/ *adj. derog.* Roman Catholic.

poplar /ˈpɒplə(r)/ *n.* tall slender tree with a straight trunk and often tremulous leaves. [Latin *populus*]

poplin /ˈpɒplɪn/ *n.* plain-woven fabric usu. of cotton, with a corded surface. [French *papeline*]

poppadam /ˈpɒpədəm/ *n.* (also **poppadom, popadam**) *Ind.* thin, crisp, spiced bread eaten with curry etc. [Tamil]

popper *n.* **1** *colloq.* press-stud. **2** thing that pops (*party popper*).

poppet /ˈpɒpɪt/ *n. colloq.* (esp. as a term of endearment) small or dainty person. [Latin *pup(p)a* doll]

popping-crease *n. Cricket* line in front of and parallel to the wicket, within which the batsman stands. [from POP[1]]

poppy /ˈpɒpɪ/ *n.* (*pl.* **-ies**) **1** plant with showy esp. scarlet flowers and a milky sap. **2** artificial poppy worn on Remembrance Sunday. [Latin *papaver*]

poppycock *n. slang* nonsense. [Dutch *pappekak*]

Poppy Day *n.* = REMEMBRANCE SUNDAY.

populace /ˈpɒpjʊləs/ *n.* the common people. [Italian: related to POPULAR]

popular /ˈpɒpjʊlə(r)/ *adj.* **1** liked by many people. **2 a** of or for the general public. **b** prevalent among the general public (*popular fallacies*). **3** (sometimes *derog.*) adapted to the understanding, taste, or means of the people (*popular science*; *the popular press*). □ **popularity** /-ˈlærɪtɪ/ *n.* **popularly** *adv.* [Anglo-Latin *populus* PEOPLE]

popular front *n.* party or coalition combining left-wing groups.

popularize *v.* (also **-ise**) (**-zing** or **-sing**) **1** make popular. **2** present (a difficult subject) in a readily understandable form. □ **popularization** /-ˈzeɪʃ(ə)n/ *n.*

popular music *n.* any music that appeals to a wide public.

populate /ˈpɒpjʊˌleɪt/ *v.* (**-ting**) **1** inhabit, form the population of. **2** supply with inhabitants. [medieval Latin: related to PEOPLE]

population /ˌpɒpjʊˈleɪʃ(ə)n/ *n.* **1** inhabitants of a place, country, etc. **2** total number of these or any group of living things.

population explosion *n.* sudden large increase of population.

◆ **population projection** *n.* forecast of the size of a population at some future date. For example, the population projection for the UK in 2001–2006 is 58 957 000, based on a 1985 projection.

◆ **population pyramid** *n.* diagram that illustrates the distribution of a population by age. The youngest and most numerous age group forms a rectangle at the base of the pyramid; the oldest and least numerous is a small rectangle at its apex.

---

populist /ˈpɒpjʊlɪst/ *n.* politician claiming to represent the ordinary people. [Latin *populus* people]

populous /ˈpɒpjʊləs/ *adj.* thickly inhabited.

pop-up *adj.* involving parts that pop up automatically (*pop-up toaster*; *pop-up book*).

p.o.r. *abbr.* **1** pay(able) on receipt. **2** port of refuge.

porcelain /ˈpɔːsəlɪn/ *n.* **1** hard fine translucent ceramic with a transparent glaze. **2** objects made of this. [Italian diminutive of *porca* sow]

porch *n.* covered entrance to a building. [Latin *porticus*]

porcine /ˈpɔːsaɪn/ *adj.* of or like pigs. [Latin: related to PORK]

porcupine /ˈpɔːkjʊˌpaɪn/ *n.* rodent with a body and tail covered with erectile spines. [Provençal: related to PORK, SPINE]

◆ **porcupine provisions** *n.pl.* (also **shark repellents**) provisions made by a company to deter take-over bids. See POISON PILL; STAGGERED DIRECTORSHIPS.

---

pore[1] *n.* esp. *Biol.* minute opening in a surface through which fluids etc. may pass. [Greek *poros*]

pore[2] *v.* (**-ring**) (foll. by *over*) **1** be absorbed in studying (a book etc.). **2** meditate on. [origin unknown]

Pori /ˈpɔːrɪ/ port in SW Finland, on the Gulf of Bothnia; it has copper-refining, wood-processing, chemical, and textile industries; pop. (1994) 76 561.

pork *n.* flesh (esp. unsalted) of a pig, used as food. [Latin *porcus* pig]

porker *n.* pig raised for food.

pork pie *n.* pie of minced pork etc. eaten cold.

pork pie hat *n.* hat with a flat crown and a brim turned up all round.

porky *adj.* (**-ier, -iest**) **1** *colloq.* fat. **2** of or like pork.

porn *–n.* (also **porno**) *colloq.* pornography. *–attrib. adj.* pornographic. [abbreviation]

pornography /pɔːˈnɒgrəfɪ/ *n.* **1** explicit representation of sexual activity in literature, films, etc., intended to stimulate erotic rather than aesthetic or emotional feelings. **2** literature etc. containing this. □ **pornographic** /-nəˈgræfɪk/ *adj.* [Greek *pornē* prostitute]

porous /ˈpɔːrəs/ *adj.* **1** full of pores. **2** letting through air, water, etc. □ **porosity** /pɔːˈrɒsɪtɪ/ *n.* [Latin: related to PORE[1]]

porphyry /ˈpɔːrfɪrɪ/ *n.* (*pl.* **-ies**) hard rock composed of crystals of white or red feldspar in a red matrix. □ **porphyritic** /-ˈrɪtɪk/ *adj.* [Greek: related to PURPLE]

porpoise /ˈpɔːpəs/ *n.* sea mammal of the whale family, with a blunt rounded snout. [Latin *porcus* pig, *piscis* fish]

porridge /ˈpɒrɪdʒ/ *n.* **1** dish of oatmeal or cereal boiled in water or milk. **2** *slang* imprisonment. [alteration of POTTAGE]

porringer /ˈpɒrɪndʒə(r)/ *n.* small bowl, often with a handle, for soup etc. [French *potager*: related to POTTAGE]

Port. *abbr.* **1** Portugal. **2** Portuguese.

port[1] *n.* **1** harbour. **2** town possessing a harbour. [Latin *portus*]

port[2] *n.* a kind of sweet fortified wine. [*Oporto* in Portugal]

port[3] *–n.* left-hand side of a ship or aircraft looking forward. *–v.* (also *absol.*) turn (the helm) to port. [probably originally the side turned to PORT[1]]

port[4] *–n.* **1** opening in the side of a ship for entrance, loading, etc. **2** porthole. **3 a** point at which a connection can be made between an input/output device and the central processor of a computer system, allowing data to be passed. **b** point through which data can enter or leave a computer network. *–v.* move (a program) from one computer system to another. [Latin *porta* gate]

portable /ˈpɔːtəb(ə)l/ *–adj.* **1** easily movable, convenient for carrying. **2 a** (of a right, opinion, etc.) capable of being transferred or adapted in altered circumstances (*portable pension*). **b** (of a computer program) readily transferable from one computer to others, usu. being written in a high-level language possessing an internationally agreed standard. *–n.* portable version of an item, e.g. a television or microcomputer. □ **portability** /ˌpɔːtəˈbɪlɪtɪ/ *n.* [Latin *porto* carry]

portage /ˈpɔːtɪdʒ/ *–n.* **1** carrying of boats or goods overland between two navigable waters. **2** place where this is necessary. *–v.* (**-ging**) convey (a boat or goods) over a portage. [Latin *porto* carry]

Portakabin /ˈpɔːtəˌkæbɪn/ *n. propr.* prefabricated room or small building. [from PORTABLE, CABIN]

portal /ˈpɔːt(ə)l/ *n.* doorway or gate etc., esp. an elaborate one. [Latin: related to PORT[4]]

Port Arthur /ˈɑːθə(r)/ see LÜDA.

Port-au-Prince /ˌpɔːtəʊˈprɪns/ capital of Haiti; coffee and sugar are exported; pop. (est. 1995) 846 594.

portcullis /pɔːtˈkʌlɪs/ *n.* strong heavy grating lowered to block a gateway in a fortress etc. [French, = sliding door]

Port Elizabeth /ɪˈlɪzəbəθ/ seaport in SE South Africa, in Eastern Cape province; ore is exported and there are fruit-canning and flour-milling industries; pop. (1991) 303 353.

portend /pɔːˈtend/ *v.* **1** foreshadow as an omen. **2** give warning of. [Latin *portendo*: related to PRO-[1], TEND[1]]

portent /ˈpɔːtent/ *n.* **1** omen, significant sign of something to come. **2** prodigy; marvellous thing. [Latin *portentum*: related to PORTEND]

portentous /pɔːˈtentəs/ *adj.* **1** like or being a portent. **2** pompously solemn.

porter[1] *n.* **1** person employed to carry luggage etc. **2** dark beer brewed from charred or browned malt. [Latin *porto* carry]

porter[2] *n.* gatekeeper or doorman, esp. of a large building. [Latin: related to PORT[4]]

porterage *n.* **1** hire of porters. **2** charge for this. [from PORTER[1]]

porterhouse steak *n.* choice cut of beef.

portfolio /pɔːtˈfəʊlɪəʊ/ *n.* (*pl.* **-s**) **1 a** folder for loose sheets of paper, drawings, etc. **b** samples of an artist's work. **2** range of investments held by a person, company, etc. In building up an investment portfolio an institution will have its own investment analysts, while an individual may make use of the services of a merchant bank that offers **portfolio management**. The choice of portfolio will depend on the mix of income and capital growth its owner expects. **3** office of a minister of state (cf. MINISTER WITHOUT PORTFOLIO). [Italian *portafogli* sheet-carrier]

♦ **portfolio insurance** *n.* use of a financial futures and options market to protect the value of a portfolio of investments. For example, a fund manager may expect the general level of prices to fall on the stock exchange. The manager could protect the portfolio by selling the appropriate number of index futures, which could then be bought back at a profit if the market falls. Alternatively, the manager could establish the value of the portfolio at current prices by buying put options, which would provide the opportunity to benefit if there was a rise in the general level of prices.

♦ **portfolio theory** *n.* analytical approach to the selection and management of a portfolio of investments. It will include a study of diversification to minimize risk, as well as a historical view of markets to survey price trends. A major aspect of portfolio theory, now that index and equity futures and options can be bought and sold, will be portfolio insurance. The theory, as well as considering risks and capital growth, will also be concerned with the structure of portfolios in relation to their expected income.

Port-Gentil /ˌpɔːʒɑ̃ˈtiː/ principal port and industrial centre of Gabon; industries include oil refining; pop. (1993) 80 841.

Port Harcourt /ˈhɑːkɔːt/ principal seaport of SE Nigeria; coal and tin are exported; pop. (est. 1995) 399 700.

Port Hedland /ˈhedlənd/ seaport in Western Australia, on the NW coast, linked by rail to the iron-ore mines at Newman; pop. (est. 1987) 13 600.

porthole *n.* aperture (esp. glazed) in a ship's side for letting in light.

portico /ˈpɔːtɪˌkəʊ/ *n.* (*pl.* **-es** or **-s**) colonnade; roof supported by columns at regular intervals, usu. attached as a porch to a building. [Latin *porticus* porch]

portion /ˈpɔːʃ(ə)n/ –*n.* **1** part or share. **2** amount of food allotted to one person. **3** one's destiny or lot. –*v.* **1** divide (a thing) into portions. **2** (foll. by *out*) distribute. [Latin *portio*]

Portland /ˈpɔːtlənd/ city in the US, an industrial river port in NW Oregon; manufactures include electronic goods, aluminium, and paper products; pop. (est. 1994) 450 777.

Portland cement *n.* cement manufactured from chalk and clay. [Isle of *Portland* in Dorset]

Portland stone *n.* building limestone from the Isle of Portland.

Port Louis /ˈluːɪ/ capital of Mauritius; pop. (est. 1994) 144 474.

portly /ˈpɔːtlɪ/ *adj.* (**-ier**, **-iest**) corpulent; stout. [Latin *porto* carry]

portmanteau /pɔːtˈmæntəʊ/ *n.* (*pl.* **-s** or **-x** /-təʊz/) trunk for clothes etc., opening into two equal parts. [Latin *porto* carry: related to MANTLE]

portmanteau word *n.* word combining the sounds and meanings of two others, e.g. *motel*, *Oxbridge*.

♦ **port mark** *n.* mark on the packages of goods destined for export, giving the name of the overseas port to which they are to be shipped or sent by air freight.

Port Moresby /ˈmɔːzbɪ/ capital and chief port of Papua New Guinea, on the S coast of the island of New Guinea; pop. (1990) 193 242.

Porto see OPORTO.

Pôrto Alegre /ˌpɔːtəʊ əˈlegrə, əˈleɪgreɪ/ major port in SE

Portugal /ˈpɔːtjʊg(ə)l/, **Republic of** country in SW Europe, occupying the W part of the Iberian peninsula, bordering on the Atlantic Ocean. As one of the poorer European countries, Portugal has benefited from membership of the European Community (which it joined in 1986): there has been strong export growth and substantial foreign investment. The agricultural sector produces olives (and olive oil), fortified wines (esp. port), and table wines for export; cereals, rice, vegetables, citrus fruits, and figs are also grown. Forestry and fishing are also important, with cork, wood products, and sardines being exported. There are deposits of iron ore, copper pyrites, uranium, kaolin, sodium, wolfram, and other minerals. Manufacturing industry is expanding and now accounts for a substantial proportion of the country's exports, including textiles, footwear, machinery, transport equipment, chemicals, processed food (e.g. canned fish), glassware, and pottery. Tourism is also a major source of revenue.

History. Portugal became an independent kingdom in the 12th century and between the 14th and 16th centuries emerged as one of the leading European colonial powers. Independence was lost to Spain in 1580 and not regained until 1688, by which time Portugal's importance in European affairs had declined. The country has been a republic since 1911, after the expulsion of the monarchy in 1910. The long and repressive dictatorship (1932–68) of Salazar was followed by a period of political instability and military rule; constitutional government was restored in 1976 and stability was further increased by reforms in the 1980s. Portugal joined the EC (now EU) in 1986. A socialist president was elected in 1996. President, Jorge Sampaio; prime minister, António Guterres; capital, Lisbon.

language	Portuguese
currency	escudo (Esc) of 100 centavos
pop. (1996)	9 927 000
GNP (1994)	US$92B
literacy	86% (m); 87% (f)
life expectancy	71 (m); 78 (f)

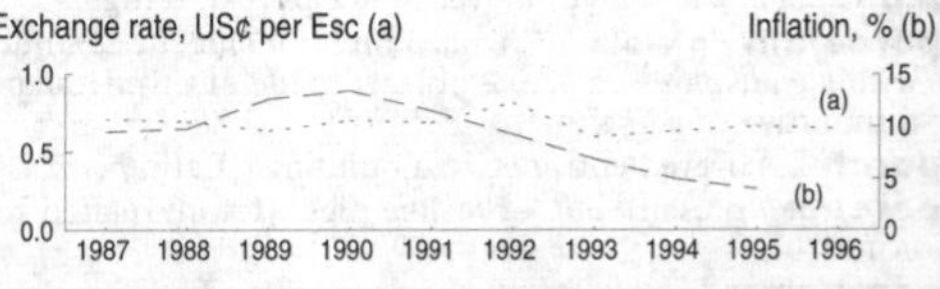

Brazil, a centre of commerce with meat-processing and textile industries; pop. (1991) 1 237 223.

port of call *n.* place where a ship or a person stops on a journey.

Port-of-Spain capital and chief port of Trinidad and Tobago, on the W coast of Trinidad; exports include sugar, rum, and petroleum products; pop. (est. 1992) 52 451.

Porto Novo /ˌpɔːtəʊ 'nəʊvəʊ/ capital of Benin, a seaport on the Gulf of Guinea; pop. (1992) 177 660.

Port Pirie /'pɪrɪ/ port in South Australia, NW of Adelaide on the Spencer Gulf; pop. (est. 1991) 12 216. Ores mined at Broken Hill in New South Wales are refined in Port Pirie.

portrait /'pɔːtrɪt/ *n.* **1** drawing, painting, photograph, etc. of a person or animal, esp. of the face. **2** description in words. □ **portraitist** *n.* [French: related to PORTRAY]

portraiture /'pɔːtrɪtʃə(r)/ *n.* **1** making portraits. **2** description in words. **3** portrait.

portray /pɔː'treɪ/ *v.* **1** make a likeness of. **2** describe in words. □ **portrayal** *n.* **portrayer** *n.* [French *portraire -trait* depict]

Port Said /saɪd/ seaport in Egypt, at the N end of the Suez Canal; pop. (est. 1994) 460 000.

Portsmouth /'pɔːtsməθ/ port and naval base in S England, on the Hampshire coast; industries include ship maintenance, aircraft engineering, electronics, and tourism; pop. (est. 1994) 189 100.

Port Stanley see STANLEY.

Port Sudan chief port of Sudan, on the Red Sea; pop. (1993) 305 385.

Portuguese /ˌpɔːtʃʊ'giːz/ *–n.* (*pl.* same) **1 a** native or national of Portugal. **b** person of Portuguese descent. **2** language of Portugal. *–adj.* of Portugal, its people, or language. [medieval Latin]

Portuguese man-of-war *n.* (*pl.* **men-**) jellyfish with a large crest and poisonous sting.

♦ **POS** *abbr.* = POINT OF SALE.

---

pose /pəʊz/ *–v.* (**-sing**) **1** assume a certain attitude of the body, esp. when being photographed or painted. **2** (foll. by *as*) pretend to be (another person etc.) (*posing as a celebrity*). **3** behave affectedly to impress others. **4** put forward or present (a question etc.). **5** place (an artist's model etc.) in a certain attitude. *–n.* **1** attitude of body or mind. **2** affectation, pretence. [Latin *pauso* PAUSE, confused with Latin *pono* place]

poser *n.* **1** poseur. **2** *colloq.* puzzling question or problem.

poseur /pəʊ'zɜː(r)/ *n.* person who behaves affectedly. [French *poser* POSE]

posh *colloq. –adj.* smart; upper-class. *–adv.* in an upper-class way (*talk posh*). □ **posh up** smarten up. □ **poshly** *adv.* **poshness** *n.* [perhaps from slang *posh* a dandy, money]

posit /'pɒzɪt/ *v.* (**-t-**) assume as a fact, postulate. [Latin: related to POSITION]

position /pə'zɪʃ(ə)n/ *–n.* **1** place occupied by a person or thing. **2** way in which a thing or its parts are placed or arranged. **3** proper place (*in position*). **4** advantage (*jockeying for position*). **5** attitude; view on a question. **6 a** situation in relation to others (*puts one in an awkward position*). **b** extent to which an investor, dealer, or speculator has made a commitment in the market by buying or selling securities, currencies, commodities, etc. See LONG POSITION; OPEN POSITION; SHORT POSITION. **7** rank, status; social standing. **8** paid employment. **9** place where troops etc. are posted for strategical purposes. *–v.* place in position. □ **in a position to** able to. □ **positional** *adj.* [Latin *pono posit-* place]

♦ **position audit** *n.* systematic assessment of the current situation of an organization. This usu. involves drawing up a report (either internally or through external consultants) of the strengths and weaknesses of the organization and the opportunities or threats that it faces (see SWOT). The position audit is a vital tool in designing the future strategies of a large organization.

---

positive /'pɒzɪtɪv/ *–adj.* **1** explicit; definite, unquestionable (*positive proof*). **2** (of a person) convinced, confident, or overconfident in an opinion. **3 a** absolute; not relative. **b** *Gram.* (of an adjective or adverb) expressing a simple quality without comparison. **4** *colloq.* downright (*it was a positive miracle*). **5** constructive (*positive thinking*). **6** marked by the presence and not absence of qualities (*positive reaction*). **7** esp. *Philos.* dealing only with matters of fact; practical. **8** tending in a direction naturally or arbitrarily taken as that of increase or progress. **9** greater than zero. **10** *Electr.* of, containing, or producing the kind of electrical charge produced by rubbing glass with silk; lacking electrons. **11** (of a photographic image) showing lights and shades or colours unreversed. *–n.* positive adjective, photograph, quantity, etc. □ **positively** *adv.* **positiveness** *n.* [Latin: related to POSITION]

positive acknowledgement see ACKNOWLEDGEMENT 4.

positive discrimination *n.* practice of making distinctions in favour of groups considered to be underprivileged.

♦ **positive economics** *n.pl.* (as *sing.*) economic analysis that is free of value judgements, i.e. independent of any particular ethical position or normative judgements (cf. NORMATIVE ECONOMICS). Milton Friedman first postulated that this is the proper field of economic analysis and it is on this postulate that the claim of economics to be a science rests. However, many have argued that a pure positive economics is not possible.

---

positive vetting *n.* inquiry into the background etc. of a candidate for a post involving national security.

positivism *n.* philosophical system recognizing only facts and observable phenomena. □ **positivist** *n.* & *adj.*

positron /'pɒzɪˌtrɒn/ *n. Physics* elementary particle with the same mass as but opposite (positive) charge to an electron. [*posi*tive elec*tron*]

posse /'pɒsɪ/ *n.* **1** strong force or company. **2** body of law-enforcers. [Latin, = be able]

possess /pə'zes/ *v.* **1** hold as property; own. **2** have (a faculty, quality, etc.). **3** occupy or dominate the mind of (*possessed by the devil*; *possessed by fear*). □ **be possessed of** own, have. **what possessed you?** an expression of incredulity. □ **possessor** *n.* [Latin *possideo possess-*]

possession /pə'zeʃ(ə)n/ *n.* **1** possessing or being possessed. **2** thing possessed. **3** holding or occupancy. **4** *Law* actual physical control of goods or land. A person may still have possession of goods that are lost or mislaid (but not abandoned), provided that no one else has physical possession of them. Possession may be divorced from ownership; for example, a thief has legal possession of stolen goods but not ownership. Possession usu. requires intention to possess – a person cannot unknowingly possess something. **5** (in *pl.*) property, wealth, subject territory, etc. **6** *Football* etc. control of the ball by a player.

possessive /pə'zesɪv/ *–adj.* **1** wanting to retain what one has, reluctant to share. **2** jealous and domineering. **3** *Gram.* indicating possession. *–n.* (in full **possessive case**) *Gram.* case of nouns and pronouns expressing possession. □ **possessiveness** *n.*

possibility /ˌpɒsɪ'bɪlɪtɪ/ *n.* (*pl.* **-ies**) **1** state or fact of being possible. **2** thing that may exist or happen. **3** (usu. in *pl.*) capability of being used; potential (*have possibilities*). [Latin *posse* be able]

possible /'pɒsɪb(ə)l/ *–adj.* **1** capable of existing, happening, being done, etc. **2** potential (*a possible way of doing it*). *–n.* **1** possible candidate, member of a team, etc. **2** highest possible score, esp. in shooting.

possibly *adv.* **1** perhaps. **2** in accordance with possibility (*cannot possibly go*).

possum /'pɒsəm/ *n.* **1** *colloq.* = OPOSSUM 1. **2** *Austral.* & *NZ colloq.* marsupial resembling an American opossum.

□ **play possum** *colloq.* pretend to be unconscious; feign ignorance. [abbreviation]

POST /pəʊst/ *abbr.* point-of-sale terminal. See ELECTRONIC POINT OF SALE.

post[1] /pəʊst/ *–n.* **1** long stout piece of timber or metal set upright in the ground etc. to support something, mark a position or boundary, etc. **2** pole etc. marking the start or finish of a race. *–v.* **1** (often foll. by *up*) attach (a notice etc.) in a prominent place. **2** announce or advertise by poster or list. [Latin *postis*]

post[2] /pəʊst/ *–n.* **1** official conveyance of parcels, letters, etc. (*send it by post*). **2** single collection or delivery of these; the letters etc. dispatched (*has the post arrived?*). **3** place where letters etc. are collected (*take it to the post*). *–v.* **1** put (a letter etc.) in the post. **2** (esp. as **posted** *adj.*) (often foll. by *up*) supply with information (*keep me posted*). **3 a** enter (an item) in a ledger, usu. from a book of prime entry. **b** (often foll. by *up*) complete (a ledger) in this way. [Latin: related to POSITION]

post[3] /pəʊst/ *–n.* **1** place where a soldier is stationed or which he or she patrols. **2** place of duty. **3 a** position taken up by a body of soldiers. **b** force occupying this. **c** fort. **4** job, paid employment. **5** = TRADING POST. *–v.* **1** place (soldiers, an employee, etc.). **2** appoint to a post or command. [French: related to POST[2]]

post- *prefix* after, behind. [Latin *post* (adv. and prep.)]

postage *n.* charge for sending a letter etc. by post.

postage stamp *n.* official stamp affixed to a letter etc., showing the amount of postage paid.

postal *adj.* of or by post. [French: related to POST[2]]

♦ **postal account** *n.* savings account with a bank or building society that can only be operated by letter or by automated teller machine. Postal accounts pay a higher rate of interest than those operated over the counter or by telephone.

---

postal code *n.* = POSTCODE.

postal order *n.* money order issued by the Post Office.

postbag *n.* = MAILBAG.

postbox *n.* public box for posting mail.

postcard *n.* card for sending by post without an envelope.

postcode *n.* group of letters and figures in a postal address to assist sorting, enabling the mail to reach the delivery postman. Mail marked with numbers-only codes will only reach a particular town. See also ZIP CODE.

post-coital /pəʊst'kəʊɪt(ə)l/ *adj. formal* occurring after sexual intercourse.

postdate /pəʊst'deɪt/ *v.* (**-ting**) **1** give a date later than the actual one to (a document etc.). A postdated (or forward-dated) cheque cannot be negotiated before the date written on it, irrespective of when it was signed. **2** follow in time.

♦ **post-entry duty** see OVER-ENTRY CERTIFICATE.

---

poster *n.* **1** placard or bill exhibited in a public place as an advertisement. Poster advertising accounts for less than 10% of the total advertising expenditure in the UK. See also FLY-POST. **2** large printed picture.

poste restante /ˌpəʊst re'stɑ̃t/ *n.* **1** service provided by the post offices of most countries in which letters, parcels, etc. are sent to a named post office in any of these countries for collection by the addressee (on providing some proof of identity). **2** department in a post office where letters etc. are kept till called for. [French]

posterior /pɒ'stɪərɪə(r)/ *–adj.* **1** later; coming after. **2** at the back. *–n.* (in *sing.* or *pl.*) buttocks. [Latin, comparative of *posterus*: related to POST-]

posterity /pɒ'sterɪtɪ/ *n.* **1** succeeding generations. **2** person's descendants. [Latin: related to POSTERIOR]

postern /'pɒst(ə)n/ *n. archaic* back door; side way or entrance. [Latin: related to POSTERIOR]

poster paint *n.* gummy opaque paint.

post-free *adj.* & *adv.* carried by post free, or with postage prepaid.

postgraduate /pəʊst'grædjʊət/ *–n.* person engaged in a course of study after taking a first degree. *–adj.* of or concerning postgraduates.

post-haste *adv.* with great speed.

posthumous /'pɒstjʊməs/ *adj.* **1** occurring after death. **2** (of a book etc.) published after the author's death. **3** (of a child) born after the death of its father. □ **posthumously** *adv.* [Latin *postumus* last]

postilion /pɒ'stɪljən/ *n.* (also **postillion**) person riding on the near horse of a team drawing a coach when there is no coachman. [Italian: related to POST[2]]

post-impressionism /ˌpəʊstɪm'preʃəˌnɪz(ə)m/ *n.* art intending to express the individual artist's conception of the objects represented. □ **post-impressionist** *n.* & *adj.*

post-industrial /ˌpəʊstɪn'dʌstrɪəl/ *adj.* of a society or economy which no longer relies on heavy industry.

♦ **post-Keynesianism** /ˌpəʊst'keɪnzɪənɪz(ə)m/ *n.* economic theory that attempts to re-establish the policy prescriptions of J. M. Keynes (see KEYNESIANISM) by the application of newer theories, e.g. the efficiency-wage theory and implicit contract theory. Sometimes more radical approaches, including Marxism, are used to defend Keynesian policies. In general, post-Keynesianism is an area in which there has been much research but limited success. □ **post-Keynesian** *n.* & *adj.*

---

postman *n.* (*fem.* **postwoman**) person employed to deliver and collect letters etc.

postmark *–n.* official mark on a letter, giving the place, date, etc., and cancelling the stamp. *–v.* mark (an envelope etc.) with this.

postmaster *n.* (*fem.* **postmistress**) official in charge of a post office.

post-modern /pəʊst'mɒd(ə)n/ *adj.* (in the arts etc.) of the movement reacting against modernism, esp. by drawing attention to former conventions. □ **post-modernism** *n.* **post-modernist** *n.* & *adj.*

post-mortem /pəʊst'mɔːtəm/ *–n.* **1** examination made after death, esp. to determine its cause. **2** *colloq.* discussion after a game, election, etc. *–adv.* & *adj.* after death. [Latin]

postnatal /pəʊst'neɪt(ə)l/ *adj.* of the period after childbirth.

Post Office *n.* **1** public department or corporation responsible for postal services. **2** (**post office**) room or building where postal business is carried on.

post-office box *n.* numbered place in a post office where letters are kept until called for.

post-paid *adj.* & *adv.* on which postage has been paid.

postpone /pəʊs'pəʊn/ *v.* (**-ning**) cause or arrange (an event etc.) to take place at a later time. □ **postponement** *n.* [Latin *pono* place]

postprandial /pəʊst'prændɪəl/ *adj. formal* or *joc.* after dinner or lunch. [Latin *prandium* a meal]

postscript /'pəʊstskrɪpt/ *n.* additional paragraph or remark, usu. at the end of a letter after the signature and introduced by 'PS'.

postulant /'pɒstjʊlənt/ *n.* candidate, esp. for admission to a religious order. [Latin: related to POSTULATE]

postulate *–v.* /'pɒstjʊˌleɪt/ (**-ting**) **1** (often foll. by *that*) assume as a necessary condition, esp. as a basis for reasoning; take for granted. **2** claim. *–n.* /'pɒstjʊlət/ **1** thing postulated. **2** prerequisite or condition. □ **postulation** /ˌpɒstjʊ'leɪʃ(ə)n/ *n.* [Latin *postulo*]

posture /'pɒstʃə(r)/ *–n.* **1** relative position of parts, esp. of the body; carriage, bearing. **2** mental attitude. **3** condition or state (of affairs etc.). *–v.* (**-ring**) **1** assume a mental or physical attitude, esp. for effect. **2** pose (a person). □ **postural** *adj.* [Latin: related to POSIT]

postwar /pəʊst'wɔː(r), 'pəʊst-/ *adj.* occurring or existing after a war.

posy /'pəʊzɪ/ *n.* (*pl.* **-ies**) small bunch of flowers. [alteration of POESY]

pot[1] *–n.* **1** rounded ceramic, metal, or glass vessel for holding liquids or solids or for cooking in. **2** flowerpot, teapot, etc. **3** contents of a pot. **4** total amount bet in a game etc. **5** (usu. in *pl.*) *colloq.* large sum (*pots of money*). **6** *slang* silver cup etc. as a trophy. *–v.* (**-tt-**) **1** place in a pot. **2** (usu. as **potted** *adj.*) preserve in a sealed pot (*potted shrimps*). **3** pocket (a ball) in billiards etc. **4** abridge or epitomize. **5** shoot at, hit, or kill (an animal) with a pot-shot. **6** seize or secure. □ **go to pot** *colloq.* deteriorate; be ruined. □ **potful** *n.* (*pl.* **-s**). [Old English from Latin]

pot[2] *n. slang* marijuana. [Mexican Spanish *potiguaya*]

potable /ˈpəʊtəb(ə)l/ *adj.* drinkable. [Latin *poto* drink]

potage /pɒˈtɑːʒ/ *n.* thick soup. [French: related to POT[1]]

potash /ˈpɒtæʃ/ *n.* an alkaline potassium compound. [Dutch: related to POT[1], ASH[1]]

potassium /pəˈtæsɪəm/ *n.* soft silver-white metallic element. [from POTASH]

potation /pəˈteɪʃ(ə)n/ *n.* **1** a drink. **2** drinking. [Latin: related to POTION]

potato /pəˈteɪtəʊ/ *n.* (*pl.* **-es**) **1** starchy plant tuber used for food. **2** plant bearing this. [Spanish *patata* from Taino *batata*]

potato crisp *n.* = CRISP *n.*

pot-belly *n.* **1** protruding stomach. **2** person with this.

pot-boiler *n.* piece of art, writing, etc. done merely to earn money.

pot-bound *adj.* (of a plant) with roots filling the flower-pot, leaving no room to expand.

poteen /pɒˈtʃiːn/ *n. Ir.* illicit alcoholic spirit. [Irish *poitín* diminutive of *pota* POT[1]]

potent /ˈpəʊt(ə)nt/ *adj.* **1** powerful; strong. **2** (of a reason) cogent; forceful. **3** (of a male) capable of sexual erection or orgasm. □ **potency** *n.* [Latin *potens -ent-*: related to POSSE]

potentate /ˈpəʊtənˌteɪt/ *n.* monarch or ruler. [Latin: related to POTENT]

potential /pəˈtenʃ(ə)l/ *–adj.* capable of coming into being or action; latent. *–n.* **1** capacity for use or development. **2** usable resources. **3** *Physics* quantity determining the energy of mass in a gravitational field or of charge in an electric field. □ **potentiality** /-ʃɪˈælɪtɪ/ *n.* **potentially** *adv.* [Latin: related to POTENT]

potential difference *n.* difference of electric potential between two points.

◆ **potential entrant** *n.* organization that is poised to enter a market and would do so if there was a small price rise or a reduction in barriers to entry. In monopoly situations, the existence of potential entrants holds potential profits in check.

◆ **potentially exempt transfer** *n.* (also **PET**) gift that is not subject to inheritance tax when it is made, although it may become taxable if the donor dies within a specified period. See LIFETIME TRANSFER.

---

pother /ˈpɒðə(r)/ *n. literary* noise, commotion, fuss. [origin unknown]

pot-herb *n.* herb grown in a kitchen garden.

pothole *n.* **1** deep hole or cave system in rock. **2** hole in a road surface. □ **potholer** *n.* **potholing** *n.*

pot-hook *n.* **1** hook over a hearth for hanging or lifting a pot. **2** curved stroke in handwriting.

pot-hunter *n.* **1** person who hunts for game at random. **2** person who competes merely for the prize.

potion /ˈpəʊʃ(ə)n/ *n.* dose of a liquid medicine, drug, poison, etc. [Latin *poto* drink]

pot luck *n.* whatever is available.

Potosí /ˌpɒtəʊˈsiː/ chief mining city and industrial centre of S Bolivia; pop. (est. 1993) 123 327.

pot plant *n.* plant grown in a flowerpot.

pot-pourri /pəʊˈpʊərɪ/ *n.* (*pl.* **-s**) **1** scented mixture of dried petals and spices. **2** musical or literary medley. [French, = rotten pot]

pot roast *n.* piece of meat cooked slowly in a covered dish. □ **pot-roast** *v.*

Potsdam /ˈpɒtsdæm/ industrial city in Germany, situated just W of Berlin; pop. (est. 1995) 138 268.

potsherd /ˈpɒtʃɜːd/ *n.* esp. *Archaeol.* broken piece of ceramic material.

pot-shot *n.* **1** random shot. **2** casual attempt.

pottage /ˈpɒtɪdʒ/ *n. archaic* soup, stew. [French: related to POT[1]]

potter[1] *v.* (*US* **putter**) **1** (often foll. by *about, around*) work or occupy oneself in a desultory manner. **2** go slowly, dawdle, loiter (*pottered up to the pub*). [dial. *pote* push]

potter[2] *n.* maker of ceramic vessels. [Old English: related to POT[1]]

potter's wheel *n.* horizontal revolving disc to carry clay during moulding.

pottery *n.* (*pl.* **-ies**) **1** vessels etc. made of fired clay. **2** potter's work. **3** potter's workshop. [French: related to POTTER[2]]

potting shed *n.* shed in which plants are potted and tools etc. are stored.

potty[1] *adj.* (**-ier, -iest**) *slang* **1** foolish, crazy. **2** insignificant, trivial. □ **pottiness** *n.* [origin unknown]

potty[2] *n.* (*pl.* **-ies**) *colloq.* chamber-pot, esp. for a child.

pouch *–n.* **1** small bag or detachable outside pocket. **2** baggy area of skin under the eyes etc. **3 a** pocket-like receptacle of marsupials. **b** similar structure in various animals, e.g. in the cheeks of rodents. *–v.* **1** put or make into a pouch. **2** take possession of; pocket. [French: related to POKE[2]]

pouffe /puːf/ *n.* large firm cushion used as a low seat or footstool. [French]

poult /pəʊlt/ *n.* young domestic fowl, turkey, pheasant, etc. [contraction of PULLET]

poulterer /ˈpəʊltərə(r)/ *n.* dealer in poultry and usu. game. [*poulter*: related to POULT]

poultice /ˈpəʊltɪs/ *–n.* soft medicated usu. heated mass applied to the body and kept in place with muslin etc., to relieve soreness and inflammation. *–v.* (**-cing**) apply a poultice to. [Latin *puls* pottage]

poultry /ˈpəʊltrɪ/ *n.* domestic fowls (ducks, geese, turkeys, chickens, etc.), esp. as a source of food. [French: related to POULT]

POUNC *abbr.* Post Office Users' National Council.

pounce *–v.* (**-cing**) **1** spring or swoop, esp. as in capturing prey. **2** (often foll. by *on, upon*) **a** make a sudden attack. **b** seize eagerly upon a remark etc. *–n.* act of pouncing. [origin unknown]

pound[1] *n.* **1** unit of weight equal to 16 oz. avoirdupois (0.4536 kg), 12 oz. troy (0.3732 kg). **2 a** (in full **pound sterling**) (*pl.* same or **-s**) standard monetary unit of the United Kingdom, the Falkland Islands, and Gibraltar. **b** standard monetary unit of Cyprus, Egypt, Lebanon, and Syria. [Latin *pondo*]

pound[2] *v.* **1** crush or beat with repeated blows. **2** (foll. by *at, on*) deliver heavy blows or gunfire. **3** (foll. by *along* etc.) make one's way heavily or clumsily. **4** (of the heart) beat heavily. [Old English]

pound[3] *n.* enclosure where stray animals or officially removed vehicles are kept until claimed. [Old English]

poundage *n.* commission, charge, tax, or fee of so much per pound sterling or weight.

pound coin *n.* coin worth one pound.

◆ **pound cost averaging** *n.* method of accumulating capital by investing a fixed sum of money in a particular share every month (or other period). When prices fall the fixed sum will buy correspondingly more shares and when prices rise fewer shares are bought. The result is that the average purchase price over a period is lower than the arithmetic average of the market prices at each purchase date (because more shares are bought at lower prices and fewer at higher prices).

---

pounder *n.* (usu. in *comb.*) **1** thing or person weighing a specified number of pounds (*a five-pounder*). **2** gun firing a shell of a specified number of pounds.

pound of flesh *n.* any legal but morally offensive demand.

pour /pɔː(r)/ *v.* **1** (usu. foll. by *down, out, over,* etc.) flow or cause to flow esp. downwards in a stream or shower. **2** dispense (a drink) by pouring. **3** rain heavily. **4** (usu. foll. by *in, out,* etc.) come or go in profusion or rapid succession (*the crowd poured out; letters poured in*). **5** discharge or send freely. **6** (often foll. by *out*) utter at length or in a rush (*poured out their story*). [origin unknown]

pourboire /pʊəˈbwɑː(r)/ *n.* gratuity, tip. [French]

pout –*v.* **1** push the lips forward as a sign of displeasure or sulking. **2** (of the lips) be pushed forward. –*n.* this action. [origin unknown]

pouter *n.* a kind of pigeon that is able to inflate its crop.

poverty /ˈpɒvətɪ/ *n.* **1** being poor; want. **2** (often foll. by *of, in*) scarcity or lack. **3** inferiority, poorness. [Latin *pauper*]

poverty line *n.* minimum income needed for the necessities of life.

poverty-stricken *adj.* very poor.

◆ **poverty trap** *n.* situation in which an increase in the income of a low-earning household causes either a loss of state benefits or an increase in taxation that approximately equals the increase in earnings, i.e. the household faces a marginal tax rate of 100% (in some instances the marginal tax rate can exceed 100%). The poverty trap creates a disincentive to earning. Most progressive tax systems create poverty traps and policies for removing them are difficult to find.

POW *abbr.* prisoner of war.

pow *int.* expressing the sound of a blow or explosion. [imitative]

powder –*n.* **1** mass of fine dry particles. **2** medicine or cosmetic in this form. **3** = GUNPOWDER. –*v.* **1** apply powder to. **2** (esp. as **powdered** *adj.*) reduce to a fine powder (*powdered milk*). □ **powdery** *adj.* [Latin *pulvis -ver-* dust]

powder blue *adj.* & *n.* (as adj. often hyphenated) pale blue.

powder-puff *n.* soft pad for applying powder to the skin, esp. the face.

powder-room *n. euphem.* women's lavatory in a public building.

power –*n.* **1** ability to do or act. **2** particular faculty of body or mind. **3 a** influence, authority. **b** ascendancy, control (*the party in power*). **4** authorization; delegated authority. **5** influential person, body, or thing. **6** state having international influence. **7** vigour, energy. **8** active property or function (*heating power*). **9** *colloq.* large number or amount (*did me a power of good*). **10** capacity for exerting mechanical force or doing work (*horsepower*). **11** (often *attrib.*) mechanical or electrical energy as distinct from manual labour. **12 a** electricity supply. **b** particular source or form of energy (*hydroelectric power*). **13** *Physics* rate of energy output. **14** product obtained when a number is multiplied by itself a certain number of times (*2 to the power of 3 = 8*). **15** magnifying capacity of a lens. **16** deity. –*v.* **1** supply with mechanical or electrical energy. **2** (foll. by *up, down*) increase or decrease the power supplied to (a device); switch on or off. □ **the powers that be** those in authority. [Latin *posse* be able]

powerboat *n.* powerful motor boat.

power cut *n.* temporary withdrawal or failure of an electric power supply.

power-fail recovery *n.* automatic procedure for dealing with the effects resulting from a loss of the incoming power supply to a computer: when the voltage is restored, the program or programs that had been running can be restarted.

powerful *adj.* having much power or influence. □ **powerfully** *adv.* **powerfulness** *n.*

powerhouse *n.* **1** = POWER STATION. **2** person or thing of great energy.

powerless *adj.* **1** without power. **2** wholly unable. □ **powerlessness** *n.*

power line *n.* conductor supplying electrical power, esp. one supported by pylons or poles.

power of attorney *n.* (also **PA**) **1** authority to act for another person in legal and financial matters. **2** formal document providing this.

powerplant *n.* installation which provides power.

power point *n.* socket in a wall etc. for connecting an electrical device to the mains.

power-sharing *n.* coalition government, esp. as preferred on principle.

power station *n.* building where electrical power is generated for distribution.

powwow –*n.* meeting for discussion (orig. among North American Indians). –*v.* hold a powwow. [Algonquian]

Powys /ˈpaʊɪs, ˈpaʊɪs/ inland county of Wales; pop. (est. 1994) 120 200; county town, Llandrindod Wells. Farming is the main occupation; there is also some tourism.

pox *n.* **1** virus disease leaving pock-marks. **2** *colloq.* = SYPHILIS. [alteration of *pocks* pl. of POCK]

poxy *adj.* (**-ier, -iest**) **1** infected by pox. **2** *slang* of poor quality; worthless.

Poznań /pɒzˈnæn/ industrial city in W Poland; chemicals and glass are manufactured; pop. (est. 1995) 582 304.

PP –*abbr.* parcel post. –*international civil aircraft marking* Brazil.

pp *abbr.* pianissimo.

pp. *abbr.* pages.

p.p. *abbr.* **1** parcel post. **2** (also **pp**) = PER PRO. **3** post-paid.

PPB *abbr.* planning-programming-budgeting (system).

PPBS *abbr.* planning-programming-budgeting system.

ppd *abbr.* **1** post-paid. **2** prepaid.

◆ **PPI** abbr. **1** = POLICY PROOF OF INTEREST. **2** = PRODUCER PRICE INDEX.

p.p.m. *abbr.* parts per million.

PPMA *abbr.* Produce Packaging and Marketing Association.

PPN *abbr. Computing* public packet network. See also PACKET SWITCHING.

PPP *abbr.* **1** personal pension plan (see PERSONAL PENSION SCHEME). **2** private patients plan. **3** = PURCHASING POWER PARITY.

PPS *abbr.* **1** Parliamentary Private Secretary. **2** additional postscript. **3** (in Australia) prescribed payments system. [sense 2 from *post-postscript*]

PR *abbr.* **1** (also **P/R**) payroll. **2** *Law* personal representative. **3** proportional representation. **4** = PUBLIC RELATIONS. **5** Puerto Rico. –*postcode* Preston. –*airline flight code* Philippine Airlines.

Pr *symb.* praseodymium.

Pr. *abbr. US Finance* preferred (stock).

pr. *abbr.* **1** pair. **2** price.

practicable /ˈpræktɪkəb(ə)l/ *adj.* **1** that can be done or used. **2** possible in practice. □ **practicability** /-ˈbɪlɪtɪ/ *n.* [French: related to PRACTICAL]

practical /ˈpræktɪk(ə)l/ –*adj.* **1** of or concerned with practice rather than theory (*practical difficulties*). **2** suited to use; functional (*practical shoes*). **3** (of a person) good at making, organizing, or mending things. **4** sensible, realistic. **5** that is such in effect, virtual (*in practical control*). –*n.* practical examination or lesson. □ **practicality** /-ˈkælɪtɪ/ *n.* (*pl.* **-ies**). [Greek *praktikos* from *prassō* do]

practical joke *n.* humorous trick played on a person.

practically *adv.* **1** virtually, almost. **2** in a practical way.

practice /ˈpræktɪs/ –*n.* **1** habitual action or performance. **2 a** repeated activity undertaken in order to improve a skill. **b** session of this. **3** action as opposed to theory. **4** the work, business, or place of business of a doctor, lawyer, etc. (*has a practice in town*). **5** procedure, esp. of a specified kind (*bad practice*). –*v.* *US* var. of PRACTISE. □ **in practice 1** when actually applied; in reality. **2** skilful from recent practice. **out of practice** lacking a former skill from lack of practice. [from PRACTISE]

practise /'præktɪs/ *v.* (*US* **practice**) (**-sing** or *US* **-cing**) **1** perform habitually; carry out in action. **2** do repeatedly as an exercise to improve a skill; exercise oneself in or on (an activity requiring skill). **3** (as **practised** *adj.*) experienced, expert. **4** (also *absol.*) be engaged in (a profession, religion, etc.). [Latin: related to PRACTICAL]

practitioner /præk'tɪʃənə(r)/ *n.* person practising a profession, esp. medicine.

praenomen /priː'nəʊmen/ *n.* ancient Roman's first or personal name (e.g. *Marcus* Tullius Cicero). [Latin: related to PRE-, NOMEN]

praetor /'priːtə(r)/ *n.* ancient Roman magistrate below consul. [Latin]

praetorian guard /priː'tɔːrɪən/ *n.* bodyguard of the ancient Roman emperor.

pragmatic /præg'mætɪk/ *adj.* dealing with matters from a practical point of view. □ **pragmatically** *adv.* [Greek *pragma -mat-* deed]

pragmatism /'prægmə,tɪz(ə)m/ *n.* **1** pragmatic attitude or procedure. **2** philosophy that evaluates assertions solely by their practical consequences and bearing on human interests. □ **pragmatist** *n.* [Greek *pragma*: related to PRAGMATIC]

Prague /prɑːg/ (Czech **Praha** /'prɑːhə/) capital of the Czech Republic, an industrial centre producing motor vehicles, aircraft, chemicals, clothing, and processed food; pop. (est. 1995) 1 213 299.

Praia /'praɪə/ capital of the Republic of Cape Verde, situated on the island of São Tiago; pop. (1990) 61 644.

prairie /'preərɪ/ *n.* large area of treeless grassland, esp. in North America. [Latin *pratum* meadow]

prairie dog *n.* North American rodent making a barking sound.

prairie oyster *n.* seasoned raw egg, swallowed without breaking the yolk.

prairie wolf *n.* = COYOTE.

praise /preɪz/ –*v.* (**-sing**) **1** express warm approval or admiration of. **2** glorify (God) in words. –*n.* praising; commendation. [French *preisier* from Latin *pretium* price]

praiseworthy *adj.* worthy of praise.

praline /'prɑːliːn/ *n.* sweet made by browning nuts in boiling sugar. [French]

pram *n.* four-wheeled conveyance for a baby, pushed by a person on foot. [abbreviation of *perambulator*]

prance /prɑːns/ –*v.* (**-cing**) **1** (of a horse) raise the forelegs and spring from the hind legs. **2** walk or behave in an elated or arrogant manner. –*n.* prancing, prancing movement. [origin unknown]

prang *slang* –*v.* **1** crash (an aircraft or vehicle). **2** damage by impact. **3** bomb (a target) successfully. –*n.* act of pranging. [imitative]

prank *n.* practical joke; piece of mischief. [origin unknown]

prankster *n.* practical joker.

praseodymium /,preɪzɪə'dɪmɪəm/ *n.* soft silvery metallic element of the lanthanide series. [Greek *prasios* green]

prat *n. slang* **1** fool. **2** buttocks. [origin unknown]

prate –*v.* (**-ting**) **1** chatter; talk too much. **2** talk foolishly or irrelevantly. –*n.* prating; idle talk. [Low German or Dutch]

prattle /'præt(ə)l/ –*v.* (**-ling**) chatter in a childish or inconsequential way. –*n.* childish or inconsequential chatter. [Low German *pratelen*: related to PRATE]

prawn *n.* edible shellfish like a large shrimp. [origin unknown]

pray *v.* (often foll. by *for* or *to* + infin. or *that* + clause) **1** say prayers; make devout supplication. **2 a** entreat. **b** ask earnestly (*prayed to be released*). **3** (as *imper.*) *archaic* please (*pray tell me*). [Latin *precor*]

prayer[1] /'preə(r)/ *n.* **1 a** request or thanksgiving to God or an object of worship. **b** formula used in praying (*the Lord's prayer*). **c** act of praying. **d** religious service consisting largely of prayers (*morning prayer*). **2** entreaty to a person. [Latin: related to PRECARIOUS]

prayer[2] /'preɪə(r)/ *n.* person who prays.

prayer-book *n.* book of set prayers.

prayer-mat *n.* small carpet on which Muslims kneel to pray.

prayer-wheel *n.* revolving cylindrical box inscribed with or containing prayers, used esp. by Tibetan Buddhists.

praying mantis see MANTIS.

pre- *prefix* before (in time, place, order, degree, or importance). [Latin *prae* before]

preach *v.* **1** (also *absol.*) deliver (a sermon); proclaim or expound (the gospel etc.). **2** give moral advice in an obtrusive way. **3** advocate or inculcate (a quality or practice etc.). □ **preacher** *n.* [Latin *praedico* proclaim]

♦ **preacquisition profit** /prɪ,ækwɪ'zɪʃ(ə)n/ *n.* retained profit of one company before it is taken over by another company. Preacquisition profits should not be distributed to the shareholders of the acquiring company by way of dividend, as such profits do not constitute income to the parent company but a partial repayment of its capital outlay on the acquisition of the shares.

---

preamble /priː'æmb(ə)l/ *n.* **1** preliminary statement. **2** introductory part of a statute or deed etc. [Latin: related to AMBLE]

pre-amp /'priːæmp/ *n.* = PREAMPLIFIER. [abbreviation]

preamplifier /priː'æmplɪ,faɪə(r)/ *n.* electronic device that amplifies a weak signal (e.g. from a microphone or pickup) and transmits it to a main amplifier.

prearrange /,priːə'reɪndʒ/ *v.* (**-ging**) arrange beforehand. □ **prearrangement** *n.*

prebend /'prebənd/ *n.* **1** stipend of a canon or member of chapter. **2** portion of land or tithe from which this is drawn. □ **prebendal** /prɪ'bend(ə)l/ *adj.* [Latin *praebeo* grant]

prebendary /'prebəndərɪ/ *n.* (*pl.* **-ies**) holder of a prebend; honorary canon. [medieval Latin: related to PREBEND]

Precambrian /priː'kæmbrɪən/ *Geol.* –*adj.* of the earliest geological era. –*n.* this era.

precarious /prɪ'keərɪəs/ *adj.* **1** uncertain; dependent on chance. **2** insecure, perilous. □ **precariously** *adv.* **precariousness** *n.* [Latin *precarius*: related to PRAY]

precast /priː'kɑːst/ *adj.* (of concrete) cast in its final shape before positioning.

precaution /prɪ'kɔːʃ(ə)n/ *n.* action taken beforehand to avoid risk or ensure a good result. □ **precautionary** *adj.* [Latin: related to CAUTION]

♦ **precautionary demand for money** *n. Econ.* amount of money that individuals or firms will wish to hold to deal with unexpected events. An element of liquidity-preference theory, the precautionary motive is affected by the prevailing interest rate, since higher interest rates will raise the opportunity cost of holding cash balances. The precautionary demand will also be affected by the level of confidence in the economy. Cf. SPECULATIVE DEMAND FOR MONEY; TRANSACTIONS DEMAND FOR MONEY.

---

precede /prɪ'siːd/ *v.* (**-ding**) **1** come or go before in time, order, importance, etc. **2** (foll. by *by*) cause to be preceded. [Latin: related to CEDE]

precedence /'presɪd(ə)ns/ *n.* **1** priority in time, order, importance, etc. **2** right of preceding others. □ **take precedence** (often foll. by *over*, *of*) have priority (over).

precedent –*n.* /'presɪd(ə)nt/ previous case etc. taken as a guide for subsequent cases or as a justification. –*adj.* /prɪ'siːd(ə)nt, 'presɪ-/ preceding in time, order, importance, etc. [French: related to PRECEDE]

♦ **preceding-year basis** *n.* basis on which UK taxes are assessed. Income or profits are charged to tax in the year in which they are assessed, which is normally the financial year following the one in which they were earned.

---

precentor /prɪ'sentə(r)/ *n.* person who leads the singing or (in a synagogue) the prayers of a congregation. [Latin *praecentor* from *cano* sing]

precept /'pri:sept/ *n.* **1** rule or guide, esp. for conduct. **2** lawful demand, esp. from one authority to another to levy rates. [Latin *praeceptum* maxim, order]

preceptor /prɪ'septə(r)/ *n.* teacher, instructor. □ **preceptorial** /ˌpri:sep'tɔ:rɪəl/ *adj.* [Latin: related to PRECEPT]

precession /prɪ'seʃ(ə)n/ *n.* slow movement of the axis of a spinning body around another axis. [Latin: related to PRECEDE]

precession of the equinoxes *n.* **1** slow retrograde motion of equinoctial points along the ecliptic. **2** resulting earlier occurrence of equinoxes in each successive sidereal year.

pre-Christian /pri:'krɪstʃ(ə)n/ *adj.* before Christianity.

precinct /'pri:sɪŋkt/ *n.* **1** enclosed area, e.g. around a cathedral, college, etc. **2** designated area in a town, esp. where traffic is excluded. **3** (in *pl.*) environs. [Latin *praecingo -cinct-* encircle]

preciosity /ˌpreʃɪ'ɒsɪtɪ/ *n.* affected refinement in art etc., esp. in the choice of words. [related to PRECIOUS]

precious /'preʃəs/ *–adj.* **1** of great value or worth. **2** beloved; much prized (*precious memories*). **3** affectedly refined. **4** *colloq.* often *iron.* **a** considerable (*a precious lot of good*). **b** expressing contempt or disdain (*keep your precious flowers!*). *–adv. colloq.* extremely, very (*had precious little left*). □ **preciousness** *n.* [Latin *pretium* price]

precious metals *n.pl.* gold, silver, and platinum.

precious stone *n.* piece of mineral of great value, esp. as used in jewellery.

precipice /'presɪpɪs/ *n.* **1** vertical or steep face of a rock, cliff, mountain, etc. **2** dangerous situation. [Latin *praeceps -cipit-* headlong]

precipitate *–v.* (**-ting**) /prɪ'sɪpɪˌteɪt/ **1** hasten the occurrence of; cause to occur prematurely. **2** (foll. by *into*) send rapidly into a certain state or condition (*was precipitated into war*). **3** throw down headlong. **4** *Chem.* cause (a substance) to be deposited in solid form from a solution. **5** *Physics* condense (vapour) into drops and so deposit it. *–adj.* /prɪ'sɪpɪtət/ **1** headlong; violently hurried (*precipitate departure*). **2** (of a person or act) hasty, rash. *–n.* /prɪ'sɪpɪtət/ **1** *Chem.* substance precipitated from a solution. **2** *Physics* moisture condensed from vapour, e.g. rain, dew.

precipitation /prɪˌsɪpɪ'teɪʃ(ə)n/ *n.* **1** precipitating or being precipitated. **2** rash haste. **3 a** rain or snow etc. falling to the ground. **b** quantity of this.

precipitous /prɪ'sɪpɪtəs/ *adj.* **1 a** of or like a precipice. **b** dangerously steep. **2** = PRECIPITATE *adj.*

précis /'preɪsi:/ *–n.* (*pl.* same /-si:z/) summary, abstract. *–v.* (**-cises** /-si:z/; **-cised** /-si:d/; **-cising** /-si:ɪŋ/) make a précis of. [French]

precise /prɪ'saɪs/ *adj.* **1 a** accurately expressed. **b** definite, exact. **2** punctilious; scrupulous in being exact. [Latin *praecido* cut short]

precisely *adv.* **1** in a precise manner; exactly. **2** (as a reply) quite so, as you say.

precision /prɪ'sɪʒ(ə)n/ *n.* **1** accuracy. **2** degree of exactness or refinement in measurement etc. **3** (*attrib.*) marked by or adapted for precision (*precision instruments*).

preclinical /pri:'klɪnɪk(ə)l/ *adj.* of the first, chiefly theoretical, stage of a medical education.

preclude /prɪ'klu:d/ *v.* (**-ding**) **1** (foll. by *from*) prevent. **2** make impossible. [Latin *praecludo*: related to CLOSE[1]]

precocious /prɪ'kəʊʃəs/ *adj.* **1** often *derog.* (of esp. a child) prematurely developed in some respect. **2** (of an action etc.) indicating such development. □ **precociously** *adv.* **precociousness** *n.* **precocity** /-'kɒsɪtɪ/ *n.* [Latin *praecox -cocis* early ripe]

precognition /ˌpri:kɒg'nɪʃ(ə)n/ *n.* supposed foreknowledge, esp. of a supernatural kind.

preconceive /ˌpri:kən'si:v/ *v.* (**-ving**) form (an idea or opinion etc.) beforehand.

preconception /ˌpri:kən'sepʃ(ə)n/ *n.* preconceived idea, prejudice.

precondition /ˌpri:kən'dɪʃ(ə)n/ *n.* condition that must be fulfilled in advance.

precursor /pri:'kɜ:sə(r)/ *n.* **1 a** forerunner. **b** person who precedes in office etc. **2** harbinger. [Latin *praecurro -curs-* run before]

predate /pri:'deɪt/ *v.* (**-ting**) precede in time.

predator /'predətə(r)/ *n.* predatory animal. [Latin]

predatory *adj.* **1** (of an animal) preying naturally upon others. **2** plundering or exploiting others.

♦ **predatory pricing** *n.* pricing of goods or services at such a low level that other firms cannot compete and are forced to leave the market. While it has long been accepted that some firms resort to predatory pricing on occasions, the application of game theory to strategic behaviour has shown that predatory pricing is unlikely to occur very often as it is at least as painful for the predator as for the victim. This encourages most potential predators to look for a more cooperative plan.

---

predecease /ˌpri:dɪ'si:s/ *v.* (**-sing**) die earlier than (another person).

predecessor /'pri:dɪˌsesə(r)/ *n.* **1** former holder of an office or position with respect to a later holder. **2** ancestor. **3** thing to which another has succeeded. [Latin *decessor*: related to DECEASE]

predestine /pri:'destɪn/ *v.* (**-ning**) **1** determine beforehand. **2** ordain in advance by divine will or as if by fate. □ **predestination** /-'neɪʃ(ə)n/ *n.* [French or Church Latin: related to PRE-]

predetermine /ˌpri:dɪ'tɜ:mɪn/ *v.* (**-ning**) **1** decree beforehand. **2** predestine.

predicament /prɪ'dɪkəmənt/ *n.* difficult or unpleasant situation. [Latin: related to PREDICATE]

predicant /'predɪkənt/ *hist. –adj.* (of a religious order) engaged in preaching. *–n.* predicant person, esp. a Dominican. [Latin: related to PREDICATE]

predicate *–v.* /'predɪˌkeɪt/ **1** (also *absol.*) assert (something) about the subject of a proposition. **2** (foll. by *on*) found or base (a statement etc.) on. *–n.* /'predɪkət/ *Gram.* & *Logic* what is said about the subject of a sentence or proposition etc. (e.g. *went home* in *John went home*). □ **predicable** /'predɪkəb(ə)l/ *adj.* **predication** /-'keɪʃ(ə)n/ *n.* [Latin *praedico -dicat-* declare]

predicative /prɪ'dɪkətɪv/ *adj.* **1** *Gram.* (of an adjective or noun) forming or contained in the predicate, as *old* in *the dog is old*. **2** that predicates. [Latin: related to PREDICATE]

predict /prɪ'dɪkt/ *v.* (often foll. by *that*) foretell, prophesy. □ **predictor** *n.* [Latin *praedico -dict-* foretell]

predictable *adj.* that can be predicted or is to be expected. □ **predictability** /-'bɪlɪtɪ/ *n.* **predictably** *adv.*

prediction /prɪ'dɪkʃ(ə)n/ *n.* **1** predicting or being predicted. **2** thing predicted.

predilection /ˌpri:dɪ'lekʃ(ə)n/ *n.* (often foll. by *for*) preference or special liking. [Latin *praediligo* prefer]

predispose /ˌpri:dɪ'spəʊz/ *v.* (**-sing**) **1** influence favourably in advance. **2** (foll. by *to*, or *to* + infin.) render liable or inclined beforehand. □ **predisposition** /-pə'zɪʃ(ə)n/ *n.*

predominant /prɪ'dɒmɪnənt/ *adj.* **1** predominating. **2** being the strongest or main element. □ **predominance** *n.* **predominantly** *adv.*

predominate /prɪ'dɒmɪˌneɪt/ *v.* (**-ting**) **1** (foll. by *over*) have control. **2** be superior. **3** be the strongest or main element.

pre-echo /pri:'ekəʊ/ *n.* (*pl.* **-es**) **1** faint copy heard just before an actual sound in a recording, caused by the accidental transfer of signals. **2** foreshadowing.

pre-embryo /pri:'embrɪəʊ/ *n.* (*pl.* **-s**) potential human embryo in the first fourteen days after fertilization.

pre-eminent /pri:'emɪnənt/ *adj.* **1** excelling others. **2** outstanding. □ **pre-eminence** *n.* **pre-eminently** *adv.*

pre-empt /pri:'empt/ *v.* **1 a** forestall. **b** appropriate in advance. **2** obtain by pre-emption. [back-formation from PRE-EMPTION]

■ **Usage** *Pre-empt* is sometimes used to mean *prevent*, but this is considered incorrect in standard English.

pre-emption /priːˈempʃ(ə)n/ *n.* **1** purchase or taking by one person or party before the opportunity is offered to others. **2** right to this; first refusal. [medieval Latin *emo empt-* buy]

◆ **pre-emption rights** *n.pl.* principle, established in company law, according to which any new shares issued by a company must first be offered to the existing shareholders as the legitimate owners of the company. To satisfy this principle a company must write to every shareholder (see RIGHTS ISSUE), involving an expensive and lengthy procedure. Newer methods of issuing shares, e.g. vendor placings or bought deals, are much cheaper and easier to effect, although they violate pre-emption rights. In the US pre-emption rights have now been largely abandoned but controversy is still widespread in the UK.

pre-emptive /priːˈemptɪv/ *adj.* **1** pre-empting. **2** (of military action) intended to prevent attack by disabling the enemy.

◆ **pre-empt spot** *n.* advertising spot for a particular period of air time on television, bought in advance at a discount for use only if another advertiser does not offer to take up that time at the full rate.

preen *v.* **1** (of a bird) tidy (the feathers or itself) with its beak. **2** (of a person) smarten or admire (oneself, one's hair, clothes, etc.). **3** (often foll. by *on*) congratulate or pride (oneself). [origin unknown]

prefab /ˈpriːfæb/ *n. colloq.* prefabricated building. [abbreviation]

prefabricate /priːˈfæbrɪˌkeɪt/ *v.* (**-ting**) manufacture sections of (a building etc.) prior to their assembly on site.

preface /ˈprefəs/ –*n.* **1** introduction to a book stating its subject, scope, etc. **2** preliminary part of a speech. –*v.* (**-cing**) **1** (foll. by *with*) introduce or begin (a speech or event). **2** provide (a book etc.) with a preface. **3** (of an event etc.) lead up to (another). □ **prefatory** /-tərɪ/ *adj.* [Latin *praefatio*]

prefect /ˈpriːfekt/ *n.* **1** chief administrative officer of a district, esp. in France. **2** senior pupil in a school, helping to maintain discipline. [Latin *praeficio -fect-* set in authority over]

prefecture /ˈpriːfektʃə(r)/ *n.* **1** district under the government of a prefect. **2** prefect's office or tenure. [Latin: related to PREFECT]

prefer /prɪˈfɜː(r)/ *v.* (**-rr-**) **1** (often foll. by *to*, or *to* + infin.) like better (*prefers coffee to tea*). **2** submit (information, an accusation, etc.) for consideration. **3** promote or advance (a person). [Latin *praefero -lat-*]

preferable /ˈprefərəb(ə)l/ *adj.* to be preferred; more desirable. □ **preferably** *adv.*

preference /ˈprefərəns/ *n.* **1** preferring or being preferred. **2** thing preferred. **3** favouring of one person etc. before others. **4** prior right, esp. to the payment of debts. □ **in preference to** as a thing preferred over (another).

◆ **preference share** *n.* share in a company yielding a fixed rate of interest rather than a variable dividend. A preference share is an intermediate form of security between an ordinary share and a debenture. Preference shares, like ordinary shares but unlike debentures, usu. confer some degree of ownership of the company. In the event of liquidation, they are less likely to be paid off than debentures, but more likely than ordinary shares. Preference shares may be redeemable at a fixed or variable date; alternatively they may be undated. Sometimes they are convertible. The rights of preference shareholders vary from company to company and are set out in the articles of association. Voting rights are normally restricted, often only being available if the interest payments are in arrears. **Participating preference shares** carry additional rights to dividends, such as a further share in the profits of the company, after the ordinary shareholders have received a stated percentage. See also PREFERRED ORDINARY SHARE.

preferential /ˌprefəˈrenʃ(ə)l/ *adj.* **1** of or involving preference. **2** giving or receiving a favour. □ **preferentially** *adv.*

◆ **preferential creditor** *n.* creditor whose debt will be met in preference to those of other creditors and who thus has the best chance of being paid in full on the bankruptcy of an individual or the winding-up of a company. Preferential creditors, who are usu. paid in full after secured debts and before ordinary creditors, include the Inland Revenue in respect of PAYE, Customs and Excise in respect of VAT and car tax, the DSS in respect of National Insurance Social Security contributions, the trustees of occupational pensions schemes, and employees in respect of any remuneration outstanding.

◆ **preferential duty** *n.* specially low import duty imposed on goods from a country that has a trade agreement of a certain kind with the importing country. For example, in the days of the British Empire, imports from member countries were granted **Imperial Preference** on imported materials, which later became **Commonwealth Preference**.

◆ **preferential payment** *n.* payment made to a preferential creditor.

preferment /prɪˈfɜːmənt/ *n. formal* promotion to a higher office.

◆ **preferred ordinary share** *n.* share issued by some companies that ranks between a preference share and an ordinary share in the payment of dividends.

◆ **preferred position** *n.* desirable position for an advertisement in a publication, for which a premium is charged.

prefigure /priːˈfɪɡə(r)/ *v. formal* (**-ring**) represent or imagine beforehand.

prefix /ˈpriːfɪks/ –*n.* **1** verbal element placed at the beginning of a word to qualify its meaning (e.g. *ex-*, *non-*). **2** title before a name (e.g. *Mr*). –*v.* (often foll. by *to*) **1** add as an introduction. **2** join (a word or element) as a prefix.

pregnant /ˈpreɡnənt/ *adj.* **1** having a child or young developing in the uterus. **2** full of meaning; significant; suggestive (*a pregnant pause*). □ **pregnancy** *n.* (*pl.* **-ies**). [Latin *praegnans*]

preheat /priːˈhiːt/ *v.* heat beforehand.

prehensile /priːˈhensaɪl/ *adj. Zool.* (of a tail or limb) capable of grasping. [Latin *prehendo -hens-* grasp]

prehistoric /ˌpriːhɪˈstɒrɪk/ *adj.* **1** of the period before written records. **2** *colloq.* utterly out of date. □ **prehistory** /-ˈhɪstərɪ/ *n.*

prejudge /priːˈdʒʌdʒ/ *v.* (**-ging**) form a premature judgement on (a person, issue, etc.).

prejudice /ˈpredʒʊdɪs/ –*n.* **1 a** preconceived opinion. **b** (foll. by *against*, *in favour of*) bias, partiality. **2** harm that results or may result from some action or judgement (*to the prejudice of*). –*v.* (**-cing**) **1** impair the validity or force of (a right, claim, statement, etc.). **2** (esp. as **prejudiced** *adj.*) cause (a person) to have a prejudice. □ **without prejudice** (often foll. by *to*) without detriment (to an existing right or claim). Used as a heading to a document or letter containing an offer etc., it indicates in addition that the offer cannot be taken as the signatory's last word, bind the signatory in any way, or be used as evidence in a court of law. [Latin: related to JUDGE]

prejudicial /ˌpredʒʊˈdɪʃ(ə)l/ *adj.* (often foll. by *to*) causing prejudice; detrimental.

prelacy /ˈpreləsɪ/ *n.* (*pl.* **-ies**) **1** church government by prelates. **2** (prec. by *the*) prelates collectively. **3** office or rank of prelate. [Anglo-French from medieval Latin: related to PRELATE]

prelate /ˈprelət/ *n.* high ecclesiastical dignitary, e.g. a bishop. [Latin: related to PREFER]

prelim /'priːlɪm/ *n. colloq.* **1** preliminary university examination. **2** (in *pl.*) pages preceding the main text of a book. [abbreviation]

preliminary /prɪ'lɪmɪnərɪ/ *–adj.* introductory, preparatory. *–n.* (*pl.* **-ies**) (usu. in *pl.*) **1** preliminary action or arrangement (*dispense with the preliminaries*). **2** preliminary trial or contest. [Latin *limen* threshold]

♦ **preliminary expenses** *n.pl.* expenses involved in the formation of a company, including the cost of producing a prospectus, issuing shares, and advertising the flotation.

---

prelude /'preljuːd/ *–n.* (often foll. by *to*) **1** action, event, or situation serving as an introduction. **2** introductory part of a poem etc. **3** *Mus.* **a** introductory piece to a fugue, suite, etc. **b** short piece of a similar type. *–v.* (**-ding**) **1** serve as a prelude to. **2** introduce with a prelude. [Latin *ludo lus-* play]

premarital /priː'mærɪt(ə)l/ *adj.* existing or (esp. of sexual relations) occurring before marriage.

premature /'premətʃə(r), -'tʃʊə(r)/ *adj.* **1 a** occurring or done before the usual or proper time (*a premature decision*). **b** too hasty. **2** (of a baby) born (esp. three or more weeks) before the end of gestation. □ **prematurely** *adv.* [Latin: related to PRE-, MATURE]

premed /priː'med/ *n. colloq.* = PREMEDICATION. [abbreviation]

premedication /ˌpriːmedɪ'keɪʃ(ə)n/ *n.* medication to prepare for an operation etc.

premeditate /priː'medɪˌteɪt/ *v.* (**-ting**) think out or plan beforehand (*premeditated murder*). □ **premeditation** /-'teɪʃ(ə)n/ *n.* [Latin: related to MEDITATE]

premenstrual /priː'menstrʊəl/ *adj.* of the time shortly before each menstruation (*premenstrual tension*).

premier /'premɪə(r)/ *–n.* prime minister or other head of government. *–adj.* first in importance, order, or time. □ **premiership** *n.* [French, = first]

première /'premɪˌeə(r)/ *–n.* first performance or showing of a play or film. *–v.* (**-ring**) give a première of. [French feminine: related to PREMIER]

premise /'premɪs/ *n.* **1** *Logic* = PREMISS. **2** (in *pl.*) **a** house or other building with its grounds, outbuildings, etc. **b** *Law* houses, lands, or tenements previously specified in a document etc. □ **on the premises** in the building etc. concerned. [Latin *praemissa* set in front]

premiss /'premɪs/ *n. Logic* previous statement from which another is inferred. [var. of PREMISE]

premium /'priːmɪəm/ *n.* **1** amount to be paid for a contract of insurance or life assurance. **2** sum added to interest, wages, price, etc. **3 a** amount in excess of the nominal value of a share or other security. **b** amount in excess of the issue price of a share or other security. **4** reward or prize. **5** (*attrib.*) (of a commodity) of the best quality and therefore more expensive. □ **at a premium 1** highly valued; above the usual or nominal price. **2** scarce and in demand. [Latin *praemium* reward]

Premium Bond *n.* (also **Premium Savings Bond**) UK government security offering no regular income or capital gain but entering weekly and monthly draws for tax-free prizes. The prize fund (calculated at 6.5% from 1988) is distributed in a range of prizes, winners being drawn by Ernie (electronic random number indicating equipment). The bonds, first issued in 1956 and now administered by the Department for National Savings, are in £1 denominations with a minimum purchase of £100 and a maximum holding of £20,000. They are repaid at their face value at any time.

♦ **premium bonus** *n.* bonus paid to workers that is related to the time they save in doing their work over a standard time set for this. Depending on the needs of the organization, a premium bonus scheme can be varied to achieve a balance between quality and speed of production; it also provides an incentive for employees. The standards were formerly set by experienced staff but more scientific attempts at classifying work units have resulted in the introduction of systematic work-study techniques. These schemes can lead to friction between employee and employer as standard times are a permanent source of conflict. In the 1960s and 1970s measured daywork became a popular alternative system. See also PIECE RATE.

♦ **premium offer** *n.* special offer of a domestic product advertised on the package of some other product. The purchaser sends a set number of package tops or labels with a small cash payment to an address given and receives the domestic product by post. Premium offers are handled by **premium houses**, who provide all the services required to distribute the products.

---

premolar /priː'məʊlə(r)/ *n.* (in full **premolar tooth**) tooth between the canines and molars.

premonition /ˌpremə'nɪʃ(ə)n/ *n.* forewarning; presentiment. □ **premonitory** /prɪ'mɒnɪtərɪ/ *adj.* [Latin *moneo* warn]

prenatal /priː'neɪt(ə)l/ *adj.* of the period before childbirth.

preoccupy /priː'ɒkjʊˌpaɪ/ *v.* (**-ies, -ied**) **1** (of a thought etc.) dominate the mind of (a person) to the exclusion of all else. **2** (as **preoccupied** *adj.*) otherwise engrossed; mentally distracted. □ **preoccupation** /-'peɪʃ(ə)n/ *n.* [Latin *praeoccupo* seize beforehand]

preordain /ˌpriːɔː'deɪn/ *v.* ordain or determine beforehand.

prep *n. colloq.* **1** homework, esp. in boarding-schools. **2** period when this is done. [abbreviation of PREPARATION]

prepack /priː'pæk/ *v.* (also **pre-package** /-'pækɪdʒ/) pack (goods) on the site of production or before retail.

prepaid *past* and *past part.* of PREPAY.

preparation /ˌprepə'reɪʃ(ə)n/ *n.* **1** preparing or being prepared. **2** (often in *pl.*) something done to make ready. **3** specially prepared substance. **4** = PREP.

preparatory /prɪ'pærətərɪ/ *–adj.* (often foll. by *to*) serving to prepare; introductory. *–adv.* (often foll. by *to*) in a preparatory manner (*was packing preparatory to departure*).

preparatory school *n.* private primary school or *US* secondary school.

prepare /prɪ'peə(r)/ *v.* (**-ring**) **1** make or get ready for use, consideration, etc. **2** assemble (a meal etc.). **3 a** make (a person or oneself) ready or disposed in some way (*prepared them for a shock*). **b** get ready (*prepare to jump*). □ **be prepared** (often foll. by *for*, or *to* + infin.) be disposed or willing to. [Latin *paro* make ready]

preparedness /prɪ'peərɪdnɪs/ *n.* readiness, esp. for war.

prepay /priː'peɪ/ *v.* (*past* and *past part.* **prepaid**) **1** pay (a charge) in advance. **2** pay postage on (a letter etc.) before posting.

♦ **prepayment** *n.* = PAYMENT IN ADVANCE.

---

preplan /priː'plæn/ *v.* (**-nn-**) plan in advance.

preponderate /prɪ'pɒndəˌreɪt/ *v.* (**-ting**) (often foll. by *over*) be greater in influence, quantity, or number; predominate. □ **preponderance** *n.* **preponderant** *adj.* [Latin *pondus -der-* weight]

preposition /ˌprepə'zɪʃ(ə)n/ *n. Gram.* word governing (and usu. preceding) a noun or pronoun and expressing a relation to another word, as in: 'the man *on* the platform', 'came *after* dinner', 'went *by* train'. □ **prepositional** *adj.* [Latin *praepono -posit-* place before]

prepossess /ˌpriːpə'zes/ *v.* **1** (usu. in *passive*) (of an idea, feeling, etc.) take possession of (a person). **2 a** prejudice (usu. favourably and spontaneously). **b** (as **prepossessing** *adj.*) attractive, appealing. □ **prepossession** /-'zeʃ(ə)n/ *n.*

preposterous /prɪ'pɒstərəs/ *adj.* **1** utterly absurd; outrageous. **2** contrary to nature, reason, or sense. □ **preposterously** *adv.* [Latin, = before behind]

preppy *n.* (*pl.* **-ies**) *US colloq.* student of an expensive private school or similar-looking person. [from PREP]

prepuce /'priːpjuːs/ *n.* **1** = FORESKIN. **2** fold of skin surrounding the clitoris. [Latin *praeputium*]

Pre-Raphaelite /priːˈræfəˌlaɪt/ *–n.* member of a group of 19th-century artists emulating Italian art before the time of Raphael. *–adj.* **1** of the Pre-Raphaelites. **2** (**pre-Raphaelite**) (esp. of a woman) like a type painted by the Pre-Raphaelites (e.g. with long thick curly auburn hair).

pre-record /ˌpriːrɪˈkɔːd/ *v.* record (esp. material for broadcasting) in advance.

prerequisite /priːˈrekwɪzɪt/ *–adj.* required as a precondition. *–n.* prerequisite thing.

■ **Usage** *Prerequisite* is sometimes confused with *perquisite* which means 'an extra profit, allowance, or right'.

prerogative /prɪˈrɒgətɪv/ *n.* right or privilege exclusive to an individual or class. [Latin *praerogo* ask first]

Pres. *abbr.* President.

presage /ˈpresɪdʒ/ *–n.* **1** omen, portent. **2** presentiment, foreboding. *–v.* (**-ging**) **1** portend, foreshadow. **2** give warning of (an event etc.) by natural means. **3** (of a person) predict or have a presentiment of. [Latin *praesagium*]

presbyopia /ˌprezbɪˈəʊpɪə/ *n.* long-sightedness caused by loss of elasticity of the eye lens, occurring esp. in old age. □ **presbyopic** /-ˈɒpɪk/ *adj.* [Greek *presbus* old man, *ōps* eye]

presbyter /ˈprezbɪtə(r)/ *n.* **1** (in the Episcopal Church) minister of the second order; priest. **2** (in the Presbyterian Church) elder. [Church Latin from Greek, = elder]

Presbyterian /ˌprezbɪˈtɪərɪən/ *–adj.* (of a church) governed by elders all of equal rank, esp. with ref. to the Church of Scotland. *–n.* member of a Presbyterian Church. □ **Presbyterianism** *n.*

presbytery /ˈprezbɪtərɪ/ *n.* (*pl.* **-ies**) **1** eastern part of a chancel. **2** body of presbyters, esp. a court next above a Kirk-session. **3** house of a Roman Catholic priest.

preschool /ˈpriːskuːl/ *adj.* of the time before a child is old enough to go to school.

prescient /ˈpresɪənt/ *adj.* having foreknowledge or foresight. □ **prescience** *n.* [Latin *praescio* know before]

prescribe /prɪˈskraɪb/ *v.* (**-bing**) **1 a** advise the use of (a medicine etc.). **b** recommend, esp. as a benefit. **2** lay down or impose authoritatively. [Latin *praescribo*]

■ **Usage** *Prescribe* is sometimes confused with *proscribe*.

prescript /ˈpriːskrɪpt/ *n.* ordinance, law, command. [Latin: related to PRESCRIBE]

prescription /prɪˈskrɪpʃ(ə)n/ *n.* **1** act of prescribing. **2 a** doctor's (usu. written) instruction for the supply and use of a medicine. **b** medicine prescribed.

prescriptive /prɪˈskrɪptɪv/ *adj.* **1** prescribing, laying down rules. **2** arising from custom.

presence /ˈprez(ə)ns/ *n.* **1** being present. **2** place where a person is (*admitted to their presence*). **3** person's appearance or bearing, esp. when imposing. **4** person or spirit that is present (*the royal presence; aware of a presence in the room*). [Latin: related to PRESENT[1]]

presence of mind *n.* calmness and quick-wittedness in sudden difficulty etc.

present[1] /ˈprez(ə)nt/ *–adj.* **1** (usu. *predic.*) being in the place in question. **2 a** now existing, occurring, or being such. **b** now being considered etc. (*in the present case*). **3** *Gram.* expressing an action etc. now going on or habitually performed (*present participle*). *–n.* (prec. by *the*) **1** the time now passing (*no time like the present*). **2** *Gram.* present tense. □ **at present** now. **by these presents** *Law* by this document. **for the present** just now; for the time being. [Latin *praesens -ent-*]

present[2] /prɪˈzent/ *v.* **1** introduce, offer, or exhibit for attention or consideration. **2 a** (with a thing as object, foll. by *to*) offer or give as a gift (to a person). **b** (with a person as object, foll. by *with*) make available to; cause to have (*that presents us with a problem*). **3 a** (of a company, producer, etc.) put (a piece of entertainment) before the public. **b** (of a performer, compère, etc.) introduce. **4** introduce (a person) formally (*may I present my fiancé?*). **5 a** (of a circumstance) reveal (some quality etc.) (*this presents some difficulty*). **b** exhibit (an appearance etc.). **6** (of an idea etc.) offer or suggest itself. **7** deliver (a cheque, bill, etc.) for acceptance or payment. **8 a** (usu. foll. by *at*) aim (a weapon). **b** hold out (a weapon) in position for aiming. □ **present arms** hold a rifle etc. vertically in front of the body as a salute. □ **presenter** *n.* (in sense 3b). [Latin *praesento*: related to PRESENT[1]]

present[3] /ˈprez(ə)nt/ *n.* thing given, gift. [French: related to PRESENT[1]]

presentable /prɪˈzentəb(ə)l/ *adj.* of good appearance; fit to be presented. □ **presentability** /-ˈbɪlɪtɪ/ *n.* **presentably** *adv.*

presentation /ˌprezənˈteɪʃ(ə)n/ *n.* **1 a** presenting or being presented. **b** thing presented. **2** manner or quality of presenting. **3** demonstration or display of materials, information, etc.; lecture.

present-day *attrib. adj.* of this time; modern.

presentiment /prɪˈzentɪmənt/ *n.* vague expectation; foreboding (esp. of misfortune).

presently *adv.* **1** soon; after a short time. **2** esp. *US* & *Scot.* at the present time; now.

◆ **present value** see FUTURE VALUE.

---

preservative /prɪˈzɜːvətɪv/ *–n.* substance for preserving perishable foodstuffs, wood, etc. *–adj.* tending to preserve.

preserve /prɪˈzɜːv/ *–v.* (**-ving**) **1** keep safe or free from decay etc. **2** maintain (a thing) in its existing state. **3** retain (a quality or condition). **4** treat (food) to prevent decomposition or fermentation. **5** keep (game etc.) undisturbed for private use. *–n.* (in *sing.* or *pl.*) **1** preserved fruit; jam. **2** place where game etc. is preserved. **3** sphere of activity regarded as a person's own. □ **preservation** /ˌprezəˈveɪʃ(ə)n/ *n.* [Latin *servo* keep]

pre-set /priːˈset/ *v.* (**-tt-**; *past* and *past part.* **-set**) set or fix (a device) in advance of its operation.

preshrunk /priːˈʃrʌŋk/ *adj.* (of fabric etc.) treated so that it shrinks during manufacture and not in use.

preside /prɪˈzaɪd/ *v.* (**-ding**) **1** (often foll. by *at*, *over*) be chairperson or president of a meeting etc. **2** exercise control or authority. [Latin *sedeo* sit]

presidency /ˈprezɪdənsɪ/ *n.* (*pl.* **-ies**) **1** office of president. **2** period of this.

president /ˈprezɪd(ə)nt/ *n.* **1** head of a republican state. **2** head of a society or council etc. **3** head of certain colleges. **4** *US* **a** head of a university etc. **b** chief executive of a company, equivalent to the chairman of the board of a UK company. **5** title sometimes given to a past chairman or managing director of a UK company, usu. for an honorary position that carries little responsibility for running the company. **6** person in charge of a meeting. □ **presidential** /-ˈdenʃ(ə)l/ *adj.*

presidium /prɪˈsɪdɪəm/ *n.* (also **praesidium**) standing committee in a Communist country. [Latin: related to PRESIDE]

press[1] *–v.* **1** apply steady force to (a thing in contact). **2 a** compress or squeeze a thing to flatten, shape, or smooth it. **b** squeeze (a fruit etc.) to extract its juice. **3** (foll. by *out of*, *from*, etc.) squeeze (juice etc.). **4** embrace or caress by squeezing (*pressed my hand*). **5** (foll. by *on*, *against*, etc.) exert pressure. **6** be urgent; demand immediate action. **7** (foll. by *for*) make an insistent demand. **8** (foll. by *up*, *round*, etc.) crowd. **9** (foll. by *on*, *forward*, etc.) hasten insistently. **10** (often in *passive*) (of an enemy etc.) bear heavily on. **11** (often foll. by *for*, or *to* + infin.) urge or entreat (*pressed me to stay; pressed me for an answer*). **12** (foll. by *on*, *upon*) **a** urge (an opinion, claim, or course of action). **b** force (an offer, a gift, etc.). **13** insist on (*did not press the point*). **14** manufacture (a gramophone record, car part, etc.) by using pressure to shape and extract from a sheet of material. *–n.* **1** act of pressing (*give it a press*). **2** device for compressing, flattening, shaping, extracting juice, etc. **3** = PRINTING-PRESS. **4** (prec. by *the*) **a** art or practice of printing. **b** newspapers etc. generally or collectively. **5** notice or publicity in newspapers etc. (*got a good press*). **6** (**Press**) printing or publishing company. **7 a** crowding. **b** crowd (of people etc.). **8** the pressure of affairs. **9** esp. *Ir.* & *Scot.* large usu. shelved cupboard. □ **be pressed for** have barely enough (time etc.). **go** (or **send) to press** go or send to be printed. [Latin *premo press-*]

press[2] *v.* **1** *hist.* force to serve in the army or navy. **2** bring into use as a makeshift (*was pressed into service*). [obsolete *prest* from French, = loan]

press agent *n.* person employed to obtain advertising and press publicity.

press conference *n.* interview given to a number of journalists.

press gallery *n.* gallery for reporters, esp. in a legislative assembly.

press-gang –*n.* **1** *hist.* body of men employed to press men into army or navy service. **2** any group using coercive methods. –*v.* force into service.

pressie /ˈprezɪ/ *n.* (also **prezzie**) *colloq.* present, gift. [abbreviation]

pressing –*adj.* **1** urgent. **2** urging strongly (*pressing invitation*). –*n.* **1** thing made by pressing, e.g. a gramophone record. **2** series of these made at one time. **3** act of pressing (*all at one pressing*). □ **pressingly** *adv.*

press release *n.* statement issued to newspapers.

press-stud *n.* small fastening device engaged by pressing its two halves together.

press-up *n.* exercise in which the prone body is raised from the ground by placing the hands on the floor and straightening the arms.

pressure /ˈpreʃə(r)/ –*n.* **1 a** exertion of continuous force on or against a body by another in contact with it. **b** force exerted. **c** amount of this (expressed by the force on a unit area) (*atmospheric pressure*). **2** urgency (*work under pressure*). **3** affliction or difficulty (*under financial pressure*). **4** constraining influence (*put pressure on us*). –*v.* (**-ring**) (often foll. by *into*) apply (esp. moral) pressure to; coerce; persuade. [Latin: related to PRESS[1]]

pressure-cooker *n.* airtight pan for cooking quickly under steam pressure. □ **pressure-cook** *v.*

pressure group *n.* group formed to influence public policy.

pressure point *n.* point where an artery can be pressed against a bone to inhibit bleeding.

pressurize *v.* (also **-ise**) (**-zing** or **-sing**) **1** (esp. as **pressurized** *adj.*) maintain normal atmospheric pressure in (an aircraft cabin etc.) at a high altitude. **2** raise to a high pressure. **3** pressure (a person). □ **pressurization** /-ˈzeɪʃ(ə)n/ *n.*

pressurized-water reactor *n.* nuclear reactor with water at high pressure as the coolant.

♦ **Prestel** /ˈprestel/ *n. propr.* public computerized visual information service operated by British Telecom. Each user has a number and password and can use either a Prestel set or a microcomputer linked to the telephone network through a modem. The service offers news, information on exports, investments, and companies, as well as tax guides etc. It is a two-way videotex system, enabling users to send messages to other users and to the information providers. Response pages enable bookings to be made and other services to be purchased. [from PRESS 1, TELECOMMUNICATION]

---

prestidigitator /ˌprestɪˈdɪdʒɪˌteɪtə(r)/ *n. formal* conjuror. □ **prestidigitation** /-ˈteɪʃ(ə)n/ *n.* [French: related to PRESTO, DIGIT]

prestige /preˈstiːʒ/ *n.* **1** respect or reputation derived from achievements, power, associations, etc. **2** (*attrib.*) having or conferring prestige. □ **prestigious** /-ˈstɪdʒəs/ *adj.* [Latin *praestigiae* juggler's tricks]

presto /ˈprestəʊ/ *Mus.* –*adv.* & *adj.* in quick tempo. –*n.* (*pl.* **-s**) presto passage or movement. [Latin *praestus* quick]

prestressed /priːˈstrest/ *adj.* (of concrete) strengthened by stretched wires within it.

presumably /prɪˈzjuːməblɪ/ *adv.* as may reasonably be presumed.

presume /prɪˈzjuːm/ *v.* (**-ming**) **1** (often foll. by *that*) suppose to be true; take for granted. **2** (often foll. by *to* + infin.) **a** take the liberty, be impudent enough (*presumed to question their authority*). **b** dare, venture (*may I presume to ask?*). **3** be presumptuous. **4** (foll. by *on*, *upon*) take advantage of or make unscrupulous use of (a person's good nature etc.). [Latin *praesumo*]

presumption /prɪˈzʌmpʃ(ə)n/ *n.* **1** arrogance, presumptuous behaviour. **2 a** presuming a thing to be true. **b** thing that is or may be presumed to be true. **3** ground for presuming. [Latin: related to PRESUME]

presumptive /prɪˈzʌmptɪv/ *adj.* giving grounds for presumption (*presumptive evidence*).

presumptuous /prɪˈzʌmptʃʊəs/ *adj.* unduly or overbearingly confident. □ **presumptuously** *adv.* **presumptuousness** *n.*

presuppose /ˌpriːsəˈpəʊz/ *v.* (**-sing**) **1** assume beforehand. **2** imply. □ **presupposition** /-ˌsʌpəˈzɪʃ(ə)n/ *n.*

pre-tax /priːˈtæks, ˈpriː-/ *adj.* **1** (of income etc.) before deduction of taxes. **2** (of company profit) before deduction of corporation tax.

pretence /prɪˈtens/ *n.* (*US* **pretense**) **1** pretending, make-believe. **2 a** pretext, excuse. **b** false show of intentions or motives. **3** (foll. by *to*) claim, esp. a false one (to merit etc.). **4** display; ostentation. [Anglo-Latin: related to PRETEND]

pretend /prɪˈtend/ –*v.* **1** claim or assert falsely so as to deceive (*pretend knowledge*; *pretended to be rich*). **2** imagine to oneself in play (*pretended it was night*). **3** (as **pretended** *adj.*) falsely claim to be such (*a pretended friend*). **4** (foll. by *to*) **a** lay claim to (a right or title etc.). **b** profess to have (a quality etc.). –*adj. colloq.* pretended; in pretence (*pretend money*). [Latin *praetendo*: related to TEND[1]]

pretender *n.* person who claims a throne, title, etc.

pretense *US* var. of PRETENCE.

pretension /prɪˈtenʃ(ə)n/ *n.* **1** (often foll. by *to*) **a** assertion of a claim. **b** justifiable claim. **2** pretentiousness. [medieval Latin: related to PRETEND]

pretentious /prɪˈtenʃəs/ *adj.* **1** making an excessive claim to merit or importance. **2** ostentatious. □ **pretentiously** *adv.* **pretentiousness** *n.*

preterite /ˈpretərɪt/ (*US* **preterit**) *Gram.* –*adj.* expressing a past action or state. –*n.* preterite tense or form. [Latin *praeteritum* past]

preternatural /ˌpriːtəˈnætʃər(ə)l/ *adj.* extraordinary, exceptional; supernatural. [Latin *praeter* beyond]

♦ **pretesting** /ˌpriːˈtestɪŋ/ *n.* use of marketing research to predict the effectiveness of an advertisement before it is issued for wide exposure. □ **pretest** *v.*

---

pretext /ˈpriːtekst/ *n.* ostensible reason; excuse offered. [Latin *praetextus*: related to TEXT]

Pretoria /prɪˈtɔːrɪə/ administrative capital of the Republic of South Africa and former capital of Transvaal; it has iron and steel, engineering, and food-processing industries; pop. (1991) 525 583.

prettify /ˈprɪtɪˌfaɪ/ *v.* (**-ies**, **-ied**) make pretty, esp. in an affected way.

pretty /ˈprɪtɪ/ –*adj.* (**-ier**, **-iest**) **1** attractive in a delicate way (*pretty girl*; *pretty dress*). **2** fine or good of its kind. **3** *iron.* considerable, fine (*a pretty penny*). –*adv. colloq.* fairly, moderately. –*v.* (**-ies**, **-ied**) (often foll. by *up*) make pretty. □ **pretty much** (or **nearly** or **well**) *colloq.* almost; very nearly. □ **prettily** *adv.* **prettiness** *n.* [Old English]

pretty-pretty *adj. colloq.* too pretty.

pretzel /ˈprets(ə)l/ *n.* crisp knot-shaped salted biscuit. [German]

prevail /prɪˈveɪl/ *v.* **1** (often foll. by *against*, *over*) be victorious or gain mastery. **2** be the more usual or predominant. **3** exist or occur in general use or experience. **4** (foll. by *on*, *upon*) persuade. [Latin *praevaleo*: related to AVAIL]

prevalent /ˈprevələnt/ *adj.* **1** generally existing or occurring. **2** predominant. □ **prevalence** *n.* [related to PREVAIL]

prevaricate /prɪˈværɪˌkeɪt/ *v.* (**-ting**) **1** speak or act evasively or misleadingly. **2** quibble, equivocate. □ **prevarication** /-ˈkeɪʃ(ə)n/ *n.* **prevaricator** *n.* [Latin, = walk crookedly]

■ **Usage** *Prevaricate* is often confused with *procrastinate*, which means 'to defer or put off action'.

prevent /prɪˈvent/ *v.* (often foll. by *from* + verbal noun) stop from happening or doing something; hinder; make impossible (*the weather prevented me from going*). □ **preventable** *adj.* (also **preventible**). **prevention** *n.* [Latin *praevenio -vent-* hinder]

■ **Usage** The use of *prevent* without 'from' as in *prevented me going* is informal. An acceptable alternative is *prevented my going*.

preventative /prɪˈventətɪv/ *adj.* & *n.* = PREVENTIVE.

preventive /prɪˈventɪv/ *–adj.* serving to prevent, esp. disease or machine failure. *–n.* preventive agent, measure, drug, etc.

preview /ˈpriːvjuː/ *–n.* showing of a film, play, exhibition, etc., before it is seen by the general public. *–v.* see or show in advance.

previous /ˈpriːvɪəs/ *–adj.* **1** (often foll. by *to*) coming before in time or order. **2** *colloq.* hasty, premature. *–adv.* (foll. by *to*) before. □ **previously** *adv.* [Latin *praevius* from *via* way]

pre-war /priːˈwɔː(r), ˈpriː-/ *adj.* existing or occurring before a war.

prey /preɪ/ *–n.* **1** animal that is hunted or killed by another for food. **2** (often foll. by *to*) person or thing that is influenced by or vulnerable to (something undesirable) (*prey to morbid fears*). *–v.* (foll. by *on, upon*) **1** seek or take as prey. **2** (of a disease, emotion, etc.) exert a harmful influence (*it preyed on his mind*). [Latin *praeda*]

prezzie var. of PRESSIE.

price *–n.* **1** amount of money for which a thing is bought or sold. The relationship between price and value has long been a source of dispute in economics. Classical economists attempted to use the labour theory of value to find a stable relationship between price and value. Subsequently Marxist economists have attempted to solve what they call the transformation problem. To neoclassical economists price and value are equal at the margin, i.e. the price will reflect the value of the last unit purchased, while the value of all other units sold will exceed the price, giving rise to a consumer surplus. **2** what is or must be given, done, sacrificed, etc. to obtain or achieve something (*peace at any price*). **3** odds in betting. *–v.* (**-cing**) **1** fix or find the price of (a thing for sale). **2** estimate the value of. □ **at a price** at a high cost. **price on a person's head** reward for a person's capture or death. **what price ...?** (often foll. by verbal noun) *colloq.* **1** what is the chance of ...? (*what price your finishing the course?*). **2** *iron.* the much boasted ... proves disappointing (*what price your friendship now?*). [Latin *pretium*]

♦ **price control** *n.* restrictions by a government on the prices of consumer goods, usu. imposed on a short-term basis as a measure to control inflation. See also PRICES AND INCOME POLICY.

♦ **price discrimination** *n.* sale of the same product at different prices to different buyers. Practised usu. by monopolists, it requires that a market can be subdivided to exploit different sets of consumers and that these divisions can be sustained. Pure price discrimination rarely exists, since sellers usu. differentiate the product slightly (as in first-class rail travel and different types of theatre seat). Governments may use price discrimination in order to redistribute wealth but usu. it is a monopolist's way of extracting a higher pure economic profit.

♦ **price–dividend ratio** *n.* (also **P/D ratio, PDR**) current market price of a company share divided by the dividend per share for the previous year. It is a measure of the investment value of the share.

♦ **price–earnings ratio** *n.* (also **P/E ratio, PER**) current market price of a company share divided by the earnings per share (e.p.s.) of the company. The P/E ratio usu. refers to the annual e.p.s. and is expressed as a number (e.g. 5 or 10), often called the **multiple** of the company. Loosely, it can be thought of as the number of years it would take the company to earn an amount equal to its market value. High multiples, usu. associated with low yields, indicate that the company is growing rapidly, while a low multiple is associated with dull no-growth stocks. The P/E ratio is one of the main indicators used by fundamental analysts to decide whether the shares in a company are expensive or cheap, relative to the market.

price-fixing *n.* maintaining of prices at a certain level by agreement between competing sellers.

♦ **price leadership** *n.* setting of the price of a product by a dominant firm in an industry in the knowledge that competitors will follow this lead in order to avoid the high cost of a price war. This practice is often found in oligopolies and has the effect of a cartel. To achieve a stable market, the price must be set at a sensible level. Cf. PRICE RING. □ **price leader** *n.*

priceless *adj.* **1** invaluable. **2** *colloq.* very amusing or absurd.

♦ **price level** *n.* average level of prices of goods and services in an economy, usu. calculated as a figure on a price index. See RETAIL PRICE INDEX.

♦ **price method** *n. US* = PIECE RATE.

♦ **price–net tangible assets ratio** *n.* current market price of a company share divided by its net tangible assets. The higher the ratio, the more attractive the share as an investment.

♦ **price ring** *n.* group of firms in the same industry that have agreed among themselves to fix a minimum retail price for their competing products, thus forming a cartel. Price rings are illegal in many countries unless they can be shown to be in the public interest. See CONSUMER PROTECTION; PRICE LEADERSHIP.

♦ **prices and income policy** *n.* government policy to curb inflation by directly imposing wage restraint and price controls. Some less interventionist governments prefer indirect methods using fiscal and monetary policies.

♦ **price support** *n.* government policy of providing support for certain basic, usu. agricultural, products to stop the price falling below an agreed level. Support prices can be administered in various ways: the government can purchase and stockpile surplus produce to support the price or it can pay producers a cash payment as a subsidy to raise the price they obtain through normal market channels. See also COMMON AGRICULTURAL POLICY.

price tag *n.* **1** label on an item showing its price. **2** cost of an undertaking.

♦ **price theory** *n. Econ.* theory that, at the microeconomic level, defines the role of prices in consumer demand and the supply of goods by the firm. At a broader level, it explains the role of prices in markets as a whole. At the macroeconomic level it treats wages and interest rates as the prices of particular goods, thus implying that governments must take market forces into account when formulating such policies as incomes policy and monetary policy.

♦ **price variance** *n.* variance arising when the actual price of goods sold or purchased differs from the standard price (see VARIANCE 3).

price war *n.* period of fierce competition between two or more firms in the same industry that are seeking to increase their shares of the market by cutting the prices of their products. Although this can give short-term advantages in some circumstances to one participant, in the longer run it is a situation from which no one profits. To avoid the perils of selling products at a loss in order to outdo the competition, in most industries prices are not allowed by competitors to fall below a certain level, competition being restricted to other methods, such as advertising, improving the packaging, etc.

pricey *adj.* (**-cier**, **-ciest**) *colloq.* expensive.

prick *–v.* **1** pierce slightly; make a small hole in. **2** (foll.

by *off*, *out*) mark with small holes or dots. **3** trouble mentally (*my conscience pricked me*). **4** tingle. **5** (foll. by *out*) plant (seedlings etc.) in small holes pricked in the soil. *–n.* **1** act of pricking. **2** small hole or mark made by pricking. **3** pain caused as by pricking. **4** mental pain. **5** *coarse slang* **a** penis. **b** *derog.* contemptible man. □ **prick up one's ears 1** (of a dog etc.) make the ears erect when alert. **2** (of a person) become suddenly attentive. [Old English]

prickle /'prɪk(ə)l/ *–n.* **1** small thorn. **2** hard-pointed spine of a hedgehog etc. **3** prickling sensation. *–v.* **(-ling)** affect or be affected with a sensation of multiple pricking. [Old English]

prickly *adj.* **(-ier, -iest) 1** having prickles. **2** (of a person) ready to take offence. **3** tingling. □ **prickliness** *n.*

prickly heat *n.* itchy inflammation of the skin, causing a tingling sensation and common in hot countries.

prickly pear *n.* **1** cactus with pear-shaped prickly fruit. **2** its fruit.

pride *–n.* **1 a** elation or satisfaction at one's achievements, qualities, possessions, etc. **b** object of this feeling; the flower or best. **2** high or overbearing opinion of one's worth or importance. **3** (in full **proper pride**) proper sense of what befits one's position; self-respect. **4** group (of certain animals, esp. lions). **5** best condition, prime. *–v.refl.* **(-ding)** (foll. by *on, upon*) be proud of. □ **take pride** (or **a pride) in 1** be proud of. **2** maintain in good condition or appearance. [Old English: related to PROUD]

pride of place *n.* most important or prominent position.

prie-dieu /priː'djɜː/ *n.* (*pl.* **prie-dieux** pronunc. same) kneeling-desk for prayer. [French, = pray God]

priest *n.* **1** ordained minister of the Roman Catholic or Orthodox Church, or of the Anglican Church (above a deacon and below a bishop). **2** (*fem.* **priestess**) official minister of a non-Christian religion. □ **priesthood** *n.* **priestly** *adj.* [Latin PRESBYTER]

prig *n.* self-righteous or moralistic person. □ **priggish** *adj.* **priggishness** *n.* [origin unknown]

prim *adj.* **(primmer, primmest)** stiffly formal and precise; prudish. □ **primly** *adv.* **primness** *n.* [French: related to PRIME[1]]

prima ballerina /ˌpriːmə ˌbælə'riːnə/ *n.* chief female dancer in a ballet. [Italian]

primacy /'praɪməsɪ/ *n.* (*pl.* **-ies**) **1** pre-eminence. **2** office of a primate. [Latin: related to PRIMATE]

prima donna /ˌpriːmə 'dɒnə/ *n.* (*pl.* **prima donnas**) **1** chief female singer in an opera. **2** temperamentally self-important person. □ **prima donna-ish** *adj.* [Italian]

prima facie /ˌpraɪmə 'feɪʃiː/ *–adv.* at first sight. *–adj.* (of evidence) appearing to be conclusive at first sight but not necessarily conclusive. [Latin]

♦ **primage** /'praɪmɪdʒ/ *n.* **1** percentage added to a freight charge to cover the cost of loading or unloading a ship. **2** extra charge for handling goods with special care when they are being loaded or unloaded from a ship, aircraft, etc. [medieval Latin: related to PRIME[2], -AGE]

primal /'praɪm(ə)l/ *adj.* **1** primitive, primeval. **2** chief, fundamental. [Latin: related to PRIME[1]]

primary /'praɪmərɪ/ *–adj.* **1 a** of the first importance; chief. **b** fundamental, basic. **2** earliest, original; first in a series. **3** of the first rank in a series; not derived. **4** designating any of the colours red, green, and blue, or (for pigments) red, blue, and yellow, of which all other colours are mixtures. **5** (of education) for children below the age of 11. **6** (**Primary**) *Geol.* of the lowest series of strata. **7** *Biol.* of the first stage of development. *–n.* (*pl.* **-ies**) **1** thing that is primary. **2** (in full **primary election**) (in the US) preliminary election to appoint party conference delegates or to select candidates for a principal (esp. presidential) election. **3** = PRIMARY FEATHER. □ **primarily** /'praɪmərɪlɪ, -'meərɪlɪ/ *adv.* [Latin: related to PRIME[1]]

primary feather *n.* large flight-feather of a bird's wing.

♦ **primary market** *n.* market in which securities are sold for the first time. Cf. SECONDARY MARKET.

♦ **primary production** see PRODUCTION 3.

primary school *n.* school for children below the age of 11.

primate /'praɪmeɪt/ *n.* **1** member of the highest order of mammals, including apes, monkeys, and man. **2** (also /-mət/) archbishop. [Latin *primas -at-* chief]

prime[1] *–adj.* **1** chief, most important. **2** first-rate, excellent. **3** primary, fundamental. **4** *Math.* **a** (of a number etc.) divisible only by itself and unity (e.g. 2, 3, 5, 7, 11). **b** (of numbers) having no common factor but unity. *–n.* **1** state of the highest perfection (*prime of life*). **2** (prec. by *the*; foll. by *of*) the best part. [Latin *primus* first]

prime[2] *v.* **(-ming) 1** prepare (a thing) for use or action. **2** prepare (a gun) for firing or (an explosive) for detonation. **3** pour (liquid) into a pump to enable it to work. **4** prepare (wood etc.) for painting by applying a substance that prevents paint from being absorbed. **5** equip (a person) with information etc. **6** ply (a person) with food or drink in preparation for something. [origin unknown]

♦ **prime costs** *n.pl.* direct costs of the production of goods or services. Prime costs usu. refer to the materials and labour immediately attributable to a particular cost unit. Cf. OVERHEAD COSTS.

♦ **prime entry book** *n.* = BOOK OF PRIME ENTRY.

prime minister *n.* head of an elected government; principal minister.

primer[1] *n.* substance used to prime wood etc.

primer[2] *n.* **1** elementary textbook for teaching children to read. **2** introductory book. [Latin: related to PRIME[1]]

♦ **prime rate** *n.* rate of interest at which US banks lend money to first-class borrowers. It is similar in operation to the base rate in the UK.

prime time *n.* (in broadcasting) time when audience figures are highest, and therefore advertising rates are highest.

primeval /praɪ'miːv(ə)l/ *adj.* **1** of the first age of the world. **2** ancient, primitive. □ **primevally** *adv.* [Latin: related to PRIME[1], *aevum* age]

primitive /'prɪmɪtɪv/ *–adj.* **1** at an early stage of civilization (*primitive man*). **2** undeveloped, crude, simple (*primitive methods*). *–n.* **1** untutored painter with a direct naïve style. **2** picture by such a painter. □ **primitively** *adv.* **primitiveness** *n.* [Latin: related to PRIME[1]]

primogeniture /ˌpraɪməʊ'dʒenɪtʃə(r)/ *n.* **1** fact of being the first-born child. **2** (in full **right of primogeniture**) right of succession belonging to the first-born. [medieval Latin: related to PRIME[1], Latin *genitura* birth]

primordial /praɪ'mɔːdɪəl/ *adj.* existing at or from the beginning, primeval. [Latin: related to PRIME[1], *ordior* begin]

primp *v.* **1** make (the hair, clothes, etc.) tidy. **2** *refl.* make (oneself) smart. [var. of PRIM]

primrose /'prɪmrəʊz/ *n.* **1 a** wild plant bearing pale yellow spring flowers. **b** its flower. **2** pale yellow colour. [French and medieval Latin, = first rose]

primrose path *n.* pursuit of pleasure.

primula /'prɪmjʊlə/ *n.* cultivated plant bearing primrose-like flowers in a wide variety of colours. [Latin diminutive: related to PRIME[1]]

Primus /'praɪməs/ *n. propr.* portable cooking stove burning vaporized oil. [Latin, = first]

prince *n.* (as a title usu. **Prince**) **1** male member of a royal family other than the reigning king. **2** ruler of a small state. **3** noble man in some countries. **4** (often foll. by *of*) chief or greatest (*the prince of novelists*). [Latin *princeps -cip-*]

Prince Consort *n.* (title conferred on) the husband of a reigning queen who is himself a prince.

Prince Edward Island smallest province of Canada, an island in the Gulf of St Lawrence; pop. (est. 1995)

136 100; capital, Charlottetown. Agriculture is important, producing esp. potatoes and livestock; other sources of revenue are fishing, food-processing industries, and tourism.

princeling /ˈprɪnslɪŋ/ *n.* young or petty prince.

princely *adj.* (**-ier, iest**) **1** of or worthy of a prince. **2** sumptuous, generous, splendid.

Prince of Wales *n.* (title conferred on) the eldest son and heir apparent of the British monarch.

Prince Regent *n.* prince who acts as regent, esp. the future George IV.

Prince Rupert's Land see RUPERT'S LAND.

princess /prɪnˈses/ *n.* (as a title usu. **Princess** /ˈprɪnses/) **1** wife of a prince. **2** female member of a royal family other than a queen. [French: related to PRINCE]

Princess Royal *n.* (title conferred on) the British monarch's eldest daughter.

principal /ˈprɪnsɪp(ə)l/ *–adj.* **1** (usu. *attrib.*) first in rank or importance; chief. **2** main, leading. *–n.* **1** chief person. **2** head of some schools, colleges, and universities. **3** leading performer in a concert, play, etc. **4** capital sum, as distinct from the interest or income derived from it. **5** person on whose behalf an agent or broker acts. **6** civil servant of the grade below Secretary. **7** person directly responsible for a crime. □ **principally** *adv.* [Latin: related to PRINCE]

principal boy *n.* leading male role in a pantomime, usu. played by a woman.

principality /ˌprɪnsɪˈpælɪtɪ/ *n.* (*pl.* **-ies**) **1** state ruled by or government of a prince. **2** (**the Principality**) Wales.

principal parts *n.pl. Gram.* parts of a verb from which all other parts can be deduced.

principle /ˈprɪnsɪp(ə)l/ *n.* **1** fundamental truth or law as the basis of reasoning or action. **2 a** personal code of conduct (*person of high principle*). **b** (in *pl.*) personal rules of conduct (*has no principles*). **3** general law in physics etc. **4** law of nature forming the basis for the construction or working of a machine etc. **5** fundamental source; primary element. □ **in principle** in theory. **on principle** on the basis of a moral code. [Latin *principium* source]

principled *adj.* based on or having (esp. praiseworthy) principles of behaviour.

◆ **principles of taxation** *n.pl.* set of criteria, largely determined by the economist Adam Smith, for determining whether a given tax or system of taxation is good or bad. The main principles are that taxes should be equitable and certain. Subsidiary principles are that they should distort choices that would otherwise be made as little as possible and that the cost of collection should be as low as possible. Some economists argue that a further principle might be that the tax should be effective in redistributing income.

---

prink *v.* **1 a** (usu. *refl.*; often foll. by *up*) smarten (oneself) up. **b** dress oneself up. **2** (of a bird) preen. [origin unknown]

print *–v.* **1** produce or cause (a book, picture, etc.) to be produced by applying inked types, blocks, or plates, to paper, etc. **2** express or publish in print. **3 a** (often foll. by *on, in*) impress or stamp (a mark on a surface). **b** (often foll. by *with*) impress or stamp (a surface with a seal, die, etc.). **4** (often *absol.*) write (letters) without joining them up. **5** (often foll. by *off, out*) produce (a photograph) from a negative. **6** (usu. foll. by *out*) (of a computer etc.) produce output in printed form. **7** mark (a textile fabric) with a coloured design. **8** (foll. by *on*) impress (an idea, scene, etc. on the mind or memory). *–n.* **1** indentation or mark on a surface left by the pressure of a thing in contact with it. **2 a** printed lettering or writing. **b** words in printed form. **c** printed publication, esp. a newspaper. **3** picture or design printed from a block or plate. **4** photograph produced on paper from a negative. **5** printed cotton fabric.□ **in print 1** (of a book etc.) available from the publisher. **2** in printed form. **out of print** no longer available from the publisher. [Latin *premo*: related to PRESS[1]]

printed circuit *n.* electric circuit with thin strips of conductor printed on one or both sides of a flat insulating sheet. The assembly of circuit plus supporting sheet is called a **printed circuit board (PCB)**. A PCB connects via an appropriate socket to the internal wiring of a computer system etc. Smaller modular PCBs may be connected to a PCB to augment its function.

printer *n.* **1** person who prints books etc. **2** owner of a printing business. **3** device that prints, esp. from a computer. A computer printer converts the coded information from a computer into a readable form printed on paper. **Impact printers**, in which the printed characters are produced by mechanical impact, include line printers, which print a whole line at a time, and character printers, of which the daisywheel printer is used for good-quality business correspondence (see also DOT MATRIX PRINTER). **Non-impact printers**, which produce characters without the use of mechanical impact, include ink jet printers, which squirt a fine stream of ink onto the paper (see also LASER PRINTER; THERMAL PRINTER).

printer format see FORMAT *n.* 3.

printing *n.* **1** production of printed books etc. **2** copies of a book printed at one time. **3** printed letters or writing imitating them.

printing-press *n.* machine for printing from types or plates etc.

printout *n.* computer output in printed form.

◆ **print run** *n.* the number of copies of a document, article, book, etc. made at a specific printing.

---

prior /ˈpraɪə(r)/ *–adj.* **1** earlier. **2** (often foll. by *to*) coming before in time, order, or importance. *–adv.* (foll. by *to*) before (*left prior to his arrival*). *–n.* (*fem.* **prioress**) **1** superior of a religious house or order. **2** (in an abbey) deputy of an abbot. [Latin, = earlier]

priority /praɪˈɒrɪtɪ/ *n.* (*pl.* **-ies**) **1** thing that is regarded as more important than others. **2** high(est) place among various things to be done (*gave priority to*). **3** right to do something before other people. **4** right to proceed ahead of other traffic. **5** (state of) being more important. □ **prioritize** *v.* (also **-ise**). (**-zing** or **-sing**). [medieval Latin: related to PRIOR]

◆ **priority date** see PATENT *n.* 1.

◆ **priority percentage** *n.* (also **prior charge**) proportion of any profit that must be paid to holders of fixed-interest capital (preference shares and loan stock) before arriving at the sums to be distributed to ordinary shareholders. These percentages help to assess the security of the income of ordinary shareholders and are related to the gearing of the company's capital (see CAPITAL GEARING).

---

priory /ˈpraɪərɪ/ *n.* (*pl.* **-ies**) monastery governed by a prior or nunnery governed by a prioress. [Anglo-French and medieval Latin: related to PRIOR]

◆ **prior-year adjustment** *n.* adjustment to the profit and loss account of an organization necessitated by matters relating to earlier years, which give a misleading view of the position. Such an adjustment might arise as a result of under- or overvaluation of assets or liabilities or because of changes in accounting policies. For the purpose of accounting standards the term is limited to material adjustments arising from either changes in accounting policies or the correction of fundamental errors. Minor adjustments to estimates are not prior-year adjustments. Prior-year adjustments are made by adjusting the opening balances of reserves.

---

prise *v.* (also **prize**) (**-sing** or **-zing**) force open or out by leverage. [French: related to PRIZE[2]]

prism /ˈprɪz(ə)m/ *n.* **1** solid figure whose two ends are equal parallel rectilinear figures, and whose sides are parallelograms. **2** transparent body in this form, usu. triangular with refracting surfaces at an acute angle with each other, which separates white light into a spectrum of colours. [Greek *prisma -mat-* thing sawn]

prismatic /prɪz'mætɪk/ *adj.* **1** of, like, or using a prism. **2** (of colours) distributed (as if) by a transparent prism. [Greek: related to PRISM]

prison /'prɪz(ə)n/ *n.* **1** place of captivity, esp. a building to which persons are committed while awaiting trial or for punishment. **2** custody, confinement. [Latin *prehendo* seize]

prisoner /'prɪznə(r)/ *n.* **1** person kept in prison. **2** (in full **prisoner at the bar**) person in custody on a criminal charge and on trial. **3** person or thing confined by illness, another's grasp, etc. **4** (in full **prisoner of war**) person captured in war. □ **take prisoner** seize and hold as a prisoner. [Anglo-French: related to PRISON]

prisoner of conscience *n.* see CONSCIENCE.

◆ **prisoners' dilemma** *n. Econ.* situation in which an individual's decision to maximize utility turns out to be detrimental both personally and for everyone else. A problem in game theory, the prisoners' dilemma has many applications in economics, in which it tends to undermine the belief in the efficiency of competitive economies (see also INVISIBLE HAND). [from the dilemma of two mythical prisoners (partners in crime) who accept that silence would be in their best interests but end up informing on each other, because they each expect their partner to do the same]

prissy /'prɪsɪ/ *adj.* (**-ier, -iest**) prim, prudish. □ **prissily** *adv.* **prissiness** *n.* [perhaps from PRIM, SISSY]

Priština /prɪʃ'tiːnə/ city in S Serbia, capital of the province of Kosovo; pop. (1991) 155 499.

pristine /'prɪstiːn/ *adj.* **1** in its original condition; unspoilt. **2** spotless; fresh as if new. **3** ancient, primitive. [Latin *pristinus* former]

■ **Usage** The use of *pristine* in sense 2 is considered incorrect by some people.

privacy /'prɪvəsɪ/ *n.* **1 a** being private and undisturbed. **b** right to this. **2** freedom from intrusion or public attention. **3** (in full **privacy of data**) protection of stored data against unauthorized reading. When privacy is required for data stored in a computer it implies that the data is confidential and that access to it should be limited. The data may be 'owned' in some way by a particular person or organization, e.g. data derived from commercial research and development. More usually it is data about a particular person or organization. Personal data is protected by legislation in many countries (see DATA PROTECTION). If a system has poor security then the privacy of data is at risk. If the integrity of the data is to be maintained in some way by the system, then the privacy is reduced because of the number of copies of the information that safe operation of a computer system demands.

private /'praɪvət/ *–adj.* **1** belonging to an individual, one's own, personal (*private property*). **2** confidential, not to be disclosed to others (*private talks*). **3** kept or removed from public knowledge or observation. **4** not open to the public. **5** (of a place) secluded. **6** (of a person) not holding public office or an official position. **7** (of education or medical treatment) conducted outside the state system, at the individual's expense. *–n.* **1** private soldier. **2** (in *pl.*) *colloq.* genitals. □ **in private** privately. □ **privately** *adv.* [Latin *privo* deprive]

◆ **private bank** *n.* **1** commercial bank owned by one person or a partnership. They have been superseded in the UK by joint-stock banks, but still exist in the US. **2** bank that is not a member of a clearing house and therefore has to use a clearing bank as an agent. **3** bank that is not owned by the state.

private bill *n.* parliamentary bill affecting an individual or corporation only.

◆ **private branch exchange** *n.* (also **PBX**) private telephone exchange in an organization that routes calls between extensions and the outside telephone network and between internal extensions. The automatic version, a **private automatic branch exchange (PABX)**, enables calls to be dialled direct from extensions. Incoming calls may be taken by an operator or callers can dial internal extensions direct.

◆ **private brand** *n.* = OWN BRAND.

◆ **private carrier** see CARRIER 2.

private company *n.* = PRIVATE LIMITED COMPANY.

private detective *n.* detective engaged privately, outside an official police force.

◆ **private enterprise** *n.* **1** (also **free enterprise**) economic system in which citizens are allowed to own capital and property and to run their own businesses with a minimum of state interference. The system encourages entrepreneurs and the making of profits by private individuals and firms. **2** business not under state control.

privateer /,praɪvə'tɪə(r)/ *n.* **1** privately owned and officered warship holding a government commission. **2** its commander.

private eye *n. colloq.* private detective.

◆ **private health insurance** *n.* form of insurance that covers private medical treatment and all normal associated costs. This includes payment for private rooms in private or National Health hospitals, fees for surgeons, anaesthetists, or physicians, and also charges for X-rays, pathology tests, and physiotherapy. Cover can be taken out on an individual basis or by a family, or a company can organize group cover with substantial discounts depending on the number of employees involved. Many large organizations offer private health insurance for senior executives and their families as a fringe benefit.

private hotel *n.* hotel not obliged to take all comers.

◆ **private limited company** *n.* (also **private company**) any limited company that is not a public limited company. Such a company is not permitted to offer its shares for sale to the public and it is free from the rules that apply to public limited companies.

private means *n.pl.* income from investments etc., apart from earned income.

private member *n.* MP not holding government office.

private member's bill *n.* bill introduced by a private member, not part of government legislation.

private parts *n.pl. euphem.* genitals.

private sector *n.* the part of an economy free of direct state control. In a mixed economy most commercial and industrial firms are in the private sector, run by private enterprise. Cf. PUBLIC SECTOR.

◆ **private-sector liquidity** see PSL.

private soldier *n.* ordinary soldier other than the officers.

◆ **private treaty** *n.* contract made by personal arrangement between the buyer and seller or their agents, i.e. not by public auction.

private view *n.* viewing of an exhibition (esp. of paintings) before it opens to the public.

privation /praɪ'veɪʃ(ə)n/ *n.* lack of the comforts or necessities of life. [Latin: related to PRIVATE]

privative /'prɪvətɪv/ *adj.* **1** consisting in or marked by loss or absence. **2** *Gram.* expressing privation. [Latin: related to PRIVATE]

◆ **privatization** /,praɪvətaɪ'zeɪʃ(ə)n/ *n.* (also **-isation**) process of selling a publicly owned company to the private sector. Privatization may be pursued for political as well as economic reasons. The economic justification for privatization is that a company will be more efficient under private ownership, although most economists would argue that privatization will only achieve this if it is accompanied by increased competition. Recently, privatizations in the form of share offers to the general public have been advo-

cated as a means of increasing the participation of individuals in the capitalist system. Cf. NATIONALIZATION 1.

privatize /'praɪvə,taɪz/ *v.* (also **-ise**) (**-zing** or **-sing**) transfer (a business etc.) from state to private ownership.

privet /'prɪvɪt/ *n.* bushy evergreen shrub used for hedges. [origin unknown]

privilege /'prɪvɪlɪdʒ/ *–n.* **1** right, advantage, or immunity, belonging to a person, class, or office. **2** special benefit or honour (*a privilege to meet you*). *–v.* (**-ging**) invest with a privilege. □ **privileged** *adj.* [Latin: related to PRIVY, *lex leg-* law]

privy /'prɪvɪ/ *–adj.* **1** (foll. by *to*) sharing in the secret of (a person's plans etc.). **2** *archaic* hidden, secret. *–n.* (*pl.* **-ies**) lavatory, esp. an outside one. [French *privé* private place]

Privy Council *n.* body of advisers appointed by the sovereign (now chiefly honorary). □ **Privy Counsellor** *n.* (also **Privy Councillor**).

privy purse *n.* allowance from the public revenue for the monarch's private expenses.

privy seal *n.* seal formerly affixed to minor state documents.

prize[1] *–n.* **1** something that can be won in a competition, lottery, etc. **2** reward given as a symbol of victory or superiority. **3** something striven for or worth striving for. **4** (*attrib.*) **a** to which a prize is awarded (*prize poem*). **b** excellent of its kind. *–v.* (**-zing**) value highly (*a much prized possession*). [French: related to PRAISE]

prize[2] *n.* ship or property captured in naval warfare. [French *prise* from Latin *prehendo* seize]

prize[3] var. of PRISE.

prizefight *n.* boxing-match fought for a prize of money. □ **prizefighter** *n.*

prize-giving *n.* awarding of prizes, esp. formally at a school etc.

prizewinner *n.* winner of a prize. □ **prizewinning** *attrib. adj.*

PRO *abbr.* **1** Public Record Office. **2** public relations officer (see PUBLIC RELATIONS).

pro[1] /prəʊ/ *n.* (*pl.* **-s**) *colloq.* professional. [abbreviation]

pro[2] /prəʊ/ *–adj.* (of an argument or reason) for; in favour. *–n.* (*pl.* **-s**) reason in favour. *–prep.* in favour of. [Latin, = for, on behalf of]

pro-[1] *prefix* **1** favouring or supporting (*pro-government*). **2** acting as a substitute or deputy for (*proconsul*). **3** forwards (*produce*). **4** forwards and downwards (*prostrate*). **5** onwards (*progress*). **6** in front of (*protect*). [Latin *pro* in front (of)]

pro-[2] *prefix* before in time, place, order, etc. [Greek *pro* before]

proactive /prəʊ'æktɪv/ *adj.* (of a person, policy, etc.) taking the initiative. [from PRO-[2], after REACTIVE]

probability /,prɒbə'bɪlɪtɪ/ *n.* (*pl.* **-ies**) **1** being probable. **2** likelihood of something happening. **3** probable or most probable event. **4** *Math.* extent to which an event is likely to occur, measured by the ratio of the favourable cases to the total number of possible cases. It can be represented on a scale by a number between 0 (zero probability of the event happening, i.e. it is certain not to) and 1 (certainty that it will occur). □ **in all probability** most probably.

probable /'prɒbəb(ə)l/ *–adj.* (often foll. by *that*) that may be expected to happen or prove true; likely (*the probable explanation*; *it is probable that they forgot*). *–n.* probable candidate, member of a team, etc. □ **probably** *adv.* [Latin: related to PROVE]

probate /'prəʊbeɪt/ *–n.* **1** official proving of a will. **2** certificate issued by the Family Division of the High Court, on the application of executors appointed by a will, to the effect that the will is valid and that the executors are authorized to administer the deceased's estate. When there is no apparent doubt about the will's validity, probate is granted in **common form** on the executors filing an affidavit. Probate granted in common form can be revoked by the court at any time on the application of an interested party who proves that the will is invalid. When the will is disputed, probate in **solemn form** is granted, but only if the court decides that the will is valid after hearing the evidence on the disputed issues in a **probate action**. **3** verified copy of a will with the certificate as handed to the executors. *–adj.* (*attrib.*) concerned with probate. [Latin *probo* PROVE]

♦ **probate price** *n.* price of shares or other securities used for inheritance-tax purposes on the death of the owner. The price is taken as either one quarter of the interval between the upper and lower quotations of the day on which the owner died added to the lower figure or as half way between the highest and lowest recorded bargains of the day, whichever is the lower.

♦ **probate value** *n.* value of the assets at the time of a person's death, agreed with the Capital Taxes Office of the Inland Revenue for the purposes of calculating inheritance tax.

probation /prə'beɪʃ(ə)n/ *n.* **1** *Law* system of supervising and monitoring the behaviour of (esp. young) offenders, as an alternative to prison. **2** period of testing the character or abilities of esp. a new employee. □ **on probation** undergoing probation. □ **probationary** *adj.* [Latin: related to PROVE]

probationer *n.* person on probation.

probation officer *n.* official supervising offenders on probation.

probative /'prəʊbətɪv/ *adj. formal* affording proof. [Latin: related to PROVE]

probe *–n.* **1** penetrating investigation. **2** small device, esp. an electrode, for measuring, testing, etc. **3** blunt-ended surgical instrument for exploring a wound etc. **4** (in full **space probe**) unmanned exploratory spacecraft transmitting information about its environment. *–v.* (**-bing**) **1** examine or enquire into closely. **2** explore with a probe. [Latin *proba*: related to PROVE]

probity /'prəʊbɪtɪ/ *n.* uprightness, honesty. [Latin *probus* good]

problem /'prɒbləm/ *n.* **1** doubtful or difficult matter requiring a solution. **2** something hard to understand or accomplish. **3** (*attrib.*) causing problems (*problem child*). **4** puzzle or question for solution; exercise. [Greek *problēma -mat-*]

problematic /,prɒblə'mætɪk/ *adj.* (also **problematical**) attended by difficulty; doubtful or questionable. □ **problematically** *adv.* [Greek: related to PROBLEM]

proboscis /prəʊ'bɒsɪs/ *n.* **1** long flexible trunk or snout of some mammals, e.g. an elephant or tapir. **2** elongated mouth parts of some insects. [Greek *boskō* feed]

proboscis monkey *n.* monkey of Borneo, the male of which has a large pendulous nose.

procedure /prə'siːdʒə(r)/ *n.* **1** way of acting or advancing, esp. in business or legal action. **2** way of performing a task. **3** series of actions conducted in a certain order or manner. **4** section of a computer program that carries out a well-defined operation on data. □ **procedural** *adj.* [French: related to PROCEED]

proceed /prə'siːd/ *v.* **1** (often foll. by *to*) go forward or on further; make one's way. **2** (often foll. by *with*, or *to* + infin.) continue with an activity; go on to do something (*proceeded with their work*; *proceeded to beg me*). **3** (of an action) be carried on or continued (*the case will now proceed*). **4** adopt a course of action (*how shall we proceed?*). **5** go on to say. **6** (foll. by *against*) start a lawsuit against (a person). **7** (often foll. by *from*) originate (*trouble proceeded from illness*). [Latin *cedo cess-* go]

proceeding *n.* **1** action or piece of conduct (*high-handed proceeding*). **2** (in *pl.*) (in full **legal proceedings**) lawsuit. **3** (in *pl.*) published report of discussions or a conference.

proceeds /'prəʊsiːdz/ *n.pl.* profits from sale etc. [pl. of obsolete *proceed* (n.) from PROCEED]

process[1] /'prəʊses/ *–n.* **1** course of action or proceeding, esp. a series of stages in manufacture etc. **2** progress or course (*in process of construction*). **3** natural or involuntary course or change (*process of growing old*). **4** action at law;

summons or writ. **5** *Computing* task currently being executed by the processor or awaiting execution. **6** natural projection of a bone, stem, etc. –*v.* **1** deal with by a particular process. **2** (as **processed** *adj.*) treat (food, esp. to prevent decay) (*processed cheese*). **3** *Computing* perform a sequence of arithmetic calculations and logical operations on (data) in accordance with instructions in a computer program. See also PROCESSOR 3. [Latin: related to PROCEED]

process[2] /prə'ses/ *v.* walk in procession. [back-formation from PROCESSION]

process control *n.* computer-based monitoring and control of a manufacturing or industrial process. Sensing instruments measure one or more variables. The input from these instruments is compared with the optimum values, and control devices are adjusted to maintain the process in an efficient and safe state. Any serious problems will cause automatic safety features to operate and human supervisors will be notified.

procession /prə'seʃ(ə)n/ *n.* **1** people or vehicles etc. advancing in orderly succession, esp. at a ceremony, demonstration, or festivity. **2** movement of such a group (*go in procession*). [Latin: related to PROCEED]

processional –*adj.* **1** of processions. **2** used, carried, or sung in processions. –*n.* *Eccl.* processional hymn or hymn book.

processor /'prəʊsesə(r)/ *n.* **1** machine that processes things. **2** = FOOD PROCESSOR. **3** *Computing* piece of hardware, or a combination of hardware and firmware, whose function is to interpret and execute instructions. It may be the principal operating part of a computer (see CENTRAL PROCESSOR). In larger or more complex computers there may be several processors, acting independently, each one performing some of the processing tasks or possibly having a specialized function. See also MICROPROCESSOR. **4** = COMPUTER.

proclaim /prə'kleɪm/ *v.* **1** (often foll. by *that*) announce or declare publicly or officially. **2** declare to be (king, a traitor, etc.). □ **proclamation** /ˌprɒklə'meɪʃ(ə)n/ *n.* [Latin: related to CLAIM]

proclivity /prə'klɪvɪtɪ/ *n.* (*pl.* **-ies**) tendency, inclination. [Latin *clivus* slope]

procrastinate /prəʊ'kræstɪˌneɪt/ *v.* (**-ting**) defer action. □ **procrastination** /-'neɪʃ(ə)n/ *n.* **procrastinator** *n.* [Latin *cras* tomorrow]

■ **Usage** *Procrastinate* is often confused with *prevaricate* which means 'to be evasive, quibble'.

procreate /'prəʊkrɪˌeɪt/ *v.* (**-ting**) (often *absol.*) produce (offspring) naturally. □ **procreation** /-'eɪʃ(ə)n/ *n.* **procreative** *adj.* [Latin: related to CREATE]

Procrustean /prəʊ'krʌstɪən/ *adj.* seeking to enforce uniformity ruthlessly or violently. [Greek *Prokroustēs*, name of a robber who fitted his victims to a bed by stretching them or cutting bits off them]

proctor /'prɒktə(r)/ *n.* disciplinary officer (usu. one of two) at certain universities. □ **proctorial** /-'tɔːrɪəl/ *adj.* **proctorship** *n.* [from PROCURATOR]

procuration /ˌprɒkjʊ'reɪʃ(ə)n/ *n.* **1** *formal* act of procuring. **2** function or authorized action of an attorney. [Latin: related to PROCURE]

procurator /'prɒkjʊˌreɪtə(r)/ *n.* agent or proxy, esp. with power of attorney. [Latin *procurator* agent]

procurator fiscal *n.* (in Scotland) local coroner and public prosecutor.

procure /prə'kjʊə(r)/ *v.* (**-ring**) **1** obtain, esp. by care or effort; acquire (*managed to procure a copy*). **2** bring about (*procured their dismissal*). **3** (also *absol.*) obtain (women) for prostitution. □ **procurement** *n.* [Latin *curo* look after]

procurer *n.* (*fem.* **procuress**) person who obtains women for prostitution. [Latin PROCURATOR]

prod –*v.* (**-dd-**) **1** poke with a finger, stick, etc. **2** stimulate to action. **3** (foll. by *at*) make a prodding motion. –*n.* **1** poke, thrust. **2** stimulus to action. [origin unknown]

prodigal /'prɒdɪg(ə)l/ –*adj.* **1** recklessly wasteful. **2** (foll. by *of*) lavish. –*n.* **1** prodigal person. **2** (in full **prodigal son**) repentant wastrel, returned wanderer, etc. (Luke 15:11–32). □ **prodigality** /-'gælɪtɪ/ *n.* [Latin *prodigus* lavish]

prodigious /prə'dɪdʒəs/ *adj.* **1** marvellous or amazing. **2** enormous. **3** abnormal. [Latin: related to PRODIGY]

prodigy /'prɒdɪdʒɪ/ *n.* (*pl.* **-ies**) **1** exceptionally gifted or able person, esp. a precocious child. **2** marvellous, esp. extraordinary, thing. **3** (foll. by *of*) wonderful example (of a quality). [Latin *prodigium* portent]

produce –*v.* /prə'djuːs/ (**-cing**) **1** manufacture or prepare (goods etc.). **2** bring forward for consideration, inspection, or use (*will produce evidence*). **3** bear, yield, or bring into existence (offspring, fruit, a harvest, etc.). **4** cause or bring about (a reaction, sensation, etc.). **5** *Geom.* extend or continue (a line). **6** supervise the production of (a play, film, broadcast, record, etc.). –*n.* /'prɒdjuːs/ **1 a** what is produced, esp. agricultural products collectively (*dairy produce*). See also COMMODITY. **b** amount of this. **2** (often foll. by *of*) result (of labour, efforts, etc.). □ **producible** /prə'djuːsɪb(ə)l/ *adj.* [Latin *duco duct-* lead]

◆ **produce broker** see COMMODITY BROKER.

producer /prə'djuːsə(r)/ *n.* **1** person who produces goods etc. **2** person who supervises the production of a play, film, broadcast, etc.

◆ **producer goods** *n.pl.* = CAPITAL GOODS.

◆ **producer price index** *n.* (also **PPI**) measure of the rate of inflation among goods purchased and manufactured by UK industry (replacing the former **wholesale price index**). It measures the movements in prices of about 10 000 goods relative to the same base year. Cf. RETAIL PRICE INDEX.

◆ **producer surplus** *n.* amount by which the market price exceeds the price at which producers would be willing to sell at least some goods. A concept analogous to consumer surplus, producer surplus is maximized in perfect competition, which is another way of saying that perfect competition shows Pareto optimality.

◆ **producer theory** *n.* branch of microeconomics that analyses the methods by which goods and services are supplied to a market by firms or entrepreneurs. The combination of producer theory and consumer theory provides an explanation of the interaction of supply and demand in a market. This combination enables predictions to be made both about the behaviour of a particular market (see PARTIAL EQUILIBRIUM ANALYSIS) and the whole economy (see GENERAL EQUILIBRIUM ANALYSIS).

product /'prɒdʌkt/ *n.* **1** thing or substance produced, esp. by manufacture. **2** result. **3** quantity obtained by multiplying. [Latin: related to PRODUCE]

◆ **product differentiation** *n.* distinction between products that fulfil the same purpose but are made by different producers and therefore compete with each other. The distinction may be real (i.e. one product is better than others) or illusory. Producers in a competitive market use packaging, advertising, etc. to enhance the illusion that differences exist where none in fact do. In economic theory, if there is product differentiation, the products are not perfectly substitutable for each other and competition between them is therefore imperfect.

◆ **product elimination** *n.* process used to withdraw a product from a market in an orderly fashion so that it does not disrupt the sale of other products marketed by the same organization.

production /prə'dʌkʃ(ə)n/ *n.* **1** producing or being produced, esp. in large quantities (*go into production*). **2** total yield. **3** *Econ.* process by which inputs (see FACTORS OF PRODUCTION) are converted into outputs (goods etc.). Neoclassical economists usu. analyse the production process by means of a production function, which establishes the combinations of inputs required to produce a set of outputs efficiently. Marxists, however, view the production process as the root of capitalist exploitation, the capitalist extracting labour power from workers and skimming off the surplus for personal use. **Primary pro-**

duction in economic theory is concerned with reaping such natural benefits as those obtained by agriculture, forestry, hunting, fishing, mining, etc. **Secondary production** involves the manufacture of goods, buildings, roads, etc. from raw materials, while **tertiary production** concerns the services provided by transport companies, banks, insurance companies, and the professions. **4** thing produced, esp. a film, play, book, etc. [Latin: related to PRODUCE]

◆ **production function** *n. Econ.* function defining the maximum possible output from different combinations and quantities of inputs; this can be represented as a curve on a graph. In producer theory, if certain assumptions are made, a unique combination of inputs exists that will minimize the cost of a given level of output; this level of output is a point on a curve representing the production function. Production functions are widely used in economic analysis; in fact, the form of the production function can represent the technological possibilities of an economy at a particular time. See also COST MINIMIZATION; PROFIT MAXIMIZATION.

production line *n.* systematized sequence of operations involved in producing a commodity.

productive /prəˈdʌktɪv/ *adj.* **1** of or engaged in the production of goods. **2** producing much (*productive writer*). **3** producing commodities of exchangeable value (*productive labour*). **4** (foll. by *of*) producing or giving rise to (*productive of great annoyance*). □ **productively** *adv.* **productiveness** *n.* [Latin: related to PRODUCE]

◆ **productive expenditure** *n.* money spent by a government on public services, schools, hospitals, etc., i.e. for benefits in the future as opposed to the immediate benefits that follow from current consumption.

productivity /ˌprɒdʌkˈtɪvɪtɪ/ *n.* **1** being productive, capacity to produce. **2** output of an organization, workforce, or economy per unit of input (labour, raw materials, capital, etc.). Economists are usu. interested in changes in productivity, particularly with respect to labour. Increasing labour productivity is one means by which an economy can enhance its competitiveness. See also UNIT LABOUR COSTS.

◆ **productivity agreement** *n.* agreement between an employer and a union in which an increase in wages is given for a measured increase in productivity. To arrive at such an agreement, **productivity bargaining** is needed to reach a compromise between the increase in wages demanded by the unions and the increase in productivity demanded by the employers.

◆ **product life cycle** *n.* (also **PLC**) marketing model that describes the changes of a product's level of sales over a specified period. The model describes four phases, each of which represents a different opportunity for the marketer. A new product starts in the **introduction phase**, characterized by low sales: buyers are unsure about the product and it is not stocked by all distributors. Sales can be increased by introductory price offers and advertising support. If purchasers are satisfied with the product, its reputation will spread and it will enter the **growth phase**: the product will become more widely available and sales will increase. Competitors' versions will then appear and eventually the **maturity phase** will be reached, in which supply and demand are matched and sales stabilize. The maturity phase is the longest period, characterized by intense competition, but eventually a better way of satisfying consumers' needs will almost certainly be provided by another new product and the **decline phase** will be entered. The duration of each phase is unique to each product. Due to the poor profitability of the introduction phase, it is common for marketing expenditure to be high to encourage a quick transition to the growth phase; however, this expenditure has to be weighed against the need to recoup product development costs in the event that the product is a failure.

◆ **product line** *n.* group of closely related products marketed by one company. See also FAMILY BRAND.

◆ **product-market strategy** *n.* (also **Ansoff matrix**) marketing planning model. Companies can sell either existing or new products; and they can sell them either in markets familiar to them (existing markets) or in new markets. The resulting two-by-two matrix gives four alternative strategies for increasing sales. One is to concentrate on selling more existing products into existing markets (i.e. increasing market penetration), by such means as price reductions and increased advertising; this is regarded as a low-risk strategy. Alternatively, an organization can modify or improve its existing products and sell these to current customers (**product development**). The third option is to sell existing products to a new market (**market development**), for example, by exporting them. These two strategies are medium-risk. The highest-risk strategy is to develop new products for new markets.

◆ **product orientation** *n.* attitude of a company that believes its product comes first and that persuading customers to buy it follows. **Market orientation** typifies the attitude of a company that will only produce what it believes it can sell.

◆ **products-guarantee insurance** *n.* insurance against financial loss as a consequence of a fault occurring in a company's product. A product-guarantee claim would be made, for example, to pay for the cost of recalling and repairing cars that are found to have a defective component. This type of policy would not pay compensation to customers or members of the public injured as a result of the defect. Such claims would be met by a products-liability insurance.

◆ **products liability** *n.* liability of manufacturers and other persons for defective products. Under the Consumer Protection Act (1987), passed to conform with the requirements of the European Community (EC) law, the producer of a defective product that causes death or personal injury or damage to property is strictly liable for the damage. A claim may only be made for damage to property if the property was for private use or consumption and the value of the damage caused exceeds £275. The persons liable for a defective product are the producer (i.e. the manufacturer, including producers of component parts and raw materials), a person who puts his or her name or trade mark on the product, a person who imports the product into the EC, and a supplier who fails, when reasonably requested to do so by the person injured, to identify the producer or importer of the product. The purchaser of a defective product may sue the seller for breach of contract in failing to supply a product that conforms to the contract. Under the same act suppliers of consumer goods must ensure that the goods comply with the general safety requirement. Otherwise they commit a criminal offence. See also CONSUMER PROTECTION.

◆ **products-liability insurance** *n.* insurance protecting against liability to pay any compensation to customers who are killed, injured, or have property damaged as a result of a defect in a product that the insured has manufactured or supplied. Costs incurred as a consequence of the defect that are not legal damages would not be covered by a policy of this kind. A products-guarantee insurance is intended to cover these costs.

◆ **product testing** *n.* anonymous testing and evaluation of a product, often used in the early stages of new product development to assess its marketability.

proem /ˈprəʊɪm/ *n.* preface etc. to a book or speech. [Latin from Greek]

Prof. *abbr.* Professor.

profane /prəˈfeɪn/ *–adj.* **1 a** irreverent, blasphemous. **b** (of language) obscene. **2** not sacred or biblical; secular. *–v.* (**-ning**) **1** treat (esp. a sacred thing) irreverently; disregard. **2** violate or pollute. □ **profanation** /ˌprɒfəˈneɪʃ(ə)n/ *n.* [Latin *fanum* temple]

profanity /prəˈfænɪtɪ/ *n.* (*pl.* **-ies**) **1** profane act or language; blasphemy. **2** swear-word.

profess /prəˈfes/ *v.* **1** claim openly to have (a quality or feeling). **2** (often foll. by *to* + infin.) pretend, declare (*profess ignorance*). **3** affirm one's faith in or allegiance to. [Latin *profiteor -fess-* declare]

professed *adj.* **1** self-acknowledged (*professed Christian*). **2** alleged, ostensible. □ **professedly** /-sɪdlɪ/ *adv.*

profession /prəˈfeʃ(ə)n/ *n.* **1** vocation or calling, esp. learned or scientific (*medical profession*). **2** people in a profession. **3** declaration or avowal. □ **the oldest profession** *colloq.* prostitution.

professional *–adj.* **1** of, belonging to, or connected with a profession. **2 a** skilful, competent. **b** worthy of a professional (*professional conduct*). **3** engaged in a specified activity as one's main paid occupation (*professional boxer*). **4** *derog.* engaged in a specified activity, esp. fanatically (*professional agitator*). *–n.* professional person. □ **professionally** *adv.*

♦ **professional-indemnity insurance** *n.* form of third-party insurance that covers a professional person (e.g. a solicitor, surveyor, or accountant) against compensation that must be paid if he or she is successfully sued for professional negligence. This can include the giving of defective advice if the businessperson has been advertising as an expert. See also PUBLIC-LIABILITY INSURANCE.

professionalism *n.* qualities associated with a profession, esp. competence, skill, etc.

♦ **professional valuation** *n.* assessment of the value of an asset (share, property, stock, etc.) in the balance sheet or prospectus of a company, by a person professionally qualified to give such a valuation. The professional qualification necessary will depend on the asset; for example, a qualified surveyor may be needed to value property, whereas unquoted shares might best be valued by a qualified accountant.

professor /prəˈfesə(r)/ *n.* **1 a** (often as a title) highest-ranking academic teaching in a university department; holder of a university chair. **b** *US* university teacher. **2** person who professes a religion etc. □ **professorial** /ˌprɒfɪˈsɔːrɪəl/ *adj.* **professorship** *n.*

proffer *v.* offer. [French: related to PRO-[1], OFFER]

proficient /prəˈfɪʃ(ə)nt/ *adj.* (often foll. by *in*, *at*) adept, expert. □ **proficiency** *n.* **proficiently** *adv.* [Latin *proficio -fect-* advance]

profile /ˈprəʊfaɪl/ *–n.* **1 a** outline, esp. of a human face, as seen from one side. **b** representation of this. **2** short biographical or character sketch. *–v.* (**-ling**) represent or describe by a profile. □ **keep a low profile** remain inconspicuous. [Italian *profilare* draw in outline]

profit /ˈprɒfɪt/ *–n.* **1** advantage or benefit. **2 a** financial gain. **b** excess of the selling price of an article or service being sold over the costs of providing it. **c** surplus of net assets at the end of a period of trading over the net assets at the start of that period, adjusted where relevant for amounts of capital injected or withdrawn by the proprietors. As profit is notoriously hard to define, it is not always possible to derive one single figure of profit for an organization from an accepted set of data. **d** (also **economic profit**) return on capital as a factor of production (see NORMAL ECONOMIC PROFIT; PURE ECONOMIC PROFIT; SUPERPROFIT). *–v.* (**-t-**) **1** (also *absol.*) be beneficial to. **2** obtain advantage or benefit (*profited by the experience*). □ **at a profit** with financial gain. [Latin *profectus*: related to PROFICIENT]

♦ **profitability** /ˌprɒfɪtəˈbɪlɪtɪ/ *n.* capacity or potential of a project or an organization to make a profit. Measures of profitability include return on capital employed, positive net cash flows, and the ratio of net profit to sales.

profitable *adj.* **1** yielding profit. **2** beneficial. □ **profitably** *adv.*

♦ **profit and loss account** *n.* **1** account in the books of an organization showing the profits (or losses) made on its business activities with the deduction of the appropriate expenses. **2** statement of the profit (or loss) of an organization derived from the account in the books. It is one of the statutory accounts that, for most limited companies, has to be filed annually with the UK Registrar of Companies. The profit and loss account usu. consists of three parts. The first is a trading account, showing the total sales income less the costs of production, etc. and any changes in the value of stock or work in progress from the last accounting period; this gives the gross profit (or loss). The second part gives any other income (apart from trading) and lists administrative and other costs to arrive at a net profit (or loss); from this net profit before taxation the appropriate corporation tax is deducted to give the net profit after taxation. In the third part, the net profit after tax is appropriated to dividends or to reserves. The UK Companies Act (1985) gives a choice of four formats, one of which must be used to file a profit and loss account for a registered company.

♦ ***profit à prendre*** /ˌprɒfiː æ ˈprɑ̃drə/ *n.* right to take something off another person's land: a form of incorporeal hereditament. The thing to be taken must consist either of part of the land (e.g. crops) or wild animals existing on it. A right to take water is therefore not a *profit à prendre*. [French, literally = 'profit to take']

♦ **profit centre** *n.* unit within an organization that is required to show a profit.

profiteer /ˌprɒfɪˈtɪə(r)/ *–n.* person who makes excessive profits by charging inflated prices for a commodity that is in short supply, esp. during a war or national disaster. *–v.* make or seek excessive profits, often illegally or on the black market.

profiterole /prəˈfɪtəˌrəʊl/ *n.* small hollow choux bun, usu. filled with cream and covered with chocolate. [French diminutive: related to PROFIT]

♦ **profit forecast** *n.* forecast by the directors of a public company of the profits to be expected in a stated period. If a new flotation is involved, the profit forecast must be reported on by the reporting accountants and the sponsor to the share issue. An existing company is not required to make a profit forecast with its accounts, but if it does it must be reported on by the company's auditors.

♦ **profit function** *n. Econ.* function relating the amount a firm chooses to produce, the costs of its inputs, and its level of profits; this can be represented as a curve on a graph. In producer theory, making certain assumptions, there will be a unique combination of inputs for a given level of output that maximizes profits; this is a point on the curve representing the profit function. However, a firm may choose to maximize some objective other than profits (see MANAGERIAL THEORY OF THE FIRM; SATISFICING BEHAVIOUR), which will lead it to pick some other point on the curve of its profit function.

♦ **profit impact of market strategy** *n.* (also **PIMS**) study of the major factors that influence profits in a wide variety of industries.

profit margin *n.* profit after the deduction of costs.

♦ **profit maximization** *n.* assumption that firms or entrepreneurs will choose outputs and inputs to gain the highest level of profit that is feasible (see PROFIT MOTIVE). Although this is one of the most frequently made assumptions in economics (because it yields simple results), there are several alternative assumptions (see SATISFICING BEHAVIOUR; MANAGERIAL THEORY OF THE FIRM). As with all the other assumptions made in microeconomics, profit maximization, in a perfectly competitive economy, will yield Pareto-optimal results.

♦ **profit motive** *n.* assumption in economics that entrepreneurs seek to maximize profits. The assumption is little more than an observation that most human beings aspire to be wealthy. See also PROFIT MAXIMIZATION.

♦ **profit-sharing** *n.* distributing part of the profits of a company to its employees, in the form of either cash or shares in the company. There are many workers' participation schemes that use profit-sharing as a means of increasing the motivation of employees; some schemes relate the share of the profit to salary or wages, others to length of service, and yet others give equal shares to all who have been employed by the company for a minimum period.

♦ **profits tax** *n.* tax on the profits of a company. See CORPORATION TAX.

♦ **profit-taking** *n.* selling commodities or securities at a profit, either after a market rise or because they show a profit at current levels but will not do so if an expected fall in prices occurs.

profligate /ˈprɒflɪgət/ *–adj.* **1** recklessly extravagant. **2** licentious, dissolute. *–n.* profligate person. □ **profligacy** *n.* **profligately** *adv.* [Latin *profligo* ruin]

♦ **pro forma** /prəʊ ˈfɔːmə/ *–adv.* & *adj.* as or being a matter of form. *–n.* (in full **pro-forma invoice**) invoice sent in advance of goods supplied, usu. before some of the invoice details are known. For example, in commodity trading a pro-forma invoice may be sent to the buyer at the time of shipment, based on a notional weight, although the contract specifies that the buyer will only pay for the weight ascertained on landing the goods at the port of destination. When the missing facts are known, in this case the landed weight, a final invoice is sent. [Latin]

profound /prəˈfaʊnd/ *adj.* **(-er, -est) 1** having or demanding great knowledge, study, or insight (*profound treatise*; *profound doctrines*). **2** intense, unqualified, thorough (*a profound sleep*; *profound indifference*). **3** deep (*profound crevasses*). □ **profoundly** *adv.* **profoundness** *n.* **profundity** /prəˈfʌndɪtɪ/ *n.* (*pl.* **-ies**). [Latin *profundus*]

profuse /prəˈfjuːs/ *adj.* **1** (often foll. by *in*, *of*) lavish; extravagant. **2** exuberantly plentiful; copious (*profuse variety*). □ **profusely** *adv.* **profusion** /-ˈfjuːʒ(ə)n/ *n.* [Latin *fundo fus-* pour]

progenitor /prəʊˈdʒenɪtə(r)/ *n.* **1** ancestor. **2** predecessor. **3** original. [Latin *progigno* beget]

progeny /ˈprɒdʒɪnɪ/ *n.* **1** offspring; descendant(s). **2** outcome, issue. [Latin: related to PROGENITOR]

progesterone /prəʊˈdʒestəˌrəʊn/ *n.* steroid hormone which stimulates the preparation of the uterus for pregnancy and maintains the uterus in the event of fertilization. [German: related to PRO-[1], GESTATION]

progestogen /prəʊˈdʒestədʒɪn/ *n.* **1** steroid hormone (e.g. progesterone) maintaining pregnancy and preventing further ovulation. **2** similar synthetic hormone.

prognosis /prɒgˈnəʊsɪs/ *n.* (*pl.* **-noses** /-siːz/) forecast, esp. of the course of a disease. [Greek *gignōskō* know]

prognostic /prɒgˈnɒstɪk/ *–n.* **1** (often foll. by *of*) advance indication, esp. of the course of a disease. **2** prediction, forecast. *–adj.* (often foll. by *of*) foretelling, predictive. [Latin: related to PROGNOSIS]

prognosticate /prɒgˈnɒstɪˌkeɪt/ *v.* **(-ting) 1** (often foll. by *that*) foretell, foresee, prophesy. **2** (of a thing) betoken, indicate. □ **prognostication** /-ˈkeɪʃ(ə)n/ *n.* **prognosticator** *n.* [medieval Latin: related to PROGNOSTIC]

program /ˈprəʊgræm/ *–n.* **1** *US* var. of PROGRAMME. **2** set of instructions or statements submitted as a unit to a computer system and used to direct the way in which that system behaves. It is expressed in a formal notation (see PROGRAMMING LANGUAGE) and must be converted into the appropriate machine code before it can be executed by the computer. There are usu. various stages in producing a program (see COMPUTER PROGRAMMING). *–v.* **(-mm-) 1** *US* var. of PROGRAMME. **2** feed a program into (a computer). **3** put (data, a problem, etc.) into an appropriate form so that it can be processed by a computer. **4** design and write computer programs. □ **programmable** *adj.* **programmer** *n.*

program file *n. Computing* file containing one or more programs or program fragments. Cf. DATA FILE.

program library *n.* organized collection of computer programs held on backing store. It may be available for general use by all users of a particular computer system, in which case it is called the **system library**. The individual programs are known as **library programs**. A typical library might contain compilers, utility programs, application packages, and procedures or subroutines. A particular library program can be automatically incorporated in a user's program.

programme /ˈprəʊgræm/ (*US* **program**) *–n.* **1** list of events, performers, etc. at a public function etc. **2** radio or television broadcast. **3** plan of events (*programme is dinner and an early night*). **4** course or series of studies, lectures, etc. **5** *Computing* var. of PROGRAM. *–v.* **(-mm-**; *US* **-m-) 1** make a programme of. **2** *Computing* var. of PROGRAM. □ **programmable** *adj.* **programmatic** /-grəˈmætɪk/ *adj.* [Greek *graphō* write]

programming *n.* = COMPUTER PROGRAMMING.

programming language *n.* notation in which a computer program is expressed. It consists of a set of letters, digits, punctuation marks, and other characters that can be assembled into various combinations, together with a strictly defined set of rules describing exactly which combinations are permitted. This set of rules is the **syntax** of the language. The meaning of text constructed according to the syntax is also strictly defined, by the **semantics** of the language. Programming languages are thus artificial languages in that there is no freedom of expression characteristic of a natural language like English. See also HIGH-LEVEL LANGUAGE; LOW-LEVEL LANGUAGE.

♦ **program trading** *n.* trading on international stock exchanges using a computer program to exploit differences between stock index futures and actual share prices on world equity markets. It is said to account for some 10% of the daily turnover (1989–90) on the New York Stock Exchange and has been partly blamed for the market crash in October 1987.

progress *–n.* /ˈprəʊgres/ **1** forward or onward movement towards a destination. **2** advance or development; improvement (*made little progress*). **3** *hist.* state tour, esp. by royalty. *–v.* /prəˈgres/ **1** move or be moved forward or onward; continue. **2** advance, develop, or improve (*science progresses*). □ **in progress** developing; going on. [Latin *progredior -gress-* go forward]

♦ **progress chaser** *n.* person who is responsible for following the progress of work being done in a factory or office and for seeing that it is completed on time.

progression /prəˈgreʃ(ə)n/ *n.* **1** progressing. **2** succession; series. [Latin: related to PROGRESS]

progressive /prəˈgresɪv/ *–adj.* **1** moving forward. **2** proceeding step by step; cumulative (*progressive drug use*). **3 a** favouring rapid political or social reform. **b** modern; efficient (*a progressive company*). **4** (of disease, violence, etc.) increasing in severity or extent. **5** (of a card-game, dance, etc.) with periodic changes of partners. **6** *Gram.* (of a tense) expressing action in progress, e.g. *am writing*, *was writing*. *–n.* (also **Progressive**) advocate of progressive political policies. □ **progressively** *adv.* [French or medieval Latin: related to PROGRESS]

♦ **progressive tax** *n.* tax in which the rate of tax increases with increases in the tax base. The most common of these is income tax but progressive rates are also applied to National Insurance contributions, inheritance tax, and to a limited extent corporation tax. Such taxes are generally linked to the ability-to-pay principle (see ABILITY-TO-PAY TAXATION). Cf. PROPORTIONAL TAX.

♦ **progress payment** *n.* instalment of a total payment made to a contractor when a specified stage of the operation has been completed.

prohibit /prəˈhɪbɪt/ *v.* **(-t-)** (often foll. by *from* + verbal noun) **1** forbid. **2** prevent. □ **prohibitor** *n.* **prohibitory** *adj.* [Latin *prohibeo -hibit-*]

prohibited degrees var. of FORBIDDEN DEGREES.

prohibition /ˌprəʊhɪˈbɪʃ(ə)n, ˌprəʊɪˈb-/ *n.* **1** forbidding or being forbidden. **2** edict or order that forbids. **3** (usu. **Prohibition**) legal ban on the manufacture and sale of alcohol, esp. in the US (1920–33). □ **prohibitionist** *n.* (in sense 3).

prohibitive /prə'hɪbɪtɪv/ *adj.* **1** prohibiting. **2** (of prices, taxes, etc.) extremely high (*prohibitive price*). □ **prohibitively** *adv.*

project *–n.* /'prɒdʒekt/ **1** plan; scheme. **2** extensive essay, piece of research, etc. by a student. *–v.* /prə'dʒekt/ **1** protrude; jut out. **2** throw; cast; impel. **3** extrapolate (results etc.) to a future time; forecast. **4** plan or contrive (a scheme etc.). **5** cause (light, shadow, images, etc.) to fall on a surface. **6** cause (a sound, esp. the voice) to be heard at a distance. **7** (often *refl.* or *absol.*) express or promote forcefully or effectively. **8** make a projection of (the earth, sky, etc.). **9 a** (also *absol.*) attribute (an emotion etc.) to an external object or person, esp. unconsciously. **b** (*refl.*) imagine (oneself) having another's feelings, being in the future, etc. [Latin *projicio -ject-* throw forth]

projectile /prə'dʒektaɪl/ *–n.* **1** missile, esp. fired by a rocket. **2** bullet, shell, etc. *–adj.* **1** capable of being projected by force, esp. from a gun. **2** projecting or impelling.

projection /prə'dʒekʃ(ə)n/ *n.* **1** projecting or being projected. **2** thing that projects or obtrudes. **3** presentation of an image etc. on a surface. **4** forecast or estimate (*projection of next year's profits*). **5 a** mental image viewed as an objective reality. **b** unconscious transfer of feelings etc. to external objects or persons. **6** representation on a plane surface of any part of the surface of the earth or a celestial sphere (*Mercator projection*). □ **projectionist** *n.* (in sense 3).

projector /prə'dʒektə(r)/ *n.* apparatus for projecting slides or film on to a screen.

prokaryote /prəʊ'kærɪət/ *n.* (also **procaryote**) organism in which the chromosomes are not separated from the cytoplasm by a membrane; bacterium. [from PRO-[2], *karyo-* from Greek *karuon* kernel, *-ote* as in ZYGOTE]

prolactin /prəʊ'læktɪn/ *n.* hormone that stimulates milk production after childbirth. [from PRO-[1], LACTATION]

prolapse /'prəʊlæps/ *–n.* (also **prolapsus** /-'læpsəs/) **1** forward or downward displacement of a part or organ. **2** prolapsed womb, rectum, etc. *–v.* (**-sing**) undergo prolapse. [Latin: related to LAPSE]

prolate /'prəʊleɪt/ *adj. Geom.* (of a spheroid) lengthened in the direction of a polar diameter. [Latin, = brought forward, prolonged]

prole *adj.* & *n. derog. colloq.* proletarian. [abbreviation]

prolegomenon /ˌprəʊlɪ'gɒmɪnən/ *n.* (*pl.* **-mena**) (usu. in *pl.*) preface to a book etc., esp. when critical or discursive. [Greek *legō* say]

proletarian /ˌprəʊlɪ'teərɪən/ *–adj.* of the proletariat. *–n.* member of the proletariat. [Latin *proles* offspring]

proletariat /ˌprəʊlɪ'teərɪət/ *n.* **1** wage-earners collectively. **2** esp. *derog.* lowest, esp. uneducated, class. [French: related to PROLETARIAN]

proliferate /prə'lɪfəˌreɪt/ *v.* (**-ting**) **1** reproduce; produce (cells etc.) rapidly. **2** increase rapidly in numbers. □ **proliferation** /-'reɪʃ(ə)n/ *n.* [Latin *proles* offspring]

prolific /prə'lɪfɪk/ *adj.* **1** producing many offspring or much output. **2** (often foll. by *of*) abundantly productive. **3** (often foll. by *in*) abounding, copious. □ **prolifically** *adv.* [medieval Latin: related to PROLIFERATE]

prolix /'prəʊlɪks/ *adj.* (of speech, writing, etc.) lengthy; tedious. □ **prolixity** /-'lɪksɪtɪ/ *n.* [Latin]

Prolog /'prəʊlɒg/ *n.* (also **PROLOG**) programming language based on symbolic logic and widely used in the field of artificial intelligence. [from *pro*gramming in *log*ic]

prologue /'prəʊlɒg/ *n.* **1** preliminary speech, poem, etc., esp. of a play. **2** (usu. foll. by *to*) introductory event. [Greek *logos* word]

prolong /prə'lɒŋ/ *v.* **1** extend in time or space. **2** (as **prolonged** *adj.*) lengthy, esp. tediously so. □ **prolongation** /ˌprəʊlɒŋ'geɪʃ(ə)n/ *n.* [Latin *longus* long]

PROM *abbr. Computing* programmable read-only memory, a type of semiconductor memory that is fabricated in a similar way to ROM. The contents required, however, are added after rather than during manufacture and cannot be altered from that time.

prom *n. colloq.* **1** = PROMENADE *n.* 1. **2** = PROMENADE CONCERT. [abbreviation]

promenade /ˌprɒmə'nɑːd/ *–n.* **1** paved public walk, esp. along the sea front at a resort. **2** walk, ride, or drive, taken esp. for display or pleasure. *–v.* (**-ding**) **1** make a promenade (through). **2** lead (a person etc.) about, esp. for display. [French]

promenade concert *n.* concert with restricted seating and a large area for standing.

promenade deck *n.* upper deck on a passenger ship.

promenader *n.* **1** person who promenades. **2** regular attender at promenade concerts.

Promethean /prə'miːθɪən/ *adj.* daring or inventive. [*Prometheus*, a mortal punished by the Greek gods for stealing fire]

promethium /prə'miːθɪəm/ *n.* radioactive metallic element of the lanthanide series, found in nuclear waste. [*Prometheus*: see PROMETHEAN]

prominence /'prɒmɪnəns/ *n.* **1** being prominent. **2** jutting outcrop, mountain, etc. [Latin: related to PROMINENT]

prominent /'prɒmɪnənt/ *adj.* **1** jutting out, projecting. **2** conspicuous. **3** distinguished, important. [Latin *promineo* project]

promiscuous /prə'mɪskjʊəs/ *adj.* **1** having frequent, esp. casual, sexual relationships. **2** mixed and indiscriminate. **3** *colloq.* carelessly irregular; casual. □ **promiscuity** /-'skjuːɪtɪ/ *n.* **promiscuously** *adv.* [Latin *misceo* mix]

promise /'prɒmɪs/ *–n.* **1** assurance that one will or will not undertake a certain action etc. (*promise of help*). **2** sign of future achievements, good results, etc. (*writer of great promise*). *–v.* (**-sing**) **1** (usu. foll. by *to* + infin., or *that* + clause; also *absol.*) make a promise (*promise not to be late*). **2** (often foll. by *to* + infin.) seem likely (to) (*promises to be a good book*). **3** *colloq.* assure (*I promise you, it will not be easy*). □ **promise well** (or **ill** etc.) hold out good (or bad etc.) prospects. [Latin *promissum* from *mitto miss-* send]

promised land *n.* (prec. by *the*) **1** *Bibl.* Canaan (Gen. 12:7 etc.). **2** any desired place, esp. heaven.

promising *adj.* likely to turn out well; hopeful, full of promise (*promising start*). □ **promisingly** *adv.*

promissory /'prɒmɪsərɪ/ *adj.* conveying or implying a promise. [medieval Latin: related to PROMISE]

♦ **promissory note** *n.* document that is a negotiable instrument and contains a promise to pay a certain sum of money to a named person, to his or her order, or to the bearer. It must be unconditional, signed by the maker, and delivered to the payee or bearer. A promissory note cannot be reissued, unless the promise is made by a banker and is payable to the bearer, i.e. unless it is a banknote. These documents are widely used in the US but not in common use in the UK.

---

promo /'prəʊməʊ/ *n.* (*pl.* **-s**) *colloq.* **1** (often *attrib.*) promotion, advertising (*promo video*). **2** promotional video, trailer, etc. [abbreviation]

promontory /'prɒməntərɪ/ *n.* (*pl.* **-ies**) point of high land jutting out into the sea etc.; headland. [Latin]

promote /prə'məʊt/ *v.* (**-ting**) **1** (often foll. by *to*) raise (a person) to a higher office, rank, etc. (*promoted to captain*). **2** help forward; encourage (a cause, process, etc.). **3** publicize and sell (a product). See SALES PROMOTION. **4** *Chess* raise (a pawn) to the rank of queen etc. □ **promotion** /-'məʊʃ(ə)n/ *n.* **promotional** /-'məʊʃən(ə)l/ *adj.* [Latin *promoveo -mot-*]

promoter *n.* **1** person who promotes, esp. a sporting event, theatrical production, etc. **2** (in full **company promoter**) person involved in setting up and funding a new company, including preparing its articles and memorandum of association, registering the company, finding directors, and raising subscriptions. The promoter is in a position of trust with regard to the new company and may not make an undisclosed profit or benefit at its expense. A promoter may be personally liable for the fulfilment of a contract entered into by, or on behalf of, the new company before it has been formed. [medieval Latin: related to PROMOTE]

prompt –*adj.* acting, made, or done with alacrity; ready (*prompt reply*). –*adv.* punctually (*at six o'clock prompt*). –*v.* **1** (usu. foll. by *to*, or *to* + infin.) incite; urge (*prompted them to action*). **2 a** (also *absol.*) supply a forgotten word etc. to (an actor etc.). **b** assist (a hesitating speaker) with a suggestion. **3** give rise to; inspire (feeling, thought, action, etc.). –*n.* **1 a** act of prompting. **b** thing said to prompt an actor etc. **c** = PROMPTER. **2** *Computing* short message or sign on a VDU screen to show that the system is waiting for input. □ **promptitude** *n.* **promptly** *adv.* **promptness** *n.* [Latin]

◆ **prompt cash** *n.* payment terms for goods or services in which payment is due within a few days (usu. not more than 14) of delivery of the goods or the rendering of the service.

◆ **prompt day** *n.* (also **prompt date**) **1** day or date on which payment is due for the purchase of goods. In some commodity spot markets it is the day payment is due and delivery of the goods may be effected. **2** date on which a contract on a commodity exchange, such as the London Metal Exchange, matures.

prompter *n.* person who prompts actors.

promulgate /'prɒməlˌgeɪt/ *v.* (**-ting**) **1** make known to the public; disseminate; promote. **2** proclaim (a decree, news, etc.). □ **promulgation** /-'geɪʃ(ə)n/ *n.* **promulgator** *n.* [Latin]

prone *adj.* **1 a** lying face downwards. **b** lying flat, prostrate. **c** having the front part downwards, esp. the palm. **2** (usu. foll. by *to*, or *to* + infin.) disposed or liable (*prone to bite his nails*). **3** (usu. in *comb.*) likely to suffer (*accident-prone*). □ **proneness** /'prəʊnnɪs/ *n.* [Latin]

PRONED /'prəʊˌnɛd/ *abbr.* Promotion of Non-Executive Directors.

prong *n.* each of two or more projecting pointed parts at the end of a fork etc. [origin unknown]

pronominal /prəʊ'nɒmɪn(ə)l/ *adj.* of, concerning, or being, a pronoun. [Latin: related to PRONOUN]

pronoun /'prəʊnaʊn/ *n.* word used instead of and to indicate a noun already mentioned or known, esp. to avoid repetition (e.g. we, their, this, ourselves). [from PRO-[1], NOUN]

pronounce /prə'naʊns/ *v.* (**-cing**) **1** (also *absol.*) utter or speak (words, sounds, etc.) in a certain, or esp. in the approved, way. **2** utter or proclaim (a judgement, sentence, etc.) officially, formally, or solemnly (*I pronounce you man and wife*). **3** state as one's opinion (*pronounced the beef excellent*). **4** (usu. foll. by *on, for, against, in favour of*) pass judgement (*pronounced for the defendant*). □ **pronounceable** *adj.* **pronouncement** *n.* [Latin *nuntio* announce]

pronounced *adj.* strongly marked; noticeable (*pronounced limp*).

pronto /'prɒntəʊ/ *adv. colloq.* promptly, quickly. [Latin: related to PROMPT]

pronunciation /prəˌnʌnsɪ'eɪʃ(ə)n/ *n.* **1** pronouncing of a word, esp. with reference to a standard. **2** act of pronouncing. **3** way of pronouncing words etc. [Latin: related to PRONOUNCE]

proof –*n.* **1** facts, evidence, reasoning, etc. establishing or helping to establish a fact (*no proof that he was there*). **2** demonstration, proving (*not capable of proof*). **3** test, trial (*put them to the proof*). **4** standard of strength of distilled alcohol. **5** trial impression from type or film, for correcting before final printing. **6** step by step resolution of a mathematical or philosophical problem. **7** photographic print made for selection etc. –*adj.* **1** (often in *comb.*) impervious to penetration, ill effects, etc., esp. by a specified agent (*proof against corruption*; *childproof*). **2** being of proof alcoholic strength. –*v.* **1** make proof, esp. make (fabric) waterproof. **2** make a proof of (a printed work). [Latin *proba*: related to PROVE]

proofread *v.* (*past* and *past part.* **-read** /-red/) read and correct (printer's proofs). □ **proofreader** *n.*

prop[1] –*n.* **1** rigid, esp. separate, support. **2** person who supports, comforts, etc. –*v.* (**-pp-**) (often foll. by *against*, *up*, etc.) support with or as if with a prop. [Low German or Dutch]

prop[2] *n. colloq.* = PROPERTY 4. [abbreviation]

prop[3] *n. colloq.* aircraft propeller. [abbreviation]

propaganda /ˌprɒpə'gændə/ *n.* **1** organized propagation of a doctrine by use of publicity, selected information, etc. **2** usu. *derog.* ideas etc. so propagated. □ **propagandist** *n.* & *adj.* [Latin: related to PROPAGATE]

propagate /'prɒpəˌgeɪt/ *v.* (**-ting**) **1 a** breed (a plant, animal, etc.) from the parent stock. **b** (*refl.* or *absol.*) (of a plant, animal, etc.) reproduce itself. **2** disseminate (a belief, theory, etc.). **3** transmit (a vibration, earthquake, etc.). □ **propagation** /-'geɪʃ(ə)n/ *n.* [Latin *propago*]

propagator *n.* **1** person or thing that propagates. **2** small heated box for germinating seeds or raising seedlings.

propane /'prəʊpeɪn/ *n.* gaseous hydrocarbon used as bottled fuel. [*propionic acid*: related to PRO-[2], Greek *piōn* fat]

propanone /'prəʊpəˌnəʊn/ *n. Chem.* = ACETONE. [from PROPANE]

propel /prə'pel/ *v.* (**-ll-**) drive or push forward; urge on. □ **propellant** *n.* & *adj.* [Latin *pello puls-* drive]

propeller *n.* revolving shaft with blades, esp. for propelling a ship or aircraft.

propene /'prəʊpiːn/ *n. Chem.* = PROPYLENE. [from PROPANE, ALKENE]

propensity /prə'pensɪtɪ/ *n.* (*pl.* **-ies**) inclination, tendency. [Latin *propensus* inclined]

proper /'prɒpə(r)/ *adj.* **1 a** accurate, correct (*gave him the proper amount*). **b** fit, suitable, right (*at the proper time*). **2** decent; respectable, esp. excessively so (*not quite proper*). **3** (usu. foll. by *to*) belonging or relating (*respect proper to them*). **4** (usu. placed after the noun) strictly so called; genuine (*this is the crypt, not the cathedral proper*). **5** *colloq.* thorough; complete (*a proper row*). [Latin *proprius* one's own]

proper fraction *n.* fraction less than unity, with the numerator less than the denominator.

properly *adv.* **1** fittingly, suitably (*do it properly*). **2** accurately, correctly (*properly speaking*). **3** rightly. **4** with decency; respectably (*behave properly*). **5** *colloq.* thoroughly (*properly puzzled*).

proper noun *n.* (also **proper name**) capitalized name for an individual person, place, animal, country, title, etc., e.g. 'Jane', 'Everest'.

propertied /'prɒpətɪd/ *adj.* having property, esp. land.

property /'prɒpətɪ/ *n.* (*pl.* **-ies**) **1** thing(s) capable of being owned (see PERSONAL PROPERTY; REAL PROPERTY) and which may be tangible (e.g. a building or work of art) or intangible (e.g. a right of way or a right under a contract). **2** possession, esp. a house, land, etc. (*has money in property*). **3** attribute, quality, or characteristic (*property of dissolving grease*). **4** movable object used on a theatre stage or in a film. [Latin *proprietas*: related to PROPER]

◆ **property bond** *n.* bond issued by a life-assurance company, the premiums for which are invested in a fund that owns property.

◆ **property income certificate** *n.* (also **PINC**) certificate giving the bearer a share in the value of a particular property and a share of the income from it. PINCs can be bought and sold.

◆ **property insurance** *n.* insurance covering loss, damage, or destruction of any form of item from personal jewellery to industrial plant and machinery. Property-insurance policies are a form of indemnity in which the insurer undertakes to make good the loss suffered by the insured. The policy may state the specific compensation payable in the event of loss or damage; if it does not, the policy will usu. pay the intrinsic value of the insured object, taking into account any appreciation or depreciation on the original cost. Such policies usu. have a maximum sum for which the insurers are liable.

◆ **property register** see LAND REGISTRATION.

◆ **property tax** *n.* tax based on the value of property owned by the taxpayer.

---

prophecy /ˈprɒfɪsɪ/ *n.* (*pl.* **-ies**) **1 a** prophetic utterance, esp. biblical. **b** prediction of future events. **2** faculty, practice, etc. of prophesying (*gift of prophecy*). [Greek: related to PROPHET]

prophesy /ˈprɒfɪˌsaɪ/ *v.* (**-ies, -ied**) **1** (usu. foll. by *that, who,* etc.) foretell (an event etc.). **2** speak as a prophet; foretell the future. [French *profecier*: related to PROPHECY]

prophet /ˈprɒfɪt/ *n.* (*fem.* **prophetess**) **1** teacher or interpreter of the supposed will of God. **2 a** person who foretells events. **b** spokesman; advocate (*prophet of the new order*). **3** (**the Prophet**) Muhammad. [Greek *prophētēs* spokesman]

prophetic /prəˈfetɪk/ *adj.* **1** (often foll. by *of*) containing a prediction; predicting. **2** of a prophet. □ **prophetically** *adv.* [Latin: related to PROPHET]

prophylactic /ˌprɒfɪˈlæktɪk/ –*adj.* tending to prevent disease etc. –*n.* **1** preventive medicine or action. **2** esp. *US* condom. [Greek, = keeping guard before]

prophylaxis /ˌprɒfɪˈlæksɪs/ *n.* preventive treatment against disease. [from PRO-², Greek *phulaxis* guarding]

propinquity /prəˈpɪŋkwɪtɪ/ *n.* **1** nearness in space; proximity. **2** close kinship. **3** similarity. [Latin *prope* near]

propitiate /prəˈpɪʃɪˌeɪt/ *v.* (**-ting**) appease (an offended person etc.). □ **propitiable** *adj.* **propitiation** /-ˈeɪʃ(ə)n/ *n.* **propitiator** *n.* **propitiatory** /-ʃətərɪ/ *adj.* [Latin: related to PROPITIOUS]

propitious /prəˈpɪʃəs/ *adj.* **1** (of an omen etc.) favourable, auspicious. **2** (often foll. by *for, to*) suitable, advantageous. [Latin *propitius*]

proponent /prəˈpəʊnənt/ *n.* person advocating a motion, theory, or proposal. [Latin: related to PROPOSE]

proportion /prəˈpɔːʃ(ə)n/ –*n.* **1 a** comparative part or share (*large proportion of the profits*). **b** comparative ratio (*proportion of births to deaths*). **2** correct or pleasing relation of things or parts of a thing (*has fine proportions; exaggerated out of all proportion*). **3** (in *pl.*) dimensions; size (*large proportions*). **4** *Math.* equality of ratios between two pairs of quantities, e.g. 3:5 and 9:15. –*v.* (usu. foll. by *to*) make proportionate (*proportion the punishment to the crime*). [Latin: related to PORTION]

proportional *adj.* in due proportion; comparable (*proportional increase in the expense*). □ **proportionally** *adv.*

proportional representation *n.* electoral system in which parties gain seats in proportion to the number of votes cast for them.

◆ **proportional spacing** *n.* feature of some typewriters, printers, and typesetting machines whereby each character occupies a space proportional to its size rather than having a uniform width.

◆ **proportional tax** *n.* tax in which the amount of tax paid is proportional to the size of the tax base, i.e. a tax with a single rate. Cf. PROGRESSIVE TAX.

---

proportionate /prəˈpɔːʃənət/ *adj.* = PROPORTIONAL. □ **proportionately** *adv.*

proposal /prəˈpəʊz(ə)l/ *n.* **1 a** act of proposing something. **b** course of action etc. proposed. **2** offer of marriage.

propose /prəˈpəʊz/ *v.* (**-sing**) **1** (also *absol.*) put forward for consideration or as a plan; suggest. **2** (usu. foll. by *to* + infin., or verbal noun) intend; purpose (*propose to open a café*). **3** (usu. foll. by *to*) offer oneself in marriage. **4** nominate (a person) as a member of a society, for an office, etc. □ **propose a toast** (or **somebody's health**) ask people to drink to someone's health. □ **proposer** *n.* [Latin *pono posit-* place]

proposition /ˌprɒpəˈzɪʃ(ə)n/ –*n.* **1** statement, assertion. **2** scheme proposed, proposal. **3** *Logic* statement subject to proof or disproof. **4** *colloq.* problem, opponent, prospect, etc. for consideration (*difficult proposition*). **5** *Math.* formal statement of a theorem or problem, often including the demonstration. **6 a** likely commercial etc. enterprise etc. **b** person regarded similarly. **7** *colloq.* sexual proposal. –*v. colloq.* make a (esp. sexual) proposal to (*he propositioned her*). [Latin: related to PROPOSE]

propound /prəˈpaʊnd/ *v.* offer for consideration; propose. [*propo(u)ne* from Latin: related to PROPOSE]

proprietary /prəˈpraɪətərɪ/ *adj.* **1 a** of or holding property (*proprietary classes*). **b** of a proprietor (*proprietary rights*). **2** held in private ownership. [Latin *proprietarius*: related to PROPERTY]

◆ **proprietary company** *n.* (in Australia & South Africa) private limited company. The abbreviation 'Pty.' must be used after the name of such a company.

---

proprietary medicine *n.* drug, medicine, etc. produced by a company, usu. under a patent.

proprietary name *n.* (also **proprietary term**) registered name of a product etc. as a trade mark.

proprietor /prəˈpraɪətə(r)/ *n.* (*fem.* **proprietress**) **1** holder of property. **2** owner of a business etc., esp. of a hotel. □ **proprietorial** /-ˈtɔːrɪəl/ *adj.* [related to PROPRIETARY]

◆ **proprietorship register** see LAND REGISTRATION.

---

propriety /prəˈpraɪɪtɪ/ *n.* (*pl.* **-ies**) **1** fitness; rightness. **2** correctness of behaviour or morals. **3** (in *pl.*) details or rules of correct conduct. [French: related to PROPERTY]

propulsion /prəˈpʌlʃ(ə)n/ *n.* **1** driving or pushing forward. **2** impelling influence. □ **propulsive** /-ˈpʌlsɪv/ *adj.* [related to PROPEL]

propylene /ˈprəʊpɪˌliːn/ *n.* gaseous hydrocarbon used in the manufacture of chemicals. [from *propyl*, a univalent radical of propane]

pro rata /prəʊ ˈrɑːtə/ –*adj.* proportional. –*adv.* proportionally. [Latin]

prorogue /prəˈrəʊg/ *v.* (**-gues, -gued, -guing**) **1** discontinue the meetings of (a parliament etc.) without dissolving it. **2** (of a parliament etc.) be prorogued. □ **prorogation** /ˌprəʊrəˈgeɪʃ(ə)n/ *n.* [Latin *prorogo* extend]

PROS *abbr.* preventive maintenance, repair, and operational services.

prosaic /prəˈzeɪɪk/ *adj.* **1** like prose, lacking poetic beauty. **2** unromantic; dull; commonplace. □ **prosaically** *adv.* [Latin: related to PROSE]

pros and cons *n.pl.* reasons or considerations for and against a proposition etc.

proscenium /prəˈsiːnɪəm/ *n.* (*pl.* **-s** or **-nia**) part of the stage in front of the curtain and the enclosing arch. [Greek: related to SCENE]

proscribe /prəˈskraɪb/ *v.* (**-bing**) **1** forbid, esp. by law. **2** reject or denounce (a practice etc.). **3** outlaw (a person). □ **proscription** /-ˈskrɪpʃ(ə)n/ *n.* **proscriptive** /-ˈskrɪptɪv/ *adj.* [Latin, = publish in writing]

■ **Usage** *Proscribe* is sometimes confused with *prescribe*.

prose /prəʊz/ –*n.* **1** ordinary written or spoken language not in verse. **2** passage of prose, esp. for translation into a foreign language. **3** dull or matter-of-fact quality (*prose of existence*). –*v.* (**-sing**) talk tediously. [Latin *prosa* from *oratio* straightforward (discourse)]

prosecute /ˈprɒsɪˌkjuːt/ *v.* (**-ting**) **1** (also *absol.*) institute legal proceedings against (a person), or with reference to (a claim, crime, etc.) (*decided not to prosecute*). **2** *formal* carry on (a trade, pursuit, etc.). □ **prosecutor** *n.* [Latin *prosequor -secut-* pursue]

prosecution /ˌprɒsɪˈkjuːʃ(ə)n/ *n.* **1 a** institution and continuation of (esp. criminal) legal proceedings. **b** prosecuting party in a court case. **2** prosecuting or being prosecuted (*in the prosecution of his hobby*).

proselyte /ˈprɒsəˌlaɪt/ *n.* **1** person converted, esp. recently, from one opinion, creed, party, etc., to another. **2** convert to Judaism. □ **proselytism** /-ləˌtɪz(ə)m/ *n.* [Latin *proselytus* from Greek]

proselytize /ˈprɒsələˌtaɪz/ *v.* (also **-ise**) (**-zing** or **-sing**) (also *absol.*) convert or seek to convert from one belief etc. to another.

prose poem *n.* piece of poetic writing in prose.

prosody /ˈprɒsədɪ/ *n.* **1** science of versification. **2** the study of speech-rhythms. □ **prosodic** /prəˈsɒdɪk/ *adj.* **prosodist** *n.* [Greek *pros* to: related to ODE]

prospect –*n.* /ˈprɒspekt/ **1 a** (often in *pl.*) expectation, esp. of success in a career etc. (*job with no prospects*). **b** something one expects (*don't relish the prospect of meeting him*). **2** extensive view of landscape etc. (*striking prospect*). **3** mental picture. **4** possible or probable customer, subscriber, etc. –*v.* /prəˈspekt/ (usu. foll. by *for*) explore, search (esp. a region) for gold etc. □ **prospector** /prəˈspektə(r)/ *n.* [Latin: related to PROSPECTUS]

prospective /prəˈspektɪv/ *adj.* some day to be; expected; future (*prospective bridegroom*). [Latin: related to PROSPECTUS]

♦ **prospective damages** see DAMAGES.

---

prospectus /prəˈspektəs/ *n.* (*pl.* **-tuses**) **1** printed document advertising or describing a school, forthcoming book, etc. **2** document that gives details about a new issue of shares and invites the public to buy shares or debentures in the company. A copy must be filed with the Registrar of Companies. The prospectus must conform to the provisions of the Companies Act (1985), describe the aims, capital structure, and any past history of the venture, and may contain future profit forecasts. There are heavy penalties for knowingly making false statements in a prospectus. [Latin, = prospect, from *prospicio -spect-* look forward]

prosper *v.* be successful, thrive. [Latin *prospero*]

prosperity /prɒˈsperɪtɪ/ *n.* prosperous state; wealth; success.

prosperous /ˈprɒspərəs/ *adj.* **1** successful; rich; thriving. **2** auspicious (*prosperous wind*). □ **prosperously** *adv.* [French from Latin]

prostate /ˈprɒsteɪt/ *n.* (in full **prostate gland**) gland round the neck of the bladder in male mammals, releasing part of the semen. □ **prostatic** /-ˈstætɪk/ *adj.* [Greek *prostatēs* one who stands before]

prosthesis /prɒsˈθiːsɪs/ *n.* (*pl.* **-theses** /-siːz/) **1** artificial leg etc; false tooth, breast, etc. **2** branch of surgery dealing with prostheses. □ **prosthetic** /-ˈθetɪk/ *adj.* [Greek, = placing in addition]

prostitute /ˈprɒstɪˌtjuːt/ –*n.* **1** woman who engages in sexual activity for payment. **2** (usu. **male prostitute**) man or boy who engages in sexual activity, esp. with homosexual men, for payment. –*v.* (**-ting**) **1** (esp. *refl.*) make a prostitute of (esp. oneself). **2** misuse or offer (one's talents, skills, name, etc.) for money etc. □ **prostitution** /-ˈtjuːʃ(ə)n/ *n.* [Latin *prostituo -tut-* offer for sale]

prostrate –*adj.* /ˈprɒstreɪt/ **1 a** lying face downwards, esp. in submission. **b** lying horizontally. **2** overcome, esp. by grief, exhaustion, etc. **3** growing along the ground. –*v.* /prɒˈstreɪt/ (**-ting**) **1** lay or throw (esp. a person) flat. **2** *refl.* throw (oneself) down in submission etc. **3** overcome; make weak. □ **prostration** /prɒˈstreɪʃ(ə)n/ *n.* [Latin *prosterno -strat-* throw in front]

prosy /ˈprəʊzɪ/ *adj.* (**-ier, -iest**) tedious, commonplace, dull (*prosy talk*). □ **prosily** *adv.* **prosiness** *n.*

protactinium /ˌprəʊtækˈtɪnɪəm/ *n.* radioactive metallic element. [German: related to ACTINIUM]

protagonist /prəˈtægənɪst/ *n.* **1** chief person in a drama, story, etc. **2** leading person in a contest etc.; principal performer. **3** (usu. foll. by *of*, *for*) advocate or champion of a cause etc. (*protagonist of women's rights*). [Greek: related to PROTO-, *agōnistēs* actor]

■ **Usage** The use of *protagonist* in sense 3 is considered incorrect by some people.

protean /prəʊˈtiːən/ *adj.* variable, taking many forms; versatile. [*Proteus*, Greek sea-god who took various shapes]

protect /prəˈtekt/ *v.* **1** (often foll. by *from*, *against*) keep (a person, thing, etc.) safe; defend, guard. **2** shield (home industry) from competition with import duties. [Latin *tego tect-* cover]

protection /prəˈtekʃ(ə)n/ *n.* **1 a** protecting or being protected; defence. **b** thing, person, or animal that protects. **2** *colloq.* **a** immunity from violence etc. obtained by payment to gangsters etc. **b** (in full **protection money**) money so paid. □ **protectionist** *n.* & *adj.*

♦ **protectionism** *n.* policy of using tariffs, import quotas, and other restrictions to shield domestic manufacturers from foreign competition. Retaliation is an obvious reason for not trying to protect domestic industries in this way. On the other hand an industry of national importance in wartime could be eliminated by peacetime foreign competition if some protection is not given. Protecting a particular industry may increase profits and maintain employment in that industry but it may do so at the expense of the consumers, who have to pay more for the products of that industry than they would if they were allowed to buy untariffed imports.

---

protective /prəˈtektɪv/ *adj.* protecting; intended or tending to protect. □ **protectively** *adv.* **protectiveness** *n.*

protective custody *n.* detention of a person for his or her own protection.

♦ **protective duty** *n.* tariff imposed on an import to protect domestic manufacturers from foreign competition. See PROTECTIONISM.

---

protector *n.* (*fem.* **protectress**) **1** person or thing that protects. **2** *hist.* regent ruling during the minority or absence of the sovereign. □ **protectorship** *n.*

protectorate /prəˈtektərət/ *n.* **1 a** state that is controlled and protected by another. **b** this relation. **2** *hist.* **a** office of the protector of a kingdom or state. **b** period of this, esp. in England 1653–9.

protégé /ˈprɒtɪˌʒeɪ/ *n.* (*fem.* **protégée** pronunc. same) person under the protection, patronage, tutelage, etc. of another. [French: related to PROTECT]

protein /ˈprəʊtiːn/ *n.* any of a group of organic compounds composed of one or more chains of amino acids and forming an essential part of all living organisms. [Greek *prōtos* first]

pro tem /prəʊ ˈtem/ *adj.* & *adv. colloq.* = PRO TEMPORE. [abbreviation]

pro tempore /prəʊ ˈtempərɪ/ *adj.* & *adv.* for the time being. [Latin]

Proterozoic /ˌprəʊtərəʊˈzəʊɪk/ *Geol.* –*adj.* of the later part of the Precambrian era. –*n.* this time. [Greek *proteros* former, *zōē* life]

protest –*n.* /ˈprəʊtest/ **1** statement or act of dissent or disapproval. **2** certificate signed by a notary public at the request of the holder of a bill of exchange that has been refused payment or acceptance. It is a legal requirement after noting the bill (see NOTING). –*v.* /prəˈtest/ **1** (usu. foll. by *against*, *at*, *about*, etc.) make a protest. **2** affirm (one's innocence etc.) solemnly. **3** *Law* write or obtain a protest in regard to (a bill of exchange). **4** *US* object to (a decision etc.). □ **under protest** unwillingly. □ **protester** *n.* (also **protestor**). [Latin *protestor* declare formally]

Protestant /ˈprɒtɪst(ə)nt/ –*n.* member or follower of any of the Churches separating from the Roman Catholic Church after the Reformation. –*adj.* of the Protestant Churches or their members etc. □ **Protestantism** *n.* [related to PROTEST]

protestation /ˌprɒtɪˈsteɪʃ(ə)n/ *n.* **1** strong affirmation. **2** protest. [Latin: related to PROTEST]

protium /ˈprəʊtɪəm/ *n.* ordinary isotope of hydrogen. [Latin: related to PROTO-]

proto- *comb. form* first. [Greek *prōtos*]

protocol /ˌprəʊtəˈkɒl/ –*n.* **1** official formality and etiquette, esp. as observed on state occasions etc. **2** original draft of esp. the terms of a treaty. **3** formal statement of a transaction. **4** agreed procedure used to exchange information between entities in a computer network. –*v.* (**-ll-**) draw up or record in a protocol. [Greek *kolla* glue]

proton /ˈprəʊtɒn/ *n.* elementary particle with a positive electric charge equal to that of an electron, and occurring in all atomic nuclei. [Greek *prōtos* first]

protoplasm /'prəʊtə,plæz(ə)m/ *n.* material comprising the living part of a cell, consisting of a nucleus in membrane-enclosed cytoplasm. □ **protoplasmic** /-'plæzmɪk/ *adj.* [Greek: related to PROTO-, PLASMA]

prototype /'prəʊtə,taɪp/ *n.* **1** original as a pattern for imitations, improved forms, representations, etc. **2** trial model or preliminary version of a vehicle, machine, etc. □ **prototypic** /-'tɪpɪk/ *adj.* **prototypical** /-'tɪpɪk(ə)l/ *adj.* [Greek: related to PROTO-]

protozoan /,prəʊtə'zəʊən/ *–n.* (also **protozoon** /-'zəʊɒn/) (*pl.* **protozoa** /-'zəʊə/ or **-s**) unicellular microscopic organism, e.g. amoebae and ciliates. *–adj.* (also **protozoic** /-'zəʊɪk/) of this group. [from PROTO-, Greek *zōion* animal]

protract /prə'trækt/ *v.* (often as **protracted** *adj.*) prolong or lengthen. □ **protraction** *n.* [Latin *traho tract-* draw]

protractor *n.* instrument for measuring angles, usu. in the form of a graduated semicircle.

protrude /prə'tru:d/ *v.* (**-ding**) thrust forward; stick out; project. □ **protrusion** *n.* **protrusive** *adj.* [Latin *trudo trus-* thrust]

protuberant /prə'tju:bərənt/ *adj.* bulging out; prominent. □ **protuberance** *n.* [Latin: related to TUBER]

proud *adj.* **1** feeling greatly honoured or pleased (*proud to know him*). **2 a** (often foll. by *of*) haughty, arrogant (*too proud to speak to us*). **b** (often in *comb.*) having a proper pride; satisfied (*house-proud*; *proud of a job well done*). **3** (of an occasion, action, etc.) justly arousing or showing pride (*proud day*; *proud smile*). **4** imposing, splendid. **5** slightly projecting (*nail stood proud of the plank*). □ **do proud** *colloq.* treat with lavish generosity or honour (*did us proud*). □ **proudly** *adv.* [French *prud* valiant]

prove /pru:v/ *v.* (**-ving**; *past part.* **proved** or **proven** /'pru:v(ə)n, 'prəʊ-/) **1** (often foll. by *that*) demonstrate the truth of by evidence or argument. **2 a** (usu. foll. by *to* + infin.) be found (*it proved to be untrue*). **b** emerge as (*will prove the winner*). **3** test the accuracy of (a calculation). **4** establish the validity of (a will). **5** (of dough) rise in bread-making. □ **not proven** (in Scottish Law) verdict that there is insufficient evidence to establish guilt or innocence. **prove oneself** show one's abilities, courage, etc. □ **provable** *adj.* [Latin *probo* test, approve]

■ **Usage** In British English it is not standard to use *proven* as the past participle (it is standard Scots and American English). It is, however, common in certain expressions, such as *of proven ability*.

provenance /'prɒvɪnəns/ *n.* origin or place of origin; history. [French *provenir* from Latin]

Provençal /,prɒvɒn'sɑ:l/ *–adj.* of Provence. *–n.* native or language of Provence. [French: related to PROVINCE]

Provence /prɒ'vɑ̃s/ district and former province in SE France, now part of the region of Provence-Côte d'Azur; pop. (est. 1990) 4 257 900; capital, Marseilles. Grapes and olives are grown, and tourism (esp. along the French Riviera) is important.

provender /'prɒvɪndə(r)/ *n.* **1** animal fodder. **2** *joc.* food. [Latin: related to PREBEND]

proverb /'prɒvɜ:b/ *n.* short pithy saying in general use, held to embody a general truth. [Latin *proverbium* from *verbum* word]

proverbial /prə'vɜ:bɪəl/ *adj.* **1** (esp. of a characteristic) well known; notorious (*his proverbial honesty*). **2** of or referred to in a proverb (*proverbial ill wind*). □ **proverbially** *adv.* [Latin: related to PROVERB]

provide /prə'vaɪd/ *v.* (**-ding**) **1** supply, furnish (*provided me with food*; *provided a chance*). **2 a** (usu. foll. by *for, against*) make due preparation. **b** (usu. foll. by *for*) take care of a person etc. with money, food, etc. (*provides for a large family*). **3** (usu. foll. by *that*) stipulate in a will, statute, etc. □ **provider** *n.* [Latin *provideo -vis-* foresee]

provided *conj.* (often foll. by *that*) on the condition or understanding that.

Providence /'prɒvɪd(ə)ns/ city and port in the US, capital of the state of Rhode Island; oil is exported, and machinery, jewellery, and rubber goods are manufactured; pop. (est. 1994) 150 639.

providence /'prɒvɪd(ə)ns/ *n.* **1** protective care of God or nature. **2** (**Providence**) God in this aspect. **3** foresight; thrift. [Latin: related to PROVIDE]

provident *adj.* having or showing foresight; thrifty. [Latin: related to PROVIDE]

providential /,prɒvɪ'denʃ(ə)l/ *adj.* **1** of or by divine foresight or interposition. **2** opportune, lucky. □ **providentially** *adv.*

Provident Society *n.* = FRIENDLY SOCIETY.

providing *conj.* = PROVIDED.

province /'prɒvɪns/ *n.* **1** principal administrative division of a country etc. **2** (**the provinces**) country outside a capital city, esp. regarded as uncultured or unsophisticated. **3** sphere of action; business (*outside my province*). **4** branch of learning etc. (*in the province of aesthetics*). **5** district under an archbishop or metropolitan. **6** territory outside Italy under an ancient Roman governor. [Latin *provincia*]

provincial /prə'vɪnʃ(ə)l/ *–adj.* **1** of a province or provinces. **2** unsophisticated or uncultured. *–n.* **1** inhabitant of a province or the provinces. **2** unsophisticated or uncultured person. □ **provincialism** *n.*

provision /prə'vɪʒ(ə)n/ *–n.* **1 a** act of providing (*provision of nurseries*). **b** preparation, esp. for the future (*made provision for their old age*). **2** (in *pl.*) food, drink, etc., esp. for an expedition. **3** legal or formal stipulation or proviso. **4** amount set aside out of profits in the accounts of an organization for a known liability (even though the specific amount might not be known) or for the diminution in value of an asset. Common provisions are for bad debts and for depreciation and also for accrued liabilities. According to the UK Companies Act (1981) notes must be given to explain every material provision in the accounts of a limited company. *–v.* supply with provisions. [Latin: related to PROVIDE]

provisional *–adj.* **1** providing for immediate needs only; temporary. **2** (**Provisional**) of the unofficial wing of the IRA, using terrorism. *–n.* (**Provisional**) member of the Provisional wing of the IRA. □ **provisionally** *adv.*

◆ **provisional liquidator** *n.* person appointed by a court after the presentation of a winding-up petition on a company (see COMPULSORY LIQUIDATION). The provisional liquidator protects the interests of all the parties involved until the winding-up order is made, but has limited powers. The official receiver is normally appointed to this post. See also LIQUIDATOR.

◆ **provision for bad debts** *n.* sum credited to an account in the books of an organization to allow for the fact that some of the debtors might not pay their debts in full. This amount is normally deducted from the total debtors in the balance sheet.

◆ **provision for depreciation** *n.* sum credited to an account in the books of an organization to allow for the depreciation of a fixed asset. The aggregate amounts set aside from year to year are deducted from the value of the asset in the balance sheet to give its net book value.

---

proviso /prə'vaɪzəʊ/ *n.* (*pl.* **-s**) **1** stipulation. **2** clause containing this. □ **provisory** *adj.* [Latin, = it being provided]

Provo /'prəʊvəʊ/ *n.* (*pl.* **-s**) *colloq.* Provisional. [abbreviation]

provocation /,prɒvə'keɪʃ(ə)n/ *n.* **1** provoking or being provoked (*did it under severe provocation*). **2** cause of annoyance.

provocative /prə'vɒkətɪv/ *adj.* **1** (usu. foll. by *of*) tending to provoke, esp. anger or sexual desire. **2** intentionally annoying or controversial. □ **provocatively** *adv.* **provocativeness** *n.*

provoke /prə'vəʊk/ *v.* (**-king**) **1** (often foll. by *to*, or *to* + infin.) rouse or incite (*provoked him to fury*). **2** call forth; instigate; cause (indignation, an inquiry, process, etc.). **3** (usu. foll. by *into* + verbal noun) irritate or stimulate (a person) (*provoked him into retaliating*). **4** tempt; allure. [Latin *provoco* call forth]

provost /ˈprɒvəst/ *n.* **1** head of some (esp. Oxbridge) colleges. **2** head of a cathedral chapter. **3** = PROVOST MARSHAL. [Latin *propositus* from *pono* place]

provost marshal /prəˈvəʊ/ *n.* head of military police in camp or on active service.

prow *n.* **1** fore-part or bow of a ship. **2** pointed or projecting front part. [French *proue* from Greek *prōira*]

prowess /ˈpraʊɪs/ *n.* **1** skill, expertise. **2** valour, gallantry. [French: related to PROUD]

prowl –*v.* (often foll. by *about*, *around*) roam (a place) esp. stealthily or restlessly or in search of prey, plunder, etc. –*n.* act of prowling. □ **on the prowl** prowling. □ **prowler** *n.* [origin unknown]

prox. *abbr.* proximo.

proximate /ˈprɒksɪmət/ *adj.* **1** nearest or next before or after (in place, order, time, causation, thought process, etc.). **2** approximate. [Latin *proximus* nearest]

♦ **proximate cause** *n.* dominant and effective cause of an event or chain of events that results in a claim on an insurance policy. The loss must be caused directly, or as a result of a chain of events initiated, by an insured peril. For example, a policy covering storm damage would also pay for items in a freezer that deteriorate because of a power cut caused by the storm, which is the proximate cause of the loss of the frozen food.

---

proximity /prɒkˈsɪmɪtɪ/ *n.* nearness in space, time, etc. (*in close proximity*). [Latin: related to PROXIMATE]

proximo /ˈprɒksɪˌməʊ/ *adj. Commerce* of next month (*the third proximo*). [Latin, = in the next (*mense* month)]

proxy /ˈprɒksɪ/ *n.* (*pl.* **-ies**) (also *attrib.*) **1** authorization given to a substitute or deputy (*proxy vote*; *married by proxy*). **2 a** person authorized to act thus. **b** person who acts in the place of a member of a company at a company meeting at which one or more votes are taken. Notices calling meetings must state that a member may appoint a proxy, and directors commonly offer themselves as proxies for shareholders who cannot attend a meeting. A **special proxy** is empowered to act at one specified meeting; a **general proxy** is authorized to vote at any meeting. **3 a** written authorization for esp. proxy voting. **b** proxy vote. [obsolete *procuracy* procuration]

PRP *abbr.* profit-related (or performance-related) pay.

PRs *symb.* Pakistani rupees.

♦ **PRT** *abbr.* = PETROLEUM REVENUE TAX.

---

prude /pruːd/ *n.* excessively (often affectedly) squeamish or sexually modest person. □ **prudery** *n.* **prudish** *adj.* **prudishly** *adv.* **prudishness** *n.* [French: related to PROUD]

♦ **prudence concept** *n.* principle of accounting designed to ensure that unrealized profits are not distributed to shareholders by way of dividend. According to this principle, unrealized profits are not taken account of until they are realized; on the other hand foreseeable losses are taken account of as soon as they can be foreseen. Although the prudence concept must give a view with a pessimistic bias, most accountants accept that taking the required 'true and fair view' means doing so in accordance with the prudence concept.

---

prudent /ˈpruːd(ə)nt/ *adj.* cautious; politic. □ **prudence** *n.* **prudently** *adv.* [Latin *prudens -ent-*: related to PROVIDENT]

prudential /pruːˈdenʃ(ə)l/ *adj.* of or showing prudence. □ **prudentially** *adv.*

prune[1] /pruːn/ *n.* dried plum. [Latin *prunum* from Greek]

prune[2] /pruːn/ *v.* (**-ning**) **1 a** (often foll. by *down*) trim (a bush etc.) by cutting away dead or overgrown branches etc. **b** (usu. foll. by *off*, *away*) lop (branches etc.) thus. **2** reduce (costs etc.) (*prune expenses*). **3 a** (often foll. by *of*) clear or remove superfluities from. **b** remove (superfluities). [French *prooignier* from Romanic: related to ROUND]

prurient /ˈprʊərɪənt/ *adj.* having or encouraging unhealthy sexual curiosity. □ **prurience** *n.* [Latin *prurio* itch]

Prussian /ˈprʌʃ(ə)n/ –*adj.* of Prussia, or esp. its rigidly militaristic tradition. –*n.* native of Prussia. [*Prussia*, former German state]

Prussian blue *n.* & *adj.* (as adj. often hyphenated) deep blue (pigment).

prussic acid /ˈprʌsɪk/ *n.* hydrocyanic acid. [French]

pry /praɪ/ *v.* (**pries, pried**) **1** (usu. foll. by *into*) inquire impertinently. **2** (usu. foll. by *into*, *about*, etc.) look or peer inquisitively. [origin unknown]

PS *abbr.* postscript.

PSA *abbr.* Property Services Agency.

psalm /sɑːm/ *n.* **1** (also **Psalm**) sacred song, esp. from the Book of Psalms, esp. metrically chanted in a service. **2** (**the Psalms** or **the Book of Psalms**) Old Testament book containing the Psalms. [Latin *psalmus* from Greek]

psalmist *n.* composer of a psalm.

psalmody /ˈsɑːmədɪ, ˈsæl-/ *n.* practice or art of singing psalms, hymns, etc., esp. in public worship. [Greek: related to PSALM]

Psalter /ˈsɔːltə(r)/ *n.* **1** the Book of Psalms. **2** (**psalter**) version or copy of this. [Old English and French from Greek *psaltērion* stringed instrument]

psaltery /ˈsɔːltərɪ/ *n.* (*pl.* **-ies**) ancient and medieval instrument like a dulcimer but played by plucking the strings. [Latin: related to PSALTER]

♦ **PSBR** *abbr.* = PUBLIC SECTOR BORROWING REQUIREMENT.

PSE *abbr.* **1** Pacific Stock Exchange. **2** *Computing* programming (or project) support environment.

psephology /sɪˈfɒlədʒɪ/ *n.* the statistical study of voting etc. □ **psephologist** *n.* [Greek *psēphos* pebble, vote]

pseud /sjuːd/ *colloq.* –*adj.* (esp. intellectually) pretentious; not genuine. –*n.* such a person; poseur. [from PSEUDO-]

pseudo /ˈsjuːdəʊ/ *adj.* & *n.* (*pl.* **-s**) = PSEUD.

pseudo- *comb. form* (also **pseud-** before a vowel) **1** false; not genuine (*pseudo-intellectual*). **2** resembling or imitating (*pseudo-acid*). [Greek *pseudēs* false]

pseudonym /ˈsjuːdənɪm/ *n.* fictitious name, esp. of an author. [Greek: related to PSEUDO-, *onoma* name]

psi /psaɪ, saɪ/ *n.* twenty-third letter of the Greek alphabet (Ψ, ψ). [Greek]

p.s.i. *abbr.* pounds per square inch.

psittacosis /ˌsɪtəˈkəʊsɪs/ *n.* contagious viral disease of esp. parrots, transmissible to human beings. [Greek *psittakos* parrot]

PSL *abbr.* **1** private-sector liquidity, formerly used as a measure of the money supply. **2** public-sector loan(s).

PSN *abbr.* **1** *Computing* packet-switching network (see PACKET SWITCHING). **2** public switched network.

psoriasis /səˈraɪəsɪs/ *n.* skin disease marked by red scaly patches. [Greek *psōra* itch]

PSS *abbr. Computing* Packet Switch Stream, the public packet network of British Telecom (see PACKET SWITCHING).

psst *int.* (also **pst**) whispered exclamation to attract a person's attention. [imitative]

PST *abbr. US* & *Canadian* Pacific Standard Time.

PSTN *abbr.* public switched telephone network.

PSU *abbr. Computing* power supply unit.

PSV *abbr.* public service vehicle.

psych /saɪk/ *v. colloq.* **1** (usu. foll. by *up*; often *refl.*) prepare (oneself or another) mentally for an ordeal etc. **2** (often foll. by *out*) intimidate or frighten (a person), esp. for one's own advantage. **3** (usu. foll. by *out*) analyse (a person's motivation etc.) for one's own advantage (*can't psych him out*). [abbreviation]

psyche /ˈsaɪkɪ/ *n.* the soul, spirit, or mind. [Latin from Greek]

psychedelia /ˌsaɪkəˈdiːlɪə/ *n.pl.* **1** psychedelic phenomena. **2** subculture associated with these.

psychedelic /ˌsaɪkəˈdelɪk/ *adj.* **1 a** expanding the mind's awareness etc., esp. with hallucinogenic drugs. **b** hallucinatory; bizarre. **c** (of a drug) producing hallucinations. **2** *colloq.* **a** producing a hallucinatory effect; vivid in colour or design etc. **b** (of colours, patterns, etc.) bright, bold, and often abstract. [Greek *psukhē* mind, *dēlos* clear]

psychiatry /saɪˈkaɪətrɪ/ *n.* the study and treatment of mental disease. □ **psychiatric** /-kɪˈætrɪk/ *adj.* **psychiatrist** *n.* [from PSYCHO-, Greek *iatros* physician]

psychic /ˈsaɪkɪk/ *–adj.* **1 a** (of a person) considered to have occult powers such as telepathy, clairvoyance, etc. **b** supernatural. **2** of the soul or mind. *–n.* person considered to have psychic powers; medium. [Greek *psukhē* soul, mind]

psychical *adj.* **1** concerning psychic phenomena or faculties (*psychical research*). **2** of the soul or mind. □ **psychically** *adv.*

psycho /ˈsaɪkəʊ/ *colloq. –n.* (*pl.* **-s**) psychopath. *–adj.* psychopathic. [abbreviation]

psycho- *comb. form* of the mind or psychology. [Greek: related to PSYCHIC]

psychoanalysis /ˌsaɪkəʊəˈnælɪsɪs/ *n.* treatment of mental disorders by bringing repressed fears and conflicts into the conscious mind over a long course of interviews. □ **psychoanalyse** /-ˈænəˌlaɪz/ *v.* (**-sing**). **psychoanalyst** /-ˈænəlɪst/ *n.* **psychoanalytic** /-ˌænəˈlɪtɪk/ *adj.* **psychoanalytical** /-ˌænəˈlɪtɪk(ə)l/ *adj.*

psychokinesis /ˌsaɪkəʊkɪˈniːsɪs/ *n.* movement of objects supposedly by telepathy or mental effort.

psychological /ˌsaɪkəˈlɒdʒɪk(ə)l/ *adj.* **1** of or arising in the mind. **2** of psychology. **3** *colloq.* (of an ailment etc.) imaginary (*her cold is psychological*). □ **psychologically** *adv.*

psychological block *n.* mental inhibition caused by emotional factors.

psychological moment *n.* best time for achieving a particular effect or purpose.

◆ **psychological tests** *n.pl.* tests designed to assess the personalities and abilities of individuals to determine their suitability for a particular job and to make best use of their talents. With the increasing use of computers to analyse information, the tests have become more and more complex in personnel selection; choosing the wrong person for a senior job can be costly and have far-reaching effects in a competitive market.

---

psychological warfare *n.* campaign directed at reducing enemy morale.

psychology /saɪˈkɒlədʒɪ/ *n.* (*pl.* **-ies**) **1** the study of the human mind. **2** treatise on or theory of this. **3 a** mental characteristics etc. of a person or group. **b** mental aspects of an activity, situation, etc. (*psychology of crime*). □ **psychologist** *n.*

psychopath /ˈsaɪkəˌpæθ/ *n.* **1** mentally deranged person, esp. showing abnormal or violent social behaviour. **2** mentally or emotionally unstable person. □ **psychopathic** /-ˈpæθɪk/ *adj.*

psychopathology /ˌsaɪkəʊpəˈθɒlədʒɪ/ *n.* **1** the study of mental disorders. **2** mentally or behaviourally disordered state.

psychopathy /saɪˈkɒpəθɪ/ *n.* psychopathic or psychologically abnormal behaviour.

psychosis /saɪˈkəʊsɪs/ *n.* (*pl.* **-choses** /-siːz/) severe mental disorder with loss of contact with reality. [Greek: related to PSYCHE]

psychosomatic /ˌsaɪkəʊsəˈmætɪk/ *adj.* **1** (of a bodily disorder) mental, not physical, in origin. **2** of the mind and body together.

psychotherapy /ˌsaɪkəʊˈθerəpɪ/ *n.* treatment of mental disorder by psychological means. □ **psychotherapeutic** /-ˈpjuːtɪk/ *adj.* **psychotherapist** *n.*

psychotic /saɪˈkɒtɪk/ *–adj.* of or suffering from a psychosis. *–n.* psychotic person.

PT *–abbr.* physical training. *–international civil aircraft marking* Brazil.

Pt *symb.* platinum.

pt. *abbr.* **1** part. **2** payment. **3** pint. **4** point. **5** *Naut.* port.

p.t. *abbr.* part time.

PTA *abbr.* **1** parent-teacher association. **2** preferential trade area.

Pta *symb.* peseta.

ptarmigan /ˈtɑːmɪgən/ *n.* game-bird with a grouselike appearance. [Gaelic]

Pte. *abbr.* **1** Private (soldier). **2** (in India etc.) private limited company.

pteridophyte /ˈterɪdəˌfaɪt/ *n.* flowerless plant, e.g. ferns, club-mosses, etc. [Greek *pteris* fern]

pterodactyl /ˌterəˈdæktɪl/ *n.* large extinct flying reptile. [Greek *pteron* wing, DACTYL]

pterosaur /ˈterəˌsɔː(r)/ *n.* flying reptile with large bat-like wings. [Greek *pteron* wing, *saura* lizard]

PTI *abbr. Computing* public tool interface.

◆ **PTN** *abbr.* = PUBLIC TELEPHONE NETWORK.

PTO *abbr.* **1** (in the US) Patent and Trademark Office. **2** please turn over. **3** public telecommunications operator. **4** Public Trust Office (see PUBLIC TRUSTEE).

Ptolemaic /ˌtɒlɪˈmeɪɪk/ *adj. hist.* of Ptolemy or his theories. [Greek *Ptolemaios*, 2nd-century astronomer]

Ptolemaic system *n.* theory that the earth is the stationary centre of the universe.

ptomaine /ˈtəʊmeɪn/ *n.* any of various esp. toxic amine compounds in putrefying matter. [Greek *ptōma* corpse]

PTT *abbr.* Postal, Telegraph, and Telephone Administration.

Pty. *abbr.* = PROPRIETARY COMPANY.

PU *airline flight code* Pluna.

Pu *symb.* plutonium.

p.u. *abbr.* paid up.

pub *n. colloq.* public house. [abbreviation]

pub-crawl *n. colloq.* drinking tour of several pubs.

puberty /ˈpjuːbətɪ/ *n.* period of sexual maturation. □ **pubertal** *adj.* [Latin *puber* adult]

pubes[1] /ˈpjuːbiːz/ *n.* (*pl.* same) lower hairy part of the abdomen at the front of the pelvis. [Latin]

pubes[2] *pl.* of PUBIS.

pubescence /pjuːˈbes(ə)ns/ *n.* **1** beginning of puberty. **2** soft down on plants, or on animals, esp. insects. □ **pubescent** *adj.* [Latin: related to PUBES[1]]

pubic /ˈpjuːbɪk/ *adj.* of the pubes or pubis.

pubis /ˈpjuːbɪs/ *n.* (*pl.* **pubes** /-biːz/) either of a pair of bones forming the two sides of the pelvis. [Latin *os pubis* bone of the PUBES[1]]

public /ˈpʌblɪk/ *–adj.* **1** of the people as a whole (*public holiday*). **2** open to or shared by all (*public baths*). **3** done or existing openly (*public apology*). **4** (of a service, funds, etc.) provided by or concerning government (*public money*; *public records*). **5** of or involved in the affairs, esp. the government or entertainment, of the community (*distinguished public career*; *public figures*). *–n.* **1** (as *sing.* or *pl.*) community, or members of it, in general. **2** specified section of the community (*reading public*; *my public*). □ **go public 1** apply to a stock exchange to become a public limited company. See FLOTATION. **2** reveal one's plans etc. **in public** openly, publicly. □ **publicly** *adv.* [Latin]

public-address system *n.* set of loudspeakers, microphones, amplifiers, etc., used in addressing large audiences.

publican /ˈpʌblɪkən/ *n.* keeper of a public house. [Latin: related to PUBLIC]

publication /ˌpʌblɪˈkeɪʃ(ə)n/ *n.* **1 a** preparation and issuing of a book, newspaper, etc. to the public. **b** book etc. so issued. **2** making something publicly known. [Latin: related to PUBLIC]

public bar *n.* least expensive bar in a public house.

♦ **public company** *n.* company whose shares are available to the public through a stock exchange. See PUBLIC LIMITED COMPANY.

public convenience *n.* public lavatory.

♦ **public corporation** *n.* state-owned organization set up either to provide a national service (as does the British Broadcasting Corporation) or to run a nationalized industry (as does the British Coal Corporation). The chairman and members of the board of a public corporation are usu. appointed by the appropriate government minister, who retains overall control and accountability to parliament. The public corporation attempts to reconcile public accountability for the use of public finance, freedom of commercial operation on a day-to-day basis, and maximum benefits for the community.

♦ **public debts** *n.pl.* debts of the public sector of the economy, including the national debt.

♦ **public deposits** *n.pl.* balances to the credit of government departments held at the Bank of England.

public enemy *n.* notorious wanted criminal.

♦ **public examination** see BANKRUPTCY.

public figure *n.* famous person.

♦ **public finance** *n.* **1** financing of the goods and services provided by national and local government through taxation or other means. **2** economic study of the issues involved in raising and spending money for the public benefit.

♦ **public finance accountant** *n.* member of the Chartered Institute of Public Finance and Accountancy. The principal function of the members of this body is to prepare the financial accounts and act as management accountants for government agencies, local authorities, nationalized industries, and such bodies as publicly owned health and water authorities. As many of these bodies are non-profit-making and are governed by special statutes, the skills required of public sector accountants differ from those required in the private sector.

♦ **public good** *n. Econ.* a good that is simultaneously available to all the individuals in an economy. The consumption of a public good by one individual does not reduce the quantity available for consumption by another individual. An example of a public good is national defence. It is usu. argued that public goods will be undersupplied by the market since a calculation of the ratio of the cost to the benefit to an individual will usu. ignore the public aspect. This is usu. considered the minimum justification for a government to intervene in the operation of a free market.

public health *n.* provision of adequate sanitation, drainage, etc. by government.

public house *n.* inn providing alcoholic drinks for consumption on the premises.

♦ **public issue** *n.* **1** method of making a new issue of shares, loan stock, etc. in which the public are invited, through advertisements in the national press, to apply for shares at a price fixed by the company. Cf. INTRODUCTION 5; ISSUE BY TENDER; OFFER FOR SALE; PLACING. **2** new issue so made.

publicist /ˈpʌblɪsɪst/ *n.* publicity agent or public relations officer.

publicity /pʌbˈlɪsɪtɪ/ *n.* **1** public exposure. **2 a** advertising. **b** material used for this. [French: related to PUBLIC]

publicize /ˈpʌblɪˌsaɪz/ *v.* (also **-ise**) (**-zing** or **-sing**) advertise; make publicly known.

public lending right *n.* (also **PLR**) right of authors to payment when their books etc. are lent by public libraries, compensating for loss of royalties. The scheme, introduced in the UK in 1983, pays authors a fee proportional to the number of times their books were borrowed in the previous year from a sample of 16 public libraries situated throughout the UK. The sum to be divided in this way is fixed by parliament. Individual authors may not earn more than £5000 from the PLR.

♦ **public-liability insurance** *n.* insurance against liability to pay compensation to a member of the public and court costs in the event of the policyholder being successfully sued for causing death, injury, or damage to property by failing to take reasonable care in his or her actions or those of his or her employees. A business whose work brings it into contact with the public must have a public-liability policy. See also EMPLOYERS'-LIABILITY INSURANCE; PROFESSIONAL-INDEMNITY INSURANCE; THIRD-PARTY INSURANCE.

♦ **public limited company** *n.* (also **plc, PLC**) company registered under the Companies Act (1980) as a public company. Its name must end with the initials 'plc'. It must have an authorized share capital of at least £50,000, of which at least £12,500 must be paid up. The company's memorandum must comply with the format in Table F of the Companies Regulations (1985). It may offer shares and securities to the public. The regulation of such companies is stricter than that of private companies. Most public companies are converted from private companies, under the re-registration procedure in the Companies Act.

public opinion *n.* views, esp. moral, generally prevalent.

public ownership *n.* state ownership of the means of production, distribution, or exchange.

♦ **public policy** *n. Law* the interests of the community. If a contract is (on common-law principles) contrary to public policy, this will usu. make it an illegal contract. In a few cases, however, such a contract is void but not illegal, and is treated slightly more leniently (e.g. by severance). Contracts that are illegal because they contravene public policy include any contract to commit a crime or a tort or to defraud the revenue, any contract that prejudices national safety or the administration of justice, and any immoral contract. Contracts that are merely void include contracts in restraint of trade.

public prosecutor *n.* law officer acting on behalf of the state or in the public interest.

public relations *n.pl.* (usu. treated as *sing.*) (also **PR**) professional promotion of a favourable public image, esp. by a company, charity, famous person, etc. Some organizations employ their own public relations officers to deal with the media, provide information in the form of handouts, and to represent their principals at press conferences, etc. Others use **public relations agencies** to fulfil these functions. PR does not involve paid advertising, which is a quite separate activity. While an advertising agent will plan an advertising campaign, charging a percentage of the money spent, PR agencies, for a flat fee (plus expenses), will seek to promote their principals by persuading newspapers to feature them in articles, TV and radio personalities to interview them or otherwise feature them in their programmes, etc.

public relations officer *n.* (also **PRO**) person employed to promote public relations.

public school *n.* **1** private fee-paying secondary school, esp. for boarders. **2** *US, Austral.*, & *Scot.* non-fee-paying school.

♦ **public sector** *n.* part of an economy in a mixed economy that covers the activities of the government and local authorities. This includes education, the National Health Service, the social services, public transport, the police, local public services, etc., as well as state-owned industries and public corporations. Cf. PRIVATE SECTOR.

♦ **Public Sector Borrowing Requirement** *n.* (also **PSBR**) amount by which UK government expenditure exceeds its income (i.e. the **public sector deficit**); this must be financed by borrowing (e.g. by selling gilt-edged securities) or by printing money. As an indicator of government fiscal policy the PSBR has acquired increased status since the late 1970s. By that time many economists had come to accept that a high PSBR is inflationary or leads to the crowding out of private expenditure; this remains a widely held view. While printing money simply causes prices to rise (see QUANTITY THEORY OF MONEY), selling gilts has the effect of raising interest rates, reducing private investment, and curbing private expenditure. See also CENTRAL GOVERNMENT BORROWING REQUIREMENT.

♦ **public sector deficit** see PUBLIC SECTOR BORROWING REQUIREMENT.

public servant *n.* state official.

public spirit *n.* willingness to engage in community action. □ **public-spirited** *adj.*

♦ **public telephone network** *n.* (also **PTN**) the telephone network provided in the UK by British Telecom. Telephone equipment in offices, factories, homes, etc. connected to this network may be bought or rented from British Telecom or from outside suppliers. However, by government order, all such equipment must be clearly marked with a green circle to show that it has been approved for connection to the network. Equipment marked with a red triangle is not approved for connection.

public transport *n.* buses, trains, etc. charging set fares and running on fixed routes.

♦ **public trustee** *n.* state official in charge of the **Public Trust Office**, a trust corporation set up for certain statutory purposes. Being a corporation sole, the office exists irrespective of the person performing it. The public trustee may act as administrator of small estates, as trustee for English trusts where required, and as receiver when directed to do so by a court. He or she may hold funds of registered Friendly Societies and trade unions.

public utility *n.* organization supplying water, gas, etc. to the community.

♦ **public warehouse** see WAREHOUSE *n.* 1.

♦ **public works** *n.pl.* government-sponsored construction work, esp. that undertaken during a recession or a depression on such activities as house building or road building. Aimed at increasing the level of employment and aggregate demand, it is an activity generally associated with Keynesianism. See also PUMP-PRIMING; INFRASTRUCTURE 1; REFLATION; EFFECTIVE DEMAND.

publish /ˈpʌblɪʃ/ *v.* **1** (also *absol.*) prepare and issue (a book, newspaper, etc.) for public sale. **2** make generally known. **3** announce formally. [Latin: related to PUBLIC]

♦ **published accounts** *n.pl.* accounts of organizations published according to UK law. The most common, according to the UK Companies Act (1981), are the accounts of limited companies, which must be provided for their shareholders and filed with the Registrar of Companies at Companies House, Cardiff. The accounts comprise the balance sheet, the profit and loss account, the statement of source and application of funds, the directors' report, and the auditors' report. In the case of groups of companies, consolidated accounts are also required. Small companies and medium-sized companies, as defined by the act, need not file some of these documents.

publisher *n.* person or (esp.) company that publishes books etc. for sale.

puce *adj.* & *n.* dark red or purple-brown. [Latin *pulex* flea]

puck[1] *n.* rubber disc used as a ball in ice hockey. [origin unknown]

puck[2] *n.* mischievous or evil sprite. □ **puckish** *adj.* **puckishly** *adv.* **puckishness** *n.* [Old English]

pucker –*v.* (often foll. by *up*) gather into wrinkles, folds, or bulges (*this seam is puckered up*). –*n.* such a wrinkle, bulge, fold, etc. [origin unknown]

pud /pʊd/ *n. colloq.* = PUDDING. [abbreviation]

pudding /ˈpʊdɪŋ/ *n.* **1 a** any of various sweet cooked dishes (*rice pudding*). **b** savoury dish containing flour, suet, etc. (*steak and kidney pudding*). **c** sweet course of a meal. **d** any of various sausages stuffed with oatmeal, spices, blood, etc. (*black pudding*). **2** *colloq.* plump, stupid, or lazy person. □ **puddingy** *adj.* [Latin *botellus* sausage]

puddle /ˈpʌd(ə)l/ –*n.* **1** small pool, esp. of rainwater. **2** clay and sand worked with water used as a watertight covering for embankments etc. –*v.* (**-ling**) **1** knead (clay and sand) into puddle. **2** stir (molten iron) to produce wrought iron by expelling carbon. □ **puddly** *adj.* [Old English]

pudendum /pjuːˈdendəm/ *n.* (*pl.* **pudenda**) (usu. in *pl.*) genitals, esp. of a woman. [Latin *pudeo* be ashamed]

pudgy /ˈpʌdʒɪ/ *adj.* (**-ier, -iest**) *colloq.* (esp. of a person) plump, podgy. □ **pudginess** *n.* [cf. PODGY]

Puebla /ˈpweblə/ **1** state in SE central Mexico; pop. (est. 1995) 4 624 239. **2** (in full **Puebla de Zaragoza**) its capital city, an important agricultural and industrial centre; pop. (1990) 1 007 170.

puerile /ˈpjʊəraɪl/ *adj.* childish, immature. □ **puerility** /-ˈrɪlɪtɪ/ *n.* (*pl.* **-ies**). [Latin *puer* boy]

puerperal /pjuːˈɜːpər(ə)l/ *adj.* of or caused by childbirth. [Latin *puer* boy, *pario* bear]

puerperal fever *n.* fever following childbirth and caused by uterine infection.

Puerto Cortés /ˌpwɜːtəʊ kɔːˈtez/ principal port of Honduras, on the Caribbean coast; pop. (1991) 32 500.

Puerto Plata /ˌpwɜːtəʊ ˈplɑːtə/ principal beach resort of the Dominican Republic, with a deep-water harbour for cruise liners; pop. (1986) 96 500.

Puerto Rico /ˌpwɜːtəʊ ˈriːkəʊ/ island of the Greater Antilles in the West Indies, a US territory with full powers of local government; pop. (1996) 3 766 000; capital, San Juan. Formerly a Spanish colony, it was ceded to the US in 1898. Manufacturing industries are important, producing esp. chemicals, metal products, and machinery; agricultural products include sugar cane, tobacco, coffee, and fruit. □ **Puerto Rican** *adj.* & *n.*

puff –*n.* **1 a** short quick blast of breath or wind. **b** sound of or like this. **c** small quantity of vapour, smoke, etc., emitted in one blast (*puff of smoke*). **2** light pastry cake containing jam, cream, etc. **3** gathered material in a dress etc. (*puff sleeve*). **4** extravagantly enthusiastic review, advertisement, etc., esp. in a newspaper. **5** = POWDER-PUFF. –*v.* **1** emit a puff of air or breath; blow with short blasts. **2** (usu. foll. by *away*, *out*, etc.) emit or move with puffs (*puffing away at his cigar; train puffed out*). **3** (usu. in *passive*; often foll. by *out*) *colloq.* put out of breath (*arrived puffed*). **4** breathe hard; pant. **5** (usu. foll. by *up*, *out*) inflate; swell (*his eye was puffed up*). **6** (usu. foll. by *out*, *up*, *away*) blow or emit (dust, smoke, etc.) with a puff. **7** smoke (a pipe etc.) in puffs. **8** (usu. as **puffed up** *adj.*) elate; make proud or boastful. **9** advertise or promote with exaggerated or false praise. □ **puff up** = sense 8 of *v.* [imitative]

puff-adder *n.* large venomous African viper which inflates the upper part of its body.

puff-ball *n.* ball-shaped fungus emitting clouds of spores.

puffin /ˈpʌfɪn/ *n.* N Atlantic and N Pacific sea bird with a large head and brightly coloured triangular bill. [origin unknown]

puff pastry *n.* leaved pastry made light and flaky by rolling and folding the dough many times.

puffy *adj.* (**-ier, -iest**) **1** swollen, puffed out. **2** *colloq.* short-winded. □ **puffily** *adv.* **puffiness** *n.*

pug *n.* (in full **pug-dog**) dog of a dwarf breed with a broad flat nose and wrinkled face. [origin unknown]

pugilist /ˈpjuːdʒɪlɪst/ *n.* (esp. professional) boxer. □ **pugilism** *n.* **pugilistic** /-ˈlɪstɪk/ *adj.* [Latin *pugil* boxer]

Puglia see APULIA.

pugnacious /pʌgˈneɪʃəs/ *adj.* quarrelsome; disposed to fight. □ **pugnaciously** *adv.* **pugnacity** /-ˈnæsɪtɪ/ *n.* [Latin *pugnax -acis* from *pugno* fight]

pug-nose *n.* short squat or snub nose. □ **pug-nosed** *adj.*

♦ **puisne mortgage** /'pju:nɪ/ *n.* legal mortgage of unregistered land that is not protected by the deposit of title deeds. It should instead be protected by registration. [French *puisné* born later]

puissance /'pwi:sɔ̃s/ *n.* competitive jumping of large obstacles in showjumping. [French: related to PUISSANT]

puissant /'pwi:sɒnt/ *adj. literary* or *archaic* powerful; mighty. [Romanic: related to POTENT]

puke *v.* & *n.* (**-king**) *slang* vomit. □ **pukey** *adj.* [imitative]

pukka /'pʌkə/ *adj. Anglo-Ind. colloq.* **1** genuine. **2** of good quality; reliable (*a pukka job*). [Hindi]

pula /'pu:lə/ *n.* standard monetary unit of Botswana. [Tswana]

pulchritude /'pʌlkrɪˌtju:d/ *n. literary* beauty. □ **pulchritudinous** /-'tju:dɪnəs/ *adj.* [Latin *pulcher* beautiful]

pule *v.* (**-ling**) *literary* cry querulously or weakly; whimper. [imitative]

pull /pʊl/ *–v.* **1** exert force upon (a thing, person, etc.) to move it to oneself or the origin of the force (*pulled it nearer*). **2** exert a pulling force (*engine will not pull*). **3** extract (a cork or tooth) by pulling. **4** damage (a muscle etc.) by abnormal strain. **5 a** move (a boat) by pulling on the oars. **b** (of a boat etc.) be caused to move, esp. in a specified direction. **6** (often foll. by *up*) proceed with effort (up a hill etc.). **7** (foll. by *on*) bring out (a weapon) for use against (a person). **8** check the speed of (a horse), esp. to lose a race. **9** attract (custom or support). **10** draw (liquor) from a barrel etc. **11** (foll. by *at*) tear or pluck at. **12** (often foll. by *on, at*) inhale or drink deeply; draw or suck (on a pipe etc.). **13** (often foll. by *up*) remove (a plant) by the root. **14 a** *Cricket* strike (the ball) to the leg side. **b** *Golf* strike (the ball) widely to the left. **15** print (a proof etc.). **16** *slang* succeed in attracting sexually. *–n.* **1** act of pulling. **2** force exerted by this. **3** influence; advantage. **4** attraction or attention-getter. **5** deep draught of liquor. **6** prolonged effort, e.g. in going up a hill. **7** handle etc. for applying a pull. **8** printer's rough proof. **9** *Cricket* & *Golf* pulling stroke. **10** suck at a cigarette. □ **pull about 1** treat roughly. **2** pull from side to side. **pull apart** (or **to pieces**) = *take to pieces* (see PIECE). **pull back** (cause to) retreat. **pull down 1** demolish (esp. a building). **2** humiliate. **pull a face** distort the features, grimace. **pull a fast one** see FAST[1]. **pull in 1** (of a bus, train, etc.) arrive to take passengers. **2** (of a vehicle) move to the side of or off the road. **3** *colloq.* earn or acquire. **4** *colloq.* arrest. **pull a person's leg** deceive playfully. **pull off 1** remove by pulling. **2** succeed in achieving or winning. **pull oneself together** recover control of oneself. **pull the other one** *colloq.* expressing disbelief (with ref. to *pull a person's leg*). **pull out 1** take out by pulling. **2** depart. **3** withdraw from an undertaking. **4** (of a bus, train, etc.) leave a station, stop, etc. **5** (of a vehicle) move out from the side of the road, or to overtake. **pull over** (of a vehicle) pull in. **pull one's punches** avoid using one's full force. **pull the plug on** put an end to (by withdrawing resources etc.). **pull rank** take unfair advantage of one's seniority. **pull round** (or **through**) (cause to) recover from an illness. **pull strings** exert (esp. clandestine) influence. **pull together** work in harmony. **pull up 1** (cause to) stop moving. **2** pull out of the ground. **3** reprimand. **4** check oneself. **pull one's weight** (often *refl.*) do one's fair share of work. [Old English]

pullet /'pʊlɪt/ *n.* young hen, esp. one less than one year old. [Latin *pullus*]

pulley /'pʊlɪ/ *n.* (*pl.* **-s**) **1** grooved wheel or wheels for a cord etc. to pass over, set in a block and used for changing the direction of a force. **2** wheel or drum fixed on a shaft and turned by a belt, used esp. to increase speed or power. [French *polie*: related to POLE[2]]

pull-in *n.* roadside café or other stopping-place.

Pullman /'pʊlmən/ *n.* (*pl.* **-s**) **1** luxurious railway carriage or motor coach. **2** sleeping-car. [*Pullman*, name of the designer]

pull-out *n.* removable section of a magazine etc.

pullover *n.* knitted garment put on over the head and covering the top half of the body.

pullulate /'pʌljʊˌleɪt/ *v.* (**-ting**) **1** (of a seed, shoot, etc.) bud, sprout. **2** swarm, teem. **3** develop; spring up. **4** (foll. by *with*) abound. □ **pullulation** /-'leɪʃ(ə)n/ *n.* [Latin *pullulo* sprout]

pulmonary /'pʌlmənərɪ/ *adj.* **1** of the lungs. **2** having lungs or lunglike organs. **3** affected with or susceptible to lung disease. [Latin *pulmo -onis* lung]

pulp *–n.* **1** soft fleshy part of fruit etc. **2** soft thick wet mass, esp. from rags, wood, etc., used in paper-making. **3** (often *attrib.*) cheap fiction etc., orig. printed on rough paper. *–v.* reduce to or become pulp. □ **pulpy** *adj.* **pulpiness** *n.* [Latin]

pulpit /'pʊlpɪt/ *n.* **1** raised enclosed platform in a church etc. from which the preacher delivers a sermon. **2** (prec. by *the*) preachers collectively; preaching. [Latin *pulpitum* platform]

pulpwood *n.* timber suitable for making paper-pulp.

pulsar /'pʌlsɑ:(r)/ *n.* cosmic source of regular rapid pulses of radiation, e.g. a rotating neutron star. [from *pulsating star*, after *quasar*]

pulsate /pʌl'seɪt/ *v.* (**-ting**) **1** expand and contract rhythmically; throb. **2** vibrate, quiver, thrill. □ **pulsation** *n.* **pulsatory** *adj.* [Latin: related to PULSE[1]]

pulse[1] *–n.* **1 a** rhythmical throbbing of the arteries as blood is propelled through them, esp. in the wrists, temples, etc. **b** each beat of the arteries or heart. **2** throb or thrill of life or emotion. **3** general feeling or opinion. **4** single vibration of sound, electric current, light, etc., esp. as a signal. **5** rhythmical beat, esp. of music. *–v.* (**-sing**) pulsate. [Latin *pello puls-* drive, beat]

pulse[2] *n.* (as *sing.* or *pl.*) **1** edible seeds of various leguminous plants, e.g. chick-peas, lentils, beans, etc. **2** plant producing these. [Latin *puls*]

pulverize /'pʌlvəˌraɪz/ *v.* (also **-ise**) (**-zing** or **-sing**) **1** reduce or crumble to fine particles or dust. **2** *colloq.* demolish, defeat utterly. □ **pulverization** /-'zeɪʃ(ə)n/ *n.* [Latin *pulvis -ver-* dust]

puma /'pju:mə/ *n.* wild American greyish-brown cat. [Spanish from Quechua]

pumice /'pʌmɪs/ *n.* (in full **pumice-stone**) **1** light porous volcanic rock used in cleaning or polishing. **2** piece of this used for removing hard skin etc. [Latin *pumex pumic-*]

pummel /'pʌm(ə)l/ *v.* (**-ll-**; *US* **-l-**) strike repeatedly, esp. with the fists. [from POMMEL]

pump[1] *–n.* **1** machine or device for raising or moving liquids, compressing gases, inflating tyres, etc. **2** act of pumping; stroke of a pump. *–v.* **1** (often foll. by *in, out, into, up,* etc.) raise or remove (liquid, gas, etc.) with a pump. **2** (often foll. by *up*) fill (a tyre etc.) with air. **3** remove (water etc.) with a pump. **4** work a pump. **5** (often foll. by *out*) (cause to) move, pour forth, etc., as if by pumping. **6** persistently question (a person) to obtain information. **7 a** move vigorously up and down. **b** shake (a person's hand) effusively. □ **pump iron** *colloq.* exercise with weights. [origin uncertain]

pump[2] *n.* **1** plimsoll. **2** light dancing shoe. **3** *US* court shoe. [origin unknown]

pumpernickel /'pʌmpəˌnɪk(ə)l/ *n.* German wholemeal rye bread. [German]

pumpkin /'pʌmpkɪn/ *n.* **1** large rounded yellow or orange fruit cooked as a vegetable. **2** large-leaved tendrilled plant bearing this. [Greek *pepōn* melon]

♦ **pump-priming** *n. Econ.* action by a government of adding to aggregate demand in order to set off the multiplier process. A policy advocated by Keynesians, it usu. involves allowing government expenditure to exceed receipts, thus creating a budget deficit. Pump-priming was widely employed by governments in the post-war era in order to maintain full employment; however, it became discredited in the 1970s when it failed to halt rising unemployment and was even held to be responsible for inflation. See also DEMAND MANAGEMENT; STAGFLATION.

pun –*n.* humorous use of a word or words with two or more meanings; play on words. –*v.* (**-nn-**) (foll. by *on*; also *absol.*) make a pun or puns with (words). [origin unknown]

punch[1] –*v.* **1** strike, esp. with a closed fist. **2 a** pierce a hole in (metal, paper, etc.) as or with a punch. **b** pierce (a hole) thus. –*n.* **1** blow with a fist. **2** ability to deliver this. **3** *colloq.* vigour, momentum; effective force. **4** tool, machine, or device for punching holes or impressing a design in leather, metal etc. □ **puncher** *n.* [var. of *pounce* emboss]

punch[2] *n.* drink of wine or spirits mixed with water, fruit juices, spices, etc., and usu. served hot. [origin unknown]

punch[3] *n.* (**Punch**) grotesque humpbacked puppet in *Punch and Judy* shows. □ **as pleased as Punch** extremely pleased. [abbreviation of *Punchinello*, name of the chief character in an Italian puppet-show]

punchball *n.* stuffed or inflated ball on a stand for punching as exercise or training.

punch-bowl *n.* **1** bowl for punch. **2** deep round hollow in a hill.

punch-drunk *adj.* stupefied from or as if from a series of heavy blows.

punched card *n.* rectangular paper card on which data is encoded in the form of holes punched in columns. A specific pattern of holes and spaces represents a particular letter, number, or other character (see also CARD READER). Punched cards are no longer used in present-day computing but were employed extensively for the input, output, and storage of data in early computers.

punched tag *n.* small tag that is attached to a product in a shop etc. and carries data on that product, encoded as a pattern of holes. When the product is sold or moved to a different location the punched data is collected mechanically for stock or production control, sales records, etc.

punched tape see PAPER TAPE.

punch-line *n.* words giving the point of a joke or story.

punch-up *n. colloq.* fist-fight; brawl.

punchy *adj.* (**-ier, -iest**) vigorous; forceful.

punctilio /pʌŋk'tɪlɪəʊ/ *n.* (*pl.* **-s**) **1** delicate point of ceremony or honour. **2** etiquette of such points. **3** petty formality. [Italian and Spanish: related to POINT]

punctilious /pʌŋk'tɪlɪəs/ *adj.* **1** attentive to formality or etiquette. **2** precise in behaviour. □ **punctiliously** *adv.* **punctiliousness** *n.* [Italian: related to PUNCTILIO]

punctual /'pʌŋktʃʊəl/ *adj.* keeping to the appointed time; prompt. □ **punctuality** /-'ælɪtɪ/ *n.* **punctually** *adv.* [medieval Latin: related to POINT]

punctuate /'pʌŋktʃʊˌeɪt/ *v.* (**-ting**) **1** insert punctuation marks in. **2** interrupt at intervals (*punctuated his tale with heavy sighs*). [medieval Latin: related to PUNCTUAL]

punctuation /ˌpʌŋktʃʊ'eɪʃ(ə)n/ *n.* **1** system of marks used to punctuate a written passage. **2** use of, or skill in using, these.

punctuation mark *n.* any of the marks (e.g. full stop and comma) used in writing to separate sentences etc. and clarify meaning.

puncture /'pʌŋktʃə(r)/ –*n.* **1** prick or pricking, esp. the accidental piercing of a pneumatic tyre. **2** hole made in this way. –*v.* (**-ring**) **1** make or undergo a puncture (in). **2** prick, pierce, or deflate (pomposity etc.). [Latin *punctura*: related to POINT]

pundit /'pʌndɪt/ *n.* **1** (also **pandit**) learned Hindu. **2** often *iron.* expert. □ **punditry** *n.* [Hindustani from Sanskrit]

Pune /'puːnə/ (formerly **Poona**) city in W India, in the state of Maharashtra; a centre of commerce and industry, it produces textiles, paper, rubber, and munitions; pop. (1991) 1 566 651.

pungent /'pʌndʒ(ə)nt/ *adj.* **1** sharp or strong in taste or smell, esp. producing a smarting or pricking sensation. **2** (of remarks) penetrating, biting, caustic. **3** mentally stimulating. □ **pungency** *n.* [Latin: related to POINT]

punish /'pʌnɪʃ/ *v.* **1** inflict retribution on (an offender) or for (an offence). **2** *colloq.* inflict severe blows on (an opponent). **3** tax, abuse, or treat severely or improperly. □ **punishable** *adj.* **punishing** *adj.* [Latin *punio*]

punishment *n.* **1** punishing or being punished. **2** loss or suffering inflicted in this. **3** *colloq.* severe treatment or suffering.

punitive /'pjuːnɪtɪv/ *adj.* **1** inflicting or intended to inflict punishment. **2** (of taxation etc.) extremely severe. [French or medieval Latin: related to PUNISH]

Punjab /pʌn'dʒɑːb, 'pʌndʒɑːb/ **1** (also **the Punjab**) region of the N Indian subcontinent, divided between India and Pakistan. It produces wheat (under irrigation), pulses, cotton, oil-seeds, and other crops. **2** province in NE Pakistan; pop. (1985) 53 840 000; capital, Lahore. **3** state in NW India; pop. (est. 1994) 21 695 000; capital, Chandigarh.

Punjabi /pʊn'dʒɑːbɪ/ –*n.* (*pl.* **-s**) **1** native of Punjab. **2** language of Punjab. –*adj.* of Punjab, its people, or language.

punk *n.* **1 a** (in full **punk rock**) anti-establishment and deliberately outrageous style of rock music. **b** (in full **punk rocker**) devotee of this. **2** esp. *US* young hooligan or petty criminal; lout. **3** soft crumbly fungus-infested wood used as tinder. [origin unknown]

punkah /'pʌŋkə/ *n.* large swinging cloth fan on a frame, worked by a cord or electrically. [Hindi]

punnet /'pʌnɪt/ *n.* small light basket or container for fruit or vegetables. [origin unknown]

punster *n.* person who makes puns, esp. habitually.

punt[1] –*n.* square-ended flat-bottomed pleasure boat propelled by a long pole. –*v.* **1** propel (a punt) with a pole. **2** travel or convey in a punt. □ **punter** *n.* [Low German or Dutch]

punt[2] –*v.* kick (a ball, esp. in Rugby) after it has dropped from the hands and before it reaches the ground. –*n.* such a kick. [origin unknown]

punt[3] *v.* **1** *colloq.* **a** bet on a horse etc. **b** speculate in shares etc. **2** (in some card-games) lay a stake against the bank. [French *ponter*]

punt[4] /pʊnt/ *n.* standard monetary unit of the Republic of Ireland. [Irish, = pound]

Punta Arenas /ˌpʊntə ə'reɪnəs/ city and port in S Chile, capital of Magallanes province on the Strait of Magellan; wool, mutton, and oil are exported; pop. (est. 1995) 117 206.

punter *n. colloq.* **1** person who gambles or lays a bet. **2** speculator on a stock exchange or commodity market, esp. one who hopes to make quick profits. **3 a** customer or client; member of an audience. **b** prostitute's client.

puny /'pjuːnɪ/ *adj.* (**-ier, -iest**) **1** undersized. **2** weak, feeble. [French *puisné* born afterwards]

pup –*n.* young dog, wolf, rat, seal, etc. –*v.* (**-pp-**) (also *absol.*) (of a bitch etc.) bring forth (young). [from PUPPY]

pupa /'pjuːpə/ *n.* (*pl.* **pupae** /-piː/) insect in the stage between larva and imago. □ **pupal** *adj.* [Latin, = doll]

pupil[1] /'pjuːpɪl/ *n.* person taught by another, esp. a schoolchild or student. [Latin *pupillus*, *-illa* diminutives of *pupus* boy, *pupa* girl]

pupil[2] *n.* dark circular opening in the centre of the iris of the eye. [related to PUPIL[1]]

puppet /'pʌpɪt/ *n.* **1** small figure moved esp. by strings as entertainment. **2** person controlled by another. □ **puppetry** *n.* [var. of POPPET]

puppet state *n.* country that is nominally independent but actually under the control of another power.

puppy /'pʌpɪ/ *n.* (*pl.* **-ies**) **1** young dog. **2** conceited or arrogant young man. [French: related to POPPET]

puppy-fat *n.* temporary fatness of a child or adolescent.

puppy love *n.* = CALF-LOVE.

purblind /'pɜːblaɪnd/ *adj.* **1** partly blind; dim-sighted. **2** obtuse, dim-witted. □ **purblindness** *n.* [from *pur(e)* (= 'utterly') *blind*]

purchase /'pɜːtʃəs/ –*v.* (**-sing**) **1** buy. **2** (often foll. by *with*) obtain or achieve at some cost. –*n.* **1** buying. **2** thing bought. **3 a** firm hold to prevent slipping; leverage. **b** device or tackle for moving heavy objects. **4** annual rent or return from land. □ **purchaser** *n.* [Anglo-French: related to PRO-[1], CHASE[1]]

◆ **purchase day book** *n.* (also **purchase journal**) book of prime entry in which the invoices of an organization's suppliers are recorded. These may only include invoices for goods supplied for resale but in most organizations they include invoices for all goods and services supplied; this often requires a number of columns to analyse the invoices into such account categories as motor expenses, light and heat, etc. Postings are made from the purchase day book to the personal accounts of the suppliers in the purchase ledger, while the totals of the analysis columns are posted to the nominal ledger.

◆ **purchased life annuity** *n.* annuity in which a single premium purchases an income to be paid from a specified future date for the rest of the policyholder's life.

◆ **purchase ledger** *n.* ledger in which the personal accounts of an organization's suppliers are recorded. The total of the balances in this ledger represents the organization's trade creditors.

◆ **purchase ledger control account** *n.* account in the nominal ledger to which the totals of the entries in the purchase day book are posted at regular intervals. With this procedure the balance on the purchase ledger control account should, at any time, equal the aggregate of the balances on all the individual accounts in the ledger. The balance also represents the total of trade creditors.

◆ **purchasing officer** *n.* person employed by a manufacturer and responsible for purchasing the raw materials used in the manufacturing process. If these include raw materials that fluctuate in price, the purchasing officer has to show that the average purchase price for the year is not excessive. He or she is also responsible for maintaining adequate stocks to tide the company over any break in the continuity of supply, without tying up excessive amounts of capital.

◆ **purchasing power parity** *n.* (also **PPP**) parity between two currencies at a rate of exchange that will give each currency exactly the same purchasing power in its own economy. The belief that exchange rates adjust to reflect PPP dates back at least to the 17th century, but in the short term, at least, is demonstrably false (see OVERSHOOTING). It may well hold in the long term, and is often used as a benchmark to indicate the levels that exchange rates should achieve (although measurement is difficult and controversial).

purdah /ˈpɜːdə/ *n. Ind.* screening of women from strangers by a veil or curtain in some Muslim and Hindu societies. [Urdu]

pure *adj.* **1** unmixed, unadulterated (*pure white*; *pure malice*). **2** of unmixed origin or descent (*pure-blooded*). **3** chaste. **4** not morally corrupt. **5** guiltless. **6** sincere. **7** (of a sound) perfectly in tune. **8** (of a subject of study) abstract, not applied. □ **pureness** *n.* [Latin *purus*]

purée /ˈpjʊəreɪ/ *–n.* smooth pulp of vegetables or fruit etc. *–v.* (**-ées, -éed**) make a purée of. [French]

◆ **pure economic profit** *n.* surplus or rent extracted by a producer or seller in exploiting a privileged position in a market. This position may be a result of monopoly, oligopoly, limited information, or even government regulations. It represents a return in excess of that required to bring an entrepreneur to the market and is therefore generally disliked. This is not the same as saying that monopoly is not Pareto optimal, although the two statements are often confused. See also SUPERPROFIT.

◆ **pure endowment assurance** *n.* insurance providing for payment of an agreed amount if the policyholder is alive on a specified future date. If the policyholder dies before the specified date no payment is made and the premium payments cease. The use of the word 'assurance' for this type of contract is questionable as there is no element of life-assurance cover.

purely *adv.* **1** in a pure manner. **2** merely, solely, exclusively.

purgative /ˈpɜːgətɪv/ *–adj.* **1** serving to purify. **2** strongly laxative. *–n.* **1** purgative thing. **2** laxative. [Latin: related to PURGE]

purgatory /ˈpɜːgətərɪ/ *–n.* (*pl.* **-ies**) **1** *RC Ch.* supposed place or state of expiation of petty sins after death and before entering heaven. **2** place or state of temporary suffering or expiation. *–adj.* purifying. □ **purgatorial** /-ˈtɔːrɪəl/ *adj.* [medieval Latin: related to PURGE]

purge *–v.* (**-ging**) **1** (often foll. by *of, from*) make physically or spiritually clean. **2** remove by cleansing. **3** rid (an organization, party, etc.) of unacceptable members. **4 a** empty (the bowels). **b** empty the bowels of (a person). **5** *Law* atone for (an offence, esp. contempt of court). *–n.* **1** act of purging. **2** purgative. [Latin *purgo* purify]

purify /ˈpjʊərɪˌfaɪ/ *v.* (**-ies, -ied**) **1** clear of extraneous elements; make pure. **2** (often foll. by *of, from*) make ceremonially pure or clean. □ **purification** /-fɪˈkeɪʃ(ə)n/ *n.* **purificatory** /-fɪˌkeɪtərɪ/ *adj.* **purifier** *n.*

purist /ˈpjʊərɪst/ *n.* advocate of scrupulous purity, esp. in language or art. □ **purism** *n.* **puristic** /-ˈrɪstɪk/ *adj.*

puritan /ˈpjʊərɪt(ə)n/ *–n.* **1** (**Puritan**) *hist.* member of a group of English Protestants who sought to simplify and regulate forms of worship after the Reformation. **2** purist member of any party. **3** strict observer of religion or morals. *–adj.* **1** (**Puritan**) *hist.* of the Puritans. **2** scrupulous and austere in religion or morals. □ **puritanism** *n.* [Latin: related to PURE]

puritanical /ˌpjʊərɪˈtænɪk(ə)l/ *adj.* strictly religious or moral in behaviour. □ **puritanically** *adv.*

purity /ˈpjʊərɪtɪ/ *n.* pureness, cleanness.

purl[1] *–n.* **1** knitting stitch made by putting the needle through the front of the previous stitch and passing the yarn round the back of the needle. **2** chain of minute loops; picot. *–v.* (also *absol.*) knit with a purl stitch. [origin unknown]

purl[2] *v.* (of a brook etc.) flow with a babbling sound. [imitative]

purler *n. colloq.* headlong fall. [*purl* overturn]

purlieu /ˈpɜːljuː/ *n.* (*pl.* **-s**) **1** person's bounds, limits, or usual haunts. **2** *hist.* tract on the border of a forest. **3** (in *pl.*) outskirts, outlying region. [Anglo-French *puralé* from *aller* go]

purlin /ˈpɜːlɪn/ *n.* horizontal beam along the length of a roof. [Anglo-Latin *perlio*]

purloin /pəˈlɔɪn/ *v. formal* or *joc.* steal, pilfer. [Anglo-French *purloigner* from *loign* far]

purple /ˈpɜːp(ə)l/ *–n.* **1** colour between red and blue. **2** (in full **Tyrian purple**) crimson dye obtained from some molluscs. **3** purple robe, esp. of an emperor or senior magistrate. **4** scarlet official dress of a cardinal. **5** (prec. by *the*) position of rank, authority, or privilege. *–adj.* of a purple colour. *–v.* (**-ling**) make or become purple. □ **purplish** *adj.* [Greek *porphura*, a shellfish yielding dye]

purple heart *n. colloq.* heart-shaped stimulant tablet, esp. of amphetamine.

purple passage *n.* (also **purple patch**) ornate or elaborate literary passage.

purport *–v.* /pəˈpɔːt/ **1** profess; be intended to seem (*purports to be an officer*). **2** (often foll. by *that*) (of a document or speech) have as its meaning; state. *–n.* /ˈpɜːpɔːt/ **1** ostensible meaning. **2** sense or tenor (of a document or statement). □ **purportedly** /pəˈpɔːtɪdlɪ/ *adv.* [Latin: related to PRO-[1], *porto* carry]

purpose /ˈpɜːpəs/ *–n.* **1** object to be attained; thing intended. **2** intention to act. **3** resolution, determination. *–v.* (**-sing**) have as one's purpose; design, intend. □ **on purpose** intentionally. **to no purpose** with no result or effect. **to the purpose 1** relevant. **2** useful. [Latin *propono* PROPOSE]

purpose-built *adj.* (also **purpose-made**) built or made for a specific purpose.

purposeful *adj.* **1** having or indicating purpose. **2** intentional. **3** resolute. □ **purposefully** *adv.* **purposefulness** *n.*

purposeless *adj.* having no aim or plan.

purposely *adv.* on purpose.

purposive /ˈpɜːpəsɪv/ *adj.* **1** having, serving, or done with a purpose. **2** purposeful; resolute.

purr /pɜː(r)/ *–v.* **1** (of a cat) make a low vibratory sound expressing contentment. **2** (of machinery etc.) run smoothly and quietly. **3** (of a person) express pleasure; utter purringly. *–n.* purring sound. [imitative]

purse *–n.* **1** small pouch for carrying money on the person. **2** *US* handbag. **3** money, funds. **4** sum as a present or prize in a contest. *–v.* (**-sing**) **1** (often foll. by *up*) pucker or contract (the lips etc.). **2** become wrinkled. □ **hold the purse-strings** have control of expenditure. [Greek, = leather bag]

purser *n.* officer on a ship who keeps the accounts, esp. the head steward in a passenger vessel.

pursuance /pəˈsjuːəns/ *n.* (foll. by *of*) carrying out or observance (of a plan, idea, etc.).

pursuant *adv.* (foll. by *to*) in accordance with. [French: related to PURSUE]

pursue /pəˈsjuː/ *v.* (**-sues, -sued, -suing**) **1** follow with intent to overtake, capture, or do harm to; go in pursuit. **2** continue or proceed along (a route or course of action). **3** follow or engage in (study or other activity). **4** proceed according to (a plan etc.). **5** seek after, aim at. **6** continue to investigate or discuss (a topic). **7** importune (a person) persistently. **8** (of misfortune etc.) persistently assail. □ **pursuer** *n.* [Latin *sequor* follow]

pursuit /pəˈsjuːt/ *n.* **1** act of pursuing. **2** occupation or activity pursued. □ **in pursuit of** pursuing. [French: related to SUIT]

pursuivant /ˈpɜːsɪv(ə)nt/ *n.* officer of the College of Arms below a herald. [French: related to PURSUE]

purulent /ˈpjʊərʊlənt/ *adj.* of, containing, or discharging pus. □ **purulence** *n.* [Latin: related to PUS]

purvey /pəˈveɪ/ *v.* provide or supply (food etc.) as one's business. □ **purveyor** *n.* [Latin: related to PROVIDE]

purview /ˈpɜːvjuː/ *n.* **1** scope or range of a document, scheme, etc. **2** range of physical or mental vision. [Anglo-French past part.: related to PURVEY]

pus *n.* thick yellowish or greenish liquid produced from infected tissue. [Latin *pus puris*]

Pusan /puːˈsæn/ seaport in South Korea, on the SE coast; pop. (1995) 3 813 814.

push /pʊʃ/ *–v.* **1** exert a force on (a thing) to move it or cause it to move away. **2** exert such a force (*do not push against the door*). **3 a** thrust forward or upward. **b** (cause to) project (*pushes out new roots*). **4** move forward or make (one's way) by force or persistence. **5** exert oneself, esp. to surpass others. **6** (often foll. by *to*, *into*, or *to* + infin.) urge, impel, or press (a person) hard; harass. **7** (often foll. by *for*) pursue or demand (a claim etc.) persistently. **8** promote, e.g. by advertising. **9** *colloq.* sell (a drug) illegally. *–n.* **1** act of pushing; shove, thrust. **2** force exerted in this. **3** vigorous effort. **4** military attack in force. **5** enterprise, ambition. **6** use of influence to advance a person. □ **be pushed for** *colloq.* have very little of (esp. time). **give** (or **get) the push** *colloq.* dismiss or send (or be dismissed or sent) away. **push about** = *push around*. **push along** (often in *imper.*) *colloq.* depart, leave. **push around** *colloq.* bully. **push one's luck 1** take undue risks. **2** act presumptuously. **push off 1** push with an oar etc. to get a boat out into a river etc. **2** (often in *imper.*) *colloq.* go away. **push through** get (a scheme, proposal, etc.) completed or accepted quickly. [Latin: related to PULSATE]

push-bike *n. colloq.* bicycle.

push-button *n.* **1** button to be pushed, esp. to operate an electrical device. **2** (*attrib.*) operated thus.

pushchair *n.* folding chair on wheels, for pushing a young child along in.

pusher *n. colloq.* seller of illegal drugs.

pushful *adj.* pushy; arrogant. □ **pushfully** *adv.*

pushing *adj.* **1** pushy. **2** *colloq.* having nearly reached (a specified age).

◆ **push money** *n.* cash inducement given to a retailer by a manufacturer or wholesaler to be used to reward sales personnel who are particularly successful in selling specified products.

pushover *n. colloq.* **1** something easily done. **2** person easily persuaded, defeated, etc.

push-start *–n.* starting of a vehicle by pushing it to turn the engine. *–v.* start (a vehicle) in this way.

Pushtu /ˈpʌʃtuː/ *n.* & *adj.* = PASHTO. [Persian]

push-up *n.* = PRESS-UP.

pushy *adj.* (**-ier, -iest**) *colloq.* excessively self-assertive. □ **pushily** *adv.* **pushiness** *n.*

pusillanimous /ˌpjuːsɪˈlænɪməs/ *adj. formal* cowardly, timid. □ **pusillanimity** /-ləˈnɪmɪtɪ/ *n.* [Church Latin *pusillanimis* from *pusillus* very small, *animus* mind]

puss /pʊs/ *n. colloq.* **1** cat (esp. as a form of address). **2** sly or coquettish girl. [Low German or Dutch]

pussy /ˈpʊsɪ/ *n.* (*pl.* **-ies**) **1** (also **pussy-cat**) *colloq.* cat. **2** *coarse slang* vulva.

pussyfoot *v. colloq.* **1** move stealthily. **2** equivocate; stall.

pussy willow *n.* willow with furry catkins.

pustulate /ˈpʌstjʊˌleɪt/ *v.* (**-ting**) form into pustules. [Latin: related to PUSTULE]

pustule /ˈpʌstjuːl/ *n.* pimple containing pus. □ **pustular** *adj.* [Latin *pustula*]

put /pʊt/ *–v.* (**-tt-**; *past* and *past part.* **put**) **1** move to or cause to be in a specified place or position (*put it in your pocket*; *put the children to bed*). **2** bring into a specified condition or state (*puts me in great difficulty*). **3** (often foll. by *on*, *to*) impose, enforce, assign, or apply (*put a tax on beer*; *where do you put the blame?*; *put a stop to it*; *put it to good use*). **4** place (a person) or (*refl.*) imagine (oneself) in a specified position (*put them at their ease*; *put yourself in my shoes*). **5** (foll. by *for*) substitute (one thing) for (another). **6** express in a specified way (*to put it mildly*). **7** (foll. by *at*) estimate (an amount etc.) at so much (*put the cost at £50*). **8** (foll. by *into*) express or translate in (words, or another language). **9** (foll. by *into*) invest (money in an asset, e.g. land). **10** (foll. by *on*) stake (money) on (a horse etc.). **11** (foll. by *to*) submit for attention (*put it to a vote*). **12** throw (esp. a shot or weight) as a sport. **13** (foll. by *back*, *off*, *out to sea*, etc.) (of a ship etc.) proceed in a specified direction. *–n.* throw of the shot etc. □ **put about 1** spread (information, a rumour, etc.). **2** *Naut.* turn round; put (a ship) on the opposite tack. **put across 1** communicate (an idea etc.) effectively. **2** (often in **put it** (or **one) across**) achieve by deceit. **put away 1** restore (a thing) to its usual or former place. **2** lay (money etc.) aside for future use. **3** imprison or commit to a home etc. **4** consume (food and drink), esp. in large quantities. **5** = *put down* 7. **put back 1** = *put away* 1. **2** change (a meeting etc.) to a later date or time. **3** move back the hands of (a clock or watch). **put a bold** etc. **face on it** see FACE. **put the boot in** see BOOT. **put by** = *put away* 2. **put down 1** suppress by force. **2** *colloq.* snub, humiliate. **3** record or enter in writing. **4** enter the name of (a person) on a list. **5** (foll. by *as*, *for*) account or reckon. **6** (foll. by *to*) attribute (*put it down to bad planning*). **7** put (an old or sick animal) to death. **8** pay as a deposit. **9** stop to let (passengers) get off. **put an end to** see END. **put one's foot down** see FOOT. **put one's foot in it** see FOOT. **put forth** (of a plant) send out (buds or leaves). **put forward 1** suggest or propose. **2** advance the time shown on (a clock or watch). **put in 1 a** enter or submit (a claim etc.). **b** (foll. by *for*) submit a claim for (a specified thing). **2** (foll. by *for*) be a candidate for (an appointment, election, etc.). **3** spend (time). **4** interpose (a remark, blow, etc.). **put it to a person** (often foll. by *that*) challenge a person to deny. **put off 1 a** postpone. **b** postpone an engagement with (a person). **2** (often foll. by *with*) evade (a person) with an excuse etc. **3** hinder, dissuade; offend, disconcert. **put on 1** clothe oneself with. **2** cause (a light etc.) to function. **3** cause (transport) to be available. **4** stage (a play, show, etc.). **5** advance the hands of (a clock or watch). **6 a** pretend to (an emotion). **b** assume, take on (a character or appearance). **c** (**put it on**) exaggerate one's feelings etc. **7** increase one's weight by (a specified amount). **8** (foll. by *to*) make aware of or put in touch with (*put us on to their new accountant*). **put on weight** increase one's weight. **put out 1 a** (often as **put out** *adj.*) disconcert or annoy. **b** (often *refl.*) inconvenience (*don't put yourself out*). **2** extinguish (a fire or light). **3** cause (a batsman or side) to be out. **4** allocate (work) to be done off the premises. **5** blind (a person's eyes). **put over** = *put across* 1. **put a sock in it** see SOCK[1]. **put through 1** carry out or complete. **2** (often foll. by *to*) connect by telephone. **put to flight** see FLIGHT[2]. **put together 1** assemble (a whole) from parts. **2** combine (parts) to form a whole. **put under** make unconscious. **put up 1** build, erect. **2** raise (a price etc.). **3** take or provide with accommodation (*put me up for the night*). **4** engage in (a defensive fight, struggle, etc.). **5** present (a proposal). **6** present oneself, or propose, for election. **7** provide (money) as a backer. **8** display (a notice). **9** offer for sale or competition. **put upon** (usu. in *passive*) *colloq.* take advantage of (a person) unfairly or excessively. **put a person up to** (usu. foll. by verbal noun) instigate a person to (*put them up to stealing*). **put up with** endure, tolerate. **put the wind up** see WIND[1]. **put a person wise** see WISE. **put words into a person's mouth** see MOUTH. [Old English]

putative /ˈpjuːtətɪv/ *adj. formal* reputed, supposed (*his putative father*). [Latin *puto* think]

put-down *n. colloq.* snub.

♦ **put-of-more option** see OPTION TO DOUBLE 1.

---

put-on *n. colloq.* deception or hoax.

♦ **put option** see OPTION 3.

---

putrefy /ˈpjuːtrɪˌfaɪ/ *v.* (**-ies, -ied**) **1** become or make putrid; go bad. **2** fester, suppurate. **3** become morally corrupt. □ **putrefaction** /-ˈfækʃ(ə)n/ *n.* **putrefactive** /-ˈfæktɪv/ *adj.* [Latin *puter putris* rotten]

putrescent /pjuːˈtres(ə)nt/ *adj.* rotting. □ **putrescence** *n.* [Latin: related to PUTRID]

putrid /ˈpjuːtrɪd/ *adj.* **1** decomposed, rotten. **2** foul, noxious. **3** corrupt. **4** *slang* of poor quality; contemptible; very unpleasant. □ **putridity** /-ˈrɪdɪtɪ/ *n.* [Latin *putreo* rot (v.)]

putsch /pʊtʃ/ *n.* attempt at political revolution; violent uprising. [Swiss German]

putt *–v.* (**-tt-**) strike (a golf ball) gently on a putting-green. *–n.* putting stroke. [from PUT]

puttee /ˈpʌtɪ/ *n. hist.* long strip of cloth wound round the leg from ankle to knee for protection and support, worn esp. by soldiers. [Hindi]

putter[1] *n.* golf club for putting.

putter[2] *US* var. of POTTER[1].

♦ **put-through** *n.* two deals made simultaneously by a market maker on the London Stock Exchange, in which a large quantity of shares is sold by one client and bought by another, the market maker taking a very small turn.

---

putting-green *n.* (in golf) smooth area of grass round a hole.

putty /ˈpʌtɪ/ *–n.* cement of whiting and linseed oil, used for fixing panes of glass, filling holes, etc. *–v.* (**-ies, -ied**) cover, fix, join, or fill with putty. [French *potée*: related to POT[1]]

put-up job *n. colloq.* fraudulent scheme.

puzzle /ˈpʌz(ə)l/ *–n.* **1** difficult or confusing problem. **2** problem or toy designed to test knowledge or ingenuity. *–v.* (**-ling**) **1** confound or disconcert mentally. **2** (usu. foll. by *over* etc.) be perplexed (about). **3** (usu. as **puzzling** *adj.*) require much mental effort (*puzzling situation*). **4** (foll. by *out*) solve or understand by hard thought. □ **puzzlement** *n.* [origin unknown]

puzzler *n.* difficult question or problem.

PVC *abbr.* polyvinyl chloride.

PW *abbr.* policewoman.

p.w. *abbr.* per week.

PX *abbr. Telephony* private exchange.

PY *international vehicle registration* Paraguay.

pyaemia /paɪˈiːmɪə/ *n.* (*US* **pyemia**) blood-poisoning caused by pus-forming bacteria in the bloodstream. [Greek *puon* pus, *haima* blood]

pygmy /ˈpɪgmɪ/ *n.* (also **pigmy**) (*pl.* **-ies**) (often *attrib.*) **1** member of a dwarf people of esp. equatorial Africa. **2** very small person, animal, or thing. **3** insignificant person. [Latin from Greek]

pyjamas /pəˈdʒɑːməz/ *n.pl.* (*US* **pajamas**) **1** suit of loose trousers and jacket for sleeping in. **2** loose trousers worn by both sexes in some Asian countries. **3** (**pyjama**) (*attrib.*) of either part of a pair of pyjamas (*pyjama jacket*). [Urdu, = leg-clothing]

pylon /ˈpaɪlən/ *n.* tall structure, esp. as a support for electric-power cables etc. [Greek *pulē* gate]

Pyongyang /pjʌŋˈjɑːŋ/ capital of North Korea, a centre of commerce and industry; pop. (est. 1987) 2 355 000.

pyorrhoea /ˌpaɪəˈrɪə/ *n.* (*US* **pyorrhea**) **1** gum disease causing loosening of the teeth. **2** discharge of pus. [Greek *puon* pus, *rheō* flow]

pyracantha /ˌpaɪərəˈkænθə/ *n.* evergreen thorny shrub with white flowers and bright red or yellow berries. [Latin from Greek]

pyramid /ˈpɪrəmɪd/ *n.* **1** monumental, esp. stone, structure, with a square base and sloping triangular sides meeting at an apex, esp. an ancient Egyptian royal tomb. **2** solid of this shape with esp. a square or triangular base. **3** pyramid-shaped thing or pile of things. □ **pyramidal** /-ˈræmɪd(ə)l/ *adj.* [Greek *puramis -mid-*]

♦ **pyramid selling** *n.* method of selling to the public using a hierarchy of part-time workers. A central instigator (at the apex of the pyramid) usu. sells a franchise to regional organizers for a certain product, together with an agreed quantity of the goods. These organizers recruit district distributors, who each take some of the stock and, in turn, recruit door-to-door sellers, who take smaller proportions of the stock. In some cases the last stage consists of people who sell the goods to their friends. As the central instigator can sell more goods by this means than are likely to be bought at the base of the pyramid, and someone on the way down is liable to be caught with unsaleable stock, the system is illegal in the UK.

---

pyre /ˈpaɪə(r)/ *n.* heap of combustible material, esp. for burning a corpse. [Greek: related to PYRO-]

pyrethrum /paɪˈriːθrəm/ *n.* **1** aromatic chrysanthemum. **2** insecticide from its dried flowers. [Latin from Greek]

pyretic /paɪˈretɪk/ *adj.* of, for, or producing fever. [Greek *puretos* fever]

Pyrex /ˈpaɪəreks/ *n. propr.* hard heat-resistant glass, used esp. for ovenware. [invented word]

pyrexia /paɪˈreksɪə/ *n. Med.* = FEVER. [Greek *purexis*]

pyrites /paɪˈraɪtiːz/ *n.* (in full **iron pyrites**) lustrous yellow mineral that is a sulphide of iron. [Greek: related to PYRE]

pyro- *comb. form* **1** denoting fire. **2** denoting a mineral etc. changed under the action of heat, or fiery in colour. [Greek *pur* fire]

pyromania /ˌpaɪərəʊˈmeɪnɪə/ *n.* obsessive desire to start fires. □ **pyromaniac** *n.* & *adj.*

pyrotechnics /ˌpaɪərəʊˈteknɪks/ *n.pl.* **1** art of making fireworks. **2** display of fireworks. **3** any brilliant display. □ **pyrotechnic** *adj.*

pyrrhic /ˈpɪrɪk/ *adj.* (of a victory) won at too great a cost. [*Pyrrhus* of Epirus, who defeated the Romans in 279 BC, but suffered heavy losses]

Pythagoras' theorem /paɪˈθægərəs/ *n.* theorem that the square on the hypotenuse of a right-angled triangle is equal to the sum of the squares on the other two sides. [Pythagoras (6th century bc), name of a Greek philosopher]

python /ˈpaɪθ(ə)n/ *n.* large tropical constricting snake. [Greek *Puthōn*, name of a monster]

pyx /pɪks/ *n.* vessel for the consecrated bread of the Eucharist. [Greek *puxis* BOX[1]]

PZ *international civil aircraft marking* Suriname.

Qq

Q[1] /kjuː/ *n.* (also **q**) (*pl.* **Qs** or **Q's**) seventeenth letter of the alphabet.

Q[2] *abbr.* (also **Q.**) **1** quarterly. **2** quarter-page (in advertisement placing). **3** Queen('s). **4** question.

Q[3] *symb.* quetzal.

q. *abbr.* **1** quarter. **2** quarterly. **3** quarto. **4** query.

QA *abbr.* quality assurance.

Qantas /ˈkwɒntəs/ *n.* Australian airline. [abbreviation, from *Q*ueensland *an*d *N*orthern *T*erritory *A*erial *S*ervice]

QC *–abbr.* **1** quality control. **2** Queen's Counsel.

QCT *abbr.* quality-control technology.

QED *abbr.* which was to be proved. [Latin *quod erat demonstrandum*]

QER *abbr.* Quarterly Economic Review.

QF *airline flight code* Qantas Airways.

Qinghai /tʃɪŋˈhaɪ/ (also **Tsinghai**) mountainous province in W central China; pop. (est. 1995) 4 740 000; capital, Xining (Sining). Products include coal, oil, iron, and salt.

♦ **QL** *abbr.* = QUERY LANGUAGE.

Qld. *abbr.* Queensland.

qlty. *abbr.* quality.

qly. *abbr.* quarterly.

QM *abbr.* quartermaster.

QP *abbr.* = QUERY PROCESSING.

QR *–abbr. Marketing* quick response. *–symb.* riyal (of Qatar).

qr. *abbr.* **1** quarter(s). **2** quarterly. **3** quire.

QRV *abbr.* Qualified Valuer, Real Estate Institute of New South Wales.

QS *abbr.* quantity surveyor.

qt. *abbr.* quart(s).

qtly. *abbr.* quarterly.

qto. *abbr.* quarto.

qtr. *abbr.* quarter.

qty. *abbr.* quantity.

QU *airline flight code* Uganda Airlines.

qua /kwɑː, kweɪ/ *conj.* in the capacity of. [Latin, = in the way in which]

quack[1] *–n.* harsh sound made by ducks. *–v.* utter this sound. [imitative]

quack[2] *n.* **1** unqualified practitioner, esp. of medicine; charlatan (often *attrib.*: *quack cure*). **2** *slang* any doctor. □ **quackery** *n.* [abbreviation of *quacksalver* from Dutch: probably related to QUACK[1], SALVE[1]]

quad[1] /kwɒd/ *n. colloq.* quadrangle. [abbreviation]

quad[2] /kwɒd/ *n. colloq.* quadruplet. [abbreviation]

quad[3] /kwɒd/ *colloq. –n.* quadraphonics. *–adj.* quadraphonic. [abbreviation]

Quadragesima /ˌkwɒdrəˈdʒesɪmə/ *n.* first Sunday in Lent. [Latin *quadragesimus* fortieth]

quadrangle /ˈkwɒdˌræŋg(ə)l/ *n.* **1** four-sided plane figure, esp. a square or rectangle. **2** four-sided court, esp. in colleges. □ **quadrangular** /-ˈræŋgjʊlə(r)/ *adj.* [Latin: related to QUADRI-, ANGLE[1]]

quadrant /ˈkwɒdrənt/ *n.* **1** quarter of a circle's circumference. **2** quarter of a circle enclosed by two radii at right angles. **3** quarter of a sphere etc. **4** any of four parts of a plane divided by two lines at right angles. **5 a** graduated quarter-circular strip of metal etc. **b** instrument graduated (esp. through an arc of 90°) for measuring angles. [Latin *quadrans -ant-*]

quadraphonic /ˌkwɒdrəˈfɒnɪk/ *adj.* (of sound reproduction) using four transmission channels. □ **quadraphonically** *adv.* **quadraphonics** *n.pl.* [from QUADRI-, STEREOPHONIC]

quadrate *–adj.* /ˈkwɒdrət/ esp. *Anat.* & *Zool.* square or rectangular. *–n.* /ˈkwɒdrət, -dreɪt/ rectangular object. *–v.* /kwɒˈdreɪt/ (**-ting**) make square. [Latin *quadro* make square]

quadratic /kwɒˈdrætɪk/ *Math. –adj.* involving the square (and no higher power) of an unknown quantity or variable (*quadratic equation*). *–n.* quadratic equation.

quadri- *comb. form* four. [Latin *quattuor* four]

quadriceps /ˈkwɒdrɪˌseps/ *n.* four-headed muscle at the front of the thigh. [from QUADRI-, BICEPS]

quadrilateral /ˌkwɒdrɪˈlætər(ə)l/ *–adj.* having four sides. *–n.* four-sided figure.

quadrille /kwɒˈdrɪl/ *n.* **1** a kind of square dance. **2** music for this. [French]

quadriplegia /ˌkwɒdrɪˈpliːdʒə/ *n.* paralysis of all four limbs. □ **quadriplegic** *adj.* & *n.* [from QUADRI-, Greek *plēgē* a blow]

quadruped /ˈkwɒdrʊˌped/ *n.* four-footed animal, esp. a mammal. [Latin: related to QUADRI-, *pes ped-* foot]

quadruple /ˈkwɒdrʊp(ə)l/ *–adj.* **1** fourfold; having four parts. **2** (of time in music) having four beats in a bar. *–n.* fourfold number or amount. *–v.* (**-ling**) multiply by four. [Latin: related to QUADRI-]

quadruplet /ˈkwɒdrʊplɪt/ *n.* each of four children born at one birth.

Qatar /ˈkætɑː(r), ˈgæ-/, **State of** sheikdom on a peninsula on the W coast of the Persian Gulf. Oil production provides a substantial proportion of national income, but the exploitation of large reserves of natural gas (which began in 1991) and the subsequent development of associated industries is expected to reduce the dependence of the country's economy on oil. Chemicals, textiles, and furniture are among the main manufactured products. Qatar is a member of OPEC. The country became a British protectorate in 1916, and until 1971 (when it became a sovereign independent state) was in special treaty relations with Britain. In 1995 Sheikh Hamad bin Khalifa Al-Thani became head of state after overthrowing his father. An attempted coup failed in 1996. Head of state, Sheikh Hamad bin Khalifa Al-Thani; capital, Doha. □ **Qatari** *adj.* & *n.*

languages	Arabic (official), English
currency	riyal (QR) of 100 dirhams
pop. (1996)	590 000
GNP (1994)	US$7.8B
literacy	79% (m); 79% (f)
life expectancy	70 (m); 74 (f)

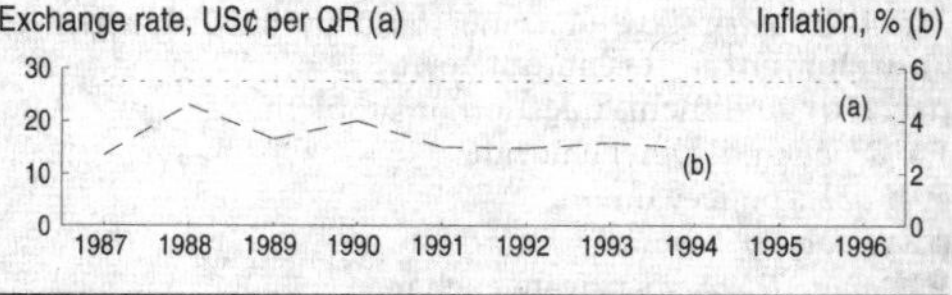

quadruplicate –*adj.* /kwɒ'dru:plɪkət/ **1** fourfold. **2** of which four copies are made. –*v.* /kwɒ'dru:plɪ,keɪt/ (**-ting**) multiply by four.

quaff /kwɒf/ *v. literary* **1** drink deeply. **2** drain (a cup etc.) in long draughts. □ **quaffable** *adj.* [perhaps imitative]

quagmire /'kwɒg,maɪə(r), 'kwæg-/ *n.* **1** muddy or boggy area. **2** hazardous situation. [from *quag* bog, MIRE]

quail[1] *n.* (*pl.* same or **-s**) small game-bird related to the partridge. [French *quaille*]

quail[2] *v.* flinch; show fear. [origin unknown]

quaint *adj.* attractively odd or old-fashioned. □ **quaintly** *adv.* **quaintness** *n.* [French *cointe* from Latin *cognosco* ascertain]

quake –*v.* (**-king**) shake, tremble. –*n. colloq.* earthquake. [Old English]

Quaker *n.* member of the Society of Friends. □ **Quakerism** *n.*

qualification /,kwɒlɪfɪ'keɪʃ(ə)n/ *n.* **1** accomplishment fitting a person for a position or purpose. **2** thing that modifies or limits (*statement had many qualifications*). **3** qualifying or being qualified. □ **qualificatory** /'kwɒl-/ *adj.* [French or medieval Latin: related to QUALIFY]

♦ **qualified acceptance** *n.* acceptance of a bill of exchange that varies the effect of the bill as drawn. The holder may refuse to take a qualified acceptance, in which case the drawer and any endorsers must be notified or they will no longer be liable. If the holder takes a qualified acceptance, all previous signatories who did not assent from liability are released.

♦ **qualified report** *n.* auditors' report in which the auditors, for one reason or another, have been unable to satisfy themselves that the accounts give a true and fair view of a company's affairs. For smaller companies, in which internal control cannot be perfect, qualified reports are not uncommon. However, it is usu. regarded as a serious matter for a public limited company to receive a qualified report.

qualify /'kwɒlɪ,faɪ/ *v.* (**-ies, -ied**) **1** (often as **qualified** *adj.*) make competent or fit for a position or purpose. **2** make legally entitled. **3** (usu. foll. by *for*) (of a person) satisfy conditions or requirements. **4** modify or limit (a statement etc.) (*qualified approval*). **5** *Gram.* (of a word) attribute a quality to esp. a noun. **6** moderate, mitigate; make less severe. **7** (foll. by *as*) be describable as, count as (*a grunt hardly qualifies as conversation*). □ **qualifier** *n.* [Latin *qualis* such as, of what kind]

♦ **qualifying distribution** *n.* distribution from a company for which advance corporation tax is paid. Qualifying distributions include dividends, issues of redeemable preference shares, bonus issues of shares, and distribution of any company assets to shareholders.

♦ **qualifying policy** *n.* life-assurance policy that the UK Inland Revenue has agreed is eligible for tax relief on the premiums and/or the payment of the sum assured. Tax relief on life-assurance premiums was abolished on 13 March 1984, therefore policies eligible for life-assurance premium relief have now disappeared. Cf. NON-QUALIFYING POLICY.

qualitative /'kwɒlɪtətɪv/ *adj.* of quality as opposed to quantity. □ **qualitatively** *adv.* [Latin: related to QUALITY]

♦ **qualitative marketing research** *n.* marketing research techniques that use small samples of respondents to gain an impression of their beliefs, motivations, perceptions, and opinions. Unstructured methods of data collection, e.g. depth interviews and group discussions, are used to explore topics in considerable detail. Qualitative marketing research is frequently used to test an advertisement's effectiveness or to explore new products (see also CONCEPT TEST). In general, it is used to show why people buy a particular product, whereas quantitative marketing research reveals how many people buy it.

quality /'kwɒlɪtɪ/ *n.* (*pl.* **-ies**) **1** degree of excellence. **2 a** general excellence (*has quality*). **b** (*attrib.*) of high quality (*a quality product*). **3** attribute, faculty (*has many good qualities*). **4** relative nature or character. **5** timbre of a voice or sound. **6** *archaic* high social standing (*people of quality*). [Latin *qualis* such as, of what kind]

quality control *n.* **1** maintaining of requisite standards in products or services. **2** systematic inspection of products, or a sample of the products on a production line, at various stages of production for this purpose. In mass production, the statistical analysis of parameters measured on a random sample of the end product is most important. The larger the sample tested, the higher will be the manufacturer's reputation for producing goods of a high standard. **Quality control charts** are frequently used in mass production; the horizontal axis of the chart (graph) is calibrated in units of time, while the vertical axis represents the values of such variables as the percentage of defective products. The cause of any sustained rise in the variable must be examined immediately.

qualm /kwɑ:m/ *n.* **1** misgiving; uneasy doubt. **2** scruple of conscience. **3** momentary faint or sick feeling. [origin uncertain]

quandary /'kwɒndərɪ/ *n.* (*pl.* **-ies**) **1** perplexed state. **2** practical dilemma. [origin uncertain]

quango /'kwæŋgəʊ/ *n.* (*pl.* **-s**) body performing some public function with financial support from and senior appointments made by the government. While not actually government agencies, they are not independent and are usu. answerable to a government minister. [abbreviation of *qua*si (or *qua*si-*a*utonomous) *n*on-*g*overnment(al) *o*rganization]

♦ **quant** /kwɒnt/ *n. colloq.* highly paid computer specialist with a background in the quantitative sciences, employed by a city institution (e.g. a portfolio management company, bond research house, or merchant bank) to develop systems that map past movements in financial markets with a view to predicting future equity, commodity, and currency values. [abbreviation of *quant*itative]

quanta *pl.* of QUANTUM.

quantify /'kwɒntɪ,faɪ/ *v.* (**-ies, -ied**) **1** determine the quantity of. **2** express as a quantity. □ **quantifiable** *adj.* **quantification** /,kwɒntɪfɪ'keɪʃ(ə)n/ *n.* [medieval Latin: related to QUANTITY]

quantitative /'kwɒntɪtətɪv/ *adj.* **1** of quantity as opposed to quality. **2** measured or measurable by quantity.

♦ **quantitative marketing research** *n.* marketing research techniques that use large samples of respondents to quantify behaviour and reactions to marketing activities. A structured questionnaire is usu. used to obtain data that quantifies the numbers and proportions of respondents falling into each predetermined category; for example, a study might show how many people per thousand of the population buy a particular product. Cf. QUALITATIVE MARKETING RESEARCH.

quantity /'kwɒntɪtɪ/ *n.* (*pl.* **-ies**) **1** property of things that is measurable. **2** size, extent, weight, amount, or number. **3** specified or considerable portion, number, or amount (*buys in quantity*; *small quantity of food*). **4** (in *pl.*) large amounts or numbers; an abundance. **5** length or shortness of vowel sounds or syllables. **6** *Math.* value, component, etc. that may be expressed in numbers. [Latin *quantus* how much]

quantity surveyor *n.* person who measures and prices building work.

♦ **quantity theory of money** *n.* theory, first proposed by the philosopher David Hume, stating that the price level is proportional to the quantity of money in the economy. Formally, it is usu. stated in the equation $MV = PT$, where M is the quantity of money, V is its velocity of circulation, P is the price level, and T the number of transactions in the period. Milton Friedman made this equation the central pivot of monetarism, with the additional assumption that V is more or less constant; thus, for a given number of transactions, the relationship between *M* and *P* is direct. This implies that any increase in the money supply will lead to an increase in the price level, i.e. to inflation. See DEMAND FOR MONEY; MONETARY POLICY.

♦ **quantity variance** *n. Econ.* variance arising when the quantities sold, purchased, or produced differ from the standard.

---

quantum /'kwɒntəm/ *n.* (*pl.* **quanta**) **1** *Physics* discrete amount of energy proportional to the frequency of radiation it represents. **2** a required or allowed amount. [Latin *quantus* how much]

quantum jump *n.* **1** (also **quantum leap**) sudden large increase or advance. **2** *Physics* abrupt transition in an atom or molecule from one quantum state to another.

quantum mechanics *n.pl.* (usu. treated as *sing.*) (also **quantum theory**) *Physics* theory assuming that energy exists in discrete units.

♦ ***quantum meruit*** /'meruːɪt/ *–n.* **1** payment for goods or services supplied in partial fulfilment of a contract, after the contract has been breached. **2** payment for goods or services supplied and accepted, although no price has been agreed between buyer and seller. *–attrib. adj.* denoting such payments. [Latin, = as much as has been earned]

---

quarantine /'kwɒrən,tiːn/ *–n.* **1** isolation imposed on persons or animals to prevent infection or contagion. **2** period of this. *–v.* (**-ning**) put in quarantine. [Italian *quaranta* forty]

quark[1] /kwɑːk/ *n. Physics* component of protons and neutrons. [word used by Joyce in *Finnegans Wake* (1939)]

quark[2] /kwɑːk/ *n.* a kind of low-fat curd cheese. [German]

quarrel /'kwɒr(ə)l/ *–n.* **1** severe or angry dispute or contention. **2** break in friendly relations. **3** cause of complaint (*have no quarrel with him*). *–v.* (**-ll-**; *US* **-l-**) **1** (often foll. by *with*) find fault. **2** dispute; break off friendly relations. [Latin *querela* from *queror* complain]

quarrelsome *adj.* given to quarrelling.

quarry[1] /'kwɒrɪ/ *–n.* (*pl.* **-ies**) place from which stone etc. may be extracted. *–v.* (**-ies, -ied**) extract (stone) from a quarry. [Latin *quadrum* square]

quarry[2] /'kwɒrɪ/ *n.* (*pl.* **-ies**) **1** intended victim or prey. **2** object of pursuit. [Latin *cor* heart]

quarry tile *n.* unglazed floor-tile.

quart /'kwɔːt/ *n.* liquid measure equal to a quarter of a gallon; two pints (0.946 litre). [Latin *quartus* fourth]

quarter /'kwɔːtə(r)/ *–n.* **1** each of four equal parts into which a thing is divided. **2** period of three months. **3** point of time 15 minutes before or after any hour. **4 a** 25 US or Canadian cents. **b** coin for this. **5** part of a town, esp. as occupied by a particular class (*residential quarter*). **6 a** point of the compass. **b** region at this. **7** direction, district, or source of supply (*help from any quarter*). **8** (in *pl.*) **a** lodgings. **b** accommodation of troops etc. **9 a** one fourth of a lunar month. **b** moon's position between the first and second (**first quarter**) or third and fourth (**last quarter**) of these. **10 a** each of the four parts into which a carcass is divided. **b** (in *pl.*) = HINDQUARTERS. **11** mercy towards an enemy etc. on condition of surrender. **12 a** grain measure equivalent to 8 bushels. **b** one-fourth of a hundredweight. **c** *colloq.* one-fourth of a pound weight. **13** each of four divisions on a shield. *–v.* **1** divide into quarters. **2** *hist.* divide (the body of an executed person) in this way. **3 a** put (troops etc.) into quarters. **b** provide with lodgings. **4** *Heraldry* place (coats of arms) on the four quarters of a shield. □ **quarter up** see PROBATE PRICE. [Latin *quartarius*: related to QUART]

quarterback *n.* player in American football who directs attacking play.

quarter day *n.* one of four days on which quarterly payments are due, tenancies begin and end, etc. In England, Wales, and Northern Ireland they are Lady Day (25 March), Midsummer Day (24 June), Michaelmas (29 September), and Christmas Day (25 December). In Scotland they are Candlemas (2 February), Whitsuntide (15 May), Lammas (1 August), and Martinmas (11 November).

quarterdeck *n.* part of a ship's upper deck near the stern, usu. reserved for officers.

quarter-final *n.* match or round preceding the semifinal.

quarter-hour *n.* **1** period of 15 minutes. **2** = QUARTER *n.* 3.

quarter-light *n.* small pivoted window in the side of a car, carriage, etc.

quarterly *–adj.* produced or occurring once every quarter of a year. *–adv.* once every quarter of a year. *–n.* (*pl.* **-ies**) quarterly journal.

quartermaster *n.* **1** regimental officer in charge of quartering, rations, etc. **2** naval petty officer in charge of steering, signals, etc.

quarter sessions *n.pl. hist.* court of limited criminal and civil jurisdiction, usu. held quarterly.

quarterstaff *n. hist.* stout pole 6–8 feet long, formerly used as a weapon.

quartet /kwɔː'tet/ *n.* **1** *Mus.* **a** composition for four performers. **b** the performers. **2** any group of four. [Latin *quartus*]

quarto /'kwɔːtəʊ/ *n.* (*pl.* **-s**) **1** size of a book or page given by folding a sheet of standard size twice to form four leaves. **2** book or sheet of this size. [Latin: related to QUART]

quartz /kwɔːts/ *n.* silica in various mineral forms. [German from Slavonic]

quartz clock *n.* (also **quartz watch**) clock or watch operated by vibrations of an electrically driven quartz crystal.

quasar /'kweɪzɑː(r)/ *n. Astron.* highly luminous object with a large red shift. [from *quas*i-stell*ar*]

quash /kwɒʃ/ *v.* **1** annul; reject as invalid, esp. by a legal procedure. **2** suppress, crush. [French *quasser* from Latin]

quasi- /'kweɪzaɪ/ *comb. form* **1** seemingly, not really. **2** almost. [Latin *quasi* as if]

♦ **quasi-contract** *n.* legally binding obligation that one party has to another, as determined by a court, although no formal contract exists between them.

---

quaternary /kwə'tɜːnərɪ/ *–adj.* **1** having four parts. **2** (**Quaternary**) *Geol.* of the most recent period in the Cenozoic era. *–n.* (**Quaternary**) *Geol.* this period. [Latin *quaterni* four each]

quatrain /'kwɒtreɪn/ *n.* four-line stanza. [French *quatre* four]

quatrefoil /'kætrə,fɔɪl/ *n.* four-pointed or -leafed figure, esp. as an architectural ornament. [Anglo-French *quatre* four: related to FOIL[2]]

quattrocento /,kwætrəʊ'tʃentəʊ/ *n.* 15th-century Italian art. [Italian, = 400, used for the years 1400–99]

quaver *–v.* **1** (esp. of a voice or sound) vibrate, shake, tremble. **2** sing or say with a quavering voice. *–n.* **1** *Mus.* note half as long as a crotchet. **2** trill in singing. **3** tremble in speech. □ **quavery** *adj.* [probably imitative]

quay /kiː/ *n.* artificial landing-place for loading and unloading ships. [French]

quayside *n.* land forming or near a quay.

Que. *abbr.* Quebec.

queasy /'kwiːzɪ/ *adj.* (**-ier, -iest**) **1 a** (of a person) nauseous. **b** (of the stomach) easily upset, weak of digestion. **2** (of the conscience etc.) overscrupulous. □ **queasily** *adv.* **queasiness** *n.* [origin uncertain]

Quebec /kwɪ'bek/ **1** province in E Canada; pop. (est. 1995) 7 334 200. Manufacturing industries are of major importance, producing paper and paper products (from the province's abundant forests), aircraft, motor vehicles, electronic goods, textiles, and clothing; gold, copper, and asbestos are mined. Quebec's culture remains predominantly French. **2** its capital city, a port on the St Lawrence river; it has service and manufacturing industries; city pop. (1991) 167 517; metropolitan area pop. 645 550.

queen –*n.* **1** (as a title usu. **Queen**) female sovereign. **2** (in full **queen consort**) king's wife. **3** woman, country, or thing pre-eminent of its kind. **4** fertile female among ants, bees, etc. **5** most powerful piece in chess. **6** court-card depicting a queen. **7** (**the Queen**) national anthem when the sovereign is female. **8** *slang offens.* male homosexual. **9** belle or mock sovereign for some event (*Queen of the May*). –*v. Chess* convert (a pawn) into a queen when it reaches the opponent's side of the board. □ **queenly** *adj.* (**-ier, -iest**). **queenliness** *n.* [Old English]

Queen-Anne *n.* (often *attrib.*) style of English architecture, furniture, etc., in the early 18th century.

queen bee *n.* **1** fertile female bee. **2** woman who behaves as if she is the most important person in a group.

Queen Charlotte Islands /'ʃɑːlət/ Canadian island group off the coast of British Columbia, noted for its timber and fishing resources; pop. (est. 1995) 5644.

queen mother *n.* dowager who is mother of the sovereign.

Queen of the May *n.* = MAY QUEEN.

queen-post *n.* either of two upright timbers between the tie-beam and main rafters of a roof-truss.

♦ **Queen's Awards** *n.pl.* two separate awards instituted by royal warrant in 1976 to replace the Queen's Award to Industry, which was instituted in 1965. The **Queen's Award for Export Achievement** is given for a sustained increase in export earnings to an outstanding level for the products or services concerned and for the size of the applicants' organizations. The **Queen's Award for Technological Achievement** is given for a significant technological advance in a production or development process in British industry. The awards are announced on the Queen's actual birthday (21 April). Awards are held for five years and entitle the holders to fly a special flag and display the emblem of the award on their packages, stationery, etc.

Queensberry Rules /'kwiːnzbərɪ/ *n.pl.* standard rules, esp. of boxing. [from the name Marquis of *Queensberry*]

Queen's Counsel *n.* counsel to the Crown, taking precedence over other barristers.

♦ **Queen's enemies** see PERIL 2.

Queen's English *n.* (prec. by *the*) English language correctly written or spoken.

Queen's evidence see EVIDENCE.

Queen's Guide *n.* Guide who has reached the highest rank of proficiency.

Queen's highway *n.* public road, regarded as being under the sovereign's protection.

Queensland /'kwiːnzlənd/ state in NE Australia; pop. (est. 1996) 3 339 000; capital, Brisbane. Coal is mined and exported, and there are also major deposits of copper, lead, silver, zinc, oil, and natural gas; forestry is important, and agriculture produces sugar cane, cotton, tobacco, beef, and wool. Much of the state's manufacturing industry is involved in the processing of primary products. □ **Queenslander** *n.*

Queen's Proctor *n.* official who has the right to intervene in probate, divorce, and nullity cases when collusion or the suppression of facts is alleged.

Queen's Scout *n.* Scout who has reached the highest standard of proficiency.

queer –*adj.* **1** strange, odd, eccentric. **2** shady, suspect, of questionable character. **3** slightly ill; faint. **4** *slang offens.* (esp. of a man) homosexual. –*n. slang offens.* homosexual. –*v. slang* spoil, put out of order. □ **in Queer Street** *slang* in difficulty, esp. in debt. **queer a person's pitch** *colloq.* spoil a person's chances. [origin uncertain]

quell *v.* **1** crush or put down (a rebellion etc.). **2** suppress (fear etc.). [Old English]

quench *v.* **1** satisfy (thirst) by drinking. **2** extinguish (a fire or light). **3** cool, esp. with water. **4** esp. *Metallurgy* cool (a hot substance) in cold water etc. **5** stifle or suppress (desire etc.). [Old English]

Querétaro /ke'reɪtə,rəʊ/ **1** state in central Mexico; pop. (est. 1995) 1 248 844. **2** its capital city; pop. (1990) 385 503.

quern *n.* hand-mill for grinding corn. [Old English]

querulous /'kwerʊləs/ *adj.* complaining, peevish. □ **querulously** *adj.* [Latin *queror* complain]

query /'kwɪərɪ/ –*n.* (*pl.* **-ies**) **1** question. **2** question mark or the word *query* as a mark of interrogation. –*v.* (**-ies, -ied**) **1** ask or inquire. **2** call in question. **3** dispute the accuracy of. [Latin *quaere* imperative of *quaero* inquire]

♦ **query language** *n.* (also **QL**) special-purpose computer programming language used to extract information from a database. In general, each database management system has its own query language.

---

query processing *n.* (also **QP**) retrieval of one or more values from a computer file or database, leaving the contents unchanged.

quest –*n.* **1** search or seeking. **2** thing sought, esp. by a medieval knight. –*v.* (often foll. by *about*) go about in search of something (esp. of dogs seeking game). [Latin *quaero quaesit-* seek]

question /'kwestʃ(ə)n/ –*n.* **1** sentence worded or expressed so as to seek information or an answer. **2 a** doubt or dispute about a matter (*no question that he is dead*). **b** raising of such doubt etc. **3** matter to be discussed or decided. **4** problem requiring a solution. –*v.* **1** ask questions of; interrogate; subject (a person) to examination. **2** throw doubt upon; raise objections to. □ **be just a question of time** be certain to happen sooner or later. **be a question of** be at issue, be a problem (*it's a question of money*). **call in** (or **into) question** express doubts about. **in question** that is being discussed or referred to (*the person in question*). **out of the question** not worth discussing; impossible. □ **questioner** *n.* **questioning** *adj.* & *n.* **questioningly** *adv.* [Latin: related to QUEST]

questionable *adj.* doubtful as regards truth, quality, honesty, wisdom, etc.

question mark *n.* punctuation mark (?) indicating a question.

question-master *n.* person presiding over a quiz game etc.

questionnaire /,kwestʃə'neə(r)/ *n.* formulated series of questions, esp. for statistical analysis. [French: related to QUESTION]

question time *n.* period in Parliament when MPs may question ministers.

Quetta /'kwetə/ city and trading centre in W Pakistan, the capital of Baluchistan province; pop. (1981) 285 000.

quetzal /'kwets(ə)l/ *n.* standard monetary unit of Guatemala. [Spanish from Nahuatl *quetzalli* tail-feather of a native bird]

queue /kjuː/ –*n.* line or sequence of persons, vehicles, etc. waiting their turn. –*v.* (**queues, queued, queuing** or **queueing**) (often foll. by *up*) form or join a queue. [Latin *cauda* tail]

queue-jump *v.* push forward out of turn in a queue.

Quezon City /'keɪsɒn/ city in the N Philippines, situated on the outskirts of Manila on the island of Luzon; industries include textiles; pop. (1994) 1 676 644.

quibble /'kwɪb(ə)l/ –*n.* **1** petty objection; trivial point of criticism. **2** evasion; argument relying on ambiguity. **3** *archaic* pun. –*v.* (**-ling**) use quibbles. □ **quibbling** *adj.* [origin uncertain]

quiche /kiːʃ/ *n.* savoury flan. [French]

quick –*adj.* **1** taking only a short time (*quick worker*). **2** arriving after a short time, prompt. **3** with only a short interval (*in quick succession*). **4** lively, intelligent, alert. **5** (of a temper) easily roused. **6** *archaic* alive (*the quick and the dead*). –*adv.* (also as *int.*) quickly. –*n.* **1** soft sensitive flesh, esp. below the nails. **2** seat of emotion (*cut to the quick*). □ **quickly** *adv.* [Old English]

♦ **quick assets** *n.pl.* = LIQUID ASSETS.

quicken *v.* **1** make or become quicker; accelerate. **2** give life or vigour to; rouse. **3 a** (of a woman) reach a stage in pregnancy when movements of the foetus can be felt. **b** (of a foetus) begin to show signs of life.

quick-fire *attrib. adj.* rapid; in rapid succession.

quick-freeze *v.* freeze (food) rapidly so as to preserve its natural qualities.

quickie *n. colloq.* thing done or made quickly.

quicklime *n.* = LIME[1] 1.

quick one *n. colloq.* drink (usu. alcoholic) taken quickly.

quicksand *n.* (often in *pl.*) **1** area of loose wet sand that sucks in anything placed on it. **2** treacherous situation etc.

quickset *–attrib. adj.* (of a hedge etc.) formed of cuttings, esp. hawthorn. *–n.* hedge formed in this way.

quicksilver *n.* mercury.

quickstep *n.* fast foxtrot.

quick-tempered *adj.* easily angered.

quick-witted *adj.* quick to grasp a situation, make repartee, etc. □ **quick-wittedness** *n.*

quid[1] *n.* (*pl.* same) *slang* one pound sterling. □ **quids in** *slang* in a position of profit. [probably from Latin *quid* what]

quid[2] *n.* lump of tobacco for chewing. [a dialect word, = CUD]

quiddity /ˈkwɪdɪtɪ/ *n.* (*pl.* **-ies**) **1** *Philos.* essence of a thing. **2** quibble; trivial objection. [Latin *quidditas* from *quid* what]

quid pro quo /ˌkwɪd prəʊ ˈkwəʊ/ *n.* (*pl.* **quid pro quos**) return made (for a gift, favour, etc.). Contracts require a quid pro quo in the form of a consideration, without which they would become unilateral agreements. [Latin, = something for something]

quiescent /kwɪˈes(ə)nt/ *adj.* inert, dormant. □ **quiescence** *n.* [related to QUIET]

quiet /ˈkwaɪət/ *–adj.* **1** with little or no sound or motion. **2** of gentle or peaceful disposition. **3** unobtrusive; not showy. **4** not overt; disguised. **5** undisturbed, uninterrupted; free or far from vigorous action. **6** informal (*quiet wedding*). **7** enjoyed in quiet (*quiet smoke*). **8** not anxious or remorseful. **9** not busy (*it is very quiet at work*). **10** peaceful (*all quiet on the frontier*). *–n.* **1** silence; stillness. **2** undisturbed state; tranquillity. *–v.* (often foll. by *down*) make or become quiet or calm. □ **be quiet** (esp. in *imper.*) cease talking etc. **keep quiet** (often foll. by *about*) say nothing. **on the quiet** secretly. □ **quietly** *adv.* **quietness** *n.* [Latin *quiesco* become calm]

quieten *v.* (often foll. by *down*) = QUIET *v.*

quietism *n.* passive contemplative attitude towards life, esp. as a form of mysticism. □ **quietist** *n.* & *adj.* [Italian: related to QUIET]

quietude /ˈkwaɪɪˌtjuːd/ *n.* state of quiet.

quietus /kwaɪˈiːtəs/ *n.* release from life; death, final riddance (*will get its quietus*). [medieval Latin: related to QUIET]

quiff *n.* **1** man's tuft of hair, brushed upward over the forehead. **2** curl plastered down on the forehead. [origin unknown]

quill *n.* **1** (in full **quill-feather**) large feather in a wing or tail. **2** hollow stem of this. **3** (in full **quill pen**) pen made of a quill. **4** (usu. in *pl.*) porcupine's spine. [probably Low German *quiele*]

quilt *–n.* coverlet, esp. of quilted material. *–v.* line a coverlet or garment with padding enclosed between layers of cloth by lines of stitching. □ **quilter** *n.* **quilting** *n.* [Latin *culcita* cushion]

quim *n. coarse slang* female genitals. [origin unknown]

quin *n. colloq.* quintuplet. [abbreviation]

quince *n.* **1** acid pear-shaped fruit used in jams etc. **2** tree bearing this. [originally a plural, from French *cooin*, from *Cydonia* in Crete]

quincentenary /ˌkwɪnsenˈtiːnərɪ/ *–n.* (*pl.* **-ies**) 500th anniversary; celebration of this. *–adj.* of this anniversary. [Latin *quinque* five]

quincunx /ˈkwɪnkʌŋks/ *n.* five objects, esp. trees, at the corners and centre of a square or rectangle. [Latin, = five-twelfths]

quinine /ˈkwɪniːn/ *n.* bitter drug obtained from cinchona bark, used as a tonic and to reduce fever. [Spanish *quina* cinchona bark, from Quechua *kina* bark]

Quinquagesima /ˌkwɪŋkwəˈdʒesɪmə/ *n.* Sunday before Lent. [Latin *quinquagesimus* fiftieth]

quinquennial /kwɪŋˈkwenɪəl/ *adj.* **1** lasting five years. **2** recurring every five years. □ **quinquennially** *adv.* [Latin *quinquennis* from *quinque* five, *annus* year]

quinquereme /ˈkwɪŋkwɪˌriːm/ *n.* ancient Roman galley with five files of oarsmen on each side. [Latin *quinque* five, *remus* oar]

Quintana Roo /kiːnˌtɑːnə ˈrəʊ/ state in SE Mexico, on the Yucatán peninsula; pop. (est. 1995) 703 442; capital, Chetumal.

quintessence /kwɪnˈtes(ə)ns/ *n.* **1** (usu. foll. by *of*) purest and most perfect form, manifestation, or embodiment of a quality etc. **2** highly refined extract. □ **quintessential** /ˌkwɪntɪˈsenʃ(ə)l/ *adj.* **quintessentially** /ˌkwɪntɪˈsenʃəlɪ/ *adv.* [Latin *quinta essentia* fifth substance (underlying the four elements)]

quintet /kwɪnˈtet/ *n.* **1** *Mus.* **a** composition for five performers. **b** the performers. **2** any group of five. [Latin *quintus*]

quintuple /ˈkwɪntjʊp(ə)l/ *–adj.* fivefold; having five parts. *–n.* fivefold number or amount. *–v.* (**-ling**) multiply by five. [Latin *quintus* fifth]

quintuplet /ˈkwɪntjʊplɪt/ *n.* each of five children born at one birth.

quintuplicate *–adj.* /kwɪnˈtjuːplɪkət/ **1** fivefold. **2** of which five copies are made. *–v.* /kwɪnˈtjuːplɪˌkeɪt/ (**-ting**) multiply by five.

QUIP /kwɪp/ *abbr. Computing* query interactive processor.

quip *–n.* clever saying; epigram. *–v.* (**-pp-**) make quips. [perhaps from Latin *quippe* forsooth]

quire *n.* 25 (formerly 24) sheets of paper. [Latin: related to QUATERNARY]

quirk *n.* **1** peculiar feature, peculiarity. **2** trick of fate. □ **quirky** *adj.* (**-ier**, **-iest**). [origin unknown]

quisling /ˈkwɪzlɪŋ/ *n.* collaborator, traitor. [*Quisling*, name of a Norwegian officer and collaborator with the Nazis]

quit *–v.* (**-tting**; *past* and *past part.* **quitted** or **quit**) **1** (also *absol.*) give up, let go, abandon (a task etc.). **2** *US* cease, stop (*quit grumbling*). **3** leave or depart from. *–predic. adj.* (foll. by *of*) rid (*glad to be quit of the problem*). [Latin: related to QUIET]

quitch *n.* (in full **quitch-grass**) = COUCH[2]. [Old English]

quite *adv.* **1** completely, entirely, wholly. **2** to some extent, rather. **3** (often foll. by *so*) said to indicate agreement. □ **quite a** (or **some**) remarkable or outstanding (thing). **quite a few** *colloq.* a fairly large number of. **quite something** *colloq.* remarkable thing or person. [var. of QUIT]

Quito /ˈkiːtəʊ/ capital of Ecuador, an industrial city in the NW of the country; pop. (est. 1996) 1 444 363.

quits *predic. adj.* on even terms by retaliation or repayment. □ **call it quits** acknowledge that things are now even; agree to stop quarrelling. [probably related to QUIT]

quitter *n.* **1** person who gives up easily. **2** shirker.

quiver[1] /ˈkwɪvə(r)/ *–v.* tremble or vibrate with a slight rapid motion. *–n.* quivering motion or sound. [obsolete *quiver* nimble]

quiver[2] /ˈkwɪvə(r)/ *n.* case for arrows. [Anglo-French from Germanic]

quixotic /kwɪkˈsɒtɪk/ *adj.* extravagantly and romantically chivalrous. □ **quixotically** *adv.* [Don *Quixote*, in Cervantes' romance]

quiz *–n.* (*pl.* **quizzes**) **1** test of knowledge, esp. as entertainment. **2** interrogation, examination. *–v.* (**-zz-**) examine by questioning. [origin unknown]

quizzical /ˈkwɪzɪk(ə)l/ *adj.* expressing or done with mild or amused perplexity. □ **quizzically** *adv.*

quod *n. slang* prison. [origin unknown]

quoin /kɔɪn/ *n.* **1** external angle of a building. **2** cornerstone. **3** wedge used in printing and gunnery. [var. of COIN]

quoit /kɔɪt/ *n.* **1** ring thrown to encircle an iron peg. **2** (in *pl.*) game using these. [origin unknown]

quondam /ˈkwɒndæm/ *attrib. adj.* that once was, sometime, former. [Latin adv., = formerly]

quorate /ˈkwɔːreɪt/ *adj.* constituting or having a quorum. [from QUORUM]

quorum /ˈkwɔːrəm/ *n.* minimum number of members that must be present to constitute a valid meeting. For a company, the quorum for a meeting is laid down in the articles of association. [Latin, = of whom]

quota /ˈkwəʊtə/ *n.* **1 a** share to be contributed to, or received from, a whole. **b** fixed amount of funds allocated by the International Monetary Fund to each of its participating member countries. **2 a** number of goods, people, etc. stipulated or permitted. **b** fixed amount of a product or commodity that may be imported into or exported from a country as laid down by a government in an attempt to control the market in that product or commodity. [Latin *quotus* from *quot* how many]

quotable /ˈkwəʊtəb(ə)l/ *adj.* worth quoting.

quotation /kwəʊˈteɪʃ(ə)n/ *n.* **1** passage or remark quoted. **2** quoting or being quoted. **3** contractor's estimate. **4** indication of the price at which a seller might be willing to offer goods for sale. It does not have the status of a firm offer. **5 a** representation of a security on a recognized stock exchange (see LISTED COMPANY). A quotation allows the shares of a company to be traded on the stock exchange and enables the company to raise new capital if it needs to do so (see FLOTATION; LISTING REQUIREMENTS; RIGHTS ISSUE). **b** = QUOTED PRICE. [medieval Latin: related to QUOTE]

quotation marks *n.pl.* inverted commas (' ' or " ") used at the beginning and end of a quotation etc.

quote –*v.* (**-ting**) **1** cite or appeal to (an author, book, etc.) in confirmation of some view. **2 a** repeat or copy out a passage from. **b** (foll. by *from*) cite (an author, book, etc.). **3** (foll. by *as*) cite (an author etc.) as proof, evidence, etc. **4 a** enclose (words) in quotation marks. **b** (as *int.*) verbal formula indicating opening quotation marks (*he said, quote, 'I shall stay'*). **5** (often foll. by *at*, also *absol.*) state the price of. –*n. colloq.* **1** passage quoted. **2** price quoted. **3** (usu. in *pl.*) quotation marks. [Latin *quoto* mark with numbers]

♦ **quoted company** *n. hist.* listed company.

♦ **quoted price** *n.* official price of a security or commodity. On the London Stock Exchange, quoted prices are given daily in the Official List. Quoted prices of commodities are given by the relevant markets and recorded in the financial press.

♦ **quote-driven** *adj.* denoting an electronic financial market system, esp. for a stock exchange, in which prices are determined by the questions made by market makers or dealers. Cf. ORDER-DRIVEN.

---

quoth /kwəʊθ/ *v.* (only in 1st and 3rd person) *archaic* said. [Old English]

quotidian /kwɒˈtɪdɪən/ *adj.* **1** occurring or recurring daily. **2** commonplace, trivial. [Latin *cotidie* daily]

quotient /ˈkwəʊʃ(ə)nt/ *n.* result of a division sum. [Latin *quotiens -ent-* how many times]

q.v. *abbr.* which see (in references). [Latin *quod vide*]

Qwaqwa /ˈkwækwə/ former Bantu homeland in South Africa.

qwerty /ˈkwɜːtɪ/ *attrib. adj.* denoting the standard keyboard on English-language typewriters etc., with *q, w, e, r, t,* and *y* as the first keys on the top row of letters.

QWL *abbr.* quality of work(ing) life.

QZ *airline flight code* Zambia Airways.

R[1] /ɑː(r)/ *n.* (also **r**) (*pl.* **Rs** or **R's**) eighteenth letter of the alphabet.

R[2] *abbr.* (also **R.**) **1** *Regina* (*Elizabeth R*). **2** *Rex*. **3** River. **4** (also ®) registered as a trade mark. **5** *Chess* rook.

R[3] *symb.* rand.

r. *abbr.* (also **r**) **1** radius. **2** *Commerce* received. **3** right.

RA *–abbr.* **1 a** Royal Academy. **b** Royal Academician. **2** Royal Artillery. *–international vehicle registration* Argentina. *–international civil aircraft marking* Russia.

R/A *abbr.* refer to acceptor (on a bill of exchange).

Ra *symb.* radium.

Rabat /rəˈbæt/ capital of Morocco, an industrial port on the Atlantic coast; pop. (1984) 556 000; with Salé (1994) 1 320 000.

Rabaul /rəˈbaʊl/ town in Papua New Guinea, the chief town and port of the island of New Britain; exports include copra; pop. (1990) 17 022.

rabbet /ˈræbɪt/ *–n.* step-shaped channel cut along the edge or face of a length of wood etc., usu. to receive the edge or tongue of another piece. *–v.* (**-t-**) **1** join or fix with a rabbet. **2** make a rabbet in. [French *rab(b)at*: related to REBATE[1]]

rabbi /ˈræbaɪ/ *n.* (*pl.* **-s**) **1** Jewish scholar or teacher, esp. of the law. **2** Jewish religious leader. □ **rabbinical** /rəˈbɪnɪk(ə)l/ *adj.* [Hebrew, = my master]

rabbit /ˈræbɪt/ *–n.* **1 a** burrowing plant-eating mammal of the hare family. **b** *US* hare. **2** its fur. *–v.* (**-t-**) **1** hunt rabbits. **2** (often foll. by *on*, *away*) *colloq.* talk pointlessly; chatter. [origin uncertain]

rabbit punch *n.* short chop with the edge of the hand to the nape of the neck.

rabble /ˈræb(ə)l/ *n.* **1** disorderly crowd, mob. **2** contemptible or inferior set of people. **3** (prec. by *the*) the lower or disorderly classes of the populace. [origin uncertain]

rabble-rouser *n.* person who stirs up the rabble or a crowd, esp. to agitate for social change.

Rabelaisian /ˌræbəˈleɪzɪən/ *adj.* **1** of or like the French satirist Rabelais or his writings. **2** marked by exuberant imagination and coarse humour.

rabid /ˈræbɪd, ˈreɪ-/ *adj.* **1** affected with rabies, mad. **2** violent, fanatical. □ **rabidity** /rəˈbɪdɪtɪ/ *n.* [Latin *rabio* rave]

rabies /ˈreɪbiːz/ *n.* contagious viral disease of esp. dogs, transmissible through saliva to humans etc. and causing madness; hydrophobia. [Latin: related to RABID]

RAC *abbr.* Royal Automobile Club.

raccoon var. of RACOON.

race[1] *–n.* **1** contest of speed between runners, horses, vehicles, ships, etc. **2** (in *pl.*) series of these for horses, dogs, etc., at a fixed time on a regular course. **3** contest between persons to be first to achieve something. **4 a** strong current in the sea or a river. **b** channel (*mill-race*). *–v.* (**-cing**) **1** take part in a race. **2** have a race with. **3** try to surpass in speed. **4** (foll. by *with*) compete in speed with. **5** cause to race. **6 a** go at full or excessive speed. **b** cause to do this. **7** (usu. as **racing** *adj.*) follow or take part in horse-racing (*a racing man*). [Old Norse]

race[2] *n.* **1** each of the major divisions of humankind, each having distinct physical characteristics. **2** fact or concept of division into races. **3** genus, species, breed, or variety of animals or plants. **4** group of persons, animals, or plants connected by common descent. **5** any great division of living creatures (*the human race*). [Italian *razza*]

racecourse *n.* ground for horse-racing.

racegoer *n.* person who frequents horse-races.

racehorse *n.* horse bred or kept for racing.

raceme /rəˈsiːm/ *n.* flower cluster with separate flowers attached by short stalks at equal distances along the stem. [Latin *racemus* grape-bunch]

race meeting *n.* sequence of horse-races at one place.

race relations *n.pl.* relations between members of different races in the same country.

race riot *n.* outbreak of violence due to racial antagonism.

racetrack *n.* **1** = RACECOURSE. **2** track for motor racing.

racial /ˈreɪʃ(ə)l/ *adj.* **1** of or concerning race. **2** on the grounds of or connected with difference in race. □ **racially** *adv.*

racialism /ˈreɪʃəˌlɪz(ə)m/ *n.* = RACISM. □ **racialist** *n.* & *adj.*

racing car *n.* motor car built for racing.

racing driver *n.* driver of a racing car.

racism *n.* **1** belief in the superiority of a particular race; prejudice based on this. **2** antagonism towards other races. □ **racist** *n.* & *adj.*

rack[1] *–n.* **1** framework, usu. with rails, bars, etc., for holding things. **2** cogged or toothed bar or rail engaging with a wheel or pinion etc. **3** *hist.* instrument of torture stretching the victim's joints. *–v.* **1** (of disease or pain) inflict suffering on. **2** *hist.* torture (a person) on the rack. **3** place in or on a rack. **4** shake violently. **5** injure by straining. □ **on the rack** suffering acute mental or physical pain. **rack one's brains** make a great mental effort. [Low German or Dutch]

rack[2] *n.* destruction (esp. *rack and ruin*). [from WRACK]

rack[3] *v.* (often foll. by *off*) draw off (wine, beer, etc.) from the lees. [Provençal *arracar* from *raca* stems and husks of grapes, dregs]

racket[1] /ˈrækɪt/ *n.* (also **racquet**) **1** bat with a round or oval frame strung with catgut, nylon, etc., used in tennis, squash, etc. **2** (in *pl.*) game like squash, played in a court of four plain walls. [French *raquette* from Arabic *rahat* palm of the hand]

racket[2] /ˈrækɪt/ *n.* **1** disturbance, uproar, din. **2** *slang* **a** scheme for obtaining money etc. by dishonest means. **b** dodge; sly game. **3** *colloq.* line of business. [perhaps imitative]

racketeer /ˌrækɪˈtɪə(r)/ *n.* person who operates a dishonest business. □ **racketeering** *n.*

rack-rent *n.* **1** high rent paid when no capital payment (premium) has been made for the lease and the rent therefore represents the full value of the land and buildings. **2** any extortionate rent.

raconteur /ˌrækɒnˈtɜː(r)/ *n.* teller of anecdotes. [French: related to RECOUNT]

racoon /rəˈkuːn/ *n.* (also **raccoon**) (*pl.* same or **-s**) **1** North American mammal with a bushy tail and sharp snout. **2** its fur. [Algonquian]

racquet var. of RACKET[1].

racy *adj.* (**-ier, -iest**) **1** lively and vigorous in style. **2** risqué. **3** of distinctive quality (*a racy wine*). □ **raciness** *n.* [from RACE[2]]

rad *n.* unit of absorbed dose of ionizing radiation. [from *r*adiation *a*bsorbed *d*ose]

RADA /ˈrɑːdə/ *abbr.* Royal Academy of Dramatic Art.

radar /ˈreɪdɑː(r)/ *n.* **1** system for detecting the direction, range, or presence of objects, by sending out pulses of high frequency electromagnetic waves which they reflect. **2** apparatus for this. [from *ra*dio *d*etection *a*nd *r*anging]

radar trap *n.* device using radar to detect speeding vehicles.

raddle /ˈræd(ə)l/ *–n.* red ochre. *–v.* (**-ling**) **1** colour with raddle or too much rouge. **2** (as **raddled** *adj.*) worn out. [related to RUDDY]

radial /ˈreɪdɪəl/ *–adj.* **1** of or in rays. **2 a** arranged like rays or radii. **b** having spokes or radiating lines. **c** acting or moving along lines diverging from a centre. **3** (in full **radial-ply**) (of a tyre) having fabric layers arranged radially and the tread strengthened. *–n.* radial-ply tyre. □ **radially** *adv.* [medieval Latin: related to RADIUS]

radian /ˈreɪdɪən/ *n.* SI unit of angle, equal to an angle at the centre of a circle the arc of which is equal in length to the radius (1 radian is approx. 57°).

radiant /ˈreɪdɪənt/ *–adj.* **1** emitting rays of light. **2** (of eyes or looks) beaming with joy, hope, or love. **3** (of beauty) splendid or dazzling. **4** (of light) issuing in rays. *–n.* point or object from which light or heat radiates. □ **radiance** *n.* **radiantly** *adv.*

radiant heat *n.* heat transmitted by radiation.

radiate *–v.* /ˈreɪdɪˌeɪt/ (**-ting**) **1 a** emit rays of light, heat, etc. **b** (of light or heat) be emitted in rays. **2** emit (light, heat, etc.) from a centre. **3** transmit or demonstrate (joy etc.). **4** diverge or spread from a centre. *–adj.* /ˈreɪdɪət/ having divergent rays or parts radially arranged.

radiation /ˌreɪdɪˈeɪʃ(ə)n/ *n.* **1** radiating or being radiated. **2** *Physics* **a** emission of energy as electromagnetic waves or as moving particles. **b** energy transmitted in this way, esp. invisibly. **3** (in full **radiation therapy**) treatment of cancer etc. using radiation, e.g. X-rays or ultraviolet light.

radiation sickness *n.* sickness caused by exposure to radiation, such as gamma rays.

radiator /ˈreɪdɪˌeɪtə(r)/ *n.* **1** device for heating a room etc., consisting of a metal case through which hot water or steam circulates. **2** engine-cooling device in a motor vehicle or aircraft.

radical /ˈrædɪk(ə)l/ *–adj.* **1** fundamental (*a radical error*). **2** far-reaching; thorough (*radical change*). **3** advocating thorough reform; holding extreme political views; revolutionary. **4** forming the basis; primary. **5** of the root of a number or quantity. **6** (of surgery etc.) seeking to ensure the removal of all diseased tissue. **7** of the roots of words. **8** *Bot.* of the root. *–n.* **1** person holding radical views or belonging to a radical party. **2** *Chem.* **a** = FREE RADICAL. **b** atom or a group of these normally forming part of a compound and remaining unaltered during the compound's ordinary chemical changes. **3** root of a word. **4** *Math.* quantity forming or expressed as the root of another. □ **radicalism** *n.* **radically** *adv.* [Latin: related to RADIX]

radicchio /rəˈdiːkɪəʊ/ *n.* (*pl.* **-s**) chicory with reddish-purple leaves. [Italian, = chicory]

radicle /ˈrædɪk(ə)l/ *n.* part of a plant embryo that develops into the primary root; rootlet. [Latin: related to RADIX]

radii *pl.* of RADIUS.

radio /ˈreɪdɪəʊ/ *–n.* (*pl.* **-s**) **1** (often *attrib.*) **a** transmission and reception of sound messages etc. by electromagnetic waves of radio-frequency. **b** apparatus for receiving, broadcasting, or transmitting radio signals. **2 a** sound broadcasting (*prefers the radio*). **b** broadcasting station or channel (*Radio One*). *–v.* (**-es, -ed**) **1 a** send (a message) by radio. **b** send a message to (a person) by radio. **2** communicate or broadcast by radio. [short for *radio-telegraphy* etc.]

radio- *comb. form* **1** denoting radio or broadcasting. **2** connected with radioactivity. **3** connected with rays or radiation.

radioactive /ˌreɪdɪəʊˈæktɪv/ *adj.* of or exhibiting radioactivity.

radioactivity /ˌreɪdɪəʊækˈtɪvɪtɪ/ *n.* spontaneous disintegration of atomic nuclei, with the emission of usu. penetrating radiation or particles.

radiocarbon /ˌreɪdɪəʊˈkɑːbən/ *n.* radioactive isotope of carbon.

radio-controlled /ˌreɪdɪəʊkənˈtrəʊld/ *adj.* controlled from a distance by radio.

radio-frequency *n.* (*pl.* **-ies**) frequency band of telecommunication, ranging from 10^4 to 10^{11} or 10^{12} Hz.

radiogram /ˈreɪdɪəʊˌgræm/ *n.* **1** combined radio and record-player. **2** picture obtained by X-rays etc. **3** telegram sent by radio.

radiograph /ˈreɪdɪəʊˌgrɑːf/ *–n.* **1** instrument recording the intensity of radiation. **2** = RADIOGRAM 2. *–v.* obtain a picture of by X-ray, gamma ray, etc. □ **radiographer** /-ˈɒgrəfə(r)/ *n.* **radiography** /-ˈɒgrəfɪ/ *n.*

radioisotope /ˌreɪdɪəʊˈaɪsəˌtəʊp/ *n.* radioactive isotope.

radiology /ˌreɪdɪˈɒlədʒɪ/ *n.* the study of X-rays and other high-energy radiation, esp. as used in medicine. □ **radiologist** *n.*

♦ **radio paging** *n.* method of contacting a person when away from base, in which a high-frequency signal received by an outside radio-paging unit carried by the person causes it to bleep and alerts the carrier to phone headquarters, the office, etc. Several messages can be stored on a pocket receiver and messages can be received from more than one source by using different bleeps for different callers. □ **radio pager** *n.*

---

radiophonic /ˌreɪdɪəʊˈfɒnɪk/ *adj.* of or relating to electronically produced sound, esp. music.

radioscopy /ˌreɪdɪˈɒskəpɪ/ *n.* examination by X-rays etc. of objects opaque to light.

radio-telegraphy /ˌreɪdɪəʊtɪˈlegrəfɪ/ *n.* telegraphy using radio.

radio-telephony /ˌreɪdɪəʊtɪˈlefənɪ/ *n.* telephony using radio. □ **radio-telephone** /-ˈtelɪˌfəʊn/ *n.*

radio telescope *n.* directional aerial system for collecting and analysing radiation in the radio-frequency range from stars etc.

radiotherapy /ˌreɪdɪəʊˈθerəpɪ/ *n.* treatment of disease by X-rays or other forms of radiation.

radish /ˈrædɪʃ/ *n.* **1** plant with a fleshy pungent root. **2** this root, eaten esp. raw. [Latin RADIX]

radium /ˈreɪdɪəm/ *n.* radioactive metallic element orig. obtained from pitchblende etc., used esp. in radiotherapy.

radius /ˈreɪdɪəs/ *n.* (*pl.* **radii** /-dɪˌaɪ/ or **radiuses**) **1 a** straight line from the centre to the circumference of a circle or sphere. **b** length of this. **2** distance from a centre (*within a radius of 20 miles*). **3 a** thicker and shorter of the two bones in the human forearm. **b** corresponding bone in a vertebrate's foreleg or a bird's wing. [Latin]

radix /ˈreɪdɪks/ *n.* (*pl.* **radices** /-dɪˌsiːz/) *Math.* number or symbol used as the basis of a numeration scale (e.g. ten in the decimal system). [Latin, = root]

radon /ˈreɪdɒn/ *n.* gaseous radioactive inert element arising from the disintegration of radium.

RAF *abbr.* /*colloq.* ræf/ Royal Air Force.

raffia /ˈræfɪə/ *n.* **1** palm-tree native to Madagascar. **2** fibre from its leaves, used for weaving and for tying plants etc. [Malagasy]

raffish /ˈræfɪʃ/ *adj.* **1** disreputable, rakish. **2** tawdry. [*raff* rubbish]

raffle /ˈræf(ə)l/ *–n.* fund-raising lottery with prizes. *–v.* (**-ling**) (often foll. by *off*) sell by means of a raffle. [French *raf(f)le*, a dice-game]

raft /rɑːft/ *n.* flat floating structure of timber or other materials for conveying persons or things. [Old Norse]

rafter /ˈrɑːftə(r)/ *n.* each of the sloping beams forming the framework of a roof. [Old English]

rag[1] *n.* **1** torn, frayed, or worn piece of woven material. **2** (in *pl.*) old or worn clothes. **3** (*collect.*) scraps of cloth used as material for paper, stuffing, etc. **4** *derog.* newspaper. □ **in rags** much torn. **rags to riches** poverty to affluence. [probably a back-formation from RAGGED]

rag[2] *slang –n.* **1** fund-raising programme of stunts, parades, and entertainment organized by students. **2** prank. **3 a** rowdy celebration. **b** noisy disorderly scene. –*v.* (**-gg-**) **1** tease; play rough jokes on. **2** engage in rough play; be noisy and riotous. [origin unknown]

rag[3] *n.* ragtime composition. [abbreviation]

ragamuffin /'rægə,mʌfɪn/ *n.* child in ragged dirty clothes. [probably from RAG[1]]

rag-and-bone man *n.* itinerant dealer in old clothes, furniture, etc.

rag-bag *n.* **1** bag for scraps of fabric etc. **2** miscellaneous collection.

rag doll *n.* stuffed cloth doll.

rage –*n.* **1** fierce or violent anger. **2** fit of this. **3** violent action of a natural force. –*v.* (**-ging**) **1** be full of anger. **2** (often foll. by *at, against*) speak furiously or madly. **3** (of wind, battle, etc.) be violent; be at its height. **4** (as **raging** *adj.*) extreme, very painful (*raging thirst*; *raging headache*). □ **all the rage** very popular, fashionable. [Latin RABIES]

ragged /'rægɪd/ *adj.* **1** torn; frayed. **2** in ragged clothes. **3** with a broken or jagged outline or surface. **4** faulty, imperfect; lacking finish, smoothness, or uniformity. [Old Norse]

ragged robin *n.* pink-flowered campion with tattered petals.

raglan /'ræglən/ –*adj.* (of a sleeve) running up to the neck of a garment. –*n.* (often *attrib.*) overcoat without shoulder seams, the sleeves running up to the neck. [Lord *Raglan*]

ragout /ræ'gu:/ *n.* meat stewed with vegetables and highly seasoned. [French]

ragtag *n.* (in full **ragtag and bobtail**) *derog.* rabble or common people. [from RAG[1]]

ragtime *n.* form of highly syncopated early jazz, esp. for the piano.

rag trade *n. colloq.* the clothing business.

Ragusa /ræ'gu:zə/ see DUBROVNIK.

ragwort /'rægwɜ:t/ *n.* yellow-flowered ragged-leaved plant.

raid –*n.* **1** rapid surprise attack, esp.: **a** in warfare. **b** in order to commit a crime, steal, or do harm. **2** surprise attack by police etc. to arrest suspected persons or seize illicit goods. –*v.* make a raid on. [Scots form of ROAD]

♦ **raider** *n.* **1** person who raids. **2** person or organization that specializes in exploiting companies with undervalued assets by initiating hostile take-over bids.

---

rail[1] –*n.* **1** level or sloping bar or series of bars: **a** used to hang things on. **b** as the top of banisters. **c** forming part of a fence or barrier as protection. **2** steel bar or continuous line of bars laid on the ground, usu. as a railway. **3** (often *attrib.*) railway. –*v.* **1** furnish with a rail or rails. **2** (usu. foll. by *in, off*) enclose with rails. □ **off the rails** disorganized; out of order; deranged. [French *reille* from Latin *regula* RULE]

rail[2] *v.* (often foll. by *at, against*) complain or protest strongly; rant. [French *railler*]

rail[3] *n.* wading bird often inhabiting marshes. [French]

railcar *n.* single powered railway coach.

railcard *n.* pass entitling the holder to reduced rail fares.

railing *n.* (usu. in *pl.*) fence or barrier made of rails.

raillery /'reɪlərɪ/ *n.* good-humoured ridicule. [French *raillerie*: related to RAIL[2]]

railman *n.* = RAILWAYMAN.

railroad –*n.* esp. *US* = RAILWAY. –*v.* (often foll. by *into, through*, etc.) coerce; rush (*railroaded into agreeing*; *railroaded through the Cabinet*).

railway *n.* **1** track or set of tracks of steel rails upon which trains run. **2** such a system worked by a single company. **3** organization and personnel required for its working.

railwayman *n.* railway employee.

raiment /'reɪmənt/ *n. archaic* clothing. [*arrayment*: related to ARRAY]

rain –*n.* **1 a** condensed atmospheric moisture falling in drops. **b** fall of such drops. **2** (in *pl.*) **a** (prec. by *the*) rainy season. **b** rainfalls. **3 a** falling liquid or solid particles or objects. **b** rainlike descent of these. –*v.* **1** (prec. by *it* as subject) rain falls. **2 a** fall like rain. **b** (prec. by *it* as subject) send in large quantities. **3** send down like rain; lavishly bestow (*rained blows upon him*). **4** (of the sky, clouds, etc.) send down rain. □ **rain off** (or *US* **out**) (esp. in *passive*) cause (an event etc.) to be cancelled because of rain. [Old English]

rainbow /'reɪnbəʊ/ –*n.* arch of colours formed in the sky by reflection, refraction, and dispersion of the sun's rays in falling rain or in spray or mist. –*adj.* many-coloured. [Old English: related to RAIN, BOW[1]]

rainbow trout *n.* large trout orig. of the Pacific coast of North America.

rain check *n.* esp. *US* ticket given for later use when an outdoor event is interrupted or postponed by rain. □ **take a rain check on** reserve the right not to take up (an offer) until convenient.

raincoat *n.* waterproof or water-resistant coat.

raindrop *n.* single drop of rain.

rainfall *n.* **1** fall of rain. **2** quantity of rain falling within a given area in a given time.

rain forest *n.* luxuriant tropical forest with heavy rainfall.

rainproof *adj.* impervious to rain.

rainstorm *n.* storm with heavy rain.

rainwater *n.* water collected from fallen rain.

rainwear *n.* clothes for wearing in the rain.

rainy *adj.* (**-ier, -iest**) (of weather, a climate, day, etc.) in or on which rain is falling or much rain usu. falls. [Old English: related to RAIN]

rainy day *n.* time of special need in the future.

raise /reɪz/ –*v.* (**-sing**) **1** put or take into a higher position. **2** (often foll. by *up*) cause to rise or stand up or be vertical. **3** increase the amount, value, or strength of. **4** (often foll. by *up*) construct or build up. **5** levy, collect, or bring together (*raise money*). **6** cause to be heard or considered (*raise an objection*). **7** set going or bring into being (*raise hopes*). **8** bring up, educate. **9** breed, grow. **10** promote to a higher rank. **11** (foll. by *to*) multiply a quantity to a power. **12** cause (bread) to rise. **13** *Cards* bet more than (another player). **14** end (a siege etc.). **15** remove (a barrier etc.). **16** cause (a ghost etc.) to appear. **17** *colloq.* get hold of, find. **18** rouse from sleep or death, or from a lair. –*n.* **1** *Cards* increase in a stake or bid. **2** esp. *US* increase in salary. □ **raise Cain** *colloq.* = *raise the roof.* **raise one's eyebrows** see EYEBROW. **raise from the dead** restore to life. **raise a laugh** cause others to laugh. **raise the roof** be very angry; cause an uproar. [Old Norse]

raisin /'reɪz(ə)n/ *n.* dried grape. [Latin: related to RACEME]

raison d'être /,reɪzɔ̃ 'detr/ *n.* (*pl.* ***raisons d'être*** pronunc. same) purpose or reason that accounts for, justifies, or originally caused a thing's existence. [French]

raj /rɑ:dʒ/ *n.* (prec. by *the*) *hist.* British sovereignty in India. [Hindi]

raja /'rɑ:dʒə/ *n.* (also **rajah**) *hist.* **1** Indian king or prince. **2** petty dignitary or noble in India. [Hindi from Sanskrit]

Rajasthan /,rɑ:dʒə'stɑ:n/ state in NW India; pop. (est. 1994) 48 040 000; capital, Jaipur. Agriculture (esp. cereals and livestock) is the main source of revenue; there are also coal and other mineral deposits, and textile, cement, and glass industries. □ **Rajasthani** *adj.* & *n.*

Rajshahi /rɑ:dʒ'ʃɑ:jɪ, 'rɑ:dʒ-/ city in W Bangladesh, a port on the Ganges; city pop. (1991) 318 000; metropolitan area pop. (1991) 517 136.

rake[1] –*n.* **1** implement consisting of a pole with a toothed crossbar at the end for drawing together hay etc. or smoothing loose soil or gravel. **2** similar implement used (e.g.) to draw in money at a gaming-table. –*v.* (**-king**) **1** collect or gather with or as with a rake. **2** make tidy or smooth with a rake. **3** use a rake. **4** search thoroughly, ransack. **5** direct gunfire along (a line) from end to end. **6** scratch or scrape. □ **rake in** *colloq.* amass (profits etc.). **rake up** revive the (unwelcome) memory of. [Old English]

rake[2] *n.* dissolute man of fashion. [*rakehell*: related to RAKE[1], HELL]

rake[3] *–v.* (**-king**) **1** set or be set at a sloping angle. **2** (of a mast or funnel) incline from the perpendicular towards the stern. *–n.* **1** raking position or build. **2** amount by which a thing rakes. [origin unknown]

rake-off *n. colloq.* commission or share.

rakish *adj.* **1** dashing; jaunty. **2** dissolute. □ **rakishly** *adv.* [from RAKE[2]]

Raleigh /ˈrɑːlɪ/ city in the US, capital of North Carolina; manufactures include computers and textiles; pop. (est. 1994) 236 707.

rallentando /ˌrælənˈtændəʊ/ *Mus. –adv.* & *adj.* with a gradual decrease of speed. *–n.* (*pl.* **-s** or **-di** /-dɪ/) passage to be performed in this way. [Italian]

rally[1] /ˈrælɪ/ *–v.* (**-ies, -ied**) **1** (often foll. by *round*) bring or come together as support or for action. **2** bring or come together again after a rout or dispersion. **3** recover after illness etc., revive. **4** revive (courage etc.). **5** (of share-prices etc.) increase after a fall. *–n.* (*pl.* **-ies**) **1** rallying or being rallied. **2** mass meeting of supporters or persons with a common interest. **3** competition for motor vehicles, mainly over public roads. **4** (in tennis etc.) extended exchange of strokes. **5** rise in prices in a market (e.g. a stock exchange or commodity market) after a fall, usu. brought about by a change of sentiment. However, if the change has occurred because there are more buyers than sellers, it is known as a **technical rally**. For example, unfavourable sentiment might cause a market to fall, in turn causing sellers to withdraw at the lower prices. The market will then be sensitive to the presence of very few buyers, who, if they show their hand, may bring about a technical rally. [French *rallier*: related to RE-, ALLY]

rally[2] /ˈrælɪ/ *v.* (**-ies, -ied**) ridicule good-humouredly. [French *railler*: related to RAIL[2]]

rallycross *n.* motor racing over roads and cross-country.

♦ **RAM**[1] *n. Computing* random-access memory, the part of main-store memory that can be both read from and written to (cf. ROM). The amount of RAM determines the amount of memory the user has in which to run programs. Most types of RAM lose their contents when the computer is turned off. See also RANDOM ACCESS; SEMICONDUCTOR MEMORY. [abbreviation]

RAM[2] *abbr.* **1** /ræm/ *US* reverse annuity mortgage. **2** Royal Academy of Music.

ram *–n.* **1** uncastrated male sheep. **2** (**the Ram**) zodiacal sign or constellation Aries. **3** *hist.* = BATTERING-RAM. **4** falling weight of a pile-driving machine. **5** hydraulically operated water pump. *–v.* (**-mm-**) **1** force or squeeze into place by pressure. **2** (usu. foll. by *down, in,* etc.) beat down or drive in by heavy blows. **3** (of a ship, vehicle, etc.) strike violently, crash against. **4** (foll. by *against, into*) dash or violently impel. [Old English]

Ramadan /ˈræməˌdæn/ *n.* ninth month of the Muslim year, with strict fasting from sunrise to sunset. [Arabic]

ramble /ˈræmb(ə)l/ *–v.* (**-ling**) **1** walk for pleasure. **2** talk or write incoherently. *–n.* walk taken for pleasure. [Dutch *rammelen*]

rambler *n.* **1** person who rambles. **2** straggling or spreading rose.

rambling *adj.* **1** wandering. **2** disconnected, incoherent. **3** (of a house, street, etc.) irregularly arranged. **4** (of a plant) straggling, climbing.

rambutan /ræmˈbuːt(ə)n/ *n.* **1** red plum-sized prickly fruit. **2** East Indian tree bearing this. [Malay]

RAMC *abbr.* Royal Army Medical Corps.

ramekin /ˈræmɪkɪn/ *n.* **1** small dish for baking and serving an individual portion of food. **2** food served in this. [French *ramequin*]

ramification /ˌræmɪfɪˈkeɪʃ(ə)n/ *n.* (usu. in *pl.*) **1** consequence. **2** subdivision of a complex structure or process. [French: related to RAMIFY]

ramify /ˈræmɪˌfaɪ/ *v.* (**-ies, -ied**) (cause to) form branches, subdivisions, or offshoots; branch out. [Latin *ramus* branch]

ramp *–n.* **1** slope, esp. joining two levels of ground, floor, etc. **2** movable stairs for entering or leaving an aircraft. **3** transverse ridge in a road making vehicles slow down. *–v.* **1** furnish or build with a ramp. **2 a** assume a threatening posture. **b** (often foll. by *about*) storm, rage. **3** boost the image of a security by buying with the object of forcing the price up and then selling to make a quick profit. □ **ramper** *n.* [French *ramper* crawl]

rampage *–v.* /ræmˈpeɪdʒ/ (**-ging**) **1** (often foll. by *about*) rush wildly or violently about. **2** rage, storm. *–n.* /ˈræmpeɪdʒ/ wild or violent behaviour. □ **on the rampage** rampaging. [perhaps from RAMP]

rampant /ˈræmpənt/ *adj.* **1** unchecked, flourishing excessively. **2** rank, luxuriant. **3** (placed after the noun) *Heraldry* (of an animal) standing on its left hind foot with its forepaws in the air (*lion rampant*). **4** violent, fanatical. □ **rampancy** *n.* [French: related to RAMP]

rampart /ˈræmpɑːt/ *n.* **1 a** defensive wall with a broad top and usu. a stone parapet. **b** walkway on top of this. **2** defence, protection. [French *remparer* fortify]

ramrod *n.* **1** rod for ramming down the charge of a muzzle-loading firearm. **2** thing that is very straight or rigid.

ramshackle /ˈræmˌʃæk(ə)l/ *adj.* tumbledown, rickety. [related to RANSACK]

ran *past* of RUN.

ranch /rɑːntʃ/ *–n.* **1** cattle-breeding establishment, esp. in the US and Canada. **2** farm where other animals are bred (*mink ranch*). *–v.* farm on a ranch. □ **rancher** *n.* [Spanish *rancho* group of persons eating together]

rancid /ˈrænsɪd/ *adj.* smelling or tasting like rank stale fat. □ **rancidity** /-ˈsɪdɪtɪ/ *n.* [Latin *rancidus* stinking]

rancour /ˈræŋkə(r)/ *n.* (*US* **rancor**) inveterate bitterness, malignant hate. □ **rancorous** *adj.* [Latin *rancor*: related to RANCID]

Rand /rænd, rɑːnt/, **the** = WITWATERSRAND.

rand *n.* standard monetary unit of South Africa and Namibia. [the RAND]

R & B *abbr.* rhythm and blues.

R & D *abbr.* = RESEARCH AND DEVELOPMENT.

Randers /ˈrɑːnəz/ port in Denmark, on the E coast of the Jutland peninsula; pop. (1995) 61 435.

R & M *abbr.* reliability and marketing.

random /ˈrændəm/ *adj.* made, done, etc., without method or conscious choice. □ **at random** without a particular aim. □ **randomize** *v.* (also **-ise**) (**-zing** or **-sing**). **randomization** /-ˈzeɪʃ(ə)n/ *n.* **randomly** *adv.* **randomness** *n.* [French *randon* from *randir* gallop]

random access *n. Computing* method of retrieval or storage of data that does not require any other stored data to be read first. The storage locations can be accessed (read or written to) in any order. There is random access with magnetic disk storage. There is also random access with main storage, i.e. with RAM and ROM, but with a much shorter access time than with disk storage.

random numbers *n.pl.* numbers that are drawn from a set of permissible numbers and that have no detectable pattern or bias. Any number in the set should therefore have an equal probability of being selected. Random numbers are required, for example, when selecting the winners of the Premium Bond scheme.

♦ **random sample** *n.* group selected from a population of people or things in such a way that every individual has an equal chance of being selected. A **stratified random sample** is obtained by dividing the total population into subgroups according to some desired criterion before selecting the random sample. For example, in selecting a random sample of people to interview one might first stratify the population by age or income.

◆ **random-walk theory** *n.* theory that share prices move, for whatever reason, without any memory of past movements and that the movements therefore follow no pattern. This theory is used to refute the predictions of chartists, who rely on past patterns of movements to predict present and future prices.

---

randy /'rændɪ/ *adj.* (**-ier**, **-iest**) eager for sexual gratification, lustful. □ **randily** *adv.* **randiness** *n.* [perhaps related to RANT]

ranee /'rɑːnɪ/ *n.* (also **rani**) (*pl.* **-s**) *hist.* raja's wife or widow. [Hindi]

rang *past* of RING[2].

range /reɪndʒ/ *–n.* **1 a** region between limits of variation, esp. scope of effective operation. **b** such limits. **2** area relevant to something. **3 a** distance attainable by a gun or projectile. **b** distance between a gun or projectile and its objective. **4** row, series, etc., esp. of mountains. **5** area with targets for shooting. **6** fireplace with ovens and hotplates for cooking. **7** area over which a thing is distributed. **8** distance that can be covered by a vehicle without refuelling. **9** distance between a camera and the subject to be photographed. **10** large area of open land for grazing or hunting. *–v.* (**-ging**) **1** reach; lie spread out; extend; be found over a specified district; vary between limits. **2** (usu. in *passive* or *refl.*) line up, arrange. **3** rove, wander. **4** traverse in all directions. [French: related to RANK[1]]

rangefinder *n.* instrument for estimating the distance of an object to be shot at or photographed.

ranger *n.* **1** keeper of a royal or national park, or of a forest. **2** member of a body of mounted soldiers. **3** (**Ranger**) senior Guide.

Rangoon /ræŋ'guːn/ (also **Yangon** /jæŋ'gɔːn/) capital of Burma, a seaport 32 km (20 miles) from the Indian Ocean on the Rangoon river; pop. (est. 1995) 3 851 000.

rangy /'reɪndʒɪ/ *adj.* (**-ier**, **-iest**) tall and slim.

rani var. of RANEE.

rank[1] *–n.* **1 a** position in a hierarchy, grade of advancement. **b** distinct social class; grade of dignity or achievement. **c** high social position. **d** place in a scale. **2** row or line. **3** single line of soldiers drawn up abreast. **4** place where taxis await customers. **5** order, array. *–v.* **1** have a rank or place. **2** classify, give a certain grade to. **3** arrange (esp. soldiers) in rank. □ **close ranks** maintain solidarity. **the ranks** common soldiers. [French *ranc*]

rank[2] *adj.* **1** luxuriant, coarse; choked with or apt to produce weeds or excessive foliage. **2 a** foul-smelling. **b** loathsome, corrupt. **3** flagrant, virulent, gross, complete (*rank outsider*). [Old English]

rank and file *n.* (usu. treated as *pl.*) ordinary members of an organization.

rankle /'ræŋk(ə)l/ *v.* (**-ling**) (of envy, disappointment, etc., or their cause) cause persistent annoyance or resentment. [French *(d)rancler* fester, from medieval Latin *dra(cu)nculus* little serpent]

ransack /'rænsæk/ *v.* **1** pillage or plunder (a house, country, etc.). **2** thoroughly search. [Old Norse *rannsaka* from *rann* house, *-saka* seek]

ransom /'rænsəm/ *–n.* **1** money demanded or paid for the release of a prisoner. **2** liberation of a prisoner in return for this. *–v.* **1** buy the freedom or restoration of; redeem. **2** = *hold to ransom* (see HOLD[1]). **3** release for a ransom. [Latin: related to REDEMPTION]

rant *–v.* speak loudly, bombastically, violently, or theatrically. *–n.* piece of ranting. □ **rant and rave** express anger noisily and forcefully. [Dutch]

ranunculus /rə'nʌŋkjʊləs/ *n.* (*pl.* **-luses** or **-li** /-ˌlaɪ/) plant of the genus including buttercups. [Latin, diminutive of *rana* frog]

RAOC *abbr.* Royal Army Ordnance Corps.

rap[1] *–n.* **1** smart slight blow. **2** knock, sharp tapping sound. **3** *slang* blame, punishment. **4 a** rhythmic monologue recited to music. **b** (in full **rap music**) style of rock music with words recited. *–v.* (**-pp-**) **1** strike smartly. **2** knock; make a sharp tapping sound. **3** criticize adversely. **4** perform a rap. □ **take the rap** suffer the consequences. □ **rapper** *n.* [probably imitative]

rap[2] *n.* small amount, the least bit (*don't care a rap*). [Irish *ropaire* counterfeit coin]

rapacious /rə'peɪʃəs/ *adj.* grasping, extortionate, predatory. □ **rapacity** /rə'pæsɪtɪ/ *n.* [Latin *rapax*: related to RAPE[1]]

rape[1] *–n.* **1 a** act of forcing a woman or girl to have sexual intercourse against her will. **b** forcible sodomy. **2** (often foll. by *of*) violent assault or plunder, forcible interference. *–v.* (**-ping**) commit rape on. [Latin *rapio* seize]

rape[2] *n.* plant grown as fodder, and for its seed from which oil is extracted. [Latin *rapum, rapa* turnip]

rapid /'ræpɪd/ *–adj.* (**-er**, **-est**) **1** quick, swift. **2** acting or completed in a short time. **3** (of a slope) descending steeply. *–n.* (usu. in *pl.*) steep descent in a river-bed, with a swift current. □ **rapidity** /rə'pɪdɪtɪ/ *n.* **rapidly** *adv.* **rapidness** *n.* [Latin: related to RAPE[1]]

rapid eye-movement *n.* type of jerky movement of the eyes during dreaming.

rapier /'reɪpɪə(r)/ *n.* **1** light slender sword for thrusting. **2** (*attrib.*) sharp (*rapier wit*). [French *rapière*]

rapine /'ræpaɪn/ *n. rhet.* plundering. [Latin: related to RAPE[1]]

rapist *n.* person who commits rape.

rapport /ræ'pɔː(r)/ *n.* relationship or communication, esp. when useful and harmonious. [Latin *porto* carry]

rapprochement /ræ'prɒʃmɑ̃/ *n.* resumption of harmonious relations, esp. between states. [French: related to APPROACH]

rapscallion /ræp'skæljən/ *n. archaic* or *joc.* rascal. [perhaps from RASCAL]

rapt *adj.* **1** fully absorbed or intent, enraptured. **2** carried away with feeling or lofty thought. [Latin *raptus*: related to RAPE[1]]

rapture /'ræptʃə(r)/ *n.* **1** ecstatic delight. **2** (in *pl.*) great pleasure or enthusiasm or the expression of it. □ **rapturous** *adj.* [French or medieval Latin: related to RAPE[1]]

rare[1] *adj.* (**rarer**, **rarest**) **1** seldom done, found, or occurring; uncommon, unusual. **2** exceptionally good. **3** of less than the usual density. □ **rareness** *n.* [Latin *rarus*]

rare[2] *adj.* (**rarer**, **rarest**) (of meat) cooked so that the inside is still red and juicy; underdone. [Old English]

rarebit *n.* = WELSH RABBIT. [from RARE[1]]

rare earth *n.* lanthanide element.

rarefy /'reərɪˌfaɪ/ *v.* (**-ies**, **-ied**) **1** make or become less dense or solid. **2** purify or refine (a person's nature etc.). **3** make (an idea etc.) subtle. □ **rarefaction** /-'fækʃ(ə)n/ *n.* [French or medieval Latin: related to RARE[1]]

rarely *adv.* **1** seldom, not often. **2** exceptionally.

raring /'reərɪŋ/ *adj. colloq.* enthusiastic, eager (*raring to go*). [participle of *rare*, dial. var. of ROAR or REAR[2]]

rarity /'reərətɪ/ *n.* (*pl.* **-ies**) **1** rareness. **2** uncommon thing. [Latin: related to RARE[1]]

Ras al Khaimah /rɑːs æl 'kaɪmə/ **1** one of the seven member states of the United Arab Emirates; pop. (1993) 148 000. **2** its capital city (Port Saqr); pop. (latest est.) 74 880.

rascal /'rɑːsk(ə)l/ *n.* dishonest or mischievous person. □ **rascally** *adj.* [French *rascaille* rabble]

rase var. of RAZE.

rash[1] *adj.* reckless, impetuous, hasty. □ **rashly** *adv.* **rashness** *n.* [probably Old English]

rash[2] *n.* **1** eruption of the skin in spots or patches. **2** (usu. foll. by *of*) sudden widespread phenomenon (*rash of strikes*). [origin uncertain]

rasher *n.* thin slice of bacon or ham. [origin unknown]

rasp /rɑːsp/ *–n.* **1** coarse kind of file having separate teeth. **2** grating noise or utterance. *–v.* **1 a** scrape with a rasp. **b** scrape roughly. **c** (foll. by *off*, *away*) remove by scraping. **2 a** make a grating sound. **b** say gratingly. **3** grate upon (a person or feelings). [French *raspe(r)*]

raspberry /ˈrɑːzbərɪ/ *n.* (*pl.* **-ies**) **1 a** red blackberry-like fruit. **b** bramble bearing this. **2** *colloq.* sound made by blowing through the lips, expressing derision or disapproval. [origin unknown]

raspberry-cane *n.* raspberry plant.

Rastafarian /ˌræstəˈfeərɪən/ (also **Rasta** /ˈræstə/) *–n.* member of a Jamaican sect, often having dreadlocks and regarding Haile Selassie of Ethiopia as God. *–adj.* of this sect. [*Ras Tafari*, title of former Emperor Haile Selassie]

rat *–n.* **1 a** rodent like a large mouse. **b** similar rodent (*muskrat; water-rat*). **2** turncoat. **3** *colloq.* unpleasant or treacherous person. **4** (in *pl.*) *slang* exclamation of annoyance etc. *–v.* (**-tt-**) **1** hunt or kill rats. **2** (also foll. by *on*) inform (on); desert, betray. [Old English]

ratable var. of RATEABLE.

ratatat (also **rat-a-tat**) var. of RAT-TAT.

ratatouille /ˌrætəˈtuːɪ, -ˈtwiː/ *n.* dish of stewed onions, courgettes, tomatoes, aubergines, and peppers. [French dial.]

ratbag *n. slang* obnoxious person.

ratchet /ˈrætʃɪt/ *n.* **1** set of teeth on the edge of a bar or wheel with a catch ensuring motion in one direction only. **2** (in full **ratchet-wheel**) wheel with a rim so toothed. [French *rochet* lance-head]

♦ **ratchet effect** *n.* irreversible change to an economic variable (e.g. prices, wages, exchange rates, etc.). For example, once a price or wage has been forced up by some temporary economic pressure, it is unlikely to fall back when the pressure is reduced. This rise may be reflected in parallel sympathetic rises throughout the economy, thus fuelling inflation.

rate[1] *–n.* **1** numerical proportion between two sets of things (*moving at a rate of 50 m.p.h.*) or as the basis of calculating an amount or value (*rate of interest*). **2** fixed or appropriate charge, cost, or value; measure of this (*postal rates; the rate for the job*). **3** pace of movement or change (*prices increasing at a great rate*). **4** (in *comb.*) class or rank (*first-rate*). **5** (in *pl.*) local-authority tax, levied on businesses (and formerly on private individuals), calculated as a poundage on the rateable value of property occupied in the area of the rating authority. The **poundage** is fixed annually by the rating authority as the number of pence that must be paid for each pound of rateable value. The **rateable value** (or **net annual rentable value**) is determined by the Board of Inland Revenue for each property by deducting, from the rack-rent that the property would earn, certain allowable costs. Domestic rates have been replaced in the UK by the council tax (see also COMMUNITY CHARGE). *–v.* (**-ting**) **1 a** estimate the worth or value of. **b** assign a value to. **2** consider, regard as. **3** (foll. by *as*) rank or be considered. **4 a** subject to the payment of a local rate. **b** value for the purpose of assessing rates. **5** be worthy of, deserve. □ **at any rate** in any case, whatever happens. **at this rate** if this example is typical. [Latin *rata*: related to RATIO]

rate[2] *v.* (**-ting**) scold angrily. [origin unknown]

rateable *adj.* (also **ratable**) liable to rates.

♦ **rateable value** see RATE[1] *n.* 5.

rate-capping *n. hist.* imposition of an upper limit on local-authority rates. □ **rate-cap** *v.*

♦ **rate card** *n.* list of prices charged for advertising space, TV or radio time, etc. See also OFF-CARD RATE.

♦ **rate of exchange** *n.* (also **exchange rate**) price of one currency in terms of another. It is usu. expressed in terms of how many units of the home country's currency are needed to buy one unit of the foreign currency, but in some cases (notably in the UK) it is expressed as the number of units of foreign currency that one unit of the home currency will buy. Two rates are usu. given, the buying and selling rates; the difference is the profit or commission charged by the organization carrying out the exchange.

♦ **rate of interest** *n.* = INTEREST RATE.

♦ **rate of return** *n.* annual amount of income from an investment, expressed as a percentage of the original investment. This rate is very important in assessing the relative merits of different investments. It is therefore important to note whether a quoted rate is before or after tax, since with most investments, the after-tax rate of return is most relevant. See also ANNUAL PERCENTAGE RATE.

♦ **rate of time preference** *n.* see TIME PREFERENCE.

♦ **rate of turnover** *n.* frequency, expressed in annual terms, with which some part of the assets of an organization is turned over. To provide a reasonable measure in terms of stock, the sales revenue (or if a more accurate estimate is needed the cost of goods sold) is divided by the average value of the stock. However, some accountants divide the sales figure by the value of the fixed assets to arrive at turnover of fixed assets. This is less realistic, although it does express the relationship of sales to the fixed assets of the organization, which in some organizations could be significant.

ratepayer *n.* person liable to pay rates.

rather /ˈrɑːðə(r)/ *adv.* **1** by preference (*would rather not go*). **2** (usu. foll. by *than*) more truly; as a more likely alternative (*is stupid rather than dishonest*). **3** more precisely (*a book, or rather, a pamphlet*). **4** slightly, to some extent (*became rather drunk*). **5** /rɑːˈðɜː(r)/ (as an emphatic response) assuredly (*Did you like it? – Rather!*). □ **had rather** would rather. [Old English comparative of *rathe* early]

ratify /ˈrætɪˌfaɪ/ *v.* (**-ies**, **-ied**) confirm or accept (an agreement made in one's name) by formal consent, signature, etc. □ **ratification** /-fɪˈkeɪʃ(ə)n/ *n.* [medieval Latin: related to RATE[1]]

rating *n.* **1** placing in a rank or class. **2** estimated standing of a person as regards credit etc. **3** non-commissioned sailor. **4** amount fixed as a local rate. **5** relative popularity of a broadcast programme as determined by the estimated size of the audience.

ratio /ˈreɪʃɪəʊ/ *n.* (*pl.* **-s**) quantitative relation between two similar magnitudes expressed as the number of times one contains the other (*in the ratio of three to two*). [Latin *reor rat-* reckon]

ratiocinate /ˌrætɪˈɒsɪˌneɪt/ *v.* (**-ting**) *literary* reason, esp. using syllogisms. □ **ratiocination** /-ˈneɪʃ(ə)n/ *n.* [Latin: related to RATIO]

ration /ˈræʃ(ə)n/ *–n.* **1** official allowance of food, clothing, etc., in a time of shortage. **2** (usu. in *pl.*) fixed daily allowance of food, esp. in the armed forces. *–v.* **1** limit (persons or provisions) to a fixed ration. **2** (usu. foll. by *out*) share out (food etc.) in fixed quantities. □ **ration by price** increase the price of goods in short supply, esp. an essential commodity, so that only the rich can afford to buy. [Latin: related to RATIO]

rational /ˈræʃən(ə)l/ *adj.* **1** of or based on reason. **2** sensible. **3** endowed with reason. **4** rejecting what is unreasonable or cannot be tested by reason in religion or custom. **5** (of a quantity or ratio) expressible as a ratio of whole numbers. □ **rationally** *adv.* [Latin: related to RATION]

rationale /ˌræʃəˈnɑːl/ *n.* fundamental reason, logical basis. [neuter of Latin *rationalis*: related to RATIONAL]

♦ **rational expectations** *n.pl. Econ.* expectations about the economy that are held by rational individuals and that utilize all the available information without systematic error. First proposed by J. F. Muth (1961), the theory of rational expectations has caused a revolution in macroeconomics. Keynesian theory, prior to Muth, did not involve rational expectations, implying that individuals used information inefficiently. In the current theory, however, when combined with the market clearing assumption, rational expectations imply that fiscal policy and monetary policy cannot influence real variables, provided that everyone has equal access to information. One direction taken by post-Keynesian theory has been to investigate the consequences of the unequal distribution of information and the economic inefficiencies that this creates.

rationalism /ˈræʃənəˌlɪz(ə)m/ *n.* practice of treating reason as the basis of belief and knowledge. □ **rationalist** *n.* & *adj.* **rationalistic** /-ˈlɪstɪk/ *adj.*

♦ **rationality** /ˌræʃəˈnælɪtɪ/ *n.* **1** condition of being rational. **2** reasoned or logical argument etc. **3** *Econ.* assumption made in neoclassical economics that individuals will compare all possible combinations of goods when making their choices and will always prefer more of a good than less. Since, in practice, rationality could involve a large amount of calculation and information gathering, the assumption has always been considered controversial. Without it, however, most of the results of consumer theory and producer theory are not valid and alternative assumptions do not appear to yield useful predictions (see also BOUNDED RATIONALITY).

♦ **rationalization** /ˌræʃənəlaɪˈzeɪʃ(ə)n/ *n.* (also **-isation**) **1** reorganization of a firm, group, or industry to increase its efficiency and profitability. This may include closing some manufacturing units and expanding others (horizontal integration), merging different stages of the production process (vertical integration), merging support units, closing units that are duplicating effort of others, etc. **2** making rational.

rationalize *v.* (also **-ise**) (**-zing** or **-sing**) **1** (often foll. by *away*) offer a rational but specious explanation of (one's behaviour or attitude). **2** make logical and consistent. **3** make (a business etc.) more efficient and profitable by reorganizing it to reduce or eliminate waste. See RATIONALIZATION.

ratline /ˈrætlɪn/ *n.* (also **ratlin**) (usu. in *pl.*) any of the small lines fastened across a sailing-ship's shrouds like ladder-rungs. [origin unknown]

rat race *n. colloq.* fiercely competitive struggle for position, power, etc.

ratsbane *n.* anything poisonous to rats, esp. a plant.

rattan /rəˈtæn/ *n.* **1** climbing palm with long thin jointed pliable stems, used for furniture etc. **2** piece of rattan stem used as a walking-stick etc. [Malay]

rat-tat /rætˈtæt/ *n.* (also **rat-tat-tat** /ˌrættætˈtæt/, **ratatat**, **rat-a-tat** /ˌrætəˈtæt/) rapping sound, esp. of a knocker. [imitative]

rattle /ˈræt(ə)l/ *–v.* (**-ling**) **1 a** give out a rapid succession of short sharp hard sounds. **b** cause to do this. **c** cause such sounds by shaking something. **2** (often foll. by *along*) **a** move with a rattling noise. **b** move or travel briskly. **3 a** (usu. foll. by *off*) say or recite rapidly. **b** (usu. foll. by *on*) talk in a lively thoughtless way. **4** *colloq.* disconcert, alarm. *–n.* **1** rattling sound. **2** device or plaything made to rattle. □ **rattly** *adj.* [probably Low German or Dutch]

rattlesnake *n.* poisonous American snake with a rattling structure of horny rings on its tail.

rattling *–adj.* **1** that rattles. **2** brisk, vigorous (*rattling pace*). *–adv. colloq.* remarkably (*rattling good story*).

ratty *adj.* (**-ier**, **-iest**) **1** relating to or infested with rats. **2** *colloq.* irritable, bad-tempered. □ **rattily** *adv.* **rattiness** *n.*

raucous /ˈrɔːkəs/ *adj.* harsh-sounding, loud and hoarse. □ **raucously** *adv.* **raucousness** *n.* [Latin]

raunchy /ˈrɔːntʃɪ/ *adj.* (**-ier**, **-iest**) *colloq.* coarse, earthy, sexually boisterous. □ **raunchily** *adv.* **raunchiness** *n.* [origin unknown]

♦ **Rausing** /ˈraʊsɪŋ/, **Hans** (1926–) Swedish businessman, managing director (1954–83), chief executive officer (1983–93), chairman (1985–93), and honorary chairman (from 1993) of Tetra Laval Group, the world's largest manufacturer of packaging. Hans sold his half of the company to his brother, **Gad Rausing**, and is now a member of the Co-ordination Council for Foreign Investments, Russia (from 1995).

ravage /ˈrævɪdʒ/ *–v.* (**-ging**) devastate, plunder. *–n.* **1** devastation. **2** (usu. in *pl.*; foll. by *of*) destructive effect. [French alteration from *ravine* rush of water]

rave *–v.* (**-ving**) **1** talk wildly or furiously in or as in delirium. **2** (usu. foll. by *about*, *over*) speak with rapturous admiration; go into raptures. **3** *colloq.* enjoy oneself freely (esp. *rave it up*). *–n.* **1** (usu. *attrib.*) *colloq.* highly enthusiastic review. **2** (also **rave-up**) *colloq.* lively party. **3** *slang* craze. [probably French dial. *raver*]

ravel /ˈræv(ə)l/ *v.* (**-ll-**; *US* **-l-**) **1** entangle or become entangled. **2** fray out. **3** (often foll. by *out*) disentangle, unravel, separate into threads. [probably Dutch *ravelen*]

raven /ˈreɪv(ə)n/ *–n.* large glossy blue-black crow with a hoarse cry. *–adj.* glossy black. [Old English]

ravening /ˈrævənɪŋ/ *adj.* hungrily seeking prey; voracious. [French *raviner* from Latin: related to RAPINE]

Ravenna /rəˈvenə/ city and port in NE central Italy, linked by canal to the Adriatic coast; industrial activity (esp. oil refining) is increasing; pop. (est. 1994) 133 604.

ravenous /ˈrævənəs/ *adj.* **1** very hungry. **2** voracious. **3** rapacious. □ **ravenously** *adv.* [obsolete *raven* plunder, from French *raviner* ravage]

raver *n. colloq.* uninhibited pleasure-loving person.

ravine /rəˈviːn/ *n.* deep narrow gorge. [Latin: related to RAPINE]

raving *–n.* (usu. in *pl.*) wild or delirious talk. *–adj.* & *adv. colloq.* as an intensifier (*a raving beauty*; *raving mad*).

ravioli /ˌrævɪˈəʊlɪ/ *n.* small pasta envelopes containing minced meat etc. [Italian]

ravish /ˈrævɪʃ/ *v.* **1** *archaic* rape (a woman). **2** enrapture. □ **ravishment** *n.* [Latin: related to RAPE[1]]

ravishing *adj.* lovely, beautiful. □ **ravishingly** *adv.*

raw *adj.* **1** uncooked. **2** in the natural state; not processed or manufactured. **3** inexperienced, untrained. **4 a** stripped of skin; with the flesh exposed, unhealed. **b** sensitive to the touch from being so exposed. **5** (of the atmosphere, day, etc.) cold and damp. **6** crude in artistic quality; lacking finish. **7** (of the edge of cloth) without hem or selvage. □ **in the raw 1** in its natural state without mitigation (*life in the raw*). **2** naked. **touch on the raw** upset (a person) on a sensitive matter. [Old English]

Rawalpindi /rɔːlˈpɪndɪ/ city in N Pakistan, a centre of commerce with oil-refining, chemical, and other industries; pop. (est. 1995) 1 290 000.

raw-boned *adj.* gaunt.

raw deal *n.* harsh or unfair treatment.

rawhide *n.* **1** untanned hide. **2** rope or whip of this.

Rawlplug /ˈrɔːlplʌg/ *n. propr.* cylindrical plug for holding a screw or nail in masonry. [*Rawl*ings, name of the engineers who introduced it]

raw material *n.* material from which manufactured goods are made.

Rawson /ˈrɔːs(ə)n/ city in S Argentina, on the Patagonian coast, capital of Chubut province; pop. (1991) 19 161.

ray[1] *n.* **1** single line or narrow beam of light from a small or distant source. **2** straight line in which radiation travels to a given point. **3** (in *pl.*) radiation of a specified type (*X-rays*). **4** trace or beginning of an enlightening or cheering influence (*ray of hope*). **5** any of a set of radiating lines, parts, or things. **6** marginal floret of a composite flower, e.g. a daisy. [Latin RADIUS]

ray[2] *n.* large edible marine fish with a flat body and a long slender tail. [Latin *raia*]

ray[3] *n.* (also **re**) *Mus.* second note of a major scale. [Latin *resonare*, word arbitrarily taken]

rayon /ˈreɪɒn/ *n.* textile fibre or fabric made from cellulose. [from RAY[1]]

raze *v.* (also **rase**) (**-zing** or **-sing**) completely destroy; tear down (esp. *raze to the ground*). [Latin *rado ras-* scrape]

razor /ˈreɪzə(r)/ *n.* instrument with a sharp blade used in cutting hair, esp. shaving. [French *rasor*: related to RAZE]

razor-bill *n.* auk with a sharp-edged bill.

razor-blade *n.* flat piece of metal with a sharp edge, used in a safety razor.

razor-edge *n.* (also **razor's edge**) **1** keen edge. **2** sharp mountain-ridge. **3** critical situation. **4** sharp line of division.

razzle-dazzle /'ræzəl,dæz(ə)l/ *n.* (also **razzle**) *colloq.* **1** **a** excitement; bustle. **b** spree. **2** extravagant publicity. [reduplication of DAZZLE]

razzmatazz /,ræzmə'tæz/ *n. colloq.* **1** glamorous excitement, bustle. **2** spree. **3** insincere actions. [probably an alteration of RAZZLE-DAZZLE]

RB *international vehicle registration* Botswana.

Rb *symb.* rubidium.

RBI *abbr.* resource-based industry.

RC *–abbr.* Roman Catholic. *–international vehicle registration* Taiwan.

RCA *–abbr.* Radio Corporation of America. *–international vehicle registration* Central African Republic.

RCB *international vehicle registration* Republic of the Congo.

RCD *abbr.* Regional Cooperation for Development (association of Asian countries).

rcd. *abbr.* received.

RCH *international vehicle registration* Chile.

RD *abbr.* (also **R/D**) refer to drawer (on a cheque).

Rd. *abbr.* (also **Rd**) Road.

r.d. *abbr. Shipping* running days.

RD&D *abbr.* research, development, and demonstration.

RD&E *abbr.* research, development, and engineering.

RDBMS *abbr. Computing* relational database management system.

RDC *abbr.* Rural District Council.

RDD *abbr. US Marketing* random digital dialing.

r.d.d. *abbr.* required delivery date.

RDE *abbr.* Research and Development Establishment.

RDI *abbr.* Royal Designer for Industry (of the Royal Society of Arts).

RDPL *international civil aircraft marking* Laos.

RDT&E *abbr.* research, development, testing, and engineering.

RE *abbr.* **1** Religious Education. **2** Royal Engineers. **3** Royal Exchange.

Re *symb.* **1** rhenium. **2** (*pl.* **Rs**) Indian rupee.

re[1] /ri:/ *prep.* **1** in the matter of (as the first word in a heading). **2** *Commerce* about, concerning (in letters). [Latin, ablative of *res* thing]

re[2] var. of RAY[3].

re- *prefix* **1** attachable to almost any verb or its derivative, meaning: **a** once more; afresh, anew. **b** back; with return to a previous state. **2** (also **red-** before a vowel, as in *redolent*) in verbs and verbal derivatives denoting: **a** in return; mutually (*react*). **b** opposition (*resist*). **c** behind or after (*relic*). **d** retirement or secrecy (*recluse*). **e** off, away, down (*recede*; *relegate*; *repress*). **f** frequentative or intensive force (*redouble*; *resplendent*). **g** negative force (*recant*; *reveal*). [Latin]

■ **Usage** In sense 1, a hyphen is normally used when the word begins with *e* (*re-enact*), or to distinguish the compound from a more familiar one-word form (*re-cover* = cover again).

reach *–v.* **1** (often foll. by *out*) stretch out, extend. **2** (often foll. by *for*) stretch out the hand etc.; make a stretch or effort. **3** get as far as. **4** get to or attain. **5** make contact with the hand etc., or by telephone etc. (*could not be reached*). **6** hand, pass (*reach me that book*). **7** take with an outstretched hand. **8** *Naut.* sail with the wind abeam or abaft the beam. *–n.* **1** extent to which a hand etc. can be reached out, influence exerted, motion carried out, or mental powers used. **2** act of reaching out. **3** continuous extent, esp. of a river between two bends or of a canal between locks. **4** proportion of a total market that an advertiser hopes to reach at least once within a given period in an advertising campaign. **5** *Naut.* distance traversed in reaching. □ **reachable** *adj.* [Old English]

reach-me-down *n. colloq.* **1** ready-made garment. **2** = HAND-ME-DOWN.

reacquaint /,ri:ə'kweɪnt/ *v.* make acquainted again. □ **reacquaintance** *n.*

react /rɪ'ækt/ *v.* **1** (often foll. by *to*) respond to a stimulus; change or behave differently due to some influence (*reacted badly to the news*). **2** (often foll. by *against*) respond with repulsion to; tend in a reverse or contrary direction. **3** (foll. by *with*) (of a substance or particle) be the cause of chemical activity or interaction with another (*nitrous oxide reacts with the metal*). **4** (foll. by *with*) cause (a substance) to react with another.

reaction /rɪ'ækʃ(ə)n/ *n.* **1** reacting, response. **2** bad physical response to a drug etc. **3** occurrence of a condition after a period of its opposite. **4** tendency to oppose change or reform. **5** interaction of substances undergoing chemical change. **6** *Finance* reversal in a market trend as a result of overselling on a falling market (when some buyers are attracted by the low prices) or overbuying on a rising market (when some buyers are willing to take profits).

reactionary *–adj.* tending to oppose (esp. political) change or reform. *–n.* (*pl.* **-ies**) reactionary person.

reactivate /rɪ'æktɪ,veɪt/ *v.* (**-ting**) restore to a state of activity. □ **reactivation** /-'veɪʃ(ə)n/ *n.*

reactive /rɪ'æktɪv/ *adj.* **1** showing reaction. **2** reacting rather than taking the initiative. **3** susceptible to chemical reaction.

reactor *n.* **1** person or thing that reacts. **2** = NUCLEAR REACTOR.

read *–v.* (*past* and *past part.* **read** /red/) **1** (also *absol.*) reproduce mentally or (often foll. by *aloud*, *out*, *off*, etc.) vocally the written or printed words of (a book, author, etc.). **2** convert or be able to convert into the intended words or meaning (written or other symbols or the things expressed in this way) (*can't read music*). **3** understand by observing; interpret (*read me like a book*; *read his silence as consent*; *read my mind*; *reads tea-leaves*). **4** find (a thing) stated in print etc. (*read that you were leaving*). **5** (often foll. by *into*) assume as intended or deducible (*read too much into it*). **6** bring into a specified state by reading (*read myself to sleep*). **7** **a** (of a recording instrument) show (a specified figure etc.). **b** interpret (a recording instrument) (*read the meter*). **8** convey meaning when read; have a certain wording (*it reads persuasively*; *reads from left to right*). **9** sound or affect a hearer or reader when read (*the book reads like a parody*). **10** study by reading (esp. a subject at university). **11** (as **read** /red/ *adj.*) versed in a subject (esp. literature) by reading (*well-read person*). **12** *Computing* **a** sense and retrieve (data) from a storage medium, e.g. magnetic disk. **b** sense and interpret (data) on a credit card, document, etc. and convert it into an electrical signal that can be fed into a computer. **13** hear and understand (over a radio) (*are you reading me?*). **14** replace (a word etc.) with the correct one(s) (*for 'this' read 'these'*). *–n.* **1** spell of reading. **2** *colloq.* book etc. as regards readability (*is a good read*). □ **read between the lines** look for or find hidden meaning. **read up** (often followed by *on*) make a special study of (a subject). **take as read** treat (a thing) as if it has been agreed. [Old English]

readable *adj.* **1** able to be read. **2** interesting to read. □ **readability** /-'bɪlɪtɪ/ *n.*

readdress /,ri:ə'dres/ *v.* **1** change the address of (an item for posting). **2** address (a problem etc.) anew. **3** speak or write to anew.

reader *n.* **1** person who reads. **2** book intended to give reading practice, esp. in a foreign language. **3** device for producing an image that can be read from microfilm etc. **4** (**Reader**) university lecturer of the highest grade below professor. **5** publisher's employee who reports on submitted manuscripts. **6** printer's proof-corrector. **7** person appointed to read aloud, esp. in church.

readership *n.* **1** readers of a newspaper etc. **2** (also **Readership**) position of Reader.

readily /'redɪlɪ/ *adv.* **1** without showing reluctance, willingly. **2** without difficulty.

readiness *n.* **1** ready or prepared state. **2** willingness. **3** facility; promptness in argument or action.

reading *n.* **1 a** act of reading (*reading of the will*). **b** matter to be read (*made exciting reading*). **2** (in *comb.*) used for reading (*reading-lamp*; *reading-room*). **3** literary knowledge. **4** entertainment at which a play, poems, etc., are read. **5** figure etc. shown by a recording instrument. **6** interpretation or view taken (*what is your reading of the facts?*). **7** interpretation made (of drama, music, etc.). **8** each of the successive occasions on which a bill must be presented to a legislature for acceptance. [Old English: related to READ]

readjust /ˌriːəˈdʒʌst/ *v.* adjust again or to a former state. □ **readjustment** *n.*

readmit /ˌriːədˈmɪt/ *v.* (**-tt-**) admit again. □ **readmission** *n.*

read-only memory see ROM.

readopt /ˌriːəˈdɒpt/ *v.* adopt again. □ **readoption** *n.*

read-out *n. Computing* **1** information retrieved from main store after processing and displayed on a screen or copied into backing store. **2** process of reading data from a memory device.

ready /ˈredɪ/ –*adj.* (**-ier, -iest**) (usu. *predic.*) **1** with preparations complete (*dinner is ready*). **2** in a fit state. **3** willing, inclined, or resolved (*he is always ready to complain*). **4** within reach; easily secured (*ready source of income*). **5** fit for immediate use. **6** immediate, unqualified (*found ready acceptance*). **7** prompt (*is always ready with excuses*). **8** (foll. by *to* + infin.) about to (*ready to burst*). **9** provided beforehand. –*adv.* (usu. in *comb.*) beforehand; so as not to require doing when the time comes for use etc. (*is ready packed*; *ready-mixed concrete*; *ready-made family*). –*n.* (*pl.* **-ies**) *slang* (prec. by *the*) = READY MONEY. –*v.* (**-ies, -ied**) make ready, prepare. □ **at the ready** ready for action. **make ready** prepare. [Old English]

ready-made *adj.* (also **ready-to-wear**) (esp. of clothes) made in a standard size, not to measure.

ready money *n.* **1** actual coin or notes. **2** payment on the spot.

ready reckoner *n.* book or table listing standard numerical calculations as used esp. in commerce.

reaffirm /ˌriːəˈfɜːm/ *v.* affirm again. □ **reaffirmation** /-ˌæfəˈmeɪʃ(ə)n/ *n.*

reafforest /ˌriːəˈfɒrɪst/ *v.* replant (former forest land) with trees. □ **reafforestation** /-ˈsteɪʃ(ə)n/ *n.*

reagent /riːˈeɪdʒ(ə)nt/ *n. Chem.* substance used to cause a reaction, esp. to detect another substance.

real[1] –*adj.* **1** actually existing or occurring. **2** genuine; rightly so called; not artificial. **3** *Law* consisting of immovable property such as land or houses (*real property*). **4** appraised by purchasing power (*real value*). **5** *Math.* (of a quantity) having no imaginary part (see IMAGINARY 2). –*adv. Scot.* & *US colloq.* really, very. □ **for real** *colloq.* seriously, in earnest. **the real thing** (of an object or emotion) genuine, not inferior. [Anglo-French and Latin *realis* from *res* thing]

real[2] /reɪˈɑːl/ *n.* **1** standard monetary unit of Brazil. **2** *hist.* coin and monetary unit in Spanish-speaking countries. [Spanish: related to ROYAL]

◆ **real account** *n.* ledger account for some types of property (e.g. land and buildings, plant, investments, stock) to distinguish it from a nominal account, which would be for revenue or expense items (e.g. sales, motor expenses, discount received, etc.). This distinction is now largely obsolete and both sets of accounts are maintained in the same ledger, usu. referred to as the nominal ledger.

real ale *n.* beer regarded as brewed in a traditional way.

◆ **real effect** see REAL TERMS.

◆ **real estate** *n.* esp. *US* = REAL PROPERTY.

realign /ˌriːəˈlaɪn/ *v.* **1** align again. **2** regroup in politics etc. □ **realignment** *n.*

◆ **real investment** *n.* investment in capital equipment (e.g. a factory, plant and machinery, etc.) or valuable social assets (e.g. a school, a dam, etc.) rather than in such paper assets as securities, debentures, etc.

realism *n.* **1** practice of regarding things in their true nature and dealing with them as they are. **2** fidelity to nature in representation; the showing of life etc. as it is. **3** *Philos.* doctrine that abstract concepts have an objective existence. □ **realist** *n.*

realistic /rɪəˈlɪstɪk/ *adj.* **1** regarding things as they are; following a policy of realism. **2** based on facts rather than ideals. □ **realistically** *adv.*

reality /rɪˈælɪtɪ/ *n.* (*pl.* **-ies**) **1** what is real or existent or underlies appearances. **2** (foll. by *of*) the real nature of. **3** real existence; state of being real. **4** resemblance to an original. □ **in reality** in fact. [medieval Latin or French: related to REAL[1]]

◆ **realizable assets** *n.pl.* = LIQUID ASSETS.

◆ **realization account** *n.* account used to record the disposal of an asset or assets and to determine the profit or loss on the disposal. The principle of realization accounts is that they are debited with the book value of the asset and credited with the sale price of the asset. Any balance therefore represents the profit or loss on disposal.

realize *v.* (also **-ise**) (**-zing** or **-sing**) **1** (often foll. by *that*) be fully aware of; conceive as real. **2** understand clearly. **3** present as real. **4** convert into actuality. **5 a** convert into money. **b** acquire (profit). **c** be sold for (a specified price). □ **realizable** *adj.* **realization** /-ˈzeɪʃ(ə)n/ *n.*

◆ **realized profit (or loss)** *n.* profit (or loss) that has arisen from a completed transaction (usu. the sale of goods or services or other assets). In accounting terms, a profit is usu. regarded as having been realized when an asset has been legally disposed of and not when the cash is received, since if an asset is sold on credit the asset being disposed of is exchanged for another asset, a debt. The debt may or may not prove good but that is regarded as a separate transaction.

real life *n.* **1** life lived by actual people. **2** (*attrib.*) (**real-life**) actual, not fictional (*her real-life husband*).

reallocate /riːˈæləˌkeɪt/ *v.* (**-ting**) allocate again or differently. □ **reallocation** /-ˈkeɪʃ(ə)n/ *n.*

really /ˈrɪəlɪ/ *adv.* **1** in reality. **2** very (*really useful*). **3** indeed, I assure you. **4** expression of mild protest or surprise.

realm /relm/ *n.* **1** *formal* kingdom. **2** sphere, domain (*the realm of myth*). [Latin REGIMEN]

real money *n.* current coin; cash.

◆ **real property** *n.* (also **realty**, **real estate** esp. *US*) property consisting of land or buildings as distinct from personal property (personalty).

real tennis *n.* original form of tennis played on an indoor court.

◆ **real terms** *n.pl.* representation of the value of a good or service in terms of money, taking into account fluctuations in the price level. Economists are usu. interested in the relationship between the prices of goods in real terms, i.e. by adjusting prices according to a price index or some other measure of inflation. In neoclassical economics, any adjustment in the relative prices of goods leads to changes in the quantities supplied and demanded: this is referred to as a **real effect**. When assessing a government policy, economists are interested in real effects.

real time *n.* **1** actual time during which a process occurs. **2** (*attrib.*) (**real-time**) *Computing* (of a system) in which the response time is the actual time during which an event occurs. Real-time operation is used when it is essential that a computer coordinates its activities with external events (e.g. in the control of industrial processes) or when any delay in response should be minimal (e.g. in such point of sale terminals as airline reservation systems).

◆ **realtor** *n. US* estate agent or land agent.

◆ **realty** /'riːəltɪ/ *n.* = REAL PROPERTY.

◆ **real value** *n.* monetary value expressed in real terms.

◆ **real wages** *n.pl.* wages expressed in real terms, i.e. the quantity of goods and services a money wage will buy at any particular time. If money wages increase faster than the price level in an economy the wage-earners are better off; otherwise they are not.

---

ream *n.* **1** twenty quires of paper. **2** (in *pl.*) large quantity of writing. [Arabic, = bundle]

reanimate /riː'ænɪˌmeɪt/ *v.* (**-ting**) **1** restore to life. **2** restore to activity or liveliness. □ **reanimation** /-'meɪʃ(ə)n/ *n.*

reap *v.* **1** cut or gather (a crop, esp. grain) as a harvest. **2** harvest the crop of (a field etc.). **3** receive as the consequence of one's own or others' actions. [Old English]

reaper *n.* **1** person who reaps. **2** reaping machine. **3** (**the Reaper** or **grim Reaper**) death personified.

reappear /ˌriːə'pɪə(r)/ *v.* appear again or as previously. □ **reappearance** *n.*

reapply /ˌriːə'plaɪ/ *v.* (**-ies, -ied**) apply again, esp. submit a further application (for a position etc.). □ **reapplication** /-æplɪ'keɪʃ(ə)n/ *n.*

reappoint /ˌriːə'pɔɪnt/ *v.* appoint to a position previously held. □ **reappointment** *n.*

reapportion /ˌriːə'pɔːʃ(ə)n/ *v.* apportion again or differently.

reappraise /ˌriːə'preɪz/ *v.* (**-sing**) appraise or assess again or differently. □ **reappraisal** *n.*

rear[1] *–n.* **1** back part of anything. **2** space behind, or position at the back of, anything. **3** *colloq.* buttocks. *–adj.* at the back. □ **bring up the rear** come last. [probably from REARWARD or REARGUARD]

rear[2] *v.* **1 a** bring up and educate (children). **b** breed and care for (animals). **c** cultivate (crops). **2** (of a horse etc.) raise itself on its hind legs. **3 a** set upright. **b** build. **c** hold upwards. **4** extend to a great height. [Old English]

rear admiral *n.* naval officer ranking below vice admiral.

rearguard *n.* body of troops detached to protect the rear, esp. in retreats. [French *reregarde*]

rearguard action *n.* **1** engagement undertaken by a rearguard. **2** defensive stand or struggle, esp. when losing.

rear-lamp *n.* (also **rear-light**) usu. red light at the rear of a vehicle.

rearm /riː'ɑːm/ *v.* (also *absol.*) arm again, esp. with improved weapons. □ **rearmament** *n.*

rearmost *adj.* furthest back.

rearrange /ˌriːə'reɪndʒ/ *v.* (**-ging**) arrange again in a different way. □ **rearrangement** *n.*

rearrest /ˌriːə'rest/ *–v.* arrest again. *–n.* rearresting or being rearrested.

rearward /'rɪəwəd/ *–n.* (esp. in prepositional phrases) rear (*to the rearward of; in the rearward*). *–adj.* to the rear. *–adv.* (also **rearwards**) towards the rear. [Anglo-French *rerewarde* = REARGUARD]

reason /'riːz(ə)n/ *–n.* **1** motive, cause, or justification. **2** fact adduced or serving as this. **3** intellectual faculty by which conclusions are drawn from premisses. **4** sanity (*lost his reason*). **5** sense; sensible conduct; what is right, practical, or practicable; moderation. *–v.* **1** form or try to reach conclusions by connected thought. **2** (foll. by *with*) use argument with (a person) by way of persuasion. **3** (foll. by *that*) conclude or assert in argument. **4** (foll. by *into, out of*) persuade or move by argument. **5** (foll. by *out*) think out (consequences etc.). **6** (often as **reasoned** *adj.*) express in logical or argumentative form. **7** embody reason in (an amendment etc.). □ **by reason of** owing to. **in** (or **within**) **reason** within the bounds of moderation. **with reason** justifiably. [Latin *ratio*]

reasonable *adj.* **1** having sound judgement; moderate; ready to listen to reason. **2** not absurd. **3 a** not greatly less or more than might be expected. **b** inexpensive. **c** tolerable, fair. □ **reasonableness** *n.* **reasonably** *adv.*

reassemble /ˌriːə'semb(ə)l/ *v.* (**-ling**) assemble again or into a former state. □ **reassembly** *n.*

reassert /ˌriːə'sɜːt/ *v.* assert again, esp. with renewed emphasis. □ **reassertion** *n.*

reassess /ˌriːə'ses/ *v.* assess again or differently. □ **reassessment** *n.*

reassign /ˌriːə'saɪn/ *v.* assign again or differently. □ **reassignment** *n.*

reassure /ˌriːə'ʃʊə(r)/ *v.* (**-ring**) **1** restore confidence to; dispel the apprehensions of. **2** confirm in an opinion or impression. □ **reassurance** *n.* **reassuring** *adj.*

reawaken /ˌriːə'weɪkən/ *v.* awaken again.

rebate[1] /'riːbeɪt/ *n.* **1** partial refund (*tax rebate*). **2 a** deduction from a sum to be paid; discount. **b** discount allowed on a bill of exchange that is paid before it matures. [French *rabattre*: related to RE-, ABATE]

rebate[2] /'riːbeɪt/ *n.* & *v.* (**-ting**) = RABBET.

rebel *–n.* /'reb(ə)l/ **1** person who fights against, resists, or refuses allegiance to, the established government. **2** person or thing that resists authority or control. *–attrib. adj.* /'reb(ə)l/ **1** rebellious. **2** of rebels. **3** in rebellion. *–v.* /rɪ'bel/ (**-ll-**; *US* **-l-**) (usu. foll. by *against*) **1** act as a rebel; revolt. **2** feel or display repugnance. [Latin: related to RE-, *bellum* war]

rebellion /rɪ'beljən/ *n.* open resistance to authority, esp. organized armed resistance to an established government. [Latin: related to REBEL]

rebellious /rɪ'beljəs/ *adj.* **1** tending to rebel. **2** in rebellion. **3** defying lawful authority. **4** (of a thing) unmanageable, refractory. □ **rebelliously** *adv.* **rebelliousness** *n.*

rebid /'riːbɪd/ *–v.* /also riː'bɪd/ (**-dd-**; *past* and *past part.* **rebid**) bid again. *–n.* **1** act of rebidding. **2** bid so made.

rebind /riː'baɪnd/ *v.* (*past* and *past part.* **rebound**) bind (esp. a book) again or differently.

rebirth /riː'bɜːθ/ *n.* **1** new incarnation. **2** spiritual enlightenment. **3** revival. □ **reborn** /riː'bɔːn/ *adj.*

reboot /riː'buːt/ *v.* (often *absol.*) *Computing* boot up (a system) again, i.e. load a new copy of the operating system from backing store and allow the system a fresh start.

rebound *–v.* /rɪ'baʊnd/ **1** spring back after impact. **2** (foll. by *upon*) (of an action) have an adverse effect upon (the doer). *–n.* /'riːbaʊnd/ act of rebounding; recoil, reaction. □ **on the rebound** while still recovering from an emotional shock, esp. rejection by a lover. [French *rebonder*: related to BOUND[1]]

rebroadcast /riː'brɔːdkɑːst/ *–v.* (*past* **-cast** or **-casted**; *past part.* **-cast**) broadcast again. *–n.* repeat broadcast.

rebuff /rɪ'bʌf/ *–n.* **1** rejection of one who makes advances, proffers help, shows interest, makes a request, etc. **2** snub. *–v.* give a rebuff to. [French from Italian]

rebuild /riː'bɪld/ *v.* (*past* and *past part.* **rebuilt**) build again or differently.

rebuke /rɪ'bjuːk/ *–v.* (**-king**) express sharp disapproval to (a person) for a fault; censure. *–n.* rebuking or being rebuked. [Anglo-French]

rebus /'riːbəs/ *n.* (*pl.* **rebuses**) representation of a word (esp. a name) by pictures etc. suggesting its parts. [Latin *rebus*, ablative pl. of *res* thing]

rebut /rɪ'bʌt/ *v.* (**-tt-**) **1** refute or disprove (evidence or a charge). **2** force or turn back; check. □ **rebuttal** *n.* [Anglo-French *rebuter*: related to BUTT[1]]

REC /rek/ *abbr.* regional electricity company.

rec *n. colloq.* recreation ground. [abbreviation]

recalcitrant /rɪ'kælsɪtrənt/ *adj.* **1** obstinately disobedient. **2** objecting to restraint. □ **recalcitrance** *n.* [Latin *recalcitro* kick out, from *calx* heel]

recall /rɪ'kɔːl/ *–v.* **1** summon to return. **2** recollect, remember. **3** bring back to memory; serve as a reminder of. **4** revoke or annul (an action or decision). **5** revive, resuscitate. **6** take back (a gift). *–n.* /also 'ri:kOl/ **1** summons to come back. **2** act of remembering. **3** ability to remember. **4** possibility of recalling, esp. in the sense of revoking (*beyond recall*).

♦ **recall test** *n.* test used in marketing research to ascertain how much consumers can remember about an advertisement. **Spontaneous tests** reveal which advertisements a respondent can remember without guidance or assistance. **Prompted** (or **aided**) **tests** indicate which advertisements respondents can remember from a series they have seen in a campaign.

recant /rɪ'kænt/ *v.* (also *absol.*) withdraw and renounce (a former belief or statement) as erroneous or heretical. □ **recantation** /ˌri:kæn'teɪʃ(ə)n/ *n.* [Latin: related to CHANT]

recap /'ri:kæp/ *colloq.* *–v.* (**-pp-**) recapitulate. *–n.* recapitulation. [abbreviation]

recapitulate /ˌri:kə'pɪtjʊˌleɪt/ *v.* (**-ting**) **1** go briefly through again; summarize. **2** go over the main points or headings of. [Latin: related to CAPITAL]

recapitulation /ˌri:kəˌpɪtjʊ'leɪʃ(ə)n/ *n.* **1** act of recapitulating. **2** *Mus.* part of a movement in which themes are restated. [Latin: related to RECAPITULATE]

recapture /ri:'kæptʃə(r)/ *–v.* (**-ring**) **1** capture again; recover by capture. **2** re-experience (a past emotion etc.). *–n.* act of recapturing.

recast /ri:'kɑ:st/ *–v.* (*past* and *past part.* **recast**) **1** cast again (a play, net, votes, etc.). **2** put into a new form; improve the arrangement of. *–n.* **1** recasting. **2** recast form.

recce /'rekɪ/ *colloq.* *–n.* reconnaissance. *–v.* (**recced, recceing**) reconnoitre. [abbreviation]

recd *abbr.* received.

recede /rɪ'si:d/ *v.* (**-ding**) **1** go or shrink back or further off. **2** be left at an increasing distance by an observer's motion. **3** slope backwards (*a receding chin*). **4** decline in force or value. [Latin *recedere -cess-*: related to CEDE]

receipt /rɪ'si:t/ *–n.* **1** receiving or being received. **2** written acknowledgement of payment received. **3** (usu. in *pl.*) amount of money etc. received. **4** *archaic* recipe. *–v.* place a written or printed receipt on (a bill). □ **in receipt of** having received. [Anglo-French *receite*: related to RECEIVE]

♦ **receivables** /rɪ'si:vəb(ə)lz/ *n.pl.* sums of money owing to a business from persons or businesses to whom goods or services have been supplied in the normal course of trade.

receive *v.* (**-ving**) **1** take or accept (a thing offered, sent, or given). **2** acquire; be provided with. **3** have conferred or inflicted on one. **4** react to (news, a play, etc.) in a particular way. **5 a** stand the force or weight of. **b** bear up against; encounter with opposition. **6** consent to hear (a confession or oath) or consider (a petition). **7** (also *absol.*) accept (stolen goods knowingly). **8** admit; consent or prove able to hold; provide accommodation for. **9** (of a receptacle) be able to hold. **10** greet or welcome, esp. in a specified manner. **11** entertain as a guest etc. **12** admit to membership. **13** convert (broadcast signals) into sound or pictures. **14** (often as **received** *adj.*) give credit to; accept as authoritative or true. □ **be at** (or **on) the receiving end** *colloq.* bear the brunt of something unpleasant. [Latin *recipio -cept-* get back again]

♦ **received bill** *n.* bill of lading that has been stamped 'Goods received for shipment'. This does not imply that they have been loaded but that they have been received for loading. Cf. SHIPPED BILL.

received pronunciation *n.* the form of educated spoken English used in southern England.

receiver *n.* **1** person or thing that receives. **2** part of a machine or instrument that receives something (esp. the part of a telephone that contains the earpiece). **3 a** = OFFICIAL RECEIVER. **b** person appointed by a court to administer property under litigation. Where there is a floating charge over the whole of a company's property and a crystallizing event has occurred, an **administrative receiver** may be appointed to manage the whole of the company's business. This person will have wide powers under the Insolvency Act to carry on the business of the company, take possession of its property, commence liquidation, etc. A receiver appointed in respect of a fixed charge can deal with the property covered by the charge only, and has no power to manage the company's business. **4** radio or television receiving apparatus. **5** person who receives stolen goods.

♦ **receivership** *n.* **1** situation in which a lender holds a mortgage or charge (esp. a floating charge) over a company's property and, in consequence of a default by the company, a receiver is appointed to realize the assets charged in order to repay the debt. **2** office or function of a receiver, esp. the official receiver.

♦ **receiving order** *n. hist.* bankruptcy order (see BANKRUPTCY).

recent /'ri:s(ə)nt/ *–adj.* **1** not long past; that happened, began to exist, or existed, lately. **2** not long established; lately begun; modern. **3** (**Recent**) *Geol.* of the most recent epoch of the Quaternary period. *–n.* (**Recent**) *Geol.* this epoch. □ **recently** *adv.* [Latin *recens -ent-*]

receptacle /rɪ'septək(ə)l/ *n.* **1** containing vessel, place, or space. **2** *Bot.* enlarged and modified area of the stem apex which bears the flower. [Latin: related to RECEIVE]

reception /rɪ'sepʃ(ə)n/ *n.* **1** receiving or being received. **2** way in which a person or thing is received (*cool reception*). **3** social occasion for receiving guests, esp. after a wedding. **4** place where guests or clients etc. report on arrival at a hotel, office, etc. **5 a** receiving of broadcast signals. **b** quality of this. [Latin: related to RECEIVE]

receptionist *n.* person employed to receive guests, clients, etc.

reception room *n.* room for receiving guests, clients, etc.

receptive /rɪ'septɪv/ *adj.* able or quick to receive impressions or ideas. □ **receptively** *adv.* **receptiveness** *n.* **receptivity** /ˌri:sep'tɪvɪtɪ/ *n.* [French or medieval Latin: related to RECEIVE]

recess /rɪ'ses, 'ri:ses/ *–n.* **1** space set back in a wall. **2** (often in *pl.*) remote or secret place. **3** temporary cessation from work, esp. of Parliament. *–v.* **1** make a recess in. **2** place in a recess. **3** *US* take a recess; adjourn. [Latin *recessus*: related to RECEDE]

recession /rɪ'seʃ(ə)n/ *n.* **1** slow-down or fall in the rate of growth of gross national product, indicating a temporary decline in economic activity or prosperity. A severe recession is called a depression. Economic growth usu. follows a cycle from boom to recession and back again (see BUSINESS CYCLE). Recession is associated with falling levels of investment, rising unemployment, and sometimes falling prices. The conditions of the major economies in the 1980s has been called **growth recession**, since despite very high levels of unemployment, economic growth continued at a reasonable pace. Interventionist economists, whether Keynesian or monetarist, advocate government intervention through fiscal or monetary stimulus during recession (see also NEW CLASSICAL MACROECONOMICS). **2** receding or withdrawal from a place or point. [Latin: related to RECESS]

recessional *–adj.* sung while the clergy and choir withdraw after a service. *–n.* recessional hymn.

recessive /rɪ'sesɪv/ *adj.* **1** tending to recede. **2** (of an inherited characteristic) appearing in offspring only when not masked by an inherited dominant characteristic.

recharge *–v.* /ri:'tʃɑ:dʒ/ (**-ging**) charge (a battery etc.) again or be recharged. *–n.* /'ri:tʃɑ:dʒ/ recharging or being recharged. □ **rechargeable** /ri:'tʃɑ:dʒəb(ə)l/ *adj.*

recheck *–v.* /ri:'tʃek/ check again. *–n.* /'ri:tʃek/ further check or inspection.

recherché /rə'ʃeəʃeɪ/ *adj.* **1** carefully sought out; rare or exotic. **2** far-fetched. [French]

rechristen /riːˈkrɪs(ə)n/ *v.* **1** christen again. **2** give a new name to.

recidivist /rɪˈsɪdɪvɪst/ *n.* person who relapses into crime. □ **recidivism** *n.* [Latin *recidivus* falling back: related to RECEDE]

Recife /rəˈsiːfeɪ/ (formerly **Pernambuco** /ˌpɜːnæmˈbuːkəʊ/) port in NE Brazil, on the Atlantic coast; there are sugar-refining and distilling industries, and sugar and cotton are exported; pop. (1991) 1 296 995.

recipe /ˈresɪpɪ/ *n.* **1** statement of the ingredients and procedure required for preparing a cooked dish. **2** (foll. by *for*) certain means to (an outcome) (*recipe for disaster*). [2nd sing. imperative of Latin *recipio* RECEIVE]

recipient /rɪˈsɪpɪənt/ *n.* person who receives something. [Italian or Latin: related to RECEIVE]

reciprocal /rɪˈsɪprək(ə)l/ –*adj.* **1** in return (*a reciprocal greeting*). **2** mutual. **3** *Gram.* (of a pronoun) expressing mutual relation (as in *each other*). –*n. Math.* expression or function so related to another that their product is unity (*$^1/_2$ is the reciprocal of 2*). □ **reciprocally** *adv.* [Latin *reciprocus* moving to and fro]

reciprocate /rɪˈsɪprəˌkeɪt/ *v.* (**-ting**) **1** requite (affection etc.). **2** (foll. by *with*) give in return. **3** give and receive mutually; interchange. **4** (of a part of a machine) move backwards and forwards. □ **reciprocation** /-ˈkeɪʃ(ə)n/ *n.*

reciprocity /ˌresɪˈprɒsɪtɪ/ *n.* **1** condition of being reciprocal. **2** mutual action. **3** form of negotiation in which one party agrees to make a concession in return for a reciprocal, or broadly equivalent, action by the other. Most international economic negotiations take this form. For example, agreements to lower protectionist barriers over markets are nearly always done on a reciprocal basis.

recital /rɪˈsaɪt(ə)l/ *n.* **1** reciting or being recited. **2** concert of classical music given by a soloist or small group. **3** (foll. by *of*) detailed account of (connected things or facts); narrative.

recitation /ˌresɪˈteɪʃ(ə)n/ *n.* **1** reciting. **2** thing recited.

recitative /ˌresɪtəˈtiːv/ *n.* musical declamation in the narrative and dialogue parts of opera and oratorio. [Italian *recitativo*: related to RECITE]

recite /rɪˈsaɪt/ *v.* (**-ting**) **1** repeat aloud or declaim (a poem or passage) from memory. **2** give a recitation. **3** enumerate. [Latin *recito* read out]

reckless /ˈreklɪs/ *adj.* disregarding the consequences or danger etc.; rash. □ **recklessly** *adv.* **recklessness** *n.* [Old English *reck* concern oneself]

reckon /ˈrekən/ *v.* **1** (often foll. by *that*) be of the considered opinion; think. **2** consider or regard (*reckoned to be the best*). **3** count or compute by calculation. **4** (foll. by *in*) count in or include in computation. **5** make calculations; add up an account or sum. **6** (foll. by *on*) rely on, count on, or base plans on. **7** (foll. by *with* or *without*) take (or fail to take) into account. [Old English]

reckoning *n.* **1** counting or calculating. **2** consideration or opinion. **3** settlement of an account.

reclaim /rɪˈkleɪm/ *v.* **1** seek the return of (one's property, rights, etc.). **2** bring (land) under cultivation, esp. from being under water. **3** win back or away from vice, error, or a waste condition.□ **reclaimable** *adj.* **reclamation** /ˌrekləˈmeɪʃ(ə)n/ *n.* [Latin *reclamare* cry out against]

reclassify /riːˈklæsɪˌfaɪ/ *v.* (**-ies, -ied**) classify again or differently. □ **reclassification** /-fɪˈkeɪʃ(ə)n/ *n.*

recline /rɪˈklaɪn/ *v.* (**-ning**) assume or be in a horizontal or relaxed leaning position. [Latin *reclino*]

reclothe /riːˈkləʊð/ *v.* (**-thing**) clothe again or differently.

recluse /rɪˈkluːs/ *n.* person given to or living in seclusion or isolation; hermit. □ **reclusive** *adj.* [Latin *recludo -clus-* shut away]

recognition /ˌrekəgˈnɪʃ(ə)n/ *n.* recognizing or being recognized. [Latin: related to RECOGNIZE]

recognizance /rɪˈkɒgnɪz(ə)ns/ *n.* **1** bond by which a person undertakes before a court or magistrate to observe some condition, e.g. to appear when summoned. **2** sum pledged as surety for this. [French: related to RE-]

recognize /ˈrekəgˌnaɪz/ *v.* (also **-ise**) (**-zing** or **-sing**) **1** identify as already known. **2** realize or discover the nature of. **3** (foll. by *that*) realize or admit. **4** acknowledge the existence, validity, character, or claims of. **5** show appreciation of; reward. **6** (foll. by *as, for*) treat. □ **recognizable** *adj.* [Latin *recognosco*]

♦ **Recognized Investment Exchange** *n.* (also **RIE**) body authorized in the UK to conduct investment management on behalf of clients, with the approval of the Securities and Investment Board. RIEs include the International Petroleum Exchange, London Commodity Exchange, London International Financial Futures and Options Exchange, London Stock Exchange, and the London Metal Exchange.

♦ **Recognized Professional Body** *n.* (also **RPB**) organization registered with the Securities and Investment Board as having statutory recognition for regulating their professions. The RPBs are the Chartered Association of Certified Accountants, Institute of Actuaries, Institute of Chartered Accountants in England and Wales, Institute of Chartered Accountants in Ireland, Institute of Chartered Accountants for Scotland, the Insurance Brokers Registration Council, the Law Society, the Law Society of Northern Ireland, and the Law Society of Scotland.

---

recoil /rɪˈkɔɪl/ –*v.* **1** suddenly move or spring back in fear, horror, or disgust. **2** shrink mentally in this way. **3** rebound after an impact. **4** (foll. by *on, upon*) have an adverse reactive effect on (the originator). **5** (of a gun) be driven backwards by its discharge. –*n.* /also ˈriːkɔɪl/ act or sensation of recoiling. [French *reculer* from Latin *culus* buttocks]

recollect /ˌrekəˈlekt/ *v.* **1** remember. **2** succeed in remembering; call to mind. [Latin *recolligo*: related to COLLECT[1]]

recollection /ˌrekəˈlekʃ(ə)n/ *n.* **1** act or power of recollecting. **2** thing recollected. **3 a** person's memory. **b** time over which memory extends (*happened within my recollection*). [French or medieval Latin: related to RECOLLECT]

recolour /riːˈkʌlə(r)/ *v.* colour again or differently.

recombine /ˌriːkəmˈbaɪn/ *v.* (**-ning**) combine again or differently.

recommence /ˌriːkəˈmens/ *v.* (**-cing**) begin again. □ **recommencement** *n.*

recommend /ˌrekəˈmend/ *v.* **1** suggest as fit for some purpose or use. **2** advise as a course of action etc. **3** (of qualities, conduct, etc.) make acceptable or desirable. **4** (foll. by *to*) commend or entrust (to a person or a person's care). □ **recommendation** /-ˈdeɪʃ(ə)n/ *n.* [medieval Latin: related to RE-]

♦ **recommended retail price** *n.* (also **RRP, manufacturer's recommended price, MRP**) price that a manufacturer recommends as the retail price for a product. The manufacturer has no legal power to enforce this recommendation unless an agreement exists under the Restrictive Trade Practices Act (1976). See also RESALE PRICE MAINTENANCE.

---

recompense /ˈrekəmˌpens/ –*v.* (**-sing**) **1** make amends to (a person) or for (a loss etc.). **2** requite; reward or punish (a person or action). –*n.* **1** reward, requital. **2** retribution. [Latin: related to COMPENSATE]

reconcile /ˈrekənˌsaɪl/ *v.* (**-ling**) **1** make friendly again after an estrangement. **2** (usu. in *refl.* or *passive*; foll. by *to*) make acquiescent or contentedly submissive to (something disagreeable). **3** settle (a quarrel etc.). **4 a** harmonize, make compatible. **b** show the compatibility of by argument or in practice. □ **reconcilable** *adj.* **reconciliation** /-ˌsɪlɪˈeɪʃ(ə)n/ *n.* [Latin: related to CONCILIATE]

recondite /ˈrekənˌdaɪt/ *adj.* **1** (of a subject or knowledge) abstruse, out of the way, little known. **2** (of an author or style) dealing in abstruse knowledge or allusions, obscure. [Latin *recondo -dit-* put away]

recondition /ˌriːkənˈdɪʃ(ə)n/ *v.* overhaul, renovate, make usable again.

reconnaissance /rɪˈkɒnɪs(ə)ns/ *n.* **1** survey of a region, esp. to locate an enemy or ascertain strategic features. **2** preliminary survey. [French: related to RECONNOITRE]

reconnect /ˌriːkəˈnekt/ *v.* connect again. □ **reconnection** *n.*

reconnoitre /ˌrekəˈnɔɪtə(r)/ *v.* (*US* **reconnoiter**) (**-ring**) make a reconnaissance (of). [French: related to RECOGNIZE]

reconquer /riːˈkɒŋkə(r)/ *v.* conquer again. □ **reconquest** *n.*

R.Econ.S. *abbr.* Royal Economic Society.

reconsider /ˌriːkənˈsɪdə(r)/ *v.* consider again, esp. for a possible change of decision. □ **reconsideration** /-ˈreɪʃ(ə)n/ *n.*

reconstitute /riːˈkɒnstɪˌtjuːt/ *v.* (**-ting**) **1** reconstruct. **2** reorganize. **3** rehydrate (dried food etc.). □ **reconstitution** /-ˈtjuːʃ(ə)n/ *n.*

reconstruct /ˌriːkənˈstrʌkt/ *v.* **1** build again. **2 a** form an impression of (past events) by assembling the evidence for them. **b** re-enact (a crime). **3** reorganize. □ **reconstruction** *n.*

reconvene /ˌriːkənˈviːn/ *v.* (**-ning**) convene again, esp. after a pause in proceedings.

reconvert /ˌriːkənˈvɜːt/ *v.* convert back to a former state. □ **reconversion** *n.*

recopy /riːˈkɒpɪ/ *v.* (**-ies**, **-ied**) copy again.

record –*n.* /ˈrekɔːd/ **1 a** piece of evidence or information constituting an (esp. official) account of something that has occurred, been said, etc. **b** document etc. preserving this. **2** state of being set down or preserved in writing etc. **3** (in full **gramophone record**) disc carrying recorded sound in grooves on each surface, for reproduction by a record-player. **4** official report of the proceedings and judgement in a court of justice. **5 a** facts known about a person's past. **b** list of a person's previous criminal convictions. **6** (often *attrib.*) best performance (esp. in sport) or most remarkable event of its kind on record. **7** object serving as a memorial; portrait. **8** *Computing* collection of related items of data treated as a unit within a data file or database. For example, a company may keep a file of payroll data, with one record per employee. Records are usu. divided into **fields**, one field for each item of data (e.g. name, salary, tax code, etc.). –*v.* /rɪˈkɔːd/ **1** set down in writing or some other permanent form for later reference. **2** convert (sound, a broadcast, etc.) into permanent form for later reproduction. □ **for the record** as an official statement etc. **go on record** state one's opinion openly, so that it is recorded. **have a record** have a recorded criminal conviction or convictions. **off the record** unofficially, confidentially. **on record** officially recorded; publicly known. [Latin *cor cordis* heart]

record-breaking *attrib. adj.* that breaks a record.

recorded delivery *n.* Post Office service in which the dispatch and receipt of an item are recorded on payment of an extra fee.

recorder /rɪˈkɔːdə(r)/ *n.* **1** apparatus for recording, esp. a video or tape recorder. **2** (also **Recorder**) barrister or solicitor of at least ten years' standing, serving as a part-time judge. **3** wooden or plastic wind instrument with holes covered by the fingers. **4** keeper of records.

record-holder *n.* person who holds a record.

recording *n.* **1** process by which audio or video signals are recorded for later reproduction. **2** material or a programme recorded.

recordist *n.* person who records sound.

record-player *n.* apparatus for reproducing sound from gramophone records.

recount /rɪˈkaʊnt/ *v.* **1** narrate. **2** tell in detail. [Anglo-French *reconter*: related to RE-, COUNT[1]]

re-count –*v.* /riːˈkaʊnt/ count again. –*n.* /ˈriːkaʊnt/ re-counting, esp. of votes in an election.

recoup /rɪˈkuːp/ *v.* **1** recover or regain (a loss). **2** compensate or reimburse for a loss. □ **recoupment** *n.* [French *recouper* cut back]

recourse /rɪˈkɔːs, ˈriː-/ *n.* **1** resort to a possible source of help. **2** person or thing resorted to. **3** right to demand payment. □ **have recourse to** turn to (a person or thing) for help. **without recourse** words written on a bill of exchange indicating that, in the event of non-payment, the holder has no recourse to the person from whom it was bought. If these words do not appear on the bill, the holder does have recourse to the drawer or endorser if the bill is dishonoured at maturity. [Latin: related to COURSE]

♦ **recourse agreement** *n.* agreement between a hire-purchase company and a retailer, in which the retailer undertakes to repossess the goods if the buyer fails to pay his regular instalments.

---

recover /rɪˈkʌvə(r)/ *v.* **1** regain possession, use, or control of. **2** return to health, consciousness, or to a normal state or position. **3** obtain or secure by legal process. **4** retrieve or make up for (a loss, setback, etc.). **5** *refl.* regain composure, consciousness, or control of one's limbs. **6** retrieve (reusable substances) from waste. □ **recoverable** *adj.* [Latin: related to RECUPERATE]

re-cover /riːˈkʌvə(r)/ *v.* **1** cover again. **2** provide (a chair etc.) with a new cover.

recovery *n.* (*pl.* **-ies**) recovering or being recovered. [Anglo-French *recoverie*: related to RECOVER]

♦ **recovery stock** *n.* share that has fallen in price but is believed to have the potential of climbing back to its original level.

---

recreant /ˈrekrɪənt/ *literary* –*adj.* craven, cowardly. –*n.* coward. [medieval Latin: related to CREED]

re-create /ˌriːkrɪˈeɪt/ *v.* (**-ting**) create over again, reproduce. □ **re-creation** *n.*

recreation /ˌrekrɪˈeɪʃ(ə)n/ *n.* **1** process or means of refreshing or entertaining oneself. **2** pleasurable activity. □ **recreational** *adj.* [Latin: related to CREATE]

recreation ground *n.* public land used for sports or games.

recriminate /rɪˈkrɪmɪˌneɪt/ *v.* (**-ting**) make mutual or counter accusations. □ **recrimination** /-ˈneɪʃ(ə)n/ *n.* **recriminatory** /-nətərɪ/ *adj.* [medieval Latin: related to CRIME]

recross /riːˈkrɒs/ *v.* cross again.

recrudesce /ˌriːkruːˈdes/ *v.* (**-cing**) *formal* (of a disease or difficulty etc.) break out again. □ **recrudescence** *n.* **recrudescent** *adj.* [Latin: related to CRUDE]

recruit /rɪˈkruːt/ –*n.* **1** newly enlisted serviceman or servicewoman. **2** new member of a society etc. **3** beginner. –*v.* **1** enlist (a person) as a recruit. **2** form (an army etc.) by enlisting recruits. **3** get or seek recruits. **4** replenish or reinvigorate (numbers, strength, etc.). □ **recruitment** *n.* [French dial. *recrute*: related to CREW[1]]

rectal /ˈrekt(ə)l/ *adj.* of or by means of the rectum.

rectangle /ˈrekˌtæŋg(ə)l/ *n.* plane figure with four straight sides and four right angles, esp. other than a square. □ **rectangular** /-ˈtæŋgjʊlə(r)/ *adj.* [French or medieval Latin]

♦ **rectification of register** *n.* **1** alteration of any of the land registers by the registrar or the court, for example when a mistake has been made as to the ownership of land or an entry has been obtained by fraud. Anyone suffering loss because of rectification or anyone who has suffered loss as a result of a refusal to rectify a mistake in the register may be entitled to state compensation. **2** alteration of the register of the members of a company by the court if any members have been omitted, a person's name has been wrongly entered, or delay has occurred in removing the name of a former member. The court may award damages as well as rectifying the register.

---

rectify /ˈrektɪˌfaɪ/ *v.* (**-ies**, **-ied**) **1** adjust or make right. **2** purify or refine, esp. by repeated distillation. **3** convert (alternating current) to direct current. □ **rectifiable** *adj.*

rectification /-fɪ'keɪʃ(ə)n/ *n.* **rectifier** *n.* [Latin *rectus* straight, right]

rectilinear /ˌrektɪ'lɪnɪə(r)/ *adj.* **1** bounded or characterized by straight lines. **2** in or forming a straight line. [Latin: related to RECTIFY]

rectitude /'rektɪˌtju:d/ *n.* **1** moral uprightness, righteousness. **2** correctness. [Latin *rectus* right]

recto /'rektəʊ/ *n.* (*pl.* **-s**) **1** right-hand page of an open book. **2** front of a printed leaf. [Latin, = on the right]

rector /'rektə(r)/ *n.* **1** (in the Church of England) incumbent of a parish where all tithes formerly passed to the incumbent (cf. VICAR). **2** *RC Ch.* priest in charge of a church or religious institution. **3** head of some universities and colleges. □ **rectorship** *n.* [Latin *rego rect-* rule]

rectory *n.* (*pl.* **-ies**) rector's house. [French or medieval Latin: related to RECTOR]

rectum /'rektəm/ *n.* (*pl.* **-s**) final section of the large intestine, terminating at the anus. [Latin, = straight]

recumbent /rɪ'kʌmbənt/ *adj.* lying down; reclining. [Latin *cumbo* lie]

recuperate /rɪ'ku:pəˌreɪt/ *v.* (**-ting**) **1** recover from illness, exhaustion, loss, etc. **2** regain (health, a loss, etc.). □ **recuperation** /-'reɪʃ(ə)n/ *n.* **recuperative** /-rətɪv/ *adj.* [Latin *recupero*]

recur /rɪ'kɜ:(r)/ *v.* (**-rr-**) **1** occur again; be repeated. **2** (foll. by *to*) go back in thought or speech. **3** (as **recurring** *adj.*) (of a decimal fraction) with the same figure(s) repeated indefinitely (*1.6 recurring*). [Latin *curro* run]

recurrent /rɪ'kʌrənt/ *adj.* recurring; happening repeatedly. □ **recurrence** *n.*

recusant /'rekjʊz(ə)nt/ *–n.* person who refuses submission to an authority or compliance with a regulation, esp. *hist.* one who refused to attend services of the Church of England. *–adj.* of or being a recusant. □ **recusancy** *n.* [Latin *recuso* refuse]

recycle /ri:'saɪk(ə)l/ *v.* (**-ling**) convert (waste) to reusable material. □ **recyclable** *adj.*

red *–adj.* (**redder, reddest**) **1** of the colour ranging from that of blood to deep pink or orange. **2** flushed in the face with shame, anger, etc. **3** (of the eyes) bloodshot or red-rimmed. **4** (of the hair) reddish-brown, tawny. **5** having to do with bloodshed, burning, violence, or revolution. **6** *colloq.* Communist or socialist. **7** (**Red**) *hist.* Russian, Soviet. *–n.* **1** red colour or pigment. **2** red clothes or material. **3** *colloq.* Communist or socialist. □ **in the red** in debt or deficit. □ **reddish** *adj.* **redness** *n.* [Old English]

red. *abbr.* **1** *Finance* redeemable. **2** reduce(d). **3** reduction.

red admiral *n.* butterfly with red bands.

red-blooded *adj.* virile, vigorous.

redbreast *n. colloq.* robin.

redbrick *adj.* (of a university) founded in the 19th or early 20th centuries.

redcap *n.* member of the military police.

red card *n. Football* card shown by the referee to a player being sent off the field.

red carpet *n.* privileged treatment of an eminent visitor.

red cell *n.* (also **red corpuscle**) erythrocyte.

redcoat *n. hist.* British soldier.

Red Crescent *n.* equivalent of the Red Cross in Muslim countries.

Red Cross *n.* international organization bringing relief to victims of war or disaster.

redcurrant *n.* **1** small red edible berry. **2** shrub bearing this.

redden *v.* **1** make or become red. **2** blush.

redecorate /ri:'dekəˌreɪt/ *v.* (**-ting**) decorate (a room etc.) again or differently. □ **redecoration** /-'reɪʃ(ə)n/ *n.*

redeem /rɪ'di:m/ *v.* **1** recover by expenditure of effort or by a stipulated payment. **2** make a single payment to cancel (a regular charge or obligation). **3** convert (tokens or bonds etc.) into goods or cash. **4** deliver from sin and damnation. **5** make up for; be a compensating factor in (*has one redeeming feature*). **6** (foll. by *from*) save from (a defect). **7** *refl.* save (oneself) from blame. **8** purchase the freedom of (a person). **9** save (a person's life) by ransom. **10** save or rescue or reclaim. **11** fulfil (a promise). □ **redeemable** *adj.* [Latin *emo* buy]

♦ **redeemable gilt** *n.* gilt that has a redemption date. See GILT-EDGED SECURITY.

♦ **redeemable preference share** *n.* preference share that a company reserves the right to redeem, either out of profits or out of the proceeds of a further issue of shares. It may or may not have a fixed redemption date.

---

redeemer *n.* **1** person who redeems. **2** (**the Redeemer**) Christ.

redefine /ˌri:dɪ'faɪn/ *v.* (**-ning**) define again or differently. □ **redefinition** /-defɪ'nɪʃ(ə)n/ *n.*

redemption /rɪ'dempʃ(ə)n/ *n.* **1** redeeming or being redeemed. **2** thing that redeems. **3** repayment at maturity of a bond (see also GILT-EDGED SECURITY) or other document certifying a loan by the borrower to the lender (or whoever owns the bond at that date). The **redemption date** specifies when repayment takes place and is usu. printed on the bond certificate itself. [Latin: related to REDEEM]

♦ **redemption date** see REDEMPTION 3.

♦ **redemption yield** see YIELD *n.* 2.

---

redeploy /ˌri:dɪ'plɔɪ/ *v.* send (troops, workers, etc.) to a new place or task. □ **redeployment** *n.*

redesign /ˌri:dɪ'zaɪn/ *v.* design again or differently.

redevelop /ˌri:dɪ'veləp/ *v.* replan or rebuild (esp. an urban area). □ **redevelopment** *n.*

red flag *n.* **1** symbol of socialist revolution. **2** warning of danger.

red-handed *adv.* in the act of committing a crime, doing wrong, etc.

red hat *n.* **1** cardinal's hat. **2** symbol of a cardinal's office.

redhead *n.* person with red hair.

red herring *n.* misleading clue; distraction.

red-hot *adj.* **1** heated until red. **2** *colloq.* highly exciting. **3** *colloq.* (of news) fresh; completely new. **4** intensely excited. **5** enraged.

red-hot poker *n.* cultivated plant with spikes of usu. red or yellow flowers.

redial /ri:'daɪəl/ *v.* (**-ll-**; *US* **-l-**) dial again.

rediffusion /ˌri:dɪ'fju:ʒ(ə)n/ *n.* relaying of broadcast programmes, esp. by cable from a central receiver.

Red Indian *n. offens.* American Indian.

redirect /ˌri:daɪ'rekt, -dɪ'rekt/ *v.* **1** direct again; send in a different direction. **2** readdress (a letter etc.).

♦ **rediscount** /ri:'dɪskaʊnt/ *v.* (esp. of a discount house) discount a bill of exchange or promissory note that has already been discounted by someone else.

---

rediscover /ˌri:dɪ'skʌvə(r)/ *v.* discover again. □ **rediscovery** *n.* (*pl.* **-ies**).

redistribute /ˌri:dɪ'strɪˌbju:t, ri:'dɪs-/ *v.* (**-ting**) distribute again or differently. □ **redistribution** /-'bju:ʃ(ə)n/ *n.*

■ **Usage** The second pronunciation given, with the stress on the second syllable, is considered incorrect by some people.

♦ **redistribution of income** see INCOME REDISTRIBUTION.

---

redivide /ˌri:dɪ'vaɪd/ *v.* (**-ding**) divide again or differently.

red lead *n.* red form of lead oxide used as a pigment.

red-letter day *n.* day that is pleasantly noteworthy or memorable (orig. a festival marked in red on the calendar).

red light *n.* **1** signal to stop on a road, railway, etc. **2** warning.

red-light district *n.* district where many prostitutes work.

red meat *n.* meat that is red when raw (e.g. beef or lamb).

redneck *n. US* often *derog.* politically conservative working-class White in the southern US.

redo /riː'duː/ *v.* (**redoing**; *3rd sing. present* **redoes**; *past* **redid**; *past part.* **redone**) **1** do again. **2** redecorate.

redolent /'redələnt/ *adj.* **1** (foll. by *of, with*) strongly reminiscent, suggestive, or smelling. **2** fragrant. □ **redolence** *n.* [Latin *oleo* smell]

redouble /riː'dʌb(ə)l/ *–v.* (**-ling**) **1** make or grow greater or more intense or numerous. **2** *Bridge* double again a bid already doubled by an opponent. *–n. Bridge* redoubling of a bid.

redoubt /rɪ'daʊt/ *n. Mil.* outwork or fieldwork without flanking defences. [French *redoute*: related to REDUCE]

redoubtable /rɪ'daʊtəb(ə)l/ *adj.* formidable.

redound /rɪ'daʊnd/ *v.* **1** (foll. by *to*) make a great contribution to (one's credit or advantage etc.). **2** (foll. by *upon, on*) come back or recoil upon. [Latin *unda* wave]

red pepper *n.* **1** cayenne pepper. **2** ripe red fruit of the capsicum plant.

redpoll *n.* finch with a red forehead, similar to a linnet.

redraft /riː'drɑːft/ *v.* draft (a text) again, usu. differently.

red rag *n.* something that excites a person's rage.

redraw /riː'drɔː/ *v.* (*past* **redrew**; *past part.* **redrawn**) draw again or differently.

redress /rɪ'dres/ *–v.* **1** remedy or rectify (a wrong or grievance etc.). **2** readjust, set straight again. *–n.* **1** reparation for a wrong. **2** (foll. by *of*) redressing (a grievance etc.). □ **redress the balance** restore equality. [French: related to DRESS]

red rose *n.* emblem of Lancashire or the Lancastrians.

Red Sea long narrow landlocked sea separating Africa from the Arabian peninsula, connected to the Arabian Sea by the Gulf of Aden and to the Mediterranean Sea by the Suez Canal.

redshank *n.* sandpiper with bright-red legs.

red shift *n.* displacement of the spectrum to longer wavelengths in the light coming from receding galaxies etc.

redskin *n. colloq. offens.* American Indian.

red squirrel *n.* native British squirrel with reddish fur.

redstart *n.* red-tailed songbird. [from RED, obsolete *steort* tail]

red tape *n.* excessive bureaucracy or formality, esp. in public business.

reduce /rɪ'djuːs/ *v.* (**-cing**) **1** make or become smaller or less. **2** (foll. by *to*) bring by force or necessity (to some undesirable state or action) (*reduced them to tears; reduced to begging*). **3** convert to another (esp. simpler) form (*reduced it to a powder*). **4** convert (a fraction) to the form with the lowest terms. **5** (foll. by *to*) bring, simplify, or adapt by classification or analysis (*the dispute may be reduced to three issues*). **6** make lower in status or rank. **7** lower the price of. **8** lessen one's weight or size. **9** weaken (*is in a very reduced state*). **10** impoverish. **11** subdue, bring back to obedience. **12** *Chem.* **a** (cause to) combine with hydrogen. **b** (cause to) undergo addition of electrons. **13 a** (in surgery) restore (a dislocated etc. part) to its proper position. **b** remedy (a dislocation etc.) in this way. □ **reducible** *adj.* [Latin *duco* bring]

reduced circumstances *n.pl.* poverty after relative prosperity.

♦ **reducing-balance depreciation** see DEPRECIATION 2.

---

reductio ad absurdum /rɪˌdʌktɪəʊ æd æb'zɜːdəm/ *n.* proof of the falsity of a premiss by showing that its logical consequence is absurd. [Latin, = reduction to the absurd]

reduction /rɪ'dʌkʃ(ə)n/ *n.* **1** reducing or being reduced. **2** amount by which prices etc. are reduced. **3** smaller copy of a picture etc. □ **reductive** *adj.*

♦ **redundancy** /rɪ'dʌndənsɪ/ *n.* (*pl.* **-ies**) **1** loss of a job by an employee because the job has ceased to exist or because there is no longer work for the person. It involves dismissal by the employer, with or without notice, for any reason other than a breach of the contract of employment by the employee, provided that no reasonable alternative employment has been offered by the same employer. In these circumstances a **redundancy payment** must be made by the employer, the amount of which will depend on the employee's age, length of service, and rate of pay (cf. COMPENSATION FOR LOSS OF OFFICE). The employer can claim back part of the redundancy payment from the government. **2** superfluity. **3** provision of additional components in an electronic or mechanical system in order to increase the reliability of the system and, in the event of faults occurring, to increase its ability to recover from such situations.

---

redundant /rɪ'dʌnd(ə)nt/ *adj.* **1** superfluous. **2** that can be omitted without any loss of significance. **3** (of a person) no longer needed at work and therefore unemployed. See REDUNDANCY 1. [Latin: related to REDOUND]

reduplicate /rɪ'djuːplɪˌkeɪt/ *v.* (**-ting**) **1** make double. **2** repeat. **3** repeat (a letter or syllable or word) exactly or with a slight change (e.g. hurly-burly, see-saw). □ **reduplication** /-'keɪʃ(ə)n/ *n.*

redwing *n.* thrush with red underwings.

redwood *n.* very large Californian conifer yielding red wood.

re-echo /riː'ekəʊ/ *v.* (**-es, -ed**) echo repeatedly; resound.

reed *n.* **1 a** water or marsh plant with a firm stem. **b** tall straight stalk of this. **2 a** strip of cane etc. vibrating to produce the sound in some wind instruments. **b** (esp. in *pl.*) such an instrument. [Old English]

reed-bed *n.* bed or growth of reeds.

re-educate /riː'edjʊˌkeɪt/ *v.* (**-ting**) educate again, esp. to change a person's views. □ **re-education** /-'keɪʃ(ə)n/ *n.*

reedy *adj.* (**-ier, -iest**) **1** full of reeds. **2** like a reed. **3** (of a voice) like a reed instrument in tone. □ **reediness** *n.*

reef[1] *n.* **1** ridge of rock or coral etc. at or near the surface of the sea. **2 a** lode of ore. **b** bedrock surrounding this. [Old Norse *rif*]

reef[2] *–n.* each of several strips across a sail, for taking it in or rolling it up to reduce its surface area in a high wind. *–v.* take in a reef or reefs of (a sail). [Dutch from Old Norse]

reefer *n.* **1** *slang* marijuana cigarette. **2** thick double-breasted jacket. [from REEF[2]]

reef-knot *n.* symmetrical double knot.

reek *–v.* (often foll. by *of*) **1** smell strongly and unpleasantly. **2** have unpleasant or suspicious associations (*reeks of corruption*). *–n.* **1** foul or stale smell. **2** esp. *Scot.* smoke. **3** vapour, visible exhalation. [Old English]

reel *–n.* **1** cylindrical device on which thread, silk, yarn, paper, film, wire, etc., are wound. **2** quantity of thread etc. wound on a reel. **3** device for winding and unwinding a line as required, esp. in fishing. **4** revolving part in various machines. **5 a** lively folk or Scottish dance. **b** music for this. *–v.* **1** wind (thread, fishing-line, etc.) on a reel. **2** (foll. by *in, up*) draw (fish etc.) in or up with a reel. **3** stand, walk, or run unsteadily. **4** be shaken mentally or physically. **5** rock from side to side, or swing violently. **6** dance a reel. □ **reel off** say or recite very rapidly and without apparent effort. [Old English]

re-elect /ˌriːɪ'lekt/ *v.* elect again, esp. to a further term of office. □ **re-election** /-ɪ'lekʃ(ə)n/ *n.*

re-embark /ˌriːɪm'bɑːk/ *v.* go or put on board ship again.

re-emerge /ˌriːɪ'mɜːdʒ/ *v.* (**-ging**) emerge again; come back out. □ **re-emergence** *n.*

re-emphasize /riː'emfəˌsaɪz/ *v.* (also **-ise**) (**-zing** or **-sing**) place renewed emphasis on.

re-employ /ˌriːɪm'plɔɪ/ *v.* employ again. □ **re-employment** *n.*

re-enact /ˌriːɪ'nækt/ *v.* act out (a past event). □ **re-enactment** *n.*

re-engage /ˌriːɪn'geɪdʒ/ *v.* (**-ging**) engage again.

re-enlist /ˌriːɪn'lɪst/ *v.* enlist again, esp. in the armed services.

re-enter /riː'entə(r)/ *v.* enter again; go back in.

re-entrant /riː'entrənt/ *adj.* (of an angle) pointing inwards, reflex.

re-entry /riː'entrɪ/ *n.* (*pl.* **-ies**) act of entering again, esp. (of a spacecraft, missile, etc.) re-entering the earth's atmosphere.

re-equip /ˌriːɪ'kwɪp/ *v.* (**-pp-**) provide or be provided with new equipment.

re-establish /ˌriːɪ'stæblɪʃ/ *v.* establish again or anew. □ **re-establishment** *n.*

reeve[1] *n. hist.* **1** chief magistrate of a town or district. **2** official supervising a landowner's estate. [Old English]

reeve[2] *v.* (*past* **rove** or **reeved**) *Naut.* **1** (usu. foll. by *through*) thread (a rope or rod etc.) through a ring or other aperture. **2** fasten (a rope or block) in this way. [probably Dutch *reven*]

reeve[3] *n.* female ruff. [origin unknown]

re-examine /ˌriːɪg'zæmɪn/ *v.* (**-ning**) examine again or further. □ **re-examination** /-'neɪʃ(ə)n/ *n.*

♦ **re-export** –*v.* /ˌriːɪk'spɔːt, riː'ek-/ export (imported goods). –*n.* /riː'ekspɔːt/ **1** (usu. in *pl.*) commodity etc. that has been imported and is then exported without having undergone any material change while in the exporting country. Countries with a major re-export or entrepôt trade distinguish re-exports from domestic exports in their balance of payments accounts. Any import duty paid on re-exports can be reclaimed (see DRAWBACK 2). **2** re-exporting.

---

ref[1] *n. colloq.* referee in sports. [abbreviation]

ref[2] *n. Commerce* reference. [abbreviation]

reface /riː'feɪs/ *v.* (**-cing**) put a new facing on (a building).

refashion /riː'fæʃ(ə)n/ *v.* fashion again or differently.

refectory /rɪ'fektərɪ/ *n.* (*pl.* **-ies**) dining-room, esp. in a monastery or college. [Latin *reficio* renew]

refectory table *n.* long narrow table.

refer /rɪ'fɜː(r)/ *v.* (**-rr-**) (usu. foll. by *to*) **1** make an appeal or have recourse to (some authority or source of information) (*referred to his notes*). **2** send on or direct (a person, or a question for decision). **3** (of a person speaking) make an allusion or direct the hearer's or reader's attention (*did not refer to our problems*). **4** (of a statement etc.) be relevant; relate (*these figures refer to last year*). **5** send (a person) to a medical specialist etc. **6** (foll. by *back to*) **a** return (a document etc.) to its sender for clarification. **b** send (a proposal etc.) back to (a lower body, court, etc.). **7** fail (a candidate in an examination). □ **refer to drawer** words written on a cheque that is being dishonoured by a bank indicating that the payee should consult the drawer, usu. because the drawer's account has insufficient funds to cover the cheque and the manager of the bank is unwilling to allow the account to be overdrawn or further overdrawn. Other reasons for referring to the drawer are that the drawer has been made bankrupt, that there is a garnishee order against the drawer, that the drawer has stopped the cheque, or that something in the cheque itself is incorrect (e.g. it is wrongly dated, words and figures don't agree, etc.). □ **referable** /rɪ'fɜːrəb(ə)l/ *adj.* [Latin *refero relat-* carry back]

referee /ˌrefə'riː/ –*n.* **1** umpire, esp. in football or boxing. **2** person referred to for a decision in a dispute etc., esp. one appointed by two arbitrators who cannot agree on the award to be made in a dispute to be settled by arbitration. **3** person willing to testify to the character of an applicant for employment etc. –*v.* (**-rees, -reed**) act as referee (for).

reference /'refərəns/ *n.* **1** referring of a matter for decision or settlement or consideration to some authority. **2** scope given to this authority. **3** (foll. by *to*) **a** relation, respect, or correspondence. **b** allusion. **c** direction to a book etc. (or a passage in it) where information may be found. **d** book or passage so cited. **4** act of looking up a passage etc., or referring to a book or person for information. **5 a** written testimonial supporting an applicant for employment etc. See also BANKER'S REFERENCE; TRADE REFERENCE. **b** person giving this. □ **with** (or **in**) **reference to** regarding; as regards; about. □ **referential** /-'renʃ(ə)l/ *adj.*

reference book *n.* book intended to be consulted for occasional information rather than to be read continuously.

♦ **reference group** *n. Advertising* group upon which consumers model their behaviour or their buying habits. It might consist of friends, neighbours, colleagues, or a more remote group of people that is admired or to which the consumer aspires. Advertisers, recognizing the influence of reference groups, often associate a product with an appropriate reference group in order to enhance its appeal.

---

referendum /ˌrefə'rendəm/ *n.* (*pl.* **-s** or **-da**) vote on an important political question open to all the electors of a state. [Latin: related to REFER]

referral /rɪ'fɜːr(ə)l/ *n.* referring of a person to a medical specialist etc.

referred pain *n.* pain felt in a part of the body other than its actual source.

refill –*v.* /riː'fɪl/ fill again. –*n.* /'riːfɪl/ **1** thing that refills, esp. another drink. **2** act of refilling. □ **refillable** /-'fɪləb(ə)l/ *adj.*

♦ **refinance** –*v.* /ˌriːfaɪ'næns, riː'faɪ-/ (**-cing**) repay some or all of the loan capital of a firm by obtaining fresh loans, usu. at a lower rate of interest. –*n.* /riː'faɪnæns/ refinancing.

♦ **refinance credit** *n.* credit facility enabling a foreign buyer to obtain credit for a purchase when the exporter does not wish to provide it. The buyer opens a credit at a branch or agent of his or her bank in the exporting country, the exporter being paid by sight draft on the buyer's credit. The bank in the exporting country accepts a bill of exchange drawn on the buyer, which is discounted and the proceeds sent to the bank issuing the credit. The buyer only has to pay when the bill on the bank in the exporting country matures.

---

refine /rɪ'faɪn/ *v.* (**-ning**) **1** free from impurities or defects. **2** make or become more polished, elegant, or cultured.

refined *adj.* polished, elegant, cultured.

refinement *n.* **1** refining or being refined. **2** fineness of feeling or taste. **3** polish or elegance in behaviour or manner. **4** added development or improvement (*car with several refinements*). **5** subtle reasoning; fine distinction.

refiner *n.* person or firm whose business is to refine crude oil, metal, sugar, etc.

refinery *n.* (*pl.* **-ies**) place where oil, sugar, etc. is refined.

refit –*v.* /riː'fɪt/ (**-tt-**) esp. *Naut.* make or become serviceable again by repairs, renewals, etc. –*n.* /'riːfɪt/ refitting.

reflate /riː'fleɪt/ *v.* (**-ting**) cause reflation of (a currency or economy etc.). [from RE-, after *inflate, deflate*]

reflation /riː'fleɪʃ(ə)n/ *n.* expanding the level of output of an economy by government stimulus, either fiscal or monetary policy. This could involve increasing the money supply and government expenditure on investment, public works, subsidies, etc., or reducing taxation and interest rates. Reflation is usu. advocated in times of increasing unemployment, and is favoured by Keynesian economists. Monetarists and new classical macroeconomists have argued that reflation can only lead to inflation. □ **reflationary** *adj.* [from RE-, after *inflation, deflation*]

reflect /rɪ'flekt/ *v.* **1** (of a surface or body) throw back (heat, light, sound, etc.). **2** (of a mirror) show an image of; reproduce to the eye or mind. **3** correspond in appearance or effect to (*their behaviour reflects their upbringing*). **4 a** (of an action, result, etc.) show or bring (credit, discredit, etc.). **b** (*absol.*; usu. foll. by *on, upon*) bring discredit on. **5 a** (often foll. by *on, upon*) meditate on; think about. **b** (foll. by *that, how*, etc.) consider; remind oneself. [Latin *flecto flex-* bend]

reflection /rɪˈflekʃ(ə)n/ *n.* (also **reflexion**) **1** reflecting or being reflected. **2 a** reflected light, heat, or colour. **b** reflected image. **3** reconsideration (*on reflection*). **4** (often foll. by *on*) discredit or thing bringing discredit. **5** (often foll. by *on, upon*) idea arising in the mind; comment.

reflective *adj.* **1** (of a surface etc.) reflecting. **2** (of mental faculties) concerned in reflection or thought. **3** (of a person or mood etc.) thoughtful; given to meditation. □ **reflectively** *adv.* **reflectiveness** *n.*

reflector *n.* **1** piece of glass or metal etc. for reflecting light in a required direction, e.g. a red one on the back of a motor vehicle or bicycle. **2 a** telescope etc. using a mirror to produce images. **b** the mirror itself.

reflex /ˈriːfleks/ –*adj.* **1** (of an action) independent of the will, as an automatic response to the stimulation of a nerve. **2** (of an angle) exceeding 180°. –*n.* **1** reflex action. **2** sign or secondary manifestation (*law is a reflex of public opinion*). **3** reflected light or image. [Latin: related to REFLECT]

reflex camera *n.* camera in which the viewed image is formed by a mirror, enabling the scene to be correctly composed and focused.

reflexion var. of REFLECTION.

reflexive /rɪˈfleksɪv/ *Gram.* –*adj.* **1** (of a word or form, esp. of a pronoun) referring back to the subject of a sentence (e.g. *myself*). **2** (of a verb) having a reflexive pronoun as its object (as in *to wash oneself*). –*n.* reflexive word or form, esp. a pronoun (e.g. *myself*).

reflexology /ˌriːflekˈsɒlədʒɪ/ *n.* massage through points on the feet, hands, and head, to relieve tension and treat illness. □ **reflexologist** *n.*

refloat /riːˈfləʊt/ *v.* set (a stranded ship) afloat again.

refocus /riːˈfəʊkəs/ *v.* (**-s-** or **-ss-**) focus again or anew.

reforest /riːˈfɒrɪst/ *v.* = REAFFOREST. □ **reforestation** /-ˈsteɪʃ(ə)n/ *n.*

reforge /riːˈfɔːdʒ/ *v.* (**-ging**) forge again or differently.

reform /rɪˈfɔːm/ –*v.* **1** make or become better by the removal of faults and errors. **2** abolish or cure (an abuse or malpractice). –*n.* **1** removal of faults or abuses, esp. moral, political, or social. **2** improvement made or suggested. □ **reformative** *adj.*

re-form /riːˈfɔːm/ *v.* form again. □ **re-formation** /-ˈmeɪʃ(ə)n/ *n.*

reformat /riːˈfɔːmæt/ *v.* (**-tt-**) format anew.

reformation /ˌrefəˈmeɪʃ(ə)n/ *n.* **1** reforming or being reformed, esp. a radical change for the better in political, religious, or social affairs. **2** (**the Reformation**) *hist.* 16th-century movement for the reform of abuses in the Roman Church ending in the establishment of the Reformed or Protestant Churches.

reformatory /rɪˈfɔːmətərɪ/ –*n.* (*pl.* **-ies**) *US* & *hist.* institution for the reform of young offenders. –*adj.* producing reform.

Reformed Church *n.* a Protestant (esp. Calvinist) Church.

reformer *n.* person who advocates or brings about (esp. political or social) reform.

reformism /rɪˈfɔːmɪz(ə)m/ *n.* policy of reform rather than abolition or revolution. □ **reformist** *n.* & *adj.*

reformulate /riːˈfɔːmjʊˌleɪt/ *v.* (**-ting**) formulate again or differently. □ **reformulation** /-ˈleɪʃ(ə)n/ *n.*

refract /rɪˈfrækt/ *v.* (of water, air, glass, etc.) deflect (a ray of light etc.) at a certain angle when it enters obliquely from another medium. □ **refraction** *n.* **refractive** *adj.* [Latin *refringo -fract-* break open]

refractor *n.* **1** refracting medium or lens. **2** telescope using a lens to produce an image.

refractory /rɪˈfræktərɪ/ *adj.* **1** stubborn, unmanageable, rebellious. **2** (of a wound, disease, etc.) not yielding to treatment. **3** (of a substance) hard to fuse or work. [Latin: related to REFRACT]

refrain[1] /rɪˈfreɪn/ *v.* (foll. by *from*) avoid doing (an action) (*refrain from smoking*). [Latin *frenum* bridle]

refrain[2] /rɪˈfreɪn/ *n.* **1** recurring phrase or lines, esp. at the ends of stanzas. **2** music accompanying this. [Latin: related to REFRACT]

refrangible /rɪˈfrændʒɪb(ə)l/ *adj.* that can be refracted. [Latin: related to REFRACT]

refreeze /riːˈfriːz/ *v.* (**-zing**; *past* **refroze**; *past part.* **refrozen**) freeze again.

refresh /rɪˈfreʃ/ *v.* **1** give new spirit or vigour to. **2** revive (the memory), esp. by consulting the source of one's information. □ **refreshing** *adj.* **refreshingly** *adv.* [French: related to FRESH]

refresher *n.* **1** something that refreshes, esp. a drink. **2** *Law* extra fee payable to counsel in a prolonged case.

refresher course *n.* course reviewing or updating previous studies.

refreshment *n.* **1** refreshing or being refreshed. **2** (usu. in *pl.*) food or drink.

refrigerant /rɪˈfrɪdʒərənt/ –*n.* substance used for refrigeration. –*adj.* cooling. [Latin: related to REFRIGERATE]

refrigerate /rɪˈfrɪdʒəˌreɪt/ *v.* (**-ting**) **1** make or become cool or cold. **2** subject (food etc.) to cold in order to freeze or preserve it. □ **refrigeration** /-ˈreɪʃ(ə)n/ *n.* [Latin *refrigero* from *frigus* cold]

refrigerator *n.* cabinet or room in which food etc. is kept cold.

refroze *past* of REFREEZE.

refrozen *past part.* of REFREEZE.

refuel /riːˈfjuːəl/ *v.* (**-ll-**; *US* **-l-**) replenish a fuel supply; supply with more fuel.

refuge /ˈrefjuːdʒ/ *n.* **1** shelter from pursuit, danger, or trouble. **2** person or place etc. offering this. [Latin *refugium* from *fugio* flee]

refugee /ˌrefjʊˈdʒiː/ *n.* person taking refuge, esp. in a foreign country from war, persecution, or natural disaster. [French *réfugié*: related to REFUGE]

♦ refugee capital *n.* hot money belonging to a foreign government, company, or individual that is invested in the country offering the highest interest rate, usu. on a short-term basis.

---

refulgent /rɪˈfʌldʒ(ə)nt/ *adj. literary* shining, gloriously bright. □ **refulgence** *n.* [Latin *refulgeo* shine brightly]

refund –*v.* /rɪˈfʌnd/ (also *absol.*) **1** pay back (money or expenses). **2** reimburse (a person). –*n.* /ˈriːfʌnd/ **1** act of refunding. **2** sum refunded. □ **refundable** /rɪˈfʌndəb(ə)l/ *adj.* [Latin *fundo* pour]

refurbish /riːˈfɜːbɪʃ/ *v.* **1** brighten up. **2** restore and redecorate. □ **refurbishment** *n.*

refurnish /riːˈfɜːnɪʃ/ *v.* furnish again or differently.

refusal /rɪˈfjuːz(ə)l/ *n.* **1** refusing or being refused. **2** (in full **first refusal**) right or privilege of deciding to take or leave a thing before it is offered to others.

refuse[1] /rɪˈfjuːz/ *v.* (**-sing**) **1** withhold acceptance of or consent to (*refuse an offer, orders*). **2** (often foll. by *to* + infin.) indicate unwillingness or inability (*I refuse to go*; *car refuses to start*; *I refuse!*). **3** (often with double object) not grant (a request) made by (a person). **4** (also *absol.*) (of a horse) be unwilling to jump (a fence etc.). [French *refuser*]

refuse[2] /ˈrefjuːs/ *n.* items rejected as worthless; waste. [French: related to REFUSE[1]]

refusenik /rɪˈfjuːznɪk/ *n. hist.* Soviet Jew who was refused permission to emigrate to Israel.

refute /rɪˈfjuːt/ *v.* (**-ting**) **1** prove the falsity or error of (a statement etc. or the person advancing it). **2** rebut by argument. **3** deny or contradict (without argument). □ **refutation** /ˌrefjʊˈteɪʃ(ə)n/ *n.* [Latin *refuto*]

■ **Usage** The use of *refute* in sense 3 is considered incorrect by some people. It is often confused in this sense with *repudiate*.

reg /redʒ/ *n. colloq.* = REGISTRATION MARK. [abbreviation]

reg. *abbr.* **1** (also **regd.**) registered. **2** registration.

regain /rɪ'geɪn/ *v.* obtain possession or use of after loss (*regain consciousness*).

regal /'riːg(ə)l/ *adj.* **1** of or by a monarch or monarchs. **2** fit for a monarch; magnificent. □ **regality** /rɪ'gælɪtɪ/ *n.* **regally** *adv.* [Latin *rex reg-* king]

regale /rɪ'geɪl/ *v.* (**-ling**) **1** entertain lavishly with feasting. **2** (foll. by *with*) entertain with (talk etc.). [French *régaler*: related to GALLANT]

regalia /rɪ'geɪlɪə/ *n.pl.* **1** insignia of royalty used at coronations. **2** insignia of an order or of civic dignity. [medieval Latin: related to REGAL]

regard /rɪ'gɑːd/ *–v.* **1** gaze on steadily (usu. in a specified way) (*regarded them suspiciously*). **2** heed; take into account. **3** look upon or think of in a specified way (*regard it as an insult*). *–n.* **1** gaze; steady or significant look. **2** (foll. by *to, for*) attention or care. **3** (foll. by *for*) esteem; kindly feeling; respectful opinion. **4** respect; point attended to (*in this regard*). **5** (in *pl.*) expression of friendliness in a letter etc.; compliments. □ **as regards** about, concerning; in respect of. **in** (or **with**) **regard to** as concerns; in respect of. [French *regard(er)*: related to GUARD]

regardful *adj.* (foll. by *of*) mindful of.

regarding *prep.* about, concerning; in respect of.

regardless *–adj.* (foll. by *of*) without regard or consideration for. *–adv.* without paying attention.

regatta /rɪ'gætə/ *n.* event consisting of rowing or yacht races. [Italian]

regency /'riːdʒənsɪ/ *n.* (*pl.* **-ies**) **1** office of regent. **2** commission acting as regent. **3 a** period of office of a regent or regency commission. **b** (**Regency**) (in the UK) 1811 to 1820. [medieval Latin *regentia*: related to REGENT]

regenerate *–v.* /rɪ'dʒenə,reɪt/ (**-ting**) **1** bring or come into renewed existence; generate again. **2** improve the moral condition of. **3** impart new, more vigorous, or spiritually higher life or nature to. **4** *Biol.* regrow or cause (new tissue) to regrow. *–adj.* /rɪ'dʒenərət/ spiritually born again, reformed. □ **regeneration** /-'reɪʃ(ə)n/ *n.* **regenerative** /-rətɪv/ *adj.*

regent /'riːdʒ(ə)nt/ *–n.* person appointed to administer a state because the monarch is a minor or is absent or incapacitated. *–adj.* (after the noun) acting as regent (*Prince Regent*). [Latin *rego* rule]

reggae /'regeɪ/ *n.* West Indian style of music with a strongly accented subsidiary beat. [origin unknown]

regicide /'redʒɪ,saɪd/ *n.* **1** person who kills or helps to kill a king. **2** killing of a king. [Latin *rex reg-* king, -CIDE]

regime /reɪ'ʒiːm/ *n.* (also **régime**) **1** method or system of government. **2** prevailing order or system of things. **3** regimen. [French: related to REGIMEN]

regimen /'redʒɪmən/ *n.* prescribed course of exercise, way of life, or diet. [Latin *rego* rule]

regiment *–n.* /'redʒɪmənt/ **1 a** permanent unit of an army, usu. commanded by a colonel and divided into several companies, troops, or batteries. **b** operational unit of artillery etc. **2** (usu. foll. by *of*) large or formidable array or number. *–v.* /'redʒɪ,ment/ **1** organize (esp. oppressively) in groups or according to a system. **2** form into a regiment or regiments. □ **regimentation** /-'teɪʃ(ə)n/ *n.* [Latin: related to REGIMEN]

regimental /,redʒɪ'ment(ə)l/ *–adj.* of a regiment. *–n.* (in *pl.*) military uniform, esp. of a particular regiment. □ **regimentally** *adv.*

Regina /rɪ'dʒaɪnə/ city in W Canada, capital of Saskatchewan; situated at the centre of wheat-growing plains, it has agriculture-related and oil-refining industries; pop. (1991) 179 178.

Regina /rɪ'dʒaɪnə/ *n.* **1** (after the name) reigning queen (*Elizabeth Regina*). **2** *Law* the Crown (*Regina v. Jones*). [Latin, = queen: related to REX]

region /'riːdʒ(ə)n/ *n.* **1** geographical area or division, having definable boundaries or characteristics (*fertile region*). **2** administrative area, esp. in Scotland. **3** part of the body (*lumbar region*). **4** sphere or realm (*region of metaphysics*). □ **in the region of** approximately. □ **regional** *adj.* **regionally** *adv.* [Latin *rego* rule]

register /'redʒɪstə(r)/ *–n.* **1** official list, e.g. of births, marriages, and deaths, of children in a class, of shipping, of professionally qualified persons, or of qualified voters in a constituency. **2** book in which items are recorded for reference. **3** device recording speed, force, etc. **4 a** compass of a voice or instrument. **b** part of this compass (*lower register*). **5** adjustable plate for widening or narrowing an opening and regulating a draught, esp. in a fire-grate. **6 a** set of organ pipes. **b** sliding device controlling this. **7** = CASH REGISTER. **8** form of a language (colloquial, literary, etc.) used in particular circumstances. **9** *Computing* storage location in the processing unit of a computer in which data has to be placed before it can be operated upon by instructions. *–v.* **1** set down (a name, fact, complaint, etc.) formally; record in writing. **2** enter or cause to be entered in a particular register. **3** commit (a letter etc.) to registered post. **4** (of an instrument) record automatically; indicate. **5 a** express (an emotion) facially or by gesture (*registered surprise*). **b** (of an emotion) show in a person's face or gestures. **6** make an impression on a person's mind. [Latin *regero -gest-* transcribe, record]

♦ **registered capital** see SHARE CAPITAL.

♦ **registered company** *n.* company incorporated in the UK by the Registrar of Companies in accordance with the Companies Act. It may be a public limited company, a private limited company, or an unlimited company.

♦ **registered land** *n.* land the title to which has been registered under the Land Registration Act (1925). See LAND REGISTRATION; RECTIFICATION OF REGISTER.

♦ **registered land certificate** *n.* document that has replaced title deeds for registered land. It provides proof of ownership of the land and is in the possession of the landowner unless the land is subject to a mortgage, in which case it is retained by the Land Registry.

♦ **registered name** *n.* name in which a UK company is registered. The name, without which a company cannot be incorporated, is stated in the memorandum of association. Some names are prohibited by law and will not be registered; these include names already registered and names that in the opinion of the Secretary of State for Trade and Industry are offensive. The name may be changed by special resolution of the company and the Secretary of State may order a company to change a misleading name. The name must be displayed at each place of business, on stationery, and on bills of exchange etc., otherwise the company and its officers will be liable to a fine.

---

registered nurse *n.* nurse with a state certificate of competence.

♦ **registered office** *n.* official premises of a UK company, to which all correspondence can be sent. Any change of address must be notified to the Registrar of Companies within 14 days and published in the *London Gazette*. Statutory registers are kept at the registered office, the address of which must be disclosed on stationery and in the company's annual return.

♦ **registered post** *n.* Post Office service, offering special precautions for safety, in which letters can be registered, a certificate of posting being given to the sender and a receipt signed on delivery. The fee is related to the compensation given if the letter is lost.

♦ **registered stock** *n.* = INSCRIBED STOCK.

♦ **register of charges** *n.* **1** register maintained by the Registrar of Companies on which certain charges must be registered by companies (see CHARGE *n.* 3). A charge is created when a company gives a creditor the right to recover his debt from specific assets. The types of charge that must be registered in this way, and the details that must be given, are set out in the Companies Act (1985). Failure to register the charge within 21 days of its creation renders it void, so that it cannot be enforced against a liquidator or creditor of the company. The underlying debt remains valid, however, but ranks only as an unsecured debt. **2** list of charges that a company must maintain at its registered address or principal place of business. Failure to do so may render the directors and company officers liable to a fine. This register must be available for inspection by other persons during normal business hours. **3** see LAND CHARGES REGISTER. **4** the charges register. See LAND REGISTRATION.

♦ **register of companies** *n.* see COMPANIES HOUSE.

♦ **register of debenture-holders** *n.* list of the holders of debentures in a UK company. There is no legal requirement for such a register to be kept but if one exists it must be kept at the company's registered office or at a place notified to the Registrar of Companies. It must be available for inspection, to debenture-holders and shareholders free of charge and to the public for a small fee.

♦ **register of directors and secretaries** *n.* register listing the directors and the secretary of a UK company, which must be kept at its registered office. It must state the full names of the directors and the company secretary, their residential addresses, the nationality of directors, particulars of other directorships held, the occupation of directors, and (in the case of a public company) their dates of birth. If the function of director or secretary is performed by another company, the name and registered office of that company must be given. The register must be available for inspection by members of the company free of charge and it may be inspected by the public for a small fee.

register office *n.* state office where civil marriages are conducted.

■ **Usage** *Register office* is the official name, although *registry office* is often heard in colloquial usage.

♦ **register of members** *n.* list of the members of a company, which all UK companies must keep at their registered office or the place where the register is made up, provided that the address of this is notified to the Registrar of Companies. It contains the names and addresses of the members, the dates on which they were registered as members, and the dates on which any ceased to be members. If the company has a share capital, the register must state the number and class of the shares held by each member and the amount paid for the shares. As legal, rather than beneficial, ownership is registered, it is not always possible to discover from the register who controls the shares. The register must be available for inspection by members free of charge for at least two normal office hours per working day. Others may inspect it on payment of a small fee. The register may be rectified by the court if it is incorrect.

registrar /ˌredʒɪ'strɑː(r)/ *n.* **1** official responsible for keeping a register. **2** chief administrator in a university, college, etc. **3** hospital doctor training as a specialist. [medieval Latin: related to REGISTER]

♦ **Registrar of Companies** *n.* official charged with the duty of registering all the companies in the UK. There is one registrar for England and Wales and one for Scotland. The registrar is responsible for carrying out a wide variety of administrative duties connected with registered companies, including maintaining the register of companies and the register of charges, issuing certificates of incorporation, and receiving annual returns. See also COMPANIES HOUSE.

registration /ˌredʒɪ'streɪʃ(ə)n/ *n.* registering or being registered. [French or medieval Latin: related to REGISTER]

♦ **registration fee** *n.* small fee charged by a company whose shares are quoted on a stock exchange when it is requested to register the name of a new owner of shares.

registration mark *n.* (also **registration number**) combination of letters and numbers identifying a vehicle etc.

registry /'redʒɪstrɪ/ *n.* (*pl.* **-ies**) place where registers or records are kept. [medieval Latin: related to REGISTER]

registry office *n.* = REGISTER OFFICE.

Regius professor /'riːdʒɪəs/ *n.* holder of a chair founded by a sovereign (esp. one at Oxford or Cambridge instituted by Henry VIII) or filled by Crown appointment. [Latin *regius* royal]

regrade /riː'greɪd/ *v.* (**-ding**) grade again or differently.

regress *–v.* /rɪ'gres/ **1** move backwards; return to a former, esp. worse, state. **2** *Psychol.* (cause to) return mentally to a former stage of life. *–n.* /'riːgres/ act of regressing. □ **regression** /rɪ'greʃ(ə)n/ *n.* **regressive** /rɪ'gresɪv/ *adj.* [Latin *regredior -gress-* go back]

♦ **regressive tax** *n.* tax levied at a rate that decreases as income increases. Indirect taxes fall into this category. Regressive taxes are said to fall more heavily on the poor than on the rich; for example, the poor spend a higher proportion of their incomes on VAT than the rich. A proportional tax may also be regressive; because of the theory of the marginal utility of money (i.e. the next pound is of more value to the poor than to the rich), it is thought that a flat rate of tax bears unfairly on the poor.

regret /rɪ'gret/ *–v.* (**-tt-**) **1** feel or express sorrow, repentance, or distress over (an action or loss etc.). **2** acknowledge with sorrow or remorse (*regret to say*). *–n.* feeling of sorrow, repentance, etc., over an action or loss etc. □ **give** (or **send) one's regrets** formally decline an invitation. [French *regretter*]

regretful *adj.* feeling or showing regret. □ **regretfully** *adv.*

regrettable *adj.* (of events or conduct) undesirable, unwelcome; deserving censure. □ **regrettably** *adv.*

regroup /riː'gruːp/ *v.* **1** group or arrange again or differently. **2** *Mil.* prepare for a fresh attack.

regrow /riː'grəʊ/ *v.* grow again, esp. after an interval. □ **regrowth** *n.*

regular /'regjʊlə(r)/ *–adj.* **1** acting, done, or recurring uniformly or calculably in time or manner; habitual, constant, orderly. **2** conforming to a rule or principle; systematic. **3** harmonious, symmetrical. **4** conforming to a standard of etiquette or procedure. **5** properly constituted or qualified; pursuing an occupation as one's main pursuit (*regular soldier*). **6** *Gram.* (of a noun, verb, etc.) following the normal type of inflection. **7** *colloq.* thorough, absolute (*a regular hero*). **8** (before or after the noun) bound by religious rule; belonging to a religious or monastic order (*canon regular*). **9** (of a person) defecating or menstruating at predictable times. *–n.* **1** regular soldier. **2** *colloq.* regular customer, visitor, etc. **3** one of the regular clergy. □ **regularity** /-'lærɪtɪ/ *n.* **regularize** *v.* (also **-ise**) (**-zing** or **-sing**). **regularly** *adv.* [Latin *regula* rule]

regulate /'regjʊˌleɪt/ *v.* (**-ting**) **1** control by rule. **2** subject to restrictions. **3** adapt to requirements. **4** alter the speed of (a machine or clock) so that it works accurately. □ **regulator** *n.* **regulatory** /-lətərɪ/ *adj.* [Latin: related to REGULAR]

♦ **regulated tenancy** *n.* tenancy on a dwelling with full rent protection under the Rent Act (1977). The maximum rent payable under such a tenancy is that agreed between landlord and tenant or a registered fair rent set by a local Rent Officer on the application of either party, with appeal to the Rent Assessment Committee. Under the Housing Act (1988), new tenancies are known as **assured tenancies**, and rents are fixed by Rent Assessment Committees if the landlord and tenant cannot agree. Previous regulated tenancies remain protected.

regulation /ˌregjʊ'leɪʃ(ə)n/ *n.* **1** regulating or being regulated. **2** prescribed rule. **3** imposition by a government of controls over the decisions of individuals or firms, esp. over industries in which there is monopoly or oligopoly, in order to prevent firms from exploiting their market power to extract pure economic profits. Regulation may be seen as an alternative to nationalization. For example, the types of industries that have formerly been nationalized in the UK have usu. been regulated in the US. The main vehicle for regulation in the UK has been the Monopolies and Mergers Commission. To an economist, the most important reason for regulation by a government is to encourage competition. See also DEREGULATE 5. **4** (*attrib.*) **a** in accordance with regulations; of the correct type etc. **b** *colloq.* usual.

regulo /'regjʊ,ləʊ/ *n.* (usu. foll. by a numeral) each of the numbers of a scale denoting temperature in a gas oven (*cook at regulo 6*). [*Regulo*, propr. term for a thermostatic gas oven control]

regurgitate /rɪ'gɜːdʒɪ,teɪt/ *v.* (**-ting**) **1** bring (swallowed food) up again to the mouth. **2** reproduce, rehash (information etc.). □ **regurgitation** /-'teɪʃ(ə)n/ *n.* [Latin *gurges -git-* whirlpool]

rehabilitate /,riːhə'bɪlɪ,teɪt/ *v.* (**-ting**) **1** restore to effectiveness or normal life by training etc., esp. after imprisonment or illness. **2** restore to former privileges or reputation or a proper condition. □ **rehabilitation** /-'teɪʃ(ə)n/ *n.* [medieval Latin: related to RE-, ABILITY]

rehang /riː'hæŋ/ *v.* (*past* and *past part.* **rehung**) hang again or differently.

rehash –*v.* /riː'hæʃ/ put (old material) into a new form without significant change or improvement. –*n.* /'riːhæʃ/ **1** material rehashed. **2** rehashing.

rehear /riː'hɪə(r)/ *v.* (*past* and *past part.* **reheard** /-'hɜːd/) hear (esp. a judicial case) again.

rehearsal /rɪ'hɜːs(ə)l/ *n.* **1** trial performance or practice of a play, music, etc. **2** process of rehearsing.

rehearse /rɪ'hɜːs/ *v.* (**-sing**) **1** practise (a play, music, etc.) for later public performance. **2** hold a rehearsal. **3** train (a person) by rehearsal. **4** recite or say over. **5** give a list of, enumerate. [Anglo-French: related to HEARSE]

reheat /riː'hiːt/ *v.* heat again.

rehouse /riː'haʊz/ *v.* (**-sing**) house elsewhere.

rehung *past* and *past part.* of REHANG.

Reich /raɪx/ *n.* the former German state, esp. the Third Reich. [German, = empire]

♦ **Reichmann** /'raɪxmən/, **Paul** (1930–) Canadian business executive, born in Vienna. With his brothers Ralph and Albert he founded the Olympia and York Construction Company, which has extensive property developments in Canada, New York, and London (including the Canary Wharf project).

---

reign /reɪn/ –*v.* **1** be king or queen. **2** prevail (*confusion reigns*). **3** (as **reigning** *attrib. adj.*) (of a winner, champion, etc.) currently holding the title etc. –*n.* **1** sovereignty, rule. **2** period during which a sovereign rules. [Latin *regnum*: related to REX]

reimburse /,riːɪm'bɜːs/ *v.* (**-sing**) **1** repay (a person who has expended money). **2** repay (a person's expenses). □ **reimbursement** *n.*

reimpose /,riːɪm'pəʊz/ *v.* (**-sing**) impose again, esp. after a lapse.

Reims /riːmz/ (also **Rheims**) ancient cathedral city in N France, capital of Champagne-Ardenne region; pop. (1990) 185 164.

rein /reɪn/ –*n.* (in *sing.* or *pl.*) **1** long narrow strap with each end attached to the bit, used to guide or check a horse etc. **2** similar device used to restrain a child. **3** means of control. –*v.* **1** check or manage with reins. **2** (foll. by *up*, *back*) pull up or back with reins. **3** (foll. by *in*) hold in as with reins. **4** govern, restrain, control. □ **give free rein to** allow freedom of action or expression. **keep a tight rein on** allow little freedom to. [French *rene* from Latin *retinēre* RETAIN]

reincarnation /,riːɪnkɑː'neɪʃ(ə)n/ *n.* rebirth of a soul in a new body. □ **reincarnate** /-'kɑːneɪt/ *v.* (**-ting**). **reincarnate** /-'kɑːnət/ *adj.*

reindeer /'reɪndɪə(r)/ *n.* (*pl.* same or **-s**) subarctic deer with large antlers. [Old Norse]

reinforce /,riːɪn'fɔːs/ *v.* (**-cing**) strengthen or support, esp. with additional personnel or material, or by an increase of numbers, quantity, or size etc. [French *renforcer*]

reinforced concrete *n.* concrete with metal bars or wire etc. embedded to increase its strength.

reinforcement *n.* **1** reinforcing or being reinforced. **2** thing that reinforces. **3** (in *pl.*) reinforcing personnel or equipment etc.

reinsert /,riːɪn'sɜːt/ *v.* insert again.

reinstate /,riːɪn'steɪt/ *v.* (**-ting**) **1** replace in a former position. **2** restore (a person etc.) to former privileges. □ **reinstatement** *n.*

♦ **reinstatement of the sum insured** *n.* payment of an additional premium to return the sum insured to its full level, after a claim has reduced it. Insurance policies are, in effect, a promise to pay money if a particular event occurs. If a claim is paid, the insurance is reduced by the claim amount (or if a total loss is paid, the policy is exhausted). If the policyholder wishes to return the cover to its full value, a premium representing the amount of cover used by the claim must be paid. In the case of a total loss the whole premium must be paid again.

♦ **reinsurance** /,riːɪn'ʃʊərəns/ *n.* (also **RI**, **R/I**) passing of all or part of an insurance risk that has been covered by an insurer to another insurer in return for a premium. The policyholder is usu. not aware that reinsurance has been arranged as no mention is made of it on the policy. Reinsurance is a similar process to the bookmaker's practice of laying off bets with other bookmakers when too much money is placed on a particular horse. Very often an insurer will only accept a risk with a high payout if a total loss occurs (e.g. for a jumbo jet) if the potential loss can be reduced by reinsurance. See also FACULTATIVE REINSURANCE. Cf. CO-INSURANCE.

---

reinsure /,riːɪn'ʃʊə(r)/ *v.* (**-ring**) insure again. See REINSURANCE.

♦ **reintermediation** /riː,ɪntə,miːdɪ'eɪʃ(ə)n/ *n.* see DISINTERMEDIATION.

---

reinterpret /,riːɪn'tɜːprɪt/ *v.* (**-t-**) interpret again or differently. □ **reinterpretation** /-'teɪʃ(ə)n/ *n.*

reintroduce /,riːɪntrə'djuːs/ *v.* (**-cing**) introduce again. □ **reintroduction** /-'dʌkʃ(ə)n/ *n.*

reinvest /,riːɪn'vest/ *v.* invest again (esp. proceeds or interest). □ **reinvestment** *n.*

reissue /riː'ɪʃuː/ –*v.* (**-ues**, **-ued**, **-uing**) issue again or in a different form. –*n.* new issue, esp. of a previously published book.

REIT *abbr. US* real-estate investment trust.

reiterate /riː'ɪtə,reɪt/ *v.* (**-ting**) say or do again or repeatedly. □ **reiteration** /-'reɪʃ(ə)n/ *n.*

reject –*v.* /rɪ'dʒekt/ **1** put aside or send back as not to be used, done, or complied with etc. **2** refuse to accept or believe in. **3** rebuff or withhold affection from (a person). **4** show an immune response to (a transplant) so that it fails. –*n.* /'riːdʒekt/ thing or person rejected as unfit or below standard. □ **rejection** /rɪ'dʒekʃ(ə)n/ *n.* [Latin *rejicio -ject-* throw back]

rejig /riː'dʒɪg/ *v.* (**-gg-**) **1** re-equip (a factory etc.) for a new kind of work. **2** rearrange.

rejoice /rɪ'dʒɔɪs/ *v.* (**-cing**) **1** feel great joy. **2** be glad. **3** (foll. by *in*, *at*) take delight. [French *rejoir*: related to JOY]

rejoin[1] /riː'dʒɔɪn/ *v.* **1** join together again; reunite. **2** join (a companion etc.) again.

rejoin[2] /rɪ'dʒɔɪn/ *v.* **1** say in answer, retort. **2** reply to a charge or pleading in a lawsuit. [French *rejoindre*: related to JOIN]

rejoinder /rɪ'dʒɔɪndə(r)/ *n.* what is said in reply; retort. [Anglo-French: related to REJOIN[2]]

rejuvenate /rɪ'dʒuːvə,neɪt/ *v.* (**-ting**) make (as if) young again. □ **rejuvenation** /-'neɪʃ(ə)n/ *n.* [Latin *juvenis* young]

rekindle /riː'kɪnd(ə)l/ *v.* (**-ling**) kindle again.

relabel /riː'leɪb(ə)l/ *v.* (**-ll-**; *US* **-l-**) label (esp. a commodity) again or differently.

relapse /rɪˈlæps/ *–v.* (**-sing**) (usu. foll. by *into*) fall back or sink again (into a worse state after improvement). *–n.* /also ˈriː-/ relapsing, esp. a deterioration in a patient's condition after partial recovery. [Latin *labor laps-* slip]

relate /rɪˈleɪt/ *v.* (**-ting**) **1** narrate or recount. **2** (usu. foll. by *to, with*) connect (two things) in thought or meaning; associate. **3** (foll. by *to*) have reference to. **4** (foll. by *to*) feel connected or sympathetic to. [Latin: related to REFER]

related *adj.* connected, esp. by blood or marriage.

relation /rɪˈleɪʃ(ə)n/ *n.* **1 a** the way in which one person or thing is related or connected to another. **b** connection, correspondence, contrast, or feeling prevailing between persons or things (*bears no relation to the facts*; *enjoyed good relations for many years*). **2** relative. **3** (in *pl.*) **a** (foll. by *with*) dealings (with others). **b** sexual intercourse. **4** = RELATIONSHIP. **5 a** narration (*his relation of the events*). **b** narrative. □ **in relation to** as regards. [Latin: related to REFER]

relationship *n.* **1** state or instance of being related. **2 a** connection or association (*good working relationship*). **b** *colloq.* emotional (esp. sexual) association between two people.

♦ **relationship banking** *n.* long-term relationship established by a bank with its corporate clients to develop an insight into the clients' businesses to improve its ability to make informal decisions regarding the making of loans to the clients.

---

relative /ˈrelətɪv/ *–adj.* **1** considered in relation to something else (*relative velocity*). **2** (foll. by *to*) proportioned to (something else) (*growth is relative to input*). **3** implying comparison or contextual relation (*'heat' is a relative word*). **4** comparative (*their relative merits*). **5** having mutual relations; corresponding in some way; related to each other. **6** (foll. by *to*) having reference or relating to (*the facts relative to the issue*). **7** *Gram.* **a** (of a word, esp. a pronoun) referring to an expressed or implied antecedent and attaching a subordinate clause to it, e.g. *which, who*. **b** (of a clause) attached to an antecedent by a relative word. *–n.* **1** person connected by blood or marriage. **2** species related to another by common origin. **3** *Gram.* relative word, esp. a pronoun. □ **relatively** *adv.* [Latin: related to REFER]

relative atomic mass *n.* the ratio of the average mass of one atom of an element to one-twelfth of the mass of an atom of carbon-12.

relative density *n.* the ratio between the mass of a substance and that of the same volume of a substance used as a standard (usu. water or air).

relative molecular mass *n.* the ratio of the average mass of one molecule of an element or compound to one-twelfth of the mass of an atom of carbon-12.

relativity /ˌreləˈtɪvɪtɪ/ *n.* **1** being relative. **2** *Physics* **a** (**special theory of relativity**) theory based on the principle that all motion is relative and that light has a constant velocity. **b** (**general theory of relativity**) theory extending this to gravitation and accelerated motion.

♦ **relaunch** *–v.* /riːˈlɔːntʃ/ reintroduce (an existing product or brand) into the market after changes have been made to it. *–n.* /ˈriːˌlɔːntʃ/ reintroduction of such a product or brand.

---

relax /rɪˈlæks/ *v.* **1** make or become less stiff, rigid, or tense. **2** make or become less formal or strict (*rules were relaxed*). **3** reduce or abate (one's attention, efforts, etc.). **4** cease work or effort. **5** (as **relaxed** *adj.*) at ease; unperturbed. [Latin *relaxo*: related to LAX]

relaxation /ˌriːlækˈseɪʃ(ə)n/ *n.* **1** relaxing or being relaxed. **2** recreation.

relay /ˈriːleɪ/ *–n.* **1** fresh set of people etc. substituted for tired ones. **2** supply of material similarly used. **3** = RELAY RACE. **4** device activating an electric circuit etc. in response to changes affecting itself. **5 a** device to receive, reinforce, and transmit a message, broadcast, etc. **b** relayed message or transmission. *–v.* also /rɪˈleɪ/ receive (a message, broadcast, etc.) and transmit it to others. [French *relai* from Latin *laxo*: see LAX]

re-lay /riːˈleɪ/ *v.* (*past* and *past part.* **re-laid**) lay again or differently.

relay race *n.* race between teams of which each member in turn covers part of the distance.

relearn /riːˈlɜːn/ *v.* learn again.

release /rɪˈliːs/ *–v.* (**-sing**) **1** (often foll. by *from*) set free; liberate, unfasten. **2** allow to move from a fixed position. **3 a** make (information, a recording, etc.) publicly available. **b** issue (a film etc.) for general exhibition. *–n.* **1** liberation from a restriction, duty, or difficulty. **2** handle or catch that releases part of a mechanism. **3** news item etc. made available for publication (*press release*). **4 a** film or record etc. that is released. **b** releasing or being released in this way. [French *relesser* from Latin *relaxo* RELAX]

relegate /ˈrelɪˌgeɪt/ *v.* (**-ting**) **1** consign or dismiss to an inferior position. **2** transfer (a sports team) to a lower division of a league etc. **3** banish. □ **relegation** /-ˈgeɪʃ(ə)n/ *n.* [Latin *relego* send away]

relent /rɪˈlent/ *v.* relax severity, abandon a harsh intention, yield to compassion. [medieval Latin *lentus* flexible]

relentless *adj.* unrelenting, oppressively constant. □ **relentlessly** *adv.*

re-let /riːˈlet/ *–v.* (**-tt-**; *past* and *past part.* **-let**) let (a property) for a further period or to a new tenant. *–n.* re-let property.

relevant /ˈrelɪv(ə)nt/ *adj.* (often foll. by *to*) bearing on or having reference to the matter in hand. □ **relevance** *n.* [Latin *relevo*: related to RELIEVE]

reliability /rɪˌlaɪəˈbɪlɪtɪ/ *n.* **1** consistency; dependability. **2** *Computing* measure of the ability of a system to provide its specified services for a given period or when demanded.

reliable /rɪˈlaɪəb(ə)l/ *adj.* of consistently good character or quality; dependable. □ **reliably** *adv.*

reliance /rɪˈlaɪəns/ *n.* (foll. by *in, on*) trust, confidence. □ **reliant** *adj.*

relic /ˈrelɪk/ *n.* **1** object that is interesting because of its age or association. **2** part of a dead holy person's body or belongings kept as an object of reverence. **3** surviving custom or belief etc. from a past age. **4** memento or souvenir. **5** (in *pl.*) what has survived. **6** (in *pl.*) dead body or remains of a person. [Latin *reliquiae* remains: related to RELINQUISH]

relict /ˈrelɪkt/ *n.* object surviving in its primitive form. [French *relicte*: related to RELIC]

relief /rɪˈliːf/ *n.* **1 a** alleviation of or deliverance from pain, distress, anxiety, etc. **b** feeling accompanying such deliverance. **2** feature etc. that diversifies monotony or relaxes tension. **3** assistance (esp. financial) given to those in special need or difficulty. **4 a** replacing of a person or persons on duty by another or others. **b** person or persons replacing others in this way. **5** (usu. *attrib.*) thing supplementing another in some service (*relief bus*). **6 a** method of moulding, carving, or stamping in which the design stands out from the surface. **b** piece of sculpture etc. in relief. **c** representation of relief given by an arrangement of line, colour, or shading. **7** vividness, distinctness (*brings the facts out in sharp relief*). **8** (foll. by *of*) reinforcement (esp. the raising of a siege) of a place. **9** esp. *Law* redress of a hardship or grievance. [French and Italian: related to RELIEVE]

relief map *n.* map indicating hills and valleys by shading etc. rather than by contour lines alone.

relief road *n.* road taking traffic around a congested area.

relieve /rɪˈliːv/ *v.* (**-ving**) **1** bring or give relief to. **2** mitigate the tedium or monotony of. **3** release (a person) from a duty by acting as or providing a substitute. **4** (foll. by *of*) take (esp. a burden or duty) away from (a person). □ **relieve one's feelings** use strong language or vigorous behaviour when annoyed. **relieve oneself** urinate or defecate. □ **relieved** *adj.* [Latin *relevo* raise again, alleviate]

relievo /rɪˈliːvəʊ/ *n.* (*pl.* **-s**) = RELIEF 6. [Italian *rilievo*: related to RELIEF]

relight /riːˈlaɪt/ *v.* (*past* and *past part.* **-lit**) light (a fire etc.) again.

religion /rɪˈlɪdʒ(ə)n/ *n.* **1** belief in a superhuman controlling power, esp. in a personal God or gods entitled to obedience and worship. **2** expression of this in worship. **3** particular system of faith and worship. **4** life under monastic vows. **5** thing that one is devoted to. [Latin *religio* bond]

religiosity /rɪˌlɪdʒɪˈɒsɪtɪ/ *n.* state of being religious or too religious. [Latin: related to RELIGIOUS]

religious /rɪˈlɪdʒəs/ *–adj.* **1** devoted to religion; pious, devout. **2** of or concerned with religion. **3** of or belonging to a monastic order. **4** scrupulous, conscientious. *–n.* (*pl.* same) person bound by monastic vows. □ **religiously** *adv.* [Latin *religiosus*: related to RELIGION]

reline /riːˈlaɪn/ *v.* (**-ning**) put a new lining in (a garment etc.).

relinquish /rɪˈlɪŋkwɪʃ/ *v.* **1** surrender or resign (a right or possession). **2** give up or cease from (a habit, plan, belief, etc.). **3** relax hold of. □ **relinquishment** *n.* [Latin *relinquo -lict-* leave behind]

reliquary /ˈrelɪkwərɪ/ *n.* (*pl.* **-ies**) esp. *Relig.* receptacle for a relic or relics. [French *reliquaire*: related to RELIC]

relish /ˈrelɪʃ/ *–n.* **1** (often foll. by *for*) great liking or enjoyment. **2 a** appetizing flavour. **b** attractive quality. **3** condiment eaten with plainer food to add flavour. **4** (foll. by *of*) distinctive taste or tinge. *–v.* **1** get pleasure out of; enjoy greatly. **2** anticipate with pleasure. [French *reles* remainder: related to RELEASE]

relive /riːˈlɪv/ *v.* (**-ving**) live (an experience etc.) over again, esp. in the imagination.

reload /riːˈləʊd/ *v.* (also *absol.*) load (esp. a gun) again.

relocate /ˌriːləʊˈkeɪt/ *v.* (**-ting**) **1** locate (an office, factory, etc.) in a new place, often as a result of a merger, take-over, etc. **2** move to a new place (esp. to live or work). □ **relocation** /-ˈkeɪʃ(ə)n/ *n.*

♦ **relocation allowance** *n.* financial incentive for an employee to remain with a relocated organization.

---

reluctant /rɪˈlʌkt(ə)nt/ *adj.* (often foll. by *to* + infin.) unwilling or disinclined. □ **reluctance** *n.* **reluctantly** *adv.* [Latin *luctor* struggle]

rely /rɪˈlaɪ/ *v.* (**-ies, -ied**) (foll. by *on, upon*) **1** depend on with confidence or assurance. **2** be dependent on. [Latin *religo* bind closely]

REM *abbr.* rapid eye-movement.

remade *past* and *past part.* of REMAKE.

remain /rɪˈmeɪn/ *v.* **1** be left over after others or other parts have been removed, used, or dealt with. **2** be in the same place or condition during further time; stay (*remained at home*). **3** (foll. by compl.) continue to be (*remained calm*; *remains President*). [Latin *remaneo*]

remainder *–n.* **1** residue. **2** remaining persons or things. **3** number left after division or subtraction. **4** copies of a book left unsold when demand has almost ceased. *–v.* dispose of (a remainder of books) at a reduced price. [Anglo-French: related to REMAIN]

remains *n.pl.* **1** what remains after other parts have been removed or used etc. **2** relics of antiquity, esp. of buildings. **3** dead body.

remake *–v.* /riːˈmeɪk/ (**-king**; *past* and *past part.* **remade**) make again or differently. *–n.* /ˈriːmeɪk/ thing that has been remade, esp. a cinema film.

remand /rɪˈmɑːnd/ *–v.* return (a prisoner) to custody, esp. to allow further inquiry. *–n.* recommittal to custody. □ **on remand** in custody pending trial. [Latin *remando*]

remand centre *n.* institution to which accused persons are remanded.

remark /rɪˈmɑːk/ *–v.* **1** (often foll. by *that*) **a** say by way of comment. **b** *archaic* take notice of; regard with attention. **2** (usu. foll. by *on, upon*) make a comment. *–n.* **1** written or spoken comment; anything said. **2 a** noticing (*worthy of remark*). **b** commenting (*let it pass without remark*). [French *remarquer*: related to MARK[1]]

remarkable *adj.* worth notice; exceptional; striking. □ **remarkably** *adv.* [French *remarquable*: related to REMARK]

remarry /riːˈmærɪ/ *v.* (**-ies, -ied**) marry again. □ **remarriage** *n.*

REME /ˈriːmiː/ *abbr.* Royal Electrical and Mechanical Engineers.

remeasure /riːˈmeʒə(r)/ *v.* (**-ring**) measure again.

remedial /rɪˈmiːdɪəl/ *adj.* **1** affording or intended as a remedy. **2** (of teaching etc.) for slow or disadvantaged pupils. [Latin: related to REMEDY]

remedy /ˈremɪdɪ/ *–n.* (*pl.* **-ies**) (often foll. by *for, against*) **1** medicine or treatment. **2** means of counteracting or removing anything undesirable. **3** redress; legal or other reparation. *–v.* (**-ies, -ied**) rectify; make good. □ **remediable** /rɪˈmiːdɪəb(ə)l/ *adj.* [Latin *remedium* from *medeor* heal]

remember /rɪˈmembə(r)/ *v.* **1** (often foll. by *to* + infin. or *that* + clause) keep in the memory; not forget. **2** (also *absol.*) bring back into one's thoughts. **3** think of or acknowledge (a person), esp. in making a gift etc. **4** (foll. by *to*) convey greetings from (one person) to (another) (*remember me to John*). [Latin: related to MEMORY]

remembrance /rɪˈmembrəns/ *n.* **1** remembering or being remembered. **2** a memory or recollection. **3** keepsake, souvenir. **4** (in *pl.*) greetings conveyed through a third person. [French: related to REMEMBER]

Remembrance Day *n.* **1** = REMEMBRANCE SUNDAY. **2** *hist.* Armistice Day.

Remembrance Sunday *n.* Sunday nearest 11 Nov., when those killed in the wars of 1914–18 and 1939–45 and later conflicts are commemorated.

remind /rɪˈmaɪnd/ *v.* (usu. foll. by *of* or *to* + infin. or *that* + clause) cause (a person) to remember or think of (*reminds me of her father*; *reminded them of the time*).

reminder *n.* **1** thing that reminds, esp. a repeat letter or bill. **2** (often foll. by *of*) memento.

reminisce /ˌremɪˈnɪs/ *v.* (**-cing**) indulge in reminiscence.

reminiscence /ˌremɪˈnɪs(ə)ns/ *n.* **1** remembering things past. **2** (in *pl.*) collection in literary form of incidents and experiences remembered. [Latin *reminiscor* remember]

reminiscent *adj.* **1** (foll. by *of*) reminding or suggestive of. **2** concerned with reminiscence.

remiss /rɪˈmɪs/ *adj.* careless of duty; lax, negligent. [Latin: related to REMIT]

remission /rɪˈmɪʃ(ə)n/ *n.* **1** reduction of a prison sentence on account of good behaviour. **2** remitting of a debt or penalty etc. **3** diminution of force, effect, or degree (esp. of disease or pain). **4** (often foll. by *of*) forgiveness (of sins etc.). [Latin: related to REMIT]

remit *–v.* /rɪˈmɪt/ (**-tt-**) **1** cancel or refrain from exacting or inflicting (a debt, punishment, etc.). **2** abate or slacken; cease partly or entirely. **3** send (money etc.) in payment. **4 a** (foll. by *to*) refer (a matter for decision etc.) to some authority. **b** send back (a case) to a lower court. **5** postpone or defer. **6** pardon (sins etc.). *–n.* /ˈriːmɪt/ **1** terms of reference of a committee etc. **2** item remitted for consideration. [Latin *remitto -miss-*]

remittance *n.* **1** money sent, esp. by post. **2** sending of money.

remittent *adj.* (of a fever or disease) abating at intervals.

remix *–v.* /riːˈmɪks/ mix again. *–n.* /ˈriːmɪks/ remixed recording.

remnant /ˈremnənt/ *n.* **1** small remaining quantity. **2** piece of cloth etc. left when the greater part has been used or sold. [French: related to REMAIN]

remodel /riːˈmɒd(ə)l/ *v.* (**-ll-**; *US* **-l-**) **1** model again or differently. **2** reconstruct.

remold *US* var. of REMOULD.

remonstrate /ˈremənˌstreɪt/ *v.* (**-ting**) (foll. by *with*) make a protest; argue forcibly. □ **remonstrance** /rɪˈmɒnstrəns/ *n.* **remonstration** /-ˈstreɪʃ(ə)n/ *n.* [medieval Latin *monstro* show]

remorse /rɪˈmɔːs/ *n.* **1** deep regret for a wrong committed. **2** compunction; compassion, mercy (*without remorse*). [medieval Latin *mordeo mors-* bite]

remorseful *adj.* filled with repentance. □ **remorsefully** *adv.*

remorseless *adj.* without compassion. □ **remorselessly** *adv.*

remortgage /riːˈmɔːɡɪdʒ/ *–v.* (**-ging**) (also *absol.*) mortgage again; revise the terms of an existing mortgage on (a property). *–n.* different or altered mortgage.

remote /rɪˈməʊt/ *adj.* (**remoter, remotest**) **1** far away, far apart, distant. **2** isolated; secluded. **3** distantly related (*remote ancestor*). **4** slight, faint (*a remote hope*; *not the remotest chance*). **5** aloof; not friendly. □ **remotely** *adv.* **remoteness** *n.* [Latin *remotus*: related to REMOVE]

remote control *n.* **1** control of an apparatus from a distance by means of signals transmitted from a radio or electronic device. **2** such a device.

♦ **remoteness of damage** *n.* extent to which a person is liable to compensate for loss or injury that has resulted from his or her actions. In the law of negligence, a person is presumed to intend the natural consequences of his or her acts. If proved negligent the person will be liable for all the direct and immediate consequences of the negligence. If, however, the consequences of a person's acts could not be reasonably foreseen or anticipated, the resulting damage is said to be too remote. Similarly, in the law of contract, damage resulting from breach of contract will be deemed too remote unless it arises directly from the breach complained of. No damages will be awarded for damage the courts deem to be too remote.

---

remould (*US* **remold**) *–v.* /riːˈməʊld/ **1** mould again; refashion. **2** re-form the tread of (a tyre). *–n.* /ˈriːməʊld/ remoulded tyre.

removal /rɪˈmuːv(ə)l/ *n.* **1** removing or being removed. **2** transfer of furniture etc. on moving house.

remove /rɪˈmuːv/ *–v.* (**-ving**) **1** take off or away from the place occupied. **2 a** convey to another place; change the situation of. **b** get rid of; dismiss. **3** cause to be no longer present or available; take away (*privileges were removed*). **4** (in *passive*; foll. by *from*) distant or remote in condition (*country is not far removed from anarchy*). **5** (as **removed** *adj.*) (esp. of cousins) separated by a specified number of steps of descent (*a first cousin twice removed* = a grandchild of a first cousin). *–n.* **1** degree of remoteness; distance. **2** stage in a gradation; degree (*several removes from what I expected*). **3** form or division in some schools. □ **removable** *adj.* [Latin *removeo -mot-*]

remunerate /rɪˈmjuːnəˌreɪt/ *v.* (**-ting**) **1** reward; pay for services rendered. **2** serve as or provide recompense for (work etc.) or to (a person). □ **remuneration** /-ˈreɪʃ(ə)n/ *n.* **remunerative** /-rətɪv/ *adj.* [Latin *munus -ner-* gift]

Renaissance /rɪˈneɪs(ə)ns/ *n.* **1** revival of art and literature in the 14th–16th centuries. **2** period of this. **3** (often *attrib.*) style of art, architecture, etc. developed during this era. **4** (**renaissance**) any similar revival. [French *naissance* birth]

Renaissance man *n.* person with many talents or pursuits, esp. in the humanities.

renal /ˈriːn(ə)l/ *adj.* of the kidneys. [Latin *renes* kidneys]

rename /riːˈneɪm/ *v.* (**-ming**) name again; give a new name to.

renascent /rɪˈnæs(ə)nt/ *adj.* springing up anew; being reborn. □ **renascence** *n.*

renationalize /riːˈnæʃənəˌlaɪz/ *v.* (also **-ise**) (**-zing** or **-sing**) nationalize again (an originally nationalized and more recently privatized industry etc.). □ **renationalization** /-ˈzeɪʃ(ə)n/ *n.*

rend *v.* (*past* and *past part.* **rent**) *archaic* tear or wrench forcibly. [Old English]

render *v.* **1** cause to be or become (*rendered us helpless*). **2** give or pay (money, service, etc.), esp. in return or as a thing due. **3** (often foll. by *to*) **a** give (assistance). **b** show (obedience etc.). **c** do (a service etc.). **4** submit; send in; present (an account, reason, etc.). **5 a** represent or portray. **b** act (a role). **c** *Mus.* perform; execute. **6** translate. **7** (often foll. by *down*) melt down (fat etc.). **8** cover (stone or brick) with a coat of plaster. □ **rendering** *n.* (esp. in senses 5, 6, and 8). [Latin *reddo* give back]

rendezvous /ˈrɒndɪˌvuː/ *–n.* (*pl.* same /-ˌvuːz/) **1** agreed or regular meeting-place. **2** meeting by arrangement. *–v.* (**rendezvouses** /-ˌvuːz/; **rendezvoused** /-ˌvuːd/; **rendezvousing** /-ˌvuːɪŋ/) meet at a rendezvous. [French, = present yourselves]

rendition /renˈdɪʃ(ə)n/ *n.* interpretation or rendering of a dramatic role, piece of music, etc. [French: related to RENDER]

renegade /ˈrenɪˌɡeɪd/ *n.* person who deserts a party or principles. [medieval Latin: related to RENEGE]

renege /rɪˈniːɡ/ *v.* (**-ging**) (often foll. by *on*) go back on (one's word etc.). [Latin *nego* deny]

renegotiate /ˌriːnɪˈɡəʊʃɪˌeɪt/ *v.* (**-ting**) (also *absol.*) negotiate again or on different terms. □ **renegotiation** /-ˈeɪʃ(ə)n/ *n.*

renew /rɪˈnjuː/ *v.* **1** revive; make new again; restore to the original state. **2** reinforce; resupply; replace. **3** repeat or re-establish, resume after an interruption (*renewed our acquaintance*). **4** (also *absol.*) grant or be granted continuation of (a licence, subscription, lease, etc.). **5** recover (strength etc.). □ **renewable** *adj.* **renewal** *n.*

♦ **renewal notice** *n.* invitation from an insurer to continue an insurance policy that is about to expire by paying the **renewal premium**. The renewal premium is shown on the notice; it may differ from the previous premium, either because insurance rates have changed or because the insured value has changed. Many insurers increase the insured value of certain objects automatically, in line with inflation.

---

renminbi /renˈmɪnbɪ/ *n.* currency used in China by the indigenous population. [Mandarin, = people's money]

Rennes /ren/ industrial city and commercial centre in NW France, in Brittany; pop. (1990) 203 533.

rennet /ˈrenɪt/ *n.* **1** curdled milk found in the stomach of an unweaned calf. **2** preparation made from the stomach-membrane of a calf or from certain fungi, used in making cheese etc. [probably Old English: related to RUN]

♦ **renounceable document** *n.* document that provides evidence of ownership, for a limited period, of unregistered shares. An allotment letter sent to shareholders when a new issue is floated is an example. Ownership of the shares can be passed to someone else by renunciation at this stage.

---

renounce /rɪˈnaʊns/ *v.* (**-cing**) **1** consent formally to abandon (a claim, right, etc.). **2** repudiate; refuse to recognize any longer. **3** decline further association or disclaim relationship with. □ **renounceable** *adj.* [Latin *nuntio* announce]

renovate /ˈrenəˌveɪt/ *v.* (**-ting**) restore to good condition; repair. □ **renovation** /-ˈveɪʃ(ə)n/ *n.* **renovator** *n.* [Latin *novus* new]

renown /rɪˈnaʊn/ *n.* fame, high distinction. [French *renomer* make famous]

renowned *adj.* famous, celebrated.

rent[1] *–n.* **1** tenant's periodical payment to an owner for the use of land or premises, usu. under a lease. See also GROUND-RENT; RACK-RENT 1; REGULATED TENANCY. **2** payment for the use of equipment etc. *–v.* **1** (often foll. by *from*) take, occupy, or use at a rent. **2** (often foll. by *out*) let or hire (a thing) for rent. **3** (foll. by *at*) be let at a specified rate. [French *rente*: related to RENDER]

rent[2] *n.* **1** large tear in a garment etc. **2** opening in clouds etc. [from REND]

rent[3] *past* and *past part.* of REND.

rental /ˈrent(ə)l/ *n.* **1** amount paid or received as rent. **2** act of renting. [Anglo-French or Anglo-Latin: related to RENT[1]]

rent-boy *n.* young male prostitute.

♦ ***rentes*** /rɑ̃t/ *n.pl.* non-redeemable government bonds issued by several European governments, notably France. The interest, which is paid annually, for ever, is called *rente.* [French]

rentier /ˈrɑ̃tɪ,eɪ/ *n.* person living on income from property, investments, etc. [French]

♦ **renting back** *n.* = LEASE-BACK.

renumber /riːˈnʌmbə(r)/ *v.* change the number or numbers given or allocated to.
renunciation /rɪ,nʌnsɪˈeɪʃ(ə)n/ *n.* **1** renouncing or giving up. **2** self-denial. **3** *Finance* **a** surrendering rights to shares in a rights issue. The person to whom the shares are allotted by allotment letter fills in the **renunciation form** (usu. attached to the letter) in favour of the person to whom the rights are to be renounced. **b** disposal of a unit-trust holding by completing the renunciation form on the reverse of the certificate and sending it to the trust managers.
reoccupy /riːˈɒkjʊ,paɪ/ *v.* (**-ies, -ied**) occupy again. □ **reoccupation** /-ˈpeɪʃ(ə)n/ *n.*
reoccur /,riːəˈkɜː(r)/ *v.* (**-rr-**) occur again or habitually. □ **reoccurrence** /-ˈkʌrəns/ *n.*
reopen /riːˈəʊpən/ *v.* open again.
reorder /riːˈɔːdə(r)/ *–v.* **1** order again. **2** put into a new order. *–n.* renewed or repeated order for goods.
reorganize /riːˈɔːgə,naɪz/ *v.* (also **-ise**) (**-zing** or **-sing**) organize differently. □ **reorganization** /-ˈzeɪʃ(ə)n/ *n.*
reorient /riːˈɔːrɪ,ent/ *v.* **1** give a new direction or outlook to (ideas, a person, etc.). **2** help (a person) find his or her bearings again. **3** (refl., often foll. by *to*) adjust oneself to or come to terms with something.
reorientate /riːˈɔːrɪən,teɪt/ *v.* (**-ting**) = REORIENT. □ **reorientation** /-ˈteɪʃ(ə)n/ *n.*
rep[1] *n. colloq.* representative, esp. a commercial traveller. [abbreviation]
rep[2] *n. colloq.* **1** repertory. **2** repertory theatre or company. [abbreviation]
repack /riːˈpæk/ *v.* pack again.
repackage /riːˈpækɪdʒ/ *v.* (**-ging**) **1** package again or differently. **2** present in a new form.
repaid *past* and *past part.* of REPAY.
repaint *–v.* /riːˈpeɪnt/ **1** paint again or differently. **2** restore the paint or colouring of. *–n.* /ˈriːpeɪnt/ act of repainting.
repair[1] /rɪˈpeə(r)/ *–v.* **1** restore to good condition after damage or wear. **2** set right or make amends for (loss, wrong, error, etc.). *–n.* **1** restoring to sound condition (*in need of repair*). **2** result of this (*the repair hardly shows*). **3** good or relative condition for working or using (*in bad repair*). □ **repairable** *adj.* **repairer** *n.* [Latin *paro* make ready]
repair[2] /rɪˈpeə(r)/ *v.* (foll. by *to*) resort; have recourse; go. [Latin: related to REPATRIATE]

♦ **repairing lease** see LEASE *n.*

repaper /riːˈpeɪpə(r)/ *v.* paper (a wall etc.) again.
reparable /ˈrepərəb(ə)l/ *adj.* (of a loss etc.) that can be made good. [Latin: related to REPAIR[1]]
reparation /,repəˈreɪʃ(ə)n/ *n.* **1** making amends. **2** (esp. in *pl.*) compensation for war damages.
repartee /,repɑːˈtiː/ *n.* **1** practice or skill of making witty retorts. **2** conversation characterized by such retorts. [French *repartie* from *repartir* reply promptly: related to PART]
repast /rɪˈpɑːst/ *n. formal* **1** meal. **2** food and drink for this. [Latin *repasco -past-* feed]
repatriate *–v.* /riːˈpætrɪ,eɪt/ (**-ting**) **1** return (a person) to his or her native land. **2** return (capital) from a foreign investment to investment in the country from which it originally came. *–n.* /riːˈpætrɪət/ repatriated person. □ **repatriation** /-ˈeɪʃ(ə)n/ *n.* [Latin *repatrio* go back home, from *patria* native land]
repay /riːˈpeɪ/ *v.* (*past* and *past part.* **repaid**) **1** pay back (money). **2** make repayment to (a person). **3** make return for; requite (a service, action, etc.) (*must repay their kindness; the book repays close study*). □ **repayable** *adj.* **repayment** *n.*

♦ **repayment mortgage** *n.* mortgage in which the borrower's regular payments consist of both capital repayments and interest.

REPC *abbr.* Regional Economic Planning Council.
repeal /rɪˈpiːl/ *–v.* revoke or annul (a law etc.). *–n.* repealing. [French: related to APPEAL]
repeat /rɪˈpiːt/ *–v.* **1** say or do over again. **2** recite, rehearse, or report (something learnt or heard). **3** recur; appear again. **4** (of food) be tasted after being swallowed due to belching. *–n.* **1 a** repeating. **b** thing repeated (often *attrib.*: *repeat prescription*). **2** repeated broadcast. **3** *Mus.* **a** passage intended to be repeated. **b** mark indicating this. **4** pattern repeated in wallpaper etc. □ **repeat itself** recur in the same form. **repeat oneself** say or do the same thing over again. □ **repeatable** *adj.* **repeatedly** *adv.* [Latin *peto* seek]
repeater *n.* **1** person or thing that repeats. **2** firearm which fires several shots without reloading. **3** watch or clock which repeats its last strike when required. **4** device for the re-transmission of an electrical message.
repel /rɪˈpel/ *v.* (**-ll-**) **1** drive back; ward off (*repel an attacker*). **2** refuse to accept (*repelled offers of help*). **3** be repulsive or distasteful to. **4** resist mixing with or admitting (*oil and water repel each other; surface repels moisture*). **5** (of a magnetic pole) push away from itself (*like poles repel*). □ **repellent** *adj.* & *n.* [Latin *repello -puls-*]
repent /rɪˈpent/ *v.* **1** (often foll. by *of*) feel deep sorrow about one's actions etc. **2** (also *absol.*) wish one had not done; resolve not to continue (a wrongdoing etc.). □ **repentance** *n.* **repentant** *adj.* [Latin *paeniteo*]
repercussion /,riːpəˈkʌʃ(ə)n/ *n.* **1** (often foll. by *of*) indirect effect or reaction following an event or act. **2** recoil after impact. **3** echo. [Latin: related to RE-]
repertoire /ˈrepə,twɑː(r)/ *n.* **1** stock of works that a performer etc. knows or is prepared to perform. **2** stock of techniques etc. (*repertoire of excuses*). [Latin: related to REPERTORY]
repertory /ˈrepətərɪ/ *n.* (*pl.* **-ies**) **1** performance of various plays for short periods by one company. **2** repertory theatres collectively. **3** store or collection, esp. of information, instances, etc. **4** = REPERTOIRE. [Latin *reperio* find]
repertory company *n.* theatrical company that performs plays from a repertoire.
repetition /,repəˈtɪʃ(ə)n/ *n.* **1 a** repeating or being repeated. **b** thing repeated. **2** copy. □ **repetitious** *adj.* **repetitive** /rɪˈpetətɪv/ *adj.*
repetitive strain injury *n.* painful esp. hand or arm condition resulting from prolonged repetitive movements.
rephrase /riːˈfreɪz/ *v.* (**-sing**) express differently.
repine /rɪˈpaɪn/ *v.* (**-ning**) (often foll. by *at, against*) fret; be discontented. [from PINE[2], after *repent*]
replace /rɪˈpleɪs/ *v.* (**-cing**) **1** put back in place. **2** take the place of; succeed; be substituted for. **3** find or provide a substitute for. **4** (often foll. by *with, by*) fill up the place of.
replacement *n.* **1** replacing or being replaced. **2** person or thing that replaces another.

♦ **replacement cost** *n.* **1** cost of replacing a damaged article etc. **2** price at which the assets of an organization could be replaced, broadly in their existing state. In current-cost accounting, instead of valuing assets at their historical cost, less depreciation where appropriate, assets are valued at their current cost, which in most cases is taken to be the replacement cost.
♦ **replacement ratio** *n.* percentage of a redundant worker's former income that is replaced by unemployment benefit or other state benefits. Supply-side economists have argued that replacement ratios have risen in

the postwar period, encouraging workers to live off the dole rather than find new jobs.

---

replant /riːˈplɑːnt/ *v.* **1** transfer (a plant etc.). **2** plant (ground) again.

replay *–v.* /riːˈpleɪ/ play (a match, recording, etc.) again. *–n.* /ˈriːpleɪ/ replaying of a match, recorded incident in a game, etc.

replenish /rɪˈplenɪʃ/ *v.* **1** (often foll. by *with*) fill up again. **2** renew (a supply etc.). □ **replenishment** *n.* [French *plenir* from *plein* full]

replete /rɪˈpliːt/ *adj.* (often foll. by *with*) **1** well-fed, gorged. **2** filled or well-supplied. □ **repletion** *n.* [Latin *pleo* fill]

replica /ˈreplɪkə/ *n.* **1** exact copy, esp. a duplicate of a work, made by the original artist. **2** copy or model, esp. on a smaller scale. [Italian *replicare* REPLY]

reply /rɪˈplaɪ/ *–v.* (**-ies**, **-ied**) **1** (often foll. by *to*) make an answer, respond in word or action. **2** say in answer. *–n.* (*pl.* **-ies**) **1** replying (*what did they say in reply?*). **2** what is replied; response. [Latin *replico* fold back]

repoint /riːˈpɔɪnt/ *v.* point (esp. brickwork) again.

repopulate /riːˈpɒpjʊˌleɪt/ *v.* (**-ting**) populate again or increase the population of.

report /rɪˈpɔːt/ *–v.* **1 a** bring back or give an account of. **b** state as fact or news, narrate or describe or repeat, esp. as an eyewitness or hearer etc. **c** relate as spoken by another. **2** make an official or formal statement about. **3** (often foll. by *to*) bring (an offender or offence) to the attention of the authorities. **4** (often foll. by *to*) present oneself to a person as having returned or arrived. **5** (also *absol.*) take down word for word, summarize, or write a description of for publication. **6** make or send in a report. **7** (foll. by *to*) be responsible to (a superior etc.). *–n.* **1** account given or opinion formally expressed after investigation or consideration. **2** description, summary, or reproduction of a scene, speech, law case, etc., esp. for newspaper publication or broadcast. **3** common talk; rumour. **4** way a person or thing is spoken of (*hear a good report of you*). **5** periodical statement on (esp. a school pupil's) work, conduct, etc. **6** sound of a gunshot etc. □ **reportedly** *adv.* [Latin *porto* bring]

reportage /ˌrepɔːˈtɑːʒ/ *n.* **1** reporting of news for the media. **2** typical style of this. **3** factual journalistic material in a book etc. [from REPORT, after French]

reported speech *n.* speaker's words with the person, tense, etc. adapted, e.g. *he said that he would go*.

reporter *n.* person employed to report news etc. for the media.

♦ **reporting accountants** *n.pl.* firm of accountants who report on the financial information provided in a company's prospectus. They may or may not be the company's own auditors.

♦ **report program generator** *n.* (also **RPG**) simple business-oriented computer programming language. RPG allows users to generate reports easily from information in computer files and simple RPG programs can perform complicated business tasks.

---

repose[1] /rɪˈpəʊz/ *–n.* **1** cessation of activity, excitement, or toil. **2** sleep. **3** peaceful or quiescent state; tranquillity. *–v.* (**-sing**) **1** (also *refl.*) lie down in rest. **2** (often foll. by *in, on*) lie, be lying or laid, esp. in sleep or death. [Latin: related to PAUSE]

repose[2] /rɪˈpəʊz/ *v.* (**-sing**) (foll. by *in*) place (trust etc.) in. [from RE-, POSE]

reposeful *adj.* showing or inducing repose. □ **reposefully** *adv.* [from REPOSE[1]]

reposition /ˌriːpəˈzɪʃ(ə)n/ *v.* **1** move or place in a different position. **2** alter one's position.

♦ **repositioning** *n.* attempt to make a product appeal to a different segment of a market, esp. a product that has not performed as profitably as expected. Repositioning usu. involves changing some of the product's features, its packaging, or its price.

---

repository /rɪˈpɒzɪtərɪ/ *n.* (*pl.* **-ies**) **1** place where things are stored or may be found, esp. a warehouse or museum. **2** receptacle. **3** (often foll. by *of*) **a** book, person, etc. regarded as a store of information etc. **b** recipient of secrets etc. [Latin: related to REPOSE[2]]

repossess /ˌriːpəˈzes/ *v.* **1** regain possession of (esp. goods on which payment instalments are in arrears under a hire-purchase agreement). **2** = FORECLOSE 1b. □ **repossession** *n.*

repot /riːˈpɒt/ *v.* (**-tt-**) move (a plant) to another, esp. larger, pot.

reprehend /ˌreprɪˈhend/ *v. formal* rebuke; find fault with. [Latin *prehendo* seize]

reprehensible /ˌreprɪˈhensɪb(ə)l/ *adj.* blameworthy.

represent[1] /ˌreprɪˈzent/ *v.* **1** stand for or correspond to. **2** (often in *passive*) be a specimen of. **3** embody; symbolize. **4** place a likeness of before the mind or senses. **5** (often foll. by *as, to be*) describe or depict as; declare. **6** (foll. by *that*) allege. **7** show, or play the part of, on stage. **8** be a substitute or deputy for; be entitled to act or speak for. **9** be elected as a member of a legislature etc. by. [Latin: related to PRESENT[2]]

represent[2] /ˌriːprɪˈzent/ *v.* submit (a cheque etc.) again for payment.

representation /ˌreprɪzenˈteɪʃ(ə)n/ *n.* **1** representing or being represented. **2** thing that represents another. **3** (esp. in *pl.*) statement made of allegations or opinions. **4** (in *pl.*) information given by a person wishing to arrange insurance about the nature of the risk that is to be covered. If it contains a material fact it must be true to the best knowledge and belief of the person wishing to be insured. See UTMOST GOOD FAITH.

representational *adj. Art* depicting a subject as it appears to the eye.

representative /ˌreprɪˈzentətɪv/ *–adj.* **1** typical of a class. **2** containing typical specimens of all or many classes (*representative sample*). **3 a** consisting of elected deputies etc. **b** based on representation by these (*representative government*). **4** (foll. by *of*) serving as a portrayal or symbol of. *–n.* **1** (foll. by *of*) sample, specimen, or typical embodiment of. **2 a** agent of a person or society. **b** commercial traveller. **3** delegate; substitute. **4** deputy etc. in a representative assembly. [French or medieval Latin: related to REPRESENT[1]]

repress /rɪˈpres/ *v.* **1 a** keep under; quell. **b** suppress; prevent from sounding, rioting, or bursting out. **2** *Psychol.* actively exclude (an unwelcome thought) from conscious awareness. **3** (usu. as **repressed** *adj.*) subject (a person) to the suppression of his or her thoughts or impulses. □ **repression** *n.* **repressive** *adj.* [Latin: related to PRESS[1]]

reprice /riːˈpraɪs/ *v.* (**-cing**) price again or differently.

reprieve /rɪˈpriːv/ *–v.* (**-ving**) **1** remit or postpone the execution of (a condemned person). **2** give respite to. *–n.* **1 a** reprieving or being reprieved. **b** warrant for this. **2** respite. [*repry* from French *reprendre -pris* take back]

reprimand /ˈreprɪˌmɑːnd/ *–n.* (esp. official) rebuke. *–v.* administer this to. [Latin: related to REPRESS]

reprint *–v.* /riːˈprɪnt/ print again. *–n.* /ˈriːprɪnt/ **1** reprinting of a book etc. **2** book etc. reprinted. **3** quantity reprinted.

reprisal /rɪˈpraɪz(ə)l/ *n.* act of retaliation. [medieval Latin: related to REPREHEND]

reprise /rɪˈpriːz/ *n.* **1** repeated passage in music. **2** repeated item in a musical programme. [French: related to REPRIEVE]

repro /ˈriːprəʊ/ *n.* (*pl.* **-s**) (often *attrib.*) *colloq.* reproduction or copy. [abbreviation]

reproach /rɪˈprəʊtʃ/ *–v.* express disapproval to (a person or oneself) for a fault. *–n.* **1** rebuke or censure. **2** (often foll. by *to*) thing that brings disgrace or discredit. **3** state of disgrace or discredit. □ **above** (or **beyond**) **reproach** perfect, blameless. [French *reprochier*]

reproachful *adj.* full of or expressing reproach. □ **reproachfully** *adv.*

reprobate /'reprə,beɪt/ *n.* unprincipled or immoral person. [Latin: related to PROVE]

reprocess /riː'prəʊses/ *v.* process again or differently.

reproduce /,riːprə'djuːs/ *v.* (**-cing**) **1** produce a copy or representation of. **2** cause to be seen or heard etc. again (*tried to reproduce the sound exactly*). **3** produce further members of the same species by natural means. **4** *refl.* produce offspring. □ **reproducible** *adj.*

reproduction /,riːprə'dʌkʃ(ə)n/ *n.* **1** reproducing or being reproduced, esp. the production of further members of the same species. **2** copy of a work of art. **3** (*attrib.*) (of furniture etc.) imitating an earlier style. **4** quality of reproduced sound.□ **reproductive** *adj.*

reprogram /riː'prəʊgræm/ *v.* (also **reprogramme**) (**-mm-**; *US* **-m-**) program (esp. a computer) again or differently. □ **reprogramable** *adj.* (also **reprogrammable**).

reproof /rɪ'pruːf/ *n. formal* **1** blame (*glance of reproof*). **2** rebuke. [French *reprove*: related to REPROVE]

reprove /rɪ'pruːv/ *v.* (**-ving**) *formal* rebuke (a person, conduct, etc.). [Latin: related to REPROBATE]

reptile /'reptaɪl/ *n.* **1** cold-blooded scaly animal of a class including snakes, lizards, crocodiles, turtles, tortoises, etc. **2** mean, grovelling, or repulsive person. □ **reptilian** /-'tɪlɪən/ *adj.* & *n.* [Latin *repo rept-* creep]

republic /rɪ'pʌblɪk/ *n.* state in which supreme power is held by the people or their elected representatives or by an elected or nominated president, not by a monarch etc. [Latin *res* concern: related to PUBLIC]

republican *–adj.* **1** of or constituted as a republic. **2** characteristic of a republic. **3** advocating or supporting republican government. *–n.* **1** person advocating or supporting republican government. **2** (**Republican**) **a** *US* supporter of the Republican Party. **b** *Ir.* supporter of the IRA or Sinn Féin. □ **republicanism** *n.*

republish /riː'pʌblɪʃ/ *v.* publish again or in a new edition etc. □ **republication** /-'keɪʃ(ə)n/ *n.*

repudiate /rɪ'pjuːdɪ,eɪt/ *v.* (**-ting**) **1 a** disown, disavow, reject. **b** refuse dealings with. **c** deny. **2** refuse to recognize or obey (authority or a treaty). **3** refuse to pay (a debt), e.g. (of a government) refuse to settle (a national debt incurred by a previous government). **4** refuse to honour (a contract). See also BREACH OF CONTRACT. □ **repudiation** /-'eɪʃ(ə)n/ *n.* [Latin *repudium* divorce]

■ **Usage** See note at *refute*.

repugnance /rɪ'pʌgnəns/ *n.* **1** antipathy; aversion. **2** inconsistency or incompatibility of ideas etc. [Latin *pugno* fight]

repugnant *adj.* **1** extremely distasteful. **2** contradictory.

repulse /rɪ'pʌls/ *–v.* (**-sing**) **1** drive back by force of arms. **2 a** rebuff. **b** refuse. *–n.* **1** repulsing or being repulsed. **2** rebuff. [Latin: related to REPEL]

repulsion /rɪ'pʌlʃ(ə)n/ *n.* **1** aversion, disgust. **2** *Physics* tendency of bodies to repel each other.

repulsive /rɪ'pʌlsɪv/ *adj.* causing aversion or loathing; disgusting. □ **repulsively** *adv.* [French *répulsif* or REPULSE]

repurchase /riː'pɜːtʃɪs/ *–v.* (**-sing**) purchase again. *–n.* **1** act of purchasing again. **2** purchase from an investor of a unit-trust holding by the trust managers.

♦ **repurchase agreement** *n.* (also **repo**) agreement in which a security is sold and later bought back at an agreed price. The seller is paid in full and makes the agreement to raise ready money without losing the holding. The buyer negotiates a suitable repurchase price to enable a profit to be earned equivalent to interest on the buyer's money. An **overnight repo** is a method of overcoming a short-term shortage of funds on the money market using a repo on an overnight basis.

---

reputable /'repjʊtəb(ə)l/ *adj.* of good repute; respectable. [French or medieval Latin: related to REPUTE]

reputation /,repjʊ'teɪʃ(ə)n/ *n.* **1** what is generally said or believed about a person's or thing's character (*reputation for honesty*; *reputation of being a crook*). **2** state of being well thought of; respectability (*lost its reputation*). [Latin: related to REPUTE]

repute /rɪ'pjuːt/ *–n.* reputation. *–v.* (as **reputed** *adj.*) **1** be generally considered (*is reputed to be the best*). **2** passing as, but probably not (*his reputed father*). □ **reputedly** *adv.* [Latin *puto* think]

♦ **reputed owner** *n.* person who acts as if he or she owns certain goods, with the consent of the true owner. If that person becomes bankrupt, the goods are divided among the creditors and the true owner may be estopped (see ESTOPPEL) from claiming them.

---

request /rɪ'kwest/ *–n.* **1** act of asking for something (*came at his request*). **2** thing asked for. *–v.* **1** ask to be given, allowed, or favoured with. **2** (foll. by *to* + infin.) ask (a person) to do something. **3** (foll. by *that*) ask that. □ **by** (or **on**) **request** in response to an expressed wish. [Latin: related to REQUIRE]

request stop *n.* bus-stop at which a bus stops only if requested.

requiem /'rekwɪəm/ *n.* **1** (**Requiem**) (also *attrib.*) chiefly *RC Ch.* mass for the repose of the souls of the dead. **2** music for this. [Latin, = rest]

require /rɪ'kwaɪə(r)/ *v.* (**-ring**) **1** need; depend on for success or fulfilment (*the work requires patience*). **2** lay down as an imperative (*required by law*). **3** command; instruct (a person etc.). **4** order; insist on (an action or measure). □ **requirement** *n.* [Latin *requiro -quisit-* seek]

requisite /'rekwɪzɪt/ *–adj.* required by circumstances; necessary to success etc. *–n.* (often foll. by *for*) thing needed (for some purpose). [Latin: related to REQUIRE]

requisition /,rekwɪ'zɪʃ(ə)n/ *–n.* **1** official or government order laying claim to the use of property or materials, usu. during a national emergency, with or without the consent of the owner. **2** formal written demand that some duty should be performed. **3** being called or put into service. *–v.* demand the use or supply of, esp. by requisition order. A property may later be **derequisitioned**, i.e. returned to its owner. [Latin: related to REQUIRE]

requite /rɪ'kwaɪt/ *v.* (**-ting**) **1** make return for (a service). **2** reward or avenge (a favour or injury). **3** (often foll. by *for*) make return to (a person). **4** reciprocate (love etc.) □ **requital** *n.* [from RE-, *quite* = QUIT]

reran *past* of RERUN.

reread /riː'riːd/ *v.* (*past* and *past part.* **reread** /-'red/) read again.

rerecord /,riːrɪ'kɔːd/ *v.* record again.

reredos /'rɪədɒs/ *n.* ornamental screen covering the wall at the back of an altar. [Anglo-French: related to ARREARS, *dos* back]

re-release /,riːrɪ'liːs/ *–v.* (**-sing**) release (a record, film, etc.) again. *–n.* re-released record, film, etc.

re-route /riː'ruːt/ *v.* (**-teing**) send or carry by a different route.

rerun *–v.* /riː'rʌn/ (**-nn-**; *past* **reran**; *past part.* **rerun**) **1** run (a race, film, etc.) again. **2** repeat (a course of action). *–n.* /'riːrʌn/ **1** act of rerunning. **2** film etc. shown again. **3** repetition (of events).

resale /riː'seɪl/ *n.* sale of a thing previously bought.

♦ **resale price maintenance** *n.* (also **RPM**) agreement between a manufacturer, wholesaler, or retailer not to sell a specified product below a fixed price, usu. one given by the manufacturer. The purpose is to ensure that all parties are allowed to make a reasonable profit without cut-throat competition. Such an agreement, however, is not in the public interest as it stifles competition; RPM contracts are now illegal in the UK unless it can be shown that they are in the public interest. See RECOMMENDED RETAIL PRICE.

---

resat *past* and *past part.* of RESIT.

reschedule /riː'ʃedjuːl, -'skedʒʊəl/ *v.* (**-ling**) alter the schedule of; replan.

rescind /rɪ'sɪnd/ *v.* abrogate, revoke, cancel. [Latin *rescindo -sciss-* cut off]

♦ **rescission** /rɪ'sɪʒ(ə)n/ *n.* **1** revoking; cancelling. **2**

Law right of a party to a contract to have it set aside and to be restored to the position he or she was in before the contract was made. This is an equitable remedy, available at the discretion of the court. The usual grounds for rescission are mistake, misrepresentation, undue influence, and unconscionable bargains (i.e. those in which the terms are very unfair). No rescission will be allowed where the party seeking it has taken a benefit under the contract (affirmation), or where it is not possible to restore the parties to their former position, or where third parties have already acquired rights under the contract.

---

rescript /riːˈskrɪpt/ *n.* **1** Roman emperor's or Pope's written reply to an appeal for a decision. **2** official edict or announcement. [Latin *rescribo -script-* reply in writing]

rescue /ˈreskjuː/ *–v.* (**-ues**, **-ued**, **-uing**) (often foll. by *from*) save or set free from danger or harm. *–n.* rescuing or being rescued. □ **rescuer** *n.* [Romanic: related to RE-, EX-[1], QUASH]

reseal /riːˈsiːl/ *v.* seal again. □ **resealable** *adj.*

research /rɪˈsɜːtʃ, ˈriːsɜːtʃ/ *–n.* (often *attrib.*) systematic investigation and study of materials, sources, etc., in order to establish facts and reach conclusions. *–v.* do research into or for. □ **researcher** *n.* [French: related to SEARCH]

■ **Usage** The second pronunciation, with the stress on the first syllable, is considered incorrect by some people.

research and development *n.* (also **R & D**) work directed towards the innovation, introduction, and improvement of products and processes by governments and industrial firms. Research may be pure (seeking clarification of scientific principles with no end product in view) or applied (using the techniques of pure research to some specified commercial end); development usu. refers to the improvement of a product or process by scientists in conjunction with engineers. R & D is the lifeblood of many industries and, indeed, provides one of the main justifications for free enterprise and the making of profits. Vast sums are spent by industrial conglomerates in seeking new products and the means of producing them cheaply, efficiently, and safely.

♦ **research brief** *n.* document that defines the objectives of a marketing research study etc. before the research is undertaken.

---

resell /riːˈsel/ *v.* (*past* and *past part.* **resold**) sell (an object etc.) after buying it.

resemblance /rɪˈzembləns/ *n.* likeness or similarity. [Anglo-French: related to RESEMBLE]

resemble /rɪˈzemb(ə)l/ *v.* (**-ling**) be like; have a similarity to, or the same appearance as. [French *sembler* seem]

resent /rɪˈzent/ *v.* feel indignation at; be aggrieved by (a circumstance, action, or person). [Latin *sentio* feel]

resentful *adj.* feeling resentment. □ **resentfully** *adv.*

resentment *n.* indignant or bitter feelings. [Italian or French: related to RESENT]

reservation /ˌrezəˈveɪʃ(ə)n/ *n.* **1** reserving or being reserved. **2** thing booked, e.g. a room in a hotel. **3** spoken or unspoken limitation or exception to an agreement etc. **4** (in full **central reservation**) strip of land between the carriageways of a road. **5** area of land reserved for occupation by American Indians etc. [Latin: related to RESERVE]

reserve /rɪˈzɜːv/ *–v.* (**-ving**) **1** put aside, keep back for a later occasion or special use. **2** order to be specially retained or allocated for a particular person or at a particular time. **3** retain or secure (*reserve the right to*). *–n.* **1** thing reserved for future use; extra amount. **2** limitation or exception attached to something. **3** self-restraint; reticence; lack of cordiality. **4** part of the capital of a company, other than the share capital, largely arising from retained profit or from the issue of share capital at more than its nominal value. Reserves are surpluses not yet distributed and, in some cases (e.g. share premium account or capital redemption reserve), not distributable (cf. PROVISION *n.* 4). The directors of a company may choose to earmark part of these funds for a special purpose (e.g. a **reserve for obsolescence** of plant). However, reserves should not be seen as specific sums of money put aside for special purposes as they are represented by the general net assets of the company. Reserves are subdivided into **revenue reserves**, which are available to be distributed to the shareholders by way of dividends, and **capital reserves**, which for various reasons are not distributable as dividends, although they may be converted into permanent share capital by way of a bonus issue (see CAPITAL RESERVES). **5** (in *sing.* or *pl.*) assets kept readily available. **6** (in *sing.* or *pl.*) **a** troops withheld from action to reinforce or protect others. **b** forces in addition to the regular army etc., but available in an emergency. **7** member of the military reserve. **8** extra player chosen as a possible substitute in a team. **9** land reserved for special use, esp. as a habitat (*nature reserve*). □ **in reserve** unused and available if required. **reserve judgement** postpone giving one's opinion. [Latin *servo* keep]

♦ **reserve capital** *n.* (also **uncalled capital**) part of the issued capital of a company that is held in reserve and is intended only to be called up if the company is wound up.

♦ **reserve currency** *n.* foreign currency that is held by a government because it has confidence in its stability and intends to use it to settle international debts. The US dollar and the pound sterling fulfilled this role for many years but the Japanese yen and the Deutschmark are now preferred by most governments.

---

reserved *adj.* **1** reticent; slow to reveal emotion or opinions; uncommunicative. **2** set apart, destined for a particular use.

reserve price *n.* lowest acceptable price stipulated for an item sold at public auction. If the reserve price is not reached by the bidding, the auctioneer is instructed to withdraw the article from sale.

♦ **reserve tranche** *n.* the 25% of its quota to which a member of the International Monetary Fund has unconditional access, for which it pays no charges, and for which there is no obligation to repay the funds. The reserve tranche corresponds to the 25% of quota that was paid not in the member's domestic currency but in Special Drawing Rights (SDRs) or currencies of other IMF members. It counts as part of the member's foreign reserves. Before 1978 it was known as the **gold tranche**, as it was paid in gold. Like all IMF facilities it is available only to avert balance of payments problems, although for the reserve tranche the IMF has no power either to challenge the member's assessment of need or to impose a corrective policy. Further funds are available through credit tranches but these are subject to certain conditions (see CONDITIONALITY). Use of the reserve tranche was heaviest in the 1970s, when members needed it to gain access to the IMF's Oil Facilities (1974–6) and the US made a record level of reserve-tranche purchases (1978).

---

reservist *n.* member of the military reserve.

reservoir /ˈrezəˌvwɑː(r)/ *n.* **1** large natural or artificial lake as a source of water supply. **2** receptacle for fluid. **3** supply of information etc. [French: related to RESERVE]

reset /riːˈset/ *v.* (**-tt-**; *past* and *past part.* **reset**) set (a bone, gems, a clock etc.) again or differently.

resettle /riːˈset(ə)l/ *v.* (**-ling**) settle again or elsewhere. □ **resettlement** *n.*

reshape /riːˈʃeɪp/ *v.* (**-ping**) shape or form again or differently.

reshuffle /riːˈʃʌf(ə)l/ *–v.* (**-ling**) **1** shuffle (cards) again. **2** change the posts of (government ministers etc.). *–n.* act of reshuffling.

reside /rɪˈzaɪd/ *v.* (**-ding**) **1** have one's home, dwell permanently. **2** (foll. by *in*) (of power, a right, etc.) be vested in. **3** (foll. by *in*) (of a quality) be present or inherent in. [Latin *sedeo* sit]

residence /ˈrezɪd(ə)ns/ *n.* **1** process of residing or being resident. **2 a** place where a person resides. **b** house, esp. one of pretension. □ **in residence** living or working at a specified place, esp. for the performance of duties (*artist in residence*).

residency /ˈrezɪdənsɪ/ *n.* (*pl.* **-ies**) **1** = RESIDENCE 1, 2a. **2** permanent or regular engagement of a musician, artist, etc., in one place.

resident *–n.* **1** (often foll. by *of*) **a** permanent inhabitant. **b** non-migratory species of bird. **2** guest in a hotel etc. staying overnight. *–adj.* **1** residing; in residence. **2** having quarters at one's workplace etc. (*resident housekeeper*). **3** located in. **4** (of birds etc.) non-migratory.

residential /ˌrezɪˈdenʃ(ə)l/ *adj.* **1** suitable for or occupied by dwellings (*residential area*). **2** used as a residence (*residential hotel*). **3** based on or connected with residence (*residential course*).

residual /rɪˈzɪdjʊəl/ *–adj.* left as a residue or residuum. *–n.* residual quantity.

◆ **residual unemployment** *n.* amount of unemployment accounted for by people in an economy that remain unemployed, even when there is full employment. They consist largely of people who are so physically or mentally handicapped that they are virtually unemployable; they therefore do not usu. feature in unemployment statistics.

residuary /rɪˈzɪdjʊərɪ/ *adj.* **1** of the residue of an estate (*residuary bequest*). **2** residual.

◆ **residuary legatee** *n.* person to whom a testator's estate is left after specific bequests have been satisfied.

residue /ˈrezɪˌdjuː/ *n.* **1** what is left over or remains; remainder. **2** what remains of an estate after the payment of charges, debts, and bequests. [Latin *residuum*: related to RESIDUUM]

residuum /rɪˈzɪdjʊəm/ *n.* (*pl.* **-dua**) **1** substance left after combustion or evaporation. **2** residue. [Latin: related to RESIDE]

resign /rɪˈzaɪn/ *v.* **1** (often foll. by *from*) give up office, one's employment, etc. **2** relinquish, surrender (a right, task, etc.). **3** *refl.* (usu. foll. by *to*) reconcile (oneself etc.) to the inevitable. [Latin *signo* sign]

re-sign /riːˈsaɪn/ *v.* sign again.

resignation /ˌrezɪgˈneɪʃ(ə)n/ *n.* **1** resigning, esp. from one's job or office. **2** letter etc. conveying this. **3** reluctant acceptance of the inevitable. [medieval Latin: related to RESIGN]

resigned *adj.* **1** (often foll. by *to*) having resigned oneself; resolved to endure. **2** indicative of this □ **resignedly** /-nɪdlɪ/ *adv.*

resilient /rɪˈzɪlɪənt/ *adj.* **1** resuming its original shape after compression etc. **2** readily recovering from a setback. □ **resilience** *n.* [Latin: related to SALIENT]

resin /ˈrezɪn/ *–n.* **1** adhesive substance secreted by some plants and trees. **2** (in full **synthetic resin**) organic compound made by polymerization etc. and used in plastics. *–v.* (**-n-**) rub or treat with resin. □ **resinous** *adj.* [Latin]

resist /rɪˈzɪst/ *–v.* **1** withstand the action or effect of. **2** stop the course or progress of. **3** abstain from (pleasure, temptation, etc.). **4** strive against; try to impede; refuse to comply with (*resist arrest*). **5** offer opposition; refuse to comply. *–n.* protective coating of a resistant substance. □ **resistible** *adj.* [Latin *sisto* stop]

resistance *n.* **1** resisting; refusal to comply. **2** power of resisting. **3** ability to withstand disease. **4** impeding or stopping effect exerted by one thing on another. **5** *Physics* property of hindering the conduction of electricity, heat, etc. **6** resistor. **7** secret organization resisting a régime, esp. in an occupied country. □ **resistant** *adj.* [Latin: related to RESIST]

resistor *n.* device having resistance to the passage of an electric current.

resit *–v.* /riːˈsɪt/ (**-tt-**; *past* and *past part.* **resat**) sit (an examination) again after failing. *–n.* /ˈriːsɪt/ **1** resitting of an examination. **2** examination specifically for this.

resold *past* and *past part.* of RESELL.

resoluble /rɪˈzɒljʊb(ə)l/ *adj.* **1** that can be resolved. **2** (foll. by *into*) analysable into. [Latin: related to RESOLVE]

resolute /ˈrezəˌluːt/ *adj.* determined, decided, firm of purpose. □ **resolutely** *adv.* [Latin: related to RESOLVE]

resolution /ˌrezəˈluːʃ(ə)n/ *n.* **1** resolute temper or character. **2** thing resolved on; intention. **3** formal expression of opinion or intention by the members of a company, a legislative body, or a public meeting. If a motion is put before the members of a company at a general meeting and the required majority vote in favour of it, the motion is passed and becomes a resolution, by which members are bound. A resolution may also be passed by unanimous informal consent of the members. An **ordinary resolution** may be passed by a bare majority of the members. The Companies Act prescribes this type of resolution for certain actions, e.g. the removal of a director. Normally, no particular length of notice is required for an ordinary resolution to be proposed, beyond the notice needed to call the meeting. However, if a director or an auditor is to be removed, or if a director who is over the statutory retirement age is to be appointed or permitted to remain in office, special notice must be given to the company (28 days) and by the company to the members (21 days). An **extraordinary resolution** is one for which 14 days' notice is required. The notice should state that it is an extraordinary resolution and for such a resolution 75% of those voting must approve it if it is to be passed. A **special resolution** requires 21 days' notice to the shareholders and a 75% majority to be effective. The type of resolution required to make a particular decision may be prescribed by the Companies Acts or by the company's articles. For example, an extraordinary resolution is required to wind up a company voluntarily, while a special resolution is required to change the company's articles of association. **4** (usu. foll. by *of*) solving of a doubt, problem, or question. **5** separation into components. **6** (foll. by *into*) conversion into another form. **7** *Mus.* causing discord to pass into concord. **8** smallest interval measurable by a scientific instrument. **9 a** amount of information or detail that can be produced by a device (e.g. a VDU) or revealed in a computer or TV image etc. The device or image can be described qualitatively as having a **high resolution** or a **low resolution** etc. **b** number of lines (e.g. of text) that can be displayed on a screen, or the number of pixels that are available in the horizontal and vertical directions of a graphics screen.

resolve /rɪˈzɒlv/ *–v.* (**-ving**) **1** make up one's mind; decide firmly (*resolved to leave, on leaving*). **2** cause (a person) to do this (*events resolved him to leave*). **3** solve, explain, or settle (a doubt, argument, etc.). **4** (foll. by *that*) (of an assembly or meeting) pass a resolution by vote. **5** (often foll. by *into*) (cause to) separate into constituent parts; analyse. **6** (foll. by *into*) reduce by mental analysis into. **7** *Mus.* convert or be converted into concord. *–n.* firm mental decision or intention; determination. [Latin: related to SOLVE]

resolved *adj.* resolute, determined.

resonant /ˈrezənənt/ *adj.* **1** (of sound) echoing, resounding; continuing to sound; reinforced or prolonged by reflection or vibration. **2** (of a body, room, etc.) tending to reinforce or prolong sounds, esp. by vibration. **3** (often foll. by *with*) (of a place) resounding. □ **resonance** *n.* [Latin: related to RESOUND]

resonate /ˈrezəˌneɪt/ *v.* (**-ting**) produce or show resonance; resound. □ **resonator** *n.* [Latin: related to RESONANT]

resort /rɪˈzɔːt/ *–n.* **1** place frequented esp. for holidays or for a specified purpose or quality (*seaside resort; health resort*). **2 a** thing to which one has recourse; expedient, measure. **b** (foll. by *to*) recourse to; use of (*without resort to violence*). *–v.* **1** (foll. by *to*) turn to as an expedient (*resorted to force*). **2** (foll. by *to*) go often or in large numbers to. □ **in the** (or **as a) last resort** when all else has failed. [French *sortir* go out]

re-sort /riːˈsɔːt/ *v.* sort again or differently.

resound /rɪˈzaʊnd/ *v.* **1** (often foll. by *with*) (of a place) ring or echo. **2** (of a voice, instrument, sound, etc.) produce echoes; go on sounding; fill a place with sound. **3 a** (of a reputation etc.) be much talked of. **b** (foll. by *through*) produce a sensation. **4** (of a place) re-echo (a sound). [Latin: related to SOUND[1]]

resounding *adj.* **1** ringing, echoing. **2** notable, emphatic (*a resounding success*).

resource /rɪ'zɔːs/ *–n.* **1** expedient or device. **2** (often in *pl.*) means available; facilities, equipment, stock, or supply that can be drawn on; asset. **3** (in *pl.*) country's collective wealth. **4** skill in devising expedients (*person of great resource*). **5** (in *pl.*) one's inner strength, ingenuity, etc. *–v.* (**-cing**) provide with resources. □ **resourceful** *adj.* (in sense 4). **resourcefully** *adv.* **resourcefulness** *n.* [French: related to SOURCE]

respect /rɪ'spekt/ *–n.* **1** deferential esteem felt or shown towards a person or quality. **2** (foll. by *of, for*) heed or regard. **3** aspect, detail, etc. (*correct in all respects*). **4** reference, relation (*with respect to*). **5** (in *pl.*) polite messages or attentions (*give her my respects*). *–v.* **1** regard with deference or esteem. **2 a** avoid interfering with or harming. **b** treat with consideration. **c** refrain from offending (a person, feelings, etc.). □ **in respect of** (or **with respect to**) as concerns. □ **respecter** *n.* [Latin *respicio -spect-* look back at]

respectable *adj.* **1** of acceptable social standing; decent and proper in appearance or behaviour. **2** fairly competent (*a respectable try*). **3** reasonably good in condition, appearance, number, size, etc. □ **respectability** /-'bɪlɪtɪ/ *n.* **respectably** *adv.*

respectful *adj.* showing deference. □ **respectfully** *adv.*

respecting *prep.* with regard to; concerning.

respective *adj.* of or relating to each of several individually (*go to your respective seats*). [French or medieval Latin: related to RESPECT]

respectively *adv.* for each separately or in turn, and in the order mentioned (*she and I gave £10 and £1 respectively*).

respell /riː'spel/ *v.* (*past* and *past part.* **respelt** or **respelled**) spell again or differently, esp. phonetically.

respiration /ˌrespə'reɪʃ(ə)n/ *n.* **1 a** breathing. **b** single breath in or out. **2** *Biol.* (in living organisms) the absorption of oxygen and the release of energy and carbon dioxide. [Latin *spiro* breathe]

respirator /'respəˌreɪtə(r)/ *n.* **1** apparatus worn over the face to warm, filter, or purify inhaled air. **2** apparatus for maintaining artificial respiration.

respire /rɪ'spaɪə(r)/ *v.* (**-ring**) **1** (also *absol.*) breathe (air etc.); inhale and exhale. **2** (of a plant) carry out respiration. □ **respiratory** /rɪ'spɪrətərɪ/ *adj.*

respite /'respaɪt/ *n.* **1** interval of rest or relief. **2** delay permitted before the discharge of an obligation or the suffering of a penalty. [Latin: related to RESPECT]

resplendent /rɪ'splend(ə)nt/ *adj.* brilliant, dazzlingly or gloriously bright. □ **resplendence** *n.* [Latin *resplendeo* shine]

respond /rɪ'spɒnd/ *v.* **1** answer, reply. **2** act or behave in a corresponding manner. **3** (usu. foll. by *to*) show sensitiveness to by behaviour or change (*does not respond to kindness*). **4** (of a congregation) make set answers to a priest etc. [Latin *respondeo -spons-*]

respondent *–n.* defendant, esp. in an appeal or divorce case. *–adj.* in the position of defendant.

♦ **respondentia** /ˌrespɒn'denʃə/ see HYPOTHECATION 2. [Latin]

---

response /rɪ'spɒns/ *n.* **1** answer given in a word or act; reply. **2** feeling, movement, or change caused by a stimulus or influence. **3** (often in *pl.*) any part of the liturgy said or sung in answer to the priest. [Latin: related to RESPOND]

responsibility /rɪˌspɒnsə'bɪlɪtɪ/ *n.* (*pl.* **-ies**) **1 a** (often foll. by *for, of*) being responsible. **b** authority; managerial freedom (*job with more responsibility*). **2** person or thing for which one is responsible; duty, commitment. **3** capacity for rational conduct (*diminished responsibility*).

responsible /rɪ'spɒnsəb(ə)l/ *adj.* **1** (often foll. by *to, for*) liable to be called to account (to a person or for a thing). **2** morally accountable for one's actions; capable of rational conduct. **3** of good credit, position, or repute; respectable; evidently trustworthy. **4** (often foll. by *for*) being the primary cause. **5** involving responsibility. □ **responsibly** *adv.*

responsive /rɪ'spɒnsɪv/ *adj.* **1** (often foll. by *to*) responding readily (to some influence). **2** sympathetic. **3 a** answering. **b** by way of answer. □ **responsiveness** *n.*

respray *–v.* /riː'spreɪ/ spray again (esp. a vehicle with paint). *–n.* /'riːspreɪ/ act of respraying.

rest[1] *–v.* **1** cease from exertion, action, etc. **2** be still or asleep, esp. to refresh oneself or recover strength. **3** give relief or repose to; allow to rest. **4** (foll. by *on, upon, against*) lie on; be supported by. **5** (foll. by *on, upon*) depend or be based on. **6** (foll. by *on, upon*) (of a look) alight or be steadily directed on. **7** (foll. by *on, upon*) place for support or foundation on. **8** (of a problem or subject) be left without further investigation or discussion (*let the matter rest*). **9 a** lie in death. **b** (foll. by *in*) lie buried in (a churchyard etc.). **10** (as **rested** *adj.*) refreshed by resting. *–n.* **1** repose or sleep. **2** cessation of exertion, activity, etc. **3** period of resting. **4** support for holding or steadying something. **5** *Mus.* **a** interval of silence. **b** sign denoting this. □ **at rest** not moving; not agitated or troubled; dead. **be resting** *euphem.* (of an actor) be out of work. **rest one's case** conclude one's argument etc. **rest on one's laurels** not seek further success. **rest on one's oars** relax one's efforts. **set at rest** settle or relieve (a question, a person's mind, etc.). [Old English]

rest[2] *–n.* (prec. by *the*) the remaining part or parts; the others; the remainder of some quantity or number. *–v.* **1** remain in a specified state (*rest assured*). **2** (foll. by *with*) be left in the hands or charge of (*the final arrangements rest with you*). □ **for the rest** as regards anything else. [French *rester* remain]

restart *–v.* /riː'stɑːt/ start again. *–n.* /'riːstɑːt/ act of restarting.

restate /riː'steɪt/ *v.* (**-ting**) express again or differently, esp. for emphasis. □ **restatement** *n.*

restaurant /'restəˌrɒnt/ *n.* public premises where meals may be bought and eaten. [French from *restaurer* RESTORE]

restaurant car *n.* dining-car.

restaurateur /ˌrestərə'tɜː(r)/ *n.* restaurant-keeper.

rest-cure *n.* rest usu. of some weeks as a medical treatment.

restful *adj.* giving rest or a feeling of rest; quiet, undisturbed. □ **restfully** *adv.* **restfulness** *n.*

rest home *n.* place where old or convalescent people are cared for.

restitution /ˌrestɪ'tjuːʃ(ə)n/ *n.* **1** restoring of a thing to its proper owner. **2** reparation for an injury (esp. *make restitution*). It is a legal principle that a person who has been unjustly enriched at the expense of another should make restitution, e.g. by returning property or money. [Latin]

restive /'restɪv/ *adj.* **1** fidgety; restless. **2** (of a horse) jibbing; refractory. **3** (of a person) resisting control. □ **restively** *adv.* **restiveness** *n.* [French: related to REST[2]]

restless *adj.* **1** without rest or sleep. **2** uneasy; agitated. **3** constantly in motion, fidgeting, etc. □ **restlessly** *adv.* **restlessness** *n.* [Old English: related to REST[1]]

restock /riː'stɒk/ *v.* (also *absol.*) stock again or differently.

restoration /ˌrestə'reɪʃ(ə)n/ *n.* **1** restoring or being restored. **2** model or representation of the supposed original form of a thing. **3** (**Restoration**) *hist.* **a** (prec. by *the*) re-establishment of the British monarchy in 1660. **b** (often *attrib.*) literary period following this (*Restoration comedy*).

restorative /rɪ'stɒrətɪv/ *–adj.* tending to restore health or strength. *–n.* restorative medicine, food, etc.

restore /rɪ'stɔː(r)/ *v.* (**-ring**) **1** bring back to the original state by rebuilding, repairing, etc. **2** bring back to health etc. **3** give back to the original owner etc. **4** reinstate. **5**

replace; put back; bring back to a former condition. **6** make a representation of the supposed original state of (a ruin, extinct animal, etc.). □ **restorer** *n.* [Latin *restauro*]

restrain /rɪˈstreɪn/ *v.* **1** (often *refl.*, usu. foll. by *from*) check or hold in; keep in check, under control, or within bounds. **2** repress, keep down. **3** confine, imprison. [Latin *restringo -strict-*]

restraint *n.* **1** restraining or being restrained. **2** restraining agency or influence. **3** moderation; self-control. **4** reserve of manner. **5** confinement, esp. because of insanity.

♦ **restraint of trade** *n.* term in a contract that restricts a person's right to carry on his or her trade or profession. An example, in a contract covering the sale of a business, would be a clause that attempts to restrict the seller's freedom to set up in competition to the buyer. Such clauses are illegal, unless they can be shown not to be contrary to the public interest.

---

restrict /rɪˈstrɪkt/ *v.* **1** confine, limit. **2** withhold from general circulation or disclosure. □ **restriction** *n.* [Latin: related to RESTRAIN]

restrictive /rɪˈstrɪktɪv/ *adj.* restricting. [French or medieval Latin: related to RESTRICT]

♦ **restrictive covenant** *n.* **1** clause in a contract that restricts the freedom of one of the parties in some way. Employment contracts, for example, sometimes include a clause in which an employee agrees not to compete with the employer for a specified period after leaving the employment. Such clauses may not be enforceable in law. See RESTRAINT OF TRADE; RESTRICTIVE TRADE PRACTICES. **2** clause in a contract affecting the use of land. See COVENANT *n.* 2.

♦ **restrictive endorsement** *n.* endorsement on a bill of exchange that restricts the freedom of the endorsee to negotiate it.

♦ **restrictive trade practices** *n.pl.* agreements between traders that are not considered to be in the public interest. Under the Restrictive Trade Practices Acts (1956, 1968, and 1976) and the Fair Trading Act (1973) any agreement between two or more suppliers of goods or services restricting prices, conditions of sale, quantities offered, processes, areas and persons to be supplied, etc. must be registered with the Director General of Fair Trading and, where appropriate, investigated by the **Restrictive Practices Court**. Such agreements are presumed to be contrary to the public interest unless the parties are able to prove to the court that the agreement is beneficial. An example of an agreement permitted by the court is the Net Book Agreement. In 1976 the service industries were included in the Restrictive Trade Practices Act. This led to an examination by the Office of Fair Trading of the London Stock Exchange and its subsequent (1986) change of rules (see BIG BANG).

---

rest room *n.* esp. *US* public lavatory.

restructure /riːˈstrʌktʃə(r)/ *v.* (**-ring**) give a new structure to; rebuild; rearrange.

restyle /riːˈstaɪl/ *v.* (**-ling**) reshape; remake in a new style.

result /rɪˈzʌlt/ *–n.* **1** consequence, issue, or outcome of something. **2** satisfactory outcome (*gets results*). **3** end product of calculation. **4** (in *pl.*) list of scores or winners etc. in examinations or sporting events. *–v.* **1** (often foll. by *from*) arise as the actual, or follow as a logical, consequence. **2** (often foll. by *in*) have a specified end or outcome (*resulted in a large profit*). [Latin *resulto* spring back]

resultant *–adj.* resulting, esp. as the total outcome of more or less opposed forces. *–n.* force etc. equivalent to two or more acting in different directions at the same point.

resume /rɪˈzjuːm/ *v.* (**-ming**) **1** begin again or continue after an interruption. **2** begin to speak, work, or use again; recommence. **3** get back; take back (*resume one's seat*). [Latin *sumo sumpt-* take]

résumé /ˈrezjʊˌmeɪ/ *n.* summary. [French: related to RESUME]

resumption /rɪˈzʌmpʃ(ə)n/ *n.* resuming. □ **resumptive** *adj.* [Latin: related to RESUME]

resurface /riːˈsɜːfɪs/ *v.* (**-cing**) **1** lay a new surface on (a road etc.). **2** return to the surface. **3** turn up again.

resurgent /rɪˈsɜːdʒ(ə)nt/ *adj.* rising or arising again. □ **resurgence** *n.* [Latin *resurgo -surrect-* rise again]

resurrect /ˌrezəˈrekt/ *v.* **1** *colloq.* revive the practice, use, or memory of. **2** raise or rise from the dead. [back-formation from RESURRECTION]

resurrection /ˌrezəˈrekʃ(ə)n/ *n.* **1** rising from the dead. **2** (**Resurrection**) Christ's rising from the dead. **3** revival after disuse, inactivity, or decay. [Latin: related to RESURGENT]

resuscitate /rɪˈsʌsɪˌteɪt/ *v.* (**-ting**) **1** revive from unconsciousness or apparent death. **2** revive, restore. □ **resuscitation** /-ˈteɪʃ(ə)n/ *n.* [Latin *suscito* raise]

retail /ˈriːteɪl/ *–n.* sale of goods in small quantities to the public, and usu. not for resale. *–adj. & adv.* by retail; at a retail price. *–v.* **1** sell (goods) by retail. **2** (often foll. by *at, of*) (of goods) be sold in this way (esp. for a specified price). **3** /also rɪˈteɪl/ recount; relate details of. [French *taillier* cut: related to TALLY]

♦ **retailer** *n.* distributor that sells goods or services to consumers (cf. WHOLESALER). There are, broadly, three categories of retailer: chain stores, cooperative retailers, and independent retailers.

♦ **retail price index** *n.* (also **RPI**) index of the prices of goods and services in retail shops purchased by average households, expressed in percentage terms relative to a base year, which is taken as 100. For example, if 1987 is taken as the base year for the UK (i.e. average prices in 1987 = 100), then in 1946 the RPI stood at 7.4, and in 1990 at 126.1. The RPI is published by the Central Statistical Office on a monthly basis and includes the prices of some 130 000 different commodities. The RPI is one of the standard measures of the rate of inflation. See also PRODUCER PRICE INDEX; TAX AND PRICE INDEX.

♦ **retail tender** *n.* application to buy a substantial number of shares in a privatization offer through a **retail tender broker**.

---

retain /rɪˈteɪn/ *v.* **1 a** keep possession of; not lose; continue to have. **b** not abolish, discard, or alter. **2** keep in one's memory. **3** keep in place; hold fixed. **4** secure the services of (a person, esp. a barrister) with a preliminary payment. [Latin *retineo -tent-*]

♦ **retained earnings** *n.pl.* (also **retentions**) profits earned to date but not yet distributed to shareholders by way of dividends. Such earnings form an important part of the capital of most companies (see RESERVE *n.* 4).

♦ **retained profits** *n.pl.* (also **ploughed-back profits**) part of the annual profits of an organization that are not distributed to its owners but are invested in the assets of the organization. Retained profits are normally the means that enable organizations to grow; it is usu. easier to retain profits than to raise new capital.

---

retainer *n.* **1** fee for securing a person's services. **2** faithful servant (esp. *old retainer*). **3** reduced rent paid to retain unoccupied accommodation. **4** person or thing that retains.

retake *–v.* /riːˈteɪk/ (**-king**; *past* **retook**; *past part.* **retaken**) **1** take (a photograph, exam, etc.) again. **2** recapture. *–n.* /ˈriːteɪk/ **1** act of filming a scene or recording music etc. again. **2** film or recording obtained in this way. **3** act of taking an exam etc. again.

retaliate /rɪˈtælɪˌeɪt/ *v.* (**-ting**) repay an injury, insult, etc. in kind; attack in return. □ **retaliation** /-ˈeɪʃ(ə)n/ *n.* **retaliatory** /-ˈtæljətərɪ/ *adj.* [Latin *talis* such]

retard /rɪˈtɑːd/ *v.* **1** make slow or late. **2** delay the progress or accomplishment of. □ **retardant** *adj.* & *n.* **retardation** /ˌriːtɑːˈdeɪʃ(ə)n/ *n.* [Latin *tardus* slow]

retarded *adj.* backward in mental or physical development.

retch *v.* make a motion of vomiting, esp. involuntarily and without effect. [Old English]

retell /riː'tel/ *v.* (*past* and *past part.* **retold**) tell again or differently.

retention /rɪ'tenʃ(ə)n/ *n.* **1** retaining or being retained. **2** condition of retaining bodily fluid (esp. urine) normally evacuated. **3** amount held back from payment by the customer of a contractor until an agreed period has elapsed as a safeguard against any faults being found in the work done. **4** (in *pl.*) = RETAINED EARNINGS. [Latin: related to RETAIN]

retentive /rɪ'tentɪv/ *adj.* **1** tending to retain. **2** (of memory etc.) not forgetful. [French or medieval Latin: related to RETAIN]

retexture /riː'tekstʃə(r)/ *v.* (**-ring**) treat (material, a garment, etc.) so as to restore its original texture.

rethink –*v.* /riː'θɪŋk/ (*past* and *past part.* **rethought**) consider again, esp. with a view to making changes. –*n.* /'riːθɪŋk/ reassessment; rethinking.

Rethymnon /'reθɪm,nɒn/ port on the Greek island of Crete, on the N coast; pop. (latest est.) 18 500.

reticence /'retɪs(ə)ns/ *n.* **1** avoidance of saying all one knows or feels, or more than is necessary. **2** disposition to silence; taciturnity. □ **reticent** *adj.* [Latin *reticeo* keep silent]

reticulate –*v.* /rɪ'tɪkjʊ,leɪt/ (**-ting**) divide or be divided in fact or appearance into a network. –*adj.* /rɪ'tɪkjʊlət/ reticulated. □ **reticulation** /-'leɪʃ(ə)n/ *n.* [Latin *reticulum* diminutive of *rete* net]

retie /riː'taɪ/ *v.* (**retying**) tie again.

retina /'retɪnə/ *n.* (*pl.* **-s** or **-nae** /-,niː/) layer at the back of the eyeball sensitive to light. □ **retinal** *adj.* [Latin *rete* net]

retinue /'retɪ,njuː/ *n.* body of attendants accompanying an important person. [French: related to RETAIN]

retire /rɪ'taɪə(r)/ *v.* (**-ring**) **1 a** leave office or employment, esp. because of age. **b** cause (a person) to retire from work. **2** withdraw, go away, retreat. **3** seek seclusion or shelter. **4** go to bed. **5** withdraw (troops). **6** *Cricket* (of a batsman) voluntarily end or be compelled to suspend one's innings. **7** *Finance* withdraw (a bill of exchange) from circulation when it has been paid on or before its due date. □ **retire into oneself** become uncommunicative or unsociable. [French *tirer* draw]

retired *adj.* **1** having retired from employment. **2** withdrawn from society or observation; secluded.

retirement *n.* **1 a** retiring from employment or office. The normal retirement age in the UK is 60 for a woman, 65 for a man. It is at these ages that state pensions begin. Other policies can nominate other pre-agreed dates, which the Inland Revenue will accept in certain cases. **b** period of one's life as a retired person. **2** seclusion.

retirement pension *n.* pension paid by the state to retired people above a certain age. See PENSION *n.* 1.

◆ **retirement relief** *n.* relief from capital-gains tax given to persons disposing of business assets at or over 60 years of age, or earlier if retiring due to ill health.

retiring *adj.* shy; fond of seclusion.

retold *past* and *past part.* of RETELL.

retook *past* of RETAKE.

retort[1] /rɪ'tɔːt/ –*n.* incisive, witty, or angry reply. –*v.* **1 a** say by way of a retort. **b** make a retort. **2** repay (an insult or attack) in kind. [Latin *retorqueo -tort-* twist]

retort[2] /rɪ'tɔːt/ –*n.* **1** vessel with a long neck turned downwards, used in distilling liquids. **2** vessel for heating coal to generate gas. –*v.* purify (mercury) by heating in a retort. [medieval Latin: related to RETORT[1]]

retouch /riː'tʌtʃ/ *v.* improve (a picture, photograph, etc.) by minor alterations.

retrace /rɪ'treɪs/ *v.* (**-cing**) **1** go back over (one's steps etc.). **2** trace back to a source or beginning. **3** recall the course of (a thing) in one's memory.

retract /rɪ'trækt/ *v.* **1** withdraw (a statement or undertaking). **2** draw or be drawn back or in. □ **retractable** *adj.* **retraction** *n.* [Latin *retraho -tract-* draw back]

retractile /rɪ'træktaɪl/ *adj.* capable of being retracted.

retrain /riː'treɪn/ *v.* train again or further, esp. for new work.

retread –*v.* /riː'tred/ **1** (*past* **retrod**; *past part.* **retrodden**) tread (a path etc.) again. **2** (*past, past part.* **retreaded**) put a fresh tread on (a tyre). –*n.* /'riːtred/ retreaded tyre.

retreat /rɪ'triːt/ –*v.* **1** (esp. of military forces) go back, retire; relinquish a position. **2** recede. –*n.* **1 a** act of retreating. **b** *Mil.* signal for this. **2** withdrawal into privacy or security. **3** place of shelter or seclusion. **4** period of seclusion for prayer and meditation. **5** *Mil.* bugle-call at sunset. [Latin: related to RETRACT]

retrench /rɪ'trentʃ/ *v.* **1** cut down expenses; introduce economies. **2** reduce the amount of (costs). □ **retrenchment** *n.* [French: related to TRENCH]

retrial /riː'traɪəl/ *n.* second or further (judicial) trial.

retribution /,retrɪ'bjuːʃ(ə)n/ *n.* requital, usu. for evil done; vengeance. □ **retributive** /rɪ'trɪbjʊtɪv/ *adj.* [Latin: related to TRIBUTE]

retrieve /rɪ'triːv/ –*v.* (**-ving**) **1 a** regain possession of. **b** recover by investigation or effort of memory. **2** obtain (information stored in a computer etc.). **3** (of a dog) find and bring in (killed or wounded game etc.). **4** (foll. by *from*) rescue (esp. from a bad state). **5** restore to a flourishing state; revive. **6** repair or set right (a loss or error etc.) (*managed to retrieve the situation*). –*n.* possibility of recovery (*beyond retrieve*). □ **retrievable** *adj.* **retrieval** *n.* [French *trouver* find]

retriever *n.* dog of a breed used for retrieving game.

retro /'retrəʊ/ *slang* –*adj.* reviving or harking back to the past. –*n.* retro fashion or style.

retro- *comb. form* **1** denoting action back or in return. **2** *Anat.* & *Med.* denoting location behind. [Latin]

retroactive /,retrəʊ'æktɪv/ *adj.* (esp. of legislation) effective from a past date.

retrod *past* of RETREAD.

retrodden *past part.* of RETREAD.

retrograde /'retrə,greɪd/ –*adj.* **1** directed backwards. **2** reverting, esp. to an inferior state; declining. **3** reversed (*retrograde order*). –*v.* **1** move backwards; recede. **2** decline, revert. [Latin *retrogradior -gress-* move backwards]

retrogress /,retrə'gres/ *v.* **1** move backwards. **2** deteriorate. □ **retrogression** /-'greʃ(ə)n/ *n.* **retrogressive** *adj.*

retrorocket /'retrəʊ,rɒkɪt/ *n.* auxiliary rocket for slowing down a spacecraft etc.

retrospect /'retrə,spekt/ *n.* □ **in retrospect** when looking back. [from RETRO-, PROSPECT]

retrospection /,retrə'spekʃ(ə)n/ *n.* looking back into the past.

retrospective /,retrə'spektɪv/ –*adj.* **1** looking back on or dealing with the past. **2** (of a statute etc.) applying to the past as well as the future. –*n.* exhibition, recital, etc. showing an artist's development over his or her lifetime. □ **retrospectively** *adv.*

retroussé /rə'truːseɪ/ *adj.* (of the nose) turned up at the tip. [French]

retroverted /'retrəʊ,vɜːtɪd/ *adj.* (of the womb) inclined backwards. [Latin: related to RETRO-, *verto* turn]

retrovirus /'retrəʊ,vaɪərəs/ *n.* any of a group of RNA viruses which form DNA during the replication of their RNA, and so transfer genetic material into the DNA of host cells. [from the initial letters of *reverse transcriptase* + VIRUS]

retry /riː'traɪ/ *v.* (**-ies, -ied**) try (a defendant or lawsuit) a second or further time.

retsina /ret'siːnə/ *n.* Greek white wine flavoured with resin. [modern Greek]

retune /riː'tjuːn/ *v.* (**-ning**) **1** tune (a musical instrument) again or differently. **2** tune (a radio etc.) to a different frequency.

return /rɪ'tɜːn/ –*v.* **1** come or go back. **2** bring, put, or send back. **3** pay back or reciprocate; give in response. **4** yield (a profit). **5** say in reply; retort. **6** (in cricket or tennis etc.) hit or send (the ball) back. **7** state, mention, or describe officially, esp. in answer to a writ or formal demand. **8** (of an electorate) elect as an MP, government, etc. *–n.* **1** coming or going back. **2 a** giving, sending, putting, or paying back. **b** (often in *pl.*) thing given or sent back, usu. because it is unsatisfactory. **Returns inwards** are goods returned to an organization by customers; **returns outwards** are goods returned by an organization to its suppliers. **3** (in full **return ticket**) ticket for a journey to a place and back to the starting-point. **4** (in *sing.* or *pl.*) **a** income or profit from an investment, undertaking, etc. **b** acquisition of these. See also RETURN ON CAPITAL EMPLOYED; RETURNS TO SCALE. **5** formal statement compiled or submitted by order (*income-tax return*). **6** (in full **return match** or **game**) second match etc. between the same opponents. **7 a** person's election as an MP etc. **b** returning officer's announcement of this. □ **by return (of post)** by the next available post in the return direction. **in return** as an exchange or reciprocal action. **many happy returns (of the day)** greeting on a birthday. □ **returnable** *adj.* [Romanic: related to TURN]

♦ **returned cheque** *n.* cheque on which payment has been refused and which has been returned to the bank on which it was drawn. If the reason is lack of funds, the bank will mark it 'refer to drawer'; if the bank wishes to give the drawer an opportunity to pay in sufficient funds to cover it, they will also mark it 'please represent'. The collecting bank will then present it for payment again, after letting the payee know that the cheque has been dishonoured.

---

returnee /ˌrɪtɜːˈniː/ *n.* person who returns home from abroad, esp. after war service.

returning officer *n.* official conducting an election in a constituency and announcing the results.

return key *n.* (also **enter key**) key on a computer keyboard that sends a carriage return character to the computer. It is often used to signal that the current line of typing is complete and may be processed.

♦ **return on capital employed** *n.* (also **ROCE**) profits of an organization expressed as a percentage of the capital employed. This is an important indicator of the efficiency with which the assets of the organization are used; it provides a useful comparison of companies in the same industry or, for the investor, a comparison between various industrial sectors. Frequently, return on capital is calculated by comparing the profits with the book value of the net assets. This tends to undervalue the assets, so that a capital figure based on market value would be more helpful, although not as readily obtainable.

♦ **returns to scale** *n.pl.* relationship between the quantities of input required to produce different levels of output. At very low levels of production, doubling the amount of input will usu. more than double the amount of output; this is called **increasing returns to scale**. At intermediate levels of production it is usu. assumed that double the amount of input will simply double the amount of output, called **constant returns to scale**. At very high levels of output it is usu. thought that doubling input leads to less than a doubling of output (for example, because it becomes increasingly difficult to manage large-scale organizations). This last stage is called **decreasing** (or **diminishing**) **returns to scale**. Assumptions concerning returns to scale are often important in micro-economic analysis.

---

retying *pres. part.* of RETIE.

retype /riːˈtaɪp/ *v.* (**-ping**) type again, esp. to correct errors.

reunify /riːˈjuːnɪˌfaɪ/ *v.* (**-ies, -ied**) restore (esp. separated territories) to a political unity. □ **reunification** /-fɪˈkeɪʃ(ə)n/ *n.*

Réunion /ˌreɪuːnˈjɔ̃/ island in the Indian Ocean, E of Madagascar, an overseas department of France; pop. (1996) 671 000; capital, Saint-Denis. Exports include sugar, molasses, and rum.

reunion /riːˈjuːnjən/ *n.* **1** reuniting or being reunited. **2** social gathering, esp. of people formerly associated.

reunite /ˌriːjuːˈnaɪt/ *v.* (**-ting**) (cause to) come together again.

reupholster /ˌriːʌpˈhəʊlstə(r)/ *v.* upholster anew.

reuse *–v.* /riːˈjuːz/ (**-sing**) use again. *–n.* /riːˈjuːs/ second or further use. □ **reusable** /-ˈjuːzəb(ə)l/ *adj.*

Rev. *abbr.* Reverend.

rev *colloq. –n.* (in *pl.*) number of revolutions of an engine per minute. *–v.* (**-vv-**) **1** (of an engine) revolve; turn over. **2** (also *absol.*; often foll. by *up*) cause (an engine) to run quickly. [abbreviation]

rev. a/c *abbr.* revenue account(s).

♦ **revalorization of currency** /riːˌvælərаɪˈzeɪʃ(ə)n/ *n.* (also **-isation**) replacement of one currency unit by another. A government often takes this step if a nation's currency has been devalued frequently or by a large amount. Cf. REVALUATION OF CURRENCY. □ **revalorize** *v.*

♦ **revaluation of assets** *n.* revaluing the assets of a company, either because they have increased in value since they were acquired or because inflation has made the balance-sheet values unrealistic. The Companies Act (1985) makes it obligatory for the directors of a company to state in the directors' report if they believe the value of land differs materially from the value in the balance sheet. The Companies Act (1980) lays down the procedures to adopt when fixed assets are revalued.

♦ **revaluation of currency** *n.* increasing the value of a currency in terms of gold or other currencies. Revaluation, usu. made by a government that has a persistent balance of payments surplus, has the effect of making imports cheaper but exports dearer and therefore less competitive in a country. It is therefore unpopular with governments. Cf. DEVALUATION 1; REVALORIZATION OF CURRENCY.

---

revalue /riːˈvæljuː/ *v.* (**-ues, -ued, -uing**) give a different, esp. higher, value to (a currency etc.). □ **revaluation** /-ˈeɪʃ(ə)n/ *n.*

revamp /riːˈvæmp/ *v.* **1** renovate, revise, improve. **2** patch up.

Revd *abbr.* Reverend.

reveal /rɪˈviːl/ *v.* **1** display or show; allow to appear. **2** (often as **revealing** *adj.*) disclose, divulge, betray (*revealing remark*). **3** (in *refl.* or *passive*) come to sight or knowledge. [Latin *velum* veil]

reveille /rɪˈvælɪ/ *n.* military waking-signal. [French *réveillez* wake up]

revel /ˈrev(ə)l/ *–v.* (**-ll-**; *US* **-l-**) **1** have a good time; be extravagantly festive. **2** (foll. by *in*) take keen delight in. *–n.* (in *sing.* or *pl.*) revelling. □ **reveller** *n.* **revelry** *n.* (*pl.* **-ies**). [Latin: related to REBEL]

revelation /ˌrevəˈleɪʃ(ə)n/ *n.* **1 a** revealing, esp. the supposed disclosure of knowledge to man by a divine or supernatural agency. **b** knowledge disclosed in this way. **2** striking disclosure. **3** (**Revelation** or *colloq.* **Revelations**) (in full **the Revelation of St John the Divine**) last book of the New Testament.

revenge /rɪˈvendʒ/ *–n.* **1** retaliation for an offence or injury. **2** act of retaliation. **3** desire for this; vindictive feeling. **4** (in games) win after an earlier defeat. *–v.* (**-ging**) **1** (in *refl.* or *passive*; often foll. by *on, upon*) inflict retaliation for (an offence). **2** avenge (a person). [Latin: related to VINDICATE]

revengeful *adj.* eager for revenge. □ **revengefully** *adv.*

revenue /ˈrevəˌnjuː/ *n.* **1 a** income, esp. a substantial one. **b** (in *pl.*) items constituting this. **2** state's annual income from which public expenses are met. **3** department of the civil service collecting this. [French *revenu* from Latin *revenio* return]

♦ **revenue account** *n.* **1** account recording the income from trading operations or the expenses incurred in these operations. **2** budgeted amount that can be spent for day-to-day operational expenses, esp. in public-sector budgeting. Cf. CAPITAL ACCOUNT 2.

♦ **revenue reserve** see RESERVE *n.* 4.

reverberate /rɪˈvɜːbəˌreɪt/ *v.* (**-ting**) **1** (of sound, light, or heat) be returned, echoed, or reflected repeatedly. **2** return (a sound etc.) in this way. **3** (of an event etc.) produce a continuing effect, shock, etc. □ **reverberant** *adj.* **reverberation** /-ˈreɪʃ(ə)n/ *n.* **reverberative** /-rətɪv/ *adj.* [Latin *verbero* beat]

revere /rɪˈvɪə(r)/ *v.* (**-ring**) hold in deep and usu. affectionate or religious respect. [Latin *vereor* fear]

reverence /ˈrevərəns/ *–n.* **1** revering or being revered. **2** capacity for revering. *–v.* (**-cing**) regard or treat with reverence. [Latin: related to REVERE]

reverend /ˈrevərənd/ *adj.* (esp. as the title of a clergyman) deserving reverence. [Latin *reverendus*: related to REVERE]

Reverend Mother *n.* Mother Superior of a convent.

reverent /ˈrevərənt/ *adj.* feeling or showing reverence. □ **reverently** *adv.* [Latin: related to REVERE]

reverential /ˌrevəˈrenʃ(ə)l/ *n.* of the nature of, due to, or characterized by reverence. □ **reverentially** *adv.* [medieval Latin: related to REVERENCE]

reverie /ˈrevərɪ/ *n.* fit of abstracted musing, day-dream. [French]

revers /rɪˈvɪə(r)/ *n.* (*pl.* same /-ˈvɪəz/) **1** turned-back edge of a garment revealing the undersurface. **2** material on this surface. [French: related to REVERSE]

reverse /rɪˈvɜːs/ *–v.* (**-sing**) **1** turn the other way round or up or inside out. **2** change to the opposite character or effect. **3** (cause to) travel backwards. **4** make (an engine etc.) work in a contrary direction. **5** revoke or annul (a decree, act, etc.). *–adj.* **1** backwards or upside down. **2** opposite or contrary in character or order; inverted. *–n.* **1** opposite or contrary (*the reverse is the case*). **2** contrary of the usual manner (*printed in reverse*). **3** piece of misfortune; disaster; defeat. **4** reverse gear or motion. **5** reverse side. **6** side of a coin etc. bearing the secondary design. **7** verso of a printed leaf. □ **reverse arms** hold a rifle with the butt upwards. **reverse the charges** have the recipient of a telephone call pay for it. □ **reversal** *n.* **reversible** *adj.* [Latin *verto vers-* turn]

reverse gear *n.* gear used to make a vehicle etc. go backwards.

♦ **reverse take-over** *n.* **1** purchasing of a public company by a private company. This may be the cheapest way that a private company can obtain a listing on a stock exchange, as it avoids the expenses of a flotation and it may be that the assets of the public company can be purchased at a discount. However, on the London Stock Exchange there are regulations stipulating that the nature of the target company's business must be compatible with that of the private company. The name of the public company is usu. changed to that of the private company, which takes over the listing. **2** buying of a larger company by a smaller company.

♦ **reverse yield gap** see YIELD GAP.

♦ **reversible lay days** see LAY DAYS.

reversing light *n.* white light at the rear of a vehicle showing that it is in reverse gear.

reversion /rɪˈvɜːʃ(ə)n/ *n.* **1** return to a previous state, habit, etc. **2** *Biol.* return to ancestral type. **3** legal right (esp. of the original owner, or his or her heirs) to possess or succeed to property on the death of the present possessor. □ **reversionary** *adj.* [Latin: related to REVERSE]

♦ **reversionary annuity** *n.* = CONTINGENT ANNUITY.

♦ **reversionary bonus** *n.* sum added to the amount payable on death or maturity of a with-profits life-assurance policy. The bonus is added if the life-assurance company has a surplus or has a profit on the investment of its life funds. Once a reversionary bonus has been made it cannot be withdrawn if the policy runs to maturity or to the death of the insured. However, if the policy is cashed, the bonus is usu. reduced by an amount that depends on the length of time the policy has to run.

revert /rɪˈvɜːt/ *v.* **1** (foll. by *to*) return to a former state, practice, opinion, etc. **2** (of property, an office, etc.) return by reversion. □ **revertible** *adj.* (in sense 2).

review /rɪˈvjuː/ *–n.* **1** general survey or assessment of a subject or thing. **2** survey of the past. **3** revision or reconsideration (*is under review*). **4** display and formal inspection of troops etc. **5** published criticism of a book, play, etc. **6** periodical with critical articles on current events, the arts, etc. *–v.* **1** survey or look back on. **2** reconsider or revise. **3** hold a review of (troops etc.). **4** write a review of (a book, play, etc.). □ **reviewer** *n.* [French *revoir*: related to VIEW]

revile /rɪˈvaɪl/ *v.* (**-ling**) abuse verbally. [French: related to VILE]

revise /rɪˈvaɪz/ *v.* (**-sing**) **1** examine or re-examine and improve or amend (esp. written or printed matter). **2** consider and alter (an opinion etc.). **3** (also *absol.*) go over (work learnt or done) again, esp. for an examination. □ **revisory** *adj.* [Latin *reviso* from *video vis-* see]

Revised Standard Version *n.* revision published in 1946–57 of the American Standard Version (itself based on the English RV).

Revised Version *n.* revision published in 1881–95 of the Authorized Version of the Bible.

revision /rɪˈvɪʒ(ə)n/ *n.* **1** revising or being revised. **2** revised edition or form. [Latin: related to REVISE]

revisionism *n.* often *derog.* revision or modification of an orthodoxy, esp. of Marxism. □ **revisionist** *n.* & *adj.*

revisit /riːˈvɪzɪt/ *v.* (**-t-**) visit again.

revitalize /riːˈvaɪtəˌlaɪz/ *v.* (also **-ise**) (**-zing** or **-sing**) imbue with new life and vitality.

revival /rɪˈvaɪv(ə)l/ *n.* **1** reviving or being revived. **2** new production of an old play etc. **3** revived use of an old practice, style, etc. **4 a** reawakening of religious fervour. **b** campaign to promote this.

revivalism *n.* promotion of a revival, esp. of religious fervour. □ **revivalist** *n.* & *adj.*

revive /rɪˈvaɪv/ *v.* (**-ving**) **1** come or bring back to consciousness, life, or strength. **2** come or bring back to existence, or to use or notice etc. [Latin *vivo* live]

revivify /rɪˈvɪvɪˌfaɪ/ *v.* (**-ies, -ied**) restore to animation, vigour, or life. □ **revivification** /-fɪˈkeɪʃ(ə)n/ *n.* [Latin: related to VIVIFY]

♦ **revocable letter of credit** see LETTER OF CREDIT.

revoke /rɪˈvəʊk/ *–v.* (**-king**) **1** rescind, withdraw, or cancel. **2** *Cards* fail to follow suit when able to do so. *–n.* *Cards* revoking. □ **revocable** /ˈrevəkəb(ə)l/ *adj.* **revocation** /ˌrevəˈkeɪʃ(ə)n/ *n.* [Latin *voco* call]

revolt /rɪˈvəʊlt/ *–v.* **1** rise in rebellion. **2 a** affect with strong disgust. **b** (often foll. by *at, against*) feel strong disgust. *–n.* **1** act of rebelling. **2** state of insurrection. **3** sense of disgust. **4** mood of protest or defiance. [Italian: related to REVOLVE]

revolting *adj.* disgusting, horrible. □ **revoltingly** *adv.*

revolution /ˌrevəˈluːʃ(ə)n/ *n.* **1** forcible overthrow of a government or social order. **2** any fundamental change or reversal of conditions. **3** revolving. **4 a** single completion of an orbit or rotation. **b** time taken for this. **5** cyclic recurrence. [Latin: related to REVOLVE]

revolutionary *–adj.* **1** involving great and often violent change. **2** of or causing political revolution. *–n.* (*pl.* **-ies**) instigator or supporter of political revolution.

revolutionize *v.* (also **-ise**) (**-zing** or **-sing**) change fundamentally.

revolve /rɪˈvɒlv/ *v.* (**-ving**) **1** (cause to) turn round, esp. on an axis; rotate. **2** move in a circular orbit. **3** ponder (a problem etc.) in the mind. **4** (foll. by *around*) have as its chief concern; be centred upon (*his life revolves around his job*). [Latin *revolvo -volut-*]

revolver *n.* pistol with revolving chambers enabling several shots to be fired without reloading.

◆ **revolving credit** *n.* bank credit that is negotiated for a specified period; it allows for drawdown and repayment within that period. Repaid amounts can be redrawn up to the agreed limit of the credit. At the end of the loan period there is a bullet repayment of the principal and any outstanding interest; alternatively, a repayment schedule is negotiated for the outstanding principal and interest.

revolving door *n.* door with usu. four partitions turning round a central axis.

◆ **revolving underwriting facility** see NOTE ISSUANCE FACILITY.

revue /rɪ'vjuː/ *n.* entertainment of short usu. satirical sketches and songs. [French: related to REVIEW]

revulsion /rɪ'vʌlʃ(ə)n/ *n.* **1** abhorrence. **2** sudden violent change of feeling. [Latin *vello vuls-* pull]

reward /rɪ'wɔːd/ *–n.* **1 a** return or recompense for service or merit. **b** requital for good or evil. **2** sum offered for the detection of a criminal, restoration of lost property, etc. *–v.* give a reward to (a person) or for (a service etc.). [Anglo-French *reward(er)* REGARD]

rewarding *adj.* (of an activity etc.) worthwhile; satisfying.

rewind /riː'waɪnd/ *v.* (*past* and *past part.* **rewound**) wind (a film or tape etc.) back.

rewire /riː'waɪə(r)/ *v.* (**-ring**) provide with new electrical wiring.

reword /riː'wɜːd/ *v.* express in different words.

rework /riː'wɜːk/ *v.* revise; refashion; remake. □ **reworking** *n.*

rewrite *–v.* /riː'raɪt/ (**-ting**; *past* **rewrote**; *past part.* **rewritten**) write again or differently. *–n.* /'riːraɪt/ **1** rewriting. **2** thing rewritten.

Rex *n.* **1** (after the name) reigning king (*George Rex*). **2** *Law* the Crown (*Rex v. Jones*). [Latin]

Reykjavik /'reɪkjəvɪk/ capital and chief port of Iceland, in the SW of the country; fish processing is a major industry; pop. (est. 1993) 104 276.

RF *symb.* Rwanda franc.

Rf *symb.* **1** rutherfordium. **2** rufiyaa.

RFC *abbr.* **1** (in the US) Reconstruction Finance Corporation. **2** Rugby Football Club.

RFQ *abbr. Commerce* request for quotation.

RFS *abbr.* Registry of Friendly Societies.

RG *–postcode* Reading. *–airline flight code* Varig Brazilian Airlines.

RGN *abbr.* Registered General Nurse.

RGNP *abbr.* real gross national product.

RH *–abbr.* (also **r.h.**) right hand. *–postcode* Redhill. *–international vehicle registration* Haiti.

Rh *symb.* rhodium.

rhapsodize /'ræpsəˌdaɪz/ *v.* (also **-ise**) (**-zing** or **-sing**) talk or write rhapsodies.

rhapsody /'ræpsədɪ/ *n.* (*pl.* **-ies**) **1** enthusiastic or extravagant speech or composition. **2** piece of music in one movement, often based on national, folk, or popular melodies. □ **rhapsodic** /ræp'sɒdɪk/ *adj.* [Greek *rhaptō* stitch: related to ODE]

rhea /'riːə/ *n.* South American flightless ostrich-like bird. [Greek *Rhea* mother name of Zeus]

Rheims see REIMS.

Rhein see RHINE.

rhenium /'riːnɪəm/ *n.* rare metallic element occurring naturally in molybdenum ores. [Latin *Rhenus* Rhine]

rheostat /'riːəˌstæt/ *n.* instrument used to control an electric current by varying the resistance. [Greek *rheos* stream]

rhesus /'riːsəs/ *n.* (in full **rhesus monkey**) small N Indian monkey. [*Rhesus*, mythical king of Thrace]

rhesus factor *n.* antigen occurring on the red blood cells of most humans and some other primates.

rhesus negative *adj.* lacking the rhesus factor.

rhesus positive *adj.* having the rhesus factor.

rhetoric /'retərɪk/ *n.* **1** art of effective or persuasive speaking or writing. **2** language designed to persuade or impress (esp. seen as overblown and meaningless). [Greek *rhētōr* orator]

rhetorical /rɪ'tɒrɪk(ə)l/ *adj.* **1** expressed artifically or extravagantly. **2** of the nature or art of rhetoric. □ **rhetorically** *adv.* [Greek: related to RHETORIC]

rhetorical question *n.* question used for effect but not seeking an answer (e.g. *who cares?* for *nobody cares*).

rheumatic /ruː'mætɪk/ *–adj.* of, suffering from, producing, or produced by rheumatism. *–n.* person suffering from rheumatism. □ **rheumatically** *adv.* **rheumaticky** *adj. colloq.* [Greek *rheuma* stream]

rheumatic fever *n.* fever with inflammation and pain in the joints.

rheumatics *n.pl.* (treated as *sing.*; often prec. by *the*) *colloq.* rheumatism.

rheumatism /'ruːməˌtɪz(ə)m/ *n.* disease marked by inflammation and pain in the joints, muscles, or fibrous tissue, esp. rheumatoid arthritis.

rheumatoid /'ruːməˌtɔɪd/ *adj.* having the character of rheumatism.

rheumatoid arthritis *n.* chronic progressive disease causing inflammation and stiffening of the joints.

Rhine /raɪn/ (German **Rhein**) river in W Europe, flowing from the Swiss Alps to the North Sea through the Netherlands. Most of its course lies within W Germany and it forms part of an important inland waterway network.

Rhineland Palatinate /'raɪnlænd pə'lætɪˌneɪt/ (German **Rheinland-Pfalz** /-fælts/) state (*Land*) in W Germany; pop. (est. 1995) 3 951 600; capital, Mainz. Wine production is important; other agricultural produce includes potatoes, cereals, and livestock. There are also chemical and engineering industries.

rhinestone *n.* imitation diamond. [RHINE]

rhino /'raɪnəʊ/ *n.* (*pl.* same or **-s**) *colloq.* rhinoceros. [abbreviation]

rhinoceros /raɪ'nɒsərəs/ *n.* (*pl.* same or **-roses**) large thick-skinned mammal with usu. one horn on its nose. [Greek *rhis rhin-* nose, *keras* horn]

rhizome /'raɪzəʊm/ *n.* underground rootlike stem bearing both roots and shoots. [Greek *rhizoma*]

rho /rəʊ/ *n.* seventeenth letter of the Greek alphabet (Ρ, ρ). [Greek]

Rhode Island /rəʊd/ state in the NE US, on the Atlantic coast; pop. (est. 1994) 990 225; capital, Providence. Industries include electronics and machine-tool manufacture.

Rhodes /rəʊdz/ Greek island in the SE Aegean, largest of the Dodecanese; tourism is important, and agriculture produces cereals, fruit, and wine; pop. (est. 1995) 92 900.

Rhodesia /rəʊ'diːʃə/ **1** former British territory in Africa S of Democratic Republic of Congo, later divided into Northern Rhodesia (now Zambia) and Southern Rhodesia (now Zimbabwe). **2** see ZIMBABWE. □ **Rhodesian** *adj.* & *n.*

rhodium /'rəʊdɪəm/ *n.* hard white metallic element used in making alloys and plating jewellery. [Greek *rhodon* rose]

rhododendron /ˌrəʊdə'dendrən/ *n.* (*pl.* **-s** or **-dra**) evergreen shrub with large clusters of trumpet-shaped flowers. [Greek *rhodon* rose, *dendron* tree]

rhomboid /'rɒmbɔɪd/ *–adj.* (also **rhomboidal** /-'bɔɪd(ə)l/) like a rhombus. *–n.* quadrilateral of which only the opposite sides and angles are equal. [Greek: related to RHOMBUS]

rhombus /'rɒmbəs/ *n.* (*pl.* **-buses** or **-bi** /-baɪ/) *Geom.* parallelogram with oblique angles and equal sides. [Greek *rhombos*]

Rhône /rəʊn/ river in W Europe, rising in the Swiss Alps and flowing W and S through France to the Mediterranean Sea. The cities of Geneva, Lyons, and Avignon lie along its course.

RHS *abbr.* Royal Horticultural Society.

rhubarb /'ru:bɑ:b/ *n.* **1 a** plant with long fleshy dark-red leaf-stalks cooked as a dessert. **b** these stalks. **2 a** *colloq.* indistinct conversation or noise, from the repeated use of the word 'rhubarb' by a crowd. **b** *slang* nonsense. [Greek *rha* rhubarb, *barbaros* foreign]

rhyme /raɪm/ *–n.* **1** identity of sound between words or their endings, esp. in verse. **2** (in *sing.* or *pl.*) verse or a poem having rhymes. **3** use of rhyme. **4** word providing a rhyme. *–v.* (**-ming**) **1 a** (of words or lines) produce a rhyme. **b** (foll. by *with*) act as or treat (a word) as a rhyme (with another). **2** make or write rhymes. **3** put or make (a story etc.) into rhyme. □ **rhyme or reason** sense, logic. [Latin: related to RHYTHM]

rhymester *n.* writer of (esp. simple) rhymes.

rhyming slang *n.* slang that replaces words by rhyming words or phrases, e.g. *suit* by *whistle and flute*.

rhythm /'rɪð(ə)m/ *n.* **1 a** periodical accent and the duration of notes in music, esp. as beats in a bar. **b** type of structure formed by this (*samba rhythm*). **2** measured regular flow of verse or prose determined by the length of and stress on syllables. **3** *Physiol.* pattern of successive strong and weak movements. **4** regularly recurring sequence of events. □ **rhythmic** *adj.* **rhythmical** *adj.* **rhythmically** *adv.* [Greek *rhuthmos*]

rhythm and blues *n.* popular music with blues themes and a strong rhythm.

rhythm method *n.* abstention from sexual intercourse near the time of ovulation, as a method of birth control.

rhythm section *n.* piano (or guitar etc.), bass, and drums in a dance or jazz band.

RI *–abbr.* **1** Railway Inspectorate. **2** (also **R/I**) = REINSURANCE. **3** Rhode Island. **4** Rotary International. *–US postcode* Rhode Island. *–international vehicle registration* Indonesia.

rial /'ri:al, 'raɪəl/ *n.* standard monetary unit of Iran and Oman. [Persian: related to RIYAL]

rib *–n.* **1** each of the curved bones joined to the spine in pairs and protecting the chest. **2** joint of meat from this part of an animal. **3** supporting ridge, timber, rod, etc. across a surface or through a structure. **4** *Knitting* combination of plain and purl stitches producing a ribbed design. *–v.* (**-bb-**) **1** provide with ribs; act as the ribs of. **2** *colloq.* make fun of; tease. **3** mark with ridges. [Old English]

RIBA *abbr.* Royal Institute of British Architects.

ribald /'rɪb(ə)ld/ *adj.* coarsely or disrespectfully humorous; obscene. [French *riber* be licentious]

ribaldry *n.* ribald talk or behaviour.

riband /'rɪbənd/ *n.* ribbon. [French *riban*]

ribbed *adj.* having ribs or riblike markings.

ribbing *n.* **1** ribs or a riblike structure. **2** *colloq.* teasing.

ribbon /'rɪbən/ *n.* **1 a** narrow strip or band of fabric, used esp. for trimming or decoration. **b** material in this form. **2** ribbon worn to indicate some honour or membership of a sports team etc. **3** long narrow strip of anything (*typewriter ribbon*). **4** (in *pl.*) ragged strips (*torn to ribbons*). [var. of RIBAND]

ribbon development *n.* building of houses one house deep along a road leading out of a town or village.

ribcage *n.* wall of bones formed by the ribs round the chest.

riboflavin /ˌraɪbəʊ'fleɪvɪn/ *n.* (also **riboflavine** /-vi:n/) vitamin of the B complex, found in liver, milk, and eggs. [*ribose* sugar, Latin *flavus* yellow]

ribonucleic acid /ˌraɪbənju:'kli:ɪk/ *n.* nucleic acid in living cells, involved in protein synthesis. [*ribose* sugar]

rib-tickler *n.* something amusing, joke.

◆ **Ricardian equivalence theorem** /rɪ'kɑ:dɪən/ *n.* *Econ.* theory that a tax cut financed by government borrowing will have no effect on an individual's wealth and therefore will not increase either consumption or investment. The reason is that additional government borrowing will need to be repaid in the future through taxation, thus offsetting the original tax cut. A form of the theory, sometimes known as **debt neutrality**, has provided a basis for the belief that government fiscal policy cannot alter such real variables as employment or output. [*Ricardo*, name of an economist]

rice *n.* **1** swamp grass cultivated in esp. Asian marshes. **2** grains of this, used as food. [French *ris* ultimately from Greek *oruza*]

rice-paper *n.* edible paper made from the bark of an oriental tree and used for painting and in cookery.

rich *adj.* **1** having much wealth. **2** splendid, costly, elaborate. **3** valuable (*rich offerings*). **4** copious, abundant, ample (*rich supply of ideas*). **5** (often foll. by *in*, *with*) (of soil or a region etc.) fertile; abundant in resources etc. (*rich in nutrients*). **6** (of food or diet) containing much fat or spice etc. **7** (of the mixture in an internal-combustion engine) containing a high proportion of fuel. **8** (of colour, sound, or smell) mellow and deep, strong and full. **9** highly amusing or ludicrous; outrageous. □ **richness** *n.* [Old English and French]

riches *n.pl.* abundant means; valuable possessions. [French *richeise*: related to RICH]

richly *adv.* **1** in a rich way. **2** fully, thoroughly (*richly deserves success*).

Richmond /'rɪtʃmənd/ city and port in the US, capital of Virginia; tobacco is the main product; pop. (est. 1994) 201 108.

Richter scale /'rɪktə/ *n.* scale of 0 to 10 for representing the strength of an earthquake. [*Richter*, name of a seismologist]

rick[1] *n.* stack of hay etc. [Old English]

rick[2] (also **wrick**) *–n.* slight sprain or strain. *–v.* sprain or strain slightly. [Low German *wricken*]

rickets /'rɪkɪts/ *n.* (treated as *sing.* or *pl.*) deficiency disease of children with softening of the bones. [origin uncertain]

rickety /'rɪkɪtɪ/ *adj.* **1** insecure, shaky. **2** suffering from rickets. □ **ricketiness** *n.*

rickrack var. of RICRAC.

rickshaw /'rɪkʃɔ:/ *n.* (also **ricksha** /-ʃə/) light two-wheeled hooded vehicle drawn by one or more persons. [abbreviation of *jinrickshaw* from Japanese]

ricochet /'rɪkəˌʃeɪ/ *–n.* **1** rebounding of esp. a shell or bullet off a surface. **2** hit made after this. *–v.* (**-cheted** /-ˌʃeɪd/; **-cheting** /-ˌʃeɪɪŋ/ or **-chetted** /-ˌʃetɪd/; **-chetting** /-ˌʃetɪŋ/) (of a projectile) make a ricochet. [French]

ricotta /rɪ'kɒtə/ *n.* soft Italian cheese. [Latin: related to RE-, *coquo* cook]

ricrac /'rɪkræk/ *n.* (also **rickrack**) zigzag braided trimming for garments. [from RACK[1]]

RICS *abbr.* = ROYAL INSTITUTION OF CHARTERED SURVEYORS.

rid *v.* (**-dd-**; *past* and *past part.* **rid**) (foll. by *of*) free (a person or place) of something unwanted. □ **be** (or **get) rid of** be freed or relieved of; dispose of. [Old Norse]

riddance /'rɪd(ə)ns/ *n.* getting rid of something. □ **good riddance** expression of relief at getting rid of something.

ridden *past part.* of RIDE.

riddle[1] /'rɪd(ə)l/ *–n.* **1** verbal puzzle or test, often with a trick answer. **2** puzzling fact, thing, or person. *–v.* (**-ling**) speak in riddles. [Old English: related to READ]

riddle[2] /'rɪd(ə)l/ *–v.* (**-ling**) (usu. foll. by *with*) **1** make many holes in, esp. with gunshot. **2** (in *passive*) fill; permeate (*riddled with errors*). **3** pass through a riddle. *–n.* coarse sieve. [Old English]

ride *–v.* (**-ding**; *past* **rode**; *past part.* **ridden** /'rɪd(ə)n/) **1** (often foll. by *on*, *in*) travel or be carried on (a bicycle etc.) or esp. *US* in (a vehicle); be conveyed (*rode her bike*; *rode on her bike*; *rode the tram*). **2** (often foll. by *on*; also *absol.*) be carried by (a horse etc.). **3** be carried or supported by (*ship rides the waves*). **4** traverse or take part in on horseback etc. (*ride 50 miles*; *rode the prairie*). **5 a** lie at anchor; float buoyantly. **b** (of the moon) seem to float. **6** yield to (a blow) so as to reduce its impact. **7** give a ride to; cause to ride (*rode me home*). **8** (of a rider) cause (a horse etc.) to move forward (*rode their horses at the fence*). **9** (as **ridden** *adj.*) (foll. by *by*, *with*, or in *comb.*) be dominated by; be infested with (*ridden with guilt*; *rat-ridden cellar*). *–n.* **1** journey or spell of riding in a vehicle, or on a horse, bicycle, person's back, etc. **2** path (esp. through woods) for riding on. **3** specified kind of ride (*bumpy ride*). **4** amusement for riding on at a fairground etc. □ **let a thing ride** leave it undisturbed. **ride again** reappear as strong etc. as ever. **ride high** be elated or successful. **ride out** come safely through (a storm, danger, etc.). **ride roughshod over** see ROUGHSHOD. **ride up** (of a garment) work upwards out of place. **take for a ride** *colloq.* hoax or deceive. [Old English]

rider *n.* **1** person who rides (esp. a horse). **2** additional remark following a statement, verdict, etc. □ **riderless** *adj.*

ridge *–n.* **1** line of the junction of two surfaces sloping upwards towards each other (*ridge of a roof*). **2** long narrow hilltop, mountain range, or watershed. **3** any narrow elevation across a surface. **4** elongated region of high barometric pressure. **5** raised strip of esp. ploughed land. *–v.* (**-ging**) mark with ridges. □ **ridgy** *adj.* [Old English]

ridge-pole *n.* horizontal roof pole of a long tent.

ridgeway *n.* road or track along a ridge.

ridicule /ˈrɪdɪˌkjuːl/ *–n.* derision, mockery. *–v.* (**-ling**) make fun of; mock; laugh at. [Latin *rideo* laugh]

ridiculous /rɪˈdɪkjʊləs/ *adj.* **1** deserving or inviting ridicule. **2** unreasonable. □ **ridiculously** *adv.* **ridiculousness** *n.*

riding¹ /ˈraɪdɪŋ/ *n.* sport or pastime of travelling on horseback.

riding² /ˈraɪdɪŋ/ *n. hist.* former administrative division (**East, North, West Riding**) of Yorkshire. [Old English from Old Norse, = third part]

riding-light *n.* light shown by a ship at anchor.

riding-school *n.* establishment teaching horsemanship.

RIE *abbr.* = RECOGNIZED INVESTMENT EXCHANGE.

riel /ˈriːəl/ *n.* standard monetary unit of Cambodia. [Khmer]

Riesling /ˈriːzlɪŋ/ *n.* **1** a kind of grape. **2** white wine made from this. [German]

rife *predic. adj.* **1** of common occurrence; widespread. **2** (foll. by *with*) abounding in. [Old English, probably from Old Norse]

riff *n.* short repeated phrase in jazz etc. [abbreviation of RIFFLE]

riffle /ˈrɪf(ə)l/ *–v.* (**-ling**) **1** (often foll. by *through*) leaf quickly through (pages). **2 a** turn (pages) in quick succession. **b** shuffle (playing-cards), esp. by flexing and combining the two halves of a pack. *–n.* **1** act of riffling. **2** *US* **a** shallow disturbed part of a stream. **b** patch of waves or ripples. [perhaps var. of RUFFLE]

riff-raff /ˈrɪfræf/ *n.* (often prec. by *the*) rabble; disreputable people. [French *rif et raf*]

rifle¹ /ˈraɪf(ə)l/ *–n.* **1** gun with a long rifled barrel, esp. one fired from the shoulder. **2** (in *pl.*) riflemen. *–v.* (**-ling**) make spiral grooves in (a gun, its barrel, or its bore) to make a projectile spin. [French]

rifle² /ˈraɪf(ə)l/ *v.* (**-ling**) (often foll. by *through*) **1** search and rob. **2** carry off as booty. [French]

rifleman *n.* soldier armed with a rifle.

rifle-range *n.* place for rifle-practice.

rifle-shot *n.* **1** shot fired with a rifle. **2** distance coverable by this.

rifling *n.* arrangement of grooves on the inside of a gun's barrel.

rift *–n.* **1** crack, split; break (in cloud etc.). **2** disagreement; breach. **3** cleft in earth or rock. *–v.* tear or burst apart. [Scandinavian: related to RIVEN]

rift-valley *n.* steep-sided valley formed by subsidence between nearly parallel faults.

rig¹ *–v.* (**-gg-**) **1** provide (a ship) with sails, rigging, etc. **2** (often foll. by *out*, *up*) fit with clothes or other equipment. **3** (foll. by *up*) set up hastily or as a makeshift. **4** assemble and adjust the parts of (an aircraft). *–n.* **1** arrangement of a ship's masts, sails, etc. **2** equipment for a special purpose, e.g. a radio transmitter. **3** = OIL RIG. **4** *colloq.* style of dress; uniform (*in full rig*). □ **rigged** *adj.* (also in *comb.*). [perhaps from Scandinavian]

rig² *–v.* (**-gg-**) manage or fix (a result etc.) fraudulently (*rigged the election*). *–n.* trick, dodge, or way of swindling. □ **rig the market** make a profit, usu. on a security or commodity market, by overriding the normal market forces. This often involves taking a long position or a short position in the market that is sufficiently substantial to influence price levels, and then supporting or depressing the market by further purchases or sales. □ **rigger** *n.* [origin unknown]

Riga /ˈriːgə/ capital of Latvia, a port on the Baltic Sea and a centre of industry; pop. (est. 1995) 839 670.

rigger *n.* **1** worker on an oil rig. **2** person who rigs or who arranges rigging.

rigging *n.* ship's spars, ropes, etc.

right /raɪt/ *–adj.* **1** (of conduct etc.) just, morally or socially correct (*do the right thing*). **2** true, correct (*which is the right way?*). **3** suitable or preferable (*right person for the job*). **4** sound or normal; healthy; satisfactory (*engine doesn't sound right*). **5** on or towards the east side of the human body, or of any object etc., when facing north. **6** (of a side of fabric etc.) meant for display or use. **7** *colloq.* real; complete (*made a right mess of it*). **8** (also **Right**) *Polit.* of the Right. *–n.* **1** that which is correct or just; fair treatment (often in *pl.*: *rights and wrongs of the case*). **2** justification or fair claim (*has no right to speak*). **3** legal or moral entitlement; authority to act (*human rights*; *right of reply*). **4** right-hand part, region, or direction. **5** *Boxing* **a** right hand. **b** blow with this. **6** (often **Right**) **a** conservative political group or section. **b** conservatives collectively. **7** side of a stage to the right of a person facing the audience. *–v.* **1** (often *refl.*) restore to a proper, straight, or vertical position. **2** correct or avenge (mistakes, wrongs, etc.); set in order; make reparation. *–adv.* **1** straight (*go right on*). **2** *colloq.* immediately (*do it right now*). **3 a** (foll. by *to*, *round*, *through*, etc.) all the way (*sank right to the bottom*). **b** (foll. by *off*, *out*, etc.) completely (*came right off its hinges*). **4** exactly, quite (*right in the middle*). **5** justly, properly, correctly, truly, satisfactorily (*not holding it right*; *if I remember right*). **6** on or to the right side. *–int. colloq.* expressing agreement or assent. □ **by right** (or **rights**) if right were done. **do right by** act dutifully towards (a person). **in one's own right** through one's own position or effort etc. **in the right** having justice or truth on one's side. **in one's right mind** sane. **of** (or **as of**) **right** having legal or moral etc. entitlement. **on the right side of** *colloq.* **1** in the favour of (a person etc.). **2** somewhat less than (a specified age). **put** (or **set**) **right 1** restore to order, health, etc. **2** correct the mistaken impression etc. of (a person). **put** (or **set**) **to rights** make correct or well ordered. **right away** (or **off**) immediately. **right oh!** (or **ho!**) = RIGHTO. **right on!** *slang* expression of strong approval or encouragement. **a right one** *colloq.* foolish or funny person. **right you are!** *colloq.* exclamation of assent. **too right** *slang* expression of agreement. □ **rightness** *n.* [Old English]

right angle *n.* angle of 90°.

right arm *n.* one's most reliable helper.

right bank *n.* bank of a river on the right facing downstream.

righten *v.* make right or correct.

righteous /ˈraɪtʃəs/ *adj.* (of a person or conduct) morally right; virtuous, law-abiding. □ **righteously** *adv.* **righteousness** *n.* [Old English]

rightful *adj.* **1 a** (of a person) legitimately entitled to (a position etc.) (*rightful heir*). **b** (of status or property etc.) that one is entitled to. **2** (of an action etc.) equitable, fair. □ **rightfully** *adv.* [Old English]

right hand *n.* = RIGHT-HAND MAN.

right-hand *attrib. adj.* **1** on or towards the right side of a person or thing. **2** done with the right hand. **3** (of a screw) = RIGHT-HANDED 4b.

right-handed *adj.* **1** naturally using the right hand for writing etc. **2** (of a tool etc.) for use by the right hand. **3** (of a blow) struck with the right hand. **4 a** turning to the right. **b** (of a screw) turned clockwise to tighten. □ **right-handedly** *adv.* **right-handedness** *n.*

right-hander *n.* **1** right-handed person. **2** right-handed blow.

right-hand man *n.* indispensable or chief assistant.

Right Honourable *n.* title given to certain high officials, e.g. Privy Counsellors.

rightism *n.* political conservatism. □ **rightist** *n.* & *adj.*

right-justified see JUSTIFY 4.

rightly *adv.* justly, properly, correctly, justifiably.

right-minded *adj.* (also **right-thinking**) having sound views and principles.

rightmost *adj.* furthest to the right.

righto /ˈraɪtəʊ/ *int. colloq.* expressing agreement or assent.

♦ **right of resale** *n.* right that the seller in a contract of sale has to resell the goods if the buyer does not pay the price as agreed. If the goods are perishable or the seller gives notice to the buyer of an intention to resell and the buyer still does not pay within a reasonable time, the seller may resell them and recover from the first buyer damages for any loss.

---

right of way *n.* **1** right established by usage to pass over another's ground. **2** path subject to such a right. **3** right of a vehicle to precedence.

Right Reverend *n.* bishop's title.

♦ **rights issue** *n.* issue of new shares to existing shareholders, who must be offered the new shares in proportion to their holding of old shares (see PRE-EMPTION RIGHTS). For example in a 1 for 4 rights issue, shareholders would be asked to buy one new share for every four they already hold. As rights are usu. issued at a discount to the market price of existing shares, those not wishing to take up their rights can sell them in the market (see RIGHTS LETTER; RENUNCIATION 3). A rights issue is one method by which quoted companies on a stock exchange can raise new capital. Cf. BOUGHT DEAL; SCRIP ISSUE; VENDOR PLACING.

♦ **rightsize** *v.* restructure and rationalize an organization to cut costs and improve effectiveness without ruthless downsizing. Rightsizing can include increasing the size of an organization to meet increased demand, but is more often a euphemism for restrained downsizing.

♦ **rights letter** *n.* document sent to an existing shareholder of a company offering shares in a rights issue on advantageous terms. If the recipient does not wish to take advantage of the offer he or she can sell the letter and the attendant rights on the stock exchange (see RENUNCIATION 3).

---

right turn *n.* turn of 90 degrees to the right.

rightward /ˈraɪtwəd/ *–adv.* (also **rightwards**) towards the right. *–adj.* going towards or facing the right.

right wing *–n.* **1** more conservative section of a political party or system. **2** right side of a football etc. team on the field. *–adj.* (**right-wing**) conservative or reactionary. □ **right-winger** *n.*

rigid /ˈrɪdʒɪd/ *adj.* **1** not flexible; unbendable. **2** (of a person, conduct, etc.) inflexible, unbending, harsh. □ **rigidity** /-ˈdʒɪdɪtɪ/ *n.* **rigidly** *adv.* **rigidness** *n.* [Latin *rigidus* from *rigeo* be stiff]

rigmarole /ˈrɪgməˌrəʊl/ *n.* **1** lengthy and complicated procedure. **2** rambling or meaningless talk or tale. [originally *ragman roll* catalogue]

rigor[1] /ˈrɪgə(r), ˈraɪgɔː(r)/ *n.* feeling of cold with shivering and a rise in temperature, preceding a fever etc. [Latin *rigeo* be stiff]

rigor[2] *US* var. of RIGOUR.

rigor mortis /ˌrɪgə ˈmɔːtɪs/ *n.* stiffening of the body after death.

rigorous /ˈrɪgərəs/ *adj.* **1** firm; strict, severe. **2** strictly exact or accurate. □ **rigorously** *adv.* **rigorousness** *n.* [related to RIGOUR]

rigour /ˈrɪgə(r)/ *n.* (*US* **rigor**) **1 a** severity, strictness, harshness. **b** (in *pl.*) harsh measures or conditions. **2** logical exactitude. **3** strict enforcement of rules etc. (*utmost rigour of the law*). **4** austerity of life. [Latin: related to RIGOR[1]]

rig-out *n. colloq.* outfit of clothes.

Rijeka /riːˈekə/ (Italian **Fiume** /fɪˈuːmeɪ/) port in Croatia, on the Adriatic coast; it has shipyards as well as oil-refining and other industries; pop. (1991) 167 964.

rile *v.* (**-ling**) *colloq.* anger, irritate. [French from Latin]

rill *n.* small stream. [probably Low German or Dutch]

RIM *international vehicle registration* Mauritania.

rim *n.* **1** edge or border, esp. of something circular. **2** outer edge of a wheel, holding the tyre. **3** part of spectacle frames around the lens. □ **rimless** *adj.* **rimmed** *adj.* (also in *comb.*). [Old English]

rime[1] *–n.* **1** frost. **2** hoar-frost. *–v.* (**-ming**) cover with rime. [Old English]

rime[2] *archaic* var. of RHYME.

rind /raɪnd/ *n.* tough outer layer or covering of fruit and vegetables, cheese, bacon, etc. [Old English]

ring[1] *–n.* **1** circular band, usu. of metal, worn on a finger. **2** circular band of any material. **3** rim of a cylindrical or circular object, or a line or band round it. **4** mark etc. resembling a ring (*rings round his eyes*; *smoke rings*). **5** ring in the cross-section of a tree, produced by one year's growth. **6 a** enclosure for a circus performance, boxing, betting at races, showing of cattle, etc. **b** (prec. by *the*) bookmakers collectively. **7 a** people or things in a circle. **b** such an arrangement. **8 a** group of manufacturers, dealers, or traders who agree among themselves to control the price or conditions of sale of a product for their own benefit. Such agreements are illegal in most countries, unless they can be shown to be in the public interest. See RESTRICTIVE TRADE PRACTICES. **b** association of dealers in an auction sale, esp. a sale of antiques or paintings, who agree not to bid against each other but to allow one of their number to buy an article being auctioned at an artificially low price, on the understanding that this person will auction it again exclusively to members of the ring. The difference between the purchase price and the final price paid is shared among the members of the ring. This is an illegal practice. **c** group of spies, politicians, etc., combined usu. covertly. **9** circular or spiral course. **10** = GAS RING. **11 a** thin disc of particles etc. round a planet. **b** halo round the moon. *–v.* **1** (often foll. by *round, about, in*) make or draw a circle round; encircle. **2** put a ring on (a bird etc.) or through the nose of (a pig, bull, etc.). □ **run** (or **make**) **rings round** *colloq.* outclass or outwit (another person). [Old English]

ring[2] *–v.* (*past* **rang**; *past part.* **rung**) **1** (often foll. by *out* etc.) give a clear resonant or vibrating sound of or as of a bell. **2 a** make (esp. a bell) ring. **b** (*absol.*) call by ringing a bell (*you rang, sir?*). **3** (also *absol.*; often foll. by *up*) call by telephone (*will ring you*). **4** (usu. foll. by *with, to*) (of a place) resound with a sound, fame, etc. (*theatre rang with applause*). **5** (of the ears) be filled with a sensation of ringing. **6 a** sound (a peal etc.) on bells. **b** (of a bell) sound (the hour etc.). **7** (foll. by *in, out*) usher in or out with bell-ringing (*rang out the Old Year*). **8** convey a specified impression (*words rang true*). *–n.* **1** ringing sound or tone. **2** act or sound of ringing a bell. **3** *colloq.* telephone call (*give me a ring*). **4** specified feeling conveyed by words etc. (*had a melancholy ring*). **5** set of esp. church bells. □ **ring back** make a return telephone call to. **ring a bell** *colloq.* begin to revive a memory. **ring down** (or **up) the curtain 1** cause the curtain to be lowered or raised. **2** (foll. by *on*) mark the end or the beginning of (an enterprise etc.). **ring in** report or make contact by telephone. **ring off** end a telephone call. **ring round** telephone several people. **ring up 1** call by telephone. **2** record (an amount etc.) on a cash register. [Old English]

ring-binder *n.* loose-leaf binder with ring-shaped clasps.

ring-dove *n.* woodpigeon.

ringer *n.* bell-ringer. □ **be a ringer** (or **dead ringer) for** *slang* resemble (a person) exactly.

ring-fence *v.* (**-cing**) protect or guarantee (funds).

ring finger *n.* third finger, esp. of the left hand, on which a wedding ring is usu. worn.

ringgit /ˈrɪŋgɪt/ *n.* standard monetary unit of Malaysia. [Malay]

ringing tone *n.* sound heard after dialling an unengaged number.

ringleader *n.* leading instigator of a crime, mischief, etc.

ringlet /ˈrɪŋlɪt/ *n.* curly lock of esp. long hair. □ **ringleted** *adj.*

ringmaster *n.* person directing a circus performance.

ring-pull *attrib. adj.* (of a tin) having a ring for pulling to break its seal.

ring road *n.* bypass encircling a town.

ringside *n.* area immediately beside a boxing or circus ring etc. (often *attrib.*: *ringside view*).

♦ **ring trading** *n.* = CALL-OVER.

---

ringworm *n.* fungal skin infection causing circular inflamed patches, esp. on the scalp.

rink *n.* **1** area of ice for skating or curling etc. **2** enclosed area for roller-skating. **3** building containing either of these. **4** strip of bowling-green. **5** team in bowls or curling. [apparently from French *renc* RANK[1]]

rinse *–v.* (**-sing**) (often foll. by *through*, *out*) **1** wash or treat with clean water etc. **2** wash lightly. **3** put (clothes etc.) through clean water after washing. **4** (foll. by *out*, *away*) clear (impurities) by rinsing. *–n.* **1** rinsing (*give it a rinse*). **2** temporary hair tint (*blue rinse*). [French *rincer*]

Rio de Janeiro /ˈriːəʊ də ʒəˈnɪəˌrəʊ/ chief port and second-largest city in Brazil; it has shipbuilding and sugar-refining industries and exports sugar, coffee, and iron ore; pop. (1991) 5 473 909.

Rioja /riːˈəʊxə/, **La** autonomous region of N Spain, in a wine-producing area; pop. (est. 1994) 263 437; capital, Logroño.

Río Muni /ˌriːəʊ ˈmuːnɪ/ the part of Equatorial Guinea that lies on the mainland of W Africa; chief town, Bata.

riot /ˈraɪət/ *–n.* **1 a** violent disturbance by a crowd of people. **b** (*attrib.*) involved in suppressing riots (*riot police*). **2** loud uncontrolled revelry. **3** (foll. by *of*) lavish display or sensation (*riot of colour and sound*). **4** *colloq.* very amusing thing or person. *–v.* make or engage in a riot. □ **read the Riot Act** act firmly to suppress insubordination; give warning. **run riot 1** throw off all restraint. **2** (of plants) grow or spread uncontrolled. □ **rioter** *n.* **riotous** *adj.* [French]

♦ **riot and civil commotion** *n.* risk not usu. covered in householders' insurance policies or commercial policies, unless a special clause has been added to cover loss or damage due to riot or civil commotion.

RIP *abbr.* may he, she, or they rest in peace. [Latin *requiesca(n)t in pace*]

rip[1] *–v.* (**-pp-**) **1** tear or cut (a thing) quickly or forcibly away or apart (*ripped out the lining*). **2 a** make (a hole etc.) by ripping. **b** make a long tear or cut in. **3** come violently apart; split. **4** rush along. *–n.* **1** long tear or cut. **2** act of ripping. □ **let rip** *colloq.* **1** (allow to) proceed or act without restraint or interference. **2** speak violently. **rip into** *colloq.* attack (a person) verbally. **rip off** *colloq.* **1** swindle. **2** steal. [origin unknown]

rip[2] *n.* stretch of rough water caused by meeting currents. [origin uncertain]

rip[3] *n.* **1** dissolute person; rascal. **2** worthless horse. [origin uncertain]

RIPA *abbr.* Royal Institute of Public Administration.

riparian /raɪˈpeərɪən/ *adj.* of or on a river-bank (*riparian rights*). [Latin *ripa* bank]

rip-cord *n.* cord for releasing a parachute from its pack.

ripe *adj.* **1** (of grain, fruit, cheese, etc.) ready to be reaped, picked, or eaten. **2** mature, fully developed (*ripe in judgement*). **3** (of a person's age) advanced. **4** (often foll. by *for*) fit or ready (*ripe for development*). □ **ripeness** *n.* [Old English]

ripen *v.* make or become ripe.

rip-off *n. colloq.* swindle, financial exploitation.

riposte /rɪˈpɒst/ *–n.* **1** quick retort. **2** quick return thrust in fencing. *–v.* (**-ting**) deliver a riposte. [Italian: related to RESPOND]

ripper *n.* **1** person or thing that rips. **2** murderer who mutilates the victims' bodies.

ripple /ˈrɪp(ə)l/ *–n.* **1** ruffling of the water's surface, small wave or waves. **2** gentle lively sound, e.g. of laughter or applause. **3** wavy appearance in hair, material, etc. **4** slight variation in the strength of a current etc. **5** ice-cream with veins of syrup (*raspberry ripple*). *–v.* (**-ling**) **1** (cause to) form or flow in ripples. **2** show or sound like ripples. □ **ripply** *adj.* [origin unknown]

rip-roaring *adj.* **1** wildly noisy or boisterous. **2** excellent, first-rate.

ripsaw *n.* coarse saw for sawing wood along the grain.

RISC /rɪsk/ *abbr.* reduced-instruction-set computer, one with a processor designed to execute a small number of simple machine instructions extremely fast.

rise /raɪz/ *–v.* (**-sing**; *past* **rose** /rəʊz/; *past part.* **risen** /ˈrɪz(ə)n/) **1** come or go up. **2** grow, project, expand, or incline upwards; become higher. **3** appear or be visible above the horizon. **4** get up from lying, sitting, kneeling, or from bed; become erect. **5** (of a meeting etc.) adjourn. **6** reach a higher position, level, amount, intensity, etc. **7** make progress socially etc. (*rose from the ranks*). **8 a** come to the surface of liquid. **b** (of a person) react to provocation (*rise to the bait*). **9** come to life again. **10** (of dough) swell by the action of yeast etc. **11** (often foll. by *up*) rebel (*rise up against them*). **12** originate (*river rises in the mountains*). **13** (of wind) start to blow. **14** (of a person's spirits) become cheerful. *–n.* **1** rising. **2** upward slope, hill, or movement (*house stood on a rise*). **3 a** increase in amount, extent, sound, pitch, etc. (*rise in unemployment*). **b** increase in salary. **4** increase in status or power; upward progress. **5** movement of fish to the surface. **6** origin. **7 a** vertical height of a step, arch, incline, etc. **b** = RISER 2. □ **get** (or **take) a rise out of** *colloq.* provoke a reaction from (a person), esp. by teasing. **on the rise** on the increase. **rise above** be superior to (petty feelings, difficulties, etc.). **rise to** develop powers equal to (an occasion). [Old English]

riser *n.* **1** person who rises from bed (*early riser*). **2** vertical section between the treads of a staircase.

risible /ˈrɪzɪb(ə)l/ *adj.* laughable, ludicrous. [Latin *rideo ris-* laugh]

rising *–adj.* **1** advancing to maturity or high standing (*rising young lawyer*). **2** approaching a specified age (*rising five*). **3** (of ground) sloping upwards. *–n.* revolt or insurrection.

rising damp *n.* moisture absorbed from the ground into a wall.

risk *–n.* **1** chance or possibility of danger, loss, injury, etc. (see also PERIL 2). If it can be described sufficiently accurately for a calculation to be made of the probability of it happening, on the basis of past records, it is called an **insurable risk**. Fire, theft, accident, etc. are all insurable risks because underwriters can assess the probability of having to pay out a claim and can therefore calculate a reasonable premium. If the risk is met so infrequently that no way of calculating the probability of the event exists, no underwriter will insure against it and it is therefore an **uninsurable risk** (see also ACTUARY). **2** possibility of suffering a loss in trading. The **credit risk** is the risk a trader takes by offering credit or the risk that a bank will withdraw credit facilities. The **systematic risk** involves the risk of a failure in a whole system, e.g. a clearing-house failure. The **delivery risk** arises because a supplier may fail to deliver as contracted. **3** person or thing causing a risk or regarded in relation to risk (*is a poor risk*). *–v.* **1** expose to risk. **2** accept the chance of (*risk getting wet*). **3** venture on. □ **at risk** exposed to danger. **at one's**

(own) risk accepting responsibility, agreeing to make no claims. **at the risk of** with the possibility of (an adverse consequence). **put at risk** expose to danger. **run a** (or **the**) **risk** (often foll. by *of*) expose oneself to danger or loss etc. **take a risk** (or **risks**) chance the possibility of danger etc. [French *risque(r)* from Italian]

♦ **risk capital** *n.* (also **venture capital**) capital invested in a project in which there is a substantial element of risk, esp. money invested in a new venture or an expanding business in exchange for shares in the business. Risk capital is usu. invested in the equity of the company; it is not a loan.

♦ **risk management** *n.* control of the chances of losing on an investment. It can involve taking out an insurance against loss, hedging a loan against a rise in interest rates, and using FINANCIAL FUTURES to protect an investment against a fall in interest rates.

---

risky *adj.* (**-ier**, **-iest**) **1** involving risk. **2** = RISQUÉ. □ **riskily** *adv.* **riskiness** *n.*

risotto /rɪˈzɒtəʊ/ *n.* (*pl.* **-s**) Italian savoury rice dish cooked in stock. [Italian]

risqué /ˈrɪskeɪ, -ˈkeɪ/ *adj.* (of a story etc.) slightly indecent. [French: related to RISK]

rissole /ˈrɪsəʊl/ *n.* cake of spiced minced meat, coated in breadcrumbs and fried. [French]

rit. *abbr. Mus.* ritardando.

ritardando /ˌrɪtɑːˈdændəʊ/ *adv.* & *n.* (*pl.* **-s** or **-di** /-dɪ/) *Mus.* = RALLENTANDO. [Italian]

rite *n.* **1** religious or solemn observance, act, or procedure (*burial rites*). **2** body of customary observances characteristic of a Church etc. (*Latin rite*). [Latin *ritus*]

rite of passage *n.* (often in *pl.*) event marking a change or stage in life, e.g. marriage.

ritual /ˈrɪtʃʊəl/ *–n.* **1 a** prescribed order of a ceremony etc. **b** solemn or colourful pageantry etc. **2** procedure regularly followed. *–adj.* of or done as a ritual or rite (*ritual murder*). □ **ritually** *adv.* [Latin: related to RITE]

ritualism *n.* regular or excessive practice of ritual. □ **ritualist** *n.* **ritualistic** /-ˈlɪstɪk/ *adj.* **ritualistically** /-ˈlɪstɪkəlɪ/ *adv.*

ritzy /ˈrɪtzɪ/ *adj.* (**-ier**, **-iest**) *colloq.* high-class, luxurious, showily smart. [from *Ritz*, name of luxury hotels]

rival /ˈraɪv(ə)l/ *–n.* (often *attrib.*) **1** person competing with another. **2** person or thing that equals another in quality. *–v.* (**-ll-**; *US* **-l-**) be, seem, or claim to be the rival of or comparable to. [Latin *rivus* stream]

rivalry *n.* (*pl.* **-ies**) being rivals; competition.

riven /ˈrɪv(ə)n/ *adj. literary* split, torn. [past part. of *rive* from Old Norse]

river /ˈrɪvə(r)/ *n.* **1** copious natural stream of water flowing to the sea or a lake etc. **2** copious flow (*rivers of blood*). □ **sell down the river** *colloq.* betray or let down. [Latin *ripa* bank]

riverside *n.* (often *attrib.*) ground along a river-bank.

rivet /ˈrɪvɪt/ *–n.* nail or bolt for joining metal plates etc., with the headless end beaten out when in place. *–v.* (**-t-**) **1 a** join or fasten with rivets. **b** beat out or press down the end of (a nail or bolt). **c** fix, make immovable. **2 a** (foll. by *on, upon*) direct intently (one's eyes or attention etc.). **b** (esp. as **riveting** *adj.*) engross (a person or the attention). [French *river* fasten]

riviera /ˌrɪvɪˈeərə/ *n.* coastal subtropical region, esp. that of SE France and NW Italy. [Italian, = sea-shore]

rivulet /ˈrɪvjʊlɪt/ *n.* small stream. [Latin *rivus* stream]

Riyadh /riːˈɑːd/ capital and commercial centre of Saudi Arabia; pop. (est. 1991) 1 800 000.

riyal /rɪˈɑːl/ *n.* standard monetary unit of Qatar, Saudi Arabia, and Yemen. [Arabic: related to REAL[2]]

RJ *airline flight code* Royal Jordanian Airlines.

RJE *abbr. Computing* remote job entry.

RK *airline flight code* Air Afrique.

RL *international vehicle registration* Lebanon.

RLO *abbr.* returned letter office.

Rls *symb.* rial (of Iran).

RM *–abbr.* **1** Royal Mail. **2** Royal Marines. *–international vehicle registration* Madagascar. *–postcode* Romford.

rm. *abbr.* room.

RMA *abbr.* Royal Military Academy.

RMB *abbr.* (also **Rmb**) renminbi.

RMM *international vehicle registration* Mali.

RMS *abbr.* **1** (also **r.m.s.**) *Math.* root mean square. **2** Royal Mail Service. **3** Royal Mail Ship (or Steamer).

RMT *abbr.* National Union of Rail, Maritime, and Transport Workers.

RN *–abbr.* Royal Navy. *–international vehicle registration* Republic of Niger.

Rn *symb.* radon.

RNA *abbr.* ribonucleic acid.

RNLI *abbr.* Royal National Lifeboat Institution.

RO *–abbr.* **1** record(s) office. **2** = REGISTERED OFFICE. *–symb.* rial (of Oman). *–international vehicle registration* Romania.

ROA *abbr.* return on assets.

roach *n.* (*pl.* same or **-es**) small freshwater fish of the carp family. [French]

road *n.* **1 a** way with a prepared surface, for vehicles, pedestrians, etc. **b** part of this for vehicles only (*step out into the road*). **2** one's way or route. **3** (usu. in *pl.*) piece of water near the shore in which ships can ride at anchor. □ **any road** *dial.* = ANYWAY 2, 3. **get out of the** (or **my** etc.) **road** *dial.* stop obstructing a person. **in the** (or **one's**) **road** *dial.* forming an obstruction. **one for the road** *colloq.* final (esp. alcoholic) drink before departure. **on the road** travelling, esp. as a firm's representative, itinerant performer, or vagrant. **the road to** way of getting to or achieving (*road to London*; *road to ruin*). [Old English: related to RIDE]

roadbed *n.* **1** foundation structure of a railway. **2** foundation material for a road. **3** *US* part of a road on which vehicles travel.

roadblock *n.* barrier set up on a road in order to stop and examine traffic.

road fund licence *n.* disc displayed on a vehicle certifying payment of road tax.

♦ **road haulage** *n.* transport of goods by road vehicles, which in Europe may carry up to 38 tonnes.

---

road-hog *n. colloq.* reckless or inconsiderate road-user.

road-holding *n.* stability of a moving vehicle.

road-house *n.* inn or club on a major road.

roadie *n. colloq.* assistant of a touring band etc., erecting and maintaining equipment.

road-metal *n.* broken stone used in road-making etc.

road sense *n.* capacity for safe behaviour in traffic etc.

roadshow *n.* **1** television or radio series broadcasting each programme from a different venue. **2** any touring political or advertising campaign or touring entertainment.

roadside *n.* (often *attrib.*) strip of land beside a road.

road sign *n.* sign giving information or instructions to road users.

roadstead *n.* = ROAD 3.

roadster *n.* open car without rear seats.

road tax *n.* periodic tax payable on road vehicles.

road test *–n.* test of a vehicle's roadworthiness. *–v.* (**road-test**) test (a vehicle) on the road.

Road Town capital of the British Virgin Islands, on the island of Tortola; pop. (est. 1991) 6330.

roadway *n.* **1** road. **2** part of a road intended for vehicles.

roadworks *n.pl.* construction, repair, etc. of roads.

roadworthy *adj.* fit to be used on the road. □ **roadworthiness** *n.*

roam *–v.* **1** ramble, wander. **2** travel unsystematically over, through, or about. *–n.* act of roaming; ramble. □ **roamer** *n.* [origin unknown]

roan *–adj.* (of esp. a horse) having a coat thickly interspersed with hairs of another colour. *–n.* roan animal. [French]

roar *–n.* **1 a** loud deep hoarse sound, as made by a lion. **b** similar sound. **2** loud laugh. *–v.* **1** (often foll. by *out*) utter loudly or make a roar, roaring laugh, etc. **2** travel in a vehicle at high speed, esp. with the engine roaring. [Old English]

roaring drunk *predic. adj.* very drunk and noisy.

roaring forties *n.pl.* stormy ocean tracts between lat. 40° and 50° S.

roaring success *n.* great success.

roaring trade *n.* (also **roaring business**) very brisk trade or business.

roaring twenties *n.pl.* decade of the 1920s.

roast *–v.* **1 a** cook (food, esp. meat) or (of food) be cooked in an oven or by open heat (*roast chestnuts*). **b** heat (coffee beans) before grinding. **2** *refl.* expose (oneself etc.) to fire or heat. **3** criticize severely, denounce. *–attrib. adj.* roasted (*roast beef*). *–n.* **1 a** roast meat. **b** dish of this. **c** piece of meat for roasting. **2** process of roasting. [French *rost(ir)* from Germanic]

roaster *n.* **1** oven, dish, apparatus, etc. for roasting. **2** fowl, potato, etc. for roasting.

roasting *–adj.* very hot. *–n.* severe criticism or denunciation.

rob *v.* (**-bb-**) (often foll. by *of*) **1** (also *absol.*) take unlawfully from, esp. by force or threat (*robbed the safe*; *robbed her of her jewels*). **2** deprive of what is due or normal (*robbed of sleep*). □ **robber** *n.* [French *rob(b)er* from Germanic]

robbery *n.* (*pl.* **-ies**) **1** act of robbing. **2** *colloq.* excessive charge or cost.

robe *–n.* **1 a** long loose outer garment. **b** (often in *pl.*) this worn as an indication of rank, office, profession, etc. **2** esp. *US* dressing-gown. *–v.* (**-bing**) clothe in a robe; dress. [French]

robin /'rɒbɪn/ *n.* **1** (also **robin redbreast**) small brown red-breasted bird. **2** *US* red-breasted thrush. [pet form of *Robert*]

Robin Hood *n.* person who steals from the rich to give to the poor.

robinia /rə'bɪnɪə/ *n.* any of various North American trees or shrubs, e.g. a locust tree or false acacia. [*Robin*, name of a French gardener]

robot /'rəʊbɒt/ *n.* **1** machine resembling or functioning like a human. **2** programmable device engineered to perform many simple repetitive tasks formerly done by human labour. It consists of one or more articulated mechanical manipulators, typically an arm and hand, that are linked to a computer and have considerable freedom of movement. In more advanced types there is also some form of sensory mechanism, such as a TV camera acting as an artificial eye. Most robots in current industrial use follow a fixed sequence of instructions but can be reprogrammed to carry out another task. They can be used, for example, for loading and unloading machines, positioning and transferring parts, and welding. **3** person who acts mechanically. □ **robotic** /-'bɒtɪk/ *adj.* **robotize** *v.* (also **-ise**) (**-zing** or **-sing**). [Czech]

robotics /rəʊ'bɒtɪks/ *n.pl.* (usu. treated as *sing.*) art, science, or study of robot design and operation.

robust /rəʊ'bʌst/ *adj.* (**-er, -est**) **1** strong and sturdy, esp. in physique or construction. **2** (of exercise, discipline, etc.) vigorous, requiring strength. **3** (of mental attitude, argument, etc.) straightforward, vigorous. **4** (of a statement, reply, etc.) bold, firm, unyielding. □ **robustly** *adv.* **robustness** *n.* [Latin *robur* strength]

roc *n.* gigantic bird of Eastern legend. [Spanish from Arabic]

ROCE *abbr.* = RETURN ON CAPITAL EMPLOYED.

rochet /'rɒtʃɪt/ *n.* surplice-like vestment of a bishop or abbot. [French from Germanic]

rock[1] *n.* **1 a** hard material of the earth's crust, often exposed on the surface. **b** similar material on other planets. **2** *Geol.* any natural material, hard or soft (e.g. clay), consisting of one or more minerals. **3 a** projecting rock forming a hill, cliff, reef, etc. **b** (**the Rock**) Gibraltar. **4** large detached stone. **5** *US* stone of any size. **6** firm and dependable support or protection. **7** hard sweet usu. in the form of a peppermint-flavoured stick. **8** *slang* precious stone, esp. a diamond. □ **get one's rocks off** *coarse slang* achieve (esp. sexual) satisfaction. **on the rocks** *colloq.* **1** short of money. **2** (of a marriage etc.) broken down. **3** (of a drink) served neat with ice-cubes. [French *roque, roche*]

rock[2] *–v.* **1** move gently to and fro; set, maintain, or be in, such motion. **2** (cause to) sway; shake, oscillate, reel. **3** distress, perturb (*rocked by the news*). *–n.* **1** rocking movement. **2** spell of this. **3 a** = ROCK AND ROLL. **b** rock and roll-influenced popular music. □ **rock the boat** *colloq.* disturb a stable situation. [Old English]

rockabilly /'rɒkə,bɪlɪ/ *n.* rock and roll combined with hill-billy music.

rock and roll *n.* (also **rock 'n' roll**) popular dance-music originating in the 1950s with a heavy beat and often a blues element.

rock-bottom *–adj.* (of prices etc.) the very lowest. *–n.* very lowest level.

rock-cake *n.* small rough-surfaced spicy currant bun.

rock-crystal *n.* transparent colourless quartz, usu. in hexagonal prisms.

rocker *n.* **1** curved bar etc. on which something can rock. **2** rocking-chair. **3** devotee of rock music, esp. a leather-clad motor cyclist. **4 a** device for rocking. **b** pivoted switch operating between 'on' and 'off' positions. □ **off one's rocker** *slang* crazy.

rockery *n.* (*pl.* **-ies**) construction of stones with soil between them for growing rock-plants on.

rocket /'rɒkɪt/ *–n.* **1** cylindrical firework or signal etc. propelled to a great height after ignition. **2** engine operating on the same principle, providing thrust but not dependent on air intake. **3** rocket-propelled missile, spacecraft, etc. **4** *slang* severe reprimand. *–v.* (**-t-**) **1 a** move rapidly upwards or away. **b** increase rapidly (*prices rocketed*). **2** bombard with rockets. [French *roquette* from Italian]

rocketry *n.* science or practice of rocket propulsion.

rock-face *n.* vertical surface of natural rock.

rockfall *n.* descent or mass of loose fallen rocks.

rock-garden *n.* = ROCKERY.

Rockhampton /rɒk'hæmpt(ə)n/ city and port in Australia, in Queensland, the centre of Australia's largest beef-producing area; pop. (1993) 65 868.

rocking-chair *n.* chair mounted on rockers or springs for gently rocking in.

rocking-horse *n.* toy horse on rockers or springs.

rock-plant *n.* plant growing on or among rocks.

rock-salmon *n.* any of several fishes, esp. the catfish and dogfish.

rock-salt *n.* common salt as a solid mineral.

rocky[1] *adj.* (**-ier, -iest**) of, like, or full of rock or rocks. □ **rockiness** *n.*

rocky[2] *adj.* (**-ier, -iest**) *colloq.* unsteady, tottering, unstable. □ **rockiness** *n.*

rococo /rə'kəʊkəʊ/ *–adj.* **1** of a late baroque style of 18th-century decoration. **2** (of literature, music, architecture, etc.) highly ornate. *–n.* this style. [French]

rod *n.* **1** slender straight cylindrical bar or stick. **2 a** cane for flogging. **b** (prec. by *the*) use of this. **3** = FISHING-ROD. **4** *hist.* (as a measure) perch or square perch (see PERCH[1] *n.* 3). □ **make a rod for one's own back** make trouble for oneself. [Old English]

♦ **Roddick** /'rɒdɪk/, **Anita** (1942–) British retailer, formerly managing director (1976–94), now chief executive (since 1994), and founder of the Body Shop, a chain store selling beauty products developed without testing on animals and packaged in easily recyclable containers. She and her husband Gordon opened the first shop in Brighton in 1976.

---

rode *past* of RIDE.

rodent /ˈrəʊd(ə)nt/ *n.* mammal with strong incisors and no canine teeth, e.g. the rat, mouse, squirrel, beaver, and porcupine. [Latin *rodo* gnaw]

rodeo /ˈrəʊdɪəʊ, rəˈdeɪəʊ/ *n.* (*pl.* **-s**) **1** exhibition of cowboys' skills in handling animals. **2** round-up of cattle on a ranch for branding etc. [Spanish]

rodomontade /ˌrɒdəmɒnˈteɪd/ *n.* boastful talk or behaviour. [French from Italian]

ROE *abbr.* return on equity.

roe[1] /rəʊ/ *n.* **1** (also **hard roe**) mass of eggs in a female fish's ovary. **2** (also **soft roe**) milt of a male fish. [Low German or Dutch]

roe[2] /rəʊ/ *n.* (*pl.* same or **-s**) (also **roe-deer**) small kind of deer. [Old English]

roebuck *n.* male roe-deer.

roentgen /ˈrʌntjən/ *n.* (also **röntgen**) former unit of ionizing radiation. [*Röntgen*, name of a physicist]

Roeselare /ˌruːsəˈlærə/ (French **Roulers** /ruːˈleə(r)/) textile-manufacturing town in W Belgium; pop. (est. 1995) 53 617.

ROG *abbr.* (also **r.o.g.**) receipt of goods.

rogation /rəʊˈgeɪʃ(ə)n/ *n.* (usu. in *pl.*) litany of the saints chanted on the three days before Ascension day. [Latin *rogo* ask]

Rogation Days *n.pl.* the three days before Ascension Day.

roger /ˈrɒdʒə(r)/ *int.* **1** your message has been received and understood (used in radio communication etc.). **2** *slang* I agree. [from the name, code for *R*]

rogue /rəʊg/ *n.* **1** dishonest or unprincipled person. **2** *joc.* mischievous person, esp. a child. **3** (usu. *attrib.*) wild fierce animal driven away or living apart from others (*rogue elephant*). **4** (often *attrib.*) inexplicably aberrant result or phenomenon; inferior or defective specimen. [origin unknown]

roguery /ˈrəʊgərɪ/ *n.* (*pl.* **-ies**) conduct or action characteristic of rogues.

rogues' gallery *n. colloq.* collection of photographs of known criminals etc., used for identification.

roguish *adj.* **1** playfully mischievous. **2** characteristic of rogues. □ **roguishly** *adv.* **roguishness** *n.*

ROI *abbr.* return on investment.

roister *–v.* (esp. as **roistering** *–adj.*) revel noisily; be uproarious. □ **roisterer** *n.* [Latin: related to RUSTIC]

ROK *international vehicle registration* South Korea.

role *n.* (also **rôle**) **1** actor's part in a play, film, etc. **2** person's or thing's function. [French: related to ROLL]

role model *n.* person on whom others model themselves.

role-playing *n.* (also **role-play**) acting of characters or situations as an aid in psychotherapy, language-teaching, etc. □ **role-play** *v.*

roll /rəʊl/ *–v.* **1** (cause to) move or go in some direction by turning on an axis (*ball rolled under the table*; *rolled the barrel into the cellar*). **2 a** make cylindrical or spherical by revolving between two surfaces or over on itself (*rolled a newspaper*). **b** make thus (*rolled a cigarette*). **c** gather into a mass or shape (*rolled the dough into a ball*; *rolled himself into a ball*). **3** (often foll. by *along*, *by*, etc.) (cause to) move, advance, or be conveyed on or (of time etc.) as if on wheels etc. (*bus rolled past*; *rolled the trolley*; *years rolled by*; *rolled by in his car*). **4** flatten or form by passing a roller etc. over or by passing between rollers (*roll the lawn*; *roll pastry*). **5** rotate (*his eyes rolled*; *he rolled his eyes*). **6 a** wallow (*dog rolled in the dust*). **b** (of a horse etc.) lie on its back and kick about. **7** (of a moving ship, aircraft, vehicle, or person) sway to and fro sideways or walk unsteadily (*rolled out of the pub*). **8 a** undulate (*rolling hills*; *rolling mist*). **b** carry or propel with undulations (*river rolls its waters to the sea*). **9** (cause to) start functioning or moving (*cameras rolled*). **10** sound or utter with vibrations or a trill (*thunder rolled*; *rolls his* rs). *–n.* **1** rolling motion or gait; undulation (*roll of the hills*). **2 a** spell of rolling (*roll in the mud*). **b** gymnastic exercise in which the body rolls in a forward or backward circle. **c** (esp. **a roll in the hay**) *colloq.* sexual intercourse etc. **3** rhythmic rumbling sound of thunder etc. **4** complete revolution of an aircraft about its longitudinal axis. **5** anything forming a cylinder by being turned over on itself without folding (*roll of carpet*; *sausage roll*). **6 a** small portion of bread individually baked. **b** this with a specified filling (*ham roll*). **7** thing cylindrical in shape (*rolls of fat*; *roll of hair*). **8 a** official list or register (*electoral roll*). **b** total numbers on this. □ **be rolling in** *colloq.* have plenty of (esp. money). **rolled into one** combined in one person or thing. **roll in** arrive in great numbers or quantity. **roll on** *v.* **1** put on or apply by rolling. **2** (in *imper.*) *colloq.* come quickly (*roll on Friday!*). **roll up 1** *colloq.* arrive in a vehicle; appear on the scene. **2** make into or form a roll. **strike off the rolls** debar (esp. a solicitor) from practising. [Latin *rotulus* diminutive: related to ROTA]

roll-call *n.* calling out a list of names to establish who is present.

rolled gold *n.* thin coating of gold applied to a base metal by rolling.

rolled oats *n.pl.* husked and crushed oats.

roller *n.* **1 a** hard revolving cylinder for smoothing, spreading, crushing, stamping, hanging a towel on, etc., used alone or in a machine. **b** cylinder for diminishing friction when moving a heavy object. **2** small cylinder on which hair is rolled for setting. **3** long swelling wave.

roller bearing *n.* bearing like a ball-bearing but with small cylinders instead of balls.

roller blind *n.* blind on a roller.

roller-coaster *n.* **1** switchback at a fair etc. **2** (*attrib.*) (of emotions etc.) uncontrollable, unstable.

roller-skate *–n.* metal frame with small wheels, fitted to shoes for riding on a hard surface. *–v.* (**-ting**) move on roller-skates. □ **roller-skater** *n.*

roller towel *n.* towel with the ends joined, hung on a roller.

rollicking /ˈrɒlɪkɪŋ/ *adj.* jovial, exuberant. [origin unknown]

rolling drunk *predic. adj.* swaying or staggering from drunkenness.

♦ **rolling launch** *n.* process of gradually introducing a new product into the market.

---

rolling-mill *n.* machine or factory for rolling metal into shape.

rolling-pin *n.* cylinder for rolling out pastry, dough, etc.

rolling-stock *n.* **1** locomotives, carriages, etc. used on a railway. **2** *US* road vehicles of a company.

rolling stone *n.* unsettled rootless person.

rollmop *n.* rolled uncooked pickled herring fillet. [German *Rollmops*]

roll-neck *adj.* (of a garment) having a high loosely turned-over neck.

roll of honour *n.* list of those honoured, esp. the dead in war.

roll-on *–attrib. adj.* (of deodorant etc.) applied by means of a rotating ball in the neck of the container. *–n.* light elastic corset.

roll-on roll-off *adj.* (of a ferry or cargo ship) in which vehicles are driven directly on and off.

♦ **roll-over credit** *n.* medium- or long-term bank loan in which the rate of interest varies with short-term money-market rates (such as LIBOR) because the bank has raised the loan by short-term money-market or interbank market borrowing.

♦ **roll-over relief** *n.* relief from capital-gains tax allowing tax on the disposal of an asset to be postponed, by deducting the capital gain from the base cost of another asset acquired by the person making the original disposal. The effect is that the gain on the disposal of the second asset will be increased because the consideration for the purchase of the asset is treated as artificially reduced by the gain on the earlier asset. This type of relief is available in a variety of transactions, in which the person disposing of the asset will not be in funds to pay the tax, e.g. the replacement of business assets, gifts of assets from one person to another, and the formation of companies in exchange for shares. See also EMPLOYEE SHARE-OWNERSHIP PLAN.

---

roll-top desk *n.* desk with a flexible cover sliding in curved grooves.

roll-up *n.* (also **roll-your-own**) hand-rolled cigarette.

roly-poly /ˌrəʊlɪˈpəʊlɪ/ *–n.* (*pl.* **-ies**) (also **roly-poly pudding**) pudding made of a rolled strip of suet pastry covered with jam etc. and boiled or baked. *–adj.* podgy, plump. [probably ROLL]

ROM /rɒm/ *n. Computing* read-only memory, the part of main-store memory whose contents are fixed during manufacture and can therefore be read but not modified. ROM generally stores the essential programs required by the computer. For example, ROM usu. contains a short program to load the operating system when the machine is switched on, and sometimes the whole operating system itself. See also EPROM; PROM; RANDOM ACCESS; SEMICONDUCTOR MEMORY. [abbreviation]

rom. *abbr.* roman (type).

ROM cartridge *n.* (also **ROM pack**) module containing software that is permanently stored as ROM. The module can easily be plugged into and later removed from a microcomputer.

Roman /ˈrəʊmən/ *–adj.* **1** of ancient Rome, its territory, people, etc. **2** of medieval or modern Rome. **3** = ROMAN CATHOLIC. **4** (**roman**) (of type) plain and upright, used in ordinary print. **5** (of the alphabet etc.) based on the ancient Roman system with letters A–Z. *–n.* **1** citizen or soldier of the ancient Roman Republic or Empire. **2** citizen of modern Rome. **3** = ROMAN CATHOLIC. **4** (**roman**) roman type. [Latin]

Roman candle *n.* firework discharging flaming coloured balls.

Roman Catholic *–adj.* of the part of the Christian Church acknowledging the Pope as its head. *–n.* member of this Church. □ **Roman Catholicism** *n.*

romance /rəʊˈmæns/ *–n.* /also ˈrəʊ-/ **1** idealized, poetic, or unworldly atmosphere or tendency. **2 a** love affair. **b** mutual attraction in this. **c** sentimental or idealized love. **3 a** literary genre concerning romantic love, stirring action, etc. **b** work of this genre. **4** medieval, esp. verse, tale of chivalry, common in the Romance languages. **5 a** exaggeration, lies. **b** instance of this. **6** (**Romance**) (often *attrib.*) languages descended from Latin. **7** *Mus.* short informal piece. *–v.* (**-cing**) **1** exaggerate, distort the truth, fantasize. **2** court, woo. [Romanic: related to ROMANIC]

■ **Usage** The alternative pronunciation given for the noun, with the stress on the first syllable, is considered incorrect by some people.

Roman Empire *n. hist.* that established by Augustus in 27 BC and divided by Theodosius in AD 395.

Romanesque /ˌrəʊməˈnesk/ *–n.* style of European architecture *c.* 900–1200, with massive vaulting and round arches. *–adj.* of this style.

Romanian /rəʊˈmeɪnɪən/ (also **Rumanian** /ruː-/) *–n.* **1 a** native or national of Romania. **b** person of Romanian descent. **2** language of Romania. *–adj.* of Romania, its people, or language.

Romanic /rəʊˈmænɪk/ *–n.* = ROMANCE *n.* 6. *–adj.* **1 a** of Romance. **b** Romance-speaking. **2** descended from, or inheriting the civilization etc. of, the ancient Romans. [Latin *Romanicus*: related to ROMAN]

romanize /ˈrəʊməˌnaɪz/ *v.* (also **-ise**) (**-zing** or **-sing**) **1** make Roman or Roman Catholic in character. **2** put into the Roman alphabet or roman type. □ **romanization** /-ˈzeɪʃ(ə)n/ *n.*

Roman law *n.* law-code of ancient Rome, forming the basis of many modern codes.

Roman nose *n.* aquiline high-bridged nose.

roman numeral *n.* any of the Roman letters representing numbers: I = 1, V = 5, X = 10, L = 50, C = 100, D = 500, M = 1000.

Romano- *comb. form* Roman; Roman and (*Romano-British*).

romantic /rəʊˈmæntɪk/ *–adj.* **1** of, characterized by, or suggestive of romance (*romantic picture*). **2** inclined towards or suggestive of romance in love (*romantic evening; romantic words*). **3** (of a person) imaginative, visionary, idealistic. **4 a** (of style in art, music, etc.) concerned more with feeling and emotion than with form and aesthetic qualities. **b** (also **Romantic**) of the 18th–19th-century romantic movement or style in the European arts. **5** (of a project etc.) unpractical, fantastic. *–n.* **1** romantic person. **2** romanticist. □ **romantically** *adv.* [French: related to ROMANCE]

romanticism *n.* (also **Romanticism**) adherence to a romantic style in art, music, etc.

romanticist *n.* (also **Romanticist**) writer or artist of the romantic school.

romanticize *v.* (also **-ise**) (**-zing** or **-sing**) **1** make romantic; exaggerate (*romanticized account*). **2** indulge in romantic thoughts or actions.

Romania /rəʊˈmeɪnɪə/ (also **Rumania** /ruː-/), **Republic of** country in SE Europe with an E coastline on the Black Sea. After the Second World War Romania's economy became increasingly industrialized but agriculture remains important, esp. as a source of employment. Principal crops include cereals, potatoes, sugar beet, vines, and fruits; sheep and cattle raising and wine production are also important. The mining industry is a major sector of the economy, exploiting oil and natural gas, coal, iron ore, salt, bauxite, lead, zinc, copper, and uranium. The manufacturing sector is based largely on the metallurgical, mechanical engineering, chemical, and timber industries; manufactured exports include petroleum products, machinery, vehicle parts, and electrical goods. Since 1990 agriculture and industry, formerly under state control, have been undergoing restructuring along free-market lines. In 1995 a mass privatization measure was passed affecting over 3000 companies.
History. Romania was formed in 1859 by the unification of the principalities of Wallachia and Moldavia and gained independence from the Ottoman Empire in 1878, becoming a kingdom in 1881. After the First World War it acquired territory in Bessarabia, Bukovina, and Transylvania, some of which it relinquished to the Soviet Union during the Second World War (see also MOLDAVIA); in 1948 Romania became a Communist state. The totalitarian presidency of Nicolae Ceauşescu (1974–89) was marked by forced economic growth, impoverishment of the population, and suppression of all political opposition; it was brought to an end by his overthrow and execution. The National Salvation Front government which succeeded it failed to solve the country's economic problems and fell in 1991. It was replaced by a coalition government that oversaw the adoption of a new constitution guaranteeing multi-party democracy and market reforms; free elections were held in 1992; however, the government continued to be dominated by ex-Communists. In presidential and legislative elections held in 1997 non-communists emerged victorious. President, Emil Constantinescu; prime minister, Rady Vasile; capital, Bucharest.

languages	Romanian (official), Hungarian, German
currency	leu (*pl.* lei) of 100 bani
pop. (1996)	22 670 000
GNP (1994)	US$27.9B
literacy	98% (m); 95% (f)
life expectancy	69 (m); 75 (f)

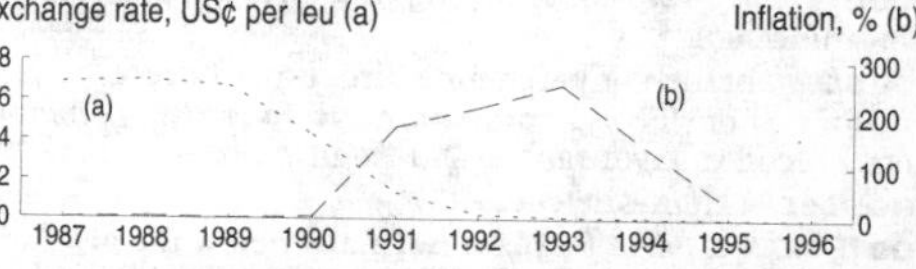

Romany /ˈrɒmənɪ/ *–n.* (*pl.* **-ies**) **1** Gypsy. **2** language of the Gypsies. *–adj.* of Gypsies or the Romany language. [Romany *Rom* gypsy]

Rome /rəʊm/ (Italian **Roma** /ˈrəʊmə/) capital of Italy, situated on the River Tiber; it is a centre of culture and classical history, with many art treasures, and tourism is of major economic importance; pop. (est. 1994) 2 687 881.

Rome, Treaty of see EUROPEAN ECONOMIC COMMUNITY.

Romeo /ˈrəʊmɪəʊ/ *n.* (*pl.* **-s**) passionate male lover or seducer. [name of a character in Shakespeare]

romp *–v.* **1** play roughly and energetically. **2** (foll. by *along, past,* etc.) *colloq.* proceed without effort. *–n.* spell of romping. □ **romp in** (or **home**) *colloq.* win easily. [perhaps from RAMP]

rompers *n.pl.* (also **romper suit**) young child's one-piece garment covering the trunk and usu. the legs.

RONA *abbr.* return on net assets.

rondeau /ˈrɒndəʊ/ *n.* (*pl.* **rondeaux** pronunc. same or /-əʊz/) poem of ten or thirteen lines with only two rhymes throughout and with the opening words used twice as a refrain. [French: related to RONDEL]

rondel /ˈrɒnd(ə)l/ *n.* rondeau, esp. one of special form. [French: related to ROUND: cf. ROUNDEL]

rondo /ˈrɒndəʊ/ *n.* (*pl.* **-s**) musical form with a recurring leading theme. [French RONDEAU]

Rondônia /rɒnˈdɒnjə/ state in NW Brazil; pop. (est. 1987) 981 800; capital, Pôrto Velho.

röntgen var. of ROENTGEN.

rood *n.* **1** crucifix, esp. one raised on a rood-screen. **2** quarter of an acre. [Old English]

rood-screen *n.* carved screen separating nave and chancel.

roof *–n.* (*pl.* **-s**) **1 a** upper covering of a building. **b** top of a covered vehicle. **c** top inner surface of an oven, refrigerator, etc. **2** overhead rock in a cave or mine etc. *–v.* **1** (often foll. by *in, over*) cover with or as with a roof. **2** be the roof of. □ **go through the roof** *colloq.* (of prices etc.) rise dramatically. **hit** (or **go through) the roof** *colloq.* become very angry. [Old English]

roof-garden *n.* garden on the flat roof of a building.

roofing *n.* material for a roof.

roof of the mouth *n.* palate.

roof-rack *n.* framework for luggage on top of a vehicle.

rooftop *n.* **1** outer surface of a roof. **2** (in *pl.*) tops of houses etc. □ **shout it from the rooftops** make a thing embarrassingly public.

roof-tree *n.* ridge-piece of a roof.

rook[1] /rʊk/ *–n.* black bird of the crow family nesting in colonies. *–v.* **1** *colloq.* charge (a customer) extortionately. **2** win money at cards etc., esp. by swindling. [Old English]

rook[2] /rʊk/ *n.* chess piece with a battlement-shaped top. [French from Arabic]

rookery *n.* (*pl.* **-ies**) colony of rooks, penguins, or seals.

rookie /ˈrʊkɪ/ *n. slang* new recruit. [corruption]

room /ruːm/ *–n.* **1** space for, or occupied by, something; capacity (*takes up too much room*; *room for improvement*). **2 a** part of a building enclosed by walls, floor, and ceiling. **b** (in *pl.*) apartments or lodgings. **c** people in a room (*room fell silent*). *–v. US* have room(s); lodge, board. [Old English]

rooming-house *n.* lodging house.

room-mate *n.* person sharing a room.

room service *n.* provision of food etc. in a hotel bedroom.

roomy *adj.* (**-ier, -iest**) having much room, spacious. □ **roominess** *n.*

roost *–n.* branch or perch for a bird, esp. to sleep. *–v.* settle for rest or sleep. □ **come home to roost** (of a scheme etc.) recoil unfavourably. [Old English *hrōst*]

rooster *n.* domestic cock.

root[1] *–n.* **1 a** part of a plant normally below the ground, conveying nourishment from the soil. **b** (in *pl.*) branches or fibres of this. **c** small plant with a root for transplanting. **2 a** plant with an edible root. **b** such a root. **3** (in *pl.*) emotional attachment or family ties to a place or community. **4 a** embedded part of a hair, tooth, nail, etc. **b** part of a thing attaching it to a greater whole. **5** (often *attrib.*) basic cause, source, nature, or origin (*root of all evil*; *roots in the distant past*; *root cause*; *the root of things*). **6 a** number that when multiplied by itself a usu. specified number of times gives a specified number or quantity (*cube root of eight is two*). **b** square root. **c** value of an unknown quantity satisfying a given equation. **7** *Philol.* core of a word, without prefixes, suffixes, etc. *–v.* **1** (cause to) take root; grow roots (*root them firmly*). **2** (esp. as **rooted** *adj.*) fix firmly; establish (*rooted objection to*; *reaction rooted in fear*). **3** (usu. foll. by *out, up*) drag or dig up by the roots. □ **root and branch** thorough(ly), radical(ly). **root out** find and get rid of. **strike** (or **take**) **root 1** begin to grow and draw nourishment from the soil. **2** become established. □ **rootless** *adj.* [Old English]

root[2] *v.* **1** (also *absol.*) (often foll. by *up*) turn up (the ground) with the snout, beak, etc., in search of food. **2 a** (foll. by *around, in,* etc.) rummage. **b** (foll. by *out* or *up*) find or extract by rummaging. **3** (foll. by *for*) *US slang* encourage by applause or support. [Old English and Old Norse]

rootstock *n.* **1** rhizome. **2** plant into which a graft is inserted. **3** primary form from which offshoots have arisen.

ROP *abbr.* = RUN OF PAPER.

rope *–n.* **1 a** stout cord made by twisting together strands of hemp, wire, etc. **b** piece of this. **2** (foll. by *of*) quantity of onions, pearls, etc. strung together. **3** (prec. by *the*) **a** halter for hanging a person. **b** execution by hanging. *–v.* (**-ping**) **1** fasten, secure, or catch with rope. **2** (usu. foll. by *off, in*) enclose with rope. **3** *Mountaineering* connect with or attach to a rope. □ **know** (or **learn** or **show**) **the ropes** know (or learn or show) how to do a thing properly. **rope in** persuade to take part. **rope into** persuade to take part in (*roped into washing up*). [Old English]

rope-ladder *n.* two ropes with crosspieces, used as a ladder.

ropy *adj.* (also **ropey**) (**-ier, -iest**) *colloq.* poor in quality. □ **ropiness** *n.*

Roquefort /ˈrɒkfɔː(r)/ *n. propr.* soft blue cheese made from ewes' milk. [*Roquefort* in France]

ro-ro /ˈrəʊrəʊ/ *attrib. adj.* roll-on roll-off. [abbreviation]

rorqual /ˈrɔːkw(ə)l/ *n.* whale with a dorsal fin. [French from Norwegian]

Rorschach test /ˈrɔːʃɑːk/ *n.* personality test based on the subject's interpretation of a standard set of ink-blots. [*Rorschach*, name of a psychiatrist]

rosaceous /rəʊˈzeɪʃəs/ *adj.* of a large plant family including the rose. [Latin: related to ROSE[1]]

Rosario /rəʊˈsɑːrɪˌəʊ/ river port in E central Argentina, a centre of commerce with sugar-refining, food-processing, and other industries; pop. (est. 1992) 1 157 372.

rosary /ˈrəʊzərɪ/ *n.* (*pl.* **-ies**) **1** *RC Ch.* repeated sequence of prayers. **2** string of beads for keeping count in this. [Latin *rosarium* rose-garden]

Roscommon /rɒsˈkɒmən/ county in the Republic of Ireland, in the province of Connaught; cattle rearing is the main agricultural activity; pop. (1991) 51 897; capital, Roscommon.

rose[1] /rəʊz/ *–n.* **1** prickly bush or shrub bearing usu. fragrant red, pink, yellow, or white flowers. **2** this flower. **3** flowering plant resembling this (*Christmas rose*). **4 a** pinkish-red colour. **b** (usu. in *pl.*) rosy complexion (*roses in her cheeks*). **5** sprinkling-nozzle of a watering-can etc. **6** circular electric light mounting on a ceiling. **7 a** representation of a rose in heraldry etc. **b** rose-shaped design. **8** (in *pl.*) used to express luck, ease, success, etc. (*roses all the way*; *everything's roses*). *–adj.* = ROSE-COLOURED 1. [Latin *rosa*]

rose[2] *past* of RISE.

rosé /ˈrəʊzeɪ/ *n.* light pink wine. [French]

Roseau /rəʊ'zəʊ/ capital of Dominica; pop. (1991) 15 853.

rosebowl *n.* bowl for cut roses, esp. as a prize in a competition.

rosebud *n.* **1** bud of a rose. **2** pretty young woman.

rose-bush *n.* rose plant.

rose-coloured *adj.* **1** pinkish-red. **2** optimistic, cheerful (*wears rose-coloured glasses*).

rose-hip *n.* = HIP[2].

rosemary /'rəʊzmərɪ/ *n.* evergreen fragrant shrub used as a herb. [*rosmarine* from Latin *ros* dew: related to MARINE]

rosette /rəʊ'zet/ *n.* **1** rose-shaped ornament of ribbon etc., esp. as a supporter's badge or as a prize in a competition. **2** rose-shaped carving. [French diminutive: related to ROSE[1]]

rose-water *n.* perfume made from roses.

rose-window *n.* circular window with roselike tracery.

rosewood *n.* any of several fragrant close-grained woods used in making furniture.

rosin /'rɒzɪn/ *–n.* resin, esp. in solid form. *–v.* (**-n-**) rub (esp. a violin bow etc.) with rosin. [alteration of RESIN]

Roskilde /'rɒskɪlə/ port in Denmark, on the island of Zealand; it has tanning, distilling, and meat-processing industries; pop. (1990) 49 080.

RoSPA /'rɒspə/ *abbr.* Royal Society for the Prevention of Accidents.

roster /'rɒstə(r)/ *–n.* list or plan of turns of duty etc. *–v.* place on a roster. [Dutch *rooster*, literally 'gridiron']

Rostock /'rɒstɒk/ industrial port in NE Germany, on the Baltic coast; fish processing and ship repairing are important; pop. (est. 1995) 232 634.

Rostov-on-Don /'rɒstɒf/ city and port in S Russia, on the River Don near its point of entry into the Sea of Azov; manufactures include agricultural machinery, textiles, and processed food; pop. (est. 1995) 1 026 000.

rostrum /'rɒstrəm/ *n.* (*pl.* **rostra** or **-s**) platform for public speaking, an orchestral conductor, etc. [Latin]

rosy /'rəʊzɪ/ *adj.* (**-ier, -iest**) **1** pink or red. **2** optimistic, hopeful (*rosy future*). □ **rosily** *adv.* **rosiness** *n.*

rot *–v.* (**-tt-**) **1** (of animal or vegetable matter) lose its original form by the chemical action of bacteria, fungi, etc.; decay. **2** gradually perish or waste away (*left to rot in prison*). **3** cause to rot, make rotten. *–n.* **1** rotting; decay. **2** *slang* nonsense (*talks rot*). **3** decline in standards etc. (*rot set in*). *–int.* expressing incredulity or ridicule. [Old English]

rota /'rəʊtə/ *n.* list of duties to be done or names of people to do them in turn; roster. [Latin, = wheel]

Rotarian /rəʊ'teərɪən/ *–n.* member of Rotary. *–adj.* of Rotary.

rotary /'rəʊtərɪ/ *–adj.* acting by rotation (*rotary drill*). *–n.* (*pl.* **-ies**) **1** rotary machine. **2** (**Rotary**) (in full **Rotary International**) worldwide charitable society of businessmen, orig. entertaining in rotation. [medieval Latin: related to ROTA]

Rotary Club *n.* local branch of Rotary.

rotate /rəʊ'teɪt/ *v.* (**-ting**) **1** move round an axis or centre, revolve. **2** take or arrange (esp. crops) in rotation. **3** act or take place in rotation (*chairmanship will rotate*). □ **rotatable** *adj.* **rotatory** /'rəʊtətərɪ, -'teɪtərɪ/ *adj.* [Latin: related to ROTA]

rotation /rəʊ'teɪʃ(ə)n/ *n.* **1** rotating or being rotated. **2** recurrence; recurrent series or period; regular succession. Under the articles of association of most UK companies, one-third of the directors are obliged to retire each year (normally at the annual general meeting), so that each director retires by rotation every three years. Retiring directors may be re-elected. **3** the growing of different crops in regular order to avoid exhausting the soil. □ **rotational** *adj.*

Rotavator /'rəʊtə,veɪtə(r)/ *n.* (also **Rotovator**) *propr.* machine with a rotating blade for breaking up or tilling the soil. [from ROTARY, CULTIVATOR]

rote *n.* (usu. prec. by *by*; also *attrib.*) mechanical or habitual repetition (in order to memorize) (*rote learning*). [origin unknown]

rot-gut *n. slang* cheap harmful alcohol.

♦ **Rothermere** /'rɒðə,mɪə(r)/, **Vere Harold Esmond Harmsworth, 3rd Viscount** (1925–) British newspaper proprietor, chairman (since 1978) of Daily Mail and General Trust plc and controller of his family's 70% stake in that company. He was also chairman (1970–92) of Associated Newspapers Ltd.

♦ **Rothschild** /'rɒθtʃaɪld/, **Sir Evelyn de** (1931–) British merchant banker, chairman of N M Rothschild & Sons Ltd. and formerly chairman of the Economist Newspaper (1972–89), United Racecourses Ltd. (1977–94), and the British Merchant Banking and Securities Houses Association (formerly Accepting Houses Committee) (1985–89). His cousin and likely successor as chairman of N M Rothschild & Sons Ltd., **Leopold David de Rothschild** (1927–), is a director (since 1970) of the family bank and heads their operations in Paris. **Edmund Leopold de Rothschild** (1916–), brother of Leopold David, was chairman (1970–75) and a director (1975–94) of the bank and of their main subsidiary, asset management company Rothschild Continuation Holdings. The bank has become a leading adviser to privatized companies, including among its clients British Telecom. The Rothschild family owns approximately 53% (worth $800 million) of Rothschild Continuation Holdings.

---

rotisserie /rəʊ'tɪsərɪ/ *n.* **1** restaurant etc. where meat is roasted or barbecued. **2** rotating spit for roasting or barbecuing meat. [French: related to ROAST]

rotor /'rəʊtə(r)/ *n.* **1** rotary part of a machine. **2** rotary aerofoil on a helicopter, providing lift. [related to ROTATE]

Rotorua /,rəʊtə'ruːə/ health resort in New Zealand, on North Island, at the centre of a region of thermal springs and geysers; pop. (1994) 54 700.

Rotovator var. of ROTAVATOR.

rotten /'rɒt(ə)n/ *adj.* (**-er, -est**) **1** rotting or rotted; fragile from age or use. **2** morally or politically corrupt. **3** *slang* **a** disagreeable, unpleasant, bad (*had a rotten time*). **b** worthless (*rotten idea*). **c** ill (*feel rotten*). □ **rottenly** *adv.* **rottenness** *n.* [Old Norse: related to ROT]

rotten borough *n. hist.* (before 1832) English borough electing an MP though having very few voters.

rotter *n. slang* nasty or contemptible person. [from ROT]

Rotterdam /'rɒtə,dæm/ chief port of the Netherlands, on the Rhine delta, linked by canal to the North Sea; pop. (1995) 599 414. The port handles much entrepôt trade from Germany; there are also engineering, shipbuilding, and oil-refining industries.

Rottweiler /'rɒt,vaɪlə(r), -,waɪlə(r)/ *n.* black-and-tan dog noted for ferocity. [*Rottweil* in Germany]

rotund /rəʊ'tʌnd/ *adj.* **1** plump, podgy. **2** (of speech etc.) sonorous, grandiloquent. □ **rotundity** *n.* [Latin *rotundus*: related to ROTA]

rotunda /rəʊ'tʌndə/ *n.* circular building, hall, or room, esp. domed. [Italian *rotonda*: related to ROTUND]

ROU *international vehicle registration* Uruguay.

rouble /'ruːb(ə)l/ *n.* (also **ruble**) standard monetary unit of Russia, Belarus, and Tajikstan. [French from Russian]

roué /'ruːeɪ/ *n.* (esp. elderly) debauchee. [French]

Rouen /ruː'ɑ̃/ port in NW France, on the River Seine, capital of the region of Upper Normandy (Haute-Normandie); industries include textiles, engineering, and electronics; pop. (1990) 105 470.

rouge /ruːʒ/ *–n.* red cosmetic for colouring the cheeks. *–v.* (**-ging**) **1** colour with or apply rouge. **2** become red, blush. [Latin *rubeus* red]

rough /rʌf/ *–adj.* **1** uneven or bumpy, not smooth, level, or polished. **2** shaggy or coarse-haired. **3** boisterous, coarse; violent, not mild, quiet, or gentle (*rough fellow; rough play; rough sea*). **4** (of wine etc.) sharp or harsh in taste. **5** harsh, insensitive (*rough words; rough treatment*). **6 a** unpleasant, severe, demanding (*had a rough time*). **b** unfortunate; undeserved (*had rough luck*). **c** (often foll.

by *on*) hard or unfair (towards). **7** lacking finish etc. **8** incomplete, rudimentary, approximate (*rough attempt*; *rough sketch*; *rough estimate*). **9** (of stationery etc.) used for rough notes etc. **10** *colloq.* unwell; depressed (*feeling rough*). –*adv.* in a rough manner (*play rough*). –*n.* **1** (usu. prec. by *the*) hardship (*take the rough with the smooth*). **2** rough ground, esp. on a golf-course (*ball went into the rough*). **3** violent person (*bunch of roughs*). **4** unfinished or natural state (*written it in rough*). –*v.* **1** (foll. by *up*) ruffle (feathers, hair, etc.), esp. by rubbing. **2** (foll. by *out*, *in*) shape, plan, or sketch roughly. □ **rough it** *colloq.* do without basic comforts. **rough up** *slang* attack violently. □ **roughish** *adj.* **roughness** *n.* [Old English]

roughage *n.* coarse fibrous material in food, stimulating intestinal action.

rough-and-ready *adj.* crude but effective; not over-particular.

rough-and-tumble –*adj.* irregular, scrambling, disorderly. –*n.* disorderly fight; scuffle.

roughcast –*n.* (often *attrib.*) plaster of lime and gravel, used on outside walls. –*adj.* (of a plan etc.) roughly formed, preliminary. –*v.* (*past* and *past part.* **-cast**) **1** coat with roughcast. **2** prepare in outline.

rough diamond *n.* **1** uncut diamond. **2** rough-mannered but honest person.

rough-dry *v.* dry (clothes) without ironing.

roughen *v.* make or become rough.

rough-hewn *adj.* uncouth, unrefined.

rough house *n. slang* disturbance or row; boisterous play.

rough justice *n.* **1** treatment that is approximately fair. **2** unjust treatment.

roughly *adv.* **1** in a rough manner. **2** approximately (*roughly 20 people*). □ **roughly speaking** approximately.

roughneck *n. colloq.* **1** worker on an oil rig. **2** rough or rowdy person.

rough-rider *n.* person who breaks in or rides unbroken horses.

roughshod *adj.* (of a horse) having shoes with nail-heads projecting to prevent slipping. □ **ride roughshod over** treat inconsiderately or arrogantly.

roulade /ruːˈlɑːd/ *n.* **1** rolled piece of meat, sponge, etc. with a filling. **2** quick succession of notes, usu. sung to one syllable. [French *rouler* roll]

Roulers see ROESELARE.

roulette /ruːˈlet/ *n.* gambling game in which a ball is dropped on to a revolving numbered wheel. [French, = little wheel]

round –*adj.* **1** shaped like a circle, sphere, or cylinder; convex; circular, curved, not angular. **2** done with or involving circular motion. **3** entire, continuous, complete (*round dozen*). **4** candid, outspoken. **5** (usu. *attrib.*) (of a number) expressed for brevity as a complete number (*£297.32, or in round figures £300*). **6** (of a voice, style, etc.) flowing, sonorous. –*n.* **1** round object or form. **2 a** revolving motion or course (*yearly round*). **b** recurring series of activities, meetings, etc. (*continuous round of pleasure*; *round of talks*). **3 a** fixed route for deliveries (*milk round*). **b** route etc. for supervision or inspection (*watchman's round*; *doctor's rounds*). **4** drinks etc. for all members of a group. **5 a** one bullet, shell, etc. **b** act of firing this. **6 a** slice from a loaf of bread. **b** sandwich made from two slices. **c** joint of beef from the haunch. **7** set, series, or sequence of actions in turn, esp.: **a** one spell of play in a game etc. **b** one stage in a competition. **8** *Golf* playing of all the holes in a course once. **9** song for unaccompanied voices overlapping at intervals. **10** rung of a ladder. **11** (foll. by *of*) circumference or extent of (*in all the round of Nature*). –*adv.* **1** with circular motion (*wheels go round*). **2** with return to the starting-point or an earlier state (*summer soon comes round*). **3** with change to an opposite position, opinion, etc. (*turned round to look*; *soon won them round*). **4** to, at, or affecting a circumference, area, group, etc. (*tea was handed round*; *may I look round?*). **5** in every direction within a radius (*spread destruction round*). **6** circuitously (*go the long way round*). **7** to a person's house, a convenient place, etc. (*ask him round*; *will be round soon*; *brought the car round*). **8** measuring (a specified distance) in girth. –*prep.* **1** so as to encircle or enclose (*a blanket round him*). **2** at or to points on the circumference of (*sat round the table*). **3** with successive visits to (*hawks them round the cafés*). **4** within a radius of (*towns round Birmingham*). **5** having as an axis or central point (*planned a book round the War*). **6 a** so as to pass in a curved course (*go round the corner*). **b** having so passed (*be round the corner*). **c** in the resulting position (*find them round the corner*). –*v.* **1** give or take a round shape. **2** pass round (a corner, cape, etc.). **3** (usu. foll. by *up*, *down*) express (a number) approximately, for brevity. □ **go the round** (or **rounds**) (of news etc.) be passed on. **in the round 1** with all features shown; all things considered. **2** with the audience on at least three sides of the stage. **3** (of sculpture) with all sides shown. **round about 1** all round; on all sides (of). **2** approximately (*round about £50*). **round and round** several times round. **round the bend** see BEND[1]. **round off** make complete or less angular. **round on** attack unexpectedly, esp. verbally. **round out 1** provide with more details. **2** complete, finish. **round the twist** see TWIST. **round up 1** collect or bring together. **2** = sense 3 of *v.* □ **roundish** *adj.* **roundness** *n.* [Latin: related to ROTUND]

roundabout –*n.* **1** road junction at which traffic circulates in one direction round a central island. **2 a** large revolving device for children to ride on in a playground. **b** = MERRY-GO-ROUND 1. –*adj.* circuitous.

round brackets *n.pl.* brackets of the form ().

round dance *n.* dance in which couples move in circles or dancers form one large circle.

roundel /ˈraʊnd(ə)l/ *n.* **1** circular mark, esp. identifying military aircraft. **2** small disc, esp. a medallion. [French *rondel(le)*: related to ROUND]

roundelay /ˈraʊndɪˌleɪ/ *n.* short simple song with a refrain. [alteration of French *rondelet* diminutive: related to ROUNDEL]

rounder *n.* **1** (in *pl.*; treated as *sing.*) ball game in which players hit the ball and run through a round of bases. **2** complete run as a unit of scoring in rounders.

Roundhead *n. hist.* member of the Parliamentary party in the English Civil War.

◆ **round lot** *n.* round number of shares or a round amount of stock for which market makers will sometimes offer better prices than for **odd lots**.

---

roundly *adv.* bluntly, severely (*told them roundly*).

round robin *n.* **1** petition, esp. with signatures in a circle to conceal the order of writing. **2** *US* tournament in which each competitor plays every other.

round-shouldered *adj.* with shoulders bent forward and a rounded back.

roundsman *n.* tradesman's employee delivering goods.

Round Table *n.* **1** international charitable association. **2** (**round table**) assembly for discussion, esp. at a conference (often *attrib.*: *round-table talks*).

round trip *n.* trip to one or more places and back again.

◆ **round-tripping** *n.* transaction that enables a company to borrow money from one source and lend it at a profit to another, by taking advantage of a short-term rise in interest rates.

---

round-up *n.* **1** systematic rounding up. **2** summary or résumé.

roundworm *n.* worm with a rounded body.

rouse /raʊz/ *v.* (**-sing**) **1** (cause to) wake. **2** (often foll. by *up*, often *refl.*) stir up, make or become active or excited (*was roused to protest*). **3** anger (*terrible when roused*). **4** evoke (feelings). [origin unknown]

rousing *adj.* exciting, stirring (*rousing song*).

Rousse see RUSE.

roustabout /ˈraʊstəˌbaʊt/ *n.* **1** labourer on an oil rig. **2** unskilled or casual labourer. [*roust* rout out, rouse]

rout[1] –*n.* **1** disorderly retreat of defeated troops (*put them* *to rout*). **2** overthrow, defeat. –*v.* put to flight, defeat. [French: related to ROUTE]

rout[2] *v.* = ROOT[2]. [var. of ROOT[2]]

route /ruːt/ –*n.* way or course taken (esp. regularly) from one place to another. –*v.* (**-teing**) send, forward, or direct by a particular route. [French *route* road, from Latin *rupta (via)*]

route march *n.* training-march for troops.

routine /ruːˈtiːn/ –*n.* **1** regular course or procedure, unvarying performance of certain acts. **2** set sequence in a dance, comedy act, etc. **3** *Computing* sequence of instructions for a particular task. –*adj.* **1** performed as part of a routine (*routine duties*). **2** of a customary or standard kind. □ **routinely** *adv.* [French: related to ROUTE]

roux /ruː/ *n.* (*pl.* same) mixture of fat and flour used in sauces etc. [French]

Rovaniemi /ˌrɒvænˈjeɪmɪ/ town in N Finland, the principal town of Finnish Lapland; pop. (1987) 32 911.

rove[1] *v.* (**-ving**) **1** wander without settling; roam, ramble. **2** (of eyes) look about. [probably Scandinavian]

rove[2] *past* of REEVE[2].

rover[1] *n.* wanderer.

rover[2] *n.* pirate. [Low German or Dutch]

roving eye *n.* tendency to infidelity.

row[1] /rəʊ/ *n.* **1** line of persons or things. **2** line of seats across a theatre etc. **3** street with houses along one or each side. □ **in a row 1** forming a row. **2** *colloq.* in succession (*two days in a row*). [Old English]

row[2] /rəʊ/ –*v.* **1** (often *absol.*) propel (a boat) with oars. **2** convey (a passenger) thus. –*n.* **1** spell of rowing. **2** trip in a rowing-boat. □ **rower** *n.* [Old English]

row[3] /raʊ/ *colloq.* –*n.* **1** loud noise or commotion. **2** fierce quarrel or dispute. **3** severe reprimand. –*v.* **1** make or engage in a row. **2** reprimand. [origin unknown]

rowan /ˈrəʊən/ *n.* (in full **rowan-tree**) **1** *Scot.* & *N.Engl.* mountain ash. **2** (in full **rowan-berry**) its scarlet berry. [Scandinavian]

row-boat *n. US* = ROWING-BOAT.

rowdy /ˈraʊdɪ/ –*adj.* (**-ier, -iest**) noisy and disorderly. –*n.* (*pl.* **-ies**) rowdy person. □ **rowdily** *adv.* **rowdiness** *n.* **rowdyism** *n.* [origin unknown]

rowel /ˈraʊəl/ *n.* spiked revolving disc at the end of a spur. [Latin *rotella* diminutive: related to ROTA]

rowing-boat *n.* small boat propelled by oars.

♦ **Rowland** /ˈrəʊlənd/, **Roland ('Tiny')** (1917–) British businessman, formerly chief executive (until 1994) and a director (until 1995) of Lonrho plc, which he joined in 1961 and developed from the London and Rhodesian Mining and Land Co. He was also chairman (1983–93) and managing director (1991–94) of The Observer Ltd.

---

rowlock /ˈrɒlək/ *n.* device on a boat's side for holding an oar in place. [*oarlock* from Old English: related to OAR, LOCK[1]]

royal /ˈrɔɪəl/ –*adj.* **1** of, suited to, or worthy of a king or queen. **2** in the service or under the patronage of a king or queen. **3** of the family of a king or queen. **4** majestic, splendid. **5** exceptional, first-rate (*had a royal time*). –*n. colloq.* member of the royal family. □ **royally** *adv.* [Latin: related to REGAL]

royal blue *adj.* & *n.* (as adj. often hyphenated) deep vivid blue.

Royal British Legion *n.* national association of ex-members of the armed forces, founded in 1921.

Royal Commission *n.* commission of inquiry appointed by the Crown at the request of the government.

royal family *n.* family of a sovereign.

royal flush *n.* straight poker flush headed by an ace.

royal icing *n.* hard white icing for cakes.

♦ **Royal Institution of Chartered Surveyors** *n.* (also **RICS**) institution, founded in 1868 and given a Royal Charter in 1881, that aims to provide education and training for surveyors and to define and control their professional conduct. Qualification as a Chartered Surveyor is part academic (passing the Institution's own professional examinations or a recognized degree or diploma) and part practical (assessed professional experience over a two-year period). A candidate is then able to apply for election as an Associate, using the initials ARICS after his or her name. After 12 years' further experience an Associate may apply for a Fellowship (FRICS).

---

royalist *n.* supporter of monarchy, or *hist.* of the royal side in the English Civil War. □ **royalism** *n.*

royal jelly *n.* substance secreted by worker bees and fed by them to future queen bees.

Royal Marine *n.* British marine (see MARINE *n.* 1).

♦ **Royal Mint** *n.* organization that has the sole right to manufacture coins in the UK. Controlled by the Chancellor of the Exchequer, it was formerly situated in the City of London but moved to Llantrisant in Wales in 1968. It also makes banknotes, UK medals, and some foreign coins.

Royal Navy *n.* British navy.

royalty *n.* (*pl.* **-ies**) **1** royal office, dignity, or power; being royal. **2 a** royal persons. **b** member of a royal family. **3** payment made for the right to use the property of another person for gain. Examples include the percentage of the profit from the sale of a book or invention paid to the author or inventor (see COPYRIGHT *n.*; PATENT *n.* 1) and the payment made to a landowner on sales of minerals that have been extracted from his or her land. A royalty is regarded as a wasting asset as copyrights, patents, and mines have limited lives. **4** royal right (now esp. over minerals) granted by the sovereign. [French: related to ROYAL]

royal warrant *n.* warrant authorizing a tradesperson to supply goods to a specified royal person.

royal 'we' *n.* use of 'we' instead of 'I' by a single person.

RP –*abbr.* **1** received pronunciation. **2** recommended price. **3** reply paid. **4** (also **R/P**) reprint. **5** repurchase. **6** *Insurance* return (of) premium. –*international vehicle registration* & *international civil aircraft marking* the Philippines.

Rp *symb.* rupiah.

RPB *abbr.* = RECOGNIZED PROFESSIONAL BODY.

♦ **RPG** *abbr.* = REPORT PROGRAM GENERATOR.

RPI *abbr.* = RETAIL PRICE INDEX.

RPM *abbr.* **1** reliability performance measure. **2** = RESALE PRICE MAINTENANCE.

r.p.m. *abbr.* revolutions per minute.

RPO *abbr.* Royal Philharmonic Orchestra.

RPQ *abbr.* request for price quotation.

RQ *abbr.* (also **R/Q**) *Commerce* request for quotation.

RRP *abbr.* = RECOMMENDED RETAIL PRICE.

Rs *symb.* Indian rupees.

RSA *abbr.* **1** Royal Society of Arts. **2** Royal Scottish Academy; Royal Scottish Academician.

RSC *abbr.* Royal Shakespeare Company.

RSFSR *abbr. hist.* Russian Soviet Federative Socialist Republic.

RSJ *abbr.* rolled steel joist.

RSM –*abbr.* regimental sergeant major. –*international vehicle registration* San Marino.

RSPB *abbr.* Royal Society for the Protection of Birds.

RSPCA *abbr.* Royal Society for the Prevention of Cruelty to Animals.

RSV *abbr.* Revised Standard Version (of the Bible).

RSVP *abbr.* (in an invitation etc.) please answer. [French *répondez s'il vous plaît*]

rt. *abbr.* right.

RTA *abbr.* reciprocal trade agreement(s).

RTBA *abbr.* rate to be agreed.

RTDS *abbr. Computing* real-time data system.

RTE *abbr. Computing* real-time execution.

Rt. Hon. *abbr.* Right Honourable.

RTL *abbr. Computing* real-time language.

rtn. *abbr.* return.

Rt. Revd. *abbr.* (also **Rt. Rev.**) Right Reverend.

RTZ *abbr.* Rio Tinto Zinc Corporation Limited.

RU *–abbr.* **1** *Computing* registered user. **2** Rugby Union. *–international vehicle registration* Burundi.

Ru *symb.* ruthenium.

rub *–v.* (**-bb-**) **1** move something, esp. one's hand, with firm pressure over the surface of. **2** (usu. foll. by *against, in, on, over*) apply (one's hand etc.) in this way. **3** clean, polish, chafe, or make dry, sore, or bare by rubbing. **4** (foll. by *in, into, through, over*) apply (polish etc.) by rubbing. **5** (often foll. by *together, against, on*) move with contact or friction or slide (objects) against each other. **6** (of cloth, skin, etc.) become frayed, worn, sore, or bare with friction. *–n.* **1** act or spell of rubbing (*give it a rub*). **2** impediment or difficulty (*there's the rub*). □ **rub along** *colloq.* cope or manage routinely. **rub down** dry, smooth, or clean by rubbing. **rub it in** (or **rub a person's nose in it**) emphasize or repeat an embarrassing fact etc. **rub off 1** (usu. foll. by *on*) be transferred by contact, be transmitted (*his attitudes have rubbed off on me*). **2** remove by rubbing. **rub out** erase with a rubber. **rub shoulders with** associate with. **rub up 1** polish. **2** brush up (a subject or one's memory). **rub up the wrong way** irritate. [Low German]

rubato /ruːˈbɑːtəʊ/ *n. Mus.* (*pl.* **-s** or **-ti** /-tɪ/) temporary disregarding of strict tempo. [Italian, = robbed]

rubber[1] *n.* **1** tough elastic substance made from the latex of plants or synthetically. **2** piece of this or a similar substance for erasing esp. pencil marks. **3** *colloq.* condom. **4** (in *pl.*) *US* galoshes. □ **rubbery** *adj.* **rubberiness** *n.* [from RUB[1]]

rubber[2] *n.* match of esp. three successive games between the same sides or persons at whist, bridge, cricket, etc. [origin unknown]

rubber band *n.* loop of rubber for holding papers etc. together.

rubberize *v.* (also **-ise**) (**-zing** or **-sing**) treat or coat with rubber.

rubberneck *colloq. –n.* inquisitive person, esp. a tourist or sightseer. *–v.* behave like a rubberneck.

rubber plant *n.* **1** evergreen tropical plant often cultivated as a house-plant. **2** (also **rubber tree**) tropical tree yielding latex.

rubber stamp *–n.* **1** device for inking and imprinting on a surface. **2 a** person who mechanically copies or endorses others' actions. **b** indication of such endorsement. *–v.* (**rubber-stamp**) approve automatically.

rubbing *n.* impression or copy made by rubbing.

rubbish /ˈrʌbɪʃ/ *–n.* **1** waste material; refuse, litter. **2** worthless material; trash. **3** (often as *int.*) nonsense. *–v. colloq.* criticize contemptuously. □ **rubbishy** *adj.* [Anglo-French *rubbous*]

rubble /ˈrʌb(ə)l/ *n.* rough fragments of stone, brick, etc., esp. from a demolished building. [French *robe* spoils]

rub-down *n.* rubbing down.

rubella /ruːˈbelə/ *n. formal* German measles. [Latin *rubellus* reddish]

Rubicon /ˈruːbɪˌkɒn/ *n.* boundary; point from which there is no going back. [*Rubicon*, river on an ancient frontier of Italy]

rubicund /ˈruːbɪˌkʌnd/ *adj.* (of a face, complexion, etc.) ruddy, high-coloured. [Latin *rubeo* be red]

rubidium /ruːˈbɪdɪəm/ *n.* soft silvery metallic element. [Latin *rubidus* red]

Rubik's cube /ˈruːbɪks/ *n.* cube-shaped puzzle in which composite faces must be restored to single colours by rotation. [*Rubik*, name of its inventor]

ruble var. of ROUBLE.

rubric /ˈruːbrɪk/ *n.* **1** heading or passage in red or special lettering. **2** explanatory words. **3** established custom or rule. **4** direction for the conduct of divine service in a liturgical book. [Latin *ruber* red]

ruby /ˈruːbɪ/ *–n.* (*pl.* **-ies**) **1** rare precious stone varying in colour from deep crimson to pale rose. **2** deep red colour. *–adj.* of this colour. [Latin *rubeus* red]

ruby wedding *n.* fortieth wedding anniversary.

RUC *abbr.* Royal Ulster Constabulary.

ruche /ruːʃ/ *n.* frill or gathering of lace etc. □ **ruched** *adj.* [French, = beehive]

ruck[1] *n.* **1** (prec. by *the*) main body of competitors not likely to overtake the leaders. **2** undistinguished crowd or group. **3** *Rugby* loose scrum. [apparently Scandinavian]

ruck[2] *–v.* (often foll. by *up*) make or become creased or wrinkled. *–n.* crease or wrinkle. [Old Norse]

rucksack /ˈrʌksæk/ *n.* bag carried on the back, esp. by hikers. [German]

ruckus /ˈrʌkəs/ *n.* esp. *US informal* row, commotion. [perhaps from RUCTION OR RUMPUS]

ruction /ˈrʌkʃ(ə)n/ *n. colloq.* **1** disturbance or tumult. **2** (in *pl.*) row, heated arguments. [origin unknown]

rudder *n.* flat piece hinged vertically to the stern of a ship or on the tailplane of an aircraft etc., for steering. □ **rudderless** *adj.* [Old English]

ruddy /ˈrʌdɪ/ *adj.* (**-ier, -iest**) **1** (of a person, complexion, etc.) freshly or healthily red. **2** reddish. **3** *colloq.* bloody, damnable. □ **ruddily** *adv.* **ruddiness** *n.* [Old English]

rude *adj.* **1** impolite or offensive. **2** roughly made or done; crude (*rude plough*). **3** primitive or uneducated (*rude simplicity*). **4** abrupt, sudden, startling (*rude awakening*). **5** *colloq.* indecent, lewd (*rude joke*). **6** vigorous or hearty (*rude health*). □ **rudely** *adv.* **rudeness** *n.* [Latin *rudis*]

rudiment /ˈruːdɪmənt/ *n.* **1** (in *pl.*) elements or first principles of a subject. **2** (in *pl.*) imperfect beginning of something undeveloped or yet to develop. **3** vestigial or undeveloped part or organ. □ **rudimentary** /-ˈmentərɪ/ *adj.* [Latin: related to RUDE]

rue[1] *v.* (**rues, rued, rueing** or **ruing**) repent of; wish to be undone or non-existent (esp. *rue the day*). [Old English]

rue[2] *n.* evergreen shrub with bitter strong-scented leaves. [Greek *rhutē*]

rueful *adj.* genuinely or humorously sorrowful. □ **ruefully** *adv.* **ruefulness** *n.* [from RUE[1]]

◆ **RUF** *abbr.* revolving underwriting facility. See NOTE ISSUANCE FACILITY.

ruff[1] *n.* **1** projecting starched frill worn round the neck, esp. in the 16th century. **2** projecting or coloured ring of feathers or hair round a bird's or animal's neck. **3** domestic pigeon. **4** (*fem.* **reeve** /riːv/) wading bird with a ruff. [perhaps = ROUGH]

ruff[2] *–v.* trump at cards. *–n.* trumping. [French *ro(u)ffle*]

ruffian /ˈrʌfɪən/ *n.* violent lawless person. [Italian *ruffiano*]

ruffle /ˈrʌf(ə)l/ *–v.* (**-ling**) **1 a** disturb the smoothness or tranquillity of. **b** undergo this. **2** gather (lace etc.) into a ruffle. **3** (often foll. by *up*) (of a bird) erect (its feathers) in anger, display, etc. *–n.* frill of lace etc., esp. round the wrist or neck. [origin unknown]

rufiyaa /ruːˈfiːjɑː/ *n.* standard monetary unit of the Maldives. [related to RUPEE]

rufous /ˈruːfəs/ *adj.* (esp. of animals) reddish-brown. [Latin *rufus*]

RUG *abbr. Computing* restricted users group.

rug *n.* **1** thick floor covering, usu. smaller than a carpet. **2** thick woollen coverlet or wrap. □ **pull the rug from under** deprive of support; weaken, unsettle. [probably Scandinavian]

Rugby /ˈrʌgbɪ/ *n.* (in full **Rugby football**) team game played with an oval ball that may be kicked or carried. [*Rugby school*, where it was first played]

Rugby League *n.* partly professional Rugby with teams of 13.

Rugby Union *n.* amateur Rugby with teams of 15.

Rügen /ˈruːgən/ German island in the Baltic Sea, linked to the mainland by a causeway; pop. (latest est.) 87 504.

rugged /ˈrʌgɪd/ *adj.* **1** (esp. of ground) rough, uneven. **2** (of features) wrinkled, furrowed, irregular. **3 a** unpolished; lacking refinement (*rugged grandeur*). **b** harsh in sound. **4** robust, hardy. □ **ruggedly** *adv.* **ruggedness** *n.* [probably Scandinavian]

rugger /ˈrʌgə(r)/ *n. colloq.* Rugby.

Ruhr /rʊə(r)/ river in W Germany, a tributary of the Rhine; it has given its name to the region of coalmining and heavy industry that lies along its course.

ruin /ˈruːɪn/ *–n.* **1** destroyed, wrecked, or spoiled state. **2** downfall or elimination (*ruin of my hopes*). **3** complete loss of one's property or position (*bring to ruin*). **4** (in *sing.* or *pl.*) remains of a building etc. that has suffered ruin. **5** cause of ruin (*the ruin of us*). *–v.* **1 a** bring to ruin (*extravagance has ruined me*). **b** spoil, damage. **2** (esp. as **ruined** *adj.*) reduce to ruins. □ **in ruins** completely wrecked (*hopes were in ruins*). [Latin *ruo* fall]

ruination /ˌruːɪˈneɪʃ(ə)n/ *n.* **1** bringing to ruin. **2** ruining or being ruined.

ruinous *adj.* **1** bringing ruin, disastrous (*ruinous expense*). **2** dilapidated. □ **ruinously** *adv.*

rule *–n.* **1** compulsory principle governing action. **2** prevailing custom or standard; normal state of things. **3** government or dominion (*under British rule*). **4** graduated straight measure; ruler. **5** code of discipline of a religious order. **6** order made by a judge or court with reference to a particular case only. **7** *Printing* thin line or dash. *–v.* (**-ling**) **1** dominate; keep under control. **2** (often foll. by *over*) have sovereign control of (*rules over a vast kingdom*). **3** (often foll. by *that*) pronounce authoritatively. **4 a** make parallel lines across (paper). **b** make (a straight line) with a ruler etc. □ **as a rule** usually. **rule out** exclude; pronounce irrelevant or ineligible. **rule the roost** be in control. [Latin *regula*]

♦ **rule against perpetuities** see PERPETUITIES AND ACCUMULATIONS ACT (1964).

---

rule of thumb *n.* rule based on experience or practice rather than theory.

ruler *n.* **1** person exercising government or dominion. **2** straight usu. graduated strip of wood, metal, or plastic used to draw or measure.

ruling *n.* authoritative pronouncement.

rum[1] *n.* spirit distilled from sugar-cane or molasses. [origin unknown]

rum[2] *adj.* (**rummer, rummest**) *colloq.* odd, strange, queer. [origin unknown]

Rumania, Rumanian see ROMANIA, ROMANIAN.

rumba /ˈrʌmbə/ *n.* **1** Latin American ballroom dance orig. from Cuba. **2** music for this. [American Spanish]

rum baba *n.* sponge cake soaked in rum syrup.

rumble /ˈrʌmb(ə)l/ *–v.* (**-ling**) **1** make a continuous deep resonant sound as of distant thunder. **2** (foll. by *along, by, past,* etc.) (esp. of a vehicle) move with a rumbling noise. **3** (often *absol.*) *slang* find out the esp. discreditable truth about. *–n.* rumbling sound. [probably Dutch *rommelen*]

rumbustious /rʌmˈbʌstʃəs/ *adj. colloq.* boisterous, noisy, uproarious. [probably var. of *robustious* from ROBUST]

ruminant /ˈruːmɪnənt/ *–n.* animal that chews the cud. *–adj.* **1** of ruminants. **2** meditative. [related to RUMINATE]

ruminate /ˈruːmɪˌneɪt/ *v.* (**-ting**) **1** meditate, ponder. **2** chew the cud. □ **rumination** /-ˈneɪʃ(ə)n/ *n.* **ruminative** /-nətɪv/ *adj.* [Latin *rumen* throat]

rummage /ˈrʌmɪdʒ/ *–v.* (**-ging**) **1** search, esp. unsystematically. **2** (foll. by *out, up*) find among other things. *–n.* **1** rummaging. **2** search of a ship or aircraft by customs officers looking for contraband, illegal drugs, etc. [French *arrumage* from *arrumer* stow cargo]

rummage sale *n.* esp. *US* jumble sale.

rummy /ˈrʌmɪ/ *n.* card-game played usu. with two packs. [origin unknown]

rumour /ˈruːmə(r)/ (*US* **rumor**) *–n.* (often foll. by *of* or *that*) general talk, assertion, or hearsay of doubtful accuracy (*heard a rumour that you are leaving*). *–v.* (usu. in *passive*) report by way of rumour (*it is rumoured that you are leaving*). [Latin *rumor* noise]

rump *n.* **1** hind part of a mammal or bird, esp. the buttocks. **2** remnant of a parliament etc. [probably Scandinavian]

rumple /ˈrʌmp(ə)l/ *v.* (**-ling**) crease, ruffle. [Dutch *rompelen*]

rump steak *n.* cut of beef from the rump.

rumpus /ˈrʌmpəs/ *n. colloq.* disturbance, brawl, row, or uproar. [origin unknown]

run *–v.* (**-nn-**; *past* **ran**; *past part.* **run**) **1** go with quick steps, never having both or all feet on the ground at once. **2** flee, abscond. **3** go or travel hurriedly or briefly (*I'll just run down to the shops*). **4 a** advance by or as by rolling or on wheels, or smoothly or easily. **b** (cause to) be in action or operation or go in a specified way (*left the engine running; ran the car into a tree*). **c** feed in and carry out (a program) on a computer. **5** be current or operative (*lease runs for 99 years*). **6** travel on its route (*train is running late*). **7** (of a play etc.) be staged or presented (*now running at the Apollo*). **8** extend; have a course, order, or tendency (*road runs by the coast; prices are running high*). **9 a** (often *absol.*) compete in (a race). **b** finish a race in a specified position. **10** (often foll. by *for*) seek election (*ran for president*). **11** flow (with) or be wet; drip (with) (*walls running with condensation*). **12 a** cause (water etc.) to flow. **b** fill (a bath) thus. **13** spread rapidly (*ink ran over the table*). **14** traverse (a course, race, or distance). **15** perform (an errand). **16** publish (an article etc.) in a newspaper etc. **17** direct or manage (a business etc.). **18** own and use (a vehicle) regularly. **19** transport in a private vehicle (*ran me to the station*). **20** enter (a horse etc.) for a race. **21** smuggle (guns etc.). **22** chase or hunt. **23** allow (an account) to accumulate before paying. **24** (of a dyed colour) spread from the dyed parts. **25 a** (of a thought, the eye, the memory, etc.) pass quickly (*ideas ran through my mind*). **b** pass (one's eye) quickly (*ran my eye down the page*). **26** (of tights etc.) ladder. **27** (of esp. the eyes or nose) exude liquid. *–n.* **1** running. **2** short excursion. **3** distance travelled. **4** general tendency. **5** regular route. **6** continuous stretch, spell, or course (*run of bad luck*). **7** (often foll. by *on*) high general demand (*run on the dollar*). **8** quantity produced at one time (*print run*). **9** average type or class (*general run of customers*). **10** point scored in cricket or baseball. **11** (foll. by *of*) free use of or access to (*run of the house*). **12 a** animal's regular track. **b** enclosure for fowls etc. **c** range of pasture. **13** ladder in tights etc. **14** *Mus.* rapid scale passage. **15** (in full **the runs**) *colloq.* diarrhoea. □ **on the run** fleeing. **run about 1** bustle, hurry. **2** (esp. of children) play freely. **run across** happen to meet or find. **run after 1** pursue at a run. **2** pursue, esp. sexually. **run along** *colloq.* depart. **run around 1** take from place to place by car etc. **2** (often foll. by *with*) *slang* engage in esp. promiscuous sexual relations. **run away 1** (often foll. by *from*) flee, abscond. **2** mentally evade (a problem etc.). **run away with 1** carry off. **2** win easily. **3** deprive of self-control, carry away. **4** consume (money etc.). **5** (of a horse) bolt with (a rider etc.). **6** leave home to have a relationship with (esp. another person's husband or wife). **run down 1** knock down. **2** reduce the numbers etc. of. **3** (of an unwound clock etc.) stop. **4** discover after a search. **5** *colloq.* disparage. **run dry 1** cease to flow. **2** = *run out* 1. **run for it** seek safety by fleeing. **run** (or **good run) for one's money 1** vigorous or close competition. **2** some return for outlay or effort. **run the gauntlet** see GAUNTLET[2]. **run high** (of feelings) be strong. **run in 1** run (an engine or vehicle) carefully when new. **2** *colloq.* arrest. **run in the family** (of a trait) be common in a family. **run into 1** collide with. **2** encounter. **3** reach as many as (a usu. high figure). **run into the ground** *colloq.* bring (a person) to exhaustion etc. **run low** (or **short**) become depleted, have too little. **run off 1** flee. **2** produce (copies etc.) on a machine. **3** decide (a race etc.) after heats or a tie. **4** (cause to) flow away. **5** write or recite fluently. **run off with** = *run away with* 6. **run on 1** continue in operation. **2** speak volubly or incessantly. **3** continue on the same line as the preceding matter. **run out 1** come to an end.

2 (foll. by *of*) exhaust one's stock of. **3** put down the wicket of (a running batsman). **run out on** *colloq.* desert (a person). **run over 1** (of a vehicle etc.) knock down or crush. **2** overflow. **3** study or repeat quickly. **run ragged** exhaust (a person). **run rings round** see RING[1]. **run riot** see RIOT. **run a** (or **the) risk** see RISK. **run through 1** examine or rehearse briefly. **2** peruse. **3** deal successively with. **4** spend money rapidly or recklessly. **5** pervade. **6** pierce with a sword etc. **run to 1** have the money, resources, or ability for. **2** reach (an amount or number). **3** (of a person) show a tendency to (*runs to fat*). **run to earth** see EARTH. **run to seed** see SEED. **run up 1** accumulate (a debt etc.). **2** build or make hurriedly. **3** raise (a flag). **run up against** meet with (a difficulty etc.). [Old English]

runabout *n.* light car or aircraft.

run-around *n.* (esp. in phr. **give a person the run-around**) *colloq.* deceit or evasion.

runaway *n.* **1** fugitive. **2** bolting animal, vehicle out of control. **3** (*attrib.*) that is running away or out of control (*runaway slave*; *runaway inflation*).

run-down *–n.* **1** reduction in numbers. **2** detailed analysis. *–adj.* **1** decayed, dilapidated. **2** exhausted (from overwork, illness, etc.).

rune *n.* **1** letter of the earliest Germanic alphabet. **2** similar mark of mysterious or magic significance. □ **runic** *adj.* [Old Norse]

rung[1] *n.* **1** step of a ladder. **2** strengthening crosspiece in a chair etc. [Old English]

rung[2] *past part.* of RING[2].

run-in *n.* **1** approach to an action or event. **2** *colloq.* quarrel.

runnel /ˈrʌn(ə)l/ *n.* **1** brook. **2** gutter. [Old English]

runner *n.* **1** person, horse, etc. that runs, esp. in a race. **2** creeping rooting plant-stem. **3** rod, groove, roller, or blade on which a thing, e.g. a sledge, slides. **4** sliding ring on a rod etc. **5** messenger. **6** (in full **runner bean**) twining bean plant with long flat green edible seed pods. **7** long narrow ornamental cloth or rug. □ **do a runner** *slang* abscond, leave hastily; flee.

runner-up *n.* (*pl.* **runners-up** or **runner-ups**) competitor or team taking second place.

running *–n.* **1** action of runners in a race etc. **2** way a race etc. proceeds. *–adj.* **1** continuous (*running battle*). **2** consecutive (*three days running*). **3** done with a run (*running jump*). □ **in** (or **out of) the running** (of a competitor) with a good (or poor) chance of success. **make** (or **take up) the running** take the lead; set the pace. **take a running jump** (esp. as *int.*) *slang* go away.

running-board *n.* footboard on either side of a vehicle.

◆ **running broker** *n.* bill broker who does not personally discount bills of exchange but acts between bill owners and discount houses or banks on a commission basis.

running commentary *n.* verbal description of an esp. sporting event.

◆ **running days** *n.pl.* consecutive days including Saturdays, Sundays, and Bank Holidays.

◆ **running-down clause** *n.* clause in a hull insurance policy covering a shipowner against liability for compensation as a result of a collision with another vessel.

running knot *n.* knot that slips along a rope etc. to allow tightening etc.

running mate *n. US* **1** candidate for vice-president etc. **2** horse intended to set the pace for another horse in a race.

running repairs *n.pl.* minor or temporary repairs etc.

running sore *n.* suppurating sore; festering situation etc.

running water *n.* flowing water, esp. on tap.

◆ **running yield** see YIELD *n.* 2.

runny *adj.* (**-ier, -iest**) **1** tending to run or flow. **2** excessively fluid.

run-off *n.* additional election, race, etc., after a tie.

◆ **run of paper** *adj.* & *adv.* (also **run-of-paper** when *attrib.*) (of an advertisement in a paper, magazine, etc.) positioned at the discretion of the editor. Such an advertisement is offered at a lower rate than one set in a specified position in the publication.

run-of-the-mill *adj.* ordinary, undistinguished.

run-out *n.* dismissal of a batsman by being run out.

Russia /ˈrʌʃə/ (officially **Russian Federation**) largest country in the world, covering N Eurasia and occupying three-quarters of the land area of the former Soviet Union. It includes 22 autonomous republics. Russia possesses some of the world's richest mineral deposits, including iron ore, coal, oil, natural gas, gold, platinum, copper, zinc, lead, and tin. Manufacturing industries are centred on Moscow and St Petersburg and include iron and steel, engineering, textiles, and chemicals. There are extensive forests; timber and associated industries are important. Agricultural products include wheat and other grains, cotton, fruit and vegetables, tobacco, and sugar beet. The country's principal exports are mineral fuels and lubricants, machinery and transport equipment, textiles and other manufactured goods, timber, and chemicals. Following the establishment of Russia as an independent state in 1992, the government introduced measures to reorganize the economy into a free-market system, including the abolition of most state subsidies, price liberalization, and the privatization of state-owned industries. Although limited financial assistance from the IMF and other sources has been granted to implement these reforms, the country faces massive inflation due to poor budgetary and monetary control.

History. The Russian empire originated from the expansion of the principality of Muscovy, initiated during the reign (1682–1725) of Peter the Great, W towards Poland and Hungary, S to the Black Sea, and E to the Pacific Ocean. From the early 18th century Russia played an increasing role in Europe and by the end of the 19th century had become a multinational empire under virtually absolute control of the monarchy. Social and economic problems, exacerbated by the First World War, led to the overthrow of the Tsar in 1917 and the establishment of a Communist government. Russia became the Russian Soviet Federative Socialist Republic and in 1922 merged with the Ukraine, Belorussia, and Transcaucasia to constitute the USSR (see UNION OF SOVIET SOCIALIST REPUBLICS). Following the breakup of the USSR in 1991 the Russian Federation was established as an independent state with Boris Yeltsin as its first president. The economic reforms instituted by Yeltsin's government were consistently opposed by the conservative parliament. However, a referendum in 1993 endorsed Yeltsin's reforms. An attempted coup in October 1993 was suppressed. A further referendum in late 1993 endorsed a new constitution. In the mid-1990s there was recurrent fighting with rebels in Chechenia. President, Boris Yeltsin; prime minister, Sergei Kiriyenko; Capital, Moscow.

language	Russian
currency	rouble of 100 copecks
population (1996)	148 070 000
GNP (1994)	US$392B
life expectancy	58 (m); 72 (f)

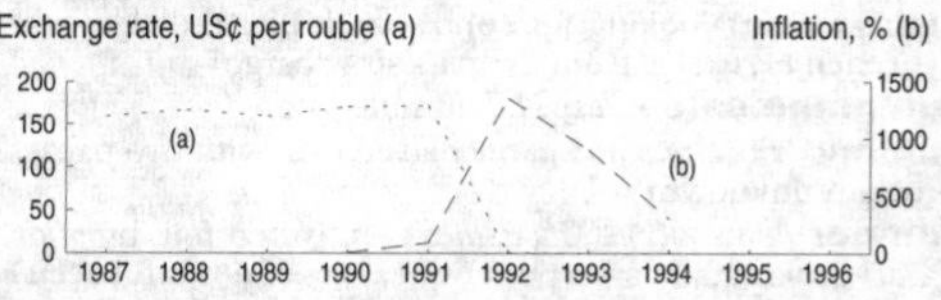

runt *n.* **1** smallest pig etc. in a litter. **2** weakling; undersized person. [origin unknown]

run-through *n.* **1** rehearsal. **2** brief survey.

run-up *n.* (often foll. by *to*) preparatory period.

runway *n.* specially prepared surface for aircraft taking off and landing.

rupee /ruːˈpiː/ *n.* standard monetary unit of India, Mauritius, Nepal, Pakistan, Seychelles, and Sri Lanka. [Hindustani]

Rupert's Land /ˈruːpəts/ (also **Prince Rupert's Land**) area of N and W Canada around Hudson Bay.

rupiah /ruːˈpiːə/ *n.* standard monetary unit of Indonesia. [related to RUPEE]

rupture /ˈrʌptʃə(r)/ *–n.* **1** breaking; breach. **2** breach in a relationship; disagreement and parting. **3** abdominal hernia. *–v.* (**-ring**) **1** burst (a cell or membrane etc.). **2** sever (a connection). **3** affect with or suffer a hernia. [Latin *rumpo rupt-* break]

rural /ˈrʊər(ə)l/ *adj.* in, of, or suggesting the country (*rural seclusion*). [Latin *rus rur-* the country]

rural dean see DEAN[1].

rural district *n. hist.* group of country parishes with an elected council.

RUS *international vehicle registration* Russia.

Ruse /ˈruːseɪ/ (also **Rousse** /ˈruːsə/) industrial city in N Bulgaria, a river port on the Danube; pop. (est. 1996) 168 051.

ruse /ruːz/ *n.* stratagem or trick. [French]

rush[1] *–v.* **1** go, move, flow, or act precipitately or with great speed. **2** move or transport with great haste (*was rushed to hospital*). **3** (foll. by *at*) **a** move suddenly towards. **b** begin or attack impetuously. **4** perform or deal with hurriedly (*don't rush your dinner*). **5** force or induce (a person) to act hastily. **6** attack or capture by sudden assault. **7** *slang* overcharge (a customer). *–n.* **1 a** rushing; violent or speedy advance or attack. **b** sudden flow, flood. **2** period of great activity. **3** (*attrib.*) done with great haste or speed (*a rush job*). **4** sudden migration of large numbers. **5** (foll. by *on, for*) sudden strong demand for a commodity. **6** (in *pl.*) *colloq.* first uncut prints of a film. [French *ruser*: related to RUSE]

rush[2] *n.* **1** marsh plant with slender tapering pith-filled stems, used for making chair-bottoms, baskets, etc. **2** stem of this. □ **rushy** *adj.* [Old English]

rush candle *n.* candle made of rush pith dipped in tallow.

rush hour *n.* time(s) each day when traffic is heaviest.

rushlight *n.* rush candle.

rusk *n.* slice of bread rebaked as a light biscuit, esp. as baby food. [Spanish or Portuguese *rosca* twist]

russet /ˈrʌsɪt/ *–adj.* reddish-brown. *–n.* **1** russet colour. **2** rough-skinned russet-coloured apple. [Latin *russus*]

Russian /ˈrʌʃ(ə)n/ *–n.* **1 a** native or national of Russia or (loosely) the former Soviet Union. **b** person of Russian descent. **2** language of Russia. *–adj.* **1** of Russia or (loosely) the former Soviet Union or its people. **2** of or in Russian.

Russian roulette *n.* firing of a revolver, with one chamber loaded, at one's head, after spinning the chamber.

Russian salad *n.* salad of mixed diced vegetables with mayonnaise.

Russo- *comb. form* Russian; Russian and.

rust *–n.* **1** reddish corrosive coating formed on iron, steel, etc. by oxidation, esp. when wet. **2** fungal plant-disease with rust-coloured spots. **3** impaired state due to disuse or inactivity. **4** reddish-brown. *–v.* **1** affect or be affected with rust. **2** become impaired through disuse. [Old English]

rustic /ˈrʌstɪk/ *–adj.* **1** of or like country people or country life. **2** unsophisticated. **3** of rude or rough workmanship. **4** made of untrimmed branches or rough timber (*rustic bench*). **5** *Archit.* with a roughened or rough-hewn surface. *–n.* country person, peasant. □ **rusticity** /-ˈtɪsɪtɪ/ *n.* [Latin *rus* the country]

rusticate /ˈrʌstɪˌkeɪt/ *v.* (**-ting**) **1** send down (a student) temporarily from university. **2** retire to or live in the country. **3** make rustic. □ **rustication** /-ˈkeɪʃ(ə)n/ *n.*

rustle /ˈrʌs(ə)l/ *–v.* (**-ling**) **1** (cause to) make a gentle sound as of dry blown leaves. **2** (also *absol.*) steal (cattle or horses). *–n.* rustling sound. □ **rustle up** *colloq.* produce at short notice. □ **rustler** *n.* (esp. in sense 2 of *v.*). [imitative]

rustproof *–adj.* not susceptible to corrosion by rust. *–v.* make rustproof.

rusty *adj.* (**-ier, -iest**) **1** rusted or affected by rust. **2** stiff with age or disuse. **3** (of knowledge etc.) impaired, esp. by neglect (*my French is rusty*). **4** rust-coloured. **5** (of black clothes) discoloured by age. □ **rustiness** *n.*

rut[1] *–n.* **1** deep track made by the passage of wheels. **2** established (esp. tedious) practice or routine (*in a rut*). *–v.* (**-tt-**) mark with ruts. [probably French: related to ROUTE]

rut[2] *–n.* periodic sexual excitement of a male deer etc. *–v.* (**-tt-**) be affected with rut. [Latin *rugio* roar]

Ruthenia /ruːˈθiːnɪə/ region of central Europe that is now part of Ukraine. □ **Ruthenian** *adj.* & *n.*

ruthenium /ruːˈθiːnɪəm/ *n.* rare hard white metallic element from platinum ores. [medieval Latin *Ruthenia* Russia]

rutherfordium /ˌrʌðəˈfɔːdɪəm/ *n.* artificial metallic element. [*Rutherford*, name of a physicist]

ruthless /ˈruːθlɪs/ *adj.* having no pity or compassion. □ **ruthlessly** *adv.* **ruthlessness** *n.* [*ruth* pity, from RUE[1]]

RV *abbr.* **1** rateable value. **2** Revised Version (of the Bible).

RWA *international vehicle registration* Rwanda.

Rwanda /ruːˈændə/, **Republic of** country in central Africa, E of Democratic Republic of Congo. The economy is based on agriculture, largely subsistence. Coffee and tea are the dominant cash crops, accounting for a major proportion of export revenue, and livestock farming is important; sugar, beans, cassava, and maize are also grown. Other exports include cassiterite (a tin ore), pyrethrum, hides, and cinchona bark. Small-scale industries under development include food processing and textiles.
History. The area was claimed by Germany from 1890, and after the First World War it became part of a Belgian trust territory, gaining independence as a republic in 1962. In 1990 the Rwanda Patriotic Front (exiled members of the minority Tutsi tribe) invaded Rwanda; in 1992 a ceasefire agreement was reached, after the adoption of a new multiparty constitution, and a coalition transitional government was formed; however, in 1994, the president was assassinated. The army responded to the assassination by massacring Tutsis and a state of civil war was resumed, from which the Rwandan Patriotic Front (Tutsis) emerged victorious. Ethnic unrest and violence has continued. In 1996 the Rwandan army attacked Hutu refugee camps in Zaïre (now Democratic Republic of Congo). President, Maj.-Gen. Juvénal Habyarimana; prime minister, Dismas Nsengiyaremye; capital, Kigali. □ **Rwandan** *adj.* & *n.*

languages	Kinyarwanda (a Bantu language), English, & French (official), Swahili
currency	franc (RF) of 100 centimes
pop. (1996)	6 853 000
GNP (1993)	US$1.4B
literacy	69% (m); 51% (f)
life expectancy	35 (m); 36 (f)

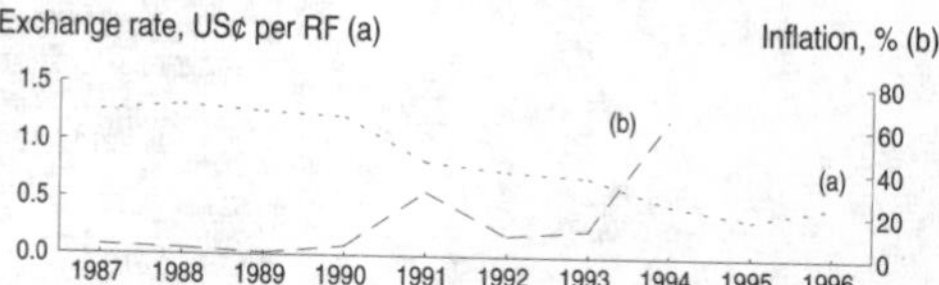

-ry *suffix* = -ERY (*infantry*; *rivalry*).

Ryazan /rɪə'zæn/ city in W central Russia; it has oil-refining and engineering industries; pop. (est. 1995) 536 000.

rye /raɪ/ *n.* **1 a** cereal plant. **b** grain of this used for bread and fodder. **2** (in full **rye whisky**) whisky distilled from fermented rye. [Old English]

ryegrass *n.* forage or coarse lawn grass. [alteration of *ray-grass*]

Ryukyu Islands /rɪ'uːkjuː/ chain of Japanese islands in the W Pacific, stretching from the S tip of Kyushu island to Taiwan; pop. (1995) 1 273 504. The economy is based on agriculture and fishing.

Ss

S[1] /es/ *n.* (also **s**) (*pl.* **Ss** or **S's**) **1** nineteenth letter of the alphabet. **2** S-shaped thing.

S[2] *abbr.* **1** (also **S.**) **1** Saint. **2** (also **S.**) South, Southern. **3** summer sea water (see LOAD LINE).

S[3] *–symb.* **1** sulphur. **2** schilling. *–international vehicle registration* Sweden. *–postcode* Sheffield.

S/. *symb.* sucre.

s. *abbr.* **1** second(s). **2** *hist.* shilling(s). **3** son. [sense 2 originally from Latin *solidus*]

-s' *suffix* denoting the possessive case of plural nouns and sometimes of singular nouns ending in *s* (*the boys' shoes*; *Charles' book*). [Old English inflection]

's *abbr.* **1** is; has (*he's*; *she's got it*; *John's*; *Charles's*). **2** us (*let's*).

-'s *suffix* denoting the possessive case of singular nouns and of plural nouns not ending in *-s* (*John's book*; *book's cover*; *children's shoes*).

S2 *international civil aircraft marking* Bangladesh.

S7 *international civil aircraft marking* Seychelles.

S9 *international civil aircraft marking* São Tomé and Príncipe.

SA *–abbr.* **1** Salvation Army. **2 a** (Spanish) sociedad anónima (= public company). **b** (Portuguese) sociedade anónima (= public company). **3** (French) société anonyme (= public limited company). **4** South Africa. **5** South America. **6** South Australia. *–postcode* Swansea. *–airline flight code* South African Airways.

S/A *abbr.* **1** subject to acceptance. **2** *US* survivorship agreement.

s.a. *abbr.* **1** safe arrival. **2** subject to approval.

SAA *abbr.* **1** South African Airways. **2** *Computing* systems application architecture.

SAAB /sɑːb/ *n.* (also **Saab**) Swedish aircraft and car company. [abbreviation, from Swedish *Svensk Aeroplan Aktiebolag*]

Saarland /ˈsɑːlænd/ state (*Land*) in W Germany; products include coal and steel; pop. (est. 1995) 1 084 200; capital, Saarbrücken.

Saba /ˈsɑːbə/ smallest island of the Netherlands Antilles; pop. (est. 1994) 1197; chief town, The Bottom.

Sabah /ˈsɑːbɑː/ state of Malaysia, comprising N Borneo and some offshore islands; pop. (est. 1993) 1 472 700; capital, Kota Kinabalu. Products include rice, rubber, and timber; copper and oil are mined.

sabbath /ˈsæbəθ/ *n.* religious day of rest kept by Christians on Sunday and Jews on Saturday. [Hebrew, = rest]

sabbatical /səˈbætɪk(ə)l/ *–adj.* (of leave) granted at intervals to a university teacher for study or travel. *–n.* period of sabbatical leave. [Greek: related to SABBATH]

Sabena /səˈbiːnə/ *n.* Belgian airline. [abbreviation, from French *Société anonyme belge d'exploitation de la navigation aérienne*]

saber *US* var. of SABRE.

sable /ˈseɪb(ə)l/ *–n.* (*pl.* same or **-s**) **1** small brown-furred mammal of N Europe and N Asia. **2** its skin or fur. *–adj.* **1** (usu. placed after noun) *Heraldry* black. **2** esp. *poet.* gloomy. [Slavonic]

sabot /ˈsæbəʊ/ *n.* **1** shoe carved from wood. **2** wooden-soled shoe. [French]

sabotage /ˈsæbəˌtɑːʒ/ *–n.* deliberate damage to productive capacity, esp. as a political act. *–v.* (**-ging**) **1** commit sabotage on. **2** destroy, spoil. [French: related to SABOT]

saboteur /ˌsæbəˈtɜː(r)/ *n.* person who commits sabotage. [French]

sabre /ˈseɪbə(r)/ *n.* (*US* **saber**) **1** curved cavalry sword. **2** light tapering fencing-sword. [French from German *Sabel*]

sabre-rattling *n.* display or threat of military force.

sac *n.* membranous bag in an animal or plant. [Latin: related to SACK[1]]

saccharin /ˈsækərɪn/ *n.* a sugar substitute. [medieval Latin *saccharum* sugar]

saccharine /ˈsækəˌriːn/ *adj.* excessively sentimental or sweet.

sacerdotal /ˌsækəˈdəʊt(ə)l/ *adj.* of priests or priestly office. [Latin *sacerdos -dot-* priest]

sachet /ˈsæʃeɪ/ *n.* **1** small bag or packet containing shampoo etc. **2** small scented bag for perfuming drawers etc. [French diminutive: related to SAC]

sack[1] *–n.* **1 a** large strong bag for storage or conveyance. **b** quantity contained in a sack. **2** (prec. by *the*) *colloq.* dismissal from employment. **3** (prec. by *the*) *US slang* bed. *–v.* **1** put into a sack or sacks. **2** *colloq.* dismiss from employment. [Latin *saccus*]

sack[2] *–v.* plunder and destroy (a captured town etc.). *–n.* such sacking. [French *mettre à* put in a sack *sac*]

sack[3] *n. hist.* white wine from Spain and the Canaries. [French *vin sec* dry wine]

sackbut /ˈsækbʌt/ *n.* early form of trombone. [French]

sackcloth *n.* **1** coarse fabric of flax or hemp used for sacks. **2** clothing for penance or mourning (esp. *sackcloth and ashes*).

sacking *n.* material for making sacks; sackcloth.

sacral /ˈseɪkr(ə)l/ *adj.* **1** *Anat.* of the sacrum. **2** of or for sacred rites. [Latin *sacrum* sacred]

sacrament /ˈsækrəmənt/ *n.* **1** symbolic Christian ceremony, e.g. baptism and Eucharist. **2** (also **Blessed** or **Holy Sacrament**) (prec. by *the*) Eucharist. **3** sacred thing. □ **sacramental** /-ˈment(ə)l/ *adj.* [Latin: related to SACRED]

Sacramento /ˌsækrəˈmentəʊ/ city in the US, capital of California, a deep-water port with food-processing and aerospace industries; pop. (est. 1994) 373 964.

sacred /ˈseɪkrɪd/ *adj.* **1 a** (often foll. by *to*) dedicated to a god. **b** connected with religion (*sacred music*). **2** safeguarded or required esp. by tradition; inviolable. [Latin *sacer* holy]

sacred cow *n. colloq.* traditionally hallowed idea or institution.

sacrifice /ˈsækrɪˌfaɪs/ *–n.* **1 a** voluntary relinquishing of something valued. **b** thing so relinquished. **c** the loss entailed. **2 a** slaughter of an animal or person or surrender of a possession, as an offering to a deity. **b** animal, person, or thing so offered. **3** loss of welfare as a result of paying a tax. One of the principles of taxation is that a tax should be formulated so that it involves **equality of sacrifice** on the part of the taxpayers. It is assumed that taxpayers with equal incomes will sacrifice equal amounts of welfare by paying identical taxes. *–v.* (**-cing**) **1** give up (a thing) as a sacrifice. **2** (foll. by *to*) devote or give over to. **3** (also *absol.*) offer or kill as a sacrifice. □ **sacrificial** /-ˈfɪʃ(ə)l/ *adj.* [Latin: related to SACRED]

sacrilege /ˈsækrɪlɪdʒ/ *n.* violation of what is regarded as sacred. □ **sacrilegious** /-ˈlɪdʒəs/ *adj.* [Latin: related to SACRED, *lego* take]

sacristan /ˈsækrɪst(ə)n/ *n.* person in charge of a sacristy and church contents. [medieval Latin: related to SACRED]

sacristy /ˈsækrɪstɪ/ *n.* (*pl.* **-ies**) room in a church where vestments, sacred vessels, etc., are kept. [medieval Latin: related to SACRED]

sacrosanct /ˈsækrəʊˌsæŋkt/ *adj.* most sacred; inviolable. □ **sacrosanctity** /-ˈsæŋkt-/ *n.* [Latin: related to SACRED, SAINT]

sacrum /ˈseɪkrəm/ *n.* (*pl.* **sacra** or **-s**) triangular bone between the two hip-bones. [Latin *os sacrum* sacred bone]

sad *adj.* (**sadder, saddest**) **1** unhappy. **2** causing sorrow. **3** regrettable. **4** shameful, deplorable. □ **sadden** *v.* **sadly** *adv.* **sadness** *n.* [Old English]

saddle /ˈsæd(ə)l/ *–n.* **1** seat of leather etc. strapped on a horse etc. for riding. **2** bicycle etc. seat. **3** joint of meat consisting of the two loins. **4** ridge rising to a summit at each end. *–v.* (**-ling**) **1** put a saddle on (a horse etc.). **2** (foll. by *with*) burden (a person) with a task etc. □ **in the saddle 1** mounted. **2** in office or control. [Old English]

saddleback *n.* **1** roof of a tower with two opposite gables. **2** hill with a concave upper outline. **3** black pig with a white stripe across the back. □ **saddlebacked** *adj.*

saddle-bag *n.* **1** each of a pair of bags laid across the back of a horse etc. **2** bag attached to a bicycle saddle etc.

saddler *n.* maker of or dealer in saddles etc.

saddlery /ˈsædlərɪ/ *n.* (*pl.* **-ies**) saddler's goods, trade, or premises.

Sadducee /ˈsædjʊˌsiː/ *n.* member of a Jewish sect of the time of Christ that denied the resurrection of the dead. [Hebrew]

sadhu /ˈsɑːduː/ *n.* (in India) holy man, sage, or ascetic. [Sanskrit]

sadism /ˈseɪdɪz(ə)m/ *n.* **1** *colloq.* enjoyment of cruelty to others. **2** sexual perversion characterized by this. □ **sadist** *n.* **sadistic** /səˈdɪstɪk/ *adj.* **sadistically** /səˈdɪstɪkəlɪ/ *adv.* [de *Sade*, name of an author]

sado-masochism /ˌseɪdəʊˈmæsəˌkɪz(ə)m/ *n.* sadism and masochism in one person. □ **sado-masochist** *n.* **sado-masochistic** /-ˈkɪstɪk/ *adj.*

s.a.e. *abbr.* stamped addressed envelope.

SAEF *abbr.* = STOCK EXCHANGE AUTOMATIC EXECUTION FACILITY.

safari /səˈfɑːrɪ/ *n.* (*pl.* **-s**) expedition, esp. in Africa, to observe or hunt animals (*go on safari*). [Swahili from Arabic *safara* to travel]

safari park *n.* park where wild animals are kept in the open for viewing from vehicles.

safe *–adj.* **1** free of danger or injury. **2** secure, not risky (*in a safe place*). **3** reliable, certain. **4** prevented from escaping or doing harm (*have got him safe*). **5** (also **safe and sound**) uninjured; with no harm done. **6** cautious, unenterprising. *–n.* **1** strong lockable cabinet etc. for valuables. **2** = MEAT SAFE. □ **on the safe side** with a margin for error. □ **safely** *adv.* [French *sauf* from Latin *salvus*]

safe conduct *n.* **1** immunity given from arrest or harm. **2** document securing this.

♦ **safe custody** *n.* service offered by most UK commercial banks, in which the bank holds valuable items belonging to its customers in its strongroom. These items are usu. documents (e.g. house deeds and bearer bonds), but they may also include jewellery etc. The bank is a bailee for these items and its liability will depend on whether or not it has charged the customer for the service and the terms of the customer's own insurance (in the case of jewellery etc.).

safe deposit *n.* building containing strongrooms and safes for hire.

safeguard *–n.* protecting proviso, circumstance, etc. *–v.* guard or protect (rights etc.).

safe house *n.* place of refuge etc. for spies, terrorists, etc.

safe keeping *n.* preservation in a safe place.

safe period *n.* time during the month when conception is least likely.

safe sex *n.* sexual activity in which precautions are taken against sexually transmitted diseases, esp. Aids.

safety *n.* being safe; freedom from danger.

safety-belt *n.* **1** = SEAT-BELT. **2** belt or strap worn to prevent injury.

safety-catch *n.* device preventing a gun-trigger or machinery from being operated accidentally.

safety curtain *n.* fireproof curtain between a stage and auditorium.

safety lamp *n.* miner's lamp so protected as not to ignite firedamp.

safety match *n.* match igniting only on a specially prepared surface.

safety net *n.* net placed to catch an acrobat etc. in case of a fall.

safety pin *n.* pin with a guarded point.

safety razor *n.* razor with a guard to prevent cutting the skin.

safety-valve *n.* **1** (in a steam boiler) automatic valve relieving excess pressure. **2** means of venting excitement etc. harmlessly.

saffron /ˈsæfrən/ *–n.* **1** deep yellow food colouring and flavouring made from dried crocus stigmas. **2** colour of this. *–adj.* deep yellow. [French from Arabic]

sag *–v.* (**-gg-**) **1** sink or subside, esp. unevenly. **2** have a downward bulge or curve in the middle. **3** fall in price. *–n.* state or extent of sagging. □ **saggy** *adj.* [Low German or Dutch]

saga /ˈsɑːgə/ *n.* **1** long heroic story, esp. medieval Icelandic or Norwegian. **2** series of connected novels concerning a family's history etc. **3** long involved story. [Old Norse: related to SAW[3]]

sagacious /səˈgeɪʃ(ə)s/ *adj.* showing insight or good judgement. □ **sagacity** /səˈgæsɪtɪ/ *n.* [Latin *sagax -acis*]

♦ **sagacity segmentation** *n.* form of MARKET SEGMENTATION that improves upon the discriminating power of income and demographic classifications. It combines life cycle, income, and socio-economic information with JICNAR data. The underlying assumption is that as people pass

---

St Kitts and Nevis /kɪts, ˈniːvɪs/, **Federation of** country in the West Indies, consisting of two adjoining islands (St Kitts and Nevis) of the Leeward Islands. The economy is based on agriculture, producing sugar (a major export), molasses, cotton, coconuts, and other products. Tourism and light industry are increasing in importance; manufactured goods include electronic components (the chief export) and knitwear. Formerly a colony consisting of St Kitts, Nevis, and Anguilla, it became a state in association with Britain (which had responsibility for defence and foreign affairs) in 1967, but Anguilla seceded within three months. St Kitts and Nevis became an independent state within the Commonwealth in 1983 and is a member of CARICOM. In 1997 the Nevis parliament voted to hold a referendum on secession from the federation. Prime minister, Dr Denzil Douglas; capital, Basseterre (on St Kitts).

language	English
currency	East Caribbean dollar (EC$) of 100 cents
pop. (1996)	39 400
GNP (1994)	US$195M
literacy	90% (m); 90% (f)
life expectancy	63 (m); 69 (f)

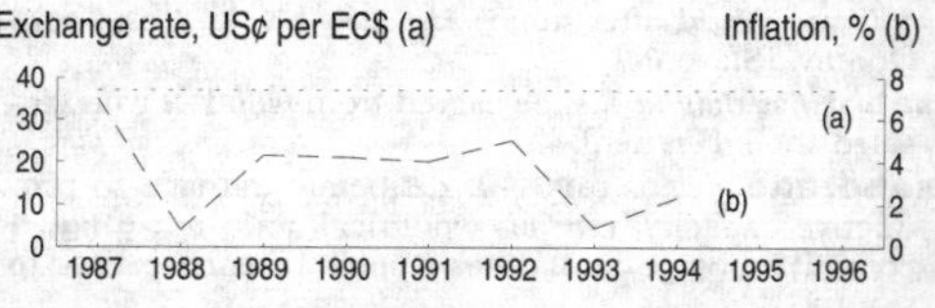

through various stages of their lives their changed aspirations and behaviour patterns are reflected in their consumption of goods and services.

sage[1] *n.* culinary herb with dull greyish-green leaves. [French from Latin SALVIA]

sage[2] *–n.* often *iron.* wise man. *–adj.* wise, judicious, experienced. □ **sagely** *adv.* [French from Latin *sapio* be wise]

sagebrush *n.* growth of shrubby aromatic plants in some semi-arid regions of W North America.

Sagittarius /ˌsædʒɪˈteərɪəs/ *n.* (*pl.* **-es**) **1** constellation and ninth sign of the zodiac (the Archer). **2** person born when the sun is in this sign. □ **Sagittarian** *adj.* & *n.* [Latin, = archer]

sago /ˈseɪgəʊ/ *n.* (*pl.* **-s**) **1** a starch used in puddings etc. **2** (in full **sago palm**) any of several tropical palms and cycads yielding this. [Malay]

Sahara /səˈhɑːrə/ desert in N Africa, the largest in the world, with deposits of oil, gas, and phosphates. See also WESTERN SAHARA.

sahib /sɑːb/ *n. hist.* (in India) form of address to European man. [Arabic, = lord]

said *past* and *past part.* of SAY.

Saida see SIDON.

Saigon /saɪˈgɒn/ see HO CHI MINH CITY.

sail *–n.* **1** piece of material extended on rigging to catch the wind and propel a boat or ship. **2** ship's sails collectively. **3** voyage or excursion in a sailing-boat. **4** ship, esp. as discerned from its sails. **5** wind-catching apparatus of a windmill. *–v.* **1** travel on water by the use of sails or engine-power. **2** begin a voyage (*sails at nine*). **3 a** navigate (a ship etc.). **b** travel on (a sea). **4** set (a toy boat) afloat. **5** glide or move smoothly or in a stately manner. **6** (often foll. by *through*) *colloq.* succeed easily (*sailed through the exams*). □ **sail close to the wind 1** sail as nearly against the wind as possible. **2** come close to indecency or dishonesty. **sail into** *colloq.* attack physically or verbally. **under sail** with sails set. [Old English]

sailboard *n.* board with a mast and sail, used in windsurfing. □ **sailboarder** *n.* **sailboarding** *n.*

sailcloth *n.* **1** material used for sails. **2** canvas-like dress material.

sailing-boat *n.* (also **sailing-ship**) vessel driven by sails.

sailor *n.* **1** member of a ship's crew, esp. one below the rank of officer. **2** person considered with regard to seasickness (*a good sailor*). [originally *sailer*: see -ER[1]]

sailplane *n.* glider designed for sustained flight.

sainfoin /ˈsænfɔɪn/ *n.* pink-flowered fodder-plant. [Latin *sanctus* holy, *foenum* hay]

◆ **Sainsbury** /ˈseɪnzbərɪ/, **David John** (1940–) British retailer, chairman and chief executive (since 1992) of J. Sainsbury plc, the supermarket group, in which he owns a 13% share; the Sainsbury family owns a further 27%. He was also a member of the Carter Committee that reviewed the activities of the Post Office (1975–7); his publications include *Government and Industry: A New Partnership* (1981).

saint /seɪnt, before a name usu. sənt/ *–n.* (*abbr.* **St** or **S**; *pl.* **Sts** or **SS**) **1** holy or (in some Churches) formally canonized person regarded as worthy of special veneration. **2** very virtuous person. *–v.* (as **sainted** *adj.*) saintly. □ **sainthood** *n.* **saintlike** *adj.* [Latin *sanctus* holy]

St Andrews /ˈændruːz/ town in E Scotland, on the coast of Fife; pop. (1991) 11 136. Its Royal and Ancient Golf Club is the ruling authority on the game of golf.

St Bernard /ˈbɜːnəd/ *n.* (in full **St Bernard dog**) very large dog of a breed orig. kept in the Alps to rescue travellers.

St Catherines /ˈkæθrɪnz/ city and port in Canada, in S Ontario, an industrial and fruit-farming centre; pop. (1991) 129 300.

St Croix /krɔɪ/ island in the West Indies, the largest of the US Virgin Islands; pop. (1990) 50 139; chief town, Christiansted. Tourism and agriculture are the main sources of revenue.

Saint-Denis /sædəˈniː/ capital of the island of Réunion in the Indian Ocean; pop. (1995) 207 158.

Saint Eustatius /juːˈsteɪʃəs/ small island of the Netherlands Antilles, in the Caribbean Sea; pop. (est. 1990) 1716; chief town, Oranjestad.

St George's /ˈdʒɔːdʒɪz/ capital of Grenada, a port and resort on the SW coast of the island; pop. (1991) 4621.

St George's Channel channel linking the Irish Sea with the Atlantic Ocean and separating Ireland from mainland Britain.

St Helena /hɪˈliːnə/ island in the S Atlantic, a British dependent territory that itself has the dependencies of Ascension Island and Tristan da Cunha; pop. (1992) 5700; capital, Jamestown.

St Helier /ˈhelɪə(r)/ capital of the Channel Islands, on the island of Jersey, a resort and market town trading in early vegetables and cattle; pop. (latest est.) 27 400.

Saint John /dʒɒn/ city and port in E Canada, a centre of commerce and heavy industry for New Brunswick; pop. (1991) 90 457.

St John island in the West Indies, one of the three principal islands of the US Virgin Islands; pop. (1990) 3504.

St John's /dʒɒnz/ **1** city in Canada, capital and commercial centre of Newfoundland; pop. (1991) 95 770. **2** capital of Antigua and Barbuda, chief port of the island of Antigua; pop. (1991) 21 514.

St John's wort *n.* yellow-flowered plant.

St Lawrence /ˈlɒrəns/ river of North America flowing from Lake Ontario to the Atlantic Ocean. The St Lawrence Seaway, which includes a number of artificial sections to bypass rapids, enables large vessels to navigate the entire length of the river.

St Leger /ˈledʒə(r)/ *n.* horse-race at Doncaster for three-year-olds. [from the name of the founder]

St Louis /ˈluːɪ/ city and port in the US, in E Missouri, a major transportation and trading centre on the Mississippi River; manufactures include aircraft, cars, and chemicals; pop. (est. 1994) 368 215.

saintly *adj.* (**-ier, -iest**) very holy or virtuous. □ **saintliness** *n.*

St Lucia /ˈluːʃə/ island country in the West Indies, one of the Windward Islands. It is predominantly agricultural; principal crops are bananas (the major export), coconut products, and cocoa beans, and mangoes, avocados, spices, cassava, and yams are also grown. The processing of these products is the chief manufacturing activity, though attempts have recently been made to diversify the industrial sector of the economy; clothing and paper products now contribute significantly to export revenue. Tourism is increasing in importance. Possession of the island was long disputed with France, and it did not pass finally into British hands until the early 19th century. Since 1979 it has been an independent state within the Commonwealth. St Lucia is a member of CARICOM. Prime minister, Kenny Anthony; capital, Castries. □ **St Lucian** *adj.* & *n.*

languages	English (official), French patois
currency	East Caribbean dollar (EC$) of 100 cents
pop. (1996)	144 000
GNP (1994)	US$501M
literacy	80%
life expectancy	67 (m); 72 (f)

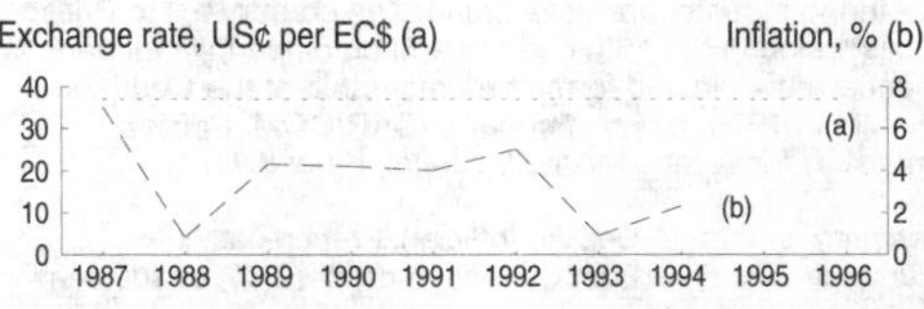

Saint Martin /sæ̃ mɑːˈtæ̃/ island in the Caribbean Sea, one of the Lesser Antilles. The S section (Dutch **Sint Maarten**) forms part of the Netherlands Antilles; pop. (est. 1994) 37 256; chief town, Philipsburg. The N section forms part of the French overseas department of Guadeloupe; pop. (est. 1990) 28 518; chief town, Marigot.

St Moritz /sæ̃ mɒˈriːts/ resort and winter sports centre in SE Switzerland; pop. (est. 1990) 5335.

St Nazaire /sæ̃ næˈzeə(r)/ seaport and industrial town in NW France, at the mouth of the River Loire; it has shipbuilding, chemical, and oil-refining industries; pop. (1990) 64 812.

Saint Nicolas /ˈnɪkələs/ (Flemish **Sint Niklaas** /sɪnt ˈnɪklɑːs/) industrial town in Belgium, in East Flanders; pop. (est. 1995) 68 397.

St Paul /pɔːl/ city in the US, capital of Minnesota, on the Mississippi River, and an important trading centre for the surrounding agricultural area, with oil-refining and food-processing industries; pop. (est. 1994) 262 071.

St Petersburg /ˈpiːtəzˌbɜːg/ (formerly (1924–91) **Leningrad**) city in Russia, on an inlet of the Gulf of Finland; a centre of commerce and culture, it has engineering, chemical, and metallurgical industries and also manufactures cars and electronic goods; pop. (est. 1994) 4 838 000.

St Pierre and Miquelon /sæ̃ pɪˈeər, ˈmiːkəˌlɔ̃/ group of eight small islands in the N Atlantic, S of Newfoundland, comprising a Territorial Collectivity of France; pop. (1990) 6392; chief settlement, St Pierre.

St Thomas /ˈtɒməs/ island in the West Indies, the second-largest of the US Virgin Islands; tourism is an important source of revenue; pop. (est. 1995) 50 744.

St Tropez /sæ̃ trəʊˈpeɪ/ fishing-port and resort in S France, on the Côte d'Azur; pop. (est. 1995) 6050.

St Vitus's dance /ˈvaɪtəsɪz/ *n.* disease producing involuntary convulsive movements of the body.

Sakai /sɑːˈkaɪ/ industrial city in Japan, on the S coast of Honshu island; pop. (1995) 802 965.

sake[1] *n.* □ **for Christ's** (or **God's** or **goodness'** or **Heaven's** or **Pete's** etc.) **sake** expression of impatience, supplication, anger, etc. **for the sake of** (or **for one's sake**) out of consideration for; in the interest of; because of; in order to please, honour, get, or keep. [Old English]

sake[2] /ˈsɑːkɪ/ *n.* Japanese rice wine. [Japanese]

Sakhalin /ˌsɑːxəˈliːn/ Russian island in the Sea of Okhotsk, off the E coast of the mainland; activities include forestry, the exploitation of coal, iron, and oil reserves, and agriculture (esp. vegetables and dairy farming); pop. (est. 1995) 673 000.

SAL *abbr.* **1** South Arabian League. **2** surface air-lifted mail.

salaam /səˈlɑːm/ –*n.* **1** (chiefly as a Muslim greeting) Peace! **2** Muslim low bow with the right palm on the forehead. **3** (in *pl.*) respectful compliments. –*v.* make a salaam (to). [Arabic]

salacious /səˈleɪʃəs/ *adj.* **1** indecently erotic. **2** lecherous. □ **salaciousness** *n.* **salacity** /səˈlæsɪtɪ/ *n.* [Latin *salax -acis*: related to SALIENT]

salad /ˈsæləd/ *n.* cold mixture of usu. raw vegetables, often with a dressing. [French *salade* from Latin *sal* salt]

salad cream *n.* creamy salad-dressing.

salad days *n.* period of youthful inexperience.

salad-dressing *n.* = DRESSING 2a.

salamander /ˈsæləˌmændə(r)/ *n.* **1** tailed newtlike amphibian once thought able to endure fire. **2** similar mythical creature. [Greek *salamandra*]

salami /səˈlɑːmɪ/ *n.* (*pl.* **-s**) highly-seasoned orig. Italian sausage. [Italian]

sal ammoniac /ˌsæl əˈməʊnɪˌæk/ *n.* ammonium chloride, a white crystalline salt. [Latin *sal* salt, *ammoniacus* of Jupiter Ammon]

salary /ˈsælərɪ/ –*n.* (*pl.* **-ies**) fixed regular (usu. monthly) payment to an employee, esp. to executive, managerial, and administrative employees who work in an office. Unlike a wage, it is unlikely to be related to hours worked or to the quantity of goods produced and it is usu. specified in annual rather than weekly terms. –*v.* (**-ies, -ied**) (usu. as **salaried** *adj.*) pay a salary to. [Latin *salarium* money for buying salt]

sale *n.* **1** exchange of a commodity for money etc.; act or instance of selling. **2** amount sold (*sales were enormous*). **3** temporary offering of goods at reduced prices. **4 a** event at which goods are sold. **b** public auction. □ **on** (or **for) sale** offered for purchase. [Old English]

saleable *adj.* fit or likely to be sold. □ **saleability** /-ˈbɪlɪtɪ/ *n.*

◆ **sale and lease-back** see LEASE-BACK.

◆ **sale as seen** *n.* sale made on the basis that the buyer has inspected the goods and is buying them as a result of this inspection and not on any guarantee of quality or condition by the seller. The seller does not guarantee or imply that the goods are suitable for any particular purpose.

◆ **sale by description** *n.* sale made on the basis that the quality of the goods sold will correspond to the description given of them in the contract of sale.

◆ **sale by instalments** see HIRE PURCHASE.

◆ **sale by sample** *n.* sale made on the basis that the quality and condition of the bulk of the goods will be at least as good as that of a representative sample. In contracts in which goods are sold by sample, the contract may stipulate how and by whom the bulk should be sampled and what tests should be used to compare it to the selling sample. The contract will also usu. lay down the procedure to be adopted if the bulk sample is not as good as the selling sample.

Salem /ˈseɪləm/ **1** city in the US, capital of Oregon; industries include food-processing; pop. (est. 1994) 115 912. **2** city and port in the US, in NE Massachusetts; pop. (1990) 38 090. **3** industrial city in S India, in Tamil Nadu; textiles are manufactured; pop. (1991) 366 712.

sale of work *n.* sale of home-made goods etc. for charity.

St Vincent and the Grenadines /ˈvɪns(ə)nt, ˈgrenəˌdiːnz/ country in the West Indies, in the Windward Islands, consisting of the island of St Vincent and some of the Grenadines. Its economy is based on agriculture and the processing of agricultural products, bananas being the principal export; other cash crops include arrowroot, taro, sweet potatoes, coconuts, and spices. Tourism and manufacturing industry are developing. The country fell to British possession in the 18th century and obtained full independence with a limited form of membership of the Commonwealth in 1979; it is a member of CARICOM. Prime minister, Sir James Mitchell; capital, Kingstown.

languages	English (official), French patois
currency	East Caribbean dollar (EC$) of 100 cents
pop. (1996)	113 000
GNP (1994)	US$235M
literacy	96%
life expectancy	71 (m); 74 (f)

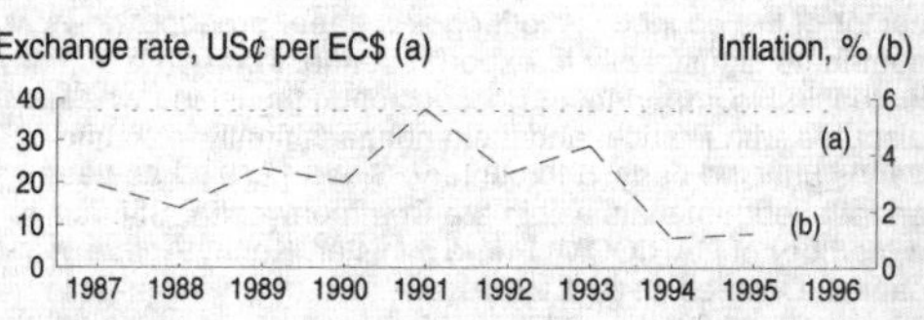

♦ **sale or return** *n.* trading agreement in which the seller agrees to take back from the buyer any goods that the buyer has failed to sell, usu. in a specified period. Some retail shops buy certain of their goods on sale or return.

saleroom *n.* room where auctions are held.

♦ **sales day book** *n.* book of prime entry in which an organization records the invoices issued to its customers for goods or services supplied in the course of its trade. Postings are made from this book to the personal accounts of the customers, while the totals of the invoices are posted to the sales account in the nominal ledger.

♦ **sales forecast** *n.* estimate of the likely sales for a product, given certain criteria and assumptions.

♦ **sales ledger** *n.* ledger that records the personal accounts of an organization's customers. The total of the balances in this ledger represents the organization's trade debtors.

salesman *n.* **1** man employed to sell goods. **2** *US* commercial traveller.

♦ **sales management** *n.* organization, direction, recruitment, training, and motivation of the sales force within a planned marketing strategy. In very large markets, such as the US, there might be a hierarchy of sales managers and district managers, reporting to regional managers, who in turn report to a national sales manager. □ **sales manager** *n.*

salesmanship *n.* skill in selling.

salesperson *n.* salesman or saleswoman.

♦ **sales promotion** *n.* activity designed to boost the sales of a product or service. It may include an advertising campaign, increased public-relations activity, a free-sample campaign, offering free gifts or trading stamps, arranging demonstrations or exhibitions, setting up competitions with attractive prizes, temporary price reductions, door-to-door calling, telephone selling, personal letters, etc.

♦ **sales quota** *n.* target set by sales management for a specific area or sales representative. Since the earnings of sales representatives are often directly related to the sales achieved, the setting of realistic quotas is imperative.

♦ **sales representative** *n.* person who sells the goods and services of an organization, either as an employee of that organization or as part of a contractual sales force. Additional responsibilities might include generating new sales leads (see COLD CALL), publicizing changes in products or prices, gathering information about competitors' activity, and merchandising products. Sales representatives often receive a commission on what they sell.

♦ **sales response function** *n.* relationship between the likely sales of a particular product during a specified period and the level of marketing support it receives. The more advertising, sales promotion, or public-relations support for a product, the higher the sales are likely to be.

sales talk *n.* persuasive talk promoting goods or an idea etc.

♦ **sales tax** *n.* tax based on the selling price of goods. Such taxes are not now generally favoured, since for goods sold on from one trader to another the amount of sales tax borne by the ultimate buyer becomes too great. VAT was largely designed to meet this objection.

♦ **sales territory** *n.* unit of organization of a sales force within a company. Each sales representative is usu. assigned a geographical area, market segment, or product group in which to develop sales, and accordingly accepts the credit for the success (or otherwise) of the product within that area.

saleswoman *n.* woman employed to sell goods.

salicylic acid /ˌsælɪ'sɪlɪk/ *n.* chemical used as a fungicide and in aspirin and dyes. □ **salicylate** /sə'lɪsɪˌleɪt/ *n.* [Latin *salix* willow]

salient /'seɪlɪənt/ *–adj.* **1** prominent, conspicuous. **2** (of an angle, esp. in fortification) pointing outwards. *–n.* salient angle or part of a fortification; outward bulge in a military line. [Latin *salio* leap]

saline /'seɪlaɪn/ *–adj.* **1** containing salt or salts. **2** tasting of salt. **3** of chemical salts. **4** of the nature of a salt. *–n.* **1** salt lake, spring, etc. **2** saline solution. □ **salinity** /sə'lɪnɪtɪ/ *n.* **salinization** /ˌsælɪnaɪ'zeɪʃ(ə)n/ *n.* [Latin *sal* salt]

Salisbury /'sɔːlzbərɪ/ **1** city in S England, in Wiltshire; there is some light industry and tourism; pop. (1991) 39 268. **2** see HARARE.

saliva /sə'laɪvə/ *n.* colourless liquid secreted into the mouth by glands. □ **salivary** /sə'laɪ-, 'sælɪ-/ *adj.* [Latin]

salivate /'sælɪˌveɪt/ *v.* (**-ting**) secrete saliva, esp. in excess. □ **salivation** /-'veɪʃ(ə)n/ *n.* [Latin *salivare*: related to SALIVA]

sallow[1] /'sæləʊ/ *adj.* (**-er, -est**) (esp. of the skin) yellowish. [Old English]

sallow[2] /'sæləʊ/ *n.* **1** low-growing willow. **2** a shoot or the wood of this. [Old English]

sally /'sælɪ/ (*pl.* **-ies**) *–n.* **1** sudden military charge; sortie. **2** excursion. **3** witticism. *–v.* (**-ies, -ied**) **1** (usu. foll. by *out, forth*) set out on a walk, journey, etc. **2** (usu. foll. by *out*) make a military sally. [French *saillie* from Latin *salio* leap]

salmon /'sæmən/ *–n.* (*pl.* usu. same or **-s**) large expensive edible fish with orange-pink flesh. *–adj.* salmon-pink. [Latin *salmo*]

salmonella /ˌsælmə'nelə/ *n.* (*pl.* **-llae** /-liː/) **1** bacterium causing food poisoning. **2** such food poisoning. [*Salmon*, name of a veterinary surgeon]

salmon pink *adj.* & *n.* (as adj. often hyphenated) orange-pink colour of salmon flesh.

salmon trout *n.* large silver-coloured trout.

salon /'sælɒn/ *n.* **1** room or establishment of a hairdresser, beautician, etc. **2** *hist.* meeting of eminent people in the home of a lady of fashion. **3** reception room, esp. of a continental house. [French: related to SALOON]

Salonica /sə'lɒnɪkə/ (Greek **Thessaloniki** /ˌθesəlɒ'niːkɪ/) seaport in NE Greece, the capital of the province of Macedonia and second-largest city of Greece; its exports comprise approximately one-third of the country's total, and there are also textile and food-processing industries; pop. (1991) 377 951.

saloon /sə'luːn/ *n.* **1 a** large room or hall on a ship, in a hotel, etc. **b** public room for a specified purpose (*billiard-saloon*). **2** (in full **saloon car**) (usu. four-seater) car with the body closed off from the luggage area. **3** *US* drinking-bar. **4** (in full **saloon bar**) more comfortable bar in a public house. [French *salon*]

salsa /'sælsə/ *n.* a kind of dance music of Cuban origin, with jazz and rock elements. [Spanish: related to SAUCE]

salsify /'sælsɪfɪ/ *n.* (*pl.* **-ies**) plant with long fleshy edible roots. [French from Italian]

SALT /sɔːlt, sɒlt/ *abbr.* Strategic Arms Limitation Talks (or Treaty).

salt /sɔːlt, sɒlt/ *–n.* **1** (also **common salt**) sodium chloride, esp. mined or evaporated from sea water, and used for seasoning or preserving food. **2** chemical compound formed from the reaction of an acid with a base. **3** piquancy; wit. **4** (in *sing.* or *pl.*) **a** substance resembling salt in taste, form, etc. (*bath salts*). **b** (esp. in *pl.*) substance used as a laxative. **5** (also **old salt**) experienced sailor. **6** = SALT-CELLAR. *–adj.* containing, tasting of, or preserved with salt. *–v.* **1** cure, preserve, or season with salt or brine. **2** sprinkle (a road etc.) with salt. □ **salt away** (or **down**) *slang* put (money etc.) by. **the salt of the earth** most admirable or honest person or people (Matt. 5:13). **take with a pinch** (or **grain) of salt** regard sceptically. **worth one's salt** efficient, capable. [Old English]

salt-cellar *n.* container for salt at table. [earlier *salt saler* from French *salier* salt-box]

salting *n.* (esp. in *pl.*) marsh overflowed by the sea.

saltire /'sɔːlˌtaɪə(r)/ *n.* X-shaped cross dividing a shield in four. [French *sautoir* stile]

Salt Lake City city in the US, capital of Utah and a centre of commerce for local mining activities; there are food-processing, oil-refining, and textile industries; pop. (est. 1994) 171 849.

salt-lick *n.* place where animals lick salt from the ground.

salt-mine *n.* mine yielding rock-salt.

salt-pan *n.* vessel, or depression near the sea, used for getting salt by evaporation.

saltpetre /ˌsɒlt'piːtə(r), ˌsɔːlt-/ *n.* (*US* **saltpeter**) white crystalline salty substance used in preserving meat and in gunpowder. [Latin *sal petrae*, = salt of rock]

salt-water *adj.* of or living in the sea.

salty *adj.* (**-ier, -iest**) **1** tasting of or containing salt. **2** (of wit etc.) piquant.□ **saltiness** *n.*

salubrious /sə'luːbrɪəs/ *adj.* health-giving; healthy. □ **salubrity** *n.* [Latin *salus* health]

saluki /sə'luːkɪ/ *n.* (*pl.* **-s**) dog of a tall slender silky-coated breed. [Arabic]

salutary /'sæljʊtərɪ/ *adj.* having a good effect. [Latin: related to SALUTE]

salutation /ˌsæljuː'teɪʃ(ə)n/ *n. formal* sign or expression of greeting.

salute /sə'luːt/ *–n.* **1** gesture of respect, homage, greeting etc. **2** *Mil.* & *Naut.* prescribed gesture or use of weapons or flags as a sign of respect etc. **3** ceremonial discharge of a gun or guns. *–v.* (**-ting**) **1 a** make a salute to. **b** (often foll. by *to*) perform a salute. **2** greet. **3** commend. [Latin *salus -ut-* health]

Salvador /ˌsælvə'dɔː(r)/ **1** (also **Bahia** /bɑː'iːə/) port in NE Brazil, on the Atlantic coast; products include processed food and tobacco; sugar, cocoa, tobacco, and diamonds are exported; pop. (1991) 2 070 296. **2** see EL SALVADOR.

salvage /'sælvɪdʒ/ *–n.* **1** rescue of property from the sea, a fire, etc. **2** goods, property, etc. saved from a shipwreck or from a fire. If a cargo is treated as a total loss for insurance purposes, there still may be salvageable items that have a **salvage value**; these may be sold by the insurers or allowed for in the settlement of their claim. **3** reward paid to persons who help to save a ship, goods, etc. voluntarily and at some danger to themselves. **Salvage money** cannot be paid to anyone responsible for the care of the ship. The reward is paid by the owners of the ship or the cargo and the salvors have a lien on the property rescued for the salvage money. **4 a** saving and use of waste materials. **b** materials salvaged. *–v.* (**-ging**) **1** save from a wreck etc. **2** retrieve from a disaster etc. (*salvaged her pride*). □ **salvageable** *adj.* [Latin: related to SAVE[1]]

salvation /sæl'veɪʃ(ə)n/ *n.* **1** saving or being saved. **2** deliverance from sin and damnation. **3** religious conversion. **4** person or thing that saves. □ **salvationist** *n.* (esp. with ref. to the Salvation Army). [Latin: related to SAVE[1]]

Salvation Army *n.* worldwide evangelical Christian quasi-military organization helping the poor.

salve[1] *–n.* **1** healing ointment. **2** (often foll. by *for*) thing that soothes or consoles. *–v.* (**-ving**) soothe. [Old English]

salve[2] *v.* (**-ving**) save from wreck or fire etc. □ **salvable** *adj.* [back-formation from SALVAGE]

salver *n.* tray, esp. silver, for drinks, letters, etc. [Spanish *salva* assaying of food]

salvia /'sælvɪə/ *n.* garden plant of the sage family with red or blue flowers. [Latin, = SAGE[1]]

salvo /'sælvəʊ/ *n.* (*pl.* **-es** or **-s**) **1** simultaneous discharge of guns etc. **2** round of applause. [Italian *salva*]

sal volatile /ˌsæl və'lætɪlɪ/ *n.* solution of ammonium carbonate used as smelling-salts. [Latin, = volatile salt]

♦ **salvor** /'sælvə(r)/ *n.* person who effects or assists in the salvage of cargo etc. See SALVAGE *n.* 3.

Salzburg /'sæltsbɜːg, 'sɑː-/ **1** province in central Austria; pop. (est. 1994) 504 258. **2** its capital city, noted for its music festivals; manufactures include textiles and leather goods; pop. (1991) 143 971.

SAM *abbr.* surface-to-air missile.

S. Am. *abbr.* South America(n).

SAMA *abbr.* Saudi Arabian Monetary Agency.

Samar /'sɑːmɑː(r)/ third-largest island in the Philippines; pop. (est. 1985) 1 300 000; chief town, Catbalogan. Rice, coconuts, and hemp are grown, and there is some mining (of copper and iron ore).

Samara /sə'mɑːrə/ (formerly (1935–91) **Kuibishev**) industrial city in SW Russia, a port on the River Volga; activities include oil refining and market gardening; pop. (est. 1995) 1 184 000.

Samarinda /ˌsæmə'rɪndə/ city in Indonesia, capital of the province of East Kalimantan; pop. (1990) 335 016.

Samaritan /sə'mærɪt(ə)n/ *n.* **1** (in full **good Samaritan**) charitable or helpful person (Luke 10:33 etc.). **2** member of an organization that listens to suicidal people. [originally = inhabitant of ancient Samaria]

samarium /sə'meərɪəm/ *n.* metallic element of the lanthanide series. [ultimately from *Samarski*, name of an official]

Samarkand /ˌsæmɑː'kænd/ city in E Uzbekistan; manufactures include cotton, silk, wine, and metal goods; pop. (1996) 368 000.

samba /'sæmbə/ *–n.* **1** ballroom dance of Brazilian origin. **2** music for this. *–v.* (**-bas, -baed** or **-ba'd** /-bəd/, **-baing** /-bəɪŋ/) dance the samba. [Portuguese]

same *–adj.* **1** (often prec. by *the*) identical; not different (*on the same bus*). **2** unvarying (*same old story*). **3** (usu. prec. by *this, these, that, those*) just mentioned (*this same man later died*). *–pron.* (prec. by *the*) **1** the same person or thing. **2** *Law* or *archaic* the person or thing just mentioned. *–adv.* (usu. prec. by *the*) similarly; in the same way

---

Samoa /sə'məʊə/, **Independent State of (formerly (1962–1997) Western Samoa)** country consisting of a group of nine islands in the SW Pacific. The economy is based on agriculture: coconut oil and cream, copra, taro, and cocoa are the chief exports. Forestry, fishing, tourism, and manufacturing industry are developing sources of revenue. Beer and cigarettes are among the chief manufactured exports. Discovered by the Dutch in the early 18th century, the islands were administered by Germany from 1900. After the First World War they were mandated to New Zealand, becoming an independent state in 1962. The country was treated as a member of the Commonwealth from 1962 until formal admission in 1970. Universal suffrage was introduced following a referendum in 1990. In 1997 the name of the country was changed to Independent State of Samoa. Head of state, HH Malietoa Tanumafili II; prime minister, Tofilau Eti Alesana; capital, Apia.

languages	Samoan, English
currency	tala (WS$) of 100 sene
pop. (1996)	167 400
GNP (1994)	US$163M
literacy	100%
life expectancy	67 (m); 71 (f)

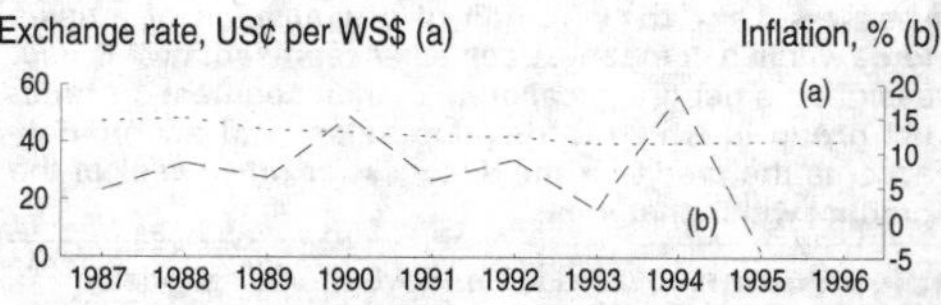

(*feel the same*). □ **all** (or **just**) **the same 1** nevertheless. **2** emphatically the same. **at the same time 1** simultaneously. **2** notwithstanding. **be all** (or **just**) the same to make no difference to. **same here** *colloq.* the same applies to me. □ **sameness** *n.* [Old Norse]

samizdat /ˌsæmɪz'dæt/ *n.* clandestine publication of banned literature. [Russian]

Samoa /sə'məʊə/ group of Polynesian islands. The E part (**American Samoa**), containing the island of Tutuila, is a US territory; pop. (est. 1990) 46 773; capital, Pago Pago. Fish canning is a major industry and canned tuna the chief export. See also SAMOA. □ **Samoan** *adj.* & *n.*

Samos /'seɪmɒs/ Greek island in the Aegean Sea; pop. (1991) 41 965.

samosa /sə'məʊsə/ *n.* fried triangular pastry containing spiced vegetables or meat. [Hindustani]

samovar /'sæməˌvɑː(r)/ *n.* Russian tea-urn. [Russian]

Samoyed /'sæməˌjed/ *n.* **1** member of a people of northern Siberia. **2** (also **samoyed**) dog of a white Arctic breed. [Russian]

sampan /'sæmpæn/ *n.* small boat used in the Far East. [Chinese]

samphire /'sæmˌfaɪə(r)/ *n.* edible maritime rock-plant. [French, = St Peter('s herb)]

sample /'sɑːmp(ə)l/ –*n.* **1** small representative part or quantity, as of a product, commodity, etc. given to potential buyers to enable them to test its suitability. See also SALE BY SAMPLE. **2** *Statistics* small group of items or people selected from a larger group to represent the characteristics of the larger group. Samples are often used in marketing research because it is not feasible to interview every member of a particular market; however, conclusions about a market drawn from a sample always contain a sampling error and must be used with caution. In general, the larger the sample, the more accurate will be the conclusions drawn from it. See also RANDOM SAMPLE; SAMPLING 2. **3** illustrative or typical example. –*v.* (**-ling**) **1** take or give samples of. **2** try the qualities of. **3** experience briefly. [Anglo-French: related to EXAMPLE]

sampler[1] *n.* piece of embroidery using various stitches as a specimen of proficiency. [French: related to EXEMPLAR]

sampler[2] *n.* **1** person or thing that samples. **2** *US* collection of representative items etc.

sampling *n.* **1** technique of digitally encoding a piece of sound and re-using it as part of a composition or recording. **2** process by which a sample of people or items are selected for a particular study. Measurements made on the sample will provide information on similar people or items not in the sample. In **quota sampling**, used in marketing research, the composition of the sample reflects the known structure of the market. Thus, if it is known that 60% of purchasers of household DIY products are men, any sample would reflect this. An alternative sampling procedure is **random sampling**, which ensures that everyone in a particular market has an equal chance of selection (see also RANDOM SAMPLE). Although more accurate than quota sampling, it is also more expensive.

Samson /'sæms(ə)n/ *n.* person of great strength. [*Samson* in the Old Testament]

samurai /'sæmʊˌraɪ/ *n.* (*pl.* same) **1** Japanese army officer. **2** *hist.* member of a Japanese military caste. [Japanese]

♦ **samurai bond** *n.* bond issued in Japan by a foreign institution. It is denominated in yen and can be bought by non-residents of Japan.

Sana'a /sæ'nɑː, 'sɑːnə/ capital of Yemen and of the former Yemen Arab Republic (North Yemen); pop. (est. 1995) 972 000.

San Antonio /sæn æn'təʊnɪˌəʊ/ industrial city in the US, in S central Texas, and a trading centre for the surrounding agricultural area; pop. (est. 1994) 998 905.

sanatorium /ˌsænə'tɔːrɪəm/ *n.* (*pl.* **-s** or **-ria**) **1** residential clinic esp. for convalescents and the chronically sick. **2** room etc. for sick people in a school etc. [Latin *sano* heal]

San Carlos de Bariloche /sæn 'kɑːlɒs deɪ ˌbærɪ'ləʊtʃɪ/ principal Andean skiing resort of Argentina, in the province of Río Negro; pop. (1980) 48 200.

sanctify /'sæŋktɪˌfaɪ/ *v.* (**-ies**, **-ied**) **1** consecrate; treat as holy. **2** free from sin. **3** justify; sanction. □ **sanctification** /-fɪ'keɪʃ(ə)n/ *n.* [Latin *sanctus* holy]

sanctimonious /ˌsæŋktɪ'məʊnɪəs/ *adj.* ostentatiously pious. □ **sanctimoniously** *adv.* **sanctimoniousness** *n.* **sanctimony** /'sæŋktɪmənɪ/ *n.* [Latin *sanctimonia* sanctity]

sanction /'sæŋkʃ(ə)n/ –*n.* **1** approval by custom or tradition; express permission. **2** confirmation of a law etc. **3** penalty for disobeying a law or rule, or a reward for obeying it. **4** *Ethics* moral force encouraging obedience to any rule of conduct. **5** (esp. in *pl.*) (esp. economic) action by a state against another to abide by an international agreement etc. See ECONOMIC SANCTIONS. –*v.* **1** authorize or agree to (an action etc.). **2** ratify; make (a law etc.) binding. [Latin *sancio sanct-* make sacred]

sanctity /'sæŋktɪtɪ/ *n.* holiness, sacredness; inviolability. [Latin *sanctus* holy]

sanctuary /'sæŋktʃʊərɪ/ *n.* (*pl.* **-ies**) **1** holy place. **2 a** holiest part of a temple etc. **b** chancel. **3** place where birds, wild animals, etc. are bred and protected. **4** place of refuge.

sanctum /'sæŋktəm/ *n.* (*pl.* **-s**) **1** holy place. **2** *colloq.* study, den.

sand –*n.* **1** fine loose grains resulting from the erosion of esp. siliceous rocks and forming the seashore, deserts, etc. **2** (in *pl.*) **a** grains of sand. **b** expanse of sand. **c** sandbank. –*v.* smooth with sandpaper or sand. [Old English]

sandal[1] /'sænd(ə)l/ *n.* shoe with an openwork upper or no upper, usu. fastened by straps. [Latin from Greek]

sandal[2] /'sænd(ə)l/ *n.* = SANDALWOOD. [Sanskrit *candana*]

sandal-tree *n.* tree yielding sandalwood.

sandalwood *n.* **1** scented wood of a sandal-tree. **2** perfume from this.

sandbag –*n.* bag filled with sand, used for temporary defences etc. –*v.* (**-gg-**) **1** defend or hit with sandbag(s). **2** *Finance* (of a target company) obstruct an unwelcome take-over bid by prolonging talks with the bidder, in the hope that a white knight will appear and make a more acceptable bid.

sandbank *n.* sand forming a shallow place in the sea or a river.

sandblast –*v.* roughen, treat, or clean with a jet of sand driven by compressed air or steam. –*n.* this jet. □ **sandblaster** *n.*

sandboy *n.* □ **happy as a sandboy** extremely happy or carefree. [probably = a boy hawking sand for sale]

sandcastle *n.* model castle made of sand at the seashore.

sand-dune *n.* (also **sand-hill**) = DUNE.

sander *n.* power tool for sanding.

S&FA *abbr.* shipping and forwarding agent(s).

S&H *abbr.* shipping and handling (charges).

San Diego /sæn dɪ'eɪgəʊ/ industrial city and naval port in the US, on the Pacific coast of S California; pop. (est. 1994) 1 151 977.

♦ **Sandilands Committee** /'sændɪˌlændz/ *n.* committee set up in 1975 by the UK government to consider the most appropriate way to account for the effects of inflation in the published accounts of companies. It recommended current-cost accounting in preference to the current-purchasing-power accounting favoured by the accountancy bodies. [*Sandilands*, name of committee chairman]

S&L *abbr.* = SAVINGS AND LOAN ASSOCIATION.

sandman *n.* imaginary person causing tiredness in children.

sand-martin *n.* bird nesting in sandy banks.

sandpaper –*n.* paper with an abrasive coating for smoothing or polishing. –*v.* rub with this.

sandpiper *n.* wading bird frequenting wet sandy areas.

sandpit *n.* pit containing sand, for children to play in.

sandstone *n.* sedimentary rock of compressed sand.

sandstorm *n.* storm with clouds of sand raised by the wind.

sandwich /ˈsænwɪdʒ/ –*n.* **1** two or more slices of bread with a filling. **2** layered cake with jam or cream. –*v.* **1** put (a thing, statement, etc.) between two of another character. **2** squeeze in between others (*sat sandwiched in the middle*). [from the Earl of *Sandwich*]

sandwich-board *n.* each of two boards worn front and back to carry advertisements.

sandwich course *n.* course with alternate periods of study at a college, university, etc. and supervised work experience in a factory or industrial organization. The course usu. lasts for five years, with six-monthly periods in both college and industry.

sandy *adj.* (**-ier**, **-iest**) **1** having much sand. **2 a** (of hair) reddish. **b** sand-coloured. □ **sandiness** *n.*

sane *adj.* **1** of sound mind; not mad. **2** (of views etc.) moderate, sensible. [Latin *sanus* healthy]

San Francisco /frænˈsɪskəʊ/ city and seaport in the US, on the coast of California, with a magnificent landlocked harbour entered by a channel called the Golden Gate; it has shipbuilding, food-processing, and petroleum-refining industries; pop. (est. 1994) 734 676.

sang *past* of SING.

sang-froid /sɑ̃ˈfrwɑː/ *n.* calmness in danger or difficulty. [French, = cold blood]

sangria /sæŋˈgriːə/ *n.* Spanish drink of red wine with lemonade, fruit, etc. [Spanish, = bleeding]

sanguinary /ˈsæŋgwɪnərɪ/ *adj.* **1** bloody. **2** bloodthirsty. [Latin *sanguis -guin-* blood]

sanguine /ˈsæŋgwɪn/ *adj.* **1** optimistic, confident. **2** (of the complexion) florid, ruddy.

Sanhedrin /ˈsænɪdrɪn/ *n.* highest court of justice and the supreme council in ancient Jerusalem. [Greek *sunedrion* council]

sanitarium /ˌsænɪˈteərɪəm/ *n.* (*pl.* **-s** or **-ria**) *US* = SANATORIUM. [related to SANITARY]

sanitary /ˈsænɪtərɪ/ *adj.* **1** (of conditions etc.) affecting health. **2** hygienic. □ **sanitariness** *n.* [Latin *sanitas*: related to SANE]

sanitary towel *n.* (*US* **sanitary napkin**) absorbent pad used during menstruation.

sanitation /ˌsænɪˈteɪʃ(ə)n/ *n.* **1** sanitary conditions. **2** maintenance etc. of these. **3** disposal of sewage and refuse etc.

sanitize /ˈsænɪˌtaɪz/ *v.* (also **-ise**) (**-zing** or **-sing**) **1** make sanitary; disinfect. **2** *colloq.* censor (information etc.) to make it more acceptable.

sanity /ˈsænɪtɪ/ *n.* **1** being sane. **2** moderation. [Latin *sanitas*: related to SANE]

San José /sæn xəʊˈzeɪ, həʊ-/ **1** capital and chief port of Costa Rica; pop. (1995) 321 193. **2** city in the US, in W California at the centre of 'Silicon Valley'; industries include electronics, aerospace, food processing, and wine; pop. (est. 1994) 816 884.

San Juan /sæn ˈxwɑːn, ˈhwɑːn/ capital and chief port of Puerto Rico; a centre of industry and tourism, it exports coffee, sugar, and tobacco; pop. (1990) 437 745.

sank *past* of SINK.

San Luis Potosí /sæn luːˈiːs ˌpɒtəʊˈsiː/ **1** state in N central Mexico; pop. (est. 1995) 2 191 712. **2** its capital, a silver-mining city; pop. (1990) 488 238.

San Pedro Sula /sæn ˌpedrəʊ ˈsuːlə/ industrial city in Honduras, a trading centre for the surrounding agricultural region (producing sugar cane and bananas); pop. (1994) 368 500.

San Salvador /sæn ˈsælvəˌdɔː(r)/ capital of El Salvador, with textile and food-processing industries; pop. (1992) 422 570.

sansculotte /ˌsænzkjʊˈlɒt/ *n.* (esp. in the French Revolution) extreme republican. [French, literally = 'without knee-breeches']

sanserif /sænˈserɪf/ *n.* (also **sans-serif**) form of type without serifs. [apparently from *sans* without, SERIF]

Sanskrit /ˈsænskrɪt/ –*n.* ancient and sacred language of the Hindus in India. –*adj.* of or in this language. [Sanskrit, = composed]

◆ ***sans recours*** /sɑ̃ rəˈkʊə(r)/ = without recourse (see RECOURSE). [French]

Santa Ana /ˌsæntə ˈænə/ city in El Salvador, a centre of the coffee trade; pop. (1992) 202 337.

Santa Claus /ˈsæntə ˌklɔːz/ *n.* person said to bring children presents on Christmas Eve. [Dutch, = St Nicholas]

Santa Cruz /ˌsæntə ˈkruːz/ commercial city in Bolivia, in the agricultural central region of the country; it has sugar-refining and cigarette-manufacturing industries; pop. (est. 1993) 767 260.

Santa Fé /ˌsæntə ˈfeɪ/ city and resort in the US, capital of New Mexico; pop. (est. 1994) 62 514.

Santander /ˌsæntænˈdeə(r)/ principal ferry port of N Spain, capital of the region of Cantabria; it has fishing and shipbuilding industries; pop. (est. 1994) 194 822.

Santiago /ˌsæntɪˈɑːgəʊ/ capital of Chile, in the centre of the country; industries include food processing, metallurgy, and textiles; pop. (est. 1995) 5 076 808.

Santiago de Compostela /deɪ ˌkɒmpɒˈstelə/ city in NW Spain, capital of Galicia region; pop. (1991) 87 472.

Santiago de Cuba /deɪ ˈkjuːbə/ second-largest city on the island of Cuba; sugar, coffee, tobacco, and metal ores are exported; pop. (est. 1994) 440 084.

Santo Domingo /ˌsæntəʊ dəˈmɪŋgəʊ/ capital and chief port of the Dominican Republic; pop. (1993) 2 138 262.

Santorini /ˌsæntɔːˈriːnɪ/ (Greek **Thera** or **Thira** /ˈθɪərə/) Greek island in the Cyclades group in the Aegean Sea; pop. (latest est.) 8000.

São Paulo /saʊ ˈpaʊləʊ/ largest city in Brazil and second-largest in South America; products include coffee, processed food, textiles, and electrical appliances; pop. (1991) 9 393 753 (metropolitan area, 1995) 16 417 000.

sap[1] –*n.* **1** vital juice circulating in plants. **2** vigour, vitality. **3** *slang* foolish person. –*v.* (**-pp-**) **1** drain or dry (wood) of sap. **2** weaken. [Old English]

sap[2] –*n.* tunnel or trench dug to get nearer to the enemy. –*v.* (**-pp-**) **1** dig saps. **2** undermine. [French *sappe* or Italian *zappa* spade]

sapient /ˈseɪpɪənt/ *adj. literary* **1** wise. **2** aping wisdom. □ **sapience** *n.* [Latin *sapio* be wise]

s.a.p.l. *abbr.* sailed as per list (i.e. Lloyd's List).

sapling *n.* young tree. [from SAP[1]]

San Marino /sæn mæˈriːnəʊ/, **Republic of** small landlocked republic in Italy, near Rimini on the Adriatic coast. The economy is based on agriculture, manufacturing industries, and tourism; exports include wine, wheat, dairy produce, wood, ceramics, furniture, textiles, and chemicals. San Marino is perhaps Europe's oldest state, claiming to have been independent almost continuously since its foundation in the 4th century; its independence was guaranteed by Italy in 1862. Heads of state, two regents elected at six-monthly intervals; capital, San Marino, pop. (est. 1991) 4179.

language	Italian
currency	Italian lira (L) of 100 centesimi
pop. (1996)	25 300
GDP (est. 1990)	L493.6B
literacy	99% (m); 97% (f)
life expectancy	77 (m); 85 (f)

---

sapper *n.* **1** person who digs saps. **2** soldier of the Royal Engineers (esp. as the official term for a private).

Sapphic /'sæfɪk/ *adj.* **1** of Sappho or her poetry. **2** lesbian. [Greek *Sappho*, poetess of Lesbos]

sapphire /'sæfaɪə(r)/ *–n.* **1** transparent blue precious stone. **2** its bright blue colour. *–adj.* (also **sapphire blue**) bright blue. [Greek *sappheiros* lapis lazuli]

Sapporo /sə'pɔːrəʊ/ city in N Japan, capital of the island of Hokkaido, a ski resort with sawmilling, flour-milling, and printing industries; pop. (1995) 1 756 968.

sappy *adj.* (**-ier, -iest**) **1** full of sap. **2** young and vigorous.

saprophyte /'sæprəˌfaɪt/ *n.* plant or micro-organism living on dead or decayed organic matter. [Greek *sapros* rotten, *phuō* grow]

saraband /'særəˌbænd/ *n.* **1** slow stately Spanish dance. **2** music for this. [Spanish *zarabanda*]

Saracen /'særəs(ə)n/ *n. hist.* Arab or Muslim at the time of the Crusades. [Greek *sarakénos*]

Saragossa /ˌsærə'gɒsə/ (Spanish **Zaragoza** /ˌθærə'gɒθə/) city in NE Spain, capital of Aragon region; products include paper and wine; pop. (est. 1994) 606 620.

Sarajevo /ˌsærə'jeɪvəʊ/ capital of the republic of Bosnia-Hercegovina; industries include brewing, sugar refining, and the manufacture of carpets and pottery, but a prolonged siege (1992–3) by Bosnian Serbs has devastated normal activities in the city; pop. (est. 1995) 250 000.

Saratov /sə'rætɒf/ industrial city in W Russia, on the River Volga; pop. (est. 1995) 895 000.

Sarawak /sə'rɑːwək/ state of Malaysia, on the NW coast of Borneo; pop. (1991) 1 648 217; capital, Kuching. The production and export of oil are major sources of revenue; agriculture produces rice, sago, pepper, and rubber, and forestry is also important.

sarcasm /'sɑːˌkæz(ə)m/ *n.* ironically scornful language. □ **sarcastic** /sɑː'kæstɪk/ *adj.* **sarcastically** /sɑː'kæstɪkəlɪ/ *adv.* [Greek *sarkazō* speak bitterly]

sarcoma /sɑː'kəʊmə/ *n.* (*pl.* **-s** or **-mata**) malignant tumour of connective tissue. [Greek *sarx sark-* flesh]

sarcophagus /sɑː'kɒfəgəs/ *n.* (*pl.* **-phagi** /-ˌgaɪ/) stone coffin. [Greek, = flesh-consumer]

sardine /sɑː'diːn/ *n.* (*pl.* same or **-s**) young pilchard etc. sold in closely packed tins. □ **like sardines** crowded close together. [French from Latin]

Sardinia /sɑː'dɪnɪə/ (Italian **Sardegna** /sɑː'deɪnjə/) large island in the Mediterranean Sea W of Italy, an autonomous region of Italy; pop. (est. 1994) 1 657 375; capital, Cagliari. Agricultural activities include sheep farming and the cultivation of cereals, vines, and olives; coal, lead, and zinc are mined, and there are chemical, petrochemical, and food-processing industries. Tourism is also important. □ **Sardinian** *adj.* & *n.*

sardonic /sɑː'dɒnɪk/ *adj.* bitterly mocking or cynical. □ **sardonically** *adv.* [Greek *sardonios* sardinian]

sardonyx /'sɑːdənɪks/ *n.* onyx in which white layers alternate with yellow or orange ones. [Greek *sardonux*]

sargasso /sɑː'gæsəʊ/ *n.* (*pl.* **-s** or **-es**) (also **sargassum**) (*pl.* **-gassa**) seaweed with berry-like air-vessels. [Portuguese]

sarge *n. slang* sergeant. [abbreviation]

Sargodha /sɑː'gəʊdə/ city in N Pakistan; pop. (1981) 294 000.

sari /'sɑːriː/ *n.* (*pl.* **-s**) length of cloth draped round the body, traditionally worn by women of the Indian subcontinent. [Hindi]

sarky /'sɑːkɪ/ *adj.* (**-ier, -iest**) *slang* sarcastic. [abbreviation]

Sarl. *abbr.* **1** (Italian) società a responsabilità limitata (= private limited company). **2** (also **Sàrl.**) (French) société à responsabilité limitée (= private limited company).

sarnie /'sɑːnɪ/ *n. colloq.* sandwich. [abbreviation]

sarong /sə'rɒŋ/ *n.* Malay and Javanese garment of a long strip of cloth tucked round the waist or under the armpits. [Malay]

sarsaparilla /ˌsɑːsəpə'rɪlə/ *n.* **1** preparation of the dried roots of various plants, esp. smilax, used to flavour some drinks and medicines and formerly as a tonic. **2** plant yielding this. [Spanish]

sarsen /'sɑːs(ə)n/ *n.* sandstone boulder carried by ice during a glacial period. [from SARACEN]

sarsenet /'sɑːsnɪt/ *n.* soft silk material used esp. for linings. [Anglo-French from *sarzin* SARACEN]

sartorial /sɑː'tɔːrɪəl/ *adj.* of men's clothes or tailoring. □ **sartorially** *adv.* [Latin *sartor* tailor]

SAS *abbr.* **1** Scandinavian Airline System. **2** Special Air Service.

Sas. *abbr.* (Italian) società in accomandita semplice (= limited partnership).

s.a.s.e. *abbr.* (also **SASE**) *US* self-addressed stamped envelope.

sash[1] *n.* strip or loop of cloth etc. worn over one shoulder or round the waist. [Arabic, = muslin]

sash[2] *n.* frame holding the glass in a sash-window. [from CHASSIS]

sashay /'sæʃeɪ/ *v.* esp. *US colloq.* walk or move ostentatiously, casually, or diagonally. [French *chassé*]

sash-cord *n.* strong cord attaching the sash-weights to a window sash.

sash-weight *n.* weight attached to each end of a window sash.

sash-window *n.* window sliding up and down in grooves.

Sask. *abbr.* Saskatchewan.

Saskatchewan /sə'skætʃɪwən/ province of central Canada; pop. (est. 1995) 1 015 600; capital, Regina. It has rich deposits of oil, natural gas, uranium, zinc, potash, copper, and other minerals; the S part of the province is an important wheat-growing area.

Saskatoon /ˌsæskə'tuːn/ industrial city in Canada, in S central Saskatchewan, at the heart of a major grain-producing region; city pop. (1991) 186 058; metropolitan area pop. 210 023. There are clothing and chemical industries, and potash and metals are produced.

sass *US colloq. –n.* impudence, cheek. *–v.* be impudent to. [var. of SAUCE]

sassafras /'sæsəˌfræs/ *n.* **1** small North American tree. **2** medicinal preparation from its leaves or bark. [Spanish or Portuguese]

Sassenach /'sæsəˌnæk/ *n. Scot. & Ir.* usu. *derog.* English person. [Gaelic *Sasunnoch*]

São Tomé and Príncipe /saʊ tʊ'meɪ, 'prɪnsɪpɪ/, **Democratic Republic of** country consisting of two islands in the Gulf of Guinea. It is primarily agricultural, producing cocoa, copra, palm oil, coffee, and bananas for export. Formerly an overseas province of Portugal, the islands became independent in 1975. President, Miguel Trovoada; prime minister, Raul Braganca Neto; capital, São Tomé, pop. (est. 1990) 25 000.

language	Portuguese
currency	dobra (Db) of 100 centavos
pop. (1996)	134 000
GNP (1994)	US$31M
literacy	70% (m); 39% (f)
life expectancy	61 (m); 65 (f)

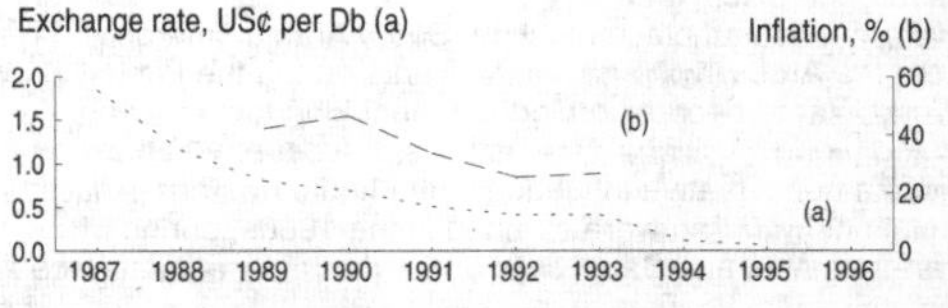

sassy *adj.* (**-ier, -iest**) esp. *US colloq.* impudent, cheeky. [var. of SAUCY]

SAT *abbr.* **1** Senior Member of the Association of Accounting Technicians. **2** /sæt/ standard assessment task.

Sat. *abbr.* Saturday.

sat *past* and *past part.* of SIT.

Satan /'seɪt(ə)n/ *n.* the Devil; Lucifer. [Hebrew, = enemy]

satanic /sə'tænɪk/ *adj.* of or like Satan; hellish; evil. □ **satanically** *adv.*

Satanism /'seɪtə,nɪz(ə)m/ *n.* **1** worship of Satan. **2** pursuit of evil. □ **Satanist** *n.* & *adj.*

satchel /'sætʃ(ə)l/ *n.* small shoulder-bag for carrying school-books etc. [Latin: related to SACK[1]]

sate *v.* (**-ting**) *formal* gratify fully; surfeit. [probably dial. *sade* satisfy]

sateen /sæ'tiːn/ *n.* glossy cotton fabric like satin. [*satin* after *velveteen*]

satellite /'sætə,laɪt/ *–n.* **1** celestial or artificial body orbiting the earth or another planet. **2** (in full **satellite state**) small country controlled by another. *–attrib. adj.* transmitted by satellite (*satellite television*). [Latin *satelles -lit-* attendant]

satellite dish *n.* dish-shaped aerial for receiving satellite television.

satiate /'seɪʃɪ,eɪt/ *v.* (**-ting**) = SATE. □ **satiable** /-ʃəb(ə)l/ *adj.* **satiation** /-'eɪʃ(ə)n/ *n.* [Latin *satis* enough]

satiety /sə'taɪɪtɪ/ *n. formal* being sated. [Latin: related to SATIATE]

satin /'sætɪn/ *–n.* silk etc. fabric glossy on one side. *–adj.* smooth as satin. □ **satiny** *adj.* [Arabic *zaitūnī*]

satinwood *n.* a kind of yellow glossy timber.

satire /'sætaɪə(r)/ *n.* **1** ridicule, irony, etc., used to expose folly or vice etc. **2** work using this. □ **satirical** /sə'tɪrɪk(ə)l/ *adj.* **satirically** /sə'tɪrɪkəlɪ/ *adv.* [Latin *satira* medley]

satirist /'sætərɪst/ *n.* **1** writer of satires. **2** satirical person.

satirize /'sætə,raɪz/ *v.* (also **-ise**) (**-zing** or **-sing**) attack or describe with satire.

satisfaction /,sætɪs'fækʃ(ə)n/ *n.* **1** satisfying or being satisfied (*derived great satisfaction*). **2** thing that satisfies (*is a great satisfaction to me*). **3** (foll. by *for*) atonement; compensation (*demanded satisfaction*).

satisfactory /,sætɪs'fæktərɪ/ *adj.* adequate; giving satisfaction. □ **satisfactorily** *adv.*

♦ **satisficing behaviour** /'sætɪs,faɪsɪŋ/ *n. Econ.* behaviour demonstrated by firms who pursue such goals as satisfactory profits and satisfactory growth when they are unable to maximize profits because of bounded rationality. This is an assumption that is probably more realistic than profit maximization. See also MANAGERIAL THEORY OF THE FIRM. [from SATISFY]

satisfy /'sætɪs,faɪ/ *v.* (**-ies, -ied**) **1 a** meet the expectations or desires of. **b** be adequate. **2** meet (an appetite or want). **3** rid (a person) of such an appetite or want. **4** pay (a debt or creditor). **5** adequately fulfil or comply with (conditions etc.). **6** (often foll. by *of, that*) convince, esp. with proof etc. □ **satisfy oneself** (often foll. by *that*) become certain. [Latin *satisfacio*]

satrap /'sætræp/ *n.* **1** provincial governor in the ancient Persian empire. **2** subordinate ruler. [Persian, = protector of the land]

satsuma /sæt'suːmə/ *n.* variety of tangerine. [*Satsuma*, province in Japan]

saturate /'sætʃə,reɪt/ *v.* (**-ting**) **1** fill with moisture. **2** (often foll. by *with*) fill to capacity. **3** cause (a substance etc.) to absorb, hold, etc. as much as possible of another substance etc. **4** supply (a market) beyond demand. **5** (as **saturated** *adj.*) (of fat molecules) containing the greatest number of hydrogen atoms. [Latin *satur* full]

saturation /,sætʃə'reɪʃ(ə)n/ *n.* saturating or being saturated.

saturation point *n.* stage beyond which no more can be absorbed or accepted.

Saturday /'sætə,deɪ/ *–n.* day of the week following Friday. *–adv. colloq.* **1** on Saturday. **2** (**Saturdays**) on Saturdays; each Saturday. [Latin: related to SATURNALIA]

saturnalia /,sætə'neɪlɪə/ *n.* (*pl.* same or **-s**) **1** (usu. **Saturnalia**) *Rom. Hist.* festival of Saturn in December, the predecessor of Christmas. **2** (as *sing.* or *pl.*) scene of wild revelry. [Latin, pl. from *Saturnus* Roman god]

saturnine /'sætə,naɪn/ *adj.* of gloomy temperament or appearance.

satyr /'sætə(r)/ *n.* **1** (in Greek and Roman mythology) woodland god with some horselike or goatlike features. **2** lecherous man. [Greek *saturos*]

sauce /sɔːs/ *–n.* **1** liquid or viscous accompaniment to a dish. **2** something adding piquancy or excitement. **3** *colloq.* impudence, impertinence, cheek. *–v.* (**-cing**) *colloq.* be impudent to; cheek. [Latin *salsus* salted]

sauce-boat *n.* jug or dish for serving sauces etc.

saucepan *n.* cooking pan, usu. round with a lid and a projecting handle, used on a hob.

saucer *n.* **1** shallow circular dish for standing a cup on. **2** thing of this shape. □ **saucerful** *n.* (*pl.* **-s**). [French *saussier*]

saucy *adj.* (**-ier, -iest**) impudent, cheeky. □ **saucily** *adv.* **sauciness** *n.*

sauerkraut /'saʊə,kraʊt/ *n.* German dish of pickled cabbage. [German]

sauna /'sɔːnə/ *n.* **1** Finnish-style steam bath. **2** building or room with this. [Finnish]

saunter /'sɔːntə(r)/ *–v.* walk slowly; stroll. *–n.* leisurely walk. [origin unknown]

Saudi Arabia /,saʊdɪ ə'reɪbɪə/, **Kingdom of** country in SW Asia occupying most of the Arabian peninsula. Since the Second World War the economy has been revolutionized by the exploitation of the area's oil resources, the export of crude oil now accounting for some 75% of the government's revenue and making Saudi Arabia the largest oil producer in the Middle East. Some of the oil is refined locally; other industries include petrochemicals, chemicals, steel production, and the manufacture of fertilizers, machinery, electrical equipment, and food products. Agriculture is largely restricted to irrigated land and the oases; livestock is reared on the pasture lands. Further mineral deposits have been discovered.

History. The birthplace of Islam, Saudi Arabia emerged from the Arab revolt against the Turks during the First World War to become an independent kingdom in 1932. Ruled along traditional Islamic lines, the country has exercised a conservative influence over Middle Eastern politics. Relations with Iran were strained in the 1980s, during the Iran-Iraq War, and Saudi support for the multinational force against Iraq in the Gulf War (1991) led to Iraqi rocket attacks on Saudi cities. Head of state and government, King Fahd Ibn Abdul Aziz; capital, Riyadh. □ **Saudi Arabian** *adj.* & *n.*

language	Arabic
currency	riyal (SRIs) of 100 halalah
pop. (1996)	18 426 000
GNP (1994)	US$126B
literacy	71% (m); 50% (f)
life expectancy	68 (m); 71 (f)

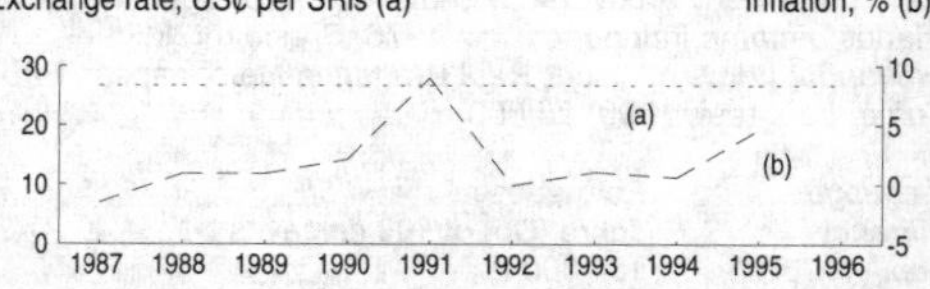

saurian /'sɔːrɪən/ *adj.* of or like a lizard. [Greek *saura* lizard]

sausage /'sɒsɪdʒ/ *n.* **1 a** seasoned minced meat etc. in a cylindrical edible skin. **b** piece of this. **2** sausage-shaped object. □ **not a sausage** *colloq.* nothing at all. [French *saussiche*]

sausage meat *n.* minced meat used in sausages etc.

sausage roll *n.* sausage meat in a pastry roll.

sauté /'səʊteɪ/ *–attrib. adj.* (esp. of potatoes) fried quickly in a little fat. *–n.* food so cooked. *–v.* (**sautéd** or **sautéed**) cook in this way. [French *sauter* jump]

Sauternes /səʊ'tɜːn/ *n.* sweet white wine from Sauternes in the Bordeaux region of France. [*Sauternes* in France]

s.a.v. *abbr.* stock at valuation.

savage /'sævɪdʒ/ *–adj.* **1** fierce; cruel. **2** wild; primitive. *–n.* **1** *derog.* member of a primitive tribe. **2** cruel or barbarous person. *–v.* (**-ging**) **1** attack and maul. **2** attack verbally. □ **savagely** *adv.* **savagery** *n.* (*pl.* **-ies**). [French from Latin *silva* a wood]

savannah /sə'vænə/ *n.* (also **savanna**) grassy plain in tropical and subtropical regions. [Spanish]

savant /'sæv(ə)nt, sæ'vɑ̃/ *n.* (*fem.* **savante** /'sæv(ə)nt/, /sæ'vɑ̃t/) learned person. [French]

save[1] *–v.* (**-ving**) **1** (often foll. by *from*) rescue or keep from danger, harm, etc. **2** (often foll. by *up*) keep (esp. money) for future use. **3 a** (often *refl.*) relieve (another or oneself) from spending (money, time, trouble, etc.); prevent exposure to (annoyance etc.). **b** obviate the need for. **4** preserve from damnation; convert. **5 a** avoid losing (a game, match, etc.). **b** prevent (a goal etc.) from being scored. *–n. Football* etc. prevention of a goal etc. □ **savable** *adj.* (also **saveable**). [Latin *salvo* from *salvus* safe]

save[2] *archaic* or *poet. –prep.* except; but. *–conj.* (often foll. by *for*) except; but. [Latin *salvo*, *salva*, ablative sing. of *salvus* safe]

◆ **save-as-you-earn** *n.* (also **SAYE**) method of making regular savings (not necessarily linked to earnings) which carries certain tax privileges. SAYE has been used to encourage tax-free savings in building societies or National Savings and also to encourage employees to acquire shares in their own organizations.

---

saveloy /'sævə,lɔɪ/ *n.* seasoned dried smoked sausage. [Italian *cervellata*]

saver *n.* **1** person who saves esp. money. **2** (often in *comb.*) thing that saves (time etc.). **3** cheap (esp. off-peak) fare.

saving *–adj.* (often in *comb.*) making economical use of (*labour-saving*). *–n.* **1** anything that is saved. **2** an economy (*a saving in expenses*). **3** (usu. in *pl.*) **a** money set aside by individuals, either for some special purpose or to provide an income at some time in the future (often after retirement). Money saved can be placed in a savings account with a bank or building society, invested in National Savings, or used to purchase securities. Savings are also used to buy pensions, annuities, various kinds of bonds, and endowment assurance. **b** *Econ.* residue remaining from income after expenditure on consumption (see also SAVINGS RATIO). Savings are an important concept in macroeconomics as the level of savings in an economy determines the resources available for investment. If, for example, firms plan to invest more than households save, in an open economy resources will have to be borrowed from overseas. Governments may also force individuals in the economy to save by means of taxation, which is subsequently used for investment. **4** act of preserving or rescuing. *–prep.* **1** except. **2** without offence to (*saving your presence*).

saving grace *n.* redeeming quality.

◆ **savings account** *n.* bank or building-society account into which personal savings are paid. Interest paid on a savings account is usu. higher than that paid on a deposit account and withdrawals are usu. restricted. Banks and building societies now offer a wide range of accounts with interest depending on the sums invested and the withdrawal terms.

◆ **savings and loan association** *n.* (also **S&L**) *US* building society. It usu. offers loans with a fixed rate of interest and has greater investment flexibility than a UK building society.

◆ **savings bank** *n.* bank paying interest on small deposits.

◆ **savings certificate** *n.* interest-bearing certificate issued by the UK government to savers. See NATIONAL SAVINGS.

◆ **savings ratio** *n. Econ.* ratio of savings by individuals and households to disposable income. Savings are estimated in the national income accounts by deducting consumers' expenditure (see CONSUMPTION 6) from disposable income. Variations in the savings ratio reflect the changing preferences of individuals between present and future consumption. Countries (e.g. Japan) with very high savings ratios have tended to experience faster growth in GDP than countries (e.g. the US) with low savings ratios.

---

saviour /'seɪvjə(r)/ *n.* (*US* **savior**) **1** person who saves from danger etc. **2** (**Saviour**) (prec. by *the*, *our*) Christ. [Latin: related to SAVE[1]]

savoir faire /,sævwɑː 'feə(r)/ *n.* ability to behave appropriately; tact. [French]

Savonlinna /,sɑːvɒn'liːnə/ (Swedish **Nyslott** /'niːslɒt/) town in SE Finland, in Mikkeli province, famous for its annual opera festival; pop. (1987) 28 510.

savor *US* var. of SAVOUR.

savory[1] /'seɪvərɪ/ *n.* (*pl.* **-ies**) aromatic herb used esp. in cookery. [Latin *satureia*]

savory[2] *US* var. of SAVOURY.

savour /'seɪvə(r)/ (*US* **savor**) *–n.* **1** characteristic taste, flavour, etc. **2** hint of a different quality etc. in something. *–v.* **1** appreciate and enjoy (food, an experience, etc.). **2** (foll. by *of*) imply or suggest (a specified quality). [Latin *sapor*]

savoury /'seɪvərɪ/ (*US* **savory**) *–adj.* **1** having an appetizing taste or smell. **2** (of food) salty or piquant, not sweet. **3** pleasant; acceptable. *–n.* (*pl.* **-ies**) savoury dish. □ **savouriness** *n.*

savoy /sə'vɔɪ/ *n.* cabbage with wrinkled leaves. [*Savoy* in SE France]

savvy /'sævɪ/ *slang –v.* (**-ies, -ied**) know. *–n.* knowingness; understanding. *–adj.* (**-ier, -iest**) *US* knowing; wise. [Pidgin alteration of Spanish *sabe usted* you know]

saw[1] *–n.* **1** hand tool with a toothed blade used to cut esp. wood with a to-and-fro movement. **2** power tool with a toothed rotating disk or moving band, for cutting. *–v.* (*past part.* **sawn** or **sawed**) **1** cut (wood etc.) or make (boards etc.) with a saw. **2** use a saw. **3 a** move with a sawing motion (*sawing away on his violin*). **b** divide (the air etc.) with gesticulations. [Old English]

saw[2] *past* of SEE[1].

saw[3] *n.* proverb; maxim. [Old English: related to SAY]

sawdust *n.* powdery wood particles produced in sawing.

sawfish *n.* (*pl.* same or **-es**) large marine fish with a toothed flat snout.

sawmill *n.* factory for sawing planks.

sawn *past part.* of SAW[1].

sawn-off *adj.* (*US* **sawed-off**) (of a shotgun) with part of the barrel sawn off.

sawtooth *adj.* (also **sawtoothed**) serrated.

sawyer *n.* person who saws timber, esp. for a living.

sax *n. colloq.* saxophone. [abbreviation]

saxe /sæks/ *n.* & *adj.* (in full **saxe blue**; as adj. often hyphenated) light greyish blue colour. [French, = Saxony]

saxifrage /'sæksɪ,freɪdʒ/ *n.* rock-plant with small white, yellow, or red flowers. [Latin *saxum* rock, *frango* break]

Saxon /'sæks(ə)n/ *–n.* **1** *hist.* **a** member of the Germanic people that conquered parts of England in the 5th–6th centuries. **b** (usu. **Old Saxon**) language of the Saxons.

2 = ANGLO-SAXON. –*adj.* **1** *hist.* of the Saxons. **2** = ANGLO-SAXON. [Latin *Saxo -onis*]

Saxony /'sæksənɪ/ **1** state (*Land*) in E Germany; pop. (est. 1990) 5 000 000; capital, Dresden. **2** see LOWER SAXONY.

Saxony-Anhalt /'ɑːnhɑːlt/ state (*Land*) in E Germany; pop. (est. 1995) 2 759 200; capital, Magdeburg.

saxophone /'sæksəˌfəʊn/ *n.* metal woodwind reed instrument used esp. in jazz. □ **saxophonist** /-'sɒfənɪst/ *n.* [*Sax*, name of the maker]

say –*v.* (*3rd sing. present* **says** /sez/; *past* and *past part.* **said** /sed/) **1** (often foll. by *that*) **a** utter (specified words); remark. **b** express (*say what you feel*). **2** (often foll. by *that*) **a** state; promise or prophesy. **b** have specified wording; indicate (*clock says ten to six*). **3** (in *passive*; usu. foll. by *to* + infin.) be asserted (*is said to be old*). **4** (foll. by *to* + infin.) *colloq.* tell to do (*he said to hurry*). **5** convey (information) (*spoke, but said little*). **6** offer as an argument or excuse (*much to be said in favour of it*). **7** (often *absol.*) give an opinion or decision as to (*hard to say*). **8** take as an example or as near enough (*paid, say, £20*). **9** recite or repeat (prayers, Mass, tables, a lesson, etc.). **10** convey (inner meaning etc.) (*what is the poem saying?*). **11** (**the said**) *Law* or *joc.* the previously mentioned. –*n.* **1** opportunity to express a view (*let him have his say*). **2** share in a decision (*had no say in it*). □ **I'll say** *colloq.* yes indeed. **I say!** exclamation of surprise etc. or drawing attention. **that is to say** in other words, more explicitly. [Old English]

SAYE *abbr.* = SAVE-AS-YOU-EARN.

saying *n.* maxim, proverb, etc. □ **go without saying** be too obvious to need mention.

◆ **Say's law** /seɪz/ *n. Econ.* law that supply creates its own demand, suggesting that there is never any barrier to achieving a perfectly competitive Pareto-optimal general equilibrium (see PARETO OPTIMALITY). The implication that in these circumstances involuntary unemployment is impossible was denied by Keynes. Say's law is generally considered too strong, since Walras' law is sufficient to demonstrate the possibility of a full employment equilibrium. [*Say*, name of an economist]

---

say-so *n. colloq.* **1** power of decision. **2** mere assertion (*his say-so is not enough*).

Sb *symb.* antimony. [Latin *stibium*]

SBA *abbr.* (in the US) Small Business Administration.

SBAC *abbr.* Society of British Aerospace Companies. [formerly *S*ociety of *B*ritish *A*ircraft *C*onstructors]

SBIC *abbr.* (in the US) small business investment company.

SBLI *abbr. US* savings bank life insurance.

SBU *abbr.* = STRATEGIC BUSINESS UNIT.

SC *abbr.* & *US postcode* South Carolina.

Sc *symb.* scandium.

sc. *abbr.* scilicet.

s.c. *abbr.* **1** salvage charges. **2** small capitals.

s/c *abbr.* (French) *Commerce* son compte (= (on) his or her account).

scab –*n.* **1** crust over a healing cut, sore, etc. **2** (often *attrib.*) *colloq. derog.* blackleg. **3** skin disease, esp. in animals. **4** fungous plant disease. –*v.* (**-bb-**) **1** *colloq. derog.* act as a blackleg. **2** form a scab, heal over. □ **scabby** *adj.* (**-ier, -iest**). [Old Norse: cf. SHABBY]

scabbard /'skæbəd/ *n. hist.* sheath of a sword etc. [Anglo-French]

scabies /'skeɪbiːz/ *n.* contagious skin disease causing itching. [Latin]

scabious /'skeɪbɪəs/ *n.* plant with esp. blue pincushion-shaped flowers. [medieval Latin *scabiosa* (*herba*) named as curing scabies]

scabrous /'skeɪbrəs/ *adj.* **1** rough, scaly. **2** indecent, salacious. [Latin]

scaffold /'skæfəʊld/ *n.* **1** *hist.* platform for the execution of criminals. **2** = SCAFFOLDING. [Romanic: related to EX-[1], CATAFALQUE]

scaffolding *n.* **1 a** temporary structure of poles, planks, etc., for building work. **b** materials for this. **2** any temporary framework.

scalar /'skeɪlə(r)/ *Math.* & *Physics* –*adj.* (of a quantity) having only magnitude, not direction. –*n.* scalar quantity. [Latin: related to SCALE[3]]

scalawag var. of SCALLYWAG.

scald /skɔːld, skɒld/ –*v.* **1** burn (the skin etc.) with hot liquid or steam. **2** heat (esp. milk) to near boiling-point. **3** (usu. foll. by *out*) clean with boiling water. –*n.* burn etc. caused by scalding. [Latin *excaldo* from *calidus* hot]

scale[1] –*n.* **1** each of the thin horny plates protecting the skin of fish and reptiles. **2** something resembling this. **3** white deposit formed in a kettle etc. by hard water. **4** tartar formed on teeth. –*v.* (**-ling**) **1** remove scale(s) from. **2** form or come off in scales. □ **scaly** *adj.* (**-ier, -iest**). [French *escale*]

scale[2] *n.* **1 a** (often in *pl.*) weighing machine. **b** (also **scale-pan**) each of the dishes on a simple balance. **2** (**the Scales**) zodiacal sign or constellation Libra. □ **tip** (or **turn) the scales 1** be the decisive factor. **2** (usu. foll. by *at*) weigh. [Old Norse *skál* bowl]

scale[3] –*n.* **1** graded classification system (*high on the social scale*). **2 a** (often *attrib.*) ratio of reduction or enlargement in a map, model, picture, etc. (*on a scale of one inch to the mile*; *a scale model*). **b** relative dimensions. **3** *Mus.* set of notes at fixed intervals, arranged in order of pitch. **4 a** set of marks on a line used in measuring etc. **b** rule determining the distances between these. **c** rod etc. on which these are marked. –*v.* (**-ling**) **1 a** climb (a wall, height, etc.). **b** climb (the social scale, heights of ambition, etc.). **2** represent proportionally; reduce to a common scale. □ **in scale** in proportion. **scale down** (or **up**) make or become smaller (or larger) in proportion. **to scale** uniformly in proportion. [Latin *scala* ladder]

◆ **scale effect** = ECONOMIES OF SCALE.

---

scalene /'skeɪliːn/ *adj.* (esp. of a triangle) having unequal sides. [Greek *skalēnos* unequal]

scallion /'skæljən/ *n.* esp. *US* shallot; spring onion etc. [Latin from *Ascalon* in ancient Palestine]

scallop /'skæləp, 'skɒl-/ (also **scollop** /'skɒl-/) –*n.* **1** edible mollusc with two fan-shaped ridged shells. **2** (in full **scallop shell**) single shell of a scallop, often used for cooking or serving food in. **3** (in *pl.*) ornamental edging of semicircular curves. –*v.* (**-p-**) ornament with scallops. □ **scalloping** *n.* (in sense 3 of *n.*). [French ESCALOPE]

scallywag /'skælɪˌwæg/ *n.* (also **scalawag** /'skælə-/) scamp, rascal. [origin unknown]

scalp –*n.* **1** skin on the head, with the hair etc. attached. **2** *hist.* this cut off as a trophy by an American Indian. –*v.* **1** *hist.* take the scalp of (an enemy). **2** *US colloq.* resell (shares etc.) at a high or quick profit. [probably Scandinavian]

scalpel /'skælp(ə)l/ *n.* surgeon's small sharp knife. [Latin *scalpo* scratch]

◆ **scalper** *n.* trader in futures or options who deals frequently and may only hold a position for minutes.

---

scam *n. US slang* trick, fraud. [origin unknown]

scamp *n. colloq.* rascal; rogue. [probably Dutch]

scamper –*v.* run and skip. –*n.* act of scampering. [perhaps from SCAMP]

scampi /'skæmpɪ/ *n.pl.* large prawns. [Italian]

scan –*v.* (**-nn-**) **1** look at intently or quickly. **2** (of a verse etc.) be metrically correct. **3 a** examine (a surface etc.) to detect radioactivity etc. **b** traverse (a particular region) with a radar etc. beam. **4** resolve (a picture) into its elements of light and shade for esp. television transmission. **5** analyse the metrical structure of (verse). **6** obtain an image of (part of the body) using a scanner. –*n.* **1** scanning. **2** image obtained by scanning. [Latin *scando* climb, scan]

scandal /'skænd(ə)l/ *n.* **1** cause of public outrage. **2**

outrage etc. so caused. **3** malicious gossip. □ **scandalous** *adj.* **scandalously** *adv.* [Greek *skandalon*, = snare]

scandalize *v.* (also **-ise**) (**-zing** or **-sing**) offend morally; shock.

scandalmonger *n.* person who habitually spreads scandal.

Scandinavia /ˌskændɪˈneɪvɪə/ peninsula in NW Europe occupied by Norway and Sweden. The name often refers to these countries together with Denmark, Finland, and Iceland, considered as a cultural unit.

Scandinavian *–n.* **1 a** native or inhabitant of Scandinavia. **b** person of Scandinavian descent. **2** family of languages of Scandinavia. *–adj.* of Scandinavia. [Latin]

scandium /ˈskændɪəm/ *n.* metallic element occurring naturally in lanthanide ores. [Latin *Scandia* Scandinavia]

scanner *n.* **1** device for scanning or systematically examining all the parts of something. **2** machine for measuring radiation, ultrasound reflections, etc. from the body as a diagnostic aid.

scansion /ˈskænʃ(ə)n/ *n.* metrical scanning of verse. [Latin: related to SCAN]

scant *adj.* barely sufficient; deficient. [Old Norse]

scanty *adj.* (**-ier, -iest**) **1** of small extent or amount. **2** barely sufficient. □ **scantily** *adv.* **scantiness** *n.*

scapegoat /ˈskeɪpgəʊt/ *n.* person blamed for others' shortcomings (with ref. to Lev. 16). [obsolete *scape* escape]

scapula /ˈskæpjʊlə/ *n.* (*pl.* **-lae** /-ˌliː/ or **-s**) shoulder-blade. [Latin]

scapular /ˈskæpjʊlə(r)/ *–adj.* of the shoulder or shoulder-blade. *–n.* short monastic cloak.

scar[1] *–n.* **1** usu. permanent mark on the skin from a wound etc. **2** emotional damage from grief etc. **3** sign of damage. **4** mark left on a plant by the loss of a leaf etc. *–v.* (**-rr-**) **1** (esp. as **scarred** *adj.*) mark with a scar or scars (*scarred for life*). **2** form a scar. [French *eschar(r)e*]

scar[2] *n.* (also **scaur**) steep craggy outcrop of a mountain or cliff. [Old Norse, = reef]

scarab /ˈskærəb/ *n.* **1 a** sacred dung-beetle of ancient Egypt. **b** a kind of beetle. **2** ancient Egyptian gem cut in the form of a beetle. [Latin *scarabaeus* from Greek]

scarce /skeəs/ *–adj.* **1** (usu. *predic.*) (esp. of food, money, etc.) in short supply. **2** rare. *–adv. archaic* or *literary* scarcely. □ **make oneself scarce** *colloq.* keep out of the way; surreptitiously disappear. [French *scars* Latin *excerpto* EXCERPT]

scarcely *adv.* **1** hardly, only just (*had scarcely arrived*). **2** surely not (*can scarcely have said so*). **3** esp. *iron.* not (*scarcely expected to be insulted*).

scarcity *n.* (*pl.* **-ies**) **1** (often foll. by *of*) lack or shortage, esp. of food. **2** *Econ.* condition that exists if more of a good or service is demanded than can be produced. As human needs are virtually unlimited and resources are finite, most goods and services are, in the economic sense, scarce. In a free economy, allocation of scarce resources is controlled by the price mechanism; in a controlled economy, central government has to decide how resources are to be allocated.

scare /skeə(r)/ *–v.* (**-ring**) **1** frighten, esp. suddenly. **2** (as **scared** *adj.*) (usu. foll. by *of*, or *to* + infin.) frightened; terrified. **3** (usu. foll. by *away*, *off*, *up*, etc.) drive away by frightening. **4** become scared (*they don't scare easily*). *–n.* **1** sudden attack of fright. **2** alarm caused by rumour etc. (*a measles scare*). [Old Norse]

scarecrow *n.* **1** human figure dressed in old clothes and set up in a field to scare birds away. **2** *colloq.* badly-dressed, grotesque-looking, or very thin person.

scaremonger *n.* person who spreads alarming rumours. □ **scaremongering** *n.*

scarf[1] *n.* (*pl.* **scarves** /skɑːvz/ or **-s**) piece of material worn esp. round the neck or over the head, for warmth or ornament. [French *escarpe*]

scarf[2] *–v.* join the ends of (timber etc.) by bevelling or notching them to fit and then bolting them etc. *–n.* (*pl.* **-s**) joint made by scarfing. [probably French *escarf*]

scarify[1] /ˈskærɪˌfaɪ/ *v.* (**-ies, -ied**) **1 a** make slight incisions in. **b** cut off skin from. **2** hurt by severe criticism etc. **3** loosen (soil). □ **scarification** /-fɪˈkeɪʃ(ə)n/ *n.* [Greek *skariphos* stylus]

scarify[2] /ˈskeərɪˌfaɪ/ *v.* (**-ies, -ied**) *colloq.* scare.

scarlatina /ˌskɑːləˈtiːnə/ *n.* = SCARLET FEVER. [Italian: related to SCARLET]

scarlet /ˈskɑːlət/ *–adj.* of brilliant red tinged with orange. *–n.* **1** scarlet colour or pigment. **2** scarlet clothes or material (*dressed in scarlet*). [French *escarlate*]

scarlet fever *n.* infectious bacterial fever with a scarlet rash.

scarlet pimpernel *n.* wild plant with small esp. scarlet flowers.

scarlet woman *n. derog.* promiscuous woman, prostitute.

scarp *–n.* steep slope, esp. the inner side of a ditch in a fortification. *–v.* make perpendicular or steep. [Italian *scarpa*]

scarper *v. slang* run away, escape. [probably Italian *scappare* escape]

scarves *pl.* of SCARF[1].

scary /ˈskeərɪ/ *adj.* (**-ier, -iest**) *colloq.* frightening.

scat[1] *v.* (**-tt-**) (usu. in *imper.*) *colloq.* depart quickly. [perhaps an abbreviation of SCATTER]

scat[2] *–n.* wordless jazz singing. *–v.* (**-tt-**) sing scat. [probably imitative]

scathing /ˈskeɪðɪŋ/ *adj.* witheringly scornful. □ **scathingly** *adv.* [Old Norse]

scatology /skæˈtɒlədʒɪ/ *n.* excessive interest in excrement or obscenity. □ **scatological** /-təˈlɒdʒɪk(ə)l/ *adj.* [Greek *skōr skat-* dung]

scatter *–v.* **1 a** throw about; strew. **b** cover by scattering. **2 a** (cause to) move in flight etc.; disperse. **b** disperse or cause (hopes, clouds, etc.) to disperse. **3** (as **scattered** *adj.*) wide apart or sporadic (*scattered villages*). **4** *Physics* deflect or diffuse (light, particles, etc.). *–n.* **1** act of scattering. **2** small amount scattered. **3** extent of distribution. [probably var. of SHATTER]

scatterbrain *n.* person lacking concentration. □ **scatterbrained** *adj.*

scatty /ˈskætɪ/ *adj.* (**-ier, -iest**) *colloq.* scatterbrained. □ **scattily** *adv.* **scattiness** *n.*

scaur var. of SCAR[2].

scavenge /ˈskævɪndʒ/ *v.* (**-ging**) (usu. foll. by *for*; also *absol.*) search for and collect (discarded items). [back-formation from SCAVENGER]

scavenger *n.* **1** person who scavenges. **2** animal feeding on carrion, refuse, etc. [Anglo-French *scawager*: related to SHOW]

Sc.D. *abbr.* Doctor of Science. [Latin *scientiae doctor*]

SCE *abbr.* Scottish Certificate of Education.

scenario /sɪˈnɑːrɪəʊ/ *n.* (*pl.* **-s**) **1** outline of the plot of a play, film, etc. **2** postulated sequence of future events. [Italian]

■ **Usage** *Scenario* should not be used to mean 'situation', as in *it was an unpleasant scenario.*

scene /siːn/ *n.* **1** place in which events, real or fictional, occur. **2 a** incident, real or fictional. **b** description of this. **3** public display of emotion, temper, etc. (*made a scene in the restaurant*). **4 a** continuous portion of a play in a fixed setting; subdivision of an act. **b** similar section of a film, book, etc. **5 a** piece of scenery used in a play. **b** these collectively. **6** landscape or view. **7** *colloq.* **a** area of interest (*not my scene*). **b** milieu (*well-known on the jazz scene*). □ **behind the scenes 1** offstage. **2** secret; secretly. **set the scene** describe the location of events. [Greek *skēnē* tent, stage]

scenery *n.* **1** natural features of a landscape, esp. when picturesque. **2** painted backcloths, props, etc., used as the background in a play etc. [Italian: related to SCENARIO]

scene-shifter *n.* person who moves scenery in a theatre.

scenic *adj.* **1 a** picturesque. **b** of natural scenery. **2** of or on the stage. □ **scenically** *adv.*

scent /sent/ *–n.* **1** distinctive, esp. pleasant, smell. **2** = PERFUME *n.* 2. **3 a** perceptible smell left by an animal. **b** clues etc. leading to a discovery. **c** power of detecting esp. smells. *–v.* **1 a** discern by scent. **b** sense (*scented danger*). **2** (esp. as **scented** *adj.*) make fragrant (*scented soap*). □ **put** (or **throw) off the scent** deceive by false clues etc. **scent out** discover by smelling or searching. [French *sentir* perceive]

scepter *US* var. of SCEPTRE.

sceptic /'skeptɪk/ *n.* (*US* **skeptic**) **1** person inclined to doubt accepted opinions. **2** person who doubts the truth of religions. **3** philosopher who questions the possibility of knowledge. □ **scepticism** /-ˌsɪz(ə)m/ *n.* [Greek *skeptomai* observe]

sceptical *adj.* (*US* **skeptical**) inclined to doubt accepted opinions; critical; incredulous. □ **sceptically** *adv.*

sceptre /'septə(r)/ *n.* (*US* **scepter**) staff as a symbol of sovereignty. [Greek *skēptō* lean on]

Sch. *abbr.* **1** *Taxation* = SCHEDULE *n.* 6 (followed by a letter). **2** schilling.

schadenfreude /'ʃɑːdənˌfrɔɪdə/ *n.* malicious enjoyment of another's misfortunes. [German *Schaden* harm, *Freude* joy]

schedule /'ʃedjuːl/ *–n.* **1 a** list of intended events, times, etc. **b** plan of work. **2** list or scale of rates or prices. **3** *US* timetable. **4** tabulated list. **5** *Law* part of the legislation that is placed at the end of an act of Parliament and contains subsidiary matter to the main sections of the act. **6** *Taxation* **a** one of several classes of income tax derived from the original income-tax legislation defining various sources of income for tax purposes. Some of the schedules are further subdivided into cases. The broad classification is: Schedule A, rents from property in the UK; Schedule B, income from commercial woodlands; Schedule C, interest paid by public bodies; Schedule D, Case 1, profits from trade; Case II, profits from professions or vocations; Case III, interest not otherwise taxed; Case IV, income from securities outside the UK; Case V, income from possessions outside the UK; Case VI, other annual profits and gains; Schedule E, Cases I, II, and III, emoluments of offices or employments (the cases depending on the residential status of the taxpayer); Schedule F, dividends paid by UK companies. **b** working papers submitted with tax returns or tax computations. *–v.* (**-ling**) **1** include in a schedule. **2** make a schedule of. **3** list (a building) for preservation. □ **according to** (or **on) schedule** as planned; on time. [Latin *schedula* slip of paper]

scheduled flight *n.* (also **scheduled service** etc.) regular public flight, service, etc.

schema /'skiːmə/ *n.* (*pl.* **schemata** or **-s**) synopsis, outline, or diagram. [Greek *skhēma -at-* form, figure]

schematic /skɪ'mætɪk/ *–adj.* of or as a scheme or schema; diagrammatic. *–n.* diagram, esp. of an electronic circuit. □ **schematically** *adv.*

schematize /'skiːməˌtaɪz/ *v.* (also **-ise**) (**-zing** or **-sing**) put in schematic form.

scheme /skiːm/ *–n.* **1** systematic plan or arrangement (*colour scheme*). **2** artful plot. **3** timetable, outline, syllabus, etc. *–v.* (**-ming**) plan, esp. secretly or deceitfully. □ **scheming** *adj.* [Greek: related to SCHEMA]

♦ **scheme of arrangement** see ARRANGEMENT 6a.

---

scherzo /'skeəˌtsəʊ/ *n.* (*pl.* **-s**) *Mus.* vigorous, often playful, piece, esp. as part of a larger work. [Italian, = jest]

schilling /'ʃɪlɪŋ/ *n.* standard monetary unit of Austria. [German, = SHILLING]

schism /'skɪz(ə)m/ *n.* division of a group (esp. religious) into sects etc., usu. over doctrine. □ **schismatic** /-'mætɪk/ *adj.* & *n.* [Greek *skhizō* to split]

schist /ʃɪst/ *n.* layered crystalline rock. [Greek *skhizō* to split]

schizo /'skɪtsəʊ/ *colloq. –adj.* schizophrenic. *–n.* (*pl.* **-s**) schizophrenic person. [abbreviation]

schizoid /'skɪtsɔɪd/ *–adj.* tending to schizophrenia but usu. without delusions. *–n.* schizoid person.

schizophrenia /ˌskɪtsə'friːnɪə/ *n.* mental disease marked by a breakdown in the relation between thoughts, feelings, and actions, and often with delusions and retreat from social life. □ **schizophrenic** /-'frenɪk/ *adj.* & *n.* [Greek *skhizō* to split, *phrēn* mind]

Schleswig-Holstein /'ʃlesvɪk 'hɒlʃtaɪn/ state (*Land*) in NW Germany; pop. (est. 1995) 2 708 400; capital, Kiel. Agriculture produces cereals, potatoes, and cattle; there are also shipbuilding and engineering industries.

schlock /ʃlɒk/ *n. US colloq.* trash. [Yiddish *shlak* a blow]

schmaltz /ʃmɔːlts/ *n. colloq.* esp. *US* sentimentality, esp. in music, drama, etc. □ **schmaltzy** *adj.* [Yiddish]

schmuck /ʃmʌk/ *n. slang* esp. *US* foolish or contemptible person. [Yiddish]

schnapps /ʃnæps/ *n.* any of various spirits drunk in N Europe. [German]

schnitzel /'ʃnɪtz(ə)l/ *n.* escalope of veal. [German]

scholar /'skɒlə(r)/ *n.* **1** learned person, academic. **2** holder of a scholarship. **3** person of specified academic ability (*poor scholar*). □ **scholarly** *adj.* [Latin: related to SCHOOL[1]]

scholarship *n.* **1 a** academic achievement, esp. of a high level. **b** standards of a good scholar (*shows great scholarship*). **2** financial award for a student etc., given for scholarly achievement.

scholastic /skə'læstɪk/ *adj.* **1** of schools, education, etc.; academic. **2** *hist.* of scholasticism. [Greek: related to SCHOOL[1]]

scholasticism /ˌskə'læstɪˌsɪz(ə)m/ *n. hist.* medieval western Church philosophy.

school[1] /skuːl/ *–n.* **1 a** educational institution for pupils up to 19 years of age, or (*US*) including college or university level. **b** (*attrib.*) of or for use in school (*school dinners*). **2 a** school buildings, pupils, staff, etc. **b** time of teaching; the teaching itself (*no school today*). **3** university department or faculty. **4 a** group of similar artists etc., esp. followers of an artist etc. **b** group of like-minded people (*belongs to the old school*). **5** group of card-players etc. **6** *colloq.* instructive circumstances etc. (*school of adversity*). *–v.* **1** send to school; educate. **2** (often foll. by *to*) discipline, train, control. **3** (as **schooled** *adj.*) (foll. by *in*) educated or trained (*schooled in humility*). □ **at** (*US* **in) school** attending lessons etc. **go to school** attend lessons. [Greek *skholē*]

school[2] /skuːl/ *n.* (often foll. by *of*) shoal of fish, whales, etc. [Low German or Dutch]

school age *n.* age-range of school attendance.

schoolboy *n.* boy attending school.

schoolchild *n.* child attending school.

schoolgirl *n.* girl attending school.

schoolhouse *n.* school building, esp. in a village.

schooling *n.* education, esp. at school.

school-leaver *n.* person finishing secondary school (esp. considered as joining the job market).

schoolmaster *n.* head or assistant male teacher.

schoolmistress *n.* head or assistant female teacher.

schoolroom *n.* room used for lessons.

schoolteacher *n.* teacher in a school.

school year *n.* period from September to July.

schooner /'skuːnə(r)/ *n.* **1** fore-and-aft rigged ship with two or more masts. **2 a** measure or glass for esp. sherry. **b** *US* & *Austral.* tall beer-glass. [origin uncertain]

schottische /ʃɒ'tiːʃ/ *n.* **1** a kind of slow polka. **2** music for this. [German, = Scottish]

Schwerin /'ʃʊeərɪn/ city in NE Germany, capital of Mecklenburg-West Pomerania; manufactures include machinery and chemicals; pop. (est. 1995) 118 291.

Schwyz /ʃviːts/ town and resort in central Switzerland, capital of a canton of the same name; pop. (1990) 12 534.

sciatic /saɪ'ætɪk/ *adj.* **1** of the hip. **2** of the sciatic nerve. **3** suffering from or liable to sciatica. [Greek *iskhion* hip]

sciatica /saɪ'ætɪkə/ *n.* neuralgia of the hip and leg. [Latin: related to SCIATIC]

sciatic nerve *n.* largest nerve, running from pelvis to thigh.

science /'saɪəns/ *n.* **1** branch of knowledge involving systematized observation and experiment. **2 a** knowledge so gained, or on a specific subject. **b** pursuit or principles of this. **3** skilful technique. [Latin *scio* know]

science fiction *n.* fiction with a scientific theme, esp. concerned with the future, space, other worlds, etc.

science park *n.* area containing science-based industries.

scientific /ˌsaɪən'tɪfɪk/ *adj.* **1 a** following the systematic methods of science. **b** systematic, accurate. **2** of, used in, or engaged in science. □ **scientifically** *adv.*

scientist /'saɪəntɪst/ *n.* student or expert in science.

Scientology /ˌsaɪən'tɒlədʒɪ/ *n.* system of religious philosophy based on self-improvement and graded courses of study and training. □ **Scientologist** *n.* & *adj.* [Latin *scientia* knowledge]

sci-fi /'saɪfaɪ/ *n.* (often *attrib.*) *colloq.* science fiction. [abbreviation]

scilicet /'saɪlɪˌset/ *adv.* that is to say (used esp. in explanation of an ambiguity). [Latin]

Scilly Islands /'sɪlɪ/ (also **Scillies**) group of about 140 small islands off the W extremity of Cornwall and administratively part of that county; pop. (1991) 1978; capital, Hugh Town (on St Mary's). Early spring flowers are grown for sale in the UK; other agricultural activities include dairy farming and market gardening. There is also an important tourist industry. □ **Scillonian** /sɪ'ləʊnɪən/ *adj.* & *n.*

scimitar /'sɪmɪtə(r)/ *n.* curved oriental sword. [French and Italian]

scintilla /sɪn'tɪlə/ *n.* trace. [Latin, = spark]

scintillate /'sɪntɪˌleɪt/ *v.* (**-ting**) **1** (esp. as **scintillating** *adj.*) talk cleverly; be brilliant. **2** sparkle; twinkle. □ **scintillation** /-'leɪʃ(ə)n/ *n.* [Latin: related to SCINTILLA]

scion /'saɪən/ *n.* **1** shoot of a plant etc., esp. one cut for grafting or planting. **2** descendant; younger member of (esp. a noble) family. [French]

scissors /'sɪzəz/ *n.pl.* (also **pair of scissors** *sing.*) hand-held cutting instrument with two pivoted blades opening and closing. [Latin *caedo* cut: related to CHISEL]

SCIT *abbr.* Special Commissioners of Income Tax.

sclerosis /sklə'rəʊsɪs/ *n.* **1** abnormal hardening of body tissue. **2** (in full **multiple** or **disseminated sclerosis**) serious progressive disease of the nervous system. □ **sclerotic** /-'rɒtɪk/ *adj.* [Greek *sklēros* hard]

scoff[1] *–v.* (usu. foll. by *at*) speak scornfully; mock. *–n.* mocking words; taunt. [perhaps from Scandinavian]

scoff[2] *colloq. –v.* eat greedily. *–n.* food; a meal. [Afrikaans *schoff* from Dutch]

scold /skəʊld/ *–v.* **1** rebuke (esp. a child). **2** find fault noisily. *–n. archaic* nagging woman. □ **scolding** *n.* [probably Old Norse]

scollop var. of SCALLOP.

sconce *n.* wall-bracket for a candlestick or light-fitting. [Latin *(ab)sconsa* covered (light)]

scone /skɒn, skəʊn/ *n.* small cake of flour, fat, and milk, baked quickly. [origin uncertain]

scoop *–n.* **1** spoon-shaped object, esp.: **a** a short-handled deep shovel for loose materials. **b** a large long-handled ladle for liquids. **c** the excavating part of a digging-machine etc. **d** an instrument for serving ice-cream etc. **2** quantity taken up by a scoop. **3** scooping movement. **4** exclusive news item. **5** large profit made quickly. *–v.* **1** (usu. foll. by *out*) hollow out (as if) with a scoop. **2** (usu. foll. by *up*) lift (as if) with a scoop. **3** forestall (a rival newspaper etc.) with a scoop. **4** secure (a large profit etc.), esp. suddenly. [Low German or Dutch]

scoot *v.* (esp. in *imper.*) *colloq.* run or dart away, esp. hastily. [origin unknown]

scooter *n.* **1** child's toy with a footboard on two wheels and a long steering-handle. **2** (in full **motor scooter**) low-powered motor cycle with a shieldlike protective front.

scope *n.* **1** range or opportunity (*beyond the scope of our research*). **2** extent of mental ability, outlook, etc. (*intellect limited in its scope*). [Greek, = target]

-scope *comb. form* forming nouns denoting: **1** device looked at or through (*telescope*). **2** instrument for observing or showing (*oscilloscope*). □ **-scopic** /'skɒpɪk/ *comb. form* forming adjectives. [Greek *skopeō* look at]

-scopy *comb. form* indicating viewing or observation, usu. with an instrument ending in *-scope* (*microscopy*).

scorbutic /skɔː'bjuːtɪk/ *adj.* of, like, or affected with scurvy. [Latin *scorbutus* scurvy]

scorch *–v.* **1** burn or discolour the surface of with dry heat. **2** become so discoloured etc. **3** (as **scorching** *adj.*) *colloq.* **a** (of the weather) very hot. **b** (of criticism etc.) stringent; harsh. *–n.* mark made by scorching. [origin unknown]

scorched earth policy *n.* **1** policy of destroying anything that might be of use to an invading enemy. **2** policy in which a company that believes it is to be the target of a take-over bid makes its balance sheet or profitability less attractive than it really is by a reversible manoeuvre, such as borrowing money at an exorbitant rate of interest. It is an extreme form of poison pill.

scorcher *n. colloq.* very hot day.

score *–n.* **1 a** number of points, goals, runs, etc., made by a player or side in some games. **b** respective numbers of points etc. at the end of a game (*score was five–nil*). **c** act of gaining esp. a goal. **2** (*pl.* same or **-s**) twenty or a set of twenty. **3** (in *pl.*) a great many (*scores of people*). **4** reason or motive (*rejected on that score*). **5** *Mus.* **a** copy of a composition showing all the vocal and instrumental parts arranged one below the other. **b** music for a film or play, esp. for a musical. **6** notch, line, etc. cut or scratched into a surface. **7** record of money owing. *–v.* (**-ring**) **1 a** win or gain (a goal, points, success, etc.). **b** count for (points in a game etc.) (*a boundary scores six*). **2 a** make a score in a game (*failed to score*). **b** keep score in a game. **3** mark with notches etc. **4** have an advantage (*that is where he scores*). **5** *Mus.* (often foll. by *for*) orchestrate or arrange (a piece of music). **6** *slang* **a** obtain drugs illegally. **b** make a sexual conquest. □ **keep score** (or **the score**) register scores as they are made. **know the score** *colloq.* be aware of the essential facts. **on that score** so far as that is concerned. **score off** (or **score points off**) *colloq.* humiliate, esp. verbally. **score out** delete. □ **scorer** *n.* [Old Norse: related to SHEAR]

scoreboard *n.* large board for displaying the score in a game or match.

score-book *n.* (also **score-card** or **-sheet**) printed book etc. for entering esp. cricket scores in.

scoria /'skɔːrɪə/ *n.* (*pl.* **scoriae** /-rɪˌiː/) **1** cellular lava, or fragments of it. **2** slag or dross of metals. □ **scoriaceous** /-'eɪʃəs/ *adj.* [Greek *skōria* refuse]

scorn *–n.* disdain, contempt, derision. *–v.* **1** hold in contempt. **2** reject or refuse to do as unworthy. [French *escarnir*]

scornful *adj.* (often foll. by *of*) contemptuous. □ **scornfully** *adv.*

Scorpio /'skɔːpɪəʊ/ *n.* (*pl.* **-s**) **1** constellation and eighth sign of the zodiac (the Scorpion). **2** person born when the sun is in this sign. [Greek *skorpios* scorpion]

scorpion /'skɔːpɪən/ *n.* **1** arachnid with pincers and a jointed stinging tail. **2** (**the Scorpion**) zodiacal sign or constellation Scorpio.

Scot *n.* **1** native of Scotland. **2** person of Scottish descent. [Latin *Scottus*]

Scot. *abbr.* **1** Scotland. **2** Scottish.

ScotBIC /'skɒtˌbɪk/ *abbr.* Scottish Business in the Community.

Scotch *–adj.* var. of SCOTTISH or SCOTS. *–n.* **1** var. of SCOTTISH or SCOTS. **2** Scotch whisky. [from SCOTTISH]

■ **Usage** *Scots* or *Scottish* is preferred to *Scotch* in Scotland, except in the compound nouns *Scotch broth, egg, fir, mist, terrier,* and *whisky*.

scotch *v.* **1** put an end to; frustrate. **2** *archaic* wound without killing. [origin unknown]

Scotch broth *n.* meat soup with pearl barley etc.

Scotch egg *n.* hard-boiled egg in sausage meat.

Scotch fir *n.* (also **Scots fir**) = SCOTS PINE.

Scotch mist *n.* thick drizzly mist.

Scotch terrier *n.* (also **Scottish terrier**) small rough-haired terrier.

Scotch whisky *n.* whisky distilled in Scotland.

SCOTEC /'skəʊtek/ *abbr.* Scottish Technical Education Council.

scot-free *adv.* unharmed, unpunished. [obsolete *scot* tax]

Scotland /'skɒtlənd/ the N part of Great Britain and of the United Kingdom; pop. (1991) 4 998 567; capital, Edinburgh. The exploitation of North Sea oil led to a boom on the E coast, but elsewhere the traditional industries of shipbuilding and steelmaking have suffered from the effects of economic recession. Agriculture (esp. sheep rearing and dairy farming) remains an important source of revenue; other activities include forestry, fishing, whisky distilling, and tourism. An independent country in the Middle Ages, Scotland was amalgamated with England as a result of the union of the crowns in 1603 and of the parliaments in 1707 (see GREAT BRITAIN). An increase in nationalist feeling in the 1960s and 1970s failed to achieve devolution in a referendum of 1979, but the Scottish Nationalist Party continues to campaign for independence. A referendum in 1997 gave a mandate for the establishment of a separate Scottish parliament with limited tax varying powers within the UK. See also UNITED KINGDOM.

Scots (also **Scotch**) esp. *Scot. –adj.* **1** = SCOTTISH *adj.* **2** in the dialect, accent, etc. of (esp. Lowlands) Scotland. *–n.* **1** = SCOTTISH *n.* **2** form of English spoken in (esp. Lowlands) Scotland. [var. of SCOTTISH]

Scots fir var. of SCOTCH FIR.

Scotsman *n.* (*fem.* **Scotswoman**) = SCOT.

Scots pine *n.* (also **Scottish pine**) a kind of pine tree.

Scottie *n.* (also **Scottie dog**) *colloq.* Scotch terrier.

Scottish (also **Scotch**) *–adj.* of Scotland or its inhabitants. *–n.* (prec. by *the*; treated as *pl.*) people of Scotland.

♦ **Scottish Development Department** *n.* (also **SDD**) department of the UK government **Scottish Office** that, with the **Industry Department for Scotland**, another department of the same office, is responsible for the development and expansion of industry in Scotland. Both departments have offices in London and Edinburgh.

Scottish pine var. of SCOTS PINE.

Scottish terrier var. of SCOTCH TERRIER.

SCOTVEC /'skɒt,vek/ *abbr.* Scottish Vocational Education Council.

scoundrel /'skaʊndr(ə)l/ *n.* unscrupulous villain; rogue. [origin unknown]

scour[1] *–v.* **1 a** cleanse by rubbing. **b** (usu. foll. by *away, off*, etc.) clear (rust, stains, etc.) by rubbing etc. **2** clear out (a pipe, channel, etc.) by flushing through. *–n.* scouring or being scoured. □ **scourer** *n.* [French *escurer*]

scour[2] *v.* search thoroughly, esp. by scanning (*scoured the streets for him*; *scoured the newspaper*). [origin unknown]

scourge /skɜːdʒ/ *–n.* **1** person or thing seen as causing suffering. **2** whip. *–v.* (**-ging**) **1** whip. **2** punish, oppress. [Latin *corrigia* whip]

Scouse *colloq. –n.* **1** Liverpool dialect. **2** native of Liverpool. *–adj.* of Liverpool. [from LOBSCOUSE]

♦ **SCOUT** /skaʊt/ *abbr.* shared currency option under tender, a currency option designed esp. for companies who are tendering for the same overseas job in a foreign currency. To save each of them having to hedge the currency risk separately, SCOUT enables them to share the cost of a single option.

---

scout *–n.* **1** soldier etc. sent ahead to get esp. military intelligence. **2** search for this. **3** = TALENT-SCOUT. **4** (also **Scout**) member of the Scout Association, an (orig. boys') association intended to develop character. **5** domestic worker at an Oxford college. *–v.* **1** (often foll. by *for*) go about searching for information etc. **2** (foll. by *about, around*) make a search. **3** (often foll. by *out*) *colloq.* explore to get information about (territory etc.). □ **scouting** *n.* [French *escoute(r)* from Latin *ausculto* listen]

Scouter *n.* adult leader of Scouts.

Scoutmaster *n.* person in charge of a group of Scouts.

scow *n.* esp. *US* flat-bottomed boat. [Dutch]

scowl *–n.* severe frowning or sullen expression. *–v.* make a scowl. [Scandinavian]

scrabble /'skræb(ə)l/ *–v.* (**-ling**) scratch or grope about, esp. in search of something. *–n.* **1** act of scrabbling. **2** (**Scrabble**) *propr.* game in which players build up words from letter-blocks on a board. [Dutch]

scrag *–n.* **1** (also **scrag-end**) inferior end of a neck of mutton. **2** skinny person or animal. *–v.* (**-gg-**) *slang* **1** strangle, hang. **2** handle roughly, beat up. [origin uncertain]

scraggy *adj.* (**-ier, -iest**) thin and bony. □ **scragginess** *n.*

scram *v.* (**-mm-**) (esp. in *imper.*) *colloq.* go away. [perhaps from SCRAMBLE]

scramble /'skræmb(ə)l/ *–v.* (**-ling**) **1** clamber, crawl, climb, etc., esp. hurriedly or anxiously. **2** (foll. by *for, at*) struggle with competitors (for a thing or share). **3** mix together indiscriminately. **4** cook (eggs) by stirring them in a pan over heat. **5** change the speech frequency of (a broadcast transmission or telephone conversation) so as to make it unintelligible without a decoding device. **6** (of fighter aircraft or pilots) take off quickly in an emergency or for action. *–n.* **1** act of scrambling. **2** difficult climb or walk. **3** (foll. by *for*) eager struggle or competition. **4** motor-cycle race over rough ground. **5** emergency take-off by fighter aircraft. [imitative]

♦ **scrambled merchandising** *n.* selling certain products in retail outlets not traditionally associated with these products. For example, some traditional clothes shops now sell food, while some supermarkets sell household goods in addition to food.

---

scrambler *n.* device for scrambling telephone conversations.

scrap[1] *–n.* **1** small detached piece; fragment. **2** rubbish or waste material. **3** discarded metal for reprocessing (often *attrib.*: *scrap metal*). **4** (with *neg.*) smallest piece or amount. **5** (in *pl.*) **a** odds and ends. **b** uneaten food. *–v.* (**-pp-**) discard as useless. [Old Norse: related to SCRAPE]

scrap[2] *colloq. –n.* fight or rough quarrel. *–v.* (**-pp-**) have a scrap. [perhaps from SCRAPE]

scrapbook *n.* blank book for sticking cuttings, drawings, etc. in.

scrape *–v.* (**-ping**) **1 a** move a hard or sharp edge across (a surface), esp. to make smooth. **b** apply (a hard or sharp edge) in this way. **2** (foll. by *away, off*, etc.) remove by scraping. **3 a** rub (a surface) harshly against another. **b** scratch or damage by scraping. **4** make (a hollow) by scraping. **5 a** draw or move with a scraping sound. **b** make such a sound. **c** produce such a sound from. **6** (often foll. by *along, by, through*, etc.) move almost touching surrounding obstacles etc. (*scraped through the gap*). **7** narrowly achieve (a living, an examination pass, etc.). **8** (often foll. by *by, through*) **a** barely manage. **b** pass an examination etc. with difficulty. **9** (foll. by *together, up*) bring, provide, or amass with difficulty. **10** be economical. **11** draw back a foot in making a clumsy bow. **12** (foll. by *back*) draw (the hair) tightly back. *–n.* **1** act or sound of scraping. **2** scraped place; graze. **3** *colloq.* predicament caused by rashness etc. □ **scrape the barrel** *colloq.* be reduced to a limited choice etc. [Old Norse]

scraper *n.* device for scraping, esp. paint etc. from a surface.

scrap heap *n.* **1** pile of scrap. **2** state of being discarded as useless.

scrapie /'skreɪpɪ/ *n.* viral disease of sheep, characterized by lack of coordination.

scraping *n.* (esp. in *pl.*) fragment produced by scraping.

scrap merchant *n.* dealer in scrap.

scrappy *adj.* (**-ier, -iest**) **1** consisting of scraps. **2** incomplete; carelessly arranged or put together.

scrapyard *n.* place where (esp. metal) scrap is collected for reuse.

scratch *–v.* **1** score, mark, or wound superficially, esp. with a sharp object. **2** (also *absol.*) scrape, esp. with the nails to relieve itching. **3** make or form by scratching. **4** (foll. by *together*, *up*, etc.) = SCRAPE 9. **5** (foll. by *out*, *off*, *through*) strike (out) (writing etc.). **6** (also *absol.*) withdraw (a competitor, oneself, etc.) from a race or competition. **7** (often foll. by *about*, *around*, etc.) **a** scratch the ground etc. in search. **b** search haphazardly (*scratching about for evidence*). *–n.* **1** mark or wound made by scratching. **2** sound of scratching. **3** spell of scratching oneself. **4** *colloq.* superficial wound. **5** line from which competitors in a race (esp. those not receiving a handicap) start. *–attrib. adj.* **1** collected by chance. **2** collected or made from whatever is available; heterogeneous. **3** with no handicap given (*scratch race*). □ **from scratch 1** from the beginning. **2** without help. **scratch one's head** be perplexed. **scratch the surface** deal with a matter only superficially. **up to scratch** up to the required standard. [origin uncertain]

scratchy *adj.* (**-ier, -iest**) **1** tending to make scratches or a scratching noise. **2** causing itching. **3** (of a drawing etc.) untidy, careless. □ **scratchily** *adv.* **scratchiness** *n.*

scrawl *–v.* **1** write or make (marks) in a hurried untidy way. **2** (foll. by *out*) cross out by scrawling over. *–n.* **1** hurried untidy manner of writing. **2** example of this. □ **scrawly** *adj.* [origin uncertain]

scrawny *adj.* (**-ier, -iest**) lean, scraggy. [dial.]

scream *–n.* **1** loud high-pitched cry of fear, pain, etc. **2** similar sound or cry. **3** *colloq.* hilarious occurrence or person. *–v.* **1** emit a scream. **2** speak or sing (words etc.) in a screaming tone. **3** make or move with a screaming sound. **4** laugh uncontrollably. **5** be blatantly obvious. [Old English]

scree *n.* (in *sing.* or *pl.*) **1** small loose stones. **2** mountain slope covered with these. [Old Norse, = landslip]

screech *–n.* harsh piercing scream. *–v.* utter with or make a screech. □ **screechy** *adj.* (**-ier, -iest**). [Old English (imitative)]

screech-owl *n.* owl that screeches, esp. a barn-owl.

screed *n.* **1** long usu. tiresome piece of writing or speech. **2** layer of cement etc. applied to level a surface. [probably from SHRED]

screen *–n.* **1** fixed or movable upright partition for separating, concealing, or protecting from heat etc. **2** thing used to conceal or shelter. **3 a** concealing stratagem. **b** protection thus given. **4 a** blank surface on which a photographic image is projected. **b** (prec. by *the*) the cinema industry; films collectively. **5** surface of a cathode-ray tube etc., esp. of a television or VDU, on which images or text appear. **6** = SIGHT-SCREEN. **7** = WINDSCREEN. **8** frame with fine netting to keep out insects etc. **9** large sieve or riddle. **10** system of checking for disease, an ability, attribute, etc. *–v.* **1** (often foll. by *from*) **a** shelter; hide. **b** protect from detection, censure, etc. **2** (foll. by *off*) conceal behind a screen. **3** show (a film, television programme, etc.). **4** prevent from causing, or protect from, electrical interference. **5** test or check (a person or group) for a disease, reliability, loyalty, etc. **6** sieve. [French]

screenplay *n.* film script.

screen printing *n.* printing process with ink forced through a prepared sheet of fine material.

screen test *n.* audition for a part in a film.

♦ **screen trading** *n.* any form of trading that relies on the use of a computer screen rather than personal contact, as in floor trading, pit trading, ring trading, etc. On the London Stock Exchange the Stock Exchange Automatic Execution Facility is an example.

---

screenwriter *n.* person who writes for the cinema.

screw /skruː/ *–n.* **1** thin cylinder or cone with a spiral ridge or thread running round the outside (**male screw**) or the inside (**female screw**). **2** (in full **wood-screw**) metal male screw with a slotted head and a sharp point. **3** (in full **screw-bolt**) blunt metal male screw on which a nut is threaded to bolt things together. **4** straight screw used to exert pressure. **5** (in *sing.* or *pl.*) instrument of torture acting in this way. **6** (in full **screw-propeller**) propeller with twisted blades acting like a screw on the water or air. **7** one turn of a screw. **8** (foll. by *of*) small twisted-up paper (of tobacco etc.). **9** (in billiards etc.) an oblique curling motion of the ball. **10** *slang* prison warder. **11** *coarse slang* **a** act of sexual intercourse. **b** partner in this. *–v.* **1** fasten or tighten with a screw or screws. **2** turn (a screw). **3** twist or turn round like a screw. **4** (of a ball etc.) swerve. **5** (foll. by *out of*) extort (consent, money, etc.) from. **6** (also *absol.*) *coarse slang* have sexual intercourse with. **7** swindle. □ **have a screw loose** *colloq.* be slightly crazy. **put the screws on** *colloq.* pressurize, intimidate. **screw up 1** contract or contort (one's face etc.). **2** contract and crush (a piece of paper etc.) into a tight mass. **3** summon up (one's courage etc.). **4** *slang* **a** bungle. **b** spoil (an event, opportunity, etc.). **c** upset, disturb mentally. [French *escroue*]

screwball *n. US slang* crazy or eccentric person.

screwdriver *n.* tool with a tip that fits into the head of a screw to turn it.

screw top *n.* (also (with hyphen) *attrib.*) screwed-on cap or lid.

screw-up *n. slang* bungle, mess.

screwy *adj.* (**-ier, -iest**) *slang* **1** crazy or eccentric. **2** absurd. □ **screwiness** *n.*

scribble /'skrɪb(ə)l/ *–v.* (**-ling**) **1** write or draw carelessly or hurriedly. **2** *joc.* be an author or writer. *–n.* **1** scrawl. **2** hasty note etc. [Latin *scribillo* diminutive: related to SCRIBE]

scribe *–n.* **1** ancient or medieval copyist of manuscripts. **2** ancient Jewish record-keeper or professional theologian and jurist. **3** pointed instrument for making marks on wood etc. **4** *colloq.* writer, esp. a journalist. *–v.* (**-bing**) mark with a scribe. □ **scribal** *adj.* [Latin *scriba* from *scribo* write]

scrim *n.* open-weave fabric for lining or upholstery etc. [origin unknown]

scrimmage /'skrɪmɪdʒ/ *–n.* tussle; brawl. *–v.* (**-ging**) engage in this. [from SKIRMISH]

scrimp *v.* skimp. [origin unknown]

♦ **scrip** *n.* **1** (*collect.*) certificates that demonstrate ownership of stocks, shares, and bonds (capital raised by subscription), esp. the certificates relating to a scrip issue. **2** such a certificate. **3** share or shares allocated in a scrip issue. [abbreviation of sub*scrip*tion receipt]

♦ **scrip issue** *n.* (also **bonus issue**, **capitalization issue**, **free issue**) issue of new share certificates to existing shareholders to reflect the accumulation of profits in the reserves of a company's balance sheet. The shareholders do not pay for the new shares and appear to be no better off. However, in a 1 for 3 scrip issue, for example, the shareholders receive one new share for every three old shares they own. This automatically reduces the price of the shares by 25%, catering to the preference of shareholders to hold cheaper shares rather than expensive ones; it also encourages them to hope that the price will gradually climb to its former value, which will, of course, make them 25% better off.

---

script *–n.* **1** text of a play, film, or broadcast. **2** handwriting; written characters. **3** type imitating handwriting. **4** alphabet or system of writing. **5** examinee's written answers. *–v.* write a script for (a film etc.). [Latin *scriptum* from *scribo* write]

scripture /'skrɪptʃə(r)/ *n.* **1** sacred writings. **2** (**Scripture** or **the Scriptures**) the Bible. □ **scriptural** *adj.* [Latin: related to SCRIPT]

scriptwriter *n.* person who writes scripts for films, TV, etc. □ **scriptwriting** *n.*

scrivener /ˈskrɪvənə(r)/ *n. hist.* **1** copyist or drafter of documents. **2** notary. [French *escrivein*]

scrofula /ˈskrɒfjʊlə/ *n.* disease with glandular swellings, probably a form of tuberculosis. □ **scrofulous** *adj.* [Latin *scrofa* a sow]

scroll /skrəʊl/ *–n.* **1** roll of parchment or paper, esp. written on. **2** book in the ancient roll form. **3** ornamental design imitating a roll of parchment. *–v.* (often foll. by *down*, *up*, *left*, or *right*) move through (text etc. displayed on a computer screen) to view parts of a file etc. that cannot fit on the screen. [originally *(sc)rowle* ROLL]

scrolled *adj.* having a scroll ornament.

Scrooge /skruːdʒ/ *n.* miser. [name of a character in Dickens]

scrotum /ˈskrəʊtəm/ *n.* (*pl.* **scrota** or **-s**) pouch of skin containing the testicles. □ **scrotal** *adj.* [Latin]

scrounge *v.* (**-ging**) (also *absol.*) obtain by cadging. □ **on the scrounge** scrounging. □ **scrounger** *n.* [dial. *scrunge* steal]

scrub[1] *–v.* (**-bb-**) **1** clean by rubbing, esp. with a hard brush and water. **2** (often foll. by *up*) (of a surgeon etc.) clean and disinfect the hands and arms before operating. **3** *colloq.* scrap or cancel. **4** use water to remove impurities from (gases etc.). *–n.* scrubbing or being scrubbed. [Low German or Dutch]

scrub[2] *n.* **1 a** brushwood or stunted forest growth. **b** land covered with this. **2** (*attrib.*) small or dwarf variety (*scrub pine*). □ **scrubby** *adj.* [from SHRUB]

scrubber *n.* **1** *slang* promiscuous woman. **2** apparatus for purifying gases etc.

scruff[1] *n.* back of the neck (esp. *scruff of the neck*). [perhaps from Old Norse *skoft* hair]

scruff[2] *n. colloq.* scruffy person. [origin uncertain]

scruffy *adj.* (**-ier**, **-iest**) *colloq.* shabby, slovenly, untidy. □ **scruffily** *adv.* **scruffiness** *n.* [*scruff* = SCURF]

scrum *n.* **1** scrummage. **2** *colloq.* = SCRIMMAGE *n.* [abbreviation]

scrum-half *n.* half-back who puts the ball into the scrum.

scrummage *n. Rugby* massed forwards on each side pushing to gain possession of the ball thrown on the ground between them. [related to SCRIMMAGE]

scrump *v. colloq.* steal from an orchard or garden. [related to SCRUMPY]

scrumptious /ˈskrʌmpʃəs/ *adj. colloq.* **1** delicious. **2** delightful. [origin unknown]

scrumpy /ˈskrʌmpɪ/ *n. colloq.* rough cider. [dial. *scrump* small apple]

scrunch *–v.* **1** (usu. foll. by *up*) crumple. **2** crunch. *–n.* crunching sound. [var. of CRUNCH]

scruple /ˈskruːp(ə)l/ *–n.* **1** (often in *pl.*) moral concern. **2** doubt caused by this. *–v.* (**-ling**) (foll. by *to* + infin.; usu. with *neg.*) hesitate because of scruples. [Latin]

scrupulous /ˈskruːpjʊləs/ *adj.* **1** conscientious, thorough. **2** careful to avoid doing wrong. **3** punctilious; over-attentive to details. □ **scrupulously** *adv.* [Latin: related to SCRUPLE]

scrutineer /ˌskruːtɪˈnɪə(r)/ *n.* person who scrutinizes ballot-papers.

scrutinize /ˈskruːtɪˌnaɪz/ *v.* (also **-ise**) (**-zing** or **-sing**) subject to scrutiny.

scrutiny /ˈskruːtɪnɪ/ *n.* (*pl.* **-ies**) **1** critical gaze. **2** close investigation. **3** official examination of ballot-papers. [Latin *scrutinium* from *scrutor* examine]

SCSI /ˈskuːzɪ/ *abbr.* small computer systems interface, a standard way of connecting peripherals to small and medium-sized computers.

scuba /ˈskuːbə/ *n.* (*pl.* **-s**) aqualung. [acronym of *s*elf-*c*ontained *u*nderwater *b*reathing *a*pparatus]

scuba-diving *n.* swimming underwater using a scuba. □ **scuba-dive** *v.* **scuba-diver** *n.*

scud *–v.* (**-dd-**) **1** move straight and fast; skim along (*scudding clouds*). **2** *Naut.* run before the wind. *–n.* **1** spell of scudding. **2** scudding motion. **3** vapoury driving clouds or shower. [perhaps an alteration of SCUT]

scuff *–v.* **1** graze or brush against. **2** mark or wear out (shoes) in this way. **3** shuffle or drag the feet. *–n.* mark of scuffing. [imitative]

scuffle /ˈskʌf(ə)l/ *–n.* confused struggle or fight at close quarters. *–v.* (**-ling**) engage in a scuffle. [probably Scandinavian: related to SHOVE]

scull *–n.* **1** either of a pair of small oars. **2** oar over the stern of a boat to propel it, usu. by a twisting motion. **3** (in *pl.*) sculling race. *–v.* (often *absol.*) propel (a boat) with sculls. [origin unknown]

sculler *n.* **1** user of sculls. **2** boat for sculling.

scullery /ˈskʌlərɪ/ *n.* (*pl.* **-ies**) back kitchen; room for washing dishes etc. [Anglo-French *squillerie*]

scullion /ˈskʌljən/ *n. archaic* **1** cook's boy. **2** person who washes dishes etc. [origin unknown]

sculpt *v.* sculpture. [shortening of SCULPTOR]

sculptor *n.* (*fem.* **sculptress**) artist who sculptures. [Latin: related to SCULPTURE]

sculpture /ˈskʌlptʃə(r)/ *–n.* **1** art of making three-dimensional or relief forms, by chiselling, carving, modelling, casting, etc. **2** work of sculpture. *–v.* (**-ring**) **1** represent in or adorn with sculpture. **2** practise sculpture. □ **sculptural** *adj.* [Latin *sculpo sculpt-* carve]

scum *–n.* **1** layer of dirt, froth, etc. at the top of liquid. **2** *derog.* worst part, person, or group (*scum of the earth*). *–v.* (**-mm-**) **1** remove scum from. **2** form a scum (on). □ **scummy** *adj.* (**-ier**, **-iest**). [Low German or Dutch]

scumbag *n. slang* contemptible person.

scupper[1] *n.* hole in a ship's side to drain water from the deck. [French *escopir* to spit]

scupper[2] *v. slang* **1** sink (a ship or its crew). **2** defeat or ruin (a plan etc.). **3** kill. [origin unknown]

scurf *n.* dandruff. □ **scurfy** *adj.* [Old English]

scurrilous /ˈskʌrɪləs/ *adj.* grossly or indecently abusive. □ **scurrility** /skəˈrɪlɪtɪ/ *n.* (*pl.* **-ies**). **scurrilously** *adv.* **scurrilousness** *n.* [Latin *scurra* buffoon]

scurry /ˈskʌrɪ/ *–v.* (**-ies**, **-ied**) run or move hurriedly, esp. with short quick steps; scamper. *–n.* (*pl.* **-ies**) **1** act or sound of scurrying. **2** flurry of rain or snow. [abbreviation of *hurry-scurry* reduplication of HURRY]

scurvy /ˈskɜːvɪ/ *–n.* disease caused by a deficiency of vitamin C. *–adj.* (**-ier**, **-iest**) paltry, contemptible. □ **scurvily** *adv.* [from SCURF]

scut *n.* short tail, esp. of a hare, rabbit, or deer. [origin unknown]

Scutari /ˈskuːtərɪ/ **1 (also Shkodër** /ˈʃkəʊdə(r)/ **a** province of NW Albania; pop. (1990) 241 549. **b** its capital city; manufactures include cement, weapons, and canned food; pop. (1990) 81 800. **2** see ÜSKÜDAR.

scutter *v.* & *n. colloq.* scurry. [perhaps an alteration of SCUTTLE[2]]

scuttle[1] /ˈskʌt(ə)l/ *n.* **1** = COAL-SCUTTLE. **2** part of a car body between the windscreen and the bonnet. [Old Norse from Latin *scutella* dish]

scuttle[2] /ˈskʌt(ə)l/ *–v.* (**-ling**) scurry; flee from danger etc. *–n.* hurried gait; precipitate flight. [perhaps related to dial. *scuddle* frequentative of SCUD]

scuttle[3] /ˈskʌt(ə)l/ *–n.* hole with a lid in a ship's deck or side. *–v.* let water into (a ship) to sink it. [Spanish *escotilla* hatchway]

Scylla and Charybdis /ˌsɪlə, kəˈrɪbdɪs/ *n.pl.* two dangers or extremes such that one can be avoided only by approaching the other. [names of a monster and a whirlpool in Greek mythology]

scythe /saɪð/ *–n.* mowing and reaping implement with a long handle and curved blade swung over the ground. *–v.* (**-thing**) cut with a scythe. [Old English]

SD *–abbr.* **1** sea-damaged. **2** send direct. **3** *Commerce* short delivery. **4** (also **S/D**) *Finance* sight draft. **5** South Dakota. **6** special delivery. **7** standard deviation. *–international vehicle registration* Swaziland. *–US postcode* South Dakota. *–airline flight code* Sudan Airways.

s.d. *abbr.* **1** *Commerce* short delivery. **2** *sine die.* **3** standard deviation.
SDA *abbr.* Scottish Development Agency.
S.Dak. *abbr.* South Dakota.
SDD *abbr.* **1** = SCOTTISH DEVELOPMENT DEPARTMENT. **2** subscriber direct dialling.
SDI *abbr.* strategic defence initiative.
SDLC *abbr. Computing* synchronous data link control, communications protocol used by IBM.
SDLP *abbr.* (in Northern Ireland) Social Democratic and Labour Party.
SDP *abbr. hist.* Social Democratic Party.
SDR *abbr.* = SPECIAL DRAWING RIGHT.
SE *–abbr.* **1 a** south-east. **b** south-eastern. **2** (also **S/E**) stock exchange. *–international civil aircraft marking* Sweden. *–postcode* south-east London.
Se *symb.* selenium.
sea *n.* **1** expanse of salt water that covers most of the earth's surface. **2** any part of this. **3** named tract of this partly or wholly enclosed by land (*North Sea*). **4** large inland lake (*Sea of Galilee*). **5** waves of the sea; their motion or state (*choppy sea*). **6** (foll. by *of*) vast quantity or expanse. **7** (*attrib.*) living or used in, on, or near the sea (often prefixed to the name of a marine animal, plant, etc., having a superficial resemblance to what it is named after) (*sea lettuce*). □ **at sea 1** in a ship on the sea. **2** perplexed, confused. **by sea** in a ship or ships. **go to sea** become a sailor. **on the sea 1** = *at sea* 1. **2** on the coast. [Old English]
sea anchor *n.* bag to retard the drifting of a ship.
sea anemone *n.* marine animal with tube-shaped body and petal-like tentacles.
seabed *n.* ocean floor.
sea bird *n.* bird living near the sea.
seaboard *n.* **1** seashore or coastline. **2** coastal region.
seaborne *adj.* transported by sea.
sea change *n.* notable or unexpected transformation.
sea cow *n.* **1** sirenian. **2** walrus.
sea dog *n.* old sailor.
seafarer *n.* **1** sailor. **2** traveller by sea. □ **seafaring** *adj.* & *n.*
seafood *n.* (often *attrib.*) edible sea fish or shellfish (*seafood restaurant*).
sea front *n.* part of a town directly facing the sea.
seagoing *adj.* (of ships) fit for crossing the sea.
sea green *adj.* & *n.* (as adj. often hyphenated) bluish-green.
seagull *n.* = GULL[1].
sea horse *n.* **1** small upright fish with a head like a horse's. **2** mythical creature with a horse's head and fish's tail.
seakale *n.* plant with young shoots used as a vegetable.
seal[1] *–n.* **1** piece of stamped wax, lead, paper, etc., attached to a document or to a receptacle, envelope, etc., to guarantee authenticity or security. **2** engraved piece of metal etc. for stamping a design on a seal. **3** substance or device used to close a gap etc. **4** anything regarded as a confirmation or guarantee (*seal of approval*). **5** decorative adhesive stamp. *–v.* **1** close securely or hermetically. **2** stamp, fasten, or fix with a seal. **3** certify as correct with a seal or stamp. **4** (often foll. by *up*) confine securely. **5** settle or decide (*their fate is sealed*). **6** (foll. by *off*) prevent entry to or exit from (an area). □ **set one's seal to** (or **on**) authorize or confirm. [Latin *sigillum*]
seal[2] *–n.* fish-eating amphibious marine mammal with flippers. *–v.* hunt for seals. [Old English]
sealant *n.* material for sealing, esp. to make airtight or watertight.
sea legs *n.pl.* ability to keep one's balance and avoid seasickness at sea.
sea level *n.* mean level of the sea's surface, used in reckoning the height of hills etc. and as a barometric standard.
sealing-wax *n.* mixture softened by heating and used to make seals.
sea lion *n.* large, eared seal.
Sea Lord *n.* naval member of the Admiralty Board.
sealskin *n.* **1** skin or prepared fur of a seal. **2** (often *attrib.*) garment made from this.
seals of office *n.pl.* seals held, esp. by the Lord Chancellor or a Secretary of State.
seam *–n.* **1** line where two edges join, esp. of cloth or boards. **2** fissure between parallel edges. **3** wrinkle. **4** stratum of coal etc. *–v.* **1** join with a seam. **2** (esp. as **seamed** *adj.*) mark or score with a seam. □ **seamless** *adj.* [Old English]
seaman *n.* **1** person whose work is at sea. **2** sailor, esp. one below the rank of officer.
seamanship *n.* skill in managing a ship or boat.
seam bowler *n. Cricket* bowler who makes the ball deviate by bouncing it off its seam.
sea mile *n.* = NAUTICAL MILE.
seamstress /'semstrɪs/ *n.* (also **sempstress**) woman who sews, esp. for a living. [Old English: related to SEAM]
seamy *adj.* (**-ier, -iest**) **1** disreputable or sordid (esp. *the seamy side*). **2** marked with or showing seams. □ **seaminess** *n.s*
seance /'seɪɑ̃s/ *n.* meeting at which a spiritualist attempts to make contact with the dead. [French]
sea pink *n.* maritime plant with bright pink flowers.
seaplane *n.* aircraft designed to take off from and land on water.
seaport *n.* town with a harbour.
SEAQ /'siːæk/ *abbr.* = STOCK EXCHANGE AUTOMATED QUOTATIONS SYSTEM.
sear *v.* **1** scorch, cauterize. **2** cause anguish to. **3** brown (meat) quickly at a high temperature to retain its juices in cooking. [Old English]
search /sɜːtʃ/ *–v.* **1** (also *absol.*) look through or go over thoroughly to find something. **2** examine or feel over (a person) to find anything concealed. **3** probe (*search one's conscience*). **4** (foll. by *for*) **a** look thoroughly in order to find. **b** *Computing* locate information held in a file etc. See also GLOBAL SEARCH. **5** (as **searching** *adj.*) (of an examination) thorough; keenly questioning (*searching gaze*). **6** (foll. by *out*) look for; seek out. *–n.* **1** act of searching. **2** investigation. □ **in search of** trying to find. **search and replace** word-processing operation in which each occurrence of a particular word or character in a document, or a section of a document, is located and the word etc. is replaced by a different one. **search me!** *colloq.* I do not know. □ **searcher** *n.* **searchingly** *adv.* [Anglo-French *cerchier*]

♦ **search engine** *n.* service provided to INTERNET users to enable them to search for items of interest. Some are free others charge a subscription in return for providing access to specialist publications, text retrieval, and other services.

---

searchlight *n.* **1** powerful outdoor electric light with a concentrated beam that can be turned in any direction. **2** light or beam from this.
search-party *n.* group of people conducting an organized search.
search warrant *n.* official authorization to enter and search a building.
sea room *n.* space at sea for a ship to turn etc.
sea salt *n.* salt produced by evaporating sea water.
seascape *n.* picture or view of the sea.
Sea Scout *n.* member of the maritime branch of the Scout Association.
seashell *n.* shell of a salt-water mollusc.
seashore *n.* land next to the sea.
seasick *adj.* nauseous from the motion of a ship at sea. □ **seasickness** *n.*
seaside *n.* sea-coast, esp. as a holiday resort.
season /'siːz(ə)n/ *–n.* **1** each of the climatic divisions of

the year (spring, summer, autumn, winter). **2** proper or suitable time. **3** time when something is plentiful, active, etc. **4** (usu. prec. by *the*) = HIGH SEASON. **5** time of year for an activity or for social life generally (*football season*; *London in the season*). **6** indefinite period. **7** *colloq.* = SEASON TICKET. *–v.* **1** flavour (food) with salt, herbs, etc. **2** enhance with wit etc. **3** moderate. **4** (esp. as **seasoned** *adj.*) make or become suitable by exposure to the weather or experience (*seasoned wood*; *seasoned campaigner*). □ **in season 1** (of food) plentiful and good. **2** (of an animal) on heat. [Latin *satio* sowing]

seasonable *adj.* **1** suitable or usual to the season. **2** opportune. **3** apt.

■ **Usage** *Seasonable* is sometimes confused with *seasonal.*

seasonal *adj.* of, depending on, or varying with the season (*seasonal rate of charging*; *seasonal discount*). □ **seasonally** *adv.*

■ **Usage** See note at *seasonable.*

♦ **seasonal unemployment** *n.* unemployment that occurs as a result of the seasonal nature of some jobs, for example in the building trade, seaside holiday trade, and agriculture. UK unemployment figures are usu. **seasonally adjusted**, i.e. adjusted to flatten the peaks and troughs of unemployment in certain seasons.

seasoning *n.* salt, herbs, etc. added to food to enhance its flavour.

season ticket *n.* ticket entitling the holder to unlimited travel, access, etc., in a given period.

seat *–n.* **1** thing made or used for sitting on. **2 a** buttocks. **b** part of a garment covering them. **3** part of a chair etc. on which the buttocks rest. **4** place for one person in a theatre etc. **5** position as an MP, committee member, etc., or the right to occupy it. **6** supporting or guiding part of a machine. **7** location (*seat of learning*). **8** country mansion. **9** manner of sitting on a horse etc. *–v.* **1** cause to sit. **2** provide sitting accommodation for (*bus seats 50*). **3** (as **seated** *adj.*) sitting. **4** put or fit in position. □ **be seated** sit down. **by the seat of one's pants** *colloq.* by instinct rather than knowledge. **take a seat** sit down. [Old Norse: related to SIT]

seat-belt *n.* belt securing car or aircraft passengers.

-seater *comb. form* having a specified number of seats.

seating *n.* **1** seats collectively. **2** sitting accommodation.

♦ **SEATS** *abbr.* = STOCK EXCHANGE ALTERNATIVE TRADING SERVICE.

Seattle /sɪˈæt(ə)l/ port and industrial city in the NW US, in the state of Washington; industries include sawmilling, shipbuilding, and aircraft manufacture; pop. (est. 1994) 520 947.

sea urchin *n.* small marine animal with a spiny shell.

sea wall *n.* wall built to stop flooding or erosion by the sea.

seaward /ˈsiːwəd/ *–adv.* (also **seawards**) towards the sea. *–adj.* going or facing towards the sea.

seaway *n.* **1** inland waterway open to seagoing ships. **2** ship's progress. **3** ship's path across the sea.

seaweed *n.* plant growing in the sea or on rocks on a shore.

seaworthy *adj.* fit to put to sea. □ **seaworthiness** *n.*

sebaceous /sɪˈbeɪʃəs/ *adj.* fatty; secreting oily matter. [Latin *sebum* tallow]

Sebastopol /sɪˈbæstəp(ə)l/ (Russian **Sevastopol** /sɪˈvæ-/) port, resort, and naval base in S Ukraine, in the Crimea; pop. (est. 1996) 365 000.

♦ **SEC** *abbr.* = SECURITIES AND EXCHANGE COMMISSION.

Sec. *abbr.* (also **sec.**) secretary.

sec[1] *abbr.* secant.

sec[2] *n. colloq.* (in phrases) second, moment (*wait a sec*). [abbreviation]

sec. *abbr.* second(s).

sec *adj.* (of wine) dry. [French]

secant /ˈsiːkənt/ *n. Math.* **1** ratio of the hypotenuse to the shorter side adjacent to an acute angle (in a right-angled triangle). **2** line cutting a curve at one or more points. [French]

secateurs /ˌsekəˈtɜːz/ *n.pl.* pruning clippers used with one hand. [French]

secede /sɪˈsiːd/ *v.* (**-ding**) withdraw formally from a political federation or religious body. [Latin *secedo -cess-*]

secession /sɪˈseʃ(ə)n/ *n.* act of seceding. □ **secessionist** *n.* & *adj.* [Latin: related to SECEDE]

seclude /sɪˈkluːd/ *v.* (**-ding**) (also *refl.*) **1** keep (a person or place) apart from others. **2** (esp. as **secluded** *adj.*) screen from view. [Latin *secludo -clus-*]

seclusion /sɪˈkluːʒ(ə)n/ *n.* secluded state or place.

second[1] /ˈsekənd/ *–adj.* **1** next after first. **2** additional (*ate a second cake*). **3** subordinate; inferior. **4** *Mus.* performing a lower or subordinate part (*second violins*). **5** such as to be comparable to (*a second Callas*). *–n.* **1** runner-up. **2** person or thing besides the first or previously mentioned one. **3** second gear. **4** (in *pl.*) inferior goods. **5** (in *pl.*) *colloq.* second helping or course. **6** assistant to a duellist, boxer, etc. *–v.* **1** support; back up. **2** formally support (a nomination, resolution, or its proposer). □ **at second hand** indirectly. □ **seconder** *n.* (esp. in sense 2 of *v.*). [Latin *secundus* from *sequor* follow]

second[2] /ˈsekənd/ *n.* **1** sixtieth of a minute of time or of an angle. **2** *colloq.* very short time (*wait a second*). [medieval Latin *secunda* (*minuta*) secondary (minute)]

second[3] /sɪˈkɒnd/ *v.* transfer (a person) temporarily to another department etc. □ **secondment** *n.* [French *en second* in the second rank]

secondary /ˈsekəndərɪ/ *–adj.* **1** coming after or next below what is primary. **2** derived from or supplementing what is primary. **3** (of education, a school, etc.) following primary, esp. from the age of 11. *–n.* (*pl.* **-ies**) secondary thing. □ **secondarily** *adv.* [Latin: related to SECOND[1]]

♦ **secondary bank** *n.* **1** finance house. **2** organization that offers some banking services, e.g. making loans, offering secondary mortgages, etc., but that does not offer the usual commercial-bank services of cheque accounts etc.

secondary colour *n.* result of mixing two primary colours.

♦ **secondary data** *n.* marketing research information available to researchers that they have not gathered themselves. Examples include data provided by a government department or extracted from company records.

♦ **secondary market** *n.* financial market in which existing securities are traded, as opposed to a **primary market**, in which securities are sold for the first time. In most cases a stock exchange largely fulfils the role of a secondary market, with the flotation of new issues representing only a small proportion of its total business. However, it is the existence of a flourishing secondary market, providing liquidity and the spreading of risks, that creates the conditions for a healthy primary market.

♦ **secondary picketing** *n.* picketing of premises of a firm not directly involved in an industrial dispute. See PICKETING.

♦ **secondary production** see PRODUCTION 3.

second-best *adj.* & *n.* next after best.

second chamber *n.* upper house of a parliament.

second class *–n.* second-best group, category, postal service, or accommodation. *–adj.* & *adv.* (**second-class**) of or by the second class (*second-class citizens*; *travelled second-class*).

second cousin *n.* son or daughter of one's parent's cousin.

second-degree *adj.* denoting burns that cause blistering but not permanent scars.

second fiddle see FIDDLE.

second-guess *v. colloq.* **1** anticipate by guesswork. **2** criticize with hindsight.

second-hand *–adj.* **1 a** having had a previous owner; not new. **b** (*attrib.*) (of a shop etc.) where such goods can be bought. **2** (of information etc.) indirect, not from one's own observation etc. *–adv.* **1** on a second-hand basis. **2** indirectly.

second lieutenant *n.* army officer next below lieutenant.

secondly *adv.* **1** furthermore. **2** as a second item.

♦ **second mortgage** *n.* mortgage taken out on a property that is already mortgaged. Second and subsequent mortgages can often be used to raise money from a finance house (but not a commercial bank or building society) if the value of the property has increased considerably since the first mortgage was taken out. As the deeds of the property are usu. held by the first mortgagee, the second mortgagee undertakes a greater risk and therefore usu. demands a higher rate of interest. The second mortgagee usu. registers the second mortgage for protection against subsequent mortgages. In the UK, the Land Registry will issue a certificate of second charge in the case of registered land.

second nature *n.* acquired tendency that has become instinctive.

♦ **second of exchange** see BILLS IN A SET.

second officer *n.* assistant mate on a merchant ship.

second person see PERSON 3.

second-rate *adj.* mediocre; inferior.

second sight *n.* clairvoyance.

second string *n.* alternative course of action etc.

second thoughts *n.pl.* revised opinion or resolution.

♦ **second-tier market** *n.* market for stocks and shares in which listing requirements for the companies are less stringent than those on a main market. Although a second-tier market needs to be effectively regulated, conditions of entry and reporting are less expensive. In the UK the unlisted securities market is a second-tier market.

second wind *n.* **1** recovery of normal breathing during exercise after initial breathlessness. **2** renewed energy to continue.

secrecy /'siːkrəsɪ/ *n.* state of being secret; habit or faculty of keeping secrets (*done in secrecy*).

secret /'siːkrɪt/ *–adj.* **1** kept or meant to be kept private, unknown, or hidden. **2** acting or operating secretly. **3** fond of secrecy. *–n.* **1** thing kept or meant to be kept secret. **2** mystery. **3** effective but not generally known method (*what's their secret?*; *the secret of success*). □ **in secret** secretly. □ **secretly** *adv.* [Latin *secerno secret-* separate]

secret agent *n.* spy.

secretaire /ˌsekrɪ'teə(r)/ *n.* escritoire. [French: related to SECRETARY]

secretariat /ˌsekrɪ'teərɪət/ *n.* **1** administrative office or department. **2** its members or premises. [medieval Latin: related to SECRETARY]

secretary /'sekrɪtərɪ/ *n.* (*pl.* **-ies**) **1** employee who assists with correspondence, records, making appointments, etc. **2** official of a society etc. who keeps minutes, writes letters, etc. **3** principal assistant of a government minister, ambassador, etc. □ **secretarial** /-'teərɪəl/ *adj.* **secretaryship** *n.* [Latin *secretarius*: related to SECRET]

secretary bird *n.* long-legged crested African bird.

Secretary-General *n.* principal administrator of an organization.

Secretary of State *n.* **1** head of a major government department. **2** *US* = FOREIGN MINISTER.

secret ballot *n.* ballot in which votes are cast in secret.

secrete /sɪ'kriːt/ *v.* (**-ting**) **1** (of a cell, organ, etc.) produce and discharge (a substance). **2** conceal. □ **secretory** *adj.* [from SECRET]

secretion /sɪ'kriːʃ(ə)n/ *n.* **1 a** process of secreting. **b** secreted substance. **2** act of concealing. [Latin: related to SECRET]

secretive /'siːkrətɪv/ *adj.* inclined to make or keep secrets; uncommunicative. □ **secretively** *adv.* **secretiveness** *n.*

secret police *n.* police force operating secretly for political ends.

♦ **secret reserve** *n.* = HIDDEN RESERVE.

secret service *n.* government department concerned with espionage.

secret society *n.* society whose members are sworn to secrecy about it.

sect *n.* **1** group sharing (usu. unorthodox) religious, political, or philosophical doctrines. **2** (esp. exclusive) religious denomination. [Latin *sequor* follow]

sectarian /sek'teərɪən/ *–adj.* **1** of a sect. **2** devoted, esp. narrow-mindedly, to one's sect. *–n.* member of a sect. □ **sectarianism** *n.* [medieval Latin *sectarius* adherent]

section /'sekʃ(ə)n/ *–n.* **1** each of the parts of a thing or out of which a thing can be fitted together. **2** part cut off. **3** subdivision. **4** *US* **a** area of land. **b** district of a town. **5** act of cutting or separating surgically. **6 a** cutting of a solid by a plane. **b** resulting figure or area. *–v.* **1** arrange in or divide into sections. **2** compulsorily commit to a psychiatric hospital. [Latin *seco sect-* cut]

sectional /'sekʃən(ə)l/ *adj.* **1 a** of a social group (*sectional interests*). **b** partisan. **2** made in sections. **3** local rather than general. □ **sectionally** *adv.*

sector /'sektə(r)/ *n.* **1** distinct part of an enterprise, society, the economy, etc. **2** military subdivision of an area. **3** plane figure enclosed by two radii of a circle, ellipse, etc., and the arc between them. **4** *Computing* subdivision of a track on a magnetic disk. A computer records data on a disk one sector at a time: each sector has a unique address that contains the track location and sector number. The disk is divided into sectors (i.e. formatted) prior to any recording of data, either at the time of manufacture or by control information written on the disk by computer program. [Latin: related to SECTION]

secular /'sekjʊlə(r)/ *adj.* **1** not concerned with religion; not sacred; worldly (*secular education*; *secular music*). **2** (of clerics) not monastic. □ **secularism** *n.* **secularize** *v.* (also **-ise**) (**-zing** or **-sing**). **secularization** /-'zeɪʃ(ə)n/ *n.* [Latin *saeculum* an age]

secure /sɪ'kjʊə(r)/ *–adj.* **1** untroubled by danger or fear. **2** safe. **3** reliable; stable; fixed. *–v.* (**-ring**) **1 a** make secure or safe. **b** make financially safe; protect financially. **2** fasten or close securely. **3** succeed in obtaining. □ **securely** *adv.* [Latin *se* without, *cura* care]

♦ **secured creditor** *n.* creditor who has a charge on the property of the debtor. See FIXED CHARGE; FLOATING CHARGE.

♦ **secured debenture** *n.* debenture secured by a charge over the property of a company, e.g. a mortgage debenture is secured on land belonging to the company. A trust deed usu. sets out the powers of the debenture holders to enforce their security in the event of the company defaulting in payment of the principal or the interest. It is usual to appoint a receiver to realize the security.

♦ **secured liability** *n.* debt against which the borrower has provided sufficient assets as security to safeguard the lender in case of non-repayment.

♦ **secured loan** *n.* loan in which the lender has an asset to which he or she can have recourse if the borrower defaults on the loan repayments.

♦ **Securities and Exchange Commission** *n.* (also **SEC**) US government agency that closely monitors the activities of stockbrokers and traders in securities. It also monitors take-overs in the US. If a person or organization acquires 5% or more of the equity of another company it must notify the SEC of the purchase within ten days. See also CREEPING TAKE-OVER.

♦ **Securities and Futures Authority Ltd.** *n.* (also **SFA**) Self-Regulating Organization formed from the merger of The Securities Association Ltd. (TSA) and the Association of Futures Brokers and Dealers Ltd. (AFBD) in April 1991. It is responsible for regulating the conduct of brokers and dealers in securities, options, and futures, including most of those on the London Stock Exchange and the London International Financial Futures and Options Exchange.

♦ **Securities and Investment Board** *n.* (also **SIB**) regulatory body set up by the Financial Services Act (1986) to oversee London's financial markets (e.g. the stock exchange, life assurance, unit trusts). Each market has its own Self-Regulating Organization (SRO), which reports to the SIB. The prime function of the SIB is to protect investors from fraud and to ensure that the rules of conduct established by the government and the SROs are followed. However, as the structure of City institutions and their regulation is not fixed for all time, the role of the SIB has to be capable of adapting to changing practices. Moreover, some City activities are outside its control; for example, take-overs remain under the supervision of the Take-over Panel (see CITY CODE ON TAKE-OVERS AND MERGERS). Members of the SIB are appointed jointly by the Secretary of State for Trade and Industry and the Governor of the Bank of England from leading City institutions; while this understandably leads to suggestions of partisanship, it is doubtful whether outsiders would have sufficient understanding of City practices to be effective as regulators. The SIB is authorized to grant recognition to investment institutions and is financed by the fees paid to achieve this recognition. In 1997 the new Labour government announced its intention to restructure the SIB, giving it greater powers over individual markets and the commercial banking system.

♦ **securitization** /sɪˌkjʊərɪtaɪˈzeɪʃ(ə)n/ *n.* (also **-isation**) process that enables borrowing and lending by banks to be replaced by the issue of such securities as Eurobonds. A bank borrows money from savers (investors) and lends to borrowers, charging fees to both for its service as well as making a turn on the interest payments. If a borrower can borrow directly from an investor, by issuing the investor with a bond (or equity), the costs to both borrower and lender can be reduced. Securitization has occurred increasingly in the 1980s as technology has improved and investors have become more sophisticated.

♦ **securitized mortgage** *n.* mortgage that has been converted into a marketable security, which can be sold to an investor. One advantage of selling on mortgages and other loans in this way is that it enables banks to move assets from their balance sheets, thus boosting their cash ratios. Securitization of mortgages is strictly controlled by the regulating authorities.

♦ **securitized paper** *n.* financial instrument (e.g. a bond or note) which results from a borrower and investor agreeing on an exchange of funds by securitization.

---

security *n.* (*pl.* **-ies**) **1** secure condition or feeling. **2** thing that guards or guarantees. **3 a** safety against espionage, theft, etc. **b** organization for ensuring this. **4** protection against access to information stored in a computer system by unauthorized recipients or unauthorized alteration or destruction of that information, as by using passwords when logging on and classifying information to restrict access to it. **5 a** thing deposited or pledged as a guarantee of an undertaking etc. **b** asset or assets to which a lender can have recourse if the borrower defaults on loan repayments. See also COLLATERAL *n.* 1. **6** (often in *pl.*) **a** financial asset, e.g. shares, government stocks, debentures, bonds, unit trusts, and rights to money lent or deposited. Securities do not include insurance policies. See also BEARER SECURITY; DATED SECURITY; FIXED-INTEREST SECURITY; GILT-EDGED SECURITY; LISTED SECURITY; MARKETABLE SECURITY. **b b** document as evidence of this.

security risk *n.* person or thing that threatens security.

Sedan /sɪˈdæn/ town in NE France; it has metallurgical, textile, and food-processing industries; pop. (1990) 22 400.

sedan /sɪˈdæn/ *n.* **1** (in full **sedan chair**) *hist.* enclosed chair for one, carried on poles by two men. **2** *US* enclosed car with four or more seats. [origin uncertain]

sedate /sɪˈdeɪt/ *–adj.* tranquil and dignified; serious. *–v.* (**-ting**) put under sedation.□ **sedately** *adv.* **sedateness** *n.* [Latin *sedo* settle, calm]

sedation /sɪˈdeɪʃ(ə)n/ *n.* act of calming, esp. by sedatives. [Latin: related to SEDATE]

sedative /ˈsedətɪv/ *–n.* calming drug or influence. *–adj.* calming, soothing. [medieval Latin: related to SEDATE]

sedentary /ˈsedəntərɪ/ *adj.* **1** sitting. **2** (of work etc.) done while sitting. **3** (of a person) disinclined to exercise. [Latin *sedeo* sit]

sedge *n.* waterside or marsh plant resembling coarse grass. □ **sedgy** *adj.* [Old English]

sediment /ˈsedɪmənt/ *n.* **1** grounds; dregs. **2** matter deposited on the land by water or wind. □ **sedimentary** /-ˈmentərɪ/ *adj.* **sedimentation** /-ˈteɪʃ(ə)n/ *n.* [Latin *sedeo* sit]

sedition /sɪˈdɪʃ(ə)n/ *n.* conduct or speech inciting to rebellion. □ **seditious** *adj.* [Latin *seditio*]

seduce /sɪˈdjuːs/ *v.* (**-cing**) **1** entice into sexual activity or wrongdoing. **2** coax or lead astray. □ **seducer** *n.* [Latin *se-* away, *duco duct-* lead]

seduction /sɪˈdʌkʃ(ə)n/ *n.* **1** seducing or being seduced. **2** thing that tempts or attracts.

seductive /sɪˈdʌktɪv/ *adj.* alluring, enticing. □ **seductively** *adv.* **seductiveness** *n.*

seductress /sɪˈdʌktrɪs/ *n.* female seducer. [obsolete *seductor* male seducer: related to SEDUCE]

sedulous /ˈsedjʊləs/ *adj.* persevering, diligent, painstaking. □ **sedulity** /sɪˈdjuːlɪtɪ/ *n.* **sedulously** *adv.* [Latin *sedulus* zealous]

sedum /ˈsiːdəm/ *n.* fleshy-leaved plant with yellow, pink, or white flowers, e.g. the stonecrop. [Latin, = houseleek]

see[1] *v.* (*past* **saw**; *past part.* **seen**) **1** perceive with the eyes. **2** have or use this power. **3** discern mentally; understand. **4** watch (a film, game, etc.). **5** ascertain, learn (*will see if he's here*). **6** imagine, foresee (*see trouble ahead*). **7** look at for information (*see page 15*). **8** meet and recognize (*I saw your mother in town*). **9 a** meet socially or on business; visit or be visited by (*is too ill to see anyone*; *must see a doctor*). **b** meet regularly as a boyfriend or girlfriend. **10** reflect, wait for clarification (*we shall have to see*). **11** experience (*I never thought to see it*). **12** find attractive (*can't think what she sees in him*). **13** escort, conduct (*saw them home*). **14** witness (an event etc.) (*see the New Year in*). **15** ensure (*see that it is done*). **16 a** (in poker etc.) equal (a bet). **b** equal the bet of (a player). □ **see about 1** attend to. **2** consider. **see the back of** *colloq.* be rid of. **see fit** see FIT[1]. **see the light 1** realize one's mistakes etc. **2** undergo religious conversion. **see off 1** be present at the departure of (a person). **2** *colloq.* ward off, get the better of. **see out 1** accompany out of a building etc. **2** finish (a project etc.) completely. **3** survive (a period etc.). **see over** inspect; tour. **see red** *colloq.* become enraged. **see stars** *colloq.* see lights as a result of a blow on the head. **see things** *colloq.* have hallucinations. **see through** detect the truth or true nature of. **see a person through** support a person during a difficult time. **see a thing through** finish it completely. **see to it** (foll. by *that*) ensure. [Old English]

see[2] *n.* **1** area under the authority of a bishop or archbishop. **2** his office or jurisdiction. [Latin *sedes* seat]

seed *–n.* **1 a** part of a plant capable of developing into another such plant. **b** seeds collectively, esp. for sowing. **2** semen. **3** prime cause, beginning. **4** offspring, descendants. **5** (in tennis etc.) seeded player. *–v.* **1 a** place seeds in. **b** sprinkle (as) with seed. **2** sow seeds. **3** produce or drop seed. **4** remove seeds from (fruit etc.). **5** place a crystal etc. in (a cloud) to produce rain. **6** *Sport* **a** so position (a strong competitor in a knockout competition) that he or she will not meet other strong competitors in early rounds. **b** arrange (the order of play) in this way. □ **go** (or **run) to seed 1** cease flowering as seed develops. **2** become degenerate, unkempt, etc. □ **seedless** *adj.* [Old English]

seed-bed *n.* **1** bed prepared for sowing. **2** place of development.

♦ **seed capital** *n.* small amount of initial capital required to fund the research and development necessary before a new company is set up. The seed capital should enable a persuasive and accurate business plan to be drawn up.

seedling *n.* young plant raised from seed rather than from a cutting etc.

seed-pearl *n.* very small pearl.

seed-potato *n.* potato kept for seed.

seedsman *n.* dealer in seeds.

seedy *adj.* (**-ier, -iest**) **1** shabby, unkempt. **2** *colloq.* unwell. **3** full of or going to seed.□ **seediness** *n.*

seeing *conj.* (usu. foll. by *that*) considering that, inasmuch as, because.

seek *v.* (*past* and *past part.* **sought** /sɔːt/) **1** (often foll. by *for, after*) search or inquire. **2 a** try or want to find or get or reach (*sought my hand*). **b** request (*sought help*). **3** endeavour (*seek to please*). □ **seek out 1** search for and find. **2** single out as a friend etc. □ **seeker** *n.* [Old English]

seem *v.* (often foll. by *to* + infin.) appear or feel (*seems ridiculous*). □ **I** etc. **can't seem to** I etc. appear unable to (*can't seem to manage it*). **it seems** (or **would seem**) (often foll. by *that*) it appears to be the case. [Old Norse]

seeming *adj.* apparent but perhaps doubtful (*his seeming interest*). □ **seemingly** *adv.*

seemly *adj.* (**-ier, -iest**) in good taste; decorous. □ **seemliness** *n.* [Old Norse: related to SEEM]

seen *past part.* of SEE[1].

See of Rome *n.* the papacy.

seep *v.* ooze out; percolate. [Old English]

seepage *n.* **1** act of seeping. **2** quantity that seeps out.

seer *n.* **1** person who sees. **2** prophet; visionary.

seersucker /'sɪəˌsʌkə(r)/ *n.* linen, cotton, etc. fabric with a puckered surface. [Persian]

see-saw /'siːsɔː/ *–n.* **1 a** long plank balanced on a central support, for children to sit on at each end and move up and down alternately. **b** this game. **2** up-and-down or to-and-fro motion. **3** close contest with alternating advantage. *–v.* **1** play on a see-saw. **2** move up and down. **3** vacillate in policy, emotion, etc. *–adj.* & *adv.* with up-and-down or backward-and-forward motion. [reduplication of SAW[1]]

seethe /siːð/ *v.* (**-thing**) **1** boil, bubble over. **2** be very angry, resentful, etc. [Old English]

see-through *adj.* (esp. of clothing) translucent.

SEG *abbr.* socio-economic grade.

segment /'segmənt/ *–n.* **1** each part into which a thing is or can be divided. **2** part of a circle or sphere etc. cut off by an intersecting line or plane. *–v.* usu. /-'ment/ divide into segments. □ **segmental** /-'ment(ə)l/ *adj.* **segmentation** /-'teɪʃ(ə)n/ *n.* [Latin *seco* cut]

segregate /'segrɪˌgeɪt/ *v.* (**-ting**) **1** put apart; isolate. **2** separate (esp. an ethnic group) from the rest of the community. [Latin *grex greg-* flock]

segregation /ˌsegrɪ'geɪʃ(ə)n/ *n.* **1** enforced separation of ethnic groups in a community etc. **2** segregating or being segregated. □ **segregationist** *n.* & *adj.*

seigneur /seɪ'njɜː(r)/ *n.* feudal lord. □ **seigneurial** *adj.* [French from Latin *senior* SENIOR]

Seine /seɪn/ river in N France, flowing from Burgundy to the English Channel near Le Havre. The cities of Paris and Rouen lie along its course.

seine /seɪn/ *–n.* fishing-net with floats at the top and weights at the bottom edge. *–v.* (**-ning**) fish or catch with a seine. [Old English *segne*]

seise var. of SEIZE 6.

seismic /'saɪzmɪk/ *adj.* of earthquakes. [Greek *seismos* earthquake]

seismogram /'saɪzməˌgræm/ *n.* record given by a seismograph.

seismograph /'saɪzməˌgrɑːf/ *n.* instrument that records the force, direction, etc., of earthquakes. □ **seismographic** /-'græfɪk/ *adj.*

seismology /saɪz'mɒlədʒɪ/ *n.* the study of earthquakes. □ **seismological** /-mə'lɒdʒɪk(ə)l/ *adj.* **seismologist** *n.*

seize /siːz/ *v.* (**-zing**) **1** (often foll. by *on, upon*) take hold of forcibly or suddenly. **2** take possession of forcibly or by legal power. **3** affect suddenly (*panic seized us*). **4** (often foll. by *on, upon*) take advantage of (an opportunity etc.). **5** (often foll. by *on, upon*) comprehend quickly or clearly. **6** (also **seise**) (usu. foll. by *of*) *Law* put in possession of. □ **seized** (or **seised) of 1** possessing legally. **2** aware or informed of. **seize up 1** (of a mechanism) become jammed. **2** (of part of the body etc.) become stiff. [French *saisir*]

seizure /'siːʒə(r)/ *n.* **1** seizing or being seized. **2** sudden attack, esp. of epilepsy or apoplexy.

Sekondi /ˌsekən'diː/ see TAKORADI.

Selangor /sə'læŋgə(r)/ state in Malaysia, on the W coast of the Malay Peninsula; pop. (est. 1993) 1 981 200; capital, Shah Alam. It is the economic centre of the country, its chief products being tin and rubber.

seldom /'seldəm/ *adv.* rarely, not often. [Old English]

select /sɪ'lekt/ *–v.* choose, esp. with care. *–adj.* **1** chosen for excellence or suitability. **2** (of a society etc.) exclusive. [Latin *seligo -lect-*]

select committee *n.* small parliamentary committee conducting a special inquiry.

selection /sɪ'lekʃ(ə)n/ *n.* **1** selecting or being selected. **2** selected person or thing. **3** things from which a choice may be made. **4** evolutionary process by which some species thrive better than others.

selective *adj.* **1** of or using selection (*selective schools*). **2** able to select. **3** (of memory etc.) selecting what is convenient. □ **selectively** *adv.* **selectivity** /-'tɪvɪtɪ/ *n.*

selector *n.* **1** person who selects, esp. a team. **2** device in a vehicle, machinery, etc. that selects the required gear etc.

selenium /sɪ'liːnɪəm/ *n.* non-metallic element occurring naturally in various metallic sulphide ores. [Greek *selēnē* moon]

self *n.* (*pl.* **selves**) **1** individuality, personality, or essence (*showed his true self; is her old self again*). **2** object of introspection or reflexive action. **3 a** one's own interests or pleasure. **b** concentration on these. **4** *Commerce* or *colloq.* myself, yourself, etc. (*cheque drawn to self*). [Old English]

self- *comb. form* expressing reflexive action: **1** of or by oneself or itself (*self-locking*). **2** on, in, for, or of oneself or itself (*self-absorbed*).

self-abasement /ˌselfə'beɪsmənt/ *n.* self-humiliation; cringing.

self-absorption /ˌselfəb'zɔːpʃ(ə)n/ *n.* absorption in oneself. □ **self-absorbed** *adj.*

self-abuse /ˌselfə'bjuːs/ *n. derog.* masturbation.

self-addressed /ˌselfə'drest/ *adj.* (of an envelope) bearing one's own address for a reply.

self-adhesive /ˌselfəd'hiːsɪv/ *adj.* (of an envelope, label, etc.) adhesive, esp. without wetting.

self-advancement /ˌselfəd'vɑːnsmənt/ *n.* advancement of oneself.

self-aggrandizement /ˌselfə'grændɪzmənt/ *n.* process of enriching oneself or making oneself powerful. □ **self-aggrandizing** /-'grændaɪzɪŋ/ *adj.*

self-analysis /ˌselfə'næləsɪs/ *n.* analysis of oneself, one's motives, character, etc.

self-appointed /ˌselfə'pɔɪntɪd/ *adj.* designated so by oneself, not by others (*self-appointed critic*).

self-assembly /ˌselfə'semblɪ/ *adj.* assembled by the buyer from a kit.

self-assertive /ˌselfə'sɜːtɪv/ *adj.* confident or aggressive in promoting oneself, one's rights, etc. □ **self-assertion** *n.*

♦ **self-assessment** *n.* system enabling taxpayers to assess their own INCOME TAX and CAPITAL GAINS TAX. This system was introduced in the UK on a voluntary basis for the year 1996–97. It was accompanied by the Board of Inland Revenue acquiring extensive audit powers.

self-assured /ˌselfəˈʃʊəd/ *n.* self-confident. □ **self-assurance** *n.*

self-aware /ˌselfəˈweə(r)/ *adj.* conscious of one's character, feelings, motives, etc. □ **self-awareness** *n.*

self-catering /selfˈkeɪtərɪŋ/ *adj.* (of a holiday, accommodation etc.) with cooking facilities provided, but no food.

self-censorship /selfˈsensəʃɪp/ *n.* censoring of oneself.

self-centred /selfˈsentəd/ *adj.* (*US* **-centered**) preoccupied with oneself; selfish. □ **self-centredly** *adv.* **self-centredness** *n.*

self-cleaning /selfˈkliːnɪŋ/ *adj.* (esp. of an oven) cleaning itself when heated.

self-conceit /ˌselfkənˈsiːt/ *n.* high or exaggerated opinion of oneself.

self-confessed /ˌselfkənˈfest/ *adj.* openly admitting oneself to be.

self-confident /selfˈkɒnfɪd(ə)nt/ *adj.* having confidence in oneself. □ **self-confidence** *n.* **self-confidently** *adv.*

self-congratulatory /ˌselfkənˌgrætjʊˌlətərɪ/ *adj.* = SELF-SATISFIED. □ **self-congratulation** /-ˈleɪʃ(ə)n/ *n.*

self-conscious /selfˈkɒnʃəs/ *adj.* nervous, shy, or embarrassed. □ **self-consciously** *adv.* **self-consciousness** *n.*

self-consistent /ˌselfkənˈsɪst(ə)nt/ *adj.* (of parts of the same whole etc.) consistent; not conflicting. □ **self-consistency** *n.*

self-contained /ˌselfkənˈteɪnd/ *adj.* **1** (of a person) uncommunicative; independent. **2** (of accommodation) complete in itself, having no shared entrance or facilities.

self-control /ˌselfkənˈtrəʊl/ *n.* power of controlling one's behaviour, emotions, etc. □ **self-controlled** *adj.*

self-critical /selfˈkrɪtɪk(ə)l/ *adj.* critical of oneself, one's abilities, etc. □ **self-criticism** /-ˌsɪz(ə)m/ *n.*

self-deception /ˌselfdɪˈsepʃ(ə)n/ *n.* deceiving of oneself, esp. about one's motives or feelings. □ **self-deceit** /-dɪˈsiːt/ *n.*

self-defeating /ˌselfdɪˈfiːtɪŋ/ *adj.* (of an action etc.) doomed to failure because of internal inconsistencies; achieving the opposite of what is intended.

self-defence /ˌselfdɪˈfens/ *n.* (*US* **-defense**) physical or verbal defence of one's body, property, rights, reputation, etc.

self-delusion /ˌselfdɪˈluːʒ(ə)n/ *n.* act of deluding oneself.

self-denial /ˌselfdɪˈnaɪəl/ *n.* asceticism, esp. to discipline oneself. □ **self-denying** *adj.*

self-deprecation /ˌselfdeprɪˈkeɪʃ(ə)n/ *n.* belittling oneself. □ **self-deprecating** /-ˈdeprɪˌkeɪtɪŋ/ *adj.*

self-destruct /ˌselfdɪˈstrʌkt/ *–v.* (of a spacecraft, bomb, etc.) explode or disintegrate automatically, esp. when pre-set to do so. *–attrib. adj.* enabling a thing to self-destruct (*self-destruct device*).

self-destruction /ˌselfdɪˈstrʌkʃ(ə)n/ *n.* **1** destroying of itself or oneself or one's chances, happiness, etc. **2** act of self-destructing. □ **self-destructive** *adj.*

self-determination /ˌselfdɪˌtɜːmɪˈneɪʃ(ə)n/ *n.* **1** nation's right to determine its own government etc. **2** ability to act with free will.

self-discipline /selfˈdɪsɪplɪn/ *n.* **1** ability to apply oneself. **2** self-control. □ **self-disciplined** *adj.*

self-discovery /ˌselfdɪˈskʌvərɪ/ *n.* process of acquiring insight into one's character, desires, etc.

self-doubt /selfˈdaʊt/ *n.* lack of confidence in oneself.

self-drive /selfˈdraɪv/ *adj.* (of a hired vehicle) driven by the hirer.

self-educated /selfˈedjʊˌkeɪtɪd/ *adj.* educated by one's own reading etc., without formal instruction.

self-effacing /ˌselfɪˈfeɪsɪŋ/ *adj.* retiring; modest. □ **self-effacement** *n.*

self-employed /ˌselfɪmˈplɔɪd/ *adj.* working as a freelance or for one's own business etc. Self-employed taxpayers who trade on their own account are taxed on the profits of their trades rather than by PAYE and their National-Insurance contributions differ from those of employees. □ **self-employment** *n.*

self-esteem /ˌselfɪˈstiːm/ *n.* good opinion of oneself.

self-evident /selfˈevɪd(ə)nt/ *adj.* obvious; without the need of proof or further explanation. □ **self-evidence** *n.* **self-evidently** *adv.*

self-examination /ˌselfɪgˌzæmɪˈneɪʃ(ə)n/ *n.* **1** the study of one's own conduct etc. **2** examining of one's body for signs of illness.

self-explanatory /ˌselfɪkˈsplænətərɪ/ *adj.* not needing explanation.

self-expression /ˌselfɪkˈspreʃ(ə)n/ *n.* artistic or free expression.

self-financing /selfˈfaɪnænsɪŋ, -ˈnænsɪŋ/ *adj.* (of an institution or undertaking) that pays for itself without subsidy.

self-fulfilling /ˌselffʊlˈfɪlɪŋ/ *adj.* (of a prophecy etc.) bound to come true as a result of its being made.

self-fulfilment /ˌselffʊlˈfɪlmənt/ *n.* fulfilment of one's ambitions etc.

self-governing /selfˈgʌvənɪŋ/ *adj.* governing itself or oneself. □ **self-government** *n.*

self-help /selfˈhelp/ *n.* (often *attrib.*) use of one's own abilities, resources, etc. to solve one's problems etc. (*formed a self-help group*).

self-image /selfˈɪmɪdʒ/ *n.* one's conception of oneself.

self-important /ˌselfɪmˈpɔːt(ə)nt/ *adj.* conceited; pompous. □ **self-importance** *n.*

self-imposed /ˌselfɪmˈpəʊzd/ *adj.* (of a task etc.) imposed on and by oneself.

self-improvement /ˌselfɪmˈpruːvmənt/ *n.* improvement of oneself or one's life etc. by one's own efforts.

self-induced /ˌselfɪnˈdjuːst/ *adj.* induced by oneself or itself.

self-indulgent /ˌselfɪnˈdʌldʒ(ə)nt/ *adj.* **1** indulging in one's own pleasure, feelings, etc. **2** (of a work of art etc.) lacking economy and control. □ **self-indulgence** *n.*

self-inflicted /ˌselfɪnˈflɪktɪd/ *adj.* inflicted by and on oneself.

self-interest /selfˈɪntrəst/ *n.* one's personal interest or advantage. □ **self-interested** *adj.*

selfish *adj.* concerned chiefly with one's own interests or pleasure; actuated by or appealing to self-interest. □ **selfishly** *adv.* **selfishness** *n.*

self-justification /ˌselfdʒʌstɪfɪˈkeɪʃ(ə)n/ *n.* justification or excusing of oneself.

self-knowledge /selfˈnɒlɪdʒ/ *n.* understanding of oneself.

selfless *adj.* unselfish. □ **selflessly** *adv.* **selflessness** *n.*

♦ **self-liquidating** /selfˈlɪkwɪˌdeɪtɪŋ/ *adj.* **1** (of an asset) earning back its original cost out of income over a fixed period. **2** (of a loan) used to finance a project that will provide sufficient yield to repay the loan and its interest and leave a profit. **3** (of a sales-promotion offer) paying for itself. For example, an offer of a free tea mug in exchange for a specified number of vouchers, each taken from a box of tea bags, will be self-liquidating if the extra sales of tea bags during the promotion pay for the costs of buying and despatching the mugs.

self-made *adj.* successful or rich by one's own effort.

self-opinionated /ˌselfəˈpɪnjəˌneɪtɪd/ *adj.* stubbornly adhering to one's opinions.

self-perpetuating /ˌselfpəˈpetjuːˌeɪtɪŋ/ *adj.* perpetuating itself or oneself without external agency.

self-pity /selfˈpɪtɪ/ *n.* feeling sorry for oneself. □ **self-pitying** *adj.*
self-pollination /ˌselfpɒlɪˈneɪʃ(ə)n/ *n.* pollination of a flower by pollen from the same plant. □ **self-pollinating** *adj.*
self-portrait /selfˈpɔːtrɪt/ *n.* portrait or description of oneself by oneself.
self-possessed /ˌselfpəˈzest/ *adj.* calm and composed. □ **self-possession** /-ˈzeʃ(ə)n/ *n.*
self-preservation /ˌselfprezəˈveɪʃ(ə)n/ *n.* **1** keeping oneself safe. **2** instinct for this.
self-proclaimed /ˌselfprəˈkleɪmd/ *adj.* proclaimed by oneself or itself to be such.
self-propelled /ˌselfprəˈpeld/ *adj.* (of a vehicle etc.) propelled by its own power. □ **self-propelling** *adj.*
self-raising /selfˈreɪzɪŋ/ *adj.* (of flour) containing a raising agent.
self-realization /ˌselfrɪəlaɪˈzeɪʃ(ə)n/ *n.* development of one's abilities etc.
self-regard /ˌselfrɪˈgɑːd/ *n.* proper regard for oneself.
self-regulating /selfˈregjʊˌleɪtɪŋ/ *adj.* regulating oneself or itself without intervention. □ **self-regulation** /-ˈleɪʃ(ə)n/ *n.* **self-regulatory** /-lətərɪ/ *adj.*

◆ **Self-Regulating Organization** *n.* (also **SRO**) any of several organizations set up in the UK under the Financial Services Act (1986) to regulate the activities of investment businesses and to draw up and enforce specific codes of conduct. The SROs recognized by the Securities and Investment Board, to whom they report, are: the Securities and Futures Authority Ltd (SFA), the Investment Managers Regulatory Organization (IMRO), which regulates any institution that offers investment management (including Friendly Societies), and the Personal Investment Authority (PIA), which regulates the activities of investment business carried out mainly with or for the private investor.

---

self-reliance /ˌselfrɪˈlaɪəns/ *n.* reliance on one's own resources etc.; independence. □ **self-reliant** *adj.*
self-reproach /ˌselfrɪˈprəʊtʃ/ *n.* reproach directed at oneself.
self-respect /ˌselfrɪˈspekt/ *n.* respect for oneself. □ **self-respecting** *adj.*
self-restraint /ˌselfrɪˈstreɪnt/ *n.* self-control.
self-righteous /selfˈraɪtʃəs/ *adj.* smugly sure of one's rightness. □ **self-righteously** *adv.* **self-righteousness** *n.*
self-rule /selfˈruːl/ *n.* self-government.
self-sacrifice /selfˈsækrɪˌfaɪs/ *n.* selflessness; self-denial. □ **self-sacrificing** *adj.*
selfsame *adj.* (prec. by *the*) very same, identical.
self-satisfied /selfˈsætɪsˌfaɪd/ *adj.* complacent; self-righteous. □ **self-satisfaction** /-ˈfækʃ(ə)n/ *n.*
self-sealing /selfˈsiːlɪŋ/ *adj.* **1** (of a tyre etc.) automatically able to seal small punctures. **2** (of an envelope) self-adhesive.
self-seed /selfˈsiːd/ *v.* (of a plant) propagate itself by seed. □ **self-seeder** *n.*
self-seeking /selfˈsiːkɪŋ/ *adj.* & *n.* selfish.
self-service /selfˈsɜːvɪs/ *–adj.* (often *attrib.*) (of a shop, restaurant, petrol station, etc.) with customers serving themselves and paying at a checkout etc., hence greatly reducing labour costs. *–n. colloq.* self-service restaurant etc.
self-starter /selfˈstɑːtə(r)/ *n.* **1** electrical appliance for starting an engine. **2** ambitious person with initiative.
self-styled *adj.* called so by oneself.
self-sufficient /ˌselfsəˈfɪʃ(ə)nt/ *adj.* **1** able to supply one's own needs; independent. **2** (of a country) having the necessary resources etc. for its economic survival independently of the rest of the world. It is not always economically sound for a self-sufficient country to use home products if they can be purchased more cheaply elsewhere, esp. if that country wishes to build up an export trade. □ **self-sufficiency** *n.*
self-supporting /ˌselfsəˈpɔːtɪŋ/ *adj.* financially self-sufficient.
self-taught /selfˈtɔːt/ *adj.* self-educated.

◆ **self-tender** *n.* tender in which a company approaches its shareholders in order to buy back some or all of its shares. There are two circumstances in which this operation can be of use. One is in the case of a hostile bid: the directors may wish to buy back shares in their company in order to reduce the chances of the bidder being able to buy a controlling interest in the company. The other circumstance is that the board may wish to show increased earnings per share; if they are unable to increase their profits it may be appropriate for them to reduce the number of shares in the company.

---

self-willed /selfˈwɪld/ *adj.* obstinately pursuing one's own wishes.
self-worth /selfˈwɜːθ/ *n.* = SELF-ESTEEM.
sell *–v.* (*past* and *past part.* **sold** /səʊld/) **1** exchange or be exchanged for money (*these sell well*). **2** stock for sale (*do you sell eggs?*). **3** (foll. by *at, for*) have a specified price (*sells at £5*). **4** (also *refl.*) betray or prostitute for money etc. **5** (also *refl.*) advertise or publicize (a product, oneself, etc.). **6** cause to be sold (*name alone will sell it*). **7** *colloq.* make (a person) enthusiastic about (an idea etc.). *–n. colloq.* **1** manner of selling (*soft sell*). **2** deception; disappointment. □ **sell down the river** see RIVER. **sell off** sell at reduced prices. **sell out 1** (also *absol.*) sell (all one's stock etc.). **2** *Stock Exch.* (of a broker) sell securities, commodities, etc. because the original buyer is unable to pay for them due to a fall in market price. The broker sells them at the best price available and the original buyer is responsible for any difference between the price realized and the original selling price, plus the costs of selling out. **3** betray; be treacherous or disloyal. **sell short 1** disparage, underestimate. **2** *Stock Exch.* sell commodities, securities, currencies, etc. that one does not have. See BEAR[2] 3. **sell up** sell one's business, house, etc. [Old English]
Sellafield /ˈseləˌfiːld/ (formerly **Windscale**) site of an atomic power station in NW England, near the coast of Cumbria, now belonging to British Nuclear Fuels.
sell-by date *n.* latest recommended date of sale.
seller *n.* **1** person who sells. **2** thing that sells well or badly. □ **sellers over** condition of a market in commodities, securities, etc. in which buyers have been satisfied but some sellers remain. Such a condition indicates a weak market, with a tendency for prices to fall.

◆ **seller's market** *n.* (also **sellers' market**) trading conditions in which the demand exceeds the supply, so that sellers can increase prices. At some point, however, buyers will cease to follow the price rises and the sellers will be forced to drop prices in order to make sales. Cf. BUYER'S MARKET.
◆ **selling costs** *n.pl.* costs incurred in selling a product or service, including advertising, display, after-sales service, promotions, and the salaries and commissions of the sales force.

---

selling-point *n.* advantageous feature.
Sellotape /ˈseləˌteɪp/ *–n. propr.* adhesive usu. transparent tape. *–v.* (**sellotape**) (**-ping**) fix with Sellotape. [from CELLULOSE]
sell-out *n.* **1** commercial success, esp. the selling of all tickets for a show. **2** betrayal.
selvage /ˈselvɪdʒ/ *n.* (also **selvedge**) fabric edging woven to prevent cloth from fraying. [from SELF, EDGE]
selves *pl.* of SELF.
semantic /sɪˈmæntɪk/ *adj.* of meaning in language. □ **semantically** *adv.* [Greek *sēmainō* to mean]

◆ **semantic differential** *n.* method of comparing the image of a product or company with the competition by asking members of the public to describe the product or company by choosing one of a pair of words or phrases that would best describe it.

---

semantics *n.pl.* (usu. treated as *sing.*) **1** branch of linguistics concerned with meaning. **2** part of the description of a programming language, concerned with specifying the meaning of statements, control structures, etc. See PROGRAMMING LANGUAGE.

semaphore /ˈseməˌfɔː(r)/ –*n.* **1** system of signalling with the arms or two flags. **2** railway signalling apparatus consisting of a post with a movable arm or arms etc. –*v.* (**-ring**) signal or send by semaphore. [Greek *sēma* sign, *pherō* bear]

Semarang /səˈmɑːræŋ/ port in Indonesia, capital of the province of Central Java; industries include textiles and shipbuilding, and sugar, coffee, rubber, copra, and kapok are exported; pop. (1990) 1 005 316.

semblance /ˈsembləns/ *n.* (foll. by *of*) appearance; show (*a semblance of anger*). [French *sembler* resemble]

semen /ˈsiːmən/ *n.* reproductive fluid of males. [Latin *semen semin-* seed]

semester /sɪˈmestə(r)/ *n.* half-year course or term in (esp. US) universities. [Latin *semestris* from *sex* six, *mensis* month]

semi /ˈsemɪ/ *n.* (*pl.* **-s**) *colloq.* semi-detached house. [abbreviation]

semi- *prefix* **1** half. **2** partly. [Latin]

semibreve /ˈsemɪˌbriːv/ *n. Mus.* note equal to four crotchets.

semicircle /ˈsemɪˌsɜːk(ə)l/ *n.* half of a circle or of its circumference. □ **semicircular** /-ˈsɜːkjʊlə(r)/ *adj.*

semicolon /ˌsemɪˈkəʊlən/ *n.* punctuation mark (;) of intermediate value between a comma and full stop.

semiconductor /ˌsemɪkənˈdʌktə(r)/ *n.* substance that in certain conditions has electrical conductivity intermediate between insulators and metals.

semiconductor memory *n. Computing* cheap compact memory composed of one or more integrated circuits fabricated in semiconductor material. The integrated circuit is composed of an array of microscopic electronic devices, each of which can store one bit of data (either a binary 1 or a binary 0). There may be thousands of these storage locations within a single integrated circuit measuring only a few square millimetres in area. Data can be accessed extremely rapidly from these locations. The categories of semiconductor memory include RAM (which is read/write memory), ROM (read-only memory), PROM (programmable ROM), and EPROM (erasable PROM). There is random access to all these types of semiconductor memory. Semiconductor RAM has been used to build the main store in computers since the early 1970s. See also RANDOM ACCESS.

semi-conscious /ˌsemɪˈkɒnʃəs/ *adj.* partly or imperfectly conscious.

semi-detached /ˌsemɪdɪˈtætʃt/ –*adj.* (of a house) joined to one other on one side only. –*n.* such a house.

semifinal /ˌsemɪˈfaɪn(ə)l/ *n.* match or round preceding the final. □ **semifinalist** *n.*

seminal /ˈsemɪn(ə)l/ *adj.* **1** of seed, semen, or reproduction; germinal. **2** (of ideas etc.) forming a basis for future development. [Latin: related to SEMEN]

seminar /ˈsemɪˌnɑː(r)/ *n.* **1** small discussion class at a university etc. **2** short intensive course of study. **3** conference of specialists. [German: related to SEMINARY]

seminary /ˈsemɪnərɪ/ *n.* (*pl.* **-ies**) training-college for priests or rabbis etc. □ **seminarist** *n.* [Latin: related to SEMEN]

semiotics /ˌsemɪˈɒtɪks/ *n.* the study of signs and symbols and their use, esp. in language. □ **semiotic** *adj.* [Greek *sēmeiōtikos* of signs]

semi-permeable /ˌsemɪˈpɜːmɪəb(ə)l/ *adj.* (of a membrane etc.) allowing small molecules to pass through.

semiprecious /ˌsemɪˈpreʃəs/ *adj.* (of a gem) less valuable than a precious stone.

semi-professional /ˌsemɪprəˈfeʃən(ə)l/ –*adj.* **1** (of a footballer, musician, etc.) paid for an activity but not relying on it for a living. **2** of semi-professionals. –*n.* semi-professional person.

semiquaver /ˈsemɪˌkweɪvə(r)/ *n. Mus.* note equal to half a quaver.

semi-skilled /ˌsemɪˈskɪld/ *adj.* (of work or a worker) needing or having some training.

semi-skimmed /ˌsemɪˈskɪmd/ *adj.* (of milk) from which some of the cream has been skimmed.

♦ **semi-solus** /ˌsemɪˈsəʊləs/ *adj.* (of an advertisement) appearing on the same page as another advertisement but not adjacent to it. Cf. SOLUS.

Semite /ˈsiːmaɪt/ *n.* member of the peoples said to be descended from Shem (Gen. 10), including esp. the Jews and Arabs. [Greek *Sēm* Shem]

Semitic /sɪˈmɪtɪk/ *adj.* **1** of the Semites, esp. the Jews. **2** of languages of the family including Hebrew and Arabic.

semitone /ˈsemɪˌtəʊn/ *n.* half a tone in the musical scale.

semitropical /ˌsemɪˈtrɒpɪk(ə)l/ *adj.* subtropical.

♦ **semivariable costs** /ˌsemɪˈveərɪəb(ə)l/ *n.pl.* (also **stepped costs**) costs that vary with levels of production but in discrete steps rather than continuously. An example might be the rent of workshop floor-space; new space will only be required when production reaches a given level and then not again until the new capacity has been exhausted.

---

semivowel /ˈsemɪˌvaʊəl/ *n.* **1** sound intermediate between a vowel and a consonant (e.g. *w*, *y*). **2** letter representing this.

semolina /ˌseməˈliːnə/ *n.* **1** hard grains left after the milling of flour, used in milk puddings etc. **2** pudding of this. [Italian *semolino*]

sempstress var. of SEAMSTRESS.

Semtex *n. propr.* malleable odourless plastic explosive. [from *Semtin* in the Czech Republic, where it was originally made]

SEN *abbr. hist.* State Enrolled Nurse.

Sen. *abbr.* **1** Senior. **2** Senator.

senate /ˈsenɪt/ *n.* **1** legislative body, esp. the upper and smaller assembly in the US, France, etc. **2** governing body of a university or (*US*) a college. **3** ancient Roman state council. [Latin *senatus* from *senex* old man]

senator /ˈsenətə(r)/ *n.* member of a senate. □ **senatorial** /-ˈtɔːrɪəl/ *adj.* [Latin: related to SENATE]

S en C *abbr.* (French) société en commandite (= limited partnership).

send *v.* (*past* and *past part.* **sent**) **1 a** order or cause to go or be conveyed. **b** propel (*sent him flying*). **c** cause to become (*sent me mad*). **2** send a message etc. (*he sent to warn me*). **3** (of God, etc.) grant, bestow, or inflict; bring about; cause to be. **4** *slang* put into ecstasy. □ **send away for** order (goods) by post. **send down 1** rusticate or expel from a university. **2** send to prison. **send for 1** summon. **2** order by post. **send in 1** cause to go in. **2** submit (an entry etc.) for a competition etc. **send off 1** dispatch (a letter, parcel, etc.). **2** attend the departure of (a person) as a sign of respect etc. **3** *Sport* (of a referee) order (a player) to leave the field. **send off for** = *send away for*. **send on** transmit further or in advance of oneself. **send up 1** cause to go up. **2** transmit to a higher authority. **3** *colloq.* ridicule by mimicking. **send word** send information. □ **sender** *n.* [Old English]

Sendai /senˈdaɪ/ city in Japan, capital of Tohoku region on the island of Honshu; pop. (1995) 971 263.

send-off *n.* party etc. at the departure of a person, start of a project, etc.

send-up *n. colloq.* satire, parody.

senescent /sɪˈnes(ə)nt/ *adj.* growing old. □ **senescence** *n.* [Latin *senex* old]

seneschal /ˈsenɪʃ(ə)l/ *n.* steward of a medieval great house. [French, = old servant]

senhor /seɪnˈjɔː(r)/ *n.* title used of or to a Portuguese or Brazilian man. [Portuguese from Latin *senior* SENIOR]

senhora /seɪnˈjɔːrə/ *n.* title used of or to a Portuguese woman or a Brazilian married woman.

senhorita /ˌseɪnjəˈriːtə/ *n.* title used of or to a Brazilian unmarried woman.

senile /ˈsiːnaɪl/ *adj.* **1** of old age. **2** mentally or physically infirm because of old age. □ **senility** /sɪˈnɪlɪtɪ/ *n.* [Latin: related to SENESCENT]

senile dementia *n.* illness of old people with loss of memory and control of bodily functions etc.

senior /ˈsiːnɪə(r)/ *–adj.* **1** more or most advanced in age, standing, or position. **2** (placed after a person's name) senior to a relative of the same name. *–n.* **1** senior person. **2** one's elder or superior. □ **seniority** /-ˈɒrɪtɪ/ *n.* [Latin comparative of *senex* old]

senior citizen *n.* old-age pensioner.

♦ **senior debt** *n.* debt taking precedence over other debts called in for repayment. Sometimes a lender to a company with other debts will stipulate that they will only lend if the loan ranks as the senior debt.

---

senior nursing officer *n.* person in charge of nursing services in a hospital.

senior school *n.* school for children esp. over the age of 11.

senior service *n.* Royal Navy.

senna /ˈsenə/ *n.* **1** cassia. **2** laxative from the dried pod of this. [Arabic]

S en NC *abbr.* (French) société en nom collectif (= partnership).

señor /senˈjɔː(r)/ *n.* (*pl.* **señores** /-rez/) title used of or to a Spanish-speaking man. [Spanish from Latin *senior* SENIOR]

señora /senˈjɔːrə/ *n.* title used of or to a Spanish-speaking married woman.

señorita /ˌsenjəˈriːtə/ *n.* title used of or to a young or unmarried Spanish-speaking woman.

sensation /senˈseɪʃ(ə)n/ *n.* **1** feeling in one's body (*sensation of warmth*). **2** awareness, impression (*sensation of being watched*). **3 a** intense interest, shock, etc. felt among a large group. **b** person, event, etc., causing this. **4** sense of touch. [medieval Latin: related to SENSE]

sensational *adj.* **1** causing or intended to cause great public excitement etc. **2** dazzling; wonderful (*you look sensational*). □ **sensationalize** *v.* (also **-ise**) (**-zing** or **-sing**). **sensationally** *adv.*

sensationalism *n.* use of or interest in the sensational. □ **sensationalist** *n.* & *adj.*

sense *–n.* **1 a** any of the five bodily faculties transmitting sensation. **b** sensitiveness of all or any of these (*good sense of smell*). **2** ability to perceive or feel. **3** (foll. by *of*) consciousness; awareness (*sense of guilt*). **4** quick or accurate appreciation, understanding, or instinct (*sense of humour*). **5** practical wisdom, common sense. **6 a** meaning of a word etc. **b** intelligibility or coherence. **7** prevailing opinion (*sense of the meeting*). **8** (in *pl.*) sanity, ability to think. *–v.* (**-sing**) **1** perceive by a sense or senses. **2** be vaguely aware of. **3** realize. **4** (of a machine etc.) detect. □ **come to one's senses 1** regain consciousness. **2** regain common sense. **in a** (or **one) sense** if the statement etc. is understood in a particular way. **make sense** be intelligible or practicable. **make sense of** show or find the meaning of. **take leave of one's senses** go mad. [Latin *sensus* from *sentio sens-* feel]

senseless *adj.* **1** pointless; foolish. **2** unconscious. □ **senselessly** *adv.* **senselessness** *n.*

sense-organ *n.* bodily organ conveying external stimuli to the sensory system.

sensibility /ˌsensɪˈbɪlɪtɪ/ *n.* (*pl.* **-ies**) **1** capacity to feel. **2 a** sensitiveness. **b** exceptional degree of this. **3** (in *pl.*) tendency to feel offended etc.

■ **Usage** *Sensibility* should not be used to mean 'possession of good sense'.

sensible /ˈsensɪb(ə)l/ *adj.* **1** having or showing wisdom or common sense. **2 a** perceptible by the senses. **b** great enough to be perceived. **3** (of clothing etc.) practical. **4** (foll. by *of*) aware. □ **sensibly** *adv.*

sensitive /ˈsensɪtɪv/ *adj.* **1** (often foll. by *to*) acutely susceptible to external stimuli or impressions; having sensibility. **2** easily offended or hurt. **3** (often foll. by *to*) (of an instrument etc.) responsive to or recording slight changes. **4** (of photographic materials) responding (esp. rapidly) to light. **5** (of a topic etc.) requiring tactful treatment or secrecy. □ **sensitively** *adv.* **sensitiveness** *n.* **sensitivity** /-ˈtɪvɪtɪ/ *n.*

♦ **sensitive market** *n.* market in commodities, securities, etc. that is sensitive to outside influences because it is basically unstable. For example, a poor crop in a commodity market may make it sensitive, with buyers anxious to cover their requirements but unwilling to show their hand and risk forcing prices up. News of a hurricane in the growing area could cause a sharp price rise in such a sensitive market.

---

sensitize /ˈsensɪˌtaɪz/ *v.* (also **-ise**) (**-zing** or **-sing**) make sensitive. □ **sensitization** /-ˈzeɪʃ(ə)n/ *n.*

sensor *n.* device for detecting or measuring a physical property. [from SENSORY]

sensory *adj.* of sensation or the senses. [Latin *sentio sens-* feel]

sensual /ˈsensjʊəl/ *adj.* **1 a** of physical, esp. sexual, pleasure. **b** enjoying or giving this, voluptuous. **2** showing sensuality (*sensual lips*). □ **sensualism** *n.* **sensually** *adv.* [Latin: related to SENSE]

■ **Usage** *Sensual* is sometimes confused with *sensuous*, which does not have the sexual overtones of *sensual*.

sensuality /ˌsensjʊˈælɪtɪ/ *n.* (esp. sexual) gratification of the senses.

sensuous /ˈsensjʊəs/ *adj.* of or affecting the senses, esp. aesthetically. □ **sensuously** *adv.* **sensuousness** *n.* [Latin: related to SENSE]

Senegal /ˌsenɪˈgɔːl/, **Republic of** country on the W coast of Africa, with Mauritania to the N and The Gambia forming a narrow enclave within its territory. Subsistence agriculture occupies a large proportion of the population; crops include peanuts and peanut oil, rice, millet, and maize. There are important deposits of phosphates, iron ore, natural gas, and offshore oil. Industries, centred on Dakar, include food processing and textiles. Cotton fabrics and fish products are major manufactured exports; other exports include fish and crustaceans, peanuts and peanut oil, phosphates, and petroleum products. Tourism is an increasing source of revenue.
History. Part of the Mali empire in the 14th and 15th centuries, the area was colonized by the French in the second half of the 19th century. Senegal became part of French West Africa in 1895, a self-governing member of the French community in 1958, and part of the Federation of Mali in 1959 before becoming an independent republic in 1960. In 1982 Senegal joined with The Gambia to form the Senegambia Confederation, which collapsed in 1989. President, Abdou Diouf; prime minister, Habib Thiam; capital, Dakar. □ **Senegalese** /-ˈliːz/ *adj.* & *n.*

languages	French (official), African dialects
currency	CFA franc (CFAF) of 100 centimes
pop. (1996)	8 532 000
GNP (1994)	US$4.9B
literacy	43% (m); 23% (f)
life expectancy	55 (m); 58 (f)

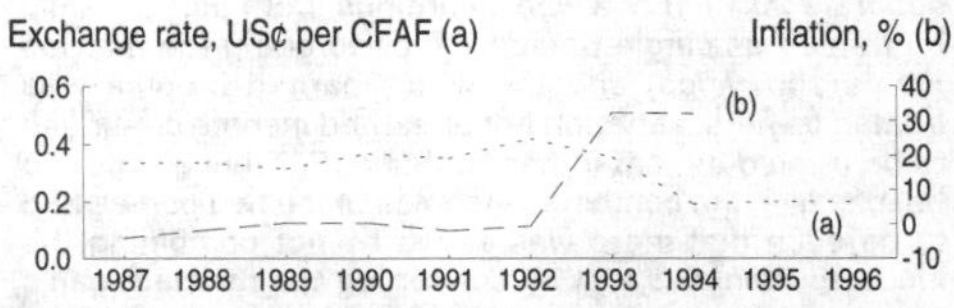

■ **Usage** See note at *sensual*.

sent *past* and *past part.* of SEND.

sentence /'sent(ə)ns/ *–n.* **1** statement, question, exclamation, or command containing or implying a subject and predicate (e.g. *I went*; *come here!*). **2 a** decision of a lawcourt, esp. the punishment allotted to a convicted criminal. **b** declaration of this. *–v.* (**-cing**) **1** declare the sentence of (a convicted criminal etc.). **2** (foll. by *to*) declare (such a person) to be condemned to (a punishment). [Latin *sententia* from *sentio* consider]

sententious /sen'tenʃəs/ *adj.* **1** pompously moralizing. **2** affectedly formal in style. **3** aphoristic; using maxims. □ **sententiousness** *n.* [Latin: related to SENTENCE]

sentient /'senʃ(ə)nt/ *adj.* capable of perception and feeling. □ **sentience** *n.* **sentiency** *n.* **sentiently** *adv.* [Latin *sentio* feel]

sentiment /'sentɪmənt/ *n.* **1** mental feeling. **2** (often in *pl.*) what one feels, opinion. **3** opinion or feeling, as distinct from its expression (*the sentiment is good*). **4** emotional or irrational view. **5** such views collectively, esp. as an influence. **6** tendency to be swayed by feeling. **7 a** mawkish or exaggerated emotion. **b** display of this.

sentimental /ˌsentɪ'ment(ə)l/ *adj.* **1** of or showing sentiment. **2** showing or affected by emotion rather than reason. □ **sentimentalism** *n.* **sentimentalist** *n.* **sentimentality** /-'tælɪtɪ/ *n.* **sentimentalize** *v.* (also **-ise**) (**-zing** or **-sing**). **sentimentally** *adv.*

sentimental value *n.* value given to a thing because of its associations.

sentinel /'sentɪn(ə)l/ *n.* sentry or lookout. [French from Italian]

sentry /'sentrɪ/ *n.* (*pl.* **-ies**) soldier etc. stationed to keep guard. [perhaps from obsolete *centrinel*, var. of SENTINEL]

sentry-box *n.* cabin for sheltering a standing sentry.

Seoul /səʊl/ capital of the Republic of Korea (South Korea), a rapidly developing centre of industry and commerce; pop. (1995) 10 229 262.

sepal /'sep(ə)l/ *n.* division or leaf of a calyx. [perhaps from SEPARATE, PETAL]

separable /'sepərəb(ə)l/ *adj.* able to be separated. □ **separability** /-'bɪlɪtɪ/ *n.* [Latin: related to SEPARATE]

separate *–adj.* /'sepərət/ forming a unit by itself, existing apart; disconnected, distinct, or individual. *–n.* /'sepərət/ (in *pl.*) trousers, skirts, etc. that are not parts of suits. *–v.* /'sepəˌreɪt/ (**-ting**) **1** make separate, sever. **2** prevent union or contact of. **3** go different ways. **4** (esp. as **separated** *adj.*) cease to live with one's spouse. **5** (foll. by *from*) secede. **6 a** divide or sort into parts or sizes. **b** (often foll. by *out*) extract or remove (an ingredient etc.). □ **separately** *adv.* **separateness** *n.* [Latin *separo* (v.)]

♦ **separate assessment** *n.* (before April 1990) an election that could be made by one party to a marriage in the UK enabling each party to pay his or her own tax. Unlike an election for separate taxation of a wife's earnings, this saved no tax. It merely allocated the total tax payable by the married couple as a single unit to the two parties for payment.

♦ **separate taxation of a wife's earnings** *n. hist.* an election that could be made by both parties to a marriage in the UK enabling the earned income of the wife to be treated separately from that of her husband. The normal principle of income tax was that a married couple were treated as one and the total income of both was deemed to be that of the husband. Thus a married woman's income was taxed at her husband's marginal rate. By separate taxation of a wife's earnings, both parties could be treated as single persons (thus forgoing the married man's allowance) and the wife's earned income was treated as hers, although her unearned income continued to be treated as that of her husband. For this election to be effective, the combined incomes of the two parties had to be such that more was saved by not combining the incomes than was lost by converting the married man's allowance to a single person's allowance. However, from April 1990 independent taxation of husband and wife was introduced in the UK. All taxpayers, married or single, have the same personal allowance, in addition to a married couple's allowance. Wives pay their own tax on their own income and make a separate tax return. At the same time other anomalies favouring unmarried cohabitation were removed from the UK tax system.

---

separation /ˌsepə'reɪʃ(ə)n/ *n.* **1** separating or being separated. **2** (in full **judicial** or **legal separation**) legal arrangement by which a couple remain married but live apart. [Latin: related to SEPARATE]

separatist /'sepərətɪst/ *n.* person who favours separation, esp. political independence. □ **separatism** *n.*

separator /'sepəˌreɪtə(r)/ *n.* **1** machine for separating, e.g. cream from milk. **2** person or thing that separates.

Sephardi /sɪ'fɑːdɪ/ *n.* (*pl.* **Sephardim**) Jew of Spanish or Portuguese descent. □ **Sephardic** *adj.* [Hebrew, = Spaniard]

sepia /'siːpɪə/ *n.* **1** dark reddish-brown colour or paint. **2** brown tint used in photography. [Greek, = cuttlefish]

SEPON /'siːpɒn/ *abbr.* = STOCK EXCHANGE POOL NOMINEES LTD.

sepoy /'siːpɔɪ/ *n. hist.* native Indian soldier under European, esp. British, discipline. [Persian *sipāhī* soldier]

sepsis /'sepsɪs/ *n.* septic condition. [Greek: related to SEPTIC]

Sept. *abbr.* September.

sept *n.* clan, esp. in Ireland. [alteration of SECT]

September /sep'tembə(r)/ *n.* ninth month of the year. [Latin *septem* seven, originally the 7th month of the Roman year]

septennial /sep'tenɪəl/ *adj.* **1** lasting for seven years. **2** recurring every seven years.

septet /sep'tet/ *n.* **1** *Mus.* **a** composition for seven performers. **b** the performers. **2** any group of seven. [Latin *septem* seven]

septic /'septɪk/ *adj.* contaminated with bacteria, putrefying. [Greek *sēpō* rot]

septicaemia /ˌseptɪ'siːmɪə/ *n.* (*US* **septicemia**) blood-poisoning. □ **septicaemic** *adj.* [from SEPTIC, Greek *haima* blood]

septic tank *n.* tank in which sewage is disintegrated through bacterial activity.

septuagenarian /ˌseptjʊədʒɪ'neərɪən/ *n.* person from 70 to 79 years old. [Latin *septuageni* 70 each]

Septuagesima /ˌseptjʊə'dʒesɪmə/ *n.* Sunday before Sexagesima. [Latin, = seventieth]

Septuagint /'septjʊəˌdʒɪnt/ *n.* Greek version of the Old Testament including the Apocrypha. [Latin *septuaginta* seventy]

septum /'septəm/ *n.* (*pl.* **septa**) partition such as that between the nostrils or the chambers of a poppy-fruit or of a shell. [Latin *s(a)eptum* from *saepio* enclose]

septuple /'septjʊp(ə)l/ *–adj.* **1** sevenfold, having seven parts. **2** being seven times as many or as much. *–n.* sevenfold number or amount. [Latin *septem* seven]

sepulchral /sɪ'pʌlkr(ə)l/ *adj.* **1** of a tomb or interment. **2** funereal, gloomy. [Latin: related to SEPULCHRE]

sepulchre /'sepəlkə(r)/ (*US* **sepulcher**) *–n.* tomb esp. cut in rock or built of stone or brick. *–v.* (**-ring**) **1** place in a sepulchre. **2** serve as a sepulchre for. [Latin *sepelio* bury]

sepulture /'sepəltʃə(r)/ *n.* burying, interment. [Latin: related to SEPULCHRE]

sequel /'siːkw(ə)l/ *n.* **1** what follows (esp. as a result). **2** novel, film, etc., that continues the story of an earlier one. [Latin *sequor* follow]

sequence /'siːkwəns/ *n.* **1** succession. **2** order of succession. **3** set of things belonging next to one another; unbroken series. **4** part of a film dealing with one scene or topic. [Latin: related to SEQUEL]

sequencer *n.* programmable electronic device for storing sequences of musical notes, chords, etc., and transmitting them when required to an electronic musical instrument. □ **sequencing** *n.*

sequential /sɪ'kwenʃ(ə)l/ *adj.* forming a sequence or consequence. □ **sequentially** *adv.* [from SEQUENCE]

sequential access *n.* = SERIAL ACCESS.

sequester /sɪ'kwestə(r)/ *v.* **1** (esp. as **sequestered** *adj.*) seclude, isolate. **2** = SEQUESTRATE. [Latin *sequester* trustee]

sequestrate /'si:kwɪˌstreɪt, sɪ'kwe-/ *v.* (**-ting**) **1** confiscate. **2** take temporary possession of (a debtor's estate etc.). □ **sequestrator** /'si:kwɪˌstreɪtə(r)/ *n.* [Latin: related to SEQUESTER]

♦ **sequestration** /ˌsi:kwɪ'streɪʃ(ə)n/ *n.* confiscation of the property of a person or organization that has not complied with a court order. This drastic remedy, which is ordered in serious cases only, is most commonly used against companies, trade unions, and in matrimonial cases.

sequin /'si:kwɪn/ *n.* circular spangle, esp. sewn on to clothing. □ **sequinned** *adj.* (also **sequined**). [Italian *zecchino* a gold coin]

sequoia /sɪ'kwɔɪə/ *n.* extremely tall Californian evergreen conifer. [*Sequoiah*, name of a Cherokee]

seraglio /sə'rɑ:lɪəʊ/ *n.* (*pl.* **-s**) **1** harem. **2** *hist.* Turkish palace. [Italian *serraglio* from Turkish]

Seraing /sə'ræ̃/ industrial town in E Belgium, SW of Liège; industries include railway engineering; pop. (1995) 61 408.

seraph /'serəf/ *n.* (*pl.* **-im** or **-s**) angelic being of the highest order of the celestial hierarchy. □ **seraphic** /sə'ræfɪk/ *adj.* [Hebrew]

Serb *–n.* **1** native of Serbia. **2** person of Serbian descent. *–adj.* = SERBIAN. [Serbian *Srb*]

Serbia /'sɜ:bɪə/ constituent republic of the Federal Republic of Yugoslavia; pop. (est. 1995) 5 806 000; capital, Belgrade. Agriculture is important, producing esp. wheat, maize, and sugar beet, and there are deposits of coal and copper. Part of the Ottoman empire from the 14th to the 19th centuries, Serbia became an independent kingdom in 1878. Subsequent Serbian ambitions to found a South Slav nation state brought the country into rivalry with the Austro-Hungarian empire and eventually contributed to the outbreak of the First World War. After the war Serbia was absorbed into the new state of Yugoslavia. Increasing Serbian nationalism in the late 1980s contributed to the breakup of Yugoslavia in 1991, and the following year Serbia and Montenegro (the two remaining constituent republics) formed a new Federal Republic of Yugoslavia. Serbian involvement in the Bosnian civil war (1992–5) led to the imposition of a trade embargo on the republic. See also YUGOSLAVIA.

Serbian /'sɜ:bɪən/ *–n.* **1** dialect of Serbo-Croat spoken in Serbia. **2** = SERB. *–adj.* of Serbia.

Serbo-Croat /ˌsɜ:bəʊ'krəʊæt/ (also **Serbo-Croatian** /-krəʊ'eɪʃ(ə)n/) *–n.* official language of the Federal Republic of Yugoslavia, combining Serbian and Croatian. *–adj.* of this language.

SERC /sɜ:k/ *abbr.* Science and Engineering Research Council.

serenade /ˌserə'neɪd/ *–n.* **1** piece of music performed at night, esp. beneath a lover's window. **2** orchestral suite for a small ensemble. *–v.* (**-ding**) perform a serenade to. □ **serenader** *n.* [Italian: related to SERENE]

serendipity /ˌserən'dɪpɪtɪ/ *n.* faculty of making happy discoveries by accident. □ **serendipitous** *adj.* [coined by Horace Walpole]

serene /sɪ'ri:n/ *adj.* (**-ner, -nest**) **1** clear and calm. **2** tranquil, unperturbed. □ **serenely** *adv.* **sereneness** *n.* **serenity** /sɪ'renɪtɪ/ *n.* [Latin]

serf *n.* **1** *hist.* labourer who was not allowed to leave the land on which he worked. **2** oppressed person, drudge. □ **serfdom** *n.* [Latin *servus* slave]

serge *n.* durable twilled worsted etc. fabric. [French *sarge*, *serge*]

sergeant /'sɑ:dʒ(ə)nt/ *n.* **1** non-commissioned Army or RAF officer next below warrant-officer. **2** police officer below inspector. [French *sergent* from Latin *serviens -ent-* servant]

sergeant-major *n.* (in full **regimental sergeant-major**) warrant-officer assisting the adjutant of a regiment or battalion.

serial /'sɪərɪəl/ *–n.* (also *attrib.*) story etc. published, broadcast, or shown in regular instalments. *–adj.* **1** of, in, or forming a series. **2** *Mus.* using transformations of a fixed series of notes (see SERIES 4). □ **serially** *adv.* [from SERIES]

serial access *n.* (also **sequential access**) *Computing* method of retrieval or storage of data that reads blocks of data from the storage medium in the order in which they occur until the required item or storage location is found. The access time thus depends on the location of the item. Cf. RANDOM ACCESS.

serialize *v.* (also **-ise**) (**-zing** or **-sing**) publish or produce in instalments. □ **serialization** /-'zeɪʃ(ə)n/ *n.*

serial number *n.* number identifying an item in a series.

serial transmission *n.* *Computing* method of sending data between devices, typically a computer and its peripherals, in which the individual bits making up a unit of data (e.g. a character) are transmitted one after another along the same path. See also PARALLEL *adj.* 3b.; HANDSHAKE 2.

series /'sɪəri:z, -rɪz/ *n.* (*pl.* same) **1** number of similar or related things, events, etc.; succession, row, or set. **2** set of related but individual programmes. **3** set of related geological strata. **4** arrangement of the twelve notes of the chromatic scale as a basis for serial music. **5** set of electrical circuits or components arranged so that the same current passes through each successively. □ **in series** in ordered succession. [Latin *sero* join]

serif /'serɪf/ *n.* slight projection at the extremities of a printed letter (as in T contrasted with T) (cf. SANSERIF). [origin uncertain]

serio-comic /ˌsɪərɪəʊ'kɒmɪk/ *adj.* combining the serious and the comic.

serious /'sɪərɪəs/ *adj.* **1** thoughtful, earnest. **2** important, demanding consideration. **3** not negligible; dangerous, frightening (*serious injury*). **4** sincere, in earnest, not frivolous. **5** (of music, literature, etc.) intellectual in content or appeal; not popular. □ **seriously** *adv.* **seriousness** *n.* [Latin *seriosus*]

♦ **Serious Fraud Office** *n.* (also **SFO**) body established in 1987 to be responsible for investigating and prosecuting complex frauds in England, Wales, and Northern Ireland. The Attorney General appoints and superintends its director. Serious and complex fraud cases can go straight to the Crown Court without committal for trial. That court can hold preparatory hearings to clarify issues for the jury and settle points of law.

serjeant /'sɑ:dʒ(ə)nt/ *n.* (in full **serjeant-at-law**, *pl.* **serjeants-at-law**) *hist.* barrister of the highest rank. [var. of SERGEANT]

serjeant-at-arms *n.* (*pl.* **serjeants-at-arms**) official of a court, city, or parliament, with ceremonial duties.

sermon /'sɜ:mən/ *n.* **1** spoken or written discourse on religion or morals etc., esp. delivered in church. **2** admonition, reproof. [Latin *sermo -onis* speech]

sermonize *v.* (also **-ise**) (**-zing** or **-sing**) moralize (to).

serous /'sɪərəs/ *adj.* **1** of or like serum; watery. **2** (of a gland or membrane) having a serous secretion. □ **serosity** /-'rɒsɪtɪ/ *n.* [related to SERUM]

serpent /'sɜ:pənt/ *n.* **1** snake, esp. large. **2** sly or treacherous person. [Latin *serpo* creep]

serpentine /'sɜ:pənˌtaɪn/ *–adj.* **1** of or like a serpent. **2** coiling, meandering. **3** cunning, treacherous. *–n.* soft usu. dark-green rock, sometimes mottled.

SERPS /sɜ:ps/ *abbr.* = STATE EARNINGS-RELATED PENSION SCHEME.

serrated /sə'reɪtɪd/ *adj.* with a sawlike edge. □ **serration** *n.* [Latin *serra* saw]

serried /'serɪd/ *adj.* (of ranks of soldiers etc.) close together. [French *serrer* to close]

serum /'sɪərəm/ *n.* (*pl.* **sera** or **-s**) **1** liquid that separates from a clot when blood coagulates, esp. used for inoculation. **2** watery fluid in animal bodies. [Latin, = whey]

servant /'sɜːv(ə)nt/ *n.* **1** person employed to do domestic duties, esp. in a wealthy household. **2** devoted follower or helper. [French: related to SERVE]

serve –*v.* (**-ving**) **1** do a service for (a person, community, etc.). **2** be a servant to. **3** carry out duties (*served on six committees*). **4** (foll. by *in*) be employed in (esp. the armed forces) (*served in the navy*). **5 a** be useful to or serviceable for. **b** meet requirements; perform a function. **6 a** go through a due period of (apprenticeship, a prison sentence, etc.). **b** go through (a due period) of imprisonment etc. **7** present (food) to eat. **8** (in full **serve at table**) act as a waiter. **9 a** attend to (a customer etc.). **b** (foll. by *with*) supply with (goods). **10** treat (a person) in a specified way. **11 a** (often foll. by *on*) deliver (a writ etc.). **b** (foll. by *with*) deliver a writ etc. to. **12** (also *absol.*) (in tennis etc.) deliver (a ball etc.) to begin or resume play. **13** (of an animal) copulate with (a female). –*n.* = SERVICE *n.* 16a, b. □ **serve a person right** be a person's deserved punishment etc. **serve up** *derog.* offer (*served up the same old excuses*). [Latin *servio*]

server *n.* **1 a** person who serves. **b** utensil for serving food. **2** celebrant's assistant at a mass etc. **3** *Computing* device in a network, usu. a local area network, that manages an expensive shared resource for the computers on the network. For example, a **file server** manages a set of disks and provides storage and archiving services.

servery *n.* (*pl.* **-ies**) room or counter from which meals etc. are served.

service /'sɜːvɪs/ –*n.* **1** work, or the doing work, for another or for a community etc. (often in *pl.*: *the services of a lawyer*). **2** work done by a machine etc. (*has given good service*). **3** assistance or benefit given. **4** provision or supplying of a public need, e.g. transport, or (often in *pl.*) of water, gas, electricity, etc. **5** economic good consisting of human worth in the form of labour, advice, managerial skill, etc., rather than a commodity (see GOOD *n.* 3). **Services to trade** include banking, insurance, transport, etc. **Professional services** encompass the advice and skill of accountants, lawyers, architects, business consultants, doctors, etc. **Consumer services** include those given by caterers, cleaners, mechanics, plumbers, etc. Industry may be divided into extractive, manufacturing, and service sectors. The **service industries** make up an increasing proportion of the national income. **6** employment as a servant. **7** state or period of employment (*resigned after 15 years' service*). See also SERVICE CONTRACT. **8** public or Crown department or organization (*civil service*). **9** (in *pl.*) the armed forces. **10** (*attrib.*) of the kind issued to the armed forces (*service revolver*). **11 a** ceremony of worship. **b** form of liturgy for this. **12 a** provision for the maintenance of a machine etc. **b** routine maintenance of a vehicle etc. **13** assistance given to customers. **14 a** serving of food, drinks, etc.; quality of this. **b** extra charge nominally made for this. **15** (in *pl.*) = SERVICE AREA (*motorway services*). **16** set of dishes, plates, etc. for serving meals (*dinner service*). **17 a** act of serving in tennis etc. **b** person's turn to serve. **c** (in full **service game**) game in which a specified player serves. –*v.* (**-cing**) **1** maintain or repair (a car, machine, etc.). **2** supply with a service. **3** pay the interest on (a loan). □ **at a person's service** ready to serve a person. **be of service** be helpful or useful. **in service 1** employed as a servant. **2** in use. **out of service** not available for use, not working. [Latin *servitium* from *servus* slave]

serviceable *adj.* **1** useful or usable; able to render service. **2** durable but plain. □ **serviceability** /-'bɪlɪtɪ/ *n.*

service area *n.* area beside a major road providing petrol, refreshments, toilet facilities, etc.

service charge *n.* additional charge for service in a restaurant etc.

◆ **service contract** *n.* (also **service agreement**) employment contract between an employer and employee, usu. a senior employee (e.g. a director, executive manager, etc.). Service contracts must be kept at the registered office of a company and be open to inspection by members of the company. The Companies Acts (1980 and 1985) prohibit service contracts that give an employee guaranteed employment for more than five years, without the company having an opportunity to break the employment as and when it needs to. This measure prevents directors with long service agreements from suing companies for loss of office in the event of a take-over or reorganization. See also COMPENSATION FOR LOSS OF OFFICE; GOLDEN PARACHUTE.

service flat *n.* flat in which domestic service and sometimes meals are provided for an extra fee.

service industry *n.* industry providing services, not goods (see SERVICE *n.* 5).

serviceman *n.* **1** man in the armed forces. **2** man providing service or maintenance.

service road *n.* road serving houses, shops, etc., lying back from the main road.

service station *n.* = GARAGE *n.* 2.

servicewoman *n.* woman in the armed forces.

serviette /ˌsɜːvɪ'et/ *n.* table-napkin. [French: related to SERVE]

servile /'sɜːvaɪl/ *adj.* **1** of or like a slave. **2** fawning; subservient. □ **servility** /-'vɪlɪtɪ/ *n.* [Latin *servus* slave]

serving *n.* quantity of food for one person.

servitor /'sɜːvɪt(ə)r/ *n. archaic* servant, attendant. [Latin: related to SERVE]

servitude /'sɜːvɪˌtjuːd/ *n.* slavery, subjection. [Latin *servus* slave]

servo /'sɜːvəʊ/ *n.* (*pl.* **-s**) **1** powered mechanism producing motion at a higher level of energy than the input level. **2** (in *comb.*) involving this. [Latin *servus* slave]

◆ **servqual** *n.* combination of service and quality, providing an important marketing strategy. A high level of service combined with high quality products has a positive effect on consumer satisfaction, which is reflected in their willingness to place repeat orders.

SES *abbr.* **1** Singapore Stock Exchange. **2** *US* socio-economic status.

sesame /'sesəmɪ/ *n.* **1** East Indian plant with oil-yielding seeds. **2** its seeds. □ **open sesame** magic phrase for opening a locked door or gaining access. [Greek]

SESDAQ /'sesdæk/ *abbr.* Stock Exchange of Singapore Dealing and Automated Quotation System.

SESI *abbr.* Stock Exchange of Singapore Index.

Sesotho /se'suːtuː/ *n.* Bantu language of Lesotho. [Bantu, = language of Sotho (people of S Africa)]

sesqui- /'seskwɪ/ *comb. form* denoting $1^1/_2$ (*sesquicentennial*). [Latin]

sessile /'sesaɪl/ *adj.* **1** (of a flower, leaf, eye, etc.) attached directly by its base without a stalk or peduncle. **2** fixed in one position; immobile. [Latin: related to SESSION]

session /'seʃ(ə)n/ *n.* **1** period devoted to an activity (*recording session*). **2** assembly of a parliament, court, etc. **3** single meeting for this. **4** period during which these are regularly held. **5** academic year. □ **in session** assembled for business; not on vacation. □ **sessional** *adj.* [Latin *sedeo sess-* sit]

sestet /ses'tet/ *n.* **1** last six lines of a sonnet. **2** sextet. [Italian *sesto* sixth]

SET /'es 'iː 'tiː or set/ *abbr. hist.* selective employment tax.

set[1] *v.* (**-tt-**; *past* and *past part.* **set**) **1** put, lay, or stand in a certain position etc. **2** apply (one thing) to (another) (*set pen to paper*). **3 a** fix ready or in position. **b** dispose suitably for use, action, or display. **4 a** adjust (a clock or watch) to show the right time. **b** adjust (an alarm clock) to sound at the required time. **5 a** fix, arrange, or mount. **b** insert (a jewel) in a ring etc. **6** make (a device) ready to operate. **7** lay (a table) for a meal. **8** style (the hair) while damp. **9** (foll. by *with*) ornament or provide (a surface). **10** make or bring into a specified state; cause to be (*set things in motion*; *set it on fire*). **11** (of jelly, cement, etc.) harden or solidify. **12** (of the sun, moon, etc.) move towards or below the earth's horizon. **13** show (a story etc.) as happening in a certain time or place. **14 a** (foll. by *to* + infin.) cause (a person or oneself) to do a specified thing. **b** (foll. by pres. part.) start (a person or thing) doing something. **15** give as work to be done or a matter to be dealt with. **16** exhibit as a model etc. (*set an example*). **17** initiate; lead (*set the fashion*; *set the pace*). **18** establish (a record etc.). **19** determine or decide. **20** appoint or establish (*set them in authority*). **21 a** put parts of (a broken or dislocated bone, limb, etc.) together for healing. **b** deal with (a fracture etc.) in this way. **22** (in full **set to music**) provide (words etc.) with music for singing. **23 a** compose (type etc.). **b** compose the type etc. for (a book etc.). **24** (of a tide, current, etc.) have a certain motion or direction. **25** (of a face) assume a hard expression. **26 a** cause (a hen) to sit on eggs. **b** place (eggs) for a hen to sit on. **27** (of eyes etc.) become motionless. **28** feel or show a certain tendency (*opinion is setting against it*). **29 a** (of blossom) form into fruit. **b** (of fruit) develop from blossom. **c** (of a tree) develop fruit. **30** (of a dancer) take a position facing one's partner. **31** (of a hunting dog) take a rigid attitude indicating the presence of game. **32** *dial.* or *slang* sit. □ **set about 1** begin or take steps towards. **2** *colloq.* attack. **set against 1** consider or reckon as a balance or compensation for. **2** cause to oppose. **set apart** separate, reserve, differentiate. **set aside 1** put to one side. **2** keep for future use. **3** disregard or reject. **set back 1** place further back in place or time. **2** impede or reverse the progress of. **3** *colloq.* cost (a person) a specified amount. **set down 1** record in writing. **2** allow to alight. **3** (foll. by *to*) attribute to. **4** (foll. by *as*) explain as. **set eyes on** see EYE. **set foot on** (or **in**) enter or go to (a place etc.). **set forth 1** begin a journey. **2** expound. **set in 1** (of weather etc.) begin, become established. **2** insert. **set off 1** begin a journey. **2** detonate (a bomb etc.). **3** initiate, stimulate. **4** cause (a person) to start laughing, talking, etc. **5** adorn; enhance. **6** (foll. by *against*) use as a compensating item (see SET-OFF). **set on** (or **upon**) **1** attack violently. **2** cause or urge to attack. **set oneself up as** pretend or claim to be. **set out 1** begin a journey. **2** (foll. by *to* + infin.) intend. **3** demonstrate, arrange, or exhibit. **4** mark out. **5** declare. **set sail** hoist the sails, begin a voyage. **set to** begin vigorously, esp. fighting, arguing, or eating. **set up 1** place in position or view. **2** start (a business etc.). **3** establish in some capacity. **4** supply the needs of. **5** begin making (a loud sound). **6** cause (a condition or situation). **7** prepare (a task etc. for another). **8** restore the health of (a person). **9** establish (a record). **10** *colloq.* frame or cause (a person) to look foolish; cheat. [Old English]

set[2] *n.* **1** group of linked or similar things or persons. **2** section of society. **3** collection of objects for a specified purpose (*cricket set*; *teaset*). **4** radio or television receiver. **5** (in tennis etc.) group of games counting as a unit towards winning a match. **6** *Math.* collection of things sharing a property. **7** direction or position in which something sets or is set. **8** slip, shoot, bulb, etc., for planting. **9** setting, stage furniture, etc., for a play or film etc. **10** styling of the hair while damp. **11** (also **sett**) badger's burrow. **12** (also **sett**) granite paving-block. [senses 1–6 from French *sette*; senses 7–12 from SET[1]]

set[3] *adj.* **1** prescribed or determined in advance; fixed (*a set meal*). **2** (of a phrase or speech etc.) having invariable or predetermined wording; not extempore. **3** prepared for action. **4** (foll. by *on*, *upon*) determined to get or achieve etc. [past part. of SET[1]]

set-back *n.* reversal or arrest of progress; relapse.

◆ **set-off** *n.* **1** thing set off against another. **2** agreement between the parties involved to set off one debt against another or one loss against a gain. A banker is empowered to set off a credit balance on one account against a debit balance on another. It is usual in these circumstances for the bank to issue a **letter of set-off**, which the customer countersigns to indicate agreement.

set piece *n.* **1** formal or elaborate arrangement, esp. in art or literature. **2** fireworks arranged on scaffolding etc.

◆ **Sets** *abbr.* Stock Exchange Electronic Trading System, a computerized order-driven system introduced on the London Stock Exchange in November 1997. Brokers enter their orders to buy or to sell shares, which are matched by the computer. The object is to cut out the middleman (market-maker) in order to reduce costs.

set square *n.* right-angled triangular plate for drawing lines, esp. at 90°, 45°, 60°, or 30°.

sett var. of SET[2] 11, 12.

settee /se'tiː/ *n.* = SOFA. [origin uncertain]

setter *n.* dog of a long-haired breed trained to stand rigid when scenting game.

set theory *n.* the study or use of sets in mathematics.

setting *n.* **1** position or manner in which a thing is set. **2** immediate surroundings of a house etc. **3** period, place, etc., of a story, drama, etc. **4** frame etc. for a jewel. **5** music to which words are set. **6** cutlery etc. for one person at a table. **7** level at which a machine is set to operate (*on a high setting*).

settle[1] /'set(ə)l/ *v.* (**-ling**) **1** (often foll. by *down*, *in*) establish or become established in an abode or lifestyle. **2** (often foll. by *down*) **a** regain calm after disturbance; come to rest. **b** adopt a regular or secure style of life. **c** (foll. by *to*) apply oneself (*settled down to work*). **3** (cause to) sit, alight, or come down to stay for some time. **4** make or become composed, certain, quiet, or fixed. **5** determine, decide, or agree upon. **6** resolve (a dispute, matter, etc.). **7** agree to terminate (a lawsuit). **8** (foll. by *for*) accept or agree to (esp. a less desirable alternative). **9** (also *absol.*) pay (a debt, account, etc.). **10** (as **settled** *adj.*) established (*settled weather*). **11** calm (nerves, the stomach, etc.). **12 a** colonize. **b** establish colonists in. **13** subside; fall to the bottom or on to a surface. □ **settle up** (also *absol.*) pay (an account, debt, etc.). **settle with 1** pay (a creditor). **2** get revenge on. [Old English: related to SIT]

settle[2] /'set(ə)l/ *n.* high-backed wooden bench, often with a box below the seat. [Old English]

settlement *n.* **1** settling or being settled. **2 a** place occupied by settlers. **b** small village. **3 a** political or financial etc. agreement. **b** arrangement ending a dispute. **4** payment of an outstanding account, invoice, charge, etc. **5 a** disposition of land or other property made by deed or will under which a trust is set up by the settlor. The settlement names the beneficiaries and the terms under which they are to acquire the property. **b** document in which such a disposition is made. **c** amount or property given.

◆ **settlement price** *n.* price at which an index futures or option contract is settled. On the London International Financial Futures and Option Exchange it is known as the EDSP (Exchange Delivery Settlement Price), which is calculated on the last day of the delivery month.

settler *n.* person who settles abroad.

◆ **settlor** /'setlə(r)/ *n. Law* person declaring or creating a settlement or trust. For tax purposes any person providing money or property for a settlement will be regarded as the settlor.

set-to *n.* (*pl.* **-tos**) *colloq.* fight, argument.

set-up *n.* **1** arrangement or organization. **2** manner, structure, or position of this. **3** instance of setting a person up (see *set up* 10).

Sevastopol see SEBASTOPOL.

seven /'sev(ə)n/ *adj.* & *n.* **1** one more than six. **2** symbol for this (7, vii, VII). **3** size etc. denoted by seven. **4** seven o'clock. [Old English]

◆ **seven-day money** *n.* money that has been invested in the money market for a term of seven days. Special interest rates are quoted for seven-day money.

sevenfold *adj.* & *adv.* **1** seven times as much or as many. **2** consisting of seven parts.

seven seas *n.* (prec. by *the*) the oceans of the world.

seventeen /ˌsevən'tiːn/ *adj.* & *n.* **1** one more than sixteen. **2** symbol for this (17, xvii, XVII). **3** size etc. denoted by seventeen. □ **seventeenth** *adj.* & *n.* [Old English]

seventh *adj.* & *n.* **1** next after sixth. **2** one of seven equal parts of a thing. □ **seventhly** *adv.*

Seventh-Day Adventists *n.pl.* sect of Adventists observing the sabbath on Saturday.

seventh heaven *n.* state of intense joy.

seventy /'sevəntɪ/ *adj.* & *n.* (*pl.* **-ies**) **1** seven times ten. **2** symbol for this (70, lxx, LXX). **3** (in *pl.*) numbers from 70 to 79, esp. the years of a century or of a person's life. □ **seventieth** *adj.* & *n.* [Old English]

sever /'sevə(r)/ *v.* divide, break, or make separate, esp. by cutting (*severed artery*). [Anglo-French *severer* from Latin *separo*]

several /'sevr(ə)l/ *–adj.* & *pron.* more than two but not many; a few. *–adj. formal* separate or respective (*went their several ways*). □ **severally** *adv.* [Latin *separ* distinct]

severance *n.* **1** act of severing. **2** severed state. **3** *Law* separation of the good parts of a contract from the bad. It applies to contracts that are not illegal but are void by statute or common law: courts will, if possible, save such contracts from complete invalidity by severance of the parts that are void.

severance pay *n.* payment made to an employee on termination of a contract. See also COMPENSATION FOR LOSS OF OFFICE.

severe /sɪ'vɪə(r)/ *adj.* **1** rigorous and harsh (*severe critic*). **2** serious (*severe shortage*). **3** forceful (*severe storm*). **4** extreme (*severe winter*). **5** exacting (*severe competition*). **6** plain in style. □ **severely** *adv.* **severity** /-'verɪtɪ/ *n.* [Latin *severus*]

Seville /'sevɪl/ (Spanish **Sevilla** /se'viːljə/) city and river port in SW Spain, capital of Andalusia; industries include textiles and engineering, and fruit (esp. oranges), wine, and olive oil are exported; pop. (1991) 714 148.

Seville orange /'sevɪl, sə'vɪl/ *n.* bitter orange used for marmalade. [SEVILLE]

sew /səʊ/ *v.* (*past part.* **sewn** or **sewed**) fasten, join, etc., with a needle and thread or a sewing-machine. □ **sew up 1** join or enclose by sewing. **2** (esp. in *passive*) *colloq.* satisfactorily arrange or finish; gain control of. [Old English]

sewage /'suːɪdʒ/ *n.* waste matter conveyed in sewers. [from SEWER]

sewage farm *n.* (also **sewage works**) place where sewage is treated.

sewer /'suːə(r)/ *n.* conduit, usu. underground, for carrying off drainage water and sewage. [Anglo-French *sever(e)*: related to EX-[1], *aqua* water]

sewerage /'suːərɪdʒ/ *n.* system of, or drainage by, sewers.

sewing /'səʊɪŋ/ *n.* material or work to be sewn.

sewing-machine *n.* machine for sewing or stitching.

sewn *past part.* of SEW.

sex *–n.* **1** each of the main groups (male and female) into which living things are categorized on the basis of their reproductive functions (*what sex is your dog?*). **2** sexual instincts, desires, etc., or their manifestation. **3** *colloq.* sexual intercourse. **4** (*attrib.*) of or relating to sex or sexual differences. *–v.* **1** determine the sex of. **2** (as **sexed** *adj.*) having a specified sexual appetite (*highly sexed*). [Latin *sexus*]

sexagenarian /ˌseksədʒɪ'neərɪən/ *n.* person from 60 to 69 years old. [Latin *-arius* from *sexaginta* sixty]

Sexagesima /ˌseksə'dʒesɪmə/ *n.* Sunday before Quinquagesima. [Latin, = sixtieth]

sex appeal *n.* sexual attractiveness.

sex change *n.* apparent change of sex by hormone treatment and surgery.

sex chromosome *n.* chromosome determining the sex of an organism.

sexism *n.* prejudice or discrimination, esp. against women, on the grounds of sex. □ **sexist** *adj.* & *n.*

sexless *adj.* **1** neither male nor female. **2** lacking sexual desire or attractiveness.

sex life *n.* person's sexual activity.

sex maniac *n. colloq.* person obsessed with sex.

sex object *n.* person regarded as an object of sexual gratification.

sex offender *n.* person who commits a sexual crime.

sexology /sek'sɒlədʒɪ/ *n.* the study of sexual relationships or practices. □ **sexologist** *n.*

sex symbol *n.* person widely noted for sex appeal.

sextant /'sekst(ə)nt/ *n.* instrument with a graduated arc of 60°, used in navigation and surveying for measuring the angular distance of objects by means of mirrors. [Latin *sextans -ntis* sixth part]

sextet /sek'stet/ *n.* **1** *Mus.* **a** composition for six performers. **b** the performers. **2** any group of six. [alteration of SESTET after Latin *sex* six]

sexton /'sekst(ə)n/ *n.* person who looks after a church and churchyard, often acting as bell-ringer and gravedigger. [French *segerstein* from Latin *sacristanus*]

sextuple /'seksˌtjuːp(ə)l/ *–adj.* **1** sixfold. **2** having six parts. **3** being six times as many or as much. *–n.* sixfold number or amount. [medieval Latin from Latin *sex* six]

sextuplet /'seksˌtjʊplɪt, -'tjuːplɪt/ *n.* each of six children born at one birth.

sexual /'sekʃʊəl/ *adj.* of sex, the sexes, or relations between them. □ **sexuality** /-'ælɪtɪ/ *n.* **sexually** *adv.*

sexual intercourse *n.* method of reproduction involv-

Seychelles /seɪ'ʃelz/, **Republic of** country in the Indian Ocean, a member state of the Commonwealth, consisting of a group of about 90 islands NE of Madagascar. Noted for their beauty, the islands attract a considerable tourist trade. The economy is also supported by the production and export of copra and cinnamon. Fishing is important; fresh and frozen fish and canned tuna are major exports; the country also re-exports petroleum products. Other products include tobacco and beer.
History. Annexed by the French in the mid-18th century, the Seychelles were captured by Britain during the Napoleonic Wars and administered from Mauritius before becoming a separate colony in 1903 and finally an independent republic in 1976. The constitution of 1979 made Seychelles a one-party state. In 1992 a new constitution, introducing a multi-party system, was approved, and multi-party elections resulted in victory for the ruling party. President, France Albert René; capital, Victoria. □ **Seychellois** /-ʃel'wɑː/ *adj.* & *n.*

languages	English, French, and Creole
currency	rupee (SR) of 100 cents
pop. (1996)	76 100
GNP (1994)	US$453M
literacy	82% (m); 85% (f)
life expectancy	66 (m); 73 (f)

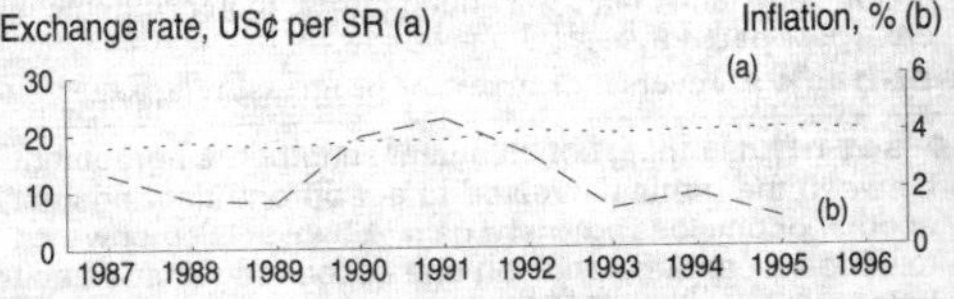

ing insertion of the penis into the vagina, usu. followed by ejaculation.

sexy *adj.* (**-ier, -iest**) **1** sexually attractive, stimulating, or aroused. **2** *colloq.* (of a project etc.) exciting, trendy. □ **sexily** *adv.* **sexiness** *n.*

SF *abbr.* **1** science fiction. **2** (also **s.f.**) sinking fund.

Sf *symb.* Suriname guilder.

sf *abbr.* sforzando.

SFA *abbr.* = SECURITIES AND FUTURES AUTHORITY LTD.

Sfax /sfæks/ second-largest city in Tunisia, a seaport on the E coast; a major centre of phosphate processing, it also exports olive oil, sponges, and cotton and woollen goods; pop. (1994) 230 900.

SFO *abbr.* **1** = SERIOUS FRAUD OFFICE. **2** = SUPERANNUATION FUNDS OFFICE.

sforzando /sfɔːˈtsændəʊ/ *–adj. & adv. Mus.* with sudden emphasis. *–n.* (*pl.* **-s** or **-di** /-dɪ/) **1** suddenly emphasized note or group of notes. **2** increase in emphasis and loudness. [Italian]

SG *–abbr.* **1** ship and goods. **2** Solicitor General. *–postcode* Stevenage.

sgd. *abbr.* signed.

S. Glam. *abbr.* South Glamorgan.

SGP *international vehicle registration* Singapore.

's-Gravenhage see The HAGUE.

Sgt. *abbr.* Sergeant.

sh *int.* = HUSH.

Shaanxi /ʃɑːnˈʃiː/ (also **Shensi** /ʃenˈsiː/) province in N central China; pop. (est. 1995) 34 810 000; capital, Xian. Crops include wheat, millet, and cotton, and there are deposits of coal, iron, and oil.

Shaba /ˈʃɑːbə/ copper-mining region in SE Democratic Republic of Congo; pop. (est. 1994) 5 602 000; capital, Lubumbashi.

shabby /ˈʃæbɪ/ *adj.* (**-ier, -iest**) **1** faded and worn, dingy, dilapidated. **2** contemptible (*a shabby trick*). □ **shabbily** *adv.* **shabbiness** *n.* [related to SCAB]

shack *–n.* roughly built hut or cabin. *–v.* (foll. by *up*) *slang* cohabit, esp. as lovers. [perhaps from Mexican *jacal* wooden hut]

shackle /ˈʃæk(ə)l/ *–n.* **1** metal loop or link, closed by a bolt, used to connect chains etc. **2** fetter for the ankle or wrist. **3** (usu. in *pl.*) restraint, impediment. *–v.* (**-ling**) fetter, impede, restrain. [Old English]

shad *n.* (*pl.* same or **-s**) large edible marine fish. [Old English]

shaddock /ˈʃædək/ *n.* **1** largest citrus fruit, with a thick yellow skin and bitter pulp. **2** tree bearing these. [Capt. *Shaddock*, who introduced it to the West Indies in the 17th century]

shade *–n.* **1** comparative darkness (and usu. coolness) given by shelter from direct light and heat. **2** area so sheltered. **3** darker part of a picture etc. **4** colour, esp. as darker or lighter than one similar. **5** comparative obscurity. **6** slight amount (*a shade better*). **7** lampshade. **8** screen against the light. **9** (in *pl.*) esp. *US colloq.* sunglasses. **10** *literary* ghost. **11** (in *pl.*; foll. by *of*) reminder of, suggesting (esp. something undesirable) (*shades of Hitler!*). *–v.* (**-ding**) **1** screen from light. **2** cover, moderate, or exclude the light of. **3** darken, esp. with parallel lines to show shadow etc. **4** (often foll. by *away, off, into*) pass or change gradually. [Old English]

shading *n.* light and shade shown on a map or drawing by parallel lines etc.

shadow /ˈʃædəʊ/ *–n.* **1** shade; patch of shade. **2** dark shape projected by a body intercepting rays of light. **3** inseparable attendant or companion. **4** person secretly following another. **5** slightest trace (*not a shadow of doubt*). **6** weak or insubstantial remnant (*a shadow of his former self*). **7** (*attrib.*) denoting members of an Opposition party holding posts parallel to those of the government (*shadow Cabinet*). **8** shaded part of a picture. **9** gloom or sadness. *–v.* **1** cast a shadow over. **2** secretly follow and watch. [Old English: related to SHADE]

shadow-boxing *n.* boxing with an imaginary opponent as training.

♦ **shadow director** *n.* person in accordance with whose instructions the directors of a company are accustomed to act although that person has not been appointed as a director. Some provisions of the Companies Acts, including wrongful trading and the regulation of loans to directors, relate to both directors and shadow directors.

♦ **shadow price** *n.* price attributed to a good or service by an economist in the absence of an explicit market price. In a perfectly competitive economy the shadow price is equal to the market price, but in general the two may differ. It is common, therefore, to attempt to estimate shadow prices when carrying out a cost-benefit analysis for government projects, since few believe that real-world economies are perfectly competitive. However, there is no generally accepted method for calculating shadow prices and they are usu. considered unreliable.

---

shadowy *adj.* **1** like or having a shadow. **2** vague, indistinct.

shady /ˈʃeɪdɪ/ *adj.* (**-ier, -iest**) **1** giving shade. **2** situated in shade. **3** disreputable; of doubtful honesty. □ **shadily** *adv.* **shadiness** *n.*

shaft /ʃɑːft/ *n.* **1** narrow usu. vertical space, for access to a mine, or (in a building) for a lift, ventilation, etc. **2** (foll. by *of*) **a** ray (of light). **b** bolt (of lightning). **3** stem or handle of a tool etc. **4** long narrow part supporting, connecting, or driving thicker part(s) etc. **5 a** *archaic* arrow, spear. **b** its long slender stem. **6** hurtful or provocative remark (*shafts of wit*). **7** each of the pair of poles between which a horse is harnessed to a vehicle. **8** central stem of a feather. **9** column, esp. between the base and capital. [Old English]

shag[1] *n.* **1** coarse kind of cut tobacco. **2 a** rough mass of hair etc. **b** (*attrib.*) (of a carpet) with a long rough pile **3** cormorant, esp. the crested cormorant. [Old English]

shag[2] *v.* (**-gg**) *coarse slang* **1** have sexual intercourse with. **2** (usu. in *passive*; often foll. by *out*) exhaust, tire out. [origin unknown]

shaggy *adj.* (**-ier, -iest**) **1** hairy, rough-haired. **2** unkempt. □ **shagginess** *n.*

shaggy-dog story *n.* long rambling joke, amusing only by its pointlessness.

shagreen /ʃæˈgriːn/ *n.* **1** a kind of untanned granulated leather. **2** sharkskin. [var. of CHAGRIN]

shah *n. hist.* former monarch of Iran. [Persian]

shake *–v.* (**-king**; *past* **shook** /ʃʊk/; *past part.* **shaken**) **1** move forcefully or quickly up and down or to and fro. **2** (cause to) tremble or vibrate. **3** agitate, shock, or upset the composure of. **4** weaken or impair in courage, effectiveness, etc. **5** (of a voice, note, etc.) tremble; trill. **6** gesture with (one's fist, a stick, etc.). **7** *colloq.* shake hands (*they shook on the deal*). *–n.* **1** shaking or being shaken. **2** jerk or shock. **3** (in *pl.*; prec. by *the*) *colloq.* fit of trembling. **4** *Mus.* trill. **5** = MILK SHAKE. □ **no great shakes** *colloq.* mediocre, poor. **shake down 1** settle or cause to fall by shaking. **2** settle down; become established. **shake hands** (often foll. by *with*) clasp hands as a greeting, farewell, in congratulation, as confirmation of a deal, etc. **shake one's head** turn one's head from side to side in refusal, denial, disapproval, or concern. **shake off** get rid of or evade (a person or thing). **shake out 1** empty by shaking. **2** open (a sail, flag, etc.) by shaking. **shake up 1** mix by shaking. **2** restore to shape by shaking. **3** disturb or make uncomfortable; rouse from apathy, conventionality, etc. [Old English]

shaker *n.* **1** person or thing that shakes. **2** container for shaking together the ingredients of cocktails etc.

Shakespearian /ʃeɪkˈspɪərɪən/ *adj.* (also **Shakespearean**) of Shakespeare.

shake-up *n.* upheaval or drastic reorganization.

shako /ˈʃækəʊ/ *n.* (*pl.* **-s**) cylindrical plumed peaked military hat. [Hungarian *csákó*]

shaky *adj.* (**-ier, -iest**) **1** unsteady; trembling. **2** unsound, infirm. **3** unreliable. □ **shakily** *adv.* **shakiness** *n.*

shale *n.* soft rock of consolidated mud or clay that splits easily. □ **shaly** *adj.* [German: related to SCALE[2]]

shall /ʃæl, ʃ(ə)l/ *v.aux.* (*3rd sing. present* **shall**; *archaic 2nd sing. present* **shalt**; *past* **should** /ʃʊd, ʃəd/) (foll. by infin. without *to*, or *absol.*; present and past only in use) **1** (in the 1st person) expressing the future tense or (with *shall* stressed) emphatic intention (*I shall return soon*). **2** (in the 2nd and 3rd persons) expressing a strong assertion, command, or duty (*they shall go to the party*; *thou shalt not steal*; *they shall obey*). **3** (in 2nd-person questions) expressing an enquiry, esp. to avoid the form of a request (*shall you go to France?*). □ **shall I?** (or **we**) do you want me (or us) to? [Old English]

shallot /ʃə'lɒt/ *n.* onion-like plant with a cluster of small bulbs. [French: related to SCALLION]

shallow /'ʃæləʊ/ *–adj.* **1** of little depth. **2** superficial, trivial. *–n.* (often in *pl.*) shallow place. □ **shallowness** *n.* [Old English]

shalom /ʃə'lɒm/ *n.* & *int.* Jewish salutation at meeting or parting. [Hebrew]

shalt *archaic 2nd person sing.* of SHALL.

sham *–v.* (**-mm-**) **1** feign, pretend. **2** pretend to be. *–n.* **1** imposture, pretence. **2** bogus or false person or thing. *–adj.* pretended, counterfeit. [origin unknown]

shaman /'ʃæmən/ *n.* witch-doctor or priest claiming to communicate with gods etc. □ **shamanism** *n.* [Russian]

shamble /'ʃæmb(ə)l/ *–v.* (**-ling**) walk or run awkwardly, dragging the feet. *–n.* shambling gait. [perhaps related to SHAMBLES]

shambles *n.pl.* (usu. treated as *sing.*) **1** *colloq.* mess, muddle. **2** butcher's slaughterhouse. **3** scene of carnage. [pl. of *shamble* table for selling meat]

shambolic /ʃæm'bɒlɪk/ *adj. colloq.* chaotic, unorganized. [from SHAMBLES after *symbolic*]

shame *–n.* **1** distress or humiliation caused by consciousness of one's guilt, dishonour, or folly. **2** capacity for feeling this. **3** state of disgrace or discredit. **4 a** person or thing that brings disgrace etc. **b** thing that is wrong or regrettable. *–v.* (**-ming**) **1** bring shame on; make ashamed; put to shame. **2** (foll. by *into, out of*) force by shame (*shamed into confessing*). □ **for shame!** reproof to a shameless person. **put to shame** humiliate by being greatly superior. [Old English]

shamefaced *adj.* **1** showing shame. **2** bashful, shy. □ **shamefacedly** /also -sɪdlɪ/ *adv.*

shameful *adj.* disgraceful, scandalous. □ **shamefully** *adv.* **shamefulness** *n.*

shameless *adj.* **1** having or showing no shame. **2** impudent. □ **shamelessly** *adv.*

shammy /'ʃæmɪ/ *n.* (*pl.* **-ies**) (in full **shammy leather**) *colloq.* = CHAMOIS 2. [representing corrupted pronunciation]

shampoo /ʃæm'puː/ *–n.* **1** liquid for washing the hair. **2** similar substance for washing cars, carpets, etc. *–v.* (**-poos, -pooed**) wash with shampoo. [Hindustani]

shamrock /'ʃæmrɒk/ *n.* trefoil, used as an emblem of Ireland. [Irish]

Shandong /ʃæn'dʌŋ/ (also **Shantung** /ʃæn'tʌŋ/) province in NE China; pop. (est. 1995) 86 710 000; capital, Jinan. It is an important trading and agricultural area, producing wheat, cotton, and other crops.

shandy /'ʃændɪ/ *n.* (*pl.* **-ies**) beer with lemonade or ginger beer. [origin unknown]

Shanghai /ʃæŋ'haɪ/ chief port and largest city in China; it has shipbuilding, engineering, textile, chemical, steel, and publishing industries; pop. (1990) 7 496 509.

shanghai /ʃæŋ'haɪ/ *v.* (**-hais, -haied, -haiing**) **1** *colloq.* trick or force someone into doing something. **2** trick or force (a person) into serving as a sailor. [SHANGHAI]

shank *n.* **1 a** leg. **b** lower part of the leg. **c** shin-bone. **2** shaft or stem, esp. the part of a tool etc. joining the handle to the working end. [Old English]

shanks's mare *n.* (also **shanks's pony**) one's own legs as transport.

Shansi see SHANXI.

shan't /ʃɑːnt/ *contr.* shall not.

Shantung see SHANDONG.

shantung /ʃæn'tʌŋ/ *n.* soft undressed Chinese silk. [SHANTUNG]

shanty[1] /'ʃæntɪ/ *n.* (*pl.* **-ies**) **1** hut or cabin. **2** shack. [origin unknown]

shanty[2] /'ʃæntɪ/ *n.* (*pl.* **-ies**) (in full **sea shanty**) sailors' work song. [probably French *chanter*: related to CHANT]

shanty town *n.* area with makeshift housing.

Shanxi /ʃæn'ʃiː/ (also **Shansi** /ʃæn'siː/) province in N central China; pop. (est. 1995) 30 450 000; capital, Taiyuan. Industry is centred on its deposits of coal and iron; cotton and cereals are grown, and metalwork and pottery are among its manufactures.

shape *–n.* **1** effect produced by a thing's outline. **2** external form or appearance. **3** specific form or guise (*in the shape of an excuse*). **4** good or specified condition (*back in shape*; *in poor shape*). **5** person or thing seen in outline or indistinctly. **6** mould or pattern. **7** moulded jelly etc. **8** piece of material, paper, etc., made or cut in a particular form. *–v.* (**-ping**) **1** give a certain shape or form to; fashion, create. **2** influence (one's life, course, etc.). **3** (usu. foll. by *up*) show signs of developing; show promise. **4** (foll. by *to*) adapt or make conform. □ **in any shape or form** in any form at all (*don't like jazz in any shape or form*). **take shape** take on a definite form. [Old English]

shapeless *adj.* lacking definite or attractive shape. □ **shapelessness** *n.*

shapely *adj.* (**-ier, -iest**) pleasing in appearance, elegant, well-proportioned. □ **shapeliness** *n.*

shard *n.* broken piece of pottery or glass etc. [Old English]

share[1] *–n.* **1** portion of a whole allotted to or taken from a person. **2** one of a number of titles of ownership in a company. Most companies are limited by shares, thus an investor can limit his or her liability if the company fails to the amount paid for (or owing on) the shares. A share confers on its owner a legal right to the part of the company's profits (usu. by payment of a dividend) and to any voting rights attaching to that share (see A SHARES; DIVIDEND 1; VOTING SHARES). Companies are obliged to keep a public record of the rights attaching to each class of share. The common classes of shares are: ordinary shares, which have no guaranteed amount of dividend but carry voting rights; and preference shares, which receive dividends (and/or repayment of capital on winding-up) before ordinary shares, but which have no voting rights. Shares in public companies may be bought and sold in an open market, e.g. a stock exchange. Shares in a private company are generally subject to restrictions on sale, e.g. they must be offered to existing shareholders first or the directors' approval must be sought before they are sold elsewhere. See also FOUNDERS' SHARES; PARTLY PAID SHARES; PREFERENCE SHARE; PREFERRED ORDINARY SHARE; SUBSCRIPTION SHARES; TERM SHARES. *–v.* (**-ring**) **1** (also *absol.*) have or use with another or others; get, have, or give a share of (*we shared a room*; *refused to share*; *shared his food*). **2** (foll. by *in*) participate. **3** (often foll. by *out*) divide and distribute (*let's share the last cake*). **4** have in common (*shared the same beliefs*). [Old English: related to SHEAR]

share[2] *n.* = PLOUGHSHARE. [Old English: related to SHARE[1]]

♦ **share account** *n.* building society deposit account with no fixed investment period. It usu. demands one month's notice for withdrawals but will often pay up to £250 without notice.

♦ **share capital** *n.* capital of a company that arises from the issue of shares. Every company must commence with some share capital (a minimum of two shares). The **authorized share capital** (or **registered capital** or **nominal capital**) of a company is the total amount of capital it is authorized to raise according to its articles of association. The **issued share capital** (or **subscribed share capital**) is the amount of the authorized capital that shareholders have subscribed. If the shareholders have subscribed the full par value of the share, this will constitute the **fully paid share capital**. If they have subscribed only a proportion of the issued share capital, this is called the **called-up capital**. Some capital may be subscribed on application or on allotment or as separate calls. The shares do not become fully paid until the last call has been made. See also RESERVE CAPITAL.

♦ **share certificate** *n.* document that provides evidence of ownership of shares in a company. It states the number and class of shares owned by the shareholder and the serial number of the shares. It is stamped by the common seal of the company and usu. signed by at least one director and the company secretary. It is not a negotiable instrument. See BEARER SECURITY.

♦ **share exchange** *n.* service offered by most unit-trust managements and life assurance companies, in which the trust or company takes over a client's shareholding and invests the proceeds in unit-trust funds etc. of the client's choice. The client is thereby saved the trouble and expense of disposing of the shares and if they are absorbed into the trust's or company's own portfolio the client may receive a better price than would be possible on the market (i.e. the offer price rather than the bid price).

♦ **share-for-share offer** *n.* takeover bid in which the directors of one company offer shares in that company as payment in acquiring the shares in the target company. If the offer is accepted the shareholders of both companies become the owners of the new combine.

♦ **shareholder** *n.* owner of shares in a limited company or limited partnership. A shareholder is a member of the company.

♦ **share index** see CHAMBRE AGENT GENERAL INDEX; DAX; DOW JONES INDUSTRIAL AVERAGE; FINANCIAL TIMES SHARE INDEXES; NIKKEI STOCK AVERAGE; HANG SENG INDEX.

♦ **share option** *n.* **1** benefit sometimes offered to employees, esp. new employees, in which they are given an option to buy shares in the company for which they work at a favourable fixed price or at a stated discount to the market price. **2** right to buy or sell shares on a particular date at a particular price. See OPTION 3.

share-out *n.* act of sharing out, distribution.

♦ **share premium** *n.* amount payable for shares in a company and issued by the company itself in excess of their par value. Share premiums received by a company must be credited to a **share premium account**, which cannot be used for paying dividends to the shareholders, although it may be used to make bonus or scrip issues.

♦ **share register** *n.* register kept by a limited company in which ownership of shares in that company is kept, together with the full names, addresses, extent of holding, and class of shares for each shareholder. Entry in the register constitutes evidence of ownership and allows missing share certificates to be replaced by the company on proof of the owner's identity.

♦ **share shop** *n.* stockbroker, bank, building society or other financial intermediary appointed by the UK government to sell shares in a PRIVATIZATION ISSUE.

♦ **share split** *n.* division of the share capital of a company into smaller units. The effect of a share split is the same as a scrip issue although the technicalities differ. Share splits are usu. carried out when the existing shares reach such a high price that trading in them becomes difficult.

♦ **share warehousing** *n.* building up a holding of the shares of a company that is to be the target for a take-over. The shares are bought in the name of nominees in relatively small lots and 'warehoused' until the purchaser has built up a significant interest in the company.

Sharjah /ˈʃɑːdʒə/ (Arabic **Ash-Shariqah** /ˌæʃʃɑːˈriːkə/) **1** third-largest of the member states of the United Arab Emirates; pop. (1993) 342 000. **2** its capital city, on the Persian Gulf.

shark[1] *n.* large voracious marine fish. [origin unknown]

shark[2] *n. colloq.* swindler, profiteer. [origin unknown]

♦ **shark repellents** *n.pl. colloq.* = PORCUPINE PROVISIONS.

sharkskin *n.* **1** skin of a shark. **2** smooth slightly shiny fabric.

♦ **shark watcher** *n. colloq.* business consultant who specializes in helping companies to identify raiders and to provide early warning of share warehousing and other manoeuvres used as preliminaries to take-overs.

sharp *–adj.* **1** having an edge or point able to cut or pierce. **2** tapering to a point or edge. **3** abrupt, steep, angular. **4** well-defined, clean-cut. **5 a** severe or intense. **b** (of food etc.) pungent, acid. **6** (of a voice etc.) shrill and piercing. **7** (of words or temper etc.) harsh. **8** acute; quick to understand. **9** artful, unscrupulous. **10** vigorous or brisk. **11** *Mus.* above the normal pitch; a semitone higher than a specified pitch (*C sharp*). *–n.* **1** *Mus.* **a** note a semitone above natural pitch. **b** sign (♯) indicating this. **2** *colloq.* swindler, cheat. *–adv.* **1** punctually (*at nine o'clock sharp*). **2** suddenly (*pulled up sharp*). **3** at a sharp angle. **4** *Mus.* above true pitch (*sings sharp*). □ **sharply** *adv.* **sharpness** *n.* [Old English]

♦ **sharp bender** *n.* firm that has been underperforming but suddenly improves as a result of new management, new products, or a major change in business strategy.

sharpen *v.* make or become sharp. □ **sharpener** *n.*

sharper *n.* swindler, esp. at cards.

sharpish *colloq. –adj.* fairly sharp. *–adv.* **1** fairly sharply. **2** quite quickly.

sharp practice *n.* dishonest or dubious dealings.

sharpshooter *n.* skilled marksman.

sharp-witted *adj.* keenly perceptive or intelligent.

shat *past* and *past. part.* of SHIT.

shatter *v.* **1** break suddenly in pieces. **2** severely damage or destroy. **3** (esp. in *passive*) greatly upset or discompose. **4** (usu. as **shattered** *adj.*) *colloq.* exhaust. [origin unknown]

shave *–v.* (**-ving**; *past part.* **shaved** or (as *adj.*) **shaven**) **1** remove (bristles or hair) with a razor. **2** (also *absol.*) remove bristles or hair with a razor from (a person, face, leg, etc.). **3** reduce by a small amount. **4** pare (wood etc.) to shape it. **5** miss or pass narrowly. *–n.* **1** shaving or being shaved. **2** narrow miss or escape. **3** tool for shaving wood etc. [Old English]

shaver *n.* **1** thing that shaves. **2** electric razor. **3** *colloq.* young lad.

Shavian /ˈʃeɪvɪən/ *–adj.* of or like the writings of G. B. Shaw. *–n.* admirer of Shaw. [*Shavius*, Latinized form of *Shaw*]

shaving *n.* thin strip cut off wood etc.

shawl *n.* large usu. rectangular piece of fabric worn over the shoulders or head, or wrapped round a baby. [Urdu from Persian *shāl*]

S/HE *abbr. Shipping* Sundays and holidays excepted.

she /ʃiː/ *–pron.* (*obj.* **her**; *poss.* **her**; *pl.* **they**) the woman, girl, female animal, ship, or country, etc. previously named or in question. *–n.* **1** female; woman. **2** (in *comb.*) female (*she-goat*). [Old English]

s/he *pron.* written representation of 'he or she' used to indicate either sex.

sheaf *–n.* (*pl.* **sheaves**) bundle of things laid lengthways together and usu. tied, esp. reaped corn or a collection of papers. *–v.* make into sheaves. [Old English]

shear *–v.* (*past* **sheared**; *past part.* **shorn** or **sheared**) **1** (also *absol.*) clip the wool off (a sheep etc.). **2** remove or take off by cutting. **3** cut with scissors or shears etc. **4** (foll. by *of*) **a** strip bare. **b** deprive. **5** (often foll. by *off*) distort, be distorted, or break, from structural strain. *–n.* **1** strain produced by pressure in the structure of a substance. **2** (in *pl.*) (also **pair of shears** *sing.*) large scissor-shaped clipping or cutting instrument. □ **shearer** *n.* [Old English]

sheath *n.* (*pl.* **-s** /ʃiːðz, ʃiːθs/) **1** close-fitting cover, esp.

for the blade of a knife or sword. **2** condom. **3** enclosing case, covering, or tissue. **4** woman's close-fitting dress. [Old English]

sheathe /ʃiːð/ *v.* (**-thing**) **1** put into a sheath. **2** encase; protect with a sheath.

sheath knife *n.* dagger-like knife carried in a sheath.

sheave *v.* (**-ving**) make into sheaves.

sheaves *pl.* of SHEAF.

shebeen /ʃɪ'biːn/ *n.* esp. *Ir.* unlicensed drinking place. [Irish]

shed[1] *n.* one-storeyed usu. wooden structure for storage or shelter, or as a workshop. [from SHADE]

shed[2] *v.* (**-dd-**; *past* and *past part.* **shed**) **1** let, or cause to, fall off (*trees shed their leaves*). **2** take off (clothes). **3** reduce (an electrical power load) by disconnection etc. **4** cause to fall or flow (*shed blood; shed tears*). **5** disperse, diffuse, radiate (*shed light*). **6** get rid of (*IBM are shedding 200 jobs; shed your inhibitions*). □ **shed light on** help to explain. [Old English]

she'd /ʃiːd/ *contr.* **1** she had. **2** she would.

sheen *n.* **1** gloss or lustre. **2** brightness. □ **sheeny** *adj.* [Old English, = beautiful]

sheep *n.* (*pl.* same) **1** mammal with a thick woolly coat, esp. kept for its wool or meat. **2** timid, silly, or easily-led person. **3** (usu. in *pl.*) member of a minister's congregation. [Old English]

sheep-dip *n.* preparation or place for cleansing sheep of vermin etc. by dipping.

sheepdog *n.* **1** dog trained to guard and herd sheep. **2** dog of a breed suitable for this.

sheepfold *n.* pen for sheep.

sheepish *adj.* embarrassed or shy; ashamed. □ **sheepishly** *adv.*

sheepshank *n.* knot for shortening a rope temporarily.

sheepskin *n.* **1** garment or rug of sheep's skin with the wool on. **2** leather from sheep's skin used in bookbinding etc.

sheer[1] *–adj.* **1** mere, complete (*sheer luck*). **2** (of a cliff etc.) perpendicular. **3** (of a textile) diaphanous. *–adv.* directly, perpendicularly. [Old English]

sheer[2] *v.* **1** esp. *Naut.* swerve or change course. **2** (foll. by *away, off*) turn away, esp. from a person or topic one dislikes or fears. [origin unknown]

sheet[1] *–n.* **1** large rectangle of cotton etc. used esp. in pairs as inner bedclothes. **2** broad usu. thin flat piece of paper, metal, etc. **3** wide expanse of water, ice, flame, falling rain, etc. **4** page of unseparated postage stamps. **5** *derog.* newspaper. *–v.* **1** provide or cover with sheets. **2** form into sheets. **3** (of rain etc.) fall in sheets. [Old English]

sheet[2] *n.* rope or chain attached to the lower corner of a sail to hold or control it. [Old English: related to SHEET[1]]

sheet anchor *n.* **1** emergency reserve anchor. **2** person or thing depended on in the last resort.

sheeting *n.* material for making bed linen.

sheet metal *n.* metal rolled or hammered etc. into thin sheets.

sheet music *n.* music published in sheets, not bound.

Sheffield /'ʃefiːld/ industrial city in N England, in South Yorkshire, noted for metalworking, esp. the production of steel and the manufacture of cutlery and silverware; pop. (1994) 530 100.

sheikh /ʃeɪk/ *n.* **1** chief or head of an Arab tribe, family, or village. **2** Muslim leader. □ **sheikhdom** *n.* [Arabic]

sheila /'ʃiːlə/ *n. Austral.* & *NZ slang* girl, young woman. [origin uncertain]

shekel /'ʃek(ə)l/ *n.* **1** standard monetary unit of modern Israel. **2** *hist.* silver coin and unit of weight in ancient Israel etc. **3** (in *pl.*) *colloq.* money; riches. [Hebrew]

shelduck /'ʃeldʌk/ *n.* (*pl.* same or **-s**; *masc.* **sheldrake**, *pl.* same or **-s**) bright-plumaged wild duck. [probably from dial. *sheld* pied, DUCK[1]]

shelf *n.* (*pl.* **shelves**) **1** wooden etc. board projecting from a wall, or as part of a unit, used to store things. **2 a** projecting horizontal ledge in a cliff face etc. **b** reef or sandbank. □ **on the shelf 1** (of a woman) regarded as too old to hope for marriage. **2** (esp. of a retired person) put aside as if no longer useful. [Low German]

shelf-life *n.* time for which a stored item remains usable.

shelf-mark *n.* code on a library book showing where it is kept.

shell *–n.* **1 a** hard outer case of many molluscs, the tortoise, etc. **b** hard but fragile case of an egg. **c** hard outer case of a nut-kernel, seed, etc. **2 a** explosive projectile for use in a big gun etc. **b** hollow container for fireworks, cartridges, etc. **3** shell-like thing, esp.: **a** a light racing-boat. **b** the metal framework of a vehicle etc. **c** the walls of an unfinished or gutted building, ship, etc. *–v.* **1** remove the shell or pod from. **2** bombard with shells. □ **come out of one's shell** become less shy and more sociable. **shell out** (also *absol.*) *colloq.* pay (money). □ **shell-less** *adj.* **shell-like** *adj.* [Old English]

she'll /ʃiːl/ *contr.* she will; she shall.

shellac /ʃə'læk/ *–n.* resin used for making varnish. *–v.* (**-ck-**) varnish with shellac. [from SHELL, LAC]

♦ **shell company** *n.* **1** non-trading company, with or without a stock-exchange listing, used as a vehicle for various company manoeuvres or kept dormant for future use in some other capacity. **2** company that has ceased to trade and is sold to new owners for a small fee to minimize the cost and trouble of setting up a new company. Some business brokers register such companies with the sole object of selling them to people setting up new businesses. The name and objects of such a company can be changed for a small charge.

---

shellfish *n.* (*pl.* same) **1** aquatic mollusc with a shell. **2** crustacean.

shell-shock *n.* nervous breakdown caused by warfare. □ **shell-shocked** *adj.*

shelter *–n.* **1** protection from danger, bad weather, etc. **2** place giving shelter or refuge. *–v.* **1** act or serve as a shelter to; protect; conceal; defend. **2** find refuge; take cover. [origin unknown]

shelve *v.* (**-ving**) **1** put aside, esp. temporarily. **2** put (books etc.) on a shelf. **3** fit with shelves. **4** (of ground etc.) slope. □ **shelving** *n.*

shelves *pl.* of SHELF.

shemozzle /ʃɪ'mɒz(ə)l/ *n. slang* **1** brawl or commotion. **2** muddle. [Yiddish]

shenanigan /ʃɪ'nænɪgən/ *n.* (esp. in *pl.*) *colloq.* mischievous or questionable behaviour, carryings-on. [origin unknown]

Shensi see SHAANXI.

Shenyang /ʃen'jæŋ/ (formerly **Mukden** /'mʊkd(ə)n/) fourth-largest city in China, capital of Liaoning province and an important centre of industry; pop. (est. 1990) 3 603 712.

Shenzhen /ʃen'ʒen/ industrial city in S China, developed as a special economic zone near Canton; pop. (est. 1990) 350 727.

♦ **Shepherd** /'ʃepəd/, **Sir Peter** (1916–96) British businessman, chairman (1958–86) of the family-owned Shepherd Building Group Ltd. founded by his grandfather in 1890.

---

shepherd /'ʃepəd/ *–n.* **1** (*fem.* **shepherdess**) person employed to tend sheep. **2** member of the clergy etc. in charge of a congregation. *–v.* **1 a** tend (sheep etc.). **b** guide (followers etc.). **2** marshal or drive (a crowd etc.) like sheep. [Old English: related to SHEEP, HERD]

shepherd's pie *n.* = COTTAGE PIE.

Sheraton /'ʃerət(ə)n/ *n.* (often *attrib.*) style of English furniture *c.*1790. [name of a furniture-maker]

sherbet /'ʃɜːbət/ *n.* **1** flavoured sweet effervescent powder or drink. **2** drink of sweet diluted fruit juices. [Turkish and Persian from Arabic]

sherd *n.* = POTSHERD. [Old English]

sheriff /'ʃerɪf/ *n.* **1 a** (also **High Sheriff**) chief executive officer of the Crown in a county, administering justice etc. **b** honorary officer elected annually in some towns. **2** *US* elected chief law-enforcing officer in a county. **3** (also **sheriff-depute**) *Scot.* chief judge of a county or district. [Old English: related to SHIRE, REEVE[1]]

Sherpa *n.* (*pl.* same or **-s**) member of a Himalayan people living on the borders of Nepal and Tibet. [native name]

sherry /'ʃerɪ/ *n.* (*pl.* **-ies**) **1** fortified wine orig. from S Spain. **2** glass of this. [*Xeres* in Andalusia]

's-Hertogenbosch /ˌseətɒxen'bɒs/ (French **Bois-le-Duc** /ˌbwɑːlə'djuːk/) city in the Netherlands, capital of North Brabant; pop. (1994) 95 448.

she's /ʃiːz, ʃɪz/ *contr.* **1** she is. **2** she has.

Shetland Islands /'ʃetlənd/ (also **Shetlands**) group of about 100 Scottish islands NNE of the Orkneys, constituting an island area (Shetland) of Scotland; pop. (est. 1996) 23 020; chief town, Lerwick. The islands are important bases for the exploitation of oil and gas in the North Sea. Other activities include fishing, salmon farming, sheep farming (esp. for wool), fish processing, and knitting. □ **Shetlander** *n.*

Shetland pony *n.* pony of a small hardy rough-coated breed. [SHETLAND ISLANDS]

shew *archaic* var. of SHOW.

SHEX *abbr. Shipping* Sundays and holidays excepted.

Sh.F. *abbr.* shareholders' funds.

shiatsu /ʃɪ'ætsuː/ *n.* Japanese therapy in which pressure is applied, chiefly with fingers and hands, to specific points on the body. [Japanese, = finger pressure]

shibboleth /'ʃɪbəˌleθ/ *n.* long-standing formula, doctrine, or phrase, etc., held to be true by a party or sect. [Hebrew (Judg. 12:6)]

shied *past* & *past part.* of SHY[2].

shield *–n.* **1 a** piece of armour held in front of the body for protection when fighting. **b** person or thing giving protection. **2** shield-shaped trophy. **3** protective plate or screen in machinery etc. **4** *Heraldry* stylized representation of a shield for displaying a coat of arms etc. *–v.* protect or screen. [Old English]

shier *compar.* of SHY[1].

shiest *superl.* of SHY[1].

shift *–v.* **1** (cause to) change or move from one position to another. **2** remove, esp. with effort. **3** *slang* **a** hurry. **b** consume (food or drink). **4** *US* change (gear) in a vehicle. *–n.* **1** act of shifting. **2 a** relay of workers. **b** time for which they work. **3 a** device, stratagem, or expedient. **b** trick or evasion. **4** woman's straight unwaisted dress or petticoat. **5** *Physics* displacement of a spectral line. **6** key on a keyboard used to switch between lower and upper case etc. **7** *US* **a** gear lever in a vehicle. **b** mechanism for this. □ **make shift** manage; get along somehow. **shift for oneself** rely on one's own efforts. **shift one's ground** take up a new position in an argument etc. [Old English]

shiftless *adj.* lacking resourcefulness; lazy.

shifty *adj. colloq.* (**-ier**, **-iest**) evasive; deceitful. □ **shiftily** *adv.* **shiftiness** *n.*

Shiite /'ʃiːaɪt/ *–n.* adherent of the branch of Islam rejecting the first three Sunni caliphs. *–adj.* of this branch. [Arabic *Shiah*, = party]

Shijiazhuang /ˌʃiːdʒɪə'dʒwæŋ/ city in NE central China, capital of Hebei province; coal is mined, and there are also textile, chemical, and engineering industries; pop. (est. 1991) 1 320 000.

Shikoku /ʃɪ'kəʊkuː/ smallest of the four main islands of Japan; pop. (1995) 4 183 000; capital, Matsuyama. Activities include copper-mining and fishing; rice, grain, tobacco, and camphor are produced.

shillelagh /ʃɪ'leɪlə/ *n.* Irish cudgel. [*Shillelagh* in Ireland]

shilling /'ʃɪlɪŋ/ *n.* **1** *hist.* former British coin and monetary unit worth one-twentieth of a pound. **2** standard monetary unit of Kenya, Somalia, Tanzania, and Uganda. [Old English]

shilly-shally /'ʃɪlɪˌʃælɪ/ *v.* (**-ies**, **-ied**) be undecided; vacillate. [from *shall I?*]

shim *–n.* thin wedge in machinery etc. to make parts fit. *–v.* (**-mm-**) fit or fill up with a shim. [origin unknown]

shimmer *–v.* shine tremulously or faintly. *–n.* tremulous or faint light. [Old English]

shin *–n.* **1** front of the leg below the knee. **2** cut of beef from this part. *–v.* (**-nn-**) (usu. foll. by *up, down*) climb quickly by clinging with the arms and legs. [Old English]

shin-bone *n.* = TIBIA.

shindig /'ʃɪndɪg/ *n. colloq.* **1** lively noisy party. **2** = SHINDY 1. [probably from SHINDY]

shindy /'ʃɪndɪ/ *n.* (*pl.* **-ies**) *colloq.* **1** brawl, disturbance, or noise. **2** = SHINDIG 1. [perhaps an alteration of SHINTY]

shine *–v.* (**-ning**; *past* and *past part.* **shone** /ʃɒn/ or **shined**) **1** emit or reflect light; be bright; glow. **2** (of the sun, a star, etc.) be visible. **3** cause (a lamp etc.) to shine. **4** (*past* and *past part.* **shined**) polish. **5** be brilliant; excel. *–n.* **1** light; brightness. **2** high polish; lustre. □ **take a shine to** *colloq.* take a fancy to. [Old English]

shiner *n. colloq.* black eye.

shingle[1] /'ʃɪŋg(ə)l/ *n.* small smooth pebbles, esp. on the sea-shore. □ **shingly** *adj.* [origin uncertain]

shingle[2] /'ʃɪŋg(ə)l/ *–n.* **1** rectangular wooden tile used on roofs etc. **2** *archaic* **a** shingled hair. **b** shingling of hair. *–v.* (**-ling**) **1** roof with shingles. **2** *archaic* **a** cut (a woman's hair) short. **b** cut the hair of (a person or head) in this way. [Latin *scindula*]

shingles /'ʃɪŋg(ə)lz/ *n.pl.* (usu. treated as *sing.*) acute painful viral inflammation of the nerve ganglia, with a rash often encircling the body. [Latin *cingulum* girdle]

Shinto /'ʃɪntəʊ/ *n.* Japanese religion with the worship of ancestors and nature-spirits. □ **Shintoism** *n.* **Shintoist** *n.* [Chinese, = way of the gods]

shinty /'ʃɪntɪ/ *n.* (*pl.* **-ies**) **1** game like hockey, but with taller goalposts. **2** stick or ball used in this. [origin uncertain]

shiny *adj.* (**-ier**, **-iest**) **1** having a shine. **2** (of clothing) with the nap worn off. □ **shininess** *n.*

ship *–n.* **1** large seagoing vessel. **2** *US* aircraft. **3** spaceship. *–v.* (**-pp-**) **1** put, take, or send away in a ship. **2 a** take in (water) over a ship's side etc. **b** lay (oars) at the bottom of a boat. **c** fix (a rudder etc.) in place. **3 a** embark. **b** (of a sailor) take service on a ship. **4** deliver (goods) to an agent for forwarding. □ **ship off** send away. **when a person's ship comes home** (or **in**) when a person's fortune is made. [Old English]

-ship *suffix* forming nouns denoting: **1** quality or condition (*friendship; hardship*). **2** status, office, etc. (*authorship; lordship*). **3** tenure of office (*chairmanship*). **4** specific skill (*workmanship*). **5** members of a group (*readership*). [Old English]

shipboard *attrib. adj.* used or occurring on board a ship.

♦ **shipbroker** *n.* broker who specializes in arranging charters, cargo space, and sometimes passenger bookings, receiving a brokerage on the business obtained. See also BALTIC EXCHANGE.

---

shipbuilder *n.* person, company, etc., that constructs ships. □ **shipbuilding** *n.*

ship-canal *n.* canal large enough for ships.

shipload *n.* as many goods or passengers as a ship can hold.

shipmate *n.* fellow member of a ship's crew.

shipment *n.* **1** amount of goods shipped. **2** act of shipping goods etc.

shipowner *n.* owner of a ship, ships, or shares in ships.

♦ **shipowner's lien** *n.* right of a shipowner to retain possession of cargo being carried if the freight charges are not paid.

♦ **shipped bill** *n.* bill of lading confirming that specified goods have been loaded onto a specified ship.

---

shipper *n.* **1** person or organization that exports goods, usu. owned by the shipper, to a foreign country by sea or by air. **2** (in some trades) importer, esp. one buying f.o.b. port of shipment and paying the freight, who sells on to merchants or users. [Old English]

shipping *n.* **1** transport of goods etc. **2** ships, esp. a navy.

♦ **shipping and forwarding agent** *n.* organization that specializes in the handling of goods sent by sea, air, rail, or road, esp. if the goods are being exported or imported. Such agents advise on the best method of transport, book freight, cover insurance, and arrange custom clearance at both ends, if necessary. They usu. do all the required paperwork and documentation. They also arrange inland transport in the exporting or importing country, arranging factory-to-factory transport, if it is required.

♦ **shipping bill** *n.* form used by HM Customs and Excise before goods can be exported from the UK. It is also required when removing goods from a bonded warehouse before drawback can be claimed.

♦ **shipping conference** *n.* association of shipowners whose liners ply the same routes. They combine to fix freight rates, passenger rates, and terms of contracts. Liners that belong to conferences are called **conference line ships**.

♦ **shipping documents** *n.pl.* documents that an exporter of goods delivers to his or her bank in the exporting country in order to obtain payment for the goods. The bank sends them to its branch or agents in the importing country, who only release them to the importer against payment. Once the importer has these documents the goods can be claimed at the port of destination. The documents usu. consist of a commercial invoice, bill of lading, insurance policy or certificate, weight note, quality certificate, and, if required, a certificate of origin, consular invoice, and export licence.

♦ **shipping ton** see TON 3.

---

ship's boat *n.* small boat carried on board a ship.

♦ **ship's certificate of registry** *n.* document that the master of a ship must always carry. It records the ship's country of registration, home port, owner's name, registered tonnage, permitted number of passengers, master's name, etc.

---

shipshape *adv.* & *predic.adj.* trim, neat, tidy.

♦ **ship's papers** *n.pl.* documents that the master of a ship must always have available for inspection if required. They include the ship's certificate of registry, bill of health, log book, the ship's articles (muster roll), the charter-party if the ship is on charter, cargo manifest and bills of lading, and passenger manifest if it is carrying passengers.

♦ **ship's report** *n.* report that the master of a ship must make to the port authorities on arrival at a port. It lists details of the ship, crew, passengers, and cargo.

---

shipwreck *–n.* **1 a** destruction of a ship by a storm, foundering, etc. **b** ship so destroyed. **2** (often foll. by *of*) ruin of hopes, dreams, etc. *–v.* **1** inflict shipwreck on. **2** suffer shipwreck.

shipwright *n.* **1** shipbuilder. **2** ship's carpenter.

shipyard *n.* place where ships are built etc.

Shiraz /ʃɪəˈræz/ city and trading centre in SW central Iran, capital of Fars province; pop. (1991) 965 117.

shire *n.* county. [Old English]

shire-horse *n.* heavy powerful draught-horse.

shirk *v.* (also *absol.*) avoid (duty, work, etc.). □ **shirker** *n.* [German *Schurke* scoundrel]

shirr *–n.* elasticated gathered threads in a garment etc. forming smocking. *–v.* gather (material) with parallel threads. □ **shirring** *n.* [origin unknown]

shirt *n.* upper-body garment of cotton etc., usu. front-opening. □ **keep one's shirt on** *colloq.* keep one's temper. **put one's shirt on** *colloq.* bet all one has on. □ **shirting** *n.* **shirtless** *adj.* [Old English]

shirtsleeve *n.* (usu. in *pl.*) sleeve of a shirt. □ **in shirt-sleeves** without one's jacket on.

shirt-tail *n.* curved part of a shirt below the waist.

shirtwaister *n.* woman's dress with a bodice like a shirt.

shirty *adj.* (**-ier**, **-iest**) *colloq.* angry; annoyed. □ **shirtily** *adv.* **shirtiness** *n.*

shish kebab /ˌʃɪʃ kɪˈbæb/ *n.* pieces of meat and vegetables grilled on skewers. [Turkish: related to KEBAB]

shit *coarse slang –n.* **1** faeces. **2** act of defecating. **3** contemptible person. **4** nonsense. *–int.* exclamation of anger etc. *–v.* (**-tt-**; *past* and *past part.* **shitted, shat** or **shit**) defecate or cause the defecation of (faeces etc.). [Old English]

shitty *adj.* (**-ier**, **-iest**) *coarse slang* **1** disgusting, contemptible. **2** covered with excrement.

shiver[1] /ˈʃɪvə(r)/ *–v.* tremble with cold, fear, etc. *–n.* **1** momentary shivering movement. **2** (in *pl.*, prec. by *the*) attack of shivering. □ **shivery** *adj.* [origin uncertain]

shiver[2] /ˈʃɪvə(r)/ *–n.* (esp. in *pl.*) small fragment or splinter. *–v.* break into shivers. [related to dial. *shive* slice]

shoal[1] *–n.* multitude, esp of fish swimming together. *–v.* (of fish) form shoals. [Dutch: cf. SCHOOL[2]]

shoal[2] *–n.* **1 a** area of shallow water. **b** submerged sandbank visible at low water. **2** (esp. in *pl.*) hidden danger. *–v.* (of water) get shallower. [Old English]

shock[1] *–n.* **1** violent collision, impact, tremor, etc. **2** sudden and disturbing effect on the emotions etc. **3** acute prostration following a wound, pain, etc. **4** = ELECTRIC SHOCK. **5** disturbance in the stability of an organization etc. *–v.* **1 a** horrify; outrage. **b** (*absol.*) cause shock. **2** affect with an electric or pathological shock. [French *choc, choquer*]

shock[2] *–n.* group of corn-sheaves in a field. *–v.* arrange (corn) in shocks. [origin uncertain]

shock[3] *n.* unkempt or shaggy mass of hair. [origin unknown]

shock absorber *n.* device on a vehicle etc. for absorbing shocks, vibrations, etc.

shocker *n. colloq.* **1** shocking person or thing. **2** sensational novel etc.

shocking *adj.* **1** causing shock; scandalous. **2** *colloq.* very bad. □ **shockingly** *adv.*

shocking pink *adj.* & *n.* (as adj. often hyphenated) vibrant shade of pink.

shockproof *adj.* resistant to the effects of (esp. physical) shock.

shock therapy *n.* (also **shock treatment**) treatment of depressive patients by electric shock etc.

shock troops *n.pl.* troops specially trained for assault.

shock wave *n.* **1** moving region of high air pressure caused by an explosion or by a supersonic body. **2** wave of emotional shock (*the news sent shock waves throughout the region*).

shod *past* and *past part.* of SHOE.

shoddy /ˈʃɒdɪ/ *adj.* (**-ier**, **-iest**) **1** poorly made. **2** counterfeit. □ **shoddily** *adv.* **shoddiness** *n.* [origin unknown]

shoe /ʃuː/ *–n.* **1** protective foot-covering of leather etc., esp. one not reaching above the ankle. **2** protective metal rim for a horse's hoof. **3** thing like a shoe in shape or use. **4** = BRAKE SHOE. *–v.* (**shoes, shoeing**; *past* and *past part.* **shod**) **1** fit (esp. a horse etc.) with a shoe or shoes. **2** (as **shod** *adj.*) (in *comb.*) having shoes etc. of a specified kind (*roughshod*). □ **be in a person's shoes** be in his or her situation, difficulty, etc. [Old English]

shoehorn *n.* curved implement for easing the heel into a shoe.

shoelace *n.* cord for lacing up shoes.

shoemaker *n.* maker of boots and shoes. □ **shoemaking** *n.*

shoestring *n.* **1** shoelace. **2** *colloq.* small esp. inadequate amount of money.

shoe-tree *n.* shaped block for keeping a shoe in shape.

♦ **shogun bond** /ˈʃəʊɡʊn/ *n.* bond sold on the Japanese market by a foreign institution and denominated in a foreign currency. Cf. SAMURAI BOND. [Japanese *shogun* a general]

Sholapur /ˌʃəʊləˈpʊə(r)/ city in W India, in the state of Maharashtra, a centre of the cotton textile industry; pop. (1991) 604 215.

shone *past* and *past part.* of SHINE.

shoo *–int.* exclamation used to frighten away animals etc. *–v.* (**shoos, shooed**) **1** utter the word 'shoo!'. **2** (usu. foll. by *away*) drive away by shooing. [imitative]

shook *past* of SHAKE.

shoot *–v.* (*past* and *past part.* **shot**) **1 a** (also *absol.*) cause (a weapon) to fire. **b** kill or wound with a bullet, arrow, etc. **2** send out, discharge, etc., esp. swiftly. **3** (often foll. by *out, along, forth,* etc.) come or go swiftly or vigorously. **4 a** (of a plant etc.) put forth buds etc. **b** (of a bud etc.) appear. **5** hunt game etc. with a gun. **6** film or photograph. **7** (also *absol.*) esp. *Football* **a** score (a goal). **b** take a shot at (the goal). **8** (of a boat) sweep swiftly down or under (a bridge, rapids, etc.). **9** (usu. foll. by *through, up,* etc.) (of a pain) seem to stab. **10** (often foll. by *up*; also *absol.*) *slang* inject (a drug). *–n.* **1 a** young branch or sucker. **b** new growth of a plant. **2 a** hunting party, expedition, etc. **b** land shot over for game. **3** = CHUTE[1]. *–int. colloq.* invitation to ask questions etc. □ **shoot down 1** kill by shooting. **2** cause (an aircraft etc.) to crash by shooting. **3** argue effectively against. **shoot one's bolt** *colloq.* do all that is in one's power. **shoot one's mouth off** *slang* talk too much or indiscreetly. **shoot up 1** grow rapidly. **2** rise suddenly. **3** terrorize by indiscriminate shooting. **the whole shoot** (or **the whole shooting match**) *colloq.* everything. [Old English]

shooting-brake *n. archaic* estate car.

shooting star *n.* small rapidly moving meteor.

shooting-stick *n.* walking-stick with a foldable seat.

shop *–n.* **1** place for the retail sale of goods or services. **2** act of going shopping (*did a big shop*). **3** place for manufacture or repair (*engineering-shop*). **4** one's profession etc. as a subject of conversation (*talk shop*). **5** *colloq.* institution, place of business, etc. *–v.* (**-pp-**) **1** go to a shop or shops to buy goods. **2** *slang* inform against (a criminal etc.). □ **all over the shop** *colloq.* **1** in disorder. **2** everywhere. **shop around** look for the best bargain. □ **shopper** *n.* [French *eschoppe*]

shop assistant *n.* person serving in a shop.

shop-floor *n.* **1** production area in a factory etc. **2** workers as distinct from management.

shopkeeper *n.* owner or manager of a shop.

shoplift *v.* steal goods while appearing to shop. □ **shoplifter** *n.*

shopping *n.* **1** (often *attrib.*) purchase of goods etc. **2** goods purchased.

shopping centre *n.* area or complex of shops.

shop-soiled *adj.* soiled or faded by display in a shop.

♦ **shop steward** *n.* employee working in a factory etc. who is the elected representative of a trade union and is responsible for negotiating with the employers on behalf of the other members of the same union in the factory etc.

shopwalker *n.* supervisor in a large shop.

shore[1] *n.* **1** land adjoining the sea, a lake etc. **2** (usu. in *pl.*) country (*foreign shores*). □ **on shore** ashore. [Low German or Dutch]

shore[2] *–n.* prop or beam set against a ship, wall, etc., as a support. *–v.* (**-ring**) (often foll. by *up*) support (as if) with a shore or shores; hold up. [Low German or Dutch]

shoreline *n.* line where shore and water meet.

shorn *past part.* of SHEAR.

short *–adj.* **1 a** measuring little from head to foot, top to bottom, or end to end; not long. **b** not long in duration. **c** seeming short (*a few short years of happiness*). **2 a** (usu. foll. by *of, on*) deficient; scanty (*short of spoons*). **b** not far-reaching; acting or being near at hand (*short range*). **3 a** concise; brief. **b** curt; uncivil. **4** (of the memory) unable to remember distant events. **5** (of a vowel or syllable) having the lesser of the two recognized durations. **6** (of pastry) easily crumbled. **7** (of stocks etc.) sold or selling when the amount is not in hand, with reliance on getting the deficit at a lower price in time for delivery. **8** (of a drink of spirits) undiluted. **9** (of odds or a chance) nearly even. *–adv.* **1** before the natural or expected time or place; abruptly. **2** rudely. *–n.* **1** short circuit. **2** *colloq.* short drink. **3** short film. **4** (in *pl.*) see SHORTS. *–v.* short-circuit. □ **be caught** (or **taken**) **short 1** be put at a disadvantage. **2** *colloq.* urgently need to use the lavatory. **be short for** be an abbreviation for. **come short of** = *fall short of*. **for short** as a short name (*Tom for short*). **in short** briefly. **short of 1** see sense 2a of *adj.* **2** less than (*nothing short of a miracle*). **3** distant from (*two miles short of home*). **4** without going so far as (*did everything short of resigning*). **short on** *colloq.* see sense 2a of *adj.* □ **shortish** *adj.* **shortness** *n.* [Old English]

shortage *n.* (often foll. by *of*) deficiency; amount lacking.

short back and sides *n.* short simple haircut.

♦ **short bill** *n.* bill of exchange that is payable at sight, on demand, or within ten days.

shortbread *n.* rich biscuit of butter, flour, and sugar.

shortcake *n.* **1** = SHORTBREAD. **2** cake of short pastry filled with fruit and cream.

short-change *v.* cheat, esp. by giving insufficient change.

short circuit *–n.* electric circuit through small resistance, esp. instead of the resistance of a normal circuit. *–v.* (**short-circuit**) **1** cause a short circuit (in). **2** shorten or avoid by taking a more direct route etc.

shortcoming *n.* deficiency; defect.

♦ **short covering** *n.* purchasing goods that one has already sold (see SHORT POSITION). Dealers in commodities, securities, or foreign exchanges hope to purchase these goods at below the price at which they sold them in order to make a profit. Dealers cover their shorts when they expect the market to turn or when it has already started to move upwards.

shortcrust *n.* (in full **shortcrust pastry**) a type of crumbly pastry.

short cut *n.* **1** route shorter than the usual one. **2** quick method.

♦ **short-dated gilt** see GILT-EDGED SECURITY.

♦ **short delivery** *n.* delivery of goods that has fewer items than invoiced or a smaller total weight than invoiced. This may be due to accidental loss, which could give rise to an insurance claim, or it may be due to some normal process (e.g. drying out during shipment), in which case the weight on arrival will be used in a final invoice. It may also be an attempt by the seller to make an extra profit, in which case the buyer would be well advised to make a claim for short delivery.

shorten *v.* become or make shorter or short.

shortening *n.* fat for pastry.

shortfall *n.* deficit.

shorthand *n.* **1** (often *attrib.*) system of rapid writing using special symbols. **2** abbreviated or symbolic mode of expression.

short-handed *adj.* understaffed.

shorthand typist *n.* typist qualified in shorthand.

shorthorn *n.* animal of a breed of cattle with short horns.

♦ **short interest** *n.* (in marine insurance) difference between the insured value of goods and their market value, when the insured value exceeds the market value. In these circumstances any excess premium paid can be reclaimed.

short list *–n.* list of selected candidates from which a final choice is made. *–v.* (**short-list**) put on a short list.

short-lived *adj.* ephemeral.

shortly *adv.* **1** (often foll. by *before, after*) soon. **2** in a few words; curtly. [Old English]

♦ **short position** *n.* position held by a dealer in securities (see MARKET MAKER), commodities, currencies, etc. in which sales exceed holdings because the dealer expects prices to fall, which will enable the shorts to be covered at a profit. Cf. LONG POSITION.

---

short-range *adj.* **1** having a short range. **2** relating to the immediate future.

♦ **short run** *n.* period in economic theory that is sufficiently short for at least one factor of production to remain unchanged. Cf. LONG RUN.

---

shorts *n.pl.* **1** trousers reaching to the knees or higher. **2** *US* underpants. **3** *Finance* **a** short-dated gilt-edged securities. **b** securities, commodities, currencies, etc. sold by a dealer who does not own them.

♦ **short sale** *n.* sale of commodities, securities, currencies, etc. that one does not have. Short sellers expect prices to fall so that they can cover their short sales at a profit before delivery has to be made. See also BEAR^2 3.

---

short shrift *n.* curt or dismissive treatment. [Old English *shrift* confession: related to SHRIVE]

short sight *n.* inability to focus on distant objects.

short-sighted *adj.* **1** having short sight. **2** lacking imagination or foresight. □ **short-sightedly** *adv.* **short-sightedness** *n.*

short temper *n.* temper easily lost. □ **short-tempered** *adj.*

short-term *adj.* of or for a short period of time.

♦ **short-term capital** *n.* capital raised for a short period to cover an exceptional demand for funds over a short period. A bank loan is an example.

♦ **short-term instrument** *n.* negotiable instrument that matures in three months or less.

♦ **short-term interest rates** *n.pl.* rates of interest on **short-term loans**, i.e. loans that are made for a short period. Banks will usu. pay higher rates for short-term loans, in which no withdrawal is permitted until the money is withdrawn on an agreed date, usu. within three months. However, when banks are asked to make loans for a short term, their interest rate charged may be lower than for a long-term loan, which will involve a higher risk.

♦ **short-term monetary support** (also **STMS**) *n.* funds available to a member country of the European Union for three months. These funds are provided by the central banks of other members.

♦ **short ton** *US* see TON 2.

---

short wave *n.* radio wave of frequency greater than 3 MHz.

short weight *n.* weight less than it is alleged to be.

short-winded *adj.* easily becoming breathless.

shorty *n.* (also **shortie**) (*pl.* **-ies**) *colloq.* person or garment shorter than average.

shot^1 *n.* **1** firing of a gun, cannon, etc. (*heard a shot*). **2** attempt to hit by shooting or throwing etc. **3 a** single non-explosive missile for a gun etc. **b** (*pl.* same or **-s**) small lead pellet used in quantity in a single charge. **c** (as *pl.*) these collectively. **4 a** photograph. **b** continuous film sequence. **5 a** stroke or a kick in a ball game. **b** *colloq.* attempt, guess (*had a shot at it*). **6** *colloq.* person of specified shooting skill (*a good shot*). **7** ball thrown by a shot-putter. **8** launch of a space rocket. **9** range etc. to or at which a thing will carry or act. **10** *colloq.* **a** drink of esp. spirits. **b** injection of a drug etc. □ **like a shot** *colloq.* without hesitation; willingly. [Old English]

shot^2 *past* and *past part.* of SHOOT. *adj.* (of coloured material) woven so as to show different colours at different angles. □ **shot through** (usu. foll. by *with*) permeated or suffused.

shotgun *n.* gun for firing small shot at short range.

shotgun wedding *n. colloq.* wedding enforced because of the bride's pregnancy.

shot in the arm *n. colloq.* stimulus or encouragement.

shot in the dark *n.* mere guess.

shot-put *n.* athletic contest in which a shot is thrown. □ **shot-putter** *n.*

should /ʃʊd, ʃəd/ *v.aux.* (*3rd sing.* **should**) *past* of SHALL, used esp.: **1** in reported speech (*I said I should be home soon*). **2 a** to express obligation or likelihood (*I should tell you; you should have read it; they should have arrived by now*). **b** to express a tentative suggestion (*I should like to add*). **3 a** expressing the conditional mood in the 1st person (*I should have been killed if I had gone*). **b** forming a conditional clause (*if you should see him*).

shoulder /ˈʃəʊldə(r)/ *–n.* **1** part of the body at which the arm, foreleg, or wing is attached. **2** either of the two projections below the neck. **3** upper foreleg of an animal as meat. **4** (often in *pl.*) shoulder regarded as supportive, comforting, etc. (*a shoulder to cry on; has broad shoulders*). **5** strip of land next to a road. **6** the part of a garment covering the shoulder. *–v.* **1 a** push with the shoulder. **b** make one's way thus. **2** take on (a burden etc.). □ **put one's shoulder to the wheel** make a great effort. **shoulder arms** hold a rifle with the barrel against the shoulder and the butt in the hand. **shoulder to shoulder 1** side by side. **2** with united effort. [Old English]

shoulder bag *n.* bag hung from the shoulder by a strap.

shoulder-blade *n.* either of the large flat bones of the upper back.

shoulder-length *adj.* (of hair etc.) reaching to the shoulders.

shoulder-pad *n.* pad in a garment to bulk out the shoulder.

shoulder-strap *n.* **1** strip of cloth going over the shoulder from front to back of a garment. **2** strap suspending a bag etc. from the shoulder. **3** strip of cloth from shoulder to collar, esp. on a military uniform.

shouldn't /ˈʃʊd(ə)nt/ *contr.* should not.

shout *–v.* **1** speak or cry loudly. **2** say or express loudly. *–n.* **1** loud cry of joy etc., or calling attention. **2** *colloq.* one's turn to buy a round of drinks etc. □ **shout down** reduce to silence by shouting. [perhaps related to SHOOT]

shove /ʃʌv/ *–v.* (**-ving**) **1** (also *absol.*) push vigorously. **2** *colloq.* put casually (*showed it in a drawer*). *–n.* act of shoving. □ **shove off 1** start from the shore in a boat. **2** *slang* depart. [Old English]

shove-halfpenny *n.* form of shovelboard played with coins etc. on a table.

shovel /ˈʃʌv(ə)l/ *–n.* **1** spadelike tool with raised sides, for shifting coal etc. **2** (part of) a machine with a similar form or function. *–v.* (**-ll-**; *US* **-l-**) **1** move (as if) with a shovel. **2** *colloq.* move in large quantities or roughly (*shovelled peas into his mouth*). □ **shovelful** *n.* (*pl.* **-s**). [Old English]

shovelboard *n.* game played esp. on a ship's deck by pushing discs over a marked surface.

shoveller /ˈʃʌvələ(r)/ *n.* (also **shoveler**) duck with a shovel-like beak.

show /ʃəʊ/ *–v.* (*past part.* **shown** or **showed**) **1** be, allow, or cause to be, visible; manifest (*buds are beginning to show; white shows the dirt*). **2** (often foll. by *to*) offer for scrutiny etc. (*show your tickets please*). **3 a** indicate (one's feelings) (*showed his anger*). **b** accord, grant (favour, mercy, etc.). **4** (of feelings etc.) be manifest (*his dislike shows*). **5 a** demonstrate; point out; prove (*showed it to be false; showed his competence*). **b** (usu. foll. by *how to* + infin.) instruct by example (*showed them how to knit*). **6** (*refl.*) exhibit oneself (as being) (*showed herself to be fair*). **7** exhibit in a show. **8** (often foll. by *in, out, up, round,* etc.) conduct or lead (*showed them to their rooms*). **9** *colloq.* = *show up* 3 (*he didn't show*). *–n.* **1** showing. **2** spectacle, display, exhibition, etc. **3** public entertainment or performance. **4 a** outward appearance or display. **b** empty appearance; mere display. **5** *colloq.* undertaking, business, etc. **6** *Med.* discharge of blood etc. at the onset of childbirth. □ **good** (or **bad** or **poor) show!** *colloq.* that was well (or badly) done. **on show** being exhibited. **show one's hand** disclose one's plans. **show off 1** display to advantage. **2** *colloq.* act pretentiously. **show up 1** make or be conspicuous or clearly visible. **2** expose or humiliate. **3** *colloq.* appear; arrive. **show willing** show a willingness to help etc. [Old English]

showbiz *n. colloq.* = SHOW BUSINESS.

show business *n. colloq.* theatrical profession.

showcase *–n.* **1** glass case for exhibiting goods etc. **2** event etc. designed to exhibit someone or something to advantage. *–v.* (**-sing**) display in or as if in a showcase.

showdown *n.* final test or confrontation.

shower *–n.* **1** brief fall of rain, snow, etc. **2 a** brisk flurry of bullets, dust, etc. **b** sudden copious arrival of gifts, honours, etc. **3** (in full **shower-bath**) **a** cubicle, bath, etc. in which one stands under a spray of water. **b** apparatus etc. used for this. **c** act of bathing in a shower. **4** *US* party for giving presents to a prospective bride etc. **5** *slang* contemptible person or group. *–v.* **1** discharge (water, missiles, etc.) in a shower. **2** take a shower. **3** (usu. foll. by *on, upon*) lavishly bestow (gifts etc.). **4** descend in a shower. □ **showery** *adj.* [Old English]

showerproof *adj.* resistant to light rain.

showgirl *n.* female singer and dancer in musicals, variety shows, etc.

show house *n.* (also **show flat**) furnished and decorated new house etc., on show to prospective buyers.

showing *n.* **1** display, performance. **2** quality of performance. **3** presentation of a case; evidence.

showjumping *n.* sport of riding horses competitively over a course of fences etc. □ **showjumper** *n.*

showman *n.* **1** proprietor or manager of a circus etc. **2** person skilled in publicity, esp. self-advertisement. □ **showmanship** *n.*

shown *past part.* of SHOW.

show-off *n. colloq.* person who shows off.

show of hands *n.* raised hands indicating a vote for or against.

show-piece *n.* **1** item presented for display. **2** outstanding specimen.

show-place *n.* tourist attraction.

showroom *n.* room used to display goods for sale.

show-stopper *n. colloq.* **1** act in a show receiving prolonged applause. **2** legal action taken by the target firm in an unwelcome take-over bid that seeks a permanent injunction to prevent the bidder from persisting in take-over activities, on the grounds that the bid is legally defective in some way.

show trial *n.* judicial trial designed to frighten or impress the public.

showy *adj.* (**-ier, -iest**) **1** brilliant; gaudy. **2** striking. □ **showily** *adv.* **showiness** *n.*

shpg. *abbr.* shipping.

shpt. *abbr.* shipment.

shr. *abbr.* share(s).

shrank *past* of SHRINK.

shrapnel /ˈʃræpn(ə)l/ *n.* **1** fragments of an exploded bomb etc. **2** shell containing pieces of metal etc., timed to burst short of impact. [*Shrapnel*, name of the inventor of the shell]

shred *–n.* **1** scrap or fragment. **2** least amount (*not a shred of evidence*). *–v.* (**-dd-**) tear or cut into shreds. □ **shredder** *n.* [Old English]

shrew /ʃruː/ *n.* **1** small mouselike long-nosed mammal. **2** bad-tempered or scolding woman. □ **shrewish** *adj.* (in sense 2). [Old English]

shrewd /ʃruːd/ *adj.* astute; clever and judicious. □ **shrewdly** *adv.* **shrewdness** *n.* [perhaps from obsolete *shrew* to curse, from SHREW]

shriek *–n.* shrill scream or sound. *–v.* make or utter in a shriek. [Old Norse]

shrike *n.* bird with a strong hooked and toothed bill. [Old English]

shrill *–adj.* **1** piercing and high-pitched in sound. **2** *derog.* sharp, unrestrained. *–v.* utter with or make a shrill sound. □ **shrillness** *n.* **shrilly** *adv.* [origin uncertain]

shrimp *–n.* **1** (*pl.* same or **-s**) small edible crustacean, turning pink when boiled. **2** *colloq.* very small person. *–v.* try to catch shrimps. [origin uncertain]

shrine *n.* **1** esp. *RC Ch.* **a** place for special worship or devotion. **b** tomb or reliquary. **2** place hallowed by some memory or association. [Latin *scrinium* bookcase]

shrink *–v.* (*past* **shrank**; *past part.* **shrunk** or (esp. as *adj.*) **shrunken**) **1** make or become smaller, esp. from moisture, heat, or cold. **2** (usu. foll. by *from*) recoil; flinch. *–n.* **1** act of shrinking. **2** *slang* psychiatrist. [Old English]

shrinkage *n.* **1** process or degree of shrinking. **2** loss of unsold goods from a retail outlet through wastage, damage, theft, etc.

shrink-wrap *v.* enclose (an article) in film that shrinks tightly on to it.

shrive *v.* (**-ving**; *past* **shrove**; *past part.* **shriven**) *RC Ch. archaic* **1** (of a priest) hear and absolve (a penitent). **2** (*refl.*) submit oneself to a priest for confession etc. [Old English *scrīfan* impose as penance]

shrivel /ˈʃrɪv(ə)l/ *v.* (**-ll-**; *US* **-l-**) contract into a wrinkled or dried-up state. [perhaps from Old Norse]

Shropshire /ˈʃrɒpʃɪə(r)/ county in the W Midlands of England; pop. (est. 1994) 416 510; county town, Shrewsbury. It is primarily agricultural, producing cereals and sugar beet; there is also cattle and sheep farming in the S part of the county and dairy farming in the N.

shroud *–n.* **1** wrapping for a corpse. **2** thing that conceals. **3** (in *pl.*) ropes supporting a mast. *–v.* **1** clothe (a body) for burial. **2** cover or conceal. [Old English, = garment]

shrove *past* of SHRIVE.

Shrovetide *n.* Shrove Tuesday and the two days preceding it.

Shrove Tuesday *n.* day before Ash Wednesday.

shrub *n.* any woody plant smaller than a tree and with branches near the ground. □ **shrubby** *adj.* [Old English]

shrubbery *n.* (*pl.* **-ies**) area planted with shrubs.

shrug *–v.* (**-gg-**) (often *absol.*) slightly and momentarily raise (the shoulders) to express indifference, doubt, etc. *–n.* act of shrugging. □ **shrug off** dismiss as unimportant. [origin unknown]

shrunk (also **shrunken**) *past part.* of SHRINK.

shudder *–v.* **1** shiver, esp. convulsively, from fear, cold etc. **2** feel strong repugnance, fear, etc. (*shudder at the thought*). **3** vibrate. *–n.* **1** act of shuddering. **2** (in *pl.*; prec. by *the*) *colloq.* state of shuddering. [Low German or Dutch]

shuffle /ˈʃʌf(ə)l/ *–v.* (**-ling**) **1** (also *absol.*) drag (the feet) in walking etc. **2** (also *absol.*) rearrange or intermingle (esp. cards or papers). **3 a** prevaricate, be evasive. **b** keep shifting one's position. *–n.* **1** act of shuffling; shuffling walk or movement. **2** change of relative positions. **3** shuffling dance. □ **shuffle off** remove, get rid of. [Low German]

shufti /ˈʃʊftɪ/ *n.* (*pl.* **-s**) *colloq.* look, glimpse. [Arabic *šaffa* try to see]

Shumen /ˈʃuːmen/ city in NE Bulgaria; industries include brewing; pop. (1990) 110 574.

shun *v.* (**-nn-**) avoid; keep clear of. [Old English]

shunt *–v.* **1** move (a train) between sidings etc.; (of a train) be shunted. **2** move or put aside; redirect. *–n.* **1** shunting or being shunted. **2** *Electr.* conductor joining two points of a circuit, through which current may be diverted. **3** *Surgery* alternative path for the circulation of the blood. **4** *slang* collision of vehicles, esp. one behind another. [perhaps from SHUN]

shush /ʃʊʃ, ʃʌʃ/ *–int.* hush! *–v.* **1** quieten (a person or people) by saying "shush". **2** fall silent. [imitative]

shut *v.* (**-tt-**; *past* and *past part.* **shut**) **1 a** move (a door, window, lid, etc.) into position to block an opening. **b** close or seal (a room, box, eye, etc.) by moving a door etc. **2** become or be capable of being closed or sealed. **3** become or make closed for trade. **4** fold or contract (a book, telescope, etc.). **5** (usu. foll. by *in*, *out*) keep in or out of a room etc. **6** (usu. foll. by *in*) catch (a finger, dress, etc.) by shutting something on it. **7** bar access to. □ **be** (or **get) shut of** *slang* be (or get) rid of. **shut down 1** stop (a factory etc.) from operating. **2** (of a factory etc.) stop operating. **shut off 1** stop the flow of (water, gas, etc.). **2** separate from society etc. **shut out 1** exclude. **2** screen from view. **3** prevent. **4** block from the mind. **shut up 1** close all doors and windows of. **2** imprison. **3** put (a thing) away in a box etc. **4** (esp. in *imper.*) *colloq.* stop talking. **shut up shop** close a business, shop, etc., temporarily or permanently. [Old English]

shut-down *n.* closure of a factory, part of an organization, etc., which incurs **shut-down costs**.

shut-eye *n. colloq.* sleep.

shutter *–n.* **1** movable hinged cover for a window. **2** device that exposes the film in a camera. *–v.* provide with shutters.

shuttle /ˈʃʌt(ə)l/ *–n.* **1 a** (in a loom) instrument pulling the weft-thread between the warp-threads. **b** (in a sewing-machine) bobbin carrying the lower thread. **2** train, bus, etc. used in a shuttle service. **3** = SPACE SHUTTLE. *–v.* (**-ling**) (cause to) move to and fro like a shuttle. [Old English: related to SHOOT]

shuttlecock *n.* cork with a ring of feathers, or a similar plastic device, struck to and fro in badminton.

shuttle diplomacy *n.* negotiations conducted by a mediator travelling between disputing parties.

shuttle service *n.* transport service operating to and fro over a short route.

shy[1] /ʃaɪ/ *–adj.* (**shyer, shyest** or **shier, shiest**) **1 a** timid and nervous in company; self-conscious. **b** (of animals etc.) easily startled. **2** (in *comb.*) disliking or fearing (*work-shy*). *–v.* (**shies, shied**) **1** (usu. foll. by *at*) (esp. of a horse) turn suddenly aside in fright. **2** (usu. foll. by *away from*, *at*) avoid involvement in. *–n.* sudden startled movement. □ **shyly** *adv.* (also **shily**). **shyness** *n.* [Old English]

shy[2] *–v.* (**shies, shied**) (also *absol.*) fling, throw. *–n.* (*pl.* **shies**) fling, throw. [origin unknown]

Shylock /ˈʃaɪlɒk/ *n.* hard-hearted money-lender. [name of a character in Shakespeare]

shyster /ˈʃaɪstə(r)/ *n.* esp. *US colloq.* unscrupulous or unprofessional person. [origin uncertain]

SI *abbr.* **1** the international metric system of units of measurement (see SI UNITS). **2** Shetland Islands. **3** South Island (New Zealand). [sense 1 from French *Système International*]

Si *symb.* silicon.

si /siː/ *n.* = TE. [French from Italian]

s.i. *abbr.* sum insured.

SIA *abbr.* Society of Investment Analysts.

SIAC *abbr.* (in the US) Securities Industry Automation Corporation.

Sialkot /sɪˈɑːlkɒt/ city in Pakistan, in Punjab province; manufactures include textiles and surgical instruments; pop. (1981) 296 000.

Siam /saɪˈæm/ see THAILAND.

Siamese /ˌsaɪəˈmiːz/ *–n.* (*pl.* same) **1** native or language of Siam (now Thailand) in Asia. **2** (in full **Siamese cat**) cat of a cream-coloured short-haired breed with dark markings and blue eyes. *–adj.* of Siam, its people, or language.

Siamese twins *n.pl.* **1** twins joined at some part of the body. **2** any closely associated pair.

SIB *abbr.* **1** = SECURITIES AND INVESTMENT BOARD. **2** Shipbuilding Industry Board.

Siberia /saɪˈbɪərɪə/ region of N Asia, forming the larger part of Russia and extending into N Kazakhstan, noted for its extremely cold winters. It has rich deposits of coal, petroleum, diamonds, and gold; forestry and hydroelectricity are also important. □ **Siberian** *adj.* & *n.*

sibilant /ˈsɪbɪlənt/ *–adj.* **1** sounded with a hiss. **2** hissing. *–n.* sibilant letter or sound. □ **sibilance** *n.* **sibilancy** *n.* [Latin]

sibling *n.* each of two or more children having one or both parents in common. [Old English, = akin]

SIBOR /ˈsiːbɔː/ *abbr.* Singapore Inter-Bank Offered Rate.

sibyl /ˈsɪbɪl/ *n.* pagan prophetess. [Greek *sibulla*]

sibylline /ˈsɪbɪˌlaɪn/ *adj.* **1** of or from a sibyl. **2** oracular; prophetic. [Latin: related to SIBYL]

SIC *abbr.* Standard Industrial Classification.

sic /sɪk/ *adv.* (usu. in brackets) used, spelt, etc. as written (confirming, or emphasizing, the quoted or copied words). [Latin, = so]

SICAV *abbr.* (French) société d'investissement à capital variable (= unit trust).

Sichuan /sɪtʃˈwɑːn/ (also **Szechwan** /setʃˈwɑːn/) province in central China; pop. (est. 1995) 112 140 000; capital, Chengdu. Rice is the most important product; other crops include wheat, maize, sugar cane, and cotton. There is also some forestry, coalmining, gas and oil production, and other industries.

Sicily /ˈsɪsɪlɪ/ large triangular island in the Mediterranean Sea, comprising (with adjacent islands) an autonomous region of Italy, from the S tip of which it is separated by the Strait of Messina; pop. (est. 1994) 5 025 280; capital, Palermo. The economy is predominantly agricultural, producing citrus fruits, wheat, rye, vegetables, and wine. Oil-refining and petrochemical industries are being developed, resulting from the exploitation of offshore oil. □ **Sicilian** /sɪˈsɪljən, -lɪən/ *adj.* & *n.*

sick *–adj.* **1** esp. *US* unwell, ill. **2** vomiting or likely to vomit. **3** (often foll. by *of*) *colloq.* **a** disgusted; surfeited. **b** angry, esp. because of surfeit. **4** *colloq.* (of a joke etc.) cruel, morbid, perverted, offensive. **5 a** mentally disordered. **b** (esp. in *comb.*) pining (*lovesick*). *–n. colloq.* vomit. *–v.* (usu. foll. by *up*) *colloq.* vomit. □ **take** (or **fall) sick** *colloq.* be taken ill. [Old English]

sickbay *n.* room, cabin, etc. for those who are sick.

sickbed *n.* invalid's bed.

sicken *v.* **1** affect with disgust etc. **2 a** (often foll. by *for*) show symptoms of illness. **b** (often foll. by *at*, or *to* + infin.) feel nausea or disgust. **3** (as **sickening** *adj.*) **a** disgusting. **b** *colloq.* very annoying. □ **sickeningly** *adv.*

sickle /ˈsɪk(ə)l/ *n.* short-handled tool with a semicircular blade, used for reaping etc. [Old English]

sick-leave *n.* leave granted because of illness.

sickle-cell *n.* sickle-shaped blood cell, esp. as found in a type of severe hereditary anaemia.

sickly *adj.* (**-ier, -iest**) **1 a** weak; apt to be ill. **b** languid, faint, or pale. **2** causing ill health. **3** sentimental or mawkish. **4** of or inducing nausea. [related to SICK]

sickness *n.* **1** being ill; disease. **2** vomiting or a tendency to vomit.

♦ **sickness and accident insurance** *n.* form of health insurance in which the benefits are paid after eight days for a total of 140 weeks after the onset of an illness or accident that prevents the insured from working. Premiums can increase each year and renewal can be refused if a claim has been made. Cf. PERMANENT HEALTH INSURANCE.

---

sick-pay *n.* pay given during sick-leave.

side *–n.* **1 a** each of the surfaces bounding an object. **b** vertical inner or outer surface. **c** such a surface as distinct from the top or bottom, front or back. **2 a** right or left part of a person or animal, esp. of the torso. **b** left or right half or a specified part of a thing. **c** (often in *comb.*) adjoining position (*seaside*; *stood at my side*). **d** direction (*from all sides*). **3 a** either surface of a thing regarded as having two surfaces. **b** writing filling one side of a sheet of paper. **4** aspect of a question, character, etc. (*look on the bright side*). **5 a** each of two competing groups in war, politics, games, etc. **b** cause etc. regarded as being in conflict with another. **6 a** part or region near the edge. **b** (*attrib.*) subordinate, peripheral, or detached part (*side-road*; *side-table*). **7** *colloq.* television channel. **8** each of the bounding lines of a plane rectilinear figure. **9** position nearer or farther than, or right or left of, a given dividing line. **10** line of descent through one parent. **11** (in full **side spin**) spin given to a billiard-ball etc. by hitting it on one side. **12** *slang* cheek; pretensions (*has no side about him*). –*v.* (**-ding**) (usu. foll. by *with*) take part or be on the same side. □ **by the side of 1** close to. **2** compared with. **let the side down** embarrass or fail one's colleagues. **on one side 1** not in the main or central position. **2** aside. **on the ... side** somewhat (*on the high side*). **on the side 1** as a sideline. **2** illicitly. **3** *US* as a side dish. **side by side** standing close together, esp. for mutual support. **take sides** support one or other cause etc. [Old English]

sideboard *n.* table or esp. a flat-topped cupboard for dishes, table linen, etc.

sideboards *n.pl. colloq.* hair grown by a man down the sides of his face.

sideburns *n.pl.* = SIDEBOARDS. [earlier *burnsides*, after General *Burnside* (d. 1881)]

side-car *n.* passenger compartment attached to the side of a motor cycle.

sided *adj.* **1** having sides. **2** (in *comb.*) having a specified number or type of sides.

♦ **side deal** *n.* private deal between two people, usu. for the personal benefit of one of them, as a subsidiary to a transaction between the officials of a company, government, etc. For example, the chairman of a public company may agree to encourage the board to welcome a take-over bid because of a personal profit agreed in some side deal with the bidder. Side deals are rigorously investigated by the Panel on Take-overs and Mergers (see CITY CODE ON TAKE-OVERS AND MERGERS).

---

side-door *n.* **1** door at the side of a building. **2** indirect means of access.

side-drum *n.* small double-headed drum.

side-effect *n.* secondary (usu. undesirable) effect.

sidekick *n. colloq.* friend, associate; henchman.

sidelight *n.* **1** light from the side. **2** small light at the side of the front of a vehicle. **3** *Naut.* light on the side of a moving ship.

sideline *n.* **1** work etc. done in addition to one's main activity. **2** (usu. in *pl.*) **a** line bounding the side of a hockey-pitch etc. **b** space next to these where spectators etc. sit. □ **on the sidelines** not directly concerned.

sidelong –*adj.* (esp. of a glance) oblique. –*adv.* obliquely.

sidereal /saɪˈdɪərɪəl/ *adj.* of the constellations or stars. [Latin *sidus sider-* star]

sidereal day *n.* time between successive meridional transits of a star etc.

side-road *n.* minor road, esp. branching from a main road.

side-saddle –*n.* saddle for a woman riding with both legs on the same side of the horse. –*adv.* riding in this position.

sideshow *n.* **1** small show or stall in an exhibition, fair, etc. **2** minor incident or issue.

sidesman *n.* assistant churchwarden who takes the collection etc.

side-splitting *adj.* causing violent laughter.

sidestep –*n.* step to the side. –*v.* (**-pp-**) **1** avoid by stepping sideways. **2** evade.

side-swipe –*n.* **1** glancing blow on or from the side. **2** incidental criticism etc. –*v.* hit (as if) with a side-swipe.

sidetrack *v.* divert or diverge from the main course or issue.

sidewalk *n. US* pavement.

sideways –*adv.* **1** to or from a side. **2** with one side facing forward. –*adj.* to or from a side.

side-whiskers *n.pl.* whiskers on the cheeks.

side wind *n.* wind from the side.

siding *n.* short track at the side of a railway line, used for shunting.

sidle /ˈsaɪd(ə)l/ *v.* (**-ling**) (usu. foll. by *along*, *up*) walk timidly or furtively. [shortening of SIDELONG]

Sidon /ˈsaɪd(ə)n/ (Arabic **Saida** /ˈsaɪdə/) city and seaport in Lebanon; pop. (est. 1990) 100 000.

SIDS *abbr.* sudden infant death syndrome; cot-death.

siege *n.* **1** surrounding and blockading of a town, castle, etc. **2** similar operation by police etc. to force an armed person out of a building. □ **lay siege to** conduct the siege of. **raise the siege of** abandon, or cause the abandonment of, an attempted siege of. [French *sege* seat]

siemens /ˈsiːmənz/ *n.* SI unit of conductance, equal to one reciprocal ohm. [von *Siemens*, name of an engineer]

Siena /sɪˈenə/ city in W central Italy, in Tuscany; noted for its medieval architecture and other attractions, it has an important tourist industry; pop. (1990) 58 278. □ **Sienese** /-ˈniːz/ *adj.* & *n.*

sienna /sɪˈenə/ *n.* **1** a kind of earth used as a pigment. **2** its colour of yellowish-brown (**raw sienna**) or reddish-brown (**burnt sienna**). [SIENA]

sierra /sɪˈerə/ *n.* long jagged mountain chain, esp. in Spain or Spanish America. [Spanish from Latin *serra* saw]

siesta /sɪˈestə/ *n.* afternoon sleep or rest, esp. in hot countries. [Spanish from Latin *sexta* (*hora*) sixth hour]

sieve /sɪv/ –*n.* perforated or meshed utensil for separat-

Sierra Leone /sɪˌerə lɪˈəʊn/, **Republic of** country on the W coast of Africa, a member state of the Commonwealth. Agriculture provides employment for a large proportion of the population: the chief cash crops are coffee, cocoa, palm kernels, and ginger, and food crops include rice, cassava, maize, and vegetables. Livestock (esp. cattle) are raised in the N of the country. Exports of minerals, including rutile, diamonds, bauxite, and gold, are a major source of revenue; iron ore is also mined. Other activities include forestry and fishing.

History. The district around Freetown on the coast became a British colony in 1807, but the large inland territory was not declared a protectorate until 1896. Sierra Leone achieved independence in 1961; it became a republic in 1971 and a one-party state in 1978. The introduction of a multi-party system was approved by referendum in 1991, but in 1992, after a military coup overthrew the interim government, a ruling council took over under Capt. Valentine Strasser. In 1996 Strasser was ousted by Brig.-Gen. Julius Maada Bio, who surrendered power to a civilian government following free elections in which Ahmad Tejan Kabbah became president. Kabbah was deposed by a military coup in 1997 but restored following an invasion by Nigerian-led forces in 1998. President, Ahmad Tejan Kabbah; capital, Freetown. □ **Sierra Leonian** *adj.* & *n.*

languages	English (official), African languages
currency	leone (Le) of 100 cents
pop. (1996)	4 617 000
GNP (1994)	US$698M
literacy	45% (m); 18% (f)
life expectancy	41 (m); 44 (f)

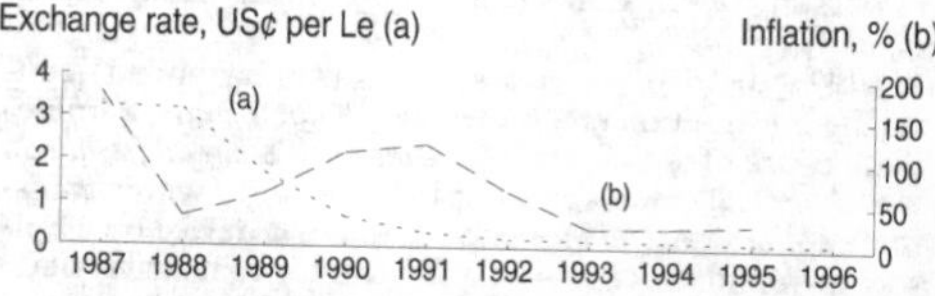

ing solids or coarse material from liquids or fine particles, or for pulping. *–v.* (**-ving**) sift. [Old English]

sift *v.* **1** put through a sieve. **2** (usu. foll. by *from, out*) separate (finer or coarser parts) from material. **3** sprinkle (esp. sugar) from a perforated container. **4** examine (evidence, facts, etc.). **5** (of snow, light, etc.) fall as if from a sieve. [Old English]

Sig. *abbr.* (Italian) Signor (= Mr).

SIGAC *abbr.* Scottish Industrial Groups Advisory Council.

sigh /saɪ/ *–v.* **1** emit an audible breath in sadness, weariness, relief, etc. **2** (foll. by *for*) yearn for. **3** express with sighs. **4** make a sighing sound. *–n.* **1** act of sighing. **2** sound made in sighing. [Old English]

sight /saɪt/ *–n.* **1 a** faculty of seeing. **b** act of seeing or being seen. **2** thing seen. **3** opinion (*in my sight*). **4** range of vision (*out of sight*). **5** (usu. in *pl.*) noteworthy features of a town etc. **6 a** device on a gun, telescope, etc. for assisting aim or observation. **b** aim or observation so gained. **7** *colloq.* unsightly person or thing (*looked a sight*). **8** *colloq.* great deal (*a sight too clever*). *–v.* **1** get sight of, observe the presence of (*they sighted land*). **2** aim (a gun etc.) with a sight. □ **after sight** words used on a bill of exchange to indicate that the period of the bill should commence from the date on which the drawee is presented with it for acceptance, i.e. has sight of it. **at first sight** on first glimpse or impression. **at sight 1** words used on a bill of exchange to indicate that payment is due on presentation. **2** (also **on sight**) as soon as a person or a thing has been seen. **catch** (or **lose) sight of** begin (or cease) to see or be aware of. **in sight 1** visible. **2** near at hand. **set one's sights on** aim at. [Old English: related to SEE[1]]

♦ **sight bill** *n.* (also **sight draft**) bill of exchange that is payable at sight, i.e. on presentation, irrespective of when it was drawn.

---

sighted *adj.* **1** not blind. **2** (in *comb.*) having specified vision (*long-sighted*).

sight for sore eyes *n. colloq.* welcome person or thing.

sightless *adj.* blind.

sightly *adj.* attractive to look at.

sight-read *v.* read (music) at sight.

sight-screen *n. Cricket* large white screen placed near the boundary in line with the wicket to help the batsman see the ball.

sightseer *n.* person visiting the sights of a place. □ **sightseeing** *n.*

sight unseen *adv.* without previous inspection.

sigma /'sɪgmə/ *n.* eighteenth letter of the Greek alphabet (Σ, σ, or, when final, ς). [Latin from Greek]

sign /saɪn/ *–n.* **1** thing indicating a quality, state, future event, etc. (*sign of weakness*). **2** mark, symbol, etc. **3** gesture or action conveying an order etc. **4** signboard; signpost. **5** each of the twelve divisions of the zodiac. *–v.* **1 a** (also *absol.*) write (one's name) on a document etc. as authorization. **b** sign (a document) as authorization. **2** communicate by gesture (*signed to me to come*). **3** engage or be engaged by signing a contract etc. (see also *sign on, sign up*). □ **sign away** relinquish (property etc.) by signing. **sign in 1** sign a register on arrival. **2** get (a person) admitted by signing a register. **sign off 1** end work, broadcasting, etc. **2** withdraw one's claim to unemployment benefit after finding work. **sign on 1** agree to a contract etc. **2** employ (a person). **3** register as unemployed. **sign out** sign a register on departing. **sign up 1** engage (a person). **2** enlist in the armed forces. **3** enrol. [Latin *signum*]

signal[1] /'sɪgn(ə)l/ *–n.* **1 a** sign (usu. prearranged) conveying information etc. **b** message of such signs. **2** immediate cause of action etc. (*her death was a signal for hope*). **3 a** electrical impulse or impulses or radio waves transmitted as a signal. **b** sequence of these. **4** device on a railway giving instructions or warnings to train-drivers etc. *–v.* (**-ll-**; *US* **-l-**) **1** make signals. **2 a** (often foll. by *to* + infin.) make signals to; direct. **b** transmit or express by signal; announce. □ **signaller** *n.* [Latin: *signum* sign]

signal[2] /'sɪgn(ə)l/ *attrib. adj.* remarkable, noteworthy. □ **signally** *adv.* [French *signalé*: related to SIGNAL[1]]

signal-box *n.* building beside a railway track from which signals are controlled.

signalize *v.* (also **-ise**) (**-zing** or **-sing**) **1** make noteworthy or remarkable. **2** indicate.

signalman *n.* railway signal operator.

signatory /'sɪgnətərɪ/ *–n.* (*pl.* **-ies**) party that has signed an agreement, esp. a treaty. *–adj.* having signed such an agreement etc. [Latin: related to SIGN]

signature /'sɪgnətʃə(r)/ *n.* **1 a** person's name, initials, etc. used in signing. **b** act of signing. **2** *Mus.* **a** = KEY SIGNATURE. **b** = TIME SIGNATURE. **3** *Printing* section of a book made from one sheet folded and cut. [medieval Latin: related to SIGNATORY]

signature tune *n.* tune used regularly to introduce a particular broadcast or performer.

signboard *n.* board displaying a name or symbol etc. outside a shop or hotel etc.

signet /'sɪgnɪt/ *n.* small seal. [French or medieval Latin: related to SIGN]

signet-ring *n.* ring with a seal set in it.

significance /sɪg'nɪfɪkəns/ *n.* **1** importance. **2** meaning. **3** being significant. **4** extent to which a result deviates from a hypothesis such that the difference is due to more than errors in sampling. [Latin: related to SIGNIFY]

significant *adj.* **1** having a meaning; indicative. **2** noteworthy; important. □ **significantly** *adv.* [Latin: related to SIGNIFY]

significant figure *n.* digit conveying information about a number containing it.

signify /'sɪgnɪˌfaɪ/ *v.* (**-ies, -ied**) **1** be a sign or indication of. **2** mean; symbolize. **3** make known. **4** be of importance; matter. □ **signification** /-fɪ'keɪʃ(ə)n/ *n.* [Latin: related to SIGN]

sign language *n.* system of communication by gestures, used esp. by the deaf.

sign of the cross *n.* Christian sign made by tracing a cross with the hand.

signor /'siːnjɔː(r)/ *n.* (*pl.* **-nori** /-'njɔːriː/) title used of or to an Italian-speaking man. [Latin *senior* SENIOR]

signora /siː'njɔːrə/ *n.* title used of or to an Italian-speaking married woman.

signorina /ˌsiːnjə'riːnə/ *n.* title used of or to an Italian-speaking unmarried woman.

signpost *–n.* **1** post on a road etc. indicating direction etc. **2** indication, guide. *–v.* provide with a signpost or signposts.

signwriter *n.* person who paints signboards etc.

Sikh /siːk, sɪk/ *n.* member of an Indian monotheistic sect. [Hindi, = disciple]

Sikkim /'sɪkɪm/ state in NE India, in the E Himalayas; pop. (est. 1994) 444 000; capital, Gangtok. It is a major producer of cardamom; other crops include mandarin oranges, cereals, pulses, and vegetables, and there is some copper-mining and timber production. □ **Sikkimese** /-'miːz/ *adj.* & *n.*

silage /'saɪlɪdʒ/ *n.* **1** green fodder stored in a silo. **2** storage in a silo. [alteration of ENSILAGE after *silo*]

silence /'saɪləns/ *–n.* **1** absence of sound. **2** abstinence from speech or noise. **3** avoidance of mentioning a thing, betraying a secret, etc. *–v.* (**-cing**) make silent, esp. by force or superior argument. □ **in silence** without speech or other sound. [Latin: related to SILENT]

silencer *n.* device for reducing the noise of a vehicle's exhaust, a gun, etc.

silent *adj.* not speaking; not making or accompanied by any sound. □ **silently** *adv.* [Latin *sileo* be silent]

silent majority *n.* the mass of allegedly moderate people who rarely express an opinion.

silhouette /ˌsɪluː'et/ *–n.* **1** picture showing the outline only, usu. in black on white or cut from paper. **2** dark shadow or outline against a lighter background. –*v.* (**-ting**) represent or (usu. in *passive*) show in silhouette. [*Silhouette*, name of a politician]

silica /'sılıkə/ *n.* silicon dioxide, occurring as quartz etc. and as a main constituent of sandstone and other rocks. □ **siliceous** /-'lıʃəs/ *adj.* [Latin *silex -lic-* flint]

silica gel *n.* hydrated silica in a hard granular form used as a drying agent.

silicate /'sılı,keıt/ *n.* compound of a metal with silicon and oxygen.

silicon /'sılıkən/ *n. Chem.* non-metallic element occurring widely in silica and silicates.

♦ **silicon chip** *n.* integrated circuit fabricated from silicon.

---

silicone /'sılı,kəʊn/ *n.* any organic compound of silicon, with high resistance to cold, heat, water, etc.

silicosis /,sılı'kəʊsıs/ *n.* lung fibrosis caused by inhaling dust containing silica.

silk *n.* **1** fine soft lustrous fibre produced by silkworms. **2** (often *attrib.*) thread or cloth from this. **3** (in *pl.*) cloth or garments of silk, esp. as worn by a jockey. **4** *colloq.* Queen's (or King's) Counsel, as having the right to wear a silk gown. **5** fine soft thread (*embroidery silk*). □ **take silk** become a Queen's (or King's) Counsel. [Old English *sioloc*]

silken *adj.* **1** made of silk. **2** soft or lustrous.

silk-screen printing *n.* = SCREEN PRINTING.

silkworm *n.* caterpillar that spins a cocoon of silk.

silky *adj.* (**-ier, -iest**) **1** soft and smooth like silk. **2** suave. □ **silkily** *adv.* **silkiness** *n.*

sill *n.* slab of stone, wood, or metal at the foot of a window or doorway. [Old English]

sillabub var. of SYLLABUB.

silly /'sılı/ –*adj.* (**-ier, -iest**) **1** foolish, imprudent. **2** weak-minded. **3** *Cricket* (of a fielder or position) very close to the batsman. –*n.* (*pl.* **-ies**) *colloq.* foolish person. □ **sillily** *adv.* **silliness** *n.* [Old English, = happy]

silo /'saıləʊ/ *n.* (*pl.* **-s**) **1** pit or airtight barn etc. in which green crops are kept for fodder. **2** pit or tower for storing grain, cement, etc. **3** underground storage chamber for a guided missile. [Spanish from Latin]

silt –*n.* sediment in a channel, harbour, etc. –*v.* (often foll. by *up*) choke or be choked with silt. [perhaps an Scandinavian]

Silurian /saı'ljʊərıən/ *Geol.* –*adj.* of the third period of the Palaeozoic era. –*n.* this period. [*Silures*, people of ancient Wales]

silvan var. of SYLVAN.

silver –*n.* **1** greyish-white lustrous precious metallic element. **2** colour of this. **3** silver or cupro-nickel coins. **4** household cutlery. **5** = SILVER MEDAL. –*adj.* of or coloured like silver. –*v.* **1** coat or plate with silver. **2** provide (a mirror-glass) with a backing of tin amalgam etc. **3** make silvery. **4** turn grey or white. [Old English]

silver band *n.* band playing silver-plated instruments.

silver birch *n.* common birch with silver-coloured bark.

silverfish *n.* (*pl.* same or **-es**) **1** small silvery wingless insect. **2** silver-coloured fish.

silver jubilee *n.* 25th anniversary.

silver lining *n.* consolation or hope in misfortune.

silver medal *n.* medal of silver, usu. awarded as second prize.

silver paper *n.* aluminium foil.

silver plate *n.* vessels, cutlery, etc., plated with silver. □ **silver-plated** *adj.*

silver sand *n.* fine pure sand used in gardening.

silver screen *n.* (usu. prec. by *the*) cinema films collectively.

silverside *n.* upper side of a round of beef.

silversmith *n.* worker in silver.

silver tongue *n.* eloquence.

silverware *n.* articles of or plated with silver.

silver wedding *n.* 25th anniversary of a wedding.

silvery *adj.* **1** like silver in colour or appearance. **2** having a clear gentle ringing sound.

silviculture /'sılvı,kʌltʃə(r)/ *n.* (also **sylviculture**) cultivation of forest trees. [Latin *silva* a wood: related to CULTURE]

simian /'sımıən/ –*adj.* **1** of the anthropoid apes. **2** like an ape or monkey. –*n.* ape or monkey. [Latin *simia* ape]

similar /'sımılə(r)/ *adj.* **1** like, alike. **2** (often foll. by *to*) having a resemblance. **3** *Geom.* shaped alike. □ **similarity** /-'lærıtı/ *n.* (*pl.* **-ies**). **similarly** *adv.* [Latin *similis* like]

simile /'sımılı/ *n.* **1** esp. poetical comparison of one thing with another using the words 'like' or 'as' (e.g. *as brave as a lion*). **2** use of this. [Latin, neuter of *similis* like]

similitude /sı'mılı,tju:d/ *n.* **1** guise, appearance. **2** comparison; expression of a comparison. [Latin: related to SIMILE]

simmer –*v.* **1** bubble or boil gently. **2** be in a state of suppressed anger or excitement. –*n.* simmering condition. □ **simmer down** become less agitated. [perhaps imitative]

simnel cake /'sımn(ə)l/ *n.* rich fruit cake, usu. with a marzipan layer and decoration, eaten esp. at Easter. [Latin *simila* fine flour]

simony /'saımənı/ *n.* buying or selling of ecclesiastical privileges. [from *Simon* Magus (Acts 8:18)]

simoom /sı'mu:m/ *n.* hot dry dust-laden desert wind. [Arabic]

simper –*v.* **1** smile in a silly or affected way. **2** express by or with simpering. –*n.* such a smile. [origin unknown]

simple /'sımp(ə)l/ *adj.* (**simpler, simplest**) **1** understood or done easily and without difficulty. **2** not complicated or elaborate; plain. **3** not compound or complex. **4** absolute, unqualified, straightforward (*the simple truth*). **5** foolish; gullible, feeble-minded. □ **simpleness** *n.* [Latin *simplus*]

simple fracture *n.* fracture of the bone only without a wound.

simple interest *n.* interest payable on a capital sum only. See also INTEREST RATE.

simple-minded *adj.* foolish; feeble-minded. □ **simple-mindedness** *n.*

simpleton *n.* gullible or halfwitted person.

simplex /'sımpleks/ *adj.* involving only one-way transmission of data between two end-points. [Latin, = onefold]

simplicity /sım'plısıtı/ *n.* fact or condition of being simple.

simplify /'sımplı,faı/ *v.* (**-ies, -ied**) make simple or simpler. □ **simplification** /-fı'keıʃ(ə)n/ *n.*

simplistic /sım'plıstık/ *adj.* excessively or affectedly simple. □ **simplistically** *adv.*

simply *adv.* **1** in a simple manner. **2** absolutely (*simply astonishing*). **3** merely (*was simply trying to please*).

simulate /'sımjʊ,leıt/ *v.* (**-ting**) **1** pretend to be, have, or feel. **2** imitate or counterfeit. **3** reproduce the conditions of (a situation etc.), e.g. for training. **4 a** produce a computer model of (a process). **b** (of a computer-controlled device) imitate the behaviour of another system, often using components of that system. □ **simulator** *n.* [Latin: related to SIMILAR]

♦ **simulation** *n.* **1** pretending, imitating. **2** acting out a marketing situation for test purposes. In **computer simulation** all the available data is fed into a computer, which enables a range of possible strategies to be compared. In **laboratory simulation** marketing situations are realistically recreated in order to assess possible results or responses.

---

simultaneous /,sıməl'teınıəs/ *adj.* (often foll. by *with*) occurring or operating at the same time. □ **simultaneity** /-tə'ni:ıtı/ *n.* **simultaneously** *adv.* [Latin *simul* at the same time]

sin[1] –*n.* **1 a** breaking of divine or moral law, esp. deliberately. **b** such an act. **2** offence against good taste or propriety etc. –*v.* (**-nn-**) **1** commit a sin. **2** (foll. by *against*) offend. [Old English]

sin[2] /saɪn/ *abbr.* sine.

Sinaloa /ˌsiːnəˈləʊə/ state in W Mexico; pop. (est. 1995) 2 424 745; capital, Culiacán Rosales.

sin bin *n. colloq. Ice Hockey* penalty box.

since –*prep.* throughout or during the period after (*has been here since June; happened since yesterday*). –*conj.* **1** during or in the time after (*what have you done since we met?*). **2** because. –*adv.* **1** from that time or event until now (*has not seen him since*). **2** ago (*many years since*). [Old English, = after that]

sincere /sɪnˈsɪə(r)/ *adj.* (**sincerer, sincerest**) **1** free from pretence. **2** genuine, honest, frank. □ **sincerity** /-ˈserɪtɪ/ *n.* [Latin]

sincerely *adv.* in a sincere manner. □ **yours sincerely** formula for ending an informal letter.

Sind /sɪnd/ province in S Pakistan; pop. (est. 1985) 21 682 000; capital, Karachi. There is some agriculture, producing esp. grain and livestock; manufactures include textiles, chemicals, and cement.

sine *n.* ratio of the side opposite a given angle (in a right-angled triangle) to the hypotenuse. [Latin SINUS]

sinecure /ˈsaɪnɪˌkjʊə(r), ˈsɪn-/ *n.* profitable or prestigious position requiring little or no work. [Latin *sine cura* without care]

sine die /ˌsaɪnɪ ˈdaɪɪ, ˌsɪneɪ ˈdiːeɪ/ *adv. formal* indefinitely (*postponed sine die*). [Latin]

sine qua non /ˌsɪneɪ kwɑː ˈnəʊn/ *n.* indispensable condition or qualification. [Latin, = without which not]

sinew /ˈsɪnjuː/ *n.* **1** tough fibrous tissue uniting muscle to bone; a tendon. **2** (in *pl.*) muscles; bodily strength. **3** (in *pl.*) strength or framework of a thing. □ **sinewy** *adj.* [Old English]

sinful *adj.* committing or involving sin. □ **sinfully** *adv.* **sinfulness** *n.*

sing –*v.* (*past* **sang**; *past part.* **sung**) **1** utter musical sounds, esp. words with a set tune. **2** utter or produce by singing. **3** (of the wind, a kettle, etc.) hum, buzz, or whistle. **4** (of the ears) hear a humming sound. **5** *slang* turn informer. **6** (foll. by *of*) *literary* celebrate in verse. –*n.* act or spell of singing. □ **sing out** shout. **sing the praises of** praise enthusiastically. □ **singer** *n.* [Old English]

singe /sɪndʒ/ –*v.* (**-geing**) **1** burn superficially; scorch. **2** burn off the tips of (hair). –*n.* superficial burn. [Old English]

singer-songwriter *n.* person who sings and writes songs.

Singhalese var. of SINHALESE.

single /ˈsɪŋg(ə)l/ –*adj.* **1** one only, not double or multiple. **2** united or undivided. **3** for or done by one person etc. **4** one by itself (*a single tree*). **5** regarded separately (*every single thing*). **6** not married. **7** (with *neg.* or *interrog.*) even one (*not a single car*). **8** (of a flower) having only one circle of petals. –*n.* **1** single thing, esp. a single room in a hotel. **2** (in full **single ticket**) ticket valid for an outward journey only. **3** pop record with one item on each side. **4** *Cricket* hit for one run. **5** (usu. in *pl.*) game with one player on each side. **6** (in *pl.*) unmarried people. –*v.* (foll. by *out*) choose for special attention etc. □ **singly** *adv.* [Latin *singulus*]

single-breasted *adj.* (of a coat etc.) having only one set of buttons and overlapping little down the front.

◆ **single-capacity system** *Stock Exch.* see DUAL-CAPACITY SYSTEM.

◆ **single column centimetre** *n.* unit used in selling advertising space in printed publications.

single combat *n.* duel.

single cream *n.* thin cream with a relatively low fat content.

single-decker *n.* bus with only one deck.

single file –*n.* line of people one behind another. –*adv.* one behind the other.

single-handed *adv.* without help. □ **single-handedly** *adv.*

◆ **single-life pension** *n.* pension or annuity that is paid for the lifetime of the beneficiary only, rather than for the lifetime of a surviving spouse.

◆ **Single Market** *n.* underlying concept of trading in the European Union which came into effect on 1 January 1993. Legislation includes: elimination of frontier controls, harmonization of VAT and product standards, open tendering for public supply contracts, free movement of capital within the Union, and a reduction of state aid for certain industries.

single-minded *adj.* having or intent on only one aim. □ **single-mindedly** *adv.* **single-mindedness** *n.*

single parent *n.* person bringing up a child or children alone.

◆ **single-premium assurance** *n.* life assurance in which the insured pays only one capital sum rather than regular premiums. See also INVESTMENT BOND.

singlet /ˈsɪŋglɪt/ *n.* sleeveless vest. [after *doublet*]

◆ **single-tax system** *n.* system of taxation proposing one major tax, usu. a comprehensive income tax, instead of several taxes (e.g. income tax, capital-gains tax, and National Insurance, as in the UK). Arguments in favour of such taxes are that they should be less avoidable and should simplify administration. On the other hand the pre-

Singapore /ˌsɪŋgəˈpɔː(r)/, **Republic of** country in SE Asia, a member state of the Commonwealth, consisting of the island of Singapore and about 54 smaller islands, lying off the S tip of the Malay Peninsula to which it is linked by a causeway carrying a road and railway. One of the largest and busiest seaports in the world, Singapore is a centre of trade and finance. It has important oil-refining, shipbuilding, and ship-repairing industries; manufactures include textiles, iron and steel, electronics, scientific instruments, footwear, and wood products. Major exports include petroleum products, office machinery, telecommunications equipment, and rubber.

History. In 1819 Sir Stamford Raffles established a trading post of the East India Company on the island. It was incorporated with Penang and Malacca to form the Straits Settlements in 1826; these became a Crown Colony in the following year. Singapore rapidly grew, by virtue of its large protected harbour, to become the most important commercial centre and naval base in SE Asia. It fell to the Japanese in 1942, and after liberation became first a British Crown Colony in 1946 and then a self-governing state in 1959. Federated with Malaysia in 1963, it regained full independence two years later. President, Ong Teng Cheong; prime minister, Goh Chok Tong. □ **Singaporean** /-ˈpɔːrɪən/ *adj.* & *n.*

languages	Malay, Chinese, Tamil, English
currency	dollar (S$) of 100 cents
pop. (1996)	3 045 000
GNP (1994)	US$65.8B
literacy	95% (m); 85% (f)
life expectancy	74 (m); 78 (f)

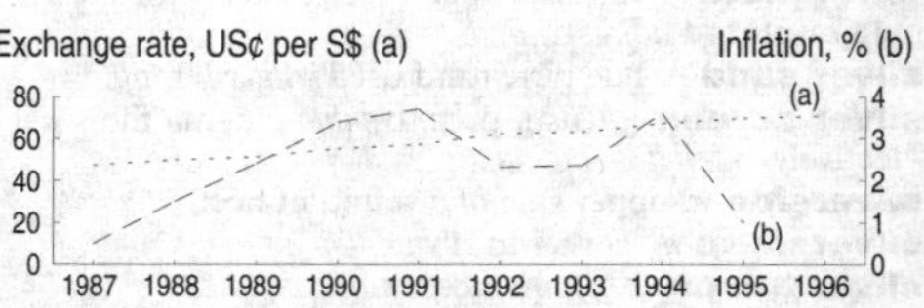

sent variety of taxes is designed for a variety of purposes and flexibility may be lost in a single-tax system.

singleton /ˈsɪŋg(ə)lt(ə)n/ *n.* **1** one card only of a suit in a player's hand. **2** single person or thing. [after *simpleton*]

singsong *–n.* informal singing party. *–adj.* monotonously rising and falling. [from SING, SONG]

singular /ˈsɪŋgjʊlə(r)/ *–adj.* **1** unique; outstanding; extraordinary, strange. **2** *Gram.* (of a word or form) denoting a single person or thing. *–n. Gram.* **1** singular word or form. **2** the singular number. □ **singularity** /-ˈlærɪtɪ/ *n.* **singularly** *adv.* [Latin: related to SINGLE]

sinh /ʃaɪn, saɪˈneɪtʃ/ *abbr. Math.* hyperbolic sine. [*sine*, *h*yperbolic]

Sinhalese /ˌsɪnhəˈliːz, ˌsɪnəˈliːz/ (also **Singhalese** /ˌsɪŋg-/) *–n.* (*pl.* same) **1** member of a N Indian people now forming the majority of the population of Sri Lanka. **2** language of this people. *–adj.* of this people or language. [Sanskrit]

sinister /ˈsɪnɪstə(r)/ *adj.* **1** evil or villainous in appearance or manner. **2** wicked, criminal. **3** ominous. **4** *Heraldry* of or on the left-hand side of a shield etc. (i.e. to the observer's right). [Latin, = left]

sink *–v.* (*past* **sank** or **sunk**; *past part.* **sunk** or as *adj.* **sunken**) **1** fall or come slowly downwards. **2** disappear below the horizon. **3 a** go or penetrate below the surface esp. of a liquid. **b** (of a ship) go to the bottom of the sea etc. **4** settle comfortably. **5 a** decline in strength etc. **b** (of the voice) descend in pitch or volume. **6** cause or allow to sink or penetrate. **7** cause (a plan, person, etc.) to fail. **8** dig (a well) or bore (a shaft). **9** engrave (a die). **10** invest (money). **11 a** knock (a ball) into a pocket or hole in billiards, golf, etc. **b** achieve this by (a stroke). **12** overlook or forget (*sank their differences*). *–n.* **1** plumbed-in basin, esp. in a kitchen. **2** place where foul liquid collects. **3** place of vice. □ **sink in 1** penetrate or permeate. **2** become understood. [Old English]

sinker *n.* weight used to sink a fishing-line or sounding-line.

Sinkiang see XINJIANG.

sinking fund *n.* **1** money set aside gradually for the eventual repayment of a debt. **2** fund set up to replace a wasting asset at the end of its useful life. A regular annual sum is usu. set aside to enable the fund to replace the exhausted asset at a specified date, taking into account interest at the expected rate. It is argued that amounts set aside for depreciation of an asset should be equal to the annual amounts needed to be placed in a notional sinking fund.

sinner *n.* person who sins, esp. habitually.

Sinn Fein /ʃɪn ˈfeɪn/ *n.* political wing of the IRA. [Irish, = we ourselves]

Sino- *comb. form* Chinese; Chinese and (*Sino-American*). [Greek *Sinai* the Chinese]

sinology /saɪˈnɒlədʒɪ/ *n.* the study of the Chinese language, Chinese history, etc. □ **sinologist** *n.*

Sint Niklaas see SAINT NICOLAS.

Sintra /ˈsiːntrə/ (also **Cintra**) town in central Portugal, a centre of tourism and agriculture; pop. (latest est.) 22 000.

sinuous /ˈsɪnjʊəs/ *adj.* with many curves; undulating. □ **sinuosity** /-ˈɒsɪtɪ/ *n.* [Latin: related to SINUS]

sinus /ˈsaɪnəs/ *n.* cavity of bone or tissue, esp. in the skull connecting with the nostrils. [Latin, = bosom, recess]

sinusitis /ˌsaɪnəˈsaɪtɪs/ *n.* inflammation of a sinus.

SIO *abbr. Computing* serial input/output.

-sion see -ION.

sip *–v.* (**-pp-**) drink in small amounts or by spoonfuls. *–n.* **1** small mouthful of liquid. **2** act of taking this. [perhaps var. of SUP[1]]

SIPC *abbr.* (in the US) Securities Investor Protection Corporation.

siphon /ˈsaɪf(ə)n/ *–n.* **1** tube shaped like an inverted V or U with unequal legs, used to convey liquid from a container to a lower level by atmospheric pressure. **2** bottle from which aerated water is forced by the pressure of gas. *–v.* (often foll. by *off*) **1** (cause to) flow through a siphon. **2** divert or set aside (funds etc.). [Greek, = pipe]

sir *n.* **1** polite form of address or reference to a man. **2** (**Sir**) title prefixed to the forename of a knight or baronet. [from SIRE]

sire *–n.* **1** male parent of an animal, esp. a stallion. **2** *archaic* form of address to a king. **3** *archaic* father or male ancestor. *–v.* (**-ring**) (esp. of an animal) beget. [French from Latin *senior* SENIOR]

siren /ˈsaɪərən/ *n.* **1 a** device for making a loud wailing or warning sound. **b** this sound. **2** (in Greek mythology) woman or winged creature whose singing lured unwary sailors on to rocks. **3** (often *attrib.*) temptress; seductress. [Greek *seirēn*]

sirloin /ˈsɜːlɔɪn/ *n.* upper and choicer part of a loin of beef. [French: related to SUR-[1], LOIN]

sirocco /sɪˈrɒkəʊ/ *n.* (also **scirocco**) (*pl.* **-s**) **1** Saharan simoom. **2** warm sultry wind in S Europe. [Arabic *sharūk*]

sirup *US* var. of SYRUP.

sis *n. colloq.* sister. [abbreviation]

sisal /ˈsaɪs(ə)l/ *n.* **1** fibre made from a Mexican agave. **2** this plant. [*Sisal*, the port of Yucatan]

siskin /ˈsɪskɪn/ *n.* yellowish-green songbird. [Dutch]

sissy /ˈsɪsɪ/ (also **cissy**) *colloq. –n.* (*pl.* **-ies**) effeminate or cowardly person. *–adj.* (**-ier, -iest**) effeminate; cowardly. [from SIS]

sister *n.* **1** woman or girl in relation to her siblings. **2** female fellow member of a trade union, feminist group, etc. **3** senior female nurse. **4** member of a female religious order. **5** (often *attrib.*) of the same type, design, or origin etc. (*sister ship*; *prose, the younger sister of verse*). □ **sisterly** *adj.* [Old English]

sisterhood *n.* **1** relationship between or as between sisters. **2** society of esp. religious or charitable women. **3** community of feeling between women.

sister-in-law *n.* (*pl.* **sisters-in-law**) **1** sister of one's wife or husband. **2** wife of one's brother.

♦ **sister-ship clause** *n.* clause used in marine insurance policies to enable the insurer to make a claim as a result of a collision between two ships both owned by the same insurer. Without this clause, the insurer may have no claim as it is not possible to sue oneself.

Sisyphean /ˌsɪsɪˈfiːən/ *adj.* (of toil) endless and fruitless like that of Sisyphus (who endlessly pushed a stone uphill in Hades). [Latin from Greek]

sit *v.* (**-tt-**; *past* and *past part.* **sat**) **1** support the body by resting the buttocks on the ground or a seat etc. **2** cause to sit; place in a sitting position. **3 a** (of a bird) perch or warm the eggs in its nest. **b** (of an animal) rest with the hind legs bent and the buttocks on the ground. **4** (of a committee etc.) be in session. **5** (usu. foll. by *for*) pose (for a portrait). **6** (foll. by *for*) be a Member of Parliament for (a constituency). **7** (often foll. by *for*) take (an examination). **8** be in a more or less permanent position or condition (*left sitting in Rome*; *parcel sitting on the doorstep*). **9** (of clothes etc.) fit or hang in a certain way. □ **be sitting pretty** be comfortably placed. **sit at a person's feet** be a person's pupil. **sit back** relax one's efforts. **sit down 1** sit after standing. **2** cause to sit. **3** (foll. by *under*) submit tamely to (an insult etc.). **sit in 1** occupy a place as a protest. **2** (foll. by *for*) take the place of. **3** (foll. by *on*) be present as a guest or observer at (a meeting etc.). **sit in judgement** be censorious or self-righteous. **sit on 1** be a member of (a committee etc.). **2** hold a session or inquiry concerning. **3** *colloq.* delay action about. **4** *colloq.* repress, rebuke, or snub. **sit on the fence** remain neutral or undecided. **sit out 1** take no part in (a dance etc.). **2** stay till the end of (esp. an ordeal). **3** sit outdoors. **sit tight** *colloq.* **1** remain firmly in one's place. **2** not yield. **sit up 1** rise from lying to sitting. **2** sit firmly upright. **3** go to bed late. **4** *colloq.* become interested or aroused etc. **sit well on** suit or fit. [Old English]

sitar /'sɪtɑː(r), sɪ'tɑː(r)/ *n.* long-necked Indian lute. [Hindi]

SITC *abbr.* Standard International Trade Classification.

sitcom *n. colloq.* situation comedy. [abbreviation]

SITC(R) *abbr.* Standard International Trade Classification (Revised).

sit-down *–attrib. adj.* **1** (of a meal) eaten sitting at a table. **2** (of a protest etc.) with demonstrators occupying their workplace or sitting down on the ground in a public place. *–n.* **1** spell of sitting. **2** sit-down protest etc.

♦ **sit-down strike** *n.* strike in which workers come to their place of work, but refuse to either work or to go home. In a **work-in**, the workers refuse to leave the place of work and continue working, usu. in spite of management instructions not to do so.

site *–n.* **1** ground chosen or used for a town or building. **2** place of or for some activity (*camping site*). *–v.* **(-ting)** locate, place. [Latin *situs*]

sit-in *n.* protest involving sitting in.

Sitka /'sɪtkə/ *n.* (in full **Sitka spruce**) fast-growing spruce yielding timber. [*Sitka* in Alaska]

SITPRO /'sɪtprəʊ/ *abbr.* Simpler Trade Procedures Board. [formerly *S*implification of *I*nternational *T*rade *Pro*cedures]

sitter *n.* **1** person who sits, esp. for a portrait. **2** babysitter (see BABYSIT). **3** *colloq.* easy catch or shot.

sitting *–n.* **1** continuous period spent engaged in an activity (*finished the book in one sitting*). **2** time during which an assembly is engaged in business. **3** session in which a meal is served. *–adj.* **1** having sat down. **2** (of an animal or bird) still. **3** (of an MP etc.) current.

sitting duck *n.* (also **sitting target**) *colloq.* easy target.

sitting-room *n.* room for relaxed sitting in.

sitting tenant *n.* tenant occupying premises.

situate /'sɪtjʊˌeɪt/ *v.* **(-ting)** (usu. in *passive*) **1** put in a certain position or circumstances. **2** establish or indicate the place of; put in a context. [Latin *situo*: related to SITE]

situation /ˌsɪtjʊ'eɪʃ(ə)n/ *n.* **1** place and its surroundings. **2** circumstances; position; state of affairs. **3** *formal* paid job. □ **situational** *adj.*

situation comedy *n.* broadcast comedy based on characters dealing with awkward domestic situations.

sit-up *n.* physical exercise of sitting up from a supine position without using the arms or hands.

sit-upon *n. colloq.* buttocks.

sit. vac. *abbr.* (*pl.* **sits vac.**) situation vacant.

♦ **SI units** *n.pl.* units used in science and increasingly for commercial purposes. There are seven basic units: metre, kilogram, second, ampere, kelvin, candela, and mole. Derived units with special names include the hertz (frequency), joule (energy), volt (potential), and watt (power). They are used with a standard set of multiples and sub-multiples, including hecto- (× 100), kilo- (× 1000), centi- (× 1/100), and milli- (× 1/1000).

six *adj.* & *n.* **1** one more than five. **2** symbol for this (6, vi, VI). **3** size etc. denoted by six. **4** *Cricket* hit scoring six runs. **5** six o'clock. □ **at sixes and sevens** in confusion or disagreement. **knock** (or **hit) for six** *colloq.* utterly surprise or overcome. [Old English]

sixer *n.* **1** *Cricket* hit for six runs. **2** Brownie or Cub in charge of a group of six.

sixfold *adj.* & *adv.* **1** six times as much or as many. **2** consisting of six parts.

sixpence /'sɪkspəns/ *n.* **1** sum of six esp. old pence. **2** *hist.* coin worth this.

sixpenny *adj.* costing or worth sixpence, esp. before decimalization.

six-shooter *n.* (also **six-gun**) revolver with six chambers.

sixteen /ˌsɪks'tiːn, 'sɪks-/ *adj.* & *n.* **1** one more than fifteen. **2** symbol for this (16, xvi, XVI). **3** size etc. denoted by sixteen. □ **sixteenth** *adj.* & *n.* [Old English]

sixth *adj.* & *n.* **1** next after fifth. **2** any of six equal parts of a thing. □ **sixthly** *adv.*

sixth form *n.* form in a secondary school for pupils over 16.

sixth-form college *n.* separate college for pupils over 16.

sixth former *n.* sixth-form pupil.

sixth sense *n.* supposed intuitive or extrasensory faculty.

sixty /'sɪkstɪ/ *adj.* & *n.* (*pl.* **-ies**) **1** six times ten. **2** symbol for this (60, lx, LX). **3** (in *pl.*) numbers from 60 to 69, esp. the years of a century or of a person's life. □ **sixtieth** *adj.* & *n.* [Old English]

sizable var. of SIZEABLE.

size[1] *–n.* **1** relative dimensions, magnitude. **2** each of the classes into which similar things are divided according to size. *–v.* **(-zing)** sort in sizes or according to size. □ **the size of it** *colloq.* the truth of the matter. **size up** *colloq.* form a judgement of. □ **sized** *adj.* (also in *comb.*). [French *sise*]

size[2] *–n.* sticky solution used in glazing paper, stiffening textiles, etc. *–v.* **(-zing)** treat with size. [perhaps = SIZE[1]]

sizeable *adj.* (also **sizable**) large or fairly large.

sizzle /'sɪz(ə)l/ *–v.* **(-ling) 1** sputter or hiss, esp. in frying. **2** *colloq.* be very hot or excited etc. *–n.* sizzling sound. □ **sizzling** *adj.* & *adv.* [imitative]

SJ *abbr.* Society of Jesus.

Sjaelland see ZEALAND.

SK *–postcode* Stockport. *–airline flight code* Scandinavian Airline System.

ska /skɑː/ *n.* a kind of fast orig. Jamaican pop music. [origin unknown]

Skagerrak /'skægəˌræk/ strait separating S Norway from N Denmark and linking the Baltic to the North Sea.

skate[1] *–n.* **1** boot with a blade attached for gliding on ice; this blade. **2** = ROLLER-SKATE *n.* *–v.* **(-ting) 1 a** move on skates. **b** perform (a specified figure) on skates. **2** (foll. by *over*) refer fleetingly to, disregard. □ **get one's skates on** *slang* make haste. **skate on thin ice** *colloq.* behave rashly, risk danger. □ **skater** *n.* [Dutch *schaats* from French]

skate[2] *n.* (*pl.* same or **-s**) large flat marine fish used as food. [Old Norse]

skateboard *–n.* short narrow board on two pairs of trucks, for riding on while standing. *–v.* ride on a skateboard. □ **skateboarder** *n.*

skedaddle /skɪ'dæd(ə)l/ *v.* **(-ling)** *colloq.* run away, depart quickly. [origin unknown]

skein /skeɪn/ *n.* **1** loosely-coiled bundle of yarn or thread. **2** flock of wild geese etc. in flight. [French *escaigne*]

skeleton /'skelɪt(ə)n/ *n.* **1** hard framework of bones etc. of an animal. **2** supporting framework or structure of a thing. **3** very thin person or animal. **4** useless or dead remnant. **5** outline sketch, epitome. **6** (*attrib.*) having only the essential or minimum number of persons, parts, etc. (*skeleton staff*). □ **skeletal** *adj.* [Greek *skellō* dry up]

skeleton in the cupboard *n.* discreditable or embarrassing secret.

skeleton key *n.* key designed to fit many locks.

skeptic *US* var. of SCEPTIC.

skerry /'skerɪ/ *n.* (*pl.* **-ies**) *Scot.* reef, rocky island. [Old Norse]

sketch *–n.* **1** rough or unfinished drawing or painting. **2** rough draft or general outline. **3** short usu. humorous play. **4** short descriptive essay etc. *–v.* **1** make or give a sketch of. **2** draw sketches. **3** (often foll. by *in, out*) outline briefly. [Greek *skhēdios* extempore]

sketch-book *n.* (also **sketch-block**) pad of drawing-paper for sketching.

sketch-map *n.* roughly-drawn map with few details.

sketchy *adj.* **(-ier, -iest) 1** giving only a rough outline, like a sketch. **2** *colloq.* unsubstantial or imperfect, esp. through haste. □ **sketchily** *adv.* **sketchiness** *n.*

skew *–adj.* oblique, slanting, set askew. *–n.* slant. *–v.* **1**

make skew. **2** distort. **3** move obliquely. □ **on the skew** askew. [French: related to ESCHEW]

skewbald /'skju:bɔ:ld/ *–adj.* (esp. of a horse) with irregular patches of white and another colour. *–n.* skewbald animal. [origin uncertain]

skewer /'skju:ə(r)/ *–n.* long pin designed for holding meat together while cooking. *–v.* fasten together or pierce (as) with a skewer. [origin uncertain]

skew-whiff *adj.* & *adv. colloq.* askew.

ski /ski:/ *–n.* (*pl.* **-s**) **1** each of a pair of long narrow pieces of wood etc., fastened under the feet for travelling over snow. **2** similar device under a vehicle or aircraft. *–v.* (**skis, ski'd** or **skied** /ski:d/; **skiing**) travel on skis. □ **skier** *n.* [Norwegian from Old Norse]

skid *–v.* (**-dd-**) **1** (of a vehicle etc.) slide on slippery ground, esp. sideways or obliquely. **2** cause (a vehicle) to skid. *–n.* **1** act of skidding. **2** runner beneath an aircraft for use when landing. □ **on the skids** *colloq.* about to be discarded or defeated. **put the skids under** *colloq.* hasten the downfall or failure of. [origin unknown]

skid-pan *n.* slippery surface for drivers to practise control of skidding.

skid row *n. US slang* part of a town frequented by vagrants etc.

skiff *n.* light rowing- or sculling-boat. [French *esquif*: related to SHIP]

ski-jump *n.* steep slope levelling off before a sharp drop to allow a skier to leap through the air. □ **ski-jumping** *n.*

skilful *adj.* (*US* **skillful**) (often foll. by *at, in*) having or showing skill. □ **skilfully** *adv.*

ski-lift *n.* device for carrying skiers up a slope, usu. a cable with hanging seats.

skill *n.* (often foll. by *in*) ability to do something well; technique, expertise. [Old Norse, = difference]

skilled *adj.* **1** (often foll. by *in*) skilful. **2** (of work or a worker) requiring or having skill or special training.

skillet /'skɪlɪt/ *n.* **1** small long-handled metal cooking-pot. **2** *US* frying-pan. [French]

skillful *US* var. of SKILFUL.

skim *–v.* (**-mm-**) **1 a** take a floating layer from the surface of (a liquid). **b** take (cream etc.) from the surface of a liquid. **2 a** barely touch (a surface) in passing over. **b** (often followed by *over*) deal with or treat (a matter) superficially. **3** (often foll. by *over, along*) go or glide lightly. **4** (often followed by *through*) read or look over cursorily. *–n.* skimming. [French: related to SCUM]

skimmia /'skɪmɪə/ *n.* evergreen shrub with red berries. [Japanese]

skim milk *n.* (also **skimmed milk**) milk from which the cream has been removed.

skimp *v.* **1** (often followed by *on*) economize; use a meagre or insufficient amount of, stint. **2** (often foll. by *in*) supply (a person etc.) meagrely with food etc. **3** do hastily or carelessly. [cf. SCRIMP]

skimpy *adj.* (**-ier, -iest**) meagre; insufficient. □ **skimpiness** *n.*

skin *–n.* **1** flexible covering of a body. **2 a** skin of a flayed animal with or without the hair etc. **b** material prepared from skins. **3** complexion of the skin. **4** outer layer or covering, esp. of a fruit, sausage, etc. **5** film like skin on a liquid etc. **6** container for liquid, made of an animal's skin. **7** *slang* skinhead. *–v.* (**-nn-**) **1** remove the skin from. **2** graze (part of the body). **3** *slang* swindle. □ **be skin and bone** be very thin. **by** (or **with**) **the skin of one's teeth** by a very narrow margin. **get under a person's skin** *colloq.* interest or annoy a person intensely. **have a thick** (or **thin**) **skin** be insensitive (or sensitive). **no skin off one's nose** *colloq.* of no consequence to one. □ **skinless** *adj.* [Old Norse]

skin-deep *adj.* superficial.

skin-diver *n.* underwater swimmer without a diving-suit, usu. with aqualung and flippers. □ **skin-diving** *n.*

skinflint *n.* miser.

skinful *n. colloq.* enough alcohol to make one drunk.

skin-graft *n.* **1** surgical transplanting of skin. **2** skin transferred in this way.

skinhead *n.* youth with a shaven head, esp. one of an aggressive gang.

skinny *adj.* (**-ier, -iest**) thin or emaciated. □ **skinniness** *n.*

skint *adj. slang* having no money left. [= *skinned*]

skin-tight *adj.* (of a garment) very close-fitting.

skip[1] *–v.* (**-pp-**) **1 a** move along lightly, esp. with alternate hops. **b** jump lightly, esp. over a skipping-rope. **c** gambol, caper, frisk. **2** (often foll. by *from, off, to*) move quickly from one point, subject, etc. to another. **3** (also *absol.*) omit parts of (a text, subject, etc.). **4** *colloq.* miss intentionally, not attend. **5** *colloq.* leave hurriedly. *–n.* skipping movement or action. □ **skip it** *colloq.* abandon a topic etc. [probably Scandinavian]

skip[2] *n.* **1** large container for building refuse etc. **2** container for transporting or raising materials in mining etc. [Old Norse]

skipjack *n.* (in full **skipjack tuna**) (*pl.* same or **-s**) small striped Pacific tuna used as food. [from SKIP[1], JACK]

skipper *–n.* **1** captain of a ship or aircraft. **2** captain of a sporting team. *–v.* be captain of. [Low German or Dutch *schipper*]

skipping-rope *n.* length of rope turned over the head and under the feet while jumping it as a game or exercise.

skirl *–n.* shrill sound, esp. of bagpipes. *–v.* make a skirl. [probably Scandinavian]

skirmish /'skɜ:mɪʃ/ *–n.* **1** minor battle. **2** short argument or contest of wit etc. *–v.* engage in a skirmish. [French from Germanic]

skirt *–n.* **1** woman's garment hanging from the waist. **2** the part of a coat etc. hanging below the waist. **3** hanging part at the base of a hovercraft. **4** (in *sing.* or *pl.*) edge, border, extreme part. **5** (also **bit of skirt**) *slang offens.* woman. **6** (in full **skirt of beef** etc.) cut of meat from the flank or diaphragm. *–v.* (often foll. by *around*) **1** go or lie along or round the edge of. **2** avoid dealing with (an issue etc.). [Old Norse: related to SHIRT]

skirting-board *n.* narrow board etc. along the bottom of a room-wall.

ski-run *n.* slope prepared for skiing.

skit *n.* light, usu. short, piece of satire or burlesque. [perhaps from Old Norse: related to SHOOT]

skittish *adj.* **1** lively, playful. **2** (of a horse etc.) nervous, inclined to shy. [perhaps related to SKIT]

skittle /'skɪt(ə)l/ *n.* **1** pin used in skittles. **2** (in *pl.*; usu. treated as *sing.*) game of trying to bowl down usu. nine wooden pins. [origin unknown]

skive *v.* (**-ving**) (often followed by *off*) *slang* evade work; play truant. □ **skiver** *n.* [Old Norse]

skivvy /'skɪvɪ/ *–n.* (*pl.* **-ies**) *colloq. derog.* female domestic servant. *–v.* (**-ies, -ied**) work as a skivvy. [origin unknown]

Skopje /'skɒpjeɪ/ capital of Macedonia; manufactures include cement, glass, brick, and steel; pop. (1994) 541 280.

Skr *symb.* Swedish krona.

skua /'skju:ə/ *n.* large predatory sea bird. [Old Norse]

skulduggery /skʌl'dʌgərɪ/ *n.* trickery; unscrupulous behaviour. [origin unknown]

skulk *v.* move stealthily; lurk, hide. [Scandinavian]

skull *n.* **1** bony case of the brain of a vertebrate. **2** bony skeleton of the head. **3** head as the seat of intelligence. [origin unknown]

skull and crossbones *n.pl.* representation of a skull with two crossed thigh-bones as an emblem of piracy or death.

skullcap *n.* peakless cap covering the crown only.

skunk *n.* (*pl.* same or **-s**) **1** black and white striped mammal emitting a powerful stench when attacked. **2** *colloq.* contemptible person. [American Indian]

sky /skaɪ/ *–n.* (*pl.* **skies**) (in *sing.* or *pl.*) atmosphere and outer space as seen from the earth. *–v.* (**skies, skied**)

Cricket etc. hit (a ball) high. □ **to the skies** without reserve (*praise to the skies*). [Old Norse, = cloud]

sky blue *adj.* & *n.* (as adj. often hyphenated) bright clear blue.

skydiving *n.* sport of performing acrobatic manoeuvres under free fall before opening a parachute. □ **skydiver** *n.*

Skye /skaɪ/ largest island of the Inner Hebrides in NW Scotland; pop. (est. 1985) 7500; chief town, Portree. There is some sheep and cattle farming, and tourism is an important source of revenue. –*n.* (in full **Skye terrier**) long-haired slate or fawn coloured variety of Scotch terrier.

sky-high *adv.* & *adj.* very high.

skyjack *v. slang* hijack (an aircraft).

skylark –*n.* lark that sings while soaring. –*v.* play tricks, frolic.

skylight *n.* window in a roof.

skyline *n.* outline of hills, buildings, etc. against the sky.

sky-rocket –*n.* = ROCKET *n.* 1. –*v.* (esp. of prices) rise very rapidly.

skyscraper *n.* very tall building.

skyward /ˈskaɪwəd/ –*adv.* (also **skywards**) towards the sky. –*adj.* moving skyward.

sky-writing *n.* writing in aeroplane smoke-trails.

SL –*abbr.* (also **s.l.**) *Insurance* salvage loss. –*international civil aircraft marking* Slovenia. –*postcode* Slough.

slab *n.* **1** flat thick esp. rectangular piece of solid material, esp. stone. **2** mortuary table. [origin unknown]

slack[1] –*adj.* **1** (of rope etc.) not taut. **2** inactive or sluggish. **3** negligent, remiss. **4** (of tide etc.) neither ebbing nor flowing. –*n.* **1** slack part of a rope (*haul in the slack*). **2** slack period. **3** (in *pl.*) informal trousers. –*v.* **1** loosen (rope etc.). **2** *colloq.* take a rest, be lazy. □ **slack off 1** loosen. **2** (also **slack up**) reduce one's level of activity; reduce speed. □ **slackness** *n.* [Old English]

slack[2] *n.* coal-dust or fragments of coal. [probably Low German or Dutch]

slacken *v.* make or become slack. □ **slacken off** = *slack off* (see SLACK[1]).

slacker *n.* shirker.

slag –*n.* **1** refuse left after smelting etc. **2** *slang derog.* prostitute; promiscuous woman. –*v.* (**-gg-**) **1** form slag. **2** (often foll. by *off*) *slang* insult, slander. □ **slaggy** *adj.* [Low German]

slag-heap *n.* hill of refuse from a coalmine, steelworks, etc.

slain *past part.* of SLAY[1].

slake *v.* (**-king**) **1** assuage or satisfy (thirst, a desire, etc.). **2** temper (quicklime) by combination with water. [Old English: related to SLACK[1]]

slalom /ˈslɑːləm/ *n.* **1** ski-race down a zigzag obstacle course. **2** obstacle race in canoes etc. [Norwegian]

slam[1] –*v.* (**-mm-**) **1** shut forcefully and loudly. **2** put down loudly. **3** put or do suddenly (*slam the brakes on*; *car slammed to a halt*). **4** *slang* criticize severely. **5** *slang* hit. **6** *slang* conquer easily. –*n.* sound or action of slamming. [probably Scandinavian]

slam[2] *n. Cards* winning of every trick in a game. [origin uncertain]

slander –*n.* **1** false and damaging utterance about a person. **2** uttering of this. –*v.* utter slander about. □ **slanderous** *adj.* [French *esclandre*: related to SCANDAL]

slang –*n.* very informal words, phrases, or meanings, not regarded as standard and often used by a specific profession, class, etc. –*v.* use abusive language (to). □ **slangy** *adj.* [origin unknown]

slanging-match *n.* prolonged exchange of insults.

slant /slɑːnt/ –*v.* **1** slope; lie or (cause to) go obliquely. **2** (often as **slanted** *adj.*) present (information) in a biased or particular way. –*n.* **1** slope; oblique position. **2** point of view, esp. a biased one. –*adj.* sloping, oblique. □ **on a** (or **the**) **slant** aslant. [Scandinavian]

slantwise *adv.* aslant.

slap –*v.* (**-pp-**) **1** strike with the palm or a flat object, or so as to make a similar noise. **2** lay forcefully (*slapped it down*). **3** put hastily or carelessly (*slap paint on*). **4** (often foll. by *down*) *colloq.* reprimand or snub. –*n.* **1** blow with the palm or a flat object. **2** slapping sound. –*adv.* suddenly, fully, directly (*ran slap into him*). [Low German, imitative]

slap and tickle *n. colloq.* sexual horseplay.

slap-bang *adv. colloq.* violently, headlong.

slapdash –*adj.* hasty and careless. –*adv.* in this manner.

slap-happy *adj. colloq.* cheerfully casual or flippant.

slap in the face *n.* rebuff or affront.

slap on the back *n.* congratulations.

slapstick *n.* boisterous comedy.

slap-up *attrib. adj. colloq.* excellent, lavish.

slash –*v.* **1** cut or gash with a knife etc. **2** (often foll. by *at*) deliver or aim cutting blows. **3** reduce (prices etc.) drastically. **4** censure vigorously. –*n.* **1** slashing cut or stroke. **2** *Printing* oblique stroke; solidus. **3** *slang* act of urinating. [origin unknown]

slat *n.* thin narrow piece of wood, plastic, or metal, esp. as in a fence or Venetian blind. [French *esclat* splinter]

slate –*n.* **1** (esp. bluish-grey) metamorphic rock easily split into flat smooth plates. **2** piece of this as a tile or *hist.* for writing on. **3** bluish-grey colour of slate. **4** *US* list of nominees for office etc. –*v.* (**-ting**) **1** roof with slates. **2** *colloq.* criticize severely. **3** *US* make arrangements for (an event etc.). **4** *US* nominate for office etc. –*adj.* of slate or the colour of slate. □ **on the slate** on (usu. informal) credit. □ **slating** *n.* **slaty** *adj.* [French *esclate*, feminine of *esclat*: related to SLAT]

slattern /ˈslæt(ə)n/ *n.* slovenly woman. □ **slatternly** *adj.* [origin uncertain]

slaughter /ˈslɔːtə(r)/ –*v.* **1** kill (animals) for food or skins or because of disease. **2** kill (people) ruthlessly or on a great scale. **3** *colloq.* defeat utterly. –*n.* act of slaughtering. □ **slaughterer** *n.* [Old Norse: related to SLAY]

slaughterhouse *n.* place for the slaughter of animals as food.

Slav /slɑːv/ –*n.* member of a group of peoples in central and E Europe speaking Slavonic languages. –*adj.* of the Slavs. [Latin *Sclavus*, ethnic name]

slave –*n.* **1** person who is owned by and has to serve another. **2** drudge, hard worker. **3** (foll. by *of*, *to*) obsessive devotee (*slave of fashion*). **4** machine, or part of one, directly controlled by another. –*v.* (**-ving**) (often foll. by *at*, *over*) work very hard. [French *esclave* from Latin *Sclavus* SLAV (captive)]

slave-driver *n.* **1** overseer of slaves. **2** demanding boss.

slave labour *n.* forced labour.

slaver[1] *n. hist.* ship or person engaged in the slave-trade.

slaver[2] /ˈslævə(r)/ –*v.* **1** dribble. **2** (foll. by *over*) drool over. –*n.* **1** dribbling saliva. **2 a** fulsome flattery. **b** drivel, nonsense. [Low German or Dutch]

slavery /ˈsleɪvərɪ/ *n.* **1** condition of a slave. **2** drudgery. **3** practice of having slaves.

slave-trade *n. hist.* dealing in slaves, esp. African Blacks.

Slavic /ˈslɑːvɪk/ *adj.* & *n.* = SLAVONIC.

slavish *adj.* **1** like slaves. **2** without originality. □ **slavishly** *adv.*

Slavonic /sləˈvɒnɪk/ –*adj.* **1** of the group of languages including Russian, Polish, and Czech. **2** of the Slavs. –*n.* Slavonic language-group. [related to SLAV]

slay *v.* (*past* **slew** /sluː/; *past part.* **slain**) **1** *literary* = KILL *v.* 1. **2** = KILL *v.* 4. □ **slayer** *n.* [Old English]

sleaze *n. colloq.* sleaziness. [back-formation from SLEAZY]

sleazy *adj.* (**-ier, -iest**) squalid, tawdry. □ **sleazily** *adv.* **sleaziness** *n.* [origin unknown]

sled *US* –*n.* sledge. –*v.* (**-dd-**) ride on a sledge. [Low German]

sledge –*n.* vehicle on runners for use on snow. –*v.* (**-ging**) travel or convey by sledge. [Dutch *sleedse*]

sledgehammer /ˈsledʒˌhæmə(r)/ *n.* **1** large heavy long-handled hammer used to break stone etc. **2** (*attrib.*) heavy or powerful (*sledgehammer blow*). [Old English *slecg*: related to SLAY]

sleek –*adj.* **1** (of hair, skin, etc.) smooth and glossy. **2** looking well-fed and comfortable. –*v.* make sleek. □ **sleekly** *adv.* **sleekness** *n.* [var. of SLICK]

sleep –*n.* **1** natural recurring condition of suspended consciousness, with the eyes closed and the muscles relaxed. **2** period of sleep (*had a sleep*). **3** state like sleep; rest, quiet, death. –*v.* (*past* and *past part.* **slept**) **1 a** be in a state of sleep. **b** fall asleep. **2** (foll. by *at*, *in*, etc.) spend the night. **3** provide beds etc. for (*house sleeps six*). **4** (foll. by *with*, *together*) have sexual intercourse, esp. in bed. **5** (foll. by *on*) put off (a decision) until the next day. **6** (foll. by *through*) fail to be woken by. **7** be inactive or dead. **8** (foll. by *off*) remedy by sleeping. □ **get to sleep** manage to fall asleep. **go to sleep 1** begin to sleep. **2** (of a limb) become numb. **put to sleep 1** anaesthetize. **2** put down (an animal). **sleep around** *colloq.* be sexually promiscuous. **sleep in** sleep later than usual in the morning. [Old English]

sleeper *n.* **1** person or animal that sleeps. **2** horizontal beam supporting a railway track. **3 a** sleeping-car. **b** berth in this. **4** ring or stud worn in a pierced ear to keep the hole open.

sleeping-bag *n.* padded bag to sleep in when camping etc.

sleeping-car *n.* (also **sleeping-carriage**) railway coach with berths.

♦ sleeping partner *n.* person who has capital in a partnership but takes no part in its commercial activities. He or she has all the legal benefits and obligations of ownership and shares in the profits of the partnership in accordance with the provisions laid down in the partnership agreement.

---

sleeping-pill *n.* pill to induce sleep.

sleeping policeman *n.* ramp etc. in the road to make traffic slow down.

sleeping sickness *n.* tropical disease causing extreme lethargy.

sleepless *adj.* **1** lacking sleep (*sleepless night*). **2** unable to sleep. **3** continually active. □ **sleeplessness** *n.*

sleepwalk *v.* walk about while asleep. □ **sleepwalker** *n.*

sleepy *adj.* (**-ier, -iest**) **1** drowsy. **2** quiet, inactive (*sleepy town*). □ **sleepily** *adv.* **sleepiness** *n.*

sleet –*n.* **1** snow and rain falling together. **2** hail or snow melting as it falls. –*v.* (prec. by *it* as subject) sleet falls (*it is sleeting*). □ **sleety** *adj.* [Old English]

sleeve *n.* **1** part of a garment that encloses an arm. **2** cover of a gramophone record. **3** tube enclosing a rod etc. □ **up one's sleeve** in reserve. □ **sleeved** *adj.* (also in *comb.*). **sleeveless** *adj.* [Old English]

sleigh /sleɪ/ –*n.* sledge, esp. for riding on. –*v.* travel on a sleigh. [Dutch *slee*: related to SLEDGE]

sleight of hand /slaɪt/ *n.* dexterity, esp. in conjuring. [Old Norse: related to SLY]

slender *adj.* (**-er, -est**) **1 a** of small girth or breadth. **b** gracefully thin. **2** relatively small, scanty, inadequate. [origin unknown]

slept *past* and *past part.* of SLEEP.

sleuth /sluːθ/ *colloq.* –*n.* detective. –*v.* investigate crime etc. [Old Norse]

slew[1] /sluː/ (also **slue**) –*v.* (often foll. by *round*) turn or swing forcibly to a new position. –*n.* such a turn. [origin unknown]

slew[2] *past* of SLAY.

SLIC *n.* (in the US) (Federal) Savings and Loan Insurance Corporation.

slice –*n.* **1** thin flat piece or wedge of esp. food cut off or out. **2** share; part. **3** long-handled kitchen utensil with a broad flat perforated blade. **4** *Sport* stroke that sends the ball obliquely. –*v.* (**-cing**) **1** (often foll. by *up*) cut into slices. **2** (foll. by *off*) cut off. **3** (foll. by *into*, *through*) cut (as) with a knife. **4** strike (a ball) with a slice. [French *esclice* from Germanic]

slick –*adj. colloq.* **1 a** skilful or efficient. **b** superficially or pretentiously smooth and dextrous; glib. **2** sleek, smooth. –*n.* large patch of oil etc., esp. on the sea. –*v. colloq.* **1** (usu. foll. by *back*, *down*) flatten (one's hair etc.). **2** (usu. foll. by *up*) make sleek or smart. □ **slickly** *adv.* **slickness** *n.* [Old English]

slide –*v.* (*past* and *past part.* **slid**) **1** move along a smooth surface with continuous contact on the same part of the thing moving. **2** move quietly or smoothly; glide. **3** glide over ice without skates. **4** (foll. by *over*) barely touch upon (a delicate subject etc.). **5** (often foll. by *into*) move quietly or unobtrusively. –*n.* **1** act of sliding. **2** rapid decline. **3** inclined plane down which children, goods, etc., slide. **4** track made by or for sliding, esp. on ice. **5** part of a machine or instrument that slides. **6 a** mounted transparency viewed with a projector. **b** piece of glass holding an object for a microscope. **7** = HAIR-SLIDE. □ **let things slide** be negligent; allow deterioration. [Old English]

slide-rule *n.* ruler with a sliding central strip, graduated logarithmically for making rapid calculations.

♦ sliding peg *n.* = CRAWLING PEG.

---

sliding scale *n.* scale of fees, taxes, wages, etc., that varies according to some other factor.

slight /slaɪt/ –*adj.* **1 a** small; insignificant. **b** inadequate. **2** slender, frail-looking. **3** (in *superl.*) any whatever (*if there were the slightest chance*). –*v.* treat disrespectfully; ignore. –*n.* act of slighting. □ **slightly** *adv.* **slightness** *n.* [Old Norse]

Sligo /ˈslaɪgəʊ/ **1** county in the W Republic of Ireland, in Connaught province; cattle and dairy farming are the main agricultural activities, and there are deposits of coal, lead, and copper; pop. (1991) 54 756. **2** its capital, a seaport on the Atlantic; pop. 17 300.

slim –*adj.* (**slimmer, slimmest**) **1** not fat, slender. **2** small, insufficient (*slim chance*). –*v.* (**-mm-**) (often foll. by *down*) **1** become slimmer by dieting, exercise, etc. **2** make smaller (*slimmed it down to 40 pages*). □ **slimmer** *n.* **slimming** *n.* & *adj.* **slimmish** *adj.* [Low German or Dutch]

slime *n.* thick slippery mud or sticky substance produced by an animal or plant. [Old English]

♦ Slim Helu /hɪluː/, **Carlos** (1939/40–) Mexican businessman, owner of the major part of Mexico City-based conglomerate Grupo Carso, through which he controls Sears Roebuck de México and (via subsidiary Carso Global Telecom) Teléfonos de México. He is regarded as the most wealthy Latin American.

---

slimline *adj.* **1** of slender design. **2** (of a drink) not fattening.

slimy *adj.* (**-ier, -iest**) **1** like, covered with, or full of slime. **2** *colloq.* disgustingly obsequious. □ **sliminess** *n.*

sling[1] –*n.* **1** strap etc. used to support or raise a thing. **2** bandage supporting an injured arm from the neck. **3** strap etc. for firing a stone etc. by hand. –*v.* (*past* and *past part.* **slung**) **1** *colloq.* throw. **2** suspend with a sling. □ **sling one's hook** *slang* go away. [Old Norse or Low German or Dutch]

sling[2] *n.* sweetened drink of spirits (esp. gin) and water. [origin unknown]

sling-back *n.* shoe held in place by a strap above the heel.

slink *v.* (*past* and *past part.* **slunk**) (often foll. by *off*, *away*, *by*) move in a stealthy or guilty manner. [Old English]

slinky *adj.* (**-ier, -iest**) (of a garment) close-fitting and sinuous.

slip[1] –*v.* (**-pp-**) **1** slide unintentionally or momentarily; lose one's footing or balance. **2** go or move with a sliding motion. **3** escape or fall from being slippery or not being held properly. **4** (often foll. by *in, out, away*) go unobserved or quietly. **5 a** make a careless or slight error. **b** fall below standard. **6** place or slide stealthily or casually (*slipped a coin to him*). **7** release from restraint or connection. **8** move (a stitch) to the other needle without knitting it. **9** (foll. by *on, off*) pull (a garment) easily or hastily on or off. **10** escape from; evade (*dog slipped its collar; slipped my mind*). –*n.* **1** act of slipping. **2** careless or slight error. **3 a** pillowcase. **b** petticoat. **4** (in *sing.* or *pl.*) = SLIPWAY. **5** *Cricket* **a** fielder stationed for balls glancing off the bat to the off side. **b** (in *sing.* or *pl.*) this position. □ **give a person the slip** escape from; evade. **let slip 1** utter inadvertently. **2** miss (an opportunity). **3** release, esp. from a leash. **slip up** *colloq.* make a mistake. [probably from Low German *slippen*]

slip[2] *n.* **1** small piece of paper, esp. for writing on. **2** piece cut from a plant for grafting or planting. □ **slip of a** small and slim (*slip of a girl*). [Low German or Dutch]

slip[3] *n.* clay and water mixture for decorating earthenware. [Old English, = slime]

slip-knot *n.* **1** knot that can be undone by a pull. **2** running knot.

slip of the pen *n.* (also **slip of the tongue**) small written (or spoken) mistake.

slip-on –*attrib. adj.* easily slipped on and off. –*n.* slip-on shoe or garment.

slippage *n.* act or an instance of slipping.

slipped disc *n.* displaced disc between vertebrae causing lumbar pain.

slipper *n.* light loose soft indoor shoe.

slippery *adj.* **1** difficult to grasp, stand on, etc. because smooth or wet. **2** unreliable, unscrupulous. □ **slipperiness** *n.* [Old English]

slippery slope *n.* course leading eventually to disaster.

slippy *adj.* (**-ier**, **-iest**) *colloq.* slippery. □ **look** (or **be**) **slippy** make haste.

slip-road *n.* road for entering or leaving a motorway etc.

slipshod *adj.* careless, slovenly.

slipstream *n.* current of air or water driven back by a revolving propeller or a moving vehicle.

slip-up *n. colloq.* mistake.

slipway *n.* ramp for building ships or landing boats.

slit –*n.* straight narrow incision or opening. –*v.* (**-tt-**; *past* and *past part.* **slit**) **1** make a slit in. **2** cut into strips. [Old English]

slither /ˈslɪðə(r)/ –*v.* slide unsteadily. –*n.* act of slithering. □ **slithery** *adj.* [var. of *slidder*: related to SLIDE]

Sliven /ˈsliːv(ə)n/ textile-manufacturing city in central Bulgaria; pop. (1990) 112 220.

sliver /ˈslɪvə(r)/ –*n.* long thin piece cut or split off. –*v.* **1** break off as a sliver. **2** break or form into slivers. [Old English]

Sloane /sləʊn/ *n.* (in full **Sloane Ranger**) *slang* fashionable and conventional upper-class young person. □ **Sloaney** *adj.* [*Sloane* Square in London, and Lone *Ranger*, cowboy hero]

slob *n. colloq. derog.* lazy, untidy, or fat person. [Irish *slab* mud]

slobber –*v.* **1** slaver. **2** (foll. by *over*) drool over. –*n.* slaver. □ **slobbery** *adj.* [Dutch]

sloe /sləʊ/ *n.* **1** = BLACKTHORN. **2** its small sour bluish-black fruit. [Old English]

slog –*v.* (**-gg-**) **1** hit hard and usu. wildly. **2** work or walk doggedly. –*n.* **1** hard random hit. **2 a** hard steady work or walk. **b** spell of this. [origin unknown]

slogan /ˈsləʊgən/ *n.* **1** catchy phrase used in advertising etc. **2** party cry; watchword. [Gaelic, = war cry]

sloop *n.* small one-masted fore-and-aft-rigged vessel. [Dutch *sloep*]

slop –*v.* (**-pp-**) **1** (often foll. by *over*) spill over the edge of a vessel. **2** wet (the floor etc.) by slopping. –*n.* **1** liquid spilled or splashed. **2** sloppy language. **3** (in *pl.*) dirty waste water or wine etc. from a kitchen, bedroom, or prison vessels. **4** (in *sing.* or *pl.*) unappetizing weak liquid food. □ **slop about** move about in a slovenly manner. **slop out** carry slops out (in prison etc.). [Old English]

slope –*n.* **1** inclined position, direction, or state. **2** piece of rising or falling ground. **3** difference in level between the two ends or sides of a thing. **4** place for skiing on a mountain etc. –*v.* (**-ping**) **1** have or take a slope, slant. **2** cause to slope. □ **slope arms** place one's rifle in a sloping position against one's shoulder. **slope off** *slang* go away, esp. to evade work etc. [*aslope* crosswise]

sloppy *adj.* (**-ier**, **-iest**) **1** wet, watery, too liquid. **2** careless, untidy. **3** foolishly sentimental. □ **sloppily** *adv.* **sloppiness** *n.*

slosh –*v.* **1** (often foll. by *about*) splash or flounder. **2** *slang* hit, esp. heavily. **3** *colloq.* **a** pour (liquid) clumsily. **b** pour liquid on. –*n.* **1** slush. **2** act or sound of splashing. **3** *slang* heavy blow. [var. of SLUSH]

sloshed *predic. adj. slang* drunk.

slot –*n.* **1** slit in a machine etc. for a thing, esp. a coin, to be inserted. **2** slit, groove, etc. for a thing. **3** allotted place in a schedule, esp. in broadcasting. –*v.* (**-tt-**) **1** (often foll. by *in, into*) place or be placed (as if) into a slot. **2** provide with slots. [French *esclot* hollow of breast]

sloth /sləʊθ/ *n.* **1** laziness, indolence. **2** slow-moving South American mammal that hangs upside down in trees. [from SLOW]

slothful *adj.* lazy. □ **slothfully** *adv.*

slot-machine *n.* machine worked by the insertion of a coin, esp. selling small items or providing amusement.

slouch –*v.* stand, move, or sit in a drooping fashion. –*n.* **1** slouching posture or movement. **2** *slang* incompetent or slovenly worker etc. [origin unknown]

slouch hat *n.* hat with a wide flexible brim.

slough[1] /slaʊ/ *n.* swamp, miry place. [Old English]

slough[2] /slʌf/ –*n.* part that an animal casts or moults, esp. a snake's cast skin. –*v.* (often foll. by *off*) cast or drop off as a slough. [origin unknown]

Slough of Despond *n.* state of hopeless depression.

Slovak /ˈsləʊvæk/ –*n.* **1** native of Slovakia. **2** language of Slovakia. –*adj.* of the Slovaks or their language. [native name]

sloven /ˈslʌv(ə)n/ *n.* untidy or careless person. [origin uncertain]

slovenly –*adj.* careless and untidy; unmethodical. –*adv.* in a slovenly manner. □ **slovenliness** *n.*

slow /sləʊ/ –*adj.* **1 a** taking a relatively long time to do a thing (also foll. by *of*: *slow of speech*). **b** acting, moving, or

---

Slovakia /sləʊˈvækɪə/ landlocked country in central Europe, formerly a federal republic of Czechoslovakia. Slovakia's economy is considerably weaker than that of the Czech Republic as it was more dependent on the now declining defence industry. Agriculture produces cereals, fruit, wine, and tobacco. Manufactured goods include machinery, transport equipment, and chemicals, all of which are exported. Iron, zinc, and copper ores are all mined. Slovakia became an independent state, officially the Slovak Republic, on 1 Jan. 1993. President, Mikal Kovac; prime minister, Vladimir Meciar; capital, Bratislava.

languages	Slovak (official), Czech, Hungarian
currency	koruna (Kčs) of 100 haléřů
pop. (1996)	5 372 000
GNP (1994)	US$11.9B
literacy	99% (m); 99% (f)
life expectancy	66 (m); 75 (f)

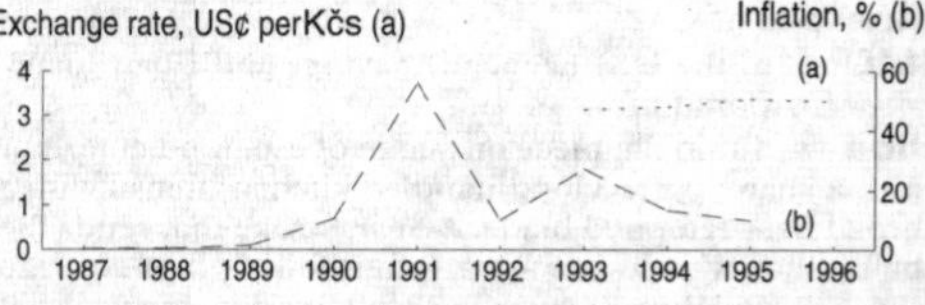

done without speed, not quick. **2** not conducive to speed (*slow route*). **3** (of a clock etc.) showing a time earlier than is correct. **4** (of a person) not understanding or learning readily. **5** dull, tedious. **6** slack, sluggish (*business is slow*). **7** (of a fire or oven) giving little heat. **8** *Photog.* (of a film) needing long exposure. **9** reluctant; not hasty (*slow to anger*). *–adv.* slowly (also in *comb.*: *slow-moving traffic*). *–v.* (usu. foll. by *down, up*) **1** reduce one's speed or the speed of (a vehicle etc.). **2** reduce one's pace of life. □ **slowish** *adj.* **slowly** *adv.* **slowness** *n.* [Old English]

slowcoach *n. colloq.* slow person.

slow-down *n.* action of slowing down.

slow motion *n.* **1** speed of a film at which actions etc. appear much slower than usual. **2** simulation of this in real action.

slow-worm *n.* small European legless lizard. [Old English *slow* uncertain]

SL Re *symb.* Sri Lanka rupee.

sludge *n.* **1** thick greasy mud or sediment. **2** sewage. □ **sludgy** *adj.* [cf. SLUSH]

slue var. of SLEW[1].

slug[1] *n.* **1** small shell-less mollusc often destroying plants. **2 a** bullet, esp. of irregular shape. **b** missile for an airgun. **3** *Printing* **a** metal bar used in spacing. **b** line of type in Linotype printing. **4** mouthful of drink (esp. spirits). [Scandinavian]

slug[2] *US –v.* (**-gg-**) hit hard. *–n.* hard blow. □ **slug it out** fight it out. [origin unknown]

sluggard /ˈslʌgəd/ *n.* lazy person. [related to SLUG[1]]

sluggish *adj.* inert; slow-moving. □ **sluggishly** *adv.* **sluggishness** *n.*

sluice /sluːs/ *–n.* **1** (also **sluice-gate, sluice-valve**) sliding gate or other contrivance for regulating the volume or flow of water. **2** water so regulated. **3** (**sluice-way**) artificial water-channel, esp. for washing ore. **4** place for rinsing. **5** act of rinsing. *–v.* (**-cing**) **1** provide or wash with a sluice or sluices. **2** rinse, esp. with running water. **3** (foll. by *out, away*) wash out or away with a flow of water. **4** (of water) rush out (as if) from a sluice. [French *escluse*]

slum *–n.* **1** house unfit for human habitation. **2** (often in *pl.*) overcrowded and squalid district in a city. *–v.* (**-mm-**) visit slums, esp. out of curiosity. □ **slum it** *colloq.* put up with conditions less comfortable than usual. □ **slummy** *adj.* [originally cant]

slumber *v.* & *n. poet.* or *joc.* sleep. [Old English]

slump *–n.* sudden severe or prolonged fall in prices and trade, usu. bringing widespread unemployment (see DEPRESSION 2). *–v.* **1** undergo a slump. **2** sit or fall heavily or limply. [imitative]

slung *past* and *past part.* of SLING[1].

slunk *past* and *past part.* of SLINK.

slur *–v.* (**-rr-**) **1** pronounce indistinctly with sounds running into one another. **2** *Mus.* perform (notes) legato. **3** *archaic* or *US* put a slur on (a person or a person's character). **4** (usu. foll. by *over*) pass over (a fact, fault, etc.) lightly. *–n.* **1** imputation of wrongdoing. **2** act of slurring. **3** *Mus.* curved line joining notes to be slurred. [origin unknown]

slurp *colloq. –v.* eat or esp. drink noisily. *–n.* sound of this. [Dutch]

slurry /ˈslʌrɪ/ *n.* thin semi-liquid cement, mud, manure, etc. [related to dial. *slur* thin mud]

slush *n.* **1** thawing muddy snow. **2** silly sentimentality. □ **slushy** *adj.* (**-ier, -iest**). [origin unknown]

♦ **slush fund** *n.* money set aside by an organization for discreet payments to influential people for preferential treatment, advance information, or other services for the benefit of the organization. Slush funds are usu. used for purposes less blatant than bribes.

slut *n. derog.* slovenly or promiscuous woman. □ **sluttish** *adj.* [origin unknown]

sly /slaɪ/ *adj.* (**slyer, slyest**) **1** cunning, crafty, wily. **2** secretive. **3** knowing; insinuating. □ **on the sly** secretly. □ **slyly** *adv.* **slyness** *n.* [Old Norse: related to SLAY]

SM *–abbr. US* service mark (registered proprietary name). *–postcode* Sutton (Surrey). *–airline flight code* Aberdeen Airways.

Sm *symb.* samarium.

smack[1] *–n.* **1** sharp slap or blow. **2** hard hit at cricket etc. **3** loud kiss. **4** loud sharp sound. *–v.* **1** slap. **2** part (one's lips) noisily in anticipation of food. **3** move, hit, etc., with a smack. *–adv. colloq.* **1** with a smack. **2** suddenly; directly; violently. **3** exactly (*smack in the centre*). □ **a smack in the eye** (or **face**) *colloq.* rebuff; setback. [imitative]

smack[2] (foll. by *of*) *–v.* **1** have a flavour of; taste of. **2** suggest (*smacks of nepotism*). *–n.* **1** flavour. **2** barely discernible quality. [Old English]

smack[3] *n.* single-masted sailing-boat. [Low German or Dutch]

smack[4] *n. slang* heroin or other hard drug. [probably alteration of Yiddish *schmeck* sniff]

smacker *n. slang* **1** loud kiss. **2 a** £1. **b** *US* $1.

small /smɔːl/ *–adj.* **1** not large or big. **2** not great in importance, amount, number, power, etc. **3** not much; little (*paid small attention*). **4** insignificant (*from small beginnings*). **5** of small particles (*small shot*). **6** on a small scale (*small farmer*). **7** poor or humble. **8** mean; ungenerous. **9** young (*small child*). *–n.* **1** slenderest part of a thing, esp. of the back. **2** (in *pl.*) *colloq.* underwear, esp. as laundry. *–adv.* into small pieces (*chop it small*). □ **feel** (or **look**) **small** be humiliated or ashamed. □ **smallish** *adj.* **smallness** *n.* [Old English]

small arms *n.pl.* portable firearms.

small beer *n.* trifling thing.

small change *n.* coins, not notes.

♦ **small claims** *n.pl.* civil actions involving relatively small sums, usu. £500 in the UK. In the county courts, such claims are dealt with by arbitration before a registrar, with a simplified procedure without incurring the expense of legal representation.

♦ **small company** *n.* company, as defined by the UK

Slovenia /sləˈviːnɪə/ republic in S central Europe, formerly a constituent republic of Yugoslavia. The economy of Slovenia has been adversely affected by its withdrawal from the centrally-planned economy of Yugoslavia, but the country is seeking new markets in the EU and is receiving aid from the EBRD. Agriculture produces wheat, fruits (including grapes), potatoes, sugar beet, and livestock; industries include metallurgy, steel, and the manufacture of furniture, textiles and clothing, machinery and transport equipment, and pharmaceutical products (all exported). Coal, lignite, mercury, zinc, and other minerals are all mined. Slovenia became an independent state in 1992. President, Milan Kucan; prime minister, Janez Drnovsek; capital, Ljubljana. □ **Slovene** /ˈsləʊviːn/ *adj.* & *n.* **Slovenian** *adj.* & *n.*

languages	Slovenian (official), Hungarian, Italian
currency	tolar (SIT) of 100 stotin
pop. (1996)	1 958 746
GNP (1994)	US$14.2B
literacy	99% (m); 99% (f)
life expectancy	69 (m); 77 (f)

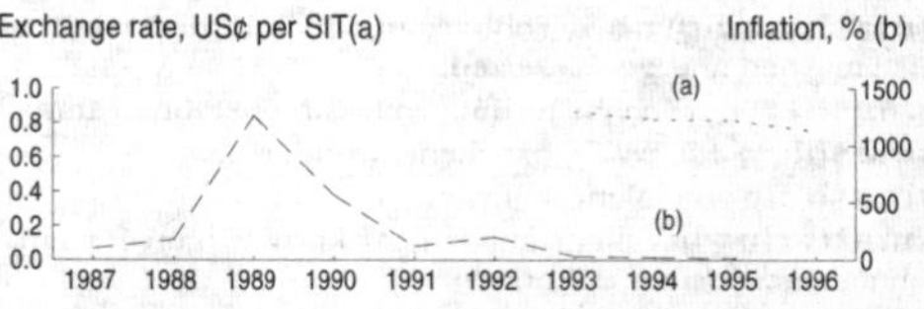

Companies Act (1981), that falls below any two of the following three size criteria: gross assets £700,000; turnover £1,400,000; average number of employees 50. These companies, if not public limited companies or banking, insurance, or shipping companies, may file very abbreviated accounts (see MODIFIED ACCOUNTS) with the Registrar of Companies (excluding even a profit and loss account), although they must provide their own shareholders with the full statutory information. In certain circumstances they pay a reduced rate of corporation tax (the **small-company rate**).

---

small fry *n.* unimportant people; children.

smallholder *n.* farmer of a smallholding.

smallholding *n.* agricultural holding smaller than a farm.

small hours *n.pl.* period soon after midnight.

small-minded *adj.* petty; narrow in outlook.

smallpox *n. hist.* acute contagious disease with fever and pustules, usu. leaving scars.

♦ **small print** *n.* printed matter on a document, e.g. a life-assurance policy or hire-purchase agreement, in which the seller sets out the conditions of the sale and the mutual liabilities of buyer and seller. The use of a very small type size and unintelligible jargon is often intended to obscure the buyer's legal rights and safeguards. This unfair practice has largely been remedied by the various acts that provide consumer protection. See also COOLING-OFF PERIOD 2.

---

small-scale *adj.* made or occurring on a small scale.

small talk *n.* light social conversation.

small-time *adj. colloq.* unimportant, petty.

smarm *–v. colloq.* **1** (often foll. by *down*) smooth, plaster flat (hair etc.). **2** be ingratiating. *–n. colloq.* obsequiousness. [dial.]

smarmy *adj.* (**-ier**, **-iest**) *colloq.* ingratiating. □ **smarmily** *adv.* **smarminess** *n.*

smart *–adj.* **1** well-groomed, neat. **2** brightly coloured, newly painted, etc. **3** stylish, fashionable. **4** (esp. *US*) clever, ingenious, quickwitted. **5** quick, brisk. **6** painfully severe; sharp, vigorous. *–v.* **1** feel or give pain. **2** rankle. **3** (foll. by *for*) suffer the consequences of. *–n.* sharp pain; stinging sensation. *–adv.* smartly. □ **smartish** *adj.* & *adv.* **smartly** *adv.* **smartness** *n.* [Old English]

smart alec *n.* (also **smart aleck**) *colloq.* conceited know-all.

♦ **smart card** *n.* plastic card similar to a credit card but having some memory and a microprocessor embedded within it. It is usu. used for obtaining cash from an automated teller machine, but can also be used as an identification card that gains the bearer access to a computer system, hotel room, office, etc.

---

smarten *v.* (usu. foll. by *up*) make or become smart.

♦ **smart money** *n.* money invested by people with expert knowledge, esp. those with inside information about a particular project or investment opportunity.

---

smash *–v.* **1** (often foll. by *up*) **a** break into pieces; shatter. **b** bring or come to sudden destruction, defeat, or disaster. **2** (foll. by *into*, *through*) move with great force. **3** (foll. by *in*) break with a crushing blow. **4** hit (a ball etc.) with great force, esp. downwards. *–n.* **1** act of smashing, collision. **2** sound of this. **3** (in full **smash hit**) very successful play, song, performer, etc. *–adv.* with a smash. [imitative]

smash-and-grab *n.* robbery in which a shop-window is smashed and goods seized.

smasher *n. colloq.* beautiful or pleasing person or thing.

smashing *adj. colloq.* excellent, wonderful.

smash-up *n.* violent collision.

smattering *n.* slight superficial knowledge of a language etc. [origin unknown]

SME *international vehicle registration* Suriname.

smear *–v.* **1** daub or mark with grease etc. **2** smudge. **3** defame. *–n.* **1** act of smearing. **2** *Med.* **a** material smeared on a microscopic slide etc. for examination. **b** specimen of this. □ **smeary** *adj.* [Old English]

smear test *n.* = CERVICAL SMEAR.

smell *–n.* **1** faculty of perceiving odours. **2** quality in substances that is perceived by this. **3** unpleasant odour. **4** act of inhaling to ascertain smell. *–v.* (*past* and *past part.* **smelt** or **smelled**) **1** perceive or examine by smell. **2** emit an odour; stink. **3** seem by smell to be (*smells sour*). **4** (foll. by *of*) **a** emit the odour of (*smells of fish*). **b** be suggestive of (*smells of dishonesty*). **5** perceive; detect (*smell a bargain*). **6** have or use a sense of smell. □ **smell a rat** suspect trickery etc. **smell out** detect by smell or investigation. [Old English]

smelling-salts *n.pl.* sharp-smelling substances sniffed to relieve faintness etc.

smelly *adj.* (**-ier**, **-iest**) having a strong or unpleasant smell. □ **smelliness** *n.*

smelt[1] *v.* **1** extract metal from (ore) by melting. **2** extract (metal) in this way. □ **smelter** *n.* [Low German or Dutch *smelten*]

smelt[2] *past* and *past part.* of SMELL.

smelt[3] *n.* (*pl.* same or **-s**) small edible green and silver fish. [Old English]

smidgen /ˈsmɪdʒ(ə)n/ *n.* (also **smidgin**) *colloq.* small bit or amount. [perhaps from *smitch* in the same sense]

smilax /ˈsmaɪlæks/ *n.* any of several climbing shrubs. [Greek, = bindweed]

smile *–v.* (**-ling**) **1** have or assume a happy, kind, or amused expression, with the corners of the mouth turned up. **2** express by smiling (*smiled a welcome*). **3** give (a smile) of a specified kind (*smiled a sardonic smile*). **4** (foll. by *on*, *upon*) favour (*fortune smiled on me*). *–n.* **1** act of smiling. **2** smiling expression or aspect. [perhaps from Scandinavian]

smirch *–v.* soil; discredit. *–n.* spot, stain. [origin unknown]

smirk *–n.* conceited or silly smile. *–v.* give a smirk. [Old English]

smite *v.* (**-ting**; *past* **smote**; *past part.* **smitten** /ˈsmɪt(ə)n/) **1** *archaic* or *literary* **a** hit. **b** chastise; defeat. **2** (in *passive*) affect strongly; seize (*smitten with regret*; *smitten by her beauty*). [Old English]

smith *n.* **1** blacksmith. **2** (esp. in *comb.*) worker in metal (*goldsmith*). **3** (esp. in *comb.*) craftsman (*wordsmith*). [Old English]

smithereens /ˌsmɪðəˈriːnz/ *n.pl.* small fragments. [dial. *smithers*]

smithy /ˈsmɪðɪ/ *n.* (*pl.* **-ies**) blacksmith's workshop, forge. [related to SMITH]

smitten *past part.* of SMITE.

SMMT *abbr.* Society of Motor Manufacturers and Traders Ltd.

smock *–n.* **1** loose shirtlike garment often ornamented with smocking. **2** loose overall. *–v.* adorn with smocking. [Old English]

smocking *n.* ornamental effect on cloth made by gathering it tightly with stitches.

smog *n.* smoke-laden fog. □ **smoggy** *adj.* (**-ier**, **-iest**). [portmanteau word]

smoke *–n.* **1** visible vapour from a burning substance. **2** act of smoking tobacco. **3** *colloq.* cigarette or cigar. *–v.* (**-king**) **1** **a** inhale and exhale the smoke of (a cigarette etc.). **b** do this habitually. **2** emit smoke or visible vapour. **3** darken or preserve with smoke (*smoked salmon*). □ **go up in smoke** *colloq.* come to nothing. **smoke out** **1** drive out by means of smoke. **2** drive out of hiding etc. [Old English]

smoke bomb *n.* bomb that emits dense smoke on exploding.

smoke-free *adj.* **1** free from smoke. **2** where smoking is not permitted.

smokeless *adj.* producing little or no smoke; free from smoke.

smokeless zone *n.* district where only smokeless fuel may be used.

smoker *n.* **1** person who habitually smokes. **2** compartment on a train where smoking is allowed.

smokescreen *n.* **1** cloud of smoke concealing (esp. military) operations. **2** ruse for disguising one's activities.

smokestack *n.* **1** chimney or funnel of a locomotive or steamer. **2** tall chimney.

♦ **smokestack industry** *n. colloq.* any of the traditional British industries, esp. heavy engineering, as opposed to modern industries, e.g. electronics.

---

smoky *adj.* (**-ier, -iest**) **1** emitting, filled with, or obscured by, smoke. **2** stained with or coloured like smoke. **3** having the flavour of smoked food. □ **smokiness** *n.*

smolder *US* var. of SMOULDER.

Smolensk /smə'lensk/ city in W Russia; industries include engineering, textiles, and the manufacture of consumer goods; pop. (est. 1995) 353 000.

smooch *colloq.* –*n.* **1** period of slow close dancing. **2** period of kissing and caressing. –*v.* engage in a smooch. □ **smoochy** *adj.* [imitative]

smooth /smu:ð/ –*adj.* **1** having an even surface; free from projections, dents, and roughness. **2** that can be traversed without check. **3** (of the sea etc.) calm, flat. **4** (of a journey etc.) easy. **5** not harsh in sound or taste. **6** suave, conciliatory; slick. **7** not jerky. –*v.* **1** (often foll. by *out, down*) make or become smooth. **2** (often foll. by *out, down, over, away*) reduce or get rid of (differences, faults, difficulties, etc.) in fact or appearance. –*n.* smoothing touch or stroke. –*adv.* smoothly. □ **smoothly** *adv.* **smoothness** *n.* [Old English]

smoothie /'smu:ðɪ/ *n. colloq.*, often *derog.* smooth person.

smooth-tongued *adj.* insincerely flattering.

smorgasbord /'smɔ:gəs,bɔ:d/ *n.* various esp. savoury dishes as hors d'œuvres or a buffet meal. [Swedish]

smote *past* of SMITE.

smother /'smʌðə(r)/ *v.* **1** suffocate, stifle. **2** (foll. by *in, with*) overwhelm or cover with (kisses, gifts, kindness, etc.). **3** extinguish (a fire) by covering it. **4 a** die of suffocation. **b** have difficulty breathing. **5** (often foll. by *up*) suppress or conceal. [Old English]

smoulder /'sməʊldə(r)/ (*US* **smolder**) –*v.* **1** burn slowly without flame or internally. **2** (of emotions) be fierce but suppressed. **3** (of a person) show silent emotion. –*n.* smouldering. [origin unknown]

♦ **SMP** *abbr.* = STATUTORY MATERNITY PAY.

SMRTB *abbr.* Ship and Marine Requirements Technology Board.

smudge –*n.* blurred or smeared line, mark, blot, etc. –*v.* (**-ging**) **1** make a smudge on or of. **2** become smeared or blurred. □ **smudgy** *adj.* [origin unknown]

smug *adj.* (**smugger, smuggest**) self-satisfied. □ **smugly** *adv.* **smugness** *n.* [Low German *smuk* pretty]

smuggle /'smʌg(ə)l/ *v.* (**-ling**) **1** (also *absol.*) import or export illegally, esp. without paying duties. **2** (foll. by *in, out*) convey secretly. □ **smuggler** *n.* **smuggling** *n.* [Low German]

smut –*n.* **1** small flake of soot etc. **2** spot or smudge made by this. **3** obscene talk, pictures, or stories. **4** fungous disease of cereals. –*v.* (**-tt-**) mark with smuts.□ **smutty** *adj.* (**-ier, -iest**). [origin unknown]

Smyrna see IZMIR.

SN –*abbr.* (also **S/N**) shipping note. –*international vehicle registration* Senegal. –*postcode* Swindon. –*airline flight code* Sabena World Airlines.

Sn *symb.* tin.

SNA *abbr. Computing* systems network architecture.

snack *n.* **1** light, casual, or hurried meal. **2** small amount of food eaten between meals. [Dutch]

snack bar *n.* place where snacks are sold.

snaffle /'snæf(ə)l/ –*n.* (in full **snaffle-bit**) simple bridle-bit without a curb. –*v.* (**-ling**) *colloq.* steal; seize. [Low German or Dutch perhaps from *snavel* beak]

snafu /snæ'fu:/ *slang* –*adj.* in utter confusion. –*n.* this state. [acronym of '*s*ituation *n*ormal: *a*ll *f*ouled (or *f*ucked) *u*p']

snag –*n.* **1** unexpected obstacle or drawback. **2** jagged projection. **3** tear in material etc. –*v.* (**-gg-**) catch or tear on a snag. [probably Scandinavian]

snail *n.* slow-moving gastropod mollusc with a spiral shell. [Old English]

snail's pace *n.* very slow movement.

snake –*n.* **1** long limbless reptile. **2** (also **snake in the grass**) traitor; secret enemy. **3** *hist.* European monetary system in which the exchange rate between the participants was restricted by a fluctuation limit of 2¼%. The participants were the Belgian franc, Danish krone, French franc, Irish punt, Dutch guilder, German Deutschmark, and Italian lira. Sterling did not participate in this arrangement, which was replaced in 1979 by the European Monetary System. –*v.* (**-king**) move or twist like a snake. [Old English]

snake-charmer *n.* person appearing to make snakes move by music etc.

snakes and ladders *n.pl.* (usu. treated as *sing.*) board-game with counters moved up 'ladders' and down 'snakes'.

snakeskin –*n.* skin of a snake. –*adj.* made of snakeskin.

snaky *adj.* **1** of or like a snake. **2** winding, sinuous. **3** cunning, treacherous.

snap –*v.* (**-pp-**) **1** break suddenly or with a cracking sound. **2** (cause to) emit a sudden sharp crack. **3** open or close with a snapping sound. **4** speak or say irritably. **5** (often foll. by *at*) make a sudden audible bite. **6** move quickly (*snap into action*). **7** photograph. –*n.* **1** act or sound of snapping. **2** crisp biscuit (*brandy snap*). **3** snapshot. **4** (in full **cold snap**) sudden brief spell of cold weather. **5 a** card-game in which players call 'snap' when two similar cards are exposed. **b** (as *int.*) on noticing an (often unexpected) similarity. **6** vigour, liveliness. –*adv.* with a snap (*heard it go snap*). –*adj.* done without forethought (*snap decision*). □ **snap out of** *slang* get rid of (a mood, etc.) by a sudden effort. **snap up** accept (an offer etc.) quickly or eagerly. [Low German or Dutch *snappen* seize]

snapdragon *n.* plant with a two-lipped flower.

snap-fastener *n.* = PRESS-STUD.

snapper *n.* any of several edible marine fish.

snappish *adj.* **1** curt; ill-tempered; sharp. **2** inclined to snap.

snappy *adj.* (**-ier, -iest**) *colloq.* **1** brisk, lively. **2** neat and elegant (*snappy dresser*). **3** snappish. □ **make it snappy** be quick. □ **snappily** *adv.*

snapshot *n.* casual or informal photograph.

snare /sneə(r)/ –*n.* **1** trap, esp. with a noose, for birds or animals. **2** trap, trick, or temptation. **3** (in *sing.* or *pl.*) twisted strings of gut, hide, or wire stretched across the lower head of a side-drum to produce a rattle. **4** (in full **snare drum**) drum fitted with snares. –*v.* (**-ring**) catch in a snare; trap. [Old Norse]

snarl[1] –*v.* **1** growl with bared teeth. **2** speak, say, or express angrily. –*n.* act or sound of snarling. [*snar* from Low German]

snarl[2] –*v.* (often foll. by *up*) twist; entangle; hamper the movement of (traffic etc.); become entangled or congested. –*n.* knot, tangle. [from SNARE]

snarl-up *n. colloq.* traffic jam; muddle.

snatch –*v.* **1** (often foll. by *away, from*) seize or remove quickly, eagerly, or unexpectedly. **2 a** steal (a handbag etc.) by grabbing. **b** *slang* kidnap. **3** secure with difficulty. **4** (foll. by *at*) **a** try to seize. **b** take (an offer etc.) eagerly. –*n.* **1** act of snatching. **2** fragment of a song or talk etc. **3** *US slang* kidnapping. **4** short spell of activity etc. [related to SNACK]

snazzy *adj.* (**-ier, -iest**) *slang* smart, stylish, showy. □ **snazzily** *adv.* **snazziness** *n.* [origin unknown]

SNB *abbr. Stock Exch.* etc. sellers no buyers.

SNCF *abbr.* French state railway authority or system. [French *Société Nationale des Chemins de Fer*]

sneak *–v.* **1** (foll. by *in, out, past, away*, etc.) go or convey furtively. **2** *slang* steal unobserved. **3** *slang* tell tales; turn informer. **4** (as **sneaking** *adj.*) **a** furtive (*sneaking affection*). **b** persistent and puzzling (*sneaking feeling*). *–n.* **1** mean-spirited underhand person. **2** *slang* tell-tale; informer. *–adj.* acting or done without warning; secret. □ **sneaky** *adj.* (**-ier, -iest**). [origin uncertain]

sneaker *n. slang* soft-soled canvas shoe.

sneak-thief *n.* thief who steals without breaking in.

Sneek /sneɪk/ market town and water-sports centre in the Netherlands, with the largest yachting harbour in the country; pop. (1987) 29 337.

sneer *–n.* contemptuous smile or remark. *–v.* **1** (often foll. by *at*) smile or speak derisively. **2** say with a sneer. □ **sneering** *adj.* **sneeringly** *adv.* [origin unknown]

sneeze *–n.* sudden loud involuntary expulsion of air from the nose and mouth caused by irritation of the nostrils. *–v.* (**-zing**) make a sneeze. □ **not to be sneezed at** *colloq.* worth having or considering. [Old English]

snick *–v.* **1** make a small notch or incision in. **2** *Cricket* deflect (the ball) slightly with the bat. *–n.* **1** small notch or cut. **2** *Cricket* slight deflection of the ball. [*snickersnee* long knife, ultimately from Dutch]

snicker *n.* & *v.* = SNIGGER. [imitative]

snide *adj.* sneering; slyly derogatory. [origin unknown]

SNIF *abbr. Finance* short-term note issuance facility.

sniff *–v.* **1** inhale air audibly through the nose. **2** (often foll. by *up*) draw in through the nose. **3** smell the scent of by sniffing. *–n.* **1** act or sound of sniffing. **2** amount of air etc. sniffed up. □ **sniff at** show contempt for. **sniff out** = *smell out.* [imitative]

sniffer *n.* person who sniffs, esp. a drug etc. (often in *comb.*: *glue-sniffer*).

sniffer-dog *n. colloq.* dog trained to sniff out drugs or explosives.

sniffle /ˈsnɪf(ə)l/ *–v.* (**-ling**) sniff slightly or repeatedly. *–n.* **1** act of sniffling. **2** (in *sing.* or *pl.*) cold in the head causing sniffling. [imitative: cf. SNIVEL]

sniffy *adj. colloq.* (**-ier, -iest**) disdainful. □ **sniffily** *adv.* **sniffiness** *n.*

snifter *n. slang* small alcoholic drink. [dial. *snift* sniff]

SNIG *abbr.* sustainable non-inflationary growth.

snigger *–n.* half-suppressed laugh. *–v.* utter this. [var. of SNICKER]

snip *–v.* (**-pp-**) (also *absol.*) cut with scissors etc., esp. in small quick strokes. *–n.* **1** act of snipping. **2** piece snipped off. **3** *slang* **a** something easily done. **b** bargain. [Low German or Dutch *snippen*]

snipe *–n.* (*pl.* same or **-s**) wading bird with a long straight bill. *–v.* (**-ping**) **1** fire shots from hiding, usu. at long range. **2** (often foll. by *at*) make a sly critical attack. □ **sniper** *n.* (in sense 1 of *v.*). [probably Scandinavian]

snippet /ˈsnɪpɪt/ *n.* **1** small piece cut off. **2** (usu. in *pl.*) **a** scrap of information etc. **b** short extract from a book etc.

snitch *slang –v.* **1** steal. **2** (often foll. by *on*) inform on a person. *–n.* informer. [origin unknown]

snivel /ˈsnɪv(ə)l/ *–v.* (**-ll-**; *US* **-l-**) **1** weep with sniffling. **2** run at the nose; sniffle. **3** show weak or tearful sentiment. *–n.* act of snivelling. [Old English]

snob *n.* person who despises those inferior in social position, wealth, intellect, taste, etc. (*intellectual snob*). □ **snobbery** *n.* **snobbish** *adj.* **snobby** *adj.* (**-ier, -iest**). [origin unknown]

SNOBOL /ˈsnəʊˌbɒl/ *n. Computing* programming language designed esp. for text manipulation.

snog *slang –v.* (**-gg-**) engage in kissing and caressing. *–n.* period of this. [origin unknown]

snood *n.* ornamental hairnet, worn usu. at the back of the head. [Old English]

snook *n. slang* contemptuous gesture with the thumb to the nose and the fingers spread. □ **cock a snook** (often foll. by *at*) **1** make this gesture. **2** register one's contempt. [origin unknown]

snooker *–n.* **1** game played on an oblong cloth-covered table with a cue-ball, 15 red, and 6 coloured balls. **2** position in this game in which a direct shot would lose points. *–v.* **1** (also *refl.*) subject (oneself or an opponent) to a snooker. **2** (esp. as **snookered** *adj.*) *slang* thwart, defeat. [origin unknown]

snoop *colloq. –v.* **1** pry into another's affairs. **2** (often foll. by *about, around*) investigate transgressions of rules, the law, etc. *–n.* act of snooping. □ **snooper** *n.* **snoopy** *adj.* [Dutch]

snooty *adj.* (**-ier, -iest**) *colloq.* supercilious; conceited; snobbish. □ **snootily** *adv.* [origin unknown]

snooze *colloq. –n.* short sleep, nap. *–v.* (**-zing**) take a snooze. [origin unknown]

snore *–n.* snorting or grunting sound of breathing during sleep. *–v.* (**-ring**) make this sound. [imitative]

snorkel /ˈsnɔːk(ə)l/ *–n.* **1** breathing-tube for an underwater swimmer. **2** device for supplying air to a submerged submarine. *–v.* (**-ll-**; *US* **-l-**) use a snorkel. [German *Schnorchel*]

snort *–n.* **1** explosive sound made esp. by horses by the sudden forcing of breath through the nose. **2** similar human sound showing contempt, incredulity, etc. **3** *colloq.* small drink of liquor. **4** *slang* inhaled dose of powdered cocaine etc. *–v.* **1** make a snort. **2** (also *absol.*) *slang* inhale (esp. cocaine). **3** express or utter with a snort. [imitative]

snot *n. slang* nasal mucus. [probably Low German or Dutch: related to SNOUT]

snotty *adj.* (**-ier, -iest**) *slang* **1** running or covered with nasal mucus. **2** snooty, contemptible. □ **snottily** *adv.* **snottiness** *n.*

snout *n.* **1** projecting nose and mouth of an animal. **2** *derog.* person's nose. **3** pointed front of a thing. [Low German or Dutch]

snow /snəʊ/ *–n.* **1** frozen atmospheric vapour falling to earth in light white flakes. **2** fall or layer of this. **3** thing resembling snow in whiteness or texture etc. **4** *slang* cocaine. *–v.* **1** (prec. by *it* as subject) snow falls (*it is snowing; if it snows*). **2** (foll. by *in, over, up*, etc.) confine or block with snow. □ **be snowed under** be overwhelmed, esp. with work. [Old English]

snowball *–n.* ball of compressed snow for throwing in play. *–v.* **1** throw or pelt with snowballs. **2** increase rapidly.

snowball-tree *n.* guelder rose.

snowberry *n.* (*pl.* **-ies**) shrub with white berries.

snow-blind *adj.* temporarily blinded by the glare from snow.

snowblower *n.* machine that clears snow by blowing.

snowbound *adj.* prevented by snow from going out or travelling.

snowcap *n.* snow-covered mountain peak. □ **snow-capped** *adj.*

snowdrift *n.* bank of snow heaped up by the wind.

snowdrop *n.* early spring plant with white drooping flowers.

snowfall *n.* **1** fall of snow. **2** amount of this.

snowflake *n.* each of the flakes in which snow falls.

snow goose *n.* white Arctic goose.

snowline *n.* level above which snow never melts entirely.

snowman *n.* human figure made of compressed snow.

snowmobile /ˈsnəʊməˌbiːl/ *n.* motor vehicle, esp. with runners or Caterpillar tracks, for travel over snow.

snowplough *n.* (*US* **snowplow**) device or vehicle for clearing roads of thick snow.

snowshoe *n.* racket-shaped attachment to a boot for walking on snow without sinking in.

snowstorm *n.* heavy fall of snow, esp. with a high wind.

snow white *adj.* & *n.* (as adj. often hyphenated) pure white.

snowy *adj.* (**-ier**, **-iest**) **1** of or like snow. **2** (of the weather etc.) with much snow.

snowy owl *n.* large white Arctic owl.

SNP *abbr.* Scottish National Party.

Snr. *abbr.* Senior.

snub *–v.* (**-bb-**) rebuff or humiliate with sharp words or coldness. *–n.* act of snubbing. *–adj.* short and blunt in shape. [Old Norse, = chide]

snub nose *n.* short turned-up nose. □ **snub-nosed** *adj.*

snuff[1] *–n.* charred part of a candle-wick. *–v.* trim the snuff from (a candle). □ **snuff it** *slang* die. **snuff out 1** extinguish (a candle flame). **2** put an end to (hopes etc.). [origin unknown]

snuff[2] *–n.* powdered tobacco or medicine taken by sniffing. *–v.* take snuff. [Dutch]

snuffbox *n.* small box for holding snuff.

snuffer *n.* device for snuffing or extinguishing a candle.

snuffle /'snʌf(ə)l/ *–v.* (**-ling**) **1** make sniffing sounds. **2** speak or say nasally or whiningly. **3** breathe noisily, esp. with a blocked nose. *–n.* snuffling sound or tone. □ **snuffly** *adj.* [Low German or Dutch *snuffelen*]

snug *–adj.* (**snugger**, **snuggest**) **1** cosy, comfortable, sheltered. **2** close-fitting. *–n.* small room in a pub. □ **snugly** *adv.* [probably Low German or Dutch]

snuggery *n.* (*pl.* **-ies**) snug place, den.

snuggle /'snʌg(ə)l/ *v.* (**-ling**) settle or draw into a warm comfortable position.

SO *–abbr.* **1** special order. **2** standing order. **3** Stationery Office. *–postcode* Southampton.

S/O *abbr.* shipowner.

so[1] /səʊ/ *–adv.* **1** to such an extent (*stop complaining so; so small as to be invisible; not so late as I expected*). **2** in this or that way; in the manner, position, or state described or implied (*place your feet so; am not cold but may become so*). **3** also (*he went and so did I*). **4** indeed, actually (*you said it was good, and so it is*). **5** very (*I am so glad*). **6** (with verbs of saying or thinking etc.) thus, this, that (*I think so; so he said*). *–conj.* (often foll. by *that*) **1** consequently (*was ill, so couldn't come*). **2** in order that (*came early so that I could see you*). **3** and then; as the next step (*so then I gave up; and so to bed*). **4** (introducing a question) then; after that (*so what did you do?*). □ **and so on** (or **forth**) **1** and others of the same kind. **2** and in other similar ways. **or so** approximately (*50 or so*). **so as to** in order to. **so be it** expression of acceptance or resignation. **so long!** *colloq.* goodbye. **so much 1** a certain amount (of). **2** nothing but (*so much nonsense*). **so much for** that is all that need be done or said about (a thing). **so so** *adj.* & *adv. colloq.* only moderately good or well. **so what?** *colloq.* that is not significant. [Old English]

so[2] var. of SOH.

s.o. *abbr.* **1** seller's option. **2** shipping order.

-so *comb. form* = -SOEVER.

soak *–v.* **1** make or become thoroughly wet through saturation. **2** (of rain etc.) drench. **3** (foll. by *in, up*) absorb (liquid, knowledge, etc.). **4** *refl.* (often foll. by *in*) steep (oneself) in a subject etc. **5** (foll. by *in, into, through*) (of liquid) go or penetrate by saturation. **6** *colloq.* extort money from. **7** *colloq.* drink heavily. *–n.* **1** act of soaking; prolonged spell in a bath. **2** *colloq.* hard drinker. [Old English]

soakaway *n.* pit into which liquids may flow and then percolate slowly into the subsoil.

soaking *adj.* (in full **soaking wet**) wet through.

so-and-so /'səʊən,səʊ/ *n.* (*pl.* **-so's**) **1** particular but unspecified person or thing. **2** *colloq.* objectionable person.

soap *–n.* **1** cleansing agent yielding lather when rubbed in water. **2** *colloq.* = SOAP OPERA. *–v.* apply soap to. [Old English]

soapbox *n.* makeshift stand for a speaker in the street etc.

soap flakes *n.pl.* thin flakes of soap for washing clothes etc.

soap opera *n.* broadcast drama serial with domestic themes (orig. sponsored in the US by soap manufacturers).

soap powder *n.* powdered soap, esp. with additives, for washing clothes etc.

soapstone *n.* steatite.

soapsuds *n.pl.* = SUDS.

soapwort *n.* plant with pink or white flowers, and leaves yielding a soapy substance.

soapy *adj.* (**-ier**, **-iest**) **1** of or like soap. **2** containing or smeared with soap. **3** unctuous, flattering. □ **soapily** *adv.* **soapiness** *n.*

soar *v.* **1** fly or rise high. **2** reach a high level or standard. **3** fly without flapping the wings or using power. [French *essorer*]

sob *–v.* (**-bb-**) **1** inhale convulsively, usu. with weeping. **2** utter with sobs. *–n.* act or sound of sobbing. [imitative]

sober *–adj.* (**soberer**, **soberest**) **1** not drunk. **2** not given to drink. **3** moderate, tranquil, sedate, serious. **4** not exaggerated. **5** (of a colour etc.) quiet; dull. *–v.* (often foll. by *down, up*) make or become sober. □ **soberly** *adv.* [French from Latin]

sobriety /sə'braɪɪtɪ/ *n.* being sober. [Latin: related to SOBER]

sobriquet /'səʊbrɪ,keɪ/ *n.* (also **soubriquet** /'su:-/) nickname. [French]

sob story *n. colloq.* story or explanation appealing for sympathy.

Soc. *abbr.* **1** Socialist. **2** Society.

so-called *adj.* commonly called, often incorrectly.

soccer /'sɒkə(r)/ *n.* Association football. [from *(As)soc(iation)*, -ER[1]]

sociable /'səʊʃəb(ə)l/ *adj.* liking company, gregarious; friendly. □ **sociability** /-'bɪlɪtɪ/ *n.* **sociably** *adv.* [Latin *socius* companion]

social /'səʊʃ(ə)l/ *–adj.* **1** of society or its organization, esp. of the relations of people or classes of people. **2** living in organized communities. **3** needing companionship; gregarious. *–n.* social gathering, esp. of a club. □ **socially** *adv.* [Latin: related to SOCIABLE]

♦ **social accounting** see SOCIAL RESPONSIBILITY REPORTING.

---

social climber *n.* person anxious to gain a higher social status.

social contract *n.* agreement between the state and population for mutual advantage.

social democracy *n.* political system favouring a mixed economy and democratic social change. □ **social democrat** *n.*

socialism *n.* **1** political and economic theory advocating state ownership and control of the means of production, distribution, and exchange. **2** social system based on this. □ **socialist** *n.* & *adj.* **socialistic** /-'lɪstɪk/ *adj.* [French: related to SOCIAL]

socialite /'səʊʃə,laɪt/ *n.* person moving in fashionable society.

socialize /'səʊʃə,laɪz/ *v.* (also **-ise**) (**-zing** or **-sing**) **1** mix socially. **2** make social. **3** organize on socialistic principles. □ **socialization** /-'zeɪʃ(ə)n/ *n.*

♦ **social overhead capital** *n.* = INFRASTRUCTURE 1b.

♦ **social responsibility reporting** *n.* reporting the costs and benefits of social accounting issues, i.e. issues regarding the impact of a company on society, which may include charitable donations, research funding, product safety, community involvement, employment of disadvantaged groups, and environmental issues, such as pollution control and energy conservation. A firm's social responsibility involves striking a balance between its profit-making goals and its responsibility to its local community and the wider community.

---

social science *n.* the study of society and social relationships. □ **social scientist** *n.*

♦ **social security** *n.* **1** government system for paying allowances to the sick and the unemployed, as well as maternity benefits and retirement pensions. Since 1988 in the UK this has been the responsibility of the Department of Social Security. **2** assistance provided by this system.

social services *n.pl.* welfare services provided by the state, esp. education, health, and housing.

social work *n.* professional or voluntary work with disadvantaged groups. □ **social worker** *n.*

♦ **societal marketing** *n.* **1** form of marketing that takes into consideration the long-term welfare of society rather than the individual needs of consumers. **2** marketing a social cause, as in an anti-apartheid campaign.

society /sə'saɪətɪ/ *n.* (*pl.* **-ies**) **1** organized and interdependent community. **2** system and organization of this. **3** aristocratic part of this; its members (*polite society; society would not approve*). **4** mixing with others; companionship, company. **5** club, association (*music society; building society*). □ **societal** *adj.* [Latin *societas*]

Society Islands group of islands in French Polynesia, divided into the Windward Islands (including Tahiti) and the Leeward Islands; products include copra, vanilla, phosphates, and mother-of-pearl; pop. (1988) 162 573.

Society of Friends *n.* pacifist Christian sect with no written creed or ordained ministers; Quakers.

Society of Jesus see JESUIT.

socio- *comb. form* of society or sociology (and) (*socio-economic*). [Latin: related to SOCIAL]

♦ **socio-economic grade** *n.* any of several grades used in classifying the population according to social and economic status. The system is based on the occupation of the head of the household and groups are designated by a letter. It was developed by Research Surveys Ltd. for the Institute of Practitioners in Advertising in 1962 for use in the national readership survey. See A[1] 6; B[1] 6; C1; C2 *n.* 1; D[1] 6; E[1] 3.

sociology /ˌsəʊsɪ'ɒlədʒɪ/ *n.* the study of society and social problems. □ **sociological** /-ə'lɒdʒɪk(ə)l/ *adj.* **sociologist** *n.* [French: related to SOCIAL]

sock[1] *n.* **1** knitted covering for the foot and lower leg. **2** insole. □ **pull one's socks up** *colloq.* make an effort to improve. **put a sock in it** *slang* be quiet. [Old English *socc* from Greek *sukkhos* slipper]

sock[2] *colloq.* –*v.* hit hard. –*n.* hard blow. □ **sock it to** attack or address (a person or people) vigorously. [origin unknown]

socket /'sɒkɪt/ *n.* hollow for something to fit into etc., esp. a device receiving an electric plug, light-bulb, etc. [Anglo-French]

Socotra /səʊ'kəʊtrə/ island belonging to Yemen in the Arabian Sea near the mouth of the Gulf of Aden; largely barren, it yields a few crops (including dates) and there is some livestock farming; capital, Tamridah.

Socratic /sə'krætɪk/ *adj.* of Socrates or his philosophy.

Socratic irony *n.* pose of ignorance to entice others into refutable statements.

Socratic method *n.* dialectic, procedure by question and answer.

sod[1] *n.* **1** turf, piece of turf. **2** surface of the ground. [Low German or Dutch]

sod[2] *coarse slang* –*n.* **1** unpleasant or awkward person or thing. **2** fellow (*lucky sod*). –*v.* (**-dd-**) **1** damn (*sod them!*). **2** (as **sodding** *adj.*) damned. □ **sod off** go away. [abbreviation of SODOMITE]

soda /'səʊdə/ *n.* **1** compound of sodium in common use. **2** (in full **soda water**) effervescent water used esp. with spirits etc. as a drink. [perhaps from Latin *sodanum* from Arabic]

soda bread *n.* bread leavened with baking-soda.

soda fountain *n.* **1** device supplying soda water. **2** shop or counter with this.

sodden /'sɒd(ə)n/ *adj.* **1** saturated; soaked through. **2** stupid or dull etc. with drunkenness. [archaic past part. of SEETHE]

sodium /'səʊdɪəm/ *n.* soft silver-white metallic element. [from SODA]

sodium bicarbonate *n.* white crystalline compound used in baking-powder.

sodium chloride *n.* common salt.

sodium hydroxide *n.* strongly alkaline compound used in soap etc.; caustic soda.

sodium lamp *n.* lamp using sodium vapour and giving a yellow light.

sodium nitrate *n.* white powdery compound used in fertilizers etc.

sodomite /'sɒdəˌmaɪt/ *n.* person who practises sodomy. [Greek: related to SODOMY]

sodomy /'sɒdəmɪ/ *n.* = BUGGERY. □ **sodomize** *v.* (also **-ise**) (**-zing** or **-sing**). [Latin from *Sodom*: Gen. 18,19]

Sod's Law *n.* = MURPHY'S LAW.

SOE *abbr.* state-owned enterprise.

soever /səʊ'evə(r)/ *adv. literary* of any kind; to any extent (*how great soever it may be*).

-soever *comb. form* of any kind; to any extent (*whatsoever, howsoever*).

sofa /'səʊfə/ *n.* long upholstered seat with a back and arms. [Arabic *shuffa*]

sofa bed *n.* sofa that can be converted into a bed.

Sofala see BEIRA.

SOFFEX /'sɒfeks/ *abbr.* Swiss Options and Financial Futures Exchange.

soffit /'sɒfɪt/ *n.* undersurface of an arch, lintel, etc. [French *soffite*, Italian *soffitta*]

Sofia /'səʊfɪə, sə'fiːə/ (also **Sophia**) capital of Bulgaria; there are engineering, textile, and food-processing industries; pop. (est. 1996) 1 116 823.

soft –*adj.* **1** not hard; easily cut or dented; malleable. **2** (of cloth etc.) smooth; fine; not rough. **3** (of wind etc.) mild, gentle. **4** (of water) low in mineral salts and lathering easily. **5** (of light or colour etc.) not brilliant or glaring. **6** (of sound) gentle, not loud. **7** (of a consonant) sibilant (as *c* in *ice*, *s* in *pleasure*). **8** (of an outline etc.) vague, blurred. **9** gentle, conciliatory. **10** compassionate, sympathetic. **11** feeble, half-witted, silly, sentimental. **12** *colloq.* (of a job etc.) easy. **13** (of drugs) not highly addictive. **14** (also **soft-core**) (of pornography) not highly obscene. **15** (of currency) likely to fall in value; not readily exchangeable into other currencies. –*adv.* softly. □ **be soft on** *colloq.* **1** be lenient towards. **2** be infatuated with. **have a soft spot for** be fond of. □ **softish** *adj.* **softly** *adv.* **softness** *n.* [Old English]

softball *n.* form of baseball using a softer and larger ball.

soft-boiled *adj.* (of an egg) boiled leaving the yolk soft.

soft-centred *adj.* **1** (of a sweet) having a soft centre. **2** soft-hearted; sentimental.

♦ **soft commodity** see COMMODITY 1.

♦ **soft currency** *n.* currency of a country that has a weak balance of payments and for which there is relatively little demand. Cf. HARD CURRENCY.

soft drink *n.* non-alcoholic drink.

soften /'sɒf(ə)n/ *v.* **1** make or become soft or softer. **2** (often foll. by *up*) **a** make weaker by preliminary attack. **b** make (a person) more receptive to persuasion. □ **softener** *n.*

soft fruit *n.* small stoneless fruit (a strawberry or currant).

soft furnishings *n.pl.* curtains, rugs, etc.

soft-hearted *adj.* tender, compassionate. □ **soft-heartedness** *n.*

softie *n.* (also **softy**) (*pl.* **-ies**) *colloq.* weak, silly, or soft-hearted person.

soft keyboard *n.* keyboard in which the meaning of each key, or of some of the keys, can be allocated and possibly changed by program control. Soft keyboards are frequently used on electronic point-of-sale terminals and in industrial data collection.

♦ **soft loan** *n.* loan with an artificially low rate of interest. Soft loans are sometimes made to developing nations by industrialized nations for political reasons.

softly-softly *adj.* (also **softly, softly**) (of strategy) cautious and cunning.
soft option *n.* easier alternative.
soft palate *n.* rear part of the palate.
soft pedal –*n.* piano pedal that softens the tone. –*v.* (**soft-pedal**) (**-ll-**; *US* **-l-**) refrain from emphasizing; be restrained.
soft roe see ROE[1].

♦ **soft sell** *n.* unobtrusive salesmanship based on implication rather than forceful statement and relentless repetition. Cf. HARD SELL.

soft soap –*n. colloq.* persuasive flattery. –*v.* (**soft-soap**) *colloq.* persuade with flattery.
soft-spoken *adj.* having a gentle voice.
soft target *n.* vulnerable person or thing.
soft touch *n. colloq.* gullible person, esp. over money.

♦ **software** *n.* programs used with a computer (together with their documentation), including program listings, program libraries, and user and programming manuals. See also APPLICATIONS SOFTWARE; SYSTEMS SOFTWARE. Cf. HARDWARE 3.

software engineering *n.* activities involved in the design and development of software. The aim is to produce programs that are reliable and efficient by following standards of quality and adhering to specifications, as is done in other engineering disciplines.
software house *n.* commercial organization whose main business is to produce software or assist in the production of software. Software houses may offer a range of services, including consultancy, the hiring out of suitably qualified personnel to work within a client's team, and a complete system design and development service.
software package *n.* = APPLICATION PACKAGE.
software tool *n.* one of a set of programs used in the development, repair, or enhancement of other programs. All the programs in the set have a common mode of use and employ files and other facilities in a well-defined standard way. A typical set of tools might consist of a text editor, compiler, link loader, and some form of debug tool.
softwood *n.* easily sawn wood of deciduous trees.
softy var. of SOFTIE.
soggy /'sɒgɪ/ *adj.* (**-ier, -iest**) sodden, saturated; too moist (*soggy bread*). □ **sogginess** *n.* [dial. *sog* marsh]
soh /səʊ/ *n.* (also **so**) *Mus.* fifth note of a major scale. [Latin *solve*, word arbitrarily taken]
soigné /'swɑːnjeɪ/ *adj.* (*fem.* ***soignée*** pronunc. same) well-groomed. [French]
soil[1] *n.* **1** upper layer of earth in which plants grow. **2** ground belonging to a nation; territory (*on French soil*). [Latin *solium* seat, *solum* ground]
soil[2] –*v.* **1** make dirty; smear or stain. **2** defile; discredit. –*n.* **1** dirty mark. **2** filth; refuse. [French *soill(i)er*]
soil pipe *n.* discharge-pipe of a lavatory.
soirée /'swɑːreɪ/ *n.* evening party, usu. for conversation or music. [French]
soixante-neuf /ˌswɑːsɑ̃t'nɜːf/ *n. slang* mutual oral stimulation of the genitals. [French, = sixty-nine]
sojourn /'sɒdʒ(ə)n/ –*n.* temporary stay. –*v.* stay temporarily. [French *sojorner*]
sol /sɒl/ *n.* standard monetary unit of Peru. [Spanish, = sun]
sola[1] /'səʊlə/ *n.* pithy-stemmed East Indian swamp plant. [Urdu]

♦ **sola**[2] /'səʊlə/ var. of SOLO *n.* 4.

solace /'sɒləs/ –*n.* comfort in sadness, disappointment, or tedium. –*v.* (**-cing**) give solace to. [Latin *solatium*]
solan /'səʊlən/ *n.* (in full **solan goose**) large gooselike gannet. [Old Norse]
solar /'səʊlə(r)/ *adj.* of or reckoned by the sun. [Latin *sol* sun]
solar battery *n.* (also **solar cell**) device converting solar radiation into electricity.
solar day *n.* interval between meridian transits of the sun.
solarium /sə'leərɪəm/ *n.* (*pl.* **-ria**) room with sun-lamps or a glass roof etc. [Latin: related to SOLAR]
solar panel *n.* panel that absorbs the sun's rays as an energy source.
solar plexus *n.* complex of nerves at the pit of the stomach.
solar system *n.* the sun and the celestial bodies whose motion it governs.
solar year *n.* time taken for the earth to travel once round the sun.
sola topi *n.* sun-helmet made from the pith of the sola plant.
sold *past* and *past part.* of SELL. *adj.* (foll. by *on*) *colloq.* enthusiastic about.
solder /'sɒldə(r), 'səʊ-/ –*n.* fusible alloy used to join metals or wires etc. –*v.* join with solder. [Latin: related to SOLID]
soldering iron *n.* heated tool for melting and applying solder.
soldier /'səʊldʒə(r)/ –*n.* **1** member of an army. **2** (in full **common soldier**) private or NCO in an army. **3** *colloq.* finger of bread for dipping into egg. –*v.* serve as a soldier. □ **soldier on** *colloq.* persevere doggedly. □ **soldierly** *adj.* [French *soulde*, originally = soldier's pay]
soldier of fortune *n.* mercenary.
soldiery *n.* soldiers, esp. of a specified character.

♦ **sold note** see CONTRACT NOTE.

sole[1] –*n.* **1** undersurface of the foot. **2** part of a shoe, sock, etc., under the foot, esp. other than the heel. **3** lower surface or base of a plough, golf-club head, etc. –*v.* (**-ling**) provide (a shoe etc.) with a sole. □ **-soled** *adj.* (in *comb.*). [Latin *solea* sandal]
sole[2] *n.* (*pl.* same or **-s**) flat-fish used as food. [Latin *solea* sandal, which the shape of fish resembles]
sole[3] *adj.* one and only; single, exclusive. [French from Latin *solus*]

♦ **sole agency** *n.* commercial agency that gives its holder exclusive rights to sell a product or service in a particular territory for a specified period.

solecism /'sɒlɪˌsɪz(ə)m/ *n.* **1** mistake of grammar or idiom. **2** offence against etiquette. □ **solecistic** /-'sɪstɪk/ *adj.* [Greek *soloikos* speaking incorrectly]
solely /'səʊllɪ/ *adv.* **1** alone (*solely responsible*). **2** only (*did it solely out of duty*).
solemn /'sɒləm/ *adj.* **1** serious and dignified. **2** formal. **3** awe-inspiring. **4** (of a person) serious or cheerless in manner. **5** grave, sober (*solemn promise*). □ **solemnly** *adv.* **solemness** *n.* [Latin *solemnis*]
solemnity /sə'lemnɪtɪ/ *n.* (*pl.* **-ies**) **1** being solemn. **2** rite, ceremony.
solemnize /'sɒləmˌnaɪz/ *v.* (also **-ise**) (**-zing** or **-sing**) **1** duly perform (esp. a marriage ceremony). **2** make solemn. □ **solemnization** /-'zeɪʃ(ə)n/ *n.*
solenoid /'səʊləˌnɔɪd/ *n.* cylindrical coil of wire acting as a magnet when carrying electric current. [French from Greek *sōlēn* tube]
sol-fa /'sɒlfɑː/ *n.* system of syllables representing musical notes. [*sol* var. of SOH, FA]
soli *pl.* of SOLO 1.
solicit /sə'lɪsɪt/ *v.* (**-t-**) **1** seek (esp. business) repeatedly or earnestly. **2** (also *absol.*) accost as a prostitute. □ **solicitation** /-'teɪʃ(ə)n/ *n.* [Latin *sollicitus* anxious]

solicitor *n.* lawyer qualified to advise clients and instruct barristers. [French: related to SOLICIT]

Solicitor-General *n.* (*pl.* **Solicitors-General**) law officer below the Attorney-General or the Lord Advocate.

♦ **solicitor's letter** *n.* letter written by a solicitor to a debtor who has failed to settle a debt. The letter usu. threatens to take the matter to court, unless payment is received by a specified date.

---

solicitous *adj.* **1** showing interest or concern. **2** (foll. by *to* + infin.) eager, anxious. □ **solicitously** *adv.* [Latin: related to SOLICIT]

solicitude *n.* being solicitous. [Latin: related to SOLICITOUS]

solid /'sɒlɪd/ *–adj.* (**-der**, **-dest**) **1** firm and stable in shape; not liquid or fluid. **2** of such material throughout, not hollow. **3** of the same substance throughout (*solid silver*). **4** sturdily built; not flimsy or slender. **5 a** three-dimensional. **b** of solids (*solid geometry*). **6 a** sound, reliable (*solid arguments*). **b** dependable (*solid friend*). **7** sound but unexciting (*solid piece of work*). **8** financially sound. **9** uninterrupted (*four solid hours*). **10** unanimous, undivided. **11** (of printing) without spaces. *–n.* **1** solid substance or body. **2** (in *pl.*) solid food. **3** *Geom.* three-dimensional body or magnitude. *–adv.* solidly (*jammed solid*). □ **solidly** *adv.* **solidness** *n.* [Latin *solidus*]

solidarity /,sɒlɪ'dærɪtɪ/ *n.* **1** unity, esp. political or in an industrial dispute. **2** mutual dependence. [French: related to SOLID]

solidify /sə'lɪdɪ,faɪ/ *v.* (**-ies**, **-ied**) make or become solid. □ **solidification** /-fɪ'keɪʃ(ə)n/ *n.*

solidity /sə'lɪdɪtɪ/ *n.* being solid; firmness.

solid-state *adj.* using the electronic properties of solids (e.g. a semiconductor) to replace those of valves.

solidus /'sɒlɪdəs/ *n.* (*pl.* **solidi** /-,daɪ/) oblique stroke (/). [Latin: related to SOLID]

soliloquy /sə'lɪləkwɪ/ *n.* (*pl.* **-quies**) **1** talking without or regardless of hearers, esp. in a play. **2** this part of a play. □ **soliloquist** *n.* **soliloquize** *v.* (also **-ise**) (**-zing** or **-sing**). [Latin *solus* alone, *loquor* speak]

solipsism /'sɒlɪp,sɪz(ə)m/ *n.* philosophical theory that the self is all that exists or can be known. □ **solipsist** *n.* [Latin *solus* alone, *ipse* self]

solitaire /,sɒlɪ'teə(r)/ *n.* **1** jewel set by itself. **2** ring etc. with this. **3** game for one player in which pegs etc. are removed from a board by jumping others over them. **4** *US* = PATIENCE 3. [French: see SOLITARY]

solitary /'sɒlɪtərɪ/ *–adj.* **1** living or being alone; not gregarious; lonely. **2** secluded. **3** single, sole. *–n.* (*pl.* **-ies**) **1** recluse. **2** *colloq.* = SOLITARY CONFINEMENT. □ **solitariness** *n.* [Latin *solitarius* from *solus* alone]

solitary confinement *n.* isolation in a separate cell.

solitude /'sɒlɪ,tjuːd/ *n.* **1** being solitary. **2** lonely place. [Latin *solitudo*: related to SOLITARY]

solo /'səʊləʊ/ *–n.* (*pl.* **-s**) **1** (*pl.* **-s** or **soli** /-lɪ/) musical piece or passage, or a dance, performed by one person. **2** thing done by one person, esp. an unaccompanied flight. **3** (in full **solo whist**) type of whist in which one player may oppose the others. **4** (also **sola**) single bill of exchange of which no other copies are in circulation. *–v.* (**-es**, **-ed**) perform a solo. *–adv.* unaccompanied, alone. [Italian from Latin: related to SOLE[3]]

soloist /'səʊləʊɪst/ *n.* performer of a solo, esp. in music.

Solomon's seal *n.* flowering plant with drooping green and white flowers. [*Solomon*, king of Israel]

solstice /'sɒlstɪs/ *n.* either of the times when the sun is furthest from the equator. [Latin *solstitium* 'the sun standing still']

soluble /'sɒljʊb(ə)l/ *adj.* **1** that can be dissolved, esp. in water. **2** solvable. □ **solubility** /-'bɪlɪtɪ/ *n.* [Latin *solvo solut-* release]

♦ **solus** /'səʊləs/ *adj.* (of an advertisement) in an isolated position on the page, poster, etc., so that it is separated from any competitive announcement. Cf. SEMI-SOLUS. [Latin, = alone]

♦ **solus site** *n.* retail outlet, e.g. a petrol station, that carries the products of only one company.

---

solute /'sɒljuːt/ *n.* dissolved substance.

solution /sə'luːʃ(ə)n/ *n.* **1** solving or means of solving a problem. **2 a** conversion of a solid or gas into a liquid by mixture with a liquid. **b** state resulting from this. **3** dissolving or being dissolved.

solve *v.* (**-ving**) answer, remove, or effectively deal with (a problem). □ **solvable** *adj.*

solvent *–adj.* **1** able to pay one's debts; not in debt. **2** able to dissolve or form a solution with something. *–n.* solvent liquid etc. □ **solvency** *n.* (in sense 2 of *adj.*).

som /sɔːm/ *n.* standard monetary unit of Kyrgyzstan.

somatic /sə'mætɪk/ *adj.* of the body, not of the mind. □ **somatically** *adv.* [Greek *sōma -mat-* body]

sombre /'sɒmbə(r)/ *adj.* (also *US* **somber**) dark, gloomy, dismal. □ **sombrely** *adv.* **sombreness** *n.* [Latin *sub ombra* under shade]

sombrero /sɒm'breərəʊ/ *n.* (*pl.* **-s**) broad-brimmed hat worn esp. in Latin America. [Spanish: related to SOMBRE]

some /sʌm/ *–adj.* **1** unspecified amount or number of (*some water*; *some apples*; *some of them*). **2** unknown or unspecified (*some day*; *some fool broke it*). **3** approximately (*some ten days*). **4** considerable (*went to some trouble*; *at some cost*). **5** (usu. stressed) **a** at least a modicum of (*have some consideration*). **b** such up to a point (*that is some help*). **c** *colloq.* remarkable (*I call that some story*). *–pron.* some people or things, some number or amount (*I have some already*). *–adv. colloq.* to some extent (*do it some more*). [Old English]

-some[1] *suffix* forming adjectives meaning: **1** producing (*fearsome*). **2** characterized by being (*gladsome*). **3** apt to (*tiresome*; *meddlesome*). **4** suitable for (*cuddlesome*). [Old English]

-some[2] *suffix* forming nouns from numerals, meaning 'a group of' (*foursome*). [Old English]

somebody *–pron.* some person. *–n.* (*pl.* **-ies**) important person.

someday *adv.* at some time in the future.

Solomon Islands /'sɒləmən/ country consisting of a group of islands in the S Pacific, SE of the Bismarck Archipelago. Timber products, fish and fish products, copra, palm oil, and cacao beans are the main exports. Discovered by the Spanish in 1568, the islands were divided between Britain and Germany in the late 19th century; the S islands became a British protectorate in 1893, to which others were added in 1898–1900. The Solomons achieved self-government in 1976 and full independence as a member state of the Commonwealth two years later, with the exception of the N part of the chain, which is now part of Papua New Guinea. Prime minister, Bartholomew Ulufa'alu; capital, Honiara.

languages	English (official), 120 Melanesian dialects
currency	dollar (SI$) of 100 cents
pop. (1996)	396 000
GNP (1994)	US$291M
literacy	62% (m); 45% (f)
life expectancy	69 (m); 74 (f)

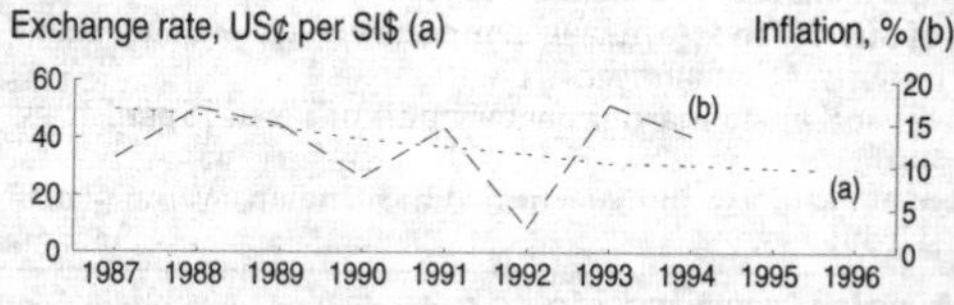

somehow *adv.* **1** for some reason or other (*somehow I don't trust him*). **2** in some way; by some means.

someone *n.* & *pron.* = SOMEBODY.

someplace *adv. US colloq.* = SOMEWHERE.

somersault /ˈsʌmə,sɒlt/ –*n.* leap or roll with the body turning through a circle. –*v.* perform this. [French *sobre* above, *saut* jump]

Somerset /ˈsʌmə,set/ county in SW England; pop. (est. 1994) 477 900; county town, Taunton. Dairy farming and cider-making are the main agricultural activities; industries include textiles, food processing, and tourism.

something *n.* & *pron.* **1** unspecified or unknown thing (*something has happened*). **2** unexpressed or intangible quantity, quality, or extent (*something strange about it*). **3** *colloq.* notable person or thing. □ **something else** *colloq.* something exceptional. **something like** approximately. **something of** to some extent (*something of an expert*). [Old English: related to SOME, THING]

sometime –*adv.* **1** at some time. **2** formerly. –*attrib. adj.* former.

sometimes *adv.* occasionally.

somewhat *adv.* to some extent.

somewhen *adv. colloq.* at some time.

somewhere –*adv.* in or to some place. –*pron.* some unspecified place.

somnambulism /sɒmˈnæmbjʊ,lɪz(ə)m/ *n.* sleepwalking. □ **somnambulant** *adj.* **somnambulist** *n.* [Latin *somnus* sleep, *ambulo* walk]

somnolent /ˈsɒmnələnt/ *adj.* **1** sleepy, drowsy. **2** inducing drowsiness. □ **somnolence** *n.* [Latin: related to SOMNAMBULISM]

♦ **Son** /sɑ̃/, **Masayoshi** (1957–) Japanese businessman, founder (1981) of Japan's largest software distributor, Softbank, which specializes in personal computer games. In partnership with Rupert Murdoch, Sony, and Fuji TV, he recently launched JSkyB, a Japanese satellite TV company. Son owns almost half the shares in Softbank.

---

son /sʌn/ *n.* **1** boy or man in relation to his parent(s). **2** male descendant. **3** (foll. by *of*) male member of a family, etc. **4** male descendent or inheritor of a quality etc. (*sons of freedom*). **5** form of address, esp. to a boy. [Old English]

sonar /ˈsəʊnɑː(r)/ *n.* **1** system for the underwater detection of objects by reflected sound. **2** apparatus for this. [*so*und *na*vigation and *r*anging]

sonata /səˈnɑːtə/ *n.* composition for one or two instruments, usu. in three or four movements. [Italian, = sounded]

sonatina /,sɒnəˈtiːnə/ *n.* simple or short sonata. [Italian, diminutive of SONATA]

son et lumière /,sɒneɪˈluːmjeə(r)/ *n.* entertainment by night at a historic building etc., using lighting effects and recorded sound to give a dramatic narrative of its history. [French, = sound and light]

song *n.* **1** words set to music or meant to be sung. **2** vocal music. **3** musical composition suggestive of a song. **4** cry of some birds. □ **for a song** *colloq.* very cheaply. [Old English: related to SING]

song and dance *n. colloq.* fuss, commotion.

songbird *n.* bird with a musical call.

songbook *n.* book of song lyrics and music.

song cycle *n.* set of linked songs.

songster *n.* (*fem.* **songstress**) **1** singer. **2** songbird.

song thrush *n.* common thrush, noted for singing.

songwriter *n.* writer of songs or the music for them.

sonic /ˈsɒnɪk/ *adj.* of or using sound or sound waves. [Latin *sonus* sound]

sonic bang *n.* (also **sonic boom**) noise made when an aircraft passes the speed of sound.

sonic barrier *n.* = SOUND BARRIER.

son-in-law *n.* (*pl.* **sons-in-law**) daughter's husband.

sonnet /ˈsɒnɪt/ *n.* poem of 14 lines with a fixed rhyme scheme and, in English, usu. ten syllables per line. [French *sonnet* or Italian *sonetto*]

sonny /ˈsʌnɪ/ *n. colloq.* familiar form of address to a young boy.

Sonora /səˈnɒrə/ state in NW Mexico; pop. (est. 1995) 2 083 630; capital, Hermosillo.

sonorous /ˈsɒnərəs/ *adj.* **1** having a loud, full, or deep sound; resonant. **2** (of language, style, etc.) imposing. □ **sonority** /səˈnɒrɪtɪ/ *n.* [Latin]

soon *adv.* **1** in a short time (*shall soon know*). **2** relatively early (*must you go so soon?*). **3** readily or willingly (*would sooner go; would as soon stay*). □ **as** (or **so**) **soon as** at the moment that; not later than; as early as (*came as soon as I could*). **sooner or later** at some future time; eventually. □ **soonish** *adv.* [Old English]

soot /sʊt/ *n.* black powdery deposit from smoke. [Old English]

sooth *n. archaic* truth. [Old English]

soothe /suːð/ *v.* (**-thing**) **1** calm (a person, feelings, etc). **2** soften or mitigate (pain etc.). [Old English]

soothsayer /ˈsuːθ,seɪə(r)/ *n.* seer, prophet.

sooty *adj.* (**-ier, -iest**) **1** covered with soot. **2** black or brownish-black.

SOP *abbr.* standard operating procedure.

sop –*n.* **1** thing given or done to pacify or bribe. **2** piece of bread etc. dipped in gravy etc. –*v.* (**-pp-**) **1** (as **sopping** *adj.*) drenched (*came home sopping; sopping wet clothes*). **2** (foll. by *up*) soak or mop up. [Old English]

Sophia see SOFIA.

sophism /ˈsɒfɪz(ə)m/ *n.* false argument, esp. one intended to deceive. [Greek *sophos* wise]

sophist /ˈsɒfɪst/ *n.* captious or clever but fallacious reasoner. □ **sophistic** /səˈfɪstɪk/ *adj.* [Greek: related to SOPHISM]

sophisticate /səˈfɪstɪkət/ *n.* sophisticated person. [medieval Latin: related to SOPHISM]

sophisticated /səˈfɪstɪ,keɪtɪd/ *adj.* **1** (of a person) worldly-wise; cultured; elegant. **2** (of a thing, idea, etc.) highly developed and complex. □ **sophistication** /-ˈkeɪʃ(ə)n/ *n.*

Somalia /səˈmɑːlɪə/ (officially **Somali Democratic Republic**) country in NE Africa, with a coastline on the Indian Ocean. The economy is largely agricultural, dependent on nomadic stock-raising and (in the S) some irrigated plantation-farming. Livestock, skins, hides, and bananas are the main exports. Other crops include sugar, maize, and sorghum. Mineral resources are limited, but there is some mining of tin, iron ore, uranium, and gypsum. Fishing is a developing industry and contributes to export earnings. *History.* The modern Somali Democratic Republic (which became an independent member of the United Nations in 1960) is a result of the unification of the former British Somaliland and Italian Somalia. Since independence, Somalia has been involved in border disputes with Kenya and Ethiopia, the latter leading to Somali invasion of the Ogaden (1977–8). Civil war broke out in Somalia in 1988 and has continued, with many casualties and widespread starvation. In 1991 the former president Siad Barré was overthrown in a military coup; this was followed by fierce fighting between rival factions and led to UN intervention in 1992. In 1993 the warring factions agreed to a ceasefire and the formation of a transitional government, to be monitored by a large UN peacekeeping force. The UN force withdrew in 1994–5 and civil war resumed. President, Hussein Aideed; capital, Mogadishu. □ **Somali** *n.* & *adj.*

languages	Somali, Arabic (official), Italian, English
currency	shilling (So.Sh.) of 100 cents
pop. (1996)	6 802 000
GNP (1990)	US$946M
literacy	42% (m); 14% (f)
life expectancy	54 (m); 55 (f)

sophistry /ˈsɒfɪstrɪ/ *n.* (*pl.* **-ies**) **1** use of sophisms. **2** a sophism.

sophomore /ˈsɒfəˌmɔː(r)/ *n. US* second-year university or high-school student. [*sophum*, obsolete var. of SOPHISM]

soporific /ˌsɒpəˈrɪfɪk/ *–adj.* inducing sleep. *–n.* soporific drug or influence. □ **soporifically** *adv.* [Latin *sopor* sleep]

sopping see SOP.

soppy *adj.* (**-ier, -iest**) *colloq.* mawkishly sentimental; silly; infatuated. □ **soppily** *adv.* **soppiness** *n.* [from SOP]

soprano /səˈprɑːnəʊ/ *n.* (*pl.* **-s**) **1 a** highest singing-voice. **b** female or boy singer with this voice. **2** instrument of a high or the highest pitch in its family. [Italian *sopra* above]

S.o.R. *abbr.* (also **SOR**) sale or return.

sorbet /ˈsɔːbeɪ/ *n.* **1** water-ice. **2** sherbet. [Arabic *sharba* to drink]

sorcerer /ˈsɔːsərə(r)/ *n.* (*fem.* **sorceress**) magician, wizard. □ **sorcery** *n.* (*pl.* **-ies**). [French *sourcier*: related to SORT]

sordid /ˈsɔːdɪd/ *adj.* **1** dirty, squalid. **2** ignoble, mercenary. □ **sordidly** *adv.* **sordidness** *n.* [Latin *sordidus*]

sore *–adj.* **1** (of a part of the body) painful. **2** suffering pain. **3** aggrieved, vexed. **4** *archaic* grievous or severe (*in sore need*). *–n.* **1** inflamed place on the skin or flesh. **2** source of distress or annoyance. *–adv. archaic* grievously, severely. □ **soreness** *n.* [Old English]

sorely *adv.* extremely (*sorely tempted*; *sorely vexed*).

sore point *n.* subject causing distress or annoyance.

sorghum /ˈsɔːgəm/ *n.* tropical cereal grass. [Italian *sorgo*]

sorority /səˈrɒrɪtɪ/ *n.* (*pl.* **-ies**) *US* female students' society in a university or college. [Latin *soror* sister]

sorrel[1] /ˈsɒr(ə)l/ *n.* sour-leaved herb. [Germanic: related to SOUR]

sorrel[2] /ˈsɒr(ə)l/ *–adj.* of a light reddish-brown colour. *–n.* **1** this colour. **2** sorrel animal, esp. a horse. [French]

Sorrento /səˈrentəʊ/ seaport and resort in central Italy, on a peninsula facing the Bay of Naples; pop. (1990) 17 500.

sorrow /ˈsɒrəʊ/ *–n.* **1** mental distress caused by loss or disappointment etc. **2** cause of sorrow. *–v.* feel sorrow, mourn. [Old English]

sorrowful *adj.* feeling, causing, or showing sorrow. □ **sorrowfully** *adv.*

sorry /ˈsɒrɪ/ *–adj.* (**-ier, -iest**) **1** pained, regretful, penitent (*sorry about the mess*). **2** (foll. by *for*) feeling pity or sympathy for. **3** (*attrib.*) wretched (*a sorry sight*). *–int.* expression of apology. □ **sorry for oneself** dejected. [Old English: related to SORE]

sort *–n.* **1** group of similar things etc.; class or kind. **2** *colloq.* person of a specified kind (*a good sort*). **3** *Computing* process of rearranging information into a desired (e.g. alphabetical) order, achieved by means of **sort keys** that are associated with each record of information. *–v.* (often foll. by *out, over*) arrange systematically; put in order. □ **of a sort** (or **of sorts**) *colloq.* barely deserving the name (*a holiday of sorts*). **out of sorts** slightly unwell; in low spirits. **sort of** *colloq.* as it were; to some extent. **sort out 1** separate into sorts. **2** select from a varied group. **3** disentangle or put into order. **4** solve. **5** *colloq.* deal with or reprimand. [Latin *sors sort-* lot]

sortie /ˈsɔːtɪ/ *–n.* **1** sally, esp. from a besieged garrison. **2** operational military flight. *–v.* (**-ties, -tied, -tieing**) make a sortie. [French]

SOS /ˌesəʊˈes/ *n.* (*pl.* **SOSs**) **1** international code-signal of extreme distress. **2** urgent appeal for help. [letters easily recognized in Morse]

So.Sh. *symb.* Somali shilling.

Sosnowiec /sɒsˈnɒvjets/ city in S Poland, centre of a coalmining region; industries include metallurgy, engineering, chemicals, and textiles; pop. (est. 1995) 248 900.

sostenuto /ˌsɒstəˈnuːtəʊ/ *Mus. –adv.* & *adj.* in a sustained or prolonged manner. *–n.* (*pl.* **-s**) passage to be played in this way. [Italian]

sot *n.* habitual drunkard. □ **sottish** *adj.* [Old English]

sotto voce /ˌsɒtəʊ ˈvəʊtʃɪ/ *adv.* in an undertone. [Italian]

sou /suː/ *n.* **1** *colloq.* very small sum of money. **2** *hist.* former French coin of low value. [French from Latin: related to SOLID]

soubrette /suːˈbret/ *n.* **1** pert maidservant etc. in a comedy. **2** actress taking this part. [French]

soubriquet var. of SOBRIQUET.

soufflé /ˈsuːfleɪ/ *n.* light spongy sweet or savoury dish usu. made with stiffly beaten egg-whites and gelatine. [French, = blown]

sough /saʊ, sʌf/ *–v.* moan or whisper like the wind in trees etc. *–n.* this sound. [Old English]

sought *past* and *past part.* of SEEK.

sought-after *adj.* generally desired.

souk /suːk/ *n.* market-place in Muslim countries. [Arabic]

soul /səʊl/ *n.* **1** spiritual or immaterial part of a person, often regarded as immortal. **2** moral, emotional, or intellectual nature of a person. **3** personification or pattern (*the very soul of discretion*). **4** an individual (*not a soul in sight*). **5** person regarded with familiarity or pity etc. (*the poor soul*; *a good soul*). **6** person regarded as an animating or essential part (*life and soul*). **7** energy or intensity, esp. in a work of art. **8** = SOUL MUSIC. □ **upon my soul** exclamation of surprise. [Old English]

soul-destroying *adj.* (of an activity etc.) tedious, monotonous.

soul food *n.* traditional food of American Blacks.

soulful *adj.* having, expressing, or evoking deep feeling. □ **soulfully** *adv.*

soulless *adj.* **1** lacking sensitivity or noble qualities. **2** undistinguished or uninteresting.

soul mate *n.* person ideally suited to another.

soul music *n.* Black American music with rhythm and blues, gospel, and rock elements.

soul-searching *n.* introspection.

sound[1] *–n.* **1** sensation caused in the ear by the vibration of the surrounding air or other medium. **2** vibrations causing this sensation. **3** what is or may be heard. **4** idea or impression conveyed by words (*don't like the sound of that*). **5** mere words. *–v.* **1** (cause to) emit sound. **2** utter, pronounce (*sound a warning note*). **3** convey an impression when heard (*sounds worried*). **4** give an audible signal for (an alarm etc.). **5** test (the lungs etc.) by the sound produced. □ **sound off** talk loudly or express one's opinions forcefully. □ **soundless** *adj.* [Latin *sonus*]

sound[2] *–adj.* **1** healthy; not diseased, injured, or rotten. **2** (of an opinion, policy, etc.) correct, well-founded. **3** financially secure. **4** undisturbed (*sound sleeper*). **5** thorough (*sound thrashing*). *–adv.* soundly (*sound asleep*). □ **soundly** *adv.* **soundness** *n.* [Old English]

sound[3] *v.* **1** test the depth or quality of the bottom of (the sea or a river etc.). **2** (often foll. by *out*) inquire (esp. discreetly) into the opinions or feelings of (a person). [French *sonder* from Latin *sub unda* under the wave]

sound[4] *n.* strait (of water). [Old English, = swimming]

sound barrier *n.* high resistance of air to objects moving at speeds near that of sound.

sound bite *n.* short pithy extract from an interview, speech, etc., as part of a news etc. broadcast.

soundbox *n.* the hollow body of a stringed musical instrument, providing resonance.

sound effect *n.* sound other than speech or music made artificially for a film, broadcast, etc.

sounding *n.* **1** measurement of the depth of water. **2** (in *pl.*) region close enough to the shore for sounding. **3** (in *pl.*) cautious investigation.

sounding-balloon *n.* balloon used to obtain information about the upper atmosphere.

sounding-board *n.* **1 a** person etc. used to test opinion. **b** means of disseminating opinions etc. **2** canopy directing sound towards an audience.

ounding-line *n.* line used in sounding.

ounding-rod *n.* rod used in sounding water in a ship's hold.

oundproof –*adj.* impervious to sound. –*v.* make soundproof.

ound system *n.* equipment for sound reproduction.

oundtrack *n.* **1** the sound element of a film or video. **2** recording of this made available separately. **3** any single track in a multi-track recording.

ound wave *n.* wave of compression and rarefaction, by which sound is transmitted in the air etc.

oup /suːp/ –*n.* liquid food made by boiling meat, fish, or vegetables. –*v.* (usu. foll. by *up*) *colloq.* **1** increase the power of (an engine). **2** enliven (*a souped-up version of the original*). □ **in the soup** *colloq.* in difficulties. [French]

oupçon /ˈsuːpsɔ̃/ *n.* small quantity; trace. [French: related to SUSPICION]

oup-kitchen *n.* place dispensing soup etc. to the poor.

oup-plate *n.* deep wide-rimmed plate.

oup-spoon *n.* large round-bowled spoon.

oupy *adj.* (**-ier, -iest**) **1** like soup. **2** sentimental.

our –*adj.* **1** acid in taste or smell, esp. because unripe or fermented. **2** morose; bitter. **3** (of a thing) unpleasant; distasteful. **4** (of the soil) dank. –*v.* make or become sour. □ **go** (or **turn) sour 1** turn out badly. **2** lose one's keenness. □ **sourly** *adv.* **sourness** *n.* [Old English]

ource /sɔːs/ *n.* **1** place from which a river or stream issues. **2** place of origination. **3** person or document etc. providing information. □ **at source** at the point of origin or issue. [French: related to SURGE]

♦ **source and application** (or **disposition**) **of funds** *n.* statement showing how an organization has raised finance for a specified period and how that finance has been applied. Sources of funds are typically trading profits, issues of shares or loan stock, sales of fixed assets, and borrowings. Applications are typically trading losses, purchases of fixed assets, dividends paid, and repayment of borrowings. Any balancing figure represents an increase or decrease in working capital.

sour grapes *n.pl.* resentful disparagement of something one covets.

sourpuss *n.* *colloq.* sour-tempered person.

souse /saʊs/ –*v.* (**-sing**) **1** immerse in pickle or other liquid. **2** (as **soused** *adj.*) *colloq.* drunk. **3** (usu. foll. by *in*) soak (a thing) in liquid. –*n.* **1 a** pickle made with salt. **b** *US* food in pickle. **2** plunge or drench in water. [French *sous*]

Sousse /suːs/ port and resort on the E coast of Tunisia; sardine fishing is important, and manufactured products include canned sardines and olive oil; pop. (1994) 125 000.

soutane /suːˈtɑːn/ *n.* cassock worn by a Roman Catholic priest. [French from Italian *sotto* under]

south –*n.* **1** point of the horizon 90° clockwise from east. **2** compass point corresponding to this. **3** direction in which this lies. **4** (usu. **the South**) part of the world, a country, or a town to the south. –*adj.* **1** towards, at, near, or facing the south. **2** from the south (*south wind*). –*adv.* **1** towards, at, or near the south. **2** (foll. by *of*) further south than. □ **to the south** (often foll. by *of*) in a southerly direction. [Old English]

South America the S half of the American land mass, connected to North America by the Isthmus of Panama, bordered by the Atlantic Ocean to the E and the Pacific Ocean to the W. Colonized largely by the Spanish in the 16th century, much of the continent remained part of Spain's overseas empire until the 1820s. Both culturally and ethnically the continent is now a mixture of native Indian and imported Hispanic influences, modified slightly by European and North American penetration in the 19th and 20th centuries. Although many South American countries are still hampered by economic underdevelopment and political instability, a minority have emerged as world industrial powers in their own right. □ **South American** *adj.* & *n.*

Southampton /saʊθˈhæmpt(ə)n/ industrial city and seaport on the S coast of England, in Hampshire; an important passenger port, it has marine-engineering and boatbuilding industries, and there is a major oil refinery at nearby Fawley; pop. (est. 1994) 211 700.

South Australia state in S central Australia; pop. (est. 1996) 1 477 700; capital, Adelaide. Agriculture produces wheat, barley, vegetables, sheep, grapes, and wine. There are deposits of iron ore, coal, natural gas, and opals, and industries include textiles, chemicals, and iron and steel.

southbound *adj.* travelling or leading southwards.

South Carolina /ˌkærəˈlaɪnə/ state in the SE US, on the

South Africa, Republic of country occupying the southernmost part of the continent of Africa. South Africa is the dominant economic power in this half of the continent, with rich deposits of gold and diamonds (the principal exports), coal, copper, iron ore, chrome, manganese, platinum, uranium, phosphates, and other minerals. Agricultural products include fruit, sugar cane, cotton, maize, wheat, peanuts, wine, meat, and wool, many of which are exported. Forestry and fishing are also important, and manufacturing industry is well developed (esp. around Pretoria, Johannesburg, and the ports), producing chemicals, pharmaceuticals, machinery, processed food, metal products, transport equipment, and textiles. Economic sanctions imposed by the US in 1985 were lifted in 1991, and the EC's trade embargo (imposed in 1986) in 1992.

History. Settled by the Dutch in the 17th century, the Cape area later came under British occupation, leading to inland expansion, the subjugation of the native population, and finally war between the British and the Boer (Dutch) settlers at the end of the 19th century. The defeated Boer republics of the Transvaal and the Orange Free State were annexed as British Crown Colonies in 1902, but joined with the colonies of Natal and the Cape to form the self-governing Union of South Africa in 1910. In 1960–1 South Africa became a republic and left the Commonwealth, partly as a result of international criticism of the country's policy of White minority rule (apartheid). Bantu homelands for the Black populations were granted limited self-government from 1963 (see HOMELAND 2). Internal opposition to apartheid led to widespread rioting and the declaration of a state of emergency in 1985, and external pressure continued in the form of economic and other sanctions. A number of reforms were instituted in 1990, leading to the effective abolition of apartheid in 1991 and talks between the government and leaders of the ANC and other Black groups. Multiracial elections held in 1994 resulted in victory for the ANC. President, Nelson Mandela; administrative capital, Pretoria; legislative capital, Cape Town. □ **South African** *adj.* & *n.*

languages	Afrikaans, English, Ndebele, Pedi, Sotho, Swazi, Tsonga, Tswana, Venda, Xhosa, Zulu (official)
currency	rand (R) of 100 cents
pop. (1996)	41 743 000
GNP (1994)	US$119B
literacy	82%
life expectancy	62 (m); 68 (f)

Exchange rate, US¢ per R (a) — Inflation, % (b)

60 / 40 / 20 / 0 — 20 / 15 / 10 / 5 / 0

(a) (b)

1987 1988 1989 1990 1991 1992 1993 1994 1995 1996

Atlantic coast; pop. (est. 1996) 3 698 746; capital, Columbia. Cotton and timber are grown, supplying the textile and furniture industries; other manufactures include chemicals and machinery.

South China Sea section of the Pacific Ocean bounded by the E Vietnamese coast, Taiwan, the Philippines, and Borneo.

South Dakota /dəˈkəʊtə/ state in the N central US; pop. (est. 1996) 732 405; capital, Pierre. It is primarily agricultural, producing livestock, and is also the site of the largest gold mine in the US.

South-East *n.* part of a country or town to the south-east.

south-east *–n.* **1** point of the horizon midway between south and east. **2** direction in which this lies. *–adj.* of, towards, or coming from the south-east. *–adv.* towards, at, or near the south-east.

southeaster /saʊθˈiːstə(r)/ *n.* south-east wind.

south-easterly *adj.* & *adv.* = SOUTH-EAST.

south-eastern *adj.* on the south-east side.

Southend-on-Sea /saʊθˌendɒnˈsiː/ resort town in SE England, in Essex on the Thames estuary; pop. (est. 1994) 167 500.

southerly /ˈsʌðəlɪ/ *–adj.* & *adv.* **1** in a southern position or direction. **2** (of a wind) from the south. *–n.* (*pl.* **-ies**) such a wind.

southern /ˈsʌð(ə)n/ *adj.* of or in the south. □ **southernmost** *adj.*

Southern Cross *n.* southern constellation in the shape of a cross.

southerner *n.* native or inhabitant of the south.

Southern hemisphere *n.* the half of the earth south of the equator.

southern lights *n.pl.* aurora australis.

Southern Ocean (also **Antarctic Ocean**) the body of water surrounding the continent of Antarctica.

Southern Rhodesia see ZIMBABWE.

South Glamorgan /gləˈmɔːgən/ former county in S Wales; its county town was Cardiff. In 1996 it was replaced by two new unitary authorities, the county of Cardiff and the county borough of Vale of Glamorgan.

southpaw *colloq. –n.* left-handed person, esp. in boxing. *–adj.* left-handed.

south pole see POLE[2] 1.

South Sea (also **Seas**) southern Pacific Ocean.

south-south-east *n.* point or direction midway between south and south-east.

south-south-west *n.* point or direction midway between south and south-west.

southward /ˈsaʊθwəd/ *–adj.* & *adv.* (also **southwards**) towards the south. *–n.* southward direction or region.

South-West *n.* part of a country or town to the south-west.

south-west *–n.* **1** point of the horizon midway between south and west. **2** direction in which this lies. *–adj.* of, towards, or coming from the south-west. *–adv.* towards, at, or near the south-west.

southwester /saʊθˈwestə(r)/ *n.* south-west wind.

south-westerly *adj.* & *adv.* = SOUTH-WEST.

south-western *adj.* on the south-west side.

South Yorkshire metropolitan county of N England; pop. (est. 1994) 1 305 400. Since 1986 administrative powers have rested with the districts of Sheffield, Rotherham, Doncaster, and Barnsley. Agricultural activities include sheep, dairy, and arable farming; coal is mined, and there are engineering and iron and steel industries.

souvenir /ˌsuːvəˈnɪə(r)/ *n.* memento of an occasion, place, etc. [French]

sou'wester /saʊˈwestə(r)/ *n.* **1** waterproof hat with a broad flap covering the neck. **2** south-west wind. [from SOUTHWESTER]

sovereign /ˈsɒvrɪn/ *–n.* **1** supreme ruler, esp. a monarch. **2** *hist.* British gold coin nominally worth £1. *–adj.* **1** supreme (*sovereign power*). **2** self-governing (*sovereign state*). **3** royal (*our sovereign lord*). **4** excellent; effective (*sovereign remedy*). **5** unmitigated (*sovereign contempt*). [French *so(u)verain*: *-g-* by association with *reign*]

sovereignty *n.* (*pl.* **-ies**) **1** supremacy. **2 a** self-government. **b** self-governing state.

Soviet /ˈsəʊvɪət, ˈsɒ-/ *–adj.* of the former USSR or its people. *–n.* **1** citizen of the former USSR. **2** (**soviet**) elected council in the former USSR. **3** *hist.* revolutionary council of workers, peasants, etc. [Russian]

Soviet Union see UNION OF SOVIET SOCIALIST REPUBLICS.

sow[1] /səʊ/ *v.* (*past* **sowed**; *past part.* **sown** or **sowed**) **1** (also *absol.*) **a** scatter (seed) on or in the earth. **b** (often foll. by *with*) plant with seed. **2** initiate (*sow hatred*). □ **sow one's wild oats** indulge in youthful excess or promiscuity. [Old English]

sow[2] /saʊ/ *n.* adult female pig. [Old English]

Soweto /səˈweɪtəʊ/ large predominantly Black urban area in South Africa, SW of Johannesburg, comprising 36 townships; pop. (1991) 596 632. It was the scene of rioting and violence in 1976 and 1985.

soy *n.* **1** (in full **soy sauce**) sauce from pickled soya beans. **2** (in full **soy bean**) = SOYA 1. [Japanese]

soya /ˈsɔɪə/ *n.* **1** (in full **soya bean**) **a** leguminous plant yielding edible oil and flour and used to replace animal protein. **b** seed of this. **2** (in full **soya sauce**) = SOY 1. [Malay: related to SOY]

sozzled /ˈsɒz(ə)ld/ *adj. colloq.* very drunk. [dial. *sozzle* mix sloppily, imitative]

SP *–abbr.* supra protest (see ACCEPTANCE SUPRA PROTEST). *–international civil aircraft marking* Poland. *–postcode* Salisbury.

SpA *abbr.* (Italian) società per azioni (= public limited company).

spa /spɑː/ *n.* **1** curative mineral spring. **2** resort with this. [*Spa* in Belgium]

space *–n.* **1 a** continuous expanse in which things exist and move. **b** amount of this taken by a thing or available. **2** interval between points or objects. **3** empty area (*make a space*). **4 a** outdoor urban recreation area (*open space*). **b** large unoccupied region (*wide open spaces*). **5** = OUTER SPACE. **6** interval of time (*in the space of an hour*). **7** amount of paper used in writing, available for advertising, etc. **8 a** blank between printed, typed, or written words, etc. **b** piece of metal providing this. **9** freedom to think, be oneself, etc. (*need my own space*). *–v.* (**-cing**) **1** set or arrange at intervals. **2** put spaces between. **3** (as **spaced** *adj.*) (often foll. by *out*) *slang* euphoric, esp. from taking drugs. □ **space out** spread out (more) widely. □ **spacer** *n.* [Latin *spatium*]

space age *–n.* era of space travel. *–attrib. adj.* (**space-age**) very modern.

spacecraft *n.* vehicle for travelling in outer space.

Space Invaders *n.pl.* (usu. treated as *sing.*) computer game in which players combat aliens.

spaceman *n.* (*fem.* **spacewoman**) astronaut.

space-saving *adj.* occupying little space or helping to save space.

spaceship *n.* spacecraft.

space shuttle *n.* spacecraft for repeated use, esp. between the earth and a space station.

space station *n.* artificial satellite as a base for operations in outer space.

spacesuit *n.* sealed pressurized suit for an astronaut in outer space.

space-time *n.* fusion of the concepts of space and time as a four-dimensional continuum.

spacious /ˈspeɪʃəs/ *adj.* having ample space; roomy. □ **spaciously** *adv.* **spaciousness** *n.* [Latin: related to SPACE]

spade[1] *n.* long-handled digging tool with a broad sharp-edged metal blade. □ **call a spade a spade** speak bluntly. □ **spadeful** *n.* (*pl.* **-s**). [Old English]

spade[2] *n.* **1 a** playing-card of a suit denoted by black inverted heart-shaped figures with short stalks. **b** (in *pl.*)

this suit. **2** *slang offens.* Black person. [Italian *spada* sword: related to SPADE[1]]

spadework *n.* hard preparatory work.

spaghetti /spəˈgetɪ/ *n.* pasta in long thin strands. [Italian]

spaghetti Bolognese /ˌbɒləˈneɪz/ *n.* spaghetti with a meat and tomato sauce.

spaghetti junction *n.* multi-level road junction, esp. on a motorway.

spaghetti western *n.* cowboy film made cheaply in Italy.

Spam *n. propr.* tinned meat made from ham. [*sp*iced *ham*]

span[1] *–n.* **1** full extent from end to end. **2** each part of a bridge between supports. **3** maximum lateral extent of an aeroplane or its wing, or a bird's wing, etc. **4 a** maximum distance between the tips of the thumb and little finger. **b** this as a measure of 9 in. *–v.* (**-nn-**) **1** stretch from side to side of; extend across. **2** bridge (a river etc.). [Old English]

span[2] see SPICK AND SPAN.

spandrel /ˈspændrɪl/ *n.* space between the curve of an arch and the surrounding rectangular moulding, or between the curves of adjoining arches and the moulding above. [origin uncertain]

spangle /ˈspæŋg(ə)l/ *–n.* small piece of glittering material, esp. one of many used to ornament a dress etc.; sequin. *–v.* (**-ling**) (esp. as **spangled** *adj.*) cover with or as with spangles (*star-spangled*). [obsolete *spang* from Dutch]

Spaniard /ˈspænjəd/ *n.* **1** native or national of Spain. **2** person of Spanish descent. [French *Espaigne* Spain]

spaniel /ˈspænj(ə)l/ *n.* dog of a breed with a long silky coat and drooping ears. [French *espaigneul* Spanish (dog)]

Spanish /ˈspænɪʃ/ *–adj.* of Spain, its people, or language. *–n.* **1** the language of Spain and Spanish America. **2** (**the Spanish**) (*pl.*) the people of Spain.

Spanish America those parts of Central and South America and the West Indies originally settled by Spaniards and where Spanish is the main language.

Spanish Main *hist.* NE coast of South America and adjoining parts of the Caribbean Sea.

Spanish omelette *n.* omelette with chopped vegetables in the mix.

Spanish onion *n.* large mild-flavoured onion.

Spanish Sahara see WESTERN SAHARA.

Spanish Town second-largest town in Jamaica, the former capital, in the SE of the country; pop. (1991) 92 383.

spank *–v.* **1** slap, esp. on the buttocks as punishment. **2** (of a horse etc.) move briskly. *–n.* slap, esp. on the buttocks. [imitative]

spanker *n. Naut.* fore-and-aft sail set on the after side of the mizen-mast.

spanking *–adj.* **1** brisk. **2** *colloq.* striking; excellent. *–adv. colloq.* very (*spanking new*). *–n.* slapping on the buttocks.

spanner *n.* tool for turning a nut on a bolt etc. [German]

spanner in the works *n. colloq.* impediment.

spar[1] *n.* **1** stout pole, esp. as a ship's mast etc. **2** main longitudinal beam of an aeroplane wing. [Old Norse *sperra* or French *esparre*]

spar[2] *–v.* (**-rr-**) **1** make the motions of boxing without heavy blows. **2** argue. *–n.* **1** sparring motion. **2** boxing-match. [Old English]

spar[3] *n.* easily split crystalline mineral. [Low German]

spare *–adj.* **1 a** not required for normal or immediate use; extra. **b** for emergency or occasional use. **2** lean; thin. **3** frugal. *–n.* spare part. *–v.* (**-ring**) **1** afford to give, do without; dispense with (*spared me ten minutes*). **2 a** refrain from killing, hurting, etc. **b** abstain from inflicting (*spare me this task*). **3** be frugal or grudging of (*no expense spared*). □ **go spare** *colloq.* become very angry or distraught. **not spare oneself** exert one's utmost efforts. **spare a person's life** not kill him or her. **to spare** left over; additional (*an hour to spare*). □ **sparely** *adv.* **spareness** *n.* [Old English]

spare part *n.* duplicate, esp. as a replacement.

spare-rib *n.* closely-trimmed ribs of esp. pork. [Low German *ribbesper*, associated with SPARE]

spare time *n.* leisure.

spare tyre *n. colloq.* roll of fat round the waist.

sparing *adj.* **1** frugal; economical. **2** restrained. □ **sparingly** *adv.*

spark *–n.* **1** fiery particle thrown from a fire, alight in ashes, or produced by a flint, match, etc. **2** (often foll. by *of*) small amount (*spark of interest*). **3 a** flash of light between electric conductors etc. **b** this serving to ignite the explosive mixture in an internal-combustion engine. **4 a** flash of wit etc. **b** (also **bright spark**) witty or lively person. *–v.* **1** emit a spark or sparks. **2** (often foll. by *off*) stir into activity; initiate. □ **sparky** *adj.* [Old English]

sparkle /ˈspɑːk(ə)l/ *–v.* (**-ling**) **1 a** emit or seem to emit sparks; glitter, glisten. **b** be witty; scintillate. **2** (of wine etc.) effervesce. *–n.* **1** glitter. **2** lively quality (*the song lacks sparkle*). □ **sparkly** *adj.*

Spain /speɪn/, **Kingdom of** country in SW Europe, occupying the greater part of the Iberian peninsula. Despite some industrialization and a massive development of the tourist trade, Spain remains predominantly agricultural and one of the poorer EC member states. Agricultural produce includes fruit and vegetables, esp. citrus fruits, olives, tomatoes, onions, potatoes, and peppers, which are among the country's chief exports; livestock, table wines, and sherry are also exported. Coal, lignite, iron ore, copper, zinc, and other minerals are mined. Manufactured exports include cars and other transport equipment, metal products, textiles, chemicals, footwear, and leather goods. Fishing is important, and tourism is a major source of revenue.
History. A dominant European power during the 16th century, Spain thereafter declined, suffering as a result of the War of the Spanish Succession and the Napoleonic Wars, and losing most of its overseas empire in the early 19th century. Endemic political instability finally resulted in the Spanish Civil War (1936–9) and the establishment of a Fascist dictatorship under Franco. Franco's death in 1975 was followed by the re-establishment of a constitutional monarchy and a pronounced liberalization of the state, but the country's political problems have yet to be finally resolved. A number of regions, including Catalonia, Valencia, and the Basque provinces, were granted provisional self-government in 1978, but this did not put an end to the terrorist activities of Basque separatists. Spain became a member of the European Community in 1986. Head of state, King Juan Carlos I de Borbón; prime minister, José Maria Aznar López; capital, Madrid.

languages	Castilian Spanish (official), Catalan, Galician, Basque
currency	peseta (Pta) of 100 céntimos
pop. (1996)	39 270 000
GNP (1994)	US$525B
literacy	85% (m); 84% (f)
life expectancy	73 (m); 81 (f)

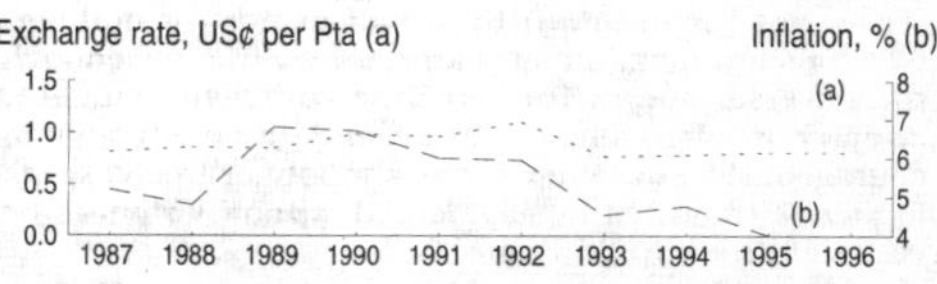

sparkler *n.* **1** hand-held sparkling firework. **2** *colloq.* diamond.

spark-plug *n.* (also **sparking-plug**) device for making a spark in an internal-combustion engine.

sparring partner *n.* **1** boxer employed to spar with another as training. **2** person with whom one enjoys arguing.

sparrow /'spærəʊ/ *n.* small brownish-grey bird. [Old English]

sparrowhawk *n.* small hawk.

sparse *adj.* thinly dispersed or scattered. □ **sparsely** *adv.* **sparseness** *n.* **sparsity** *n.* [Latin *spargo spars-* scatter]

Sparta /'spɑːtə/ town in Greece, in the S Peloponnese, administrative centre of Laconia; pop. (latest est.) 15 900. The modern town lies to the S of the ruins of the ancient city of Sparta, chief rival of Athens in the 5th century BC.

Spartan /'spɑːt(ə)n/ *–adj.* **1** of Sparta in ancient Greece. **2** austere, rigorous, frugal. *–n.* citizen of Sparta. [Latin]

spasm /'spæz(ə)m/ *n.* **1** sudden involuntary muscular contraction. **2** convulsive movement or emotion etc. **3** (usu. foll. by *of*) *colloq.* brief spell. [Greek *spasma* from *spaō* pull]

spasmodic /spæz'mɒdɪk/ *adj.* of or in spasms, intermittent. □ **spasmodically** *adv.* [Greek: related to SPASM]

spastic /'spæstɪk/ *–adj.* of or having cerebral palsy. *–n.* **1** spastic person. **2** *slang offens.* stupid or incompetent person. [Greek: related to SPASM]

spat[1] *past* and *past part.* of SPIT[1].

spat[2] *n.* (usu. in *pl.*) *hist.* short gaiter covering a shoe. [abbreviation of *spatterdash*: related to SPATTER]

spat[3] *n. colloq.* petty or brief quarrel. [probably imitative]

spat[4] *n.* spawn of shellfish, esp. the oyster. [Anglo-French, of unknown origin]

spate *n.* **1** river-flood (*river in spate*). **2** unexpected occurrence of similar events (*spate of car thefts*). [origin unknown]

spathe /speɪð/ *n.* large bract(s) enveloping a flower-cluster. [Greek *spathē* broad blade]

spatial /'speɪʃ(ə)l/ *adj.* of space. □ **spatially** *adv.* [Latin: related to SPACE]

spatter *–v.* splash or scatter in drips. *–n.* **1** splash. **2** pattering. [imitative]

spatula /'spætjʊlə/ *n.* broad-bladed flexible implement used for spreading, stirring, mixing paints, etc. [Latin diminutive: related to SPATHE]

spawn *–v.* **1 a** (of a fish, frog, etc.) produce (eggs). **b** be produced as eggs or young. **2** produce or generate in large numbers. *–n.* **1** eggs of fish, frogs, etc. **2** mycelium of mushrooms or other fungi. [Anglo-French *espaundre*: related to EXPAND]

spay *v.* sterilize (a female animal) by removing the ovaries. [Anglo-French: related to ÉPÉE]

SPDA *abbr.* single-premium deferred annuity.

SPDL *abbr. Computing* standard page description language.

speak *v.* (*past* **spoke**; *past part.* **spoken**) **1** utter words in an ordinary voice. **2** utter (words, the truth, etc.). **3 a** converse; talk (*spoke to her earlier*; *had to speak to the children about rudeness*). **b** (foll. by *of*, *about*) mention in writing etc. **c** (foll. by *for*) act as spokesman for. **4** (foll. by *to*) speak with reference to; support in words (*spoke to the resolution*). **5** make a speech. **6** use or be able to use (a specified language). **7 a** convey an idea (*actions speak louder than words*). **b** (usu. foll. by *to*) communicate feeling etc.; affect, touch (*the sunset spoke to her*). □ **generally** (or **strictly** etc.) **speaking** in the general (or strict etc.) sense. **not** (or **nothing**) **to speak of** not (or nothing) worth mentioning. **on speaking terms** friendly enough to converse. **speak for itself** be sufficient evidence. **speak out** (often followed by *against*) give one's opinion courageously. **speak up 1** speak loudly or freely; speak louder. **2** (followed by *for*) defend. **speak volumes** be very significant. [Old English]

-speak *comb. form* jargon (*Newspeak*; *computer speak*).

speakeasy *n.* (*pl.* **-ies**) *US hist. slang* place where alcoholic liquor was sold illicitly.

speaker *n.* **1** person who speaks, esp. in public. **2** person who speaks a specified language (esp. in *comb.*: *a French-speaker*). **3** (**Speaker**) presiding officer in a legislative assembly, esp. the House of Commons. **4** = LOUDSPEAKER.

speaking clock *n.* telephone service announcing the correct time.

spear *–n.* **1** thrusting or throwing weapon with a long shaft and a pointed usu. steel tip. **2 a** tip and stem of asparagus, broccoli, etc. **b** blade of grass etc. *–v.* pierce or strike (as) with a spear. [Old English]

spearhead *–n.* **1** point of a spear. **2** person or group leading an attack etc. *–v.* act as the spearhead of (an attack etc.).

spearmint *n.* common garden mint, used in cookery and to flavour chewing-gum etc.

spearwort *n.* aquatic plant with narrow spear-shaped leaves and yellow flowers.

spec[1] *n. colloq.* speculation. □ **on spec** as a gamble. [abbreviation]

spec[2] *n. colloq.* detailed working description; specification. [abbreviation of SPECIFICATION]

special /'speʃ(ə)l/ *–adj.* **1 a** exceptional. **b** peculiar; specific. **2** for a particular purpose. **3** for children with special needs (*special school*). *–n.* special constable, train, edition of a newspaper, dish on a menu, etc. □ **specially** *adv.* **specialness** *n.* [Latin: related to SPECIES]

◆ special agent see AGENT 1.

Special Branch *n.* police department dealing with political security.

special character see CHARACTER SET 2.

◆ **special clearing** *n.* passage of a cheque through the UK banking system in less than the normal three days, for a small additional charge. A cheque for which a special clearing has been arranged can usu. be passed through the system in one day.

◆ **Special Commissioners** *n.pl.* body of civil servants who are specialized tax lawyers appointed by the Lord Chancellor to hear appeals against assessments to income tax, corporation tax, and capital-gains tax. A taxpayer may choose to appeal to the Special Commissioners, rather than the General Commissioners, esp. in cases in which legal matters rather than questions of fact are at issue.

special constable *n.* person trained to assist the police in routine duties or in an emergency.

special correspondent *n.* journalist writing on special events or a special subject.

◆ **special crossing** *n.* crossing on a cheque in which the name of a bank is written between the crossing lines. A cheque so crossed can only be paid into the named bank.

special delivery *n.* delivery of mail outside the normal delivery schedule.

◆ **special deposits** *n.pl.* deposits that the UK government may instruct the clearing banks to make at the Bank of England, as a means of restricting credit in the economy. The less money the clearing banks have at their disposal, the less they are able to lend to businesses. A similar system has been used by the Federal Reserve System in the US.

◆ **special drawing right** *n.* (also **SDR**) standard unit of account used by the International Monetary Fund (IMF). In 1970 members of the IMF were allocated SDRs in proportion to the quotas of currency that they had subscribed to the fund on its formation. There have since been further allocations. SDRs can be used to settle international trade balances and to repay debts to the IMF itself. On the instructions of the IMF a member country must supply its own currency to another member, in exchange for SDRs, unless it already holds more than three times its original allocation. The value of SDRs was originally expressed in terms of gold, but since 1974 it has been valued in terms of its members' currencies. SDRs provide a credit facility for IMF members in addition to their existing credit facilities (hence the name); unlike these existing facilities they do not have to be repaid, thus forming a permanent addition to members' reserves and functioning as an international reserve currency. Cf. EUROPEAN CURRENCY UNIT.

---

special edition *n.* extra late edition of a newspaper.

special effects *n.pl.* illusions created by props, camera-work, etc.

specialist *n.* **1** person trained in a particular branch of a profession, esp. medicine. **2** person who specially studies a subject or area.

speciality /ˌspeʃɪˈælɪtɪ/ *n.* (*pl.* **-ies**) **1** special subject, product, activity, etc. **2** special feature or skill.

specialize /ˈspeʃəˌlaɪz/ *v.* (also **-ise**) (**-zing** or **-sing**) **1** (often foll. by *in*) **a** be or become a specialist. **b** devote oneself to an interest, skill, etc. (*specializes in insulting people*). **2** (esp. in *passive*) adapt for a particular purpose (*specialized organs*). **3** (as **specialized** *adj.*) of a specialist (*specialized work*). □ **specialization** /-ˈzeɪʃ(ə)n/ *n.* [French: related to SPECIAL]

special licence *n.* licence allowing immediate marriage without banns.

♦ **special Lombard rate** *n.* day-to-day rate of interest fixed by the German Bundesbank when its normal rates (see LOMBARD RATE) have been suspended for any reason.

♦ **special manager** *n.* person appointed by the court in the liquidation of a company or bankruptcy of an individual to assist the liquidator or official receiver to manage the business of the company or individual. A special manager has whatever powers the court invests in him or her.

---

special pleading *n.* biased reasoning.

♦ **special resolution** see RESOLUTION 3.

♦ **special sort** *n.* character in printing that is not part of a normal fount.

---

specialty /ˈspeʃəltɪ/ *n.* (*pl.* **-ies**) esp. *US* = SPECIALITY.

specie /ˈspiːʃiː, -ʃɪ/ *n.* money in the form of coins as opposed to banknotes or bullion. [related to SPECIES]

species /ˈspiːʃɪz, -ʃiːz, -siːz/ *n.* (*pl.* same) **1** class of things having some common characteristics. **2** group of animals or plants within a genus, differing only slightly from others and capable of interbreeding. **3** kind, sort. [Latin *specio* look]

specific /spəˈsɪfɪk/ *–adj.* **1** clearly defined (*a specific purpose*). **2** relating to a particular subject; peculiar. **3** exact, giving full details (*was specific about his wishes*). **4** *archaic* (of medicine etc.) having a distinct effect in curing a certain disease. *–n.* **1** *archaic* specific medicine or remedy. **2** specific aspect or factor (*discussed specifics*; *from the general to the specific*). □ **specifically** *adv.* **specificity** /-ˈfɪsɪtɪ/ *n.* [Latin: related to SPECIES]

specification /ˌspesɪfɪˈkeɪʃ(ə)n/ *n.* **1** act of specifying. **2** (esp. in *pl.*) detail of the design and materials etc. of work done or to be done. [medieval Latin: related to SPECIFY]

♦ **specific charge** *n.* = FIXED CHARGE.

♦ **specific damages** see DAMAGES.

---

specific gravity *n.* former name for RELATIVE DENSITY.

specific heat capacity *n.* heat required to raise the temperature of the unit mass of a given substance by a given amount (usu. one degree).

♦ **specific performance** *n.* equitable legal remedy requiring the parties to carry out the contract they have entered into. This will be granted by a court only if damages are an inadequate remedy and if it is possible to perform the contract. It is the usual remedy in cases in which there is a breach of contract for the sale of land.

---

specify /ˈspesɪˌfaɪ/ *v.* (**-ies, -ied**) **1** (also *absol.*) name or mention expressly or as a condition (*specified a two-hour limit*). **2** include in specifications. [Latin: related to SPECIFIC]

specimen /ˈspesɪmɪn/ *n.* **1** individual or sample taken as an example of a class or whole, esp. in experiments etc. **2** sample of urine for testing. **3** *colloq.* usu. *derog.* person of a specified sort. [Latin *specio* look]

specious /ˈspiːʃəs/ *adj.* plausible but wrong (*specious argument*). [Latin: related to SPECIES]

speck *–n.* **1** small spot or stain. **2** particle. *–v.* (esp. as **specked** *adj.*) marked with specks. [Old English]

speckle /ˈspek(ə)l/ *–n.* speck, esp. one of many markings. *–v.* (**-ling**) (esp. as **speckled** *adj.*) mark with speckles. [Dutch *spekkel*]

specs *n.pl. colloq.* spectacles. [abbreviation]

spectacle /ˈspektək(ə)l/ *n.* **1** striking, impressive, or ridiculous sight. **2** public show. **3** object of public attention. [Latin *specio spect-* look]

spectacled *adj.* wearing spectacles.

spectacles *n.pl.* pair of lenses in a frame resting on the nose and ears, used to correct defective eyesight.

spectacular /spekˈtækjʊlə(r)/ *–adj.* striking, impressive, lavish. *–n.* spectacular show. □ **spectacularly** *adv.*

spectator *n.* person who watches a show, game, incident, etc. □ **spectate** *v.* (**-ting**) *informal.* [Latin: related to SPECTACLE]

spectator sport *n.* sport attracting many spectators.

specter *US* var. of SPECTRE.

spectra *pl.* of SPECTRUM.

spectral /ˈspektr(ə)l/ *adj.* **1 a** of spectres. **b** ghostly. **2** of spectra. □ **spectrally** *adv.*

spectre /ˈspektə(r)/ *n.* (*US* **specter**) **1** ghost. **2** haunting presentiment (*spectre of war*). [Latin *spectrum* from *specio* look]

spectrometer /spekˈtrɒmɪtə(r)/ *n.* instrument for measuring observed spectra.

spectroscope /ˈspektrəˌskəʊp/ *n.* instrument for recording spectra for examination. □ **spectroscopic** /-ˈskɒpɪk/ *adj.* **spectroscopy** /-ˈtrɒskəpɪ/ *n.*

spectrum /ˈspektrəm/ *n.* (*pl.* **-tra**) **1** band of colours as seen in a rainbow etc. **2** entire or wide range of a subject, emotion, etc. **3** distribution of electromagnetic radiation in which the parts are arranged according to wavelength. [Latin *specio* look]

specula *pl.* of SPECULUM.

speculate /ˈspekjʊˌleɪt/ *v.* (**-ting**) **1** (usu. foll. by *on, upon, about*) theorize, conjecture. **2** deal in a commodity or asset in the hope of profiting from fluctuating prices. □ **speculative** /-lətɪv/ *adj.* **speculator** *n.* [Latin *specula* watch-tower, from *specio* look]

♦ **speculation** /ˌspekjʊˈleɪʃ(ə)n/ *n.* **1** conjecture, theory. **2** purchase or sale of something for the sole purpose of making a capital gain. For professional speculators the security, commodity, and foreign exchange markets are natural venues as they cater for speculation as well as investment and trading. Indeed, speculators help to make a viable market and thus smooth out price fluctuations, esp. in commodity futures markets. Left to producers and users alone, these markets would be much more volatile than they are with speculators taking part.

♦ **speculative demand for money** *n. Econ.* demand for money based on the conviction of speculators that interest rates are about to rise, causing bond prices to fall; it will therefore be prudent to hold money, awaiting these falls before investing. A crucial part of Keynes' theory of liquidity preference, it suggests that if speculative demand is great enough there will be a shortage of funds for investment, causing recession. The theory has been severely criticized on the grounds that speculators (investors) in this case would not exhibit rational expectations, since their expectations are based on past movements in interest rates or bond prices, not the present state of supply and demand. Cf. PRECAUTIONARY DEMAND FOR MONEY; TRANSACTIONS DEMAND FOR MONEY.

---

speculum /ˈspekjʊləm/ *n.* (*pl.* **-la**) **1** instrument for dilating orifices of the body. **2** mirror of polished metal in a telescope. [Latin, = mirror]

sped *past* and *past part.* of SPEED.

speech *n.* **1** faculty, act, or manner of speaking. **2** formal public address. **3** language of a nation, group, etc. [Old English: related to SPEAK]

speech day *n.* school celebration with speeches, prize-giving, etc.

speech generation device *n.* means of producing spoken messages, usu. artificial in origin, in response to signals from a data-processing or control system.

speechify /ˈspiːtʃɪˌfaɪ/ *v.* (**-ies, -ied**) *joc.* make esp. boring or long speeches.

speechless *adj.* temporarily silent because of emotion etc.

speech recognition *n.* process whereby a computer interprets spoken words in order to determine their data content. See also VOICE INPUT DEVICE.

speech therapy *n.* treatment for defective speech.

speed *–n.* **1** rapidity of movement. **2** rate of progress or motion. **3** gear appropriate to a range of speeds of a bicycle. **4** *Photog.* **a** sensitivity of film to light. **b** light-gathering power of a lens. **c** duration of an exposure. **5** *slang* amphetamine drug. **6** *archaic* success, prosperity. *–v.* (*past* and *past part.* **sped**) **1** go or send quickly. **2** (*past* and *past part.* **speeded**) travel at an illegal or dangerous speed. **3** *archaic* be or make prosperous or successful. □ **at speed** moving quickly. **speed up** move or work faster. □ **speeder** *n.* [Old English]

speedboat *n.* high-speed motor boat.

speed limit *n.* maximum permitted speed on a road etc.

speedo /ˈspiːdəʊ/ *n.* (*pl.* **-s**) *colloq.* = SPEEDOMETER. [abbreviation]

speedometer /spiːˈdɒmɪtə(r)/ *n.* instrument on a vehicle indicating its speed.

speedway *n.* **1 a** motor-cycle racing. **b** arena for this. **2** *US* road or track for fast traffic.

speedwell *n.* small plant with bright blue flowers. [from SPEED, WELL[1]]

speedy *adj.* (**-ier, -iest**) **1** rapid. **2** done without delay; prompt. □ **speedily** *adv.* **speediness** *n.*

speleology /ˌspiːlɪˈɒlədʒɪ/ *n.* the study of caves. [Greek *spēlaion* cave]

spell[1] *v.* (*past* and *past part.* **spelt** or **spelled**) **1** (also *absol.*) write or name correctly the letters of (a word etc.). **2 a** (of letters) form (a word etc.). **b** result in (*spell ruin*). □ **spell out 1** make out (words etc.) letter by letter. **2** explain in detail. □ **speller** *n.* [French *espeller* related to SPELL[2]]

spell[2] *n.* **1** words used as a charm or incantation etc. **2** effect of these. **3** fascination exercised by a person, activity, etc. [Old English]

spell[3] *n.* **1** short or fairly short period (*a cold spell*). **2** period of some activity or work. [Old English, = substitute]

spellbind /ˈspelbaɪnd/ *v.* (*past* and *past part.* **spellbound**) **1** (esp. as **spellbinding** *adj.*) hold the attention as if with a spell; entrance. **2** (as **spellbound** *adj.*) entranced, fascinated.

♦ **spell check** *n.* (also **spell checker**) computer program, usu. a component of a word-processing system, used to check the spelling of the words in a document. The program includes a dictionary against which each word in the document is checked and alternative spellings suggested.

---

spelling *n.* **1** way a word is spelt. **2** ability to spell.

spelt[1] *past* and *past part.* of SPELL[1].

spelt[2] *n.* a kind of wheat giving very fine flour. [Old English]

spend *v.* (*past* and *past part.* **spent**) **1** pay out (money). **2 a** use or consume (time or energy). **b** use up (material etc.). **3** (as **spent** *adj.*) having lost its original force or strength; exhausted. □ **spend a penny** *colloq.* go to the lavatory. □ **spender** *n.* [Latin: related to EXPEND]

spendthrift *–n.* extravagant person. *–adj.* extravagant.

sperm *n.* (*pl.* same or **-s**) **1** = SPERMATOZOON. **2** semen. [Greek *sperma -mat-*]

spermaceti /ˌspɜːməˈsetɪ/ *n.* white waxy substance from the sperm whale, used for ointments etc. [medieval Latin, = whale sperm]

spermatozoon /ˌspɜːmətəʊˈzəʊən/ *n.* (*pl.* **-zoa**) mature sex cell in semen. [from SPERM, Greek *zōion* animal]

sperm bank *n.* store of semen for artificial insemination.

sperm count *n.* number of spermatozoa in one ejaculation or a measured amount of semen.

spermicide /ˈspɜːmɪˌsaɪd/ *n.* substance able to kill spermatozoa. □ **spermicidal** /-ˈsaɪd(ə)l/ *adj.*

sperm whale *n.* large whale yielding spermaceti.

spew *v.* (also **spue**) **1** (often foll. by *up*) vomit. **2** (often foll. by *out*) (cause to) gush. [Old English]

sphagnum /ˈsfægnəm/ *n.* (*pl.* **-na**) (in full **sphagnum moss**) moss growing in bogs, used as packing etc. [Greek *sphagnos*]

sphere *n.* **1** solid figure with every point on its surface equidistant from its centre; its surface. **2** ball, globe. **3 a** field of action, influence, etc. **b** social class. **4** *hist.* each of the revolving shells in which celestial bodies were thought to be set. [Greek *sphaira* ball]

spherical /ˈsferɪk(ə)l/ *adj.* **1** shaped like a sphere. **2** of spheres. □ **spherically** *adv.*

spheroid /ˈsfɪərɔɪd/ *n.* spherelike but not perfectly spherical body. □ **spheroidal** /-ˈrɔɪd(ə)l/ *adj.*

sphincter /ˈsfɪŋktə(r)/ *n.* ring of muscle surrounding and closing an opening in the body. [Greek *sphiggō* bind tight]

sphinx /sfɪŋks/ *n.* **1** (**Sphinx**) (in Greek mythology) winged monster with a woman's head and a lion's body, whose riddle Oedipus guessed. **2** *Antiq.* **a** ancient Egyptian stone figure with a lion's body and a human or animal head. **b** (**the Sphinx**) huge sphinx near the Pyramids at Giza. **3** inscrutable person. [Greek]

spice *–n.* **1** aromatic or pungent vegetable substance used to flavour food. **2** spices collectively. **3 a** piquant quality. **b** (foll. by *of*) slight flavour or suggestion. *–v.* (**-cing**) **1** flavour with spice. **2** (foll. by *with*) enhance (*spiced with wit*). [French *espice*]

Spice Islands see MOLUCCA ISLANDS.

spick and span *adj.* **1** neat and clean. **2** smart and new. [earlier *span and span new*, fresh and new like a shaved chip]

spicy *adj.* (**-ier, -iest**) **1** of or flavoured with spice. **2** piquant; sensational, improper. □ **spiciness** *n.*

spider /ˈspaɪdə(r)/ *n.* eight-legged arthropod of which many species spin webs esp. to capture insects as food. [Old English: related to SPIN]

spider crab *n.* crab with long thin legs.

spider monkey *n.* monkey with long limbs and a prehensile tail.

spider plant *n.* house plant with long narrow striped leaves.

spidery *adj.* elongated and thin (*spidery handwriting*).

spiel /ʃpiːl/ *n.* *slang* glib speech or story; sales pitch. [German, = game]

spigot /ˈspɪgət/ *n.* **1** small peg or plug, esp. in a cask. **2** device for controlling the flow of liquid in a tap. [related to SPIKE[2]]

spike[1] *–n.* **1 a** sharp point. **b** pointed piece of metal, esp. the top of an iron railing. **2 a** metal point in the sole of a running-shoe to prevent slipping. **b** (in *pl.*) spiked running-shoes. **3** pointed metal rod used for filing rejected news items. **4** large nail. *–v.* (**-king**) **1** put spikes on or into. **2** fix on a spike. **3** *colloq.* **a** lace (a drink) with alcohol etc. **b** contaminate with something added. **4** *colloq.* reject (a newspaper story). □ **spike a person's guns** spoil his or her plans. [Low German or Dutch: related to SPOKE[1]]

spike[2] *n.* cluster of flower-heads on a long stem. [Latin *spica*]

spikenard /'spaɪknɑːd/ *n.* **1** tall sweet-smelling Indian plant. **2** *hist.* perfumed ointment formerly made from this. [medieval Latin *spica nardi*]

spiky *adj.* (**-ier, -iest**) **1** like a spike; having or sticking up in spikes. **2** *colloq.* touchy, irritable. □ **spikily** *adv.* **spikiness** *n.*

spill[1] *–v.* (*past* and *past part.* **spilt** or **spilled**) **1** fall or run or cause (liquid, powder, etc.) to fall or run out of a container, esp. accidentally. **2 a** throw from a vehicle, saddle, etc. **b** (foll. by *into, out* etc.) (esp. of a crowd) leave a place quickly. **3** *slang* disclose (information etc.). **4** shed (blood). *–n.* **1** spilling or being spilt. **2** tumble, esp. from a horse, bicycle, etc. □ **spill the beans** *colloq.* divulge information etc. **spill over** overflow. □ **spillage** *n.* [Old English]

spill[2] *n.* thin strip of wood or paper etc. for lighting a fire, pipe, etc. [Low German or Dutch]

spillikin /'spɪlɪkɪn/ *n.* **1** splinter of wood etc. **2** (in *pl.*) game in which thin rods are removed one at a time from a heap without moving the others. [from SPILL[2]]

spillway *n.* passage for surplus water from a dam.

spin *–v.* (**-nn-**; *past* and *past part.* **spun**) **1** (cause to) turn or whirl round quickly. **2** (also *absol.*) **a** draw out and twist (wool, cotton, etc.) into threads. **b** make (yarn) in this way. **3** (of a spider, silkworm, etc.) make (a web, cocoon, etc.) by extruding a fine viscous thread. **4** (esp. of the head) be dizzy through excitement etc. **5** tell or write (a story etc.). **6** (as **spun** *adj.*) made into threads (*spun glass; spun gold*). **7** toss (a coin). **8** (see SPIN-DRIER). *–n.* **1** spinning motion; whirl. **2** rotating dive of an aircraft. **3** secondary twisting motion, e.g. of a ball in flight. **4** *colloq.* brief drive, esp. in a car. □ **spin out** prolong. **spin a yarn** tell a story. [Old English]

spina bifida /ˌspaɪnə 'bɪfɪdə/ *n.* congenital spinal defect in which part of the spinal cord protrudes. [Latin, = cleft spine]

spinach /'spɪnɪdʒ/ *n.* green vegetable with edible leaves. [French *espinache*]

spinal /'spaɪn(ə)l/ *adj.* of the spine. [Latin: related to SPINE]

spinal column *n.* spine.

spinal cord *n.* cylindrical nervous structure within the spine.

spin bowler *n. Cricket* bowler who imparts spin to a ball.

spindle /'spɪnd(ə)l/ *n.* **1** slender rod or bar, often tapered, for twisting and winding thread. **2** pin or axis that revolves or on which something revolves. **3** turned piece of wood used as a banister, chair leg, etc. [Old English: related to SPIN]

spindle tree *n.* tree with hard wood used for spindles.

spindly *adj.* (**-ier, -iest**) long or tall and thin; thin and weak.

spin-drier *n.* (also **spin-dryer**) machine for drying clothes by spinning them in a rapidly revolving drum. □ **spin-dry** *v.*

spindrift /'spɪndrɪft/ *n.* spray on the surface of the sea. [Scots var. of *spoondrift* from obsolete *spoon* scud]

spine *n.* **1** vertebrae extending from the skull to the coccyx; backbone. **2** needle-like outgrowth of an animal or plant. **3** part of a book enclosing the page-fastening. **4** sharp ridge or projection. [Latin *spina*]

spine-chiller *n.* frightening and usu. exciting story, film, etc. □ **spine-chilling** *adj.*

spineless *adj.* **1** having no spine; invertebrate. **2** lacking resolve, feeble.

spinet /spɪ'net/ *n. hist.* small harpsichord with oblique strings. [Italian *spinetta*]

spinnaker /'spɪnəkə(r)/ *n.* large triangular sail opposite the mainsail of a racing-yacht. [*Sphinx*, name of the yacht first using it]

spinner *n.* **1** spin bowler. **2** person or thing that spins, esp. a manufacturer engaged in cotton-spinning. **3** revolving bait.

spinneret /'spɪnəˌret/ *n.* **1** spinning-organ in a spider etc. **2** device for forming synthetic fibre.

spinney /'spɪnɪ/ *n.* (*pl.* **-s**) small wood; thicket. [Latin *spinetum* from *spina* thorn]

spinning-jenny *n. hist.* machine for spinning fibres with more than one spindle at a time.

spinning wheel *n.* household device for spinning yarn or thread, with a spindle driven by a wheel with a crank or treadle.

spin-off *n.* incidental result or benefit, esp. from technology.

spinster *n.* **1** *formal* unmarried woman. **2** woman, esp. elderly, thought unlikely to marry. □ **spinsterish** *adj.* [originally = woman who spins]

spiny *adj.* (**-ier, -iest**) having many spines.

spiny anteater *n.* = ECHIDNA.

spiraea /ˌspaɪ'rɪə/ *n.* (*US* **spirea**) shrub with clusters of small white or pink flowers. [Greek: related to SPIRAL]

spiral /'spaɪər(ə)l/ *–adj.* **1** coiled in a plane or as round a cylinder or cone. **2** having this shape. *–n.* **1** spiral curve or thing (*spiral of smoke*). **2** progressive rise or fall of two or more quantities alternately because each depends on the other(s). *–v.* (**-ll-**; *US* **-l-**) **1** move in a spiral course. **2** (of prices, wages, etc.) rise or fall continuously. □ **spirally** *adv.* [Greek *speira* coil]

spiral staircase *n.* circular staircase round a central axis.

spirant /'spaɪərənt/ *–adj.* uttered with a continuous expulsion of breath. *–n.* such a consonant. [Latin *spiro* breathe]

spire *n.* **1** tapering structure, esp. on a church tower. **2** any tapering thing. [Old English]

spirea *US* var. of SPIRAEA.

spirit /'spɪrɪt/ *–n.* **1** person's essence or intelligence; soul. **2 a** rational or intelligent being without a material body. **b** ghost. **3 a** person's character (*an unbending spirit*). **b** attitude (*took it in the wrong spirit*). **c** type of person (*is a free spirit; a kindred spirit*). **d** prevailing tendency (*spirit of the age*). **4 a** (usu. in *pl.*) strong distilled liquor, e.g. whisky or gin. **b** distilled volatile liquid (*wood spirit*). **c** purified alcohol (*methylated spirit*). **5 a** courage, vivacity. **b** (in *pl.*) state of mind, mood (*in high spirits; his spirits were dashed*). **6** essential as opposed to formal meaning (*the spirit of the law*). *–v.* (**-t-**) (usu. foll. by *away, off*, etc.) convey rapidly or mysteriously. □ **in spirit** inwardly. [Latin *spiritus*: related to SPIRANT]

spirited *adj.* **1** lively, courageous. **2** (in *comb.*) in a specified mood (*high-spirited*). □ **spiritedly** *adv.*

spirit gum *n.* quick-drying gum for attaching false hair.

spirit-lamp *n.* lamp burning methylated spirit etc. instead of oil.

spiritless *adj.* lacking vigour.

spirit-level *n.* device with a glass tube nearly filled with alcohol, used to test horizontality.

spiritual /'spɪrɪtʃʊəl/ *–adj.* **1** of the spirit or soul (*spiritual relationship; spiritual home*). **2** religious, divine, inspired. **3** refined, sensitive. *–n.* (also **Negro spiritual**) religious song orig. of American Blacks. □ **spirituality** /-'ælɪtɪ/ *n.* **spiritually** *adv.*

spiritualism *n.* belief in, and supposed practice of, communication with the dead, esp. through mediums. □ **spiritualist** *n.* **spiritualistic** /-'lɪstɪk/ *adj.*

spirituous /'spɪrɪtʃʊəs/ *adj.* **1** very alcoholic. **2** distilled as well as fermented.

spirochaete /'spaɪərəʊˌkiːt/ *n.* any of various flexible spiral-shaped bacteria. [Latin from Greek *speira* coil, *khaitē* long hair]

spirogyra /ˌspaɪərəʊ'dʒaɪərə/ *n.* freshwater alga containing spiral bands of chlorophyll. [Greek *speira* coil, *guros* round]

spit[1] *–v.* (**-tt-**; *past* and *past part.* **spat** or **spit**) **1 a** (also *absol.*) eject (esp. saliva) from the mouth. **b** do this in contempt or anger. **2** utter vehemently. **3** (of a fire, gun, etc.) throw out with an explosion. **4** (of rain) fall lightly. **5** make a spitting noise. *–n.* **1** spittle. **2** act of spitting. □ **spit it out** *colloq.* say it quickly and concisely. [Old English]

spit[2] *–n.* **1** rod for skewering meat for roasting on a fire etc. **2** point of land projecting into the sea. *–v.* (**-tt-**) pierce (as) with a spit. [Old English]

spit and polish *n. colloq.* esp. military cleaning and polishing.

spite *–n.* ill will, malice. *–v.* (**-ting**) hurt, harm, or frustrate (a person) through spite. □ **in spite of** notwithstanding. [French: related to DESPITE]

spiteful *adj.* malicious. □ **spitefully** *adv.*

spitfire *n.* person of fiery temper.

spit-roast *v.* roast on a spit.

Spitsbergen /ˈspɪtsbɜːgən/ largest island of a Norwegian archipelago in the Arctic Ocean (see SVALBARD).

spitting distance *n. colloq.* very short distance.

spitting image *n.* (foll. by *of*) *colloq.* double of (a person).

spittle /ˈspɪt(ə)l/ *n.* saliva. [related to SPIT[1]]

spittoon /spɪˈtuːn/ *n.* vessel to spit into.

spiv *n. colloq.* man, esp. a flashily-dressed one, living from shady dealings. □ **spivvish** *adj.* **spivvy** *adj.* [origin unknown]

splash *–v.* **1** scatter or cause (liquid) to scatter in drops. **2** wet with spattered liquid etc. **3 a** (usu. foll. by *across, along, about*, etc.) move while spattering liquid etc. **b** jump or fall into water etc. with a splash. **4** display (news) prominently. **5** decorate with scattered colour. **6** spend (money) ostentatiously. *–n.* **1** act or noise of splashing. **2** quantity of liquid splashed. **3** mark etc. made by splashing. **4** prominent news feature, display, etc. **5** patch of colour. **6** *colloq.* small quantity of soda water etc. (in drink). □ **make a splash** attract attention. **splash out** *colloq.* spend money freely. □ **splashy** *adj.* (**-ier**, **-iest**). [imitative]

splashback *n.* panel behind a sink etc. to protect the wall from splashes.

splashdown *n.* landing of a spacecraft on the sea. □ **splash down** *v.*

splat *colloq. –n.* sharp splattering sound. *–adv.* with a splat. *–v.* (**-tt-**) fall or hit with a splat. [abbreviation of SPLATTER]

splatter *–v.* splash esp. with a continuous noisy action; spatter. *–n.* noisy splashing sound. [imitative]

splay *–v.* **1** spread apart. **2** (of an opening) have its sides diverging. **3** construct (an opening) with divergent sides. *–n.* surface at an oblique angle to another. *–adj.* splayed. [from DISPLAY]

spleen *n.* **1** abdominal organ regulating the quality of the blood. **2** moroseness, irritability (from the earlier belief that the spleen was the seat of such feelings). [Greek *splēn*]

spleenwort *n.* evergreen fern formerly used as a remedy.

splendid /ˈsplendɪd/ *adj.* **1** magnificent, sumptuous. **2** impressive, glorious, dignified (*splendid isolation*). **3** excellent; fine. □ **splendidly** *adv.* [Latin: related to SPLENDOUR]

splendiferous /splenˈdɪfərəs/ *adj. colloq.* splendid. [from SPLENDOUR]

splendour /ˈsplendə(r)/ *n.* (*US* **splendor**) dazzling brightness; magnificence. [Latin *splendeo* shine]

splenetic /splɪˈnetɪk/ *adj.* bad-tempered; peevish. □ **splenetically** *adv.* [Latin: related to SPLEEN]

splenic /ˈsplenɪk, ˈspliː-/ *adj.* of or in the spleen. [Latin from Greek: related to SPLEEN]

splice *–v.* (**-cing**) **1** join (ropes) by interweaving strands. **2** join (pieces of wood or tape etc.) by overlapping. **3** (esp. as **spliced** *adj.*) *colloq.* join in marriage. *–n.* join made by splicing. □ **splice the main brace** *Naut. hist. slang* issue an extra tot of rum. [probably Dutch *splissen*]

splint *–n.* strip of wood etc. bound to a broken limb while it sets. *–v.* secure with a splint. [Low German or Dutch]

splinter *–n.* small sharp fragment of wood, stone, glass, etc. *–v.* break into splinters; shatter. □ **splintery** *adj.* [Dutch: related to SPLINT]

splinter group *n.* breakaway political group.

Split /splɪt/ seaport in SE Croatia, on the Adriatic coast; pop. (1991) 200 459.

split *–v.* (**-tt-**; *past* and *past part.* **split**) **1 a** break, esp. with the grain or into halves; break forcibly. **b** (often foll. by *up*) divide into parts, esp. equal shares (*they split the money*). **2** (often foll. by *off, away*) remove or be removed by breaking or dividing. **3 a** (usu. foll. by *on, over*, etc.) divide into disagreeing or hostile parties (*split on the question of picketing*). **b** (foll. by *with*) quarrel or cease association with. **4** cause the fission of (an atom). **5** *slang* leave, esp. suddenly. **6** (usu. foll. by *on*) *colloq.* inform. **7 a** (as **splitting** *adj.*) (of a headache) severe. **b** (of the head) suffer from a severe headache, noise, etc. *–n.* **1** act or result of splitting. **2** disagreement; schism. **3** (in *pl.*) feat of leaping in the air or sitting down with the legs at right angles to the body in front and behind or on either side. **4** dish of split bananas etc. with ice-cream. **5** see SHARE SPLIT. □ **split the difference** take the average of two proposed amounts. **split hairs** make insignificant distinctions. **split one's sides** laugh uncontrollably. **split up** separate, end a relationship. [Dutch]

split infinitive *n.* infinitive with an adverb etc. inserted between *to* and the verb.

split-level *adj.* (of a room etc.) with more than one level.

split pea *n.* pea dried and split in half for cooking.

split personality *n.* condition in which a person seems to have two alternating personalities.

split pin *n.* metal cotter passed through a hole and held by the pressing back of the two ends.

split-screen *n.* screen on which two or more separate images are displayed. In word processing, for example, one area may be devoted to the text being processed with a second area showing such data as the number of words or lines. Cf. WINDOW 6.

split second *–n.* **1** very brief moment. **2** (of timing) very accurate. *–attrib. adj.* (**split-second**) **1** very rapid. **2** (of timing) very accurate.

♦ **split trust** *n.* investment trust divided into holdings expected to provide growth and holdings providing a good income. All income from the combined holdings is paid into one trust and all capital gains into the other, in order to cater for the preferences of investors.

---

splodge *colloq. –n.* daub, blot, or smear. *–v.* (**-ging**) make a splodge on. □ **splodgy** *adj.* [alteration of SPLOTCH]

splosh *colloq. –v.* move with a splashing sound. *–n.* **1** splashing sound. **2** splash of water etc. [imitative]

splotch *n.* & *v.* = SPLODGE. □ **splotchy** *adj.* [origin uncertain]

splurge *colloq. –n.* **1** sudden extravagance. **2** ostentatious display or effort. *–v.* (**-ging**) (usu. foll. by *on*) spend large sums of money or make a great effort. [probably imitative]

splutter *–v.* **1 a** speak, say, or express in a choking manner. **b** emit spitting sounds. **2** speak rapidly or incoherently. *–n.* spluttering speech or sound. [from SPUTTER]

spoil *–v.* (*past* and *past part.* **spoilt** or **spoiled**) **1 a** make or become useless or unsatisfactory. **b** reduce the enjoyment etc. of (*the news spoiled his dinner*). **2** make (esp. a child) unpleasant by over-indulgence. **3** (of food) go bad. **4** render (a ballot-paper) invalid by improper marking. *–n.* (usu. in *pl.*) **1** plunder, stolen goods. **2** profit or advantage from success or position. □ **be spoiling for** aggressively seek (a fight etc.). **spoilt for choice** having so many choices that it is difficult to choose. [Latin *spolio*]

spoilage *n.* **1** paper spoilt in printing. **2** spoiling of food etc. by decay.

spoiler *n.* **1** retarding device on an aircraft, interrupting the air flow. **2** similar device on a vehicle to increase contact with the ground at speed.

spoilsport *n.* person who spoils others' enjoyment.

spoilt *past* and *past part.* of SPOIL.

spoke[1] *n.* each of the rods running from the hub to the rim of a wheel. □ **put a spoke in a person's wheel** thwart or hinder a person. □ **spoked** *adj.* [Old English]

spoke[2] *past* of SPEAK.

spoken *past part.* of SPEAK. *adj.* (in *comb.*) speaking in a specified way (*well-spoken*). □ **spoken for** claimed (*this seat is spoken for*).

spokeshave *n.* tool for planing curved surfaces. [from SPOKE[1]]

spokesman *n.* (*fem.* **spokeswoman**) person speaking for a group etc. [from SPOKE[2]]

spokesperson *n.* (*pl.* **-s** or **-people**) spokesman or spokeswoman.

Spoleto /spəˈleɪtəʊ/ town in central Italy, in Umbria, noted for its annual festival of music, art, and drama; pop. (est. 1990) 36 500.

spoliation /ˌspəʊlɪˈeɪʃ(ə)n/ *n.* plundering, pillage. [Latin: related to SPOIL]

spondee /ˈspɒndiː/ *n.* metrical foot consisting of two long syllables (¯¯). □ **spondaic** /-ˈdeɪɪk/ *adj.* [Greek *spondē* libation, with which songs in this metre were associated]

sponge /spʌndʒ/ *–n.* **1** sea animal with a porous body wall and a rigid internal skeleton. **2** this skeleton or a piece of porous rubber etc. used in bathing, cleaning, etc. **3** thing like a sponge in consistency etc., esp. a sponge cake. **4** act of sponging. *–v.* (**-ging**) **1** wipe or cleanse with a sponge. **2** (often foll. by *out*, *away*, etc.) wipe off or efface (as) with a sponge. **3** (often foll. by *up*) absorb (as) with a sponge. **4** (often foll. by *on*, *off*) live as a parasite. □ **spongiform** *adj.* (esp. in senses 1, 2 of the *n.*). [Latin *spongia*]

sponge bag *n.* waterproof bag for toilet articles.

sponge cake *n.* (also **sponge pudding**) light spongy cake or pudding.

sponger *n.* parasitic person.

sponge rubber *n.* porous rubber.

spongy *adj.* (**-ier, -iest**) like a sponge, porous, elastic, absorbent. □ **sponginess** *n.*

sponsor /ˈspɒnsə(r)/ *–n.* **1** person who pledges money to a charity etc. in return for another person fulfilling a sporting etc. challenge. **2 a** patron of an artistic or sporting activity etc. **b** company etc. promoting a broadcast in return for advertising time. **3** person who introduces legislation. **4** *Finance* issuing house that handles a new issue for a company. It supervises the preparation of the prospectus and makes sure that the company is aware of the benefits and obligations of being a public company. **5** godparent at a baptism or (esp. *RC Ch.*) person who presents a candidate for baptism. *–v.* be a sponsor for. □ **sponsorial** /-ˈsɔːrɪəl/ *adj.* **sponsorship** *n.* [Latin *spondeo spons-* pledge]

spontaneous /spɒnˈteɪnɪəs/ *adj.* **1** acting, done, or occurring without external cause. **2** instinctive, automatic, natural. **3** (of style or manner) gracefully natural. □ **spontaneity** /ˌspɒntəˈneɪətɪ, -ˈniːɪtɪ/ *n.* **spontaneously** *adv.* [Latin *sponte* of one's own accord]

spontaneous combustion *n.* ignition of a substance from internal heat.

spoof *n.* & *v. colloq.* **1** parody. **2** hoax, swindle. [invented word]

spook *–n. colloq.* ghost. *–v.* esp. *US* frighten, unnerve. [Low German or Dutch]

spooky *adj.* (**-ier, -iest**) *colloq.* ghostly, eerie. □ **spookily** *adv.* **spookiness** *n.*

spool *–n.* **1** reel for winding magnetic tape, yarn, etc., on. **2** revolving cylinder of an angler's reel. *–v.* wind on a spool. [French *espole* or Germanic *spole*]

spoon *–n.* **1 a** utensil with a bowl and a handle for lifting food to the mouth, stirring, etc. **b** spoonful, esp. of sugar. **2** spoon-shaped thing, esp. (in full **spoon-bait**) a revolving metal fish-lure. *–v.* **1** (often foll. by *up*, *out*) take (liquid etc.) with a spoon. **2** hit (a ball) feebly upwards. **3** *colloq.* kiss and cuddle. □ **spoonful** *n.* (*pl.* **-s**). [Old English]

spoonbill *n.* wading bird with a broad flat-tipped bill.

spoonerism /ˈspuːnəˌrɪz(ə)m/ *n.* (usu. accidental) transposition of the initial letters etc. of two or more words. [*Spooner*, name of a scholar]

spoonfeed *v.* (*past* and *past part.* **-fed**) **1** feed with a spoon. **2** give such extensive help etc. to (a person) that he or she need make no effort.

spoor *n.* animal's track or scent. [Dutch]

Sporades /ˈspɒrəˌdiːz/ (Greek **Sporádhes** /spɒˈrɑːdiːz/) two separate groups of Greek islands in the Aegean Sea. The Northern Sporades, which lie to the E of mainland Greece, include Euboea and Skiros; the Southern Sporades, off the W coast of Turkey, include the Dodecanese.

sporadic /spəˈrædɪk/ *adj.* occurring only sparsely or occasionally. □ **sporadically** *adv.* [Greek *sporas -ad-* scattered]

spore *n.* reproductive cell of many plants and microorganisms. [Greek *spora* seed]

sporran /ˈspɒrən/ *n.* pouch worn in front of the kilt. [Gaelic *sporan*]

sport *–n.* **1 a** game or competitive activity, usu. played outdoors and involving physical exertion, e.g. cricket, football, racing. **b** these collectively. **2** (in *pl.*) meeting for competing in sports, esp. athletics. **3** amusement, fun. **4** *colloq.* **a** fair, generous, or sporting person. **b** person with a specified attitude to games, rules, etc. **5** animal or plant deviating from the normal type. *–v.* **1** amuse oneself, play about. **2** wear or exhibit, esp. ostentatiously. □ **in sport** jestingly. **make sport of** ridicule. [from DISPORT]

sporting *adj.* **1** interested or concerned in sport. **2** generous, fair. □ **a sporting chance** some possibility of success. □ **sportingly** *adv.*

sportive *adj.* playful.

sports car *n.* low-built fast car.

sports coat *n.* (also **sports jacket**) man's informal jacket.

sportsman *n.* (*fem.* **sportswoman**) **1** person who takes part in sport, esp. professionally. **2** fair and generous person. □ **sportsmanlike** *adj.* **sportsmanship** *n.*

sportswear *n.* clothes for sports or informal wear.

sporty *adj.* (**-ier, -iest**) *colloq.* **1** fond of sport. **2** rakish, showy. □ **sportily** *adv.* **sportiness** *n.*

spot *–n.* **1** small roundish area or mark differing in colour, texture, etc., from the surface it is on. **2** pimple or blemish. **3** moral blemish or stain. **4** particular place, locality. **5** particular part of one's body or aspect of one's character. **6** *colloq.* one's esp. regular position in an organization, programme, etc. **7 a** *colloq.* small quantity (*spot of trouble*). **b** drop (*spot of rain*). **8** = SPOTLIGHT. **9** (usu. *attrib.*) money paid or goods delivered immediately after a sale (*spot cash*). *–v.* (**-tt-**) **1** *colloq.* pick out, recognize, catch sight of. **2** watch for and take note of (trains, talent, etc.). **3** (as **spotted** *adj.*) marked or decorated with spots. **4** make spots, rain slightly. □ **in a spot** (or **in a tight** etc. **spot**) *colloq.* in difficulty. **on the spot 1** at the scene of an event. **2** *colloq.* in a position demanding response or action. **3** without delay. **4** without moving forwards or backwards (*running on the spot*). [perhaps from Low German or Dutch]

spot check *n.* sudden or random check.

♦ **spot currency market** *n.* market in which currencies are traded for delivery within two days, as opposed to the forward dealing exchange market in which deliveries are arranged for named months in the future.

♦ **spot goods** *n.pl.* commodities that are available for

immediate delivery, as opposed to futures in which deliveries are arranged for named months in the future. The price of spot goods (the **spot price**) is usu. higher than the forward price, unless there is a glut of that particular commodity but an expected shortage in the future.

---

spotless *adj.* absolutely clean or pure. □ **spotlessly** *adv.*

spotlight *–n.* **1** beam of light directed on a small area. **2** lamp projecting this. **3** full publicity. *–v.* (*past* and *past part.* **-lighted** or **-lit**) **1** direct a spotlight on. **2** draw attention to.

spot on *adj. colloq.* precise; on target.

spotted dick *n.* suet pudding containing currants.

spotter *n.* **1** (often in *comb.*) person who spots people or things (*train-spotter*). **2** (in full **spotter plane**) aircraft used to locate enemy positions etc.

spotty *adj.* (**-ier**, **-iest**) **1** marked with spots. **2** patchy, irregular. □ **spottiness** *n.*

spot-weld *v.* join (two metal surfaces) by welding at discrete points. □ **spot weld** *n.* **spot welder** *n.* **spot welding** *n.*

spouse /spaʊz/ *n.* husband or wife. [Latin *sponsus sponsa* betrothed]

spout *–n.* **1** projecting tube or lip used for pouring from a teapot, kettle, jug, etc., or on a fountain, roof-gutter, etc. **2** jet or column of liquid etc. *–v.* **1** discharge or issue forcibly in a jet. **2** utter or speak at length or pompously. □ **up the spout** *slang* **1** useless, ruined, broken down. **2** pregnant. [Dutch]

SPQR *abbr.* small profits and quick returns.

sprain *–v.* wrench (an ankle, wrist, etc.), causing pain or swelling. *–n.* such a wrench. [origin unknown]

sprang *past* of SPRING.

sprat *n.* small edible marine fish. [Old English]

Spratly Islands /'sprætlɪ/ group of islets and coral reefs in the South China Sea between Vietnam and Borneo, claimed in whole or in part by China, Taiwan, Vietnam, the Philippines, and Malaysia.

sprawl *–v.* **1 a** sit, lie, or fall with limbs flung out untidily. **b** spread (one's limbs) thus. **2** (of writing, a plant, a town, etc.) be irregular or straggling. *–n.* **1** sprawling movement, position, or mass. **2** straggling urban expansion. [Old English]

spray[1] *–n.* **1** water etc. flying in small drops. **2** liquid sprayed with an aerosol etc. **3** device for this. *–v.* **1** (also *absol.*) throw (liquid) as spray. **2** (also *absol.*) sprinkle (an object) thus, esp. with insecticide. **3** (of a tom-cat) mark its environment with urine, to attract females. □ **sprayer** *n.* [origin uncertain]

spray[2] *n.* **1** sprig of flowers or leaves, or a small branch; decoratively arranged bunch of flowers. **2** ornament in a similar form. [Old English]

spray-gun *n.* device for spraying paint etc.

spread /spred/ *–v.* (*past* and *past part.* **spread**) **1** (often foll. by *out*) **a** open, extend, or unfold. **b** cause to cover a surface or larger area. **c** display thus. **2** (often foll. by *out*) have a wide, specified, or increasing extent. **3** become or make widely known, felt, etc. (*rumours are spreading*). **4 a** cover (*spread the wall with paint*). **b** lay (a table). *–n.* **1** act of spreading. **2** capability or extent of spreading (*has a large spread*). **3** diffusion (*spread of learning*). **4** breadth. **5** increased girth (*middle-aged spread*). **6** *Finance* **a** difference between the buying and selling price made by a market maker on the stock exchange. **b** diversity of the investments in a portfolio: the greater the spread of a portfolio the less volatile it will be. **c** simultaneous purchase and sale of commodity futures in the hope that movement in their relative prices will enable a profit to be made. This may include a purchase and sale of the same commodity for the same delivery, but on different commodity exchanges (see STRADDLE *n.*), or a purchase and sale of the same commodity for different deliveries. **7** *colloq.* elaborate meal. **8** paste for spreading on bread etc. **9** bedspread. **10** printed matter spread across more than one column. □ **spread oneself** be lavish or discursive. **spread one's wings** develop one's powers fully. [Old English]

spread eagle *–n.* figure of an eagle with legs and wings extended as an emblem. *–v.* (**spread-eagle**) **1** (usu. as **spread-eagled** *adj.*) place (a person) with arms and legs spread out. **2** defeat utterly.

♦ **spreadsheet** *n.* computer program for the manipulation of numerical information, which is displayed as a table on a computer screen. Spreadsheets are used for financial forecasting and planning, for storing and amending accounts, etc. The tables consist of rows and columns of 'cells', each cell containing numerical information and formulae, or text. The value in a numerical cell is either typed in or is calculated from a formula in the cell; this formula can involve other cells. Each time the value of a cell is changed by the user, the values of all other dependent cells are recalculated. The ability of the cells to store text is used to annotate the table with column headings, titles, etc.

---

spree *n. colloq.* **1** extravagant outing (*shopping spree*). **2** bout of fun or drinking etc. [origin unknown]

sprig *–n.* **1** small branch or shoot. **2** ornament resembling this, esp. on fabric. *–v.* (**-gg-**) ornament with sprigs (*sprigged muslin*). [Low German *sprick*]

sprightly /'spraɪtlɪ/ *adj.* (**-ier**, **-iest**) vivacious, lively, brisk. □ **sprightliness** *n.* [from *spright*, var. of SPRITE]

spring *–v.* (*past* **sprang**; *past part.* **sprung**) **1** rise rapidly or suddenly, leap, jump. **2** move rapidly by or as by the action of a spring. **3** (usu. foll. by *from*) originate (from ancestors, a source, etc.). **4** act or appear suddenly or unexpectedly (*a breeze sprang up*; *spring to mind*; *spring to life*). **5** (often foll. by *on*) present (a thing or circumstance etc.) suddenly or unexpectedly (*sprang it on me*). **6** *slang* contrive the escape of (a person from prison etc.). **7** rouse (game) from a covert etc. **8** (usu. as **sprung** *adj.*) provide (a mattress etc.) with springs. *–n.* **1** jump, leap. **2** recoil. **3** elasticity. **4** elastic device, usu. of coiled metal, used esp. to drive clockwork or for cushioning in furniture or vehicles. **5 a** (often *attrib.*) the first season of the year, in which new vegetation begins to appear. **b** (often foll. by *of*) early stage of life etc. **6** place where water, oil, etc., wells up from the earth; basin or flow so formed. **7** motive for or origin of an action, custom, etc. □ **spring a leak** develop a leak. **spring up** come into being, appear. □ **springlike** *adj.* [Old English]

spring balance *n.* balance that measures weight by the tension of a spring.

springboard *n.* **1** flexible board for leaping or diving from. **2** source of impetus.

springbok /'sprɪŋbɒk/ *n.* (*pl.* same or **-s**) S African gazelle. [Afrikaans]

spring chicken *n.* **1** young fowl for eating. **2** youthful person.

spring-clean *–n.* (also **spring-cleaning**) thorough cleaning of a house, esp. in spring. *–v.* clean (a house) thus.

spring equinox *n.* (also **vernal equinox**) equinox about 20 March.

springer *n.* small spaniel of a breed used to spring game.

spring fever *n.* restlessness or lethargy associated with spring.

Springfield /'sprɪŋfi:ld/ city in the US, capital of Illinois and a centre of commerce and industry; pop. (est. 1994) 105 938.

spring greens *n.pl.* young cabbage leaves.

spring onion *n.* young onion eaten raw.

spring roll *n.* Chinese fried pancake filled with vegetables.

spring tide *n.* tide just after the new and the full moon when there is the greatest difference between high and low water.

springtime *n.* season of spring.

springy *adj.* (**-ier**, **-iest**) springing back quickly when squeezed, bent, or stretched; elastic. □ **springiness** *n.*

sprinkle /ˈsprɪŋk(ə)l/ –*v.* (**-ling**) **1** scatter in small drops or particles. **2** (often foll. by *with*) subject to sprinkling with liquid etc. **3** (of liquid etc.) fall on in this way. **4** distribute in small amounts. –*n.* (usu. foll. by *of*) **1** light shower. **2** = SPRINKLING. [origin uncertain]

sprinkler *n.* device for sprinkling a lawn or extinguishing fires.

sprinkling *n.* small sparse number or amount.

sprint –*v.* **1** run a short distance at full speed. **2** run (a specified distance) thus. –*n.* **1** such a run. **2** short burst in cycling, swimming, etc. □ **sprinter** *n.* [Old Norse]

sprit *n.* small diagonal spar from the mast to the upper outer corner of a sail. [Old English]

sprite *n.* elf, fairy. [*sprit*, contraction of SPIRIT]

spritsail /ˈsprɪts(ə)l/ *n.* sail extended by a sprit.

spritzer /ˈsprɪtsə(r)/ *n.* drink of wine with soda water. [German, = a splash]

sprocket /ˈsprɒkɪt/ *n.* each of several teeth on a wheel engaging with links of a chain. [origin unknown]

sprout –*v.* **1** put forth (shoots, hair, etc.). **2** begin to grow. –*n.* **1** shoot of a plant. **2** = BRUSSELS SPROUT. [Old English]

spruce[1] /spruːs/ –*adj.* neatly dressed etc.; smart. –*v.* (**-cing**) (usu. foll. by *up*) make or become smart. □ **sprucely** *adv.* **spruceness** *n.* [perhaps from SPRUCE[2]]

spruce[2] /spruːs/ *n.* **1** conifer with dense conical foliage. **2** its wood. [obsolete *Pruce* Prussia]

sprung see SPRING.

spry /spraɪ/ *adj.* (**spryer, spryest**) lively, nimble. □ **spryly** *adv.* [origin unknown]

spud –*n.* **1** *colloq.* potato. **2** small narrow spade for weeding. –*v.* (**-dd-**) (foll. by *up, out*) remove with a spud. [origin unknown]

spue var. of SPEW.

spumante /spuːˈmæntɪ/ *n.* Italian sparkling white wine. [Italian, = sparkling]

spume *n.* & *v.* (**-ming**) froth, foam. □ **spumy** *adj.* (**-ier, -iest**). [Latin *spuma*]

spun *past* and *past part.* of SPIN.

spunk *n.* **1** *colloq.* courage, mettle, spirit. **2** *coarse slang* semen. **3** touchwood. [origin unknown]

spunky *adj.* (**-ier, -iest**) *colloq.* brave, spirited.

spun silk *n.* cheap material containing waste silk.

spur –*n.* **1** small spike or spiked wheel worn on a rider's heel for urging on a horse. **2** stimulus, incentive. **3** spur-shaped thing, esp.: **a** a projection from a mountain or mountain range. **b** a branch road or railway. **c** a hard projection on a cock's leg. –*v.* (**-rr-**) **1** prick (a horse) with spurs. **2** incite or stimulate. □ **on the spur of the moment** on impulse. [Old English]

spurge *n.* plant with an acrid milky juice. [Latin *expurgare* to clean out]

spurious /ˈspjʊərɪəs/ *adj.* not genuine, fake. [Latin]

spurn *v.* reject with disdain or contempt. [Old English]

spurt –*v.* **1** (cause to) gush out in a jet or stream. **2** make a sudden effort. –*n.* **1** sudden gushing out, jet. **2** short burst of speed, growth, etc. [origin unknown]

sputnik /ˈspʊtnɪk, ˈspʌt-/ *n.* Russian artificial satellite orbiting the earth. [Russian]

sputter –*v.* make a series of quick explosive sounds, splutter. –*n.* this sound. [Dutch (imitative)]

sputum /ˈspjuːtəm/ *n.* (*pl.* **sputa**) **1** saliva. **2** expectorated matter, used esp. in diagnosis. [Latin]

spy /spaɪ/ –*n.* (*pl.* **spies**) **1** person who secretly collects and reports information for a government, company, etc. **2** person watching others secretly. –*v.* (**spies, spied**) **1** discern, see. **2** (often foll. by *on*) act as a spy. **3** (often foll. by *into*) pry. □ **spy out** explore or discover, esp. secretly. [French *espie*, *espier*]

spyglass *n.* small telescope.

spyhole *n.* peep-hole.

SQ *airline flight code* Singapore Airlines.

sq. *abbr.* square.

SQA *abbr. Computing* software quality assurance.

SQL *abbr. Computing* standard query language.

Sqn. Ldr. *abbr.* squadron leader.

squab /skwɒb/ –*n.* **1** young (esp. unfledged) pigeon or other bird. **2** short fat person. **3** stuffed cushion, esp. as part of a car-seat. **4** sofa, ottoman. –*adj.* short and fat, squat. [perhaps from Scandinavian]

squabble /ˈskwɒb(ə)l/ –*n.* petty or noisy quarrel. –*v.* (**-ling**) engage in this. [probably imitative]

squad /skwɒd/ *n.* **1** small group sharing a task etc., esp. of soldiers or policemen (*drug squad*). **2** *Sport* team. [French *escouade*]

squad car *n.* police car.

squaddie *n.* (also **squaddy**) (*pl.* **-ies**) *slang* recruit; private.

squadron /ˈskwɒdrən/ *n.* **1** unit of the RAF with 10 to 18 aircraft. **2** detachment of warships employed on a particular duty. **3** organized group etc., esp. a cavalry division of two troops. [Italian *squadrone*: related to SQUAD]

Squadron Leader *n.* commander of an RAF squadron, next below Wing Commander.

squalid /ˈskwɒlɪd/ *adj.* **1** filthy, dirty. **2** mean or poor in appearance. [Latin]

squall /skwɔːl/ –*n.* **1** sudden or violent wind, esp. with rain, snow, or sleet. **2** discordant cry; scream (esp. of a baby). –*v.* **1** utter a squall; scream. **2** utter with a squall. □ **squally** *adj.* [probably alteration of SQUEAL after BAWL]

squalor /ˈskwɒlə(r)/ *n.* filthy or squalid state. [Latin]

squander /ˈskwɒndə(r)/ *v.* spend wastefully. [origin unknown]

square /skweə(r)/ –*n.* **1** rectangle with four equal sides. **2** object of (approximately) this shape. **3** open (usu. four-sided) area surrounded by buildings. **4** product of a number multiplied by itself (*16 is the square of 4*). **5** L- or T-shaped instrument for obtaining or testing right angles. **6** *slang* conventional or old-fashioned person. –*adj.* **1** square-shaped. **2** having or in the form of a right angle (*square corner*). **3** angular, not round. **4** designating a unit of measure equal to the area of a square whose side is one of the unit specified (*square metre*). **5** (often foll. by *with*) level, parallel. **6** (usu. foll. by *to*) at right angles. **7** sturdy, squat (*a man of square frame*). **8** arranged; settled (*get things square*). **9** (also **all square**) **a** with no money owed. **b** (of scores) equal. **10** fair and honest. **11** direct (*met with a square refusal*). **12** *slang* conventional or old-fashioned. –*adv.* **1** squarely (*hit me square on the jaw*). **2** fairly, honestly. –*v.* (**-ring**) **1** make square. **2** multiply (a number) by itself. **3** (usu. foll. by *to, with*) adjust; make or be suitable or consistent; reconcile. **4** mark out in squares. **5** settle or pay (a bill etc.). **6** place (one's shoulders etc.) squarely facing forwards. **7** *colloq.* pay or bribe (a person). **8** (also *absol.*) make the scores of (a match etc.) equal. □ **back to square one** *colloq.* back to the starting-point with no progress made. **out of square** not at right angles. **square the circle 1** construct a square equal in area to a given circle. **2** do what is impossible. **square peg in a round hole** see PEG. **square up** settle an account etc. **square up to 1** move threateningly towards (a person). **2** face and tackle (a difficulty etc.) resolutely. □ **squarely** *adv.* **squareness** *n.* **squarish** *adj.* [French *esquare*, Latin *quadra*]

square-bashing *n. slang* military drill on a barrack-square.

square brackets *n.pl.* brackets of the form [ ].

square dance *n.* dance with usu. four couples facing inwards from four sides.

square deal *n.* fair bargain or treatment.

square leg *n.* fielding position in cricket at some distance on the batsman's leg side and nearly opposite the stumps.

square meal *n.* substantial meal.

square measure *n.* measure expressed in square units.

square-rigged *adj.* with the principal sails at right angles to the length of the ship.

square root *n.* number that multiplied by itself gives a specified number.

squash[1] /skwɒʃ/ *–v.* **1** crush or squeeze, esp. flat or into pulp. **2** (often foll. by *into*) *colloq.* put or make one's way by squeezing. **3** belittle, bully (a person). **4** suppress (a proposal, allegation, etc.). *–n.* **1** crowd; crowded state. **2** drink made of crushed fruit. **3** (in full **squash rackets**) game played with rackets and a small ball in a closed court. □ **squashy** *adj.* (**-ier, -iest**). [French *esquasser*: related to EX-[1], QUASH]

squash[2] /skwɒʃ/ *n.* (*pl.* same or **-es**) **1** trailing annual plant. **2** edible gourd of this. [Narragansett]

squat /skwɒt/ *–v.* (**-tt-**) **1** sit on one's heels or on the ground with the knees drawn up. **2** *colloq.* sit down. **3** occupy a building as a squatter. *–adj.* (**squatter, squattest**) short and thick, dumpy. *–n.* **1** squatting posture. **2** place occupied by squatters. [French *esquatir* flatten]

squatter *n.* person who inhabits unoccupied premises without permission.

squaw *n.* North American Indian woman or wife. [Narragansett]

squawk *–n.* **1** loud harsh cry, esp. of a bird. **2** complaint. *–v.* utter a squawk. [imitative]

squeak *–n.* **1** short high-pitched cry or sound. **2** (also **narrow squeak**) narrow escape. *–v.* **1** make a squeak. **2** utter (words) shrilly. **3** (foll. by *by*, *through*) *colloq.* pass narrowly. **4** *slang* turn informer. [imitative: related to SQUEAL, SHRIEK]

squeaky *adj.* (**-ier, -iest**) making a squeaking sound. □ **squeakily** *adv.* **squeakiness** *n.*

squeaky clean *adj.* (usu. hyphenated when *attrib.*) *colloq.* **1** completely clean. **2** above criticism.

squeal *–n.* prolonged shrill sound or cry. *–v.* **1** make, or utter with, a squeal. **2** *slang* turn informer. **3** *colloq.* protest vociferously. [imitative]

squeamish /ˈskwiːmɪʃ/ *adj.* **1** easily nauseated or disgusted. **2** fastidious. □ **squeamishly** *adv.* **squeamishness** *n.* [Anglo-French *escoymos*]

squeegee /ˈskwiːdʒiː/ *n.* rubber-edged implement on a handle, for cleaning windows etc. [*squeege*, alteration of SQUEEZE]

squeeze *–v.* (**-zing**) **1** (often foll. by *out*) **a** exert pressure on, esp. to extract moisture etc. **b** extract (moisture) by squeezing. **2** reduce in size or alter in shape by squeezing. **3** force or push into or through a small or narrow space. **4 a** harass or pressure (a person). **b** (usu. foll. by *out of*) obtain by extortion, entreaty, etc. **5** press (a person's hand) in sympathy etc. *–n.* **1** squeezing or being squeezed. **2** close embrace. **3** crowd, crowded state. **4** small quantity produced by squeezing (*squeeze of lemon*). **5** control imposed by a government to restrict inflation. An **income** (or **pay**) **squeeze** limits increases in wage and salaries, a **credit squeeze** limits the amounts that banks and other moneylenders can lend, a **dividend** (or **profits**) **squeeze** restricts increases in dividends. **6** any action on a market that forces buyers to come into the market and prices to rise. In a **bear squeeze,** bears are forced to cover in order to deliver. It may be restricted to a particular commodity or security or a particular delivery month may be squeezed, pushing its price up against the rest of the market. □ **put the squeeze on** *colloq.* coerce or pressure. [origin unknown]

squeeze-box *n. colloq.* accordion or concertina.

squelch *–v.* **1 a** make a sucking sound as of treading in thick mud. **b** move with a squelching sound. **2** disconcert, silence. *–n.* act or sound of squelching. □ **squelchy** *adj.* [imitative]

squib *n.* **1** small hissing firework that finally explodes. **2** satirical essay. [perhaps imitative]

squid *n.* (*pl.* same or **-s**) ten-armed marine cephalopod used as food. [origin unknown]

squidgy /ˈskwɪdʒɪ/ *adj.* (**-ier, -iest**) *colloq.* squashy, soggy. [imitative]

squiffy /ˈskwɪfɪ/ *adj.* (**-ier, -iest**) *slang* slightly drunk. [origin unknown]

squiggle /ˈskwɪg(ə)l/ *n.* short curly line, esp. in handwriting. □ **squiggly** *adj.* [imitative]

squill *n.* bulbous plant resembling a bluebell. [Latin *squilla*]

squint *–v.* **1** have eyes that do not move together but look in different directions. **2** (often foll. by *at*) look obliquely or with half-closed eyes. *–n.* **1** condition causing squinting. **2** stealthy or sidelong glance. **3** *colloq.* glance, look. **4** oblique opening in a church wall affording a view of the altar. [obsolete *asquint*, perhaps from Dutch *schuinte* slant]

squire *–n.* **1** country gentleman, esp. the chief landowner of a district. **2** *hist.* knight's attendant. *–v.* (**-ring**) (of a man) attend or escort (a woman). [related to ESQUIRE]

squirearchy /ˈskwaɪəˌrɑːkɪ/ *n.* (*pl.* **-ies**) landowners collectively.

squirm *–v.* **1** wriggle, writhe. **2** show or feel embarrassment. *–n.* squirming movement. [imitative]

squirrel /ˈskwɪr(ə)l/ *–n.* **1** bushy-tailed usu. tree-living rodent. **2** its fur. **3** hoarder. *–v.* (**-ll-**; *US*, **-l-**) **1** (often foll. by *away*) hoard. **2** (often foll. by *around*) bustle about. [Greek *skiouros*, from *skia* shade, *oura* tail]

squirt *–v.* **1** eject (liquid etc.) in a jet. **2** be ejected in this way. **3** splash with a squirted substance. *–n.* **1 a** jet of water etc. **b** small quantity squirted. **2** syringe. **3** *colloq.* insignificant but self-assertive person. [imitative]

squish *colloq. –n.* slight squelching sound. *–v.* move with a squish. □ **squishy** *adj.* (**-ier, -iest**). [imitative]

SR *–symb.* Seychelles rupee. *–postcode* Sunderland. *–airline flight code* Swissair.

S/R *abbr.* sale or return.

Sr *symb.* strontium.

Sri Lanka /ʃriː ˈlæŋkə, ʃrɪ, sr-/, **Democratic Socialist Republic of** (formerly, until 1972, **Ceylon**) island country off the SE coast of India. Tea, rubber, and coconuts (and coconut products) are important exports. Rice is also grown, and there are plans for the cultivation of cotton, sugar cane, and citrus fruits on a large scale. The developing industrial sector manufactures textiles (an important export), ceramics, paper, chemicals, fertilizers, leather goods, and petroleum products. Fishing also contributes to the economy, with fish products and pearls being exported. The country's chief mineral resources are gemstones, which are mined and exported.

History. The island was successively dominated by the Portuguese, Dutch, and British from the 16th century and finally annexed by the British in 1815. A Commonwealth state from 1948, the country became an independent republic under its present name in 1972. A system of proportional representation was introduced in 1978. The political stability of the island has been continually threatened by conflict between the Sinhalese and Tamil elements of the population, despite intervention by a peacekeeping force from India (1987–90). President, Chandrika Bandaranaike Kumaratunga; capital, Colombo. □ **Sri Lankan** *adj.* & *n.*

languages	Sinhalese & Tamil (official), English
currency	rupee (SL Re; *pl.* SL Rs) of 100 cents
pop. (1996)	18 318 000
GNP (1994)	US$11.6B
literacy	90% (m); 83% (f)
life expectancy	71 (m); 75 (f)

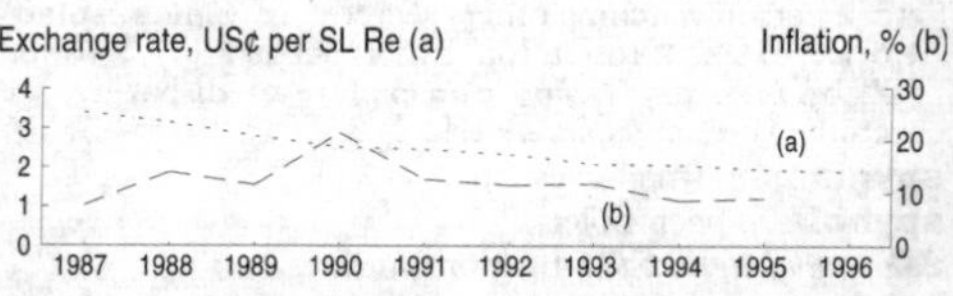

Sr. *abbr.* **1** Senhor. **2** Senior. **3** Señor. **4** Signor.
Sra. *abbr.* **1** Senhora. **2** Señora.
SRAM *abbr. Computing* static random access memory.
SRC *abbr.* (Spanish) sociedad regular colectiva (= partnership).
SRG *abbr.* Strategic Research Group (marketing research company).
Srinagar /'sri:nəgə(r)/ city in NW India, summer capital of the state of Jammu and Kashmir; manufactures include carpets, silk, silver, and leather goods; pop. (1991) 586 038.
Srl. *abbr.* (Italian) società a responsabilità limitata (= private limited company).
SRls *symb.* Saudi riyal.
SRN *abbr. hist.* State Registered Nurse.
SRNA *abbr.* Shipbuilders and Repairers National Association.
SRO *abbr.* SELF-REGULATING ORGANIZATION.
SRP *abbr.* suggested retail price.
Srta. *abbr.* **1** Senhorita. **2** Señorita.
SS *–abbr.* **1** steamship. **2** *hist.* Nazi special police force. **3** Saints. **4** social security. *–postcode* Southend-on-Sea. [sense 2 from German *Schutz-Staffel*]
SSA *abbr.* **1** (in the US) Social Security Administration. **2** (in local government) standard spending assessment.
SSADM *abbr. Computing* structured systems analysis and design method, standard UK government analysis and design methodology.
SSAP *abbr.* = STATEMENT OF STANDARD ACCOUNTING PRACTICE.
SSC *abbr. US* small-saver certificate.
SSE *abbr.* south-south-east.
SSI *abbr.* **1** Social Services Inspectorate. **2** *US* supplemental security income.
SSN *abbr.* Standard Serial Number.
SSP *abbr.* = STATUTORY SICK PAY.
SSR *abbr. hist.* Soviet Socialist Republic.
SSW *abbr.* south-south-west.
ST *–abbr.* **1** spring tide. **2** standard time. *–international civil aircraft marking* Sudan. *–postcode* Stoke-on-Trent.
St *abbr.* Saint.
St. *abbr.* Street.
st. *abbr.* stone (in weight).
stab *–v.* (**-bb-**) **1** pierce or wound with a knife etc. **2** (often foll. by *at*) aim a blow with such a weapon. **3** cause a sensation like being stabbed (*stabbing pain*). **4** hurt or distress (a person, feelings, etc.). *–n.* **1** act of stabbing. **2** wound from this. **3** *colloq.* attempt. [origin unknown]
stability /stə'bɪlɪtɪ/ *n.* being stable. [Latin: related to STABLE]
stabilize /'steɪbɪ,laɪz/ *v.* (also **-ise**) (**-zing** or **-sing**) make or become stable. □ **stabilization** /-'zeɪʃ(ə)n/ *n.*
stabilizer *n.* (also **-iser**) **1** device used to keep esp. a ship, aircraft, or (in *pl.*) child's bicycle stable. **2** food additive for preserving texture. **3** (usu. in *pl.*) *Econ.* measure used in a free economy to restrict swings in prices, production, employment, etc. Such measures include progressive income tax, control of interest rates, government spending, unemployment benefits, and government retraining schemes.
stab in the back *–n.* treacherous attack. *–v.* betray.
stable /'steɪb(ə)l/ *–adj.* (**-bler, -blest**) **1** firmly fixed or established; not likely to move or change. **2** (of a person) not easily upset or disturbed. *–n.* **1** building for keeping horses. **2** establishment for training racehorses. **3** racehorses from one stable. **4** persons, products, etc., having a common origin or affiliation. **5** such an origin or affiliation. *–v.* (**-ling**) put or keep in a stable. □ **stably** *adv.* [Latin *stabilis* from *sto* to stand]
stable-companion *n.* (also **stable-mate**) **1** horse of the same stable. **2** member of the same organization.
stabling *n.* accommodation for horses.
staccato /stə'kɑ:təʊ/ esp. *Mus. –adv.* & *adj.* with each sound or note sharply distinct. *–n.* (*pl.* **-s**) staccato passage or delivery. [Italian]
stack *–n.* **1** (esp. orderly) pile or heap. **2** = HAYSTACK. **3** *colloq.* large quantity (*a stack of work*; *stacks of money*). **4 a** = CHIMNEY-STACK. **b** = SMOKESTACK. **c** tall factory chimney. **5** stacked group of aircraft. **6** part of a library where books are compactly stored. **7** high detached rock, esp. off the coast of Scotland. *–v.* **1** pile in a stack or stacks. **2 a** arrange (cards) secretly for cheating. **b** manipulate (circumstances etc.) to suit one. **3** cause (aircraft) to fly in circles while waiting to land. [Old Norse]
stadium /'steɪdɪəm/ *n.* (*pl.* **-s**) athletic or sports ground with tiered seats for spectators. [Greek *stadion*]
staff /stɑ:f/ *–n.* **1 a** stick or pole for use in walking or as a weapon. **b** stick or rod as a sign of office etc. **c** person or thing that supports. **2 a** people employed in a business etc. **b** those in authority in a school etc. **c** body of officers assisting an officer in high command (*general staff*). **3** (*pl.* **-s** or **staves**) *Mus.* set of usu. five parallel lines on or between which notes are placed to indicate their pitch. *–v.* provide (an institution etc.) with staff. [Old English]
staff college *n.* college where officers are trained for staff duties.

◆ **staff management** see LINE AND STAFF MANAGEMENT.

---

staff nurse *n.* nurse ranking just below a sister.
Staffordshire /'stæfəd,ʃɪə(r)/ county in central England; pop. (est. 1994) 1 054 400; county town, Stafford. Dairy farming and pottery manufacture are important; coalmining has declined.
Staffs. *abbr.* Staffordshire.
staff sergeant *n.* senior sergeant of a non-infantry company.
stag *n.* **1** adult male deer. **2** *Stock Exch. slang* person who applies for a new issue of shares, intending to sell at once for a profit if the market price exceeds the issue price. [Old English]
stag beetle *n.* beetle with branched mandibles like antlers.
stage *–n.* **1** point or period in a process or development. **2 a** raised platform, esp. for performing plays etc. on. **b** (prec. by *the*) theatrical profession, drama. **c** scene of action. **3 a** regular stopping-place on a route. **b** distance between two of these. **4** *Astronaut.* section of a rocket with a separate engine. *–v.* (**-ging**) **1** present (a play etc.) on stage. **2** arrange, organize (*staged a demonstration*). [French *estage*, ultimately from Latin *sto* stand]
stagecoach *n. hist.* large closed horse-drawn coach running on a regular route by stages.
stagecraft *n.* theatrical skill or experience.
stage direction *n.* instruction in a play as to actors' movements, sound effects, etc.
stage fright *n.* performer's fear of an audience.
stage-hand *n.* person moving stage scenery etc.
stage-manage *v.* **1** be the stage-manager of. **2** arrange and control for effect.
stage-manager *n.* person responsible for lighting and mechanical arrangements etc. on stage.
stage-struck *adj.* obsessed with becoming an actor.
stage whisper *n.* **1** an aside. **2** loud whisper meant to be overheard.

◆ **stagflation** /stæg'fleɪʃ(ə)n/ *n. Econ.* state of inflation without a corresponding increase of demand and employment, as occurred in the 1970s. At that time governments generally pursued Keynesian policies, giving credence to monetarist views that government fiscal and monetary policies can only influence the price level. [blend of *stagnation, inflation*]

---

stagger *–v.* **1** (cause to) walk unsteadily. **2** shock, confuse. **3** arrange (events etc.) so that they do not coincide. **4** arrange (objects) so that they are not in line. *–n.* **1** tottering movement. **2** (in *pl.*) disease, esp. of horses and cattle, causing staggering. [Old Norse]

◆ **staggered directorships** *n.pl.* measure used as a defence against unwanted take-over bids in which a company resolves that the terms of office served by its directors are to be staggered and that no director can be removed from office without due cause. A bidder cannot then gain control of the board for some years, even with a controlling interest of the shares. See POISON PILL.

staggering *adj.* astonishing, bewildering. □ **staggeringly** *adv.*
staghound *n.* large dog used for hunting deer.
staging /ˈsteɪdʒɪŋ/ *n.* **1** presentation of a play etc. **2 a** platform or support, esp. temporary. **b** shelves for plants in a greenhouse.
staging post *n.* regular stopping-place, esp. on an air route.
stagnant /ˈstægnənt/ *adj.* **1** (of liquid) motionless, having no current. **2** dull, sluggish. □ **stagnancy** *n.* [Latin *stagnum* pool]
stagnate /stægˈneɪt/ *v.* (**-ting**) be or become stagnant. □ **stagnation** *n.*

◆ **stagnation theory** *n. Econ.* theory, not widely accepted, that business cycles arise in industrial economies because savings increase as people become more affluent but the opportunities for investing them decline (see BUSINESS CYCLE). Supporters of this theory believe that in the course of the boom period of the cycle investment opportunities should be provided by governments.

stag-party *n. colloq.* all-male celebration held esp. for a man about to marry.

◆ **STAGS** *n.pl.* European sterling bonds backed by a holding of Treasury stock. They are deep-discount bonds paying no interest. [abbreviation of *S*terling *T*ransferable *A*ccruing *G*overnment *S*ecurities]

stagy /ˈsteɪdʒɪ/ *adj.* (**-ier**, **-iest**) theatrical, artificial, exaggerated.
staid *adj.* of quiet and steady character; sedate. [= stayed, past part. of STAY[1]]
stain *–v.* **1** discolour or be discoloured by the action of liquid sinking in. **2** spoil, damage (a reputation, character, etc.). **3** colour (wood, glass, etc.) with a penetrating substance. **4** impregnate (a specimen) with a colouring agent for microscopic examination. *–n.* **1** discoloration; spot, mark. **2** blot, blemish; damage to a reputation etc. **3** substance used in staining. [earlier *distain* from French *desteindre*]
stained glass *n.* coloured glass in a leaded window etc.
stainless *adj.* **1** without stains. **2** not liable to stain.
stainless steel *n.* chrome steel resisting rust or tarnish.
stair *n.* **1** each of a set of fixed indoor steps. **2** (usu. in *pl.*) set of these. [Old English]
staircase *n.* flight of stairs and the supporting structure.
stair-rod *n.* rod securing a carpet between two steps.
stairway *n.* = STAIRCASE.
stairwell *n.* shaft for a staircase.
stake[1] *–n.* **1** stout sharpened stick driven into the ground as a support, boundary mark, etc. **2** *hist.* **a** post to which a condemned person was tied to be burnt alive. **b** (prec. by *the*) such death as a punishment. *–v.* (**-king**) **1** secure or support with a stake or stakes. **2** (foll. by *off*, *out*) mark off (an area) with stakes. **3** establish (a claim). □ **stake out** *colloq.* place under surveillance. [Old English]
stake[2] *–n.* **1** sum of money etc. wagered on an event. **2** (often foll. by *in*) interest or concern, esp. financial. **3** (in *pl.*) **a** prize-money, esp. in a horse-race. **b** such a race. *–v.* **1** wager. **2** *US colloq.* support, esp. financially. □ **at stake** risked, to be won or lost. [Old English]
stakeholder *n.* independent party with whom money etc. wagered is deposited.

◆ **stakeholder theory** *n.* theory that widens the view that a firm is responsible only to its owners. Instead employees, customers, suppliers, and the wider community are regarded as included in the responsibilities of a firm.

stake-out *n.* esp. *US colloq.* period of surveillance.
Stakhanovite /stəˈkɑːnəˌvaɪt/ *n.* (often *attrib.*) exceptionally productive worker. [*Stakhanov*, name of a Russian coalminer]
stalactite /ˈstæləkˌtaɪt/ *n.* icicle-like deposit of calcium carbonate hanging from the roof of a cave etc. [Greek *stalaktos* dripping]
stalagmite /ˈstæləgˌmaɪt/ *n.* icicle-like deposit of calcium carbonate rising from the floor of a cave etc. [Greek *stalagma* a drop]
stale *–adj.* **1 a** not fresh. **b** musty, insipid, or otherwise the worse for age or use. **2** trite, unoriginal (*stale joke*). **3** (of an athlete or performer) impaired by excessive training. *–v.* (**-ling**) make or become stale. □ **staleness** *n.* [Anglo-French *estaler* halt]

◆ **stale bull** *n.* dealer or speculator who has a long position in something, usu. a commodity, which is showing a paper profit but which the dealer cannot realize as there are no buyers at the higher levels. The dealer may be fully committed financially and unable to increase his or her bull position so that no further trading is possible.

◆ **stale cheque** *n.* cheque that has not been presented for payment within six months of being written. The bank will not honour it, returning it marked 'out of date'.

stalemate *–n.* **1** *Chess* position counting as a draw, in which a player cannot move except into check. **2** deadlock. *–v.* (**-ting**) **1** *Chess* bring (a player) to a stalemate. **2** bring to a deadlock. [obsolete *stale*: related to STALE, MATE[2]]
Stalingrad see VOLGOGRAD.
Stalinism /ˈstɑːlɪˌnɪz(ə)m/ *n.* rigid centralized authoritarian form of socialism associated with Stalin. □ **Stalinist** *n.* & *adj.* [*Stalin*, name of a Soviet statesman]
stalk[1] /stɔːk/ *n.* **1** main stem of a herbaceous plant. **2** slender attachment or support of a leaf, flower, fruit, etc. **3** similar support for an organ etc. in an animal. [diminutive of (now dial.) *stale* rung]
stalk[2] /stɔːk/ *–v.* **1** pursue (game or an enemy) stealthily. **2** stride, walk in a haughty manner. **3** *formal* or *rhet.* move silently or threateningly through (a place) (*fear stalked the land*). *–n.* **1** stalking of game. **2** haughty gait. [Old English: related to STEAL]
stalking-horse *n.* **1** horse concealing a hunter. **2** pretext concealing one's real intentions or actions. **3** weak political candidate forcing an election in the hope of a more serious contender coming forward.
stall[1] /stɔːl/ *–n.* **1** trader's booth or table in a market etc. **2** compartment for one animal in a stable or cowhouse. **3** fixed, usu. partly enclosed, seat in the choir or chancel of a church. **4** (usu. in *pl.*) each of the seats on the ground floor of a theatre. **5 a** compartment for one person in a shower-bath etc. **b** compartment for one horse at the start of a race. **6 a** stalling of an engine or aircraft. **b** condition resulting from this. *–v.* **1** (of a vehicle or its engine) stop because of an overload on the engine or an inadequate supply of fuel to it. **2** (of an aircraft or its pilot) lose control because the speed is too low. **3** cause to stall. [Old English]
stall[2] /stɔːl/ *v.* **1** play for time when being questioned etc. **2** delay, obstruct. [*stall* 'decoy': probably related to STALL[1]]
stallholder *n.* person in charge of a stall at a market etc.
stallion /ˈstæljən/ *n.* uncastrated adult male horse. [French *estalon*]
stalwart /ˈstɔːlwət/ *–adj.* **1** strong, sturdy. **2** courageous, resolute, reliable. *–n.* stalwart person, esp. a loyal comrade. [Old English, = place, WORTH]
stamen /ˈsteɪmən/ *n.* organ producing pollen in a flower. [Latin, = warp, thread]

stamina /'stæmɪnə/ *n.* physical or mental endurance. [Latin, pl. of STAMEN]

stammer *–v.* **1** speak haltingly, esp. with pauses or rapid repetitions of the same syllable. **2** (often foll. by *out*) utter (words) in this way. *–n.* **1** tendency to stammer. **2** instance of stammering. [Old English]

stamp *–v.* **1 a** bring down (one's foot) heavily, esp. on the ground. **b** (often foll. by *on*) crush or flatten in this way. **c** walk heavily. **2 a** impress (a design, mark, etc.) on a surface. **b** impress (a surface) with a pattern etc. **3** affix a postage or other stamp to. **4** assign a specific character to; mark out. *–n.* **1** instrument for stamping. **2 a** mark or design made by this. **b** impression of an official mark required to be made on deeds, bills of exchange, etc., as evidence of payment of tax. **3** small adhesive piece of paper indicating that payment has been made, esp. a postage stamp. **4** mark or label etc. on a commodity as evidence of quality etc. **5** act or sound of stamping the foot. **6** characteristic mark or quality. □ **stamp on 1** impress (an idea etc.) on (the memory etc.). **2** suppress. **stamp out 1** produce by cutting out with a die etc. **2** put an end to, destroy. [Old English]

stamp-collector *n.* philatelist.

♦ **stamp-duty** *n.* tax on specific transactions collected by stamping the legal documents giving rise to the transactions. The most common UK stamp-duty is that on the transfer of land. From 1998–9, the duty is 1% from houses valued at £60,000 to £250,000, 2% over £250,000, and 3% over £500,000. The stamp-duty on the transfer of securities was abolished in 1992.

---

stampede /stæm'piːd/ *–n.* **1** sudden flight or hurried movement of animals or people. **2** response of many persons at once to a common impulse. *–v.* (**-ding**) (cause to) take part in a stampede. [Spanish *estampida* crash, uproar]

stamping-ground *n. colloq.* favourite haunt.

stance /stɑːns, stæns/ *n.* **1** standpoint; attitude. **2** attitude or position of the body, esp. when hitting a ball etc. [Italian *stanza* standing]

stanch /stɑːntʃ, stɔːntʃ/ *v.* (also **staunch**) **1** restrain the flow of (esp. blood). **2** restrain the flow from (esp. a wound). [French *estanchier*]

stanchion /'stɑːnʃ(ə)n/ *n.* **1** upright post or support. **2** upright bar or frame for confining cattle in a stall. [Anglo-French]

stand *–v.* (*past* and *past part.* **stood** /stʊd/) **1** have, take, or maintain an upright position, esp. on the feet or a base. **2** be situated (*here once stood a village*). **3** be of a specified height. **4** be in a specified state (*stands accused*; *it stands as follows*). **5** set in an upright or specified position (*stood it against the wall*). **6 a** move to and remain in a specified position (*stand aside*). **b** take a specified attitude (*stand aloof*). **7** maintain a position; avoid falling, moving, or being moved. **8** assume a stationary position; cease to move. **9** remain valid or unaltered. **10** *Naut.* hold a specified course. **11** endure, tolerate. **12** provide at one's own expense (*stood him a drink*). **13** (often foll. by *for*) be a candidate (for office etc.) (*stood for Parliament*). **14** act in a specified capacity (*stood proxy*). **15** undergo (trial). *–n.* **1** cessation from progress, stoppage. **2 a** *Mil.* halt made to repel an attack. **b** resistance to attack or compulsion (esp. *make a stand*). **c** *Cricket* prolonged period at the wicket by two batsmen. **3** position taken up; attitude adopted. **4** rack, set of shelves, etc. for storage. **5** open-fronted stall or structure for a trader, exhibitor, etc. **6** standing-place for vehicles. **7 a** raised structure to sit or stand on. **b** *US* witness-box. **8** each halt made for a performance on a tour. **9** group of growing plants (*stand of trees*). □ **as it stands 1** in its present condition. **2** in the present circumstances. **stand by 1** stand nearby; look on without interfering. **2** uphold, support (a person). **3** adhere to (a promise etc.). **4** be ready for action. **stand a chance** see CHANCE. **stand corrected** accept correction. **stand down** withdraw from a position or candidacy. **stand for 1** represent, signify, imply. **2** *colloq.* endure, tolerate. **stand one's ground** not yield. **stand in** (usu. foll. by *for*) deputize. **stand off 1** move or keep away. **2** temporarily dismiss (an employee). **stand on** insist on, observe scrupulously. **stand on one's own feet** (or **two feet**) be self-reliant or independent. **stand out 1** be prominent or outstanding. **2** (usu. foll. by *against*, *for*) persist in opposition or support. **stand to 1** *Mil.* stand ready for an attack. **2** abide by. **3** be likely or certain to. **stand to reason** be obvious. **stand up 1 a** rise to one's feet. **b** come to, remain in, or place in a standing position. **2** (of an argument etc.) be valid. **3** *colloq.* fail to keep an appointment with. **stand up for** support, side with. **stand up to 1** face (an opponent) courageously. **2** be resistant to (wear, use, etc.). **take one's stand on** base one's argument etc. on, rely on. [Old English]

stand-alone system *n.* computer or computer program whose operation is independent of any other device or program.

standard /'stændəd/ *–n.* **1** object, quality, or measure serving as a basis, example, or principle to which others conform or should conform or by which others are judged. **2 a** level of excellence etc. required or specified (*not up to standard*). **b** average quality (*of a low standard*). **3** ordinary procedure etc. **4** distinctive flag. **5 a** upright support. **b** upright pipe. **6 a** tree or shrub that stands without support. **b** shrub grafted on an upright stem and trained in tree form. **7** tune or song of established popularity. *–adj.* **1** serving or used as a standard. **2** of a normal or prescribed quality, type, or size. **3** of recognized and permanent value; authoritative (*standard book on jazz*). **4** (of language) conforming to established educated usage. [Anglo-French: related to EXTEND, and in senses 5 and 6 of *n.* influenced by STAND]

♦ **Standard and Poor's 500 Stock Index** *n.* US index of 425 shares in US industrial companies and 75 stocks in railway and public-utility corporations. [*Standard and Poor*, name of US credit-rating agency that produced it]

---

standard assessment task *n.* standard test given to schoolchildren.

standard-bearer *n.* **1** soldier who carries a standard. **2** prominent leader in a cause.

♦ **standard costing** *n.* method of budgetary control in which standard costs are fixed in advance for such items as raw material prices, labour rates, machine costs, fixed overheads, etc. Entries in the costing records are made at the agreed standard costs so that the accounts will show variances when the actual costs differ from the standard costs. This enables management to take up the matter of the differences with those responsible.

---

standard deviation *n.* measure of the amount of variation within a group of numerical values, such as measurements of a quantity.

standardize *v.* (also **-ise**) (**-zing** or **-sing**) cause to conform to a standard. □ **standardization** /-'zeɪʃ(ə)n/ *n.*

standard lamp *n.* lamp on a tall upright with a base.

standard of living *n.* degree of material comfort of a person or group.

standard time *n.* uniform time for places in approximately the same longitude, established in a country or region by law or custom.

stand-by *n.* (*pl.* **-bys**) **1** (often *attrib.*) person or thing ready if needed in an emergency etc. **2** readiness for duty (*on stand-by*).

♦ **stand-by agreement** *n.* agreement between the International Monetary Fund and a member state, enabling the member to arrange for immediate drawing rights in addition to its normal drawing rights in such cases of emergency as a temporary balance of payments crisis.

---

stand-in *n.* deputy or substitute.

standing *–n.* **1** esteem or repute, esp. high; status. **2** duration (*of long standing*). *–adj.* **1** that stands, upright. **2** established, permanent (*a standing rule*; *a standing army*).

3 (of a jump, start, etc.) performed with no run-up. **4** (of water) stagnant.

standing committee *n.* committee that is permanent during the existence of the appointing body.

standing joke *n.* object of permanent ridicule.

♦ **standing order** *n.* **1** instruction by a customer to a bank (**banker's order**) or building society to pay a specified amount of money on a specified date or dates to a specified payee. Standing orders are widely used for such regular payments as insurance premiums, subscriptions, etc. See also CREDIT TRANSFER. **2** instruction to a retailer for a regular supply of goods.

---

standing orders *n.pl.* rules governing procedure in a parliament, council, etc.

standing ovation *n.* prolonged applause from an audience which has risen to its feet.

standing-room *n.* space to stand in.

stand-off half *n. Rugby* half-back forming a link between the scrum-half and the three-quarters.

standoffish /stænd'ɒfɪʃ/ *adj.* cold or distant in manner.

standpipe *n.* vertical pipe extending from a water supply, esp. one connecting a temporary tap to the mains.

standpoint *n.* point of view.

standstill *n.* stoppage; inability to proceed.

♦ **standstill agreement** *n.* **1** agreement between two countries in which a debt owed by one to the other is held in abeyance until a specified date in the future. **2** agreement between an unwelcome bidder for a company and the company, in which the bidder agrees to buy no more of the company's shares for a specified period.

---

stand-up *attrib. adj.* **1** (of a meal) eaten standing. **2** (of a fight) violent and thorough. **3** (of a collar) not turned down. **4** (of a comedian) telling jokes to an audience.

stank *past* of STINK.

Stanley /'stænlɪ/ (also **Port Stanley**) capital and chief port of the Falkland Islands, situated on the island of East Falkland; pop. (1991) 1557.

stanza /'stænzə/ *n.* basic metrical unit of a poem etc., typically of four to twelve rhymed lines. [Italian]

staphylococcus /ˌstæfɪlə'kɒkəs/ *n.* (*pl.* **-cocci** /-kaɪ/) bacterium sometimes forming pus. □ **staphylococcal** *adj.* [Greek *staphulē* bunch of grapes, *kokkos* berry]

staple[1] /'steɪp(ə)l/ *–n.* U-shaped metal bar or piece of wire with pointed ends for driving into and holding papers together, or holding an electrical wire in place, etc. *–v.* (**-ling**) fasten or provide with a staple. □ **stapler** *n.* [Old English]

staple[2] /'steɪp(ə)l/ *–n.* **1** principal or important article of commerce (*staples of British industry*). **2** chief element or main component. **3** fibre of cotton or wool etc. with regard to its quality (*cotton of fine staple*). *–attrib. adj.* **1** main or principal (*staple diet*). **2** important as a product or export. [French *estaple* market]

star /stɑː(r)/ *–n.* **1** celestial body appearing as a luminous point in the night sky. **2** large naturally luminous gaseous body such as the sun. **3** celestial body regarded as influencing fortunes etc. **4** thing like a star in shape or appearance. **5** decoration or mark of rank or excellence etc., usu. with radiating points. **6 a** famous or brilliant person; principal performer (*star of the show*). **b** (*attrib.*) outstanding (*star pupil*). *–v.* (**-rr-**) **1** appear or present as principal performer(s). **2** (esp. as **starred** *adj.*) mark, set, or adorn with a star or stars. □ **stardom** *n.* [Old English]

Stara Zagora /ˌstɑːrə zə'gɔːrə/ manufacturing city in E central Bulgaria; pop. (est. 1996) 149 666.

starboard /'stɑːbəd, -bɔːd/ *–n.* right-hand side of a ship or aircraft looking forward. *–v.* (also *absol.*) turn (the helm) to starboard. [Old English, = *steer board*]

starch *–n.* **1** polysaccharide obtained chiefly from cereals and potatoes. **2** preparation of this for stiffening fabric. **3** stiffness of manner; formality. *–v.* stiffen (clothing) with starch. [Old English: related to STARK]

starchy *adj.* (**-ier, -iest**) **1** of, like, or containing starch. **2** prim, formal. □ **starchily** *adv.* **starchiness** *n.*

stardust *n.* **1** multitude of stars looking like dust. **2** romance, magic feeling.

stare /steə(r)/ *–v.* (**-ring**) **1** (usu. foll. by *at*) look fixedly, esp. in curiosity, surprise, horror, etc. **2** reduce (a person) to a specified condition by staring (*stared me into silence*). *–n.* staring gaze. □ **stare a person in the face** be evident or imminent. **stare a person out** stare at a person until he or she looks away. [Old English]

starfish *n.* (*pl.* same or **-es**) echinoderm with five or more radiating arms.

star-gazer *n. colloq.* usu. *derog.* or *joc.* astronomer or astrologer.

stark *–adj.* **1** sharply evident (*in stark contrast*). **2** desolate, bare. **3** absolute (*stark madness*). *–adv.* completely, wholly (*stark naked*). □ **starkly** *adv.* **starkness** *n.* [Old English]

starkers /'stɑːkəz/ *predic. adj. slang* stark naked.

starlet /'stɑːlɪt/ *n.* promising young performer, esp. a film actress.

starlight *n.* light of the stars.

starling /'stɑːlɪŋ/ *n.* gregarious bird with blackish speckled lustrous plumage. [Old English]

starlit *adj.* **1** lit by stars. **2** with stars visible.

Star of David *n.* two interlaced equilateral triangles used as a Jewish and Israeli symbol.

starry *adj.* (**-ier, -iest**) **1** full of stars. **2** like a star.

starry-eyed *adj. colloq.* **1** enthusiastic but impractical. **2** euphoric.

Stars and Stripes *n.pl.* national flag of the US.

star-studded *adj.* covered with stars; featuring many famous performers.

START /stɑːt/ *abbr.* Strategic Arms Reduction Treaty (or Talks).

start *–v.* **1** begin. **2** set in motion or action (*started a fire*). **3** set oneself in motion or action. **4** begin a journey etc. **5** (often foll. by *up*) (cause to) begin operating. **6 a** cause or enable (a person) to make a beginning (*started me in business*). **b** (foll. by pres. part.) cause (a person) to begin (*started me coughing*). **7** (often foll. by *up*) establish. **8** give a signal to (competitors) to start in a race. **9** (often foll. by *up*, *from*, etc.) jump in surprise, pain, etc. **10** spring out, up, etc. **11** conceive (a baby). **12** rouse (game etc.). **13 a** (of timbers etc.) spring out; give way. **b** cause (timbers etc.) to do this. *–n.* **1** beginning. **2** place from which a race etc. begins. **3** advantage given at the beginning of a race etc. **4** advantageous initial position in life, business, etc. **5** sudden movement of surprise, pain, etc. □ **for a start** *colloq.* as a beginning. **start off** begin; begin to move. **start out** begin a journey. **start up** arise; occur. [Old English]

starter *n.* **1** device for starting a vehicle engine etc. **2** first course of a meal. **3** person giving the signal for the start of a race. **4** horse or competitor starting in a race.

starting-block *n.* shaped block for a runner's feet at the start of a race.

starting price *n.* odds ruling at the start of a horse-race.

startle /'stɑːt(ə)l/ *v.* (**-ling**) shock or surprise. [Old English]

star turn *n.* main item in an entertainment etc.

starve *v.* (**-ving**) **1** (cause to) die of hunger or suffer from malnourishment. **2** *colloq.* feel very hungry (*I'm starving*). **3 a** suffer from mental or spiritual want. **b** (foll. by *for*) feel a strong craving for. **4** (foll. by *of*) deprive of. **5** compel by starving (*starved into surrender*). □ **starvation** /-'veɪʃ(ə)n/ *n.* [Old English, = die]

starveling /'stɑːvlɪŋ/ *n. archaic* starving person or animal.

Star Wars *n.pl. colloq.* strategic defence initiative.

stash *colloq. –v.* (often foll. by *away*) **1** conceal; put in a safe place. **2** hoard. *–n.* **1** hiding-place. **2** thing hidden. [origin unknown]

stasis /'steɪsɪs/ *n.* (*pl.* **stases** /-siːz/) **1** inactivity; stagnation. **2** stoppage of circulation. [Greek]

state –*n.* **1** existing condition or position of a person or thing. **2** *colloq.* **a** excited or agitated mental condition (esp. *in a state*). **b** untidy condition. **3** (often **State**) **a** political community under one government. **b** this as part of a federal republic. **4** (often **State**) (*attrib.*) **a** of, for, or concerned with the state. **b** reserved for or done on occasions of ceremony. **5** (usu. **State**) civil government. **6** pomp. **7** (**the States**) USA. –*v.* (**-ting**) **1** express in speech or writing. **2** fix, specify. **3** *Mus.* play (a theme etc.), esp. for the first time. □ **in state** with all due ceremony. **lie in state** be laid in a public place of honour before burial. [partly from ESTATE, partly from Latin STATUS]

♦ **state bank** *n.* US commercial bank established by state charter rather than federal charter (cf. NATIONAL BANK). The rules governing the trading of state banks are controlled by state laws and there are therefore differences in practices from state to state. State banks are not compelled to join the Federal Reserve System, although national banks are.

♦ **state earnings-related pension scheme** *n.* (also **SERPS**) scheme, started in 1978, run by the UK government to provide a pension for every employed person in addition to the basic state flat-rate pension. The contributions are paid from part of the National-Insurance payments made by employees and employers. Payment of the pension starts at the state retirement age (65 for men, 60 for women) and the amount of pension received is calculated using a formula based on a percentage of the person's earnings. Persons who wish to contract out of SERPS may subscribe to an occupational pension scheme or a personal pension scheme.

stateless *adj.* having no nationality or citizenship.

stately *adj.* (**-ier, -iest**) dignified; imposing. □ **stateliness** *n.*

stately home *n.* large historic house, esp. one open to the public.

statement *n.* **1** stating or being stated; expression in words. **2** thing stated. **3** formal account of facts. **4** = BANK STATEMENT. **5** = STATEMENT OF ACCOUNT. **6** basic building block of a computer programming language, used in a program for a particular purpose or function, for example to specify some operation to be performed by a computer. A program consists of a sequence of statements.

♦ **statement of account** *n.* document recording the transactions of an organization with its customer for a specified period and usu. showing the indebtedness of one to the other. Many firms issue statements to their customers every month to draw attention to any unpaid invoices.

♦ **statement of affairs** *n.* statement showing the assets and liabilities of a person who is bankrupt or of a company in liquidation.

♦ **statement of standard accounting practice** *n.* (also **SSAP**) any of the statements issued by the Combined Accountancy Bodies to guide accountants on how to deal with such matters as depreciation, stock, mergers, leases, etc. in accounts in order to minimize disparity of treatment of the same transactions in different companies. These statements do not have the force of law but they represent the best accountancy practice; auditors are expected to follow them as presenting a 'true and fair view', unless it would be misleading to do so.

state of emergency *n.* condition of danger or disaster in a country, with normal constitutional procedures suspended. [medieval Latin: related to EMERGE]

state of the art –*n.* current stage of esp. technological development. –*attrib. adj.* (usu. **state-of-the-art**) absolutely up-to-date (*state-of-the-art weaponry*).

♦ **state ownership** see PUBLIC SECTOR.

stateroom *n.* **1** state apartment. **2** large private cabin in a passenger ship.

state school *n.* school largely managed and funded by the public authorities.

statesman *n.* (*fem.* **stateswoman**) distinguished and capable politician or diplomat. □ **statesmanlike** *adj.* **statesmanship** *n.*

static /ˈstætɪk/ –*adj.* **1** stationary; not acting or changing. **2** *Physics* concerned with bodies at rest or forces in equilibrium. –*n.* **1** static electricity. **2** atmospherics. □ **statically** *adv.* [Greek *statikos* from *sta-* stand]

static electricity *n.* electricity not flowing as a current.

statics *n.pl.* (usu. treated as *sing.*) **1** science of bodies at rest or of forces in equilibrium. **2** = STATIC *n.*

station /ˈsteɪʃ(ə)n/ –*n.* **1 a** regular stopping-place on a railway line. **b** buildings of this. **c** (in *comb.*) centre where vehicles of a specified type depart and arrive (*coach station*). **2** person or thing's allotted place or building etc. **3** centre for a particular service or activity. **4** establishment involved in broadcasting. **5 a** military or naval base. **b** inhabitants of this. **6** position in life; rank, status. **7** *Austral.* & *NZ* large sheep or cattle farm. –*v.* **1** assign a station to. **2** put in position. [Latin *statio* from *sto stat-* stand]

stationary *adj.* **1** not moving. **2** not meant to be moved. **3** unchanging. [Latin: related to STATION]

stationer *n.* dealer in stationery.

stationery *n.* writing-materials, office supplies, etc.

♦ **Stationery Office** *n.* (in full **Her Majesty's Stationery Office**) central government organization, founded in 1786, that supplies printing, binding, office supplies, and office machinery for the home and overseas public services. It also publishes and sells government publications, such as White Papers, acts of Parliament, Central Statistical Office information, Hansard, etc., at its own bookshops in London, Edinburgh, Manchester, Bristol, Birmingham, and Belfast.

stationmaster *n.* official in charge of a railway station.

station of the cross *n.* *RC Ch.* each of a series of images representing the events in Christ's Passion before which prayers are said.

station-wagon *n.* esp. *US* estate car.

statistic /stəˈtɪstɪk/ *n.* statistical fact or item. [German: related to STATE]

statistical *adj.* of statistics. □ **statistically** *adv.*

statistics *n.pl.* **1** (usu. treated as *sing.*) science concerned with the collection, classification, and presentation of information in numerical form. It is based on the assumption that if a group is sufficiently large, it will, unlike an individual, behave in a regular and reproducible manner. For groups that are not large enough for this assumption to be true, a measure of the likelihood of an event happening is its probability. Much of statistics is concerned with calculating and interpreting probabilities. **2** the numerical information so expressed. See also CENTRAL STATISTICAL OFFICE. □ **statistician** /ˌstætɪˈstɪʃ(ə)n/ *n.*

statuary /ˈstætʃʊərɪ/ –*adj.* of or for statues (*statuary art*). –*n.* (*pl.* **-ies**) **1** statues collectively. **2** making statues. **3** sculptor. [Latin: related to STATUE]

statue /ˈstætʃuː/ *n.* sculptured figure of a person or animal, esp. life-size or larger. [Latin *statua*]

statuesque /ˌstætʃʊˈesk/ *adj.* like, or having the dignity or beauty of, a statue.

statuette /ˌstætʃʊˈet/ *n.* small statue.

stature /ˈstætʃə(r)/ *n.* **1** height of a (esp. human) body. **2** calibre, esp. moral; eminence. [Latin *statura*]

status /ˈsteɪtəs/ *n.* **1** rank, social position, relative importance. **2** superior social etc. position. [Latin: related to STATURE]

status quo /ˌsteɪtəs ˈkwəʊ/ *n.* existing state of affairs. [Latin]

status symbol *n.* a possession etc. intended to indicate the owner's superiority.

statute /ˈstætʃuːt/ *n.* **1** written law passed by a legislative body. **2** rule of a corporation, founder, etc., intended to be permanent. [Latin *statutum* from *statuo* set up]

♦ **statute-barred debt** *n.* debt that has not been collected within the period allowed by law. See LIMITATION OF ACTIONS.

statute-book *n.* **1** book(s) containing the statute law. **2** body of a country's statutes.
statute law *n.* **1** (*collect.*) body of principles and rules of law laid down in statutes. **2** a statute.
statute mile see MILE 1.
statutory /ˈstatʃʊtərɪ/ *adj.* required or enacted by statute. □ **statutorily** *adv.*

♦ **statutory books** *n.pl.* books of account that the Companies Act (1985) requires a company to keep. They must show and explain the company's transactions, disclose with reasonable accuracy the company's financial position at any time, and enable the directors to ensure that any accounts prepared therefrom comply with the provisions of the act. They must also include entries from day to day of all money received and paid out together with a record of all assets and liabilities and statements of stockholding (where appropriate).
♦ **statutory company** *n.* company formed by special act of Parliament. Such companies are usu. public utilities that were either not nationalized or have been privatized. Their powers and privileges depend on the act under which they were formed.
♦ **statutory damages** see DAMAGES.
♦ **statutory maternity pay** *n.* (also **SMP**) pay for pregnant women who have been employed for at least six months and earned at least the lower earnings limit for National Insurance contributions. It is paid by the employer at a standard rate for 18 weeks for those who have been employed for between six months and two years. For those employed for over two years SMP is related to earnings for the first six weeks, followed by twelve weeks at the standard rate.
♦ **statutory meeting** *n.* meeting required to be held by statute, esp. one held in accordance with the Companies Act (1985), usu. the annual general meeting of the shareholders.
♦ **statutory report** *n.* report required to be made by statute, esp. the annual report and accounts required to be laid before the members of a company by the Companies Act (1985).
♦ **statutory sick pay** *n.* (also **SSP**) pay for employees absent from work due to sickness or injury. It is paid by the employer for a maximum of 28 weeks in any year and can be recovered from National Insurance contributions.

staunch[1] /stɔːntʃ/ *adj.* **1** loyal. **2** (of a ship, joint, etc.) strong, watertight, airtight, etc. □ **staunchly** *adv.* [French *estanche*]
staunch[2] var. of STANCH.
Stavanger /stəˈvæŋgə(r)/ seaport in SW Norway, centre of the country's North Sea oil industry; pop. (1996) 104 322.
stave –*n.* **1** each of the curved slats forming the sides of a cask, pail, etc. **2** = STAFF *n.* 3. **3** stanza or verse. –*v.* (**-ving**; *past* and *past part.* **stove** or **staved**) (usu. foll. by *in*) break a hole in, damage, crush by forcing inwards. □ **stave off** avert or defer (danger etc.). [from STAFF]
Stavropol see TOGLIATTI.
stay[1] –*v.* **1** continue in the same place or condition; not depart or change. **2** (often foll. by *at*, *in*, *with*) reside temporarily. **3** *archaic* or *literary* **a** stop or check. **b** (esp. in *imper.*) pause. **4** postpone (judgement etc.). **5** assuage (hunger etc.), esp. temporarily. –*n.* **1** act or period of staying. **2** suspension or postponement of a sentence, judgement, etc. **3** prop, support. **4** (in *pl.*) *hist.* (esp. boned) corset. □ **stay the course** endure to the end. **stay in** remain indoors. **stay the night** remain overnight. **stay put** *colloq.* remain where it is placed or where one is. **stay up** not go to bed (until late). [Anglo-French from Latin *sto* stand: sense 3 of *n.* from French, formed as STAY[2]]
stay[2] *n.* **1** *Naut.* rope or guy supporting a mast, flagstaff, etc. **2** supporting cable on an aircraft etc. [Old English from Germanic]
stay-at-home –*attrib. adj.* rarely going out. –*n.* such a person.
stayer *n.* person or animal with great endurance.
staying power *n.* endurance.
staysail /ˈsteɪseɪl, -s(ə)l/ *n.* sail extended on a stay.
STC *abbr.* Standard Telephones and Cables Ltd.
STD *abbr.* = SUBSCRIBER TRUNK DIALLING.
STE *abbr.* Society of Telecom Executives (trade union).
S[té] *abbr.* (French) société (= company, society).
stead /sted/ *n.* □ **in a person's or thing's stead** as a substitute; in a person's or thing's place. **stand a person in good stead** be advantageous or useful to him or her. [Old English, = place]
steadfast /ˈstedfɑːst/ *adj.* constant, firm, unwavering. □ **steadfastly** *adv.* **steadfastness** *n.* [Old English: related to STEAD]
steady /ˈstedɪ/ –*adj.* (**-ier**, **-iest**) **1** firmly fixed or supported; unwavering. **2** uniform and regular (*steady pace*; *steady increase*). **3 a** constant. **b** persistent. **4** (of a person) serious and dependable. **5** regular, established (*steady girlfriend*). –*v.* (**-ies**, **-ied**) make or become steady. –*adv.* steadily. –*n.* (*pl.* **-ies**) *colloq.* regular boyfriend or girlfriend. □ **go steady** (often foll. by *with*) *colloq.* have as a regular boyfriend or girlfriend. **steady on!** be careful! □ **steadily** *adv.* **steadiness** *n.* [from STEAD]
steady state *n.* unvarying condition, esp. in a physical process.
steak /steɪk/ *n.* **1** thick slice of meat (esp. beef) or fish, usu. grilled or fried. **2** beef cut for stewing or braising. [Old Norse]
steak-house *n.* restaurant specializing in beefsteaks.
steal –*v.* (*past* **stole**; *past part.* **stolen**) **1** (also *absol.*) take (another's property) illegally or without right or permission, esp. in secret. **2** obtain surreptitiously, insidiously, or artfully (*stole a kiss*). **3** (foll. by *in*, *out*, *away*, *up*, etc.) move, esp. silently or stealthily. –*n.* **1** *US colloq.* act of stealing or theft. **2** *colloq.* easy task or good bargain. □ **steal a march on** get an advantage over by surreptitious means. **steal the show** outshine other performers, esp. unexpectedly. **steal a person's thunder** take away the attention due to someone else by using his or her words, ideas, etc. [Old English]
stealth /stelθ/ *n.* secrecy, secret behaviour. [Old English: related to STEAL]
stealthy *adj.* (**-ier**, **-iest**) done or moving with stealth; furtive. □ **stealthily** *adv.* **stealthiness** *n.*
steam –*n.* **1 a** gas into which water is changed by boiling. **b** condensed vapour formed from this. **2 a** power obtained from steam. **b** *colloq.* power or energy. –*v.* **1 a** cook (food) in steam. **b** treat with steam. **2** give off steam. **3 a** move under steam power. **b** (foll. by *ahead*, *away*, etc.) *colloq.* proceed or travel fast or with vigour. **4** (usu. foll. by *up*) **a** cover or become covered with condensed steam. **b** (as **steamed up** *adj.*) *colloq.* angry or excited. [Old English]
steamboat *n.* steam-driven boat.
steam engine *n.* **1** engine which uses steam to generate power. **2** locomotive powered by this.
steamer *n.* **1** steamship. **2** vessel for steaming food in.
steam hammer *n.* forging-hammer powered by steam.
steam iron *n.* electric iron that emits steam.
steamroller –*n.* **1** heavy slow-moving vehicle with a roller, used to flatten new-made roads. **2** a crushing power or force. –*v.* crush or move forcibly or indiscriminately; force.
steamship *n.* steam-driven ship.
steam train *n.* train pulled by a steam engine.
steamy *adj.* (**-ier**, **-iest**) **1** like or full of steam. **2** *colloq.* erotic. □ **steamily** *adv.* **steaminess** *n.*
steatite /ˈstɪətaɪt/ *n.* impure form of talc, esp. soapstone. [Greek *stear steat-* tallow]
steed *n.* *archaic* or *poet.* horse. [Old English]

steel –*n.* **1** strong malleable alloy of iron and carbon, used esp. for making tools, weapons, etc. **2** strength, firmness (*nerves of steel*). **3** steel rod for sharpening knives. –*adj.* of or like steel. –*v.* (also *refl.*) harden or make resolute. [Old English]

steel band *n.* band playing chiefly calypso-style music on percussion instruments made from oil drums.

steel wool *n.* abrasive substance consisting of a mass of fine steel shavings.

steelworks *n.pl.* (usu. treated as *sing.*) factory producing steel. □ **steelworker** *n.*

steely *adj.* (**-ier, -iest**) **1** of or like steel. **2** severe; resolute. □ **steeliness** *n.*

steelyard *n.* balance with a graduated arm along which a weight is moved.

steep[1] –*adj.* **1** sloping sharply. **2** (of a rise or fall) rapid. **3** (*predic.*) *colloq.* **a** exorbitant; unreasonable. **b** exaggerated; incredible. –*n.* steep slope; precipice. □ **steepen** *v.* **steepish** *adj.* **steeply** *adv.* **steepness** *n.* [Old English]

steep[2] –*v.* soak or bathe in liquid. –*n.* **1** act of steeping. **2** liquid for steeping. □ **steep in 1** pervade or imbue with. **2** make deeply acquainted with (a subject etc.). [Old English]

steeple /'stiːp(ə)l/ *n.* tall tower, esp. with a spire, above the roof of a church. [Old English: related to STEEP[1]]

steeplechase *n.* **1** horse-race with ditches, hedges, etc., to jump. **2** cross-country foot-race. □ **steeplechasing** *n.*

steeplejack *n.* repairer of tall chimneys, steeples, etc.

steer[1] *v.* **1** (also *absol.*) guide (a vehicle, ship, etc.) with a wheel or rudder etc. **2** direct or guide (one's course, other people, a conversation, etc.) in a specified direction. □ **steer clear of** avoid. □ **steering** *n.* [Old English]

steer[2] *n.* = BULLOCK. [Old English]

steerage *n.* **1** act of steering. **2** *archaic* cheapest part of a ship's accommodation.

steering-column *n.* column on which a steering-wheel is mounted.

steering committee *n.* committee deciding the order of business, the course of operations, etc.

steering-wheel *n.* wheel by which a vehicle etc. is steered.

steersman *n.* person who steers a ship.

stegosaurus /ˌstegə'sɔːrəs/ *n.* (*pl.* **-ruses**) plant-eating dinosaur with a double row of bony plates along the spine. [Greek *stegē* covering, *sauros* lizard]

Steiermark see STYRIA.

stela /'stiːlə/ *n.* (*pl.* **stelae** /-liː/) (also **stele** /stiːl, 'stiːlɪ/) *Archaeol.* upright slab or pillar usu. inscribed and sculpted, esp. as a gravestone. [Latin and Greek]

stellar /'stelə(r)/ *adj.* of a star or stars. [Latin *stella* star]

stem[1] –*n.* **1** main body or stalk of a plant. **2** stalk of a fruit, flower, or leaf. **3** stem-shaped part, as: **a** the slender part of a wineglass. **b** the tube of a tobacco-pipe. **c** a vertical stroke in a letter or musical note. **4** *Gram.* root or main part of a noun, verb, etc., to which inflections are added. **5** main upright timber at the bow of a ship (*from stem to stern*). –*v.* (**-mm-**) (foll. by *from*) spring or originate from. [Old English]

stem[2] *v.* (**-mm-**) check or stop. [Old Norse]

stench *n.* foul smell. [Old English: related to STINK]

stencil /'stensɪl/ –*n.* **1** (in full **stencil-plate**) thin sheet in which a pattern is cut, placed on a surface and printed or inked over etc. to reproduce the pattern. **2** pattern so produced. **3** waxed sheet etc. from which a stencil is made by a typewriter. –*v.* (**-ll-**; *US* **-l-**) **1** (often foll. by *on*) produce (a pattern) with a stencil. **2** mark (a surface) in this way. [French *estanceler* sparkle, from Latin *scintilla* spark]

Sten gun *n.* lightweight sub-machine-gun. [*S* and *T* (initials of its inventors' surnames) + *-en* after BREN]

stenographer /ste'nɒgrəfə(r)/ *n.* esp. *US* shorthand typist. [Greek *stenos* narrow]

stentorian /sten'tɔːrɪən/ *adj.* loud and powerful. [*Stentor*, name of a herald in Homer's *Iliad*]

step –*n.* **1 a** complete movement of one leg in walking or running. **b** distance so covered. **2** unit of movement in dancing. **3** measure taken, esp. one of several in a course of action. **4** surface of a stair, stepladder, etc.; tread. **5** short distance. **6** sound or mark made by a foot in walking etc. **7** manner of walking etc. **8** degree in the scale of promotion or precedence etc. **9 a** stepping in unison or to music (esp. *in* or *out of step*). **b** state of conforming (*refuses to keep step with the team*). **10** (in *pl.*) (also **pair of steps**) = STEPLADDER. –*v.* (**-pp-**) **1** lift and set down one's foot or alternate feet in walking. **2** come or go in a specified direction by stepping. **3** make progress in a specified way (*stepped into a new job*). **4** (foll. by *off, out*) measure (distance) by stepping. **5** perform (a dance). □ **mind** (or **watch) one's step** be careful. **step by step** gradually; cautiously. **step down** resign. **step in 1** enter. **2** intervene. **step on it** *colloq.* accelerate; hurry up. **step out 1** be active socially. **2** take large steps. **step out of line** behave inappropriately or disobediently. **step up** increase, intensify. [Old English]

step- *comb. form* denoting a relationship resulting from a parent's later marriage. [Old English, = orphaned]

Stepanakert /ˌstepənə'kɜːt/ city in Azerbaijan, capital of the autonomous region of Nagorno-Karabakh; pop. (1990) 33 000.

stepbrother *n.* son of one's step-parent by a previous partner.

stepchild *n.* one's husband's or wife's child by a previous partner.

stepdaughter *n.* female stepchild.

stepfather *n.* male step-parent.

stephanotis /ˌstefə'nəʊtɪs/ *n.* fragrant tropical climbing plant. [Greek]

stepladder *n.* short folding ladder with flat steps.

stepmother *n.* female step-parent.

step-parent *n.* mother's or father's spouse who is not one's own parent.

steppe *n.* level grassy unforested plain. [Russian]

♦ **stepped costs** *n.pl.* = SEMIVARIABLE COSTS.

---

stepping-stone *n.* **1** large stone in a stream etc. helping one to cross. **2** means of progress.

stepsister *n.* daughter of one's step-parent by a previous partner.

stepson *n.* male stepchild.

ster. *abbr.* sterling.

-ster *suffix* denoting a person engaged in or associated with a particular activity or quality (*brewster; gangster; youngster*). [Old English]

stereo /'sterɪəʊ, 'stɪə-/ –*n.* (*pl.* **-s**) **1 a** stereophonic record-player etc. **b** stereophonic sound reproduction (see STEREOPHONIC). **2** = STEREOSCOPE. –*adj.* **1** = STEREOPHONIC. **2** stereoscopic (see STEREOSCOPE). [abbreviation]

stereo- *comb. form* solid; having three dimensions. [Greek *stereos* solid]

stereophonic /ˌsterɪəʊ'fɒnɪk, ˌstɪə-/ *adj.* using two or more channels, giving the effect of naturally distributed sound.

stereoscope /'sterɪəˌskəʊp, 'stɪə-/ *n.* device for producing a three-dimensional effect by viewing two slightly different photographs together. □ **stereoscopic** /-'skɒpɪk/ *adj.*

stereotype /'sterɪəʊˌtaɪp, 'stɪə-/ –*n.* **1 a** person or thing seeming to conform to a widely accepted type. **b** such a type, idea, or attitude. **2** printing-plate cast from a mould of composed type. –*v.* (**-ping**) **1** (esp. as **stereotyped** *adj.*) cause to conform to a type; standardize. **2 a** print from a stereotype. **b** make a stereotype of. [French: related to STEREO-]

sterile /'steraɪl/ *adj.* **1** unable to produce a crop, fruit, or young; barren. **2** unproductive (*sterile discussion*). **3** free from living micro-organisms etc. □ **sterility** /stəˈrɪlɪtɪ/ *n.* [Latin]

♦ **sterilization** /ˌsterɪlaɪˈzeɪʃ(ə)n/ *n.* (also **-isation**) **1** making sterile. **2** sterilized condition. **3** *Econ.* offsetting the inflationary-deflationary effects that result when a government intervenes in foreign-exchange markets. If a nation's currency is depreciating and its government wishes to intervene to stabilize the exchange rate, it can sell its reserves of foreign currency and buy its own currency. However, buying its own currency will take money out of circulation, which could cause interest rates to rise, followed by recession. Sterilization is the process of expanding the money supply in these circumstances to prevent increases in interest rates and any consequent recession. Conversely, if a government intervenes to prevent a currency from appreciating, sterilization would involve reducing the money supply.

sterilize /ˈsterɪˌlaɪz/ *v.* (also **-ise**) (**-zing** or **-sing**) **1** make sterile. **2** deprive of reproductive powers.

sterling /ˈstɜːlɪŋ/ *–adj.* **1** of or in British money (*pound sterling*). **2** (of a coin or precious metal) genuine; of standard value or purity. **3** (of a person etc.) genuine, reliable. *–n.* British money, esp. the UK pound as distinguished from the pounds of other countries. [Old English, = penny]

sterling silver *n.* silver of 92½% purity.

stern[1] *adj.* severe, grim; authoritarian. □ **sternly** *adv.* **sternness** *n.* [Old English]

stern[2] *n.* rear part, esp. of a ship or boat. [Old Norse: related to STEER[1]]

sternum /ˈstɜːnəm/ *n.* (*pl.* **-s** or **sterna**) breastbone. [Greek *sternon* chest]

steroid /ˈstɪərɔɪd, ˈste-/ *n.* any of a group of organic compounds including many hormones, alkaloids, and vitamins. [from STEROL]

sterol /ˈsterɒl/ *n.* naturally occurring steroid alcohol. [from CHOLESTEROL, etc.]

stertorous /ˈstɜːtərəs/ *adj.* (of breathing etc.) laboured and noisy. [Latin *sterto* snore]

stet *v.* (**-tt-**) (usu. written on a proof-sheet etc.) ignore or cancel (the alteration); let the original stand. [Latin, = let it stand]

stethoscope /ˈsteθəˌskəʊp/ *n.* instrument used in listening to the heart, lungs, etc. [Greek *stēthos* breast]

stetson /ˈstets(ə)n/ *n.* slouch hat with a very wide brim and high crown. [*Stetson*, name of a hat-maker]

Stettin see SZCZECIN.

stevedore /ˈstiːvəˌdɔː(r)/ *n.* person employed in loading and unloading ships. [Spanish *estivador*]

stew *–v.* **1** cook by long simmering in a closed vessel. **2** fret, be anxious. **3** *colloq.* swelter. **4** (of tea etc.) become bitter or strong from infusing too long. **5** (as **stewed** *adj.*) *colloq.* drunk. *–n.* **1** dish of stewed meat etc. **2** *colloq.* agitated or angry state. □ **stew in one's own juice** suffer the consequences of one's actions. [French *estuver*]

steward /ˈstjuːəd/ *–n.* **1** passengers' attendant on a ship, aircraft, or train. **2** official supervising a meeting, show, etc. **3** person responsible for supplies of food etc. for a college or club etc. **4** property manager. *–v.* act as a steward (of). □ **stewardship** *n.* [Old English, = house-warden]

stewardess /ˌstjuːəˈdes, ˈstjuːədɪs/ *n.* female steward, esp. on a ship or aircraft.

Stewart Island /ˈstjuːət/ island of New Zealand, off the S coast of South Island; pop. (est. 1994) 700; chief settlement, Oban.

stg. *abbr.* sterling.

STI *abbr.* Straits Times Index (of the Singapore Stock Exchange).

stick[1] *n.* **1 a** short slender length of wood. **b** this as a support or weapon. **2** thin rod of wood etc. for a particular purpose (*cocktail stick*). **3** implement used to propel the ball in hockey or polo etc. **4** gear lever. **5** conductor's baton. **6** sticklike piece of celery, dynamite, etc. **7** (often prec. by *the*) punishment, esp. by beating. **8** *colloq.* adverse criticism. **9** *colloq.* piece of wood as part of a house or furniture. **10** *colloq.* person, esp. when dull or unsociable. [Old English]

stick[2] *v.* (*past* and *past part.* **stuck**) **1** (foll. by *in*, *into*, *through*) insert or thrust (a thing or its point). **2** stab. **3** (foll. by *in*, *into*, *on*, etc.) **a** fix or be fixed on a pointed thing. **b** fix or be fixed (as) by a pointed end. **4** fix or be fixed (as) by adhesive etc. **5** remain (in the mind). **6** lose or be deprived of movement or action through adhesion, jamming, etc. **7** *colloq.* **a** put in a specified position or place. **b** remain in a place. **8** *colloq.* (of an accusation etc.) be convincing or regarded as valid. **9** *colloq.* endure, tolerate. **10** (foll. by *at*) *colloq.* persevere with. □ **be stuck for** be at a loss for or in need of. **be stuck on** *colloq.* be infatuated with. **be stuck with** *colloq.* be unable to get rid of. **get stuck in** (or **into** a thing) *slang* begin in earnest. **stick around** *colloq.* linger; remain. **stick at nothing** be absolutely ruthless. **stick by** (or **with**) stay loyal or close to. **stick in one's throat** be against one's principles. **stick it out** *colloq.* endure a burden etc. to the end. **stick one's neck out** be rashly bold. **stick out** (cause to) protrude. **stick out for** persist in demanding. **stick to 1** remain fixed on or to. **2** remain loyal to. **3** keep to (a subject etc.). **stick together** *colloq.* remain united or mutually loyal. **stick up 1** be or make erect or protruding upwards. **2** fasten to an upright surface. **3** *colloq.* rob or threaten with a gun. **stick up for** support or defend. [Old English]

sticker *n.* **1** adhesive label. **2** persistent person.

sticking-plaster *n.* adhesive plaster for wounds etc.

stick insect *n.* insect with a twiglike body.

stick-in-the-mud *n. colloq.* unprogressive or old-fashioned person.

stickleback /ˈstɪk(ə)lˌbæk/ *n.* small spiny-backed fish. [Old English, = thorn-back]

stickler *n.* (foll. by *for*) person who insists on something (*stickler for accuracy*). [obsolete *stickle* be umpire]

stick-up *n. colloq.* robbery using a gun.

sticky *adj.* (**-ier**, **-iest**) **1** tending or intended to stick or adhere. **2** glutinous, viscous. **3** humid. **4** *colloq.* difficult, awkward; unpleasant, painful (*sticky problem*; *came to a sticky end*). □ **stickily** *adv.* **stickiness** *n.*

sticky wicket *n. colloq.* difficult circumstances.

stiff *–adj.* **1** rigid; inflexible. **2** hard to bend, move, or turn etc. **3** hard to cope with; needing strength or effort (*stiff climb*). **4** severe or strong (*stiff penalty*). **5** formal, constrained. **6** (of a muscle, limb, or person etc.) aching owing to exertion, injury, etc. **7** (of esp. an alcoholic drink) strong. **8** (foll. by *with*) *colloq.* abounding in. *–adv. colloq.* utterly, extremely (*bored stiff*; *worried stiff*). *–n. slang* **1** corpse. **2** foolish or useless person. □ **stiffish** *adj.* **stiffly** *adv.* **stiffness** *n.* [Old English]

stiffen *v.* make or become stiff. □ **stiffening** *n.*

stiff-necked *adj.* obstinate; haughty.

stiff upper lip *n.* appearance of being calm in adversity.

stifle /ˈstaɪf(ə)l/ *v.* (**-ling**) **1** suppress. **2** feel or make unable to breathe easily; suffocate. **3** kill by suffocating. □ **stifling** *adj.* & *adv.* [origin uncertain]

stigma /ˈstɪgmə/ *n.* (*pl.* **-s** or, esp. in sense 3, **stigmata** /-mətə, -ˈmɑːtə/) **1** shame, disgrace. **2** part of the pistil that receives the pollen in pollination. **3** (in *pl.*) (in Christian belief) marks like those on Christ's body after the Crucifixion. [Greek *stigma -mat-* brand, dot]

stigmatize /ˈstɪgməˌtaɪz/ *v.* (also **-ise**) (**-zing** or **-sing**) (often foll. by *as*) brand as unworthy or disgraceful. [Greek *stigmatizō*: related to STIGMA]

stile *n.* steps allowing people but not animals to climb over a fence or wall. [Old English]

stiletto /stɪˈletəʊ/ *n.* (*pl.* **-s**) **1** short dagger. **2** (in full **stiletto heel**) **a** long tapering heel of a shoe. **b** shoe with such a heel. **3** pointed instrument for making eyelets etc. [Italian diminutive: related to STYLE]

still[1] *–adj.* **1** not or hardly moving. **2** with little or no sound; calm and tranquil. **3** (of a drink) not effervescing. *–n.* **1** deep silence (*still of the night*). **2** static photograph (as opposed to a motion picture), esp. a single shot from a cinema film. *–adv.* **1** without moving (*sit still*). **2** even now or at a particular time (*is he still here?*). **3** nevertheless. **4** (with *compar.*) even, yet, increasingly (*still greater efforts*). *–v.* make or become still; quieten. □ **stillness** *n.* [Old English]

still[2] *n.* apparatus for distilling spirits etc. [obsolete *still* (v.) = DISTIL]

stillbirth *n.* birth of a dead child.

stillborn *adj.* **1** born dead. **2** abortive.

still life *n.* (*pl.* **lifes**) painting or drawing of inanimate objects, e.g. fruit or flowers.

still-room *n.* **1** room for distilling. **2** housekeeper's store-room or pantry.

stilt *n.* **1** either of a pair of poles with foot supports for walking at a distance above the ground. **2** each of a set of piles or posts supporting a building etc. [Low German or Dutch]

stilted *adj.* **1** (of literary style etc.) stiff and unnatural; bombastic. **2** standing on stilts.

Stilton /ˈstɪlt(ə)n/ *n. propr.* strong rich esp. blue-veined cheese. [*Stilton* in England]

stimulant /ˈstɪmjʊlənt/ *–adj.* stimulating, esp. bodily or mental activity. *–n.* stimulant substance or influence. [Latin: related to STIMULATE]

stimulate /ˈstɪmjʊˌleɪt/ *v.* (**-ting**) **1** act as a stimulus to. **2** animate, excite, arouse. □ **stimulation** /-ˈleɪʃ(ə)n/ *n.* **stimulative** /-lətɪv/ *adj.* **stimulator** *n.* [Latin: related to STIMULUS]

stimulus /ˈstɪmjʊləs/ *n.* (*pl.* **-li** /-ˌlaɪ/) thing that rouses to activity. [Latin, = goad]

sting *–n.* **1** sharp wounding organ of an insect, snake, nettle, etc. **2 a** act of inflicting a wound with this. **b** the wound itself or the pain caused by it. **3** painful quality or effect. **4** pungency, vigour. **5** *slang* swindle. *–v.* (*past* and *past part.* **stung**) **1 a** wound or pierce with a sting. **b** be able to sting. **2** feel or give a tingling physical or sharp mental pain. **3** (foll. by *into*) incite, esp. painfully (*stung into replying*). **4** *slang* swindle, charge exorbitantly. □ **sting in the tail** unexpected final pain or difficulty. [Old English]

stinger *n.* stinging animal or thing, esp. a sharp blow.

stinging-nettle *n.* nettle with stinging hairs.

stingray *n.* broad flat-fish with a poisonous spine at the base of its tail.

stingy /ˈstɪndʒɪ/ *adj.* (**-ier, -iest**) *colloq.* niggardly, mean. □ **stingily** *adv.* **stinginess** *n.* [perhaps from STING]

stink *–v.* (*past* **stank** or **stunk**; *past part.* **stunk**) **1** emit a strong offensive smell. **2** (often foll. by *out*) fill (a place) with a stink. **3** (foll. by *out* etc.) drive (a person) out etc. by a stink. **4** *colloq.* be or seem very unpleasant. *–n.* **1** strong or offensive smell. **2** *colloq.* row or fuss. [Old English]

stink bomb *n.* device emitting a stink when opened.

stinker *n. slang* objectionable or difficult person or thing.

stinking *–adj.* **1** that stinks. **2** *slang* very objectionable. *–adv. slang* extremely and usu. objectionably (*stinking rich*).

stint *–v.* **1** supply (food or aid etc.) meanly or grudgingly. **2** (often *refl.*) supply (a person etc.) in this way. *–n.* **1** limitation of supply or effort (*without stint*). **2** allotted amount of work (*do one's stint*). **3** small sandpiper. [Old English]

stipend /ˈstaɪpend/ *n.* salary, esp. of a clergyman. [Latin *stipendium*]

stipendiary /staɪˈpendjərɪ, stɪ-/ *–adj.* receiving a stipend. *–n.* (*pl.* **-ies**) person receiving a stipend. [Latin: related to STIPEND]

stipendiary magistrate *n.* paid professional magistrate.

stipple /ˈstɪp(ə)l/ *–v.* (**-ling**) **1** draw or paint or engrave etc. with dots instead of lines. **2** roughen the surface of (paint, cement, etc.). *–n.* **1** stippling. **2** effect of stippling. [Dutch]

stipulate /ˈstɪpjʊˌleɪt/ *v.* (**-ting**) demand or specify as part of a bargain etc. □ **stipulation** /-ˈleɪʃ(ə)n/ *n.* [Latin *stipulari*]

stir[1] *–v.* (**-rr-**) **1** move a spoon etc. round and round in (a liquid etc.), esp. to mix ingredients. **2 a** cause to move, esp. slightly. **b** be or begin to be in motion. **3** rise from sleep. **4** arouse, inspire, or excite (the emotions, a person, etc.). **5** *colloq.* cause trouble between people by gossiping etc. *–n.* **1** act of stirring. **2** commotion, excitement. □ **stir in** add (an ingredient) by stirring. **stir up 1** mix thoroughly by stirring. **2** stimulate, excite. □ **stirrer** *n.* [Old English]

stir[2] *n. slang* prison. [origin unknown]

stir-fry *–v.* fry rapidly while stirring. *–n.* stir-fried dish.

Stirling /ˈstɜːlɪŋ/ market town in central Scotland, capital of Central region; industries include textiles, chemicals, and the manufacture of agricultural machinery; pop. (1991) 30 515.

stirrup /ˈstɪrəp/ *n.* metal loop supporting a horse-rider's foot. [Old English, = climbing-rope]

stirrup-cup *n.* cup of wine etc. offered to a departing traveller, orig. a rider.

stirrup-leather *n.* (also **stirrup-strap**) strap attaching a stirrup to a saddle.

stirrup-pump *n.* hand-operated water-pump with a foot-rest, used to extinguish small fires.

stitch *–n.* **1 a** (in sewing, knitting, or crocheting) single pass of a needle, or the resulting thread or loop etc. **b** particular method of sewing etc. **2** least bit of clothing (*hadn't a stitch on*). **3** sharp pain in the side induced by running etc. *–v.* sew; make stitches (in). □ **in stitches** *colloq.* laughing uncontrollably. **stitch up 1** join or mend by sewing. **2** *slang* trick, cheat, betray. [Old English: related to STICK[2]]

stitch in time *n.* timely remedy.

STMS *abbr.* SHORT-TERM MONETARY SUPPORT.

stoat *n.* mammal of the weasel family with brown fur turning mainly white in the winter. [origin unknown]

stock *–n.* **1** store of goods etc. ready for sale or distribution etc. **2** supply or quantity of anything for use. **3** collection of assets, e.g. plant and machinery owned by a company, equipment or raw material for manufacture or trade, etc. **4** farm animals or equipment. **5 a** fixed-interest security issued by the government, a local authority, or a company in fixed units, often of £100 each. Stocks usu. have a redemption date on which the par value of the unit price is repaid in full. They are dealt in on stock exchanges at prices that fluctuate, but depend on such factors as their yield and the time they have to run before redemption. **b** *US* = ORDINARY SHARE. **6** reputation or popularity (*his stock is rising*). **7 a** money lent to a government at fixed interest. **b** right to receive such interest. **8** line of ancestry (*comes of Cornish stock*). **9** liquid basis for soup etc. made by stewing bones, vegetables, etc. **10** fragrant-flowered cruciferous cultivated plant. **11** plant into which a graft is inserted. **12** main trunk of a tree etc. **13** (in *pl.*) *hist.* timber frame with holes for the feet in which offenders were locked as a public punishment. **14** base, support, or handle for an implement or machine. **15** butt of a rifle etc. **16** (in *pl.*) supports for a ship during building or repair. **17** band of cloth worn round the neck. *–attrib. adj.* **1** kept in stock and so regularly available. **2** hackneyed, conventional. *–v.* **1** have (goods) in stock. **2** provide (a shop or a farm etc.) with goods, livestock, etc. **3** fit (a gun etc.) with a stock. □ **in** (or **out of) stock** available (or not available) immediately for sale etc. **stock up** (often foll. by *with*) provide with or get stocks or supplies (of). **take stock 1** make an inventory of one's stock. **2** (often foll. by *of*) review (a situation etc.). [Old English]

stockade /stɒˈkeɪd/ *–n.* line or enclosure of upright stakes. *–v.* (**-ding**) fortify with this. [Spanish *estacada*]

♦ **stock appreciation** *n.* amount by which the value of the stock-in-trade of an organization has increased over any given period. This may refer to an increase in value due to inflation, which will be recorded in the accounts as a profit, although it is not a real profit as when the goods are sold they need to be replaced at an inflated price. To counteract this situation, adjustments have been made in the tax system, through stock relief, and in the accounting system, through current-cost accounting. Stock-in-trade may also appreciate (or depreciate) genuinely as a result of market fluctuations, esp. of raw materials.

stockbreeder *n.* livestock farmer.

♦ **stockbroker** *n.* agent who buys and sells securities on a stock exchange on behalf of clients and receives remuneration for this service in the form of a commission. Before October 1986 (see BIG BANG), stockbrokers on the London Stock Exchange were not permitted by the rules of the Stock Exchange to act as principals (unlike stockjobbers) and they worked for a fixed commission laid down by the Stock Exchange. Since October 1986, however, many London stockbrokers have taken advantage of the new rules, which allow them to buy and sell as principals, in which capacity they are now known as market makers. This change has been accompanied by the formal abolition of fixed commissions, enabling stockbrokers to vary their commission in competition with each other. Stockbrokers have traditionally offered investment advice, esp. for their institutional investors, but this service has been reduced. □ **stockbroking** *n.*

♦ **stock-building** *n.* accumulating stocks of goods for future sale. Most firms retain a certain level of stocks of finished products as a precaution against sudden increases in demand or loss of production because of strikes, etc. (see STOCK CONTROL). Stock-building represents an investment by the firm in its own goods, although unlike other forms of investment stock levels tend to increase in a recession and to fall during a boom. Stock-building can have an important effect on the behaviour of the macroeconomy; in the UK, stocks are equivalent to about 30% of the value of the gross domestic product.

stock-car *n.* specially strengthened car for use in racing with deliberate bumping.

♦ **stock control** *n.* regulation of the stock-in-trade of a company so that all components or items are available without delay but without tying up unnecessarily large sums of money. Many large manufacturers, retailers, etc. have a computerized stock-control system with automatic reordering when the stock of an item reaches a predetermined low level. In retail supermarkets, for example, the act of registering a sale at the checkout reduces the quantity of that item on the computer-held stock record; new deliveries are entered as they arrive. Thus, the stock at any instant can be read from the computer. A periodic check of the actual stock reveals the extent of pilfering.

♦ **stock cover** *n.* time for which a company's stock of raw materials would last, without replenishment at the current rate of sale or use.

♦ **stock depreciation** *n.* amount by which the value of the stock-in-trade of an organization has decreased over any given period. See also STOCK APPRECIATION.

♦ **stock exchange** *n.* **1** (also **stock market**) place in which stocks, shares, and other securities are bought and sold, prices being controlled by supply and demand. Stock exchanges have developed hand in hand with capitalism since the 17th century, constantly growing in importance and complexity. The basic function of a stock exchange is to enable public companies, governments, and local authorities to raise capital by selling securities to investors. The secondary market function of a stock exchange is to enable these investors to sell their securities to others, providing liquidity and reducing the risks attached to investment. Most countries now have stock markets; the major international stock exchanges are based in the US, Japan, and the UK. **2** (**Stock Exchange**) = LONDON STOCK EXCHANGE.

♦ **Stock Exchange Alternative Trading Service** *n.* (also **SEATS**) London Stock Exchange system for trading in less liquid securities, which commenced in November 1992. It replaced the Company Bulletin Board Service (commenced in April 1992), and allows for the registration of single market makers. By enabling a combination of quote and order displays, SEATS complements the competing Stock Exchange Automated Quotations System.

♦ **Stock Exchange Automated Quotations System** *n.* (also **SEAQ**) computerized system used on the London Stock Exchange to record the prices at which transactions in securities have been struck, thus establishing the market prices for these securities; these prices are made available to brokers through TOPIC. When a bargain is concluded, the details must be notified to the central system within certain set periods during the day.

♦ **Stock Exchange Automatic Execution Facility** *n.* (also **SAEF**) computerized system used on the London Stock Exchange to enable a broker to execute a transaction in a security through a SAEF terminal, which automatically completes the bargain at the best price with a market maker, whose position is automatically adjusted. The price of the transaction is then automatically recorded on a trading report and also passes into the settlement system. The system has greatly reduced the administrative burden on brokers and market makers but has been criticized for eliminating the personal element between brokers and market makers on the floor of the exchange.

♦ **Stock Exchange Daily Official List** *n.* = OFFICIAL LIST 2.

♦ **Stock Exchange Pool Nominees Ltd.** *n.* (also **SEPON**) official nominee company that holds all stocks and shares sold during the course of settlement on the London Stock Exchange, to facilitate the allocation of holdings. See TALISMAN.

stockholder *n.* owner of stocks or shares.

Stockholm /'stɒkhəʊm/ capital of Sweden, a major port with shipbuilding, engineering, sugar-refining, and brewing industries; pop. (est. 1996) 711 119.

stockinet /ˌstɒkɪ'net/ *n.* (also **stockinette**) elastic knitted fabric. [probably from *stocking-net*]

stocking *n.* **1** long knitted covering for the leg and foot, of nylon, wool, silk, etc. **2** differently-coloured lower leg of a horse etc. □ **in one's stocking** (or **stockinged) feet** without shoes. [from STOCK]

stocking-stitch *n.* alternate rows of plain and purl.

♦ **stock-in-trade** *n.* **1** (*US* **inventory**) goods that an organization has in hand for the purposes of its trade; trading stock. This includes raw materials, components, work-in-progress, and finished products. **2** goods or services that an organization usu. offers for sale. **3** characteristic or essential product; characteristic behaviour, actions, etc.

stockist *n.* dealer in specified types of goods.

♦ **stockjobber** *n. hist.* (also **jobber**) market maker on the London Stock Exchange prior to the Big Bang (October 1986). Stockjobbers were only permitted to deal with the general public through the intermediary of a stockbroker. This single-capacity system was replaced by the dual-capacity system of market makers after the Big Bang. Formerly, jobbers, whose liability was traditionally unlimited, earned their living by the **jobbers' turn**, the difference between the prices at which they were prepared to buy and sell. After the Big Bang most of the London firms of stockjobbers were absorbed into larger financial institutions, usu. banks.

stock market *n.* **1** = STOCK EXCHANGE 1. **2** transactions on this. **3** market in which livestock are bought and sold.

stockpile –*n.* accumulated stock of goods etc. held in reserve. –*v.* (**-ling**) accumulate a stockpile of.

♦ **stock policy** *n.* insurance policy covering the goods stocked and sold by a commercial company for specified risks or for all risks (see ALL-RISKS POLICY). Policies are usu. based on the price paid for the stock, not the price at which it might be sold, i.e. the insurance does not cover loss of profit or mark-up on the stock.

stockpot *n.* pot for making soup stock.

♦ **stock provision** *n.* bookkeeping entry made in the books of account to charge the profit and loss account of an organization with an amount to compensate for the loss in value that some items of stock may have suffered (through price falls, obsolescence, etc.). The corresponding amount is deducted from the value of the stock-in-trade in the balance sheet.

♦ **stock relief** *n. hist.* method of giving relief to traders through the tax system to allow for any overstatement of their profits as a result of stock appreciation caused by inflation. The relief was removed in 1984, when inflation began to decline.

stockroom *n.* room for storing goods.

♦ **stock split** *n. US* = SCRIP ISSUE.

stock-still *adj.* motionless.

♦ **stocktaking** *n.* **1** counting and evaluating stock-in-trade, usu. at an organization's year end in order to value the total stock for preparation of the accounts. In more sophisticated organizations, in which permanent stock records are maintained, stock is counted on a random basis throughout the year to compare quantities counted with the quantities that appear in computerized records. **2** review of one's position etc.

♦ **stock turnover** *n.* number of times in a year that the stock-in-trade of an organization is deemed to have been sold, often calculated by dividing the total cost of the goods sold in a year by an average value of the stock-in-trade. The faster the stock is turned over, the more opportunities there are to make profits on it and therefore the lower the margins that are required.

♦ **stock watering** *n.* creation of more new shares in a company than is justified by its tangible assets, even though the company may be making considerable profits. The consequences of this could be that the dividend may not be maintained at the old rate on the new capital and that if the company were to be liquidated its shareholders may not be paid out in full.

stocky *adj.* (**-ier, -iest**) short and sturdy. □ **stockily** *adv.* **stockiness** *n.*

stockyard *n.* enclosure for the sorting or temporary keeping of cattle.

stodge /stɒdʒ/ *n. colloq.* heavy fattening food. [imitative, after *stuff* and *podge*]

stodgy *adj.* (**-ier, -iest**) **1** (of food) heavy and glutinous. **2** dull and uninteresting. □ **stodgily** *adv.* **stodginess** *n.*

Stoic /ˈstəʊɪk/ *–n.* **1** member of the ancient Greek school of philosophy which sought virtue as the greatest good and taught control of one's feelings and passions. **2** (**stoic**) stoical person. *–adj.* **1** of or like the Stoics. **2** (**stoic**) = STOICAL. [Greek *stoa* portico]

stoical *adj.* having or showing great self-control in adversity. □ **stoically** *adv.*

Stoicism /ˈstəʊɪˌsɪz(ə)m/ *n.* **1** philosophy of the Stoics. **2** (**stoicism**) stoical attitude.

stoke *v.* (**-king**) (often foll. by *up*) **1** feed and tend (a fire or furnace etc.). **2** *colloq.* fill oneself with food. [back-formation from STOKER]

stokehold *n.* compartment in a steamship containing its boilers and furnace.

stokehole *n.* space for stokers in front of a furnace.

Stoke-on-Trent /ˌstəʊkɒnˈtrent/ pottery-manufacturing city in the N Midlands of England, in Staffordshire; there are also engineering and various other manufacturing industries; pop. (est. 1994) 254 200.

stoker *n.* person who tends a furnace, esp. on a steamship. [Dutch]

STOL *abbr.* short take-off and landing.

stole[1] *n.* **1** woman's garment like a long wide scarf, worn over the shoulders. **2** strip of silk etc. worn similarly by a priest. [Greek *stolē* equipment, clothing]

stole[2] *past* of STEAL.

stolen *past part.* of STEAL.

stolid /ˈstɒlɪd/ *adj.* not easily excited or moved; impassive, unemotional. □ **stolidity** /-ˈlɪdɪtɪ/ *n.* **stolidly** *adv.* [Latin]

stoma /ˈstəʊmə/ *n.* (*pl.* **-s** or **stomata**) **1** minute pore in the epidermis of a leaf. **2** small mouthlike artificial orifice made in the stomach. [Greek *stoma* mouth]

stomach /ˈstʌmək/ *–n.* **1 a** internal organ in which digestion occurs. **b** any of several such organs in animals. **2** lower front of the body. **3** (usu. foll. by *for*) **a** appetite. **b** inclination. *–v.* **1** find palatable. **2** endure (usu. with *neg.*: *cannot stomach it*). [Greek *stoma* mouth]

stomach-ache *n.* pain in the belly or bowels.

stomacher *n. hist.* pointed bodice of a dress, often jewelled or embroidered. [probably French: related to STOMACH]

stomach-pump *n.* syringe for forcing liquid etc. into or out of the stomach.

stomach upset *n.* temporary digestive disorder.

stomp *–v.* tread or stamp heavily. *–n.* lively jazz dance with heavy stamping. [var. of STAMP]

stone *–n.* **1 a** solid non-metallic mineral matter; rock. **b** small piece of this. **2** (often in *comb.*) piece of stone of a definite shape or for a particular purpose. **3 a** thing resembling stone, e.g. the hard case of the kernel in some fruits. **b** (often in *pl.*) hard morbid concretion in the body. **4** (*pl.* same) unit of weight equal to 14 lb. **5** = PRECIOUS STONE. **6** (*attrib.*) made of stone. *–v.* (**-ning**) **1** pelt with stones. **2** remove the stones from (fruit). □ **cast** (or **throw) stones** speak ill of a person. **leave no stone unturned** try all possible means. **a stone's throw** a short distance. [Old English]

Stone Age *n.* prehistoric period when weapons and tools were made of stone.

stonechat *n.* small brown bird with black and white markings.

stone-cold *adj.* completely cold.

stone-cold sober *predic. adj.* completely sober.

stonecrop *n.* succulent rock-plant.

stoned *adj. slang* drunk or drugged.

stone-dead *adj.* completely dead.

stone-deaf *adj.* completely deaf.

stone-fruit *n.* fruit with flesh enclosing a stone.

stoneground *adj.* (of flour) ground with millstones.

stonemason *n.* person who cuts, prepares, and builds with stone.

stonewall *v.* **1** obstruct (a discussion or investigation) with evasive answers etc. **2** *Cricket* bat with excessive caution.

stoneware *n.* ceramic ware which is impermeable and partly vitrified but opaque.

stonewashed *adj.* (esp. of denim) washed with abrasives to give a worn or faded look.

stonework *n.* masonry.

stonker /ˈstɒŋkə(r)/ *n. slang* excellent person or thing. □ **stonking** *adj.* [20th century: origin unknown]

stony *adj.* (**-ier, -iest**) **1** full of stones. **2 a** hard, rigid. **b** unfeeling, uncompromising. □ **stonily** *adv.* **stoniness** *n.*

stony-broke *adj. slang* entirely without money.

stood *past* and *past part.* of STAND.

stooge *colloq.* *–n.* **1** butt or foil, esp. for a comedian. **2** assistant or subordinate, esp. for routine or unpleasant work. *–v.* (**-ging**) **1** (foll. by *for*) act as a stooge for. **2** (foll. by *about*, *around*, etc.) move about aimlessly. [origin unknown]

stook /stuːk, stʊk/ *–n.* group of sheaves of grain stood on end in a field. *–v.* arrange in stooks. [related to Low German *stūke*]

stool *n.* **1** single seat without a back or arms. **2** = FOOTSTOOL. **3** (usu. in *pl.*) = FAECES. [Old English]

stoolball *n.* team game with pairs of batters scoring runs between two bases.

stool-pigeon *n.* **1** person acting as a decoy. **2** police informer.

stoop[1] *–v.* **1** lower the body, sometimes bending the knee; bend down. **2** stand or walk with the shoulders habitually bent forward. **3** (foll. by *to* + infin.) condescend. **4** (foll. by *to*) descend to (some conduct). *–n.* stooping posture. [Old English]

stoop[2] *n. US* porch, small veranda, or steps in front of a house. [Dutch *stoep*]

stop *–v.* (**-pp-**) **1 a** put an end to the progress, motion, or operation of. **b** effectively hinder or prevent. **c** discontinue (*stop playing*). **2** come to an end (*supplies suddenly stopped*). **3** cease from motion, speaking, or action. **4** defeat. **5** *slang* receive (a blow etc.). **6** remain; stay for a short time. **7** (often foll. by *up*) block or close up (a hole, leak, etc.). **8** not permit or supply as usual (*stop their wages*). **9** (in full **stop payment of** or **on**) instruct a bank to withhold payment on (a cheque). **10** fill (a tooth). **11** press (a violin etc. string) to obtain the required pitch. *–n.* **1** stopping or being stopped. **2** designated stopping-place for a bus or train etc. **3** = FULL STOP. **4** device for stopping motion at a particular point. **5** change of pitch effected by stopping a string. **6 a** (in an organ) row of pipes of one character. **b** knob etc. operating these. **7** *Optics & Photog.* = DIAPHRAGM 3a. **8 a** effective diameter of a lens. **b** device for reducing this. **9** (of sound) = PLOSIVE *adj.* □ **pull out all the stops** make extreme effort. **put a stop to** cause to end. **stop at nothing** be ruthless. **stop off** (or **over**) break one's journey. [Old English]

stopcock *n.* externally operated valve regulating the flow through a pipe etc.

stopgap *n.* temporary substitute.

stop-go *n.* **1** alternate stopping and restarting. **2** vacillation in the economic policies of a government between those intended to reflate the economy in times of high unemployment and those intended to deflate it when it has overheated.

♦ **stop-loss order** *n.* order placed with a broker in a security or commodity market to close an open position at a specified price in order to limit a loss. It may be used in a volatile market, esp. by a speculator, if the market looks as if it might move strongly.

♦ **stop notice** *n.* court procedure available to protect those who have an interest in shares but have not been registered as company members. The notice prevents the company from registering a transfer of the shares or paying a dividend upon them without informing the server of the notice.

---

stopoff *n.* break in a journey.

stopover *n.* break in a journey, esp. overnight.

stoppage *n.* **1** interruption of work owing to a strike etc. **2** (in *pl.*) sum deducted from pay, for tax, national insurance, etc. **3** condition of being blocked or stopped.

♦ **stoppage *in transitu*** /træn'sɪtjuː/ *n. Law* remedy available to an unpaid seller of goods when the buyer has become insolvent and the goods are still in course of transit. If the seller gives notice of stoppage to the carrier or other bailee of the goods, the seller is entitled to have the goods redelivered and may then retain possession of them until the price is paid. If the right is not exercised, the goods will fall into the insolvent buyer's estate and go towards satisfying the creditors. [Latin *in transitu* in transit]

---

stopper *–n.* plug for closing a bottle etc. *–v.* close with this.

stop press *n.* (often *attrib.*) late news inserted in a newspaper after printing has begun.

stopwatch *n.* watch that can be stopped and started, used to time races etc.

storage /'stɔːrɪdʒ/ *n.* **1 a** storing of goods etc. **b** method of or space for storing. **2** cost of storing. **3** storing of data in a computer etc.

storage battery *n.* (also **storage cell**) battery (or cell) for storing electricity.

storage capacity *n. Computing* amount of information that can be held in a storage device, usu. measured in bytes or bits.

♦ **storage device** *n.* device used with a computer to receive data and retain it for subsequent use. Examples include magnetic disks used as backing store and the semiconductor devices used as main store. Such devices cover a wide range of storage capacities and speeds of access.

---

storage heater *n.* electric heater releasing heat stored outside peak hours.

storage location *n. Computing* = LOCATION 4.

storage protection *n. Computing* facility that limits and hence controls access to a storage device or to one or more storage locations. The intention is to prevent inadvertent interference by users and to provide system security. It is achieved by prohibiting unauthorized reading or writing of data, or both.

store *–n.* **1** quantity of something kept available for use. **2** (in *pl.*) **a** articles gathered for a particular purpose. **b** supply of, or place for keeping, these. **3 a** = DEPARTMENT STORE. **b** esp. *US* shop. **c** (often in *pl.*) shop selling basic necessities. **4** warehouse for keeping furniture etc. temporarily. **5** (also **memory**) device or medium in which data and program instructions can be placed and held for subsequent use by a computer. The two basic types are main store and backing store. See also STORAGE DEVICE. *–v.* (**-ring**) **1** (often foll. by *up, away*) accumulate for future use. **2** put (furniture etc.) in a store. **3** stock or provide with something useful. **4** enter or retain (data or instructions) for subsequent use by a computer. □ **in store 1** kept in readiness. **2** coming in the future. **3** (foll. by *for*) awaiting. **set store by** consider important. [French *estore(r)* from Latin *instauro* renew]

♦ **store audit** *n.* measurement of what is being purchased in a shop. Such audits are regularly conducted by retail stores for their own purposes but they are also particularly useful to marketing, advertising, and brand managers in assessing the performance of their goods and services.

---

storehouse *n.* storage place.

storekeeper *n.* **1** storeman. **2** *US* shopkeeper.

storeman *n.* person in charge of a store of goods.

♦ **store of value** *n. Econ.* a function of money, enabling the acquisition of goods to be delayed. In a barter economy, goods are exchanged more or less simultaneously but in a monetary economy the selection of goods can be delayed, the value of the goods parted with being stored in the money received. To be a satisfactory store of value money must be used in a stable economy; in an inflationary economy its stored value declines.

---

storeroom *n.* storage room.

storey /'stɔːrɪ/ *n.* (*pl.* **-s**) **1** = FLOOR *n.* 3. **2** thing forming a horizontal division. □ **-storeyed** *adj.* (in *comb.*). [Anglo-Latin: related to HISTORY, perhaps originally meaning a tier of painted windows]

storied /'stɔːrɪd/ *adj. literary* celebrated in or associated with stories or legends.

stork *n.* long-legged usu. white wading bird. [Old English]

storm *–n.* **1** violent atmospheric disturbance with strong winds and usu. thunder, rain, or snow. **2** violent political etc. disturbance. **3** (foll. by *of*) **a** violent shower of missiles or blows. **b** outbreak of applause, hisses, etc. **4 a** direct assault by troops on a fortified place. **b** capture by such an assault. *–v.* **1** attack or capture by storm. **2** (usu. foll. by *in, out of,* etc.) move violently or angrily (*stormed out*). **3** (often foll. by *at, away*) talk violently, rage, bluster. □ **take by storm 1** capture by direct assault. **2** rapidly captivate. [Old English]

storm centre *n.* **1** point to which the wind spirals inward in a cyclonic storm. **2** centre of controversy etc.

storm cloud *n.* **1** heavy rain-cloud. **2** threatening situation.

storm-door *n.* additional outer door.

storm in a teacup *n.* great excitement over a trivial matter.

storm petrel *n.* (also **stormy petrel**) **1** small black and white N Atlantic petrel. **2** person causing unrest.

storm trooper *n.* member of the storm troops.

storm troops *n.pl.* **1** = SHOCK TROOPS. **2** *hist.* Nazi political militia.

stormy *adj.* (**-ier, -iest**) **1** of or affected by storms. **2** (of a wind etc.) violent. **3** full of angry feeling or outbursts (*stormy meeting*). □ **stormily** *adv.* **storminess** *n.*

stormy petrel var. of STORM PETREL.

story /ˈstɔːrɪ/ *n.* (*pl.* **-ies**) **1** account of imaginary or past events; tale, anecdote. **2** history of a person or institution etc. **3** (in full **story-line**) narrative or plot of a novel, play, etc. **4** facts or experiences worthy of narration. **5** *colloq.* fib. [Anglo-French *estorie* from Latin: related to HISTORY]

♦ **storyboard** *n.* sequence of sketches and cartoons to show the main elements in a television or cinema advertisement etc.

storyteller *n.* **1** person who tells stories. **2** *colloq.* liar. □ **storytelling** *n.* & *adj.*

stoup /stuːp/ *n.* **1** basin for holy-water. **2** *archaic* flagon, beaker. [Old Norse]

stout *–adj.* **1** rather fat, corpulent, bulky. **2** thick or strong. **3** brave, resolute. *–n.* strong dark beer. □ **stoutly** *adv.* **stoutness** *n.* [Anglo-French from Germanic]

stout-hearted *adj.* courageous.

stove[1] *n.* closed apparatus burning fuel or using electricity for heating or cooking. [Low German or Dutch]

stove[2] *past* and *past part.* of STAVE *v.*

stove-pipe *n.* pipe carrying smoke and gases from a stove to a chimney.

stow /stəʊ/ *v.* pack (goods, cargo, etc.) tidily and compactly. □ **stow away 1** place (a thing) out of the way. **2** be a stowaway on a ship etc. [from BESTOW]

stowage *n.* **1** stowing. **2** place for this.

♦ **stowage plan** *n.* plan of a ship showing where all the cargo on a particular voyage was stowed.

stowaway *n.* person who hides on a ship or aircraft etc. to travel free.

Strabane /strəˈbæn/ **1** town in Northern Ireland, in Co. Tyrone; pop. (1991) 11 981. **2** district of Northern Ireland, in Co. Tyrone; pop. (1991) 36 141.

strabismus /strəˈbɪzməs/ *n. Med.* squinting, squint. [Greek *strabos* squinting]

♦ **straddle** /ˈstræd(ə)l/ *–v.* (**-ling**) **1 a** sit or stand across (a thing) with the legs spread. **b** be situated on both sides of. **2** part (one's legs) widely. *–n.* strategy used by dealers in traded options or futures. In the traded option market it involves simultaneously purchasing put and call options; it is most profitable when the price of the underlying security is very volatile (cf. BUTTERFLY 3). In commodity and currency futures a straddle may involve buying and selling options or both buying and selling the same commodity or currency for delivery in the future, often on different markets. Undoing half the straddle is known as **breaking a leg**. [from STRIDE]

strafe /strɑːf, streɪf/ *v.* (**-fing**) bombard; attack with gunfire. [German, = punish]

straggle /ˈstræg(ə)l/ *–v.* (**-ling**) **1** lack compactness or tidiness. **2** be dispersed or sporadic. **3** trail behind in a race etc. *–n.* straggling or scattered group. □ **straggler** *n.* **straggly** *adj.* (**-ier, -iest**). [origin uncertain]

straight /streɪt/ *–adj.* **1** extending uniformly in the same direction; not bent or curved. **2** successive, uninterrupted (*three straight wins*). **3** ordered; level; tidy (*put things straight*). **4** honest, candid. **5** (of thinking etc.) logical. **6** (of theatre, music, etc.) serious, classical, not popular or comic. **7 a** unmodified. **b** (of a drink) undiluted. **8** *colloq.* **a** (of a person etc.) conventional, respectable. **b** heterosexual. **9** direct, undeviating. *–n.* **1** straight part, esp. the concluding stretch of a racetrack. **2** straight condition. **3** sequence of five cards in poker. **4** *colloq.* conventional person; heterosexual. **5** *Finance* see EUROBOND. *–adv.* **1** in a straight line; direct. **2** in the right direction. **3** correctly. □ **go straight** (of a criminal) become honest. **straight away** immediately. **straight off** *colloq.* without hesitation. □ **straightish** *adj.* **straightness** *n.* [originally a past part. of STRETCH]

straightaway /ˌstreɪtəˈweɪ/ *adv.* = *straight away*.

straighten /ˈstreɪt(ə)n/ *v.* **1** (often foll. by *out*) make or become straight. **2** (foll. by *up*) stand erect after bending.

straight eye *n.* ability to detect deviation from the straight.

straight face *n.* intentionally expressionless face. □ **straight-faced** *adj.*

straight fight *n. Polit.* contest between two candidates only.

straight flush *n.* flush in numerical sequence.

straightforward /streɪtˈfɔːwəd/ *adj.* **1** honest or frank. **2** (of a task etc.) simple.

♦ **straight-line depreciation** see DEPRECIATION 2.

straight man *n.* comedian's stooge.

strain[1] *–v.* **1** stretch tightly; make or become taut or tense. **2** injure by overuse or excessive demands. **3** exercise (oneself, one's senses, a thing, etc.) intensely; press to extremes. **4** strive intensively. **5** (foll. by *at*) tug, pull. **6** distort from the true intention or meaning. **7 a** clear (a liquid) of solid matter by passing it through a sieve etc. **b** (foll. by *out*) filter (solids) out from a liquid. *–n.* **1 a** act of straining. **b** force exerted in this. **2** injury caused by straining a muscle etc. **3** severe mental or physical demand or exertion (*suffering from strain*). **4** snatch of music or poetry. **5** tone or tendency in speech or writing (*more in the same strain*). [French *estrei(g)n-* from Latin *stringo*]

strain[2] *n.* **1** breed or stock of animals, plants, etc. **2** tendency; characteristic. [Old English, = begetting]

strained *adj.* **1** constrained, artificial. **2** (of a relationship) mutually distrustful or tense.

strainer *n.* device for straining liquids etc.

strait *n.* **1** (in *sing.* or *pl.*) narrow channel connecting two large bodies of water. **2** (usu. in *pl.*) difficulty or distress. [French *estreit* from Latin *strictus* narrow]

straitened /ˈstreɪt(ə)nd/ *adj.* of or marked by poverty.

strait-jacket *–n.* **1** strong garment with long sleeves for confining a violent prisoner etc. **2** restrictive measures. *–v.* (**-t-**) **1** restrain with a strait-jacket. **2** severely restrict.

strait-laced *adj.* puritanical.

strand[1] *–v.* **1** run aground. For the purposes of marine insurance, stranding a ship does not include running it aground and refloating it; it might involve driving a ship onto rocks when taking avoiding action etc. **2** (as **stranded** *adj.*) in difficulties, esp. without money or transport. *–n.* foreshore; beach. [Old English]

strand[2] *n.* **1** each of the twisted threads or wires making a rope or cable etc. **2** single thread or strip of fibre. **3** lock of hair. **4** element; component. [origin unknown]

strange /streɪndʒ/ *adj.* **1** unusual, peculiar, surprising, eccentric. **2** (often foll. by *to*) unfamiliar, foreign. **3** (foll. by *to*) unaccustomed. **4** not at ease. □ **strangely** *adv.* **strangeness** *n.* [French *estrange* from Latin *extraneus*]

stranger *n.* **1** person new to a particular place or company. **2** (often foll. by *to*) person one does not know. **3** (foll. by *to*) person unaccustomed to (*no stranger to controversy*).

strangle /ˈstræŋg(ə)l/ *v.* (**-ling**) **1** squeeze the windpipe or neck of, esp. so as to kill. **2** hamper, suppress. □ **strangler** *n.* [Latin *strangulo*]

stranglehold *n.* **1** throttling hold in wrestling. **2** deadly grip. **3** complete control.

strangulate /ˈstræŋgjʊˌleɪt/ *v.* (**-ting**) compress (a vein, intestine, etc.), preventing circulation. [Latin: related to STRANGLE]

strangulation /ˌstræŋgjʊˈleɪʃ(ə)n/ *n.* **1** strangling or being strangled. **2** strangulating.

strap –*n.* **1** strip of leather etc., often with a buckle, for holding things together etc. **2** narrow strip of fabric worn over the shoulders as part of a garment. **3** loop for grasping to steady oneself in a moving vehicle. **4** *Finance* triple option on a share or commodity market, consisting of one put option and two call options at the same price and for the same period. Cf. STRIP^2 2. **5** (**the strap**) punishment by beating with a leather strap. –*v.* (**-pp-**) **1** (often foll. by *down, up,* etc.) secure or bind with a strap. **2** beat with a strap. □ **strapless** *adj.* [dial., = STROP]

straphanger *n. slang* standing passenger in a bus, train, etc. □ **straphang** *v.*

strapping *adj.* large and sturdy.

Strasbourg /ˈstræzbʊəg/ city in NE France, capital of Alsace region; an inland port, trading in wine and iron ore, it also has chemical, textile, and oil-refining industries; pop. (1990) 255 937. Meetings of the Council of Europe and sessions of the European Parliament are held in this city.

strata *pl.* of STRATUM.

■ **Usage** It is incorrect to use *strata* as the singular noun instead of *stratum.*

stratagem /ˈstrætədʒəm/ *n.* **1** cunning plan or scheme. **2** trickery. [Greek *stratēgos* a general]

strategic /strəˈtiːdʒɪk/ *adj.* **1** of or promoting strategy. **2** (of materials) essential in war. **3** (of bombing or weapons) done or for use as a longer-term military objective. □ **strategically** *adv.*

♦ **strategic behaviour** *n. Econ.* behaviour of firms or individuals that is aimed at influencing the structure of a market. In traditional economics, such situations as monopoly or oligopoly were seen as the outcome of technological conditions and the state of demand. More recently, it has been observed that a particular firm or individual can influence its competitors in the market in various ways, for example by threatening a price war if other firms attempt to enter the market; this will clearly influence the structure of the market. See also BARGAINING THEORY; GAME THEORY; PREDATORY PRICING.

♦ **strategic business unit** *n.* (also **SBU**) autonomous division within a company responsible for planning the marketing of a particular range of products.

---

strategy /ˈstrætɪdʒɪ/ *n.* (*pl.* **-ies**) **1** long-term plan or policy (*economic strategy*). **2** art of war. **3** art of moving troops, ships, aircraft, etc. into favourable positions. □ **strategist** *n.*

Stratford-upon-Avon /ˈstrætfədəˌpɒnˈeɪv(ə)n/ market town in central England, in Warwickshire, where William Shakespeare was born and is buried; industries include tourism, boatbuilding, and canning; pop. (1991) 22 231.

Strathclyde /stræθˈklaɪd/ former local government region in W Scotland. It was abolished in 1996 and its administrative powers passed to 12 unitary authorities.

strathspey /stræθˈspeɪ/ *n.* **1** slow Scottish dance. **2** music for this. [*Strathspey*, valley of the river Spey]

♦ **stratified random sample** see RANDOM SAMPLE.

---

stratify /ˈstrætɪˌfaɪ/ *v.* (**-ies, -ied**) (esp. as **stratified** *adj.*) arrange in strata or grades etc. □ **stratification** /-fɪˈkeɪʃ(ə)n/ *n.* [French: related to STRATUM]

stratigraphy /strəˈtɪgrəfɪ/ *n. Geol. & Archaeol.* **1** relative position of strata. **2** the study of this. □ **stratigraphic** /ˌstrætɪˈgræfɪk/ *adj.* [from STRATUM]

stratosphere /ˈstrætəˌsfɪə(r)/ *n.* layer of atmosphere above the troposphere, extending to about 50 km from the earth's surface. □ **stratospheric** /-ˈsferɪk/ *adj.* [from STRATUM]

stratum /ˈstrɑːtəm/ *n.* (*pl.* **strata**) **1** layer or set of layers of any deposited substance, esp. of rock. **2** atmospheric layer. **3** social class. [Latin *sterno* strew]

straw *n.* **1** dry cut stalks of grain as fodder or material for bedding, packing, etc. **2** single stalk of straw. **3** thin tube for sucking drink through. **4** insignificant thing. **5** pale yellow colour. □ **clutch at straws** try any remedy in desperation. **straw in the wind** indication of future developments. [Old English]

strawberry /ˈstrɔːbərɪ/ *n.* (*pl.* **-ies**) **1** pulpy red fruit with a seed-studded surface. **2** plant with runners and white flowers bearing this. [Old English: related to STRAW, for unknown reason]

strawberry mark *n.* reddish birthmark.

straw vote *n.* (also **straw poll**) unofficial ballot as a test of opinion.

stray –*v.* **1** wander from the right place or from one's companions; go astray. **2** deviate morally or mentally. –*n.* strayed person, animal, or thing. –*adj.* **1** strayed, lost. **2** isolated, occasional. **3** *Physics* wasted or unwanted. [Anglo-French *strey*: related to ASTRAY]

streak –*n.* **1** long thin usu. irregular line or band, esp. of colour. **2** strain in a person's character. **3** spell or series (*winning streak*). –*v.* **1** mark with streaks. **2** move very rapidly. **3** *colloq.* run naked in public. □ **streaker** *n.* [Old English, = pen-stroke]

streaky *adj.* (**-ier, -iest**) **1** full of streaks. **2** (of bacon) with streaks of fat.

stream –*n.* **1** flowing body of water, esp. a small river. **2** flow of a fluid or of a mass of people. **3** current or direction in which things are moving or tending (*against the stream*). **4** group of schoolchildren of similar ability taught together. –*v.* **1** move as a stream. **2** run with liquid. **3** be blown in the wind. **4** emit a stream of (blood etc.). **5** arrange (schoolchildren) in streams. □ **on stream** in operation or production. [Old English]

streamer *n.* **1** long narrow strip of ribbon or paper. **2** long narrow flag. **3** banner headline.

streamline *v.* (**-ning**) **1** give (a vehicle etc.) the form which presents the least resistance to motion. **2** make simple or more efficient.

street *n.* **1 a** public road in a city, town, or village. **b** this with the houses etc. on each side. **2** people who live or work in a particular street. □ **on the streets** living by prostitution. **streets ahead** (often foll. by *of*) *colloq.* much superior (to). **up** (or **right up) one's street** *colloq.* what one likes, knows about, etc. [Old English]

streetcar *n. US* tram.

street credibility *n.* (also **street cred**) *slang* familiarity with a fashionable urban subculture.

♦ **street-name stocks** *n.pl. US* nominee stocks (see NOMINEE SHAREHOLDING).

---

streetwalker *n.* prostitute seeking customers in the street.

streetwise *n.* knowing how to survive modern urban life.

strength *n.* **1** being strong; degree or manner of this. **2 a** person or thing giving strength. **b** positive attribute. **3** number of people present or available; full number. □ **from strength to strength** with ever-increasing success. **in strength** in large numbers. **on the strength of** on the basis of. [Old English: related to STRONG]

strengthen /ˈstreŋθ(ə)n/ *v.* make or become stronger.

strenuous /ˈstrenjʊəs/ *adj.* **1** requiring or using great effort. **2** energetic. □ **strenuously** *adv.* [Latin]

streptococcus /ˌstreptəˈkɒkəs/ *n.* (*pl.* **-cocci** /-kaɪ/) bacterium of a type often causing infectious diseases. □ **streptococcal** *adj.* [Greek *streptos* twisted, *kokkos* berry]

streptomycin /ˌstreptəʊˈmaɪsɪn/ *n.* antibiotic effective against many disease-producing bacteria. [Greek *streptos* twisted, *mukēs* fungus]

stress –*n.* **1 a** pressure or tension. **b** quantity measuring this. **2 a** physical or mental strain. **b** distress caused by this. **3 a** emphasis. **b** emphasis on a syllable or word. –*v.*

1 emphasize. **2** subject to stress. □ **lay stress on** emphasize. [shortening of DISTRESS]

stressful *adj.* causing stress.

stretch *–v.* **1** draw, be drawn, or be able to be drawn out in length or size. **2** make or become taut. **3** place or lie at full length or spread out. **4** (also *absol.*) **a** extend (a limb etc.). **b** thrust out one's limbs and tighten one's muscles after being relaxed. **5** have a specified length or extension; extend. **6** strain or exert extremely; exaggerate (*stretch the truth*). *–n.* **1** continuous extent, expanse, or period. **2** stretching or being stretched. **3** (*attrib.*) elastic (*stretch fabric*). **4** *colloq.* period of imprisonment etc. **5** *US* straight side of a racetrack. □ **at a stretch** in one period. **stretch one's legs** exercise oneself by walking. **stretch out 1** extend (a limb etc.). **2** last; prolong. **stretch a point** agree to something not normally allowed. □ **stretchy** *adj.* (**-ier, -iest**). [Old English]

stretcher *n.* **1** two poles with canvas etc. between, for carrying a person in a lying position. **2** brick etc. laid along the face of a wall.

strew /stru:/ *v.* (*past part.* **strewn** or **strewed**) **1** scatter or spread about over a surface. **2** (usu. foll. by *with*) spread (a surface) with scattered things. [Old English: related to STRAW]

'strewth var. of 'STRUTH.

stria /'straɪə/ *n.* (*pl.* **striae** /-i:/) slight ridge or furrow. [Latin]

striate *–adj.* /'straɪɪt/ (also **striated** /-eɪtɪd/) marked with striae. *–v.* /'straɪeɪt/ (**-ting**) mark with slight ridges. □ **striation** /straɪ'eɪʃ(ə)n/ *n.*

stricken /'strɪkən/ *adj.* overcome with illness or misfortune etc. [archaic past part. of STRIKE]

strict *adj.* **1** precisely limited or defined; undeviating (*strict diet*). **2** requiring complete obedience or exact performance. □ **strictly speaking** applying words or rules in their strict sense.□ **strictly** *adv.* **strictness** *n.* [Latin *stringo strict-* draw tight]

stricture /'strɪktʃə(r)/ *n.* (usu. in *pl.*; often foll. by *on, upon*) critical or censorious remark. [Latin: related to STRICT]

stride *–v.* (**-ding**; *past* **strode**; *past part.* **stridden** /'strɪd(ə)n/) **1** walk with long firm steps. **2** cross with one step. **3** bestride. *–n.* **1 a** single long step. **b** length of this. **2** gait as determined by the length of stride. **3** (usu. in *pl.*) progress (*great strides*). **4** steady progress (*get into one's stride*). □ **take in one's stride** manage easily. [Old English]

strident /'straɪd(ə)nt/ *adj.* loud and harsh. □ **stridency** *n.* **stridently** *adv.* [Latin *strido* creak]

strife *n.* conflict; struggle. [French *estrif*: related to STRIVE]

strike *–v.* (**-king**; *past* **struck**; *past part.* **struck** or *archaic* **stricken**) **1** deliver (a blow) or inflict a blow on; hit. **2** come or bring sharply into contact with (*ship struck a rock*). **3** propel or divert with a blow. **4** (cause to) penetrate (*struck terror into him*). **5** ignite (a match) or produce (sparks etc.) by friction. **6** make (a coin) by stamping. **7** produce (a musical note) by striking. **8 a** (also *absol.*) (of a clock) indicate (the time) with a chime etc. **b** (of time) be so indicated. **9 a** attack suddenly. **b** (of a disease) afflict. **10** cause to become suddenly (*struck dumb*). **11** reach or achieve (*strike a balance*). **12** agree on (a bargain). **13** assume (an attitude) suddenly and dramatically. **14** discover or find (oil etc.) by drilling etc. **15** occur to or appear to (*strikes me as silly*). **16** (of employees) engage in a strike. **17** lower or take down (a flag or tent etc.). **18** take a specified direction. **19** (also *absol.*) secure a hook in the mouth of (a fish) by jerking the tackle. *–n.* **1** act of striking. **2** organized refusal of a group of employees to work, in an attempt to force their employers to concede to their demands for higher pay, shorter hours, better working conditions, etc. An **official strike** takes place on the instructions of a trade union, whereas an **unofficial strike** takes place without union backing. A **wildcat strike** is called at short notice in contravention of an agreement not to strike and it does not have union backing. In a **sympathetic strike** one union calls its members out on strike to support another union, although it is not in dispute with its own employers. A **token strike** is a short withdrawal of labour to threaten employers of more serious action to come if the employees' demands are not met. In a **general strike** most of the trade unions in a country call out their members, virtually bringing the country to a standstill. **3** sudden find or success. **4** attack, esp. from the air. □ **on strike** taking part in an industrial etc. strike. **strike home 1** deal an effective blow. **2** have the intended effect. **strike off 1** remove with a stroke. **2** delete (a name etc.) from a list, esp. a professional register. **strike out 1** hit out. **2** act vigorously. **3** delete (an item or name etc.). **4** set off (*struck out eastwards*). **strike up 1** start (an acquaintance, conversation, etc.), esp. casually. **2** (also *absol.*) begin playing (a tune etc.). **struck on** *colloq.* infatuated with. [Old English, = go, stroke]

strikebreaker *n.* person working or employed in place of strikers.

strike pay *n.* allowance paid to strikers by their union during an official strike.

striker *n.* **1** employee on strike. **2** *Football* attacking player positioned forward.

striking *adj.* impressive; attracting attention. □ **strikingly** *adv.*

♦ **striking price** *n.* **1** price fixed by the sellers of a security after receiving bids in a tender offer (for example, in the sale of gilt-edged securities or a new stock market issue). Those who bid below the striking price usu. receive nothing, while those who bid at or above it receive some proportion of the amount they have bid for. **2** = EXERCISE PRICE.

Strine *n.* **1** comic transliteration of Australian pronunciation. **2** (esp. uneducated) Australian English. [= *Australian* in Strine]

string *–n.* **1** twine or narrow cord. **2** piece of this or of similar material used for tying or holding together, pulling, forming the head of a racket, etc. **3** length of catgut or wire etc. on a musical instrument, producing a note by vibration. **4 a** (in *pl.*) stringed instruments in an orchestra etc. **b** (*attrib.*) of stringed instruments (*string quartet*). **5** (in *pl.*) condition or complication (*no strings attached*). **6** set of things strung together; series, list, or line. **7** tough side of a bean-pod etc. *–v.* (*past* and *past part.* **strung**) **1** fit (a racket, violin, archer's bow, etc.) with a string or strings, or (a violin etc. bow) with horsehairs etc. **2** tie with string. **3** thread on a string. **4** arrange in or as a string. **5** remove the strings from (a bean). □ **on a string** under one's control. **string along** *colloq.* **1** deceive. **2** (often foll. by *with*) keep company (with). **string out** extend; prolong. **string up 1** hang up on strings etc. **2** kill by hanging. **3** (usu. as **strung up** *adj.*) make tense. [Old English]

string-course *n.* raised horizontal band of bricks etc. on a building.

stringed *adj.* (of musical instruments) having strings.

stringent /'strɪndʒ(ə)nt/ *adj.* (of rules etc.) strict, precise; leaving no loophole for discretion. □ **stringency** *n.* **stringently** *adv.* [Latin: related to STRICT]

stringer *n.* **1** longitudinal structural member in a framework, esp. of a ship or aircraft. **2** *colloq.* freelance newspaper correspondent.

string vest *n.* vest with large meshes.

stringy *adj.* (**-ier, -iest**) like string, fibrous. □ **stringiness** *n.*

strip[1] *–v.* (**-pp-**) **1** (often foll. by *of*) remove the clothes or covering from. **2** (often foll. by *off*) undress oneself. **3** (often foll. by *of*) deprive (a person) of property or titles. **4** leave bare. **5** (often foll. by *down*) remove the accessory fittings of or take apart (a machine etc.). **6** damage the thread of (a screw) or the teeth of (a gearwheel). **7** remove (paint) or remove paint from (a surface) with solvent. **8** (often foll. by *from*) pull (a covering etc.) off (*stripped the masks from their faces*). *–n.* **1** act of stripping, esp. in striptease. **2** *colloq.* distinctive outfit worn by a sports team. [Old English]

strip[2] *n.* **1** long narrow piece. **2** *Finance* triple option on a share or commodity market, consisting of one call option and two put options at the same price and for the same period. Cf. STRAP *n.* 4. □ **tear a person off a strip** *colloq.* rebuke a person. [Low German *strippe* strap]

strip cartoon *n.* = COMIC STRIP.

strip club *n.* club at which striptease is performed.

stripe *n.* **1** long narrow band or strip differing in colour or texture from the surface on either side of it. **2** *Mil.* chevron etc. denoting military rank. [perhaps from Low German or Dutch]

striped *adj.* marked with stripes.

strip light *n.* tubular fluorescent lamp.

stripling *n.* youth not yet fully grown. [from STRIP[2]]

♦ **stripped bond** *n.* bond or stock that has been subjected to dividend stripping.

---

stripper *n.* **1** person or thing that strips something. **2** device or solvent for removing paint etc. **3** striptease performer.

strip-search *–n.* search involving the removal of all a person's clothes. *–v.* search in this way.

striptease /ˈstrɪptiːz/ *n.* entertainment in which the performer slowly and erotically undresses.

stripy *adj.* (**-ier**, **-iest**) striped.

STRIVE *abbr.* Society for the Preservation of Rural Industries and Village Enterprises.

strive *v.* (**-ving**; *past* **strove**; *past part.* **striven** /ˈstrɪv(ə)n/) **1** try hard (*strive to succeed*). **2** (often foll. by *with*, *against*) struggle. [French *estriver*]

strobe *n. colloq.* stroboscope. [abbreviation]

stroboscope /ˈstrəʊbəˌskəʊp/ *n.* **1** *Physics* instrument for determining speeds of rotation etc. by shining a bright light at intervals so that a rotating object appears stationary. **2** lamp made to flash intermittently, esp. for this purpose. □ **stroboscopic** /-ˈskɒpɪk/ *adj.* [Greek *strobos* whirling]

strode *past* of STRIDE.

stroke *–n.* **1** act of striking; blow, hit. **2** sudden disabling attack caused esp. by thrombosis; apoplexy. **3 a** action or movement, esp. as one of a series. **b** slightest action (*stroke of work*). **4** single complete motion of a wing, oar, etc. **5** (in rowing) the mode or action of moving the oar (*row a fast stroke*). **6** whole motion of a piston in either direction. **7** specified mode of swimming. **8** specially successful or skilful effort (*a stroke of diplomacy*). **9** mark made by a single movement of a pen, paintbrush, etc. **10** detail contributing to the general effect. **11** sound of a striking clock. **12** (in full **stroke oar**) oar or oarsman nearest the stern, setting the time of the stroke. **13** act or spell of stroking. *–v.* (**-king**) **1** pass one's hand gently along the surface of (hair or fur etc.). **2** act as the stroke of (a boat or crew). □ **at a stroke** by a single action. **on the stroke (of)** punctually (at). [Old English: related to STRIKE]

stroll /strəʊl/ *–v.* walk in a leisurely way. *–n.* short leisurely walk. [probably from German *Strolch* vagabond]

strolling players *n.pl. hist.* travelling actors etc.

strong *–adj.* (**stronger** /ˈstrɒŋgə(r)/; **strongest** /ˈstrɒŋgɪst/) **1** able to resist; not easily damaged, overcome, or disturbed. **2** healthy. **3** capable of exerting great force or of doing much; muscular, powerful. **4** forceful in effect (*strong wind*). **5** firmly held (*strong suspicion*). **6** (of an argument etc.) convincing. **7** intense (*strong light*). **8** formidable (*strong candidate*). **9** (of a solution or drink etc.) not very diluted. **10** of a specified number (*200 strong*). **11** *Gram.* (of a verb) forming inflections by a change of vowel within the stem (e.g. *swim*, *swam*). *–adv.* strongly. □ **come on strong** behave aggressively. **going strong** *colloq.* continuing vigorously; in good health etc. □ **strongish** *adj.* **strongly** *adv.* [Old English]

strong-arm *attrib. adj.* using force (*strong-arm tactics*).

strongbox *n.* small strongly made chest for valuables.

stronghold *n.* **1** fortified place. **2** secure refuge. **3** centre of support for a cause etc.

strong language *n.* swearing.

strong-minded *adj.* determined.

strong point *n.* (also **strong suit**) thing at which one excels.

strongroom *n.* room, esp. in a bank, for keeping valuables safe from fire and theft.

strontium /ˈstrɒntɪəm/ *n.* soft silver-white metallic element. [*Strontian* in Scotland]

strontium-90 *n.* radioactive isotope of strontium found in nuclear fallout and concentrated in bones and teeth when ingested.

strop *–n.* device, esp. a strip of leather, for sharpening razors. *–v.* (**-pp-**) sharpen on a strop. [Low German or Dutch]

stroppy /ˈstrɒpɪ/ *adj.* (**-ier**, **-iest**) *colloq.* bad-tempered; awkward to deal with. [origin uncertain]

strove *past* of STRIVE.

struck *past* and *past part.* of STRIKE.

structural /ˈstrʌktʃər(ə)l/ *adj.* of a structure. □ **structurally** *adv.*

structuralism *n.* doctrine that structure rather than function is important. □ **structuralist** *n.* & *adj.*

♦ **structural unemployment** *n.* unemployment caused by changes in the structure of an industry as a result of changes in technology or tastes. For example, increasing automation in manufacturing industry, encouraged by recent developments in computer technology, has made many skills obsolete. Thus whole communities may become unemployed until new skills have been acquired. Governments aim to relieve structural unemployment through regional policies. They may also stimulate aggregate demand if it is believed that the loss of employment has had multiplier effects.

---

structure /ˈstrʌktʃə(r)/ *–n.* **1 a** constructed unit, esp. a building. **b** way in which a building etc. is constructed. **2** framework (*new wages structure*). *–v.* (**-ring**) give structure to; organize. [Latin *struo struct-* build]

♦ **structured interview** *n.* interview used in marketing research in which the interviewer asks the questions exactly as they appear on the questionnaire, adding and explaining nothing to the respondent. The questions can only be answered 'yes', 'no', or 'don't know'. This produces easily tabulated data quickly, but the questionnaire requires careful designing to ensure that the data is not misleading.

---

strudel /ˈstruːd(ə)l/ *n.* thin leaved pastry rolled round a filling and baked. [German]

struggle /ˈstrʌg(ə)l/ *–v.* (**-ling**) **1** violently try to get free of restraint. **2** (often foll. by *for*, or *to* + infin.) try hard under difficulties (*struggled for power*; *struggled to win*). **3** (foll. by *with*, *against*) contend; fight. **4** (foll. by *along*, *up*, etc.) progress with difficulty. **5** (esp. as **struggling** *adj.*) have difficulty in gaining recognition or a living (*struggling artist*). *–n.* **1** act or spell of struggling. **2** hard or confused contest. [origin uncertain]

strum *–v.* (**-mm-**) **1** (often foll. by *on*; also *absol.*) play on (a guitar, piano, etc.), esp. carelessly or unskilfully. **2** play (a tune etc.) in this way. *–n.* sound or spell of strumming. [imitative: cf. THRUM[1]]

strumpet /ˈstrʌmpɪt/ *n. archaic* or *rhet.* prostitute. [origin unknown]

strung *past* and *past part.* of STRING.

strut *–n.* **1** bar in a framework, designed to resist compression. **2** strutting gait. *–v.* (**-tt-**) **1** walk stiffly and pompously. **2** brace with struts. [Old English]

'struth /struːθ/ *int.* (also **'strewth**) *colloq.* exclamation of surprise. [*God's truth*]

strychnine /ˈstrɪkniːn/ *n.* highly poisonous alkaloid used in small doses as a stimulant. [Greek *strukhnos* nightshade]

Sts *abbr.* Saints.

stub *–n.* **1** remnant of a pencil or cigarette etc. **2** counterfoil of a cheque or receipt etc. **3** stump. *–v.* (**-bb-**) **1** strike (one's toe) against something. **2** (usu. foll. by *out*) extinguish (a cigarette) by pressure. [Old English]

stubble /ˈstʌb(ə)l/ *n.* **1** stalks of corn etc. left in the ground after the harvest. **2** short stiff hair or bristles. □ **stubbly** *adj.* [Latin *stupula*]

stubborn /ˈstʌbən/ *adj.* obstinate, inflexible. □ **stubbornly** *adj.* **stubbornness** *n.* [origin unknown]

stubby *adj.* (**-ier**, **-est**) short and thick.

stucco /ˈstʌkəʊ/ *–n.* (*pl.* **-es**) plaster or cement for coating walls or moulding into decorations. *–v.* (**-es**, **-ed**) coat with stucco. [Italian]

stuck *past* and *past part.* of STICK².

stuck-up *adj.* conceited, snobbish. [STICK²]

stud¹ *–n.* **1** large-headed projecting nail, boss, or knob, esp. for ornament. **2** double button, esp. for use with two buttonholes in a shirt-front. *–v.* (**-dd-**) **1** set with or as with studs. **2** (as **studded** *adj.*) (foll. by *with*) thickly set or strewn. [Old English]

stud² *n.* **1 a** number of horses kept for breeding etc. **b** place where these are kept. **2** stallion. **3** *colloq.* young man, esp. one noted for sexual prowess. **4** (in full **stud poker**) form of poker with betting after the dealing of cards face up. □ **at stud** (of a stallion) hired out for breeding. [Old English]

stud-book *n.* book containing the pedigrees of horses.

studding-sail /ˈstʌns(ə)l/ *n.* extra sail set in light winds. [Low German or Dutch]

student /ˈstjuːd(ə)nt/ *n.* **1** person who is studying, esp. at a place of higher or further education. **2** (*attrib.*) studying in order to become (*student nurse*). □ **studentship** *n.* [Latin: related to STUDY]

stud-farm *n.* place where horses are bred.

studio /ˈstjuːdɪəʊ/ *n.* (*pl.* **-s**) **1** workroom of a painter, photographer, etc. **2** place for making films, recordings, or broadcast programmes. [Italian]

studio couch *n.* couch convertible into a bed.

studio flat *n.* one-roomed flat.

studious /ˈstjuːdɪəs/ *adj.* **1** assiduous in study. **2** painstaking. □ **studiously** *adv.* [Latin: related to STUDY]

study /ˈstʌdɪ/ *–n.* (*pl.* **-ies**) **1** acquisition of knowledge, esp. from books. **2** (in *pl.*) pursuit of academic knowledge. **3** private room used for reading, writing, etc. **4** piece of work, esp. a drawing, done for practice or as an experiment. **5** portrayal in literature etc. of behaviour or character etc. **6** musical composition designed to develop a player's skill. **7** thing worth observing (*his face was a study*). **8** thing that is or deserves to be investigated. *–v.* (**-ies**, **-ied**) **1** make a study of; investigate (a subject) (*study law*). **2** (often foll. by *for*) apply oneself to study. **3** scrutinize closely (a visible object). **4** learn (one's role etc.). **5** take pains to achieve (a result) or pay regard to (a subject or principle etc.). **6** (as **studied** *adj.*) deliberate, affected (*studied politeness*). [Latin *studium*]

stuff *–n.* **1** material; fabric. **2** substance or things not needing to be specified (*lot of stuff on the news*). **3** particular knowledge or activity (*know one's stuff*). **4** woollen fabric. **5** trash, nonsense. **6** (prec. by *the*) **a** *colloq.* supply, esp. of drink or drugs. **b** *slang* money. *–v.* **1** pack (a receptacle) tightly (*stuff a cushion with feathers*). **2** (foll. by *in*, *into*) force or cram (a thing). **3** fill out the skin of (an animal etc.) with material to restore the original shape. **4** fill (food, esp. poultry) with a mixture, esp. before cooking. **5** (also *refl.*) fill with food; eat greedily. **6** push, esp. hastily or clumsily. **7** (usu. in *passive*; foll. by *up*) block up (the nose etc.). **8** *slang* (expressing contempt) dispose of (*you can stuff the job*). **9** *coarse slang offens.* have sexual intercourse with (a woman). □ **get stuffed** *slang* exclamation of dismissal, contempt, etc. **stuff and nonsense** exclamation of incredulity or ridicule. [French *estoffe*]

stuffed shirt *n. colloq.* pompous person.

stuffing *n.* **1** padding for cushions etc. **2** mixture used to stuff food, esp. before cooking.

stuffy *adj.* (**-ier**, **-iest**) **1** (of a room etc.) lacking fresh air. **2** dull or uninteresting. **3** (of the nose etc.) stuffed up. **4** dull and conventional. □ **stuffily** *adv.* **stuffiness** *n.*

stultify /ˈstʌltɪˌfaɪ/ *v.* (**-ies**, **-ied**) make ineffective or useless, esp. by routine. □ **stultification** /-fɪˈkeɪʃ(ə)n/ *n.* [Latin *stultus* foolish]

stumble /ˈstʌmb(ə)l/ *–v.* (**-ling**) **1** involuntarily lurch forward or almost fall. **2** (often foll. by *along*) walk with repeated stumbles. **3** speak haltingly. **4** (foll. by *on*, *upon*, *across*) find by chance. *–n.* act of stumbling. [related to STAMMER]

stumbling-block *n.* obstacle.

stump *–n.* **1** part of a cut or fallen tree still in the ground. **2** similar part (e.g. of a branch or limb) cut off or worn down. **3** *Cricket* each of the three uprights of a wicket. **4** (in *pl.*) *joc.* legs. *–v.* **1** (of a question etc.) be too hard for; baffle. **2** (as **stumped** *adj.*) at a loss, baffled. **3** *Cricket* put (a batsman) out by touching the stumps with the ball while he is out of the crease. **4** walk stiffly or noisily. **5** (also *absol.*) *US* traverse (a district) making political speeches. □ **stump up** *colloq.* pay or produce (the money required). [Low German or Dutch]

stumpy *adj.* (**-ier**, **-iest**) short and thick. □ **stumpiness** *n.*

stun *v.* (**-nn-**) **1** knock senseless; stupefy. **2** bewilder, shock. [French: related to ASTONISH]

stung *past* and *past part.* of STING.

stunk *past* and *past part.* of STINK.

stunner *n. colloq.* stunning person or thing.

stunning *adj. colloq.* extremely attractive or impressive. □ **stunningly** *adv.*

stunt¹ *v.* retard the growth or development of. [obsolete *stunt* foolish, short]

stunt² *n.* **1** something unusual done for publicity. **2** trick or daring feat. [origin unknown]

stunt man *n.* man employed to perform dangerous stunts in place of an actor.

stupefy /ˈstjuːpɪˌfaɪ/ *v.* (**-ies**, **-ied**) **1** make stupid or insensible. **2** astonish, amaze. □ **stupefaction** /-ˈfækʃ(ə)n/ *n.* [French from Latin *stupeo* be amazed]

stupendous /stjuːˈpendəs/ *adj.* amazing or prodigious, esp. in size. □ **stupendously** *adv.* [Latin: related to STUPEFY]

stupid /ˈstjuːpɪd/ *adj.* (**stupider**, **stupidest**) **1** unintelligent, foolish (*a stupid fellow*). **2** typical of stupid persons (*stupid mistake*). **3** uninteresting, boring. **4** in a stupor. □ **stupidity** /-ˈpɪdɪtɪ/ *n.* (*pl.* **-ies**). **stupidly** *adv.* [Latin: related to STUPENDOUS]

stupor /ˈstjuːpə(r)/ *n.* dazed, torpid, or helplessly amazed state. [Latin: related to STUPEFY]

sturdy /ˈstɜːdɪ/ *adj.* (**-ier**, **-iest**) **1** robust; strongly built. **2** vigorous (*sturdy resistance*). □ **sturdily** *adv.* **sturdiness** *n.* [French *esturdi*]

sturgeon /ˈstɜːdʒ(ə)n/ *n.* (*pl.* same or **-s**) large sharklike fish yielding caviare. [Anglo-French from Germanic]

stutter *–v.* **1** stammer, esp. by involuntary repetition of the initial consonants of words. **2** (often foll. by *out*) utter (words) in this way. *–n.* act or habit of stuttering. [dial. *stut*]

Stuttgart /ˈʃtʊtgɑːt/ motor-manufacturing city in SW Germany, capital of Baden-Württemberg; other industries include metallurgy and the manufacture of electrical goods; pop. (est. 1995) 588 482.

sty¹ /staɪ/ *n.* (*pl.* **sties**) = PIGSTY. [Old English]

sty² /staɪ/ *n.* (also **stye**) (*pl.* **sties** or **styes**) inflamed swelling on the edge of an eyelid. [Old English]

Stygian /ˈstɪdʒɪən/ *adj. literary* dark, gloomy. [literally = of the *Styx*, a river round Hades in Greek mythology]

style /staɪl/ *–n.* **1** kind or sort, esp. in regard to appearance and form (*elegant style of house*). **2** manner of writing, speaking, or performing. **3** distinctive manner of a person, artistic school, or period. **4** correct way of designating a person or thing. **5** superior quality or manner (*do it in style*). **6** fashion in dress etc. **7** pointed tool for scratching or engraving. **8** *Bot.* narrow extension of the ovary supporting the stigma. *–v.* (**-ling**) **1** design or make etc. in a particular (esp. fashionable) style. **2** designate in a specified way. [Latin *stilus*]

stylish *adj.* **1** fashionable; elegant. **2** superior. □ **stylishly** *adv.* **stylishness** *n.*

stylist /'staɪlɪst/ *n.* **1 a** designer of fashionable styles etc. **b** hairdresser. **2** stylish writer or performer.

stylistic /staɪ'lɪstɪk/ *adj.* of esp. literary style. □ **stylistically** *adv.*

stylized /'staɪlaɪzd/ *adj.* (also **-ised**) painted, drawn, etc. in a conventional non-realistic style.

stylus /'staɪləs/ *n.* (*pl.* **-luses**) **1** sharp needle following a groove in a gramophone record and transmitting the recorded sound for reproduction. **2** pointed writing tool. [Latin: related to STYLE]

stymie /'staɪmɪ/ (also **stimy**) *–n.* (*pl.* **-ies**) **1** *Golf* situation where an opponent's ball lies between one's ball and the hole. **2** difficult situation. *–v.* (**-mies**, **-mied**, **-mying** or **-mieing**) **1** obstruct; thwart. **2** *Golf* block with a stymie. [origin unknown]

styptic /'stɪptɪk/ *–adj.* checking bleeding. *–n.* styptic substance. [Greek *stuphō* contract]

styrene /'staɪəri:n/ *n.* liquid hydrocarbon easily polymerized and used in making plastics etc. [Greek *sturax* a resin]

Styria /'stɪrɪə/ (German **Steiermark** /'ʃtaɪə,mɑ:k/) state of SE Austria; pop. (est. 1994) 1 203 993; capital, Graz. It has important deposits of iron ore, lignite, magnesite, and other minerals.

SU *–international civil aircraft marking* Egypt. *–airline flight code* Aeroflot.

suasion /'sweɪʒ(ə)n/ *n. formal* persuasion (*moral suasion*). [Latin *suadeo suas-* urge]

suave /swɑ:v/ *adj.* smooth; polite; sophisticated. □ **suavely** *adv.* **suavity** /-vɪtɪ/ *n.* [Latin *suavis*]

SUB *abbr. US* supplemental unemployment benefits.

sub *colloq. –n.* **1** submarine. **2** subscription. **3** substitute. **4** sub-editor. *–v.* (**-bb-**) **1** (usu. foll. by *for*) act as a substitute. **2** sub-edit. [abbreviation]

sub- *prefix* **1** at, to, or from a lower position (*subordinate*; *submerge*; *subtract*). **2** secondary or inferior position (*subclass*; *subtotal*). **3** nearly; more or less (*subarctic*). [Latin]

♦ **subagent** /sʌb'eɪdʒ(ə)nt/ *n.* person or firm that is employed to buy or sell goods as an agent of an agent. A firm may hold the agency for certain goods in a particular country, region, etc. and employ subagents to represent it in outlying districts of that country etc.

---

subaltern /'sʌbəlt(ə)n/ *n.* officer below the rank of captain, esp. a second lieutenant. [Latin: related to ALTERNATE]

sub-aqua /sʌb'ækwə/ *adj.* of underwater swimming or diving.

subaquatic /,sʌbə'kwætɪk/ *adj.* underwater.

subatomic /,sʌbə'tɒmɪk/ *adj.* occurring in, or smaller than, an atom.

subcommittee *n.* committee formed from a main committee for a special purpose.

subconscious /sʌb'kɒnʃəs/ *–adj.* of the part of the mind which is not fully conscious but influences actions etc. *–n.* this part of the mind. □ **subconsciously** *adv.*

subcontinent /'sʌb,kɒntɪnənt/ *n.* large land mass, smaller than a continent.

subcontract *–v.* /,sʌbkən'trækt/ **1** employ another contractor to do (work) as part of a larger project. **2** make or carry out a subcontract. *–n.* /sʌb'kɒntrækt/ secondary contract. □ **subcontractor** /-'træktə(r)/ *n.*

subculture /'sʌb,kʌltʃə(r)/ *n.* distinct cultural group within a larger culture.

subcutaneous /,sʌbkju:'teɪnɪəs/ *adj.* under the skin.

subdivide /,sʌbdɪ'vaɪd/ *v.* (**-ding**) divide again after a first division. □ **subdivision** /-,vɪʒ(ə)n/ *n.*

subdue /səb'dju:/ *v.* (**-dues**, **-dued**, **-duing**) **1** conquer, subjugate, or tame. **2** (as **subdued** *adj.*) softened; lacking in intensity; toned down. [Latin *subduco*]

sub-editor /sʌb'edɪtə(r)/ *n.* **1** assistant editor. **2** person who edits material for printing. □ **sub-edit** *v.* (**-t-**).

subfusc /'sʌbfʌsk/ *–adj. formal* dull; dusky. *–n.* formal clothing at some universities. [Latin *fuscus* dark brown]

subgroup /'sʌbgru:p/ *n.* subset of a group.

subheading /'sʌb,hedɪŋ/ *n.* subordinate heading or title.

subhuman /sʌb'hju:mən/ *adj.* (of behaviour, intelligence, etc.) less than human.

subject *–n.* /'sʌbdʒɪkt/ **1 a** matter, theme, etc. to be discussed, described, represented, etc. **b** (foll. by *for*) person, circumstance, etc., giving rise to a specified feeling, action, etc. (*subject for congratulation*). **2** field of study. **3** *Logic* & *Gram.* noun or its equivalent about which a sentence is predicated and with which the verb agrees. **4** any person, except a monarch, living under a government. **5** *Philos.* **a** thinking or feeling entity; the conscious mind esp. as opposed to anything external to it. **b** central substance of a thing as opposed to its attributes. **6** *Mus.* theme; leading phrase or motif. **7** person of specified tendencies (*a hysterical subject*). *–adj.* /'sʌbdʒɪkt/ **1** (foll. by *to*) conditional upon (*subject to your approval*). **2** (foll. by *to*) liable or exposed to (*subject to infection*). **3** (often foll. by *to*) owing obedience to a government etc.; in subjection. *–adv.* /'sʌbdʒɪkt/ (foll. by *to*) conditionally upon (*subject to your consent, I shall go*). *–v.* /səb'dʒekt/ **1** (foll. by *to*) make liable; expose (*subjected us to hours of waiting*). **2** (usu. foll. by *to*) subdue to one's sway etc. □ **subjection** /səb'dʒekʃ(ə)n/ *n.* [Latin *subjectus* placed under]

subjective /səb'dʒektɪv/ *adj.* **1** (of art, written history, an opinion, etc.) not impartial or literal; personal. **2** esp. *Philos.* of the individual consciousness or perception; imaginary, partial, or distorted. **3** *Gram.* of the subject. □ **subjectively** *adv.* **subjectivity** /,sʌbdʒek'tɪvɪtɪ/ *n.* [Latin: related to SUBJECT]

subjoin /sʌb'dʒɔɪn/ *v.* add (an illustration, anecdote, etc.) at the end. [Latin *subjungo -junct-*]

sub judice /sʌb 'dʒu:dɪsɪ/ *adj. Law* under judicial consideration and therefore prohibited from public discussion elsewhere. [Latin]

subjugate /'sʌbdʒʊ,geɪt/ *v.* (**-ting**) bring into subjection; vanquish. □ **subjugation** /-'geɪʃ(ə)n/ *n.* **subjugator** *n.* [Latin *jugum* yoke]

subjunctive /səb'dʒʌŋktɪv/ *Gram. –adj.* (of a mood) expressing what is imagined, wished, or possible (e.g. *if I were you*; *be that as it may*). *–n.* this mood or form. [Latin: related to SUBJOIN]

sublease *–n.* /'sʌbli:s/ lease granted by a tenant to a subtenant. See also HEAD LEASE. *–v.* /sʌb'li:s/ (**-sing**) lease to a subtenant.

sublet *–n.* /'sʌblet/ = SUBLEASE *n.* *–v.* /sʌb'let/ (**-tt-**; *past* and *past part.* **-let**) = SUBLEASE *v.*

sub-lieutenant /,sʌblef'tenənt/ *n.* officer ranking next below lieutenant.

sublimate *–v.* /'sʌblɪ,meɪt/ (**-ting**) **1** divert (esp. sexual energy) into socially more acceptable activity. **2** convert (a substance) from the solid state directly to vapour by heat, and usu. allow it to solidify again. **3** refine; purify; idealize. *–n.* /'sʌblɪmət/ sublimated substance. □ **sublimation** /-'meɪʃ(ə)n/ *n.* [Latin: related to SUBLIME]

sublime /sə'blaɪm/ *–adj.* (**sublimer**, **sublimest**) **1** of the most exalted or noble kind; awe-inspiring. **2** arrogantly unruffled (*sublime indifference*). *–v.* **1** = SUBLIMATE *v.* 2. **2** purify or elevate by or as if by sublimation; make sublime. **3** become pure (as if) by sublimation. □ **sublimely** *adv.* **sublimity** /-'lɪmɪtɪ/ *n.* [Latin *sublimis*]

subliminal /səb'lɪmɪn(ə)l/ *adj. Psychol.* (of a stimulus etc.) below the threshold of sensation or consciousness. □ **subliminally** *adv.* [Latin *limen -min-* threshold]

sub-machine-gun /,sʌbmə'ʃi:ngʌn/ *n.* hand-held lightweight machine-gun.

submarine /,sʌbmə'ri:n, 'sʌb-/ *–n.* vessel, esp. an armed warship, capable of operating under water. *–attrib. adj.*

existing, occurring, done, or used under the sea. □ **submariner** /-'mærɪnə(r)/ *n.*

submerge /səb'mɜːdʒ/ *v.* (**-ging**) **1** place, go, or dive under water. **2** inundate with work, problems, etc. □ **submergence** *n.* **submersion** /-'mɜːʃ(ə)n/ *n.* [Latin *mergo mers-* dip]

submersible /səb'mɜːsɪb(ə)l/ *–n.* submarine operating under water for short periods. *–adj.* capable of submerging.

submicroscopic /sʌb,maɪkrə'skɒpɪk/ *adj.* too small to be seen by an ordinary microscope.

submission /səb'mɪʃ(ə)n/ *n.* **1 a** submitting or being submitted. **b** thing submitted. **2** submissiveness. [Latin *submissio*: related to SUBMIT]

submissive /səb'mɪsɪv/ *adj.* humble, obedient. □ **submissively** *adv.* **submissiveness** *n.*

submit /səb'mɪt/ *v.* (**-tt-**) **1** (usu. foll. by *to*) **a** cease resistance; yield. **b** *refl.* surrender (oneself) to the control of another etc. **2** present for consideration. **3** (usu. foll. by *to*) subject (a person or thing) to a process, treatment, etc. [Latin *mitto miss-* send]

subnormal /sʌb'nɔːm(ə)l/ *adj.* below or less than normal, esp. in intelligence.

suborder *n.* taxonomic category between an order and a family.

subordinate *–adj.* /sə'bɔːdɪnət/ (usu. foll. by *to*) of inferior importance or rank; secondary, subservient. *–n.* /sə'bɔːdɪnət/ person working under another. *–v.* /sə'bɔːdɪ,neɪt/ (**-ting**) (usu. foll. by *to*) make or treat as subordinate. □ **subordination** /-'neɪʃ(ə)n/ *n.* [Latin: related to ORDAIN]

subordinate clause *n.* clause serving as an adjective, adverb, or noun in a main sentence.

◆ **subordinated debt** *n.* debt that can only be claimed by an unsecured creditor, in the event of a liquidation, after the claims of secured creditors have been met. In **subordinated unsecured loan stocks** loans are issued by such institutions as banks, in which the rights of the holders of the stock are subordinate to the interests of the depositors.

suborn /sə'bɔːn/ *v.* induce by bribery etc. to commit perjury etc. [Latin *orno* equip]

sub-plot *n.* secondary plot in a play etc.

◆ **subpoena** /sə'piːnə/ *–n.* order made by a court instructing a person to appear in court on a specified date to give evidence or to produce specified documents. The party calling for the witness must pay his or her reasonable expenses. Failure to comply with a subpoena is contempt of court. *–v.* (*past* and *past part.* **-naed** or **-na'd**) serve a subpoena on. [Latin, = under penalty]

◆ **subrogation** /,sʌbrə'geɪʃ(ə)n/ *n. Law* substitution of one person for another so that the person substituted succeeds to the rights of the other. In insurance, an insurer who has paid a claim has the right to take over any other methods the policyholder may have for obtaining compensation for the same event. For example, if a neighbour is responsible for breaking a person's window and an insurance claim is paid for the repair, the insurers may, if they wish, take over the policyholder's legal right to claim the cost of repair from the neighbour. □ **subrogate** *v.* [Latin *subrogare* choose as substitute]

sub rosa /sʌb 'rəʊzə/ *adj.* & *adv.* in secrecy or confidence. [Latin, = under the rose]

subroutine *n. Computing* section of code designed to perform a frequently used operation within a program.

subscribe /səb'skraɪb/ *v.* (**-bing**) **1** (usu. foll. by *to, for*) **a** pay (a specified sum), esp. regularly, for membership of an organization, receipt of a publication, etc. **b** contribute money to a fund, for a cause, etc. **2** (usu. foll. by *to*) agree with an opinion etc. (*I subscribe to that*). □ **subscribe to** arrange to receive (a periodical etc.) regularly. [Latin *scribo script-* write]

◆ **subscribed share capital** see SHARE CAPITAL.

◆ **subscriber** *n.* **1** person who subscribes. **2** person or organization hiring a telephone line. **3** person who signs the memorandum of association of a new company and who joins with other members in the company in paying for a specified quantity of shares in the company, signing the articles of association, and appointing the first directors of the company.

subscriber trunk dialling *n.* (also **STD**) automatic connection of trunk calls by dialling, a system now used in most countries for both national and international telephone calls.

subscript /'sʌbskrɪpt/ *–adj.* written or printed below the line. *–n.* subscript number etc.

subscription /səb'skrɪpʃ(ə)n/ *–n.* **1 a** act of subscribing. **b** money subscribed. **2** membership fee, esp. paid regularly. *–attrib. adj.* paid for mainly by advance sales of tickets (*subscription concert*).

◆ **subscription shares** *n.pl.* **1** shares in a building society that are paid for by instalments. Such shares often pay the highest interest rates. **2** shares bought by the initial subscribers to a company.

subsection *n.* division of a section.

subsequent /'sʌbsɪkwənt/ *adj.* (usu. foll. by *to*) following, esp. as a consequence. □ **subsequently** *adv.* [Latin *sequor* follow]

subservient /səb'sɜːvɪənt/ *adj.* **1** servile. **2** (usu. foll. by *to*) instrumental. **3** (usu. foll. by *to*) subordinate. □ **subservience** *n.* [Latin *subservio*]

subset *n.* set of which all the elements are contained in another set.

subside /səb'saɪd/ *v.* (**-ding**) **1** become tranquil; abate (*excitement subsided*). **2** (of water etc.) sink. **3** (of the ground) cave in; sink. □ **subsidence** /-'saɪd(ə)ns, 'sʌbsɪd(ə)ns/ *n.* [Latin *subsido*]

subsidiary /səb'sɪdɪərɪ/ *–adj.* **1** supplementary; auxiliary. **2** (of a company) controlled by another. See GROUP OF COMPANIES. *–n.* (*pl.* **-ies**) subsidiary thing, person, or company. [Latin: related to SUBSIDY]

subsidize /'sʌbsɪ,daɪz/ *v.* (also **-ise**) (**-zing** or **-sing**) **1** pay a subsidy to. **2** partially pay for by subsidy.

◆ **subsidy** /'sʌbsɪdɪ/ *n.* (*pl.* **-ies**) **1** money granted by the state to producers of certain goods to enable them to sell the goods to the public at a low price, to compete with foreign competition, to avoid making redundancies and creating unemployment, etc. In general, subsidies distort international trade and are unpopular but they are sometimes used by governments to help to establish a new industry in a country. **2** any monetary grant. [Latin *subsidium* help]

subsist /səb'sɪst/ *v.* **1** (often foll. by *on*) keep oneself alive; be kept alive. **2** remain in being; exist. [Latin *subsisto*]

subsistence /səb'sɪst(ə)ns/ *n.* **1** state or instance of subsisting. **2 a** means of support; livelihood. **b** (often *attrib.*) minimal level of existence or income.

subsistence farming *n.* farming that produces crops (**subsistence crops**) which support the farmer's household but produces no surplus for sale.

◆ **subsistence wage** *n.* lowest wage upon which a worker and the worker's family can survive. 19th-century economists, such as Malthus and Marx, believed that the long-term wages would not rise above this level, as any better standard of living would promote a population increase, which would bring the level of wages down again. This view has been shown to be fallacious in industrial countries, where workers share in national prosperity, attaining a high standard of living comparable to that of members of professions and of entrepreneurs.

subsoil /'sʌbsɔɪl/ *n.* soil immediately under the surface soil.

subsonic /sʌb'sɒnɪk/ *adj.* of speeds less than that of sound.

substance /'sʌbst(ə)ns/ *n.* **1** particular kind of material having uniform properties. **2** reality; solidity. **3** content or essence as opposed to form etc. (*substance of his remarks*). **4** wealth and possessions (*woman of substance*). □ **in substance** generally; essentially. [Latin *substantia*]

substandard /sʌb'stændəd/ *adj.* of less than the required or normal quality or size.

substantial /səb'stænʃ(ə)l/ *adj.* **1 a** of real importance or value. **b** large in size or amount. **2** solid; sturdy. **3** commercially successful; wealthy. **4** essential; largely true. **5** real; existing. □ **substantially** *adv.* [Latin: related to SUBSTANCE]

substantiate /səb'stænʃɪˌeɪt/ *v.* (**-ting**) prove the truth of (a charge, claim, etc.). □ **substantiation** /-'eɪʃ(ə)n/ *n.*

substantive /'sʌbstəntɪv/ *–adj.* /also səb'stæntɪv/ **1** genuine, actual, real. **2** not slight; substantial. *–n. Gram.* = NOUN. □ **substantively** *adv.*

♦ **substantive motion** *n.* amended motion put before a meeting.

---

substitute /'sʌbstɪˌtjuːt/ *–n.* **1** (also *attrib.*) person or thing acting or used in place of another. **2** artificial alternative to a food etc. **3** *Econ.* a good for which the demand changes in the opposite direction to the demand for some other good whose price has changed. The price elasticity of the demand for the substitute with respect to the other good is thus greater than zero. Cf. COMPLEMENT *n.* 5. *–v.* (**-ting**) (often foll. by *for*) (cause to) act as a substitute. □ **substitution** /-'tjuːʃ(ə)n/ *n.* [Latin *substituo -tut-*]

♦ **substitution effect** *n. Econ.* the change in the quantity of a good demanded when the price falls (cf. INCOME EFFECT). A change in the price of a good is usu. expected to have a negative substitution effect on the good itself, i.e. a fall in price will lead to an increase in demand. The effect of a change in price on other goods will depend on whether they are complements (in which case, the effect is negative) or substitutes (the effect is positive).

---

substratum /'sʌbˌstrɑːtəm/ *n.* (*pl.* **-ta**) underlying layer or substance.

substructure *n.* underlying or supporting structure.

subsume /səb'sjuːm/ *v.* (**-ming**) (usu. foll. by *under*) include (an instance, idea, category, etc.) in a rule, class, etc. [Latin *sumo* take]

subtenant /'sʌbˌtenənt/ *n.* person renting a room etc. from its tenant. □ **subtenancy** *n.* (*pl.* **-ies**).

subtend /sʌb'tend/ *v.* (of a line) be opposite (an angle or arc). [Latin: related to TEND[1]]

subterfuge /'sʌbtəˌfjuːdʒ/ *n.* **1** attempt to avoid blame or defeat esp. by lying or deceit. **2** statement etc. used for such a purpose. [Latin]

subterranean /ˌsʌbtə'reɪnɪən/ *adj.* underground. [Latin *terra* land]

subtext *n.* underlying theme.

subtitle /'sʌbˌtaɪt(ə)l/ *–n.* **1** secondary or additional title of a book etc. **2** caption on a film etc., esp. translating dialogue. *–v.* (**-ling**) provide with a subtitle or subtitles.

subtle /'sʌt(ə)l/ *adj.* (**subtler, subtlest**) **1** elusive, mysterious; hard to grasp. **2** (of scent, colour, etc.) faint, delicate. **3 a** perceptive (*subtle intellect*). **b** ingenious (*subtle device*). □ **subtlety** *n.* (*pl.* **-ies**). **subtly** *adv.* [Latin *subtilis*]

subtotal *n.* total of one part of a group of figures to be added.

subtract /səb'trækt/ *v.* (often foll. by *from*) deduct (a number etc.) from another. □ **subtraction** /-'trækʃ(ə)n/ *n.* [Latin *subtraho* draw away]

subtropics /sʌb'trɒpɪks/ *n.pl.* regions adjacent to the tropics. □ **subtropical** *adj.*

suburb /'sʌbɜːb/ *n.* outlying district of a city. [Latin *urbs* city]

suburban /sə'bɜːbən/ *adj.* **1** of or characteristic of suburbs. **2** *derog.* provincial in outlook. □ **suburbanite** *n.*

suburbia /sə'bɜːbɪə/ *n.* often *derog.* suburbs, their inhabitants, and their way of life.

subvention /səb'venʃ(ə)n/ *n.* subsidy. [Latin *subvenio* assist]

subversive /səb'vɜːsɪv/ *–adj.* seeking to subvert (esp. a government). *–n.* subversive person. □ **subversion** *n.* **subversively** *adv.* **subversiveness** *n.* [medieval Latin *subversivus*: related to SUBVERT]

subvert /səb'vɜːt/ *v.* overthrow or weaken (a government etc.). [Latin *verto vers-* turn]

subway /'sʌbweɪ/ *n.* **1** pedestrian tunnel beneath a road etc. **2** esp. *US* underground railway.

subzero /sʌb'zɪərəʊ/ *adj.* (esp. of temperature) lower than zero.

suc- *prefix* assim. form of SUB- before *c*.

succeed /sək'siːd/ *v.* **1 a** (often foll. by *in*) have success. **b** be successful. **2** follow; come next after. **3** (often foll. by *to*) come into an inheritance, office, title, or property (*succeeded to the throne*). [Latin *succedo -cess-* come after]

success /sək'ses/ *n.* **1** accomplishment of an aim; favourable outcome. **2** attainment of wealth, fame, or position. **3** successful thing or person. [Latin: related to SUCCEED]

successful *adj.* having success; prosperous. □ **successfully** *adv.*

succession /sək'seʃ(ə)n/ *n.* **1 a** process of following in order; succeeding. **b** series of things or people one after another. **2 a** right of succeeding to the throne, an office, inheritance, etc. **b** act or process of so succeeding. **c** those having such a right. □ **in succession** one after another. **in succession to** as the successor of.

successive /sək'sesɪv/ *adj.* following one after another; consecutive. □ **successively** *adv.*

successor /sək'sesə(r)/ *n.* (often foll. by *to*) person or thing that succeeds another.

succinct /sək'sɪŋkt/ *adj.* brief; concise. □ **succinctly** *adv.* **succinctness** *n.* [Latin *cingo cinct-* gird]

succour /'sʌkə(r)/ (*US* **succor**) *–n.* aid, esp. in time of need. *–v.* give succour to. [Latin *succurro* run to help]

succubus /'sʌkjʊbəs/ *n.* (*pl.* **-buses** or **-bi** /-ˌbaɪ/) female demon formerly believed to have sexual intercourse with sleeping men. [Latin, = prostitute]

succulent /'sʌkjʊlənt/ *–adj.* **1** juicy; palatable. **2** *Bot.* (of a plant, its leaves, or stems) thick and fleshy. *–n. Bot.* succulent plant. □ **succulence** *n.* [Latin *succus* juice]

succumb /sə'kʌm/ *v.* (usu. foll. by *to*) **1** surrender (*succumbed to temptation*). **2** die (from) (*succumbed to his injuries*). [Latin *cumbo* lie]

such *–adj.* **1** (often foll. by *as*) of the kind or degree indicated (*such people*; *people such as these*). **2** so great or extreme (*not such a fool as that*). **3** of a more than normal kind or degree (*such awful food*). *–pron.* such a person or persons; such a thing or things. □ **as such** as being what has been indicated or named; in itself (*there is no theatre as such*). **such as** for example. [Old English, = so like]

such-and-such *–attrib. adj.* of a particular kind but not needing to be specified. *–n.* such a person or thing.

suchlike *colloq. –attrib. adj.* of such a kind. *–n.* things, people, etc. of such a kind.

suck *–v.* **1** draw (a fluid) into the mouth by suction. **2** (also *absol.*) draw fluid from (a thing) in this way. **3** roll the tongue round (a sweet etc.). **4** make a sucking action or sound. **5** (usu. foll. by *down, in*) engulf or drown in a sucking movement. *–n.* act or period of sucking. □ **suck dry** exhaust the contents of by sucking. **suck in 1** absorb. **2** involve (a person) esp. against his or her will. **suck up 1** (often foll. by *to*) *colloq.* behave obsequiously. **2** absorb. [Old English]

sucker /'sʌkə(r)/ *n.* **1 a** gullible person. **b** (foll. by *for*) person susceptible to. **2 a** rubber cup etc. adhering by suction. **b** similar organ of an organism. **3** shoot springing from a root or stem below ground.

suckle /'sʌk(ə)l/ *v.* (**-ling**) **1** feed (young) from the breast or udder. **2** feed by sucking the breast etc.

suckling *n.* unweaned child or animal.

Sucre /'su:kreɪ/ legal capital and seat of the judiciary of Bolivia; pop. (est. 1993) 144 994.

sucre /'su:kreɪ/ *n.* standard monetary unit of Ecuador. [*Sucre*, name of a South American revolutionary]

sucrose /'su:krəʊz/ *n.* sugar from sugar cane, sugar beet, etc. [French *sucre* SUGAR]

suction /'sʌkʃ(ə)n/ *n.* **1** act of sucking. **2 a** production of a partial vacuum by the removal of air etc. so that liquid etc. is forced in or adhesion is procured. **b** force so produced. [Latin *sugo suct-* suck]

Sudbury /'sʌdbərɪ/ city in E Canada, in Ontario, at the centre of Canada's largest mining region, the world's largest source of nickel; other products include copper and timber; pop. (1991) 92 884; metropolitan area pop. 157 613.

sudden /'sʌd(ə)n/ *adj.* done or occurring unexpectedly or abruptly. □ **all of a sudden** suddenly. □ **suddenly** *adv.* **suddenness** *n.* [Latin *subitaneus*]

sudden death *n. colloq.* decision in a tied game etc. dependent on one move, card, etc.

sudden infant death syndrome *n.* = COT-DEATH.

sudorific /ˌsu:də'rɪfɪk/ *–adj.* causing sweating. *–n.* sudorific drug. [Latin *sudor* sweat]

suds *n.pl.* froth of soap and water. □ **sudsy** *adj.* [Low German *sudde* or Dutch *sudse* marsh, bog]

sue /su:, sju:/ *v.* (**sues, sued, suing**) **1** (also *absol.*) begin a law suit against. **2** (often foll. by *to, for*) make application to a lawcourt for redress. **3** (often foll. by *to, for*) make entreaty to a person for a favour. [Anglo-French *suer* from Latin *sequor* follow]

◆ **sue and labour clause** *n.* clause in a marine insurance policy extending the insurance to cover costs incurred by the policyholder in preventing a loss from occurring or minimizing one that could not be avoided. Without this clause the policy would only cover damage that had actually occurred.

---

suede /sweɪd/ *n.* (often *attrib.*) **1** leather with the flesh side rubbed to a nap. **2** cloth imitating it. [French, = Sweden]

suet /'su:ɪt/ *n.* hard white fat on the kidneys or loins of oxen, sheep, etc. □ **suety** *adj.* [Anglo-French *seu*, from Latin *sebum*]

suf- *prefix* assim. form of SUB- before *f*.

suffer /'sʌfə(r)/ *v.* **1** undergo pain, grief, damage, etc. **2** undergo, experience, or be subjected to (pain, loss, grief, defeat, change, etc.). **3** tolerate (*does not suffer fools gladly*). **4** (usu. foll. by *to* + infin.) *archaic* allow. □ **sufferer** *n.* [Latin *suffero*]

sufferance *n.* tacit consent. □ **on sufferance** tolerated but not encouraged. [Latin: related to SUFFER]

suffice /sə'faɪs/ *v.* (**-cing**) **1** (often foll. by *for*, or *to* + infin.) be adequate. **2** satisfy. □ **suffice it to say** I shall say only this. [Latin *sufficio*]

sufficiency /sə'fɪʃənsɪ/ *n.* (*pl.* **-ies**) (often foll. by *of*) adequate amount.

sufficient *adj.* sufficing, adequate. □ **sufficiently** *adv.*

suffix /'sʌfɪks/ *–n.* letter(s) added at the end of a word to form a derivative. *–v.* append, esp. as a suffix. [Latin *figo fix-* fasten]

suffocate /'sʌfəˌkeɪt/ *v.* (**-ting**) **1** choke or kill by stopping breathing, esp. by pressure, fumes, etc. **2** (often foll. by *by, with*) produce a choking or breathlessness in. **3** be or feel suffocated. □ **suffocating** *adj.* **suffocation** /-'keɪʃ(ə)n/ *n.* [Latin *suffoco* from *fauces* throat]

Suffolk /'sʌfək/ county in E England; pop. (est. 1994) 649 500; county town, Ipswich. Primarily agricultural, it produces cereals, sugar beet, and horses (Suffolk punches).

suffragan /'sʌfrəgən/ *n.* **1** bishop assisting a diocesan bishop. **2** bishop in relation to his archbishop or metropolitan. [medieval Latin *suffraganeus*]

suffrage /'sʌfrɪdʒ/ *n.* right of voting in political elections. [Latin *suffragium*]

suffragette /ˌsʌfrə'dʒet/ *n. hist.* woman seeking suffrage through organized protest.

suffuse /sə'fju:z/ *v.* (**-sing**) (of colour, moisture, etc.) spread throughout from within. □ **suffusion** /-'fju:ʒ(ə)n/ *n.* [Latin *suffundo* pour over]

Sufi /'su:fɪ/ *n.* (*pl.* **-s**) Muslim mystic. □ **Sufic** *adj.* **Sufism** *n.* [Arabic]

sug- *prefix* assim. form of SUB- before *g*.

◆ **Sugar** /'ʃʊgə(r)/, **Alan** (1947–) British entrepreneur, founder and chairman (since 1968) of the computer company Amstrad plc. In 1991 he sold some of his shares in Amstrad, investing some of the proceeds in Tottenham Hotspur football club, of which he has been chairman since 1991.

---

sugar /'ʃʊgə(r)/ *–n.* **1** sweet crystalline substance esp. from sugar cane and sugar beet, used in cookery etc.; sucrose. **2** *Chem.* soluble usu. sweet crystalline carbohydrate, e.g. glucose. **3** esp. *US colloq.* darling (as a term of address). *–v.* sweeten or coat with sugar. [French *sukere*, from Arabic *sukkar*]

sugar beet *n.* beet yielding sugar.

sugar cane *n.* tropical grass yielding sugar.

sugar-daddy *n. slang* elderly man who lavishes gifts on a young woman.

sugar loaf *n.* conical moulded mass of sugar.

sugar soap *n.* alkaline compound for cleaning or removing paint.

sugary *adj.* **1** containing or like sugar. **2** excessively sweet or esp. sentimental. □ **sugariness** *n.*

Sudan /su:'dɑ:n, sʊ-/, **Republic of the** country in NE Africa, S of Egypt, with a coastline on the Red Sea. The economy, heavily dependent on agriculture, is periodically affected by drought, famine, and civil disorder. Cotton, grown in the irrigated areas of the S, forms the country's most important export; other cash crops include sorghum, sesame, and peanuts. Wheat, millet, and sugar are also grown and livestock reared and exported. Forestry is important, esp. for the production and export of gum arabic. There are deposits of gold (which is exported), iron ore, and manganese, and a few manufacturing industries, producing textiles, processed food, shoes, and cigarettes. *History.* Under Arab rule from the 13th century, the country was conquered by Egypt in 1820–2. After the suppression of the Sudanese Mahdist revolt of 1881–98, the Sudan was administered as an Anglo-Egyptian condominium. It became an independent republic in 1956, but has suffered as a result of tension between N and S, where opposition to the government is led by the Sudanese People's Liberation Army. After 17 years of military government, the country was restored to civilian rule following multi-party elections in 1986, but in 1989 the government was overthrown and the constitution suspended until 1996, when legislative elections were held. Prime minister, Lieutenant-General Omar Hassan Ahmad al-Bashir; capital, Khartoum. □ **Sudanese** /ˌsu:də'ni:z/ *adj.* & *n.*

languages	Arabic (official), tribal languages
currency	dinar (Sd)
pop. (1996)	31 065 000
GNP (1992)	US$8.1B
literacy	57% (m); 34% (f)
life expectancy	53 (m); 55 (f)

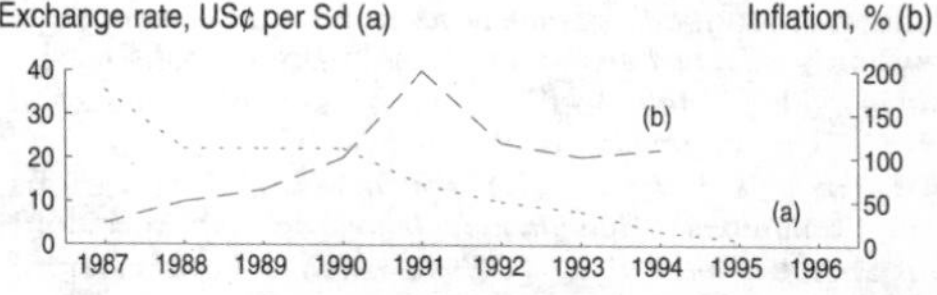

suggest /sə'dʒest/ *v.* **1** (often foll. by *that*) propose (a theory, plan, etc.). **2 a** evoke (an idea etc.). **b** hint at. □ **suggest itself** (of an idea etc.) come into the mind. [Latin *suggero -gest-*]

suggestible *adj.* **1** easily influenced. **2** capable of being suggested. □ **suggestibility** /-'bɪlɪtɪ/ *n.*

suggestion /sə'dʒestʃ(ə)n/ *n.* **1** suggesting or being suggested. **2** theory, plan, etc., suggested. **3** slight trace, hint. **4** *Psychol.* insinuation of a belief etc. into the mind. [Latin: related to SUGGEST]

suggestive /sə'dʒestɪv/ *adj.* **1** (usu. foll. by *of*) hinting (at). **2** (of a remark, joke, etc.) indecent. □ **suggestively** *adv.*

suicidal /ˌsuːɪ'saɪd(ə)l/ *adj.* **1** inclined to commit suicide. **2** of suicide. **3** self-destructive; rash. □ **suicidally** *adv.*

suicide /'suːɪˌsaɪd/ *n.* **1 a** intentional killing of oneself. **b** person who commits suicide. **2** self-destructive action or course (*political suicide*). [Latin *sui* of oneself, -CIDE]

sui generis /ˌsjuːaɪ 'dʒenərɪs, ˌsuːɪ 'gen-/ *adj.* of its own kind; unique. [Latin]

suit /suːt, sjuːt/ *–n.* **1** set of matching clothes, usu. a jacket and trousers or skirt. **2** (esp. in *comb.*) clothes for a special purpose (*swimsuit*). **3** any of the four sets (spades, hearts, diamonds, clubs) making up a pack of cards. **4** lawsuit. **5 a** petition, esp. to a person in authority. **b** *archaic* courting a woman (*paid suit to her*). *–v.* **1** go well with (a person's appearance etc.). **2** (also *absol.*) meet the demands or requirements of; satisfy; agree with. **3** make fitting; accommodate; adapt. **4** (as **suited** *adj.*) appropriate; well-fitted (*not suited to be a nurse*). □ **suit oneself** do as one chooses. [Anglo-French *siute*]

suitable *adj.* (usu. foll. by *to, for*) well-fitted; appropriate. □ **suitability** /-'bɪlɪtɪ/ *n.* **suitably** *adv.*

suitcase *n.* case for carrying clothes etc., with a handle and a flat hinged lid.

suite /swiːt/ *n.* **1** set, esp. of rooms in a hotel etc. or a sofa and armchairs. **2** *Mus.* set of instrumental pieces performed as a unit. **3** *Computing* set of programs or program modules designed to meet some overall requirement, each program or module meeting some part of that requirement. For example, an accounting suite might consist of separate programs for stock control, inventory, payroll, etc. [French: related to SUIT]

suitor /'suːtə(r), 'sjuː-/ *n.* **1** man wooing a woman. **2** plaintiff or petitioner in a lawsuit. [Anglo-French from Latin]

Sukkur /sʊ'kʊə(r)/ city in SE Pakistan, on the Indus River; pop. (1981) 191 000. Nearby is the Sukkar Barrage, built across the river and feeding irrigation canals which direct its water to the Indus valley.

Sulawesi /ˌsʊlə'weɪsɪ/ (formerly **Celebes**) Indonesian island, E of Borneo, with important deposits of nickel and other minerals; copra is also produced; pop. (1990) 12 520 711.

sulfa *US* var. of SULPHA.

sulfate *US* var. of SULPHATE.

sulfide *US* var. of SULPHIDE.

sulfite *US* var. of. SULPHITE.

sulfonamide *US* var. of SULPHONAMIDE.

sulfur etc. *US* var. of SULPHUR etc.

sulk *–v.* be sulky. *–n.* (also in *pl.*, prec. by *the*) period of sullen resentful silence. [perhaps a back-formation from SULKY]

sulky *adj.* (**-ier**, **-iest**) sullen or silent, esp. from resentment or bad temper. □ **sulkily** *adv.* **sulkiness** *n.* [perhaps from obsolete *sulke* hard to dispose of]

sullen /'sʌlən/ *adj.* passively resentful, sulky, morose. □ **sullenly** *adv.* **sullenness** *n.* [Anglo-French *sol* SOLE[3]]

sully /'sʌlɪ/ *v.* (**-ies, -ied**) disgrace or tarnish (a reputation etc.). [French *souiller*: related to SOIL[2]]

sulpha /'sʌlfə/ *n.* (*US* **sulfa**) any of various sulphonamides (often *attrib.*: *sulpha drug*). [abbreviation]

sulphate /'sʌlfeɪt/ *n.* (*US* **sulfate**) salt or ester of sulphuric acid. [Latin SULPHUR]

sulphide /'sʌlfaɪd/ *n.* (*US* **sulfide**) binary compound of sulphur.

sulphite /'sʌlfaɪt/ *n.* (*US* **sulfite**) salt or ester of sulphurous acid. [French: related to SULPHATE]

sulphonamide /sʌl'fɒnəˌmaɪd/ *n.* (*US* **sulfonamide**) any of a class of antibiotic drugs containing sulphur. [German *Sulfon* (related to SULPHUR), *amide* a derivative of AMMONIA]

sulphur /'sʌlfə(r)/ *n.* (*US* **sulfur**) **1** pale-yellow non-metallic element burning with a blue flame and a suffocating smell. **2** pale greenish-yellow colour. [Anglo-French from Latin]

sulphur dioxide *n.* colourless pungent gas formed by burning sulphur in air and dissolving in water.

sulphureous /sʌl'fjʊərɪəs/ *adj.* (*US* **sulfureous**) of or like sulphur.

sulphuric /sʌl'fjʊərɪk/ *adj.* (*US* **sulfuric**) *Chem.* containing sulphur with a valency of six.

sulphuric acid *n.* dense oily highly corrosive acid.

sulphurous /'sʌlfərəs/ *adj.* (*US* **sulfurous**) **1** of or like sulphur. **2** *Chem.* containing sulphur with a valency of four.

sulphurous acid *n.* unstable weak acid used as a reducing and bleaching acid.

sultan /'sʌlt(ə)n/ *n.* Muslim sovereign. □ **sultanate** *n.* [Arabic]

sultana /sʌl'tɑːnə/ *n.* **1** seedless raisin. **2** sultan's mother, wife, concubine, or daughter. [Italian]

sultry /'sʌltrɪ/ *adj.* (**-ier, -iest**) **1** (of weather etc.) hot and close. **2** (of a person etc.) passionate, sensual. □ **sultrily** *adv.* **sultriness** *n.* [obsolete *sulter* (v.): related to SWELTER]

Sulu Sea /'suːluː/ arm of the South China Sea separating the islands of the Philippines from NE Borneo.

sum *–n.* **1** total resulting from addition. **2** amount of money (*a large sum*). **3 a** arithmetical problem. **b** (esp. *pl.*) *colloq.* arithmetic work, esp. elementary. *–v.* (**-mm-**) find the sum of. □ **in sum** in brief. **sum up 1** (esp. of a judge) give a summing-up. **2** form or express an opinion of (a person, situation, etc.). **3** summarize. [Latin *summa*]

sum /sʌm/ *n.* (*pl.* **sumy** /'sʌmɪ/) standard monetary unit of Uzbekistan.

sumac /'suːmæk, 'ʃuː-/ *n.* (also **sumach**) **1** shrub with reddish conical fruits used as a spice. **2** dried and ground leaves of this used in tanning and dyeing. [French from Arabic]

Sumatra /sʊ'mɑːtrə/ (also **Sumatera**) second-largest island of Indonesia, separated from the Malay Peninsula by the Strait of Malacca; products include rubber, oil, coffee, tea, and pepper; pop. (est. 1995) 22 706 200.

Sumgait /ˌsʊmgɑː'iːt/ industrial city in Azerbaijan, on the W shore of the Caspian Sea; pop. (est. 1991) 236 200.

♦ **sum insured** *n.* maximum amount the insurers will pay in the event of a claim.

---

summarize /'sʌməˌraɪz/ *v.* (also **-ise**) (**-zing** or **-sing**) make or be a summary of.

summary /'sʌmərɪ/ *–n.* (*pl.* **-ies**) brief account. *–adj.* without details or formalities; brief. □ **summarily** *adv.* [Latin: related to SUM]

summation /sə'meɪʃ(ə)n/ *n.* **1** finding of a total. **2** a summing-up.

summer /'sʌmə(r)/ *n.* **1** (often *attrib.*) warmest season of the year. **2** (often foll. by *of*) mature stage of life etc. □ **summery** *adj.* [Old English]

summer-house *n.* light building in a garden etc. for sitting in in fine weather.

summer pudding *n.* pudding of soft fruit pressed in a bread case.

summer school *n.* course of summer lectures etc. held esp. at a university.

summer solstice *n.* solstice about 21 June.

summertime *n.* season or period of summer.

summer time *n.* period from March to October when clocks are advanced an hour.

summing-up *n.* **1** judge's review of evidence given to a jury. **2** recapitulation of the main points of an argument etc.

summit /'sʌmɪt/ *n.* **1** highest point, top. **2** highest degree of power, ambition, etc. **3** (in full **summit meeting, talks**, etc.) conference of heads of government. [Latin *summus* highest]

summon /'sʌmən/ *v.* **1** order to come or appear, esp. in a lawcourt. **2** (usu. foll. by *to* + infin.) call upon (*summoned her to assist*). **3** call together. **4** (often foll. by *up*) gather (courage, spirits, resources, etc.). [Latin *summoneo*]

summons –*n.* (*pl.* **summonses**) authoritative call to attend or do something, esp. to appear in court. –*v.* esp. *Law* serve with a summons.

sumo /'su:məʊ/ *n.* Japanese wrestling in which a wrestler is defeated by touching the ground with any part of the body except the soles of the feet or by moving outside the ring. [Japanese]

sump *n.* **1** casing holding the oil in an internal-combustion engine. **2** pit, well, hole, etc. in which superfluous liquid collects. [Low German or Dutch]

sumptuary /'sʌmptʃʊərɪ/ *adj. Law* regulating (esp. private) expenditure. [Latin *sumptus* cost]

sumptuous /'sʌmptʃʊəs/ *adj.* rich, lavish, costly. □ **sumptuously** *adv.* **sumptuousness** *n.* [Latin: related to SUMPTUARY]

Sun. *abbr.* Sunday.

sun –*n.* **1 a** the star round which the earth orbits and from which it receives light and warmth. **b** this light or warmth. **2** any star. –*v.* (**-nn-**) *refl.* bask in the sun. □ **under the sun** anywhere in the world. □ **sunless** *adj.* [Old English]

sunbathe *v.* (**-thing**) bask in the sun, esp. to tan the body. □ **sunbather** *n.*

sunbeam *n.* ray of sunlight.

sunbed *n.* **1** long lightweight, usu. folding, chair for sunbathing. **2** bed for lying on under a sun-lamp.

sunblock *n.* lotion protecting the skin from the sun.

sunburn *n.* inflammation and tanning of the skin from exposure to the sun. □ **sunburnt** *adj.* (also **sunburned**).

sundae /'sʌndeɪ/ *n.* ice-cream with fruit, nuts, syrup, etc. [perhaps from SUNDAY]

Sunda Islands /'sʌndə/ Indonesian islands of the Malay Archipelago, divided into two groups. The **Greater Sunda Islands** include Borneo, Sumatra, Java, and Sulawesi; the **Lesser Sunda Islands** (or **Nusa Tenggara**) lie to the E of Java and include Flores and Timor.

Sunday /'sʌndeɪ/ –*n.* **1** first day of the week, a Christian holiday and day of worship. **2** *colloq.* newspaper published on Sundays. –*adv. colloq.* **1** on Sunday. **2** (**Sundays**) on Sundays; each Sunday. [Old English]

Sunday best *n. joc.* person's best clothes, esp. for Sunday use.

Sunday school *n.* religious class on Sundays for children.

sunder *v. archaic* or *literary* separate. [Old English: cf. ASUNDER]

Sunderland /'sʌndələnd/ industrial city in NE England, in Tyne and Wear, a port at the mouth of the River Wear; there are engineering and other industries; manufactures include glass, pottery, chemicals, and paper; pop. (est. 1994) 292 200.

sundew *n.* small insect-consuming bog-plant.

sundial *n.* instrument showing the time by the shadow of a pointer in sunlight.

sundown *n.* sunset.

sundry /'sʌndrɪ/ –*adj.* various; several. –*n.* (*pl.* **-ies**) (in *pl.*) items or oddments not mentioned individually. [Old English: related to SUNDER]

sunfish *n.* (*pl.* same or **-es**) any of various almost spherical fish.

sunflower *n.* tall plant with large golden-rayed flowers.

sung *past part.* of SING.

sun-glasses *n.pl.* glasses tinted to protect the eyes from sunlight or glare.

sunk *past* and *past part.* of SINK.

♦ **sunk capital** *n.* the amount of an organization's funds that has been spent and is therefore no longer available to the organization, frequently because it has been spent on unrealizable or valueless assets.

♦ **sunk costs** *n.pl.* past expenditure, which is often thought to be irrelevant to future decisions as the best decisions tend to maximize future cash flow.

---

sunken *adj.* **1** at a lower level; submerged. **2** (of the cheeks etc.) hollow, depressed. [past part. of SINK]

sun-lamp *n.* lamp giving ultraviolet rays for therapy, to tan, etc.

sunlight *n.* light from the sun.

sunlit *adj.* illuminated by sunlight.

sun lounge *n.* room with large windows to receive sunlight.

Sunni /'sʌnɪ/ –*n.* (*pl.* same or **-s**) **1** one of the two main branches of Islam, accepting law based not only on the Koran, but on Muhammad's words and acts. **2** adherent of this branch. –*adj.* (also **Sunnite**) of or relating to Sunni. [Arabic *Sunna* = way, rule]

sunny *adj.* (**-ier, -iest**) **1** bright with or warmed by sunlight. **2** cheery, bright. □ **sunnily** *adv.* **sunniness** *n.*

sunrise *n.* **1** sun's rising. **2** time of this.

sun-roof *n.* panel in a car's roof that can be opened.

sunset *n.* **1** sun's setting. **2** time of this.

sunshade *n.* parasol; awning.

sunshine *n.* **1 a** light of the sun. **b** area lit by the sun. **2** fine weather. **3** cheerfulness. **4** *colloq.* form of address.

sunspot *n.* dark patch on the sun's surface.

♦ **sunspot theory** *n. Econ.* theory that expectations can influence an economy. The economist W. S. Jevons proposed that trade cycles seemed to coincide with changes in sunspot activity. This somewhat eccentric hypothesis is in itself of no importance but has been used as an example of the economics of expectations. For example, if sufficient people believe that sunspots influence share prices, the supporters of this theory believe that they will do so. Keynes suggested that self-fulfilling expectations of this kind could provide one explanation for economic depressions. The literature on rational expectations was thought to have refuted this view, but recent articles on sunspot theory have attempted to show that this is not the case.

---

sunstroke *n.* acute prostration from excessive exposure to the sun.

suntan *n.* brownish skin colour caused by exposure to the sun. □ **suntanned** *adj.*

suntrap *n.* sunny, esp. sheltered, place.

sun-up *n.* esp. *US* sunrise.

sup[1] –*v.* (**-pp-**) **1** take by sips or spoonfuls. **2** esp. *N.Engl. colloq.* drink (alcohol). –*n.* sip of liquid. [Old English]

sup[2] *v.* (**-pp-**) *archaic* take supper. [French]

sup- *prefix* assim. form of SUB- before *p*.

super /'su:pə(r)/ –*adj.* (also as *int.*) *colloq.* excellent; splendid. –*n. colloq.* **1** superintendent. **2** supernumerary. [shortening of words beginning *super-*]

super- *comb. form* forming nouns, adjectives, and verbs, meaning: **1** above, beyond, or over (*superstructure*; *supernormal*). **2** to an extreme degree (*superabundant*). **3** extra good or large of its kind (*supertanker*). **4** of a higher kind (*superintendent*). [Latin]

superabundant /ˌsu:pərə'bʌnd(ə)nt/ *adj.* abounding beyond what is normal or right. □ **superabundance** *n.* [Latin: related to SUPER-, ABOUND]

superannuate /ˌsu:pər'ænjʊˌeɪt/ *v.* (**-ting**) **1** pension (a person) off. **2** dismiss or discard as too old. **3** (as **superannuated** *adj.*) too old for work or use. [Latin *annus* year]

superannuation /ˌsuːpərˌænjʊˈeɪʃ(ə)n/ *n.* **1** occupational pension provided by contributions deducted from an employee's salary by the employer and passed to an insurance company or the trustees of a pension fund. **2** payment towards this.

◆ **Superannuation Funds Office** *n.* (also **SFO**) department of the UK Inland Revenue that deals with all forms of pension funds and benefits from pensions.

superb /suːˈpɜːb/ *adj.* **1** *colloq.* excellent. **2** magnificent. □ **superbly** *adv.* [Latin, = proud]

supercargo /ˈsuːpəˌkɑːgəʊ/ *n.* (*pl.* **-es**) officer in a merchant ship managing sales etc. of cargo. [Spanish *sobrecargo*]

supercharge /ˈsuːpəˌtʃɑːdʒ/ *v.* (**-ging**) **1** (usu. foll. by *with*) charge (the atmosphere etc.) with energy, emotion, etc. **2** use a supercharger on.

supercharger *n.* device supplying air or fuel to an internal-combustion engine at above atmospheric pressure to increase efficiency.

supercilious /ˌsuːpəˈsɪlɪəs/ *adj.* contemptuous; haughty. □ **superciliously** *adv.* **superciliousness** *n.* [Latin *supercilium* eyebrow]

supercomputer /ˈsuːpəkəmˌpjuːtə(r)/ *n.* powerful computer that is capable of working at very great speed, and can thus process a very large amount of data, esp. numerical data, within an acceptable time.

superconductivity /ˌsuːpəˌkɒndʌkˈtɪvɪtɪ/ *n. Physics* property of zero electrical resistance in some substances at very low temperatures. □ **superconducting** /-kənˈdʌktɪŋ/ *adj.*

superconductor /ˌsuːpəkənˈdʌktə(r)/ *n. Physics* substance having superconductivity.

superego /ˌsuːpərˈiːgəʊ/ *n.* (*pl.* **-s**) *Psychol.* part of the mind that acts as a conscience and responds to social rules.

supererogation /ˌsuːpərˌerəˈgeɪʃ(ə)n/ *n.* doing more than duty requires. [Latin *supererogo* pay in addition]

superficial /ˌsuːpəˈfɪʃ(ə)l/ *adj.* **1** of or on the surface; lacking depth. **2** swift or cursory (*superficial examination*). **3** apparent but not real (*superficial resemblance*). **4** (esp. of a person) shallow. □ **superficiality** /-ʃɪˈælɪtɪ/ *n.* **superficially** *adv.* [Latin: related to FACE]

superfine /ˈsuːpəˌfaɪn/ *adj. Commerce* of extra quality. [Latin: related to FINE[1]]

superfluity /ˌsuːpəˈfluːɪtɪ/ *n.* (*pl.* **-ies**) **1** state of being superfluous. **2** superfluous amount or thing. [Latin *fluo* to flow]

superfluous /suːˈpɜːflʊəs/ *adj.* more than is needed or wanted; useless. [Latin *fluo* to flow]

superglue /ˈsuːpəˌgluː/ *n.* exceptionally strong glue.

supergrass /ˈsuːpəˌgrɑːs/ *n. colloq.* police informer implicating many people.

superhuman /ˌsuːpəˈhjuːmən/ *adj.* exceeding normal human capability.

superimpose /ˌsuːpərɪmˈpəʊz/ *v.* (**-sing**) (usu. foll. by *on*) lay (a thing) on something else. □ **superimposition** /-pəˈzɪʃ(ə)n/ *n.*

superintend /ˌsuːpərɪnˈtend/ *v.* supervise, direct. □ **superintendence** *n.*

superintendent /ˌsuːpərɪnˈtend(ə)nt/ *n.* **1** police officer above the rank of chief inspector. **2 a** person who superintends. **b** director of an institution etc.

superior /suːˈpɪərɪə(r)/ *–adj.* **1** in a higher position; of higher rank. **2 a** high-quality (*superior leather*). **b** supercilious (*had a superior air*). **3** (often foll. by *to*) better or greater in some respect. **4** written or printed above the line. *–n.* **1** person superior to another esp. in rank. **2** head of a monastery etc. (*Mother Superior*). □ **superiority** /-ˈɒrɪtɪ/ *n.* [Latin comparative of *superus* above]

superlative /suːˈpɜːlətɪv/ *–adj.* **1** of the highest quality or degree; excellent. **2** *Gram.* (of an adjective or adverb) expressing the highest degree of a quality (e.g. *bravest*, *most fiercely*). *–n.* **1** *Gram.* superlative form of an adjective or adverb. **2** (in *pl.*) high praise; exaggerated language. [French from Latin]

◆ **supermajority provisions** /ˌsuːpəməˈdʒɒrɪtɪ/ *n.pl.* provisions in the bylaws of a company that call for more than a simple majority of its members when voting on certain motions, e.g. the approval of a merger or whether or not to agree to a take-over. In these circumstances the provisions may call for a supermajority of between 70% and 80% of the votes cast.

superman /ˈsuːpəˌmæn/ *n.* **1** *colloq.* man of exceptional strength or ability. **2** *Philos.* ideal person not subject to conventional morality etc.

supermarket /ˈsuːpəˌmɑːkɪt/ *n.* large self-service store selling food, household goods, etc.

supernatural /ˌsuːpəˈnætʃər(ə)l/ *–adj.* not attributable to, or explicable by, the laws of nature; magical; mystical. *–n.* (prec. by *the*) supernatural forces, effects, etc. □ **supernaturally** *adv.*

supernova /ˌsuːpəˈnəʊvə/ *n.* (*pl.* **-vae** /-viː/ or **-s**) exploding star observed to increase suddenly in brightness.

supernumerary /ˌsuːpəˈnjuːmərərɪ/ *–adj.* **1** in excess of the normal number; extra. **2** engaged for extra work. **3** (of an actor) appearing on stage but not speaking. *–n.* (*pl.* **-ies**) supernumerary person or thing. [Latin: related to NUMBER]

superphosphate /ˌsuːpəˈfɒsfeɪt/ *n.* fertilizer made from phosphate rock.

superpower /ˈsuːpəˌpaʊə(r)/ *n.* extremely powerful nation.

◆ **superprofit** /ˈsuːpəˌprɒfɪt/ *n.* profit in excess of a normal economic profit. See also PURE ECONOMIC PROFIT.

superscript /ˈsuːpəskrɪpt/ *–adj.* written or printed above. *–n.* superscript number or symbol. [Latin *scribo* write]

supersede /ˌsuːpəˈsiːd/ *v.* (**-ding**) **1** take the place of. **2** replace with another person or thing. □ **supersession** /-ˈseʃ(ə)n/ *n.* [Latin *supersedeo*]

supersonic /ˌsuːpəˈsɒnɪk/ *adj.* of or having a speed greater than that of sound. □ **supersonically** *adv.*

superstar /ˈsuːpəˌstɑː(r)/ *n.* extremely famous or renowned actor, musician, etc.

superstition /ˌsuːpəˈstɪʃ(ə)n/ *n.* **1** belief in the supernatural; irrational fear of the unknown. **2** practice, belief, or religion based on this. □ **superstitious** *adj.* **superstitiously** *adv.* [Latin]

superstore /ˈsuːpəˌstɔː(r)/ *n.* large supermarket.

superstructure /ˈsuːpəˌstrʌktʃə(r)/ *n.* structure built on top of another.

supertanker /ˈsuːpəˌtæŋkə(r)/ *n.* very large tanker ship.

supertax /ˈsuːpəˌtæks/ *n. hist.* additional tax on incomes above a certain level.

supervene /ˌsuːpəˈviːn/ *v.* (**-ning**) *formal* occur as an interruption or change. □ **supervention** /-ˈvenʃ(ə)n/ *n.* [Latin *supervenio*]

supervise /ˈsuːpəˌvaɪz/ *v.* (**-sing**) superintend, oversee. □ **supervision** /-ˈvɪʒ(ə)n/ *n.* **supervisor** *n.* **supervisory** *adj.* [Latin *supervideo -vis-*]

superwoman /ˈsuːpəˌwʊmən/ *n. colloq.* woman of exceptional strength or ability.

supine /ˈsuːpaɪn/ *–adj.* **1** lying face upwards. **2** inert, indolent. *–n.* Latin verbal noun used only in the accusative and ablative. [Latin]

supper *n.* **1** late evening snack. **2** evening meal, esp. light. [French *souper*]

supplant /səˈplɑːnt/ *v.* take the place of, esp. by underhand means. [Latin *supplanto* trip up]

supple /ˈsʌp(ə)l/ *adj.* (**suppler, supplest**) flexible, pliant. □ **suppleness** *n.* [Latin *supplex*]

supplement *–n.* /ˈsʌplɪmənt/ **1** thing or part added to improve or provide further information. **2** separate section, esp. a colour magazine, of a newspaper etc. *–v.* /ˈsʌplɪmənt, -ˌment/ provide a supplement for. □ **supplemental** /-ˈment(ə)l/ *adj.* **supplementary** /-ˈmentərɪ/

adj. **supplementation** /-ˈteɪʃ(ə)n/ *n.* [Latin *suppleo* supply]

suppliant /ˈsʌplɪənt/ *–adj.* supplicating. *–n.* supplicating person. [Latin: related to SUPPLICATE]

supplicate /ˈsʌplɪˌkeɪt/ *v.* **(-ting)** *literary* **1** petition humbly to (a person) or for (a thing). **2** (foll. by *to, for*) make a petition. □ **supplicant** *adj.* & *n.* **supplication** /-ˈkeɪʃ(ə)n/ *n.* **supplicatory** /-kətərɪ/ *adj.* [Latin *supplico*]

supply /səˈplaɪ/ *–v.* **(-ies, -ied) 1** provide (a thing needed). **2** (often foll. by *with*) provide (a person etc. with a thing). **3** meet or make up for (a deficiency or need etc.). *–n.* (*pl.* **-ies**) **1** providing of what is needed. **2** stock, store, amount, etc., of something provided or obtainable. **3** (in *pl.*) provisions and equipment for an army, expedition, etc. **4** (often *attrib.*) schoolteacher etc. acting as a temporary substitute for another. □ **in short supply** scarce. **supply and demand** *Econ.* quantities available and required, as factors regulating price. See MARKET FORCES; PRICE THEORY. □ **supplier** *n.* [Latin *suppleo* fill up]

♦ **supply chain management** *n.* management of the links between an organization and its supplier and customers to achieve strategic advantage. Supply chain management includes; materials management, distribution management, purchasing and supply managment, and management of the flow of information.

♦ **supply curve** *n. Econ.* curve on a graph relating the quantity of a good supplied to its price. Economists usu. expect a supply curve to slope upwards, i.e. an increase in price will be associated with an increase in the amount supplied. The intersection of the market supply curve and the market demand curve gives the market price and the total amount sold. See also DEMAND CURVE; SUPPLY THEORY.

♦ **supply-side economics** *n.* approach to macroeconomics that emphasizes the importance of the conditions under which goods and services (including labour) are supplied to the market in determining the level of employment and output in an economy. The growth of output and employment, according to this approach, can be enhanced by measures to reduce government involvement in the economy and by allowing the free market to operate. This includes such controversial measures as reducing unemployment benefits, restricting the power of trade unions, and cutting both taxes and government expenditure. Supply-side economists, who gained in popularity in the 1970s and 1980s, generally reject as ineffectual Keynesian policies aimed at increasing aggregate demand (see MONETARISM; NEW CLASSICAL MACROECONOMICS).

♦ **supply theory** *n. Econ.* theory, largely based on producer theory, analysing the way in which goods and services are brought to the market by firms or entrepreneurs. For every seller in a market there will be a supply curve relating the amount he or she is willing to sell at each possible price. Adding these curves together will enable a market supply curve to be constructed; the point at which this curve intersects the market demand curve will determine the market price and the total amount sold. Adding together all the market supply curves for an economy will give an aggregate supply curve, a concept used in macroeconomics.

---

support /səˈpɔːt/ *–v.* **1** carry all or part of the weight of; keep from falling, sinking, or failing. **2** provide for (a family etc.). **3** strengthen, encourage. **4** bear out; tend to substantiate. **5** give help or approval to (a person, team, sport, etc.); further (a cause etc.). **6** speak in favour of (a resolution etc.). **7** (also *absol.*) take a secondary part to (a principal actor etc.); perform a secondary act to (the main act) at a pop concert etc. *–n.* **1** supporting or being supported. **2** person or thing that supports. **3** secondary act at a pop concert etc.□ **in support of** so as to support. [Latin *porto* carry]

supporter *n.* person or thing that supports a cause, team, etc.

supporting film *n.* (also **supporting picture** etc.) less important film in a cinema programme.

supportive *adj.* providing (esp. emotional) support or encouragement. □ **supportively** *adv.* **supportiveness** *n.*

suppose /səˈpəʊz/ *v.* **(-sing)** (often foll. by *that*) **1** assume; be inclined to think. **2** take as a possibility or hypothesis (*suppose you are right*; *supposing you are right*). **3** (in *imper.*) as a formula of proposal (*suppose we try again*). **4** (of a theory or result etc.) require as a condition (*that supposes we're on time*). **5** (in *imper.* or *pres. part.* forming a question) in the circumstances that; if (*suppose he won't let you?*). **6** (as **supposed** *adj.*) presumed (*his supposed brother*). **7** (in *passive*; foll. by *to* + infin.) **a** be expected or required (*was supposed to write to you*). **b** (with *neg.*) ought not; not be allowed to (*you are not supposed to go in there*). □ **I suppose so** expression of hesitant agreement. [French: related to POSE]

supposedly /səˈpəʊzɪdlɪ/ *adv.* allegedly; as is generally believed.

supposition /ˌsʌpəˈzɪʃ(ə)n/ *n.* **1** thing supposed. **2** act of supposing.

suppositious /ˌsʌpəˈzɪʃəs/ *adj.* hypothetical.

suppository /səˈpɒzɪtərɪ/ *n.* (*pl.* **-ies**) medical preparation melting in the rectum or vagina. [Latin *suppositorius* placed underneath]

suppress /səˈpres/ *v.* **1** put an end to, esp. forcibly. **2** prevent (information, feelings, a reaction, etc.) from being seen, heard, or known. **3 a** partly or wholly eliminate (electrical interference etc.). **b** equip (a device) to reduce the interference caused by it. □ **suppressible** *adj.* **suppression** *n.* **suppressor** *n.* [Latin: related to PRESS[1]]

suppurate /ˈsʌpjʊˌreɪt/ *v.* **(-ting) 1** form pus. **2** fester. □ **suppuration** /-ˈreɪʃ(ə)n/ *n.* [Latin: related to PUS]

supra /ˈsuːprə/ *adv.* above or earlier (in a book etc.). [Latin]

supra- *prefix* above.

supranational /ˌsuːprəˈnæʃən(ə)l/ *adj.* transcending national limits.

♦ **supra protest** see ACCEPTANCE SUPRA PROTEST.

---

supremacy /suːˈpreməsɪ/ *n.* (*pl.* **-ies**) **1** being supreme. **2** highest authority.

supreme /suːˈpriːm/ *adj.* **1** highest in authority or rank. **2** greatest; most important. **3** (of a penalty or sacrifice etc.) involving death. □ **supremely** *adv.* [Latin]

Supreme Court *n.* highest judicial court in a state etc.

supremo /suːˈpriːməʊ/ *n.* (*pl.* **-s**) person in overall charge. [Spanish, = SUPREME]

sur-[1] *prefix* = SUPER- (*surcharge*; *surrealism*). [French]

sur-[2] *prefix* assim. form of SUB- before *r*.

Surabaya /ˌsʊərəˈbaɪə/ seaport, second-largest city, and principal naval base of Indonesia, capital of the province of East Java; it has shipbuilding, oil-refining, and rubber-processing industries; pop. (1990) 2 421 016.

Surat /ˈsʊərət, sʊˈrɑːt/ city and port in W central India, in the state of Gujarat; pop. (1991) 1 498 817.

surcease /sɜːˈsiːs/ *literary –n.* cessation. *–v.* **(-sing)** cease. [French *sursis* delayed, omitted]

surcharge *–n.* /ˈsɜːtʃɑːdʒ/ additional charge or payment. *–v.* /ˈsɜːtʃɑːdʒ, -ˈtʃɑːdʒ/ **(-ging)** exact a surcharge from. [French: related to SUR-[1]]

surd *Math. –adj.* (of a number) irrational. *–n.* surd number, esp. the root of an integer. [Latin, = deaf]

sure /ʃʊə(r), ʃɔː(r)/ *–adj.* **1** (often foll. by *of* or *that*) convinced. **2** having adequate reason for a belief or assertion. **3** (foll. by *of*) confident in anticipation or knowledge of. **4** reliable or unfailing. **5** (foll. by *to* + infin.) certain. **6** undoubtedly true or truthful. *–adv. colloq.* certainly. □ **be sure** (in *imper.* or *infin.*; foll. by *that* + clause or *to* + infin.) take care to; not fail to. **for sure** *colloq.* certainly. **make sure** make or become certain; ensure. **sure enough** *colloq.* in fact; certainly. **to be sure** admittedly; indeed, certainly. □ **sureness** *n.* [French from Latin *securus*]

sure-fire *attrib. adj. colloq.* certain to succeed.

sure-footed *adj.* never stumbling or making a mistake.

surely *adv.* **1** with certainty or safety (*slowly but surely*). **2** as an appeal to likelihood or reason (*surely that can't be right*).

surety /ˈʃʊərətɪ, ˈʃɔː-/ *n.* (*pl.* **-ies**) **1** money given as a guarantee of performance etc. or as evidence of good faith. **2** (esp. in phr. **stand surety for**) person who takes responsibility for another's debt, obligation, etc.; guarantor. [French from Latin]

surf *–n.* foam of the sea breaking on the shore or reefs. *–v.* practise surfing. □ **surfer** *n.* [origin unknown]

surface /ˈsɜːfɪs/ *–n.* **1 a** the outside of a thing. **b** area of this. **2** any of the limits of a solid. **3** top of a liquid or of the ground etc. **4** outward or superficial aspect. **5** *Geom.* set of points with length and breadth but no thickness. **6** (*attrib.*) **a** of or on the surface. **b** superficial. *–v.* (**-cing**) **1** give the required surface to (a road, paper, etc.). **2** rise or bring to the surface. **3** become visible or known. **4** *colloq.* wake up; get up. □ **come to the surface** become perceptible. [French: related to SUR-[1]]

surface mail *n.* mail carried by land or sea.

surface tension *n.* tension of the surface-film of a liquid, tending to minimize its surface area.

surfboard *n.* long narrow board used in surfing.

surfeit /ˈsɜːfɪt/ *–n.* **1** an excess, esp. in eating or drinking. **2** resulting fullness. *–v.* (**-t-**) **1** overfeed. **2** (foll. by *with*) (cause to) be wearied through excess. [French: related to SUR-[1], FEAT]

surfing *n.* sport of riding the surf on a board.

surge *–n.* **1** sudden rush. **2** heavy forward or upward motion. **3** sudden increase in price, activity, etc. **4** sudden increase in voltage of an electric current. **5** swell of the sea. *–v.* (**-ging**) **1** move suddenly and powerfully forwards. **2** (of an electric current etc.) increase suddenly. **3** (of the sea etc.) swell. [Latin *surgo* rise]

surgeon /ˈsɜːdʒ(ə)n/ *n.* **1** medical practitioner qualified in surgery. **2** naval or military medical officer.

surgery /ˈsɜːdʒərɪ/ *n.* (*pl.* **-ies**) **1** treatment of bodily injuries or disorders by incision or manipulation etc. as opposed to drugs. **2** place where or time when a doctor, dentist, etc. treats patients, or an MP, lawyer, etc. holds consultations. [Latin *chirurgia*, from Greek *kheir* hand, *ergō* work]

surgical /ˈsɜːdʒɪk(ə)l/ *adj.* **1** of or by surgeons or surgery. **2 a** used in surgery. **b** worn to correct a deformity etc. **3** (esp. of military action) swift and precise. □ **surgically** *adv.*

surgical spirit *n.* methylated spirit used for cleansing etc.

surly /ˈsɜːlɪ/ *adj.* (**-ier, -iest**) bad-tempered; unfriendly. □ **surliness** *n.* [obsolete *sirly* haughty: related to SIR]

surmise /səˈmaɪz/ *–n.* conjecture. *–v.* (**-sing**) (often foll. by *that*) infer doubtfully; guess; suppose. [Latin *supermitto -miss-* accuse]

surmount /səˈmaʊnt/ *v.* **1** overcome (a difficulty or obstacle). **2** (usu. in *passive*) cap or crown. □ **surmountable** *adj.* [French: related to SUR-[1]]

surname /ˈsɜːneɪm/ *n.* family name, usu. inherited or acquired by marriage. [obsolete *surnoun* from Anglo-French: related to SUR-[1]]

surpass /səˈpɑːs/ *v.* **1** be greater or better than, outdo. **2** (as **surpassing** *adj.*) pre-eminent. [French: related to SUR-[1]]

surplice /ˈsɜːplɪs/ *n.* loose white vestment worn by clergy and choristers. [Anglo-French *surplis*]

surplus /ˈsɜːpləs/ *–n.* **1** amount left over. **2** excess of revenue over expenditure. *–adj.* exceeding what is needed or used. [Anglo-French]

♦ **surplus value** *n. Econ.* excess of value produced by the labour of workers over the wages they are paid. A key concept in Marxist economics, it is the basis for the Marxist view that a 'just' economic system will only be achieved when workers control the process of production and so receive their own surplus value. This has been more successful as a political doctrine than as a description of an economic process.

---

surprise /səˈpraɪz/ *–n.* **1** unexpected or astonishing thing. **2** emotion caused by this. **3** catching or being caught unawares. **4** (*attrib.*) unexpected; made or done etc. without warning. *–v.* (**-sing**) **1** affect with surprise; turn out contrary to the expectations of. **2** (usu. in *passive*; foll. by *at*) shock, scandalize. **3** capture or attack by surprise. **4** come upon (a person) unawares. **5** (foll. by *into*) startle (a person) into an action etc. □ **take by surprise** affect with surprise, esp. by an unexpected encounter or statement. □ **surprising** *adj.* **surprisingly** *adv.* [French]

surreal /səˈrɪəl/ *adj.* unreal; dreamlike; bizarre. [back-formation from SURREALISM]

surrealism *n.* 20th-century movement in art and literature, attempting to express the subconscious mind by dream imagery, bizarre juxtapositions, etc. □ **surrealist** *n.* & *adj.* **surrealistic** /-ˈlɪstɪk/ *adj.* **surrealistically** /-ˈlɪstɪkəlɪ/ *adv.* [French: related to SUR-[1], REAL[1]]

surrender /səˈrendə(r)/ *–v.* **1** hand over; relinquish. **2** submit, esp. to an enemy. **3** *refl.* (foll. by *to*) yield to a habit, emotion, influence, etc. **4** give up rights under (a life-insurance policy) in return for a smaller sum received immediately. **5** abandon (hope etc.). *–n.* act of surrendering. □ **surrender to bail** duly appear in court after release on bail. [Anglo-French: related to SUR-[1]]

♦ **surrender value** *n.* sum of money given by an insurance company to the insured on a life policy that is cancelled before it has run its full term. The amount is calculated approximately by deducting from the total value of the premiums paid any costs, administration expenses, and a charge for the life-assurance cover up to the can-

---

Suriname /ˌsʊərɪˈnæm/, **Republic of** (formerly, until 1948, **Dutch Guiana**) country on the NE coast of South America. Suriname has large timber resources, but the economy is chiefly dependent on alumina, which makes up a substantial proportion of its exports. Aluminium is also processed and exported, and fishing (esp. for shrimps) is a further source of revenue. The country's agricultural potential is underdeveloped, apart from the production of rice and sugar cane, its main crops. The economy has been adversely affected by political instability in recent years. *History*. Settled by the English in 1650, the country was ceded to the Dutch in 1667 but twice returned to British control before finally reverting to the Netherlands in 1815. It attained a measure of autonomy in 1950 and 1954 followed by full independence in 1975. A military government took power in 1980; democracy and civilian rule were gradually restored, but friction continued between the army and the government, which was overthrown after a further military coup in 1990. The coalition government of President Dr Ronald Venetiaan (1991–6) amended the constitution to restrict the power of the military. President, Jules Wijdenbosch; capital, Paramaribo. □ **Surinamer** *n.* **Surinamese** /-ˈmiːz/ *adj.* & *n.*

languages	Dutch (official), English, Sranan (a native language)
currency	guilder (Sf) of 100 cents
pop. (1996)	436 000
GNP (1994)	US$364M
literacy	95% (m); 91% (f)
life expectancy	67 (m); 72 (f)

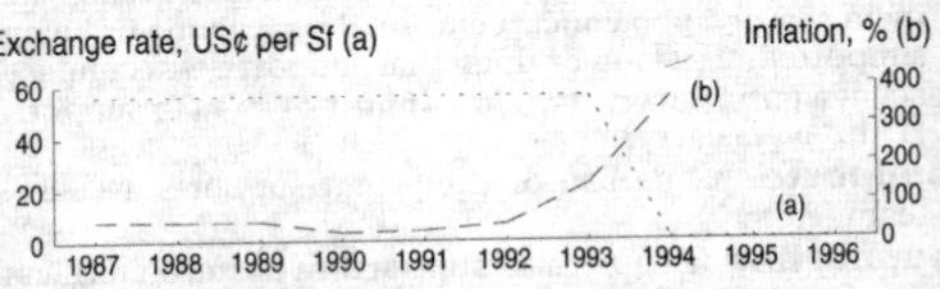

cellation date. There is little or no surrender value to a life policy in its early years.

---

surreptitious /ˌsʌrəp'tɪʃəs/ *adj.* done by stealth; clandestine. □ **surreptitiously** *adv.* [Latin *surripio* seize secretly]

Surrey /'sʌrɪ/ county in SE England; pop. (est. 1994) 1 041 200; county town, Guildford. It is mainly residential, with some industry in the NE and agriculture in the S.

surrogate /'sʌrəgət/ *n.* **1** substitute. **2** deputy, esp. of a bishop in granting marriage licences. □ **surrogacy** *n.* [Latin *rogo* ask]

surrogate mother *n.* woman who bears a child on behalf of another woman, usu. by artificial insemination of her own egg by the other woman's partner.

surround /sə'raʊnd/ *–v.* come or be all round; encircle, enclose. *–n.* **1** border or edging, esp. an area of floor between the walls and carpet of a room. **2** surrounding area or substance. [Latin: related to SUR-[1], *unda* wave]

surroundings *n.pl.* objects or conditions around or affecting a person or thing; environment.

♦ **surtax** /'sɜːtæks/ *n. hist.* **separate UK tax raised progressively on the higher incomes. This tax has now been incorporated into income tax by means of the higher rates. [French: related to SUR-[1]]**

---

surtitle /'sɜːˌtaɪt(ə)l/ *n.* explanatory caption projected on to a screen above the stage during an opera.

surveillance /sɜː'veɪləns/ *n.* close observation undertaken by the police etc. [French: related to SUR-[1], *veiller* watch]

survey *–v.* /sə'veɪ/ **1** view or consider as a whole. **2** examine the condition of (a building etc.). **3** determine the boundaries, extent, ownership, etc. of (a district etc.). *–n.* /'sɜːveɪ/ **1** general view or consideration. **2 a** act of surveying property. **b** statement etc. resulting from this. **3** investigation of public opinion etc. **4** map or plan made by surveying. [Latin: related to SUPER-, *video* see]

surveyor /sə'veɪə(r)/ *n.* person who surveys land and buildings, esp. for a living.

survival /sə'vaɪv(ə)l/ *n.* **1** surviving. **2** relic.

survive /sə'vaɪv/ *v.* (**-ving**) **1** continue to live or exist. **2** live or exist longer than. **3** remain alive after or continue to exist in spite of (a danger, accident, etc.). □ **survivor** *n.* [Anglo-French *survivre* from Latin *supervivo*]

sus var. of SUSS.

sus- *prefix* assim. form of SUB- before *c, p, t.*

susceptibility /səˌseptə'bɪlɪtɪ/ *n.* (*pl.* **-ies**) **1** being susceptible. **2** (in *pl.*) person's feelings.

susceptible /sə'septəb(ə)l/ *adj.* **1** impressionable, sensitive, emotional. **2** (*predic.*) **a** (foll. by *to*) liable or vulnerable to. **b** (foll. by *of*) allowing; admitting of (proof etc.). □ **susceptibly** *adv.* [Latin *suscipio -cept-* take up]

sushi /'suːʃɪ/ *n.* Japanese dish of balls of cold rice topped with raw fish etc. [Japanese]

♦ **sushi bond** *n.* **bond issued in Japan in a foreign currency but which is classified as a domestic Japanese bond. It is useful for institutions whose holdings of foreign bonds are limited.**

---

suspect *–v.* /sə'spekt/ **1** be inclined to think. **2** have an impression of the existence or presence of. **3** (often foll. by *of*) mentally accuse. **4** doubt the genuineness or truth of. *–n.* /'sʌspekt/ suspected person. *–adj.* /'sʌspekt/ subject to or deserving suspicion. [Latin *suspicio -spect-*]

suspend /sə'spend/ *v.* **1** hang up. **2** keep inoperative or undecided for a time. **3** debar temporarily from a function, office, etc. **4** (as **suspended** *adj.*) (of particles or a body in a fluid) floating between the top and bottom. [Latin *suspendo -pens-*]

suspended animation *n.* temporary deathlike condition.

suspended sentence *n.* judicial sentence left unenforced subject to good behaviour during a specified period.

suspender *n.* **1** attachment to hold up a stocking or sock by its top. **2** (in *pl.*) *US* braces.

suspender belt *n.* woman's undergarment with suspenders.

suspense /sə'spens/ *n.* state of anxious uncertainty or expectation. □ **suspenseful** *adj.* [French, = delay]

♦ **suspense account** *n.* **temporary account in the books of an organization for recording balances to correct mistakes or balances that have not yet been finalized (e.g. because a particular deal has not been concluded).**

---

suspension /sə'spenʃ(ə)n/ *n.* **1** suspending or being suspended. **2** springs etc. supporting a vehicle on its axles. **3** substance consisting of particles suspended in a medium.

suspension bridge *n.* bridge with a roadway suspended from cables supported by towers.

suspicion /sə'spɪʃ(ə)n/ *n.* **1** unconfirmed belief; distrust. **2** suspecting or being suspected. **3** (foll. by *of*) slight trace of. □ **above suspicion** too obviously good etc. to be suspected. **under suspicion** suspected. [Latin: related to SUSPECT]

suspicious /sə'spɪʃəs/ *adj.* **1** prone to or feeling suspicion. **2** causing suspicion. □ **suspiciously** *adv.*

suss *v. slang* (also **sus**) (**-ss-**) (usu. foll. by *out*) **1** investigate, inspect. **2** work out; realize. □ **on suss** on suspicion (of having committed a crime). [abbreviation]

Sussex /'sʌsɪks/ former county in S England, now divided into East Sussex and West Sussex.

sustain /sə'steɪn/ *v.* **1** support, bear the weight of, esp. for a long period. **2** encourage, support. **3** (of food) nourish. **4** endure, stand. **5** suffer (defeat or injury etc.). **6** (of a court etc.) uphold or decide in favour of (an objection etc.). **7** corroborate (a statement or charge). **8** maintain (effort etc.). □ **sustainable** *adj.* [Latin *sustineo* keep up]

sustenance /'sʌstɪnəns/ *n.* **1** nourishment, food. **2** means of support. [Anglo-French: related to SUSTAIN]

suttee /sʌ'tiː, 'sʌtɪ/ *n.* esp. *hist.* **1** Hindu custom of a widow's suicide on her husband's funeral pyre. **2** widow undergoing this. [Sanskrit *satī* faithful wife]

suture /'suːtʃə(r)/ *–n.* **1** stitching of the edges of a wound or incision. **2** thread or wire used for this. *–v.* (**-ring**) stitch (a wound or incision). [Latin *suo sut-* sew]

Suva /'suːvə/ capital of Fiji, situated on the island of Viti Levu; products include coconut oil and soap, and tourism is also important; pop. (est. 1990) 200 000.

suzerain /'suːzərən/ *n.* **1** *hist.* feudal overlord. **2** *archaic* sovereign or state partially controlling another state that is internally autonomous. □ **suzerainty** *n.* [French]

SV *airline flight code* Saudia-Saudi Arabian Airlines.

s.v. *abbr.* surrender value.

Svalbard /'svɑːlbɑːd/ group of Norwegian islands, comprising Spitsbergen, Edgeøya, Nordaustlandet, and others, in the Arctic Ocean N of Norway; pop. (1994) 2906. There are important coal and mineral deposits.

svelte /svelt/ *adj.* slender, lissom, graceful. [French from Italian]

Sverdlovsk see EKATERINBURG.

SW *–abbr.* **1** south-west. **2** south-western. *–postcode* south-west London.

S/W *abbr. Computing* software.

Sw. *abbr.* **1** Sweden. **2** Swedish.

SWA *international vehicle registration* Namibia.

swab /swɒb/ *–n.* **1 a** absorbent pad used in surgery. **b** specimen of a secretion taken for examination. **2** mop etc. for cleaning or mopping up. *–v.* (**-bb-**) **1** clean with a swab. **2** (foll. by *up*) absorb (moisture) with a swab. **3** mop clean (a ship's deck) [Dutch]

swaddle /'swɒd(ə)l/ *v.* (**-ling**) wrap (esp. a baby) tightly. [from SWATHE]

swaddling-clothes *n.pl.* narrow bandages formerly used to wrap and restrain a baby.

swag *n.* **1** *slang* booty of burglars etc. **2** *Austral.* & *NZ* traveller's bundle. **3** festoon of flowers, foliage, drapery, etc. □ **swagged** *adj.* [probably Scandinavian]

swagger –*v.* walk or behave arrogantly. –*n.* swaggering gait or manner. [from SWAG]

swagger stick *n.* short cane carried by a military officer.

Swahili /swəˈhiːlɪ/ *n.* (*pl.* same) **1** member of a Bantu people of Zanzibar and adjacent coasts. **2** their language. [Arabic]

swain *n.* **1** *archaic* country youth. **2** *poet.* young lover or suitor. [Old Norse, = lad]

swallow[1] /ˈswɒləʊ/ –*v.* **1** cause or allow (food etc.) to pass down the throat. **2** perform the muscular movement required to do this. **3** accept meekly or credulously. **4** repress (a feeling etc.) (*swallow one's pride*). **5** articulate (words etc.) indistinctly. **6** (often foll. by *up*) engulf or absorb; exhaust. –*n.* **1** act of swallowing. **2** amount swallowed. [Old English]

swallow[2] /ˈswɒləʊ/ *n.* migratory swift-flying bird with a forked tail. [Old English]

swallow-dive *n.* & *v.* dive with the arms outspread until close to the water.

swallow-tail *n.* **1** deeply forked tail. **2** butterfly etc. with this.

swam *past* of SWIM.

swami /ˈswɑːmɪ/ *n.* (*pl.* **-s**) Hindu male religious teacher. [Hindi *svami*]

swamp /swɒmp/ –*n.* (area of) waterlogged ground. –*v.* **1** overwhelm, flood, or soak with water. **2** overwhelm or make invisible etc. with an excess or large amount of something. □ **swampy** *adj.* (**-ier**, **-iest**). [origin uncertain]

swan /swɒn/ –*n.* large usu. white water-bird with a long flexible neck. –*v.* (**-nn-**) (usu. foll. by *about*, *off*, etc.) *colloq.* move or go aimlessly, casually, or with a superior air. [Old English]

swank *colloq.* –*n.* ostentation, swagger. –*v.* show off. □ **swanky** *adj* (**-ier**, **-iest**). [origin uncertain]

Swansea /ˈswɒnzɪ/ city and port in S Wales; industries include oil refining and the manufacture of tinplate, both these products being exported, along with coal, coke, ironwork, and cement; pop. (est. 1994) 189 300.

swansong *n.* person's last work or act before death or retirement etc.

◆ **swap** /swɒp/ (also **swop**) –*v.* (**-pp-**) exchange or barter. –*n.* **1** act of swapping. **2** thing for swapping or swapped. **3** *Finance* means by which a borrower can exchange the type of funds most easily raised for the type of funds required, usu. through the intermediary of a bank. For example, a UK company may find it easy to raise a sterling loan when it really wants to borrow Deutschmarks; a German company may have exactly the opposite problem. A swap will enable the companies to exchange the currency they possess for the currency they need. An **interest-rate swap** is one in which borrowers exchange fixed- for floating-interest rates. Swaps are most common in the Eurocurrency markets. [originally = 'hit', imitative]

SWAPO /ˈswɑːpəʊ/ *abbr.* (also **Swapo**) South West Africa People's Organization.

sward /swɔːd/ *n. literary* expanse of turf. [Old English, = skin]

S/WARE *abbr. Computing* software.

swarf /swɔːf/ *n.* fine chips or filings of stone, metal, etc. [Old Norse]

swarm[1] /swɔːm/ –*n.* **1** cluster of bees leaving the hive with the queen to establish a new colony. **2** large cluster of insects, birds, or people. **3** (in *pl.*; foll. by *of*) great numbers. –*v.* **1** move in or form a swarm. **2** (foll. by *with*) (of a place) be overrun, crowded, or infested with. [Old English]

swarm[2] /swɔːm/ *v.* (foll. by *up*) climb (a rope or tree etc.) by clinging with the hands and knees etc. [origin unknown]

swarthy /ˈswɔːðɪ/ *adj.* (**-ier**, **-iest**) dark, dark-complexioned. [obsolete *swarty* from *swart* black, from Old English]

swashbuckler /ˈswɒʃˌbʌklə(r)/ *n.* swaggering adventurer. □ **swashbuckling** *adj.* & *n.* [*swash* strike noisily, BUCKLER]

swastika /ˈswɒstɪkə/ *n.* **1** ancient symbol formed by an equal-armed cross with each arm continued at a right angle. **2** this with clockwise continuations as the symbol of Nazi Germany. [Sanskrit]

swat /swɒt/ –*v.* (**-tt-**) **1** crush (a fly etc.) with a sharp blow. **2** hit hard and abruptly. –*n.* swatting blow. [dial. var. of SQUAT]

swatch /swɒtʃ/ *n.* **1** sample, esp. of cloth. **2** collection of samples. [origin unknown]

swath /swɔːθ/ *n.* (also **swathe** /sweɪð/) (*pl.* **-s** /swɔːθs, swɔːðs, sweɪðz/) **1** ridge of cut grass or corn etc. **2** space left clear by a mower etc. **3** broad strip. [Old English]

swathe /sweɪð/ –*v.* (**-thing**) bind or wrap in bandages or garments etc. –*n.* bandage or wrapping. [Old English]

sway –*v.* **1** (cause to) lean or move unsteadily from side to side. **2** oscillate; waver. **3 a** control the motion or direction of. **b** influence; rule over. –*n.* **1** rule, influence, or government (*hold sway*). **2** swaying motion. [origin uncertain]

Swazi /ˈswɑːzɪ/ *n.* (*pl.* same or **-s**) **1** member of a S African people of Swaziland and parts of Transvaal. **2** language of Swaziland. [native name]

swear /sweə(r)/ –*v.* (*past* **swore**; *past part.* **sworn**) **1 a** (often foll. by *to* + infin. or *that* + clause) state or promise

---

Swaziland /ˈswɑːzɪˌlænd/, **Kingdom of** small landlocked country of S Africa, bounded by South Africa and Mozambique. Agriculture is still a major source of employment, although manufacturing industry is increasing in importance. Maize is the chief subsistence crop and sugar the principal export; citrus and canned fruits are also exported, and other crops include rice and cotton. Forests yield wood and wood products for export and the country's mineral deposits include asbestos (a further source of export revenue), coal, and iron ore. Manufacturing includes food processing, paper products, textiles, clothing, and machinery. Hydroelectric installations supply power and irrigation.

History. Occupied by Swazis from the mid-18th century, it was a South African protectorate from 1894 and came under British rule in 1902 after the second Boer War. In 1968 it became a fully independent kingdom within the Commonwealth. A constitution was introduced in 1978, banning all political parties and increasing the power of the monarch. In 1992 demands for greater democracy led the king to amend the constitution; following further protests in 1996 the king undertook to review the ban on political parties. Head of state, King Mswati III; prime minister, Sibusiso Dlamini; capital, Mbabane.

languages	Swazi, English
currency	lilangeni (*pl.* emalangeni, E) of 100 cents
pop. (1996)	934 000
GNP (1994)	US$1.04B
literacy	78% (m); 75% (f)
life expectancy	52 (m); 61 (f)

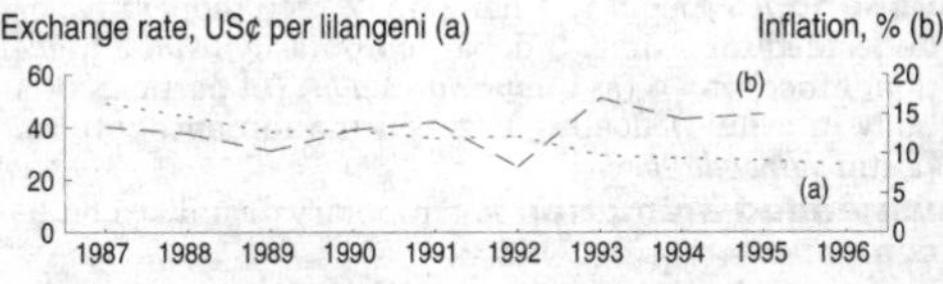

solemnly or on oath. **b** (cause to) take (an oath) (*swore them to secrecy*). **2** *colloq.* insist (*swore he was fit*). **3** (often foll. by *at*) use profane or obscene language. **4** (foll. by *by*) **a** appeal to as a witness in taking an oath (*swear by Almighty God*). **b** *colloq.* have great confidence in (*swears by yoga*). **5** (foll. by *to*; usu. in *neg.*) say certainly (*could not swear to it*). *–n.* spell of swearing. □ **swear blind** *colloq.* affirm emphatically. **swear in** induct into office etc. with an oath. **swear off** *colloq.* promise to abstain from (drink etc.). [Old English]

swear-word *n.* profane or indecent word.

sweat /swet/ *–n.* **1** moisture exuded through the pores, esp. from heat or nervousness. **2** state or period of sweating. **3** *colloq.* state of anxiety (*in a sweat*). **4** *colloq.* **a** drudgery, effort. **b** laborious task. **5** condensed moisture on a surface. *–v.* (*past* and *past part.* **sweated** or *US* **sweat**) **1** exude sweat. **2** be terrified or suffer. **3** (of a wall etc.) exhibit surface moisture. **4** (cause to) drudge or toil. **5** emit like sweat. **6** make (a horse, athlete, etc.) sweat by exercise. **7** (as **sweated** *adj.*) (of goods, labour, etc.) produced by or subjected to exploitation. □ **no sweat** *colloq.* no bother, no trouble. **sweat blood** *colloq.* **1** work strenuously. **2** be very anxious. **sweat it out** *colloq.* endure a difficult experience to the end. □ **sweaty** *adj.* (**-ier, -iest**). [Old English]

sweat-band *n.* band fitted inside a hat or worn round a wrist etc. to absorb sweat.

sweater *n.* jersey or pullover.

sweatshirt *n.* sleeved cotton sweater.

sweatshop *n.* factory where sweated labour is used.

Swede *n.* **1 a** native or national of Sweden. **b** person of Swedish descent. **2** (**swede**) large yellow-fleshed turnip orig. from Sweden. [Low German or Dutch]

Swedish *–adj.* of Sweden, its people, or language. *–n.* language of Sweden.

sweep *–v.* (*past* and *past part.* **swept**) **1** clean or clear (a room or area etc.) (as) with a broom. **2** (often foll. by *up*) clean a room etc. in this way. **3** (often foll. by *up*) collect or remove (dirt etc.) by sweeping. **4** (foll. by *aside, away,* etc.) **a** push (as) with a broom. **b** dismiss abruptly. **5** (foll. by *along, down,* etc.) carry or drive along with force. **6** (foll. by *off, away,* etc.) remove or clear forcefully. **7** traverse swiftly or lightly. **8** impart a sweeping motion to. **9** swiftly cover or affect. **10 a** glide swiftly; speed along. **b** go majestically. **11** (of landscape etc.) be rolling or spacious. *–n.* **1** act or motion of sweeping. **2** curve in the road, sweeping line of a hill, etc. **3** range or scope. **4** = CHIMNEY-SWEEP. **5** sortie by aircraft. **6** *colloq.* = SWEEPSTAKE. □ **make a clean sweep of 1** completely abolish or expel. **2** win all the prizes etc. in (a competition etc.). **sweep away** abolish swiftly. **sweep the board 1** win all the money at stake. **2** win all possible prizes etc. **sweep under the carpet** see CARPET. [Old English]

sweeper *n.* **1** person who cleans by sweeping. **2** manual device for sweeping carpets etc. **3** *Football* defensive player positioned close to the goalkeeper.

◆ **sweep facility** *n.* service provided by a bank which automatically transfers funds above a certain level from a current account to a high-interest earning account. The process can work in reverse when funds in the current account fall below a certain level. The purpose is to provide the customer with the greatest amount of interest, with the minimum personal intervention.

sweeping *–adj.* **1** wide in range or effect (*sweeping changes*). **2** generalized, arbitrary (*sweeping statement*). *–n.* (in *pl.*) dirt etc. collected by sweeping.

sweepstake *n.* **1** form of gambling in which all stakes are pooled and paid to the winners. **2** race with betting of this kind. **3** prize(s) won in a sweepstake.

sweet *–adj.* **1** tasting of sugar. **2** smelling pleasant like roses or perfume etc.; fragrant. **3** (of sound etc.) melodious or harmonious. **4** fresh; not salt, sour, bitter, etc. **5** gratifying or attractive. **6** amiable, pleasant. **7** *colloq.* pretty, charming. **8** (foll. by *on*) *colloq.* fond of; in love with. *–n.* **1** small shaped piece of sweet substance, usu. made with sugar or chocolate. **2** sweet dish or course of a meal. □ **sweetish** *adj.* **sweetly** *adv.* [Old English]

sweet-and-sour *attrib. adj.* cooked in a sauce containing sugar and vinegar or lemon etc.

sweetbread *n.* pancreas or thymus of an animal, esp. as food.

sweet-brier *n.* wild rose with small fragrant leaves.

sweet corn *n.* sweet-flavoured maize kernels.

sweeten *v.* **1** make or become sweet or sweeter. **2** make agreeable or less painful. □ **sweetening** *n.*

sweetener *n.* **1** substance used to sweeten food or drink. **2** *colloq.* bribe or inducement.

sweetheart *n.* **1** lover or darling. **2** term of endearment.

sweetie *n. colloq.* **1** = SWEET *n.* 1. **2** sweetheart.

sweetmeal *n.* sweetened wholemeal.

sweetmeat *n.* **1** = SWEET *n.* 1. **2** small fancy cake.

sweetness *n.* being sweet; fragrance. □ **sweetness and light** (esp. uncharacteristic) mildness and reason.

sweet pea *n.* climbing plant with fragrant flowers.

sweet pepper *n.* mild pepper.

sweet potato *n.* **1** tropical climbing plant with sweet tuberous roots used for food. **2** root of this.

sweetshop *n.* confectioner's shop.

sweet talk *colloq.* *–n.* flattery, blandishment. *–v.* (**sweet-talk**) flatter in order to persuade.

Sweden /'swi:d(ə)n/, **Kingdom of** country occupying the E part of the Scandinavian peninsula. Sweden's rich natural resources form the basis of its prosperous economy, in which heavy industry is important. Deposits of iron ore supply the iron and steel, metalworking, engineering, and shipbuilding industries; copper, zinc, and lead are also mined. Manufactures include cars, machinery, electrical equipment, and chemicals, which are among the country's major exports. Forestry is also important, producing wood, pulp, and paper for processing and export. Financial services are also important to the economy. Hydroelectricity provides much of the country's power, supplemented by nuclear power and imported fuel. The agricultural sector of the economy is relatively unimportant: barley, wheat, oats, and potatoes are grown in the S, and livestock are reared in the N.

History. Sweden was united with Denmark and Norway from 1397 until its re-emergence as an independent state in 1523. The following two centuries saw the country's rise and fall as the prominent Baltic power, influence on the European mainland peaking in the early 17th century and collapsing at the beginning of the 18th century. United with Norway between 1814 and 1905, Sweden maintained its neutrality in the two World Wars, while the economy prospered through increasing industrialization, and the political hegemony of the Social Democratic party led to the creation of an extensive system of social security. Sweden is a member of Efta and became a member of the EU in 1994. Head of state, King Carl XVI Gustaf; prime minister, Göran Persson; capital, Stockholm.

languages	Swedish (official), Finnish, Lapp
currency	krona (Skr) of 100 øre
pop. (1996)	8 858 000
GNP (1994)	US$206B
literacy	99% (m); 99% (f)
life expectancy	75 (m); 80 (f)

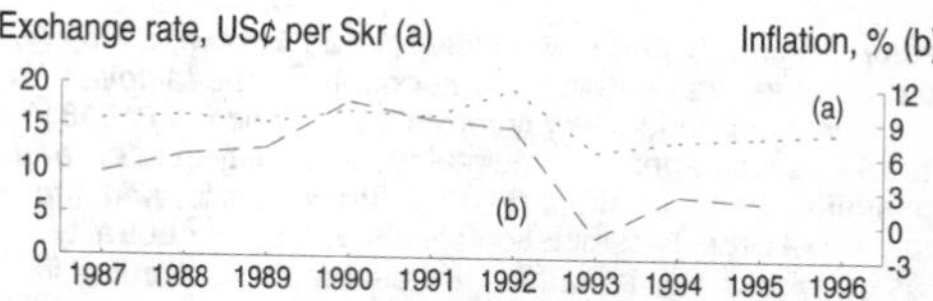

sweet tooth *n.* liking for sweet-tasting things.

sweet william *n.* cultivated plant with clusters of vivid fragrant flowers.

swell –*v.* (*past part.* **swollen** /ˈswəʊlən/ or **swelled**) **1** (cause to) grow bigger, louder, or more intense. **2** (often foll. by *up*) rise or raise up from the surrounding surface. **3** (foll. by *out*) bulge. **4** (of the heart etc.) feel full of joy, pride, relief, etc. **5** (foll. by *with*) be hardly able to restrain (pride etc.). –*n.* **1** act or the state of swelling. **2** heaving of the sea with unbreaking waves. **3 a** crescendo. **b** mechanism in an organ etc. for producing a crescendo or diminuendo. **4** *colloq.* dandy. **5** protuberance. –*adj. colloq.* **1** esp. *US* fine, excellent. **2** smart, fashionable. [Old English]

swelled head *n.* (also **swollen head**) *colloq.* conceit.

swelling *n.* abnormal bodily protuberance.

swelter –*v.* be uncomfortably hot. –*n.* sweltering condition. [Old English]

swept *past* and *past part.* of SWEEP.

swerve –*v.* (**-ving**) (cause to) change direction, esp. abruptly. –*n.* swerving movement. [Old English, = scour]

SwF *symb.* Swiss franc.

SWIFT *abbr.* Society for Worldwide Interbank Financial Transmission.

swift –*adj.* **1** quick, rapid. **2** prompt. –*n.* swift-flying migratory bird with long wings. □ **swiftly** *adv.* **swiftness** *n.* [Old English]

swig –*v.* (**-gg-**) *colloq.* drink in large draughts. –*n.* swallow of drink, esp. large. [origin unknown]

swill –*v.* **1** (often foll. by *out*) rinse or flush. **2** drink greedily. –*n.* **1** act of rinsing. **2** mainly liquid refuse as pigfood. [Old English]

swim –*v.* (**-mm-**; *past* **swam**; *past part.* **swum**) **1** propel the body through water with limbs, fins, or tail. **2** traverse (a stretch of water or distance) by swimming. **3** perform (a stroke) by swimming. **4** float on a liquid. **5** appear to undulate, reel, or whirl. **6** feel dizzy (*my head swam*). **7** (foll. by *in, with*) be flooded. –*n.* period or act of swimming. □ **in the swim** *colloq.* involved in or aware of what is going on. □ **swimmer** *n.* [Old English]

swimming-bath *n.* (also **swimming-pool**) artificial pool for swimming.

swimming-costume *n.* = BATHING-COSTUME.

swimmingly *adv. colloq.* smoothly, without impediment.

swimsuit *n.* swimming-costume, esp. one-piece for women and girls.

swimwear *n.* clothing for swimming in.

swindle /ˈswɪnd(ə)l/ –*v.* (**-ling**) (often foll. by *out of*) **1** cheat of money etc. **2** cheat a person of (money etc.) (*swindled £200 out of him*). –*n.* **1** act of swindling. **2** fraudulent person or thing. □ **swindler** *n.* [back-formation from *swindler* from German]

swine *n.* (*pl.* same) **1** *formal* or *US* pig. **2** *colloq.* (*pl.* same or **-s**) **a** contemptible person. **b** unpleasant or difficult thing. □ **swinish** *adj.* [Old English]

SWING *abbr. Finance* sterling warrant into gilt-edged stock.

swing –*v.* (*past* and *past part.* **swung**) **1 a** (cause to) move with a to-and-fro or curving motion, as of an object attached at one end and hanging free at the other; sway. **b** hang so as to be free to swing. **2** oscillate or revolve. **3** move by gripping something and leaping etc. (*swung from tree to tree*). **4** walk with a swing. **5** (foll. by *round*) move to face the opposite direction. **6** change one's opinion or mood. **7** (foll. by *at*) attempt to hit. **8** (also **swing it**) play (music) with a swing rhythm. **9** *colloq.* (of a party etc.) be lively etc. **10** have a decisive influence on (voting etc.). **11** *colloq.* achieve, manage. **12** *colloq.* be executed by hanging. –*n.* **1** act, motion, or extent of swinging. **2** swinging or smooth gait, rhythm, or action. **3 a** seat slung by ropes etc. for swinging on or in. **b** period of swinging on this. **4 a** jazz or dance music with an easy flowing rhythm. **b** rhythmic feeling or drive of this. **5** discernible change, esp. in votes or points scored etc. □ **swings and roundabouts** situation affording equal gain and loss. □ **swinger** *n.* [Old English]

swing-boat *n.* boat-shaped swing at fairs.

swing-bridge *n.* bridge that can be swung aside to let ships pass.

swing-door *n.* self-closing door opening both ways.

swingeing /ˈswɪndʒɪŋ/ *adj.* **1** (of a blow) forcible. **2** huge or far-reaching (*swingeing economies*). [archaic *swinge* strike hard, from Old English]

swing-wing *n.* aircraft wing that can move from a right-angled to a swept-back position.

swipe *colloq.* –*v.* (**-ping**) **1** (often foll. by *at*) hit hard and recklessly. **2** steal. –*n.* reckless hard hit or attempted hit. [perhaps var. of SWEEP]

swirl –*v.* move, flow, or carry along with a whirling motion. –*n.* **1** swirling motion. **2** twist or curl. □ **swirly** *adj.* [perhaps from Low German or Dutch]

swish –*v.* **1** swing (a thing) audibly through the air, grass, etc. **2** move with or make a swishing sound. –*n.* swishing action or sound. –*adj. colloq.* smart, fashionable. [imitative]

Swiss –*adj.* of Switzerland or its people. –*n.* (*pl.* same) **1** native or national of Switzerland. **2** person of Swiss descent. [French *Suisse*]

Swiss roll *n.* cylindrical sponge cake with a jam etc. filling.

switch –*n.* **1** device for completing and breaking an elec-

---

Switzerland /ˈswɪtsələnd/, **Confederation of** small landlocked country in central Europe, bordered by France, Italy, Austria, and Germany. The country's position has enabled it to become an international centre for trade and finance (esp. banking and insurance). Tourism is also a major source of revenue, the chief attractions being the Alps, which dominate the S of the country, and the Swiss lakes. The rivers of the Alps supply hydroelectric power for the important industrial sector, which manufactures machinery, chemicals, textiles, food products, precision instruments, clocks, watches, and jewellery. The country's principal exports are industrial machinery, pharmaceuticals, and precision instruments, such as clocks and watches. Dairy farming is the chief agricultural activity; cereals, fruit, vegetables, flax, hemp, and tobacco are grown and wine is produced.

History. Formerly part of the Holy Roman Empire, Switzerland emerged as an independent country in the Middle Ages; its independence was formally recognized in 1648. The Swiss Confederation maintained neutrality in international affairs through the 17th and 18th centuries, and after a period of French domination (1798–1815), its neutrality was guaranteed by the other European powers. Neutral in both World Wars, Switzerland has emerged as the headquarters of such international organizations as the Red Cross. Switzerland is a member of Efta, but has voted against joining the European Economic Area (see EUROPEAN FREE TRADE ASSOCIATION). President, Arnold Koller; capital, Berne.

languages	German, French, Italian, Romansch
currency	franc (SwF) of 100 centimes (or rappen)
pop. (1996)	7 087 000
GNP (1994)	US$264.9B
literacy	99% (m); 99% (f)
life expectancy	75 (m); 81 (f)

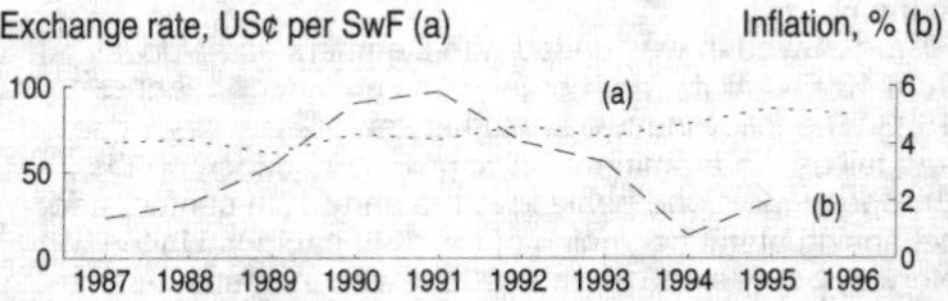

tric circuit. **2 a** transfer, change-over, or deviation. **b** exchange. **3** flexible shoot cut from a tree. **4** light tapering rod. **5** *US* railway points. *–v.* **1** (foll. by *on, off*) turn (an electrical device) on or off. **2** change or transfer. **3** exchange. **4** whip or flick with a switch. **5** use the cash from the sale of one investment to purchase another. This may, or may not, involve a liability for capital-gains tax, depending on the circumstances. **6** close an open position in a commodity market and open a similar position in the same commodity but for a different delivery period. For example, a trader may switch a holding of sugar for October delivery f.o.b. to an equal quantity of sugar for March delivery f.o.b. for the next year. □ **switch off** *colloq.* cease to pay attention. [Low German]

switchback *n.* **1** ride at a fair etc., with extremely steep ascents and descents. **2** (often *attrib.*) such a railway or road.

switchboard *n.* apparatus for making connections between electric circuits, esp. in telephony.

switched-on *adj. colloq.* **1** up to date; aware of what is going on. **2** excited; under the influence of drugs.

swivel /ˈswɪv(ə)l/ *–n.* coupling between two parts enabling one to revolve without turning the other. *–v.* (**-ll-**; *US* **-l-**) turn on or as on a swivel. [Old English]

swivel chair *n.* chair with a revolving seat.

swizz *n.* (also **swiz**) *colloq.* **1** something unfair or disappointing. **2** swindle. [origin unknown]

swizzle /ˈswɪz(ə)l/ *n.* **1** *colloq.* frothy mixed alcoholic drink esp. of rum or gin and bitters. **2** *slang* = SWIZZ. [origin unknown]

swizzle-stick *n.* stick used for frothing or flattening drinks.

swollen *past part.* of SWELL.

swoon *v.* & *n. literary* faint. [Old English]

swoop *–v.* **1** (often foll. by *down*) descend rapidly like a bird of prey. **2** (often foll. by *on*) make a sudden attack. *–n.* swooping movement or action. [Old English]

swop var. of SWAP.

sword /sɔːd/ *n.* **1** weapon with a long blade and hilt with a handguard. **2** (prec. by *the*) **a** war. **b** military power. □ **put to the sword** kill. [Old English]

sword dance *n.* dance with the brandishing of swords or with swords laid on the ground.

swordfish *n.* (*pl.* same or **-es**) large marine fish with swordlike upper jaw.

sword of Damocles /ˈdæməˌkliːz/ *n.* an immediate danger. [from *Damokles*, who had a sword hung by a hair over him]

swordplay *n.* **1** fencing. **2** repartee; lively argument.

swordsman *n.* person of (usu. specified) skill with a sword. □ **swordsmanship** *n.*

swordstick *n.* hollow walking-stick containing a blade that can be used as a sword.

swore *past* of SWEAR.

sworn *past part.* of SWEAR. *attrib. adj.* bound (as) by an oath (*sworn enemies*).

swot *colloq.* *–v.* (**-tt-**) **1** study hard. **2** (usu. foll. by *up, up on*) study (a subject) hard or hurriedly. *–n.* usu. *derog.* person who swots. [dial. var. of SWEAT]

♦ **SWOT analysis** *n.* analysis made by a company in planning the marketing of a new product to assess its strengths and weaknesses (internally) and the opportunities and threats facing it (externally). Internal strengths could be a good distribution system and adequate cash flow. Weaknesses might be identified as an already extended product line or poor servicing facilities. Opportunities could be consumer demand for a particular product or the vulnerability of a competitor, while threats might be forthcoming government legislation or diversification by a competitor. A SWOT analysis is also the main feature of an organization's managerial position audit. [*S*trengths, *W*eaknesses, *O*pportunities, *T*hreats]

SWPA *abbr.* South-West Pacific Area.

swum *past part.* of SWIM.

swung *past* and *past part.* of SWING.

SX *–abbr. Shipping* Sundays excepted. *–international civil aircraft marking* Greece.

SY *–international vehicle registration* Seychelles. *–postcode* Shrewsbury.

sybarite /ˈsɪbəˌraɪt/ *n.* self-indulgent or voluptuous person. □ **sybaritic** /-ˈrɪtɪk/ *adj.* [*Sybaris*, ancient city in S Italy]

sycamore /ˈsɪkəˌmɔː(r)/ *n.* **1** large maple or its wood. **2** *US* plane-tree or its wood. [Greek *sukomoros*]

sycophant /ˈsɪkəˌfænt/ *n.* flatterer; toady. □ **sycophancy** *n.* **sycophantic** /-ˈfæntɪk/ *adj.* [Greek *sukophantēs*]

Sydney /ˈsɪdnɪ/ largest city and chief port of Australia, capital of New South Wales and a centre of culture, finance, commerce, and industry; wheat and wool are exported, and manufactures include chemicals and consumer goods; pop. (est. 1995) 3 772 700.

syl- *prefix* assim. form of SYN- before *l*.

syllabary /ˈsɪləbərɪ/ *n.* (*pl.* **-ies**) list of characters representing syllables. [related to SYLLABLE]

syllabic /sɪˈlæbɪk/ *adj.* of or in syllables. □ **syllabically** *adv.*

syllable /ˈsɪləb(ə)l/ *n.* **1** unit of pronunciation forming the whole or part of a word and usu. having one vowel sound often with consonant(s) before or after (e.g. *water* has two, *inferno* three). **2** character(s) representing a syllable. **3** the least amount of speech or writing. □ **in words of one syllable** plainly, bluntly. [Greek *sullabē*]

syllabub /ˈsɪləˌbʌb/ *n.* (also **sillabub**) dessert of flavoured, sweetened, and whipped cream or milk. [origin unknown]

syllabus /ˈsɪləbəs/ *n.* (*pl.* **-buses** or **-bi** /-ˌbaɪ/) programme or outline of a course of study, teaching, etc. [misreading of Greek *sittuba* label]

syllepsis /sɪˈlepsɪs/ *n.* (*pl.* **syllepses** /-siːz/) figure of speech in which a word is applied to two others in different senses (e.g. *caught the train and a cold*) or to two others of which it grammatically suits one only (e.g. *neither you nor he knows*) (cf. ZEUGMA). [Greek: related to SYLLABLE]

syllogism /ˈsɪləˌdʒɪz(ə)m/ *n.* reasoning in which a conclusion is drawn from two given or assumed propositions. □ **syllogistic** /-ˈdʒɪstɪk/ *adj.* [Greek *logos* reason]

sylph /sɪlf/ *n.* **1** elemental spirit of the air. **2** slender graceful woman or girl. □ **sylphlike** *adj.* [Latin]

sylvan /ˈsɪlv(ə)n/ *adj.* (also **silvan**) **1 a** of the woods. **b** having woods. **2** rural. [Latin *silva* a wood]

sylviculture var. of SILVICULTURE.

sym- *prefix* assim. form of SYN- before *b, m, p*.

symbiosis /ˌsɪmbaɪˈəʊsɪs, ˌsɪmbɪ-/ *n.* (*pl.* **-bioses** /-siːz/) **1** interaction between two different organisms living in close physical association, usu. to the advantage of both. **2** mutually advantageous association between persons. □ **symbiotic** /-ˈɒtɪk/ *adj.* [Greek, = living together]

symbol /ˈsɪmb(ə)l/ *n.* **1** thing regarded as typifying or representing something (*white is a symbol of purity*). **2** mark, sign, etc. representing an object, idea, function, or process; logo. □ **symbolic** /-ˈbɒlɪk/ *adj.* **symbolically** /-ˈbɒlɪkəlɪ/ *adv.* [Greek *sumbolon*]

symbolism *n.* **1 a** use of symbols. **b** symbols collectively. **2** artistic and poetic movement or style using symbols to express ideas, emotions, etc. □ **symbolist** *n.*

symbolize *v.* (also **-ise**) (**-zing** or **-sing**) **1** be a symbol of. **2** represent by symbols. [French: related to SYMBOL]

♦ **symbol retailer** *n.* (also **voluntary retailer**) voluntary group of independent retailers formed to buy in large quantities from wholesalers at lower prices than they could achieve independently. Originally a defensive move by independents to counter the increasing dominance and expansion of the chain stores, supermarkets, hypermarkets, etc., these groups can also provide each other with such services as promotional support and management advice. The members of a group often use a common name or symbol to identify themselves.

---

symmetry /ˈsɪmɪtrɪ/ *n.* (*pl.* **-ies**) **1 a** correct proportion of parts. **b** beauty resulting from this. **2 a** structure allowing an object to be divided into parts of an equal shape and size. **b** possession of such a structure. **3** repetition of exactly similar parts facing each other or a centre. □ **symmetrical** /-ˈmetrɪk(ə)l/ *adj.* **symmetrically** /-ˈmetrɪkəlɪ/ *adv.* [Greek *summetria*]

sympathetic /ˌsɪmpəˈθetɪk/ *adj.* **1** of or expressing sympathy. **2** pleasant, likeable. **3** (foll. by *to*) favouring (a proposal etc.). □ **sympathetically** *adv.*

♦ **sympathetic strike** see STRIKE *n.* 2.

sympathize /ˈsɪmpəˌθaɪz/ *v.* (also **-ise**) (**-zing** or **-sing**) (often foll. by *with*) **1** feel or express sympathy. **2** agree. □ **sympathizer** *n.*

sympathy /ˈsɪmpəθɪ/ *n.* (*pl.* **-ies**) **1 a** sharing of another's feelings. **b** capacity for this. **2 a** (often foll. by *with*) sharing or tendency to share (with a person etc.) in an emotion, sensation, or condition. **b** (in *sing.* or *pl.*) compassion or commiseration; condolences. **3** (often foll. by *for*) approval. **4** (in *sing.* or *pl.*; often foll. by *with*) agreement (with a person etc.) in opinion or desire. □ **in sympathy** (often foll. by *with*) having, showing, or resulting from sympathy. [Greek, = fellow-feeling]

symphony /ˈsɪmfənɪ/ *n.* (*pl.* **-ies**) **1** large-scale composition for full orchestra in several movements. **2** instrumental interlude in a large-scale vocal work. **3** = SYMPHONY ORCHESTRA. □ **symphonic** /-ˈfɒnɪk/ *adj.* [from SYN-, Greek *phōnē* sound]

symphony orchestra *n.* large orchestra suitable for playing symphonies etc.

symposium /sɪmˈpəʊzɪəm/ *n.* (*pl.* **-sia**) **1** conference, or collection of essays, on a particular subject. **2** philosophical or other friendly discussion. [Greek *sumpotēs* fellow-drinker]

symptom /ˈsɪmptəm/ *n.* **1** physical or mental sign of disease. **2** sign of the existence of something. □ **symptomatic** /-ˈmætɪk/ *adj.* [Greek *piptō* fall]

syn- *prefix* with, together, alike. [Greek *sun* with]

synagogue /ˈsɪnəˌgɒg/ *n.* **1** building for Jewish religious observance and instruction. **2** Jewish congregation. [Greek, = assembly]

synapse /ˈsaɪnæps, ˈsɪn-/ *n. Anat.* junction of two nerve-cells. [Greek *haptō* join]

sync /sɪŋk/ (also **synch**) *colloq.* –*n.* synchronization. –*v.* synchronize. □ **in** (or **out of**) **sync** (often foll. by *with*) according or agreeing well (or badly). [abbreviation]

synchromesh /ˈsɪŋkrəʊˌmeʃ/ *n.* (often *attrib.*) system of gear-changing, esp. in vehicles, in which the gearwheels revolve at the same speed during engagement. [abbreviation of *synchronized mesh*]

synchronic /sɪŋˈkrɒnɪk/ *adj.* concerned with a subject as it exists at one point in time. □ **synchronically** *adv.* [from SYN-, Greek *khronos* time]

synchronism /ˈsɪŋkrəˌnɪz(ə)m/ *n.* **1** being or treating as synchronic or synchronous. **2** process of synchronizing sound and picture.

synchronize /ˈsɪŋkrəˌnaɪz/ *v.* (also **-ise**) (**-zing** or **-sing**) **1** (often foll. by *with*) make or be synchronous (with). **2** make the sound and picture of (a film etc.) coincide. **3** cause (clocks etc.) to show the same time. □ **synchronization** /-ˈzeɪʃ(ə)n/ *n.*

■ **Usage** *Synchronize* should not be used to mean 'coordinate' or 'combine'.

synchronous /ˈsɪŋkrənəs/ *adj.* (often foll. by *with*) existing or occurring at the same time.

syncopate /ˈsɪŋkəˌpeɪt/ *v.* (**-ting**) **1** displace the beats or accents in (music). **2** shorten (a word) by dropping interior letters. □ **syncopation** /-ˈpeɪʃ(ə)n/ *n.* [Latin: related to SYNCOPE]

syncope /ˈsɪŋkəpɪ/ *n.* **1** *Gram.* syncopation. **2** fainting through a fall in blood pressure. [Greek *sunkopē* cutting off]

syncretize /ˈsɪŋkrəˌtaɪz/ *v.* (also **-ise**) (**-zing** or **-sing**) attempt, esp. inconsistently, to unify or reconcile differing schools of thought. □ **syncretic** /-ˈkretɪk/ *adj.* **syncretism** *n.* [Greek]

syndic /ˈsɪndɪk/ *n.* any of various university or government officials. [Greek *sundikos*, = advocate]

syndicalism /ˈsɪndɪkəˌlɪz(ə)m/ *n. hist.* movement for transferring industrial ownership and control to workers' unions. □ **syndicalist** *n.* [French: related to SYNDIC]

syndicate –*n.* /ˈsɪndɪkət/ **1** combination of individuals or businesses to promote a common interest. **2** group of Lloyd's underwriters who accept insurance risks as a group; each syndicate is run by a syndicate manager or agent. The **names** in the syndicate are those members who accept an agreed share of each risk in return for the same proportion of the premium, but do not take part in organizing the underwriting business. Although a syndicate underwrites as a group, each member is financially responsible for only his or her own share. In 1993, after several years of heavy losses, Lloyd's permitted limited companies to become names. **3** agency supplying material simultaneously to a number of newspapers etc. **4** group of people who gamble, organize crime, etc. **5** committee of syndics. –*v.* /ˈsɪndɪˌkeɪt/ (**-ting**) **1** form into a syndicate. **2** publish (material) through a syndicate. □ **syndication** /-ˈkeɪʃ(ə)n/ *n.* [Latin: related to SYNDIC]

♦ **syndicated loan** *n.* very large loan made to one borrower by a group of banks headed by one lead bank, which usu. takes only a small percentage of the loan itself, syndicating the rest to other banks and financial institutions.

♦ **syndicated research** *n.* large-scale marketing research project undertaken by market-research companies and subsequently offered for sale to interested parties. It is not therefore undertaken on behalf of a client.

syndrome /ˈsɪndrəʊm/ *n.* **1** group of concurrent symptoms of a disease. **2** characteristic combination of opinions, emotions, behaviour, etc. [Greek *sundromē* running together]

synecdoche /sɪˈnekdəkɪ/ *n.* figure of speech in which a part is made to represent the whole or vice versa (e.g. *new faces at the club*; *England lost to India*). [Greek, = taking together]

♦ **synergy** *n.* added value created by joining two separate firms, i.e. an overall gain in return that is greater than the sum of its parts. Often optimistically sought, synergy is hard to achieve because of resistance to change and the difficulty of merging two corporate cultures.

synod /ˈsɪnəd/ *n.* Church council of delegated clergy and sometimes laity. [Greek, = meeting]

synonym /ˈsɪnənɪm/ *n.* word or phrase that means the same as another (e.g. *shut* and *close*). [Greek *onoma* name]

synonymous /sɪˈnɒnɪməs/ *adj.* (often foll. by *with*) **1** having the same meaning. **2** suggestive of; associated with (*his name is synonymous with terror*).

synopsis /sɪˈnɒpsɪs/ *n.* (*pl.* **synopses** /-siːz/) summary or outline. [Greek *opsis* view]

synoptic /sɪˈnɒptɪk/ *adj.* of or giving a synopsis. [Greek: related to SYNOPSIS]

Synoptic Gospels *n.pl.* Gospels of Matthew, Mark, and Luke.

synovia /saɪˈnəʊvɪə, sɪ-/ *n. Physiol.* viscous fluid lubricating joints etc. □ **synovial** *adj.* [medieval Latin]

syntax /ˈsɪntæks/ *n.* **1** grammatical arrangement of words. **2** rules or analysis of this. **3** *Computing* see PROGRAMMING LANGUAGE. □ **syntactic** /-ˈtæktɪk/ *adj.* **syntactically** /-ˈtæktɪkəlɪ/ *adv.* [Greek, = arrangement]

synth /sɪnθ/ *n. colloq.* = SYNTHESIZER.

synthesis /ˈsɪnθəsɪs/ *n.* (*pl.* **-theses** /-ˌsiːz/) **1 a** combining of elements into a whole. **b** result of this. **2** *Chem.* artificial production of compounds from their constituents as distinct from extraction from plants etc. [Greek, = placing together]

synthesize /ˈsɪnθəˌsaɪz/ *v.* (also **-ise**) (**-zing** or **-sing**) make a synthesis of.

synthesizer *n.* electronic usu. keyboard instrument producing a wide variety of sounds.

synthetic /sɪn'θetɪk/ *–adj.* **1** made by chemical synthesis, esp. to imitate a natural product. **2** affected, insincere. *–n.* synthetic substance. □ **synthetically** *adv.*

syphilis /'sɪfəlɪs/ *n.* contagious venereal disease. □ **syphilitic** /-'lɪtɪk/ *adj.* [*Syphilus*, name of a character in a poem of 1530]

SYR *international vehicle registration* Syria.

Syracuse /'saɪrə,kjuːz/ (Italian **Siracusa** /,sɪərə'kuːzə/) port in Italy, on the SE coast of Sicily; agricultural produce is processed, and there is some light industry; pop. (est. 1994) 127 496.

Syriac /'sɪrɪ,æk/ *–n.* language of ancient Syria, western Aramaic. *–adj.* of or in Syriac.

syringa /sɪ'rɪŋgə/ *n.* **1** = MOCK ORANGE. **2** lilac or similar related plant. [related to SYRINGE]

syringe /sɪ'rɪndʒ, 'sɪ-/ *–n.* device for sucking in and ejecting liquid in a fine stream. *–v.* (**-ging**) sluice or spray with a syringe. [Greek *surigx* pipe]

syrup /'sɪrəp/ *n.* (*US* **sirup**) **1 a** sweet sauce of sugar dissolved in boiling water. **b** similar fluid as a drink, medicine, etc. **2** condensed sugar-cane juice; molasses, treacle. **3** excessive sweetness of manner or style. □ **syrupy** *adj.* [Arabic *sharab*]

system /'sɪstəm/ *n.* **1** complex whole; set of connected things or parts; organized body of things. **2 a** set of organs in the body with a common structure or function. **b** human or animal body as a whole. **3** *Computing* **a** related set of hardware units, often together with the associated software (see SYSTEMS SOFTWARE), that make up a working computer installation. **b** set of programs that jointly control the operation of a computer (see OPERATING SYSTEM) or that are used or required for a particular application. **4** method; scheme of action, procedure, or classification. **5** orderliness. **6** (prec. by *the*) prevailing political or social order, esp. regarded as oppressive. □ **get a thing out of one's system** *colloq.* get rid of a preoccupation or anxiety. [Greek *sustēma -mat-*]

systematic /,sɪstə'mætɪk/ *adj.* **1** methodical; according to a system. **2** regular, deliberate. □ **systematically** *adv.*

systematize /'sɪstəmə,taɪz/ *v.* (also **-ise**) (**-zing** or **-sing**) make systematic. □ **systematization** /-'zeɪʃ(ə)n/ *n.*

system crash *n.* = CRASH[1] *n.* 5a.

systemic /sɪ'stemɪk/ *adj.* **1** *Physiol.* of the whole body. **2** (of an insecticide etc.) entering the plant via the roots or shoots and freely transported within its tissues. □ **systemically** *adv.*

system library *Computing* see PROGRAM LIBRARY.

◆ **systems analysis** *n.* examination or analysis of the objectives and problems of a system for the purpose of developing and improving the system by the use of computers. Systems analysis entails producing a precise statement of what is to be accomplished, determining the methods of achieving the objectives that are most cost-effective, and preparing a feasibility study. If the study is accepted by the customer, the systems analysts will advise on the hardware and software needed, provide programmers with the details they need to write the programs, produce documentation describing the system, plan staff training on it, and monitor the system once it is installed. □ **systems analyst** *n.*

---

systems programming see SYSTEMS SOFTWARE.

◆ **systems selling** *n.* selling of a total system rather than an individual product. For example, some computer manufacturers sell VDUs, keyboards, printers, and the necessary software for their computers, while other companies might only supply the software for these computers.

---

systems software *n.* (also **system software**) software required to produce a computer system acceptable to end-users, providing a good environment for writing, testing, running, and storing users' programs, and including programs that are essential to the effective use of the system. Operating systems, compilers, utility programs, database management systems, and communication systems are examples of systems software. Systems software is usu. provided by the computer manufacturer and is bought together with the computer. The production, documentation, maintenance, and modification of systems software is known as **systems programming**. Cf. APPLICATIONS SOFTWARE.

Szczecin /'ʃtetsiːn/ (also **Stettin** /ʃte'tiːn/) city in NW Poland, a major port on the Oder River; coal is exported, and there are shipbuilding, engineering, chemical, and textile industries; pop. (est. 1995) 419 600.

Szechwan see SICHUAN.

Szeged /'seged/ industrial city and river port in S Hungary; pop. (1996) 167 000.

Syria /'sɪrɪə/ country in SW Asia with a coastline on the E Mediterranean Sea. Agriculture is a major source of employment, producing cotton and cereals for export; tobacco is also grown and livestock are reared. Syria is becoming increasingly industrialized: manufactures include textiles, processed food, chemicals, plastics, cement, glass, and leather goods. The exploitation of the country's high-quality oil reserves is of major importance, and the economy has benefited from increasing oil exports, which now account for over half of export earnings. There are also important deposits of phosphates, which are mined and exported.

History. The present countries of Lebanon, Israel, Jordan, and adjacent parts of Iraq and Saudi Arabia were formerly part of Syria. It became a centre of Islamic power and civilization from the 7th century and a province of the Ottoman empire in 1516. After the Turkish defeat in the First World War, Syria was mandated to France and achieved full independence in 1946. It briefly formed part of the United Arab Republic (1958–61). The country's recent history has been dominated by continuing involvement in Middle Eastern affairs, esp. in the peace settlement in Lebanon, and antagonism towards Israel, despite a declared commitment to regional peace talks. President, Lieutenant-General Hafez al-Assad; prime minister, Mahmoud Al Zubi; capital, Damascus. □ **Syrian** *adj.* & *n.*

languages	Arabic (official), Kurdish, Armenian
currency	pound (LS) of 100 piastres
pop. (1996)	14 798 000
GNP (1991)	US$16.2B
literacy	85% (m); 55% (f)
life expectancy	68 (m); 71 (f)

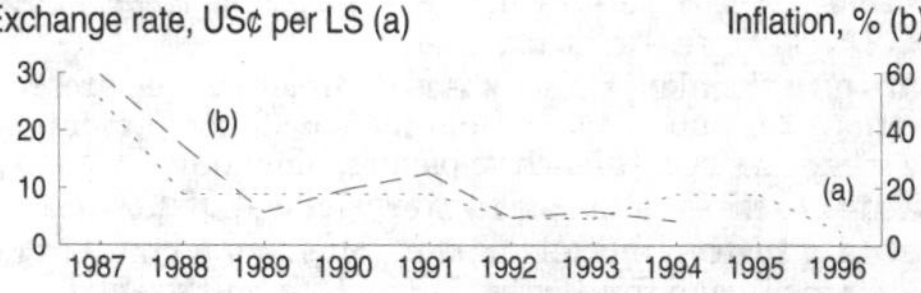

Tt

T[1] /tiː/ *n.* (also **t**) (*pl.* **Ts** or **T's**) **1** twentieth letter of the alphabet. **2** T-shaped thing (esp. *attrib.*: *T-joint*). □ **to a T** exactly; to a nicety.

T[2] *abbr.* (also **T.**) **1** *Advertising* third of a page (type area). **2** *Shipping* tropical sea water (see LOAD LINE).

T[3] *–symb.* tritium. *–international vehicle registration* Thailand.

t. *abbr.* **1** ton(s). **2** (also **t**) tonne(s). **3** *Commerce* tare.

T2 *international civil aircraft marking* Tuvalu.

T3 *international civil aircraft marking* Kiribati.

T7 *international civil aircraft marking* San Marino.

TA *–abbr.* **1** *Taxation* table of allowances. **2** Territorial Army. **3** travelling allowance. *–postcode* Taunton.

Ta *symb.* tantalum.

ta /tɑː/ *int. colloq.* thank you. [infantile form]

TAB *abbr.* tabulator (on a typewriter etc.).

tab[1] *–n.* **1** small flap or strip of material attached for grasping, fastening, or hanging up, or for identification. **2** *US colloq.* bill (*picked up the tab*). **3** distinguishing mark on a staff officer's collar. *–v.* (**-bb-**) provide with a tab or tabs. □ **keep tabs** (or **a tab) on** *colloq.* **1** keep account of. **2** have under observation or in check. [probably dial.]

tab[2] *n.* = TABULATOR 2. [abbreviation]

tabard /'tæbəd/ *n.* **1** herald's official coat emblazoned with royal arms. **2** woman's or girl's sleeveless jerkin. **3** *hist.* knight's short emblazoned garment worn over armour. [French]

Tabasco /tə'bæskəʊ/ state in E Mexico; pop. (est. 1995) 1 748 664; capital, Villahermosa.

tabasco /tə'bæskəʊ/ *n.* **1** pungent pepper. **2** (**Tabasco**) *propr.* sauce made from this. [TABASCO]

tabby /'tæbɪ/ *n.* (*pl.* **-ies**) **1** grey or brownish cat with dark stripes. **2** a kind of watered silk. [French from Arabic]

tabernacle /'tæbə,næk(ə)l/ *n.* **1** *hist.* tent used as a sanctuary by the Israelites during the Exodus. **2** niche or receptacle, esp. for the Eucharistic elements. **3** Nonconformist meeting-house. [Latin: related to TAVERN]

tabla /'tæblə/ *n. Ind.* pair of small drums played with the hands. [Arabic, = drum]

table /'teɪb(ə)l/ *–n.* **1** flat surface on a leg or legs, used for eating, working at, etc. **2 a** food provided in a household (*keeps a good table*). **b** group seated for dinner etc. **3 a** set of facts or figures in columns etc. (*table of contents*). **b** matter contained in this. **c** = MULTIPLICATION TABLE. *–v.* (**-ling**) **1** bring forward for discussion etc. at a meeting. **2** esp. *US* postpone consideration of (a matter). □ **at table** taking a meal at a table. **on the table** offered for discussion. **turn the tables** (often foll. by *on*) reverse circumstances to one's advantage (against). **under the table** *colloq.* **1** very drunk. **2** = *under the counter* (see COUNTER[1]). [Latin *tabula* board]

tableau /'tæbləʊ/ *n.* (*pl.* **-x** /-əʊz/) **1** picturesque presentation. **2** group of silent motionless people representing a scene on stage. [French, = picture, diminutive of TABLE]

tablecloth *n.* cloth spread over a table, esp. for meals.

table d'hôte /,tɑːb(ə)l 'dəʊt/ *n.* (often *attrib.*) meal from a set menu at a fixed price. [French, = host's table]

tableland *n.* elevated plateau.

table licence *n.* licence to serve alcoholic drinks with meals only.

table linen *n.* tablecloths, napkins, etc.

tablespoon *n.* **1** large spoon for serving food. **2** amount held by this. □ **tablespoonful** *n.* (*pl.* **-s**).

tablet /'tæblɪt/ *n.* **1** small solid dose of a medicine etc. **2** bar of soap etc. **3** flat slab of esp. stone, usu. inscribed. **4** *US* writing-pad. [Latin diminutive: related to TABLE]

table talk *n.* informal talk at table.

table tennis *n.* indoor ball game played with small bats on a table divided by a net.

tabletop *n.* surface of a table.

tableware *n.* dishes, plates, etc., for meals.

table wine *n.* wine of ordinary quality.

tabloid /'tæblɔɪd/ *n.* small-sized, often popular or sensational, newspaper. [from TABLET]

taboo /tə'buː/ (also **tabu**) *–n.* (*pl.* **-s**) **1** ritual isolation of a person or thing as sacred or accursed. **2** prohibition imposed by social custom. *–adj.* avoided or prohibited, esp. by social custom (*taboo words*). *–v.* (**-oos, -ooed** or **-us, -ued**) **1** put under taboo. **2** exclude or prohibit, esp. socially. [Tongan]

tabor /'teɪbə(r)/ *n. hist.* small drum, esp. used to accompany a pipe. [French]

tabu var. of TABOO.

tabular /'tæbjʊlə(r)/ *adj.* of or arranged in tables or lists. [Latin: related to TABLE]

tabulate /'tæbjʊ,leɪt/ *v.* (**-ting**) arrange (figures or facts) in tabular form. □ **tabulation** /-'leɪʃ(ə)n/ *n.*

tabulator *n.* **1** person or thing that tabulates. **2** device on a typewriter etc. for advancing to a sequence of set positions in tabular work.

TAC *abbr.* Trades Advisory Council.

♦ **tachistoscope** /tə'kɪstə,skəʊp/ *n.* projection device used in advertising and marketing research to measure the extent to which the features of an advertisement or brand are registered by consumers. The tachistoscope shows a package or advertisement for a brief period (which can be varied), enabling researchers to test the effectiveness of the design, colour, layout, or name. Tachistoscope tests are often undertaken before the product or advertisement is released. □ **tachistoscopic** /-'skɒpɪk/ *adj.* [Greek *takhistos* swiftest]

tacho /'tækəʊ/ *n.* (*pl.* **-s**) *colloq.* = TACHOMETER. [abbreviation]

tachograph /'tækə,grɑːf/ *n.* device in a vehicle recording speed and travel time. [Greek *takhos* speed]

tachometer /tə'kɒmɪtə(r)/ *n.* instrument measuring velocity or rate of rotation of a shaft (esp. in a vehicle).

tacit /'tæsɪt/ *adj.* understood or implied without being stated (*tacit consent*). □ **tacitly** *adv.* [Latin *taceo* be silent]

taciturn /'tæsɪ,tɜːn/ *adj.* saying little; uncommunicative. □ **taciturnity** /-'tɜːnɪtɪ/ *n.* [Latin: related to TACIT]

tack[1] *–n.* **1** small sharp broad-headed nail. **2** *US* drawing-pin. **3** long stitch for joining fabrics etc. lightly or temporarily together. **4** (in sailing) direction, or temporary change of direction, esp. taking advantage of a side wind (*starboard tack*). **5** course of action or policy (*change tack*). **6** sticky condition of varnish etc. *–v.* **1** (often foll. by *down* etc.) fasten with tacks. **2** stitch lightly together. **3** (foll. by *to, on, on to*) add or append. **4 a** change a ship's course by turning its head to the wind. **b** make a series of such tacks. [probably related to French *tache* clasp, nail]

tack[2] *n.* saddle, bridle, etc., of a horse. [from TACKLE]

tack[3] *n. colloq.* cheap or shoddy material; tat, kitsch. [back formation from TACKY[2]]

tackle /'tæk(ə)l/ *–n.* **1** equipment for a task or sport. **2** mechanism, esp. of ropes, pulley-blocks, hooks, etc., for lifting weights, managing sails, etc. **3** windlass with its ropes and hooks. **4** act of tackling in football etc. *–v.* (**-ling**) **1** try to deal with (a problem or difficulty). **2** grapple with (an opponent). **3** confront (a person) in discussion or argument. **4** intercept or stop (a player running with the ball). □ **tackler** *n.* [Low German]

tackle-block *n.* pulley over which a rope runs.

tacky[1] *adj.* (**-ier, -iest**) slightly sticky. □ **tackiness** *n.* [from TACK[1]]

tacky[2] *adj.* (**-ier, -iest**) *colloq.* **1** in poor taste, cheap. **2** tatty, shabby. □ **tackiness** *n.* [origin unknown]

taco /'tækəʊ/ *n.* (*pl.* **-s**) Mexican dish of meat etc. in a folded tortilla. [Mexican Spanish]

tact *n.* **1** skill in dealing with others, esp. in delicate situations. **2** intuitive perception of the right thing to do or say. [Latin *tango tact-* touch]

tactful *adj.* having or showing tact. □ **tactfully** *adv.*

tactic /'tæktɪk/ *n.* **1** tactical manoeuvre. **2** = TACTICS. [Greek from *tasso* arrange]

tactical *adj.* **1** of tactics (*tactical retreat*). **2** (of bombing etc.) done in direct support of military or naval operations. **3** adroitly planning or adroitly planned. □ **tactically** *adv.*

tactics *n.pl.* **1** (also treated as *sing.*) disposition of armed forces, esp. in warfare. **2** short-term procedure adopted in carrying out a scheme or achieving an end. □ **tactician** /tæk'tɪʃ(ə)n/ *n.*

tactile /'tæktaɪl/ *adj.* **1** of the sense of touch. **2** perceived by touch; tangible. □ **tactility** /-'tɪlɪtɪ/ *n.* [Latin: related to TACT]

tactless *adj.* having or showing no tact. □ **tactlessly** *adv.*

Tadjikistan var. of TAJIKISTAN.

tadpole *n.* larva, esp. of a frog, toad, or newt. [related to TOAD, POLL]

Taegu /'taɪguː/ city in SE South Korea, an important textile centre; pop. (1995) 2 449 139.

TAFE /'tæfɪ/ *abbr.* technical and further education.

taffeta /'tæfɪtə/ *n.* fine lustrous silk or silklike fabric. [French or medieval Latin from Persian]

taffrail /'tæfreɪl/ *n.* rail round a ship's stern. [Dutch *taffereel* panel]

Taffy /'tæfɪ/ *n.* (*pl.* **-ies**) *colloq.* often *offens.* Welshman. [a supposed pronunciation of *Davy* = *David*]

tag[1] *–n.* **1** label, esp. on an object to show its address, price, etc. **2** metal etc. point on a shoelace etc. **3** loop or flap for handling or hanging a thing. **4** loose or ragged end. **5** trite quotation or stock phrase. *–v.* (**-gg-**) **1** provide with a tag or tags. **2** (often foll. by *on, on to*) join or attach. □ **tag along** (often foll. by *with*) go along, accompany passively. [origin unknown]

tag[2] *–n.* children's chasing game. *–v.* (**-gg-**) touch in a game of tag. [origin unknown]

tag end *n.* esp. *US* last remnant.

tagliatelle /ˌtæljə'telɪ/ *n.* narrow ribbon-shaped pasta. [Italian]

Tahiti /tə'hiːtɪ/ largest of the Society Islands in the S Pacific, part of French Polynesia; pop. (1988) 115 820; capital, Papeete. Tourism is important; exports include copra, sugar cane, and vanilla. □ **Tahitian** /-ʃ(ə)n/ *adj.* & *n.*

t'ai chi /taɪ 'tʃiː/ *n.* (in full **t'ai chi chu'an** /'tʃwɑːn/) Chinese martial art and system of callisthenics with slow controlled movements. [Chinese, = great ultimate boxing]

Ta'if /'tɑːɪf/ city in Saudi Arabia, SE of Mecca, the unofficial seat of government during the summer; pop. (est. 1991) 410 000.

tail[1] *–n.* **1** hindmost part of an animal, esp. extending beyond the body. **2 a** thing like a tail, esp. an extension at the rear. **b** rear of a procession etc. **3** rear part of an aeroplane, vehicle, or rocket. **4** luminous trail following a comet. **5** inferior, weaker, or last part of anything. **6** part of a shirt or coat below the waist at the back. **7** (in *pl.*) *colloq.* **a** tailcoat. **b** evening dress including this. **8** (in *pl.*) reverse of a coin as a choice when tossing. **9** *colloq.* person following another. *–v.* **1** remove the stalks of (fruit). **2** (often foll. by *after*) *colloq.* follow closely. □ **on a person's tail** closely following a person. **tail off** (or **away**) gradually decrease or diminish; end inconclusively. **with one's tail between one's legs** dejected, humiliated. □ **tailless** *adj.* [Old English]

tail[2] *Law –n.* limitation of ownership, esp. of an estate limited to a person and that person's heirs. *–adj.* so limited (*estate tail*). □ **in tail** under such a limitation. [French *taillier* cut: related to TALLY]

tailback *n.* long line of traffic caused by an obstruction.

tailboard *n.* hinged or removable flap at the rear of a lorry etc.

tailcoat *n.* man's coat with a long divided flap at the back, worn as part of formal dress.

tail-end *n.* hindmost, lowest, or last part.

tailgate *n.* **1** esp. *US* = TAILBOARD. **2** rear door of an estate car or hatchback.

tail-light *n.* (also **tail-lamp**) *US* rear light on a vehicle etc.

tailor /'teɪlə(r)/ *–n.* maker of clothes, esp. men's outer garments to measure. *–v.* **1** make (clothes) as a tailor. **2**

Taiwan /taɪ'wæn/ (formerly **Formosa**) island off the SE coast of China, comprising (with a number of nearby islands) the Republic of China. Since the 1950s Taiwan has undergone steady economic growth, particularly in its export-oriented industries. Machinery, chemicals, metals and metal products, synthetic textiles, plastic goods, televisions, and radios are manufactured and exported; other industries include iron and steel and fishing. Timber is the chief natural resource of this mountainous and densely forested island, but there are also small deposits of coal, oil, natural gas, gold, and other minerals. Agriculture remains important, producing sugar, rice, tea, bananas, pineapples, and tobacco.

History. Settled for centuries by the Chinese, the island was ceded to Japan by China in 1895 but returned to China after the Second World War. General Chiang Kai-shek withdrew there in 1949 with 500 000 troops, after the defeat of his government by the Communist regime, and it became the headquarters of the Chinese Nationalists. In 1971 Taiwan lost its seat in the United Nations to the People's Republic of China, which regards the island as one of its provinces, and in 1979 the US severed diplomatic relations with Taiwan. However, commercial relations were maintained with the US and other non-communist countries, and in 1993 closer economic ties with China were agreed. Relations with China declined during 1995–96 following the first democratic presidential elections and Chinese military exercises in waters close to the island. President, Lee Teng-hui; prime minister, Vincent Siew; capital, Taipei. □ **Taiwanese** /-'niːz/ *adj.* & *n.*

languages	Mandarin Chinese (official), Taiwanese dialects
currency	dollar (NT$) of 100 cents
pop. (1996)	21 463 000
GNP (1995)	US$264B
literacy	97% (m); 89% (f)
life expectancy	71 (m); 77 (f)

Exchange rate, US¢ per NT$ (a) Inflation, % (b)

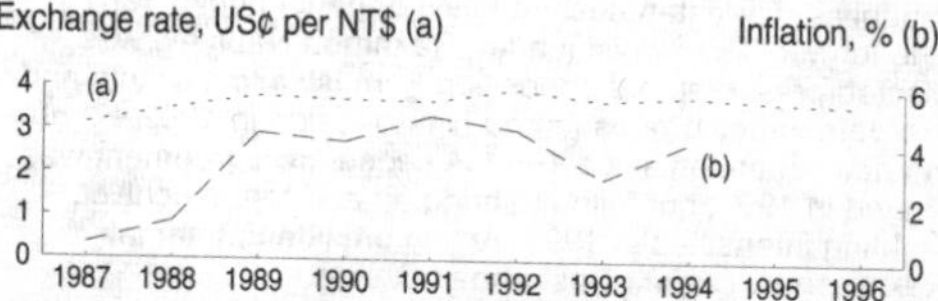

make or adapt for a special purpose. **3** work as or be a tailor. [Anglo-French *taillour*: related to TAIL[2]]

tailored *adj.* **1** (of clothing) well or closely fitted. **2** = TAILOR-MADE.

tailor-made *adj.* **1** made to order by a tailor. **2** made or suited for a particular purpose.

tailpiece *n.* **1** rear appendage. **2** final part of a thing. **3** decoration in a blank space at the end of a chapter etc.

tailpipe *n.* rear section of an exhaust-pipe.

tailplane *n.* horizontal aerofoil at the tail of an aircraft.

tailspin *n.* **1** spin by an aircraft with the tail spiralling. **2** state of chaos or panic.

tail wind *n.* wind blowing in the direction of travel.

taint *–n.* **1** spot or trace of decay, infection, corruption, etc. **2** corrupt condition or infection. *–v.* **1** affect with a taint; become tainted. **2** (foll. by *with*) affect slightly. [Latin: related to TINGE]

Taipei /taɪˈpeɪ/ capital of Taiwan; industries include textile and machinery manufacturing and food processing; pop. (est. 1996) 2 626 138.

Taiyuan /ˌtaɪʊˈɑːn/ city in NE China, capital of Shanxi province and a centre of technology and heavy industry; coalmining is also important; pop. (est. 1989) 1 900 000.

Ta'iz /tæˈɪz/ town and agricultural trading centre in Yemen, administrative capital from 1948 to 1962; pop. (est. 1995) 178 043.

taka /ˈtɑːkɑː/ *n.* standard monetary unit of Bangladesh. [Bengali]

take *–v.* (**-king**; *past* **took** /tʊk/; *past part.* **taken**) **1** lay hold of; get into one's hands. **2** acquire, capture, earn, or win. **3** get by purchase, hire, or formal agreement (*take lodgings*; *took a taxi*). **4** (in a recipe) use. **5** regularly buy (a newspaper etc.). **6** obtain after qualifying (*take a degree*). **7** occupy (*take a chair*). **8** make use of (*take the next turning on the left*; *take the bus*). **9** consume (food or medicine). **10 a** be effective (*inoculation did not take*). **b** (of a plant, seed, etc.) begin to grow. **11** require or use up (*will only take a minute*). **12** carry or accompany (*take the book home*; *bus will take you*). **13** remove; steal (*someone has taken my pen*). **14** catch or be infected with (fire or fever etc.). **15 a** experience, seek, or be affected by (*take fright*; *take pleasure*). **b** exert (*take no notice*). **16** find out and note (*took his address*; *took her temperature*). **17** understand; assume (*I took you to mean yes*). **18** treat, deal with, or regard in a specified way (*took it badly*; *took the corner too fast*). **19** (foll. by *for*) regard as being (*do you take me for an idiot?*). **20 a** accept, receive (*take the offer*; *take a call*; *takes boarders*). **b** hold (*takes 3 pints*). **c** submit to; tolerate (*take a joke*). **21** wear (*takes size 10*). **22** choose or assume (*took a job*; *took the initiative*). **23** derive (*takes its name from the inventor*). **24** (foll. by *from*) subtract (*take 3 from 9*). **25** perform or effect (*take notes*; *take an oath*; *take a look*). **26** occupy or engage oneself in (*take a rest*). **27** conduct (*took prayers*). **28** teach, be taught, or be examined in (a subject). **29 a** make (a photograph). **b** photograph (a person etc.). **30** (in *imper.*) use as an example (*take Napoleon*). **31** *Gram.* have or require as part of a construction (*this verb takes an object*). **32** have sexual intercourse with (a woman). **33** (in *passive*; foll. by *by*, *with*) be attracted or charmed by. *–n.* **1** amount taken or caught at a time etc. **2** scene or film sequence photographed continuously at one time. □ **be taken ill** become ill, esp. suddenly. **have what it takes** *colloq.* have the necessary qualities etc. for success. **take account of** see ACCOUNT. **take advantage of** see ADVANTAGE. **take after** resemble (a parent etc.). **take against** begin to dislike. **take aim** see AIM. **take apart 1** dismantle. **2** *colloq.* beat or defeat. **3** *colloq.* criticize severely. **take away 1** remove or carry elsewhere. **2** subtract. **3** buy (hot food etc.) for eating elsewhere. **take back 1** retract (a statement). **2** convey to an original position. **3** carry in thought to a past time. **4 a** return (goods) to a shop. **b** (of a shop) accept such goods. **5** accept (a person) back into one's affections, into employment, etc. **take the biscuit** (or **bun** or **cake**) *colloq.* be the most remarkable. **take down 1** write down (spoken words). **2** remove or dismantle. **3** lower (a garment worn below the waist). **take effect** see EFFECT. **take for granted** see GRANT. **take fright** see FRIGHT. **take heart** be encouraged. **take in 1** receive as a lodger etc. **2** undertake (work) at home. **3** make (a garment etc.) smaller. **4** understand; observe (*did you take that in?*). **5** cheat. **6** include. **7** *colloq.* visit (a place) on the way to another (*took in Bath*). **8** absorb into the body. **take in hand 1** undertake; start doing or dealing with. **2** undertake to control or reform (a person). **take into account** see ACCOUNT. **take it 1** (often foll. by *that*) assume. **2** *colloq.* endure in a specified way (*took it badly*). **take it easy** see EASY. **take it into one's head** see HEAD. **take it on one** (or **oneself**) (foll. by *to* + infin.) venture or presume. **take it or leave it** (esp. in *imper.*) accept it or not. **take it out of 1** exhaust the strength of. **2** have revenge on. **take it out on** relieve one's frustration by treating aggressively. **take off 1 a** remove (clothing) from the body. **b** remove or lead away. **c** withdraw (transport, a show, etc.). **2** deduct. **3** depart, esp. hastily. **4** *colloq.* mimic humorously. **5** begin a jump. **6** become airborne. **7** (of a scheme, enterprise, etc.) become successful. **8** have (a period) away from work. **take oneself off** go away. **take on 1** undertake (work etc.). **2** engage (an employee). **3** be willing or ready to meet (an opponent etc.). **4** acquire (new meaning etc.). **5** *colloq.* show strong emotion. **take out 1** remove; extract. **2** escort on an outing or as a sexual partner. **3** get (a licence, summons, etc.) issued. **4** *US* = *take away* 3. **5** *slang* murder or destroy. **take a person out of himself** or **herself** make a person forget his or her worries. **take over 1** succeed to the management or ownership of. **2** take control. **take part** see PART. **take place** see PLACE. **take shape** assume a distinct form; develop. **take one's time** not hurry. **take to 1** begin or fall into the habit of (*took to smoking*). **2** have recourse to. **3** adapt oneself to. **4** form a liking for. **take up 1** become interested or engaged in (a pursuit). **2** adopt as a protégé. **3** occupy (time or space). **4** begin (residence etc.). **5** resume after an interruption. **6** (often foll. by *on*) interrupt or question

---

Tajikistan /ˌtædʒɪkɪˈstɑːn/, **Republic of** (also **Tadjikistan**) country in central Asia, bordered by Uzbekistan, Kirghizia, China, and Afghanistan. Agriculture is a major source of employment; cotton is the principal crop and cattle, sheep, goats, and pigs are reared. Deposits of oil, lead, zinc, uranium, and other minerals are exploited; base metals are a major export. Industries include mineral processing, the manufacture of textiles, carpets, and clothing, and food processing. The poorest of the former Soviet republics, Tajikistan declared its independence in 1991. The former Communist leader, Rakhmon Nabiyev, was elected president, but opposition from Islamic militants and pro-democracy groups forced him to resign in 1992. Fighting has continued since 1992. A cease-fire agreement was signed in 1994, but failed to bring an end to the conflict. Fighting intensified in 1996. Acting president, Imamali Rakhmanov; capital, Dushanbe.

languages	Tajik (official), Russian
currency	Tajik rouble of 100 tanga
pop. (1996)	5 945 000
GNP (1994)	US$2.07B
literacy	98% (m); 96% (f)
life expectancy	65 (m); 71 (f)

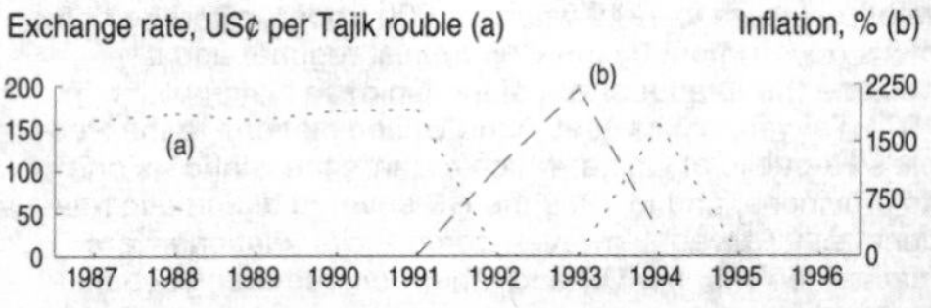

(a speaker) (on a point). **7** accept (an offer etc.). **8** shorten (a garment). **9** lift up. **10** absorb. **11** pursue (a matter etc.) further, esp. with those in authority. **take a person up on** accept (a person's offer etc.). **take up with** begin to associate with. [Old English from Old Norse]

take-away *–attrib. adj.* (of food) bought cooked for eating elsewhere. *–n.* **1** this food. **2** establishment selling this.

take-home pay *n.* employee's pay after the deduction of tax etc.

take-off *n.* **1** act of becoming airborne. **2** act of mimicking.

take-over *n.* assumption of control (esp. of a business); buying-out.

♦ **take-over bid** *n.* (also **offer to purchase**) offer made to the shareholders of a company by an individual or organization to buy their shares at a specified price in order to gain control of that company. In a welcome take-over bid the directors of the company will advise shareholders to accept the terms of the bid (see MERGER). If the bid is unwelcome, or the terms are unacceptable, the board will advise against acceptance. In the ensuing **take-over battle**, the bidder may improve the terms offered and will then usu. write to shareholders outlining the advantages that will follow from the successful take-over. In the meantime bids from other sources may be made (see GREY KNIGHT; WHITE KNIGHT) or the original bidder may withdraw as a result of measures taken by the board of the target company (see POISON PILL; PORCUPINE PROVISIONS). In an **unconditional bid**, the bidder will pay the offered price irrespective of the number of shares acquired, while the bidder of a **conditional bid** will only pay the price offered if sufficient shares are received to provide a controlling interest. Take-overs in the UK are subject to the rules and disciplines of the City Code on Take-overs and Mergers.

♦ **Take-over Panel** see CITY CODE ON TAKE-OVERS AND MERGERS.

---

taker *n.* person who takes a bet, accepts an offer, buys a traded option, etc.

take-up *n.* acceptance of a thing offered.

taking *–adj.* attractive, captivating. *–n.* (in *pl.*) amount of money taken at a show, in a shop, etc.

Takoradi /ˌtɑːkəˈrɑːdɪ/ major seaport in W Ghana, on the Gulf of Guinea; it is linked with the nearby port of Sekondi to form the joint urban area of Sekondi-Takoradi, which exports bauxite and has food-processing industries; pop. (est. 1988) 103 600.

tala /ˈtɑːlə/ *n.* standard monetary unit of Samoa. [Samoan, = eastern DOLLAR]

talc *n.* **1** talcum powder. **2** magnesium silicate formed as soft flat plates, used as a lubricator etc. [Arabic from Persian *talk*]

talcum /ˈtælkəm/ *n.* **1** = TALC 2. **2** (in full **talcum powder**) powdered talc applied to the skin, usu. perfumed. [medieval Latin: see TALC]

tale *n.* **1** (usu. fictitious) narrative or story. **2** allegation, often malicious or in breach of confidence. [Old English]

talent /ˈtælənt/ *n.* **1** special aptitude or faculty (*talent for music*). **2** high mental ability. **3 a** person or persons of talent. **b** *colloq.* attractive members of the opposite sex (*plenty of local talent*). **4** ancient esp. Greek weight and unit of currency. □ **talented** *adj.* [Greek *talanton*]

talent-scout *n.* (also **talent-spotter**) person seeking new talent, esp. in sport or entertainment.

♦ **TALISMAN** /ˈtælɪzmən/ *abbr.* Transfer Accounting Lodgement for Investors and Stock Management. The former London Stock Exchange computerized transfer system, which was replaced by CREST in 1996.

---

talisman /ˈtælɪzmən/ *n.* (*pl.* **-s**) ring, stone, etc. thought to have magic powers, esp. to bring good luck. □ **talismanic** /-ˈmænɪk/ *adj.* [French and Spanish from Greek]

talk /tɔːk/ *–v.* **1** (often foll. by *to, with*) converse or communicate verbally. **2** have the power of speech. **3** (often foll. by *about*) **a** discuss; express; utter (*talked cricket; talking nonsense*). **b** (in *imper.*) *colloq.* as an emphatic statement (*talk about expense!*). **4** use (a language) in speech (*talking Spanish*). **5** (foll. by *at*) address pompously. **6** (usu. foll. by *into, out of*) bring into a specified condition etc. by talking (*talked himself hoarse; did you talk them into it?*). **7** betray secrets. **8** gossip (*people will talk*). **9** have influence (*money talks*). *–n.* **1** conversation, talking. **2** particular mode of speech (*baby-talk*). **3** informal address or lecture. **4 a** rumour or gossip (*talk of a merger*). **b** its theme (*the talk was all babies*). **5** empty promises; boasting. **6** (often in *pl.*) discussions or negotiations. □ **now you're talking** *colloq.* I like what you say, suggest, etc. **talk back** reply defiantly. **talk down to** speak condescendingly to. **talk a person** etc. **down 1** silence by loudness or persistence. **2** bring (a pilot or aircraft) to landing by radio. **talk of 1** discuss or mention. **2** (often foll. by verbal noun) express some intention of (*talked of moving to London*). **talk out** block (a bill in Parliament) by prolonging discussion to the time of adjournment. **talk over** discuss at length. **talk a person over** (or **round**) gain agreement by talking. **talk shop** talk about one's occupation etc. **talk to** rebuke, scold. □ **talker** *n.* [from TALE or TELL]

talkative /ˈtɔːkətɪv/ *adj.* fond of or given to talking.

talkback *n.* (often *attrib.*) system of two-way communication by loudspeaker.

talkie *n. colloq.* (esp. early) film with a soundtrack.

talking *–adj.* **1** that talks, or is able to talk (*talking parrot*). **2** expressive (*talking eyes*). *–n.* in senses of TALK *v.* □ **talking of** as we are discussing.

talking book *n.* recorded reading of a book, esp. for the blind.

talking-point *n.* topic for discussion.

talking-shop *n. derog.* arena or opportunity for empty talk.

talking-to *n. colloq.* reproof, reprimand.

tall /tɔːl/ *–adj.* **1** of more than average height. **2** of a specified height (*about six feet tall*). **3** higher than the surrounding objects (*tall building*). *–adv.* as if tall; proudly (*sit tall*). □ **tallish** *adj.* **tallness** *n.* [Old English, = swift]

tallboy *n.* tall chest of drawers.

Tallinn /ˈtælɪn/ capital of Estonia, a port on the Gulf of Finland with shipbuilding and other industries; pop. (est. 1995) 434 763.

tall order *n.* unreasonable demand.

tallow /ˈtæləʊ/ *n.* hard (esp. animal) fat melted down to make candles, soap, etc. □ **tallowy** *adj.* [Low German]

tall ship *n.* sailing-ship with a high mast.

tall story *n. colloq.* extravagant story that is difficult to believe.

tally /ˈtælɪ/ *–n.* (*pl.* **-ies**) **1** reckoning of a debt or score. **2** total score or amount. **3** mark registering the number of objects delivered or received. **4** *hist.* **a** piece of notched wood for keeping account. **b** account kept thus. **5** identification ticket or label. **6** corresponding thing, counterpart, or duplicate. *–v.* (**-ies, -ied**) (often foll. by *with*) agree or correspond. [Latin *talea* rod]

tally-ho /ˌtælɪˈhəʊ/ *–int.* huntsman's cry on sighting a fox. *–n.* (*pl.* **-s**) cry of this. *–v.* (**-hoes, -hoed**) **1** utter a cry of 'tally-ho'. **2** indicate (a fox) or urge (hounds) with this cry. [cf. French *taïaut*]

♦ **tallyman** /ˈtælɪmən/ *n.* (also **tally clerk**) worker at a port or airport who checks that the goods unloaded from a ship or aircraft tally with the documents covering them and the ship's or aircraft's manifest.

Talmud /ˈtælmʊd, -məd/ *n.* body of Jewish civil and ceremonial law and legend. □ **Talmudic** /-ˈmʊdɪk/ *adj.* **Talmudist** *n.* [Hebrew, = instruction]

talon /ˈtælən/ *n.* **1** claw, esp. of a bird of prey. **2** *Finance* printed form attached to a bearer security that enables the holder to apply for a new sheet of coupons when the existing coupons have been used up. [Latin *talus* ankle]

talus /'teɪləs/ *n.* (*pl.* **tali** /-laɪ/) ankle-bone supporting the tibia. [Latin, = ankle]

TAM /tæm/ *abbr.* Television Audience Measurement (*TAM rating*).

tamarind /'tæmərɪnd/ *n.* **1** tropical evergreen tree. **2** fruit pulp from this used as food and in drinks. [Arabic, = Indian date]

tamarisk /'tæmərɪsk/ *n.* seashore shrub usu. with small pink or white flowers. [Latin]

Tamaulipas /ˌtæmaʊ'liːpæs/ state in NE Mexico; pop. (est. 1995) 2 526 387; capital, Ciudad Victoria.

tambour /'tæmbʊə(r)/ *n.* **1** drum. **2** circular frame holding fabric taut for embroidering. [French: related to TABOR]

tambourine /ˌtæmbə'riːn/ *n.* small shallow drum with jingling discs in its rim, shaken or banged as an accompaniment. [French, diminutive of TAMBOUR]

tame *–adj.* **1** (of an animal) domesticated; not wild or shy. **2** insipid; dull (*tame entertainment*). **3** (of a person) amenable. *–v.* (**-ming**) **1** make tame; domesticate. **2** subdue, curb. □ **tameable** *adj.* **tamely** *adv.* **tameness** *n.* **tamer** *n.* (also in *comb.*). [Old English]

Tamil /'tæmɪl/ *–n.* **1** member of a people of S India and Sri Lanka. **2** language of this people. *–adj.* of this people or language. [native name]

Tamil Nadu /'tæmɪl næ'duː/ (formerly **Madras**) state in SE India; pop. (est. 1994) 58 840 000; capital, Madras. Agriculture produces rice, cotton, and coffee; manufactures include machinery, electrical goods, cotton textiles, and leather goods.

Tammerfors see TAMPERE.

tam-o'-shanter /ˌtæmə'ʃæntə(r)/ *n.* floppy round esp. woollen beret, of Scottish origin. [hero of a poem by Burns]

tamp *v.* ram down hard or tightly. [*tampion* stopper for gun-muzzle, from French *tampon*]

tamper *v.* (foll. by *with*) **1** meddle with or change illicitly. **2** exert a secret or corrupt influence upon; bribe. [var. of TEMPER]

Tampere /'tæmpəˌreɪ/ (Swedish **Tammerfors** /'tɑːməˌfɔːs/) second-largest city in Finland; its many industries, powered by an abundant supply of hydroelectricity, include railway engineering, textiles, pulp and paper, and the manufacture of footwear; pop. (est. 1996) 182 742.

Tampico /tæm'piːkəʊ/ major seaport in Mexico, on the Gulf of Mexico; oil-refining is important; pop. (1990) 272 690.

tampon /'tæmpɒn/ *n.* plug of soft material used esp. to absorb menstrual blood. [French: related to TAMP]

tam-tam /'tæmtæm/ *n.* large metal gong. [Hindi]

tan[1] *–n.* **1** = SUNTAN. **2** yellowish-brown colour. **3** bark, esp. of oak, used to tan hides. *–adj.* yellowish-brown. *–v.* (**-nn-**) **1** make or become brown by exposure to sunlight. **2** convert (raw hide) into leather. **3** *slang* beat, thrash. [medieval Latin *tanno*, perhaps from Celtic]

tan[2] *abbr.* tangent.

T & E *abbr.* **1** test and evaluation. **2** trial and error.

tandem /'tændəm/ *–n.* **1** bicycle with two or more seats one behind another. **2** group of two people etc. with one behind or following the other. **3** carriage driven tandem. *–adv.* with two or more horses harnessed one behind another (*drive tandem*). □ **in tandem 1** one behind another. **2** alongside each other; together. [Latin, = at length]

T & G *abbr. colloq.* Transport and General Workers' Union.

tandoor /'tændʊə(r)/ *n.* clay oven. [Hindustani]

tandoori /tæn'dʊərɪ/ *n.* food spiced and cooked over charcoal in a tandoor (often *attrib.*: *tandoori chicken*). [Hindustani]

t. & p. *abbr. Insurance* theft and pilferage.

tang *n.* **1** strong taste or smell. **2** characteristic quality. **3** projection on the blade of esp. a knife, by which it is held firm in the handle. [Old Norse *tange* point]

Tanga /'tæŋgə/ second-largest seaport in Tanzania; pop. (1988) 187 155.

Tanganyika /ˌtæŋgə'njiːkə/ see TANZANIA.

tangent /'tændʒ(ə)nt/ *n.* **1** (often *attrib.*) straight line, curve, or surface that meets a curve at a point, but does not intersect it. **2** ratio of two sides (other than the hypotenuse) opposite and adjacent to an acute angle in a right-angled triangle. □ **at a tangent** diverging from a previous course or from what is relevant or central (*go off at a tangent*). [Latin *tango tact-* touch]

tangential /tæn'dʒenʃ(ə)l/ *adj.* **1** of or along a tangent. **2** divergent. **3** peripheral. □ **tangentially** *adv.*

tangerine /ˌtændʒə'riːn/ *n.* **1** small sweet thin-skinned citrus fruit like an orange; mandarin. **2** deep orange-yellow colour. [TANGIER]

tangible /'tændʒɪb(ə)l/ *adj.* **1** perceptible by touch. **2** definite; clearly intelligible; not elusive (*tangible proof*). □ **tangibility** /-'bɪlɪtɪ/ *n.* **tangibleness** *n.* **tangibly** *adv.* [Latin: related to TANGENT]

♦ **tangible assets** *n.pl.* fixed assets of an organization, as opposed to such assets as goodwill, patents, and trade marks. They usu. include leases and company shares, as well as assets that can be touched, i.e. physical objects.

Tangier /tæn'dʒɪə(r)/ seaport in Morocco, situated nearly opposite Gibraltar and commanding the W entrance to the Mediterranean; industries include fishing, market gardening, textile manufacturing, and tourism; pop. (est. 1993) 307 000.

tangle /'tæŋg(ə)l/ *–v.* (**-ling**) **1** intertwine (threads or hairs etc.) or become entwined in a confused mass; entangle. **2** (foll. by *with*) *colloq.* become involved (esp. in conflict) with (*don't tangle with me*). **3** complicate (*tangled affair*). *–n.* **1** confused mass of intertwined threads etc. **2** confused state. [origin uncertain]

tangly *adj.* (**-ier, -iest**) tangled.

tango /'tæŋgəʊ/ *–n.* (*pl.* **-s**) **1** slow South American ballroom dance. **2** music for this. *–v.* (**-goes, -goed**) dance the tango. [American Spanish]

tangy *adj.* (**-ier, -iest**) having a strong usu. acid tang.

tanh /θæn, tænʃ, tæn'eɪtʃ/ *abbr.* hyperbolic tangent.

Tanjungkarang /ˌtændʒʊŋkə'ræŋ/ city in Indonesia, capital of the province of Lampung at the S tip of the island of Sumatra; pop. (1980) 284 275.

tank *–n.* **1** large container, usu. for liquid or gas. **2** heavy armoured fighting vehicle moving on continuous tracks. *–v.* (usu. foll. by *up*) fill the tank of (a vehicle etc.) with fuel. □ **tankful** *n.* (*pl.* **-s**). [originally Indian, = pond, from Gujarati]

tankard /'tæŋkəd/ *n.* **1** tall beer mug with a handle. **2** contents of or amount held by this (*drank a tankard of ale*). [probably Dutch *tankaert*]

tanked up *predic. adj. colloq.* drunk.

tank engine *n.* steam engine with integral fuel and water containers.

tanker *n.* ship, aircraft, or road vehicle for carrying liquids, esp. oil, in bulk.

tanner *n.* person who tans hides.

tannery *n.* (*pl.* **-ies**) place where hides are tanned.

tannic /'tænɪk/ *adj.* of tan (sense 3). [French *tannique*: related to TANNIN]

tannic acid *n.* natural yellowish organic compound used as a mordant and astringent.

tannin /'tænɪn/ *n.* any of various organic compounds found in tree-barks and oak-galls, used in leather production. [French *tanin*: related to TAN[1]]

Tannoy /'tænɔɪ/ *n. propr.* type of public-address system. [origin uncertain]

tansy /'tænzɪ/ *n.* (*pl.* **-ies**) plant with yellow flowers and aromatic leaves. [Greek *athanasia* immortality]

tantalize /'tæntəˌlaɪz/ *v.* (also **-ise**) (**-zing** or **-sing**) **1** torment or tease by the sight or promise of the unobtainable. **2** raise and then dash the hopes of. □ **tantalization** /-'zeɪʃ(ə)n/ *n.* [*Tantalus*, mythical king punished in Hades with sight of water and fruit which drew back when he tried to reach them]

tantalum /ˈtæntələm/ *n.* rare hard white metallic element. □ **tantalic** *adj.* [related to TANTALIZE]

tantalus /ˈtæntələs/ *n.* stand in which spirit-decanters may be locked up but visible. [see TANTALIZE]

tantamount /ˈtæntəˌmaʊnt/ *predic. adj.* (foll. by *to*) equivalent to. [Italian *tanto montare* amount to so much]

tantra /ˈtæntrə/ *n.* any of a class of Hindu or Buddhist mystical or magical writings. [Sanskrit, = doctrine]

tantrum /ˈtæntrəm/ *n.* (esp. child's) outburst of bad temper or petulance. [origin unknown]

Taoiseach /ˈtiːʃəx/ *n.* prime minister of the Irish Republic. [Irish, = chief, leader]

Taoism /ˈtaʊɪz(ə)m, ˈtɑːəʊ-/ *n.* Chinese philosophy advocating humility and religious piety. □ **Taoist** *n.* [Chinese *dao* right way]

Taormina /ˌtɑːɔːˈmiːnə/ town and resort on the E coast of Sicily; pop. (1990) 10 905.

TAP *abbr.* Transportes Aéreos Portugueses (Portuguese Airlines).

tap[1] *–n.* **1** device by which a flow of liquid or gas from a pipe or vessel can be controlled. **2** tapping of a telephone etc. **3** taproom. *–v.* **(-pp-) 1** provide (a cask) or let out (liquid) with a tap. **2** draw sap from (a tree) by cutting into it. **3** obtain information or supplies from. **4** extract or obtain; discover and exploit (*mineral wealth waiting to be tapped*; *tap skills of young people*). **5** connect a listening device to (a telephone etc.). □ **on tap 1** ready to be drawn off by tap. **2** *colloq.* freely available. [Old English]

tap[2] *–v.* **(-pp-) 1** (foll. by *at*, *on*) strike a gentle but audible blow. **2** (often foll. by *against*, *on*, etc.) strike or cause (a thing) to strike lightly (*tapped me on the shoulder*). **3** (often foll. by *out*) make by a tap or taps (*tapped out the rhythm*). **4** tap-dance. *–n.* **1 a** light blow; rap. **b** sound of this. **2 a** tap-dancing. **b** metal attachment on a tap-dancer's shoe. [imitative]

tapas /ˈtæpæs/ *n.pl.* (often *attrib.*) small savoury esp. Spanish dishes. [Spanish]

tap-dance *–n.* rhythmic dance performed with shoes with metal taps. *–v.* perform a tap-dance. □ **tap-dancer** *n.* **tap-dancing** *n.*

tape *–n.* **1** narrow strip of woven material for tying up, fastening, etc. **2** this across the finishing line of a race. **3** (in full **adhesive tape**) strip of adhesive plastic etc. for fastening, masking, insulating, etc. **4 a** = MAGNETIC TAPE. **b** tape recording, reel, or cassette. **5** = TAPE-MEASURE. *–v.* **(-ping) 1 a** fasten or join etc. with tape. **b** apply tape to. **2** (foll. by *off*) seal or mark off with tape. **3** record on magnetic tape. **4** measure with tape. □ **have** (or **get**) **a person** or **thing taped** *colloq.* understand (him, it, etc.) fully. [Old English]

tape deck *n.* **1** machine for using audiotape (separate from the amplifier, speakers, etc.). **2** = TAPE UNIT.

tape drive *n.* = TAPE UNIT.

tape machine *n.* **1** machine for recording telegraph messages. **2** = TAPE RECORDER.

tape-measure *n.* strip of marked tape or flexible metal for measuring.

taper *–n.* **1** wick coated with wax etc. for conveying a flame. **2** slender candle. *–v.* (often foll. by *off*) **1** diminish or reduce in thickness towards one end. **2** make or become gradually less. [Old English]

tape recorder *n.* apparatus for recording and replaying sounds on magnetic tape. □ **tape-record** *v.* **tape recording** *n.*

tape streamer *n.* *Computing* tape unit specifically designed for the rapid backup of magnetic disks using tape cartridges.

tapestry /ˈtæpɪstrɪ/ *n.* (*pl.* **-ies**) **1 a** thick fabric in which coloured weft threads are woven to form pictures or designs. **b** (usu. wool) embroidery imitating this. **c** piece of this. **2** events or circumstances etc. seen as interwoven etc. (*life's rich tapestry*). □ **tapestried** *adj.* [*tapissery* from French *tapis* carpet]

tape unit *n.* (also **tape drive, tape deck**) *Computing* peripheral device containing a mechanism for moving magnetic tape and controlling its movement (see MAGNETIC TAPE), together with recording and sensing heads that cause data to be written to and read from the tape. Magnetic tape is held on reels or in cartridges or cassettes. The reel, cassette, or cartridge is mounted in the tape unit, and the tape is driven past the heads.

tapeworm *n.* parasitic intestinal flatworm with a segmented body.

tapioca /ˌtæpɪˈəʊkə/ *n.* starchy substance in hard white grains, obtained from cassava and used for puddings etc. [Tupi-Guarani]

tapir /ˈteɪpə(r), -pɪə(r)/ *n.* nocturnal Central and South American or Malaysian hoofed mammal with a short flexible snout. [Tupi]

♦ **tap issue** *n.* issue of UK government securities or bills to selected market makers, usu. to influence the price of gilts. The government can control their volume and price.

tappet /ˈtæpɪt/ *n.* lever or projecting part in machinery giving intermittent motion. [from TAP[2]]

taproom *n.* room in a pub serving drinks on tap.

tap root *n.* tapering root growing vertically downwards.

♦ **tap stock** *n.* gilt-edged security from an issue that has not been fully subscribed and is released onto the market slowly when its market price reaches predetermined levels. **Short taps** are short-dated stocks and **long taps** are long-dated taps.

tar[1] *–n.* **1** dark thick inflammable liquid distilled from wood or coal etc., used as a preservative of wood and

Tanzania /ˌtænzəˈniːə/, **United Republic of** country in E Africa with a coastline on the Indian Ocean, consisting of a mainland area (the former republic of Tanganyika) and the island of Zanzibar. The country is largely dependent on agriculture, exporting coffee, tea, cotton, sisal, tobacco, cashew nuts, and cloves. Subsistence farming is also important: food crops include rice, maize, bananas, and cassava. Diamonds are mined and exported; there are also deposits of gold, tin, iron, salt, coal, sapphires, and rubies. Tourism is a major source of revenue. There is a small amount of manufacturing industry, producing footwear, foodstuffs, cement, textiles, and cigarettes.

History. A German colony from the late 19th century, Tanganyika became a British mandate after the First World War and a trust territory, administered by Britain, after the Second. It achieved independence as a member state of the Commonwealth in 1961 and joined Zanzibar to form the United Republic of Tanzania in 1964. The ruling parties of the two countries merged in 1977 to form the Revolutionary Party. An amendment to the constitution, legalizing multi-party politics, was endorsed by the president in 1992. President, Benjamin Mkapa; prime minister, Frederick Sumaye; capital, Dodoma. □ **Tanzanian** *adj.* & *n.*

languages	Swahili, English
currency	shilling (TSh) of 100 cents
pop. (1996)	29 058 000
GNP (1993)	US$2.5B
literacy	79% (m); 56% (f)
life expectancy	41 (m); 45 (f)

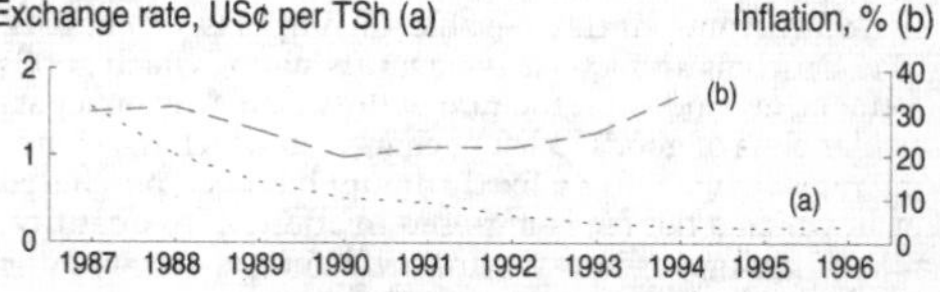

iron, in making roads, as an antiseptic, etc. **2** similar substance formed in the combustion of tobacco etc. –*v.* (**-rr-**) cover with tar. □ **tar and feather** smear with tar and then cover with feathers as a punishment. **tarred with the same brush** having the same faults. [Old English]

tar[2] *n. colloq.* sailor. [from TARPAULIN]

taramasalata /ˌtærəməsə'lɑːtə/ *n.* (also **taramosalata**) pâté made from roe with olive oil, seasoning, etc. [Greek *taramas* roe, *salata* SALAD]

Taranaki /ˌtærə'nækɪ/ administrative region in New Zealand, on North Island; pop. (1996) 105 317; chief town, New Plymouth. Dairy farming is important.

tarantella /ˌtærən'telə/ *n.* **1** whirling S Italian dance. **2** music for this. [Italian from TARANTO]

Taranto /tə'ræntəʊ/ seaport and naval base in SE Italy, in Apulia; products include iron and steel; pop. (est. 1994) 213 933.

tarantula /tə'ræntjʊlə/ *n.* **1** large hairy tropical spider. **2** large black S European spider. [medieval Latin: related to TARANTELLA]

Tarawa /'tærəwə, tə'rɑːwə/ capital of Kiribati, on the Pacific atoll of Tarawa; pop. (1990) 29 028.

tarboosh /tɑː'buːʃ/ *n.* cap like a fez. [Arabic from Persian]

tardy /'tɑːdɪ/ *adj.* (**-ier, -iest**) **1** slow to act, come, or happen. **2** delaying or delayed. □ **tardily** *adv.* **tardiness** *n.* [Latin *tardus* slow]

tare[1] *n.* **1** vetch, esp. as a cornfield weed or fodder. **2** (in *pl.*) *Bibl.* an injurious cornfield weed (Matt. 13:24-30). [origin unknown]

tare[2] *n.* **1** allowance made for the weight of packing or wrapping around goods. **2** weight of a vehicle without fuel or load. See also GROSS WEIGHT. [Arabic *tarha*]

target /'tɑːgɪt/ –*n.* **1** mark fired or aimed at, esp. a round object marked with concentric circles. **2** person or thing aimed or fired at etc. (*an easy target*). **3** objective or result aimed at. The targets of an economic policy pursued by a government usu. include full employment, stable prices, and a high rate of growth of gross domestic product. Debate in macroeconomics centres on the targets it is feasible for a government to pursue, the instruments that are suitable to implement them, and the indicators that are appropriate to assess the success or failure of the policy. For example, a new classical macroeconomist might argue that the money supply is the correct instrument for achieving stable prices and the growth of a particular monetary aggregate is the proper indicator. **4** butt for criticism, abuse, etc. –*v.* (**-t-**) **1** identify or single out as a target. **2** aim or direct (*missiles targeted on major cities*). [French *targe* shield]

♦ **target company** *n.* company that is subject to a take-over bid.

♦ **Target Group Index** *n.* (also **TGI**) annual report compiled from the returned questionnaires of a random sample of 24 000 respondents on their use of hundreds of products and thousands of brands. The questionnaires are completed with no interviewer present. The TGI is an example of syndicated research.

♦ **target marketing** *n.* selection of one or more segments of a market at which companies direct their marketing thrust. Since it has become almost impossible to market products that will satisfy everyone, target marketing enables companies to aim the products at specific groups of consumers.

♦ **target price** see COMMON AGRICULTURAL POLICY.

---

tariff /'tærɪf/ *n.* **1** table of fixed charges (*hotel tariff*). **2 a** list of customs duties payable on imports or exports. The Customs and Excise issue tariffs stating which goods attract duty and what the rate of duty is. **b** duty on a particular class of goods. **3** list of charges in which the charging rate changes after a fixed amount has been purchased or in which a flat fee is imposed in addition to quantity-related charge, as in two-part tariffs for gas or telephone services. [Arabic, = notification]

♦ **tariff office** *n.* insurance company that bases its premiums on a tariff arranged with other insurance companies. A **non-tariff office** is free to quote its own premiums.

---

tarlatan /'tɑːlət(ə)n/ *n.* thin stiff open-weave muslin. [French; probably originally Indian]

Tarmac /'tɑːmæk/ –*n. propr.* **1** = TARMACADAM. **2** runway etc. made of this. –*v.* (**tarmac**) (**-ck-**) apply tarmacadam to. [abbreviation]

tarmacadam /ˌtɑːmə'kædəm/ *n.* stone or slag bound with bitumen, used in paving roads etc. [from TAR[1], MACADAM]

tarn *n.* small mountain lake. [Old Norse]

tarnish /'tɑːnɪʃ/ –*v.* **1** (cause to) lose lustre. **2** impair (one's reputation etc.). –*n.* **1** loss of lustre, esp. as a film on a metal's surface. **2** blemish, stain. [French *ternir* from *terne* dark]

taro /'tɑːrəʊ/ *n.* (*pl.* **-s**) tropical plant with tuberous roots used as food. [Polynesian]

tarot /'tærəʊ/ *n.* (often *attrib.*) **1** (in *sing.* or *pl.*) **a** pack of mainly picture cards used in fortune-telling. **b** any game played with a similar pack of 78 cards. **2** any card from a tarot pack. [French]

tarpaulin /tɑː'pɔːlɪn/ *n.* **1** heavy-duty cloth waterproofed esp. with tar. **2** sheet or covering of this. [from TAR[1], PALL[1]]

tarragon /'tærəgən/ *n.* bushy herb used in salads, stuffings, vinegar, etc. [medieval Latin from Greek]

tarry[1] /'tɑːrɪ/ *adj.* (**-ier, -iest**) of, like, or smeared with tar.

tarry[2] /'tærɪ/ *v.* (**-ies, -ied**) *archaic* linger, stay, wait. [origin unknown]

tarsal /'tɑːs(ə)l/ –*adj.* of the ankle-bones. –*n.* tarsal bone. [from TARSUS]

tarsus /'tɑːsəs/ *n.* (*pl.* **tarsi** /-saɪ/) **1** bones of the ankle and upper foot. **2** shank of a bird's leg. [Greek]

tart[1] *n.* **1** open pastry case containing jam etc. **2** pie with a fruit or other sweet filling. □ **tartlet** *n.* [French *tarte*]

tart[2] –*n. slang* **1** prostitute; promiscuous woman. **2** *slang offens.* girl or woman. –*v.* (foll. by *up*) *colloq.* (usu. *refl.*) smarten or dress up, esp. gaudily. [probably abbreviation of SWEETHEART]

tart[3] *adj.* **1** sharp or acid in taste. **2** (of a remark etc.) cutting, bitter. □ **tartly** *adv.* **tartness** *n.* [Old English]

tartan /'tɑːt(ə)n/ *n.* **1** pattern of coloured stripes crossing at right angles, esp. denoting a Scottish Highland clan. **2** woollen cloth woven in this pattern (often *attrib.*: *tartan scarf*). [origin uncertain]

Tartar /'tɑːtə(r)/ –*n.* **1 a** member of a group of central Asian peoples including Mongols and Turks. **b** Turkic language of these peoples. **2** (**tartar**) harsh or formidable person. –*adj.* **1** of Tartars. **2** of central Asia east of the Caspian Sea. [French or medieval Latin]

tartar /'tɑːtə(r)/ *n.* **1** hard deposit that forms on the teeth. **2** deposit that forms a hard crust in wine. [medieval Latin from Greek]

tartare /tɑː'tɑː(r)/ *adj.* (in full **sauce tartare**) = TARTAR SAUCE. [French]

tartaric /tɑː'tærɪk/ *adj.* of or from tartar.

tartaric acid *n.* natural acid found esp. in unripe grapes, used in baking powders etc.

tartar sauce *n.* sauce of mayonnaise and chopped gherkins, capers, etc. [from TARTAR]

tartrazine /'tɑːtrəˌziːn/ *n.* brilliant yellow dye from tartaric acid, used to colour food etc.

tarty *adj. colloq.* (**-ier, -iest**) (esp. of a woman) vulgar, gaudy; promiscuous. [from TART[2]]

Tarzan /'tɑːz(ə)n/ *n. colloq.* agile muscular man. [name of a character in stories by E. R. Burroughs]

Tas. *abbr.* Tasmania.

Tashkent /tæʃ'kent/ capital of Uzbekistan, a centre of industry and communications; manufactures include textiles, processed food, tobacco, and chemicals; pop. (est. 1994) 2 106 000.

task /tɑːsk/ *–n.* piece of work to be done. *–v.* make great demands on (a person's powers etc.). □ **take to task** rebuke, scold. [medieval Latin *tasca,* probably = *taxa* TAX]

task force *n.* (also **task group**) armed force or other group organized for a specific operation or task.

taskmaster *n.* (*fem.* **taskmistress**) person who makes others work hard.

Tasmania /tæz'meɪnɪə/ (formerly **Van Diemen's Land**) state of Australia, consisting of one large and several smaller islands SE of the mainland; pop. (est. 1996) 473 200; capital, Hobart. Agricultural activities include dairy and sheep farming, and apples and hops are grown. Forestry is also important, producing wood chips for export, and there are deposits of iron ore, tin, lead, zinc, copper, and tungsten. □ **Tasmanian** *adj.* & *n.*

Tasman Sea the part of the S Pacific that lies between Australia and New Zealand.

Tass *n.* Russian (formerly Soviet) news agency. [abbreviation of Russian *Telegrafnoye Agentsvo Sovetskovo Soyuza*]

tassel /'tæs(ə)l/ *n.* **1** tuft of loosely hanging threads or cords etc. as decoration. **2** tassel-like flower-head of some plants, esp. maize. □ **tasselled** *adj.* (*US* **taseled**). [French *tas(s)el* clasp]

taste /teɪst/ *–n.* **1 a** sensation caused in the mouth by contact with a soluble substance. **b** faculty of perceiving this (*bitter to the taste*). **2** small sample of food or drink. **3** slight experience (*taste of success*). **4** (often foll. by *for*) liking or predilection (*expensive tastes*). **5** aesthetic discernment in art, clothes, conduct, etc. (*in poor taste*). *–v.* (**-ting**) **1** sample the flavour of (food etc.) by taking it into the mouth. **2** (also *absol.*) perceive the flavour of (*cannot taste with a cold*). **3** (esp. with *neg.*) eat or drink a small portion of (*had not tasted food for days*). **4** experience (*never tasted failure*). **5** (often foll. by *of*) have a specified flavour (*tastes of onions*). □ **to one's taste** pleasing, suitable. [French from Romanic]

taste bud *n.* cell or nerve-ending on the surface of the tongue by which things are tasted.

tasteful *adj.* having, or done in, good taste. □ **tastefully** *adv.* **tastefulness** *n.*

tasteless *adj.* **1** lacking flavour. **2** having, or done in, bad taste. □ **tastelessly** *adv.* **tastelessness** *n.*

taster *n.* **1** person employed to test food or drink by tasting. **2** small sample.

tasting *n.* gathering at which food or drink is tasted and evaluated.

tasty *adj.* (**-ier, -iest**) **1** pleasing in flavour; appetizing. **2** *colloq.* attractive. □ **tastily** *adv.* **tastiness** *n.*

tat[1] *n. colloq.* tatty things; rubbish, junk. [back-formation from TATTY]

tat[2] *v.* (**-tt-**) do, or make by, tatting. [origin unknown]

tat[3] see TIT[2].

ta-ta /tæ'tɑː/ *int. colloq.* goodbye. [origin unknown]

♦ **tatonnement** /tæ'tɒnəmɑ̃/ *n. Econ.* process by which prices reach equilibrium, esp. in Walras' general equilibrium model. The process may be thought of as an auction, in which buyers and sellers bid until equilibrium is reached at a unique price. In a free market, tatonnement will ensure that an economy will reach a perfectly competitive Pareto-optimal equilibrium. [French *tâtonnement* groping]

---

tatter *n.* (usu. in *pl.*) rag; irregularly torn cloth or paper etc. □ **in tatters** *colloq.* **1** torn in many places. **2** destroyed, ruined. [Old Norse]

tattered *adj.* in tatters.

tatting /'tætɪŋ/ *n.* **1** a kind of handmade knotted lace used for trimming etc. **2** process of making this. [origin unknown]

tattle /'tæt(ə)l/ *–v.* (**-ling**) prattle, chatter, gossip. *–n.* gossip; idle talk. [Flemish *tatelen,* imitative]

tattoo[1] /tə'tuː, tæ-/ *n.* **1** evening drum or bugle signal recalling soldiers to quarters. **2** elaboration of this with music and marching as an entertainment. **3** rhythmic tapping or drumming. [earlier *tap-too* from Dutch *taptoe,* literally 'close the tap' (of the cask)]

tattoo[2] /tə'tuː, tæ-/ *–v.* (**-oos, -ooed**) **1** mark (skin) indelibly by puncturing it and inserting pigment. **2** make (a design) in this way. *–n.* such a design. □ **tattooer** *n.* **tattooist** *n.* [Polynesian]

tatty /'tætɪ/ *adj.* (**-ier, -iest**) *colloq.* **1** tattered; shabby. **2** inferior. **3** tawdry. □ **tattily** *adv.* **tattiness** *n.* [originally Scots, = shaggy, apparently related to TATTER]

tau /taʊ, tɔː/ *n.* nineteenth letter of the Greek alphabet (Τ, τ). [Greek]

taught *past* and *past part.* of TEACH.

taunt /tɔːnt/ *–n.* insult; provocation. *–v.* insult; provoke contemptuously. [French *tant pour tant* tit for tat, smart rejoinder]

taupe /təʊp/ *adj.* & *n.* grey tinged with esp. brown. [French, = MOLE[1]]

Taupo /'taʊpəʊ/ town in New Zealand, capital of Tongariro region, North Island; pop. (1986) 15 900.

Tauranga /taʊ'ræŋə/ seaport in New Zealand, on North Island; exports include dairy produce, meat, and fruit; pop. (1994) 76 100.

Taurus /'tɔːrəs/ *n.* (*pl.* **-es**) **1** constellation and second sign of the zodiac (the Bull). **2** person born when the sun is in this sign. □ **Taurean** *adj.* & *n.* [Latin, = bull]

taut /tɔːt/ *adj.* **1** (of a rope etc.) tight; not slack. **2** (of nerves etc.) tense. **3** (of a ship etc.) in good condition. □ **tauten** *v.* **tautly** *adv.* **tautness** *n.* [perhaps = TOUGH]

tautology /tɔː'tɒlədʒɪ/ *n.* (*pl.* **-ies**) repetition using different words, esp. as a fault of style (e.g. *arrived one after the other in succession*). □ **tautological** /-tə'lɒdʒɪk(ə)l/ *adj.* **tautologous** /-ləgəs/ *adj.* [Greek *tauto* the same]

tavern /'tæv(ə)n/ *n. archaic* or *literary* inn, pub. [Latin *taberna*]

taverna /tə'vɜːnə/ *n.* Greek restaurant. [modern Greek: related to TAVERN]

tawdry /'tɔːdrɪ/ *adj.* (**-ier, -iest**) showy but worthless; gaudy. □ **tawdrily** *adv.* **tawdriness** *n.* [*tawdry lace* from *St Audrey's lace*]

tawny /'tɔːnɪ/ *adj.* (**-ier, -iest**) orange-brown or yellow-brown. [Anglo-French *tauné*: related to TAN[1]]

tawny owl *n.* reddish-brown European owl.

tax *–n.* **1** money compulsorily levied by the state or local authorities on individuals, property, or businesses. See also TAXATION. **2** (usu. foll. by *on, upon*) strain, heavy demand, or burdensome obligation. *–v.* **1** impose a tax on. **2** deduct tax from (income etc.). **3** make heavy demands on (*taxes my patience*). **4** (often foll. by *with*) confront (a person) with a fault etc; call to account. □ **taxable** *adj.* [Latin *taxo* censure, compute]

taxa *pl.* of TAXON.

♦ **taxable income** *n.* income liable to taxation. It is calculated by deducting income-tax allowances and any other tax-deductible expenses from the taxpayer's gross income.

♦ **tax and price index** *n.* (also **TPI**) measure of the increase in taxable income needed to compensate taxpayers for any increase in retail prices. As an index of the rate of inflation, it is similar to the retail price index, but in addition to measuring price changes it includes changes in average tax liability; for example, a cut in income tax will cause the TPI to rise by less than the RPI.

♦ **taxation** /tæk'seɪʃ(ə)n/ *n.* **1** imposition of tax on individuals or corporate bodies by central or local government in order to finance the expenditure of that government and also as a means of implementing its fiscal policy. Payments for specific services rendered to or for the payer are not regarded as taxation. In the UK, an individual's income is taxed by means of an income tax, while corporations pay a corporation tax. Capital profits are taxed by means of capital-gains tax, while gifts made during an individual's lifetime or on death are taxed by means of an inheritance tax. See also COUNCIL TAX; DIRECT TAXATION; INCOME TAX; INDIRECT TAXATION; PAYE; VAT. **2** payment of tax. [Latin: related to TAX]

◆ **taxation brackets** *n.pl.* figures between which taxable income or wealth is taxed at a specified rate. For example, taxable incomes between £2001 and £23,700 attract tax at 25%, while income in excess of £23,700 is taxed at 40%. See also BRACKET INDEXATION.

◆ **tax avoidance** *n.* minimizing tax liabilities legally and by means of full disclosure to the tax authorities. Cf. TAX EVASION.

◆ **tax base** *n.* specified domain on which a tax is levied, e.g. an individual's income for income tax, the estate of a deceased person for inheritance tax, the profits of a company for corporation tax.

◆ **tax burden** *n.* amount of tax suffered by an individual or organization. This may not be the same as the tax actually paid because of the possibility of shifting tax or the normal incidence of taxation. As an example of the latter case, inheritance tax is paid by the personal representatives of the deceased but the tax burden falls on the heirs, since their inheritance is reduced.

◆ **tax clearance** *n.* assurance, obtained from the UK Inland Revenue, that a proposed transaction (e.g. the reorganization of a company's share capital) will, if executed, not attract tax.

◆ **tax credit** *n.* amount deductible from an amount of tax payable, usu. because tax has already been paid on an element of the tax base. The most common tax credit in the UK is for income tax that has already been deducted at source.

◆ **tax credit system** *n.* taxation system in which individuals are given tax allowances dependent on their needs; if tax on their income is less than the total of their tax credits, they can be paid the excess credits. See also NEGATIVE INCOME TAX.

tax-deductible *adj.* (of a payment, allowance, benefit, etc.) legally deductible from income before tax assessment. See also TAXABLE INCOME.

◆ **tax deposit certificate** *n.* certificate issued by the UK Inland Revenue to a company that has deposited a sum of money with the collector of taxes, usu. as an advance against future corporation tax or against corporation tax that has not been finally agreed. The deposit earns interest until it is used to settle a tax liability.

tax disc *n.* road tax receipt displayed on the windscreen of a vehicle.

tax evasion *n.* illegal non-payment or underpayment of tax, usu. by not disclosing that one is liable to tax or by giving false information to the authorities. Cf. TAX AVOIDANCE.

◆ **tax exempt special savings account** *n.* (also **TESSA**, **Tessa**) UK account with a bank or building society, the interest or bonus on which is exempt from UK income tax provided special conditions are met. The tax exemption is lost if: (1) the deposits to the account exceed £3000 in the first year, more than £1800 in any subsequent year, or a maximum of £9000 in total; (2) the account holders' rights are assigned or used as security for a loan; (3) withdrawals exceed 75% of the interest or bonuses credited to the account prior to the withdrawal. In 1997 it was announced that TESSAs will be replaced by ISAS in April 1999.

◆ **tax exile** *n.* person with a high income or considerable wealth who chooses to live in a tax haven in order to avoid the high taxation of his or her native country. For such people the cost of living in their own country may be extremely high.

tax-free *adj.* exempt from tax.

◆ **tax haven** *n.* country or independent area that has a low rate of tax and therefore offers advantages to retired wealthy individuals or to companies that can arrange their affairs so that their tax liability falls at least partly in the tax haven. In the case of individuals, the cost of the tax saving is usu. residence in the tax haven for a majority of the year (see TAX EXILE). For multinational companies, an office in the tax haven, with some real or contrived business passing through it, is required. Monaco, Liechtenstein, the Bahamas, and the Cayman Islands are examples of tax havens.

◆ **tax holiday** *n.* period during which a company, in certain countries, is excused from paying corporation tax or profits tax (or pays them on only part of its profits) as an export incentive or an incentive to start up a new industry.

taxi /ˈtæksɪ/ *–n.* (*pl.* **-s**) (in full **taxi-cab**) car licensed to ply for hire and usu. fitted with a taximeter. *–v.* (**-xis, -xied, -xiing** or **-xying**) **1** (of an aircraft or pilot) drive on the ground before take-off or after landing. **2** go or convey in a taxi. [abbreviation of *taximeter cab*]

taxidermy /ˈtæksɪˌdɜːmɪ/ *n.* art of preparing, stuffing, and mounting the skins of animals. □ **taxidermist** *n.* [Greek *taxis* arrangement, *derma* skin]

taximeter /ˈtæksɪˌmiːtə(r)/ *n.* automatic fare-indicator fitted to a taxi. [French: related to TAX]

◆ **tax invoice** *n.* invoice for goods or services rendered by a trader who is registered for VAT, showing the selling price of the goods or services and the VAT charged on them. This invoice is an authority for the purchaser (if registered for VAT) to reclaim the VAT as input tax. Unregistered persons are prohibited by law from issuing tax invoices.

taxi rank *n.* (*US* **taxi stand**) place where taxis wait to be hired.

◆ **tax loss** *n.* amount deemed to be a loss for tax purposes, which can be set against an amount of profit, thus reducing the amount of the profit on which tax is payable. The loss may arise from trading at a loss or it may arise even when trade is profitable because such tax reliefs as capital allowances exceed the profits; this creates a loss for tax purposes only. Tax losses can usu. be set against profits of a similar and sometimes of a different type according to stringent rules.

taxman *n. colloq.* inspector or collector of taxes.

taxon /ˈtæks(ə)n/ *n.* (*pl.* **taxa**) any taxonomic group. [back-formation from TAXONOMY]

taxonomy /tækˈsɒnəmɪ/ *n.* classification of living and extinct organisms. □ **taxonomic** /-səˈnɒmɪk/ *adj.* **taxonomical** /-səˈnɒmɪk(ə)l/ *adj.* **taxonomically** /-səˈnɒmɪkəlɪ/ *adv.* **taxonomist** *n.* [Greek *taxis* arrangement, *-nomia* distribution]

taxpayer *n.* person who pays taxes.

◆ **tax relief** *n.* deduction from a taxable amount, usu. given by statute. In the UK, income-tax reliefs are given in respect of income from tax-exempt sources (e.g. PEPs, TESSAs, NSCs), as well as tax-deductible expenses, personal allowances, mortgage interest (see MORTGAGE INTEREST RELIEF), and covenants. The reliefs against capital-gains tax include the annual exemption, exemption from the proceeds of the sale of an only or a principal private residence, and retirement relief. For inheritance tax there is an annual relief as well as relief in respect of gifts between spouses and gifts to political parties and charities; agricultural and business reliefs are also available.

◆ **tax return** *n.* **1** form upon which a taxpayer makes an annual statement of income and personal circumstances enabling claims to be made for personal allowances. Statements of any capital gains, inheritances, etc. are also required in the return. The return is used by the tax authorities to assess the taxpayer's liability for tax. **2** statement so made.

◆ **tax schedule** see SCHEDULE *n.* 6.

◆ **tax shelter** *n.* financial arrangement made in order to avoid or minimize taxes.

◆ **tax wedge** *n. Econ.* difference between the marginal cost to the seller or producer of a good and the price paid by the purchaser. This difference represents the amount of tax paid.

◆ **tax year** *n.* = FISCAL YEAR.

tayberry /ˈteɪbərɪ/ *n.* (*pl.* **-ies**) hybrid fruit between the blackberry and raspberry. [River *Tay* in Scotland]

Tayside /ˈteɪsaɪd/ former local government region in E Scotland; its capital was Dundee. Tayside was abolished in 1996 and replaced by three unitary authorities: Perth and Kinross, Angus, and Dundee.

TB *abbr.* **1** training board. **2** treasury bill. **3** *Bookkeeping* trial balance. **4** tubercle bacillus. **5** tuberculosis.

Tb *symb.* terbium.

t.b. *abbr. Bookkeeping* trial balance.

t.b.a. *abbr.* **1** *Commerce* to be advised. **2** to be agreed. **3** to be announced.

Tbilisi /təbɪˈliːsɪ/ (formerly **Tiflis** /ˈtɪflɪs/) capital of Georgia; industries include engineering, textiles, and wine and food production; pop. (1994) 1 253 100.

T-bill *abbr.* treasury bill.

TBM *abbr. Computing* terabit memory.

T-bond *abbr.* treasury bond.

T-bone /ˈtiːbəʊn/ *n.* T-shaped bone, esp. in steak from the thin end of a loin.

tbsp. *abbr.* tablespoonful.

TC *–abbr.* **1** *Law* Tax Cases. **2** traveller's cheque. *–international civil aircraft marking* Turkey.

Tc *symb.* technetium.

TCP *abbr. propr.* a disinfectant and germicide. [*tr*ichloro-*p*henylmethyliodasalicyl]

TCU *abbr.* (in the US) Transportation, Communications, International Union.

TD *–abbr.* **1** (in the US) Treasury Department. **2** trust deed. *–symb.* Tunisian dinar. *–postcode* Galashiels.

TDDL *abbr. Telecom.* time-division data link.

TDM *abbr. Telecom.* time-division multiplexing.

TDMA *abbr. Telecom.* time-division multiple access.

TDR *abbr. Finance* Treasury deposit receipt.

t.d.r. *abbr.* (French) tous droits réservés (= all rights reserved).

Te *symb.* tellurium.

te /tiː/ *n.* (also **ti**) seventh note of a major scale. [earlier *si*: French from Italian]

tea *n.* **1 a** (in full **tea plant**) Asian evergreen shrub or small tree. **b** its dried leaves. **2** drink made by infusing tea-leaves in boiling water. **3** infusion of other leaves etc. (*camomile tea*; *beef tea*). **4 a** light afternoon meal of tea, bread, cakes, etc. **b** = HIGH TEA. [probably Dutch *tee* from Chinese]

♦ **tea auction** *n.* auction of Indian and Sri Lankan tea, held in Plantation House, Mincing Lane, in the City of London. The tea is shipped to the UK and handled by selling brokers, who provide sampling facilities for the buyers prior to the auction.

---

tea bag *n.* small perforated bag of tea for infusion.

tea break *n.* pause in work etc. to drink tea.

TEAC *abbr.* Technical Educational Advisory Council.

tea caddy *n.* container for tea-leaves.

teacake *n.* light usu. toasted sweet bun eaten at tea.

teach *v.* (*past* and *past part.* **taught** /tɔːt/) **1 a** give systematic information, instruction, or training to (a person) or about (a subject or skill) (*taught me to swim*). **b** (*absol.*) practise this professionally. **c** communicate, instruct in (*suffering taught me patience*). **2** advocate as a moral etc. principle (*taught forgiveness*). **3** (foll. by *to* + infin.) **a** instruct (a person) by example or punishment (*that will teach you not to disobey*). **b** *colloq.* discourage (a person) from (*that will teach you to laugh*). □ **teachable** *adj.* [Old English]

teacher *n.* person who teaches, esp. in a school.

tea chest *n.* light metal-lined plywood box for transporting tea-leaves.

teaching *n.* **1** profession of a teacher. **2** (often in *pl.*) what is taught; doctrine.

tea cloth *n.* = TEA TOWEL.

tea cosy *n.* cover to keep a teapot warm.

teacup *n.* **1** cup from which tea is drunk. **2** amount held by this. □ **teacupful** *n.* (*pl.* **-s**).

tea dance *n.* afternoon tea with dancing.

teak *n.* **1** a hard durable timber. **2** large Indian or SE Asian deciduous tree yielding this. [Portuguese from Malayalam]

teal *n.* (*pl.* same) small freshwater duck. [origin unknown]

tea lady *n.* woman employed to make tea in offices etc.

tea-leaf *n.* **1** dried leaf of tea. **2** (esp. in *pl.*) these as dregs. **3** *rhyming slang* thief.

team *–n.* **1** set of players forming one side in a game. **2** two or more people working together. **3** set of draught animals. *–v.* **1** (usu. foll. by *up*) join in a team or in common action (*teamed up with them*). **2** (foll. by *with*) match or coordinate (clothes). [Old English]

team-mate *n.* fellow-member of a team.

team spirit *n.* willingness to act for the communal good.

teamster *n.* **1** *US* lorry-driver. **2** driver of a team of animals.

teamwork *n.* combined action; co-operation.

tea-planter *n.* proprietor or cultivator of a tea plantation.

teapot *n.* pot with a handle, spout, and lid, for brewing and then pouring tea.

tear[1] /teə(r)/ *–v.* (*past* **tore**; *past part.* **torn**) **1** (often foll. by *up*) pull apart or to pieces with some force (*tore up the letter*). **2 a** make a hole or rent in this way; undergo this (*have torn my coat*; *curtain tore*). **b** make (a hole or rent). **3** (foll. by *away*, *off*, *at*, etc.) pull violently (*tore off the cover*; *tore down the notice*). **4** violently disrupt or divide (*torn by guilt*). **5** *colloq.* go hurriedly (*tore across the road*). *–n.* **1** hole etc. caused by tearing. **2** torn part of cloth etc. □ **be torn between** have difficulty in choosing between. **tear apart 1** search (a place) exhaustively. **2** criticize forcefully. **3** destroy; divide utterly; distress greatly. **tear one's hair out** *colloq.* behave with extreme desperation. **tear into** *colloq.* **1** severely reprimand. **2** start (an activity) vigorously. **tear oneself away** leave reluctantly. **tear to shreds** *colloq.* refute or criticize thoroughly. **that's torn it** *colloq.* that has spoiled things etc. [Old English]

tear[2] /tɪə(r)/ *n.* **1** drop of clear salty liquid secreted by glands from the eye, and shed esp. in grief. **2** tearlike thing; drop. □ **in tears** crying. [Old English]

tearaway *n. colloq.* unruly young person.

tear-drop *n.* single tear.

tear-duct *n.* drain for carrying tears to or from the eye.

tearful *adj.* **1** crying or inclined to cry. **2** sad (*tearful event*). □ **tearfully** *adv.*

tear-gas *n.* gas causing severe irritation to the eyes.

tearing hurry *n. colloq.* great hurry.

tear-jerker *n. colloq.* sentimental story, film, etc.

tearoom *n.* small unlicensed café serving tea etc.

tea rose *n.* hybrid shrub with a tealike scent.

tease /tiːz/ *–v.* (**-sing**) (also *absol.*) **1 a** make fun of playfully, unkindly, or annoyingly; irritate. **b** allure, esp. sexually, while withholding satisfaction. **2** pick (wool etc.) into separate fibres. **3** dress (cloth) esp. with teasels. *–n.* **1** *colloq.* person fond of teasing. **2** act of teasing (*only a tease*). □ **tease out** separate by disentangling. [Old English]

teasel /ˈtiːz(ə)l/ *n.* (also **teazel, teazle**) **1** plant with large prickly heads that are dried and used to raise the nap on woven cloth. **2** other device used for this purpose. □ **teaseler** *n.* [Old English: related to TEASE]

teaser *n.* **1** person who teases. **2** *colloq.* hard question or task.

teaset *n.* set of crockery for serving tea.

teashop *n.* = TEAROOM.

teaspoon *n.* **1** small spoon for stirring tea. **2** amount held by this. □ **teaspoonful** *n.* (*pl.* **-s**).

teat *n.* **1** mammary nipple, esp. of an animal. **2** rubber nipple for sucking from a bottle. [French from Germanic]

teatime *n.* time in the afternoon when tea is served.

tea towel *n.* towel for drying washed crockery etc.

tea trolley *n.* (*US* **tea wagon**) small trolley from which tea is served.

teazel (also **teazle**) var. of TEASEL.

TEC /tek/ *abbr.* Training and Enterprise Council.

tec *n. colloq.* detective. [abbreviation]

tech *n.* (also **tec**) *colloq.* technical college. [abbreviation]

technetium /tek'ni:ʃ(ə)m/ *n.* artificially produced radioactive metallic element. [Greek *tekhnētos* artificial]

technic /'teknɪk/ *n.* **1** (usu. in *pl.*) **a** technology. **b** technical terms, details, methods, etc. **2** technique. [Greek *tekhnē* art]

technical *adj.* **1** of the mechanical arts and applied sciences (*technical college*). **2** of a particular subject or craft etc. or its techniques (*technical terms*). **3** (of a book or discourse etc.) using technical language; specialized. **4** due to mechanical failure (*technical hitch*). **5** strictly or legally interpreted (*lost on a technical point*). □ **technically** *adv.*

technicality /ˌteknɪ'kælɪtɪ/ *n.* (*pl.* **-ies**) **1** being technical. **2** technical expression. **3** technical point or detail (*acquitted on a technicality*).

technical knockout *n.* ruling by the referee that a boxer has lost because he is not fit to continue.

♦ **technical rally** see RALLY[1] *n.* 5.

---

technician /tek'nɪʃ(ə)n/ *n.* **1** person doing practical or maintenance work in a laboratory etc. **2** person skilled in artistic etc. technique. **3** expert in practical science.

Technicolor /'teknɪˌkʌlə(r)/ *n.* (often *attrib.*) **1** *propr.* process of colour cinematography. **2** (usu. **technicolor**) *colloq.* **a** vivid colour. **b** artificial brilliance.

technique /tek'ni:k/ *n.* **1** mechanical skill in art. **2** skilful manipulation of a situation, people, etc. **3** manner of artistic execution in music, painting, etc. [French: related to TECHNIC]

technocracy /tek'nɒkrəsɪ/ *n.* (*pl.* **-ies**) **1** rule or control by technical experts. **2** instance or application of this. [Greek *tekhnē* art]

technocrat /'teknəˌkræt/ *n.* exponent or advocate of technocracy. □ **technocratic** /-'krætɪk/ *adj.*

♦ **technological change** *n.* increase in the level of output resulting from automation and computerized methods of production. Apart from increasing output, technological change can affect the ratio of capital to labour used in a factory. If it involves reducing the labour force it can lead to **technological unemployment** in an area or industry.

♦ **technological unemployment** see TECHNOLOGICAL CHANGE.

---

technology /tek'nɒlədʒɪ/ *n.* (*pl.* **-ies**) **1** knowledge or use of the mechanical arts and applied sciences (*lacked the technology*). **2** these subjects collectively. □ **technological** /-nə'lɒdʒɪk(ə)l/ *adj.* **technologically** /-nə'lɒdʒɪkəlɪ/ *adv.* **technologist** *n.* [Greek *tekhnologia* systematic treatment, from *tekhnē* art]

tectonic /tek'tɒnɪk/ *adj.* **1** of building or construction. **2** of the deformation and subsequent structural changes of the earth's crust (see PLATE TECTONICS). [Greek *tektōn* craftsman]

tectonics *n.pl.* (usu. treated as *sing.*) study of the earth's large-scale structural features (see PLATE TECTONICS).

Ted *n.* (also **ted**) *colloq.* Teddy boy. [abbreviation]

teddy /'tedɪ/ *n.* (also **Teddy**) (*pl.* **-ies**) (in full **teddy bear**) soft toy bear. [*Teddy*, pet form of *Theodore* Roosevelt]

Teddy boy /'tedɪ/ *n. colloq.* youth, esp. of the 1950s, wearing Edwardian-style clothes, hairstyle, etc. [*Teddy*, pet form of *Edward*]

tedious /'ti:dɪəs/ *adj.* tiresomely long; wearisome. □ **tediously** *adv.* **tediousness** *n.* [Latin: related to TEDIUM]

tedium /'ti:dɪəm/ *n.* tediousness. [Latin *taedium* from *taedet* it bores]

tee[1] *n.* = T[1]. [phonetic spelling]

tee[2] /ti:/ –*n.* **1 a** cleared space from which the golf ball is struck at the start of play for each hole. **b** small wooden or plastic support for a golf ball used then. **2** mark aimed at in bowls, quoits, curling, etc. –*v.* (**tees, teed**) (often foll. by *up*) place (a ball) on a golf tee. □ **tee off 1** play a ball from a tee. **2** *colloq.* start, begin. [origin unknown]

tee-hee /ti:'hi:/ (also **te-hee**) –*int.* expressing esp. derisive amusement. –*n.* titter, giggle. –*v.* (**-hees, -heed**) titter, giggle. [imitative]

teem[1] *v.* **1** be abundant. **2** (foll. by *with*) be full of or swarming with (*teeming with ideas*). [Old English, = give birth to]

teem[2] *v.* (often foll. by *down*) (of water etc.) flow copiously; pour (*teeming with rain*). [Old Norse]

teen *attrib. adj.* = TEENAGE. [abbreviation]

-teen *suffix* forming numerals from 13 to 19. [Old English]

teenage *attrib. adj.* of or characteristic of teenagers. □ **teenaged** *adj.*

teenager *n.* person from 13 to 19 years of age.

teens /ti:nz/ *n.pl.* years of one's age from 13 to 19 (*in his teens*).

teensy /'ti:nzɪ/ *adj.* (**-ier, -iest**) *colloq.* = TEENY.

teeny /'ti:nɪ/ *adj.* (**-ier, -iest**) *colloq.* tiny. [var. of TINY]

teeny-bopper *n. colloq.* young teenager, usu. a girl, who follows the latest fashions.

teeny-weeny *adj.* (also **teensy-weensy**) very tiny.

teepee var. of TEPEE.

teeter *v.* totter; move unsteadily. [dial. *titter*]

teeth *pl.* of TOOTH.

teethe /ti:ð/ *v.* (**-thing**) grow or cut teeth, esp. milk teeth.

teething-ring *n.* ring for an infant to bite on while teething.

teething troubles *n.pl.* initial difficulties in an enterprise etc.

teetotal /ti:'təʊt(ə)l/ *adj.* of or advocating total abstinence from alcohol. □ **teetotalism** *n.* **teetotaller** *n.* [reduplication of TOTAL]

teff *n.* an African cereal. [Amharic]

TEFL /'tef(ə)l/ *abbr.* teaching of English as a foreign language.

Teflon /'teflɒn/ *n. propr.* non-stick coating for kitchen utensils. [from *tetra-*, *fluor-*, *-on*]

Tegucigalpa /teˌgu:sɪ'gælpə/ capital of Honduras; pop. (1994) 775 300.

te-hee var. of TEE-HEE.

Tehran /teə'rɑ:n/ capital of Iran, a centre of commerce and industry; pop. (est. 1994) 11 000 000.

Tel. *abbr.* (also **tel.**) telephone.

Tel Aviv /tel ə'vi:v/ city in Israel, on the Mediterranean coast, united with the port of Jaffa (of which it was originally a suburb); pop. (est. 1996) 355 900 (with Jaffa).

tele- *comb. form* **1** at or to a distance (*telekinesis, telescope*). **2** television (*telecast*). **3** by telephone (*telesales*). [Greek *tēle* far off]

tele-ad /'telɪˌæd/ *n.* advertisement telephoned to a newspaper etc.

telecast –*n.* television broadcast. –*v.* transmit by television. □ **telecaster** *n.*

telecommunication /ˌtelɪkəˌmju:nɪ'keɪʃ(ə)n/ *n.* **1** communication over a distance by circuits using cable, fibre optics, satellites, radio etc. **2** (usu. in *pl.*) technology of this.

teleconference /'telɪˌkɒnfərəns/ *n.* conference with participants linked by telephone or with access to computer terminals interconnected by communication lines. □ **teleconferencing** *n.*

telefax /ˈtelɪˌfæks/ *n.* = FAX. [abbreviation of *telefacsimile*]

telegram /ˈtelɪˌgræm/ *n.* message sent by telegraph and delivered in printed form.

■ **Usage** Since 1981 *telegram* has not been in UK official use, except for international messages. See also *telemessage.*

telegraph /ˈtelɪˌgrɑːf/ –*n.* (often *attrib.*) device or system for transmitting messages or signals to a distance, esp. by making and breaking an electrical connection (*telegraph wire*). –*v.* **1** (often followed by *to*) send a message by telegraph to. **2** send or communicate by telegraph (*telegraphed my concern*). **3** give advance indication of (*telegraphed his punch*). □ **telegraphist** /tɪˈlegrəfɪst/ *n.*

telegraphic /ˌtelɪˈgræfɪk/ *adj.* **1** of or by telegraphs or telegrams. **2** economically worded. □ **telegraphically** *adv.*

♦ **telegraphic address** *n.* single word used to identify a company in a specified city. It is used in cables to reduce the cost of transmitting a complete name and address. Telegraphic addresses are registered by post offices throughout the world but are now much less used than formerly as a result of instant communication by telex and fax.

♦ **telegraphic transfer** *n.* (also **TT**) method of transmitting money overseas by means of a transfer between banks by cable or telephone. The transfer is usu. made in the currency of the payee and may be credited to the payee's account at a specified bank or paid in cash to the payee on application and identification.

telegraphy /tɪˈlegrəfɪ/ *n.* communication by telegraph.

telekinesis /ˌtelɪkaɪˈniːsɪs, -kɪˈniːsɪs/ *n.* supposed paranormal force moving objects at a distance. □ **telekinetic** /-ˈnetɪk/ *adj.* [Greek *kineō* move]

♦ **telemarketing** /ˈtelɪˌmɑːkɪtɪŋ/ *n.* (also **telephone selling**) direct marketing of goods etc. by unsolicited telephone calls. See also COLD CALL.

telemessage /ˈtelɪˌmesɪdʒ/ *n.* message sent by telephone or telex and delivered in printed form.

■ **Usage** *Telemessage* has been in UK official use since 1981 for inland messages, replacing *telegram.*

telemetry /tɪˈlemətrɪ/ *n.* process of recording the readings of an instrument and transmitting them by radio. □ **telemeter** /tɪˈlemɪtə(r)/ *n.*

teleology /ˌtiːlɪˈɒlədʒɪ, ˌte-/ *n.* (*pl.* **-ies**) *Philos.* **1** explanation of phenomena by the purpose they serve. **2** *Theol.* doctrine of design and purpose in the material world. □ **teleological** /-əˈlɒdʒɪk(ə)l/ *adj.* [Greek *telos* end]

telepathy /tɪˈlepəθɪ/ *n.* supposed paranormal communication of thoughts. □ **telepathic** /ˌtelɪˈpæθɪk/ *adj.* **telepathically** /ˌtelɪˈpæθɪkəlɪ/ *adv.*

telephone /ˈtelɪˌfəʊn/ –*n.* **1** apparatus for transmitting sound (esp. speech) to a distance, esp. by using optical or electrical signals. **2** handset etc. used in this. **3** system of communication using a network of telephones. –*v.* (**-ning**) **1** speak to or send (a message) by telephone. **2** make a telephone call. □ **on the telephone** having or using a telephone. **over the telephone** using the telephone. □ **telephonic** /-ˈfɒnɪk/ *adj.* **telephonically** /-ˈfɒnɪkəlɪ/ *adv.*

♦ **telephone banking** *n.* facility enabling customers to use banking services by means of a 24-hour telephone service and a personal identification number. See ELECTRONIC BANKING.

telephone book *n.* = TELEPHONE DIRECTORY.

telephone booth *n.* (also **telephone kiosk, telephone box**) booth etc. with a telephone for public use.

telephone directory *n.* book listing telephone subscribers and numbers.

telephone number *n.* number used to call a particular telephone.

♦ **telephone research** *n.* marketing research technique in which **telephone interviews** are conducted. It is cheaper than personal interviewing and, perhaps because it avoids face-to-face confrontations, seems to be more popular with respondents.

♦ **telephone selling** *n.* = TELEMARKETING.

telephonist /tɪˈlefənɪst/ *n.* operator in a telephone exchange or at a switchboard.

telephony /tɪˈlefənɪ/ *n.* transmission of sound by telephone.

telephoto /ˌtelɪˈfəʊtəʊ/ *n.* (*pl.* **-s**) (in full **telephoto lens**) lens used in telephotography.

telephotography /ˌtelɪfəˈtɒgrəfɪ/ *n.* photographing of distant objects with a system of lenses giving a large image. □ **telephotographic** /-ˌfəʊtəˈgræfɪk/ *adj.*

teleprinter /ˈtelɪˌprɪntə(r)/ *n.* device for transmitting, receiving, and printing telegraph messages.

teleprompter /ˈtelɪˌprɒmptə(r)/ *n.* device beside a television or cinema camera that slowly unrolls a speaker's script out of sight of the audience.

telesales /ˈtelɪˌseɪlz/ *n.pl.* selling by telephone.

telescope /ˈtelɪˌskəʊp/ –*n.* **1** optical instrument using lenses or mirrors to magnify distant objects. **2** = RADIO TELESCOPE. –*v.* (**-ping**) **1** press or drive (sections of a tube, colliding vehicles, etc.) together so that one slides into another. **2** close or be capable of closing in this way. **3** compress so as to occupy less space or time.

telescopic /ˌtelɪˈskɒpɪk/ *adj.* **1** of or made with a telescope (*telescopic observations*). **2** (esp. of a lens) able to focus on and magnify distant objects. **3** consisting of sections that telescope. □ **telescopically** *adv.*

telescopic sight *n.* telescope on a rifle etc. used for sighting.

telesoftware /ˌtelɪˈsɒftweə(r)/ *n.* software transmitted by teletext.

♦ **Teletex** /ˈtelɪˌteks/ *n. propr.* international telecommunications service using as terminals electronic typewriters with Teletex adaptors, electronic telephone exchanges, or computers. Messages can be transmitted up to a thousand times faster than by telex. Teletex was expected to replace telex, but has had limited success because of the rapid spread of fax.

♦ **teletext** /ˈtelɪˌtekst/ *n.* computerized news and information service transmitted to suitably adapted TV sets. Both text and primitive graphics can be transmitted. A number of 'pages' of information (including latest stock exchange prices) are broadcast in a continuous cycle at the same time as the normal TV signal. Having chosen teletext mode on the control pad, a page number can then be selected and that page is displayed on the screen. The teletext services available in the UK are **Ceefax** (BBC) and **Teletext** (ITV). See also TOPIC.

♦ **Teletext Output Price Information Computer** see TOPIC.

telethon /ˈtelɪˌθɒn/ *n.* exceptionally long television programme, esp. to raise money for charity. [from TELE-, MARATHON]

Teletype /ˈtelɪˌtaɪp/ *n. propr.* a kind of teleprinter.

televise /ˈtelɪˌvaɪz/ *v.* (**-sing**) broadcast on television.

television /ˈtelɪˌvɪʒ(ə)n, -ˈvɪʒ(ə)n/ *n.* **1** system for reproducing on a screen visual images transmitted (usu. with sound) by radio signals or cable. **2** (in full **television set**) device with a screen for receiving these signals. **3** television broadcasting. □ **televisual** /-ˈvɪʒʊəl/ *adj.*

television monitor *n.* = MONITOR *n.* 3a.

♦ **television rating** *n.* (also **TVR**) measurement of the popularity of a television programme based on survey research. Equipment attached to sets in selected homes records which channel the set is tuned to, while diary panels are used to determine how many people are watching the set. In this way ratings can be calculated for each programme and expressed as a percentage of the total households that can receive TV. Survey research is undertaken in the UK by the Broadcasters Audience Research Board (BARB).

♦ **telex** /'teleks/ (also **Telex**) *–n.* **1** method of communicating written messages over the international telephone network, using a teleprinter. Telex calls are made by direct dialling, a hard copy of the message being provided for both sender and recipient. Telex messages may be received by unattended machines and a tape of a message may be prepared for sending to several different recipients at any time required. The recipient's call-back signal appears on the sender's copy as proof that the message has reached the recipient's teleprinter. **2** message transmitted by telex. **3** teleprinter used in telex. *–v.* send, or communicate with, by telex. [from TELEPRINTER, EXCHANGE]

---

tell *v.* (*past* and *past part.* **told** /təʊld/) **1** relate in speech or writing (*tell me a story*). **2** make known; express in words (*tell me your name*). **3** reveal or signify to (a person) (*your face tells me everything*). **4** utter (*tell lies*). **5 a** (often foll. by *of, about*) divulge information etc.; reveal a secret, the truth etc. (*told her about Venice*; *book tells you how to cook*; *promise you won't tell*; *time will tell*). **b** (foll. by *on*) *colloq.* inform against. **6** (foll. by *to* + infin.) direct; order (*tell them to wait*). **7** assure (*it's true, I tell you*). **8** decide, determine, distinguish (*tell one from the other*). **9** (often foll. by *on*) produce a noticeable effect or influence (*strain told on me*; *evidence tells against you*). **10** (often *absol.*) count (votes) at a meeting, election, etc. □ **tell apart** distinguish between (*could not tell them apart*). **tell off** *colloq.* scold. **tell tales** make known another person's faults etc. **tell the time** read the time from a clock or watch. **you're telling me** *colloq.* I agree wholeheartedly. [Old English: related to TALE]

teller *n.* **1** person working at the counter of a bank etc. **2** person who counts votes. **3** person who tells esp. stories (*teller of tales*).

telling *adj.* having a marked effect; striking; impressive. □ **tellingly** *adv.*

telling-off *n.* (*pl.* **tellings-off**) *colloq.* scolding.

tell-tale *n.* **1** person who reveals secrets about another. **2** (*attrib.*) that reveals or betrays (*tell-tale smile*). **3** automatic monitoring or registering device.

tellurium /te'ljʊərɪəm/ *n.* rare lustrous silver-white element used in semiconductors. □ **telluric** *adj.* [Latin *tellus -ur-* earth]

telly /'telɪ/ *n.* (*pl.* **-ies**) *colloq.* **1** television. **2** television set. [abbreviation]

TELNET /'telnet/ *abbr.* teletype network.

TEMA *abbr.* Telecommunications Engineering and Manufacturing Association.

temerity /tɪ'merɪtɪ/ *n.* rashness; audacity. [Latin *temere* rashly]

temp *colloq. –n.* temporary employee, esp. a secretary. *–v.* work as a temp. [abbreviation]

temper *–n.* **1** mental disposition, mood (*placid temper*). **2** irritation or anger (*fit of temper*). **3** tendency to lose one's temper (*have a temper*). **4** composure, calmness (*lose one's temper*). **5** hardness or elasticity of metal. *–v.* **1** bring (metal or clay) to a proper hardness or consistency. **2** (foll. by *with*) moderate, mitigate (*temper justice with mercy*). □ **in a bad** (or **out of**) **temper** irritable, angry. **in a good temper** amicable, happy. [Latin *tempero* mingle]

tempera /'tempərə/ *n.* **1** method of painting using an emulsion, e.g. of pigment with egg-yolk and water, esp. on canvas. **2** this emulsion. [Italian]

temperament /'temprəmənt/ *n.* person's or animal's nature and character (*nervous temperament*). [Latin: related to TEMPER]

temperamental /ˌtemprə'ment(ə)l/ *adj.* **1** of temperament. **2 a** (of a person) unreliable; moody. **b** *colloq.* (of esp. a machine) unreliable, unpredictable. □ **temperamentally** *adv.*

temperance /'tempərəns/ *n.* **1** moderation, esp. in eating and drinking. **2** (often *attrib.*) abstinence, esp. total, from alcohol (*temperance hotel*). [Latin: related to TEMPER]

temperate /'tempərət/ *adj.* **1** avoiding excess. **2** moderate. **3** (of a region or climate) mild. [Latin: related to TEMPER]

temperature /'temprɪtʃə(r)/ *n.* **1** measured or perceived degree of heat or cold of a thing, region, etc. **2** *colloq.* body temperature above the normal (*have a temperature*). **3** degree of excitement in a discussion etc. [Latin: related to TEMPER]

tempest /'tempɪst/ *n.* violent storm. [Latin *tempus* time]

tempestuous /tem'pestʃʊəs/ *adj.* stormy; turbulent. □ **tempestuously** *adv.*

tempi *pl.* of TEMPO.

template /'templɪt, -pleɪt/ *n.* piece of thin board or metal plate etc., used as a pattern in cutting or drilling etc. [originally *templet*, diminutive of *temple*, device in a loom to keep the cloth stretched]

temple[1] /'temp(ə)l/ *n.* building for the worship, or seen as the dwelling-place, of a god or gods etc. [Latin *templum*]

temple[2] /'temp(ə)l/ *n.* flat part of either side of the head between the forehead and the ear. [French from Latin]

tempo /'tempəʊ/ *n.* (*pl.* **-s** or **-pi** /-piː/) **1** speed at which music is or should be played. **2** speed or pace. [Latin *tempus -por-* time]

temporal /'tempər(ə)l/ *adj.* **1** worldly as opposed to spiritual; secular. **2** of time. **3** *Gram.* denoting time or tense (*temporal conjunction*). **4** of the temples of the head (*temporal artery*). [Latin *tempus -por-* time]

temporary /'tempərərɪ/ *–adj.* lasting or meant to last only for a limited time. *–n.* (*pl.* **-ies**) person employed temporarily. □ **temporarily** *adv.* **temporariness** *n.*

♦ **temporary assurance** *n.* = TERM ASSURANCE.

---

temporize /'tempəˌraɪz/ *v.* (also **-ise**) (**-zing** or **-sing**) **1** avoid committing oneself so as to gain time; procrastinate. **2** comply temporarily; adopt a time-serving policy.

tempt *v.* **1** entice or incite (a person) to do what is wrong or forbidden (*tempted him to steal it*). **2** allure, attract. **3** risk provoking (fate etc.). □ **be tempted to** be strongly disposed to. □ **tempter** *n.* **temptress** *n.* [Latin *tempto, tento* try, test]

temptation /temp'teɪʃ(ə)n/ *n.* **1** tempting or being tempted; incitement, esp. to wrongdoing. **2** attractive thing or course of action. **3** *archaic* putting to the test.

tempting *adj.* attractive, inviting. □ **temptingly** *adv.*

tempura /tem'pʊərə/ *n.* Japanese dish of fish, shellfish, etc., fried in batter. [Japanese]

ten *adj.* & *n.* **1** one more than nine. **2** symbol for this (10, x, X). **3** size etc. denoted by ten. **4** ten o'clock. □ **ten to one** very probably. [Old English]

tenable /'tenəb(ə)l/ *adj.* **1** maintainable or defensible against attack or objection (*tenable position*). **2** (foll. by *for, by*) (of an office etc.) that can be held for (a specified period) or by (a specified class of person). □ **tenability** /-'bɪlɪtɪ/ *n.* [French *tenir* hold]

tenacious /tɪ'neɪʃəs/ *adj.* **1** (often foll. by *of*) keeping a firm hold. **2** persistent, resolute. **3** (of memory) retentive. □ **tenaciously** *adv.* **tenacity** /tɪ'næsɪtɪ/ *n.* [Latin *tenax -acis* from *teneo* hold]

tenancy /'tenənsɪ/ *n.* (*pl.* **-ies**) **1** status of or possession as a tenant. **2** duration of this.

♦ **tenancy agreement** *n.* agreement to let land. See LEASE *n.*

♦ **tenancy in common** *n.* tenancy involving two or more persons having an interest in the same piece of land. Each person can choose how to bequeath his or her interest, although the land itself has not been physically divided. Trustees must hold the legal estate and the tenancy in common exists in equity. See also JOINT TENANTS.

---

tenant /'tenənt/ *n.* **1** person who rents land or property from a landlord. **2** (often foll. by *of*) occupant of a place. [French: related to TENABLE]

tenant farmer *n.* person who farms rented land.

tenantry *n.* tenants of an estate etc.

tench *n.* (*pl.* same) European freshwater fish of the carp family. [Latin *tinca*]

Ten Commandments *n.pl.* (prec. by *the*) rules of conduct given by God to Moses (Exod. 20:1–17).

tend[1] *v.* **1** (often foll. by *to*) be apt or inclined (*tends to lose his temper*; *tends to fat*). **2** be moving; hold a course (*tends in our direction*). [Latin *tendo tens-* or *tent-* stretch]

tend[2] *v.* take care of, look after (an invalid, sheep, a machine etc.). [from ATTEND]

tendency /'tendənsɪ/ *n.* (*pl.* **-ies**) (often foll. by *to, towards*) leaning or inclination. [medieval Latin: related to TEND[1]]

tendentious /ten'denʃəs/ *adj. derog.* calculated to promote a particular cause or viewpoint; biased; controversial. □ **tendentiously** *adv.* **tendentiousness** *n.*

tender[1] *adj.* (**tenderer, tenderest**) **1** easily cut or chewed, not tough (*tender steak*). **2** susceptible to pain or grief; vulnerable; compassionate (*tender heart*). **3** sensitive; fragile; delicate (*tender skin*; *tender reputation*). **4** loving, affectionate. **5** requiring tact (*tender subject*). **6** (of age) early, immature (*of tender years*). □ **tenderly** *adv.* **tenderness** *n.* [Latin *tener*]

tender[2] *–v.* **1** offer, present (one's services, resignation, money as payment, etc.). **2** (often foll. by *for*) offer a tender. *–n.* **1** means of auctioning an item of value to the highest bidder. Tenders are used in many circumstances, e.g. for allocating valuable construction contracts, for selling shares on a stock market (see OFFER FOR SALE; ISSUE BY TENDER), or for the sale of government securities. **2** offer, esp. in writing, to execute work or supply goods at a stated price. **3** see LEGAL TENDER. □ **put out to tender** seek competitive tenders for (work etc.). □ **tenderer** *n.* [French: related to TEND[1]]

tender[3] *n.* **1** person who looks after people or things. **2** supply ship attending a larger one etc. **3** truck coupled to a steam locomotive to carry fuel and water. [from TEND[2]]

tenderfoot *n.* (*pl* **-s** or **-feet**) newcomer, novice.

tender-hearted /ˌtendə'hɑːtɪd/ *adj.* easily moved; compassionate. □ **tender-heartedness** *n.*

tenderize /'tendəˌraɪz/ *v.* (also **-ise**) (**-zing** or **-sing**) make (esp. meat) tender by beating, hanging, marinading, etc. □ **tenderizer** *n.*

tenderloin *n.* **1** middle part of pork loin. **2** *US* undercut of sirloin.

tender mercies *n.pl. iron.* harsh treatment.

◆ **tender offer** *n.* US practice of offering securities to the public by inviting them to tender a price. The securities are then sold to the highest bidder.

---

tender spot *n.* subject on which a person is touchy.

tendon /'tend(ə)n/ *n.* cord of strong connective tissue attaching a muscle to a bone etc. □ **tendinitis** /-'naɪtɪs/ *n.* [Latin *tendo* stretch]

tendril /'tendrɪl/ *n.* slender leafless shoot by which some climbing plants cling. [probably from French *tendrillon*]

tenebrous /'tenɪbrəs/ *adj. literary* dark, gloomy. [Latin *tenebrosus*]

tenement /'tenɪmənt/ *n.* **1** room or flat within a house or block of flats. **2** (also **tenement-house** or **-block**) house or block so divided. [Latin *teneo* hold]

Tenerife /ˌtenə'riːf/ Spanish island, the largest of the Canary Islands; pop. (1991) 725 815; capital, Santa Cruz. It produces bananas, tomatoes, and other fruit and vegetables; tourism is also important.

tenet /'tenɪt/ *n.* doctrine, principle. [Latin, = he holds]

tenfold *adj.* & *adv.* **1** ten times as much or as many. **2** consisting of ten parts.

ten-gallon hat *n.* cowboy's large broad-brimmed hat.

tenge /tɛŋ/ *n.* standard monetary unit of Kazakhstan.

Tenn. *abbr.* Tennessee.

Tennant Creek /'tenənt/ mining town in Australia, in Northern Territory, producing gold, silver, and copper; pop. (1986) 3300.

tenner *n. colloq.* ten-pound or ten-dollar note.

Tennessee /ˌtenɪ'siː/ state in the central SE US; pop. (est. 1996) 5 319 654; capital, Nashville. Products include tobacco, soya beans, cotton, hardwood, zinc, and stone; there are also chemical, textile, and food-processing industries.

tennis /'tenɪs/ *n.* game in which two or four players strike a ball with rackets over a net stretched across a court. [probably French *tenez* take! (as a server's call)]

tennis elbow *n.* sprain caused by overuse of forearm muscles.

tenon /'tenən/ *n.* wooden projection made for insertion into a cavity, esp. a mortise, in another piece. [Latin: related to TENOR]

tenor /'tenə(r)/ *n.* **1 a** male singing-voice between baritone and alto or counter-tenor. **b** singer with this voice. **2** (often *attrib.*) instrument with a similar range. **3** (usu. foll. by *of*) general meaning. **4** (usu. foll. by *of*) prevailing course, esp. of a person's life or habits. **5** *Finance* time that must elapse before a bill of exchange or promissory note becomes due for payment, as stated on the bill or note. [Latin *teneo* hold]

tenosynovitis /ˌtenəʊˌsaɪnəʊ'vaɪtɪs/ *n.* injury of esp. a wrist tendon resulting from repetitive strain. [Greek *tenōn* tendon, SYNOVIA]

tenpin *n.* pin used in tenpin bowling.

tenpin bowling *n.* game in which ten pins or skittles are bowled at in an alley.

tense[1] *–adj.* **1** stretched tight, strained. **2** causing tenseness (*tense moment*). *–v.* (**-sing**) make or become tense. □ **tense up** become tense. □ **tensely** *adv.* **tenseness** *n.* [Latin *tensus*: related to TEND[1]]

tense[2] *n.* **1** form of a verb indicating the time (also the continuance or completeness) of the action etc. **2** set of such forms as a paradigm. [Latin *tempus* time]

tensile /'tensaɪl/ *adj.* **1** of tension. **2** capable of being stretched. □ **tensility** /-'sɪlɪtɪ/ *n.* [medieval Latin: related to TENSE[1]]

tensile strength *n.* resistance to breaking under tension.

tension /'tenʃ(ə)n/ *–n.* **1** stretching or being stretched; tenseness. **2** mental strain or excitement. **3** strained (political, social, etc.) state or relationship. **4** stress produced by forces pulling apart. **5** degree of tightness of stitches in knitting and machine sewing. **6** voltage (*high tension*; *low tension*). *–v.* subject to tension. □ **tensional** *adj.* [Latin: related to TEND[1]]

tent *n.* **1** portable canvas etc. shelter or dwelling supported by poles and cords attached to pegs driven into the ground. **2** tentlike enclosure, e.g. supplying oxygen to a patient. [Latin: related to TEND[1]]

tentacle /'tentək(ə)l/ *n.* **1** long slender flexible appendage of an (esp. invertebrate) animal, used for feeling, grasping, or moving. **2** channel for gathering information, exercising influence, etc. □ **tentacled** *adj.* [Latin: related to TEMPT]

tentative /'tentətɪv/ *adj.* **1** experimental. **2** hesitant, not definite (*tentative suggestion*). □ **tentatively** *adv.* **tentativeness** *n.* [medieval Latin: related to TEMPT]

tenter *n.* machine for stretching cloth to dry in shape. [medieval Latin *tentorium*: related to TEND[1]]

tenterhook *n.* hook to which cloth is fastened on a tenter. □ **on tenterhooks** in a state of suspense or agitation due to uncertainty.

tenth *adj.* & *n.* **1** next after ninth. **2** any of ten equal parts of a thing. □ **tenthly** *adv.*

tent-stitch *n.* **1** series of parallel diagonal stitches. **2** such a stitch.

tenuous /'tenjʊəs/ *adj.* **1** slight, insubstantial (*tenuous connection*). **2** (of a distinction etc.) oversubtle. **3** thin, slender, small. **4** rarefied. □ **tenuity** /-'juːɪtɪ/ *n.* **tenuously** *adv.* [Latin *tenuis*]

tenure /'tenjə(r)/ *n.* **1** condition, or form of right or title, under which (esp. real) property is held. **2** (often foll. by *of*) **a** holding or possession of an office or property. **b** period of this. **3** guaranteed permanent employment, esp. as a teacher or lecturer. □ **tenured** *adj.* [Latin *teneo*]

tepee /'ti:pi:/ *n.* (also **teepee**) North American Indian's conical tent. [Dakota]

tepid /'tepɪd/ *adj.* **1** lukewarm. **2** unenthusiastic. □ **tepidity** /tɪ'pɪdɪtɪ/ *n.* **tepidly** *adv.* [Latin]

tequila /tɪ'ki:lə/ *n.* Mexican liquor made from an agave. [*Tequila* in Mexico]

tera- *comb. form* denoting a factor of 10^{12}. [Greek *teras* monster]

terbium /'tɜ:bɪəm/ *n.* silvery metallic element of the lanthanide series. [*Ytterby* in Sweden]

tercel /'tɜ:s(ə)l/ *n.* (also **tiercel** /'tɪəs(ə)l/) male hawk, esp. a peregrine or goshawk. [Latin *tertius* third]

tercentenary /ˌtɜ:sen'ti:nərɪ/ *n.* (*pl.* **-ies**) **1** three-hundredth anniversary. **2** celebration of this. [Latin *ter*, = three times]

teredo /tə'ri:dəʊ/ *n.* (*pl.* **-s**) bivalve mollusc that bores into submerged timbers of ships etc. [Latin from Greek]

Terengganu see TRENGGANU.

tergiversate /'tɜ:dʒɪvəˌseɪt/ *v.* (**-ting**) **1** change one's party or principles; apostatize. **2** make conflicting or evasive statements. □ **tergiversation** /-'seɪʃ(ə)n/ *n.* **tergiversator** *n.* [Latin *tergum* back, *verto* turn]

term *–n.* **1** word for a definite concept, esp. specialized (*technical term*). **2** (in *pl.*) language used; mode of expression (*in no uncertain terms*). **3** (in *pl.*) relation, footing (*on good terms*). **4** (in *pl.*) **a** stipulations (*accepts your terms*). **b** charge or price (*reasonable terms*). **5 a** limited, usu. specified, period (*term of five years*; *in the short term*). **b** period of weeks during which instruction is given or during which a lawcourt holds sessions. **6** *Logic* word or words that may be the subject or predicate of a proposition. **7** *Math.* **a** each of the quantities in a ratio or series. **b** part of an algebraic expression. **8** completion of a normal length of pregnancy. *–v.* call, name (*was termed a bigot*). □ **bring to terms** cause to accept conditions. **come to terms** yield, give way. **come to terms with** reconcile oneself to (a difficulty etc.). **in terms of** in the language peculiar to; referring to. □ **termly** *adj.* & *adv.* [Latin TERMINUS]

termagant /'tɜ:məgənt/ *n.* overbearing woman; virago. [French *Tervagan* from Italian]

◆ **term assurance** *n.* (also **temporary assurance**) form of life assurance that operates for a specified period of time. No benefit is paid if the insured person dies outside the period. Term assurance is often used to cover the period of a loan, mortgage, etc. If the insured person dies before the loan has been repaid, it is settled by the insurance company. See also DECREASING TERM ASSURANCE.

◆ **term bill** *n.* = PERIOD BILL.

---

terminable /'tɜ:mɪnəb(ə)l/ *adj.* able to be terminated.

terminal /'tɜ:mɪn(ə)l/ *–adj.* **1 a** (of a condition or disease) fatal. **b** (of a patient) dying. **2** of or forming a limit or terminus (*terminal station*). *–n.* **1** terminating thing; extremity. **2** terminus for trains or long-distance buses. **3** = AIR TERMINAL. **4** point of connection for closing an electric circuit. **5** apparatus used for communication with a computer from a remote site, the two being linked by cable or telephone line. It is usu. a VDU paired with a keyboard. Terminals can be designed for a particular application, e.g. electronic point-of-sale terminals and automated teller machines at banks. An **intelligent terminal** is one with a built-in capability to store and manipulate data, i.e. it contains a microcomputer. □ **terminally** *adv.* [Latin: related to TERMINUS]

◆ **terminal bonus** *n.* additional amount of money added to payments made on the maturity of an insurance policy or on the death of an insured person, because the investments of the insurer have produced a profit or surplus. Bonuses of this kind are paid at the discretion of the life office and usu. take the form of a percentage of the sum assured.

◆ **terminal loss relief** *n.* tax loss made in the closing year of a business's life, which may be carried back and set against profits of earlier years.

◆ **terminal market** *n.* commodity market in a trading centre, such as London or New York, rather than a market in a producing centre, such as Calcutta or Singapore. The trade in terminal markets is predominantly in futures, but spot goods may also be bought and sold.

---

terminate /'tɜ:mɪˌneɪt/ *v.* (**-ting**) **1** bring or come to an end. **2** (foll. by *in*) (of a word) end in (a specified letter etc.).

termination /ˌtɜ:mɪ'neɪʃ(ə)n/ *n.* **1** terminating or being terminated. **2** induced abortion. **3** ending or result. **4** word's final syllable or letter.

termini *pl.* of TERMINUS.

terminology /ˌtɜ:mɪ'nɒlədʒɪ/ *n.* (*pl.* **-ies**) **1** system of specialized terms. **2** science of the use of terms. □ **terminological** /-nə'lɒdʒɪk(ə)l/ *adj.* [German: related to TERMINUS]

terminus /'tɜ:mɪnəs/ *n.* (*pl.* **-ni** /-ˌnaɪ/ or **-nuses**) **1** station at the end of a railway or bus route. **2** point at the end of a pipeline etc. [Latin, = end, limit, boundary]

termite /'tɜ:maɪt/ *n.* small tropical antlike social insect destructive to timber. [Latin *termes -mitis*]

◆ **term shares** *n.pl.* shares that cannot be sold for a given period, usu. shares in a building society that cannot be cashed on demand and consequently carry a higher rate of interest.

---

terms of reference *n.pl.* scope of an inquiry etc.; definition of this.

◆ **terms of trade** *n.pl.* measure of the trading prospects of a country in terms of the prices of its imports in relation to the prices of its exports. It may be expressed as the ratio of an index of export prices to an index of import prices, or as a change of this ratio relative to a base year. Thus, the terms of trade of a country improve if its export prices rise faster than the price of its imports. A fall in the rate of exchange, other things being equal, will lead to a deterioration in the terms of trade.

◆ **term structure** *n.* (of interest rates) relationship between the yields on fixed-interest securities (e.g. government bonds) and their maturity dates. One important factor affecting the term structure relates to expectations of changes in interest rates. For example, if both short-term and long-term bonds have the same yield initially and subsequently investors expect interest rates to fall, long-term bonds will appear relatively attractive, because, being fixed-interest securities, they will continue to pay their stated rates of interest for a long period, after market interest rates have declined. Arbitrage will then ensure that their prices will rise and their yields will fall; thus yields on short-term bonds will exceed those on long-term bonds. A graph showing the relationship between the number of years to maturity and the yield is called the yield curve. Other factors that may also affect the term structure include liquidity preference and hedging pressure.

---

tern *n.* marine gull-like bird with a long forked tail. [Scandinavian]

ternary /'tɜ:nərɪ/ *adj.* composed of three parts. [Latin *terni*, = three each]

terrace /'terəs/ *–n.* **1** flat area made on a slope for cultivation. **2** level paved area next to a house. **3** row of houses built in one block of uniform style. **4** tiered standing accommodation for spectators at a sports ground. *–v.* (**-cing**) form into or provide with a terrace or terraces. [Latin *terra* earth]

terrace house *n.* (also **terraced house**) house in a terrace.

terracotta /ˌterə'kɒtə/ *n.* **1 a** unglazed usu. brownish-red earthenware. **b** statuette of this. **2** its colour. [Italian, = baked earth]

terra firma /ˌterə ˈfɜːmə/ *n.* dry land, firm ground. [Latin]

terrain /təˈreɪn/ *n.* tract of land, esp. in geographical or military contexts. [Latin: related to TERRENE]

terra incognita /ˌterə ɪŋˈkɒgnɪtə, ˌɪnkɒgˈniːtə/ *n.* unexplored region. [Latin, = unknown land]

terrapin /ˈterəpɪn/ *n.* **1** North American edible freshwater turtle. **2** (**Terrapin**) *propr.* type of prefabricated one-storey building. [Algonquian]

terrarium /təˈreərɪəm/ *n.* (*pl.* **-s** or **-ria**) **1** place for keeping small land animals. **2** sealed transparent globe etc. containing growing plants. [Latin *terra* earth, after *aquarium*]

terrazzo /teˈrætsəʊ/ *n.* (*pl.* **-s**) smooth flooring-material of stone chips set in concrete. [Italian, = terrace]

terrene /teˈriːn/ *adj.* **1** of the earth; worldly. **2** of earth, earthy. **3** terrestrial. [Latin *terrenus* from *terra* earth]

terrestrial /təˈrestrɪəl/ *adj.* **1** of or on the earth; earthly. **2** of or on dry land. [Latin *terrestris*: related to TERRENE]

terrible /ˈterɪb(ə)l/ *adj.* **1** *colloq.* very great or bad (*terrible bore*). **2** *colloq.* very incompetent (*terrible at maths*). **3** causing or likely to cause terror; dreadful, formidable. [Latin *terreo* frighten]

terribly *adv.* **1** *colloq.* very, extremely (*terribly nice*). **2** in a terrible manner.

terrier /ˈterɪə(r)/ *n.* small dog of various breeds originally used for digging out foxes etc. [French *chien terrier* dog that chases to earth]

terrific /təˈrɪfɪk/ *adj.* **1** *colloq.* **a** huge; intense (*terrific noise*). **b** excellent (*did a terrific job*). **2** causing terror. □ **terrifically** *adv.* [Latin: related to TERRIBLE]

terrify /ˈterɪˌfaɪ/ *v.* (**-ies, -ied**) fill with terror (*terrified of dogs*). □ **terrifying** *adj.* **terrifyingly** *adv.*

terrine /təˈriːn/ *n.* **1** pâté or similar food. **2** earthenware vessel, esp. for pâté. [Latin *terra* earth]

territorial /ˌterɪˈtɔːrɪəl/ *–adj.* **1** of territory or a district (*territorial possessions; territorial right*). **2** tending to defend one's territory. *–n.* (**Territorial**) member of the Territorial Army. □ **territorially** *adv.* [Latin: related to TERRITORY]

Territorial Army *n.* local volunteer reserve force.

◆ **territorial waters** *n.pl.* area of sea around a country's coastline over which it has jurisdiction according to international law, esp. within a stated distance of the shore. Since disputes have arisen over fishing rights, offshore oil mining, and mineral rights below the ocean, the universal three-mile rule has been abrogated and various nations have made different claims, some (but not all) of which have been accepted internationally. Ten to fifteen miles is now quite common in definitions of territorial waters. The Territorial Sea Act (1987) fixes the UK territorial waters at 12 nautical miles. A UN convention proposes a new 200-mile **exclusive economic zone**, which would give a country sovereign rights over all the resources of the sea, seabed, and subsoil within this zone. Fishing rights extending to 200 miles are also claimed by many nations, including the UK.

---

territory /ˈterɪtərɪ/ *n.* (*pl.* **-ies**) **1** extent of the land under the jurisdiction of a ruler, state, etc. **2** (**Territory**) organized division of a country, esp. one not yet admitted to the full rights of a state. **3** sphere of action etc.; province. **4** commercial traveller's sales area. **5** animal's or human's defended space or area. **6** area defended by a team or player in a game. [Latin *terra* land]

terror /ˈterə(r)/ *n.* **1** extreme fear. **2 a** terrifying person or thing. **b** *colloq.* formidable or troublesome person or thing, esp. a child. **3** organized intimidation; terrorism. [Latin *terreo* frighten]

terrorist *n.* (often *attrib.*) person using esp. organized violence against a government etc. □ **terrorism** *n.* [French: related to TERROR]

terrorize /ˈterəˌraɪz/ *v.* (also **-ise**) (**-zing** or **-sing**) **1** fill with terror. **2** use terrorism against. □ **terrorization** /-ˈzeɪʃ(ə)n/ *n.*

terror-stricken *adj.* (also **terror-struck**) affected with terror.

terry /ˈterɪ/ *n.* (often *attrib.*) looped pile fabric used esp. for towels and nappies. [origin unknown]

terse *adj.* (**terser, tersest**) **1** brief, concise. **2** curt, abrupt. □ **tersely** *adv.* **terseness** *n.* [Latin *tergo ters-* wipe]

tertiary /ˈtɜːʃərɪ/ *–adj.* **1** third in order or rank etc. **2** (**Tertiary**) of the first period in the Cenozoic era. *–n.* (**Tertiary**) Tertiary period. [Latin *tertius* third]

◆ **tertiary production** see PRODUCTION 3.

---

tervalent /tɜːˈvələnt, -ˈveɪlənt/ *adj.* having a valency of three. [from TERCENTENARY, VALENCE[1]]

Terylene /ˈterɪˌliːn/ *n. propr.* synthetic textile fibre of polyester. [from *terephthalic* acid, ETHYLENE]

TESL /ˈtes(ə)l/ *abbr.* teaching of English as a second language.

tesla /ˈteslə/ *n.* SI unit of magnetic induction. [*Tesla*, name of a scientist]

TESSA /ˈtesə/ *abbr.* (also **Tessa**) = TAX EXEMPT SPECIAL SAVINGS ACCOUNT.

tessellated /ˈtesəˌleɪtɪd/ *adj.* **1** of or resembling a mosaic. **2** regularly chequered. [Latin *tessella* diminutive of TESSERA]

tessellation /ˌtesəˈleɪʃ(ə)n/ *n.* close arrangement of polygons, esp. in a repeated pattern.

tessera /ˈtesərə/ *n.* (*pl.* **tesserae** /-ˌriː/) small square block used in mosaic. [Latin from Greek]

tessitura /ˌtesɪˈtʊərə/ *n.* range of a singing voice or vocal part. [Italian, = TEXTURE]

test[1] *–n.* **1** critical examination or trial of a person's or thing's qualities. **2** means, procedure, or standard for so doing. **3** minor examination, esp. in school (*spelling test*). **4** *colloq.* test match. *–v.* **1** put to the test. **2** try or tax severely. **3** examine by means of a reagent. □ **put to the test** cause to undergo a test. **test out** put to a practical test. □ **testable** *adj.* [Latin *testu(m)* earthen pot: related to TEST[2]]

test[2] *n.* shell of some invertebrates. [Latin *testa* pot, tile, shell]

testa /ˈtestə/ *n.* (*pl.* **testae** /-tiː/) seed-coat. [Latin: related to TEST[2]]

testaceous /teˈsteɪʃəs/ *adj.* having a hard continuous shell.

testament /ˈtestəmənt/ *n.* **1** will (esp. *last will and testament*). **2** (usu. foll. by *to*) evidence, proof (*is testament to his loyalty*). **3** *Bibl.* **a** covenant, dispensation. **b** (**Testament**) division of the Bible (see OLD TESTAMENT, NEW TESTAMENT). [Latin *testamentum* will: related to TESTATE]

testamentary /ˌtestəˈmentərɪ/ *adj.* of, by, or in a will.

testate /ˈtesteɪt/ *–adj.* having left a valid will at death. *–n.* testate person. □ **testacy** *n.* (*pl.* **-ies**). [Latin *testor* testify, from *testis* witness]

testator /teˈsteɪtə(r)/ *n.* (*fem.* **testatrix** /teˈsteɪtrɪks/) (esp. deceased) person who has made a will. [Latin: related to TESTATE]

test card *n.* still television picture outside normal programme hours used for adjusting brightness, definition, etc.

test case *n. Law* case setting a precedent for other similar cases.

test drive *n.* drive taken to judge the performance of a vehicle. □ **test-drive** *v.*

tester *n.* **1** person or thing that tests. **2** bottle etc. containing a cosmetic for trial in a shop.

testes *pl.* of TESTIS.

test flight *n.* aircraft flight for evaluation purposes. □ **test-fly** *v.*

testicle /ˈtestɪk(ə)l/ *n.* male organ that produces spermatozoa etc., esp. one of a pair in the scrotum in man and most mammals. [Latin, diminutive of *testis* witness]

testify /ˈtestɪˌfaɪ/ *v.* (**-ies, -ied**) **1** (often foll. by *to*) (of a person or thing) bear witness; be evidence of (*testified to the facts*). **2** give evidence. **3** affirm or declare. [Latin *testificor* from *testis* witness]

testimonial /ˌtestɪˈməʊnɪəl/ *n.* **1** certificate of character, conduct, or qualifications. **2** gift presented to a person (esp. in public) as a mark of esteem etc. [French: related to TESTIMONY]

♦ **testimonial advertisement** *n.* advertisement that makes use of the implied or explicit patronage of a product by a well-known person or organization.

---

testimony /ˈtestɪmənɪ/ *n.* (*pl.* **-ies**) **1** witness's statement under oath etc. **2** declaration or statement of fact. **3** evidence, demonstration (*produce testimony*). [Latin *testimonium* from *testis* witness]

testis /ˈtestɪs/ *n.* (*pl.* **testes** /-tiːz/) *Anat.* & *Zool.* testicle. [Latin, = witness (cf. TESTICLE)]

♦ **test marketing** *n.* (also **market testing**) procedure for launching a new product in a restricted geographical area to test consumers' reactions. If the product is unsuccessful, the company will have minimized its costs and can make the necessary changes before a wider launch. Test marketing is usu. undertaken in large towns or in areas served by a particular commercial television company. It has the disadvantage that competitors learn about the new product before its full launch. See also NEW PRODUCT DEVELOPMENT.

---

test match *n.* international cricket or Rugby match, usu. in a series.

testosterone /teˈstɒstəˌrəʊn/ *n.* male sex hormone formed in the testicles. [from TESTIS, STEROL]

test paper *n.* **1** minor examination paper. **2** paper impregnated with a substance changing colour under known conditions.

test pilot *n.* pilot who test-flies aircraft.

test run *n.* preliminary operational test to check that a computer, machine, etc. is performing in the desired manner.

test-tube *n.* thin glass tube closed at one end, used for chemical tests etc.

test-tube baby *n. colloq.* baby conceived by *in vitro* fertilization.

testy *adj.* (**-ier, -iest**) irritable, touchy. □ **testily** *adv.* **testiness** *n.* [French *teste* head: related to TEST[2]]

tetanus /ˈtetənəs/ *n.* bacterial disease causing painful spasm of the voluntary muscles. [Greek *teinō* stretch]

tetchy /ˈtetʃɪ/ *adj.* (also **techy**) (**-ier, -iest**) peevish, irritable. □ **tetchily** *adv.* **tetchiness** *n.* [*teche* blemish, fault]

tête-à-tête /ˌteɪtɑːˈteɪt/ *–n.* (often *attrib.*) private conversation between two persons. *–adv.* privately without a third person (*dined tête-à-tête*). [French, literally 'head-to-head']

tether /ˈteðə(r)/ *–n.* rope etc. confining a grazing animal. *–v.* tie with a tether. □ **at the end of one's tether** at the limit of one's patience, resources, etc. [Old Norse]

Tétouan /teɪˈtwɑːn/ city and port in N Morocco; it has light-manufacturing and textile industries and exports agricultural produce; pop. (est. 1993) 272 000.

tetra- *comb. form* four. [Greek *tettares* four]

tetrad /ˈtetræd/ *n.* group of four. [Greek: related to TETRA-]

tetragon /ˈtetrəˌgɒn/ *n.* plane figure with four angles and sides. □ **tetragonal** /tɪˈtrægən(ə)l/ *adj.* [Greek *-gōnos* -angled]

tetrahedron /ˌtetrəˈhiːdrən/ *n.* (*pl.* **-dra** or **-s**) four-sided solid; triangular pyramid. □ **tetrahedral** *adj.* [Greek *hedra* base]

tetralogy /teˈtrælədʒɪ/ *n.* (*pl.* **-ies**) group of four related literary, dramatic, or operatic works.

tetrameter /teˈtræmɪtə(r)/ *n. Prosody* verse of four measures.

TEU *abbr. Shipping* twenty-foot equivalent unit.

Teuton /ˈtjuːt(ə)n/ *n.* member of a Teutonic nation, esp. a German. [Latin *Teutones*, ancient tribe of N Europe]

Teutonic /tjuːˈtɒnɪk/ *adj.* **1** of the Germanic peoples or languages. **2** German. [Latin: related to TEUTON]

Tex. *abbr.* Texas.

Texas /ˈteksəs/ state in the S US, bordering on the Gulf of Mexico; pop. (est. 1996) 19 128 261; capital, Austin. It is a major producer of oil, natural gas, and sulphur, with chemical and other oil-related industries. Agriculture produces cotton, rice, peanuts, and livestock.

text *n.* **1** main body of a book as distinct from notes etc. **2** original book or document, esp. as distinct from a paraphrase etc. **3** passage from Scripture, esp. as the subject of a sermon. **4** subject, theme. **5** (in *pl.*) books prescribed for study. **6** data in textual form, esp. as stored, processed, or displayed in a word processor etc. [Latin *texo text-* weave]

textbook *–n.* book for use in studying, esp. a standard account of a subject. *–attrib. adj.* **1** exemplary, accurate. **2** instructively typical.

text editor *n. Computing* system or program allowing the user to enter and modify text. For example, a document can be keyed into a computer and a text editor used to create a file. A text editor can also be used to inspect the contents of a file by enabling a particular portion of the file to be displayed on a screen. The screen cursor can then be positioned at points where insertions, deletions, and other editing functions are to be performed. There is a considerable overlap between text editors and word-processing systems.

textile /ˈtekstaɪl/ *–n.* **1** (often in *pl.*) fabric, cloth, or fibrous material, esp. woven. **2** fibre, yarn. *–adj.* **1** of weaving or cloth (*textile industry*). **2** woven (*textile fabrics*). [Latin: related to TEXT]

text processing *n. Computing* manipulation of text, esp. transforming it from one format to another.

textual /ˈtekstʃʊəl/ *adj.* of, in, or concerning a text. □ **textually** *adv.*

texture /ˈtekstʃə(r)/ *–n.* **1** feel or appearance of a surface or substance. **2** arrangement of threads etc. in textile fabric. *–v.* (**-ring**) (usu. as **textured** *adj.*) **1** provide with a texture. **2** (of vegetable protein) provide with a texture resembling meat. □ **textural** *adj.* [Latin: related to TEXT]

TF *–abbr. Shipping* tropical fresh water (see LOAD LINE). *–international civil aircraft marking* Iceland. *–postcode* Telford.

TG *–abbr.* training group. *–international vehicle registration* Togo. *–international civil aircraft marking* Guatemala. *–airline flight code* Thai Airways International.

♦ **TGI** *abbr.* = TARGET GROUP INDEX.

TGV *abbr.* high-speed French passenger train. [French *train à grande vitesse*]

TGWU *abbr.* Transport and General Workers' Union.

Th *symb.* thorium.

-th *suffix* (also **-eth**) forming ordinal and fractional numbers from *four* onwards. [Old English]

Thai /taɪ/ *–n.* (*pl.* same or **-s**) **1 a** native or national of Thailand. **b** person of Thai descent. **2** language of Thailand. *–adj.* of Thailand. [Thai, = free]

Thailand, Gulf of inlet of the South China Sea between the Malay Peninsula to the W and Thailand and Cambodia to the E.

thalidomide /θəˈlɪdəˌmaɪd/ *n.* sedative drug found in 1961 to cause foetal malformation when taken early in pregnancy. [from ph*thali*mido*glutarimide*]

thallium /ˈθælɪəm/ *n.* rare soft white metallic element. [Greek *thallos* green shoot]

Thames /temz/ river in S England, flowing E from the Cotswolds in Gloucestershire through London to the North Sea. A flood barrier across the river to protect London from high tides was completed in 1982.

than /ðən, ðæn/ *conj.* introducing a comparison (*plays better than he did before*; *more bread than meat in these sausages*;

cost more than £100; you are older than he). [Old English, originally = THEN]

■ **Usage** With reference to the last example, it is also legitimate to say *you are older than him*, with *than* treated as a preposition, esp. in less formal contexts.

thane *n. hist.* **1** man who held land from an English king or other superior by military service. **2** man who held land from a Scottish king and ranked with an earl's son; chief of a clan. [Old English]

thank *–v.* **1** express gratitude to (*thanked him for the present*). **2** hold responsible (*you can thank yourself for that*). *–n.* (in *pl.*) **1** gratitude. **2** expression of gratitude. **3** (as a formula) thank you (*thanks for your help*). □ **thank goodness** (or **God** or **heavens** etc.) *colloq.* expression of relief etc. **thanks to** as the result of (*thanks to my foresight; thanks to your obstinacy*). **thank you** polite formula expressing gratitude. [Old English]

thankful *adj.* **1** grateful, pleased. **2** expressive of thanks.

thankfully *adv.* **1** in a thankful manner. **2** let us be thankful (that) (*thankfully, it didn't rain*).

■ **Usage** The use of *thankfully* in sense 2 is common but considered incorrect by some people.

thankless *adj.* **1** not expressing or feeling gratitude. **2** (of a task etc.) giving no pleasure or profit; unappreciated.

thanksgiving *n.* **1** expression of gratitude, esp. to God. **2** (**Thanksgiving** or **Thanksgiving Day**) fourth Thursday in November (a national holiday in the US).

that /ðæt/ *–demons. pron.* (*pl.* **those** /ðəʊz/) **1** person or thing indicated, named, or understood (*I heard that; who is that in the garden?*). **2** contrasted with *this* (*this is much better than that*). **3** (esp. in relative constructions) the one, the person, etc. (*a table like that described above*). **4** /ðət/ (*pl.* **that**) used instead of *which* or *whom* to introduce a defining clause (*the book that you sent me; there is nothing here that matters*). *–demons. adj.* (*pl.* **those** /ðəʊz/) designating the person or thing indicated, named, understood, etc. (cf. sense 1 of *pron.*). *–adv.* **1** to such a degree; so (*have done that much*). **2** *colloq.* very (*not that good*). *–conj.* /ðət/ introducing a subordinate clause indicating: **1** statement or hypothesis (*they say that he is better*). **2** purpose (*we eat that we may live*). **3** result (*am so sleepy that I cannot work*). □ **all that** very (*not all that good*). **that is** (or **that is to say**) formula introducing or following an explanation of a preceding word or words. **that's that** formula indicating conclusion or completion. [Old English]

■ **Usage** In sense 4 of the pronoun, *that* usu. specifies or identifies something referred to, whereas *who* or *which* need not: compare *the book that you sent me is lost* with *the book, which I gave you, is lost*. *That* is often omitted in senses 1 and 3 of the conjunction: *they say he is ill*.

thatch *–n.* **1** roof-covering of straw, reeds, etc. **2** *colloq.* hair of the head. *–v.* (also *absol.*) cover with thatch. □ **thatcher** *n.* [Old English]

thaw *–v.* **1** (often foll. by *out*) pass from a frozen into a liquid or unfrozen state. **2** (usu. prec. by *it* as subject) (of the weather) become warm enough to melt ice etc. **3** become warm enough to lose numbness etc. **4** become or make genial. **5** (often foll. by *out*) cause to thaw. *–n.* **1** thawing. **2** warmth of weather that thaws. [Old English]

THE *abbr.* Technical Help to Exporters (division of the British Standards Institute).

the /before a vowel ðɪ, before a consonant ðə, when stressed ðiː/ *–adj.* (called the definite article) **1** denoting person(s) or thing(s) already mentioned, under discussion, implied, or familiar (*gave the man a wave*). **2** describing as unique (*the Thames*). **3 a** (foll. by defining adj.) which is, who are, etc. (*Edward the Seventh*). **b** (foll. by adj. used *absol.*) denoting a class described (*from the sublime to the ridiculous*). **4** best known or best entitled to the name (with *the* stressed: *do you mean* the *Kipling?*). **5** indicating a following defining clause or phrase (*the book that you borrowed*). **6 a** indicating that a singular noun represents a species etc. (*the cat is a mammal*). **b** used with a noun which figuratively represents an occupation etc. (*went on the stage*). **c** (foll. by the name of a unit) a, per (*5p in the pound*). *–adv.* (preceding comparatives in expressions of proportional variation) in or by that (or such a) degree; on that account (*the more the merrier; the more he has the more he wants*). [Old English]

theatre /ˈθɪətə(r)/ *n.* (*US* **theater**) **1** building or outdoor area for dramatic performances. **2** writing and production of plays. **3** room or hall for lectures etc. with seats in tiers. **4** operating theatre. **5 a** scene or field of action (*the theatre of war*). **b** (*attrib.*) designating weapons intermediate between tactical and strategic. [Greek *theatron*]

theatrical /θɪˈætrɪk(ə)l/ *–adj.* **1** of or for the theatre or acting. **2** (of a manner or person etc.) calculated for effect; showy. *–n.* (in *pl.*) dramatic performances (*amateur theatricals*). □ **theatricality** /-ˈkælɪtɪ/ *n.* **theatrically** *adv.*

thee *objective case of* THOU[1].

theft *n.* act of stealing. [Old English: related to THIEF]

Thailand /ˈtaɪlænd/, **Kingdom of** (former name, until 1939, **Siam**) country in SE Asia on the Gulf of Thailand, with Burma on its W border. Rice is the main agricultural export and the chief subsistence crop; tapioca is also exported and rubber, sugar, maize, tobacco, and jute are grown. Mining is important: deposits of tin, tungsten, zinc, antimony, manganese, lead, coal, and iron are exploited, and the economy has been boosted by the discovery of oil and natural gas. Tourism is a major source of foreign currency, and manufacturing industry is rapidly developing: manufactured products, esp. electrical equipment and machinery, textiles, processed food, and integrated circuit boards, are now a major source of export revenue. Fishing remains important, but the forestry industry has been adversely affected by a ban on the export of hardwoods. *History*. A powerful Thai kingdom emerged in the area in the 14th century; increasing exposure to European powers in the 19th century resulted in the loss of territory in the E to France and in the S to Britain, though Thailand itself succeeded in retaining its independence. It became a constitutional monarchy in 1932. Politically unstable for much of the 20th century, Thailand was occupied by the Japanese in the Second World War; in recent years it has had border difficulties with Cambodia and Laos. A military coup in 1991 overthrew the civilian government, but the new military government was brought down by violent demonstrations in 1992. Free elections later that year resulted in victory for parties not allied to the military. Following the elections a number of constitutional reforms were implemented. Snap elections were held in 1996 following numerous allegations of government corruption, resulting in Chavalit Yongchaiyndh becoming prime minister. However, a massive financial crisis in 1997 forced the prime minister to resign and a new coalition government was formed under Chuan Leekpai, a former prime minister (1992–95). Head of state, King Bhumibol Adulyadej; prime minister, Chuan Leekpai; capital, Bangkok. □ **Thailander** *n.*

languages	Thai (official), Chinese, Malay, regional dialects
currency	baht (B) of 100 satang
pop. (1996)	60 003 000
GNP (1994)	US$129.8B
literacy	93% (m); 84% (f)
life expectancy	67 (m); 72 (f)

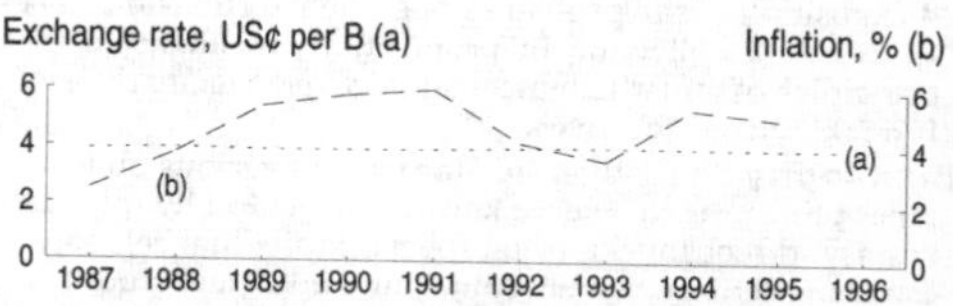

their /ðeə(r)/ *poss. pron.* (*attrib.*) of or belonging to them. [Old Norse]

theirs /ðeəz/ *poss. pron.* the one or ones of or belonging to them (*it is theirs*; *theirs are over here*). □ **of theirs** of or belonging to them (*a friend of theirs*).

theism /ˈθiːɪz(ə)m/ *n.* belief in gods or a god, esp. a god supernaturally revealed to man. □ **theist** *n.* **theistic** /-ˈɪstɪk/ *adj.* [Greek *theos* god]

them /ð(ə)m, or, when stressed, ðem/ *–pron.* **1** *objective case* of THEY. **2** *colloq.* they (*it's them again*). *–demons. adj. slang* or *dial.* those. [Old Norse]

theme *n.* **1** subject or topic of a talk, book, etc. **2** *Mus.* prominent melody in a composition. **3** *US* school exercise on a given subject. □ **thematic** /θɪˈmætɪk/ *adj.* **thematically** /θɪˈmætɪkəlɪ/ *adv.* [Greek *thema -mat-*]

theme park *n.* amusement park organized round a unifying idea.

theme song *n.* (also **theme tune**) **1** recurrent melody in a musical play or film. **2** signature tune.

themselves /ðəmˈselvz/ *pron.* **1** *emphat. form* of THEY or THEM. **2** *refl. form* of THEM. □ **be themselves** act in their normal, unconstrained manner. **by themselves** see *by oneself*.

then /ðen/ *–adv.* **1** at that time. **2 a** next; after that. **b** and also. **3 a** in that case (*then you should have said so*). **b** implying grudging or impatient concession (*all right then, if you must*). **c** used parenthetically to resume a narrative etc. (*the policeman, then, knocked on the door*). *–attrib. adj.* such at the time in question (*the then King*). *–n.* that time (*until then*). □ **then and there** immediately and on the spot. [Old English]

thence /ðens/ *adv.* (also **from thence**) *archaic* or *literary* **1** from that place. **2** for that reason. [Old English]

thenceforth /ðensˈfɔːθ/ *adv.* (also **thenceforward** /-ˈfɔːwəd/) *archaic* or *literary* from that time onward.

theo- *comb. form* God or god(s). [Greek *theos* god]

theocracy /θɪˈɒkrəsɪ/ *n.* (*pl.* **-ies**) form of government by God or a god directly or through a priestly order etc. □ **theocratic** /θɪəˈkrætɪk/ *adj.*

theodolite /θɪˈɒdəˌlaɪt/ *n.* surveying-instrument for measuring horizontal and vertical angles with a rotating telescope. [origin unknown]

theologian /θɪəˈləʊdʒɪən, -dʒ(ə)n/ *n.* expert in theology. [French: related to THEOLOGY]

theology /θɪˈɒlədʒɪ/ *n.* (*pl.* **-ies**) the study or a system of theistic (esp. Christian) religion. □ **theological** /θɪəˈlɒdʒɪk(ə)l/ *adj.* **theologically** /θɪəˈlɒdʒɪkəlɪ/ *adv.* [Greek: related to THEO-]

theorem /ˈθɪərəm/ *n.* esp. *Math.* **1** general proposition that is not self-evident but is proved by reasoning. **2** rule in algebra etc., esp. one expressed by symbols or formulae. [Greek *theōreō* look at]

theoretical /θɪəˈretɪk(ə)l/ *adj.* **1** concerned with knowledge but not with its practical application. **2** based on theory rather than experience. □ **theoretically** *adv.*

theoretician /ˌθɪərəˈtɪʃ(ə)n/ *n.* person concerned with the theoretical aspects of a subject.

theorist /ˈθɪərɪst/ *n.* holder or inventor of a theory.

theorize /ˈθɪəraɪz/ *v.* (also **-ise**) (**-zing** or **-sing**) evolve or indulge in theories.

theory /ˈθɪərɪ/ *n.* (*pl.* **-ies**) **1** supposition or system of ideas explaining something, esp. one based on general principles independent of the particular things to be explained (*atomic theory*; *theory of evolution*). **2** speculative (esp. fanciful) view (*one of my pet theories*). **3** abstract knowledge or speculative thought (*all very well in theory*). **4** exposition of the principles of a science etc. (*the theory of music*). **5** collection of propositions to illustrate the principles of a mathematical subject (*probability theory*). [Greek: related to THEOREM]

theosophy /θɪˈɒsəfɪ/ *n.* (*pl.* **-ies**) any of various philosophies professing to achieve knowledge of God by spiritual ecstasy, direct intuition, or special individual relations, esp. a modern movement following Hindu and Buddhist teachings and seeking universal brotherhood. □ **theosophical** /θɪəˈsɒfɪk(ə)l/ *adj.* **theosophist** *n.* [Greek *theosophos* wise concerning God]

Thera see SANTORINI.

therapeutic /ˌθerəˈpjuːtɪk/ *adj.* **1** of, for, or contributing to, the cure of disease. **2** soothing, conducive to well-being. □ **therapeutically** *adv.* [Greek *therapeuō* wait on, cure]

therapeutics *n.pl.* (usu. treated as *sing.*) branch of medicine concerned with cures and remedies.

therapy /ˈθerəpɪ/ *n.* (*pl.* **-ies**) non-surgical treatment of disease or disability. □ **therapist** *n.* [Greek *therapeia* healing]

there /ðeə(r)/ *–adv.* **1** in, at, or to that place or position (*lived there for a year*; *goes there daily*). **2** at that point (in speech, performance, writing, etc.). **3** in that respect (*I agree with you there*). **4** used for emphasis in calling attention (*you there!*). **5** used to indicate the fact or existence of something (*there is a house on the corner*). *–n.* that place (*lives near there*). *–int.* **1** expressing confirmation, triumph, etc. (*there! what did I tell you?*). **2** used to soothe a child etc. (*there, there, never mind*). □ **there and then** = *then and there*. [Old English]

thereabouts *adv.* (also **thereabout**) **1** near that place. **2** near that number, quantity, etc.

thereafter *adv. formal* after that.

thereby *adv.* by that means, as a result of that. □ **thereby hangs a tale** much could be said about that.

therefore /ˈðeəfɔː(r)/ *adv.* for that reason; accordingly, consequently.

therein *adv. formal* **1** in that place etc. **2** in that respect.

thereof *adv. formal* of that or it.

thereto *adv. formal* **1** to that or it. **2** in addition.

thereupon *adv.* **1** in consequence of that. **2** immediately after that.

therm *n.* unit of heat, esp. as the statutory unit of gas supplied, equivalent to 100 000 British thermal units (1.055×10^8 joules). [Greek *thermē* heat]

thermal /ˈθɜːm(ə)l/ *–adj.* **1** of, for, or producing heat. **2** promoting the retention of heat (*thermal underwear*). *–n.* rising current of warm air (used by gliders etc. to gain height). □ **thermally** *adv.* [French: related to THERM]

♦ **thermal printer** *n.* non-impact computer printer that uses special heat-sensitive paper. The printing head contains heated needles that are pressed against the paper to form dot matrix characters. The paper darkens where it is heated by the needles. Thermal printers are cheap and quiet in operation.

---

thermal unit *n.* unit for measuring heat.

thermionic /ˌθɜːmɪˈɒnɪk/ *adj.* of electrons emitted from a very hot substance. [from THERMO-, ION]

thermionic valve *n.* device giving a controlled flow of electrons in one direction, formerly used as a rectifier, esp. in radio.

thermo- *comb. form* heat. [Greek]

thermocouple /ˈθɜːməʊˌkʌp(ə)l/ *n.* device for measuring temperatures by means of a pair of different metals in contact at a point and generating a thermoelectric voltage.

thermodynamics /ˌθɜːməʊdaɪˈnæmɪks/ *n.pl.* (usu. treated as *sing.*) science of the relations between heat and other forms of energy. □ **thermodynamic** *adj.*

thermoelectric /ˌθɜːməʊɪˈlektrɪk/ *adj.* producing electricity by a difference of temperatures.

thermometer /θəˈmɒmɪtə(r)/ *n.* instrument for measuring temperature, esp. a graduated glass tube containing mercury or alcohol. [French: related to THERMO-, -METER]

thermonuclear /ˌθɜːməʊˈnjuːklɪə(r)/ *adj.* **1** relating to nuclear reactions that occur only at very high temperatures. **2** (of weapons) using thermonuclear reactions.

thermoplastic /ˌθɜːməʊˈplæstɪk/ *–adj.* that becomes plastic on heating and hardens on cooling. *–n.* thermoplastic substance.

Thermos /'θɜːməs/ *n.* (in full **Thermos flask**) *propr.* vacuum flask. [Greek: related to THERMO-]

thermosetting /'θɜːməʊˌsetɪŋ/ *adj.* (of plastics) setting permanently when heated.

thermosphere /'θɜːməˌsfɪə(r)/ *n.* region of the atmosphere beyond the mesosphere.

thermostat /'θɜːməˌstæt/ *n.* device that automatically regulates or responds to temperature. □ **thermostatic** /-'stætɪk/ *adj.* **thermostatically** /-'stætɪkəlɪ/ *adv.* [from THERMO-, Greek *statos* standing]

thesaurus /θɪ'sɔːrəs/ *n.* (*pl.* **-ri** /-raɪ/ or **-ruses**) book that lists words in groups of synonyms and related concepts. [Greek: related to TREASURE]

these *pl.* of THIS.

thesis /'θiːsɪs/ *n.* (*pl.* **theses** /-siːz/) **1** proposition to be maintained or proved. **2** dissertation, esp. by a candidate for a higher degree. [Greek, = putting]

Thespian /'θespɪən/ –*adj.* of drama. –*n.* actor or actress. [Greek *Thespis*, name of a Greek tragedian]

Thessalonica, Thessaloniki see SALONICA.

Thessaly /'θesəlɪ/ region of NE Greece; pop. (1991) 734 846. □ **Thessalian** /θe'seɪlɪən/ *adj.* & *n.*

theta /'θiːtə/ *n.* eighth letter of the Greek alphabet (Θ, θ). [Greek]

they /ðeɪ/ *pron.* (*obj.* **them**; *poss.* **their, theirs**) **1** *pl.* of HE, SHE, IT[1]. **2** people in general (*so they say*). **3** those in authority (*they have raised taxes*). [Old Norse]

they'd /ðeɪd/ *contr.* **1** they had. **2** they would.

they'll /ðeɪl, ðel/ *contr.* **1** they will. **2** they shall.

they're /ðe(r), 'ðeɪə(r)/ *contr.* they are.

they've /ðeɪv/ *contr.* they have.

THF *abbr.* Trusthouse Forte plc.

thiamine /'θaɪəmɪn, -ˌmiːn/ *n.* (also **thiamin**) B vitamin found in unrefined cereals, beans, and liver, a deficiency of which causes beriberi. [Greek *theion* sulphur, *amin* from VITAMIN]

thick –*adj.* **1** of great or specified extent between opposite surfaces. **2** (of a line etc.) broad; not fine. **3** arranged closely; crowded together; dense. **4** (usu. foll. by *with*) densely covered or filled (*air thick with smoke*). **5 a** firm in consistency; containing much solid matter. **b** made of thick material (*a thick coat*). **6 a** muddy, cloudy; impenetrable by sight. **b** (of one's head) suffering from a hangover, headache, etc. **7** *colloq.* stupid. **8 a** (of a voice) indistinct. **b** (of an accent) very marked. **9** *colloq.* intimate, very friendly. –*n.* thick part of anything. –*adv.* thickly (*snow was falling thick*). □ **a bit thick** *colloq.* unreasonable or intolerable. **in the thick of** at the busiest part of. **through thick and thin** under all conditions; in spite of all difficulties. □ **thickish** *adj.* **thickly** *adv.* [Old English]

thicken *v.* **1** make or become thick or thicker. **2** become more complicated (*plot thickens*). □ **thickener** *n.*

thickening *n.* **1** becoming thick or thicker. **2** substance used to thicken liquid. **3** thickened part.

thicket /'θɪkɪt/ *n.* tangle of shrubs or trees. [Old English: related to THICK]

thickhead *n. colloq.* stupid person. □ **thickheaded** *adj.*

thickness *n.* **1** being thick. **2** extent of this. **3** layer of material (*use three thicknesses*).

thickset *adj.* **1** heavily or solidly built. **2** set or growing close together.

thick-skinned *adj.* not sensitive to criticism.

thief *n.* (*pl.* **thieves** /θiːvz/) person who steals, esp. secretly. [Old English]

thieve *v.* (**-ving**) **1** be a thief. **2** steal (a thing). [Old English: related to THIEF]

thievery *n.* stealing.

thievish *adj.* given to stealing.

thigh /θaɪ/ *n.* part of the leg between the hip and the knee. [Old English]

thigh-bone *n.* = FEMUR.

thimble *n.* metal or plastic cap worn to protect the finger and push the needle in sewing. [Old English: related to THUMB]

thimbleful *n.* (*pl.* **-s**) small quantity, esp. of drink.

Thimphu /'tɪmpuː/ capital of Bhutan; pop. (est. 1993) 30 340.

thin –*adj.* (**thinner, thinnest**) **1** having opposite surfaces close together; of small thickness or diameter. **2** (of a line) narrow or fine. **3** made of thin material (*thin dress*). **4** lean; not plump. **5** not dense or copious (*thin hair*). **6** of slight consistency. **7** weak; lacking an important ingredient (*thin blood*; *a thin voice*). **8** (of an excuse etc.) flimsy or transparent. –*adv.* thinly (*cut the bread very thin*). –*v.* (**-nn-**) **1** (often foll. by *down*) make or become thin or thinner. **2** (often foll. by *out*) make or become less dense or crowded or numerous. □ **have a thin time** *colloq.* have a wretched or uncomfortable time. **thin on the ground** few in number. **thin on top** balding. □ **thinly** *adv.* **thinness** *n.* **thinnish** *adj.* [Old English]

♦ **thin capitalization** *n.* form of company capitalization in which the capital of a company consists of too few shares and too much loan stock in the view of the tax authority. Some countries reserve the right in such cases to treat some of the interest on the loan stock as if it were a dividend, thus denying the right to a tax deduction on the interest payment.

---

thine /ðaɪn/ *poss. pron. archaic* **1** (*predic.* or *absol.*) of or belonging to thee. **2** (*attrib.* before a vowel) = THY. [Old English]

thin end of the wedge see WEDGE.

thing *n.* **1** entity, idea, action, etc., that exists or may be thought about or perceived. **2** inanimate material object (*take that thing away*). **3** unspecified item (*a few things to buy*). **4** act, idea, or utterance (*silly thing to do*). **5** event (*unfortunate thing to happen*). **6** quality (*patience is a useful thing*). **7** person regarded with pity, contempt, or affection (*poor thing!*). **8** specimen or type (*latest thing in hats*). **9** *colloq.* one's special interest (*not my thing*). **10** *colloq.* something remarkable (*there's a thing!*). **11** (prec. by *the*) *colloq.* **a** what is proper or fashionable. **b** what is needed (*just the thing*). **c** what is to be considered (*the thing is, shall we go or not?*). **d** what is important. **12** (in *pl.*) personal belongings or clothing (*where are my things?*). **13** (in *pl.*) equipment (*painting things*). **14** (in *pl.*) affairs in general (*not in the nature of things*). **15** (in *pl.*) circumstances, conditions (*things look good*). **16** (in *pl.* with a following adjective) all that is so describable (*things Greek*). □ **do one's own thing** *colloq.* pursue one's own interests or inclinations. **have a thing about** *colloq.* be obsessed or prejudiced about. **make a thing of** *colloq.* **1** regard as essential. **2** cause a fuss about. [Old English]

thingummy /'θɪŋəmɪ/ *n.* (*pl.* **-ies**) (also **thingumabob** /-məˌbɒb/, **thingumajig** /-məˌdʒɪg/) *colloq.* person or thing whose name one has forgotten or does not know.

think –*v.* (*past* and *past part.* **thought** /θɔːt/) **1** be of the opinion (*think that they will come*). **2** judge or consider (*is thought to be a fraud*). **3** exercise the mind (*let me think for a moment*). **4** (foll. by *of* or *about*) **a** consider; be or become aware of. **b** form or entertain the idea of; imagine. **5** have a half-formed intention (*I think I'll stay*). **6** form a conception of. **7** recognize the presence or existence of (*thought no harm in it*). –*n. colloq.* act of thinking (*have a think*). □ **think again** revise one's plans or opinions. **think aloud** utter one's thoughts as soon as they occur. **think better of** change one's mind about (an intention) after reconsideration. **think fit** see FIT[1]. **think little** (or **nothing**) **of** consider to be insignificant. **think much** (or **a lot** or **highly**) **of** have a high opinion of. **think out 1** consider carefully. **2** produce (an idea etc.) by thinking. **think over** reflect upon in order to reach a decision. **think through** reflect fully upon (a problem etc.). **think twice** use careful consideration, avoid hasty action, etc. **think up** *colloq.* devise. [Old English]

thinker *n.* **1** person who thinks, esp. in a specified way (*an original thinker*). **2** person with a skilled or powerful mind.

thinking –*attrib. adj.* using thought or rational judgement. –*n.* opinion, judgement.

think-tank *n. colloq.* body of experts providing advice and ideas on national or commercial problems.

thinner *n.* solvent used to dilute paint etc.

thin-skinned *adj.* sensitive to criticism.

Thira see SANTORINI.

third *adj.* & *n.* **1** next after second. **2** each of three equal parts of a thing. □ **thirdly** *adv.* [Old English: related to THREE]

third degree –*n.* long and severe questioning, esp. by police to obtain information or a confession. –*adj.* (**third-degree**) denoting burns of the most severe kind, affecting lower layers of tissue.

♦ **third-line forcing** *n.* forcing a buyer to take a supply of something not wanted as a condition of supplying a product that is wanted. The practice is deprecated by the Restrictive Practices Court.

---

third man *n.* fielder positioned near the boundary behind the slips.

third party *n.* **1** another party besides the two principals. **2** bystander etc.

♦ **third-party insurance** *n.* insurance of a person's legal liabilities to others. The insurer and the policyholder are the two parties to the insurance contract, any other person to whom there is a legal obligation is therefore a third party. Some forms of third-party insurance are compulsory, e.g. motorists must have third-party cover for any loss or damage suffered by members of the public as a result of their driving and employers must cover against any results of injury to employees at work. Professional indemnity insurance is a form of third-party insurance that is optional.

---

third person *n.* **1** = THIRD PARTY. **2** *Gram.* see PERSON 3.

third-rate *adj.* inferior; very poor.

third reading *n.* third presentation of a bill to a legislative assembly.

Third Reich *n.* the Nazi regime, 1933–45.

Third World (usu. prec. by *the*) see DEVELOPING COUNTRY.

thirst –*n.* **1** need to drink; discomfort caused by this. **2** desire, craving. –*v.* (often foll. by *for* or *after*) **1** feel thirst. **2** have a strong desire. [Old English]

thirsty *adj.* (**-ier, -iest**) **1** feeling thirst. **2** (of land, a season, etc.) dry or parched. **3** (often foll. by *for* or *after*) eager. **4** *colloq.* causing thirst (*thirsty work*). □ **thirstily** *adv.* **thirstiness** *n.* [Old English: related to THIRST]

thirteen /θɜːˈtiːn/ *adj.* & *n.* **1** one more than twelve. **2** symbol for this (13, xiii, XIII). **3** size etc. denoted by thirteen. □ **thirteenth** *adj.* & *n.* [Old English: related to THREE]

thirty /ˈθɜːtɪ/ *adj.* & *n.* (*pl.* **-ies**) **1** three times ten. **2** symbol for this (30, xxx, XXX). **3** (in *pl.*) numbers from 30 to 39, esp. the years of a century or of a person's life. □ **thirtieth** *adj.* & *n.* [Old English: related to THREE]

Thirty-nine Articles *n.pl.* points of doctrine assented to by those taking orders in the Church of England.

this /ðɪs/ –*demons. pron.* (*pl.* **these** /ðiːz/) **1** person or thing close at hand or indicated or already named or understood (*can you see this?*; *this is my cousin*). **2** (contrasted with *that*) the person or thing nearer to hand or more immediately in mind. –*demons. adj.* (*pl.* **these** /ðiːz/) **1** designating the person or thing close at hand etc. (cf. senses 1, 2 of *pron.*). **2** (of time) the present or current (*am busy all this week*). **3** *colloq.* (in narrative) designating a person or thing previously unmentioned (*then up came this policeman*). –*adv.* to the degree or extent indicated (*knew him when he was this high*). □ **this and that** *colloq.* various unspecified things. [Old English]

thistle /ˈθɪs(ə)l/ *n.* **1** prickly plant, usu. with globular heads of purple flowers. **2** this as the Scottish national emblem. [Old English]

thistledown *n.* light down containing thistle-seeds and blown about in the wind.

thistly *adj.* overgrown with thistles.

thither /ˈðɪðə(r)/ *adv. archaic* or *formal* to or towards that place. [Old English]

tho' (also **tho**) var. of THOUGH.

thole *n.* (in full **thole-pin**) **1** pin in the gunwale of a boat as the fulcrum for an oar. **2** each of two such pins forming a rowlock. [Old English]

♦ **Thomson** /ˈtɒms(ə)n/, **Kenneth Roy, Baron Thomson of Fleet** (1923–) Canadian newspaper proprietor. Chairman (1968–70) and co-president (1971–81) of Times Newspapers, he is chairman of the Thomson Corporation, of which he owns 73%, and a director of IBM (Canada) Ltd. and Toronto-Dominion Bank.

---

thong *n.* narrow strip of hide or leather. [Old English]

thorax /ˈθɔːræks/ *n.* (*pl.* **-races** /-rəˌsiːz/ or **-raxes**) *Anat.* & *Zool.* part of the trunk between the neck and the abdomen. □ **thoracic** /θɔːˈræsɪk/ *adj.* [Latin from Greek]

thorium /ˈθɔːrɪəm/ *n. Chem.* radioactive metallic element. [*Thor*, name of Scandinavian god of thunder]

thorn *n.* **1** sharp-pointed projection on a plant. **2** thorn-bearing shrub or tree. □ **thorn in one's flesh** (or **side**) constant nuisance. □ **thornless** *adj.* [Old English]

thorny *adj.* (**-ier, -iest**) **1** having many thorns. **2** problematic, causing disagreement. □ **thornily** *adv.* **thorniness** *n.* [Old English: related to THORN]

thorough /ˈθʌrə/ *adj.* **1** complete and unqualified; not superficial. **2** acting or done with great care and completeness. **3** absolute (*thorough nuisance*). □ **thoroughly** *adv.* **thoroughness** *n.* [related to THROUGH]

thoroughbred –*adj.* **1** of pure breed. **2** high-spirited. –*n.* thoroughbred animal, esp. a horse.

thoroughfare *n.* road or path open at both ends, esp. for traffic.

thoroughgoing *attrib. adj.* thorough; complete.

those *pl.* of THAT.

thou[1] /ðaʊ/ *pron.* (*obj.* **thee** /ðiː/; *poss.* **thy** or **thine**; *pl.* **ye** or **you**) *archaic* second person singular pronoun. [Old English]

■ **Usage** *Thou* has now been replaced by *you* except in some formal, liturgical, dialect, and poetic uses.

thou[2] /θaʊ/ *n.* (*pl.* same or **-s**) *colloq.* **1** thousand. **2** one thousandth. [abbreviation]

though /ðəʊ/ (also **tho'**) –*conj.* **1** despite the fact that; in spite of being (*though it was early we left*; *though annoyed, I agreed*). **2** (introducing a possibility) even if (*ask him though he may refuse*). **3** and yet; nevertheless. –*adv. colloq.* however; all the same. [Old Norse]

thought[1] /θɔːt/ *n.* **1** process or power of thinking; faculty of reason. **2** way of thinking associated with a particular time, group, etc. **3** sober reflection or consideration. **4** idea or piece of reasoning produced by thinking. **5** (foll. by *of* + verbal noun or *to* + infin.) partly formed intention (*had no thought to go*). **6** (usu. in *pl.*) what one is thinking; one's opinion. **7** (prec. by *a*) somewhat (*a thought arrogant*). □ **in thought** meditating. [Old English: related to THINK]

thought[2] *past* and *past part.* of THINK.

thoughtful *adj.* **1** engaged in or given to meditation. **2** (of a book, writer, etc.) giving signs of serious thought. **3** (often foll. by *of*) (of a person or conduct) considerate. □ **thoughtfully** *adv.* **thoughtfulness** *n.*

thoughtless *adj.* **1** careless of consequences or of others' feelings. **2** due to lack of thought. □ **thoughtlessly** *adv.* **thoughtlessness** *n.*

thought-reader *n.* person supposedly able to perceive another's thoughts.

thousand /ˈθaʊz(ə)nd/ *adj.* & *n.* (*pl.* **thousands** or (in sense 1) **thousand**) (in *sing.* prec. by *a* or *one*) **1** ten hundred. **2** symbol for this (1000, m, M). **3** (in *sing.* or *pl.*) *colloq.* large number. □ **thousandfold** *adj.* & *adv.* **thousandth** *adj.* & *n.* [Old English]

Thousand Islands **1** group of about 1500 islands in

North America, in the St Lawrence River. Some of the islands belong to Canada and some to the US. **2** group of about 100 Indonesian islands in the SW Java Sea.

Thrace /θreɪs/ region of SE Europe, an empire in ancient times now divided between Turkey, Greece, and Bulgaria. □ **Thracian** /ˈθreɪʃ(ə)n/ *adj.* & *n.*

thrall /θrɔːl/ *n. literary* **1** (often foll. by *of*, *to*) slave (of a person, or of a power or influence). **2** slavery (*in thrall*). □ **thraldom** *n.* [Old English from Old Norse]

thrash *v.* **1** beat or whip severely. **2** defeat thoroughly. **3** deliver repeated blows. **4** (foll. by *about*, *around*) move or fling (esp. the limbs) about violently. **5** = THRESH 1. □ **thrash out** discuss to a conclusion. [Old English]

thread /θred/ *–n.* **1 a** spun-out cotton, silk, or glass etc.; yarn. **b** length of this. **2** thin cord of twisted yarns used esp. in sewing and weaving. **3** continuous aspect of a thing (*the thread of life*; *thread of his argument*). **4** spiral ridge of a screw. *–v.* **1** pass a thread through (a needle). **2** put (beads) on a thread. **3** insert (a strip of material, e.g. film or magnetic tape) into equipment. **4** make (one's way) carefully through a crowded place, over a difficult route, etc. [Old English: related to THROW]

threadbare *adj.* **1** (of cloth) with the nap worn away and the thread visible. **2** (of a person) wearing such clothes. **3** hackneyed.

Threadneedle Street see OLD LADY OF THREADNEEDLE STREET.

threadworm *n.* parasitic threadlike worm.

threat /θret/ *n.* **1** declaration of an intention to punish or hurt if an order etc. is not obeyed. **2** indication of something undesirable coming (*threat of war*). **3** person or thing as a likely cause of harm etc. [Old English]

threaten *v.* **1** make a threat or threats against. **2** be a sign of (something undesirable). **3** (foll. by *to* + infin.) announce one's intention to do an undesirable thing. **4** (also *absol.*) warn of the infliction of (harm etc.). **5** (as **threatened** *adj.*) (of a species etc.) likely to become extinct. [Old English]

three *adj.* & *n.* **1 a** one more than two. **b** symbol for this (3, iii, III). **2** size etc. denoted by three. [Old English]

three-cornered *adj.* **1** triangular. **2** (of a contest etc.) between three parties.

three-decker *n.* **1** warship with three gun-decks. **2** thing with three levels or divisions.

three-dimensional *adj.* having or appearing to have length, breadth, and depth.

threefold *adj.* & *adv.* **1** three times as much or as many. **2** consisting of three parts.

3i *abbr.* Investors in Industry.

three-legged race *n.* running-race between pairs, one member of each pair having the left leg tied to the right leg of the other.

three-line whip *n.* written notice to MPs from their leader insisting on attendance at a debate and voting a certain way.

3M *abbr.* Minnesota Mining and Manufacturing Company.

threepence /ˈθrepəns, ˈθrʊp-/ *n.* sum of three pence.

threepenny /ˈθrepənɪ, ˈθrʊp-/ *attrib. adj.* costing three pence.

three-piece *–n.* three-piece suit or suite. *–attrib. adj.* (esp. of a suit or suite) consisting of three items.

three-ply *–adj.* of three strands or layers etc. *–n.* **1** three-ply wool. **2** three-ply wood.

three-point turn *n.* method of turning a vehicle round in a narrow space by moving forwards, backwards, and forwards again.

three-quarter *n.* (also **three-quarter back**) *Rugby* any of three or four players just behind the half-backs.

three-quarters *n.pl.* three parts out of four.

three Rs *n.pl.* (prec. by *the*) reading, writing, and arithmetic.

threescore *n.* & *adj. archaic* sixty.

threesome *n.* group of three persons.

three-way *adj.* involving three directions or participants.

threnody /ˈθrenədɪ/ *n.* (*pl.* **-ies**) song of lamentation or mourning. [Greek]

thresh *v.* **1** beat out or separate grain from (corn etc.). **2** = THRASH *v.* 4. □ **thresher** *n.* [Old English]

threshing-floor *n.* hard level floor for threshing esp. with flails.

threshold /ˈθreʃəʊld/ *n.* **1** strip of wood or stone forming the bottom of a doorway and crossed in entering a house etc. **2** point of entry or beginning. **3** limit below which a stimulus causes no reaction. [Old English: related to THRASH in the sense 'tread']

◆ **threshold agreement** *n.* agreement between an employer and employees (or their union) that pay will increase by a specified amount if the rate of inflation exceeds a specified figure in a specified period. Threshold agreements are seen by some as providing an inflationary pressure of their own but others claim that they reduce inflation by making it unnecessary for unions to press for excessive settlements to protect their members against inflation.

◆ **threshold effect** *n.* point at which advertising begins to show signs of increasing sales. As advertising is expensive, the threshold effect is important because it sets the minimum level for an advertising budget.

◆ **threshold price** see COMMON AGRICULTURAL POLICY.

---

threw *past* of THROW.

thrice *adv. archaic* or *literary* **1** three times. **2** (esp. in *comb.*) highly (*thrice-blessed*). [related to THREE]

thrift *n.* **1** frugality; careful use of money etc. **2** the sea pink. [Old Norse: related to THRIVE]

thriftless *adj.* wasteful.

thrifty *adj.* (**-ier**, **-iest**) economical. □ **thriftily** *adv.* **thriftiness** *n.*

thrill *–n.* **1** wave or nervous tremor of emotion or sensation (*a thrill of joy*). **2** throb, pulsation. *–v.* **1** (cause to) feel a thrill. **2** quiver or throb with or as with emotion. [Old English, = pierce: related to THROUGH]

thriller *n.* exciting or sensational story or play etc., esp. about crime or espionage.

thrips *n.* (*pl.* same) an insect harmful to plants. [Greek, = woodworm]

thrive *v.* (**-ving**; *past* **throve** or **thrived**; *past part.* **thriven** /ˈθrɪv(ə)n/ or **thrived**) **1** prosper, flourish. **2** grow rich. **3** (of a child, animal, or plant) grow vigorously. [Old Norse]

thro' var. of THROUGH.

throat *n.* **1 a** windpipe or gullet. **b** front part of the neck containing this. **2** *literary* narrow passage, entrance, or exit. □ **cut one's own throat** harm oneself or one's interests. **ram** (or **thrust**) **down a person's throat** force on a person's attention. [Old English]

throaty *adj.* (**-ier**, **-iest**) (of a voice) hoarsely resonant. □ **throatily** *adv.* **throatiness** *n.*

throb *–v.* (**-bb-**) **1** pulsate, esp. with more than the usual force or rapidity. **2** vibrate with a persistent rhythm or with emotion. *–n.* **1** throbbing. **2** (esp. violent) pulsation. [imitative]

throe *n.* (usu. in *pl.*) violent pang, esp. of childbirth or death. □ **in the throes of** struggling with the task of. [Old English, alteration of original *throwe*, perhaps by association with *woe*]

thrombosis /θrɒmˈbəʊsɪs/ *n.* (*pl.* **-boses** /-siːz/) coagulation of the blood in a blood-vessel or organ. [Greek, = curdling]

throne *–n.* **1** chair of State for a sovereign or bishop etc. **2** sovereign power (*came to the throne*). *–v.* (**-ning**) enthrone. [Greek *thrones*]

throng *–n.* (often foll. by *of*) crowd, esp. of people. *–v.* **1** come in great numbers (*crowds thronged to the stadium*). **2** flock into or crowd round; fill with or as with a crowd. [Old English]

throstle /ˈθrɒs(ə)l/ *n.* song thrush. [Old English]

throttle /ˈθrɒt(ə)l/ *–n.* **1 a** valve controlling the flow of fuel or steam etc. in an engine. **b** (in full **throttle-lever**) lever or pedal operating this valve. **2** throat, gullet, or windpipe. *–v.* (**-ling**) **1** choke or strangle. **2** prevent the utterance etc. of. **3** control (an engine or steam etc.) with a throttle. □ **throttle back** (or **down**) reduce the speed of (an engine or vehicle) by throttling. [perhaps from THROAT]

through /θruː/ (also **thro'**, *US* **thru**) *–prep.* **1 a** from end to end or side to side of. **b** going in one side or end and out the other of. **2** between or among (*swam through the waves*). **3** from beginning to end of (*read through the letter; went through many difficulties*). **4** because of; by the agency, means, or fault of (*lost it through carelessness*). **5** *US* up to and including (*Monday through Friday*). *–adv.* **1** through a thing; from side to side, end to end, or beginning to end. **2** so as to be connected by telephone (*will put you through*). *–attrib. adj.* **1** (of a journey, route, etc.) done without a change of line or vehicle etc. or with one ticket. **2** (of traffic) going through a place to its destination. **3** (of a road) open at both ends. □ **be through** *colloq.* **1** (often foll. by *with*) have finished. **2** (often foll. by *with*) cease to have dealings. **3** have no further prospects. **through and through** thoroughly, completely. [Old English]

throughout /θruːˈaʊt/ *–prep.* right through; from end to end of. *–adv.* in every part or respect.

throughput *n.* amount of material, work, etc. put through a process in a given period, esp. in manufacturing or computing.

throve *past* of THRIVE.

throw /θrəʊ/ *–v.* (*past* **threw** /θruː/; *past part.* **thrown**) **1** propel with force through the air. **2** force violently into, or compel to be in, a specified position or state (*thrown on the rocks; threw themselves down; thrown out of work*). **3** turn or move (part of the body) quickly or suddenly (*threw an arm out*). **4** project or cast (light, a shadow, etc.). **5 a** bring to the ground in wrestling. **b** (of a horse) unseat (its rider). **6** *colloq.* disconcert (*the question threw me*). **7** (foll. by *on, off,* etc.) put (clothes etc.) hastily on or off etc. **8 a** cause (dice) to fall on a table etc. **b** obtain (a specified number) by throwing dice. **9** cause to pass or extend suddenly to another state or position (*threw a bridge across the river*). **10** operate (a switch or lever). **11** form on a potter's wheel. **12** have (a fit or tantrum etc.). **13** give (a party). *–n.* **1** act of throwing or being thrown. **2** distance a thing is or may be thrown. **3** (prec. by *a*) *slang* each; per item (*sold at £10 a throw*). □ **throw a page** *Computing* print next line on a new page. **throw away 1** discard as useless or unwanted. **2** waste or fail to make use of (an opportunity etc.). **throw back 1** revert to ancestral character. **2** (usu. in *passive*; foll. by *on*) compel to rely on. **throw in 1** interpose (a word or remark). **2** include at no extra cost. **3** throw (a football) from the edge of the pitch where it has gone out of play. **throw in the towel** (or **sponge**) admit defeat. **throw off 1** discard; contrive to get rid of. **2** write or utter in an offhand manner. **throw oneself at** seek blatantly as a sexual partner. **throw oneself into** engage vigorously in. **throw oneself on** (or **upon**) rely completely on. **throw open** (often foll. by *to*) **1** cause to be suddenly or widely open. **2** make accessible. **throw out 1** put out forcibly or suddenly. **2** discard as unwanted. **3** reject (a proposal). **throw over** desert, abandon. **throw together 1** assemble hastily. **2** bring into casual contact. **throw up 1** abandon. **2** resign from. **3** *colloq.* vomit. **4** erect hastily. **5** bring to notice. [Old English, = twist]

throw-away *attrib. adj.* **1** meant to be thrown away after (one) use. **2** spoken in a deliberately casual way. **3** disposed to throwing things away (*throw-away society*).

throwback *n.* **1** reversion to ancestral character. **2** instance of this.

throw-in *n.* throwing in of a football during play.

thru *US* var. of THROUGH.

thrum[1] *–v.* (**-mm-**) **1** play (a stringed instrument) monotonously or unskilfully. **2** (often foll. by *on*) drum idly. *–n.* **1** such playing. **2** resulting sound. [imitative]

thrum[2] *n.* **1** unwoven end of a warp-thread, or the whole of such ends, left when the finished web is cut away. **2** any short loose thread. [Old English]

thrush[1] *n.* any of various songbirds, esp. the song thrush and mistle thrush. [Old English]

thrush[2] *n.* **1** fungous disease, esp. of children, affecting the mouth and throat. **2** similar disease of the vagina. [origin unknown]

thrust *–v.* (*past* and *past part.* **thrust**) **1** push with a sudden impulse or with force. **2** (foll. by *on*) impose (a thing) forcibly; enforce acceptance of (a thing). **3** (foll. by *at, through*) pierce, stab; lunge suddenly. **4** make (one's way) forcibly. **5** (as **thrusting** *adj.*) aggressive, ambitious. *–n.* **1** sudden or forcible push or lunge. **2** propulsive force produced by a jet or rocket engine. **3** strong attempt to penetrate an enemy's line or territory. **4** remark aimed at a person. **5** stress between the parts of an arch etc. **6** (often foll. by *of*) chief theme or gist of remarks etc. [Old Norse]

thud *–n.* low dull sound as of a blow on a non-resonant surface. *–v.* (**-dd-**) make or fall with a thud. [probably Old English]

thug *n.* **1** violent ruffian. **2** (**Thug**) *hist.* member of a religious organization of robbers and assassins in India. □ **thuggery** *n.* **thuggish** *adj.* [Hindi]

thulium /ˈθjuːlɪəm/ *n.* metallic element of the lanthanide series. [Latin *Thule*, name of a region in the remote north]

thumb /θʌm/ *–n.* **1** short thicker finger on the human hand, set apart from the other four. **2** part of a glove etc. for a thumb. *–v.* **1** wear or soil (pages etc.) with a thumb. **2** turn over pages with or as with a thumb (*thumbed through the directory*). **3** request or get (a lift) by signalling with a raised thumb. **4** use the thumb in a gesture. □ **thumb one's nose** = *cock a snook* (see SNOOK). **thumbs down** indication of rejection. **thumbs up** indication of satisfaction or approval. **under a person's thumb** completely dominated by a person. [Old English]

thumb index *n.* set of lettered grooves cut down the side of a book for easy reference.

thumbnail *n.* **1** nail of a thumb. **2** (*attrib.*) concise (*thumbnail sketch*).

thumbprint *n.* impression of a thumb esp. for identification.

thumbscrew *n.* instrument of torture for crushing the thumbs.

thump *–v.* **1** beat or strike heavily, esp. with the fist. **2** throb strongly. **3** (foll. by *at, on,* etc.) knock loudly. *–n.* **1** heavy blow. **2** dull sound of this. [imitative]

thumping *adj. colloq.* (esp. as an intensifier) huge (*a thumping lie; a thumping great house*).

thunder /ˈθʌndə(r)/ *–n.* **1** loud noise caused by lightning and due to the expansion of rapidly heated air. **2** resounding loud deep noise (*thunders of applause*). **3** strong censure or denunciation. *–v.* **1** (prec. by *it* as subject) thunder sounds (*it is thundering; if it thunders*). **2** make or proceed with a noise like thunder. **3** utter (threats, compliments, etc.) loudly. **4** (foll. by *against* etc.) make violent threats etc. against. □ **steal a person's thunder** see STEAL. □ **thundery** *adj.* [Old English]

Thunder Bay city and major port in E Canada, in SW Ontario on an inlet of Lake Superior; wheat is exported, and industries include shipbuilding, timber, pulp and paper, mining, and the manufacture of aircraft and buses; pop. (1991) 113 746.

thunderbolt *n.* **1** flash of lightning with a simultaneous crash of thunder. **2** unexpected occurrence or announcement. **3** supposed bolt or shaft as a destructive agent, esp. as an attribute of a god.

thunderclap *n.* **1** crash of thunder. **2** something startling or unexpected.

thundercloud *n.* cumulus cloud charged with electricity and producing thunder and lightning.

thunder-fly *n.* = THRIPS.

thundering *adj. colloq.* (esp. as an intensifier) huge (*a thundering nuisance*; *a thundering great bruise*).

thunderous *adj.* **1** like thunder. **2** very loud.

thunderstorm *n.* storm with thunder and lightning and usu. heavy rain or hail.

thunderstruck *predic. adj.* amazed.

Thur. *abbr.* (also **Thurs.**) Thursday.

thurible /'θjʊərɪb(ə)l/ *n.* censer. [Latin *thus thur-* incense]

Thuringia /θjʊə'rɪndʒɪə/ densely forested state (*Land*) in central Germany; pop. (est. 1995) 2 517 800; capital, Erfurt.

Thursday /'θɜːzdeɪ/ –*n.* day of the week following Wednesday. –*adv. colloq.* **1** on Thursday. **2** (**Thursdays**) on Thursdays; each Thursday. [Old English]

thus /ðʌs/ *adv. formal* **1 a** in this way. **b** as indicated. **2 a** accordingly. **b** as a result or inference. **3** to this extent; so (*thus far*; *thus much*). [Old English]

thwack –*v.* hit with a heavy blow. –*n.* heavy blow. [imitative]

thwart /θwɔːt/ –*v.* frustrate or foil (a person, plan, etc.). –*n.* rower's seat. [Old Norse, = across]

thy /ðaɪ/ *poss. pron.* (*attrib.*) (also **thine** *predic.* or before a vowel) *archaic* of or belonging to thee. [from THINE]

■ **Usage** *Thy* has now been replaced by *your* except in some formal, liturgical, dialect, and poetic uses.

thyme /taɪm/ *n.* any of several herbs with aromatic leaves. [Greek *thumon*]

thymol /'θaɪmɒl/ *n.* antiseptic obtained from oil of thyme.

thymus /'θaɪməs/ *n.* (*pl.* **thymi** /-maɪ/) lymphoid organ situated in the neck of vertebrates. [Greek]

thyroid /'θaɪrɔɪd/ *n.* (in full **thyroid gland**) **1** large ductless gland in the neck of vertebrates, secreting a hormone which regulates growth and development. **2** extract prepared from the thyroid gland of animals and used in treating goitre etc. [Greek *thureos* oblong shield]

thyroid cartilage *n.* large cartilage of the larynx, forming the Adam's apple.

thyself *pron. archaic* emphat. & refl. form of THOU[1], THEE.

TI –*international civil aircraft marking* Costa Rica.

Ti *symb.* titanium.

ti var. of TE.

Tianjin /ˌtɪen'dʒɪn/ (also **Tientsin** /-'tsɪn/) port and third-largest city in China, in Hubei province; manufactures include textiles (esp. carpets), chemicals, and machinery; pop. (est. 1991) 5 770 000.

tiara /tɪ'ɑːrə/ *n.* **1** jewelled ornamental band worn on the front of a woman's hair. **2** three-crowned diadem worn by a pope. □ **tiaraed** *adj.* [Latin from Greek]

Tibet /tɪ'bet/ (Chinese **Xizang** /ʃiː'zæŋ/) autonomous region of China, on a high plateau surrounded by mountains, on the N frontier of India; pop. (est. 1995) 2 360 000; capital, Lhasa. Agriculture, concentrated in the valleys, is based on the cultivation of barley. Tibet was independent from 1911 to 1950, when China invaded the country and established a Communist administration; it was made an autonomous region in 1965.

tibia /'tɪbɪə/ *n.* (*pl.* **tibiae** /-bɪˌiː/) *Anat.* inner of two bones extending from the knee to the ankle. □ **tibial** *adj.* [Latin]

TIBOR /'tiːbɔː(r)/ *abbr. Finance* Tokyo Inter Bank Offered Rate.

tic *n.* (in full **nervous tic**) occasional involuntary contraction of the muscles, esp. of the face. [French from Italian]

tick[1] –*n.* **1** slight recurring click, esp. that of a watch or clock. **2** *colloq.* moment. **3** mark ( ) to denote correctness, check items in a list, etc. **4** (also **point**) smallest increment of price fluctuation in a commodity market. –*v.* **1** (of a clock etc.) make ticks. **2 a** mark with a tick. **b** (often foll. by *off*) mark (an item) with a tick in checking. □ **tick off** *colloq.* reprimand. **tick over 1** (of an engine etc.) idle. **2** (of a person, project, etc.) be functioning at a basic level. **what makes a person tick** *colloq.* person's motivation. [probably imitative]

tick[2] *n.* **1** parasitic arachnid on the skin of dogs, cattle, etc. **2** parasitic insect on sheep and birds etc. [Old English]

tick[3] *n. colloq.* credit (*buy goods on tick*). [apparently an abbreviation of TICKET in *on the ticket*]

tick[4] *n.* **1** cover of a mattress or pillow. **2** = TICKING. [Greek *thēkē* case]

ticker *n. colloq.* **1** heart. **2** watch. **3** *US* = TAPE MACHINE 1.

ticker-tape *n.* **1** paper strip from a tape machine. **2** this or similar material thrown from windows etc. to greet a celebrity.

ticket /'tɪkɪt/ –*n.* **1** written or printed piece of paper or card entitling the holder to enter a place, participate in an event, travel by public transport, etc. **2** notification of a traffic offence etc. (*parking ticket*). **3** certificate of discharge from the army. **4** certificate of qualification as a ship's master, pilot, etc. **5** price etc. label. **6** esp. *US* **a** list of candidates put forward by one group, esp. a political party. **b** principles of a party. **7** (prec. by *the*) *colloq.* what is correct or needed. –*v.* (**-t-**) attach a ticket to. [obsolete French *étiquet*]

ticking *n.* stout usu. striped material used to cover mattresses etc. [from TICK[4]]

tickle /'tɪk(ə)l/ –*v.* (**-ling**) **1 a** touch or stroke (a person etc.) playfully or lightly so as to produce laughter and spasmodic movement. **b** produce this sensation. **2** excite agreeably; amuse. **3** catch (a trout etc.) by rubbing it so that it moves backwards into the hand. –*n.* **1** act of tickling. **2** tickling sensation. □ **tickled pink** (or **to death**) *colloq.* extremely amused or pleased. □ **tickly** *adj.* [probably frequentative of TICK[1]]

ticklish *adj.* **1** sensitive to tickling. **2** (of a matter or person) difficult to handle.

tick-tack *n.* a kind of manual semaphore used by racecourse bookmakers.

tick-tock *n.* ticking of a large clock etc.

tidal /'taɪd(ə)l/ *adj.* relating to, like, or affected by tides. □ **tidally** *adv.*

tidal wave *n.* **1** exceptionally large ocean wave, esp. one caused by an underwater earthquake. **2** widespread manifestation of feeling etc.

tidbit *US* var. of TITBIT.

tiddler *n. colloq.* **1** small fish, esp. a stickleback or minnow. **2** unusually small thing. [perhaps related to TIDDLY[2] and *tittlebat*, a childish form of *stickleback*]

tiddly[1] *adj.* (**-ier, -iest**) *colloq.* slightly drunk. [origin unknown]

tiddly[2] *adj.* (**-ier, -iest**) *colloq.* little.

tiddly-wink /'tɪdlɪwɪŋk/ *n.* **1** counter flicked with another into a cup etc. **2** (in *pl.*) this game. [perhaps related to TIDDLY[1]]

tide *n.* **1 a** periodic rise and fall of the sea due to the attraction of the moon and sun. **b** water as affected by this. **2** time or season (usu. in *comb.*: *Whitsuntide*). **3** marked trend of opinion, fortune, or events. □ **tide over** (**-ding**) provide (a person) with what is needed during a difficult period etc. [Old English, = TIME]

tidemark *n.* **1** mark made by the tide at high water. **2 a** line left round a bath by the dirty water. **b** *colloq.* line between washed and unwashed parts of a person's body.

tidetable *n.* table indicating the times of high and low tides.

tideway *n.* tidal part of a river.

tidings /'taɪdɪŋz/ *n.* (as *sing.* or *pl.*) *archaic* or *joc.* news. [Old English, probably from Old Norse]

tidy –*adj.* (**-ier, -iest**) **1** neat, orderly. **2** (of a person) methodical. **3** *colloq.* considerable (*a tidy sum*). –*n.* (*pl.* **-ies**) **1** receptacle for holding small objects etc. **2** esp. *US* cover for a chair-back etc. –*v.* (**-ies, -ied**) (also *absol.*; often foll. by *up*) put in good order; make (oneself, a room, etc.) tidy. □ **tidily** *adv.* **tidiness** *n.* [originally = timely etc., from TIDE]

tie /taɪ/ *–v.* (**tying**) **1** attach or fasten with string or cord etc. **2 a** form (a string, ribbon, shoelace, necktie, etc.) into a knot or bow. **b** form (a knot or bow) in this way. **3** (often foll. by *down*) restrict (a person) in some way (*is tied to his job*). **4** (often foll. by *with*) achieve the same score or place as another competitor (*tied with her for first place*). **5** hold (rafters etc.) together by a crosspiece etc. **6** *Mus.* unite (written notes) by a tie. *–n.* **1** cord or wire etc. used for fastening. **2** strip of material worn round the collar and tied in a knot at the front. **3** thing that unites or restricts persons (*family ties*). **4** draw, dead heat, or equality of score among competitors. **5** match between any pair from a group of competing players or teams. **6** (also **tie-beam** etc.) rod or beam holding parts of a structure together. **7** *Mus.* curved line above or below two notes of the same pitch indicating that they are to be played without a break between them. □ **tie in** (foll. by *with*) bring into or have a close association or agreement. **tie up 1** bind securely with cord etc. **2** invest or reserve (capital etc.) so that it is not immediately available for use. **3** (often foll. by *with*) = *tie in*. **4** (usu. in *passive*) fully occupy (a person). **5** bring to a satisfactory conclusion. [Old English]

tie-break *n.* (also **tie-breaker**) means of deciding a winner from competitors who have tied.

tied *attrib. adj.* **1** (of a house) occupied subject to the tenant's working for its owner. **2** (of a public house etc.) bound to supply the products of a particular brewery only.

◆ **tied loan** *n.* loan made by one nation to another on condition that the money loaned is spent buying goods or services in the lending nation. It thus helps the lending nation, by providing employment, as well as the borrowing nation.

◆ **tied outlet** *n.* retail outlet that is obliged to sell only the products of one producer (and possibly other non-competing products). The outlet is usu. owned by the producer; in other cases the outlet agrees to become tied in return for financial concessions.

tie-dye *n.* (also **tie and dye**) method of producing dyed patterns by tying string etc. to keep the dye away from parts of the fabric.

tie-in *n.* **1** connection or association. **2** joint promotion of related commodities etc. (e.g. a book and a film).

Tientsin see TIANJIN.

tie-pin *n.* ornamental pin for holding a tie in place.

tier *n.* row, rank, or unit of a structure, as one of several placed one above another (*tiers of seats*). □ **tiered** *adj.* [French *tire* from *tirer* draw, elongate]

tiercel var. of TERCEL.

Tierra del Fuego /tɪˌerə del ˈfweɪgəʊ/ archipelago separated from the S tip of South America by the Strait of Magellan and divided between Chile and Argentina; sheep farming and oil are the main sources of revenue.

tie-up *n.* connection, association.

TIF *abbr.* **1** telephone interference (or influence) factor. **2** (French) Transports Internationaux par Chemin de Fer (= International Rail Transport).

tiff *n.* slight or petty quarrel. [origin unknown]

tiffin /ˈtɪfɪn/ *n. Ind.* light meal, esp. lunch. [apparently from *tiffing* sipping]

Tiflis see TBILISI.

tiger /ˈtaɪgə(r)/ *n.* **1** large Asian animal of the cat family, with a yellow-brown coat with black stripes. **2** fierce, energetic, or formidable person. **3** (**Tigers**) *colloq.* see TIGR. [Greek *tigris*]

tiger-cat *n.* any moderate-sized feline resembling the tiger, e.g. the ocelot.

tiger lily *n.* tall garden lily with dark-spotted orange flowers.

◆ **tiger markets** *n.pl. colloq.* the four most important markets in the Pacific Basin after Japan. They are Hong Kong, South Korea, Singapore, and Taiwan. Cf. DRAGON MARKETS.

tiger moth *n.* moth with richly spotted and streaked wings.

tight /taɪt/ *–adj.* **1** closely held, drawn, fastened, fitting, etc. (*tight hold*; *tight skirt*). **2** too closely fitting. **3** impermeable, impervious, esp. (in *comb.*) to a specified thing (*watertight*). **4** tense; stretched. **5** *colloq.* drunk. **6** *colloq.* stingy. **7** (of money or materials) not easily obtainable. **8 a** (of precautions, a programme, etc.) stringent, demanding. **b** presenting difficulties (*tight situation*). **9** produced by or requiring great exertion or pressure (*tight squeeze*). *–adv.* tightly (*hold tight!*). □ **tightly** *adv.* **tightness** *n.* [Old Norse]

tight corner *n.* (also **tight place** or **spot**) difficult situation.

tighten *v.* make or become tighter.

tight-fisted *adj.* stingy.

tight-lipped *adj.* with or as with the lips compressed to restrain emotion or speech; determinedly reticent.

◆ **tight money** *n.* = DEAR MONEY.

tightrope *n.* rope stretched tightly high above the ground, on which acrobats perform.

tights *n.pl.* **1** thin close-fitting wool or nylon etc. garment covering the legs, feet, and the lower part of the torso, worn by women and girls. **2** similar garment worn by a dancer, acrobat, etc.

◆ **TIGR** /ˈtaɪgə/ *abbr.* Treasury Investment Growth Receipts, zero-coupon bonds linked to US Treasury bonds. Denominated in dollars, their semi-annual compounding yield is taxed in the UK as income in the year of encashment or redemption. These bonds are often known as **Tigers**.

Tigre /ˈtiːgreɪ/ (also **Tigray**) autonomous region in N Ethiopia; pop. (est. 1993) 2 999 948; capital, Mekele. Crops include cereals, coffee, and cotton, but agriculture is often badly affected by drought. Secessionist rebels succeeded in overthrowing the Ethiopian government in 1991 and established a transitional administration (see ETHIOPIA).

tigress /ˈtaɪgrɪs/ *n.* female tiger.

Tijuana /tɪˈwɑːnə/ town and resort in NW Mexico, just S of the US frontier; pop. (1990) 698 752.

tike var. of TYKE.

tilde /ˈtɪldə/ *n.* mark (˜) put over a letter, e.g. over a Spanish *n* when pronounced *ny* (as in *señor*). [Latin: related to TITLE]

tile *–n.* **1** thin slab of concrete or baked clay etc. used for roofing or paving etc. **2** similar slab of glazed pottery, cork, linoleum, etc., for covering a wall, floor, etc. **3** thin flat piece used in a game (esp. in mah-jong). *–v.* (**-ling**) cover with tiles. □ **on the tiles** *colloq.* having a spree. □ **tiler** *n.* [Latin *tegula*]

tiling *n.* **1** process of fixing tiles. **2** area of tiles.

till[1] *–prep.* **1** up to or as late as (*wait till six o'clock*). **2** up to the time of (*faithful till death*). *–conj.* **1** up to the time when (*wait till I return*). **2** so long that (*laughed till I cried*). [Old Norse: related to TILL[3]]

■ **Usage** In all senses, *till* can be replaced by *until* which is more formal in style.

till[2] *n.* drawer for money in a shop or bank etc., esp. with a device recording the amount of each purchase. [origin unknown]

till[3] *v.* cultivate (land). □ **tiller** *n.* [Old English, = strive for]

tillage *n.* **1** preparation of land for growing crops. **2** tilled land.

tiller *n.* bar fitted to a boat's rudder to turn it in steering. [Anglo-French *telier* weaver's beam]

tilt *–v.* **1** (cause to) assume a sloping position; heel over. **2** (foll. by *at*) strike, thrust, or run at, with a weapon. **3** (foll. by *with*) engage in a contest. *–n.* **1** tilting. **2** sloping position. **3** (of medieval knights etc.) charging with a lance against an opponent or at a mark. **4** attack, esp. with argument or satire (*have a tilt at*). □ **full** (or **at full**)

tilt 1 at full speed. **2** with full force. **tilt at windmills** see WINDMILL. [Old English, = unsteady]

tilth *n.* **1** tillage, cultivation. **2** tilled soil. [Old English: related to TILL[3]]

Timaru /ˈtɪməˌruː/ seaport and resort in New Zealand, on the E coast of South Island; exports include wool, grain, and meat from the surrounding agricultural region; pop. (1994) 27 000.

timber *n.* **1** wood prepared for building, carpentry, etc. **2** piece of wood or beam, esp. as the rib of a vessel. **3** large standing trees. **4** (esp. as *int.*) warning cry that a tree is about to fall. [Old English, = building]

timbered *adj.* **1** made wholly or partly of timber. **2** (of country) wooded.

timberline *n.* line or level above which no trees grow.

timbre /ˈtæmbə(r), ˈtæ̃brə/ *n.* distinctive character of a musical sound or voice apart from its pitch and volume. [Greek: related to TYMPANUM]

timbrel /ˈtɪmbr(ə)l/ *n. archaic* tambourine. [French: related to TIMBRE]

Timbuktu /ˌtɪmbʌkˈtuː/ (also **Tombouctou**) town in Mali; pop. (1987) 31 925.

time –*n.* **1** indefinite continued progress of existence, events, etc., in the past, present, and future, regarded as a whole. **2** progress of this as affecting persons or things. **3** portion of time belonging to particular events or circumstances (*the time of the Plague*; *prehistoric times*). **4** allotted or available portion of time (*had no time to eat*). **5** point of time, esp. in hours and minutes (*the time is 7.30*). **6** (prec. by *a*) indefinite period. **7** time or an amount of time as reckoned by a conventional standard (*eight o'clock New York time*; *the time allowed is one hour*). **8** occasion (*last time*). **9** moment etc. suitable for a purpose etc. (*the time to act*). **10** (in *pl.*) expressing multiplication (*five times six is thirty*). **11** lifetime (*will last my time*). **12** (in *sing.* or *pl.*) conditions of life or of a period (*hard times*). **13** *slang* prison sentence (*is doing time*). **14** apprenticeship (*served his time*). **15** period of gestation. **16** date or expected date of childbirth or death. **17** measured time spent in work. **18 a** any of several rhythmic patterns of music. **b** duration of a note. –*v.* (**-ming**) **1** choose the time for. **2** do at a chosen or correct time. **3** arrange the time of arrival of. **4** ascertain the time taken by. □ **against time** with utmost speed, so as to finish by a specified time. **ahead of time** earlier than expected. **all the time 1** during the whole of the time referred to (often despite some contrary expectation etc.). **2** constantly. **at one time 1** in a known but unspecified past period. **2** simultaneously. **at the same time 1** simultaneously. **2** nevertheless. **at times** intermittently. **for the time being** until some other arrangement is made. **half the time** *colloq.* as often as not. **have no time for 1** be unable or unwilling to spend time on. **2** dislike. **have a time of it** undergo trouble or difficulty. **in no time 1** very soon. **2** very quickly. **in time 1** not late, punctual. **2** eventually. **3** in accordance with a given rhythm. **keep time** move or sing etc. in time. **pass the time of day** *colloq.* exchange a greeting or casual remarks. **time after time 1** on many occasions. **2** in many instances. **time and** (or **time and time) again** on many occasions. **the time of one's life** period of exceptional enjoyment. **time out of mind** a longer time than anyone can remember. **time was** there was a time. [Old English]

time and a half *n.* one and a half times the normal rate of payment.

◆ **time-and-motion study** *n.* method of finding the most efficient way of performing a complex task by breaking the task into small steps and measuring the time taken to perform each step. This enables standards of performance to be set. These standards can then be used to plan and control production, estimate prices and delivery times, and devise incentive schemes.

◆ **time bargain** *n. Finance* contract in which securities have to be delivered at some date in the future.

time bomb *n.* bomb designed to explode at a pre-set time.

time capsule *n.* box etc. containing objects typical of the present time, buried for future discovery.

◆ **time card** *n.* card used with a time clock to record arrival and departure times and hence the number of hours an employee spends at work. Wages are paid on the basis of hours spent at work as shown on the time card.

◆ **time charter** *n.* hire of a ship or aircraft for a specified period of time rather than for a specified number of voyages.

time clock *n.* clock with a device for recording workers' hours of work.

◆ **time deposit** *n.* deposit of money in an interest-bearing account for a specified period.

time division multiplexing (also **TDM**) see MULTIPLEXER.

time exposure *n.* exposure of photographic film for longer than the slowest normal shutter setting.

time-honoured *adj.* esteemed by tradition or through custom.

timekeeper *n.* **1** person who records time, esp. of workers or in a game. **2 a** watch or clock as regards accuracy (*a good timekeeper*). **b** person as regards punctuality. □ **timekeeping** *n.*

time-lag *n.* interval of time between a cause and effect.

timeless *adj.* not affected by the passage of time. □ **timelessly** *adv.* **timelessness** *n.*

time-limit *n.* limit of time within which a task must be done.

timely *adj.* (**-ier, -iest**) opportune; coming at the right time. □ **timeliness** *n.*

timeout *n. Computing* condition that occurs when a process waiting for either an external event or the expiry of a pre-set time interval reaches the end of the time interval before the external event has been detected. If, for example, the process has sent a message and no acknowledgement has been detected at the end of the pre-set time period, then the process may take appropriate action, e.g. retransmitting the message.

timepiece *n.* clock or watch.

◆ **time preference** *n. Econ.* tendency of individuals to prefer current consumption rather than consumption in the future. It has been quantified as the sum required by an individual as compensation for postponing consumption, expressed as a percentage of income. The **rate of time preference** can be expressed as the interest rate required.

timer *n.* person or device that measures or records time taken.

◆ **time rate** *n.* rate of pay expressed as a sum of money paid to an individual for the time worked.

time-served *adj.* having completed a period of apprenticeship or training.

time-server *n. derog.* person who changes his or her view to suit the prevailing circumstances, fashion, etc. □ **time-serving** *adj.*

time-share *n.* share in a property under a time-sharing scheme.

time-sharing *n.* **1** use of a holiday home at contractually agreed different times by several joint owners. **2** operation of a computer system whereby the time of a computer can be shared among several jobs, a brief period being allocated (by the operating system) to each job in turn. During such a period the job is permitted to use the resources of the computer, i.e. the processor, main store, etc. A multi-access system relies on time-sharing.

time sheet *n.* sheet of paper for recording hours of work etc.

time-shift –*v.* move from one time to another, esp. record (a television programme) for later viewing. –*n.* movement from one time to another (*the continual time-shifts make the plot difficult to follow*).

time signal *n.* audible signal of the exact time of day.

time signature *n. Mus.* indication of tempo following a clef.

time switch *n.* switch acting automatically at a pre-set time.

timetable –*n.* list of times at which events are scheduled to take place, esp. the arrival and departure of transport or a sequence of lessons. –*v.* (**-ling**) include in or arrange to a timetable; schedule.

♦ **time value** *n. Finance* market value of an option over and above its intrinsic value.

---

time zone *n.* range of longitudes where a common standard time is used.

timid *adj.* (**timider, timidest**) easily frightened; apprehensive. □ **timidity** /-ˈmɪdɪtɪ/ *n.* **timidly** *adv.* [Latin *timeo* fear]

timing *n.* **1** way an action or process is timed. **2** regulation of the opening and closing of valves in an internal-combustion engine.

Timişoara /ˌtɪmɪˈʃwɑːrə/ industrial city and centre of commerce in W Romania; pop. (est. 1993) 325 359.

Timor /ˈtiːmɔː(r)/ Indonesian island, the largest of the Lesser Sunda Islands in the S Malay Archipelago; products include coffee, coconuts, and sandalwood. The island was formerly divided into Dutch West Timor and Portuguese East Timor. In 1950 West Timor was absorbed into the newly formed Republic of Indonesia and in 1976 East Timor was annexed by Indonesia following its unilateral declaration of independence the previous year. Severe repression of continuing East Timorese demonstrations against Indonesian rule have been widely condemned. □ **Timorese** /-ɔːˈriːz/ *adj.* & *n.*

timorous /ˈtɪmərəs/ *adj.* **1** timid. **2** frightened. □ **timorously** *adv.* [medieval Latin: related to TIMID]

timpani /ˈtɪmpənɪ/ *n.pl.* (also **tympani**) kettledrums. □ **timpanist** *n.* [Italian, pl. of *timpano* = TYMPANUM]

TIMS *abbr.* The Institute of Management Sciences.

TIN *abbr. US* taxpayer identification number.

tin –*n.* **1** silvery-white metallic element, used esp. in alloys and in making tin plate. **2** container made of tin or tinned iron, esp. airtight for preserving food. **3** = TIN PLATE. –*v.* (**-nn-**) **1** seal (food) in a tin for preservation. **2** cover or coat with tin. [Old English]

tin can *n.* tin container, esp. an empty one.

tincture /ˈtɪŋktʃə(r)/ –*n.* (often foll. by *of*) **1** slight flavour or trace. **2** tinge (of a colour). **3** medicinal solution (of a drug) in alcohol (*tincture of quinine*). –*v.* (**-ring**) **1** colour slightly; tinge, flavour. **2** (often foll. by *with*) affect slightly (with a quality). [Latin: related to TINGE]

tinder *n.* dry substance that readily catches fire from a spark. □ **tindery** *adj.* [Old English]

tinder-box *n. hist.* box containing tinder, flint, and steel, formerly used for kindling fires.

tine *n.* prong, tooth, or point of a fork, comb, antler, etc. [Old English]

tin foil *n.* foil made of tin, aluminium, or tin alloy, used for wrapping food.

ting –*n.* tinkling sound as of a bell. –*v.* (cause to) emit this sound. [imitative]

tinge –*v.* (**-ging**) (often foll. by *with*; often in *passive*) **1** colour slightly. **2** affect slightly. –*n.* **1** tendency towards or trace of some colour. **2** slight admixture of a feeling or quality. [Latin *tingo tinct-* dye]

tingle /ˈtɪŋg(ə)l/ –*v.* (**-ling**) **1** feel a slight prickling, stinging, or throbbing sensation. **2** cause this (*the reply tingled in my ears*). –*n.* tingling sensation. □ **tingly** *adj.* [probably from TINKLE]

tin hat *n. colloq.* military steel helmet.

tinker –*n.* **1** itinerant mender of kettles and pans etc. **2** *Scot.* & *Ir.* gypsy. **3** *colloq.* mischievous person or animal. **4** spell of tinkering. –*v.* **1** (foll. by *at, with*) work in an amateurish or desultory way. **2** work as a tinker. [origin unknown]

tinkle /ˈtɪŋk(ə)l/ –*v.* (**-ling**) (cause to) make a succession of short light ringing sounds. –*n.* **1** tinkling sound. **2** *colloq.* telephone call. □ **tinkly** *adj.* [imitative]

tinnitus /tɪˈnaɪtəs/ *n. Med.* condition with ringing in the ears. [Latin *tinnio tinnit-* ring, tinkle]

tinny *adj.* (**-ier, -iest**) **1** of or like tin. **2** flimsy, insubstantial. **3** (of sound) thin and metallic.

tin-opener *n.* tool for opening tins.

tin-pan alley *n.* world of composers and publishers of popular music.

tin plate *n.* sheet iron or sheet steel coated with tin.

tinpot *attrib. adj.* cheap, inferior.

tinsel /ˈtɪns(ə)l/ *n.* **1** glittering metallic strips, threads, etc., used as decoration. **2** superficial brilliance or splendour. **3** (*attrib.*) gaudy, flashy. □ **tinselled** *adj.* **tinselly** *adj.* [Latin *scintilla* spark]

tinsmith *n.* worker in tin and tin plate.

tinsnips *n.* clippers for cutting sheet metal.

tint –*n.* **1** variety of a colour, esp. made by adding white. **2** tendency towards or admixture of a different colour (*red with a blue tint*). **3** faint colour spread over a surface. –*v.* apply a tint to; colour. [*tinct*: related to TINGE]

tin-tack *n.* iron tack.

tintinnabulation /ˌtɪntɪˌnæbjʊˈleɪʃ(ə)n/ *n.* ringing or tinkling of bells. [Latin *tintinnabulum* bell]

tin whistle *n.* = PENNY WHISTLE.

tiny /ˈtaɪnɪ/ *adj.* (**-ier, -iest**) very small or slight. □ **tinily** *adv.* **tininess** *n.* [origin unknown]

-tion see -ION.

tip[1] –*n.* **1** extremity or end, esp. of a small or tapering thing. **2** small piece or part attached to the end of a thing. **3** leaf-bud of tea. –*v.* (**-pp-**) provide with a tip. □ **on the tip of one's tongue** about to be said or remembered. **tip of the iceberg** small evident part of something much larger. [Old Norse]

tip[2] –*v.* (**-pp-**) **1** (often foll. by *over, up*) **a** lean or slant. **b** cause to do this. **2** (foll. by *into* etc.) **a** overturn or cause to overbalance. **b** discharge the contents of (a container etc.) in this way. –*n.* **1 a** slight push or tilt. **b** light stroke. **2** place where material (esp. refuse) is tipped. □ **tip the scales** see SCALE[2]. [origin uncertain]

tip[3] –*v.* (**-pp-**) **1** make a small present of money to, esp. for a service given. **2** name as the likely winner of a race or contest etc. **3** strike or touch lightly. –*n.* **1** small money present, esp. for a service given. **2** piece of private or special information, esp. regarding betting or investment. **3** small or casual piece of advice. □ **tip off** give (a person) a hint or piece of special information or warning. **tip a person the wink** give a person private information. [origin uncertain]

tip-off *n.* hint or warning etc.

tipper *n.* (often *attrib.*) road haulage vehicle that tips at the back to discharge its load.

Tipperary /ˌtɪpəˈreərɪ/ county in the central Republic of Ireland, in the province of Munster; pop. (1991) 132 772; capital, Clonmel. It is mainly agricultural, with some agriculture-related industries.

tippet /ˈtɪpɪt/ *n.* **1** long piece of fur etc. worn by a woman round the shoulders. **2** similar garment worn by judges, clergy, etc. [probably from TIP[1]]

tipple /ˈtɪp(ə)l/ –*v.* (**-ling**) **1** drink intoxicating liquor habitually. **2** drink (liquor) repeatedly in small amounts. –*n. colloq.* alcoholic drink. □ **tippler** *n.* [origin unknown]

tipstaff *n.* **1** sheriff's officer. **2** metal-tipped staff carried as a symbol of office. [from TIP[1]]

tipster *n.* person who gives tips, esp. about betting at horse-races.

tipsy /ˈtɪpsɪ/ *adj.* (**-ier, -iest**) **1** slightly drunk. **2** caused by or showing intoxication (*a tipsy lurch*). □ **tipsily** *adv.* **tipsiness** *n.* [from TIP[2]]

tiptoe –*n.* the tips of the toes. –*v.* (**-toes, -toed, -toeing**) walk on tiptoe, or very stealthily. –*adv.* (also **on tiptoe**) with the heels off the ground.

tiptop *colloq.* –*adj.* highest in excellence. –*n.* highest point of excellence. –*adv.* most excellently.

tip-up *attrib. adj.* able to be tipped, e.g. of a theatre seat.

TIR *abbr.* (French, on continental lorries) transport international routier (= international road transport).

tirade /taɪˈreɪd/ *n.* long vehement denunciation or declamation. [French from Italian]

Tirana /tɪˈrɑːnə/ (Albanian **Tiranë**) capital of Albania, an industrial city producing metallurgical products, textiles, and soap; pop. (1991) 251 000.

tire[1] *v.* (**-ring**) **1** make or grow weary. **2** exhaust the patience or interest of; bore. **3** (in *passive*; foll. by *of*) have had enough of; be fed up with. [Old English]

tire[2] *n.* **1** band of metal placed round the rim of a wheel to strengthen it. **2** *US* var. of TYRE. [perhaps = archaic *tire* 'headdress']

tired *adj.* **1** weary; ready for sleep. **2** (of an idea etc.) hackneyed. □ **tiredly** *adv.* **tiredness** *n.*

tireless *adj.* not tiring easily, energetic. □ **tirelessly** *adv.* **tirelessness** *n.*

tiresome *adj.* **1** wearisome, tedious. **2** *colloq.* annoying. □ **tiresomely** *adv.* **tiresomeness** *n.*

tiro /ˈtaɪəˌrəʊ/ *n.* (also **tyro**) (*pl.* **-s**) beginner, novice. [Latin, = recruit]

Tirol see TYROL.

Tiruchirapalli /ˌtɪrətʃɪˈrɑːpəlɪ/ city in S India, in Tamil Nadu state; pop. (1991) 387 223.

'tis /tɪz/ *archaic* it is. [contraction]

tissue /ˈtɪʃuː, ˈtɪsjuː/ *n.* **1** any of the coherent collections of specialized cells of which animals or plants are made (*muscular tissue*). **2** = TISSUE-PAPER. **3** disposable piece of thin soft absorbent paper for wiping, drying, etc. **4** fine woven esp. gauzy fabric. **5** (foll. by *of*) connected series (*tissue of lies*). [French *tissu* woven cloth]

tissue-paper *n.* thin soft paper for wrapping etc.

tit[1] *n.* any of various small birds. [probably from Scandinavian]

tit[2] *n.* □ **tit for tat** blow for blow; retaliation. [= earlier *tip* in *tip for tap*: see TIP[2]]

tit[3] *n.* **1** *coarse slang* woman's breast. **2** *colloq.* nipple. [Old English]

Titan /ˈtaɪt(ə)n/ *n.* (often **titan**) person of very great strength, intellect, or importance. [Greek, = member of a race of giants]

titanic /taɪˈtænɪk/ *adj.* gigantic, colossal. □ **titanically** *adv.* [Greek: related to TITAN]

titanium /taɪˈteɪnɪəm, tɪ-/ *n.* grey metallic element. [Greek: related to TITAN]

titbit *n.* (*US* **tidbit**) **1** dainty morsel. **2** piquant item of news etc. [perhaps from dial. *tid* tender]

titchy *adj.* (**-ier, -iest**) *colloq.* very small. [*titch* small person, from *Tich*, name of a comedian]

titfer *n. slang* hat. [abbreviation of *tit for tat*, rhyming slang]

tithe /taɪð/ –*n.* **1** one-tenth of the annual produce of land or labour, formerly taken as a tax for the Church. **2** tenth part. –*v.* (**-thing**) **1** subject to tithes. **2** pay tithes. [Old English, = tenth]

tithe barn *n.* barn built to hold tithes paid in kind.

Titian /ˈtɪʃ(ə)n/ *adj.* (of hair) bright auburn. [*Titian*, name of a painter]

titillate /ˈtɪtɪˌleɪt/ *v.* (**-ting**) **1** excite, esp. sexually. **2** tickle. □ **titillation** /-ˈleɪʃ(ə)n/ *n.* [Latin]

titivate /ˈtɪtɪˌveɪt/ *v.* (**-ting**) (often *refl.*) *colloq.* smarten up; put the finishing touches to. □ **titivation** /-ˈveɪʃ(ə)n/ *n.* [earlier *tidivate*, perhaps from TIDY after *cultivate*]

title /ˈtaɪt(ə)l/ *n.* **1** name of a book, work of art, etc. **2** heading of a chapter, document, etc. **3 a** = TITLE-PAGE. **b** book, magazine, etc., in terms of its title (*brought out two new titles*). **4** (usu. in *pl.*) caption or credit in a film etc. **5** name indicating a person's status (e.g. *professor, queen*) or used as a form of address or reference (e.g. *Lord, Mr, Your Grace*). **6** championship in sport. **7** *Law* **a** right to ownership of property with or without possession. **b** facts constituting this. **c** (foll. by *to*) just or recognized claim. [Latin *titulus*]

titled *adj.* having a title of nobility or rank.

♦ **title-deed** *n.* document proving the ownership of land. The document must go back at least 15 years to give a good root of title. If the land is registered, the land certificate now takes the place of the title-deed. See ABSTRACT OF TITLE.

---

title-holder *n.* person who holds a title, esp. a sporting champion.

title-page *n.* page at the beginning of a book giving the title, author, etc.

title role *n.* part in a play etc. that gives it its name (e.g. *Othello*).

titmouse *n.* (*pl.* **titmice**) small active tit. [Old English *tit* little, *māse* titmouse, assimilated to MOUSE]

Titograd /ˈtiːtəʊˌgræd/ see PODGORICA.

titrate /taɪˈtreɪt/ *v.* (**-ting**) *Chem.* ascertain the amount of a constituent in (a solution) by reaction with a known concentration of reagent. □ **titration** /-ˈtreɪʃ(ə)n/ *n.* [French *titre* title]

titter –*v.* laugh covertly; giggle. –*n.* covert laugh. [imitative]

tittle /ˈtɪt(ə)l/ *n.* **1** small written or printed stroke or dot. **2** particle; whit (*not one jot or tittle*). [Latin: related to TITLE]

tittle-tattle /ˈtɪt(ə)lˌtæt(ə)l/ –*n.* petty gossip. –*v.* (**-ling**) gossip, chatter. [reduplication of TATTLE]

tittup /ˈtɪtəp/ –*v.* (**-p-** or **-pp-**) go about friskily or jerkily; bob up and down; canter. –*n.* such a gait or movement. [perhaps imitative]

titular /ˈtɪtjʊlə(r)/ *adj.* **1** of or relating to a title. **2** existing, or being, in name or title only (*titular ruler*). [French: related to TITLE]

tizzy /ˈtɪzɪ/ *n.* (*pl.* **-ies**) *colloq.* state of agitation (*in a tizzy*). [origin unknown]

TJ *international civil aircraft marking* Cameroon.

T-junction *n.* road junction at which one road joins another at right angles without crossing it.

TK *airline flight code* Turkish Airlines.

Tk *symb. Currency* taka.

TL –*abbr.* **1** *Insurance* total loss. **2** Turkish lira. –*international civil aircraft marking* Central African Republic.

T/L *abbr.* **1** *Banking* time loan. **2** *Insurance* total loss.

Tl *symb.* thallium.

t.l. *abbr.* **1** *Insurance* total loss. **2** trade list.

Tlaxcala /tlɑːsˈkɑːlə/ **1** state in E central Mexico; pop. (est. 1995) 883 630. **2** its capital city; pop. (est. 1990) 25 000.

TLC *abbr.* (in Australia) Trades and Labor Council.

TLF *abbr.* = TRANSFERABLE LOAN FACILITY.

t.l.o. *abbr. Insurance* total loss only.

TLS *abbr.* typed letter, signed.

TM *abbr.* **1** trade mark. **2** training manual.

Tm *symb.* thulium.

TMO *abbr.* telegraph(ic) money order.

TN –*international vehicle registration* Tunisia. –*international civil aircraft marking* Republic of the Congo. –*US postcode* Tennessee. –*postcode* Tonbridge. –*airline flight code* Australian Airlines.

TNC *abbr.* transnational corporation.

T-note *abbr. Finance* Treasury note.

TNT *abbr.* trinitrotoluene, a high explosive formed from toluene.

TO *abbr.* **1** *Management* table of organization. **2** telegraph office. **3** telephone office. **4** telephone order.

T/O *abbr.* (also **t.o.**) turnover.

to /tə/, *before a vowel* /tʊ/, *emphat.* /tuː/ –*prep.* **1** introducing a noun expressing: **a** what is reached, approached, or touched (*fell to the ground*; *went to Paris*; *five minutes to six*). **b** what is aimed at (*throw it to me*). **c** as far as (*went on to the end*). **d** what is followed (*made to order*). **e** what is considered or affected (*am used to that*; *that is nothing to me*). **f** what is caused or produced (*turn to stone*). **g** what is compared (*nothing to what it once was*; *equal to the occasion*). **h** what is increased (*add it to mine*). **i** what is involved or composed as specified (*there is nothing to it*). **2** introducing the infinitive: **a** as a verbal noun (*to get there is the priority*). **b** expressing purpose, consequence, or cause (*we eat to live*; *left him to starve*; *I'm sorry to hear that*). **c** as a substitute for *to* + infinitive (*wanted to come but was unable to*). *–adv.* **1** in the normal or required position or condition (*come to*; *heave to*). **2** (of a door) in a nearly closed position. □ **to and fro 1** backwards and forwards. **2** repeatedly between the same points. [Old English]

toad *n.* **1** froglike amphibian breeding in water but living chiefly on land. **2** repulsive person. [Old English]

toadflax *n.* plant with yellow or purple flowers.

toad-in-the-hole *n.* sausages baked in batter.

toadstool *n.* fungus, usu. poisonous, with a round top and slender stalk.

toady *–n.* (*pl.* **-ies**) sycophant. *–v.* (foll. by *to*) (**-ies, -ied**) behave servilely to; fawn upon. □ **toadyism** *n.* [contraction of *toad-eater*]

toast *–n.* **1** sliced bread browned on both sides by radiant heat. **2 a** person or thing in whose honour a company is requested to drink. **b** call to drink or an instance of drinking in this way. *–v.* **1** brown by radiant heat. **2** warm (one's feet, oneself, etc.) at a fire etc. **3** drink to the health or in honour of (a person or thing). [French *toster* roast]

toaster *n.* electrical device for making toast.

toasting-fork *n.* long-handled fork for making toast.

toastmaster *n.* (*fem.* **toastmistress**) person responsible for announcing toasts at a public occasion.

toast rack *n.* rack for holding slices of toast at table.

tobacco /tə'bækəʊ/ *n.* (*pl.* **-s**) **1** plant of American origin with narcotic leaves used for smoking, chewing, or snuff. **2** its leaves, esp. as prepared for smoking. [Spanish *tabaco*, of American Indian origin]

tobacconist /tə'bækənɪst/ *n.* dealer in tobacco, cigarettes, etc.

♦ **Tobin's Q** /'təʊbɪnz/ *n.* theory stating that the level of investment is determined by the ratio of the stock-market valuation of the physical capital of firms and the current replacement cost of those items. Investment will rise if the former is greater than the latter and vice versa. The theory provides an improvement on both the accelerator theory (which is theoretically weak) and the user-cost-of-capital theory (which is weak in practice). [*Tobin*, name of an economist]

---

toboggan /tə'bɒgən/ *–n.* long light narrow sledge for sliding downhill over snow or ice. *–v.* ride on a toboggan. [Canadian French from Algonquian]

Tobruk /tə'brʊk/ (Arabic **Tubruq**) port in NE Libya, on the Mediterranean coast; pop. (1984) 94 000.

toby jug /'təʊbɪ/ *n.* jug or mug in the form of a stout man wearing a three-cornered hat. [familiar form of the name *Tobias*]

toccata /tə'kɑːtə/ *n.* musical composition for a keyboard instrument, designed to exhibit the performer's touch and technique. [Italian, = touched]

tocsin /'tɒksɪn/ *n.* alarm bell or signal. [Provençal *tocasenh*]

tod *n. slang* □ **on one's tod** alone; on one's own. [rhyming slang *on one's Tod Sloan*]

today /tə'deɪ/ *–adv.* **1** on this present day. **2** nowadays. *–n.* **1** this present day. **2** modern times. [Old English]

toddle /'tɒd(ə)l/ *–v.* (**-ling**) **1** walk with short unsteady steps like a small child. **2** *colloq.* **a** walk, stroll. **b** (usu. foll. by *off* or *along*) depart. *–n.* act of toddling. [origin unknown]

toddler *n.* child who is just learning to walk.

toddy /'tɒdɪ/ *n.* (*pl.* **-ies**) drink of spirits with hot water and sugar etc. [Hindustani *tār* palm]

to-do /tə'duː/ *n.* (*pl.* **-s**) commotion or fuss.

toe *–n.* **1** any of the five terminal projections of the foot. **2** corresponding part of an animal. **3** part of a shoe etc. that covers the toes. **4** lower end or tip of an implement etc. *–v.* (**toes, toed, toeing**) touch (a starting-line etc.) with the toes. □ **on one's toes** alert. **toe the line** conform, esp. under pressure. [Old English]

toecap *n.* (usu. strengthened) outer covering of the toe of a boot or shoe.

toe-hold *n.* **1** small foothold. **2** small beginning or advantage.

toenail *n.* nail of each toe.

TOFC *abbr.* trailer on flat car (type of freight container).

toff *n. slang* upper-class person. [perhaps from *tuft*, = titled undergraduate]

toffee /'tɒfɪ/ *n.* **1** firm or hard sweet made by boiling sugar, butter, etc. together. **2** this substance. □ **for toffee** *slang* (prec. by *can't* etc.) (denoting incompetence) at all (*they couldn't sing for toffee*). [origin unknown]

toffee-apple *n.* apple with a coating of toffee.

toffee-nosed *adj. slang* snobbish, superior.

tofu /'təʊfuː/ *n.* curd of mashed soya beans. [Japanese]

tog[1] *colloq. –n.* (usu. in *pl.*) item of clothing. *–v.* (**-gg-**) (foll. by *out*, *up*) dress. [apparently originally cant: ultimately related to Latin TOGA]

tog[2] *n.* unit of thermal resistance used to express the insulating properties of clothes and quilts. [arbitrary, probably from TOG[1]]

toga /'təʊgə/ *n. hist.* ancient Roman citizen's loose flowing outer garment. □ **togaed** *adj.* (also **toga'd**). [Latin]

together /tə'geðə(r)/ *–adv.* **1** in company or conjunction (*walking together*; *were at school together*). **2** simultaneously (*both shouted together*). **3** one with another (*talking together*). **4** into conjunction; so as to unite (*tied them together*; *put two and two together*). **5** into company or companionship. **6** uninterruptedly (*he could talk for three hours together*). *–adj. colloq.* well-organized; self-assured; emotionally stable□ **together with** as well as. [Old English: related to TO, GATHER]

togetherness *n.* **1** being together. **2** feeling of comfort from this.

toggle /'tɒg(ə)l/ *n.* **1** fastener for a garment consisting of a crosspiece which passes through a hole or loop. **2** *Computing* switch action that is operated the same way but with opposite effect on successive occasions. [origin unknown]

toggle switch *n.* electric switch with a lever to be moved usu. up and down.

Togliatti /tɒl'jætɪ/ (formerly **Stavropol** /'stævrəˌpɒl/) city in W central Russia, with ship-repairing, engineering, and food-processing industries; pop. (est. 1995) 702 000.

Tohoku /təʊ'həʊkuː/ largest of the five regions on Honshu island, Japan; pop. (1995) 9 834 223; capital, Sendai.

toil *–v.* **1** work laboriously or incessantly. **2** make slow painful progress. *–n.* intensive labour; drudgery. [Anglo-French *toil(er)* dispute]

toilet /'tɔɪlɪt/ *n.* **1** = LAVATORY. **2** process of washing oneself, dressing, etc. (*at one's toilet*). [French *toilette* diminutive of *toile* cloth]

toilet paper *n.* paper for cleaning oneself after excreting.

toilet roll *n.* roll of toilet paper.

toiletry /'tɔɪlɪtrɪ/ *n.* (*pl.* **-ies**) (usu. in *pl.*) article or cosmetic used in washing, dressing, etc.

toilet soap *n.* soap for washing oneself.

toilette /twɑː'let/ *n.* = TOILET 2. [French]

toilet-training *n.* training of a young child to use the lavatory. □ **toilet-train** *v.*

toilet water *n.* dilute perfume used after washing.

toils /tɔɪlz/ *n.pl.* net, snare. [*toil* from French: related to TOILET]

toilsome /ˈtɔɪlsəm/ *adj.* involving toil.

toing and froing /ˌtuːɪŋ ənd ˈfrəʊɪŋ/ *n.* constant movement to and fro; bustle; dispersed activity. [from TO, FRO]

Tokay /təˈkeɪ/ *n.* a sweet Hungarian wine. [*Tokaj* in Hungary]

Tokelau /ˌtəʊkəˈlaːuː/ group of three islands in the W Pacific Ocean, forming an overseas territory of New Zealand; copra and woven goods are exported; pop. (1991) 1577.

token /ˈtəʊkən/ *n.* **1** thing serving as a symbol, reminder, or mark (*as a token of affection*; *in token of my esteem*). **2** voucher. **3** thing equivalent to something else, esp. money. **4** (*attrib.*) **a** perfunctory (*token effort*). **b** conducted briefly to demonstrate strength of feeling (*token strike*). **c** chosen by tokenism to represent a group (*token woman*). □ **by this** (or **the same**) **token 1** similarly. **2** moreover. [Old English]

tokenism *n.* **1** granting of minimum concessions, esp. to minority groups. **2** making of only a token effort.

♦ **tokkin** /ˈtəʊkɪn/ *n.* special investment fund on the Japanese stock markets owned by companies using their cash surpluses to generate extra income, although their main business is not in the financial markets. [Japanese]

Tokyo /ˈtəʊkjəʊ/ capital of Japan, on the island of Honshu; pop. (est. 1995) 11 771 819. It has undergone rapid industrial growth since the Second World War and is now one of the world's major commercial and financial centres.

♦ **Tokyo round** *n.* sixth bargaining session between contracting parties to General Agreement on Tariffs and Trade, held in Tokyo. The round lasted from 1973 to 1979 and sought to build on the successes in multilateral tariff reduction in the previous Kennedy round. It continued to make progress on tariff reduction while also tackling the problems of **non-tariff barriers (NTBs)**, which were a common way of replacing tariffs. Various codes of conduct on NTBs were agreed, including government procurement, import valuation, and technical standards. The Tokyo round was followed by the Uruguay round, which began in 1986. See GENERAL AGREEMENT ON TARIFFS AND TRADE.

---

tolar /ˈtɒlaː(r)/ *n.* standard monetary unit of Slovenia. [Slovenian]

Tolbukhin /tɒlˈbuːxɪn/ agricultural centre in NE Bulgaria; pop. (1990) 115 786.

told *past* and *past part.* of TELL[1].

Toledo 1 /təˈleɪdəʊ/ city in central Spain, famous for metalwork, esp. the manufacture of finely-tempered sword-blades and knives; pop. (1991) 63 560. **2** /təˈliːdəʊ/ industrial city in the US, in NW Ohio, a shipping centre on Lake Erie; industries include shipbuilding, oil refining, and coalmining, and oil and coal are exported; pop. (est. 1994) 322 550.

tolerable /ˈtɒlərəb(ə)l/ *adj.* **1** endurable. **2** fairly good. □ **tolerably** *adv.* [Latin: related to TOLERATE]

tolerance /ˈtɒlərəns/ *n.* **1** willingness or ability to tolerate; forbearance. **2** allowable variation in any measurable property.

tolerant *adj.* **1** disposed to tolerate others or their acts or opinions. **2** (foll. by *of*) enduring or patient.

tolerate /ˈtɒləˌreɪt/ *v.* (**-ting**) **1** allow the existence or occurrence of without authoritative interference. **2** endure (suffering etc.). **3** find or treat as endurable. **4** be able to take or undergo (drugs, treatment, etc.) without adverse effects. [Latin *tolero*]

toleration /ˌtɒləˈreɪʃ(ə)n/ *n.* tolerating or being tolerated, esp. the allowing of religious differences without discrimination. [Latin: related to TOLERATE]

toll[1] /təʊl, tɒl/ *n.* **1** charge to use a bridge, road, etc. **2** cost or damage caused by a disaster etc. □ **take its toll** be accompanied by loss, injury, etc.

toll[2] /təʊl/ *–v.* **1 a** (of a bell) sound with slow uniform strokes. **b** ring (a bell) in this way. **c** (of a bell) announce or mark (a death etc.) in this way. **2** strike (the hour). *–n.* **1** tolling. **2** stroke of a bell. [(now dial.) *toll* entice, pull, from an Old English root]

toll-bridge *n.* bridge at which a toll is charged.

toll-gate *n.* gate preventing passage until a toll is paid.

toll-road *n.* road maintained by the tolls collected on it.

toluene /ˈtɒljʊˌiːn/ *n.* colourless aromatic liquid hydrocarbon derivative of benzene, used in the manufacture of explosives etc. [*Tolu* in Colombia]

tom *n.* (in full **tom-cat**) male cat. [abbreviation of the name *Thomas*]

tomahawk /ˈtɒməˌhɔːk/ *n.* North American Indian war-axe. [Renape]

tomato /təˈmaːtəʊ/ *n.* (*pl.* **-es**) **1** glossy red or yellow pulpy edible fruit. **2** plant bearing this. [ultimately from Mexican *tomatl*]

tomb /tuːm/ *n.* **1** burial-vault. **2** grave. **3** sepulchral monument. [Greek *tumbos*]

tombola /tɒmˈbəʊlə/ *n.* lottery with tickets drawn from a drum for immediate prizes. [French or Italian]

Tombouctou see TIMBUKTU.

tomboy *n.* boisterous girl who enjoys activities tradi-

Togo /ˈtəʊgəʊ/, **Republic of** country in W Africa, between Ghana and Benin, with a short coastline on the Gulf of Guinea. The economy is mainly agricultural: crops include cotton, coffee, and cocoa, which are among the country's principal exports, cassava, maize, and rice. Rich deposits of phosphates provide a major source of export revenue. Other industries include forestry (producing timber, palm products, and dyewoods), oil refining, textile manufacture, and food processing.

History. Annexed by Germany in 1884, the district called Togoland was divided between France and Britain after the First World War. The British section joined Ghana on the latter's independence (1957). The remainder of the area became a United Nations mandate under French administration after the Second World War and achieved independence as the Republic of Togo in 1960. The first president of the republic was assassinated in 1963, and Lieutenant Colonel Eyadéma came to power after a military coup in 1967. Violent unrest in 1991, provoked by the slow progress of democratic reform, caused Eyadéma to be stripped of all his powers and an interim government to be installed; continuing political instability delayed the introduction of the new multi-party constitution, which was approved by a referendum in 1992. Eyadéma won presidential elections in 1993; however there were allegations of vote rigging. A coalition government was formed in 1994.

President, General Gnassingbé Eyadéma; prime minister, Kwasi Klutse; capital, Lomé. □ **Togolese** /-gəˈliːz/ *adj.* & *n.*

languages	French (official), local languages
currency	CFA franc (CFAF) of 100 centimes
pop. (1996)	4 269 000
GNP (1994)	US$1.2B
literacy	67% (m); 37% (f)
life expectancy	53 (m); 56 (f)

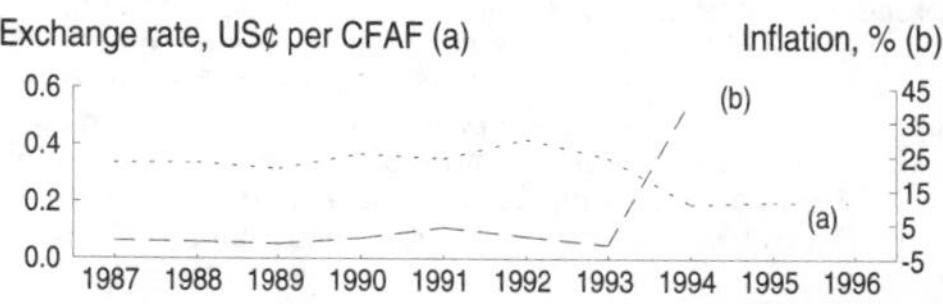

tionally associated with boys. □ **tomboyish** *adj.* [from TOM]

tombstone *n.* **1** memorial stone over a grave, usu. with an epitaph. **2** newspaper or magazine advertisement showing the parties involved in an acquisition, merger, new issue, large syndicated loan, or other major financial deal. The advertisements are simple and resemble the brief information usu. found on a gravestone.

Tom, Dick, and Harry *n.* (also **Tom, Dick, or Harry**) (usu. prec. by *any* or *every*) person taken at random (*any Tom, Dick, or Harry can walk in*).

tome *n.* heavy book or volume. [Greek *temnō* cut]

tomfool –*n.* foolish person. –*attrib. adj.* silly, foolish.

tomfoolery /tɒm'fuːlərɪ/ *n.* foolish behaviour.

Tommy /'tɒmɪ/ *n.* (*pl.* **-ies**) *colloq.* British private soldier. [*Tommy Atkins*, name used in specimens of completed official forms]

tommy-gun *n.* sub-machine-gun. [*Thompson*, name of its co-inventor]

tommy-rot *n. slang* nonsense. [from TOM]

tomography /tə'mɒgrəfɪ/ *n.* method of radiography displaying details in a selected plane within the body. [Greek *tomē* a cutting]

tomorrow /tə'mɒrəʊ/ –*adv.* **1** on the day after today. **2** at some future time. –*n.* **1** the day after today. **2** the near future. [from TO, MORROW]

Tomsk /tɒmsk/ industrial city and port in Russia, on the River Tom in W central Siberia; pop. (est. 1995) 470 000.

tomtit *n.* tit, esp. a blue tit.

tom-tom /'tɒmtɒm/ *n.* **1** primitive drum beaten with the hands. **2** tall drum used in jazz bands etc. [Hindi *tamtam*, imitative]

ton /tʌn/ *n.* **1** (in full **long ton**) unit of mass equal to 2240 lb (1016.05 kg). The ton may no longer be used for trade, having been replaced by the **metric ton** or **tonne** (1000 kg). **2** *US* (in full **short ton**) unit of mass equal to 2000 lb (907.19 kg) and consisting of 20 short hundredweights, each of 100 lb. **3** (in full **shipping ton**) measure that is used for light cargoes and consists of 100 cubic feet of space; the tonne is usu. used for heavy cargoes (see also TONNAGE 1). **4** (in full **displacement ton**) unit of measurement of a ship's mass or volume (see TONNAGE). **5** (usu. in *pl.*) *colloq.* large number or amount (*tons of people*). **6** *slang* **a** speed of 100 m.p.h. **b** £100. □ **weigh a ton** *colloq.* be very heavy. [originally the same word as TUN]

tonal /'təʊn(ə)l/ *adj.* of or relating to tone or tonality. □ **tonally** *adv.* [medieval Latin: related to TONE]

tonality /tə'nælɪtɪ/ *n.* (*pl.* **-ies**) **1** *Mus.* **a** relationship between the tones of a musical scale. **b** observance of a single tonic key as the basis of a composition. **2** colour scheme of a picture.

tone –*n.* **1** musical or vocal sound, esp. with reference to its pitch, quality, and strength. **2** (often in *pl.*) modulation of the voice expressing a particular feeling or mood (*a cheerful tone*). **3** manner of expression in writing or speaking. **4** *Mus.* **a** musical sound, esp. of a definite pitch and character. **b** interval of a major second, e.g. C–D. **5** **a** general effect of colour or of light and shade in a picture. **b** tint or shade of a colour. **6** prevailing character of the morals and sentiments etc. in a group. **7** proper firmness of the body. **8** state of good or specified health. **9** *Finance* prevailing sentiment of a market. If a stock exchange or commodity market has a firm or strong tone, prices are tending upwards, whereas if the tone is weak, nervous, or unsettled, prices are tending to fall. –*v.* (**-ning**) **1** give the desired tone to. **2** modify the tone of. **3** (often foll. by *to*) attune. **4** (foll. by *with*) (esp. of colour) be in harmony with. □ **tone down** make or become softer in tone. **tone up** make or become stronger in tone. □ **toneless** *adj.* **tonelessly** *adv.* **toner** *n.* [Greek *tonos* from *teinō* stretch]

tone-deaf *adj.* unable to perceive differences of musical pitch accurately.

tone poem *n.* orchestral composition with a descriptive or rhapsodic theme.

Tongariro /ˌtɒŋgə'rɪəˌrəʊ/ former administrative region in New Zealand, on North Island. It was abolished in 1989.

tongs *n.pl.* implement with two arms for grasping coal, sugar, etc. [Old English]

tongue /tʌŋ/ –*n.* **1** fleshy muscular organ in the mouth used in tasting, licking, and swallowing, and (in man) for speech. **2** tongue of an ox etc. as food. **3** faculty of or tendency in speech (*a sharp tongue*). **4** particular language (*the German tongue*). **5** thing like a tongue in shape or position, esp.: **a** a long low promontory. **b** a strip of leather etc. under the laces in a shoe. **c** the clapper of a bell. **d** the pin of a buckle. **e** a projecting strip on a board etc. fitting into the groove of another. –*v.* (**-guing**) use the tongue to articulate (notes) in playing a wind instrument.□ **find** (or **lose) one's tongue** be able (or unable) to express oneself after a shock etc. **hold one's tongue** see HOLD[1]. **with one's tongue in one's cheek** insincerely or ironically. [Old English]

tongue-and-groove –*n.* (often *attrib.*) planking etc. with a projecting strip down one side and a groove down the other. –*v.* **1** panel with tongue-and-groove. **2** (as **tongued and grooved** *adj.*) having a tongue-and-groove joint.

tongue-in-cheek –*adj.* ironic. –*adv.* insincerely or ironically.

tongue-tie *n.* speech impediment due to a malformation of the tongue.

tongue-tied *adj.* **1** too shy or embarrassed to speak. **2** having a tongue-tie.

tongue-twister *n.* sequence of words difficult to pronounce quickly and correctly.

tonic /'tɒnɪk/ –*n.* **1** invigorating medicine. **2** anything serving to invigorate. **3** = TONIC WATER. **4** *Mus.* keynote. –*adj.* invigorating. [Greek: related to TONE]

tonic sol-fa *n. Mus.* system of notation used esp. in teaching singing.

tonic water *n.* carbonated water flavoured with quinine.

tonight /tə'naɪt/ –*adv.* on the present or approaching evening or night. –*n.* the evening or night of the present day. [Old English]

Tonga /'tɒŋə/, **Kingdom of** (also **Friendly Islands**) country in the S Pacific consisting of over 150 small volcanic and coral islands, SE of Fiji. The economy is based on agriculture: the main exports are squash, coconut products (esp. copra), bananas, vanilla, and cassava and other root crops. Tourism and manufacturing industry (esp. food processing) are additional sources of revenue. The country's other exports include textiles, leather goods, and knitwear. Discovered by the Dutch in the early 17th century, the islands became a British protectorate in 1900, gaining independence as a member state of the Commonwealth in 1970. Head of state, King Taufa'ahau Tupou IV; prime minister, Baron Vaea of Houma; capital, Nuku'alofa. □ **Tongan** *adj.* & *n.*

languages	Tongan, English
currency	pa'anga (T$) of 100 seniti
pop. (1996)	101 100
GNP (1994)	US$160M
literacy	92% (m); 92% (f)
life expectancy	67 (m); 72 (f)

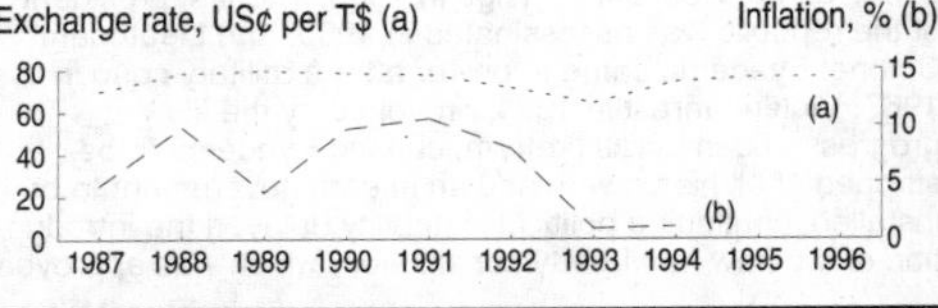

tonn. *abbr.* tonnage.

◆ **tonnage** /'tʌnɪdʒ/ *n.* **1** ship's internal cubic capacity or freight-carrying capacity, measured in various ways. The **gross register tonnage (GRT)** is the volume of a ship below the upper deck measured in shipping tons of 100 cubic feet (see TON 3). The **net register tonnage (NRT)** is the GRT less the space occupied by engines, fuel, stores, and accommodation for crew and passengers. Harbour and port dues are usu. based on the NRT and dry dock dues are usu. based on the GRT. The **deadweight tonnage** is the number of tonnes or (formerly) tons of cargo, stores, and fuel that a ship can carry. The **lightweight tonnage** is the weight of the ship in tonnes or tons, without any cargo, fuel, or stores. The **displacement tonnage** is the weight in tons of the water displaced by a ship, taking one displacement ton as the weight of 35 cubic feet of water. **2** charge per ton on freight or cargo. [related to TON]

tonne /tʌn/ *n.* (also **metric ton**) unit of mass equal to 1000 kg (2205 lb). See also TONNAGE 1; TON 1. [French: related to TON]

tonsil /'tɒns(ə)l/ *n.* either of two small organs, one on each side of the root of the tongue. [Latin]

tonsillectomy /ˌtɒnsə'lektəmɪ/ *n.* (*pl.* **-ies**) surgical removal of the tonsils.

tonsillitis /ˌtɒnsə'laɪtɪs/ *n.* inflammation of the tonsils.

tonsorial /tɒn'sɔːrɪəl/ *adj.* usu. *joc.* of a hairdresser or hairdressing. [Latin *tondeo tons-* shave]

tonsure /'tɒnʃə(r)/ *–n.* **1** shaving of the crown of the head or the entire head, esp. of a person entering the priesthood or a monastic order. **2** bare patch made in this way. *–v.* (**-ring**) give a tonsure to. [Latin: related to TONSORIAL]

◆ **tontine** /'tɒntiːn/ *n.* former name for LAST-SURVIVOR POLICY 2. [*Tonti*, name of a banker]

ton-up *attrib. adj. slang* (of a motor cyclist) achieving a speed of 100 m.p.h., esp. habitually.

TOO *abbr. Commerce* to order only.

too *adv.* **1** to a greater extent than is desirable or permissible (*too large*). **2** *colloq.* very (*not too sure*). **3** in addition (*I'm coming too*). **4** moreover (*food was bad, and expensive too*). □ **none too** rather less than (*feeling none too good*). **too bad** see BAD. **too much** intolerable. **too much for 1** more than a match for. **2** beyond what is endurable by. **too right** see RIGHT. [stressed form of TO]

took *past* of TAKE.

tool *–n.* **1** implement used to carry out mechanical functions by hand or by machine. **2** thing used in an occupation or pursuit (*tools of one's trade*). **3** *Computing* see SOFTWARE TOOL. **4** person merely used by another. **5** *coarse slang* penis. *–v.* **1** dress (stone) with a chisel. **2** impress a design on (leather). **3** (foll. by *along*, *around*, etc.) *slang* drive or ride, esp. in a casual or leisurely manner. [Old English]

toolmaker *n.* person who makes precision tools. □ **toolmaking** *n.*

tool-pusher *n.* worker directing the drilling on an oil rig.

toot *–n.* short sharp sound as made by a trumpet. *–v.* **1** sound (a trumpet etc.) with a short sharp sound. **2** give out such a sound. [probably imitative]

tooth *n.* (*pl.* **teeth**) **1** each of a set of hard bony enamel-coated structures in the jaws of most vertebrates, used for biting and chewing. **2** toothlike part or projection, e.g. the cog of a gearwheel, the point of a saw or comb, etc. **3** (often foll. by *for*) taste; appetite. **4** (in *pl.*) force, effectiveness. □ **armed to the teeth** completely and elaborately armed. **fight tooth and nail** fight very fiercely. **get one's teeth into** devote oneself seriously to. **in the teeth of 1** in spite of (opposition or difficulty etc.). **2** contrary to (instructions etc.). **3** directly against (the wind etc.). □ **toothed** *adj.* (also in *comb.*). **toothless** *adj.* [Old English]

toothache *n.* pain in a tooth or teeth.

toothbrush *n.* brush for cleaning the teeth.

tooth-comb *n.* = FINE-TOOTH COMB.

toothpaste *n.* paste for cleaning the teeth.

toothpick *n.* small sharp stick for removing food lodged between the teeth.

tooth powder *n.* powder for cleaning the teeth.

toothsome *adj.* (of food) delicious.

toothy *adj.* (**-ier**, **-iest**) having large, numerous, or prominent teeth.

tootle /'tuːt(ə)l/ *v.* (**-ling**) **1** toot gently or repeatedly. **2** (usu. foll. by *along*, *around*, etc.) *colloq.* move casually.

tootsy /'tʊtsɪ/ *n.* (*pl.* **-ies**) *slang* usu. *joc.* foot. [origin uncertain]

Toowoomba /tuː'wuːmbə/ agricultural centre in NE Australia, in Queensland; dairy and sheep farming are the chief activities; pop. (est. 1991) 83 776.

TOP /tɒp/ *abbr. Computing* technical office protocol.

top[1] *–n.* **1** highest point or part. **2 a** highest rank or place. **b** person occupying this. **c** upper end or head (*top of the table*). **3** upper surface or part of a thing. **4** stopper of a bottle, lid of a jar, etc. **5** garment for the upper part of the body. **6** utmost degree; height (*at the top of his voice*). **7** (in *pl.*) *colloq.* person or thing of the best quality. **8** (esp. in *pl.*) leaves etc. of a plant grown esp. for its root (*turnip-tops*). **9** *Naut.* platform round the head of the lower mast. **10** = TOP GEAR (*climbed the hill in top*). *–attrib. adj.* **1** highest in position. **2** highest in degree or importance. *–v.* (**-pp-**) **1** provide with a top, cap, etc. **2** be higher or better than; surpass; be at the top of (*topped the list*). **3** reach the top of (a hill etc.). **4** *slang* kill. **5** *Golf* hit (a ball) above the centre. □ **off the top of one's head** see HEAD. **on top** in a superior position; above. **on top of 1** fully in command of. **2** in close proximity to. **3** in addition to. **on top of the world** *colloq.* exuberant. **over the top 1** over the parapet of a trench (and into battle). **2** beyond what is normally acceptable (*that joke was over the top*). **top off** (or **up**) put an end or the finishing touch to. **top up 1** complete (an amount or number). **2** fill up (a partly full container). **3** top up something for (a person) (*may I top you up with sherry?*). **4** increase the benefits due under an existing insurance scheme, esp. to provide for a pension when a salary increase enables the insured to pay increased premiums. □ **topmost** *adj.* [Old English]

top[2] *n.* toy spinning on a point when set in motion. [Old English]

topaz /'təʊpæz/ *n.* transparent mineral, usu. yellow, used as a gem. [Greek *topazos*]

top brass *n. colloq.* highest-ranking officers.

topcoat *n.* **1** overcoat. **2** outer coat of paint etc.

top dog *n. colloq.* victor; master.

top drawer *n. colloq.* high social position or origin.

top-dress *v.* apply fertilizer on the top of (earth) instead of ploughing it in. □ **top-dressing** *n.*

tope *v.* (**-ping**) *archaic* or *literary* drink alcohol to excess, esp. habitually. □ **toper** *n.* [origin uncertain]

topee var. of TOPI.

Topeka /tə'piːkə/ city in the US, capital of Kansas, a centre of agricultural processing and trade; pop. (est. 1994) 120 646.

top-flight *adj.* of the highest rank of achievement.

topgallant /tɒp'gælənt/ *n.* mast, sail, yard, or rigging immediately above the topmast and topsail.

top gear *n.* highest gear.

top hat *n.* tall silk hat.

◆ **top-hat scheme** *n. colloq.* pension plan for a senior executive of a company. See EXECUTIVE PENSION PLAN.

top-heavy *adj.* disproportionately heavy at the top.

topi /'təʊpɪ/ *n.* (also **topee**) (*pl.* **-s**) hat, esp. a sola topi. [Hindi, = hat]

topiary /'təʊpɪərɪ/ *–adj.* concerned with or formed by clipping shrubs, trees, etc. into ornamental shapes. *–n.* topiary art. [Greek *topos* place]

♦ **TOPIC** /ˈtɒpɪk/ *abbr.* Teletext Output Price Information Computer, computerized communication system providing brokers and market makers on the London Stock Exchange with information about share price movements and bargains as they are transacted. Input is from SEAQ (see STOCK EXCHANGE AUTOMATED QUOTATIONS SYSTEM).

topic /ˈtɒpɪk/ *n.* subject of a discourse, conversation, or argument. [Greek *topos* place, commonplace]

topical *adj.* dealing with the news, current affairs, etc. □ **topicality** /-ˈkælɪtɪ/ *n.* **topically** *adv.*

topknot *n.* knot, tuft, crest, or bow of ribbon, worn or growing on the head.

topless *adj.* **1** without a top. **2 a** (of clothes) having no upper part. **b** (of esp. a woman) bare-breasted. **c** (of a place) where women go topless; employing bare-breasted women.

top-level *adj.* of the highest level of importance, prestige, etc.

♦ **top management** see MANAGEMENT 3.

topmast *n.* mast next above the lower mast.

top-notch *adj. colloq.* first-rate.

topography /təˈpɒgrəfɪ/ *n.* **1** detailed description, representation on a map, etc., of the features of a town, district, etc. **2** such features. □ **topographer** *n.* **topographical** /ˌtɒpəˈgræfɪk(ə)l/ *adj.* [Greek *topos* place]

topology /təˈpɒlədʒɪ/ *n.* the study of geometrical properties unaffected by changes of shape or size. □ **topological** /ˌtɒpəˈlɒdʒɪk(ə)l/ *adj.* [Greek *topos* place]

topper *n. colloq.* = TOP HAT.

topping *–adj. archaic slang* excellent. *–n.* thing that tops another thing, esp. sauce on a dessert etc.

topple /ˈtɒp(ə)l/ *v.* **(-ling) 1** (often foll. by *over, down*) (cause to) fall as if top-heavy. **2** overthrow. [from TOP[1]]

TOPS /tɒps/ *abbr.* Training Opportunities Scheme.

topsail /ˈtɒpseɪl, -s(ə)l/ *n.* square sail next above the lowest; fore-and-aft sail on a gaff.

top secret *adj.* of the highest secrecy.

topside *n.* **1** outer side of a round of beef. **2** side of a ship above the water-line.

♦ **top slicing** *n.* method of assessing the taxable gain on a life-assurance policy. The proceeds of the policy plus all capital withdrawals, less the premiums paid, are divided by the number of years for which the policy has been in force. This amount is added to any other income for the year in which the chargeable event occurred; if this places the taxpayer in a higher tax band, the whole gain is charged at the appropriate marginal rate, i.e. the tax rate in that band less the basic rate of tax. If the sum does not exceed the basic rate tax, no further tax is due.

topsoil *n.* top layer of soil.

topspin *n.* spinning motion imparted to a ball in tennis etc. by hitting it forward and upward.

topsy-turvy /ˌtɒpsɪˈtɜːvɪ/ *adv.* & *adj.* **1** upside down. **2** in utter confusion. [from TOP[1], obsolete *terve* overturn]

top-up *n.* addition; something that serves to top up.

toque /təʊk/ *n.* woman's small brimless hat. [French]

tor *n.* hill or rocky peak. [Old English]

torch *n.* **1** portable battery-powered electric lamp. **2** thing lit for illumination. **3** source of heat, illumination, or enlightenment. □ **carry a torch for** suffer from unrequited love for. [Latin: related to TORT]

torchlight *n.* light of a torch or torches. □ **torchlit** *adj.*

torch song *n.* popular song of unrequited love.

tore *past* of TEAR[1].

toreador /ˈtɒrɪəˌdɔː(r)/ *n.* bullfighter, esp. on horseback. [Latin *taurus*]

Torino see TURIN.

torment *–n.* /ˈtɔːment/ **1** severe physical or mental suffering. **2** cause of this. *–v.* /tɔːˈment/ **1** subject to torment. **2** tease or worry excessively. □ **tormentor** /-ˈmentə(r)/ *n.* [Latin *tormentum*: related to TORT]

tormentil /ˈtɔːməntɪl/ *n.* low-growing plant with bright yellow flowers. [French from medieval Latin]

torn *past part.* of TEAR[1].

tornado /tɔːˈneɪdəʊ/ *n.* (*pl.* **-es**) violent storm of small extent with whirling winds. [Spanish *tronada* thunderstorm]

Tornio /ˈtɔːnɪəʊ/ (Swedish **Tornea**) town in NW Finland, at the head of the Gulf of Bothnia; pop. (1994) 23 274.

Toronto /təˈrɒntəʊ/ largest city in Canada, the capital of Ontario and a centre of business, finance, and industry; its manufactures include chemicals, electrical goods, wood products, food, and clothing; city pop. (1986) 612 300; metropolitan area pop. (1995) 4 338 400.

torpedo /tɔːˈpiːdəʊ/ *–n.* (*pl.* **-es**) **1** cigar-shaped self-propelled underwater missile that explodes on impact with a ship. **2** similar device dropped from an aircraft. *–v.* **(-es, -ed) 1** destroy or attack with a torpedo. **2** destroy or damage (a policy, institution, plan, etc.). [Latin, = electric ray: related to TORPOR]

torpedo-boat *n.* small fast warship armed with torpedoes.

torpid /ˈtɔːpɪd/ *adj.* **1** sluggish, inactive, apathetic. **2** numb. **3** (of a hibernating animal) dormant. □ **torpidity** /-ˈpɪdɪtɪ/ *n.* [Latin: related to TORPOR]

torpor /ˈtɔːpə(r)/ *n.* torpid condition. [Latin *torpeo* be sluggish]

torque /tɔːk/ *n.* **1** *Mech.* twisting or rotating force, esp. in a machine. **2** *hist.* necklace of twisted metal, esp. of the ancient Gauls and Britons. [Latin: related to TORT]

torr /tɔː(r)/ *n.* (*pl.* same) unit of pressure equal to 133.32 pascals ($^1/_{760}$ of one atmosphere). [*Torricelli*, name of a physicist]

torrent /ˈtɒrənt/ *n.* **1** rushing stream of liquid. **2** (in *pl.*) great downpour of rain. **3** (usu. foll. by *of*) violent or copious flow (*torrent of abuse*). □ **torrential** /təˈrenʃ(ə)l/ *adj.* [French from Italian]

Torres Strait /ˈtɒrɪs/ channel separating the N tip of Queensland, Australia, from the island of New Guinea.

torrid /ˈtɒrɪd/ *adj.* **1 a** (of the weather) very hot and dry. **b** (of land etc.) parched by such weather. **2** passionate, intense. [Latin *torreo tost-* parch]

torrid zone *n.* the part of the earth between the Tropics of Cancer and Capricorn.

Tórshavn /ˈtɔːshaʊn/ capital of the Faeroe Islands, situated on the island of Strømø; pop. (1986) 15 300.

torsion /ˈtɔːʃ(ə)n/ *n.* twisting, esp. of one end of a body while the other is held fixed. □ **torsional** *adj.* [Latin: related to TORT]

torso /ˈtɔːsəʊ/ *n.* (*pl.* **-s**) **1** trunk of the human body. **2** statue of this. [Latin *thyrsus* rod]

♦ **tort** *n. Law* civil wrong other than one relating to a contract. The law of tort is concerned with providing damages for personal injury and damage to property resulting from negligence. It is also concerned with protecting against defamation of character and preserving personal freedom, enjoyment of property, and commercial interests. □ **tortious** /ˈtɔːʃəs/ *adj.* [Latin *torqueo tort-* twist]

tortfeasor /ˈtɔːtˌfiːzə(r)/ *n.* person who commits a tort. [French: related to TORT]

tortilla /tɔːˈtiːjə/ *n.* thin flat orig. Mexican maize cake eaten hot. [Spanish diminutive of *torta* cake]

tortoise /ˈtɔːtəs/ *n.* slow-moving reptile with a horny domed shell. [medieval Latin *tortuca*]

tortoiseshell /ˈtɔːtəˌʃel/ *–n.* **1** yellowish-brown mottled or clouded outer shell of some turtles. **2 a** = TORTOISESHELL CAT. **b** = TORTOISESHELL BUTTERFLY. *–adj.* having the colouring or appearance of tortoiseshell.

tortoiseshell butterfly *n.* butterfly with wings mottled like tortoiseshell.

tortoiseshell cat *n.* domestic cat with markings resembling tortoiseshell.

Tortola /tɔːˈtəʊlə/ principal island of the British Virgin Islands (see VIRGIN ISLANDS).

tortuous /'tɔːtʃʊəs/ *adj.* **1** full of twists and turns. **2** devious, circuitous. □ **tortuously** *adv.* [Latin: related to TORT]

■ **Usage** *Tortuous* should not be confused with *torturous* which means 'involving torture, excruciating'.

torture /'tɔːtʃə(r)/ *–n.* **1** infliction of severe bodily pain, esp. as a punishment or means of persuasion. **2** severe physical or mental suffering. *–v.* (**-ring**) subject to torture. □ **torturer** *n.* **torturous** *adj.* [Latin *tortura* twisting: related to TORT]

Tory /'tɔːrɪ/ *–n.* (*pl.* **-ies**) **1** *colloq.* = CONSERVATIVE *n.* 2. **2** *hist.* member of the party that gave rise to the Conservative party (opp. WHIG). *–adj. colloq.* = CONSERVATIVE *adj.* 3. □ **Toryism** *n.* [originally = Irish outlaw]

tosa /'təʊsə/ *n.* dog of a breed of mastiff, orig. kept for dog-fighting. [Japanese]

Toscana see TUSCANY.

tosh *n. colloq.* rubbish, nonsense. [origin unknown]

toss *–v.* **1** throw up (a ball etc.), esp. with the hand. **2** roll about, throw, or be thrown, restlessly or from side to side. **3** (usu. foll. by *to*, *away*, *aside*, *out*, etc.) throw (a thing) lightly or carelessly. **4 a** throw (a coin) into the air to decide a choice etc. by the side on which it lands. **b** (also *absol.*; often foll. by *for*) settle a question or dispute with (a person) in this way. **5** (of a bull etc.) throw (a person etc.) up with the horns. **6** coat (food) with dressing etc. by shaking it. *–n.* **1** act of tossing (a coin, the head, etc.). **2** fall, esp. from a horse. □ **toss one's head** throw it back esp. in anger, impatience, etc. **toss off 1** drink off at a draught. **2** dispatch (work) rapidly or without effort. **3** *coarse slang* masturbate. **toss up** toss a coin. [origin unknown]

toss-up *n.* **1** doubtful matter. **2** tossing of a coin.

tot[1] *n.* **1** small child. **2** dram of liquor. [originally dial.]

tot[2] *v.* (**-tt-**) **1** (usu. foll. by *up*) add (figures etc.). **2** (foll. by *up*) (of items) mount up. □ **tot up to** amount to. [abbreviation of TOTAL or of Latin *totum* the whole]

total /'təʊt(ə)l/ *–adj.* **1** complete, comprising the whole (*total number of votes*). **2** absolute, unqualified (*in total ignorance*). *–n.* total number or amount. *–v.* (**-ll-**; *US* **-l-**) **1 a** amount in number to. **b** find the total of. **2** (foll. by *to*, *up to*) amount to. [medieval Latin *totus* entire]

♦ **total-absorption costing** *n.* method of arriving at the cost of producing goods and services that allocates to them not only such direct costs as labour and materials but also the other costs of the organization, e.g. general overheads and head-office costs. This method ensures, if the goods can be sold at the resulting price, that all costs will be covered. However, opportunities may be lost to make some contribution to overheads if they are not fully covered. Cf. MARGINAL COSTING.

♦ **total income** *n.* (also **statutory total income**) income of a taxpayer from all sources, consisting of income from sources based on the income of the current year and income from other sources based on income of the preceding year. This artificial concept is used to calculate a person's income tax for a given year.

---

totalitarian /təʊˌtælɪ'teərɪən/ *adj.* of a one-party form of government requiring complete subservience to the state. □ **totalitarianism** *n.*

totality /təʊ'tælɪtɪ/ *n.* **1** complete amount. **2** time during which an eclipse is total.

totalizator /'təʊtəlaɪˌzeɪtə(r)/ *n.* (also **totalisator**) **1** device showing the number and amount of bets staked on a race, to facilitate the division of the total among those backing the winner. **2** system of betting based on this.

totalize /'təʊtəˌlaɪz/ *v.* (also **-ise**) (**-zing** or **-sing**) collect into a total; find the total of.

totally *adv.* completely.

♦ **total profits** *n.pl.* income of a company from all sources, including capital gains. This figure, after deduction of annual charges, is used to calculate the corporation tax payable by the company. Dividends from UK companies are not included in the figure.

---

tote[1] *n. slang* totalizator. [abbreviation]

tote[2] *v.* (**-ting**) esp. *US colloq.* carry, convey (*toting a gun*). [originally US, probably of dial. origin]

tote bag *n.* woman's large bag for shopping etc.

totem /'təʊtəm/ *n.* **1** natural object, esp. an animal, adopted esp. by North American Indians as an emblem of a clan or individual. **2** image of this. □ **totemic** /-'temɪk/ *adj.* [Algonquian]

totem-pole *n.* pole on which totems are carved or hung.

t'other /'tʌðə(r)/ *adj. & pron. dial.* or *joc.* the other. [*thet other* 'that other']

totter *–v.* **1** stand or walk unsteadily or feebly. **2 a** (of a building etc.) shake as if about to collapse. **b** (of a system of government etc.) be about to fall. *–n.* unsteady or shaky movement or gait. □ **tottery** *adj.* [Dutch]

totting-up *n.* **1** adding of separate items. **2** adding up of convictions for driving offences, possibly resulting in disqualification.

toucan /'tuːkən/ *n.* tropical American fruit-eating bird with an immense beak. [Tupi]

touch /tʌtʃ/ *–v.* **1** come into or be in physical contact with (a thing, each other, etc.). **2** (often foll. by *with*) bring the hand etc. into contact with. **3** bring (two things) into mutual contact. **4** rouse tender or painful feelings in. **5** strike lightly. **6** (usu. with *neg.*) **a** disturb, harm, or affect. **b** have any dealings with. **c** consume, use (*I don't touch alcohol*). **7** concern. **8 a** reach as far as, esp. momentarily. **b** (usu. with *neg.*) approach in excellence etc. (*can't touch him for style*). **9** modify (*pity touched with fear*). **10** (as **touched** *adj.*) *colloq.* slightly mad. **11** (usu. foll. by *for*) *slang* ask for and get money etc. from (a person) (*touched him for £5*). *–n.* **1** act of touching (*felt a touch on my arm*). **2** faculty of perception through physical contact, esp. with the fingers. **3 a** small amount; slight trace. **b** (prec. by *a*) slightly (*a touch too salty*). **4 a** manner of playing keys or strings. **b** response of the keys or strings. **c** style of workmanship, writing, etc. **5** distinguishing manner or detail (*a professional touch*). **6** special skill (*have lost my touch*). **7** (esp. in *pl.*) light stroke with a pencil etc. **8** *slang* **a** act of getting money etc. from a person by asking. **b** = SOFT TOUCH. **9** *Football* part of the field outside the side limits. □ **in touch** (often foll. by *with*) **1** in communication. **2** aware. **lose touch** (often foll. by *with*) **1** cease to be informed. **2** cease to be in contact. **out of touch** (often foll. by *with*) **1** not in correspondence. **2** not up to date. **3** lacking in awareness. **touch at** (of a ship) call at (a port etc.). **touch bottom 1** reach the bottom of water with one's feet. **2** be at the lowest or worst point. **touch down** (of an aircraft) make contact with the ground in landing. **touch off 1** explode by touching with a match etc. **2** initiate (a process) suddenly. **touch on** (or **upon**) **1** refer to or mention briefly or casually. **2** verge on. **touch up 1** give finishing touches to or retouch. **2** *slang* sexually molest. **touch wood** touch something wooden to avert ill luck. [French *tochier*]

touch-and-go *adj.* critical, risky.

touchdown *n.* act of touching down by an aircraft.

touché /tuː'ʃeɪ/ *int.* **1** acknowledgement of a justified accusation or retort. **2** acknowledgement of a hit by a fencing-opponent. [French, = *touched*]

touching *–adj.* moving; pathetic. *–prep. literary* concerning. □ **touchingly** *adv.*

touch-line *n.* (in various sports) either of the lines marking the side boundaries of the pitch.

touch pad see TOUCH-SENSITIVE DEVICE.

touch-paper *n.* paper impregnated with nitre, for igniting etc.

touch-sensitive device *n. Computing* device that responds to the touch of a finger by transmitting the coordinates of the touched point (i.e. its position) to a computer. The touch-sensitive area may be the VDU screen itself, in which case it is called a **touch-sensitive screen**. Alternatively it may be part of the keyboard or a separate unit that can be placed on a desk, and movement of the finger across the **touch pad** can cause the cursor to move around the screen.

touchstone *n.* **1** dark schist or jasper used for testing alloys by marking it with them. **2** criterion.

touch-type *v.* type without looking at the keys. □ **touch-typist** *n.*

touchwood *n.* readily inflammable wood etc., esp. when made soft by fungi.

touchy *adj.* (**-ier, -iest**) apt to take offence; over-sensitive. □ **touchily** *adv.* **touchiness** *n.*

tough /tʌf/ *–adj.* **1** hard to break, cut, tear, or chew. **2** able to endure hardship; hardy. **3** unyielding, stubborn, difficult (*it was a tough job*). **4** *colloq.* **a** acting sternly; hard (*get tough with*). **b** (of circumstances, luck, etc.) severe, hard. **5** *colloq.* criminal or violent. *–n.* tough person, esp. a ruffian. □ **toughen** *v.* **toughness** *n.* [Old English]

Toulon /tuːˈlɔ̃/ port and naval base in S France, on the Mediterranean coast; industries include marine engineering, chemicals, and textiles; pop. (1990) 170 167.

Toulouse /tuːˈluːz/ city in SW France, capital of the Midi-Pyrénées region; a centre of the aerospace industry, it also produces armaments, chemicals, and textiles; pop. (1990) 608 427.

toupee /ˈtuːpeɪ/ *n.* hairpiece to cover a bald spot. [French]

tour /tʊə(r)/ *–n.* **1 a** journey from place to place as a holiday; sightseeing excursion. **b** a walk round; inspection (*made a tour of the garden*). **2** spell of duty on military or diplomatic service. **3** series of performances, matches, etc., at different places. *–v.* **1** (usu. foll. by *through*) make a tour. **2** make a tour of (a country etc.). □ **on tour** (esp. of a team, theatre company, etc.) touring. [Latin: related to TURN]

tour de force /ˌtʊə də ˈfɔːs/ *n.* (*pl.* ***tours de force***) outstanding feat or performance. [French]

tourer *n.* car or caravan for touring in.

tourism *n.* commercial organization and operation of holidays.

tourist *n.* **1** holiday-maker, esp. abroad (often *attrib.*: *tourist season*). **2** member of a touring sports team.

tourist class *n.* lowest class of passenger accommodation in a ship, aircraft, etc.

touristy *adj.* usu. *derog.* appealing to or visited by many tourists.

tourmaline /ˈtʊərməˌliːn/ *n.* mineral of various colours used as a gemstone. [French from Sinhalese]

Tournai /tʊəˈneɪ/ (Flemish **Doornik** /ˈdɔːniːk/) textile-manufacturing town in Belgium, near the Belgian–French frontier; pop. (est. 1995) 68 086.

tournament /ˈtʊənəmənt/ *n.* **1** large contest of many rounds (*chess tournament*). **2** display of military exercises etc. (*Royal Tournament*). **3** *hist.* pageant with jousting. [French: related to TOURNEY]

tournedos /ˈtʊənəˌdəʊ/ *n.* (*pl.* same /-ˌdəʊz/) small round thick cut from a fillet of beef. [French]

tourney /ˈtʊənɪ/ *–n.* (*pl.* **-s**) tournament. *–v.* (**-eys, -eyed**) take part in a tournament. [French: related to TURN]

tourniquet /ˈtʊənɪˌkeɪ/ *n.* device for stopping the flow of blood through an artery by constriction. [French]

tour operator *n.* travel agent specializing in package holidays.

Tours /tʊə(r)/ industrial city and tourist centre in W central France; pop. (1990) 133 403.

tousle /ˈtaʊz(ə)l/ *v.* (**-ling**) **1** make (esp. the hair) untidy. **2** handle roughly. [dial. *touse*]

tout *–v.* **1** (usu. foll. by *for*) solicit custom persistently; pester customers. **2** solicit the custom of (a person) or for (a thing), esp. sell (tickets) at a price higher than the official one. **3** spy out the movements and condition of racehorses in training. *–n.* person who touts, esp. tickets. [Old English, = peep]

tow[1] /təʊ/ *–v.* pull (a boat, vehicle, etc.) along by a rope etc. *–n.* towing or being towed. □ **have in** (or **on) tow 1** be towing. **2** be accompanied by and often in charge of (a person). **on tow** being towed. [Old English]

tow[2] *n.* coarse part of flax or hemp prepared for spinning. [Low German *touw*]

toward /təˈwɔːd/ *prep.* = TOWARDS.

towards /təˈwɔːdz/ *prep.* **1** in the direction of (*set out towards town*). **2** as regards; in relation to (*attitude towards death*). **3** as a contribution to; for (*put it towards her holiday*). **4** near (*towards the end of our journey*). [Old English, = future: related to TO, -WARD]

tow-bar *n.* bar for towing esp. a caravan.

towel /ˈtaʊəl/ *–n.* absorbent cloth or paper etc. used for drying after washing. *–v.* (**-ll-**; *US* **-l-**) (often *refl.*) wipe or dry with a towel. [French *toail(l)e* from Germanic]

towelling *n.* thick soft absorbent cloth, used esp. for towels.

tower *–n.* **1** tall structure, often part of a church, castle, etc. **2** fortress etc. with a tower. **3** tall structure housing machinery etc. (*cooling tower; control tower*). *–v.* **1** (usu. foll. by *above, up*) reach or be high or above; be superior. **2** (as **towering** *adj.*) **a** high, lofty (*towering intellect*). **b** violent (*towering rage*). [Greek *turris*]

tower block *n.* tall building containing offices or flats.

tower of strength *n.* person who gives strong emotional support.

tow-headed *adj.* having very light or unkempt hair.

town *n.* **1 a** densely populated built-up defined area, between a city and a village in size. **b** densely populated area, esp. as opposed to the country. **2 a** London or the chief city or town in an area (*went up to town*). **b** central business area in a neighbourhood. □ **go to town** *colloq.* do something with great energy or enthusiasm. **on the town** *colloq.* enjoying night-life in a town. [Old English]

◆ **Town Clearing** see ASSOCIATION FOR PAYMENT CLEARING SERVICES.

---

town clerk *n. US* & *hist.* official in charge of the records etc. of a town.

town crier *n.* = CRIER 2.

townee var. of TOWNIE.

town gas *n.* manufactured gas for domestic and commercial use.

town hall *n.* headquarters of local government, with public meeting rooms etc.

town house *n.* **1** town residence, esp. of a person with a house in the country. **2** terrace house. **3** house in a planned group in a town.

townie /ˈtaʊnɪ/ *n.* (also **townee** /-ˈniː/) *derog.* town inhabitant ignorant of country life.

town planning *n.* planning of the construction and growth of towns. □ **town planner** *n.*

townscape *n.* **1** visual appearance of a town or towns. **2** picture of a town.

townsfolk *n.* inhabitants of a town or towns.

township *n.* **1** *S.Afr.* urban area set aside for Black occupation. **2** *US* & *Can.* **a** division of a county. **b** district six miles square. **3** *hist.* small town or village forming part of a large parish. **4** *Austral.* & *NZ* small town.

townsman *n.* (*fem.* **townswoman**) inhabitant of a town.

townspeople *n.pl.* people of a town.

Townsville /ˈtaʊnzvɪl/ industrial port, commercial centre, and resort in NE Australia, in Queensland; it has copper-refining, sugar-processing, and meat-packing industries; pop. (est. 1995) 124 900.

tow-path *n.* path by a river or canal, orig. used for towing a boat by horse.

toxaemia /tɒkˈsiːmɪə/ *n.* (*US* **toxemia**) **1** blood-poisoning. **2** increased blood pressure in pregnancy. [related to TOXIC, Greek *haima* blood]

toxic /ˈtɒksɪk/ *adj.* **1** poisonous. **2** of poison. □ **toxicity** /-ˈsɪsɪtɪ/ *n.* [Greek *toxikon* poison for arrows]

toxicology /ˌtɒksɪˈkɒlədʒɪ/ *n.* the study of poisons. □ **toxicological** /-kəˈlɒdʒɪk(ə)l/ *adj.* **toxicologist** *n.*

toxin /ˈtɒksɪn/ *n.* poison produced by a living organism.

toxocara /ˌtɒksəˈkɑːrə/ *n.* parasitic worm in dogs and cats.

toxocariasis /ˌtɒksəkəˈraɪəsɪs/ *n.* disease resulting from infection by the toxocara.

toy *–n.* **1** plaything. **2** thing regarded as providing amusement. **3** (usu. *attrib.*) diminutive breed of dog etc. *–v.* (usu. foll. by *with*) **1** trifle, amuse oneself, flirt. **2** move a thing idly. [origin unknown]

toy boy *n. colloq.* woman's much younger boyfriend.

♦ **Toyoda** /tɔɪˈəʊdæ/, **Shoichiro** (1925–) Japanese businessman, president (1982–92) and chairman (from 1992) of the Toyota Motor Corporation, which was founded by his grandfather. He is also chairman (from 1994) of Keidansen, Japan's elite Federation of Industrial Organizations. His brother, **Tasuro Toyoda** (1929–), was president of Toyota from 1992 to 1995.

toyshop *n.* shop selling toys.

TP *–abbr.* **1** *Insurance* third party. **2** *Computing* transaction processing. *–airline flight code* TAP Air Portugal.

t.p. *abbr. Commerce* (French) tout payé (= all expenses paid).

TPC *abbr.* (in Australia) Trade Practices Commission.

t.p.d. *abbr.* (also **TPD**) tonnes per day.

t.p.h. *abbr.* (also **TPH**) tonnes per hour.

TPI *abbr.* **1** = TAX AND PRICE INDEX. **2** Tropical Products Institute.

TPM *abbr.* **1** *Computing* etc. third-party maintenance. **2** (also **t.p.m.**) tonnes per minute.

TQ *–abbr.* **1** (also **t.q.**) *Banking* tel quel (exchange rate). **2** (in manufacturing) total quality. *–postcode* Torquay.

TQM *abbr.* total quality management.

TR *–abbr.* **1** tariff reform. **2** tonnes registered. *–international vehicle registration* Turkey. *–international civil aircraft marking* Gabon. *–postcode* Truro.

Trabzon /ˈtræbz(ə)n/ (formerly **Trebizond** /ˈtrebɪˌzɒnd/) city and port in Turkey, on the Black Sea; pop. (est. 1994) 145 400.

trace[1] *–v.* (**-cing**) **1 a** observe or find vestiges or signs of by investigation. **b** (often foll. by *along*, *through*, *to*, etc.) follow or mark the track or position of. **c** (often foll. by *back*) follow to its origins. **2** copy (a drawing etc.) by drawing over its lines on superimposed translucent paper. **3** (often foll. by *out*) mark out, delineate, sketch, or write, esp. laboriously. **4** make one's way along (a path etc.). *–n.* **1 a** indication of something having existed; vestige. **b** very small quantity. **2** track or footprint. **3** track left by the moving pen of an instrument etc. □ **traceable** *adj.* [Latin *traho* draw]

trace[2] *n.* each of the two side-straps, chains, or ropes by which a horse draws a vehicle. □ **kick over the traces** become insubordinate or reckless. [French *trais*, pl. of TRAIT]

trace element *n.* chemical element required only in minute amounts by living organisms for normal growth.

tracer *n.* **1** bullet etc. that is visible in flight because of flames etc. emitted. **2** artificial radioactive isotope which can be followed through the body by the radiation it produces.

tracery *n.* (*pl.* **-ies**) **1** ornamental stone openwork, esp. in the upper part of a Gothic window. **2** fine decorative pattern.

trachea /trəˈkiːə/ *n.* (*pl.* **-cheae** /-ˈkiːiː/) windpipe. [Latin from Greek]

tracheotomy /ˌtrækɪˈɒtəmɪ/ *n.* (*pl.* **-ies**) incision of the trachea to relieve an obstruction.

tracing *n.* **1** traced copy of a drawing etc. **2** act of tracing.

tracing-paper *n.* translucent paper for making tracings.

track *–n.* **1 a** mark(s) left by a person, animal, vehicle, etc. **b** (in *pl.*) such marks, esp. footprints. **2** rough path, esp. one beaten by use. **3** continuous railway line. **4 a** racecourse; circuit. **b** prepared course for runners etc. **5 a** groove on a gramophone record. **b** section of a record, CD, or magnetic tape containing one song etc. **c** *Computing* portion of a magnetic storage medium along which data is recorded. With hard disks and floppy disks the tracks form concentric circles (see also SECTOR 4). With magnetic tape, DAT, etc. the tracks run lengthwise. **6** line of travel (*track of the comet*). **7** band round the wheels of a tank etc. **8** line of thought or action. *–v.* **1** follow the track of. **2** trace (a course, development, etc.) by vestiges. **3** (often foll. by *back*, *in*, etc.) (of a film or television camera) move in relation to the subject being filmed. □ **in one's tracks** *colloq.* where one stands, instantly (*stopped him in his tracks*). **keep** (or **lose**) **track of** follow (or fail to follow) the course of. **make tracks** *colloq.* depart. **make tracks for** *colloq.* go in pursuit of or towards. **off the track** away from the subject. **track down** reach or capture by tracking. □ **tracker** *n.* [French *trac*]

tracker ball *n. Computing* ball that is held in a socket with less than half its surface exposed and can be rotated by the operator's fingers. The direction of rotation produces a corresponding movement of the cursor on a screen.

tracker dog *n.* police dog tracking by scent.

track events *n.pl.* running-races as opposed to jumping etc.

track record *n.* person's past performance.

track shoe *n.* runner's spiked shoe.

track suit *n.* loose warm suit worn for exercising etc.

tract[1] *n.* **1** stretch or extent of territory, esp. large. **2** bodily organ or system (*digestive tract*). [Latin *traho tract-* pull]

tract[2] *n.* pamphlet, esp. propagandist. [apparently Latin *tractatus* from *tracto* handle]

tractable *adj.* (of a person or material) easily handled; manageable. □ **tractability** /-ˈbɪlɪtɪ/ *n.* [Latin *tracto* handle]

traction /ˈtrækʃ(ə)n/ *n.* **1** act of hauling or pulling a thing over a surface. **2** sustained therapeutic pulling on a limb etc. with pulleys, weights, etc. [French or medieval Latin: related to TRACT[1]]

traction-engine *n.* steam or diesel engine for drawing heavy loads on roads, fields, etc.

tractor /ˈtræktə(r)/ *n.* **1** vehicle used for pulling farm machinery etc. **2** traction-engine. [related to TRACTION]

trad *colloq. –n.* traditional jazz. *–adj.* traditional. [abbreviation]

trade *–n.* **1 a** buying and selling. **b** this between nations etc. **2 a** activity of selling goods or services in order to make a profit. Profits from trade are taxed under income tax or corporation tax on income, rather than under capital-gains tax or corporation tax on capital gains. The Royal Commission on the Taxation of Profits and Income in 1955 identified six 'badges of trade': the subject matter of the transaction, length of ownership of the asset traded, frequency of similar transactions, work done on the asset to make it marketable, the circumstances responsible for its realization, and the motive to make a profit. However, none of these individually establishes a transaction as trading. **b** business of a specified nature or time (*Christmas trade*; *tourist trade*). **3** skilled craft practised professionally. **4** (usu. prec. by *the*) people engaged in a specific trade (*the trade will never agree*). **5** *US* transaction, esp. a swap. **6** (usu. in *pl.*) trade wind. *–v.* (**-ding**) **1** (often foll. by *in*, *with*) engage in trade; buy and sell. **2 a** exchange in commerce. **b** exchange (insults, blows, etc.). **c** *US* swap. **3** (usu. foll. by *with*, *for*) have a transaction with a person for a thing. □ **trade in** (often foll. by *for*) exchange (esp. a used car) in part payment for another. **trade off** exchange, esp. as a compromise. **trade on** take advantage of. □ **tradable** *adj.* **tradeable** *adj.* [Low German, = track: related to TREAD]

♦ **trade advertising** *n.* advertising aimed at members of the distribution channel of a product or service rather than at the consumer. It is sometimes advantageous to draw the attention of the trade to a product either in addition to consumer advertising or instead of it (usu. because it is much cheaper).

♦ **trade agreement** *n.* commercial treaty between two

(**bilateral trade agreement**) or more (**multilateral trade agreement**) nations.

♦ **trade association** *n.* association of companies in the same trade, formed to represent them in negotiations with governments, unions, other trade associations, etc., and to keep members informed of new developments affecting the trade. Trade associations also frequently draw up contracts for their members to use and provide arbitration procedures to settle disputes between members.

♦ **trade barrier** *n.* action by a government that restricts free trading between organizations within that country and the world outside. Tariffs, quotas, embargoes, sanctions, and restrictive regulations all present barriers to free trade.

♦ **trade bill** *n.* bill of exchange used to pay for goods. Trade bills are usu. either held until they mature, as they do not command a favourable discount rate compared to bank bills, or they are discounted by banks.

♦ **trade bloc** *n.* group of nations, e.g. the EC countries, that are united by trade agreements.

♦ **trade creditor** *n.* person who is owed money by an organization for having provided goods or services to that organization.

♦ **trade cycle** *n.* = BUSINESS CYCLE.

♦ **trade description** *n.* direct or indirect indication of certain characteristics of goods or of any part of them, such as their quantity, size, fitness for their purpose, time or place of origin, method of manufacture or processing, and price. Under the Trade Descriptions Act (1968), it is a criminal offence to apply a false trade description to goods or to supply or offer any goods to which a false description is applied.

♦ **trade discount** *n.* (also **trade terms**) reduction of the recommended retail price of a product or service that is offered to distributors because they buy regularly in bulk. The difference between the retail price and the discounted price provides the retailer's overheads and profit. The amount of the trade discount will often depend on the size of an order. Thus, a supermarket chain buying goods in very large quantities expects a higher trade discount than a corner shop buying in small quantities. It is also usual for members of the same trade to offer each other trade terms as a matter of course.

♦ **trade dispute** *n.* (also **industrial dispute**) dispute between an employer and employees (or their trade union), usu. about wages or conditions of working. Under the Trade Union and Labour Relations Act (1974), a person cannot be sued in tort for an act that is committed in furtherance of a trade dispute on the grounds that it induces or threatens any breach of or interference with the performance of a contract. Generally, such immunity extends only to the acts of employees against their own employer. Picketing may be unlawful when it is directed against an employer who is neither a party to the dispute nor the customer or supplier of the employer in dispute. Moreover, there is no immunity in respect of action taken to enforce a closed-shop agreement. The act, as amended by the Employment Acts (1982 and 1988) and the Trade Union Act (1984), gives similar immunity to trade unions for their actions committed in contemplation or furtherance of a trade dispute provided the action concerned is authorized by a majority vote in favour of the action in a secret ballot of the union's members. Under the Employment Act (1988) a trade union member can obtain a court order preventing industrial action being taken if it has not been authorized by a ballot. Under the Employment Act (1982), when a trade union's immunity does not apply and it is ordered to pay damages (other than for causing personal injury or for breach of duty concerning the ownership, control, or use of property, or for products liability under the Consumer Protection Act (1987)), the amount awarded may not exceed specified limits. These range from £10,000 for a union with under 5000 members to £250,000 for a union with 100 000 or more members.

♦ **traded option** see OPTION 3.

♦ **trade gap** *n.* deficit in a nation's balance of payments.

trade-in *n.* thing given in part exchange for another.

♦ **trade investment** *n.* shares in or loans made to another company with a view to facilitating trade with the other company.

♦ **trade mark** *n.* **1** symbol secured by law or custom as representing a company, product, etc. It may consist of a device, words, or a combination of these. A trader who registers a trade mark at the Register of Trade Marks, which is at the Patent Office, enjoys the exclusive right to use the trade mark in connection with the goods for which it was registered. Any manufacturer, dealer, importer, or retailer may register a trade mark. Registration is initially for seven years and is then renewable. The right to remain on the register may be lost if the trade mark is not used or is misused. The owner of a trade mark may assign it or, subject to the Registrar's approval, allow others to use it. If anyone uses a registered trade mark without the owner's permission, or uses a mark that is likely to be confused with a registered trade mark, the owner can sue for an injunction and damages or an account of profits. The owner of a trade mark that is not registered in the Register of Trade Marks but is identified with particular goods through established use may bring an action for passing off in the case of infringement. **2** distinctive characteristic etc.

trade name *n.* **1** name by which a thing is called in a trade. **2** name given to a product. **3** name under which a business trades.

trade-off *n.* balance, compromise.

♦ **Tradepoint Investment Exchange** Recognized Investment Exchange for securities in London. The London Clearing House acts as the central counterparty and all deals are settled through CREST.

♦ **trade price** *n.* price paid for goods to a wholesaler or manufacturer by a retailer, usu. the recommended retail price less the trade discount.

trader *n.* **1** person engaged in trade. **2** merchant ship.

♦ **trade reference** *n.* reference concerning the creditworthiness of a trader given by another member of the same trade, usu. to a supplier. If a firm wishes to purchase goods on credit from a supplier, the supplier will usu. ask for a trade reference from another member of the same trade, in addition to a banker's reference.

tradescantia /ˌtrædɪˈskæntɪə/ *n.* (usu. trailing) plant with large blue, white, or pink flowers. [*Tradescant*, name of a naturalist]

♦ **trade secret** *n.* **1** knowledge of some process or product belonging to a business, disclosure of which would harm the business's interests. In the UK, the courts will usu. grant injunctions to prohibit any threatened disclosure of trade secrets by employees, former employees, and others to whom the secrets have been disclosed in confidence. See also INDUSTRIAL ESPIONAGE. **2** *joc.* any secret.

tradesman *n.* (*fem.* **tradeswoman**) person engaged in trade, esp. a shopkeeper.

tradespeople *n.pl.* people engaged in trade.

♦ **Trades Union Congress** *n.* (also **TUC**) official representative body of British trade unions, to which most unions belong. It represents the trade-union movement in negotiations with the government and such bodies as the Confederation of British Industry. It also acts as an arbitrator in disputes between member unions.

♦ **trade terms** *n.pl.* = TRADE DISCOUNT.

♦ **trade union** *n.* (also **trades union**) organized association of employees in a trade, profession, etc., formed to protect and further their rights and interests and to regulate relations between employees and employers or employers' associations. A **house** (or **company**) **union** is an association of employees all belonging to the same company, which will probably have no connection with the trade-union movement. An **industrial** (or **general**) **union** has members who work in the same industry; it is usu. very large. A **craft union** is a small union of skilled workers. Unions' affairs are regulated by the Trade Union Act (1984) and the Employment Act (1988). These provide that secret ballots must be held for election of unions' executive committees and before any industrial action backed by the union is taken. The Employment Act (1988) gives a right to trade-union members not to be unjustifiably disciplined by their union (for example for failing to take industrial action). A member can apply to an industrial tribunal for a declaration that he or she has been unjustifiably disciplined. □ **trade-unionism** *n.* **trade-unionist** *n.*

♦ **trade-union official** *n.* officer of a trade union (or of a branch or section of it) or a person elected or appointed in accordance with the union's rules to represent a group of its members. An employee who is a trade-union official and whose normal working week in employment is of 16 hours or more is entitled to time off work, paid at the normal rate, for certain purposes. These must be official union duties concerning industrial relations between his or her employer and any associated employer and their employees or training approved by the Trade Union Congress and relevant to the official's union duties.

---

trade wind *n.* wind blowing continually towards the equator and deflected westward.

trading *n.* act of engaging in trade.

♦ **trading account** *n.* part of a profit and loss account in which the cost of goods sold is compared with the money raised by their sale in order to arrive at the gross profit.

♦ **trading estate** *n.* (also **industrial estate**) specially-designed industrial and commercial area, usu. sited some distance from residential areas and where premises can be acquired at low rentals. Some are developed by private companies, which buy the land cheaply from the government in areas in which the government wishes to encourage development; others are run by the government itself.

---

trading post *n.* store etc. in a remote or unsettled region.

♦ **trading profit** *n.* profit of an organization before deductions for such items as interest, directors' fees, auditors' remuneration, etc.

♦ **trading-stamps** *n.pl.* stamps bought from a trading-stamp company by a retailer and given, in proportion to the goods purchased, to customers, who can exchange them for goods or for cash from the trading-stamp company. The issue of trading-stamps is regulated by the Trading Stamp Act (1964). Each stamp must be clearly marked with a monetary value and the name of the issuing company. The retailer aims to cover the cost of the stamps by profits from any resulting increased custom.

♦ **trading stock** see STOCK-IN-TRADE 1, 2.

---

tradition /trəˈdɪʃ(ə)n/ *n.* **1 a** custom, opinion, or belief handed down to posterity. **b** this process of handing down. **2** artistic, literary, etc. principles based on experience and practice; any one of these. [Latin *trado -dit-* hand on, betray]

traditional *adj.* **1** of, based on, or obtained by tradition. **2** (of jazz) in the style of the early 20th century. □ **traditionally** *adv.*

traditionalism *n.* respect or support for tradition. □ **traditionalist** *n.* & *adj.*

♦ **traditional option** *Finance* see OPTION 3.

---

traduce /trəˈdjuːs/ *v.* (**-cing**) speak ill of; misrepresent. □ **traducement** *n.* **traducer** *n.* [Latin *traduco*, = disgrace]

traffic /ˈtræfɪk/ *–n.* **1** vehicles moving on a public highway or in the air or at sea. **2** (usu. foll. by *in*) trade, esp. illegal (*drugs traffic*). **3** coming and going of people or goods by road, rail, air, sea, etc. **4** dealings between people etc. (*had no traffic with them*). **5** messages etc. transmitted through a communications system; volume of this. *–v.* (**-ck-**) **1** (usu. foll. by *in*) deal in something, esp. illegally. **2** deal in; barter. □ **trafficker** *n.* [French from Italian]

traffic island *n.* raised area in a road to divide traffic streams and for pedestrians to use in crossing.

traffic jam *n.* traffic at a standstill because of road-works, an accident, etc.

traffic-light *n.* (also **traffic-lights** *n.pl.*) signal controlling road traffic by coloured lights.

traffic warden *n.* official employed to help control road traffic and esp. parking.

tragedian /trəˈdʒiːdɪən/ *n.* **1** writer of tragedies. **2** (*fem.* **tragedienne** /-dɪˈen/) actor in tragedy. [French: related to TRAGEDY]

tragedy /ˈtrædʒɪdɪ/ *n.* (*pl.* **-ies**) **1** serious accident, disaster, etc.; sad event. **2 a** play dealing with tragic events and ending unhappily, esp. with the downfall of the protagonist. **b** such plays as a genre. [Greek *tragōidia*]

tragic /ˈtrædʒɪk/ *adj.* **1** disastrous; greatly distressing; very sad. **2** of tragedy. □ **tragically** *adv.*

tragicomedy /ˌtrædʒɪˈkɒmədɪ/ *n.* (*pl.* **-ies**) play or situation with a mixture of comedy and tragedy. □ **tragicomic** *adj.*

trail *–n.* **1** track or scent left by a moving thing, person, etc. **2** beaten path, esp. through a wild region. **3** long line of people or things following behind something. **4** part dragging behind a thing or person. *–v.* **1** draw or be drawn along behind, esp. on the ground. **2** (often foll. by *behind*) walk wearily. **3** follow the trail of; pursue. **4** be losing in a contest (*trailing by three points*). **5** (usu. foll. by *away*, *off*) peter out; tail off. **6 a** (of a plant etc.) grow or hang over a wall, along the ground, etc. **b** hang loosely. **7** (often *refl.*) drag (oneself, one's limbs, etc.) along wearily etc. [French or Low German]

trail-blazer *n.* **1** person who marks a new track through wild country. **2** pioneer. □ **trail-blazing** *n.*

trailer *n.* **1** set of brief extracts from a film etc., used to advertise it in advance. **2** vehicle towed by another, esp.: **a** the rear section of an articulated lorry. **b** an open cart. **c** a platform for transporting a boat etc. **d** *US* a caravan.

trailing edge *n.* rear edge of an aircraft's wing etc.

train *–v.* **1 a** (often foll. by *to* + infin.) teach (a person, animal, oneself, etc.) a specified skill, esp. by practice. **b** undergo this process (*trained as a teacher*). **2** bring or come to physical efficiency by exercise, diet, etc. **3** (often foll. by *along*, *up*) guide the growth of (a plant). **4** (usu. as **trained** *adj.*) make (the mind, eye, etc.) discerning through practice etc. **5** (often foll. by *on*) point or aim (a gun, camera, etc.) at an object etc. *–n.* **1** series of railway carriages or trucks drawn by an engine. **2** thing dragged along behind or forming the back part of a dress, robe, etc. **3** succession or series of people, things, events, etc. (*train of thought*). **4** body of followers; retinue. □ **in train** properly arranged or directed. □ **trainee** /-ˈniː/ *n.* [Latin *traho* draw]

train-bearer *n.* person holding up the train of a robe etc.

trainer *n.* **1** person who trains horses, athletes, footballers, etc. **2** aircraft or simulator used to train pilots. **3** soft running shoe.

training *n.* process of teaching or learning a skill etc.

♦ **Training Agency** *n.* organization that came into existence in 1989 to replace the Training Commission, which itself replaced the **Manpower Services Commission**. It is separate from the government but is responsible to the Secretary of State for Employment and, with government support, provides opportunities for training and retraining and for unemployed 16–17-year-olds to join its **Youth Training Scheme** (**YTS**). This gives a two-year vocational training, 20 weeks of which is spent in a college or training centre, the rest being devoted to planned work experience; it usu. leads to a vocational qualification. Entrants receive a tax-free weekly allowance. The Training Agency is also responsible for skills training and adult training. See also TRAINING AND ENTERPRISE COUNCIL.

♦ **Training and Enterprise Council** *n.* (also **TEC**) one of a network of some 80 employer-led councils set up in 1989 under contracts with the Training Agency to foster economic growth in England and Wales. Their specific objectives are promoting effective training by employers to meet local requirements, providing Youth Training Schemes (see TRAINING AGENCY), developing employment training to enable unemployed people to train for local jobs, providing support for new and expanding businesses, and stimulating enterprise and economic growth by means of the Enterprise Allowance Scheme. The office staff of an area's Training Agency is available to TECs. A separate framework for training and enterprise is available in Scotland.

---

train-spotter *n.* person who collects locomotive numbers as a hobby. □ **train-spotting** *n.*

traipse *colloq.* –*v.* (**-sing**) tramp or trudge wearily. –*n.* tedious journey on foot. [origin unknown]

trait /treɪ, treɪt/ *n.* characteristic. [Latin *tractus*: related to TRACT[1]]

traitor /'treɪtə(r)/ *n.* (*fem.* **traitress**) (often foll. by *to*) person who is treacherous or disloyal, esp. to his or her country. □ **traitorous** *adj.* [Latin *traditor*: related to TRADITION]

trajectory /trə'dʒektərɪ/ *n.* (*pl.* **-ies**) path of an object moving under given forces. [Latin *traicio -ject-* throw across]

tram *n.* **1** (also **tramcar**) electrically-powered passenger road vehicle running on rails. **2** four-wheeled vehicle used in coalmines. [Low German and Dutch *trame* beam]

tramlines *n.pl.* **1** rails for a tramcar. **2** *colloq.* pair of long parallel lines at the sides of a tennis or badminton court.

trammel /'træm(ə)l/ –*n.* **1** (usu. in *pl.*) impediment; hindrance (*trammels of domesticity*). **2** triple drag-net for fishing. –*v.* (**-ll-**; *US* **-l-**) hamper. [medieval Latin *tremaculum*]

tramp –*v.* **1 a** walk heavily and firmly. **b** go on foot, esp. a distance. **2 a** cross on foot, esp. wearily or reluctantly. **b** cover (a distance) in this way. **3** (often foll. by *down*) tread on; trample; stamp on. **4** live as a tramp. –*n.* **1** itinerant vagrant or beggar. **2** sound of a person, or esp. people, walking, marching, etc. **3** long walk. **4** (in full **tramp ship**) cargo-carrying ship that does not have a planned itinerary but carries its cargo to any ports for which its charterers can find cargo. Tramps are available for voyage charter or time charter (the latter is now more common) and many are tankers. Some chartering of tramps is arranged through London's Baltic Exchange but much is now done direct through shipping agents and brokers. **5** *slang derog.* promiscuous woman. [Germanic]

trample /'træmp(ə)l/ *v.* (**-ling**) **1** tread under foot. **2** press down or crush in this way. □ **trample on 1** tread heavily on. **2** treat roughly or with contempt. [from TRAMP]

trampoline /'træmpə,liːn/ –*n.* strong fabric sheet connected by springs to a horizontal frame, used for gymnastic jumping. –*v.* (**-ning**) use a trampoline. [Italian *trampolino*]

tramway *n.* rails for a tram.

trance /trɑːns/ *n.* **1 a** sleeplike state without response to stimuli. **b** hypnotic or cataleptic state. **2** such a state as entered into by a medium. **3** rapture, ecstasy. [Latin *transeo* pass over]

♦ **tranche** /trɑːnʃ/ *n.* part or instalment of a large sum of money. In the International Monetary Fund the first 25% of a loan is known as the **reserve** (formerly **gold**) **tranche**. In **tranche funding**, successive sums of money become available on a prearranged basis to a new company, often linked to the progress of the company and its ability to reach the targets set in its business plan. [French, = slice]

---

tranny /'trænɪ/ *n.* (*pl.* **-ies**) *colloq.* transistor radio. [abbreviation]

tranquil /'træŋkwɪl/ *adj.* calm, serene, undisturbed. □ **tranquillity** /-'kwɪlɪtɪ/ *n.* **tranquilly** *adv.* [Latin]

tranquillize *v.* (*US* **tranquilize**, **-ise**) (**-zing** or **-sing**) make tranquil, esp. by a drug etc.

tranquillizer *n.* (*US* **tranquilizer**, **-iser**) drug used to diminish anxiety.

trans. *abbr.* **1** transfer(red). **2** transit.

trans- *prefix* **1** across, beyond. **2** on or to the other side of. **3** through. [Latin]

transact /træn'zækt/ *v.* perform or carry through (business). [Latin: related to ACT]

transaction /træn'zækʃ(ə)n/ *n.* **1 a** piece of esp. commercial business done. **b** transacting of business etc. **2** (in *pl.*) published reports of discussions, papers read, etc., at the meetings of a learned society. **3** *Computing* **a** single message fed into a system. It could be a request for information from a file or database or could involve the updating of a particular piece of information, or both. **b** updating or retrieval process initiated by a transaction.

transaction processing *n.* method of organizing a data-processing system in which computer transactions are processed to completion as they arise, rather than being collected together for subsequent processing (cf. BATCH PROCESSING). An on-line computer is therefore required. Transaction processing is used, for example, by travel agents to check the availability of airline seats, accommodation, etc.: if acceptable, a booking can be made and the booking record updated on the spot.

♦ **transactions demand for money** *n. Econ.* demand for money to finance current expenditure. A component of Keynes' theory of liquidity preference, it is essentially similar to the quantity theory of money. Keynes argued that transactions demand would be related positively to the level of activity in an economy but negatively to the rate of interest. Cf. PRECAUTIONARY DEMAND FOR MONEY; SPECULATIVE DEMAND FOR MONEY.

♦ **transactions velocity of circulation** see VELOCITY OF CIRCULATION.

---

transalpine /trænz'ælpaɪn/ *adj.* on the north side of the Alps. [Latin]

transatlantic /,trænzət'læntɪk/ *adj.* **1** beyond the Atlantic, esp.: **a** American. **b** *US* European. **2** crossing the Atlantic.

Transcaucasia /,trænzkɔː'keɪzɪə/ region of central Asia lying to the S of the Caucasus, now divided between Georgia, Azerbaijan, and Armenia. It has oil deposits and is an important agricultural region. □ **Transcaucasian** *adj.*

transceiver /træn'siːvə(r)/ *n.* combined radio transmitter and receiver.

transcend /træn'send/ *v.* **1** be beyond the range or grasp of (human experience, reason, belief, etc.). **2** excel; surpass. [Latin *scando* climb]

transcendent *adj.* **1** excelling, surpassing. **2** transcending human experience. **3** (esp. of God) existing apart from, not subject to the limitations of, the material universe. □ **transcendence** *n.* **transcendency** *n.*

transcendental /,trænsen'dent(ə)l/ *adj.* **1** *Philos.* a priori, not based on experience; intuitively accepted; innate in the mind. **2 a** visionary, abstract. **b** vague, obscure. □ **transcendentally** *adv.*

transcendentalism *n.* transcendental philosophy. □ **transcendentalist** *n.*

Transcendental Meditation *n.* method of detaching oneself from problems, anxiety, etc., by silent meditation and repetition of a mantra.

transcontinental /,trænzkɒntɪ'nent(ə)l/ *adj.* extending across a continent.

transcribe /træn'skraɪb/ *v.* (**-bing**) **1** copy out. **2** write out (shorthand, notes, etc.) in full. **3** record for subsequent reproduction. **4** arrange (music) for a different instrument etc. □ **transcriber** *n.* **transcription** /-'skrɪpʃ(ə)n/ *n.* [Latin *transcribo -script-*]

transcript /'trænskrɪpt/ *n.* written copy.

transducer /trænz'dju:sə(r)/ *n.* any device for converting a non-electrical signal into an electrical one, e.g. pressure into voltage. [Latin: related to DUCT]

transept /'trænsept/ *n.* **1** part of a cross-shaped church at right angles to the nave. **2** either arm of this. [Latin: related to SEPTUM]

transexual var. of TRANSSEXUAL.

transfer –*v.* /træns'fɜ:(r)/ (**-rr-**) **1** (often foll. by *to*) **a** convey, remove, or hand over (a thing etc.). **b** make over the possession of (property, a ticket, rights, etc.) to a person. **2** change or move to another group, club, department, etc. **3** change from one station, route, etc., to another on a journey. **4** convey (a design) from one surface to another. **5** change (meaning) by extension or metaphor. –*n.* /'trænsfɜ:(r)/ **1** transferring or being transferred. **2** design etc. conveyed or to be conveyed from one surface to another. **3** football player etc. who is transferred. **4** document effecting conveyance of property, a right, etc. □ **transferable** /-'fɜ:rəb(ə)l/ *adj.* [Latin *fero lat-* bear]

♦ **transferable loan facility** *n.* (also **TLF**) bank loan facility that can be traded between lenders in order to reduce the credit risk of the bank that provided the loan.

♦ **Transfer Accounting Lodgement for Investors and Stock Management** see TALISMAN.

♦ **transfer deed** *n.* deed used to transfer property from one person to another. On the London Stock Exchange a **stock transfer form** has to be signed by the seller of registered securities to legalize the transaction. This will be dealt with by the computerized TALISMAN system.

---

transference /'trænsfərəns/ *n.* **1** transferring or being transferred. **2** *Psychol.* redirection of childhood emotions to a new object, esp. to a psychoanalyst.

♦ **transfer form** see TRANSFER DEED.

♦ **transfer of value** *n.* reduction in the value of a person's estate by a gratuitous transfer. Such transfers are subject to inheritance tax in most cases if made in a given period before the date of the donor's death.

♦ **transfer payment** *n.* (also **transfer income**) payment made or income received in which no goods or services are being paid for. Pensions, unemployment benefits, subsidies to farmers, etc. are transfer payments; they are excluded in calculating gross national product.

♦ **transferred charge call** *n.* telephone call in which the caller asks the operator to ask the party called to pay for the call. In addition to the charge for the call, a transfer charge has also to be paid.

♦ **transfer stamp** *n.* impressed stamp on documents relating to the transfer of land or (formerly) securities, as an acknowledgement that the stamp duty has been paid.

---

transfiguration /ˌtrænsfɪgə'reɪʃ(ə)n/ *n.* **1** change of form or appearance. **2 a** Christ's appearance in radiant glory to three of his disciples (Matt. 17:2, Mark 9:2–3). **b** (**Transfiguration**) festival of Christ's transfiguration, 6 August. [Latin: related to TRANSFIGURE]

transfigure /træns'fɪgə(r)/ *v.* (**-ring**) change in form or appearance, esp. so as to elevate or idealize. [Latin]

transfix /træns'fɪks/ *v.* **1** paralyse with horror or astonishment. **2** pierce with a sharp implement or weapon. [Latin: related to FIX]

transform /træns'fɔ:m/ *v.* **1** make a thorough or dramatic change in the form, appearance, character, etc., of. **2** change the voltage etc. of (an alternating current). □ **transformation** /-fə'meɪʃ(ə)n/ *n.* [Latin]

transformer *n.* apparatus for reducing or increasing the voltage of an alternating current.

transfuse /træns'fju:z/ *v.* (**-sing**) **1 a** transfer (blood) from one person or animal to another. **b** inject (liquid) into a blood-vessel to replace lost fluid. **2** permeate. □ **transfusion** *n.* [Latin: related to FOUND[3]]

transgress /trænz'gres/ *v.* (also *absol.*) go beyond the bounds or limits set by (a commandment, law, etc.); sin. □ **transgression** *n.* **transgressor** *n.* [Latin *transgredior -gress-*]

tranship var. of TRANSSHIP.

transient /'trænzɪənt/ *adj.* of short duration; passing. □ **transience** *n.* [Latin: related to TRANCE]

♦ **transire** /træn'saɪə(r)/ *n.* two-part document in which the cargo loaded onto a coaster is detailed. It is supplied by the Customs at the port of shipment; one part has to be handed to the Customs at the port of destination to prove that the cargo comes from a home port rather than an overseas port. [Latin: related to TRANCE]

---

transistor /træn'zɪstə(r)/ *n.* **1** semiconductor device with three connections, capable of amplification in addition to rectification. **2** (in full **transistor radio**) portable radio with transistors. [from TRANSFER, RESISTOR]

transistorize *v.* (also **-ise**) (**-zing** or **-sing**) equip with transistors (rather than valves).

transit /'trænzɪt/ *n.* **1** going, conveying, or being conveyed, esp. over a distance. **2** passage or route. **3** apparent passage of a celestial body across the meridian of a place, or across the sun or a planet. □ **in transit** while going or being conveyed. [Latin: related to TRANCE]

transit camp *n.* camp for the temporary accommodation of soldiers, refugees, etc.

transition /træn'zɪʃ(ə)n/ *n.* **1** passing or change from one place, state, condition, etc., to another. **2** *Art* change from one style to another, esp. *Archit.* from Norman to Early English. □ **transitional** *adj.* **transitionally** *adv.* [Latin: related to TRANSIT]

transitive /'trænsɪtɪv/ *adj.* (of a verb) taking a direct object (whether expressed or implied), e.g. *saw* in *saw the donkey, saw that she was ill.* [Latin: related to TRANSIT]

transitory /'trænsɪtərɪ/ *adj.* not permanent; brief, transient. □ **transitorily** *adv.* **transitoriness** *n.* [Latin: related to TRANSIT]

Transkei /træn'skaɪ/ former Bantu homeland in South Africa, designated an independent republic in 1976 but not recognized as such outside South Africa. It was abolished following free democratic elections held in 1994 and became part of the province of Eastern Cape.

translate /træn'sleɪt/ *v.* (**-ting**) **1** (also *absol.*) (often foll. by *into*) express the sense of (a word, text, etc.) in another language or in another, esp. simpler, form. **2** be translatable, bear translation (*does not translate well*). **3** interpret (*translated his silence as dissent*). **4** move or change, esp. from one person, place, or condition, to another. □ **translatable** *adj.* **translation** *n.* **translator** *n.* [Latin: related to TRANSFER]

transliterate /trænz'lɪtəˌreɪt/ *v.* (**-ting**) represent (a word etc.) in the closest corresponding letters of a different script. □ **transliteration** /-'reɪʃ(ə)n/ *n.* [Latin *littera* letter]

translucent /træns'lu:s(ə)nt/ *adj.* allowing light to pass through; semi-transparent. □ **translucence** *n.* **translucency** *n.* [Latin *luceo* shine]

transmigrate /ˌtrænzmaɪ'greɪt/ *v.* (**-ting**) **1** (of the soul) pass into a different body. **2** migrate. □ **transmigration** /-'greɪʃ(ə)n/ *n.* [Latin]

transmission /trænz'mɪʃ(ə)n/ *n.* **1** transmitting or being transmitted. **2** broadcast programme. **3** mechanism transmitting power from the engine to the axle in a vehicle.

transmission line *n.* telephone line, electric cable, optical fibre, radio beam, etc. used to carry information between different locations.

transmit /trænz'mɪt/ *v.* (**-tt-**) **1 a** pass or hand on; transfer (*transmitted the message; how diseases are transmitted*). **b** communicate (ideas, emotions, etc.). **2 a** allow (heat, light, sound, electricity, etc.) to pass through. **b** be a medium for (ideas, emotions, etc.) (*his message transmits hope*). **3 a** broadcast (a radio or television programme). **b** send (information or computer data) over a transmission line. □ **transmissible** *adj.* **transmittable** *adj.* [Latin *mitto miss-* send]

transmitter *n.* **1** person or thing that transmits. **2** equipment used to transmit radio or other electronic signals.

transmogrify /trænz'mɒgrɪˌfaɪ/ *v.* (**-ies, -ied**) *joc.* transform, esp. in a magical or surprising manner. □ **transmogrification** /-fɪ'keɪʃ(ə)n/ *n.* [origin unknown]

transmute /trænz'mjuːt/ *v.* (**-ting**) **1** change the form, nature, or substance of. **2** *hist.* change (base metals) into gold. □ **transmutation** /-'teɪʃ(ə)n/ *n.* [Latin *muto* change]

transoceanic /ˌtrænzəʊʃɪ'ænɪk/ *adj.* **1** beyond the ocean. **2** crossing the ocean.

transom /'trænsəm/ *n.* **1** horizontal bar of wood or stone across a window or the top of a door. **2** *US* = TRANSOM WINDOW. [French *traversin*: related to TRAVERSE]

transom window *n.* window above a transom.

transparency /træns'pærənsɪ/ *n.* (*pl.* **-ies**) **1** being transparent. **2** picture, esp. a photograph, to be viewed by light passing through it. **3** essential condition of a free market in securities, in which transaction prices and volumes traded are visible for all to see. [medieval Latin: related to TRANSPARENT]

transparent /træns'pærənt/ *adj.* **1** allowing light to pass through so that bodies can be distinctly seen. **2 a** (of a disguise, pretext, etc.) easily seen through. **b** (of a quality etc.) evident; obvious. **3** easily understood; frank. □ **transparently** *adv.* [Latin *pareo* appear]

transpire /træn'spaɪə(r)/ *v.* (**-ring**) **1** (usu. prec. by *it* as subject) (of a secret or fact) come to be known; turn out; prove to be the case (*it transpired he knew nothing about it*). **2** occur; happen. **3** emit (vapour or moisture), or be emitted, through the skin, lungs, or leaves; perspire. □ **transpiration** /-spɪ'reɪʃ(ə)n/ *n.* (in sense 3). [Latin *spiro* breathe]

■ **Usage** Use of *transpire* in sense 2 is considered incorrect by some people.

transplant –*v.* /træns'plɑːnt/ **1** plant in another place (*transplanted the daffodils*). **2** transfer (living tissue or an organ) to another part of the body or to another body. –*n.* /'trænsplɑːnt/ **1 a** transplanting of an organ or tissue. **b** such an organ etc. **2** thing, esp. a plant, transplanted. □ **transplantation** /-'teɪʃ(ə)n/ *n.* [Latin]

transponder /træn'spɒndə(r)/ *n.* device for receiving a radio signal and automatically transmitting a different signal. [from TRANSMIT, RESPOND]

transport –*v.* /træns'pɔːt/ **1** take or carry (a person, goods, etc.) to another place. **2** *hist.* deport (a criminal) to a penal colony. **3** (as **transported** *adj.*) (usu. foll. by *with*) affected with strong emotion. –*n.* /'trænspɔːt/ **1 a** system of conveying people, goods, etc., from place to place. **b** means of this (*our transport has arrived*). **2** ship, aircraft, etc. used to carry soldiers, stores, etc. **3** (esp. in *pl.*) vehement emotion (*transports of joy*). □ **transportable** /-'pɔːtəb(ə)l/ *adj.* [Latin *porto* carry]

transportation /ˌtrænspɔː'teɪʃ(ə)n/ *n.* **1** conveying or being conveyed. **2 a** system of conveying. **b** esp. *US* means of this. **3** *hist.* deportation of convicts.

transport café *n.* roadside café for (esp. commercial) drivers.

transporter *n.* vehicle used to transport other vehicles or heavy machinery etc. by road.

transporter bridge *n.* bridge carrying vehicles etc. across water on a suspended moving platform.

transpose /træns'pəʊz/ *v.* (**-sing**) **1 a** cause (two or more things) to change places. **b** change the position of (a thing) in a series. **2** change the order or position of (words or a word) in a sentence. **3** put (music) into a different key. □ **transposition** /-pə'zɪʃ(ə)n/ *n.* [French: related to POSE]

transputer /træns'pjuːtə(r)/ *n.* microprocessor with integral memory designed for parallel processing. [from TRANSISTOR, COMPUTER]

transsexual /træn'sekʃʊəl/ (also **transexual**) –*adj.* having the physical characteristics of one sex and an overwhelming psychological identification with the other. –*n.* **1** transsexual person. **2** person who has had a sex change.

transship /træns'ʃɪp/ *v.* (also **tranship**) (**-pp-**) **1** ship (goods) from one port to another with a change of ship at an intermediate port. **2** transfer from one form of transport to another. □ **transshipment** *n.*

transubstantiation /ˌtrænsəbˌstænʃɪ'eɪʃ(ə)n/ *n. RC Ch.* conversion of the Eucharistic elements wholly into the body and blood of Christ. [medieval Latin: related to TRANS-, SUBSTANCE]

transuranic /ˌtrænsjʊə'rænɪk/ *adj.* (of a chemical element) having a higher atomic number than uranium.

Transvaal /trænz'vɑːl/ former province in the Republic of South Africa; its capital was Pretoria. The province was abolished following free democratic elections held in 1994.

transverse /'trænzvɜːs/ *adj.* situated, arranged, or acting in a crosswise direction. □ **transversely** *adv.* [Latin *transverto -vers-* turn across]

transvestite /trænz'vestaɪt/ *n.* man deriving sexual pleasure from dressing in women's clothes. □ **transvestism** *n.* [Latin *vestio* clothe]

Transylvania /ˌtrænsɪl'veɪnɪə/ large tableland region of NW Romania. Formerly part of Hungary, Transylvania was annexed by Romania in 1918. □ **Transylvanian** *adj.*

trap[1] –*n.* **1** device, often baited, for catching animals. **2** trick betraying a person into speech or an act. **3** arrangement to catch an unsuspecting person. **4** device for hurling an object, e.g. a clay pigeon, into the air to be shot at. **5** compartment from which a greyhound is released at the start of a race. **6** device that sends a ball into the air. **7** curve in a downpipe etc. that fills with liquid and forms a seal against the return of gases. **8** two-wheeled carriage (*pony and trap*). **9** = TRAPDOOR. **10** *slang* mouth (esp. *shut one's trap*). –*v.* (**-pp-**) **1** catch (an animal) in a trap. **2** catch or catch out (a person) by means of a trick etc. **3** stop and retain in or as in a trap. **4** provide (a place) with traps. [Old English]

trap[2] *n.* (in full **trap-rock**) dark-coloured igneous rock. [Swedish]

trapdoor *n.* door in a floor, ceiling, or roof.

trapeze /trə'piːz/ *n.* crossbar suspended by ropes as a swing for acrobatics etc. [Latin: related to TRAPEZIUM]

trapezium /trə'piːzɪəm/ *n.* (*pl.* **-zia** /-zɪə/ or **-s**) **1** quadrilateral with only one pair of sides parallel. **2** *US* = TRAPEZOID 1. [Greek *trapezion*]

trapezoid /'træpɪˌzɔɪd/ *n.* **1** quadrilateral with no two sides parallel. **2** *US* = TRAPEZIUM 1. [Greek: related to TRAPEZIUM]

trapper *n.* person who traps wild animals, esp. for their fur.

trappings *n.pl.* **1** ornamental accessories. **2** harness of a horse, esp. when ornamental. [*trap* from French *drap* cloth]

Trappist –*n.* monk of an order vowed to silence. –*adj.* of this order. [*La Trappe* in Normandy]

trash –*n.* **1** esp. *US* worthless or waste stuff; rubbish. **2** worthless person or persons. –*v. slang* wreck, vandalize. □ **trashy** *adj.* (**-ier, -iest**). [origin unknown]

trash can *n. US* dustbin.

trattoria /ˌtrætə'riːə/ *n.* Italian restaurant. [Italian]

trauma /'trɔːmə/ *n.* (*pl.* **traumata** /-mətə/ or **-s**) **1** profound emotional shock. **2** physical injury. **3** physical shock syndrome following this. □ **traumatize** *v.* (also **-ise**) (**-zing** or **-sing**). [Greek, = wound]

traumatic /trɔː'mætɪk/ *adj.* **1** of or causing trauma. **2** *colloq.* distressing (*traumatic experience*). □ **traumatically** *adv.* [Greek: related to TRAUMA]

travail /'træveɪl/ *literary* –*n.* **1** painful effort. **2** pangs of childbirth. –*v.* make a painful effort, esp. in childbirth. [French *travaillier*]

travel /'træv(ə)l/ –*v.* (**-ll-**; *US* **-l-**) **1** go from one place to another; make a journey, esp. a long one or abroad. **2 a** journey along or through (a country). **b** cover (a distance) in travelling. **3** *colloq.* withstand a long journey (*wines that do not travel*). **4** go from place to place as a salesman. **5** move or proceed as specified (*light travels faster than sound*). **6** *colloq.* move quickly. **7** pass, esp. in a deliberate manner, from point to point (*her eye travelled over the* *scene*). **8** (of a machine or part) move or operate in a specified way. –*n.* **1 a** travelling, esp. in foreign countries. **b** (often in *pl.*) spell of this. **2** range, rate, or mode of motion of a part in machinery. [originally = TRAVAIL]

travel agency *n.* agency that makes the necessary arrangements for travellers. □ **travel agent** *n.*

travelled *adj.* experienced in travelling (also in *comb.*: *much-travelled*).

traveller *n.* (*US* **traveler**) **1** person who travels or is travelling. **2** travelling salesman. **3** Gypsy.

◆ **traveller's cheque** *n.* (*US* **traveler's check**) cheque for a fixed amount that is issued by a bank, building society, travel agency, etc., and may be cashed abroad on proof of identity. The traveller has to sign the cheque twice, once in the presence of the issuer and again in the presence of the paying bank, agent, etc. Most traveller's cheques are covered against loss.

traveller's joy *n.* wild clematis.

traveller's tale *n.* incredible and probably untrue story.

travelling salesman *n.* = COMMERCIAL TRAVELLER.

travelogue /ˈtrævəˌlɒg/ *n.* film or illustrated lecture about travel. [from TRAVEL, after *monologue*]

travel-sick *adj.* suffering from nausea caused by motion in travelling.

traverse –*v.* /trəˈvɜːs/ (**-sing**) **1** travel or lie across (*traversed the country*; *pit traversed by a beam*). **2** consider or discuss the whole extent of (a subject). –*n.* /ˈtrævɜːs/ **1** sideways movement. **2** traversing. **3** thing that crosses another. □ **traversal** *n.* [French: related to TRANSVERSE]

travesty /ˈtrævɪstɪ/ –*n.* (*pl.* **-ies**) grotesque misrepresentation or imitation (*travesty of justice*). –*v.* (**-ies, -ied**) make or be a travesty of. [French *travestir* disguise, from Italian]

trawl –*v.* **1** fish with a trawl or seine. **2 a** catch by trawling. **b** (often foll. by *through*) search thoroughly (*trawled her memory for their names*). –*n.* **1** act of trawling. **2** (in full **trawl-net**) large wide-mouthed fishing-net dragged by a boat along the sea bottom. [probably Dutch *traghel* dragnet]

trawler *n.* boat used for trawling.

tray *n.* **1** flat board, usu. with a raised rim, for carrying dishes. **2** shallow lidless box for papers or small articles, sometimes forming a drawer in a cabinet etc. [Old English]

TRDA *abbr.* Timber Research and Development Association.

treacherous /ˈtretʃərəs/ *adj.* **1** guilty of or involving treachery. **2** (of the weather, ice, the memory, etc.) likely to fail or give way. □ **treacherously** *adv.* [French from *trichier* cheat: related to TRICK]

treachery /ˈtretʃərɪ/ *n.* (*pl.* **-ies**) violation of faith or trust; betrayal.

treacle /ˈtriːk(ə)l/ *n.* **1** syrup produced in refining sugar. **2** molasses. □ **treacly** *adj.* [French from Latin *theriaca* antidote against a snake-bite, from *thērion* wild animal]

tread /tred/ –*v.* (*past* **trod**; *past part.* **trodden** or **trod**) **1** (often foll. by *on*) set down one's foot; walk, step. **2 a** walk on. **b** (often foll. by *down*) press or crush with the feet. **3** perform (steps etc.) by walking. **4** (often foll. by *in, into*) press down into the ground with the feet (*trod dirt into the carpet*). –*n.* **1** manner or sound of walking. **2** top surface of a step or stair. **3** thick moulded part of a vehicle tyre for gripping the road. **4 a** part of a wheel that touches the ground or rail. **b** part of a rail that the wheels touch. **5** part of the sole of a shoe that rests on the ground. □ **tread the boards** be an actor. **tread on air** feel elated. **tread on a person's toes** offend a person; encroach on a person's privileges etc. **tread water** maintain an upright position in water by moving the feet and hands. [Old English]

treadle /ˈtred(ə)l/ *n.* lever worked by the foot and imparting motion to a machine. [Old English: related to TREAD]

treadmill *n.* **1** device for producing motion by the weight of persons or animals stepping on steps attached to a revolving upright wheel. **2** similar device used for exercise. **3** monotonous routine work.

treadwheel *n.* = TREADMILL 1, 2.

treason /ˈtriːz(ə)n/ *n.* violation by a subject of allegiance to the sovereign or state. [Latin: related to TRADITION]

■ **Usage** The crime of *petty treason* was abolished in 1828. This is why *high treason*, originally distinguished from *petty treason*, now means the same as *treason*.

treasonable *adj.* involving or guilty of treason.

treasure /ˈtreʒə(r)/ –*n.* **1 a** precious metals or gems. **b** hoard of these. **c** accumulated wealth. **2** thing valued for its rarity, workmanship, associations, etc. (*art treasures*). **3** *colloq.* much loved or highly valued person. –*v.* (**-ring**) **1** value highly. **2** (often foll. by *up*) store up as valuable. [Greek *thēsauros*]

treasure hunt *n.* **1** search for treasure. **2** game in which players seek a hidden object from a series of clues.

◆ **treasurer** *n.* **1** person employed by a large organization, e.g. a company, charity, club, etc., to look after the funds of the organization and to make appropriate investments of surplus funds. **2** person in charge of the funds of a society etc.

treasure trove *n.* gold or silver of unknown ownership found hidden on land. Treasure trove belongs to the Crown but the finder is recompensed for its value.

treasury *n.* (*pl.* **-ies**) **1** place or building where treasure is stored. **2** funds or revenue of a state, institution, or society. **3** (**Treasury**) **a** department managing the public revenue of a country. The UK Treasury is responsible for the country's financial policies and management of the economy. **b** offices and officers of this. In the UK, the First Lord of the Treasury is the prime minister, but the Treasury is run by the Chancellor of the Exchequer.

Treasury bench *n.* front bench in the House of Commons occupied by Cabinet ministers etc.

◆ **treasury bill** *n.* bill of exchange issued by the Bank of England on the authority of the UK government to raise money for temporary needs. It is repayable in three months. Treasury bills are issued by tender each week to the discount houses in units of £5000 to £100,000. They bear no interest, the yield being the difference between the purchase price and the redemption value. The US Treasury also issues treasury bills.

◆ **Treasury Investment Growth Receipts** see TIGR.

◆ **Treasury stocks** see GILT-EDGED SECURITY.

treat –*v.* **1** act or behave towards or deal with (a person or thing) in a certain way (*treated me kindly*; *treat it as a joke*). **2** apply a process to (*treat it with acid*). **3** apply medical care or attention to. **4** present or deal with (a subject) in literature or art. **5** (often foll. by *to*) provide with food, drink, or entertainment at one's own expense (*treated us to dinner*). **6** (often foll. by *with*) negotiate terms (with a person). **7** (often foll. by *of*) give a spoken or written exposition. –*n.* **1** event or circumstance (esp. when unexpected or unusual) that gives great pleasure. **2** meal, entertainment, etc., designed to do this. **3** (prec. by *a*) extremely good or well (*they looked a treat*; *has come on a treat*). □ **treatable** *adj.* [Latin *tracto* handle]

treatise /ˈtriːtɪz/ *n.* a written work dealing formally and systematically with a subject. [Anglo-French: related to TREAT]

treatment *n.* **1** process or manner of behaving towards or dealing with a person or thing. **2** medical care or attention. **3** manner of treating a subject in literature or art. **4** (prec. by *the*) *colloq.* the customary way of dealing with a person, situation, etc. (*got the full treatment*).

◆ **treaty** /ˈtriːtɪ/ *n.* (*pl.* **-ies**) **1** formal agreement between nations. A **commercial treaty** relates to trade between the signatories. **2** transaction in which a sale is negotiated between the parties involved (**by private treaty**) rather than by auction. **3** agreement in reinsurance in which a reinsurer agrees automatically to accept risks from an insurer, either when a certain sum insured is exceeded or on the basis of a percentage of every risk accepted. With such a treaty an insurer has the confidence and capacity to accept larger risks than would otherwise be possible, as the necessary reinsurance is already arranged. [Latin: related to TREAT]

Trebizond see TRABZON.

treble /'treb(ə)l/ *–adj.* **1 a** threefold. **b** triple. **c** three times as much or many (*treble the amount*). **2** high-pitched. *–n.* **1** treble quantity or thing. **2** hit on the narrow band between the two middle circles of a dartboard, scoring treble. **3 a** *Mus.* = SOPRANO (esp. a boy's voice or part, or an instrument). **b** high-pitched voice. **4** high-frequency output of a radio, record-player, etc. *–v.* (**-ling**) make or become three times as much or many; increase threefold; multiply by three. □ **trebly** *adv.* [Latin: related to TRIPLE]

treble chance *n.* method of competing in a football pool in which the chances of winning depend on the number of draws and home and away wins predicted by the competitors.

treble clef *n.* clef placing the G above middle C on the second lowest line of the staff.

tree *–n.* **1** perennial plant with a woody self-supporting main stem or trunk and usu. unbranched for some distance above the ground. **2** piece or frame of wood etc. for various purposes (*shoe-tree*). **3** = FAMILY TREE. *–v.* (**trees**; **treed**) force to take refuge in a tree. □ **grow on trees** (usu. with *neg.*) be plentiful. □ **treeless** *adj.* [Old English]

treecreeper *n.* small creeping bird feeding on insects in tree-bark.

tree-fern *n.* large fern with an upright trunklike stem.

tree line *n.* = TIMBERLINE.

tree ring *n.* ring in a cross-section of a tree, from one year's growth.

tree surgeon *n.* person who treats decayed trees in order to preserve them.

treetop *n.* topmost part of a tree.

trefoil /'trefɔɪl/ *n.* **1** leguminous plant with leaves of three leaflets, esp. clover. **2** three-lobed ornamentation, esp. in tracery windows. [Anglo-French: related to TRI-, FOIL[2]]

trek orig. *S.Afr.* *–v.* (**-kk-**) **1** travel or make one's way arduously. **2** esp. *hist.* migrate or journey with one's belongings by ox-wagon. *–n.* **1 a** long or arduous journey or walk (*quite a trek to the launderette*). **b** each stage of this. **2** organized migration of a body of people. □ **trekker** *n.* [Dutch, = draw]

trellis /'trelɪs/ *n.* (in full **trellis-work**) lattice of light wooden or metal bars, esp. as a support for climbing plants. [French *trelis*]

trematode /'tremə,təʊd/ *n.* a kind of parasitic flatworm. [Greek *trēma* hole]

tremble /'tremb(ə)l/ *–v.* (**-ling**) **1** shake involuntarily from emotion, weakness, etc. **2** be in a state of extreme apprehension. **3** quiver (*leaves trembled in the breeze*). *–n.* trembling; quiver (*tremble in his voice*). [medieval Latin: related to TREMULOUS]

trembler *n.* automatic vibrator for making and breaking an electrical circuit.

trembly *adj.* (**-ier, -iest**) *colloq.* trembling.

trem card *n.* card carried by a chemical tank vehicle and giving information that could be required in the case of an accident etc. [abbreviation of *tr*ansport *em*ergency]

tremendous /trɪ'mendəs/ *adj.* **1** *colloq.* remarkable, considerable, excellent. **2** awe-inspiring, overpowering. □ **tremendously** *adv.* [Latin *tremendus* to be trembled at: related to TREMOR]

tremolo /'tremə,ləʊ/ *n.* tremulous effect in music. [Italian: related to TREMULOUS]

tremor /'tremə(r)/ *n.* **1** shaking, quivering. **2** thrill (of fear, exultation, etc.). **3** (in full **earth tremor**) slight earthquake. [Latin *tremo* tremble]

tremulous /'tremjʊləs/ *adj.* trembling. □ **tremulously** *adv.* [Latin *tremulus*: related to TREMOR]

trench *–n.* **1** long narrow usu. deep ditch. **2** *Mil.* this dug by troops as a shelter from enemy fire. *–v.* **1** dig a trench or trenches in (the ground). **2** turn over the earth of (a field, garden, etc.) by digging a succession of ditches. [French *trenche, -ier* cut]

trenchant /'trentʃ(ə)nt/ *adj.* (of style or language etc.) incisive, terse, vigorous. □ **trenchancy** *n.* **trenchantly** *adv.* [French: related to TRENCH]

trench coat *n.* **1** soldier's lined or padded waterproof coat. **2** loose belted raincoat.

trencher *n. hist.* wooden or earthenware platter for serving food. [Anglo-French: related to TRENCH]

trencherman *n.* person who eats well, or in a specified manner.

trench warfare *n.* war carried on from trenches.

trend *–n.* general direction and tendency (esp. of events, fashion, or opinion). *–v.* **1** bend or turn away in a specified direction. **2** have a general tendency. [Old English]

trend-setter *n.* person who leads the way in fashion etc.

trendy *colloq.*; often *derog.* *–adj.* (**-ier, -iest**) fashionable. *–n.* (*pl.* **-ies**) fashionable person. □ **trendily** *adv.* **trendiness** *n.*

Trengganu /treŋ'gɑːnuː/ (also **Terengganu**) state in Malaysia, on the E coast of the Malay Peninsula; pop. (est. 1993) 752 000; capital, Kuala Terengganu. Products include rice, rubber, copra, and fish.

Trentino-Alto Adige /tren'tiːnəʊ,æltəʊ 'ædɪ,dʒeɪ/ region in NE Italy; products include timber, wine, fruit, and dairy produce; manufacturing industry and tourism are also important; pop. (est. 1994) 903 598; capital, Trento.

Trento /'trentəʊ/ (German **Trent**) city in N Italy, capital of Trentino-Alto Adige region; manufactures include chemicals, electrical goods, and silk; pop. (est. 1994) 103 063.

Trenton /'trent(ə)n/ city in the US, capital of New Jersey; manufactures include pottery, cable, rope, and metal; pop. (est. 1994) 84 441.

trepan /trɪ'pæn/ *–n.* cylindrical saw formerly used by surgeons for removing part of the skull. *–v.* (**-nn-**) perforate (the skull) with a trepan. [Greek *trupanon* auger]

trepidation /,trepɪ'deɪʃ(ə)n/ *n.* fear, anxiety. [Latin *trepidus* flurried]

trespass /'trespəs/ *–v.* **1** (usu. foll. by *on, upon*) make an unlawful or unauthorized intrusion (esp. on land or property). **2** (foll. by *on*) make unjustifiable claims on; encroach on (*trespass on your hospitality*). *–n.* **1** *Law* act of trespassing. **2** *archaic* sin, offence. □ **trespasser** *n.* [medieval Latin: related to TRANS-, PASS[1]]

tress *n.* **1** long lock of human (esp. female) hair. **2** (in *pl.*) woman's or girl's head of hair. [French]

trestle /'tres(ə)l/ *n.* **1** supporting structure for a table etc., consisting of two frames fixed at an angle or hinged, or of a bar with two divergent pairs of legs. **2** (in full **trestle-table**) table of a board or boards on trestles etc. **3** (in full **trestle-work**) open braced framework to support a bridge etc. [Latin *transtrum* cross-beam]

trews /truːz/ *n.pl.* close-fitting usu. tartan trousers. [Irish and Gaelic: related to TROUSERS]

tri- *comb. form* three or three times. [Latin and Greek]

triad /'traɪæd/ *n.* **1** group of three (esp. notes in a chord). **2** the number three. **3** (also **Triad**) Chinese secret society, usu. criminal. □ **triadic** /-'ædɪk/ *adj.* [Latin from Greek]

trial /'traɪəl/ *n.* **1** judicial examination and determination of issues between parties by a judge with or without a jury. **2** test (*will give you a trial*). **3** trying thing or person (*trials of old age*). **4** match held to select players for a team. **5** (often in *pl.*) contest involving performance by horses, dogs, motor cycles, etc. □ **on trial 1** being tried in a court of law. **2** being tested; to be chosen or retained only if suitable. [Anglo-French: related to TRY]

trial and error *n.* repeated (usu. unsystematic) attempts continued until successful.

♦ **trial balance** *n.* listing of the balances on all the accounts of an organization with debit balances in one column and credit balances in the other. If the processes of double-entry bookkeeping have been accurate, the totals of each column should be the same. If they are not the same, checks must be carried out to find the discrepancy. The figures in the trial balance after some adjustments, e.g. for closing stocks, prepayments and accruals, depreciation, etc., are used to prepare the final accounts (profit and loss account and balance sheet).

trial run *n.* preliminary operational test.

triangle /ˈtraɪˌæŋg(ə)l/ *n.* **1** plane figure with three sides and angles. **2** any three things not in a straight line, with imaginary lines joining them. **3** implement of this shape. **4** musical instrument consisting of a steel rod bent into a triangle, struck with a small steel rod. **5** situation, esp. an emotional relationship, involving three people. □ **triangular** /-ˈæŋgjʊlə(r)/ *adj.* [Latin: related to TRI-]

triangulate /traɪˈæŋgjʊˌleɪt/ *v.* (**-ting**) measure and map out (an area) by dividing it into triangles. □ **triangulation** /-ˈleɪʃ(ə)n/ *n.*

Triassic /traɪˈæsɪk/ *Geol.* –*adj.* of the earliest period of the Mesozoic era. –*n.* this period. [related to TRIAD]

triathlon /traɪˈæθlən/ *n.* athletic contest of three events for all competitors. [from TRI- after DECATHLON]

tribe *n.* **1** group of (esp. primitive) families or communities, linked by social, religious, or blood ties, and usu. having a common culture and dialect and a recognized leader. **2** any similar natural or political division. **3** usu. *derog.* set or number of persons, esp. of one profession etc. or family. □ **tribal** *adj.* **tribalism** *n.* [Latin *tribus*]

tribesman *n.* (*fem.* **-woman**) member of a tribe.

tribology /traɪˈbɒlədʒɪ/ *n.* the study of friction, wear, lubrication, and the design of bearings. [Greek *tribō* rub]

tribulation /ˌtrɪbjʊˈleɪʃ(ə)n/ *n.* great affliction. [Latin *tribulum* threshing-sledge]

tribunal /traɪˈbjuːn(ə)l/ *n.* **1** board appointed to adjudicate in some matter. **2** court of justice. **3** seat or bench for a judge or judges. [Latin: related to TRIBUNE]

tribune /ˈtrɪbjuːn/ *n.* **1** popular leader or demagogue. **2** (in full **tribune of the people**) official in ancient Rome chosen by the people to protect their interests. [Latin *tribunus*: related to TRIBE]

tributary /ˈtrɪbjʊtərɪ/ –*n.* (*pl.* **-ies**) **1** river or stream flowing into a larger river or lake. **2** *hist.* person or state paying or subject to tribute. –*adj.* **1** (of a river etc.) that is a tributary. **2** *hist.* **a** paying tribute. **b** serving as tribute. [Latin: related to TRIBUTE]

tribute /ˈtrɪbjuːt/ *n.* **1** thing said or done or given as a mark of respect or affection etc. **2** (foll. by *to*) indication of (some praiseworthy quality) (*their success is a tribute to their perseverance*). **3** *hist.* **a** periodic payment by one state or ruler to another, esp. as a sign of dependence. **b** obligation to pay this. [Latin *tributum* neuter past part. of *tribuo -ut-* assign, originally divide between TRIBES]

trice *n.* □ **in a trice** in an instant. [*trice* haul up, from Low German and Dutch]

triceps /ˈtraɪseps/ *n.* muscle (esp. in the upper arm) with three points of attachment. [Latin *caput* head]

triceratops /traɪˈserəˌtɒps/ *n.* dinosaur with three sharp horns on the forehead and a wavy-edged collar round the neck. [Greek, = three-horned face]

Trichinopoly see TIRUCHIRAPALLI.

trichinosis /ˌtrɪkɪˈnəʊsɪs/ *n.* disease caused by hairlike worms usu. ingested in meat. [Greek *thrix trikh-* hair]

trichology /trɪˈkɒlədʒɪ/ *n.* the study of hair. □ **trichologist** *n.*

trichromatic /ˌtraɪkrəˈmætɪk/ *adj.* **1** having or using three colours. **2** (of vision) having the normal three colour-sensations, i.e. red, green, and purple.

trick –*n.* **1** action or scheme undertaken to deceive or outwit. **2** illusion (*trick of the light*). **3** special technique; knack. **4 a** feat of skill or dexterity. **b** unusual action (e.g. begging) learned by an animal. **5** foolish or discreditable act; practical joke (*a mean trick to play*). **6** idiosyncrasy (*has a trick of repeating himself*). **7 a** cards played in one round of a card-game. **b** point gained in this. **8** (*attrib.*) done to deceive or mystify (*trick photography; trick question*). –*v.* **1** deceive by a trick; outwit. **2** (often foll. by *out of*) swindle (*tricked out of his savings*). **3** (foll. by *into*) cause to do something by trickery (*tricked into marriage; tricked me into agreeing*). **4** foil, baffle; take by surprise. □ **do the trick** *colloq.* achieve the required result. **how's tricks?** *colloq.* how are you? **trick or treat** esp. *US* children's custom of calling at houses at Hallowe'en with the threat of pranks if they are not given a small gift. **trick out** (or **up**) dress or deck out. [French]

trickery *n.* deception, use of tricks.

trickle /ˈtrɪk(ə)l/ –*v.* (**-ling**) **1** (cause to) flow in drops or a small stream. **2** come or go slowly or gradually (*information trickles out*). –*n.* trickling flow. [probably imitative]

trickle charger *n.* electrical charger for batteries that works at a steady slow rate.

trickster *n.* deceiver, rogue.

tricksy *adj.* (**-ier, -iest**) full of tricks; playful.

tricky *adj.* (**-ier, -iest**) **1** requiring care and adroitness (*tricky job*). **2** crafty, deceitful. □ **trickily** *adv.* **trickiness** *n.*

tricolour /ˈtrɪkələ(r)/ *n.* (*US* **tricolor**) flag of three bands of different colours, esp. the French or Irish national flags. [French: related to TRI-]

tricot /ˈtrɪkəʊ/ *n.* knitted fabric. [French]

tricycle /ˈtraɪsɪk(ə)l/ *n.* three-wheeled pedal-driven vehicle similar to a bicycle.

trident /ˈtraɪd(ə)nt/ *n.* three-pronged spear. [Latin *dens dent-* tooth]

Tridentine /traɪˈdentaɪn/ *adj.* of the Council of Trent, held at Trento in Italy 1545–63, esp. as the basis of Roman Catholic orthodoxy. [medieval Latin *Tridentum* Trento]

tried *past* and *past part.* of TRY.

triennial /traɪˈenɪəl/ *adj.* lasting, or recurring every, three years. [Latin *annus* year]

Trier /ˈtrɪə(r)/ industrial city in W Germany, at the centre of the wine-producing Moselle region of Rhineland-Palatinate; pop. (1991) 98 750.

trier /ˈtraɪə(r)/ *n.* **1** person who perseveres. **2** tester, esp. of foodstuffs.

Trieste /trɪˈest/ city in NE Italy, the largest seaport on the Adriatic and capital of Friuli-Venezia Giulia region; industries include oil refining and steel; pop. (est. 1994) 226 707.

trifle /ˈtraɪf(ə)l/ –*n.* **1** thing of slight value or importance. **2 a** small amount, esp. of money. **b** (prec. by *a*) somewhat (*a trifle annoyed*). **3** dessert of sponge cake with custard, jelly, fruit, cream, etc. –*v.* (**-ling**) **1** talk or act frivolously. **2** (foll. by *with*) treat or deal with frivolously; flirt heartlessly with. [originally *trufle* from French = *truf(f)e* deceit]

trifling *adj.* **1** unimportant, petty. **2** frivolous.

triforium /traɪˈfɔːrɪəm/ *n.* (*pl.* **-ria**) gallery or arcade above the arches of the nave, choir, and transepts of a church. [Anglo-Latin]

trig *n. colloq.* trigonometry. [abbreviation]

trigger –*n.* **1** movable device for releasing a spring or catch and so setting off a mechanism (esp. that of a gun). **2** event, occurrence, etc., that sets off a chain reaction. –*v.* (often foll. by *off*) set (an action or process) in motion; precipitate. □ **quick on the trigger** quick to respond. [*tricker* from Dutch *trekker* from *trekken* pull]

trigger-happy *adj.* apt to shoot on the slightest provocation.

trigonometry /ˌtrɪgəˈnɒmətrɪ/ *n.* branch of mathematics dealing with the relations of the sides and angles of triangles and with the relevant functions of any angles. □ **trigonometric** /-nəˈmetrɪk/ *adj.* **trigonometrical** /-nəˈmetrɪk(ə)l/ *adj.* [Greek *trigōnon* triangle]

trig point *n.* reference point on high ground, used in triangulation.

trike *n. colloq.* tricycle. [abbreviation]

trilateral /traɪˈlætər(ə)l/ *adj.* **1** of, on, or with three sides. **2** involving three parties. [Latin: related to TRI-]

trilby /ˈtrɪlbɪ/ *n.* (*pl.* **-ies**) soft felt hat with a narrow brim and indented crown. [*Trilby*, name of a character in a novel by G. du Maurier]

trilingual /traɪˈlɪŋgw(ə)l/ *adj.* **1** able to speak three languages. **2** spoken or written in three languages.

trill *–n.* **1** quavering sound, esp. a rapid alternation of sung or played notes. **2** bird's warbling. **3** pronunciation of *r* with vibration of the tongue. *–v.* **1** produce a trill. **2** warble (a song) or pronounce (*r* etc.) with a trill. [Italian]

trillion /ˈtrɪljən/ *n.* (*pl.* same) **1** a million million (10^{12}). **2** (now less often) a million million million (10^{18}). □ **trillionth** *adj.* & *n.* [French or Italian: related to TRI-, MILLION, after *billion*]

trilobite /ˈtraɪləˌbaɪt/ *n.* a kind of fossil marine arthropod. [from TRI-, Greek *lobos* lobe]

trilogy /ˈtrɪlədʒɪ/ *n.* (*pl.* **-ies**) group of three related novels, plays, operas, etc.

trim *–v.* (**-mm-**) **1 a** make neat or of the required size or form, esp. by cutting away irregular or unwanted parts. **b** set in good order. **2** (foll. by *off*, *away*) cut off (unwanted parts). **3** ornament, decorate. **4** adjust the balance of (a ship or aircraft) by arranging its cargo etc. **5** arrange (sails) to suit the wind. **6 a** associate oneself with currently prevailing views, esp. to advance oneself. **b** hold a middle course in politics or opinion. **7** *colloq.* **a** rebuke sharply. **b** thrash. **c** get the better of in a bargain etc. *–n.* **1** state of readiness or fitness (*in perfect trim*). **2** ornament or decorative material. **3** trimming of a person's hair. *–adj.* (**trimmer, trimmest**) **1** neat or spruce. **2** in good order; well arranged or equipped. [Old English, = make firm]

trimaran /ˈtraɪməˌræn/ *n.* vessel like a catamaran, with three hulls side by side. [from CATAMARAN]

trimeter /ˈtrɪmɪtə(r)/ *n.* *Prosody* line of verse of three measures. [Greek: see TRI-, -METER]

trimming *n.* **1** ornamentation or decoration, esp. for clothing. **2** (in *pl.*) *colloq.* usual accompaniments, esp. of the main course of a meal.

Trincomalee /ˌtrɪŋkəməˈliː/ principal seaport of Sri Lanka; pop. (1981) 44 913.

Trinitarian /ˌtrɪnɪˈteərɪən/ *–n.* believer in the Trinity. *–adj.* of this belief. □ **Trinitarianism** *n.*

trinitrotoluene /traɪˌnaɪtrəˈtɒljʊˌiːn/ *n.* (also **trinitrotoluol** /-ˈtɒljʊˌɒl/) = TNT.

trinity /ˈtrɪnɪtɪ/ *n.* (*pl.* **-ies**) **1** state of being three. **2** group of three. **3** (**the Trinity** or **Holy Trinity**) *Theol.* the three persons of the Christian Godhead (Father, Son, and Holy Spirit). [Latin *trinitas* from *trinus* threefold]

♦ **Trinity House** *n.* UK corporation responsible for lighthouses, aids to navigation maintained by local harbours, dealing with wrecks that present a hazard to navigation, and, until 1988, for pilotage, which was transferred to harbour authorities by the Pilotage Act (1987).

Trinity Sunday *n.* Sunday next after Whit Sunday.

Trinity term *n.* university and law term beginning after Easter.

trinket /ˈtrɪŋkɪt/ *n.* trifling ornament, esp. a piece of jewellery. □ **trinketry** *n.* [origin unknown]

trio /ˈtriːəʊ/ *n.* (*pl.* **-s**) **1** group of three. **2** *Mus.* **a** composition for three performers. **b** the performers. [French and Italian from Latin]

trip *–v.* (**-pp-**) **1 a** (often foll. by *up*) (cause to) stumble, esp. by catching the feet. **b** (foll. by *up*) (cause to) make a slip or blunder. **2 a** move with quick light steps. **b** (of a rhythm etc.) run lightly. **3** make an excursion to a place. **4 a** operate (a mechanism) suddenly by knocking aside a catch etc. **b** automatically cut out. **5** *slang* have a hallucinatory experience caused by a drug. *–n.* **1** journey or excursion, esp. for pleasure. **2 a** stumble or blunder. **b** tripping or being tripped up. **3** nimble step. **4** *slang* drug-induced hallucinatory experience. **5** device for tripping a mechanism etc. [Dutch *trippen* skip, hop]

tripartite /traɪˈpɑːtaɪt/ *adj.* **1** consisting of three parts. **2** shared by or involving three parties. [Latin *partior* divide]

tripe *n.* **1** first or second stomach of a ruminant, esp. an ox, as food. **2** *colloq.* nonsense, rubbish. [French]

triple /ˈtrɪp(ə)l/ *–adj.* **1** consisting of three usu. equal parts or things; threefold. **2** involving three parties. **3** three times as much or many. *–n.* **1** threefold number or amount. **2** set of three. *–v.* (**-ling**) multiply by three. □ **triply** *adv.* [Latin *triplus* from Greek]

triple crown *n.* winning of all three of a group of sporting events, esp. in Rugby.

triple jump *n.* athletic contest comprising a hop, step, and jump.

triplet /ˈtrɪplɪt/ *n.* **1** each of three children or animals born at one birth. **2** set of three things, esp. three equal notes played in the time of two of the same value.

triplex /ˈtrɪpleks/ *adj.* triple, threefold. [Latin]

triplicate *–adj.* /ˈtrɪplɪkət/ **1** existing in three examples or copies. **2** having three corresponding parts. **3** tripled. *–n.* /ˈtrɪplɪkət/ each of a set of three copies or corresponding parts. *–v.* /ˈtrɪplɪˌkeɪt/ (**-ting**) **1** make in three copies. **2** multiply by three. □ **in triplicate** in three copies. □ **triplication** /-ˈkeɪʃ(ə)n/ *n.* [Latin: related to TRIPLEX]

tripod /ˈtraɪpɒd/ *n.* **1** three-legged stand for a camera etc. **2** stool, table, or utensil resting on three feet or legs. [Greek, = three-footed]

Tripoli /ˈtrɪpəlɪ/ **1** capital and chief port of Libya; fruit and olive oil are exported; pop. (est. 1991) 1 000 000. **2** seaport in NW Lebanon; oil from Iraq is refined; pop. (est. 1991) 240 000.

tripos /ˈtraɪpɒs/ *n.* (at Cambridge University) honours examinations for primary degrees. [related to TRIPOD]

tripper *n.* person who goes on a pleasure trip.

triptych /ˈtrɪptɪk/ *n.* picture or relief carving on three panels, usu. hinged together at the sides. [after DIPTYCH]

Tripura /ˈtrɪpʊrə/ state in NE India; pop. (est. 1994)

Trinidad and Tobago /ˈtrɪnɪˌdæd, təˈbeɪgəʊ/, **Republic of** country in the West Indies consisting of the main island of Trinidad, off the NE coast of Venezuela, and the much smaller island of Tobago (further to the NE). A substantial part of the national income is generated by the export of oil and petroleum products. There are also significant reserves of natural gas. Industries include iron and steel, aluminium smelting, electronics, and the manufacture of fertilizers, ammonia, food products, and rum. Tourism is also an important source of revenue. The chief crops are sugar and cocoa. The islands were ceded to Britain by Spain in 1802 and were formally amalgamated as a Crown Colony in 1888. After four years as a member of the West Indies Federation, Trinidad and Tobago became an independent member state of the Commonwealth in 1962 and a republic in 1976. It is a member of CARICOM. President, Arthur Robinson; prime minister, Basdeo Panday; capital, Port of Spain. □ **Trinidadian** /-ˈdeɪdɪən/ *adj.* & *n.* **Tobagan** *adj.* & *n.* **Tobagonian** /-ˈgəʊnɪən/ *adj.* & *n.*

languages	English (official), Hindi, French, Spanish
currency	dollar (TT$) of 100 cents
pop. (1996)	1 262 000
GNP (1994)	US$4.8B
literacy	97%
life expectancy	67 (m); 72 (f)

Exchange rate, US¢ per TT$ (a) Inflation, % (b)

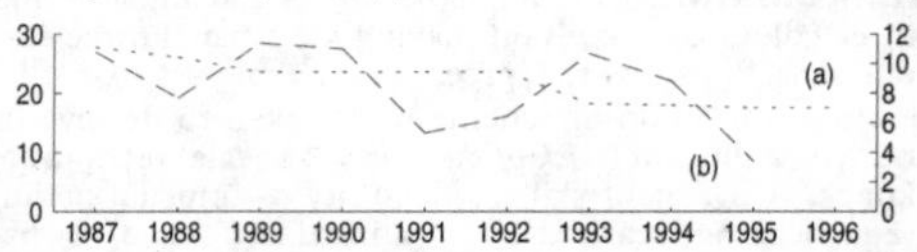

3 055 000; capital, Agartala. Crops include rice, jute, tea, and bamboo.

trip-wire *n.* wire stretched close to the ground to trip up an intruder or to operate an alarm or other device when disturbed.

trireme /'traɪriːm/ *n.* ancient Greek warship, with three files of oarsmen on each side. [Latin *remus* oar]

trisect /traɪ'sekt/ *v.* divide into three (usu. equal) parts. □ **trisection** *n.* [Latin *seco sect-* cut]

Tristan da Cunha /ˌtrɪst(ə)n də 'kuːnjə/ largest of a small group of volcanic islands in the S Atlantic, a dependency of St Helena; crayfish fishing and fish processing are the main industries; pop. (1991) 288.

trite *adj.* (of a phrase, observation, etc.) hackneyed. □ **tritely** *adv.* **triteness** *n.* [Latin *tero trit-* rub]

tritium /'trɪtɪəm/ *n.* radioactive isotope of hydrogen with a mass about three times that of ordinary hydrogen. [Greek *tritos* third]

triumph /'traɪʌmf/ –*n.* **1 a** state of victory or success (*returned in triumph*). **b** a great success or achievement. **2** supreme example (*a triumph of engineering*). **3** joy at success; exultation (*triumph in her face*). **4** processional entry of a victorious general into ancient Rome. –*v.* **1** (often foll. by *over*) gain a victory; be successful. **2** (of an ancient Roman general) ride in triumph. **3** (often foll. by *over*) exult. □ **triumphal** /-'ʌmf(ə)l/ *adj.* [French from Latin]

■ **Usage** *Triumphal*, meaning 'of or used in celebrating a triumph' as in *triumphal arch* should not be confused with *triumphant* meaning 'victorious' or 'exultant'.

triumphalism /traɪ'ʌmfəˌlɪz(ə)m/ *n.* excessive exultation over the victories of one's own party etc. □ **triumphalist** *adj.* & *n.*

triumphant /traɪ'ʌmf(ə)nt/ *adj.* **1** victorious, successful. **2** exultant. □ **triumphantly** *adv.*

■ **Usage** See note at *triumph*.

triumvirate /traɪ'ʌmvərət/ *n.* ruling group of three men, esp. in ancient Rome. [Latin *tres* three, *vir* man]

trivalent /traɪ'veɪlənt/ *adj. Chem.* having a valency of three. □ **trivalency** *n.*

Trivandrum /trɪ'vændrəm/ city in SW India, capital of the state of Kerala and a centre of commerce and communications; pop. (1991) 524 006.

trivet /'trɪvɪt/ *n.* iron tripod or bracket for a pot or kettle to stand on. [apparently from Latin *tripes* three-footed]

trivia /'trɪvɪə/ *n.pl.* trifles or trivialities.

trivial /'trɪvɪəl/ *adj.* **1** of small value or importance; trifling. **2** (of a person etc.) concerned only with trivial things. □ **triviality** /-'ælɪtɪ/ *n.* (*pl.* **-ies**). **trivially** *adv.* [Latin *trivialis* commonplace, from *trivium* three-way street corner]

trivialize *v.* (also **-ise**) (**-zing** or **-sing**) make or treat as trivial; minimize. □ **trivialization** /-'zeɪʃ(ə)n/ *n.*

trochee /'trəʊkiː/ *n. Prosody* metrical foot consisting of one long followed by one short syllable (-⏑). □ **trochaic** /trə'keɪɪk/ *adj.* [Greek, = running]

trod *past* and *past part.* of TREAD.

trodden *past part.* of TREAD.

troglodyte /'trɒgləˌdaɪt/ *n.* cave-dweller. [Greek *trōglē* hole]

troika /'trɔɪkə/ *n.* **1 a** Russian vehicle with a team of three horses abreast. **b** this team. **2** group of three people, esp. as an administrative council. [Russian]

Trojan /'trəʊdʒ(ə)n/ –*adj.* of ancient Troy in Asia Minor. –*n.* **1** native or inhabitant of Troy. **2** person who works, fights, etc. courageously. [Latin *Troia* Troy]

Trojan Horse *n.* **1** hollow wooden horse used by the Greeks to enter Troy. **2** person or device planted to bring about an enemy's downfall. **3** (also **trojan**) computer program designed to circumvent the security of a computer system.

troll[1] *n.* (in Scandinavian folklore) fabulous being, esp. a giant or dwarf dwelling in a cave. [Old Norse]

troll[2] *v.* fish by drawing bait along in the water. [perhaps related to French *troller* to quest]

trolley /'trɒlɪ/ *n.* (*pl.* **-s**) **1** table, stand, or basket on wheels or castors for serving food, transporting luggage etc., gathering purchases in a supermarket, etc. **2** low truck running on rails. **3** (in full **trolley-wheel**) wheel attached to a pole etc. used for collecting current from an overhead electric wire to drive a vehicle. [dial., perhaps from TROLL[2]]

trolley bus *n.* electric bus using a trolley-wheel.

trollop /'trɒləp/ *n.* disreputable girl or woman. [perhaps related to archaic *trull* prostitute]

trombone /trɒm'bəʊn/ *n.* brass wind instrument with a sliding tube. □ **trombonist** *n.* [French or Italian *tromba* TRUMPET]

trompe-l'œil /trɔ̃p'lɜːɪ/ *n.* (often *attrib.*) painting etc. designed to give an illusion of reality. [French, literally 'deceives the eye']

Tromsø /'trɒmsɜː/ principal city of Arctic Norway, situated on an island just W of the mainland; it has fishing and fish-processing industries; pop. (1990) 51 218.

-tron *suffix Physics* forming nouns denoting: **1** elementary particle (*positron*). **2** particle accelerator. [from ELECTRON]

Trondheim /'trɒndhaɪm/ city and fishing-port in Norway; activities include fishing, shipbuilding, and the export of timber, wood pulp, fish, and metal goods; pop. (1996) 143 746.

troop –*n.* **1** assembled company; assemblage of people or animals. **2** (in *pl.*) soldiers, armed forces. **3** cavalry unit under a captain. **4** unit of artillery or armoured vehicles. **5** grouping of three or more Scout patrols. –*v.* (foll. by *in*, *out*, *off*, etc.) come together or move in large numbers. □ **troop the colour** transfer a flag ceremonially at a public mounting of garrison guards. [French *troupe*]

trooper *n.* **1** private soldier in a cavalry or armoured unit. **2** *Austral.* & *US* mounted or state police officer. **3** cavalry horse. **4** troop-ship.

troop-ship *n.* ship used for transporting troops.

trope *n.* figurative use of a word. [Greek *tropos* from *trepō* turn]

trophy /'trəʊfɪ/ *n.* (*pl.* **-ies**) **1** cup etc. as a prize in a contest. **2** memento or souvenir of success in hunting, war, etc. [Greek *tropaion*]

tropic /'trɒpɪk/ –*n.* **1** parallel of latitude 23°27′ north (**tropic of Cancer**) or south (**tropic of Capricorn**) of the Equator. **2** each of two corresponding circles on the celestial sphere where the sun appears to turn when at its greatest declination. **3** (**the Tropics**) region between the tropics of Cancer and Capricorn. –*adj.* = TROPICAL. [Greek *tropē* turn]

tropical *adj.* of or typical of the Tropics.

troposphere /'trɒpəˌsfɪə(r)/ *n.* lowest layer of atmosphere extending about 6–10 km upwards from the earth's surface. [Greek *tropos* turn]

Trot *n. colloq.* usu. *derog.* Trotskyite. [abbreviation]

trot –*v.* (**-tt-**) **1** (of a person) run at a moderate pace. **2** (of a horse) proceed at a steady pace faster than a walk, lifting each diagonal pair of legs alternately. **3** *colloq.* walk, go. **4** cause (a horse or person) to trot. **5** traverse (a distance) at a trot. –*n.* **1** action or exercise of trotting (*proceed at a trot*; *went for a trot*). **2** (**the trots**) *slang* diarrhoea. □ **on the trot** *colloq.* **1** in succession (*six days on the trot*). **2** continually busy (*kept me on the trot*). **trot out 1** *colloq.* introduce (an opinion etc.) tediously or repeatedly. **2** cause (a horse) to trot to show his paces. [French]

troth /trəʊθ/ *n. archaic* **1** faith, loyalty. **2** truth. □ **pledge** (or **plight**) **one's troth** pledge one's word, esp. in marriage or betrothal. [Old English: related to TRUTH]

Trotskyism /'trɒtskɪˌɪz(ə)m/ *n.* political principles of L. Trotsky, esp. as urging worldwide socialist revolution. □ **Trotskyist** *n.* **Trotskyite** *n. derog.*

trotter *n.* **1** (usu. in *pl.*) animal's foot as food. **2** horse bred or trained for trotting.

troubadour /'truːbəˌdʊə(r)/ *n.* **1** singer or poet. **2** French medieval lyric poet singing of courtly love. [Provençal *trobar* find, compose]

trouble /'trʌb(ə)l/ –*n.* **1** difficulty or distress; vexation, affliction (*had trouble with my car*). **2 a** inconvenience; unpleasant exertion; bother. **b** cause of this (*she was no trouble*). **3** perceived failing (*the trouble with me is that I can't say no*). **4** dysfunction (*kidney trouble*; *engine trouble*). **5 a** disturbance (*crowd trouble*; *don't want any trouble*). **b** (in *pl.*) political or social unrest, public disturbances, esp. (**the Troubles**) in Northern Ireland. –*v.* (**-ling**) **1** cause distress or anxiety to; disturb. **2** be disturbed or worried (*don't trouble about it*). **3** afflict; cause pain etc. to. **4** (often *refl.*) subject or be subjected to inconvenience or unpleasant exertion (*sorry to trouble you*; *don't trouble yourself*). □ **ask** (or **look) for trouble** *colloq.* invite trouble by one's actions, behaviour, etc.; be rash or indiscreet. **in trouble 1** involved in a matter likely to bring censure or punishment. **2** *colloq.* pregnant while unmarried. [Latin: related to TURBID]

troublemaker *n.* person habitually causing trouble. □ **troublemaking** *n.*

troubleshooter *n.* **1** mediator in a dispute. **2** person who traces and corrects faults in machinery or in an organization etc. □ **troubleshooting** *n.*

troublesome *adj.* causing trouble, annoying.

trough /trɒf/ *n.* **1** long narrow open receptacle for water, animal feed, etc. **2** channel or hollow like this. **3** elongated region of low barometric pressure. [Old English]

trounce *v.* (**-cing**) **1** defeat heavily. **2** beat, thrash. **3** punish severely. [origin unknown]

troupe /tru:p/ *n.* company or band, esp. of artistes. [French, = TROOP]

trouper *n.* **1** member of a theatrical troupe. **2** staunch colleague.

trousers /'traʊzəz/ *n.pl.* **1** two-legged outer garment reaching from the waist usu. to the ankles. **2** (**trouser**) (*attrib.*) designating part of this (*trouser leg*). □ **wear the trousers** (esp. of a wife) dominate in a marriage. □ **trousered** *adj.* [in pl. after *drawers*: Irish and Gaelic *triubhas* trews]

trouser suit *n.* woman's suit of trousers and jacket.

trousseau /'tru:səʊ/ *n.* (*pl.* **-s** or **-x** /-səʊz/) bride's collection of clothes etc. [French: related to TRUSS]

trout *n.* (*pl.* same or **-s**) fish related to the salmon, valued as food. [Latin *tructa*]

trove *n.* = TREASURE TROVE. [Anglo-French *trové* from *trover* find]

trowel /'traʊəl/ *n.* **1** small flat-bladed tool for spreading mortar etc. **2** scoop for lifting small plants or earth. [Latin *trulla*]

troy *n.* (in full **troy weight**) system of weights used for precious metals and gems, with a pound of 12 ounces or 5760 grains; 1 oz. troy = 31.1035 g. [probably *Troyes* in France]

truant /'tru:ənt/ –*n.* **1** child who stays away from school. **2** person who avoids work etc. –*adj.* shirking, idle, wandering. –*v.* (also **play truant**) be a truant. □ **truancy** *n.* [French, probably from Celtic]

truce /tru:s/ *n.* temporary agreement to cease hostilities. [originally *trewes* pl.: Old English, = covenant: related to TRUE]

Trucial States /'tru:ʃ(ə)l/ see UNITED ARAB EMIRATES.

truck[1] *n.* **1** lorry. **2** open railway wagon for freight. [perhaps from TRUCKLE]

truck[2] *n.* dealings. □ **have no truck with** avoid dealing with. [French *troquer*]

trucker *n.* esp. *US* long-distance lorry-driver.

truckle /'trʌk(ə)l/ –*n.* (in full **truckle-bed**) low bed on wheels, stored under a larger bed. –*v.* (**-ling**) (foll. by *to*) submit obsequiously. [Latin *trochlea* pulley]

truculent /'trʌkjʊlənt/ *adj.* aggressively defiant. □ **truculence** *n.* **truculently** *adv.* [Latin *trux truc-* fierce]

trudge –*v.* (**-ging**) **1** go on foot, esp. laboriously. **2** traverse (a distance) in this way. –*n.* trudging walk. [origin unknown]

true /tru:/ –*adj.* (**truer, truest**) **1** in accordance with fact or reality (*a true story*). **2** genuine; rightly or strictly so called. **3** (often foll. by *to*) loyal, faithful. **4** (foll. by *to*) accurately conforming to (a type or standard) (*true to form*). **5** correctly positioned or balanced; upright, level. **6** exact, accurate (*a true copy*). –*adv.* **1** *archaic* truly (*tell me true*). **2** accurately (*aim true*). **3** without variation (*breed true*). □ **come true** actually happen. **out of true** out of alignment. **true to life** accurately representing reality. [Old English]

♦ **true and fair view** *n.* accurate representation of the state of an organization's affairs in terms of its published accounts. Auditors of the accounts of companies both in the UK and internationally are required by law to form an opinion as to whether the accounts they audit show a true and fair view. 'True' implies that the accounts contain no false statements; 'fair' implies that the aggregate of facts shown by the 'true' statements is not misleading because, for instance, of omissions.

---

true-blue –*adj.* extremely loyal or orthodox. –*n.* such a person, esp. a Conservative.

true-love *n.* sweetheart.

true north *n.* north according to the earth's axis, not magnetic north.

truffle /'trʌf(ə)l/ *n.* **1** edible rich-flavoured underground fungus. **2** sweet made of a chocolate mixture covered with cocoa etc. [probably Dutch from French]

trug *n.* shallow oblong garden-basket usu. of wood strips. [perhaps a dial. var. of TROUGH]

truism /'tru:ɪz(ə)m/ *n.* statement too hackneyed to be worth making, e.g. 'Nothing lasts for ever'.

truly /'tru:lɪ/ *adv.* **1** sincerely (*am truly grateful*). **2** really, indeed (*truly, I do not know*). **3** loyally (*served them truly*). **4** accurately (*is not truly depicted*). **5** properly (*well and truly*). [Old English: related to TRUE]

trump[1] –*n.* **1 a** playing-card of a suit temporarily ranking above the others. **b** (in *pl.*) this suit (*hearts are trumps*). **2** *colloq.* generous or loyal person. –*v.* **1** defeat (a card or its player) with a trump. **2** *colloq.* outdo. □ **come** (or **turn) up trumps** *colloq.* **1** turn out better than expected. **2** be greatly successful or helpful. **trump up** fabricate or invent (an accusation etc.) (*trumped-up charge*). [corruption of TRIUMPH in the same (now obsolete) sense]

trump[2] *n. archaic* trumpet-blast. [French *trompe*]

trump card *n.* **1** card belonging to, or turned up to determine, a trump suit. **2** *colloq.* valuable resource, esp. kept in reserve.

trumpery /'trʌmpərɪ/ –*n.* (*pl.* **-ies**) **1** worthless finery. **2** worthless thing; rubbish. –*adj.* showy but worthless; trashy; shallow. [French *tromperie* deceit]

trumpet /'trʌmpɪt/ –*n.* **1** brass instrument with a flared bell and bright penetrating tone. **2** trumpet-shaped thing (*ear-trumpet*). **3** sound of or like a trumpet. –*v.* (**-t-**) **1 a** blow a trumpet. **b** (of an enraged elephant etc.) make a trumpet-like cry. **2** proclaim loudly. □ **trumpeter** *n.* [French diminutive: related to TRUMP[2]]

trumpet-call *n.* urgent summons to action.

truncate /trʌŋ'keɪt/ *v.* (**-ting**) cut the top or the end from; shorten (*a truncated decimal*). □ **truncation** /-'keɪʃ(ə)n/ *n.* [Latin: related to TRUNK]

truncheon /'trʌntʃ(ə)n/ *n.* short club carried by a police officer. [French *tronchon* stump: related to TRUNK]

trundle /'trʌnd(ə)l/ *v.* (**-ling**) roll or move, esp. heavily or noisily. [var. of obsolete or dial. *trendle*: related to TREND]

trunk –*n.* **1** main stem of a tree. **2** body without the limbs and head. **3** large box with a hinged lid for luggage, storage, etc. **4** *US* boot of a car. **5** elephant's elongated prehensile nose. **6** (in *pl.*) men's close-fitting shorts worn for swimming etc. –*v.* deliver (goods) by road over long distances, usu. by means of a service that has local distribution depots from which collections and deliveries are made. [Latin *truncus* cut short]

trunk call *n.* long-distance telephone call.

trunk line *n.* main line of a railway, telephone system, etc.

trunk road *n.* important main road.

truss –*n.* **1** framework supporting a roof, bridge, etc. **2** surgical appliance worn to support a hernia. **3** bundle of hay or straw. **4** compact terminal cluster of flowers or fruit. –*v.* **1** tie up (a fowl) for cooking. **2** (often foll. by *up*) tie (a person) up with the arms to the sides. **3** support (a roof or bridge etc.) with a truss or trusses. [French]

trust –*n.* **1** firm belief in the reliability, truth, or strength etc. of a person or thing. **2** confident expectation. **3** responsibility (*position of great trust*). **4** commercial credit (*obtained goods on trust*). **5** *Law* **a** arrangement enabling property to be held by a person or persons (the trustees) for the benefit of some other person or persons (the beneficiaries). The trustee is the legal owner of the property but the beneficiary has an equitable interest in it. A trust may be intentionally created or it may be imposed by law (e.g. if a trustee gives away trust property, the recipient will hold that property as constructive trustee for the beneficiary). Trusts are commonly used to provide for families and in commercial situations (e.g. pensions trusts). **b** property so held. **c** body of trustees. **6** association of companies for reducing competition etc. –*v.* **1** place trust in; believe in; rely on the character or behaviour of. **2** (foll. by *with*) allow (a person) to have or use (a thing) from confidence in its careful use (*trusted her with my car*). **3** (often foll. by *that*) have faith, confidence, or hope that a thing will take place (*I trust you will come*). **4** (foll. by *to*) consign (a thing) to (a person) with trust. **5** (foll. by *in*) place reliance in (*we trust in you*). **6** (foll. by *to*) place (esp. undue) reliance on (*trust to luck*). □ **in trust** (of property) managed by one or more persons on behalf of another. **take on trust** accept (an assertion etc.) without evidence or investigation. [Old Norse]

♦ **trust deed** *n. Law* document creating and setting out the terms of a trust. It will usu. contain the names of the trustees, the identity of the beneficiaries, and the nature of the trust property, as well as the powers and duties of the trustees. Trusts of land must be declared in writing; trusts of other property need not be although there is often a trust deed to avoid uncertainty.

♦ **trustee** /trʌsˈtiː/ *n.* person or company that holds the legal title to property but is not its beneficial owner (see TRUST *n.* 5); there are usu. two or more trustees of a trust. Trustees may not profit from their position and must act for the benefit of the beneficiary, who may be regarded as the real owner of the property. They may be personally liable to beneficiaries for loss of trust property. □ **trusteeship** *n.*

♦ **trustee in bankruptcy** *n.* person who administers a bankrupt's estate and realizes it for the benefit of the creditors (see BANKRUPTCY).

♦ **trustee investments** *n.pl.* investments in which trustees are authorized to invest trust property. In the UK the Trustees Investment Act (1961) regulates the investments of trust property that may be made by trustees. The act applies unless excluded by a trust deed executed after the act was passed. Half of the trust fund must be invested in **narrow-range securities**, largely specified in fixed-interest investments. The other half may be invested in **wider-range securities**, most importantly ordinary shares in companies quoted on the London Stock Exchange. In some cases, trustees must take advice before investing. The act considerably enlarged the range of trustee investments.

---

trustful *adj.* full of trust or confidence. □ **trustfully** *adv.*

♦ **trust fund** *n.* fund consisting of the assets belonging to a legal trust, including money and property, that is held by the trustees for the beneficiaries.

---

trusting *adj.* having trust; trustful. □ **trustingly** *adv.*

trustworthy *adj.* deserving of trust; reliable. □ **trustworthiness** *n.*

trusty –*adj.* (**-ier, -iest**) *archaic* or *joc.* trustworthy (*a trusty steed*). –*n.* (*pl.* **-ies**) prisoner given special privileges for good behaviour.

truth /truːθ/ *n.* (*pl.* **truths** /truːðz, truːθs/) **1** quality or state of being true. **2** what is true. □ **in truth** *literary* truly, really. [Old English: related to TRUE]

truthful *adj.* **1** habitually speaking the truth. **2** (of a story etc.) true. □ **truthfully** *adv.* **truthfulness** *n.*

try /traɪ/ –*v.* (**-ies, -ied**) **1** make an effort with a view to success (often foll. by *to* + infin.; *colloq.* foll. by *and* + infin.: *tried to be on time; try and be early*). **2** make an effort to achieve (*tried my best*). **3 a** test by use or experiment. **b** test the qualities of. **4** make severe demands on (*tries my patience*). **5** examine the effectiveness of for a purpose (*try cold water; have you tried kicking it?*). **6** ascertain the state of fastening of (a door, window, etc.). **7 a** investigate and decide (a case or issue) judicially. **b** (often foll. by *for*) subject (a person) to trial (*tried for murder*). **8** (foll. by *for*) apply or compete for; seek to reach or attain (*try for a gold medal*). –*n.* (*pl.* **-ies**) **1** effort to accomplish something. **2** *Rugby* touching-down of the ball behind the opposing goal-line, scoring points and entitling the scoring side to a kick at the goal. □ **try one's hand** test how skilful one is, esp. at the first attempt. **try it on** *colloq.* try to get away with an unreasonable request etc. **try on** put on (clothes etc.) to see if they fit etc. **try out** put to the test, test thoroughly. [originally = separate, distinguish, from French *trier* sift]

■ **Usage** Use of the verb with *and* (see sense 1) is uncommon in negative contexts (except in the imperative, e.g. *don't try and get the better of me*) and in the past tense.

trying *adj.* annoying, vexatious; hard to endure.

try-on *n. colloq.* **1** act of trying it on or trying on (clothes etc.). **2** attempt to deceive.

try-out *n.* experimental test.

tryst /trɪst/ *n. archaic* meeting, esp. of lovers. [French]

TS –*postcode* Cleveland. –*international civil aircraft marking* Tunisia.

T/S *abbr.* transshipment.

♦ **TSA** *abbr.* The Securities Association Ltd. (see SECURITIES AND FUTURES AUTHORITY LTD.; SELF-REGULATING ORGANIZATION).

---

tsar /zɑː(r)/ *n.* (also **czar**) (*fem.* **tsarina** /-ˈriːnə/) *hist.* title of the former emperors of Russia. □ **tsarist** *n.* (usu. *attrib.*). [Latin *Caesar*]

♦ **TSB Group plc** see COMMERCIAL BANK. [abbreviation of *T*rustee *S*avings *B*ank]

TSE *abbr.* **1** Tokyo Stock Exchange. **2** Toronto Stock Exchange.

tsetse /ˈtsetsɪ, ˈtetsɪ/ *n.* African fly feeding on blood and transmitting esp. sleeping-sickness. [Tswana]

TSh *symb.* Tanzanian shilling.

T-shirt /ˈtiːʃɜːt/ *n.* short-sleeved casual top having the form of a T when spread out.

Tsinghai see QINGHAI.

TSO *abbr.* Trading Standards Officer.

tsp. *abbr.* (*pl.* **tsps.**) teaspoonful.

T-square /ˈtiːskweə(r)/ *n.* T-shaped instrument for drawing right angles.

TSR *abbr. Computing* terminate and stay resident, a program that is loaded into memory and is available even when another application is running.

TSRB *abbr.* Top Salaries Review Body.

TSSA *abbr.* Transport Salaried Staffs' Association (trade union).

tsunami /tsuːˈnɑːmɪ/ *n.* (*pl.* **-s**) long high sea wave caused by underwater earthquakes etc. [Japanese]

TT –*abbr.* **1** Tourist Trophy. **2** tuberculin-tested. **3 a** teetotal. **b** teetotaller. **4** = TELEGRAPHIC TRANSFER. **5** Trust Territories. –*international vehicle registration* Trinidad and Tobago. –*international civil aircraft marking* Chad.

TTC *abbr.* technical training centre.

TTF *abbr.* Timber Trade Federation.

TTL *abbr.* transistor-transistor logic, a family of high-speed logic circuits that are all fabricated with a similar structure by the same integrated-circuit techniques.

TU *–abbr.* **1** trade union. **2** training unit. *–international civil aircraft marking* Côte d'Ivoire (Ivory Coast). *–airline flight code* Tunis Air.

tub *–n.* **1** open flat-bottomed usu. round vessel. **2** tub-shaped (usu. plastic) carton. **3** *colloq.* bath. **4** *colloq.* clumsy slow boat. *–v.* (**-bb-**) plant, bathe, or wash in a tub. [probably Low German or Dutch]

tuba /'tju:bə/ *n.* (*pl.* **-s**) low-pitched brass wind instrument. [Latin, = trumpet]

tubby /'tʌbɪ/ *adj.* (**-ier, -iest**) short and fat. □ **tubbiness** *n.*

tube *–n.* **1** long hollow cylinder. **2** soft metal or plastic cylinder sealed at one end and holding a semi-liquid substance (*tube of toothpaste*). **3** hollow cylindrical organ in the body. **4** (often prec. by *the*) *colloq.* London underground (*went by tube*). **5 a** cathode-ray tube, esp. in a television set. **b** (prec. by *the*) esp. *US colloq.* television. **6** = INNER TUBE. **7** *Austral. slang* can of beer. *–v.* (**-bing**) **1** equip with tubes. **2** enclose in a tube. [Latin]

tuber *n.* **1** thick rounded part of a stem or rhizome, usu. found underground and covered with modified buds, e.g. in a potato. **2** similar root of a dahlia etc. [Latin, = hump, swelling]

tubercle /'tju:bək(ə)l/ *n.* small rounded swelling on the body or in an organ, esp. as characteristic of tuberculosis. □ **tuberculous** /-'bɜ:kjʊləs/ *adj.* [Latin *tuberculum*, diminutive of TUBER]

tubercle bacillus *n.* bacterium causing tuberculosis.

tubercular /tjʊ'bɜ:kjʊlə(r)/ *adj.* of or having tubercles or tuberculosis.

tuberculin /tjʊ'bɜ:kjʊlɪn/ *n.* sterile liquid from cultures of tubercle bacillus, used in the diagnosis and treatment of tuberculosis.

tuberculin-tested *adj.* (of milk) from cows shown to be free of tuberculosis.

tuberculosis /tjʊˌbɜ:kjʊ'ləʊsɪs/ *n.* infectious bacterial disease marked by tubercles, esp. in the lungs.

tuberose /'tju:bəˌrəʊz/ *n.* plant with scented white funnel-like flowers.

tuberous /'tju:bərəs/ *adj.* having tubers; of or like a tuber.

tubing *n.* length of tube or quantity of tubes.

Tubruq see TOBRUK.

tub-thumper *n. colloq.* ranting preacher or orator.

Tubuai Islands /tu:'bwaɪ/ (also **Austral Islands**) group of islands in the S Pacific Ocean forming part of French Polynesia; products include coffee, copra, and arrowroot; pop. (1988) 6509.

tubular /'tju:bjʊlə(r)/ *adj.* **1** tube-shaped. **2** having or consisting of tubes. **3** (of furniture etc.) having a tubular framework.

tubular bells *n.pl.* orchestral instrument of vertically suspended brass tubes struck with a hammer.

tubule /'tju:bju:l/ *n.* small tube in a plant or animal body. [Latin *tubulus*, diminutive: related to TUBE]

TUC *abbr.* = TRADES UNION CONGRESS.

tuck *–v.* **1** (often foll. by *in, up*) **a** draw, fold, or turn the outer or end parts of (cloth or clothes etc.) close together so as to be held; push in the edge of (a thing) so as to confine it (*tucked his shirt into his trousers*). **b** push in the edges of bedclothes around (a person) (*came to tuck me in*). **2** draw together into a small space (*tucked its head under its wing*). **3** stow (a thing) away in a specified place or way (*tucked it in a corner; tucked it out of sight*). **4** make a stitched fold in (cloth etc.). *–n.* **1** flattened usu. stitched fold in cloth etc. **2** *colloq.* food, esp. cakes and sweets (also *attrib.*: *tuck box*). □ **tuck in** *colloq.* eat heartily. **tuck into** (or **away**) *colloq.* eat (food) heartily (*tucked into their dinner; could really tuck it away*). [Low German or Dutch]

tucker *–n.* **1** *hist.* piece of lace or linen etc. in or on a woman's bodice. **2** *Austral. & NZ slang* food. *–v.* (esp. in *passive*; often foll. by *out*) *US & Austral. colloq.* tire.

tuck-in *n. colloq.* large meal.

tuck shop *n.* small shop selling sweets etc. to schoolchildren.

Tucson /'tu:sɒn/ resort city in the US, in SE Arizona, industrial centre for the surrounding mining and agricultural area; pop. (est. 1994) 434 726.

-tude *suffix* forming abstract nouns (*altitude*; *solitude*). [Latin *-tudo*]

Tudor /'tju:də(r)/ *adj.* **1** of the royal family of England 1485–1603 or this period. **2** of the architectural style of this period, esp. with half-timbering. [Owen *Tudor*, name of the grandfather of Henry VII]

Tues. *abbr.* (also **Tue.**) Tuesday.

Tuesday /'tju:zdeɪ/ *–n.* day of the week following Monday. *–adv.* **1** *colloq.* on Tuesday. **2** (**Tuesdays**) on Tuesdays; each Tuesday. [Old English]

tufa /'tju:fə/ *n.* **1** porous limestone rock formed round mineral springs. **2** = TUFF. [Italian: related to TUFF]

tuff *n.* rock formed from volcanic ash. [Latin *tofus*]

tuffet /'tʌfɪt/ *n.* clump of grass; small mound. [var. of TUFT]

tuft *n.* bunch or collection of threads, grass, feathers, hair, etc., held or growing together at the base. □ **tufted** *adj.* **tufty** *adj.* [probably French *tofe*]

TUG *abbr.* Telephone Users' Group.

tug *–v.* (**-gg-**) **1** (often foll. by *at*) pull hard or violently; jerk. **2** tow (a ship etc.) by a tugboat. *–n.* **1** hard, violent, or jerky pull. **2** sudden strong emotion. **3** small powerful boat for towing ships. [related to TOW[1]]

tugboat *n.* = TUG *n.* 3.

tug of love *n. colloq.* dispute over the custody of a child.

tug of war *n.* **1** trial of strength between two sides pulling opposite ways on a rope. **2** decisive or severe contest.

tugrik /'tu:ˌgri:k/ *n.* standard monetary unit of Mongolia. [Mongolian]

tuition /tju:'ɪʃ(ə)n/ *n.* **1** teaching, esp. if paid for. **2** fee for this. [Latin *tueor tuit-* look after]

Tula /'tu:lə/ industrial city in W central Russia, S of Moscow; industries include ironworking and food processing; pop. (est. 1995) 532 000.

tulip /'tju:lɪp/ *n.* **1** bulbous spring-flowering plant with showy cup-shaped flowers. **2** its flower. [Turkish *tul(i)band* TURBAN (from its shape), from Persian]

tulip-tree *n.* tree producing tulip-like flowers.

tulle /tju:l/ *n.* soft fine silk etc. net for veils and dresses. [*Tulle* in France]

Tulsa /'tʌlsə/ city in the US, in NE Oklahoma, a port linked by waterway to the Gulf of Mexico; it is a major oil-producing centre; pop. (est. 1994) 374 851.

tum *n. colloq.* stomach. [abbreviation of TUMMY]

tumble /'tʌmb(ə)l/ *–v.* (**-ling**) **1** (cause to) fall suddenly, clumsily, or headlong. **2** fall rapidly in amount etc. (*prices tumbled*). **3** (often foll. by *about, around*) roll or toss to and fro. **4** move or rush in a headlong or blundering manner. **5** (often foll. by *to*) *colloq.* grasp the meaning behind an idea, circumstance, etc. (*he quickly tumbled to our plan*). **6** overturn; fling or push roughly or carelessly. **7** perform acrobatic feats, esp. somersaults. **8** rumple or disarrange. *–n.* **1** sudden or headlong fall. **2** somersault or other acrobatic feat. **3** untidy or confused state. [Low German *tummeln*]

tumbledown *adj.* falling or fallen into ruin; dilapidated.

tumble-drier *n.* (also **tumble-dryer**) machine for drying washing in a heated rotating drum. □ **tumble-dry** *v.*

tumbler *n.* **1** drinking-glass with no handle or foot. **2** acrobat. **3** part of a lock that holds the bolt until lifted by a key. **4** a kind of pigeon that turns over backwards in flight.

tumbrel /'tʌmbr(ə)l/ *n.* (also **tumbril**) *hist.* open cart in which condemned persons were taken to the guillotine in the French Revolution. [French *tomber* fall]

tumescent /tjʊ'mes(ə)nt/ *adj.* swelling. □ **tumescence** *n.* [Latin: related to TUMOUR]

tumid /ˈtjuːmɪd/ *adj.* **1** swollen, inflated. **2** (of style etc.) inflated, bombastic. □ **tumidity** /-ˈmɪdɪtɪ/ *n.*

tummy /ˈtʌmɪ/ *n.* (*pl.* **-ies**) *colloq.* stomach. [a childish pronunciation]

tummy-button *n.* navel.

tumour /ˈtjuːmə(r)/ *n.* (*US* **tumor**) a swelling, esp. from an abnormal growth of tissue. □ **tumorous** *adj.* [Latin *tumeo* swell]

tumult /ˈtjuːmʌlt/ *n.* **1** uproar or din, esp. of a disorderly crowd. **2** angry demonstration by a mob; riot. **3** conflict of emotions in the mind. [Latin: related to TUMOUR]

tumultuous /tjʊˈmʌltʃʊəs/ *adj.* noisy; turbulent; violent.

tumulus /ˈtjuːmjʊləs/ *n.* (*pl.* **-li** /-ˌlaɪ/) ancient burial mound. [Latin: related to TUMOUR]

tun *n.* **1** large beer or wine cask. **2** brewer's fermenting-vat. [Old English]

tuna /ˈtjuːnə/ *n.* (*pl.* same or **-s**) **1** large edible marine fish. **2** (in full **tuna-fish**) its flesh as food. [American Spanish]

tundra /ˈtʌndrə/ *n.* vast level treeless Arctic region with underlying permafrost. [Lappish]

tune –*n.* melody. –*v.* (**-ning**) **1** put (a musical instrument) in tune. **2 a** adjust (a radio etc.) to the frequency of a signal. **b** (foll. by *in*) adjust a radio receiver to the required signal. **3** adjust (an engine etc.) to run efficiently. □ **in** (or **out of**) **tune 1** having (or not having) the correct pitch or intonation (*sings in tune*). **2** (usu. foll. by *with*) harmonizing (or clashing) with one's company, surroundings, etc. **to the tune of** *colloq.* to the considerable sum of. **tuned in** (often foll. by *to*) *colloq.* acquainted; in rapport; up to date. **tune up 1** bring one's instrument to the proper pitch. **2** bring to the most efficient condition. [var. of TONE]

tuneful *adj.* melodious, musical. □ **tunefully** *adv.*

tuneless *adj.* unmelodious, unmusical. □ **tunelessly** *adv.*

tuner *n.* **1** person who tunes musical instruments, esp. pianos. **2 a** part of a radio or television receiver for tuning. **b** radio receiver as a separate unit in a high-fi system. **3** electronic device for tuning a guitar etc.

tungsten /ˈtʌŋst(ə)n/ *n.* dense metallic element with a very high melting-point. [Swedish, = heavy stone]

tunic /ˈtjuːnɪk/ *n.* **1** close-fitting short coat of police or military etc. uniform. **2** loose often sleeveless garment reaching to the knees. [Latin]

tuning-fork *n.* two-pronged steel fork giving a particular note when struck.

Tunis /ˈtjuːnɪs/ capital of Tunisia, with chemical, lead-smelting, and textile industries; pop. (1994) 674 100.

tunnel /ˈtʌn(ə)l/ –*n.* **1** underground passage dug through a hill or under a road, river, etc., esp. for a railway or road. **2** underground passage dug by an animal. –*v.* (**-ll-**; *US* **-l-**) **1** (foll. by *through, into*, etc.) make a tunnel through. **2** make (one's way) by tunnelling. [French diminutive of *tonne* TUN]

tunnel vision *n.* **1** vision which is poor or lost outside the centre of the normal field of vision. **2** *colloq.* inability to grasp a situation's wider implications.

tunny /ˈtʌnɪ/ *n.* (*pl.* same or **-ies**) = TUNA. [Greek *thunnos*]

tup –*n.* ram. –*v.* (**-pp-**) (of a ram) copulate with (a ewe). [origin unknown]

Tupi /ˈtuːpɪ/ –*n.* (*pl.* same or **-s**) **1** member of an American Indian people of the Amazon valley. **2** their language. –*adj.* of this people or language. [Tupi]

tuppence /ˈtʌpəns/ *n.* = TWOPENCE. [phonetic spelling]

tuppenny /ˈtʌpənɪ/ *adj.* = TWOPENNY. [phonetic spelling]

Tupperware /ˈtʌpəˌweə(r)/ *n. propr.* range of plastic containers for storing food. [*Tupper*, name of the manufacturer]

turban /ˈtɜːbən/ *n.* **1** man's headdress of fabric wound round a cap or the head, worn esp. by Muslims and Sikhs. **2** woman's hat resembling this. □ **turbaned** *adj.* [Persian: cf. TULIP]

turbid /ˈtɜːbɪd/ *adj.* **1** (of a liquid or colour) muddy, thick; not clear. **2** (of style etc.) confused, disordered. □ **turbidity** /-ˈbɪdɪtɪ/ *n.* [Latin *turba* crowd]

■ **Usage** *Turbid* is sometimes confused with *turgid* which means 'swollen, inflated; pompous'.

turbine /ˈtɜːbaɪn/ *n.* rotary motor driven by a flow of water, steam, gas, wind, etc. [Latin *turbo -in-* spinning-top, whirlwind]

turbo /ˈtɜːbəʊ/ *n.* (*pl.* **-s**) = TURBOCHARGER.

turbo- *comb. form* turbine.

turbocharger *n.* supercharger driven by a turbine powered by the engine's exhaust gases.

turbofan *n.* jet engine in which a turbine-driven fan provides additional thrust.

turbojet *n.* **1** jet engine in which the jet also operates a turbine-driven air-compressor. **2** aircraft powered by this.

turboprop *n.* **1** jet engine in which a turbine is used as in a turbojet and also to drive a propeller. **2** aircraft powered by this. [from PROP[3]]

turbot /ˈtɜːbət/ *n.* (*pl.* same or **-s**) large European flat-fish prized as food. [French from Swedish]

turbulent /ˈtɜːbjʊlənt/ *adj.* **1** disturbed; in commotion. **2** (of a flow of air etc.) varying irregularly. **3** restless; riotous. □ **turbulence** *n.* **turbulently** *adv.* [Latin *turba* crowd]

Turco- *comb. form* (also **Turko-**) Turkish; Turkish and. [medieval Latin: related to TURK]

turd *n. coarse slang* **1** lump of excrement. **2** contemptible person. [Old English]

tureen /tjʊəˈriːn/ *n.* deep covered dish for soup. [from TERRINE]

Tunisia /tjuːˈnɪsɪə/, **Republic of** country in N Africa, on the Mediterranean Sea. Agriculture is important to the economy; mining is important in the coastal strip. Crops include wheat, barley, citrus fruits, dates, vines, and olives; livestock (esp. cattle, sheep, and goats) are also raised in the N. There are rich deposits of phosphates; other minerals include oil, iron ore, and lead. Manufacturing industry is centred on the processing of the country's natural resources; the chief exports are oil and petroleum products, phosphates, clothing, fish, and olive oil. Tourism is a major source of foreign revenue.

History. Part of the Ottoman empire from the 16th century, Tunisia became a French protectorate in 1881. The rise of nationalist activity after the Second World War led to independence in 1956 and the establishment of a republic the following year. In 1987 Habib Bourguiba, who had been elected president for life in 1975, was deposed in a bloodless coup by Zine al-Abidine Ben Ali. Ben Ali was elected president in 1989 and re-elected in 1994. President, Zine el-Abidine Ben Ali; prime minister, Hamed Karoui; capital, Tunis. □ **Tunisian** *adj.* & *n.*

languages	Arabic (official), French
currency	dinar (TD) of 1000 millimes
pop. (1996)	9 057 000
GNP (1994)	US$15.8B
literacy	78% (m); 54% (f)
life expectancy	66 (m); 68 (f)

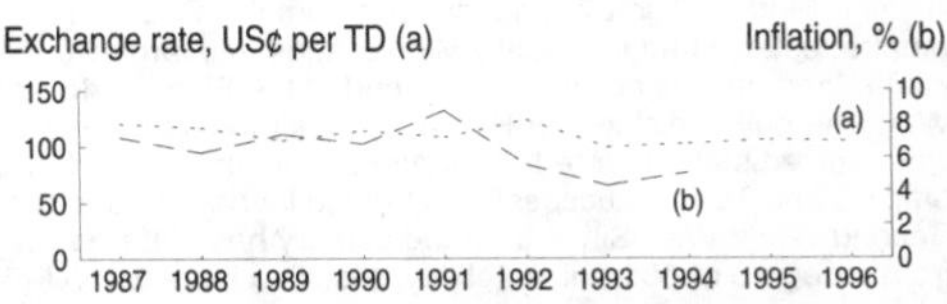

---

turf –*n.* (*pl.* **-s** or **turves**) **1 a** layer of grass etc. with earth and matted roots as the surface of grassland. **b** piece of this cut from the ground. **2** slab of peat for fuel. **3** (prec. by *the*) **a** horse-racing generally. **b** general term for racecourses. –*v.* **1** cover (ground) with turf. **2** (foll. by *out*) *colloq.* expel or eject (a person or thing). □ **turfy** *adj.* [Old English]

turf accountant *n.* bookmaker.

turgescent /tɜːˈdʒes(ə)nt/ *adj.* becoming turgid. □ **turgescence** *n.* [Latin: related to TURGID]

turgid /ˈtɜːdʒɪd/ *adj.* **1** swollen, inflated. **2** (of language) pompous, bombastic. □ **turgidity** /-ˈdʒɪdɪtɪ/ *n.* [Latin *turgeo* swell]

■ **Usage** *Turgid* is sometimes confused with *turbid* which means 'muddy, not clear; confused'.

Turin /tjʊəˈrɪn/ (Italian **Torino** /tɒˈriːnəʊ/) city in NW Italy, capital of Piedmont region and an industrial and commercial centre; manufactures include motor vehicles, textiles, paper, leather goods, wine, and chocolate; pop. (est. 1994) 945 551.

Turk *n.* **1 a** native or national of Turkey. **b** person of Turkish descent. **2** member of a central Asian people from whom the Ottomans derived, speaking a Turkic language. **3** *offens.* ferocious or wild person. [origin unknown]

turkey /ˈtɜːkɪ/ *n.* (*pl.* **-s**) **1** large orig. American bird bred for food. **2** its flesh as food. **3** *US slang* theatrical failure; flop. □ **talk turkey** *US colloq.* talk frankly; get down to business. [originally of the guinea-fowl, imported from TURKEY]

turkeycock *n.* male turkey.

Turki /ˈtɜːkɪ/ –*adj.* of a group of languages and peoples including Turkish. –*n.* this group. □ **Turkic** *adj.* [Persian: related to TURK]

Turkish –*adj.* of Turkey, the Turks, or their language. –*n.* this language.

Turkish bath *n.* **1** hot-air or steam bath followed by washing, massage, etc. **2** (in *sing.* or *pl.*) building for this.

Turkish carpet *n.* wool carpet with a thick pile and traditional bold design.

Turkish coffee *n.* strong black coffee.

Turkish delight *n.* sweet of lumps of flavoured gelatine coated in powdered sugar.

Turkish towel *n.* towel made of cotton terry.

Turko- var. of TURCO-.

Turks and Caicos Islands /tɜːks, ˈkeɪkɒs/ British dependency comprising a group of over 30 islands in the Caribbean, SE of the Bahamas; pop. (est. 1993) 14 000; capital, Grand Turk, pop. (est. 1990) 3720. Fishing is the chief source of revenue, lobsters and conchs forming the main exports; tourism and offshore banking are also important.

Turk's head *n.* turban-like ornamental knot.

Turku /ˈtʊəkuː/ (Swedish **Åbo** /ˈɔːbuː/) industrial port in SW Finland, on the Gulf of Bothnia; pop. (est. 1996) 164 744.

turmeric /ˈtɜːmərɪk/ *n.* **1** East Indian plant of the ginger family. **2** its powdered rhizome used as a spice in curry etc. or for yellow dye. [perhaps from French *terre mérite*]

turmoil /ˈtɜːmɔɪl/ *n.* **1** violent confusion; agitation. **2** din and bustle. [origin unknown]

turn /tɜːn/ –*v.* **1** move around a point or axis; give or receive a rotary motion (*turned the wheel*; *the wheel turns*). **2** change in position so that a different side, end, or part becomes outermost or uppermost etc.; invert or reverse (*it turned inside out*; *turned it upside down*). **3 a** give a new direction to (*turn your face this way*). **b** take a new direction (*turn left here*). **4** aim in a certain way (*turned the hose on them*). **5** (foll. by *into*) change in nature, form, or condition to (*turned into a frog*; *turned the book into a play*). **6** (foll. by *to*) **a** set about (*turned to doing the ironing*). **b** have recourse to (*turned to drink*; *turned to me for help*). **c** go on to consider next (*let us now turn to your report*). **7** become (*turned nasty*). **8 a** (foll. by *against*) make or become hostile to (*has turned her against us*). **b** (foll. by *on*, *upon*) become hostile to; attack (*suddenly turned on them*). **9** (of hair or leaves) change colour. **10** (of milk) become sour. **11** (of the stomach) be nauseated. **12** cause (milk) to become sour or (the stomach) to be nauseated. **13** (of the head) become giddy. **14** translate (*turn it into French*). **15** move to the other side of; go round (*turned the corner*). **16** pass the age or time of (*he has turned 40*; *it has turned 4 o'clock*). **17** (foll. by *on*) depend on; be determined by. **18** send or put; cause to go (*was turned loose*; *turned the water out into a basin*). **19** perform (a somersault etc.). **20** remake (esp. a sheet) putting the less worn outer side on the inside. **21** make (a profit). **22** divert (a bullet). **23** blunt (a knife etc.). **24** shape (an object) on a lathe. **25** give an (esp. elegant) form to (*turn a compliment*). **26** (of the tide) change direction. –*n.* **1** turning; rotary motion. **2** changed or a change of direction or tendency (*took a sudden turn to the left*). **3** point at which a turning or change occurs. **4** turning of a road. **5** change of direction of the tide. **6** change in the course of events (*a turn for the worse*). **7** *Stock Exch.* difference between the price at which a market maker will buy a security and the price at which he or she will sell it, i.e. the market maker's profit. **8** tendency or disposition; facility of forming (*is of*

Turkey /ˈtɜːkɪ/, **Republic of** country comprising Anatolia in SW Asia, between the Black Sea and the Mediterranean Sea, and a small enclave (E Thrace) in SE Europe. Agriculture provides employment for a large proportion of the working population: the chief agricultural exports are cotton, tobacco, citrus fruits, figs, grapes, and nuts, cultivated in fertile coastal regions, and livestock and livestock products (esp. skins, wool, and mohair). The country is rich in mineral resources, including chromium, borax, copper, bauxite, oil, and coal. Manufacturing industry produces textiles, food products, iron and steel, glass, cement, chemicals, and rubber and plastic goods. Products of Turkey's mining and manufacturing industries together provide a large amount of export revenue. Turkey entered a full customs union with the EU in 1996. However, Greece managed successfully to suspend an EU aid package later that year.

History. Modern Turkey is descended from the Ottoman empire, established in the late Middle Ages and largely maintained until its collapse at the end of the First World War. The nationalist leader Kemal Ataturk moulded a new westernized state, centred on Anatolia, from the ruins of the empire, and Turkey successfully avoided involvement in the Second World War. Since then the country has suffered from a degree of political instability, resulting in the imposition of military rule in 1960, 1971–3, and 1980–3. There has been friction with Greece (over Cyprus), and, since 1984, internal tension between Turks and Kurds (who are demanding autonomy) is a continuing problem: Kurdish terrorist activities are threatening Turkey's tourist industry. Turkey is seeking to expand its influence in the central Asian states of the former Soviet Union. During the 1990s Turkey's secular form of government has been increasingly challenged by Islamic fundamentalists. President, Suleyman Demirel; prime minister, Mesut Yilmaz; capital, Ankara.

languages	Turkish (official), Kurdish, Arabic
currency	lira (lT) of 100 kurus
pop. (1996)	62 650 000
GNP (1994)	US$149B
literacy	91% (m); 72% (f)
life expectancy	69 (m); 74 (f)

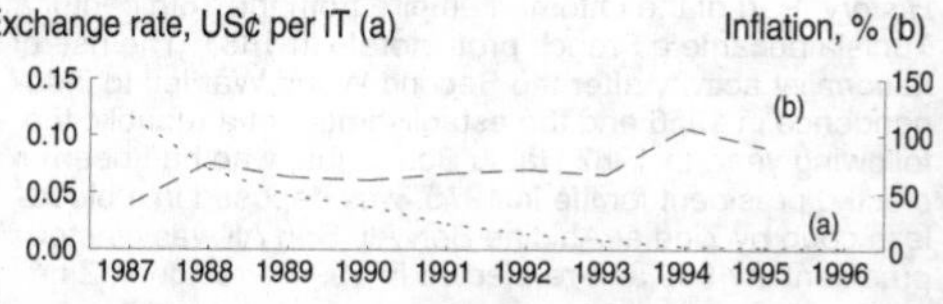

a mechanical turn of mind; has a neat turn of phrase). **9** opportunity or obligation etc. that comes successively to each of several persons etc. (*my turn to pay*). **10** short walk or ride (*took a turn in the park*). **11** short performance, variety act. **12** service of a specified kind (*did me a good turn*). **13** purpose (*served my turn*). **14** *colloq.* momentary nervous shock (*gave me a turn*). **15** *Mus.* ornament consisting of the principal note with those above and below it. □ **at every turn** continually. **by turns** in rotation; alternately. **in turn** in succession. **in one's turn** when one's turn comes. **not know which way** (or **where) to turn** be at a loss, unsure how to act, etc. **out of turn 1** when it is not one's turn. **2** inappropriately (*did I speak out of turn?*). **take turns** (or **take it in turns**) act alternately. **to a turn** (esp. cooked) perfectly. **turn about** move so as to face in a new direction. **turn and turn about** alternately. **turn around** esp. *US* = *turn round*. **turn away 1** turn to face in another direction. **2** reject. **3** send away. **turn back 1** begin or cause to retrace one's steps. **2** fold back. **turn down 1** reject (a proposal etc.). **2** reduce the volume or strength of (sound, heat, etc.) by turning a knob etc. **3** fold down. **turn one's hand to** see HAND. **turn a person's head** see HEAD. **turn in 1** hand in or return. **2** achieve or register (a performance, score, etc.). **3** *colloq.* go to bed for the night. **4** incline inwards. **5** hand over (a suspect etc.) to the authorities. **6** *colloq.* abandon (a plan etc.). **turn off 1 a** stop the flow or operation of (water, electricity, etc.) by a tap, switch, etc. **b** operate (a tap, switch, etc.) to achieve this. **2** enter a side-road. **3** *colloq.* cause to lose interest. **turn on 1 a** start the flow or operation of (water, electricity, etc.) by means of a tap, switch, etc. **b** operate (a tap, switch, etc.) to achieve this. **2** *colloq.* excite; stimulate, esp. sexually. **turn on one's heel** see HEEL[1]. **turn out 1** expel. **2** extinguish (an electric light etc.). **3** dress or equip (*well turned out*). **4** produce (goods etc.). **5** empty or clean out (a room etc.). **6** empty (a pocket). **7** *colloq.* assemble; attend a meeting etc. **8** (often foll. by *to* + infin. or *that* + clause) prove to be the case; result (*turned out to be true; see how things turn out*). **turn over 1** reverse the position of (*turn over the page*). **2 a** cause (an engine) to run. **b** (of an engine) start running. **3** consider; ponder. **4** (foll. by *to*) **a** transfer the care or conduct of (a person or thing) to (a person) (*shall turn it all over to my deputy*). **b** = *turn in* 5. **5** do business to the gross value of (*turns over £5000 a week*). **turn over a new leaf** reform one's conduct. **turn round 1** turn so as to face in a new direction. **2 a** unload and reload (a ship etc.). **b** receive, process, and send out again; cause to progress through a system. **3** adopt new opinions or policy. **turn the tables** see TABLE. **turn tail** turn one's back; run away. **turn to** set about one's work. **turn turtle** see TURTLE. **turn up 1** increase the volume or strength of by turning a knob etc. **2** discover or reveal. **3** be found, esp. by chance. **4** happen or present itself; (of a person) arrive (*people turned up late*). **5** shorten (a garment) by raising its hem. **6** fold over or upwards. [Old English *tyruan*, from Greek *tornos* lathe]

turn-about *n.* **1** turning about. **2** abrupt change of policy etc.

turn-buckle *n.* threaded device for tightly connecting parts of a metal rod or wire.

turncoat *n.* person who changes sides.

turner *n.* person who works with a lathe.

turnery *n.* **1** objects made on a lathe. **2** work with a lathe.

turning *n.* **1 a** road that branches off another. **b** place where this occurs. **2 a** use of a lathe. **b** (in *pl.*) chips or shavings from a lathe.

turning-circle *n.* smallest circle in which a vehicle can turn without reversing.

turning-point *n.* point at which a decisive change occurs.

turnip /ˈtɜːnɪp/ *n.* **1** plant with a globular root. **2** its root as a vegetable. □ **turnipy** *adj.* [dial. *neep* (Old English from Latin *napu*)]

turnip-top *n.* turnip leaves as a vegetable.

turnkey *n.* (*pl.* **-s**) *archaic* jailer.

♦ **turnkey system** *n.* **1** computer system that is ready to start work on its assigned task as soon as it is installed. All the necessary programs and pieces of equipment are supplied with the system. **2** planning and operation of a major capital project, in which the company is responsible for its overall management so that the client has only 'to turn the key' to start the operation.

turn-off *n.* **1** turning off a main road. **2** *colloq.* something that repels or causes a loss of interest.

turn-on *n. colloq.* person or thing that causes (esp. sexual) excitement.

turnout *n.* **1** number of people attending a meeting, voting at an election, etc. **2** set or display of equipment, clothes, etc.

turnover *n.* **1** act of turning over. **2** total sales figure of an organization for a stated period. **3** rate at which a particular asset is sold and replaced; for example, the turnover of stock is obtained by dividing the total sales figure by the value of the particular asset. **4** rate at which people enter and leave employment etc. **5** small pie made by folding pastry over a filling.

♦ **turnover ratio** *n.* accounting ratio showing the number of times an item of working capital has been replaced by others of the same class within a financial period.

♦ **turnover tax** *n.* tax on the sales made by a business, i.e. on its turnover. See SALES TAX.

turnpike *n.* **1** *hist.* **a** toll-gate. **b** road on which a toll was charged. **2** *US* motorway on which a toll is charged.

turn-round *n.* **1 a** unloading and reloading between trips. **b** receiving, processing, and sending out again; progress through a system. **2** reversal of an opinion or tendency.

Turkmenistan /tɜːkmenɪˈstɑːn/, **Republic of** country in central Asia, lying between the Caspian Sea and Afghanistan. Agriculture is an important source of employment, producing cotton, livestock, and livestock products (esp. wool and karakul skins). The country's rich mineral resources, esp. natural gas and oil, are a major source of export revenue for which the country is seeking new markets in Europe: to this end a gas pipeline is being constructed through Iran and Turkey to Europe. New industries being developed include chemical processing and textiles. Until 1991 Turkmenistan was a constituent republic of the Soviet Union and is still under the control of the former Communist party. In 1992 Turkmenistan became a member of the UN. President Niyazov was elected in 1990, being subsequently re-elected in 1992. In 1993 the legislature voted to extend his term until 2002, a decision that was endorsed overwhelmingly in a referendum held in 1994. There is little effective political opposition. Turkmenistan became a member of the CIS in 1993. President, Saparmurad Niyazov; capital, Ashkhabad. □ **Turkmen** *n.*

languages	Turkmen (official), Russian, Uzbek
currency	manat
pop. (1996)	4 574 000
GNP (1993)	US$4.8B
life expectancy	62 (m); 69 (f)

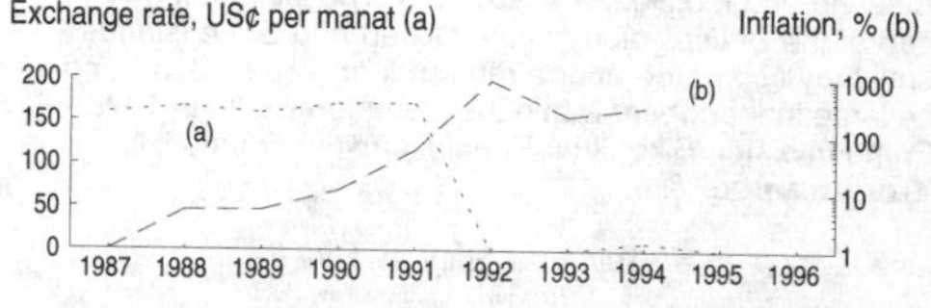

turnstile *n.* gate with revolving arms allowing people through singly.

turntable *n.* **1** circular revolving plate on which records are played. **2** circular revolving platform for turning a railway locomotive.

turn-up *n.* **1** turned up end of a trouser leg. **2** *colloq.* unexpected happening.

turpentine /ˈtɜːpən,taɪn/ *n.* resin from any of various trees. [Latin: related to TEREBINTH]

turpentine substitute *n.* = WHITE SPIRIT.

turpitude /ˈtɜːpɪ,tjuːd/ *n. formal* depravity, wickedness. [Latin *turpis* disgraceful]

turps *n. colloq.* oil of turpentine. [abbreviation]

turquoise /ˈtɜːkwɔɪz/ *–n.* **1** semiprecious stone, usu. opaque and greenish- or sky-blue. **2** greenish-blue colour. *–adj.* of this colour. [French, = Turkish]

turret /ˈtʌrɪt/ *n.* **1** small tower, esp. decorating a building. **2** low flat usu. revolving armoured tower for a gun and gunners in a ship, aircraft, fort, or tank. **3** rotating holder for tools in a lathe etc. □ **turreted** *adj.* [French diminutive: related to TOWER]

turtle /ˈtɜːt(ə)l/ *n.* **1** aquatic reptile with flippers and a horny shell. **2** its flesh, used for soup. □ **turn turtle** capsize. [alteration of earlier *tortue*: related to TORTOISE]

turtle-dove /ˈtɜt(ə)l,dʌv/ *n.* wild dove noted for its soft cooing and affection for its mate. [Latin *turtur*]

turtle-neck *n.* high close-fitting neck on a knitted garment.

Tuscan /ˈtʌskən/ *–n.* **1** inhabitant of Tuscany. **2** form of Italian spoken in Tuscany; standard Italian. *–adj.* **1** of Tuscany or the Tuscans. **2** *Archit.* of the plainest of the classical orders. [Latin]

Tuscany /ˈtʌskənɪ/ (Italian **Toscana** /tɒsˈkɑːnə/) region in W central Italy; pop. (est. 1994) 3 528 225; capital, Florence. Agriculture produces cereals, fruit, olives, and wine (Chianti); there are also iron, steel, and shipbuilding industries, and marble, lignite, mercury, salt, and borax are mined.

tusk *n.* long pointed tooth, esp. protruding from a closed mouth, as in the elephant, walrus, etc. □ **tusked** *adj.* [Old English]

tussle /ˈtʌs(ə)l/ *–n.* struggle, scuffle. *–v.* (**-ling**) engage in a tussle. [originally Scots and Northern English, perhaps diminutive of *touse*: related to TOUSLE]

tussock /ˈtʌsək/ *n.* clump of grass etc. □ **tussocky** *adj.* [perhaps from dial. *tusk* tuft]

tut var. of TUT-TUT.

tutelage /ˈtjuːtɪlɪdʒ/ *n.* **1** guardianship. **2** being under this. **3** tuition. [Latin *tutela*: related to TUTOR]

tutelary /ˈtjuːtɪlərɪ/ *adj.* **1 a** serving as guardian. **b** of a guardian. **2** giving protection. [Latin: related to TUTELAGE]

tutor /ˈtjuːtə(r)/ *–n.* **1** private teacher. **2** university teacher supervising the studies or welfare of assigned undergraduates. *–v.* **1** act as tutor to. **2** work as a tutor. □ **tutorship** *n.* [Latin *tueor tut-* watch]

tutorial /tjuːˈtɔːrɪəl/ *–adj.* of a tutor or tuition. *–n.* period of undergraduate tuition individually or in a small group. [Latin *tutorius*: related to TUTOR]

tutti /ˈtʊtɪ/ *Mus. –adj.* & *adv.* with all voices or instruments together. *–n.* (*pl.* **-s**) such a passage. [Italian, pl. of *tutto* all]

tutti-frutti /,tuːtɪˈfruːtɪ/ *n.* (*pl.* **-s**) ice-cream containing small pieces of mixed glacé fruit. [Italian, = all fruits]

tut-tut /tʌtˈtʌt/ (also **tut**) *–int.* expressing disapproval or impatience. *–n.* such an exclamation. *–v.* (**-tt-**) exclaim this. [imitative of a click of the tongue]

tutu /ˈtuːtuː/ *n.* ballet dancer's short skirt of stiffened frills. [French]

tu-whit, tu-whoo /tʊ,wɪt tʊˈwuː/ *n.* representation of the cry of an owl. [imitative]

tux *n. US colloq.* = TUXEDO. [abbreviation]

tuxedo /tʌkˈsiːdəʊ/ *n.* (*pl.* **-s** or **-es**) *US* **1** dinner-jacket. **2** suit of clothes including this. [*Tuxedo* Park in US]

TV *abbr.* television.

TVA *abbr.* (French) taxe à (or sur) la valeur ajoutée (= value-added tax).

TVEI *abbr.* Technical and Vocational Educational Initiative.

Tver /tveə/ (formerly **Kalinin**) port in central Russia; industries include engineering and textiles; pop. (est. 1994) 454 000.

♦ **TVR** *abbr.* = TELEVISION RATING.

TW *–postcode* Twickenham. *–airline flight code* Trans World Airways.

TWA *abbr.* **1** Thames Water Authority. **2** time-weighted average. **3** Trans-World Airlines.

twaddle /ˈtwɒd(ə)l/ *n.* silly writing or talk; nonsense. [earlier *twattle*, alteration of TATTLE]

twain *adj.* & *n. archaic* two. [Old English, masculine form of TWO]

twang *–n.* **1** sound made by a plucked string or released bowstring. **2** nasal quality of a voice. *–v.* (cause to) emit this sound. □ **twangy** *adj.* [imitative]

'twas /twɒz/ *archaic* it was. [contraction]

twat /twɒt/ *n. coarse slang* **1** female genitals. **2** contemptible person. [origin unknown]

tweak *–v.* **1** pinch and twist sharply; jerk. **2** make fine adjustments to (a mechanism). *–n.* act of tweaking. [probably dial. *twick*, TWITCH]

twee *adj.* (**tweer** /ˈtwiːə(r)/; **tweest** /ˈtwiːɪst/) *derog.* affectedly dainty or quaint. [a childish pronunciation of SWEET]

tweed *n.* **1** rough-surfaced woollen cloth, usu. of mixed flecked colours. **2** (in *pl.*) clothes made of tweed. [alteration of *tweel* (Scots var. of TWILL)]

tweedy *adj.* (**-ier, -iest**) **1** of or dressed in tweed. **2** characteristic of country gentry; heartily informal.

'tween *prep. archaic* = BETWEEN. [abbreviation]

tweet *–n.* chirp of a small bird. *–v.* make this noise. [imitative]

tweeter *n.* loudspeaker for high frequencies.

tweezers /ˈtwiːzəz/ *n.pl.* small pair of pincers for taking

Tuvalu /tuːˈvɑːluː/ (former name, until 1976, **Ellice Islands**) small country in the SW Pacific, consisting of a group of nine islands. The economy is dominated by subsistence agriculture and fishing, and the country is heavily dependent on foreign aid. The chief crop is coconuts, from which copra is produced for export; the sale of postage stamps and handicrafts is an additional source of revenue. Clothing and footwear are exported. The islands formed part of the British colony of the Gilbert and Ellice Islands until they separated after a referendum (see KIRIBATI) and became independent within the Commonwealth in 1978. Prime minister, Bikenibeu Paeniu; capital, Funafuti. □ **Tuvaluan** *adj.* & *n.*

languages	Tuvaluan, English
currency	Australian dollar ($A) of 100 cents
pop. (1996)	9482
GNP (1993)	US$7.4M
literacy	95%
life expectancy	61 (m); 64 (f)

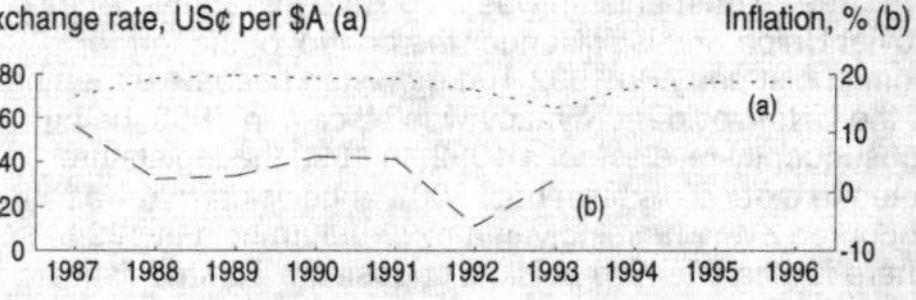

up small objects, plucking out hairs, etc. [originally *tweezes* pl. of obsolete *tweeze*, a case for small instruments]

twelfth *adj.* & *n.* **1** next after eleventh. **2** each of twelve equal parts of a thing. [Old English: related to TWELVE]

Twelfth Night *n.* 5 Jan., eve of Epiphany.

twelve *adj.* & *n.* **1** one more than eleven. **2** symbol for this (12, xii, XII). **3** size etc. denoted by twelve. **4** twelve o'clock. **5** (**the Twelve**) the apostles. [Old English]

twelvefold *adj.* & *adv.* **1** twelve times as much or as many. **2** consisting of twelve parts.

twelvemonth *n. archaic* year.

twenty /ˈtwentɪ/ *adj.* & *n.* (*pl.* **-ies**) **1** product of two and ten. **2** symbol for this (20, xx, XX). **3** (in *pl.*) numbers from 20 to 29, esp. the years of a century or of a person's life. □ **twentieth** *adj.* & *n.* [Old English]

twenty-twenty vision *n.* (also **20/20 vision**) **1** vision of normal acuity. **2** *colloq.* good eyesight.

'twere /twɜː(r)/ *archaic* it were. [contraction]

twerp *n.* (also **twirp**) *slang* stupid or objectionable person. [origin unknown]

twice *adv.* **1** two times; on two occasions. **2** in double degree or quantity (*twice as good*). [Old English: related to TWO]

twiddle /ˈtwɪd(ə)l/ –*v.* (**-ling**) twirl, adjust, or play randomly or idly. –*n.* act of twiddling. □ **twiddle one's thumbs 1** make them rotate round each other. **2** have nothing to do. □ **twiddly** *adj.* [probably imitative]

twig[1] *n.* very small thin branch of a tree or shrub. □ **twiggy** *adj.* [Old English]

twig[2] *v.* (**-gg-**) *colloq.* understand; realize. [origin unknown]

twilight /ˈtwaɪlaɪt/ *n.* **1** light from the sky when the sun is below the horizon, esp. in the evening. **2** period of this. **3** faint light. **4** period of decline or destruction. [from TWO, LIGHT[1]]

twilight zone *n.* **1** decrepit urban area. **2** undefined or intermediate zone or area.

twilit /ˈtwaɪlɪt/ *adj.* dimly illuminated by twilight.

twill *n.* fabric so woven as to have a surface of diagonal parallel ridges. □ **twilled** *adj.* [Old English, = two-thread]

'twill *archaic* it will. [contraction]

twin –*n.* **1** each of a closely related or associated pair, esp. of children or animals born at a birth. **2** exact counterpart of a person or thing. **3** (**the Twins**) zodiacal sign or constellation Gemini. –*adj.* forming, or being one of, such a pair (*twin brothers*). –*v.* (**-nn-**) **1 a** join intimately together. **b** (foll. by *with*) pair. **2** bear twins. **3** link (a town) with one in a different country, for friendship and cultural exchange. □ **twinning** *n.* [Old English: related to TWO]

twin bed *n.* each of a pair of single beds.

twine –*n.* **1** strong coarse string of twisted strands of fibre. **2** coil, twist. –*v.* (**-ning**) **1** form (a string etc.) by twisting strands. **2** weave (a garland etc.). **3** (often foll. by *with*) garland (a brow etc.). **4** (often foll. by *round*, *about*) coil or wind. **5** *refl.* (of a plant) grow in this way. [Old English]

twin-engined *adj.* having two engines.

twinge /twɪndʒ/ *n.* sharp momentary local pain or pang. [Old English]

twinkle /ˈtwɪŋk(ə)l/ –*v.* (**-ling**) **1** (of a star or light etc.) shine with rapidly intermittent gleams. **2** (of the eyes) sparkle. **3** (of the feet) move lightly and rapidly. –*n.* **1** sparkle or gleam of the eyes. **2** twinkling light. **3** light rapid movement. □ **in a twinkle** (or **a twinkling** or **the twinkling of an eye**) in an instant. □ **twinkly** *adj.* [Old English]

twin set *n.* woman's matching cardigan and jumper.

twin town *n.* town twinned with another.

twirl –*v.* spin, swing, or twist quickly and lightly round. –*n.* **1** twirling motion. **2** flourish made with a pen. [origin uncertain]

twirp var. of TWERP.

twist –*v.* **1 a** change the form of by rotating one end and not the other or the two ends in opposite directions. **b** undergo such a change. **c** wrench or pull out of shape with a twisting action (*twisted my ankle*). **2 a** wind (strands etc.) about each other. **b** form (a rope etc.) in this way. **3 a** give a spiral form to. **b** take a spiral form. **4** (foll. by *off*) break off by twisting. **5** misrepresent the meaning of (words). **6 a** take a winding course. **b** make (one's way) in a winding manner. **7** *colloq.* cheat. **8** (as **twisted** *adj.*) *derog.* (of a person or mind) neurotic; perverted. **9** dance the twist. –*n.* **1** act of twisting. **2** twisted state. **3** thing formed by twisting. **4** point at which a thing twists or bends. **5** usu. *derog.* peculiar tendency of mind or character etc. **6** unexpected development of events, esp. in a story etc. **7** (prec. by *the*) popular 1960s dance with a twisting movement of the hips. □ **round the twist** *slang* crazy. **twist a person's arm** *colloq.* coerce, esp. using moral pressure. **twist round one's finger** easily persuade or dominate (a person). □ **twisty** *adj.* (**-ier, -iest**). [related to TWIN, TWINE]

twister *n. colloq.* swindler.

twit[1] *n. slang* foolish person. [originally dial., perhaps from TWIT[2]]

twit[2] *v.* (**-tt-**) reproach or taunt, usu. good-humouredly. [Old English]

twitch –*v.* **1** (of features, muscles, etc.) move or contract spasmodically. **2** pull sharply at. –*n.* **1** sudden involuntary contraction or movement. **2** sudden pull or jerk. **3** *colloq.* state of nervousness. □ **twitchy** *adj.* (**-ier, -iest**) (in sense 3 of *n.*). [probably Old English]

twitcher *n. colloq.* bird-watcher seeking sightings of rare birds.

twitter –*v.* **1** (esp. of a bird) emit a succession of light tremulous sounds. **2** utter or express in this way. –*n.* **1** act of twittering. **2** *colloq.* tremulously excited state. □ **twittery** *adj.* [imitative]

'twixt *prep. archaic* = BETWIXT. [contraction]

two /tuː/ *adj.* & *n.* **1** one more than one. **2** symbol for this (2, ii, II). **3** size etc. denoted by two. **4** two o'clock. □ **in two** in or into two pieces. **put two and two together** infer from known facts. [Old English]

two-bit *attrib. adj. US colloq.* cheap, petty.

two-dimensional *adj.* **1** having or appearing to have length and breadth but no depth. **2** lacking substance; superficial.

two-edged *adj.* double-edged.

two-faced *adj.* insincere; deceitful.

twofold *adj.* & *adv.* **1** twice as much or as many. **2** consisting of two parts.

two-handed *adj.* **1** having, using, or requiring the use of two hands. **2** (of a card-game) for two players.

twopence /ˈtʌpəns/ *n.* **1** sum of two pence. **2** (esp. with *neg.*) *colloq.* thing of little value (*don't care twopence*).

twopenny /ˈtʌpənɪ/ *attrib. adj.* **1** costing two pence. **2** *colloq.* cheap, worthless.

twopenny-halfpenny /ˌtʌpnɪˈheɪpnɪ/ *attrib. adj.* cheap, insignificant.

two-piece –*adj.* (of a suit etc.) consisting of two matching items. –*n.* two-piece suit etc.

two-ply –*adj.* of two strands or layers etc. –*n.* **1** two-ply wool. **2** two-ply wood.

twosome *n.* two persons together.

two-step *n.* dance in march or polka time.

two-stroke –*attrib. adj.* (of an internal-combustion engine) having its power cycle completed in one up-and-down movement of the piston. –*n.* two-stroke engine.

♦ **two-tier tender offer** *n.* tender offer in a take-over in which shareholders are offered a high initial offer for sufficient shares to give the bidder a controlling interest in the company, followed by an offer to acquire the remaining shares at a lower price. Bidders use this technique in order to provide an incentive to shareholders to accept the initial offer quickly. Such offers are usu. for a combination of cash and shares in the bidder's own company.

---

two-time *v. colloq.* **1** be unfaithful to (a lover). **2** swindle. □ **two-timer** *n.*

two-tone *adj.* having two colours or sounds.

'twould /twʊd/ *archaic* it would. [contraction]

two-way *adj.* **1** involving two directions or participants. **2** (of a radio) capable of transmitting and receiving signals.

two-way mirror *n.* panel of glass that can be seen through from one side and is a mirror on the other.

TWX *abbr. US* teletypewriter exchange service.

TX *US postcode* Texas.

TY *international civil aircraft marking* Benin.

Ty. *abbr.* Territory.

-ty[1] *suffix* forming nouns denoting quality or condition (*cruelty*; *plenty*). [French from Latin *-tas -tatis*]

-ty[2] *suffix* denoting tens (*ninety*). [Old English *-tig*]

tycoon /taɪ'kuːn/ *n.* business magnate. [Japanese, = great lord]

tying *pres. part.* of TIE.

tyke /taɪk/ *n.* (also **tike**) **1** unpleasant or coarse man. **2** small child. [Old Norse]

tympani var. of TIMPANI.

tympanum /'tɪmpənəm/ *n.* (*pl.* **-s** or **-na**) **1** middle ear. **2** eardrum. **3** *Archit.* **a** vertical triangular space forming the centre of a pediment. **b** similar space over a door between the lintel and the arch. [Greek *tumpanon* drum]

Tyne and Wear /taɪn, wɪə(r)/ metropolitan county of NE England; in 1986 the county council was abolished and its administrative powers were devolved to the districts of Gateshead, Newcastle upon Tyne, North Tyneside, South Tyneside, and Sunderland.

Tynwald /'tɪnwɒld/ *n.* parliament of the Isle of Man. [Old Norse, = assembly-field]

type /taɪp/ *–n.* **1** sort, class, or kind. **2** person, thing, or event exemplifying a class or group. **3** (in *comb.*) made of, resembling, or functioning as (*ceramic-type material*; *Cheddar-type cheese*). **4** *colloq.* person, esp. of a specified character (*a quiet type*; *not my type*). **5** object, conception, or work of art, serving as a model for subsequent artists. **6** *Printing* **a** piece of metal etc. with a raised letter or character on its upper surface for printing. **b** kind or size of such pieces (*printed in large type*). **c** set or supply of these (*ran short of type*). *–v.* (**-ping**) **1** write with a typewriter. **2** typecast. **3** esp. *Biol.* & *Med.* assign to a type; classify. [Greek *tupos* impression]

typecast *v.* (*past* and *past part.* **-cast**) assign (an actor or actress) repeatedly to the same type of role.

typeface *n. Printing* **1** inked surface of type. **2** set of characters in one design.

typescript *n.* typewritten document.

typesetter *n. Printing* **1** person who composes type. **2** composing-machine. □ **typesetting** *n.*

typewriter *n.* machine with keys for producing printlike characters one at a time on paper inserted round a roller.

typewritten *adj.* produced on a typewriter.

typhoid /'taɪfɔɪd/ *n.* (in full **typhoid fever**) infectious bacterial fever attacking the intestines.

typhoon /taɪ'fuːn/ *n.* violent hurricane in E Asian seas. [Chinese, = great wind, and Arabic]

typhus /'taɪfəs/ *n.* infectious fever with a purple rash, headaches, and usu. delirium. [Greek, = stupor]

typical /'tɪpɪk(ə)l/ *adj.* **1** serving as a characteristic example; representative (*a typical English pub*). **2** (often foll. by *of*) characteristic of a particular person, thing, or type (*typical of him to refuse*). □ **typicality** /-'kælɪtɪ/ *n.* **typically** *adv.* [medieval Latin: related to TYPE]

typify /'tɪpɪˌfaɪ/ *v.* (**-ies, -ied**) **1** be typical of. **2** represent by or as a type or symbol. □ **typification** /-fɪ'keɪʃ(ə)n/ *n.* [Latin: related to TYPE]

typist /'taɪpɪst/ *n.* person who types, esp. for a living.

typo /'taɪpəʊ/ *n.* (*pl.* **-s**) *colloq.* typographical error. [abbreviation]

typography /taɪ'pɒgrəfɪ/ *n.* **1** printing as an art. **2** style and appearance of printed matter. □ **typographer** *n.* **typographical** /-pə'græfɪk(ə)l/ *adj.* **typographically** /-pə'græfɪkəlɪ/ *adv.* [French: related to TYPE]

tyrannical /tɪ'rænɪk(ə)l/ *adj.* despotic; unjustly severe. □ **tyrannically** *adv.* [Greek: related to TYRANT]

tyrannize /'tɪrəˌnaɪz/ *v.* (also **-ise**) (**-zing** or **-sing**) (often foll. by *over*) treat despotically or cruelly. [French: related to TYRANT]

tyrannosaurus /tɪˌrænə'sɔːrəs/ *n.* (*pl.* **-ruses**) (also **tyrannosaur**) dinosaur with very short front legs and a long well-developed tail. [from TYRANT, after *dinosaur*]

tyranny /'tɪrənɪ/ *n.* (*pl.* **-ies**) **1** cruel and arbitrary use of authority. **2 a** rule by a tyrant. **b** period of this. **c** state ruled by a tyrant. □ **tyrannous** *adj.* [Greek: related to TYRANT]

tyrant /'taɪərənt/ *n.* **1** oppressive or cruel ruler. **2** person exercising power arbitrarily or cruelly. [Greek *turannos*]

Tyre /taɪə(r)/ city and seaport in Lebanon; pop. (est. 1991) 70 000.

tyre /'taɪə(r)/ *n.* (*US* **tire**) rubber covering, usu. inflated, placed round a wheel to form a soft contact with the road. [var. of TIRE[2]]

Tyrian /'tɪrɪən/ *–adj.* of ancient Tyre in Phoenicia. *–n.* native or citizen of Tyre. [Latin *Tyrus* Tyre]

Tyrian purple see PURPLE *n.* 2.

tyro var. of TIRO.

Tyrol /'tɪr(ə)l, -'rɒl/ (German **Tirol**) Alpine state in W Austria; pop. (est. 1994) 654 753; capital, Innsbruck. Tourism (esp. winter sports) is important; other activities include agriculture, forestry, mining, and manufacturing industry. □ **Tyrolean** /-'liːən/ *adj.* **Tyrolese** /-'liːz/ *adj.* & *n.*

Tyrone /tɪ'rəʊn/ county in Northern Ireland; county town, Omagh. Agriculture produces barley, potatoes, turnips, flax, cattle, and sheep.

Tyrrhenian Sea /tɪ'riːnɪən/ part of the Mediterranean Sea bounded by mainland Italy, Sicily, Sardinia, Corsica, and the Ligurian Sea.

TZ *international civil aircraft marking* Mali.

tzatziki /tsæt'siːkɪ/ *n.* Greek side dish of yoghurt with cucumber. [modern Greek]

Uu

U¹ /juː/ *n.* (also **u**) (*pl.* **Us** or **U's**) **1** twenty-first letter of the alphabet. **2** U-shaped object or curve.

U² /juː/ *adj. colloq.* upper class or supposedly upper class. [abbreviation]

U³ *abbr.* (also **U.**) universal (of films classified as suitable for all).

U⁴ *symb.* uranium.

UA *airline flight code* United Airlines.

UAE *abbr.* United Arab Emirates.

UART /'juːˌɑːt/ *abbr. Computing* universal asynchronous receiver/transmitter, used in the interfaces of data transmission lines and peripherals.

UAW *abbr.* (in the US) United Automobile Workers (trade union).

u.A.w.g. *abbr.* (German) um Antwort wird gebeten (= an answer is requested).

UB *postcode* Southall.

UB40 *abbr.* **1** card issued to people claiming unemployment benefit. **2** *colloq.* unemployed person. [*u*nemployment *b*enefit]

◆ ***uberrima fides*** /'juːbəˌriːmə 'faɪdiːz, ˌjuː'berɪmə/ *n.* = UTMOST GOOD FAITH. [Latin]

UBI *abbr.* Understanding British Industry (organization).

ubiquitous /juː'bɪkwɪtəs/ *adj.* **1** (seemingly) present everywhere simultaneously. **2** often encountered. □ **ubiquity** *n.* [Latin *ubique* everywhere]

U-boat /'juːbəʊt/ *n. hist.* German submarine. [German *Untersee* undersea]

UBR *abbr.* uniform business rate.

u.c. *abbr.* upper case.

u/c *abbr. Commerce* undercharge.

UCATT /'juːkət/ *abbr.* Union of Construction, Allied Trades, and Technicians.

UCC *abbr.* **1** Union Carbide Corporation. **2** Universal Copyright Convention.

UCCA /'ʌkə/ *abbr.* Universities Central Council on Admissions.

UCITS *abbr.* Undertakings for Collective Investment in Transferable Securities.

UCW *abbr.* Union of Communication Workers.

UDA *abbr.* Ulster Defence Association (a loyalist paramilitary organization).

UDC *abbr.* **1** Urban Development Corporation. **2** Urban District Council.

udder *n.* baglike mammary organ of cattle etc., with several teats. [Old English]

UDI *abbr.* unilateral declaration of independence.

UDM *abbr.* Union of Democratic Mineworkers.

UDR *abbr.* Ulster Defence Regiment.

UEFA /juː'eɪfə/ *abbr.* Union of European Football Associations.

Ufa /uː'fɑː/ city in W central Russia, capital of the autonomous republic of Bashkir; industries include oil refining and chemicals; pop. (est. 1995) 1 094 000.

UFO /'juːfəʊ/ *n.* (also **ufo**) (*pl.* **-s**) unidentified flying object.

ugh /əx, ʌg/ *int.* **1** expressing disgust etc. **2** sound of a cough or grunt. [imitative]

Ugli /'ʌglɪ/ *n.* (*pl.* **-lis** or **-lies**) *propr.* mottled green and yellow hybrid of a grapefruit and a tangerine. [from UGLY]

uglify /'ʌglɪˌfaɪ/ *v.* (**-ies, -ied**) make ugly.

ugly /'ʌglɪ/ *adj.* (**-lier, -liest**) **1** unpleasant to the eye, ear, or mind etc. (*ugly scar; ugly snarl*). **2** unpleasantly suggestive; discreditable (*ugly rumours*). **3** threatening, dangerous (*an ugly look*). **4** morally repulsive (*ugly vices*). □ **ugliness** *n.* [Old Norse]

ugly customer *n.* threatening or violent person.

ugly duckling *n.* person lacking early promise but blossoming later.

UHF *abbr.* ultrahigh frequency.

uh-huh /'ʌhʌ/ *int. colloq.* yes; indeed. [imitative]

UHT *abbr.* ultra heat treated (esp. of milk, for long keeping).

UI *abbr.* **1** *US* unemployment insurance. **2** = USER INTERFACE.

Uganda /juː'gændə/, **Republic of** landlocked country in E Africa, a member state of the Commonwealth. The Ugandan economy is chiefly agricultural. Coffee (the principal export), cotton, tea, and tobacco are grown as cash crops and maize, millet, bananas, sweet potatoes, and yams as food crops; livestock farming and freshwater fishing are also important. Hydroelectricity is a major source of power and is exported to neighbouring Kenya. Copper extraction virtually ceased in the late 1970s but attempts are being made to restore production; tungsten, tin ore, and gold are mined. Manufacturing industries include food processing, brewing, and the production of textiles, cement, and fertilizers.

History. First explored by Europeans in the mid-19th century, Uganda became a British protectorate in 1894 and achieved full independence in 1962. The repressive dictator Idi Amin, who came to power in 1971, was overthrown in a coup aided by Tanzanian troops in 1979. The following years were marked by civil war: the rebel National Resistance Movement, from N Kenya, eventually took control of the country and established a government in 1986, since when stability has been largely restored and Uganda, with aid from the IMF and other donors, has seen some economic growth. A debt relief programme by the World Bank is to begin in 1998. A new constitution, legalizing political parties (banned since 1986), was due to be finalized in 1994; however, the ban has been extended until 2000. A new constitution was promulgated in 1995. President, Yoweri Museveni; prime minister, Kintu Musoke; capital, Kampala. □ **Ugandan** *adj.* & *n.*

languages	English (official), Swahili, Luganda (a Bantu language)
currency	Uganda shilling (USh) of 100 cents
pop. (1996)	19 136 000
GNP (1994)	US$3.7B
literacy	68% (m); 40% (f)
life expectancy	51 (m); 54 (f)

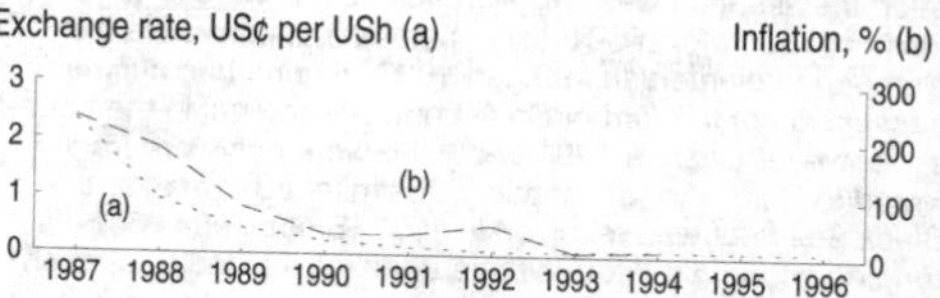

UIL *abbr.* (Italian) Unione Italiana del Lavoro (= Italian Federation of Trade Unions).

UIT *abbr.* unit investment trust.

Ujjain /uːˈdʒeɪn/ city in W central India, in the state of Madhya Pradesh; an agricultural trading centre, it also has textile industries; pop. (1991) 362 266.

Ujung Padang /uːˌdʒʊŋ pæˈdæŋ/ (formerly **Macassar** /məˈkæsə(r)/) chief seaport of the island of Sulawesi, Indonesia; coffee, copra, resins, and vegetable oils are exported; pop. (1990) 913 196.

UK *–abbr.* United Kingdom. *–airline flight code* Air UK.

UKAEA *abbr.* United Kingdom Atomic Energy Authority.

♦ ***UK Balance of Payments*** *n.* (also **Pink Book**) annual publication of the Central Statistical Office.

UKFBPW *abbr.* United Kingdom Federation of Business and Professional Women.

UKISC *abbr.* United Kingdom Industrial Space Committee.

♦ ***UK National Accounts*** *n.* (also **Blue Book**) monthly publication of the Central Statistical Office. It provides figures for the gross domestic product and separate accounts of production, income, and expenditure.

UKOOA *abbr.* United Kingdom Offshore Operators Association.

UKPIA *abbr.* United Kingdom Petroleum Industry Association Ltd.

Ukrainian /juːˈkreɪnɪən/ *–n.* **1** native or language of Ukraine. **2** person of Ukrainian descent. *–adj.* of Ukraine, its people, or language.

UKSMA *abbr.* United Kingdom Sugar Merchant Association Ltd.

ukulele /ˌjuːkəˈleɪlɪ/ *n.* small four-stringed Hawaiian guitar. [Hawaiian]

UL *airline flight code* Air Lanka.

ULA *abbr. Computing* uncommitted logic array.

Ulan Bator /ʊˌlɑːn ˈbɑːtɔː(r)/ capital of Mongolia, the country's chief industrial centre; pop. (est. 1994) 680 000.

ULCC *abbr.* ultra-large crude carrier (oil tanker).

ulcer *n.* **1** open sore on or in the body, often forming pus. **2** corrupting influence etc. □ **ulcerous** *adj.* [Latin *ulcus -cer-*]

ulcerate /ˈʌlsəˌreɪt/ *v.* (**-ting**) form into or affect with an ulcer. □ **ulceration** /-ˈreɪʃ(ə)n/ *n.*

-ule *suffix* forming diminutive nouns (*globule*). [Latin *-ulus*]

Uleåborg see OULU.

Ulhasnagar /ˌuːlhəsˈnɑːgə(r)/ city in W India, in the state of Maharashtra; pop. (1991) 369 000.

ullage /ˈʌlɪdʒ/ *n.* **1** amount by which the full capacity of a barrel etc. exceeds the volume of the contents, as a result of evaporation or leakage. **2** loss by evaporation or leakage. **3** (as defined by HM Customs and Excise) actual contents of a barrel or similar container at the time of importation into the UK. The difference between this volume and the full capacity is called the **vacuity**. [French from Latin]

Ulm /ʊlm/ industrial city in Germany, in Baden-Württemberg; pop. (est. 1995) 115 124.

ulna /ˈʌlnə/ *n.* (*pl.* **ulnae** /-niː/) **1** thinner and longer bone in the forearm, opposite to the thumb. **2** corresponding bone in an animal's foreleg or a bird's wing. □ **ulnar** *adj.* [Latin]

ULS *abbr.* unsecured loan stock. See UNSECURED DEBENTURE.

Ulster /ˈʌlstə(r)/ **1** former province of Ireland comprising the present Northern Ireland and the counties of Cavan, Donegal, and Monaghan (which are now in the Republic of Ireland). **2** (*loosely*) Northern Ireland.

ulster *n.* man's long loose overcoat of rough cloth. [ULSTER]

Ulsterman *n.* (*fem.* **Ulsterwoman**) native of Ulster.

ult. *abbr.* ultimo.

ulterior /ʌlˈtɪərɪə(r)/ *adj.* not evident or admitted; hidden, secret (esp. *ulterior motive*). [Latin, = further]

ultimate /ˈʌltɪmət/ *–adj.* **1** last or last possible, final. **2** fundamental, primary, basic (*ultimate truths*). *–n.* **1** (prec. by *the*) best achievable or imaginable. **2** final or fundamental fact or principle. □ **ultimately** *adv.* [Latin *ultimus* last]

ultimatum /ˌʌltɪˈmeɪtəm/ *n.* (*pl.* **-s**) final statement of terms, the rejection of which could cause hostility etc. [Latin: related to ULTIMATE]

ultimo /ˈʌltɪˌməʊ/ *adj. Commerce* of last month (*the 28th ultimo*). [Latin, = in the last (*mense* month)]

ultra /ˈʌltrə/ *–adj.* extreme, esp. in religion or politics. *–n.* extremist. [see ULTRA-]

ultra- *comb. form* **1** extreme(ly), excessive(ly) (*ultra-modern*). **2** beyond. [Latin *ultra* beyond]

ultrahigh /ˌʌltrəˈhaɪ/ *adj.* (of a frequency) in the range 300 to 3000 megahertz.

ultramarine /ˌʌltrəməˈriːn/ *–n.* **1** brilliant blue pigment orig. from lapis lazuli. **2** colour of this. *–adj.* of this colour. [Italian and medieval Latin, = beyond the sea, from where lapis lazuli was brought]

ultramicroscopic /ˌʌltrəˌmaɪkrəˈskɒpɪk/ *adj.* too small to be seen by an ordinary optical microscope.

ultramontane /ˌʌltrəˈmɒnteɪn/ *–adj.* **1** situated beyond

Ukraine /juːˈkreɪn/ country in SE Europe, N of the Black Sea. The economy is based on heavy industry and the exploitation of the country's rich mineral resources. There are large coalfields and deposits of iron ore, which support a major iron and steel industry; other industries include engineering, chemicals, textiles, shipbuilding, food processing, and the manufacture of consumer goods. Agriculture produces wheat, sugar beet, cotton, flax, tobacco, and livestock. Metals and minerals are the chief export. Ukraine was a constituent republic of the Soviet Union from 1922 until 1991. The conservative (former Communist) government initially resisted free-market reforms, but a programme of privatization was begun in 1992. A new constitution was promulgated in 1996. In 1992 the region of Crimea declared independence, which caused some political tension; however, the situation was largely resolved following a huge loss of support for pro-Russian parties in elections to the Crimean parliament in 1995. In 1993 Ukraine had claimed possession of the former Soviet nuclear arsenal in the country; however under a 1994 treaty the weapons were transferred to Russia for dismantling. A similar quarrel over the Black Sea fleet was resolved in 1997. Since 1994 wide-ranging economic reforms have been introduced and much foreign aid has been given, including compensation for the scheduled closure of the nuclear power plant at Chernobyl, which suffered a partial meltdown in 1986. However, economic and political progress has been hampered by continuing conflict between president and parliament. President, Leonid Kuchma; prime minister, Valery Pustovoitenko; capital, Kiev.

languages	Ukrainian (official), Russian
currency	hryvnia of 100 kopiykas (replaced the karbovanets coupon in 1996)
pop. (1996)	51 273 000
GNP (1994)	US$80.9B
literacy	99% (m); 97% (f)
life expectancy	62 (m); 73 (f)

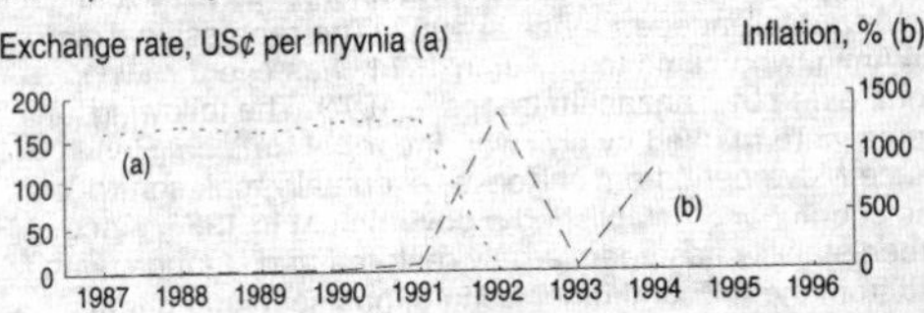

the Alps. **2** advocating supreme papal authority. *–n.* **1** person living beyond the Alps. **2** advocate of supreme papal authority. [medieval Latin: related to MOUNTAIN]

ultrasonic /ˌʌltrəˈsɒnɪk/ *adj.* of or using sound waves pitched above the range of human hearing. □ **ultrasonically** *adv.*

ultrasonics *n.pl.* (usu. treated as *sing.*) science of ultrasonic waves.

ultrasound /ˈʌltrəˌsaʊnd/ *n.* ultrasonic waves.

ultraviolet /ˌʌltrəˈvaɪələt/ *adj.* **1** having a wavelength (just) beyond the violet end of the visible spectrum. **2** of or using such radiation.

♦ ***ultra vires*** /ˌʌltrə ˈvaɪəˌriːz/ *adv. & predic.adj.* beyond one's legal power or authority. The powers of officials exercising administrative duties and of companies are limited by the instrument from which their powers are derived. If they act *ultra vires*, their action may be challenged in the courts. A company's powers are limited by the objects clause in its memorandum of association. It it enters into an agreement outside these objects, the agreement may be unenforceable, although a third party may have a remedy under the Companies Act (1985) if it was dealing with the company in good faith (or there may be other equitable remedies). [Latin]

---

ululate /ˈjuːlʊˌleɪt/ *v.* (**-ting**) howl, wail. □ **ululation** /-ˈleɪʃ(ə)n/ *n.* [Latin]

Ulyanovsk /ʊlˈjɑːnɒfsk/ (formerly **Simbirsk**) city and port in W central Russia, on the River Volga; manufactures include motor vehicles, vodka, and processed food; pop. (est. 1995) 678 000.

UM *symb. Currency* ouguiya.

um *int.* expressing hesitation or a pause in speech. [imitative]

u/m *abbr.* undermentioned.

umbel /ˈʌmb(ə)l/ *n.* flower-cluster with stalks springing from a common centre and forming a flat or curved surface. □ **umbellate** *adj.* [Latin *umbella* sunshade]

umbelliferous /ˌʌmbəˈlɪfərəs/ *adj.* (of a plant) bearing umbels, such as parsley and carrot.

umber /ˈʌmbə(r)/ *–n.* **1** natural pigment like ochre but darker and browner. **2** colour of this. *–adj.* of this colour. [Latin *umbra* shadow]

umbilical /ʌmˈbɪlɪk(ə)l/ *adj.* of the navel. [from UMBILICUS]

umbilical cord *n.* cordlike structure attaching a foetus to the placenta.

umbilicus /ʌmˈbɪlɪkəs/ *n.* (*pl.* **-ci** /-ˌsaɪ/ or **-cuses**) navel. [Latin]

umbra /ˈʌmbrə/ *n.* (*pl.* **-s** or **-brae** /-briː/) total shadow, esp. that cast on the earth by the moon during a solar eclipse. [Latin, = shadow]

umbrage /ˈʌmbrɪdʒ/ *n.* offence taken (esp. *take umbrage at*). [Latin: related to UMBRA]

umbrella /ʌmˈbrelə/ *n.* **1** collapsible cloth canopy on a central stick, used against rain, strong sun, etc. **2** protection, patronage. **3** (often *attrib.*) coordinating agency (*umbrella organization*). [Italian diminutive: related to UMBRA]

♦ **umbrella fund** *n.* offshore fund consisting of a fund of funds that invests in other offshore funds.

Umbria /ˈʌmbrɪə/ region of central Italy; pop. (est. 1994) 819 172; capital, Perugia. Cereals, vines, and olives are grown; there are also iron, steel, chemical, engineering, and food-processing industries, powered by hydroelectricity. □ **Umbrian** *adj.* & *n.*

umlaut /ˈʊmlaʊt/ *n.* **1** mark (¨) used over a vowel, esp. in Germanic languages, to indicate a vowel change. **2** such a vowel change, e.g. German *Mann, Männer* /ˈmenə(r)/, English *man, men.* [German]

Umm al-Qaiwain /ʊm æl kaɪˈwaɪn/ second-smallest of the seven states of the United Arab Emirates; pop. (1985) 29 229; capital, Umm al-Qaiwain.

umpire /ˈʌmpaɪə(r)/ *–n.* person enforcing rules and settling disputes in esp. cricket or between disputants. See also ARBITRATION. *–v.* (**-ring**) (often foll. by *for*, *in*, etc.) act as umpire (in). [French *nonper* not equal: related to PEER[2]]

umpteen /ˈʌmptiːn, -ˈtiːn/ *colloq. –adj.* indefinitely many; a lot of. *–pron.* indefinitely many. □ **umpteenth** *adj.* [jocular formation on -TEEN]

UN *abbr.* United Nations.

un-[1] *prefix* **1** added to adjectives and participles and their derivative nouns and adverbs, meaning: **a** not (*unusable*). **b** reverse of (esp. with implied approval etc.) (*unselfish*; *unsociable*). **2** (less often) added to nouns, meaning 'a lack of', 'the reverse of' (*unrest*; *untruth*). [Old English]

■ **Usage** The number of words that can be formed with this prefix (and with *un-*[2]) is virtually unlimited; consequently only a selection can be given here.

un-[2] *prefix* added to verbs and (less often) nouns, forming verbs denoting: **1** reversal (*undress*; *unsettle*). **2** deprivation (*unmask*). **3** release from (*unburden*; *uncage*). **4** causing to be no longer (*unman*). [Old English]

■ **Usage** See note at *un-*[1].

un-[3] *prefix Chem.* denoting 'one', combined with other numerical roots *nil* (= 0), *un* (= 1), *bi* (= 2), etc., to form the names of elements based on the atomic number, and terminated with *-ium*, e.g. *unnilquadium* = 104, *ununbium* = 112. [Latin *unus* one]

unabashed /ˌʌnəˈbæʃt/ *adj.* not abashed.

unabated /ˌʌnəˈbeɪtɪd/ *adj.* not abated; undiminished.

unable /ʌnˈeɪb(ə)l/ *predic. adj.* (usu. foll. by *to* + infin.) not able.

unabridged /ˌʌnəˈbrɪdʒd/ *adj.* complete; not abridged.

♦ **unabsorbed cost** /ˌʌnəbˈzɔːbd/ *n.* part of the overhead costs of a production process that is not covered by its revenue when the output falls below a specified level. Overheads are sometimes added to the direct costs of a process and divided by the output to give a unit cost. The output for this calculation is often set at such a level that the whole of the overheads are absorbed by the unit cost. If, in fact, the output falls below this level, the whole of the overheads will not be absorbed, the deficit being the unabsorbed cost.

---

unacademic /ˌʌnækəˈdemɪk/ *adj.* (of a person, book, etc.) not academic.

unacceptable /ˌʌnəkˈseptəb(ə)l/ *adj.* not acceptable. □ **unacceptably** *adv.*

unaccompanied /ˌʌnəˈkʌmpənɪd/ *adj.* **1** not accompanied. **2** *Mus.* without accompaniment.

unaccomplished /ˌʌnəˈkʌmplɪʃt/ *adj.* **1** uncompleted. **2** lacking accomplishments.

unaccountable /ˌʌnəˈkaʊntəb(ə)l/ *adj.* **1** without explanation; strange. **2** not answerable for one's actions. □ **unaccountably** *adv.*

unaccounted /ˌʌnəˈkaʊntɪd/ *adj.* (often foll. by *for*) unexplained; excluded.

unaccustomed /ˌʌnəˈkʌstəmd/ *adj.* **1** (usu. foll. by *to*) not accustomed. **2** unusual (*unaccustomed silence*).

unacknowledged /ˌʌnəkˈnɒlɪdʒd/ *adj.* not acknowledged.

unacquainted /ˌʌnəˈkweɪntɪd/ *adj.* (usu. foll. by *with*) not acquainted.

unadopted /ˌʌnəˈdɒptɪd/ *adj.* (of a road) not maintained by a local authority.

unadorned /ˌʌnəˈdɔːnd/ *adj.* plain.

unadulterated /ˌʌnəˈdʌltəˌreɪtɪd/ *adj.* **1** pure. **2** complete, utter.

unadventurous /ˌʌnədˈventʃərəs/ *adj.* not adventurous.

unadvised /ˌʌnədˈvaɪzd/ *adj.* **1** indiscreet; rash. **2** without advice. □ **unadvisedly** /-zɪdlɪ/ *adv.*

unaffected /ˌʌnəˈfektɪd/ *adj.* **1** (usu. foll. by *by*) not affected. **2** free from affectation. □ **unaffectedly** *adv.*

unaffiliated /ˌʌnəˈfɪlɪˌeɪtɪd/ *adj.* not affiliated.

unafraid /ˌʌnəˈfreɪd/ *adj.* not afraid.

unaided /ʌn'eɪdɪd/ *adj.* without help.
unalike /ˌʌnə'laɪk/ *adj.* not alike; different.
unalloyed /ˌʌnə'lɔɪd/ *adj.* **1** complete; utter (*unalloyed joy*). **2** pure.
unalterable /ʌn'ɔːltərəb(ə)l/ *adj.* not alterable.
unaltered /ʌn'ɔːltəd/ *adj.* not altered; remaining the same.
unambiguous /ˌʌnæm'bɪgjʊəs/ *adj.* not ambiguous; clear or definite in meaning. □ **unambiguously** *adv.*
unambitious /ˌʌnæm'bɪʃəs/ *adj.* not ambitious.
un-American /ˌʌnə'merɪkən/ *adj.* **1** uncharacteristic of Americans. **2** contrary to US interests, treasonable.
unamused /ˌʌnə'mjuːzd/ *adj.* not amused.
unanimous /juː'nænɪməs/ *adj.* **1** all in agreement (*committee was unanimous*). **2** (of an opinion, vote, etc.) by all without exception (*unanimous choice*). □ **unanimity** /-nə'nɪmɪtɪ/ *n.* **unanimously** *adv.* [Latin *unus* one, *animus* mind]
unannounced /ˌʌnə'naʊnst/ *adj.* not announced; without warning (of arrival etc.).
unanswerable /ʌn'ɑːnsərəb(ə)l/ *adj.* **1** irrefutable (*unanswerable case*). **2** unable to be answered (*unanswerable question*).
unanswered /ʌn'ɑːnsəd/ *adj.* not answered.
unanticipated /ˌʌnæn'tɪsɪˌpeɪtɪd/ *adj.* not anticipated.
unappealing /ˌʌnə'piːlɪŋ/ *adj.* unattractive.
unappetizing /ʌn'æpɪˌtaɪzɪŋ/ *adj.* not appetizing.
unappreciated /ˌʌnə'priːʃɪˌeɪtɪd/ *adj.* not appreciated.
unappreciative /ˌʌnə'priːʃətɪv/ *adj.* not appreciative.
unapproachable /ˌʌnə'prəʊtʃəb(ə)l/ *adj.* **1** inaccessible. **2** (of a person) unfriendly.

♦ unappropriated profit /ˌʌnə'prəʊprɪˌeɪtɪd/ *n.* part of an organization's profit that is neither allocated to a specific purpose nor paid out in dividends.

---

unarmed /ʌn'ɑːmd/ *adj.* not armed; without weapons.
unashamed /ˌʌnə'ʃeɪmd/ *adj.* **1** feeling no guilt. **2** blatant; bold. □ **unashamedly** /-mɪdlɪ/ *adv.*
unassailable /ˌʌnə'seɪləb(ə)l/ *adj.* unable to be attacked; impregnable.
unassuming /ˌʌnə'sjuːmɪŋ/ *adj.* not pretentious; modest.
unattached /ˌʌnə'tætʃt/ *adj.* **1** not engaged, married, etc. **2** (often foll. by *to*) not attached, esp. to a particular organization etc.
unattainable /ˌʌnə'teɪnəb(ə)l/ *adj.* not attainable.
unattended /ˌʌnə'tendɪd/ *adj.* **1** (usu. foll. by *to*) not attended. **2** (of a person, vehicle, etc.) alone.
unattractive /ˌʌnə'træktɪv/ *adj.* not attractive. □ **unattractively** *adv.*
unattributable /ˌʌnə'trɪbjʊtəb(ə)l/ *adj.* (esp. of published information) not attributed to a source etc.
unauthorized /ʌn'ɔːθəˌraɪzd/ *adj.* (also **-ised**) not authorized.
unavailable /ˌʌnə'veɪləb(ə)l/ *adj.* not available. □ **unavailability** /-'bɪlɪtɪ/ *n.*
unavailing /ˌʌnə'veɪlɪŋ/ *adj.* achieving nothing. □ **unavailingly** *adv.*
unavoidable /ˌʌnə'vɔɪdəb(ə)l/ *adj.* inevitable. □ **unavoidably** *adv.*
unaware /ˌʌnə'weə(r)/ –*adj.* **1** (usu. foll. by *of* or *that*) not aware. **2** unperceptive. –*adv.* = UNAWARES. □ **unawareness** *n.*
unawares *adv.* **1** unexpectedly. **2** inadvertently.
unbalanced /ʌn'bælənst/ *adj.* **1** emotionally unstable. **2** biased (*unbalanced report*).
unban /ʌn'bæn/ *v.* **(-nn-)** remove prohibited status from; allow.
unbar /ʌn'bɑː(r)/ *v.* **(-rr-) 1** unlock, open. **2** remove a bar from (a gate etc.).
unbearable /ʌn'beərəb(ə)l/ *adj.* unendurable. □ **unbearably** *adv.*
unbeatable /ʌn'biːtəb(ə)l/ *adj.* not beatable; excelling.
unbeaten /ʌn'biːt(ə)n/ *adj.* **1** not beaten. **2** (of a record etc.) not surpassed.
unbecoming /ˌʌnbɪ'kʌmɪŋ/ *adj.* **1** unflattering (*unbecoming hat*). **2** (usu. foll. by *to*, *for*) not fitting; indecorous. □ **unbecomingly** *adv.*
unbeknown /ˌʌnbɪ'nəʊn/ *adj.* (also **unbeknownst** /-'nəʊnst/) (foll. by *to*) without the knowledge of (*unbeknown to us*).
unbelief /ˌʌnbɪ'liːf/ *n.* lack of esp. religious belief. □ **unbeliever** *n.* **unbelieving** *adj.*
unbelievable /ˌʌnbɪ'liːvəb(ə)l/ *adj.* not believable; incredible. □ **unbelievably** *adv.*
unbend /ʌn'bend/ *v.* (*past* and *past part.* **unbent**) **1** straighten. **2** relax; become affable.
unbending *adj.* **1** inflexible. **2** firm; austere.
unbiased /ʌn'baɪəst/ *adj.* (also **unbiassed**) impartial.
unbidden /ʌn'bɪd(ə)n/ *adj.* not commanded or invited (*arrived unbidden*).
unbind /ʌn'baɪnd/ *v.* (*past* and *past part.* **unbound**) release; unfasten, untie.
unbleached /ʌn'bliːtʃt/ *adj.* not bleached.
unblemished /ʌn'blemɪʃt/ *adj.* not blemished.
unblinking /ʌn'blɪŋkɪŋ/ *adj.* **1** not blinking. **2** steadfast; stolid.
unblock /ʌn'blɒk/ *v.* remove an obstruction from.
unblushing /ʌn'blʌʃɪŋ/ *adj.* **1** shameless. **2** frank.
unbolt /ʌn'bəʊlt/ *v.* release the bolt of (a door etc.).
unborn /ʌn'bɔːn/ *adj.* not yet, or never to be, born (*unborn child*; *unborn hopes*).
unbosom /ʌn'bʊz(ə)m/ *v.* (often *refl.*) disclose (thoughts etc.); unburden oneself.
unbothered /ʌn'bɒðəd/ *predic. adj.* not bothered; unconcerned.
unbound[1] /ʌn'baʊnd/ *adj.* **1** not bound. **2** unconstrained. **3 a** (of a book) without a binding. **b** having paper covers.
unbound[2] *past* and *past part.* of UNBIND.
unbounded /ʌn'baʊndɪd/ *adj.* infinite (*unbounded optimism*).
unbreakable /ʌn'breɪkəb(ə)l/ *adj.* not breakable.
unbridgeable /ʌn'brɪdʒəb(ə)l/ *adj.* unable to be bridged.
unbridle /ʌn'braɪd(ə)l/ *v.* **(-ling)** remove a bridle, constraints, etc., from (a horse, one's tongue, etc.) (*unbridled insolence*).
unbroken /ʌn'brəʊkən/ *adj.* **1** not broken. **2** untamed (*unbroken horse*). **3** uninterrupted (*unbroken sleep*). **4** unsurpassed (*unbroken record*).
unbuckle /ʌn'bʌk(ə)l/ *v.* **(-ling)** release the buckle of (a strap, shoe, etc.).

♦ unbundling /ʌn'bʌnd(ə)lɪŋ/ *n.* **1** take-over of a large conglomerate with a view to retaining the core business as a going concern and selling off some or all of the subsidiary businesses to help pay for the take-over. **2** separation of systems software charges from hardware charges in the marketing of computer systems. Originally systems software was included in the purchase price as it represented only a small part of the total cost of the system, but this is no longer the case. Many microcomputer systems, however, include a number of programs (e.g. word processors or spreadsheets) in the purchase price as an incentive to buy.

---

unburden /ʌn'bɜːd(ə)n/ *v.* (often *refl.*; often followed by *to*) relieve (oneself, one's conscience, etc.) by confession etc.
unbusinesslike /ʌn'bɪznɪsˌlaɪk/ *adj.* not businesslike.
unbutton /ʌn'bʌt(ə)n/ *v.* **1** unfasten the buttons of (a garment, person, etc.). **2** (*absol.*) *colloq.* relax.

♦ uncalled capital /ʌn'kɔːld/ *n.* = RESERVE CAPITAL.

---

uncalled-for *adj.* (of a remark, action, etc.) rude, unnecessary.

uncanny /ʌn'kænɪ/ *adj.* (**-ier, -iest**) seemingly supernatural; mysterious. □ **uncannily** *adv.* **uncanniness** *n.*

uncapped /ʌn'kæpt/ *adj. Sport* (of a player) not yet awarded his cap or never having been selected to represent his country.

uncared-for /ʌn'keədfɔː(r)/ *adj.* disregarded; neglected.

uncaring /ʌn'keərɪŋ/ *adj.* neglectful, lacking compassion.

UNCDF *abbr.* United Nations Capital Development Fund.

unceasing /ʌn'siːsɪŋ/ *adj.* not ceasing; continuous (*unceasing effort*).

uncensored /ʌn'sensəd/ *adj.* not censored.

unceremonious /ˌʌnserɪ'məʊnɪəs/ *adj.* **1** abrupt; discourteous. **2** informal. □ **unceremoniously** *adv.*

uncertain /ʌn'sɜːt(ə)n/ *adj.* **1** not certainly knowing or known (*result is uncertain*). **2** unreliable. **3** changeable, erratic (*uncertain weather*). □ **in no uncertain terms** clearly and forcefully. □ **uncertainly** *adv.* **uncertainty** *n.* (*pl.* **-ies**).

♦ **uncertificated units** /ˌʌnsə'tɪfɪˌkeɪtɪd/ *n.pl.* small number of units purchased for an investor in a unit trust by reinvestment of dividends. If the number of units is too small to warrant the issue of a certificate they are held on account for the investor and added to the total when the holding is sold.

---

unchain /ʌn'tʃeɪn/ *v.* remove the chain(s) from; release.

unchallengeable /ʌn'tʃælɪndʒəb(ə)l/ *adj.* not challengeable; unassailable.

unchallenged /ʌn'tʃælɪndʒd/ *adj.* not challenged.

unchangeable /ʌn'tʃeɪndʒəb(ə)l/ *adj.* unable to be changed.

unchanged /ʌn'tʃeɪndʒd/ *adj.* not changed; unaltered.

unchanging /ʌn'tʃeɪndʒɪŋ/ *adj.* not changing; remaining the same.

unchaperoned /ʌn'ʃæpəˌrəʊnd/ *adj.* without a chaperone.

uncharacteristic /ˌʌnkærɪktə'rɪstɪk/ *adj.* not characteristic. □ **uncharacteristically** *adv.*

uncharitable /ʌn'tʃærɪtəb(ə)l/ *adj.* censorious, severe in judgement. □ **uncharitably** *adv.*

uncharted /ʌn'tʃɑːtɪd/ *adj.* not mapped or surveyed.

unchecked /ʌn'tʃekt/ *adj.* **1** not checked. **2** unrestrained (*unchecked violence*).

unchivalrous /ʌn'ʃɪvəlrəs/ *adj.* not chivalrous. □ **unchivalrously** *adv.*

unchristian /ʌn'krɪstʃ(ə)n/ *adj.* contrary to Christian principles, esp. uncaring or selfish.

uncial /'ʌnsɪəl/ *–adj.* of or written in rounded unjoined letters similar to capitals, found in manuscripts of the 4th–8th centuries. *–n.* uncial letter, style, or MS. [Latin *uncia* inch]

uncircumcised /ʌn'sɜːkəmˌsaɪzd/ *adj.* not circumcised.

UNCITRAL *abbr.* United Nations Commission on International Trade Law.

uncivil /ʌn'sɪvɪl/ *adj.* ill-mannered; impolite. □ **uncivilly** *adv.*

uncivilized /ʌn'sɪvɪˌlaɪzd/ *adj.* (also **-ised**) **1** not civilized. **2** rough; uncultured.

unclaimed /ʌn'kleɪmd/ *adj.* not claimed.

unclasp /ʌn'klɑːsp/ *v.* **1** loosen the clasp(s) of. **2** release the grip of (a hand etc.).

unclassified /ʌn'klæsɪˌfaɪd/ *adj.* **1** not classified. **2** (of state information) not secret.

uncle /'ʌŋk(ə)l/ *n.* **1 a** brother of one's father or mother. **b** aunt's husband. **2** *colloq.* (form of address by a child to) parent's male friend. **3** *slang* esp. *hist.* pawnbroker. [Latin *avunculus*]

-uncle *suffix* forming nouns, usu. diminutives (*carbuncle*). [Latin *-unculus*]

unclean /ʌn'kliːn/ *adj.* **1** not clean. **2** unchaste. **3** religiously impure; forbidden.

unclear /ʌn'klɪə(r)/ *adj.* **1** not clear or easy to understand. **2** (of a person) uncertain (*I'm unclear as to what you mean*).

unclench /ʌn'klentʃ/ *v.* **1** release (clenched hands etc.). **2** (of hands etc.) become relaxed or open.

Uncle Sam *n. colloq.* US government.

UNCLOS *abbr.* United Nations Conference on the Law of the Sea.

unclothe /ʌn'kləʊð/ *v.* (**-thing**) **1** remove clothes, leaves, etc. from. **2** expose, reveal.

unclouded /ʌn'klaʊdɪd/ *adj.* **1** clear; bright. **2** untroubled (*unclouded serenity*).

uncluttered /ʌn'klʌtəd/ *adj.* not cluttered; austere, simple.

uncoil /ʌn'kɔɪl/ *v.* unwind.

uncoloured /ʌn'kʌləd/ *adj.* **1** having no colour. **2** not influenced; impartial.

uncombed /ʌn'kəʊmd/ *adj.* (of hair or a person) not combed.

uncomfortable /ʌn'kʌmftəb(ə)l/ *adj.* **1** not comfortable. **2** uneasy; disquieting (*uncomfortable silence*). □ **uncomfortably** *adv.*

uncommercial /ˌʌnkə'mɜːʃ(ə)l/ *adj.* not commercial.

uncommitted /ˌʌnkə'mɪtɪd/ *adj.* **1** not committed. **2** not politically attached.

♦ **uncommitted facility** *n.* agreement between a bank and a company in which the bank agrees to make a loan to the company but is under obligation to provide a specified amount.

---

uncommon /ʌn'kɒmən/ *adj.* **1** unusual. **2** remarkably great etc. (*uncommon appetite*). □ **uncommonly** *adv.*

uncommunicative /ˌʌnkə'mjuːnɪkətɪv/ *adj.* taciturn.

♦ **uncompensated demand function** /ʌn'kɒmpenˌseɪtɪd/ *n.* = MARSHALLIAN DEMAND FUNCTION.

---

uncompetitive /ˌʌnkəm'petɪtɪv/ *adj.* not competitive.

uncomplaining /ˌʌnkəm'pleɪnɪŋ/ *adj.* not complaining; resigned. □ **uncomplainingly** *adv.*

uncompleted /ˌʌnkəm'pliːtɪd/ *adj.* not completed; incomplete.

uncomplicated /ʌn'kɒmplɪˌkeɪtɪd/ *adj.* simple; straightforward.

uncomplimentary /ˌʌnkɒmplɪ'mentərɪ/ *adj.* insulting.

uncomprehending /ˌʌnkɒmprɪ'hendɪŋ/ *adj.* not comprehending.

uncompromising /ʌn'kɒmprəˌmaɪzɪŋ/ *adj.* stubborn; unyielding. □ **uncompromisingly** *adv.*

unconcealed /ˌʌnkən'siːld/ *adj.* not concealed; obvious.

unconcern /ˌʌnkən'sɜːn/ *n.* calmness; indifference; apathy. □ **unconcerned** *adj.* **unconcernedly** /-nɪdlɪ/ *adv.*

unconditional /ˌʌnkən'dɪʃən(ə)l/ *adj.* not subject to conditions; complete (*unconditional surrender*). □ **unconditionally** *adv.*

♦ **unconditional bid** see TAKE-OVER BID.

---

unconditioned reflex *n.* instinctive response to a stimulus.

unconfined /ˌʌnkən'faɪnd/ *adj.* not confined; boundless.

unconfirmed /ˌʌnkən'fɜːmd/ *adj.* not confirmed.

♦ **unconfirmed letter of credit** see LETTER OF CREDIT.

---

uncongenial /ˌʌnkən'dʒiːnɪəl/ *adj.* not congenial.

unconnected /ˌʌnkə'nektɪd/ *adj.* **1** not physically joined. **2** not connected or associated. **3** disconnected (*unconnected ideas*).

unconquerable /ʌn'kɒŋkərəb(ə)l/ *adj.* not conquerable.

unconscionable /ʌn'kɒnʃənəb(ə)l/ *adj.* **1** without or contrary to conscience. **2** excessive (*unconscionable waste*). [from UN-[1], CONSCIENCE]

♦ **unconscionable bargain** *n.* = CATCHING BARGAIN.

unconscious /ʌn'kɒnʃəs/ *–adj.* not conscious (*fell unconscious; unconscious prejudice*). *–n.* normally inaccessible part of the mind affecting the emotions etc. □ **unconsciously** *adv.* **unconsciousness** *n.*

unconsidered /ˌʌnkən'sɪdəd/ *adj.* **1** not considered; disregarded. **2** not premeditated.

unconstitutional /ˌʌnkɒnstɪ'tjuːʃən(ə)l/ *adj.* in breach of a political constitution or procedural rules. □ **unconstitutionally** *adv.*

unconstrained /ˌʌnkən'streɪnd/ *adj.* not constrained or compelled.

uncontaminated /ˌʌnkən'tæmɪˌneɪtɪd/ *adj.* not contaminated.

uncontested /ˌʌnkən'testɪd/ *adj.* not contested.

uncontrollable /ˌʌnkən'trəʊləb(ə)l/ *adj.* not controllable. □ **uncontrollably** *adv.*

uncontrolled /ˌʌnkən'trəʊld/ *adj.* not controlled; unrestrained.

uncontroversial /ˌʌnkɒntrə'vɜːʃ(ə)l/ *adj.* not controversial.

unconventional /ˌʌnkən'venʃən(ə)l/ *adj.* unusual; unorthodox. □ **unconventionally** *adv.*

unconvinced /ˌʌnkən'vɪnst/ *adj.* not convinced.

unconvincing /ˌʌnkən'vɪnsɪŋ/ *adj.* not convincing. □ **unconvincingly** *adv.*

uncooked /ʌn'kʊkt/ *adj.* not cooked; raw.

uncooperative /ˌʌnkəʊ'ɒpərətɪv/ *adj.* not cooperative.

uncoordinated /ˌʌnkəʊ'ɔːdɪˌneɪtɪd/ *adj.* **1** not coordinated. **2** clumsy.

uncork /ʌn'kɔːk/ *v.* **1** draw the cork from (a bottle). **2** vent (feelings etc.).

uncorroborated /ˌʌnkə'rɒbəˌreɪtɪd/ *adj.* (esp. of evidence etc.) not corroborated.

uncountable /ʌn'kaʊntəb(ə)l/ *adj.* **1** inestimable, immense (*uncountable wealth*). **2** (of a noun) not used in the plural or with the indefinite article (e.g. *happiness, milk*).

uncouple /ʌn'kʌp(ə)l/ *v.* (**-ling**) release from couplings or couples.

uncouth /ʌn'kuːθ/ *adj.* uncultured, rough. [Old English, = unknown]

uncover /ʌn'kʌvə(r)/ *v.* **1** remove a cover or covering from. **2** disclose (*uncovered the truth*).

uncritical /ʌn'krɪtɪk(ə)l/ *adj.* **1** not critical; complacently accepting. **2** not in accordance with the principles of criticism. □ **uncritically** *adv.*

uncross /ʌn'krɒs/ *v.* **1** remove from a crossed position. **2** (as **uncrossed** *adj.*) (of a cheque) not crossed.

uncrown /ʌn'kraʊn/ *v.* **1** deprive of a crown, a position, etc. **2** (as **uncrowned** *adj.*) **a** not crowned. **b** having the status but not the name of (*uncrowned king of boxing*).

UNCSTD *abbr.* United Nations Conference on Science and Technology for Development.

♦ **UNCTAD** /'ʌŋkˌtæd/ *abbr.* (also **Unctad**) = UNITED NATIONS CONFERENCE ON TRADE AND DEVELOPMENT.

unction /'ʌŋkʃ(ə)n/ *n.* **1 a** anointing with oil etc. as a religious rite or medical treatment. **b** oil, ointment, etc. so used. **2 a** soothing words or thought. **b** excessive or insincere flattery. **3 a** emotional fervency. **b** pretence of this. [Latin *ungo unct-* anoint]

unctuous /'ʌŋktʃʊəs/ *adj.* **1** unpleasantly flattering; oily. **2** greasy or soapy. □ **unctuously** *adv.* [medieval Latin: related to UNCTION]

uncultivated /ʌn'kʌltɪˌveɪtɪd/ *adj.* not cultivated.

uncured /ʌn'kjʊəd/ *adj.* **1** not cured. **2** (of pork etc.) not salted or smoked.

uncurl /ʌn'kɜːl/ *v.* straighten out, untwist.

uncut /ʌn'kʌt/ *adj.* **1** not cut. **2** (of a book) with the pages sealed or untrimmed. **3** (of a book, film, etc.) complete; uncensored. **4** (of esp. a diamond) not shaped. **5** (of fabric) with a looped pile.

undamaged /ʌn'dæmɪdʒd/ *adj.* intact.

undated /ʌn'deɪtɪd/ *adj.* without a date.

♦ **undated security** *n.* fixed-interest security that has no redemption date. See CONSOLS.

undaunted /ʌn'dɔːntɪd/ *adj.* not daunted.

undeceive /ˌʌndɪ'siːv/ *v.* (**-ving**) (often foll. by *of*) free (a person) from a misconception, deception, or error.

undecided /ˌʌndɪ'saɪdɪd/ *adj.* **1** not settled. **2** irresolute.

undeclared /ˌʌndɪ'kleəd/ *adj.* not declared.

undefeated /ˌʌndɪ'fiːtɪd/ *adj.* not defeated.

undefended /ˌʌndɪ'fendɪd/ *adj.* not defended.

undefined /ˌʌndɪ'faɪnd/ *adj.* not defined; vague, indefinite.

undemanding /ˌʌndɪ'mɑːndɪŋ/ *adj.* not demanding; easily done or satisfied (*undemanding reading*).

undemocratic /ˌʌndemə'krætɪk/ *adj.* not democratic.

undemonstrative /ˌʌndɪ'mɒnstrətɪv/ *adj.* not emotionally expressive; reserved.

undeniable /ˌʌndɪ'naɪəb(ə)l/ *adj.* indisputable; certain. □ **undeniably** *adv.*

under *–prep.* **1 a** in or to a position lower than; below; beneath (*under the table*). **b** on the inside of (*vest under his shirt*). **2** inferior to; less than (*no-one under a major; is under 18; was under £20*). **3 a** subject to; controlled by (*under constraint; born under Saturn; prospered under him*). **b** undergoing (*is under repair*). **c** classified or subsumed in (*under two headings*). **4** at the foot of or sheltered by (*under the cliff*). **5** planted with (a crop). **6** powered by (sail, steam, etc.). *–adv.* **1** in or to a lower position or condition (*kept him under*). **2** *colloq.* in or into unconsciousness (*put him under*). *–adj.* lower (*under jaw*). □ **under arms** see ARM[2]. **under one's belt** see BELT. **under one's breath** see BREATH. **under a cloud** see CLOUD. **under control** see CONTROL. **under the counter** see COUNTER[1]. **under fire** see FIRE. **under a person's nose** see NOSE. **under the sun** anywhere in the world. **under way** in motion; in progress. **under the weather** see WEATHER. □ **undermost** *adj.* [Old English]

under- *prefix* in senses of UNDER: **1** below, beneath (*underground*). **2** lower; subordinate (*under-secretary*). **3** insufficiently, incompletely (*undercook; underdeveloped*).

underachieve /ˌʌndərə'tʃiːv/ *v.* (**-ving**) do less well than might be expected (esp. academically). □ **underachiever** *n.*

under-age *adj.* (also **under age**) not old enough.

underarm *–adj.* & *adv. Sport*, esp. *Cricket* with the arm below shoulder-level. *–attrib. adj.* **1** under the arm (*underarm seam*). **2** in the armpit.

underbelly *n.* (*pl.* **-ies**) undersurface of an animal, vehicle, etc., esp. as vulnerable to attack.

underbid *–v.* /ˌʌndə'bɪd/ (**-dd-**; *past* and *past part.* **-bid**) **1** make a lower bid than. **2** (also *absol.*) *Bridge* etc. bid less on (one's hand) than warranted. *–n.* /'ʌndəˌbɪd/ such a bid.

♦ **undercapitalized** /ˌʌndə'kæpɪt(ə)laɪzd/ *adj.* denoting an organization that has insufficient capital or reserves for the amount of business it undertakes.

undercarriage *n.* **1** wheeled retractable structure beneath an aircraft, used for landing etc. **2** supporting frame of a vehicle.

undercharge /ˌʌndə'tʃɑːdʒ/ *v.* (**-ging**) **1** charge too little to (a person). **2** give too little charge to (a gun, electric battery, etc.).

underclothes *n.pl.* clothes worn under others, esp. next to the skin.

underclothing *n.* underclothes collectively.

undercoat *n.* **1 a** layer of paint under a topcoat. **b** paint for this. **2** animal's under layer of hair etc.

undercook /ˌʌndə'kʊk/ *v.* cook insufficiently.

undercover /ˌʌndə'kʌvə(r)/ *adj.* (usu. *attrib.*) **1** surreptitious. **2** spying incognito, esp. by infiltration (*undercover agent*).

undercroft *n.* crypt. [obsolete *croft* from Latin]
undercurrent *n.* **1** current below the surface. **2** underlying often contrary feeling, influence, etc. (*undercurrent of protest*).
undercut –*v.* /ˌʌndəˈkʌt/ (**-tt-**; *past* and *past part.* **-cut**) **1** sell or work at a lower price than. **2** strike (a ball) to make it rise high. **3** cut away the part below. **4** undermine. –*n.* /ˈʌndəˌkʌt/ underside of sirloin.
underdeveloped /ˌʌndədɪˈveləpt/ *adj.* **1** not fully developed; immature. **2** (of a country etc.) with unexploited potential. □ **underdevelopment** *n.*
underdog *n.* **1** oppressed person. **2** loser in a fight.
underdone /ˌʌndəˈdʌn/ *adj.* undercooked.
underemployed /ˌʌndərɪmˈplɔɪd/ *adj.* not fully occupied. □ **underemployment** *n.*
underestimate –*v.* /ˌʌndərˈestɪˌmeɪt/ (**-ting**) form too low an estimate of. –*n.* /ˌʌndərˈestɪmət/ estimate that is too low. □ **underestimation** /-ˈmeɪʃ(ə)n/ *n.*
underexpose /ˌʌndərɪkˈspəʊz/ *v.* (**-sing**) expose (film) for too short a time etc. □ **underexposure** *n.*
underfed /ˌʌndəˈfed/ *adj.* malnourished.
underfelt *n.* felt laid under a carpet.
underfloor *attrib. adj.* beneath the floor (*underfloor heating*).
underfoot /ˌʌndəˈfʊt/ *adv.* (also **under foot**) **1** under one's feet. **2** on the ground.
underfunded *adj.* provided with insufficient money.
undergarment *n.* piece of underclothing.
undergo /ˌʌndəˈgəʊ/ *v.* (*3rd sing. present* **-goes**; *past* **-went**; *past part.* **-gone**) be subjected to; suffer; endure.
undergraduate /ˌʌndəˈgrædjʊət/ *n.* person studying for a first degree.
underground –*adv.* /ˌʌndəˈgraʊnd/ **1** beneath the ground. **2** in or into secrecy or hiding. –*adj.* /ˈʌndəˌgraʊnd/ **1** situated underground. **2** secret, subversive. **3** unconventional (*underground literature*). –*n.* /ˈʌndəˌgraʊnd/ **1** underground railway. **2** secret subversive group or activity.
undergrowth *n.* dense shrubs etc., esp. in a wood.
underhand *adj.* **1** deceitful; crafty; secret. **2** *Sport*, esp. *Cricket* underarm.
underlay[1] –*v.* /ˌʌndəˈleɪ/ (*past* and *past part.* **-laid**) lay something under (a thing) to support or raise it. –*n.* /ˈʌndəˌlaɪ/ thing so laid (esp. under a carpet).
underlay[2] *past* of UNDERLIE.
underlie /ˌʌndəˈlaɪ/ *v.* (**-lying**; *past* **-lay**; *past part.* **-lain**) **1** (also *absol.*) lie under (a stratum etc.). **2** (also *absol.*) (esp. as **underlying** *adj.*) be the basis of (a doctrine, conduct, etc.). **3** exist beneath the superficial aspect of.
underline /ˌʌndəˈlaɪn/ *v.* (**-ning**) **1** draw a line under (a word etc.) to give emphasis, indicate italic type, etc. **2** emphasize, stress.
underling /ˈʌndəlɪŋ/ *n.* usu. *derog.* subordinate.
underlying *pres. part.* of UNDERLIE.
undermanned /ˌʌndəˈmænd/ *adj.* having an insufficient crew or staff.
undermentioned /ˌʌndəˈmenʃ(ə)nd/ *adj.* mentioned later in a book etc.
undermine /ˌʌndəˈmaɪn/ *v.* (**-ning**) **1** injure (a person, reputation, health, etc.) secretly or insidiously. **2** wear away the base of (*banks were undermined*). **3** make an excavation under.
underneath /ˌʌndəˈniːθ/ –*prep.* **1** at or to a lower place than, below. **2** on the inside of. –*adv.* **1** at or to a lower place. **2** inside. –*n.* lower surface or part. –*adj.* lower. [Old English: related to NETHER]
undernourished /ˌʌndəˈnʌrɪʃt/ *adj.* insufficiently nourished. □ **undernourishment** *n.*
underpaid *past* and *past part.* of UNDERPAY.
underpants *n.pl.* undergarment, esp. men's, covering the genitals and buttocks.
underpart *n.* lower or subordinate part.
underpass *n.* **1** road etc. passing under another. **2** subway.
underpay /ˌʌndəˈpeɪ/ *v.* (*past* and *past part.* **-paid**) pay too little to (a person) or for (a thing). □ **underpayment** *n.*
underpin /ˌʌndəˈpɪn/ *v.* (**-nn-**) **1** support from below with masonry etc. **2** support, strengthen.
underplay /ˌʌndəˈpleɪ/ *v.* **1** make little of. **2** *Theatr.* underact.
underpopulated /ˌʌndəˈpɒpjʊˌleɪtɪd/ *adj.* having an insufficient or very small population.
underprice /ˌʌndəˈpraɪs/ *v.* (**-cing**) price lower than what is usual or appropriate.
underprivileged /ˌʌndəˈprɪvɪlɪdʒd/ *adj.* less privileged than others; having below average income, rights, etc.
underrate /ˌʌndəˈreɪt/ *v.* (**-ting**) have too low an opinion of.
underscore /ˌʌndəˈskɔː(r)/ *v.* (**-ring**) = UNDERLINE.
undersea *adj.* below the sea or its surface.
underseal –*v.* seal the underpart of (esp. a vehicle against rust etc.). –*n.* protective coating for this.
under-secretary /ˌʌndəˈsekrətərɪ/ *n.* (*pl.* **-ies**) subordinate official, esp. a junior minister or senior civil servant.
undersell /ˌʌndəˈsel/ *v.* (*past* and *past part.* **-sold**) sell at a lower price than (another seller).
undersexed /ˌʌndəˈsekst/ *adj.* having unusually weak sexual desires.
undershirt *n.* esp. *US* man's or boy's vest.
undershoot /ˌʌndəˈʃuːt/ *v.* (*past* and *past part.* **-shot**) land short of (a runway etc.).
undershot *adj.* **1** (of a water-wheel) turned by water flowing under it. **2** (of a lower jaw) projecting beyond the upper jaw.
underside *n.* lower or under side or surface.
undersigned /ˌʌndəˈsaɪnd/ *adj.* (usu. *absol.*) whose signature is appended (*we, the undersigned*).
undersized /ˌʌndəˈsaɪzd/ *adj.* smaller than average.
underskirt *n.* petticoat.
underslung /ˌʌndəˈslʌŋ/ *adj.* supported from above.
undersold *past* and *past part.* of UNDERSELL.
underspend /ˌʌndəˈspend/ *v.* (*past* and *past part.* **-spent**) (usu. *absol.*) spend less than (the expected amount), or too little.
understaffed /ˌʌndəˈstɑːft/ *adj.* having too few staff.
understand /ˌʌndəˈstænd/ *v.* (*past* and *past part.* **-stood**) **1** perceive the meaning of (words, a person, a language, a subject, etc.) (*understood you perfectly*; *cannot understand algebra*). **2** perceive the significance or cause of (*do not understand why he came*). **3** (often *absol.*) sympathize with, know how to deal with (*quite understand your difficulty*; *ask her, she understands*). **4** (often foll. by *that* or *absol.*) infer, take as implied (*am I to understand that you refuse?*; *he is old, I understand*). **5** supply (an implied missing word) mentally. □ **understand each other 1** know each other's views. **2** agree or collude. □ **understandable** *adj.* **understandably** *adv.* [Old English: related to STAND]
understanding –*n.* **1** ability to understand or think; intelligence. **2** individual's perception of a situation etc. **3** agreement, esp. informal (*had an understanding*). **4** sympathy; tolerance. –*adj.* **1** having understanding or insight. **2** sympathetic. □ **understandingly** *adv.*
understate /ˌʌndəˈsteɪt/ *v.* (**-ting**) **1** express mildly or in a restrained way. **2** represent as less than it actually is. □ **understatement** *n.*
understeer *n.* tendency of a vehicle not to turn sharply enough.
understood *past* and *past part.* of UNDERSTAND.
understudy esp. *Theatr.* –*n.* (*pl.* **-ies**) person ready to take on another's role etc. when required. –*v.* (**-ies, -ied**) **1** study (a role etc.) thus. **2** act as an understudy to.
undersubscribed /ˌʌndəsəbˈskraɪbd/ *adj.* without sufficient subscribers, participants, investors, etc. See also OVERSUBSCRIBE. □ **undersubscription** /-ˈskrɪpʃ(ə)n/ *n.*
undersurface *n.* lower or under surface.
undertake /ˌʌndəˈteɪk/ *v.* (**-king**; *past* **-took**; *past part.*

-taken) **1** agree to perform or be responsible for; engage in, enter upon (work, a responsibility, etc.). **2** (usu. foll. by *to* + infin.) promise. **3** guarantee (*undertake that he is innocent*).

undertaker /'ʌndə,teɪkə(r)/ *n.* professional funeral organizer.

undertaking /,ʌndə'teɪkɪŋ/ *n.* **1** work etc. undertaken, enterprise (*serious undertaking*). **2** promise. **3** /'ʌn-/ professional funeral management.

underthings *n.pl.* underclothes.

undertone *n.* **1** subdued tone or colour. **2** underlying quality or feeling.

undertook *past* of UNDERTAKE.

undertow *n.* current below the surface of the sea contrary to the surface current.

underused /,ʌndə'ju:zd/ *adj.* not used to capacity.

undervalue /,ʌndə'vælju:/ *v.* (**-ues, -ued, -uing**) **1** value insufficiently. **2** underestimate.

undervest *n.* vest.

underwater /,ʌndə'wɔ:tə(r)/ *–adj.* situated or done under water. *–adv.* under water.

underwear *n.* underclothes.

underweight *–adj.* /,ʌndə'weɪt/ below normal weight. *–n.* /'ʌndə,weɪt/ insufficient weight.

underwent *past* of UNDERGO.

underwhelm /,ʌndə'welm/ *v. joc.* fail to impress. [alteration of OVERWHELM]

underworld *n.* **1** those who live by organized crime and vice. **2** mythical abode of the dead under the earth.

underwrite /,ʌndə'raɪt/ *v.* (**-ting**; *past* **-wrote**; *past part.* **-written**) **1 a** sign and accept liability under (an insurance policy, esp. on shipping etc.). **b** accept (liability) in this way. **2** undertake to finance or support. **3** engage to buy all the unsold stock in (a company etc.).

◆ **underwriter** /'ʌndə,raɪtə(r)/ *n.* **1** person who examines a risk, decides whether or not it can be insured, and, if it can, works out the premium to be charged, usu. on the basis of the frequency of past claims for similar risks. Underwriters are either employed by insurance companies or are members of Lloyd's. See also LLOYD'S; INSTITUTE OF LONDON UNDERWRITERS. **2** financial institution, usu. an issuing house or merchant bank, that guarantees to buy a proportion of any unsold shares when a new issue is offered to the public. Underwriters usu. work for a commission (usu. 2%), and a number may combine together to buy all the unsold shares, provided that the minimum subscription stated in the prospectus has been sold to the public.

---

undescended /,ʌndɪ'sendɪd/ *adj.* (of a testicle) not descending normally into the scrotum.

undeserved /,ʌndɪ'zɜ:vd/ *adj.* not deserved. □ **undeservedly** /-vɪdlɪ/ *adv.*

undeserving /,ʌndɪ'zɜ:vɪŋ/ *adj.* not deserving.

undesigned /,ʌndɪ'zaɪnd/ *adj.* unintentional.

undesirable /,ʌndɪ'zaɪərəb(ə)l/ *–adj.* objectionable, unpleasant. *–n.* undesirable person. □ **undesirability** /-'bɪlɪtɪ/ *n.*

undetectable /,ʌndɪ'tektəb(ə)l/ *adj.* not detectable.

undetected /,ʌndɪ'tektɪd/ *adj.* not detected.

undetermined /,ʌndɪ'tɜ:mɪnd/ *adj.* = UNDECIDED.

undeterred /,ʌndɪ'tɜ:d/ *adj.* not deterred.

undeveloped /,ʌndɪ'veləpt/ *adj.* not developed.

undid *past* of UNDO.

undies /'ʌndɪz/ *n.pl. colloq.* (esp. women's) underclothes. [abbreviation]

undifferentiated /,ʌndɪfə'renʃɪ,eɪtɪd/ *adj.* not differentiated; amorphous.

◆ **undifferentiated marketing** *n.* marketing of a product aimed at the widest possible market. An early example was the Model T Ford, which was mass-produced, aimed at a very wide market, and only available in black.

---

undigested /,ʌndaɪ'dʒestɪd/ *adj.* **1** not digested. **2** (of facts etc.) not properly arranged or considered.

undignified /ʌn'dɪgnɪ,faɪd/ *adj.* lacking dignity.

undiluted /,ʌndaɪ'lju:tɪd/ *adj.* not diluted.

undiminished /,ʌndɪ'mɪnɪʃt/ *adj.* not diminished or lessened.

undine /'ʌndi:n/ *n.* female water-spirit. [Latin *unda* wave]

undiplomatic /,ʌndɪplə'mætɪk/ *adj.* tactless.

◆ **undischarged bankrupt** /,ʌndɪs'tʃɑ:dʒd/ *n.* person whose bankruptcy has not been discharged. Undischarged bankrupts must not obtain credit (above £250) without first informing their creditors of their position, and they must not become directors of companies or trade under another name. They may not hold office as a JP, MP, mayor, or councillor, and peers who are undischarged bankrupts may not sit in the House of Lords.

---

undisciplined /ʌn'dɪsɪplɪnd/ *adj.* lacking discipline; not disciplined.

undisclosed /,ʌndɪs'kləʊzd/ *adj.* not revealed or made known.

◆ **undisclosed factoring** *n.* form of factoring in which the seller of goods does not wish to disclose that a factor is being used. In these circumstances, the factor buys the goods that have been sold (rather than the debt their sale incurred) and, as an undisclosed principal, appoints the original seller to act as agent to recover the debt. The factor assumes responsibility in the case of non-payment so that from the point of view of the seller, the factor offers the same service as in normal factoring.

◆ **undisclosed principal** *n.* person who buys or sells through an agent or broker and remains anonymous. The agent or broker must disclose that such deals are being made on behalf of an undisclosed principal, otherwise he or she may be treated in law as the principal and in some circumstances the contract may be made void.

---

undiscovered /,ʌndɪ'skʌvəd/ *adj.* not discovered.

undiscriminating /,ʌndɪ'skrɪmɪ,neɪtɪŋ/ *adj.* lacking good judgement.

undisguised /,ʌndɪs'gaɪzd/ *adj.* not disguised; open.

undismayed /,ʌndɪs'meɪd/ *adj.* not dismayed.

undisputed /,ʌndɪ'spju:tɪd/ *adj.* not disputed or called in question.

undistinguished /,ʌndɪ'stɪŋgwɪʃt/ *adj.* not distinguished; mediocre.

◆ **undistributable reserves** /,ʌndɪ'strɪbjʊtəb(ə)l/ *n.pl.* = CAPITAL RESERVES.

◆ **undistributed profit** /,ʌndɪ'strɪbjʊtɪd/ *n.* profit earned by an organization but not distributed to its shareholders by way of dividends. Such sums are available for later distribution but are frequently used by companies to finance their trade.

---

undisturbed /,ʌndɪ'stɜ:bd/ *adj.* not disturbed or interfered with.

undivided /,ʌndɪ'vaɪdɪd/ *adj.* not divided or shared; whole, entire (*undivided attention*).

undo /ʌn'du:/ *v.* (*3rd sing. present* **-does**; *past* **-did**; *past part.* **-done**; *partic.* **-doing**) **1** unfasten (a coat, button, parcel, etc.), or the clothing of (a person). **2** annul, cancel (*cannot undo the past*). **3** ruin the prospects, reputation, or morals of.

undoing *n.* **1** ruin or cause of ruin. **2** reversing of an action etc. **3** opening or unfastening.

undone /ʌn'dʌn/ *adj.* **1** not done. **2** not fastened. **3** *archaic* ruined.

undoubted /ʌn'daʊtɪd/ *adj.* certain, not questioned. □ **undoubtedly** *adv.*

UNDP *abbr.* United Nations Development Programme.

undreamed /ʌn'dri:md, ʌn'dremt/ *adj.* (also **undreamt** /ʌn'dremt/) (often foll. by *of*) not dreamed, thought, or imagined.

undress /ʌn'dres/ *–v.* **1** take off one's clothes. **2** take the clothes off (a person). *–n.* **1** ordinary or casual dress, esp. as opposed to full dress or uniform. **2** naked or scantily clad state.

undressed /ʌn'drest/ *adj.* **1** not, or no longer, dressed. **2** (of food) without a dressing. **3** (of leather etc.) not treated.

undrinkable /ʌn'drɪŋkəb(ə)l/ *adj.* unfit for drinking.

undue /ʌn'djuː/ *adj.* excessive, disproportionate. □ **unduly** *adv.*

♦ **undue influence** *n.* unfair pressure exerted on a person so that he or she signs a contract that is not a true expression of that person's aims or requirements at the time, but is to the advantage of another party (either a party to the contract or a third party). Such a contract may be set aside by a court.

undulate /'ʌndjʊˌleɪt/ *v.* (**-ting**) (cause to) have a wavy motion or look. □ **undulation** /-'leɪʃ(ə)n/ *n.* [Latin *unda* wave]

undying /ʌn'daɪɪŋ/ *adj.* immortal (*undying love*).

unearned /ʌn'ɜːnd/ *adj.* not earned.

♦ **unearned income** *n.* income from investments etc. rather than from a trade, profession, or vocation or from the emoluments of office. In the UK, until 1984, it was thought that as investment income was more permanent than earned income and did not depend on the labours of the taxpayer, it should be taxed more heavily than earned income. This was achieved by an investment-income surcharge, which was an extra 15% over the normal rate of income tax. In the UK both earned and unearned income are now taxed at the same rates.

unearth /ʌn'ɜːθ/ *v.* discover by searching, digging, or rummaging.

unearthly /ʌn'ɜːθlɪ/ *adj.* **1** supernatural, mysterious. **2** *colloq.* absurdly early or inconvenient (*unearthly hour*). □ **unearthliness** *n.*

unease /ʌn'iːz/ *n.* nervousness, anxiety.

uneasy /ʌn'iːzɪ/ *adj.* (**-ier, -iest**) **1** nervous, anxious. **2** disturbing (*uneasy suspicion*). □ **uneasily** *adv.* **uneasiness** *n.*

uneatable /ʌn'iːtəb(ə)l/ *adj.* not able to be eaten (cf. INEDIBLE).

uneaten /ʌn'iːt(ə)n/ *adj.* left not eaten.

UNECA *abbr.* United Nations Economic Commission for Asia.

uneconomic /ˌʌniːkə'nɒmɪk, ˌʌnek-/ *adj.* not economic; unprofitable.

uneconomical *adj.* not economical; wasteful.

UNEDA *abbr.* United Nations Economic Development Administration.

unedifying /ʌn'edɪˌfaɪɪŋ/ *adj.* distasteful, degrading.

unedited /ʌn'edɪtɪd/ *adj.* not edited.

uneducated /ʌn'edjʊˌkeɪtɪd/ *adj.* not educated.

unembarrassed /ˌʌnɪm'bærəst/ *adj.* not embarrassed.

unemotional /ˌʌnɪ'məʊʃən(ə)l/ *adj.* not emotional; lacking emotion.

unemphatic /ˌʌnɪm'fætɪk/ *adj.* not emphatic.

unemployable /ˌʌnɪm'plɔɪəb(ə)l/ *adj.* unfit for paid employment. □ **unemployability** /-'bɪlɪtɪ/ *n.*

unemployed /ˌʌnɪm'plɔɪd/ *–adj.* **1** out of work. **2** not in use. *–n.* (prec. by *the*) those out of work, esp. those claiming unemployment benefit.

♦ **unemployment** /ˌʌnɪm'plɔɪmənt/ *n.* **1** being unemployed. **2** lack of employment in a country etc. This has been a persistent problem in industrial economies during recession over the last 200 years. Keynes' solution of government intervention, proposed in the 1930s, seemed successful in the postwar era; however, since then Keynesianism has lost ground both theoretically and in practice, largely as a result of the extent to which governments have seen the control of inflation as their first priority and have begun to doubt their ability to control long-term unemployment (see PHILLIPS CURVE). In the 1980s and 1990s large-scale unemployment has again become a problem in most Western economies, with economists more divided than ever as to possible solutions. See also INVOLUNTARY UNEMPLOYMENT; NAIRU; NATURAL RATE OF UNEMPLOYMENT; SEASONAL UNEMPLOYMENT.

unemployment benefit *n.* state payment made to an unemployed person.

unencumbered /ˌʌnɪn'kʌmbəd/ *adj.* **1** (of an estate) not having liabilities (e.g. a mortgage). **2** free; not burdened.

unending /ʌn'endɪŋ/ *adj.* endless or seemingly endless.

unendurable /ˌʌnɪn'djʊərəb(ə)l/ *adj.* too bad to be borne.

unenlightened /ˌʌnɪn'laɪt(ə)nd/ *adj.* not enlightened.

unenterprising /ʌn'entəˌpraɪzɪŋ/ *adj.* not enterprising.

unenthusiastic /ˌʌnɪnˌθjuːzɪ'æstɪk/ *adj.* not enthusiastic. □ **unenthusiastically** *adv.*

unenviable /ʌn'envɪəb(ə)l/ *adj.* not enviable.

unequal /ʌn'iːkw(ə)l/ *adj.* **1** (often foll. by *to*) not equal. **2** of varying quality. **3** unfair (*unequal contest*). □ **unequally** *adv.*

unequalled *adj.* (*US* **-aled**) superior to all others.

unequivocal /ˌʌnɪ'kwɪvək(ə)l/ *adj.* not ambiguous, plain, unmistakable. □ **unequivocally** *adv.*

unerring /ʌn'ɜːrɪŋ/ *adj.* not erring; true, certain. □ **unerringly** *adv.*

UNESCO /juː'neskəʊ/ *abbr.* (also **Unesco**) United Nations Educational, Scientific, and Cultural Organization.

unethical /ʌn'eθɪk(ə)l/ *adj.* not ethical, esp. unscrupulous or unprofessional. □ **unethically** *adv.*

uneven /ʌn'iːv(ə)n/ *adj.* **1** not level or smooth. **2** of variable quality etc. **3** (of a contest) unequal. □ **unevenly** *adv.* **unevenness** *n.*

uneventful /ˌʌnɪ'ventfʊl/ *adj.* not eventful. □ **uneventfully** *adv.*

unexampled /ˌʌnɪg'zɑːmp(ə)ld/ *adj.* without precedent.

unexceptionable /ˌʌnɪk'sepʃənəb(ə)l/ *adj.* entirely satisfactory.

■ **Usage** See note at *exceptionable.*

unexceptional /ˌʌnɪk'sepʃən(ə)l/ *adj.* usual, normal, ordinary.

unexciting /ˌʌnɪk'saɪtɪŋ/ *adj.* not exciting; dull.

unexpected /ˌʌnɪk'spektɪd/ *adj.* not expected; surprising. □ **unexpectedly** *adv.* **unexpectedness** *n.*

unexplained /ˌʌnɪk'spleɪnd/ *adj.* not explained.

unexplored /ˌʌnɪk'splɔːd/ *adj.* not explored.

unexposed /ˌʌnɪk'spəʊzd/ *adj.* not exposed.

unexpressed /ˌʌnɪk'sprest/ *adj.* not expressed or made known (*unexpressed fears*).

unexpurgated /ʌn'ekspəˌgeɪtɪd/ *adj.* (esp. of a text etc.) complete.

unfailing /ʌn'feɪlɪŋ/ *adj.* not failing or dwindling; constant; reliable. □ **unfailingly** *adv.*

unfair /ʌn'feə(r)/ *adj.* not fair, just, or impartial. □ **unfairly** *adv.* **unfairness** *n.*

♦ **unfair dismissal** *n.* dismissal of an employee that the employer cannot show to be fair. Under the Employment Protection (Consolidation) Act (1978) employees have the right not to be unfairly dismissed, provided they have served the required period of continuous employment (52 weeks for full-time employment) and are not over 65 or the normal retirement age for an employee in that particular job. An employee who considers he or she has been unfairly dismissed can apply within three months after the effective date of termination of the employment contract to an industrial tribunal for reinstatement, re-engagement, or compensation. The tribunal will make an award unless the employer shows that the principal reason for the dismissal was the employee's incapability, lack of qualifications, or conduct; redundancy; the fact that it would be illegal to continue employing the person; or some other substantial reason. The employer must also show that he or she acted reasonably in dismissing the employee. The statutory protection does not apply to members of the police and armed forces and certain other employees.

◆ **unfair prejudice** *n.* conduct in the running of a company's affairs that may entitle members to a remedy under the Companies Act (1985). In small companies, the unfairness may consist of a failure by some members to honour a common understanding reached when the company was formed, e.g. that a member be allowed to assist in the management and be paid accordingly. The usual remedy sought is for the purchase of the member's shares at a fair price. See also MINORITY PROTECTION.

◆ **unfair trading** see CONSUMER PROTECTION.

---

unfaithful /ʌn'feɪθfʊl/ *adj.* **1** not faithful, esp. adulterous. **2** treacherous; disloyal. □ **unfaithfully** *adv.* **unfaithfulness** *n.*

unfamiliar /ˌʌnfə'mɪljə(r)/ *adj.* not familiar. □ **unfamiliarity** /-lɪ'ærɪtɪ/ *n.*

UNFAO *abbr.* United Nations Food and Agriculture Organization.

unfashionable /ʌn'fæʃənəb(ə)l/ *adj.* not fashionable. □ **unfashionably** *adv.*

unfasten /ʌn'fɑːs(ə)n/ *v.* **1** make or become loose. **2** open the fastening(s) of. **3** detach.

unfathomable /ʌn'fæðəməb(ə)l/ *adj.* incapable of being fathomed.

unfavourable /ʌn'feɪvərəb(ə)l/ *adj.* (*US* **unfavorable**) not favourable; adverse, hostile. □ **unfavourably** *adv.*

◆ **unfavourable balance** *n.* balance of trade or balance of payments deficit.

---

unfeasible /ʌn'fiːzɪb(ə)l/ *adj.* not feasible; impractical.

unfeeling /ʌn'fiːlɪŋ/ *adj.* unsympathetic, harsh.

unfeigned /ʌn'feɪnd/ *adj.* genuine, sincere.

unfertilized /ʌn'fɜːtɪˌlaɪzd/ *adj.* (also **-ised**) not fertilized.

unfetter /ʌn'fetə(r)/ *v.* release from fetters.

unfilled /ʌn'fɪld/ *adj.* not filled.

unfinished /ʌn'fɪnɪʃt/ *adj.* not finished; incomplete.

unfit /ʌn'fɪt/ *adj.* (often foll. by *for*, or *to* + infin.) not fit.

unfitted /ʌn'fɪtɪd/ *adj.* **1** not fit. **2** not fitted or suited. **3** having no fittings.

unfitting /ʌn'fɪtɪŋ/ *adj.* not suitable, unbecoming.

unfix /ʌn'fɪks/ *v.* release, loosen, or detach.

unflagging /ʌn'flægɪŋ/ *adj.* tireless, persistent.

unflappable /ʌn'flæpəb(ə)l/ *adj. colloq.* imperturbable; calm. □ **unflappability** /-'bɪlɪtɪ/ *n.*

unflattering /ʌn'flætərɪŋ/ *adj.* not flattering. □ **unflatteringly** *adv.*

unfledged /ʌn'fledʒd/ *adj.* **1** (of a person) inexperienced. **2** (of a bird) not yet fledged.

unflinching /ʌn'flɪntʃɪŋ/ *adj.* not flinching. □ **unflinchingly** *adv.*

unfold /ʌn'fəʊld/ *v.* **1** open the fold or folds of, spread out. **2** reveal (thoughts etc.). **3** become opened out. **4** develop.

unforced /ʌn'fɔːst/ *adj.* **1** easy, natural. **2** not compelled or constrained.

unforeseeable /ˌʌnfɔː'siːəb(ə)l/ *adj.* not foreseeable.

unforeseen /ˌʌnfɔː'siːn/ *adj.* not foreseen.

unforgettable /ˌʌnfə'getəb(ə)l/ *adj.* that cannot be forgotten; memorable, wonderful.

unforgivable /ˌʌnfə'gɪvəb(ə)l/ *adj.* that cannot be forgiven.

unforgiving /ˌʌnfə'gɪvɪŋ/ *adj.* not forgiving.

unformed /ʌn'fɔːmd/ *adj.* **1** not formed; undeveloped. **2** shapeless.

unforthcoming /ˌʌnfɔːθ'kʌmɪŋ/ *adj.* not forthcoming.

unfortunate /ʌn'fɔːtʃənət/ –*adj.* **1** unlucky. **2** unhappy. **3** regrettable. –*n.* unfortunate person.

unfortunately *adv.* **1** (qualifying a sentence) it is unfortunate that. **2** in an unfortunate manner.

unfounded /ʌn'faʊndɪd/ *adj.* without foundation (*unfounded rumour*).

◆ **unfranked income** /ʌn'fræŋkt/ *n.* income from investments that is not franked investment income.

---

unfreeze /ʌn'friːz/ *v.* (**-zing**; *past* **unfroze**; *past part.* **unfrozen**) **1** (cause to) thaw. **2** derestrict (assets, credits, etc.).

unfriendly /ʌn'frendlɪ/ *adj.* (**-ier, -iest**) not friendly; hostile.

unfrock /ʌn'frɒk/ *v.* = DEFROCK.

unfroze *past* of UNFREEZE.

unfrozen *past part.* of UNFREEZE.

unfulfilled /ˌʌnfʊl'fɪld/ *adj.* not fulfilled.

unfunny /ʌn'fʌnɪ/ *adj.* (**-ier, -iest**) failing to amuse.

unfurl /ʌn'fɜːl/ *v.* **1** unroll, spread out (a sail, umbrella, etc.). **2** become unrolled.

unfurnished /ʌn'fɜːnɪʃt/ *adj.* **1** (usu. foll. by *with*) not supplied. **2** without furniture.

ungainly /ʌn'geɪnlɪ/ *adj.* awkward, clumsy. □ **ungainliness** *n.* [obsolete *gain* straight, from Old Norse]

ungenerous /ʌn'dʒenərəs/ *adj.* mean. □ **ungenerously** *adv.*

ungentlemanly /ʌn'dʒentəlmənlɪ/ *adj.* not gentlemanly.

unget-at-able /ˌʌnget'ætəb(ə)l/ *adj. colloq.* inaccessible.

ungird /ʌn'gɜːd/ *v.* release the girdle, belt, etc. of.

ungodly /ʌn'gɒdlɪ/ *adj.* **1** impious, wicked. **2** *colloq.* outrageous (*ungodly hour*).

ungovernable /ʌn'gʌvənəb(ə)l/ *adj.* uncontrollable, violent.

ungraceful /ʌn'greɪsfʊl/ *adj.* lacking grace or elegance. □ **ungracefully** *adv.*

ungracious /ʌn'greɪʃəs/ *adj.* discourteous; grudging. □ **ungraciously** *adv.*

ungrammatical /ˌʌngrə'mætɪk(ə)l/ *adj.* contrary to the rules of grammar. □ **ungrammatically** *adv.*

ungrateful /ʌn'greɪtfʊl/ *adj.* not feeling or showing gratitude. □ **ungratefully** *adv.*

ungreen /ʌn'griːn/ *adj.* not concerned with the protection of the environment; harmful to the environment.

ungrudging /ʌn'grʌdʒɪŋ/ *adj.* not grudging.

unguarded /ʌn'gɑːdɪd/ *adj.* **1** incautious, thoughtless (*unguarded remark*). **2** not guarded.

unguent /'ʌŋgwənt/ *n.* soft ointment or lubricant. [Latin *unguo* anoint]

ungulate /'ʌŋgjʊlət/ –*adj.* hoofed. –*n.* hoofed mammal. [Latin *ungula* hoof, claw]

unhallowed /ʌn'hæləʊd/ *adj.* **1** not consecrated. **2** not sacred, wicked.

unhampered /ʌn'hæmpəd/ *adj.* not hampered.

unhand /ʌn'hænd/ *v. rhet.* or *joc.* take one's hands off (a person); release.

unhappy /ʌn'hæpɪ/ *adj.* (**-ier, -iest**) **1** miserable. **2** unfortunate. **3** disastrous. □ **unhappily** *adv.* **unhappiness** *n.*

unharmed /ʌn'hɑːmd/ *adj.* not harmed.

unharness /ʌn'hɑːnɪs/ *v.* remove a harness from.

unhealthy /ʌn'helθɪ/ *adj.* (**-ier, -iest**) **1** in poor health. **2 a** harmful to health. **b** unwholesome. **c** *slang* dangerous. □ **unhealthily** *adv.* **unhealthiness** *n.*

unheard /ʌn'hɜːd/ *adj.* **1** not heard. **2** (usu. **unheard-of**) unprecedented.

unheeded /ʌn'hiːdɪd/ *adj.* disregarded.

unhelpful /ʌn'helpfʊl/ *adj.* not helpful. □ **unhelpfully** *adv.*

unhesitating /ʌn'hezɪˌteɪtɪŋ/ *adj.* without hesitation. □ **unhesitatingly** *adv.*

unhindered /ʌn'hɪndəd/ *adj.* not hindered.

unhinge /ʌn'hɪndʒ/ *v.* (**-ging**) **1** take (a door etc.) off its hinges. **2** (esp. as **unhinged** *adj.*) make mad or crazy.

unhistorical /ˌʌnhɪ'stɒrɪk(ə)l/ *adj.* not historical.

unhitch /ʌn'hɪtʃ/ *v.* **1** release from a hitched state. **2** unhook, unfasten.

unholy /ʌn'həʊlɪ/ *adj.* (**-ier, -iest**) **1** impious, wicked. **2** *colloq.* dreadful (*unholy row*).

unhook /ʌn'hʊk/ *v.* **1** remove from a hook or hooks. **2** unfasten the hook(s) of.

unhoped-for /ʌn'həʊptfɔː(r)/ *adj.* not hoped for or expected.

unhorse /ʌn'hɔːs/ *v.* (**-sing**) throw (a rider) from a horse.

unhurried /ʌn'hʌrɪd/ *adj.* not hurried.

unhurt /ʌn'hɜːt/ *adj.* not hurt.

unhygienic /ˌʌnhaɪ'dʒiːnɪk/ *adj.* not hygienic.

uni /'juːnɪ/ *n.* (*pl.* **-s**) esp. *Austral.* & *NZ colloq.* university. [abbreviation]

uni- *comb. form* one; having or consisting of one. [Latin *unus* one]

Uniat /'juːnɪˌæt/ (also **Uniate** /-ət/) *–adj.* of the Church in E Europe or the Near East, acknowledging papal supremacy but retaining its own liturgy etc. *–n.* member of such a Church. [Latin *unio* UNION]

unicameral /ˌjuːnɪ'kæmər(ə)l/ *adj.* with a single legislative chamber. [related to CHAMBER]

UNICEF /'juːnɪˌsef/ *abbr.* United Nations Children's (orig. International Children's Emergency) Fund.

unicellular /ˌjuːnɪ'seljʊlə(r)/ *adj.* (of an organism etc.) consisting of a single cell.

unicorn /'juːnɪˌkɔːn/ *n.* mythical horse with a single straight horn. [Latin *cornu* horn]

unicycle /'juːnɪˌsaɪk(ə)l/ *n.* single-wheeled cycle, esp. as used by acrobats. □ **unicyclist** *n.*

unidentified /ˌʌnaɪ'dentɪˌfaɪd/ *adj.* not identified.

UNIDO /juː'niːdəʊ/ *abbr.* = UNITED NATIONS INDUSTRIAL DEVELOPMENT ORGANIZATION.

unification /ˌjuːnɪfɪ'keɪʃ(ə)n/ *n.* unifying or being unified. □ **unificatory** *adj.*

Unification Church *n.* religious organization founded by Sun Myung Moon.

uniform /'juːnɪˌfɔːm/ *–adj.* **1** unvarying (*uniform appearance*). **2** conforming to the same standard, rules, etc. **3** constant over a period (*uniform acceleration*). *–n.* distinctive clothing worn by soldiers, police, schoolchildren, etc. □ **uniformed** *adj.* **uniformity** /-'fɔːmɪtɪ/ *n.* **uniformly** *adv.* [Latin: related to FORM]

unify /'juːnɪˌfaɪ/ *v.* (**-ies, -ied**) make or become united or uniform. [Latin: related to UNI-]

unilateral /ˌjuːnɪ'lætər(ə)l/ *adj.* done by or affecting only one person or party (*unilateral disarmament*). □ **unilaterally** *adv.*

unilateralism *n.* unilateral disarmament. □ **unilateralist** *n.* & *adj.*

unimaginable /ˌʌnɪ'mædʒɪnəb(ə)l/ *adj.* impossible to imagine.

unimaginative /ˌʌnɪ'mædʒɪnətɪv/ *adj.* lacking imagination; stolid, dull. □ **unimaginatively** *adv.*

unimpaired /ˌʌnɪm'peəd/ *adj.* not impaired.

unimpeachable /ˌʌnɪm'piːtʃəb(ə)l/ *adj.* beyond reproach or question.

unimpeded /ˌʌnɪm'piːdɪd/ *adj.* not impeded.

unimportant /ˌʌnɪm'pɔːt(ə)nt/ *adj.* not important.

unimpressed /ˌʌnɪm'prest/ *adj.* not impressed.

unimpressive /ˌʌnɪm'presɪv/ *adj.* not impressive.

uninformed /ˌʌnɪn'fɔːmd/ *adj.* not informed; ignorant.

uninhabitable /ˌʌnɪn'hæbɪtəb(ə)l/ *adj.* unfit for habitation.

uninhabited /ˌʌnɪn'hæbɪtɪd/ *adj.* not inhabited.

uninhibited /ˌʌnɪn'hɪbɪtɪd/ *adj.* not inhibited.

uninitiated /ˌʌnɪ'nɪʃɪˌeɪtɪd/ *adj.* not initiated, admitted, or instructed.

uninjured /ʌn'ɪndʒəd/ *adj.* not injured.

uninspired /ˌʌnɪn'spaɪəd/ *adj.* not inspired; commonplace, pedestrian.

uninspiring /ˌʌnɪn'spaɪərɪŋ/ *adj.* not inspiring.

◆ **uninsurable risk** /ˌʌnɪn'ʃʊərəb(ə)l/ see RISK *n.* 1.

unintelligent /ˌʌnɪn'telɪdʒ(ə)nt/ *adj.* not intelligent.

unintelligible /ˌʌnɪn'telɪdʒɪb(ə)l/ *adj.* not intelligible.

unintended /ˌʌnɪn'tendɪd/ *adj.* not intended.

unintentional /ˌʌnɪn'tenʃən(ə)l/ *adj.* not intentional. □ **unintentionally** *adv.*

uninterested /ʌn'ɪntrəstɪd/ *adj.* not interested; indifferent.

uninteresting /ʌn'ɪntrəstɪŋ/ *adj.* not interesting.

uninterrupted /ˌʌnɪntə'rʌptɪd/ *adj.* not interrupted.

uninvited /ˌʌnɪn'vaɪtɪd/ *adj.* not invited.

uninviting /ˌʌnɪn'vaɪtɪŋ/ *adj.* unattractive, repellent.

union /'juːnjən/ *n.* **1** uniting or being united. **2 a** whole formed from parts or members. **b** political unit so formed. **3** = TRADE UNION. **4** marriage. **5** concord (*perfect union*). **6** (**Union**) **a** university social club and (at Oxbridge) debating society. **b** buildings of this. **7** *Math.* totality of the members of two or more sets. **8** mixed fabric, e.g. cotton with linen or silk. [Latin *unus* one]

union-bashing *n. colloq.* media or government campaign against trade unions.

unionist *n.* **1 a** member of a trade union. **b** advocate of trade unions. **2** (usu. **Unionist**) member of a party advocating continued union between Great Britain and Northern Ireland. □ **unionism** *n.*

unionize *v.* (also **-ise**) (**-zing** or **-sing**) organize in or into a trade union. □ **unionization** /-'zeɪʃ(ə)n/ *n.*

Union Jack *n.* (also **Union flag**) national ensign of the United Kingdom.

Union of Soviet Socialist Republics (also **USSR, Soviet Union**) former country comprising 15 constituent republics occupying the N half of Asia and part of E Europe. It was formed in 1922, after a period of civil war following the Russian Revolution (see RUSSIA), by the

---

United Arab Emirates (former name, until 1971, **Trucial States**) federation in the Middle East, on the S coast of the Persian Gulf and the Gulf of Oman, comprising seven sheikhdoms: Abu Dhabi, Ajman, Dubai, Fujairah, Ras al-Khaimah, Sharjah, and Umm al-Qaiwain. Oil, chiefly from Abu Dhabi and Dubai, is the chief product and export; there are also large reserves of natural gas. The major heavy industries, which are related to hydrocarbons, include production of liquefied petroleum gas and oil refining. Sulphur, gypsum, and lime are also mined. Agricultural produce includes dates, tomatoes, watermelons, and tobacco, and there is a fishing industry. Food and livestock are exported. From 1892 until 1971 the emirates were British protectorates. The UAE is governed by a Supreme Council composed of the seven rulers of the member states. President, Sheikh Zayed bin Sultan al-Nahyan (of Abu Dhabi); prime minister, Sheikh Maktoum bin Rashid al-Maktoum (of Dubai); capital, Abu Dhabi.

languages	Arabic (official), Farsi, Hindi, Urdu
currency	dirham (Dh) of 100 fils
pop. (1996)	2 500 000
GNP (1993)	US$38.7B
literacy	78% (m); 79% (f)
life expectancy	69 (m); 75 (f)

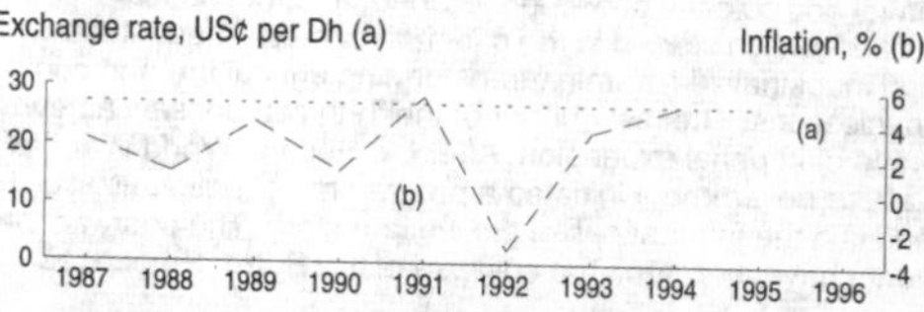

---

merging of Russia, Ukraine, Belarus, and Transcaucasia, which became constituent republics of the USSR. By 1936 the number of republics had increased to 11 by the addition of the Uzbek, Turkmen, Tajik, Kazakh, and Kirghiz SSRs (previously autonomous republics) and the separation of Transcaucasia into the Armenian, Azerbaijan, and Georgian SSRs. Between the wars Stalin ruthlessly suppressed all political opposition and reorganized the country's economy along communist lines, including state ownership of industry, collectivization of farms, and strong central planning with targets for investment, output, and construction. The German invasion of 1941 led to a long and bloody campaign in the W USSR, and by the end of the Second World War Moldavia and the Baltic States (Lithuania, Latvia, and Estonia) had become incorporated as SSRs and most E European countries were under Soviet control. In the postwar era, the USSR emerged as one of two antagonistic superpowers, rivalling the US, in the polarization of the communist and non-communist worlds. From the mid-1980s Mikhail Gorbachev sought to reform the whole communist system, with increased liberalization (glasnost) and economic changes (perestroika) that would lead to the establishment of a market economy: in 1990 the Communist Party relinquished its right to total political control. The late 1980s saw a rise in nationalist feeling and growing separatist movements in the constituent republics. In September 1991 the USSR recognized the independence of the Baltic States; by the end of the year the remaining republics had declared their independence and the USSR ceased to exist.

unique /juːˈniːk/ *adj.* **1** being the only one of its kind; having no like, equal, or parallel. **2** remarkable (*unique opportunity*). □ **uniquely** *adv.* [Latin *unicus* from *unus* one]

■ **Usage** In sense 1, *unique* cannot be qualified by adverbs such as *absolutely*, *most*, and *quite*. The use of *unique* in sense 2 is regarded as incorrect by some people.

♦ **unique selling proposition** *n.* (also **USP**) benefit that can be regarded as unique to a product and therefore can be used in advertising to differentiate it from the competition.

unisex /ˈjuːnɪˌseks/ *adj.* (of clothing, hairstyles, etc.) designed for both sexes.

unison /ˈjuːnɪs(ə)n/ *n.* **1** concord (*acted in perfect unison*). **2** coincidence in pitch of sounds or notes (*sung in unison*). [Latin *sonus* SOUND[1]]

unit /ˈjuːnɪt/ *n.* **1 a** individual thing, person, or group, esp. for calculation. **b** smallest component of a complex whole. **2** quantity as a standard of measurement (*unit of heat; SI unit*). **3** smallest share in a unit trust. **4** part of a mechanism with a specified function. **5** fitted item of furniture, esp. as part of a set. **6** subgroup with a special function. **7** group of buildings, wards, etc., in a hospital. **8 a** single-digit number. **b** the number 'one'. [Latin *unus* one]

UNITAR *abbr.* United Nations Institute for Training and Research.

Unitarian /ˌjuːnɪˈteərɪən/ –*n.* **1** person who believes that God is one, not a Trinity. **2** member of a religious body so believing. –*adj.* of Unitarians. □ **Unitarianism** *n.* [Latin *unitas* UNITY]

unitary /ˈjuːnɪtərɪ/ *adj.* **1** of a unit or units. **2** marked by unity or uniformity. [from UNIT or UNITY]

♦ **unit cost** *n.* cost of a unit of production. Examples include the cost of one refrigerator made by a refrigerator manufacturer or, in the case of a manufacturer who makes components, the cost of one component. In the case of a railway, it might be the cost of one passenger mile.

unite /jʊˈnaɪt/ *v.* (**-ting**) **1** join together; combine, esp. for a common purpose or action (*united in their struggle*). **2** join in marriage. **3** (cause to) form a physical or chemical whole (*oil will not unite with water*). [Latin *unio -it-* from *unus* one]

United Nations *n.pl.* (as *sing.* or *pl.*) (also **UN**) supranational peace-seeking organization formed in 1945.

♦ **United Nations Common Fund for Commodities** (also **CFC**) see UNITED NATIONS CONFERENCE ON TRADE AND DEVELOPMENT.

♦ **United Nations Conference on Trade and Development** *n.* (also **UNCTAD**) permanent organization set up by the UN in 1964 to encourage international trade, esp. to help developing countries to finance

United Kingdom (also **UK**, in full **United Kingdom of Great Britain and Northern Ireland**) country in NW Europe, comprising Great Britain and Northern Ireland. The economy is based on manufacturing industry. The traditional heavy industries, such as shipbuilding, coalmining, steelmaking, and motor-vehicle manufacture, have declined as a result of falling demand, an increase in imports, and foreign competition. Modern light industries, esp. making use of advanced technology, have been developed or expanded to replace them. Financial services are also important to the economy. Natural resources include coal, iron ore, tin, lead ore, potash, china clay, and salt; production of North Sea oil and gas, which began in the 1970s, remains an important source of revenue. The agricultural sector has benefited from an increase in productivity due to intensive farming methods; sheep and cattle are reared in the N and W (including Scotland and Wales), while arable farming (producing cereals, vegetables, fruit, sugar beet, etc.) and horticulture are concentrated in the E and SE. Other industries include fishing (esp. on the NE coast), forestry (in Scotland and Wales), and tourism.
History. Great Britain and Ireland were united in 1801 to form the United Kingdom of Great Britain and Ireland; the country assumed its present name in 1922, after the partition of Ireland. In the 18th century Great Britain had been the leading naval and colonial power in the world, and the Industrial Revolution, which started in the mid-18th century, made it the first industrialized country, transforming agriculture and communications. The last quarter of the 19th century saw a new wave of imperial expansion. After the Second World War the Labour government initiated a programme of nationalization and laid the foundations of the welfare state. The postwar years have also seen the collapse of the British Empire, as former colonies have gained independence, and immigration from Commonwealth countries has made Britain a multiracial society. The UK became a member of the EC (now EU) in 1973. The Conservative government, elected in 1979, pursued a policy of privatization and restructuring of the provisions of the welfare state. A period of economic prosperity in the 1980s was followed by severe recession in the early 1990s. The mid-1990s saw some measure of economic recovery. In 1997 the Labour Party enjoyed a landslide victory in the general election. Referendums held in 1997 endorsed plans for a separate Scottish parliament and a Welsh assembly. In 1998 a new settlement for the strife-torn province of Northern Ireland was agreed by most of the Northern Irish parties: it will now be put to referendums on both sides of the Irish border. Head of state, Queen Elizabeth II; prime minister, Anthony Blair; capital, London. See also ENGLAND; IRELAND; NORTHERN IRELAND; SCOTLAND; WALES.

languages	English (official), Welsh, Gaelic
currency	pound (£) of 100 pence
pop. (1996)	58 784 000
GNP (1994)	US$1069.4B
literacy	99%
life expectancy	74 (m); 79 (f)

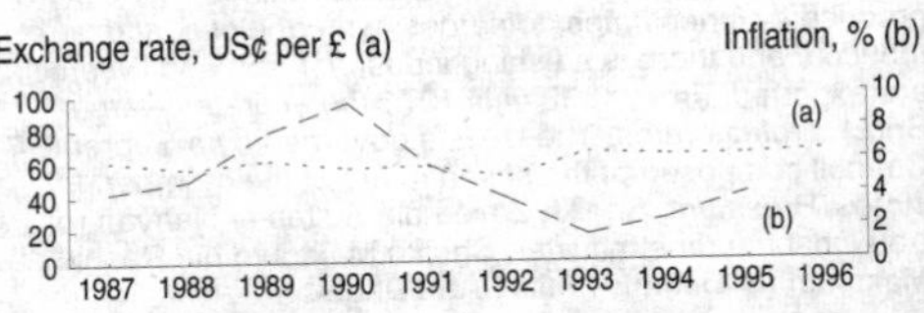

their exports. Under its auspices the **UN Common Fund for Commodities (CFC)** was established in 1989 to provide finance for international commodity organizations to enable buffer stocks to be maintained and to carry out research into the development of commodity markets.

♦ **United Nations Industrial Development Organization** *n.* (also **UNIDO**) international organization that became a specialized agency of the UN in 1986, having developed from the Centre for Industrial Development, set up in 1961. With headquarters in Vienna, its aim is to promote the industrialization of developing countries, with special emphasis on the manufacturing sector. It provides planning policies and technical advice and assistance for Third World countries.

United Reformed Church *n.* Church formed in 1972 from the English Presbyterian and Congregational Churches.

♦ **unitize** /ˈjuːnɪˌtaɪz/ *v.* (also **-ise**) (**-zing** or **-sing**) convert an investment trust into a unit trust. □ **unitization** /-ˈzeɪʃ(ə)n/ *n.*

♦ **unit labour costs** *n.pl.* total expenditure on labour per unit of output. A comparison between changes in productivity and unit labour costs in different countries enables economists to make predictions about changes in their competitiveness. For example, if unit labour costs and productivity both rise by the same amount in the UK, UK producers do not have to change the prices of their goods; if, however, Japanese unit labour costs rise by less than productivity, Japanese prices could fall, making them increasingly competitive.

♦ **unit-linked policy** *n.* life-assurance policy in which the benefits depend on the performance of a portfolio of shares. Each premium paid by the insured person is split: one part is used to provide life-assurance cover, while the balance (after the deduction of costs, expenses, etc.) is used to buy units in a unit trust. In this way a small investor can benefit from investment in a managed fund without making a large financial commitment. As they are linked to the value of shares, unit-linked policies can go up or down in value. Policyholders can surrender the policy at any time and the surrender value is the selling price of the units purchased by the date of cancellation (less expenses). Until the 1970s the profits on with-profits life-assurance policies were determined by the size of the bonus given at the discretion of the life-assurance company; this depended on their investment success and their profits in any particular year. Unit-linked policies, involving unitized portfolios, have produced higher benefits for policyholders than those that rely on with-profits bonuses. There has therefore been a widespread increase in **unit-linked savings plans**, both with and without life-assurance cover.

♦ **unit of account** *n.* **1** *Econ.* a function of money enabling its users to calculate the value of their transactions and to keep accounts (cf. STORE OF VALUE). **2** standard unit of currency of a country. **3** artificial currency used only for accounting purposes; the EC employs such a unit for fixing its farm prices (see GREEN CURRENCIES).

---

unit price *n.* price charged for each unit of goods supplied, e.g. per item, per pound, per container, etc.

♦ **unit pricing** *n.* practice of showing the price of a single unit of a product in order that shoppers can see the advantage of buying a multipack.

♦ **unit profit (**or **loss)** *n.* profit (or loss) attributable to one unit of production. See UNIT COST.

♦ **unit trust** *n.* trust formed to manage a portfolio of stock-exchange securities, in which small investors can buy units. This gives the small investor access to a diversified portfolio of securities, chosen and managed by professional fund managers, who seek either high capital gains or high yields, within the parameters of reasonable security. The trustees, usu. a commercial bank, are the legal owners of the securities and responsible for ensuring that the managers keep to the terms laid down in the trust deed. Prices of unit trusts are quoted daily, the difference between the bid and offer prices providing a margin for the management costs and the costs of buying and selling on the London Stock Exchange. Basic-rate tax is deducted from the dividends paid by unit trusts and capital gains on the sale of a holding are subject to capital-gains tax, although transactions involved in creating the portfolio are free of capital-gains tax. UK unit trusts are authorized and controlled by the Department of Trade and

---

United States (also **US**, in full **United States of America**) country occupying most of the S half of North America and also including Alaska in the N and Hawaii in the Pacific Ocean. It comprises 50 states and the Federal District of Columbia. The economy is based on manufacturing industry and the exploitation of the country's rich natural resources, which have until recently provided nearly all the raw materials required for industrial and domestic use. These include coal, oil, natural gas, iron ore, zinc ore, aluminium, lead, copper, sulphur, and phosphates; petroleum is increasingly imported. Manufacturing industry produces motor vehicles, aircraft, machinery, consumer goods, and chemicals for export. The agricultural sector of the economy is also important, with highly mechanized farming methods and efficient pest-control techniques. Cereals are the main agricultural export; cotton, tobacco, soya beans, potatoes, and oranges are also grown, and livestock (including cattle, sheep, pigs, and chickens) are raised. In 1992 the US concluded a free-trade agreement with Canada and Mexico (NAFTA: see NORTH AMERICAN FREE TRADE AGREEMENT).

History. The E coast of North America was colonized by the British in the 17th century, while the S was penetrated by the Spanish from Mexico and the centre taken possession of by the French. The modern US grew out of the successful rebellion of the E coast colonies against British rule in 1775–83. The Louisiana territory was purchased from France in 1803 and the SW was taken from Mexico after the war of 1846–8. The second half of the 19th century saw the gradual opening up of the W half of the country. In the 20th century the United States has been the world's principal economic power, participating on the Allied side in both World Wars and becoming one of the two antagonistic superpowers, dominating the non-communist world in the era following the Second World War until the end of the Cold War in 1990; during the period 1945–90 US opposition to Communism resulted in engagement in two wars (Korea and Vietnam) and investment of vast amounts of money in armaments. Domestic problems of recent years have included racial unrest and economic decline, which began in the 1970s and was exacerbated by the worldwide recession of the early 1990s; however, the economy had recovered somewhat by the mid-1990s, despite the relocation of many American manufacturers to other countries (such as Mexico) in search of cheaper labour. In 1997–8 Bill Clinton, elected president in 1993 and subsequently reelected in 1996, faced persistent allegations of sexual impropriety, but remained generally popular. President, Bill Clinton; capital, Washington, DC.

languages	English (official), Spanish
currency	dollar (US$) of 100 cents
pop. (1996)	265 455 000
GNP (1994)	US$7237.5B
literacy	99%
life expectancy	70 (m); 77 (f)

Inflation, %

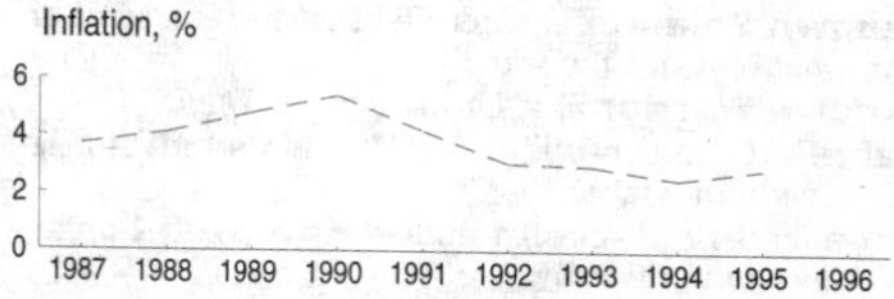

6
4
2
0
1987 1988 1989 1990 1991 1992 1993 1994 1995 1996

Industry and most belong to the Unit Trust Association. Many trusts are now available, specializing in various sectors of the market, both at home and abroad; there is also a wide spectrum of trusts catering for both those seeking growth and those seeking income. See also UNIT-LINKED POLICY.

♦ **Unit Trust Association** *n.* (also **UTA**) association formed to agree standards of practice for the managers of unit trusts for the protection of unit-trust holders and to act as the representative body of **Managers of Authorized Unit Trusts** in dealings with the government and other authorities. It also coordinates control of commissions and charges and has a register of approved agents for selling unit trusts as intermediaries.

---

unity /'juːnɪtɪ/ *n.* (*pl.* **-ies**) **1 a** oneness; being one; interconnected parts constituting a whole (*national unity*). **b** such a complex whole (*person regarded as a unity*). **2** harmony (*lived together in unity*). **3** the number 'one'. [Latin *unus* one]

univalent /ˌjuːnɪ'veɪlənt/ *adj.* having a valency of one. [from UNI-, VALENCE[1]]

univalve /'juːnɪˌvælv/ *Zool.* –*adj.* having one valve. –*n.* univalve mollusc.

universal /ˌjuːnɪ'vɜːs(ə)l/ –*adj.* of, belonging to, or done etc. by all; applicable to all cases. –*n.* term, characteristic, or concept of general application. □ **universality** /-'sælɪtɪ/ *n.* **universally** *adv.* [Latin: related to UNIVERSE]

♦ **universal banking** *n.* banking that involves not only services related to loans and savings but also those involved in making investments.

---

universal coupling *n.* (also **universal joint**) coupling or joint which can transmit rotary power by a shaft at any angle.

universal time *n.* = GREENWICH MEAN TIME.

universe /'juːnɪˌvɜːs/ *n.* **1** all existing things; Creation. **2** all mankind. **3** *Statistics* & *Logic* all the objects under consideration. [Latin *universus* combined into one]

university /ˌjuːnɪ'vɜːsɪtɪ/ *n.* (*pl.* **-ies**) **1** educational institution of advanced learning and research conferring degrees. **2** members of this. [Latin: related to UNIVERSE]

UNIX /'juːnɪks/ *n. propr.* computer operating system used on a very wide range of computer systems. See OPERATING SYSTEM.

unjust /ʌn'dʒʌst/ *adj.* not just, not fair. □ **unjustly** *adv.* **unjustness** *n.*

unjustifiable /ʌn'dʒʌstɪˌfaɪəb(ə)l/ *adj.* not justifiable. □ **unjustifiably** *adv.*

unjustified /ʌn'dʒʌstɪˌfaɪd/ *adj.* not justified.

unkempt /ʌn'kempt/ *adj.* untidy, dishevelled. [= *uncombed*]

unkind /ʌn'kaɪnd/ *adj.* not kind; harsh, cruel. □ **unkindly** *adv.* **unkindness** *n.*

unknot /ʌn'nɒt/ *v.* (**-tt-**) release the knot(s) of, untie.

unknowable /ʌn'nəʊəb(ə)l/ –*adj.* that cannot be known. –*n.* **1** unknowable thing. **2** (**the Unknowable**) the postulated absolute or ultimate reality.

unknowing /ʌn'nəʊɪŋ/ *adj.* (often foll. by *of*) not knowing; ignorant, unconscious. □ **unknowingly** *adv.*

unknown /ʌn'nəʊn/ –*adj.* (often foll. by *to*) not known, unfamiliar. –*n.* unknown thing, person, or quantity. □ **unknown to** without the knowledge of (*did it unknown to me*).

unknown quantity *n.* mysterious or obscure person or thing.

Unknown Soldier *n.* unidentified soldier etc. symbolizing a nation's dead in war.

Unknown Warrior *n.* = UNKNOWN SOLDIER.

unlabelled /ʌn'leɪb(ə)ld/ *adj.* (*US* **unlabeled**) not labelled; without a label.

unlace /ʌn'leɪs/ *v.* (**-cing**) **1** undo the lace(s) of. **2** unfasten or loosen in this way.

unladen /ʌn'leɪd(ə)n/ *adj.* not laden.

unladen weight *n.* weight of a vehicle etc. when not loaded.

unladylike /ʌn'leɪdɪˌlaɪk/ *adj.* not ladylike.

unlatch /ʌn'lætʃ/ *v.* **1** release the latch of. **2** open in this way.

unlawful /ʌn'lɔːfʊl/ *adj.* illegal, not permissible. □ **unlawfully** *adv.*

unleaded /ʌn'ledɪd/ *adj.* (of petrol etc.) without added lead.

unlearn /ʌn'lɜːn/ *v.* (*past* and *past part.* **unlearned** or **unlearnt**) **1** forget deliberately. **2** rid oneself of (a habit, false information, etc.).

unlearned[1] /ʌn'lɜːnɪd/ *adj.* not well educated; ignorant.

unlearned[2] /ʌn'lɜːnd/ *adj.* (also **unlearnt** /-'lɜːnt/) not learnt.

unleash /ʌn'liːʃ/ *v.* **1** release from a leash or restraint. **2** set free to engage in pursuit or attack.

unleavened /ʌn'lev(ə)nd/ *adj.* not leavened; made without yeast etc.

unless /ʌn'les/ *conj.* if not; except when (*shall go unless I hear from you*). [= *on less*]

unlettered /ʌn'letəd/ *adj.* illiterate; not well educated.

unlicensed /ʌn'laɪs(ə)nst/ *adj.* not licensed, esp. to sell alcohol.

unlike /ʌn'laɪk/ –*adj.* **1** not like; different from. **2** uncharacteristic of (*greed is unlike her*). **3** dissimilar, different. –*prep.* differently from (*acts quite unlike anyone else*).

unlikely /ʌn'laɪklɪ/ *adj.* (**-ier, -iest**) **1** improbable (*unlikely tale*). **2** (foll. by *to* + infin.) not expected (*unlikely to die*). **3** unpromising (*unlikely candidate*). □ **unlikeliness** *n.*

unlike signs *n.pl. Math.* plus and minus.

unlimited /ʌn'lɪmɪtɪd/ *adj.* unrestricted; enormous (*unlimited expanse*).

♦ **unlimited company** *n.* company in which the liability of the members for the company's debts is not limited in any way. Cf. LIMITED COMPANY.

---

unlined[1] /ʌn'laɪnd/ *adj.* without lines or wrinkles.

unlined[2] /ʌn'laɪnd/ *adj.* without a lining.

♦ **unliquidated damages** see DAMAGES.

---

unlisted /ʌn'lɪstɪd/ *adj.* not in a published list, esp. of Stock Exchange prices or telephone numbers.

♦ **unlisted securities** *n.pl.* securities (usu. equities) in companies that are not on an official stock-exchange list. They are therefore not required to satisfy the standards set for listing (see LISTED SECURITY). Unlisted securities are usu. issued in relatively small companies and their shares usu. carry a high degree of risk. In London, unlisted securities are traded on the unlisted securities market (USM). For full listing a company has to have a capital of at least £700,000 and 25% of the equity has to be available to the public. For unlisted securities the capital may be below this figure and only 10% of the equity need by available for purchase on the USM.

♦ **unlisted securities market** *n.* (also **USM**) former market established by the London Stock Exchange to trade in the shares of small companies. It was replaced by the ALTERNATIVE INVESTMENT MARKET in 1995.

---

unlit /ʌn'lɪt/ *adj.* not lit.

unload /ʌn'ləʊd/ *v.* **1** (also *absol.*) remove a load from (a vehicle etc.). **2** remove (a load) from a vehicle etc. **3** remove the ammunition from (a gun etc.). **4** *colloq.* get rid of.

unlock /ʌn'lɒk/ *v.* **1 a** release the lock of (a door, box, etc.). **b** release or disclose by unlocking. **2** release thoughts, feelings, etc. from (one's mind etc.).

unlooked-for /ʌn'lʊktfɔː(r)/ *adj.* unexpected.

unloose /ʌn'luːs/ *v.* (**-sing**) (also **unloosen**) loose; set free.

unlovable /ʌn'lʌvəb(ə)l/ *adj.* not lovable.

unloved /ʌn'lʌvd/ *adj.* not loved.

unlovely /ʌn'lʌvlɪ/ *adj.* not attractive; unpleasant.

unloving /ʌn'lʌvɪŋ/ *adj.* not loving.

unlucky /ʌn'lʌkɪ/ *adj.* (**-ier, -iest**) **1** not fortunate or successful. **2** wretched. **3** bringing bad luck. **4** ill-judged. □ **unluckily** *adv.*

unmade /ʌn'meɪd/ *adj.* (esp. of a bed) not made.

unmake /ʌn'meɪk/ *v.* (**-king**; *past* and *past part.* **unmade**) undo; destroy, depose, annul.

unman /ʌn'mæn/ *v.* (**-nn-**) make weak, cowardly, etc.; cause to weep etc.

unmanageable /ʌn'mænɪdʒəb(ə)l/ *adj.* not easily managed or controlled.

unmanly /ʌn'mænlɪ/ *adj.* not manly.

unmanned /ʌn'mænd/ *adj.* **1** not manned. **2** overcome by emotion etc.

unmannerly /ʌn'mænəlɪ/ *adj.* ill-mannered. □ **unmannerliness** *n.*

unmarked /ʌn'mɑːkt/ *adj.* **1** not marked. **2** not noticed.

unmarried /ʌn'mærɪd/ *adj.* not married, single.

unmask /ʌn'mɑːsk/ *v.* **1 a** remove the mask from. **b** expose the true character of. **2** remove one's mask.

unmatched /ʌn'mætʃt/ *adj.* not matched or equalled.

unmentionable /ʌn'menʃənəb(ə)l/ *–adj.* unsuitable for polite conversation. *–n.* (in *pl.*) *joc.* undergarments.

unmerciful /ʌn'mɜːsɪˌfʊl/ *adj.* merciless. □ **unmercifully** *adv.*

unmerited /ʌn'merɪtɪd/ *adj.* not merited.

unmet /ʌn'met/ *adj.* (of a demand, goal, etc.) not achieved or fulfilled.

unmethodical /ˌʌnmɪ'θɒdɪk(ə)l/ *adj.* not methodical.

unmindful /ʌn'maɪndfʊl/ *adj.* (often foll. by *of*) not mindful.

unmissable /ʌn'mɪsəb(ə)l/ *adj.* that cannot or should not be missed.

unmistakable /ˌʌnmɪ'steɪkəb(ə)l/ *adj.* clear, obvious, plain. □ **unmistakably** *adv.*

unmitigated /ʌn'mɪtɪˌgeɪtɪd/ *adj.* not mitigated; absolute (*unmitigated disaster*).

unmixed /ʌn'mɪkst/ *adj.* not mixed.

unmodified /ʌn'mɒdɪˌfaɪd/ *adj.* not modified.

unmoral /ʌn'mɒr(ə)l/ *adj.* not concerned with morality (cf. IMMORAL). □ **unmorality** /ˌʌnmə'rælɪtɪ/ *n.*

unmoved /ʌn'muːvd/ *adj.* **1** not moved. **2** constant in purpose. **3** unemotional.

unmusical /ʌn'mjuːzɪk(ə)l/ *adj.* **1** discordant. **2** unskilled in or indifferent to music.

unnameable /ʌn'neɪməb(ə)l/ *adj.* too bad to be named or mentioned.

unnamed /ʌn'neɪmd/ *adj.* not named.

unnatural /ʌn'nætʃər(ə)l/ *adj.* **1** contrary to nature; not normal. **2** lacking natural feelings, esp. cruel or wicked. **3** artificial. **4** affected. □ **unnaturally** *adv.*

unnecessary /ʌn'nesəsərɪ/ *adj.* **1** not necessary. **2** superfluous. □ **unnecessarily** *adv.*

unneeded /ʌn'niːdɪd/ *adj.* not needed.

unnerve /ʌn'nɜːv/ *v.* (**-ving**) deprive of confidence etc.

unnoticeable /ʌn'nəʊtɪsəb(ə)l/ *adj.* not easily seen or noticed.

unnoticed /ʌn'nəʊtɪst/ *adj.* not noticed.

unnumbered /ʌn'nʌmbəd/ *adj.* **1** without a number. **2** not counted. **3** countless.

unobjectionable /ˌʌnəb'dʒekʃənəb(ə)l/ *adj.* not objectionable; acceptable.

unobservant /ˌʌnəb'zɜːv(ə)nt/ *adj.* not observant.

unobserved /ˌʌnəb'zɜːvd/ *adj.* not observed.

unobtainable /ˌʌnəb'teɪnəb(ə)l/ *adj.* that cannot be obtained.

unobtrusive /ˌʌnəb'truːsɪv/ *adj.* not making oneself or itself noticed. □ **unobtrusively** *adv.*

unoccupied /ʌn'ɒkjʊˌpaɪd/ *adj.* not occupied.

unofficial /ˌʌnə'fɪʃ(ə)l/ *adj.* not officially authorized or confirmed. □ **unofficially** *adv.*

unofficial strike *n.* strike not ratified by the strikers' trade union.

unopened /ʌn'əʊpənd/ *adj.* not opened.

unopposed /ˌʌnə'pəʊzd/ *adj.* not opposed.

unorganized /ʌn'ɔːgəˌnaɪzd/ *adj.* (also **-ised**) not organized.

unoriginal /ˌʌnə'rɪdʒɪn(ə)l/ *adj.* lacking originality; derivative.

unorthodox /ʌn'ɔːθəˌdɒks/ *adj.* not orthodox.

unpack /ʌn'pæk/ *v.* **1** (also *absol.*) open and empty (a package, luggage, etc.). **2** take (a thing) from a package etc.

unpaid /ʌn'peɪd/ *adj.* (of a debt or a person) not paid.

unpainted /ʌn'peɪntɪd/ *adj.* not painted.

unpaired /ʌn'peəd/ *adj.* **1** not being one of a pair. **2** not united or arranged in pairs.

unpalatable /ʌn'pælətəb(ə)l/ *adj.* (of food, an idea, suggestion, etc.) disagreeable, distasteful.

unparalleled /ʌn'pærəˌleld/ *adj.* unequalled.

unpardonable /ʌn'pɑːdənəb(ə)l/ *adj.* that cannot be pardoned. □ **unpardonably** *adv.*

unparliamentary /ˌʌnpɑːlə'mentərɪ/ *adj.* contrary to proper parliamentary usage.

unparliamentary language *n.* oaths or abuse.

unpasteurized /ʌn'pɑːstʃəˌraɪzd/ *adj.* (also **-ised**) not pasteurized.

unpatriotic /ˌʌnpætrɪ'ɒtɪk/ *adj.* not patriotic.

unperson /'ʌnˌpɜːs(ə)n/ *n.* person said not to exist, esp. by the state.

unperturbed /ˌʌnpə'tɜːbd/ *adj.* not perturbed.

unpick /ʌn'pɪk/ *v.* undo the sewing of (stitches, a garment, etc.).

unpin /ʌn'pɪn/ *v.* (**-nn-**) unfasten or detach by removing or opening a pin or pins.

unplaced /ʌn'pleɪst/ *adj.* not placed, esp. not one of the first three in a race etc.

unplanned /ʌn'plænd/ *adj.* not planned.

unplayable /ʌn'pleɪəb(ə)l/ *adj.* **1** *Sport* (of a ball) too fast etc. to be returned. **2** that cannot be played.

unpleasant /ʌn'plez(ə)nt/ *adj.* not pleasant, disagreeable. □ **unpleasantly** *adv.* **unpleasantness** *n.*

unpleasing /ʌn'pliːzɪŋ/ *adj.* not pleasing.

unplug /ʌn'plʌg/ *v.* (**-gg-**) **1** disconnect (an electrical device) by removing its plug from the socket. **2** unstop.

unplumbed /ʌn'plʌmd/ *adj.* **1** not plumbed. **2** not fully explored or understood.

unpointed /ʌn'pɔɪntɪd/ *adj.* **1** having no point or points. **2** not punctuated. **3** (of brickwork etc.) not pointed.

unpolished /ʌn'pɒlɪʃt/ *adj.* not polished or refined; rough.

unpolitical /ˌʌnpə'lɪtɪk(ə)l/ *adj.* not concerned with politics.

unpopular /ʌn'pɒpjʊlə(r)/ *adj.* not popular; disliked. □ **unpopularity** /-'lærɪtɪ/ *n.*

unpopulated /ʌn'pɒpjʊˌleɪtɪd/ *adj.* not populated.

unpractical /ʌn'præktɪk(ə)l/ *adj.* **1** not practical. **2** (of a person) without practical skill.

unpractised /ʌn'præktɪst/ *adj.* (*US* **unpracticed**) **1** not experienced or skilled. **2** not put into practice.

unprecedented /ʌn'presɪˌdentɪd/ *adj.* having no precedent; unparalleled. □ **unprecedentedly** *adv.*

unpredictable /ˌʌnprɪ'dɪktəb(ə)l/ *adj.* that cannot be predicted. □ **unpredictability** /-'bɪlɪtɪ/ *n.* **unpredictably** *adv.*

unprejudiced /ʌn'predʒʊdɪst/ *adj.* not prejudiced.

unpremeditated /ˌʌnpriː'medɪˌteɪtɪd/ *adj.* not deliberately planned, unintentional.

unprepared /ˌʌnprɪ'peəd/ *adj.* not prepared; not ready.

unprepossessing /ˌʌnpriːpə'zesɪŋ/ *adj.* unattractive.

unpretentious /ˌʌnprɪ'tenʃəs/ *adj.* simple, modest, unassuming.

unpriced /ʌn'praɪst/ *adj.* not having a price fixed, marked, or stated.

unprincipled /ʌn'prɪnsɪp(ə)ld/ *adj.* lacking or not based on moral principles.

unprintable /ʌn'prɪntəb(ə)l/ *adj.* too offensive or indecent to be printed.

unproductive /ˌʌnprə'dʌktɪv/ *adj.* not productive.

unprofessional /ˌʌnprə'feʃən(ə)l/ *adj.* **1** contrary to professional standards. **2** unskilled, amateurish. □ **unprofessionally** *adv.*

unprofitable /ʌn'prɒfɪtəb(ə)l/ *adj.* not profitable.

unprogressive /ˌʌnprə'gresɪv/ *adj.* not progressive, old-fashioned.

unpromising /ʌn'prɒmɪsɪŋ/ *adj.* not likely to turn out well.

unprompted /ʌn'prɒmptɪd/ *adj.* spontaneous.

unpronounceable /ˌʌnprə'naʊnsəb(ə)l/ *adj.* that cannot be pronounced.

unpropitious /ˌʌnprə'pɪʃəs/ *adj.* not propitious.

unprotected /ˌʌnprə'tektɪd/ *adj.* not protected.

unprovable /ʌn'pruːvəb(ə)l/ *adj.* that cannot be proved.

unproved /ʌn'pruːvd/ *adj.* (also **unproven** /-v(ə)n/) not proved.

unprovoked /ˌʌnprə'vəʊkt/ *adj.* without provocation.

unpublished /ʌn'pʌblɪʃt/ *adj.* not published.

unpunctual /ʌn'pʌŋktʃʊəl/ *adj.* not punctual.

unpunished /ʌn'pʌnɪʃt/ *adj.* not punished.

unputdownable /ˌʌnpʊt'daʊnəb(ə)l/ *adj. colloq.* (of a book) compulsively readable.

unqualified /ʌn'kwɒlɪˌfaɪd/ *adj.* **1** not legally or officially qualified. **2** complete (*unqualified success*). **3** not competent (*unqualified to say*).

unquenchable /ʌn'kwentʃəb(ə)l/ *adj.* that cannot be quenched.

unquestionable /ʌn'kwestʃənəb(ə)l/ *adj.* that cannot be disputed or doubted. □ **unquestionably** *adv.*

unquestioned /ʌn'kwestʃ(ə)nd/ *adj.* not disputed or doubted; definite, certain.

unquestioning /ʌn'kwestʃənɪŋ/ *adj.* **1** asking no questions. **2** (of obedience etc.) absolute. □ **unquestioningly** *adv.*

unquiet /ʌn'kwaɪət/ *adj.* **1** restless, agitated. **2** anxious.

unquote /ʌn'kwəʊt/ *v.* (as *int.*) verbal formula indicating closing quotation marks.

♦ **unquoted securities** *n.pl.* securities that are not dealt in on any stock exchange. On the London Stock Exchange there are rules for occasional unofficial trading in unquoted securities of small companies or new ventures. Unquoted securities are usu. shown in balance sheets valued at cost or market value (if this can be ascertained).

---

unravel /ʌn'ræv(ə)l/ *v.* (**-ll-**; *US* **-l-**) **1** make or become disentangled, unknitted, unknotted, etc. **2** probe and solve (a mystery etc.). **3** undo (esp. knitted fabric).

unread /ʌn'red/ *adj.* **1** (of a book etc.) not read. **2** (of a person) not well-read.

unreadable /ʌn'riːdəb(ə)l/ *adj.* too dull, bad, or difficult to read.

unready /ʌn'redɪ/ *adj.* **1** not ready. **2** hesitant.

unreal /ʌn'rɪəl/ *adj.* **1** not real. **2** imaginary. **3** *slang* incredible. □ **unreality** /-ɪ'ælɪtɪ/ *n.*

unrealistic /ˌʌnrɪə'lɪstɪk/ *adj.* not realistic. □ **unrealistically** *adv.*

unrealizable /ʌn'rɪəlaɪzəb(ə)l/ *adj.* (also **-isable**) that cannot be realized.

unrealized /ʌn'rɪəlaɪzd/ *adj.* (also **-ised**) not realized.

unreason /ʌn'riːz(ə)n/ *n.* madness; chaos; disorder.

unreasonable /ʌn'riːzənəb(ə)l/ *adj.* **1** excessive (*unreasonable demands*). **2** not heeding reason. □ **unreasonably** *adv.*

unreasoning /ʌn'riːzənɪŋ/ *adj.* not reasoning.

unrecognizable /ʌn'rekəgˌnaɪzəb(ə)l/ *adj.* (also **-isable**) that cannot be recognized.

unrecognized /ʌn'rekəgˌnaɪzd/ *adj.* (also **-ised**) not acknowledged.

unrecorded /ˌʌnrɪ'kɔːdɪd/ *adj.* not recorded.

unreel /ʌn'riːl/ *v.* unwind from a reel.

unrefined /ˌʌnrɪ'faɪnd/ *adj.* not refined.

unreflecting /ˌʌnrɪ'flektɪŋ/ *adj.* not thoughtful.

unreformed /ˌʌnrɪ'fɔːmd/ *adj.* not reformed.

unregenerate /ˌʌnrɪ'dʒenərət/ *adj.* obstinately wrong or bad.

unregistered /ʌn'redʒɪstəd/ *adj.* not registered.

unregulated /ʌn'regjʊˌleɪtɪd/ *adj.* not regulated.

unrehearsed /ˌʌnrɪ'hɜːst/ *adj.* not rehearsed.

unrelated /ˌʌnrɪ'leɪtɪd/ *adj.* not related.

unrelenting /ˌʌnrɪ'lentɪŋ/ *adj.* not abating, yielding, or relaxing; unmerciful. □ **unrelentingly** *adv.*

unreliable /ˌʌnrɪ'laɪəb(ə)l/ *adj.* not reliable; erratic. □ **unreliability** /-'bɪlɪtɪ/ *n.*

unrelieved /ˌʌnrɪ'liːvd/ *adj.* monotonously uniform.

unremarkable /ˌʌnrɪ'mɑːkəb(ə)l/ *adj.* not remarkable; uninteresting, ordinary.

unremarked /ˌʌnrɪ'mɑːkt/ *adj.* not mentioned or remarked upon.

unremitting /ˌʌnrɪ'mɪtɪŋ/ *adj.* incessant. □ **unremittingly** *adv.*

unremunerative /ˌʌnrɪ'mjuːnərətɪv/ *adj.* not, or not very, profitable.

unrepeatable /ˌʌnrɪ'piːtəb(ə)l/ *adj.* **1** that cannot be done, made, or said again. **2** too indecent to repeat.

unrepentant /ˌʌnrɪ'pent(ə)nt/ *adj.* not repentant, impenitent. □ **unrepentantly** *adv.*

unrepresentative /ˌʌnreprɪ'zentətɪv/ *adj.* not representative.

unrepresented /ˌʌnreprɪ'zentɪd/ *adj.* not represented.

unrequited /ˌʌnrɪ'kwaɪtɪd/ *adj.* (of love etc.) not returned.

unreserved /ˌʌnrɪ'zɜːvd/ *adj.* **1** not reserved. **2** total; without reservation. □ **unreservedly** /-vɪdlɪ/ *adv.*

unresisting /ˌʌnrɪ'zɪstɪŋ/ *adj.* not resisting.

unresolved /ˌʌnrɪ'zɒlvd/ *adj.* **1** irresolute, undecided. **2** (of questions etc.) undetermined.

unresponsive /ˌʌnrɪ'spɒnsɪv/ *adj.* not responsive.

unrest /ʌn'rest/ *n.* disturbed or dissatisfied state (*industrial unrest*).

unrestrained /ˌʌnrɪ'streɪnd/ *adj.* not restrained.

unrestricted /ˌʌnrɪ'strɪktɪd/ *adj.* not restricted.

unrewarded /ˌʌnrɪ'wɔːdɪd/ *adj.* not rewarded.

unrewarding /ˌʌnrɪ'wɔːdɪŋ/ *adj.* not rewarding or satisfying.

unrighteous /ʌn'raɪtʃəs/ *adj.* wicked.

unripe /ʌn'raɪp/ *adj.* not ripe.

unrivalled /ʌn'raɪv(ə)ld/ *adj.* (*US* **unrivaled**) having no equal.

unroll /ʌn'rəʊl/ *v.* **1** open out from a rolled-up state. **2** display or be displayed like this.

unromantic /ˌʌnrə'mæntɪk/ *adj.* not romantic.

unruffled /ʌn'rʌf(ə)ld/ *adj.* calm.

unruly /ʌn'ruːlɪ/ *adj.* (**-ier, -iest**) undisciplined, disorderly. □ **unruliness** *n.* [related to RULE]

unsaddle /ʌn'sæd(ə)l/ *v.* (**-ling**) **1** remove the saddle from. **2** unhorse.

unsafe /ʌn'seɪf/ *adj.* not safe.

unsaid /ʌn'sed/ *adj.* not uttered or expressed (*left it unsaid*).

unsaleable /ʌn'seɪləb(ə)l/ *adj.* not saleable.

unsalted /ʌn'sɔːltɪd/ *adj.* not salted.

unsatisfactory /ˌʌnsætɪs'fæktərɪ/ *adj.* poor, unacceptable.

unsatisfied /ʌn'sætɪsˌfaɪd/ *adj.* not satisfied.

unsatisfying /ʌn'sætɪsˌfaɪɪŋ/ *adj.* not satisfying.

unsaturated /ʌn'sætʃəˌreɪtɪd/ *adj. Chem.* (of esp. a fat or oil) having double or triple bonds in its molecule and therefore capable of further reaction.

unsavoury /ʌn'seɪvərɪ/ *adj.* (*US* **unsavory**) **1** disgusting, unpleasant. **2** morally offensive.

unsay /ʌn'seɪ/ *v.* (*past* and *past part.* **unsaid**) retract (a statement).

unscalable /ʌn'skeɪləb(ə)l/ *adj.* that cannot be scaled.

unscarred /ʌn'skɑːd/ *adj.* not scarred or damaged.

unscathed /ʌn'skeɪðd/ *adj.* without injury.

unscheduled /ʌn'ʃedjuːld/ *adj.* not scheduled.

unschooled /ʌn'skuːld/ *adj.* uneducated, untrained.

unscientific /ˌʌnsaɪən'tɪfɪk/ *adj.* not scientific in method etc. □ **unscientifically** *adv.*

unscramble /ʌn'skræmb(ə)l/ *v.* (**-ling**) make plain, decode, interpret (a scrambled transmission etc.).

unscreened /ʌn'skriːnd/ *adj.* **1 a** (esp. of coal) not passed through a screen or sieve. **b** not checked, esp. for security or medical problems. **2** not having a screen. **3** not shown on a screen.

unscrew /ʌn'skruː/ *v.* **1** unfasten by removing a screw or screws. **2** loosen (a screw or screw-top).

unscripted /ʌn'skrɪptɪd/ *adj.* (of a speech etc.) delivered impromptu.

unscrupulous /ʌn'skruːpjʊləs/ *adj.* having no scruples, unprincipled. □ **unscrupulously** *adv.* **unscrupulousness** *n.*

unseal /ʌn'siːl/ *v.* break the seal of; open (a letter, receptacle, etc.).

unseasonable /ʌn'siːzənəb(ə)l/ *adj.* **1** not seasonable. **2** untimely, inopportune. □ **unseasonably** *adv.*

unseasonal /ʌn'siːzən(ə)l/ *adj.* not typical or appropriate to the time or season. □ **unseasonally** *adv.*

unseat /ʌn'siːt/ *v.* **1** remove from (esp. a parliamentary) seat. **2** dislodge from a seat, esp. on horseback.

♦ **unsecured creditor** /ˌʌnsɪ'kjʊəd/ *n.* person who is owed money by an organization but who has not arranged that in the event of non-payment specific assets would be available as a fund out of which he or she could be paid in priority to other creditors.

♦ **unsecured debenture** *n.* debenture or loan stock in which no specific assets have been set aside as a fund out of which the debenture holders could be paid in priority to other creditors in the event of non-payment.

---

unseeded /ʌn'siːdɪd/ *adj. Sport* (of a player) not seeded.

unseeing /ʌn'siːɪŋ/ *adj.* **1** unobservant. **2** blind. □ **unseeingly** *adv.*

unseemly /ʌn'siːmlɪ/ *adj.* (**-ier**, **-iest**) **1** indecent. **2** unbecoming. □ **unseemliness** *n.*

unseen /ʌn'siːn/ *–adj.* **1** not seen. **2** invisible. **3** (of a translation) to be done without preparation. *–n.* unseen translation.

unselfconscious /ˌʌnself'kɒnʃəs/ *adj.* not self-conscious. □ **unselfconsciously** *adv.* **unselfconsciousness** *n.*

unselfish /ʌn'selfɪʃ/ *adj.* concerned about others; sharing. □ **unselfishly** *adv.* **unselfishness** *n.*

unsentimental /ˌʌnsentɪ'ment(ə)l/ *adj.* not sentimental.

unsettle /ʌn'set(ə)l/ *v.* (**-ling**) **1** disturb; discompose. **2** derange.

unsettled /ʌn'set(ə)ld/ *adj.* **1** restless, disturbed; unpredictable, changeable. **2** open to change or further discussion. **3** (of a bill etc.) unpaid.

unsex /ʌn'seks/ *v.* deprive (a person, esp. a woman) of the qualities of her or his sex.

UNSF *abbr.* United Nations Special Fund for Economic Development.

unshackle /ʌn'ʃæk(ə)l/ *v.* (**-ling**) **1** release from shackles. **2** set free.

unshakeable /ʌn'ʃeɪkəb(ə)l/ *adj.* firm; obstinate. □ **unshakeably** *adv.*

unshaken /ʌn'ʃeɪkən/ *adj.* not shaken.

unshaven /ʌn'ʃeɪv(ə)n/ *adj.* not shaved.

unsheathe /ʌn'ʃiːð/ *v.* (**-thing**) remove (a knife etc.) from a sheath.

unshockable /ʌn'ʃɒkəb(ə)l/ *adj.* unable to be shocked.

unshrinking /ʌn'ʃrɪŋkɪŋ/ *adj.* unhesitating, fearless.

unsighted /ʌn'saɪtɪd/ *adj.* **1** not sighted or seen. **2** prevented from seeing.

unsightly /ʌn'saɪtlɪ/ *adj.* ugly. □ **unsightliness** *n.*

unsigned /ʌn'saɪnd/ *adj.* not signed.

unsinkable /ʌn'sɪŋkəb(ə)l/ *adj.* unable to be sunk.

unskilful /ʌn'skɪlfʊl/ *adj.* (*US* **unskillful**) not skilful.

unskilled /ʌn'skɪld/ *adj.* lacking, or (of work) not needing, special skill or training.

unsliced /ʌn'slaɪst/ *adj.* (esp. of a loaf of bread) not sliced.

unsmiling /ʌn'smaɪlɪŋ/ *adj.* not smiling.

unsmoked /ʌn'sməʊkt/ *adj.* not cured by smoking (*unsmoked bacon*).

unsociable /ʌn'səʊʃəb(ə)l/ *adj.* not sociable, disliking company.

■ **Usage** See note at *unsocial.*

unsocial /ʌn'səʊʃ(ə)l/ *adj.* **1** not social; not suitable for or seeking society. **2** antisocial.

■ **Usage** *Unsocial* is sometimes confused with *unsociable.*

♦ **unsocial hours** *n.pl.* working hours, other than normal office or factory hours, that prevent an employee from enjoying the usual social activities. Shift workers and workers who have to work unsocial hours are often paid at higher rates than those who work normal hours.

---

unsoiled /ʌn'sɔɪld/ *adj.* not soiled or dirtied.

unsold /ʌn'səʊld/ *adj.* not sold.

unsolicited /ˌʌnsə'lɪsɪtɪd/ *adj.* not asked for; voluntary.

unsolved /ʌn'sɒlvd/ *adj.* not solved.

unsophisticated /ˌʌnsə'fɪstɪˌkeɪtɪd/ *adj.* artless, simple, natural.

unsorted /ʌn'sɔːtɪd/ *adj.* not sorted.

unsought /ʌn'sɔːt/ *adj.* **1** not sought for. **2** without being requested.

unsound /ʌn'saʊnd/ *adj.* **1** unhealthy, not sound. **2** rotten, weak; unreliable. **3** ill-founded. □ **of unsound mind** insane. □ **unsoundness** *n.*

unsparing /ʌn'speərɪŋ/ *adj.* **1** lavish. **2** merciless.

unspeakable /ʌn'spiːkəb(ə)l/ *adj.* **1** that cannot be expressed in words. **2** indescribably bad. □ **unspeakably** *adv.*

unspecific /ˌʌnspə'sɪfɪk/ *adj.* not specific; general, inexact.

unspecified /ʌn'spesɪˌfaɪd/ *adj.* not specified.

unspectacular /ˌʌnspek'tækjʊlə(r)/ *adj.* not spectacular; dull.

unspoiled /ʌn'spɔɪld/ *adj.* (also **unspoilt**) not spoilt.

unspoken /ʌn'spəʊkən/ *adj.* **1** not expressed in speech. **2** not uttered as speech.

unsporting /ʌn'spɔːtɪŋ/ *adj.* not fair or generous.

unsportsmanlike /ʌn'spɔːtsmənˌlaɪk/ *adj.* unsporting.

unstable /ʌn'steɪb(ə)l/ *adj.* (**unstabler**, **unstablest**) **1** not stable; likely to fall. **2** not stable emotionally. **3** changeable.□ **unstably** *adv.*

unstained /ʌn'steɪnd/ *adj.* not stained.

unstated /ʌn'steɪtɪd/ *adj.* not stated or declared.

unsteady /ʌn'stedɪ/ *adj.* (**-ier**, **-iest**) **1** not steady or firm. **2** changeable. **3** not uniform or regular. □ **unsteadily** *adv.* **unsteadiness** *n.*

unstick /ʌn'stɪk/ *v.* (*past* and *past part.* **unstuck**) separate (a thing stuck to another). □ **come unstuck** *colloq.* come to grief, fail.

unstinted /ʌn'stɪntɪd/ *adj.* not stinted.

unstinting /ʌn'stɪntɪŋ/ *adj.* lavish; limitless. □ **unstintingly** *adv.*

unstitch /ʌn'stɪtʃ/ *v.* undo the stitches of.

unstop /ʌn'stɒp/ *v.* (**-pp-**) **1** unblock. **2** remove the stopper from.

unstoppable /ʌn'stɒpəb(ə)l/ *adj.* that cannot be stopped or prevented.

unstrap /ʌn'stræp/ *v.* (**-pp-**) undo the strap(s) of.

unstressed /ʌn'strest/ *adj.* not pronounced with stress.

unstring /ʌn'strɪŋ/ *v.* (*past* and *past part.* **unstrung**) **1** remove or relax the string(s) of (a bow, harp, etc.). **2** remove (beads etc.) from a string. **3** (esp. as **unstrung** *adj.*) unnerve.

unstructured /ʌn'strʌktʃəd/ *adj.* **1** not structured. **2** informal.

unstuck *past* and *past part.* of UNSTICK.

unstudied /ʌn'stʌdɪd/ *adj.* easy, natural, spontaneous.

unsubstantial /ˌʌnsəb'stænʃ(ə)l/ *adj.* = INSUBSTANTIAL.

unsubstantiated /ˌʌnsəb'stænʃɪˌeɪtɪd/ *adj.* not substantiated.

unsubtle /ʌn'sʌt(ə)l/ *adj.* not subtle; obvious; clumsy.

unsuccessful /ˌʌnsək'sesfʊl/ *adj.* not successful. □ **unsuccessfully** *adv.*

unsuitable /ʌn'suːtəb(ə)l, ʌn'sjuːt-/ *adj.* not suitable. □ **unsuitability** /-'bɪlɪtɪ/ *n.* **unsuitably** *adv.*

unsuited /ʌn'suːtɪd, ʌn'sjuːt-/ *adj.* **1** (usu. foll. by *for*) not fit. **2** (usu. foll. by *to*) not adapted.

unsullied /ʌn'sʌlɪd/ *adj.* not sullied.

unsung /ʌn'sʌŋ/ *adj.* not celebrated, unrecognized (*unsung heroes*).

unsupervised /ʌn'suːpəˌvaɪzd/ *adj.* not supervised.

unsupported /ˌʌnsə'pɔːtɪd/ *adj.* not supported.

unsure /ʌn'ʃʊə(r)/ *adj.* not sure.

unsurpassed /ˌʌnsə'pɑːst/ *adj.* not surpassed.

unsurprised /'ʌnsə'praɪzd/ *adj.* not surprised.

unsurprising /ˌʌnsə'praɪzɪŋ/ *adj.* not surprising. □ **unsurprisingly** *adv.*

unsuspecting /ˌʌnsə'spektɪŋ/ *adj.* not suspecting. □ **unsuspected** *adj.*

unsustainable /'ʌnsə'teɪnəb(ə)l/ *adj.* that cannot be sustained.

unsweetened /ʌn'swiːt(ə)nd/ *adj.* not sweetened.

unswept /ʌn'swept/ *adj.* not swept.

unswerving /ʌn'swɜːvɪŋ/ *adj.* steady, constant. □ **unswervingly** *adv.*

unsymmetrical /ˌʌnsɪ'metrɪk(ə)l/ *adj.* not symmetrical.

unsympathetic /ˌʌnsɪmpə'θetɪk/ *adj.* not sympathetic. □ **unsympathetically** *adv.*

unsystematic /ˌʌnsɪstə'mætɪk/ *adj.* not systematic. □ **unsystematically** *adv.*

untainted /ʌn'teɪntɪd/ *adj.* not tainted.

untalented /ʌn'tæləntɪd/ *adj.* not talented.

untameable /ʌn'teɪməb(ə)l/ *adj.* that cannot be tamed.

untamed /ʌn'teɪmd/ *adj.* not tamed, wild.

untangle /ʌn'tæŋg(ə)l/ *v.* (**-ling**) disentangle.

untapped /ʌn'tæpt/ *adj.* not (yet) tapped or used (*untapped resources*).

untarnished /ʌn'tɑːnɪʃt/ *adj.* not tarnished.

untaught /ʌn'tɔːt/ *adj.* (of a person, knowledge, etc.) not taught.

untaxed /ʌn'tækst/ *adj.* (of a person, commodity, etc.) not taxed.

unteachable /ʌn'tiːtʃəb(ə)l/ *adj.* (of a person, subject, etc.) incapable of being taught.

untenable /ʌn'tenəb(ə)l/ *adj.* (of a theory etc.) not tenable.

untested /ʌn'testɪd/ *adj.* not tested or proved.

untether /ʌn'teðə(r)/ *v.* release (an animal) from a tether.

unthinkable /ʌn'θɪŋkəb(ə)l/ *adj.* **1** unimaginable, inconceivable. **2** *colloq.* highly unlikely or undesirable. □ **unthinkably** *adv.*

unthinking /ʌn'θɪŋkɪŋ/ *adj.* **1** thoughtless. **2** unintentional, inadvertent. □ **unthinkingly** *adv.*

unthread /ʌn'θred/ *v.* take the thread out of (a needle etc.).

unthrone /ʌn'θrəʊn/ *v.* (**-ning**) dethrone.

untidy /ʌn'taɪdɪ/ *adj.* (**-ier, -iest**) not neat or orderly. □ **untidily** *adv.* **untidiness** *n.*

untie /ʌn'taɪ/ *v.* (**untying**) **1** undo (a knot, package, etc.). **2** release from bonds or attachment.

until /ən'tɪl/ *prep.* & *conj.* = TILL[1]. [earlier *untill*: *un* from Old Norse *und* as far as]

■ **Usage** *Until*, as opposed to *till*, is used esp. at the beginning of a sentence and in formal style, e.g. *until you told me, I had no idea; he resided there until his decease.*

untimely /ʌn'taɪmlɪ/ *adj.* **1** inopportune. **2** (of death) premature. □ **untimeliness** *n.*

untiring /ʌn'taɪərɪŋ/ *adj.* tireless. □ **untiringly** *adv.*

untitled /ʌn'taɪt(ə)ld/ *adj.* having no title.

unto /'ʌntʊ/ *prep. archaic* = TO (in all uses except signalling the infinitive). [from UNTIL, with *to* replacing *til*]

untold /ʌn'təʊld/ *adj.* **1** not told. **2** immeasurable (*untold misery*).

untouchable /ʌn'tʌtʃəb(ə)l/ *–adj.* that may not be touched. *–n.* member of a hereditary Hindu group held to defile members of higher castes on contact. □ **untouchability** /-'bɪlɪtɪ/ *n.*

■ **Usage** The use of this term, and social restrictions accompanying it, were declared illegal under the Indian constitution in 1949.

untouched /ʌn'tʌtʃt/ *adj.* **1** not touched. **2** not affected physically, emotionally, etc. **3** not discussed.

untoward /ˌʌntə'wɔːd/ *adj.* **1** inconvenient, unlucky. **2** awkward. **3** perverse, refractory.

untraceable /ʌn'treɪsəb(ə)l/ *adj.* that cannot be traced.

untrained /ʌn'treɪnd/ *adj.* not trained.

untrammelled /ʌn'træm(ə)ld/ *adj.* not trammelled, unhampered.

untranslatable /ˌʌntræns'leɪtəb(ə)l/ *adj.* that cannot be translated satisfactorily.

untreated /ʌn'triːtɪd/ *adj.* not treated.

untried /ʌn'traɪd/ *adj.* **1** not tried or tested. **2** inexperienced.

untroubled /ʌn'trʌb(ə)ld/ *adj.* calm, tranquil.

untrue /ʌn'truː/ *adj.* **1** not true. **2** (often foll. by *to*) not faithful or loyal. **3** deviating from an accepted standard.

untrustworthy /ʌn'trʌstˌwɜːðɪ/ *adj.* not trustworthy. □ **untrustworthiness** *n.*

untruth /ʌn'truːθ/ *n.* **1** being untrue. **2** lie.

untruthful /ʌn'truːθfʊl/ *adj.* not truthful. □ **untruthfully** *adv.*

untuck /ʌn'tʌk/ *v.* free (bedclothes etc.) from being tucked in or up.

untutored /ʌn'tjuːtəd/ *adj.* uneducated, untaught.

untwine /ʌn'twaɪn/ *v.* (**-ning**) untwist, unwind.

untwist /ʌn'twɪst/ *v.* open from a twisted or spiralled state.

unusable /ʌn'juːzəb(ə)l/ *adj.* not usable.

unused *adj.* **1** /ʌn'juːzd/ **a** not in use. **b** never having been used. **2** /ʌn'juːst/ (foll. by *to*) not accustomed.

unusual /ʌn'juːʒʊəl/ *adj.* **1** not usual. **2** remarkable. □ **unusually** *adv.*

unutterable /ʌn'ʌtərəb(ə)l/ *adj.* inexpressible; beyond description. □ **unutterably** *adv.*

◆ **unvalued policy** *n.* insurance policy for property that has a sum insured shown for each item although the insurers do not acknowledge that this figure is its actual value. As a result, if a claim is made the insured must provide proof of the value of the item lost, damaged, or stolen before a payment will be made.

---

unvarnished /ʌn'vɑːnɪʃt/ *adj.* **1** not varnished. **2** plain and straightforward (*the unvarnished truth*).

unvarying /ʌn'veərɪɪŋ/ *adj.* not varying.

unveil /ʌn'veɪl/ *v.* **1** uncover (a statue etc.) ceremonially. **2** reveal. **3** remove a veil from; remove one's veil.

unverified /ʌn'verɪˌfaɪd/ *adj.* not verified.

unversed /ʌn'vɜːst/ *adj.* (usu. foll. by *in*) not experienced or skilled.

unviable /ʌn'vaɪəb(ə)l/ *adj.* not viable.

unvoiced /ʌn'vɔɪst/ *adj.* **1** not spoken. **2** (of a consonant etc.) not voiced.

unwaged /ʌn'weɪdʒd/ *adj.* not receiving a wage; unemployed.

unwanted /ʌn'wɒntɪd/ *adj.* not wanted.

unwarrantable /ʌn'wɒrəntəb(ə)l/ *adj.* unjustifiable. □ **unwarrantably** *adv.*

unwarranted /ʌn'wɒrəntɪd/ *adj.* **1** unauthorized. **2** unjustified.

unwary /ʌn'weərɪ/ *adj.* (often foll. by *of*) not cautious. □ **unwarily** *adv.* **unwariness** *n.*

unwashed /ʌn'wɒʃt/ *adj.* not washed or clean. □ **the great unwashed** *colloq.* the rabble.

unwavering /ʌn'weɪvərɪŋ/ *adj.* not wavering. □ **unwaveringly** *adv.*

unweaned /ʌn'wi:nd/ *adj.* not yet weaned.

unwearying /ʌn'wɪərɪɪŋ/ *adj.* persistent.

unwelcome /ʌn'welkəm/ *adj.* not welcome or acceptable.

unwell /ʌn'wel/ *adj.* ill.

unwholesome /ʌn'həʊlsəm/ *adj.* **1** detrimental to physical or moral health. **2** unhealthy-looking.

unwieldy /ʌn'wi:ldɪ/ *adj.* (**-ier, -iest**) cumbersome or hard to manage, owing to size, shape, etc. □ **unwieldily** *adv.* **unwieldiness** *n.* [*wieldy* active, from WIELD]

unwilling /ʌn'wɪlɪŋ/ *adj.* not willing or inclined; reluctant. □ **unwillingly** *adv.* **unwillingness** *n.*

unwind /ʌn'waɪnd/ *v.* (*past* and *past part.* **unwound**) **1** draw out or become drawn out after having been wound. **2** *colloq.* relax.

unwinking /ʌn'wɪŋkɪŋ/ *adj.* **1** not winking. **2** vigilant.

unwise /ʌn'waɪz/ *adj.* foolish, imprudent. □ **unwisely** *adv.*

unwished /ʌn'wɪʃt/ *adj.* (usu. foll. by *for*) not wished for.

unwitting /ʌn'wɪtɪŋ/ *adj.* **1** not knowing or aware (*an unwitting offender*). **2** unintentional. □ **unwittingly** *adv.* [Old English: related to WIT]

unwonted /ʌn'wəʊntɪd/ *adj.* not customary or usual.

unworkable /ʌn'wɜ:kəb(ə)l/ *adj.* not workable; impracticable.

unworkmanlike /ʌn'wɜ:kmən,laɪk/ *adj.* badly done or made.

unworldly /ʌn'wɜ:ldlɪ/ *adj.* spiritual; naïve. □ **unworldliness** *n.*

unworn /ʌn'wɔ:n/ *adj.* not worn or impaired by wear.

unworried /ʌn'wʌrɪd/ *adj.* not worried; calm.

unworthy /ʌn'wɜ:ðɪ/ *adj.* (**-ier, -iest**) **1** (often foll. by *of*) not worthy of or befitting a person etc. **2** discreditable, unseemly. □ **unworthily** *adv.* **unworthiness** *n.*

unwound *past* and *past part.* of UNWIND.

unwrap /ʌn'ræp/ *v.* (**-pp-**) **1** remove the wrapping from. **2** open, unfold. **3** become unwrapped.

unwritten /ʌn'rɪt(ə)n/ *adj.* **1** not written. **2** (of a law etc.) based on custom or judicial decision, not on statute.

unyielding /ʌn'ji:ldɪŋ/ *adj.* **1** not yielding. **2** firm, obstinate.

unzip /ʌn'zɪp/ *v.* (**-pp-**) unfasten the zip of.

up *–adv.* **1** at, in, or towards a higher place or a place regarded as higher, e.g. the north, a capital or a university (*up in the air; up in Scotland; went up to London; came up in 1989*). **2 a** to or in an erect or required position or condition (*stood it up; wound up the watch*). **b** in or into an active condition (*stirred up trouble; the hunt is up*). **3** in a stronger or leading position (*three goals up; am £10 up; is well up in class*). **4** to a specified place, person, or time (*a child came up to me; fine up till now*). **5** higher in price or value (*our costs are up; shares are up*). **6 a** completely (*burn up; eat up*). **b** more loudly or clearly (*speak up*). **7** completed (*time is up*). **8** into a compact, accumulated, or secure state (*pack up; save up; tie up*). **9** out of bed, having risen (*are you up yet?; sun is up*). **10** happening, esp. unusually (*something is up*). **11** (usu. foll. by *before*) appearing for trial etc. (*up before the magistrate*). **12** (of a road etc.) being repaired. **13** (of a jockey) in the saddle. *–prep.* **1** upwards and along, through, or into (*climbed up the ladder; went up the road*). **2** from the bottom to the top of. **3 a** at or in a higher part of (*is up the street*). **b** towards the source of (a river). *–adj.* **1** directed upwards (*up stroke*). **2** of travel towards a capital or centre (*the up train*). *–n.* spell of good fortune. *–v.* (**-pp-**) **1** *colloq.* start, esp. abruptly, to speak or act (*upped and hit him*). **2** raise (*upped their prices*). □ **be all up with** be hopeless for (a person). **on the up** (or **up and up**) *colloq.* steadily improving. **up against 1** close to. **2** in or into contact with. **3** *colloq.* confronted with (a problem etc.). **up and about** (or **doing**) having risen from bed; active. **up and down 1** to and fro (along). **2** *colloq.* in varying health or spirits. **up for** available for or standing for (office etc.) (*up for sale*). **up to 1** until. **2** below or equal to. **3** incumbent on (*it is up to you to say*). **4** capable of. **5** occupied or busy with. **up to date** see DATE[1]. [Old English]

up- *prefix* in senses of UP, added: **1** as an adverb to verbs and verbal derivations, = 'upwards' (*upcurved; update*). **2** as a preposition to nouns forming adverbs and adjectives (*up-country; uphill*). **3** as an adjective to nouns (*upland; upstroke*).

up-and-coming *adj. colloq.* (of a person) promising; progressing.

up-and-over *adj.* (of a door) opening by being raised and pushed back into a horizontal position.

upbeat *–n.* unaccented beat in music. *–adj. colloq.* optimistic, cheerful.

upbraid /ʌp'breɪd/ *v.* (often foll. by *with, for*) chide, reproach. [Old English: related to BRAID = brandish]

upbringing *n.* rearing of a child. [obsolete *upbring* to rear]

UPC *abbr.* universal product code (bar code).

up-country *adv.* & *adj.* inland.

update *–v.* /ʌp'deɪt/ (**-ting**) bring up to date. *–n.* /'ʌpdeɪt/ **1** updating. **2** updated information etc.

up-end /ʌp'end/ *v.* set or rise up on end.

upfield *adv.* in or to a position nearer to the opponents' end of a field.

upfront /ʌp'frʌnt/ *colloq. –adv.* (usu. **up front**) **1** at the front; in front. **2** (of payments) in advance. *–adj.* **1** honest, frank, direct. **2** (of payments) made in advance.

upgrade *v.* /ʌp'greɪd/ (**-ding**) **1** raise in rank etc. **2** improve (equipment etc.).

upheaval /ʌp'hi:v(ə)l/ *n.* violent or sudden change or disruption. [from *upheave*, = heave or lift up]

uphill *–adv.* /ʌp'hɪl/ up a slope. *–adj.* /'ʌphɪl/ **1** sloping up; ascending. **2** arduous.

uphold /ʌp'həʊld/ *v.* (*past* and *past part.* **upheld**) **1** confirm (a decision etc.). **2** support, maintain (a custom etc.). □ **upholder** *n.*

upholster /ʌp'həʊlstə(r)/ *v.* provide (furniture) with upholstery. [back formation from UPHOLSTERER]

upholsterer *n.* person who upholsters, esp. for a living. [obsolete *upholster* from UPHOLD in sense 'keep in repair']

upholstery *n.* **1** covering, padding, springs, etc. for furniture. **2** upholsterer's work.

UPI *abbr.* United Press International.

upkeep *n.* **1** maintenance in good condition. **2** cost or means of this.

upland /'ʌplənd/ *–n.* (usu. in *pl.*) higher or inland parts of a country. *–adj.* of these parts.

uplift *–v.* /ʌp'lɪft/ **1** raise. **2** (esp. as **uplifting** *adj.*) elevate morally or emotionally. *–n.* /'ʌplɪft/ **1** *colloq.* elevating influence. **2** support for the bust etc.

up-market *adj.* & *adv.* of or directed at the upper end of the market; classy.

upmost var. of UPPERMOST.

upon /ə'pɒn/ *prep.* = ON. [from *up on*]

■ **Usage** *Upon* is sometimes more formal than *on*, but is standard in *once upon a time* and *upon my word*.

upper[1] *–attrib. adj.* **1** higher in place; situated above another part. **2** higher in rank etc. (*upper class*). *–n.* part of a boot or shoe above the sole. □ **on one's uppers** *colloq.* very short of money.

upper[2] *n. slang* amphetamine or other stimulant.

Upper Austria state in N Austria; pop. (est. 1994) 1 383 620; capital, Linz.

upper case *n.* capital letters.

upper crust *n. colloq.* (prec. by *the*) the aristocracy.

upper-cut *–n.* upwards blow delivered with the arm bent. *–v.* hit upwards with the arm bent.

upper hand *n.* (prec. by *the*) dominance, control.

Upper House *n.* higher house in a legislature, esp. the House of Lords.

uppermost *–adj.* (also **upmost**) **1** highest. **2** predominant. *–adv.* at or to the uppermost position.

uppish *adj. colloq.* uppity.

uppity /'ʌpɪtɪ/ *adj. colloq.* self-assertive, arrogant.

Uppsala /ʊp'sɑːlə/ city in E Sweden; there is some light industry; pop. (est. 1996) 101 337.

UPR *abbr. Insurance* unearned premiums reserve.

upright *–adj.* **1** erect, vertical. **2** (of a piano) with vertical strings. **3** honourable or honest. *–n.* **1** upright post or rod, esp. as a structural support. **2** upright piano. [Old English]

uprising *n.* insurrection.

uproar *n.* tumult; violent disturbance. [Dutch, = commotion]

uproarious /ʌp'rɔːrɪəs/ *adj.* **1** very noisy. **2** provoking loud laughter; very funny. □ **uproariously** *adv.*

uproot /ʌp'ruːt/ *v.* **1** pull (a plant etc.) up from the ground. **2** displace (a person). **3** eradicate.

uprush *n.* upward rush.

UPS *abbr.* **1** uninterruptible power supply (to computers etc.). **2** *propr. US* United Parcel Service.

ups-a-daisy var. of UPSY-DAISY.

ups and downs *n.pl.* **1** rises and falls. **2** mixed fortune.

upset *–v.* /ʌp'set/ (**-tt-**; *past* and *past part.* **upset**) **1** overturn. **2** disturb the composure or digestion of. **3** disrupt. *–n.* /'ʌpset/ **1** emotional or physical disturbance. **2** surprising result. *–adj.* /ʌp'set, 'ʌp-/ disturbed (*upset stomach*).

upshot *n.* outcome, conclusion.

upside down /ˌʌpsaɪd 'daʊn/ *adv.* & *adj.* **1** with the upper and lower parts reversed; inverted. **2** in or into total disorder. [from *up so down*, perhaps = 'up as if down']

upsilon /'juːpsɪˌlɒn, ʌp'saɪlən/ *n.* twentieth letter of the Greek alphabet (Υ, υ). [Greek, = slender U, from *psilos* slender, with ref. to its later coincidence in sound with Greek *oi*]

upstage /ʌp'steɪdʒ/ *–adj.* & *adv.* nearer the back of a theatre stage. *–v.* (**-ging**) **1** move upstage to make (another actor) face away from the audience. **2** divert attention from (a person) to oneself.

upstairs *–adv.* /ʌp'steəz/ to or on an upper floor. *–attrib. adj.* /'ʌpsteəz/ situated upstairs. *–n.* /ʌp'steəz/ upper floor.

upstanding /ʌp'stændɪŋ/ *adj.* **1** standing up. **2** strong and healthy. **3** honest.

upstart *–n.* newly successful, esp. arrogant, person. *–adj.* **1** that is an upstart. **2** of upstarts.

upstate *US –n.* provincial, esp. northern, part of a State. *–attrib. adj.* of this part. *–adv.* in or to this part.

upstream *adv.* & *adj.* **1** in the direction contrary to the flow of a stream etc. **2** denoting a loan from a subsidiary company to its parent.

upsurge *n.* upward surge.

upswept *adj.* (of hair) combed to the top of the head.

upswing *n.* upward movement or trend.

upsy-daisy /'ʌpsɪˌdeɪzɪ/ *int.* (also **ups-a-daisy**) expressing encouragement to a child who is being lifted or has fallen. [earlier *up-a-daisy*]

uptake *n.* **1** *colloq.* understanding (esp. *quick* or *slow on the uptake*). **2** taking up (of an offer etc.).

upthrust *n.* **1** upward thrust. **2** upward displacement of part of the earth's crust.

uptight /ʌp'taɪt/ *adj. colloq.* **1** nervously tense or angry. **2** *US* rigidly conventional.

uptown *US –attrib. adj.* of the residential part of a town or city. *–adv.* in or into this part. *–n.* this part.

upturn *–n.* /'ʌptɜːn/ upward trend; improvement. *–v.* /ʌp'tɜːn/ turn up or upside down.

UPU *abbr.* Universal Postal Union (UN agency).

UPVC *abbr.* unplasticized polyvinyl chloride.

upward /'ʌpwəd/ *–adv.* (also **upwards**) towards what is higher, more important, etc. *–adj.* moving or extending upwards. □ **upwards of** more than (*upwards of forty*).

upward compatible *Computing* see COMPATIBILITY 2.

upwardly *adv.* in an upward direction.

upwardly mobile *adj.* aspiring to advance socially or professionally.

upwind /ʌp'wɪnd/ *adj.* & *adv.* in the direction from which the wind is blowing.

UR *international civil aircraft marking* Ukraine.

Ural Mountains /'jʊər(ə)l/ (also **Urals**) mountain range in W central Russia. It extends S from within the Arctic Circle to Kazakhstan, and forms a natural boundary between Europe and Asia.

uranium /jʊ'reɪnɪəm/ *n.* radioactive grey dense metallic element, capable of nuclear fission and used as a source of nuclear energy. [*Uranus*, name of a planet]

urban /'ɜːbən/ *adj.* of, living in, or situated in a town or city. [Latin *urbs* city]

urbane /ɜː'beɪn/ *adj.* suave; elegant. □ **urbanity** /-'bænɪtɪ/ *n.* [Latin: related to URBAN]

urban guerrilla *n.* terrorist operating in an urban area.

urbanize /'ɜːbəˌnaɪz/ *v.* (also **-ise**) (**-zing** or **-sing**) make urban, esp. by destroying the rural quality of (a district). □ **urbanization** /-'zeɪʃ(ə)n/ *n.*

urchin /'ɜːtʃɪn/ *n.* **1** mischievous, esp. ragged, child. **2** = SEA URCHIN. [Latin *ericius* hedgehog]

Urdu /'ʊəduː, 'ɜː-/ *n.* language related to Hindi but with many Persian words, used esp. in Pakistan. [Hindustani]

-ure *suffix* forming: **1** nouns of action (*seizure*). **2** nouns of result (*creature*). **3** collective nouns (*nature*). [Latin *-ura*]

urea /jʊə'riːə/ *n.* soluble nitrogenous compound contained esp. in urine. [French *urée* from Greek *ouron* urine]

ureter /jʊə'riːtə(r)/ *n.* duct conveying urine from the kidney to the bladder. [Greek *oureō* urinate]

urethra /jʊə'riːθrə/ *n.* (*pl.* **-s**) duct conveying urine from the bladder. [Greek: related to URETER]

URF *abbr.* (French) Union des services routiers des chemins de fer européens (= Union of European Railways Road Services).

urge *–v.* (**-ging**) **1** (often foll. by *on*) drive forcibly; hasten. **2** encourage or entreat earnestly or persistently. **3** (often foll. by *on, upon*) advocate (an action or argument etc.) emphatically (to a person). *–n.* **1** urging impulse or tendency. **2** strong desire. [Latin *urgeo*]

urgent *adj.* **1** requiring immediate action or attention. **2** importunate. □ **urgency** *n.* **urgently** *adv.* [French: related to URGE]

uric /'jʊərɪk/ *adj.* of urine. [French *urique*: related to URINE]

uric acid *n.* constituent of urine.

urinal /jʊə'raɪn(ə)l/ *n.* place or receptacle for urination by men. [Latin: related to URINE]

urinary /'jʊərɪnərɪ/ *adj.* of or relating to urine.

urinate /'jʊərɪˌneɪt/ *v.* (**-ting**) discharge urine. □ **urination** /-'neɪʃ(ə)n/ *n.*

urine /'jʊərɪn/ *n.* waste fluid secreted by the kidneys and discharged from the bladder. [Latin *urina*]

urn *n.* **1** vase with a foot and usu. a rounded body, used esp. for the ashes of the dead. **2** large vessel with a tap, in which tea or coffee etc. is made or kept hot. [Latin *urna*]

urogenital /ˌjʊərə'dʒenɪt(ə)l/ *adj.* of the urinary and reproductive systems. [Greek *ouron* urine]

urology /jʊə'rɒlədʒɪ/ *n.* the study of the urinary system. □ **urological** /-rə'lɒdʒɪk(ə)l/ *adj.*

Ursa Major /ˌɜːsə/ *n.* = *Great Bear* (see BEAR²). [Latin]

Ursa Minor *n.* = *Little Bear* (see BEAR²). [Latin]

ursine /'ɜːsaɪn/ *adj.* of or like a bear. [Latin *ursus* bear]

URTU *abbr.* United Road Transport Union.

Uru. *abbr.* Uruguay(an).

♦ **Uruguay round** see GENERAL AGREEMENT ON TARIFFS AND TRADE.

Urumqi /ʊ'rʊmtʃɪ/ (also **Urumchi**) city in NW China, capital of Xinjiang autonomous region; there are iron, steel, and machine-building industries; pop. (est. 1991) 1 160 000.

US *–abbr.* United States. *–airline flight code* US Air.

U/S *abbr.* **1** unserviceable. **2** useless.

us /əs, ʌs/ *pron.* **1** *objective case* of WE (*they saw us*). **2** *colloq.* = WE (*it's us again*). **3** *colloq.* = ME¹ (*give us a kiss*). [Old English]

USA *abbr.* & *international vehicle registration* United States of America.

usable /'juːzəb(ə)l/ *adj.* that can be used.

USAEC *abbr.* United States Atomic Energy Commission.

USAF *abbr.* United States Air Force.

usage /'juːsɪdʒ/ *n.* **1** use, treatment (*damaged by rough usage*). **2** customary practice, esp. in the use of a language or as creating a precedent in law.

USAID *abbr.* United States Agency for International Development.

♦ **usance** /'juːz(ə)ns/ *n.* **1** time allowed for the payment of short-term foreign bills of exchange. It varies from country to country but is often 60 days. **2** *hist.* rate of interest on a loan. [related to USE]

USCG *abbr.* United States Coast Guard.

♦ **US customary units** *n.pl.* units of measurement in use in the US. They are based on imperial units but the US gallon is equal to 0.8327 imperial gallons and the hundredweight is taken as 100 lb, making the ton 2000 lb (instead of the imperial 2240 lb). The US has fallen behind Europe in converting to metric units but intends to do so.

USDAW /'ʌzˌdɔː/ *abbr.* (also **Usdaw**) Union of Shop, Distributive, and Allied Workers.

use *–v.* /juːz/ (**using**) **1** cause to act or serve for a purpose; bring into service. **2** treat in a specified manner (*used him shamefully*). **3** exploit for one's own ends. **4** /juːs/ did or had habitually (*I used to drink; it used not* (or *did not use*) *to rain so often*). **5** (as **used** *adj.*) second-hand. **6** (as **used** /juːst/ *predic. adj.*) (foll. by *to*) familiar by habit; accustomed (*used to hard work*). *–n.* /juːs/ **1** using or being used. **2** right or power of using (*lost the use of his legs*). **3** benefit, advantage (*a torch would be of use; it's no use talking*). **4** custom or usage (*established by long use*). □ **have no use for 1** not need. **2** dislike, be contemptuous of. **in use** being used. **make use of 1** use. **2** benefit from. **out of use** not being used. **use up 1** consume completely. **2** find a use for (leftovers etc.). [French *us, user*, ultimately from Latin *utor us-*]

USECC *abbr.* United States Employees' Compensation Commission.

useful *adj.* **1** that can be used to advantage; helpful; beneficial. **2** *colloq.* creditable, efficient (*useful footballer*). □ **make oneself useful** help. □ **usefully** *adv.* **usefulness** *n.*

useless *adj.* **1** serving no purpose; unavailing. **2** *colloq.* feeble or ineffectual (*useless at swimming*). □ **uselessly** *adv.* **uselessness** *n.*

user *n.* person who uses a thing.

♦ **user-cost-of-capital theory** *n. Econ.* theory that the level of investment is determined by the economic costs of the investment balanced against the potential returns. The costs are represented by the rate of interest that must be paid on borrowings and the price of investment goods. The returns are the flow of income from production. The calculation of costs and returns yields a net present value. While more theoretically acceptable than such models as the accelerator theory, this theory is difficult to test in practice or to use as a basis for predicting the level of investment in an economy. See also TOBIN'S Q.

♦ **user-friendly** *adj.* (of a computer etc.) easy to use, convenient. A user-friendly computer system can usu. be started up with a minimum of trouble and provides on-screen guidance to the user, usu. in the form of menus. If the user becomes confused, a help menu lists the action to be taken to correct all common mistakes. Some input devices, e.g. the mouse, are considered easier to use than the normal keyboard, and user-friendly machines therefore make use of them.

user interface *n.* (also **UI**) means of communication between a person and a computer system, esp. input/output devices used with supporting software.

user port *n.* electrical socket in a microcomputer that, with associated circuitry, allows the computer user to connect additional peripheral devices.

USES *abbr.* United States Employment Service.

USh *symb.* Uganda shilling.

usher *–n.* **1** person who shows people to their seats in a

Uruguay /'jʊərəˌgwaɪ/, **Oriental Republic of** country in South America lying S of Brazil, with a coastline on the Atlantic Ocean. The Uruguayan economy has traditionally been dependent on the livestock industry, esp. cattle and sheep, and meat and by-products, live animals, hides and skins, and wool are among the principal exports; Brazil, Argentina, and the US are the country's major trading partners. Crops grown include rice (which is also exported), barley, maize, and wheat, and there is an important fishing industry. Manufacturing industry, which is mainly concentrated on the processing of agricultural produce, includes meat-packing, textiles and clothing (important exports), leather curing, construction, rubber, chemicals, and plastics. *History*. Not permanently settled by Europeans until the 17th century, Uruguay became an area of long-standing Spanish–Portuguese rivalry. Liberated in 1825, it was declared an independent state in 1828 and became a republic in 1830. During the early part of the 20th century, despite its size (it is the smallest of the South American republics), Uruguay emerged as one of the most prosperous and literate nations in the continent, with an extensive social welfare system. During the 1950s and 1960s the economy deteriorated, which led to political unrest and urban guerrilla activity; the country came under military rule in 1973 until this was officially ended in 1985 following general elections in 1984. The first entirely free presidential elections were held in 1989. Some constitutional amendments were made in 1996. Uruguay is a member of LAIA. President, Dr Luis Alberto Lacalle; capital, Montevideo. □ **Uruguayan** *adj.* & *n.*

language	Spanish
currency	peso (NUr$) of 100 centésimos
pop. (1996)	3 140 000
GNP (1994)	US$14.7B
literacy	94% (m); 95% (f)
life expectancy	70 (m); 77 (f)

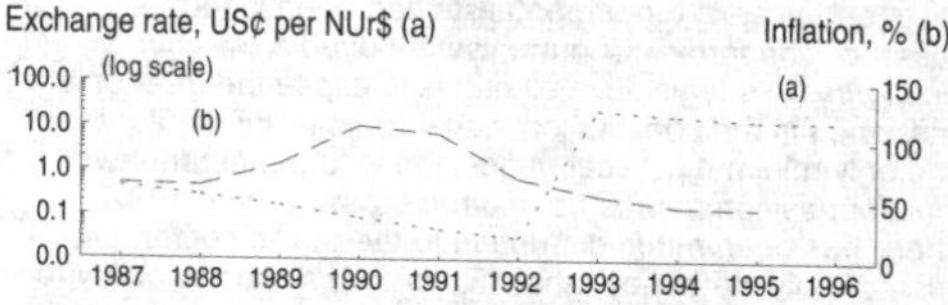

cinema, church, etc. **2** doorkeeper at a court etc. *–v.* **1** act as usher to. **2** (usu. foll. by *in*) announce, herald, or show in. [Latin *ostium* door]

usherette /ˌʌʃəˈret/ *n.* female usher, esp. in a cinema.

Ushuaia /uːˈswaɪə/ port in Tierra del Fuego, capital of the Argentinian section of the archipelago; pop. (1991) 29 166.

USITC *abbr.* United States International Trade Commission.

Üsküdar /ˌuːskuːˈdɑː/ (formerly **Scutari**) town in NW Turkey, a suburb of Istanbul on the Asian side of the Bosporus; pop. (1990) 395 620. It was a British Army base during the Crimean War.

USM *abbr.* **1** United States Mail. **2** United States Mint. **3** = UNLISTED SECURITIES MARKET.

◆ **USP** *abbr.* **1** = UNIQUE SELLING PROPOSITION. **2** (also **USPat.**) United States Patent.

USS *abbr.* **1** United States Senate. **2** United States Ship.

USSB *abbr.* United States Shipping Board.

USSR *abbr. hist.* Union of Soviet Socialist Republics.

USTC *abbr.* United States Tariff Commission.

usual /ˈjuːʒʊəl/ *adj.* **1** customary, habitual (*went as usual*). **2** (*absol.*, prec. by *the*, *my*, etc.) *colloq.* person's usual drink etc. □ **usually** *adv.* [Latin: related to USE]

usurer /ˈjuːʒərə(r)/ *n.* person who practises usury.

usurp /jʊˈzɜːp/ *v.* seize (a throne or power etc.) wrongfully. □ **usurpation** /ˌjuːzəˈpeɪʃ(ə)n/ *n.* **usurper** *n.* [French from Latin]

usury /ˈjuːʒərɪ/ *n.* **1** lending of money at interest, esp. at an exorbitant or illegal rate. **2** interest at this rate. □ **usurious** /-ˈʒʊərɪəs/ *adj.* [Anglo-French or medieval Latin: related to USE]

UT *–abbr.* universal time. *–airline flight code* UTA French Airlines. *–US postcode* Utah.

Ut. *abbr.* Utah.

UTA *abbr.* **1** Union de Transports Aériens (French airline). **2** = UNIT TRUST ASSOCIATION.

Utah /ˈjuːtɑː, *US* -tɔː/ state in the SW US; pop. (est. 1996) 2 000 494; capital, Salt Lake City. Manufactures include food products, steel, spacecraft, and electronics equipment; copper, oil, natural gas, and uranium are mined; there is also some agriculture and tourism.

utensil /juːˈtens(ə)l/ *n.* implement or vessel, esp. for kitchen use. [medieval Latin: related to USE]

uterine /ˈjuːtəˌraɪn/ *adj.* of the uterus.

uterus /ˈjuːtərəs/ *n.* (*pl.* **uteri** /-ˌraɪ/) womb. [Latin]

utilitarian /ˌjuːtɪlɪˈteərɪən/ *–adj.* **1** designed to be useful rather than attractive; severely practical. **2** of utilitarianism. *–n.* adherent of utilitarianism.

utilitarianism *n.* doctrine that actions are right if they are useful or benefit a majority.

utility /juːˈtɪlɪtɪ/ *n.* (*pl.* **-ies**) **1** usefulness. **2** useful thing. **3** = PUBLIC UTILITY. **4** *Econ.* subjective benefit derived by an individual from consumption of a good or service. In the Classical school of economics, utility referred to the usefulness of an item, which was contrasted with its value (see LABOUR THEORY OF VALUE). It was the Marginalists who laid the basis for the neoclassical school of economics, by observing that the value of a good is related to the subjective utility derived from that good, taking into account its scarcity. Thus, water has utility but little value, since it is generally not scarce. Both general and partial equilibrium analysis are based on utility and the assumption that consumers maximize utility. However, because of its subjectivity, it is difficult to measure utility and economists usu. have to assume that consumers are rational and therefore do maximize utility. See also CONSUMER PREFERENCE; CONSUMER THEORY. **5** (*attrib.*) basic and standardized (*utility furniture*). [Latin *utilis* useful: related to USE]

◆ **utility function** *n. Econ.* function that relates the different goods and services in an economy to the preferences of individuals (see CONSUMER PREFERENCE). By making certain assumptions, the utility function can be used to analyse the behaviour of consumers and markets. See also DIRECT UTILITY FUNCTION; INDIRECT UTILITY FUNCTION.

utility program *n.* any of a collection of programs that forms part of every computer system and provides a variety of generally useful functions. Examples of utility programs are loaders, text editors, link editors, programs for copying files from one storage device to another, for file deletion and file maintenance, for searching and sorting, and for debugging of programs.

utility room *n.* room for domestic appliances, e.g. a washing-machine, boiler, etc.

utility vehicle *n.* vehicle serving various functions.

utilize /ˈjuːtɪˌlaɪz/ *v.* (also **-ise**) (**-zing** or **-sing**) use; turn to account. □ **utilization** /-ˈzeɪʃ(ə)n/ *n.* [Italian: related to UTILITY]

utmost /ˈʌtməʊst/ *–attrib. adj.* furthest, extreme, greatest. *–n.* utmost point or degree etc. □ **do one's utmost** do all that one can. [Old English, = *outmost*]

◆ **utmost good faith** *n.* (also ***uberrima fides***) fundamental principle of insurance practice, requiring that a person wishing to take out an insurance cover must provide all the information the insurer needs to calculate the correct premium for the risk involved. Nothing must be withheld from the insurers, even if they do not actually ask for the information on an application form. The principle is essential because an insurer usu. has no knowledge of the facts involved in the risk they are being asked to cover; the only source of information is the person requiring the insurance. If an insured person is found to have withheld

Uzbekistan /ˌʊzbekɪˈstɑːn, ˌʌ-/, **Republic of** country in central Asia, lying S and SE of the Aral Sea. Agriculture is important, esp. the cultivation and processing of cotton; other crops include rice, vegetables, and grapes. There are rich mineral resources, including natural gas, oil, coal, gold, copper, lead, and zinc. Industry is concentrated on the processing of minerals and the manufacture of chemicals, textiles, agricultural machinery, and iron and steel. Gas, oil, and electricity are all exported. Uzbekistan was a constituent republic of the Soviet Union until 1991, when it declared its independence. The government is controlled by former Communists, and opposition from Uzbek nationalists and Islamic fundamentalists has been vigorously suppressed. The former Communists enjoyed a massive victory in 1994 legislative elections. Despite the freedoms enshrined in the constitution, censorship is still widespread and only minimal political opposition is tolerated: the two main opposition parties have been banned since 1992. There has been much disruption to the public sector, previously mainly staffed by ethnic Russians, since the ability to speak Uzbek became necessary for civil service jobs. The president's term of office was extended, by referendum in 1995, until the year 2000. President, Islam Karimov; prime minister, Utkur Sultanov; capital, Tashkent.

languages	Uzbek (official), Russian
currency	sum
pop. (1996)	23 206 000
GNP (1994)	US$21.1B
literacy	98% (m); 96% (f)
life expectancy	66 (m); 72 (f)

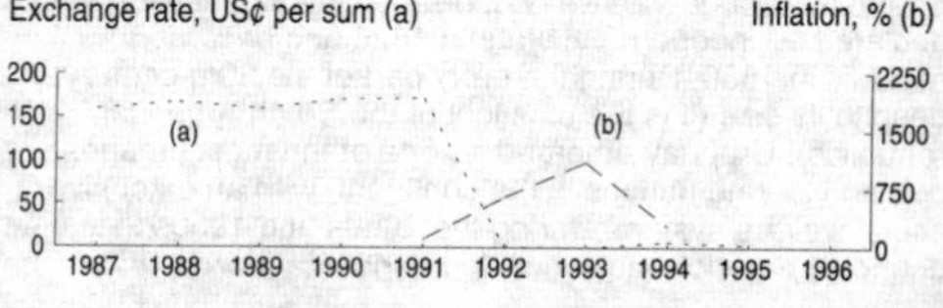

information or given false information, the insurer can treat the policy as void and the courts will support the insurer's refusal to pay claims.

Utopia /juːˈtəʊpɪə/ *n.* imagined perfect place or state of things. □ **Utopian** *adj.* (also **utopian**). [title of a book by Thomas More, from Greek *ou* not, *topos* place]

Utrecht /juːˈtrext/ city in the Netherlands, capital of the province of Utrecht; it has textile, chemical, and metallurgical industries; pop. (est. 1995) 235 357.

Uttar Pradesh /ˌʊtɑː prəˈdeʃ/ state in N India, bordering on Tibet and Nepal; pop. (est. 1994) 150 695 000; capital, Lucknow. Cereals, pulses, and sugar cane are grown; forestry is also important.

utter[1] *attrib. adj.* complete, absolute. □ **utterly** *adv.* [Old English, comparative of OUT]

utter[2] *v.* **1** emit audibly. **2** express in words. **3** *Law* put (esp. forged money) into circulation. [Dutch]

utterance *n.* **1** act of uttering. **2** thing spoken. **3** power or manner of speaking.

uttermost *attrib. adj.* utmost.

U-turn /ˈjuːtɜːn/ *n.* **1** U-shaped turn of a vehicle so as to face in the opposite direction. **2** abrupt reversal of policy.

UV *abbr.* ultraviolet.

uvula /ˈjuːvjʊlə/ *n.* (*pl.* **uvulae** /-ˌliː/) fleshy part of the soft palate hanging above the throat. □ **uvular** *adj.* [Latin diminutive of *uva* grape]

U/W *abbr.* **1** *Law* under will. **2** (also **U/w**) underwriter.

uxorial /ʌkˈsɔːrɪəl/ *adj.* of a wife. [Latin *uxor* wife]

uxorious /ʌkˈsɔːrɪəs/ *adj.* greatly or excessively fond of one's wife.

Uzbek /ˈʌzbek/ *n.* **1** native of Uzbekistan. **2** language of Uzbekistan.

Vv

V[1] /viː/ *n.* (also **v**) (*pl.* **Vs** or **V's**) **1** twenty-second letter of the alphabet. **2** V-shaped thing. **3** (as a Roman numeral) 5.

V[2] *abbr.* volt(s).

V[3] *–symb.* vanadium. *–international vehicle registration* Vatican City.

v. *abbr.* **1** verse. **2** versus. **3** very. **4** vide.

V2 *international civil aircraft marking* Antigua.

V3 *international civil aircraft marking* Belize.

V5 *international civil aircraft marking* Namibia.

V8 *international civil aircraft marking* Brunei.

VA *–abbr. Commerce* value analysis. *–US postcode* Virginia. *–airline flight code* VIASA.

Va. *abbr.* Virginia (US).

Vaasa /ˈvɑːsə/ (Swedish **Vasa**) **1** province in W Finland; pop. (est. 1995) 449 366. **2** its capital, a port on the Gulf of Bothnia; industries include ship repairing and food processing; pop. (1994) 55 089.

vac *n. colloq.* vacation. [abbreviation]

vacancy /ˈveɪkənsɪ/ *n.* (*pl.* **-ies**) **1** being vacant. **2** unoccupied job. **3** available room in a hotel etc.

vacant *adj.* **1** not filled or occupied. **2** not mentally active; showing no interest. □ **vacantly** *adv.* [Latin: related to VACATE]

vacant possession *n.* ownership of an unoccupied house etc.

vacate /vəˈkeɪt/ *v.* (**-ting**) leave vacant, cease to occupy (a house, post, etc.). [Latin *vaco* be empty]

vacation /vəˈkeɪʃ(ə)n/ *–n.* **1** fixed holiday period, esp. in universities and lawcourts. **2** *US* holiday. **3** vacating or being vacated. *–v. US* take a holiday. [Latin: related to VACATE]

vaccinate /ˈvæksɪˌneɪt/ *v.* (**-ting**) inoculate with a vaccine to immunize against a disease. □ **vaccination** /-ˈneɪʃ(ə)n/ *n.* **vaccinator** *n.*

vaccine /ˈvæksiːn/ *n.* preparation, orig. cowpox virus, used in vaccination. [Latin *vacca* cow]

vacillate /ˈvæsɪˌleɪt/ *v.* (**-ting**) be irresolute; fluctuate. □ **vacillation** /-ˈleɪʃ(ə)n/ *n.* **vacillator** *n.* [Latin]

vacuity /vəˈkjuːɪtɪ/ *n.* **1** lack of intelligence or expression. **2 a** empty space; void. **b** see ULLAGE 3.

vacuole /ˈvækjʊˌəʊl/ *n.* tiny space in an organ or cell, containing air, fluid, etc. [Latin *vacuus* empty]

vacuous /ˈvækjʊəs/ *adj.* **1** expressionless. **2** showing absence of thought or intelligence, inane. □ **vacuously** *adv.* [Latin *vacuus* empty]

vacuum /ˈvækjʊəm/ *–n.* (*pl.* **-s** or **-cua**) **1** space entirely devoid of matter. **2** space or vessel from which all or some of the air has been pumped out. **3** absence of the normal or previous content, activities, etc. **4** (*pl.* **-s**) *colloq.* vacuum cleaner. *–v. colloq.* clean with a vacuum cleaner. [Latin *vacuus* empty]

vacuum brake *n.* brake worked by the exhaustion of air.

vacuum cleaner *n.* machine for removing dust etc. by suction. □ **vacuum-clean** *v.*

vacuum flask *n.* vessel with a double wall enclosing a vacuum, ensuring that the contents remain hot or cold.

vacuum-packed *adj.* sealed after the partial removal of air.

vacuum tube *n.* tube with a near-vacuum for the free passage of electric current.

vade-mecum /ˌvɑːdɪˈmeɪkəm/ *n.* handbook etc. used constantly. [Latin, = go with me]

Vadodara /wəˈdəʊdərə/ (formerly **Baroda**) city in India, in the state of Gujarat; industries include oil refining (at Kouali) and the manufacture of petrochemicals, cotton textiles, wood, and tobacco; pop. (1991) 1 031 346.

Vaduz /væˈdʊts/ capital of Liechtenstein, a centre of tourism; pop. (est. 1995) 5067.

vagabond /ˈvægəˌbɒnd/ *–n.* wanderer, esp. an idle one. *–attrib. adj.* wandering, roving. [Latin *vagor* wander]

vagary /ˈveɪgərɪ/ *n.* (*pl.* **-ies**) caprice, whim. [Latin *vagor* wander]

vagina /vəˈdʒaɪnə/ *n.* (*pl.* **-s** or **-nae** /-niː/) canal from the uterus to the vulva in female mammals. □ **vaginal** *adj.* [Latin, = sheath]

vagrant /ˈveɪgrənt/ *–n.* unemployed itinerant. *–adj.* wandering, roving. □ **vagrancy** *n.* [Anglo-French]

vague /veɪg/ *adj.* **1** uncertain or ill-defined. **2** (of a person or mind) imprecise; inexact in thought, expression, or understanding. □ **vaguely** *adv.* **vagueness** *n.* [Latin *vagus* wandering]

vain *adj.* **1** having too high an opinion of one's looks, abilities, etc. **2** empty, trivial (*vain triumphs*). **3** useless; futile (*in the vain hope of finding it*). □ **in vain 1** without success. **2** lightly or profanely (*take his name in vain*). □ **vainly** *adv.* [Latin *vanus*]

vainglory /veɪnˈglɔːrɪ/ *n.* boastfulness; extreme vanity. □ **vainglorious** *adj.* [French *vaine gloire*]

valance /ˈvæləns/ *n.* (also **valence**) short curtain round the frame or canopy of a bedstead, above a window, etc. [Anglo-French *valer* descend]

vale *n.* (*archaic* except in place-names) valley. [Latin *vallis*]

valediction /ˌvælɪˈdɪkʃ(ə)n/ *n. formal* **1** bidding farewell. **2** words used in this. □ **valedictory** *adj.* & *n.* (*pl.* **-ies**). [Latin *vale* farewell]

valence[1] /ˈveɪləns/ *n.* = VALENCY.

valence[2] var. of VALANCE.

Valencia /vəˈlensɪə/ **1** city and port in E Spain, trading in oranges, rice, and silk; pop. (est. 1994) 764 293. **2** autonomous region in E Spain, on the Mediterranean; pop. (est. 1994) 3 909 047.

valency /ˈveɪlənsɪ/ *n.* (*pl.* **-ies**) combining power of an atom measured by the number of hydrogen atoms it can displace or combine with. [Latin *valentia* power]

valentine /ˈvælənˌtaɪn/ *n.* **1** card sent, often anonymously, as a mark of love on St Valentine's Day (14 Feb.). **2** sweetheart chosen on this day. [*Valentine*, name of two saints]

valerian /vəˈlɪərɪən/ *n.* any of various flowering herbs, esp. used as a sedative. [French from medieval Latin]

valet /ˈvælɪt, -leɪ/ *–n.* gentleman's personal servant. *–v.* (**-t-**) **1** work as a valet (for). **2** clean or clean out (a car). [French *va(s)let*, related to VARLET, VASSAL]

valetudinarian /ˌvælɪˌtjuːdɪˈneərɪən/ *–n.* person of poor health or who is unduly anxious about health. *–adj.* of a valetudinarian. □ **valetudinarianism** *n.* [Latin *valetudo* health]

valiant /ˈvæljənt/ *adj.* brave. □ **valiantly** *adv.* [Latin *valeo* be strong]

valid /ˈvælɪd/ *adj.* **1** (of a reason, objection, etc.) sound, defensible. **2 a** executed with the proper formalities, legally acceptable (*valid contract*; *valid passport*). **b** not yet expired. □ **validity** /vəˈlɪdɪtɪ/ *n.* [Latin *validus* strong: related to VALIANT]

validate /ˈvælɪˌdeɪt/ *v.* (**-ting**) **1** make valid; ratify. **2** check (computer data) for correctness or for compliance with the restrictions imposed on it. □ **validation** /-'deɪʃ(ə)n/ *n.*

valise /və'liːz/ *n. US* small portmanteau. [French from Italian]

Valium /'vælɪəm/ *n. propr.* drug diazepam used as a tranquillizer. [origin uncertain]

♦ **Valium holiday** *n. colloq.* non-trading day on a stock exchange or other commercial market; market holiday.

Valladolid /ˌvælədə'liːd/ city in N Spain, capital of Castilla-León region; a centre of industry, it produces beer, textiles, and other manufactures; pop. (est. 1994) 336 917.

Valle d'Aosta /ˌvæleɪ dɑː'ɒstə/ autonomous region in NW Italy; pop. (est. 1994) 118 239; capital, Aosta. Industry, powered by hydroelectricity, is becoming more important than agriculture; tourism is another source of revenue.

Valletta /və'letə/ capital of Malta, a commercial port on the N coast; pop. (est. 1995) 9129.

valley /'vælɪ/ *n.* (*pl.* **-s**) low area between hills, usu. with a stream or river flowing through it. [French: related to VALE]

Valona see VLORË.

♦ **valorization** /ˌvæləraɪ'zeɪʃ(ə)n/ *n.* (also **-isation**) raising or stabilization of the value of a commodity or currency by artificial means, usu. by a government. For example, if a government wishes to increase the price of a commodity that it exports it may attempt to decrease the supply of that commodity by encouraging producers to produce less, by stockpiling the commodity itself, or, in extreme cases, by destroying part of the production. □ **valorize** /'vælər-/ *v.*

valour /'vælə(r)/ *n.* (*US* **valor**) courage, esp. in battle. □ **valorous** *adj.* [Latin *valeo* be strong]

Valparaiso /ˌvælpə'raɪzəʊ/ principal port of Chile and terminus of the trans-Andean railway; it is a centre of commerce and industry, manufacturing chemicals, textiles, and vegetable oils; pop. (est. 1995) 282 168.

valuable /'væljʊəb(ə)l/ *–adj.* of great value, price, or worth. *–n.* (usu. in *pl.*) valuable thing. □ **valuably** *adv.*

valuation /ˌvæljʊ'eɪʃ(ə)n/ *n.* **1** estimation (esp. professional) of a thing's worth. **2** worth so estimated.

value /'væljuː/ *–n.* **1** worth, desirability, or utility, or the qualities on which these depend. In economic terms, value is now usu. regarded as a subjective quality depending on the scarcity of something that is desired at a particular time (see NEOCLASSICAL SCHOOL). However, Classical and Marxist economists regard value as an objective reality that can be quantified as the input of labour into goods or services (see CLASSICAL SCHOOL; MARXIST ECONOMICS). **2** worth as estimated (*set a high value on my time*). **3** amount for which a thing can be exchanged in the open market. **4** equivalent of a thing. **5** (in full **value for money**) something well worth the money spent. **6** effectiveness (*news value*). **7** (in *pl.*) one's principles, priorities, or standards. **8** *Mus.* duration of a note. **9** *Math.* amount denoted by an algebraic term. *–v.* (**-ues, -ued, -uing**) **1** estimate the value of, esp. professionally. **2** have a high or specified opinion of. □ **value received** words on a bill of exchange indicating that the bill is a means of paying for goods or services to the value of the bill. However, these words need not appear on a UK bill as everyone who has signed a UK bill is deemed to have been a party to it for value. **valueless** *adj.* **valuer** *n.* [French past part. of *valoir* be worth, from Latin *valeo*]

♦ **value added** *n.* value added to goods or services by a step in the chain of original purchase, manufacture or other enhancement, and retail. For example, if a manufacturer acquires a partly made component, the value added will be the combination of labour and profit that increase the value of the part before it is sold. See also GROSS DOMESTIC PRODUCT; VAT.

♦ **value added tax** see VAT.

♦ **value analysis** *n.* (also **VA**) examination of every feature of a product to ensure that its cost is no greater than is necessary to carry out its functions. Value analysis can be applied to a new product idea at the design stage and also to existing products.

♦ **valued policy** *n.* insurance policy in which the value of the subject matter is agreed when the cover starts. As a result, the amount to be paid in the event of a total-loss claim is already decided and does not need to be negotiated.

♦ **value for money audit** *n.* audit of a government department, charity, or other non-profit-making organization to assess whether or not it is functioning efficiently and giving value for the money it spends.

value judgement *n.* subjective estimate of worth etc.

valve *n.* **1** device controlling flow through a pipe etc., esp. allowing movement in one direction only. **2** structure in an organ etc. allowing a flow of blood etc. in one direction only. **3** = THERMIONIC VALVE. **4** device to vary the effective length of the tube in a trumpet etc. **5** half-shell of an oyster, mussel, etc. □ **valvular** /'vælvjʊlə(r)/ *adj.* [Latin *valva* leaf of a folding door]

vamoose /və'muːs/ *v. US slang* depart hurriedly. [Spanish *vamos* let us go]

vamp[1] *–n.* upper front part of a boot or shoe. *–v.* **1** (often foll. by *up*) repair or furbish. **2** (foll. by *up*) make by patching or from odds and ends. **3** improvise a musical accompaniment. [French *avantpié* front of the foot]

vamp[2] *colloq. –n.* woman who uses sexual attraction to exploit men. *–v.* allure and exploit (a man). [abbreviation of VAMPIRE]

vampire /'væmpaɪə(r)/ *n.* **1** supposed ghost or reanimated corpse sucking the blood of sleeping persons. **2** person who preys ruthlessly on others. **3** (in full **vampire bat**) tropical (esp. South American) bloodsucking bat. [French or German from Magyar]

VAN *abbr.* value added network, communications network with computer control to provide extra or specialized facilities.

van[1] *n.* **1** small covered goods vehicle. **2** railway carriage for luggage and for the guard. [abbreviation of CARAVAN]

van[2] *n.* vanguard, forefront. [abbreviation]

vanadium /və'neɪdɪəm/ *n.* hard grey metallic element used to strengthen steel. [Old Norse *Vanadís* name of the Scandinavian goddess Freyja]

Vancouver /væn'kuːvə(r)/ city and seaport in Canada, in British Columbia, a centre of commerce, tourism, and international trade, with food-processing, ship-repairing, fishing, and timber-related industries; city pop. (1991) 471 844; metropolitan area pop. (1995) 1 826 800.

Vancouver Island Canadian island off the Pacific coast, opposite Vancouver, containing the provincial capital, Victoria; timber, mining, fishing, and tourism are the chief sources of revenue; pop. (1986) 485 000.

Vanda see VANTAA.

vandal /'vænd(ə)l/ *n.* person who wilfully or maliciously damages property. □ **vandalism** *n.* [*Vandals*, name of a Germanic people that sacked Rome and destroyed works of art in the 5th century: Latin from Germanic]

vandalize /'vændəˌlaɪz/ *v.* (also **-ise**) (**-zing** or **-sing**) wilfully or maliciously destroy or damage (esp. public property).

Van Diemen's Land /væn 'diːmənz/ see TASMANIA.

V & V *abbr. Computing* verification and validation.

vane *n.* **1** weather-vane. **2** blade of a screw propeller or windmill etc. [dial. var. of obsolete *fane* banner]

vanguard /'vængɑːd/ *n.* **1** foremost part of an advancing army etc. **2** leaders of a movement etc. [French *avan(t)garde* from *avant* before: related to GUARD]

vanilla /və'nɪlə/ *n.* **1 a** tropical fragrant climbing orchid. **b** (in full **vanilla-pod**) fruit of this. **2** extract from the vanilla-pod, or a synthetic substance, used as flavouring. [Spanish diminutive of *vaina* pod]

vanish /ˈvænɪʃ/ *v.* **1** disappear. **2** cease to exist. [Latin: related to VAIN]

vanishing cream *n.* skin ointment that leaves no visible trace.

vanishing-point *n.* **1** point at which receding parallel lines appear to meet. **2** stage of complete disappearance.

vanity /ˈvænɪtɪ/ *n.* (*pl.* **-ies**) **1** conceit about one's appearance or attainments. **2** futility, unsubstantiality, unreal thing (*the vanity of human achievement*). **3** ostentatious display. [Latin: related to VAIN]

vanity bag *n.* (also **vanity case**) woman's make-up bag or case.

vanity unit *n.* wash-basin set into a unit with cupboards beneath.

vanquish /ˈvæŋkwɪʃ/ *v. literary* conquer, overcome. [Latin *vinco*]

Vantaa /ˈvæntɑː/ (Swedish **Vanda**) city in Finland, a former suburb of Helsinki; pop. (1994) 164 379.

vantage /ˈvɑːntɪdʒ/ *n.* **1** (also **vantage point**) place giving a good view. **2** *Tennis* = ADVANTAGE. [French: related to ADVANTAGE]

vapid /ˈvæpɪd/ *adj.* insipid; dull; flat. □ **vapidity** /vəˈpɪdɪtɪ/ *n.* [Latin *vapidus*]

vapor *US* var. of VAPOUR.

vaporize /ˈveɪpəˌraɪz/ *v.* (also **-ise**) (**-zing** or **-sing**) change into vapour. □ **vaporization** /-ˈzeɪʃ(ə)n/ *n.*

vapour /ˈveɪpə(r)/ *n.* (*US* **vapor**) **1** moisture or other substance diffused or suspended in air, e.g. mist, smoke. **2** gaseous form of a substance. **3** medicinal inhalant. □ **vaporous** *adj.* **vapoury** *adj.* [Latin *vapor* steam]

vapour trail *n.* trail of condensed water from an aircraft etc.

VAR *abbr. Computing* value added reseller, which increases the value of basic equipment with additional hardware and/or software.

Varanasi /vəˈrɑːnəsɪ/ (formerly **Benares** /bɪˈnɑːrɪz/) city in India, on the Ganges in the state of Uttar Pradesh, a place of pilgrimage for Hindus; pop. (1991) 929 270.

variable /ˈveərɪəb(ə)l/ *–adj.* **1** changeable, adaptable. **2** apt to vary; not constant. **3** *Math.* (of a quantity) indeterminate; able to assume different numerical values. *–n.* variable thing or quantity. □ **variability** /-ˈbɪlɪtɪ/ *n.* **variably** *adv.*

♦ **variable costs** see OVERHEAD COSTS.

♦ **variable-rate mortgage** *n.* (also **VRM**) mortgage in which the rate of interest is varied from time to time by the lender according to market conditions.

♦ **variable-rate note** *n.* (also **VRN**) bond, usu. with a fixed maturity, in which the interest is adjusted at regular intervals to reflect prevailing interest rates. It differs from a floating rate note in that the margin is not fixed but is adjusted at each coupon setting date.

♦ **variable-rate security** *n.* security in which the interest rate varies with market rates. Floating-rate notes, Eurobonds, and 90-day certificates of deposit are examples of variable-rate securities.

---

variance /ˈveərɪəns/ *n.* **1** (usu. prec. by *at*) difference of opinion; dispute (*we were at variance*). **2** discrepancy. **3** *Accounting* amount by which an actual cost differs from a standard cost (see STANDARD COSTING). Variances may be analysed into their causes, e.g. price variances, quantity variances, efficiency variances, sales mix variances, etc.

variant *–adj.* **1** differing in form or details from a standard (*variant spelling*). **2** having different forms (*forty variant types*). *–n.* variant form, spelling, type, etc.

variation /ˌveərɪˈeɪʃ(ə)n/ *n.* **1** varying. **2** departure from the normal kind, amount, a standard, etc. (*prices are subject to variation*). **3** extent of this. **4** variant thing. **5** *Mus.* theme in a changed or elaborated form.

♦ **variation margins** *n.pl.* gains or losses on open contracts in futures markets, calculated on the basis of the closing price at the end of each day. They are credited by the clearing-house to its members' accounts and by its members to their customers' accounts.

---

varicoloured /ˈveərɪˌkʌləd/ *adj.* (*US* **varicolored**) **1** variegated in colour. **2** of various colours. [Latin *varius* VARIOUS]

varicose /ˈværɪˌkəʊs/ *adj.* (esp. of a vein etc.) permanently and abnormally dilated. [Latin *varix* varicose vein]

varied /ˈveərɪd/ *adj.* showing variety.

variegated /ˈveərɪˌgeɪtɪd/ *adj.* **1** with irregular patches of different colours. **2** having leaves of two or more colours. □ **variegation** /-ˈgeɪʃ(ə)n/ *n.* [Latin: related to VARIOUS]

variety /vəˈraɪətɪ/ *n.* (*pl.* **-ies**) **1** diversity; absence of uniformity; many-sidedness. **2** quantity or collection of different things (*for a variety of reasons*). **3 a** class of things that differ from the rest in the same general class. **b** member of such a class. **4** (foll. by *of*) different form of a thing, quality, etc. **5** *Biol.* subdivision of a species. **6** series of dances, songs, comedy acts, etc. (*variety show*). [Latin: related to VARIOUS]

Varig /ˈværɪg/ *n.* Brazilian airline. [abbreviation of Portuguese *Viação Aérea Rio Grandense*]

various /ˈveərɪəs/ *adj.* **1** different, diverse (*from various backgrounds*). **2** several (*for various reasons*). □ **variously** *adv.* [Latin *varius*]

■ **Usage** *Various* (unlike *several*) cannot be used with *of*, as (wrongly) in *various of the guests arrived late.*

varlet /ˈvɑːlɪt/ *n. archaic* menial; rascal. [French var. of *vaslet* VALET]

Varna /ˈvɑːnə/ port and resort in Bulgaria, on the Black Sea; industries include engineering and boatbuilding, and it exports processed food and livestock; pop. (est. 1996) 301 421.

varnish /ˈvɑːnɪʃ/ *–n.* **1** resinous solution used to give a hard shiny transparent coating. **2** similar preparation (*nail varnish*). **3** deceptive outward appearance or show. *–v.* **1** apply varnish to. **2** give a deceptively attractive appearance to. [French *vernis*, probably ultimately from *Berenice* in Cyrenaica]

varsity /ˈvɑːsɪtɪ/ *n.* (*pl.* **-ies**) *colloq.* (esp. with ref. to sports) university. [abbreviation]

vary /ˈveərɪ/ *v.* (**-ies, -ied**) **1** be or become different; be

---

Vanuatu /ˌvænwɑːˈtuː/, **Republic of** (formerly, until 1980, **New Hebrides**) country consisting of a group of islands in the SW Pacific. Most of the labour force is engaged in agriculture: copra (the chief export), beef, cocoa, and coffee are the principal agricultural exports and yams, taro, cassava, breadfruit, and vegetables are grown as subsistence crops. There are also important fishing and timber industries, and tourism is expanding as an additional source of revenue. Discovered by the Portuguese in the early 17th century, the islands were administered jointly by Britain and France as a condominium until they became independent within the Commonwealth in 1980. President, Frederick Karlomuana Timakata; prime minister, Maxime Carlot Korman; capital, Vila (on Efate).

languages	English, French, and Bislama (all official)
currency	vatu (VT) of 100 centimes
pop. (1996)	172 000
GNP (1994)	US$189M
literacy	57% (m); 47% (f)
life expectancy	65 (m); 69 (f)

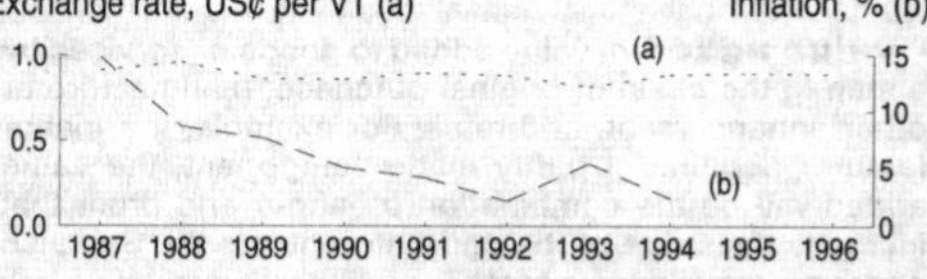

of different kinds; change. **2** make different; modify. [Latin *vario*: related to VARIOUS]

vas *n.* (*pl.* **vasa** /'veɪsə/) vessel or duct. [Latin, = vessel]

vascular /'væskjʊlə(r)/ *adj.* of or containing vessels for conveying blood, sap, etc. [Latin *vasculum* diminutive of VAS]

vas deferens /væs 'defəˌrenz/ *n.* (*pl.* **vasa deferentia** /ˌveɪsə ˌdefə'renʃɪə/) sperm duct of the testicle.

vase /vɑːz/ *n.* vessel used as an ornament or container for flowers. [Latin: related to VAS]

vasectomy /və'sektəmɪ/ *n.* (*pl.* **-ies**) removal of part of each vas deferens, esp. for sterilization.

Vaseline /'væsɪˌliːn/ *n. propr.* type of petroleum jelly used as an ointment etc. [German *Wasser* water, Greek *elaion* oil]

vassal /'væs(ə)l/ *n.* **1** *hist.* feudal tenant of land. **2** humble dependant. □ **vassalage** *n.* [medieval Latin *vassallus* retainer]

vast /vɑːst/ *adj.* immense, huge. □ **vastly** *adv.* **vastness** *n.* [Latin]

Västerås /'vɑːstərɜːs/ city in E Sweden, a port on Lake Mälaren and a centre of the electrical industry; pop. (est. 1996) 123 728.

♦ **VAT** /ˌviːeɪ'tiː, væt/ *abbr.* value added tax. Theoretically a tax on value added, in practice it resembles a sales tax in that each trader adds the tax to sale invoices and accounts for the tax so collected to Customs and Excise. However, the trader is permitted to deduct the amount of tax paid on the invoices received for goods and services (but not for wages and salaries). Thus the tax is an indirect tax, its burden being borne not by traders but by the ultimate consumers of their goods and services. The system is designed to avoid the cascade in which tax is paid on tax, as goods and services pass through long chains of activity; in VAT, all goods and services ultimately bear only the rate of tax applicable to the final sale to the consumer. VAT was introduced in the UK in 1973 to comply with its partners in the EC. In the UK all goods and services bear VAT at a rate of 17½% unless they are zero-rated or exempt.

---

vat *n.* tank, esp. for holding liquids in brewing, distilling, food manufacture, dyeing, and tanning. [dial. var. of *fat*, from Old English]

Vatican /'vætɪkən/ *n.* palace or government of the Pope in Rome. [name of a hill in Rome]

Vatican City State independent papal state in Rome, the seat of government of the Roman Catholic Church; head of government, Pope John Paul II; pop. (1996) 978. It has its own police force, diplomatic service, postal service, currency (the Vatican lira, interchangeable with the Italian lira), and radio station. The former papal states became incorporated into a unified Italy in 1870, and the temporal power of the pope was in suspense until 1929, when the Italian government recognized the full and independent sovereignty of the Holy See in the City of the Vatican.

vatu /'vɑːtuː/ *n.* standard monetary unit of Vanuatu.

vaudeville /'vɔːdəvɪl/ *n.* esp. *US* **1** variety entertainment. **2** light stage play with interspersed songs. □ **vaudevillian** /-'vɪlɪən/ *adj.* & *n.* [French]

vault /vɔːlt/ *–n.* **1** arched roof. **2** vaultlike covering (*vault of heaven*). **3** underground storage chamber or place of interment beneath a church or in a cemetery etc. **4** act of vaulting. *–v.* **1** leap, esp. using the hands or a pole. **2** spring over in this way. **3** (esp. as **vaulted**) **a** make in the form of a vault. **b** provide with a vault or vaults. [Latin *volvo* roll]

vaulting *n.* arched work in a vaulted roof or ceiling.

vaulting-horse *n.* wooden box for vaulting over.

vaunt /vɔːnt/ *v.* & *n. literary* boast. [Latin: related to VAIN]

VAX *abbr. propr.* range of computers manufactured by DEC. [*v*irtual *a*ddress e*x*tension]

VB *airline flight code* Birmingham European Airways.

VC *abbr.* **1** venture capital. **2** Victoria Cross.

VCR *abbr.* video cassette recorder.

VCT *abbr.* = VENTURE-CAPITAL TRUST.

VD *abbr.* venereal disease.

VDI *abbr.* (in computer graphics) virtual device interface.

VDT *abbr.* visual display terminal. See VISUAL DISPLAY UNIT.

♦ **VDU** *abbr.* = VISUAL DISPLAY UNIT.

VE *abbr.* Victory in Europe (in 1945).

've *abbr.* (usu. after pronouns) have (*I've*; *they've*).

veal *n.* calf's flesh as food. [French from Latin *vitulus* calf]

vector /'vektə(r)/ *n.* **1** *Math.* & *Physics* quantity having direction as well as magnitude. **2** carrier of disease. [Latin *veho vect-* convey]

vector graphics *n. Computing* method of producing pictorial images in which each line of the image is produced by a continuous movement of the spot on a VDU screen or the pen of a plotter.

Veda /'veɪdə/ *n.* (in *sing.* or *pl.*) oldest Hindu scriptures. □ **Vedic** *adj.* [Sanskrit, = knowledge]

VE day *n.* 8 May, the day marking Victory in Europe (in 1945).

veer /vɪə(r)/ *–v.* **1** change direction, esp. (of the wind) clockwise. **2** change in course or opinion etc. *–n.* change of direction. [French *virer*]

veg /vedʒ/ *n. colloq.* vegetable(s). [abbreviation]

vegan /'viːgən/ *–n.* person who does not eat animals or animal products. *–adj.* using or containing no animal products. [shortening of VEGETARIAN]

vegeburger var. of VEGGIE BURGER.

vegetable /'vedʒtəb(ə)l/ *–n.* **1** plant, esp. a herbaceous plant used for food, e.g. a cabbage, potato, or bean. **2** *colloq. derog.* **a** *offens.* person who is severely mentally incapacitated, esp. through brain injury etc. **b** dull or inactive person. *–adj.* of, derived from, or relating to plant life or vegetables as food. [Latin: related to VEGETATE]

vegetable marrow see MARROW 1.

vegetal /'vedʒɪt(ə)l/ *adj.* of or like plants. [medieval Latin: related to VEGETATE]

vegetarian /ˌvedʒɪ'teərɪən/ *–n.* person who does not eat meat or fish. *–adj.* excluding animal food, esp. meat (*vegetarian diet*). □ **vegetarianism** *n.* [from VEGETABLE]

vegetate /'vedʒɪˌteɪt/ *v.* (**-ting**) **1** live an uneventful or monotonous life. **2** grow as plants do. [Latin *vegeto* animate]

vegetation /ˌvedʒɪ'teɪʃ(ə)n/ *n.* plants collectively; plant life. [medieval Latin: related to VEGETATE]

vegetative /'vedʒɪtətɪv/ *adj.* **1** concerned with growth and development as distinct from sexual reproduction. **2** of vegetation. [French or medieval Latin: related to VEGETATE]

veggie /'vedʒɪ/ *n.* (also **vegie**) *colloq.* vegetarian. [abbreviation]

veggie burger *n.* (also **vegeburger**) flat cake like a hamburger but containing vegetables or soya protein instead of meat.

vehement /'viːəmənt/ *adj.* showing or caused by strong feeling; ardent (*vehement protest*). □ **vehemence** *n.* **vehemently** *adv.* [Latin]

vehicle /'viːɪk(ə)l/ *n.* **1** conveyance used on land or in space. **2** thing or person as a medium for expression or action. **3** liquid etc. as a medium for suspending pigments, drugs, etc. □ **vehicular** /vɪ'hɪkjʊlə(r)/ *adj.* [Latin *veho* carry]

veil /veɪl/ *–n.* **1** piece of usu. transparent fabric attached to a woman's hat etc., esp. to conceal or protect the face. **2** piece of linen etc. as part of a nun's headdress. **3** thing that hides or disguises (*a veil of silence*). *–v.* **1** cover with a veil. **2** (esp. as **veiled** *adj.*) partly conceal (*veiled threats*). □ **beyond the veil** in the unknown state of life after death. **draw a veil over** avoid discussing; hush up. **take the veil** become a nun. [Latin *velum*]

vein /veɪn/ *n.* **1 a** any of the tubes conveying blood to the heart. **b** (in general use) any blood-vessel. **2** rib of an insect's wing or leaf. **3** streak of a different colour in wood, marble, cheese, etc. **4** fissure in rock filled with ore. **5** specified character or tendency; mood (*spoke in a sarcastic vein*). □ **veined** *adj.* **veiny** *adj.* (**-ier, -iest**). [Latin *vena*]

Velcro /'velkrəʊ/ *n. propr.* fastener consisting of two strips of fabric which cling when pressed together. [French *velours croché* hooked velvet]

veld /velt/ *n.* (also **veldt**) *S.Afr.* open country. [Afrikaans: related to FIELD]

veleta /və'liːtə/ *n.* ballroom dance in triple time. [Spanish, = weather-vane]

vellum /'veləm/ *n.* **1 a** fine parchment, orig. calfskin. **b** manuscript on this. **2** smooth writing-paper imitating vellum. [French *velin*: related to VEAL]

velocity /vɪ'lɒsɪtɪ/ *n.* (*pl.* **-ies**) speed, esp. of inanimate things (*wind velocity*; *velocity of light*). [Latin *velox* swift]

♦ **velocity of circulation** *n. Econ.* average number of times that a unit of money is used in a specified period, approximately equal to the total amount of money spent in that period divided by the total amount of money in circulation. The **income velocity of circulation** is the number of times that a particular unit of currency forms part of a person's income in a specified period. It is given by the ratio of the gross national product to the amount of money in circulation. The **transactions velocity of circulation** is the number of times that a particular unit of currency is spent in a money transaction in a specified period, i.e. the ratio of the total amount of money spent in sales of goods or services to the amount of money in circulation.

---

velodrome /'veləˌdrəʊm/ *n.* place or building with a track for cycle-racing. [French *vélo* bicycle]

velour /və'lʊə(r)/ *n.* (also **velours** pronunc. same) plush-like fabric. [French]

velvet /'velvɪt/ *–n.* **1** soft fabric with a thick short pile on one side. **2** furry skin on a growing antler. *–adj.* of, like, or soft as velvet. □ **on velvet** in an advantageous or prosperous position. □ **velvety** *adj.* [Latin *villus* tuft, down]

velveteen /ˌvelvɪ'tiːn/ *n.* cotton fabric with a pile like velvet.

velvet glove *n.* outward gentleness, esp. cloaking firmness.

Ven. *abbr.* Venerable (as the title of an archdeacon).

venal /'viːn(ə)l/ *adj.* corrupt; able to be bribed; involving bribery. □ **venality** /-'nælɪtɪ/ *n.* **venally** *adv.* [Latin *venum* thing for sale]

■ **Usage** *Venal* is sometimes confused with *venial*, which means 'pardonable'.

vend *v.* offer (small wares) for sale. □ **vendible** *adj.* [Latin *vendo* sell]

Venda /'vendə/ former Bantu homeland in South Africa, designated an independent republic in 1979 but not recognized as such outside South Africa (see HOMELAND 2). Venda was abolished in 1994 following free democratic elections. Venda was amalgamated into Northern Province.

vendetta /ven'detə/ *n.* **1** blood feud. **2** prolonged bitter quarrel. [Latin: related to VINDICTIVE]

vending-machine *n.* slot-machine selling small items.

vendor *n. Law* seller, esp. of property. [Anglo-French: related to VEND]

♦ **vendor placing** *n.* sale of shares by a company (see PLACING) used as a means of acquiring another company or business. For example, if company X wishes to buy a business from company Y, it issues company X shares to company Y as payment with the prearranged agreement that these shares are then placed with investors in exchange for cash. Vendor placings have been popular with companies in recent years as a cheaper alternative to a rights issue. See also BOUGHT DEAL.

---

veneer /vɪ'nɪə(r)/ *–n.* **1** thin covering of fine wood etc. **2** (often foll. by *of*) deceptively pleasing appearance. *–v.* **1** apply a veneer to (wood etc.). **2** disguise. [German *furnieren* to furnish]

venerable /'venərəb(ə)l/ *adj.* **1** entitled to deep respect on account of character, age, associations, etc. (*venerable priest*; *venerable relics*). **2** title of an archdeacon in the Church of England. [Latin: related to VENERATE]

venerate /'venəˌreɪt/ *v.* (**-ting**) respect deeply. □ **veneration** /-'reɪʃ(ə)n/ *n.* **venerator** *n.* [Latin *veneror* revere]

venereal /vɪ'nɪərɪəl/ *adj.* **1** of sexual desire or intercourse. **2** of venereal disease. [Latin *venus veneris* sexual love]

venereal disease *n.* disease contracted by sexual intercourse with an infected person or congenitally.

Venetian /vɪ'niːʃ(ə)n/ *–n.* native, citizen, or dialect of Venice. *–adj.* of Venice. [from French or medieval Latin *Venetia* Venice]

venetian blind *n.* window-blind of adjustable horizontal slats.

Veneto /'veneˌtəʊ/ region in NE Italy; pop. (est. 1994) 4 415 309; capital, Venice.

Venezia see VENICE.

vengeance /'vendʒ(ə)ns/ *n.* punishment inflicted for wrong to oneself or one's cause. □ **with a vengeance** to a high or excessive degree (*punctuality with a vengeance*). [French *venger* from Latin *vindico* avenge]

Venezuela /ˌvene'zweɪlə/, **Republic of** country on the N coast of South America, with a coastline on the Caribbean Sea. Venezuela, a member of OPEC and LAIA, is one of the world's largest producers of oil, which contributes about three-quarters of export earnings and forms the basis of the country's economy. Aluminium and iron ore are also exported, and there are substantial deposits of natural gas, coal, diamonds, gold, zinc, copper, lead, and silver. There is an extensive beef and dairy farming industry; sugar cane, bananas, maize, rice, coffee, and cocoa are among the principal crops grown. Manufacturing industries include iron and steel, petrochemicals, textiles, clothing, plastics, and food processing.

History. Settled by the Spanish in the 16th century, Venezuela achieved independence in 1821 but did not finally emerge as a separate nation until its secession from the Federation of Grand Colombia in 1830. The country was then ruled by a succession of dictators. Following the Second World War wealth from its oil industry contributed to increased political stability and democracy. During the 1980s a decline in oil revenues led to economic crisis and serious rioting occurred in 1989 following price rises. Two unsuccessful coups took place in 1992, and the following year President Carlos Andrés Pérez was suspended pending trial for corruption charges. In late 1993 presidential elections were held; a former president was elected. Interim president, Rafael Caldera Rodríguez; Velásquez; capital, Caracas. □ **Venezuelan** *adj.* & *n.*

languages	Spanish (official), Indian languages
currency	bolívar (B) of 100 céntimos
pop. (1996)	22 311 000
GNP (1994)	US$59B
literacy	93% (m); 91% (f)
life expectancy	70 (m); 76 (f)

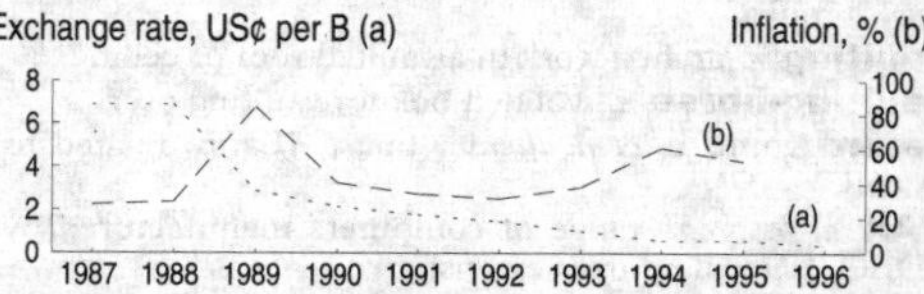

vengeful *adj.* vindictive; seeking vengeance. □ **vengefully** *adv.* [obsolete *venge* avenge: related to VENGEANCE]

venial /ˈviːnɪəl/ *adj.* (of a sin or fault) pardonable; not mortal. □ **veniality** /-ˈælɪtɪ/ *n.* **venially** *adv.* [Latin *venia* forgiveness]

■ **Usage** *Venial* is sometimes confused with *venal*, which means 'corrupt'.

Venice /ˈvenɪs/ (Italian **Venezia** /veˈnetsɪə/) city in NE Italy, built on numerous islands that are separated by canals and linked by bridges; it is a centre of tourism and commerce, manufacturing glassware, textiles, and lace; pop. (est. 1994) 306 439.

venison /ˈvenɪs(ə)n/ *n.* deer's flesh as food. [Latin *venatio* hunting]

Venn diagram *n.* diagram using overlapping and intersecting circles etc. to show the relationships between mathematical sets. [*Venn*, name of a logician]

venom /ˈvenəm/ *n.* **1** poisonous fluid of esp. snakes. **2** malignity; virulence. □ **venomous** *adj.* **venomously** *adv.* [Latin *venenum*]

venous /ˈviːnəs/ *adj.* of, full of, or contained in, veins. [Latin: related to VEIN]

vent[1] *–n.* **1** opening allowing the passage of air etc. **2** outlet; free expression (*gave vent to my anger*). **3** anus, esp. of a lower animal. *–v.* **1** make a vent in (a cask etc.). **2** give free expression to. □ **vent one's spleen on** scold or ill-treat without cause. [Latin *ventus* wind]

vent[2] *n.* slit in a garment, esp. in the lower edge of the back of a jacket. [French *fente* from Latin *findo* cleave]

ventilate /ˈventɪˌleɪt/ *v.* **(-ting) 1** cause air to circulate freely in (a room etc.). **2** air (a question, grievance, etc.). **3** *Med.* **a** oxygenate (the blood). **b** admit or force air into (the lungs). □ **ventilation** /-ˈleɪʃ(ə)n/ *n.* [Latin *ventilo* blow, winnow: related to VENT[1]]

ventilator *n.* **1** appliance or aperture for ventilating a room etc. **2** *Med.* = RESPIRATOR 2.

ventral /ˈventr(ə)l/ *adj.* of or on the abdomen. [*venter* abdomen, from Latin]

ventricle /ˈventrɪk(ə)l/ *n.* **1** cavity in the body. **2** hollow part of an organ, esp. the brain or heart. □ **ventricular** /-ˈtrɪkjʊlə(r)/ *adj.* [Latin *ventriculus* diminutive of *venter* belly]

ventriloquism /venˈtrɪləˌkwɪz(ə)m/ *n.* (also **ventriloquy**) skill of speaking without moving the lips, esp. as entertainment with a dummy. □ **ventriloquist** *n.* [Latin *venter* belly, *loquor* speak]

venture /ˈventʃə(r)/ *–n.* **1** risky undertaking. **2** commercial speculation. *–v.* **(-ring) 1** dare; not be afraid. **2** dare to go, make, or put forward (*venture out*; *venture an opinion*). **3 a** expose to risk; stake. **b** take risks. [from ADVENTURE]

♦ **venture capital** *n.* = RISK CAPITAL.

♦ **venture-capital trust** n. (also **VCT**) trust that provides capital for businesses. Investors can pay money into such trusts, which have the same tax advantages as PERSONAL EQUITY PLANS.

Venture Scout *n.* senior Scout.

venturesome *adj.* **1** disposed to take risks. **2** risky.

venue /ˈvenjuː/ *n.* place for a match, meeting, concert, etc. [French, from *venir* come]

Venus fly-trap /ˈviːnəs/ *n.* insectivorous plant. [Latin *Venus* goddess of love]

veracious /vəˈreɪʃəs/ *adj. formal* **1** truthful by nature. **2** (of a statement etc.) true. □ **veracity** /vəˈræsɪtɪ/ *n.* [Latin *verax* from *verus* true]

Veracruz /ˌveərəˈkruːz/ **1** state in E Mexico; pop. (est. 1995) 6 734 545; capital, Jalapa Enriquez. **2** city and port in Mexico, on the Gulf of Mexico; coffee, chicle, and tobacco are exported, and there are iron and steel and sugar-refining industries; pop. (1990) 438 821.

veranda /vəˈrændə/ *n.* (usu. covered) platform along the side of a house. [Hindi from Portuguese *varanda*]

verb *n.* word used to indicate action, a state, or an occurrence (e.g. *hear, be, happen*). [Latin *verbum* word]

verbal *–adj.* **1** of words. **2** oral, not written. **3** of a verb. **4** (of a translation) literal. **5** talkative. *–n.* **1** *slang* verbal statement to the police. **2** *slang* stream of abuse. □ **verbally** *adv.* [Latin: related to VERB]

■ **Usage** Some people reject sense 2 of *verbal* as illogical, and prefer *oral*. However, *verbal* is the usual term in expressions such as *verbal communication*, *verbal contract*, and *verbal evidence*.

verbalize *v.* (also **-ise**) (**-zing** or **-sing**) put into words.

verbal noun *n.* noun derived from a verb (e.g. *smoking* in *smoking is forbidden*: see -ING[1]).

verbatim /vɜːˈbeɪtɪm/ *adv.* & *adj.* in exactly the same words. [medieval Latin: related to VERB]

verbena /vɜːˈbiːnə/ *n.* (*pl.* same) plant of a genus of usu. annual or biennial plants with clusters of fragrant flowers. [Latin]

verbiage /ˈvɜːbɪɪdʒ/ *n. derog.* too many words or unnecessarily difficult words. [French: related to VERB]

verbose /vɜːˈbəʊs/ *adj.* using more words than are needed. □ **verbosity** /-ˈbɒsɪtɪ/ *n.* [Latin *verbosus* from *verbum* word]

verdant /ˈvɜːd(ə)nt/ *adj.* **1** (of grass, a field, etc.) green, lush. **2** (of a person) unsophisticated, green. □ **verdancy** *n.* [perhaps from French *verdeant* from *viridis* green]

verdict /ˈvɜːdɪkt/ *n.* **1** decision of a jury in a civil or criminal case. **2** decision; judgement. [Anglo-French *verdit* from *ver* true, *dit* saying]

verdigris /ˈvɜːdɪˌgriː/ *n.* greenish-blue substance that forms on copper or brass. [French, = green of Greece]

Verdun /vɜːˈdʌn/ fortified town in NE France, on the River Meuse; industries include brewing, textiles, and metallurgy; pop. (1990) 23 430.

verdure /ˈvɜːdjə(r)/ *n. literary* green vegetation or its colour. [French *verd* green]

Vereeniging /fəˈriːnɪkɪŋ/ city in South Africa, with coalmining and iron and steel industries; pop. (1991) 773 594 (with Vanderbijlpark and Sasolburg).

verge[1] *n.* **1** edge or border. **2** brink (*on the verge of tears*). **3** grass edging of a road etc. [Latin *virga* rod]

verge[2] *v.* **(-ging) 1** (foll. by *on*) border on. **2** incline downwards or in a specified direction. [Latin *vergo* bend]

verger *n.* **1** church caretaker and attendant. **2** officer preceding a bishop etc. with a staff. [Anglo-French: related to VERGE[1]]

verify /ˈverɪˌfaɪ/ *v.* **(-ies, -ied) 1** establish the truth, correctness, or validity of by examination etc. (*verified the keyboarded data*; *verify my figures*). **2** (of an event etc.) bear out (a prediction or promise). □ **verifiable** *adj.* **verification** /-fɪˈkeɪʃ(ə)n/ *n.* [medieval Latin: related to VERY]

verily /ˈverɪlɪ/ *adv. archaic* really, truly. [from VERY]

verisimilitude /ˌverɪsɪˈmɪlɪˌtjuːd/ *n.* appearance of being true or real. [Latin *verus* true, *similis* like]

veritable /ˈverɪtəb(ə)l/ *adj.* real; rightly so called (*a veritable feast*). □ **veritably** *adv.* [French: related to VERITY]

verity /ˈverɪtɪ/ *n.* (*pl.* **-ies**) **1** a fundamental truth. **2** *archaic* truth. [Latin *veritas* truth]

vermicelli /ˌvɜːmɪˈtʃelɪ/ *n.* **1** pasta in long slender threads. **2** shreds of chocolate as cake decoration etc. [Latin *vermis* worm]

vermicide /ˈvɜːmɪˌsaɪd/ *n.* drug that kills intestinal worms. [Latin *vermis* worm]

vermiculite /vəˈmɪkjʊˌlaɪt/ *n.* a hydrous silicate mineral used esp. as a moisture-holding medium for plant growth. [Latin *vermiculatus* worm-eaten, from *vermis* worm]

vermiform /ˈvɜːmɪˌfɔːm/ *adj.* worm-shaped. [medieval Latin: related to VERMICIDE]

vermiform appendix *n.* small blind tube extending from the caecum in man and some other mammals.

vermilion /vəˈmɪljən/ *–n.* **1** cinnabar. **2 a** brilliant red pigment made esp. from this. **b** colour of this. *–adj.* of this colour. [Latin *vermiculus* diminutive of *vermis* worm]

vermin /ˈvɜːmɪn/ *n.* (usu. treated as *pl.*) **1** mammals and birds harmful to game, crops, etc., e.g. foxes and rats. **2**

parasitic worms or insects. **3** vile people. □ **verminous** *adj.* [Latin *vermis* worm]

Vermont /vɜːˈmɒnt/ state in the NE US, bordering on Canada; pop. (est. 1996) 588 654; capital, Montpelier. Tourism and manufacturing industry are the chief sources of revenue; stone, sand, gravel, and asbestos are mined, and agriculture produces potatoes, corn, hay, dairy products, and maple syrup.

vermouth /ˈvɜːməθ/ *n.* wine flavoured with aromatic herbs. [German: related to WORMWOOD]

vernacular /vəˈnækjʊlə(r)/ *–n.* **1** language or dialect of a particular country. **2** language of a particular class or group. **3** homely speech. *–adj.* (of language) native; not foreign or formal. [Latin *vernaculus* native]

vernal /ˈvɜːn(ə)l/ *adj.* of or in spring. [Latin *ver* spring]

vernal equinox var. of SPRING EQUINOX.

vernier /ˈvɜːnɪə(r)/ *n.* small movable graduated scale for obtaining fractional parts of subdivisions on a fixed scale. [*Vernier*, name of a mathematician]

Verona /vəˈrəʊnə/ city in NE Italy, a centre of tourism, manufacturing textiles, leather goods, furniture, and paper; pop. (est. 1994) 256 756.

veronal /ˈverən(ə)l/ *n.* sedative drug. [German from VERONA]

veronica /vəˈrɒnɪkə/ *n.* speedwell. [medieval Latin, probably from St *Veronica*]

verruca /vəˈruːkə/ *n.* (*pl.* **verrucae** /-siː/ or **-s**) wart or similar growth, esp. on the foot. [Latin]

Versailles /veəˈsaɪ/ town in France, SW of Paris, noted for its royal palace; pop. (1990) 87 789.

versatile /ˈvɜːsəˌtaɪl/ *adj.* **1** adapting easily to different subjects or occupations; skilled in many subjects or occupations. **2** having many uses. □ **versatility** /-ˈtɪlɪtɪ/ *n.* [Latin *verto vers-* turn]

verse *n.* **1** poetry. **2** stanza of a poem or song. **3** each of the short numbered divisions of the Bible. **4** poem. [Latin *versus*: related to VERSATILE]

versed /vɜːst/ *adj.* (foll. by *in*) experienced or skilled in. [Latin *versor* be engaged in]

versicle /ˈvɜːsɪk(ə)l/ *n.* each of a priest's short sentences in a liturgy, answered by the congregation. [Latin diminutive: related to VERSE]

versify /ˈvɜːsɪˌfaɪ/ *v.* (**-ies, -ied**) **1** turn into or express in verse. **2** compose verses. □ **versification** /-fɪˈkeɪʃ(ə)n/ *n.* **versifier** *n.*

version /ˈvɜːʃ(ə)n/ *n.* **1** account of a matter from a particular point of view. **2** book etc. in a particular edition or translation (*Authorized Version*). **3** form or variant. [Latin *verto vers-* turn]

verso /ˈvɜːsəʊ/ *n.* (*pl.* **-s**) **1** left-hand page of an open book. **2** back of a printed leaf. [Latin *verso* (*folio*) on the turned (leaf)]

versus /ˈvɜːsəs/ *prep.* against (esp. in law and sport). [Latin: related to VERSE]

vertebra /ˈvɜːtɪbrə/ *n.* (*pl.* **-brae** /-ˌbriː/) each segment of a backbone. □ **vertebral** *adj.* [Latin *verto* turn]

vertebrate /ˈvɜːtɪbrət/ *–adj.* (of an animal) having a backbone. *–n.* vertebrate animal. [Latin *vertebratus* jointed: related to VERTEBRA]

vertex /ˈvɜːteks/ *n.* (*pl.* **-tices** /-tɪˌsiːz/ or **-texes**) **1** highest point; top, apex. **2 a** each angular point of a triangle, polygon, etc. **b** meeting-point of lines that form an angle. [Latin, = whirlpool, crown of a head, from *verto* turn]

vertical /ˈvɜːtɪk(ə)l/ *–adj.* **1** at right angles to a horizontal plane. **2** in a direction from top to bottom of a picture etc. **3** of or at the vertex. *–n.* vertical line or plane. □ **vertically** *adv.* [Latin: related to VERTEX]

♦ **vertical integration** (of companies) see INTEGRATION 3.

♦ **vertical mobility** see MOBILITY OF LABOUR.

---

vertical take-off *n.* take-off of an aircraft directly upwards.

vertiginous /vɜːˈtɪdʒɪnəs/ *adj.* of or causing vertigo. [Latin: related to VERTIGO]

vertigo /ˈvɜːtɪˌgəʊ/ *n.* dizziness caused esp. by heights. [Latin, = whirling, from *verto* turn]

vervain /ˈvɜːveɪn/ *n.* any of several verbenas, esp. one with small blue, white, or purple flowers. [Latin: related to VERBENA]

verve *n.* enthusiasm, vigour, spirit. [French]

Verviers /ˈveəvɪˌeɪ/ manufacturing town in Belgium, in the province of Liège; pop. (est. 1995) 53 940.

very /ˈverɪ/ *–adv.* **1** in a high degree (*did it very easily*). **2** in the fullest sense (foll. by *own* or superl. adj.: *do your very best*; *my very own room*). *–adj.* actual; truly such (*the very thing we need*; *his very words*; *the very same*). □ **not very** in a low degree, far from being. **very good** (or **well**) formula of consent or approval. **very high frequency** (in radio) 30-300 megahertz. **Very Reverend** title of a dean. [Latin *verus* true]

Very light /ˈvɪərɪ/ *n.* flare projected from a pistol for signalling or illuminating part of a battlefield etc. [*Very*, name of its inventor]

vesicle /ˈvesɪk(ə)l/ *n.* small bladder, bubble, or blister. [Latin]

vespers *n.pl.* evensong. [Latin *vesper* evening]

vessel /ˈves(ə)l/ *n.* **1** hollow receptacle, esp. for liquid. **2** ship or boat, esp. a large one. **3** duct or canal etc. holding or conveying blood or sap, etc., esp. = BLOOD-VESSEL. [Latin diminutive: related to VAS]

vest *–n.* **1** undergarment worn on the trunk. **2** *US* & *Austral.* waistcoat. *–v.* **1** (foll. by *with*) bestow (powers, authority, etc.) on. **2** (foll. by *in*) confer (property or power) on (a person) with an immediate fixed right of future possession. **3** clothe (oneself), esp. in vestments. [Latin *vestis* garment]

vestal virgin *n. Rom. Antiq.* virgin consecrated to Vesta and vowed to chastity. [*Vesta*, Roman goddess of the hearth and home]

♦ **vested interest** *n.* **1** personal interest in a state of affairs, the outcome of a transaction, etc., usu. with an expectation of gain. **2** *Law* interest (usu. in land or money held in trust) that is certain to come about rather than one dependent upon some event that may not happen. For example, a gift to 'A for life and then to B' means that A's interest is **vested in possession**, because A has the property now. B's gift is also vested (but not in possession) because A will certainly die sometime and then B (or B's estate if B is dead) will inherit the property. A gift to C 'if C reaches the age of 30' is not vested, because C may die before reaching that age. An interest that is not vested is known as a **contingent interest.**

---

vestibule /ˈvestɪˌbjuːl/ *n.* **1** hall or lobby of a building. **2** *US* enclosed space between railway-carriages. [Latin]

vestige /ˈvestɪdʒ/ *n.* **1** trace; sign. **2** slight amount; particle. **3** atrophied part or organ of an animal or plant that was well developed in ancestors. □ **vestigial** /-ˈtɪdʒɪəl/ *adj.* [Latin *vestigium* footprint]

vestment /ˈvestmənt/ *n.* ceremonial garment, esp. a chasuble. [Latin: related to VEST]

vestry /ˈvestrɪ/ *n.* (*pl.* **-ies**) church room or building for keeping vestments etc. in.

vet[1] *–n. colloq.* veterinary surgeon. *–v.* (**-tt-**) make a careful and critical examination of (a scheme, work, candidate, etc.). [abbreviation]

vet[2] *n. US* veteran. [abbreviation]

vetch *n.* plant of the pea family used largely for fodder. [Latin *vicia*]

veteran /ˈvetərən/ *n.* **1** (often *attrib.*) old soldier or long-serving member of any group (*war veteran*; *veteran actor*). **2** *US* ex-serviceman or servicewoman. [Latin *vetus -er-* old]

veteran car *n.* car made before 1916, or (strictly) before 1905.

veterinarian /ˌvetərɪˈneərɪən/ *n. formal* veterinary surgeon.

veterinary /ˈvetəˌrɪnərɪ/ *–adj.* of or for the diseases and injuries of animals. *–n.* (*pl.* **-ies**) veterinary surgeon. [Latin *veterinae* cattle]

veterinary surgeon *n.* person qualified to treat animals.

veto /ˈviːtəʊ/ *–n.* (*pl.* **-es**) **1** right to reject a measure, resolution, etc. unilaterally. **2** rejection, prohibition. *–v.* (**-oes, -oed**) **1** reject (a measure etc.). **2** forbid, prohibit. [Latin, = I forbid]

vex *v.* **1** anger, irritate. **2** *archaic* grieve, afflict. [Latin *vexo* afflict]

vexation /vekˈseɪʃ(ə)n/ *n.* **1** vexing or being vexed. **2** annoying or distressing thing.

vexatious /vekˈseɪʃ(ə)s/ *adj.* **1** causing vexation. **2** *Law* (of litigation) lacking sufficient grounds and seeking only to annoy the defendant.

vexed *adj.* (of a question) much discussed; problematic.

VFM *abbr.* value for money (audit).

VGA *abbr. Computing* video graphics array (type of colour graphics adaptor).

v.g.c. *abbr.* very good condition.

VH *international civil aircraft marking* Australia.

VHF *abbr.* very high frequency.

VHS *abbr. propr.* Video Home System (video cassette recording system).

VI *abbr.* Virgin Islands.

via /ˈvaɪə/ *prep.* through (*London to Rome via Paris; send it via your son*). [Latin, ablative of *via* way]

viable /ˈvaɪəb(ə)l/ *adj.* **1** (of a plan etc.) feasible, esp. economically. **2** (esp. of a foetus) capable of developing and surviving independently. □ **viability** /-ˈbɪlɪtɪ/ *n.* [French *vie* life]

viaduct /ˈvaɪəˌdʌkt/ *n.* long bridge, esp. a series of arches, carrying a road or railway across a valley or hollow. [Latin *via* way, after AQUEDUCT]

vial /ˈvaɪəl/ *n.* small (usu. cylindrical glass) vessel, esp. for holding medicines. [related to PHIAL]

viand /ˈvaɪənd/ *n. formal* (usu. in *pl.*) article of food. [Latin *vivo* live]

VIASA *abbr.* Venezuelan International Airways. [Spanish *Venezolana Internacional de Aviácion, SA*]

viaticum /vaɪˈætɪkəm/ *n.* (*pl.* **-ca**) Eucharist given to a dying person. [Latin *via* road]

vibes *n.pl. colloq.* **1** vibrations, esp. feelings communicated. **2** = VIBRAPHONE. [abbreviation]

vibrant /ˈvaɪbrənt/ *adj.* **1** vibrating. **2** (often foll. by *with*) thrilling, lively. **3** (of sound) resonant. **4** (of colours) bright and striking. □ **vibrancy** *n.* **vibrantly** *adv.* [Latin: related to VIBRATE]

vibraphone /ˈvaɪbrəˌfəʊn/ *n.* instrument like a xylophone but with motor-driven resonators under the metal bars giving a vibrato effect. [from VIBRATO]

vibrate /vaɪˈbreɪt/ *v.* (**-ting**) **1** move rapidly to and fro. **2** (of a sound) throb; resonate. **3** (foll. by *with*) quiver, thrill. **4** swing to and fro, oscillate. [Latin *vibro* shake]

vibration /vaɪˈbreɪʃ(ə)n/ *n.* **1** vibrating. **2** (in *pl.*) **a** mental, esp. occult, influence. **b** atmosphere or feeling communicated.

vibrato /vɪˈbrɑːtəʊ/ *n.* rapid slight variation in musical pitch producing a tremulous effect. [Italian: related to VIBRATE]

vibrator /vaɪˈbreɪtə(r)/ *n.* device that vibrates, esp. an instrument for massage or sexual stimulation. □ **vibratory** *adj.*

viburnum /vaɪˈbɜːnəm/ *n.* a shrub, usu. with white flowers. [Latin, = wayfaring-tree]

Vic. *abbr.* Victoria (Australia).

vicar /ˈvɪkə(r)/ *n.* clergyman of a Church of England parish where he formerly received a stipend rather than tithes: cf. RECTOR 1. [Latin *vicarius* substitute: related to VICE[3]]

vicarage *n.* vicar's house.

vicarious /vɪˈkeərɪəs/ *adj.* **1** experienced indirectly or second-hand. **2** acting or done for another. **3** deputed, delegated. □ **vicariously** *adv.* [Latin: related to VICAR]

vice[1] *n.* **1** immoral conduct. **2** form of this (*the vice of gluttony*). **3** weakness; indulgence (*brandy is my one vice*). [Latin *vitium*]

vice[2] *n.* (*US* **vise**) clamp with two jaws holding an object so as to leave the hands free to work on it. [*vis* screw, from Latin *vitis* vine]

vice[3] /ˈvaɪsɪ/ *prep.* in the place of; succeeding. [Latin, ablative of (*vix*) *vicis* change]

vice- *comb. form* forming nouns meaning: **1** substitute, deputy (*vice-president*). **2** next in rank to (*vice admiral*). [related to VICE[3]]

vice-chancellor /vaɪsˈtʃɑːnsələ(r)/ *n.* deputy chancellor (esp. administrator of a university).

vice-president /vaɪsˈprezɪd(ə)nt/ *n.* official ranking below and deputizing for a president. □ **vice-presidency** *n.* (*pl.* **-ies**). **vice-presidential** /-ˈdenʃ(ə)l/ *adj.*

viceregal /vaɪsˈriːg(ə)l/ *adj.* of a viceroy.

vicereine /ˈvaɪsreɪn/ *n.* **1** viceroy's wife. **2** woman viceroy. [French: related to VICE-, *reine* queen]

vice ring *n.* group of criminals organizing prostitution.

viceroy /ˈvaɪsrɔɪ/ *n.* sovereign's deputy ruler in a colony, province, etc. [French: related to VICE-, *roy* king]

vice squad *n.* police department concerned with prostitution etc.

vice versa /ˌvaɪsɪ ˈvɜːsə, vaɪs ˈvɜːsə/ *adj.* with the order of the terms changed; the other way round. [Latin, = the position being reversed]

vichyssoise /ˌviːʃiːˈswɑːz/ *n.* (usu. chilled) creamy soup of leeks and potatoes. [French, = of Vichy]

Vichy water /ˈviːʃiː/ *n.* effervescent mineral water from Vichy in France.

vicinity /vɪˈsɪnɪtɪ/ *n.* (*pl.* **-ies**) **1** surrounding district. **2** (foll. by *to*) nearness. □ **in the vicinity** (often foll. by *of*) near (to). [Latin *vicinus* neighbour]

vicious /ˈvɪʃəs/ *adj.* **1** bad-tempered, spiteful (*vicious dog, remark*). **2** violent (*vicious attack*). **3** corrupt, depraved. **4** (of reasoning etc.) faulty, unsound. □ **viciously** *adv.* **viciousness** *n.* [Latin: related to VICE[1]]

vicious circle *n.* self-perpetuating, harmful sequence of cause and effect.

vicious spiral *n.* vicious circle, esp. as causing inflation.

vicissitude /vɪˈsɪsɪˌtjuːd/ *n. literary* change, esp. of fortune. [Latin: related to VICE[3]]

Vicksburg /ˈvɪksbɜːg/ city in the US, in Mississippi, a distribution centre for cotton, timber, and livestock; pop. (1990) 20 908.

victim /ˈvɪktɪm/ *n.* **1** person or thing injured or destroyed (*road victim; victim of greed*). **2** prey; dupe (*fell victim to his charm*). **3** creature sacrificed to a deity or in a religious rite. [Latin]

victimize *v.* (also **-ise**) (**-zing** or **-sing**) **1** single out for punishment or discrimination. **2** make (a person etc.) a victim. □ **victimization** /-ˈzeɪʃ(ə)n/ *n.*

victor /ˈvɪktə(r)/ *n.* winner in a battle or contest. [Latin *vinco vict-* conquer]

Victoria /vɪkˈtɔːrɪə/ **1** state in SE Australia; pop. (est. 1996) 4 533 300; capital, Melbourne. Agriculture produces fruit, vines, wheat, sheep, and dairy products. Coal is mined, and there are engineering, oil-refining, and textile industries. **2** city and port in W Canada, capital of British Columbia on Vancouver Island; pop. (1991) 287 897. **3** capital of Seychelles, a seaport on the island of Mahé; pop. (est. 1993) 25 000.

Victoria Cross /vɪkˈtɔːrɪə/ *n.* highest decoration for conspicuous bravery in the armed services. [Queen *Victoria*]

Victorian *–adj.* **1** of the time of Queen Victoria. **2** prudish; strict. *–n.* person of this time.

Victoriana /vɪkˌtɔːrɪˈɑːnə/ *n.pl.* articles, esp. collectors' items, of the Victorian period.

Victoria sponge /vɪkˈtɔːrɪə/ *n.* sandwich sponge cake with a jam filling.

victorious /vɪk'tɔːrɪəs/ *adj.* **1** conquering, triumphant. **2** marked by victory. □ **victoriously** *adv.* [Latin: related to VICTOR]

victory /'vɪktərɪ/ *n.* (*pl.* **-ies**) defeat of an enemy or opponent.

victual /'vɪt(ə)l/ *–n.* (usu. in *pl.*) food, provisions. *–v.* (**-ll-**; *US* **-l-**) **1** supply with victuals. **2** obtain stores. **3** eat victuals. [Latin *victus* food]

victualler /'vɪtlə(r)/ *n.* (*US* **victualer**) **1** person etc. who supplies victuals. **2** (in full **licensed victualler**) publican etc. licensed to sell alcohol.

vicuña /vɪ'kjuːnə/ *n.* **1** South American mammal like a llama, with fine silky wool. **2 a** cloth from its wool. **b** imitation of this. [Spanish from Quechua]

vide /'vaɪdɪ/ *v.* (in *imper.*) see, consult (a passage in a book etc.). [Latin *video* see]

videlicet /vɪ'delɪˌset/ *adv.* = VIZ. [Latin *video* see, *licet* allowed]

video /'vɪdɪəʊ/ *–adj.* **1** of the recording (or reproduction) of moving pictures esp. on magnetic tape. **2** of the broadcasting of television pictures. *–n.* (*pl.* **-s**) **1** such recording or broadcasting. **2** *colloq.* = VIDEO RECORDER. **3** *colloq.* a film on videotape. *–v.* (**-oes, -oed**) record on videotape. [Latin, = I see]

video cassette *n.* cassette of videotape.

♦ **videoconferencing** *n.* communications facility enabling people at different locations to see and speak to each other, and hence hold meetings etc. In **Confravision**, public videoconferencing facilities, with studios in several major cities, are offered by British Telecom.

videodisc *n.* laser disc for recording moving pictures and sound and other data.

video game *n.* computer game played on a television screen.

video nasty *n. colloq.* horrific or pornographic video film.

video recorder *n.* (also **video cassette recorder**) apparatus for recording and playing videotapes.

videotape *–n.* magnetic tape for recording moving pictures and sound. *–v.* (**-ping**) record on this.

videotape recorder *n.* = VIDEO RECORDER.

♦ **videotex** /'vɪdɪəʊˌteks/ *n.* computer-based system providing information to users, esp. in business, via telephone links. Both text and primitive graphics can be transmitted. Special videotex terminals are available for professional use (e.g. by travel agents) and include a colour monitor, a keyboard, and a modem (for connection to the telephone network). The user selects information by typing in numbers, and the information is transmitted as a coded telephone signal and displayed on the screen, one 'page' at a time. Videotex provides interactive access to one or more sources of information; dialogue between the user and the videotex computers is conducted by means of the keyboard. See also PRESTEL; TELETEXT.

vie /vaɪ/ *v.* (**vies; vied; vying**) (often foll. by *with*) compete; strive for superiority. [probably French: related to ENVY]

Vienna /vɪ'enə/ (German **Wien** /viːn/) capital of Austria, on the River Danube; tourism is important, but the economy is based on trade and industry: manufactures include textiles, chemicals, machinery, and furniture; pop. (1991) 1 539 848. □ **Viennese** /ˌvɪə'niːz/ *adj.* & *n.*

Vientiane /vɪˌentɪ'ɑːn/ capital and chief port of Laos, on the Mekong River; pop. (est. 1990) 422 000.

Vietnamese /ˌvɪetnə'miːz/ *–adj.* of Vietnam. *–n.* (*pl.* same) native or language of Vietnam.

view /vjuː/ *–n.* **1** range of vision (*came into view*). **2 a** what is seen; prospect, scene, etc. **b** picture etc. of this. **3 a** opinion. **b** manner of considering a thing (*took a long-term view*). **4** inspection by the eye or mind (*private view*). *–v.* **1** look at; inspect with the idea of purchasing; survey visually or mentally. **2** form a mental impression or opinion of; consider. **3** watch television. □ **have in view 1** have as one's object. **2** bear (a circumstance) in mind. **in view of** considering. **on view** being shown or exhibited. **with a view to** with the hope or intention of. [Latin *video* see]

viewdata *n.* former name for VIDEOTEX.

viewer *n.* **1** person who views, esp. television. **2** device for looking at film transparencies etc.

viewfinder *n.* device on a camera showing the borders of the proposed photograph.

viewpoint *n.* point of view.

vigil /'vɪdʒɪl/ *n.* **1** keeping awake during the night etc., esp. to keep watch or pray. **2** eve of a festival or holy day. [Latin *vigilia*]

vigilance *n.* watchfulness, caution. □ **vigilant** *adj.* [Latin: related to VIGIL]

vigilante /ˌvɪdʒɪ'læntɪ/ *n.* member of a self-appointed group maintaining order etc. [Spanish, = vigilant]

vignette /viː'njet/ *n.* **1** short description, character

Vietnam /vjet'næm/, **Socialist Republic of** country in SE Asia, with its E coastline on the South China Sea. Vietnam's economy is predominantly agricultural: rice (an important export), rubber, coffee, tea, cotton, and soya-beans are grown. Sea fishing (contributing to exports) and livestock rearing are also important. The principal mineral export is crude petroleum; coal, tin, zinc, iron, antimony, and other minerals are also extracted. Manufacturing industry, concentrated mainly in the N, includes food processing, textiles, and the production of cement and fertilizers. In 1986 the government began to introduce reforms aimed at liberalizing the economy. Vietnam has suffered considerable economic problems in recent years due to the US trade embargo and consequent reduction in Western aid (as a result of Vietnam's invasion of Cambodia in 1978) and, since 1991, the collapse of its markets and sources of aid in the former Soviet Union and E Europe. However, the economy began to recover following loans in 1993 from the IMF and the World Bank. In 1995 Vietnam became a member of ASEAN.

History. Traditionally dominated by China, Vietnam came under increasing French influence in the second half of the 19th century. The country was occupied by the Japanese during the Second World War, and postwar hostilities between the French and the Communist Vietminh ended with French defeat and the partition of Vietnam along the 17th parallel in 1954. A prolonged war between North and South Vietnam, fought largely as a guerrilla campaign in the S, ended with the withdrawal of direct US military assistance to South Vietnam and its conquest by Communist forces in 1975, after which a reunited socialist republic was proclaimed (1976). Vietnamese forces invaded Cambodia in 1978–79, and in 1979 China invaded Vietnam, causing a large number of refugees (known as "boat people") to flee the country. In the 1980s there were armed clashes with Thailand. In 1989 Vietnamese troops withdrew from Cambodia. Head of state, Tran Duc Luong; prime minister, Phan Van Khai; capital, Hanoi.

languages	Vietnamese (official), French, English, Khmer, Chinese
currency	đông (D) of 10 hao, 100 xu, or 1000 trinh
pop. (1996)	76 151 000
GNP (1994)	US$13.7B
literacy	96% (m); 91% (f)
life expectancy	65 (m); 69 (f)

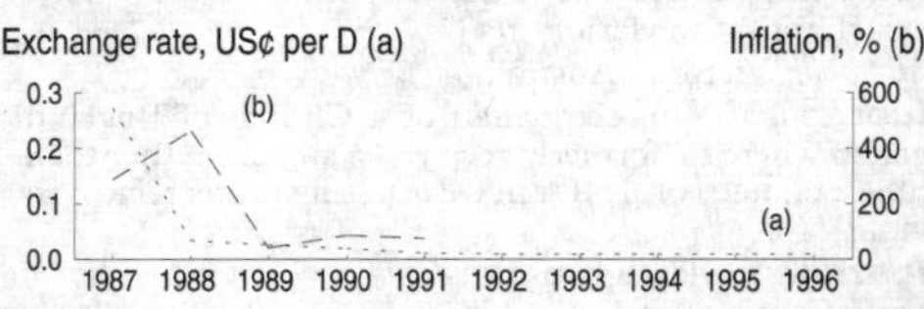

sketch. **2** book illustration not in a definite border. **3** photograph etc. with the background shaded off. [French, diminutive: related to VINE]

Vigo /ˈviːgəʊ/ seaport in NW Spain, on the Atlantic coast of Galicia; pop. (est. 1994) 288 573.

vigour /ˈvɪgə(r)/ *n.* (*US* **vigor**) **1** physical or mental strength or energy. **2** healthy growth. **3** forcefulness; trenchancy, animation. □ **vigorous** *adj.* **vigorously** *adv.* [French from Latin *vigeo* be lively]

Viking /ˈvaɪkɪŋ/ *n.* Scandinavian pirate and raider of the 8th–11th centuries. [Old Norse]

Vila /ˈviːlə/ (also **Port Vila**) capital of Vanuatu, on the SW coast of the island of Efate; pop. (est. 1993) 26 100.

vile *adj.* **1** disgusting. **2** depraved. **3** *colloq.* abominable (*vile weather*). □ **vilely** *adv.* **vileness** *n.* [Latin *vilis* cheap, base]

vilify /ˈvɪlɪˌfaɪ/ *v.* (**-ies**, **-ied**) defame; malign. □ **vilification** /-fɪˈkeɪʃ(ə)n/ *n.* [Latin: related to VILE]

villa /ˈvɪlə/ *n.* **1** country house; mansion. **2** rented holiday home, esp. abroad. **3** (usu. as part of an address) detached or semi-detached house in a residential district. [Italian and Latin]

village /ˈvɪlɪdʒ/ *n.* **1** country settlement, larger than a hamlet and smaller than a town. **2** self-contained village-like community within a city etc. (*Greenwich village*; *Olympic village*). □ **villager** *n.* [Latin: related to VILLA]

villain /ˈvɪlən/ *n.* **1** wicked person. **2** chief evil character in a play, story, etc. **3** *colloq.* professional criminal. **4** *colloq.* rascal. [Latin: related to VILLA]

villainous *adj.* wicked.

villainy *n.* (*pl.* **-ies**) wicked behaviour or act. [French: related to VILLAIN]

villein /ˈvɪlɪn/ *n. hist.* feudal tenant entirely subject to a lord or attached to a manor. □ **villeinage** *n.* [var. of VILLAIN]

Vilnius /ˈvɪlnɪəs/ capital of Lithuania, a centre of commerce and manufacturing industry; pop. (1995) 575 700.

vim *n. colloq.* vigour. [perhaps from Latin, accusative of *vis* energy]

VIN *abbr. US* vehicle identification number.

vinaigrette /ˌvɪnɪˈgret/ *n.* **1** salad dressing of oil, wine vinegar, and seasoning. **2** small bottle for smelling-salts. [French, diminutive: related to VINEGAR]

vindicate /ˈvɪndɪˌkeɪt/ *v.* (**-ting**) **1** clear of blame or suspicion. **2** establish the existence, merits, or justice of (something disputed etc.). **3** justify by evidence or argument. □ **vindication** /-ˈkeɪʃ(ə)n/ *n.* **vindicator** *n.* **vindicatory** *adj.* [Latin *vindico* claim]

vindictive /vɪnˈdɪktɪv/ *adj.* vengeful. □ **vindictively** *adv.* **vindictiveness** *n.* [Latin *vindicta* vengeance: related to VINDICATE]

vine *n.* **1** climbing or trailing plant with a woody stem, esp. bearing grapes. **2** stem of this. [Latin *vinea* vineyard]

vinegar /ˈvɪnɪgə(r)/ *n.* sour liquid got from malt, wine, cider, etc., by fermentation and used as a condiment or for pickling. □ **vinegary** *adj.* [French, = sour wine: related to EAGER]

vineyard /ˈvɪnjəd/ *n.* plantation of grapevines, esp. for wine-making.

vingt-et-un /ˌvæ̃teɪˈɜː/ *n.* = PONTOON[1]. [French, = twenty-one]

vino /ˈviːnəʊ/ *n. slang* wine, esp. of an inferior kind. [Italian, = wine]

vinous /ˈvaɪnəs/ *adj.* **1** of, like, or due to wine. **2** addicted to wine. [Latin *vinum* wine]

vintage /ˈvɪntɪdʒ/ *–n.* **1 a** season's produce of grapes. **b** wine from this. **2 a** gathering of grapes for wine-making. **b** season of this. **3** wine of high quality from a particular year and district. **4 a** year etc. when a thing was made etc. **b** thing made etc. in a particular year etc. *–adj.* **1** of high or peak quality. **2** of a past season. [Latin *vinum* wine]

vintage car *n.* car made 1917–30.

vintner *n.* wine-merchant. [Anglo-Latin from French, ultimately from Latin *vinetum* vineyard, from *vinum* wine]

vinyl /ˈvaɪnɪl/ *n.* plastic made by polymerization, esp. polyvinyl chloride. [Latin *vinum* wine]

viol /ˈvaɪəl/ *n.* medieval stringed instrument of various sizes, like a violin but held vertically. [French from Provençal]

viola[1] /vɪˈəʊlə/ *n.* instrument larger than the violin and of lower pitch. [Italian and Spanish: related to VIOL]

viola[2] /ˈvaɪələ/ *n.* any plant of the genus including the pansy and violet, esp. a cultivated hybrid. [Latin, = violet]

viola da gamba /vɪˌəʊlə də ˈgæmbə/ *n.* viol held between the player's legs.

violate /ˈvaɪəˌleɪt/ *v.* (**-ting**) **1** disregard; break (an oath, treaty, law, etc.). **2** treat (a sanctuary etc.) profanely; disrespect. **3** disturb (a person's privacy etc.). **4** rape. □ **violable** *adj.* **violation** /-ˈleɪʃ(ə)n/ *n.* **violator** *n.* [Latin *violo*]

violence /ˈvaɪələns/ *n.* **1** being violent. **2** violent conduct or treatment. **3** unlawful use of force. □ **do violence to** act contrary to; outrage. [Latin: related to VIOLENT]

violent /ˈvaɪələnt/ *adj.* **1** involving or using great physical force (*violent person*; *violent storm*). **2 a** intense, vehement (*violent pain*; *violent dislike*). **b** lurid (*violent colours*). **3** (of death) resulting from violence or poison. □ **violently** *adv.* [French from Latin]

violet /ˈvaɪələt/ *–n.* **1** sweet-scented plant with usu. purple, blue, or white flowers. **2** bluish-purple colour at the end of the spectrum opposite red. **3** pigment or clothes or material of this colour. *–adj.* of this colour. [French diminutive of *viole* VIOLA[2]]

violin /ˌvaɪəˈlɪn/ *n.* high-pitched stringed instrument played with a bow. □ **violinist** *n.* [Italian diminutive of VIOLA[1]]

violist /ˈvaɪəlɪst/ *n.* viol- or viola-player.

violoncello /ˌvaɪələnˈtʃeləʊ/ *n.* (*pl.* **-s**) *formal* = CELLO. [Italian, diminutive of *violone* bass viol]

VIP *abbr.* very important person.

viper /ˈvaɪpə(r)/ *n.* **1** small venomous snake. **2** malignant or treacherous person. [Latin]

virago /vɪˈrɑːgəʊ/ *n.* (*pl.* **-s**) fierce or abusive woman. [Latin, = female warrior]

viral /ˈvaɪər(ə)l/ *adj.* of or caused by a virus.

virgin /ˈvɜːdʒɪn/ *–n.* **1** person who has never had sexual intercourse. **2** (**the Virgin**) Christ's mother Mary. **3** (**the Virgin**) sign or constellation Virgo. *–adj.* **1** not yet used etc. **2** virginal. [Latin *virgo -gin-*]

virginal *–adj.* of or befitting a virgin. *–n.* (usu. in *pl.*) *Mus.* legless spinet in a box. [Latin: related to VIRGIN]

virgin birth *n.* **1** (usu. preceded by *the*) doctrine of Christ's birth from a virgin mother. **2** parthenogenesis.

Virginia /vəˈdʒɪnɪə/ state in the US, on the Atlantic coast; pop. (est. 1996) 6 675 451; capital, Richmond. Industries include chemicals, tobacco processing, coalmining, fishing, and tourism; agriculture produces corn, hay, tobacco, apples, and peaches. *–n.* **1** tobacco from Virginia. **2** cigarette made of this. □ **Virginian** *n.* & *adj.*

Virginia creeper *n.* ornamental vine. [VIRGINIA]

Virgin Islands group of Caribbean islands in the Lesser Antilles, divided between British and US administration. The **British Virgin Islands** comprise a dependency of about 42 islands (the largest is Tortola); pop. (1993) 17 000; capital, Road Town. Tourism is the principal industry; exports include fresh fish, sand and gravel, rum, and fruit and vegetables. The **Virgin Islands of the United States** (comprising St Croix, St Thomas, St John, and about 50 smaller islands) constitute an overseas territory of the US; pop. (1991) 99 404; capital, Charlotte Amalie. Industries include tourism, finance, and petroleum refining.

virginity /vəˈdʒɪnɪtɪ/ *n.* state of being a virgin.

Virgo /ˈvɜːgəʊ/ *n.* (*pl.* **-s**) **1** constellation and sixth sign of the zodiac (the Virgin). **2** person born when the sun is in this sign. [Latin: related to VIRGIN]

virile /ˈvɪraɪl/ *adj.* **1** (of a man) vigorous or strong. **2** sexually potent. **3** of a man as distinct from a woman or child. □ **virility** /vɪˈrɪlɪtɪ/ *n.* [Latin *vir* man]

virology /vaɪˈrɒlədʒɪ/ *n.* the study of viruses. □ **virologist** *n.*

virtual /ˈvɜːtʃʊəl/ *adj.* being so in practice though not strictly or in name (*the virtual manager*; *a virtual promise*). [medieval Latin: related to VIRTUE]

virtually *adv.* in effect, nearly, almost.

virtual reality *n.* simulation of the real world by a computer.

virtual storage *n.* means of effectively extending the amount of storage space available in the main store of a (usu. large) computer.

virtue /ˈvɜːtʃuː/ *n.* **1** moral excellence; goodness. **2** particular form of this. **3** (esp. female) chastity. **4** good quality (*has the virtue of speed*). **5** efficacy (*no virtue in such drugs*). □ **by** (or **in**) **virtue of** on account of, because of. [Latin: related to VIRILE]

virtuoso /ˌvɜːtʃʊˈəʊsəʊ/ *n.* (*pl.* **-si** /-siː/ or **-s**) (often *attrib.*) highly skilled artist, esp. a musician (*virtuoso performance*). □ **virtuosic** /-ˈɒsɪk/ *adj.* **virtuosity** /-ˈɒsɪtɪ/ *n.* [Italian: related to VIRTUOUS]

virtuous /ˈvɜːtʃʊəs/ *adj.* **1** morally good. **2** *archaic* chaste. □ **virtuously** *adv.* [Latin: related to VIRTUE]

virulent /ˈvɪrʊlənt/ *adj.* **1** strongly poisonous. **2** (of a disease) violent. **3** bitterly hostile. □ **virulence** *n.* **virulently** *adv.* [Latin: related to VIRUS]

virus /ˈvaɪərəs/ *n.* **1** microscopic organism often causing diseases. **2** = COMPUTER VIRUS. [Latin, = poison]

visa /ˈviːzə/ *n.* endorsement on a passport etc., esp. allowing entrance to or exit from a country. [Latin, = seen]

visage /ˈvɪzɪdʒ/ *n. literary* face. [Latin *visus* sight]

Visakhapatnam /vɪˌʃækəˈpʌtnəm/ seaport in SE India, on the coast of Andhra Pradesh; pop. (1991) 752 037.

vis-à-vis /ˌviːzəˈviː/ *–prep.* **1** in relation to. **2** in comparison with. *–adv.* opposite. [French, = face to face: related to VISAGE]

viscera /ˈvɪsərə/ *n.pl.* internal organs of the body. [Latin]

visceral *adj.* **1** of the viscera. **2** of feelings rather than reason.

viscid /ˈvɪsɪd/ *adj.* glutinous, sticky. [Latin: related to VISCOUS]

viscose /ˈvɪskəʊz/ *n.* **1** cellulose in a highly viscous state, used for making rayon etc. **2** fabric made from this. [Latin: related to VISCOUS]

viscount /ˈvaɪkaʊnt/ *n.* British nobleman ranking between an earl and a baron. □ **viscountcy** *n.* (*pl.* **-ies**). [Anglo-French: related to VICE-, COUNT^{2}]

viscountess *n.* **1** viscount's wife or widow. **2** woman holding the rank of viscount.

viscous /ˈvɪskəs/ *adj.* **1** glutinous, sticky. **2** semifluid. **3** not flowing freely. □ **viscosity** /-ˈkɒsɪtɪ/ *n.* (*pl.* **-ies**). [Latin *viscum* birdlime]

vise *US* var. of VICE^{2}.

visibility /ˌvɪzɪˈbɪlɪtɪ/ *n.* **1** being visible. **2** range or possibility of vision as determined by the light and weather.

visible /ˈvɪzɪb(ə)l/ *–adj.* **1** able to be seen, perceived, or ascertained. **2** (of exports etc.) consisting of actual goods. *–n.* (in *pl.*) earnings from exports and payments for imports of goods, as opposed to services (e.g. banking and insurance). The balance of trade is made up of visibles and is sometimes called the **visible balance.** □ **visibly** *adv.* [Latin: related to VISION]

vision /ˈvɪʒ(ə)n/ *n.* **1** act or faculty of seeing, sight. **2** thing or person seen in a dream or trance. **3** mental picture (*visions of hot toast*). **4** imaginative insight. **5** statesmanlike foresight. **6** beautiful person etc. **7** television or cinema picture, esp. of specified quality (*poor vision*). [Latin *video vis-* see]

visionary *–adj.* **1** given to seeing visions or to fanciful theories. **2** having vision or foresight. **3** not real, imaginary. **4** not practicable. *–n.* (*pl.* **-ies**) visionary person.

visit /ˈvɪzɪt/ *–v.* (**-t-**) **1** (also *absol.*) go or come to see or inspect (a person, place, etc.). **2** stay temporarily with (a person) or at (a place). **3** (of a disease, calamity, etc.) attack. **4 a** (foll. by *with*) punish (a person). **b** (often foll. by *upon*) inflict punishment for (a sin). *–n.* **1 a** act of visiting. **b** temporary stay, esp. as a guest. **2** (foll. by *to*) occasion of going to a doctor etc. **3** formal or official call. [Latin: related to VISION]

visitant /ˈvɪzɪt(ə)nt/ *n.* **1** visitor, esp. a ghost etc. **2** migratory bird resting temporarily in an area.

visitation /ˌvɪzɪˈteɪʃ(ə)n/ *n.* **1** official visit of inspection. **2** trouble etc. seen as divine punishment. **3** (**Visitation**) **a** visit of the Virgin Mary to Elizabeth. **b** festival of this.

visitor *n.* **1** person who visits. **2** migrant bird staying for part of the year.

visitors' book *n.* book for visitors to a hotel, church, etc., to sign, make remarks in, etc.

visor /ˈvaɪzə(r)/ *n.* (also **vizor**) **1** movable part of a helmet covering the face. **2** shield for the eyes, esp. one at the top of a vehicle windscreen. [Anglo-French *viser*: related to VISAGE]

VISS *abbr. Computing* VHS index search system.

vista /ˈvɪstə/ *n.* **1** long narrow view as between rows of trees. **2** mental view of a long series of events. [Italian]

visual /ˈvɪʒʊəl/ *adj.* of or used in seeing. □ **visually** *adv.* [Latin *visus* sight]

visual aid *n.* film etc. as a teaching aid.

visual display unit *n.* (also **VDU**) device that displays computer output (in written or pictorial form) temporarily on a screen. It typically consists of a television-like cathode-ray tube and is usu. paired with a keyboard, by which information can be fed into the computer. The screen can usu. display 80 characters on each of 24 lines, but these numbers vary from one machine to another. A screen with graphics capability is divided into a much larger number of tiny rectangular areas (see PIXEL 1).

visualize *v.* (also **-ise**) (**-zing** or **-sing**) imagine visually. □ **visualization** /-ˈzeɪʃ(ə)n/ *n.*

vital /ˈvaɪt(ə)l/ *–adj.* **1** of or essential to organic life (*vital functions*). **2** essential, indispensable (*of vital importance*). **3** full of life or activity. **4** fatal (*vital error*). *–n.* (in *pl.*) the body's vital organs, e.g. the heart and brain. □ **vitally** *adv.* [Latin *vita* life]

vitality /vaɪˈtælɪtɪ/ *n.* **1** liveliness, animation. **2** ability to survive or endure. [Latin: related to VITAL]

vitalize /ˈvaɪtəˌlaɪz/ *v.* (also **-ise**) (**-zing** or **-sing**) **1** endow with life. **2** make lively or vigorous. □ **vitalization** /-ˈzeɪʃ(ə)n/ *n.*

vital statistics *n.pl.* **1** *joc.* measurements of a woman's bust, waist, and hips. **2** statistics relating to a nation's or region's population, including its birth rate, death rate, marriage rate, etc.

vitamin /ˈvɪtəmɪn/ *n.* any of various substances present in many foods and essential to health and growth (*vitamin A, B, C,* etc.). [Latin *vita* life, AMINE]

vitamin B complex *n.* any of a group of vitamins often found together in the same foods.

vitaminize /ˈvɪtəmɪˌnaɪz/ *v.* (also **-ise**) (**-zing** or **-sing**) add vitamins to.

vitiate /ˈvɪʃɪˌeɪt/ *v.* (**-ting**) **1** impair, debase. **2** make invalid or ineffectual. □ **vitiation** /-ˈeɪʃ(ə)n/ *n.* [Latin: related to VICE^{1}]

viticulture /ˈvɪtɪˌkʌltʃə(r)/ *n.* cultivation of grapes. [Latin *vitis* vine]

Viti Levu /ˌviːtiː ˈleɪvuː/ largest of the islands of Fiji; pop. (1986) 340 561; chief settlement, Suva (capital of Fiji). Crops include rice, cotton, sugar, and pineapples, and gold is mined.

Vitoria /vɪˈtɔːrɪə/ town in NE Spain, capital of the Basque provinces; it is a centre of commerce and manufacturing industry, trading in cereals and wine; pop. (1991) 258 243.

vitreous /ˈvɪtrɪəs/ *adj.* of or like glass. [Latin *vitrum* glass]

vitreous humour *n.* clear fluid in the eye between the lens and the retina.

vitrify /ˈvɪtrɪˌfaɪ/ *v.* (**-ies, -ied**) change into glass or a glasslike substance, esp. by heat. □ **vitrifaction**

/-'fækʃ(ə)n/ *n.* **vitrification** /-fɪ'keɪʃ(ə)n/ *n.* [French or medieval Latin: related to VITREOUS]

vitriol /'vɪtrɪəl/ *n.* **1** sulphuric acid or a sulphate. **2** caustic or hostile speech or criticism. [Latin *vitrum*]

vitriolic /ˌvɪtrɪ'ɒlɪk/ *adj.* caustic, hostile.

vituperate /vaɪ'tju:pəˌreɪt/ *v.* (**-ting**) criticize abusively. □ **vituperation** /-'reɪʃ(ə)n/ *n.* **vituperative** /-rətɪv/ *adj.* [Latin]

viva[1] /'vaɪvə/ *colloq.* –*n.* (*pl.* **-s**) = VIVA VOCE. –*v.* (**vivas, vivaed, vivaing**) = VIVA-VOCE. [abbreviation]

viva[2] /'vi:və/ –*int.* long live. –*n.* cry of this as a salute etc. [Italian, = let live]

vivace /vɪ'vɑ:tʃɪ/ *adv. Mus.* in a lively manner. [Latin: related to VIVACIOUS]

vivacious /vɪ'veɪʃəs/ *adj.* lively, animated. □ **vivacity** /vɪ'væsɪtɪ/ *n.* [Latin *vivax* from *vivo* live]

vivarium /vaɪ'veərɪəm/ *n.* (*pl.* **-ria** or **-s**) **1** glass bowl etc. for keeping animals for scientific study. **2** enclosure for keeping animals in (nearly) their natural state. [Latin]

viva voce /ˌvaɪvə 'vəʊtʃɪ/ –*adj.* oral. –*adv.* orally. –*n.* oral examination. –*v.* (**viva-voce**) (**-vocees, -voceed, -voceing**) examine orally. [medieval Latin, = with the living voice]

vivid /'vɪvɪd/ *adj.* **1** (of light or colour) strong, intense. **2** (of a memory, description, the imagination, etc.) clear, lively, graphic. □ **vividly** *adv.* **vividness** *n.* [Latin]

vivify /'vɪvɪˌfaɪ/ *v.* (**-ies, -ied**) enliven, animate, give life to. [French from Latin]

viviparous /vɪ'vɪpərəs/ *adj. Zool.* bringing forth young alive. [Latin *vivus* alive, *pario* produce]

vivisect /'vɪvɪˌsekt/ *v.* perform vivisection on.

vivisection /ˌvɪvɪ'sekʃ(ə)n/ *n.* surgical experimentation on living animals for scientific research. □ **vivisectional** *adj.* **vivisectionist** *n.* & *adj.* **vivisector** /'vɪvɪˌsektə(r)/ *n.* [Latin *vivus* living, DISSECTION]

vixen /'vɪks(ə)n/ *n.* **1** female fox. **2** spiteful woman. [Old English: related to FOX]

viz. /vɪz, or by substitution 'neɪmlɪ/ *adv.* namely; that is to say; in other words. [abbreviation of VIDELICET, *z* = medieval Latin symbol for abbreviation of *-et*]

vizier /vɪ'zɪə(r)/ *n. hist.* high official in some Muslim countries. [ultimately from Arabic]

vizor var. of VISOR.

Vladivostok /ˌvlædɪ'vɒstɒk/ principal seaport of Russia, on the Pacific E coast; it is an important naval base, and the terminus of the Trans-Siberian railway, with shipbuilding and food-processing industries; pop. (est. 1995) 632 000.

VLBC *abbr.* very large bulk carrier (ship).

VLCC *abbr.* very large crude carrier (oil tanker).

Vlorë /'vlɔ:rə/ (also **Vlona** /'vləʊnə/, Italian **Valona**) port in SW Albania, on the Adriatic coast; activities include fishing and olive-oil refining; pop. (est. 1991) 76 000.

VLSI *abbr. Electronics* very large-scale integration (on integrated circuits).

VMS *abbr. Computing* voice messaging system.

VN *abbr.*, *international vehicle registration*, & *international civil aircraft marking* Vietnam.

V-neck *n.* (often *attrib.*) V-shaped neckline on a pullover etc.

vocable /'vəʊkəb(ə)l/ *n.* word, esp. with reference to form not meaning. [Latin *voco* call]

vocabulary /və'kæbjʊlərɪ/ *n.* (*pl.* **-ies**) **1** words used by a particular language, book, branch of science, or author. **2** list of these, in alphabetical order with definitions or translations. **3** individual's stock of words (*limited vocabulary*). **4** set of artistic or stylistic forms or techniques. [medieval Latin: related to VOCABLE]

vocal /'vəʊk(ə)l/ –*adj.* **1** of or uttered by the voice. **2** outspoken (*very vocal about his rights*). –*n.* (in *sing.* or *pl.*) sung part or piece of music. □ **vocally** *adv.* [Latin: related to VOICE]

vocal cords *n.* voice-producing part of the larynx.

vocalist *n.* singer.

vocalize *v.* (also **-ise**) (**-zing** or **-sing**) **1** form (a sound) or utter (a word) with the voice. **2** articulate, express. □ **vocalization** /-'zeɪʃ(ə)n/ *n.*

vocation /vəʊ'keɪʃ(ə)n/ *n.* **1 a** strong feeling of suitability for a particular career. **b** this regarded as a divine call to a career in the Church. **2** employment, trade, profession. □ **vocational** *adj.* [Latin *voco* call]

♦ **vocational training** *n.* training in a trade or occupation. In the UK, the Business and Technology Education Council (BTEC) was set up in 1983 to develop a national system of vocational training. It awards a National Vocational Qualification (NVQ), for competence in job skills at five levels, and a General National Vocational Qualification (GNVQ), for completing a broadly-based job-related school course.

---

vocative /'vɒkətɪv/ *Gram.* –*n.* case of a noun used in addressing a person or thing. –*adj.* of or in this case.

vociferate /və'sɪfəˌreɪt/ *v.* (**-ting**) **1** utter noisily. **2** shout, bawl. □ **vociferation** /-'reɪʃ(ə)n/ *n.* **vociferator** *n.* [Latin: related to VOICE, *fero* bear]

vociferous /və'sɪfərəs/ *adj.* **1** noisy, clamorous. **2** insistently and forcibly outspoken. □ **vociferously** *adv.*

vodka /'vɒdkə/ *n.* alcoholic spirit distilled esp. in Russia from rye etc. [Russian]

vogue /vəʊg/ *n.* **1** (prec. by *the*) prevailing fashion. **2** (often *attrib.*) popular use (*had a great vogue*). □ **in vogue** in fashion. □ **voguish** *adj.* [French from Italian]

voice –*n.* **1 a** sound formed in the larynx and uttered by the mouth, esp. by a person speaking, singing, etc. **b** power of this (*lost her voice*). **2 a** use of the voice; spoken or written expression (esp. *give voice*). **b** opinion so expressed. **c** right to express an opinion. **d** medium for expression. **3** *Gram.* set of verbal forms showing whether a verb is active or passive. –*v.* (**-cing**) **1** express. **2** (esp. as **voiced** *adj.*) utter with vibration of the vocal cords (e.g. *b*, *d*). □ **in good voice** singing or speaking well or easily. **with one voice** unanimously. [Latin *vox voc-*]

voice-box *n.* larynx.

voice input device *n.* device in which speech is used to feed data or system commands directly into a computer system. Such equipment involves the use of speech recognition processes, and can replace or supplement other input devices.

voice in the wilderness *n.* unheeded advocate of reform.

voiceless *adj.* **1** dumb, speechless. **2** uttered without vibration of the vocal cords (e.g. *f*, *p*).

voice-over *n.* commentary in a film etc. by an unseen narrator.

void –*adj.* **1** empty, vacant. **2** (of a contract etc.) invalid, not legally binding (*null and void*). –*n.* empty space, vacuum. –*v.* **1** render void. **2** excrete; empty (the bowels etc.). □ **void of** lacking, free from. [French]

voile /vɔɪl, vwɑ:l/ *n.* fine semi-transparent fabric. [French, = VEIL]

Vojvodina /ˌvɔɪvə'di:nə/ province of NE Serbia; pop. (est. 1995) 2 114 000; capital, Novi Sad. Agriculture is important, producing cereals, fruit, and vegetables. Formerly self-governing, the province, which has a large Hungarian minority, was stripped of its autonomy in 1990.

vol. *abbr.* volume.

volatile /'vɒləˌtaɪl/ *adj.* **1** changeable in mood; fickle. **2** (of trading conditions etc.) unstable. **3** (of a political situation etc.) likely to erupt in violence. **4** *Chem.* evaporating rapidly. **5** (of computer memory) not retaining stored contents when the power supply is switched off. □ **volatility** /-'tɪlɪtɪ/ *n.* [Latin *volo* fly]

volatilize /və'lætɪˌlaɪz/ *v.* (also **-ise**) (**-zing** or **-sing**) turn into vapour. □ **volatilization** /-'zeɪʃ(ə)n/ *n.*

vol-au-vent /'vɒləʊˌvɑ̃/ *n.* small puff pastry case with a savoury filling. [French, literally 'flight in the wind']

volcanic /vɒl'kænɪk/ *adj.* of, like, or from a volcano. □ **volcanically** *adv.*

volcano /vɒl'keɪnəʊ/ *n.* (*pl.* **-es**) **1** mountain or hill from which lava, steam, etc. escape through openings in the earth's crust. **2** volatile situation. [Latin *Volcanus* Vulcan, Roman god of fire]

vole *n.* small plant-eating rodent. [originally *vole-mouse* from Norwegian *voll* field]

Volga /'vɒlgə/ river in W Russia, the longest river in Europe, rising in the NW of the country and flowing to the Caspian Sea. It has been dammed at several points to provide a water supply and hydroelectric power.

Volgograd /'vɒlgə,græd/ (formerly (1925–61) **Stalingrad**) industrial city in SW Russia, at the junction of the Don and Volga rivers; manufactures include steel, machinery, footwear, and food; pop. (est. 1995) 1 003 000.

volition /və'lɪʃ(ə)n/ *n.* act or power of willing. □ **of one's own volition** voluntarily. □ **volitional** *adj.* [Latin *volo* wish]

volley /'vɒlɪ/ –*n.* (*pl.* **-s**) **1 a** simultaneous firing of a number of weapons. **b** bullets etc. so fired. **2** (usu. foll. by *of*) torrent (of abuse etc.). **3** playing of a ball in tennis, football, etc., before it touches the ground. –*v.* (**-eys, -eyed**) return or send by or in a volley. [French *volée* from Latin *volo* fly]

volleyball *n.* game for two teams of six hitting a large ball by hand over a high net.

Volos /'vɒlɒs/ port in E Greece, on an inlet of the Aegean Sea in Thessaly; pop. (est. 1991) 115 732.

volt /vəʊlt/ *n.* SI unit of electromotive force, the difference of potential that would carry one ampere of current against one ohm resistance. [*Volta*, name of a physicist]

Volta /'vɒltə/ river in W Africa, formed in central Ghana by the junction of the headwaters, the Black and White Volta, which rise in Burkina Faso. At Akosombo in SE Ghana the river has been dammed, creating the **Volta Dam**, a major source of hydroelectric power for industrial and domestic use, as well as for export.

voltage *n.* electromotive force expressed in volts.

volte-face /vɒlt'fɑːs/ *n.* sudden reversal of one's attitude or opinion. [French from Italian]

voltmeter *n.* instrument measuring electric potential in volts.

voluble /'vɒljʊb(ə)l/ *adj.* speaking or spoken fluently or at length. □ **volubility** /-'bɪlɪtɪ/ *n.* **volubly** *adv.* [Latin *volvo* roll]

volume /'vɒljuːm/ *n.* **1** single book forming part or all of a work. **2 a** solid content, bulk. **b** space occupied by a gas or liquid. **c** (foll. by *of*) amount or quantity. **d** measure of the amount of trade that has taken place, usu. in a specified period. On the London Stock Exchange, for example, the number of shares traded in a day is called the volume and the value of these shares is called the **turnover**. In commodity markets, the daily volume is usu. the number of lots traded in a day. **3** strength of sound, loudness. **4** (foll. by *of*) **a** moving mass of water etc. **b** (usu. in *pl.*) mass of smoke etc. [Latin *volumen*: related to VOLUBLE, ancient books being in roll form]

volumetric /,vɒljʊ'metrɪk/ *adj.* of measurement by volume. □ **volumetrically** *adv.* [from VOLUME, METRIC]

voluminous /və'luːmɪnəs/ *adj.* **1** (of drapery etc.) loose and ample. **2** written or writing at great length. [Latin: related to VOLUME]

voluntary /'vɒləntrɪ/ –*adj.* **1** acting, done, or given willingly; not compulsory; intentional. **2** unpaid (*voluntary work*). **3** (of an institution) supported by charity. **4** (of a school) built by a charity but maintained by a local education authority. **5** brought about by voluntary action. **6** (of a movement, muscle, or limb) controlled by the will. –*n.* (*pl.* **-ies**) organ solo played before or after a church service. □ **voluntarily** *adv.* **voluntariness** *n.* [Latin *voluntas* will]

♦ **voluntary arrangement** *n.* procedure provided for by the Insolvency Act (1986), in which a company may come to an arrangement with its creditors to pay off its debts and to manage its affairs so that it resolves its financial difficulties. This arrangement may be proposed by the directors, an administrator acting under an administration order, or a liquidator. A qualified insolvency practitioner must be appointed to supervise the arrangement. This practitioner may be the administrator or liquidator, in which case a meeting of the company and its creditors must be called to consider the arrangement. The proposals may be modified or approved at this meeting but, once approved, they bind all those who had notice of the meeting. The court may make the necessary orders to bring the arrangement into effect. The arrangement may be challenged in court in the case of any irregularity. The aim of this legislation is to assist the company to solve its financial problems without the need for a winding-up (see LIQUIDATION 1).

♦ **voluntary liquidation** (also **voluntary winding-up**) see CREDITORS' VOLUNTARY LIQUIDATION; MEMBERS' VOLUNTARY LIQUIDATION.

♦ **voluntary retailer** *n.* = SYMBOL RETAILER.

---

volunteer /,vɒlən'tɪə(r)/ –*n.* person who voluntarily undertakes a task or enters military etc. service. –*v.* **1** (often foll. by *to* + infin.) undertake or offer (one's services, a remark, etc.) voluntarily. **2** (often foll. by *for*) be a volunteer. [French: related to VOLUNTARY]

voluptuary /və'lʌptʃʊərɪ/ *n.* (*pl.* **-ies**) person who seeks luxury and sensual pleasure. [Latin: related to VOLUPTUOUS]

voluptuous /və'lʌptʃʊəs/ *adj.* **1** of, tending to, occupied with, or derived from, sensuous or sensual pleasure. **2** (of a woman) curvaceous and sexually desirable. □ **voluptuously** *adv.* [Latin *voluptas* pleasure]

volute /və'luːt/ *n.* spiral stonework scroll as an ornament of esp. Ionic capitals. [Latin *volvo -ut-* roll]

vomit /'vɒmɪt/ –*v.* (**-t-**) **1** eject (contents of the stomach) through the mouth; be sick. **2** (of a volcano, chimney, etc.) eject violently, belch forth. –*n.* matter vomited from the stomach. [Latin]

voodoo /'vuːduː/ –*n.* religious witchcraft as practised esp. in the West Indies. –*v.* (**-doos, -dooed**) affect by voodoo; bewitch. [Dahomey]

voracious /və'reɪʃəs/ *adj.* **1** gluttonous, ravenous. **2** very eager (*voracious reader*). □ **voraciously** *adv.* **voracity** /və'ræsɪtɪ/ *n.* [Latin *vorax* from *voro* devour]

Vorarlberg /'fɔːrɑːl,beək/ Alpine state in W Austria; pop. (est. 1994) 342 461; capital, Bregenz.

Voronezh /və'rɒnjeʒ/ industrial city in W Russia, NE of Kharkov; manufactures include aircraft, electronic goods, chemicals, and construction machinery; pop. (est. 1995) 908 000.

Voroshilovgrad /,vɒrə'ʃiːlɒf,græd/ see LUGANSK.

vortex /'vɔːteks/ *n.* (*pl.* **-texes** or **-tices** /-tɪ,siːz/) **1** whirlpool, whirlwind. **2** whirling motion or mass. **3** thing viewed as destructive or devouring (*the vortex of society*). □ **vortical** *adj.* [Latin: related to VERTEX]

vorticist /'vɔːtɪsɪst/ *n.* futuristic painter, writer, etc., of a school based on the so-called 'vortices' of modern civilization. □ **vorticism** *n.*

♦ **vostro account** /'vɒstrəʊ/ *n.* bank account held by a foreign bank with a UK bank, usu. in sterling. Cf. NOSTRO ACCOUNT. [Italian *vostro* your]

---

votary /'vəʊtərɪ/ *n.* (*pl.* **-ies**; *fem.* **votaress**) (usu. foll. by *of*) **1** person dedicated to the service of a god or cult. **2** devotee of a person, occupation, etc. [Latin: related to VOTE]

vote –*n.* **1** formal expression of choice or opinion by a ballot, show of hands, etc., in an election etc. **2** (usu. prec. by *the*) right to vote, esp. in a state election. **3** opinion expressed by a vote (*vote of no confidence*). **4** votes given by or for a particular group (*the Welsh vote*; *the Labour vote*). –*v.* (**-ting**) **1** (often foll. by *for, against*) give a vote. **2 a** enact or resolve by a majority of votes. **b** grant (a sum of money) by vote. **3** *colloq.* pronounce by general consent. **4** (often foll. by *that*) suggest, urge. □ **vote down** defeat (a proposal etc.) in a vote. **vote in** elect by voting. **vote off** dismiss from (a committee etc.) by voting. **vote out** dismiss from office etc. by voting. **vote with one's feet** *colloq.* indicate an opinion by one's presence or absence. [Latin *votum* from *voveo vot-* vow]

voter *n.* person voting or with the right to vote at an election.

♦ **voting shares** *n.pl.* shares in a company that entitle their owner to vote at the annual general meeting and any extraordinary meetings of the company. Shares that carry **voting rights** are usu. ordinary shares, rather than A shares or debentures. The company's articles of association will state which shares carry voting rights.

---

votive /ˈvəʊtɪv/ *adj.* offered or consecrated in fulfilment of a vow (*votive offering*). [Latin: related to VOTE]

vouch *v.* (foll. by *for*) answer for, be surety for (*will vouch for the truth of this*; *can vouch for him*). [French *vo(u)cher* summon, invoke]

voucher *n.* **1** document exchangeable for goods or services. **2** receipt for money or any document that supports an entry in a book of account. [from Anglo-French, or from VOUCH]

vouchsafe /vaʊtʃˈseɪf/ *v.* (**-fing**) *formal* **1** condescend to grant. **2** (foll. by *to* + infin.) condescend.

vow *–n.* solemn, esp. religious, promise (*monastic vows*; *marriage vows*). *–v.* **1** promise solemnly. **2** *archaic* declare solemnly. [French *vou(er)*: related to VOTE]

vowel /ˈvaʊəl/ *n.* **1** speech-sound made with vibration of the vocal cords but without audible friction. **2** letter(s) representing this, as *a*, *e*, *i*, *o*, *u*, *aw*, *ah*. [Latin: related to VOCAL]

vox pop *n.* (often *attrib.*) *colloq.* popular opinion as represented by informal comments from the public. [abbreviation of VOX POPULI]

vox populi /ˌvɒks ˈpɒpjʊˌlaɪ/ *n.* public opinion, popular belief. [Latin, = the people's voice]

voyage /ˈvɔɪɪdʒ/ *–n.* journey, esp. a long one by sea or in space. *–v.* (**-ging**) make a voyage. □ **voyager** *n.* [Latin VIATICUM]

♦ **voyage charter** *n.* charter of a ship or of cargo space for a fixed number of voyages rather than for a fixed period (cf. TIME CHARTER). The shipowner usu. warrants that the ship will arrive at an agreed port on an agreed day, will be in seaworthy condition, and will be properly equipped. The charterer agrees to load and unload in the agreed number of lay days.

---

voyeur /vwɑːˈjɜː(r)/ *n.* **1** person who derives sexual pleasure from secretly observing others' sexual activity or organs. **2** (esp. covert) spectator. □ **voyeurism** *n.* **voyeuristic** /-ˈrɪstɪk/ *adj.* [French *voir* see]

VPC *abbr.* (French) vente par correspondence (= mail order).

VP-F *international civil aircraft marking* Falkland Islands.

VP-LA *international civil aircraft marking* Anguilla.

VP-LMA *international civil aircraft marking* Montserrat.

VP-LV *international civil aircraft marking* Virgin Islands.

VQ-T *international civil aircraft marking* Turks and Caicos Islands.

VRAM *abbr. Computing* video random access memory.

VR-B *international civil aircraft marking* Bermuda.

VR-C *international civil aircraft marking* Cayman Islands.

VR-G *international civil aircraft marking* Gibraltar.

VR-H *international civil aircraft marking* Hong Kong.

VRM *abbr.* = VARIABLE-RATE MORTGAGE.

VRN *abbr.* = VARIABLE-RATE NOTE.

VS *airline flight code* Virgin Atlantic Airways.

vs. *abbr.* versus.

VSAM *abbr. Computing* virtual storage access method.

V-sign /ˈviːsaɪn/ *n.* **1** sign of the letter V made with the first two fingers pointing up and the back of the hand facing outwards, as a gesture of abuse etc. **2** similar sign made with the palm of the hand facing outwards, as a symbol of victory.

VSO *abbr.* Voluntary Service Overseas.

VSOP *abbr.* Very Special Old Pale (brandy).

VT *–symb. Currency* vatu. *–international civil aircraft marking* India. *–US postcode* Vermont.

Vt. *abbr.* Vermont.

VTC *abbr. US* voting trust certificate.

VTO *abbr.* vertical take-off.

VTOL /ˈviːtɒl/ *abbr.* vertical take-off and landing.

VTR *abbr.* videotape recorder.

vulcanite /ˈvʌlkəˌnaɪt/ *n.* hard black vulcanized rubber. [related to VULCANIZE]

vulcanize /ˈvʌlkəˌnaɪz/ *v.* (also **-ise**) (**-zing** or **-sing**) treat (rubber etc.) with sulphur at a high temperature to strengthen it. □ **vulcanization** /-ˈzeɪʃ(ə)n/ *n.* [*Vulcan*: related to VOLCANO]

vulcanology /ˌvʌlkəˈnɒlədʒɪ/ *n.* the study of volcanoes. □ **vulcanological** /-nəˈlɒdʒɪk(ə)l/ *adj.* **vulcanologist** *n.*

vulgar /ˈvʌlgə(r)/ *adj.* **1 a** coarse; indecent; tasteless. **b** of or characteristic of the common people. **2** common; prevalent (*vulgar errors*). □ **vulgarly** *adv.* [Latin *vulgus* common people]

vulgar fraction *n.* fraction expressed by numerator and denominator, not decimally.

vulgarian /vʌlˈgeərɪən/ *n.* vulgar (esp. rich) person.

vulgarism *n.* vulgar word, expression, action, or habit.

vulgarity /vʌlˈgærɪtɪ/ *n.* (*pl.* **-ies**) vulgar act, expression, or state.

vulgarize /ˈvʌlgəˌraɪz/ *v.* (also **-ise**) (**-zing** or **-sing**) **1** make vulgar. **2** spoil by popularizing. □ **vulgarization** /-ˈzeɪʃ(ə)n/ *n.*

vulgar tongue *n.* (prec. by *the*) national or vernacular language.

Vulgate /ˈvʌlgeɪt/ *n.* 4th-century Latin version of the Bible. [Latin: related to VULGAR]

vulnerable /ˈvʌlnərəb(ə)l/ *adj.* **1** easily wounded or harmed. **2** (foll. by *to*) exposed to damage, temptation, etc. □ **vulnerability** /-ˈbɪlɪtɪ/ *n.* **vulnerably** *adv.* [Latin *vulnus -er-* wound]

vulpine /ˈvʌlpaɪn/ *adj.* **1** of or like a fox. **2** crafty, cunning. [Latin *vulpes* fox]

vulture /ˈvʌltʃə(r)/ *n.* **1** large carrion-eating bird of prey, reputed to gather with others in anticipation of a death. **2** rapacious person. [Anglo-French from Latin]

vulva /ˈvʌlvə/ *n.* (*pl.* **-s**) external female genitals. [Latin]

vv. *abbr.* **1** verses. **2** volumes.

v.v. *abbr.* vice versa.

vying *pres. part.* of VIE.

W[1] /ˈdʌb(ə)l,juː/ *n.* (also **w**) (*pl.* **Ws** or **W's**) twenty-third letter of the alphabet.

W[2] *abbr.* **1** watt(s). **2** (also **W.**) West; Western. **3** *Shipping* winter sea water (see LOAD LINE).

W[3] *–symb.* **1** tungsten. **2** *Currency* won. *–postcode* west London. [for sense 1, *wolframium*, Latinized name]

w. *abbr.* **1** wicket(s). **2** wide(s). **3** with.

WA *–abbr.* **1** Western Australia. **2** *Insurance* with average (see AVERAGE *n.* 4). *–postcode* Warrington. *–US postcode* Washington (state).

WACCC *abbr.* Worldwide Air Cargo Commodity Classification.

wacky *adj.* (**-ier**, **-iest**) *slang* crazy. [originally dial., = left-handed]

wad /wɒd/ *–n.* **1** lump of soft material used esp. to keep things apart or in place or to block a hole. **2** bundle of banknotes or documents. *–v.* (**-dd-**) **1** stop up or keep in place with a wad. **2** line, stuff, or protect with wadding. [origin uncertain]

wadding *n.* soft fibrous material used in quilt-making etc., or to pack fragile articles.

waddle /ˈwɒd(ə)l/ *–v.* (**-ling**) walk with short steps and a swaying motion. *–n.* waddling gait. [from WADE]

wade *–v.* (**-ding**) **1** walk through water, mud, etc., esp. with difficulty. **2** (foll. by *through*) go through (a tedious task, book, etc.). **3** (foll. by *into*) *colloq.* attack (a person or task) vigorously. *–n.* spell of wading. □ **wade in** *colloq.* make a vigorous attack or intervention. [Old English]

wader *n.* **1** long-legged water-bird that wades. **2** (in *pl.*) high waterproof boots.

wadi /ˈwɒdɪ/ *n.* (*pl.* **-s**) rocky watercourse in N Africa etc., dry except in the rainy season. [Arabic]

Wadi Halfa /ˌwɒdɪ ˈhælfə/ town in N Sudan, a railway and steamship terminus; activities include commerce and agriculture; pop. (latest est.) 11 000.

WADS *abbr. Computing* wide-area data service.

wafer *n.* **1** very thin light crisp sweet biscuit. **2** disc of unleavened bread used in the Eucharist. **3** (in full **wafer seal**) disc of red paper stuck on a legal document to represent a seal. [Anglo-French *wafre* from Germanic]

wafer-thin *adj.* very thin.

waffle[1] /ˈwɒf(ə)l/ *colloq. –n.* verbose but aimless or ignorant talk or writing. *–v.* (**-ling**) indulge in waffle. [dial., = yelp]

waffle[2] /ˈwɒf(ə)l/ *n.* small crisp batter cake. [Dutch]

waffle-iron *n.* utensil, usu. of two shallow metal pans hinged together, for baking waffles.

waft /wɒft/ *–v.* convey or travel easily and smoothly as through air or over water. *–n.* (usu. foll. by *of*) whiff or scent. [originally 'convoy (ship etc.)' from Dutch or Low German *wachter* from *wachten* to guard]

WAG *international vehicle registration* The Gambia.

wag[1] *–v.* (**-gg-**) shake or wave to and fro. *–n.* single wagging motion (*with a wag of his tail*). □ **tongues wag** there is talk. [Old English]

wag[2] *n.* facetious person. [Old English]

wage *–n.* (in *sing.* or *pl.*) fixed regular payment to an employee, esp. a manual worker. *–v.* (**-ging**) carry on (a war etc.). [Anglo-French from Germanic]

waged *adj.* in regular paid employment.

◆ **wage differential** *n.* difference in earnings between workers with similar skills in different industries or between workers with different skills in the same industry. There may also be differentials between urban and non-urban wages or between regions (wages in the UK are highest in the South-East, where the cost of living is highest). The Equal Pay Act (1970) makes it illegal for a differential to exist between the pay of men and women doing like work in the same employment.

◆ **wage drift** *n.* difference between earnings and wage rates as a result of overtime pay and bonuses. In a period of wage freeze, employers can circumvent the effects of the freeze by means of bonuses and overtime, thus defeating the anti-inflationary purpose of the freeze.

---

wage-earner *n.* person who works for wages.

◆ **wage freeze** *n.* attempt by a government to counter inflation by fixing wages at their existing level for a specified period. For various reasons, including the wage drift, this is no longer considered an effective policy. **Wage restraint** is a less rigidly applied attempt to control prices by obtaining union agreement to make only modest and essential claims for wage increases.

---

wager *n.* & *v.* = BET. [Anglo-French: related to WAGE]

◆ **wage restraint** see WAGE FREEZE.

◆ **wagering contract** see GAMING CONTRACT.

◆ **wages council** *n.* UK statutory body empowered by the Wages Council Act (1954) and the Wages Act (1986) to prescribe minimum rates of pay in a particular industry. Each council consists of representatives of employers and employees in the industry concerned and independent members. Councils have usu. been established for industries in which employees' collective bargaining power is comparatively weak. The Wages Act (1986) abolished the power to create new wages councils.

Wagga Wagga /ˌwɒgə ˈwɒgə/ city and agricultural centre in Australia, in New South Wales; pop. (est. 1991) 50 930.

waggish *adj.* playful, facetious. □ **waggishly** *adv.* **waggishness** *n.*

waggle /ˈwæg(ə)l/ *v.* (**-ling**) *colloq.* wag.

waggly *adj.* unsteady; waggling.

wagon /ˈwægən/ *n.* (also **waggon**) **1** four-wheeled vehicle for heavy loads. **2** railway vehicle, esp. an open truck. **3** tea trolley. □ **on the wagon** (or **water-wagon**) *slang* teetotal. [Dutch: related to WAIN]

wagoner *n.* (also **waggoner**) driver of a wagon.

wagon-load *n.* as much as a wagon can carry.

wagtail *n.* small bird with a long tail in frequent motion.

Wahran see ORAN.

waif *n.* **1** homeless and helpless person, esp. an abandoned child. **2** ownerless object or animal. [Anglo-French, probably from Scandinavian]

waifs and strays *n.pl.* **1** homeless or neglected children. **2** odds and ends.

Waikato /waɪˈkɑːtəʊ/ **1** longest river in New Zealand, a source of hydroelectricity, flowing N and NW from the centre of North Island to the Tasman Sea. **2** administrative region of New Zealand, on North Island; pop. (1996) 356 267; chief town, Hamilton.

wail *–n.* **1** prolonged plaintive high-pitched cry of pain, grief, etc. **2** sound like this. *–v.* **1** utter a wail. **2** lament or complain persistently or bitterly. [Old Norse]

wain *n. archaic* wagon. [Old English]

wainscot /ˈweɪnskət/ *n.* boarding or wooden panelling

on the lower part of a room-wall. [Low German *wagenschot* from *wagen* WAGON]

wainscoting *n.* **1** wainscot. **2** material for this.

Wairarapa /ˌwaɪrəˈrɑːpə/ former administrative region of New Zealand, on North Island.

waist *n.* **1 a** part of the human body below the ribs and above the hips; narrower middle part of the normal human figure. **b** circumference of this. **2** narrow middle of a violin, wasp, etc. **3 a** part of a garment encircling the waist. **b** *US* blouse, bodice. **4** part of a ship between the forecastle and the quarterdeck. □ **waisted** *adj.* (also in *comb.*). [Old English: related to WAX[2]]

waistband *n.* strip of cloth forming the waist of a garment.

waistcoat *n.* close-fitting waist-length garment without sleeves or collar, worn usu. over a shirt and under a jacket.

waist-deep *adj.* & *adv.* (also **waist-high**) up to the waist.

waistline *n.* outline or size of a person's body at the waist.

wait *–v.* **1 a** defer action or departure for a specified time or until some event occurs (*wait a minute; wait till I come; wait for a fine day*). **b** be expectant. **2** await (an opportunity, one's turn, etc.). **3** defer (a meal etc.) until a person's arrival. **4** (usu. as **waiting** *n.*) park a vehicle for a short time. **5** act as a waiter or attendant. **6** (foll. by *on, upon*) **a** await the convenience of. **b** serve as an attendant to. **c** pay a respectful visit to. *–n.* **1** period of waiting. **2** (usu. foll. by *for*) watching for an enemy (*lie in wait*). **3** (in *pl.*) *archaic* street singers of Christmas carols. □ **wait and see** await the progress of events. **wait up** (often foll. by *for*) not go to bed until a person arrives or an event happens. **you wait!** used to imply a threat, warning, etc. [Germanic: related to WAKE[1]]

waiter *n.* **1** man who serves at table in a hotel or restaurant etc. **2** attendant at the London Stock Exchange and at Lloyd's who carries messages and papers etc.: the modern equivalent of the waiters in the 17th-century London coffee-houses from which these institutions grew, who also performed these functions.

waiting game *n.* the delaying of action in order to have a greater effect later.

waiting-list *n.* list of people waiting for a thing not immediately available.

waiting-room *n.* room for people to wait in, esp. to see a doctor etc. or at a station.

waitress *n.* woman who serves at table in a hotel or restaurant etc.

waive *v.* (**-ving**) refrain from insisting on or using (a right, claim, opportunity, etc.). [Anglo-French *weyver*: related to WAIF]

♦ **waiver** *n. Law* **1** setting aside or non-enforcement of a right. This may be done deliberately or it may happen by the operation of law. For example, if a tenant is in breach of a covenant in his or her lease and the tenant's landlord demands rent in spite of knowing of the breach, the landlord may be held to have waived his right to terminate the lease. **2** document recording this.

---

wake[1] *–v.* (**-king**; *past* **woke** or **waked**; *past part.* **woken** or **waked**) **1** (often foll. by *up*) (cause to) cease to sleep. **2** (often foll. by *up*) (cause to) become alert or attentive. **3** *archaic* (except as **waking** *adj.* & *n.*) be awake (*waking hours*). **4** disturb with noise. **5** evoke (an echo). *–n.* **1** watch beside a corpse before burial; attendant lamentation and (less often) merrymaking. **2** (usu. in *pl.*) annual holiday in (industrial) northern England. [Old English]

wake[2] *n.* **1** track left on the water's surface by a moving ship. **2** turbulent air left behind a moving aircraft etc. □ **in the wake of** following, as a result of. [Low German from Old Norse]

wakeful *adj.* **1** unable to sleep. **2** (of a night etc.) sleepless. **3** vigilant. □ **wakefully** *adv.* **wakefulness** *n.*

waken *v.* make or become awake. [Old Norse]

WAL *international vehicle registration* Sierra Leone.

Walachia see WALLACHIA.

wale *n.* **1** = WEAL[1]. **2** ridge on corduroy etc. **3** *Naut.* a broad thick timber along a ship's side. [Old English]

Wales /weɪlz/ the W part of Great Britain, comprising a division of the United Kingdom; pop. (1991) 2 835 073; capital, Cardiff. The decline in the traditional industries of coalmining and steelmaking in S Wales have been partly alleviated by diversification into light industry; other activities include tourism (in the N), forestry, and agriculture (esp. livestock). Wales was conquered by England in the late 13th century but continued a sporadic resistance to English rule until it was finally incorporated in 1536 (see GREAT BRITAIN). Wales has retained a distinct cultural identity, and the Welsh nationalist movement is attempting to increase the use of the Welsh language. The nationalist party Plaid Cymru remains active, despite the rejection of devolution in a referendum of 1979. A referendum on Welsh devolution in 1997 narrowly voted in favour of a separate assembly. See also UNITED KINGDOM.

walk /wɔːk/ *–v.* **1 a** progress by lifting and setting down each foot in turn, never having both feet off the ground at once. **b** (of a quadruped) go with the slowest gait. **2 a** travel or go on foot. **b** take exercise in this way. **3** traverse on foot at walking speed, tread the floor or surface of. **4** cause to walk with one (*walk the dog*). *–n.* **1 a** act of walking, the ordinary human gait. **b** slowest gait of an animal. **c** person's manner of walking. **2 a** distance which can be walked in a (usu. specified) time (*ten minutes' walk from here*). **b** excursion on foot. **3** place or track intended or suitable for walking. □ **walk all over** *colloq.* **1** defeat easily. **2** take advantage of. **walk away from 1** easily outdistance. **2** refuse to become involved with. **walk away with** *colloq.* = *walk off with*. **walk into** *colloq.* **1** encounter through unwariness. **2** get (a job) easily. **walk off with** *colloq.* **1** steal. **2** win easily. **walk on air** feel elated. **walk out 1** depart suddenly or angrily. **2** stop work in protest. **walk out on** desert, abandon. **walk the streets** be a prostitute. □ **walkable** *adj.* [Old English]

walkabout *n.* **1** informal stroll among a crowd by a visiting dignitary. **2** period of wandering in the bush by an Australian Aboriginal.

walker *n.* **1** person or animal that walks. **2 a** framework in which a baby can walk unaided. **b** = WALKING FRAME.

walkie-talkie /ˌwɔːkɪˈtɔːkɪ/ *n.* two-way radio carried on the person.

walk-in *attrib. adj.* (of a storage area) large enough to walk into.

walking *n.* & *adj.* in senses of WALK *n.*

walking frame *n.* tubular metal frame for disabled or old people to help them walk.

walking-stick *n.* stick carried for support when walking.

Walkman *n.* (*pl.* **-s**) *propr.* type of personal stereo.

walk of life *n.* occupation, profession.

walk-on *n.* **1** (in full **walk-on part**) non-speaking dramatic role. **2** player of this.

walk-out *n.* sudden angry departure, esp. as a protest or strike.

walk-over *n.* easy victory.

walkway *n.* passage or path (esp. raised) for walking along.

wall /wɔːl/ *–n.* **1** continuous vertical narrow structure of usu. brick or stone, esp. enclosing or dividing a space or supporting a roof. **2** thing like a wall, esp.: **a** a steep side of a mountain. **b** *Anat.* the outermost layer or enclosing membrane etc. of an organ etc. *–v.* **1** (esp. as **walled** *adj.*) surround with a wall. **2 a** (usu. foll. by *up, off*) block (a space etc.) with a wall. **b** (foll. by *up*) enclose within a sealed space. □ **go to the wall** be defeated or pushed aside. **up the wall** *colloq.* crazy or furious. **walls have ears** beware of eavesdroppers. □ **wall-less** *adj.* [Latin *vallum* rampart]

wallaby /ˈwɒləbɪ/ *n.* (*pl.* **-ies**) marsupial similar to but smaller than a kangaroo. [Aboriginal]

Wallachia /wɒ'leɪkɪə/ (also **Walachia**) former principality of SE Europe, united in 1859 with Moldavia to form Romania. □ **Wallachian** *adj.* & *n.*

wallah /'wɒlə/ *n. slang* person concerned with or in charge of a usu. specified thing, business, etc. [Hindi]

wall bar *n.* one of a set of parallel bars attached to the wall of a gymnasium, on which exercises are performed.

wallet /'wɒlɪt/ *n.* small flat esp. leather case for holding banknotes etc. [Anglo-French]

wall-eye /'wɔːlaɪ/ *n.* **1** eye with a streaked or opaque white iris. **2** eye squinting outwards. □ **wall-eyed** *adj.* [Old Norse]

wallflower *n.* **1** fragrant spring garden plant. **2** *colloq.* woman sitting out at a dance for lack of partners.

wall game *n.* form of football played at Eton.

Wallis and Futuna Islands /'wɒlɪs, fə'tjuːnə/ overseas territory of France comprising two groups of islands W of Samoa in the central Pacific; pop. (est. 1993) 14 400; capital, Mata-Utu. Products include copra and timber.

Walloon /wɒ'luːn/ *–n.* **1** member of a people inhabiting S and E Belgium and neighbouring France. **2** French dialect spoken by this people. *–adj.* of or concerning the Walloons or their language. [medieval Latin *Walls*]

wallop /'wɒləp/ *colloq.* *–v.* **(-p-) 1** thrash; beat. **2** (as **walloping** *adj.*) huge. *–n.* **1** heavy blow. **2** beer. [earlier senses 'gallop', 'boil', from French *waloper* from Germanic: cf. GALLOP]

wallow /'wɒləʊ/ *–v.* **1** (esp. of an animal) roll about in mud etc. **2** (usu. foll. by *in*) indulge in unrestrained pleasure, misery, etc. *–n.* **1** act of wallowing. **2** place used by buffalo etc. for wallowing. [Old English]

wallpaper *–n.* **1** paper for pasting on to interior walls as decoration. **2** usu. *derog.* trivial background noise, music, etc. *–v.* decorate with wallpaper.

♦ **Wall Street** *n.* **1** financial institutions, collectively, of New York, including the New York Stock Exchange, banks, money markets, commodity markets, etc. **2** the New York Stock Exchange. [street in New York in which the stock exchange is situated]

wall-to-wall *adj.* **1** (of a carpet) fitted to cover a whole room etc. **2** *colloq.* ubiquitous (*wall-to-wall pop music*).

wally /'wɒlɪ/ *n.* (*pl.* **-ies**) *slang* foolish or inept person. [origin uncertain]

walnut /'wɔːlnʌt/ *n.* **1** tree with aromatic leaves and drooping catkins. **2** nut of this tree. **3** its timber. [Old English, = foreign nut]

♦ **Walras' law** /'vælræz/ *n. Econ.* law that the value of goods demanded in an economy is equal to the value of goods sold. This follows from the simple idea that for each individual, income equals expenditure (including borrowing and saving). This is an important step in proving the existence of a perfectly competitive equilibrium, which is Pareto efficient in general equilibrium theory. [*Walras*, name of an economist]

walrus /'wɔːlrəs/ *n.* (*pl.* same or **-es**) large amphibious long-tusked arctic mammal. [Dutch]

walrus moustache *n.* long thick drooping moustache.

Walsall /'wɔːls(ə)l/ industrial town in England, in West Midlands; manufactures include machine tools, aircraft components, leather goods, and hardware, and there are also engineering, chemical, and electronics industries; pop. (est. 1994) 263 900.

waltz /wɔːls/ *–n.* **1** ballroom dance in triple time performed by couples revolving with sliding steps. **2** music for this. *–v.* **1** dance a waltz. **2** (often foll. by *in, out, round,* etc.) *colloq.* move easily, lightly, casually, etc. □ **waltz off with** *colloq.* **1** steal. **2** win easily. [German *Walzer* from *walzen* revolve]

Walvis Bay /'wɒlvɪs/ port on the Atlantic coast of Namibia. Previously an enclave of Cape Province, South Africa, Walvis Bay became part of Namibia in 1994. Fishing is important; pop. (est. 1992) 23 000.

wampum /'wɒmpəm/ *n.* beads made from shells and strung together for use as money, decoration, etc. by North American Indians. [Algonquian]

WAN *–abbr. Computing* = WIDE AREA NETWORK. *–international vehicle registration* Nigeria.

wan /wɒn/ *adj.* (**wanner, wannest**) pale; exhausted-looking. □ **wanly** *adv.* **wanness** *n.* [Old English, = dark]

wand /wɒnd/ *n.* **1** supposedly magic stick used by a fairy, magician, etc. **2** staff as a symbol of office. **3** *colloq.* conductor's baton. **4** hand-held device connected to a computer and used to read printed bar codes etc. It is moved steadily over the surface of the printing, and an audible or visual signal is produced if the data has been sensed satisfactorily. [Old Norse]

wander /'wɒndə(r)/ *v.* **1** (often foll. by *in, off,* etc.) go about from place to place aimlessly. **2 a** wind about; meander. **b** stray from a path etc. **3** talk or think incoherently; be inattentive or delirious. □ **wanderer** *n.* [Old English: related to WEND]

wandering Jew *n.* person who never settles down.

wanderlust *n.* eagerness for travelling or wandering; restlessness. [German]

wane *–v.* **(-ning) 1** (of the moon) decrease in apparent size. **2** decrease in power, vigour, importance, size, etc. *–n.* process of waning. □ **on the wane** waning; declining. [Old English]

Wanganui /ˌwɒŋgə'nuːɪ/ seaport in New Zealand, on the W coast of North Island; pop. (est. 1995) 42 200.

wangle /'wæŋg(ə)l/ *colloq.* *–v.* **(-ling)** (often *refl.*) contrive to obtain (a favour etc.). *–n.* act of wangling. [origin unknown]

wank *coarse slang* *–v.* masturbate. *–n.* act of masturbating. [origin unknown]

Wankel engine /'wæŋk(ə)l/ *n.* internal-combustion engine with a continuously rotated and eccentrically pivoted shaft. [*Wankel*, name of an engineer]

wanker *n. coarse slang* contemptible or ineffectual person.

Wankie see HWANGE.

wannabe /'wɒnəbɪ/ *n. slang* **1** avid fan who tries to emulate the person he or she admires. **2** anybody who would like to be someone else. [corruption of *want to be*]

want /wɒnt/ *–v.* **1 a** (often foll. by *to* + infin.) desire; wish for possession of; need (*wants a drink; wants it done immediately*). **b** require to be attended to; need (*garden wants weeding*). **c** (foll. by *to* + infin.) *colloq.* ought; should (*you want to be careful*). **2** (usu. foll. by *for*) lack; be deficient. **3** be without or fall short by. **4** (as **wanted** *adj.*) (of a suspected criminal etc.) sought by the police. *–n.* **1** (often foll. by *of*) lack, absence, or deficiency (*could not go for want of time*). **2** poverty; need. [Old Norse]

wanting *adj.* **1** lacking (in quality or quantity); not equal to requirements. **2** absent, not supplied.

wanton /'wɒnt(ə)n/ *–adj.* **1** licentious; sexually promiscuous. **2** capricious; arbitrary; motiveless (*wanton wind; wanton destruction*). **3** luxuriant; unrestrained (*wanton profusion*). *–n. literary* licentious person. □ **wantonly** *adv.* [from obsolete *wantowen*, = undisciplined]

wapiti /'wɒpɪtɪ/ *n.* (*pl.* **-s**) North American deer. [a Cree word]

War. *abbr.* Warwickshire.

war /wɔː(r)/ *–n.* **1 a** armed hostilities between esp. nations; conflict. **b** specific instance or period of this. **c** suspension of international law etc. during this. **2** hostility or contention between people, groups, etc. **3** (often foll. by *on*) sustained campaign against crime, poverty, etc. *–v.* **(-rr-) 1** (as **warring** *adj.*) rival; fighting. **2** make war. □ **at war** (often foll. by *with*) engaged in a war. **go to war** declare or begin a war. **have been in the wars** *colloq.* appear injured etc. [Anglo-French from Germanic]

warble /'wɔːb(ə)l/ *–v.* **(-ling) 1** sing in a gentle trilling manner. **2** speak in a warbling manner. *–n.* warbled song or utterance. [French *werble(r)*]

warbler *n.* bird that warbles.

war crime *n.* crime violating the international laws of war. □ **war criminal** *n.*

war cry *n.* **1** phrase or name shouted to rally one's troops. **2** party slogan etc.

ward /wɔːd/ *n.* **1** separate part of a hospital or room for a particular group of patients. **2** administrative division of a constituency. **3 a** minor under the care of a guardian or court. **b** (in full **ward of court**) minor or mentally deficient person placed under the protection of a court. **4** (in *pl.*) the corresponding notches and projections in a key and a lock. **5** *archaic* guardian's control. □ **ward off 1** parry (a blow). **2** avert (danger etc.). [Old English]

-ward *suffix* (also **-wards**) added to nouns of place or destination and to adverbs of direction and forming: **1** adverbs (usu. **-wards**) meaning 'towards' (*backwards*; *homewards*). **2** adjectives (usu. **-ward**) meaning 'turned or tending towards' (*downward*; *onward*). **3** (less commonly) nouns meaning 'the region towards or about' (*look to the eastward*). [Old English]

war dance *n.* dance performed by primitive peoples etc. before a battle or to celebrate victory.

warden /'wɔːd(ə)n/ *n.* **1** (often in *comb.*) supervising official (*traffic warden*). **2** president or governor of a college, hospital, etc. [Anglo-French and French: related to GUARDIAN]

warder /'wɔːdə(r)/ *n.* (*fem.* **wardress**) prison officer. [French: related to GUARD]

wardrobe /'wɔːdrəʊb/ *n.* **1** large cupboard for storing clothes. **2** person's stock of clothes. **3** costume department of a theatre etc. [French]

wardrobe mistress *n.* (*masc.* **wardrobe master**) person in charge of a theatrical wardrobe.

wardroom *n.* mess in a warship for commissioned officers.

-wards var. of -WARD.

wardship *n.* tutelage.

ware *n.* **1** (esp. in *comb.*) things of a specified kind made usu. for sale (*chinaware*; *hardware*). **2** (usu. in *pl.*) articles for sale. **3** ceramics etc. of a specified kind (*Delft ware*). [Old English]

♦ **warehouse** –*n.* **1** building in which goods are stored. A **public warehouse** is one at or near a port in which goods are stored after being unloaded from a ship or before being loaded onto a ship (see also BONDED WAREHOUSE). When goods are taken into a public warehouse a warehouse warrant is issued, which must be produced before the goods can be removed. **2** wholesale or large retail store. –*v.* /also -haʊz/ (**-sing**) store temporarily in a repository. □ **at warehouse** denoting delivery terms for goods that are available for immediate delivery, in which the buyer pays for delivery of the goods, including the cost of loading them onto the road or rail transport. Cf. EX WAREHOUSE.

♦ **warehouse keeper** *n.* person in charge of a warehouse. A bonded warehouse also has a **warehouse officer**, employed by HM Customs and Excise, to inspect goods entering and leaving the warehouse.

♦ **warehousing** *n.* building up a holding of shares in a company prior to making a take-over bid, by buying small lots of the shares in the name of nominees. The purpose is for the bidder to remain anonymous and to avoid having to make the statutory declaration of interest. This practice is contrary to the City Code on Take-overs and Mergers.

---

warfare *n.* waging war, campaigning.

war-game *n.* **1** military training exercise. **2** battle etc. conducted with toy soldiers.

warhead *n.* explosive head of a missile.

warhorse *n.* **1** *hist.* trooper's powerful horse. **2** *colloq.* veteran soldier, politician, etc.

warlike *adj.* **1** hostile. **2** soldierly. **3** military.

♦ **war loan** *n.* government stock issued during wartime, which has no redemption date, pays only 3½% interest, and stands at less than half its face value.

---

warlock /'wɔːlɒk/ *n.* *archaic* sorcerer. [Old English, = traitor]

warlord *n.* military commander or commander-in-chief.

warm /wɔːm/ –*adj.* **1** of or at a fairly high temperature. **2** (of clothes etc.) affording warmth. **3 a** sympathetic, friendly, loving. **b** hearty, enthusiastic. **4** *colloq. iron.* dangerous, difficult, hostile. **5** *colloq.* **a** (in a game) close to the object etc. sought. **b** near to guessing. **6** (of a colour etc.) reddish or yellowish; suggestive of warmth. **7** *Hunting* (of a scent) fresh and strong. –*v.* **1** make warm. **2 a** (often foll. by *up*) warm oneself. **b** (often foll. by *to*) become animated or sympathetic. –*n.* **1** act of warming. **2** warmth of the atmosphere etc. □ **warm up 1** make or become warm. **2** prepare for a performance etc. by practising. **3** reach a temperature for efficient working. **4** reheat (food). □ **warmly** *adv.* **warmth** *n.* [Old English]

warm-blooded *adj.* **1** having blood temperature well above that of the environment. **2** ardent.

war memorial *n.* monument to those killed in a war.

warm-hearted *adj.* kind, friendly. □ **warm-heartedness** *n.*

warming-pan *n. hist.* container for live coals with a flat body and a long handle, used for warming a bed.

warmonger *n.* person who promotes war. □ **warmongering** *n.* & *adj.*

warm-up *n.* period of preparatory exercise.

warm work *n.* **1** work etc. that makes one warm through exertion. **2** dangerous conflict etc.

warn /wɔːn/ *v.* **1** (also *absol.*) **a** (often foll. by *of* or *that*) inform of danger, unknown circumstances, etc. **b** (foll. by *to* + infin.) advise (a person) to take certain action. **c** (often foll. by *against*) inform (a person etc.) about a specific danger. **2** (usu. with *neg.*) admonish. □ **warn off** tell (a person) to keep away (from). [Old English]

warning *n.* **1** in senses of WARN. **2** thing that warns. [Old English]

war of nerves *n.* attempt to wear down an opponent psychologically.

warp /wɔːp/ –*v.* **1 a** make or become distorted, esp. through heat, damp, etc. **b** make or become perverted or strange (*warped sense of humour*). **2** haul (a ship) by a rope attached to a fixed point. –*n.* **1 a** warped state, esp. of timber. **b** perversion of the mind. **2** lengthwise threads in a loom. **3** rope used in warping a ship. [Old English]

warpaint *n.* **1** paint used to adorn the body before battle, esp. by North American Indians. **2** *colloq.* make-up.

warpath *n.* □ **on the warpath 1** (of North American Indians) going to war. **2** *colloq.* seeking a confrontation.

warrant /'wɒrənt/ –*n.* **1** thing that authorizes an action. **2 a** written authorization, money voucher, etc. **b** written authorization allowing police to search premises, arrest a suspect, etc. **3** document that serves as proof that goods have been deposited in a public warehouse. The document identifies specific goods and can be transferred by endorsement. Warrants are frequently used as security against a bank loan. Warehouse warrants for warehouses attached to a wharf are known as **dock warrants** or **wharfinger's warrants**. **4** certificate of service rank held by a warrant-officer. **5** *Finance* security that offers the owner the right to subscribe for the ordinary shares of a company at a fixed date, usu. at a fixed price. Warrants are themselves bought and sold on stock exchanges and are equivalent to stock options. Subscription prices usu. exceed the market price, as the purchase of a warrant is a gamble that a company will prosper. They have proved increasingly popular in recent years as a company can issue them without including them in the balance sheet. –*v.* **1** serve as a warrant for; justify. **2** guarantee or attest to esp. the genuineness of. □ **I** (or **I'll**) **warrant** I am certain; no doubt. [French *warant*, from Germanic]

warrant-officer *n.* officer ranking between commissioned officers and NCOs.

♦ **warranty** *n.* (*pl.* **-ies**) **1** statement made clearly in a contract (**express warranty**) or, if not stated clearly, understood between the parties to the contract (**implied**

warranty). An unfulfilled warranty does not invalidate the contract (as it would in the case of an unfulfilled condition) but could lead to the payment of damages. See also FLOATING WARRANTY. **2** condition in an insurance policy that confirms that something will or will not be done or that a certain situation exists or does not exist. If a warranty is breached, the insurer is entitled to refuse to pay claims, even if they are unconnected with the breach. For example, if a policy insuring the contents of a house has a warranty that certain locks are to be used on the doors and windows and these are found not to have been used, the insurers could decline to settle a claim for a burst pipe. In practice, however, this does not happen as insurers have agreed that they will only refuse to pay claims if the breach of warranty has affected the circumstances of the claim. **3** (also **guarantee**) manufacturer's written promise to repair or replace a faulty product, usu. free of charge, during a specified period subsequent to the date of purchase. **4** (usu. foll. by *for* + verbal noun) authority or justification. [Anglo-French *warantie*: related to WARRANT]

---

warren /ˈwɒrən/ *n.* **1** network of rabbit burrows. **2** densely populated or labyrinthine building or district. [Anglo-French *warenne* from Germanic]

warring see WAR *v.*

warrior /ˈwɒrɪə(r)/ *n.* **1** person experienced or distinguished in fighting. **2** fighting man, esp. of primitive peoples. **3** (*attrib.*) martial (*warrior nation*). [French *werreior*: related to WAR]

Warsaw /ˈwɔːsɔː/ (Polish **Warszawa** /vɑːˈʃævə/) capital of Poland, a centre of industry and communications; pop. (est. 1995) 1 640 700.

warship *n.* ship used in war.

wart /wɔːt/ *n.* **1** small hard round growth on the skin. **2** protuberance on the skin of an animal, surface of a plant, etc. □ **warts and all** *colloq.* with no attempt to conceal blemishes. □ **warty** *adj.* [Old English]

wart-hog *n.* African wild pig.

wartime *n.* period during which a war is being waged.

Warwickshire /ˈwɒrɪkˌʃɪə(r)/ county in England, in the Midlands; pop. (est. 1994) 496 300; county town, Warwick. Agriculture (esp. dairy farming) is the main activity; there is also some light industry.

wary /ˈweərɪ/ *adj.* (**-ier, -iest**) **1** on one's guard; circumspect. **2** (foll. by *of*) cautious. **3** showing caution. □ **warily** *adv.* **wariness** *n.* [*ware* look out for, avoid]

was *1st* & *3rd sing. past* of BE.

Wash. *abbr.* Washington.

wash /wɒʃ/ *–v.* **1** cleanse with liquid, esp. water. **2** (foll. by *out, off, away*, etc.) **a** remove (a stain) in this way. **b** (of a stain etc.) be removed by washing. **3** wash oneself or one's hands and face. **4** wash clothes, dishes, etc. **5** (of fabric or dye) bear washing without damage. **6** (of an argument etc.) stand scrutiny; be believed or acceptable. **7** (of a river, waters, etc.) touch. **8** (of liquid) carry along in a specified direction (*was washed overboard*; *washed up on the shore*). **9** (foll. by *over, along*, etc.) sweep, move, or splash. **10** (foll. by *over*) occur all around without greatly affecting (a person). **11** sift (ore) by the action of water. **12** brush watery paint or ink over. **13** *poet.* moisten, water. *–n.* **1 a** washing or being washed. **b** (prec. by *the*) a laundry etc. (*sent them to the wash*). **2** clothes etc. for washing or just washed. **3** motion of agitated water or air, esp. from the passage of a ship etc. or aircraft. **4** kitchen slops given to pigs. **5 a** thin, weak, or inferior liquid food. **b** liquid food for animals. **6** liquid to spread over a surface to cleanse, heal, or colour. **7** thin coating of water-colour. □ **come out in the wash** *colloq.* be resolved in the course of time. **wash one's dirty linen in public** let private quarrels or difficulties become generally known. **wash down 1** wash completely. **2** (usu. foll. by *with*) accompany or follow (food) with a drink. **wash one's hands of** renounce responsibility for. **wash out 1** clean the inside of by washing. **2** clean (a garment etc.) by brief washing. **3** *colloq.* rain off. **4** = sense 2 of *v.* **wash up 1** (also *absol.*) wash (dishes etc.) after use. **2** *US* wash one's face and hands. **3** carry on to a shore. □ **washable** *adj.* [Old English]

wash-basin *n.* plumbed-in basin for washing one's hands etc.

washboard *n.* **1** ribbed board on which clothes are scrubbed. **2** this as a percussion instrument.

washed out *adj.* (also **washed-out**) **1** faded; pale. **2** *colloq.* pale, exhausted.

washed up *adj.* (also **washed-up**) esp. *US slang* defeated, having failed.

washer *n.* **1** person or machine that washes. **2** flat ring inserted at a joint to tighten it and prevent leakage or under the head of a screw etc., or under a nut, to disperse its pressure.

washer-up *n.* (*pl.* **washers-up**) (also **washer-upper**) person who washes up dishes etc.

washerwoman *n.* laundress.

washing *n.* clothes etc. for washing or just washed.

washing-machine *n.* machine for washing clothes.

washing-powder *n.* soap powder or detergent for washing clothes.

washing-soda *n.* sodium carbonate, used dissolved in water for washing and cleaning.

Washington /ˈwɒʃɪŋt(ə)n/ **1** capital and administrative centre of the US, coterminous with the District of Columbia; pop. (1994) 567 094. **2** state in the US, the most northerly of the Pacific states; pop. (est. 1996) 5 532 939; capital, Olympia. Aircraft construction is the most important industry; other activities include nuclear research, timber production, mining (of gold, silver, and uranium), fishing, and tourism. Agriculture produces wheat, potatoes, fruit (esp. apples), and dairy products.

washing-up *n.* **1** process of washing dishes etc. **2** used dishes etc. for washing.

wash-out *n. colloq.* complete failure, non-event.

washroom *n.* esp. *US* public toilet.

◆ **wash sale** *n.* (in the US) sale or purchase by a simple investor (or group) of a block of securities to establish a loss or gain or to create the impression that the securities are trading actively.

---

washstand *n.* piece of furniture to hold a basin, jug, soap, etc.

washy *adj.* (**-ier, -iest**) **1** too watery or weak. **2** lacking vigour or intensity. □ **washily** *adv.* **washiness** *n.*

wasn't /ˈwɒz(ə)nt/ *contr.* was not.

Wasp /wɒsp/ *n.* (also **WASP**) *US* usu. *derog.* middle-class American White Protestant. [*W*hite *A*nglo-*S*axon *P*rotestant]

wasp /wɒsp/ *n.* stinging insect with black and yellow stripes. [Old English]

waspish *adj.* irritable, snappish.

wasp-waist *n.* very slender waist.

wassail /ˈwɒseɪl, -s(ə)l/ *archaic –n.* festive occasion; drinking-bout. *–v.* make merry. [Old Norse *ves heill* be in health: related to WHOLE]

wastage /ˈweɪstɪdʒ/ *n.* **1** amount wasted. **2** loss by use, wear, or leakage. **3** (also **natural wastage**) loss of employees other than by redundancy.

waste *–v.* (**-ting**) **1** use to no purpose or with inadequate result or extravagantly. **2** fail to use (esp. an opportunity). **3** (often foll. by *on*) **a** give (advice etc.) without effect. **b** (often in *passive*) fail to be appreciated or used properly (*she was wasted on him*; *feel wasted in this job*). **4** wear gradually away; make or become weak. **5** devastate. *–adj.* **1** superfluous; no longer needed. **2** not inhabited or cultivated. *–n.* **1** act of wasting. **2** waste material. **3** waste region. **4** being used up; diminution by wear. **5** = WASTE PIPE. □ **go** (or **run) to waste** be wasted. [Latin: related to VAST]

waste disposal unit *n.* device fitted to a sink etc. for disposing of household waste.

wasteful *adj.* **1** extravagant. **2** causing or showing waste. □ **wastefully** *adv.*

wasteland *n.* **1** unproductive or useless area of land. **2** place or time considered spiritually or intellectually barren.

waste paper *n.* used or valueless paper.

waste-paper basket *n.* receptacle for waste paper.

waste pipe *n.* pipe to carry off waste material.

waste product *n.* useless by-product of manufacture or of an organism.

waster *n.* **1** wasteful person. **2** *colloq.* wastrel.

♦ **wasting asset** *n.* asset that has a finite life. Examples include a lease, which may lose value throughout its life and become valueless when it terminates, and plant and machinery, which wear out during their life and therefore lose value.

---

wastrel /'weɪstr(ə)l/ *n.* good-for-nothing person.

watch /wɒtʃ/ –*v.* **1** keep the eyes fixed on. **2** keep under observation; follow observantly. **3** (often foll. by *for*) be in an alert state; be vigilant. **4** (foll. by *over*) look after; take care of. –*n.* **1** small portable timepiece for carrying on the wrist or in a pocket. **2** state of alert or constant observation or attention. **3** *Naut.* **a** usu. four-hour spell of duty. **b** (in full **starboard** or **port watch**) each of the halves into which a ship's crew is divided to take alternate watches. **4** *hist.* watchman or watchmen. □ **on the watch for** waiting for (an anticipated occurrence). **watch it** (or **oneself**) *colloq.* be careful. **watch out** (often foll. by *for*) be on one's guard. □ **watcher** *n.* (also in *comb.*). [Old English: related to WAKE[1]]

watchdog *n.* **1** dog guarding property etc. **2** person or body monitoring others' rights etc.

watchful *adj.* **1** accustomed to watching, alert. **2** on the watch. □ **watchfully** *adv.* **watchfulness** *n.*

watching brief *n.* brief of a barrister who follows a case for a client not directly concerned.

watchmaker *n.* person who makes and repairs watches and clocks.

watchman *n.* man employed to look after an empty building etc. at night.

watch-night service *n.* religious service held on the last night of the year.

watch-tower *n.* tower for keeping watch from.

watchword *n.* phrase summarizing a guiding principle.

water /'wɔːtə(r)/ –*n.* **1** colourless transparent liquid compound of oxygen and hydrogen. **2** liquid consisting chiefly of this and found in seas and rivers, in rain, and in secretions of organisms. **3** expanse of water; a sea, lake, river, etc. **4** (in *pl.*) part of a sea or river. **5** (often as **the waters**) mineral water at a spa etc. **6** state of a tide. **7** solution of a specified substance in water (*lavender-water*). **8** transparency and brilliance of a gem. **9** (*attrib.*) **a** found in or near water. **b** of, for, or worked by water. **c** involving, using, or yielding water. **10** (usu. in *pl.*) amniotic fluid, released during labour. –*v.* **1** sprinkle or soak with water. **2** supply (a plant) with water. **3** give water to (an animal). **4** secrete water. **5** (as **watered** *adj.*) (of silk etc.) having irregular wavy glossy markings. **6** take in a supply of water. □ **by water** using a ship etc. for transport. **like water** in great quantity, profusely. **make one's mouth water** cause one's saliva to flow, stimulate one's appetite or anticipation. **of the first water** of the finest quality or extreme degree. **water down 1** dilute. **2** make less forceful or horrifying. **water under the bridge** past events accepted as irrevocable. [Old English]

Water-bearer var. of WATER-CARRIER.

water-bed *n.* mattress filled with water.

water-biscuit *n.* thin crisp unsweetened biscuit.

water-buffalo *n.* common domestic Indian buffalo.

water bus *n.* boat carrying passengers on a regular run on a river, lake, etc.

water-cannon *n.* device using a jet of water to disperse a crowd etc.

Water-carrier *n.* (also **Water-bearer**) (prec. by *the*) zodiacal sign or constellation Aquarius.

water chestnut *n.* corm from a sedge, used in Chinese cookery.

water-clock *n.* clock measuring time by the flow of water.

water-closet *n.* lavatory that can be flushed.

water-colour *n.* (*US* **water-color**) **1** artists' paint made of pigment to be diluted with water and not oil. **2** picture painted with this. **3** art of painting with water-colours. □ **water-colourist** *n.*

water-cooled *adj.* cooled by the circulation of water.

watercourse *n.* **1** brook or stream. **2** bed of this.

watercress *n.* pungent cress growing in running water and used in salad.

water-diviner *n.* dowser.

♦ **watered stock** *n.* shares created by stock watering.

---

waterfall *n.* stream flowing over a precipice or down a steep hillside.

Waterford /'wɔːtəˌfəd/ **1** county in the S Republic of Ireland, in the province of Munster; dairy farming and cattle rearing are important; pop. (1991) 91 624. **2** its capital city, a port, noted for its clear colourless flint glass; pop. (1991) 40 345.

waterfowl *n.* (usu. collect. as *pl.*) birds frequenting water.

waterfront *n.* part of a town adjoining a river etc.

water-glass *n.* solution of sodium or potassium silicate used esp. for preserving eggs.

water-hammer *n.* knocking noise in a water-pipe when a tap is suddenly turned off.

water-hole *n.* shallow depression in which water collects.

water-ice *n.* flavoured and frozen water and sugar etc.

watering-can *n.* portable container with a long spout, for watering plants.

watering-hole *n.* **1** = WATERING-PLACE 1. **2** *slang* bar.

watering-place *n.* **1** pool from which animals regularly drink. **2** spa or seaside resort.

water jump *n.* jump over water in a steeplechase etc.

water-level *n.* **1 a** surface of the water in a reservoir etc. **b** height of this. **2** level below which the ground is saturated with water. **3** level using water to determine the horizontal.

water lily *n.* aquatic plant with floating leaves and flowers.

water-line *n.* line along which the surface of water touches a ship's side.

waterlogged *adj.* saturated or filled with water.

Waterloo /ˌwɔːtə'luː/ *n.* decisive defeat or contest. [*Waterloo* in Belgium, where Napoleon was defeated]

water main *n.* main pipe in a water-supply system.

waterman *n.* **1** boatman plying for hire. **2** oarsman as regards skill in keeping the boat balanced.

watermark –*n.* faint design in some paper identifying the maker etc. –*v.* mark with this.

water-meadow *n.* meadow periodically flooded by a stream.

water melon *n.* large dark-green melon with red pulp and watery juice.

water-mill *n.* mill worked by a water-wheel.

water-pistol *n.* toy pistol shooting a jet of water.

water polo *n.* game played by swimmers, with a ball like a football.

water-power *n.* mechanical force derived from the weight or motion of water.

waterproof –*adj.* impervious to water. –*n.* waterproof garment or material. –*v.* make waterproof.

water-rat *n.* = WATER-VOLE.

water-rate *n.* charge made for the use of the public water-supply.

watershed *n.* **1** line of separation between waters flowing to different rivers, basins, etc. **2** turning-point in affairs. [from *shed* ridge]

waterside *n.* edge of a sea, lake, or river.

water-ski –*n.* each of a pair of skis for skimming the surface of the water when towed by a motor boat. –*v.* travel on water-skis. □ **water-skier** *n.*

water-softener *n.* apparatus for softening hard water.

waterspout *n.* gyrating column of water and spray between sea and cloud.

water-table *n.* = WATER-LEVEL 2.

watertight *adj.* **1** closely fastened or fitted so as to prevent the passage of water. **2** (of an argument etc.) unassailable.

water-tower *n.* tower with an elevated tank to give pressure for distributing water.

water-vole *n.* aquatic vole.

waterway *n.* navigable channel.

water-wheel *n.* wheel driven by water to work machinery, or to raise water.

water-wings *n.pl.* inflated floats fixed on the arms of a person learning to swim.

waterworks *n.* **1** establishment for managing a water-supply. **2** *colloq.* shedding of tears. **3** *colloq.* urinary system.

watery *adj.* **1** containing too much water. **2** too thin in consistency. **3** of or consisting of water. **4** vapid, uninteresting. **5** (of colour) pale. **6** (of the sun, moon, or sky) rainy-looking. **7** (of eyes) moist; tearful.□ **wateriness** *n.*

WATS *abbr. US* Wide Area Telecommunications Service.

♦ **Watson** /'wɒts(ə)n/, **Thomas, Jr.** (1914–) US business executive, president (1952–61), chairman (1961–79), and chairman emeritus (since 1981) of International Business Machines Corporation (IBM), the world's largest computer manufacturer. Founded by his father in 1924, IBM began by selling tabulators, time clocks, and electric typewriters. Watson Jr. brought out the first IBM computer in 1952.

---

watt /wɒt/ *n.* SI unit of power, equivalent to one joule per second, corresponding to the rate of energy in an electric circuit where the potential difference is one volt and the current one ampere. [*Watt*, name of an engineer]

wattage *n.* amount of electrical power expressed in watts.

watt-hour *n.* energy used when one watt is applied for one hour.

wattle[1] /'wɒt(ə)l/ *n.* **1** structure of interlaced rods and sticks used for fences etc. **2** Australian acacia with pliant branches and golden flowers used as the national emblem. [Old English]

wattle[2] /'wɒt(ə)l/ *n.* fleshy appendage on the head or throat of a turkey or other birds. [origin unknown]

wattle and daub *n.* network of rods and twigs plastered with clay or mud as a building material.

wave –*v.* (**-ving**) **1 a** (often foll. by *to*) move a hand etc. to and fro in greeting or as a signal. **b** move (a hand etc.) in this way. **2 a** show a sinuous or sweeping motion as of a flag, tree, corn, etc. in the wind. **b** impart a waving motion to. **3** direct (a person) by waving (*waved them away*; *waved them to follow*). **4** express (a greeting etc.) by waving. **5** give an undulating form to (hair etc.). **6** (of hair etc.) have such a form. –*n.* **1** ridge of water between two depressions. **2** long body of water curling into an arch and breaking on the shore. **3** thing compared to this, e.g. a body of persons in one of successive advancing groups. **4** gesture of waving. **5 a** process of waving the hair. **b** undulating form produced by this. **6** temporary occurrence or increase of a condition or influence (*wave of enthusiasm*; *heat wave*). **7** *Physics* **a** disturbance of the particles of a fluid medium to form ridges and troughs for the propagation or direction of motion, heat, light, sound, etc. **b** single curve in this motion. **8** undulating line or outline. □ **make waves** *colloq.* cause trouble. **wave aside** dismiss as intrusive or irrelevant. **wave down** wave to (a vehicle or driver) to stop. [Old English]

waveband *n.* range of radio wavelengths between certain limits.

wave-form *n. Physics* curve showing the shape of a wave at a given time.

wavelength *n.* **1** distance between successive crests of a wave. **2** this as a distinctive feature of radio waves from a transmitter. **3** *colloq.* particular mode or range of thought.

wavelet *n.* small wave.

wave machine *n.* device at a swimming-pool producing waves.

waver *v.* **1** be or become unsteady; begin to give way. **2** be irresolute. **3** (of a light) flicker. [Old Norse: related to WAVE]

wavy *adj.* (**-ier, -iest**) having waves or alternate contrary curves. □ **waviness** *n.*

wax[1] –*n.* **1** sticky plastic yellowish substance secreted by bees as the material of honeycomb. **2** this bleached and purified, used for candles, modelling, etc. **3** any similar substance, e.g. the yellow substance secreted by the ear. –*v.* **1** cover or treat with wax. **2** remove unwanted hair from (legs etc.) using wax. □ **waxy** *adj.* (**-ier, -iest**). [Old English]

wax[2] *v.* **1** (of the moon) increase in apparent size. **2** become larger or stronger. **3** pass into a specified state or mood (*wax lyrical*). □ **wax and wane** undergo alternate increases and decreases. [Old English]

waxen *adj.* **1** smooth or pale like wax. **2** *archaic* made of wax.

waxwing *n.* any of various birds with tips like red sealing-wax to some wing-feathers.

waxwork *n.* **1** object, esp. a lifelike dummy, modelled in wax. **2** (in *pl.*) exhibition of wax dummies.

way –*n.* **1** road, track, path, etc., for passing along. **2** course or route for reaching a place (*asked the way to London*; *the way out*). **3** method or plan for attaining an object. **4** style, manner (*I like the way you dress*). **5** person's chosen or habitual course of action. **6** normal course of events (*that is always the way*). **7** travelling distance; length traversed or to be traversed. **8** unimpeded opportunity or space to advance (*make way*). **9** advance in some direction; impetus, progress (*under way*). **10** being engaged in movement from place to place; time spent in this (*on the way home*). **11** specified direction (*step this way*). **12** *colloq.* scope or range. **13** line of occupation or business. **14** specified condition or state (*things are in a bad way*). **15** respect (*is useful in some ways*). **16** (in *pl.*) part into which a thing is divided (*split it three ways*). **17** (in *pl.*) structure of timber etc. down which a new ship is launched. –*adv. colloq.* far (*way off*). □ **by the way** incidentally. **by way of 1** by means of. **2** as a form of. **3** passing through. **come one's way** become available to one. **get out of the** (or **my** etc.) **way** stop obstructing a person. **go out of one's way** make a special effort. **in a way** to some extent. **in the** (or **one's**) **way** forming an obstruction. **lead the way** act as guide or leader. **look the other way** ignore what one should notice. **on the** (or **one's**) **way 1** in the course of a journey etc. **2** having progressed. **3** *colloq.* (of a child) conceived but not yet born. **on the way out** *colloq.* going out of fashion or favour. **out of the way 1** no longer an obstacle. **2** disposed of. **3** unusual. **4** (of a place) remote. [Old English]

way back *adv. colloq.* long ago.

waybill *n.* **1** list of passengers or parcels on a vehicle. **2** = CONSIGNMENT NOTE. See also AIR WAYBILL.

wayfarer *n.* traveller, esp. on foot. □ **wayfaring** *n.* & *adj.*

waylay *v.* (*past* and *past part.* **waylaid**) **1** lie in wait for. **2** stop to talk to or rob.

way of life *n.* principles or habits governing all one's actions etc.

way-out *adj. colloq.* unusual; eccentric.

-ways *suffix* forming adjectives and adverbs of direction or manner (*sideways*).

ways and means *n.pl.* **1** methods of achieving something. **2** methods of raising government revenue.

wayside *n.* **1** side of a road. **2** land at the side of a road.

wayward *adj.* childishly self-willed; capricious. □ **waywardness** *n.* [from AWAY, -WARD]

WB *abbr.* **1** (also **W/B**) waybill. **2** World Bank.

Wb *abbr.* weber(s).

WC –*abbr.* water-closet. –*postcode* west central London.

w.c. *abbr.* without charge.

W/Cdr. *abbr.* Wing Commander.

WCL *abbr.* World Confederation of Labour.

WD –*international vehicle registration* Dominica. –*postcode* Watford.

W/D *abbr. Banking* withdrawal.

w/d *abbr.* (also **wd.**) warranted.

WDA *abbr. Taxation* writing-down allowance.

WDV *abbr. Taxation* written-down value.

we /wiː, wɪ/ *pron.* (*obj.* **us**; *poss.* **our, ours**) **1** *pl.* of I². **2** used for or by a royal person in a proclamation etc. or by an editor etc. in a formal context. [Old English]

WEA *abbr.* Workers' Educational Association.

weak *adj.* **1** deficient in strength, power, vigour, resolution, or number. **2** unconvincing. **3** *Gram.* (of a verb) forming inflections by the addition of a suffix to the stem. □ **weakish** *adj.* [Old Norse]

weaken *v.* make or become weak or weaker.

weak-kneed *adj. colloq.* lacking resolution.

weakling *n.* feeble person or animal.

weakly –*adv.* in a weak manner. –*adj.* (**-ier, -iest**) sickly, not robust.

weak-minded *adj.* **1** mentally deficient. **2** lacking in resolution.

weak moment *n.* time when one is unusually compliant or susceptible.

weakness *n.* **1** being weak. **2** weak point. **3** (foll. by *for*) self-indulgent liking (*weakness for chocolate*).

weak point *n.* (also **weak spot**) **1** place where defences are assailable. **2** flaw in an argument or character or in resistance to temptation.

weal¹ –*n.* ridge raised on the flesh by a stroke of a rod or whip. –*v.* mark with a weal. [var. of WALE]

weal² *n. literary* welfare. [Old English]

wealth /welθ/ *n.* **1** riches. **2** being rich. **3** *Econ.* value of the assets owned by an individual or group of individuals. Economics began as the study of wealth (e.g. Adam Smith's *The Wealth of Nations*) and how it changes during a given period. Keynesian theory tended to place a greater emphasis on income as the object of study in macroeconomics but it has since been accepted that income only tends to affect the behaviour of individuals as it affects their wealth. **4** (foll. by *of*) abundance. [Old English]

♦ **wealth effect** *n.* (also **Pigou effect**) *Econ.* change in the value of the assets held by an individual as a result of a change in the price level (inflation or deflation). Keynes argued that falling prices would reduce the level of aggregate demand and therefore create unemployment. However, if there is a wealth effect, falling prices will raise the value of money held and enhance aggregate demand, implying that the effect of money on the economy is neutral. See INSIDE MONEY; NEUTRALITY OF MONEY; OUTSIDE MONEY.

♦ **wealth tax** *n.* tax used in some European countries consisting of an annual levy on a person's wealth.

---

wealthy *adj.* (**-ier, -iest**) having an abundance, esp. of money.

wean *v.* **1** accustom (an infant or other young mammal) to food other than (esp. its mother's) milk. **2** (often foll. by *from, away from*) disengage (from a habit etc.) by enforced discontinuance. [Old English, = accustom]

weapon /ˈwepən/ *n.* **1** thing designed, used, or usable for inflicting bodily harm. **2** means for gaining the advantage in a conflict. [Old English]

weaponry *n.* weapons collectively.

wear /weə(r)/ –*v.* (*past* **wore**; *past part.* **worn**) **1** have on one's person as clothing or an ornament etc. **2** exhibit or present (a facial expression etc.) (*wore a frown*). **3** *colloq.* (usu. with *neg.*) tolerate. **4** (often foll. by *away, down*) **a** injure the surface of, or partly obliterate or alter, by rubbing, stress, or use. **b** undergo such injury or change. **5** (foll. by *off, away*) rub or be rubbed off. **6** make (a hole etc.) by constant rubbing or dripping etc. **7** (often foll. by *out*) exhaust. **8** (foll. by *down*) overcome by persistence. **9** (foll. by *well* etc.) endure continued use or life. **10** (of time) pass, esp. tediously. **11** (of a ship) fly (a flag). –*n.* **1** wearing or being worn. **2** things worn; fashionable or suitable clothing (*sportswear; footwear*). □ **wear one's heart on one's sleeve** show one's feelings openly. **wear off** lose effectiveness or intensity. **wear out 1** use or be used until useless. **2** tire or be tired out. **wear thin** (of patience, excuses, etc.) begin to fail. **wear the trousers** see TROUSERS. □ **wearer** *n.* [Old English]

♦ **wear and tear** *n.* normal damage that occurs to assets in the course of their useful lives, causing them to depreciate in value (unless steps are taken to make good the damage).

---

wearisome /ˈwɪərɪsəm/ *adj.* tedious; tiring by monotony or length.

weary /ˈwɪərɪ/ –*adj.* (**-ier, -iest**) **1** very tired after exertion or endurance. **2** (foll. by *of*) no longer interested in, tired of. **3** tiring, tedious. –*v.* (**-ies, -ied**) make or grow weary. □ **wearily** *adv.* **weariness** *n.* [Old English]

weasel /ˈwiːz(ə)l/ *n.* small flesh-eating mammal related to the stoat and ferret. [Old English]

weasel word *n.* (usu. in *pl.*) word that is intentionally ambiguous or misleading.

weather /ˈweðə(r)/ –*n.* **1** state of the atmosphere at a place and time as regards heat, cloudiness, dryness, sunshine, wind, and rain etc. **2** (*attrib.*) *Naut.* windward. –*v.* **1** expose to or affect by atmospheric changes; season (wood). **2** be discoloured or worn in this way. **3 a** come safely through (a storm). **b** survive (a difficult period etc.). **4** get to the windward of (a cape etc.). □ **keep a weather eye open** be watchful. **make heavy weather of** *colloq.* exaggerate the difficulty presented by. **under the weather** *colloq.* indisposed. [Old English]

weather-beaten *adj.* affected by exposure to the weather.

weatherboard *n.* **1** sloping board attached to the bottom of an outside door to keep out the rain etc. **2** each of a series of overlapping horizontal boards on a wall. □ **weatherboarding** *n.* (in sense 2 of *n.*).

weathercock *n.* **1** weather-vane in the form of a cock. **2** inconstant person.

weather forecast *n.* assessment of likely weather.

♦ **weather insurance** *n.* = PLUVIAL INSURANCE.

---

weatherman *n.* meteorologist, esp. one who broadcasts a weather forecast.

weatherproof *adj.* resistant to the effects of bad weather, esp. rain.

weather-vane *n.* **1** revolving pointer on a church spire etc. to show the direction of the wind. **2** inconstant person.

♦ **weather working days** *n.pl.* working days on which the weather permits work to be carried out. See also LAY DAYS.

---

weave¹ –*v.* (**-ving**; *past* **wove**; *past part.* **woven** or **wove**) **1 a** form (fabric) by interlacing long threads in two directions. **b** form (thread) into fabric in this way. **2** make fabric in this way. **3 a** (foll. by *into*) make (facts etc.) into a story or connected whole. **b** make (a story) in this way. –*n.* style of weaving. [Old English]

weave² *v.* (**-ving**) move repeatedly from side to side; take an intricate course to avoid obstructions. □ **get weaving** *slang* begin action; hurry. [Old Norse: related to WAVE]

weaver *n.* **1** person who weaves fabric. **2** (in full **weaver-bird**) tropical bird building elaborately woven nests.

web *n.* **1 a** woven fabric. **b** amount woven in one piece. **2** complex series (*web of lies*). **3** cobweb, gossamer, or a similar product of a spinning creature. **4** membrane between the toes of a swimming animal or bird. **5** large roll of paper used in printing. **6** thin flat connecting part in machinery etc. □ **webbed** *adj.* [Old English]

webbing *n.* strong narrow closely-woven fabric used for belts etc.

weber /'veɪbə(r)/ *n.* the SI unit of magnetic flux. [*Weber*, name of a physicist]

web-footed *adj.* having the toes connected by webs.

Wed. *abbr.* (also **Weds.**) Wednesday.

wed *v.* (**-dd-**; *past* and *past part.* **wedded** or **wed**) **1** usu. *formal* or *literary* marry. **2** unite. **3** (as **wedded** *adj.*) of or in marriage (*wedded bliss*). **4** (as **wedded** *adj.*) (foll. by *to*) obstinately attached or devoted to (a pursuit etc.). [Old English, = pledge]

we'd /wiːd, wɪd/ *contr.* **1** we had. **2** we should; we would.

wedding /'wedɪŋ/ *n.* marriage ceremony. [Old English: related to WED]

wedding breakfast *n.* meal etc. between a wedding and departure for the honeymoon.

wedding cake *n.* rich iced cake served at a wedding reception.

wedding ring *n.* ring worn by a married person.

wedge –*n.* **1** piece of tapering wood or metal etc. driven between two objects or parts to secure or separate them. **2** anything resembling a wedge. **3** golf club with a wedge-shaped head. –*v.* (**-ging**) **1** secure or fasten with a wedge. **2** force open or apart with a wedge. **3** (foll. by *in, into*) pack or thrust (a thing or oneself) tightly in or into. □ **thin end of the wedge** *colloq.* thing of little importance in itself, but likely to lead to more serious developments. [Old English]

Wedgwood /'wedʒwʊd/ *n. propr.* **1** a kind of fine stoneware usu. with a white cameo design. **2** its characteristic blue colour. [*Wedgwood*, name of a potter]

wedlock /'wedlɒk/ *n.* the married state. □ **born in** (or **out of**) **wedlock** born of married (or unmarried) parents. [Old English, = marriage vow]

Wednesday /'wenzdeɪ/ –*n.* day of the week following Tuesday. –*adv. colloq.* **1** on Wednesday. **2** (**Wednesdays**) on Wednesdays; each Wednesday. [Old English]

Weds. *abbr.* var. of WED.

wee[1] *adj.* (**weer** /'wiːə(r)/; **weest** /'wiːɪst/) **1** esp. *Scot.* little. **2** *colloq.* tiny. [Old English]

wee[2] *n. colloq.* = WEE-WEE.

weed –*n.* **1** wild plant growing where it is not wanted. **2** thin weak-looking person or horse. **3** (prec. by *the*) *slang* **a** marijuana. **b** tobacco. –*v.* **1 a** clear (an area) of weeds. **b** remove unwanted parts from. **2** (foll. by *out*) **a** sort out and remove (inferior or unwanted parts etc.). **b** rid of inferior parts, unwanted members, etc. **3** cut off or uproot weeds. [Old English]

weed-killer *n.* chemical used to destroy weeds.

weeds /wiːdz/ *n.pl.* (in full **widow's weeds**) *archaic* deep mourning worn by a widow. [Old English, = garment]

weedy *adj.* (**-ier, -iest**) **1** weak, feeble. **2** having many weeds.

week *n.* **1** period of seven days reckoned usu. from midnight on Saturday. **2** any period of seven days. **3** the six days between Sundays. **4 a** the five days Monday to Friday. **b** time spent working in this period (*35-hour week*; *three-day week*). [Old English]

weekday *n.* day other than Sunday or Saturday and Sunday.

weekend *n.* **1** Sunday and Saturday or part of Saturday. **2** this period extended slightly esp. for a holiday or visit etc.

weekender *n.* person who spends the weekend away from home; weekend visitor.

weekly –*adj.* done, produced, or occurring once a week. –*adv.* once a week. –*n.* (*pl.* **-ies**) weekly newspaper or periodical.

weeny /'wiːnɪ/ *adj.* (**-ier, -iest**) *colloq.* tiny. [from WEE[1]]

weep –*v.* (*past* and *past part.* **wept**) **1** shed tears. **2** (often foll. by *for*) bewail, lament over. **3 a** be covered with or send forth drops. **b** come or send forth in drops; exude liquid. **4** (as **weeping** *adj.*) (of a tree) having drooping branches. –*n.* spell of weeping. [Old English]

weepie *n. colloq.* sentimental or emotional film, play, etc.

weepy *adj.* (**-ier, -iest**) *colloq.* inclined to weep; tearful.

weevil /'wiːvɪl/ *n.* destructive beetle feeding esp. on grain. [Low German]

wee-wee /'wiːwiː/ *colloq.* –*n.* **1** act of urinating. **2** urine. –*v.* (**-wees, -weed**) urinate. [origin unknown]

weft *n.* **1** threads woven across a warp to make fabric. **2** yarn for these. **3** thing woven. [Old English: related to WEAVE[1]]

weigh /weɪ/ *v.* **1** find the weight of. **2** balance in the hands to guess or as if to guess the weight of. **3** (often foll. by *out*) take a definite weight of (a substance); measure out (a specified weight) (*weigh out the flour*; *weigh out 6 oz*). **4 a** estimate the relative value, importance, or desirability of. **b** (foll. by *with, against*) compare. **5** be equal to (a specified weight). **6** have (esp. a specified) importance; exert an influence. **7** (often foll. by *on*) be heavy or burdensome (to); be depressing (to). □ **weigh down 1** bring down by exerting weight. **2** be oppressive to. **weigh in** (of a boxer before a contest, or a jockey after a race) be weighed. **weigh in with** *colloq.* advance (an argument etc.) boldly. **weigh out** (of a jockey) be weighed before a race. **weigh up** *colloq.* form an estimate of. **weigh one's words** carefully choose the way one expresses something. [Old English, = carry]

weighbridge *n.* weighing-machine for vehicles.

weigh-in *n.* weighing of a boxer before a fight.

weight /weɪt/ –*n.* **1** force experienced by a body as a result of the earth's gravitation. **2** heaviness of a body regarded as a property of it. **3 a** quantitative expression of a body's weight. **b** scale of such weights (*troy weight*). **4** body of a known weight for use in weighing or weight training. **5** heavy body, esp. as used in a mechanism etc. **6** load or burden. **7** influence, importance. **8** *Athletics* = SHOT[1] 7. –*v.* **1 a** attach a weight to. **b** hold down with a weight. **2** (foll. by *with*) impede or burden. □ **throw one's weight about** (or **around**) *colloq.* be unpleasantly self-assertive. **worth one's weight in gold** very useful or helpful. [Old English]

◆ **weighted average** *n.* arithmetic average that takes into account the importance of the items making up the average. For example, if a person buys a commodity on three occasions, 100 tonnes at £70 per tonne, 300 tonnes at £80 per tonne, and 50 tonnes at £95 per tonne, the purchases total 450 tonnes; the simple average price would be (70 + 80 + 95)/3 = £81.7. The weighted average, taking into account the amount purchased on each occasion, would be [(100 × 70) + (300 × 80) + (50 × 95)]/450 = £79.4 per tonne.

◆ **weighted ballot** *n. Finance* ballot held if a new issue of shares has been oversubscribed, in which the allocation of shares is based on the number of shares applied for and biased towards either the smaller investor or the larger investor.

---

weighting *n.* extra allowance paid in special cases.

weightless *adj.* (of a body, esp. in an orbiting spacecraft etc.) not apparently acted on by gravity. □ **weightlessness** *n.*

weightlifting *n.* sport of lifting heavy weights. □ **weightlifter** *n.*

◆ **weight note** *n.* document produced by a seller of goods in which the gross weights of the packages are listed. It also gives the marks and numbers of the packages and an indication of the average tare.

◆ **weight or measurement** see FREIGHT *n.* 3.

---

weight training *n.* physical training using weights.

weighty *adj.* (**-ier, -iest**) **1** heavy. **2** momentous. **3** (of utterances etc.) deserving consideration. **4** influential, authoritative. □ **weightily** *adv.* **weightiness** *n.*

♦ **Weinstock** /ˈwaɪnstɒk/, **Arnold, Baron Weinstock** (1924–) British business executive, managing director (since 1963) of General Electric Company (GEC), which he has built up to a major international force in the electronics industry. Criticized in the 1980s for accumulating a cash mountain, he is now highly regarded for his management of the group and their steady profits.

weir /wɪə(r)/ *n.* dam across a river to raise the level of water upstream or regulate its flow. [Old English]

weird *adj.* **1** uncanny, supernatural. **2** *colloq.* queer, incomprehensible. □ **weirdly** *adv.* **weirdness** *n.* [Old English *wyrd* destiny]

weirdo /ˈwɪədəʊ/ *n.* (*pl.* **-s**) *colloq.* odd or eccentric person.

welch var. of WELSH.

welcome /ˈwelkəm/ *–n.* act of greeting or receiving gladly; kind or glad reception. *–int.* expressing such a greeting. *–v.* (**-ming**) receive with a welcome. *–adj.* **1** that one receives with pleasure (*welcome guest*; *welcome news*). **2** (foll. by *to*, or *to* + infin.) cordially allowed or invited (*you are welcome to use my car*). □ **make welcome** receive hospitably. **outstay one's welcome** stay too long as a visitor etc. **you are welcome** there is no need for thanks. [Old English]

weld *–v.* **1 a** hammer or press (pieces of iron or other metal usu. heated but not melted) into one piece. **b** join by fusion with an electric arc etc. **c** form by welding into some article. **2** fashion into an effectual or homogeneous whole. *–n.* welded joint. □ **welder** *n.* [alteration of WELL[2], probably influenced by the form *welled*]

welfare /ˈwelfeə(r)/ *n.* **1** well-being, happiness; health and prosperity (of a person or community etc.). **2** (**Welfare**) **a** welfare centre or office. **b** financial support given by the state. [from WELL[1], FARE]

♦ **welfare economics** *n.* branch of economics that is concerned with normative questions (see NORMATIVE ECONOMICS) relating to the well-being of society as a whole; in particular, it seeks to establish a ranking in terms of welfare between different allocations of resources. Unfortunately, the only widely agreed criterion for judging between alternatives is Pareto optimality, which is very weak. Thus, although welfare economics concerns itself with such important questions as taxation, distribution, regulation of externalities, and government policy, it has been of limited practical use.

welfare state *n.* **1** system whereby the state undertakes to protect the health and well-being of its citizens by means of grants, pensions, etc. **2** country practising this system.

welfare work *n.* organized effort for the welfare of the poor, disabled, etc.

welkin *n. poet.* sky. [Old English, = cloud]

well[1] *–adv.* (**better, best**) **1** in a satisfactory way (*works well*). **2** with some distinction (*plays the piano well*). **3** in a kind way (*treated me well*). **4** thoroughly, carefully (*polish it well*). **5** with heartiness or approval (*speak well of*). **6** probably, reasonably (*you may well be right*). **7** to a considerable extent (*is well over forty*). *–adj.* (**better, best**) **1** (usu. *predic.*) in good health. **2** (*predic.*) **a** in a satisfactory state or position. **b** advisable (*it would be well to enquire*). *–int.* expressing surprise, resignation, etc., or continuation of talk after a pause. □ **leave well alone** avoid needless change or disturbance. **well and truly** decisively, completely. **well away 1** having made considerable progress. **2** *colloq.* fast asleep or drunk. **well done!** expressing praise for something done. **well worth** certainly worth. [Old English]

well[2] *–n.* **1** shaft sunk into the ground to obtain water, oil, etc. **2** enclosed space like a well-shaft, e.g. in the middle of a building for stairs or a lift, or for light or ventilation. **3** (foll. by *of*) source. **4** (in *pl.*) spa. **5** = INK-WELL. **6** *archaic* water-spring. **7** railed space in a lawcourt. *–v.* (foll. by *out*, *up*) spring as from a fountain. [Old English]

we'll /wiːl, wɪl/ *contr.* we shall; we will.

well-adjusted *adj.* **1** mentally and emotionally stable. **2** in a good state of adjustment.

well-advised *adj.* (usu. foll. by *to* + infin.) prudent.

well-appointed *adj.* having all the necessary equipment.

well-balanced *adj.* sane, sensible.

well-behaved *adj.* habitually behaving well.

well-being *n.* state of being contented, healthy, etc.

well-born *adj.* of noble family.

well-bred *adj.* having or showing good breeding or manners.

well-built *adj.* big, strong, and well-proportioned.

well-connected *adj.* associated, esp. by birth, with persons of good social position.

well-disposed *adj.* (often foll. by *towards*) friendly or sympathetic.

well-dressed *adj.* fashionably smart.

well-earned *adj.* fully deserved.

well-founded *adj.* (of suspicions etc.) based on good evidence.

well-groomed *adj.* with carefully tended hair, clothes, etc.

well-head *n.* source.

well-heeled *adj. colloq.* wealthy.

wellies /ˈwelɪz/ *n.pl. colloq.* wellingtons. [abbreviation]

well-informed *adj.* having much knowledge or information about a subject.

Wellington /ˈwelɪŋt(ə)n/ capital of New Zealand, situated at the S end of North Island; there are engineering, food-processing, and textile industries, and wool, meat, dairy products, and fruit are exported; pop. (est. 1995) 331 100.

wellington /ˈwelɪŋt(ə)n/ *n.* (in full **wellington boot**) waterproof boot usu. reaching the knee. [Duke of *Wellington*]

well-intentioned *adj.* having or showing good intentions.

well-judged *adj.* opportunely, skilfully, or discreetly done.

well-kept *adj.* kept in good order or condition.

well-known *adj.* known to many.

well-made *adj.* **1** strongly manufactured. **2** having a good build.

well-mannered *adj.* having good manners.

well-meaning *adj.* (also **well-meant**) well-intentioned (but ineffective).

wellnigh *adv.* almost (*wellnigh impossible*).

well off *adj.* (also **well-off**) **1** having plenty of money. **2** in a fortunate situation.

well-oiled *adj. colloq.* very drunk.

well-paid *adj.* **1** (of a job) that pays well. **2** (of a person) amply rewarded for a job.

well-preserved *adj.* **1** in good condition. **2** (of an old person) showing little sign of age.

well-read *adj.* knowledgeable through much reading.

well-received *adj.* welcomed; favourably received.

well-rounded *adj.* complete and symmetrical.

well-spoken *adj.* articulate or refined in speech.

well-spring *n.* = WELL-HEAD.

well-to-do *adj.* prosperous.

well-tried *adj.* often tested with good results.

well-trodden *adj.* much frequented.

well-wisher *n.* person who wishes one well.

well-worn *adj.* **1** much worn by use. **2** (of a phrase etc.) trite.

Welsh *–adj.* of or relating to Wales or its people or language. *–n.* **1** the Celtic language of Wales. **2** (prec. by *the*; treated as *pl.*) the people of Wales. [Old English, ultimately from Latin *Volcae*, name of a Celtic people]

welsh *v.* (also **welch**) **1** (of a loser of a bet, esp. a bookmaker) decamp without paying. **2** evade an obligation. **3**

(foll. by *on*) **a** fail to carry out a promise to (a person). **b** fail to honour (an obligation). [origin unknown]

Welshman *n.* man who is Welsh by birth or descent.

Welsh rabbit *n.* (also, by folk etymology, **Welsh rarebit**) dish of melted cheese etc. on toast.

Welshwoman *n.* woman who is Welsh by birth or descent.

welt *–n.* **1** leather rim sewn round the edge of a shoe-upper for the sole to be attached to. **2** = WEAL[1]. **3** ribbed or reinforced border of a garment. **4** heavy blow. *–v.* **1** provide with a welt. **2** raise weals on; thrash. [origin unknown]

welter[1] *–v.* **1** roll, wallow. **2** (foll. by *in*) lie prostrate or be soaked in. *–n.* **1** general confusion. **2** (foll. by *of*) disorderly mixture or contrast. [Low German or Dutch]

welter[2] *n.* heavy rider or boxer. [origin unknown]

welterweight *n.* **1** weight in certain sports intermediate between lightweight and middleweight, in the amateur boxing scale 63.5–67 kg. **2** sportsman of this weight.

wen *n.* benign tumour on the skin, esp. on the scalp. [Old English]

wench *n. joc.* girl or young woman. [abbreviation of *wenchel*, from Old English, = child]

wend *v.* □ **wend one's way** make one's way. [Old English, = turn]

Wendy house /ˈwendɪ/ *n.* children's small houselike tent or structure for playing in. [*Wendy*, name of a character in Barrie's *Peter Pan*]

went *past* of GO[1].

wept *past* of WEEP.

were *2nd sing. past, pl. past*, and *past subjunctive* of BE.

we're /wɪə(r)/ *contr.* we are.

weren't /wɜːnt/ *contr.* were not.

werewolf /ˈweəwʊlf/ *n.* (*pl.* **-wolves**) mythical being who at times changes from a person to a wolf. [Old English]

Wesleyan /ˈwezlɪən/ *–adj.* of or relating to a Protestant denomination founded by John Wesley. *–n.* member of this denomination.

west *–n.* **1 a** point of the horizon where the sun sets at the equinoxes. **b** compass point corresponding to this. **c** direction in which this lies. **2** (usu. **the West**) **a** European civilization. **b** states of western Europe and North America. **c** western part of a country, town, etc. *–adj.* **1** towards, at, near, or facing the west. **2** from the west (*west wind*). *–adv.* **1** towards, at, or near the west. **2** (foll. by *of*) further west than. □ **go west** *slang* be killed or destroyed etc. **to the west** (often followed by *of*) in a westerly direction. [Old English]

West Bank region in the Middle East, W of the River Jordan and NW of the Dead Sea; pop. (est. 1994) 1 122 900. It became part of Jordan in 1948 and was under Israeli occupation from 1967; in 1988 Jordan severed legal and administrative ties with the West Bank and the Palestine Liberation Organization declared it a Palestinian state, leading to violent conflict with the Israelis. In 1993 an agreement signed by Israel and the PLO handed over the administration of the West Bank to the new Palestinian National Authority (from 1994).

West Bengal state in E India, comprising the Hindu area of former Bengal; pop. (est. 1994) 73 600 000; capital, Calcutta. Crops include rice, jute, and tea; fishing, forestry, and mining are among the other economic activities of the state.

westbound *adj.* travelling or leading westwards.

West Country *n.* south-western England.

West End *n.* main entertainment and shopping area of London.

westering *adj.* (of the sun) nearing the west.

westerly *–adj.* & *adv.* **1** in a western position or direction. **2** (of a wind) from the west. *–n.* (*pl.* **-ies**) such a wind.

western *–adj.* of or in the west. *–n.* film or novel about cowboys in western North America. □ **westernmost** *adj.*

Western Australia state in W Australia; pop. (est. 1996) 1 755 500; capital, Perth. Agriculture produces wheat, vines, citrus fruits, and dairy products; there are also important deposits of ferrous minerals, bauxite, nickel, and gold. Industry, centred on Perth, includes chemicals, textiles, oil-refining, and iron and steel.

westerner *n.* native or inhabitant of the west.

Western Isles island area of Scotland consisting of the Outer Hebrides; pop. (est. 1989) 31 384; chief town, Stornoway.

westernize *v.* (also **-ise**) (**-zing** or **-sing**) influence with, or convert to, the ideas and customs etc. of the West.

Western Sahara Moroccan desert territory in NW Africa, on the Atlantic coast; it is rich in phosphates; pop. (est. 1993) 214 000; capital, La'youn (El Aaiún). A former Spanish colony (Spanish Sahara), it was annexed by Morocco and Mauritania in 1976; when Mauritania withdrew from the territory in 1979, Morocco extended its control over the entire region. A liberation movement (the Polisario Front) continued its struggle against Morocco in an attempt to establish an independent Saharawi Arab Democratic Republic; a UN peacekeeping force arrived in 1991.

Western Somalia see OGADEN.

West Glamorgan /gləˈmɔːg(ə)n/ former county in S Wales; its county town was Swansea. In 1996 the county was abolished and replaced by two unitary authorities.

West Indies chain of islands, including the Greater Antilles, the Lesser Antilles, and the Bahamas, extending from the coast of Florida in North America to that of Venezuela in South America, enclosing the Caribbean Sea. Cultivation of sugar cane is of major importance; other crops include tobacco, coffee, bananas, and spices. □ **West Indian** *adj.* & *n.*

Westman Islands /ˈwestmən/ group of 15 volcanic islands S of Iceland; pop. (1987) 4700.

Westmeath /westˈmiːð/ county in the Republic of Ireland, in the province of Leinster; pop. (1991) 61 880; capital, Mullingar. Dairy farming and cattle fattening are the main agricultural activities.

West Midlands metropolitan county in central England; pop. (est. 1994) 2 627 800; county town, Birmingham. Since 1986 administrative power has been devolved to the districts of Wolverhampton, Walsall, Dudley, Sandwell, Birmingham, Solihull, and Coventry.

west-north-west *n.* point or direction midway between west and north-west.

♦ **Weston** /ˈwest(ə)n/, **Garfield Howard** (1927–) Canadian business executive, chairman (since 1967) of Associated British Foods plc, founded by his grandfather in 1882. Joining the company in 1951, Weston developed his own management style, to which the success of the group has been attributed. Associated British Foods now owns Fortnum & Mason (acquired in 1979) and British Sugar plc (bought in 1991 for £880 million).

Westphalia /westˈfeɪlɪə/ former province of NW Germany, now part of the state (*Land*) of North Rhine-Westphalia. □ **Westphalian** *adj.* & *n.*

West Side *n. US* western part of Manhattan.

west-south-west *n.* point or direction midway between west and south-west.

West Sussex /ˈsʌsɪks/ county in SE England; pop. (est. 1994) 722 100; county town, Chichester. Agriculture produces cereals, root crops, and dairy products; tourism is also important, esp. along the coast.

West Virginia /vəˈdʒɪnɪə/ state in the E central US, W of Virginia; pop. (est. 1996) 1 825 754; capital, Charleston. Agriculture (esp. livestock products) is important, as are coalmining and the manufacture of chemicals, metals, and stone and clay products.

westward /ˈwestwəd/ *–adj.* & *adv.* (also **westwards**) towards the west. *–n.* westward direction or region.

West Yorkshire metropolitan county in N England; pop. (est. 1994) 2 104 100; county town, Wakefield. Industries include coalmining and the manufacture of wool textiles. In 1986 the administrative powers of the county were devolved to the districts of Bradford, Leeds, Calderdale, Kirkless, and Wakefield.

WET *abbr.* West(ern) European Time.

wet *–adj.* (**wetter, wettest**) **1** soaked or covered with water or other liquid. **2** (of the weather etc.) rainy. **3** (of paint etc.) not yet dried. **4** used with water (*wet shampoo*). **5** *colloq.* feeble, inept. *–v.* (**-tt-**; *past* and *past part.* **wet** or **wetted**) **1** make wet. **2 a** urinate in or on (*wet the bed*). **b** *refl.* urinate involuntarily. *–n.* **1** liquid that wets something. **2** rainy weather. **3** *colloq.* feeble or inept person. **4** *colloq.* Conservative with liberal tendencies. **5** *colloq.* drink. □ **wet behind the ears** *colloq.* immature, inexperienced. **wet through** (or **to the skin**) with one's clothes soaked. □ **wetly** *adv.* **wetness** *n.* [Old English]

wet blanket *n. colloq.* gloomy person hindering others' enjoyment.

wet dream *n.* erotic dream with the involuntary ejaculation of semen.

wether /'weðə(r)/ *n.* castrated ram. [Old English]

wetland *n.* (often in *pl.*) swamps and other damp areas of land.

wet-nurse *–n.* woman employed to suckle another's child. *–v.* **1** act as a wet-nurse to. **2** *colloq.* treat as if helpless.

wet suit *n.* rubber garment worn by skin-divers etc. to keep warm.

WEU *abbr.* Western European Union.

we've /wi:v/ *contr.* we have.

Wexford /'weksfəd/ **1** county in the SE Republic of Ireland, in the province of Leinster; agriculture (esp. cattle rearing) is important; pop. (1991) 102 069. **2** its capital city, a seaport with food-processing and other industries; pop. (1991) 9540.

WF *postcode* Wakefield.

WFTU *abbr.* World Federation of Trade Unions.

WG *international vehicle registration* Grenada.

Wg. Cdr. *abbr.* Wing Commander.

W. Glam. *abbr.* West Glamorgan.

whack *colloq. –v.* **1** strike or beat forcefully. **2** (as **whacked** *adj.*) tired out. *–n.* **1** sharp or resounding blow. **2** *slang* share. □ **have a whack at** *slang* attempt. [imitative]

whacking *colloq. –adj.* very large. *–adv.* very.

whale *–n.* (*pl.* same or **-s**) very large marine mammal with a streamlined body and horizontal tail. *–v.* (**-ling**) hunt whales. □ **a whale of a** *colloq.* an exceedingly good or fine etc. [Old English]

whalebone *n.* elastic horny substance in the upper jaw of some whales.

whale-oil *n.* oil from the blubber of whales.

whaler *n.* whaling ship or seaman.

wham *int. colloq.* expressing forcible impact. [imitative]

Whangarei /ˌwæŋgə'reɪ/ port in New Zealand, on North Island, the site of New Zealand's only oil refinery; pop. (1994) 44 800.

◆ **wharf** /wɔ:f/ *–n.* (*pl.* **wharves** /wɔ:vz/ or **-s**) quay at which ships dock in a port, together with the adjacent warehouses in which goods are stored before loading or after unloading. *–v.* **1** moor (a ship) at a wharf. **2** store (goods) on a wharf. [Old English]

◆ **wharfage** *n.* **1** accommodation at a wharf. **2** charge made by a wharfinger for the use of a wharf for loading or unloading cargo.

◆ **wharfinger** /'wɔ:fɪndʒə(r)/ *n.* firm or individual responsible for running a wharf.

◆ **wharfinger's receipt** *n.* = DOCK RECEIPT.

◆ **wharfinger's warrant** see WARRANT *n.* 3.

---

what /wɒt/ *–interrog. adj.* **1** asking for a choice from an indefinite number or for a statement of amount, number, or kind (*what books have you read?*). **2** *colloq.* = WHICH *interrog. adj.* (*what book have you chosen?*). *–adj.* (usu. in exclam.) how great or remarkable (*what luck!*). *–rel. adj.* the or any ... that (*will give you what help I can*). *–pron.* (corresp. to the functions of the *adj.*) **1** what thing or things? (*what is your name?*; *I don't know what you mean*). **2** (asking for a remark to be repeated) = what did you say? **3** how much (*what you must have suffered!*). **4** (as *rel. pron.*) that or those which; a or the or any thing which (*what followed was worse*; *tell me what you think*). *–adv.* to what extent (*what does it matter?*). □ **what about** what is the news or your opinion of. **what-d'you-call-it** *colloq.* substitute for a name not recalled. **what ever** what at all or in any way (*what ever do you mean?*) (see also WHATEVER). **what for** *colloq.* **1** for what reason? **2** severe reprimand (esp. *give a person what for*). **what have you** (prec. by *or* or *and*) *colloq.* anything else similar. **what not** (prec. by *and*) other similar things. **what's-his** (or **-her** or **-its**) **-name** *colloq.* substitute for a name not recalled. **what's what** *colloq.* what is useful or important etc. **what with** *colloq.* because of (usu. several things). [Old English]

whatever /wɒt'evə(r)/ *adj.* & *pron.* **1** = WHAT (in relative uses) with the emphasis on indefiniteness (*lend me whatever you can*; *whatever money you have*). **2** though anything (*we are safe whatever happens*). **3** (with *neg.* or *interrog.*) at all; of any kind (*there is no doubt whatever*).

whatnot *n. colloq.* indefinite or trivial thing.

whatsoever /ˌwɒtsəʊ'evə(r)/ *adj.* & *pron.* = WHATEVER.

wheat *n.* **1** cereal plant bearing dense four-sided seed-spikes. **2** its grain, used in making flour etc. [Old English]

wheatear *n.* small migratory bird. [related to WHITE, ARSE]

wheaten *adj.* made of wheat.

wheat germ *n.* embryo of the wheat grain, extracted as a source of vitamins.

wheatmeal *n.* flour made from wheat with some of the bran and germ removed.

wheedle /'wi:d(ə)l/ *v.* (**-ling**) **1** coax by flattery or endearments. **2** (foll. by *out*) get (a thing) out of a person or cheat (a person) out of a thing by wheedling. [origin uncertain]

wheel *–n.* **1** circular frame or disc which revolves on an axle and is used for vehicular or other mechanical motion. **2** wheel-like thing. **3** motion as of a wheel, esp. the movement of a line of soldiers with one end as a pivot. **4** (in *pl.*) *slang* car. **5** = STEERING-WHEEL. *–v.* **1 a** turn on an axis or pivot. **b** swing round in line with one end as a pivot. **2 a** (often foll. by *about, round*) change direction or face another way. **b** cause to do this. **3** push or pull (a wheeled thing, or its load or occupant). **4** go in circles or curves. □ **at the wheel 1** driving a vehicle. **2** directing a ship. **3** in control. **on wheels** (or **oiled wheels**) smoothly. **wheel and deal** engage in political or commercial scheming. **wheels within wheels 1** intricate machinery. **2** *colloq.* indirect or secret agencies. □ **wheeled** *adj.* (also in *comb.*). [Old English]

wheelbarrow *n.* small handcart with one wheel and two shafts.

wheelbase *n.* distance between the axles of a vehicle.

wheelchair *n.* chair on wheels for an invalid or disabled person.

wheel-clamp see CLAMP[1] *n.* 2.

-wheeler *comb. form* vehicle with a specified number of wheels (*three-wheeler*).

wheeler-dealer *n.* person who wheels and deals.

wheel-house *n.* steersman's shelter.

wheelie *n. slang* stunt of riding a bicycle or motor cycle with the front wheel off the ground.

wheel-spin *n.* rotation of a vehicle's wheels without traction.

wheelwright *n.* person who makes or repairs wheels.

wheeze *–v.* (**-zing**) **1** breathe with an audible whistling sound. **2** utter with this sound. *–n.* **1** sound of wheezing. **2** *colloq.* clever scheme. □ **wheezy** *adj.* (**-ier, -iest**). **wheezily** *adv.* **wheeziness** *n.* [probably from Old Norse, = hiss]

whelk *n.* marine mollusc with a spiral shell. [Old English]

whelm *v. poet.* **1** engulf. **2** crush with weight. [Old English]

whelp *–n.* **1** young dog; puppy. **2** *archaic* cub. **3** ill-mannered child or youth. *–v.* (also *absol.*) give birth to (a whelp or whelps or (*derog.*) a child). [Old English]

when *–interrog. adv.* **1** at what time? **2** on what occasion? **3** how soon? *–rel. adv.* (prec. by *time* etc.) at or on which (*there are times when I could cry*). *–conj.* **1** at the or any time that; as soon as (*come when you like*; *come when ready*). **2** although (*why stand when you could sit?*). **3** after which; and then; but just then (*was nearly asleep when the bell rang*). *–pron.* what time?; which time (*till when can you stay?*; *since when it has improved*). *–n.* time, occasion (*fixed the where and when*). [Old English]

whence *formal –interrog. adv.* from what place? *–conj.* **1** to the place from which (*return whence you came*). **2** (often prec. by *place* etc.) from which. **3** and thence (*whence it follows that*). [Old English: related to WHEN]

■ **Usage** The use of *from whence* rather than simply *whence* (as in *the place from whence they came*), though common, is generally considered incorrect.

whenever /wen'evə(r)/ *conj.* & *adv.* **1** at whatever time; on whatever occasion. **2** every time that.

whensoever /ˌwensəʊ'evə(r)/ *conj.* & *adv. formal* = WHENEVER.

where /weə(r)/ *–interrog. adv.* **1** in or to what place or position? **2** in what respect? (*where does it concern us?*). *–rel. adv.* (prec. by *place* etc.) in or to which (*places where they meet*). *–conj.* **1** in or to the or any place, direction, or respect in which (*go where you like*; *tick where applicable*). **2** and there (*reached Crewe, where the car broke down*). *–pron.* what place? (*where do you come from?*). *–n.* place; scene of something (see WHEN *n.*). [Old English]

whereabouts *–interrog. adv.* /ˌweərə'baʊts/ approximately where? *–n.* /'weərəˌbaʊts/ (as *sing.* or *pl.*) person's or thing's location.

whereas /weər'æz/ *conj.* **1** in contrast or comparison with the fact that. **2** (esp. in legal preambles) taking into consideration the fact that.

whereby /weə'baɪ/ *conj.* by what or which means.

wherefore *–adv. archaic* **1** for what reason? **2** for which reason. *–n.* see WHY.

wherein /weər'ɪn/ *conj. formal* in what or which place or respect.

whereof /weər'ɒv/ *conj. formal* of what or which.

whereupon /ˌweərə'pɒn/ *conj.* immediately after which.

wherever /weər'evə(r)/ *–adv.* in or to whatever place. *–conj.* in every place that.

wherewithal /'weəwɪˌðɔːl/ *n. colloq.* money etc. needed for a purpose.

wherry /'werɪ/ *n.* (*pl.* **-ies**) **1** light rowing-boat usu. for carrying passengers. **2** large light barge. [origin unknown]

whet *v.* (**-tt-**) **1** sharpen (a tool). **2** stimulate (the appetite or a desire etc.). [Old English]

whether /'weðə(r)/ *conj.* introducing the first or both of alternative possibilities (*I doubt whether it matters*; *I do not know whether they have arrived or not*). □ **whether or no** whether it is so or not. [Old English]

whetstone *n.* tapered stone used with water to sharpen tools.

whew /hwjuː/ *int.* expressing surprise, consternation, or relief. [imitative]

whey /weɪ/ *n.* watery liquid left when milk forms curds. [Old English]

which *–interrog. adj.* asking for choice from a definite set of alternatives (*which John do you mean?*; *say which book you prefer*). *–rel. adj.* being the one just referred to; and this or these (*ten years, during which time they admitted nothing*). *–interrog. pron.* **1** which person or persons? (*which of you is responsible?*). **2** which thing or things? (*say which you prefer*). *–rel. pron.* (*poss.* **of which, whose** /huːz/) **1** which thing or things, usu. introducing a clause not essential for identification (*the house, which is empty, has been damaged*). **2** used in place of *that* after *in* or *that* (*there is the house in which I was born*; *that which you have just seen*). [Old English]

whichever /wɪtʃ'evə(r)/ *adj.* & *pron.* any which (*take whichever you like*).

whiff *n.* **1** puff or breath of air, smoke, etc. **2** smell. **3** (foll. by *of*) trace of scandal etc. **4** small cigar. [imitative]

Whig *n. hist.* member of the British reforming and constitutional party succeeded in the 19th century by the Liberal Party. □ **Whiggery** *n.* **Whiggish** *adj.* **Whiggism** *n.* [*whiggamer, -more*, nickname of 17th-century Scots rebels]

while *–n.* period of time (*a long while ago*; *waited a while*; *all this while*). *–conj.* **1** during the time that; for as long as; at the same time as (*while I was away, the house was burgled*; *fell asleep while reading*). **2** in spite of the fact that; whereas (*while I want to believe it, I cannot*). *–v.* (**-ling**) (foll. by *away*) pass (time etc.) in a leisurely or interesting way. *–rel. adv.* (prec. by *time* etc.) during which (*the summer while I was abroad*). □ **between whiles** in the intervals. **for a while** for some time. **in a while** soon. **the while** in the meantime. **worth while** (or **one's while**) worth the time or effort spent. [Old English]

■ **Usage** *Worth while* (two words) is used only predicatively, as in *thought it worth while to ring the police*, whereas *worthwhile* is used both predicatively and attributively.

whilst /waɪlst/ *adv.* & *conj.* while. [from WHILE]

whim *n.* **1** sudden fancy; caprice. **2** capriciousness. [origin unknown]

whimper *–v.* make feeble, querulous, or frightened sounds. *–n.* such a sound. [imitative]

whimsical /'wɪmzɪk(ə)l/ *adj.* capricious, fantastic. □ **whimsicality** /-'kælɪtɪ/ *n.* **whimsically** *adv.*

whimsy /'wɪmzɪ/ *n.* (*pl.* **-ies**) = WHIM. [origin uncertain]

whin *n.* (in *sing.* or *pl.*) gorse. [Scandinavian]

whinchat *n.* small songbird.

whine *–n.* **1** complaining long-drawn wail as of a dog. **2** similar shrill prolonged sound. **3** querulous tone or complaint. *–v.* (**-ning**) emit or utter a whine; complain. [Old English]

whinge /wɪndʒ/ *v.* (**-geing** or **-ging**) *colloq.* whine; grumble peevishly. [Old English]

whinny /'wɪnɪ/ *–n.* (*pl.* **-ies**) gentle or joyful neigh. *–v.* (**-ies, -ied**) give a whinny. [imitative]

whip *–n.* **1** lash attached to a stick for urging on animals or punishing etc. **2 a** member of a political party in Parliament appointed to control its discipline and tactics. **b** whips' written notice requesting or requiring attendance for voting at a division etc., variously underlined according to the degree of urgency (*three-line whip*). **c** (prec. by *the*) party discipline and instructions (*asked for the Labour whip*). **3** dessert made with whipped cream etc. **4** = WHIPPER-IN. *–v.* (**-pp-**) **1** beat or urge on with a whip. **2** beat (cream or eggs etc.) into a froth. **3** take or move suddenly, unexpectedly, or rapidly (*whipped out a knife*; *whipped behind the door*). **4** *slang* steal. **5** *slang* **a** excel. **b** defeat. **6** bind with spirally wound twine. **7** sew with overcast stitches. □ **whip in** bring (hounds) together. **whip on** urge into action. **whip up** excite or stir up. [Low German or Dutch]

whipcord *n.* tightly twisted cord.

whip hand *n.* **1** hand that holds the whip (in riding etc.). **2** (usu. prec. by *the*) advantage or control in a situation.

whiplash *n.* flexible end of a whip.

whiplash injury *n.* injury to the neck caused by a jerk of the head, esp. as in a motor accident.

whipper-in /ˌwɪpə'rɪn/ *n.* (*pl.* **whippers-in**) huntsman's assistant who manages the hounds.

whippersnapper /'wɪpəˌsnæpə(r)/ *n.* **1** small child. **2** insignificant but presumptuous person.

whippet /'wɪpɪt/ *n.* cross-bred dog of the greyhound type used for racing. [probably from obsolete *whippet* move briskly, from *whip it*]

whipping boy *n.* scapegoat.

whipping-top *n.* top kept spinning by blows of a lash.

whippoorwill /ˈwɪpʊəwɪl/ *n.* American nightjar. [imitative]

whip-round *n. colloq.* informal collection of money among a group of people.

whipstock *n.* handle of a whip.

whirl *–v.* **1** swing round and round; revolve rapidly. **2** (foll. by *away*) convey or go rapidly in a vehicle etc. **3** send or travel swiftly in an orbit or a curve. **4** (of the brain etc.) seem to spin round. *–n.* **1** whirling movement. **2** state of intense activity (*the social whirl*). **3** state of confusion (*in a whirl*). □ **give it a whirl** *colloq.* attempt it. [Old Norse, and Low German or Dutch]

whirligig /ˈwɜːlɪɡɪɡ/ *n.* **1** spinning or whirling toy. **2** merry-go-round. **3** revolving motion.

whirlpool *n.* powerful circular eddy of water.

whirlwind *n.* **1** rapidly whirling mass or column of air. **2** (*attrib.*) very rapid.

whirr *–n.* continuous rapid buzz or soft clicking sound. *–v.* (**-rr-**) make this sound. [Scandinavian]

whisk *–v.* **1** (foll. by *away, off*) **a** brush with a sweeping movement. **b** take suddenly. **2** whip (cream, eggs, etc.). **3** convey or go (esp. out of sight) lightly or quickly. **4** wave or lightly brandish. *–n.* **1** whisking action or motion. **2** utensil for whisking eggs or cream etc. **3** bunch of grass, twigs, bristles, etc., for removing dust or flies. [Scandinavian]

whisker *n.* **1** (usu. in *pl.*) hair growing on a man's face, esp. on the cheek. **2** each of the bristles on the face of a cat etc. **3** *colloq.* small distance (*within a whisker of*). □ **whiskered** *adj.* **whiskery** *adj.* [from WHISK]

whisky /ˈwɪskɪ/ *n.* (*Ir.* & *US* **whiskey**) (*pl.* **-ies** or **-eys**) spirit distilled esp. from malted grain, esp. barley or rye. [abbreviation of *usquebaugh* from Gaelic, = water of life]

whisper *–v.* **1 a** speak very softly without vibration of the vocal cords. **b** talk or say in a barely audible tone or in a secret or confidential way. **2** rustle or murmur. *–n.* **1** whispering speech or sound. **2** thing whispered. □ **it is whispered** there is a rumour. [Old English]

whist *n.* card-game usu. for two pairs of players. [earlier *whisk*, perhaps from WHISK (with ref. to whisking away the tricks): perhaps associated with *whist!* (= silence)]

whist drive *n.* social occasion with the playing of progressive whist.

whistle /ˈwɪs(ə)l/ *–n.* **1** clear shrill sound made by forcing breath through a small hole between nearly closed lips. **2** similar sound made by a bird, the wind, a missile, etc. **3** instrument used to produce such a sound. *–v.* (**-ling**) **1** emit a whistle. **2 a** give a signal or express surprise or derision by whistling. **b** (often foll. by *up*) summon or give a signal to (a dog etc.) by whistling. **3** (also *absol.*) produce (a tune) by whistling. **4** (foll. by *for*) vainly seek or desire. [Old English]

whistle-stop *n.* **1** *US* small unimportant town on a railway. **2** politician's brief pause for an electioneering speech on tour.

Whit *–n.* = WHITSUNTIDE. *–attrib. adj.* of Whitsuntide or Whit Sunday. [Old English, = white]

whit *n.* particle; least possible amount (*not a whit better*). [apparently = WIGHT]

◆ **Whitbread** /ˈwɪtbred/, **Samuel Charles** (1937–) British business executive, chairman (1984–92) of Whitbread plc, the brewing group founded in the mid-18th century by his great-great-great-great-grandfather. He was High Sheriff of Bedfordshire (1973–4) and is now Lord-Lieutenant (since 1991) of the same county.

---

white *–adj.* **1** resembling a surface reflecting sunlight without absorbing any of the visible rays; of the colour of milk or snow. **2** nearly this colour; pale, esp. in the face. **3** (**White**) **a** of the human group having light-coloured skin. **b** of or relating to White people. **4** albino (*white mouse*). **5** (of hair) having lost its colour, esp. in old age. **6** (of coffee) with milk or cream. *–n.* **1** white colour or pigment. **2 a** white clothes or material. **b** (in *pl.*) white garments as worn in cricket, tennis, etc. **3 a** (in a game or sport) white piece, ball, etc. **b** player using these. **4** = EGG-WHITE. **5** whitish part of the eyeball round the iris. **6** (**White**) member of a light-skinned race. □ **bleed white** drain of wealth etc. □ **whiteness** *n.* **whitish** *adj.* [Old English]

white ant *n.* termite.

whitebait *n.* (*pl.* same) (usu. in *pl.*) small silvery-white young of herrings and sprats, esp. as food.

white cell *n.* leucocyte.

white-collar *attrib. adj.* (of a worker or work) non-manual; clerical, administrative, managerial, or professional.

white corpuscle *n.* = WHITE CELL.

white elephant *n.* useless possession.

white feather *n.* symbol of cowardice.

white flag *n.* symbol of surrender.

White Friar *n.* Carmelite.

◆ **white goods** *n.pl.* washing-machines, dishwashers, refrigerators, tumble-driers, deep-freezes, etc., which are usu. finished in white enamel paint. Cf. BROWN GOODS.

---

whitehead *n. colloq.* white or white-topped skin-pustule.

white heat *n.* **1** temperature at which metal emits white light. **2** state of intense passion or activity. □ **white-hot** *adj.*

white hope *n.* person expected to achieve much.

Whitehorse /ˈwaɪthɔːs/ city in NW Canada, capital of Yukon Territory and an administrative, tourist, and distribution centre; pop. (est. 1995) 22 884.

white horses *n.pl.* white-crested waves at sea.

◆ **white knight** *n.* person or firm that makes a welcome take-over bid for a company on improved terms to replace an unacceptable and unwelcome bid from a black knight. If a company is the target for a take-over bid from a source of which it does not approve or on terms that it does not find attractive, it will often seek a white knight. Cf. BLACK KNIGHT; GREY KNIGHT.

---

white lead *n.* mixture of lead carbonate and hydrated lead oxide used as pigment.

white lie *n.* harmless or trivial untruth.

white light *n.* colourless light, e.g. ordinary daylight.

white magic *n.* magic used for beneficent purposes.

white meat *n.* poultry, veal, rabbit, and pork.

whiten *v.* make or become white. □ **whitener** *n.*

white noise *n.* noise containing many frequencies with equal intensities.

white-out *n.* dense blizzard, esp. in polar regions.

White Paper *n.* government report giving information.

white pepper *n.* pepper made by grinding a ripe or husked berry.

White Russian *n.* = BELARUSSIAN.

white sauce *n.* sauce of flour, melted butter, and milk or cream.

White Sea inlet of the Barents Sea on the NW coast of Russia, connected to the Gulf of Finland by inland waterways. Its chief port is Archangel.

white slave *n.* woman tricked or forced into prostitution.

white spirit *n.* light petroleum as a solvent.

white sugar *n.* purified sugar.

white tie *n.* man's white bow-tie as part of full evening dress.

whitewash *–n.* **1** solution of quicklime or whiting for whitening walls etc. **2** means employed to conceal mistakes or faults. *–v.* **1** cover with whitewash. **2** attempt to clear the reputation of by concealing facts.

white wedding *n.* wedding at which the bride wears a formal white wedding dress.

white whale *n.* northern cetacean, white when adult.

whitewood *n.* pale wood, esp. prepared for staining etc.

whither /ˈwɪðə(r)/ *archaic –adv.* **1** to what place or state? **2** (prec. by *place* etc.) to which. *–conj.* **1** to the or any place to which (*go whither you will*). **2** and thither. [Old English]

whiting[1] *n.* (*pl.* same) small white-fleshed fish used as food. [Dutch: related to WHITE]

whiting[2] *n.* ground chalk used in whitewashing etc.

whitlow /'wɪtləʊ/ *n.* inflammation near a fingernail or toenail. [originally *white* FLAW[1]]

Whitsun /'wɪts(ə)n/ *–n.* = WHITSUNTIDE. *–adj.* = WHIT. [*Whitsun Day* = Whit Sunday]

Whit Sunday *n.* seventh Sunday after Easter, commemorating Pentecost.

Whitsuntide *n.* weekend or week including Whit Sunday.

whittle /'wɪt(ə)l/ *v.* (**-ling**) **1** (often foll. by *at*) pare (wood etc.) with repeated slicing with a knife. **2** (often foll. by *away, down*) reduce by repeated subtractions. [dial. *thwittle*]

whiz (also **whizz**) *–n.* sound made by a body moving through the air at great speed. *–v.* (**-zz-**) move with or make a whiz. [imitative]

whiz-kid *n. colloq.* brilliant or highly successful young person.

WHO *abbr.* World Health Organization.

who /hu:/ *pron.* (*obj.* **whom** /hu:m/ or *colloq.* **who**; *poss.* **whose** /hu:z/) **1 a** what or which person or persons? (*who called?*; *you know who it was*). **b** what sort of person or persons? (*who am I to object?*). **2** (a person) that (*anyone who wishes can come*; *the woman whom you met*; *the man who you saw*). **3** and or but he, they, etc. (*gave it to Tom, who sold it to Jim*). [Old English]

■ **Usage** In the last two examples of sense 2 *whom* is correct, but *who* is common in less formal contexts.

whoa /wəʊ/ *int.* used to stop or slow a horse etc. [var. of HO]

who'd /hu:d/ *contr.* **1** who had. **2** who would.

whodunit /hu:'dʌnɪt/ *n.* (also **whodunnit**) *colloq.* detective story, play, or film. [= *who done* (illiterate for *did*) *it?*]

whoever /hu:'evə(r)/ *pron.* (*obj.* **whoever** or *formal* **whomever** /hu:m-/; *poss.* **whosever** /hu:z-/) **1** the or any person or persons who (*whoever comes is welcome*). **2** though anyone (*whoever else objects, I do not*).

whole /həʊl/ *–adj.* **1** uninjured, unbroken, intact, or undiminished. **2** not less than; all there is of. **3** (of blood or milk etc.) with no part removed. *–n.* **1** thing complete in itself. **2** all there is of a thing. **3** (foll. by *of*) all members etc. of (*the whole of London knows it*). □ **as a whole** as a unity; not as separate parts. **on the whole** taking everything relevant into account. **whole lot** see LOT. □ **wholeness** *n.* [Old English]

wholefood *n.* food which has not been unnecessarily processed or refined.

wholegrain *attrib. adj.* made with or containing whole grains (*wholegrain rice*).

wholehearted *adj.* **1** completely devoted. **2** done with all possible effort or sincerity. □ **wholeheartedly** *adv.*

wholemeal *n.* (usu. *attrib.*) meal or flour with none of the bran or germ removed.

whole number *n.* number without fractions; integer.

♦ **whole (of) life policy** *n.* life-assurance policy that pays a specified amount on the death of the life assured. Benefits are not made for any other reason and the cover continues until the death of the life assured, provided the premiums continue to be paid, either for life or until a specified date. They may be with-profits or unit-linked policies.

---

wholesale *–n.* selling of goods in large quantities to be retailed by others. *–adj.* & *adv.* **1** by wholesale. **2** on a large scale. *–v.* (**-ling**) sell wholesale. [*by whole sale*]

♦ **wholesale banking** *n.* (in the US) provision of banking services to large corporate businesses at special rates.

♦ **wholesale price index** see PRODUCER PRICE INDEX.

♦ **wholesaler** *n.* distributor that sells goods in large quantities, usu. to other distributors. Typically, a wholesaler buys and stores large quantities of several producers' goods and breaks into the bulk deliveries to supply retailers with smaller amounts assembled and sorted to order.

---

wholesome *adj.* **1** promoting physical, mental, or moral health. **2** prudent (*wholesome respect*). [Old English: related to WHOLE]

wholewheat *n.* (usu. *attrib.*) wheat with none of the bran or germ removed.

wholism var. of HOLISM.

wholly /'həʊllɪ/ *adv.* **1** entirely; without limitation. **2** purely.

whom *objective case* of WHO.

whomever *objective case* of WHOEVER.

whomsoever *objective case* of WHOSOEVER.

whoop /hu:p, wu:p/ *–n.* **1** loud cry of or as of excitement etc. **2** long rasping indrawn breath in whooping cough. *–v.* utter a whoop. □ **whoop it up** *colloq.* **1** engage in revelry. **2** *US* make a stir. [imitative]

whoopee /wʊ'pi:/ *int.* expressing exuberant joy. □ **make whoopee** /'wʊpɪ/ *colloq.* **1** have fun, make merry. **2** make love. [imitative]

whooping cough /'hu:pɪŋ/ *n.* infectious bacterial disease, esp. of children, with a series of short violent coughs followed by a whoop.

whoops /wʊps/ *int. colloq.* expressing surprise or apology, esp. on losing balance or making an obvious mistake. [var. of OOPS]

whop *v.* (**-pp-**) *slang* **1** thrash. **2** defeat. [origin unknown]

whopper *n. slang* **1** something big of its kind. **2** great lie.

whopping *adj. colloq.* (esp. as an intensifier) huge (*a whopping success*; *a whopping great lie*).

whore /hɔ:(r)/ *n.* **1** prostitute. **2** *derog.* promiscuous woman. [Old English]

whore-house *n.* brothel.

whorl /wɜ:l/ *n.* **1** ring of leaves etc. round a stem. **2** one turn of a spiral. [apparently var. of WHIRL]

whortleberry /'wɜ:t(ə)l,berɪ/ *n.* (*pl.* **-ies**) bilberry. [origin unknown]

whose /hu:z/ *–pron.* of or belonging to which person (*whose is this book?*). *–adj.* of whom or which (*whose book is this?*; *the man, whose name was Tim*; *the house whose roof was damaged*).

whosoever /,hu:səʊ'evə(r)/ *pron.* (*obj.* **whomsoever** /,hu:m-/; *poss.* **whosesoever** /,hu:z-/) *archaic* = WHOEVER.

who's who *n.* **1** who or what each person is (*know who's who*). **2** list with facts about notable persons.

whs. *abbr.* (also **w'hse.**) warehouse.

why /waɪ/ *–adv.* **1** for what reason or purpose (*why did you do it?*; *I do not know why you came*). **2** (prec. by *reason* etc.) for which (*the reasons why I did it*). *–int.* expressing: **1** surprised discovery or recognition (*why, it's you!*). **2** impatience (*why, of course I do!*). **3** reflection (*why, yes, I think so*). **4** objection (*why, what is wrong with it?*). □ **whys and wherefores** reasons; explanation. [Old English: related to WHAT]

Whyalla /waɪ'ælə/ steel-manufacturing town in South Australia, a port on the Spencer Gulf; pop. (1991) 25 526.

WI *abbr.* **1** West Indian. **2** West Indies. **3** Women's Institute. *–US postcode* Wisconsin.

wick *n.* strip or thread feeding a flame with fuel. □ **get on a person's wick** *colloq.* annoy a person. [Old English]

wicked /'wɪkɪd/ *adj.* (**-er, -est**) **1** sinful, iniquitous, immoral. **2** spiteful. **3** playfully malicious. **4** *colloq.* very bad. **5** *slang* excellent. □ **wickedly** *adv.* **wickedness** *n.* [origin uncertain]

wicker *n.* plaited osiers etc. as material for baskets etc. [Scandinavian]

wickerwork *n.* **1** wicker. **2** things made of wicker.

wicket /'wɪkɪt/ *n.* **1** *Cricket* **a** three stumps with the bails in position defended by a batsman. **b** ground between two wickets. **c** state of this. **d** instance of a batsman being got out (*bowler has taken four wickets*). **2** (in full **wicket-door** or **-gate**) small door or gate, esp. beside or in a larger one or closing the lower part only of a doorway. [Anglo-French *wiket* = French *guichet*]

wicket-keeper *n.* fieldsman stationed close behind a batsman's wicket.

Wicklow /ˈwɪkləʊ/ **1** county in the E Republic of Ireland, in the province of Leinster; agriculture is the main source of revenue; pop. (1991) 97 265. **2** its capital city, on the Irish Sea; pop. (1991) 5850.

widdershins /ˈwɪdəʃɪnz/ *adv.* (also **withershins** /ˈwɪð-/) esp. *Scot.* **1** in a direction contrary to the sun's course (considered unlucky). **2** anticlockwise. [German, = contrary]

wide *–adj.* **1** having sides far apart, broad, not narrow (*wide river; wide sleeve; wide angle*). **2** (following a measurement) in width (*a metre wide*). **3 a** extending far (*wide range; wide experience*). **b** considerable (*wide margin*). **4** not restricted (*a wide public*). **5 a** liberal; unprejudiced (*takes wide views*). **b** not specialized; general. **6** open to the full extent (*wide eyes*). **7** (foll. by *of*) not within a reasonable distance of, far from (*wide shot; wide of the target*). **8** (in *comb.*) extending over the whole of (*nationwide*). *–adv.* **1** widely. **2** to the full extent. **3** far from the target etc. (*shooting wide*). *–n.* = WIDE BALL. □ **give a wide berth to** see BERTH. **wide of the mark** see MARK[1]. **wide open** (often foll. by *to*) exposed (to attack etc.). **the wide world** all the world, great as it is. [Old English]

wide area network *n.* (also **WAN**) **1** computer network that provides long-distance communications, covering, for example, a whole country or including the sites of a large multinational organization. The communications are usu. provided by one or more national or international governmental entities. The facilities offered by such bodies include data communications over telephone lines or over dedicated lines (special high-quality lines reserved for the purpose). More recently national and international packet switching services have been provided. Cf. LOCAL AREA NETWORK. **2** public packet switching service of a particular country or region.

wide awake *adj.* **1** fully awake. **2** *colloq.* wary, knowing.

wide ball *n. Cricket* ball judged to be beyond the batsman's reach, so scoring a run.

wide-eyed *adj.* surprised; naïve.

widely *adv.* **1** to a wide extent; far apart. **2** extensively. **3** by many people (*it is widely thought that*). **4** considerably; to a large degree (*holds a widely different view*).

widen *v.* make or become wider.

♦ **wider-range securities** see TRUSTEE INVESTMENTS.

widespread *adj.* widely distributed.

widgeon /ˈwɪdʒ(ə)n/ *n.* (also **wigeon**) a kind of wild duck. [origin uncertain]

widow /ˈwɪdəʊ/ *–n.* **1** woman who has lost her husband by death and not married again. **2** woman whose husband is often away on a specified activity (*golf widow*). *–v.* **1** make into a widow or widower. **2** (as **widowed** *adj.*) bereft by the death of a spouse. □ **widowhood** *n.* [Old English]

widower *n.* man who has lost his wife by death and not married again.

widow's peak *n.* V-shaped growth of hair towards the centre of the forehead.

width *n.* **1** measurement from side to side. **2** large extent. **3** liberality of views etc. **4** strip of material of full width. □ **widthways** *adv.* [from WIDE]

wield *v.* hold and use; command, exert (a weapon, tool, power, etc.). [Old English]

Wiener schnitzel /ˈviːnə ˌʃnɪts(ə)l/ *n.* veal cutlet breaded, fried, and garnished. [German]

Wiesbaden /ˈviːsbɑːd(ə)n/ city and spa in SW Germany, capital of the state of Hesse and a centre of the wine industry; manufactures include chemicals and plastics; pop. (est. 1995) 266 081.

wife *n.* (*pl.* **wives**) **1** married woman, esp. in relation to her husband. **2** *archaic* woman. □ **wifely** *adj.* [Old English, = woman]

♦ **wife's earnings** see SEPARATE TAXATION OF A WIFE'S EARNINGS.

wig *n.* artificial head of hair. [abbreviation of PERIWIG]

wigeon var. of WIDGEON.

wigging *n. colloq.* reprimand. [origin uncertain]

wiggle /ˈwɪg(ə)l/ *colloq. –v.* (**-ling**) move from side to side etc. *–n.* act of wiggling; kink in a line etc. □ **wiggly** *adj.* (**-ier, -iest**). [Low German or Dutch *wiggelen*]

wight /waɪt/ *n. archaic* person. [Old English, = thing, creature]

wigwam /ˈwɪgwæm/ *n.* North American Indian's hut or tent. [Ojibwa]

wilco /ˈwɪlkəʊ/ *int. colloq.* expressing compliance or agreement. [abbreviation of *will comply*]

wild /waɪld/ *–adj.* **1** in its original natural state; not domesticated, cultivated, or civilized (*wild cat; wild strawberry*). **2** unrestrained, disorderly, uncontrolled (*wild youth; wild hair*). **3** tempestuous (*wild night*). **4** intensely eager, frantic (*wild excitement; wild delight*). **5** (foll. by *about*) *colloq.* enthusiastically devoted to. **6** *colloq.* infuriated. **7** haphazard, ill-aimed, rash (*wild guess; wild venture*). **8** *colloq.* exciting, delightful. *–adv.* in a wild manner. *–n.* **1** wild tract of land. **2** desert. □ **in the wild** in an uncultivated etc. state. **in the wilds** *colloq.* far from towns etc. **run wild** grow or stray unchecked or undisciplined. □ **wildly** *adv.* **wildness** *n.* [Old English]

wild card *n.* **1** card having any rank chosen by the player holding it. **2** *Computing* character that will match any character or combination of characters. **3** person or thing that can be used in several different ways.

wildcat *–n.* **1** hot-tempered or violent person. **2** exploratory oil well. *–adj.* (*attrib.*) **1** (of a strike) sudden and unofficial. See STRIKE *n.* 2. **2** reckless; financially unsound.

wildebeest /ˈwɪldəˌbiːst/ *n.* (*pl.* same or **-s**) = GNU. [Afrikaans: related to WILD, BEAST]

wilderness /ˈwɪldənɪs/ *n.* **1** desert; uncultivated region or garden area. **2** (foll. by *of*) confused assemblage. [Old English: related to WILD, DEER]

wildfire *n. hist.* combustible liquid used in war. □ **spread like wildfire** spread with great speed.

wildfowl *n.* (*pl.* same) game-bird.

wild-goose chase *n.* foolish or hopeless quest.

wild hyacinth *n.* = BLUEBELL.

wildlife *n.* wild animals collectively.

Wild West *n.* western US before the establishment of law and order.

wile *–n.* (usu. in *pl.*) stratagem, trick. *–v.* (**-ling**) (foll. by *away, into*, etc.) lure. [perhaps from Scandinavian]

wilful /ˈwɪlfʊl/ *adj.* (*US* **willful**) **1** intentional, deliberate (*wilful murder; wilful neglect*). **2** obstinate. □ **wilfully** *adv.* [from WILL[2]]

will[1] *v.aux.* (*3rd sing. present* **will**; *past* **would** /wʊd/) **1** (strictly only in the 2nd and 3rd persons: see SHALL) expressing a future statement, command, etc. (*you will regret this; they will leave at once*). **2** expressing the speaker's intention (*I will return soon*). **3** wish or desire (*will you have a drink?; come when you will*). **4** expressing a request as a question (*will you please open the window?*). **5** be able to (*the jar will hold a kilo*). **6** have a habit or tendency to (*accidents will happen; will sit there for hours*). **7** expressing probability or expectation (*that will be my wife*). [Old English]

will[2] *–n.* **1** faculty by which a person decides what to do. **2** strong desire or intention (*will to live*). **3** determination, will-power (*has a strong will*). **4** legal document giving directions as to the disposal of a person's property after death. It has no effect until death and may be altered as many times as the person (the testator) wishes. To be binding, it must be executed in accordance with statutory formalities. It must be in writing, signed by the testator or at the testator's direction and in his or her presence. It must appear that the signature was intended to give effect to the will (usu. it is signed at the end, close to the last words dealing with the property). The will must be witnessed by two persons, who must also sign the will. The witnesses must not be beneficiaries. **5** disposition towards others (*good will*). **6** *archaic* what one desires or ordains. *–v.* **1** try to cause by will-power (*willed her to win*). **2** intend; desire. **3** bequeath by a will. □ **at will** whenever one wishes. **with a will** energetically or resolutely. [Old English]

Willemstadt /ˈvɪləm,stɑːt/ capital of the Netherlands Antilles, a port on the S coast of the island of Curaçao; Venezuelan oil is refined; pop. (est. 1993) 197 019.

willful *US* var. of WILFUL.

willie var. of WILLY.

willies /ˈwɪlɪz/ *n.pl. colloq.* nervous discomfort (*gives me the willies*). [origin unknown]

willing *adj.* **1** ready to consent or undertake. **2** given or done etc. by a willing person. □ **willingly** *adv.* **willingness** *n.*

will-o'-the-wisp /ˌwɪləðəˈwɪsp/ *n.* **1** phosphorescent light seen on marshy ground. **2** elusive person. [= *William of the torch*]

willow /ˈwɪləʊ/ *n.* tree with pliant branches yielding osiers and timber for cricket-bats etc., usu. growing near water. [Old English]

willow-herb *n.* plant with leaves like a willow.

willow-pattern *n.* conventional Chinese design of blue on white porcelain etc.

willow-warbler *n.* small woodland bird with a tuneful song.

willowy *adj.* **1** lithe and slender. **2** having willows.

will-power *n.* control by deliberate purpose over impulse.

willy /ˈwɪlɪ/ *n.* (also **willie**) (*pl.* **-ies**) *colloq.* penis. [diminutive of *William*]

willy-nilly /ˌwɪlɪˈnɪlɪ/ *adv.* whether one likes it or not. [later spelling of *will I, nill I* I am willing, I am unwilling]

wilt *–v.* **1** wither, droop. **2** lose energy, flag. *–n.* plant-disease causing wilting. [originally dial.]

Wilts. /wɪlts/ *abbr.* Wiltshire.

Wiltshire /ˈwɪltʃɪə(r)/ county in SW England; pop. (est. 1994) 586 300; county town, Trowbridge. Mainly agricultural, it produces wheat, barley, oats, sheep, and pigs.

wily /ˈwaɪlɪ/ *adj.* (**-ier, -iest**) crafty, cunning. □ **wiliness** *n.*

WIMP /wɪmp/ *abbr.* (also **wimp**) *Computing* windows icons menus pointers, type of user interface found on microcomputers and workstations. Separate tasks are each represented by a window on the screen. A window may display a menu and an option on the menu may be selected by means of a mouse or other pointing device. Windows not required at a particular time may be overlaid by other windows or reduced to a small symbol or icon.

wimp *n. colloq.* feeble or ineffectual person. □ **wimpish** *adj.* [origin uncertain]

wimple /ˈwɪmp(ə)l/ *n.* headdress also covering the neck and the sides of the face, worn by some nuns. [Old English]

win *–v.* (**-nn-**; *past* and *past part.* **won** /wʌn/) **1** secure as a result of a fight, contest, bet, effort, etc. **2** be the victor; be victorious in. *–n.* victory in a game etc. □ **win the day** be victorious in battle, argument, etc. **win over** persuade, gain the support of. **win one's spurs** *colloq.* gain distinction or fame. **win through** (or **out**) overcome obstacles. **you can't win** *colloq.* there is no way to succeed or to please. □ **winnable** *adj.* [Old English, = toil]

wince *–n.* start or involuntary shrinking movement of the face, showing pain or distress. *–v.* (**-cing**) give a wince. [Germanic: related to WINK]

wincey /ˈwɪnsɪ/ *n.* (*pl.* **-s**) lightweight fabric of wool and cotton or linen. [apparently an alteration of *woolsey* in LINSEY-WOOLSEY]

winceyette /ˌwɪnsɪˈet/ *n.* lightweight flannelette.

winch *–n.* **1** crank of a wheel or axle. **2** windlass. *–v.* lift with a winch. [Old English]

Winchester[1] /ˈwɪntʃɪstə(r)/ cathedral city in S England, county town of Hampshire; pop. (1991) 36 121.

♦ **Winchester**[2] /ˈwɪntʃɪstə(r)/ *n.* (in full **Winchester disk**) *Computing* hard-disk system of large storage capacity in which the disks are permanently sealed, together with the read/write heads and their supporting mechanism, in an airtight container to keep dust out. The module is itself permanently fixed within the disk drive. Introduced by IBM in 1973, this design is now used by many manufacturers, esp. for microcomputers. [*Winchester* rifle (orig. IBM number of the disk corresponded to the rifle's calibre)]

wind[1] *–n.* **1** air in natural motion, esp. a current of this. **2 a** breath, esp. as needed in exercise or playing a wind instrument. **b** power of breathing easily. **3** empty talk. **4** gas generated in the bowels etc. **5** wind instruments of an orchestra etc. **6** scent carried by the wind. *–v.* **1** cause to be out of breath by exertion or a blow. **2** make (a baby) bring up wind after feeding. **3** detect the presence of by a scent. □ **get wind of** begin to suspect the existence of. **get** (or **have**) **the wind up** *colloq.* be alarmed or frightened. **in the wind** about to happen. **like the wind** swiftly. **put the wind up** *colloq.* alarm, frighten. **take the wind out of a person's sails** frustrate a person by anticipating an action or remark etc. □ **windless** *adj.* [Old English]

wind[2] /waɪnd/ *–v.* (*past* and *past part.* **wound**) **1** (often as **winding** *adj.*) go in a spiral, curved, or crooked course. **2** make (one's way) thus. **3** wrap closely; coil. **4 a** provide with a coiled thread etc. **b** surround with or as with a coil. **5** wind up (a clock etc.). *–n.* **1** bend or turn in a course. **2** single turn when winding. □ **wind down 1** lower by winding. **2** unwind. **3** draw gradually to a close. **wind off** unwind. **wind up 1** coil the whole of. **2** tighten the coiling or coiled spring of (esp. a clock). **3** *colloq.* **a** increase the intensity of (feelings etc.), excite. **b** provoke (a person) to anger etc. **4** bring to a conclusion; end. **5 a** arrange the affairs of and dissolve (a company). **b** cease business and go into liquidation. **6** *colloq.* arrive finally. [Old English]

windbag *n. colloq.* person who talks a lot but says little of any value.

♦ **windbill** *n. colloq.* = ACCOMMODATION BILL.

wind-break *n.* thing serving to break the force of the wind.

windburn *n.* inflammation of the skin caused by exposure to the wind.

windcheater *n.* wind-resistant jacket.

wind-cone *n.* = WIND-SOCK.

wind-down *n. colloq.* gradual lessening of excitement or activity.

winder *n.* winding mechanism, esp. of a clock or watch.

windfall *n.* **1** fruit, esp. an apple, blown to the ground by the wind. **2** unexpected good fortune, esp. a legacy.

Windhoek /ˈvɪnthuːk/ capital of Namibia; products include bone-meal, canned meat, and karakul skin; pop. (est. 1992) 161 000.

winding-sheet *n.* sheet in which a corpse is wrapped for burial.

♦ **winding-up** *n.* = LIQUIDATION.

wind instrument *n.* musical instrument sounded by an air-current, esp. the breath.

wind-jammer *n.* merchant sailing-ship.

windlass /ˈwɪndləs/ *n.* machine with a horizontal axle for hauling or hoisting. [Old Norse, = winding-pole]

windmill *n.* **1** mill worked by the wind acting on its sails. **2** toy consisting of a stick with curved vanes that revolve in a wind. **3** *colloq.* = ACCOMMODATION BILL. □ **tilt at windmills** attack an imaginary enemy.

window /ˈwɪndəʊ/ *n.* **1 a** opening in a wall etc., usu. with glass to admit light etc. **b** the glass itself. **2** space for display behind the window of a shop. **3** window-like opening. **4** opportunity to learn from observation. **5**

transparent part in an envelope showing an address. **6** rectangular area of a computer screen inside which part of a stored file or image can be displayed. Typically, two or more windows are displayed at once. For example, a word processor may show two different parts of a document in separate windows, or one window may be set aside for a special purpose (e.g. displaying calculations) while the rest of the screen is devoted to the main task. Some modern operating systems, esp. on microcomputers, use windows to facilitate multi-tasking. □ **windowless** *adj.* [Old Norse, = wind-eye]

window-box *n.* box placed outside a window for growing flowers.

window-dressing *n.* **1** art of arranging a display in a shop-window etc. **2** adroit presentation of facts etc. to give a deceptively favourable impression. It has been used by accountants to improve the look of balance sheets, although the practice is now deprecated.

window-pane *n.* pane of glass in a window.

window-seat *n.* **1** seat below a window, esp. in an alcove. **2** seat next to a window in an aircraft, train, etc.

window-shop *v.* look at goods displayed in shop-windows, without buying anything.

window-sill *n.* sill below a window.

windpipe *n.* air-passage from the throat to the lungs.

Windscale /'windskeɪl/ see SELLAFIELD.

windscreen *n.* screen of glass at the front of a motor vehicle.

windscreen wiper *n.* blade moving in an arc to keep a windscreen clear of rain etc.

windshield *n.* *US* = WINDSCREEN.

wind-sock *n.* canvas cylinder or cone on a mast to show the direction of the wind at an airfield etc.

windsurfing *n.* sport of riding on water on a sailboard. □ **windsurf** *v.* **windsurfer** *n.*

windswept *adj.* exposed to or swept back by the wind.

wind-tunnel *n.* tunnel-like device producing an airstream past models of aircraft etc. for the study of aerodynamics.

wind-up /'waɪndʌp/ *–n.* **1** conclusion; finish. **2** *colloq.* attempt to provoke. *–attrib. adj.* (of a mechanism) operating by being wound up.

windward /'wɪndwəd/ *–adj.* & *adv.* on the side from which the wind is blowing. *–n.* windward direction.

Windward Islands group of islands in the E Caribbean Sea, constituting the S part of the Lesser Antilles. The largest are Dominica, Martinique, St Lucia, St Vincent, and Grenada.

windy *adj.* (**-ier, -iest**) **1** stormy with or exposed to wind. **2** generating or characterized by flatulence. **3** *colloq.* wordy. **4** *colloq.* nervous, frightened. □ **windiness** *n.* [Old English: related to WIND[1]]

wine *–n.* **1** fermented grape juice as an alcoholic drink. **2** fermented drink resembling this made from other fruits etc. **3** dark-red colour of red wine. *–v.* (**-ning**) (esp. in phr. **wine and dine**) **1** drink wine. **2** entertain with wine. [Old English]

wine bar *n.* bar or small restaurant where wine is the main drink available.

winebibber *n.* tippler.

wine cellar *n.* **1** cellar for storing wine. **2** its contents.

wineglass *n.* glass for wine, usu. with a stem and foot.

wine list *n.* list of wines available in a restaurant etc.

winepress *n.* press in which grapes are squeezed in making wine.

wine vinegar *n.* vinegar made from wine as distinct from malt etc.

wine waiter *n.* waiter responsible for serving wine.

wing *–n.* **1** each of the limbs or organs by which a bird etc. is able to fly. **2** winglike structure supporting an aircraft. **3** part of a building etc. extended in a certain direction. **4 a** forward player at either end of a line in football, hockey, etc. **b** side part of a playing-area. **5** (in *pl.*) sides of a theatre stage. **6** polarized section of a political party in terms of its views. **7** flank of a battle array. **8** the part of a vehicle over a wheel. **9** air-force unit of several squadrons or groups. *–v.* **1** travel or traverse on wings. **2** wound in a wing or an arm. **3** equip with wings. **4** enable to fly; send in flight. □ **on the wing** flying, in flight. **take under one's wing** treat as a protégé. **take wing** fly away. □ **winged** *adj.* **winglike** *adj.* [Old Norse]

wing-case *n.* horny cover of an insect's wing.

wing-chair *n.* chair with side-pieces at the top of a high back.

wing-collar *n.* man's high stiff collar with turned-down corners.

wing commander *n.* RAF officer next below group captain.

winger *n.* **1** (in football etc.) wing player. **2** (in *comb.*) member of a specified political wing.

wing-nut *n.* nut with projections for the fingers to turn it.

wing-span *n.* (also **wing-spread**) measurement right across the wings.

wink *–v.* **1** (often foll. by *at*) close and open one eye quickly, esp. as a signal. **2** close and open (one or both eyes) quickly. **3** (of a light etc.) twinkle; (of an indicator) flash on and off. *–n.* **1** act of winking. **2** *colloq.* short sleep. □ **in a wink** very quickly. **wink at** purposely avoid seeing; pretend not to notice. □ **winker** *n.* (in sense 3 of *v.*). [Old English]

winkle /'wɪŋk(ə)l/ *–n.* small edible sea snail. *–v.* (**-ling**) (foll. by *out*) extract with difficulty. [abbreviation of PERIWINKLE[2]]

winkle-picker *n. slang* long pointed shoe.

winner *n.* **1** person etc. that wins. **2** *colloq.* successful or highly promising idea etc.

winning *–adj.* **1** having or bringing victory. **2** attractive (*winning smile*). *–n.* (in *pl.*) money won. □ **winningly** *adv.*

winning-post *n.* post marking the end of a race.

Winnipeg /'wɪnɪ,peg/ city in W Canada, capital of Manitoba, a distribution, manufacturing, and transportation centre; city pop. (1986) 594 550; metropolitan area pop. (1991) 616 790.

winnow /'wɪnəʊ/ *v.* **1** blow (grain) free of chaff etc. by an air-current. **2** (foll. by *out, away, from,* etc.) get rid of (chaff etc.) from grain. **3** sift, examine (evidence etc.). [Old English: related to WIND[1]]

wino /'waɪnəʊ/ *n.* (*pl.* **-s**) *slang* alcoholic.

winsome *adj.* attractive, engaging. □ **winsomely** *adv.* **winsomeness** *n.* [Old English, = joyous]

winter *–n.* **1** coldest and last season of the year. **2** (*attrib.*) characteristic of or fit for winter. *–v.* (usu. foll. by *at, in*) pass the winter. [Old English]

winter garden *n.* garden or conservatory of plants flourishing in winter.

wintergreen *n.* a kind of plant remaining green all winter.

winter jasmine *n.* jasmine with yellow flowers in winter.

winter solstice *n.* about 22 Dec.

winter sports *n.pl.* sports performed on snow or ice.

wintertime *n.* season or period of winter.

wintry *adj.* (**-ier, -iest**) **1** characteristic of winter. **2** lacking warmth; unfriendly. □ **wintriness** *n.*

winy *adj.* (**-ier, -iest**) wine-flavoured.

♦ **WIP** *abbr.* = WORK IN PROGRESS.

---

wipe *–v.* (**-ping**) **1** clean or dry the surface of by rubbing. **2** rub (a cloth) over a surface. **3** spread (a liquid etc.) over a surface by rubbing. **4** (often foll. by *away, off,* etc.) **a** clear or remove by wiping. **b** erase or eliminate completely. *–n.* **1** act of wiping. **2** piece of specially treated material for wiping (*antiseptic wipes*). □ **wipe down** clean (a wall etc.) by wiping. **wipe the floor with** *colloq.* inflict a humiliating defeat on. **wipe off** annul (a debt etc.). **wipe out 1** destroy, annihilate, obliterate. **2** clean the inside of. **wipe up 1** dry (dishes etc.). **2** take up (a liquid etc.) by wiping. [Old English]

wiper *n.* = WINDSCREEN WIPER.

wire *–n.* **1 a** metal drawn out into a thread or thin flexible rod. **b** piece of this. **c** (*attrib.*) made of wire. **2** length of this for fencing or to carry an electric current etc. **3** *colloq.* telegram. *–v.* (**-ring**) **1** provide, fasten, strengthen, etc., with wire. **2** (often foll. by *up*) install electrical circuits in (a building, equipment, etc.). **3** *colloq.* telegraph. □ **get one's wires crossed** become confused and misunderstood. [Old English]

wire-haired *adj.* (esp. of a dog) with stiff or wiry hair.

wireless *n.* radio; radio receiving set.

wire netting *n.* netting of meshed wire.

wire-tapping *n.* tapping of telephone lines to eavesdrop.

wire wool *n.* mass of fine wire for scouring or rubbing down.

wireworm *n.* destructive larva of a kind of beetle.

wiring *n.* system or installation of wires providing electrical circuits.

wiry *adj.* (**-ier**, **-iest**) **1** sinewy, untiring. **2** like wire; tough, coarse. □ **wiriness** *n.*

Wis. *abbr.* Wisconsin.

Wisconsin /wɪs'kɒnsɪn/ state in the N US; pop. (est. 1996) 5 159 795; capital, Madison. The economy is based on manufacturing industry, which produces machinery, electrical equipment, metal goods, and paper products. Agriculture (esp. livestock and dairy farming) is also important.

wisdom /'wɪzdəm/ *n.* **1** experience and knowledge together with the power of applying them. **2** prudence; common sense. **3** wise sayings. [Old English: related to WISE[1]]

wisdom tooth *n.* hindmost molar usu. cut at about 20 years of age.

wise[1] /waɪz/ *adj.* **1** having, showing, or dictated by wisdom. **2** prudent, sensible. **3** having knowledge (often in *comb.*: *streetwise*; *worldly-wise*). **4** suggestive of wisdom. **5** *US colloq.* alert, crafty. □ **be** (or **get) wise to** *colloq.* be (or become) aware of. **none the wiser** knowing no more than before. **put wise** (often foll. by *to*) *colloq.* inform (of). **wise up** esp. *US colloq.* put or get wise. □ **wisely** *adv.* [Old English]

wise[2] /waɪz/ *n. archaic* way, manner, or degree. □ **in no wise** not at all. [Old English]

-wise *suffix* forming adjectives and adverbs of manner (*clockwise*; *lengthwise*) or respect (*moneywise*).

■ **Usage** More fanciful phrase-based combinations, such as *employment-wise* (= as regards employment) are restricted to informal contexts.

wiseacre /'waɪzˌeɪkə(r)/ *n.* person who affects a wise manner. [Dutch *wijsseggher* soothsayer]

wisecrack *colloq. –n.* smart pithy remark. *–v.* make a wisecrack.

wise guy *n. colloq.* know-all.

wise man *n.* wizard, esp. one of the Magi.

wisent /'wi:z(ə)nt/ *n.* European bison. [German: cf. BISON]

wish *–v.* **1** (often foll. by *for*) have or express a desire or aspiration for (*wish for happiness*). **2** have as a desire or aspiration (*I wish I could sing*). **3** want or demand (*I wish to go*; *I wish you to do it*). **4** express one's hopes for (*wish you success*). **5** (foll. by *on*, *upon*) *colloq.* foist on. *–n.* **1 a** desire, request. **b** expression of this. **2** thing desired. □ **best** (or **good) wishes** hopes felt or expressed for another's happiness etc. [Old English]

wishbone *n.* forked bone between the neck and breast of a fowl often broken between two people, the longer portion entitling the holder to make a wish.

wishful *adj.* (often foll. by *to* + infin.) desiring. □ **wishfully** *adv.*

wish-fulfilment *n.* tendency for subconscious desire to be satisfied in fantasy.

wishful thinking *n.* belief founded on wishes rather than facts.

wishing-well *n.* well into which coins are dropped and a wish is made.

wishy-washy /'wɪʃɪˌwɒʃɪ/ *adj. colloq.* **1** feeble in quality or character. **2** weak, watery. [from WASH]

wisp *n.* **1** small bundle or twist of straw etc. **2** small separate quantity of smoke, hair, etc. **3** small thin person etc. □ **wispy** *adj.* (**-ier**, **-iest**). [origin uncertain]

wisteria /wɪ'stɪərɪə/ *n.* (also **wistaria**) climbing plant with blue, purple, or white hanging flowers. [*Wistar*, name of an anatomist]

wistful *adj.* yearning, mournfully expectant or wishful. □ **wistfully** *adv.* **wistfulness** *n.* [apparently an assimilation of obsolete *wistly* 'intently' to *wishful*]

wit *n.* **1** (in *sing.* or *pl.*) intelligence; quick understanding. **2 a** unexpected combining or contrasting of ideas or expressions. **b** power of giving pleasure by this. **3** person possessing such power. □ **at one's wit's** (or **wits') end** utterly at a loss or in despair. **have** (or **keep) one's wits about one** be alert. **live by one's wits** live by ingenious or crafty expedients, without a settled occupation. **out of one's wits** mad. **to wit** that is to say, namely. [Old English]

witch *n.* **1** sorceress, woman supposed to have dealings with the Devil or evil spirits. **2** old hag. **3** fascinating girl or woman. [Old English]

witchcraft *n.* **1** use of magic. **2** bewitching charm.

witch-doctor *n.* tribal magician of primitive people.

witchery *n.* = WITCHCRAFT.

witches' sabbath *n.* supposed midnight orgy of the Devil and witches.

witch-hazel *n.* (also **wych-hazel**) **1** American shrub with bark yielding an astringent lotion. **2** this lotion.

witch-hunt *n.* campaign against persons suspected of unpopular or unorthodox views, esp. Communists.

with /wɪð/ *prep.* expressing: **1** instrument or means used (*cut with a knife*). **2 a** association or company (*lives with his mother*; *works with Shell*). **b** parting of company (*dispense with*). **3** cause (*shiver with fear*). **4** possession (*man with dark hair*; *filled with water*). **5** circumstances (*sleep with the window open*). **6** manner (*handle with care*). **7** agreement (*sympathize with*). **8** disagreement, antagonism (*incompatible with*; *quarrel with*). **9** understanding (*are you with me?*). **10** reference or regard (*be patient with them*; *how are things with you?*). □ **away** (or **in** or **out** etc.) **with** (as *int.*) take, send, or put (a person or thing) away (or in or out etc.). **with average** see AVERAGE *n.* 4. **with it** *colloq.* **1** up to date. **2** alert and comprehending. **with that** thereupon. [Old English]

withdraw /wɪð'drɔ:/ *v.* (*past* **withdrew**; *past part.* **withdrawn**) **1** pull or take aside or back. **2** discontinue, cancel, retract. **3** remove; take away. **4** take (money) out of an account. **5** retire or move apart. **6** (as **withdrawn** *adj.*) abnormally shy and unsociable; mentally detached. [from WITH = away]

withdrawal *n.* **1** withdrawing or being withdrawn. **2** process of ceasing to take an addictive drug etc., often with an unpleasant reaction (*withdrawal symptoms*). **3** = COITUS INTERRUPTUS.

withe /wɪθ, wɪð, waɪð/ *n.* (also **withy** /'wɪðɪ/) (*pl.* **withes** or **withies**) tough flexible shoot, esp. of willow, used for binding, basketwork, etc. [Old English]

wither /'wɪðə(r)/ *v.* **1** (often foll. by *up*) make or become dry and shrivelled. **2** (often foll. by *away*) deprive of or lose vigour or freshness. **3** (esp. as **withering** *adj.*) blight with scorn etc. □ **witheringly** *adv.* [apparently var. of WEATHER]

withers /'wɪðəz/ *n.pl.* ridge between a horse's shoulder-blades. [obsolete *wither* against (the collar)]

withershins var. of WIDDERSHINS.

withhold /wɪð'həʊld/ *v.* (*past* and *past part.* **-held**) **1** hold back; restrain. **2** refuse to give, grant, or allow. [from WITH = away]

♦ **withholding tax** *n.* (also **WT**) tax deducted at source from dividends or other income paid to non-residents of a country. If there is a double-taxation agreement between the country in which the income is paid and the country in which the recipient is resident, the tax can be reclaimed.

within /wɪ'ðɪn/ *–adv.* **1** inside. **2** indoors. **3** in spirit (*pure within*). *–prep.* **1** inside. **2 a** not beyond or out of. **b** not transgressing or exceeding. **3** not further off than (*within three miles; within ten days*). □ **within one's grasp** close enough to be obtained. **within reach** (or **sight) of** near enough to be reached or seen. [Old English: related to WITH, IN]

without /wɪ'ðaʊt/ *–prep.* **1** not having or feeling or showing. **2** with freedom from. **3** in the absence of. **4** with neglect or avoidance of. **5** *archaic* outside. *–adv. archaic* or *literary* **1** outside. **2** out of doors. □ **without prejudice** see PREJUDICE. **without recourse** see RECOURSE. [Old English: related to WITH, OUT]

♦ **with-profits bond** *n.* investment bond that has a cash-in value to some extent protected by the payment and accrual of bonuses.

♦ **with-profits policy** *n.* life-assurance policy that has additional amounts added to the sum assured, or paid separately as cash bonuses, as a result of a surplus or profit made on the investment of the fund or funds of the life-assurance office. Cf. UNIT-LINKED POLICY.

withstand /wɪð'stænd/ *v.* (*past* and *past part.* **-stood**) oppose, hold out against. [Old English: related to WITH, STAND]

withy var. of WITHE.

witless *adj.* foolish, crazy. [Old English: related to WIT]

witness /'wɪtnɪs/ *–n.* **1** = EYEWITNESS. **2 a** person giving sworn testimony. **b** person attesting another's signature to a document. **3** (foll. by *to, of*) person or thing whose existence etc. attests or proves something. **4** testimony, evidence, confirmation. *–v.* **1** be an eye-witness of. **2** be witness to the authenticity of (a signature etc.). **3** serve as evidence or an indication of. **4** (foll. by *against, for, to*) give or serve as evidence. □ **bear witness to** (or **of**) **1** attest the truth of. **2** state one's belief in. **call to witness** appeal to for confirmation etc. [Old English: related to WIT]

witness-box *n.* (*US* **witness-stand**) enclosure in a lawcourt from which witnesses give evidence.

Wittenberg /'vɪtən,bɜːg/ town in E Germany, on the River Elbe, a centre of industry; pop. (1991) 87 000.

witter /'wɪtə(r)/ *v.* (often foll. by *on*) *colloq.* chatter on annoyingly or on trivial matters. [origin unknown]

witticism /'wɪtɪ,sɪz(ə)m/ *n.* witty remark. [from WITTY]

wittingly /'wɪtɪŋlɪ/ *adv.* aware of what one is doing; intentionally. [from WIT]

witty *adj.* (**-ier, -iest**) showing esp. verbal wit. □ **wittily** *adv.* **wittiness** *n.* [Old English: related to WIT]

Witwatersrand /wɪt'wɔːtəz,rænd/ (also **the Rand**) series of parallel ridges in NE South Africa. It is South Africa's chief centre of gold mining.

wives *pl.* of WIFE.

wizard /'wɪzəd/ *–n.* **1** sorcerer; magician. **2** person of remarkable powers, genius. *–adj. slang* wonderful. □ **wizardry** *n.* [from WISE[1]]

wizened /'wɪz(ə)nd/ *adj.* shrivelled-looking. [Old English]

WL *international vehicle registration* St Lucia.

W/M *abbr.* (also **w/m**) *Shipping* weight or measurement (see FREIGHT *n.* 3).

WN *postcode* Wigan.

WNA *abbr. Shipping* winter North Atlantic (see LOAD LINE).

WNW *abbr.* west-north-west.

WO *abbr.* **1** Warrant-Officer. **2** (also **w.o.**) *Commerce* written order.

w/o *abbr.* **1** without. **2** *Accounting* written off.

WOA *abbr.* Wharf Owners' Association.

woad *n.* **1** plant yielding a blue dye. **2** dye from this. [Old English]

wobble /'wɒb(ə)l/ *–v.* (**-ling**) **1** sway from side to side. **2** stand or go unsteadily; stagger. **3** waver, vacillate. *–n.* state or instance of wobbling. [cf. Low German *wabbeln*]

wobbly *adj.* (**-ier, -iest**) **1** tending to wobble. **2** wavy (*wobbly line*). **3** weak after illness. **4** wavering, insecure (*the economy was wobbly*). □ **throw a wobbly** *slang* have a tantrum or fit of nerves.

w.o.c. *abbr.* without compensation.

wodge *n. colloq.* chunk, lump. [alteration of WEDGE]

woe /wəʊ/ *n.* **1** affliction; bitter grief. **2** (in *pl.*) calamities. □ **woe betide** see BETIDE. **woe is me** alas. [Old English]

woebegone /'wəʊbɪ,gɒn/ *adj.* dismal-looking. [from WOE, *begone* = surrounded]

woeful *adj.* **1** sorrowful. **2** causing or feeling affliction. **3** very bad. □ **woefully** *adv.*

wog *n. slang offens.* foreigner, esp. a non-White one. [origin unknown]

w.o.g. *abbr.* with other goods.

woggle /'wɒg(ə)l/ *n.* leather etc. ring through which the ends of a Scout's neckerchief are passed at the neck. [origin unknown]

wok *n.* bowl-shaped frying-pan used in esp. Chinese cookery. [Chinese]

woke *past* of WAKE[1].

woken *past part.* of WAKE[1].

wold /wəʊld/ *n.* high open uncultivated land or moor. [Old English]

wolf /wʊlf/ *–n.* (*pl.* **wolves** /wʊlvz/) **1** wild animal related to the dog, usu. hunting in packs. **2** *slang* man who seduces women. *–v.* (often foll. by *down*) devour greedily. □ **cry wolf** raise false alarms. **keep the wolf from the door** avert starvation. □ **wolfish** *adj.* [Old English]

wolfhound *n.* dog of a kind used orig. to hunt wolves.

wolf in sheep's clothing *n.* hostile person who pretends friendship.

wolfram /'wʊlfrəm/ *n.* **1** tungsten. **2** tungsten ore. [German]

wolfsbane *n.* aconite.

wolf-whistle *n.* whistle made by a man to a sexually attractive woman.

Wolverhampton /,wʊlvə'hæmpt(ə)n/ industrial town in central England, in the West Midlands; industries include metalworking, engineering, and the manufacture of tools, bicycles, and chemicals; pop. (est. 1994) 245 100.

wolverine /'wʊlvə,riːn/ *n.* North American animal of the weasel family. [related to WOLF]

wolves *pl.* of WOLF.

woman /'wʊmən/ *n.* (*pl.* **women** /'wɪmɪn/) **1** adult human female. **2** the female sex. **3** *colloq.* wife or girlfriend. **4** (prec. by *the*) feminine characteristics (*brought out the woman in him*). **5** (*attrib.*) female (*woman doctor*). **6** (in *comb.*) woman of a specified nationality, skill, etc. (*Englishwoman*; *horsewoman*). **7** *colloq.* charwoman. [Old English]

womanhood *n.* **1** female maturity. **2** womanly instinct. **3** womankind.

womanish *adj. derog.* effeminate, unmanly.

womanize *v.* (also **-ise**) (**-zing** or **-sing**) chase after women; philander. □ **womanizer** *n.*

womankind *n.* (also **womenkind**) women in general.

womanly *adj.* having or showing qualities associated with women. □ **womanliness** *n.*

womb /wuːm/ *n.* organ of conception and gestation in a woman and other female mammals. [Old English]

wombat /'wɒmbæt/ *n.* burrowing plant-eating Australian marsupial. [Aboriginal]

women *pl.* of WOMAN.

womenfolk *n.* **1** women in general. **2** the women in a family.

womenkind var. of WOMANKIND.

women's libber *n. colloq.* supporter of women's liberation.

women's liberation *n.* (also **women's lib**) *colloq.* movement urging the liberation of women from domestic duties and subservient status.

women's rights *n.pl.* position of legal and social equality with men.

won[1] /wʌn/ *past* and *past part.* of WIN.

won[2] /wɒn/ *n.* standard monetary unit of North Korea and South Korea. [Korean]

wonder /ˈwʌndə(r)/ *–n.* **1** emotion, esp. admiration, excited by what is unexpected, unfamiliar, or inexplicable. **2** strange or remarkable thing, specimen, event, etc. **3** (*attrib.*) having marvellous or amazing properties etc. (*wonder drug*; *wonder woman*). *–v.* **1** be filled with wonder or great surprise. **2** (foll. by *that*) be surprised to find. **3** desire or be curious to know (*I wonder what the time is*). □ **I shouldn't wonder** *colloq.* I think it likely. **no** (or **small) wonder** one cannot be surprised. **work** (or **do) wonders 1** do miracles. **2** be remarkably effective. [Old English]

wonderful *adj.* very remarkable or admirable. □ **wonderfully** *adv.* [Old English]

wonderland *n.* **1** fairyland. **2** land of surprises or marvels.

wonderment *n.* surprise, awe.

wondrous /ˈwʌndrəs/ *poet. –adj.* wonderful. *–adv.* wonderfully (*wondrous kind*).

wonky /ˈwɒŋkɪ/ *adj.* (**-ier, -iest**) *slang* **1** crooked, askew. **2** loose, unsteady. **3** unreliable. [fanciful]

wont /wəʊnt/ *–predic. adj. archaic* or *literary* (foll. by *to* + infin.) accustomed. *–n. formal* or *joc.* what is customary, one's habit. [Old English]

won't /wəʊnt/ *contr.* will not.

wonted /ˈwəʊntɪd/ *attrib. adj.* habitual, usual.

woo *v.* (**woos, wooed**) **1** court; seek the hand or love of. **2** try to win (fame, fortune, etc.). **3** seek the favour or support of. **4** coax or importune. □ **wooer** *n.* [Old English]

wood /wʊd/ *n.* **1 a** hard fibrous substance of the trunk or branches of a tree or shrub. **b** this for timber or fuel. **2** (in *sing.* or *pl.*) growing trees densely occupying a tract of land. **3** wooden cask for wine etc. **4** wooden-headed golf club. **5** = BOWL[2] *n.* 1. □ **not see the wood for the trees** fail to grasp the main issue from over-attention to details. **out of the wood** (or **woods**) out of danger or difficulty. [Old English]

wood anemone *n.* a wild spring-flowering anemone.

woodbine *n.* honeysuckle.

woodchuck *n.* North American marmot. [American Indian name]

woodcock *n.* game-bird related to the snipe.

woodcraft *n.* **1** knowledge of woodland, esp. in camping etc. **2** skill in woodwork.

woodcut *n.* **1** relief cut on wood. **2** print made from this.

woodcutter *n.* person who cuts timber.

wooded *adj.* having woods or many trees.

wooden /ˈwʊd(ə)n/ *adj.* **1** made of wood. **2** like wood. **3 a** stiff, clumsy. **b** expressionless. □ **woodenly** *adv.* **woodenness** *n.*

woodland *n.* (often *attrib.*) wooded country, woods.

woodlouse *n.* (*pl.* **-lice**) small land crustacean with many legs.

woodman *n.* forester.

woodpecker *n.* bird that taps tree-trunks in search of insects.

woodpigeon *n.* dove with white patches like a ring round its neck.

woodpile *n.* pile of wood, esp. for fuel.

wood pulp *n.* wood-fibre prepared for paper-making.

woodruff *n.* white-flowered plant with fragrant leaves.

woodshed *n.* shed where wood for fuel is stored. □ **something nasty in the woodshed** *colloq.* shocking thing kept secret.

woodwind *n.* **1** wind instruments that were (mostly) orig. made of wood, e.g. the flute, clarinet, oboe, and saxophone. **2** one such instrument.

woodwork *n.* **1** making of things in wood. **2** things made of wood. □ **crawl out of the woodwork** *colloq.* (of something distasteful) appear.

woodworm *n.* **1** wood-boring larva of a kind of beetle. **2** condition of wood affected by this.

woody *adj.* (**-ier, -iest**) **1** wooded. **2** like or of wood. □ **woodiness** *n.*

woodyard *n.* yard where wood is used or stored.

woody nightshade *n.* a kind of nightshade with poisonous red berries.

woof[1] /wʊf/ *–n.* gruff bark of a dog. *–v.* give a woof. [imitative]

woof[2] /wuːf/ *n.* = WEFT 1. [Old English: related to WEB]

woofer /ˈwuːfə(r)/ *n.* loudspeaker for low frequencies. [from WOOF[1]]

wool /wʊl/ *n.* **1** fine soft wavy hair from the fleece of sheep etc. **2** woollen yarn or cloth or clothing. **3** wool-like substance (*steel wool*). □ **pull the wool over a person's eyes** deceive a person. [Old English]

wool-gathering *n.* absent-mindedness.

woollen (*US* **woolen**) *–adj.* made wholly or partly of wool. *–n.* **1** woollen fabric. **2** (in *pl.*) woollen garments. [Old English]

woolly *–adj.* (**-ier, -iest**) **1** bearing wool. **2** like wool. **3** woollen (*a woolly cardigan*). **4** (of a sound) indistinct. **5** (of thought) vague or confused. *–n.* (*pl.* **-ies**) *colloq.* woollen garment, esp. a pullover. □ **woolliness** *n.*

Woolsack *n.* **1** Lord Chancellor's wool-stuffed seat in the House of Lords. **2** his position.

woozy *adj.* (**-ier, -iest**) *colloq.* **1** dizzy or unsteady. **2** slightly drunk. □ **woozily** *adv.* **wooziness** *n.* [origin unknown]

wop *n. slang offens.* Italian or other S European. [origin uncertain]

Worcester /ˈwʊstə(r)/ city in W central England, county town of Hereford and Worcester, noted for its porcelain; pop. (1991) 82 661.

Worcester sauce *n.* a pungent sauce. [WORCESTER]

Worcs. *abbr.* Worcestershire.

word /wɜːd/ *–n.* **1** meaningful element of speech, usu. shown with a space on either side of it when written or printed. **2** speech, esp. as distinct from action. **3** one's promise or assurance. **4** (in *sing.* or *pl.*) thing said, remark, conversation. **5** (in *pl.*) text of a song or an actor's part. **6** (in *pl.*) angry talk (*have words*). **7** news, message (*send word*). **8** command (*gave the word to begin*). **9** *Computing* collection of bits, usu. 32 or 16 in number, that is treated as a single unit by the hardware of a computer. Main store is divided into either words or bytes. In the former case, each storage location holds one word, and the word is thus the smallest unit to be identified by an address. *–v.* put into words; select words to express. □ **in other words** expressing the same thing differently. **in so many words** in those very words; explicitly. **in a** (or **one) word** briefly. **my** (or **upon my) word** exclamation of surprise etc. **take a person at his** or **her word** interpret a person's words literally. **take a person's word for it** believe a person's statement without investigation etc. **the Word** (or **Word of God**) the Bible. **word for word** in exactly the same or (of translation) corresponding words. □ **wordless** *adj.* [Old English]

word-blindness *n.* = DYSLEXIA.

word-game *n.* game involving the making or selection etc. of words.

wording *n.* form of words used.

word of mouth *n.* (also *attrib.* **word-of-mouth**) speech (only).

♦ **word-of-mouth advertising** *n.* process in which the purchaser of a product or service tells friends, neighbours, and associates about its virtues, esp. in advance of media advertising.

WordPerfect *n. propr.* popular word-processing program for microcomputers.

word-perfect *adj.* knowing one's part etc. by heart.

wordplay *n.* witty use of words, esp. punning.

♦ **word processor** *n.* (also **WP, w.p.**) computerized text-processing system consisting of a computer unit with a typewriter keyboard, display screen, printer, and disk-memory unit. Words typed on the keyboard are displayed on the screen. Any mistakes can be corrected immediately and, when finalized, a document can be output on the printer. The document can also be stored on the disk unit for future reuse. There are usu. extensive facilities for editing text: words or blocks of text can be moved or deleted; margins and line spacings can be adjusted; and many word processors have a spelling-check routine. Some can automatically incorporate names and addresses from a separate file into a letter, a technique known as **mail merge**. Word processors may be specialized systems; however, they are increasingly general-purpose microcomputers using word-processing software. See also DESKTOP PUBLISHING. □ **word-process** *v.* **word processing** *n.*

Wordstar *n. propr.* popular word-processing program for microcomputers.

♦ **wordwrap** *n.* facility available on most word processors that causes a word at the end of a typed line to move automatically to the next line if it cannot fit within the maximum line length.

wordy *adj.* (**-ier, -iest**) using or expressed in too many words. □ **wordily** *adv.* **wordiness** *n.*

wore *past* of WEAR.

work /wɜːk/ *–n.* **1** application of mental or physical effort to a purpose; use of energy. **2** task to be undertaken. **3** thing done or made by work; result of an action. **4** employment or occupation etc., esp. as a means of earning income. **5** literary or musical composition. **6** actions or experiences of a specified kind (*nice work!*). **7** (in *comb.*) things made of a specified material or with specified tools etc. (*ironwork*; *needlework*). **8** (in *pl.*) operative part of a clock or machine. **9** *Physics* the exertion of force overcoming resistance or producing molecular change. **10** (in full **the works**) *colloq.* **a** all that is available or needed. **b** full, esp. harsh, treatment. **11** (in *pl.*) operations of building or repair (*road works*). **12** (in *pl.*; often treated as *sing.*) factory. **13** (usu. in *pl.*) *Theol.* meritorious act. **14** (usu. in *pl.* or in *comb.*) defensive structure (*earthworks*). *–v.* **1** do work; be engaged in bodily or mental activity. **2** be employed in certain work (*works in industry*). **3** make efforts (*works for peace*). **4** (foll. by *in*) be a craftsman in (a material). **5** operate or function, esp. effectively (*how does this machine work?*; *your idea will not work*). **6** operate, manage, control (*cannot work the machine*). **7 a** put or keep in operation or at work; cause to toil (*works the staff hard*). **b** cultivate (land). **8 a** bring about; produce as a result (*worked miracles*). **b** *colloq.* arrange (matters) (*worked it so that we could go*; *can you work things for us?*). **9** knead, hammer; bring to a desired shape or consistency. **10** do, or make by, needlework etc. **11** (cause to) progress or penetrate, or make (one's way), gradually or with difficulty in a specified way (*worked the peg into the hole*; *worked our way through the crowd*). **12** (foll. by *loose* etc.) gradually become (loose etc.) by constant movement. **13** artificially excite (*worked themselves into a rage*). **14 a** purchase with one's labour instead of money (*work one's passage*). **b** obtain by labour the money for (*worked my way through university*). **15** (foll. by *on, upon*) have influence. **16** be in motion or agitated; ferment. □ **at work** in action, engaged in work. **get worked up** become angry, excited, or tense. **have one's work cut out** be faced with a hard task. **work in** find a place for. **work off** get rid of by work or activity. **work out 1 a** solve (a sum) or find (an amount) by calculation. **b** solve, understand (a problem, person, etc.). **2** (foll. by *at*) be calculated. **3** give a definite result (*this sum will not work out*). **4** have a result (*the plan worked out well*). **5** provide for the details of (*has worked out a scheme*). **6** engage in physical exercise or training. **work over 1** examine thoroughly. **2** *colloq.* treat with violence. **work through** arrive at an understanding of (a problem) etc. **work to rule** (as a protest) follow official working rules exactly in order to reduce output. **work up 1** bring gradually to an efficient or (of a painting etc.) advanced state. **2** (foll. by *to*) advance gradually to a climax etc. **3** elaborate or excite by degrees. **4** mingle (ingredients). **5** learn (a subject) by study. **work wonders** see WONDER. [Old English]

workable *adj.* that can be worked, will work, or is worth working. □ **workability** /-'bɪlɪtɪ/ *n.*

workaday *adj.* ordinary, everyday, practical.

workaholic /ˌwɜːkə'hɒlɪk/ *n. colloq.* person addicted to working.

work-basket *n.* basket for sewing materials.

workbench *n.* bench for manual work, esp. carpentry.

workbook *n.* student's book with exercises.

workbox *n.* box for tools, needlework, etc.

work camp *n.* camp at which community work is done, esp. by young volunteers.

workday *n.* day on which work is usu. done.

worker *n.* **1** person who works, esp. for an employer. **2** neuter bee or ant. **3** person who works hard.

♦ **workers' participation** see INDUSTRIAL DEMOCRACY.

work experience *n.* scheme intended to give young people temporary experience of employment.

workforce *n.* **1** workers engaged or available. **2** number of these.

workhouse *n. hist.* public institution for the poor of a parish.

♦ **work-in** see SIT-DOWN STRIKE.

working *–attrib. adj.* **1 a** engaged in work (*working mother*; *working man*). **b** while so engaged (*all his working life*; *in working hours*). **2** functioning or able to function (*working model*). *–n.* **1** activity of work. **2** functioning. **3** mine or quarry. **4** (usu. in *pl.*) machinery, mechanism.

♦ **working assets** see WORKING CAPITAL.

♦ **working capital** *n.* capital of a company that is employed in its day-to-day trading operations. It consists of current assets (mainly trading stock, debtors, and cash) less current liabilities (mainly trade creditors). In the normal trade cycle (the supply of goods by suppliers, the sale of stock to debtors, payments of debts in cash, and the use of cash to pay suppliers) the working capital is the aggregate of the net assets involved, sometimes called the **working assets**.

working class *n.* social class employed, esp. in manual or industrial work, for wages. □ **working-class** *adj.*

working day *n.* **1** day on which work is usu. done. See also LAY DAYS; WEATHER WORKING DAYS. **2** part of the day devoted to work.

♦ **working director** *n.* = EXECUTIVE DIRECTOR.

working hypothesis *n.* hypothesis as a basis for action.

working knowledge *n.* knowledge adequate to work with.

working lunch *n.* lunch at which business is conducted.

working order *n.* condition in which a machine works.

working party *n.* group of people appointed to study and advise on a particular problem.

♦ **work in progress** *n.* (also **WIP**) partly manufactured goods or partly completed contracts. For accounting purposes, work in progress is usu. valued at its cost by keeping records of the cost of the materials and labour put into it, together with some estimate of allocated overheads. In the case of long-term contracts, the figure might also include an element of profit.

workload *n.* amount of work to be done.

workman *n.* **1** man employed to do manual labour. **2** person with regard to skill in a job (*a good workman*).

workmanlike *adj.* competent, showing practised skill.

workmanship *n.* degree of skill in doing a task or of finish in the product made.

workmate *n.* person working alongside another.

◆ **work measurement** see WORK STUDY.

---

work of art *n.* fine picture, poem, building, etc.

workout *n.* session of physical exercise or training.

workpiece *n.* thing worked on with a tool or machine.

workplace *n.* place at which a person works.

workroom *n.* room for working in.

worksheet *n.* **1** paper for recording work done or in progress. **2** paper listing questions or activities for students etc. to work through.

workshop *n.* **1** room or building in which goods are manufactured. **2** place or meeting for concerted discussion or activity (*dance workshop*).

work-shy *adj.* disinclined to work.

workstation *n.* **1** location of a stage in a manufacturing process. **2** position in an office etc. equipped with all the facilities required to perform a particular task that involves a computer, including a keyboard and a VDU and possibly a printer, disk drive, mouse, and communication line.

◆ **work study** *n.* assessment of methods of working so as to achieve maximum productivity. It consists of a **method study** to compare existing methods with proposed methods and **work measurement** to establish the time required by a qualified worker to do the job to a specified standard.

---

work table *n.* table for working at.

worktop *n.* flat surface for working on, esp. in a kitchen.

◆ **work-to-rule** *n.* form of industrial action in which employees pay a slavish obedience to employers' regulations in order to dislocate working procedures, without resorting to a strike. It usu. involves an overtime ban.

---

world /wɜːld/ *n.* **1 a** the earth, or a planetary body like it. **b** its countries and people. **2** the universe, all that exists. **3 a** the time, state, or scene of human existence. **b** (prec. by *the, this*) mortal life. **4** secular interests and affairs. **5** human affairs; active life. **6** average, respectable, or fashionable people or their customs or opinions. **7** all that concerns or all who belong to a specified class or sphere of activity (*the world of sport*). **8** (foll. by *of*) vast amount. **9** (*attrib.*) affecting many nations, of all nations (*world politics; world champion*). □ **bring** (or **come) into the world** give birth (or be born). **for all the world** (foll. by *like, as if*) precisely. **in the world** of all; at all (*what in the world is it?*). **man** (or **woman) of the world** person experienced and practical in human affairs. **out of this world** *colloq.* extremely good etc. **think the world of** have a very high regard for. [Old English]

◆ **World Bank** see INTERNATIONAL BANK FOR RECONSTRUCTION AND DEVELOPMENT.

---

world-beater *n.* person or thing surpassing all others.

world-class *adj.* of a quality or standard regarded as high throughout the world.

World Cup *n.* competition between football teams from various countries.

world-famous *adj.* known throughout the world.

worldly *adj.* (**-ier, -iest**) **1** of the affairs of the world, temporal, earthly (*worldly goods*). **2** experienced in life, sophisticated, practical. □ **worldliness** *n.*

worldly-wise *adj.* prudent or shrewd in one's dealings with the world.

world music *n.* pop music that incorporates local or ethnic elements (esp. from the developing world).

◆ **World Trade Organization** *n.* (also **WTO**) world trading system set up in 1995 at the Uruguay round of GATT, which superseded GATT.

---

world war *n.* war involving many major nations.

world-weary *adj.* bored with human affairs. □ **world-weariness** *n.*

worldwide *–adj.* occurring in or known in all parts of the world. *–adv.* throughout the world.

worm[1] /wɜːm/ *–n.* **1** any of various types of creeping invertebrate animals with long slender bodies and no limbs. **2** larva of an insect, esp. in fruit or wood. **3** (in *pl.*) intestinal parasites. **4** insignificant or contemptible person. **5** spiral part of a screw. *–v.* **1** (often *refl.*) move with a crawling motion. **2** *refl.* (foll. by *into*) insinuate oneself into favour etc. **3** (foll. by *out*) obtain (a secret etc.) by cunning persistence. **4** rid (a dog etc.) of worms. [Old English]

worm[2] /wɜːm/ *n.* (also **WORM**) *Computing* type of storage device in which information once written cannot be erased or overwritten. See also OPTICAL DISK. [acronym of *w*rite *o*nce *r*ead *m*any times]

worm-cast *n.* convoluted mass of earth left on the surface by a burrowing earthworm.

wormeaten *adj.* **1** eaten into by worms; decayed. **2** old and dilapidated.

worm-hole *n.* hole left by the passage of a worm.

Worms /wɜːmz, vɔːmz/ industrial town in SW Germany, on the Rhine; pop. (1991) 77 430.

worm's-eye view *n.* view from below or from a humble position.

wormwood /ˈwɜːmwʊd/ *n.* **1** plant with a bitter aromatic taste. **2** bitter mortification; source of this. [Old English: cf. VERMOUTH]

wormy *adj.* (**-ier, -iest**) **1** full of worms. **2** wormeaten. □ **worminess** *n.*

worn /wɔːn/ *past part.* of WEAR[1]. *adj.* **1** damaged by use or wear. **2** looking tired and exhausted.

worrisome /ˈwʌrɪsəm/ *adj.* causing worry.

worry /ˈwʌrɪ/ *–v.* (**-ies, -ied**) **1** give way to anxiety. **2** harass, importune; be a trouble or anxiety to. **3** (of a dog etc.) shake or pull about with the teeth. **4** (as **worried** *adj.*) uneasy. *–n.* (*pl.* **-ies**) **1** thing that causes anxiety or disturbs tranquility. **2** disturbed state of mind; anxiety. □ **worrier** *n.* [Old English, = strangle]

worry beads *n.pl.* string of beads manipulated with the fingers to occupy or calm oneself.

worse /wɜːs/ *–adj.* **1** more bad. **2** (*predic.*) in or into worse health or a worse condition (*is getting worse*). *–adv.* more badly; more ill. *–n.* **1** worse thing or things (*you might do worse than accept*). **2** (prec. by *the*) worse condition (*a change for the worse*). □ **none the worse** (often foll. by *for*) not adversely affected (by). **the worse for wear 1** damaged by use. **2** injured. **worse luck** unfortunately. **worse off** in a worse (esp. financial) position. [Old English]

worsen *v.* make or become worse.

worship /ˈwɜːʃɪp/ *–n.* **1 a** homage or service to a deity. **b** acts, rites, or ceremonies of this. **2** adoration, devotion. **3** (**Worship**) (prec. by *His, Her, Your*) forms of description or address for a mayor, certain magistrates, etc. *–v.* (**-pp-**; *US* **-p-**) **1** adore as divine; honour with religious rites. **2** idolize or regard with adoration. **3** attend public worship. **4** be full of adoration. □ **worshipper** *n.* [Old English: related to WORTH, -SHIP]

worshipful *adj.* (also **Worshipful**) *archaic* (esp. in old titles of companies or officers) honourable, distinguished.

worst /wɜːst/ *–adj.* most bad. *–adv.* most badly. *–n.* worst part or possibility (*prepare for the worst*). *–v.* get the better of; defeat. □ **at its** etc. **worst** in the worst state. **at worst** (or **the worst**) in the worst possible case. **do your worst** expression of defiance. **get the worst of it** be defeated. **if the worst comes to the worst** if the worst happens. [Old English: related to WORSE]

worsted /ˈwʊstɪd/ *n.* **1** fine woollen yarn. **2** fabric made from this. [*Worste(a)d* in Norfolk]

wort /wɜːt/ *n.* **1** *archaic* (except in names) plant (*liver-*

wort). **2** infusion of malt before it is fermented into beer. [Old English]

worth /wɜːθ/ *–predic. adj.* (*used like a preposition*) **1** of a value equivalent to (*is worth £50; is worth very little*). **2** such as to justify or repay (*worth doing; not worth the trouble*). **3** possessing or having property amounting to (*is worth a million pounds*). *–n.* **1** what a person or thing is worth; the (usu. high) merit of (*of great worth*). **2** equivalent of money in a commodity (*ten pounds' worth of petrol*). □ **for all one is worth** *colloq.* with one's utmost efforts. **for what it is worth** without a guarantee of its truth or value. **worth it** *colloq.* worth while. **worth one's salt** see SALT. **worth one's weight in gold** see WEIGHT. **worth while** (or **one's while**) see WHILE. [Old English]

worthless *adj.* without value or merit. □ **worthlessness** *n.*

worthwhile *adj.* that is worth the time, effort, or money spent.

■ **Usage** See note at *while*.

worthy /ˈwɜːðɪ/ *–adj.* (**-ier, -iest**) **1** deserving respect, estimable (*lived a worthy life*). **2** entitled to (esp. condescending) recognition (*a worthy old couple*). **3 a** (foll. by *of* or *to* + infin.) deserving (*worthy of a mention*). **b** (foll. by *of*) adequate or suitable to the dignity etc. of (*words worthy of the occasion*). *–n.* (*pl.* **-ies**) **1** worthy person. **2** person of some distinction. □ **worthily** *adv.* **worthiness** *n.*

-worthy *comb. form* forming adjectives meaning: **1** deserving of (*noteworthy*). **2** suitable for (*roadworthy*).

would /wʊd, wəd/ *v.aux.* (*3rd sing.* **would**) *past* of WILL[1], used esp.: **1** in reported speech (*he said he would be home by evening*). **2** to express a condition (*they would have been killed if they had gone*). **3** to express habitual action (*would wait every evening*). **4** to express a question or polite request (*would they like it?; would you come in, please?*). **5** to express probability (*she would be over fifty by now*). **6** to express consent (*they would not help*).

would-be *attrib. adj.* desiring or aspiring to be.

wouldn't /ˈwʊd(ə)nt/ *contr.* would not.

wound[1] /wuːnd/ *–n.* **1** injury done to living tissue by a deep cut or heavy blow etc. **2** pain inflicted on one's feelings; injury to one's reputation. *–v.* inflict a wound on. [Old English]

wound[2] *past* and *past part.* of WIND[2].

wound up *adj.* excited; tense; angry.

wove *past* of WEAVE[1].

woven *past part.* of WEAVE[1].

wow[1] /waʊ/ *–int.* expressing astonishment or admiration. *–n. slang* sensational success. *–v. slang* impress greatly. [imitative]

wow[2] /waʊ/ *n.* slow pitch-fluctuation in sound-reproduction, perceptible in long notes. [imitative]

WP *abbr.* (also **w.p.**) **1** *Law* without prejudice (see PREJUDICE). **2** word processor (or processing).

WPA *abbr. Insurance* with particular average.

WPC *abbr.* woman police constable.

WPI *abbr. hist.* wholesale price index. See PRODUCER PRICE INDEX.

w.p.m. *abbr.* words per minute.

WR *–abbr.* warehouse receipt. *–postcode* Worcester.

WRAC *abbr.* Women's Royal Army Corps.

wrack *n.* **1** seaweed cast up or growing on the shore. **2** destruction. [Low German or Dutch *wrak*: cf. WRECK]

WRAF *abbr.* Women's Royal Air Force.

wraith *n.* **1** ghost. **2** spectral appearance of a living person supposed to portend that person's death. [origin unknown]

wrangle /ˈræŋg(ə)l/ *–n.* noisy argument or dispute. *–v.* (**-ling**) engage in a wrangle. [Low German or Dutch]

wrap *–v.* (**-pp-**) **1** (often foll. by *up*) envelop in folded or soft encircling material. **2** (foll. by *round, about*) arrange or draw (a pliant covering) round (a person). **3** (foll. by *round*) *slang* crash (a vehicle) into (a stationary object). *–n.* **1** shawl, scarf, etc. **2** esp. *US* wrapping material. □ **take the wraps off** disclose. **under wraps** in secrecy. **wrapped up in** engrossed or absorbed in. **wrap up 1** *colloq.* finish off (a matter). **2** put on warm clothes (*wrap up well*). **3** (in *imper.*) *slang* be quiet. [origin unknown]

wraparound *adj.* (also **wrapround**) **1** (esp. of clothing) designed to wrap round. **2** curving or extending round at the edges.

wrap-over *–attrib. adj.* (of a garment) overlapping when worn. *–n.* such a garment.

wrapper *n.* **1** cover for a sweet, book, posted newspaper, etc. **2** loose enveloping robe or gown.

wrapping *n.* (esp. in *pl.*) material used to wrap; wraps, wrappers.

wrapping paper *n.* strong or decorative paper for wrapping parcels.

wrapround var. of WRAPAROUND.

wrasse /ræs/ *n.* bright-coloured marine fish. [Cornish *wrach*]

wrath /rɒθ/ *n. literary* extreme anger. [Old English: related to WROTH]

wrathful *adj. literary* extremely angry. □ **wrathfully** *adv.*

wreak *v.* **1** (usu. foll. by *upon*) give play to (vengeance or one's anger etc.). **2** cause (damage etc.) (*wreak havoc*). [Old English, = avenge]

wreath /riːθ/ *n.* (*pl.* **-s** /riːðz/) **1** flowers or leaves fastened in a ring, esp. as an ornament for the head or for laying on a grave etc. **2** curl or ring of smoke, cloud, or soft fabric. [Old English: related to WRITHE]

wreathe /riːð/ *v.* (**-thing**) **1** encircle or cover as, with, or like a wreath. **2** (foll. by *round*) wind (one's arms etc.) round (a person etc.). **3** (of smoke etc.) move in wreaths.

wreck *–n.* **1** the sinking or running aground of a ship. **2** ship that has suffered a wreck. **3** greatly damaged building, thing, or person. **4** (foll. by *of*) wretched remnant. *–v.* **1 a** seriously damage (a vehicle etc.). **b** ruin (hopes, a life, etc.). **2** cause the wreck of (a ship). [Anglo-French *wrec* from Germanic]

wreckage *n.* **1** wrecked material. **2** remnants of a wreck. **3** act of wrecking.

wrecker *n.* **1** person or thing that wrecks or destroys. **2** esp. *US* person employed in demolition or breaking up damaged vehicles. **3** esp. *hist.* person on the shore who tries to bring about a shipwreck for plunder or profit.

Wren *n.* member of the Women's Royal Naval Service. [from the abbreviation WRNS]

wren *n.* small usu. brown short-winged songbird with an erect tail. [Old English]

wrench *–n.* **1** violent twist or oblique pull or tearing off. **2** tool like a spanner for gripping and turning nuts etc. **3** painful uprooting or parting. *–v.* **1** twist or pull violently round or sideways. **2** (often foll. by *off, away*, etc.) pull off with a wrench. [Old English]

wrest *v.* **1** wrench away from a person's grasp. **2** (foll. by *from*) obtain by effort or with difficulty. [Old English]

wrestle /ˈres(ə)l/ *–n.* **1** contest in which two opponents grapple and try to throw each other to the ground, esp. as an athletic sport. **2** hard struggle. *–v.* (**-ling**) **1** (often foll. by *with*) take part or fight in a wrestle. **2 a** (foll. by *with, against*) struggle. **b** (foll. by *with*) do one's utmost to deal with (a task, difficulty, etc.). □ **wrestler** *n.* **wrestling** *n.* [Old English]

wretch *n.* **1** unfortunate or pitiable person. **2** (often as a playful term of depreciation) reprehensible person. [Old English, = outcast]

wretched /ˈretʃɪd/ *adj.* (**wretcheder, wretchedest**) **1** unhappy, miserable; unwell. **2** of bad quality; contemptible. **3** displeasing, hateful. □ **wretchedly** *adv.* **wretchedness** *n.*

wrick var. of RICK[2].

wriggle /ˈrɪg(ə)l/ *–v.* (**-ling**) **1** (of a worm etc.) twist or turn its body with short writhing movements. **2** make wriggling motions. **3** (foll. by *along, through*, etc.) go thus (*wriggled through the gap*). **4** be evasive. *–n.* act of wriggling. □ **wriggle out of** *colloq.* avoid on a pretext. □ **wriggly** *adj.* [Low German *wriggelen*]

wright /raɪt/ *n.* maker or builder (usu. in *comb.*: *playwright*; *shipwright*). [Old English: related to WORK]

wring *–v.* (*past* and *past part.* **wrung**) **1 a** squeeze tightly. **b** (often foll. by *out*) squeeze and twist, esp. to remove liquid. **2** break by twisting. **3** distress, torture. **4** extract by squeezing. **5** (foll. by *out*, *from*) obtain by pressure; extort. *–n.* act of wringing. □ **wring one's hands** clasp them as a gesture of distress. **wring the neck of** kill (a chicken etc.) by twisting its neck. [Old English]

wringer *n.* device for wringing water from washed clothes etc.

wringing *adj.* (in full **wringing wet**) so wet that water can be wrung out.

wrinkle /ˈrɪŋk(ə)l/ *–n.* **1** crease in the skin, esp. caused by age. **2** similar mark in another flexible surface. **3** *colloq.* useful tip or clever expedient. *–v.* (**-ling**) **1** make wrinkles in. **2** form wrinkles. [probably related to Old English *gewrinclod* sinuous]

wrinkly *–adj.* (**-ier, -iest**) having wrinkles. *–n. slang offens.* old or middle-aged person.

wrist *n.* **1** joint connecting the hand with the arm. **2** part of a garment covering this. [Old English]

wristlet *n.* band to strengthen, guard, or adorn the wrist.

wrist-watch *n.* watch worn on a strap etc. round the wrist.

◆ **writ**[1] *n.* form of written command issued by a court. A **writ of summons** is an order by which an action in the High Court is started. It commands the defendant to appear before the court to answer the claim made in the writ by the plaintiff. It is used in actions in tort, claims alleging fraud, and claims for damages in respect of personal injuries, death, or infringement of patent. A **writ of execution** is used to enforce a judgement; it instructs a court officer to collect money, seize property, or carry out some other act. A **writ of delivery** is a writ of execution directing a sheriff to seize goods and deliver them to the plaintiff or to obtain their value in money, according to an agreed assessment. If the defendant has no option to pay the assessed value, the writ is a **writ of specific delivery**. [Old English: related to WRITE]

---

writ[2] *archaic past part.* of WRITE. □ **writ large** in magnified or emphasized form.

write *v.* (**-ting**; *past* **wrote**; *past part.* **written**) **1** mark paper or some other surface with symbols, letters, or words. **2** form or mark (such symbols etc.). **3** form or mark the symbols of (a word or sentence, or document etc.). **4** fill or complete (a sheet, cheque, etc.) with writing. **5** transfer (data) into a computer store. **6** (esp. in *passive*) indicate (a quality or condition) by one's or its appearance (*guilt was written on his face*). **7** compose for written or printed reproduction or publication. **8** (usu. foll. by *to*) write and send a letter (to a person). **9** *US* write and send a letter to (a person). **10** convey (news etc.) by letter. **11** state in a book etc. **12** (foll. by *into*, *out of*) include or exclude (a character or episode) in a story by changing the text. **13** (of an underwriter) cover an insurance risk, accepting liability, under an insurance contract. □ **write down** record in writing. **write in** send a suggestion, query, etc. in writing to esp. a broadcasting station. **write off 1** (foll. by *for*) = *send away for* (see SEND). **2** *Accounting* **a** reduce the value of (an asset, e.g. an expired lease) to zero in a balance sheet. **b** reduce (a bad debt) to zero in a profit and loss account. **3** acknowledge the loss of. **4** completely destroy (a vehicle etc.). **5** dismiss as insignificant. **write out** write in full or in finished form. **write up 1** write a full account of; bring (a diary etc.) up to date. **2** praise in writing. [Old English]

write-off *n.* thing written off, esp. a vehicle too badly damaged to be repaired.

writer *n.* **1** person who writes or has written something. **2** author of books etc. **3** seller of a traded option.

writer's cramp *n.* muscular spasm due to excessive writing.

write-up *n.* written or published account, review.

writhe /raɪð/ *v.* (**-thing**) **1** twist or roll oneself about in or as in acute pain. **2** suffer mental torture or embarrassment (*writhed with shame*). [Old English]

writing *n.* **1** written words etc. **2** handwriting. **3** (usu. in *pl.*) author's works. □ **in writing** in written form. **the writing on the wall** ominously significant event etc.

writing-desk *n.* desk for writing at, esp. with compartments for papers etc.

writing-paper *n.* paper for writing (esp. letters) on.

written *past part.* of WRITE.

◆ **written-down value** *n. Accounting* value of an asset after deducting amounts for depreciation or, in the case of tax computations, for capital allowances.

WRNS *abbr.* Women's Royal Naval Service.

Wroclaw /ˈvrɒtswɑːf/ (German **Breslau** /ˈbreslaʊ/) port and industrial city in W Poland, on the River Oder; it has electronics, engineering, and food-processing industries; pop. (est. 1995) 642 900.

wrong *–adj.* **1** mistaken; not true; in error. **2** unsuitable; less or least desirable (*the wrong road*; *a wrong decision*). **3** contrary to law or morality (*it is wrong to steal*). **4** amiss; out of order, in a bad or abnormal condition (*something wrong with my heart*; *has gone wrong*). *–adv.* (usu. placed last) in a wrong manner or direction; with an incorrect result (*guessed wrong*). *–n.* **1** what is morally wrong. **2** unjust action (*suffer a wrong*). *–v.* **1** treat unjustly. **2** mistakenly attribute bad motives to. □ **do wrong** sin. **do wrong to** malign or mistreat (a person). **get wrong 1** misunderstand (a person etc.). **2** obtain an incorrect answer to. **get** (or **get hold of**) **the wrong end of the stick** misunderstand completely. **go wrong 1** take the wrong path. **2** stop functioning properly. **3** depart from virtuous behaviour. **in the wrong** responsible for a quarrel, mistake, or offence. **on the wrong side of 1** out of favour with (a person). **2** somewhat more than (a stated age). **wrong side out** inside out. **wrong way round** in the reverse of the normal or desirable orientation or sequence etc. □ **wrongly** *adv.* **wrongness** *n.* [Old English]

wrongdoer *n.* person who behaves immorally or illegally. □ **wrongdoing** *n.*

wrong-foot *v. colloq.* **1** (in tennis, football, etc.) catch (an opponent) off balance. **2** disconcert; catch unprepared.

wrongful *adj.* unwarranted, unjustified (*wrongful arrest*). □ **wrongfully** *adv.*

◆ **wrongful dismissal** *n.* termination of an employee's contract of employment not in accordance with that contract. Thus when an employee is dismissed without due notice (in circumstances that do not justify summary dismissal) or when the employer prematurely terminates the employee's fixed-term contract, the employee is entitled to claim damages in the courts for wrongful dismissal. The court's jurisdiction concerns only the parties' contractual rights and not their statutory rights under the employment protection legislation (cf. UNFAIR DISMISSAL). The Employment Protection (Consolidation) Act (1978) empowers the Secretary of State for Employment to give industrial tribunals jurisdiction to hear claims of wrongful dismissal.

◆ **wrongful trading** *n.* trading during a period in which a company had no reasonable prospect of avoiding insolvent liquidation. The liquidator of a company may petition the court for an order instructing a director of a company that has gone into insolvent liquidation to make a contribution to the company's assets. The court may order any contribution it thinks proper if the director knew, or ought to have known, of the company's situation. A director would be liable if a reasonably diligent person carrying out the same function in the company would have realized the situation: no intention to defraud need be shown. See FRAUDULENT TRADING.

---

wrong-headed *adj.* perverse and obstinate.

wrong side *n.* worse or unusable side of esp. fabric.

wrote *past* of WRITE.

wroth /rəʊθ/ *predic. adj. archaic* angry. [Old English]

wrought /rɔːt/ *archaic past* and *past part.* of WORK. *adj.* (of metals) beaten out or shaped by hammering.

wrought iron *n.* tough malleable form of iron suitable for forging or rolling, not cast.

wrung *past* and *past part.* of WRING.

WRVS *abbr.* Women's Royal Voluntary Service.

wry /raɪ/ *adj.* (**wryer**, **wryest** or **wrier**, **wriest**) **1** distorted or turned to one side. **2** (of a face, smile, etc.) contorted in disgust or mockery. **3** (of humour) dry and mocking. □ **wryly** *adv.* **wryness** *n.* [Old English]

wryneck *n.* small woodpecker able to turn its head over its shoulder.

WS *–postcode* Walsall.

WSW *abbr.* west-south-west.

WT *–abbr.* = WITHHOLDING TAX. *–airline flight code* Nigeria Airlines.

wt. *abbr.* weight.

WTO *abbr.* = WORLD TRADE ORGANIZATION.

Wuhan /wuːˈhæn/ port in E China, on the Yangtze River, a centre of commerce and industry (esp. iron and steel); pop. (est. 1991) 3 750 000.

Wuppertal /ˈvʊpəˌtɑːl/ industrial city in W Germany, in North Rhine-Westphalia; manufactures include textiles; pop. (est. 1995) 383 776.

WV *–international vehicle registration* St Vincent and the Grenadines. *–postcode* Wolverhampton. *–US postcode* West Virginia.

W.Va. *abbr.* West Virginia.

WW *abbr.* (also **W/W**) warehouse warrant.

WWDSHEX *abbr. Shipping* weather working days, Sundays and holidays excluded.

WWW *abbr.* World Wide Web.

WY *US postcode* Wyoming.

wych- *comb. form* in names of trees with pliant branches (*wych-alder*, *wych-elm*). [Old English, = bending]

wych-hazel var. of WITCH-HAZEL.

Wykehamist /ˈwɪkəmɪst/ *–adj.* of Winchester College. *–n.* past or present member of Winchester College. [William of *Wykeham*, name of the founder]

Wyo. *abbr.* Wyoming.

Wyoming /waɪˈəʊmɪŋ/ state in the W central US; pop. (est. 1996) 481 400; capital, Cheyenne. There are deposits of oil, coal, natural gas, uranium, iron ore, and other minerals. Activities include agriculture (esp. livestock production), tourism, oil refining, and food processing.

WYSIWYG /ˈwɪzɪwɪg/ *adj.* (also **wysiwyg**) *Computing* denoting a form of text onscreen exactly corresponding to its printout. [acronym of *w*hat *y*ou *s*ee *i*s *w*hat *y*ou *g*et]

X[1] /eks/ *n.* (also **x**) (*pl.* **Xs** or **X's**) **1** twenty-fourth letter of the alphabet. **2** (as a roman numeral) ten. **3** (usu. **x**) *Math.* **a** first unknown quantity. **b** a Cartesian coordinate (*x-axis*). **4** unknown or unspecified number or person etc. **5** cross-shaped symbol used esp. to indicate position (*X marks the spot*) or incorrectness, or to symbolize a kiss or a vote, or as the signature of a person who cannot write.

X[2] *symb.* (of films) classified as suitable for adults only.

■ **Usage** This symbol was superseded in the UK in 1983 by *18*, but it is still used in the US.

x. *abbr. Finance* = EX[1] 2.

XA *international civil aircraft marking* Mexico.

x.a. *abbr. Finance* ex all. See EX[1] 2.

XB *international civil aircraft marking* Mexico.

x.b. *abbr. Finance* ex bonus. See EX[1] 2.

XC *international civil aircraft marking* Mexico.

x.c. *abbr. Finance* **1** ex capitalization. **2** ex coupon. See EX[1] 2.

X-chromosome /'eks,krəʊmə,səʊm/ *n.* (in humans and some other mammals) sex chromosome of which the number in female cells is twice that in male cells. [*X* as an arbitrary label]

x.cp. *abbr. Finance* ex coupon. See EX[1] 2.

x.d. *abbr.* (also **x.div.**) *Finance* ex dividend. See EX[1] 2.

Xe *symb.* xenon.

xenon /'zenɒn, 'ziː-/ *n.* heavy inert gaseous element. [Greek, neuter of *xenos* strange]

xenophobia /,zenə'fəʊbɪə/ *n.* hatred or fear of foreigners. □ **xenophobic** *adj.* [Greek *xenos* strange, stranger]

♦ **xerography** /zɪə'rɒgrəfɪ/ *n.* dry copying process in which powder adheres to areas remaining electrically charged after exposure of the surface to light from an image of the document to be copied. The process is also used in printing computer output with a laser printer. In a **plain-paper photocopier** an image is formed on a selenium-coated plate or cylinder. This is dusted with a resinous toner, which sticks selectively to the charged areas, the image so formed being transferred to a sheet of paper, on which it is fixed by heating. [Greek *xērosdry*]

Xerox /'zɪərɒks/ *–n. propr.* **1** machine for copying by xerography. **2** copy thus made. *–v.* (**xerox**) reproduce by this process.

xi /saɪ, ksaɪ/ *n.* fourteenth letter of the Greek alphabet (Ξ, ξ). [Greek]

Xian /ʃiː'æn/ industrial city in N China, capital of Shaanxi province; manufactures include chemicals, textiles, steel, and electronic equipment; pop. (est. 1989) 2 710 000.

x. in. *abbr. Banking* ex (i.e. without) interest.

♦ **X-inefficiency** *n.* amount by which the efficiency of a firm falls below the maximum possible. For example, in 1981 two completely identical Ford plants were compared, one in Germany and one in the UK: the German plant was found to produce 50% more cars with 22% fewer workers. The X-inefficiency of the British plant could have been due to any of several causes, including inertia, incomplete information, insulation from free competition, poor labour relations, or managerial incompetence.

Xinjiang /,ʃɪntʃɪ'æŋ/ (also **Sinkiang**) autonomous region in NW China; pop. (est. 1995) 16 320 000; capital, Urumqi. Crops include wheat, cotton, and fruit, and there are deposits of oil and minerals.

-xion see -ION.

Xizang see TIBET.

Xmas /'krɪsməs, 'eksməs/ *n. colloq.* = CHRISTMAS. [abbreviation, with X for the initial chi of Greek *Khristos* Christ]

XMS *abbr. Computing* extended memory specification.

x.n. *abbr.* = EX NEW.

x.r. *abbr. Finance* ex rights. See EX[1] 2.

X-ray /'eksreɪ/ *–n.* **1** (in *pl.*) electromagnetic radiation of short wavelength, able to pass through opaque bodies. **2** photograph made by X-rays, esp. showing the position of bones etc. by their greater absorption of the rays. *–v.* photograph, examine, or treat with X-rays. [X, originally with ref. to the unknown nature of the rays]

xs. *abbr.* **1** excess. **2** expenses.

XT *international civil aircraft marking* Burkina Faso.

XU *international civil aircraft marking* Cambodia.

X Windows *n. propr. Computing* precisely defined form of windowing mechanism.

XY *international civil aircraft marking* Burma.

xylem /'zaɪləm/ *n. Bot.* woody tissue. [Greek]

xylophone /'zaɪlə,fəʊn/ *n.* musical instrument of graduated wooden or metal bars struck with small wooden hammers. □ **xylophonist** *n.* [Greek *xulon* wood]

Y[1] /waɪ/ *n.* (also **y**) (*pl.* **Ys** or **Y's**) **1** twenty-fifth letter of the alphabet. **2** (usu. **y**) *Math.* **a** second unknown quantity. **b** a Cartesian coordinate (*y-axis*). **3** Y-shaped thing.

Y[2] *symb.* **1** *Currency* yuan. **2** yttrium.

-y[1] *suffix* forming adjectives: **1** from nouns and adjectives, meaning: **a** full of; having the quality of (*messy*). **b** addicted to (*boozy*). **2** from verbs, meaning 'inclined to', 'apt to' (*sticky*). [Old English]

-y[2] *suffix* (also **-ey, -ie**) forming diminutive nouns, pet names, etc. (*granny*; *Sally*; *nightie*). [originally *Scottish*]

-y[3] *suffix* forming nouns denoting state, condition, or quality (*orthodoxy*). [Latin *-ia*, Greek *-eia*]

YA *–abbr.* (also **Y/A**) York–Antwerp (see YORK–ANTWERP RULES). *–international civil aircraft marking* Afghanistan.

yacht /jɒt/ *–n.* **1** light sailing-vessel. **2** larger usu. power-driven vessel for cruising. *–v.* race or cruise in a yacht. [Dutch *jaghtschip*, literally 'pursuit-ship']

yachtsman *n.* (*fem.* **yachtswoman**) person who sails yachts.

yack *slang –n.* trivial or unduly persistent conversation. *–v.* engage in this. [imitative]

yah /jɑː/ *int.* (also **yah boo**) expressing derision or defiance. [imitative]

yahoo /jɑːˈhuː/ *n.* bestial person. [name of a race of brutes in *Gulliver's Travels*]

Yahweh /ˈjɑːweɪ/ *n.* (also **Yahveh** /-veɪ/) = JEHOVAH.

yak *n.* long-haired Tibetan ox. [Tibetan]

Yale lock *n. propr.* type of lock with a revolving barrel, used for doors etc. [*Yale*, name of its inventor]

Yalta /ˈjæltə/ port and resort in S Ukraine, on the Black Sea; pop. (est. 1988) 89 000.

yam *n.* **1 a** tropical or subtropical climbing plant. **b** edible starchy tuber of this. **2** *US* sweet potato. [Portuguese or Spanish]

yammer /ˈjæmə(r)/ *colloq.* or *dial. –n.* **1** lament, wail, grumble. **2** voluble talk. *–v.* utter a yammer. [Old English]

Yamoussoukro /ˌjæmuːˈsuːkrəʊ/ capital of Côte d'Ivoire, chosen to replace Abidjan as the capital in 1983; pop. (1988) 106 786.

yang *n.* (in Chinese philosophy) the active male principle of the universe (cf. YIN).

Yangtze Kiang /ˈjæŋtsɪ ˈkjæŋ/ principal river in China, rising in Tibet and flowing through central China to the East China Sea.

Yank *n. colloq.* often *derog.* American. [abbreviation of YANKEE]

yank *v.* & *n. colloq.* pull with a jerk. [origin unknown]

Yankee /ˈjæŋkɪ/ *n. colloq.* **1** often *derog.* = YANK. **2** *US* inhabitant of New England or of the northern states. [origin uncertain: perhaps from Dutch *Janke*, diminutive of *Jan* John, as a nickname]

♦ **Yankee bond** *n. Finance* bond issued in the US by a foreign borrower.

Yaoundé /jæˈʊndeɪ/ capital of Cameroon; industries include oil refining and light manufacturing; pop. (est. 1992) 800 000.

yap *–v.* (**-pp-**) **1** bark shrilly or fussily. **2** *colloq.* talk noisily, foolishly, or complainingly. *–n.* sound of yapping. □ **yappy** *adj.* (**-ier, -iest**) in sense 1 of *v.* [imitative]

YAR *abbr.* = YORK–ANTWERP RULES.

yarborough /ˈjɑːbərə/ *n.* whist or bridge hand with no card above a 9. [Earl of *Yarborough*, said to have betted against it]

yard[1] *n.* **1** unit of linear measure (3 ft, 0.9144 metre). **2** this length of material. **3** square or cubic yard. **4** spar slung across a mast for a sail to hang from. **5** (in *pl.*; foll. by *of*) *colloq.* a great length. **6** *colloq.* a billion. [Old English, = stick]

yard[2] *n.* **1** piece of enclosed ground, esp. attached to a building or used for a particular purpose. **2** *US* & *Austral.* garden of a house. [Old English, = enclosure]

yardage *n.* number of yards of material etc.

yard-arm *n.* either end of a ship's yard.

Yardie /ˈjɑːdɪ/ *n. slang* member of a Jamaican or West Indian gang engaging in organized crime, esp. drug-trafficking. [Jamaican English, = house, home]

yardstick *n.* **1** standard of comparison. **2** measuring rod a yard long, usu. divided into inches etc.

yarmulke /ˈjɑːməlkə/ *n.* (also **yarmulka**) skullcap worn by Jewish men. [Yiddish]

yarn *–n.* **1** spun thread, esp. for knitting, weaving, etc. **2** *colloq.* story, traveller's tale, anecdote. *–v. colloq.* tell yarns. [Old English]

yarrow /ˈjærəʊ/ *n.* perennial plant, esp. milfoil. [Old English]

yashmak /ˈjæʃmæk/ *n.* veil concealing the face except the eyes, worn by some Muslim women. [Arabic]

yaw *–v.* (of a ship or aircraft etc.) fail to hold a straight course; go unsteadily. *–n.* yawing of a ship etc. from its course. [origin unknown]

yawl *n.* a kind of ship's boat or sailing- or fishing-boat. [Low German *jolle* or Dutch *jol*]

yawn *–v.* **1** open the mouth wide and inhale, esp. when sleepy or bored. **2** gape, be wide open. *–n.* **1** act of yawning. **2** *colloq.* boring idea, activity, etc. [Old English]

yaws /jɔːz/ *n.pl.* (usu. treated as *sing.*) contagious tropical skin-disease with large red swellings. [origin unknown]

Yb *symb.* ytterbium.

Y-chromosome /ˈwaɪˌkrəʊməˌsəʊm/ *n.* (in humans and some other mammals) sex chromosome occurring only in male cells. [*Y* as an arbitrary label]

YD *symb.* Yemeni dinar.

yd. *abbr.* (*pl.* **yds.**) yard (measure).

ye[1] /jiː/ *pron. archaic pl.* of THOU[1] (*ye gods!*).

ye[2] /jiː/ *adj. pseudo-archaic* = THE (*ye olde tea-shoppe*). [from the obsolete *y*-shaped letter for *th*]

yea /jeɪ/ *archaic –adv.* **1** yes. **2** indeed (*ready, yea eager*). *–n.* utterance of 'yea'; 'yes' vote. [Old English]

yeah /jeə/ *adv. colloq.* yes. [a casual pronunciation of YES]

year /jɪə(r)/ *n.* **1** time occupied by the earth in one revolution round the sun, approx. 365¼ days. **2** (also **calendar year**) period from 1 Jan. to 31 Dec. inclusive. **3** period of twelve months, starting at any point (*four years ago*; *tax year*). **4** (in *pl.*) age, time of life (*young for his years*). **5** (usu. in *pl.*) *colloq.* very long time. **6** group of students entering college etc. in the same academic year. [Old English]

yearbook *n.* annual publication dealing with events or aspects of the (usu. preceding) year.

yearling *n.* animal between one and two years old.

♦ **yearling bond** *n.* UK local authority bond that is redeemable one year after issue.

yearly *–adj.* **1** done, produced, or occurring once a year. **2** of or lasting a year. *–adv.* once a year.

♦ **yearly savings plans** *n.pl.* (in full **National Savings Yearly Plans**) saving scheme introduced by the Department for National Savings in 1984. Savers make 12 monthly payments of between £20 and £400; this entitles them to a **Yearly Plan Certificate**, which earns maximum tax-free interest if held for four years, annual interest being compounded.

yearn /jɜːn/ *v.* be filled with longing, compassion, or tenderness. □ **yearning** *n.* & *adj.* [Old English]

♦ **year of assessment** *n.* = FISCAL YEAR.

yeast *n.* greyish-yellow fungus obtained esp. from fermenting malt liquors and used as a fermenting agent, to raise bread, etc. [Old English]

yeasty *adj.* (**-ier**, **-iest**) **1** of, like, or tasting of yeast; frothy. **2** in a ferment. **3** working like yeast. **4** (of talk etc.) light and superficial.

yell *–n.* loud sharp cry; shout. *–v.* cry, shout. [Old English]

yellow /ˈjeləʊ/ *–adj.* **1** of the colour of buttercups, lemons, egg-yolks, etc. **2** having a yellow skin or complexion. **3** *colloq.* cowardly. *–n.* **1** yellow colour or pigment. **2** yellow clothes or material. *–v.* turn yellow. □ **yellowish** *adj.* **yellowness** *n.* **yellowy** *adj.* [Old English: related to GOLD]

yellow-belly *n. colloq.* coward.

♦ **Yellow Book** *n. colloq.* publication, entitled *Admission of Securities to Listing*, issued by the Council of the London Stock Exchange. It sets out the regulations for admission to the Official List and the obligations of companies with listed securities.

yellow card *n.* card shown by the referee to a football-player being cautioned.

yellow fever *n.* tropical virus disease with fever and jaundice.

yellow flag *n.* flag displayed by a ship in quarantine.

yellowhammer *n.* bunting of which the male has a yellow head, neck, and breast.

Yellowknife /ˈjeləʊˌnaɪf/ city in N Canada, capital of the Northwest Territories; pop. (1991) 15 179.

Yellow Pages *propr.* see CLASSIFIED DIRECTORY.

yellow pepper *n.* ripe yellow fruit of the capsicum plant.

Yellow River (Chinese **Huang Ho** /hwæŋ ˈhəʊ/) second-largest river in China, rising in the mountains of W central China and flowing NE, S, and E to enter the Bo Hai Gulf.

yellow spot *n.* point of acutest vision in the retina.

yellow streak *n. colloq.* trait of cowardice.

yelp *–n.* sharp shrill cry as of a dog in pain or excitement. *–v.* utter a yelp. [Old English]

yen[1] *n.* (*pl.* same) standard monetary unit of Japan. [Japanese from Chinese]

yen[2] *colloq. –n.* longing or yearning. *–v.* (**-nn-**) feel a longing. [Chinese]

yeoman /ˈjəʊmən/ *n.* **1** esp. *hist.* man holding and cultivating a small landed estate. **2** member of the yeomanry force. □ **yeomanly** *adj.* [from earlier *yoman*, *yeman*, etc., probably = young man]

Yeoman of the Guard *n.* member of the sovereign's bodyguard.

yeomanry *n.* (*pl.* **-ies**) **1** body or class of yeomen. **2** *hist.* volunteer cavalry force raised from the yeoman class.

Yeoman Warder *n.* (correct term for) a 'beefeater' at the Tower of London.

yep *adv.* & *n.* (also **yup**) *US colloq.* = YES.

YER *abbr.* (also **y.e.r.**) *Finance* yearly effective rate (of interest).

Yerevan /ˌjerɪˈvæn/ capital of Armenia; industries include chemicals, textiles, and food processing; pop. (est. 1994) 1 226 000.

YES *abbr.* Youth Enterprise Scheme.

yes *–adv.* **1** indicating that the answer to the question is affirmative, the statement etc. made is correct, the request or command will be complied with, or the person summoned or addressed is present. **2** (**yes?**) **a** indeed? is that so? **b** what do you want? *–n.* **1** an utterance of the word *yes*. **2** affirmation or assent. **3** 'yes' vote. □ **say yes** grant a request, confirm a statement. [Old English, = *yea let it be*]

yes-man *n. colloq.* weakly acquiescent person.

yesterday /ˈjestəˌdeɪ/ *–adv.* **1** on the day before today. **2** in the recent past. *–n.* **1** the day before today. **2** the recent past. [Old English]

yesteryear /ˈjestəˌjɪə(r)/ *n. archaic* or *rhet.* **1** last year. **2** the recent past. [Old English *yester-* that is last past, YEAR]

Yemen /ˈjemən/, **Republic of** country in the S and SW of the Arabian peninsula, formerly divided into the People's Democratic Republic of Yemen (South Yemen) and the Yemen Arab Republic (North Yemen). The economy is predominantly agricultural: cotton, coffee, and livestock products (esp. hides and skins) are exported, and wheat, barley, sesame, millet, sorghum, tobacco, fruit, and vegetables are also grown. The fishing industry is important, producing dried and salted fish for export. Oil is the major export and accounts for three-quarters of export revenue. There are reserves of natural gas. There is some light industry, producing textiles, cigarettes, soft drinks, and handicrafts, and shipping services provided by Aden contribute to the commercial economy, but the country is dependent on foreign aid and revenue from nationals working in Saudi Arabia and elsewhere. In 1995 Yemen began implementation of a number of economic reforms to satisfy criteria for World Bank and IMF aid.

History. Part of the Ottoman empire from the 16th century, Yemen came under increasing British influence in the 19th century as a result of the strategic importance of Aden at the mouth of the Red Sea. The state of North Yemen, established in 1934, became a republic in 1962. South Yemen declared its independence in 1967, becoming the People's Democratic Republic of Yemen in 1970. After several years of border fighting, negotiations towards unification of the two republics began in 1979 and culminated in the establishment of a multi-party state in 1990; the country's first multi-party parliamentary elections were held in 1993. In 1994 rebels in the south of the country attempted to break away, but the rebellion collapsed after a few months. Following this a coalition government was formed and the constitution was amended. President, Ali Abdullah Saleh; prime minister, Dr. Faraj Saeed Bin Ghanem; administrative capital, Sana'a; commercial capital, Aden. □ **Yemeni** *adj.* & *n.*

language	Arabic
currency	riyal (YRls) of 100 fils, dinar (YD) of 1000 fils
pop. (1996)	16 600 200
GNP (1994)	US$3.8B
literacy	68% (m); 23% (f)
life expectancy	55 (m); 59 (f)

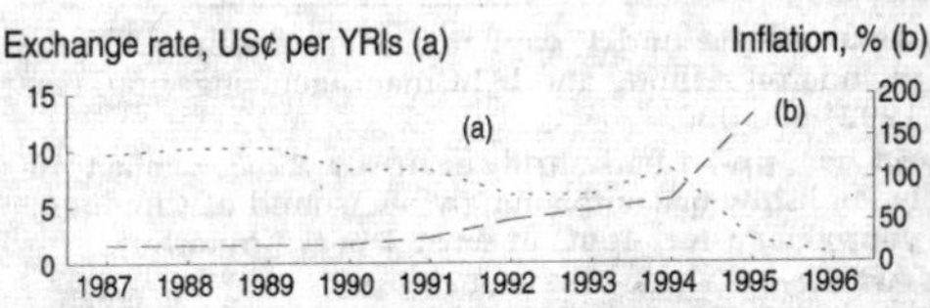

yet –*adv.* **1** as late as, or until, now or then (*there is yet time; your best work yet*). **2** (with *neg.* or *interrog.*) so soon as, or by, now or then (*it is not time yet; have you finished yet?*). **3** again; in addition (*more and yet more*). **4** in the remaining time available (*I will do it yet*). **5** (foll. by *compar.*) even (*a yet more difficult task*). **6** nevertheless; and or but in spite of that. –*conj.* but at the same time; but nevertheless. [Old English]

yeti /ˈjetɪ/ *n.* = ABOMINABLE SNOWMAN. [Tibetan]

yew *n.* **1** dark-leaved evergreen tree bearing berry-like cones. **2** its wood. [Old English]

Y-fronts /ˈwaɪfrʌnts/ *n. propr.* men's or boys' briefs with a Y-shaped seam at the front.

YHA *abbr.* Youth Hostels Association.

YI *international civil aircraft marking* Iraq.

Yid *n. slang offens.* Jew. [back-formation from YIDDISH]

Yiddish /ˈjɪdɪʃ/ –*n.* language used by Jews in or from Europe, orig. a German dialect with words from Hebrew etc. –*adj.* of this language. [German *jüdisch* Jewish]

yield –*v.* **1** produce or return as a fruit, profit, or result. **2** give up; surrender, concede. **3 a** (often foll. by *to*) surrender; submit; defer to. **b** (as **yielding** *adj.*) compliant; submissive; soft and pliable. **4** (foll. by *to*) give right of way to (other traffic). **5** (foll. by *to*) be inferior or confess inferiority to (*I yield to none in this matter*). –*n.* **1** amount yielded or produced. **2** income from an investment. The **nominal yield** of a fixed-interest security is the interest it pays expressed as a percentage of its par value. For example, a £100 stock quoted as paying 8% interest will yield £8 per annum for every £100 of stock held. However, the **current yield** (or **interest yield** or **running yield** or **earnings yield** or **flat yield**) will depend on the market price of the stock. If the 8% £100 stock mentioned above was standing at a market price of £90, the current yield would be 100/90 × 8 = 8.9%. As interest rates rise, so the market values of fixed-interest stocks (not close to redemption) fall in order that they should give a competitive current yield. The capital gain (or loss) on redemption of a stock, which is normally redeemable at £100, can also be taken into account. This is called the **yield to redemption** (or **redemption yield**). The redemption yield consists approximately of the current yield plus the capital gain (or loss) divided by the number of years to redemption. Thus, if the above stock had nine years to run to redemption, its redemption yield would be about 8.9 + 10/9 = 10%. The yields of the various stocks on offer are usu. listed in commercial papers as both current yields and redemption yields, based on the current market price. However, for an investor who actually owns stock, the yield will be calculated not on the market price but the price the investor paid for it. The annual yield on a fixed-interest stock can be stated exactly once it has been purchased. This is not the case with equities, however, where neither the dividend yield (see DIVIDEND 1) nor the capital gain (or loss) can be forecast, reflecting the greater degree of risk attaching to investments in equities. Yields on fixed-interest securities and equities are usu. quoted gross, i.e. before deduction of tax. **3** income obtained from a tax. [Old English, = pay]

♦ **yield curve** *n.* curve on a graph in which the yield of fixed-interest securities is plotted against the length of time they have to run to maturity. The yield curve usu. slopes upwards, indicating that investors expect to receive a premium for holding securities that have a long time to run. However, when there are expectations of changes in interest rate, the slope of the yield curve may change (see TERM STRUCTURE).

♦ **yield gap** *n.* difference between the average annual dividend yield on equities and the average annual yield on long-dated gilt-edged securities. Before the 1960s equity yields usu. exceeded gilt yields, reflecting the greater degree of risk involved in an investment in equities. In the 1960s rising equity prices led to falling dividend yields, causing a **reverse yield gap**. This was accepted as equities were seen to provide a better hedge against inflation than fixed-interest securities; thus their greater risk element is compensated by the possibility of higher capital gains.

♦ **yield to redemption** see YIELD *n.* 2.

---

yin *n.* (in Chinese philosophy) the passive female principle of the universe (cf. YANG).

yippee /jɪˈpiː/ *int.* expressing delight or excitement. [natural exclamation]

YJ *international civil aircraft marking* Vanuatu.

YK –*international civil aircraft marking* Syria. –*airline flight code* Cyprus Turkish Airlines.

YL *international civil aircraft marking* Latvia.

YMCA *abbr.* Young Men's Christian Association.

YN *international civil aircraft marking* Nicaragua.

YO *postcode* York.

yob /jɒb/ *n. slang* lout, hooligan. □ **yobbish** *adj.* [back slang for BOY]

yobbo /ˈjɒbəʊ/ *n.* (*pl.* **-s**) *slang* = YOB.

yodel /ˈjəʊd(ə)l/ –*v.* (**-ll-**; *US* **-l-**) sing with melodious inarticulate sounds and frequent changes between falsetto and normal voice in the manner of Swiss mountain-dwellers. –*n.* yodelling cry. □ **yodeller** *n.* [German]

yoga /ˈjəʊgə/ *n.* **1** Hindu system of meditation and asceticism designed to effect reunion with the universal spirit. **2** system of physical exercises and breathing control used in yoga. [Sanskrit, = union]

yoghurt /ˈjɒgət/ *n.* (also **yogurt**) semi-solid sourish food made from milk fermented by added bacteria. [Turkish]

yogi /ˈjəʊgɪ/ *n.* (*pl.* **-s**) devotee of yoga. [Hindustani: related to YOGA]

Yogyakarta see JOGJAKARTA.

yoicks *int.* cry used by fox-hunters to urge on the hounds. [origin unknown]

yoke –*n.* **1** wooden crosspiece fastened over the necks of two oxen etc. and attached to the plough or wagon to be pulled. **2** (*pl.* same or **-s**) pair (of oxen etc.). **3** object like a yoke in form or function, e.g. a wooden shoulder-piece for carrying a pair of pails, the top section of a garment from which the rest hangs. **4** sway, dominion, or servitude. **5** bond of union, esp. of marriage. –*v.* (**-king**) **1** put a yoke on. **2** couple or unite (a pair). **3** (foll. by *to*) link (one thing) to (another). **4** match or work together. [Old English]

yokel /ˈjəʊk(ə)l/ *n.* rustic; country bumpkin. [perhaps dial.]

Yokohama /ˌjəʊkəʊˈhɑːmə/ seaport and second-largest city in Japan, on Honshu island; it has shipbuilding, oil-refining, chemical, textile, and steel industries; pop. (1995) 3 307 408.

yolk /jəʊk/ *n.* yellow inner part of an egg. [Old English: related to YELLOW]

Yom Kippur /jɒm ˈkɪpə(r)/ *n.* most solemn religious fast day of the Jewish year, Day of Atonement. [Hebrew]

yon *adj.* & *adv. literary* & *dial.* yonder. [Old English]

yonder –*adv.* over there; at some distance in that direction; in the place indicated. –*adj.* situated yonder.

yonks *n.pl. slang* a long time (*yonks ago*). [origin unknown]

yoo-hoo /ˈjuːhuː/ *int.* used to attract a person's attention. [natural exclamation]

yore *n.* □ **of yore** a long time ago. [Old English, = long ago]

York /jɔːk/ city in N England, in North Yorkshire; industries include railway engineering, the manufacture of chocolate, sugar, and glass, and tourism; pop. (1991) 124 609.

york *v. Cricket* bowl out with a yorker. [back-formation from YORKER]

♦ **York–Antwerp rules** *n.pl.* (also **YA rules**, **YAR**) set of rules drawn up in 1877, at conferences held in York and Antwerp, to facilitate the task of working out shares in general average losses in marine insurance (see AVERAGE *n.* 4).

---

yorker *n. Cricket* ball that pitches immediately under the bat. [probably with ref. to the practice of Yorkshire cricketers]

Yorkist /ˈjɔːkɪst/ *–n. hist.* follower of the House of York, esp. in the Wars of the Roses. *–adj.* of the House of York.

Yorks. *abbr.* Yorkshire.

Yorkshire pudding /ˈjɔːkʃə/ *n.* baked batter eaten with roast beef.

Yorkshire terrier /ˈjɔːkʃə/ *n.* small long-haired blue and tan kind of terrier.

you /juː/ *pron.* (*obj.* **you**; *poss.* **your, yours**) **1** the person or persons addressed. **2** (as *int.* with a noun) in an exclamatory statement (*you fools!*). **3** (in general statements) one, a person, people (*you get used to it*). □ **you and yours** you and your family, property, etc. [Old English, originally objective case of YE[1]]

you'd /juːd/ *contr.* **1** you had. **2** you would.

you'll /juːl/ *contr.* you will; you shall.

young /jʌŋ/ *–adj.* (**younger** /ˈjʌŋgə(r)/; **youngest** /ˈjʌŋgɪst/) **1** not far advanced in life, development, or existence; not yet old. **2 a** immature, inexperienced. **b** youthful. **3** of or characteristic of youth (*young love*). **4** representing young people (*Young Farmers*). **5 a** distinguishing a son from his father (*young George*). **b** as a familiar or condescending form of address (*listen, young lady*). **6** (**younger**) distinguishing one person from another of the same name (*the younger Pitt*). *–n.* (*collect.*) offspring, esp. of animals. □ **youngish** *adj.* [Old English]

young person *n. Law* person aged between 14 and 17 years.

youngster *n.* child, young person.

your /jɔː(r)/ *poss. pron.* **1** of or belonging to you. **2** *colloq.* often *derog.* much talked of; well known (*your typical professor*). [Old English]

you're /jɔː(r)/ *contr.* you are.

yours /jɔːz/ *poss. pron.* **1** the one or ones belonging to you (*it is yours; yours are over there*). **2** your letter (*yours of the 10th*). **3** introducing a formula ending a letter (*yours ever; yours truly*). □ **of yours** of or belonging to you (*friend of yours*).

yourself /jɔːˈself/ *pron.* (*pl.* **yourselves**) **1 a** *emphat. form* of YOU. **b** *refl. form* of YOU. **2** in your normal state of body or mind (*are quite yourself again*). □ **be yourself** see ONESELF.

youth /juːθ/ *n.* (*pl.* **-s** /juːðz/) **1** being young; period between childhood and adult age. **2** vigour, enthusiasm, inexperience, or other characteristic of this period. **3** young man. **4** (as *pl.*) young people collectively (*the youth of the country*). [Old English: related to YOUNG]

youth club *n.* place for young people's leisure activities.

youthful *adj.* young or still having the characteristics of youth. □ **youthfully** *adv.* **youthfulness** *n.*

youth hostel *n.* any of a chain of cheap lodgings for holiday-makers, esp. walkers and cyclists.

◆ **Youth Training Scheme** (also **YTS**) see TRAINING AGENCY.

you've /juːv/ *contr.* you have.

yowl *–n.* loud wailing cry of or as of a cat or dog in distress. *–v.* utter a yowl. [imitative]

yo-yo /ˈjəʊjəʊ/ *n.* (*pl.* **yo-yos**) **1** toy consisting of a pair of discs with a deep groove between them in which string is attached and wound, and which can be made to fall and rise. **2** thing that repeatedly falls and rises. [origin unknown]

YR *international civil aircraft marking* Romania.

yr. *abbr.* **1** year(s). **2** younger. **3** your.

YRls *symb.* Yemen riyal.

yrs. *abbr.* **1** years. **2** yours.

YS *international civil aircraft marking* El Salvador.

YTD *abbr. Accounting* year to date.

YTS *abbr.* Youth Training Scheme. See TRAINING AGENCY.

ytterbium /ɪˈtɜːbɪəm/ *n.* metallic element of the lanthanide series. [*Ytterby* in Sweden]

yttrium /ˈɪtrɪəm/ *n.* metallic element resembling the lanthanides. [related to YTTERBIUM]

YU *international vehicle registration* & *international civil aircraft marking* Yugoslavia.

yuan /juːˈɑːn/ *n.* (*pl.* same) standard monetary unit of China. [Chinese]

Yucatán /ˌjuːkəˈtɑːn/ state in SE Mexico, at the N tip of the Yucatán peninsula (separating the Gulf of Mexico from the Caribbean Sea); pop. (est. 1995) 1 555 733; capital, Mérida.

yucca /ˈjʌkə/ *n.* subtropical white-flowered plant with swordlike leaves, often grown as a house-plant. [Carib]

yuck /jʌk/ *int.* (also **yuk**) *slang* expression of strong distaste. [imitative]

yucky *adj.* (also **yukky**) (**-ier, -iest**) *slang* **1** messy, repellent. **2** sickly, sentimental.

Yugoslavia /ˌjuːgəʊˈslɑːvɪə/, **Federal Republic of** country in SE Europe, with a coastline on the Adriatic Sea, comprising the two constituent republics of Serbia and Montenegro. Manufacturing industries are important, producing clothing, textiles, machinery, transport equipment, chemicals, and foodstuffs, all of which are normally exported. Copper ore, lead-zinc ore, magnesite, asbestos ore, and silver are all mined. The chief agricultural products are maize, wheat, tobacco, sugar beet, and livestock (esp. pigs, sheep, and cattle). A trade embargo, imposed in 1992 because of Serbia's involvement in the Bosnian civil war, banned the import and export of all goods except food and medicines and has crippled the country's economy.
Although the embargo was lifted in late 1996, most of the republic's foreign assets remain frozen and economic reconstruction has scarcely begun.
History. The country was formed, as a kingdom, in 1918 as a result of the peace settlement at the end of the First World War: it comprised Serbia, Montenegro, and the former Slavic provinces of the Austro-Hungarian empire (Croatia, Slovenia, and Bosnia-Hercegovina) and assumed the name of Yugoslavia in 1929. Invaded by the Axis powers during the Second World War, in 1945 Yugoslavia emerged from a long guerrilla war as a Communist state, the Socialist Federal Republic of Yugoslavia, under Marshal Tito. Tito's death in 1980 was followed by the growth of nationalist movements in the constituent republics: independence was declared by Slovenia and Croatia in 1991 and by Bosnia-Hercegovina and Macedonia the following year. The republic in its present form was established by Serbia and Montenegro in April 1992 but this has not so far been recognized by many other countries, mainly because of Serbian involvement in the civil war in Bosnia (1992–5). The period 1997–8 has seen growing tension between Serbia and Montenegro and renewed violence in the predominantly Albanian province of Kosovo. President, Slobodan Milosevic; prime minister, Radoje Kontic; capital, Belgrade. □ **Yugoslav** /ˈjuː-/ *adj.* & *n.*, **Yugoslavian** *adj.* & *n.*

language	Serbo-Croat
currency	new dinar (Din) of 100 paras
pop. (1996)	10 473 000
GNP (1995)	US$15.9B
literacy	97% (m); 88% (f)
life expectancy	69 (m); 74 (f)

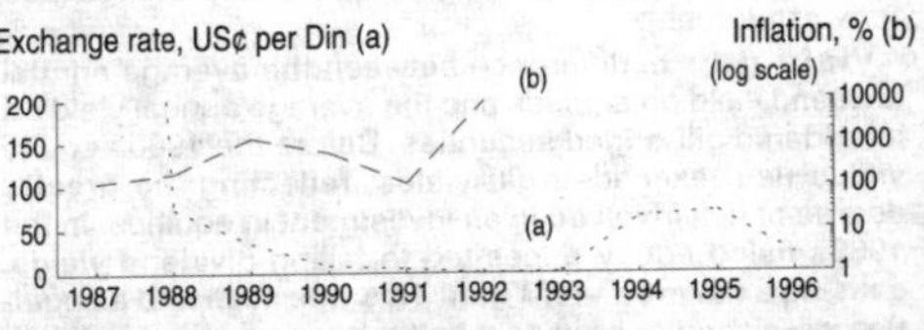

yuk var. of YUCK.

yukky var. of YUCKY.

Yukon Territory territory in NW Canada; pop. (est. 1995) 30 100; capital, Whitehorse. Mining, esp. of lead, zinc, silver, and gold, is the principal industry and there is some tourism.

yule *n.* (in full **yule-tide**) *archaic* the Christmas festival. [Old English]

yule-log *n.* **1** large log traditionally burnt on Christmas Eve. **2** log-shaped chocolate cake eaten at Christmas.

yummy /ˈjʌmɪ/ *adj.* (**-ier, -iest**) *colloq.* tasty, delicious. [from YUM-YUM]

yum-yum *int.* expressing pleasure from eating or the prospect of eating. [natural exclamation]

Yunnan /juːˈnæn/ province in S China; pop. (est. 1995) 39 390 000; capital, Kunming. It is an important producer of tin; other products include rice and timber.

yup var. of YEP.

yuppie /ˈjʌpɪ/ *n.* (also **yuppy**) (*pl.* **-ies**) (often *attrib.*) *colloq.*, usu. *derog.* young ambitious professional person, esp. one from the business world. [from *y*oung *u*rban *p*rofessional]

YV *international vehicle registration* & *international civil aircraft marking* Venezuela.

YWCA *abbr.* Young Women's Christian Association.

Zz

Z[1] /zed/ *n.* (also **z**) (*pl.* **Zs** or **Z's**) **1** twenty-sixth letter of the alphabet. **2** (usu. **z**) *Math.* **a** third unknown quantity. **b** a Cartesian coordinate (*z-axis*).

Z[2] *–international vehicle registration* Zambia. *–international civil aircraft marking* Zimbabwe.

ZA *–international vehicle registration* South Africa. *–international civil aircraft marking* Albania.

zabaglione /ˌzæbəˈljəʊnɪ/ *n.* Italian dessert of whipped and heated egg-yolks, sugar, and wine. [Italian]

Zacatecas /ˌzækəˈteɪkəs/ **1** state in N central Mexico; pop. (est. 1995) 1 336 348. **2** its capital city; pop. (1990) 100 051.

Zagreb /ˈzɑːgreb/ capital of Croatia; manufactures include machinery, textiles, and paper; pop. (1991) 867 717.

Zaïre /ˈzɑːˈɪə(r)/, **Republic of** former name (1971–97) of Democratic Republic of CONGO.

Zaïre River see CONGO RIVER.

Zákinthos /ˈzækɪnˌθɒs/ **1** the most southerly of the Greek islands in the Ionian Sea; pop. (latest est.) 31 000. **2** its capital city; pop. (latest est.) 10 000.

Zakopane /ˌzækəʊˈpænə/ winter sports resort in S Poland, in the Tatra Mountains; pop. (1990) 28 630.

Zambezi River /zæmˈbiːzɪ/ river in Africa, flowing through Angola, Zambia, and Mozambique to the Indian Ocean. It forms the border between Zambia and Zimbabwe.

Zamboanga /ˌsæmbəʊˈæŋgə/ port and resort in the S Philippines, on the W coast of the island of Mindanao; brass and bronze goods are manufactured, and exports include copra, hemp, and hardwood; pop. (est. 1994) 464 466.

zany /ˈzeɪnɪ/ *adj.* (**-ier, -iest**) comically idiotic; crazily ridiculous. [French or Italian]

Zanzibar /ˌzænzɪˈbɑː(r)/ **1** Tanzanian island off the coast of E Africa; cloves and copra are exported; pop. (1994) 444 000; chief town, Zanzibar, pop. (1988) 157 634. **2** former British protectorate consisting of the islands of Zanzibar and Pemba, which became an independent sultanate in 1963. The following year the sultan was overthrown and Zanzibar united with Tanganyika to form Tanzania.

zap *slang –v.* (**-pp-**) **1 a** kill or destroy; attack. **b** hit hard (*zapped the ball over the net*). **2** move quickly. **3** overwhelm emotionally. *–int.* expressing the sound or impact of a bullet, ray gun, etc., or any sudden event. [imitative]

Zaporozhye /ˌzæpəˈrɒʒjɪ/ industrial city in E Ukraine, on the Dnieper River, site of a dam providing hydroelectric power; pop. (est. 1996) 882 000.

zappy *adj.* (**-ier, -iest**) *colloq.* lively, energetic.

Zaragoza see SARAGOSSA.

Zarathustrian var. of ZOROASTRIAN.

ZB *–airline flight code* Monarch Airlines.

ZBB *abbr. US* zero-base(d) budgeting.

ZE *postcode* Lerwick.

zeal *n.* earnestness or fervour; hearty persistent endeavour. [Greek *zēlos*]

Zealand /ˈziːlənd/ (Danish **Sjælland** /ˈʃelənd/) principal island of Denmark, situated between the Jutland peninsula and the S tip of Sweden; pop. (est. 1988) 2 000 254; chief city, Copenhagen. Arable and dairy farming are important.

zealot /ˈzelət/ *n.* extreme partisan; fanatic. □ **zealotry** *n.*

zealous /ˈzeləs/ *adj.* full of zeal; enthusiastic. □ **zealously** *adv.*

♦ Zebra /ˈzebrə, ˈziː-/ *n.* **discounted zero-coupon bond, in which the accrued income is taxed annually rather than on redemption. [possibly after *Tiger* (see TIGR)]**

---

zebra /ˈzebrə, ˈziː-/ *n.* (*pl.* same or **-s**) black-and-white striped African animal of the family including the ass and horse. [Italian or Portuguese from Congolese]

zebra crossing *n.* striped street-crossing where pedestrians have precedence.

zebu /ˈziːbuː/ *n.* (*pl.* same or **-s**) humped ox of Asia and Africa. [French]

zed *n.* letter Z. [Greek ZETA]

zee /ziː/ *n. US* letter Z. [var. of ZED]

Zeebrugge /ziːˈbrʊgə/ seaport on the coast of Belgium, linked by canal to Bruges and by ferry to Hull and Dover in England.

Zeeland /ˈziːlənd/ agricultural province in the SE Netherlands, at the estuary of the Maas, Scheldt, and Rhine rivers; crops include wheat, sugar beet, and fruit; pop. (1995) 365 846; capital, Middelburg.

Zeitgeist /ˈtsaɪtgaɪst/ *n.* the spirit of the times. [German]

Zen *n.* form of Buddhism emphasizing meditation and intuition. [Japanese, = meditation]

Zend *n.* an interpretation of the Avesta. [Persian]

Zend-Avesta *n.* Zoroastrian sacred writings of the Avesta (or text) and Zend (or commentary).

zenith /ˈzenɪθ/ *n.* **1** point of the heavens directly above an

---

Zambia /ˈzæmbɪə/, **Republic of** (formerly (1911–64) **Northern Rhodesia**) landlocked country in central Africa, a member state of the Commonwealth. The economy is based on revenue from the mining sector, esp. copper, of which Zambia is one of the world's major producers; cobalt, zinc, and lead are also exported. Agriculture, which employs a large proportion of the population, produces tobacco for export, maize, sugar, cotton, peanuts, vegetables, and livestock; there are also transport and construction industries. Since the end of one-party rule in 1991 the previously state-controlled economy has experienced a number of free market economic reforms.
History. The area was administered by the British South Africa Company from 1889 until taken over as a protectorate by the British government in 1924. After ten years (1953–63) as part of the Federation of Rhodesia and Nyasaland, it gained full independence in 1964, as a republic under President Kenneth Kaunda. One-party rule, introduced in 1973, was replaced in 1991 by a multi-party electoral system after violent protests by opposition groups in 1990. In the subsequent elections (1991) Kaunda was defeated by Frederick J. Chiluba, who was re-elected in 1996 amid allegations of electoral fraud. President, Frederick J. Chiluba; capital, Lusaka. □ **Zambian** *adj.* & *n.*

languages	English (official), Bantu dialects
currency	kwacha (k) of 100 ngwee
pop. (1996)	9 715 000
GNP (1994)	US$3.2B
literacy	85% (m); 71% (f)
life expectancy	45 (m); 46 (f)

observer. **2** highest point (of power or prosperity etc.). [Latin from Arabic]

zephyr /ˈzefə(r)/ *n. literary* mild gentle breeze. [Greek, = west wind]

Zeppelin /ˈzepəlɪn/ *n.* large dirigible German airship of the early 20th century. [Count F. von *Zeppelin*, name of an airman]

Zermatt /ˈzɜːmæt/ Alpine ski resort and mountaineering centre in S Switzerland, near the Matterhorn; pop (est. 1989) 4200.

zero /ˈzɪərəʊ/ *n.* (*pl.* **-s**) **1** figure 0; nought; nil. **2** point on the scale of a thermometer etc. from which a positive or negative quantity is reckoned. **3** (*attrib.*) no, not any (*zero growth*). **4** (in full **zero-hour**) **a** hour at which a planned, esp. military, operation is timed to begin. **b** crucial moment. **5** lowest or earliest point (*down to zero; the year zero*). □ **zero in on** (**-oes, -oed**) **1** take aim at. **2** focus one's attention on. [Arabic: related to CIPHER]

♦ **zero-coupon bond** *n. Finance* bond that offers no interest payments. In effect, the interest is paid at maturity in the redemption value of the bond. Investors sometimes prefer zero-coupon bonds as they may confer more favourable tax treatment. See also DEEP-DISCOUNT BOND; TIGR; ZEBRA.

zero option *n.* disarmament proposal for the total removal of certain types of weapons on both sides.

♦ **zero-rated** *adj.* (of goods or services) taxable for VAT but with a tax rate of zero. A distinction is made between exempt goods and services (e.g. postage stamps) and zero-rated goods or services (e.g. food, books, and children's clothes) as exempt goods are outside the VAT system and there is no opportunity to offset input tax, whereas zero-rated goods and services are within the system, providing an opportunity for offsetting input tax.

♦ **zero-sum game** *n.* game or contest between two or more individuals in which the winnings of one equal the losses of the other, i.e. gains minus losses equal zero. An example of a zero-sum game is an argument over who pays a taxi fare: one person's gain is another's loss. The prisoners' dilemma is a non-zero-sum game that demonstrates the benefits of cooperation (see PRISONERS' DILEMMA). Both zero- and non-zero-sum games have a wide range of applications in economics.

zest *n.* **1** piquancy; stimulating flavour or quality. **2 a** keen enjoyment or interest. **b** (often foll. by *for*) relish. **c** gusto. **3** scraping of orange or lemon peel as flavouring. □ **zestful** *adj.* **zestfully** *adv.* [French]

zeta /ˈziːtə/ *n.* sixth letter of the Greek alphabet (Z, ζ). [Greek]

zeugma /ˈzjuːgmə/ *n.* figure of speech using a verb or adjective with two nouns, to one of which it is strictly applicable while the word appropriate to the other is not used (e.g. *with weeping eyes and* [sc. *grieving*] *hearts*) (cf. SYLLEPSIS). [Greek, = a yoking, from *zugon* yoke]

z.H. *abbr.* (also **z.Hd.**) (German) zu Händen (= for the attention of, or care of).

Zhejiang /ˌdʒɜːdʒɪˈæŋ/ (also **Chekiang** /ˌtʃekɪˈæŋ/) province in E China; pop. (est. 1995) 42 940 000; capital, Hangzhou. Agriculture, silk production, and fishing are the main economic activities.

Zhengzhou /dʒeŋˈdʒəʊ/ (also **Chengchow** /tʃeŋˈtʃaʊ/) city in NE central China, capital of Henan province; pop. (1990) 1 159 679.

ziggurat /ˈzɪgəˌræt/ *n.* rectangular stepped tower in ancient Mesopotamia, surmounted by a temple. [Assyrian]

zigzag /ˈzɪgzæg/ *–adj.* with abrupt alternate right and left turns (*zigzag line*). *–n.* zigzag line; thing having the form of a zigzag or having sharp turns. *–adv.* with a zigzag course. *–v.* (**-gg-**) move in a zigzag course. [French from German]

zilch *n.* esp. *US slang* nothing. [origin uncertain]

zillion /ˈzɪljən/ *n. colloq.* indefinite large number. [probably after *million*]

Zimmer frame *n. propr.* a kind of walking-frame. [*Zimmer*, name of the maker]

zinc *n.* greyish-white metallic element used as a component of brass and in galvanizing sheet iron. [German *Zink*]

zing *colloq. –n.* vigour, energy. *–v.* move swiftly, esp. with a high-pitched ringing sound. [imitative]

zinnia /ˈzɪnɪə/ *n.* garden plant with showy flowers. [*Zinn*, name of a physician and botanist]

Zion /ˈzaɪən/ *n.* **1** ancient Jerusalem; its holy hill. **2 a** the Jewish people or religion. **b** the Christian Church. **3** the Kingdom of Heaven. [Hebrew *ṣīyôn*]

Zionism *n.* movement for the re-establishment and development of a Jewish nation in what is now Israel. □ **Zionist** *n.* & *adj.*

zip *–n.* **1** light fast sound. **2** energy, vigour. **3 a** (in full **zip-fastener**) fastening device of two flexible strips with interlocking projections, closed or opened by sliding a

---

Zimbabwe /zɪmˈbɑːbwɪ/, **Republic of** (formerly (1911–64) **Southern Rhodesia**) landlocked country in SE Africa, a member state of the Commonwealth, bordered by Zambia, Botswana, South Africa, and Mozambique. Agriculture remains an important sector of the economy, and the principal agricultural exports include tobacco, cotton, sugar, and maize (also the chief subsistence crop); tea, coffee, groundnuts, wheat, and millet are also grown. The mining and export of gold, nickel, copper, asbestos, chrome, tin, and other minerals is a major source of foreign revenue. Industries include food processing, metallurgy, engineering, chemical production, and textiles; forestry and fishing are also important. Tourism is becoming increasingly important. Economic sanctions (1965–79) led to diversification of the economy, which has been adversely affected in recent years by drought and by internal financial crises. In 1990 a series of economic reforms began under a World Bank programme.

History. Administered by the British South Africa company from 1889, Southern Rhodesia became a self-governing British colony in 1923. It was temporarily reunited with Northern Rhodesia (now Zambia) to form part of the Federation of Rhodesia and Nyasaland (1953–63). The following year the ruling White minority of what was now known as Rhodesia sought independence, but Britain refused to grant this unless Black majority rule was to be guaranteed within a definite period. Led by its prime minister, Ian Smith, Rhodesia issued a unilateral declaration of independence (UDI) in 1965, which was countered by the imposition of economic sanctions by Britain and the UN. Smith was eventually forced to concede the principle of Black majority rule (1979), and after an unsuccessful attempt to introduce this under the moderate Bishop Muzorewa, whose government was opposed by the other two nationalist parties (ZANU and ZAPU), elections were held under British supervision in 1980. These resulted in victory for the ZANU party and the formal granting of independence to the country. The merging of ZANU and ZAPU in 1987 was designed to create a one-party state. The late 1990s have seen strikes, food riots, and growing pressure for constitutional reform. In 1998 international pressure forced Mugabe to abandon plans to confiscate White farms without compensation. President, Robert Gabriel Mugabe; capital, Harare. □ **Zimbabwean** *adj.* & *n.*

languages	English (official), Shona, Sindebele
currency	dollar (Z$) of 100 cents
pop. (1996)	11 515 000
GNP (1994)	US$5.4B
literacy	90% (m); 79% (f)
life expectancy	58 (m); 62 (f)

clip along them. **b** (*attrib.*) having a zip-fastener (*zip bag*). –*v.* (**-pp-**) **1** (often foll. by *up*) fasten with a zip-fastener. **2** move with zip or at high speed. [imitative]

♦ **Zip code** *n. US* postcode consisting of a five- or nine-digit code, the first five digits indicating the state and postal zone or post office, the last four digits the rural route, building, or other delivery location. [*z*one *i*mprovement *p*lan]

zipper *n.* esp. *US* = ZIP 3a.

zippy *adj.* (**-ier, -iest**) *colloq.* lively, speedy.

zircon /ˈzɜːkən/ *n.* zirconium silicate of which some translucent varieties are cut into gems. [German *Zirkon*]

zirconium /zəˈkəʊnɪəm/ *n.* grey metallic element.

zit *n.* esp. *US slang* pimple. [origin unknown]

zither /ˈzɪðə(r)/ *n.* stringed instrument with a flat soundbox, placed horizontally and played with the fingers and a plectrum. [Latin: related to GUITAR]

ZK *international civil aircraft marking* New Zealand.

Zl *symb.* zloty.

zloty /ˈzlɒtɪ/ *n.* (*pl.* same or **-s**) standard monetary unit of Poland. [Polish]

Zn *symb.* zinc.

zodiac /ˈzəʊdɪˌæk/ *n.* **1** belt of the heavens including all apparent positions of the sun, moon, and planets as known to ancient astronomers, and divided into twelve equal parts (**signs of the zodiac**). **2** diagram of these signs. □ **zodiacal** /zəˈdaɪək(ə)l/ *adj.* [Greek *zōion* animal]

zombie /ˈzɒmbɪ/ *n.* **1** *colloq.* person who acts mechanically or lifelessly. **2** corpse said to have been revived by witchcraft. [West African]

zone –*n.* **1** area having particular features, properties, purpose, or use (*danger zone*; *smokeless zone*). **2** well-defined region of more or less beltlike form. **3** area between two concentric circles. **4** encircling band of colour etc. **5** *archaic* belt, girdle. –*v.* (**-ning**) **1** encircle as or with a zone. **2** arrange or distribute by zones. **3** assign as or to a particular area. □ **zonal** *adj.* [Greek *zōnē* girdle]

zonked /zɒŋkt/ *adj. slang* (often foll. by *out*) exhausted; intoxicated. [*zonk* hit]

zoo *n.* zoological garden. [abbreviation]

zoological /ˌzəʊəˈlɒdʒɪk(ə)l, ˌzuːə-/ *adj.* of zoology.

■ **Usage** See note at *zoology*.

zoological garden *n.* (also **zoological gardens** *n.pl.*) public garden or park with a collection of animals for exhibition and study.

zoology /zəʊˈɒlədʒɪ, ˌzuːˈɒl-/ *n.* the study of animals. □ **zoologist** *n.* [Greek *zōion* animal]

■ **Usage** The second pronunciation given for *zoology*, *zoological*, and *zoologist*, with the first syllable pronounced as in *zoo*, although extremely common, is considered incorrect by some people.

zoom –*v.* **1** move quickly, esp. with a buzzing sound. **2** cause an aeroplane to mount at high speed and a steep angle. **3** (often foll. by *in* or *in on*) (of a camera) change rapidly from a long shot to a close-up (of). **4** (of prices etc.) rise sharply. –*n.* **1** aeroplane's steep climb. **2** zooming camera shot. [imitative]

zoom lens *n.* lens allowing a camera to zoom by varying the focal length.

zoophyte /ˈzəʊəˌfaɪt/ *n.* plantlike animal, esp. a coral, sea anemone, or sponge. [Greek *zōion* animal, *phuton* plant]

Zoroastrian /ˌzɒrəʊˈæstrɪən/ (also **Zarathustrian** /ˌzærəˈθʊstrɪən/) –*adj.* of Zoroaster (or Zarathustra) or the dualistic religious system taught by him. –*n.* follower of Zoroaster. □ **Zoroastrianism** *n.* [*Zoroaster*, Persian founder of the religion]

ZP *international civil aircraft marking* Paraguay.

ZQ *airline flight code* Ansett New Zealand.

Zr *symb.* zirconium.

ZS *international civil aircraft marking* South Africa.

zucchini /zuːˈkiːnɪ/ *n.* (*pl.* same or **-s**) esp. *US* & *Austral.* courgette. [Italian, pl. of *zucchino*, diminutive of *zucca* gourd]

Zuider Zee /ˌzaɪdə ˈziː/ large shallow inlet of the North Sea in the Netherlands, large parts of which have been reclaimed for agricultural use.

Zulu /ˈzuːluː/ –*n.* (*pl.* **-s**) **1** member of a S African Bantu people. **2** their language. –*adj.* of this people or language. [native name]

Zululand see KWAZULU.

Zürich /ˈzjʊərɪk/ largest city in Switzerland, a centre of commerce, banking, and insurance with heavy engineering and other industries; pop. (est. 1995) 342 872.

ZW *international vehicle registration* Zimbabwe.

Zwickau /ˈtsvɪkaʊ/ mining and industrial city in SE Germany; manufactures include motor vehicles, chemicals, and machinery; pop. (est. 1995) 104 921.

zygote /ˈzaɪgəʊt/ *n. Biol.* cell formed by the union of two gametes. [Greek *zugōtos* yoked: related to ZEUGMA]

APPENDICES

Appendix I

Checklist for a Business Plan

A business plan would usually be expected to provide information about:

1. The nature, objectives, and (if appropriate) the history of the business
2. The personnel employed (or to be employed)
3. The product(s) or service(s) to be sold in relation to the market
4. The prospective premises
5. The plant and/or equipment required
6. A forecast of the sales, year by year, or month by month (as appropriate), for three, five, or ten years
7. A financial summary giving the source of funds, expected setting-up expenses, and running expenses in a detailed cash-flow projection covering, for example, three years in detail and a further two years in outline.
8. A forecast of the profitability of the enterprise.

1. The business

The following details could be given:

a. Personal details For the founder, proprietor, partners, directors, or other instigators of the business state each person's name, address, age, and profession if it is relevant to the business. Some details of their background and experience should also be given.

b. Structure of the business State whether the business is or will be set up as a sole trader, a partnership, or a limited company.

c. Description of the business activities Describe the product or service the business will offer for sale and to what extent (if at all) it will manufacture the product.

d. Commencement date State the date on which trading will start (for a new business) and why this date has been selected.

e. Objectives State what the business is expected to achieve in general terms of sales and profitability, referring to a more detailed analysis in sections 6 and 7.

f. History of the business A new business will probably have no history; however, something should be said of how it came into being. A restructured business or a business seeking new capital will have a history and this should be given here, paying special attention to any mergers or takeovers.

2. Personnel

State the number of employees (other than directors, partners, founders, etc). For all senior personnel give names, ages, qualifications, position within the company, and salary. If no staff are currently employed but some will be required for the business to trade, state the numbers it is proposed to recruit and their salaries as accurately as possible. An overall plan of staff requirements, together with any further recruitment or redundancies, should be given. If this requires considerable detail it should be given in an appendix.

3. The product(s) or service(s) in relation to the market

a. Product or service details Provide details of all products and their proposed sale prices. State the pricing policy, taking into account the price and quality of competing products or services.

b. Market details State the nature of the market; whether it is growing, declining, static, or seasonal. Give brief details of any market testing undertaken and profiles of intended customers. If substantial orders, or letters stating an intent to place substantial orders, have been received, copies should be attached. State if any market research has been undertaken.

c. The competition Give the names of major competitors, their pricing policy, strengths, weaknesses, location, etc. State the way in which the company's products or services will be better than those of competitors and any other salient information on overcoming competition.

d. Proposed marketing methods Give details of proposed methods of marketing your products or services and the cost of implementation. Include in your budgeted expenditure a figure for advertising. If advertising and PR are important to your sales plan, give details in an appendix.

e. Suppliers Give details of your principal suppliers as well as alternative sources of supply. Give a brief account of the justifications and advantages in using the chosen supplier. If you have any letters from suppliers that could be of interest to a possible backer, attach copies.

4. The Premises

a. Property type State whether the premises of both offices and any manufacturing or storage units will be leased or bought. If the premises are to be leased, state the length of the lease, whether there is an option to renew, the present rent, and the frequency of rent reviews. Mention should also be made of who bears responsibility for internal and external repairs. If the premises are owned state the purchase price and when it was bought.

If a valuer's report has been obtained for either leasehold or freehold property, a copy should be provided. If the property is freehold its written-down value in the balance sheet should be given. In both leasehold and freehold property the amounts payable in rates should be stated.

b. Specifications State the overall size of the premises and how it is (or is to be) subdivided, e.g. production space, storage space, retailing space, office space. If appropriate, supply a plan.

5. Equipment required

If the business manufactures or is intended to manufacture its product(s), it may be useful to give a brief outline here of the process involved.

a. Manufacturing equipment Details should be given of equipment already owned, including the purchase price, depreciation, and current value. Also give financial details of any manufacturing equipment currently hired, leased, or borrowed. Add a note concerning the cost of servicing equipment owned (mentioning any guarantees) or (if appropriate) leased.

b. General trading equipment Give details of any equipment owned for trading purposes, e.g. cash tills, company vans or cars, including the depreciation, present value, and purchase price. Mention any such items leased or borrowed, stating rental paid and terms of leasing.

c. Equipment on hire purchase Give details of any equipment currently being bought on hire purchase, the date and terms of the contract, and the amounts already paid.

d. Equipment required Give details of all equipment that it is intended to purchase, either to commence trading or to increase existing production. State the prices, leasing arrangements, and source of funds.

6. Sales forecasts

The business plan should state how the sales are to be achieved, with details of any distribution network. Discounts and agency fees should be stated and a breakdown of the sale price in the form of a pie chart is often useful. Provide a detailed forecast of sales either on a monthly basis, if this is feasible, or on a quarterly or annual basis if this is more appropriate. The sales forecasts should be projected as far into the future as possible (certainly three years but longer if a sensible forecast can be made). These figures will form the all-important basis of the cash-flow projections (see 7. below)

7. Financial Summary

The financial summary of a new business will consist of three documents:

a. a statement of the source of funds

b. a cash-flow projection for at least three years

c. a projection of profits for at least three years.

For a restructured business or a business seeking new capital the supporting documents should also include:

d. copies of the balance sheets and profit and loss accounts for at least the past three years.

a. Source of funds

For an existing business the capital structure should be given. This may consist of shares, loan stock, and debt. The long-term debt may consist of debentures, while the short-term debt may be in the form of bank loans. For a new business, the intended capital structure should be outlined together with a list of shareholders, stock and debenture holders, etc.

For a business seeking new capital, the requirements should be stated precisely and the form of security offered should be given.

b. Cash-flow projection

This is probably the most important part of the business plan. If the plan is to be credible, it is essential that the cash-flow projection should not contain any estimates or items that cannot be substantiated at least as fair and likely. For a convincing business plan the cash-flow projection might cover the first three years in detail and the next two years in less detail. If an outline projection for ten years can be provided the picture becomes increasingly credible.

c. An estimate of the profitability over at least three years should be given. This should be realistic, even if it shows that the venture is unlikely to be profitable in its initial year (or two).

Useful addresses (UK)

The Registrar of Companies & Ltd Partnerships
(Board of Trade)
Companies House
City Road
London
EC1
tel 0171 253 9393

Department of Trade and Industry
1 Victoria Street
London
SW1H 0ET
tel 0171 215 5000

Most High-Street banks now run small-business schemes, which will be able to offer some advice. In addition there are 82 independent Training and Enterprise Councils in England and Wales. In Scotland there are 22 Local Enterprise Companies.

Appendix II

Compiling Graphs and Charts

Graphs and charts are of great use in simplifying the presentation of large amounts of complex data. Graphs and charts may either be drawn by hand or generated by computer software from data entered in tabular form. For business users simple graphical facilities are provided by spreadsheet packages, which enable the data in a spreadsheet to be represented graphically.

Before compiling a chart or graph it is necessary to choose the type of pictorial representation that best suits the information to be imparted, as some graphs or charts are better suited to certain purposes than others.

When preparing a graph or chart it is advisable to concentrate on important points of information and avoid unnecessary detail; a fussy or ill-prepared graph can be more difficult to interpret than the original data. The main types of graphs and charts are:

Line graphs

This type of graph is especially useful for displaying large amounts of information and for simultaneous monitoring of several related pieces of data, such as sales. A simple line graph may look like this:

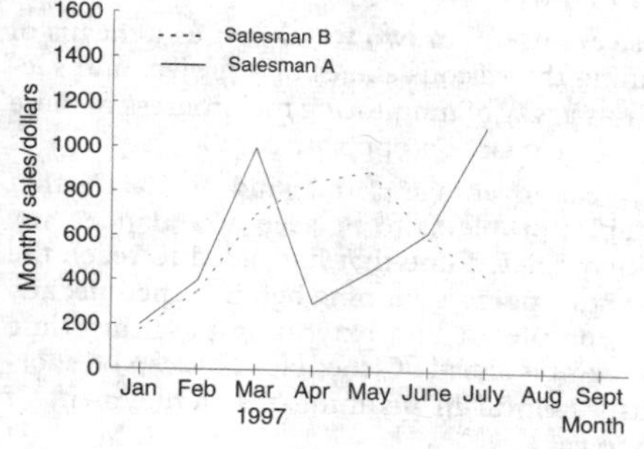

In all cases the clear labelling of the axes of a graph is essential. Always give the precise units in which the quantity is measured. If a mathematical or scientific analysis is likely to be involved, the relationship

quantity = number × unit

should be borne in mind. For example,

monthly sales = 500 dollars

Treating this statement as an equation, the axis showing the monthly sales should be marked:

monthly sales/dollars

Pictogram

This type of pictorial representation is valuable when presenting figures to the general public because of its clarity and simplicity. To be truly effective, however, the icons used should all be of equal size – increasing amounts should be represented by additional, rather than larger, icons. For example:

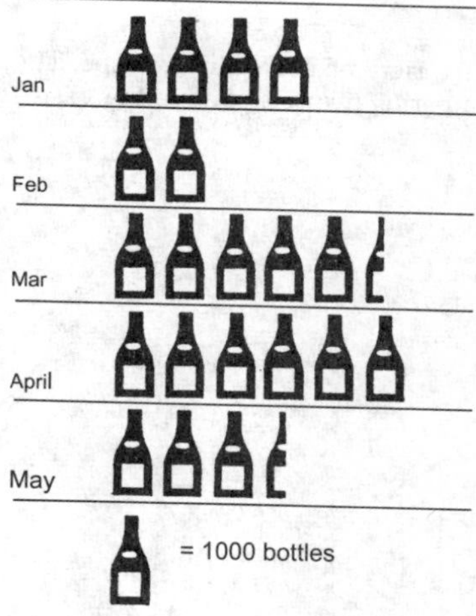

Pie charts

These are especially useful when it is necessary to show the parts of something in relation to the whole. Pie charts do not cope well with large amounts of information and it is best not to overcrowd them; using any more than five or six divisions involves a loss of visual impact. For example, the age range of all the customers of a particular shop could be shown by a pie chart (Fig. A).

Fig. A. Customers' range of ages

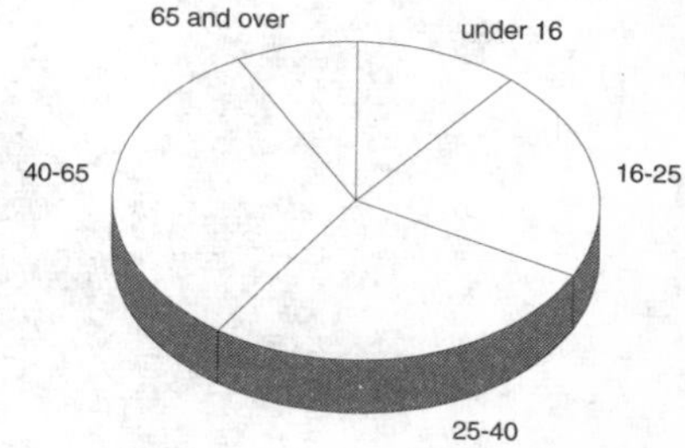

There are two possible ways of highlighting sections of a pie chart: by tinting a section, or by extracting one of the sections (as in Fig. B).

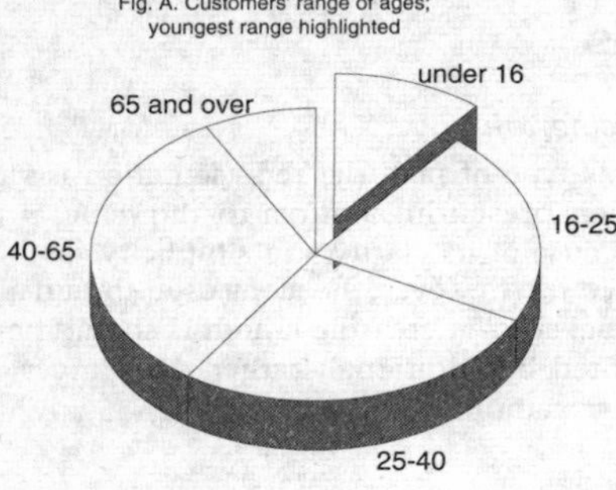

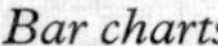

Bar charts

These have a variety of uses, but are especially useful for comparing two sets of data. For example, sales.

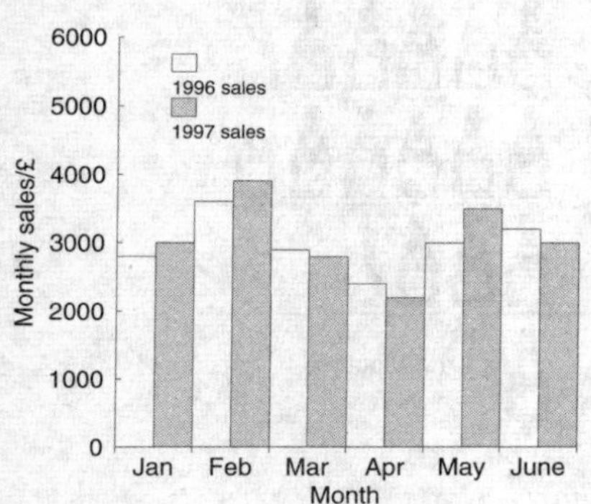

Clear labelling of the diagram itself and of the axes is again essential.

Deviation charts

These are useful for data comparison and have the advantage of being able to show negative performance: for example, the profitability of sales teams.

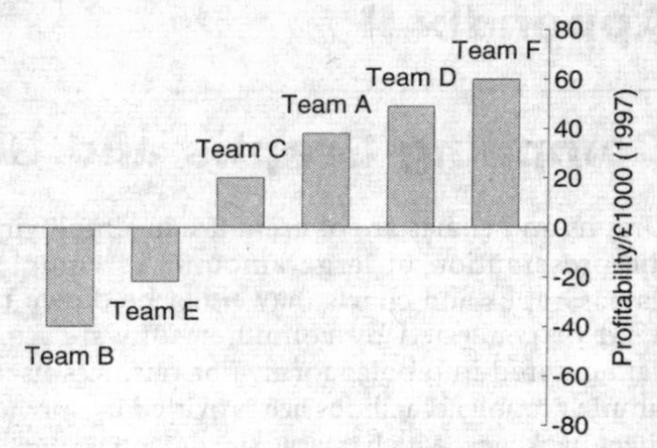

Histogram

This specialized form of chart is most useful for displaying frequency distribution: for example, time taken for orders to be dispatched in a specified period.

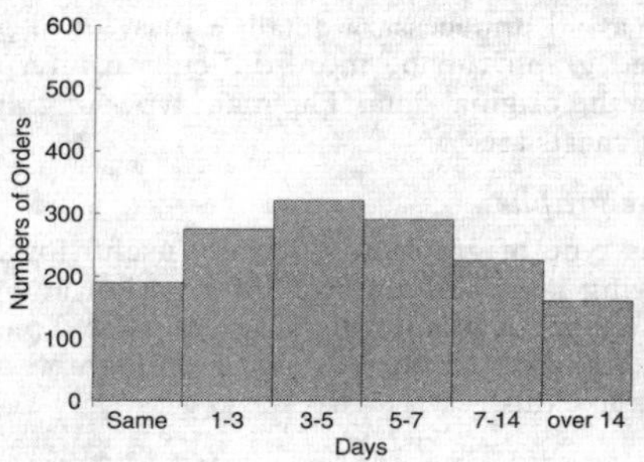

Gantt charts

These are useful in two ways, first as a means of planning the various stages of a project and secondly as a way of monitoring the progress of these stages (see chart on opposite page).

The great advantage of this kind of chart is that it enables problems to be seen at a glance. Any work-completed line that has failed to reach the 'time now' point is running behind schedule; any work-completed line extending past the 'time now' point is ahead of schedule. This can be enormously helpful in planning the deployment of manpower.

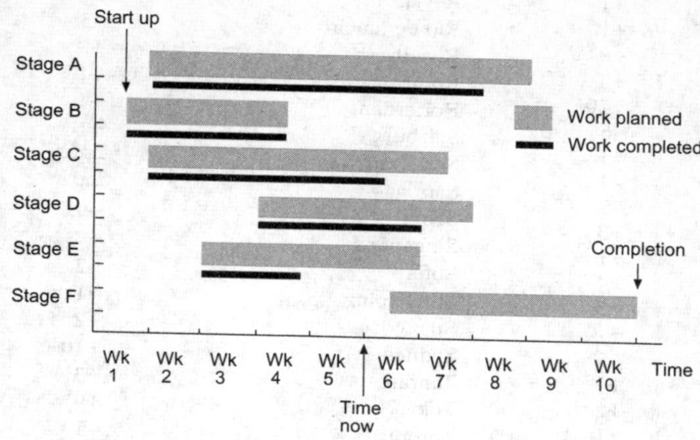

Appendix III

World Times *Deviations from* Greenwich Mean Time (GMT)

Abu Dhabi	+4
Accra	0
Adelaide	+9½
Algiers	0
Amman	+2
Amsterdam	+1
Ankara	+1
Athens	+1
Auckland	+12
Baghdad	+3
Bahrain	+3
Bangkok	+5
Barbados	–4
Barcelona	+1
Beirut	+2
Belgrade	+1
Berlin	+1
Bermuda	–4
Berne	+1
Bombay	+5½
Bonn	+1
Brindisi	+1
Brisbane	+10
Brussels	+1
Bucharest	+2
Budapest	+1
Buenos Aires	–3
Cairo	+2
Calcutta	+5½
Canberra	+10
Cape Town	+2
Caracas	–4
Chicago	–6
Copenhagen	+1
Dallas	–6½
Damascus	+3
Darwin	+9½
Delhi	+5½
Detroit	–5
Dhaka	+6½
Doha	+3
Dubai	+4
Dublin	0
Dusseldorf	+1
Frankfurt	+1
Geneva	+1
Gibraltar	+1
Gothenburg	+1
Hanoi	+7
Helsinki	+2
Hobart	+10
Hong Kong	+8
Honolulu	–10
Islamabad	+5
Istanbul	+3
Jakarta	+8
Jamaica	–5
Jerusalem	+2
Johannesburg	+2
Karachi	+5½
Kuala Lumpur	+7½
Kuwait	+3
Lagos	+1
Lima	–5
Lisbon	0
London	0
Los Angeles	–8
Luxembourg	+1
Madeira	–1
Madras	+5½

Madrid	+1
Malta	+1
Manila	+8
Mauritius	+4
Melbourne	+10
Mexico City	−6
Milan	+1
Montevideo	−3
Montreal	−5
Moscow	+3
Munich	+1
Muscat	+4
Nairobi	+3
Naples	+1
New York	−5
Nice	+1
Nicosia	+2
Oslo	+1
Ottawa	−5
Palma	+1
Panama	−5
Paris	+1
Peking	+8
Perth	+8
Prague	+1
Pretoria	+2
Quebec	−5
Rabat	0
Rangoon	+6½
Rawalpindi	+5
Reykjavik	0
Rio de Janeiro	−3
Riyadh	+3
Rome	+1
Rotterdam	+1
Salzburg	+1
San Francisco	−8
Santiago	−4
Seoul	+9
Singapore	+7½
Sofia	+2
Stockholm	+1
Suez	+2
Sydney	+10
Tehran	+3½
Tokyo	+9
Toronto	−5
Tripoli	+2
Tunis	+1
Turin	+1
Vancouver	−8
Venice	+1
Vienna	+1
Warsaw	+1
Washington	−5
Wellington	+12
Winnipeg	−6
Zürich	+1

Appendix IV

Some Points of English Usage

1. Meanings

The following words are often used wrongly or carelessly, or confused with other similar words.

affect/effect

Both these words are both verbs and nouns, but only **effect** is common as a noun, usually meaning 'a result, consequence, impression, etc.', e.g. *My father's strictness had no effect on my desire to learn.* As verbs they are used differently. **Affect** means 'to produce an effect upon', e.g. *Smoking during pregnancy can affect a baby's development.* **Effect** means 'to bring about', e.g. *Alterations were effected with some sympathy for the existing fabric.*

aggravate

This word is commonly used in informal contexts to mean 'to annoy or exasperate', rather than 'to make worse or more serious'; this is considered incorrect by many people. An example of correct usage is *The psychological stress aggravates the horse's physical stress.*

alibi

The chief meaning of this word is 'evidence that when something took place one was elsewhere', e.g. *He has no alibi for Wednesday afternoon.* It is also sometimes used informally to mean 'an excuse, pretext, or justification'; this is considered incorrect by many people.

all right/alright

Although found widely, **alright** remains non-standard, even where standard spelling is somewhat cumbersome, e.g. *I wanted to make sure it was all all right.*

all together/altogether

These variants are used in different contexts. **All together** means 'all at once' or 'all in one place or in one group', e.g. *They came all together*; *We managed to get three bedrooms all* *together* (i.e. near each other). **Altogether** means 'in total', e.g. *The hotel has twenty rooms altogether.*

alternate/alternative

These words should not be confused. In British English **alternate** means 'every other', e.g. *There will be a dance on alternate Saturdays*, whereas **alternative** means 'available as another choice', e.g. *an alternative route*. In American usage, however, **alternate** can be used to mean 'available as another choice'.

altogether see all together.

amend/emend

Amend, meaning 'to make improvements or corrections in', is often confused with **emend**, a more technical word used in the context of textual correction. Examples of each are: *The policy, in popular and amended form, was offered to the electorate in early 1929; The poems have been collected, arranged, and emended.*

anticipate

Anticipate in the sense 'to expect, foresee' is well-established in informal use (e.g. *He anticipated a restless night*), but is regarded as incorrect by some people. The formal sense, 'to deal with or use before the proper time', is illustrated by the sentence *The specialist would find that the thesis he had been planning had already been anticipated.*

antisocial, unsociable, unsocial

These words are often confused. There is some overlap in meaning but, in general, **antisocial** is used to describe behaviour which harms society, **unsociable** refers to a person who dislikes being in the company of others, and **unsocial** is used in the phrase *unsocial hours* meaning 'hours outside normal working hours'. **Unsociable** can also be used in the phrase *unsociable hours*, but *unsocial hours* is preferable.

anyone/any one

Anyone is written as two words only to emphasize a numerical sense, e.g. *Any one of us can do it.* Otherwise it is written as one word (e.g. *Anyone who wants to can come*).

Arab/Arabian

Arab is now the usual term for a native of Arabia. **Arabian** is generally used as an adjective, especially in geographical contexts (e.g. *Arabian peninsula*).

baluster/banister

These words are sometimes confused. A **baluster** is usually part of a balustrade, whereas a **banister** supports the handrail of a staircase.

beg the question

This phrase is often used to mean (1) to evade a difficulty, or (2) to pose or invite the question (that ...), instead of (3) to assume the truth of an argument or proposition to be proved. (1) and (2) are considered incorrect by many people.

born/borne

Born is used with reference to birth (e.g. *was born in Dublin*), except for *borne by* followed by the name of the mother (e.g. *was borne by Mary*). **Borne** is used in other senses (e.g. *a litter borne by four slaves*).

censor/censure

Both these words are both verbs and nouns, but **censor** is used to mean 'to cut unacceptable parts out of a book, film, etc.' or 'a person who does this', while **censure** means 'to criticize harshly' or 'harsh criticism'.

chronic

This word is sometimes used to mean 'very bad', e.g. *The film was chronic*, or 'habitual, inveterate', e.g. *a chronic liar*. The former use is extremely informal whereas the latter is considered to be incorrect by some people. The correct meaning of this word is 'persisting for a long time' and it is used chiefly of illnesses or other problems, e.g. *Over one million people in the UK have chronic bronchitis.*

complacent/complaisant

Complacent means 'smugly self-satisfied', e.g. *The British are still largely complacent about their eating habits*, while **complaisant**, a much rarer word, means 'deferential, willing to please', e.g. *When unharnessed, the dogs are very peaceful and complaisant.*

compose/comprise

Both these words can be used to mean 'to constitute or make up' but **compose** is preferred in this sense, e.g. *Citizens act as witnesses in the courts and finally may compose the jury.* **Comprise** is correctly used to mean 'to be composed of, consist of', e.g. *Each crew comprises a commander, a gunner, and a driver.*

condole/console

Condole is sometimes confused with **console** but is much rarer. It is usually used with *with* and means 'to express sympathy with', e.g. *Her friends came to condole with her.* **Console** means 'to comfort in grief or disappointment', e.g. *They consoled themselves with the thought that they wouldn't have enjoyed the concert anyway.*

continual/continuous

Continual is used of something that happens very frequently, e.g. *There were continual interruptions,* whereas **continuous** is used of something that happens without pause, e.g. *There was a dull, continuous background noise.*

credible/credulous

The adjective **credible** means 'believable' or 'convincing' and can be applied to a situation, statement, policy, or threat to a person. **Credulous** means 'too ready to believe, gullible' and is usually used to describe a person.

crucial

Crucial is used in formal contexts to mean 'decisive, critical', e.g. *The first five years of a child's life are crucial.* Its use to mean 'very important', as in *It is crucial not to forget your passport,* should be restricted to informal contexts.

decimate

The usual sense of this word is now 'to destroy a large proportion of'. This use is considered inappropriate by some people because the original and literal sense is 'to kill or remove one in ten of'. In any case, this word should not be used to mean 'to defeat utterly'.

definite/definitive

Definitive in the sense '(of an answer, verdict, etc.) decisive, unconditional, final' is sometimes confused with **definite**. However, **definite** does not have the connotations of authority: *a definite no* is simply a firm refusal, whereas *a definitive no* is an authoritative judgement or decision that something is not the case.

deprecate/depreciate

Deprecate means 'to express disapproval of, to deplore', e.g. *The establishment magazines began by deprecating the film's free and easy attitudes to drugs and sex,* while **depreciate** (apart from its financial senses) means 'to disparage or belittle', e.g. *Writing to her sister soon after the auction, Virginia was already depreciating her own aesthetic taste.*

dilemma

This word should be used with regard to situations in which a difficult choice has to be made between undesirable alternatives, as in *You see his dilemma? Whatever he did next, his wife would find out, divorce him, and get custody of the child.* Its use to mean simply 'a difficult situation' is considered incorrect by some people.

disinterested/uninterested

Disinterested is sometimes used in informal contexts to mean 'not interested or uninterested', but this is widely regarded as incorrect. The proper meaning is 'impartial', e.g. *I for one am making a disinterested search for information.* The use of the noun **disinterest** to mean 'a lack of interest' is also objected to, but it is rarely used in any other sense and the alternative **uninterest** is rare.

effect see affect.

emend see amend.

emotional/emotive

Although the senses of these two words overlap, **emotive** is more common in the sense 'arousing emotion', e.g. *Drug use is an emotive issue,* and is not used at all to describe a person as being liable to excessive emotion.

enormity

This word is commonly used to mean 'great size', e.g. *wilting under the enormity of the work,* but this is regarded as incorrect by some people. The original and preferred meaning is 'extreme wickedness', as in *the enormity of the crime.*

exceptionable/exceptional

Exceptionable means 'open to objection', e.g. *There was nothing exceptionable in her behaviour,* and is usually found in negative contexts. It is sometimes confused with the much commoner word **exceptional** meaning 'unusual, outstanding'.

feasible

The correct meaning of this word is 'practicable' or 'possible', e.g. *Walking all night was not feasible without the aid of moon or torch.* It should not be used to mean 'likely' or 'probable'.

flammable see inflammable.

flaunt/flout

These words are often confused because both suggest an element of arrogance or showing off. However, **flaunt** means 'to display ostentatiously', e.g. *He liked to flaunt his wealth,* while **flout** means 'to express contempt for or disobey (laws, convention, etc.)', e.g. *The fine is too low for those who flout the law continuously.*

-fuls/-s full

The combining form **-ful** is used to form nouns meaning 'the amount needed to fill', e.g. *cupful, spoonful.* The plural form of such words is **-s**, (*cupfuls, spoonfuls,* etc.). *Three cups full* would denote the individual cups rather than a quantity regarded in terms of a cup used as a measure, and would be used in contexts such as *They brought us three cups full of water.*

fulsome

This word means 'excessive, cloying, or insincere', but is sometimes misunderstood as meaning 'generous' in the phrase *fulsome praise.*

hoi polloi

This phrase is usually preceded by *the*, e.g. *The hoi polloi grew weary and sat on the floor.* Strictly speaking, the *the* is unnecessary because *hoi* means 'the' (in Greek).

hopefully

Strictly speaking, this word should be used only to mean 'in a hopeful manner', e.g. *Robert peered hopefully into the fridge.* However, it is also very commonly used to mean 'it is to be hoped', e.g. *Hopefully, all the details will be in this evening's newspapers.* This usage is considered incorrect by some people.

impedance/impediment

Impedance is a specialized electrical term, while **impediment** is an everyday term meaning 'a hindrance or obstruction', e.g. *He would have to write by hand but that was no impediment.*

imply see **infer.**

inchoate

This word means 'just begun or rudimentary, undeveloped', e.g. *All was as yet in an inchoate state*, but it is often used incorrectly to mean 'chaotic' or 'incoherent'.

infer/imply

Infer should be used to mean 'to deduce or conclude', as in *We can infer from these studies that* .... Its use to mean 'to imply or suggest' is widely considered incorrect.

inflammable/flammable/non-flammable

Both **inflammable** and **flammable** mean 'easily set on fire or excited'. The opposite is **non-flammable**. Where there is a danger of **inflammable** being understood to mean the opposite, i.e. 'not easily set on fire', **flammable** can be used to avoid confusion.

ingenious/ingenuous

These words are sometimes confused. **Ingenious** means 'clever, skilful, or resourceful', e.g. *an ingenious device*, while **ingenuous** means 'artless' or 'frank', e.g. *She is both ingenuous and sophisticated by turns.*

intense/intensive

Intense is sometimes wrongly used instead of **intensive** to describe a course of study which consists in covering a large amount of material in a short space of time.

interface

The use of **interface** to mean 'a place or means of interaction', e.g. *Experts looked at the crucial interface between broadcasters and independents*, or as a verb meaning 'to interact', e.g. *courses where business executives interface with nature at great expense*, is deplored by some people.

interment/internment

Interment means 'the burial of a corpse', while **internment** means 'the confining of a prisoner, etc.'.

latter

This word means 'the second-mentioned of two'. Its use to mean 'the last-mentioned of three or more' is common, but considered incorrect by some people since *latter* means 'later' rather than 'latest'. **Last** or **last-mentioned** is to be preferred where three or more things are involved.

laudable/laudatory

These words are sometimes confused. **Laudable** is the more common and means 'commendable' or 'praiseworthy', e.g. *The Orthodox Palestinian Society pursued a laudable charitable programme which involved the foundation and maintenance of schools and hospitals.* **Laudatory** means 'expressing praise', e.g. *The new manifesto enjoyed a good reception – including a laudatory front-page endorsement from London's only daily newspaper.*

lay/lie

In standard English **lay** is a transitive verb and **lie** intransitive. The intransitive use of **lay**, as in *It gave him the opportunity of laying on the grass at lunchtime*, is incorrect. Similarly, the transitive use of **lie**, as in *Lie it on the table*, is also incorrect. In the first example *laying* should be *lying* and in the second *lie* should be *lay*. The noun meaning 'a prolonged stay in bed in the morning' is **lie-in**; **lay-in** is incorrect.

leading question

This phrase means 'a question that prompts the answer wanted' and was originally a legal term. In weakened use it tends to mean 'an awkward, pointed, or loaded question', or even 'principal question', but these usages are considered incorrect by some people.

liable

This word is commonly used with *to* to mean 'likely to do something undesirable', e.g. *Without his glasses he's liable to smash into a tree.* This usage is considered incorrect by some people. Correct usage is exemplified by the sentence *You could be liable for a heavy fine if you are caught out.*

lie see lay.

like

The use of **like** as a conjunction meaning 'as' or 'as if', e.g. *I don't have a posh set of in-laws like you do*; *They sit up like they're begging for food*, is considered incorrect by some people.

locate

In standard English it is not acceptable to use **locate** to mean merely 'to find', e.g. *It drives him out of his mind when he can't locate something.* **Locate** should be used more precisely to mean 'to discover the exact place or position of', e.g. *One club member was proposing to use an echo sounder to help locate fish in the lake.*

luxuriant/luxurious

These words are sometimes confused. **Luxuriant** means 'lush, profuse, or prolific', e.g. *forests of dark luxuriant foliage*; *luxuriant black eyelashes.* **Luxurious**, a much commoner word, means 'supplied with luxuries, extremely comfortable', e.g. *a luxurious hotel.*

masterful/masterly

These words overlap in meaning and are sometimes confused. Apart from meaning 'domineering', **masterful** also means 'masterly' or 'very skilful'. However, **masterful** is generally used in this sense to describe a person, e.g. *He's just got a marginal talent he's masterful at exploiting*, while **masterly** usually describes and achievement or action, e.g. *This was a masterly realization of the score.*

militate/mitigate

These words are often confused but have quite different meanings. **Militate** means 'to have force or effect' and is usually used with *against*, e.g. *The rules militated against the weak, the infirm, or even the well-mannered.* **Mitigate**, on the other hand, means 'to make milder or less severe', e.g. *His disappointment was mitigated by the generous offer of a free holiday.*

mutual

This word is sometimes used with no sense of reciprocity, simply to mean 'common to two or more people', as in *a mutual friend*; *a mutual interest.* Such use is considered incorrect by some people, for whom **common** is preferable.

non-inflammable see inflammable.

off/off of

The use of **off of** to mean **off**, e.g. *He took the cup off of the table*, is non-standard and to be avoided.

perquisite/prerequisite

These words are sometimes confused. **Perquisite** usually means 'an extra benefit or privilege', e.g. *There were no perquisites attached to their offices, apart from one or two special privileges.* **Prerequisite** means 'something required as a precondition', e.g. *An education in the sciences is a prerequisite of medical training.*

plus

The use of **plus** as a conjunction meaning 'and furthermore', e.g. *plus we will be pleased to give you personal financial advice*, is considered incorrect by many people.

prerequisite see perquisite.

prescribe/proscribe

These words are sometimes confused, but they are opposite in meaning. **Prescribe** means 'to advise the use of' or 'impose authoritatively', whereas **proscribe** means 'to reject, denounce, or ban'. Examples of each are as follows:

The teachers would prescribe topics to be dealt with.

She proscribed all religious, philosophical, or psychological books for village libraries.

A regime which both prescribes and proscribes literature.

prevaricate/procrastinate

Prevaricate means 'to act or speak evasively', e.g. *When I was asked what subject I was reading, I knew I would have to prevaricate or face problems.* It is sometimes confused with **procrastinate** which means 'to postpone or put off an action', e.g. *He hesitates and procrastinates until the time for action is over.*

proscribe see prescribe.

protagonist

The correct meaning of this word is 'chief or leading person', e.g. *The choreographer must create movements which display each protagonist's particular behaviour and reactions.* However, it is also used, usually with *of* or *for*, to mean 'an advocate or champion of a cause etc.', e.g. … *the flawed economics of the nuclear protagonists' case.*

proved/proven

The usual past participle of *prove* is **proved**.

Proven is uncommon except in certain expressions such as *of proven ability, proven reliability*, and *proven success*. It is, however, standard in Scots and American English.

refute/repudiate

Strictly speaking, **refute** means 'to prove (a person or statement) to be wrong', e.g. *No amount of empirical research can either confirm or refute it*. However, it is also sometimes used to mean 'to deny or repudiate'. This usage is considered incorrect by some people.

scenario

The proper meaning of this word is 'an outline of a plot' or 'a postulated sequence of events'. It should not be used in standard English to mean 'situation', e.g. *a nightmare scenario*.

Scotch/Scots/Scottish

In Scotland the term **Scots** and **Scottish** are preferred to **Scotch** and they mean the same (e.g. *a Scots/Scottish accent, miner, farmer*, etc.). **Scotch** is used in various compound nouns such as *Scotch broth, egg, fir, mist, terrier*, and *whisky*. Similarly, **Scotsman** and **Scotswoman** are preferred to **Scotchman** and **Scotchwoman**.

seasonable/seasonal

Seasonable means 'usual or suitable for the season' or 'opportune', e.g. *Although seasonable, the weather was not suitable for picnics*. **Seasonal** means 'of, depending on, or varying with the season', e.g. *Seasonal changes posed problems for mills situated on larger rivers*.

sensual/sensuous

These two words are of similar meaning and are often, therefore, confused. Both mean 'of the senses', but **sensual** means 'of the senses as opposed to the intellect or spirit' and has sexual overtones while **sensuous** is used with regard to the senses aesthetically rather than physically. Examples illustrate this difference:

The smoke-filled room was invaded by sexy, sensual snarls of guitars and harmonicas.

The shadowy interior is a sensuous baroque mix of gilt and candle wax.

thankfully

The most common use of this word is in the sense 'fortunately, let us be thankful', e.g. *Thankfully, the damage was minimal*. This usage is still considered incorrect by some people (cf. **hopefully**). The strict sense of this word is 'in a thankful or grateful manner', e.g. *He heaped a plate for him and Cameron took it thankfully*.

'til/till see until.

tortuous/torturous

These words sound similar but have different meanings. **Tortuous** means 'full of twists and turns' or 'devious, circuitous', e.g. *Both paths have proved tortuous and are strewn with awkward boulders; He got into a tortuous discussion about the cubic capacity of the engine of the car*.

Torturous is the adjective which relates to *torture* and means 'involving torture, excruciating', e.g. *The experience had become pure music, each note torturous yet unbearably sweet*.

triumphal/triumphant

These words are sometimes confused. The more common, **triumphant**, means 'victorious' or 'exultant', e.g. *She had chaired a difficult meeting through to its triumphant conclusion; Rosie returned triumphant with the file and the man went away*.

Triumphal means 'used in or celebrating a triumph', e.g. *The last element to be added was the magnificent triumphal arch; Any prospect of retaking the Falklands as an uninterrupted triumphal procession was illusory*.

turbid/turgid

Turbid is used of a liquid or colour to mean 'muddy, not clear', or of literary style etc. to mean 'confused', e.g. *the turbid utterances and twisted language of Carlyle*.

Turgid means 'swollen, inflated, or enlarged' but is also often used to describe literary style which is pompous or bombastic, e.g. *Communications arriving at the orderly room were largely turgid documents in "Whitehallese" from the War Office*.

unexceptionable see exceptionable.

unsociable/unsocial see antisocial.

until/till/'til

Until is more formal than **till**, and is more usual at the beginning of a sentence, e.g. *Until 1921 some elements among the peasantry had kept a certain independence of outlook*.

'Til is considered incorrect in standard English and should be avoided.

venal/venial

These words are sometimes confused. **Venal** means 'corrupt, able to be bribed, or involving bribery', e.g. *The lawcourts are venal and can take decades to decide a case*.

Venial is used among Christians to describe a certain type of sin and means 'pardonable, excusable, not mortal', e.g. *The Reformation had renounced purgatory as an intermediate stage, in which those who had committed venial sins might work their passage to a better world*.

worth while/worthwhile

Worth while (two words) is used only predicatively, e.g. *Nobody had thought it worth while to ring the police*, and means 'worth the time or effort spent'.

Worthwhile (one word) also has this meaning but can be used both predicatively and attributively, e.g. *Only in unusual circumstances would investment be worthwhile* (predicative); *He was a worthwhile subject for the 'cure'* (attributive). In addition, **worthwhile** has the sense 'of value or importance', e.g. *It's great to be doing such a worthwhile job.*

2. Plurals

The most common mistake with regard to the following words is the use of the plural form as if it were the singular.

bacterium (plural **bacteria**)

Bacteria is often used incorrectly instead of **bacterium** for the singular form. Correct usage is as follows:

A close relative of E. coli *is salmonella, a bacterium whose primary habitat is the intestines of birds* (singular); *New close-up filming techniques reveal lice, mites, and bacteria stalking the landscape of the human body* (plural).

criterion (plural **criteria**)

Many people use **criteria** as if it were the singular form. Examples of correct usage are:

Many borrowers choose an appealing discount deal as the sole criterion when they take out a loan (singular); *Aesthetic criteria are also clearly important* (plural).

datum (plural **data**)

In general, the singular form is **datum**, not **data**, as shown by the following examples:

The object under scrutiny is compared with an observed or preconceived datum (singular); *The data support a trend that has so far been supported only by anecdotal evidence* (plural).

In the context of computers, **data** is now often used as if it were a singular collective noun (like 'information'), e.g. *You can guarantee that the data is accurate and charges reach you faster than they normally would on the paper system.* This use is acceptable.

In other contexts, **data** should be used (like 'facts') with a plural verb, e.g. *These data do lend some support to the prevailing public opinion.*

die/dice

The form **dice** is now standard for both the singular and plural in the sense 'a cube used in games', e.g. *There was a furry dice hanging from the mirror; The dice were loaded against the Gorbachev reforms.*

Die (plural **dies**) means 'a device for stamping, cutting, or moulding', e.g. *The dies used to make Roman bronze medallions might last for ten years.*

Die (plural **dice**) is an architectural term meaning 'the cubical part of a pedestal between the base and the cornice'.

-fuls/-s full

See Section 1 (**Meanings**).

graffito (plural **graffiti**)

Strictly speaking, **graffiti** should be used only with a plural construction, e.g. *The graffiti were aggressive and insulting.* The singular and collective use is considered incorrect by many people, but is often found, e.g. *The most common graffiti is 'Vive le Roi'.* **Graffito** is the correct singular form, e.g. *The meanest graffito, if fully understood, can be a treasure of human expressiveness.*

medium (plural **media**)

A very common mistake is the use of **media** as a collective noun with a singular verb, especially in the sense 'a means of communication'. Correct usage is as follows: *Loads of my friends are miserable over the way they look, and the media are basically saying, 'Yes, you're right to be miserable'.* INCORRECT usage is shown by the example *I have always found councillors very approachable – very different from the image the media gives them.* In the second example, *gives* should be *give*.

An example of the correct use of the singular is as follows:

Television is the most important medium for getting known by the general public.

phenomenon (plural **phenomena**)

Phenomena is often used wrongly, as if it were the singular form rather than the plural. The following examples illustrate correct usage:

This phenomenon can best be observed in Santander, that most elegant of ferry ports.

Men began to regard these phenomena with more composure.

stratum (plural **strata**)

Strata is often used wrongly, as if it were the singular form rather than the plural. Examples of correct usage are as follows:

Very occasionally a coin can be dated from the other objects in the same stratum.

Below all these strata lay the immemorial peasant base of straight barter.

See also sections ***f* to *v*** and **plural formation** in Section 4 (**Word Formation**).

3. Grammar

as

In the following sentences, formal usage requires the *subjective* case (*I, he, she, we, they*) because the pronoun would be the subject if a verb were supplied:

> *You are just as intelligent as* he (in full, *as he is*)
>
> *He ... might not have heard the motif so often as* I (in full, *as I had*)

Informal usage permits *You are just as intelligent as* him.

Formal English uses the *objective* case (*me, him, her, us, them*) only when the pronoun would be the object if a verb were supplied:

> *I thought you preferred John to Mary, but I see that you like her just as much as* him (which means ... *just as much as you like him*).

collective nouns

Collective nouns are singular words that denote many individuals, e.g. *audience, government, orchestra, the clergy, the public.*

It is normal for collective nouns, being singular, to be followed by singular verbs and pronouns (*is, has, consists*, and *it* in the examples below):

> *The Government* is *determined to beat inflation,* as it has *promised*
>
> *Their family* is *huge*: it consists *of five boys and three girls*
>
> *The bourgeoisie* is *despised for not being proletarian*

The singular verb and pronouns are preferable unless the collective is clearly and unmistakably used to refer to separate individuals rather than to a united body, e.g.

> *The Cabinet has made* its *decision*, but
>
> *The Cabinet* are *resuming* their *places around the table at Number 10 Downing Street*

The singular should always be used if the collective noun is qualified by a singular word like *this, that, every*, etc.:

> *This family* is *divided*
>
> *Every team* has its *chance to win*

• Do not mix singular and plural, as (wrongly) in

> *The congregation* were *now dispersing.* It *tended to form knots and groups*

comparison of adjectives and adverbs

Whether to use *-er, -est* or *more, most.*

The two ways of forming the comparative and superlative of adjectives and adverbs are:

(*a*) The addition of the comparative and superlative suffixes *-er* and *-est.* Monosyllabic adjectives and adverbs almost always require these suffixes, e.g. *big* (*bigger, biggest*), *soon* (*sooner, soonest*), and so normally do many adjectives of two syllables, e.g. *narrow* (*narrower, narrowest*), *silly* (*sillier, silliest*).

(*b*) The placing of the comparative and superlative adverbs *more* and *most* before the adjective or adverb. These are used with adjectives of three syllables or more (e.g. *difficult, memorable*), participles (e.g. *bored, boring*), many adjectives of two syllables (e.g. *afraid, awful, childish, harmless, static*), and adverbs ending in *-ly* (e.g. *highly, slowly*). Adjectives with two syllables vary between the use of the suffixes and of the adverbs.

There are many which never take the suffixes, e.g.

antique	*breathless*	*futile*
bizarre	*constant*	*steadfast*

There is also a large class which is acceptable with either, e.g.

clever	*handsome*	*polite*
common	*honest*	*solemn*
cruel	*pleasant*	*tranquil*
extreme		

The choice is largely a matter of style.

group possessive

The group possessive is the construction by which the ending *-'s* of the possessive case can be added to the last word of a noun phrase, which is regarded as a single unit, e.g.

> *The king of Spain's daughter*
>
> *John and Mary's baby*
>
> *Somebody else's umbrella*
>
> *A quarter of an hour's drive*

Expressions like these are natural and acceptable. Informal language, however, permits the extension of the construction to long and complicated phrases:

> *The people in the house opposite's geraniums*
>
> *The man who called last week's umbrella is still in the hall*

In these, the connection between the words forming the group possessive is much looser and more complicated than in the earlier examples. The effect is often somewhat ludicrous.

• Expressions of this sort should not be used in serious prose. Substitute:

> *The geraniums of the people in the house opposite*
>
> *The umbrella of the man who called last week is still in the hall*

-ics, nouns in

Nouns ending in *-ics* denoting subjects or disciplines are sometimes treated as singular and sometimes as plural. Examples are:

apologetics	*genetics*	*optics*
classics (as a study)	*linguistics*	*phonetics*
	mathematics	*physics*
dynamics	*mechanics*	*politics*
economics	*metaphysics*	*statistics*

electronics *obstetrics* *tactics*
ethics

When used strictly as the name of a discipline they are treated as singular:

Psychometrics is *unable to investigate the nature of intelligence*

So also when the complement is singular:

Mathematics is *his strong point*

When used more loosely, to denote a manifestation of qualities, often accompanied by a possessive, they are treated as plural:

His politics were *a mixture of fear, greed, and envy*

I don't understand the mathematics of it, which are *complicated*

The acoustics in this hall are *dreadful*

So also when they denote a set of activities or pattern of behaviour, as commonly with words like:

acrobatics *dramatics* *heroics*
athletics *gymnastics* *hysterics*

E.g. *The mental gymnastics required to believe this* are *beyond me.*

I or *me*, *we* or *us*, etc.

There is often confusion about which case of a personal pronoun to use when the pronoun stands alone or follows the verb *to be*.

1. When the personal pronoun stands alone, as when it forms the answer to a question, formal usage requires it to have the case it would have if the verb were supplied:

Who killed Cock Robin?—I (in full, *I killed him*)

Which of you did he approach?—Me (in full, *he approached me*)

Informal usage permits the objective case in both kinds of sentence, but this is not acceptable in formal style. It so happens that the subjective case often sounds stilted. It is then best to avoid the problem by providing the substitute verb *do*, or, if the preceding sentence contains an auxiliary, by repeating the auxiliary, e.g.

Who likes cooking?—I do

Who can cook?—I can

2. When a personal pronoun follows *it is*, *it was*, *it may be*, *it could have been*, etc., it should always have the subjective case:

Nobody could suspect that it was she

We are given no clues as to what it must have felt like to be he

Informal usage favours the objective case:

I thought it might have been him *at the door*

Don't tell me it's them *again!*

• This is not acceptable in formal usage.

When *who* or *whom* follows, the subjective case is obligatory in formal usage and quite usual informally:

It was I *who painted the back door purple*

The informal use of the objective case often sounds substandard:

It was her *who would get into trouble*

(For agreement between the personal pronoun antecedent and the verb in *It is I who* etc., see ***I who, you who,* etc.**)

In constructions that have the form *I am* + noun or noun phrase + *who*, the verb following *who* agrees with the noun (the antecedent of *who*) and is therefore always in the third person (singular or plural):

I am the sort of person who likes *peace and quiet*

You are the fourth of my colleagues who's *told me that* (*'s* = *has*, agreeing with *the fourth*)

I should or *I would*

There is often uncertainty whether to use *should* or *would* in the first person singular and plural before verbs such as *like* or *think* and before the adverbs *rather* and *sooner.*

1. *Should* is correct before verbs of liking, e.g. *be glad, be inclined, care, like,* and *prefer*:

Would you like a beer?—I should prefer *a cup of coffee, if you don't mind*

2. *Should* is correct in tentative statements of opinion, with verbs such as *guess, imagine, say,* and *think*:

I should imagine *that you are right*

I shouldn't have thought *it was difficult*

3. *Would* is correct before the adverbs *rather* and *sooner*, e.g.

I would *truly* rather *be in the middle of this than sitting in that church in a tight collar*

Would is always correct with persons other than the first person singular and plural.

I who, you who, etc.

The verb following a personal pronoun (*I, you, he,* etc.) + *who* should agree with the pronoun and should not be in the third person singular unless the third person singular pronoun precedes *who*:

I, who have *no savings to speak of, had to pay for the work*

This remains so even if the personal pronoun is in the objective case:

They made me, who have *no savings at all, pay for the work* (not *who has*)

When *it is* (*it was*, etc.) precedes *I who*, etc., the same rule applies: the verb agrees with the personal pronoun:

It's I who have *done it*

It could have been we who were *mistaken*

Informal usage sometimes permits the third person to be used (especially when the verb *to be* follows *who*):

You who's *supposed to be so practical!*

Is it me who's *supposed to be keeping an eye on you?*

• This is not acceptable in formal usage.

may or might

There is sometimes confusion about whether to use *may* or *might* with the perfect infinitive referring to a past event, e.g. *He may have done* or *He might have done.*

1. If uncertainty about the action or state denoted by the perfect infinitive remains, i.e. at the time of speaking or writing the truth of the event is still unknown, then either *may* or *might* is acceptable:

As they all wore so many different clothes of identically the same kind ... there may *have been several more or several less*

For all we knew we were both bastards, although of course there might *have been a ceremony*

2. If there is no longer uncertainty about the event, or the matter was never put to the test, and therefore the event did not in fact occur, use *might*:

If that had come ten days ago my whole life might *have been different*

You should not have let him come home alone; he might *have got lost*

• It is a common error to use *may* instead of *might* in these circumstances:

If he (President Galtieri) *had not invaded, then eventually the islands* may *have fallen into their lap*

I am grateful for his intervention without which they may *have remained in the refugee camp indefinitely*

Schoenberg may *never have gone atonal but for the break-up of his marriage*

(These are all from newspaper articles. *Might* should be substituted for *may* in each.)

none (pronoun)

The pronoun *none* can be followed either by singular verb and singular pronouns, or by plural ones. Either is acceptable, although the plural tends to be more common.

Singular: *None of them* was *allowed to forget for a moment*

Plural: *None of the fountains ever* play

None of the authors expected their *books to become best-sellers*

ought

Oughtn't or *didn't ought*?

The standard form of the negative of *ought* is *ought not* or *oughtn't*:

A look from Claudia showed me I ought not *to have begun it*

Being an auxiliary verb, *ought* can precede *not* and does not require the verb *do*. It is non-standard to form the negative with *do* (*didn't ought*):

I hope that none here will say I did anything I didn't ought. *For I only done my duty*

When the negative is used to reinforce a question in a short extra clause or 'question tag', the negative should be formed according to the rule above:

You ought to be pleased, oughtn't you? (not *didn't you?*)

In the same way *do* should not be used as a substitute verb for *ought*, e.g.

Ought he to go?—Yes, he ought (not *he did*)

You ought not to be pleased, ought *you?* (not *did you?*)

shall and will

'The horror of that moment,' the King went on, 'I shall never, never *forget!' 'You will, though,' the Queen said, 'if you don't make a memorandum of it.'*

There is considerable confusion about when to use *shall* and *will.* Put simply, the traditional rule in standard British English is:

1. In the first person, singular and plural.

(*a*) *I shall, we shall* express the simple future, e.g.

I am not a manual worker and please God I never shall *be one*

In the following pages we shall *see good words ... losing their edge*

(*b*) *I will, we will* express intention or determination on the part of the speaker (especially a promise made by him or her), e.g.

I will *take you to see her tomorrow morning*

I will *no longer accept responsibility for the fruitless loss of life*

'I don't think we will *ask Mr. Fraser's opinion,' she said coldly*

2. For the second and third persons, singular and plural, the rule is exactly the converse.

(*a*) *You, he, she, it,* or *they will* express the simple future, e.g.

Will *it disturb you if I keep the lamp on for a bit?*

Serapina will *last much longer than a car. She'll probably last longer than you* will

(*b*) *You, he, she, it,* or *they shall* express intention or determination on the part of the speaker or someone other than the actual subject of the verb, especially a promise made by the speaker to or about the subject, e.g.

Today you shall *be with me in Paradise*

One day you shall *know my full story*

Shall *the common man be pushed back into the mud, or* shall *he not?*

The two uses of *will*, and one of those of *shall*, are well illustrated by:

'I will follow you to the ends of the earth,' replied Susan, passionately. 'It will *not be necessary,' said*

George. 'I am only going down to the coal-cellar. I shall *spend the next half-hour or so there.'*

In informal usage *I will* and *we will* are quite often used for the simple future, e.g.

I will *be a different person when I live in England*

More often the distinction is covered up by the contracted form *'ll*, e.g.

I don't quite know when I'll *get the time to write again*

• The use of *will* for *shall* in the first person is not regarded as fully acceptable in formal usage.

singular or plural

1. When subject and complement are different in number (i.e. one is singular, the other plural), the verb normally agrees with the subject, e.g.

(Plural subject)

Their wages were *a mere pittance*

Liqueur chocolates are *our speciality*

The biblical *The wages of sin is death* reflects an obsolete idiom by which *wages* took a singular verb.

(Singular subject)

What we need is *customers*

Our speciality is *liqueur chocolates*

2. A plural word or phrase used as a name, title, or quotation counts as singular, e.g.

Sons and Lovers has *always been one of Lawrence's most popular novels*

3. A singular phrase that happens to end with a plural word should nevertheless be followed by a singular verb, e.g.

Everyone except the French wants (not *want*) *Britain to join*

One in six has (not *have*) *this problem*

See also ***-ics*, *-s* plural or singular**

-s plural or singular

Some nouns, though they have the plural ending *-s*, are nevertheless usually treated as singulars, taking singular verbs and pronouns referring back to them.

1. *News*

2. Diseases:

measles *mumps* *rickets* *shingles*

Measles and *rickets* can also be treated as ordinary plural nouns.

3. Games:

billiards	*dominoes*	*ninepins*
bowls	*draughts*	*skittles*
darts	*fives*	

4. Countries:

the Bahamas	*the Philippines*
the Netherlands	*the United States*

These are treated as singular when considered as a unit, which they commonly are in a political context, or when the complement is singular, e.g.

The Philippines is *a predominantly agricultural country*

The United States has *withdrawn its ambassador*

The Bahamas and *the Philippines* are also the geographical names of the groups of islands which the two nations comprise, and in this use can be treated as plurals, e.g.

The Bahamas were *settled by British subjects*

See also ***-ics***.

used to

The negative and interrogative of *used to* can be formed in two ways:

(i) Negative: *used not to*
Interrogative: *used X to?*

This formation follows the pattern of the other auxiliary verbs.

Examples:

Used you to beat your mother?

You used not to have a moustache, used you?

(ii) Negative: *did not use to, didn't use to*
Interrogative: *did X use to?*

This formation is the same as that used with regular verbs.

Examples:

She didn't use to find sex revolting

Did you use to be a flirt?

• Either form is acceptable. On the whole *used you to, used he to*, etc. tend to sound rather stilted.

• The correct spellings of the negative forms are:

usedn't to and *didn't use to*

not:

usen't to and *didn't used to*

we (with phrase following)

Expressions consisting of *we* or *us* followed by a qualifying word or phrase, e.g. *we English, us English*, are often misused with the wrong case of the first person plural pronoun. In fact the rules are exactly the same as for *we* or *us* standing alone.

If the expression is the subject, *we* should be used:

(Correct) *Not always laughing as heartily as* we English *are supposed to do*

(Incorrect) *We all make mistakes, even* us anarchists (Substitute *we anarchists*)

If the expression is the object or the complement of a preposition, *us* should be used:

(Correct) *To* us English, *Europe is not a very vivid conception*

(Incorrect) *The Manchester Guardian has said some nice things about* we in the North-East

you and *I* or *you* and *me*

When a personal pronoun is linked by *and* or *or* to a noun or another pronoun there is often confusion about which case to put the pronoun in. In fact the rule is exactly as it would be for the pronoun standing alone.

1. If the two words linked by *and* or *or* constitute the subject, the pronoun should be in the subjective case, e.g.

Only she *and her mother cared for the old house*

That's what we would do, that is, John and I

Who could go?—Either you or he

The use of the objective case is quite common in informal speech, but it is non-standard, e.g. (examples from the speech of characters in novels)

Perhaps only her *and Mrs Natwick had stuck to the christened name*

That's how we look at it, me *and Martha*

Either Mary had to leave or me

2. If the two words linked by *and* or *or* constitute the object of the verb, or the complement of a preposition, the objective case must be used:

The afternoon would suit her *and John better*

It was time for Sebastian and me *to go down to the drawing-room*

The use of the subjective case is very common informally. It probably arises from an exaggerated fear of the error indicated under 1 above.

• It remains, however, non-standard, e.g.

It was this that set Charles and I *talking of old times*

Why is it that people like you and I *are so unpopular?*

Between you and I

This last expression is very commonly heard. *Between you and me* should always be substituted.

4. Word Formation

-able and *-ible*

Words ending in *-able* generally owe their form to the Latin termination *-abilis* or the Old French *-able* (or both), and words in *-ible* to the Latin *-ibilis.* The suffix *-able* is also added to words of distinctly French or English origin, and as a living element to English roots.

A. Words ending in *-able*. The following alterations are made to the stem:

1. Silent *-e* is dropped, e.g. *adorable, imaginable.*

Exceptions: words whose stem ends in *-ce, -ee, -ge, -le*, and the following:

blameable	*rateable*
dyeable	*ropeable*
giveable (but *forgivable*)	*saleable*
hireable	*shareable*
holeable	*sizeable*
likeable	*tameable*
liveable	*tuneable*
nameable	*unshakeable*

• American spelling tends to omit *-e-* in the words above.

2. Final *-y* becomes *-i-* (see ***y* to *i*** B).

Exception: *flyable.*

3. A final consonant may be doubled, e.g. *clubbable.*

Exceptions:

inferable	*referable*
preferable (but *conferrable*)	*transferable*

4. Most verbs of more than two syllables ending in *-ate* drop this ending when forming adjectives in *-able*, e.g. *alienable, calculable, demonstrable,* etc. Verbs of two syllables ending in *-ate* form adjectives in *-able* regularly, e.g. *creatable, debatable, dictatable,* etc.

B. Words ending in *-ible.* These are fewer, since *-ible* is not a living suffix. Below is a list of the commonest. Almost all form their negative in *in-, il-,* etc., so that the negative form can be inferred from the positive in the list below; the exceptions are indicated by (*un*).

accessible	*edible*	*perfectible*
adducible	*eligible*	*permissible*
admissible	*exhaustible*	*persuasible*
audible	*expressible*	*plausible*
avertible	*extensible*	*possible*
collapsible	*fallible*	*reducible*
combustible	(*un*)*feasible*	*repressible*
compatible	*flexible*	*reproducible*
comprehensible	*forcible*	*resistible*
contemptible	*fusible*	*responsible*
corrigible	*gullible*	*reversible*
corruptible	*indelible*	*risible*
credible	(*un*)*intelligible*	*sensible*
defensible	*irascible*	(*un*)*susceptible*
destructible	*legible*	*tangible*
digestible	*ostensible*	*vincible*
negligible	*vendible*	*dirigible*
discernible	*perceptible*	*visible*
divisible		

-ant or *-ent*

-ant is the noun ending, *-ent* the adjective ending in the following:

dependant	*dependent*
descendant	*descendent*
pendant	*pendent*
propellant	*propellent*

independent is both adjective and noun; *dependence, independence* are the abstract nouns.

The following are correct spellings:

ascendant, -nce, -ncy	*relevant, -nce*
attendant, -nce	*repellent*
expellent	*superintendent, -ncy*
impellent	*tendency*
intendent, -ncy	*transcendent, -nce*

-ative or *-ive*

Correct are:

(*a*) *authoritative*	*qualitative*

interpretative *quantitative*
(b) *assertive* *preventive*
exploitive

c and *ck*

Words ending in *-c* interpose *k* before suffixes which otherwise would indicate a soft *c*, chiefly *-ed*, *-er*, *-ing*, *-y*, e.g.:

bivouacker, -ing	*panicky*
colicky	*picnicked, -er, -ing*
frolicked, -ing	*plasticky*
mimicked, -ing	*trafficked, -ing*

Exceptions: *arced*, *-ing*, *zinced*, *zincify*, *zincing.*

Before *-ism*, *-ist*, and *-ize c* (chiefly occurring in the suffix *-ic*) remains and is pronounced soft, e.g. *Anglicism*, *physicist*, *domesticity*, *italicize*.

-cede or *-ceed*

Exceed, *proceed*, *succeed*; the other verbs similarly formed have *-cede*, e.g. *concede*, *intercede*, *recede.* Note also *supersede.*

-ce or *-se*

Advice, *device*, *licence*, and *practice* are nouns; the related verbs are spelt with *-se*: *advise*, *devise*, *license*, *practise.* Similarly *prophecy* (noun), *prophesy* (verb).

• American spelling favours *licence*, *practice* for both noun and verb; but the nouns *defence*, *offence*, *pretence* are spelt with *c* in Britain, *s* in America.

en- or *in-*

The following pairs of words can give trouble:

encrust (verb)	*incrustation*
engrain (verb) to dye in the raw state	*ingrain* (adjective) dyed in the yarn
	ingrained deeply rooted
enquire ask	*inquire* undertake a formal investigation
enquiry question	*inquiry* official investigation
ensure make sure	*insure* take out insurance (against risk: note *assurance* of life)

-erous or *-rous*

The ending *-erous* is normal in adjectives related to nouns ending in *-er*, e.g. *murderous*, *slanderous*, *thunderous.* The exceptions are:

ambidextrous	*disastrous*	*monstrous*
cumbrous	*leprous*	*slumbrous*
dextrous	*meandrous*	*wondrous*

for- and *fore-*

The prefix *for-* means 'away, out, completely', or implies prohibition or abstention. *Fore-* is the same as the ordinary word so spelt, = 'beforehand, in front'.

Note especially:

forbear refrain	*forebear* ancestor
forgather	*foreclose*
forgo abstain from	*forego* (esp. in *foregoing* (*list*), *foregone* (*conclusion*))
forfeit	

f to *v*

Certain nouns that end in *f* or *f* followed by silent *e* change this *f* to *v* in some derivatives. Most are familiar, but with a few derivatives there is variation between *f* and *v* or uncertainty about which consonant is correct; only these are dealt with below.

beef: plural *beeves* oxen, *beefs* kinds of beef.

calf (young bovine animal): *calfish* calflike; *calves-foot jelly.*

calf (of leg): *(enormously) calved* having (enormous) calves.

corf (basket): plural *corves.*

dwarf: plural usually *dwarfs*, but *dwarves* is commonly found.

elf: *elfish* and *elvish* are both acceptable; *elfin* but *elven.*

handkerchief: plural usually *handkerchiefs*, but *handkerchieves* is commonly found.

hoof: plural usually *hoofs*, but *hooves* is commonly found; adjective *hoofed* or *hooved.*

knife: verb *knife.*

leaf: *leaved* having leaves (*broad-leaved* etc.) but *leafed* as past of *leaf* (*through a book* etc.).

life: *lifelong* lasting a lifetime; *livelong* (*day* etc., poetic: the *i* is short); the plural of *still life* is *still lifes.*

oaf: plural *oafs.*

roof: plural *roofs.* • *Rooves* is commonly heard and sometimes written. Its written use should be avoided.

scarf (garment): plural usually *scarves*, but *scarfs* is commonly found.

scarf (joint): plural and verb keep *f.*

sheaf: plural *sheaves*; verb *sheaf* or *sheave*; *sheaved* made into a sheaf.

shelf: plural *shelves*; *shelvy* having sandbanks.

staff: plural *staffs* but archaic and musical *staves.*

turf: plural *turfs* or *turves*; verb *turf*; *turfy.*

wharf: plural *wharfs* or *wharves.*

wolf: *wolfish* of a wolf.

-ize and *-ise*

-ize should be preferred to *-ise* as a verbal ending in words in which both are in use.

1. The choice arises only where the ending is pro-

nounced *eyes*, not where it is *ice*, *iss*, or *eez*. So: *precise*, *promise*, *expertise*, *remise*.

2. The choice applies only to the verbal suffix (of Greek origin), added to nouns and adjectives with the sense 'make into, treat with, or act in the way of (that which is indicated by the stem word)'.

Hence are eliminated

(*a*) nouns in *-ise*:

compromise	*exercise*	*revise*
demise	*franchise*	*surmise*
disguise	*merchandise*	*surprise*
enterprise		

(*b*) verbs corresponding to a noun which has *-is-* as part of the stem (e.g. in the syllables *-vis-*, *-cis-*, *mis-*), or identical with a noun in *-ise*. Some of the more common verbs in *-ise* are:

advertise	*despise*	*incise*
advise	*devise*	*merchandise*
apprise	*disguise*	*premise*
arise	*emprise*	*prise* (*open*)
chastise	*enfranchise*	*revise*
circumcise	*enterprise*	*supervise*
comprise	*excise*	*surmise*
compromise	*exercise*	*surprise*
demise	*improvise*	*televise*

3. In most cases, *-ize* verbs are formed on familiar English stems, e.g. *authorize*, *familiarize*, *symbolize*; or with a slight alteration to the stem, e.g. *agonize*, *dogmatize*, *sterilize*. A few words have no such immediate stem: *aggrandize* (cf. *aggrandizement*), *appetize* (cf. *appetite*), *baptize* (cf. *baptism*), *catechize* (cf. *catechism*), *recognize* (cf. *recognition*), and *capsize*.

-or and *-er*

These two suffixes, denoting 'one who or that which performs (the action of the verb)' are from Latin (through French) and Old English respectively, but their origin is not a sure guide to their distribution.

1. *-er* is the living suffix, forming most newly-coined agent nouns; but *-or* is frequently used with words of Latin origin to coin technical terms.

2. *-er* is usual after doubled consonants (except *-ss-*), after soft *c* and *g*, after *-i-*, after *ch* and *sh*, and after *-er*, *-graph*, *-ion*, and *-iz-*, e.g.

chopper, *producer*, *avenger*, *qualifier*, *launcher*, *furnisher*, *discoverer*, *photographer*, *executioner*, *organizer*.

Principal exceptions: *counsellor*, *carburettor*, *conqueror*.

3. *-or* follows *-at-* to form a suffix *-ator*, often but not always in words related to verbs in *-ate*, e.g. *duplicator*, *incubator*.

Exception: *debater*.

Note: nouns in *-olater*, as *idolater*, do not contain the agent suffix.

4. No rule can predict whether a given word having *-s-*, *-ss-*, or *-t-* (apart from *-at-*) before the suffix requires *-or* or *-er*. So *supervisor*, *compressor*, *prospector*, but *adviser*, *presser*, *perfecter*. *-tor* usually follows *c*, unstressed *i*, and *u*, e.g. *actor*, *compositor*, *executor*; *-ter* usually follows *f*, *gh*, *l*, *r*, and *s*, e.g. *drifter*, *fighter*, *defaulter*, *exporter*, *protester*; but there are numerous exceptions.

5. A functional distinction is made between *-or* and *-er* in the following:

accepter one who accepts	*acceptor* (in scientific use)
adapter one who adapts	*adaptor* electrical device
caster one who casts, casting machine	*castor* beaver; plant giving oil; sugar (sprinkler); wheel
censer vessel for incense	*censor* official
conveyer one who conveys	*conveyor* device
resister one who resists	*resistor* electrical device
sailer ship of specified power	*sailor* seaman

6. A number of words have *-er* in normal use but *-or* in Law:

abetter	*mortgager* (*mortgagor*)
accepter	*settler*
granter	

-our or *-or*

1. In agent nouns, only *-or* occurs as the ending (cf. ***-or* and *-er***), e.g. *actor*, *counsellor*.

Exception: *saviour*.

2. In abstract nouns, *-our* is usual, e.g. *colour*, *favour*, *humour*. Only the following end in *-or*:

error	*pallor*	*terror*
horror	*squalor*	*torpor*
languor	*stupor*	*tremor*
liquor		

• In American English *-or* is usual in nearly all words in which British English has *-our* (*glamour* and *saviour* are the main exceptions).

3. Nouns in *-our* change this to *-or* before the suffixes *-ation*, *-iferous*, *-ific*, *-ize*, and *-ous*, e.g.

coloration, *humorous*, *odoriferous*, *soporific*, *vaporize*, *vigorous*.

But *-our* keeps the *u* before *-able*, *-er*, *-ful*, *-ism*, *-ist*, *-ite*, and *-less*, e.g.

armourer, *behaviourism*, *colourful*, *favourite*, *honourable*, *labourite*, *odourless*, *behaviourist*.

Exception: *humorist*.

plural formation

Most nouns simply add *-s*, e.g. *cats*, *dogs*, *horses*, *cameras*.

A. The regular plural suffix *-s* is preceded by *-e-*:

1. After sibilant consonants, where ease of pronunciation requires a separating vowel, i.e. after

ch: e.g. *branches*, *coaches*, *matches* (but

note *conchs, lochs, stomachs* where the *ch* has a different sound)

s: e.g. *buses, gases, pluses, yeses* (note that single *s* is not doubled)
sh: e.g. *ashes, bushes*
ss: e.g. *grasses, successes*
x: e.g. *boxes, sphinxes*
z: e.g. *buzzes, waltzes* (note *quizzes* with doubling of *z*)

Proper names follow the same rule, e.g. *the Joneses, the Rogerses, the two Charleses.*

• *-es* should not be replaced by an apostrophe, as *the Jones'*.

2. After *-y* (not preceded by a vowel), which changes to *i*, e.g. *ladies, soliloquies, spies.*

Exceptions: proper names, e.g. *the Willoughbys, the three Marys*; also *trilbys, lay-bys, standbys, zlotys* (Polish currency).

3. After *-o* in certain words:

buffaloes *haloes* *stuccoes*
calicoes *heroes* *tomatoes*
dingoes *mosquitoes* *tornadoes*
dominoes *mottoes* *torpedoes*
echoes *Negroes* *vetoes*
embargoes *noes* *volcanoes*
goes *potatoes*

Words not in this list add only *-s*. Some words (e.g. *cargo, grotto, innuendo, mango, memento, peccadillo,* and *portico*) are found with either plural form.

It is helpful to remember that *-e-* is never inserted:

(*a*) when the *o* is preceded by another vowel, e.g. *cuckoos, embryos, ratios.*

(*b*) when the word is an abbreviation, e.g. *hippos, kilos.*

(*c*) with proper names, e.g. *Lotharios, Figaros, the Munros.*

4. With words which change final *f* to *v* (see ***f* to *v***), e.g. *calves, scarves.*

B. Plural of compound nouns.

1. Compounds made up of a noun followed by an adjective, a prepositional phrase, or an adverb attach *-s* to the noun, e.g.

(*a*) *courts martial* *heirs presumptive*
cousins-german *poets laureate*

But *brigadier-generals, lieutenant-colonels, sergeant-majors.*

(*b*) *men-of-war* *tugs of war*
sons-in-law
(*c*) *hangers-on* *whippers-in*
runners-up

Note: In informal usage *-s* is not infrequently transferred to the second element of compounds of type (*a*).

2. Compounds which contain no noun, or in which the noun element is now disguised, add *-s* at the end. So also do nouns formed from phrasal verbs and compounds ending in *-ful*, e.g.

(*a*) *ne'er-do-wells* *will-o'-the-wisps*
forget-me-nots
(*b*) *pullovers* *set-ups*
run-throughs
(*c*) *handfuls* *spoonfuls*

(See also **-ful/-s full** in Section **1 Meanings**)

3. Compounds containing *man* or *woman* make both elements plural, as usually do those made up of two words linked by *and*, e.g.

(*a*) *gentlemen ushers* *women doctors*
menservants
(*b*) *pros and cons* *ups and downs*

C. The plural of the following nouns with a singular in *-s* is unchanged:

biceps *means* *species*
congeries *mews* *superficies*
forceps *series* *thrips*
innings

The following are mass nouns, not plurals:

bona fides (= 'good faith'), *kudos*

• The singulars *bona-fide* (as a noun; there is an adjective *bona-fide*), *congery, kudo*, sometimes seen, are erroneous.

D. Plural of nouns of foreign origin. The terminations that may form their plurals according to a foreign pattern are given in alphabetical order below; to each is added a list of the words that normally follow this pattern, although some of these (marked *) are found with *-s* or *-es* if they are considered to be sufficiently assimilated into English. It is recommended that the regular plural (in *-s*) should be used for all the other words with these terminations, even though some are found with either type of plural.

1. *-a* (Latin and Greek) becomes *-ae* (or **-as*):

alga *lamina* *nebula**
alumina *larva* *papilla*

Note: *formula* has *-ae* in mathematical and scientific use.

2. *-eau, -eu* (French) add *-x* (or **-e(a)us*)

*beau** *château* *plateau**
*bureau** *milieu** *tableau*

3. *-ex, -ix* (Latin) become *-ices*:

appendix *cortex* *matrix*
calix *helix* *radix*

Note: *index, vortex* have *-ices* in mathematical and scientific use (otherwise regular).

4. *-is* (Greek and Latin) becomes *-es* (pronounced eez):

amanuensis *crisis* *oasis*
analysis *ellipsis* *parenthesis*
antithesis *hypothesis* *synopsis*
axis *metamorphosis* *thesis*
basis

5. *-o* (Italian) becomes *-i* (or **-os*):

*concerto grosso** (or *concerti grossi*)
graffito *ripieno**
*maestro** *virtuoso**

Note: *solo* and *soprano* sometimes have *-i* in technical contexts (otherwise regular).

6. *-on* (Greek) becomes *-a*:

criterion *parhelion* *phenomenon*

Note: The plural of *automaton* is in *-a* when used collectively (otherwise regular).

7. *-s* (French) is unchanged in the plural (note: it is silent in the singular, but pronounced *-z* in the plural):

chamois	*corps*	*fracas*
chassis	*faux pas*	*patois*

Also (not a noun in French): *rendezvous.*

8. *-um* (Latin) becomes *-a* (or **-ums*):

addendum	*datum*	*maximum*
bacterium	*desideratum*	*minimum*
candelabrum	*dictum**	*quantum*
*compendium**	*effluvium*	*scholium*
corrigendum	*emporium**	*spectrum*
*cranium**	*epithalamium**	*speculum*
crematorium	*erratum*	*stratum*
curriculum		

Note: *medium* in scientific use, and in the sense 'a means of communication' (as *mass medium*) has plural in *-a*; the collective plural of *memorandum* 'things to be noted' is in *-a*; *rostrum* has *-a* in technical use; otherwise these words are regular. In the technical sense 'starting-point' *datum* has a regular plural.

9. *-us* (Latin) becomes *-i* (or **-uses*):

alumnus	*fungus**	*nucleus*
bacillus	*gladiolus**	*radius**
bronchus	*locus*	*stimulus*
*cactus**	*narcissus**	*terminus**
*calculus**		

Note: *focus* has plural in *-i* in scientific use, but otherwise is regular; *genius* has plural *genii* when used to mean 'guardian spirit', but in its usual sense is regular; *genus* becomes *genera*, while *corpus* becomes *corpora* or *corpuses*, and *opus* becomes *opera* or *opuses*.

• The following words of foreign origin are plural nouns; they should normally not be construed as singulars (see also Section 2, **Plurals**, where some of these are treated as separate entries).

bacteria	*graffiti*	*phenomena*
candelabra	*insignia*	*regalia*
criteria	*media*	*strata*
data		

E. There is no need for an apostrophe before *-s*:

1. After figures: *the 1890s.*

2. After abbreviations: *MPs, SOSs.*

But it is needed in: *dot the i's and cross the t's.*

possessive case

To form the possessive:

1. Normally, add *-'s* in the singular and *-s'* (i.e. apostrophe following the plural suffix *-s*) in the plural, e.g.

Bill's book	*the Johnsons' dog*
his master's voice	*a girls' school*

Nouns that do not form plural in *-s* add *-'s* to the plural form, e.g.

children's books *women's liberation*

2. Nouns ending in *s* add *-'s* for the singular possessive, e.g.

boss's	*Hicks's*
Burns's	*St James's Square*
Charles's	*Tess's*
Father Christmas's	*Thomas's*

To form the plural possessive, they add an apostrophe to the *s* of the plural in the normal way, e.g.

bosses'	*the octopuses' tentacles*
the Joneses' dog	*the Thomases' dog*

French names ending in silent *s* or *x* add *-'s*, which is pronounced as *z*, e.g.

Dumas's (= Dumah's) *Crémieux's*

Names ending in *-es* pronounced *iz* are treated like plurals and take only an apostrophe (following the pronunciation, which is *iz*, not *iziz*), e.g.

Bridges'	*Moses'*
Hodges'	*Riches'*

Polysyllables not accented on the last or second last syllable can take the apostrophe alone, but the form with *-'s* is equally acceptable, e.g.

Barnabas'	or	*Barnabas's*
Nicholas'	or	*Nicholas's*

It is the custom in classical works to use the apostrophe only, irrespective of pronunciation, for ancient classical names ending in *-s*, e.g.

Ceres'	*Herodotus'*	*Venus'*
Demosthenes'	*Mars'*	*Xerxes'*

Jesus' is an accepted liturgical archaism. But in non-liturgical use, *Jesus's* is acceptable.

With the possessive preceding the word *sake*, be guided by the pronunciation, e.g.

for goodness' sake	but	*for God's sake*
for conscience' sake	but	*for Charles's sake*

After *-x* and *-z*, use *-'s*, e.g. *Ajax's, Berlioz's music, Liebniz's law, Lenz's law.*

3. Expressions such as:

a fortnight's holiday	*two weeks' holiday*
a pound's worth	*two pounds' worth*
your money's worth	

contain possessives and should have apostrophes correctly placed.

4. In *I'm going to the butcher's, grocer's*, etc. there is a possessive with ellipsis of the word 'shop'. The same construction is used in *I'm going to Brown's, Green's*, etc., so that properly an apostrophe is called for. Where a business calls itself *Brown, Green*, or the like (e.g. *Marks and Spencer, J. Sainsbury*) the apostrophe would be expected before *-s*. But many businesses use the title *Browns, Greens*, etc., without an apostrophe (e.g. *Debenhams, Barclays Bank*). No apostrophe is necessary in *a Debenhams store* or in (*go to* or *take to*) *the cleaners.*

5. The apostrophe must not be used:

(*a*) with the plural non-possessive *-s*: notices such as *TEA'S* are often seen, but are wrong.

(*b*) with the possessive of pronouns: *hers, its, ours, theirs, yours*; the possessive of *who* is *whose.*

• *it's = it is; who's = who is.*

• There are no words *her's, our's, their's, your's.*

-re or -er

The principal words in which the ending *-re* (with the unstressed 'ə' sound – there are others with the sound 'rə', e.g. *macabre*, or 'ray', e.g. *padre*) is found are:

accoutre	*_lucre_	*_ogre_
*_acre_	_lustre_	_philtre_
amphi-theatre	_manoeuvre_	_reconnoitre_
	*_massacre_	_sabre_
*_cadre_	*_meagre_	_sceptre_
calibre	*_mediocre_	_sepulchre_
centre	_metre_ (_note meter_ the measuring device)	_sombre_
*_euchre_		_spectre_
fibre		_theatre_
goitre	_mitre_	_titre_
litre	_nitre_	*_wiseacre_
louvre	_ochre_	

• All but those marked * are spelt with *-er* in American English.

re- prefix

This prefix is followed by a hyphen:

1. Before another *e*, e.g. *re-echo, re-entry.*

2. So as to distinguish the compound so formed from the more familiar identically spelt word written solid, e.g.

re-cover (put new cover on): *recover*
re-form (form again): *reform*
re-sign (sign again): *resign*

-s suffix

A. As the inflection of the plural of nouns: see **plural formation.**

B. As the inflection of the third person singular present indicative of verbs, it requires the same changes in the stem as the plural ending, namely the insertion of *-e-*:

1. After sibilants (*ch, s, sh, x, z*), e.g. *catches, tosses, pushes, fixes, buzzes*; note that single *s* and *z* are subject to doubling of final consonant, though the forms in which they occur are rare, e.g. *gasses, nonplusses, quizzes, whizzes.*

2. After *y*, which is subject to the change of *y* to *i*, e.g. *cries, flies, carries, copies.*

3. After *o*: *echo, go, torpedo, veto*, like the corresponding nouns, insert *-e-* before *-s.*

-xion or -ction

Complexion, crucifixion, effluxion, fluxion all have *-x*; *connection, reflection* (which formerly sometimes had *-x-*) have *-ct-*; *deflexion* is increasingly being replaced by *deflection, genuflexion* by *genuflection*, and *inflexion* by *inflection.*

• In American spelling *-ction* is more usual in *connection, deflection, genuflection, inflection, reflection.*

-y or -ey adjectives

When *-y* is added to a word to form an adjective, the following changes in spelling occur:

1. Doubling of final consonant, e.g. *shrubby.*

2. Dropping of silent *-e*, e.g. *bony, chancy, mousy.*

Exceptions:

(*a*) After *u*:

bluey *gluey* *tissuey*

(*b*) In words that are not well established in the written language, where the retention of *-e* helps to clarify the sense:

cottagey *dicey* *dikey*
pacey *villagey*

Note also *holey* (distinguished from *holy*); *phoney* (of unknown origin).

3. Insertion of *-e-* when *-y* is also the final letter of the stem:

clayey *skyey* *sprayey* *wheyey*

Also in *gooey.*

4. Adjectives ending in unstressed *-ey* (2 (*a*) and (*b*) and 3 above) change this *-ey* to *-i-* before the comparative and superlative suffixes *-er* and *-est* and the adverbial suffix *-ly*, e.g.

dicey: *dicier* *gooey*: *gooier* *pacey*: *pacier*
phoney: phonily

Before *-ness* there is variation, e.g.

clayey: *clayeyness* *phoney*: *phoniness* *wheyey*: *wheyiness*

y or i

There is often uncertainty about whether *y* or *i* should be written in the following words:

Write i in:	Write y in:
cider	*dyke* (*dike* is also found)
cipher (*cypher* is also found)	*Gypsy* (*Gipsy* is also found)
Libya	*lyke-wake*
lich-gate (*lych-* is also found)	*lynch law*
linchpin	*pygmy* (*pigmy* is also found)
sibyl (classical)	*style* (manner)
	stylus
siphon (*syphon* is also found)	*stymie* (*stymy* is also found)
siren	*Sybil* (frequently as Christian name)
stile (in fence)	
timpani (drums; *tympani* is also found)	*syllabub* (*sillabub* is also found)
tiro (*tyro* is also found)	*sylvan* (*silvan* is also found)

witch-hazel (wych-hazel is also found)
syrup
tyke (*tike* is also found)
tympanum (ear-drum)
tyre (of wheel)
wych-elm

-yse or -yze

This verbal ending (e.g. in *analyse, catalyse, paralyse*) is not a suffix but part of the Greek stem *-lyse*. It should not be written with *z* (though *z* is normally used in such words in America).

y to i

Words that end in *-y* change this to *-i-* before certain suffixes. The conditions are:

A. The *-y* does not change to *-i-* when preceded by a vowel (other than *u* in *-guy, -quy*). So *enjoyable, conveyed, parleyed, gayer, gayest, donkeys, buys, employer, joyful, coyly, enjoyment, greyness.*

Exceptions: *daily, gaily,* and adjectives ending in unstressed *-ey* (see **-y or -*ey* adjectives** 4).

B. When the suffix is:

1. *-able*, e.g. *deniable, justifiable, variable.*

Exception: *flyable.*

2. *-ed* (the past tense and past participle), e.g. *carried, denied, tried.*

3. *-er* (agent-noun suffix), e.g. *carrier, crier, supplier.*

Exceptions: *flyer, fryer, shyer* (one who, a horse which, shies), *skyer* (in cricket). Note that *drier, prier, trier* (one who tries) are regular.

4. *-er, -est* (comparative and superlative); e.g. *drier, driest; happier, happiest.*

5. *-es* (noun plural and third person singular present indicative), e.g. *ladies, soliloquies, spies; carries, denies, tries.*

Exceptions: see **plural formation** A2.

6. *-ful* (adjectives), e.g. *beautiful, fanciful.* (*Bellyful* is a noun, not an adjective.)

7. *-less* (adjectives), e.g. *merciless, remediless.*

Exceptions: some rare compounds, e.g. *countryless, hobbyless, partyless.*

8. *-ly* (adverbs), e.g. *drily, happily, plaguily.*

Exceptions: *shyly, slyly, spryly, wryly.*

9. *-ment* (nouns), e.g. *embodiment, merriment.*

10. *-ness* (nouns), e.g. *happiness, cliquiness.*

Exceptions: *dryness, flyness, shyness, slyness, spryness, wryness; busyness* (distinguished from *business*).

5. Pronunciation

The following words are often mispronounced:

	Preferred:	*Not preferred:*
comparable	/ˈkɒmˈpərəb(ə)l/	/kɒmˈpærəb(ə)l/
contribute	/kənˈtrɪbjuːt/	/ˈkɒntrɪbjuːt/
controversy	/ˈkɒntrəvɜːsɪ/	/kənˈtrɒvəsɪ/
decade	/ˈdekeɪd/	/dɪˈkeɪd/
deity	/ˈdiːɪtɪ/	/ˈdeɪɪtɪ/
diphtheria	/dɪfˈθɪərɪə/	/dɪpˈθɪərɪə/
dispute	/dɪˈspjuːt/	/ˈdɪspjuːt/
distribute	/dɪˈstrɪbjuːt/	/ˈdɪstrɪbjuːt/
exquisite	/ˈekskwɪzɪt/	/ɪkˈskwɪzɪt/
formidable	/ˈfɔːmɪdəb(ə)l/	/fɔːˈmɪdəb(ə)l/
harass(ment)	/ˈhærəs(mənt)/	/həˈræs(mənt)/
integral adj.	/ˈɪntɪgr(ə)l/	/ɪnˈtegr(ə)l/
irreparable	/ɪˈrepərəb(ə)l/	/ɪrɪˈpærəb(ə)l/
irrevocable	/ɪˈrevəkəb(ə)l/	/ɪrɪˈvəʊkəb(ə)l/
kilometre	/ˈkɪləˌmiːtə(r)/	/kɪˈlɒmɪtə(r)/
lamentable	/ˈlæməntəb(ə)l/	/ləˈmentəbl/
length	/leŋθ/	/leŋkθ/
preferable	/ˈprefərəb(ə)l/	/prɪˈfɜːrəb(ə)l/
primarily	/ˈpraɪmərɪlɪ/	/praɪˈmeərɪlɪ/
reputable	/ˈrepjʊtəb(ə)l/	/rɪˈpjuːtəb(ə)l/
research	/rɪˈsɜːtʃ/	/ˈriːsɜːtʃ/
romance	/rəʊˈmæns/	/ˈrəʊmæns/
secretary	/ˈsekrɪtərɪ/ or /sekrətrɪ/	/ˈsekɪteərɪ/
strength	/streŋθ/	/streŋkθ/
surveillance	/sɜːˈveɪləns/	/sɜːˈveɪjəns/
temporarily	/ˈtempərərɪlɪ/	/tempəˈreərɪlɪ/
trait	/treɪ/	/treɪt/
vulnerable	/ˈvʌlnərəb(ə)l/	/ˈvʌnərəb(ə)l/
zoology	/zəʊˈɒlədʒɪ/	/zuːˈɒlədʒɪ/

Appendix V

Punctuation Marks

Punctuation is a complicated subject, and only the main principles can be discussed here. The explanations are based on practice in British English; usage in American English differs in some instances. The main headings are as follows:

1. General remarks
2. Capital letter
3. Full stop
4. Semicolon
5. Comma
6. Colon
7. Question mark
8. Exclamation mark
9. Apostrophe
10. Quotation marks
11. Brackets
12. Dash
13. Hyphen

1. General remarks

The purpose of punctuation is to mark out strings of words into manageable groups and help clarify their meaning (or in some cases to prevent a wrong meaning being deduced). The marks most commonly used to divide a piece of prose or other writing are the full stop, the semicolon, and the comma, with the strength of the dividing or separating role diminishing from the full stop to the comma. The full stop therefore marks the main division into sentences; the semicolon joins sentences (as in this sentence); and the comma (which is the most flexible in use and causes most problems) separates smaller elements with the least loss of continuity. Brackets and dashes also serve as separators – often more strikingly than commas, as in this sentence.

2. Capital letter C

1.1 This is used for the first letter of the word beginning a sentence in most cases:

He decided not to come. Later he changed his mind.

1.2 A sentence or clause contained in a subordinate or parenthetic role within a larger one does not normally begin with a capital letter:

I have written several letters (there are many to be written) and hope to finish them tomorrow.

1.3 In the following, however, the sentence is a separate one and therefore does begin with a capital letter:

There is more than one possibility. (I have said this often before.) So we should think carefully before acting.

1.4 A capital letter also begins sentences that form quoted speech:

The assistant turned and replied, 'There are no more left.'

2 It is used in proper names (*Paris*, *John Smith*), names of people and languages and related adjectives (*Englishman*, *Austrian*, *French*), names of institutions and institutional groups (*the British Museum*, *Protestants*, *Conservatives*), and names of days and months (*Tuesday*, *March*) and related words (*Easter Sunday*). It is also used by convention in names that are trade marks (*Biro*, *Jacuzzi*).

3 It is used in titles of books, newspapers, plays, films, television programmes, etc., and in headings and captions.

4 It is used in designations of rank or relationship when used as titles (*King John*, *Aunt Mabel*, *Pope Gregory*), and to designate divinity (*God*, *the Almighty*, etc.).

5 Lines of verse often begin with a capital letter.

6 Many abbreviations consist partly or entirely of the initial letters of words in capital letters (with or without a full stop): *BBC*, *DoE*, *M.Litt.*

3. Full stop .

1 This is used to mark the end of a sentence when it is a statement (and not a question or exclamation). In prose, sentences marked by full stops normally represent a discrete or distinct statement; more closely connected or complementary statements are joined by a semicolon (as here).

2.1 Full stops are used to mark many abbreviations (*Weds.*, *Gen.*, *p.m.*). They are often omitted in abbreviations that are familiar or very common (*Dr*, *Mr*, *Mrs*, etc.), in abbreviations that consist entirely of capital letters (*BBC*, *GMT*, etc.), and in acronyms that are pronounced as a word rather than a sequence of letters (*Nato*, *Ernie*, etc.).

2.2 If an abbreviation with a full stop comes at the end of a sentence, another full stop is not added when the full stop of the abbreviation is the last character:

They have a collection of many animals, including dogs, cats, tortoises, snakes, etc.

but

They have a collection of many animals (dogs, cats, tortoises, snakes, etc.).

3 A sequence of three full stops is used to mark an ellipsis or omission in a sequence of words, especially when forming an incomplete quotation. When the omission occurs at the end of a sentence, a fourth point is added as the full stop of the whole sentence:

He left the room, banged the door,...and went out.

The report said: 'There are many issues to be considered, of which the chief are money, time, and personnel.... Let us consider personnel first.'

4 A full stop is used as a decimal point (*10.5 per cent*; *£1.65*), and to divide hours and minutes in giving time (*6.15 p.m.*), although a colon is usual in American use (*6:15 p.m.*).

4. Semicolon ;

1.1 The main role of the semicolon is to unite sentences that are closely associated or that complement or parallel each other in some way, as in the following:

In the north of the city there is a large industrial area with little private housing; further east is the university.

To err is human; to forgive, divine.

1.2 It is often used as a stronger division in a sentence that already includes divisions by means of commas:

He came out of the house, which lay back from the road, and saw her at the end of the path; but instead of continuing towards her, he hid until she had gone.

2 It is used in a similar way in lists of names or other items, to indicate a stronger division:

I should like to thank the managing director, Stephen Jones; my secretary, Mary Cartwright; and my assistant, Kenneth Sloane.

5. Comma ,

1 Use of the comma is more difficult to describe than other punctuation marks, and there is much variation in practice. Essentially, its role is to give detail to the structure of sentences, especially longer ones, and make their meaning clear. Too many commas can be distracting; too few can make a piece of writing difficult to read or, worse, difficult to understand.

2.1 The comma is widely used to separate the main clauses of a compound sentence when they are not sufficiently close in meaning or content to form a continuous unpunctuated sentence, and are not distinct enough to warrant a semicolon. A conjunction such as *and, but, yet,* etc. is normally used:

The road runs through a beautiful wooded valley, and the railway line follows it closely.

2.2 It is considered incorrect to join the clauses of a compound sentence without a conjunction. In the following sentence, the comma should either be replaced by a semicolon, or be retained and followed by *and*:

I like swimming very much, I go to the pool every week.

2.3 It is also considered incorrect to separate a subject from its verb with a comma:

Those with the smallest incomes and no other means, should get most support.

3.1 Commas are usually inserted between adjectives coming before a noun:

An enterprising, ambitious person.

A cold, damp, badly heated room.

3.2 But the comma is omitted when the last adjective has a closer relation to the noun than the others:

A distinguished foreign politician.

A little old lady.

4 An important role of the comma is to prevent ambiguity or (momentary) misunderstanding, especially after a verb used intransitively where it might otherwise be taken to be transitive:

With the police pursuing, the people shouted loudly.

Other examples follow:

He did not want to leave, from a feeling of loyalty.

In the valley below, the houses appeared very small.

However, much as I should like to I cannot agree.

(compare *However much I should like to I cannot agree.*)

5.1 The comma is used in pairs to separate elements in a sentence that are not part of the main statement:

I should like you all, ladies and gentlemen, to raise your glasses.

There is no sense, as far as I can see, in this suggestion.

It appears, however, that we were wrong.

5.2 It is also used to separate a relative clause from its antecedent when the clause is not serving an identifying function:

The book, which was on the table, was a present.

In the above sentence, the information in the *which* clause is incidental to the main statement; without the commas, it would form an essential part of it in identifying which book is being referred to (and could be replaced by *that*):

The book which/that was on the table was a present.

6.1 Commas are used to separate items in a list or sequence. Usage varies as to the inclusion of a comma before *and* in the last item; the practice in this dictionary is to include it:

The following will report at 9.30 sharp: Jones, Smith, Thompson, and Williams.

6.2 A final comma before *and*, when used regularly and consistently, has the advantage of clarifying the grouping at a composite name occurring at the end of a list:

We shall go to Smiths, Boots, Woolworths, and Marks and Spencer.

6. Colon :

1 The main role of the colon is to separate main clauses when there is a step forward from the first to the second, especially from introduction to main point, from general statement to example, from cause to effect, and from premiss to conclusion:

There is something I want to say: I should like you all to know how grateful I am to you.

It was not easy: to begin with I had to find the right house.

The weather was bad: so we decided to stay at home.

(In this example, a comma could be used, but the emphasis on cause and effect would be much reduced.)

2 It also introduces a list of items. In this use a dash should not be added:

The following will be needed: a pen, pencil, rubber, piece of paper, and ruler.

3 It is used to introduce, more formally and emphatically than a comma would, speech or quoted material:

I told them last week: 'Do not in any circumstances open this door.'

7. Question mark ?

1.1 This is used in place of the full stop to show that the preceding sentence is a question:

Do you want another piece of cake?

He really is her husband?

1.2 It is not used when the question is implied by indirect speech:

I asked you whether you wanted another piece of cake.

2 It is used (often in brackets) to express doubt or uncertainty about a word or phrase immediately following or preceding it:

Julius Caesar, born (?) 100 BC.

They were then seen boarding a bus (to London?).

8. Exclamation mark !

This is used after an exclamatory word, phrase, or sentence expressing any of the following:

1 Absurdity:	*What an idea!*
2 Command or warning:	*Go to your room!* *Be careful!*
3 Contempt or disgust:	*They are revolting!*
4 Emotion or pain:	*I hate you!* *That really hurts!* *Ouch!*
5 Enthusiasm:	*I'd love to come!*
6 Wish or regret:	*Let me come!* *If only I could swim!*
7 Wonder, admiration, or surprise:	*What a good idea!* *Aren't they beautiful!*

9. Apostrophe '

1.1 The main use is to indicate the possessive case, as in *John's book*, *the girls' mother*, etc. It comes before the *s* in singular and plural nouns not ending in *s*, as in *the boy's games* and *the women's games*. It comes after the *s* in plural nouns ending in *s*, as in *the boys' games*.

1.2 In singular nouns ending in *s* practice differs between (for example) *Charles'* and *Charles's*; in some cases the shorter form is preferable for reasons of sound, as in *Xerxes' fleet*.

1.3 It is also used to indicate a place or business, e.g. *the butcher's*. In this use it is often omitted in some names, e.g. *Smiths*, *Lloyds Bank*.

2 It is used to indicate a contraction, e.g. *he's*, *wouldn't*, *bo's'n*, *o'clock*.

3 It is sometimes used to form a plural of individual letters or numbers, although this use is diminishing. It is helpful in *cross your t's* but unnecessary in *MPs* and *1940s*.

4 For its use as a quotation mark, see section 10.

10. Quotation marks "

1 The main use is to indicate direct speech and quotations. A single turned comma (') is normally used at the beginning, and a single apostrophe (') at the end of the quoted matter:

She said, 'I have something to ask you.'

2 The closing quotation mark should come after any punctuation mark which is part of the quoted matter, but before any mark which is not:

They shouted, 'Watch out!'

They were described as 'an unruly bunch'.

Did I hear you say 'go away!'?

3 Punctuation dividing a sentence of direct speech is put inside the quotation marks:

'Go away,' he said, 'and don't ever come back.'

4 Quotation marks are also used around cited words and phrases:

What does 'integrated circuit' mean?

5 A quotation within a quotation is put in double quotation marks:

'Have you any idea,' he said, 'what "integrated circuit" means?'

11. Brackets ([ ])

1 The types of brackets used in normal punctuation are round brackets ( ) and square brackets [ ].

2 The main use of round brackets is to enclose explanations and extra information or comment:

He is (as he always was) a rebel.

Zimbabwe (formerly Rhodesia).

They talked about Machtpolitik *(power politics).*

3 They are used to give references and citations:

Thomas Carlyle (1795–1881).

A discussion of integrated circuits (see p. 38).

4 They are used to enclose reference letters or figures, e.g. *(1) (a)*.

5 They are used to enclose optional words:

There are many (apparent) difficulties.

(In this example, the difficulties may or may not be only apparent.)

6.1 Square brackets are used less often. The main use is to enclose extra information attributable to someone (normally an editor) other than the writer of the surrounding text:

The man walked in, and his sister [Sarah] greeted him.

6.2 They are used in some contexts to convey special kinds of information, especially when round brackets are also used for other purposes: for example, in this dictionary they are used to give the etymologies at the end of entries.

12. Dash —

1 A single dash is used to indicate a pause, whether a hesitation in speech or to introduce an explanation or expansion of what comes before it:

'I think you should have—told me,' he replied.

We then saw the reptiles—snakes, crocodiles, that sort of thing.

2 A pair of dashes is used to indicate asides and parentheses, like the use of commas as explained at 5.5.1 above, but forming a more distinct break:

People in the north are more friendly—and helpful—than those in the south.

There is nothing to be gained—unless you want a more active social life—in moving to the city.

3 It is sometimes used to indicate an omitted word: for example, a coarse word in direct speech:

'—you all,' he said.

13. Hyphen -

1 The hyphen has two main functions: to link words or elements of words into longer words and compounds, and to mark the division of a word at the end of a line in print or writing.

2.1 The use of the hyphen to connect words to form compound words is diminishing in English, especially when the elements are of one syllable as in *birdsong*, *eardrum*, and *playgroup*, and also in some longer formations such as *figurehead* and *nationwide*. The hyphen is used more often in routine and occasional couplings, especially when reference to the senses of the separate elements is considered important or unavoidable, as in *boiler-room*. It is often retained to avoid awkward collisions of letters, as in *breast-stroke*.

2.2 The hyphen serves to connect words that have a syntactic link, as in *hard-covered books* and *French-speaking people*, where the reference is to books with hard covers and people who speak French, rather than hard books with covers and French people who can speak (which would be the senses conveyed if the hyphens were omitted). It is also used to avoid more extreme kinds of ambiguity, as in *twenty-odd people*.

2.3 A particularly important use of the hyphen is to link compounds and phrases used attributively, as in *a well-known man* (but *the man is well known*), and *Christmas-tree lights* (but *the lights on the Christmas tree*).

2.4 It is also used to connect elements to form words in cases such as *re-enact* (where the collision of two *e*s would be awkward), *re-form* (= to form again, to distinguish it from *reform*), and some other prefixed words such as those in *anti-*, *non-*, *over-*, and *post-*. Usage varies in this regard, and much depends on how well established and clearly recognizable the resulting formation is. When the second element is a name, a hyphen is usual (as in *anti-Darwinian*).

2.5 It is used to indicate a common second element in all but the last of a list, e.g. *two-, three-, or fourfold.*

3 The hyphen used to divide a word at the end of a line is a different matter, because it is not a permanent feature of the spelling. It is more common in print, where the text has to be accurately spaced and the margin justified; in handwritten and typed or word-processed material it can be avoided altogether. In print, words need to be divided carefully and consistently, taking account of the appearance and structure of the word. Detailed guidance on word-division may be found in the *Oxford Spelling Dictionary*.

Appendix VI

Royal Mail Services

1st and 2nd class services

The price of postage for both of these services is determined by weight. 1st class post has no weight limit, however, 2nd class post has an upper weight limit of 750g.

Certificate of posting

A certificate can be obtained free of charge from the Post Office at the time of posting if documentary proof of postage is required.

Caller service

If an urgently required letter or package is thought to be at the local delivery office it can be collected in person. The Post Office will require proof of identity and address. There is a fee for the search (26p, 1998).

Business collection and delivery

Collection

There is a free collection service for most types of post, including Registered, Recorded Delivery, and Special Delivery, providing 1000 letters or letters to the value of £200 are posted. Smaller amounts of post will be collected for a fee (£5, 1998) and annual fees are negotiable.

Delivery

Daily deliveries (Monday to Saturday) are made free of charge to the ground floor, for every additional floor up or down there is an annual charge (£42 p.a., 1998). The Royal Mail will negotiate tailor-made collection and delivery services for business customers.

Selectapost

A service offered on a yearly basis with payments to be made quarterly in advance. Selectapost subdivides a firm's mail before delivery so that separate bundles can be delivered to separate departments in a company.

Redirection

A service to forward mail to a new permanent or temporary address from an old address. The service operates for a maximum of two years.

Premium services

Recorded Delivery

A service in which a certificate of postage is provided and a signature on delivery is required. It is suitable for items worth £26 or less. The service can be used with 1st and 2nd class post. A small charge (60p, 1998) is made in addition to the standard postage.

Special Delivery

Items sent by Special Delivery will be delivered on the next working day; if the Royal Mail fails to make delivery on the next working day, the cost of posting will be refunded to the sender. It is suitable for items worth £50 or less and weighing a maximum of 30 kg. The price starts at £3.20 for items weighing 100 g or less and increases on a sliding scale (1998).

Registered Post

A similar service to Special Delivery but extra security is provided and compensation is available up to £500, if the package is lost or damaged. Registered post can only be used with 1st class post. For items between £500 and £2,200, there exists a new service, *Registered Plus.*

Consequential Loss Insurance

A service that provides extra insurance on Registered Post items. The scheme insures a business against consequential loss of business, profits, or sales as a result of lost, damaged, or delayed post. The upper limit for compensation is £10,000, with fees being charged on a sliding scale.

Electronic Post

A service in which the Royal Mail delivers to an unlimited number of addresses a text, invoice, etc. (the main text) supplied by a customer. The main text is sent to the Electronic Mail Centre by means of a modem, floppy disk, or magnetic tape. Personal details of the addressees can subsequently be added through the same channels. The personalized text will then be printed, inserted into 'telegram' style envelopes, and delivered by 1st class post. Data can be accepted until 6pm for the same night's post. Technical advice and help is available from the Electronic Mail Centre. Prices currently range from 15p to 25p per item, inclusive of basic stationery, plus a flat fee of £70 per hour, and postage at the normal rate per item. The service can be used to despatch mail to foreign destinations.

Faxmail

The Royal Mail's fax courier service is a combination of fax transmission and a courier service, making it possible for a fax to be sent from a fax owner to a non-fax owner, from a non-fax owner to a fax owner, and between two non-fax owners. Same-day service is possible within most of the UK, with services also available to Europe, North America, and other foreign destinations. Prices vary according to the number of pages and the delivery speed required: the fax cover sheet, however, is free.

International Services

Surface mail

This is slightly cheaper than airmail, delivery is usually within two weeks in Western Europe, eight weeks in rest of Europe, and up to twelve weeks elsewhere. Letters to Europe cannot be sent by surface mail.

Airmail

This service is more expensive than surface mail but provides faster delivery. Delivery to cities in Western Europe is usually within three working days with other worldwide destinations taking between four and eight working days.

International Unsorted

A service specially designed for businesses spending £2,500 p.a. or more on international mail. The service offers the advantages of Airmail in addition to simpler procedures since there are only two weight categories (under 20g, over 20g) and two destination classifications (within Europe, rest of the world). Discount rates are charged and considerable savings can be made. Businesses not qualifying for an International Unsorted contract may use *International Unsorted on Demand* for one-off postings amounting to over £100. An efficient and economical *International Sorted* service is available to customers who can presort their mail to the requirements of the Royal Mail.

Printflow

A range of services designed to deliver printed material to any destination in the world. The service has three streams depending upon the importance of cost or delivery speed. It is suitable for businesses spending a minimum of £10,000 p.a. on international mail.

Swiftair Airmail

An express airmail service, one to two days faster than standard Airmail, offering delivery to 140 countries. The service is available as part of regular business collections. A standard charge of £2.70 (1998) per item is made in addition to postage. *Swiftair plus Recorded* and *Swiftair plus Registered* services are also available.

International Registration

A service offering additional security on international mail. A registered item will be signed for at every stage of its journey. Insurance cover for loss or damage is available, up to £2,200. If advice of delivery is required it has to be requested at the time of posting.

International Business Reply

A service enabling customers overseas to respond to promotions at no cost to themselves by supplying pre-paid reply material pre-printed with a UK address.

Customs, VAT and prohibited items

Declaration forms Letters and packages to destinations outside the EU are liable to overseas customs examinations and must be declared on special forms. For gifts or goods up to the value of £270, the Green label (CN22) should be used; for goods in excess of £270, CN23 should be used in addition to the top section of the Green label (CN22). All contents must be fully and accurately described.

Customs clearance fees (inward) Charges are made for presenting and clearing packages from abroad through H. M. Customs. Items from the EU are not charged.

VAT requirements Goods (not including gifts) exported by post are zero rated for VAT. However, each item valued at more than £100 must have a VAT label 444 attached. Businesses are required to supply H. M. Customs with a certificate of posting (form C & E 132, which is available from any Customs Office) signed by a postal officer.

Export licences Certain goods may not be exported without an export licence from the Department of Trade and Industry. Information on goods requiring licences is availabe from:

Department of Trade and Industry
1 Victoria Street
London
SW1H 0ET
tel 0171 215 5000

Infectious, perishable, and biological substances Such goods may only be sent by the Royal Mail to certain countries and then only by authorized senders and by special arrangement. A fee for this service is charged in addition to postage and registration.

Prohibited items Packets sent abroad must not contain articles or substances that are not allowed to be imported by the country of destination. Regulations vary from country to country and occasionally apply to such ordinary items as playing cards (in Greece). These regulations can be checked at a local post office.

Dangerous items and substances Dangerous substances must not be sent through the Royal Mail International services. Nine classes of dangerous substances exist and details may be found in *Post Office Guide*.

Bulk mailing

Mailsort

A range of mailsort services exist offering discounts on standard postage rates of between 13% and 15% (with a further 2% discount if barcoding is used). Discounts vary depending upon the time of postage and amount of presorting done by the customer. The service can be an advantage to a business mailing a minimum of 4000 letters at a time. Royal Mail provides some free help and advice.

Presstream

A service offering discounts of between 13% and 15% on 1st and 2nd class postage on customer-sorted newspapers, magazines, and journals. Qualification is a minimum mailing of 1000 packages twice annually. Royal Mail provides some free help and advice.

PacketPost Daily Rate

A service provided for a minimum posting of 10,000 packets per annum, with no daily quota. Essentially a time saving service, it eliminates the need to weigh and stamp individual packets. The service works by dividing the total weight of each day's packets by the number of items to give an average weight. The service may work out slightly cheaper.

PacketPost Flat Rate

A service similar to *PacketPost Daily Rate*, qualification is a minimum posting of 10,000 packets per annum, with no daily quota. Packets should be of a relatively stable weight, enabling each package to be charged at a single prearranged flat rate.

Direct Mail

Household Delivery

This service provides a nationwide door-to-door delivery of unaddressed leaflets and promotional material. Distribution can be arranged by postcode area, district or sector, TV region, geodemographic breakdown, or by selecting residential addresses only. The cost of the service depends on volume and weight.

See also *Mailsort* under **Bulk Mailing**.

Response Services

Business Reply

A service to encourage customers to respond to advertisements, circulars, etc., by using pre-paid self-addressed envelopes. The service can use either 1st or 2nd class mail.

Freepost

A similar service to Business Reply except that a business's address may be supplied through such media as television, radio, and the press, as well as pre-printed envelopes. Only 2nd class post is used.

Admail

A redirection service enabling advertisers to use a local or prestigious address but to have replies redirected to another address anywhere in the UK. The service can be used in conjunction with Business Reply. Admail works on fixed term contracts, which can range from 30 days to 1 year. Discounts are available if a business uses more than one Admail contract.

Parcelforce

Parcelforce Datapost

A parcel-delivery service that offers a guaranteed next-morning delivery with choice of times (by 10 am or noon). A refund of the difference between the charge for the service level selected and that for the service level provided may be claimed if delivery is delayed. There is compensation of up to £500 for loss or damage and consequential loss cover from £100 to £5,000. Supplements apply for certain outlying areas and Saturday delivery is subject to a 100% supplement.

Parcelforce 24, Parcelforce 48

Services offering a guaranteed 24- and 48-hour parcel delivery service to most UK addresses. Supplements and refunds for delayed delivery are as for *Parcelforce Datapost*. Compensation up to £250 is payable for any loss or damage. No consequential loss insurance is available.

Parcelforce standard

A parcel-delivery service that provides reliable, though not guaranteed, delivery within 3 days of despatch in the UK. Basic compensation of £20 per parcel is payable in the event of loss or damage, provided the Certificate of Posting can be produced. Additional compensation is available up to £500 for an additional fee. No consequential loss insurance is available.

International Datapost

A parcel-delivery service that offers express guaranteed delivery to 206 destinations throughout the world. A next-day service, with delivery by 8.30 am or 10.30 am, is available to many popular European destinations. Compensation levels for any damage, loss, or consequential loss are identical to those offered by Parcelforce Datapost. An *Ireland 24* service (only available in Northern Ireland) guarantees next-day delivery to the Republic of Ireland, with compensation of up to £250 for loss or damage. A *Euro 48* service guarantees delivery within two days to most European cities (three days to other areas), with compensation of up to £500 for loss or damage. All *International Datapost* services offer a refund in the event of delay.

International Standard Service

A parcel-delivery service that offers more destinations than International Datapost and is considerably cheaper. However, delivery times are longer (from three working days for Europe, from five for outside Europe) and there is no consequential loss insurance included; the maximum compensation for loss or damage is £250.

International Economy Service

A basic international parcel-delivery service offering only discretionary compensation in case of loss or damage. Delivery takes from 10 working days for Europe and from 20 for outside Europe, but, depending on destination, can take anything up to 73 days.

All prices given are correct at the time of going to press.

Appendix VII

Paper Sizes and Types

International paper sizes

International paper sizes are based upon a rectangle of paper with an area of one square metre, the sides of which are in the proportion 1:√2. This geometrical relationship is used so that any lengthways halfing of the original rectangle of paper produces another rectangle of paper with the same geometric relationship. For example, the A series is shown opposite.

There are three series of international paper size; A, B, and C. A is the most common series, with A4 being the favoured size for business correspondence. The B series is often used for posters, wall charts, other large items and where circumstances dictate a size of paper intermediate between any two adjacent sizes of the A series. The C series is used mainly when it is necessary to fit an envelope inside another envelope. The range and sizes of the three series are as follows:

A series (mm)

A0	841 × 1189	A6	105 × 148
A1	594 × 841	A7	74 × 105
A2	420 × 594	A8	52 × 74
A3	297 × 420	A9	37 × 52
A4	210 × 297	A10	26 × 37
A5	148 × 210		

B series (mm)

B0	1000 × 1414	B6	125 × 176
B1	707 × 1000	B7	88 × 125
B2	500 × 707	B8	62 × 88
B3	353 × 500	B9	44 × 62
B4	250 × 353	B10	31 × 44
B5	176 × 250		

C series (mm)

C4	324 × 229
C5	229 × 162
C6	162 × 114

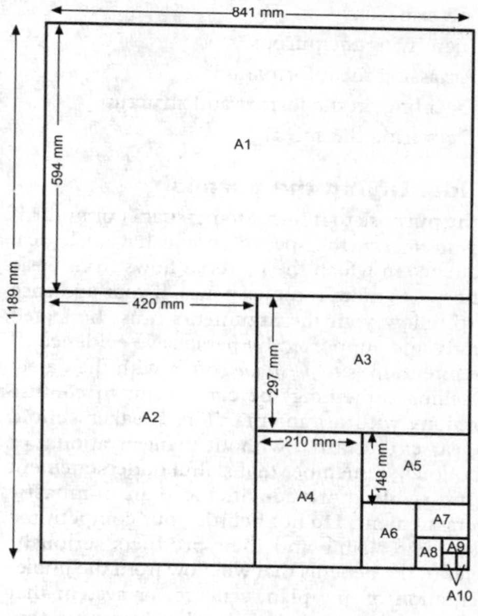

Types of paper

The most common types of business paper are:

Bond

This is a good quality, durable paper, usually weighing 70–90 grams per square metre (gsm). Available in a range of colours it is normally used for top copies and business correspondence.

Bank

This is a flimsy paper, easily creased and torn, usually weighing 40–50 gsm. It is normally used for carbon copies and sets of forms and is available in a variety of colours.

No Carbon Required (NCR)

This paper is specially treated to produce copies without the need for carbon paper. It is normally used in sets of forms.

Air mail

This is a very lightweight paper, usually blue, and is normally used on overseas mail to reduce postage costs when charge depends on weight.

There are many other types of paper, for writing, printing, drawing, and wrapping; it is wise to consult a good quality stationer for advice on these.

Paper measures

Printing paper	*Writing paper*
516 sheets = 1 ream	*480 sheets = 1 ream*
2 reams = 1 bundle	*24 sheets = 1 quire*
5 bundles = 1 bale	*20 quires = 1 ream*

Appendix VIII

Checklist for a Business Speech

There are four key areas in planning a business speech:

1. Identifying the purpose
2. Amassing the information
3. Deciding on the format and structure
4. Delivering the speech.

1. Identifying the purpose

Is the purpose to inform, to persuade, or both? If it is *to inform*, the speech should have a logical sequence in which the material flows from basic concepts to more complex issues. If your audience is to follow you, the arguments must be stated clearly and supported by persuasive evidence. If the intention is *to persuade* (often with the object of selling something) be careful not to confuse opinions with arguments. The speaker should appear enthusiastic, without being irrational or emotional; remember that skilful understatement is invariably more convincing than bombastic overstatement. Do not belittle your competitors: take their claims and their products seriously. Refer to the benefits that will flow from the implementation of any plan, scheme, or system that you are advocating and the disadvantages that will stem from not implementing them.

2. Amassing information

Gather as much information as possible that has a direct bearing on your subject. If the speech is designed to persuade, the speaker must have the necessary information required to convince the audience that any objections they might raise are not valid. If this can be done in the speech rather than in subsequent questions and answers, the speaker will be in a stronger position.

Once information has been gathered, it can usefully be sorted into three categories:

- what must be discussed
- what should be discussed
- what could be discussed.

The main body of the speech should be built round the first two categories; the third category should be included only if sufficient time remains – but the material should be prepared in case it is needed.

3. Forming a structure

Often a structure will suggest itself as material is being sorted. Bear in mind, however, that the format will depend on the venue, the time, and the size of the audience. Clearly, a speech in a lecture hall will need to be more formal than a more personal account given in a small boardroom. An audience before lunch is subject to different distractions from those that make the minds of an audience wander after lunch. Research has shown that an audience often requires a minute or two to settle down, they are then very receptive for three or four minutes; attention subsequently falls until the closing three or four minutes of the speech. Many professional speakers structure their speeches to begin with a short preamble, then summarize the main points of the speech in the peak receptive period, elucidate these points, draw conclusions, and recap on the central points in the last minutes.

Some experienced speakers suggest writing the closing section first, as this helps to focus the speech on the main points and provides a target to work towards.

4. Delivering the speech

Different speakers use different techniques. Some speak entirely from memory, some from notes or prompt cards, and some have a text fully written out. Reading a fully written-out speech makes it practically impossible to dry up and confers clarity; however, the speaker must learn to look up and address the audience and not simply read with his or her head down. Speaking from cards adds an element of spontaneity, especially if the cards only contain headings and key sentences. In the end, each speaker should use the method that suits him or her best.

The personal mannerisms of the speaker are less important than the enthusiasm and sincerity with which the speech is delivered.

Many professional speakers emphasize the need to look at the audience rather than the back of the room (a common habit among novices). If an audience feels that a speaker is deliberately avoiding looking at them they may assume that the speaker is not personally convinced by what he or she is saying; however, direct eye contact with members of the audience can appear confrontational. By looking at people's ears or shoulders one can give an impression of personal contact without appearing too challenging. This also has the effect of making the speech appear more personal – the members of the audience feel that they are being spoken *to* rather than *at*. Another popular method of creating a sense of intimacy is to deliver a speech as though speaking to a particular person.

If you are intending to use quotations, be sure that

you get them right, that they are absolutely appropriate, and that the audience will understand their relevance. Inappropriate literary quotations merely look pompous and misquotations and wrong attributions make a fool of the speaker. ("As Shakespeare said: 'they also serve who only stand and wait'!")

If you intend to tell a joke, be sure that you know how to tell it – especially how to get the timing right. If you can make the audience laugh they are likely to warm to you and to your cause. If the joke falls flat or you muff it, you may have lost them for good. Be careful, too, that your jokes do not offend or victimize members of the audience.

Avoid engaging hecklers in argument: rely on the chairperson to restore order. It is unwise to take a stance against a member of the audience unless it is apparent that the audience feels hostile towards that individual.